Collins

Diccionario
Español-Inglés
Inglés-Español

Spanish-English
English-Spanish
Dictionary

Collins Universal

Español-Inglés
English-Spanish

Collins

Collins Spanish Dictionary

HarperCollins Publishers
Westerhill Road
Bishopbriggs
Glasgow
G64 2QT
Great Britain

Eighth Edition 2005

Latest Reprint 2006

ISBN-13 978-0-00-718374-6
ISBN-10 0-00-718374-7

www.collins.co.uk

A catalogue record for this book is available from the British Library

Grupo Editorial Random House Mondadori S.L.
Travessera de Gràcia 47-49
08021 Barcelona

www.diccionarioscollins.com

ISBN 84-253-3940-5

HarperCollins Publishers,
10 East 53rd Street, New York, NY 10022

HARPERCOLLINS SPANISH UNABRIDGED DICTIONARY.
Eighth US Edition 2005

ISBN-13 978-0-06-074896-8
ISBN-10 0-06-074896-6

Library of Congress Cataloging-in-Publication Data has been applied for

www.harpercollins.com

HarperCollins books may be purchased for educational, business, or sales promotional use. For information, please write to:
Special Markets Department, HarperCollins Publishers, 10 East 53rd Street, New York, NY 10022

Typeset by Morton Word Processing Ltd, Scarborough

Printed in Italy by Legoprint S.P.A.

Acknowledgements
We would like to thank those authors and publishers who kindly gave permission for copyright material to be used in the Collins Word Web. We would also like to thank Times Newspapers Ltd for providing valuable data.

SIXTH, SEVENTH AND EIGHTH EDITIONS
EDICIONES SEXTA, SÉPTIMA Y OCTAVA

Series Editor **Directora de publicaciones**

Lorna Sinclair Knight

General Editor **Dirección general**

Jeremy Butterfield

Project Management **Dirección editorial**

Gerard Breslin

Senior Editors **Responsables de redacción**

Teresa Álvarez García Cordelia Lilly

Editorial Coordination **Coordinación editorial**

Emma Aeppli Sharon Hunter Joyce Littlejohn Val McNulty

Senior Contributors **Equipo de redacción**

Fernando León Solís Julie Muleba
Victoria Ordóñez Diví José María Ruiz Vaca
Alison Sadler

Contributors **Colaboradores**

Tom Bartlett Joaquín Blasco Diarmuid Bradley Michael Britton
Claire Calder Harry Campbell Malihé Forghani-Nowbari José Martín Galera
Nerea Gandarias Mendieta Elena García Álvarez Ben Goldstein Bob Grossmith
Jane Horwood Lesley Kingsley Ana Cristina Llompart Mª Ángeles Pérez Alonso
Ana Ramos Mar Rodríguez Vázquez Victoria Romero Cerro Carol Styles Carvajal
Palmira Sullivan Eduardo Vallejo Stephen Waller

Editorial Assistance **Ayudantes de redacción**

Elspeth Anderson Susan Dunsmore Alice Grandison Angela Jack
Irene Lakhani Cindy Mitchell Maggie Seaton

Data Management **Informática**

Jane Creevy Paul Hassett Sorcha Lenagh

FIFTH EDITION QUINTA EDICIÓN

Editorial Staff **Redacción**

Teresa Álvarez García Gerard Breslin Jeremy Butterfield
Sharon Hunter Cordelia Lilly José María Ruiz Vaca

Contributors **Colaboradores**

Professor I. F. Ariza Diarmuid Bradley José Ramón Parrondo

Computing **Informática**

Robert McMillan

THIRD AND FOURTH EDITIONS
EDICIONES TERCERA Y CUARTA

by/por

Colin Smith

in collaboration with **en colaboración con**

Diarmuid Bradley Teresa de Carlos Louis Rodrigues
José Ramón Parrondo

Editorial Management **Dirección editorial**

Jeremy Butterfield

Coordinating Editor **Coordinador de la obra**

Gerard Breslin

Assistant Editors **Ayudantes de redacción**

Sharon Hunter
Lesley Johnston

SECOND EDITION SEGUNDA EDICIÓN

by/por

Colin Smith

in collaboration with en colaboración con

María Boniface Hugo Pooley Arthur Montague
Mike Gonzalez

FIRST EDITION PRIMERA EDICIÓN

by/por

Colin Smith

in collaboration with en colaboración con

Manuel Bermejo Marcos Eugenio Chang-Rodríguez

Colin Smith

In this, the first edition of the Spanish Dictionary not to have benefited from the contribution of the late Colin Smith, we would like to acknowledge his pioneering work in the field of English-Spanish lexicography. Not only was the first edition of the dictionary in 1971 the result of many years of devoted, scholarly labour on his part, he was also the main contributor to the second and third editions. In his memory and in his honour we have retained, with some slight changes, the section on word formation in Spanish which he wrote for the third edition. We in the editorial team are all indebted to him for the breadth of his vision and his constant encouragement, and hope that this latest edition is a fitting tribute to him, "il miglior fabbro".

Colin Smith

En esta primera edición del diccionario de inglés que no se ha beneficiado de la colaboración del desaparecido Colin Smith, quisiéramos dejar constancia de nuestro reconocimiento a su labor pionera en el campo de la lexicografía bilingüe de inglés-español. No sólo fue la primera edición del diccionario de 1971 el resultado de muchos años de trabajo riguroso y erudito por su parte, si no que además su contribución a la segunda y tercera ediciones fue primordial. En su memoria y en su honor hemos mantenido, con alguna pequeña variación, la sección dedicada a la formación de palabras en español que escribió para la tercera edición. Nuestro equipo editorial se halla en deuda con él por su amplitud de miras y continuo apoyo, por lo que esperamos que esta nueva edición sea un tributo apropiado para "il miglior fabbro".

Acknowledgements

Agradecimientos

Guillermo Arce, Pamela Bacarisse, David Balagué, Jennie Bachelor, Clive Bashleigh, Peter Beardsell, William Bidgood, Tom Bookless, Everett L. Boyd, T.R.M. Bristow, Prof R.F. Brown, John Butt, Max Cawdron, Nick Gardner, A. Bryson Gerrard, Robert Burakoff, Trevor Chubb, Sabine Citron, G.T. Colegate, Joe Cremona, Dr G.A. Davies, Eve Degnen, Maureen Dolan, Carmen and Pablo Domínguez, Fr Carlos Elizalde C.P., John England, María Jesús Fernández Prieto, José Miguel Galván Déniz, G.C. Gilham, Paul Gomez, Isobel Gordon, H.B. Hall, Stephen Harrison, Patrick Harvey, Tony Heathcote, David Henn, Leo Hickey, Ian Jacob, Leonor del Pino Jiménez, Concepción and Pilar Jiménez Bautista, A. Johnson, F. Killoran, Norman Lamb, Emilio Lorenzo, A. Madigan, A. McCallum, Rosa María Manchón, Rodney Mantle, Duncan Marshall, María Martín, Hazel Mills, Alan Morley, Brian Morris, Brian Mott, Bernard Murphy, Ana Newton, Patrick Nield, Richard Nott, Hugh O'Donnell, Chantal Pérez Hernández, Dan Quilter, Hugo Pooley, Chris Pratt, Brian Powell, Robert Pring-Mill, M. Dolores Ramis, Sr J. and Sra M. del Río, Brian Steel, C.H. Stevenson, Diana Streeten, Sra A. Espinosa de Walker, Sra M.J. Fernández de Wangermann, Ian Weetman, G. Weston, Richard Wharton, Roger Wright, Alan Yates

William Collins' dream of knowledge for all began with the publication of his first book in 1819. A self-educated mill worker, he not only enriched millions of lives, but also founded a flourishing publishing house. Today, staying true to this spirit, Collins books are packed with inspiration, innovation, and practical expertise.
They place you at the centre of a world of possibility and give you exactly what you need to explore it.

Language is the key to this exploration, and at the heart of Collins Dictionaries is language as it is really used. New words, phrases, and meanings spring up every day, and all of them are captured and analysed by the Collins Word Web. Constantly updated, and with over 2.5 billion entries, this living language resource is unique to our dictionaries.

Words are tools for life. And a Collins Dictionary makes them work for you.

Collins. Do more.

CONTENTS

Introduction	xii
Using the dictionary	xvi
Complex entries and language notes	xxxiii
Cultural notes	xxxiv
Pronunciation and spelling	xxxv
SPANISH-ENGLISH	1-1036
Language in Use: a grammar of communication in Spanish and English	1-63
ENGLISH-SPANISH	1041-2113
The Spanish verb	2117
The English verb	2126
Aspects of word formation in Spanish	2131
Numerals	2135
Weights and measures	2138
Time and date	2141

ÍNDICE DE MATERIAS

Introducción	xiv
Cómo utilizar el diccionario	xvi
Entradas complejas y notas lingüísticas	xxxiii
Notas culturales	xxxiv
Pronunciación y ortografía	xxxv
ESPAÑOL-INGLÉS	1-1036
Lengua y Uso: gramática comunicativa del inglés y del español	1-63
INGLÉS-ESPAÑOL	1041-2113
El verbo español	2117
El verbo inglés	2126
La formación de palabras en español	2131
Números	2135
Pesos y medidas	2138
Hora y fecha	2141

INTRODUCTION

Since it was first published to great critical acclaim in 1971, the COLLINS SPANISH DICTIONARY has become one of the most highly-respected reference works of its kind. The extent of its coverage together with the clarity and accuracy of the information it gives have made it a recognized authority in the field of Spanish-English English-Spanish lexicography.

While building on all the strengths that have made the COLLINS SPANISH DICTIONARY so popular, including features such as the Language in Use guide to self-expression and the recent innovative encyclopaedic and usage boxes, this latest edition marks an exciting new step forward. As well as adding a wealth of new words and expressions which have come into the language since the last edition, we have used the huge English and Spanish databases developed through the groundbreaking research into computational linguistics carried out by COLLINS in partnership with the University of Birmingham since the 1970s to refine existing entries, senses and phrases. These multi-million-word corpora are collections of texts held on computer, which provide numerous examples of how words are actually used in the widest possible variety of contexts, be it in newspapers, in literature, in official reports or in ordinary spoken language. In much the same way as scientists who analyse objective data to confirm their hypotheses, dictionary editors now have access to vast databases of hard facts and evidence to back up their own linguistic intuition. The result is a degree of accuracy and depth of coverage that would be impossible to achieve using traditional methods alone. Here is an example of how authentic usage, as documented in our corpora, be it the Bank of English or the Banco de español, is reflected in our dictionary entries:

disc. If the problem is	severe	and does not settle spontaneously
British system of justice took a	severe	blow. Let's hope that the
depressed and confidence has taken a	severe	blow from the turmoil in the
slow and tedious. I suffered from	severe	bouts of depression, migraine, fits
Pete suffered a fractured skull and	severe	brain damage. He went into a coma
Bosnia to Sarajevo because of the	severe	cold. Priorities will be blankets
the deeply damaged system. The	severe	conditions, which shocked EC
substantial loss of ozone could have	severe	consequences for life on Earth,
dictatorship here would be a very	severe	consequences in terms of trade,
and it will have especially	severe	consequences for the nations of the
his residence. This, at a time when	severe	constraints have been applied to
But at the same time he was a	severe	critic of American policy on the
said: "This bomb would have caused	severe	damage, injury and death within a
month, hurricane-force winds caused	severe	damage to property across much of
exploding under the bows, caused	severe	damage and slowed up the
Apart from anything else, the	severe	decline in Test-match crowds is
in the open and inflicting a	severe	defeat upon him, the pursuit of a
situation. The effect of the two	severe	defeats, and the continuous attack
interests adequately because of the	severe	defeats suffered in the preceding
Republic, has suffered several	severe	defeats and its very survival is
like cost, loss of child labour,	severe	discipline, outweigh the
Water companies claim that	severe	droughts are freak occurrences
to note that, despite its own	severe	economic problems, Turkey had
out at Warren after his son suffered	severe	facial injuries after beating
of sickness can therefore result in	severe	financial problems. With a PHI
City came to a virtual stop today.	Severe	flooding trapped people in their
to a new pipe-laying programme. The	severe	frost and rapid thaw caused small
and many families suffered	severe	hardship as a consequence. Little
the people continued to suffer	severe	hardship. Free-market policies
illness and yesterday awoke with a	severe	headache and stomach pains which
Hingham when he apparently died of a	severe	illness. The two were blindfolded
conditions such as TB or other	severe	illnesses; disorders of the
14, was airlifted to hospital with	severe	injuries. He was undergoing an
as he walked his dog. She had	severe	injuries to the head. The

severe [sɪˈvɪəʳ] ADJ (*compar* **severer**; *superl* **severest**) [1] (= *serious*) [*problem, consequence, damage*] grave, serio; [*injury, illness*] grave; [*defeat, setback, shortage*] serio; [*blow, reprimand*] fuerte, duro; [*pain, headache*] fuerte; **I suffered from ~ bouts of depression** padecía profundas *or* serias depresiones; **many families suffered ~ hardship as a consequence** muchas familias sufrieron enormes penurias a consecuencia de ello; **we have been under ~ pressure to cut costs** nos han presionado mucho para reducir gastos; **to suffer a ~ loss of blood** sufrir gran pérdida de sangre; **~ losses** (*Fin*) enormes *or* cuantiosas pérdidas *fpl*
[2] (= *harsh*) [*weather, conditions, winter*] duro, riguroso; [*cold*] extremo; [*storm, flooding, frost*] fuerte
[3] (= *strict*) [*person, penalty*] severo; [*discipline*] estricto; **I was his ~st critic** yo era su crítico más severo; **to be ~ with sb** ser severo con algn
[4] (= *austere*) [*person, appearance, expression*] severo, adusto; [*clothes, style*] austero; [*hairstyle*] (de corte) serio; [*architecture*] sobrio

One of our greatest challenges, given the sheer wealth of information to be presented, was to make such a sophisticated reference work simple and quick to use. The result is a completely new layout, designed to make different senses, set structures and idioms easier to locate even in the longest entries, which have been given a special treatment all their own.

By combining the tried-and-tested strengths of the existing dictionary with a new and innovative approach, we feel we have taken the most significant step forward in Spanish-English lexicography since our first edition in 1971. We are confident that the COLLINS SPANISH DICTIONARY will continue to be a valued companion for students, teachers, translators and language enthusiasts alike.

Introducción

Desde la primera edición, aparecida en 1971, el diccionario COLLINS de inglés-español ha sido una de las obras de consulta más respetadas e influyentes en su campo. La extensión del vocabulario incluido, junto a la claridad y la fiabilidad de su contenido han hecho de él un diccionario cuya calidad es ampliamente reconocida en el mundo de la lexicografía de español-inglés.

Profundizando en la línea trazada por anteriores ediciones y además de elementos tan destacados como la guía de expresión "Lengua y uso" y las innovadoras notas enciclopédicas y gramaticales, hemos dado con esta edición un importante paso adelante. No sólo hemos añadido una profusión de neologismos y expresiones que han entrado en la lengua desde la última edición, sino que hemos refinado el tratamiento de las entradas explorando en profundidad sus distintas acepciones y usos gracias a las bases de datos de inglés y español creadas a partir de la investigación en lingüística computacional llevada a cabo por COLLINS en colaboración con la universidad de Birmingham desde los años 70. Estas colecciones de textos son poderosas herramientas informáticas de análisis que muestran cómo funcionan las palabras en el mayor número de contextos posibles, tales como el periodístico, el de la administración, la literatura o la lengua hablada. Al igual que en las ciencias, en las que los investigadores analizan información objetiva para confirmar sus hipótesis, los lexicógrafos tienen ahora acceso a vastos bancos de datos con las pruebas que confirman sus propias intuiciones lingüísticas. El resultado es un nivel de exactitud y profundidad en el vocabulario incluido que sería imposible conseguir utilizando únicamente métodos tradicionales. Aquí abajo puede verse un ejemplo de cómo el uso real, documentado en nuestros corpus, bien del Bank of English o del Banco de español, se refleja en las entradas de nuestro diccionario:

y cuántos son productos de un apoyo	decidido	a otro candidato, como es usted en este
gobierno # El ministro mostró su apoyo	decidido	a que el Gobierno agote los plazos del
El portavoz de ciu manifestó un apoyo	decidido	a la resolución del Consejo General del
del teatro infantil y juvenil, el apoyo	decidido	a la autoría dramática autóctona y a la
municipal de Madrid ha dado apoyo	decidido	a la Escuela Normal de Ballet de Adolfo
Reclamamos de las instituciones un apoyo	decidido	al ballet clásico y denunciamos
Reserva Federal, dé una muestra de apoyo	decidido	al dólar, elevando los tipos de interés
sino también recompensas políticas: un	decidido	apoyo diplomático español y de la UE
Moscú, por su parte, critica a Bonn el	decidido	apoyo a la extensión de la Organización
cerealista y ganadera, encontramos un	decidido	apoyo a los demás sectores de la
momentos, Calvo Sotelo encontró un	decidido	apoyo a su propuesta entre la derecha.
a un alzamiento pacífico, vigoroso y	decidido	contra la injusticia, la corrupción, la
una pronta y pacífica conclusión con el	decidido	concurso de la OEA # dijo ayer el
de cinco millones de espectadores y el	decidido	elogio de la mayoría. De otro modo, el
Durante algunos minutos camino con paso	decidido,	contemplando de soslayo el desamparo
y de súbito le invade un sentimiento	decidido	de aversión por esta oscuridad helada,
sus comentaristas proviene de que este	decidido	adversario de las armas nucleares
como un hábil negociador y un	decidido	defensor del comercio multilateral y de
firmadas bajo tortura. Se mostró firme,	decidido,	defensor de otra justicia. El juez le
contemporáneo. Así lo vio ese otro	decidido	gnóstico, André Breton, por intermedio
nos podíamos esperar es que fuese un	decidido	impulsor de las matemáticas. En
que las cosas mismas". Santayana es un	decidido	materialista o, si se prefiere, un
de que aquél naciera), Jámblico, era	decidido	partidario de la teurgia, y su obra Los
de tensiones entre Felipe V, partidario	decidido	del reconocimiento, y el Consejo de
él. Simultáneamente, comenzaba a ser un	decidido	promotor del diálogo entre ETA y el
a San Sebastián, se ha dicho que era	decidido,	valiente, temperamental, vehemente.
verdadero y continuo, joven y vigoroso,	decidido	y leal, con un mundo soñado para la paz
clave dentro del equipo que parece estar	decidido	a abandonar el club cuando concluya su
durante una parte del día. No estaba nada	decidido	a abonarme. Me parecía mucho dinero,
al público, porque el Gobierno está	decidido	a asumir este compromiso, con y por la
que antes de partir y estaba totalmente	decidido	a casarme con tal de recuperarla,
evidentes dificultades, el padre está	decidido	a llevar adelante la división familiar,
defenderlo en la sesión próxima, y esta	decidido	a marcharse del Gobierno si se vota el
de tanta animadversión: el actor está	decidido	a montar un supercasino en la reserva
que jugarse la existencia. Que yo estoy	decidido	a sacar el asunto adelante y las
estadounidense, Bill Clinton, está	decidido	a seguir adelante con un proyecto de
que debe sufrir un artista cuando está	decidido	a seguir sin concesiones su verdadera
su segunda mujer. Les anunció que estaba	decidido	a suicidarse y todos los que le
de que me reconcilie, no lo haría. Estoy	decidido	a terminar con el matrimonio". El
crisis místicas, pero, sobre todo,	decidido	a convertirse en pintor, hizo progresos

que le reafirme en su posición de líder.	decidido	a luchar por el título, su trabajo ha
en esquí de fondo, un joven triatleta	decidido	a ser bombero o un empleado de artes
la categoría social de la dama.	decidido	a seguir el juego, el dueño del hotel
la oportuna aclimatación. Me levanté	decidido	a comenzar el suplicio de la escalada
asomó la cabeza por la ventanilla	decidido	a echar una mano y, cuando se quiso dar
en el caso, acudió ayer a la Audiencia	decidido	a declarar. Pero esta mañana (por
exploré el terreno diplomático,	decidido	a intentar por mi cuenta y riesgo lo
sesteando, pero el Zaragoza salió	decidido	a resolver el partido y supo aprovechar
de los encuestados afirma no estar	decidido	del todo. Conviene saber que la
pero él está ya practicamente	decidido.	Se presentará como candidato
hablando dos o tres minutos y se dirigió	decidido	hacia mí. Cuando pasó al lado de Celia
refleja sentimentalmente quien cabalga	decidido	hacia el poder. Chirac tiene la lista
de asalto. Salió de su casa, se encaminó	decidido	y enfiló la mirada hacia la oficina de
me dirigí a la terminal. La cruzé	decidido	y salí al exterior. Tomé un taxi. Pasé

decidido ADJ 1 (= *firme*) [*apoyo*] wholehearted; [*paso, gesto*] purposeful; [*esfuerzo, intento*] determined; [*defensor, partidario*] staunch, strong; [*actitud, persona*] resolute; **dio su apoyo ~ al proyecto** he gave his solid *o* wholehearted support to the project; **hubo un ~ apoyo a su propuesta entre la derecha** there was solid support for his proposal from the right; **andaba con paso ~** she walked purposefully *o* with a purposeful stride; **los más ~s saltaron al agua** the most resolute jumped into the water
2 **estar ~: voy a dejar el trabajo, ya estoy ~** I'm going to leave my job, I've made up my mind *o* I've decided; **estar ~ a hacer algo** to be resolved *o* determined to do sth; **estaba decidida a irse con él** she'd made up her mind to go with him, she was resolved *o* determined to go with him

Frente a tan abundante información, uno de nuestros mayores desafíos era convertir esta herramienta de consulta tan sofisticada en una obra sencilla y fácil de usar. El resultado es una presentación totalmente nueva, diseñada para que las distintas acepciones, locuciones y modismos puedan localizarse fácilmente incluso en las entradas más largas, a las que se ha dado un tratamiento especial.
La combinación de estas innovaciones tecnológicas con los puntos fuertes tradicionales de este diccionario constituyen en nuestra opinión el avance más significativo en el campo de la lexicografía bilingüe desde la publicación de la primera edición del 71. Estamos convencidos de que el diccionario COLLINS de inglés-español continuará siendo un valioso compañero para estudiantes, traductores, lingüistas y para todos los amantes de la lengua.

Using the Dictionary

Word order

Alphabetical order is followed except in the cases mentioned below. For easier reference, abbreviations, acronyms and proper names are given alphabetically in the wordlist. Although traditionally **CH** and **LL** have been considered separate letters in Spanish and words containing them used to be given after other **C/L** combinations on the Spanish side, it is now the policy of the Association of Spanish Language Academies to order such words according to the universal Latin alphabet as in English. This is the policy followed in this dictionary. **Ñ** continues to be considered a separate letter and is therefore given between **N** and **O**.

If two or more variants follow one another alphabetically, they are usually treated in the same entry and the more common form given first.

If variant spellings are not alphabetically adjacent, each is treated as a separate headword and there is a cross-reference to the form treated in depth. Note, however, that English words whose endings can be spelt either **-ize** or **-ise**, **-ization** or **-isation** etc are always included at the **z** spelling.

For the alphabetical order of compounds see **Compounds** and for that of phrasal verbs see **Phrasal verbs**.

Cross-referring of headwords

Cross-references include alternative spellings, parts of irregular verbs, irregular plural forms, contracted forms and some prefixes and suffixes.

armor [ˈɑːməʳ] N (*US*) = **armour**

voy *ver* **ir**

gave [geɪv] PT *of* **give**

Homonyms

Superscript numbers are used to separate unrelated words which have the same spelling and pronunciation, e.g. **port**[1], **port**[2], **choclo**[1], **choclo**[2].

Pronunciation

As Spanish pronunciation is generally entirely predictable, pronunciation rules are given on pages xxxv-xxxviii and IPA phonetic transcriptions are only included on the Spanish side where the pronunciation of a given word or its inflections is at odds with these, as is the case for some words of foreign origin, e.g. **camping**.

camping [ˈkampin] SM (*pl* **campings** [ˈkampin])

Since English pronunciation is far less predictable, phonetic transcriptions are included for all headwords on the English side and for irregular plural inflections where appropriate.

amoeba [əˈmiːbə] N (*pl* **amoebas**, **amoebae** [əˈmiːbiː])

For the pronunciation of two-word compounds, see the phonetic transcription given under each headword.

Special entries

Complex entries

Entries that are very long - often function words, delexical verbs or words which are used in a large number of set structures (**back**, **dar**) - are given special treatment in this dictionary. Complex entries with more than one part of speech begin with a special "menu" which shows how they are structured. Special notes inside the entry either explain important points of grammar and usage which cannot be properly demonstrated by examples alone, or refer you to another part of the dictionary. In entries on the English side the word BUT introduces exceptions to general translations which have been suggested. The beginning of each semantic category is clearly signposted with indicators in boxes, and set structures have been given special prominence to make them easy to locate. Finally, in entries where there are long sequences of examples containing

Cómo utilizar el diccionario

Orden alfabético

Se sigue siempre el orden alfabético, excepto en los casos mencionados más abajo. Para facilitar la consulta del diccionario se incluyen en el texto las abreviaturas, siglas y nombres propios en el lugar que les corresponde alfabéticamente. Aunque **CH** y **LL** se consideraban tradicionalmente letras, la Asociación de Academias de la Lengua Española ya no las considera como tales, de acuerdo al alfabeto latino universal, por lo que se encontrarán alfabetizadas como **C+H** y **L+L**. La **Ñ** continúa siendo una letra independiente.

Si dos o más variantes van una a continuación de otra en el orden alfabético, aparecen normalmente en la misma entrada y la variante más frecuente suele ir primero.

Las variantes ortográficas que no van una a continuación de otra aparecen como entradas independientes y se da una remisión a la variante en la que se desarrolla la entrada. Las palabras inglesas que pueden escribirse con las terminaciones **-ize** o **-ise, -ization** o **-isation**, etc, aparecen siempre escritas con **z**.

Para el orden alfabético de los compuestos, véase **Compuestos** y para los verbos frasales, véase **Verbos frasales**.

Remisiones de una entrada a otra

Se envían a otras entradas las variantes ortográficas, las formas irregulares de los verbos, los plurales irregulares de las palabras inglesas, las formas contraídas y algunos prefijos y sufijos.

Homónimos

Se usan cifras voladitas para separar las palabras que tienen la misma grafía y pronunciación, p.ej. **port**[1], **port**[2], **choclo**[1], **choclo**[2].

Pronunciación

Al ser la pronunciación española por lo general previsible, se dan simplemente las normas de pronunciación en las páginas xxxv-xxxviii y sólo se incluyen las transcripciones en el alfabeto fonético internacional de aquellas palabras cuya pronunciación puede estar poco clara para los no hablantes de español, como es el caso de los extranjerismos, por ej. **camping**.

En la sección de inglés se incluye la transcripción fonética de todas las entradas, así como la del plural si es irregular, ya que la pronunciación inglesa es mucho menos previsible.

Para la pronunciación de los compuestos formados por dos palabras, véase la transcripción fonética de cada palabra.

Entradas especiales

Entradas complejas

A las entradas más largas, tales como algunos de los verbos más básicos y aquellas palabras que se usan en un gran número de expresiones fijas (**back**, **dar**), se les ha dado una presentación especial en este diccionario. Si tienen más de una categoría gramatical aparece un recuadro al comienzo de la entrada con todas ellas. En algunas de las entradas se verán o bien notas que explican puntos gramaticales importantes que no pueden aclararse sólo con ejemplos o bien remisiones a otra parte del diccionario. La palabra BUT en las entradas inglesas introduce las excepciones a las traducciones generales dadas. Al comienzo de cada acepción aparece un recuadro con un indicador para dicha acepción. Las estructuras fijas aparecen resaltadas de forma especial para que sean fácilmente localizables. Por último, en las entradas en las que hay párrafos largos con importantes

significant grammatical or lexical collocations, a key word is underlined and the examples are alphabetized on this word.

colocaciones gramaticales o léxicas, una palabra clave en la frase aparece subrayada y gobierna el orden alfabético de dichas frases.

Cultural notes

Extra information on culturally significant events, institutions, traditions and customs which cannot be given in an ordinary translation or gloss is given in the form of shaded boxed notes following the relevant entry. See index on page xxxiv.

Notas culturales

Se ha dado una información adicional sobre aquellos acontecimientos, instituciones, costumbres y tradiciones culturales importantes a los que no puede darse una traducción normal o una pequeña explicación. Dicha información aparece en un recuadro tras la entrada correspondiente. Véase el índice en la página xxxiv.

Language notes

These boxed notes are aimed at tackling certain areas of difficulty where even an advanced student may benefit from further explanation. They are designed to complement the dictionary entry in a clear and succinct fashion and to provide further helpful examples. The points covered in these notes were selected on the advice of practising teachers and academics. See index on page xxxiii.

Notas lingüísticas

Estas notas lingüísticas, cuyo objetivo es aclarar y explicar aquellas dificultades que pueda tener incluso un estudiante avanzado, están diseñadas para complementar la entrada del diccionario de una forma clara y esquemática, proporcionando para ello más ejemplos ilustrativos. Los puntos que se han tratado en dichas notas se han seleccionado con la ayuda de profesores de ambos idiomas. Véase el índice en la página xxxiii.

Finding your way through entries

Part-of-speech categories

Grammatical functions are distinguished by bold face letters and abbreviations, for example:

Cómo orientarse dentro de una entrada

Categorías gramaticales

Las categorías gramaticales vienen marcadas por letras en negrita y por abreviaturas, por ej.:

arder ▸conjug 2a◂ Ⓐ VT ...
Ⓑ VI ...

See list of abbreviations used inside the front and back cover.

Sometimes two or more parts of speech are treated together on the Spanish side if the translations apply equally to each, for example:

Véase la lista de abreviaturas en el interior de las cubiertas del libro.

En algunas ocasiones dos o más categorías gramaticales aparecen juntas en las entradas españolas si la traducción es válida para todas ellas, por ej.:

moldavo/a ADJ, SM/F Moldavian, Moldovan

Meaning categories

The diverse meanings of the headword within each entry or part-of-speech category are separated by numbers in blue face, [1] ... [2] ..., occasionally subdivided into [1.1], [1.2], etc. A certain order is normally followed: basic and concrete senses first, figurative and familiar ones later.

Categorías semánticas

Las distintas acepciones de una entrada están separadas por números en azul, [1] ... [2] ... y en ocasiones aparecen subdivididas en [1.1], [1.2], etc. Se sigue normalmente un cierto orden: primero los significados básicos y concretos, después los figurados y familiares.

Highlighting

To enable you to home in quickly on the phrase you are looking for in entries or categories over a certain length, where it makes semantic sense we have underlined a key element in phrases and structures and alphabetized such phrases and structures accordingly.

Subrayado

Para que sea posible localizar inmediatamente la frase buscada en entradas o categorías de mayor tamaño, hemos subrayado un elemento clave en diversas frases y estructuras en aquellos casos en los que tiene sentido semánticamente hacerlo. Dichas frases aparecen alfabetizadas siguiendo el elemento subrayado.

sail [seɪl] Ⓐ N [1] (*Naut*) (= *cloth*) vela *f*; **the age of ~** la época de la navegación a vela; **in** *or* **under full ~** a toda vela, a vela llena; **to lower the ~s** arriar las velas; **to set ~** [*ship, person*] hacerse a la vela, zarpar; **we set ~ from Portsmouth** nos hicimos a la vela en Portsmouth; **to set ~ for Liverpool** zarpar hacia Liverpool, hacerse a la vela con rumbo a Liverpool; **to take in the ~s** amainar las velas; **under ~** a vela; ✦***IDIOM*** **to take the wind out of sb's ~s** bajarle los humos a algn
[2] (*Naut*) (= *trip*) paseo *m* en barco; **it's three days' ~ from here** desde aquí se tarda tres días en barco; **to go for a ~** dar una vuelta en barco

Idioms, proverbs and set phrases

On the English side idioms are preceded by the label ✦***IDIOM*** or ✦***IDIOMS*** and proverbs by ✦***PROV*** or ✦***PROVS*** while on the Spanish side idioms are labelled ✦***MODISMO*** or ✦***MODISMOS*** and proverbs ✦***REFRÁN*** or ✦***REFRANES***. Both types of phrase are generally grouped at the end of the relevant sense category of the first invariable element in the phrase: e.g. **to ring the changes** and **to ring true/false** are all included under **ring**. Other types of set phrase are similarly given under the first lexical element, e.g. **red in the face** is given under **red**.
The only exception to this is where certain very common English and Spanish verbs such as **make** or **tener** form the basis

Modismos, refranes y estructuras

En la parte de inglés los modismos aparecen precedidos de las marcas ✦***IDIOM*** o ✦***IDIOMS*** y los refranes de las marcas ✦***PROV*** o ✦***PROVS***. En la parte de español las marcas correspondientes son ✦***MODISMO*** o ✦***MODISMOS*** y ✦***REFRÁN*** o ✦***REFRANES***. Ambos tipos de expresiones se hallarán agrupados normalmente al final de la categoría semántica correspondiente del primer elemento invariable de cada expresión. Por ej.: **to ring the changes** y **to ring true/false** aparecen en la entrada **ring**. Otros tipos de expresiones fijas aparecen también bajo el primer elemento léxico, por ej. se incluye **red in the face** en la entrada **red**.

of a very large number of phrases, e.g. **to make an appointment**, **to make hay while the sun shines**, **to make sense**, **tener la impresión de que ..**, **tener sentido**, **tener interés**.

Since the entries for these verbs are very long, phrases are treated under the second element so that the user will find them more easily in the shorter entry; **to make an appointment** is thus under **appointment** and **tener interés** under **interés**.

There is, however, also intentional duplication of phrases where appropriate. Thus **año bisiesto** belongs under **año** under the first rule we have given; but it is also the sole phrase under the headword **bisiesto**. In many other cases phrases are duplicated because they illustrate something about both headwords.

En el caso de verbos muy frecuentes en ambas lenguas, tales como **make** o **tener**, que se usan con numerosas expresiones, dichas expresiones suelen aparecer en el segundo elemento, por ej.: **to make an appointment**, **to make hay while the sun shines**, **to make sense**, **tener la impresión de que ...**, **tener sentido**, **tener interés**.

Dado el tamaño de las entradas de estos verbos, la frase aparece bajo el segundo elemento para que sea más fácil de encontrar. Así, **to make an appointment** aparece bajo **appointment** y **tener interés** bajo **interés**.

Hay, sin embargo, muchos casos en los que dichas expresiones aparecen en ambas entradas. Es el caso de **año bisiesto**, que según la norma mencionada debe ir bajo la entrada **año**, pero que es también la única frase en **bisiesto**. En otras ocasiones se duplican las expresiones si ilustran algo sobre ambas entradas.

Repetition of the headword in the entry

To save space, where the headword occurs in its full form within the entry it is replaced by ~. Where it might otherwise be confusing or the phrase is a common sign, the full form is used.

Repetición del lema en la entrada

Para ahorrar espacio, el lema se substituye por ~ cuando aparece completo dentro de la entrada. Se usa, sin embargo, la palabra completa en las frases cuando no hacerlo puede dar lugar a confusión o si dicha frase es un letrero.

smoking ['sməʊkɪŋ] Ⓐ N **~ is bad for you** el fumar te perjudica; **~ or non-~?** ¿fumador o no fumador?; **to give up ~** dejar de fumar; **"no smoking"** "prohibido fumar"; **no ~ area** zona *f* de no fumadores

pisar ▸conjug 1a◂ Ⓐ VT [1] (= *andar sobre*) to walk on; **¿se puede ~ el suelo de la cocina?** can I walk on the kitchen floor?
[2] (= *poner el pie encima de*) to tread on, step on; **perdona, te he pisado** sorry, I trod *o* stepped on your foot; **vio una cucaracha y la pisó** she saw a cockroach and trod *o* stood on it; **~ el acelerador a fondo** to step on the accelerator, put one's foot down*; **"prohibido pisar el césped"** "keep off the grass";

Compounds in both languages are given in full, as are pronominal verbs in Spanish and phrasal verbs in English.

Los compuestos nominales aparecen completos en ambos idiomas, así como los verbos pronominales en español y los verbos frasales en inglés.

red [red] Ⓐ ADJ (*compar* **redder**; *superl* **reddest**)
Ⓒ CPD ► **red admiral** N vanesa *f* roja ► **red alert** N alerta *f* roja; **to be on ~ alert** estar en alerta roja ► **the Red Army** N el Ejército Rojo ► **red blood cell** N glóbulo *m* rojo ► **red cabbage** N col *f* lombarda, lombarda *f*

call ...
►**call off** VT + ADV [1] (= *cancel*) [+ *meeting, race*] cancelar, suspender; [+ *deal*] anular; [+ *search*] abandonar, dar por terminado; **the strike was ~ed off** se desconvocó la huelga
[2] [+ *dog*] llamar (*para que no ataque*)

levantar ...
Ⓒ **levantarse** VPR [1] (= *alzarse*) [1·1] (*de la cama, del suelo*) to get up; **me levanto todos los días a las ocho** I get up at eight every day;

Compounds

On the English-Spanish side of this dictionary, some entries include as their last category a section headed CPD or COMPOUND(S). In these will be found nouns made up of two or more separate words such as **sand dune** (under **sand**), **fast food** (under **fast**), **ear, nose and throat specialist** (under **ear**).

Each compound is preceded by a blue triangle ►, and the order is alphabetical.

Single-word nouns such as **blackbird**, and words usually written with a hyphen such as **by-your-leave**, appear as headwords in their own right.

Only compound words functioning as nouns are shown in compound categories. Adjective compounds which can be written with a hyphen or without, usually depending on whether they precede or follow a noun, are shown as headwords in their hyphenated form.

Compuestos

En la sección de inglés-español de este diccionario, algunas entradas incluyen una última categoría gramatical denominada CPD o COMPOUND(S). En ella se encontrarán los sustantivos formados por dos o más palabras como **sand dune** (bajo **sand**), **fast food** (bajo **fast**), **ear, nose and throat specialist** (bajo **ear**).

Los sustantivos compuestos (p. ej. **blackbird**) que gráficamente forman una sola palabra y aquellos escritos normalmente con guión (p. ej. **by-your-leave**) aparecen como entradas independientes.

Sólo aparecen bajo la categoría de compuestos aquellos que funcionan como sustantivo. Los compuestos que funcionan como adjetivo (que pueden escribirse con guión o sin él, según precedan o sigan a un sustantivo), aparecen como entradas independientes escritos con guión.

hard [hɑ:d] Ⓐ ADJ ...
► **the hard core** N (= *intransigents*) los incondicionales, el núcleo duro; *see also* **hard-core**

hard-core ['hɑ:dkɔ:ʳ] ADJ [*pornography*] duro; [*supporter, militant, activist*] acérrimo; [*conservative, communist*] acérrimo, empedernido; *see also* **hard**

Compounds which are used as both nouns and adjectives and are never hyphenated (**North American**, **West Indian**) are given as separate entries.

On the Spanish-English side compounds made up of a noun plus two or more separate words are shown within the relevant sense category of the first word preceded by a blue triangle ►.

A los compuestos que se usan como adjetivo y sustantivo y que no llevan guión (**North American**, **West Indian**) se les considera entradas independientes.

En la sección de español-inglés los compuestos nominales formados por un sustantivo más una o más palabras aparecen por orden alfabético al final de la categoría semántica correspondiente y precedidos de un triángulo azul ►.

copa SF 1 (= *recipiente*) (*para bebidas*) glass; (*para postres*) dessert glass; **huevo a la ~** (*Andes, Cono Sur*) boiled egg ► **copa balón** balloon glass, brandy glass ► **copa de champán** champagne glass ...
4 (*Dep*) (= *trofeo, competición*) cup ► **Copa de Europa** European Cup ► **Copa del Mundo** World Cup ► **Copa del Rey** (*Esp*) *Spanish FA Cup*

Phrasal verbs

Phrasal verbs like **light up**, **show off** etc are listed in their own alphabetical sequence at the end of the entry for the main verb and are highlighted by a triangle symbol ►.

They are classified according to the following part of speech categories:-

VT + ADV	phrasal verbs with the patterns: **he took the lid off** **he took off the lid**
VI + ADV	phrasal verbs with the pattern: **the seat comes off**
VT + PREP	phrasal verbs with the pattern: **her new hairstyle takes ten years off her**
VI + PREP	phrasal verbs with the pattern: **she came off her bike**

Where the phrasal verb form is identical in one meaning to a category of the main verb, it may be included in the main verb entry.

Verbos frasales

Los verbos frasales como **light up**, **show off**, etc aparecen por orden alfabético al final de la entrada del verbo principal, marcados por un triángulo azul ►.

Se les clasifica según las siguientes categorías gramaticales:

VT + ADV	verbos frasales con las estructuras: **he took the lid off** **he took off the lid**
VI + ADV	verbos frasales con la estructura: **the seat comes off**
VT + PREP	verbos frasales con la estructura: **her new hairstyle takes ten years off her**
VI + PREP	verbos frasales con la estructura: **she came off her bike**

Cuando el verbo frasal tiene el mismo significado que una de las categorías del verbo principal, puede ir incluido en la entrada de este último. Por ej., véase

hobble ['hɒbl] ...
Ⓒ VI (*also* **to ~ along**) cojear, andar cojeando; **to ~ to the door** ir cojeando a la puerta

Literal verb and preposition combinations are usually included in the entry for the main verb.

La combinación literal de verbo más preposición suele aparecer incluida en la entrada del verbo principal.

pound[2]
Ⓑ VI ...
2 (= *strike*) **the sea ~ed against** *or* **on the rocks** el mar azotaba las rocas *or* batía contra las rocas; **somebody began ~ing at** *or* **on the door** alguien empezó a aporrear la puerta;

In the case of less common adverbs and prepositions the phrase may well appear under the adverb or preposition.

En el caso de los adverbios y preposiciones menos frecuentes la expresión puede estar en la entrada del adverbio o de la preposición.

astern [ə'stɜ:n] ADV (*Naut*) a popa; **to fall ~** quedarse atrás; **to go ~** ciar, ir hacia atrás; **to make a boat fast ~** amarrar un barco por la popa; **~ of** detrás de

Plurals

Irregular plural forms of English nouns are given on the English-Spanish side while those of Spanish nouns are given on the Spanish-English side.

Plural inflections for Spanish nouns are shown where the following rules do not apply:

a) If a Spanish noun ends in a vowel it takes **-s** in the plural (e.g. **casa-s**, **tribu-s**).

Plurales

Los plurales irregulares de las entradas inglesas aparecen en la sección de inglés-español, mientras que los plurales irregulares de las entradas españolas aparecen en la sección de español-inglés.

Se han incluido los plurales de los sustantivos españoles que no siguen las siguientes normas:

a) Si el sustantivo termina en vocal se añade **-s** para formar el plural (p.ej. **casa-s**, **tribu-s**).

b) If it ends in a consonant (including for this purpose **y**) it takes **-es** in the plural (e.g. **pared-es**, **árbol-es**).

c) Nouns that end in stressed **í** take **-es** in the plural (e.g. **rubí-rubíes**). Exception: **esquí-esquís**.

d) Nouns that end in **-z** change this to **c** and add **-es** in the plural (e.g. **luz-luces**; **paz-paces**). The pronunciation is not affected.

e) The accent which is written on a number of endings of singular nouns is not needed in the plural (e.g. **nación-naciones**, **patán-patanes**, **inglés-ingleses**). Some words having no written accent in the singular need one in the plural (e.g. **crimen-crímenes**, **joven-jóvenes**).

There is little agreement about the plural of recent anglicisms and gallicisms, and some latinisms. Each case is treated separately in the dictionary.

Noun plurals in English are indicated after the headword only when they are truly irregular (e.g. **ox-oxen**), and in the few cases where a word in **-o** takes a plural in **-oes** (e.g. **potato-es**). In all other cases the basic rules apply:

a) Most English nouns take **-s** in the plural: **bed-s**, **site-s**, **photo-s**.

b) Nouns that end in **-s**, **-x**, **-z**, **-sh** and some in **-ch** [tʃ] take **-es** in the plural: **boss-es**, **box-es**, **dish-es**, **patch-es**.

c) Nouns that end in **-y** not preceded by a vowel change the **-y** to **-ies** in the plural: **lady-ladies**, **berry-berries** (but **tray-s**, **key-s**).

b) Si termina en consonante (la **y** se considera como consonante en esta posición) se añade **-es** para formar el plural (p.ej. **pared-es**, **árbol-es**).

c) Los sustantivos que terminan en **-í** acentuada forman el plural añadiendo **-es** (p.ej. **rubí-rubíes**). Excepción: **esquí-esquís**.

d) Los sustantivos que terminan en **-z** la cambian en **c** en plural (p.ej. **luz-luces; paz-paces**). Esto no afecta a la pronunciación.

e) La tilde de algunas terminaciones de los sustantivos en singular se suprime en el plural (p.ej. **nación-naciones**, **patán-patanes**, **inglés-ingleses**). Algunas palabras que no llevan tilde en singular la tienen en plural (p.ej. **crimen-crímenes**).

Debido a la confusión reinante en cuanto a la forma plural de los anglicismos y galicismos de reciente acuñación y de algún latinismo, se trata separadamente cada caso.

Los plurales de los sustantivos ingleses se incluyen tras el lema sólo cuando son irregulares (p.ej. **ox-oxen**), y en los pocos casos en los que una palabra terminada en **-o** forma el plural en **-oes** (p.ej. **potato-es**). En los demás casos se aplican las siguientes reglas:

a) La mayor parte de los sustantivos en inglés forman el plural añadiendo **-s**: **bed-s**, **site-s**, **photo-s**.

b) Los sustantivos terminados en **-s, -x, -z, -sh** y algunos en **-ch** [tʃ] forman el plural añadiendo **-es**: **boss-es**, **box-es**, **dish-es**, **patch-es**.

c) Los sustantivos terminados en **-y** no precedida por vocal forman el plural cambiando la **-y** en **-ies**: **lady-ladies**, **berry-berries** (pero **tray-s**, **key-s**).

Plural forms of the headword which differ substantially from the singular form are listed in their alphabetical place in the word list with a cross-reference, and repeated under the singular form.

Cuando es radicalmente distinto del singular, el plural aparece como entrada independiente con una remisión al singular, en donde aparecen ambas formas.

children ['tʃɪldrən] NPL *of* **child**

Spanish nouns which are invariable in the plural are marked INV or inv.

Los sustantivos españoles cuyo plural es idéntico al singular llevan la marca INV o inv.

campus SM INV (*Univ*) campus

bottle ... ► **bottle opener** N abrebotellas *m inv*, destapador *m*

Verbs

All Spanish verb headwords are referred by number and letter (e.g. ▸1a◂, ▸2e◂) to the table of verb paradigms on pages 2118-2125. In a few cases in which verbs have slight irregularities or are defective, the fact is noted after the headword. English irregular or strong verbs have their principal parts noted in bold face after the headword; these are also listed on pages 2128-2129. Minor variations of spelling are listed on page 2130.

Verbos

Los verbos españoles llevan una remisión en número y letra (p.ej.▸1a◂, ▸2e◂) al cuadro de conjugaciones en las págs. 2118-2125. En los casos en los que el verbo es ligeramente irregular o defectivo, se nota tal hecho en la entrada. El pretérito y el participio de pasado de los verbos irregulares ingleses aparecen tras el lema en negrita y puede verse la lista de dichos verbos en las págs. 2128-2129. Las irregularidades ortográficas de los verbos ingleses constan en la pág. 2130.

Comparatives and superlatives

Where English adjectives have common inflected comparative and superlative forms, these are shown in the entry on the English-Spanish side.

Comparativos y superlativos

El comparativo y el superlativo de los adjetivos ingleses se incluyen en la entrada en la sección de inglés-español si son de uso frecuente.

easy ['i:zɪ] Ⓐ ADJ (*compar* **easier**; *superl* **easiest**)

Masculine and feminine nouns

On the Spanish-English side, parallel senses of nouns which change their endings predictably depending on whether they refer to a male or a female (e.g. **abuelo/abuela**, **profesor/profesora**) are treated under the entry for the masculine form even if there is also a separate entry for the feminine form in which other senses are treated.

Sustantivos masculinos y femeninos

Si el sustantivo tiene terminaciones de masculino y femenino, se incluyen bajo la forma del masculino las acepciones comunes (por ej.: **abuelo/abuela**, **profesor/profesora**). Las acepciones específicas del femenino aparecen como entradas independientes.

prima SF [1] [*de seguro*] premium
[2] (= *gratificación*)

primo/a Ⓐ ADJ [1] [*número*] prime
Ⓑ SM/F [1] (= *pariente*) cousin;

Where a translation of a Spanish noun referring to a person varies depending on whether the referent is male or female, the masculine translation is separated from the feminine translation by a slash where this is not confusing.

Cuando las traducciones para el masculino y el femenino son distintas, aparecen separadas por una barra si la traducción así dada no lleva a confusión.

francés/esa ...
Ⓑ SM/F Frenchman/Frenchwoman

Gender information

On both sides of the dictionary gender information is given for Spanish nouns.

English side

masculine noun (e.g. coche *m*)	m	sustantivo masculino (p.ej.: coche *m*)
feminine noun (e.g. aceituna *f*)	f	sustantivo femenino (p.ej.: aceituna *f*)
noun which is identical for masculine and feminine (e.g. hablante *mf*)	mf	sustantivo invariable en género (p.ej.: hablante *mf*)
masculine or feminine noun depending on the ending selected (e.g. profesor(a) *m/f*, niño/a *m/f*)	m/f	sustantivo masculino o femenino, según la terminación (p.ej.: profesor(a) *m/f*, niño/a *m/f*)
noun which can be either masculine or feminine (e.g. azúcar *m or f*)	m or f	sustantivo que puede ser masculino o femenino (p.ej.: azúcar *m or f*)
masculine noun used in the singular unlike the English (e.g. **capital assets** NPL activo *msing* fijo)	msing	sustantivo masculino usado en singular, a diferencia del inglés (p.ej.: **capital assets** NPL activo *msing* fijo)
feminine noun used in the singular unlike the English (e.g. **cash reserves** NPL reserva *fsing* en efectivo)	fsing	sustantivo femenino usado en singular, a diferencia del inglés (p.ej.: **cash reserves** NPL reserva *fsing* en efectivo)
masculine plural noun (e.g. consejos *mpl*)	mpl	sustantivo masculino plural (p.ej.: consejos *mpl*)
feminine plural noun (e.g. golosinas *fpl*)	fpl	sustantivo femenino plural (p.ej.: golosinas *fpl*)
masculine noun optionally used in the plural with the same meaning (e.g. remordimiento(s) *m(pl)*)	m (pl)	sustantivo masculino usado en ocasiones en plural con el mismo significado (p.ej.: remordimiento(s) *m(pl)*)
feminine noun optionally used in the plural with the same meaning (e.g. pasta(s) *f(pl)*)	f (pl)	sustantivo femenino usado en ocasiones en plural con el mismo significado (p.ej.: pasta(s) *f(pl)*)

Spanish side

masculine noun (e.g. **coche** SM)	SM	sustantivo masculino (p.ej.: **coche** SM)
feminine noun (e.g. **aceituna** SM)	SF	sustantivo femenino (p.ej.: **aceituna** SF)
noun which is identical for masculine and feminine (e.g. **hablante** SMF)	SMF	sustantivo invariable en género (p.ej.: **hablante** SMF)
masculine or feminine noun depending on the ending selected (e.g. **profesor(a)** SM/F, **tío/a** SM/F)	SM/F	sustantivo masculino o femenino, según la terminación (p.ej.: **profesor(a)** SM/F, **tío/a** SM/F)
masculine or feminine noun (e.g. **azúcar** SM O SF)	SM O SF	sustantivo masculino o femenino (p.ej.: **azúcar** SM O SF)
masculine plural noun (e.g. **alicates** SMPL)	SMPL	sustantivo masculino plural (p.ej.: **alicates** SMPL)
feminine plural noun (e.g. **afueras** SFPL)	SFPL	sustantivo femenino plural (p.ej.: **afueras** SFPL)

Gender in examples

Where a Spanish example is ambiguous as to the gender of the subject of a verb in the third person singular, either "he" or "she" may have been used in the translation to try to reflect the gender balance in the real world.

Attributive use

Where a Spanish adjective is translated by a noun modifier in English which can only be used before the noun, this is labelled *antes de s*.

papelero/a Ⓐ ADJ **1** (*Com*) paper *antes de s*

Regional labels

Words and expressions which are restricted to particular areas of the English- or Spanish-speaking worlds are marked as such:

ENGLISH REGIONAL LABELS

Australia
Brit (= Britain)
Canada
EEUU[1] (= United States of America)
Engl (= England)
Escocia[1] (= Scotland)
Irl (= Ireland)
N Engl (= North of England)
New Zealand (= New Zealand)
Scot[2] (= Scotland)
US[2] (= United States of America)

[1] Spanish-English side only
[2] English-Spanish side only

El género

Se da información sobre el género de los sustantivos españoles en ambas partes del diccionario.

El género en los ejemplos

Cuando el género es ambiguo en los ejemplos españoles en los que se usa la forma de tercera persona del singular, la traducción al inglés puede ser tanto "he" como "she", en un intento de reflejar de esta forma el uso del género existente en la realidad.

Uso aposicional

Cuando un adjetivo español se traduce por un sustantivo inglés que funciona como modificador de otro sustantivo y por lo tanto sólo puede ir antes del mismo, este hecho se indica tras la traducción.

Marcas de región

Aparecen marcadas como tales aquellas palabras y expresiones cuyo uso en el mundo anglófono o hispanohablante es restringido a una región determinada.

MARCAS DE REGIÓN PARA EL INGLÉS

Australia
Brit (= Reino Unido)
Canada
EEUU[1] (= Estados Unidos de América)
Engl (= Inglaterra)
Escocia[1]
Irl (= Irlanda)
N Engl (= norte de Inglaterra)
New Zealand (= Nueva Zelanda)
Scot[2] (Escocia)
US[2] (= Estados Unidos de América)

[1] en la sección de español-inglés
[2] en la sección de inglés-español

SPANISH REGIONAL LABELS

And (= Andes region: Bolivia, Chile, Colombia, Ecuador, Peru)
Ant (= Antilles)
Arg (= Argentina)
Bol (= Bolivia)
CAm (= Central America: Costa Rica, El Salvador, Guatemala, Honduras, Nicaragua)
Caribe (Caribbean: Cuba, Puerto Rico, Santo Domingo, Panama, Venezuela)
Chile
Col (= Colombia)
Cono Sur[1] (= Southern Cone: Argentina, Chile, Paraguay, Uruguay)
Costa Rica
Cuba
Ecu (= Ecuador)
El Salvador
Esp[1] (= Spain)
Guat (= Guatemala)
Hond (= Honduras)
LAm (= Latin America: generally applicable to the whole region)
Mex[2]/Méx[1] (= Mexico)
Nic (= Nicaragua)
Pan (= Panama)
Par (= Paraguay)
Peru[2]
Puerto Rico
Santo Domingo
S. Cone[2] (= Southern Cone: Argentina, Chile, Paraguay, Uruguay)
Sp[2] (= Spain)
Uru (= Uruguay)
Ven (= Venezuela)

[1] Spanish-English side only
[2] English-Spanish side only

If the word is used particularly in a region, the regional label includes *esp* for especially: *esp LAm, esp Brit*

MARCAS DE REGIÓN PARA EL ESPAÑOL

And (= región andina: Bolivia, Chile, Colombia, Ecuador, Perú)
Ant (= Antillas)
Arg (= Argentina)
Bol (= Bolivia)
CAm (= Centroamérica: Costa Rica, El Salvador, Guatemala, Honduras, Nicaragua)
Caribe (Caribe: Cuba, Puerto Rico, Santo Domingo, Panamá, Venezuela)
Chile
Col (= Colombia)
Cono Sur[1] (= Cono Sur: Argentina, Chile, Paraguay, Uruguay)
Costa Rica
Cuba
Ecu (= Ecuador)
El Salvador
Esp[1] (= España)
Guat (= Guatemala)
Hond (= Honduras)
LAm (= Latinoamérica)
Mex[2]/Méx[1] (= México)
Nic (= Nicaragua)
Pan (= Panamá)
Par (= Paraguay)
Perú[1]
Puerto Rico
Santo Domingo
S. Cone[2] (= Cono Sur : Argentina, Chile, Paraguay, Uruguay)
Sp[2] (= España)
Uru (= Uruguay)
Ven (= Venezuela)

[1] en la sección de español-inglés
[2] en la sección de inglés-español

Si una palabra o expresión se usa especialmente en una región, la marca de región puede incluir la abreviatura *esp: esp LAm, esp Brit*

Indicating material

General indicating material takes the following forms:

In square brackets [ ]

1. Within verb entries, typical noun subjects of the headword.

Material indicador

Puede aparecer de las siguientes formas:

Entre corchetes [ ]

1. Dentro de los verbos, para los sustantivos que funcionan como sujeto de los mismos.

stop [stɒp] …
Ⓒ VI [1] (= *stop moving*) [*person, vehicle*] pararse, detenerse; [*clock, watch*] pararse;

parir ▸conjug 3a◂ Ⓐ VI [*mujer*] to give birth, have a baby; [*yegua*] to foal; [*vaca*] to calve; [*cerda*] to farrow; [*perra*] to pup;

2. Within noun entries, typical noun complements of the headword.

2. Dentro de los sustantivos, para los complementos nominales de dichos sustantivos.

bottom [ˈbɒtəm] Ⓐ N [1] [*of box, cup, sea, river, garden*] fondo *m*; [*of stairs, page, mountain, tree*] pie *m*; [*of list, class*] último/a *m/f*; [*of foot*] planta *f*; [*of shoe*] suela *f*; [*of chair*] asiento *m*;

tapa SF [1] [*de caja, olla, piano*] lid; [*de frasco*] top; [*de depósito de gasolina*] cap;
[2] [*de libro*] cover;
[3] [*de zapato*] heelplate

3. Typical noun complements of adjectives.

3. Dentro de los adjetivos, para los sustantivos a los que suelen modificar dichos adjetivos.

soft [sɒft] Ⓐ ADJ …
[1] (= *not hard*) [*ground, water, cheese, pencil, contact lens*] blando; [*bed, mattress, pillow*] blando, mullido; [*metal*] maleable, dúctil;

duro/a Ⓐ ADJ [1] (= *resistente*) [*material, superficie, cama, agua*] hard; [*cable, alambre*] stiff; [*pan*] hard, stale; [*carne*] tough; [*legumbres*] hard; [*articulación, mecanismo*] stiff; [*músculo*] firm, hard;

4. Typical verb or adjective complements of adverbs.

4. Dentro de los adverbios, para los verbos o adjetivos a los que suelen modificar dichos adverbios.

softly ['sɒftlɪ] ADV [1] (= *quietly*) [*walk, move*] silenciosamente, sin hacer ruido; [*say*] bajito, en voz baja; [*whistle*] bajito;

dulcemente ADV [*sonreír, cantar*] sweetly; [*acariciar*] gently; [*amar*] tenderly, fondly; [*contestar*] gently, softly

In square brackets with +

Typical objects of verbs or of prepositions.

Entre corchetes con el signo +

Complemento nominal de verbos o preposiciones.

water ...
Ⓑ VT [+ *garden, plant*] regar; [+ *horses, cattle*] abrevar, dar de beber a; [+ *wine*] aguar, diluir,

crear ▸conjug 1a◂ VT [1] (= *hacer, producir*) [+ *obra, objeto, empleo*] to create; ...
[2] (= *establecer*) [+ *comisión, comité, fondo, negocio, sistema*] to set up; [+ *asociación, cooperativa*] to form, set up;

►**abide by** VI + PREP [+ *rules*] atenerse a, obrar de acuerdo con; [+ *promise*] cumplir con; [+ *decision*] respetar, atenerse a; [+ *rules of competition*] ajustarse a, aceptar

In parentheses with =

Synonyms and mini-definitions.

Entre paréntesis con el signo =

Sinónimos y mini-definiciones.

wood ... Ⓐ N [1] (= *material*)
[2] (= *firewood*) leña *f*
[3] (= *forest*) bosque *m*;

oliva Ⓐ SF [1] (= *aceituna*) olive;
[2] (= *árbol*) olive tree

In parentheses ( )

Other information and hints which guide the user.

Entre paréntesis ( )

Otro tipo de información que oriente al usuario.

rise ... Ⓐ N [1] ...
(*in tone, pitch*) subida *f*, elevación *f*; ...
[2] (= *increase*) (*in number, rate, value*) aumento *m*; (*in price, temperature*) subida *f*, aumento *m*; (*Brit*) (*in salary*) aumento *m* (de sueldo);

pintar ... Ⓐ VT [1] (*Arte*) (*con óleo, acuarela*) to paint; (*con lápices, rotuladores*) (= *dibujar*) to draw;

Other indicators

Cultural equivalent sign ≈: is used when the source language headword or phrase has no precise equivalent in the target language and is therefore untranslatable. In such cases the nearest cultural equivalent is given.

Otros indicadores

Signo de equivalencia cultural ≈: usado cuando la entrada en la lengua origen no tiene un equivalente preciso en la traducción, por lo que es intraducible. En tal caso se da el equivalente cultural más próxima.

national ...
► **National Insurance** N (*Brit*) ≈ Seguridad *f* Social; ... ► **the National Lottery** N (*Brit*) ≈ la lotería primitiva

ITV SF ABR (*Esp*) (= **Inspección Técnica de Vehículos**) ≈ MOT

An explanatory gloss (in italics) is given in cases where there is no cultural equivalent in the target language.

Si no hay un equivalente cultural en la lengua término se da una explicación en cursiva en dicha lengua.

RP Ⓐ N ABBR ... *pronunciación estándar del inglés*; ...

N² ... **20-N** *20th November, day of Franco's death*

Field labels

Labels indicating subject fields occur in the following cases:

Marcas de campo semántico

Se usan dichas marcas en los siguientes casos:

muñeca SF [1] (*Anat*) wrist

1. To differentiate various meanings of the headword.
2. When the meaning in the source language is clear but may be ambiguous in the target language.

1. Para diferenciar distintas acepciones de una palabra.
2. Cuando el significado en la lengua origen está claro pero puede ser ambiguo en la traducción.

retention [rɪ'tenʃən] N retención *f* (*also Med*)

cimera SF crest (*tb Heráldica*)

3. When a word is a technical word in the field in question.

3. Cuando se trata de una acepción técnica.

veer ... VI ... [*wind*] cambiar de dirección, rolar (*Met, Naut*);

A full list of the abbreviated field labels is given on the inside covers of the dictionary.

Puede verse la lista completa de las abreviaturas de campo semántico en el interior de las cubiertas del diccionario.

Style labels

A dozen or so indicators of register are used to mark non-neutral words and expressions. These indicators are given for both source and target language and serve mainly as a warning to the reader using the foreign language. The following paragraphs explain the meaning of the most common style labels, of which a complete list is given with explanations on the inside covers of the dictionary.

(i) The abbreviation *frm* (for formal) denotes formal language such as that used on an official form, in pronouncements and other formal communications.

Marcas de estilo

Se usan una serie de indicadores de registro como marcas de palabras y expresiones sin un registro neutro para la lengua origen y para la traducción. Estas marcas sirven principalmente de advertencia para el lector que use el idioma extranjero. Los siguientes párrafos explican el significado de las marcas de estilo más frecuentes, cuya lista completa puede verse en el interior de las cubiertas del diccionario.

(i) La abreviatura *frm* (de formal) denota un lenguaje usado en contextos formales como impresos oficiales, declaraciones y comunicados.

heretofore [ˌhɪətʊ'fɔːʳ] ADV (*frm*) (= *up to specified point*) hasta aquí; (= *up to now*) hasta ahora, hasta este momento; (= *previously*) con anterioridad

colegir ▸conjug 3c, 3k◂ (*frm*) VT [1] (= *juntar*) to collect, gather

(ii) * indicates that the expression, while not forming part of standard language, is used by all educated speakers in a relaxed situation, but would not be used in a formal essay or letter, or on an occasion when the speaker wishes to impress.

(ii) El asterisco * indica que la expresión no forma parte del lenguaje neutro, pero es usada en conversaciones y en la vida privada por todos los hablantes, aunque no se usaría en un ensayo, una carta oficial o en una ocasión en la que el hablante desee crear una impresión especial.

bomb ...
►**bomb along** * VI + ADV ir a toda marcha*, ir a toda hostia (*Sp**);

chollo* SM [1] (= *buena oportunidad*) snip*, bargain;

(iii) ⁑ indicates that the expression is used by some but not all educated speakers in a very relaxed situation. Such words should be handled with extreme care by the non-native speaker unless they are very fluent in the language and very sure of their company.

(iii) Dos asteriscos ⁑ indican que no todos los hablantes cultos usan en la vida privada la expresión a la que se refieren. Tales palabras o expresiones han de ser usadas con precaución por los hablantes no nativos a no ser que tengan un amplio dominio del idioma y conozcan bien a sus interlocutores.

clink[2]⁑ [klɪŋk] N (= *jail*) trena⁑ *f*

agua SF ... **mear ~ bendita**⁑ to be a holy Joe*;

(iv) ⁂ means "Danger!" Such words are liable to offend in any situation, and therefore are to be avoided by the non-native speaker.

(iv) Tres asteriscos ⁂ indican ¡peligro!. Tales palabras o expresiones pueden resultar ofensivas en una situación determinada y por lo tanto es preferible que los hablantes no nativos las eviten.

dick ... N...
[2] (⁂) polla *f* (*Sp*⁂), verga⁂ *f*

polla SF ...
[2] (⁂) (= *pene*) prick⁂;

(v) † denotes old-fashioned terms which are no longer in wide current use but which the foreign user will certainly find in reading, or may encounter in humorous use.

(v) † indica que un término es anticuado, apenas se usa en el lenguaje de hoy día, aunque pueden encontrarse en la literatura o en contextos humorísticos.

dashed†* [dæʃt] ADJ (*euph*) = **damned A2**

edad SF ... **estar en ~ de merecer**† to be of courting age†;

(vi) †† denotes obsolete words which the user will normally find in literature, or may encounter in humorous use.

(vi) †† denota palabras arcaicas que se pueden encontrar en la literatura o en contextos humorísticos.

amancebado†† ADJ **estar** *o* **vivir ~s** to live together, cohabit

(vii) *liter* denotes an expression which belongs to literary language.

(vii) *liter* indica que una expresión pertenece al lenguage literario.

past ...
Ⓒ ADJ **...**
[4] (*= over*) **... in <u>times</u> ~** antiguamente, antaño (*liter*)

(viii) The labels and symbols above are used to mark either an individual word or phrase, or a whole category, or even a complete entry. Where a headword is marked with asterisks, any phrases in the entry will only have asterisks if they are of a different register from the headword. All English compounds are marked even if their register is the same as that of the headword.

Where individual phrases rather than the whole entry or category are stylistically marked, the style label is included after the phrase in question.

(viii) Las marcas y símbolos que se acaban de explicar pueden ir acompañando a una palabra, una expresión, una categoría o toda una entrada. Si el lema lleva asteriscos, las frases incluidas en esa entrada sólo llevan asteriscos si tienen un registro diferente del lema. Todos los compuestos ingleses llevan la marca de registro aunque este sea el mismo que el del lema.

Si se trata de expresiones individuales, no de toda la entrada o categoría, la marca de estilo aparece al final de dichas expresiones.

eye ... Ⓐ N [1] **... to make (sheep's) ~s at sb*** lanzar miraditas insinuantes a algn, hacer ojitos a algn*; **...**

Note that the second informal * refers only to *hacer ojitos a algn* and not to the translation given before the comma.

Where a phrase contains alternatives and both/all are stylistically marked, the register is shown at the end of the phrase.

El segundo asterisco sólo se refiere a *hacer ojitos a algn* y no a la traducción dada antes de la coma.

Si la frase incluye otras alternativas, se marca el registro al final de la frase si este se aplica a todas las variantes.

cabeza ... SF **... andar** *o* **ir de ~***

Where a phrase contains alternatives and only one is stylistically marked, the register is shown as follows.

Si sólo una de las variantes necesita la marca de registro, ésta aparece como sigue:

apurada* SF (*LAm*) **¿por qué no te echas** *o* **pegas una ~?** why don't you get a move on* *o* hurry up?;

(only the first is informal)

(sólo la primera es informal)

acostumbrado ADJ **... ya estoy ~ a que no me entiendan** I'm used to *o* (*frm*) accustomed to not being understood

(only the second is formal)

The user should not confuse the style label *liter* with the field label *Literat* which indicates that the term or expression so labelled belongs to the field of literature. Similarly, the user should note that the abbreviation *lit* indicates the literal as opposed to the figurative meaning of a word.

(sólo la segunda es formal)

Conviene tener en cuenta que no significan lo mismo la marca de estilo *liter* y la marca de campo semántico *Literat*, que indica que se trata de un término o expresión perteneciente al campo de la literatura. Del mismo modo, hay que recordar que la abreviatura *lit* indica que se trata del sentido literal de una palabra, no del figurado.

Punctuation

A comma is used to separate translations which have the same or very similar meanings.

Puntuación

Se usa una coma para separar las traducciones que tienen el mismo significado, o con un significado muy similar.

perhaps ... ADV quizá(s), tal vez;
claro Ⓐ ADJ **...** [*color*] light, pale;

A semi-colon separates translations which are not interchangeable. Indicators are given to differentiate between non-interchangeable translations.

El punto y coma separa traducciones que no son intercambiables. Se dan indicadores para diferenciar estas traducciones.

chair ... (*gen*) silla *f*; (*= armchair*) sillón *m*, butaca *f*; (*= wheelchair*) silla *f* (de ruedas); (*= seat*) lugar *m*, asiento *m*;
asesinar ... VT [1] (*= matar*) to murder; (*Pol*) to assassinate

Alternative parts of phrases and translations are preceded by *or* (English-Spanish side) or *o* (Spanish-English side).

Las variantes de una frase o traducción aparecen precedidas de *or* en la sección de inglés-español y de *o* en la sección de español-inglés.

fall ...
Ⓑ VI [1] **... to ~ to** *or* **on one's <u>knees</u>** arrodillarse, caer de rodillas;
cabeza ... SF **... andar** *o* **ir de ~***

An oblique / indicates alternatives in source language which are reflected exactly in the target language.

La barra indica alternativas en la lengua origen que se ven reflejadas igualmente en la lengua término.

fact-finding ... ADJ **on a ~ tour/mission**
en viaje/misión de reconocimiento;

On the Spanish-English side an oblique is also used to indicate that the translation differs depending on whether the referent is male or female.

También se usa para separar las traducciones de masculino y femenino en la sección de español-inglés.

inglés/esa ...
Ⓑ SM/F Englishman/Englishwoman;

Parentheses within illustrative phrases or their translations indicate that the material contained within them is optional.

El paréntesis dentro de las frases ilustrativas o de sus traducciones indica que el material contenido en ellos es opcional.

Fahrenheit ...
CPD ► **Fahrenheit thermometer** N termómetro *m* de (grados) Fahrenheit

Equivalent phrases are separated by a lozenge ◊.

Las frases equivalentes aparecen separadas por un rombo ◊.

charge ... to ~ sth (up) to sb ◊ ~ sth (up) to sb's account

Cross-references

These are used to refer the user to the headword under which a certain compound, idiom or phrase has been treated (see **Idioms, proverbs and set phrases** above).

Remisiones

Se usan para enviar al usuario a las entradas en las que se encuentran otros compuestos, modismos y expresiones que incluyen la palabra en cuestión (véase más arriba **Modismos, refranes y expresiones**).

purse ... N ... *see also* **public A1, silk C**

lechuga SF ... *ver tb* **fresco A6**

They are also used to draw the user's attention to the full treatment of such words as numerals, days of the week and months of the year under certain key words.

También se usan para llamar la atención sobre las entradas en las que podrán encontrarse más frases y ejemplos relacionados con los numerales, los días de la semana y los meses del año.

January ... N enero *m*; *see* **July** *for usage*

The key words which are treated in depth are:
English: **five**, **fifth**, **Tuesday**, **July**
Spanish: **seis**, **seiscientos**, **sexto**, **sábado**, **septiembre**

Dichas entradas son:
Inglés: **five**, **fifth**, **Tuesday**, **July**
Español: **seis**, **seiscientos**, **sexto**, **sábado**, **septiembre**

References at the foot of the page

If a word you are looking up has a triangle ▼ next to it in the margin, you will find the word repeated at the foot of the page, together with a number or numbers referring you to relevant topics in **Language in Use**. For example:

Remisiones a pie de página

Si la palabra que se busca tiene un triángulo ▼ junto a ella al margen, se encontrará a pie de página una remisión de dicha palabra a una sección de **Lengua y Uso** en la que se tratan aspectos relevantes a ella. Por ej.:

▼ **abrazo** ...

➤ LENGUA Y USO: **abrazo 2** 48.2

synonym

sinónimo

IPA phonetics

transcripción fonética

homograph number

número de homógrafo

phrasal verb marked by ►

verbo frasal marcado con ►

~ replaces headword

~ sustituye al lema

cross-reference

remisión a otra entrada

compounds marked by ►

compuestos marcados con ►

old-fashioned

anticuado

American English

inglés americano

⁑ very informal

⁑ muy familiar

dally ['dælɪ] VI [1] (= *dawdle*) tardar; **to ~ over sth** perder el tiempo con algo; *see also* **dilly-dally**

[2] (= *amuse o.s.*) divertirse; **to ~ with** [+ *lover*] coquetear con, tener escarceos amorosos con; [+ *idea*] entretenerse con

Dalmatia [dæl'meɪʃə] N Dalmacia *f*

Dalmatian [dæl'meɪʃən] Ⓐ N (= *person*) dálmata *mf*

Ⓑ ADJ dálmata

dalmatian [dæl'meɪʃən] N (= *dog*) perro *m* dálmata

daltonism ['dɔːltənɪzəm] N daltonismo *m*

dam[1] [dæm] Ⓐ N (= *wall*) dique *m*, presa *f*; (= *reservoir*) presa *f*, embalse *m*

Ⓑ VT (*also* **~ up**) poner un dique a, represar; (*fig*) reprimir, contener

► **dam up** VT + ADV = **dam B**

dam[2]⁑ [dæm] ADJ = **damn D, damned A2**

dam[3] [dæm] N (*Zool*) madre *f*

damage ['dæmɪdʒ] Ⓐ N [1] (*gen*) daño *m*; (*visible, eg on car*) desperfectos *mpl*; (*to building, area*) daños *pl*; **to do** *or* **cause ~ to** [+ *building*] causar daños a; [+ *machine*] causar desperfectos en; **the bomb did a lot of ~** la bomba causó muchos daños; **not much ~ was caused to the car** el coche no sufrió grandes desperfectos

[2] (*fig*) (*to chances, reputation etc*) perjuicio *m*, daño *m*; **to do** *or* **cause ~ to sth/sb** causar perjuicio a algo/algn, perjudicar algo/a algn; **the ~ is done** el daño ya está hecho; ✦*IDIOM* **what's the ~?*** (= *cost*) ¿cuánto va a ser?, ¿qué se debe?

[3] **damages** (*Jur*) daños *mpl* y perjuicios; *see also* **recover A2**

Ⓑ VT (= *harm*) dañar; [+ *machine*] averiar, causar desperfectos en; [+ *health, chances, reputation*] perjudicar; **to be ~d in a collision** sufrir daños en un choque

Ⓒ CPD ► **damage limitation exercise** N campaña *f* para minimizar los daños

damaging ['dæmɪdʒɪŋ] ADJ (*gen*) dañino; (*fig*) perjudicial (**to** para)

damascene ['dæməsiːn] Ⓐ ADJ damasquinado, damasquino

Ⓑ VT damasquinar

Damascus [də'mɑːskəs] N Damasco *m*

damask ['dæməsk] Ⓐ ADJ [*cloth*] adamascado; [*steel*] damasquinado

Ⓑ N (= *cloth*) damasco *m*; (= *steel*) acero *m* damasquinado

Ⓒ VT [+ *cloth*] adamascar; [+ *steel*] damasquinar

Ⓓ CPD ► **damask rose** N rosa *f* de Damasco

dame [deɪm] N [1] **Dame** (*Brit*) (= *title*) *título aristocrático para mujeres equivalente a "sir"*

[2] (*esp Brit*†) dama *f*, señora *f*; (*Brit Theat*) *personaje de mujer anciana en las pantomimas británicas interpretado por un actor*; → PANTOMIME

[3] (*US*†*) (= *woman*) tía* *f*, gachí *f* (*Sp*⁑)

damfool⁑ ['dæm'fuːl] ADJ = **damn-fool**

dammit⁑ ['dæmɪt] EXCL ¡maldita sea!*; ✦*IDIOM* **as near as ~** (*Brit*) casi, por un pelo

damn [dæm] Ⓐ VT [1] (*Rel*) (= *condemn*) condenar; **the effort was ~ed from the start** desde el principio el intento estaba condenado a fracasar; **the critics ~ed the book** los críticos pusieron *or* tiraron el libro por los suelos; **I'll see him ~ed first** antes lo veré colgado; ✦*IDIOM* **to ~ sth/sb with faint praise** despachar algo/a algn con tímidos elogios

[2] (= *swear at*) maldecir

[3] (⁑) (*in exclamations*) **~ it!** ¡maldita sea!*; **him/you!** ¡maldito sea/seas!*; **~ this car!** ¡al diablo con este coche!; **well I'll be ~ed!** ¡ca-

Spanish gender

género en español

letters for different parts of speech

letras para las distintas categorías gramaticales

numbers for different senses

números para las distintas acepciones

typical objects of verb

típicos objetos del verbo

cross-reference to cultural note

remisión a nota cultural

Peninsular Spanish

español peninsular

British English

inglés británico

remisión a la tabla de conjugaciones

reference to verb tables

inglés americano

American English

refrán

proverb

* familiar

* informal

= sinónimo

= synonym

expresión fija con una palabra subrayada

highlighted word in set expression

modismos

idioms

español de América

Latin American Spanish

compuestos marcados con ►

compounds marked by ►

aclaración de la traducción

translation clarified

remisiones a otra entrada

cross-references

~ sustituye al lema

~ replaces the headword

callana SF 1 (*LAm Culin*) flat earthenware pan 2 (*Cono Sur hum*) (= *reloj*) pocket watch

callandito* ADV, **callandico*** ADV (= *sin ruido*) softly, very quietly; (= *furtivamente*) stealthily

callar ▸conjug 1a◂ Ⓐ VI 1 (= *dejar de hablar*) to be quiet; **¡calla, que no puedo oír la radio!** be *o* keep quiet, I can't hear the radio!, shut up *o* (*EEUU*) hush up, I can't hear the radio!*; **su madre le mandó ~** his mother ordered him to be quiet, his mother told him to shut up; **—Ernesto se casa —¡calla! ¡eso no puede ser!** "Ernesto is getting married" — "you're joking! that can't be true!"

2 (= *no hablar*) to say nothing, keep quiet; **al principio optó por ~** initially he decided to say nothing *o* keep quiet; **✦REFRÁN quien calla, otorga** silence is *o* gives *o* implies consent

Ⓑ VT 1 (= *hacer callar*) **calló a los niños con un cuento** he got the children to be *o* keep quiet by reading them a story; **reparten dinero para ~ las protestas** they're giving out money to silence *o* quell complaints; **¡calla *o* cállate la boca!*** shut your mouth!*, shut your face!*

2 (= *ocultar*) to keep to o.s., keep quiet; **será mejor ~ este asunto** it's best to keep this matter to ourselves *o* keep this matter quiet

Ⓒ **callarse** VPR 1 (= *dejar de hablar*) to stop talking, go quiet; **al entrar el profesor todos se ~on** when the teacher came in, everyone stopped talking *o* went quiet; **¡cállense, por favor!** please be quiet!; **si empieza a hablar, ya no se calla** once he starts talking, he doesn't stop

2 (= *no decir nada*) to say nothing, keep quiet; **en esas circunstancias es mejor ~se** in those circumstances, it would be best to say nothing *o* keep quiet

calle SF 1 (= *vía pública*) street; (*con más tráfico*) road; **una ~ muy céntrica** a street right in the centre of town; **~ abajo** down the street; **~ arriba** up the street; **✦MODISMOS abrir ~** to make way, clear the way; **echar por la ~ de en medio** to push on, press on regardless; **se los lleva a todos de ~*** they just can't stay away from her, they find her irresistible; **llevar *o* traer a algn por la ~ de la amargura*** to make sb's life a misery* ► **calle cerrada** (*Ven, Col, Méx*), **calle ciega** (*Ven, Col*), **calle cortada** (*Cono Sur*) dead end, dead-end street, cul-de-sac ► **calle de doble sentido** two-way street ► **calle de sentido único, calle de una mano** (*Cono Sur*), **calle de una sola vía** (*Col*), **calle de un solo sentido** (*Chile*) one-way street ► **calle peatonal** pedestrianized street, pedestrian street ► **calle principal** main street ► **calle residencial** residential street (*with low speed limit and priority for pedestrians*) ► **calle sin salida** cul-de-sac, dead end, dead end street; *ver tb* **aplanar A1**, **cabo 2**

2 (= *no casa*) 2.1 **la ~: he estado todo el día en la ~** I've been out all day; **se sentaba en la ~ a ver pasar a la gente** he used to sit out in the street *o* outside watching the people go by; **a los dos días de su detención ya estaba otra vez en la ~** two days after his arrest he was back on the streets again; **el grupo tiene ya tres discos en la ~** the group already have three records out; **irse a la ~** to go out, go outside; **¡iros a la ~ a jugar!** go and play outside!; **salir a la ~** (= *per-*

Ⓓ CPD ► **harvest festival** N fiesta *f* de la cosecha ► **harvest home** N (= *festival*) ≈ fiesta *f* de la cosecha; (= *season*) cosecha *f* ► **harvest moon** N luna *f* llena ► **harvest time** N cosecha *f*, siega *f*

equivalent in Spanish-speaking countries / equivalencia en países hispanohablantes

harvester ['hɑːvɪstəʳ] N 1 (= *person*) [*of cereals*] segador(a) *m/f*; [*of fruit, vegetables*] recolector(a) *m/f*; [*of grapes*] vendimiador(a) *m/f*
2 (= *machine*) cosechadora *f*; (= *combine harvester*) segadora-trilladora *f*

harvesting ['hɑːvɪstɪŋ] N = **harvest A1**

has [hæz] 3RD PERS SING PRESENT *of* **have**

cross-reference / remisión a otra entrada

has-been* ['hæzbiːn] N vieja gloria *f*

• informal / • familiar

hash¹ [hæʃ] Ⓐ N 1 (*Culin*) picadillo *m*
2 (*) lío* *m*, embrollo *m*; **to make a ~ of sth** hacer algo muy mal; **he made a complete ~ of the interview** la entrevista le fue fatal; ✦*IDIOM* **to settle sb's ~** cargarse a algn*
Ⓑ CPD ► **hash browns** NPL *croquetas de patata hervida y cebolla*

explanation (no Spanish equivalent) / explicación (sin equivalencia en español)

hash²* [hæʃ] N (= *hashish*) hachís *m*, chocolate‡ *m* (*Sp*), mota *f* (*CAm**)

Central American Spanish / español de Centroamérica

hash³ [hæʃ] N (*Typ*) almohadilla *f*

specialist field / campo semántico

hashish ['hæʃɪʃ] N hachís *m*

hasn't ['hæznt] = **has not**

hasp [hɑːsp] N (*for padlock*) hembrilla *f*; (*on window*) falleba *f*; (*on box, book*) cierre *m*

Hassidic [hə'sɪdɪk] ADJ hasídico

hassle ['hæsl] Ⓐ N (*) (= *problem, difficulty*) lío *m*, problema *m*; **no ~!** ¡no hay problema!; **it's not worth the ~** no vale la pena
Ⓑ VT molestar, fastidiar

hassock ['hæsək] N (*Rel*) cojín *m*

hast†† [hæst] *see* **have**

archaic / arcaico

haste [heɪst] N prisa *f*, apuro *m* (*LAm*); **to do sth in ~** hacer algo precipitadamente *or* de prisa; **to make ~** darse prisa, apurarse (*LAm*); **to make ~ to do sth** apresurarse a hacer algo; ✦*PROVS* **more ~ less speed** ◊ **make ~ slowly** vísteme despacio que tengo prisa

Latin American Spanish / español de América

proverbs / refranes

hasten ['heɪsn] Ⓐ VT [+ *process*] acelerar; [+ *sb's end, downfall*] precipitar; **to ~ sb's departure** acelerar la partida *or* marcha de algn; **to ~ one's steps** apretar el paso; **to ~ death** precipitar *or* adelantar la muerte
Ⓑ VI apresurarse, darse prisa; **to ~ to do sth** apresurarse a hacer algo; **I ~ to add that …** me apresuro a añadir que …; **she ~ed to assure me that nothing was wrong** se apresuró a asegurarme que no pasaba nada

examples / ejemplos

►**hasten away** VI + ADV marcharse precipitadamente (**from** de)

preposition often used / preposición usada normalmente

►**hasten back** VI + ADV volver con toda prisa

►**hasten on** VI + ADV seguir adelante con toda prisa

hastily ['heɪstɪlɪ] ADV 1 (= *hurriedly*) de prisa, apresuradamente; **I ~ suggested that …** me apresuré a sugerir que …
2 (= *rashly*) [*speak*] precipitadamente; [*judge*] a la ligera

words which commonly co-occur / palabras que se usan a menudo juntas

hasty ['heɪstɪ] ADJ (*compar* **hastier**; *superl* **hastiest**) 1 (= *hurried*) apresurado, precipitado
2 (= *rash*) precipitado; **don't be so ~** no te precipites

common comparative and superlative forms / formas del comparativo y superlativo

hat [hæt] Ⓐ N sombrero *m*; **to raise one's ~** (*in greeting*) descubrirse; **to take off one's ~** quitarse el sombrero; ✦*IDIOMS* **to eat one's ~: I'll eat my ~ if …** que me maten si …; **to hang one's ~ up** jubilarse; **my ~!** ¡caramba!; **that's old ~** eso no es nada nuevo; **to pass the ~ round** pasar el platillo; **to take one's ~ off to sb** quitarse el sombrero *or* descubrirse ante algn; **I take my ~ off to him** me descubro ante él; **to talk through one's ~*** decir

idioms / modismos

creador(a) Ⓐ ADJ creative

Ⓑ SM/F [1] [*de movimiento, organización, personaje*] creator

[2] (= *artista*) artist; (= *diseñador*) designer; **los grandes ~es del Renacimiento** the great artists of the Renaissance; **los ~es de moda juvenil** designers of youth fashion

Ⓒ SM **el Creador** (*Rel*) the Creator

campo semántico / specialist field

crear ▸conjug 1a◂ VT [1] (= *hacer, producir*) [+ *obra, objeto, empleo*] to create; **el hombre fue creado a imagen de Dios** man was created in the image of God; **~on una ciudad de la nada** they created a city out of nothing

[2] (= *establecer*) [+ *comisión, comité, fondo, negocio, sistema*] to set up; [+ *asociación, cooperativa*] to form, set up; [+ *cargo, puesto*] to create; [+ *movimiento, organización*] to create, establish, found; **¿qué se necesita para ~ una empresa?** what do you need in order to set up *o* start a business?; **esta organización se creó para defender los derechos humanos** this organization was created *o* established *o* founded to defend human rights; **aspiraban a ~ un estado independiente** they aimed to create *o* establish *o* found an independent state

objetos típicos del verbo / typical objects of verb

números para las distintas acepciones / numbers for different senses

[3] (= *dar lugar a*) [+ *condiciones, clima, ambiente*] to create; [+ *problemas*] to cause, create; [+ *expectativas*] to raise; **el bloqueo ha creado una situación insostenible** the blockade has created an untenable situation; **el vacío creado por su muerte** the gap left *o* created by her death; **la nicotina crea adicción** nicotine is addictive

[4] (*liter*) (= *nombrar*) to make, appoint; **fue creado papa** he was made pope

creatividad SF creativity

creativo/a Ⓐ ADJ creative

Ⓑ SM/F (*tb* ~ **de publicidad**) copywriter

crece SM *o* SF (*Cono Sur*) = **crecida**

remisión a otra entrada / cross-reference

crecepelo SM hair-restorer

crecer ▸conjug 2d◂ Ⓐ VI [1] (= *desarrollarse*) [*animal, planta, objeto*] to grow; **el jazmín ha dejado de ~** the jasmine has stopped growing; **te ha crecido mucho el pelo** your hair's grown a lot; **me he dejado ~ la barba** I've grown a beard; **crecí en Sevilla** I grew up in Seville; **la princesa fue creciendo en belleza y sabiduría** the princess grew in beauty and wisdom

[2] (= *aumentar*) [*cantidad, producción, sentimiento*] to grow; [*gastos*] to increase, rise; [*inflación*] to rise; [*desempleo*] to increase, grow, rise; **el número de heridos seguía creciendo** the number of wounded continued to grow; **la economía española ~á un 4%** the Spanish economy will grow by 4%; **crece el temor de un conflicto armado** there are growing fears of an armed conflict; **el viento fue creciendo en intensidad** the wind increased *o* grew in intensity; **~ en importancia** to grow in importance

sujetos típicos del verbo / typical subjects of verb

ejemplos / examples

[3] (= *extenderse*) [*ciudad*] to grow; [*río, marea*] to rise; [*luna*] to wax

Ⓑ **crecerse** VPR [1] (= *tomar fuerza*) **pocos jugadores saben ~se ante la adversidad** there are few players who can stand up and be counted in the face of adversity

[2] (*) (= *engreírse*) to get full of o.s.; **con nada que le digas ya se crece** whatever you say to him he still gets all full of himself *o* his head still starts to swell

letras para las distintas categorías gramaticales / letters for different parts of speech

verbo pronominal / pronominal verb

in [ɪn]

[A] PREPOSITION	[C] ADJECTIVE
[B] ADVERB	[D] NOUN

menu

menú

(A) PREPOSITION

*When **in** is the second element in a phrasal verb, eg **ask in, fill in, look in**, etc, look up the verb. When it is part of a set combination, eg **in the country, in ink, in danger, covered in**, look up the other word.*

where to look

envío a otra entrada

[1] [***in expressions of place***] en; (= *inside*) dentro de; **it's in London/Scotland/Galicia** está en Londres/Escocia/Galicia; **in the garden** en el jardín; **in the house** en casa; (= *inside*) dentro de la casa; **our bags were stolen, and our passports were in them** nos robaron los bolsos, y nuestros pasaportes iban dentro

language tip

nota de uso

*When phrases like **in Madrid, in Germany** are used to identify a particular group, **de** is the usual translation:*

our colleagues in Madrid nuestros colegas de Madrid; **the chairs in the room** las sillas de la habitación, las sillas que hay en la habitación *or* dentro de la habitación; **in here/there** aquí/allí dentro; **it's hot in here** aquí dentro hace calor

meaning indicator

indicador de acepción

[2] [***in expressions of time***] [2·1] (= *during*) en; **in 1986** en 1986; **in May/spring** en mayo/primavera; **in the eighties/the 20th century** en los años ochenta/el siglo 20; **in the morning(s)/evening(s)** por la mañana/la tarde; **at four o'clock in the morning/afternoon** a las cuatro de la mañana/la tarde

[2·2] (= *for*) **she hasn't been here in years** hace años que no viene

[2·3] (= *in the space of*) en; **I did it in 3 hours/days** lo hice en 3 horas/días; **it was built in a week** fue construido en una semana

[2·4] (= *within*) dentro de; **I'll see you in three weeks' time** *or* **in three weeks** te veré dentro de tres semanas; **he'll be back in a moment/a month** volverá dentro de un momento/un mes

[3] [***indicating manner, medium***] en; **in a loud/soft voice** en voz alta/baja; **in Spanish/English** en español/inglés; **to pay in dollars** pagar en dólares; **it was underlined in red** estaba subrayado en rojo; **a magnificent sculpture in marble and copper** una magnífica escultura de *or* en mármol y cobre

[4] [*= clothed in*] **she opened the door in her dressing gown** abrió la puerta en bata; **they were all in shorts** todos iban en *or* llevaban pantalón corto; **he went out in his new raincoat** salió con el impermeable nuevo; **you look nice in that dress** ese vestido te sienta bien

*When phrases like **in the blue dress, in the glasses** are used to identify a particular person, **de** is the usual translation:*

the man in the hat el hombre del sombrero; **the boy in the checked trousers** el chico de los pantalones de cuadros; [*BUT*] **the girl in green** la chica vestida de verde; *see also* **dressed**

translation exception

ejemplo con una traducción distinta a la general

[5] [***giving ratio, number***] **one person in ten** una persona de cada diez; **one in five pupils** uno de cada cinco alumnos; **he had only a one in fifty chance of survival** sólo tenía una posibilidad entre cincuenta de sobrevivir; **what happened was a chance in a million** había una posibilidad entre un millón de que pasara lo que pasó; **20 pence in the pound** veinte peniques por (cada) libra; **once in a hundred years** una vez cada cien años; **in twos** de dos en dos; **these jugs are produced in their millions** estas jarras se fabri-

decir

▸conjug 3o◂
A VERBO TRANSITIVO
B VERBO INTRANSITIVO
C VERBO PRONOMINAL
D SUSTANTIVO MASCULINO
Para otras expresiones con el participio, ver ***dicho***.

menú

menu

remisión a otra entrada

where to look

Ⓐ VERBO TRANSITIVO

1 *= afirmar* to say; **ya sabe ~ varias palabras** she can already say several words, she already knows several words; **—tengo prisa —dijo** "I'm in a hurry," she said; **viene y dice: —estás despedido*** he goes "you're fired"*; **olvídalo, no he dicho nada** forget I said anything; **¿decía usted?** you were saying?; **como dicen los madrileños** as they say in Madrid; **como decía mi abuela** as my grandmother used to say; **como iba diciendo ...** as I was saying ...; **¿cómo ha dicho usted?** pardon?, what did you say?; **~ para** *o* **entre sí** to say to o.s.

expresión fija con una palabra subrayada

highlighted word in set expression

- **decir que** to say (that); **mi amigo dice que eres muy guapa** my friend says (that) you're very pretty; **dicen que ...** they say (that) ..., people say (that) ...; **el cartel dice claramente que ...** the sign says clearly *o* clearly states that ...; **~ que sí/no** to say yes/no; —**¿viene? —dice que sí** "is she coming?" — "she says she is *o* she says so"; **la miré y me dijo que sí/no con la cabeza** I looked at her and she nodded/shook her head; *ver tb* **adiós B**

2

- **decir algo a algn** to tell sb sth; **¿quién te lo dijo?** who told you?; **se lo dije bien claro, pero no me hizo caso** I told her quite clearly, but she didn't take any notice of me; **tengo algo que ~te** there's something I want to tell you, I've got something to tell you; **hoy nos dicen las notas** they're telling *o* giving us our results today
- **decir a algn que** + *INDIC* to tell sb (that); **me dijo que no vendría** he told me (that) he wouldn't come; **ya te dije que no tiene ni idea** I told you he hasn't got a clue; **¿no te digo que no puedo ir?** I've already told you I can't go
- **decir a algn que** + *SUBJUN* (= *ordenar*) to tell sb to do sth; (= *pedir*) to ask sb to do sth; **la profesora me dijo que esperara fuera** the teacher told me to wait outside; **le dije que fuera más tarde** I told her to go later; **dile que venga a cenar mañana con nosotros** ask him to come and have supper with us tomorrow; **te digo que te calles** I said shut up

estructuras fijas

set structures

3 *= contar* [+ *mentiras, verdad, secreto*] to tell; **~ tonterías** to talk nonsense; *ver tb* **verdad 1**

4 *= llamar* to call; **¿cómo le dicen a esto en Perú?** what do they call this in Peru?; **se llama Francisco, pero le dicen Paco** his name is Francisco, but he's known as Paco; **le dicen "el torero"** he's known as "el torero";

indicador de acepción

meaning indicator

Complex entries

all
any
as
ask
back
be
by
charge
do
for
get
give
go
good
hang
have
how
in
just
keep
know
make
mind
off
over
press
put
some
that
to
up
what
when
where
which
with

Entradas complejas

caer
coger
dar
de
decir
dejar
echar
estar
hacer
ir
llegar
llevar
mano
más
pasar
poder
poner
por
quedar
querer
sacar
salir
ser
tener
tirar
tomar
valer
venir
ver
vuelta

Language notes

ABLE, CAN
AFTER
AND
ASK
AVERAGE, HALF
BAD
BE
BECOME, GO, GET
BEFORE
BOTH
BUT
COME, GO
EASY, DIFFICULT, IMPOSSIBLE
ENOUGH
FORGET
GREAT, BIG, LARGE
GROUP
HOWEVER
HUNDRED
IF
LESS THAN, FEWER THAN
LET
LIKE
LOOK FOR
LOVE
MAJORITY, MOST
MINORITY
MORE THAN
NEW
OFTEN
OLD
OR
POOR
PURE
REMEMBER
SAD
SINCE
SMALL
AS SOON AS
STILL
STRANGE, RARE
TAKE
THEN
THERE IS, THERE ARE
THIS
UNTIL
USED TO
WEAR
WHO, WHOM
WHOSE
WHY
YET
YOU

Notas lingüísticas

ABURRIDO
ACONSEJAR
ACOSTUMBRAR
ACUSAR
ALGUNO, ALGO
APENAS
ATENTAMENTE
AUNQUE
AYUDAR
BAJAR
CADA
CALIENTE
CANSADO
CANTIDAD
CÁRCEL
CASA
CASI
CIEN, CIENTO
CLÁSICO
COLEGIO
COLGAR
CÓMICO
CONOCER
CONSEJO
CUÁNTO
DECIR
DEJAR
DEMASIADO
DESDE
DIVERTIDO
DOS
DURANTE
ECONÓMICO
ELÉCTRICO
EN
ENFERMEDAD
ENTRAR
ESPERAR
EXPLICAR
HABLAR
HASTA
HOSPITAL
HÚMEDO
IGLESIA
KILOS, METROS, AÑOS
LLEGAR
MANERA, FORMA, MODO
MASCULINO
MUEBLE
NINGUNO
NOTICIA
OLVIDAR
PANTALONES, ZAPATOS, GAFAS
PAPEL
PAR
PAREJA
PASAR
PEDIR
PERSONA
PREFERIR
SABER
SALADO
SALIR
SER
SI
SUBIR
TODAVÍA
TODO
VACACIONES
VENIR
VIAJE

Cultural notes

A LEVELS
ACLU
ACT OF PARLIAMENT
AFFIRMATIVE ACTION
ALL-AMERICAN
FIFTH AMENDMENT
AMERICAN DREAM
ANGLO-SAXON
APRIL FOOLS' DAY
ARCHBISHOP
ASCOT
ATTORNEY
AULD LANG SYNE
BACKBENCHER
BANK HOLIDAY
BASEBALL
BED AND BREAKFAST
BEST MAN
BILL OF RIGHTS
BOOKER PRIZE
BOXING DAY
BRITAIN
BRITISH COUNCIL
BUDGET
BUREAU OF INDIAN AFFAIRS
BURNS' NIGHT
BY-ELECTION
CABINET
CAJUN
CAPITOL
CAR BOOT SALE
CHECKS AND BALANCES
CHILDREN IN NEED
CHRISTMAS DINNER
CHURCHES OF ENGLAND/ SCOTLAND
CITIZENS' ADVICE BUREAU
CITY NICKNAMES
COCKNEY
COLLEGE
COMIC RELIEF
COMMON LAW
COMMONWEALTH
COMPREHENSIVE SCHOOLS
CONGRESS
CONSTITUTION
CRICKET
DAR
DC – DISTRICT OF COLUMBIA
DEAN'S LIST
DEGREE
DIXIE
DOWNING STREET
DRIVE-IN
DRIVING LICENCE/ DRIVER'S LICENSE
DUDE RANCH
EDINBURGH FESTIVAL
EISTEDDFOD
ELECTORAL COLLEGE
ENGLISH
ESTABLISHMENT
EXECUTIVE PRIVILEGE
STATE FAIR
FAIRNESS DOCTRINE
FCC
FDA
FOURTH OF JULY
FREEDOM OF INFORMATION ACT
FRONT BENCH
FULBRIGHT
GCSE
GLASTONBURY
GRADE
GRAMMAR SCHOOL
GRAND JURY
GRANT-MAINTAINED SCHOOL
GREEN-WELLIE BRIGADE
GREYHOUND RACING
GROUNDHOG DAY
GUY FAWKES NIGHT
HALLOWE'EN
HIGH SCHOOL
HIGHLAND GAMES
HOGMANAY
HOME COUNTIES
HONOURS LIST
IMPERIAL SYSTEM
IVY LEAGUE
LABOR DAY
LAND OF HOPE AND GLORY
LAWYERS
LEADER OF THE HOUSE
LEGION
LIBRARY OF CONGRESS
LIMERICK
LOLLIPOP LADY/MAN
LORD
MACY'S THANKSGIVING PARADE
MARGINAL SEAT
MASON-DIXON LINE
NAACP
NATIONAL GUARD
NATIONAL TRUST
NRA
NVQ
OFF-BROADWAY
OMBUDSMAN
OPEN UNIVERSITY
WE SHALL OVERCOME
OXBRIDGE
OXFAM
PAGE THREE
PANTOMIME
PEP RALLY
PHI BETA KAPPA
PILGRIM FATHERS
PLEDGE OF ALLEGIANCE
POET LAUREATE
POLITICALLY CORRECT
POPPY DAY
PREPARATORY SCHOOL
PRIMARIES
PRIVY COUNCIL
PROM
PUBLIC ACCESS TELEVISION
PULITZER
QC/KC
QUANGO
QUEEN'S/KING'S SPEECH
RA – ROYAL ACADEMY OF ARTS
RAG WEEK
REDBRICK UNIVERSITY
RHYMING SLANG
RSC – ROYAL SHAKESPEARE COMPANY
RUGBY
RULE BRITANNIA
SAVE THE CHILDREN
SLOANE RANGER
SMALL TOWN
SMITHSONIAN INSTITUTION
SORORITY/FRATERNITY
SPEAKER
SQUARE DANCE
STATE OF THE UNION ADDRESS
STATES' RIGHTS
SUNBELT
SUNDAY PAPERS
TABLOIDS AND BROADSHEETS
TEFL/EFL, TESL/ESL, ELT, TESOL/ESOL
TERRITORIAL ARMY
THANKSGIVING
THREE RS
V-E DAY
VICTORIAN
WASP
WESTMINSTER
WHIP
WHITEHALL
YANKEE
YEARBOOK
ZERO

Notas culturales

ACADEMIA
APELLIDO
APERTURISMO
ARAUCANO
ARPILLERA
BARAJA ESPAÑOLA
BOE
CABALGATA DE REYES
CAMINO DE SANTIAGO
CARLISMO
CARNAVAL
CARPA
CASA DE CONTRATACIÓN
CASTELLANO
CATALÁN
CAVA
CCOO
CHICHA
CHURROS
COCA
COMEDIA
COMUNIDAD AUTÓNOMA
CONGRESO DE LOS DIPUTADOS
LA CONSTITUCIÓN ESPAÑOLA
CORRIDO
CORTES GENERALES
COSTUMBRISMO
CRIANZA
CULTERANISMO, CONCEPTISMO
DENOMINACIÓN DE ORIGEN
LOS DESAPARECIDOS
DIADA NACIONAL DE CATALUNYA
DNI
DON/DOÑA
ENCOMIENDA
ENTREMÉS
EP – EDUCACIÓN PRIMARIA
ERTZAINTZA
ESCUELA OFICIAL DE IDIOMAS
ESO
ESPERPENTO
ESTANCO
EUSKERA
23-F
FALANGE ESPAÑOLA
FALLAS
FIESTAS
FOLLETÍN
FRANQUISMO
FUEROS
GALLEGO
GAUCHO
GENERACIÓN DEL 27/ DEL 98
GENERALITAT
GESTORÍA
EL GORDO
GRINGO
GUARANÍ
GUARDIA CIVIL
GUERRA CIVIL ESPAÑOLA
DÍA DE LA HISPANIDAD
DÍA DE LOS (SANTOS) INOCENTES
INSUMISO
JEREZ
LEÍSMO, LOÍSMO, LAÍSMO
LENGUAS COOFICIALES
LICENCIATURA
LOGSE
LOTERÍA
CONJUNTO MARIACHI
MARTES Y TRECE
MILI
MOVIDA MADRILEÑA
DÍA DE LOS MUERTOS
20-N
NÁHUATL
NOCHEBUENA
NOCHEVIEJA
OBJETOR DE CONCIENCIA
ONCE
OPOSICIONES
OPUS DEI
PACTOS DE LA MONCLOA
PAGA EXTRAORDINARIA
PARADOR NACIONAL
PELADO
PERONISMO
PÍCARO
POLICÍA
PRENSA DEL CORAZÓN
PRESIDENTE DEL GOBIERNO
PRESTACIÓN SOCIAL SUSTITUTORIA
PROVINCIA
HACER PUENTE
PULQUE
QUECHUA
QUINIELA
RAE
REALISMO MÁGICO
RECONQUISTA
RESERVA
DÍA DE REYES
ROMERÍA
SACRA
SAINETE
SANFERMINES
SAN ISIDRO
SAN JUAN
SANTO
SEMANA SANTA
SENADO
SOBREMESA
SOLERA
TERTULIA
LA TRANSICIÓN
TRIBUNAL CONSTITUCIONAL
TUNA
TURRÓN
ZARZUELA

Spanish Pronunciation and Spelling

Pronouncing European Spanish

1 The pronunciation of European Spanish is generally quite clear from its spelling and the notes below should be sufficient for an English speaker to understand what written Spanish actually sounds like. Because Spanish pronunciation is so regular you will find that in Part I of the dictionary (Spanish into English) most of the headwords are not transcribed phonetically in IPA (International Phonetic Alphabet). Any words that do have a phonetic transcription are pronounced in a way that you would not expect, such as *reloj* [re'lo] for example, or they have been taken from another language and given a Spanish sound, often while keeping the original spelling.
The pronunciation described below could be called 'educated' Castilian. Pronunciation often heard in the Spanish regions, for example Andalusia, has not been covered. There are separate notes on the pronunciation of Latin American Spanish on p.xxxviii.

2 Placing the stress

There are simple rules for placing stress on Spanish words:

Ⓐ If a word ends in a vowel, or in *n* or *s* (often an indication of the plural of verbs and nouns respectively), the penultimate syllable is stressed: *zap**a**to, zap**a**tos, div**i**de, div**i**den, dividi**e**ron, antiviviseccion**i**sta, telefon**e**a, hist**o**ria, diluvi**a**ba.*

Ⓑ If the word ends in a consonant other than *n* or *s*, the last syllable is stressed: *verd**a**d, practic**a**r, decib**e**l, virr**e**y, coñ**a**c, pesad**e**z.*

Ⓒ If the word needs to be stressed in some way contrary to rules Ⓐ and Ⓑ, an acute accent is written over the vowel to be stressed: *habl**ará**, guar**aní**, rub**í**, est**é**, roco**có**, **má**quina, **mé**todos, **vié**ndolo, para**lí**tico, **hú**ngaro.* The same syllable is stressed in the singular and plural forms of each word, but an accent may have to be added or suppressed in the plural: *cr**i**men, cr**í**menes, naci**ó**n, naci**o**nes.* There are a few exceptions to this rule, e.g. *car**á**cter, caract**e**res,* and *r**é**gimen, reg**í**menes.* Only in a few verb forms does the stress fall further back than the antepenultimate syllable: *c**á**ntamelo, proh**í**baselo.*

3 Dividing syllables

You will have seen in 2Ⓐ above that in cases like *telefonea* and *historia* not all vowels count equally when dividing and stressing syllables. The convention is that *a, e* and *o* are 'strong' vowels while *i* and *u* are 'weak'. Bearing this in mind we can apply four rules:

Ⓐ Where there is a combination of weak + strong vowels, forming a single syllable (called a diphthong), the stress falls on the strong vowel: *b**a**ila, ci**e**rra, pu**e**sto, p**e**ine, c**a**usa.*

Ⓑ In a combination of weak + weak vowels, again forming a diphthong, the stress falls on the second element: *ru**i**do, fu**i**mos, vi**u**da.*

Ⓒ Where two strong vowels are combined they are pronounced as two distinct syllables, the stress falling according to rules Ⓐ and Ⓑ in section 2 above: *ma/**e**s/tro* (three syllables), *con/tra/**e**r* (three syllables), *cre/**e**r* (two syllables).

Ⓓ Any word that has a combination of vowels whose parts are not stressed according to the above rules is given an acute accent on the stressed part: *cre**í**do, per**í**odo, ba**ú**l, r**í**e, t**í**o.*

Note that in cases where IPA transcriptions are given for Spanish words, the stress mark ['] is inserted in the same way as explained for English. See **La pronunciación del inglés británico**, section 2.

4 Spanish letters and their sounds

All the examples given below are pronounced as in British English.

Vowels

Spanish vowels are pronounced clearly and quite sharply, and unlike English are not extended to form diphthongs (e.g. **side** [saɪd], **know** [nəʊ]). Unstressed vowels are relaxed only slightly (compare English **natural** ['nætʃrəl] with Spanish natural [natu'ral]). Stressed vowels are pronounced slightly more open and short before **rr** (compare **carro** with **caro**, **perro** with **pero**).

a	[a]	Not so short as **a** in English *p**a**t, b**a**tter*, but not so long as in *r**a**ther, b**a**r*	**pata** **amara**
e	[e]	In an open syllable (one which ends in a vowel) like **e** in English *th**e**y*, but without the sound of the **y**. In a closed syllable (one which ends in a consonant) the sound is shorter, like the **e** in *s**e**t, w**e**t*	**me** **pelo** **sangre** **peldaño**
i	[i]	Not so short as **i** in the English *b**i**t, t**i**p*, but not so long as in *mach**i**ne*	**iris** **filo**
o	[o]	In an open syllable (one which ends in a vowel) like **o** in the English *n**o**te*, but without the sound of [ʊ] which ends the vowel in this word. In a closed syllable (one which ends in a consonant) it is a shorter sound, but not quite so short as in the English *p**o**t, c**o**t*	**poco** **cosa** **bomba** **conté**
u	[u]	Like **u** in the English *r**u**le* or **oo** in *f**oo**d*. Silent after **q** and in the groups **gue**, **gui**, unless marked by a diaeresis (*arg**ü**ir, frag**ü**e, antig**ü**edad*)	**luna** **pula** **aquel** **pague**
y	[i]	When used as a vowel – i.e. in the conjunction **y** meaning 'and', as well as at the end of words such as *vo**y**, le**y*** – it is pronounced like **i**	

Diphthongs

(Single syllables consisting of two vowels. See also section 3 above)

ai, ay	[ai]	like **i** in the English *s**i**de*	**baile** **hay**
au	[au]	like **ou** in English *s**ou**nd*	**áureo** **causa**

ei, ey	[ei]	like **ey** in the English *th**ey***	**reina** **rey**
eu	[eu]	like the vowel sounds in the English **may-you**, without the sound of the **y**	**deuda** **feudo**
oi, oy	[oi]	like **oy** in the English *b**oy***	**oiga** **soy**

Semiconsonants

There are two semiconsonants in Spanish which appear in a variety of combinations as the first element. Not all the combinations are listed here.

i, y	[j]	like **y** in the English ***y**es*, *yacht* (See also the note under **y** in the list of consonants)	**bien** **hielo** **yunta** **apoyo**
u	[w]	like **w** in the English ***w**ell*	**huevo** **fuente** **agua** **guardar**

Consonants

b, v		These two letters have the same value in Spanish. There are two distinct pronunciations depending on position and context:	
	[b]	At the start of the breath group and after the written letters **m** and **n** (pronounced [m]) the sound is like the English **b**	**bomba** **boda** **enviar**
	[β]	In all other positions the sound is between an English **b** and **v** in which the lips do not quite meet (called a bilabial fricative, a sound unknown in English)	**haba** **severo** **yo voy** **de Vigo**
c		This letter has two different values:	
	[k]	**c** before **a**, **o**, **u** or a consonant is like the English **k** in keep, but without the slight aspiration which accompanies it	**calco** **acto** **cuco**
	[θ]	**c** before **e**, **i** is like the English **th** in ***th**in*. In parts of Andalusia and Latin America this is pronounced like **s** in English ***s**ame,* and is known as **seseo**. In words like *acción*, *se**cc**ión* both types of c sound are heard [kθ]	**celda** **hacer** **cinco** **cecear**
ch	[tʃ]	like **ch** in the English ***ch**ur**ch***	**mucho** **chorro**
d		This letter has three different values depending on position and context:	
	[d]	At the start of the breath-group, and after **l**, **n** the sound is like the English **d**	**dama** **aldea** **andar**
	[ð]	Between vowels and after consonants other than **l**, **n** the sound is relaxed and similar to the English sound **th** [ð] in ***th**is*. In parts of Spain and in casual speech it is further relaxed and even disappears, especially in the **-ado** ending	**pide** **cada** **pardo** **sidra**
		In the final position, the second type of [ð] is further relaxed or completely omitted. In eastern parts of Spain this final **d** may be heard as a **t**	**verdad** **usted** **Madrid** **callad**
f	[f]	like the English **f** in ***f**or*	**fama** **fofo**
g		This letter has three different values depending on position and context:	
	[x]	Before **e**, **i** it is the same as Spanish **j** (see below)	**Gijón** **general**
	[g]	At the start of the breath group and after **n** the sound is that of the English **g** in ***g**et*	**gloria** **rango** **pingüe**
	[ɣ]	In other positions the sound is as in the second type above, but it is fricative and not plosive	**haga** **agosto**
		Note that in the group **gue**, **gui** the **u** is silent (*guerra*, *guindar*) except when marked by a diaeresis (*antigüedad*, *argüir*). In the group **gua** all the letters are sounded (***gua**rdia*, ***gua**po*)	
h		always silent	
j	[x]	a strong guttural sound not found in the English of England, but like the **ch** of Scots *lo**ch***, Welsh *ba**ch***, or German *Aa**ch**en*, *A**ch**tung*. It is silent at the end of a word (*reloj*)	**jota** **jején** **baraja**

k	[k]	like the English letter **k** in ***k**ick*, but without the slight aspiration which accompanies it	**kilo**
l	[l]	like English letter **l** in ***l**ove*	**lelo** **pañal**
ll	[ʎ]	similar to the English **lli** in *mi**lli**on*. In parts of Spain and most parts of Latin America it is pronounced as [j] and in other parts as [ʒ]. The pronunciation as [j] is rapidly becoming more widely accepted in Spain.	**calle** **ella** **lluvia** **millón**
m	[m]	like the letter **m** in English ***m**ade*	**mano** **mamá**
n	[n]	like the letter **n** in English ***n**one*, but before **v** is pronounced as **m**, the group making [mb] (e.g. *e**nv**iar, si**n v**alor*)	**nadie** **pan** **pino**
ñ	[ɲ]	similar to the English sound **ni** [nj] in *o**ni**on*	**uña** **ñoño**
p	[p]	like English letter **p** in ***p**ut*, but without the slight aspiration which accompanies it. It is often silent in *se**p**tiembre, sé**p**timo*	**padre** **patata**
q	[k]	like English **k** in ***k**ick*, but without the slight aspiration which accompanies it. Always written in combination with **u**, which is silent	**que** **quinqué** **bosque** **quiosco**
r	[r]	a single trill or vibration stronger than any **r** in the English of England, but like the Scots **r**. It is more relaxed in the final position and is silent in parts of Spain and Latin America. Pronounced like **rr** at the start of a word and also after **l**, **n**, **s**	**coro** **quiere** **rápido** **real**
rr	[rr]	strongly trilled in a way that does not exist in English	**torre** **burro** **irreal**
s		Two pronunciations:	
	[s]	Except in the instances mentioned next, it is like the letter **s** in English ***s**ame*	**casa** **Isabel** **soso**
	[z]	Before a voiced consonant (**b**, **d**, **g**, **l**, **m**, **n**) it is usually pronounced like **s** in English *ro**s**e, pha**s**e*	**desde** **asgo** **mismo** **asno**
t	[t]	like English **t** in ***t**ame*, but without the slight aspiration which accompanies it	**título** **pata**
v		see **b**	
w		found in a few recent loanwords only; usually pronounced like Spanish **b**, **v** or like an English **v**, or kept as English **w**	**wáter** **week-end** **wolframio**
x		There are several possible pronunciations:	
	[ks]	Between vowels, **x** is pronounced like English **x** in *bo**x*** [ks], or	**máximo**
	[gs]	like **gs** in big stick [gs]	**examen**
	[s]	In a few words the **x** is pronounced between vowels like English **s** in ***s**ame*, but not by all Spanish speakers	**exacto** **auxilio**
	[s]	Before a consonant **x** is pronounced like English **s** in ***s**ame*, but not by all Spanish speakers	**extra** **sexto**
y	[j]	as a consonant or semiconsonant, **y** is pronounced as in English ***y**es, **y**outh*. In emphatic speech in Spain and Latin America this is similar to **j** in the English word jam [dʒ]. In Argentina, Chile etc this **y** is pronounced like the **s** in English *lei**s**ure* [ʒ]	**mayo** **yo** **mayor** **ya**
z	[θ]	like the English **th** in ***th**in*. In parts of Andalusia and Latin America this is pronounced like the English **s** in ***s**ame*, and is known as **seseo**	**zapato** **zorro** **zumbar** **luz**

5 Additional notes on pronunciation

(A) The letter **b** is usually not pronounced in groups with **s** such as **obscuro**, **substituir**. In practice, such words are generally written **oscuro**, **sustituir** etc and this is the spelling under which they are treated in the dictionary.

(B) With one exception there are no real double consonants in Spanish speech. **cc** in words like **acción** is two separate sounds [kθ], while **ll** and **rr** have their own values (see table).
The exception is the **nn** group found in words with the prefix **in**-, e.g. **innato**, or occasionally **con**-, **sin**- as in **connatural**, **sinnúmero**. In these cases the **n** is pronounced double [nn].

(C) When taking loanwords from other languages the majority of Spanish speakers will adapt the pronunciation of these words, usually while keeping the original spelling. For some examples of this, see the main dictionary text under **chalet, jazz** and **shock**.

(D) No well-established Spanish word begins with what is called 'impure s', i.e. **s** plus a consonant as an initial group. When Spanish speakers have to pronounce a foreign word or name they will almost always add an initial e-sound, so that Smith becomes [ez'miθ] or [es'mis]. More recent anglicisms tend to be written in Spanish as **slip, slogan** etc, but are pronounced [ez'lip] and [ez'loɣan], while more established English loanwords are written **esnob, esplín** etc and are pronounced accordingly.

6 The letters of the Spanish alphabet

When letters of the alphabet are spoken one at a time, or when a word is spelled out letter by letter etc, the names of the letters are as follows:

a	[a]	**j**	['xota]	**r**	['ere]
b	[be] (*in LAm* [be'larɣa])	**k**	[ka]	**rr***	['erre]
c	[θe] *or* [se]	**l**	['ele]	**s**	['ese]
ch*	[tʃe]	**ll***	['eʎe]	**t**	[te]
d	[de]	**m**	['eme]	**u**	[u]
e	[e]	**n**	['ene]	**v**	['uβe] (*in LAm* [be'korta])
f	['efe]	**ñ**	['eɲe]	**w**	['uβe 'doβle] (*in LAm* ['doβle be])
g	[xe]	**o**	[o]	**x**	['ekis]
h	['atʃe]	**p**	[pe]	**y**	[i'ɣrjeɣa]
i	[i]	**q**	[ku]	**z**	['θeta] *or* ['seta]

The gender of the letters is feminine: '¿esto es una c o una t?' You also say 'una a' and 'la a', 'una h' and 'la h' (i.e. you do not apply the rule as in un ave, el agua).

*Though not strictly letters of the alphabet, these are considered separate sounds in Spanish.

Pronouncing Latin American Spanish

The pronunciation of Latin American Spanish varies widely from place to place, so the following notes are intended to give a general picture only. As a rule, the Spanish spoken in the upland areas of Latin America is similar to Castilian Spanish, while the lowland and coastal areas have many features of Andalusian pronunciation. Vowel sounds are all roughly the same, but there are differences in the way consonants are pronounced.
These are listed below:

1 The Castilian [θ] sound (like the **th** in the English word ***th**in*) which is written **c** or **z** is pronounced as various kinds of **s** [s] throughout Latin America. This is known as **seseo**.

2 At the end of a syllable or a word, **s** is a slight aspiration, e.g. **las dos** [lah'doh], mosca ['mohka], but in parts of the Andes, upland Mexico and Peru the [s] sound is retained as in Castilian Spanish.

3 The Castilian written **ll** [ʎ] (like **lli** in the English word *mi**lli**on*) is pronounced in three different ways in Latin America. In parts of Colombia, all Peru, Bolivia, N. Chile and Paraguay it remains [ʎ]. In Argentina, Uruguay, upland Ecuador and part of Mexico it is pronounced [ʒ]. In the remaining areas it is pronounced [j]. When this last kind [j] is in contact with the vowels **e** and **i** it disappears altogether, and one finds incorrect written forms such as **gaína** (for **gallina**) and **biete** (for **billete**).

4 In all parts of Latin America you will often find confusion between the letters **l** and **r**: **clin** (for **crin**), **carma** (for **calma**) etc.

5 Written **h** is silent in Castilian, but in parts of Mexico and Peru this **h** is aspirated at the start of a word, so you may find incorrectly spelt forms such as **jarto** (for **harto**) and **jablar** (for **hablar**). Compare **halar/jalar** and other cases in the main dictionary text.

Spanish Spelling

1 Use of capitals

As in English, capital letters are used to begin words in the following cases:
– for the first letter of the first word in a sentence
– for proper names (but see also below)

María, el Papa, el Rey, la Real Academia Española,
Viernes Santo, el Partido Laborista, Dios

Note that where the article is an integral part of the proper name, it also begins with a capital – **El Escorial, La Haya, La Habana** – but where the article is generally or optionally used with the name of a country, it does not begin with a capital – **la India, la Argentina**
– for abbreviations of titles:

Sr., D., Excmª

In the following cases usage differs from English:
– names of days and months:

lunes, mayo

– the pronoun **yo**, unless it begins a sentence
– while capitals are used for names of countries, they are not used for the adjectives derived therefrom:

Francia, but **francés**

Similarly, adjectives derived from proper names do not begin with a capital:

... en los estudios lorquianos, las teorías einsteinianas

– in the titles of books, films, plays etc, only the first word begins with a capital letter:

Lo que el viento se llevó, Cien años de soledad

– points of the compass begin with lower case:

norte, sur etc

(though they are capitalized if part of a name: **Korea del Sur**)
– official and noble titles:

el duque de Alba, el ministro de Interior

Note that capital letters can be accentuated in the same way as lower case letters.

2 Punctuation

Other than the differences listed below, punctuation in English and Spanish is very similar.

(A) Exclamation marks and question marks

An inverted exclamation mark (¡) or question mark (¿) is required at the start of the exclamation or question in addition to the standard exclamation mark or question mark at the end. The position of these marks does not always coincide with the beginning of the sentence:

¡Qué calor hace!
Pues, ¿vamos o no vamos?
Son trece en total, ¿verdad?

Ⓑ **Full stops**

These are used very much as in English, except that:

– they are generally used after abbreviations:

Sr. Solís

They are used in numbers where English uses a comma:

English	*Spanish*
10,587	10.587

Ⓒ **Commas**

A comma is used instead of the decimal point:

English	*Spanish*
10.1	10,1 *(diez coma uno)*

Ⓓ **Colons**

These are used instead of a comma after the name of the recipient of a letter, though nowadays the colon is often left out altogether in these contexts

Querida Dolores:

Muy Señor mío:

Ⓔ **Semicolons**

These are sometimes used where a comma or a full stop would be expected in English, to denote a longer pause between phrases:

Me habló de la familia, los amigos, el trabajo; sin embargo, no mencionó a su hijo.

Ⓕ **Hyphens**

These are used very sparingly, since the tendency is for compound nouns and adjectives to be written as a single word:

antifranquista, proeuropeo, antihistamínico

When the two adjectives refer to different things, the hyphen is used:

el eje franco-alemán, el pensamiento anglo-americano

Hyphens are also used as in English to join nouns:

misiles tierra-aire, el eje Roma-Berlín

Confusion reigns in the use or absence of the hyphen in such combinations: **hombre rana, hombre-rana**. If the combination is brief there is a tendency to use the hyphen: **granja-escuela, grúa-puente, dos grúas-puente**. The Academy appears to rule against the hyphen but has hardly put its mind as yet to this relatively new and rapidly developing usage.

Ⓖ **The dash**

1. The dash is often used to insert parenthetical material where English would use a comma:

la moción de censura fue aprobada por unanimidad — algo cada vez más raro en el parlamento — a últimas horas de la sesión.

2. The dash is used to represent continuous dialogue where English would use inverted commas. It is used both to show a change of speaker and the resumption of dialogue after a pause:

—¿Vas a venir? —dijo suavemente

—No puedo —contesté

Note that punctuation in direct speech is placed after the dash.

Ⓗ **Quotation marks**

Traditionally "*comillas*" «...» were used to enclose quotations, unusual words, and so on. However, the tendency in some media these days is to use standard inverted commas, and the *El País* style guide, which is widely followed in Spain, recommends this.

3 Word division

The rules for splitting words in Spanish are not the same as for English. The main points are:

Ⓐ A single consonant between vowels is grouped with the second of them: **pa-lo, Barcelo-na**.

Ⓑ In a group of two consonants between vowels, the first is grouped with the preceding vowel and the second with the following vowel: **in-nato, des-mochar, paten-te**. But groups having **l** or **r** as the second element are considered as units and join the following vowel only: **re-probar, de-clarar**.

Ⓒ A group consisting of consonant + **h** may be split: **ex-hibición, Al-hambra**.

Ⓓ Remember that **ch**, **ll** and **rr** are considered as individual letters and must therefore never be split: **aprove-char, aga-lla, contra-rrevolucionario.**

Ⓔ In a group of three consonants, the first two join the preceding vowel: **trans-porte, cons-tante**. The exception to this rule is if the third consonant in this group is **l** or **r** only the first consonant joins the preceding vowel while the second and third join the following vowel: **som-bra, des-preciar, con-clave.**

Ⓕ Two vowels should never be separated, even where they form one syllable: **rui-do, maes-tro, pro-veer.**

Ⓖ Where it is obvious that a word is made up of two more words which have an independent existence of their own, the composite word can be split in ways that contradict the above rules: **latino-americano, re-examinar, vos-otros.** The same applies to some prefixes: **des-animar, ex-ánime.**

Pronunciación y ortografía

La pronunciación del inglés británico

Como es sabido, la ortografía del inglés se ajusta a criterios históricos y etimológicos y en muchos puntos apenas ofrece indicaciones ciertas de cómo ha de pronunciarse cada palabra. Por ello nos ha parecido aconsejable y de utilidad para los hispanohablantes dar para cada palabra inglesa una pronunciación figurada o transcripción. Al tratar de explicar en estas notas los sonidos del inglés mediante comparaciones con los sonidos del español en un espacio reducido nos damos cuenta de que realizamos una labor que no pasa de ser aproximativa.

1 Sistema de signos

Se emplean los signos de la IPA (International Phonetic Association). Hemos seguido en general las transcripciones de Daniel Jones, *English Pronouncing Dictionary*, London, Dent, 14th ed., 1989. En el prólogo de esta obra el autor explica los principios que le han guiado en su trabajo.

2 Acentuación

En las transcripciones el signo [ˈ] se coloca delante de la sílaba acentuada. El signo [ˌ] se pone delante de la sílaba que lleva el acento secundario o más ligero en las palabras largas, p.ej. **acceleration** [ækˌseləˈreɪʃən]. Dos signos de acento principal [ˈ ˈ] indican que las dos sílabas, o bien dos de las sílabas, se acentúan igualmente, p.ej. **A 1** [ˈeɪˈwʌn], **able-bodied** [ˈeɪblˈbɒdɪd].

3 Signos impresos en cursiva

En la palabra ***annexation*** [ˌænekˈseɪʃ*ə*n], la [*ə*] en cursiva indica que este sonido puede o no pronunciarse; bien porque muchos hablantes la pronuncian pero otros muchos no, o bien porque es un sonido que se oye en el habla lenta y cuidada pero que no se oye en el habla corriente y en el ritmo de la frase entera.

4 Transcripciones alternativas

En los casos donde se dan dos transcripciones, ello indica que ambas pronunciaciones son igualmente aceptables en el uso culto, p.ej. **medicine** [ˈmeds*ɪ*n,ˈmedɪs*ɪ*n], o bien que la pronunciación varía bastante según la posición de la palabra en la frase y el contexto fonético, p.ej. **an** [æn, ən, n].

5 Véase también la nota sobre la pronunciación del inglés norteamericano (pág. xlii).

6 El orden en que se explican los signos abajo es más o menos ortográfico y no estrictamente fonético.

Vocales

[æ]	sonido breve, bastante abierto, parecido al de **a** en *c**a**rro*	**bat** **apple**	[bæt] [ˈæpl]
[ɑː]	sonido largo parecido al de **a** en *c**a**ro*	**farm** **calm**	[fɑːm] [kɑːm]
[e]	sonido breve, bastante abierto, parecido al de **e** en *p**e**rro*	**set** **less**	[set] [les]
[ə]	'vocal neutra', siempre átona; parecida a la **e** del artículo francés *l**e*** y a la **a** final del catalán (p.ej. *cas**a**, port**a***)	**above** **porter** **convey**	[əˈbʌv] [ˈpɔːtəʳ] [kənˈveɪ]
[ɜː]	forma larga del anterior, en sílaba acentuada; algo parecido al sonido de **eu** en la palabra francesa *l**eu**r*	**fern** **work** **murmur**	[fɜːn] [wɜːk] [ˈmɜːməʳ]
[ɪ]	sonido breve, abierto, parecido al de **i** en *esb**i**rro, **i**rreal*	**tip** **pity**	[tɪp] [ˈpɪtɪ]
[iː]	sonido largo parecido al de **i** en *v**i**no*	**see** **bean** **ceiling**	[siː] [biːn] [ˈsiːlɪŋ]
[ɒ]	sonido breve, bastante abierto, parecido al de **o** en *c**o**rra, t**o**rre*	**rot** **wash**	[rɒt] [wɒʃ]
[ɔː]	sonido largo, bastante cerrado, algo parecido al de **o** en *p**o**r*	**ball** **board**	[bɔːl] [bɔːd]
[ʊ]	sonido muy breve, más cerrado que la **u** en *b**u**rro*	**soot** **full**	[sʊt] [fʊl]
[uː]	sonido largo, parecido al de **u** en ***u**no, s**u**pe*	**root** **fool**	[ruːt] [fuːl]
[ʌ]	sonido abierto, breve y algo oscuro, sin correspondencia en español; se pronuncia en la parte anterior de la boca sin redondear los labios	**come** **rum** **blood** **nourish**	[kʌm] [rʌm] [blʌd] [ˈnʌrɪʃ]

Diptongos

[aɪ]	sonido parecido al de **ai** en *fr**ai**le, v**ai**s*	**lie** **fry**	[laɪ] [fraɪ]
[aʊ]	sonido parecido al de **au** en *p**au**sa, s**au**ce*	**sow** **plough**	[saʊ] [plaʊ]
[eɪ]	sonido medio abierto, pero más cerrado que la **e** de *casé*; suena como si le siguiese una [i] débil, especialmente en sílaba acentuada	**fate** **say** **waiter** **straight**	[feɪt] [seɪ] [ˈweɪtəʳ] [streɪt]

[əʊ]	sonido que es una especie de **o** larga, sin redondear los labios ni levantar la lengua; suena como si le siguiese una [u] débil	**ago** **also** **atrocious** **note**	[əˈgəʊ] [ˈɔːlsəʊ] [əˈtrəʊʃəs] [nəʊt]
[ɛə]	sonido que se encuentra únicamente delante de la **r**: el primer elemento se parece a la ***e*** de *p**e**rro,* pero es más abierto y breve; el segundo elemento es una forma débil de la 'vocal neutra' [ə]	**there** **rare** **fair** **ne'er**	[ðɛəʳ] [rɛəʳ] [fɛəʳ] [nɛəʳ]
[ɪə]	sonido cuyo primer elemento es una **i** medio abierta; el segundo elemento es una forma débil de la 'vocal neutra' [ə]	**here** **interior** **fear** **beer**	[hɪəʳ] [ɪnˈtɪərɪəʳ] [fɪəʳ] [bɪəʳ]
[ɔɪ]	sonido cuyo primer elemento es una **o** abierta; seguido de una **i** abierta pero débil; parecido al sonido de **oy** en *v**oy*** o de **oi** en *c**oi**me*	**toy** **destroy** **voice**	[tɔɪ] [dɪsˈtrɔɪ] [vɔɪs]
[ʊə]	sonido cuyo primer elemento es una **u** medio larga; el segundo elemento es una forma débil de la 'vocal neutra' [ə]	**allure** **sewer** **pure**	[əˈljʊəʳ] [sjʊəʳ] [pjʊəʳ]

Consonantes

[b]	como la **b** de *tum**b**ar, um**b**río*	**bet** **able**	[bet] [ˈeɪbl]
[d]	como la **d** de *con**d**e, an**d**ar*	**dime** **mended**	[daɪm] [ˈmendɪd]
[f]	como la **f** de *fo**f**o, in**f**lar*	**face** **snaffle**	[feɪs] [ˈsnæfl]
[g]	como la **g** de ***g**rande, ran**g**o*	**go** **agog**	[gəʊ] [əˈgɒg]
[h]	es una aspiración fuerte, algo así como la jota castellana [x] pero sin la aspereza gutural de aquélla	**hit** **reheat**	[hɪt] [ˈriːˈhiːt]
[j]	como la **y** de *cu**y**o, re**y**es*	**you** **pure** **million**	[juː] [pjʊəʳ] [ˈmɪljən]
[k]	como la **c** de ***c**ama* o la **k** de ***k**ilómetro,* pero acompañada por una ligera aspiración inexistente en español	**catch** **kiss** **chord** **box**	[kætʃ] [kɪs] [kɔːd] [bɒks]
[l]	como la **l** de ***l**eer, pa**l**a*	**lick** **place**	[lɪk] [pleɪs]
[m]	como la **m** de ***m**es, co**m**er*	**mummy** **roam**	[ˈmʌmɪ] [rəʊm]
[n]	como la **n** de ***n**ada, habla**n***	**nut** **sunny**	[nʌt] [ˈsʌnɪ]
[ŋ]	como el sonido que tiene la **n** en *ba**n**co, ra**n**go*	**bank** **sinker** **singer**	[bæŋk] [ˈsɪŋkəʳ] [ˈsɪŋəʳ]
[p]	como la **p** de ***p**alo, ro**p**a,* pero acompañada por una ligera aspiración inexistente en español	**pope** **pepper**	[pəʊp] [ˈpepəʳ]
[r]	Es un sonido muy débil, casi semivocal, que no tiene la vibración fuerte que caracteriza la **r** española. Se articula elevando la punta de la lengua hacia el paladar duro. (NB: En el inglés de Inglaterra la **r** escrita se pronuncia únicamente delante de vocal; en las demás posiciones es muda. Véase abajo).	**rate** **pear** **fair** **blurred** **sorrow**	[reɪt] [pɛəʳ] [fɛəʳ] [blɜːd] [ˈsɒrəʊ]
[ʳ]	Este signo en las transcripciones indica que la **r** escrita en posición final de palabra se pronuncia en el inglés británico en muchos casos cuando la palabra siguiente empieza con vocal. En algún dialecto inglés y sobre todo en los Estados Unidos esta **r** se pronuncia siempre, así cuando la palabra se pronuncia aislada como cuando la siguen otras (empezando con vocal o sin ella)	**bear** **humour** **after**	[bɛəʳ] [ˈhjuːməʳ] [ˈɑːftəʳ]
[s]	como la **s** (sorda) de *ca**s**a, **s**esión*	**sit** **scent** **cents** **pox**	[sɪt] [sent] [sents] [pɒks]
[t]	como la **t** de ***t**ela, ra**t**a,* pero acompañada por una ligera aspiración inexistente en español	**tell** **strut** **matter**	[tel] [strʌt] [ˈmætəʳ]
[v]	Inexistente en español (aunque se encuentra en catalán y valenciano). En inglés es sonido labiodental, y se produce juntando el labio inferior con los dientes superiores	**vine** **river** **cove**	[vaɪn] [ˈrɪvəʳ] [kəʊv]
[w]	como la **u** de *h**u**evo, p**u**ede*	**wine** **bewail**	[waɪn] [bɪˈweɪl]

[z]	como la **s** (sonora) de *desde, mismo*	**zero** **roses** **buzzer**	[ˈzɪərəʊ] [ˈrəʊzɪz] [ˈbʌzəʳ]
[ʒ]	Inexistente en español, pero como la **j** de las palabras francesas ***j**our, **j**alousie,* o como la **g** de las palabras portuguesas ***g**ente, **g**eral*	**rouge** **leisure** **azure**	[ruːʒ] [ˈleʒəʳ] [ˈeɪʒəʳ]
	Este sonido aparece a menudo en el grupo [dʒ], parecido al grupo **dj** de la palabra francesa *a**dj**acent*	**page** **edge** **jail**	[peɪdʒ] [edʒ] [dʒeɪl]
[ʃ]	Inexistente en español, pero como la **ch** de las palabras francesas ***ch**ambre, fi**ch**e,* o como la **x** de la palabra portuguesa *ro**x**o*	**shame** **ocean** **ration** **sugar**	[ʃeɪm] [ˈəʊʃən] [ˈræʃən] [ˈʃʊgəʳ]
	Este sonido aparece a menudo en el grupo [tʃ], parecido al grupo **ch** del español *mu**ch**o, **ch**o**ch**o*	**much** **chuck** **natural**	[mʌtʃ] [tʃʌk] [ˈnætʃrəl]
[θ]	como la **z** de ***z**umbar,* o la **c** de ***c**iento*	**thin** **maths**	[θɪn] [mæθs]
[ð]	forma sonorizada del anterior, algo parecido a la **d** de *to**d**o, habla**d**o*	**this** **other** **breathe**	[ðɪs] [ˈʌðəʳ] [briːð]
[x]	sonido que en rigor no pertenece al inglés de Inglaterra, pero que se encuentra en el inglés de Escocia y en palabras escocesas usadas en Inglaterra etc; es como la **j** de ***j**oven, ro**j**o*	**loch**	[lɔx]

7 Sonidos extranjeros

El grado de corrección con que un hablante de inglés pronuncia las palabras extranjeras que acaban de incorporarse al idioma depende – como en español – de su nivel cultural y de los conocimientos que pueda tener del idioma de donde se ha tomado la palabra. Las transcripciones que damos de tales palabras representan una pronunciación más bien culta. En las transcripciones la tilde [˜] indica que la vocal tiene timbre nasal (en muchas palabras de origen francés). En las pocas palabras tomadas del alemán aparece a veces la [x], para cuya explicación véase el cuadro de las consonantes.

8 Las letras del alfabeto inglés

Cuando se citan una a una, o cuando se deletrea una palabra para mayor claridad, o cuando se identifica un avión etc por una letra y su nombre, las letras suenan así:

a	[eɪ]	**j**	[dʒeɪ]	**s**	[s]
b	[biː]	**k**	[keɪ]	**t**	[tiː]
c	[siː]	**l**	[el]	**u**	[juː]
d	[diː]	**m**	[em]	**v**	[viː]
e	[iː]	**n**	[en]	**w**	[ˈdʌbljuː]
f	[ef]	**o**	[əʊ]	**x**	[eks]
g	[dʒiː]	**p**	[piː]	**y**	[waɪ]
h	[eɪtʃ]	**q**	[kjuː]	**z**	[zed] (*en EEUU* [ziː])
i	[aɪ]	**r**	[ɑːʳ]		

La pronunciación del inglés norteamericano

Empleamos las abreviaturas (*Brit*) (British) y (*US*) (United States).

1 Acentuación

Las palabras que tienen dos sílabas o más después del acento principal llevan en inglés americano un acento secundario que no tienen en inglés británico, p.ej.

	(*US*)	(*Brit*)
dictionary	ˈdɪkʃəˌnerɪ	ˈdɪkʃənrɪ
secretary	ˈsekrəˌterɪ	ˈsekrətrɪ

En algunos casos se acentúa en inglés americano una sílaba distinta de la que lleva el acento en inglés británico, p.ej:

primarily	praɪˈmærɪlɪ	ˈpraɪmərɪlɪ

Este cambio de acento se percibe ahora también, por influencia norteamericana, en el inglés de Inglaterra.

2 Entonación

El inglés americano se habla con un ritmo más lento y en un tono más monótono que en Inglaterra, debido en parte al alargamiento de las vocales que se apunta abajo.

3 Sonidos

Muchas de las vocales breves acentuadas en inglés británico se alargan mucho en inglés americano, y alguna vocal inacentuada en inglés británico se oye con más claridad en inglés americano, p.ej.

rapid	ˈræːpɪd	ˈræpɪd
capital	ˈkæːbɪdəl	ˈkæpɪtl

Una peculiaridad muy notable del inglés americano es la nasalización de las vocales antes y después de las consonantes nasales [m, n, ŋ].

En las vocales individuales también hay diferencias. El sonido [ɑː] en inglés británico en muchas palabras se pronuncia en inglés americano como [æ] o bien [æː], p.ej.

	(*US*)	(*Brit*)
grass	græs græːs	grɑːs
answer	ˈænsər ˈæːnsər	ˈɑːnsəʳ

El sonido [ɒ] en inglés británico se pronuncia en inglés americano casi como una [ɑ] oscura, p.ej.

dollar	ˈdɑlər	ˈdɒləʳ
hot	hɑt	hɒt
topic	ˈtɑpɪk	ˈtɒpɪk

El diptongo que se pronuncia en inglés británico [juː] en sílaba acentuada se pronuncia en la mayor parte de inglés americano sin [j], p.ej.

Tuesday	ˈtuːzdɪ	ˈtjuːzdɪ
student	ˈstuːdənt	ˈstjuːdənt

Pero muchas palabras de este tipo se pronuncian en inglés americano igual que en inglés británico, p.ej. **music, pure, fuel**.

En último lugar entre las vocales, se nota que la sílaba final **-ile** que se pronuncia en inglés británico [aɪl] es a menudo en inglés americano [əl] o bien [ɪl], p.ej.

missile	ˈmɪsəl ˈmɪsɪl	ˈmɪsaɪl

Existen otras diferencias en la pronunciación de las vocales de palabras individuales, p.ej. **tomato**, pero éstas se tratan individualmente en el texto del diccionario.

En cuanto a las consonantes, hay que destacar dos diferencias. La consonante sorda [t] entre vocales suele sonorizarse bastante en inglés americano, p.ej.

	(*US*)	(*Brit*)
united	jʊ'naɪdɪd	juː'naɪtɪd

o sufre lenición [t].

La *r* escrita en posición final después de vocal o entre vocal y consonante es por la mayor parte muda en inglés británico, pero se pronuncia a menudo en inglés americano, p.ej.

where	wɛər	wɛəʳ
sister	'sɪstər	'sɪstəʳ

Hemos tomado esto en cuenta en las transcripciones en el texto del diccionario. También en posición final de sílaba (no sólo de palabra) se nota esta pronunciación de la *r* escrita:

	(*US*)	(*Brit*)
burden	'bɜːrdn	'bɜːdn
jersey	'dʒɜːrzɪ	'dʒɜːzɪ

Conviene advertir que aun dentro del inglés de Estados Unidos hay notables diferencias regionales; la lengua de Nueva Inglaterra difiere bastante de la del Sur, la del Medio Oeste no es la de California, etc. Los datos que constan arriba no son más que indicaciones muy someras.

La ortografía del inglés

Vamos a hablar aquí de una serie de reglas ortográficas del inglés que pueden resultar de utilidad para los hablantes de español, así como de las diferencias ortográficas entre el inglés británico y el norteamericano. Nos referiremos, en primer lugar, al inglés británico.

1 Consonantes dobles

Ⓐ En las palabras monosílabas que acaban en una sola consonante, esta consonante se dobla cuando se añade un sufijo que empieza por vocal.

Ej: **knot** + **-ed** = **knotted**; **cut** + **-er** = **cutter**; **hit** + **-ing** = **hitting**

EXCEPCIONES:
Cuando en la palabra hay dos vocales juntas.

Ej: **feel** → **feeling**

Cuando la consonante final es doble.

Ej: **hand** → **handed**

Ⓑ En las palabras de dos o tres sílabas acabadas en consonante precedida de una sola vocal, esta consonante se dobla al añadírsele un sufijo, siempre que el énfasis de la raíz recaiga en la última sílaba.

Ej: **regret** + **-ing** = **regretting**; **transfer** + **-ed** = **transferred**; **begin** + **-er** = **beginner**

NOTA: cuando la última sílaba no va acentuada esto no ocurre.

Ej: **enter** + **-ed** = **entered**, **answer** + **-ing** = **answering**, **count** + **-er** = **counter**.

Sin embargo, existen algunas excepciones como:

kidnap → **kidnapper**, **kidnapped** etc; **worship** → **worshipping**, **worshipped** etc; **handicap** → **handicapped**, **handicapping**

Ⓒ En algunas palabras acabadas en **-l**, esta **l** se suele hacer doble en los dos casos siguientes:

– en las palabras acabadas por **-l** precedida de una sola vocal.

Ej: **equal** → **equalling**; **instil** → **instilled**; **repel** → **repellent**

– en las palabras acabadas en dos vocales que formen un diptongo.

Ej: **real** → **really**; **fuel** → **fuelled**

2 Cuando desaparece la -e final

Ⓐ En las palabras acabadas en una sola **-e** precedida de consonante, la **-e** desaparece cuando se añade un sufijo que empiece por vocal.

Ej: **care** → **cared**; **retrieve** → **retrieving**; **love** → **lovable**

NOTA: La excepción a esta regla la constituye la palabra **likeable** – aunque también existe la forma "likable" – así como algunas palabras que terminan por **-ce** o **-ge** (ver más abajo).

Ⓑ Cuando se añade a la palabra un sufijo que empiece por consonante, la **-e** final se mantiene.

Ej: **hate** → **hateful**

EXCEPCIONES:

1. Cuando la palabra acaba en **-able** o **-ible** y se le añade el sufijo adverbial **-ly**.

Ej: **possible** → **possibly**; **arguable** → **arguably**

2. En determinadas palabras, entre las que cabe destacar:

whole → **wholly**; **argue** → **argument**; **judge** → **judgment**; **true** → **truly**; **due** → **duly**

3 Palabras terminadas en -ce y -ge

Ⓐ Tanto en las palabras que terminan por **-ce** como en las que terminan por **-ge**, la **-e** final se mantiene al añadirles un sufijo que empiece por **a** o por **o**, a fin de que se mantenga el sonido suave de la **c** y la **g**.

Ej: **change** → **changeable**; **replace** → **replaceable**; **outrage** → **outrageous**

Ⓑ En las palabras que terminan en **-ce**, la **-e** se convierte en **i** antes del sufijo **-ous**.

Ej: **space** → **spacious**; **malice** → **malicious**

4 Palabras terminadas en -y

Ⓐ Cuando las palabras que terminan por **-y** van precedidas de una consonante, la **y** se convierte en **i** al añadírseles cualquier sufijo que empiece por vocal.

Ej: **try** → **tried**; **carry** → **carried**; **funny** → **funnier**; **easy** → **easily**

NOTA: Esto ocurre también en los sustantivos en singular acabados en **y** precedida de consonante, que forman el plural añadiendo el sufijo **-es**. Así: **baby** → **babies**; **lorry** → **lorries**. Y lo mismo en la formación de la tercera persona del presente: **hurry** → **she hurries**; **cry** → **she cries**.

EXCEPCIÓN: La única excepción a esta regla la constituye el sufijo **-ing**.

Ej: **try** + **ing** = **trying**; **carry** + **ing** = **carrying**.

Ⓑ Cuando la **-y** va precedida de vocal, esta **y** se mantiene.

Ej: **convey** → **conveyed**; **lay** → **layer**

NOTA: Los sustantivos que acaban en **y** precedida de vocal tienen un plural regular. Así: **boy** → **boys**; **key** → **keys**. En los verbos acabados en **y** precedida de vocal la tercera persona del presente se forma añadiendo solamente una **s**: **say** → **she says**; **stay** → **he stays**.

5 Grupos vocálicos -ie- y -ei-

En la mayoría de los casos, el orden de las letras de estos grupos vocálicos en el interior de una palabra es **-ie-**, a menos que la **i** vaya precedida de **c**, en cuyo caso ocurre lo contrario.

Ej: **retrieve, believe** pero **receive, deceipt**

Sin embargo, existen unas cuantas excepciones a esta regla, que son, entre otras, las siguientes palabras:

beige	height	seize	weigh
eight	leisure	sleigh	weight
either	neighbour	their	weird
foreign	neither	veil	
freight	rein	vein	

6 Sustantivos terminados en -o

Estos sustantivos forman el plural añadiendo el sufijo **-es**.

Ej: **tomato, tomatoes**; **hero, heroes**; **potato, potatoes**.

EXCEPCIONES:
Cuando terminan en dos vocales.

Ej: **studio, studios**; **radio, radios**.

Cuando los sustantivos son, en origen, palabras abreviadas.

Ej: **kilo, kilos**; **photo, photos**.

7 Palabras terminadas en -ence y -ense

En inglés británico los verbos derivados de ciertos sustantivos que se escriben con **-c-** se escriben con **-s-**. Pero, como veremos más adelante, esto no ocurre en inglés americano.

Ej: **a licence** pero **to license**
the practice pero **to practise**

8 Mayúsculas

Las mayúsculas se emplean más en inglés que en español. Se emplean como en español al principio de palabra en los siguientes casos: en la primera palabra de la frase; en los nombres propios de toda clase; en los nombres, sobrenombres y pronombres posesivos de Dios, Jesucristo, la Virgen etc; en las graduaciones y títulos de las autoridades del estado, del ejército, de la iglesia y de las empresas.

Las mayúsculas se emplean en inglés en los siguientes casos donde se escribe minúscula en español:

Ⓐ Los nombres de los días y meses: **Monday, Tuesday, May, June**

Ⓑ El pronombre personal de sujeto, primera persona: **I** (yo). Pero, a diferencia del español, en que se escribe Vd., Vds., el pronombre de segunda persona (igual que el resto de los pronombres) se escribe siempre con minúscula.

Ⓒ Los gentilicios: **I like the French, two Frenchwomen, French cheese, to talk French, a text in old Castilian**. Sin embargo, el adjetivo de nacionalidad puede escribirse con minúscula en algún caso cuando se refiere a una cosa corriente u objeto conocido de todos, p. ej. **a french window, french beans, german measles, venetian blinds**.

Ⓓ En los nombres y adjetivos derivados de otras clases de nombres propios: **a Darwinian explanation, a Thatcherite, the Elizabethans**.

Ⓔ En los sustantivos y adjetivos principales en los títulos de libros, películas, artículos etc: **A Clockwork Orange, Gone with the Wind**.

9 Apóstrofes

El apóstrofe se usa fundamentalmente en inglés:

Ⓐ En la formación del posesivo (el llamado posesivo sajón), para la que se añade una **s** precedida de apóstrofe al singular de cualquier sustantivo o al plural que no acabe en **-s**.

Ej: **my father's car**; **women's talk**

En los plurales de los sustantivos acabados en **-s** se añade solamente un apóstrofe.

Ej: **their friends' house; my daughters' social life**

Ⓑ En determinadas contracciones de palabras, para señalar la omisión de una o más letras.

Ej: **I am** → **I'm**; **you are** → **you're**; **he is** → **he's**; **I had/ I would** → **I'd**; **you have** → **you've**; **does not** → **doesn't**; **I shall/will** → **I'll** etc

10 Diferencias ortográficas entre el inglés británico y el norteamericano

Palabras con el grupo vocálico -ou-

Ⓐ En las palabras terminadas en **-our** en inglés británico derivadas del latín, la **u** se suprime en inglés americano. Así, por ejemplo: inglés británico **colour** = inglés americano **color**; inglés británico **labour** = inglés americano **labor**. (Esto no afecta a los monosílabos como **dour, flour, sour,** donde no hay diferencia).

Ⓑ En inglés americano también se suprime la **u** cuando este grupo de letras se encuentra en el interior de la palabra. Así: inglés británico **mould** = inglés americano **mold**; inglés británico **smoulder** = inglés americano **smolder**.

Palabras terminadas en -re *(Brit)*

Cuando esta terminación va precedida de consonante y el énfasis no recae en esta sílaba en inglés británico, normalmente cambia a **-er** en inglés americano: inglés británico **centre** = inglés americano **center**; inglés británico **metre** = inglés americano **meter**; inglés británico **theatre** = inglés americano **theater**. (Pero no existe diferencia en **acre, genre, lucre, massacre, mediocre, ogre**).

Vocales finales

Ciertas vocales finales, que no tienen valor en la pronunciación, se escriben en inglés británico pero se suprimen en inglés americano: inglés americano **catalog** = inglés británico **catalogue**; inglés americano **prolog** = inglés británico **prologue**; inglés americano **program** = inglés británico **programme**; inglés americano **kilogram** = inglés británico **kilogramme**.

Diptongos de origen griego o latino

En inglés americano se suele simplificar los diptongos de origen griego o latino **ae, oe,** escribiéndose sencillamente **e**: inglés americano **anemia** = inglés británico **anaemia**; inglés americano **anesthesia** = inglés británico **anaesthesia**. En inglés americano se duda entre **subpoena** y **subpena**; en inglés británico se mantiene siempre el primero.

Palabras terminadas en -ence *(Brit)*

En algunos casos las palabras que en inglés británico terminan en **-ence** se escriben **-ense** en inglés americano: inglés británico **defence** = inglés americano **defense**; inglés británico **offence** = inglés americano **offense**.

Consonantes dobles

Algunas consonantes que en inglés británico se escriben dobles, en inglés americano se escriben sencillas: inglés británico **waggon** = inglés americano **wagon** (aunque **wagon** se admite también en el Reino Unido). Pero esto ocurre sobre todo en formas verbales, al añadirse sufijos a verbos que acaban en consonante (ver más arriba). Así, por ejemplo: inglés británico **kidnapped** = inglés americano **kidnaped**; inglés británico **worshipped** = inglés americano **worshiped**.

En el caso de la **l** o **ll** intervocálicas, mientras en inglés británico la **l** se hace doble antes de un sufijo en las palabras que terminan en **l** precedida de una sola vocal o de dos vocales que forman un diptongo (ver más arriba), en inglés americano estas palabras se escriben con una sola **l**. Así, por ejemplo: inglés británico **councillor** = inglés americano **councilor**; inglés británico **traveller** = inglés americano **traveler**. Sin embargo, en posición de final de sílaba o de palabra, la **l** en inglés británico es a menudo **ll** en inglés americano: así inglés americano **enroll, enrolls** = inglés británico **enrol, enrols**; inglés americano **skillful** = inglés británico **skilful**.

Uso familiar

En inglés americano se modifica algún otro grupo ortográfico del inglés, pero sólo en la escritura de tono familiar: inglés americano **tho** = inglés británico **though**; inglés americano **thru** = inglés británico **through**. También son más corrientes en inglés americano las formas como **Peterboro** (o bien **Peterboro'**), aunque éstas no son desconocidas en inglés británico.

Algunas palabras aisladas

Existe una serie de palabras aisladas que se escriben de modo diferente:

(US)	*(Brit)*	*(US)*	*(Brit)*
ax	axe	mustache	moustache
check	cheque	pajamas	pyjamas
cozy	cosy	plow	plough
disk	disc	skeptic	sceptic
gray	grey	tire	tyre
gypsy	gipsy		

Es importante observar, sin embargo, que existen algunas palabras que en inglés británico se escriben con ortografía americano, aunque en general su significado queda restringido a determinados contextos. Así, por ejemplo, encontramos **disk** y **program** con ortografía norteamericana, pero referidos exclusivamente a la Informática, mientras que en todos los demás casos se escribe **disc** y **programme**.

11 La puntuación

Se usan los mismos signos que en español, con las siguientes excepciones:

Ⓐ Los signos de admiración e interrogación

Los signos de apertura de admiración e interrogación (¡¿) no se emplean en inglés.

Ej.: **What is her name?**
Help!

Ⓑ El paréntesis

En inglés el paréntesis se prefiere en muchos casos a la doble raya con función parentética (—...—).

Ej.: **Old people think that the pace of modern life (i.e. from 1940 onwards) is far too fast.**

Ⓒ Las comillas

Se utilizan para abrir y cerrar el diálogo y la oración directa, en lugar de la raya.

Ej.: **"Would you like a cup of coffee?" she asked, smiling shyly.**

Ⓓ La raya

En inglés informal se usa a menudo, en lugar de los dos puntos o del punto y coma, para indicar que lo que sigue es conclusión o resumen de lo anterior.

Ej.: **Everybody was trying to speak at the same time — the noise was deafening.**

Y también bien para separar un comentario o una idea del resto de la frase.

Ej.: **She told me everything she knew — at least that's what I thought at the time.**

Ⓔ El guión

Se usa, como en español, para formar palabras compuestas de otras dos o más palabras, así como para dividir palabras al final de renglón (ver más abajo).

También se usa en ocasiones en inglés británico para separar determinados prefijos, en los siguientes casos:

– cuando el prefijo acaba en la misma vocal con la que empieza la siguiente palabra.

Ej.: **co-opting, pre-eminent**

– cuando va delante de una palabra escrita con mayúscula.

Ej.: **anti-American, pre-Victorian**

– siempre que se trate de los prefijos **ex-** y **non-**.

Ej.: **ex-husband, non-proliferation**

12 La división de la palabra

Las reglas para dividir una palabra en final de renglón son menos estrictas en inglés que en español. En general se prefiere cortar la palabra tras vocal, **hori-zontal, vindi-cation**, pero se prefiere mantener como unidades ciertos sufijos comunes, **vindica-tion, glamor-ous**. De acuerdo con esto se divide la palabra dejando separada la desinencia **-ing**, p.ej. **sicken-ing**, pero si ésta está precedida por un grupo de consonantes, una de ellas se deja unida a **-ing**, p.ej. **tick-ling**. Los grupos de dos consonantes iguales se dividen: **pat-ter, yel-low, disap-pear**, así como los demás grupos consonánticos, que lo hacen de acuerdo con los elementos separables que forman la palabra: **dis-count, per-turb**.

DICCIONARIO ESPAÑOL~INGLÉS

SPANISH~ENGLISH DICTIONARY

A a

A, a SF (= *letra*) A, a

a PREP 1 (*indicando dirección*) 1·1 (*hacia alguna parte*) to; **voy a la tienda/al parque** I'm going to the shop/to the park; **ir a trabajar** *o* **al trabajo** to go to work; **de aquí a Sevilla se tarda una hora** it's an hour from here to Seville; **mirar al norte** to look north(wards); **de cara al norte** facing north; **torcer a la derecha** to turn (to the) right; **ir a casa** to go home

1·2 (*hacia dentro*) into; **me caí al río/mar** I fell into the river/sea; **mirarse a los ojos** to look into each other's eyes; **subir a un avión** to get into a plane; **subirse a un tren** to get on a train

1·3 **llegar a** [+ *ciudad, país*] to arrive in; [+ *edificio*] to arrive at; **¿cuándo llegaste a Londres?** when did you arrive in London?; **no ha llegado todavía a la oficina** she still hasn't arrived at the office

1·4 (= *encima de*) onto; **se subieron al tejado** they climbed onto the roof; **bajaron del tren al andén** they stepped out of the train onto the platform

2 (*indicando situación, distancia*) **al final de la calle** at the end of the street; **a la orilla del río** on the riverbank; **al lado del cine** next to the cinema; **siéntate a mi lado** sit next to me, sit beside me; **nos pusimos a la sombra** we moved into the shade; **está a siete km de aquí** it is seven km (away) from here; **de éste a aquél no hay mucha diferencia** there's not much difference between this one and that one; **a lo lejos** in the distance; **a la derecha** on the right; **a la izquierda** on the left; **estar a la mesa** to be at table; **estaba sentado a su mesa de trabajo** he was sitting at his desk

3 (*con expresiones de tiempo*) 3·1 (*en un momento concreto*) at; **a las ocho** at eight o'clock; **a los 55 años** at the age of 55; **¿a qué hora llega el tren?** what time *o* when does the train arrive?; **estamos a tres de julio** it's the third of July; **a la mañana siguiente** the following morning; **a medianoche** at midnight; **a mediodía** at noon; **a la noche** at night; **a la tarde** in the afternoon; *ver tb* **tiempo**

3·2 (*con tiempo transcurrido*) **a la semana** a week later; **al año** a year later; **al año de vivir en Caracas** after living in Caracas for a year; **a los pocos días** after a few days, a few days later; **"Cervantes, a los 400 años de su muerte"** "Cervantes 400 years after his death", "Cervantes 400 years on"; **a los 18 minutos de juego** in the 18th minute, 18 minutes into the game; **a la que te descuidas ...** if you're not careful ..., before you know where you are ...

3·3 (*indicando frecuencia*) **dos veces al día** twice a day; **una vez a la semana** once a week; **día a día vamos mejorando** we're improving with every day, we're improving day by day

3·4 **al** (+ *INFIN*): **al entrar yo** when I came in; **al verlo, lo reconocí inmediatamente** when I saw him, I recognized him immediately; **nos cruzamos al salir** we bumped into each other as we were going out; **estar al llegar** to be about to arrive; **al no llegar a tiempo, quedamos fuera de la prueba** since we didn't arrive on time, we were eliminated from the race

4 (*indicando modo*) **a la americana** American-style; **una cocina a gas** a gas stove; **funciona a pilas y a la red** it runs on batteries and on mains electricity; **una camisa a cuadros** a check *o* checked shirt; **una camisa a rayas** a striped shirt; **a pie/caballo** on foot/horseback; **fui a pie** I walked; **fui a caballo** I rode; **a oscuras** in the dark; **a lápiz** in pencil; **lo derribó a puñetazos** she knocked him to the ground; **lo mataron a navajazos** they stabbed him to death; **sabe a queso** it tastes of cheese; **huele a vino** it smells of wine; **es muy agradable al tacto** it feels very nice; **beber algo a sorbos** to sip sth; **despertarse al menor ruido** to wake at the slightest sound; **a mano** by hand; **hay que lavarlo a mano** it should be washed by hand; **escrito a mano** hand-written; **hecho a mano** handmade; **una sábana bordada a mano** a hand-embroidered sheet

5 (*indicando cantidad, precio, velocidad*) **a un precio elevado** at a high price; **a 3 euros el kilo** at *o* for 3 euros a kilo; **los huevos están a un euro la docena** eggs are a euro a dozen; **al 5 por ciento** at 5 per cent; **íbamos a más de 120km por hora** we were going at *o* doing over 120km an hour; **poco a poco** little by little

6 (*indicando finalidad*) 6·1 (*tras verbos*) to; **voy a verla** I'm going to see her; **ha ido a por agua a la fuente** she's gone to get some water from the fountain; **empezó a cantar** he began to sing, he started singing; **ha salido a tomar el aire** she's gone out for a breath of fresh air; **vengo a que me den un impreso** I've come to get a form

6·2 (*tras sustantivos*) **el criterio a adoptar** the criterion to be adopted; **asuntos a tratar** items to be discussed; **"precio a convenir"** "price negotiable"; **¿cuál es la cantidad a pagar?** what do we have to pay?; **éste será el camino a seguir** this must be the path to take

7 (*con complemento de persona*) 7·1 (*como complemento indirecto*) to; **¿le has dado el libro a él?** did you give him the book?, did you give the book to him?; **le enseñé a Pablo el libro que me dejaste** I showed Pablo the book you lent me, I showed the book you lent me to Pablo; **el Barcelona marcó cinco goles al Madrid** Barcelona scored five against Madrid

7·2 (*como complemento directo*) *no se traduce*; **vi al jefe** I saw the boss; **llamé al médico** I called the doctor

7·3 (*indicando procedencia*) from; **se lo compré a él** I bought it from him

8 (*indicando condición*) **a no ser esto así, me iría** if this were not the case, I'd leave

9 (*indicando desafío*) **a que** I bet; **¿a que no sabes quién ha llamado?** (I) bet you can't guess who called; **¿a que no te atreves a tirarte de cabeza?** (I) bet you don't dare dive in headfirst

10 (*uso imperativo*) **¡a callar!** be quiet!; **¡a trabajar!** down to work!; **¡a comer!** lunch is ready!

11 (= *en cuanto a*) **a supersticioso no hay quien le gane** when it comes to being superstitious, there's nobody quite like him

A. ABR = **aprobado**

AA ABR (*Aer*) = **Aerolíneas Argentinas**

A.A. ABR (= **Alcohólicos Anónimos**) AA

AA.AA. ABR (= **Antiguos Alumnos**) FPs

AAE SF ABR (= **Asociación de Aerolíneas Europeas**) AEA

AA.EE. ABR = **Asuntos Exteriores**

ab. ABR (= **abril**) Apr

abacá SM abaca, Manilla hemp

abacado SM (*Caribe*) avocado pear

abacería SF grocer's (shop), grocery store

abacero/a SM/F grocer

ábaco SM abacus

abacora SF (*LAm*) *type of tuna*

abacorar ▸conjug 1a◂ VT 1 (*Andes, Caribe*) (= *acosar*) to harass, bother; (= *sorprender*) to catch, surprise

2 (*Caribe*) (= *acometer*) to undertake boldly; (= *seducir*) to entice away

3 (*LAm Com*) to monopolize

abad SM abbot

abadejo SM 1 (= *pez*) [*de mar*] cod, codfish; [*de agua dulce*] ling; (*Caribe*) (= *pez espada*)

swordfish
[2] (= *insecto*) Spanish fly
[3] (*Culin*) dried salted cod
[4] (= *ave*) kinglet

abadengo Ⓐ ADJ abbatial, of an abbot
Ⓑ SM abbacy

abadesa SF [1] (*Rel*) abbess
[2] (*LAm**) madame, brothel keeper

abadía SF [1] (= *convento*) abbey
[2] (= *oficio*) abbacy

abajadero SM slope, incline

abajar ▸conjug 1a◂ VT (*LAm*) = **bajar**

abajeño/a (*LAm*) Ⓐ ADJ lowland, coastal
Ⓑ SM/F lowlander, coastal dweller

abajera SF (*Cono Sur*) saddlecloth

abajero ADJ (*LAm*) lower, under

abajino/a (*Cono Sur*) Ⓐ ADJ northern
Ⓑ SM/F northerner

abajo Ⓐ ADV [1] (*indicando posición*) [1·1] (*gen*) down; **~ en el río** down at the river; **ahí** *o* **allá** *o* **allí ~** down there; **aquí ~** down here; **de ~** lower, bottom; **yo duermo en la litera de ~** I sleep in the lower *o* bottom bunk; **la sábana de ~** the bottom sheet; **la parte de ~** the bottom; **el piso de ~** (= *planta inferior*) the next floor down; (= *planta baja*) the ground floor; **desde ~** from below; **más ~** (*en distancia*) further down; (*en altura*) lower down; **dos kilómetros más ~** two kilometres further down; **hay una farmacia un poco más ~** there's a chemist's further down the road; **unos escalones más ~** a few steps lower down; **vivo tres pisos más ~** I live three floors below; **de cintura para ~** from the waist down; **por ~** (= *en la parte inferior*) at the bottom; (= *por debajo*) underneath; **el abrigo está lleno de barro por ~** the bottom of the coat is all muddy; **tenía telarañas por ~** it had cobwebs underneath; **~ del todo** right at the bottom, at the very bottom; *ver tb* **boca**
[1·2] (*en edificio, casa*) downstairs; **~ están la cocina y el salón** the kitchen and lounge are downstairs; **te están esperando ~** they're waiting for you downstairs; **los vecinos de ~** the downstairs neighbours; **hay una fiesta en el apartamento de ~** there's a party in the flat downstairs
[2] (*indicando dirección*) [2·1] (*con sustantivos*) **aguas ~** downriver, downstream; **continuaron aguas ~ durante un rato** they continued downriver *o* downstream for a while; **sigamos aguas ~ del río** let's carry on down the river; **calle ~** down the street; **seguimos calle ~, hasta la plaza** we followed the street down to the square; **estuvimos calle arriba, calle ~, buscando al niño** we went up and down the street, looking for the child; **cuesta ~** down the hill; **escaleras ~** downstairs; **ladera ~** down the hillside; **río ~** downstream, downriver
[2·2] (*con preposición*) **hacia ~** downward(s), down; **se iban deslizando hacia ~** they were sliding downward(s) *o* down; **caminaba con la cabeza hacia ~** he walked with his head bent down; **para ~**: **me voy para ~** I'm going down; **no mires para ~** don't look down; **la economía va para ~** the economy is going downhill
[2·3] (*con verbo*) **echar ~** [+ *puerta, barricada*] to break down; [+ *gobierno*] to bring down; [+ *paz*] to break up; **venirse ~** [*edificio, estructura, economía*] to collapse; [*planes, sueños*] to come to nothing; [*persona*] to go to pieces; **después del divorcio se vino ~** after the divorce he went to pieces; **este país se ha venido ~ por culpa de la guerra** this country has been ruined by war, war has brought this country to its knees
[3] (*en un texto*) below; **en la foto de ~** in the photo below; **el ~ firmante** the undersigned
[4] (*en una escala*) the bottom; **los cambios deben empezar por ~, a nivel local** change should begin at the bottom, at local level; **los de ~ siempre salimos perdiendo** those of us at the bottom (of the pile) are always the losers; **una revolución tiene que empezar desde ~** a revolution must start from the bottom up; **para ~**: **los responsables, de ministro para ~, deben dimitir** those responsible, from the minister down, should resign; **de 30 años para ~** 30 years old and under
[5] (*esp LAm*) (= *debajo*) underneath
[6] **~ de** (*LAm*) under; **~ de la camisa** under the shirt
Ⓑ EXCL down with!; **¡~ el gobierno!** down with the government!

abajofirmante SMF **el ~** ◊ **la ~** the undersigned

abalanzadero SM (*Méx*) ford, cattle crossing

abalanzar ▸conjug 1f◂ Ⓐ VT [1] (= *lanzar*) to hurl, throw
[2] (= *impeler*) to impel
[3] (= *pesar*) to weigh
[4] (= *equilibrar*) to balance
Ⓑ **abalanzarse** VPR [1] (= *lanzarse*) to rush forward; [*multitud*] to surge forward; **todos se ~on hacia la salida** everyone rushed towards the exit; **~se sobre** to spring at, rush at; [*ave*] to pounce on
[2] (*Cono Sur*) [*caballo*] to rear up

abaldonar ▸conjug 1a◂ VT (†) (= *degradar*) to degrade, debase; (= *insultar*) to affront

abalear* ▸conjug 1a◂ Ⓐ VT (*LAm*) to fire at, shoot up*; (*Andes*) (= *fusilar*) to shoot, execute
Ⓑ VI (*LAm*) to shoot off one's gun, fire in the air

abaleo* SM (*LAm*) shooting

abalorio SM glass bead; ✦**MODISMO no vale un ~** it's worthless

abalumar* ▸conjug 1a◂ VT (*Méx*), **abalumbar*** ▸conjug 1a◂ VT (*Méx*) to pile up, stack

abanarse* ▸conjug 1a◂ VPR (*Cono Sur*) to show off

abanderado/a SM/F [1] (= *portaestandarte*) standard bearer
[2] [*de un movimiento*] champion, leader
[3] (*LAm*) (= *representante*) representative
[4] (*Méx*) (= *linier*) linesman, assistant referee

abanderar ▸conjug 1a◂ VT [1] (*Náut*) to register
[2] [+ *causa*] to champion; [+ *campaña*] to take a leading role in

abanderizar ▸conjug 1f◂ Ⓐ VT to organize into bands
Ⓑ **abanderizarse** VPR to band together; (*Cono Sur Pol*) to take sides, adopt a position

abandonado ADJ [1] (= *sin gente*) [*pueblo, vivienda vacía*] abandoned, deserted; [*fábrica, cantera*] disused; [*edificio en ruinas*] derelict
[2] (= *desatendido*) [*jardín, terreno*] neglected; **la casa estaba muy abandonada, toda cubierta de polvo** the house was really neglected, completely covered in dust; **tienes ~s a los amigos** you've neglected your friends; **¡~ me tenías!** you'd forgotten all about me!; **tienen el negocio muy ~** they've allowed their business to decline; **dejar ~** [+ *cónyuge, hijo*] to abandon, desert; [+ *animal, casa, vehículo*] to abandon; **huyeron dejando abandonadas sus armas** they fled abandoning their weapons; **el autobús nos dejó ~s en la carretera** the bus left us stranded *o* abandoned us by the roadside
[3] (= *despreocupado*) slack; **es muy ~ para las cosas de la casa** he's very slack about everything to do with the house
[4] (= *desaliñado*) scruffy, shabby; **a ver si no eres tan ~ y te arreglas un poco** come on, tidy yourself up a bit and stop looking so scruffy *o* shabby
[5] (= *solitario*) desolate, forlorn (*frm*)

abandonamiento SM = **abandono**

abandonar ▸conjug 1a◂ Ⓐ VT [1] (= *dejar abandonado*) [+ *cónyuge, hijo*] to abandon, desert; [+ *animal, casa, posesiones*] to abandon; [+ *obligaciones*] to neglect; **la abandonó por otra mujer** he abandoned *o* deserted her for another woman; **no me abandones nunca** never leave me; **tuvimos que ~ nuestras pertenencias en la huida** we had to abandon all our belongings when we fled; **no debes ~ las labores de la casa** you shouldn't neglect the housework; **~ el barco** to abandon ship; ✦**MODISMO ~ a algn a su suerte** *o* **a la buena de Dios** to abandon *o* leave sb to their fate
[2] (= *marcharse de*) [+ *lugar, organización*] to leave; **pronto podrán ~ el hospital** they will soon be able to leave the hospital; **abandonó la reunión hecho una furia** he stormed out of the meeting; **miles de refugiados han abandonado la ciudad** thousands of refugees have abandoned the city
[3] (= *renunciar a*) [+ *estudios, proyecto*] to give up, abandon; [+ *costumbre, cargo*] to give up; [+ *privilegio, título*] to renounce, relinquish; **hemos abandonado la idea de montar un negocio** we have given up *o* abandoned the idea of starting a business; **he decidido ~ la política** I've decided to give up *o* abandon politics; **si el tratamiento no da resultado lo ~emos** if the treatment doesn't work, we'll abandon it; **no es fácil ~ el tabaco** it's not easy to give up smoking; **la guerrilla ha prometido ~ las armas** the guerrillas have promised to lay down their arms; **se comprometieron a ~ sus reivindicaciones territoriales** they promised to renounce *o* relinquish their territorial claims
[4] [*buen humor, suerte*] to desert; **el valor la abandonó** her courage deserted her; **nunca los abandona la alegría** they are always happy
Ⓑ VI [1] (*Atletismo*) (*antes de la prueba*) to pull out, withdraw; (*durante la prueba*) to pull out, retire
[2] (*Boxeo*) to concede defeat, throw in the towel* *o* (*EEUU*) sponge
[3] (*Ajedrez*) to resign, concede
[4] (*Inform*) to quit
Ⓒ **abandonarse** VPR [1] (= *no cuidarse*) to let o.s. go; **no deberías ~te aunque estés deprimida** you shouldn't let yourself go even though you're depressed; **aunque no se abandona nada parece cada vez más viejo** although he looks after himself very well he looks older every day
[2] (= *entregarse*) to abandon o.s.; **nos aban-**

donamos en manos de la suerte we abandoned ourselves to the hand of fate; **~se a** [+ *alcohol, droga*] to give o.s. over *o* up to, abandon o.s. to; [+ *destino, suerte*] to abandon o.s. to; [+ *sueño*] to surrender to, give in to; **no te abandones a la desesperación** don't give in to despair
3 (= *desanimarse*) to lose heart, get discouraged

abandonismo SM defeatism

abandonista ADJ, SMF defeatist

abandono SM 1 (= *acción*) 1·1 [*de lugar*] **ordenaron el ~ de la isla** they ordered people to abandon *o* leave the island; **el ~ de la zona por las tropas de ocupación** the withdrawal of the occupying forces from the region
1·2 [*de actividad, proyecto*] abandonment; **votaron a favor del ~ del leninismo** they voted in favour of renouncing Leninism, they voted for the abandonment of Leninism; **ofrecen ayudas a los agricultores para el ~ de la producción** they are offering aid to farmers to cease production; **mi ~ del cargo se debió a problemas internos** I gave up the post because of internal problems
1·3 (*Jur*) [*de cónyuge*] desertion; [*de hijos*] abandonment; **en caso de ~ de uno de los cónyuges** in the event of the desertion of either partner
► **abandono de deberes** dereliction of duty
► **abandono de la escuela** = **abandono escolar** ► **abandono del domicilio conyugal**, **abandono del hogar** desertion
► **abandono de tierras** land set aside, set-aside ► **abandono escolar** leaving school (*before school-leaving age*); **problemas causados por el ~ escolar** problems caused by students leaving school early
2 (*Dep*) (*antes de la prueba*) withdrawal; (*durante la prueba*) retirement; (*Ajedrez*) resignation; **ganar por ~** to win by default (*thanks to an opponent's withdrawal*)
3 (= *descuido*) neglect, abandon (*frm*); **la iglesia se encontraba en un terrible estado de ~** the church was in a terrible state of neglect *o* abandon (*frm*); **es lamentable el ~ que sufre la sanidad pública desde hace años** it's dreadful how public health has been so neglected for years; **darse al ~** to go downhill
4 (= *vicio*) indulgence; **llevaba una vida de excesos y ~** she led a life of excess and indulgence; **viven en el mayor ~** they live in utter degradation
5 (= *soledad*) desolation; **me invadió una sensación de ~** I was overcome by a feeling of desolation; **el pueblo presentaba un aspecto de ~** the town had a forlorn look about it
6 (*Méx*) (= *ligereza*) abandon, ease

abanicada SF fanning, fanning action

abanicar ▸conjug 1g◂ Ⓐ VT to fan
Ⓑ **abanicarse** VPR to fan o.s.; ✦*MODISMO* **~se con algo** (*Cono Sur*‡) not to give a damn about sth*

abanico SM 1 (*para darse aire*) fan; **extender las cartas en ~** to fan out one's cards; **con hojas en ~** with leaves arranged like a fan
► **abanico de chimenea** fire screen
► **abanico eléctrico** (*Méx*) (= *ventilador*) electric fan
2 (= *gama*) range ► **abanico de posibilidades** range of possibilities ► **abanico de salarios**, **abanico salarial** wage scale
3 (*Náut*) derrick
4 (*Caribe Ferro*) points signal

abaniquear ▸conjug 1a◂ (*LAm*) Ⓐ VT to fan
Ⓑ **abaniquearse** VPR to fan o.s.

abaniqueo SM (*con abanico*) fanning, fanning movement; (= *manoteo*) gesticulation

abaniquero/a SM/F (= *fabricante*) fan maker; (= *comerciante*) dealer in fans

abarajar* ▸conjug 1a◂ VT (*Cono Sur*) [+ *golpe*] to parry, counter

abaratamiento SM price reduction

abaratar ▸conjug 1a◂ Ⓐ VT [+ *artículo*] to make cheaper, lower the price of; [+ *precio*] to lower
Ⓑ **abaratarse** VPR to get cheaper, come down (in price)

abarca SF sandal

abarcar ▸conjug 1g◂ VT 1 (*con los brazos*) to get one's arms round
2 (= *comprender*) to include, take in; (= *contener*) to contain, comprise; **el capítulo abarca tres siglos** the chapter covers three centuries; **sus conocimientos abarcan todo el campo de ...** his knowledge ranges over the whole field of ...; **abarca una hectárea** it takes up a hectare, it's a hectare in size
3 [+ *tarea*] to undertake, take on; ✦*REFRÁN* **quien mucho abarca poco aprieta** don't bite off more than you can chew
4 (*LAm*) (= *acaparar*) to monopolize, corner the market in
5 (*con la vista*) to take in; **desde aquí se abarca todo el valle** you can take in the whole valley from here

abarque SM (*Andes*) (= *huevos*) clutch

abarquillar ▸conjug 1a◂ Ⓐ VT (= *arrollar*) to curl up, roll up; (= *arrugar*) to wrinkle
Ⓑ **abarquillarse** VPR (= *arrollarse*) to curl up, roll up; (= *arrugarse*) to crinkle

abarraganarse ▸conjug 1a◂ VPR to live together, set up home together

abarrajado* ADJ (*Cono Sur*) (= *libertino*) dissolute, free-living; (= *peleón*) quarrelsome, argumentative

abarrajar* ▸conjug 1a◂ Ⓐ VI (*Cono Sur*) to run away, flee
Ⓑ **abarrajarse** VPR 1 (*Andes*) (= *caer de bruces*) to fall flat on one's face
2 (*Andes, Cono Sur*) (= *prostituirse*) to prostitute o.s., sell o.s.; (= *envilecerse*) to become corrupt, be perverted

abarrajo SM (*Andes*) fall, stumble

abarrancadero SM tight spot, jam

abarrancar ▸conjug 1g◂ Ⓐ VT to make cracks in, open up fissures in
Ⓑ **abarrancarse** VPR 1 (= *caer*) to fall into a ditch *o* pit
2 (= *atascarse*) to get stopped up
3 (*Náut*) to run aground
4 (= *meterse en un lío*) to get into a jam

abarrotar ▸conjug 1a◂ Ⓐ VT 1 (= *llenar*) to pack; **el público abarrotaba la sala** the hall was packed with people; **el cine estaba abarrotado (de gente)** the cinema was packed; **abarrotado de** bursting with, stuffed full of
2 (*Náut*) to stow, pack tightly
3 (*Com*) to overstock
Ⓑ **abarrotarse** VPR 1 (= *llenarse*) to get packed
2 (*LAm Com*) to become saturated; **~se de** (*Méx*) to be stuffed with, be bursting with

abarrote SM 1 (*Náut*) packing
2 **abarrotes** (*LAm*) (= *ultramarinos*) groceries; **tienda de ~s** grocer's (shop), grocery store

abarrotería SF (*LAm*) grocer's (shop), grocery store

abarrotero/a SM/F (*LAm*) grocer

abastar ▸conjug 1a◂ VT to supply

abastardar ▸conjug 1a◂ Ⓐ VT to degrade, debase
Ⓑ VI to degenerate

abastecedor(a) Ⓐ ADJ supplying
Ⓑ SM/F 1 (= *proveedor*) supplier, purveyor (*frm*)
2 (*Méx*) (= *carnicero*) wholesale butcher, meat supplier

abastecer ▸conjug 2d◂ VT to supply, provide (**de** with)

abastecimiento SM (= *acto*) supplying, provision; (= *servicio*) supply, provision; (= *víveres*) provisions *pl* ► **abastecimiento de agua** water supply

abastero SM (*Cono Sur, Méx*) wholesale butcher

abasto SM 1 (= *provisión*) supply; **dar ~ a** to supply; **dar ~ a un pedido** to fill an order, meet an order; **no da ~** there isn't enough (to go round); **no puedo dar ~ (a)** (*fig*) I can't cope *o* keep up (with)
2 (*Cono Sur*) public meat market
3 (*Caribe*) grocer's (shop), grocery store

abatanado ADJ skilled, skilful, skillful (*EEUU*)

abatanar ▸conjug 1a◂ VT [+ *paño*] to beat, full; (= *maltratar*) to beat

abatatado ADJ (*Cono Sur*) shy, coy

abatatarse ▸conjug 1a◂ VPR (*Cono Sur*) to be shy, be bashful

abate SM (*Rel frec hum*) father, abbé

abatí SM (*Andes, Cono Sur*) maize, Indian corn (*EEUU*)

abatible ADJ **asiento ~** tip-up seat; (*Aut*) reclining seat; **mesa de alas ~s** gate-leg(ged) table

abatido ADJ 1 (= *deprimido*) depressed, dejected; **estar muy ~** to be very depressed; **estar ~ por el dolor** to be writhing in pain; **tener la cara abatida** to be crestfallen, look dejected
2 (= *despreciable*) despicable, contemptible
3 (*Com, Fin*) depreciated

abatimiento SM 1 (= *derribamiento*) demolition, knocking down
2 (= *depresión*) depression, dejection
3 (= *moral*) contemptible nature

abatir ▸conjug 3a◂ Ⓐ VT 1 (= *derribar*) to demolish, knock down; [+ *tienda de campaña*] to take down; [+ *árbol*] to cut down, fell; [+ *ave*] to shoot down, bring down; [+ *bandera*] to lower, strike; [+ *persona*] to knock down
2 [*enfermedad, dolor*] to lay low, prostrate (*frm*)
3 (= *desanimar*) to depress, discourage; (= *humillar*) to humble, humiliate
Ⓑ **abatirse** VPR 1 (= *caerse*) to drop, fall; [*pájaro, avión*] to swoop, dive; **~se sobre** to swoop on
2 (= *desanimarse*) to be depressed, get discouraged

abayuncar ▸conjug 1g◂ (*Méx*) Ⓐ VT [+ *vaca*] to

throw, ground; **~ a algn*** to put sb on the spot
Ⓑ **abayuncarse** VPR (*) to become countrified

abbasí ADJ, SMF Abbasid

ABC SM ABR, **abc** SM ABR = **abecé 2**

Abderramán SM Abd-al-Rahman

abdicación SF abdication

abdicar ▸conjug 1g◂ Ⓐ VT to renounce, relinquish; **~ la corona** to give up the crown, abdicate
Ⓑ VI to abdicate; **~ de algo** to renounce *o* relinquish sth; **~ en algn** to abdicate in favour of sb

abdomen SM abdomen

abdominal Ⓐ ADJ abdominal
Ⓑ SM sit-up

abducción SF (*Med*) abduction

abductor SM (*Anat*) abductor

abecé SM 1 (= *abecedario*) ABC, alphabet
2 (= *lo básico*) rudiments *pl*, basic elements *pl*

abecedario SM alphabet; (= *libro*) primer, spelling book

abedul SM birch ► **abedul plateado** silver birch

abeja SF 1 bee ► **abeja asesina** killer bee ► **abeja machiega** queen bee ► **abeja macho** male bee, drone ► **abeja maestra** queen bee ► **abeja neutra**, **abeja obrera** worker bee ► **abeja reina** queen bee
2 (*fig*) (= *hormiguita*) hard worker

abejar SM apiary

abejarrón SM bumblebee

abejaruco SM bee-eater

abejera SF beehive

abejón SM 1 (= *abejorro*) drone; (*Méx*) buzzing insect
2 **hacer ~*** (*CAm*) (= *cuchichear*) to whisper; (*Caribe*) (= *silbar*) to boo, hiss

abejonear ▸conjug 1a◂ (*) VI (*Caribe*) to mumble, whisper

abejorro SM (= *insecto volador*) bumblebee; (= *coleóptero*) cockchafer

abejucarse ▸conjug 1g◂ VPR (*Méx*) to twist up, climb

abellacado ADJ villainous

abellacar ▸conjug 1g◂ VT to lower, degrade

aberenjenado ADJ violet-coloured, violet-colored (*EEUU*)

aberración SF aberration; **es una ~ bañarse cinco veces al día** it's crazy to have a bath five times a day

aberrante ADJ aberrant

aberrar ▸conjug 1a◂ VI to be mistaken, err

aberrear ▸conjug 1a◂ VT (*Andes*) to anger, annoy

Aberri Eguna SM *Basque national holiday*, ≈ Easter Sunday

abertura SF 1 (*gen*) opening, gap; (= *agujero*) hole; (= *grieta*) crack; (= *corte*) slit; (= *brecha*) gap
2 (*Geog*) (= *cala*) cove; (= *valle*) wide valley, gap; (= *puerto*) pass
3 (*Cos*) vent
4 (= *franqueza*) openness, frankness

abertzale Ⓐ ADJ **movimiento ~** (Basque) nationalist movement
Ⓑ SMF Basque nationalist

abetal SM fir plantation, fir wood

abeto SM fir, fir tree ► **abeto blanco** silver fir ► **abeto del norte**, **abeto falso**, **abeto rojo** spruce

abetunado ADJ dark-skinned

abetunar ▸conjug 1a◂ VT (*LAm*) to polish, clean

abey SM (*Caribe*) jacaranda tree

abiertamente ADV openly; **ha condenado ~ el terrorismo** she has openly condemned terrorism

abiertazo ADJ (*CAm*) generous, open-handed

abierto Ⓐ PP *de* **abrir**
Ⓑ ADJ 1 [*puerta, armario, boca, herida*] open; **tenía el libro ~ por la página 23** she had the book open at page 23; **la puerta estaba un poco abierta** the door was ajar; **me miró con los ojos muy ~s** he looked at me with his eyes wide-open, he looked at me with wide-open eyes; **llevas la bragueta abierta** your flies are undone *o* open; **dejar ~** [+ *ventana, cortina, válvula*] to leave open; [+ *grifo*] to leave running, leave on; **dejó el tarro ~** he left the top off the jar; *ver tb* **boca, brazo, libro**
2 [*comercio, museo, oficina*] open; **"abierto"** "open"; **estar ~ las 24 horas** to be open 24 hours; **estar ~ al público** to be open to the public
3 (= *sin obstáculos*) [*competición, billete*] open; **un campeonato ~ a todos los menores de 25 años** a championship open to all those under 25; **en campo ~** in the open
4 (= *extrovertido*) [*persona*] open, outgoing; [*carácter, mentalidad*] open; **tiene una mentalidad muy abierta** he's very open-minded, he's got a very open mind
5 **estar ~ a** [+ *sugerencias, ideas*] to be open to; **tienen una actitud abierta al diálogo** they are open to dialogue
6 (= *directo*) [*contradicción, oposición*] open; [*desafío*] direct; **se encuentran en ~ desacuerdo con él** they openly disagree with him
7 (*TV*) **en ~: emitir un programa en ~** to broadcast a programme unscrambled; **emisión en ~** unscrambled programme
8 (*Ling*) [*vocal, sonido*] open
Ⓒ SM (*Dep*) **el Abierto** the Open

abigarrado ADJ 1 (= *de diversos colores*) multi-coloured, multi-colored (*EEUU*); [*animal*] piebald, brindled; [*escena*] vivid, colourful, colorful (*EEUU*)
2 (= *heterogéneo, variopinto*) motley
3 [*habla*] disjointed, uneven

abigarramiento SM 1 [*de colores*] variety
2 [*de ideas, objetos*] chaos

abigarrar ▸conjug 1a◂ VT *to paint etc in a variety of colours*

abigeato SM (*Méx*) cattle rustling

abigeo SM (*Méx*) cattle rustler

-abilidad *ver* **Aspects of Word Formation in Spanish 2**

abintestato ADJ intestate

abiótico ADJ abiotic

abiselar ▸conjug 1a◂ VT to bevel

Abisinia SF Abyssinia

abisinio/a ADJ, SM/F Abyssinian

abismado ADJ 1 (= *abstraído*) lost (*in thought*); **estaba ~ en su lectura** he was engrossed in his reading; **estaba ~ en sus pensamientos** he was lost *o* deep in thought
2 (= *sorprendido*) astonished, amazed

abismal ADJ (= *enorme*) vast, enormous; [*diferencia*] irreconcilable

abismalmente ADV abysmally

abismante* ADJ (*LAm*) amazing, astonishing

abismar ▸conjug 1a◂ Ⓐ VT 1 (= *hundir*) **~ a algn en la tristeza** to plunge sb into sadness
2 (= *humillar*) to cast down, humble
Ⓑ **abismarse** VPR 1 **~se en** to plunge into; **~se en el dolor** to abandon o.s. to grief
2 (*LAm*) (= *asombrarse*) to be amazed, be astonished

abismo SM 1 (= *sima*) abyss, chasm; **de sus ideas a las mías hay un ~** our views are worlds *o* poles apart
2 (= *profundidad*) depth(s); (*Rel*) hell; **desde los ~s de la Edad Media** from the dark depths of the Middle Ages; **estar al borde del ~** to be on the brink of ruin

abizcochado ADJ (*LAm*) spongy

Abjacia SF, **Abjasia** SF Abkhazia

abjacio/a ADJ, SM/F, **abjasio/a** ADJ, SM/F, **abjaso/a** ADJ, SM/F Abkhaz, Abkhazi, Abkhazian

abjuración SF (*Jur*) abjuration

abjurar ▸conjug 1a◂ Ⓐ VT to abjure, forswear
Ⓑ VI **~ de** to abjure, forswear

ablación SF [*de órgano*] removal ► **ablación del clítoris**, **ablación femenina** female circumcision

ablactación SF (*Med*) weaning

ablactar ▸conjug 1a◂ VT (*Med*) to wean

ablandabrevas* SMF INV useless person, good-for-nothing

ablandador SM ► **ablandador de agua** water softener ► **ablandador de carnes** (*Méx*) meat tenderizer

ablandahigos* SMF INV = **ablandabrevas**

ablandamiento SM (*gen*) softening (up); (= *moderación*) moderation

ablandar ▸conjug 1a◂ Ⓐ VT 1 (= *poner blando*) to soften; (*Culin*) to tenderize; [+ *vientre*] to loosen
2 (= *conmover*) to touch; (= *mitigar*) to mitigate, temper; (= *calmar*) to soothe
3 (*LAm Aut*) to run in, break in (*EEUU*)
Ⓑ VI (*Meteo*) [*frío*] to become less severe; [*viento*] to moderate; [*elementos*] decrease in force, die down
Ⓒ **ablandarse** VPR (= *ponerse blando*) to soften (up), get soft(er); [*persona*] to relent, soften; (*con la edad*) to mellow

ablande SM (*LAm Aut*) running-in

ablativo Ⓐ ADJ ablative
Ⓑ SM ablative ► **ablativo absoluto** ablative absolute

-able *ver* **Aspects of Word Formation in Spanish 2**

ablución SF ablution

ablusado Ⓐ ADJ (= *no tallado*) loose
Ⓑ SM (*Cono Sur*) loose garment

abnegación SF self-denial, abnegation (*frm*)

abnegado ADJ self-denying, self-sacrificing

abnegarse ▸conjug 1h, 1j◂ VPR to deny o.s., go without

abobado ADJ (= *que parece tonto*) stupid-looking; (= *asombrado*) bewildered

abobamiento SM (= *estupidez*) silliness, stupidity; (= *asombro*) bewilderment

abobar ▸conjug 1a◂ Ⓐ VT (= *entontecer*) to

make stupid; (= *asombrar*) to daze, bewilder
Ⓑ **abobarse** VPR to become stupid

abocado ADJ [*vino*] smooth, pleasant; [*jerez*] medium-sweet

abocar ▸conjug 1g◂ Ⓐ VT to pour out, decant
Ⓑ VI 1 (*Náut*) to enter a river/channel
2 (= *ir a parar*) **~ a** to lead to, result in, end up in; **estar abocado al desastre** to be heading for disaster; **verse abocado a un peligro** to see danger looming ahead
3 **estar abocado a hacer algo** to be designed to do sth; **esta medida está abocada a mejorar la situación** this measure is designed to *o* is intended to improve the situation
Ⓒ **abocarse** VPR 1 (= *aproximarse*) to approach; **~se con algn** to meet sb, have an interview with sb
2 **~se a** (*Cono Sur*) to confront, face up to

abocardo SM (*Téc*) drill

abocastro SM (*Andes, Cono Sur*) ugly devil

abocetar ▸conjug 1a◂ VT to sketch

abochornado ADJ embarrassed

abochornante ADJ = **bochornoso 2**

abochornar ▸conjug 1a◂ Ⓐ VT (= *sofocar*) to suffocate; (= *avergonzar*) to shame, embarrass
Ⓑ **abochornarse** VPR to get flushed; [*planta*] to wilt; **~se de** to get embarrassed about

abocinado ADJ trumpet-shaped

abocinar ▸conjug 1a◂ Ⓐ VT (= *dar forma de bocina*) to shape like a trumpet; (*Cos*) to flare
Ⓑ **abocinarse** VPR (*) to fall flat on one's face

abodocarse ▸conjug 1g◂ VPR 1 (*CAm*) [*líquido*] to go lumpy
2 (*Méx**) to come out in boils

abofado ADJ (*Caribe, Méx*) swollen

abofarse ▸conjug 1g◂ VPR (*Méx*) to stuff o.s.

abofetear ▸conjug 1a◂ VT to slap, hit (in the face)

abogacía SF (= *abogados*) legal profession; (= *oficio*) the law

abogaderas SFPL (*LAm*), **abogaderías** SFPL (*LAm pey*) specious arguments, false arguments

abogado/a SM/F 1 lawyer, attorney(-at-law) (*EEUU*); **ejercer de ~** to practise *o* (*EEUU*) practice law; **recibirse de ~** (*esp LAm*) to qualify as a lawyer ► **abogado/a auxiliar** (*Méx*) junior lawyer ► **abogado/a criminalista** criminal lawyer ► **abogado/a defensor(a)** defending counsel ► **abogado/a del Estado** public prosecutor, attorney general (*EEUU*) ► **abogado del diablo** devil's advocate ► **abogado/a de oficio** court-appointed counsel, duty solicitor, public defender (*EEUU*) ► **abogado/a de secano** barrack-room lawyer ► **abogado/a laboralista** labour lawyer, labor lawyer (*EEUU*) ► **abogado/a matrimonialista** divorce lawyer ► **abogado/a penalista** (*Méx*) criminal lawyer
2 (= *defensor, partidario*) champion, advocate

abogar ▸conjug 1h◂ VI to plead; **~ por** (= *defender en juicio*) to plead for, defend; (= *propugnar*) to advocate, champion

abolengo SM (= *linaje*) ancestry, lineage; (= *patrimonio*) inheritance; **de rancio ~** of ancient lineage

abolición SF abolition

abolicionismo SM abolitionism

abolicionista SMF abolitionist

abolir ▸conjug 3a; defectivo◂ VT to abolish

abolladura SF 1 (*en metal*) dent
2 (= *hinchazón*) bump; (= *cardenal*) bruise
3 (*Arte*) embossing

abollar ▸conjug 1a◂ Ⓐ VT 1 [+ *metal*] to dent
2 (*Med*) to raise a bump on
3 (*Arte*) to emboss, do repoussé work on
Ⓑ **abollarse** VPR 1 [*metal*] to get dented
2 [*persona*] to get bruised

abollón SM dent

abollonar ▸conjug 1a◂ VT to emboss

abolsado ADJ baggy

abolsarse ▸conjug 1a◂ VPR to become baggy

abombachado ADJ baggy

abombado ADJ 1 (= *convexo*) convex; (= *abovedado*) domed; (= *saltón*) bulging
2 (*LAm*) (= *aturdido*) stunned
3 (*Méx**) (= *borracho*) tight*
4 (*LAm*) [*comida*] rotten; **estar ~** to smell bad, stink

abombar ▸conjug 1a◂ Ⓐ VT 1 (= *hacer convexo*) to make convex; (= *deformar*) to cause to bulge
2 (*) (= *aturdir*) to stun; (= *desconcertar*) to disconcert, confuse
Ⓑ **abombarse** VPR (*LAm*) 1 (= *pudrirse*) to decompose, go off*
2 (*) (= *emborracharse*) to get tight*

abominable ADJ abominable

abominablemente ADV abominably

abominación SF abomination; **es una ~** it's an abomination, it's detestable

abominar ▸conjug 1a◂ Ⓐ VT to abominate, detest
Ⓑ VI **~ de** to curse

abonable ADJ payable, due

abonado/a Ⓐ ADJ 1 (*Com*) paid, paid-up
2 (*Agr*) fertilised
Ⓑ SM/F (*Telec*) (*a revista*) subscriber; (*Teat, Ferro*) season-ticket holder; **los ~s a la televisión por cable** cable TV subscribers

abonamiento SM = **abono**

abonanzar ▸conjug 1f◂ Ⓐ VI to grow calm, become settled
Ⓑ **abonanzarse** VPR to grow calm, become settled

abonar ▸conjug 1a◂ Ⓐ VT 1 (*Agr*) to fertilize; **abonan los campos cada primavera** they fertilize *o* put fertilizer on the fields every spring; **han abonado el jardín con estiércol** they've manured *o* put manure on the garden; **están abonando el terreno para cambiar la ley** they're preparing the ground for a change in the law
2 (= *pagar*) [+ *cuota, salario, renta*] to pay; [+ *cheque, giro*] to cash; **abonamos una cuota anual de ochenta euros** we pay an annual fee of eighty euros; **no nos han abonado las horas extras** we haven't been paid (for our) overtime; **"abonen al ser servidos"** "please pay as soon as you are served"; **la cajera no me quiso ~ el cheque** the cashier refused to cash the cheque; **tengo varios cheques para ~ en cuenta** I've got a few cheques to pay in; **me ~on los intereses en mi cuenta** the interest was credited to *o* paid into my account
3 (= *fomentar*) [+ *hipótesis, teoría*] to lend weight to, lend credence to; [+ *esperanza*] to add to, fuel; **eso abona nuestras sospechas** that adds to our suspicions
Ⓑ **abonarse** VPR **~se a una revista** to subscribe to a magazine, take out a subscription to a magazine; **me he abonado a la ópera** I have bought a season ticket for the opera

abonaré SM promissory note, IOU

abonero/a SM/F 1 (*Méx*) (= *vendedor a plazos*) *street credit salesperson*
2 (*LAm*) (= *que recoge abonos*) collector

abono SM 1 (*Agr*) (= *fertilizante*) manure, fertilizer; (= *acto*) fertilizing, manuring ► **abono químico** chemical fertilizer, artificial manure
2 (*Com*) (= *pago*) payment; (= *plazo*) instalment, installment (*EEUU*); (= *crédito*) credit; (*LAm*) (= *entrega inicial*) down payment, deposit; **pagar por** *o* **en ~s** to pay by instalments *o* (*EEUU*) installments
3 (*a periódico, revista, etc*) subscription; (*Teat, Ferro*) season ticket
4 (= *aval*) guarantee
5 (*Méx*) (= *recibo*) receipt

aboquillado ADJ tipped, filter-tipped

abordable ADJ 1 [*lugar*] accessible; [*tarea*] manageable; [*precio*] reasonable
2 [*persona*] approachable; **no es nada ~** he's a difficult man

abordaje SM 1 (*Náut*) (= *choque*) collision; (= *invasión*) boarding; **¡al ~!** all aboard!
2 [*de problema*] approach (**de** to); (*a persona*) accosting, approach

abordar ▸conjug 1a◂ Ⓐ VT 1 (= *acometer*) to tackle; **el libro aborda temas controvertidos** the book tackles some controversial subjects; **pidió más dinero para ~ el problema de la vivienda** he requested more money to tackle *o* deal with the housing problem
2 (= *tratar*) to deal with; **el ministro se negó a ~ la cuestión en la rueda de prensa** the minister refused to deal with the subject at the press conference
3 **~ a algn** to approach sb; **abordó al profesor en el pasillo** he approached the teacher in the corridor; **una multitud de periodistas la abordó al salir** a crowd of journalists accosted her as she was leaving
4 (*Náut*) (= *atacar*) to board; (= *chocar con*) to ram
5 (*Méx*) [+ *bus*] to board, get on; (*Caribe Aer*) to board
Ⓑ VI (*Náut*) to dock

aborigen Ⓐ ADJ aboriginal
Ⓑ SMF aborigine, aboriginal

aborrascarse ▸conjug 1g◂ VPR to get stormy

aborrecer ▸conjug 2d◂ VT 1 (= *odiar*) to loathe, detest; (= *aburrirse con*) to become bored by
2 [+ *crías*] to desert, abandon

aborrecible ADJ loathsome, detestable

aborrecido ADJ hated, loathed

aborrecimiento SM (= *odio*) hatred, abhorrence; (= *aburrimiento*) boredom

aborregado ADJ **cielo ~** mackerel sky

aborregarse ▸conjug 1h◂ VPR 1 (*) (= *seguir*) to follow like a sheep/like sheep, tag along
2 (*Meteo*) to cloud over
3 (*LAm**) to be silly, get silly

abortar ▸conjug 1a◂ Ⓐ VI (*accidentalmente*) to have a miscarriage; (*deliberadamente*) to have an abortion; **se puede ~ gratuitamente** you can have a free abortion
Ⓑ VT 1 (= *abandonar*) [+ *plan, aterrizaje*] to abort

2 (= *frustrar*) [+ *complot*] to foil, frustrate; [+ *motín, protesta*] to quell, put down; **el portero abortó el intento de gol** the goalkeeper frustrated the attempt at a goal
3 (*Inform*) to abort

abortero/a SM/F abortionist

abortista Ⓐ ADJ [*clínica*] abortion *antes de s*; [*política*] pro-abortion
Ⓑ SMF 1 (= *partidario*) abortion campaigner
2 (= *criminal*) abortionist; **~ ilegal** backstreet abortionist
Ⓒ SF *woman who has had an abortion*

abortivo Ⓐ ADJ abortive
Ⓑ SM abortifacient

aborto SM 1 (*Med*) (*accidental*) miscarriage; (*provocado*) abortion; (*Jur*) (criminal) abortion ► **aborto clandestino** backstreet abortion ► **aborto espontáneo** miscarriage ► **aborto eugenésico** eugenic abortion ► **aborto habitual** repeated miscarriage ► **aborto ilegal** illegal abortion ► **aborto libre y gratuito** free abortion on demand
2 (*Biol*) monster, freak
3 (= *fracaso*) failure
4 (‡) ugly man/woman; (*aplicado a mujer*) old cow‡

abortón SM (*Vet*) premature calf

abotagado ADJ swollen, bloated

abotagamiento SM swelling

abotagarse ▸conjug 1h◂ VPR to swell up, become bloated

abotargado ADJ = **abotagado**

abotargamiento SM = **abotagamiento**

abotargarse ▸conjug 1h◂ VPR = **abotagarse**

abotonador SM buttonhook

abotonar ▸conjug 1a◂ Ⓐ VT 1 (= *abrochar*) to button up, do up
2 (*Méx*) (= *tapar*) to block, obstruct
Ⓑ VI [*planta*] to bud
Ⓒ **abotonarse** VPR (= *abrocharse*) to button up, do up

abovedado Ⓐ ADJ vaulted, arched
Ⓑ SM vaulting

abovedar ▸conjug 1a◂ VT to vault, arch

aboyar ▸conjug 1a◂ VT 1 (*Náut*) to mark with buoys
2 (*Méx*) to float

abozalar ▸conjug 1a◂ VT to muzzle

abr. ABR (= **abril**) Apr

abra[1] SF 1 (*Geog*) (= *cala*) inlet; (*entre montañas*) (mountain) pass
2 (*Geol*) (= *grieta*) fissure
3 (*LAm*) (= *claro*) clearing

abra[2] SF (*LAm*) panel, leaf (of a door)

abracadabra SM abracadabra

abracadabrante ADJ (= *aparatoso*) spectacular; (= *atractivo*) enchanting, captivating; (= *insólito*) unusual; (= *raro*) extravagant

abracar ▸conjug 1g◂ VT (*Méx*) = **abrazar**

Abraham SM, **Abrahán** SM Abraham

abrasado ADJ 1 (= *quemado*) burnt, burned (*EEUU*), burnt up
2 **estar ~** (= *avergonzado*) to burn with shame; **estar ~ en cólera** to be in a raging temper

abrasador ADJ, **abrasante** ADJ burning, scorching

abrasar ▸conjug 1a◂ Ⓐ VT 1 (= *quemar*) to burn (up); (*con lejía*) to scorch; **murieron abrasados** they burned to death
2 [+ *plantas*] [*sol*] to dry up, parch; [*viento*] to sear; [*helada*] to cut, nip
3 (= *derrochar*) to squander, waste
4 (= *avergonzar*) to fill with shame
Ⓑ VI **esta sopa abrasa** this soup's boiling
Ⓒ **abrasarse** VPR 1 (= *quemarse*) to burn (up); [*tierra*] to be parched
2 **~se de amores** to be passionately in love; **~se de calor** to be roasting *o* sweltering; **~se de sed** to be parched, have a raging thirst

abrasión SF (= *erosión*) abrasion; (*Med*) graze

abrasivo ADJ, SM abrasive

abrazadera SF (= *soporte*) bracket, clamp; (*Tip*) (= *corchete*) bracket ► **abrazadera para papeles** paper clip

abrazar ▸conjug 1f◂ Ⓐ VT 1 [+ *persona*] to embrace, hug, hold
2 (= *adoptar*) [+ *fe*] to adopt, embrace; [+ *doctrina*] to espouse; [+ *oportunidad*] to seize; [+ *profesión*] to adopt, enter, take up
3 [+ *empresa*] to take charge of
4 (= *abarcar*) to include, take in
Ⓑ **abrazarse** VPR to embrace (each other), hug (each other); **~se a** [*persona*] to embrace, hug; [*niño*] to cling to, clutch

▼**abrazo** SM 1 (= *acción*) hug, embrace
2 (*en cartas*) **un ~ afectuoso** *o* **cordial** with best wishes *o* kind regards; **un fuerte ~ (de)** love from

abreboca (*LAm*) Ⓐ ADJ absent-minded
Ⓑ SM appetizer

abrebotellas SM INV bottle opener

abrecartas SM INV letter opener, paper knife

ábrego SM south-west wind

abrelatas SM INV tin opener, can opener (*EEUU*)

abrenuncio EXCL not for me!

abrevadero SM (*Zool*) (*natural*) watering place; (*Agr*) (= *pilón*) drinking trough

abrevar ▸conjug 1a◂ Ⓐ VT [+ *animal*] to water; [+ *tierra*] to water, irrigate; [+ *pieles*] to soak
Ⓑ VI (*Zool*) to drink
Ⓒ **abrevarse** VPR (= *regodearse*) **~se en sangre** to wallow in blood

abreviación SF abridgement, shortening

abreviadamente ADV (= *sucintamente*) briefly, succinctly; (= *en forma resumida*) in an abridged form

abreviado ADJ (= *breve*) brief; (= *reducido*) shortened, abridged; **la palabra es forma abreviada de ...** the word is short for ...

abreviar ▸conjug 1b◂ Ⓐ VT 1 (= *acortar*) [+ *palabra*] to abbreviate; [+ *texto*] to abridge, reduce; [+ *discurso, estancia, etc*] to shorten, cut short
2 (= *acercar*) [+ *fecha*] to bring forward; [+ *acontecimiento*] to hasten
Ⓑ VI (= *apresurarse*) to be quick; **bueno, para ~ ...** well, to cut a long story short ...

abreviatura SF abbreviation, contraction

abriboca ADJ INV (*Arg*) open-mouthed

abridor SM [*de botellas*] bottle opener; [*de latas*] tin opener, can opener (*EEUU*)

abrigada SF, **abrigadero** SM shelter, windbreak; **abrigadero de ladrones** (*Méx*) den of thieves

abrigado ADJ 1 (= *cubierto de ropa*) wrapped up (**con** in); **iba ~ con una chaqueta** he was wrapped up in a jacket; **tengo los pies bien ~s** my feet are nice and warm
2 (= *que abriga*) [*ropa*] warm
3 (= *protegido*) [*lugar*] sheltered, protected (**de** from)

abrigador(a) Ⓐ ADJ (*Andes, Méx*) warm
Ⓑ SM/F *person who covers up for another*

abrigar ▸conjug 1h◂ Ⓐ VT 1 (*del frío*) [*persona*] to wrap up; [*ropa, manta*] to keep warm; **abriga bien a los niños** wrap the kids up well; **este gorro de lana te ~á las orejas** this woolly hat will keep your ears warm
2 (= *resguardar*) to shelter, protect (**de** from); **los árboles nos abrigaban del viento** the trees sheltered *o* protected us from the wind
3 (= *ayudar*) to support; **tiene un buen equipo que le abriga** he's got a good team supporting him
4 (= *albergar*) [+ *ambición, sospecha, temor*] to harbour, harbor (*EEUU*); [+ *duda*] to entertain, harbour, harbor (*EEUU*); [+ *esperanza, ilusión*] to cherish, harbour, harbor (*EEUU*); [+ *opinión*] to hold
Ⓑ VI [*ropa, manta*] to be warm; **esta manta no abriga nada** this blanket isn't warm at all; **este jersey abriga mucho** this jumper is nice and warm
Ⓒ **abrigarse** VPR 1 (*con ropa*) to wrap (o.s.) up; **salió a la nieve sin ~se** he went out in the snow without wrapping himself up; **¡abrígate bien!** wrap up well!; **usaban una manta para ~se** they used a blanket to keep themselves warm; **abrígate el cuello con la bufanda** cover your neck up with the scarf
2 (= *resguardarse*) to shelter, take shelter (**de** from); **nos abrigamos de la tormenta bajo un árbol** we took shelter *o* sheltered from the storm under a tree; **se abrigaba en la presunción de inocencia** he sheltered behind the presumption of innocence

abrigo SM 1 (= *prenda*) coat; **un ~ de pieles** a fur coat; **un ~ de visón** a mink coat
2 (= *protección*) 2.1 (*contra el frío*) **¿tienes suficiente ~?** are you warm enough?; **esta manta te servirá de ~** this blanket will keep you warm; **esta capa es un buen ~ para el invierno** this cloak is lovely and warm for the winter; **ropa de ~** warm clothes
2.2 (*contra el viento, la lluvia*) shelter; **las rocas nos sirvieron de ~** the rocks sheltered us, the rocks gave us shelter; ✦***MODISMO*** **de ~** (*Esp*) [*gastos, presupuesto, pelea*] huge; **tiene una bronquitis de ~** she has really bad bronchitis; **ten cuidado porque es un tipo de ~** be careful — he's a dodgy character*
3 **al ~ de** 3.1 (= *protegido por*) [*seto, roca*] in the shelter of; [*noche, oscuridad*] under cover of; [*ley, poder*] under, under the protection of; **la ciudad está situada al ~ de unas colinas** the town is sheltered by hills; **charlamos al ~ de la lumbre** we chatted by the fireside; **escaparon al ~ de la noche** they escaped under cover of darkness; **crearon empresas al ~ de la nueva ley** they set up companies under the protection of the new law; **se crearon pequeños bancos al ~ del proceso de industrialización** the process of industrialization led to the creation of small banks
3.2 (= *protegido de*) [*tormenta, viento*] sheltered from; [*escándalo, desgracias*] protected from; **nos pusimos al ~ del viento** we took shelter *o* we sheltered from the wind; **por su posición estaba al ~ de semejantes infortunios** the nature of his position protected him from such misfortunes; **al ~ de las miradas indiscretas** away from prying eyes; **una so-**

➤ LENGUA Y USO: **abrazo 2** 48.2

ciedad al ~ de amenazas externas a society immune to outside threats

[4] (*Náut*) natural harbour, natural harbor (*EEUU*), haven

abril SM April; **en el ~ de la vida** in the springtime of one's life; **una chica de 15 ~es** a girl of 15 summers (*liter*); ✦*MODISMO* **estar hecho un ~** to look very handsome; ✦*REFRÁN* **en ~ aguas mil** April showers bring May flowers; *ver tb* **septiembre**

abrileño ADJ April *antes de s*

abrillantado Ⓐ ADJ [*superficie*] polished; (*Culin*) glazed

Ⓑ SM [*de superficie*] polish(ing); (*Culin*) glaze, glazing

abrillantadora SF floor polisher

abrillantamuebles SM INV furniture polish

abrillantar ▸conjug 1a◂ VT (= *pulir*) to polish; [+ *piedra*] to cut; (*Culin*) to glaze; (= *mejorar*) to enhance, jazz up*

abrir ▸conjug 3a◂ (*pp* **abierto**) Ⓐ VT [1] (*algo que estaba cerrado*) [1·1] [+ *puerta, armario, libro, ojos*] to open; [+ *cremallera, bragueta*] to undo; **abre la ventana** open the window; **~ una puerta/ventana de par en par** to open a door/window wide; **le abrían las cartas** they were opening his letters; **abre la boca** open your mouth; (*en el dentista*) open wide; **no encuentro la llave para ~ la puerta** I can't find the key to open *o* unlock the door; **abrid el libro por la página 50** turn to page 50 in the book, open the book at page 50; ✦*MODISMO* **en un ~ y cerrar de ojos** in the twinkling of an eye

[1·2] (*desplegando*) [+ *mapa, mantel*] to spread out; [+ *paraguas*] to open, put up; [+ *mano, abanico, paracaídas*] to open

[1·3] (*haciendo una abertura*) [+ *pozo*] to sink; [+ *foso, cimientos*] to dig; [+ *agujero, perforación*] to make, bore; [+ *camino*] to clear; (*LAm*) [+ *bosque*] to clear; **tuvimos que ~ camino cortando ramas** we had to cut a path through the branches; **he abierto un sendero en el jardín** I've made a path in the garden; **la explosión abrió una brecha en la pared** the explosion blew a hole in the wall; **las lluvias han abierto socavones en las calles** the rain has caused potholes to appear on the streets

[1·4] (*haciendo un corte*) [+ *sandía*] to cut open; [+ *herida*] to open; **abre el pan por la mitad** cut the loaf in half

[1·5] [+ *grifo, luz, agua*] to turn on; [+ *válvula*] to open; **abre el grifo del agua caliente** turn the hot water tap on; **abre un poco más el grifo** open the tap a bit more; **¿has abierto el gas?** have you turned the gas on?

[2] (= *encabezar*) [+ *manifestación, desfile*] to lead, head; [+ *baile*] to open, lead off; [+ *lista*] to head

[3] (= *inaugurar*) [3·1] [+ *acto, ceremonia*] to open; **se acaban de volver a ~ las negociaciones con los sindicatos** negotiations with the unions have been reopened; **el plazo para las solicitudes se abre en abril** applications may be made from April; **ya han abierto el plazo de matrícula** registration has already started

[3·2] (*Com*) [+ *negocio*] to set up, start; [+ *cuenta*] to open; **ha decidido ~ su propio negocio** she has decided to set up *o* start her own business; **han abierto un centro de atención al cliente** they've opened a customer service centre; **he abierto la cuenta con 400 euros** I opened the account with 400 euros; **~ un expediente a algn** (*investigación*) to open a file on sb; (*proceso*) to begin proceedings against sb; **~ una información** to open *o* start an inquiry

[3·3] (*Tip*) **~ comillas** to open quotes; **~ paréntesis** to open brackets

[3·4] (*Mil*) **¡abran fuego!** (open) fire!

[4] (= *ampliar*) [+ *perspectivas*] to open up; **este acuerdo abre nuevas perspectivas de paz** this agreement offers new hope of peace; **vivir en el extranjero le abrió la mente** living abroad opened up his mind *o* made him more open-minded; **estos países han abierto sus economías** these countries have opened their economy up

[5] [+ *apetito*] **las vitaminas te ~án el apetito** taking vitamins will improve your appetite; **ese olor me esta abriendo el apetito** that smell is making me hungry; **esta selección abre el apetito a los lectores** this selection is intended to whet the readers' appetite

Ⓑ VI [1] [*puerta, cajón*] to open; **esta puerta no abre** this door won't open

[2] [*persona*] to open the door, open up; **¡abre, soy yo!** open the door *o* open up, it's me!; **llamé pero no abrió nadie** I knocked at the door, but nobody answered; **esta llave no abre bien** this key is a bit stiff

[3] [*comercio, museo*] to open; **las tiendas abren a las diez** the shops open at ten o'clock; **los sábados no abrimos al público** we're not open to the public on Saturdays; **el banco abre de 9 a 1** the bank is open from 9 to 1; **el almacén volverá a ~ en septiembre** the warehouse will reopen in September

[4] [*flor*] to open

[5] (*en operación quirúrgica*) **vamos a tener que ~** we're going to have to open him up

[6] (*Meteo*) to clear up; **parece que está empezando a ~** it looks like it's starting to clear up

[7] (*Bridge*) to open; **~ de tres a un palo** to open three in a suit; **~ de corazones** to open (with a bid in) hearts

[8] (*Caribe**) (= *huir*) to escape, run off

Ⓒ **abrirse** VPR [1] [*paracaídas, paraguas, ventana, libro*] to open; **de repente se abrió la puerta** suddenly, the door opened; **se están abriendo las costuras** it's coming apart at the seams; **la madera se está abriendo** the wood is splitting

[2] (= *extenderse*) **ante nosotros se abría todo un mundo de posibilidades** a whole world of possibilities was opening up before us; **~se a algo** to open out onto sth; **la avenida se abre a una magnífica plaza** the avenue opens out onto a magnificent square

[3] [*persona*] [3·1] **no te abras tanto en las curvas** stay a bit closer to the side of the road when going round bends; **el delantero se abrió hacia la banda** the forward went wide

[3·2] **intentaron ~se paso entre la muchedumbre** they tried to make their way through the crowd; ✦*MODISMO* **~se camino en la vida** to make one's way in life

[3·3] (*‡*) (= *largarse*) **¡me abro!** I'm off!; **¡ábrete!** shove off!*

[4] **~se a: tenemos que ~nos más al progreso** we have to open up more to progress; **~se a *o* con algn** to confide in sb

[5] (= *romperse, rajarse*) **se le ha abierto la herida** his wound has opened; **~se la cabeza** to crack one's head open; **~se el tobillo** to twist one's ankle, sprain one's ankle; **~se las venas** to slash one's wrists

[6] (*Meteo*) to clear, clear up

[7] (*Méx*) (= *echar marcha atrás*) to backtrack, back-pedal

abrita SF (*CAm*) short dry spell

abrochador SM [1] (= *abotonador*) buttonhook

[2] (*LAm*) (= *grapadora*) stapler, stapling machine

abrochar ▸conjug 1a◂ Ⓐ VT [1] [+ *botón, cremallera, vestido*] to do up; [+ *broche, hebilla*] to fasten; **¿me abrochas el vestido?** can you do up my dress?; **abróchale el abrigo al niño** do up the boy's coat; **¿me abrochas?** can you do me up?; **llevas los botones sin ~** your buttons are undone

[2] (*LAm*) [+ *papeles*] to staple (together)

[3] (*Méx*) (= *atar*) to tie up; (= *agarrar*) to grab hold of

[4] (*Andes*) (= *reprender*) to reprimand

Ⓑ **abrocharse** VPR **abróchate la camisa** do up your shirt; **el vestido se abrocha delante con cremallera** the dress does up at the front with a zip; **abróchate los zapatos** tie up your (shoe)laces; **abróchense el cinturón de seguridad** fasten your seat belts

abrogación SF abrogation, repeal

abrogar ▸conjug 1h◂ VT to abrogate, repeal

abrojo SM [1] (*Bot*) thistle; (*Mil*) caltrop

[2] **abrojos** (*Náut*) submerged rocks, reefs; (*Méx*) (= *matorral*) thorn bushes

abroncar* ▸conjug 1g◂ Ⓐ VT (= *avergonzar*) to shame, make ashamed; (= *ridiculizar*) to ridicule; (= *aburrir*) to bore; (= *molestar*) to annoy; [+ *orador*] to boo, heckle, barrack; (= *reprender*) to give a lecture to, tick off

Ⓑ **abroncarse** VPR (= *enfadarse*) to get angry

abroquelarse ▸conjug 1a◂ VPR **~ con** *o* **de** to shield o.s. with, defend o.s. with

abrumador ADJ [1] (= *agobiante*) crushing; (= *pesado*) burdensome; **es una responsabilidad ~a** it's a heavy responsibility

[2] (= *importante*) [*mayoría*] overwhelming; [*superioridad*] crushing, overwhelming

abrumadoramente ADV [1] (= *de forma agobiante*) crushingly

[2] (= *enormemente*) vastly, overwhelmingly

abrumar ▸conjug 1a◂ Ⓐ VT (= *agobiar*) to overwhelm; (= *oprimir*) to oppress, weigh down; (= *cansar*) to wear out, exhaust; **~ a algn de trabajo** to overload *o* swamp sb with work; **le ~on con atenciones** they made too much of a fuss of him

Ⓑ **abrumarse** VPR (*Meteo*) to get foggy, get misty

abrupto ADJ [1] [*cuesta*] steep; [*terreno*] rough, rugged

[2] [*tono*] abrupt

[3] [*cambio*] sudden

abrutado ADJ brutish, brutalized

ABS SM ABR (= **antilock braking system**) ABS

absceso SM abscess

abscisión SF incision

absenta SF absinth(e)

absentismo SM [*de obreros*] absenteeism; [*de terrateniente*] absentee landlordism ▸ **absentismo laboral** absenteeism from work

absentista SMF (= *obrero*) absentee; (= *terrateniente*) absentee landlord

ábside SM [*de iglesia*] apse; [*de tienda de campaña*] bell, bell end

absintio SM absinth(e)

absolución SF (*Rel*) absolution; (*Jur*) acquittal

absoluta SF 1 (= *declaración*) dogmatic statement, authoritative assertion
2 (*Mil*) discharge; **tomar la ~** to take one's discharge, leave the service

absolutamente ADV 1 (= *completamente*) absolutely; **es ~ imposible** it's absolutely impossible; **está ~ prohibido** it is absolutely forbidden; **el puente estaba ~ destruido** the bridge was completely destroyed
2 (*con negativos*) not at all, by no means; **~ nada** nothing at all; **—¿así que no viene nadie? —absolutamente** "so nobody is coming?" — "nobody at all"

absolutismo SM absolutism ► **absolutismo ilustrado** enlightened dictatorship

absolutista ADJ, SMF absolutist

absolutizar ▸conjug 1f◂ VT to pin down, be precise about

absoluto ADJ 1 (= *no relativo*) absolute; **los nacionalistas lograron mayoría absoluta** the nationalists got an absolute majority; **lo ~** the absolute
2 (= *máximo*) [*prioridad*] top; [*reposo, fe*] complete; [*verdad*] absolute; **tengo la absoluta certeza de que vino** I'm absolutely certain that he came; **son de absoluta necesidad** they are absolutely necessary *o* essential; **guardaron el más ~ silencio** they remained absolutely silent; **nunca lo supe con certeza absoluta** I never knew for sure; **viven en la miseria más absoluta** they live in the most abject poverty; **existe compenetración absoluta entre los dos** there is a perfect understanding between them, they understand each other perfectly
3 [*monarquía, poder*] absolute
4 **en ~** not at all; **—¿es verdad? —no, en ~** "is it true?" — "no, absolutely not *o* no, not at all"; **—¿te importa? —en ~** "do you mind?" — "no, absolutely not *o* no, not at all"; **esa idea no me atrae en ~** that idea doesn't appeal to me at all *o* in the slightest; **no dijo nada en ~** he said absolutely nothing (at all); **no es en ~ extraño** it is by no means odd

absolutorio ADJ **fallo ~** verdict of not guilty

absolver ▸conjug 2h◂ (*pp* **absuelto**) VT (*Rel*) to absolve; (*Jur*) to acquit, clear (**de** of)

absorbencia SF absorbency

absorbente Ⓐ ADJ 1 (*Quím*) absorbent
2 (= *interesante*) interesting, absorbing; [*tarea*] demanding; [*amor*] possessive, tyrannical
Ⓑ SM absorbent ► **absorbente higiénico** sanitary towel, sanitary napkin (*EEUU*)

absorber ▸conjug 2a◂ Ⓐ VT 1 [+ *líquido*] to absorb, soak up
2 [+ *información*] to absorb, take in; [+ *recursos*] to use up; [+ *energías*] to take up; [+ *atención*] to command
Ⓑ **absorberse** VPR **~se en** to become absorbed *o* engrossed in

absorbible ADJ absorbable

absorbidad SF absorbency

absorción SF 1 [*de líquidos*] absorption
2 (= *atracción*) absorption
3 (*Com*) takeover

absorto ADJ absorbed, engrossed; **estar ~** (= *extasiado*) to be entranced; (= *pasmado*) to be amazed; **estar ~ (en sus pensamientos)** to be lost in thought; **estar ~ en un proyecto** to be engrossed in *o* taken up with a scheme

abstemio/a Ⓐ ADJ teetotal
Ⓑ SM/F teetotaller

abstención SF abstention

abstencionismo SM abstentionism

abstencionista SMF abstainer

abstenerse ▸conjug 2k◂ VPR (*gen*) to abstain; **~ de hacer algo** to refrain from doing sth; **en la duda, abstente** when in doubt, don't; **"abstenerse intermediarios"** "no dealers"; **"abstenerse si no cumplen los requisitos"** "those without the necessary qualifications need not apply"

abstinencia SF (*gen*) abstinence; (*Rel*) fasting; [*de drogas*] withdrawal

abstinente ADJ (*Rel*) abstinent, observing abstinence

abstracción SF 1 (= *acto*) abstraction; (*pey*) (= *despiste*) absent-mindedness
2 **hacer ~ de** to leave aside, except

abstractar ▸conjug 1a◂ VT [+ *publicaciones*] to abstract, make abstracts of

abstracto ADJ abstract; **en ~** in the abstract

abstraer ▸conjug 2o◂ Ⓐ VT to abstract
Ⓑ **abstraerse** VPR to be lost in thought, be preoccupied; **~se de** to detach o.s. from

abstraído ADJ (= *ensimismado*) withdrawn; (= *inquieto*) preoccupied

abstruso ADJ abstruse

absuelto PP *de* **absolver**

absurdamente ADV absurdly

absurdez SF absurdity

absurdidad SF absurdity

absurdo Ⓐ ADJ absurd; **es ~ que** it is absurd that; **lo ~ es que ...** the ridiculous thing is that ...; **teatro del ~** theatre *o* (*EEUU*) theater of the absurd
Ⓑ SM absurdity, (piece of) nonsense; **decir ~s** to talk nonsense

abubilla SF hoopoe

abucharar* ▸conjug 1a◂ VT (= *abuchear*) to boo, jeer; (= *excluir*) to ostracize, marginalize; (= *criticar*) to slate*, criticize; (= *avergonzar*) to put to shame; **quedarse abucharado** to be left out, be ostracized

abuchear ▸conjug 1a◂ VT to boo, jeer at; **ser abucheado** (*Teat*) to be booed, be hissed (at)

abucheo SM booing, jeering; **ganarse un ~** (*Teat*) to be booed, be hissed (at)

abuelado* ADJ (*Cono Sur*) spoiled by one's grandparents

abuelita SF 1 (*Cono Sur*) (= *gorra*) baby's bonnet
2 (*Andes*) (= *cuna*) cradle

abuelito/a* SM/F granddad/granny*, grandpa/grandma*; (*Méx*) grandfather/grandmother

abuelo/a SM/F 1 (= *pariente*) grandfather/grandmother; **mis ~s** my grandparents; **¡tu abuela!*** rubbish!; ✦***MODISMOS*** **¡cuéntaselo a tu abuela!*** pull the other one!*, go tell that to the marines! (*EEUU*); **no necesitar abuela*** to blow one's own trumpet; **(éramos pocos) y parió la abuela*** and that was the last straw, and that was all we needed; **no tener abuela*** to be full of o.s.
2 (= *anciano*) old man/old woman; **está hecho un ~** he looks like an old man
3 (= *antepasado*) ancestor, forbear

abulense Ⓐ ADJ of/from Ávila
Ⓑ SMF native/inhabitant of Ávila; **los ~s** the people of Ávila

abulia SF total apathy

abúlico ADJ apathetic

abulón SM (*esp Méx*) abalone

abultado ADJ 1 (= *voluminoso*) bulky, unwieldy; [*labios, libro*] thick; (*Med*) swollen
2 (= *exagerado*) exaggerated

abultamiento SM 1 (= *voluminosidad*) bulkiness, (large) size; (*Med*) swelling
2 (= *exageración*) exaggeration

abultar ▸conjug 1a◂ Ⓐ VT 1 (= *aumentar*) to increase; (= *agrandar*) to enlarge; (= *hacer abultado*) to make bulky
2 (= *exagerar*) to exaggerate
Ⓑ VI 1 (= *tener bulto*) to be bulky, be big
2 (= *tener más importancia*) to increase in importance

abundamiento SM abundance, plenty; **a** *o* **por mayor ~** furthermore

abundancia SF 1 (= *multitud*) abundance; **hay gran ~ de olivos** there is a great abundance of olive trees; **en ~: hay copas en ~** there are plenty of glasses; **había bebida en ~** there was plenty to drink
2 (= *copiosidad*) abundance; **bendijo la ~ de la cosecha** he blessed the abundance of the harvest
3 (= *prosperidad*) **su familia vive en la ~** his family are very well-off; **la sociedad de la ~** the affluent society; ✦***MODISMO*** **nadar en la ~** to be rolling in money; *ver tb* **cuerno**

abundante ADJ 1 (= *copioso*) abundant, plentiful; **el agua es ~ en toda la zona** water is abundant *o* plentiful throughout the area; **la fauna es ~ en el parque nacional** ◊ **el parque nacional es ~ en fauna** there is abundant wildlife in the national park, there is a wealth of fauna in the national park; **un país ~ en minerales** a country which is rich in minerals, a country which abounds in minerals; **una ~ ración de calamares** a generous portion of squid; **teníamos ~ comida** we had plenty of food; **tienes que hervirlos en agua ~** you have to boil them in plenty of water; **la nubosidad será ~ en Galicia** there will be extensive cloud in Galicia
2 (*en plural*) a great many; **un texto con ~s citas** a text with a great many *o* numerous quotations; **los flamencos son muy ~s en toda la zona** there are a great many flamingos throughout the area; **existen ~s pruebas** there is plenty of proof

abundantemente ADV [*llover, sangrar*] heavily; [*crecer*] abundantly

abundar ▸conjug 1a◂ VI 1 (= *existir en abundancia*) to be plentiful; **el olivo abunda en el sur** olive trees are plentiful in the south; **este tipo de cáncer abunda entre personas sedentarias** this type of cancer is very common in *o* among sedentary people
2 (*frm*) (= *tener en abundancia*) **~ en algo: la zona abunda en gas natural** the area is rich in natural gas, natural gas is plentiful in the area; **los periódicos abundan en anglicismos** the newspapers abound in *o* with anglicisms
3 (= *profundizar*) **~ en algo** (*frm*) to elaborate on sth; **me gustaría ~ en ese comentario**

I'd like to elaborate on this remark; **no quiso ~ más en el asunto** he declined to elaborate [4] (= *estar de acuerdo*) **yo abundo en esa opinión** I absolutely *o* wholeheartedly agree

Abundio SM *ver* **tonto A1.2**

abundoso ADJ (*LAm*) abundant

abur* EXCL so long!

aburguesado ADJ **un barrio ~** a gentrified area; **un hombre ~** a man who has become bourgeois, a man who has adopted middle-class ways

aburguesamiento SM embourgeoisement

aburguesar ▸conjug 1a◂ Ⓐ VT to gentrify
Ⓑ **aburguesarse** VPR [*persona*] to become bourgeois, adopt middle-class ways

aburrición SF (*LAm*) = **aburrimiento**

aburridamente ADV in a boring manner, boringly

aburrido ADJ (= *que aburre*) boring, tedious; (= *que siente aburrimiento*) bored; **un libro ~** a boring book; **una espera aburrida** a tedious wait; **¡estoy ~ de decírtelo!** I'm tired of telling you!

> **ABURRIDO**
>
> **¿"Bored" o "boring"?**
>
> • Usamos **bored** para referirnos al hecho de *estar* aburrido, es decir, de sentir aburrimiento:
>
> Si estás aburrida podrías ayudarme con este trabajo
>
> ***If you're bored you could help me with this work***
>
> • Usamos **boring** con personas, actividades y cosas para indicar que alguien o algo *es* aburrido, es decir, que produce aburrimiento:
>
> ¡Qué novela más aburrida!
>
> ***What a boring novel!***
>
> No me gusta salir con él; es muy aburrido
>
> ***I don't like going out with him; he's very boring***

aburridón ADJ (*Andes*) rather boring

aburrimiento SM boredom, tedium; **¡qué ~!** what a bore!

aburrir ▸conjug 3a◂ Ⓐ VT [1] (*gen*) to bore; (= *cansar*) to tire, weary
[2] (‡) [+ *dinero*] to blow*; [+ *tiempo*] to waste
Ⓑ **aburrirse** VPR to be bored, get bored (**con, de, por** with); **~se como una ostra** to be bored stiff

abusado/a (*Méx*) Ⓐ EXCL (*) (= *cuidado*) look out!, careful!
Ⓑ ADJ [1] (= *astuto*) sharp, cunning
[2] (= *cauteloso*) watchful, wary
Ⓒ SM/F swot*, grind (*EEUU**)

abusador ADJ (*Cono Sur*) abusive

abusar ▸conjug 1a◂ VI [1] (= *extralimitarse*) to take advantage; **es muy generoso pero no debéis ~** he's very generous but you mustn't take advantage; **~ de** [+ *persona*] to take advantage of; [+ *amistad, hospitalidad, amabilidad, privilegio*] to abuse; **de los débiles todo el mundo abusa** everyone takes advantage of the weak; **el acusado abusó de su condición de policía** the defendant abused his position as a policeman; **no quiero ~ de su tiempo** I don't want to take up too much of your time; **si siguen abusando de mi paciencia, un día estallaré** if they continue to try my patience, one of these days I'm going to explode; **~ de la confianza de algn** (= *aprovecharse*) to take advantage of sb's good will; (= *traicionar*) to betray sb's trust
[2] (= *usar en exceso*) **está bien beber de vez en cuando pero sin ~** drinking every so often is fine as long as you don't overdo it; **~ de**: **~ del tabaco** to smoke too much; **no conviene ~ de las grasas** it's not good to eat too much fat; **abusan de la jerga técnica** they use too much technical jargon
[3] (= *usar mal*) **~ de** [+ *dinero*] to misuse
[4] (*sexualmente*) **~ de algn** to (sexually) abuse sb

abusión SF (= *abuso*) abuse; (= *superstición*) superstition

abusivamente ADV unfairly

abusivo ADJ unfair; [*precio*] exorbitant, outrageous

abuso SM [1] (= *extralimitación*) [*de privilegios, cargo, fondos*] abuse; **se siguen cometiendo ~s en los derechos humanos** human rights abuses are still being committed; **cuando hay ~ de amistad** when unfair demands are made on friendship, when there are impositions made on friendship; **lo que te han cobrado es un ~** it's outrageous what they've charged you ▸ **abuso de autoridad** abuse of authority ▸ **abuso de confianza** (*Pol, Fin*) breach of trust, betrayal of trust; **su actitud me parece un ~ de confianza** I think he's taking liberties ▸ **abuso de poder** abuse of power
[2] (= *uso excesivo*) [*de tabaco, drogas*] abuse; [*de disolventes, pesticidas*] overuse; **el ~ del alcohol puede traer consecuencias fatales** alcohol abuse can have fatal consequences; **especies en peligro por el ~ de la caza** endangered species through overhunting; **había un ~ de adjetivos en el texto** there was too much *o* excessive use of adjectives in the text; **recibió varias quejas por ~ de fuerza** he received several complaints of excessive use of force; **no es recomendable el ~ de la sal en la comida** it's not advisable to put too much salt in your food; **hicieron uso y ~ del teléfono** they used the phone to excess
[3] (*tb* **~ sexual**) sexual abuse ▸ **abuso de menores** child abuse ▸ **abusos deshonestos** indecent assault *sing*

abusón/ona* Ⓐ ADJ (= *egoísta*) selfish; (= *engreído*) big-headed*; (= *insolente*) abusive
Ⓑ SM/F selfish person, bighead*; **eres un ~** you're a selfish pig*

abute‡ ADV **vivir de ~** to live well, live like a prince; *ver tb* **dabuti**

abyección SF wretchedness, abjectness

abyecto ADJ wretched, abject

a.C. ABR (= **antes de Cristo**) BC

a/c. ABR [1] = **a cuenta**
[2] (= **al cuidado de**) c/o

acá ADV [1] (*esp LAm*) (= *aquí*) here, over here; **~ y allá** *o* **acullá** here and there; **pasearse de ~ para allá** to walk up and down *o* to and fro; **¡ven** *o* **vente para ~!** come over here!; **¡más ~!** more over this way!; **más ~ de** on this side of; **tráelo más ~** move it this way, bring it closer; **está muy ~** it's right here; **no tan ~** not so close, not so far this way
[2] (= *ahora*) at this time, now; **de** *o* **desde ayer ~** since yesterday; **de ~ a poco** of late; **¿de cuándo ~?** since when?
[3] (*LAm*) (= *como demostrativo*) this person *etc* here; **~ le contará** he'll tell you about it; **~ es mi señora** and this is my wife

acabada SF finish

acabadero* SM (*Méx*) **el ~** the limit, the last straw

acabado Ⓐ ADJ [1] (= *completo*) finished
[2] (= *viejo*) old, worn out; **estar ~** (*de salud*) to be a wreck; **está ~ como futbolista** he's finished as a footballer, his footballing days are over
[3] (*LAm*) (= *flaco*) thin; (*Méx*) (= *rendido*) exhausted; **está muy ~** (*Méx*) he's looking very old
Ⓑ SM (*Téc*) finish; **buen ~** high finish ▸ **acabado brillo** gloss finish ▸ **acabado satinado** matt finish

acabador(a) SM/F (*Téc*) finisher

acabalar ▸conjug 1a◂ VT to complete

acaballadero SM stud farm

acaballado* ADJ (*Cono Sur*) clumsy, gauche

acaballar ▸conjug 1a◂ VT to cover

acabamiento SM (= *acto*) finishing, completion; (= *final*) end; (= *muerte*) death; (*LAm*) (= *agotamiento*) exhaustion

acabar ▸conjug 1a◂ Ⓐ VT [1] (= *terminar*) [+ *actividad, trabajo*] (*gen*) to finish; (= *dar el toque final a*) to finish off; **¿habéis acabado la instalación de la antena?** have you finished installing the aerial?; **me falta poco para ~ el jersey** I've nearly finished the jumper; **me quedan sólo un par de horas para ~ este cuadro** it'll only take me another couple of hours to finish off this painting; **acabó sus días en prisión** he ended his days in prison
[2] (= *consumir*) to finish; **ya hemos acabado el aceite** we've used up *o* finished the oil; **cuando acabe esta cerveza me voy** when I've finished this beer I'm going
[3] (*LAm*) (= *hablar mal de*) **~ a algn** to speak ill of sb
Ⓑ VI [1] (= *terminar*) to finish, end; **¿te falta mucho para ~?** are you nearly finished?, have you got long to go?; **la crisis lleva años y no acaba** the recession has been going on for years and there's no sign of it ending; **es cosa de nunca ~** there's no end to it; ✦***MODISMO*** **acabáramos**: **acabáramos, ¿así que se trata de tu hijo?** oh, I see, so it's your son, then?; *ver tb* **cuento 1**, **rosario 1**
[2] **~ con** [2·1] [+ *comida*] to finish off; [+ *injusticia*] to put an end to, stop; [+ *relación*] to end; [+ *reservas*] to exhaust, use up; [+ *esperanzas*] to put paid to; **acabaron con la tarta en un minuto** they finished off the cake within a minute; **¿todavía no has acabado con la carta?** haven't you finished the letter yet?; **hay que ~ con tanto desorden** we must put an end to all this confusion; **hemos acabado con todas las provisiones** we've exhausted *o* used up all our supplies
[2·2] [+ *persona*] (= *atender*) to finish with; (= *matar*) to do away with; **cuando acabe con ella, te lavo la cabeza** when I'm done *o* finished with her, I'll wash your hair; **¡acabemos con él!** let's do away with him!*; **esto acabará conmigo** this will be the end of me
[3] **~ de hacer algo** [3·1] (*cuando se ha terminado*) **acabo de llamarla por teléfono** I have just phoned her; **acababa de entrar cuando sonó el teléfono** I had just come in when the phone rang
[3·2] (*cuando se está haciendo*) **cuando acabemos de pagarlo** when we finish paying for it; ✦***MODISMOS*** **para ~ de arreglarlo**: **para ~ de**

arreglarlo, se fue sin despedirse on top of everything, she left without even saying good-bye; **¡acaba de parir!*** spit it out!*

3·3 **no acabo de entender por qué lo hizo** I just can't understand why she did it; **no acabo de entender este concepto** I just can't seem to understand this concept; **ese candidato no me acaba de convencer** I'm not too sure about that candidate

4 (*con complemento de modo*) **la película acaba bien** the film has a happy ending; **su relación acabó mal** their relationship came to an unhappy end; **si sigues así vas a ~ mal** if you carry on like that you'll come to a sticky end; **acabé harto de tantas fiestas** I ended up getting fed up of all those parties; **la palabra acaba con** *o* **por "z"** the word ends in a "z"; **~ en algo** to end in sth; **espero que no acabe en tragedia** I hope it won't end in tragedy; **el palo acaba en punta** the stick ends in a point; **unos zapatos que acaban en punta** a pair of pointed shoes; **la fiesta acabó en un baile** the party ended with everyone dancing; **después de tanto hablar, todo acabó en nada** after all that talk, it all came to nothing

5 **~ haciendo algo** ◊ **~ por hacer algo** to end up doing sth; **acabó aceptándolo** he ended up accepting it

6 (*en una relación*) to finish, split up; **hemos acabado** we've finished, we've split up; **¿cuánto hace que acabaste con ella?** how long is it since you split up with *o* finished with her?

7 (*LAm***) (= *eyacular*) to come**

Ⓒ **acabarse** VPR 1 (= *terminarse*) [*acto, reunión*] to finish, come to an end; [*reservas*] to run out; **la impresora te avisa cuando se acaba el papel** the printer tells you when the paper runs out; **todo se acabó para él*** he's had it*; **¡se acabó!** that's it!; **¡un minuto más y se acabó!** one more minute and that will be it!; **¡te quedas aquí y se acabó!** you're staying here and that's that!; **le das el dinero y se acabó** just give her the money and be done with it; ✦**MODISMO ... y (san) se acabó** ... and that's the end of the matter

2 (*con complemento indirecto*) **se me ha acabado el tabaco** I'm out of cigarettes; **pronto se nos acabará la gasolina** we'll soon be out of petrol; **se me acabó la paciencia** my patience is exhausted *o* at an end, I've run out of patience

3 (*con valor enfático*) **acábate el café y nos vamos** drink your coffee up and we'll go

4 [*persona*] (= *morir*) to die; (*esp LAm*) (= *cansarse*) to wear o.s. out

acabildar ▸conjug 1a◂ VT to get together, organize into a group

acabóse SM, **acabose** SM **esto es el ~** this is the last straw; **la fiesta fue el ~** it was the party to end all parties, it was the best party ever

acachetear ▸conjug 1a◂ VT to slap, punch

acachihuite SM (*Méx*) (= *paja*) straw, hay; (= *cesto*) straw basket

acacia SF acacia ▸ **acacia falsa** locust tree

acacito ADV (*LAm*) = **acá**

academia SF 1 (= *establecimiento*) academy; (*Escol*) (private) school; **la Real Academia** the Spanish Academy; **la Real Academia de la Historia** the Spanish Academy of History ▸ **academia de baile** dance school ▸ **academia de comercio** business school ▸ **academia de idiomas** language school ▸ **academia de música** school of music, conservatoire ▸ **academia militar** military academy

2 (= *sociedad*) learned society

> **ACADEMIA**
>
> *In Spain* **academias** *are private schools catering for students of all ages and levels outside normal school and working hours. Some specialize in particular skills such as computing, languages and dressmaking while others offer extra tuition in core school subjects and syllabuses. For people hoping to do well enough in the* **oposiciones** *to get a post in the public sector, there are* **academias** *offering special preparatory courses for these notoriously difficult competitive examinations.*
>
> ⇨ *See also* OPOSICIONES

académico/a Ⓐ ADJ academic

Ⓑ SM/F academician, member (of an academy) ▸ **académico/a de número** full member (*of an academy*)

acaecer ▸conjug 2d◂ VI to happen, occur; **acaeció que ...** it came about that ...

acaecimiento SM happening, occurrence

acahual SM (*Méx*) (= *girasol*) sunflower; (= *yerba*) tall grass

acáis* SMPL peepers*, eyes

acalambrarse ▸conjug 1a◂ VPR to get cramp

acalaminado ADJ (*Cono Sur*) rough, uneven, bumpy

acalenturarse ▸conjug 1a◂ VPR to get feverish

acallamiento SM (= *silenciamiento*) silencing, quietening; (= *apaciguamiento*) pacification

acallar ▸conjug 1a◂ VT 1 (= *silenciar*) to silence, quieten, quiet (*EEUU*)

2 (= *calmar*) [+ *furia*] to assuage, pacify; [+ *crítica, duda*] to silence

acaloradamente ADV heatedly, excitedly

acalorado ADJ 1 (= *con calor*) heated, hot

2 (= *enardecido*) [*discusión*] heated; [*partidario*] passionate; (= *agitado*) agitated

acaloramiento SM 1 (= *calor*) heat

2 (= *enardecimiento*) vehemence, passion

acalorar ▸conjug 1a◂ Ⓐ VT 1 (= *calentar*) to make hot, warm up; (= *sobrecalentar*) to overheat

2 (= *enardecer*) to inflame, excite; [+ *pasiones*] to inflame; [+ *audiencia*] to work up; [+ *ambición*] to stir up, encourage

Ⓑ **acalorarse** VPR 1 (= *sofocarse*) to get hot, become overheated

2 (= *enardecerse*) [*persona*] (*al actuar*) to get excited, get worked up (**por** about); (*al hablar*) to get worked up; [*discusión*] to become heated

acalórico ADJ low-calorie *antes de s*, low in calories

acaloro SM anger

acalote SM (*Méx*) channel

acamar ▸conjug 1a◂ VT to beat down, lay

acamastronarse ▸conjug 1a◂ VPR (*LAm*) to get crafty, become artful

acampada SF camping; **ir de** *o* **hacer una ~** to go camping ▸ **acampada libre** camping rough, camping in the wild

acampado/a SM/F camper, motorhome (*EEUU*)

acampanado ADJ bell-shaped; [*pantalón*] flared, bell-bottomed

acampar ▸conjug 1a◂ Ⓐ VI to camp; (*Mil*) to encamp

Ⓑ **acamparse** VPR to camp

acampo SM pasture, common pasture

acanalado ADJ 1 (= *con canales*) grooved, furrowed

2 (*Arquit*) fluted

3 (*Téc*) [*hierro*] corrugated

acanaladura SF (= *canal*) groove, furrow; (*Arquit*) fluting

acanalar ▸conjug 1a◂ VT 1 (= *hacer canales*) to groove, furrow

2 (*Arquit*) to flute

3 (*Téc*) [+ *hierro*] to corrugate

acanallado ADJ disreputable, low

acanelado ADJ cinnamon-flavoured *o* (*EEUU*) -flavored, cinnamon-coloured *o* (*EEUU*) -colored

acantilado Ⓐ ADJ [*risco*] steep, sheer; [*costa*] rocky; [*fondo del mar*] shelving

Ⓑ SM cliff

acanto SM acanthus

acantonamiento SM 1 (= *lugar*) cantonment

2 (= *acto*) billeting, quartering

acantonar ▸conjug 1a◂ VT (*Mil*) (= *colocar*) to station; (*en domicilio privado*) to billet

acaparación SF = **acaparamiento**

acaparador(a) Ⓐ ADJ 1 (= *acumulador*) **las hormigas son animales ~es** ants are hoarders; **instintos ~es** acquisitive instincts

2 (= *egoísta*) (*con cosas*) selfish; (*con personas*) possessive

Ⓑ SM/F 1 [*de objetos, mercancías*] hoarder

2 (= *egoísta*) (*con cosas*) selfish person; (*con personas*) possessive person

acaparamiento SM 1 (= *acumulación*) hoarding, stockpiling; **hizo ~ de víveres** he hoarded *o* stockpiled provisions

2 (*Com*) (= *monopolio*) [*de ventas*] monopolizing; [*del mercado*] cornering

3 (= *apropiamiento*) **se quejaron del ~ del teléfono por uno de ellos** they complained that one of them was hogging* *o* monopolizing the phone; **consiguió el ~ de todas las miradas** he managed to capture everyone's attention

acaparar ▸conjug 1a◂ VT 1 (= *acumular*) [+ *víveres, bienes*] to hoard; **~ provisiones para el invierno** to hoard food supplies for the winter

2 (= *tener la totalidad de*) 2·1 [+ *producción, poder, conversación*] to monopolize; **acaparan la distribución de gasolina en la zona** they have a monopoly on the distribution of petrol in the area; **~ el mercado de algo** to corner the market in sth; **han acaparado el mercado del vino** they have cornered the wine market

2·2 (*pey*) to hog*, monopolize; **a ver si no acaparas el teléfono** don't hog* *o* monopolize the telephone, will you?

3 (= *quedarse con*) to take; **la película que acaparó todos los premios** the film which took all the prizes; **han acaparado un 25% del mercado de ventas a domicilio** they have captured *o* taken a 25% share of the home sales market; **la industria acapara la mayor parte de las ayudas del gobierno** industry gets most of the government aid

4 (= *poseer*) to hold; **la izquierda acapara**

todos los puestos en el ayuntamiento the left holds all of the council posts; **la empresa acapara el 40% de la tierra** the company owns 40% of the land

5 (= *ocupar*) to take up; **el accidente acaparó las primeras páginas de todos los periódicos** the accident took up the front pages in all the newspapers; **el cantante acapara los titulares estos días** the singer is front page news these days

6 [+ *atención, interés*] to capture; **este asunto acaparó la atención de todos los políticos** this issue captured the attention of all the politicians; **le gustaba ~ las miradas de todo el mundo** he liked to hog the limelight*

acapetate SM (*Méx*) straw mat

acapillar‡ ▸conjug 1a◂ VT (*Méx*) to grab, take hold of

acápite SM (*LAm*) (= *párrafo*) paragraph; (= *título*) subheading; **punto ~** full stop, new paragraph

a cappella [aka'pela] ADV a cappella

acapullado ADJ in bud

acapulqueño/a Ⓐ ADJ of/from Acapulco
Ⓑ SM/F native/inhabitant of Acapulco; **los ~s** the people of Acapulco

acaracolado ADJ spiral *antes de s*, winding, twisting

acaramelado ADJ 1 (*Culin*) **con sabor ~** toffee-flavoured *o* (*EEUU*) -flavored; **de color ~** toffee-coloured *o* (*EEUU*) -colored

2 (*fig*) (= *dulce*) sugary, oversweet; (= *correcto*) over-polite; **estaban ~s** [*amantes*] they were all lovey-dovey*

acaramelar ▸conjug 1a◂ Ⓐ VT to coat with caramel
Ⓑ **acaramelarse** VPR to become besotted with each other

acardenalar ▸conjug 1a◂ Ⓐ VT to bruise
Ⓑ **acardenalarse** VPR to get bruised, go black and blue

acar(e)ar ▸conjug 1a◂ VT (= *carear*) to bring face to face; (= *afrontar*) to face, face up to

acariciador ADJ caressing

acariciar ▸conjug 1b◂ VT 1 (= *hacer caricias*) to caress, stroke; (= *sobar*) to fondle; [+ *animal*] to pat, stroke; (= *rozar*) to brush

2 [+ *esperanzas*] to cherish, cling to; [+ *proyecto*] to have in mind

acaricida SM (*Cono Sur*) insecticide

ácaro SM mite

acarraladura* SF (*Andes, Cono Sur*) run, ladder

acarreadizo ADJ transportable, that can be transported

acarreado/a SM/F (*Méx*) *peasant bussed in by the government in order to vote*

acarrear ▸conjug 1a◂ VT 1 (= *transportar*) to transport, carry; (= *arrastrar*) to cart

2 (= *causar*) to cause, bring in its train *o* wake; **le acarreó muchos disgustos** it caused *o* brought him lots of problems; **acarreó la caída del gobierno** it led to the fall of the government

acarreo SM (= *flete*) haulage, carriage; **gastos de ~** transport charges

acarreto SM (*Caribe, Méx*) = **acarreo**

acartonado ADJ [*superficie*] like cardboard; (= *enjuto*) wizened

acartonar ▸conjug 1a◂ Ⓐ VT [+ *piel*] to weather
Ⓑ **acartonarse** VPR (= *ponerse rígido*) to grow stiff; (= *quedarse enjuto*) to become wizened

acartuchado* ADJ (*Cono Sur*) stuffy, stuck-up*

acarvamiento SM erosion

acaserarse* ▸conjug 1a◂ VPR (*Andes*††) to become attached; (*Com*) to become a regular customer (*of a shop*); (= *sentar la cabeza*) to settle down; (*Andes, Caribe*) (= *quedarse en casa*) to stay at home

acaso Ⓐ ADV 1 (*en preguntas retóricas*) **¿~ no te lo he dicho cien veces?** haven't I told you a hundred times?; **¿~ tengo yo la culpa de lo que haga mi hermana?** (how) am I to blame for what my sister does?; **¿~ yo lo sé?** how would I know?

2 (*frm*) (= *quizá*) perhaps; **~ no es verdad lo que dicen** perhaps what they say is not true; **es ~ el más prestigioso galardón de poesía** it is perhaps the most prestigious poetry award; **~ venga** perhaps he will come

3 **si ~: no quiero nada, si ~ algo de fruta** I don't want anything, except maybe *o* perhaps some fruit; **está bueno, si ~ un poco dulce** it's quite good, if perhaps a bit too sweet; **no tienes que ir, si ~ lo llamas por teléfono** you don't have to go, just give him a phone call; **si ~ llama, dímelo** if by any chance he phones, let me know

4 **por si ~** just in case; **yo por si ~ llevo impermeable** I'm wearing a raincoat just in case; **llévalo por si ~ hace falta** take it, just in case you need it; **por si ~ viniera** just in case he should come *o* were to come

Ⓑ SM (*frm*) chance; **al ~** at random; **por ~** ◊ **por un ~** by (any) chance

acastañado ADJ hazel

acatamiento SM [*de ley*] observance (**de** of), compliance (**de** with); (= *respeto*) respect (**a** for)

acatar ▸conjug 1a◂ VT 1 (= *respetar*) to respect; [+ *ley*] to observe, comply with

2 (= *subordinarse a*) to defer to

3 (*LAm*) (= *notar*) to notice, observe

4 (*Cono Sur, Méx*) (= *molestar*) to annoy

acatarrado ADJ **estar ~** to have a cold

acatarrar ▸conjug 1a◂ Ⓐ VT (*LAm*) (= *molestar*) to annoy, bother
Ⓑ **acatarrarse** VPR 1 (= *resfriarse*) to catch a cold

2 (*Cono Sur**) (= *emborracharse*) to get boozed up*

acato SM = **acatamiento**

acatólico/a ADJ, SM/F non-Catholic

acaudalado ADJ well-off, affluent

acaudalar ▸conjug 1a◂ VT to acquire, accumulate

acaudillar ▸conjug 1a◂ VT to lead, command

➤ **acceder** ▸conjug 2a◂ VI 1 (= *aceptar*) to agree; **se lo propuse y accedieron** I suggested it and they agreed; **~ a algo** to agree to sth; **el director ha accedido a nuestra petición** the director agreed *o* acceded (*frm*) to our request; **~ a hacer algo** to agree to do sth

2 **~ a** (= *entrar*) 2·1 [+ *lugar*] to gain access to; [+ *grupo social, organización*] to be admitted to; **por esta puerta se accede al salón** you can gain access to the lounge through this door; **no pueden ~ al mercado laboral por no tener estudios** they have no access to the labour market because they have no qualifications; **este examen os permitirá ~ a la universidad** this exam will enable you to gain admittance to the university; **si ganan este partido, acceden a la final** if they win this match they go through to the final

2·2 (*Inform*) [+ *fichero, Internet*] to access; **no está autorizado a ~ a la base de datos** he is not authorized to access the database

3 (= *conseguir*) **~ a** [+ *información*] to gain access to, access; **fue la primera mujer en ~ a este puesto** she was the first woman to assume this post; **accedió a la secretaría general** he became secretary general; **las personas que no pueden ~ a una vivienda digna** people who have no access to decent housing; **los jóvenes tienen dificultades para ~ a un puesto de trabajo** young people have problems finding a job; **para ~ a estas becas es necesario ser europeo** only European citizens are eligible for these grants; **accedió a una graduación superior** he attained a higher rank, he was promoted to a higher rank; **~ al poder** to assume power; **~ a la propiedad de algo** to become the owner of sth; **~ al trono** to succeed to the throne

accesibilidad SF accessibility (**to** a)

accesible ADJ 1 [*lugar, texto, lenguaje, estilo*] accessible

2 [*persona*] approachable

3 [*precio, producto*] affordable

accesión SF 1 (= *consentimiento*) assent (**a** to), acquiescence (**a** in)

2 (= *accesorio*) accessory

3 (*Med*) attack

accésit SM (*pl* **accésits**) second prize

acceso SM 1 (= *posibilidad de entrar*) (*a edificio, institución, mercado, documentos*) access; (*a competición*) entry; **tenemos libre ~ a la biblioteca** we have free access to the library; **hay que garantizar el ~ público a la educación** we must guarantee public access to education; **tiene ~ a la información confidencial** she has access to confidential information; **"acceso prohibido"** ◊ **"prohibido el acceso"** "no entry", "no admittance"; **(código de) ~ internacional** (*Telec*) international (dialling) code; **eso coincidió con su ~ al poder** this coincided with his assuming power; **dar ~ a** [+ *lugar*] to lead to; [+ *institución*] to give entry to; [+ *competición*] to provide a place in; [+ *información*] to give access to; **de fácil ~: un puerto de fácil ~** a port with easy access; **los controles son de fácil ~** the controls are easily accessible; **~ gratuito** free admission ► **acceso al trono** accession

2 (= *llegada*) 2·1 (*en coche*) access; **no es posible el ~ por carretera** there is no access by road *o* no road access; **las inundaciones han cortado los ~s a la finca** floods have cut off access *o* the approaches to the estate; **carretera** *o* **vía de ~** (*a ciudad*) approach road; (*a autovía*) slip road

2·2 [*de avión*] approach

3 (= *entrada*) entrance; **el ~ principal del museo** the main entrance to the museum; **puerta de ~** entrance gate *o* door

4 (*Univ*) (= *ingreso*) entrance; **le negaron el ~ a la carrera que quería** they didn't let him join the course he wished; **curso de ~** access course; **prueba de ~** entrance exam

5 (*Inform*) access ► **acceso aleatorio** random access ► **acceso directo** direct access ► **acceso en serie** serial access ► **acceso múltiple** multi-access ► **acceso remoto** re-

➤ LENGUA Y USO: **acceder** 38.2, 38.3, 39.3

mote access ► **acceso secuencial** sequential access

[6] (= *ataque*) [6·1] (*Med*) [*de asma, fiebre*] attack; [*de tos*] fit

[6·2] [*de celos, cólera*] fit; [*de generosidad*] display; **en un ~ de ira** in a fit of rage

accesoria SF annex, outbuilding

accesorio Ⓐ ADJ accessory; [*gastos*] incidental

Ⓑ SM [1] (*gen*) accessory, attachment, extra; **accesorios** (*Téc*) accessories, spare parts; (*Aut*) spare parts; (*Teat*) props

[2] (*de vestir*) accessory

accidentado/a Ⓐ ADJ [1] [*terreno*] rough, uneven

[2] (= *turbado*) [*vida*] troubled, eventful; [*historial*] variable, up-and-down; [*viaje*] eventful

[3] (*Med*) injured

[4] (*Caribe Aut*) broken down; (*LAm euf*) (= *giboso*) hunchbacked

Ⓑ SM/F accident victim, casualty

accidental ADJ [1] (= *contingente*) accidental; (= *no deliberado*) unintentional; (= *fortuito*) [*encuentro*] casual, chance *antes de s*

[2] (= *fugaz*) brief, transient; **un empleo ~** a temporary job

accidentalidad SF accident rate, number of accidents

accidentalmente ADV (= *por casualidad*) by chance; (= *sin querer*) accidentally, unintentionally

accidentarse ▸conjug 1a◂ VPR to have an accident; (*Méx Aut*) to (have a) crash

accidente SM [1] (= *suceso*) accident; **por ~** by accident, by chance; **una vida sin ~s** an uneventful life; **sufrir un ~** to have *o* meet with an accident; **hay ~s que no se pueden prever** accidents will happen ► **accidente aéreo** plane crash ► **accidente de carretera** road accident ► **accidente de circulación** traffic accident ► **accidente de trabajo, accidente laboral** industrial accident ► **accidente múltiple** multiple accident, pile-up

[2] (*Med*) faint, swoon

[3] (*Ling*) accidence

[4] **~s** [*de terreno*] unevenness *sing*, roughness *sing*

[5] **~ de la cara** (*Méx*) (= *rasgo*) feature

acción SF [1] (= *actividad*) action; **es hora de pasar a la ~** it's time to take action; **¡luces, cámara, ~!** lights, camera, action!; **el programa de ~** the programme of action; **en ~** in action; **puso el plan en ~** he put the plan in action; **ponerse en ~** to go into action; **estar en ~** (*Cuba**) to be busy; **hombre de ~** man of action; **película de ~** action film, action movie (*esp EEUU*) ► **acción directa** (*Pol*) direct action

[2] (= *acto*) act; **llevaron a cabo una ~ condenable** they committed a reprehensible act; **deben ser juzgados por sus acciones y no por sus palabras** they should be judged by their deeds, not by their words; **buena ~** good deed; **mala ~**: **sufrirán justo castigo por sus malas acciones** they will receive fair punishment for their evil deeds; **es incapaz de una mala ~** he would never do anything bad; ✦***REFRÁN*** **unir la ~ a la palabra** to suit the deed to the word ► **acción de gracias** thanksgiving

[3] (= *efecto*) [*de medicamento, viento*] action; **su ~ sobre el sistema nervioso** its action on the nervous system; **por ~ química** by chemical action; **una crema adelgazante de ~ rápida** a fast-acting slimming cream; **lo recomiendan por su ~ relajante** it is recommended for its relaxing effect; **de ~ retardada** [*bomba, mecanismo*] delayed-action *antes de s*

[4] (*Mil*) (*gen*) action; (= *operación*) operation; **han condenado la ~ militar estadounidense** the American military action has been condemned; **una de las zonas de ~ de la guerrilla** one of the areas where the guerrillas are active; **una ~ que dejó varios heridos** an operation which left several wounded; **muerto en ~** killed in action; **fuerza** *o* **brigada de ~ rápida** rapid action force ► **acción de guerra** military operation

[5] (*Teat, Literat, Cine*) (= *trama*) action; **la ~ se desarrolla en Italia** the action takes place in Italy ► **acción aparte** by-play

[6] (= *movimiento*) [*de la cara, cuerpo*] movement; **sus acciones eran cada vez más lentas** her movements were slower and slower

[7] (*Jur*) action ► **acción judicial, acción legal** (*gen*) legal action; (= *pleito*) lawsuit; **van a emprender acciones legales** they are going to take legal action; **han presentado una ~ judicial contra el periódico** they have taken out a lawsuit against the newspaper ► **acción penal** criminal action ► **acción popular** (*Jur*) people's action

[8] (*Com, Fin*) share; **capital en acciones** share capital; **emisión de acciones** share issue, stock issue ► **acción cotizada en bolsa** listed share, quoted share ► **acción liberada** fully-paid share ► **acción ordinaria** ordinary share, common stock (*EEUU*) ► **acción preferente** preference share, preferred stock (*EEUU*) ► **acción primitiva** ordinary share, common stock (*EEUU*) ► **acción prioritaria** priority share ► **acción sin voto** non-voting share

accionado SM shares *pl*, shareholding; **~ mayoritario** majority shareholding

accionamiento SM (*Mec*) operation; **el mecanismo que controla el ~ del motor** the mechanism which controls the operation of the engine; **una capota de ~ eléctrico** an electrically-operated top; **un motor con ~ a distancia** a remote-controlled engine

accionar ▸conjug 1a◂ Ⓐ VT [1] (*Mec*) [*+ mecanismo, motor, alarma*] to activate, operate; [*+ bomba, misil*] to activate, trigger; [*+ interruptor*] to switch; [*+ palanca*] to pull

[2] (*Inform*) to drive

Ⓑ VI to gesticulate

accionariado SM [1] (= *acciones*) shares *pl*, total of shares, shareholding

[2] (= *personas*) shareholders *pl*

accionarial ADJ share *antes de s*; **paquete ~** ◊ **participación ~** shareholding

accionario ADJ share *antes de s*, of stocks and shares, relating to stocks and shares

accionista SMF shareholder, stockholder; **~ mayoritario** majority shareholder

accisa SF excise duty

ACE SF ABR (= **Acción Católica Española**) *charitable and campaigning organization*

acebo SM holly, holly tree

acebuche SM [1] (= *árbol*) wild olive tree; (= *madera*) olive wood

[2] (*) (= *simplón*) yokel, hillbilly (*EEUU*)

acechadera SF (= *escondite*) hiding place; (*Caza*) hide, blind (*EEUU*)

acechador(a) SM/F spy, watcher

acechanza SF = **acecho**

acechar ▸conjug 1a◂ VT (= *observar*) to spy on, watch; (= *esperar*) to lie in wait for; [*+ caza*] to stalk; (= *amenazar*) to threaten, beset; **~ la ocasión** to wait one's chance

acecho SM (= *acto de espiar*) spying, watching; (*Mil*) ambush; **estar al** *o* **en ~** to lie in wait; **cazar al ~** to stalk

acechón* ADJ spying, prying; **hacer la acechona** to spy, pry

acecinar ▸conjug 1a◂ Ⓐ VT [*+ carne*] to salt, cure

Ⓑ **acecinarse** VPR (= *quedarse enjuto*) to get very thin

acedar ▸conjug 1a◂ Ⓐ VT (= *poner agrio*) [1] to turn sour, make bitter

[2] (= *amargar*) to sour, embitter

Ⓑ **acedarse** VPR (= *ponerse agrio*) to turn sour; [*planta*] to wither, yellow

acedera SF sorrel

acedía SF [1] (*Culin*) acidity, sourness

[2] (*Med*) heartburn

[3] (*fig*) (= *desabrimiento*) unpleasantness

[4] (= *pez*) plaice

acedo ADJ (= *agrio*) acid, sour; (= *desagradable*) sour, unpleasant, disagreeable

acéfalo ADJ (= *sin cabeza*) headless; (= *sin líder*) leaderless

aceitada‡ SF (*Cono Sur*) bribe, backhander*, sweetener (*EEUU*)

aceitar ▸conjug 1a◂ VT [1] (= *untar con aceite*) to oil

[2] **~ a algn** (*Caribe, Cono Sur**) (= *sobornar*) to bribe sb, grease sb's palm*

aceite SM [1] (*Culin, Med, Téc*) oil; ✦***MODISMO*** **echar ~ al fuego** to add fuel to the flames ► **aceite alcanforado** camphorated oil ► **aceite combustible** fuel oil ► **aceite de algodón** cottonseed oil ► **aceite de almendra** almond oil ► **aceite de ballena** whale oil ► **aceite de cacahuete** peanut oil ► **aceite de coco** coconut oil ► **aceite de colza** rapeseed oil ► **aceite de girasol** sunflower oil ► **aceite de hígado de bacalao** cod-liver oil ► **aceite de linaza** linseed oil ► **aceite de maíz** corn oil ► **aceite de oliva** olive oil ► **aceite de oliva refinado** refined olive oil ► **aceite de oliva virgen** virgin olive oil ► **aceite de ricino** castor oil ► **aceite de soja** soya oil ► **aceite lubricante** lubricating oil ► **aceite vegetal** vegetable oil

[2] (‡) (= *droga*) hash*; (*Méx*) LSD

aceitera SF (*Culin*) oil bottle; (*Aut*) oilcan; **~s** oil and vinegar set

aceitero/a Ⓐ ADJ oil *antes de s*

Ⓑ SM/F oil merchant

aceitón SM thick oil, dirty oil

aceitoso ADJ oily

aceituna SF olive ► **aceituna rellena** stuffed olive

aceitunado ADJ (= *verdoso*) olive *antes de s*, olive-coloured *o* (*EEUU*) -colored; (= *de tez aceitunada*) olive-skinned

aceitunero/a SM/F (*Com*) dealer in olives; (*Agr*) olive picker

aceituno Ⓐ ADJ (*LAm*) [*color*] olive; **(de) color ~** olive-coloured o (*EEUU*) -colored
Ⓑ SM [1] (= *árbol*) olive tree
[2] (‡) (= *guardia civil*) Civil Guard

aceleración SF (*Mec*) acceleration; (= *agilización*) speeding-up, hastening

acelerada SF acceleration, speed-up

aceleradamente ADV [1] (= *rápidamente*) rapidly
[2] (= *precipitadamente*) hastily

acelerado ADJ [1] (= *rápido*) [*avance, crecimiento, ritmo*] rapid; **con el corazón ~** with her heart racing o beating fast; **andaban con paso ~** they walked at a brisk pace; **los ochenta fueron una década muy acelerada** the eighties was a decade of hectic activity
[2] [*curso*] intensive, crash *antes de s*
[3] (*) [*persona*] hyper*; **se le ve muy ~ últimamente** he's been very hyper lately*

acelerador SM accelerator, gas pedal (*EEUU*); **apretar** o **pisar el ~** (*lit*) to put one's foot down, step on the gas (*esp EEUU**); (*fig*) to step up the pace ► **acelerador de partículas** particle accelerator

acelerar ▸conjug 1a◂ Ⓐ VT [1] (*Aut*) [+ *coche*] to accelerate; [+ *motor*] to rev, rev up
[2] (= *apresurar*) [+ *cambio, proceso*] to speed up; [+ *acontecimiento*] to hasten; **deben ~ los trámites de aduana** they must speed up customs procedures; **las conversaciones ~on el final de la guerra** the talks hastened the end of the war; **~ la marcha** to go faster; **~ el paso** to quicken one's pace, speed up; **~ el ritmo de algo** to speed sth up
[3] (*Fís*) [+ *partícula, velocidad*] to accelerate
Ⓑ VI [1] (*Aut*) [*coche, conductor*] to accelerate; **no aceleres en las curvas** don't accelerate on the bends; **aceleró a fondo** he put his foot to the floor
[2] (*) (= *darse prisa*) to get a move on*, hurry up; **venga, acelera, que nos están esperando** come on, get a move on* o hurry up, they're waiting for us
Ⓒ **acelerarse** VPR [1] (= *apresurarse*) [*cambio, proceso*] to speed up; **el proceso se acelera si se eleva la temperatura** the process speeds up if the temperature is raised; **eso no será posible si se acelera la inflación** this will not be possible if inflation goes up any faster; **el corazón se le aceleró** her heart beat faster, her heart started racing; **~se a hacer algo** to hurry to do sth, hasten to do sth
[2] (*) (= *ponerse nervioso*) to get over-excited
[3] (*Fís*) (= *aumentar la velocidad*) to accelerate; **los objetos se aceleran en la caída** objects accelerate as they fall

acelerón SM [1] (*Aut*) sudden acceleration
[2] (*fig*) (= *gran paso*) leap forward; (= *aumento*) rapid increase; (= *mejora*) rapid improvement

acelga SF Swiss chard

acémila SF [1] (= *mula*) beast of burden, mule
[2] (= *persona torpe*) thick-headed person

acemilero SM muleteer

acendrado ADJ pure, unblemished; **de ~ carácter español** typically o thoroughly Spanish in nature

acendrar ▸conjug 1a◂ VT (= *purificar*) to purify; (*Téc*) (= *refinar*) to refine; (*Literat*) (= *pulir*) to refine

acensuar ▸conjug 1d◂ VT to tax

acento SM [1] (*Ling*) (*escrito*) accent; (*hablado*) stress, emphasis; **pon un ~ sobre la o** put an accent on the o; **el ~ cae en la segunda sílaba** the stress o emphasis is on the second syllable ► **acento agudo** acute accent ► **acento circunflejo** circumflex (accent) ► **acento ortográfico** written accent ► **acento tónico** tonic accent
[2] (= *deje*) accent; **tiene ~ francés** he has French accent; **tiene un ~ muy cerrado** he has a very strong o broad accent; **con (un) fuerte ~ andaluz** with a strong Andalusian accent; **hablan inglés sin nada de ~** they speak English without a trace of an accent; **un hombre de ~ sudamericano** a man with a South American accent
[3] (= *énfasis*) emphasis; **un programa de jazz con ~ latino** a jazz programme with the emphasis on Latin American jazz; **ha sido una campaña con ~ bipartidista** it has been a campaign with a two-party emphasis; **poner el ~ en algo** to put the emphasis on sth, emphasize o stress sth
[4] (*frm*) (= *tono*) tone (of voice); **lo anunció con ~ triunfal** he announced it with a note of triumph in his voice, he announced it in a triumphant tone of voice, he announced it triumphantly

acentor SM ► **acentor común** hedgesparrow, dunnock

acentuación SF accentuation

acentuado ADJ accented, stressed

acentuamiento SM increase

acentuar ▸conjug 1e◂ Ⓐ VT [1] (*Ling*) to accent, stress; **esta palabra se acentúa en la u** this word is stressed on the u
[2] (= *subrayar*) to emphasize, accentuate
[3] (*Inform*) to highlight
Ⓑ **acentuarse** VPR to become more noticeable, be accentuated; **se acentúa la tendencia a la baja en la Bolsa** the downward trend in the Stock Exchange is becoming more pronounced

aceña SF water mill

aceñero SM miller

acepción SF [1] (*Ling*) sense, meaning
[2] (*en el trato*) preference; **sin ~ de persona** impartially

acepilladora SF planing machine

acepilladura SF wood shaving

acepillar ▸conjug 1a◂ VT [1] (= *cepillar*) to brush; (*Téc*) to plane, shave
[2] (*LAm**) (= *adular*) to suck up to*

aceptabilidad SF acceptability

▼ **aceptable** ADJ acceptable, passable

aceptación SF (= *acto*) acceptance; (= *aprobación*) approval; (= *popularidad*) popularity, standing; **mandar algo a la ~** (*Com*) to send sth on approval; **este producto tendrá una ~ enorme** this product will be widely welcomed; **no tener ~** to be unsuccessful

▼ **aceptar** ▸conjug 1a◂ VT [1] [+ *oferta, propuesta, dimisión*] to accept; [+ *cheque, moneda, tarjeta, trabajo*] to accept, take; [+ *condición*] to accept, agree to; **aceptó las tareas que se le asignaron** he accepted the tasks he was assigned; **la impresora sólo acepta este tipo de papel** the printer only takes this type of paper; **se niega a ~ los hechos** he refuses to face the facts; **no han aceptado mi solicitud de trabajo** they have rejected my job application; **"no aceptamos devoluciones"** "no refunds given"
[2] **~ hacer algo** to agree to do sth; **aceptó rebajarnos el alquiler** he agreed to reduce our rent; **no ~ hacer algo** to refuse to do sth; **no acepta pagar su parte** he refuses to pay his share; **por fin ~on que se publicara** they finally agreed for it to be published, they finally allowed it to be published; **no acepta que las mujeres trabajen** he doesn't accept o agree that women should work
[3] **~ a algn** to accept sb; **no me ~on en la carrera de medicina** I wasn't accepted on the medical course; **me ~on muy bien en mi nuevo trabajo** I was made to feel very welcome in my new job; **¿aceptas a María por esposa?** do you take María to be your lawful wedded wife?

acepto ADJ acceptable, agreeable (**a, de** to), welcomed (**a, de** by)

acequia SF [1] (*Agr*) irrigation ditch, irrigation channel
[2] (*LAm*) (= *riachuelo*) stream; (= *alcantarilla*) sewer

acera SF pavement, sidewalk (*EEUU*); **los de la ~ de enfrente*** the gays

acerado ADJ [1] (*Téc*) steel *antes de s*; (*con punta de acero*) steel-tipped
[2] (= *mordaz*) sharp, cutting

acerar ▸conjug 1a◂ Ⓐ VT [1] (*Téc*) to make into steel
[2] (= *vigorizar*) to harden; (= *hacer mordaz*) [+ *estilo*] to sharpen up, make more incisive
Ⓑ **acerarse** VPR to toughen o.s., harden o.s.

acerbamente ADV (*fig*) harshly, scathingly

acerbidad SF acerbity, harshness

acerbo ADJ [*sabor*] bitter, sour; (= *cruel*) harsh, scathing; **tener un odio ~ a algo** to despise o detest sth

acerca de PREP about

acercamiento SM [1] (*a un lugar*) approach; **maniobras de ~ a la pista** runway approach manoeuvres; **golpe de ~** (*Golf*) approach shot
[2] (*a un tema*) introduction; **el documental es un excelente ~ a la mitología** the documentary is an excellent introduction to mythology
[3] (= *reconciliación*) (*entre personas*) reconciliation; (*entre países, posiciones*) rapprochement; **su muerte fue motivo de ~ entre los hermanos** her death led to a reconciliation between the brothers; **la obra trata de conseguir el ~ con el público** the play seeks to forge a closer relationship with the audience; **fue el artífice del ~ entre China y EE.UU.** he was the architect of the rapprochement between China and the US

acercar ▸conjug 1g◂ Ⓐ VT [1] (= *aproximar*) (*gen*) to move closer; (*al hablante*) to bring closer; **acerca la silla a la mesa** move your chair closer to the table; **acercó la cámara a uno de los actores** he moved the camera up to one of the actors; **acerca un poco la silla** bring your chair a bit closer; **acercó sus labios a los míos** he brought his lips close to mine; **un intento de ~ la cultura al pueblo** an attempt to bring culture to the people
[2] (= *dar*) (*sin moverse*) to pass; (*desde más lejos*) to bring over; **acércame las tijeras** pass the scissors; **¿puedes ~me aquel paquete?** can you bring me over that parcel?

➤ LENGUA Y USO: **aceptable** 38.2 **aceptar** 39.1, 46.6, 52.1, 52.5

[3] (= *llevar en coche*) to take; **¿me puedes ~ a casa?** can you take me home?; **¿quieres que te acerque al aeropuerto?** do you want me to take you to the airport?

[4] (= *unir*) [+ *culturas, países, puntos de vistas*] to bring closer (together); **hay intereses comunes que nos acercan** there are common interests that bring us closer (together); **van a celebrar una nueva reunión para intentar ~ posturas** they are having another meeting to try and bring the two sides closer (together)

Ⓑ **acercarse** VPR [1] (= *aproximarse*) [1·1] (*al hablante*) to come closer; (*a algo alejado del hablante*) to get closer; **acércate, que te vea** come closer so that I can see you; **no te acerques más, que te puedes quemar** don't get any closer, you could burn yourself; **al ver que se acercaban, el conductor se paró** when he saw them coming closer *o* approaching, the driver stopped; **unos pasos femeninos se acercaban por el pasillo** a woman's footsteps were coming up the corridor; **~se a: no te acerques tanto a la mesa** don't get so close to the table; **los periodistas no pudieron ~se al avión** the journalists couldn't get near the plane; **me acerqué a la ventana** I went up *o* over to the window; **señores pasajeros, nos estamos acercando a Heathrow** ladies and gentlemen, we're approaching Heathrow; **el paro se acerca al 10%** unemployment is approaching 10%

[1·2] (= *abordar*) **~se a algn** (*al hablante*) to come up to sb; (*lejos del hablante*) to go up to sb; **se me acercó por la espalda** she came up behind me; **se le ~on para pedirle autógrafos** they went up to her to ask for autographs

[1·3] **~se algo al oído** to put sth to one's ear

[2] (*en el tiempo*) [*acontecimiento, momento*] to get closer, get nearer; **ya se acercan las vacaciones** the holidays are nearly here, the holidays are getting closer *o* nearer; **se acercaba la hora de despedirnos** it was nearly time to say goodbye; **~se a** [+ *fecha*] to approach; [+ *situación*] to get closer to; **se acercan a la edad de la jubilación** they are approaching retirement age; **nos acercábamos a la solución** we were getting closer to finding a answer

[3] (= *ir*) **acércate a la tienda y trae una botella de agua** go over to the shop and get a bottle of water; **tengo que ~me a comprar el periódico** I just have to go and buy the paper; **ya me ~é un día a visitaros** one of these days I'll pay you a visit *o* I'll come and see you; **acércate por la oficina cuando puedas** call by the office when you get the chance

[4] (= *parecerse*) **~se a algo**: **nuestros gustos se acercan más a la ópera** our tastes tend more towards opera; **los resultados se acercan bastante a lo que esperábamos** the results are fairly close to what we expected; **eso se acerca a la herejía** that is verging on heresy

ácere SM maple

acería SF steelworks, steel mill

acerico SM pincushion

acero SM steel; **tener buenos ~s** (= *aguante*) to have guts*; (= *hambre*) to be ravenously hungry ► **acero al carbono** carbon steel ► **acero al manganeso** manganese steel ► **acero bruto** crude steel ► **acero colado** cast steel ► **acero fundido** cast steel ► **acero inoxidable** stainless steel ► **aceros especiales** special steels

acerote SM (= *holgazán*) idler, loafer

acérrimo ADJ [*partidario*] staunch; [*enemigo*] bitter

acerrojar ▸conjug 1a◂ VT to bolt

acertado ADJ [1] (= *correcto*) [*diagnóstico, respuesta*] right, correct; [*descripción, resumen*] accurate; **han sido tres respuestas acertadas** you had three right *o* correct answers; **estuvieron ~s en su elección** they made the right *o* correct choice; **el portero estuvo muy ~ en la segunda mitad** the goalkeeper didn't put a foot wrong in the second half

[2] (= *apropiado*) [*comentario, título, regalo*] appropriate; **la música del funeral no fue muy acertada** the music was not very appropriate for a funeral; **tu contestación estuvo muy acertada** your reply was very appropriate; **fue la compra más acertada de mi vida** it was the best purchase of my life; **creo que tu elección ha sido muy acertada** I think you've made a very good choice

[3] (= *sensato*) [*juicio, consejo, idea*] wise; **seguí el ~ consejo de mi padre** I followed my father's wise advice; **estuviste muy poco ~ al decir eso** that wasn't a very wise thing to say

acertante Ⓐ ADJ [*quiniela, boleto*] winning

Ⓑ SMF [*de quiniela, concurso*] winner; **esta semana han aparecido tres máximos ~s** this week three winners got the top prize

acertar ▸conjug 1j◂ Ⓐ VT [+ *respuesta*] to get right; [+ *adivinanza*] to guess; **gana el que acierte antes cinco preguntas** the winner is the first one to get five answers right *o* to answer five questions correctly; **¿cuántos números has acertado esta semana?** how many numbers did you get this week?; **a ver si aciertas lo que traigo** see if you can guess what I've brought you

Ⓑ VI [1] (*al disparar*) to hit the target; **rara vez aciertan** they rarely hit their targets; **la bala le acertó de lleno en el corazón** the bullet hit him right in the heart; **disparó a matar pero no acertó** he shot to kill but he missed

[2] (= *adivinar*) to get it right; **¡has acertado!** you got it right!; ✦***REFRÁN*** **piensa mal y ~ás** think the worst and you won't be far wrong

[3] (*al decir, hacer algo*) to be right; **aciertan cuando dicen que la corrupción no tiene solución** they're right when they say that there's no solution to corruption; **acertó al quedarse callado** he did the right thing keeping quiet, he was right to keep quiet; **~ con algo** (*al escoger*) to get sth right; **han acertado de pleno con el nuevo modelo de coche familiar** they've scored a real winner* *o* they've got it just right with their new family car; **habéis acertado con el regalo** you made just the right choice with that present; **~ en algo**: **habéis acertado en la elección** you have made the right choice; **~on de pleno en sus pronósticos** their forecasts were totally accurate *o* correct

[4] **~ a hacer algo** (= *conseguir*) to manage to do sth; (*casualmente*) to happen to do sth; **acerté a encontrar la salida** I managed to find the exit; **no acerté a expresarme con claridad** I didn't manage to express myself clearly; **los médicos no aciertan a dar con lo que tiene** the doctors can't find out what's wrong with him; **no acierto a comprenderlo** I fail to understand it; **acertamos a pasar por delante de su casa** we happened to pass by his house

[5] **~ con** (= *encontrar*) to manage to find; **acerté con el interruptor** I managed to find the switch; **tras mucho pensarlo acertamos con la solución** after a lot of thought we managed to find the solution

[6] [*planta*] to flourish, do well

acertijo SM riddle, puzzle

acervo SM [1] (*Jur*) undivided estate, common property; **aportar algo a nuestro ~ común** to contribute sth to our collective heritage ► **acervo arqueológico** arch(a)eological wealth, arch(a)eological riches *pl* ► **acervo cultural** cultural heritage

[2] (= *montón*) heap, pile; (= *provisión*) stock, store

acetato SM acetate ► **acetato de vinilo** vinyl acetate

acético ADJ acetic

acetilénico ADJ acetylene *antes de s*

acetileno SM acetylene

acetona SF acetone

acetre SM (= *vasija*) small pail; (*Rel*) holy water vessel, portable stoup

acezar ▸conjug 1f◂ VI to puff, pant

achacable ADJ **~ a** attributable to

achacar ▸conjug 1g◂ VT [1] **~ algo a** to attribute sth to, put sth down to; **~ la culpa a algn** to lay the blame on sb

[2] (*LAm**) (= *robar*) to pinch*, nick‡; (= *saquear*) to pillage, loot

achacoso ADJ sickly, ailing

achaflanar ▸conjug 1a◂ VT to chamfer, bevel

achafranar** ▸conjug 1a◂ VI (*Méx*) to fuck**, screw**

achahuistlarse ▸conjug 1a◂ VPR (*Méx*) to get depressed

achalay EXCL, **achachay** EXCL (*Andes*) **¡achalay!** brr!

achampañado ADJ champagne-flavoured *o* (*EEUU*) -flavored

achamparse ▸conjug 1a◂ VPR (*Cono Sur*) **~ algo** to keep sth which does not belong to one

achancharse* ▸conjug 1a◂ VPR [1] (*Andes*) (= *ponerse perezoso*) to get lazy

[2] (*Cono Sur*) (= *engordar*) to get fat

[3] (*Andes*) (= *ponerse violento*) to become embarrassed

achantado* ADJ (*CAm*) bashful, shy

achantar ▸conjug 1a◂ Ⓐ VT (= *intimidar*) to intimidate; (= *humillar*) to take down a peg; (*) (= *asustar*) to scare, frighten

Ⓑ **achantarse** VPR [1] (= *intimidarse*) to back down, eat one's words; **~se por las buenas** to be easily intimidated

[2] (= *esconderse*) to hide away

achaparrado ADJ [*árbol*] stunted; [*persona*] stocky, thickset

achapinarse ▸conjug 1a◂ VPR (*CAm*) to adopt the local customs

achaque SM [1] (*Med*) ailment, malady ► **achaques de la vejez** ailments *o* infirmities of old age ► **achaques mañaneros** morning sickness

[2] (= *defecto*) defect, fault, weakness

[3] (= *asunto*) matter, subject; **en ~ de** in the matter of, on the subject of

4 (= *pretexto*) pretext; **con ~ de** under the pretext of

achara EXCL (*CAm*) what a pity!

achares* SMPL jealousy; **dar ~ a algn** to make sb jealous

acharolado ADJ polished, varnished

achatamiento SM 1 (= *allanamiento*) flattening

2 (*LAm*) (= *desmoralización*) loss of moral fibre; **sufrieron un ~** they lost heart, they felt down

achatar ▸conjug 1a◂ Ⓐ VT to flatten

Ⓑ **achatarse** VPR 1 (= *allanarse*) to flatten, become flat

2 (*Cono Sur, Méx*) (= *declinar*) to grow weak, decline; (*LAm*) (= *desmoralizarse*) to lose heart, feel down

3 (*Cono Sur, Méx*) (= *avergonzarse*) to be overcome with shame, be embarrassed; **quedarse achatado** to be ashamed, be embarrassed

achicado ADJ childish, childlike

achicador SM scoop, baler

achicalado ADJ (*Méx*) sugared, honeyed

achicalar ▸conjug 1a◂ VT (*Méx*) to cover in honey, soak in honey

achicanado ADJ Chicano, characteristic of Mexican-Americans

achicar ▸conjug 1g◂ Ⓐ VT 1 (= *empequeñecer*) to make smaller; (= *hacer de menos*) to dwarf; [+ *espacios*] to reduce; (*Cos*) to shorten, take in; (= *descontar*) to minimize

2 (= *desaguar*) to bale *o* (*EEUU*) bail out; (*con bomba*) to pump out

3 (*fig*) (= *humillar*) to humiliate; (= *intimidar*) to intimidate, browbeat

4 (*Andes*) (= *matar*) to kill

5 (*Andes, Caribe*) (= *sujetar*) to fasten, hold down

Ⓑ **achicarse** VPR 1 (= *empequeñecerse*) to get smaller; [*ropa*] to shrink

2 (*esp LAm*) (= *rebajarse*) to be intimidated, belittle o.s.

achicharradero SM inferno

achicharrante ADJ **calor ~** sweltering heat

achicharrar ▸conjug 1a◂ Ⓐ VT 1 (= *quemar*) to scorch; (*Culin*) to fry to a crisp; (*demasiado*) to burn; **el sol achicharraba la ciudad** the city was roasting in the heat

2 (*) (= *fastidiar*) to bother, plague, pester

3 (*Chile**) (= *aplastar*) to flatten, crush

4 (‡) (= *matar*) to shoot, riddle with bullets

Ⓑ VI **hace un sol que achicharra** it's absolutely roasting

Ⓒ **achicharrarse** VPR to get burnt; **¡me estoy achicharrando!** I'm getting burnt to a cinder!

achicharronar ▸conjug 1a◂ VT (*LAm*) to flatten, crush

achichiguar ▸conjug 1i◂ VT 1 (*Méx**) (= *mimar*) to cosset, spoil

2 (*Agr*) to shade

achichincle* SM (*Méx*) minion

achichuncle‡ SMF (*Méx*) creep‡, crawler‡, brown-nose (*EEUU*‡)

achicopalado* ADJ (*Méx*) depressed, gloomy

achicoria SF chicory, endive (*EEUU*)

achiguado* ADJ (*Méx*) spoiled

achiguarse ▸conjug 1i◂ VPR (*Cono Sur*) [*pared*] to bulge, sag; [*persona*] to get very fat

achilarse ▸conjug 1a◂ VPR (*Andes*) to turn cowardly

achimero SM (*CAm*) pedlar, peddler (*EEUU*), hawker

achimes SMPL (*CAm*) cheap goods, trinkets

achín SM (*CAm*) pedlar, peddler (*EEUU*), hawker

achinado ADJ 1 (*LAm*) (= *mestizo*) half-caste; (= *burdo*) coarse, common

2 [*aspecto*] Chinese-like, oriental; [*ojos*] slanting

achinar* ▸conjug 1a◂ Ⓐ VT to scare

Ⓑ **achinarse** VPR (*Cono Sur*) to become coarse

achipolarse* ▸conjug 1a◂ VPR (*Méx*) to grow sad, get gloomy

achique SM 1 (= *empequeñecimiento*) making smaller; [*de espacios*] reduction

2 (= *desagüe*) baling; (*con bomba*) pumping

achiquillado ADJ (*esp Méx*) childish

achiquitar ▸conjug 1a◂ VT (*LAm*) to make smaller, reduce

achirarse ▸conjug 1a◂ VPR (*Andes*) (= *nublarse*) to cloud over; (= *oscurecerse*) to get dark

achís EXCL atishoo!

achispado ADJ tipsy

achispar* ▸conjug 1a◂ Ⓐ VT (*LAm*) to cheer up, liven up

Ⓑ **achisparse** VPR to get tipsy

-acho, -acha *ver* **Aspects of Word Formation in Spanish 2**

achocar ▸conjug 1g◂ VT 1 (= *tirar*) to throw against a wall, dash against a wall

2 (= *pegar*) to hit, bash*

3 (*) (= *guardar*) to hoard, stash away*

achocharse ▸conjug 1a◂ VPR to get doddery, begin to dodder

achoclonarse ▸conjug 1a◂ VPR (*LAm*) to crowd together

achocolatado ADJ 1 [*color*] chocolate-brown

2 **estar ~‡** (= *borracho*) to be canned‡

acholado ADJ (*LAm*) 1 half-caste, part-Indian

2 (= *acobardado*) cowed; (= *avergonzado*) abashed

acholar ▸conjug 1a◂ (*LAm*) Ⓐ VT (= *avergonzar*) to embarrass; (= *intimidar*) to intimidate, scare

Ⓑ **acholarse** VPR 1 (= *acriollarse*) [*indígenas*] to have mestizo *o* half-breed ways, adopt mestizo *o* half-breed ways

2 (= *acobardarse*) to be cowed; (= *avergonzarse*) to be abashed, become shy; (= *sonrojarse*) to blush

acholo SM (*LAm*) embarrassment

-achón, -achona *ver* **Aspects of Word Formation in Spanish 2**

achoramiento‡ SM (*Cono Sur*) threat

achubascarse ▸conjug 1g◂ VPR to become threatening, cloud over

achuchado* ADJ 1 (= *difícil*) hard, difficult

2 **estar ~** (*Cono Sur*) (= *palúdico*) to have malaria; (= *acatarrado*) to have a chill; (= *febril*) to be feverish; (= *asustado*) to be scared, be frightened

achuchar ▸conjug 1a◂ Ⓐ VT 1 (= *aplastar*) to crush, squeeze flat

2 (= *empujar*) to shove, jostle; (= *acosar*) to harass, pester

3 **~ un perro contra algn** to set a dog on sb

Ⓑ **achucharse** VPR 1 [*amantes*] to cuddle, fondle (one another), pet*

2 (*Cono Sur*) (*paludismo*) to catch malaria; (= *acatarrarse*) to catch a chill; (= *tener fiebre*) to get feverish; (= *asustarse*) to get scared

achuchón SM 1 (= *abrazo*) squeeze

2 (= *empujón*) shove, push

3 **tener un ~** (*Med*) to be ill, be poorly

achucutado ADJ (*LAm*) (= *avergonzado*) abashed, ashamed; (= *deprimido*) gloomy, depressed; (= *agobiado*) overwhelmed

achucutarse ▸conjug 1a◂ VPR (*LAm*) (= *avergonzarse*) to be abashed, be ashamed; (= *estar afligido*) to be dismayed; (= *deprimirse*) to be depressed; (= *marchitarse*) to wilt

achucuyarse ▸conjug 1a◂ VPR (*CAm*) = **achucutarse**

achuicarse ▸conjug 1g◂ VPR (*Cono Sur*) (= *avergonzarse*) to be embarrassed; (= *apocarse*) to feel small

achulado ADJ, **achulapado** ADJ 1 (= *presumido*) cocky

2 (= *grosero*) coarse, uncouth

achumado* ADJ (*LAm*) drunk

achumarse* ▸conjug 1a◂ VPR (*LAm*) to get drunk

achunchar ▸conjug 1a◂ Ⓐ VT 1 (*Andes, Chile*) (= *avergonzar*) to shame

2 (*LAm*) (= *intimidar*) to scare

Ⓑ **achuncharse** VPR 1 (*Andes, Chile*) (= *avergonzarse*) to be ashamed

2 (*LAm*) (= *intimidarse*) to get scared

achuntar ▸conjug 1a◂ (*Cono Sur*) Ⓐ VT (= *hacer bien*) to do properly, get right

Ⓑ VI (= *acertar*) to guess right; (= *dar en el clavo*) to hit the nail on the head

achuñuscar* ▸conjug 1g◂ VT (*Cono Sur*) to squeeze

achupalla SF (*LAm*) pineapple

achura SF (*Cono Sur*) offal

achurar ▸conjug 1a◂ Ⓐ VT (*Cono Sur*) [+ *animal*] to gut; [+ *persona*] to kill

Ⓑ VI (*LAm*) (= *salir ganando*) to benefit from *o* do well out of

achurrucarse ▸conjug 1g◂ VPR (*CAm*) (= *marchitarse*) to wilt

achurruscado* ADJ rumpled, crumpled up

achurruscar ▸conjug 1g◂ VT (*Andes, Cono Sur*) to rumple, crumple up

aciago ADJ ill-fated, fateful, black*

aciano SM cornflower

acíbar SM 1 (= *jugo*) aloes

2 (= *amargura*) sorrow, bitterness

acibarar ▸conjug 1a◂ VT 1 (= *poner acíbar*) to add bitter aloes to, make bitter

2 (= *amargar*) to embitter; **~ la vida a algn** to make sb's life a misery

acicalado ADJ 1 [*persona*] smart, spruce; (*pey*) tarted up*, overdressed

2 [*metal*] polished, bright and shiny

acicalar ▸conjug 1a◂ Ⓐ VT 1 [+ *persona*] to dress up, bedeck

2 [+ *metal*] to polish, burnish, shine

Ⓑ **acicalarse** VPR to smarten o.s. up, spruce o.s. up

acicate SM incentive

acicatear ▸conjug 1a◂ VT [+ *persona*] to spur on; [+ *imaginación*] to fire

acícula SF (*Bot*) needle

acidez SF (*Quím*) acidity; (*Culin*) sourness

acidia SF indolence, apathy, sloth

acidificar ▸conjug 1g◂ Ⓐ VT to acidify

Ⓑ **acidificarse** VPR to acidify

acidillo ADJ slightly sour

ácido Ⓐ ADJ 1 [*sabor, olor*] sour, acid
2 **estar ~** (*LAm**) (= *fabuloso*) to be great*, be fabulous*
Ⓑ SM 1 (*Quím*) acid ► **ácido acético** acetic acid ► **ácido ascórbico** ascorbic acid ► **ácido carbólico** carbolic acid ► **ácido carbónico** carbonic acid ► **ácido cianhídrico** hydrocyanic acid ► **ácido clorhídrico** hydrochloric acid ► **ácido lisérgico** lysergic acid ► **ácido nicotínico** nicotinic acid ► **ácido nítrico** nitric acid ► **ácido nitroso** nitrous acid ► **ácido nucleico** nucleic acid ► **ácido oxálico** oxalic acid ► **ácido ribonucleico** ribonucleic acid ► **ácido sulfúrico** sulphuric acid ► **ácido úrico** uric acid
2 (*) (= *droga*) LSD, acid*; (= *pastilla*) acid tab*, LSD tab*

acidófilo ADJ acidophilous

acidulante SM acidulant, acidifier

acídulo ADJ acidulous

acierto SM 1 (= *respuesta correcta*) (*en concurso, examen*) correct answer; (*en quiniela, diagnóstico*) correct forecast; **cuenta los ~s y los errores** count the correct and incorrect answers; **una quiniela con 15 ~s** a coupon with 15 correct forecasts
2 (= *buena decisión*) good move, good decision; **fue un ~ invitarla a la fiesta** it was a good move *o* decision to invite her to the party
3 (= *cualidad*) **dudo del ~ de esa decisión** I doubt the wisdom of that decision; **con ~** (= *hábilmente*) skilfully, skillfully (*EEUU*); (= *correctamente*) rightly; **resolvió la situación con ~** she resolved the situation skilfully; **el periódico que con tanto ~ dirige** the paper which he edits so competently; **lo que con tanto ~ denominaron realismo** what they so rightly called realism; **tener el ~ de hacer algo** to have the good sense to do sth
4 (= *éxito*) success; **es una historia de ~s y fracasos** it's a story of successes and failures
5 (*Ftbl*) fine shot; **el gol llegó en un ~ de Cardeñosa** the goal came from a fine shot by Cardeñosa

aciguatado* ADJ (*Méx*) silly, stupid

aciguatarse ▸conjug 1a◂ VPR (*Caribe, Méx*) to grow stupid; (*) (= *enloquecer*) to go crazy, lose one's head

acitrón SM 1 (*Culin*) candied citron
2 (*LAm Bot*) bishop's weed, goutweed

acizañar* ▸conjug 1a◂ VT to stir things*, cause trouble

aclamación SF acclamation; **elegir a algn por ~** to elect sb by acclamation; **aclamaciones** applause *sing*, acclaim *sing*; **entre las aclamaciones del público** amid applause from the audience

aclamar ▸conjug 1a◂ VT (= *proclamar*) to acclaim; (= *aplaudir*) to applaud; **~ a algn por jefe** to acclaim sb as leader, hail sb as leader

aclaración SF (*para hacer entender*) clarification; (*para dar razones*) explanation; **quisiera hacerles una ~** I'd like to clarify something; **exijo una ~ de tu comportamiento** I demand an explanation for your behaviour ► **aclaración marginal** marginal note

aclarado SM (*Esp*) rinse

aclarar ▸conjug 1a◂ Ⓐ VT 1 (= *explicar*) [+ *suceso, motivo*] to clarify; [+ *duda, malentendido*] to clear up; [+ *misterio*] to solve; **están tratando de ~ las circunstancias de su muerte** they are trying to clarify the circumstances surrounding her death; **todavía no se ha aclarado quién lo hizo** it is still not clear who did it; **con esto ya queda todo aclarado** with this now everything is clear; **dejaremos cinco minutos para ~ dudas** we'll leave five minutes to clear up any queries; **~ algo a algn** to explain sth to sb; **no pudo ~nos el motivo de su comportamiento** she couldn't explain the reasons for her behaviour; **me lo explicó dos veces pero no consiguió aclarármelo** she explained it to me twice but couldn't manage to make it clear; **le he escrito para ~ las cosas** I've written to him to make things clear; **~ que** to make it clear that; **quiero ~ que no soy racista** I want to make it clear that I am not a racist
2 (*Esp*) [+ *ropa, vajilla, pelo*] to rinse; **se debe ~ con agua fría** it should be rinsed in cold water
3 (= *diluir*) [+ *pintura, salsa*] to thin, thin down
4 (= *hacer más claro*) [+ *color, pelo*] to make lighter, lighten
5 [+ *bosque*] to clear
Ⓑ VI 1 (= *amanecer*) to get light; **ya estaba aclarando** it was already getting light
2 (= *despejarse las nubes*) to clear up; **en cuanto aclare, saldremos** as soon as it clears up, we'll go out
3 (*Esp*) (= *enjuagar*) to rinse
Ⓒ **aclararse** VPR 1 [*día, cielo*] to clear up
2 (= *hacerse más claro*) [*pelo, color*] to go lighter; [*mancha*] to fade
3 **~se la voz** to clear one's throat
4 (*Esp**) [*persona*] **con tantas instrucciones no me aclaro** I'm confused by all these instructions; **explícamelo otra vez, a ver si me aclaro** explain it to me again and let's see if I understand; **¡a ver si te aclaras!** (= *decídete*) make up your mind!; (= *explícate*) what are you on about?*

aclaratorio ADJ explanatory

aclayos: SMPL (*Méx*) eyes

aclimatación SF acclimatization, acclimation (*EEUU*); (= *aire acondicionado*) air conditioning

aclimatar ▸conjug 1a◂ Ⓐ VT to acclimatize, acclimate (*EEUU*)
Ⓑ **aclimatarse** VPR to acclimatize o.s., get acclimatized; **~se a algo** to get used to sth

acné SF, **acne** SF acne

ACNUR SM ABR (= **Alto Comisariado de las Naciones Unidas para los Refugiados**) UNHCR

-aco, -aca *ver* **Aspects of Word Formation in Spanish 2**

acobardamiento SM intimidation

acobardar ▸conjug 1a◂ Ⓐ VT (= *intimidar*) to intimidate, cow; (= *atemorizar*) to overawe, unnerve
Ⓑ **acobardarse** VPR (= *asustarse*) to be intimidated, get frightened; (= *echarse atrás*) to flinch, shrink back (**ante** from, at)

acobe* SM (*Caribe*) iron

acobrado ADJ copper-coloured *o* (*EEUU*) -colored, coppery

acocear ▸conjug 1a◂ VT (= *cocear*) to kick; (= *maltratar*) to ill-treat, trample on; (= *insultar*) to insult

acochambrar* ▸conjug 1a◂ VT (*Méx*) to make filthy

acocharse ▸conjug 1a◂ VPR to squat, crouch

acochinar: ▸conjug 1a◂ VT to bump off:

acocil SM (*Méx*) freshwater shrimp; **estar como un ~** to be red in the face

acodado ADJ bent

acodalar ▸conjug 1a◂ VT to shore up, prop up

acodar ▸conjug 1a◂ Ⓐ VT [+ *brazo*] to lean, rest; [+ *tubo*] to bend; [+ *planta*] to layer
Ⓑ **acodarse** VPR to lean (**en** on); **acodado en** leaning on; **~se hacia** to bend towards, curve towards

acodiciarse ▸conjug 1b◂ VPR **~ a** to covet

acodo SM layer

acogedizo ADJ gathered at random

acogedor ADJ (= *hospitalario*) welcoming; [*ambiente*] friendly, cosy, cozy (*EEUU*), warm; [*cuarto*] snug, cosy, cozy (*EEUU*)

acoger ▸conjug 2c◂ Ⓐ VT 1 (= *albergar*) [+ *huésped, refugiado*] to take in; [+ *visitante*] to receive; [+ *fugitivo*] to harbour, harbor (*EEUU*), shelter; **nuestro país acogió a los exiliados** our country took in the exiles; **muchas familias acogen a estudiantes** many families provide accommodation for *o* take in students; **la ciudad acoge todos los años a miles de visitantes** the city receives thousands of visitors every year; **que Dios la acoja en su seno** may God receive her soul; **niños acogidos en centros públicos** children housed *o* accommodated in public centres; **el hotel que acoge a los periodistas extranjeros** the hotel where the foreign journalists are staying; **acogen en sus filas a antiguos terroristas** they number former terrorists among their ranks
2 (= *recibir*) [+ *noticia, idea, propuesta*] to receive; **acogieron la noticia con sorpresa** they were surprised at the news, they received the news with surprise; **nos acogieron con muestras de afecto** they received us with demonstrations of affection; **acogieron el plan como una oportunidad de reconvertir la industria** they welcomed the plan as an opportunity to restructure industry
3 (= *ser sede de*) [*ciudad*] to host; [*edificio, auditorio*] to be the venue for; **Atenas acogió por segunda vez los Juegos Olímpicos** Athens hosted the Olympics for the second time; **el palacio acoge un ciclo de conciertos** the palace is the venue for a concert season
4 (= *contener*) 4·1 [+ *espectadores*] to seat, hold; **el teatro podrá ~ a 100.000 espectadores** the theatre will be able to seat *o* hold 100,000 people
4·2 [+ *obras*] **este edificio acoge al Museo de la Ciencia** this building houses the Science Museum; **los pasillos del nuevo centro ~án una exposición fotográfica** the corridors of the new centre will accommodate a photographic exhibition; **la exposición acoge obras religiosas** the exhibition includes *o* contains religious works
Ⓑ **acogerse** VPR 1 (= *acudir*) **~se a** [+ *ley, derecho*] to invoke; **se han acogido al derecho a no declarar** they have invoked the right not to testify; **se acogieron a la protección del santo** they turned to the saint for protection
2 (= *beneficiarse*) **~se a**: **los trabajadores**

que lo deseen podrán ~se a las bajas incentivadas any workers who wish to may take voluntary redundancy; **~se a la amnistía** to accept the offer of amnesty

acogible ADJ (*Cono Sur*) acceptable

acogida SF [1] (= *recibimiento*) [*de noticia, producto, propuesta*] reception; **Madrid dispensó una fría ~ al espectáculo** Madrid afforded the show a very cold reception; **una calurosa ~** a warm welcome; **la ~ del disco fue muy favorable** the record was very favourably received; **tener buena/mala ~** to be well/poorly received; **¿qué ~ tuvo la idea?** how was the idea received?; **el centro de ~ de visitantes** the visitors' centre

[2] (= *albergue*) [2·1] (*Pol*) [*de refugiado, emigrante*] **tras la ~ de miles de refugiados** after accepting thousands of refugees; **un centro de ~** a reception centre; **país de ~** host country

[2·2] [*de personas necesitadas*] **un centro de ~ de personas sin hogar** a homeless hostel, a shelter for the homeless; **un centro de ~ de menores** a children's refuge; **dar ~ a algn** to accept sb; **familia de ~** host family

► **acogida familiar** (*Jur*) fostering; *ver tb* **casa 1**

[3] [*de ríos*] meeting place

acogimiento SM ► **acogimiento familiar, acogimiento judicial** fostering

acogollar ▸conjug 1a◂ (*Agr*) Ⓐ VT to cover up, protect

Ⓑ VI to sprout

acogotar ▸conjug 1a◂ VT (= *derribar*) to knock down, fell, poleaxe, polеax (*EEUU*); (= *dejar sin sentido*) to lay out; (*LAm*) (= *dominar*) to have at one's mercy; (= *agarrar*) to grab round the neck; **~ a algn** (*Cono Sur*) to harass sb for payment

acohombrar ▸conjug 1a◂ VT (*Agr*) to earth up

acojinar ▸conjug 1a◂ VT (*Téc*) to cushion

acojonador‡ ADJ (*esp Esp*) = **acojonante**

acojonamiento‡ SM (*esp Esp*) funk*, fear

acojonante‡ ADJ (*esp Esp*) (= *impresionante*) tremendous, brilliant*

acojonar‡ ▸conjug 1a◂ (*esp Esp*) Ⓐ VT [1] (= *atemorizar*) to put the wind up*, intimidate

[2] (= *impresionar*) to impress; (= *asombrar*) to amaze, overwhelm

Ⓑ **acojonarse** VPR [1] (= *acobardarse*) to back down; (= *inquietarse*) to get the wind up*; **¡no te acojones!** take it easy!*

[2] (= *asombrarse*) to be amazed, be overwhelmed

[3] (**) (*de miedo*) to freak out*, shit o.s.**

acojone‡ SM, **acojono**‡ SM (*esp Esp*) funk*, fear

acolada SF accolade

acolchado Ⓐ ADJ [*tela*] quilted, padded; [*sobre*] padded

Ⓑ SM [1] [*de tela*] quilting; [*de sobre*] padding

[2] (*Cono Sur*) eiderdown

acolchar ▸conjug 1a◂ VT [1] [+ *tela*] to quilt, pad

[2] (= *amortiguar*) [+ *sonido*] to muffle; [+ *golpe*] to soften

acólito SM (*Rel*) acolyte; (= *monaguillo*) server, altar boy; (*fig*) (= *adlátere*) acolyte, minion

acollador SM (*Náut*) lanyard

acollar ▸conjug 1l◂ VT (*Agr*) to earth up; (*Náut*) to caulk

acollarar ▸conjug 1a◂ VT [1] [+ *bueyes*] to yoke, harness; [+ *perro*] to put a collar on; (= *atar*) to tie by the neck

[2] (*Cono Sur*) to trap into marriage

acollerar ▸conjug 1a◂ Ⓐ VT, VI to gather, herd together

Ⓑ **acollerarse** VPR = **A**

acomedido ADJ (*LAm*) (= *generoso*) helpful, obliging; (= *solícito*) concerned, solicitous

acomedirse ▸conjug 3k◂ VPR (*LAm*) to offer to help; **~ a hacer algo** to do sth willingly

acometedor ADJ (= *emprendedor*) energetic, enterprising; [*toro*] fierce

acometer ▸conjug 2a◂ VT [1] (= *atacar*) to attack, set upon; [*toro*] to charge

[2] [+ *tarea*] to undertake, attempt; [+ *asunto*] to tackle, deal with; [+ *construcción*] to begin, start on

[3] [*sueño*] to overcome; [*miedo*] to seize, take hold of; [*dudas*] to assail; [*enfermedad*] to attack; **le acometieron dudas** he was assailed by doubts, he began to have doubts; **me acometió la tristeza** I was overcome with sadness

acometida SF [1] (= *ataque*) attack, assault; [*de toro*] charge

[2] (*Elec*) connection

acometimiento SM attack ► **acometimiento y agresión** (*Méx Jur*) assault and battery

acometividad SF [1] (= *energía*) energy, enterprise

[2] (= *agresividad*) aggressiveness; [*de toro*] fierceness; **mostrar ~** to show some fight *o* pluck

[3] (*Cono Sur*) (= *susceptibilidad*) touchiness

acomodable ADJ (= *adaptable*) adaptable; (= *que sirve*) suitable

acomodación SF (*gen*) accommodation; (= *adaptación*) adaptation; (= *arreglo*) arrangement

acomodadizo ADJ (= *complaciente*) accommodating, obliging; (= *manejable*) pliable

acomodado ADJ [1] (= *apropiado*) suitable, fit; [*precio*] moderate; [*artículo*] moderately priced

[2] (= *rico*) well-to-do, well-off

acomodador(a) SM/F usher/usherette

acomodamiento SM [1] (= *cualidad*) suitability, convenience

[2] (= *acto*) arrangement, agreement

acomodar ▸conjug 1a◂ Ⓐ VT [1] [+ *visitante, huésped*] to put up; **nos ~on en diferentes cuartos** they put us up in different rooms; **~on a los evacuados en la escuela** they put up *o* accommodated the evacuees in the school

[2] (= *sentar*) **nos ~on en nuestros asientos** they showed us to our seats

[3] (= *poner cómodo*) to make comfortable

[4] (= *albergar*) [*local*] to seat; [*vehículo*] to take; **una sala con capacidad para ~ a mil personas** a hall with a capacity of one thousand, a hall which can seat one thousand people

[5] (*frm*) (= *adaptar*) **~ algo a algo** to adapt sth to (suit) sth; **~on la historia a sus necesidades políticas** they adapted history to suit their political requirements; **tendrán que ~ la ley a la directiva europea** they will have to bring the law into line with the European directive; **tienes que ~ tus gastos a tus ingresos** you need to adjust your expenditure to your income

[6] (*frm*) (= *conciliar*) [+ *colores*] to match; [+ *enemigos, rivales*] to reconcile

[7] (*frm*) (= *suministrar*) **~ a algn con algo** to supply o provide sb with sth

[8] (*LAm*) (= *colocar*) to put; **acomoda aquí los libros** put the books here

[9] (*Cono Sur, Méx*) (= *dar trabajo a*) to get a job for, fix up (with a job)*; **acomodó a su primo en la oficina** he got his cousin a job in the office, he fixed his cousin up (with a job) in the office*

[10] (*Caribe*) (= *estafar*) to con*, trick

Ⓑ **acomodarse** VPR [1] (= *ponerse cómodo*) **¡acomódate!** make yourself comfortable; **se acomodó en el sillón** he settled down in the armchair; **se ~on en una mesa contigua a la nuestra** (*frm*) they sat at the next table to us

[2] (= *adaptarse*) **~se a algo** to adapt to sth; **yo me acomodo a todo** I'm easy*

[3] (*) (= *casarse*) to marry into money

[4] (*frm*) **~se de** to provide o.s. with

[5] (*LAm*) (= *ajustarse*) [+ *ropa, gafas*] to adjust

acomodaticio ADJ = **acomodadizo**

acomodo SM [1] (= *arreglo*) arrangement; (= *acuerdo*) agreement, understanding

[2] (= *puesto*) post, job; (*LAm pey*) (= *enchufe*) soft job, plum job

[3] (*LAm*) (= *soborno*) bribe

acompañado/a Ⓐ ADJ [1] [*persona*] **está ~** he's with someone; **los invitados no podrán ir ~s a la boda** guests can't take someone else along with them to the wedding; **~ de: entró acompañada de su padre** she came in with her father, she came in accompanied by her father; **la enciclopedia viene acompañada de un diccionario** the encyclopaedia comes with a dictionary; **bien/mal ~** in good/bad company; *ver tb* **solo**

[2] [*lugar*] busy, frequented

[3] **con falda acompañada** with skirt to match, with a skirt of the same colour *o* pattern

[4] **estar ~** (*Caribe**) to be drunk

Ⓑ SM/F (*LAm*) (= *amante*) lover; (= *cónyuge*) common-law husband/wife

acompañamiento SM [1] (= *cortejo*) (*como escolta*) escort; [*de rey*] retinue; [*de sepelio*] funeral procession; [*de boda*] wedding party

[2] (*Mús*) accompaniment; **con ~ de piano** with piano accompaniment; **cantar sin ~** to sing unaccompanied

[3] (= *acción*) accompaniment; **esta salsa sirve como ~ de pescados** this sauce makes a good accompaniment to fish; **filete y patatas como ~** steak served with potatoes

[4] (= *consecuencias*) aftermath; **el terremoto y su ~** the earthquake and its aftermath

[5] (*Teat*) (*en acotaciones escénicas*) retinue; (*en títulos de crédito*) supporting cast; **Macbeth y ~** Macbeth and his retinue

acompañanta SF (= *señora de compañía*) female companion, female chaperon; (*Mús*) accompanist

acompañante SMF (= *que acompaña*) companion, escort; (*Mús*) accompanist

acompañar ▸conjug 1a◂ Ⓐ VT [1] (*a alguna parte*) (*gen*) to go with, accompany (*frm*); **no quiero que me acompañe nadie** I don't want anyone to go with me; **¿quieres que te acompañe al médico?** do you want me to go to the doctor's with you?; **¡te acompaño!** I'll come with you!; **iba acompañado de dos guardaespaldas** he had two bodyguards with him, he was accompanied by two bodyguards; **su abogado lo acompañó en la rueda de prensa** his lawyer was with him at the press conference; **~ a algn a casa** to see sb home; **~ a algn a la puerta** to see sb to the door, see sb out

2 (= *hacer compañía*) (*por un rato*) to keep company; (*como pareja*) to be companion to; **nos quedamos un rato para ~ a la abuela** we stayed a while to keep grandmother company; **su hermana la acompañó durante toda su enfermedad** her sister stood by her side throughout the illness; **la mujer que lo acompañó en sus últimos años** the woman who was his companion *o* who was companion to him in his last years; **~ a algn en algo** to join sb in sth; **se ofrecieron a ~me en la búsqueda** they offered to join me in the search; **le acompaño en el sentimiento** (*en un entierro*) please accept my condolences

3 (= *ocurrir al mismo tiempo*) to accompany; **el escándalo que acompañó al estreno de la ópera** the scandal that accompanied the opening of the opera

4 [*comida*] **este vino acompaña bien al queso** this wine goes well with cheese; **~ algo con** *o* **de algo** to serve sth with sth; **se puede ~ de una salsa** it can be served with a sauce

5 [*documentos*] **la solicitud debe ir acompañada de un certificado** the application should be accompanied by a certificate

6 (*Mús*) to accompany (**a, con** on); **estuvo acompañado a la guitarra por Juan Maya** he was accompanied on the guitar by Juan Maya

7 (= *ser favorable*) **a ver si la suerte nos acompaña** let's hope we're lucky, let's hope our luck's in; **parece que nos acompaña la mala suerte** we seem to be dogged by *o* to be having a lot of bad luck; **el tiempo no nos acompañó** we were unlucky with the weather

Ⓑ VI 1 (= *hacer compañía*) to be company; **un perro acompaña mucho** a dog is good company

2 [*comida*] **¿quieres un poco de pan para ~?** would you like some bread to go with it?

3 [*ser favorable*] to be favourable *o* (EEUU) favorable; **si la coyuntura económica acompaña** if the economic climate is favourable; **es una pena que el tiempo no ~a** it's a shame the weather wasn't more favourable; **si el tiempo acompaña** weather permitting

Ⓒ **acompañarse** VPR (*Mús*) to accompany o.s. (**con, de** on); **se acompaña con la guitarra** she accompanies herself on the guitar

acompaño SM (*CAm, Méx*) meeting, group, crowd

acompasado ADJ 1 (*Mús*) (= *rítmico*) rhythmic, regular; (= *medido*) measured

2 (= *pausado*) slow, deliberate

acompasar ▸conjug 1a◂ VT 1 (*Mús*) to mark the rhythm of; **~ la dicción** to speak with a marked rhythm

2 (*Mat*) to measure with a compass

3 (= *ajustarse a*) to match, keep in step with

acomplejado ADJ neurotic, hung-up*; **está ~ por su nariz** he's got a complex about his nose, he's got a thing about his nose

acomplejante ADJ (*Cono Sur*) inhibiting, embarrassing

acomplejar ▸conjug 1a◂ Ⓐ VT **~ a algn** to give sb a complex

Ⓑ **acomplejarse** VPR to get a complex (**con, por** about); **¡no te acomplejes!** don't get so worked up!

acompletadores* SMPL (*Méx*) beans

acomunarse ▸conjug 1a◂ VPR to join forces

aconchabar* ▸conjug 1a◂ Ⓐ VT (*LAm*) to take on, hire

Ⓑ **aconchabarse** VPR to gang up*

aconchado/a* SM/F (*Méx*) sponger*, scrounger*

aconchar ▸conjug 1a◂ Ⓐ VT 1 (= *poner a salvo*) to push to safety

2 (*Náut*) (= *encallar*) to beach, run aground; [*viento*] to drive ashore

3 (*Méx**) (= *reprender*) to tell off*

Ⓑ **aconcharse** VPR 1 (*Náut*) (= *volcarse*) to keel over; (= *encallarse*) run aground

2 (*Cono Sur*) [*líquido*] to settle, clarify

3 (*) (= *vivir de otro*) to sponge*, live off somebody else

acondicionado ADJ **bien ~** [*persona*] genial, affable, nice; [*objeto*] in good condition; **mal ~** [*persona*] bad-tempered, difficult; [*objeto*] in bad condition; **aire ~** air conditioning; **un laboratorio bien ~** a well-equipped laboratory

acondicionador SM conditioner ► **acondicionador de aire** air conditioner

acondicionamiento SM (*gen*) conditioning; (*Com*) shopfitting ► **acondicionamiento de aire** air conditioning

acondicionar ▸conjug 1a◂ VT 1 (= *arreglar*) to arrange, prepare; [+ *pelo*] to condition

2 (*Com*) to fit out

3 (= *aclimatar*) to air-condition

acongojado ADJ distressed, anguished

acongojar ▸conjug 1a◂ Ⓐ VT to distress, grieve

Ⓑ **acongojarse** VPR to become distressed; **¡no te acongojes!** don't distress yourself!, don't get upset!

acónito SM (*Bot*) aconite, monkshood

▼ **aconsejable** ADJ (= *conveniente*) advisable; (= *sensato*) sensible, politic; **nada** *o* **poco ~** inadvisable; **eso no es ~** that is not advisable; **no sería ~ que usted viniera** you would be ill-advised to come

aconsejado ADJ **bien ~** sensible; **mal ~** ill-advised

▼ **aconsejar** ▸conjug 1a◂ Ⓐ VT 1 (= *dar consejos a*) to advise; **~ a algn hacer algo** to advise sb to do sth

2 [+ *cuidado*] to advise, recommend; [+ *virtud*] to preach

Ⓑ **aconsejarse** VPR to seek advice, take advice; **~ con** *o* **de** to consult; **~ mejor** to think better of it

aconsonantar ▸conjug 1a◂ VT, VI to rhyme (**con** with)

acontecedero† ADJ which could happen, possible

acontecer ▸conjug 2d◂ VI to happen, occur

acontecimiento SM event; **fue realmente un ~** it was an event of some importance; **fue todo un ~** it was quite an affair

acopiar ▸conjug 1b◂ VT (= *juntar*) to gather, gather together, collect; (*Com*) to buy up, get a monopoly of; [+ *miel*] to collect, hive

> **ACONSEJAR**
>
> **Aconsejar a algn que haga algo** se traduce al inglés con **advise** + **OBJETO** + **INFINITIVO** *con* **to**, es decir: **advise sb to do sth**:
>
> Le aconsejé que (no) cambiase de trabajo
> ***I advised her (not) to change jobs***
> Le aconsejaré a mi hermana que se lo piense dos veces
> ***I'll advise my sister to think it over carefully***
>
> **NOTA:** Cuando se quiere aconsejar a una persona, en inglés se suele utilizar el condicional para que no parezca un mandato, como se ve en los siguientes ejemplos:
>
> Le aconsejo que consulte a un abogado
> ***I would advise you to see a lawyer***
> Te aconsejo que lo hagas
> ***I'd advise you to do it***
>
> *Para otros usos y ejemplos ver la entrada.*

acopio SM 1 (= *acto*) gathering, collecting

2 (= *cantidad*) collection; (= *suministro*) store, stock; [*de madera*] stack; (*Cono Sur*) (= *abundancia*) abundance; **hacer ~** to stock up (**de** with), lay in stocks (**de** of)

acoplable ADJ attachable

acoplado Ⓐ ADJ **un equipo bien ~** a well coordinated team

Ⓑ SM 1 (*Cono Sur Aut*) (= *remolque*) trailer, semitrailer (EEUU)

2 (*Cono Sur**) (= *parásito*) hanger-on*, sponger*; (= *intruso*) gatecrasher

acoplador SM ► **acoplador acústico** acoustic coupler

acoplamiento SM (*Mec*) coupling; (*Elec*) connection; (*Telec, TV*) link-up, hook-up; [*de astronaves*] docking, link-up; (*Zool*) mating ► **acoplamiento de manguito** sleeve coupling ► **acoplamiento en serie** series connection ► **acoplamiento universal** universal joint

acoplar ▸conjug 1a◂ Ⓐ VT 1 (= *unir*) (*Téc*) to couple; (*Elec*) to connect, join up; [+ *carros*] to join up, hook up; [+ *astronaves*] to dock, link up; (*LAm Ferro*) to couple (up)

2 (*Zool*) [+ *animales*] to mate, pair; [+ *bueyes*] to yoke, hitch

3 (*Dep*) to coordinate; [+ *personas*] to associate, bring together; [+ *opiniones*] to reconcile; [+ *proyectos, esfuerzos*] to coordinate

Ⓑ **acoplarse** VPR 1 (*Zool*) to mate, pair

2 (*Aer*) to dock

3 (*Elec*) to cause feedback

4 (= *hacer las paces*) to make it up, be reconciled

acoplo SM (*Elec*) feedback

acoquinamiento SM intimidation

acoquinar ▸conjug 1a◂ Ⓐ VT to scare, intimidate, cow

Ⓑ **acoquinarse** VPR to get scared, take fright

acorar ▸conjug 1a◂ VT to distress, afflict, upset

acorazado Ⓐ ADJ [*cámara*] security *antes de s*; [*vehículo*] reinforced, armoured, armored (EEUU), armour-plated, armor-plated (EEUU)

Ⓑ SM battleship

acorazar ▸conjug 1f◂ Ⓐ VT to armour-plate, armor-plate (EEUU)

Ⓑ **acorazarse** VPR (= *armarse de valor*) to steel o.s. (**contra** against); (= *hacerse insensible*) to become inured (**contra** to)

➤ LENGUA Y USO: **aconsejable** 29.2 **aconsejar** 28.2, 29.1, 29.2

acorazonado ADJ heart-shaped

acorchado ADJ [1] (= *esponjoso*) spongy, cork-like
[2] (*Med*) (= *insensible*) numb; [*boca*] furry

acorchar ▸conjug 1a◂ Ⓐ VT to cover with cork
Ⓑ **acorcharse** VPR [1] [*patata*] to go spongy
[2] (*Med*) [*pierna, dedos*] to go numb

acordada SF decree

acordadamente ADV unanimously, by common consent

acordar ▸conjug 1l◂ Ⓐ VT [1] (= *decidir*) [+ *precio, fecha*] to agree, agree on; **eso no es lo que acordamos** that is not what we agreed; **han acordado la suspensión provisional de las obras** it was agreed that the works should be suspended temporarily; **~ hacer algo** to agree to do sth; **~on retrasar la reunión** they agreed to put back the meeting; **~ que** to agree that; **acordamos que nadie saliera de la sala** we agreed that no one should leave the room
[2] [+ *opiniones*] to reconcile; [+ *instrumentos*] to tune; [+ *colores*] to blend, harmonize
[3] (= *recordar*) **~ algo a algn**†† to remind sb of sth; **~ a algn de hacer algo** ◊ **~ a algn que haga algo** (*Andes, Chile*) to remind sb to do sth
[4] (*LAm*) (= *conceder*) to grant, accord (*frm*)
Ⓑ VI **~ con algo** to go with sth, match sth
Ⓒ **acordarse** VPR to remember; **no me acuerdo** I don't *o* can't remember; **ya te lo traeré, si me acuerdo** I'll bring it for you, if I remember (to); **no quiero ni ~me** I don't even want to think about it; **ahora que me acuerdo** now that I think of it, come to think of it; **~se de algo/algn** to remember sth/sb; **¿te acuerdas de mí?** do you remember me?; **nadie se acordaba del número** nobody could think of *o* remember the number; **ya no me acordaba de que tenía una reunión** I'd completely forgotten that I had a meeting; **no quiero ni ~me del frío que pasamos** I can hardly bear to think of how cold we were; **el otro día me acordé de ti cuando ...** I thought of you the other day when ...; **me acuerdo mucho de mi infancia** I often think about *o* recall my childhood; **desde que te has ido, me acuerdo mucho de ti** since you left, I've missed you a lot; **¡te ~ás de ésta!** I'll teach you!, I'll give you something to remember me by!; **~se de hacer algo** to remember to do sth; **acuérdate de comprar pan** don't forget *o* remember to buy some bread; **~se de haber hecho algo** to remember doing sth; **me acuerdo de haber leído un artículo sobre eso** I remember reading an article about that; ✦***MODISMO*** **no se acuerda ni del santo de su nombre** he can hardly remember *o* he has trouble remembering his own name

acorde Ⓐ ADJ [1] **~ a** *o* **con** [+ *situación, posición*] appropriate to; [+ *ley, directiva*] in conformity *o* compliance with; **su comportamiento fue ~ a** *o* **con las circunstancias** her behaviour was appropriate to the circumstances; **un motor ~ a** *o* **con las normas ecológicas** an engine that complies with environmental regulations
[2] (*frm*) (= *coincidente*) **estar ~s** to be agreed, be in agreement
[3] (*Mús*) harmonious
Ⓑ SM (*Mús*) chord; **a los ~s de la marcha nupcial** to the strains of the wedding march

acordeón SM accordion ► **acordeón de botones** button accordion ► **acordeón de teclas, acordeón piano** piano accordion

acordeonista SMF accordionist

acordonado ADJ [1] (*Cos*) ribbed
[2] [*calle*] cordoned-off; [*moneda, borde*] milled
[3] (*LAm*) [*animal*] thin

acordonamiento SM [1] (*Cos*) ribbing
[2] (= *acción*) [*de calle*] cordoning off; [*de moneda, borde*] milling

acordonar ▸conjug 1a◂ VT [1] [+ *zapatos*] to do up, lace up
[2] [+ *lugar*] (*con guardias*) to cordon off; (*con cerca*) to surround
[3] [+ *moneda, borde*] to mill
[4] (*LAm*) [+ *terreno*] to prepare

acornar ▸conjug 1l◂ VT, **acornear** ▸conjug 1a◂ VT to gore

acorralamiento SM (= *cercamiento*) enclosing; (= *arrinconamiento*) cornering, trapping

acorralar ▸conjug 1a◂ VT (*Agr*) [+ *ganado*] to pen, corral; (= *arrinconar*) to corner; (= *intimidar*) to intimidate

acorrer ▸conjug 2a◂ Ⓐ VT to help, go to the aid of
Ⓑ VI to run up; **~ a algn** to hasten to sb

acortamiento SM shortening, reduction

acortar ▸conjug 1a◂ Ⓐ VT [+ *vestido, falda, traje*] to take up, shorten; [+ *artículo, texto*] to shorten, cut down; [+ *periodo, duración*] to shorten, reduce; **esta carretera ~á la distancia entre las dos ciudades** this road will shorten the distance between the two cities; **yendo por aquí acortamos camino** it's shorter if we go this way; **tuve que ~ las vacaciones y volver a casa** I had to cut short my holidays and go home; **el Barcelona está acortando distancias con el Real Madrid** Barcelona is catching up with Real Madrid
Ⓑ **acortarse** VPR to get shorter; **empiezan a ~se los días** the days are getting shorter

acosar ▸conjug 1a◂ VT [1] (= *atosigar*) to hound, harass; **~ a algn a preguntas** to pester sb with questions; **ser acosado sexualmente** to suffer (from) sexual harassment, be sexually harassed
[2] (= *perseguir*) to pursue relentlessly; [+ *animal*] to urge on

acosijar ▸conjug 1a◂ VT (*Méx*) = **acosar**

acoso SM [1] (= *atosigamiento*) harassment; **es víctima del ~ de la prensa** she's a victim of press harassment; **operación de ~ y derribo** (*Mil*) search and destroy operation; **una operación de ~ y derribo contra el presidente** a campaign to hound the president out of office ► **acoso sexual** sexual harassment
[2] (= *persecución*) relentless pursuit

acostar ▸conjug 1l◂ Ⓐ VT [1] (= *tender*) to lay down
[2] (*en cama*) to put to bed
[3] (*Náut*) to bring alongside
Ⓑ **acostarse** VPR [1] (= *tumbarse*) to lie down; (= *ir a dormir*) to go to bed; (*LAm*) (= *dar a luz*) to give birth; **nos acostamos tarde** we went to bed late; **Pilar se acostó con Juan** Pilar went to bed *o* slept with Juan; **ella se acuesta con cualquiera** she sleeps around; **es hora de ~se** it's bedtime
[2] (= *inclinarse*) to lean, bend

acostillado ADJ ribbed, with ribs

acostumbrado ADJ [1] (= *normal*) usual, customary (*frm*); **se vieron en el lugar ~** they met at the usual *o* (*frm*) customary place; **se acostó antes de lo ~** she went to bed earlier than usual
[2] **~ a algo** used to sth; **no estoy acostumbrada al calor** I'm not used to the heat; **está ~ a trabajar de noche** he's used to working at night; **ya estoy ~ a que no me entiendan** I'm used to *o* (*frm*) accustomed to not being understood
[3] **bien ~: su marido está muy bien ~** her husband is very well trained; **mal ~: sus hijos están muy mal ~s** her children are very spoilt; **su mujer lo tiene muy mal ~** his wife spoils him (rotten)

acostumbrar ▸conjug 1a◂ Ⓐ VT **~ a algn a algo** to get sb used to sth; **~ a algn a las dificultades** to get sb used to the problems; **~ a algn a hacer algo** to accustom sb to doing sth
Ⓑ VI **~ (a) hacer algo** to be used *o* accustomed to doing sth, be in the habit of doing sth; **los sábados acostumbra (a) ir al cine** on Saturdays he usually goes to the cinema
Ⓒ **acostumbrarse** VPR [1] **~se a algo** to get accustomed *o* used to sth; **se acostumbró a tomar chocolate** he got into the habit of drinking chocolate; **está acostumbrado a verlas venir** he's not easily fooled
[2] (*esp LAm*) **aquí no se acostumbra decir eso** people don't say that *o* that isn't said here; **no se acostumbra** it isn't customary *o* usual

ACOSTUMBRAR

- La forma pronominal **acostumbrarse a hacer algo** se traduce al inglés por **get used to** + **-ING**:

  Te acostumbrarás a trabajar aquí
  You'll get used to working here
  Con el tiempo me acostumbré a estar sin él
  In time I got used to being without him

- La expresión **estar acostumbrado a hacer algo** se traduce por **to be used to** + **-ING**:

  Está acostumbrado a levantarse temprano
  He's used to getting up early

NOTA: Otra forma de traducir esta estructura al inglés es con la construcción **to be accustomed to** + **-ING**, aunque tiene un registro formal:

  He's accustomed to getting up early

- Cuando el verbo **acostumbrar** equivale a **soler**, se puede traducir de dos formas distintas en inglés, dependiendo de si la acción a la que se refiere ocurre en el pasado o en el presente.
- En el *pasado*, lo traducimos por **used to** + **INFINITIVO**:

  Cuando era niña acostumbraba a rezar todas las noches
  When I was a child I used to pray every night
  El año pasado acostumbrábamos a vernos todos los viernes
  Last year we used to meet every Friday

- En el *presente* se traduce por el adverbio **usually** + **PRESENTE SIMPLE**:

  Los domingos acostumbro a levantarme tarde
  I usually get up late on Sundays

Para otros usos y ejemplos ver la entrada.

acotación SF [1] (= *linde*) boundary mark; (*Geog*) elevation mark

2 (*Tip*) (= *anotación*) marginal note
3 (*Teat*) stage direction

acotado Ⓐ ADJ enclosed, fenced
Ⓑ SM (*tb* ~ **de caza**) game preserve

acotamiento SM (*Méx*) hard shoulder, berm (*EEUU*), emergency lane

acotar ▸conjug 1a◂ VT 1 [+ *terreno*] (= *marcar*) to survey, mark out; (= *poner cotos en*) to limit, set bounds to; [+ *caza*] to fence in, protect
2 [+ *página*] to annotate; [+ *mapa*] to mark elevations on
3 [+ *árboles*] to lop
4 (= *aceptar*) to accept, adopt; (= *elegir*) to choose; (= *avalar*) to vouch for; (= *comprobar*) to check, verify

acotejar ▸conjug 1a◂ Ⓐ VT (*LAm*) [+ *cosas*] to put in order, arrange
Ⓑ **acotejarse** VPR (*LAm*) (= *acomodarse*) to come to an arrangement

acotillo SM sledgehammer

acoyundar ▸conjug 1a◂ VT to yoke

acr. ABR (= **acreedor**) Cr

acracia SF anarchy

ácrata Ⓐ ADJ anarchist(ic), libertarian
Ⓑ SMF anarchist, libertarian

acrático ADJ = **ácrata A**

acre[1] ADJ 1 [*sabor*] sharp, bitter; [*olor*] acrid, pungent
2 [*temperamento*] sour; [*crítica*] sharp, biting, mordant

acre[2] SM acre

acrecencia SF 1 (*Jur*) accretion
2 = **acrecentamiento**

acrecentamiento SM increase, growth

acrecentar ▸conjug 1j◂ Ⓐ VT (= *aumentar*) to increase, augment; (= *ascender*) [+ *persona*] to advance, promote
Ⓑ **acrecentarse** VPR to increase, grow

acrecer ▸conjug 2d◂ VT to increase

acrecimiento SM increase, growth

acreditación SF (= *acto*) accreditation; (= *autorización*) authorization, sanctioning

acreditado ADJ (*Pol*) accredited; (= *estimado*) reputable; **nuestro representante ~** our official agent; **una casa acreditada** a reputable firm

acreditar ▸conjug 1a◂ Ⓐ VT 1 (= *dar reputación a*) to do credit to, give credit to; **y virtudes que le acreditan** and qualities which do him credit
2 (= *avalar*) to vouch for, guarantee; (= *probar*) to prove; (= *autorizar*) to sanction, authorize; **~ su personalidad** to establish one's identity
3 (*Pol*) [+ *embajador*] to accredit
4 (*Com*) to credit; (*Andes*) (= *fiar*) to sell on credit
Ⓑ **acreditarse** VPR to prove one's worth; **~se como** to get a reputation for; **~se en** to get a reputation in

acreditativo ADJ **documentos ~s** supporting documents

acreedor(a) Ⓐ ADJ **~ a** worthy of, deserving of
Ⓑ SM/F creditor ► **acreedor(a) común** unsecured creditor ► **acreedor(a) con garantía** secured creditor ► **acreedor(a) diferido/a** deferred creditor ► **acreedor(a) hipotecario/a** mortgagee

➤ LENGUA Y USO: **actitud** 33.1

acreencia SF (*LAm*) (= *saldo acreedor*) credit balance; (= *deuda*) debt, amount owing *o* owed

acremente ADV sharply, bitterly

acribadura SF sifting, sieving

acribar ▸conjug 1a◂ VT to sift, riddle

acribillado ADJ [*superficie*] pitted, pockmarked; **~ a** riddled with, peppered with; **~ de** filled with; **~ de picaduras** covered with stings

acribillar ▸conjug 1a◂ VT 1 to riddle, pepper; **~ a balazos** to riddle with bullets; **~ a puñaladas** to cover with stab wounds
2 (= *fastidiar*) to pester, badger; **~ a algn a preguntas** to bombard sb with questions

acridio SM (*LAm*) locust

acrílico ADJ acrylic

acrilonitrilo SM acrylonitrile

acriminación SF incrimination, accusation

acriminador(a) Ⓐ ADJ incriminating
Ⓑ SM/F accuser

acriminar ▸conjug 1a◂ VT (*Jur*) to incriminate, accuse; (*fig*) [+ *falta*] to exaggerate

acrimonia SF 1 (= *olor*) acridness, pungency; (= *sabor*) sharpness, sourness
2 (= *desabrimiento*) acrimony, bitterness

acrimonioso ADJ acrimonious

acriollado ADJ (*esp Cono Sur*) *adapted or adjusted to the customs of a Latin American country*

acriollarse ▸conjug 1a◂ VPR (*esp Cono Sur*) to go native

acrisolado ADJ (= *refinado*) pure; **una fe acrisolada** a faith tried and tested; **el patriotismo más ~** the noblest kind of patriotism; **de acrisolada honradez** of unquestionable honesty

acrisolar ▸conjug 1a◂ VT 1 (*Téc*) (= *purificar*) to purify, refine
2 (= *acendrar*) to bring out, prove

acristalado ADJ glazed

acristalamiento SM glazing; **los ~s** the windows, the glazing; **doble ~** double glazing

acristalar ▸conjug 1a◂ VT to glaze

acristianar ▸conjug 1a◂ VT (= *hacer cristiano*) to christianize; [+ *niño*] to baptize

acritud SF = **acrimonia**

acrobacia SF acrobatics *sing* ► **acrobacia aérea** aerobatics *sing*, aerial acrobatics *sing*

acróbata SMF acrobat

acrobático ADJ acrobatic

acrobatismo SM acrobatics *sing*

acrónimo SM acronym

Acrópolis SF Acropolis

acróstico ADJ, SM acrostic

acta SF 1 [*de reunión*] minutes *pl*; **constar en ~**: **las pruebas documentales constan en ~** the documentary proof is in the minutes; **pidieron que su oposición al plan constara en ~** they asked for their opposition to the plan to be noted; **que conste en ~** let it be noted in the record; **levantar ~ de** [+ *reunión, sesión parlamentaria*] to write up the minutes of; [+ *acontecimiento, delito*] to make a(n official) report on; **tomar ~ de algo** (*Cono Sur*) to take note of sth, bear sth in mind
2 [*de congreso*] proceedings *pl*; [*de organismo*] records *pl*
3 (*Educ*) [*de notas*] student's achievement record
4 (= *certificado*) certificate ► **acta de bautismo** certificate of baptism ► **acta de defunción** death certificate ► **acta de diputado** (*Pol*) certificate of election ► **acta de matrimonio** marriage certificate ► **acta de nacimiento** birth certificate ► **acta matrimonial** marriage certificate
5 [*de acuerdo*] ► **acta constitutiva** charter ► **acta orgánica** (*LAm*) constitution ► **Acta Única Europea** Single European Act
6 (*Jur*) **el juez levantó ~ del accidente** the judge drew up an official report on the accident ► **acta de acusación** bill of indictment ► **acta notarial** affidavit
7 (*Rel*) (= *relato*) ► **actas de los mártires** lives of the martyrs ► **actas de un santo** life of a saint
8 (*LAm*) (= *ley*) act, law

actinia SF actinia, sea anemone

actínico ADJ actinic

actinio SM actinium

actitud SF 1 (= *comportamiento, disposición*) attitude; **no vas a conseguir nada con esa ~** you won't get anywhere with that attitude; **tienes que cambiar tu ~ ante la vida** you must change your attitude to life; **han adoptado una ~ firme** they have taken a firm stand *o* a tough stance
2 (= *postura física*) posture; **tenía el mentón levantado, en ~ desafiante** he had his chin raised in a defiant posture; **adoptó una ~ pensativa** she adopted a thoughtful pose; **en ~ de**: **estaba en ~ de absoluta concentración** he was in state of total concentration; **las encontré en ~ de oración** I found them at prayer; **se incorporó en ~ de despedirse** he stood up as if he was going to leave
3 (= *estado de ánimo*) frame of mind, mood; **en ~ resignada** in a resigned mood *o* frame of mind

activación SF [*de mecanismo*] activation; [*de gestión, actividad*] expediting, speeding-up

activador SM (*Téc*) activator; (= *estímulo*) stimulus

activamente ADV actively

activar ▸conjug 1a◂ VT (= *poner en marcha*) to activate; [+ *trabajo*] to expedite, speed up, hurry along; [+ *fuego*] to brighten up, poke; [+ *mercado*] to stimulate

actividad SF 1 (= *acción*) activity; **ha habido una intensa ~ diplomática** there has been intense diplomatic activity; **estos son meses de escasa ~ en el sector hotelero** these months are not very busy in the hotel sector; **ha sido una jornada de escasa ~ bursátil** trading was slow *o* sluggish on the stock exchange today; **en ~**: **el volcán aún está en ~** the volcano is still active; **estuvo en ~ hasta su muerte** he worked right up until his death; **la recolección está en plena ~** the harvest is in full swing
2 (= *tarea profesional*) work; **los pescadores han reanudado su ~** the fishermen have gone back to work ► **actividad docente** teaching ► **actividad lucrativa** gainful employment
3 **actividades** (= *actos*) activities *pl*; **es sospechoso de ~es terroristas** he is suspected of terrorist activities; **~es culturales** cultural activities; **~es deportivas** sporting activities; *ver tb* **extraescolar**

activismo SM activism

activista SMF activist

activo Ⓐ ADJ [1] (= *que obra*) active; (= *vivo*) lively, energetic; (= *ocupado*) busy
[2] (*Ling*) active
Ⓑ SM [1] (*Com*) assets *pl* ► **activo circulante** circulating assets *pl* ► **activo corriente** current assets *pl* ► **activo de la quiebra** bankrupt's estate ► **activo fijo** fixed assets *pl* ► **activo flotante** floating assets *pl* ► **activo inmaterial** intangible assets *pl* ► **activo intangible** intangible assets *pl* ► **activo invisible** invisible assets *pl* ► **activo líquido** liquid assets *pl* ► **activo neto** net worth ► **activo oculto** hidden assets *pl* ► **activo operante** operating assets *pl* ► **activo realizable** liquid assets *pl* ► **activos bloqueados** frozen assets ► **activos congelados** frozen assets ► **activos inmobiliarios** property assets, real-estate assets ► **activo tangible** tangible assets *pl* ► **activo y pasivo** assets and liabilities *pl*
[2] (*Mil*) **oficial en ~** serving officer; **estar en ~** to be on active service

acto SM [1] (= *acción*) act, action; **el ~ de escribir es un tipo de terapia** the act *o* action of writing is a kind of therapy; **no es responsable de sus ~s** he's not responsible for his actions; **la atraparon en el ~ de falsificar la firma** they caught her in the act of forging the signature; **hacer ~ de presencia** (= *asistir*) to attend, be present; (= *aparecer*) to appear; (= *dejarse ver brevemente*) put in an appearance; **morir en ~ de servicio** to die on active service; **el ~ sexual** the sexual *o* sex act ► **acto carnal** carnal act ► **acto de contrición** act of contrition ► **acto de desagravio** act of atonement ► **acto de fe** act of faith ► **acto de habla** speech act ► **acto reflejo** reflex action ► **Actos de los Apóstoles** Acts (of the Apostles)
[2] (= *ceremonia*) **celebrar un ~** to hold a function ► **acto inaugural** opening ceremony ► **acto oficial** official function ► **acto público** public engagement ► **acto religioso** (religious) service
[3] (*Teat*) act
[4] **en el ~** (= *inmediatamente*) there and then; **la ingresaron y la operaron en el ~** she was admitted and operated on there and then *o* on the spot; **murió en el ~** he died instantly; **"reparaciones en el acto"** "repairs while you wait"
[5] **~ seguido** ◊ **~ continuo** (*frm*) immediately after(wards)

actor Ⓐ ADJ (*Jur*) **parte ~a** prosecution
Ⓑ SM [1] (*Teat, Cine*) actor; **primer ~** leading man ► **actor cinematográfico, actor de cine** film actor, movie actor (*EEUU*) ► **actor de doblaje** dubber ► **actor de reparto** supporting actor
[2] (*Jur*) (= *demandante*) plaintiff

actriz SF actress; **primera ~** leading lady ► **actriz cinematográfica** film actress ► **actriz de doblaje** dubber ► **actriz de reparto** supporting actress

actuación SF [1] (= *intervención*) [*de cantante, deportista*] performance; [*de actor*] acting; **la primera ~ pública de la banda** the band's first public performance; **su ~ es lo peor de la película** the worst thing in the film is his acting ► **actuación en directo, actuación en vivo** live performance
[2] (= *espectáculo*) **todas sus actuaciones tuvieron un gran éxito de público** all his shows were a great success with the public; **habrá dos actuaciones de jazz** there will be two jazz sessions
[3] (= *acción*) action; **sus líneas de ~** their plan of action; **las actuaciones policiales fueron vanas** police action was to no avail; **criticaron la ~ del presidente ante la crisis** they criticized the president's handling of the crisis
[4] (= *conducta*) behaviour, behavior (*EEUU*), conduct; **la ~ de la policía en la manifestación** the behaviour *o* conduct of the police at the demonstration
[5] **actuaciones** (*Jur*) (legal) proceedings

actual ADJ [1] (= *de ahora*) [*situación, sistema, gobernante*] current, present; [*sociedad*] contemporary, present-day; [*moda*] current, modern; **el ~ campeón de Europa** the reigning *o* current *o* present European champion; **en el momento ~** at the present moment; **la ~ literatura francesa** French literature today, present-day French literature; **eso no le interesa a la juventud ~** that doesn't interest young people today; **el 6 del ~** the 6th of this month
[2] (= *de actualidad*) [*cuestión, tema*] topical; **en la reunión trataron temas muy ~es** they dealt with highly topical issues in the meeting
[3] (= *moderno*) up-to-date, fashionable; **ha cambiado su peinado por otro algo más ~** he's changed his hairstyle for a more up-to-date *o* fashionable one; **corbatas de diseño muy ~** very fashionable-looking ties; **emplean las técnicas más ~es** they use the most up-to-date *o* up-to-the-minute techniques, they use the latest techniques

actualidad SF [1] **en la ~** (= *hoy día*) nowadays; (= *en este momento*) currently, at present, presently (*EEUU*); **es un juego muy de moda en la ~** it's a very popular game nowadays; **hay en la ~ más de dos millones de parados** there are currently over two million unemployed, there are over two million unemployed at present
[2] (= *cualidad*) **las obras de Shakespeare no han perdido ~** the works of Shakespeare have not lost their topicality; **de ~** [*noticia, tema*] topical; [*modelo, diseño*] up-to-date, up-to-the-minute; **una cuestión de palpitante ~** a highly topical question; **poner algo de ~** to focus attention on sth; **eso ha puesto de ~ un problema olvidado** that has focused attention on a forgotten problem
[3] (*Periodismo*) **la ~** (= *asuntos*) current affairs *pl*; (= *noticias*) news, current news; **una revista sobre la ~ francesa** a magazine on French current affairs; **y ahora vamos a pasar a la ~ internacional** and now (for) international news
[4] **actualidades** (*en periódico*) current affairs; (*en cine*) newsreel *sing*

actualización SF (= *acto*) updating; (*Inform*) update, updating; (*Contabilidad*) discounting

actualizador ADJ modernizing

actualizar ▸conjug 1f◂ VT (= *poner al día*) to bring up to date, update; (*Inform*) to update; (*Contabilidad*) to discount

actualmente ADV [1] (= *en este momento*) currently, at present, presently (*EEUU*); **~ está rodando una nueva película** he's currently making a new film, he's making a new film at present
[2] (= *hoy día*) nowadays; **~ se usan métodos más eficaces** nowadays more efficient methods are used

actuar ▸conjug 1e◂ Ⓐ VI [1] [*actor*] to act; [*cantante, banda, compañía, equipo*] to perform; **~ en una película** to act *o* be in a film
[2] (= *obrar*) to act; **actúa como** *o* **de mediador en el conflicto** he's acting as a mediator in the conflict; **actúa de manera rara** he's acting *o* behaving strangely; **la indecisión no le dejaba ~** indecision prevented him from taking any action; **el árbitro actuó bien en el partido** the referee did a good job in the match
[3] (*Jur*) (= *proceder*) to institute (legal) proceedings; [*abogado*] to act; **el abogado que actúa en nombre de mi familia** the lawyer acting for my family
[4] (= *tener efecto*) to act; **la crema actúa directamente sobre la herida** the cream acts directly on the wound; **el freno actúa sobre la rueda trasera** the brake acts on the back wheel
Ⓑ VT (= *hacer funcionar*) to work, operate

actuarial ADJ actuarial

actuario/a SM/F [1] (*Jur*) clerk (of the court)
[2] (*Fin*) actuary

acuache* SM, **acuachi*** SM (*Méx*) mate, buddy (*EEUU**), pal*

acuadrillar ▸conjug 1a◂ Ⓐ VT (= *juntar en cuadrilla*) to form into a band; (*Chile*) (= *acometer*) to set upon
Ⓑ **acuadrillarse** VPR to band together, gang up

acuanauta SMF deep-sea diver

acuaplano SM surfboarding

acuarela SF watercolour, watercolor (*EEUU*); **pintor(a) a la ~** watercolourist, watercolorist (*EEUU*)

acuarelista SMF watercolourist, watercolorist (*EEUU*)

Acuario SM Aquarius

acuario SM aquarium

acuárium SM aquarium

acuartelado ADJ (*Heráldica*) quartered

acuartelamiento SM (*Mil*) quartering, billeting; (= *disciplina*) confinement to barracks

acuartelar ▸conjug 1a◂ Ⓐ VT (*Mil*) to quarter, billet; (= *disciplinar*) to confine to barracks
Ⓑ **acuartelarse** VPR to withdraw to barracks

acuático ADJ aquatic, water *antes de s*

acuátil ADJ aquatic, water *antes de s*

acuatinta SF aquatint

acuatizaje SM touchdown (*on water*), landing (*on water*)

acuatizar ▸conjug 1f◂ VI to come down (*on water*), land (*on water*)

acuchamado ADJ (*Caribe*) (= *triste*) sad, depressed

acuchamarse ▸conjug 1a◂ VPR (*Caribe*) to get depressed

acuchillado ADJ [1] [*vestido*] slashed
[2] (= *escarmentado*) wary, schooled by bitter experience

acuchillar ▸conjug 1a◂ Ⓐ VT [1] (= *cortar*) to knife, stab; [+ *vestido*] to slash
[2] [+ *persona*] to stab (to death), knife
[3] (*Téc*) to plane down, smooth

Ⓑ **acuchillarse** VPR **se ~on** they fought with knives, they slashed at each other

acuchucar ▸conjug 1g◂ VT (*Cono Sur*) to crush, flatten

acucia SF (= *diligencia*) diligence, keenness; (= *prisa*) haste; (= *anhelo*) keen desire, longing

acuciadamente ADV (= *diligentemente*) diligently, keenly; (= *con prisa*) hastily; (= *con deseo*) longingly

acuciador ADJ = **acuciante**

acuciante ADJ pressing; **necesidad ~** dire necessity, urgent *o* pressing need

acuciar ▸conjug 1b◂ VT 1 (= *estimular*) to urge on; (= *dar prisa a*) to hasten; (= *acosar*) to harass; [*problema*] to press, worry; **acuciado por el hambre** driven on by hunger
2 (= *anhelar*) to yearn for, long for

acucioso ADJ (= *diligente*) keen, diligent

acuclillarse ▸conjug 1a◂ VPR to squat down

ACUDE SF ABR = **Asociación de Consumidores y Usuarios de España**

acudir ▸conjug 3a◂ VI 1 (*indicando movimiento*) (= *ir*) to go; (= *venir*) to come; **señor Martínez, acuda a información por favor** Mr Martínez, please go to the information desk; **dijo que ~ía a declarar voluntariamente** he said that he would testify voluntarily; **el perro acude cuando lo llamo** the dog comes when I call; **muchos profesores acuden cada año a nuestro congreso** every year many teachers come to *o* attend our conference; **miles de personas acudieron al aeropuerto** thousands of people turned up at *o* came to the airport; **sólo diez trabajadores acudieron a sus puestos** only ten workers showed up for work; **acudieron en su ayuda** they went to his aid; **no acudió a la cita** he did not keep the appointment, he did not turn up (for the appointment); **~ a una llamada** to answer a call; **~ al médico** to consult a doctor; **~ a la mente** to come to (one's) mind; **esta imagen acude a la mente de muchas personas** for many people this is the image that comes to mind; **~ a las urnas** to go to the polls
2 (= *participar*) to take part; **el pasado año acudieron 130 expositores** last year 130 exhibitors took part
3 (= *recurrir*) **~ a** to turn to; **no tenemos a quién ~** we have nobody to turn to; **acudo a ustedes para quejarme sobre …** I am writing to complain about …; **~ a los tribunales** to go to court
4 (*Agr*) to produce, yield

acueducto SM aqueduct

ácueo ADJ aqueous

▼ **acuerdo** SM 1 (= *decisión conjunta*) agreement; (*implícito, informal*) understanding; (*de negocios*) deal; **ambas partes quieren llegar a un ~** both parties wish to come to *o* reach an agreement; **tenemos una especie de ~ para no hacernos la competencia** we have a sort of understanding that we will not become competitors; **llegaron a un ~ sin necesidad de acudir a juicio** they settled out of court; **de común ~** by mutual agreement, by mutual consent; **de *o* por mutuo ~** by mutual agreement, by mutual consent; **tomar un ~: no tomaron ni un solo ~ en la reunión** nothing was agreed on in the meeting; **se tomó el ~ de ofrecer ayuda a los países afectados** it was agreed to give aid to the affected countries ► **acuerdo de desarme** disarmament agreement, arms agreement ► **acuerdo de pago respectivo** (*Com*) knock-for-knock agreement, no-fault agreement (*EEUU*) ► **acuerdo de paz** peace agreement ► **acuerdo de pesca** fishing agreement ► **acuerdo de principio** agreement in principle ► **acuerdo entre caballeros** gentlemen's agreement ► **Acuerdo General sobre Aranceles Aduaneros y Comercio** General Agreement on Tariffs and Trade ► **acuerdo marco** framework agreement ► **acuerdo prematrimonial** prenuptial agreement ► **acuerdo tácito** unspoken agreement, tacit agreement ► **acuerdo verbal** verbal agreement
2 **de ~** 2·1 (*independiente*) OK, all right; **sí, de ~** yes, OK, yes, all right; **cada uno pondremos 40 euros ¿de ~?** we'll each put in 40 euros, OK *o* all right?
2·2 **estar de ~** to agree, be in agreement (*frm*); **en eso estamos de ~** we agree on that, we're in agreement on that (*frm*); **sigo sin estar de ~** I still don't agree; **estoy totalmente de ~ contigo** I totally agree with you; **estoy de ~ con que deberíamos mudarnos de casa** I agree that we should move house
2·3 **ponerse de ~** to come to an agreement, reach (an) agreement; **aún no nos hemos puesto de ~** we still haven't come to an agreement, we still haven't reached (an) agreement; **no se ponían de ~ en nada** they couldn't agree on anything
2·4 **de ~ con** according to, in accordance with (*frm*); **todo se hizo de ~ con las reglas** everything was done according to *o* (*frm*) in accordance with the regulations; **de ~ con el artículo 27** as laid down in article 27, in accordance with article 27 (*frm*); **de ~ con estas fuentes, las dos mujeres fueron secuestradas** according to these sources, the two women were kidnapped; **una casa de ~ con sus necesidades** a house to suit their needs

acuícola ADJ aquatic

acuicultor(a) SM/F fish farmer

acuicultura SF aquaculture

acuidad SF sharpness

acuífero Ⓐ ADJ aquiferous, water-bearing
Ⓑ SM aquifer

acuilmarse ▸conjug 1a◂ VPR (*CAm*) (= *deprimirse*) to get depressed; (= *acobardarse*) to lose one's nerve

acuitadamente ADV sorrowfully, with regret

acuitar ▸conjug 1a◂ Ⓐ VT to afflict, distress, grieve
Ⓑ **acuitarse** VPR to grieve, be grieved (**por** at, by)

acular* ▸conjug 1a◂ Ⓐ VT 1 [+ *caballo*] to back (**a** against, into)
2 (= *acorralar*) to corner, force into a corner
Ⓑ VI (*Andes*) to back away

acullá ADV over there, yonder (*liter*)

acullicar ▸conjug 1g◂ VI (*Andes, Cono Sur*) to chew coca (leaves)

aculturación SF acculturation

aculturar ▸conjug 1a◂ VT to acculturate

acumuchar ▸conjug 1a◂ VT (*Cono Sur*) to pile up, accumulate

acumulación SF (= *acto*) accumulation; (= *reserva*) pile, stock; **una ~ de gas** a build-up of gas

acumulador Ⓐ ADJ accumulative
Ⓑ SM (= *batería*) storage battery; [*de calor*] storage heater

acumular ▸conjug 1a◂ Ⓐ VT [+ *posesiones*] to accumulate; [+ *datos*] to amass, gather
Ⓑ **acumularse** VPR to accumulate, gather, pile up; **se me acumula el trabajo** the work is piling up (on me)

acumulativo ADJ cumulative

acúmulo SM accumulation, build-up

acunar ▸conjug 1a◂ VT to rock, rock to sleep

acuñación SF [*de moneda*] minting; [*de frase*] coining

acuñar ▸conjug 1a◂ Ⓐ VT 1 [+ *moneda*] to mint; [+ *medalla*] to strike; [+ *frase*] to coin; [+ *rueda*] to wedge
2 (*Caribe*) (= *llevar a cabo*) to finish successfully
Ⓑ **acuñarse** VPR (*CAm*) to hit o.s., sustain a blow

acuosidad SF (= *calidad*) wateriness; [*de fruta*] juiciness

acuoso ADJ (= *con agua*) watery; [*fruta*] juicy

acupuntor(a) SM/F acupuncturist

acupuntura SF acupuncture

acupunturista SMF acupuncturist

acurrado ADJ 1 (*Caribe, Méx*) (= *guapo*) handsome
2 (*CAm*) (= *rechoncho*) squat, chubby

acurrucarse ▸conjug 1g◂ VPR to snuggle up, curl up

acusación SF (= *inculpación*) accusation; (*Jur*) (= *cargo*) charge, indictment; (= *acusador*) prosecution; **negar la ~** to deny the charge

acusado/a Ⓐ ADJ 1 (*Jur*) accused
2 (= *marcado*) (*gen*) marked, pronounced; [*acento*] strong; [*contraste*] marked, striking; [*característica, rasgo, personalidad*] strong; [*color*] deep
Ⓑ SM/F accused, defendant

acusador(a) Ⓐ ADJ accusing, reproachful; **los letrados ~es** prosecuting counsel; **la parte ~a** the plaintiff
Ⓑ SM/F accuser ► **acusador(a) público/a** public prosecutor, procurator fiscal (*Escocia*), prosecuting *o* district attorney (*EEUU*)

acusar ▸conjug 1a◂ Ⓐ VT 1 (= *culpar*) to accuse; **~ a algn de algo** to accuse sb of sth; **nos acusan de racistas** they are accusing us of being racists; **~ a algn de hacer algo** to accuse sb of doing sth; **le acusan de promover la violencia** he is being accused of promoting violence
2 (*Jur*) (= *incriminar*) charge; **~ a algn de algo** to charge sb with sth; **le han acusado de asesinato** he has been charged with murder; **~ a algn de hacer algo** to charge sb with doing sth; **le acusan de malversar fondos** he is being charged with embezzling funds
3 (= *mostrar*) **sus caras acusaban el cansancio** tiredness showed in their faces; **la empresa acusaba cierta desorganización** the company was showing signs of disorganization
4 (= *registrar*) to pick up, register; **este sismógrafo acusa la menor vibración** this seismometer picks up *o* registers the least vibra-

➤ LENGUA Y USO: **acuerdo 2·2** 38.1, 39.1, 40.1, 40.3

tion

[5] (*Correos*) **~ recibo de algo** to acknowledge receipt of sth

Ⓑ **acusarse** VPR [1] (= *confesarse*) to confess; **~se de (haber hecho) algo** to confess to (having done) sth

[2] (= *registrarse*) **mañana se ~á un aumento de las temperaturas** temperatures will rise tomorrow, tomorrow there will be a rise in temperature; **esta deficiencia se acusa aquí claramente** this deficiency is clearly noticeable here, this deficiency shows clearly here

ACUSAR

- Traducimos **acusar (de)** por **accuse (of)** en la mayoría de los casos:

  Me acusó de haber mentido
  He accused me of lying
  ¿De qué me estás acusando?
  What are you accusing me of?

- Traducimos **acusar (de)** por **charge (with)** cuando se trata de una acusación formal que llevará a la celebración de un juicio:

  No lo han acusado de ninguno de los cargos
  He hasn't been charged with anything
  Hasta ahora, la policía lo ha acusado solamente de uno de los asesinatos
  So far, the police have only charged him with one of the murders

NOTA: El verbo **indict** tiene un significado parecido a **charge**, pero sólo se usa en contextos legales muy especializados.

Para otros usos y ejemplos ver la entrada.

acusativo ADJ, SM accusative

acusatorio ADJ accusatory, accusing

acuse SM ► **acuse de recibo** acknowledgement of receipt

acusetas* SMF INV (*Andes, Cono Sur*) telltale, sneak, tattler (*EEUU**)

acusete* SMF, **acusica*** SMF (*Esp*), **acusique*** SMF telltale, sneak, tattler (*EEUU**)

acusón/ona* Ⓐ ADJ telltale, sneaking
Ⓑ SM/F telltale, sneak, tattler (*EEUU**)

acústica SF acoustics

acústico Ⓐ ADJ acoustic Ⓑ SM hearing aid

acutí SM (*LAm*) guinea pig

AD SF ABR (*Ven*) = **Acción Democrática**

ADA SF ABR (= **Ayuda del Automovilista**) ≈ AA, ≈ RAC, ≈ AAA (*EEUU*)

-ada *ver* **Aspects of Word Formation in Spanish 2**

ADAC SM ABR (= **avión de despegue y aterrizaje cortos**) VTOL

adagio SM (= *proverbio*) adage, proverb; (*Mús*) adagio

adalid SM leader, champion

adamado ADJ [*hombre*] effeminate, soft; [*mujer*] elegant, chic; (*pey*) flashy

adamascado ADJ damask

adamascar ▸conjug 1g◂ VT to damask

Adán SM Adam

adán SM (= *sucio*) scruffy fellow; (= *vago*) lazy fellow; ✦***MODISMO*** **estar hecho un ~** to be terribly shabby

adaptabilidad SF adaptability, versatility

adaptable ADJ (= *versátil*) adaptable, versatile; (*Tip*) compatible

adaptación SF adaptation

adaptador SM adapter, adaptor ► **adaptador universal** universal adapter *o* adaptor

adaptar ▸conjug 1a◂ Ⓐ VT [1] (= *acomodar*) to adapt; (= *encajar*) to fit, make suitable (**para** for); (= *ajustar*) to adjust

[2] (*Inform*) to convert (**para** to)

Ⓑ **adaptarse** VPR to adapt (**a** to); **saber ~se a las circunstancias** to be able to adapt to the circumstances

adaptativo ADJ adaptive

adaraja SF toothing

adarga SF *leather oval shield*

adarme SM **ni un ~** not a whit; **no me importa un ~** I couldn't care less; **sin un ~ de educación** with no manners at all; **por ~s** in dribs and drabs

a. de C. ABR (= **antes de Cristo**) BC

adecentar ▸conjug 1a◂ Ⓐ VT to tidy up
Ⓑ **adecentarse** VPR to tidy o.s. up

adecuación SF adaptation

adecuadamente ADV suitably

adecuado ADJ [1] (= *apropiado*) [*actitud, respuesta, ropa, tratamiento*] appropriate; [*documento, requisito*] appropriate, relevant; **los medios ~s para resolver el problema** the appropriate means to solve the problem; **es el traje más ~ para la primavera** it is the most suitable *o* appropriate outfit for spring; **exigen un uso ~ de los recursos** they are demanding that resources be used appropriately *o* properly; **una actitud poco adecuada** an inappropriate attitude; **estar en el momento y el lugar ~s** to be in the right place at the right time; **esta no es la pieza adecuada** this is not the right part; **el hombre ~ para el puesto** the right man for the job; **lo más ~ sería ...** the best thing *o* the most appropriate thing would be to ...

[2] (= *acorde*) **~ a algo**: **un precio ~ a mis posibilidades** a price within my budget *o* reach

[3] (= *suficiente*) [*dinero, tiempo*] sufficient

adecuamiento SM adjustment

adecuar ▸conjug 1d◂ Ⓐ VT to adapt; **han adecuado el planteamiento a la nueva situación** they've adapted their approach to the new situation *o* in line with the new situation; **adecuó su charla a la edad de su audiencia** he adapted *o* tailored his speech to suit the age of the audience; **han adecuado los impuestos a la directiva europea** taxes have been adjusted in line with the European directive

Ⓑ **adecuarse** VPR [1] (= *adaptarse*) to adapt; **no se adecuó a las nuevas circunstancias** he failed to adapt to the new circumstances; **tenemos que ~nos a los avances técnicos** we have to keep up with *o* keep abreast of technical progress

[2] (*frm*) (= *ser apropiado*) to be suitable *o* right for sth; **este producto no se adecúa a lo que busco** this product is not suitable *o* right for what I want

adefesiero* ADJ (*Andes, Cono Sur*) (= *cómico*) comic, ridiculous; (= *torpe*) clumsy; (*en el vestido*) overdressed, camp*

adefesio SM [1] (= *persona rara*) queer bird, oddball*; (= *persona fea*) disaster*; (= *objeto feo*) monstrosity; (= *ropa fea*) outlandish attire, ridiculous attire; **estaba hecha un ~** she looked a sight

[2] (= *disparate*) piece of nonsense, absurdity; **hablar ~s** to talk nonsense

adefesioso ADJ (*Andes, Cono Sur*) nonsensical, ridiculous

adehala SF (= *propina*) gratuity, tip; [*de sueldo*] bonus

a. de J.C. ABR (= **antes de Jesucristo**) BC

adela SF (*CAm*) bittersweet

adelaida SF (*Méx*) fuchsia

adelantado/a Ⓐ ADJ [1] (= *avanzado*) [*país, método, trabajo*] advanced; **las obras están ya muy adelantadas** the work is now very advanced; **lleva la tesis bastante adelantada** she's quite well ahead with her thesis; **estar** *o* **ir ~ en los estudios** to be well ahead in one's studies; **sus ideas eran bastante adelantadas entonces** his ideas were quite ahead of their time

[2] [*reloj*] fast; **el despertador va unos minutos ~** the alarm clock is a few minutes fast

[3] (= *precoz*) [*persona*] advanced, ahead of one's age; **está muy ~ para su edad** he's very advanced for his age, he's well ahead of his age

[4] (= *prematuro*) [*cosecha, elecciones*] early; **es un regalo ~ de tu cumpleaños** it's an early birthday present

[5] (= *de antemano*) [*pago*] advance; **por ~** in advance; **hay que sacar el billete por ~** you need to buy the ticket in advance

[6] (= *atrevido*) forward, bold

[7] (*Dep*) (*en una posición*) **vio al portero ~ y disparó** he saw the goalkeeper out of goal and took a shot; **un pase ~** a forward pass

Ⓑ SM/F [1] (= *pionero*) pioneer; **ser un ~ en algo** to be a pioneer in sth

[2] (*Hist*) governor (*of a frontier province*)

adelantamiento SM [1] (*Aut*) overtaking, passing (*esp EEUU*); **realizó un ~ en una curva peligrosa** he overtook on a dangerous bend

[2] (= *en el tiempo*) **el ~ de las elecciones no ha sido posible** it has not been possible to bring forward the elections

[3] (= *progreso*) progress

adelantar ▸conjug 1a◂ Ⓐ VT [1] (= *pasar por delante*) [+ *vehículo, rival*] to overtake, pass (*esp EEUU*); **adelantó al resto del pelotón** he overtook the rest of the pack; **la oposición ha adelantado al gobierno en las encuestas** the opposition has overtaken the government in the polls

[2] (= *mover de sitio*) [+ *ficha, meta*] to move forward; **~on la meta 300 metros** they moved the finishing line 300 metres forward

[3] (*en el tiempo*) [3·1] [+ *fecha, acto*] to bring forward; **no van a ~ las elecciones** there is not going to be an early election, the election is not going to be brought forward; **no adelantemos acontecimientos** let's not get ahead of ourselves, let's not jump the gun*

[3·2] [+ *reloj*] to put forward; **hoy se adelantan los relojes una hora** today the clocks go forward (by) one hour

[4] (= *conseguir*) **no adelantamos nada con decírselo** we'll get nowhere by telling him; **¿qué adelantas con enfadarte?** getting upset won't get you anywhere

[5] (= *anticipar*) [5·1] [+ *sueldo, dinero*] to pay in advance, advance; **me ~on parte de la paga de Navidad** they paid me some of my Christmas bonus in advance, they advanced me some of my Christmas bonus; **el dinero es**

para ~ pagas a las tropas the money is for making advance payments to the troops

5·2 [+ *información*] to disclose, reveal; **ha adelantado las líneas generales de su plan** he has disclosed *o* revealed the outline of his plan; **como adelantó este periódico, ha aumentado la tasa de paro** as this newspaper revealed, the unemployment rate has gone up; **lo único que puedo ~te es que se trata de una buena noticia** the only thing that I can tell you now is that it is good news

6 (= *apresurar*) [+ *trabajo*] to speed up; **yo voy poniendo la mesa para ~ trabajo** I'll start laying the table to speed things up; **~ el paso** to speed up, quicken one's pace

7 (*Dep*) [+ *balón*] to pass forward

Ⓑ VI 1 (*Aut*) to overtake, pass (*EEUU*); **"prohibido ~"** "no overtaking", "no passing" (*EEUU*)

2 (= *avanzar*) to make progress; **por el atajo ~emos más** we'll make better progress if we take the shortcut; **llevamos un mes negociando sin ~ nada** we have spent a month negotiating without making any progress *o* headway

3 [*reloj*] to gain time; **ese reloj adelanta dos minutos diarios** that clock gains two minutes a day

Ⓒ **adelantarse** VPR 1 (= *avanzar*) to go forward, move forward; **se adelantó para darle dos besos** she stepped *o* went *o* moved forward to kiss him; **nos adelantamos a su encuentro** we went forward to meet him; **se adelantó a codazos** she elbowed her way forward

2 (= *ir por delante*) to go ahead; **me ~é a inspeccionar el camino** I'll go ahead and check the way; **~se en el marcador** (*Dep*) to go ahead

3 (= *anticiparse*) [*cosecha, primavera*] to come early; **el calor se ha adelantado este año** the hot weather has come early this year

4 **~se a** 4·1 [+ *deseos, preguntas*] to anticipate; **se adelantó a posibles preguntas** he anticipated possible questions

4·2 [+ *persona*] (= *hacer antes*) to get in before; (= *dejar atrás*) to get ahead of; **yo iba a comprarlo pero alguien se me adelantó** I was going to buy it but someone beat me to it *o* got in before me; **un grupo de 19 corredores se adelantó al pelotón** a group of 19 runners got ahead of the pack; **es un diseñador que se adelanta a su tiempo** as a designer he is ahead of his time

5 [*reloj*] to gain time

adelante ADV 1 (*indicando dirección*) forward; **tráelo para ~** bring it forward; **echado para ~** (= *inclinado*) leaning forward; (= *seguro de sí mismo*) self-assured; **hacia ~** forward; **el espejo estaba inclinado hacia ~** the mirror was tilted forward; **un paso (hacia) ~** a step forward; **mirar hacia ~** to look ahead; **llevar ~ un proyecto** to carry out a project; **sacar ~ una empresa/un espectáculo** to get a company/a show off the ground; **sacar ~ a los hijos** to give one's children a good education in life; **salir ~** [*proyecto, propuesta*] to go ahead; **hay que trabajar mucho para salir ~** you have to work hard to get on (in life); **si trabajamos juntos saldremos ~** if we all work together we'll get through this; **la orquesta no podrá salir ~ sin subvenciones** the orchestra won't be able to survive without subsidies; **seguir ~** to go on; **tuvimos una avería y no pudimos seguir ~** we broke down and couldn't go on any further; **mis hijos me dan fuerzas para seguir ~** my children give me the strength to keep going; **decidieron seguir ~ con sus proyectos** they decided to go ahead *o* carry on with their plans; **antes de seguir ~, ¿hay alguna pregunta?** before I go on, are there any questions?; *ver tb* **paso 3**

2 (*indicando posición*) **la fila dos es demasiado ~** row two is too near the front *o* too far forward; **está más ~** it's further on; **la parte de ~** the front; **más ~** (*en una sala*) further forward; (*en texto*) below; **prefiero sentarme más ~** I'd rather sit further forward; **véase nota más ~** see note below

3 (*indicando tiempo*) **en ~** from now on, in future; **en ~ las reuniones serán cada dos años** from now on *o* in future the meetings will be every two years; **desde el 13 de agosto en ~** from 13th August (onwards); **de ahora en ~** ◊ **de aquí en ~** from now on; **de hoy en ~** as from today; **más ~** later; **volveré a referirme al tema más ~** I will refer to the subject again later (on); **decidimos dejar la reunión para más ~** we decided to leave the meeting till a later date *o* till later

4 (*indicando cantidad*) **en ~** upwards; **de 50 euros en ~** from 50 euros (upwards); **para niños de tres años en ~** for children of three and upwards

5 **¡adelante!** (*autorizando a entrar*) come in!; (*animando a seguir*) go on!, carry on!; (*Mil*) forward!

6 **~ de** (*LAm*) in front of; **se sentó ~ de mí** he sat in front of me

adelanto SM 1 (= *progreso*) 1·1 (= *acción*) advancement; (= *resultado*) step forward; **esa ley supone un gran ~** that law marks a great step forward; **eso representa un ~ sobre el método actual** that is an improvement on the current method

1·2 **adelantos** (= *descubrimientos*) advances; **los ~s de la ciencia** the advances of science; **una cocina con los últimos ~s** a kitchen with the latest mod cons*

2 (*en tiempo*) **piden el ~ de las elecciones** they are asking for the elections to be brought forward; **han conseguido el ~ de la edad de jubilación** they have managed to get the retirement age lowered; **el tren llegó con un ~ de 15 minutos** the train arrived 15 minutes early; **de ~**: **con una hora de ~** an hour early; **su agenda está repleta con seis meses de ~** her diary is full six months ahead; **el reloj lleva diez minutos de ~** the clock is ten minutes fast; **llevaba tres minutos de ~ sobre el segundo corredor** he had a three-minute lead over the runner in second place

3 [*de información*] **facilitaron un ~ de los resultados** they released some of the results in advance; **el artículo es sólo un ~ de su próximo libro** the article is just a taster of his latest book

4 [*de dinero*] (= *anticipo*) advance; (= *depósito*) deposit; **solicitó un ~ de quinientos euros** he asked for an advance of five hundred euros; **hay que hacer un ~ en metálico** it is necessary to make a cash deposit

5 (*Ajedrez*) (= *movimiento*) forward move

adelfa SF rosebay, oleander

adelgazador ADJ slimming, weight-reducing

adelgazamiento SM slimming

adelgazante Ⓐ ADJ slimming, weight-reducing

Ⓑ SM slimming product

adelgazar ▸conjug 1f◂ Ⓐ VT 1 (= *reducir el grosor*) to make thin, make slender; [+ *kilos*] to lose, take off; [+ *persona, figura*] to slim, reduce, slenderize (*EEUU*); [+ *palo*] to pare, whittle; [+ *punta*] to sharpen; [+ *voz*] to raise the pitch of

2 (*fig*) (= *purificar*) to purify, refine; [+ *entendimiento*] to sharpen

Ⓑ VI (= *perder peso*) to grow thin; (*con régimen*) to slim, lose weight

Adelpha [a'ðelfa] SF ABR (*Esp*) = **Asociación de Defensa Ecológica y del Patrimonio Histórico-artístico**

ademán SM 1 [*de mano*] gesture, movement; (= *postura*) posture, position; **en ~ de hacer algo** as if to do sth, getting ready to do sth; **hacer ~ de hacer** to make as if to do, make a move to do; **hacer ademanes** to gesture, make signs

2 **ademanes** (= *modales*) manners

además ADV 1 (= *también*) (*para añadir otro elemento*) also, in addition (*frm*); (*para reforzar un comentario*) what's more, besides, furthermore (*frm*), moreover (*frm*); **hay, ~, pistas de tenis y campos de golf** there are also tennis courts and golf courses, in addition, there are tennis courts and golf courses (*frm*); **y ~, me dijo que no me quería** and what's more, *o* and besides, he told me he didn't love me; **estoy cansado y, ~, no me apetece** I'm tired, and what's more, *o* besides, I don't feel like it; **quiero decirle, ~, que ésa no era mi intención** furthermore, *o* moreover I want to tell you that that was not my intention (*frm*)

2 **~ de** as well as, besides, in addition to (*frm*); **~ del alojamiento, necesitamos la comida** as well as *o* besides somewhere to stay we need food; **~ de una fotocopia, se requiere el documento original** as well as *o* (*frm*) in addition to a photocopy, we require the original document; **el examen fue largo, ~ de difícil** the exam was long as well as difficult; **~ de que** (+ *INDIC*) as well as + *ger*; **~ de que estaba cansado, no había comido** as well as being tired he hadn't eaten

Adén SM Aden

ADENA SF ABR (*Esp*) = **Asociación para la Defensa de la Naturaleza**

adenoideo ADJ adenoidal

adentellar ▸conjug 1a◂ VT to sink one's teeth into

adentrarse ▸conjug 1a◂ VPR **~ en** to go into, get inside; (= *penetrar*) to penetrate into; **~ en la selva** to go deep(er) into the forest; **~ en sí mismo** to become lost in thought

adentro Ⓐ ADV 1 (*esp LAm*) = **dentro 1**

2 **mar ~** out at sea, out to sea; **tierra ~** inland; **¡adentro!** come in!

Ⓑ PREP **~ de** (*LAm*) (= *dentro de*) inside; **~ mío** inside myself

Ⓒ SM 1 (*Cono Sur*) indoors, inside the house

2 **adentros** (*de persona*) innermost being *sing*, innermost thoughts; **dijo para sus ~s** he said to himself; **reírse para sus ~s** to laugh inwardly

➤ LENGUA Y USO: además 53.5

adepto/a SM/F (= *partidario*) follower, supporter; (*Rel*) adept, initiate; (*LAm**) (= *drogadicto*) drug addict

aderezado ADJ favourable, favorable (*EEUU*), suitable

aderezar ▸conjug 1f◂ Ⓐ VT [1] (= *preparar*) to prepare, get ready; (= *vestir*) to dress up; (= *adornar*) to embellish, adorn
[2] (*Culin*) (= *sazonar*) to season, garnish; [+ *ensalada*] to dress; [+ *bebidas*] to prepare, mix; [+ *vinos*] to blend
[3] [+ *máquina*] to repair; [+ *tela*] to gum, size
Ⓑ **aderezarse** VPR (= *prepararse*) to dress up, get ready

aderezo SM [1] (= *preparación*) preparation; (= *adorno*) decoration; **dar el ~ definitivo a algo** to put the finishing touch to sth ► **aderezo de casa** household equipment ► **aderezo de mesa** dinner service
[2] (*Culin*) (= *aliño*) seasoning, dressing; (*Cos*) adornment; (= *reparación*) repair
[3] (= *joyas*) set of jewels ► **aderezo de diamantes** set of diamonds

adeudado ADJ in debt

adeudar ▸conjug 1a◂ Ⓐ VT [+ *dinero*] to owe; [+ *impuestos*] to be liable for; **~ una suma en una cuenta** to debit an account for a sum
Ⓑ VI (= *emparentar*) to become related by marriage
Ⓒ **adeudarse** VPR to run into debt

adeudo SM (= *deuda*) debt; (*en aduana*) customs duty; (*en cuenta*) debit, charge

adeveras (*LAm*): **de ~** ADV = **veras 2**

ADEVIDA SF ABR (*Esp*) = **Asociación en Defensa de la Vida Humana**

a.D.g. ABR (= **a Dios gracias**) D.G.

adherencia SF [1] (= *calidad*) adherence; (= *acción*) adhesion
[2] (= *vínculo*) bond, connection
[3] (*Aut*) road holding
[4] **tener ~s** to have connections

adherente ADJ adhesive, sticky; **~ a** (*fig*) adhering to

adherido/a SM/F adherent, follower

adherir ▸conjug 3i◂ Ⓐ VT (= *pegar*) to adhere, stick (**a** to)
Ⓑ VI, **adherirse** VPR (= *pegarse*) to adhere, stick (**a** to); **~se a** (= *seguir*) to follow; (= *afiliarse*) to join, become a member of

adhesión SF (*Téc*) adhesion; (= *apoyo*) adherence, support; (= *afiliación*) membership

adhesividad SF adhesiveness

adhesivo Ⓐ ADJ adhesive, sticky
Ⓑ SM adhesive

adicción SF addiction

adición SF [1] (*Mat*) addition; (= *sumar*) adding, adding up
[2] (*Jur*) acceptance
[3] (*Cono Sur*) (= *cuenta*) bill, check (*EEUU*)

adicional ADJ (= *complementario*) additional, extra; (*Inform*) add-on

adicionalidad SF additionality

adicionar ▸conjug 1a◂ VT (= *añadir*) to add (**a** to); (*Mat*) (= *sumar*) to add, add up

adictivo ADJ addictive

adicto/a Ⓐ ADJ [1] **~ a algo** addicted to sth; **es ~ a la heroína** he's addicted to heroin, he's a heroin addict; **soy ~ a las ostras** I'm addicted to oysters; **es ~ al trabajo** he's a workaholic
[2] (= *fiel*) [*admirador, amigo*] devoted; **un público ~ llenaba la sala** a devoted audience filled the hall
[3] (= *partidario*) loyal; **la prensa adicta al Gobierno** sections of the press loyal to *o* supportive of the government; **las personas adictas al régimen franquista** supporters of the Franco regime
Ⓑ SM/F [1] (*a la droga, tele*) addict
[2] (= *seguidor*) follower, supporter; (*LAm Dep*) supporter, fan

adiestrado ADJ trained

adiestrador(a) SM/F trainer

adiestramiento SM [*de animal*] training; (*Mil, Dep*) drilling, practice ► **adiestramiento con armas** weapons training

adiestrar ▸conjug 1a◂ Ⓐ VT [+ *animal*] to train; (*Mil*) (= *entrenar*) to drill; (= *guiar*) to guide, lead
Ⓑ **adiestrarse** VPR to practise, practice (*EEUU*), train o.s.; **~se a hacer** to teach o.s. to do

adifés ADV [1] (*CAm*) (= *con dificultad*) with difficulty
[2] (*Caribe*) (= *a propósito*) on purpose, deliberately

adinerado ADJ wealthy, well-off

adinerarse ▸conjug 1a◂ VPR to get rich

ad infinitum ADV ad infinitum

adiós Ⓐ EXCL (*al irse*) goodbye!; (*al saludar*) hello!; **✦MODISMO ¡~ Madrid, que te quedas sin gente!** good riddance!
Ⓑ SM goodbye, farewell; **decir(se) los adioses** to say one's farewells; **ir a decir ~ a algn** to go to say goodbye to sb; **decir ~ a algo** (= *renunciar*) to wave sth goodbye, give sth up

adiosito* EXCL (*esp LAm*) bye-bye!, cheerio!

adiposidad SF, **adiposis** SF INV adiposity

adiposo ADJ adipose, fat

aditamento SM (= *complemento*) complement, addition; (= *accesorio*) accessory

aditivo SM additive ► **aditivo alimenticio** food additive

adivinación SF (= *predicción*) prophecy, divination; (= *conjeturas*) guessing; (= *solución*) solving; **por ~** by guesswork ► **adivinación de pensamientos** mind-reading

adivinador(a) SM/F fortune teller

adivinanza SF riddle, conundrum

adivinar ▸conjug 1a◂ Ⓐ VT [1] (= *acertar*) [+ *acertijo, adivinanza*] to solve; **¡adivina quién ha llamado!** guess who called!; **¡adivina por qué no vino!** guess why he didn't come!; **~ el pensamiento a algn** to read sb's mind *o* thoughts; **~ las intenciones a algn** to second-guess sb
[2] (= *predecir*) to foresee; **~ el futuro** to foresee the future; **es fácil ~ lo que ocurrirá** it's easy to foresee *o* see what will happen
[3] (= *entrever*) (*frm*) **a lo lejos adivinó la figura de un hombre** in the distance he could just make out the figure of a man; **su primera novela deja ~ su genio** her first novel gives a glimpse of *o* hints at her genius
Ⓑ **adivinarse** VPR (*frm*) **su silueta se adivinaba en la ventana** one could make out her silhouette in the window, her silhouette was just visible in the window; **en este texto se adivina su sensibilidad** in this text one gets a glimpse of his sensitivity; **en los parques ya se adivina la primavera** in the parks you can see the first signs of spring

adivino/a SM/F fortune-teller

adj. ABR (= **adjunto**) enc, encl

adjetivar ▸conjug 1a◂ VT (*Gram*) (= *dar valor de adjetivo*) to use adjectivally, use attributively; (= *modificar*) to modify

adjetivo Ⓐ ADJ adjectival
Ⓑ SM adjective

adjudicación SF [1] [*de premio*] award; (*en subasta*) knocking down, sale
[2] (*Méx Jur*) adjudication, award

adjudicado EXCL sold!

adjudicador(a) Ⓐ ADJ adjudicating
Ⓑ SM/F adjudicator

adjudicar ▸conjug 1g◂ Ⓐ VT to award (**a** to); **~ algo al mejor postor** to knock sth down to the highest bidder
Ⓑ **adjudicarse** VPR **~se algo** to appropriate sth; **~se el premio** to win (the prize)

adjudicatorio/a SM/F (= *premiado*) award winner; (*en subasta*) successful bidder

▼**adjuntar** ▸conjug 1a◂ VT (= *incluir*) to append, attach; (*en carta*) to enclose; **adjuntamos factura** we enclose our account

▼**adjunto/a** Ⓐ ADJ [1] [*información*] attached; **rellene el formulario ~** please complete the attached form; **un órgano consultivo ~ a la Presidencia** a consultative body attached to the presidency; **en el documento ~ a esta carta** in the enclosed document
[2] (= *ayudante*) assistant; **profesor(a) ~/a** assistant lecturer; **director(a) ~/a** assistant director
Ⓑ ADV (*en carta*) **remitir** *o* **enviar algo ~** to enclose sth; **le envío ~ mi CV** I enclose my CV, please find enclosed my CV
Ⓒ SM/F [1] (= *ayudante*) **el ~ al** *o* **del director** the assistant to the director, the director's assistant
[2] (*en carta*) enclosure; **~s: un folleto informativo y un contrato** enc: one information leaflet and one contract
[3] (*Ling*) adjunct

adlátere SM (= *compañero*) companion, associate; (*pey*) (= *subordinado*) minion, minder

adminículo SM accessory, gadget; **adminículos** emergency kit

administración SF [1] (= *organización*) administration; (= *dirección*) management, running; **en ~** in trust; **obras en ~** books handled by us, books for which we are agents ► **Administración de Correos** General Post Office ► **administración empresarial**, **administración de empresas** (= *curso*) business administration, business management ► **administración de lotería** lottery outlet ► **administración financiera** financial management ► **administración militar** commissariat ► **administración pública** civil service, public administration (*EEUU*)
[2] (*Pol*) government, administration ► **administración central** central government ► **administración territorial** local government
[3] (= *oficina*) headquarters *pl*, central office; (*Andes*) [*de hotel*] reception
[4] (*Caribe Rel*) extreme unction

administrador(a) SM/F [*de bienes, distrito*] administrator; [*de organización, empresa*] manager; [*de tierras*] agent, land agent; **es buena ~a**

➤ LENGUA Y USO: **adjuntar** 46.4, 47.1, 47.2, 47.5 **adjunto A1** 47.2

de la casa she uses the housekeeping money very efficiently ► **administrador(a) de aduanas** chief customs officer, collector of customs ► **administrador(a) de correos** postmaster/postmistress ► **administrador(a) de fincas** land agent ► **administrador(a) de redes** system administrator ► **administrador(a) judicial** (*Méx*) receiver

administrar ▸conjug 1a◂ Ⓐ VT [1] (= *organizar*) to administer; (*Com*) to manage, run [2] [+ *justicia, sacramento*] to administer Ⓑ **administrarse** VPR to manage one's own affairs

administrativo/a Ⓐ ADJ administrative; (*Com*) managerial; (= *del gobierno*) of the government, of the administration Ⓑ SM/F (= *funcionario*) clerk, office worker; (= *encargado*) administrator, administrative officer

admirable ADJ admirable

▼**admiración** SF [1] (= *aprecio*) admiration; **es conocida su ~ por el rey** his admiration for the king is well known; **un gesto digno de ~** an admirable gesture; **causar** *o* **despertar ~** to be (much) admired; **ganarse la ~ de algn** to win sb's admiration; **sentir** *o* **tener ~ a** *o* **por algn** to admire sb; **siento** *o* **tengo mucha ~ por él** I admire him greatly *o* very much; **le tengo mucha ~** I admire him greatly *o* very much [2] (= *asombro*) amazement; **ante la ~ de todos** to everyone's amazement [3] (*Tip*) exclamation mark

admirador(a) SM/F admirer

admirar ▸conjug 1a◂ Ⓐ VT [1] (= *estimar*) to admire; **~ algo/a algn** to admire sth/sb; **lo admiran por su coraje** he is admired for his courage; **sus progresos son de ~** his progress is admirable [2] (= *contemplar*) [+ *cuadro, panorama*] to admire; **admiramos el paisaje desde la cima** we admired the scenery from the top of the hill [3] (*frm*) (= *asombrar*) to amaze, astonish; **su descaro admiró a todos** everyone was amazed *o* astonished at *o* by his nerve; **me admira tu ingenuidad** your ingenuity amazes *o* astonishes me; **no es de ~ que haya triunfado** it's hardly surprising that she has won Ⓑ **admirarse** VPR (*frm*) (= *asombrarse*) to be amazed, be astonished

admirativo ADJ admiring, full of admiration

admisibilidad SF admissibility

admisible ADJ [*conducta, crítica, propuesta*] acceptable, admissible (*frm*); [*excusa, nivel*] acceptable; **no es ~ que continúe esta situación** we cannot allow this situation to continue

admisión SF [1] (= *entrada*) (*en club, organización*) admission; (*en universidad*) acceptance; **"reservado el derecho de admisión"** "the management reserves the right to refuse admission"; **se ha ampliado el plazo de ~ de solicitudes** the closing date for applications has been extended; **las condiciones de ~ al concurso** the conditions of entry to the competition; **acto de ~** (*Jur*) validation (*of a suit*); **prueba de ~** entrance examination [2] [*de error*] acceptance [3] (*Mec*) intake, inlet; **válvula de ~** inlet valve ► **admisión de aire** air intake

admitido ADJ [1] [*candidato, alumno*] admitted [2] [*opinión, teoría, vocablo*] accepted [3] [*producto*] permitted

▼**admitir** ▸conjug 3a◂ VT [1] (= *dejar entrar*) (*en organización*) to admit, accept; (*en hospital*) to admit; **el club no admite mujeres** the club does not admit *o* accept women members; **los extranjeros no son admitidos en la comunidad** foreigners are not accepted into the community; **fue admitido en la universidad** he was accepted for university [2] (= *aceptar*) [+ *opinión, regalo*] to accept; **se admiten apuestas** all bets accepted; **¿ha admitido la Academia esa palabra?** has the Academy accepted that word?; **"se admiten tarjetas de crédito"** "we take *o* accept credit cards"; **"no se admiten propinas"** "no tipping"; **el juez admitió la demanda a trámite** the judge granted leave to file a lawsuit [3] (= *permitir*) to allow, permit (*frm*); **el contenido de plomo admitido en las gasolinas** the permitted lead content of petrol, the amount of lead allowed *o* permitted (*frm*) in petrol; **mi presupuesto no admite grandes despilfarros** my budget won't run to *o* does not allow extravagances; **este asunto no admite medias tintas** there's no room for half measures here; **la calidad de este vino no admite comparaciones** this is a wine of incomparable quality; **esto no admite demora** this cannot be put off, this will brook no delay (*frm*); **no admite discusión** it is indisputable; **no admite duda(s)** it leaves no room for doubt; **no admite otra explicación** it allows of no other explanation [4] (= *reconocer*) [+ *culpabilidad, error*] to admit; **admito que la culpa ha sido mía** I admit that it was my fault; **admitió que había sido testigo** he admitted being a witness; **hay que ~ que no hay nada mejor** it has to be said that there's nothing better [5] (= *tener cabida para*) to hold; **la sala admite 500 personas** the hall holds 500 people

admón. ABR (= **administración**) admin

admonición SF warning ► **admonición escrita** written warning ► **admonición oral** verbal warning

admonitorio ADJ warning *antes de s*

ADN Ⓐ SM ABR (= **ácido desoxirribonucleico**) DNA; **prueba del ~** DNA test Ⓑ SF ABR (*Bol*) = **Acción Democrática Nacionalista**

adnominal ADJ, SM adnominal

-ado *ver* **Aspects of Word Formation in Spanish 2**

adobado SM pickled pork

adobar ▸conjug 1a◂ VT (= *preparar*) to prepare, dress; (= *cocinar*) to cook; [+ *carne*] to season, pickle; [+ *pieles*] to tan; [+ *narración*] to twist

adobe SM [1] (= *tabique*) adobe, sun-dried brick [2] (*Cono Sur hum*) (= *pie*) big foot [3] **descansar haciendo ~s** (*Méx*) to moonlight, do work on the side

adobera SF [1] (*para ladrillos*) mould *o* (*EEUU*) mold for making adobes [2] (*Cono Sur, Méx**) (= *queso*) brick-shaped cheese; (= *molde*) cheese mould, cheese mold (*EEUU*) [3] (*Cono Sur hum*) (= *pie*) big foot

adobo SM [1] (= *preparación*) preparation, dressing; [*de pieles*] tanning [2] (= *salsa*) pickle, sauce; (*Méx*) (*picante*) red chili sauce; (*para pieles*) tanning mixture

adocenado ADJ common-or-garden*

adocenarse ▸conjug 1a◂ VPR [1] (= *hacerse común*) to become commonplace [2] (= *decaer*) to become mediocre [3] (= *estancarse*) to remain stagnant, become fossilized

adoctrinación SF indoctrination

adoctrinador ADJ indoctrinating, indoctrinatory

adoctrinamiento SM indoctrination

adoctrinar ▸conjug 1a◂ VT to indoctrinate (**en** with)

adolecer ▸conjug 2d◂ VI **~ de** (*Med*) to be ill with; (*fig*) to suffer from

adolescencia SF adolescence

adolescente Ⓐ ADJ adolescent Ⓑ SMF (*Med*) adolescent; (= *joven*) teenager, teen (*EEUU**)

Adolfo SM Adolphus, Adolph, Adolf

adolorido ADJ (*LAm*) = **dolorido**

adonde CONJ (*esp LAm*) where

adónde (*esp LAm*) Ⓐ ADV INTERROG where? Ⓑ CONJ where

adondequiera ADV wherever

Adonis SM Adonis; **es un ~** he's gorgeous*

adopción SF [1] [*de niño*] adoption [2] [*de medidas, decisiones*] **es necesaria la ~ de medidas contra la crisis** we need to take *o* adopt measures against the crisis; **consiguió la ~ de un acuerdo** he managed to get an agreement adopted [3] [*de nacionalidad*] adoption, taking; **es español de ~** he's Spanish by adoption

adoptado/a Ⓐ ADJ adopted Ⓑ SM/F adopted child

adoptar ▸conjug 1a◂ VT [1] [+ *niño*] to adopt; **lo adoptó como hijo** she adopted him as her son [2] (= *tomar*) [+ *medida, decisión, postura, actitud*] to take; [+ *papel*] to take on; **~ una postura crítica frente al gobierno** to take a critical stance towards the government; **han adoptado el papel de víctimas** they have taken on the role of victims; **en la reunión no se adoptó ningún acuerdo concreto** nothing definite was agreed on in the meeting [3] [+ *postura física*] **durante el sueño adopta una mala postura** he sleeps in a bad position; **deberías ~ una postura mejor al sentarte** you should sit better *o* with a better posture; **adoptó una postura provocativa con el cigarrillo** she struck a provocative pose with her cigarette [4] (= *empezar a usar*) [+ *nombre, nacionalidad*] to take, adopt; [+ *costumbres*] to adopt; [+ *sistema*] to adopt, introduce

adoptivo ADJ [*padres*] adoptive; [*hijo*] adopted; **patria adoptiva** country of adoption; **hijo ~ de la ciudad** honorary citizen

adoquín SM [1] (*para pavimentar*) paving stone, flagstone, cobble [2] (*) (= *tonto*) idiot, clod

adoquinado SM paving, cobbles, flagstones

adoquinar ▸conjug 1a◂ VT to pave, cobble

adorable ADJ adorable

adoración SF adoration, worship; **una mirada llena de ~** an adoring look ► **Adoración de los Reyes** Epiphany

➤ LENGUA Y USO: **admiración 1** 40.4 **admitir 4** 45.2

adorador ADJ adoring

adorar ▸conjug 1a◂ VT to adore, worship

adormecedor ADJ (= *soporífero*) that sends one to sleep, soporific; [*droga*] sedative; [*música, tono*] lulling, dreamy

adormecer ▸conjug 2d◂ Ⓐ VT (= *dar sueño*) to make sleepy, send to sleep; (= *sosegar*) to calm, lull
Ⓑ **adormecerse** VPR [1] (= *amodorrarse*) to become sleepy, become drowsy; (= *dormirse*) to fall asleep, go to sleep; [*pierna, mano*] to go numb
[2] **~se en** (*fig*) to persist in

adormecido ADJ [*persona*] sleepy, drowsy; (= *aletargado*) inactive; [*miembro*] numb

adormecimiento SM (= *somnolencia*) sleepiness, drowsiness; [*de un miembro*] numbness

adormidera SF poppy

adormilarse ▸conjug 1a◂ VPR, **adormitarse** ▸conjug 1a◂ VPR to doze

adornar ▸conjug 1a◂ VT [1] (= *decorar*) to adorn, decorate (**de** with); (*Cos*) to trim (**de** with); (*Culin*) to garnish (**de** with)
[2] [+ *persona*] (= *dotar*) to endow, bless (**de** with); **le adornan mil virtudes** he is blessed with every virtue

adornista SMF decorator

adorno SM [1] (= *objeto*) ornament; **una casa llena de ~s** a house full of ornaments ► **adornos de navidad** Christmas decorations
[2] (= *decoración*) ornamentation, adornment; **un estilo literario sin ~ superfluo** a literary style with no superfluous ornamentation *o* adornment; **de ~** decorative; **macetas de ~** decorative plant pots; **no se puede comer, está de ~** you can't eat it, it's just for decoration; **no funciona, está** *o* **es de ~** it doesn't work, it's just for show
[3] (*Cos*) trim, trimming
[4] (*Culin*) garnish

adosado Ⓐ ADJ **casa adosada** ◊ **chalet ~** semi-detached house, duplex (*EEUU*)
Ⓑ SM semi-detached house

adosar ▸conjug 1a◂ VT [1] **~ algo a una pared** to lean sth against a wall, place sth with its back against a wall
[2] (*LAm*) (= *juntar*) to join firmly; (= *adjuntar*) to attach, enclose (*with a letter*)

adquirido ADJ **mal ~** ill-gotten

adquiriente SMF purchaser

adquirir ▸conjug 3i◂ VT [1] (= *comprar*) [+ *vivienda, billete*] to purchase; (*Fin*) [+ *derechos, acciones, empresa*] to acquire, purchase; **pueden ~se en cualquier tienda especializada** they are available in any specialist shop
[2] (= *conseguir*) [+ *cultura, conocimientos, dinero*] to acquire; [+ *fama*] to gain, achieve; **viajando adquirió una gran experiencia** she gained great experience travelling; **ha adquirido renombre con una biografía de Stalin** he became renowned for his biography of Stalin
[3] (= *adoptar*) [+ *costumbre*] to adopt; [+ *carácter, identidad*] to take on, acquire; [+ *nacionalidad*] to acquire, obtain; [+ *compromiso*] to undertake; [+ *color*] to take on; **adquirieron las costumbres locales** they adopted the local customs; **el problema adquirió proporciones de crisis** the problem took on *o* acquired crisis proportions; **la palabra "enchufe" adquirió el sentido que todos conocemos** the word "enchufe" took on *o* acquired the sense we are all familiar with; **deberían cumplir los compromisos adquiridos** they should fulfill the commitments they have undertaken; **el cielo adquirió un color rosado** the sky took on a pinkish colour; **el partido comenzó a ~ importancia** the party began to grow in importance; **hay que impedir que esas ideas adquieran fuerza** we have to prevent these ideas gaining a hold

adquisición SF [1] (= *compra*) acquisition, purchase; **he hecho unas nuevas adquisiciones** I've made some new acquisitions *o* purchases; **una casa de reciente ~** a newly-purchased house; *ver tb* **oferta**
[2] (= *artículo comprado*) acquisition; **una de las mejores adquisiciones del museo** one of the museum's finest acquisitions; **este televisor ha sido una buena ~** the television has been a good buy
[3] (= *persona*) acquisition; **la última ~ del Atlético** Atlético's latest signing *o* acquisition; **la cocinera ha sido una auténtica ~*** the cook is a real find*
[4] [*de conocimientos, datos*] acquisition; **problemas en la ~ de un idioma extranjero** problems in foreign language acquisition
[5] [*de costumbres*] adoption

adquisidor(a) SM/F buyer, purchaser

adquisitivo ADJ acquisitive; **poder ~** ◊ **valor ~** purchasing power

adquisividad SF acquisitiveness

adral SM rail, sideboard (*of a cart etc*)

adrede ADV on purpose, deliberately

adredemente ADV (*LAm*) = **adrede**

adrenalina SF adrenalin

Adriano SM Hadrian

Adriático SM **(Mar) ~** Adriatic (Sea)

adscribir ▸conjug 3a◂ (*pp* **adscrito**) VT **~ a** to appoint to, assign to; **estuvo adscrito al servicio de ...** he was attached to ...

aduana SF [1] (= *institución*) customs; (= *oficina*) customs house; (= *impuesto*) customs duty; **derecho de ~** customs duty; **libre de ~** duty-free; **pasar por la ~** to go through customs
[2] (‡) (= *escondite*) pad‡, hide-out; (= *refugio*) safe house; (*Méx*) (= *burdel*) brothel

aduanal ADJ customs *antes de s*

aduanero/a Ⓐ ADJ customs *antes de s*
Ⓑ SM/F customs officer

aducir ▸conjug 3n◂ VT (= *alegar*) to adduce, offer as proof; [+ *prueba*] to provide, furnish

adueñarse ▸conjug 1a◂ VPR **~ de** (= *apropiarse*) to take possession of; (*fig*) to master

adujar ▸conjug 1a◂ VT to coil

adulación SF flattery, adulation

adulada* SF (*Méx*) flattery

adulador(a) Ⓐ ADJ flattering, fawning
Ⓑ SM/F flatterer

adular ▸conjug 1a◂ VT to flatter

adulate ADJ, SM (*LAm*) = **adulón**

adulón/ona* Ⓐ ADJ fawning
Ⓑ SM/F toady, creep*, brown-nose (*EEUU*‡)

adulonería SF flattering, fawning

adulteración SF adulteration

adulterado ADJ adulterated

adulterar ▸conjug 1a◂ Ⓐ VT (= *viciar*) to adulterate
Ⓑ VI (= *cometer adulterio*) to commit adultery

adulterino ADJ (*gen*) adulterous; [*moneda*] spurious, counterfeit

adulterio SM adultery

adúltero/a Ⓐ ADJ adulterous
Ⓑ SM/F adulterer/adulteress

adultez SF adulthood

adulto/a ADJ, SM/F adult, grown-up

adunar ▸conjug 1a◂ VT (*liter*) to join, unite

adunco ADJ bent, curved

adustez SF harshness, severity

adusto ADJ [1] (= *desabrido*) harsh, severe
[2] (= *inexorable*) grim, stern
[3] (= *hosco*) sullen
[4] (= *caliente*) scorching hot

advenedizo/a Ⓐ ADJ (= *del extranjero*) foreign, from outside
Ⓑ SM/F (= *forastero*) foreigner, outsider; (*pey*) (= *arribista*) upstart; (*LAm*) (= *novato*) novice

advenimiento SM advent, arrival ► **advenimiento al trono** accession to the throne

adventicio ADJ adventitious

adverbial ADJ adverbial; **locución ~** ◊ **oración ~** adverbial phrase

adverbialización SF adverbialization

adverbialmente ADV adverbially

adverbio SM adverb

adversario/a Ⓐ ADJ opposing, rival
Ⓑ SM/F adversary, opponent

adversativo ADJ adversative

adversidad SF (= *problemas*) adversity; (= *revés*) setback, mishap

adverso ADJ [*lado*] opposite, facing; [*resultado etc*] adverse; [*suerte*] bad

▼**advertencia** SF [1] (= *aviso*) warning; **hizo caso omiso de mis ~s** he ignored my warnings; **un disparo de ~** a warning shot; **hacer una ~** to give a warning; **espero que esto os sirva de ~** let this be a warning to you; ✦*REFRÁN* **sobre ~ no hay engaño** forewarned is forearmed
[2] (= *consejo*) **hacer una ~** to give some advice, give a piece of advice; **una ~: conviene llevar ropa de abrigo** a word of advice: take warm clothes with you
[3] (= *prefacio*) preface, foreword

advertido ADJ sharp

advertimiento SM = **advertencia**

▼**advertir** ▸conjug 3i◂ Ⓐ VT [1] (= *avisar*) to warn; **es la última vez que te lo advierto** that's the last time I'm going to warn you; **estás advertido** you have been warned; **~ a algn de algo** to warn sb about sth; **~ a algn que haga algo** to warn sb to do sth; **nos advirtió que no nos fiáramos de él** she warned us not to trust him; **te advierto que es la última vez que tolero que me insultes** I'm warning you that's the last time I'll allow you to insult me; **sí, iré, pero te advierto que tengo que estar de vuelta en casa pronto** yes, I'll go, but remember that I have to be back home early; **te advierto que no pienso ir** I have to let you know that I'm not going; **te advierto que tal vez habría sido mejor que no lo hubiera sabido** mind you, perhaps it would have been better if she hadn't found it
[2] (= *aconsejar*) to advise, tell; **adviértele**

➤ LENGUA Y USO: **advertencia** 29.3 **advertir A1** 29.3

que se lleve el paraguas advise *o* tell him to take his umbrella; **ya les advertí que si había algún problema me lo dijeran** I already told them to let me know if there were any problems
[3] (= *notar*) [+ *olor, error*] to notice; **advertí en él un extraño comportamiento** I noticed some strange behaviour on his part; **el perro advirtió nuestra presencia** the dog noticed us; **en sus últimas obras se advierten una serie de cambios** one can see *o* observe some changes in her latest works; **~ que** to notice that; **¿ha advertido que su coche pierde aceite?** have you noticed that your car's leaking oil?; **advertimos que ya no corríamos peligro** we realised that we were no longer in danger
(B) VI **~ de** *o* **sobre algo** to warn of sth; **las señales advertían del peligro** the signs warned of danger
Adviento SM Advent
advocación SF (*Rel*) name, dedication; **una iglesia bajo la ~ de San Felipe** a church dedicated to St Philip
advocar ▸conjug 1g◂ VT (*LAm*) to advocate
ADVP (A) ADJ ABR (= **adicto a drogas por vía parenteral**) *who uses drugs intravenously*
(B) SM ABR IV drug user
adyacencia SF nearness, proximity; **en las ~s** in the vicinity
adyacente ADJ adjacent
AEDAVE SF ABR (= **Asociación Empresarial de Agencias de Viajes Españoles**) ≈ ABTA
AEE SF ABR (= **Agencia Europea del Espacio**) ESA
aeración SF aeration
aéreo ADJ (*Fot*) aerial; [*tráfico*] air; (*Ferro*) overhead, elevated
aero... PREF aero...
aerobic SM aerobics
aeróbico ADJ aerobic
aerobismo SM (*Cono Sur*) aerobics
aerobús SM [1] (*Aer*) airbus
[2] (*Caribe*) long-distance bus, coach, bus (*EEUU*)
aeroclub SM flying club
aerodeslizador SM, **aerodeslizante** SM hovercraft
aerodinámica SF aerodynamics *sing*
aerodinámico ADJ (*Fís*) aerodynamic; [*forma*] streamlined
aerodinamismo SM streamlining
aerodinamizar ▸conjug 1f◂ VT to streamline
aeródromo SM aerodrome, airdrome (*EEUU*)
aeroenviar ▸conjug 1c◂ VT to send by air
aeroescuela SF flying school
aeroespacial ADJ aerospace *antes de s*
aeroestación SF air terminal
aerofaro SM beacon
aerofobia SF fear of flying
aerofoto SF aerial photograph
aerofotográfico ADJ aerial photographic
aerofumigación SF crop dusting
aerogenerador SM wind turbine
aerografía SF spray painting, airbrushing
aerografiado (A) ADJ spray-painted, airbrushed
(B) SM spray painting, airbrushing
aerografista SMF spray paint artist
aerógrafo SM airbrush
aerograma SM aerogram, airmail letter
aeroligero SM microlight
aerolínea SF airline
aerolito SM meteorite
aeromodelismo SM aeromodelling, making model aeroplanes
aeromodelista SMF model aeroplane enthusiast
aeromodelístico ADJ model aeroplane *antes de s*
aeromodelo SM model aeroplane
aeromotor SM aero-engine
aeromozo/a SM/F (*LAm*) steward/stewardess, air steward/stewardess, flight attendant (*EEUU*)
aeronauta SMF aeronaut
aeronáutica SF aeronautics *sing*
aeronáutico ADJ aeronautical
aeronaval ADJ air-sea *antes de s*; **base ~** air-sea base
aeronave SF airship ► **aeronave espacial** spaceship
aeronavegabilidad SF airworthiness
aeronavegable ADJ airworthy
aeroparque SM (*Arg*) small airport
aeroplano SM aeroplane, airplane (*EEUU*)
aeroportuario ADJ airport *antes de s*
aeroposta SF (*LAm*) airmail
aeropuerto SM airport ► **aeropuerto de escala, aeropuerto de paso** stopover airport
aerosol SM aerosol
aerostática SF ballooning
aeróstato SM balloon, aerostat
aerotaxi SM air taxi
aeroterrestre ADJ air-ground *antes de s*
aerotransportado ADJ airborne
aerotransporte SM air transport
aerotransportista SM carrier, air carrier
aeroturbina SF wind turbine
aerovía SF (= *ruta*) airway; (= *compañía*) airline
AES SM ABR (*Econ*) (= **Acuerdo Económico Social**) *wages pact*
a/f ABR = **a favor**
afabilidad SF affability, geniality
afable ADJ affable, genial
afablemente ADV affably, genially
afamado ADJ famous, noted (**por** for)
afamar ▸conjug 1a◂ (A) VT to make famous
(B) **afamarse** VPR to become famous, make a reputation
afán SM [1] (= *deseo*) eagerness; **en su ~ de marcar un gol** in his eagerness to score a goal; **con ~ de**: **con ~ de agradar, repartió regalos para todos** in his eagerness to please he gave everyone presents; **por ~ de**: **lo hizo por ~ de superarse** she did out of a desire to better herself; **lo hicieron por ~ de ganar tiempo** they did it in a bid to gain time; **tener ~ de algo** to be eager for sth ► **afán de conocimiento** thirst for knowledge ► **afán de lucro**: **el ~ de lucro** the profit motive; **actuaron sin ~ de lucro** they didn't do it to make money ► **afán de protagonismo**: **un juez con ~ de protagonismo** a judge who loves publicity *o* always wants to be in the limelight; **tu hermano tiene mucho ~ de protagonismo** your brother always wants to be the centre of attention ► **afán de superación** desire to better oneself ► **afán de venganza** thirst for revenge ► **afán de victoria** will to win, desire to win
[2] (= *ahínco*) **hacer algo con ~** to do sth eagerly; **rebuscó con ~ en los archivos** he searched eagerly through the files
[3] (*frm*) (= *intención*) **una obra con ~ didáctico** an educational work; **sin ~ efectista** with no desire for dramatic effect
[4] (*LAm*) (= *prisa*) hurry; **tengo muchísimo ~** I'm in a tearing hurry; **ir con ~** to be in a hurry
afanador(a) SM/F (= *ladrón*) thief; (*Méx*) (= *obrero*) menial worker; [*de limpieza*] cleaner
afanaduría SF (*Méx*) casualty ward
afanar ▸conjug 1a◂ (A) VT [1] (*) (= *birlar*) to pinch*, swipe*
[2] (*CAm*) [+ *dinero*] to earn, make
[3] (= *acosar*) to press, harass, bother; (*LAm*) (= *empujar*) to hustle
(B) **afanarse** VPR [1] (= *trabajar*) to toil, labour, labor (*EEUU*) (**en** at); **~se por hacer algo** to strive to do sth
[2] (*Andes*) (= *enfadarse*) to get angry
afanosamente ADV (= *con esmero*) diligently; (= *apasionadamente*) feverishly
afanoso ADJ [1] [*trabajo*] hard, heavy
[2] (= *concienzudo*) [*temperamento*] industrious; [*actividad, búsqueda*] feverish, hectic
afantasmado ADJ conceited
afarolado ADJ (*LAm*) (= *emocionado*) excited, worked up
afarolarse ▸conjug 1a◂ VPR (*LAm*) (= *emocionarse*) to get excited, get worked up
afasia SF aphasia
afásico ADJ (*Psic*) aphasic; (= *mudo*) mute, dumb
AFE SF ABR (= **Asociación de Futbolistas Españoles**) ≈ FA, ≈ SFA
afeamiento SM [1] (*físicamente*) defacing, disfigurement
[2] (= *censura*) condemnation, censure
afear ▸conjug 1a◂ VT [1] (= *hacer feo*) to make ugly, disfigure; **los errores que afean el texto** the mistakes which disfigure the text
[2] (= *censurar*) to condemn, censure
afección SF [1] (= *cariño*) affection, fondness; (= *inclinación*) inclination; **afecciones del alma** emotions
[2] (*Med*) trouble, disease ► **afección cardíaca** heart trouble ► **afección hepática** liver complaint ► **afección lumbar** back trouble
afeccionarse ▸conjug 1a◂ VPR (*Cono Sur*) **~ a** to take a liking to, become fond of
afectación SF affectation
afectadamente ADV affectedly
afectado ADJ [1] (= *forzado*) [*acento, persona*] affected; [*estilo*] stilted, precious
[2] (*Med*) (= *aquejado*) **estar ~ del corazón** to have heart trouble; **estar ~** (*Méx*) to be consumptive; (*Cono Sur*) to be hurt
afectante ADJ (*Cono Sur*) disturbing, distressing
afectar ▸conjug 1a◂ (A) VT [1] (= *repercutir sobre*) to affect; **el paro afecta especialmente a los jóvenes** unemployment affects young people in particular; **la falta de oxígeno afecta al cerebro** lack of oxygen affects the brain; **por lo que afecta al tema de la**

contaminación as far as the question of pollution is concerned

2 (= *entristecer*) to sadden; (= *conmover*) to move; **su muerte nos afectó mucho** we were terribly saddened by his death; **me ~on mucho las imágenes del documental** I was very moved by the pictures in the documentary

3 (*frm*) (= *fingir*) to affect, feign; **~ ignorancia** to affect *o* feign ignorance

4 (*Jur*) to tie up, encumber

5 (*LAm*) [+ *forma*] to take, assume

6 (*LAm*) (= *destinar*) to allocate

Ⓑ **afectarse** VPR (*LAm*) (= *enfermar*) to fall ill

afectísimo ADJ affectionate; **suyo ~** yours truly

afectividad SF emotional nature, emotion; **falta de ~** (*en persona*) unemotional nature; (*en relación*) lack of emotion

afectivo ADJ affective

afecto Ⓐ ADJ 1 (= *apegado*) affectionate; **~ a** attached to

2 **~ a** (*Jur*) (= *sujeto*) subject to, liable for

3 **~ de** (*Med*) afflicted with

Ⓑ SM 1 (= *cariño*) affection, fondness (**a** for); **tomar ~ a algn** to become attached to sb

2 (= *emoción*) feeling, emotion

afectuosamente ADV affectionately; (*en carta*) yours affectionately

afectuosidad SF affection

afectuoso ADJ affectionate

afeitada SF = **afeitado 1**

afeitado SM 1 [*de barba*] shave

2 (*Taur*) blunting of the horns, trimming of the horns

afeitadora SF electric razor, electric shaver

afeitar ▸conjug 1a◂ Ⓐ VT 1 (= *rasurar*) to shave; [+ *cola, planta*] to trim; (*Taur*) [+ *cuernos*] to blunt, trim; [+ *toro*] to blunt the horns of, trim the horns of; **¡que te afeiten!*** get your head seen to!*

2 (*) (= *pasar*) to brush, brush past, shave

3 (= *maquillar*) to make up, paint, apply cosmetics to

Ⓑ **afeitarse** VPR 1 (= *rasurarse*) to shave, have a shave

2 (= *maquillarse*) to make o.s. up, put one's make-up on

afeite SM make-up, cosmetic, cosmetics *pl*

afelpado ADJ plush, velvety

afeminación SF effeminacy

afeminado Ⓐ ADJ effeminate

Ⓑ SM effeminate man, poof*, fag (*EEUU**)

afeminamiento SM effeminacy

afeminarse ▸conjug 1a◂ VPR to become effeminate

aferrado ADJ stubborn; **seguir ~ a** to stick to, stand by

aferrar ▸conjug 1j◂ Ⓐ VT 1 (= *asir*) to grasp, seize

2 (*Náut*) [+ *barco*] to moor; [+ *vela*] furl

Ⓑ **aferrarse** VPR 1 (= *agarrarse*) to cling, hang on

2 **~se a** *o* **en** (= *obstinarse en*) to stick to, stand by; **~se a un principio** to stick to a principle; **~se a una esperanza** to cling to a hope; **~se a su opinión** to remain firm in one's opinion

3 (*Náut*) [*barco*] to anchor, moor

afestonado ADJ festooned

affaire SM (SF *en Cono Sur*) affair, affaire

affidávit SM affidavit, sworn statement

affmo./a ABR = **afectísimo/a**

Afganistán SM Afghanistan

afgano/a ADJ, SM/F Afghan

afianzado/a SM/F (*LAm*) (= *novio*) fiancé; (= *novia*) fiancée

afianzamiento SM 1 (*Téc*) strengthening, securing

2 (*Fin*) guarantee, security

3 (*Jur*) surety, bond

afianzar ▸conjug 1f◂ Ⓐ VT 1 (= *reforzar*) to strengthen, secure; (= *sostener*) to support, prop up; (*fig*) (= *apoyar*) to support, back

2 (*Com*) (= *avalar*) to guarantee, vouch for; (= *ser fiador*) to stand surety for

Ⓑ **afianzarse** VPR (= *sostenerse*) to steady o.s.; (*fig*) (= *establecerse*) to become strong, become established; **~se a** to catch hold of; **la reacción se afianzó después de la guerra** the reaction set in after the war

afiche SM (*esp LAm*) poster

afición SF 1 (= *apego*) fondness, liking (**a** for); (= *inclinación*) inclination (**a** towards); **cobrar ~ a** ◊ **tomar ~ a** to take a liking to; **tener ~ a** to like, be fond of

2 (= *pasatiempo*) hobby, pastime; **¿qué aficiones tiene?** what are his interests?; **pinta por ~** he paints as a hobby

3 **la ~** (*Dep*) the fans; **aquí hay una gran ~** support is strong here

aficionado/a Ⓐ ADJ 1 (= *entusiasta*) keen, enthusiastic; **es muy ~** he's very keen; **es muy aficionada a la pintura** she's very keen on painting

2 (= *no profesional*) amateur; **un equipo de fútbol ~** an amateur football team

Ⓑ SM/F 1 (= *entusiasta*) (*de hobby*) enthusiast; (*como espectador*) lover; **un libro para los ~s al bricolaje** a book for DIY enthusiasts; **los ~s al teatro** theatre lovers; **todos los ~s a la música** all music lovers

2 (= *no profesional*) amateur; **tenis para ~s** amateur tennis; **partido de ~s** amateur game; **función de ~s** amateur performance; **somos simples ~s** we're just amateurs

3 [*de equipo, grupo*] fan, supporter; **gritaban los ~s** the fans were shouting

aficionar ▸conjug 1a◂ Ⓐ VT **~ a algn a algo** to interest sb in sth

Ⓑ **aficionarse** VPR **~se a algo** to get fond of sth, take a liking to sth

afidávit SM affidavit, sworn statement

áfido SM aphid

afiebrado ADJ feverish

afijo SM affix

afiladera SF grindstone, whetstone

afilado ADJ [*borde*] sharp; [*punta*] tapering, sharp

afilador SM (= *persona*) knife-grinder; (*Téc*) steel sharpener; (= *correa*) razor strop ► **afilador de lápices** pencil sharpener

afiladura SF sharpening

afilalápices SM INV pencil sharpener

afilar ▸conjug 1a◂ Ⓐ VT 1 [+ *herramienta*] (= *hacer más cortante*) to sharpen, put an edge on; (= *sacar punta*) to put a point on; [+ *cuchillo*] to whet, grind; [+ *navaja*] to strop

2 (*Cono Sur*) (= *flirtear*) to flatter, court; (*Chile***) (= *joder*) to fuck**, screw**

Ⓑ **afilarse** VPR 1 [*cara*] to sharpen, grow thin; [*dedos*] to taper

2 (*LAm*) (= *prepararse*) to get ready

afiliación SF (*Pol*) affiliation; [*de sindicatos*] membership

afiliado/a Ⓐ ADJ affiliated (**a** to), member *antes de s*; (*Com*) subsidiary; **los países ~s** the member countries

Ⓑ SM/F member

afiliarse ▸conjug 1b◂ VPR **~ a** to affiliate to, join

afiligranado ADJ 1 (*Cos*) filigreed

2 (= *delicado*) delicate, fine; [*persona*] dainty

afilón SM (= *correa*) strop; (= *chaira*) steel

afilorar ▸conjug 1a◂ VT (*Caribe*) to adorn

afín Ⓐ ADJ 1 (= *lindante*) bordering, adjacent

2 (= *relacionado*) similar; [*persona*] related

Ⓑ SMF (= *pariente*) relation by marriage

afinación SF 1 (*Mús*) tuning

2 (*Aut*) tuning(-up)

3 (= *perfeccionamiento*) refining, polishing; (= *fin*) completion

afinado ADJ 1 (*Mús*) in tune

2 (= *acabado*) finished, polished

afinador(a) Ⓐ SM (*Mús*) tuning key

Ⓑ SM/F (= *persona*) tuner ► **afinador(a) de pianos** piano tuner

afinar ▸conjug 1a◂ Ⓐ VT 1 (*Mús*) to tune

2 (*Aut*) to tune up

3 (= *perfeccionar*) to put the finishing touch to, complete; (= *pulir*) to polish; (*Téc*) to purify, refine; [+ *puntería*] to sharpen, make more precise

Ⓑ VI to sing in tune, play in tune

Ⓒ **afinarse** VPR (= *pulirse*) to become polished

afincado/a Ⓐ ADJ settled

Ⓑ SM/F (*Cono Sur*) landowner

afincarse ▸conjug 1g◂ VPR [*persona*] to settle; [*creencia*] to take root

afinidad SF 1 (= *atracción*) affinity; (= *semejanza*) similarity; (= *parentesco*) relationship; **parentesco por ~** relationship by marriage

2 (*Quím*) affinity

▼ **afirmación** SF affirmation

afirmado SM (*Aut*) road surface; (*Cono Sur*) (= *acera*) paving, paved surface

▼ **afirmar** ▸conjug 1a◂ Ⓐ VT 1 (= *reforzar*) to make secure, strengthen

2 (= *declarar*) to assert, state; [+ *lealtad*] to declare, protest; **~ que** to affirm that; **~ bajo juramento** to swear under oath

3 (*LAm*) [+ *golpe*] to deal, give

Ⓑ **afirmarse** VPR 1 (= *recobrar el equilibrio*) to steady o.s.; **~se en los estribos** (= *sujetarse*) to settle one's feet firmly in the stirrups; (*Cono Sur*) (= *aguantarse*) to grit one's teeth

2 **~se en lo dicho** to stand by what one has said

afirmativa SF affirmative answer, yes*

afirmativamente ADV affirmatively; **contestar ~** to answer in the affirmative

afirmativo ADJ affirmative, positive; **en caso ~** if that is the case; **voto ~** vote in favour, vote for

aflatarse ▸conjug 1a◂ VPR (*LAm*) to be sad

aflautado ADJ high, fluty

aflicción SF affliction, sorrow

aflictivo ADJ distressing

afligente ADJ (*CAm, Méx*) distressing, upsetting

afligido Ⓐ ADJ 1 (= *apenado*) grieving, heartbroken; **los ~s padres** the bereaved parents

➤ LENGUA Y USO: **afirmación** 53.6 **afirmar A2** 53.1, 53.3, 53.5

2 (*Med*) ~ **por** stricken with
Ⓑ SM **los ~s** (*que padecen*) the afflicted; (*por deceso*) the bereaved

afligir ▸conjug 3c◂ Ⓐ VT 1 (= *afectar*) to afflict; (= *apenar*) to pain, distress
2 (*LAm*) (= *golpear*) to beat, hit
Ⓑ **afligirse** VPR to get upset; **no te aflijas** don't get upset, don't upset yourself (over it); **no te aflijas tanto** you must not let it affect you like this, don't get so worked up*

aflojamiento SM (= *acto*) loosening, slackening; [*de esfuerzo, presión*] weakening

aflojar ▸conjug 1a◂ Ⓐ VT 1 (= *dejar suelto*) [+ *corbata, cinturón, nudo*] to loosen; [+ *tuerca, rosca*] to slacken, loosen; [+ *disciplina, restricción, política, presión*] to relax; **se sentó y se aflojó (el nudo de) la corbata** he sat down and loosened (the knot in) his tie
2 (= *relajar*) [+ *cuerda*] to slacken; [+ *músculo*] to relax
3 (= *ralentizar*) **caminamos sin ~ el paso** *o* **la marcha** *o* **el ritmo** we walked without slackening our pace *o* without slowing down; **nuevas medidas para ~ la marcha de la economía** new measures to slow down the economy
4 (*) [+ *vientre*] to loosen
5 (*) [+ *dinero*] to fork out*, cough up*
Ⓑ VI 1 (*Meteo*) [*viento*] to drop; [*lluvia*] to ease off; [*calor*] to let up
2 [*fiebre*] to subside; [*tensión*] to ease, subside
3 [*ventas*] to tail off; **el negocio afloja en agosto** business slows down *o* eases up in August
4 (*al andar, correr, competir*) to ease up, let up; **no aflojó hasta conseguir la victoria** he did not ease up *o* let up until he won
Ⓒ **aflojarse** VPR 1 [*algo apretado, cinturón, corbata*] to loosen; [*nudo, tuerca, rosca*] to come *o* work loose
2 [*algo tenso, cuerda*] to slacken
3 [*fiebre, interés*] to subside
4 (*Caribe***) (= *ensuciarse*) to shit o.s.**

afloración SF outcrop

aflorado ADJ fine, elegant

afloramiento SM = **afloración**

aflorar ▸conjug 1a◂ VI (*Geol*) to crop out, outcrop; (= *surgir*) to come to the surface, emerge

afluencia SF 1 (= *aflujo*) influx; **la ~ de turistas** the influx of tourists; **la ~ de capital extranjero** the influx of foreign capital; **hubo gran ~ de público** there was a good turnout; **la ~ a las urnas fue escasa** there was a low turnout at the polls
2 (*frm*) (= *elocuencia*) eloquence, fluency

afluente Ⓐ ADJ 1 [*agua, líquido*] inflowing
2 [*discurso*] eloquent, fluent
Ⓑ SM (*Geog*) tributary

afluir ▸conjug 3g◂ VI [*agua, líquido*] to flow (**a** into); [*gente*] to flock (**a** into, to)

aflujo SM (*Med*) afflux, congestion; (*Mec*) inflow, inlet

aflús* ADJ (*LAm*) broke*, flat (*EEUU**)

afluxionarse ▸conjug 1a◂ VPR (*LAm*) to catch a cold

afmo./a ABR = **afectísimo/a**

afoetear†† ▸conjug 1a◂ VT (*Andes, Caribe*) to whip, beat

afonía SF loss of voice, aphonia

afónico ADJ 1 (= *sin voz*) voiceless; (= *ronco*) hoarse; **estar ~** to have lost one's voice
2 [*letra*] silent, mute

aforado/a Ⓐ ADJ [*provincia, territorio*] *with a regional charter*; **persona aforada** *ver* **B**
Ⓑ SM/F *person with parliamentary immunity who can only be tried by the Supreme Court*

aforador SM gauger

aforar ▸conjug 1a◂ VT 1 (*Téc*) to gauge
2 (= *valorar*) to appraise, value

aforismo SM aphorism

aforístico ADJ aphoristic

aforjudo* ADJ (*Cono Sur*) silly, stupid

aforo SM 1 (*Téc*) gauging
2 (*Teat*) capacity; **el teatro tiene un ~ de 2.000** the theatre can seat 2,000
3 (= *valoración*) appraisal, valuation
4 (*Com*) import duty

aforrar ▸conjug 1a◂ Ⓐ VT 1 (= *forrar*) to line
2 (*Cono Sur**) (= *golpear*) to smack, punch
Ⓑ **aforrarse** VPR 1 (= *abrigarse*) to wrap up warm, put on warm underclothes
2 (*) (= *atiborrarse*) to stuff o.s.*, tuck it away*

afortunadamente ADV fortunately, luckily

afortunado ADJ (= *con suerte*) fortunate, lucky; (= *feliz*) happy; **poco ~** unsuccessful; **un comentario poco ~** a rather inappropriate comment

AFP SF ABR (= **alfa-fetoproteína**) AFP, afp

afrailado* ADJ (*LAm*) churchy*

afrancesado/a Ⓐ ADJ (*pey*) (= *que imita lo francés*) frenchified; (*Pol*) pro-French, supporting the French
Ⓑ SM/F (*pey*) (= *imitador de lo francés*) frenchified person; (*Pol*) pro-French person

afrancesamiento SM (= *sentimiento*) francophilism, pro-French feeling; (= *proceso*) gallicization, frenchification (*pey*)

afrancesarse ▸conjug 1a◂ VPR (= *asemejarse a lo francés*) to go French, become gallicized, acquire French habits; (*Pol*) to become a francophile

afrechillo SM (*Cono Sur*) bran

afrecho SM (= *salvado*) bran; (*LAm*) (= *serrín*) sawdust ▸ **afrecho remojado** mash

afrenta SF affront, insult

afrentar ▸conjug 1a◂ Ⓐ VT (= *insultar*) to affront, insult; (= *desacreditar*) to dishonour, dishonor (*EEUU*) Ⓑ **afrentarse** VPR (= *avergonzarse*) to be ashamed (**de** of)

afrentoso ADJ (= *insultante*) insulting, outrageous; (= *vergonzoso*) shameful

África SF Africa ▸ **África Austral** Southern Africa ▸ **África del Norte** North Africa ▸ **África del Sur** South Africa ▸ **África negra** Black Africa

africaans SM Afrikaans

africado ADJ affricate

africanidad SF Africanness

africanista SMF (= *experto*) specialist in African affairs; (= *aficionado*) person interested in Africa

africano/a ADJ, SM/F African

afrijolar ▸conjug 1a◂ VT (*Andes*) to bother, annoy; **~ una tarea a algn** to give sb an unpleasant job to do

afrikaner ADJ, SMF (*pl* **afrikaners**) Afrikaner

afro ADJ Afro; **peinado ~** Afro hairstyle

afroamericano ADJ Afro-American

afroasiático ADJ Afro-Asian

afrobrasileño ADJ Afro-Brazilian

afrocaribeño ADJ Afro-Caribbean

afrocubano ADJ Afro-Cuban

afrodisíaco ADJ, SM, **afrodisiaco** ADJ, SM aphrodisiac

Afrodita SF Aphrodite

afronegrismo SM (*LAm*) *word borrowed from an African language*

afrontamiento SM confrontation

afrontar ▸conjug 1a◂ VT 1 [+ *dos personas*] to bring face to face
2 [+ *peligro*] to confront, face up to; [+ *problema*] to deal with, tackle

afrutado ADJ fruity

afta SF (*Med*) sore

after ['after] SM (*pl* **afters** *o* **after**), **afterhours** [after'auars] SM INV after-hours club

aftershave SM INV, **after-shave** [after'ʃeif] SM INV aftershave

aftersun SM INV, **after sun** SM INV [after'san] aftersun

aftosa SF (*tb* **fiebre ~**) foot-and-mouth disease

afuera Ⓐ ADV (*esp LAm*) out, outside; **¡afuera!** out of the way!, get out!; **de ~** from outside; **por ~** on the outside; **las hojas de ~** the outer leaves, the outside leaves Ⓑ PREP **~ de** (*LAm*) outside Ⓒ **afueras** SFPL outskirts

afuerano/a (*Chile*), **afuereño/a** (*Chile*), **afuerino/a** (*Chile*) Ⓐ ADJ strange, outside
antes de s
Ⓑ SM/F [*de afuera*] outsider, stranger; (= *trabajador*) itinerant worker, casual worker

afuetear ▸conjug 1a◂ VT (*LAm*) to whip, beat

afufa‡ SF flight, escape; **tomar las ~s** to beat it*

afufar‡ ▸conjug 1a◂ VI, **afufarse** VPR to beat it*, get out quick

afufón‡ SM flight, escape

afusilar ▸conjug 1a◂ VT (*Méx*) to shoot

afutrarse ▸conjug 1a◂ VPR (*Cono Sur*) to dress up

ag. ABR (= **agosto**) Aug

agachada* SF trick, dodge*

agachadiza SF (= *ave*) snipe; **hacer la ~** to duck, try not to be seen

agachado/a* SM/F (*LAm*) down-and-out, bum (*EEUU**)

agachar ▸conjug 1a◂ Ⓐ VT [+ *cabeza*] to bend, bow; **~ las orejas*** to hang one's head
Ⓑ **agacharse** VPR 1 (= *agazaparse*) to stoop, bend down, bend over; (= *acuclillarse*) to squat; (= *bajar la cabeza*) to duck; (= *encogerse*) to cower
2 (*fig*) (= *esconderse*) to go into hiding, lie low
3 (*LAm*) (= *ceder*) to give in, submit
4 (*Méx*) (= *callarse*) **~se algo** to keep sth under one's hat
5 **~se con algo** (*Andes, Méx*) (= *robar*) to make off with sth, pocket sth
6 (*LAm*) (= *prepararse*) to get ready

agache SM (*Andes*) (= *embuste*) fib, tale; **andar de ~** to be on the run

agachón‡ ADJ (*LAm*) weak-willed, submissive

agafar‡ ▸conjug 1a◂ VT to pinch*, nick*

agalbanado ADJ lazy, shiftless

agalla SF 1 (*Bot*) gall ▸ **agalla de roble** oak apple
2 [*de pez*] gill

3 **agallas*** (= *valor*) pluck, guts*; **tener (muchas) ~s** to be brave, have guts*; **es hombre de ~s** he's got guts*
4 (*LAm*) **tener ~s** (= *ser glotón*) to be greedy; (= *ser tacaño*) to be mean; (= *ser descarado*) to have lots of cheek*
5 **tener ~s** (*Cono Sur*) (= *ser astuto*) to be sharp, be smart
6 **agallas** (= *amígdalas*) tonsils; (= *anginas*) tonsillitis

agalludo (*Cono Sur*) ADJ 1 (= *valiente*) daring, bold
2 (= *tacaño*) mean, stingy
3 (= *glotón*) greedy

Agamenón SM Agamemnon

ágape SM banquet, feast

agareno/a Ⓐ ADJ Moslem
Ⓑ SM/F Moslem

agarrada SF 1 (= *pelea*) scrap, brawl; (= *riña*) row, run-in*
2 (*Dep*) tackle

agarradera SF (*LAm*), **agarradero** SM 1 (= *asidero*) handle, grip; [*de cortina*] cord
2 (= *amparo*) protection
3 **agarraderas** (= *influencias*) pull *sing*, influence *sing*; **tener buenas ~s** to have friends in the right places

agarrado ADJ 1 mean, stingy
2 **baile ~** slow dance

agarrador ADJ (*Andes, Cono Sur*) strong

agarrafar ▸conjug 1a◂ VT to grab hold of

agarrao* SM slow dance

agarrar ▸conjug 1a◂ Ⓐ VT 1 (= *asir*) 1·1 (*sujetando*) to hold (on to); **agarra bien el bolso** hold on to your handbag firmly; **le señalaron falta por ~ a un jugador contrario** a free kick was given against him for holding on to one of the opposition; **lo tuvo bien agarrado hasta que llegó la policía** she held him until the police arrived; **entró agarrada del brazo de su padre** she came in holding her father's arm; **iban agarrados del brazo** they were walking arm in arm; **me agarró del brazo** he took me by the arm
1·2 (*con violencia*) to grab; **agarró al niño por el hombro** he grabbed the child by the shoulder; **la agarró de los pelos y no la soltaba** she grabbed her hair and refused to let her go
1·3 (*con fuerza*) to grip; **la agarró fuertemente del brazo** he gripped her arm tightly
2 (= *capturar*) to catch; **ya han agarrado al ladrón** they've already caught the thief
3 [+ *resfriado*] to catch; **he agarrado un buen resfriado** I've caught a nasty cold; **lo tiene bien agarrado al pecho** she's got a nasty chesty cough; ✦*MODISMO* **~la*** (= *emborracharse*) to get plastered*
4 (*) (= *conseguir*) to get, wangle*
5 (*esp LAm*) (= *coger*) **agarré otro pedazo de pastel** I took another piece of cake; **agarra el libro del estante** take the book off the shelf; **~ una flor** to pick a flower; **~ un tren** to catch a train; **la casa tiene tanto trabajo que no sé por dónde ~la** the house needs such a lot doing to it, I don't know where to start; **~ el vuelo** (= *despegar*) to take off
6 (*CAm, Caribe, Méx**) (= *captar*) to get*, understand
7 (*Cono Sur*) **~ a palos a algn*** to beat sb up*
8 (*Caribe***) to fuck**
Ⓑ VI 1 (= *asir*) **agarra por este extremo** hold it by this end, take hold of it by this end
2 (*Bot*) [*planta*] to take (root)
3 [*color*] to take
4 (*esp LAm*) (= *coger*) **agarre por esta calle** take this street; **agarró y se fue*** he upped and went*; **~ para** (= *salir*) to set out for
Ⓒ **agarrarse** VPR 1 (= *asirse*) to hold on; **¡agárrate bien!** hold (on) tight!; **~se a** *o* **de algo** to hold on to sth; **agárrate bien a la barandilla** hold on tight to the rail; **necesita algo adonde ~se** she needs something to hold on to; **me agarré al asiento con todas mis fuerzas** I held on to *o* gripped the seat with all my strength; **se ~on de los pelos** they tore at each other's hair; ✦*MODISMO* **¡agárrate!*** wait for it!, listen to this!; **pues ahora agárrate, porque lo que te voy a contar es mucho peor** I hope you're sitting down, because what I'm going to tell you now is much worse; **—¿sabes que le ha tocado la quiniela? —¡agárrate!** "did you know she won the pools?" — "never!"
2 (*Aut*) [*coche, neumático*] to hold the road; **este coche se agarra muy bien en las curvas** this car holds the road very well on bends; **estos neumáticos se agarran con fuerza al asfalto** these tyres have excellent grip
3 (*como excusa*) **~se a algo**: **se agarra a cualquier excusa** any (old) excuse will do him; **se agarra a su mala salud para conseguir lo que quiere** she uses her poor health as an excuse to get whatever she wants; **se agarró a que era el mayor para hacerse cargo de la expedición** he used the fact that he was the oldest to take charge of the expedition
4 (*) (= *cogerse*) **se agarró una buena borrachera** he got well and truly plastered*; **me agarré un cabreo tremendo** I got really narked*; **se agarró un buen berrinche cuando se enteró** she threw a tantrum *o* fit when she found out
5 (*esp LAm*) (= *pelear*) to have a fight; **se ~on a tiros** they started shooting at each other; **se ~on a puñetazos** they started hitting each other; **la tenía agarrada conmigo** he had it in for me*
6 (*Culin*) (= *pegarse*) to stick

agarre SM 1 (*LAm*) (= *agarro*) hold; (*Aut*) road-holding, road-holding quality
2 (*Andes*) (= *asidero*) handle
3 (= *valor*) guts* *pl*
4 **tener ~*** (= *tener influencia*) to have pull, be able to pull strings

agarrete ADJ (*Andes*) mean, stingy

agarro SM grasp, hold, clutch

agarroch(e)ar ▸conjug 1a◂ VT [+ *animal*] to jab with a goad; (*Taur*) to prick with a pike

agarrón SM 1 (= *tirón*) jerk, pull, tug
2 = **agarrada 1**

agarroso ADJ (*CAm*) sharp, acrid, bitter

agarrotamiento SM (= *apretón*) tightening; [*de músculos*] stiffening; (*Aut*) seizing up

agarrotar ▸conjug 1a◂ Ⓐ VT (= *atar*) to tie tight; [+ *persona*] to squeeze tight, press tightly; [+ *criminal*] to garrotte; [+ *músculos*] to stiffen; **esta corbata me agarrota** this tie is strangling me; **tengo los músculos agarrotados** I'm all stiff
Ⓑ **agarrotarse** VPR (*Med*) to stiffen, get numb; (*Aut*) to seize up

agasajado/a SM/F chief guest, guest of honour *o* (*EEUU*) honor

agasajador ADJ warm, welcoming

agasajamiento SM = **agasajo**

agasajar ▸conjug 1a◂ VT to entertain, fête

agasajo SM (= *acogida*) royal welcome; (= *regalo*) gift; **~s** hospitality

ágata SF agate

agatas ADV (*Cono Sur*) 1 (= *con dificultad*) with great difficulty, only with great difficulty
2 (= *apenas*) hardly, scarcely; **~ llegó, empezó a cantar** no sooner had he arrived than he started to sing

agauchado ADJ (*Cono Sur*) like a gaucho

agaucharse ▸conjug 1a◂ VPR (*Cono Sur*) *to imitate or dress like a gaucho*

agave SF agave, American aloe

agavilladora SF binder

agavillar ▸conjug 1a◂ Ⓐ VT [+ *trigo*] to bind, bind in sheaves; [+ *libro*] to bind
Ⓑ **agavillarse** VPR to gang up, band together

agazapar ▸conjug 1a◂ Ⓐ VT (*) to grab, grab hold of, nab*
Ⓑ **agazaparse** VPR (= *ocultarse*) to hide; (= *agacharse*) to crouch down, squat; **estaba agazapada tras las rocas** she was hidden behind the rocks; **tras esto se agazapa otra cosa** something else is concealed behind this

agencia SF 1 (= *empresa*) agency; (= *oficina*) office, bureau ▸ **agencia de cobro** debt-collecting agency ▸ **agencia de colocaciones** employment agency ▸ **agencia de contactos** dating agency ▸ **agencia de créditos** credit agency ▸ **agencia de damas de compañía** escort agency ▸ **agencia de información** news agency ▸ **agencia de noticias** news agency ▸ **agencia de patentes** patents office ▸ **agencia de prensa** news agency ▸ **agencia de promoción** development agency ▸ **Agencia de Protección de Datos** (*Esp*) *data protection agency* ▸ **agencia de publicidad** advertising agency ▸ **agencia de seguridad** security company ▸ **agencia de transportes** haulage company ▸ **agencia de turismo**, **agencia de viajes** travel agent's, travel agency ▸ **agencia exclusiva** exclusive agency ▸ **agencia inmobiliaria** estate agent's (office), real estate agency (*EEUU*) ▸ **agencia tributaria** Inland Revenue, Internal Revenue (*EEUU*) ▸ **agencia única** sole agency
2 (*Chile*) (= *montepío*) pawnshop

agenciar ▸conjug 1b◂ Ⓐ VT 1 (= *lograr*) to bring about, effect, engineer
2 (= *procurar*) to obtain, procure (**algo a algn** sth for sb); (*pey*) to wangle*, fiddle*
3 [+ *trato*] to negotiate
Ⓑ **agenciarse** VPR 1 (= *apañarse*) to look after o.s.; **yo me las ~é para llegar allí** I'll manage to get there somehow, I'll work out how to get there; **bien sabe agenciárselas** he takes good care of number one
2 (= *proporcionarse*) **~se algo** to get hold of sth, obtain sth

agenciero SM (*Cono Sur*) (= *agente*) agent, representative; [*de lotería*] lottery agent; (*Chile*) [*de montepío*] pawnbroker

agencioso ADJ active, diligent

agenda SF 1 (= *libro*) [*de citas, anotaciones*] diary, datebook (*EEUU*), notebook; [*de direcciones*] address book ▸ **agenda de bolsillo** pocket diary ▸ **agenda de despacho**,

agenda de mesa desk diary ► **agenda de trabajo** engagement book ► **agenda electrónica** PDA
[2] [*de reunión*] agenda
[3] [*de actividades*] agenda, schedule; **una ~ apretada** a very busy agenda *o* schedule

agente Ⓐ SMF (= *representante*) agent; (= *policía*) policeman/policewoman; (*LAm*) (= *oficial*) officer, official ► **agente acreditado** accredited agent ► **agente comercial** business agent ► **agente de bolsa** stockbroker ► **agente de exportación** export agent ► **agente de negocios** business agent, broker ► **agente de prensa** press agent ► **agente de publicidad** (*Com*) advertising agent; (*Teat*) publicity agent ► **agente de seguridad** (*en vuelos comerciales*) sky marshal ► **agente de seguros** insurance agent ► **agente de transportes** carrier ► **agente de turismo** travel agent, courier ► **agente de ventas** sales agent, sales rep, sales representative ► **agente de viajes** travel agent ► **agente especial** special agent ► **agente extranjero** foreign agent ► **agente inmobiliario** estate agent, real estate agent *o* broker (*EEUU*), realtor (*EEUU*) ► **agente literario** literary agent ► **agente marítimo** shipping agent ► **agente oficial** official agent, authorized agent ► **agente provocador** agent provocateur ► **agente secreto** secret agent ► **agentes sociales** social partners (*employers and unions*) ► **agente tributario** tax inspector ► **agente único** sole agent ► **agente viajero** commercial traveller, salesman Ⓑ SM (*Quím*) agent ► **agente químico** chemical agent

agible ADJ feasible, workable

agigantado ADJ gigantic, huge; **a pasos ~s** by leaps and bounds

agigantar ▸conjug 1a◂ Ⓐ VT to enlarge, increase greatly; **~ algo** to exaggerate sth
Ⓑ **agigantarse** VPR (*gen*) to seem huge; [*crisis*] to get much bigger, get out of proportion

ágil ADJ (= *ligero*) agile, nimble; (= *flexible*) flexible, adaptable

agilidad SF [1] (= *ligereza*) agility, nimbleness; (= *flexibilidad*) flexibility, adaptability; **con ~** nimbly, quickly
[2] (*Aut*) manoeuvrability, maneuverability (*EEUU*), handling

agilipollado* ADJ stupid, daft

agilipollarse* ▸conjug 1a◂ VPR to get all confused, act like an idiot

agilitar ▸conjug 1a◂ Ⓐ VT (= *hacer ágil*) to make agile; (= *facilitar*) to help, make it easy for; (*LAm*) (= *activar*) to activate, set in motion
Ⓑ **agilitarse** VPR (= *hacerse ágil*) to limber up

agilización SF (= *aceleración*) speeding-up; (= *mejora*) improvement

agilizar ▸conjug 1f◂ Ⓐ VT (= *acelerar*) to speed up; (= *mejorar*) to improve, make more flexible
Ⓑ **agilizarse** VPR to speed up

ágilmente ADV nimbly, quickly

agio SM (= *especulación*) speculation, agio; (*Méx*) (= *usura*) usury

agiotaje SM speculation

agiotista SMF (= *especulador*) speculator; (*Méx*) (= *usurero*) usurer

agitación SF [1] [*de mano*] waving, flapping; [*de bebida*] shaking, stirring; [*de mar*] roughness
[2] (*Pol*) agitation; (= *bullicio*) bustle, stir; (= *intranquilidad*) nervousness; (= *emoción*) excitement

agitado Ⓐ ADJ [1] [*mar*] rough, choppy; [*aire*] turbulent; [*vuelo*] bumpy
[2] (*fig*) (= *trastornado*) agitated, upset; (= *emocionado*) excited; [*vida*] hectic
Ⓑ SM stirring, mixing

agitador(a) Ⓐ SM (*Mec*) agitator, shaker; (*Culin*) stirrer
Ⓑ SM/F (*Pol*) agitator

agitanado ADJ gipsy-like, gypsy-like (*EEUU*)

agitar ▸conjug 1a◂ Ⓐ VT [1] [+ *mano, bandera, arma*] to wave; **agitaba un pañuelo** she was waving a handkerchief; **el viento agitaba las hojas** the wind stirred the leaves; **el pájaro agitaba las alas** the bird was flapping its wings
[2] [+ *botella, líquido*] to shake; **agítese antes de usar** shake well before use; **agité al herido para que volviera en sí** I shook the injured man *o* I gave the injured man a shake to bring him round; **agitó el café con una cuchara** he stirred the coffee with a spoon
[3] (= *inquietar*) to worry, upset; **los rumores del accidente la ~on** the rumours about the accident worried *o* upset her
[4] (= *convulsionar*) [+ *multitud*] to stir up; **su asesinato agitó al país** his assassination stirred up the country
[5] (= *esgrimir*) to use; **agitan el miedo a la guerra para ganar votos** they use the fear of war to win votes
Ⓑ **agitarse** VPR [1] (= *moverse*) [*ramas*] to stir; [*bandera, toldo*] to flap; [*mar*] to get rough; [*barco*] to toss
[2] (= *inquietarse*) to get worried *o* upset
[3] (= *moverse inquieto*) **el enfermo se agitaba en la cama** the patient was tossing and turning; **la acusada se agitaba nerviosa** the defendant shifted uneasily

aglomeración SF agglomeration ► **aglomeración de gente** mass of people ► **aglomeración de tráfico** traffic jam ► **aglomeración urbana** urban sprawl

aglomerado Ⓐ ADJ massed together, in a mass; **viven ~s** they live on top of each other
Ⓑ SM (= *madera*) chipboard, Masonite® (*EEUU*); (*Téc*) agglomeration ► **aglomerado asfáltico** asphalt, blacktop (*EEUU*)

aglomerar ▸conjug 1a◂ Ⓐ VT to agglomerate, crowd together
Ⓑ **aglomerarse** VPR (= *juntarse*) to agglomerate, form a mass; (= *apiñarse*) to crowd together

aglutinación SF agglutination

aglutinador ADJ agglutinative, cohesive; **fuerza ~a** unifying force, force that draws things together

aglutinadora SF unifying force

aglutinante ADJ agglutinative

aglutinar ▸conjug 1a◂ Ⓐ VT [1] (*Med*) to agglutinate
[2] (= *unir*) to draw together, bring together
Ⓑ **aglutinarse** VPR [1] (*Med*) to agglutinate
[2] (= *unirse*) to come together, gel

agnosticismo SM agnosticism

agnóstico/a ADJ, SM/F agnostic

agobiado ADJ [1] [*persona*] **estar ~**: **estamos ~s de trabajo** we're up to our eyes in work*; **estaba agobiada por tantas visitas** she found all these visitors overwhelming *o* a bit too much*; **no puedo hacerlo porque estoy ~ con otras cosas** I can't do it, I'm rushed off my feet with other things* *o* I've got too much else on*
[2] [*lugar*] cluttered; **el dormitorio queda muy ~ con tantos muebles** the bedroom is very cluttered with all the furniture
[3] **ser ~ de hombros** (*Cono Sur*) to have a stoop

agobiador ADJ = **agobiante**

agobiante ADJ [1] [*calor, ambiente, lugar*] oppressive; **un día de verano ~** a stifling *o* sweltering summer's day
[2] (= *insoportable*) [*trabajo, día*] stressful; [*pena, ritmo*] unbearable; [*responsabilidad*] overwhelming; **es ~ verla sufrir y no poder hacer nada** it's unbearable watching her suffer and being unable to do anything; **una ~ sensación de soledad** an overwhelming sense of loneliness

agobiar ▸conjug 1b◂ Ⓐ VT [1] (= *oprimir*) [*problemas, responsabilidad, pena*] to overwhelm; [*ropa*] to stifle; **estamos agobiados por las incesantes llamadas telefónicas** we're overwhelmed with constant phone calls; **agobiado por las deudas, tuvo que volver a trabajar** weighed down by debts, he was forced to go back to work; **este bochorno me agobia** I find this close weather oppressive *o* stifling
[2] (= *angustiar*) **le agobian mucho los espacios cerrados** he gets really anxious in enclosed spaces; **me agobian las grandes ciudades** big cities are too much for me*, I find big cities very stressful; **me agobia un montón oír el fútbol por la radio*** hearing football on the radio really gets to me*
[3] (= *molestar*) to pester, harass; **estaban agobiándola con tantas preguntas** they were pestering *o* harassing her with so many questions
[4] (*) (= *meter prisa*) **no me agobies, ya terminaré el trabajo cuando pueda** please, give me a break *o* get off my back, I'll finish the work when I can*
Ⓑ **agobiarse** VPR (*) **no se agobia con nada** he doesn't let anything get on top of him *o* get to him*; **me agobié del calor que hacía** the heat was too much for me

agobio SM [1] (= *malestar*) **el calor y el ~ provocaron algunos mareos entre el público** it was so hot and crowded that some of the audience fainted
[2] (= *angustia*) **soñaban con unas vacaciones lejos del ~ del trabajo doméstico** they dreamed of holidays away from the stress of housework; **¡cuántos deberes! ¡qué ~!*** so much homework! it's a nightmare!*

agolpamiento SM throng, crush

agolparse ▸conjug 1a◂ VPR (= *apiñarse*) to throng, crowd together; (= *acumularse*) [*problemas*] to come one on top of another; [*lágrimas*] to come in a flood; **~ en torno a algn** to crowd round sb

agonía SF [1] [*de muerte*] death agony, death throes *pl*; (= *últimos momentos*) dying moments *pl*; **la época está en su ~** the period is in its death throes; **en su ~** on his death-bed; **acortar la ~ a un animal** to put an animal out of its misery
[2] (= *angustia*) anguish; (= *deseo*) desire, yearning

agonías* SMF INV moaner, misery guts*

agónico ADJ (= *moribundo*) dying; (= *angustiante*) agonizing

agonioso ADJ (*LAm*) (= *egoísta*) selfish; (= *fastidioso*) bothersome; **es tan ~** he's such a pest

agonizante Ⓐ ADJ (= *moribundo*) dying; [*luz*] failing
Ⓑ SMF dying person

agonizar ▸conjug 1f◂ VI to be dying, be in one's death throes; **~ por hacer algo** to be dying to do sth

agonizos SMPL (*Méx*) worries, troubles

agora†† ADV (*LAm*) = **ahora**

ágora SF main square

agorafobia SF agoraphobia

agorafóbico/a SM/F agoraphobe

agorar ▸conjug 1m◂ VT to predict, prophesy

agorero/a Ⓐ ADJ (= *que presagia*) prophetic; (= *que presagia males*) ominous; **ave agorera** bird of ill omen
Ⓑ SM/F (= *adivino*) soothsayer, fortune teller

agostar ▸conjug 1a◂ Ⓐ VT [1] (= *quemar*) to parch, burn up
[2] (= *marchitar*) to wither, kill before time
[3] (*Méx*) (= *pastar*) to graze on rough ground
Ⓑ **agostarse** VPR [1] (= *secarse*) to dry up, shrivel
[2] (= *marchitarse*) to die, fade away

agosteño ADJ August *antes de s*

agosto SM August; (= *cosecha*) harvest; (= *época*) harvest time; **hacer su ~** to feather one's nest, make one's pile; *ver tb* **septiembre**

agotado ADJ [1] (= *cansado*) **estar ~** to be exhausted, be worn out
[2] (= *acabado*) [*mercancía, producto*] sold out; [*existencias, provisión*] finished, exhausted; [*libro*] out of stock
[3] [*pila*] flat

agotador ADJ exhausting

agotamiento SM [1] (= *cansancio*) exhaustion
▸ **agotamiento nervioso** nervous strain
▸ **agotamiento por calor** heat exhaustion
[2] [*de reservas*] depletion, draining

agotar ▸conjug 1a◂ Ⓐ VT [1] (= *cansar*) wear out, tire out; **las vacaciones me agotan** holidays wear *o* tire me out, holidays are exhausting; **este niño me agota las fuerzas** this child wears *o* tires me out
[2] (= *terminar con*) [+ *recursos naturales, reservas*] to use up, exhaust; [+ *posibilidades*] to exhaust; **el público agotó las entradas en dos horas** all the tickets (were) sold out within two hours; **las jugueterías ~on sus existencias** the toyshops sold out; **han agotado todas las vías legales** they have exhausted all legal avenues; **antes de eso prefieren ~ la vía diplomática** they prefer to try all diplomatic options first; **agoté todos mis argumentos intentando convencerle** I ran out of arguments trying to persuade him; **agotamos todos los temas de conversación** we ran out of topics of conversation; **tanto papeleo me agota la paciencia** I lose patience with *o* get impatient with all this paperwork
[3] **he decidido ~ el plazo** I decided to take as much time as I was allowed; **he agotado todas las prórrogas** all my extensions have run out, I've used up all my extensions; **el gobierno pretende ~ la legislatura** the government aims to last out its term
Ⓑ VI (= *cansar*) **correr cuando hace calor agota** running in the heat tires you out, running in the heat is exhausting
Ⓒ **agotarse** VPR [1] (= *cansarse*) to get exhausted, tire o.s. out, wear o.s. out; **me agoto pronto nadando** I soon get exhausted when I swim, I soon tire *o* wear myself out when I swim, swimming soon tires *o* wears me out
[2] [*mercancía, artículo, género*] sell out; **se han agotado las entradas para el concierto** tickets for the concert have sold out; **ese producto se nos ha agotado** we've sold out of that product, that product is *o* has sold out
[3] [*recursos, reservas*] to run out; **se me agotó la gasolina** I ran out of petrol; **se me ~on los argumentos para defender mi tesis** I ran out of arguments to defend my thesis; **se me está agotando la paciencia** my patience is running out *o* wearing thin
[4] [*prórroga, tiempo*] to run out; **el tiempo se iba agotando** time was running out; **el plazo se agota mañana** the deadline is tomorrow

agraceño ADJ tart, sour

agraciado/a Ⓐ ADJ [1] (= *atractivo*) graceful, attractive; (= *encantador*) charming; **poco ~** plain
[2] (= *con suerte*) lucky; **ser ~ con** to be blessed with; **salir ~** to be lucky, be the winner
Ⓑ SM/F lucky winner

agraciar ▸conjug 1b◂ VT [1] (= *adornar*) to adorn; (= *ceder*) to grace; (= *hacer más atractivo*) to make more attractive
[2] [+ *preso*] to pardon
[3] **~ a algn con algo** to bestow sth on sb

agradable ADJ (= *grato*) pleasant, agreeable; **es un sitio ~** it's a nice place; **el cadáver no era muy ~ para la vista** the body was not a pretty sight; **ser ~ al gusto** to taste good, be tasty

agradablemente ADV pleasantly, agreeably

agradar ▸conjug 1a◂ Ⓐ VT to please, be pleasing to; **esto no me agrada** I don't like this
Ⓑ VI to please; **su presencia siempre agrada** your presence is always welcome; **si le agrada le traeré más café** if you wish I'll bring you more coffee
Ⓒ **agradarse** VPR to like each other

▼ **agradecer** ▸conjug 2d◂ Ⓐ VT (= *dar las gracias a*) to thank; (= *sentirse agradecido*) to be grateful for; **(te) agradezco tu ayuda** thanks for your help; **se lo agradezco** thank you, I am much obliged to you (*frm*); **un favor que él no ~ía nunca lo bastante** a favour *o* (*EEUU*) favor he can never thank you enough for; **le ~ía me enviara** I would be grateful if you would send me; **eso no lo tiene que ~ a nadie** he has nobody to thank for that, he owes nobody thanks for that
Ⓑ **agradecerse** VPR **¡se agradece!** much obliged!, thanks very much!; **una copita de jerez siempre se agradece** a glass of sherry is always welcome

agradecido ADJ [1] **estar ~ (por algo)** to be grateful (for sth); **estamos muy ~s** we are very grateful; **me miró agradecida** she looked at me gratefully; **¡muy ~!** many thanks!, I'm very grateful!, I appreciate it!; **le quedaría muy ~ si me enviara un ejemplar** I should be very grateful if you would send me a copy
[2] **ser ~** [*persona*] to be appreciative; **es muy agradecida, cualquier cosita la pone contenta** she's very appreciative, any little thing makes her happy
[3] [*planta, tierra*] **son terrenos muy ~s** this land is easy to grow things on, this land is very easy to cultivate; **los olivos son árboles muy ~s** olive trees are very easy to grow
[4] (= *bien recibido*) **tu visita es siempre agradecida** you're always welcome here

▼ **agradecimiento** SM (= *gratitud*) gratitude; (= *aprecio*) appreciation

agrado SM [1] (= *cualidad*) affability; **con ~** willingly
[2] (= *gusto*) **ser del ~ de algn** to be to sb's liking; **tengo el ~ de informarle que ...** (*LAm*) I have pleasure in informing you that ..., I am glad to tell you that ...

ágrafo/a ADJ, SM/F illiterate

agramatical ADJ ungrammatical

agrandamiento SM enlargement

agrandar ▸conjug 1a◂ Ⓐ VT (= *hacer más grande*) to make bigger, enlarge; (= *exagerar*) to exaggerate, magnify
Ⓑ **agrandarse** VPR to get bigger

agranijado ADJ pimply

agrario ADJ agrarian; **política agraria** agricultural policy; **reforma agraria** land reform

agrarismo SM (*Méx*) agrarian reform movement

agrarista (*Méx*) Ⓐ ADJ **movimiento ~** agrarian reform movement
Ⓑ SMF supporter of land reform

agravación SF, **agravamiento** SM (= *empeoramiento*) worsening; (*Med*) change for the worse

agravado SM **robo con ~** robbery with aggravation

agravante Ⓐ ADJ aggravating
Ⓑ SM *o* SF additional problem; (*Jur*) aggravating circumstance; **con la ~ de que** with the further difficulty that; **robo con ~** robbery with aggravation; **con la ~ de la nocturnidad** (*Jur*) made more serious by the fact that it was done at night

agravar ▸conjug 1a◂ Ⓐ VT [1] (= *hacer más grave*) [+ *pena*] to increase; [+ *dolor*] to make worse; [+ *situación*] to aggravate; (*fig*) (= *oprimir*) to oppress, burden (**con** with)
[2] (= *hacer más pesado*) to weigh down, make heavier
Ⓑ VI, **agravarse** VPR (= *empeorarse*) to worsen, get worse

agraviar ▸conjug 1b◂ Ⓐ VT (= *dañar*) to wrong; (= *insultar*) to offend, insult
Ⓑ **agraviarse** VPR to be offended, take offence, take offense (*EEUU*) (**de, por** at)

agravio SM (= *daño*) wrong, injury; (= *insulto*) offence, offense (*EEUU*), insult; (*Jur*) grievance, injustice ▸ **agravio comparativo** inequality, resentment arising from inequality
▸ **agravios de hecho** assault and battery

agravión ADJ (*Cono Sur*) touchy, quick to take offence

agravioso ADJ offensive, insulting

agraz SM [1] (= *uva*) sour grape; (= *jugo*) sour grape juice; **en ~** prematurely, before time
[2] (*fig*) (= *amargura*) bitterness, ill-feeling

agrazar ▸conjug 1f◂ Ⓐ VT [1] (= *amargar*) to embitter
[2] (= *fastidiar*) to vex, annoy
Ⓑ VI (= *saber amargo*) to taste sour, have a sharp taste

➤ LENGUA Y USO: **agradecer A** 31, 40.4, 46.1, 46.5, 47.1, 47.2, 47.5, 49, 52.1 **agradecimiento** 49

agrazón SM [1] (= *uva*) wild grape; (= *grosellero*) gooseberry bush
[2] (*fig*) (= *enfado*) vexation, annoyance

agredir ▸conjug 3a◂ VT (*físicamente*) to assault, set upon; (*verbalmente*) to attack

agregado/a Ⓐ SM/F [1] (= *profesor*) assistant
[2] (*Pol*) ► **agregado/a comercial** commercial attaché ► **agregado/a cultural** cultural attaché ► **agregado/a de prensa** press attaché ► **agregado/a militar** military attaché
[3] (*LAm*) (= *aparcero*) sharecropper; (*Cono Sur*) (= *inquilino*) paying guest; (*Caribe*) (= *jornalero*) day labourer, day laborer (*EEUU*)
Ⓑ SM [1] (*Téc*) aggregate
[2] (= *bloque*) concrete block

agregaduría SF (*Pol*) office of attaché; (*Escol*) assistantship

agregar ▸conjug 1h◂ Ⓐ VT [1] (= *añadir*) to add; **~ algo a algo** to add sth to sth; **agregue el azúcar y remueva** add the sugar and stir; **—y no me satisface, agregó** "and I'm not satisfied," she added
[2] [+ *trabajador, empleado*] to appoint; **fue agregado a la oficina de prensa** he was appointed to the press office
Ⓑ **agregarse** VPR **~se a algo** to join sth; **se ~on a la fiesta** they joined the party

agremiar ▸conjug 1b◂ Ⓐ VT to form into a union, unionize
Ⓑ **agremiarse** VPR to form a union

agresión SF (= *acometida*) aggression; (*contra persona*) attack, assault; **pacto de no ~** non-aggression pact ► **agresión sexual** sexual assault

agresivamente ADV aggressively

agresividad SF (= *violencia*) aggressiveness; (= *vigor*) drive, punch, vigour, vigor (*EEUU*)

agresivo ADJ (= *violento*) aggressive; (= *vigoroso*) forceful, vigorous

agresor(a) Ⓐ ADJ **país ~** aggressor country
Ⓑ SM/F (= *atacante*) aggressor, attacker; (*Jur*) assailant

agreste ADJ [1] (= *campestre*) rural, country
[2] [*paisaje*] wild
[3] (*fig*) (= *tosco*) rough, uncouth

agrete ADJ sourish

agriado ADJ [1] [*persona*] (= *resentido*) sour, resentful; (= *exasperado*) angry, irritated
[2] (*Cono Sur*) (= *agrio*) sour, sharp

agriar ▸conjug 1b *o* 1c◂ Ⓐ VT [1] (= *avinagrar*) to turn sour
[2] (*fig*) (= *amargar*) to sour; (= *fastidiar*) to vex, annoy
Ⓑ **agriarse** VPR [1] (= *avinagrarse*) to turn sour
[2] (= *amargarse*) to become embittered; (= *fastidiarse*) to get cross, get exasperated; **se le ha agriado el carácter** he's turned into a right creep*

agrícola ADJ agricultural, farming *antes de s*

agricultor(a) Ⓐ ADJ agricultural, farming *antes de s*
Ⓑ SM/F farmer ► **agricultor(a) de montaña** hill farmer

agricultura SF agriculture, farming ► **agricultura biodinámica, agricultura biológica** organic farming ► **agricultura de montaña** hill farming ► **agricultura de rozas y quema** slash-and-burn agriculture ► **agricultura de subsistencia** subsistence farming ► **agricultura ecológica** organic farming ► **agricultura intensiva** intensive farming ► **agricultura orgánica** organic farming

agricultural ADJ (*LAm*) agricultural, farming *antes de s*

agridulce ADJ bittersweet; **cerdo ~** sweet and sour pork

agriera SF (*LAm*) heartburn

agrietado ADJ (= *con grietas*) cracked; [*piel*] chapped

agrietar ▸conjug 1a◂ Ⓐ VT (= *resquebrajar*) to crack, crack open; [+ *piel*] to chap
Ⓑ **agrietarse** VPR (= *resquebrajarse*) to crack; [*piel*] to become chapped

agrifolio SM holly

agrimensor(a) SM/F surveyor

agrimensura SF surveying

agringado ADJ (*LAm*) like a gringo, like a foreigner

agringarse ▸conjug 1h◂ VPR (*LAm*) to act *o* behave like a gringo, act *o* behave like a foreigner

agrio Ⓐ ADJ [1] (*al gusto*) sour, tart; (*fig*) (= *desabrido*) bitter, disagreeable
[2] [*camino*] rough, uneven; [*materia*] brittle; [*color*] garish
Ⓑ SM (= *zumo*) sour juice; **agrios** (= *frutas*) citrus fruits

agriparse ▸conjug 1a◂ VPR (*Cono Sur*) (= *coger gripe*) to get flu, get the flu (*esp EEUU*); **estar agripado** to have flu *o* (*esp EEUU*) the flu

agriura SF (*LAm*) sourness, tartness

agro SM agriculture

agroalimentario ADJ food and agriculture *antes de s*

agrobiología SF agrobiology

agrobiológico ADJ agrobiological

agrobiólogo/a SM/F agrobiologist

agroenergética SF *use of agricultural products as sources of energy*

agroforestal ADJ agroforestry *antes de s*

agro-industria SF agro-industry

agronegocios SMPL agribusiness

agronomía SF agronomy, agriculture

agrónomo/a Ⓐ ADJ **ingeniero ~** agricultural scientist
Ⓑ SM/F agronomist, agricultural expert

agropecuario ADJ farming *antes de s*; **sector ~** agriculture and fishing; **política agropecuaria** farming policy; **riqueza agropecuaria** agricultural wealth

agropesquero ADJ *relating to farming and fishing*

agroproducto SM farm produce

agroquímico ADJ, SM agrochemical

agrosistema SM agricultural ecosystem, farming ecosystem

agroturismo SM rural tourism

agroturístico ADJ rural tourism *antes de s*

agrupación SF [1] (= *grupo*) group, association; (= *reunión*) gathering; (= *unión*) union; (*Mús*) ensemble
[2] (= *acción*) grouping; (= *reunión*) coming together

agrupamiento SM grouping

agrupar ▸conjug 1a◂ Ⓐ VT (= *reunir en grupo*) to group, group together; [+ *gente, datos etc*] to gather, assemble; (= *amontonar*) to crowd together
Ⓑ **agruparse** VPR (*Pol*) to form a group; (= *juntarse*) to gather together, come together (**en torno a** round)

agrura SF [1] (= *sabor agrio*) sourness, tartness
[2] **agruras** (*Méx Med*) heartburn

agua SF [1] (*para beber, lavar*) water; **lavar en ~ fría** wash in cold water; **dame ~** give me a drink of water; **un motor refrigerado por ~** a water-cooled engine; **dos ~s con gas y una sin gas, por favor** two sparkling mineral waters and one still one, please; **ha sido un invierno de mucha ~** it's been a very wet winter, we've had a lot of rain this winter; **¡hombre al ~!** man overboard!; **lanzar un barco al ~** to launch a boat; **caer ~** to rain; **hace falta que caiga mucha ~** we need a lot of rain; **cayó ~ a mares** it poured down; **echarse al ~** (*lit*) to dive in; (*fig*) to take the plunge; **¡~ va!** look out!, careful!; **sin decir ~ va** without (any) warning; ✦*MODISMOS* **bailar el ~ a algn** (*Esp*) (= *adular*) to dance attendance on sb; (*Méx**) (= *coquetear*) to flirt with sb; **bañarse en ~ de rosas** to see the world through rose-tinted spectacles; **hacérsele la boca ~ a algn** (*Esp*) ◊ **hacérsele ~ la boca a algn** (*LAm*): **se me hace la boca ~ sólo de pensar en la sopa** just thinking about the soup makes my mouth water, my mouth is watering just thinking about the soup; **se le hace la boca ~ de pensar en los beneficios** he's drooling at the thought of the profit he'll make; **quedar en ~ de borrajas** [*promesas, proyectos*] to come to nothing; **cambiar el ~ al canario** *o* **a las aceitunas*** to take a leak*; **coger ~ en cesto** to labour in vain, be wasting one's time; **como ~ para chocolate** (*Méx**) furious; **estar con el ~ al cuello** to be in it up to one's neck*; **¿me da para mis ~s?** (*Méx*) how about a little something for me?; **echar a algn al ~** (*Chile**) to give sb away; **gastar el dinero como ~** to spend money like water; **como ~ de mayo** (*Esp*): **esperan la privatización como ~ de mayo** they are eagerly awaiting privatization; **la noticia fue recibida como ~ de mayo en los mercados financieros** the news was welcomed with open arms on the financial markets; **este dinero nos viene como ~ de mayo** this money is a godsend, this money couldn't have come at a better time; **llevar el ~ a su molino** to turn things to one's own advantage; **mear ~ bendita**‡ to be a holy Joe*; **es ~ pasada** that's all water under the bridge; **pescar en ~ turbia** to fish in troubled waters; **sacar ~ de las piedras** to work miracles; **de primera ~** (*Chile*) first hand; **ser como el ~ por San Juan** to be harmful, be unwelcome; ✦*REFRANES* **~ que no has de beber déjala correr** don't be a dog in the manger; **nunca digas de esta ~ no beberé** never say never; **de las ~s mansas me libre Dios** still waters run deep; **~ pasada no mueve molino** it's no good crying over spilt milk; **lo que por ~ viene, por ~ se va** (*Col*) easy come, easy go* ► **agua bendita** holy water ► **agua blanda** soft water ► **agua corriente** running water ► **agua (de) cuba** (*Chile*) bleach ► **agua de cebada** barley water ► **agua de colonia** eau de cologne ► **agua de espliego** lavender water ► **agua de fregar** dishwater ► **agua de fuego** firewater ► **agua de fusión de la nieve** meltwater ► **agua de lavanda** lavender water ► **agua del grifo** tap water ► **agua de lluvia** rainwater ► **agua de mar**

sea water ► **agua de rosas** rosewater ► **agua de seltz** seltzer, soda (water), seltzer water (*EEUU*) ► **agua destilada** distilled water ► **agua dulce** fresh water; **un pez de ~ dulce** a freshwater fish ► **agua dura** hard water ► **agua fuerte** *nitric acid solution* ► **agua Jane®** (*Uru*) bleach ► **agua mineral** mineral water; **~ mineral con gas** sparkling mineral water; **~ mineral sin gas** still mineral water ► **agua nieve** sleet; **cayó ~ nieve** it was sleeting ► **agua oxigenada** hydrogen peroxide ► **agua (de) panela** (*Col, Ven*) hot lemon ► **agua perra** (*Chile*) boiled water (*drunk for its cleansing properties*) ► **agua pesada** heavy water ► **agua potable** drinking water ► **agua salada** salt water; **un pez de ~ salada** a saltwater fish ► **agua tónica** tonic water; *ver tb* **claro**, **grabado**, **vía**

[2] (*CAm, Andes*) (= *gaseosa*) fizzy drink, soda (*EEUU*); (= *infusión*) herbal tea; **~ de manzanilla** camomile tea

[3] (*CAm*) (= *zumo*) juice; **~ de pera** pear juice

[4] **aguas** [*de mar, río*] waters; [*de la marea*] tide *sing*; **las frías ~s del Atlántico** the cold waters of the Atlantic; **Dios creó las ~s** God created the seas and the oceans; **~s abajo** downstream, downriver; **~s arriba** upstream, upriver; **hacer ~s** [*barco*] to take in water; [*explicación, teoría*] to be full of holes, not to hold water; [*relación, organización, proyecto*] to founder; **nuestro mercado interno hacía ~** our domestic market was foundering *o* in trouble; **romper ~s**: **rompió ~s camino del hospital** her waters broke on the way to the hospital; **tomar las ~s** to take the waters; ✦*MODISMOS* **estar** *o* **nadar entre dos ~s** to sit on the fence; **volver las ~s a su cauce**: **las ~s están volviendo a su cauce** things are returning to normal ► **aguas amnióticas** amniotic fluid *sing* ► **aguas de consumo** drinking water *sing* ► **aguas de escorrentía** runoff water *sing* ► **aguas de pantoque** bilge water *sing* ► **aguas fecales** sewage *sing* ► **aguas internacionales** international waters ► **aguas jurisdiccionales** territorial waters ► **aguas litorales** coastal waters ► **aguas llenas** high tide *sing* ► **aguas mayores** (*euf*) faeces *sing* (*frm*), feces *sing* (*EEUU frm*); **hacer ~s mayores** to have a bowel movement ► **aguas menores** (*euf*) urine *sing*; **hacer ~s menores** to pass water ► **aguas muertas** neap tide *sing* ► **aguas negras**, **aguas residuales**, **aguas servidas** (*Cono Sur*) sewage *sing* ► **aguas subterráneas** groundwater *sing* ► **aguas superficiales** surface water *sing* ► **aguas termales** thermal springs ► **aguas territoriales** territorial waters

[5] **aguas** (= *ondulación*) [5·1] [*de piedra preciosa*] veins; **la malaquita tenía unas ~s blancas** the malachite had white veins in it; **un papel azul haciendo ~s** a blue paper with a marbled design

[5·2] [*de tejado*] pitch, slope; **cubrir ~s** to put the roof on, top out; **tejado a dos ~s** gabled roof; **tejado a cuatro ~s** hipped roof

[6] **aguas** (= *destello*) sparkle *sing*; **el diamante tenía unas ~s preciosas** the diamond sparkled beautifully, the diamond had a wonderful sparkle

aguacate SM [1] (= *fruto*) avocado pear; (= *árbol*) avocado pear tree

[2] (*CAm**) (= *idiota*) idiot, fool

[3] **aguacates** (*Méx***) balls**, bollocks**

aguacatero SM avocado tree

aguacero SM shower, heavy shower, downpour

aguacha SF foul water, stagnant water

aguachacha SF (*CAm*) weak drink, nasty drink

aguachado ADJ (*Cono Sur*) tame

aguachento ADJ (*Andes, Cono Sur*) (= *aguado*) watery

aguachinado ADJ (*Caribe*) (= *acuoso*) watery; (= *blando*) soft

aguachinarse ▸conjug 1a◂ VPR (*Méx*) to be flooded

aguachirle SF [1] (= *bebida*) slops *pl*, dishwater

[2] (= *bagatela*) trifle, mere nothing

aguacil SM (*Cono Sur*) dragonfly

aguacola SF (*Méx*) fish glue

aguada SF [1] (*Agr*) watering place

[2] (*Náut*) water supply

[3] (*Min*) flood

[4] (*Arte*) watercolour, watercolor (*EEUU*), wash

aguadilla SF ducking; **hacer una ~ a algn** to duck sb, hold sb's head under water

aguado ADJ [1] (= *diluido*) [*sopa*] thin, watery; [*leche, vino*] watered down; [*café*] weak

[2] (*) (= *abstemio*) teetotal

[3] (*LAm*) (= *débil*) weak

[4] (*Méx*) (= *perezoso*) lazy, idle

aguador(a) SM/F water carrier, water seller

aguaducho SM [1] (= *arroyo*) freshet

[2] (= *quiosco*) refreshment stall, small open-air café

aguafiestas SMF INV spoilsport, killjoy

aguafuerte SF [1] (*Quím*) nitric acid

[2] (*Arte*) etching; **grabar algo al ~** to etch sth

aguafuertista SMF etcher

aguaitada SF (*LAm*) look, glance; **echar una ~ a** to take a look at

aguaitar ▸conjug 1a◂ Ⓐ VT [1] (*LAm*) (= *mirar*) to watch; (= *espiar*) to spy on, observe; (= *acechar*) to lie in wait for

[2] (*Andes, Caribe*) (= *esperar*) to wait for

[3] (*Cono Sur*) (= *ver*) to look, see

Ⓑ VI (*LAm*) **~ por la ventana** to look out of the window

aguaje SM [1] (= *marea*) tide, spring tide; (= *corriente*) current; (= *estela*) wake

[2] (= *provisión*) water supply; (*Agr*) watering trough

[3] (*CAm*) (= *aguacero*) downpour

aguajirado ADJ (*Caribe*) withdrawn, timid

aguajirarse ▸conjug 1a◂ VPR (*Caribe*) (= *tomar costumbres campesinas*) to become countrified, acquire peasant's habits *etc*; (= *ser reservado*) to be withdrawn, be reserved

agualotal SM (*CAm*) swamp, marsh

aguamala SF (*Andes*) jellyfish

aguamanil SM (= *jarro*) water jug; (= *jofaina*) washbasin, bathroom sink

aguamar SM jellyfish

aguamarina SF aquamarine

aguamarse ▸conjug 1a◂ VPR (*Andes*) to get scared, be intimidated

aguamiel SF [1] (= *hidromiel*) sugared water

[2] (*CAm, Méx*) (= *jugo del maguey*) fermented maguey juice, fermented agave juice

aguamuerta SF (*Cono Sur*) jellyfish

aguanieve SF sleet

aguano SM (*Andes*) mahogany

aguanoso ADJ [1] (= *lleno de agua*) wet, watery; [*tierra*] waterlogged

[2] (*Méx*) (= *insípido*) [*persona*] wet*

aguantable ADJ bearable, tolerable

aguantaderas SFPL **tener ~** to be patient, put up with a lot

aguantadero* SM (*Cono Sur*) hide-out

aguantador(a) Ⓐ ADJ (*LAm*) = **aguantón** Ⓐ

Ⓑ SM/F (*) fence*, receiver, receiver of stolen goods

aguantar ▸conjug 1a◂ Ⓐ VT [1] (= *soportar deliberadamente*) to put up with, endure; **aguanté el dolor como pude** I bore *o* put up with *o* endured the pain as best as I could; **tenemos que estar aguantando continuas ofensas** we have to put up with *o* endure continual insults; **no ~é tus impertinencias ni un minuto más** I won't stand for *o* take *o* put up with your cheek a minute longer; ✦*MODISMO* **~ el chaparrón** to weather the storm

[2] (= *tener capacidad de resistir*) to stand up to; **esta planta aguanta bien el calor** this plant withstands *o* can take heat well, this plant stands up well to heat; **aguanta bastante bien el trabajo en la mina** he stands up pretty well to the work in the mine; **no sé si podré ~ ese ritmo** I don't know if I'll be able to stand the pace; **sabe ~ bien las bromas** he can take a joke; **no ~**: **no aguanto a los cotillas** I can't bear *o* stand gossips; **no aguanto ver sufrir a un animal** I can't bear *o* stand to see an animal suffering; **no aguantaba la rutina de los entrenamientos** he couldn't cope with *o* take the training programme; **no hay quien te aguante** you're impossible *o* insufferable; **este frío no hay quien lo aguante** this cold is just unbearable; **no hay quien aguante una ópera tan larga** who could sit through an opera that long?

[3] (= *sostener*) [*persona*] to hold; [*muro, columna*] to support, hold up; **aguanta un momento el paquete** hold the parcel a minute; **la pierna que aguanta la guitarra** the leg that supports the guitar; **se rompió el cable que aguantaba la antena** the cable holding up *o* supporting the aerial broke; **estas vigas pueden ~ cualquier peso** these beams can take any weight; **esta estantería no podrá ~ tantos libros** these shelves won't take so many books

[4] (= *contener*) [+ *respiración*] to hold; [+ *risa, llanto*] to hold back; **soy capaz de ~ la respiración durante dos minutos** I can hold my breath for two minutes; **el mundo aguantó la respiración temiendo un desastre** the world waited with bated breath, fearing a disaster; **apenas podía ~ la risa** she couldn't hold back her laughter; **~ las ganas de hacer algo** to resist the urge to do sth; **no pude ~ las ganas de decirle lo que pensaba** I couldn't resist telling her what I thought, I couldn't resist the urge to tell her what I thought; **se tuvo que ~ las ganas de llorar** she had to stifle her desire to cry

[5] (= *durar*) to last; **este abrigo no ~á otro invierno** this coat won't last another winter

Ⓑ VI [1] [*persona*] **ya no aguanto más** I can't bear it *o* stand it *o* take it any longer, I can't bear *o* stand *o* take any more; **cuando empe-**

zaba a correr no aguantaba más de diez minutos when she started running she couldn't keep going *o* last for more than ten minutes; **~é en Madrid hasta que pueda** I'll hang on *o* hold on in Madrid as long as I can; **yo me emborracho enseguida, pero él aguanta mucho** I get drunk straight away but he can really hold his drink; **tienes que ~ hasta el año que viene con esos zapatos** you'll have to make do with those shoes until next year; **yo ya no aguanto mucho, a las diez estoy en la cama** I can't take the pace any more, I'm in bed by ten; **aguantan poco sin aburrirse** they have a low boredom threshold, they're easily bored; **bailaremos hasta que el cuerpo aguante** we'll dance till we drop; **es de guapo que no se puede ~*** he's drop dead gorgeous*, he's to die for*
[2] [*clavo, columna*] to hold; **¿crees que este clavo ~á?** do you think this nail will hold?; **esa columna va a ~ poco** that pillar won't hold (out) much longer
[3] (*LAm**) (= *esperar*) to hang on*, hold on; **¡aguanta!** hang on* *o* hold on a minute!
Ⓒ **aguantarse** VPR [1] (= *mantenerse*) **estaba tan cansado que ya no me aguantaba de pie** I was so tired I could hardly stand; **~se de algo** to hang onto sth, hang on by sth; **me aguanté de una cuerda hasta que llegaron los bomberos** I hung onto a rope *o* I hung on by a rope until the firefighters came
[2] (= *contenerse*) **¿por qué tenemos que ~nos y no responder?** why do we have to keep quiet and not respond?; **¿no puedes ~te hasta que lleguemos a casa?** can't you hold on until we get home?; **~se de hacer algo** to hold back from doing sth
[3] (= *conformarse*) **no quería ir a la boda, pero me tuve que ~** I didn't want to go to the wedding but I had to grin and bear it; **¡si no te gusta el helado, ahora te aguantas!** if you don't like the ice cream, that's tough! *o* you can lump it!*
[4] (= *soportarse*) **cuando me duele la cabeza no me aguanto ni yo** when I have a headache I'm unbearable; **no sé cómo te aguantas** you're impossible *o* insufferable
[5] (*Méx*) (= *callarse*) to keep quiet, keep one's mouth shut*; **¡aguántate!** calm down!

aguante SM [1] (= *paciencia*) patience; **no tengo ningún ~ con los niños** I have no patience with children; **no tiene ninguna capacidad de ~** she has no capacity for patience
[2] (= *resistencia*) (*ante el dolor*) endurance; (*ante el cansancio*) stamina, staying power; **¿ya estás cansado? ¡qué poco ~ tienes!** are you tired already? you've no staying power *o* stamina!; **no pongas libros en esa mesa, que tiene muy poco ~** don't put books on that table, it can't take much weight
[3] (*Caribe**) **al ~ de algn** behind sb's back

aguantón Ⓐ ADJ (*Caribe, Méx*) long-suffering, extremely patient
Ⓑ SM (*Caribe**) **te darás un ~** you'll have a long wait

aguapié SM weak wine, plonk*

aguar ▸conjug 1i◂ VT [1] [+ *vino*] to water, water down
[2] (*fig*) (= *estropear*) to spoil, mar; **~ la fiesta a algn** to spoil sb's fun
[3] (*CAm, Cono Sur*) [+ *ganado*] to water

aguarana SMF (*Andes*) primitive jungle Indian

aguardada SF wait, waiting

aguardadero SM, **aguardado** SM hide, blind (*EEUU*)

aguardar ▸conjug 1a◂ Ⓐ VT (= *esperar*) to wait for, await; (*con ansias*) to expect; **no sabemos el futuro que nos aguarda** we don't know what's in store for us
Ⓑ VI (= *esperar*) to wait; **aguarde usted** I'm coming to that; **¡aguarda te digo!** hold your horses!*

aguardentería SF liquor store

aguardentero/a SM/F liquor seller

aguardentoso ADJ [*licor, bebida*] alcoholic; [*voz*] husky, gruff

aguardiente SM brandy, liquor ▸ **aguardiente de caña** rum ▸ **aguardiente de cerezas** cherry brandy ▸ **aguardiente de manzana** applejack

aguardientoso ADJ (*LAm*) = **aguardentoso**

aguardo SM hide, blind (*EEUU*)

aguarrás SM turpentine

aguate SM (*Méx*) (= *espina*) prickle, spine

aguatero/a SM/F (*Méx*) (= *aguador*) water carrier, water seller

aguatocha SF pump

aguatoso ADJ (*Méx*) prickly

aguaturma SF Jerusalem artichoke

aguaviva SF (*Cono Sur*) jellyfish

aguayo SM (*Andes*) multicoloured *o* (*EEUU*) multicolored woollen cloth (*for adornment, or carried as shoulder bag*)

aguaza SF (*Med*) liquid (*from a tumour*); (*Bot*) sap

aguazal SM (= *charco*) puddle; (= *pantano*) swamp

aguazar ▸conjug 1f◂ Ⓐ VT to flood, waterlog
Ⓑ **aguazarse** VPR to flood, become waterlogged

agudeza SF [1] [*de los sentidos, de la mente*] acuteness, sharpness; **con una enorme ~ visual** with very keen *o* sharp vision
[2] (= *ingenio*) wit, wittiness
[3] (= *comentario, golpe*) witticism

agudización SF [*de los sentidos, de la mente*] sharpening; [*de crisis*] deterioration, worsening

agudizar ▸conjug 1f◂ Ⓐ VT [+ *los sentidos, la mente*] to sharpen, make more acute; [+ *crisis*] to aggravate
Ⓑ **agudizarse** VPR [*los sentidos, la mente*] to sharpen; (= *empeorarse*) worsen; **el problema se agudiza** the problem is becoming more acute; **la competencia se agudiza** competition is intensifying

agudo ADJ [1] (= *afilado*) [*filo*] sharp; [*instrumento*] sharp, pointed
[2] (= *intenso*) [*enfermedad, dolor*] acute; [*acento*] acute
[3] [*ángulo*] acute
[4] (= *incisivo*) [*mente, sentido*] sharp, keen; [*ingenio*] ready, lively; [*crítica*] penetrating; [*observación*] smart, clever; [*pregunta*] acute, searching
[5] (= *gracioso*) witty
[6] (*Mús*) [*nota*] high, high-pitched; [*voz, sonido*] piercing

agué EXCL (*CAm*) hello!

agüeitar ▸conjug 1a◂ (*LAm*) = **aguaitar**

agüera SF irrigation ditch

agüero SM omen, sign; **de buen ~** lucky; **ser de buen ~** to augur well; **de mal ~** of ill omen, unlucky; **pájaro de mal ~** bird of ill omen

aguerrido ADJ hardened, veteran

aguerrir ▸conjug 3a; imperfecto◂ VT to inure, harden

agüevar‡ ▸conjug 1a◂ Ⓐ VT (*CAm, Méx*) to put down, shame
Ⓑ **agüevarse** VPR to cower, shrink

aguijada SF, **aguijadera** SF goad

aguijar ▸conjug 1a◂ Ⓐ VT [+ *buey, mula, etc*] to goad; (*fig*) (= *incitar*) to urge, spur on
Ⓑ VI (= *acelerar el paso*) to hurry along, make haste

aguijón SM [1] (= *puya*) goad; [*de insecto*] sting; [*de planta*] prickle, spine; **dar coces contra el ~** to kick against the pricks, struggle in vain
[2] (= *incitación*) stimulus, incitement; **el ~ de la carne** sexual desire

aguijonazo SM prick, prick with a goad, jab; (*Zool, Bot*) sting

aguijonear ▸conjug 1a◂ VT = **aguijar A**

aguijoneo SM goading, provocation

águila SF [1] (= *ave*) eagle ▸ **águila calzada** booted eagle ▸ **águila culebrera** short-toed eagle ▸ **águila perdicera** Bonelli's eagle ▸ **águila pescadora** osprey ▸ **águila ratonera** buzzard ▸ **águila real** golden eagle; ✦***MODISMO*** **ser un ~** to be a genius, be terribly clever
[2] (*Cono Sur*) (= *estafador*) cheat, swindler; **andar a palos con el ~*** to be broke
[3] [*de moneda*] **¿~ o sol?** (*Méx*) heads or tails?

aguileña SF columbine

aguileño ADJ [*nariz*] aquiline; [*rostro*] sharp-featured; [*persona*] hawk-nosed

aguilera SF eagle's nest, eyrie

aguilillo/a SM/F (*LAm*) fast horse

aguilón SM (= *ave*) large eagle; [*de grúa*] jib; (*Arquit*) gable, gable end; (*Andes*) (= *caballo*) large heavy horse

aguilucho SM (= *cría*) eaglet, young eagle; (*LAm*) (= *halcón*) hawk, falcon

aguinaldo SM [1] (= *propina*) Christmas box; (= *plus*) Christmas bonus
[2] (*LAm*) (= *villancico*) Christmas carol

aguita‡ SF (*Andes*) cash, dough‡, bread‡

agüita SF (*Chile*) [*de menta*] herb tea, herbal tea

agüitado ADJ (*Méx*) depressed, gloomy

aguja SF [1] (*Cos, Med*) needle; [*de sombrero*] hatpin; **darle a la ~*** to shoot up‡; ✦***MODISMO*** **buscar una ~ en un pajar** to look for a needle in a haystack ▸ **aguja capotera** darning needle ▸ **aguja de arria** (*LAm*) pack needle ▸ **aguja de gancho** crochet hook ▸ **aguja de hacer punto** knitting needle ▸ **aguja de marear** compass, compass needle; **conocer la ~ de marear** to know one's way around ▸ **aguja de media, aguja de tejer** (*LAm*) knitting needle ▸ **aguja de zurcir** darning needle ▸ **aguja hipodérmica** hypodermic needle ▸ **aguja imantada, aguja magnética** compass, compass needle
[2] (= *indicador*) [*de reloj*] hand; (*Téc*) pointer, hand; (*Mil*) firing pin; [*de tocadiscos*] stylus, needle; **tumbar la ~*** (*Aut*) to step on the gas*, go full out
[3] (*LAm Agr*) (= *estaca*) fence post

[4] ► **aguja de pino** (*Bot*) pine needle
[5] (= *chapitel*) spire, steeple
[6] **agujas** (*Culin*) (= *costillas*) shoulder *sing*, rib *sing*
[7] **agujas** (*Ferro*) points, switch *sing* (*EEUU*)
[8] (= *pez*) garfish
[9] (*CAm, Méx*) (= *carne*) beef

agujazo SM prick, jab

agujereado ADJ full of holes

agujerear ▸conjug 1a◂ VT (= *hacer agujeros en*) to make holes in; (= *penetrar*) to pierce

agujero SM [1] (= *abertura*) hole; **hacer un ~ en** to make a hole in ► **agujero de hombre** manhole ► **agujero de ozono** ozone hole, hole in the ozone layer ► **agujero negro** black hole
[2] (*Cos*) (*para agujas*) needle case; (*para alfileres*) pincushion
[3] (*Fin*) (= *deuda*) hole, drain, deficit

agujetas SFPL [1] (= *rigidez*) stiffness *sing*; **tengo ~ en las piernas después del partido** my legs are stiff after the game
[2] (*Méx*) (= *cordones*) shoelaces

agujetero SM (*LAm*) (= *alfiletero*) pincushion

agujón SM hatpin

agur* EXCL cheerio!*, so long!

agusanado ADJ maggoty, wormy

agusanarse ▸conjug 1a◂ VPR to get maggoty

Agustín SM Augustine

agustino ADJ, SM, **agustiniano** ADJ, SM Augustinian

agutí SM (*LAm*) guinea pig

aguzado ADJ (*LAm*) sharp, on the ball*

aguzamiento SM sharpening

aguzanieves SF INV wagtail

aguzar ▸conjug 1f◂ VT [1] (= *afilar*) to sharpen
[2] (*fig*) (= *incitar*) to incite, stir up; [+ *ingenio*] to sharpen; [+ *apetito*] to whet; **~ el oído** to prick up one's ears; **~ la vista** to keep one's eyes peeled*

ah EXCL [1] (*para expresar sorpresa*) ah!, ha!, oh!; **¡ah del barco!** ship ahoy!
[2] (*LAm*) (*para interrogar*) **¿ah?** what?

a.h. ABR (= **año de la Hégira**) AH

ahechaduras SFPL chaff *sing*

ahechar ▸conjug 1a◂ VT to sift

aherrojamiento SM oppression

aherrojar ▸conjug 1a◂ VT (= *encadenar*) to put in irons, fetter; (*fig*) (= *someter*) to oppress

aherrumbrarse ▸conjug 1a◂ VPR [*metal*] to rust, get rusty; [*color*] to take on the colour of iron

ahí ADV [1] (*en un lugar*) there; **ponlo ~** put it there; **~ está Antonio** there's Antonio; **~ llega el pelotón** here comes the pack; **ésa de ~ es mi madre** that woman over there is my mother; **¿Nina, estás ~?** Nina, are you there?; **de un salto puedo llegar hasta ~ enfrente** I can get over there in one jump; **~ abajo** down there; **~ arriba** up there; **~ dentro** in there, inside; **~ fuera** out there, outside; **~ mero** (*Méx*) ◊ **~ mismo** right there; **vivo ~ mismo** I live right there; **~ no más** (*LAm*) right (near) here; **por ~** (*indicando dirección*) that way; (*indicando posición*) over there; **entra por ~** go in that way; **busca por ~** look over there; **las tijeras deben de estar por ~** the scissors must be around somewhere; **hoy podemos ir a cenar por ~** we can go out for dinner tonight, we can eat out tonight; **¿no dicen por ~ que vivimos en un país libre?** don't they say we live in a free country?; **lleva muchos años viviendo por ~ fuera** he has been living abroad for many years; **debe de tener unos cincuenta años o por ~** she must be about fifty or so; **por ~ se le ocurre llamar** (*Cono Sur*) he might think to phone; **~ tiene** there you are; **~ tiene sus libros** there are your books; **¡~ va!**: **~ va el balón, ¡cógelo!** there goes the ball, catch it!; **¡~ va, qué bonito!** wow, it's lovely!; **¡~ va, no me había dado cuenta de que eras tú!** well well! I didn't realise it was you; ✦**MODISMO ~ donde lo ves** believe it or not; **~ donde lo ves, come más que tú y yo juntos** believe it or not he eats more than you and me put together
[2] (*en una situación*) **la injusticia no acaba ~** the injustice doesn't end there; **~ está la clave de todo** that's the key to everything; **¡~ está el problema!** that's the problem!; **~ está, por ejemplo, el caso de Luis** there's the case of Luis, for example; **~ estaba yo, con casi cincuenta años, y todavía soltero** there was I, about to turn fifty, and still a bachelor; **—¿está mejor tu mujer? —~ anda** *o* (*LAm*) **~ va** "is your wife better?" — "she's doing all right"; **¡hombre, haber empezado por ~!** why didn't you say so before?; **de ~** that's why; **de ~ las quejas de los inquilinos** that's why the tenants are complaining, hence the tenants' complaints (*frm*); **de ~ que me sintiera un poco decepcionado** that's why I felt a bit let down; **de ~ se deduce que ...** from that it follows that ...; **hasta ~**: **hasta ~ llego yo** I can work that much out for myself; **bueno, hasta ~ de acuerdo** well, I agree with you up to there *o* that point; **¡hasta ~ podíamos llegar!** what a nerve!, that's the limit!, can you credit it!; **he ~ el dilema** that's the dilemma, there you have the dilemma; **~ sí que** (*LAm*): **si hubiéramos ido más rápido, ~ sí que nos matamos** if we'd gone any faster, we'd definitely have been killed; **~ sí que me pillaste** you've really got me there; ✦**MODISMOS ¡~ es nada!** imagine!, wow!; **~ está el meollo** *o* **el quid de la cuestión** that's the crux of the matter, that's the whole problem; **hasta por ~ no más** (*Cono Sur*) up to a point
[3] (*en el tiempo*) **~ mismo** (*LAm*) ◊ **~ no más** (*Chile*) there and then; **a partir de ~** from then on

ahijado/a SM/F (= *hijo adoptivo*) godson/goddaughter; (*fig*) (= *protegido*) protégé/protégée

ahijar ▸conjug 1a◂ VT [1] [+ *niño*] to adopt; [+ *animal*] to adopt, mother
[2] **~ algo a algn** (= *imputar*) to impute sth to sb

ahijuna** EXCL (*LAm*) you bastard!**

ahilar ▸conjug 1a◂ Ⓐ VT (= *poner en fila*) to line up
Ⓑ VI (= *andar en fila*) to go in single file
Ⓒ **ahilarse** VPR (= *desmayarse*) to faint with hunger; [*planta*] to grow poorly; [*vino*] to turn sour, go off

ahincadamente ADV hard, earnestly

ahincado ADJ earnest

ahincar ▸conjug 1g◂ Ⓐ VT (= *instar*) to press, urge
Ⓑ **ahincarse** VPR (= *apresurarse*) to hurry up, make haste

ahinco SM, **ahínco** SM (= *seriedad*) earnestness, intentness; (= *énfasis*) emphasis; (= *empeño*) effort; (= *resolución*) determination, perseverance; **con ~** eagerly, hard, earnestly

ahitar ▸conjug 1a◂ Ⓐ VT to cloy, surfeit
Ⓑ **ahitarse** VPR (= *empacharse*) to stuff o.s. (**de** with), give o.s. a surfeit (**de** of); (*Med*) (= *indigestarse*) give o.s. indigestion

ahíto Ⓐ ADJ [1] (= *empachado*) gorged, satiated
[2] (*fig*) (= *harto*) **estar ~ de** to be fed up with
[3] (= *lleno*) full, packed tight
Ⓑ SM (= *empacho*) surfeit, satiety; (*Med*) (= *indigestión*) indigestion

AHN SM ABR (*Esp*) = **Archivo Histórico Nacional**

ahogadero SM [1] [*de animal*] throatband; [*de verdugo*] hangman's rope
[2] (= *lugar caluroso*) **esto es un ~** it's stifling in here

ahogado/a Ⓐ ADJ [1] [*persona*] (*en agua*) drowned; (*por falta de aire*) suffocated; **morir ~** (*en agua*) to drown; (*por falta de aire*) to suffocate
[2] (= *apagado*) [*voz, llanto*] stifled; [*grito*] muffled
[3] [*lugar*] cluttered; **la cocina está ahogada con tantos muebles** the kitchen looks cluttered with so much furniture
[4] (= *sin dinero*) **el club está ~ económicamente** the club is going under; **nos vimos ~s por las deudas** we were up to our eyes in debt
[5] (*Méx**) (= *borracho*) drunk
Ⓑ SM/F drowned man/woman
Ⓒ SM (*Andes*) (= *salsa*) *sauce made with tomatoes, onions and peppers*; (= *guisado*) *stew made with tomatoes, onions and peppers*

ahogador SM (*Méx*) choke

ahogar ▸conjug 1h◂ Ⓐ VT [1] (= *matar*) (*en agua*) to drown; (*quitando el aire*) to suffocate; **lo ahogó en la bañera** she drowned him in the bath; **si riegas tanto el cactus lo vas a ~** if you keep watering the cactus so much you'll drown it; ✦**MODISMO ~ las penas** to drown one's sorrows
[2] (= *asfixiar*) [*humo, espina, emoción*] to choke; [*angustia, pena*] to overcome; **el cuello de la camisa me está ahogando** the neck of this shirt is choking me; **su voz tiembla, ahogada por la emoción** her voice trembles, choked with emotion; **este calor me ahoga** this heat is suffocating me *o* is stifling; **la angustia me ahoga** I am overcome with anguish
[3] (*económicamente*) [+ *empresa, país*] to cripple; **los impuestos ahogan a la pequeña empresa** taxation is crippling small businesses; **intentan ~ a Cuba con el bloqueo económico** they are trying to cripple Cuba with the economic blockade
[4] (= *reprimir*) [+ *bostezo, tos*] to stifle; [+ *llanto*] to stifle, choke back
[5] (= *detener*) [+ *fuego, llamas*] to smother; [+ *lucha, rebelión*] to crush, put down; [+ *voces, protestas*] to stifle; [+ *derechos, libertades*] to curtail; [+ *desarrollo, posibilidades, plan*] to hinder, block; **~on la rebelión en sangre** they crushed the rebellion with bloodshed; **las malas comunicaciones ahogan la expansión económica** bad communications are hindering *o* blocking economic expansion; **los aplausos ahogaban sus palabras** her words were drowned (out) by the applause; **el Bar-**

celona ahogó las esperanzas del Deportivo Barcelona put paid to *o* dashed Deportivo's hopes

6 (= *bloquear*) to block; **las hojas ahogan las alcantarillas** the drains were blocked (up) with leaves

7 (*Aut*) [+ *motor*] to flood

8 (*Ajedrez*) [+ *rey*] to stalemate

Ⓑ **ahogarse** VPR 1 (*en agua*) (*accidentalmente*) to drown; (*suicidándose*) to drown o.s.; **se les ahogó el hijo en una piscina** their son drowned in a swimming pool; **no hay que regar tanto las plantas, porque se ahogan** you shouldn't water the plants so much, they'll get waterlogged; ✦*MODISMO* **~se en un vaso de agua** to make a mountain out of a molehill

2 (= *asfixiarse*) 2·1 (*por falta de aire*) **subió la cuesta ahogándose** she climbed the hill gasping for breath; **si subo las escaleras deprisa me ahogo** if I go up the stairs too quickly I get out of breath

2·2 (*por el calor*) to suffocate; **me ahogo de calor** I'm suffocating with this heat, the heat is stifling

2·3 (*con humo, espina*) to choke (**con** on)

3 (= *agobiarse*) **me ahogo en los ascensores** I get claustrophobic in lifts; **se ahoga en un mar de indecisiones** she is drowning in a sea of indecision

4 (*Aut*) [*motor*] to flood

ahogo SM 1 (= *asfixia*) breathlessness; **una sensación de ~ le impedía hablar** a feeling of breathlessness prevented him from speaking; **el asma le produce ~** asthma makes him breathless

2 (= *angustia*) feeling of distress

3 (= *apuro económico*) financial difficulty; **hemos pasado unos ~s tremendos para comprar el piso** we went through tremendous difficulties to buy the flat

ahoguío SM (*Med*) = **ahogo 2**

ahondar ▸conjug 1a◂ Ⓐ VT to deepen, make deeper

Ⓑ VI **~ en** to study thoroughly, explore

Ⓒ **ahondarse** VPR to go in more deeply, sink in more deeply

ahora Ⓐ ADV 1 (= *en este momento*) now; **hace ~ un mes** a month ago now; **~ o nunca** now or never; **ese color se lleva mucho ~** people wear that colour a lot these days *o* now; **el ~ primer ministro** the present prime minister; **de ~ en adelante** from now on; **de ~** of today; **la juventud de ~** the youth of today, today's youth; **no es una cosa de ~** it's not a recent thing; **desde ~** from now on; **hasta ~** up to now, so far; **~ mismo** right now; **~ mismo están reunidos** they're in a meeting at the moment *o* right now; **a partir de ~** from now on; **por ~** for the moment, for now; **es todo lo que podemos hacer por ~** it's all we can do for the moment *o* for now; **por ~ ha dirigido sólo dos películas** up to now he has only directed two films; **~ que** now that; **~ que lo dices** now that you mention it; **~ que lo pienso** come to think of it, now that I think of it; **~ resulta que …** now it turns out that …; **~ sí que me voy** I'm definitely going this time; **~ sí que os habéis equivocado** this time you're definitely wrong

2 (= *hace poco*) just now; **me lo acaban de decir ~** they've just told me; **acaban de llegar ~ mismito** they've just this minute arrived; **~ tiempo** (*Chile*) a while ago; **~ último** (*Chile*) recently

3 (= *enseguida*) in a minute; **~ lo apunto** I'll write it down in a minute; **~ mismo voy** I'll be right there, I'll be there in a minute; **¡hasta ~!** see you in a minute!

Ⓑ CONJ 1 (= *sin embargo*) **~, yo entiendo que eso no fue lo acordado** I understand, though, that that is not what was agreed; **es muy barato; ~, si no te gusta no lo compro** it's very cheap; then again, if you don't like it I won't buy it; **~ bien** however; **~ que** although; **es listo, ~ que bastante vago** he's bright, although quite lazy

2 (*uso distributivo*) **~ la quitan, ~ la ponen** one minute they take it away, the next they put it back; **la ducha escocesa, ~ caliente, ~ fría** the Scottish shower — one minute hot, the next cold

ahorcado/a Ⓐ ADJ (*Cono Sur**) flat broke*

Ⓑ SM/F hanged person

ahorcadura SF hanging

ahorcajarse ▸conjug 1a◂ VPR to sit astride; **~ en** to straddle

ahorcamiento SM hanging

ahorcar ▸conjug 1g◂ Ⓐ VT to hang; **a la fuerza ahorcan** there is no alternative; **¡que me ahorquen!** cross my heart!

Ⓑ **ahorcarse** VPR to hang o.s.

ahorita ADV (*esp LAm*), **ahoritica** ADV (*LAm*), **ahoritita** ADV (*Méx*) (= *en este momento*) right now, this very minute; (= *hace poco*) a minute ago, just now; (= *dentro de poco*) in a minute; **¡~ voy!** I'm just coming!, I'll be with you in a minute!

ahormar ▸conjug 1a◂ VT 1 (= *ajustar*) to fit, adjust (**a** to); (= *formar*) to shape, mould, to mold (*EEUU*); [+ *zapatos*] to break in, stretch; [+ *carácter*] to mould, mold (*EEUU*)

2 **~ a algn** (= *poner en razón*) to make sb see sense

ahorquillado ADJ forked

ahorquillar ▸conjug 1a◂ Ⓐ VT 1 (= *apoyar*) to prop up

2 (= *formar*) to shape like a fork

Ⓑ **ahorquillarse** VPR to fork, become forked

ahorrador ADJ thrifty

ahorrar ▸conjug 1a◂ Ⓐ VT 1 [+ *dinero, energía, tiempo, trabajo*] to save; **así podrás ~ algo de electricidad** this way you will be able to save some electricity; **tienen bastante dinero ahorrado** they have quite a lot of money saved up *o* put by

2 (= *evitar*) [+ *disgustos, molestias, problemas*] to save; [+ *peligro*] to avoid; **me gustaría ~te las molestias** I'd like to save you the trouble; **te ~é los detalles** I'll spare you the details; **lo contó sin ~ detalles** she told it in great detail; **no ~ ataques/críticas contra algn** to show no mercy in one's attacks/criticism of sb; **no ~ elogios con algn** to be unstinting in one's praise of sb; **no ~ esfuerzos** to spare no effort, be unstinting in one's efforts

3 (††) [+ *esclavo*] to free

Ⓑ VI to save; **está ahorrando para comprarse un coche** he's saving (up) to buy a car; **no encienden la calefacción para ~** they don't put the heating on to save money *o* to economize

Ⓒ **ahorrarse** VPR 1 [+ *dinero, tiempo*] to save; **al comprar esa casa se ahorró bastante dinero** buying that house saved him quite a lot of money; ✦*MODISMO* **no ahorrárselas con nadie** to be afraid of nobody

2 (= *evitarse*) to save o.s.; **así te ahorras tener que ir al médico** this will save you *o* you'll save yourself having to go to the doctor's; **un regalo que te ahorras** it saves you having to buy a present, you save yourself having to buy a present; **podías haberte ahorrado los comentarios** I could have done without your comments; **por mí puedes ~te las molestias** as far as I'm concerned you can save yourself the trouble

ahorrativo ADJ (= *que no derrocha*) thrifty; (*pey*) (= *tacaño*) stingy, mean

ahorrillos SMPL small savings

ahorrista SMF saver

ahorro SM 1 (= *acto*) [*de dinero, energía, trabajo*] saving; **una política que fomenta el ~** a policy which promotes saving; **un plan de ~ energético** an energy saving scheme

2 **ahorros** (= *dinero*) savings; **he gastado todos mis ~s** I've spent all my savings; **con el tiempo he conseguido reunir unos ahorrillos** over time I've managed to get some savings together; *ver tb* **caja, libreta**

3 (= *cualidad*) thrift

ahoyar ▸conjug 1a◂ VT to dig holes in

ahuchar[1] ▸conjug 1a◂ VT to hoard, put by

ahuchar[2] ▸conjug 1a◂ VT (*Andes, Méx*) = **azuzar 2**

ahuecado ADJ **voz ahuecada** deep voice

ahuecar ▸conjug 1g◂ Ⓐ VT 1 (= *excavar*) to hollow, hollow out; **~ la mano** to cup one's hand

2 (*Agr*) to loosen, soften; (*Cos*) to fluff out

3 [+ *voz*] to deepen

4 **~ el ala** to make o.s. scarce

Ⓑ VI **¡ahueca!*** beat it!*

Ⓒ **ahuecarse** VPR to show off

ahuesarse ▸conjug 1a◂ VPR (*Andes, Cono Sur*) 1 (*) (= *pasar de moda*) to go out of fashion; [*alimentos*] to go off, go bad; [*mercancías*] to get spoiled

2 [*persona*] to get thin

ahuevado ADJ (*LAm*) silly, stupid

ahuizote SM 1 (*CAm, Méx*) (= *persona*) pain*, pain in the neck*, nuisance

2 (= *maleficio*) evil spell, curse

ahulado SM (*CAm, Méx*) oilskin; **~s** rubber shoes

ahumado Ⓐ ADJ 1 (*Culin*) smoked; (= *lleno de humo*) smoky; [*vidrio*] tinted

2 (*) (= *borracho*) tight*, tipsy

Ⓑ SM 1 (= *acción*) smoking, curing

2 (*) (= *borracho*) drunk

ahumar ▸conjug 1a◂ Ⓐ VT 1 (*Culin*) to smoke, cure

2 [+ *superficie*] to make smoky; [+ *sala*] to fill with smoke

3 [+ *colmena*] to smoke out

Ⓑ VI to smoke, give out smoke

Ⓒ **ahumarse** VPR 1 [*comida*] to acquire a smoky flavour *o* (*EEUU*) flavor

2 [*cuarto*] to be smoky

3 (*) (= *emborracharse*) to get tight*

ahusado ADJ tapering

ahusarse ▸conjug 1a◂ VPR to taper

ahuyentar ▸conjug 1a◂ Ⓐ VT 1 (= *espantar*) to frighten off, frighten away; (= *mantener a distancia*) to keep off

2 [+ *temores, dudas, etc*] to banish, dispel; ~

las penas con vino to drown one's sorrows in wine
Ⓑ **ahuyentarse** VPR to run away; (*Méx*) to stay away

AI SF ABR (= **Amnistía Internacional**) AI

AID SF ABR (= **Agencia Internacional para el Desarrollo**) AID

AIF SF ABR (= **Asociación Internacional de Fomento**) IDA

AIH [ai'atʃe] SF ABR = **Asociación Internacional de Hispanistas**

aimara, aimará (*pl* **aimaraes**) Ⓐ ADJ, SMF Aymara, Aymara Indian
Ⓑ SM (*Ling*) Aymara

aína ADV (*liter*) speedily

aindiado ADJ (*LAm*) Indian-like, Indianized

airadamente ADV angrily

airado ADJ [1] (= *enojado*) angry; (= *violento*) wild, violent; **joven ~** angry young man; **salió ~ del cuarto** he stormed out of the room
[2] [*vida*] immoral, depraved

airar ▸conjug 1a◂ Ⓐ VT (= *enojar*) to anger; (= *irritar*) to annoy
Ⓑ **airarse** VPR to get angry (**de, por** at)

airbag ['erβag] SM (*pl* **airbags**) airbag

aire SM [1] (= *elemento*) air; **una bocanada de ~ fresco** a breath of fresh air; **parece que me falta el ~** I feel as if I can't breathe; **ir a la montaña a respirar ~ puro** to go to the hills where the air is pure; **¡fuera de aquí, aire!*** get out of here! scram!*; **al ~**: **lanzar algo al ~** to throw sth into the air; **la fruta se deja secar al ~** the fruit is left to dry uncovered; **un vestido con la espalda al ~** a backless dress; **estar en el ~** [*balón, paracaidista*] to be in the air; (*Radio*) to be on (the) air; **todo está en el ~ hasta que se conozcan los resultados** it's all up in the air until the results are known; **la polémica estaba en el ~** controversy hung in the air; **dejar una pregunta/problema en el ~** to leave a question/issue up in the air; **al ~ libre** (*con verbo*) outdoors, in the open air; (*con sustantivo*) outdoor *antes de s*, open-air *antes de s*; **el concierto se celebró al ~ libre** the concert was held outdoors *o* in the open air; **una piscina al ~ libre** an outdoor *o* open-air pool; **le gusta la vida al ~ libre** she loves the outdoor life; **actividades al ~ libre** outdoor activities; **salir al ~** (*Radio*) to go on (the) air; **saltar por los ~s** to blow up, explode; **tomar el ~** to get some fresh air; **salió a tomar un poco el ~** he went out to get *o* for some fresh air; **¡vete a tomar el ~!*** scram!*, clear off!*; **~ viciado** (*en habitación cerrada*) stale air; (*en fábrica, ciudad contaminada*) foul air; **volar por los ~s** to blow up, explode; **todas las esperanzas de paz han volado por los ~s** all hopes of peace have been dashed; ✦*MODISMOS* **a mi/tu/su ~**: **aprendieron a su ~** they learned in their own way; **le gusta hacer las cosas a su ~** he likes to do things his own way; **eso le permitió trabajar a su ~** that enabled her to work the way she wanted; **ir a su ~** to go one's own way, do one's own thing*; **beber los ~s por algn** to be madly in love with sb; **darle un ~ a algn**: **le dio un ~ y perdió el habla** he had a stroke and lost the power of speech; **estar de buen/mal ~** to be in a good/bad mood; **mantenerse del ~** to live on thin air; **mudarse a cualquier ~** to change from one minute to the next; **ofenderse del ~** to be really touchy; **seguir el ~ a algn** to humour sb; **vivir del ~** to live on thin air ► **aire acondicionado** air conditioning; **un vehículo con ~ acondicionado** an air-conditioned vehicle ► **aire colado** cold draught, cold draft (*EEUU*) ► **aire comprimido** compressed air; **una escopeta de ~ comprimido** an air rifle ► **aire detonante** firedamp ► **aire líquido** liquid air
[2] (*Meteo*) (= *viento*) wind; (= *corriente*) draught, draft (*EEUU*); **no corre nada de ~** there isn't a breath of wind; **entra mucho ~ por la puerta** there's a strong draught coming in through the door; **hoy hace mucho ~** it's very windy today; **entraba un ~ muy agradable de la calle** there was a lovely breeze coming in from the street; **dar ~ a algn** to fan sb; **la prensa no da ~ al éxito del gobierno** the press is giving no coverage to the government's success; **darse ~** to fan o.s.; ✦*MODISMOS* **¿qué ~s te traen por aquí?** what brings you here?; **cambiar *o* mudar de ~s** to have a change (of scene) ► **aires de cambio** (*Pol*) winds of change
[3] (= *aspecto*) air; **los techos altos le daban un ~ señorial a la casa** high ceilings gave a stately air to the house; **le respondió con ~ cansado** he replied wearily; **su cara tiene un ~ familiar** there's something familiar about his face; **tienen ~ de no haber roto un plato en su vida** they look as if butter wouldn't melt in their mouths; ✦*MODISMO* **darse ~s** to put on airs; **eso te pasa por darte ~s de superioridad** that's what happens when you think you're better than everyone else *o* when you put on airs; **no te des esos ~s de suficiencia conmigo** don't get on your high horse with me
[4] (= *parecido*) **¿no le notas un ~ con Carlos?** don't you think he looks a bit like Carlos?; **darse un ~ a algn** to look a bit like sb ► **aire de familia** family resemblance, family likeness
[5] (= *aerofagia*) wind; **las lentejas me provocan mucho ~** lentils give me a lot of wind
[6] (= *garbo*) style, panache; **lleva la ropa con mucho ~** she wears her clothes with great style *o* panache; **dio unos pases de muleta con buen ~** he did a few stylish passes with the cape
[7] (*Mús*) air; **música con ~s populares** music with popular airs

aireación SF ventilation

aireado SM (= *ventilación*) ventilation; [*de vino*] aeration

aire-aire ADJ **misil ~** air-to-air missile

airear ▸conjug 1a◂ Ⓐ VT [1] (= *ventilar*) to air, ventilate; [+ *ropa*] to air; **~ la atmósfera** to clear the air
[2] (= *difundir*) [+ *idea, cuestión*] to air; (*en prensa*) to discuss at length, give a lot of coverage to
[3] (= *publicar*) to gossip about
Ⓑ **airearse** VPR (= *tomar el aire*) to take the air; (= *resfriarse*) to catch a chill

airecito SM breeze, gentle wind

aireo SM ventilation

aire-tierra ADJ INV **misil ~** air-to-ground missile

airón SM [1] (= *ave*) heron
[2] (= *penacho*) tuft, crest

airosamente ADV gracefully, elegantly; **salir ~ de algo** to come through sth unscathed

airosidad SF grace, elegance

airoso ADJ [1] (= *elegante*) graceful, elegant; **quedar ~ ◊ salir ~** to be successful, come out with flying colours; **salir ~ de algo** to come through sth unscathed
[2] (= *ventilado*) airy; [*cuarto*] draughty; [*lugar expuesto*] windy; [*tiempo*] windy, blowy

aislación SF insulation ► **aislación de sonido** soundproofing ► **aislación térmica** insulation

aislacionismo SM isolationism

aislacionista ADJ, SMF isolationist

aislado ADJ [1] (= *remoto*) isolated
[2] (= *incomunicado*) cut off; **quedamos ~s por las inundaciones** we were cut off by the floods; **están ~s de la civilización** they are cut off *o* isolated from civilization
[3] (= *suelto*) **un caso ~** an isolated case
[4] (*Elec*) insulated

aislador Ⓐ ADJ (*Elec*) insulating
Ⓑ SM (*Elec*) insulator

aislamiento SM [1] (= *acción*) isolation; (= *soledad*) loneliness, lonesomeness (*EEUU*) ► **aislamiento sensorial** sensory deprivation
[2] (*Elec*) insulation ► **aislamiento acústico** soundproofing ► **aislamiento térmico** insulation

aislante Ⓐ ADJ insulating
Ⓑ SM (*Elec*) insulator; (= *suelo impermeable*) groundsheet

aislar ▸conjug 1a◂ Ⓐ VT [1] (= *dejar solo*) to isolate; (= *separar*) to separate, detach
[2] [+ *ciudad, fortaleza*] to cut off
[3] (*Elec*) to insulate
Ⓑ **aislarse** VPR to isolate o.s., cut o.s. off (**de** from)

AITA SF ABR (= **Asociación Internacional del Transporte Aéreo**) IATA

ajá EXCL (= *¡estupendo!*) splendid!; (*indicando sorpresa*) aha!

ajajay EXCL = **ajay**

ajamonarse* ▸conjug 1a◂ VPR to get plump, run to fat

ajar¹ SM garlic field, garlic patch

ajar² ▸conjug 1a◂ Ⓐ VT [1] (= *arrugar*) to crumple, crush
[2] (= *despreciar*) to abuse, disparage
Ⓑ **ajarse** VPR (= *arrugarse*) [*piel*] to get wrinkled; [*planta*] to wither, fade; [*chaqueta, vestido*] to get crumpled

ajarabezado ADJ **vino ~** wine with syrup added

ajarafe SM (*Geog*) tableland; (*Arquit*) terrace, flat roof

ajardinar ▸conjug 1a◂ VT to landscape; **zona ajardinada** landscaped area

ajay EXCL (*LAm*) (*risa*) ha!

-aje *ver* **Aspects of Word Formation in Spanish 2**

ajedrea SF savory

ajedrecista SMF chess player

ajedrez SM chess; **un ~** a chess set

ajedrezado ADJ chequered, checkered (*EEUU*)

ajenjo SM (= *planta*) wormwood; (= *bebida*) absinth, absinthe

ajeno ADJ [1] (= *de otro*) **con el dinero ~** with other people's money; **puso los huevos en un nido ~** it laid its eggs in another bird's nest; **esta semana juegan en campo ~** this week they are playing away from home; **a**

costa ajena at sb else's expense; **por cuenta ajena**: **trabaja por cuenta ajena** he works for someone else; **trabajador por cuenta ajena** employed worker; **es matón por cuenta ajena** he's a hired thug; **meterse en lo ~** to interfere in other people's affairs; *ver tb* **vergüenza 1**

2 (= *no relacionado*) **~ a** outside; **según fuentes ajenas a la empresa** according to sources outside the company; **"prohibido el paso a toda persona ajena a la obra"** "authorized staff only past this point"; **hablaron de cosas ajenas al trabajo** they talked about things unconnected with work; **el malhumor es ~ a su carácter** he's not at all bad-tempered in character, being bad-tempered is quite alien to his character (*frm*); **reacciones ajenas a la racionalidad** irrational reactions; **el juez declaró que se mantendría ~ a la política** the judge declared that he would remain outside of politics; **por razones ajenas a nuestra voluntad** for reasons beyond our control

3 (= *indiferente*) **no es ajena a los problemas de los ciudadanos** she is not indifferent to the population's problems; **nada de lo humano le es ~** (*liter*) everything human is his concern (*liter*); **siguió leyendo, ~ a lo que sucedía** she carried on reading, oblivious to what was happening

4 (= *extraño*) strange; **todo le era ~ y desconocido** everything was strange and unknown

ajerezado ADJ sherry-flavoured *o* (*EEUU*) -flavored

ajete SM young garlic

ajetreado ADJ busy

ajetrearse ▸conjug 1a◂ VPR (= *atarearse*) to bustle about, be busy; (= *fatigarse*) to tire o.s. out

ajetreo SM (= *actividad*) hustle and bustle; (= *labor*) drudgery, hard work; **es un continuo ~** there's constant coming and going

ají SM (*pl* **ajíes, ajises**) (*LAm*) (= *pimiento picante*) chili; (= *pimiento dulce*) red pepper; (= *salsa*) chili sauce; ✦*MODISMOS* **estar hecho un ~** to be hopping mad; **ponerse como un ~** to go bright red, go bright red in the face; **refregarle a algn el ~** to criticize sb

ajiaceite SM *sauce of garlic and olive oil*

ajiaco SM (*LAm*) 1 (*Culin*) potato and chili stew; **meterse el ~*** to eat

2 (= *lío*) mess, mix-up

ajibararse ▸conjug 1a◂ VPR (*Caribe*) = **aguajirarse**

ajigolones SMPL (*CAm, Méx*) troubles, difficulties

ajilar ▸conjug 1a◂ VI (*CAm, Méx*) to set out somewhere; (*Caribe*) to walk quickly

ajilimoje SM, **ajilimójili** SM *sauce of garlic and pepper*; **~s*** bits and pieces, things, odds and ends; **ahí está el ~*** that's the point, that's the trouble

ajillo SM chopped garlic; **al ~** with garlic, cooked in garlic

ajimez SM mullioned window

ajiseco SM (*Andes*) mild red pepper

ajises* SMPL (*LAm*) *de* **ají**

ajizarse* ▸conjug 1f◂ VPR (*Cono Sur*) to lose one's temper, get mad

ajo SM 1 (*Bot, Culin*) garlic; **un ~** a clove of garlic; (= *salsa*) garlic sauce; ✦*MODISMOS* **¡~ y agua!*** you've just got to put up with it!; **harto de ~s** ill-bred, common; **(tieso) como un ~** high and mighty, stuck-up*; **estar como el ~** (*Cono Sur*) to feel miserable; **andar en el ~** ◊ **estar en el ~** (= *involucrado*) to be mixed up in it; (= *enterado*) to be in on the secret; **revolver el ~** to stir up trouble ▸ **ajo tierno** young garlic

2 (*) (= *palabrota*) swearword, oath, curse; ✦*MODISMOS* **echar ~s y cebollas** ◊ **soltar ~s y cebollas** to swear like a trooper, let fly*

-ajo, -aja *ver* **Aspects of Word Formation in Spanish 2**

ajoaceite SM *sauce of garlic and oil*

ajoarriero SM *dish of cod with oil, garlic and peppers*

ajobar ▸conjug 1a◂ VT to carry on one's back, hump*

ajoblanco SM *cold garlic and almond soup*

ajobo SM (= *carga*) load; (= *pesadumbre*) burden

ajochar ▸conjug 1a◂ VT (*Andes*) = **azuzar**

ajonje SM, **ajonjo** SM birdlime

ajonjeo SM (*Andes*) compliment, nice remark

ajonjolí SM sesame

ajorca SF bracelet, bangle

ajornalar ▸conjug 1a◂ VT to employ by the day

ajotar ▸conjug 1a◂ VT (*CAm*) = **azuzar** (*Caribe*) (= *desdeñar*) to scorn; (= *rechazar*) to rebuff

ajoto SM (*Caribe*) rebuff

ajuar SM 1 [*de novia*] (= *objetos*) trousseau; (= *dote*) dowry

2 [*de niño*] layette

3 (= *muebles*) household furnishings *pl*

ajuarar ▸conjug 1a◂ VT to furnish, fit up

ajuiciado ADJ sensible

ajuiciar ▸conjug 1b◂ VT to bring to one's senses

ajumado/a* Ⓐ ADJ tight*, tipsy

Ⓑ SM/F drunk, drunkard

ajumarse* ▸conjug 1a◂ VPR to get tight*, get tipsy

ajuntar* ▸conjug 1a◂ Ⓐ VT (*entre niños*) to make friends with, be friends with; **¡ya no te ajunto!** I'm not your friend any more!

Ⓑ **ajuntarse** VPR (= *amancebarse*) to live together, live in sin; (*entre niños*) **¡no me ajunto contigo!** I'm not your friend any more!

Ajuria Enea SF (= *residencia*) *residence of chief minister of Basque autonomous government*; (= *gobierno*) *Basque autonomous government*

ajurídico ADJ (*Cono Sur*) illegal

ajustado ADJ 1 (= *ceñido*) tight, tight-fitting; **unos vaqueros ~s** a pair of tight *o* tight-fitting jeans; **la blusa le quedaba muy ajustada** the blouse was very tight on her

2 (= *con poco margen*) [*presupuesto*] tight; [*resultado*] tight, close; **tienen los precios más ~s del mercado** they have the most competitive prices in the market; **hemos tenido que venderlo todo a un precio muy ~** we had to sell everything at a very low profit; **los resultados de las elecciones han sido muy ~s** the election results were very tight *o* close; **la victoria fue muy ajustada** it was a very close victory

3 (= *acertado*) accurate; **un ~ retrato de la sociedad española** an accurate portrait of Spanish society; **~ a algo** in keeping with sth; **usó un lenguaje ~ a la ocasión** his language was in keeping with the occasion; **~ a la ley** in accordance with the law

ajustador SM 1 (*Téc*) fitter; (*Tip*) compositor

2 (*Col*) (= *sujetador*) (*tb* **~es**) bra

3 (= *chaleco*) bodice

ajustamiento SM 1 [*de pieza, grifo*] (*al colocarla*) fitting; (*al apretarla*) tightening

2 (*Fin*) settlement

ajustar ▸conjug 1a◂ Ⓐ VT 1 (*Téc*) 1·1 [+ *pieza, grifo*] (*colocando*) to fit; (*apretando*) to tighten; **¿cómo se ajusta la baca al vehículo?** how does the roof rack fit onto the vehicle?; **necesito unos alicates para ~ la válvula** I need some pliers to tighten the valve

1·2 (= *regular*) [+ *volumen, temperatura*] to adjust, regulate; [+ *asiento, retrovisor*] to adjust; [+ *cinturón*] to tighten

1·3 (*Chile, Méx*) [+ *motor*] to fix; **hay que ~le el motor a la moto** we need to fix the motorbike's engine

2 (= *pactar*) [+ *acuerdo, trato*] to reach; [+ *boda*] to arrange; [+ *precio*] to agree on; **ya hemos ajustado el presupuesto con los albañiles** we have already agreed on the price with the builders; **el precio ha quedado ajustado en 500 euros** the price has been fixed *o* set at 500 euros; **~ cuentas con algn** (*lit*) to settle accounts with sb; (*fig*) to settle one's scores with sb

3 (= *adaptar*) to adjust (**a** to); **deben ~ la producción a la demanda** they must adjust production to demand; **tuvieron una reunión para ~ diferencias** they had a meeting to settle their differences

4 (*euf*) (= *reducir*) **han tenido que ~ el número de sucursales** the number of branches had to be rationalized (*euf*); **este año hemos tenido que ~ drásticamente el presupuesto** this year we have had to sharply reduce our budget

5 (*Cos*) [+ *cintura, manga*] to take in; **hay que ~ la cintura** the waist needs taking in

6 (*Tip*) to compose

7 (†) [+ *criado*] to hire, engage

8 (*CAm, Méx, Chile, Ven*) **~ un golpe a algn** to deal sb a blow; **~ un garrotazo a algn** to beat sb with a club

Ⓑ VI 1 (= *encajar*) to fit; **este corcho no ajusta en la botella** this cork doesn't fit in the bottle; **rellena con masilla los empalmes que no ajusten** fill the joints that don't fit together with putty

2 (*Ven*) (= *agudizarse*) to get worse; **durante la noche me ajustó el dolor** the pain got worse during the night; **por el camino ajustó el aguacero** on the way, there was a sudden downpour

Ⓒ **ajustarse** VPR 1 (= *ceñirse*) 1·1 [*persona*] **¿me ayudas a ~me la corbata?** can you help me adjust my tie?; **salió del baño ajustándose los pantalones** he came out of the bathroom doing up his trousers

1·2 [*zapato*] to fit; [*pantalón, vestido*] to cling; **el zapato debe ~se al pie lo mejor posible** the shoe should fit the foot as well as possible; **se ajusta al cuerpo como una segunda piel** it clings to the body like a second skin; *ver tb* **cinturón**

2 (= *encajarse*) to fit; **el tapón no se ajustaba** the top didn't fit

3 (= *adaptarse*) **~se a** [+ *situación, estilo*] to adapt to; [+ *necesidades*] to meet; [+ *presupuesto*] to be within; [+ *norma, regla*] to comply with; **los precios bajan para ~se a las demandas del mercado** prices go down

to meet the demands of the market; **el motor se ajusta a la nueva normativa europea** the engine complies with the new European standards; **este contrato se ajusta al presupuesto de nuestro club** this contract is within our club's budget; **tendrán que ~se al guión** they will have to keep to *o* follow the script; **(no) se ajusta a derecho** it is (not) legally admissible
[4] (= *coincidir*) **la narración se ajusta a la verdad** the story agrees with the facts; **los rumores no siempre se ajustan a la realidad** rumours do not always reflect the real situation
[5] (= *llegar a un acuerdo*) to come to an agreement (**con** with)

ajuste SM [1] (*Téc*) adjustment; **~ de zoom eléctrico** electric zoom adjustment; **estos tornillos necesitan algo de ~** these screws need a little tightening; **¿cómo se hace el ~ del brillo en este televisor?** how do you adjust the brightness on this television?; **~ fino** fine tuning; *ver tb* **carta 7**
[2] (= *adaptación*) adjustment; **se producirán ~s de precios** price adjustments will occur; **mal ~** maladjustment ► **ajuste económico** economic adjustment ► **ajuste estructural** structural adjustment ► **ajuste financiero** financial settlement ► **ajuste de plantilla** (*Esp*) redeployment of labour *o* (*EEUU*) labor ► **ajuste laboral** redeployment of labour *o* (*EEUU*) labor ► **ajuste presupuestario** budget settlement ► **ajuste salarial** wage adjustment
[3] (= *pacto*) **ha habido un ~ de costes** there has been an adjustment in costs; **tras el ~ del precio** after fixing the price ► **ajuste de cuentas** settling of scores
[4] (*Cos*) **necesita unos pequeños ~s en la cintura** it needs to be taken in a little at the waist
[5] (*Tip*) composition, make-up
[6] (*Jur*) (= *honorarios*) retaining fee; (= *sobrepaga*) bonus ► **ajuste por aumento del costo de la vida** cost-of-living bonus
[7] (*Méx*) [*de motor*] overhaul

ajusticiable SMF *person who may face capital punishment*

ajusticiamiento SM execution

ajusticiar ▸conjug 1b◂ VT to execute, put to death

ajustón SM (*Andes*) (= *castigo*) punishment; (= *mal trato*) ill-treatment

al *ver* **a**

ala Ⓐ SF [1] [*de insecto, pájaro*] wing; **de cuatro ~s** four-winged; **de ~s azules** blue-winged
[2] [*de avión*] wing; **con ~s en delta** delta-winged; **con ~s en flecha** swept-wing ► **ala delta** hang glider
[3] (*Pol*) wing; **el ~ izquierda del partido** the left wing of the party
[4] (*Mil*) wing, flank
[5] [*de edificio*] wing
[6] (= *parte sobresaliente*) [*de sombrero*] brim; [*de corazón*] auricle; [*del techo*] eaves *pl*; [*de mesa*] leaf, flap
[7] (*Dep*) (= *banda*) wing ► **ala derecha** outside-right ► **ala izquierda** outside-left
[8] ✦*MODISMOS* **ahuecar el ~*** to beat it*; **arrastrar el ~** (= *cortejar*) to be courting; (= *estar deprimido*) to be depressed; **se le cayeron las ~s del corazón** his heart sank; **cortar las ~s a algn** to clip sb's wings; **dar ~s a algn** to encourage sb; **del ~** (*Esp**) **las 100 euros del ~** a cool 100 euros*; **ser como ~ de mosca** to be paper thin, be transparent; **quedar tocado de ~** to be a lame duck; **tomar ~s*** to get cheeky*; **volar con las propias ~s** to stand on one's own two feet
Ⓑ SMF (*Dep*) winger; **medio ~** half-back, wing-half

Alá SM Allah

alabado SM [1] **al ~** (*Cono Sur*) (= *amanecer*) at dawn
[2] **al ~** (*Méx*) (= *anochecer*) at nightfall

alabador ADJ eulogistic

alabamiento SM praise

alabancioso ADJ boastful

alabanza SF (*tb* **~s**) praise; **en ~ de** in praise of; **cantar las ~s de algn** to sing sb's praises; **digno de toda ~** thoroughly praiseworthy, highly commendable

alabar ▸conjug 1a◂ Ⓐ VT to praise; **~ a algn de** *o* **por algo** to praise sb for sth
Ⓑ **alabarse** VPR to boast; **~se de** to boast of being; **se alaba de** *o* **por prudente** he prides himself on being sensible

alabarda SF halberd

alabardero SM (*Hist*) halberdier; (*Teat*) member of the claque, paid applauder

alabastrado ADJ, **alabastrino** ADJ alabastrine, alabaster *antes de s*

alabastro SM alabaster

álabe SM (*Mec*) wooden cog, tooth; [*de noria*] bucket; [*de árbol*] drooping branch

alabear ▸conjug 1a◂ Ⓐ VT to warp
Ⓑ **alabearse** VPR to warp

alabeo SM warp, warping; **tomar ~** to warp

alacalufe SMF (*Cono Sur*) *Indian inhabitant of Tierra del Fuego*

alacena SF cupboard, closet (*EEUU*)

alacrán SM [1] (= *escorpión*) scorpion
[2] (*Cono Sur*) (= *chismoso*) gossip, scandalmonger

alacranear ▸conjug 1a◂ VI to gossip, spread scandal

alacraneo SM (*Cono Sur*) gossip, scandal

alacre ADJ (*Méx*) ready and willing

alacridad SF alacrity, readiness; **con ~** with alacrity, readily

alada SF flutter, fluttering

ALADI SF ABR = **Asociación Latinoamericana de Integración**

Aladino SM Aladdin

alado ADJ (= *con alas*) winged; (= *ligero*) swift

alafia SF (*CAm*) verbosity, wordiness

alafre (*Caribe*) Ⓐ ADJ wretched, miserable
Ⓑ SM wretch

alagartado ADJ motley, variegated, many-colored (*EEUU*)

alalá SM *traditional song in parts of northern Spain*

ALALC SF ABR (= **Asociación Latinoamericana de Libre Comercio**) LAFTA

alambicado ADJ [1] (= *destilado*) distilled
[2] (= *intrincado*) [*proceso, estilo*] intricate; [*teoría, misterio*] complex
[3] (= *afectado*) [*estilo*] precious; [*modales*] affected
[4] (= *sutil*) subtle
[5] (= *dado con escasez*) given sparingly, given grudgingly
[6] (= *reducido*) **precios ~s** rock-bottom prices

alambicamiento SM [1] (= *destilación*) distilling
[2] (= *rebuscamiento*) preciosity, affectation

alambicar ▸conjug 1g◂ VT [1] (= *destilar*) to distil, distill (*EEUU*)
[2] [+ *estilo*] to complicate unnecessarily
[3] (= *escudriñar*) to scrutinize, investigate
[4] (= *reducir*) (*gen*) to minimize, reduce to a minimum; [+ *precio*] to reduce to the minimum

alambique SM still; ✦*MODISMOS* **dar algo por ~** to give sth sparingly *o* grudgingly; **pasar algo por ~** to go through sth with a fine-tooth comb

alambiquería SF (*Caribe*) distillery

alambiquero SM (*Caribe*) distiller

alambrada SF (= *red*) wire netting; (= *cerca*) wire fence; (*Mil*) barbed-wire entanglement ► **alambrada de espino**, **alambrada de púas** barbed-wire fence

alambrado SM (= *red*) wire netting; (= *cerca*) wire fence, wire fencing; (*Elec*) wiring, wiring system

alambrar ▸conjug 1a◂ VT (*Elec*) to wire; (*Agr*) to fence with wire

alambre SM wire; ✦*MODISMO* **estar hecho un ~** to be as thin as a rake ► **alambre cargado** live wire ► **alambre de espino**, **alambre de púas** barbed wire ► **alambre de tierra** earth wire, ground wire (*EEUU*) ► **alambre espinoso** barbed wire ► **alambre forrado** covered wire

alambrera SF (= *red*) wire netting, chicken wire; (= *cobertera*) wire cover; (*para chimenea*) fireguard

alambrista SMF tightrope walker

alambrito SM (*LAm*) tall thin person

alambrón SM wire rod

alameda SF (*Bot*) poplar grove; (= *avenida*) avenue, boulevard

álamo SM poplar ► **álamo blanco** white poplar ► **álamo de Italia** Lombardy poplar ► **álamo negro** black poplar ► **álamo temblón** aspen

alamparse ▸conjug 1a◂ VPR **~ por** to crave, have a craving for

alancear ▸conjug 1a◂ VT to spear, lance

alano[1] SM mastiff

alano[2] (*Hist*) Ⓐ ADJ of the Alani
Ⓑ **alanos** SMPL Alani

alar SM [1] [*de tejado*] eaves *pl*
[2] (*LAm*) (= *acera*) pavement, sidewalk (*EEUU*)

alarde SM [1] display; **un ~ de patriotismo** a display of patriotism; **la decisión fue todo un ~ de serenidad** the decision was a feat of cool-headedness; **en un ~ de generosidad, me pagaron la cena** in a show *o* display of generosity they paid for my dinner; **en un ~ de falsa modestia** in a show of false modesty; **hacer ~ de**: **siempre hace ~ de sus riquezas** he is always showing off his wealth; **siempre está haciendo ~ de sus triunfos sexuales** he's always boasting about *o* of his sexual prowess; **el grupo hizo ~ de su poder de convocatoria** the band demonstrated *o* displayed their pulling power, it was a demonstration of the pulling power of the band
[2] (*Mil*†) review
[3] **alardes** (*esp LAm*) (= *jactancias*) boasts

alardeado ADJ much-vaunted

alardear ▸conjug 1a◂ VI to boast, brag (**de** about)

alardeo SM boasting, bragging

alargadera SF (*Quím*) adapter; (*Téc*) extension

alargado ADJ long, extended

alargador SM (*Cono Sur*) extension lead

alargamiento SM (*gen*) lengthening; (= *prórroga*) extension; (*Arquit*) extension

alargar ▸conjug 1h◂ Ⓐ VT [1] (*en longitud*) [+ *cuerda, goma*] to stretch; [+ *pista de aterrizaje*] to lengthen; [+ *cuello*] to crane; [+ *mano*] to stretch out; [+ *vestido*] to lengthen, let down
[2] (*en tiempo*) [+ *visita*] to prolong, extend; [+ *discurso, espera*] to prolong; [+ *relato*] to spin out; **esto alargó nuestra espera** this prolonged our wait, this forced us to wait longer
[3] [+ *cable de escalada*] to pay out
[4] (= *dar*) to hand, pass (**a** to)
[5] [+ *sueldo*] to increase, raise
[6] [+ *paso*] to quicken
Ⓑ **alargarse** VPR [1] (*en longitud*) to lengthen, get longer [2] (*en tiempo*) [*días*] to grow longer; [*relato*] to drag out; [*orador*] to go on for a long time; **~se en algo** to expatiate on sth, enlarge upon sth; **se alargó en la charla** he spun his talk out [3] (= *divagar*) to digress

alargo SM extension, lead

alarido SM shriek, yell; **dar ~s** to shriek, yell

alarife SMF [1] (*Constr*) (= *arquitecto*) master builder; (= *albañil*) bricklayer
[2] (*Cono Sur*) (= *tipo listo*) sharp customer*; (= *mujer de vida alegre*) loose woman

alarma SF alarm; **falsa ~** false alarm; **dar la ~** to raise the alarm; **con creciente ~** with growing alarm, with growing concern; **timbre de ~** alarm bell; **voz de ~** warning note; **señal de ~** alarm signal ▸ **alarma aérea** air-raid warning ▸ **alarma antiincendios** fire alarm ▸ **alarma antirrobo** [*de coche*] car alarm, anti-theft alarm; [*de casa*] burglar alarm ▸ **alarma de incendios** fire alarm ▸ **alarma de ladrones** burglar alarm ▸ **alarma social** public alarm; **no había motivo para la ~ social** there was no cause for panic *o* public alarm

alarmante ADJ alarming

alarmantemente ADV alarmingly

alarmar ▸conjug 1a◂ Ⓐ VT (= *dar alarma*) to alarm; (= *asustar*) to frighten; (*Mil*) to alert, rouse
Ⓑ **alarmarse** VPR to get alarmed, be alarmed; **¡no te alarmes!** don't be alarmed!

alarmismo SM alarmism

alarmista Ⓐ ADJ alarmist
Ⓑ SMF alarmist

alauí ADJ, **alauita** ADJ Moroccan

Álava SF Álava

alavense = **alavés**

alavés/esa Ⓐ ADJ of/from Álava
Ⓑ SM/F native/inhabitant of Álava; **los alaveses** the people of Álava

alazán/ana Ⓐ ADJ sorrel
Ⓑ SM/F sorrel, sorrel horse

alazor SM safflower; **aceite de ~** safflower oil

alba SF [1] (= *amanecer*) dawn, daybreak; **al ~** at dawn; **al rayar** *o* **romper el ~** at daybreak
[2] (*Rel*) alb

albacea SMF executor/executrix

Albacete SM Albacete

albacetense = **albaceteño**

albaceteño/a Ⓐ ADJ of/from Albacete
Ⓑ SM/F native/inhabitant of Albacete; **los ~s** the people of Albacete

albacora SF albacore, long fin tunny

albahaca SF basil

albanega SF hairnet

albanés/esa Ⓐ ADJ, SM/F Albanian
Ⓑ SM (*Ling*) Albanian

Albania SF Albania

albano = **albanés**

albanokosovar ADJ, SMF Kosovar Albanian

albañal SM (= *cloaca*) drain, sewer; (= *estercolero*) dung heap; (*fig*) (= *sitio sucio*) mess, muck heap*

albañil SMF builder, construction worker

albañilería SF (= *oficio*) bricklaying, building; **trabajo de ~** brickwork

albaquía SF balance due, remainder

albar ADJ white

albarán SM [1] (*Com*) delivery note, invoice
[2] (= *señal*) "to let" sign

albarda SF (*para la carga*) packsaddle; (*CAm*) (= *silla de montar*) saddle; **~ sobre ~** piling it on, with a lot of unnecessary repetition; **✦MODISMO ¡como ahora llueven ~s!*** not on your life!

albardar ▸conjug 1a◂ VT to saddle, put a packsaddle on

albardear* ▸conjug 1a◂ VT (*CAm*) to bother, vex

albardilla SF [1] (= *silla de montar*) small saddle; (= *almohadilla*) cushion, pad
[2] (*Arquit*) coping
[3] (*Culin*) lard

albareque SM sardine net

albaricoque SM apricot

albaricoquero SM apricot tree

albariño SM (*type of*) *Galician wine*

albarrada SF [1] (= *muro*) wall
[2] (*Andes*) (= *cisterna*) cistern

albatros SM INV albatross, double eagle (*EEUU*)

albayalde SM white lead

albazo SM [1] (*Andes, Méx*) dawn raid
[2] (*Cono Sur*) dawn visit

albeador(a)* SM/F (*Cono Sur*) early riser

albear* ▸conjug 1a◂ VI (*Cono Sur*) to get up at dawn, get up early

albedrío SM (= *voluntad*) will; (= *capricho*) whim; (= *gusto*) pleasure; **libre ~** free will; **¡hágalo a su ~!** have it your way!

albéitar SM veterinary surgeon, veterinarian (*EEUU*)

albeitería SF veterinary medicine

alberca SF (= *depósito*) tank, reservoir; (*Méx*) (= *piscina*) swimming pool

albérchigo SM (= *fruto*) peach, clingstone peach; (= *árbol*) peach tree, clingstone peach tree

albergar ▸conjug 1h◂ Ⓐ VT [1] (= *acomodar*) [+ *visitante, refugiado, inmigrante*] to provide accommodation for; [+ *criminal, fugitivo*] to harbour; **fue condenado por ~ a un terrorista** he was found guilty of harbouring a terrorist
[2] (= *dar cabida a*) [+ *espectadores, público*] to accommodate, hold; [+ *evento, celebración*] to host; **el estadio puede ~ a 30.000 personas** the stadium can accommodate *o* hold 30,000 people, the stadium has a capacity of 30,000; **el edificio que alberga la sede del partido** the building which houses the party's headquarters; **este terreno ~á 300 chalets** this land will provide space for 300 houses
[3] [+ *esperanza*] to cherish; [+ *dudas*] to have; **aún alberga los rencores de la infancia** he still harbours childhood resentments
Ⓑ **albergarse** VPR [1] (= *refugiarse*) to shelter
[2] (= *alojarse*) to stay

albergue SM (= *refugio*) shelter, refuge; (= *alojamiento*) lodging; [*de montaña*] refuge, mountain hut; (*Zool*) lair, den; **dar ~ a algn** to take sb in ▸ **albergue de animales** animal refuge ▸ **albergue de carretera** roadhouse ▸ **albergue juvenil** youth hostel ▸ **albergue nacional** state-owned tourist hotel

alberguista SMF youth hosteller

albero Ⓐ ADJ white
Ⓑ SM [1] (*Geol*) pipeclay
[2] (= *paño*) dishcloth, tea towel

Alberto SM Albert

albillo ADJ white

albina SF salt lake, salt marsh

albinismo SM albinism

albino/a ADJ, SM/F albino

Albión SF Albion; **la pérfida ~** perfidious Albion

albis ADV **quedarse en ~** not to know a thing, not have a clue; **me quedé en ~** my mind went blank

albo ADJ (*liter*) white

albogue SM (= *flauta*) rustic flute, shepherd's flute; (= *gaita*) bagpipes; **~s** (= *platillos*) cymbals

albóndiga SF meatball

albondigón SM large meatball

albor SM [1] (= *color*) whiteness
[2] (= *luz*) dawn, dawn light ▸ **albor de la vida** childhood, youth
[3] (*liter*) **albores** dawn; **a los ~es** at dawn; **en los ~es de la ciencia** at the dawn of science

alborada SF (= *alba*) daybreak, dawn; (*Mil*) reveille; (*Mús poét*) aubade, dawn song; (*Méx Rel*) night procession

alborear ▸conjug 1a◂ VI to dawn

albornoz SM [1] (= *de baño*) bathrobe
[2] (= *prenda árabe*) burnous, burnouse

alborotadamente ADV (= *ruidosamente*) noisily; (= *con excitación*) excitedly

alborotadizo ADJ excitable

alborotado ADJ [1] [*persona*] (= *excitado*) agitated, excited; (= *ruidoso*) noisy; (= *precipitado*) hasty; (= *impetuoso*) reckless; (= *amotinado*) riotous
[2] [*período*] troubled, eventful
[3] [*mar*] rough

alborotador(a) Ⓐ ADJ (= *ruidoso*) boisterous, noisy; (*Pol*) (= *sedicioso*) seditious
Ⓑ SM/F (= *agitador*) agitator, troublemaker; (= *alumno*) troublemaker

alborotar ▸conjug 1a◂ Ⓐ VT (= *agitar*) to disturb, agitate; (= *amotinar*) to incite to rebel; (= *excitar*) to excite
Ⓑ VI to make a racket, make a row
Ⓒ **alborotarse** VPR [1] [*individuo*] to get excited, get worked up; [*multitud*] to riot; [*mar*] to get rough
[2] (*CAm*) (= *ponerse amoroso*) to become amo-

rous
3 (*Cono Sur*) [*caballo*] to rear up
alboroto SM 1 (= *disturbio*) disturbance; (= *vocerío*) racket, row; (= *jaleo*) uproar; (= *motín*) riot; (= *pelea*) brawl; **armar un ~** to cause a commotion
2 (= *susto*) scare, alarm
3 **alborotos** (*CAm*) (= *rosetas de maíz*) popcorn *sing*
alborotoso/a (*Andes, Caribe*) Ⓐ ADJ troublesome, riotous
Ⓑ SM/F troublemaker
alborozado ADJ jubilant, overjoyed
alborozar ▸conjug 1f◂ Ⓐ VT to gladden, fill with joy
Ⓑ **alborozarse** VPR to be overjoyed, rejoice
alborozo SM joy, jubilation, rejoicing
albricias SFPL 1 (*como excl*) (= *¡felicidades!*) congratulations; **¡albricias! ¡lo conseguí!** whoopee! I got it!
2 (= *regalo*) gift *sing*, reward *sing* (*to sb bringing good news*)
albufera SF lagoon
álbum SM (*pl* **álbums, álbumes**) album; (*Mús*) (= *disco*) album; (= *elepé*) LP ▸ **álbum de recortes** scrapbook ▸ **álbum de sellos** stamp album ▸ **álbum doble** double album
albumen SM (= *clara*) white of egg; (*Bot*) albumen
albúmina SF albumin
albuminoso ADJ albuminous
albur SM 1 (*Esp*) (= *pez*) bleak
2 (= *riesgo*) chance, risk
3 (*Méx*) (= *juego de palabras*) pun
4 (*Caribe*) (= *mentira*) lie
albura SF (= *blancura*) whiteness; [*de huevo*] white of egg
alburear ▸conjug 1a◂ Ⓐ VT (*CAm*) to disturb, upset
Ⓑ VI 1 (*Andes*) (= *enriquecerse*) to make money, get rich
2 (*Caribe*) (= *barrer para dentro*) to line one's pockets
3 (*Méx*) (= *decir albores*) to pun, play with words
ALCA SF ABR (= **Área de Libre Comercio de las Américas**) FTAA
alca SF razorbill
alcabala SF 1 (*Hist*) (= *tributo*) sales tax
2 (*LAm*) [*de policía*] roadblock
alcachofa SF 1 artichoke
2 ▸ **alcachofa de (la) ducha, alcachofa de la ducha** shower head ▸ **alcachofa de regadera** rose
3 (*Radio**) microphone
alcahué* SM = **cacahuete**
alcahuete/a Ⓐ SM/F 1 (= *proxeneta*) (*hombre*) procurer, pimp; (*mujer*) procuress, go-between
2 (= *chismoso*) gossip
Ⓑ SM (*Teat*) drop curtain
alcahuetear ▸conjug 1a◂ VI to procure, pimp, to act as a go-between
alcahuetería SF procuring, pimping; **alcahueterías** pimping
alcaide SM (*Hist*) [*de castillo*] governor; [*de cárcel*] warder, guard (*EEUU*), jailer
alcaidía SF (= *cargo*) governorship; (= *edificio*) governor's residence
alcaldable SMF *candidate for mayor*
alcaldada SF abuse of authority
alcalde SM 1 [*de ayuntamiento*] mayor; (= *juez*) magistrate; **tener el padre ~** to have influence
2 (*LAm**) (= *alcahuete*) procurer, pimp
alcaldear* ▸conjug 1a◂ VI to lord it, be bossy
alcaldesa SF mayoress
alcaldía SF (= *oficio*) mayoralty, office of mayor; (= *oficina*) mayor's office; (= *edificio*) town hall, city hall (*EEUU*)
alcalducho* SM jumped-up mayor, power-mad mayor
álcali SM alkali
alcalino ADJ alkaline
alcaloide SM alkaloid
alcaloideo ADJ alkaloid
alcamonero ADJ (*Caribe*) meddlesome
alcamonías SFPL 1 (*Culin*) aromatic seeds (*for seasoning*)
2 (*) (= *alcahuetería*) pimping
alcance SM 1 (= *posibilidad de acceso*) [*de brazo, persona*] reach; [*de pensamiento*] scope; **el escaso ~ de la mente humana** the limited scope of the human mind; **al ~ de algn** available to sb; **empleó todos los medios a su ~** she used all the means available to her; **no tenía el dinero a su ~** he didn't have access to the money, he didn't have the money available; **estar al ~ de algn** to be within sb's reach; **vi que estaba a mi ~ y lo cogí** I saw that it was within my reach and I grabbed it; **el récord estaba a nuestro ~** the record was within our grasp *o* reach; **estas joyas no están al ~ de cualquiera** not everyone can afford these jewels; **hizo lo que estaba a su ~ por ayudarme** he did what he could to help me; **estar fuera del ~ de algn** (= *alejado, imposible*) to be out of sb's reach, be beyond sb's reach; (= *incomprensible*) to be over sb's head; (= *caro*) to be beyond sb's means; **"manténgase fuera del alcance de los niños"** "keep out of reach of children"; **quiero estar fuera del ~ de esas miradas** I don't want to be the object of those looks; **se encontraban fuera del ~ de los disparos** they were out of the gunfire; **al ~ de la mano** at hand, within arm's reach; **al ~ del oído** within earshot; **poner algo al ~ de algn** to make sth available to sb; **un intento de poner la cultura al ~ de todos** an attempt to make culture available to everyone; **al ~ de la vista** within sight; **cuando el faro estuvo al ~ de nuestra vista** when the lighthouse came into view *o* was within sight; **al ~ de la voz** within call
2 (= *distancia*) (*Mil*) range; **al ~** within range; **de corto ~** [*arma, misil*] short-range *antes de s*; [*objetivo, proyecto*] short-term *antes de s*; **de gran** *o* **largo ~** [*faros*] full beam *antes de s*, high beam *antes de s* (*EEUU*); [*arma, misil, micrófono*] long-range *antes de s*; [*vuelo*] long haul *antes de s*; [*efecto, repercusiones*] far-reaching; **de medio** *o* **mediano ~** [*arma, misil*] medium-range; *ver tb* **buzón 1**
3 (= *importancia*) [*de problema*] extent; [*de noticia, suceso*] importance, significance; **el ~ del problema** the extent of the problem; **esta huelga tiene mayor ~ para los trabajadores** this strike has greater importance *o* significance for the workers; **comprendió el verdadero ~ de lo ocurrido** she understood the true significance of what had happened; **una crisis de ~ planetario** a worldwide crisis
4 (= *persecución*) pursuit; **andar** *o* **ir a los ~s de algn** to press close on sb; **dar ~ a algn** (= *capturar*) to capture sb; (= *llegar a la altura*) to catch up with sb; **cuando la policía le dio ~** when the police captured him; **a punto estuvo de dar ~ al líder de la carrera** he was on the point of catching (up with) the leader of the race; **el Barcelona ha dado ~ al Madrid en el número de puntos** Barcelona have caught up with Madrid in number of points; **andar** *o* **ir en los ~s a algn** to spy on sb; **seguir el ~ a algn** (*Mil*) to pursue sb
5 (*Fin*) adverse balance, deficit
6 (*Tip*) stop-press, stop-press news
7 **alcances** 7·1 (= *inteligencia*) grasp *sing*; **ideas superiores a sus ~s** ideas beyond his grasp; **de cortos** *o* **pocos ~s** not very bright; **es hombre de cortos ~s** he's not a very intelligent man, he's not too bright
7·2 (*CAm*) (= *calumnias*) calumnies, malicious accusations
8 (*Chile*) **hacer un ~** to clear sth up, clarify sth ▸ **alcance de nombres**: **no es su padre, es sólo un ~ de nombres** he's not his father, it just happens that their names coincide
alcancía SF 1 (= *hucha*) money box; (*LAm*) (= *cepillo*) collection box, poor box
2 (*Méx**) (= *cárcel*) nick*, slammer*, can (*EEUU**)
alcancil SM (*Cono Sur*) procurer, pimp
alcándara SF (*para ropa*) clothes rack; (*para aves*) perch
alcandora SF beacon
alcanfor SM camphor
alcanforado ADJ camphorated
alcanforar ▸conjug 1a◂ Ⓐ VT to camphorate
Ⓑ **alcanforarse** VPR (*Andes, CAm, Caribe*) to disappear, make o.s. scarce*
alcantarilla SF 1 (*para aguas de desecho*) (= *boca*) drain; (= *cloaca*) sewer; (= *conducto*) culvert, conduit
2 (*Caribe, Méx*) (= *fuente*) public fountain; (*Andes*) (*para goma*) *vessel for collecting latex*
alcantarillado SM sewer system, drains *pl*
alcantarillar ▸conjug 1a◂ VT to lay drains in
alcanzadizo ADJ easy to reach, easily reachable, accessible
alcanzado ADJ 1 (*) (= *necesitado*) hard up*, broke*; **salir ~** to make a loss
2 (*Andes*) (= *fatigado*) tired; (= *atrasado*) slow, late
alcanzar ▸conjug 1f◂ Ⓐ VT 1 (*en carrera*) 1·1 [+ *persona*] (= *llegar a la altura de*) to catch up (with); **la alcancé cuando salía por la puerta** I caught up with her *o* I caught her up just as she was going out of the door; **están a punto de ~ al grupo de cabeza** they are about to catch (up with) the leading group; **dentro de poco ~á a su padre en altura** he'll soon be as tall as his father
1·2 [+ *ladrón, autobús, tren*] to catch; **no nos ~án nunca** they'll never catch us
2 (= *llegar a*) [+ *cima, límite, edad*] to reach; **por fin ~on la cima** they finally reached the summit; **alcanzó las cajas con un palo** she reached the boxes with a stick; **puede ~ una velocidad de 200km/h** it can reach speeds of up to 200km/h; **alcanzó el rango de general** he reached the rank of general; **la producción ha alcanzado las 20 toneladas** production has reached 20 tons; **el libro ha**

alcanzado ya las seis ediciones the book is already in its sixth edition; **las montañas alcanzan los 5.000m** the mountains rise to 5,000m; **el termómetro llegó a ~ los cuarenta grados** temperatures rose as high as forty degrees; **~ la mayoría de edad** to come of age; **alcanzó la orilla a nado** he made it to the shore by swimming, he swam back to the shore; **no llegó a ~ la pubertad** he never made it as far as puberty
3 (= *conseguir*) [+ *acuerdo*] to reach; [+ *éxito, objetivo*] to achieve; **el acuerdo fue alcanzado tras muchos meses de conversaciones** the agreement was reached after many months of talks; **las expectativas no se corresponden con los resultados alcanzados** the expectations are out of proportion with the results that have been achieved; **~ la fama** to find fame, become famous; **~ la paz** to achieve peace
4 (= *afectar*) to affect; **el cambio nos ~á a todos** the change will affect us all; **una ley que alcanza sobre todo a los jubilados** a law which mainly affects *o* hits pensioners
5 [*bala*] to hit; **uno de los dos disparos alcanzó al presidente** the president was hit by one of the two shots; **la lancha fue alcanzada por un obús** the launch was hit by a shell
6 (*esp LAm*) (= *dar*) to pass; **alcánzame la sal, por favor** could you pass (me) the salt, please?; **¿me alcanzas las tijeras?** could you pass me the scissors?
7 (*) (= *entender*) to grasp, understand; **no alcanza más allá de lo que le han enseñado** he's only capable of understanding what he's been taught
Ⓑ VI 1 (= *llegar*) to reach (**a, hasta** as far as); **no alcanzo** I can't reach; **no alcanzaba al timbre** she couldn't reach (as far as) the doorbell; **hasta donde alcanza la vista** as far as the eye can see
2 **~ a hacer algo** to manage to do sth; **no alcancé a verlo** I didn't manage to see him; **no alcanzo a ver cómo pudo suceder** I can't see how it can have happened; **no alcanzo a comprender sus razones** I just can't understand her reasons
3 (= *ser suficiente*) to be enough; **con dos botellas ~á para todos** two bottles will be enough for everyone; **el sueldo no me alcanza para nada** I can't make ends meet on my salary; **¿te alcanza para el tren?** (*esp LAm*) have you got enough money for the train?
4 (*LAm*) (= *ascender*) **¿a cuánto alcanza todo?** how much does it all come to?

alcanzativo ADJ (*CAm*) suspicious

alcaparra SF caper

alcaraván SM stone curlew

alcaravea SF caraway

alcarreño/a Ⓐ ADJ of/from La Alcarria
Ⓑ SM/F native/inhabitant of La Alcarria; **los ~s** the people of La Alcarria

alcatraz SM gannet

alcaucil SM 1 (*Cono Sur*) artichoke
2 (*Cono Sur‡*) (= *informador*) informer, nark*; (= *alcahuete*) pimp

alcaudón SM shrike

alcayata SF meat hook, spike

alcayota SF squash, vegetable marrow

alcazaba SF citadel, castle

alcázar SM (*Mil*) fortress, citadel; (= *palacio*) royal palace; (*Náut*) quarter-deck

alcazuz SM liquorice

alce[1] SM (*Zool*) elk, moose; **~ de América** moose

alce[2] SM (*Naipes*) cut; **no dar ~ a algn** (*Cono Sur*) to give sb no respite, give sb no rest

alción SM (*Orn*) kingfisher; (*Mit*) halcyon

alcista (*Com, Fin*) Ⓐ ADJ **mercado ~** bull market, rising market; **la tendencia ~** the upward trend
Ⓑ SMF bull, speculator

alcoba SF 1 (= *dormitorio*) bedroom; (*Méx Ferro*) couchette, sleeping compartment ► **alcoba de huéspedes** spare room, guest room
2 (= *mobiliario*) suite of bedroom furniture

alcohol SM alcohol; **lámpara de ~** spirit lamp ► **alcohol absoluto** absolute alcohol, pure alcohol ► **alcohol de quemar**, **alcohol desnaturalizado**, **alcohol metílico** methylated spirit ► **alcohol vínico** vinic alcohol

alcoholemia SF alcohol level of the blood; **control de ~** ◊ **prueba de ~** ◊ **test de ~** breath test, Breathalyser® test, Breathalyzer® (*EEUU*)

alcoholero ADJ alcohol *antes de s*

alcohólico/a Ⓐ ADJ alcoholic; **no ~** [*bebida*] non-alcoholic, soft
Ⓑ SM/F alcoholic

alcoholímetro SM Breathalyser®, Breathalyzer® (*EEUU*)

alcoholismo SM alcoholism

alcoholista* SMF (*Cono Sur*) drunk

alcoholizado ADJ **está ~** he's an alcoholic; **morir ~** to die of alcoholism

alcoholizar ▸conjug 1f◂ Ⓐ VT to alcoholize
Ⓑ **alcoholizarse** VPR to become an alcoholic

alcor SM hill

Alcorán SM Koran

alcornoque SM 1 (= *árbol*) cork tree
2 (*) (= *tonto*) idiot

alcorza SF 1 (*Culin*) icing, sugar paste
2 (*Cono Sur**) (= *tipo sensible*) crybaby, sensitive soul

alcorzar ▸conjug 1f◂ VT to ice

alcotán SM hobby

alcotana SF pickaxe, pickax (*EEUU*)

alcubilla SF cistern, reservoir

alcucero ADJ sweet-toothed

alcurnia SF ancestry, lineage; **de ~** of noble family, of noble birth

alcurniado ADJ aristocratic, noble

alcuza SF (*para aceite*) olive-oil bottle; (*LAm*) (= *vinagreras*) cruet, cruet stand

alcuzcuz SM couscous

aldaba SF 1 (*de puerta*) knocker, door knocker; (*para caballo*) hitching ring; **tener buenas ~s** to have friends in the right places
2 **~s‡** (= *tetas*) tits**

aldabada SF knock, knock on the door; **dar ~s en** to knock at

aldabilla SF latch

aldabón SM (= *aldaba*) large knocker, large door knocker; (= *asa*) handle

aldabonazo SM bang, loud knock, loud knock on the door; **dar ~s en** to bang at

aldea SF small village, hamlet

aldeanismo SM provincialism, parish-pump attitudes

aldeano/a Ⓐ ADJ 1 (= *de pueblo*) village *antes de s*; (= *de campo*) rustic; **gente aldeana** country people
2 (*pey*) (= *pueblerino*) provincial, parish-pump *antes de s*; **actitud aldeana** parish-pump attitude
Ⓑ SM/F villager; **los ~s** the villagers

aldehuela SF hamlet

aldeorrio SM backward little place, rural backwater

alderredor ADV = **alrededor**

aldosterona SF aldosterone

aldrina SF aldrin

aleación SF (= *proceso*) alloying; (= *efecto*) alloy ► **aleación ligera** light alloy

aleado ADJ alloyed, alloy *antes de s*

alear[1] ▸conjug 1a◂ VT (*Téc*) to alloy

alear[2] ▸conjug 1a◂ VI 1 [*ave*] to flutter, flap, flap its wings; [*persona*] to move one's arms up and down
2 (= *cobrar fuerzas*) to improve; **ir aleando** to be improving

aleatoriamente ADV randomly, at random

aleatoriedad SF randomness

aleatorio ADJ (*Estadística*) random, contingent; (= *fortuito*) accidental, fortuitous

aleatorizar ▸conjug 1f◂ VT to randomize

alebrarse ▸conjug 1j◂ VPR 1 (= *pegarse al suelo*) to lie flat
2 (= *acobardarse*) to cower

alebrestar ▸conjug 1a◂ Ⓐ VT (*LAm*) (= *poner nervioso*) to excite, make nervous; (= *alterar*) to distress, disturb
Ⓑ **alebrestarse** VPR 1 (= *ponerse nervioso*) to get excited; (= *alterarse*) to get distressed, become agitated; (= *rebelarse*) to rebel
2 (*Andes*) [*caballo*] to rear up

aleccionador ADJ (= *instructivo*) instructive, enlightening; [*castigo*] exemplary

aleccionamiento SM (= *instrucción*) instruction, enlightenment; (*Pol euf*) repression

aleccionar ▸conjug 1a◂ VT (= *instruir*) to instruct, enlighten; (= *castigar*) to teach a lesson to; (= *regañar*) to lecture

alechado ADJ (*LAm*) milky

alechugado ADJ (= *plisado*) pleated; (= *de volantes*) frilled, frilly

alechugar ▸conjug 1h◂ VT (= *doblar con pliegues*) to fold, pleat; (= *rizar*) to frill

aledaño Ⓐ ADJ adjoining, bordering
Ⓑ SM boundary, limit; **los aledaños** the outskirts

alefra* EXCL (*Caribe*) touch wood!, knock on wood! (*EEUU*)

alegación SF (*Jur*) declaration, declaration in court; (*Caribe, Cono Sur, Méx*) (= *discusión*) argument ► **alegación de culpabilidad** (*Méx Jur*) plea of guilty ► **alegación de inocencia** (*Méx Jur*) plea of not guilty

alegador(a) Ⓐ ADJ (*Cono Sur*) argumentative
Ⓑ SM/F argumentative person

alegal ADJ (*Cono Sur*) illegal

alegar ▸conjug 1h◂ Ⓐ VT 1 (*Jur*) to allege; (= *citar*) [+ *dificultad*] to plead; [+ *autoridad*] to quote; [+ *razones*] to put forward, adduce; [+ *méritos*] to cite, adduce; **~ que** to claim that, assert that; **alegando que …** claiming that …, on the grounds that …

[2] (*LAm*) (= *discutir*) to argue against, dispute
Ⓑ VI (*LAm*) to argue; (= *protestar*) to complain loudly, kick up a fuss

alegata SF (*LAm*) fight

alegato SM [1] (*Jur*) (*escrito*) indictment; (*oral*) allegation; (= *declaración*) statement, assertion
[2] (*LAm*) (= *discusión*) argument, dispute

alegoría SF allegory

alegóricamente ADV allegorically

alegórico ADJ allegoric, allegorical

alegorizar ▸conjug 1f◂ VT to allegorize

alegrador ADJ cheering

▼ **alegrar** ▸conjug 1a◂ Ⓐ VT [1] (= *poner contento*) to cheer up; **le mandamos flores para ~la un poco** we sent her some flowers to cheer her up a bit; **me alegra que me preguntes eso** I'm glad you asked me that; **nos alegra saber que ha aprobado** we're pleased to hear that you passed
[2] (= *animar*) [+ *fiesta, reunión*] to liven up; [+ *casa, cuarto*] to brighten up, cheer up; **el rojo te alegra la cara** red gives your face a bit of colour; **¡alegra esa cara!** cheer up!; **los niños alegran el hogar con sus risas** the children liven up *o* cheer up the house with their laughter
[3] [+ *fuego*] to poke
[4] [+ *toro*] to excite, stir up
[5] (*Náut*) [+ *cuerda*] to slacken
Ⓑ **alegrarse** VPR [1] (= *complacerse*) to be happy, be pleased; **siempre se alegra cuando la visitamos** she's always happy *o* pleased when we go and visit her; **nos alegramos de *o* por tu decisión** we're very happy *o* pleased with your decision; **me alegro de verte** I'm pleased to see you, it's good to see you; **me alegro por ella** I'm happy *o* pleased for her; **—he aprobado —¡me alegro!** "I passed" — "I'm pleased to hear it!"; **me alegro muchísimo** I'm delighted; **—¿te importa que haya venido? —no, me alegro mucho** "do you mind me coming?" — "not at all, I'm pleased you've come"; **—ya puedo devolverte el dinero —me alegro de saberlo** "I can pay you back now" — "I'm glad to hear it"; **me alegro de que hayas venido, necesito tu ayuda** I'm glad you've come, I need your help; **me alegro de que saques el tema** I'm glad you mentioned that
[2] (*) (= *emborracharse*) to get merry *o* tipsy*

alegre ADJ [1] (= *feliz*) [*persona*] happy; [*cara, carácter*] happy, cheerful; **recibimos una ~ noticia** we received some happy news; **estar ~ (por algo)** to be happy (about sth); **ser ~** to be cheerful *o* happy; **María es muy ~** María's a very cheerful *o* happy person
[2] (= *luminoso*) [*día, habitación, color*] bright
[3] [*música, fiesta*] lively
[4] (*) (= *borracho*) **estar ~** to be merry *o* tipsy*
[5] (= *irresponsable*) thoughtless
[6] (= *inmoral*) [*vida*] fast; (†) [*chiste*] risqué, blue; *ver tb* **mujer 1**

alegremente ADV [1] (= *felizmente*) happily, cheerfully
[2] (= *irresponsablemente*) gaily; **se lo gastó todo ~** he spent it all without a thought for tomorrow

alegría SF [1] (= *felicidad*) happiness, joy; (= *satisfacción*) gladness; (= *optimismo*) cheerfulness; (= *regocijo*) merriment; **¡qué ~!** how marvellous!, that's splendid!; **saltar de ~** to jump for joy ► **alegría vital** joie de vivre
[2] (*pey*) (= *irresponsabilidad*) recklessness, irresponsibility
[3] (*Bot*) ► **alegría de la casa** balsam
[4] **alegrías** (*Mús*) *Andalusian song or dance*; (*Esp*⁑) (= *genitales*) naughty bits⁑

alegro SM allegro

alegrón SM [1] [*de felicidad*] thrill; **¡me dio un ~!** what a thrill I got!
[2] [*de fuego*] sudden blaze, flare-up

alegrona SF (*LAm*) prostitute

alehop EXCL hup!

alejado ADJ [1] (= *distanciado*) remote; **en un pueblecito ~** in a remote little village; **vivimos algo ~s** we live quite far away, we live quite a distance away; **~ de** [*lugar*] distant from; [*persona*] away from; **un planeta muy ~ del sol** a planet very distant from the sun; **vive ~ de todo** he lives away from it all; **una lesión lo mantuvo ~ del fútbol** an injury kept him out of football; **ha pasado varios años alejada de los escenarios** she has spent several years off the stage; **viven completamente ~s de la realidad** they live completely cut off from the real world *o* from reality; **una sentencia muy alejada de la realidad actual** a sentence out of line with current thinking
[2] (= *diferente*) removed (**de** from); **muy ~ de nuestro concepto de libertad** very far removed from our concept of freedom

alejamiento SM [1] (= *distanciamiento*) (*gen*) distance; (*como actividad*) distancing; **se ha producido un pequeño ~ entre los dos planetas** the two planets have shifted slightly apart *o* away from each other; **la obra supone un ~ de la tradición teatral** the work represents a break with *o* a distancing from theatrical tradition
[2] (*entre personas*) **unos meses de ~ nos sentarán bien a los dos** a few months away from each other will do us both good, a few months apart will do us good; **se produjo un ~ entre el gobierno y los ciudadanos** there was a rift between the government and the people
[3] [*de cargo*] removal
[4] (= *actitud distante*) detachment

Alejandría SF Alexandria

alejandrino SM alexandrine

Alejandro SM Alexander ► **Alejandro Magno** Alexander the Great

alejar ▸conjug 1a◂ Ⓐ VT [1] (= *distanciar*) to move away (**de** from); **aleja un poco más el jarrón** move the vase away a little
[2] (= *hacer abandonar*) (*de lugar*) to keep away (**de** from); (*de puesto*) to remove (**de** from); **ese olor aleja a los mosquitos** that smell keeps the mosquitoes away; **una enfermedad lo alejó de la vida pública** illness forced him to withdraw from public life; **lo hice para ~los de la tentación** I did it to keep them out of temptation's way; **~ a algn de algn** (= *distanciar*) to keep sb away from sb; (= *causar ruptura*) to cause a rift between sb and sb; **intentó ~la de mí** he tried to keep her away from me; **aquel asunto los alejó definitivamente** that matter caused a permanent rift between them
[3] (= *desviar*) [+ *atención*] to distract; [+ *sospechas*] to remove; [+ *amenaza, peligro*] to remove; **tratan de ~ nuestra atención de los problemas** they are trying to distract our attention from the problems; **aleja de ti las tentaciones** stay out of temptation's way; **eso alejó el fantasma de la crisis** that removed the spectre of a crisis
Ⓑ **alejarse** VPR [1] (= *irse lejos*) to go away, move away (**de** from); **alejémonos un poco más** let's get *o* go *o* move a bit further away; **un coche rojo se alejaba del lugar** a red car was leaving the scene; **vieron ~se corriendo a dos jóvenes** they saw two youths running away; **se alejó lentamente** he walked off slowly; **no conviene ~se de la orilla** it's better not to go too far from the shore; **~se del buen camino** (*lit*) to lose one's way; (*fig*) to go *o* stray off the straight and narrow
[2] (= *separarse*) **~se de algo: la carretera se aleja de la costa** the road veers away from the coast; **en esta obra se aleja de los problemas sociales** in this work she moves away from social problems; **cada vez se alejan más del descenso** they are moving further away from relegation; **después de su divorcio se alejó de la vida social** after her divorce she withdrew from social life; **poco a poco se fueron alejando de sus amigos** they gradually drifted apart from their friends; **~se del tema** to get off the subject
[3] (= *desaparecer*) [*peligro*] to recede; [*ruido*] to grow fainter; **la amenaza de una guerra se fue alejando poco a poco** the threat of war gradually receded; **se aleja la posibilidad de un nuevo recorte de los tipos de interés** the possibility of a new cut in interest rates is becoming increasingly unlikely
[4] (= *diferir*) **su comportamiento se aleja de lo normal** his behaviour is far from being normal; **lo que te he contado no se aleja de la verdad** what I have told you is not far from the truth; **la centralización del poder se aleja del espíritu de las sociedades cooperativas** the centralization of power is alien to the spirit of cooperative societies

alelado ADJ (= *aturdido*) stupefied, bewildered; (= *bobo*) foolish, stupid

alelamiento SM (= *aturdimiento*) bewilderment; (= *insensatez*) foolishness, stupidity

alelar ▸conjug 1a◂ Ⓐ VT to stupefy, bewilder
Ⓑ **alelarse** VPR to be stupefied, be bewildered

aleluya Ⓐ EXCL hallelujah!, hurray!
Ⓑ SM *o* SF (*Mús, Rel*) hallelujah, alleluia
Ⓒ SM [1] (= *Pascua*) Easter time
[2] **ir al ~** (*Caribe**) (= *pagar a escote*) to go Dutch*, share costs
Ⓓ SF [1] (= *alegría*) **estar de ~** to rejoice
[2] (*Arte*) (= *estampa*) Easter print, strip cartoon with rhyming couplets (*originally on religious themes*); (= *pintura mala*) (*) daub, bad painting
[3] (*LAm*) (= *excusa*) frivolous excuse
[4] (*poét*, *) doggerel

alelúyico* ADJ evangelical

alemán/ana Ⓐ ADJ, SM/F German
Ⓑ SM (*Ling*) German

Alemania SF Germany

alentada SF big breath, deep breath; **de una ~** in one breath

alentado ADJ [1] (= *valiente*) brave; (= *orgulloso*) proud, haughty
[2] (*Cono Sur*) (= *sano*) healthy
[3] (*CAm, Méx*) (= *mejorado*) improved, better

➤ LENGUA Y USO: **alegrar A1** 48.1, 51.1, 51.2 **B1** 51.3, 52.4

alentador ADJ encouraging

alentar ▸conjug 1j◂ Ⓐ VT [1] (= *animar*) to encourage, hearten; [+ *oposición*] to stiffen; [+ *esperanzas*] to raise; **en su pecho alienta la esperanza de ...** he cherishes the hope of ...; **~ a algn a hacer algo** to encourage sb to do sth
[2] (*LAm*) (= *aplaudir*) to clap, applaud
Ⓑ VI (= *brillar*) to burn, glow
Ⓒ **alentarse** VPR [1] (= *animarse*) to take heart, cheer up
[2] (*esp LAm Med*) to get better
[3] (*Andes, CAm*) (= *dar a luz*) to give birth (**de** to)

aleonarse ▸conjug 1a◂ VPR (*Cono Sur*) to get excited, get worked up

aleoyota SF (*Cono Sur*) pumpkin

alepantado ADJ (*Andes*) absent-minded

alerce SM larch, larch tree

alergeno SM, **alérgeno** SM allergen

alergia SF allergy; **tener ~ a** to be allergic to (*tb fig*) ► **alergia al polen, alergia polínica** pollen allergy, allergy to pollen ► **alergia primaveral** hay fever

alérgico/a Ⓐ ADJ allergic (**a** to)
Ⓑ SM/F allergic person

alergista SMF, **alergólogo/a** SM/F allergist, specialist in allergies

alergológico ADJ allergy *antes de s*

alero SM [1] (*Arquit*) eaves; (*Aut*) mudguard, fender (*EEUU*), wing; ✦***MODISMO*** **estar** *o* **en el ~** (= *indeciso*) to be unsure, remain undecided
[2] (*Dep*) winger

alerón SM aileron

alerta Ⓐ EXCL watch out!
Ⓑ ADJ, ADV alert, watchful; **estar ~** ◊ **estar ojo ~** to be on the alert; **todos los servicios de auxilio están ~(s)** all the rescue services are on stand-by
Ⓒ SF alert; **dar la ~** ◊ **dar la voz de ~** to raise the alarm; **en estado de ~** on the alert; **en ~ de 24 horas** on 24-hour stand-by ► **alerta previa** early warning ► **alerta roja** red alert

alertar ▸conjug 1a◂ Ⓐ VT to alert; **~ a algn de algo** to alert sb to sth
Ⓑ VI to be alert, keep one's eyes open

alesnado ADJ (*Caribe*) brave, intrepid

aleta SF [1] (*Zool*) [*de pez*] fin; [*de foca*] flipper; [*de pájaro*] wing, small wing; [*de natación*] flipper ► **aleta dorsal** dorsal fin
[2] (*Mec*) [*de coche*] wing, fender (*EEUU*); [*de hélice*] blade

aletargado ADJ drowsy, lethargic

aletargamiento SM drowsiness, lethargy

aletargar ▸conjug 1h◂ Ⓐ VT (= *causar letargo*) to make drowsy, make lethargic
Ⓑ **aletargarse** VPR (= *padecer letargo*) to grow drowsy, become lethargic; (= *hibernar*) to become dormant, hibernate

aletazo SM [1] [*de ave*] wingbeat, flap, flap of the wing; [*de pez*] movement of the fin
[2] (*Cono Sur*) (= *bofetada*) punch, slap
[3] (*CAm*) (= *hurto*) robbery; (= *estafa*) swindle

aletear ▸conjug 1a◂ VI [*ave*] to flutter, flap its wings; [*pez*] to move its fins; [*persona*] to wave one's arms

aleteo SM [1] [*de ave*] fluttering, flapping of the wings; [*de pez*] movement of the fins
[2] (*Med*) (= *palpitación*) palpitation

aleudar ▸conjug 1a◂ Ⓐ VT to leaven, ferment with yeast
Ⓑ **aleudarse** VPR to rise

aleve ADJ treacherous, perfidious

alevín SM, **alevino** SM [1] (= *cría de pez*) fry, young fish
[2] (= *joven principiante*) youngster, novice

alevosía SF [1] (= *traición*) treachery
[2] (*Jur*) premeditation; **con ~** in a cold-blooded manner

alevoso/a Ⓐ ADJ treacherous
Ⓑ SM/F traitor

alfa[1] SF (= *letra*) alpha

alfa[2] SF (*LAm*) (= *alfalfa*) lucerne, alfalfa

alfabéticamente ADV alphabetically

alfabético ADJ alphabetic, alphabetical

alfabetismo SM literacy

alfabetización SF teaching people to read and write; **campaña de ~** literacy campaign

alfabetizado ADJ literate, that can read and write

alfabetizador(a) SM/F literacy tutor

alfabetizar ▸conjug 1f◂ VT [1] (= *clasificar*) to arrange alphabetically
[2] (= *enseñar*) to teach to read and write

alfabeto SM alphabet ► **alfabeto Morse** Morse code ► **alfabeto romano** Roman alphabet

alfajor SM (*Cono Sur*) *sweet biscuit with filling*; (*Esp*) (= *polvorón*) *cake eaten at Christmas*

alfalfa SF lucerne, alfalfa

alfalfar SM lucerne field

alfandoque SM [1] (*LAm Culin*) cheesecake
[2] (*Andes, Cono Sur Mús*) maraca

alfanje SM (= *sable*) cutlass; (= *pez*) swordfish

alfanumérico ADJ alphanumeric

alfaque SM (*Náut*) bar, sandbank

alfaquí SM Moslem doctor, ulema, expounder of the Law

alfar SM [1] (= *taller*) potter's workshop
[2] (= *arcilla*) clay

alfarería SF (= *arte*) pottery; (= *tienda*) pottery shop

alfarero/a SM/F potter

alfarjía SF batten (*esp for door or window frames*)

alféizar SM (*Arquit*) (= *corte del muro*) splay, embrasure; [*de ventana*] window sill

alfeñicado* ADJ [1] (= *débil*) weakly, delicate
[2] (= *afectado*) affected

alfeñicarse* ▸conjug 1g◂ VPR [1] (= *enflaquecerse*) to get terribly thin, look frail
[2] (= *remilgarse*) to act affectedly, be overnice

alfeñique SM [1] (= *persona débil*) weakling
[2] (= *afectación*) affectation
[3] (*Culin*) toffee-like paste, almond-flavoured *o* (*EEUU*) -flavored sugar paste

alferecía SF epilepsy

alférez SMF (*Mil*) second lieutenant, subaltern; (*Rel*) official standard bearer (*in processions*) ► **alférez de fragata** midshipman, middie (*EEUU**) ► **alférez de navío** sub-lieutenant, ensign (*EEUU*)

alfil SM bishop

alfiler SM [1] (*Cos*) pin; (= *broche*) brooch, clip; **aquí ya no cabe ni un ~** you can't squeeze anything else in; **prendido con ~es** shaky, hardly hanging together; **puesto con 25 ~es** dressed up to the nines ► **alfiler de corbata** tiepin ► **alfiler de gancho** (*Arg*) safety pin ► **alfiler de seguridad** (*LAm*) safety pin ► **alfiler de sombrero** hatpin
[2] (= *propina*) **~es** pin money, dress allowance; **pedir para ~es** to ask for a tip

alfilerar ▸conjug 1a◂ VT to pin together, pin up

alfilerazo SM (= *punzada*) pinprick; **tirar ~s a algn** (= *criticar*) to have a dig at sb

alfilerillo SM (*Andes, Cono Sur*) *type of spikenard used for animal feeding*

alfiletero SM (= *estuche*) needle case; (= *acerico*) pincushion

alfolí SM [*de granos*] granary; [*de sal*] salt warehouse

alfombra SF (*grande*) carpet; (*pequeña*) rug, mat ► **alfombra de baño** bath mat ► **alfombra de oración** prayer mat ► **alfombra mágica** magic carpet ► **alfombra voladora** flying carpet

alfombrado SM carpeting

alfombrar ▸conjug 1a◂ VT to carpet

alfombrero/a SM/F carpet maker

alfombrilla SF [1] rug, mat ► **alfombrilla roja** red carpet
[2] (*Med*) (= *sarampión*) German measles; (*Caribe*) (= *sarpullido*) rash; (*Méx*) (= *viruela*) smallpox

alfonsí ADJ Alphonsine (*esp re Alfonso X, 1252-84*)

alfonsino ADJ Alphonsine (*esp re recent kings of Spain named Alfonso*)

Alfonso SM Alphonso; **~ X el Sabio** Alphonso the Wise (*1252-84*)

alforfón SM buckwheat

alforja SF [*de jinete*] saddlebag; (*en bicicleta*) pannier; (= *mochila*) knapsack; **~s** (= *provisión*) provisions (*for a journey*); **sacar los pies de las ~s** to go off on a different tack; **para ese viaje no hacían falta ~s** there was no point in bringing all this stuff, you didn't have to go to such trouble; **pasarse a la otra ~** (*Cono Sur*) to overstep the mark, go too far

alforjudo ADJ (*Cono Sur*) silly, stupid

alforza SF (= *pliegue*) pleat, tuck; (= *cicatriz*) slash, scar

alforzar ▸conjug 1f◂ VT to pleat, tuck

Alfredo SM Alfred

alga SF seaweed, alga; **~ tóxica** toxic alga

algaida SF (*Bot*) bush, undergrowth; (*Geog*) dune

algalia SF [1] (= *perfume*) civet
[2] (*Med*) catheter

algara SF (*Hist*) raid

algarabía SF [1] (= *griterío*) hullabaloo
[2] (*Ling*) Arabic
[3] (*Bot*) cornflower

algarada SF [1] (= *griterío*) outcry; **hacer** *o* **levantar una ~** to kick up a tremendous fuss
[2] (*Hist*) cavalry raid, cavalry troop

Algarbe SM **el ~** the Algarve

algarero ADJ noisy, rowdy

algarroba SF carob, carob bean

algarrobo SM carob tree, locust tree

algazara SF din, uproar

álgebra SF algebra ► **álgebra de Boole** Boolean algebra

algebraico ADJ algebraic

algecireño/a Ⓐ ADJ of/from Algeciras
Ⓑ SM/F native/inhabitant of Algeciras; **los ~s** the people of Algeciras

álgido ADJ (= *muy frío*) icy, chilly; [*momento*] crucial, decisive

algo Ⓐ PRON [1] (*en oraciones afirmativas*) something; **estaba buscando ~ más barato** I was looking for something cheaper; **—¿no habéis comido nada? —sí, ~ hemos picado** "haven't you eaten anything?" — "yes, we've had a little snack"; **~ así: es músico o ~ así** he's a musician or something like that; **dura ~ así como tres horas** it's about three hours long; **~ de: tuve ~ de miedo** I was a bit scared; **sé ~ de inglés** I know a little English; **nos dieron ~ de comer** they gave us something to eat; **hay ~ de verdad en lo que dicen** there is some truth in what they say; **tenía ~ de revolucionario** there was something of the revolutionary in him; **tengo ~ de prisa** I'm in a bit of a hurry; **tienen ~ de razón** they are right to a certain extent *o* in a way; **en ~: queríamos ser útiles en ~** we wanted to be of some use; **se ha cambiado en ~ el plan** the plan has been changed slightly; **las dos hermanas se parecen en ~** there is a certain likeness between the two sisters; **estar en ~** (= *implicado*) to be involved in sth; (*Ven*‡) to be high on sth; **llegar a ser ~** to be something; **tomar ~** (*de beber*) to have a drink; (*de comer*) to have a bite (to eat); **¿quieres tomarte ~?** would you like a drink?; **llegamos a las tres y ~** we arrived at three something; **al nacer pesó tres kilos y ~** she weighed just over three kilos at birth; ✦***MODISMOS*** **~ es ~** it's better than nothing; **creerse ~** to think one is somebody; **darle ~ a algn***: **casi me da ~ cuando falló el penalti** I nearly died when he missed the penalty; **si no deja de comer dulces un día le va a dar ~** if he doesn't stop eating sweet things something will happen to him one day; **cuando le da por ~ ...** when he gets something into his head ...; **por ~ será** there must be a reason for it; **si lo dice el director, por ~ será** if the manager says so, he must have his reasons *o* there must be a reason for it; **ya es ~: ha logrado un estilo propio, lo que ya es ~** she has achieved her own style, which is quite something

[2] (*en oraciones interrogativas, condicionales*) (*gen*) anything; (*esperando respuesta afirmativa*) something; **¿hay ~ para mí?** is there anything *o* something for me?; **¿puedes darme ~?** can you give me something?; **¿le has dado ~ más de dinero?** have you given him any more money?; **¿no le habrá pasado ~?** nothing has happened to him, has it?

Ⓑ ADV [1] (*con adjetivo*) rather, a little; **estos zapatos son ~ incómodos** these shoes are rather *o* a little uncomfortable; **puede parecer ~ ingenuo** he may seem slightly *o* rather *o* a little *o* somewhat (*frm*) naive

[2] (*con verbos*) a little; **me recuerda ~ a mi padre** he reminds me a little of my father; **la inflación ha subido ~ más de dos puntos** inflation has gone up by a little over two points

Ⓒ SM [1] **un ~: tiene un ~ que atrae** there's something attractive about him *o* there's something about him that's attractive; **había un ~ de tristeza en su expresión** there was something sad in his expression

[2] (*Col*) *mid-afternoon snack*; → ALGUNO, ALGO

algodón SM [1] (*Cos*) (= *material*) cotton; (= *planta*) cotton plant ✦***MODISMO*** **se crió entre algodones** he was always pampered ► **algodón en rama** raw cotton; ► **algodón labrado** patterned cotton ► **algodón pólvora** gun cotton

[2] (*Med*) swab ► **algodón hidrófilo** cotton wool, absorbent cotton (*EEUU*)

[3] [*de azúcar*] candy floss, cotton candy (*EEUU*)

algodonal SM cotton plantation

algodonar ▸conjug 1a◂ VT to stuff with cotton wool, wad

algodoncillo SM milkweed

algodoncito SM cotton wool bud, cotton bud, Q-tip® (*EEUU*)

algodonero/a Ⓐ ADJ cotton *antes de s*

Ⓑ SM/F (= *persona*) (= *cultivador*) cotton grower; (= *comerciante*) cotton dealer

Ⓒ SM (= *planta*) cotton plant

algodonosa SF cotton grass

algodonoso ADJ cottony

algorítmica SF algorithms *pl*

algoritmo SM algorithm

algoterapia SF seaweed wrap treatment

alguacil SM (*Jur*) bailiff, constable (*EEUU*); (*Taur*) (*tb* **alguacilillo**) mounted official

alguicida SM algicide

alguien PRON (*gen*) somebody, someone; (*en frases interrogativas*) anybody, anyone; **si viene ~** if somebody comes, if anybody comes; **¿viste a ~?** did you see anybody?; **para ~ que conozca la materia** for anybody who is familiar with the subject; **~ se lo habrá dicho** somebody or other must have told him; **se cree ~** he thinks he's somebody

alguita‡ SF (*Andes*) money, dough‡

alguito (*LAm*) = **algo**

alguno/a Ⓐ ADJ (*before masc sing* **algún**) [1] (*antes de s*) (*en oraciones afirmativas*) some; (*en oraciones interrogativas, condicionales*) any; **algún día lo comprenderás** some day you'll understand; **tuvimos algunas dificultades** we had a few *o* some difficulties; **llámame si tienes algún problema** call me if you have any problems; **¿conoces algún hotel barato?** do you know a cheap hotel?; **hubo alguna que otra nube** there were one or two clouds, there was the odd cloud; **objetos de alguna importancia** objects of some importance; **en alguna parte** somewhere; **alguna vez** (*en oraciones afirmativas*) at some point; (*en oraciones interrogativas, condicionales*) ever; **todos lo hemos hecho alguna vez** we've all done it at one time or another *o* at some point; **alguna vez le he oído hablar de ella** I have heard him mention her sometimes; **¿has estado alguna vez en Nueva York?** have you ever been to New York?

[2] (*después de s*) **no tiene talento ~** he has no talent at all; **nos atacaron sin motivo ~** they attacked us for no reason at all; **sin interés ~** without the slightest interest; **sin valor ~** completely worthless; *ver tb* **duda**

[3] **algunos** (= *varios*) several; **salvaron ~s cientos de vidas** they saved several hundred lives

Ⓑ PRON [1] (= *objeto*) one; **estará en ~ de esos cajones** it must be in one of those drawers; **de entre tantas camisas, seguro que alguna te gustará** out of all these shirts, there's bound to be one that you like; **~ que otro** one or two

[2] (= *persona*) someone, somebody; **siempre hay ~ que protesta** there is always one *o* someone *o* somebody who complains; **~ de ellos** one of them

[3] **algunos** (= *cosas*) some, some of them; (= *personas*) some, some of us, you *etc*; **vinieron ~s, pero no todos** some of them came, but not all; **~s no se han enterado todavía** some (people) haven't found out yet

> **ALGUNO, ALGO**
>
> **"Some" y "any" en oraciones afirmativas e interrogativas**
>
> **Frases Afirmativas**
>
> • En frases afirmativas debe usarse **some** o las formas compuestas de **some**:
>
> He leído algunos artículos interesantes sobre el tema
> ***I have read some interesting articles on the subject***
>
> Algunos no están de acuerdo
> ***Some people disagree***
>
> He comprado algo para ti
> ***I've bought something for you***
>
> **Frases Interrogativas**
>
> • En frases interrogativas que expresan algún tipo de ofrecimiento o petición y cuya respuesta se espera que sea positiva, también debe emplearse la forma **some**, *etc*:
>
> Tienes muchos libros. ¿Me dejas alguno?
> ***You've got lots of books. Can I borrow some?***
>
> • En el resto de las frases interrogativas, empléese **any** o las formas compuestas de **any**:
>
> ¿Se te ocurre alguna otra idea?
> ***Do you have any other ideas?***
>
> ¿Hay algún sitio donde podamos escondernos?
> ***Is there anywhere we can hide?***
>
> **Frases Condicionales**
>
> • La construcción **si** + **verbo** + **algo** o **algún/alguna**, *etc* se traduce al inglés por **if** + **sujeto** + **verbo** + **any** o **some**, *etc*:
>
> Si necesitas algo, dímelo
> ***If you need anything, let me know***
>
> Si quiere algunas cintas, no deje de pedirlas
> ***If you would like some tapes, don't hesitate to ask***
>
> **NOTA:** Hay que tener en cuenta que **some** se utiliza cuando tenemos más certeza de que la condición se vaya a cumplir.
>
> ⇨ *Ver tb* NINGUNO
>
> *Para otros usos y ejemplos ver las entradas* ***algo*** *y* ***alguno.***

alhaja SF [1] (= *joya*) jewel, gem; (= *objeto precioso*) precious object, treasure; (= *mueble*) fine piece (of furniture)

[2] (= *persona*) treasure, gem; **¡buena ~!** (*iró*) she's a fine one!

alhajado ADJ (*Andes*) wealthy

alhajar ▸conjug 1a◂ VT [+ *persona*] to adorn (*with jewels*); [+ *habitación*] to furnish, appoint, appoint in delicate taste

alhajera SF (*Cono Sur*) jewel box

alharaca SF fuss; **hacer ~s** to make a fuss, make a great song and dance

alharaquiento ADJ demonstrative, highly emotional

alhelí SM wallflower, stock

alheña SF [1] (*Bot*) (= *arbusto*) privet; (= *flor*) privet flower

[2] (= *hongo*) blight, mildew

[3] (*para teñir*) henna

alheñar ▸conjug 1a◂ Ⓐ VT to dye with henna

Ⓑ **alheñarse** VPR to become mildewed, get covered in mildew

alhóndiga SF corn exchange

alhucema SF lavender

aliacán SM jaundice

aliado/a Ⓐ ADJ allied

Ⓑ SM/F ally; **los Aliados** the Allies

Ⓒ SM (*Cono Sur*) (= *emparedado*) toasted sandwich; (= *bebida*) mixed drink

aliaga SF = **aulaga**

aliancista (*Esp Pol, Hist*) Ⓐ ADJ **política ~** policy of Alianza Popular

Ⓑ SMF member of Alianza Popular

alianza SF [1] (= *pacto*) alliance; **la Alianza** (*Rel*) the Covenant; **Santa Alianza** Holy Alliance ► **la Alianza Atlántica** the Atlantic Alliance, NATO ► **Alianza para el Progreso** Alliance for Progress

[2] (= *anillo*) wedding ring

aliar ▸conjug 1c◂ Ⓐ VT to ally, bring into an alliance

Ⓑ **aliarse** VPR to form an alliance; **~se con** to ally o.s. with, side with

alias ADV, SM INV alias

alicaído ADJ (= *débil*) drooping, weak; (= *triste*) downcast, depressed

Alicante SM Alicante

alicantina SF trick, ruse

alicantino/a Ⓐ ADJ of/from Alicante

Ⓑ SM/F native/inhabitant of Alicante; **los ~s** the people of Alicante

alicatado SM tiling

alicatar ▸conjug 1a◂ VT [+ *pared*] to tile; [+ *azulejo*] to shape, cut

alicate SM [1] = **alicates**

[2] (*Arg*) (= *cortaúñas*) nail clippers *pl*

alicates SMPL pliers, pincers; **~ de corte** wire cutters

Alicia SF Alice; **"~ en el país de las maravillas"** "Alice in Wonderland"; **"~ a través del espejo"** "Alice through the Looking-glass"

aliciente SM (= *incentivo*) incentive, inducement; (= *atractivo*) attraction; **ofrece el ~ de** it has the attraction of; **ofrecer un ~** to hold out an inducement

alicorarse* ▸conjug 1a◂ VPR (*Andes*) to get boozed*

alicorear ▸conjug 1a◂ VT (*CAm*) to decorate, adorn

alicrejo SM (*CAm*) (= *animal feo*) *spider-like creature*; (*hum*) (= *rocín*) old horse, nag

alicurco ADJ (*Cono Sur*) sly, cunning

alienación SF (= *enajenación*) alienation; (*Psic*) alienation, mental derangement

alienado/a Ⓐ ADJ (= *marginado*) alienated; (*Psic*) insane, mentally ill

Ⓑ SM/F (= *marginado*) alienated person; (*Psic*) mentally ill person

alienador ADJ, **alienante** ADJ alienating, dehumanizing, inhuman

alienar ▸conjug 1a◂ VT = **enajenar**

alienígena Ⓐ ADJ (= *extranjero*) alien, foreign; (= *extraterrestre*) alien, extraterrestrial

Ⓑ SMF (= *extranjero*) alien, foreigner; (= *extraterrestre*) alien, extraterrestrial being

alienista SMF specialist in mental illness, psychiatrist, alienist (*EEUU*)

aliento SM [1] (= *hálito*) breath; **tiene mal ~** he has bad breath; **le huele el ~ a ajo** his breath smells of garlic

[2] (= *respiración*) **el ejercicio me dejó sin ~** the exercise left me breathless *o* out of breath; **contener el ~** to hold one's breath; **dar los últimos ~s** (*liter*) to breathe one's last (*liter*); **faltar el ~**: **me falta el ~** I'm out of breath; **recobrar** *o* **recuperar el ~** to get one's breath back; **tomar ~**: **paró, tomó ~ y continuó hablando** he stopped to get his breath back, then went on talking; ✦*MODISMOS* **cortar a algn el ~** to take sb's breath away; **de un ~** (*frm*) (= *de una vez*) in one go

[3] (*frm*) (= *ánimo*) courage, spirit; **cobrar ~** to take heart; **dar ~ a algn** to encourage sb

[4] (= *tono*) **una novela de hondo ~ patriótico** a novel with a deeply patriotic spirit, a profoundly patriotic novel

alifafe* SM ailment

aligación SF (= *aleación*) alloy; (= *vínculo*) bond, tie

aligeramiento SM (= *reducción de peso*) lightening; (= *aliviamiento*) easing, alleviation; (= *aceleración*) speeding-up

aligerar ▸conjug 1a◂ Ⓐ VT (= *hacer ligero*) to lighten; [+ *dolor*] to ease, relieve, alleviate; (= *abreviar*) to shorten; (= *acelerar*) to quicken; **voy a dar un paseo para ~ las piernas** I'm going for a walk to stretch my legs

Ⓑ VI (= *darse prisa*) to hurry, hurry up

Ⓒ **aligerarse** VPR [*carga*] to get lighter; **~se de ropa** to put on lighter clothing

aligustre SM privet

alijar¹ ▸conjug 1a◂ VT (*Téc*) to sandpaper

alijar² ▸conjug 1a◂ VT [+ *carga*] to lighten; [+ *barco*] to unload; [+ *contrabando*] to land, smuggle ashore

alijo SM [1] (= *aligeramiento*) lightening; (= *descarga*) unloading

[2] (= *contrabando*) contraband, smuggled goods; **un ~ de armas** an arms cache, an arms haul; **un ~ de drogas** a drugs shipment, a consignment of drugs

alilaya Ⓐ SF (*Andes, Caribe*) (= *excusa*) lame excuse, flimsy excuse

Ⓑ SMF (*Méx*) (= *persona astuta*) cunning person, sharp character*

alimaña SF [1] (*Zool*) pest; **~s** vermin

[2] (= *persona*) bloodsucker*

alimañero SM gamekeeper, vermin destroyer

alimentación SF [1] (= *acción*) feeding; (= *comida*) food; **el coste de la ~** the cost of food; **la ~ de los niños** the feeding of children ► **alimentación insuficiente** malnutrition ► **alimentación natural** natural food, health foods

[2] (*Téc*) feed; (*Elec*) supply; **bomba de ~** feed pump ► **alimentación a la red** mains supply ► **alimentación automática de hojas** automatic sheet feeder ► **alimentación automática de papel** (automatic) paper feeder ► **alimentación por fricción** friction feed

alimentador SM (*Téc*) feeder ► **alimentador automático de hojas** automatic sheet feeder ► **alimentador automático de papel** (automatic) paper feeder ► **alimentador de red** mains power supply

alimentar ▸conjug 1a◂ Ⓐ VT [1] (= *dar de comer a*) to feed; **alimentan el ganado con piensos** they feed the cattle with animal fodder; **tengo una familia que ~** I've got a family to feed

[2] (= *nutrir*) to be nutritious *o* nourishing; **la comida rápida no te alimenta nada** fast food is not at all nutritious *o* nourishing

[3] [+ *imaginación*] to fire, fuel; [+ *esperanzas, pasiones*] to feed, fuel; [+ *sentimiento, idea*] to foster; **ese tipo de comentario alimenta el rencor** that sort of remark fosters resentment; **sus historias ~on mi deseo de ir a Perú** her stories strengthened *o* fuelled my desire to go to Peru

[4] [+ *hoguera, horno doméstico, fuego*] to feed, add fuel to; [+ *horno industrial*] to stoke; **el operario alimenta la máquina de** *o* **con combustible** the operator feeds fuel into the machine

[5] (*Elec*) to supply

Ⓑ VI to be nutritious, be nourishing; **esta comida no alimenta nada** this food is not at all nutritious *o* nourishing; ✦*MODISMO* **huele que alimenta*** it smells delicious

Ⓒ **alimentarse** VPR [1] [*animal*] to feed; **se alimentan de carroña** they feed on carrion

[2] [*persona*] **en este país se alimentan fatal** people eat very poorly in this country; **se alimenta sólo de productos naturales** she eats only natural foods; **durante el naufragio se ~on sólo de fruta** while shipwrecked they lived *o* survived on fruit

[3] (*Mec*) **el motor se alimenta de gasoil** the engine runs on diesel

alimentario ADJ food *antes de s*; **la industria alimentaria** the food industry

alimenticio ADJ [1] (= *nutritivo*) nourishing, nutritive

[2] (= *relativo a comida*) food *antes de s*; **productos ~s** foodstuffs; **valor ~** food value, nutritional value

alimento SM [1] (= *comida*) food; **de mucho ~** nourishing; **de poco ~** of little nutritional value ► **alimento de primera necesidad** staple food ► **alimentos integrales** whole foods ► **alimentos naturales** health foods

[2] (= *apoyo*) encouragement, support; (= *incentivo*) incentive; [*de pasión*] fuel

[3] **alimentos** (*Jur*) maintenance allowance *sing*, alimony *sing* (*EEUU*)

alimentoso ADJ nourishing

alimoche SM Egyptian vulture

alimón: **al ~** ADV together, jointly, in collaboration

alindado ADJ foppish, dandified

alindar¹ ▸conjug 1a◂ VT (= *adornar*) to embellish, make pretty, make look nice; [+ *persona*] to doll up, prettify

alindar² ▸conjug 1a◂ Ⓐ VT [+ *tierra*] to mark off, mark out

Ⓑ VI (= *estar contiguo*) to adjoin, be adjacent

alinderar ▸conjug 1a◂ VT (*CAm, Cono Sur*) to mark out the boundaries of

alineación SF [1] (*Téc*) alignment; **estar fuera de ~** to be out of alignment, be out of true

[2] (*Dep*) line-up

alineado ADJ **países no ~s** non-aligned countries; **está ~ con el partido** he is in line with the party

alineamiento SM alignment; **no ~** non-alignment

alinear ▸conjug 1a◂ Ⓐ VT (*Téc*) to align; [+ *alumnos*] to line up, put into line; [+ *soldados*] to form up; (*Dep*) [+ *equipo*] to select, pick (**con** with)
Ⓑ **alinearse** VPR (= *ponerse en fila*) to line up; (*Mil*) to fall in; (*Inform*) to justify; **se ~on a lo largo de la calle** they lined up along the street

aliñador SM (*Cono Sur*) bonesetter

aliñar ▸conjug 1a◂ VT 1 (*Culin*) [+ *ensalada*] to dress; [+ *guiso*] to season
2 (= *adornar*) to adorn, embellish; (= *preparar*) to prepare
3 (*Cono Sur*) [+ *hueso*] to set

aliño SM 1 (*Culin*) [*de ensalada*] dressing; [*de guiso*] seasoning
2 (= *adorno*) adornment, embellishment

alioli SM (*Culin*) *sauce of garlic and oil*

alionar ▸conjug 1a◂ VT (*Cono Sur*) to stir up

alionín SM blue tit

alipego SM (*CAm*) 1 (= *plus*) extra, bonus (*added as part of a sale*)
2 (*) (= *persona no invitada*) gatecrasher, intruder

aliquebrado ADJ crestfallen

alirón Ⓐ EXCL (= *¡bien!*) hurray!
Ⓑ SM **cantar el ~** (*lit*) *to sing a chant celebrating one's team's victory*; (*fig*) to celebrate

alisado Ⓐ ADJ (= *liso*) smooth; (*Téc*) polished
Ⓑ SM (= *acción*) smoothing; (*Téc*) polishing, finishing

alisador SM (= *persona*) polisher; (= *herramienta*) smoothing blade, smoothing tool

alisadura SF (= *acción*) smoothing; (*Téc*) polishing; **~s** (= *raspaduras*) cuttings, shavings

alisar[1] ▸conjug 1a◂ VT 1 [+ *vestido*] to smooth, smooth down; [+ *pelo*] to smooth, sleek
2 (*Téc*) to polish, finish

alisar[2] SM, **aliseda** SF alder grove

alíscafo SM, **aliscafo** SM hydrofoil

alisios SMPL **vientos ~** trade winds

aliso SM alder, alder tree

alistamiento SM (= *matrícula*) enrolment, enrollment (*EEUU*); (*Mil*) enlistment

alistar ▸conjug 1a◂ Ⓐ VT 1 (= *registrar*) to list, put on a list; (= *matricular*) to enrol, enroll (*EEUU*); (*Mil*) to enlist
2 (= *disponer*) to prepare, get ready
3 (*CAm*) [+ *zapato*] to sew, sew up
Ⓑ **alistarse** VPR 1 (= *matricularse*) to enrol *o* (*EEUU*) enroll; (*Mil*) to enlist, join up
2 (*LAm*) (= *vestirse*) to dress up; (= *prepararse*) to get ready

aliteración SF alliteration

aliterado ADJ alliterative

alitranca SF (*Andes, Cono Sur*) brake, braking device

aliviadero SM overflow channel

aliviador ADJ comforting, consoling

alivianarse* ▸conjug 1a◂ VPR (*Méx*) to play it cool, be cool, be laid-back*

aliviar ▸conjug 1b◂ Ⓐ VT 1 [+ *dolor, sufrimiento, problema*] to ease, relieve; **medidas para ~ los efectos de la catástrofe** measures to ease *o* relieve the effects of the disaster
2 [+ *carga, peso*] to lighten
3 (= *consolar*) to soothe; **el vino alivia las penas** wine soothes away your troubles; **me alivia saberlo** I'm pleased to hear it
4 (*frm*) **~ el paso** to quicken one's step
5 (†) (= *robar*) **~ a algn de algo** to relieve sb of sth (*hum*)
Ⓑ VI (= *darse prisa*) to speed up
Ⓒ **aliviarse** VPR 1 [*dolor*] to ease
2 [*enfermo*] to get better; **¡que te alivies!** get well soon!

alivio SM 1 (= *consuelo*) relief; **es un gran ~ haber aprobado por fin** it's a great relief to have passed at last, I'm relieved that I've passed at last; **¡qué ~!** what a relief!; **dio un suspiro de ~** he gave a sigh of relief
2 [*de un dolor*] **los paños calientes le servirán de ~** the hot towels will ease *o* relieve his pain; **¡que siga el ~!** I hope you continue to improve!
3 (*Esp*) **de ~*** awful, frightful; **me dio un susto de ~** he gave me an awful fright
4 ► **alivio de luto** half-mourning

aljaba SF 1 (*para flechas*) quiver
2 (*Cono Sur Bot*) fuchsia

aljama SF (*Hist*) 1 (= *barrio*) [*de moros*] Moorish quarter; [*de judíos*] Jewish quarter, ghetto
2 (= *mezquita*) mosque; (= *sinagoga*) synagogue
3 (= *reunión*) [*de moros*] gathering of Moors; [*de judíos*] gathering of Jews

aljamía SF *Spanish written in Arabic characters (14th-16th centuries)*

aljamiado ADJ **texto ~** *text of Spanish written in Arabic characters*

aljibe SM 1 (= *tanque*) cistern, tank; (*Náut*) water tender; (*Aut*) oil tanker
2 (*Andes*) (= *pozo*) well; (= *calabozo*) dungeon, underground prison

aljofaina SF washbasin, washbowl

aljófar SM (= *perla*) pearl; [*de rocío*] dewdrop

aljofarar ▸conjug 1a◂ VT to bedew, cover with pearls of moisture

aljofifa SF floorcloth

aljofifar ▸conjug 1a◂ VT to wash, mop, mop up

allá ADV 1 (*indicando posición*) there, over there; (*dirección*) (over) there; **~ arriba** up there; **~ abajo** down there; **~ en Sevilla** down in Seville, over in Seville; **~ mismo** right there; **~ lejos** way off in the distance, away over there; **no tan ~** not so far; **más ~** further away, further over; **más ~ de** beyond; **más ~ de los límites** beyond the limits; **cualquier número más ~ de siete** any number higher than seven; **no sabe contar más ~ de diez** she can't count above ten, she can't count beyond ten; **por ~** thereabouts; **vamos ~** let's go there; **¡~ voy!** I'm coming!; ✦**MODISMOS** **el más ~** the beyond, the great beyond; **no muy ~*** (= *valer poco*) not much cop*; **no está muy ~** (*de salud*) he isn't very well; **~ lo veremos** we'll see when we get there, we'll sort that one out later
2 **~ tú** that's up to you, that's your problem; **¡~ él!** that's his lookout!*, that's his problem!; **~ cada uno** that's for the individual to decide
3 (*indicando tiempo*) **~ en 1600** back in 1600, way back in 1600, as long ago as 1600; **~ por el año 1960** round about 1960; **~ en mi niñez** in my childhood days

allacito ADV (*LAm*) = **allá**

allanamiento SM 1 (= *nivelación*) levelling, leveling (*EEUU*); (= *alisadura*) smoothing; (*Mil*) razing
2 [*de obstáculos*] removal
3 (*Jur*) submission (**a** to)
4 (*esp LAm*) [*de policía*] raid; **el juez dispuso el ~ del domicilio** the judge granted the police a search warrant for the house
► **allanamiento de morada** breaking and entering
5 (= *pacificación*) pacification

allanar ▸conjug 1a◂ Ⓐ VT 1 (= *nivelar*) to level, level out, make even; (= *alisar*) to smooth, smooth down; (*Mil*) to raze (to the ground)
2 [+ *problema*] to iron out
3 (*Jur*) [+ *casa*] (= *robar*) to break into, burgle, burglarize (*EEUU*); (*esp LAm*) [*policía*] to raid
4 [+ *país*] to pacify, subdue
Ⓑ **allanarse** VPR 1 (= *nivelarse*) to level out, level off
2 (= *derrumbarse*) to fall down, tumble down
3 (*fig*) (= *acceder*) to submit, give way; **~se a** to accept, agree to; **se allana a todo** he agrees to everything

allegadizo ADJ gathered at random, put together unselectively

allegado/a Ⓐ ADJ 1 (= *afín*) near, close; **según fuentes allegadas al ministro** according to sources close to the minister
2 [*pariente*] close; **los más ~s y queridos** one's nearest and dearest; **las personas allegadas a …** those closest to …
Ⓑ SM/F 1 (= *pariente*) relation, relative
2 (= *partidario*) follower

allegar ▸conjug 1h◂ Ⓐ VT 1 (= *reunir*) to gather (together), collect
2 (= *acercar*) **~ una cosa a otra** to put something near something else
3 (= *añadir*) to add
Ⓑ **allegarse** VPR 1 (*fig*) (= *adherirse*) **~se a una opinión** to adopt a view; **~se a una secta** to become attached to a sect
2 (= *llegar*) to arrive, approach; **~se a algn** to go up to sb

allende (*liter*) Ⓐ ADV on the other side
Ⓑ PREP beyond; **~ los mares** beyond the seas; **~ los Pirineos** on the other side of the Pyrenees; **~ lo posible** impossible

allí ADV 1 (*indicando posición*) there; **~ arriba** up there; **~ dentro** in there; **~ cerca** near there; **de ~** from there; **de ~ para acá** back and forth; **por ~** over there, round there; **hasta ~** as far as that, up to that point; **~ donde va despierta admiración** wherever he goes he makes a favourable impression; **está tirado por ~*** he's hanging around somewhere
2 (*indicando tiempo*) **de ~ a poco** shortly afterwards
3 (*expresiones*) **de ~** (= *por lo tanto*) and so, and thus (*frm o liter*); **de ~ que …** (= *por eso*) that is why …, hence ... (*frm*); **de ~ a decir que es un timo** but that's a long way from calling it a swindle; **hasta ~ no más** (*LAm*) that's the limit

allicito ADV (*LAm*) = **allí**

alma SF 1 (= *espíritu*) soul; **una oración por su ~** a prayer for his soul; **no había ni un ~ en la iglesia** there wasn't a soul in the church; **un pueblo de 2.000 ~s** a village of 2,000 souls; **tenía ~ de poeta** she had a poetic spirit; **es mi amigo del ~** he's my soulmate; **ni ~ viviente** not a single living soul ► **alma bendita** kind soul ► **alma cándida** poor innocent ► **¡alma de cántaro!** you idiot! ► **alma caritativa**, **alma de Dios**

kind soul ► **alma en pena** lost soul ► **almas gemelas** soul mates, kindred spirits (*más frm*)

2 ✦*MODISMOS* **tener el ~ en su almario** to have what it takes; **le arrancó el ~** he was devastated; **estaba con el ~ en la boca** my heart was in my mouth; **se le cayó el ~ a los pies** his heart sank; **huir** *o* **ir como ~ que lleva el diablo** to flee *o* go like a bat out of hell; **se echó el ~ a las espaldas** he abandoned all scruples; **en el ~: te lo agradezco en el ~** I'm eternally *o* deeply grateful; **se me clavó en el ~** = **me llegó al alma**; **me dolió en el ~** it broke my heart; **lo siento en el ~** I am truly sorry; **entregar el ~ (a Dios)** (*euf*) to depart this life; **hasta el ~: me mojé hasta el ~** I got soaked to the skin; **vomitó hasta el ~** she was violently sick; **estar con** *o* **tener el ~ en un hilo** to have one's heart in one's mouth *o* (*EEUU*) throat; **en lo más hondo de mi ~** from the bottom of my heart, in my heart of hearts; **irse el ~ tras algo/algn** to fall in love with sth/sb, fall for sth/sb; **me llegó al ~** (= *me dolió*) I was deeply hurt; (= *me conmovió*) I found it deeply moving *o* touching; **de mi ~: ¡madre mía de mi ~! ◊ ¡Dios mío de mi ~!** good God!, good grief!; **¡hijo de mi ~!** (*con cariño*) my darling boy!, my precious child!; (*con ironía*) my dear child!; **¡mi ~!** *o* **¡~ mía!, ¿qué te ha pasado?** my love! what's wrong?; **partir el ~ a algn** (= *hacer sufrir*) to break sb's heart; (= *golpear*) (*) to beat sb up; **partirse el ~: se parten el ~ trabajando** they work themselves into the ground; **se me parte el ~** it breaks my heart; **no puedo con mi ~** (*Esp**) I'm completely shattered*, I'm ready to drop*; **rendir el ~** to give up the ghost; **romper el ~ a algn** = **partir el alma a algn**; **romperse el ~** (*LAm*) to break one's neck; **me salió del ~** I just said it without thinking, it just came out; **no tener ~** to have no soul; **con toda el ~: lo deseo con toda el ~** I want it desperately; **la quiero con toda mi ~** I love her with all my heart; **lo odio con toda mi ~** I detest him, I hate his guts*; **tiró fuerte, con toda su ~** he pulled hard, with all his might; **vender el ~ al diablo** to sell one's soul to the devil; **con el ~ en vilo** = **con el alma en un hilo**; **le volvió el ~ al cuerpo** he recovered his composure

3 (= *parte vital*) [*de grupo, organización*] driving force; [*de asunto*] heart, crux; **hasta que no lleguemos al ~ del asunto** until we get to the heart *o* crux of the matter; **es el ~ de la fiesta** she's the life and soul of the party

4 (*Téc*) [*de cable*] core; [*de cuerda*] core, central strand; [*de cañón*] bore; [*de raíl*] web

5 (*Bot*) pith

6 (*Andes*) (= *cadáver*) corpse

almacén SM 1 [*de mercancías*] warehouse, store; **tener algo en ~** (= *de reserva*) to have sth in store; (*Com*) to stock sth ► **almacén de depósito** bonded warehouse ► **almacén depositario** (*Com*) depository

2 (*Mec, Mil*) magazine

3 (= *tienda*) shop, store; **almacenes ◊ grandes almacenes** department store *sing*; **Almacenes Pérez** Pérez Department Store ► **almacén frigorífico** cold store

4 (*LAm*) (= *tienda de comestibles*) grocer's (shop)

almacenable ADJ that can be stored, storable

almacenado SM storage, warehousing

almacenaje SM 1 (= *servicio*) storage, storing ► **almacenaje de larga duración** long-term storage ► **almacenaje frigorífico** cold storage

2 (= *gastos*) storage charge

almacenamiento SM (*en almacén, depósito*) warehousing; (*Inform*) storage ► **almacenamiento de datos** data storage ► **almacenamiento primario** primary storage ► **almacenamiento secundario** secondary storage ► **almacenamiento temporal en disco** spooling, disk spooling

almacenar ▸conjug 1a◂ VT 1 (*como negocio*) to store, warehouse

2 [*cliente*] to put into storage; [+ *víveres*] to stock up (with)

3 (= *guardar*) to keep, collect; [+ *rencor, odio*] to store up

4 (*Inform*) to store

almacenero/a SM/F (*en almacén*) storekeeper; (*LAm*) (*en tienda*) shopkeeper, grocer, storekeeper (*EEUU*)

almacenista SM (= *dueño*) warehouse owner; (= *vendedor*) wholesaler; (*LAm*) (*en tienda*) shopkeeper, grocer, storekeeper (*EEUU*)

almáciga SF, **almácigo** SM plantation, nursery

almádena SF sledgehammer

almadía SF raft

almadiarse ▸conjug 1c◂ VPR to be sick, vomit

almadraba SF (= *acto, arte*) tunny fishing; (= *lugar*) tunny fishery; (= *redes*) tunny net, tunny nets *pl*

almadreña SF wooden shoe, clog

almagre SM red ochre, red ocher (*EEUU*)

almajara SF hotbed, forcing frame

alma máter SF 1 (= *impulsor*) driving force

2 (*Univ*) alma mater

almanaque SM almanac; ✦*MODISMOS* **hacer ~s** to muse; **echar a algn vendiendo ~s** (*Andes, Cono Sur*) to send sb away with a flea in his ear

almariarse ▸conjug 1c◂ VPR (*CAm, Cono Sur*) to be sick, vomit

almazara SF oil mill, oil press

almeja SF 1 (*Zool*) clam

2 (**) [*de mujer*] cunt**; **mojar la ~** to have a screw**

almenado ADJ battlemented, crenellated

almenara SF (= *fuego*) beacon; (= *araña*) chandelier

almenas SFPL battlements

almendra SF 1 (*Bot*) almond; ✦*MODISMO* **ser ~** (*Caribe*) (= *encanto*) to be a love, be a peach; ► **almendra amarga** bitter almond ► **almendra garapiñada** sugared almond ► **almendra tostada** toasted almond

2 (= *semilla*) kernel, stone

3 [*de vidrio*] cut-glass drop (*of chandelier*)

almendrada SF almond milk shake, *drink made with milk and almonds*

almendrado Ⓐ ADJ 1 [*forma*] almond-shaped; **de ojos ~s** almond-eyed

2 [*sabor*] nutty

Ⓑ SM (= *dulce*) macaroon

almendral SM almond orchard

almendrera SF almond tree

almendrillo SM (*LAm*) almond tree

almendro SM almond tree

almendruco SM green almond

Almería SF Almería

almeriense Ⓐ ADJ of/from Almería

Ⓑ SMF native/inhabitant of Almería; **los ~s** the people of Almería

almete SM helmet

almez SM hackberry

almiar SM hayrick

almíbar SM syrup; **peras en ~** pears in syrup; **estar hecho un ~** (= *amable*) to be all sweetness and light; (*pey*) (= *meloso*) to overdo the flattery ► **almíbar de pelo** (*LAm*) heavy syrup

almibarado ADJ 1 (= *con almíbar*) syrupy; (= *dulce*) honeyed, oversweet

2 (= *meloso*) sugary

almibarar ▸conjug 1a◂ VT (= *bañar en almíbar*) to preserve in syrup; **~ las palabras** to use honeyed words

almidón SM (= *fécula*) starch; (*Méx*) (= *engrudo*) paste

almidonado ADJ 1 [*ropa*] starched

2 [*persona*] (= *estirado*) stiff, starchy; (= *pulcro*) dapper, spruce

almidonar ▸conjug 1a◂ VT to starch; **los prefiero sin ~** I prefer them unstarched

almilla SF 1 (= *jubón*) bodice

2 (*Téc*) tenon

3 (*Culin*) breast of pork

alminar SM minaret

almirantazgo SM admiralty

almirante SMF admiral

almirez SM mortar

almizcle SM musk

almizcleño ADJ musky

almizclera SF muskrat, musquash

almizclero SM musk deer

almo ADJ (*poét*) (= *vivificador*) nourishing; (= *digno de veneración*) sacred, venerable

almocafre SM weeding hoe

almodrote SM 1 (= *salsa*) cheese and garlic sauce

2 (*fig*) (= *baturrillo*) hotchpotch, hodgepodge (*EEUU*)

almofré SM (*LAm*), **almofrez** SM (*LAm*) sleeping bag, bedroll

almohada SF [*de cama*] pillow; (= *funda*) pillowcase; (= *cojín*) cushion; **consultar algo con la ~** to sleep on sth ► **almohada mariposa** butterfly pillow ► **almohada neumática** air cushion

almohade ADJ, SMF Almohad

almohadilla SF 1 (= *almohada pequeña*) small pillow

2 (= *cojincillo*) (*para alfileres*) pincushion; (*para sellos*) inkpad ► **almohadilla de entintar** inkpad

3 (*LAm*) (= *agarrador*) holder (*for iron*)

4 (*Arquit*) boss

almohadillado Ⓐ ADJ (= *acolchado*) padded, stuffed; (*Arquit*) dressed

Ⓑ SM dressed stone

almohadón SM (= *almohada grande*) large pillow, bolster; (*Rel*) hassock

almohaza SF currycomb

almohazar ▸conjug 1f◂ VT [+ *caballo*] to brush down, groom; [+ *piel*] to dress

almoneda SF (= *subasta*) auction; (= *liquidación*) clearance sale

almoned(e)ar ▸conjug 1a◂ VT to auction

almorávide ADJ, SMF Almoravid

almorranas SFPL piles

almorta SF vetch

almorzar ▸conjug 1f, 1l◂ Ⓐ VT (*a mediodía*) to have for lunch, lunch on (*frm*); (*a media mañana*) to have for breakfast, have for brunch
Ⓑ VI (*a mediodía*) to have lunch, lunch (*frm*); (*a media mañana*) to have breakfast; **vengo almorzado** I've had lunch

almuecín SM, **almuédano** SM muezzin

almuerzo SM (*a mediodía*) lunch; (*a media mañana*) breakfast, brunch; [*de boda*] wedding breakfast ► **almuerzo de gala** official luncheon ► **almuerzo de negocios** business lunch ► **almuerzo de trabajo** working lunch

alnado/a SM/F stepchild

aló EXCL (*esp LAm Telec*) hello!

alobado‡ ADJ dim*, thick*

alocado/a Ⓐ ADJ (= *loco*) crazy, mad; (= *irresponsable*) wild; (= *distraído*) scatterbrained
Ⓑ SM/F madcap

alocar ▸conjug 1g◂ (*LAm*) Ⓐ VT to drive mad; **me alocan las pizzas** I love pizzas, I'm mad for pizzas*
Ⓑ **alocarse** VPR to fly off the handle*, go crazy

alocución SF speech, address, allocution (*frm*)

áloe SM (*Bot*) aloe; (*Farm*) aloes

alojado/a SM/F (*LAm*) guest, lodger, roomer (*EEUU*)

alojamiento SM (= *lugar de hospedaje*) lodging, lodgings *pl*; (*Mil*) billet, quarters *pl*; (*Andes*) (= *pensión*) small hotel, boarding house; **buscar ~** to look for accommodation; **dar ~** to put up, accommodate

alojar ▸conjug 1a◂ Ⓐ VT (= *hospedar*) to put up, accommodate; (*Mil*) to billet, quarter
Ⓑ **alojarse** VPR to stay; (*Mil*) to be billeted, be quartered; **~se en** to stay at, put up at; **la bala se alojó en el pulmón** the bullet lodged in the lung

alón Ⓐ ADJ (*LAm*) (= *de ala grande*) large-winged; [*sombrero*] broad-brimmed
Ⓑ SM wing (*of chicken*)

alondra SF lark, skylark

alongar ▸conjug 1l◂ Ⓐ VT = **alargar A**
Ⓑ **alongarse** VPR to move away

alopecia SF alopecia

alpaca SF alpaca

alpargata SF rope-soled sandal, espadrille; **turismo de ~** travelling on the cheap*, tourism on a shoestring

alpargatería SF sandal shop

alpargatero/a Ⓐ ADJ (*) (= *de poca categoría*) low-class, down-market; (= *barato*) done on the cheap*
Ⓑ SM/F (= *fabricante*) *maker of canvas sandals*; (= *vendedor*) *seller of canvas sandals*

alpargatilla SMF crafty person

alpende SM shed, lean-to

Alpes SMPL Alps

alpestre ADJ (= *de los Alpes*) Alpine; (= *montañoso*) mountainous

alpinismo SM mountaineering, climbing

alpinista SMF mountaineer, climber

alpinístico ADJ mountaineering *antes de s*, climbing *antes de s*

alpino ADJ Alpine

alpiste SM [1] (= *semillas*) birdseed, canary seed
[2] (*) (= *alcohol*) drink, booze*
[3] (*LAm**) (= *dinero*) brass*

Al Qaeda SM *o* SF Al Qaeda

alquería SF farmhouse, farmstead

alquiladizo/a Ⓐ ADJ (= *que se alquila*) for rent, for hire; (= *que se puede alquilar*) that can be rented, that can be hired; (*pey*) (= *asalariado*) hireling
Ⓑ SM/F hireling

alquilado/a SM/F (*Caribe*) tenant

alquilador(a) SM/F (= *propietario*) renter, hirer; (= *usuario*) tenant, lessee

alquilar ▸conjug 1a◂ Ⓐ VT [1] [*propietario*] [+ *inmueble*] to let, rent, rent out; [+ *coche, autocar*] to hire, hire out; (*TV*) to rent, rent out; **"se alquila"** "to let", "for rent" (*EEUU*); **aquí no se alquila casa alguna** there is no house to let here
[2] [*usuario*] [+ *inmueble*] to rent; [+ *coche, autocar*] to hire; (*TV*) to rent; **turba alquilada** rent-a-mob*; **"por ~"** "to let", "for rent" (*EEUU*)
Ⓑ **alquilarse** VPR [1] [*persona*] (*como asalariado*) to hire o.s. out; (*Caribe*) (*como sirviente*) to go into service
[2] [*taxi*] to be for hire

alquiler SM [1] (= *acción*) [*de inmueble*] letting, renting; (*Téc*) plant hire; [*de coche, autocar*] hire, hiring; **coche de ~** hire car; **"alquiler sin conductor"** (*Esp*) "self-drive" ► **alquiler de úteros** surrogate motherhood, womb-leasing
[2] (= *precio*) [*de inmueble*] rent, rental; [*de coche, autocar*] hire charge; **contrato de ~** tenancy agreement; **control de ~es** rent control; **exento de ~es** rent-free; **madre de ~** surrogate mother; **pagar el ~** to pay the rent; **subir el ~ a algn** to raise sb's rent; **vivir de ~** to live in rented accommodation

alquimia SF alchemy

alquimista SM alchemist

alquitara SF still

alquitarar ▸conjug 1a◂ VT to distil

alquitrán SM tar ► **alquitrán de hulla** coal tar ► **alquitrán mineral** coal tar

alquitranado Ⓐ ADJ tarred, tarry
Ⓑ SM [*de carretera*] tarmac; (= *lienzo*) tarpaulin, tarp (*EEUU*)

alquitranar ▸conjug 1a◂ VT (= *untar con alquitrán*) to tar; [+ *carretera*] to tarmac

alrededor Ⓐ ADV [1] around; **todo ~** all around
[2] **~ mío,** *etc* (*Cono Sur*) around me, *etc*
[3] **~ de** (= *en torno a*) around; **todo ~ de la iglesia** all around the church; **mirar ~ de sí** ◊ **mirar ~ suyo** to look around *o* about one
[4] **~ de** (= *aproximadamente*) about, in the region of; **~ de 200** about 200
Ⓑ SM (= *contorno*) **mirar a su ~** to look around *o* about one; **~es** (*de un lugar*) surroundings, neighbourhood *sing*, neighborhood *sing* (*EEUU*); [*de ciudad*] outskirts; **en los ~es de Londres** in the area round London, on the outskirts of London

Alsacia SF Alsace

Alsacia-Lorena SF Alsace-Lorraine

alsaciano/a ADJ, SM/F Alsatian

alt. ABR [1] (= **altura**) ht
[2] (= **altitud**) alt.

alta SF [1] (*Med*) (*tb* **~ médica**) certificate of discharge; **dar a algn el ~ (médica)** ◊ **dar de ~ a algn** to discharge sb
[2] (*en club, organismo*) membership; **solicitó el ~ en el club de golf** he applied for membership of the golf club, he applied to be a member of the golf club; **solicité el ~ de la línea telefónica** I applied for a phone line; **causar ~** ◊ **darse de ~** to join; **doce nuevos miembros han causado ~** twelve new members have joined; **darse de ~ en la empresa** to join the company; **nos dimos de ~ en la Seguridad Social** we registered with Social Security
[3] (*Jur*) **dar una propiedad de ~** to register a property at the Land Registry
[4] (*Mil*) **dar a algn de ~** to pass sb (as) fit

altamente ADV highly; **es ~ venenoso** it's highly poisonous; **documentos ~ secretos** top secret documents

altanería SF [1] (= *altivez*) haughtiness, arrogance
[2] (*Caza*) hawking, falconry
[3] (*Meteo*) upper air

altanero ADJ [1] (= *altivo*) haughty, arrogant
[2] [*ave*] high-flying

altar SM altar; **llevar a algn al ~** to lead sb to the altar; ✦**MODISMOS poner a algn en un ~** to put sb on a pedestal; **quedarse para adornar ~es** to be left on the shelf; **subir a los ~es** to be beatified, be canonized ► **altar mayor** high altar

altaricón* ADJ big-built, large

altavoz SM (*Radio*) loudspeaker; (*Elec*) amplifier

altea SF mallow

altear ▸conjug 1a◂ VT (*Cono Sur*) to order to stop, order to halt

alterabilidad SF changeability

alterable ADJ changeable

alteración SF [1] (= *cambio*) alteration, change
[2] (= *aturdimiento*) upset, disturbance; (*Med*) irregularity of the pulse ► **alteración del orden público** breach of the peace
[3] (= *riña*) quarrel, dispute
[4] (= *agitación*) strong feeling, agitation

alterado ADJ (= *cambiado*) changed; [*orden*] disturbed; (= *enfadado*) angry; (*Med*) upset, disordered

alterar ▸conjug 1a◂ Ⓐ VT [1] (= *cambiar*) to modify, alter; **tuvimos que ~ los planes por la huelga** we had to modify *o* alter our plans because of the strike
[2] (= *estropear*) [+ *alimentos*] to spoil; [+ *leche*] to sour; **la humedad alteró los alimentos** the humidity spoiled the food, the humidity made the food go bad
[3] (= *conmocionar*) to shake, upset; **la noticia del accidente la alteró visiblemente** she was visibly shaken *o* upset by the news of the accident
[4] **~ el orden** to disturb the peace
[5] (= *distorsionar*) [+ *verdad*] to distort, twist
Ⓑ **alterarse** VPR [1] (= *estropearse*) [*alimentos*] to spoil, go bad; [*leche*] to go sour
[2] [*voz*] to falter
[3] (= *turbarse*) to be shaken, be upset; **se alteró con la noticia de su muerte** he was shaken *o* upset by the news of her death; **¡tranquila, no te alteres!** keep calm!, don't get upset!; **continuó hablando sin ~se** he continued speaking unperturbed

altercado SM, **altercación** SF argument, altercation

altercar ▸conjug 1g◂ VI to argue, quarrel, wrangle

álter ego SM alter ego

alteridad SF otherness

alternación SF alternation

alternadamente ADV alternately

alternado ADJ alternate

alternador SM alternator

alternancia SF alternation ► **alternancia de cultivos** crop rotation ► **alternancia en el poder** power switching, taking turns in office

alternante ADJ alternating

alternar ▸conjug 1a◂ Ⓐ VT (*gen*) to alternate, vary; [+ *cultivos*] to rotate

Ⓑ VI [1] (= *turnar*) to alternate (**con** with); (*Téc*) to alternate, reciprocate

[2] (= *relacionarse*) to mix, socialize; (*) (= *ir a bares*) to go on a pub crawl*, go boozing*; **~ con un grupo** to mix with a group, go around with a group; **~ con la gente bien** to hobnob with top people; **tiene pocas ganas de ~** he doesn't want to mix, he is not inclined to be sociable; **~ de igual a igual** to be on an equal footing

Ⓒ **alternarse** VPR (= *hacer turnos*) to take turns, change about; **~se a los mandos** to take turns at the controls; **~se en el poder** to take turns in office

▼ **alternativa** SF [1] (= *opción*) alternative, option, choice; **no tener ~** to have no alternative *o* option *o* choice; **tomar una ~** to make a choice

[2] (= *sucesión*) alternation; (= *trabajo*) shift work, work done in relays ► **alternativa de cosechas** crop rotation

[3] (*Taur*) *ceremony by which a novice becomes a fully qualified bullfighter*; **tomar la ~** *to become a fully qualified bullfighter*

[4] **alternativas** (*en actitud*) ups and downs, vicissitudes, fluctuations; **las ~s de la política** the ups and downs *o* vicissitudes of politics

alternativamente ADV alternately

alternativo ADJ (*Elec*) alternating; [*cultura, prensa*] alternative; **fuentes alternativas de energía** alternative energy sources

alterne SM (*con gente*) mixing, socializing; (*euf*) (= *relaciones sexuales*) sexual contact, sexual contacts *pl*; **club de ~** singles club; **estas chicas no son de ~** these girls don't sleep around*, these girls are not easy lays‡; *ver tb* **chica**

alterno ADJ (*Bot, Mat*) alternate; (*Elec*) alternating; **tiempo con nubes alternas** there will be patches of clouds

altero SM (*Méx*), **alterón** SM (*Andes*) heap, pile

alteza SF [1] (= *altura*) height

[2] (= *título*) **Alteza** Highness; **Su Alteza Real** His/Her Royal Highness; **sí, Alteza** yes, your Highness

[3] (= *elevación*) sublimity ► **alteza de miras** high-mindedness

altibajos SMPL ups and downs

altillo SM [1] (*Geog*) small hill, hillock

[2] (*LAm*) (= *desván*) attic

[3] (= *entreplanta*) mezzanine

altilocuencia SF grandiloquence

altilocuente ADJ, **altílocuo** ADJ grandiloquent

altímetro SM altimeter

➤ LENGUA Y USO: **alternativa 1** 45.4

altimontano ADJ high mountain *antes de s*, upland *antes de s*

altinal SM (*Méx*) pillar, column

altiplanicie SF high plateau

altiplánico ADJ high plateau *antes de s*

altiplano SM (= *meseta*) high plateau; (*LAm*) [*de los Andes*] high Andean plateau, altiplano

altísimo ADJ very high; **el Altísimo** the Almighty

altisonancia SF high-flown style

altisonante ADJ, **altísono** ADJ high-flown, high-sounding

altitud SF (*Aer*) height, altitude; (*Geog*) elevation; **a una ~ de** at a height *o* altitude of

altivamente ADV haughtily, arrogantly

altivarse ▸conjug 1a◂ VPR to give o.s. airs

altivez SF, **altiveza** SF haughtiness, arrogance

altivo ADJ haughty, arrogant

alto[1] Ⓐ ADJ [1] (*en altura*) [1·1] [*edificio, persona*] tall; [*monte*] high; **está muy ~ para su edad** he is very tall for his age; **los pisos ~s tienen más luz natural** the top flats have more natural light; **jersey de cuello ~** polo neck jumper, turtleneck; **camino de alta montaña** high mountain path; **zapatos de tacón** *o* (*Cono Sur, Perú*) **taco ~** high-heeled shoes, high heels; *ver tb* **mar**[1] **1**

[1·2] **lo ~**: **una casa en lo ~ de la cuesta** a house on top of the hill; **desde lo ~ del árbol** from the top of the tree; **lanzar algo de** *o* **desde lo ~** to throw sth down, throw sth down from above; ✦*MODISMO* **por todo lo ~**: **lo celebraron por todo lo ~** they celebrated it in style

[2] (*en nivel*) [*grado, precio, riesgo*] high; [*clase, cámara*] upper; **se han alcanzado muy altas temperaturas** there have been very high temperatures; **tiene la tensión alta** he has high blood pressure; **los alumnos de los niveles más ~s** the highest level students; **la marea estaba alta** it was high tide, the tide was in; **ha pagado un precio muy ~ por su descaro** he paid a very high price for his cheekiness; **una familia de clase alta** an upper class family; **la cámara alta del Parlamento ruso** the upper house of the Russian parliament; **ocupa una alta posición en el gobierno** he occupies a high-ranking position in the government; **tiene un ~ sentido del deber** he has a strong sense of duty; **alta burguesía** upper-middle class; **~ cargo** (*puesto*) high-ranking position; (*persona*) senior official, high-ranking official; **alta cocina** haute cuisine; **~/a comisario/a** High Commissioner; **Alto Comisionado** High Commission; **alta costura** high fashion, haute couture; **de alta definición** high-definition *antes de s*; **~/a ejecutivo/a** top executive; **alta escuela** (*Hípica*) dressage; **un jugador de alta escuela** a top quality player; **altas esferas** upper echelons; **alta fidelidad** high fidelity, hi-fi; **altas finanzas** high finance; **alta frecuencia** high frequency; **~ funcionario** senior official, high-ranking official; **oficiales de alta graduación** senior officers, high-ranking officers; **~s hornos** blast furnace; **~s mandos** senior officers, high-ranking officers; **de altas miras**: **es un chico de altas miras** he is a boy of great ambition; **alta presión** (*Téc, Meteo*) high pressure; **hoy continuarán las altas presiones** the high pressure system will continue today; **alta sociedad** high society; **alta tecnología** high technology; **temporada alta** high season; **alta tensión** high tension, high voltage; **alta traición** high treason; **alta velocidad** high speed; **Alta Velocidad Española** (*Esp*) *name given to high speed train system*

[3] (*en intensidad*) **el volumen está muy ~** the volume is very loud; **la calefacción está muy alta** the heating is very high; **en voz alta** [*leer*] out loud; [*hablar*] in a loud voice

[4] (*en el tiempo*) **hasta altas horas de la madrugada** until the early hours

[5] [*estilo*] lofty, elevated

[6] (= *revuelto*) **estar ~** [*río*] to be high; [*mar*] to be rough

[7] (*Geog*) upper; **el Alto Rin** the Upper Rhine

[8] (*Mús*) [*nota*] sharp; [*instrumento, voz*] alto

[9] (*Hist, Ling*) high; **~ antiguo alemán** Old High German; **la alta Edad Media** the high Middle Ages

Ⓑ ADV [1] (= *arriba*) high; **sube un poco más ~** go up a little higher; **ha llegado muy ~ en su carrera profesional** he's reached the top in his professional career; **lanzar algo ~** to throw sth high

[2] (= *en voz alta*) **gritar ~** to shout out loud; **hablar ~** (= *en voz alta*) to speak loudly; (= *con franqueza*) to speak out, speak out frankly; **¡más ~, por favor!** louder, please!; **pon la radio un poco más ~** turn the radio up a little; **pensar (en) ~** to think out loud, think aloud; *ver tb* **volar**

Ⓒ SM [1] (= *altura*) **el muro tiene 5 metros de ~** the wall is 5 metres high; **mide 1,80 de ~** he is 1.80 metres tall; **en ~**: **coloque los pies en ~** put your feet up; **con las manos en ~** (*en atraco, rendición*) with one's hands up; (*en manifestación*) with one's hands in the air; ✦*MODISMO* **dejar algo en ~**: **el resultado deja muy en ~ su reputación como el mejor del mundo** the result has boosted his reputation as the best in the world; **estas cosas dejan en ~ el buen nombre de un país** these things contribute to maintaining the country's good name

[2] (*Geog*) hill; **el pueblo está en un ~** the town lies on a hill ► **Altos del Golán** Golan Heights

[3] (*Arquit*) upper floor

[4] (*Mús*) alto

[5] ► **altos y bajos** ups and downs

[6] **pasar por ~** [+ *detalle, problema*] to overlook

[7] (*Chile*) [*de ropa, cartas*] pile

[8] (*Chile*) [*de tela*] length

[9] **los ~s** (*Cono Sur, Méx*) [*de casa*] upstairs; (*Geog*) the heights; **los ~s de Jalisco** the Jalisco heights

alto[2] Ⓐ SM [1] (= *parada*) stop; **dar el ~ a algn** to order sb to halt, stop sb; **hacer un ~** (*en viaje*) to stop off; (*en actividad*) to take a break; **a este bar vienen los camioneros que hacen un ~ en el camino** the lorry drivers stop off at this bar on the way; **hicieron un ~ en el trabajo para comer un bocadillo** they took a break from work to eat a sandwich; **poner el ~ a algo** (*Méx*) to put an end to sth ► **alto el fuego** (*Esp*) ceasefire

[2] (*Aut*) (= *señal*) stop sign; (= *semáforo*) lights *pl*

Ⓑ EXCL **¡alto!** halt!, stop!; **¡~ ahí!** stop there!; **¡~ el fuego!** cease fire!

altocúmulo SM altocumulus

altomedieval ADJ early medieval, of the High Middle Ages

altoparlante SM (*LAm*) loudspeaker

altorrelieve SM high relief

altostrato SM altostratus

altozanero SM (*Col*) porter

altozano SM 1 (= *otero*) small hill, hillock; [*de ciudad*] upper part
2 (*Andes, Caribe*) (= *atrio*) cathedral forecourt, church forecourt

altramuz SM lupin

altruismo SM altruism

altruista Ⓐ ADJ altruistic
Ⓑ SMF altruist

altura SF 1 [*de edificio, techo, persona*] height; **el agua llegó hasta una ~ de 30cms** the water reached a height of 30cms; **las dos estanterías tienen la misma ~** the two bookshelves are the same height; **se necesita tener una ~ superior a 1,80** you have to be over 1.80 metres tall; **hubo olas de hasta tres metros de ~** there were waves up to three metres high, there were waves of up to three metres in height; **a la ~ de algo**: **la ventana quedaba a la ~ de mi cabeza** the window was level with my head; **sentí un dolor a la ~ de los riñones** I felt a pain around my kidneys; **se hizo un corte a la ~ del tobillo** he cut himself on the ankle ► **altura de caída** [*de cascada*] fall ► **altura de la vegetación** timber line
2 (*en el aire*) height, altitude; **el avión subió a una ~ de 10.000 pies** the plane rose to a height *o* an altitude of 10,000 feet; **nos encontramos a 3.000 metros de ~ sobre el nivel del mar** we are 3,000 metres above sea level; **volaba a muy poca ~ del suelo** it was flying just above the ground; **ganar** *o* **tomar ~** to climb, gain height; **el globo empezó a perder ~** the balloon began to lose height; ► **altura de crucero** cruising height; *ver tb* **mal**
3 (= *nivel*) **no llegó a la ~ que se exigía** he did not measure up to the standard required; **si lo insultas te estás rebajando a su ~** if you insult him you are just lowering yourself to his level; **no encuentra ningún rival a su ~** she can't find a rival to match her, she can't find a rival in her league; **un partido de gran ~** a really excellent game; **estar a la ~ de** [+ *persona*] to be in the same league as, be on a par with; [+ *tarea*] to be up to, be equal to; **no estamos a la ~ de los trabajadores japoneses** we are not in the same league as Japanese workers, we are not on a par with Japanese workers; **su último artículo no estaba a la ~ de los anteriores** his last article did not match up to the previous ones; **la novela no estaba a la ~ del concurso** the novel was not up to the standard set by the competition, the novel did not measure up to the competition standards; **supo estar a la ~ de las circunstancias** he managed to rise to the occasion; **no estábamos a la ~ de los acontecimientos** we didn't keep abreast of events; ✦**MODISMOS** **dejar** *o* **poner a algn a la ~ del betún** *o* (*Arg, Uru*) **de un felpudo** *o* (*Chile*) **del unto*** (*estando presente*) to make sb feel small; (*estando ausente*) to lay into sb; **quedar a la ~ del betún** (*Esp*): **si no los invitamos quedaremos a la ~ del betún** if we don't invite them, it'll look really bad
4 (*Geog*) **a la ~ de** on the same latitude as; **a la ~ de Cádiz** on the same latitude as Cádiz; **a la ~ del km 8** at the 8th km, at the 8th km point; **hay retenciones a la ~ de Burgos** there are tailbacks near Burgos; **¿a qué ~ de la calle quiere que pare?** how far along the street do you want me to stop?
5 (*Náut*) **buque de ~** seagoing vessel; **pesca de ~** deep-sea fishing; **remolcador de ~** deep-sea tug, ocean-going tug
6 (*Dep*) (= *salto*) high jump; (= *distancia del suelo*) height; **acaban de superar la ~ de 1,90** they have managed to beat the height of 1.90
7 (*Mús*) pitch
8 [*de ideas, sentimientos*] sublimity, loftiness
9 **alturas** 9·1 (= *lugar elevado*) (*Geog*) heights; (*Rel*) heaven *sing*; **en las ~s de Sierra Nevada** on the heights of Sierra Nevada; **¡Gloria a Dios en las ~s!** Glory to God in Heaven!; **estar en las ~s** (*Rel*) to be on high
9·2 [*de organización*] upper echelons; **en las ~s abundan las intrigas palaciegas** court intrigues are plentiful in the upper echelons
9·3 **a estas ~s** [*de edad*] at my/your/his/*etc* age; [*de tiempo*] at this stage; **a estas ~s no me preocupan las arrugas** at my age, wrinkles don't worry me; **a estas ~s del año las playas están casi vacías** at this stage of the year the beaches are almost empty; **a estas ~s nadie te va a preguntar nada** at this stage no one is going to ask you anything; **¿todavía no confías en mí a estas ~s?** you still don't trust me after all this time?; **a estas ~s no podemos volvernos atrás** having come this far we can't go back now, we can't go back at this stage
9·4 (†) (= *pisos*) storey, story (*EEUU*); **una casa de cinco ~s** a five-storey house

alubia SF kidney bean
► **alubia pinta** pinto bean

alucinación SF hallucination

alucinado ADJ 1 (= *trastornado*) suffering hallucinations
2 (*) (= *fascinado*) gobsmacked*; **me quedé ~** I was gobsmacked

alucinador ADJ hallucinatory, deceptive

alucinante Ⓐ ADJ 1 (*Med*) hallucinatory
2 (*Esp**) (= *fascinante*) attractive, beguiling; (= *misterioso*) mysterious; (*) (= *genial*) great, fantastic*
3 (*Esp**) (= *inconcebible*) absurd; **es ~** it's mind-blowing*
Ⓑ SM (*Méx*) hallucinogenic drug

alucinar ▸conjug 1a◂ Ⓐ VT 1 (= *engañar*) to delude, deceive
2 (*Esp**) (= *fascinar*) **me alucinó lo que pasó** I was gobsmacked at what happened‡
Ⓑ VI 1 (= *padecer alucinaciones*) to hallucinate
2 (*Esp**) (= *delirar*) **¡tú alucinas!** you're seeing things!; **¡este tío alucina!** this guy must be joking!*; **yo alucino con esa canción** I love this song; **yo alucinaba al ver tanta cosa** I was gobsmacked at all the stuff I saw‡
Ⓒ **alucinarse** VPR to delude o.s.; **~se de algo*** to be gobsmacked at sth‡

alucine* SM delusion; **de ~** (= *genial*) fantastic*, great*; **¡qué ~!** (= *¡es genial!*) this is brill!*

alucinógeno/a Ⓐ ADJ hallucinogenic
Ⓑ SM/F (*) acid head‡
Ⓒ SM (*Med*) hallucinogen

alucinosis SF INV hallucinosis

alud SM 1 [*de nieve*] avalanche
2 (= *afluencia*) wave

aludido ADJ aforesaid, above-mentioned; **darse por ~** to take the hint; **no darse por ~** to pretend not to hear; **no te des por ~** don't take it personally

aludir ▸conjug 3a◂ VI **~ a** to allude to, mention

aluego ADV *etc* (*LAm*) = **luego**

alujado ADJ (*CAm, Méx*) bright, shining

alujar ▸conjug 1a◂ VT (*CAm, Méx*) to polish, shine

alumbrado/a Ⓐ ADJ (*) drunk
Ⓑ SM lighting ► **alumbrado de emergencia** emergency lighting ► **alumbrado de gas** gas lighting ► **alumbrado eléctrico** electric lighting ► **alumbrado fluorescente** fluorescent lighting ► **alumbrado público** street lighting
Ⓒ SM/F (*Rel*) illuminist; **los Alumbrados** the Illuminati

alumbramiento SM 1 (*Elec*) (= *acción*) lighting up; (= *sistema*) lighting, illumination
2 (*Med*) childbirth; **tener un feliz ~** to have a safe delivery

alumbrar ▸conjug 1a◂ Ⓐ VT 1 (= *iluminar*) [+ *cuarto, calle, ciudad*] to light; [+ *estadio, edificio, monumento*] to light up; **una sola bombilla alumbraba el cuarto** the room was lit by a single bulb; **la felicidad alumbró su rostro** his face lit up with happiness; **el sol alumbra la tierra** the sun illuminates the earth
2 (= *enfocar*) (*con linterna, foco*) **ve delante y alumbra el camino** you go ahead and light the way; **alumbra aquí** shine the light here
3 (*frm*) [+ *asunto*] to shed light on
4 (*frm*) (= *instruir*) to enlighten
5 [+ *agua*] to find
6 (*Rel*) [+ *ciego*] to give sight to
Ⓑ VI 1 (= *dar luz*) to give light, shed light; **esta bombilla alumbra bien** this bulb gives a good light
2 (*frm*) (= *dar a luz*) to give birth
Ⓒ **alumbrarse** VPR (†) (= *emborracharse*) to get lit up*

alumbre SM alum

aluminio SM aluminium, aluminum (*EEUU*); **papel de ~** cooking foil, kitchen foil, silver foil

aluminosis SF INV (*Constr*) *degeneration of cement used in construction*

alumnado SM 1 (*Univ*) student body; (*Escol*) roll, pupils
2 (*LAm*) (= *colegio*) college, school

alumno/a SM/F 1 (*Escol*) pupil; (*Univ*) student; **antiguo ~** (*Escol*) old boy, former pupil, alumnus (*EEUU*); (*Univ*) old student, former student, alumnus (*EEUU*) ► **alumno/a externo/a** day pupil ► **alumno/a interno/a** boarder
2 (*Jur*) ward, foster child

alunarse ▸conjug 1a◂ VPR (*CAm*) to get saddle-sore (*horse*)

alunizaje SM 1 (= *aterrizaje en la luna*) landing on the moon, moon landing
2 (*) (= *robo*) smash-and-grab raid

alunizar ▸conjug 1f◂ VI to land on the moon

alusión SF (= *mención*) allusion, reference; (= *indirecta*) hint; **hacer ~ a** to allude to, refer to

alusivo ADJ allusive

aluvial ADJ alluvial

aluvión SM 1 (*Geol*) alluvium ► **tierras de aluvión** alluvial soil *sing*, alluvial soils
2 (*fig*) (= *alud*) flood; **llegan en incontenible ~** they come in an unstoppable flood ► **aluvión de improperios** stream *o* torrent of abuse

aluvionado SM alluviation

álveo SM riverbed, streambed

alveolar ADJ alveolar

alvéolo SM, **alveolo** SM (*Anat*) alveolus; [*de panal*] cell; (*fig*) (= *laberinto*) network, honeycomb

alverja SF 1 (= *arveja*) vetch
2 (*LAm*) (= *guisante*) pea

alverjilla SF sweet pea

alza SF 1 (= *subida*) [*de precio, temperatura*] rise; **el ~ de los tipos de interés** the rise in interest rates; **la bolsa ha experimentado una fuerte ~** the stock market has risen sharply; **al ~** [*tendencia*] upward; [*inflación, precio*] rising; **revisar los precios al ~** to put prices up; **la Bolsa se mantuvo ayer al ~** the stock market continued its upward trend yesterday; **en ~** [*acciones, precio*] on the rise; **las acciones están en ~** the shares are rising *o* on the rise; **un artista en ~** a rising star; **un joven escritor en ~** an up-and-coming writer; **jugar al ~** (*Fin*) to speculate on a rising market; ✦*MODISMO* **hacer algo por la pura ~** to do sth just for the sake of it
2 (*Mil, Caza*) sights *pl* ► **alzas fijas** fixed sights ► **alzas graduables** adjustable sights
3 (*en zapato*) raised insole

alzacristales SM INV ► **alzacristales eléctrico** electric windows *pl*

alzacuello SM, **alzacuellos** SM INV clerical collar, dog collar

alzada SF 1 [*de caballos*] height
2 (*Arquit*) elevation, side view
3 (*Jur*) appeal

alzado/a Ⓐ ADJ 1 (= *levantado*) raised; **con el puño ~** with a raised fist; *ver tb* **votación**
2 (*Fin*) [*cantidad, precio*] fixed; [*quiebra*] fraudulent; [*persona*] fraudulently bankrupt; **por un precio ~** for a lump sum; *ver tb* **tanto D1**
3 (*Méx, Ven*) (= *engreído*) big-headed
4 (*Chile, Col, Perú, Ven*) (= *sublevado*) arrogant, cocky*
5 (*LAm*) [*animal*] (= *arisco*) wild; **estar ~** (*Cono Sur*) to be on heat
6 (*Andes*) (= *borracho*) drunk
Ⓑ SM/F (= *persona sublevada*) rebel ► **alzado/a en armas** armed insurgent
Ⓒ SM 1 (*Arquit*) elevation
2 (*Tip*) gathering

alzamiento SM 1 (= *acción*) raising, lifting; **en el ~ del coche** in the raising *o* lifting of the car; **el juez ordenó el ~ del cadáver** the judge ordered the removal of the corpse
2 (= *sublevación*) revolt, uprising; **~ en armas** armed revolt, armed uprising
3 (*Com*) (*de precio*) rise, increase; (*en subasta*) higher bid ► **alzamiento de bienes** concealment of assets

alzaprima SF 1 (= *palanca*) lever, crowbar; (= *calce*) wedge
2 (*Mús*) bridge
3 (*Cono Sur*) (= *carro pesado*) heavy trolley, flat truck

alzaprimar ▸conjug 1a◂ VT (= *levantar*) to lever up, raise with a lever; (*fig*) (= *avivar*) to arouse, stir up

alzar ▸conjug 1f◂ Ⓐ VT 1 (= *levantar*) 1·1 [+ *objeto, persona*] to lift; [+ *objeto muy pesado*] to hoist; [+ *copa*] to raise; **no podía ~la del suelo** he could not lift her off the floor; **los manifestantes ~on sus banderas** the demonstrators raised *o* lifted up their flags; **alcemos nuestras copas por la victoria** let us raise our glasses to victory; **~on el telón unos minutos más tarde** the curtain went up a few minutes later
1·2 [+ *brazo, cabeza, cejas*] to raise; **alzó los brazos al cielo** he raised up his arms to heaven; **alzó la mano para pedir la palabra** he put up *o* raised his hand to ask permission to speak; **~ la mirada** *o* **los ojos** *o* **la vista** to look up; **ni siquiera alzó la vista cuando entramos** she didn't even look up when we came in; **no alzó la mirada del libro ni un momento** he didn't look up *o* avert his gaze (*más frm*) from the book for one moment; **~ la voz** to raise one's voice; **a tu padre no le alces la voz** don't raise your voice at your father; **alza un poco más la voz, que no te oigo** speak up a little, I can't hear you; **alzan su voz contra la injusticia** they speak out against injustice; **siempre se ~án voces llamando a la unidad** there will always be calls for unity; *ver tb* **vuelo² 1**
2 (= *erigir*) [+ *monumento*] to raise; [+ *edificio*] to erect
3 [+ *mantel*] to put away
4 [+ *prohibición*] to lift
5 [+ *cosecha*] to gather in, bring in
6 (*Rel*) [+ *cáliz, hostia*] to elevate
7 (*Tip*) to gather
8 (= *recoger*) (*Méx*) (*del suelo*) to pick up; (*LAm*) (*a un bebé*) to pick up
9 (*Méx*) (= *ordenar*) [+ *casa, recámara*] to tidy up; **~ la mesa** to clear the table; **~ los trastes** to clear away the dishes
10 (*Méx*) [+ *dinero*] to save
Ⓑ **alzarse** VPR 1 (= *ponerse en pie*) to rise; **cuando entró la novia todos se ~on** when the bride entered everyone stood up *o* rose to their feet
2 [*edificio, monte, monumento*] (= *tener una altura determinada*) to rise; (= *estar situado*) to stand; **la cordillera se alza 2.500m sobre el nivel del mar** the mountain range rises 2,500m above sea level; **en la plaza se alzaba la iglesia** the church stood in the square; **el rascacielos se alza por encima del parque** the skyscraper rises *o* towers over the park
3 (= *aumentar*) [*precio, temperatura*] to rise
4 (= *rebelarse*) to rise up, rise, revolt (**contra** against); **~se en armas** to take up arms, rise up in arms
5 (= *llevarse*) **~se con** [+ *premio, votos*] to win; [+ *dinero*] to run off with; **el Barcelona se alzó con el título de Liga** Barcelona won *o* took the League title; **se ~on con la mayoría absoluta** they won an absolute majority; **~se con el poder** to take power; **~se con la victoria** to win; **era el favorito indiscutible para ~se con la victoria** he was the undisputed favourite to win; **los primeros comicios en que los socialistas se han alzado con la victoria** the first elections in which the socialists have been victorious *o* have won; ✦*MODISMO* **~se con el santo y la limosna** to make a clean sweep
6 (*Com*) to go fraudulently bankrupt
7 (*Andes*) (= *emborracharse*) to get drunk
8 (*Méx, Ven*) (= *volverse engreído*) to get bigheaded
9 (*Chile, Col, Perú, Ven*) (= *rebelarse*) **le llamé la atención a la muchacha y se me alzó** I told the maid off and she answered me back; **por nada se alza** he gets bolshy at the slightest thing*
10 **~se de hombros** (*Méx*) to shrug one's shoulders
11 (*LAm*) [*animal*] (= *volverse arisco*) to run wild; (= *entrar en celo*) to be on heat

alzaválvulas SM INV tappet

alzo SM (*CAm*) theft

A.M. SF ABR (= **amplitud modulada**) AM

a.m. ABR (= **ante meridiem**) a.m., am

ama SF ► **ama de brazos** nurse, nursemaid ► **ama de cría** wet nurse ► **ama de cura** priest's housekeeper ► **ama de gobierno**, **ama de llaves** housekeeper ► **ama de leche** wet nurse ► **ama seca** nurse, nursemaid; *ver tb* **amo**

▼**amabilidad** SF (= *generosidad*) kindness; (= *cortesía*) courtesy; **tuvo la ~ de acompañarme** he was kind enough to come with me, he was good enough to come with me; **tenga la ~ de** (+ *INFIN*) please be so kind as to + *infin*

amabilísimo ADJ SUPERL *de* **amable**

▼**amable** ADJ kind, nice; **es usted muy ~** you are very kind; **si es tan ~** if you would be so kind; **ser ~ con algn** to be kind to sb, be nice to sb; **¡qué ~ ha sido usted trayéndolo!** how kind of you to bring it!; **¡muy ~!** thanks very much, that's very kind, that's very kind of you; **sea tan ~ (como para)** ◊ **si es tan ~ (como para)** (*LAm*) please be so kind as to

amablemente ADV kindly; **muy ~ me ayudó** he very kindly helped me

amachambrarse ▸conjug 1a◂ VPR (*Cono Sur*) = **amachinarse**

amacharse ▸conjug 1a◂ VPR (*LAm*) [*persona*] to dig one's heels in, refuse to be moved; [*caballo*] to refuse

amachinarse ▸conjug 1a◂ VPR (*LAm*) (= *amancebarse*) to set up house together; **~ con algn** to become sb's lover; **estar** *o* **vivir amachinado con** to live with

amacho ADJ (*CAm, Cono Sur*) (= *destacado*) outstanding; (= *fuerte*) strong, vigorous

amaderado ADJ woody

amado/a Ⓐ ADJ dear, beloved
Ⓑ SM/F lover, sweetheart

amador(a) Ⓐ ADJ loving, fond
Ⓑ SM/F lover

amadrigar ▸conjug 1h◂ Ⓐ VT to take in, give shelter to
Ⓑ **amadrigarse** VPR [*animal*] to go into its hole, burrow; [*persona*] (= *retraerse*) to go into retirement, hide o.s. away

amadrinar ▸conjug 1a◂ VT [+ *niño*] to be godmother to; [+ *soldado, regimiento*] to be patron to

amaestrado ADJ 1 [*animal*] trained; (*de circo*) performing
2 [*plan*] well-thought out, artful

amaestrador(a) SM/F trainer

amaestramiento SM training

➤ LENGUA Y USO: amabilidad 31 amable 48.1

amaestrar ▸conjug 1a◂ VT [+ *persona*] to train, teach; [+ *animal*] to train; [+ *caballo*] to break in

amagar ▸conjug 1h◂ Ⓐ VT (= *amenazar*) to threaten, portend (*liter*); (= *dar indicios de*) to show signs of
Ⓑ VI (= *estar próximo*) to threaten, be impending; (*Med*) (= *manifestarse*) to show the first signs; (*Esgrima*) to feint; **~ a hacer algo** to threaten to do sth, show signs of doing sth
Ⓒ **amagarse** VPR [1] (*) (= *esconderse*) to hide
[2] (*Cono Sur*) (= *tomar una postura amenazante*) to adopt a threatening posture

amago SM [1] (= *amenaza*) threat; (*fig*) (= *inicio*) beginning
[2] (*Med*) (= *señal*) sign, symptom; (= *indicio*) hint; **un ~ de mapa** a rough map; **con un ~ de sonrisa** with the suggestion of a smile, with a faint smile ► **amago tormentoso** outbreak of bad weather
[3] (*Esgrima*) feint

amainar ▸conjug 1a◂ Ⓐ VT [+ *vela*] to take in, shorten; [+ *furia*] to calm
Ⓑ VI, **amainarse** VPR [*viento*] to abate, die down; [*ira*] to subside; [*esfuerzo*] to slacken

amaine SM [1] [*de velas*] shortening
[2] [*de ira, viento*] abatement, moderation; [*de esfuerzo*] lessening, slackening

amaitinar ▸conjug 1a◂ VT to spy on

amaizado ADJ (*Andes*) rich

amalaya EXCL (*LAm*) = **ojalá**

amalayar ▸conjug 1a◂ VT (*Andes, CAm, Méx*) to covet, long for; **~ hacer algo** to long to do sth

amalgama SF amalgam

amalgamación SF amalgamation

amalgamar ▸conjug 1a◂ Ⓐ VT (*Quím*) to amalgamate; (*fig*) (= *combinar*) to combine, blend
Ⓑ **amalgamarse** VPR to amalgamate

Amalia SF Amelia

amamantar ▸conjug 1a◂ VT [1] (= *dar el pecho a*) to suckle, nurse
[2] (*Caribe*) (= *mimar*) to spoil

amancebado†† ADJ **estar** o **vivir ~s** to live together, cohabit

amancebamiento SM common-law union, cohabitation

amancebarse†† ▸conjug 1a◂ VPR to live together, cohabit

amancillar ▸conjug 1a◂ VT (= *manchar*) to stain; (= *deslustrar*) tarnish, dishonour, dishonor (*EEUU*)

amanecer ▸conjug 2d◂ Ⓐ VI [1] [*día*] to dawn; **el día amaneció lloviendo** at daybreak it was raining; **amanece a las siete** it gets light at seven; **nos amaneció en Granada** the next morning found us in Granada, the next morning we woke up in Granada
[2] [*persona, ciudad*] to wake up (in the morning); **amanecimos en Vigo** the next morning found us in Vigo, the next morning we woke up in Vigo; **amaneció acatarrado** he woke up with a cold; **el pueblo amaneció cubierto de nieve** morning saw the village covered in snow, when the next day dawned the village was covered in snow; **amaneció rey** (*liter*) he woke up to find himself king; **amanecieron bailando** (*LAm*) they danced all night, they were still dancing at dawn; **¿cómo amaneció?** (*LAm*) how are you this morning?
Ⓑ SM dawn, daybreak; **al ~** at dawn, at daybreak

amanecida SF dawn, daybreak

amanerado ADJ (= *afectado*) mannered, affected; (*LAm*) (= *demasiado correcto*) excessively polite

amaneramiento SM affectation

amanerarse ▸conjug 1a◂ VPR to become affected

amanezca SF (*Caribe, Méx*) (= *alba*) dawn; (= *desayuno*) breakfast

amanezquera SF (*Caribe, Méx*) early morning, daybreak

amanita SF amanita

amanojar ▸conjug 1a◂ VT to gather by the handful, gather in bunches

amansa SF (*Cono Sur*) [*de fieras*] taming; [*de caballos*] breaking-in

amansado ADJ tame

amansador(a) SM/F (= *domador*) tamer; (*Méx*) [*de caballos*] horse breaker, horse trainer

amansadora SF (*Arg*) [1] (= *sala*) waiting room
[2] (*) (= *espera*) long wait (*at government office*)

amansamiento SM [1] (= *acto*) [*de fieras*] taming; [*de caballos*] breaking-in
[2] (= *cualidad*) tameness

amansar ▸conjug 1a◂ Ⓐ VT [+ *caballo*] to break in; [+ *fiera*] to tame; [+ *persona*] to tame, subdue; [+ *pasión*] to soothe
Ⓑ **amansarse** VPR [*persona*] to calm down; [*pasión*] to moderate

amanse SM (*Andes, Méx*) [*de caballos*] breaking-in; [*de fieras*] taming

amante Ⓐ ADJ loving, fond; **nación ~ de la paz** peace-loving nation
Ⓑ SMF (= *hombre, mujer*) lover; (= *mujer*) mistress; **tuvo muchas ~s** he had many mistresses

amanuense SMF (= *escribiente*) scribe, amanuensis; (= *copista*) copyist; (*Pol*) secretary

amañado ADJ [1] (= *falso*) fake, faked
[2] (= *diestro*) skilful, skillful (*EEUU*), clever
[3] [*resultado, pelea*] fixed, rigged

amañador(a) Ⓐ ADJ (*Andes, Caribe*) having a pleasant climate
Ⓑ SM/F (*) fixer*

amañamiento SM (= *manipulación*) fiddling, trickery; (*Pol*) rigging, gerrymandering

amañanar ▸conjug 1a◂ VI [*persona*] to wake up; [*día*] to dawn

amañar ▸conjug 1a◂ Ⓐ VT [1] (*pey*) (= *manipular*) [+ *resultado*] to alter, tamper with; [+ *elección*] to rig; [+ *foto*] to fake; [+ *partido, jurado*] to fix; [+ *cuentas*] to cook*; [+ *excusa*] to cook up
[2] (= *hacer bien*) to do skilfully, do skillfully (*EEUU*), do cleverly
Ⓑ **amañarse** VPR [1] [*ser diestro*] to be skilful o (*EEUU*) skillful, be expert; (= *adquirir destreza*) to become expert, get the hang of it
[2] (= *acostumbrarse*) to become accustomed to; **ya se amaña en Quito** he's beginning to feel at home in Quito
[3] (= *llevarse bien con*) **~se con** to get along with
[4] (*Caribe*) (= *mentir*) to tell lies, lie

amaño SM [1] (= *destreza*) skill, expertness, cleverness; **tener ~ para** to have an aptitude for
[2] (= *ardid*) trick, guile
[3] **amaños** (= *herramientas*) tools; (*Cono Sur*) (= *mañas*) underhand means

amapola SF poppy; **ponerse como una ~** to turn as red as a beetroot

amar ▸conjug 1a◂ VT to love

amaraje SM [*de hidroavión*] landing (*on the sea*); [*de nave espacial*] splashdown, touchdown ► **amaraje forzoso** ditching

amaranto SM amaranth

amarar ▸conjug 1a◂ VI [*hidroavión*] to land (*on the sea*); [*nave espacial*] to splash down, touch down; (*forzosamente*) to ditch

amarchantarse ▸conjug 1a◂ VPR (*Caribe, Méx*) **~ en** to deal regularly with

amargado ADJ bitter, embittered; **estar ~** to be bitter

amargamente ADV bitterly

amargar ▸conjug 1h◂ Ⓐ VT [+ *comida*] to make bitter, sour; [+ *persona*] to embitter; [+ *ocasión*] to spoil; **~ la vida a algn** to make sb's life a misery; **a nadie le amarga un dulce** something's better than nothing
Ⓑ VI to be bitter, taste bitter
Ⓒ **amargarse** VPR [1] [*comida*] to get bitter
[2] [*persona*] to become bitter o embittered

amargo/a Ⓐ ADJ [1] [*sabor*] bitter, tart; **más ~ que tueras** ◊ **más ~ que la hiel** terribly bitter
[2] (*fig*) (= *apenado*) bitter, embittered
[3] (*Cono Sur*) (= *cobarde*) cowardly; (*Caribe*) (= *poco servicial*) unhelpful, offhand
Ⓑ SM [1] [*de sabor*] bitterness, tartness
[2] **amargos** (= *licor*) bitters
[3] (*Cono Sur*) (= *mate*) bitter tea, *bitter Paraguayan tea*
Ⓒ SM/F (*Cono Sur**) [*de mal genio*] grouch*; (= *vago*) shirker, skiver*

amargón SM dandelion

amargor SM, **amargura** SF [1] (= *sabor*) bitterness, tartness
[2] (*fig*) (= *aflicción*) bitterness; (= *pena*) grief, sorrow

amargoso ADJ (*LAm*) = **amargo A**

amariconado‡, **amaricado**‡ Ⓐ ADJ effeminate
Ⓑ SM nancy boy‡, pansy*

Amarilis SF Amaryllis

amarilla SF (*Dep*) yellow card; *ver tb* **amarillo**

amarillear ▸conjug 1a◂ VI [1] (= *tirar a amarillo*) to be yellowish; (= *mostrarse amarillo*) to show yellow, look yellow
[2] (= *volverse amarillo*) to go o turn yellow
[3] (= *palidecer*) to pale

amarillecer ▸conjug 2d◂ VI to yellow, turn yellow

amarillejo ADJ yellowish

amarillento ADJ (= *que tira a amarillo*) yellowish; [*tez*] pale, sallow

amarillez SF (= *cualidad*) yellow, yellowness; [*de tez*] paleness, sallowness

amarillismo SM [1] (*Prensa*) sensationalist journalism
[2] (*Pol**) *trade unionism which is in league with the bosses*

amarillista ADJ [1] [*prensa*] sensationalist
[2] [*sindicato*] pro-management

amarillo Ⓐ ADJ [*color*] yellow; [*semáforo*] amber, yellow (*EEUU*); *ver tb* **prensa**, **sindicato**
Ⓑ SM [1] (= *color*) yellow ► **amarillo canario** canary yellow ► **amarillo limón** lemon yellow ► **amarillo mostaza** mustard yellow

► **amarillo paja** straw colour *o* (*EEUU*) color
[2] (*Caribe*) ripe banana; *ver tb* **amarilla**

amarilloso ADJ (*LAm*) yellowish

amariposado* ADJ effeminate

amarra SF [1] (*Náut*) mooring line; (*LAm*) (= *cuerda*) rope, line, cord; (*Méx*) (= *rienda*) rein, lead
[2] **amarras** (*Náut*) moorings; **cortar** *o* **romper las ~s** to break loose, cut adrift; **echar las ~s** to moor
[3] **amarras** (= *protección*) protection *sing*; **tener buenas ~s** to have good connections

amarradera SF (*Andes*) (*para barcos*) mooring; (*Méx*) (= *cuerda*) rope, line, tether

amarradero SM (= *poste*) post, bollard; (*para barco*) berth, mooring

amarrado ADJ (*LAm*) mean, stingy

amarradura SF mooring

amarraje SM mooring charges *pl*

amarrar ▸conjug 1a◂ Ⓐ VT [1] (= *asegurar*) (*esp LAm*) to fasten, tie up; [+ *barco*] to moor, tie up; [+ *cuerda*] to lash, belay; (*Naipes*) to stack; **está de ~** he's raving mad; ✦***MODISMO*** **tener a algn bien amarrado** to have sb under one's thumb
[2] (*) (= *empollar*) to swot*, mug up*
Ⓑ VI (*) to get down to it in earnest
Ⓒ **amarrarse** VPR (*) **amarrársela** (*Andes, CAm*) to get tight*

amarre SM (= *acto*) fastening, tying; (= *lugar*) berth, mooring

amarrete/a* (*Cono Sur*) Ⓐ ADJ mean, stingy*
Ⓑ SM/F miser, skinflint, tightwad (*EEUU**)

amarro SM (*Andes*) (= *cuerda*) knotted string, knotted rope; (= *nudos*) mass of knots; (= *paquete*) bundle, packet, package (*EEUU*) ► **amarro de cigarrillos** packet of cigarettes

amarrocar ▸conjug 1g◂ VI (*Cono Sur*) to scrimp and save

amarronado ADJ chestnut, brownish

amarroso ADJ (*CAm*) acrid, sharp

amartelado ADJ lovesick; **andar** *o* **estar ~ con** to be in love with; **andan muy ~s** they're deeply in love

amartelamiento SM lovesickness, infatuation

amartelar ▸conjug 1a◂ Ⓐ VT [1] (= *dar celos a*) to make jealous
[2] (= *enamorar*) to make fall in love; [+ *corazón*] to win, conquer
Ⓑ **amartelarse** VPR to fall in love (**de** with)

amartillar ▸conjug 1a◂ VT (= *martillar*) to hammer; [+ *rifle*] to cock

amartizaje SM Mars landing, landing on Mars

amasadera SF kneading trough

amasado ADJ (*Caribe*) [1] [*sustancia*] doughy
[2] [*persona*] plump

amasador(a) SM/F kneader, baker

amasadora SF kneading machine

amasadura SF [1] (= *acto*) kneading
[2] (= *hornada*) batch

amasamiento SM (*Culin*) kneading; (*Med*) massage

amasandería SF (*Andes, Cono Sur*) ≈ bakery

amasandero/a SM/F (*Andes, Cono Sur*) ≈ baker

amasar ▸conjug 1a◂ VT [1] (*Culin*) [+ *masa*] to knead; [+ *harina, yeso*] to mix, prepare
[2] [+ *dinero*] to amass
[3] (*Med*) to massage
[4] (*) (= *tramar*) to cook up*, concoct

amasiato SM (*Méx, Perú*) cohabitation, common-law marriage; **su ~ duró mucho tiempo** they lived together for a long time

amasigado ADJ (*Andes*) dark, swarthy

amasijar‡ ▸conjug 1a◂ VT (*Cono Sur*) to do in*

amasijo SM [1] (*Culin*) (= *acción*) kneading; (*Téc*) mixing
[2] (= *material*) mixture; (= *mezcla*) hotchpotch, hodgepodge (*EEUU*), medley
[3] (= *plan*) plot, scheme
[4] (*Caribe*) (= *pan*) wheat bread

amasio/a SM/F (*CAm, Méx*) (= *amante*) lover; (= *mujer*) mistress

amate SM (*LAm*) fig tree

amateur ADJ, SMF amateur

amateurismo SM amateurism

amatista SF amethyst

amatorio ADJ love *antes de s*; **poesía amatoria** love poetry

amauta SM (*Andes*) Inca elder

amayorado ADJ (*Andes*) precocious, forward

amazacotado ADJ (= *pesado*) heavy, awkward; (= *informe*) shapeless, formless; (*Literat*) ponderous, stodgy; **~ de detalles** crammed with details

amazona SF [1] (*Literat*) amazon; (*Dep*) horsewoman, rider; (= *mujer varonil*) (*pey*) mannish woman
[2] (= *traje*) riding suit

Amazonas SM Amazon; **el río ~** the Amazon

Amazonia SF Amazonia

amazónico ADJ Amazon *antes de s*, Amazonian

ambages SMPL **hablar sin ~** to come straight to the point

ambagioso ADJ involved, circuitous, roundabout

ámbar SM amber ► **ámbar gris** ambergris

ambareado ADJ (*Andes**) chestnut, auburn

ambarino ADJ amber, yellow (*EEUU*)

Amberes SM Antwerp

➤ **ambición** SF ambition

➤ **ambicionar** ▸conjug 1a◂ VT (= *desear*) to aspire to, seek; (= *codiciar*) to lust after, covet; **~ ser algo** to have an ambition to be sth

ambiciosamente ADV ambitiously

ambicioso/a Ⓐ ADJ [1] (= *que tiene ambición*) ambitious
[2] (*pey*) (= *egoísta*) proud, self-seeking
Ⓑ SM/F (*gen*) ambitious person; (= *oportunista*) careerist; **~ de figurar** social climber

ambidextro ADJ, **ambidiestro** ADJ ambidextrous

ambientación SF [1] (= *estilo*) setting; **una novela de ~ oriental** a novel set in the Far East, a novel with an oriental setting; **la ~ estaba muy bien conseguida** they captured the atmosphere very well ► **ambientación musical** incidental music
[2] (*Radio*) sound effects
[3] (= *adaptación*) **le cuesta bastante la ~ a los sitios nuevos** he finds it hard to adjust to new places

ambientado ADJ [1] [*película, obra*] **un relato ~ en los años veinte** a story set in the twenties; **la película está muy bien ambientada** the film has a very good atmosphere
[2] [*persona*] **estar ~** to be settled in, be at home
[3] (*Méx*) (= *climatizado*) air-conditioned

ambientador(a) Ⓐ SM/F (*Cine, TV*) dresser
Ⓑ SM air freshener

ambiental ADJ [1] (= *del aire*) **hay un 70% de humedad ~** there is 70% humidity; **la luz ~ era insuficiente** the lighting was not strong enough; *ver tb* **música 1**
[2] (= *medioambiental*) environmental; **contaminación ~** environmental pollution; **su entorno ~ fue muy negativo** he was in a very negative environment

ambientalismo SM environmentalism

ambientalista ADJ, SMF environmentalist

ambientalmente ADV environmentally; **una zona ~ protegida** an environmentally protected area

ambientar ▸conjug 1a◂ Ⓐ VT [1] (= *dar ambiente a*) **los fans ambientaban el partido** the fans gave the match some atmosphere; **~on la entrada del hotel con decorados exóticos** they livened up the hotel foyer with exotic decoration
[2] [+ *película, obra*] to set
[3] (= *orientar*) to orientate, direct
Ⓑ **ambientarse** VPR [1] (= *adaptarse*) to settle in, adjust; **donde quiera que va, se ambienta rápidamente** wherever he goes, he manages to settle in *o* adjust quickly; **pondré un poco de música para que nos vayamos ambientando** I'll put some music on to get some atmosphere going
[2] (= *orientarse*) to orientate o.s., get one's bearings

ambiente Ⓐ ADJ INV **medio ~** environment; **ruido ~** environmental noise; **trabajamos con 120 decibelios de ruido ~** we work at a noise level of 120 decibels; **temperatura ~** room temperature; **"sírvase a temperatura ~"** "serve at room temperature"
Ⓑ SM [1] (= *aire*) **el ~ de la sala estaba muy cargado de humo** there was a very smoky atmosphere in the room, the air was really smoky in the room; **habrá ~ soleado en la costa** it will be sunny on the coast, there will be sunny weather on the coast ► **ambiente artificial** air conditioning
[2] (*creado por el entorno, la decoración*) atmosphere; **en medio de un ~ festivo** amid a festive atmosphere; **la madera da un ~ cálido al despacho** wood gives a warm feeling to *o* creates a warm atmosphere in the study; **no había un buen ~ en la oficina** there wasn't a good atmosphere in the office; **se respiraba un ~ de tensión** there was a feeling of tension; **cambiar de ~** to have a change of scene; **crónica de ~** background report; **micrófono de ~** field microphone; *ver tb* **música**
[3] (= *animación*) **¡qué ambientazo había en la plaza de toros!** what a great atmosphere there was in the bullring!; **el espléndido ~ cultural de París** the wonderful cultural life *o* ambience of Paris
[4] (= *entorno*) environment; **con su familia se siente en su ~** with her family, she really feels in her element; **~ familiar** home environment; **~ laboral** work environment
[5] **ambientes** (= *grupo social*) circles; **en ~s universitarios** in the university world, in university circles
[6] (‡) (*tb* **~ homosexual**) **el ~** the gay scene, the scene‡; **de ~** [*bar, discoteca*] gay *antes de s*
[7] (*Cono Sur*) (= *habitación*) room

ambigú SM buffet

➤ LENGUA Y USO: **ambición** 35.2 **ambicionar** 35.4

ambiguamente ADV ambiguously
ambigüedad SF ambiguity
ambiguo ADJ [1] (= *impreciso*) ambiguous; (= *incierto*) doubtful, uncertain; (= *equívoco*) noncommittal, equivocal
[2] (*) (= *bisexual*) bisexual
[3] (*Ling*) common
ambilado ADJ (*Caribe*) **estar** *o* **quedar ~** (= *boquiabierto*) to be left open-mouthed; (= *embobado*) to be distracted
ámbito SM [1] (= *campo*) field; (= *límite*) boundary, limit; **dentro del ~ de** within the limits of, in the context of; **en el ~ nacional** on a nationwide basis, on a nationwide scale; **en todo el ~ nacional** over the whole nation, throughout the country; **en el ~ nacional y extranjero** at home and abroad
[2] (*fig*) (= *esfera*) scope, range; **buscar mayor ~** to look for greater scope ► **ámbito de acción** sphere of activity
ambivalencia SF ambivalence
ambivalente ADJ ambivalent
ambladura SF **a paso de ~** at an amble
amblar ▸conjug 1a◂ VI to amble, walk in a leisurely manner
ambo SM (*Arg*) two-piece suit
ambos ADJ, PRON both; **vinieron ~** they both came; **~ tenéis los ojos azules** you've both got blue eyes; **~ a dos** both, both (of them) together
ambrosía SF ambrosia
Ambrosio SM Ambrose
ambucia SF (*Cono Sur*) (= *codicia*) greed, greediness; (= *hambre*) voracious hunger
ambuciento ADJ (*Cono Sur*) (= *codicioso*) greedy; (= *hambriento*) voracious
ambulancia SF (= *vehículo*) ambulance; (*Mil*) field hospital ► **ambulancia de correos** (*Esp*) post-office coach
ambulanciero/a SM/F ambulance man/woman
ambulante Ⓐ ADJ (= *que anda*) walking; [*circo, vendedor*] travelling, traveling (*EEUU*); [*biblioteca*] mobile; [*músico*] itinerant; [*actor*] strolling
Ⓑ SMF (= *vendedor callejero*) street seller, street vendor
ambulatoriamente ADV **tratar un paciente ~** to treat sb as an out-patient
ambulatorio Ⓐ SM (= *clínica*) national health clinic; (= *sección*) out-patients department
Ⓑ ADJ **tratar a algn en régimen ~** to treat sb as an out-patient
ameba SF amoeba, ameba (*EEUU*)
amedrentador ADJ frightening, menacing
amedrentar ▸conjug 1a◂ Ⓐ VT (= *asustar*) to scare, frighten; (= *intimidar*) to intimidate
Ⓑ **amedrentarse** VPR to be scared, be intimidated
amejoramiento SM (*LAm*) = **mejoramiento**
amejorar ▸conjug 1a◂ VT (*LAm*) = **mejorar A**
amelcocharse ▸conjug 1a◂ VPR [1] (*Caribe*) to fall in love
[2] (*Méx*) [*azúcar*] to harden, set
[3] (= *ser coqueta*) to be coy, be prim
amelonado ADJ [1] (= *forma*) melon-shaped
[2] **estar ~*** (= *enamorado*) to be lovesick
amén Ⓐ SM INV [1] (*Rel*) amen; ✦***MODISMOS*** **decir ~ a todo** to agree to everything; **en un decir ~** in a trice
[2] **~ de** (= *salvo*) except for, aside from (*EEUU*); (= *además de*) in addition to, besides
[3] **~ de que** (= *a pesar de*) in spite of the fact that
Ⓑ EXCL amen!
-amen *ver* **Aspects of Word Formation in Spanish 2**
amenaza SF threat ► **amenaza amarilla** yellow peril ► **amenaza de bomba** bomb scare ► **amenaza de muerte** death threat
amenazador ADJ, **amenazante** ADJ threatening, menacing
amenazar ▸conjug 1f◂ Ⓐ VT to threaten; **~ a algn de muerte** to threaten to kill sb; **me amenazó con despedirme** he threatened to fire me; **una especie amenazada de extinción** a species threatened with extinction; **la tarde amenazaba lluvia** it looked like rain in the evening; **~ violencia** to threaten violence
Ⓑ VI to threaten, impend; **~ con hacer algo** to threaten to do sth
amenguar ▸conjug 1i◂ VT [1] (= *disminuir*) to lessen, diminish
[2] (= *despreciar*) to belittle
[3] (= *deshonrar*) to dishonour, dishonor (*EEUU*)
amenidad SF pleasantness, agreeableness
amenización SF (= *mejoramiento*) improvement; [*de conversación*] enlivening; [*de estilo*] brightening up; [*de una reunión*] entertainment
amenizar ▸conjug 1f◂ VT (= *hacer agradable*) to make pleasant; [+ *conversación*] to enliven, liven up; [+ *estilo*] to brighten up; [+ *reunión*] to provide entertainment for, entertain
ameno ADJ (= *agradable*) pleasant, agreeable, nice; [*estilo*] engaging; [*libro*] enjoyable, readable; [*lectura*] light; **prefiero una lectura más amena** I prefer lighter reading; **es un sitio ~** it's a nice spot; **la vida aquí es más amena** life is more pleasant here
amento SM catkin
América SF (= *continente, Norteamérica*) America; (*LAm*) (= *Hispanoamérica*) South America, Spanish America, Latin America; **hacerse la ~** (*Cono Sur*) to make a fortune ► **América Central** Central America ► **América del Norte** North America ► **América del Sur** South America ► **América Latina** Latin America
americana SF coat, jacket ► **americana de sport** sports jacket; *ver tb* **americano**
americanada SF typically American thing, typically American thing to do
americanismo SM [1] (*Ling*) Americanism; (*LAm*) (= *imperialismo*) Yankee imperialism
[2] (*Caribe, Méx*) (= *apego a lo americano*) *liking for North American ways etc*
americanista SMF [1] (= *estudioso*) Americanist, specialist in indigenous American culture; (= *literato*) specialist in American literature
[2] (*CAm, Méx*) (= *aficionado*) *person with a liking for North American ways etc*
americanización SF americanization
americanizar ▸conjug 1f◂ Ⓐ VT to americanize
Ⓑ **americanizarse** VPR to become americanized
americano/a ADJ, SM/F (= *del continente, de Norteamérica*) American; (= *de Hispanoamérica*) Latin American, South American, Spanish American; *ver tb* **americana**
americio SM (*Quím*) americium
amerindio/a ADJ, SM/F American Indian, Amerindian
ameritado ADJ (*LAm*) worthy
ameritar ▸conjug 1a◂ VT (*LAm*) to deserve
amerizaje SM [*de hidroavión*] landing (*on the sea*); [*de nave espacial*] splashdown, touchdown
amerizar ▸conjug 1f◂ VI [*hidroavión*] to land (*on the sea*); [*nave espacial*] to splash down, touch down
amestizado ADJ *like a half breed*
ametrallador(a) SM/F machine gunner
ametralladora SF machine gun
ametrallamiento SM machine-gunning, machine-gun attack
ametrallar ▸conjug 1a◂ VT to machine-gun
amianto SM asbestos
amiba SF, **amibo** SM amoeba, ameba (*EEUU*)
amigable ADJ (= *amistoso*) friendly, sociable; (*Jur*) **~ componedor** arbitrator
amigablemente ADV amicably
amigacho* SM (*pey*) mate, buddy (*EEUU*), bachelor friend; **ha salido con los ~s** he's out with the boys; **esos ~s tuyos** those cronies of yours
amigarse ▸conjug 1h◂ VPR (= *hacerse amigos*) to get friendly, become friends; [*amantes*] to set up house together
amigazo* SM (*Cono Sur*) pal*, buddy (*EEUU*), close friend
amígdala SF tonsil
amigdalitis SF INV tonsillitis
amigdalotomía SF tonsillectomy
amigo/a Ⓐ SM/F [1] friend; **Manuel es un ~ mío** Manuel is a friend of mine; **es una amiga de Sofía** she is a friend of Sofía's *o* of Sofía; **es un ~ de la infancia** he's a childhood friend; **es una amiga del colegio** she's a school friend; **el perro es el mejor ~ del hombre** a dog is a man's best friend; **hacer ~s** to make friends ► **amigo/a de confianza** very close friend, intimate friend ► **amigo/a del alma** soulmate ► **amigo/a de lo ajeno** (*hum*) thief ► **amigo/a en la prosperidad** fair-weather friend ► **amigo/a íntimo/a** very close friend, intimate friend ► **amigo/a por correspondencia** penfriend
[2] (= *novio*) boyfriend/girlfriend
[3] (*en oración directa*) **pero, ~, ya no se puede hacer nada** there's nothing more we can do, my friend; **¡amigo! en ese tema ya no entro** hold on, I'm not getting mixed up in that!
Ⓑ ADJ [1] **son muy ~s** they are good *o* close friends; **Gonzalo es muy ~ de Pepe** Gonzalo is a good *o* close friend of Pepe's *o* of Pepe; **hacerse ~s** to become friends; **al final me hice muy ~ de Antonio** in the end Antonio and I became good friends; **se perdonaron y quedaron tan ~s** they made it up and everything was fine; **lo pagamos a medias y todos tan ~s** we'll go halves on it and that'll be fine
[2] **ser ~ de algo** to be fond of sth; **soy ~ del buen vino** I'm fond of good wine; **no soy muy ~ de las multitudes** I'm not very fond of *o* keen on crowds; **soy ~ de hablar con franqueza** I like straight talking
[3] [*país, fuego*] friendly

amigote SM mate*, sidekick*, buddy (*EEUU**); (*pey*) sidekick*, crony

amiguero ADJ (*LAm*) friendly

amiguete* SM (= *amigo*) mate, buddy (*EEUU*); (*con influencias*) influential friend, friend in the right place

amiguismo SM old-boy network, jobs for the boys

amiguito/a SM/F (= *novio*) boyfriend/girlfriend; (= *amante*) lover

amiláceo ADJ starchy

amilanar ▸conjug 1a◂ Ⓐ VT to scare, intimidate
Ⓑ **amilanarse** VPR to get scared, be intimidated (**ante, por** at)

aminoácido SM amino acid

aminorar ▸conjug 1a◂ VT [+ *precio*] to cut, reduce; [+ *velocidad*] to reduce

amistad SF [1] (= *cariño*) friendship; (= *relación amistosa*) friendly relationship, friendly connection; **hacer** *o* **trabar ~ con** to strike up a friendship with, become friends with; **llevar ~ con** to be on friendly terms with; **hacer las ~es** to make it up; **romper las ~es** to fall out
[2] **amistades** (= *amigos*) friends; (= *relaciones*) acquaintances; **invitar a las ~es** to invite one's friends

amistar ▸conjug 1a◂ Ⓐ VT [1] (= *hacer amigos*) to bring together, make friends of; (= *reconciliar*) to bring about a reconciliation between
[2] (*Méx*) (= *hacerse amigo de*) to befriend
Ⓑ **amistarse** VPR (= *hacerse amigos*) to become friends (**con** with), establish a friendship (**con** with); (= *reconciliarse*) to make it up

amistosamente ADV amicably, in a friendly way; **la carta termina ~** the letter ends in a friendly tone; **ayudémonos ~** let's help each other as friends

amistoso Ⓐ ADJ (= *amigable*) friendly, amicable; (*Dep*) friendly; (*Inform*) user-friendly
Ⓑ SM (*Dep*) friendly, friendly game

amnesia SF amnesia ► **amnesia temporal** blackout

amnésico/a ADJ, SM/F amnesiac, amnesic; **es ~** he suffers from memory loss *o* amnesia

amniocentesis SF INV amniocentesis

amniótico ADJ amniotic; **líquido ~** amniotic fluid

amnistía SF amnesty ► **Amnistía Internacional** Amnesty International

amnistiado/a Ⓐ ADJ amnestied
Ⓑ SM/F *person granted an amnesty*

amnistiar ▸conjug 1c◂ VT to amnesty, grant an amnesty to

amo/a Ⓐ SM/F [1] (= *de casa*) master/mistress; **¿está el ~?** is the master in? ► **amo/a de casa** house-husband/housewife
[2] (= *propietario*) owner
Ⓑ SM (= *jefe*) boss; **ser el ~** to be the boss; **ese corredor es el ~ de la pista** that runner rules the track; *ver tb* **ama**

amoblado (*LAm*) Ⓐ ADJ furnished
Ⓑ SM furniture

amoblamiento SM (*LAm*) furnishing

amoblar ▸conjug 1l◂ VT (*LAm*) to furnish

amodorramiento SM sleepiness, drowsiness

amodorrarse ▸conjug 1a◂ VPR [1] (= *adormecerse*) to get sleepy, get drowsy
[2] (= *dormirse*) to go to sleep

amohinar ▸conjug 1a◂ Ⓐ VT to vex, annoy
Ⓑ **amohinarse** VPR to sulk

amohosado ADJ (*Cono Sur*) rusty

amojonar ▸conjug 1a◂ VT to mark out, mark the boundary of

amojosado ADJ (*Bol*) rusty

amoladera SF [1] (= *piedra*) whetstone, grindstone
[2] (*LAm**) (= *tipo pesado*) nuisance, pain*

amolado ADJ [1] (*Cono Sur*) (= *fastidiado*) bothered, irritated
[2] (*Andes, Méx*) (= *ofendido*) offended; (= *que molesta*) irritating, annoying
[3] (*Andes*) (= *dañado*) damaged, ruined

amolador Ⓐ ADJ annoying
Ⓑ SM knife grinder

amoladura SF grinding, sharpening

amolar ▸conjug 1l◂ Ⓐ VT [1] (*Téc*) to grind, sharpen
[2] (= *fastidiar*) to pester, annoy; (= *perseguir*) to harass, pester
[3] (= *estropear*) to damage, ruin
[4] (*Méx***) (= *arruinar*) to screw up**, fuck up**; **¡lo amolaste!** you screwed it up!**, you fucked it up!**
Ⓑ **amolarse** VPR [1] (*esp LAm*) (= *enojarse*) to get cross, take offence *o* (*EEUU*) offense; (= *estropearse*) to be ruined
[2] (**) = **joder C**
[3] (= *enflaquecer*) to get thinner

amoldable ADJ adaptable

amoldar ▸conjug 1a◂ Ⓐ VT [1] (= *formar*) to mould, mold (*EEUU*) (**a, según** on)
[2] (= *ajustar*) to adapt (**a** to), adjust (**a** to)
Ⓑ **amoldarse** VPR to adapt o.s., adjust o.s. (**a** to)

amonal SM ammonal

amonarse* ▸conjug 1a◂ VPR to get tight*

amondongado ADJ fat, flabby

amonedación SF coining, minting

amonedar ▸conjug 1a◂ VT to coin, mint

amonestación SF [1] (= *reprimenda*) reprimand; (= *advertencia*) warning; (= *consejo*) piece of advice; (*Ftbl*) caution, yellow card; (*Jur*) caution
[2] **amonestaciones** (*Rel*) marriage banns; **correr las amonestaciones** to publish the banns

amonestador ADJ warning, cautionary

amonestar ▸conjug 1a◂ VT [1] (= *reprender*) to reprimand; (= *advertir*) to warn; (= *avisar*) to advise; (*Dep*) to caution, book; (*Jur*) to caution
[2] (*Rel*) to publish the banns of

amoniacal ADJ [*nitrógeno, cloruro*] ammoniacal; [*compuesto, disolución*] ammonia *antes de s*

amoniaco, **amoníaco** Ⓐ ADJ [*nitrógeno, cloruro*] ammoniacal; [*compuesto, disolución*] ammonia *antes de s*
Ⓑ SM ammonia ► **amoniaco líquido** liquid ammonia

amononar ▸conjug 1a◂ VT (*Cono Sur*) to improve the appearance of, smarten up; (*pey*) to prettify

amontillado SM amontillado, amontillado wine

amontonadamente ADV in heaps

amontonado ADJ heaped, heaped up, piled up; **viven ~s** they live on top of each other

amontonamiento SM [1] (= *acción*) [*de mercancías, cajas*] piling up, heaping; [*de dinero*] hoarding; [*de datos*] accumulation; [*de gente*] crowding, overcrowding; [*de coches*] traffic jam
[2] (= *montón*) [*de cajas*] heap, pile; [*de dinero*] stash; [*de gente*] crowd

amontonar ▸conjug 1a◂ Ⓐ VT [1] (= *apilar*) to pile (up), heap (up); [+ *datos*] to gather, collect; [+ *dinero*] to hoard; [+ *nieve, nubes*] to bank up; **viene amontonando fichas** he's been collecting data in large quantities; **~ alabanzas sobre algn** to heap praises on sb
[2] (*Andes*) (= *insultar*) to insult
Ⓑ **amontonarse** VPR [1] (= *apilarse*) to pile up; [*nubes*] to gather; [*hojas, nieve*] to drift; [*datos*] to accumulate; [*desastres*] to come one on top of another; [*gente*] to crowd, crowd together; **viven amontonados*** they're shacked up together*; **la gente se amontonó en la salida** people crowded into the exit, people jammed the exit; **se ~on los coches** the cars got into a jam
[2] (*) (= *enfadarse*) to fly off the handle*
[3] (*Andes*) [*terreno*] to revert to scrub

amor SM [1] (= *pasión*) love (**a** for); **por el ~ al arte** (*hum*) just for the fun of it; **hacer algo por ~ al arte** to do sth for nothing, do sth for free; **por el ~ de** for the love of; **por (el) ~ de Dios** for God's sake; **hacer algo con ~** to do sth lovingly, do sth with love; **lo hizo por ~** he did it for love; **casarse por ~** to marry for love; **matrimonio sin ~** loveless marriage; **una relación de ~-odio** a love-hate relationship; **hacer el ~** to make love; **hacer el ~ a** (= *cortejar*) to court; (= *hacer sexo*) to make love to ► **amor a primera vista** love at first sight ► **amor cortés** courtly love ► **amor de madre** mother love ► **amor fracasado** disappointment in love ► **amor interesado** cupboard love ► **amor libre** free love ► **amor maternal** mother love ► **amor platónico** platonic love ► **amor propio** amour propre, self-respect; **es cuestión de ~ propio** it's a matter of pride; **picarle a algn en el ~ propio** to wound sb's pride
[2] (= *persona*) love, lover; **mi ~** ◊ **~ mío** my love, my darling; **¡eres un ~!** you're a love!, you are sweet!; **primer ~** first love; **buscar un nuevo ~** to look for a new love; **tiene un ~ en la ciudad** he's carrying on an affair in town
[3] ✦*MODISMOS* **ir al ~ del agua** to go with the current; **estar al ~ de la lumbre** to be close to the fire; **~ con el ~ se paga** one good turn deserves another; (*iró*) an eye for an eye
[4] **amores** (= *amoríos*) love affair *sing*, romance *sing*; **tener mal de ~es** to be lovesick; **¡de mil ~es!** ◊ **¡con mil ~es!** I'd love to!, gladly!; **los mil ~es de don Juan** Don Juan's countless affairs; **requebrar a algn de ~es** to court sb

amoral ADJ amoral

amoralidad SF amorality

amoratado ADJ (= *morado*) purple, purplish; (*de frío*) blue; (= *golpeado*) black and blue, bruised; **ojo ~** black eye, shiner*

amoratarse ▸conjug 1a◂ VPR (= *ponerse morado*) to turn purple, go purple; (*de frío*) to turn blue; (*por golpes*) to turn black and blue

amorcillo SM [1] (= *amorío*) flirtation, lighthearted affair
[2] (= *Cupido*) Cupid

amordazar ▸conjug 1f◂ VT [+ *persona*] to gag; [+ *perro*] to muzzle; (*fig*) (= *hacer callar*) to gag, silence

amorfo ADJ amorphous, shapeless

amorío SM (*tb* ~**s**) love affair, romance

amorochado ADJ (*LAm*) = **morocho A1**

amorosamente ADV lovingly, affectionately

amoroso ADJ [1] (= *cariñoso*) [*persona*] loving, affectionate; [*mirada*] amorous; [*carta*] love *antes de s*; **poesía amorosa** love poetry; **en tono ~** in an affectionate tone; **empezar a sentirse ~** to begin to feel amorous
[2] (*fig*) [*tierra*] workable; [*metal*] malleable; [*tiempo*] mild
[3] (*Cono Sur*) (= *dulce*) sweet, pretty, cute

amorrar ▸conjug 1a◂ VI (= *inclinar la cabeza*) to hang one's head; (*fig*) (= *enfurruñarse*) to be sullen, sulk; (*Náut*) to pitch, dip the bows under

amortajar ▸conjug 1a◂ VT to shroud

amortecer ▸conjug 2d◂ Ⓐ VT [+ *ruido*] to deaden, muffle; [+ *luz*] to dim; [+ *fuego*] to damp down; [+ *pasión*] to curb, control
Ⓑ VI (*Med*) to faint, swoon; [*ruido*] to become muffled, die away

amortecido ADJ **caer ~** to fall in a swoon, faint away

amortecimiento SM [1] [*de ruido*] deadening, muffling; [*de luz*] dimming
[2] [*de pasión*] controlling
[3] (*Med*) fainting

amortiguación SF = **amortiguamiento**

amortiguador Ⓐ ADJ (*de ruido*) deadening, muffling; (*de luz*) softening
Ⓑ SM (*Mec, Aut*) shock absorber; (*Ferro*) buffer; (*Elec*) damper ► **amortiguador de luz** dimmer (switch) ► **amortiguador de ruido** silencer, muffler (*EEUU*)

amortiguamiento SM [1] [*de ruido*] deadening, muffling; [*de choque, golpe*] cushioning, absorption; [*de color*] toning down; [*de luz*] dimming, softening
[2] (*Elec*) damping

amortiguar ▸conjug 1i◂ Ⓐ VT [1] [+ *ruido*] to deaden, muffle; [+ *choque*] to cushion, absorb; [+ *color*] to tone down; [+ *luz*] to dim, soften; [+ *fuego*] to damp down; (*Elec*) to damp
[2] (*fig*) (= *mitigar*) to alleviate
Ⓑ **amortiguarse** VPR [1] [*luz*] to grow dim; [*ruido*] to die down
[2] (*Cono Sur*) [*planta*] to wither
[3] (*Cono Sur*) (= *deprimirse*) to get depressed

amortizable ADJ redeemable

amortización SF [1] (*Fin*) [*de bono*] redemption; [*de préstamo*] repayment; [*de bienes*] depreciation; [*de puesto*] abolition
[2] (*Jur*) amortization

amortizar ▸conjug 1f◂ VT [1] (*Fin*) [+ *capital*] to write off; [+ *bono*] to redeem; [+ *préstamo*] to pay off, repay; [+ *puesto*] to abolish; **~ algo por desvalorización** to write sth off for depreciation
[2] (*Jur*) to amortize

amos: EXCL *ver* **ir A12**

amoscarse* ▸conjug 1g◂ VPR [1] (= *enojarse*) to get cross, be peeved*
[2] (*Caribe, Méx*) (= *aturdirse*) to get confused; (= *avergonzarse*) to get embarrassed

amostazar* ▸conjug 1f◂ Ⓐ VT to make cross, peeve*
Ⓑ **amostazarse** VPR [1] (= *enojarse*) to get cross, get peeved*
[2] (*LAm*) (= *avergonzarse*) to be embarrassed, get embarrassed

amotinado/a Ⓐ ADJ (= *rebelde*) riotous; (*Mil, Náut*) mutinous
Ⓑ SM/F (*civil*) rioter; (*Pol*) rebel; (*Mil, Náut*) rebel, mutineer

amotinador(a) ADJ, SM/F = **amotinado**

amotinamiento SM [*civil*] riot; (*Pol*) rising, insurrection; (*Mil, Náut*) mutiny

amotinar ▸conjug 1a◂ Ⓐ VT to incite to riot, mutiny, *etc*
Ⓑ **amotinarse** VPR (= *causar disturbios*) to riot; (*Pol*) to rise up; (*Mil, Náut*) to mutiny

amover ▸conjug 2h◂ VT to dismiss, remove, remove from office

amovible ADJ [*pieza*] removable, detachable; [*empleo*] temporary

amparador(a) Ⓐ ADJ protecting, protective
Ⓑ SM/F (= *protector*) protector/protectress; [*de criminal*] harbourer, harborer (*EEUU*)

amparar ▸conjug 1a◂ Ⓐ VT [1] (= *proteger*) to protect (**de** from), shelter; (= *ayudar*) to help; **~ a los pobres** to help the poor; **lo ampara el ministro** the minister protects him; **la ley nos ampara** the law is there to protect us
[2] (*Jur*) [+ *criminal*] to harbour, harbor (*EEUU*)
[3] (*Caribe*) (= *pedir prestado*) to borrow
Ⓑ **ampararse** VPR [1] (= *buscar protección*) to seek protection, seek help; **~se con** *o* **de** *o* **en** to seek the protection of
[2] (*de la lluvia*) to shelter

amparo SM [1] (= *protección*) **buscó ~ en la familia** he sought refuge in his family; **mis nietos son mi único ~** my grandchildren are all I have; **al ~ de la ley** under the protection of the law; **actuaron al ~ de la oscuridad** they acted under cover of darkness; **viven al ~ de las donaciones de caridad** they live on *o* off charitable donations
[2] (= *refugio*) shelter, refuge; **la cabaña da ~ contra la nieve** the hut provides shelter from the snow, the hut gives refuge from the snow; **dio ~ a los terroristas** she sheltered the terrorists
[3] (*Jur*) **recurso de ~** *appeal on the grounds of unconstitutionality*

ampáyar SM, **ampáyer** SM (*LAm*) referee, umpire

ampe EXCL (*Andes*) please!

amperímetro SM ammeter

amperio SM ampère, amp

ampliable ADJ (= *extensible*) extendable, which can be extended (**a** to); (*Inform*) expandable (**a** to)

ampliación SF (= *acción*) extension; (*Fot*) enlargement; (= *expansión*) expansion ► **ampliación de capital**, **ampliación de capitales** increase of capital

ampliado SM (*LAm Pol*) general meeting

ampliadora SF enlarger

ampliamente ADV (= *cumplidamente*) amply; (= *extensamente*) extensively; **satisfará ~ la demanda** it will more than meet the demand

ampliar ▸conjug 1c◂ VT [1] (*en tamaño*) to extend; **queremos ~ el salón** we want to extend the living room, we want to make the living room bigger; **lee mucho para ~ su vocabulario** he reads a lot in order to extend *o* expand his vocabulary; **se fue a Inglaterra a ~ sus estudios** he went to England to broaden his studies
[2] (*en número*) to increase; **van a ~ las plazas de profesor** they are going to increase the number of teaching posts; **no ~án la plantilla** they are not going to increase *o* expand the headcount *o* the payroll
[3] [+ *prórroga, período*] to extend; **han ampliado el plazo de matrícula** they have put back the closing date for enrolment, they have extended the period for enrolment
[4] (*Fot*) to enlarge
[5] (*Com*) [+ *empresa, compañía*] to expand, grow; [+ *capital*] to increase; **deseamos ~ el campo de acción de la empresa** we want to extend *o* expand *o* broaden the company's area of business
[6] [+ *sonido*] to amplify
[7] [+ *idea, explicación*] to elaborate on
[8] [+ *poderes*] to extend, widen

amplificación SF (*Téc*) amplification; (*LAm Fot*) enlargement

amplificador SM amplifier

amplificar ▸conjug 1g◂ VT (*Téc*) to amplify; (*LAm Fot*) to enlarge

amplio ADJ [1] (= *espacioso*) [*habitación, interior*] spacious; [*avenida, calle*] wide; **el terremoto afectó a una amplia zona del sur** the earthquake affected a wide area in the south; **compró una amplia extensión de terreno** he bought a vast tract *o* stretch of land
[2] [*ropa*] loose(-fitting), roomy*; [*falda*] full
[3] [*margen*] wide; **un ~ margen a ambos lados** a wide margin on each side; **los socialistas ganaron las elecciones por amplia mayoría** the socialists won the election with a large majority
[4] [*conocimiento, vocabulario, poder, gama*] wide, extensive; **un ~ surtido de productos** a wide *o* extensive range of products
[5] [*sentido*] broad; **en el sentido ~ de la expresión** in the broad sense of the term
[6] [*repercusión*] far-reaching; **la noticia tuvo amplia difusión** *o* **~ eco en la prensa** the news was widely *o* extensively reported; **su novela tuvo amplia resonancia entre los intelectuales** his novel had great influence among the intellectuals
[7] [*informe*] full, detailed

amplitud SF [1] (= *espaciosidad*) [*de sala, habitación, interior*] spaciousness; [*de avenida, calle*] wideness; [*de terreno*] expanse, extent; **retiramos el sofá para dar ~ al cuarto** we moved the sofa to make the room bigger
[2] [*de ropa*] looseness; [*de falda*] fullness
[3] [*de conocimientos, vocabulario, poder, variedad*] extent ► **amplitud de criterio**, **amplitud de horizontes**, **amplitud de miras** broadmindedness
[4] **de gran ~** [*reforma, proyecto*] wide-ranging, far-reaching
[5] (*Radio*) ► **amplitud de banda** bandwidth ► **amplitud de onda** amplitude

ampo SM (= *blancura*) dazzling whiteness; (= *copo de nieve*) snowflake; **como el ~ de la nieve** as white as the driven snow

ampolla SF (*en la piel*) blister; (*de inyección*) ampoule; (= *frasco*) flask; **la decisión levantó ~s entre los ministros** the decision got a few backs up in the Cabinet

ampollarse ▸conjug 1a◂ VPR to blister, form blisters

ampolleta SF [1] [*de arena*] hourglass; [*de termómetro*] bulb
[2] (*LAm*) (= *bombilla*) bulb; ✦*MODISMO* **encendérsele a algn la ~*** to have a brainwave

ampón ADJ (= *voluminoso*) bulky; [*persona*] stout, tubby

ampulosamente ADV bombastically, pompously

ampulosidad SF bombast, pomposity

ampuloso ADJ bombastic, pompous

amputación SF amputation

amputado/a SM/F amputee

amputar ▸conjug 1a◂ VT to amputate, cut off

amuchachado ADJ boyish

amuchar* ▸conjug 1a◂ VT (*Andes, Cono Sur*) to increase, multiply

amueblado Ⓐ ADJ furnished (**con, de** with)
Ⓑ SM (*Cono Sur*) hotel, hotel room (*used for sexual encounters and paid for by the hour*)

amueblamiento SM furnishing

amueblar ▸conjug 1a◂ VT to furnish (**de** with); **sin ~** unfurnished

amuermado* ADJ bored

amuermante* ADJ (= *aburrido*) boring, dull; (= *ordinario*) banal, mundane

amuermar* ▸conjug 1a◂ Ⓐ VT to bore
Ⓑ **amuermarse** VPR [1] (= *tener sueño*) to feel sleepy (*after a meal*); (*fig*) (= *aburrirse*) to get bored; (= *deprimirse*) to get depressed
[2] (= *ponerse pesado*) to get very dull

amuinar* ▸conjug 1a◂ (*Méx*) Ⓐ VT to make cross, irritate
Ⓑ **amuinarse** VPR to get cross

amujerado ADJ effeminate

amularse ▸conjug 1a◂ VPR (*Méx*) [*persona*] to get stubborn, dig one's heels in; (*Com*) to become unsaleable, become a glut on the market

amulatado ADJ mulatto-like

amuleto SM amulet, charm

amunicionar ▸conjug 1a◂ VT to supply with ammunition

amuñecado ADJ doll-like

amura SF (*Náut*) (= *proa*) bow; (= *cabo*) tack

amurallado ADJ walled, fortified

amurallar ▸conjug 1a◂ VT to wall, fortify

amurar ▸conjug 1a◂ VI to tack

amurrarse ▸conjug 1a◂ VPR (*LAm*) to get depressed, become sad

amurriarse ▸conjug 1b◂ VPR (*Esp*) to get sad, get depressed

amurruñarse ▸conjug 1a◂ VPR (*Caribe*) (= *abrazarse*) to nestle together, cuddle up; (= *hacerse un ovillo*) to curl up

amusgar ▸conjug 1h◂ Ⓐ VT [+ *orejas*] to lay back, throw back; [+ *ojos*] to screw up, narrow
Ⓑ **amusgarse** VPR (*CAm*) to feel ashamed

Ana SF Ann, Anne

anabólico ADJ anabolic

anabolizante SM anabolic steroid

anacarado ADJ mother-of-pearl *antes de s*

anacardo SM (= *fruto*) cashew, cashew nut; (= *árbol*) cashew tree

anaco SM (*Andes*) poncho, Indian blanket

anacoluto SM anacoluthon

anaconda SF anaconda

anacoreta SMF anchorite

Anacreonte SM Anacreon

anacronía SF anachronism

anacrónico ADJ anachronistic

anacronismo SM anachronism

ánade SM duck ► **ánade friso** gadwall ► **ánade rabudo** pintail ► **ánade real** mallard ► **ánade silbón** wigeon

anadear ▸conjug 1a◂ VI to waddle

anadeo SM waddle, waddling

anadón SM duckling

anaeróbico ADJ, **anaerobio** ADJ anaerobic

anafe SM portable cooker

anáfora SF anaphora

anafórico ADJ anaphoric, anaphorical

anagrama SM anagram

anal ADJ anal

analcohólico ADJ non-alcoholic, soft

anales SMPL annals

analfa* ADJ, SMF = **analfabeto**

analfabetismo SM illiteracy ► **analfabetismo funcional** functional illiteracy

analfabeto/a Ⓐ ADJ illiterate
Ⓑ SM/F illiterate, illiterate person

analgesia SF analgesia

analgésico Ⓐ ADJ analgesic, painkilling
Ⓑ SM analgesic, painkiller

análisis SM INV [1] (= *examen*) analysis; (*detallado*) breakdown
[2] (*Fin*) ► **análisis de costos** cost analysis ► **análisis de costos-beneficios** cost-benefit analysis ► **análisis de mercados** market research ► **análisis de viabilidad** feasibility study ► **análisis financiero** financial analysis
[3] (*Med, Quím, Fís*) ► **análisis de sangre** blood test ► **análisis espectral** spectrum analysis ► **análisis orgánico** organic analysis
[4] (*Ling*) analysis, parsing ► **análisis del discurso** discourse analysis ► **análisis funcional** functional analysis
[5] (*Inform*) ► **análisis de la voz** speech analysis ► **análisis de sistemas** systems analysis

analista SMF (= *analizador*) analyst; (= *escritor de anales*) chronicler, annalist ► **analista de inversiones** investment consultant ► **analista de sistemas** systems analyst ► **analista financiero** financial analyst, market analyst

analista-programador(a) SM/F computer analyst and programmer

analítico ADJ analytic, analytical; **cuadro ~** analytic table

analizable ADJ analysable, analyzable (*EEUU*); **fácilmente ~** easy to analyse

analizador(a) SM/F analyst

analizar ▸conjug 1f◂ VT to analyse

analogía SF (= *correspondencia*) analogy; (= *semejanza*) similarity; **por ~ con** on the analogy of

analógico ADJ (= *que se corresponde*) analogical; (*Inform*) analog

análogo Ⓐ ADJ analogous, similar (**a** to)
Ⓑ SM analogue; **limpiar con alcohol o ~** clean with alcohol or similar substance

ananá SM, **ananás** SM INV, **ananasa** SF (*Andes*) pineapple

anapesto SM anapaest

anaquel SM shelf

anaquelería SF shelves *pl*, shelving

anaranjado Ⓐ ADJ orange, orange-coloured, orange-colored (*EEUU*)
Ⓑ SM orange, orange colour, orange color (*EEUU*)

anarco/a* SM/F anarchist

anarcosindicalismo SM anarcho-syndicalism

anarcosindicalista Ⓐ ADJ anarcho-syndical
Ⓑ SMF anarcho-syndicalist

anarquía SF anarchy

anárquico ADJ anarchic, anarchical

anarquismo SM anarchism

anarquista Ⓐ ADJ anarchist, anarchistic
Ⓑ SMF anarchist

anarquizante ADJ anarchic

anarquizar ▸conjug 1f◂ VT to cause anarchy in, cause complete chaos in

anatema SM anathema

anatematizante ADJ **palabras ~s** words of condemnation

anatematizar VT, **anatemizar** ▸conjug 1f◂ VT
[1] (*Rel*) to anathematize
[2] (= *maldecir*) to curse

anatomía SF [1] (= *ciencia, cuerpo*) anatomy
[2] (= *análisis*) anatomy

anatómico ADJ anatomical; **asiento ~** anatomically designed seat

anatomizar ▸conjug 1f◂ VT [1] (= *diseccionar*) to anatomize; (*Arte*) [+ *huesos, músculos*] to bring out, emphasize
[2] (= *analizar*) to anatomize, dissect

anca SF [1] (= *cacha*) rump, haunch; **no sufre ~s*** he can't take a joke; ✦*MODISMO* **llevar a algn a las ~s** *o* **en ~(s)** (*LAm*) to let sb ride pillion; **esto lleva el desastre en ~** (*LAm*) this spells disaster ► **ancas de rana** frog's legs
[2] **ancas*** (= *posaderas*) behind *sing*
[3] (*Andes*) (= *maíz*) toasted maize

ancestral ADJ (*de los antepasados*) ancestral; (= *antiguo*) ancient

ancestro SM (*esp LAm*) (= *persona*) ancestor; (= *linaje*) ancestry

anchamente ADV widely

ancheta SF [1] (= *lote*) small lot of goods; (= *negocio*) small business
[2] (= *ganancia*) gain, profit; (*Andes, Méx*) (= *ganga*) bargain; (= *negocio*) profitable deal; (= *oportunidad*) chance to make easy money; **¡vaya ~!** ◊ **¡buena ~!** some deal this turned out to be!
[3] (*Andes, Cono Sur*) (= *palabrería*) prattle, babble
[4] (*Caribe*) (= *broma*) joke; (= *estafa*) hoax

ancho Ⓐ ADJ [1] (= *amplio*) [*camino, puente, habitación*] wide; [*calle, sonrisa, manos*] broad; [*muro*] thick; **el salón es más ~ que largo** the living room is wider than it is long; **un tarro de boca ancha** a wide-necked bottle; **tenía las espaldas anchas** he had a broad back; **era muy ~ de hombros** he was very broad-shouldered; **plantas de hoja ancha** broad-leaved plants; **a lo ~ de algo** across sth; **colocaron una cuerda a lo ~ de la calle** they put a rope across the street; **había manifestantes a todo lo ~ de la avenida** there were demonstrators the length and breadth of the avenue; **por todo el ~ mundo** throughout the whole wide world, the world over; *ver tb* **Castilla, largo A6**
[2] (= *holgado*) [*chaqueta, pantalón*] loose, loose-fitting; [*falda*] full; [*manga*] wide; **que-**

dar *o* (*Esp*) **estar** *o* (*Esp*) **venir ~ a algn** to be too wide for sb; **la chaqueta le quedaba muy ancha** the jacket was too wide for him; **esta camisa me viene ancha** this shirt is too big for me, this shirt is on the big side*; **le viene muy ~ el cargo** the job is too much for him; ✦*MODISMO* **a sus anchas**: **puedes hojear a tus anchas todos los libros** you can leaf through all the books at your leisure; **con ellos podrá discutir a sus anchas** you can discuss things freely with them; **aquí estoy a mis anchas** I feel at ease here; **ponerse a sus anchas** to make o.s. comfortable, spread o.s.; *ver tb* **manga 1**

3 (*Esp*) (= *cómodo, confortable*) **aquí te puedes sentir bien ancha** you can make yourself comfortable *o* at home here; **en dos coches iremos más ~s** we'll be more comfortable in two cars, we'll have more room if we go in two cars; ✦*MODISMOS* **quedarse tan ~** ◊ **quedarse más ~ que largo**: **le dijo cuatro verdades y se quedó tan ~** he gave him a piece of his mind and felt very pleased with himself; **no sabes lo ~ que me he quedado después de decírselo** it feels such a weight off my shoulders to have told him; *ver tb* **pancho**

4 (= *liberal*) liberal, broad-minded; **~ de conciencia** (*Esp*) not overscrupulous; **~ de miras** broad-minded

5 (= *orgulloso*) proud; **iba todo ~ con su traje nuevo** he was very proud in his new suit; **ponerse ~** to get conceited

Ⓑ SM 1 (= *anchura*) [*de camino, ventana*] width; [*de río*] width, breadth; **¿cuál es el ~ de la mesa?** what is the width of the table?; **todo el ~ de la habitación** the whole width of the room; **de ~**: **tiene doce metros de ~** it is twelve metres wide; **las dos mesas tienen lo mismo de ~** both tables are the same width; **4 metros de largo por 2 de ~** 4 metres long by 2 metres wide ► **ancho de banda** band width; *ver tb* **doble**

2 (*Ferro*) (*tb* **~ de vía**) gauge, gage (*EEUU*); **~ europeo** European gauge; **~ internacional** international gauge; **~ normal** standard gauge

anchoa SF anchovy

anchor SM = **anchura**

anchote ADJ burly

anchoveta SF (*Andes*) anchovy (*for fishmeal*)

anchura SF 1 (= *amplitud*) [*de camino, ventana*] width; [*de río*] width, breadth; **de ~**: **un tronco de un metro de ~** a metre wide trunk; **tiene dos metros de ~** it is two metres wide ► **anchura alar** wingspan ► **anchura de banda** band width

2 (*Cos*) [*de falda*] fullness

3 (*Esp**) (= *descaro*) cheek*; **me habló con tanta ~** he talked to me with such a cheek *o* nerve* ► **anchura de conciencia** lack of scruple

anchuroso ADJ (= *ancho*) wide, broad; (= *espacioso*) spacious

ancianidad SF old age

anciano/a Ⓐ ADJ old, aged

Ⓑ SM/F [*de mucha edad*] old man/woman, elderly man/woman; (*Rel*) elder

ancilar ADJ ancillary

ancla SF anchor; **echar ~s** to drop anchor; **levar ~s** to weigh anchor ► **ancla de la esperanza** (*Náut*) sheet anchor; (*fig*) (= *única esperanza*) last hope

ancladero SM anchorage

anclaje SM 1 (*Náut*) (= *acción*) anchoring, anchorage; (= *fondeadero*) anchorage; (= *tributo*) mooring charge

2 (*Aut*) catch, clamp (*of a seat belt*)

anclar ▸conjug 1a◂ Ⓐ VT to anchor

Ⓑ VI to anchor, drop anchor; **estar anclado a/en algo** to be anchored to/in sth

ancón SM 1 (*Náut*) cove

2 (*Méx*) (= *rincón*) corner

3 (*Andes*) (= *camino*) mountain pass

áncora SF anchor ► **áncora de salvación** sheet anchor, last hope

andadas SFPL (*Caza*) tracks; (= *aventuras*) adventures; (*Chile, Méx*) walk *sing*, stroll *sing*; **volver a las ~** to backslide, go back to one's old ways

andaderas SFPL baby walker *sing*

andadero ADJ passable, easy to traverse

andado ADJ (= *trillado*) worn, well-trodden; (= *corriente*) common, ordinary; [*ropa*] old, worn

andador(a) Ⓐ ADJ 1 (= *que anda rápido*) fast-walking; **es ~** he's a good walker

2 (= *viajero*) fond of travelling, fond of gadding about

3 (*Cono Sur*) [*caballo*] well-paced, long-striding

Ⓑ SM/F walker

Ⓒ SM 1 (*para niños*) baby walker; (*para enfermos*) Zimmer® frame

2 **andadores** [*de niño*] reins

Ⓓ SF (*Méx*) prostitute, streetwalker, hustler (*EEUU**)

andadura SF 1 (= *acción*) walking; (= *manera*) gait, walk; (= *de caballo*) pace

2 (*fig*) (= *camino*) path, course; (= *progreso*) progress; (= *avance*) advance; **comenzar nuevas ~s** to start again

ándale EXCL (*esp Méx*) come on!, hey!; *ver tb* **ándele**, **andar A11**

andalón ADJ (*Méx*) well-paced, long-striding

Andalucía SF Andalusia

andalucismo SM 1 (*Ling*) andalusianism, *word or phrase etc peculiar to Andalusia*

2 (= *sentimiento*) *sense of the differentness of Andalusia*; (*Pol*) *doctrine of or belief in Andalusian autonomy*

andaluz(a) Ⓐ ADJ, SM/F Andalusian

Ⓑ SM (*Ling*) Andalusian

andaluzada* SF (= *cuento*) tall story, *piece of typical Andalusian exaggeration*; (= *acto*) *the sort of thing one expects from an Andalusian*

andamiaje SM, **andamiada** SF (*Constr*) scaffolding; (*fig*) (= *estructura*) framework, structure

andamio SM (*Constr*) scaffold; **~s** scaffolding *sing* ► **andamio óseo** skeleton, bone structure

andana SF row, line; ✦*MODISMO* **llamarse ~** to go back on one's word

andanada SF 1 (*Mil*) broadside; (*fig*) (= *reprensión*) reprimand, rocket*; **soltar la ~ a algn** to give sb a rocket*; **soltar una ~** to say sth unexpected, drop a bombshell*; **por ~s** (*Cono Sur*) in excess, to excess ► **andanada verbal** verbal broadside

2 (*Dep*) stand, grandstand; (*Taur*) *section of cheap seats*

3 (= *andana*) [*de ladrillos*] layer, row

andante Ⓐ ADJ (= *que anda*) walking; **caballero ~** knight errant

Ⓑ SM (*Mús*) andante

andanza SF (= *suerte*) fortune; **~s** (= *vicisitudes*) deeds, adventures

andar ▸conjug 1p◂ Ⓐ VI 1 (= *ir a pie*) to walk; (= *moverse*) to move; (= *viajar*) to travel around; **iremos andando a la estación** we'll walk to the station; **vinimos andando** we walked here, we came on foot; **el tren empezó a ~** the train started moving; **la máquina empezó a ~** the machine started up; **anduvieron por Jamaica y Cuba** they travelled around Jamaica and Cuba; **~ a caballo** to ride; **~ tras algo/algn** to be after sth/sb; **~ tras una chica** to be *o* chase after a girl

2 (= *funcionar*) to go, work; **el reloj no anda** the clock won't go, the clock isn't working; **el reloj anda bien** the clock keeps good time; **¿cómo anda esto?** how does this work?

3 (*) (= *estar*) to be; **no sé por dónde anda** I don't know where he is; **anda por aquí** it's around here somewhere; **seguro que ése anda por Brasil** he's bound to be somewhere in Brazil; **~ alegre** to be *o* feel cheerful; **hay que ~ con cuidado** you have to be careful; **últimamente ando muy liado** I've been very busy lately; **~ bien de salud** to be well, be in good health; **andamos mal de dinero** we're badly off for money, we're short of money; **¿cómo andan las cosas?** how are things?; **¿cómo anda eso?** how are things going?; **¿qué tal andas?** how are you?; **¿cómo andas de tabaco?** how are you off for cigarettes?; **ando escaso de tiempo** I am pushed for time; **de ~ por casa**: **ropa de ~ por casa** clothes for wearing around the house; **un montaje muy de ~ por casa** a rough-and-ready production; **justicia de ~ por casa** rough-and-ready justice; ✦*MODISMO* **andan como Pedro por su casa** they act as if they owned the place; ✦*REFRÁN* **quien mal anda, mal acaba** you get what you deserve

4 (= *rebuscar*) **¡no andes ahí!** keep away from there!; **~ en** to rummage around in; **han estado andando en el armario** they've been rummaging around in the cupboard; **no andes en mis cosas** keep out of my things

5 **~ a**: **siempre andan a gritos** they're always shouting; **andan a la greña** *o* **a la gresca** they're at each other's throats

6 **~ con algn** to go around with sb; **anda con una chica francesa** he goes around with a French girl; ✦*REFRÁN* **dime con quién andas y te diré quién eres** a man is known by the company he keeps

7 **~ en** (= *estar implicado en*) to be involved in; **~ en pleitos** to be engaged *o* involved in lawsuits; **anda en la droga** he's involved with drugs; **sospecho que anda en ello Rosa** I suspect Rosa is involved; **¿en qué andas?** what are you up to?

8 **~ haciendo algo** to be doing sth; **¿qué andas buscando?** what are you looking for?; **ando buscando un socio** I'm looking for a partner; **no andes criticándolo todo el tiempo** stop criticizing him all the time

9 **~ por** (= *rondar*): **anda por los 50** he's about 50; **el pueblo anda por los 1.000 habitantes** the village has about 1,000 inhabitants; **anda por los 700 euros** it's around 700 euros

10 ✦*MODISMO* **andando el tiempo**: **un niño**

que, andando el tiempo, sería rey a child who, in time, would become king; **andando el tiempo la pena de muerte desaparecerá** the death penalty will eventually disappear

[11] (*exclamaciones*) **¡anda!** (= *¡no me digas!*) well I never!; (= *¡vamos!*) come on!; **¡anda!, no lo sabía** well I never, I didn't know that!; **anda, dímelo** go on, tell me; **anda, no me molestes** just stop annoying me, will you?; **anda, no te lo tomes tan a pecho** come on, there's no need to take it to heart like that; **¡anda, anda!** come on!; **¡ándale (pues)!** (*Méx**) (= *apúrese*) come on!, hurry up!; (= *adiós*) cheerio!; (= *gracias*) thanks!; (*encontrando algo*) that's it!; **¡andando!** right, let's get on with it!; **andando, que todavía hay mucho que hacer** let's get moving, there's still a lot to do; **¡anda ya!**: **anda ya, no nos vengas con esnobismos** come on, don't be such a snob; **—dile que te gusta —¡anda ya, para que me suba el precio!** "tell her you like it" — "oh sure, so she can charge me more!"

Ⓑ VT [1] (= *recorrer a pie*) [+ *trecho*] to walk; **anduvimos varios kilómetros** we walked several kilometres; **me conocía muy bien el camino por haberlo andado varias veces** I knew the path very well, as I'd been down *o* walked it several times before

[2] (*LAm*) (= *llevar*) [+ *ropa*] to wear; [+ *objeto*] to carry; **yo no ando reloj** I don't wear a watch

Ⓒ **andarse** VPR [1] (= *irse*) to go off, go away; **✦*MODISMO*** **~se por las ramas** to beat about the bush

[2] **~se con**: **ándate con cuidado** take care; **no puedes ~te con tonterías** you can't afford to mess about; **no ~se con contemplaciones** *o* **remilgos** not to stand on ceremony; **no podía ~se con demasiados remilgos a la hora de elegir marido** she couldn't be too fussy when choosing a husband; **no podemos ~nos con contemplaciones a la hora de buscar una solución a la crisis** we can't afford to worry about the niceties when looking for a solution to the crisis; **no se anda con chiquitas** he doesn't mess about; **no ~se con rodeos** not to beat about the bush

[3] **~se en** [+ *herida, nariz*] to pick; (= *permitirse*) to indulge in; **no te andes en la nariz** don't pick your nose; **se andaba en la herida** he was picking at his wound

[4] **todo se andará** all in good time

Ⓓ SM walk, gait; **es de ~es rápidos** he walks quickly; **a más** *o* **todo ~** at full speed, as quickly as possible; **✦*MODISMOS*** **a largo ~†** (= *al final*) in the end; (= *a largo plazo*) in the long run; **estar en un ~†** to be on the same level

andaras SM (*Andes*) Indian flute

andarica SF (*Asturias*) crab

andariego ADJ fond of travelling, restless

andarilla SF (*Andes*) *type of flute*

andarín SM walker; **es muy ~** he is a great walker

andarivel SM [1] (*Téc*) cable ferry

[2] (*Náut*) (= *salvavidas*) lifeline

[3] (*esp LAm*) (= *puente*) rope bridge; (= *cerco*) rope barrier; [*de piscina*] lane

[4] (*Andes*) (= *adornos*) adornments *pl*, trinkets *pl*

andas SFPL [1] (*Med*) (= *camilla*) stretcher *sing*; (= *silla*) litter *sing*, sedan chair *sing*; **llevar a algn en ~** (*lit*) to carry sb on a platform; (*fig*) to treat sb with great deference

[2] (*Rel*) portable platform *sing*; (= *féretro*) bier *sing*

ándele EXCL (*Méx*) (= *¡venga!*) come on!, hurry up!; (= *¡ya ves!*) see what I mean!; (= *¡ya lo creo!*) get away!*; (= *correcto*) exactly!

andén SM [1] (*Ferro*) platform ► **andén de salida** departure platform ► **andén de vacío** arrival platform

[2] (*Náut*) quayside

[3] (*CAm, Col*) (= *acera*) pavement, sidewalk (*EEUU*)

Andes SMPL Andes

andinismo SM (*LAm*) mountaineering, climbing; **hacer ~** to go mountaineering, go climbing

andinista SMF (*LAm*) mountaineer, climber

andino ADJ Andean, of/from the Andes

ándito SM (= *pasillo*) outer walk, corridor; (= *acera*) pavement, sidewalk (*EEUU*)

andoba* SM guy*, chap*

andolina SF swallow

andón ADJ (*LAm*) = **andador A3**

andonear ▸conjug 1a◂ VI (*Caribe*) [*persona*] to amble along, stroll along; [*caballo*] to trot

andorga* SF belly

andorina SF swallow

Andorra SF Andorra

andorrano/a ADJ, SM/F Andorran

andorrear* ▸conjug 1a◂ VI (= *ajetrearse*) to bustle about, fuss around; (= *ir de acá para allá*) to gad about, move about a lot

andorrero/a Ⓐ ADJ bustling, busy

Ⓑ SM/F busy sort, gadabout

Ⓒ SF (*pey*) streetwalker, hustler (*EEUU**)

andrajo SM [1] rag, tatter; **~s** rags, tatters; **estar en ~s** ◊ **estar hecho un ~** to be in rags; **ser un ~ humano** to be a wreck*

[2] (= *pillo*) rascal, good-for-nothing

[3] (= *bagatela*) trifle, mere nothing

andrajoso ADJ ragged, in tatters

Andrés SM Andrew

androcéntrico ADJ male-centred, androcentric

androcentrismo SM male-centredness, androcentricity

androfobia SF hatred of men

androgénico ADJ androgenic

andrógeno SM androgen

androginia SF androgyny

andrógino/a Ⓐ ADJ androgynous

Ⓑ SM/F androgyne

androide SM android

Andrómaca SF Andromache

andrómina* SF fib*, tale

andropausia SF male menopause

androsterona SF androsterone

andullo SM (*Cuba, Méx*) plug of tobacco

andurrial SM [1] (= *lodazal*) bog, quagmire; (= *zanja*) ditch; (= *descampado*) piece of waste ground

[2] **andurriales** (= *lugar extraviado*) out-of-the way place *sing*; **en esos ~es** in that godforsaken place

anduve, anduviera *etc ver* **andar**

anea SF bulrush

aneblar ▸conjug 1j◂ Ⓐ VT (= *cubrir de niebla*) to cover with mist; (= *anublar*) to obscure, darken, cast a cloud over

Ⓑ **aneblarse** VPR (= *cubrirse de niebla*) to get misty; (= *anublarse*) to get dark

anécdota SF anecdote, story; **este cuadro tiene una ~** there's a tale attached to this picture

anecdotario SM collection of stories

anecdótico ADJ (= *de anécdota*) anecdotal; (= *trivial*) trivial; **contenido ~** story content; **valor ~** story value, value as a story; **el estudio se queda en lo ~** the study does not rise above the merely superficial

anecdotismo SM anecdotal nature, anecdotal quality, merely anecdotal quality

anega SF (*Cono Sur*) = **fanega**

anegación SF flooding

anegadizo ADJ [*tierra*] subject to flooding, frequently flooded; [*madera*] heavier than water

anegar ▸conjug 1h◂ Ⓐ VT [1] (= *ahogar*) to drown

[2] (= *inundar*) to flood; (*fig*) (= *abrumar*) to overwhelm

Ⓑ **anegarse** VPR [1] (= *ahogarse*) to drown

[2] (= *inundarse*) to flood, be flooded; **~se en llanto** to dissolve into tears

[3] (*Náut*) to sink, founder

anejo Ⓐ ADJ attached, joined on (**a** to)

Ⓑ SM (*Arquit*) annexe, outbuilding; [*de libro*] supplement, appendix

anemia SF anaemia, anemia (*EEUU*)

anémico ADJ anaemic, anemic (*EEUU*)

anemómetro SM anemometer, wind gauge ► **anemómetro registrador** wind-speed indicator

anémona SF, **anémone** SF anemone ► **anémona de mar** sea anemone

aneroide ADJ aneroid

anestesia SF anaesthesia, anesthesia (*EEUU*); **me operaron con ~** I was operated on under anaesthetic; **operar sin ~** to operate without (an) anaesthetic ► **anestesia general** general anaesthetic, general anesthetic (*EEUU*) ► **anestesia local** local anaesthetic, local anesthetic (*EEUU*)

anestesiante ADJ, SM anaesthetic, anesthetic (*EEUU*)

anestesiar ▸conjug 1b◂ VT to anaesthetize, anesthetize (*EEUU*), give an anaesthetic to, give an anesthetic to (*EEUU*)

anestésico ADJ, SM anaesthetic, anesthetic (*EEUU*)

anestesista SMF anaesthetist, anesthetist (*EEUU*)

anexar ▸conjug 1a◂ VT [1] (*Pol*) to annex

[2] [+ *documento*] to attach, append

anexión SF, **anexionamiento** SM annexation

anexionar ▸conjug 1a◂ Ⓐ VT to annex

Ⓑ **anexionarse** VPR to annex

anexo Ⓐ ADJ (= *anejo*) attached; (*en carta*) enclosed; **llevar** *o* **algo ~** ◊ **tener algo ~** to have sth attached; **~ a la presente ...** (*Méx*) please find enclosed ...

Ⓑ SM (*Arquit*) annexe; (*Rel*) dependency; [*de carta*] enclosure

anfeta* SF = **anfetamina**

anfetamina SF amphetamine

anfetamínico/a SM/F [1] (= *adicto*) amphetamine addict, speed freak*

[2] (*) (= *pesado*) bore, pain*; (= *imbécil*) idiot

anfibio Ⓐ ADJ (*Zool*) amphibious; [*avión, vehículo*] amphibian
Ⓑ SM amphibian; **los ~s** the amphibia

anfibología SF ambiguity

anfibológico ADJ ambiguous

anfiteatro SM amphitheatre, amphitheater (*EEUU*); (*Univ*) lecture theatre *o* (*EEUU*) theater; (*Teat*) dress circle ► **anfiteatro anatómico** dissecting room

Anfitrión SM Amphitryon

anfitrión/ona SM/F host/hostess

ánfora SF [1] (= *cántaro*) amphora; (*Cono Sur**) [*de marihuana*] marijuana pouch
[2] (*Méx Pol*) ballot box

anfractuosidad SF [1] (= *aspereza*) roughness, unevenness; [*de camino*] bend; **~es** rough places
[2] (*Anat*) (*de cerebro*) sulcus anfractuosity

anfractuoso ADJ rough, uneven

angarillas SFPL [*de albañil*] handbarrow *sing*; (*en bicicleta*) panniers; (*Culin*) cruet (stand) *sing*

angarrio ADJ (*Andes, Caribe*) terribly thin, thin as a rake*

angas SMPL ✦**MODISMO por ~ o por mangas** (*Andes*) like it or not

ángel SM [1] angel; **pasó un ~** (*silencio*) there was a sudden silence; (*en charla*) there was a lull in the conversation ► **ángel caído** fallen angel ► **ángel custodio, ángel de la guarda** guardian angel ► **ángel del infierno** hell's angel ► **ángel exterminador** angel of death
[2] (= *gracia*) **tener ~** to have charm, be very charming; **tener mal ~** to be a nasty piece of work*

angélica SF angelica

angelical ADJ, **angélico** ADJ angelic, angelical

angelino/a Ⓐ ADJ of/from Los Angeles
Ⓑ SM/F native/inhabitant of Los Angeles; **los ~s** the people of Los Angeles

angelito SM (= *niño*) little angel; (*LAm*) (= *niño fallecido*) dead child; **¡angelito!** (*Cono Sur*) don't play the innocent!, pull the other one!*; **¡no seas ~!** (*Cono Sur*) don't be silly!

angelón* SM ► **angelón de retablo** fat old thing

angelopolitano/a (*Méx*) Ⓐ ADJ of/from Puebla
Ⓑ SM/F native/inhabitant of Puebla; **los ~s** the people of Puebla

angelote SM [1] (= *niño*) chubby child
[2] (*LAm*) (= *persona*) decent person
[3] (= *pez*) angel fish

ángelus SM INV angelus

angina SF [1] (*Med*) angina; (*Méx, Ven*) tonsil; **tener ~s** to have tonsillitis; (*gen*) to have a sore throat ► **angina de pecho** angina pectoris
[2] **~s** (*Esp***) (= *pecho*) tits**

angiosperma SF angiosperm

anglicanismo SM Anglicanism

anglicano/a ADJ, SM/F Anglican

anglicismo SM anglicism

anglicista Ⓐ ADJ **tendencia ~** anglicizing tendency
Ⓑ SMF anglicist

angliparla SF (*hum*) Spanglish

anglo... PREF anglo...

anglófilo/a ADJ, SM/F anglophile

anglofobia SF anglophobia

anglófobo/a Ⓐ ADJ anglophobe, anglophobic
Ⓑ SM/F anglophobe

anglófono/a Ⓐ ADJ English-speaking
Ⓑ SM/F English speaker

anglonormando/a Ⓐ ADJ Anglo-Norman; **Islas Anglonormandas** Channel Isles
Ⓑ SM/F Anglo-Norman
Ⓒ SM (*Ling*) Anglo-Norman

angloparlante, **anglohablante** Ⓐ ADJ English-speaking
Ⓑ SMF English speaker

anglosajón/ona Ⓐ ADJ, SM/F Anglo-Saxon
Ⓑ SM (*Ling*) Anglo-Saxon

Angola SF Angola

angoleño/a ADJ, SM/F Angolan

angolés = **angoleño**

angora SF angora

angorina SF artificial angora

angostar ▸conjug 1a◂ Ⓐ VT (= *estrechar*) to narrow; (*Cono Sur*) (= *hacer pequeño*) to make smaller; [+ *ropa*] to take in
Ⓑ **angostarse** VPR to narrow, get narrow, get narrower

angosto ADJ narrow

angostura SF [1] (= *estrechez*) narrowness
[2] (*Náut*) narrows *pl*, strait; (*Geog*) narrow pass
[3] (= *bebida*) angostura

angra SF cove, creek

ángstrom SM (*pl* **ángstroms**) angstrom

anguila SF (= *pez*) eel; **~s** (*Náut*) slipway *sing*

angula SF elver, baby eel

angulación SF camera angle

angular Ⓐ ADJ angular; *ver* **piedra A1**
Ⓑ SM **gran ~** wide-angle lens

Angulema SF Angoulême

ángulo SM (*Mat*) angle; (= *esquina*) corner; (= *curva*) bend, turning; (*Mec*) knee, bend; **de ~ ancho** (*Fot*) wide-angle; **en ~** at an angle; **está inclinado con un ~ de 45 grados** it is leaning at an angle of 45 degrees; **formar ~ con** to be at an angle to ► **ángulo agudo** acute angle ► **ángulo alterno** alternate angle ► **ángulo del ojo** corner of one's eye ► **ángulo de mira** angle of sight ► **ángulo de subida** (*Aer*) angle of climb ► **ángulo de toma** (*Fot*) angle of shooting ► **ángulo muerto** (*Aut*) blind spot ► **ángulo oblicuo** oblique angle ► **ángulo obtuso** obtuse angle ► **ángulo recto** right angle; **de** *o* **en ~ recto** right-angled

anguloso ADJ [*cara*] angular, sharp; [*camino*] winding, zigzagging

angurria SF (*esp LAm*) [1] (= *hambre*) desperate hunger; **comer con ~** to eat greedily
[2] (= *angustia*) extreme anxiety
[3] (= *tacañería*) stinginess*

angurriento ADJ (*esp LAm*), **angurrioso** (*Cono Sur*) ADJ [1] (= *glotón*) greedy
[2] (= *ansioso*) anxious
[3] (*) (= *tacaño*) mean, stingy*

angustia Ⓐ SF [1] (= *miedo*) anguish, distress; **una mirada/sensación de ~** a look/feeling of anguish *o* distress; **un grito de ~** a cry of anguish, an anguished cry; **sentía un nudo de ~ en la garganta** I could feel a knot in my throat, from anguish; **¡estuve a punto de caerme por el acantilado! ¡qué ~!** I was just about to fall off the cliff! what an ordeal!; **da ~ ver esos niños tan delgados** it's distressing to see children as thin as that ► **angustia de muerte** death throes
[2] (= *ansiedad*) (*por estrés, miedo*) anxiety; (*por inseguridad*) angst; **cada vez que voy en metro noto una terrible sensación de ~** every time I travel by underground I feel terribly anxious *o* I feel a terrible anxiety; **no podía contener la ~** he could not contain his anxiety; **su vejez estuvo llena de ~** he had an angst-ridden old age; **ataque de ~** anxiety attack, panic attack ► **angustia adolescente** adolescent angst ► **angustia existencial**, **angustia vital** (*Med*) state of anxiety; (*Psic*) angst
[3] (*) (= *náuseas*) **me da ~ cuando como** I feel sick if I eat
Ⓑ SMF INV **ser un ~s*** to be a worrier

angustiado ADJ [1] (= *asustado*) [*persona*] distressed; [*expresión, mirada*] anguished; **están muy ~s por la desaparición de su hija** they are very distressed about their daughter's disappearance; **recordaba el rostro ~ de su familia** I recalled the anguished look *o* look of anguish of their family; **nos hizo una súplica angustiada** he let out an anguished plea
[2] (= *preocupado*) anxious; **está ~ por no tener trabajo** he is very worried *o* he is anxious about not having a job
[3] (= *avaro*) grasping, mean

angustiante ADJ distressing

angustiar ▸conjug 1b◂ Ⓐ VT [1] (= *agobiar*) to distress; **la angustiaba verlo sufrir** she was distressed to see him suffer, seeing him suffer distressed her
[2] (= *preocupar*) to make anxious; **los exámenes no me angustian** exams don't make me anxious
Ⓑ **angustiarse** VPR [1] (= *agobiarse*) to be distressed (**por** at, on account of)
[2] (= *preocuparse*) to get anxious; **no deberías ~te por un pequeño dolor** you shouldn't worry *o* get anxious about a slight pain

angustiosamente ADV [1] (= *con pena*) in an anguished voice; **—no iré —dijo ~** "I won't go," she said in an anguished voice; **estuvo llorando ~** he was crying inconsolably
[2] (= *con preocupación*) anxiously

angustioso ADJ [1] (= *angustiado*) [*sensación*] distressed, anguished; [*voz, mirada*] anguished; **tres horas de angustiosa espera** three hours of anxious waiting
[2] (= *agobiante*) [*habitación, espacio*] oppressive; [*problema, recuerdo, situación*] distressing; **tomar decisiones es siempre ~** taking decisions always makes one anxious; **pasamos unos momentos muy ~s** we went through moments of great anguish
[3] (= *doloroso*) (*lit*) agonizing; (*fig*) heartbreaking; **sintió un ~ dolor** he felt an agonizing pain; **momentos de angustiosa soledad** moments of heartbreaking solitude

anhá EXCL (*Cono Sur*) = **anjá**

anhelación SF [1] (*Med*) panting
[2] (= *ansia*) longing, yearning

anhelante ADJ [1] (= *jadeante*) panting
[2] (= *ansioso*) eager; **esperar ~ algo** to long for sth

anhelar ▸conjug 1a◂ Ⓐ VT to long for, yearn for; **~ hacer algo** to be eager to do sth, long

to do sth
Ⓑ VI (*Med*) to gasp, pant

▼**anhelo** SM longing, desire (**de, por** for); **con ~** longingly; **tener ~s de** to be eager for, long for ▸ **anhelo de superación** urge to do better

anheloso ADJ [1] (*Med*) [*persona*] gasping, panting; [*respiración*] heavy, difficult, laboured, labored (*EEUU*)
[2] (= *ansioso*) eager, anxious

anhídrido SM ▸ **anhídrido carbónico** carbon dioxide

Aníbal SM Hannibal

anidación SF, **anidada** SF nesting

anidamiento SM nesting

anidar ▸conjug 1a◂ Ⓐ VT to take in, shelter
Ⓑ VI [1] (*Orn*) to nest, make its nest; (*Inform*) to nest
[2] (= *morar*) to live, make one's home; **la maldad anida en su alma** his heart is full of evil

anieblar ▸conjug 1a◂ = **aneblar**

aniego SM (*Andes, Cono Sur*), **aniegue** SM (*Méx*) flood

anilina SF aniline

anilla SF [1] [*de cortina*] curtain ring; [*de puro*] cigar band ▸ **anilla de desgarre** ring pull
[2] (*Orn*) ring
[3] **anillas** (*Gimnasia*) rings

anillado Ⓐ ADJ ringed, banded (*EEUU*), ring-shaped
Ⓑ SM ringing (*of birds*)

anillamiento SM ringing (*of birds*)

anillar ▸conjug 1a◂ VT (= *dar forma de anillo a*) to make into a ring, make rings in; (= *sujetar*) to fasten with a ring; (*Orn*) to ring

anillejo SM, **anillete** SM small ring, ringlet

anillo SM (*gen*) ring; [*de puro*] cigar band; **no creo que se me caigan los ~s por eso** I don't feel it's in any way beneath my dignity; **venir como ~ al dedo** to be just right, suit to a tee ▸ **anillo de boda** wedding ring ▸ **anillo de compromiso** engagement ring ▸ **anillo de crecimiento** growth ring ▸ **anillo de pedida** engagement ring ▸ **anillo pastoral** bishop's ring

ánima SF [1] (*Rel*) soul; **las ~s** (= *oración*) the Angelus *sing* ▸ **ánima bendita, ánima del purgatorio, ánima en pena** soul in purgatory
[2] (*Mil*) bore
[3] (*Cono Sur*) (= *santuario*) wayside shrine

animación SF [1] (= *alegría*) life; **a la fiesta le faltaba un poco de ~** the party lacked a bit of life, the party was a bit dead*; **hemos logrado darle un poco de ~ al bar** we have managed to liven up the bar, we have managed to put some life into the bar; **su poesía goza de cierta ~** his poetry possesses a certain liveliness
[2] (= *bullicio*) activity; **una intensa ~ en la Bolsa** an intense activity on the Stock Market; **una plaza con muchísima ~** a square with a lot of bustle *o* activity, a very lively square ▸ **animación suspendida** suspended animation
[3] (= *impulso*) **una campaña de ~ a la lectura** a reading promotion campaign; **coordinador de ~ social** social activities coordinator ▸ **animación (socio)cultural**: **en verano aumenta la ~ cultural** there are more cultural things going on in the summer; **departamento de ~ sociocultural** department of culture
[4] (*Cine*) animation ▸ **animación por ordenador** computer animation

animadamente ADV [*charlar*] animatedly, in a lively way; [*bailar*] in a lively way

animado ADJ [1] (= *con ánimo*) **no está muy ~ últimamente** he hasn't been in very high spirits recently; **estar ~ a hacer algo** to be keen to do sth
[2] (= *alentado*) **~ de** *o* **por algo/algn** encouraged by sth/sb, urged on by sth/sb; **~s por los hinchas** encouraged *o* urged on by the fans; **~s por el fanatismo** driven by fanaticism
[3] [*lugar*] (= *alegre*) lively; (= *concurrido*) [*bar, mercado*] bustling, busy; **una fiesta muy animada** a very lively party; **una mañana muy animada en la Bolsa** a very lively morning on the Stock Market; **la boda estuvo animada por un grupo de música** the wedding was livened up by a band
[4] (= *con vida*) animate; **un cortometraje ~** a short animation film; *ver tb* **dibujo 2**
[5] (*Ling*) animate

animador(a) SM/F (*TV*) host/hostess, presenter ▸ **animador(a) cultural** (*en ayuntamiento*) events organiser; (*en hotel*) entertainment manager ▸ **animador(a) turístico(a)** tourist coordinator

animadora SF [1] (= *cantante*) night-club singer
[2] (*Dep*) cheerleader

animadversión SF ill will, antagonism

animal Ⓐ ADJ [1] (= *de los animales*) animal; **instinto ~** animal instinct
[2] (*) (= *estúpido*) stupid; **el muy ~ no sabe la capital de España** he's so stupid he doesn't know what the capital of Spain is
[3] (*) (= *bruto*) **¡deja ya de empujar, no seas tan ~!** stop pushing, you great oaf *o* brute; **no seas ~, trátala con cariño** don't be such a brute, be kind to her; **¡el muy ~ se comió tres platos!** he had three helpings, the oaf *o* pig!
Ⓑ SM animal; **los ~es salvajes** wild animals; **soy un ~ político** I am a political animal; **ser ~ de costumbres** to be a creature of habit; ✦*MODISMOS* **ser un ~ de bellota*** to be as thick as two short planks*; **comer como un ~*** to eat like a pig; **trabajar como un ~*** to work like a slave, work all the hours God sends* ▸ **animal de carga** (= *burro, buey*) beast of burden; **¡me tratas como a un ~ de carga!** what did your LAST servant die of?* ▸ **animal de compañía** pet ▸ **animal de laboratorio** laboratory animal ▸ **animal de tiro** draught animal, draft animal (*EEUU*) ▸ **animal doméstico** [*de compañía*] pet; [*de granja*] domestic animal
Ⓒ SMF (*) [1] (= *estúpido*) fool, moron*; **¡animal!, tres y dos son cinco** you fool *o* moron*, three plus two makes five
[2] (= *bruto*) brute; **el ~ de Juan seguía pegándole** that brute Juan kept on hitting him; **el ~ de Antonio se comió su plato y el mío** that pig Antonio ate all his own dinner and mine too; **eres un ~, lo has roto** you're so rough you've gone and broken it

animalada SF [1] (= *disparate*) silly thing (*to do o say*); (= *ultraje*) disgrace; (= *atrocidad*) outrage
[2] (*LAm*) (= *rebaño*) group of animals, herd of animals

animalaje SM (*Cono Sur*) group of animals, herd of animals

animalejo SM (= *animal*) odd-looking creature, nasty animal; (= *bicho*) creepy-crawly*

animalidad SF animality

animalizarse ▸conjug 1f◂ VPR to become brutalized

animalote SM big animal

animalucho SM (= *animal*) ugly brute; (= *bicho*) creepy-crawly*

animar ▸conjug 1a◂ Ⓐ VT [1] (= *alegrar*) [+ *persona triste*] to cheer up; [+ *habitación*] to brighten up; **unas flores la ~án** some flowers will cheer her up; **una sonrisa de ilusión animaba sus ojos** an excited smile brightened the look in her eyes
[2] (= *entretener*) [+ *persona aburrida*] to liven up; [+ *charla, fiesta, reunión*] to liven up, enliven; **un humorista animó la velada** a comedian livened up *o* enlivened the evening
[3] (= *alentar*) [+ *persona*] to encourage; [+ *proyecto*] to inspire; [+ *fuego*] to liven up; **había pancartas animando al equipo nacional** there were banners cheering on the national team; **te estaré animando desde las gradas** I'll be rooting for you *o* cheering you on from the crowd; **~ a algn a hacer** *o* **a que haga algo** to encourage sb to do sth; **esas noticias nos ~on a pensar que ...** that news encouraged us to think that ...; **ignoramos las razones que lo ~on a dimitir** we are unaware of the reasons for his resignation *o* the reasons that led him *o* prompted him to resign; **me animan a que siga** they're encouraging *o* urging me to carry on
[4] (*Econ*) [+ *mercado, economía*] to stimulate, inject life into
[5] (*Bio*) to animate, give life to
Ⓑ **animarse** VPR [1] (= *alegrarse*) [1·1] [*persona*] to cheer up; [*cara, ojos*] to brighten up; **necesito una copa para ~me** I need a drink to cheer me *o* myself up; **¡venga, anímate!** come on, cheer up!; **se le animó la cara al verme** her face brightened up when she saw me
[1·2] [*charla, fiesta, reunión*] to liven up; **hace falta más alcohol si quieres que la fiesta se anime** we need more alcohol if you want the party to get going *o* liven up
[2] (= *decidirse*) **si te animas, hemos quedado en el cine** if you feel like it, we're meeting at the cinema; **cuando la economía va bien, la gente se anima y gasta** when the economy is doing well people feel more like spending; **si tú te animas, yo también** I'm game if you are; **nos vamos a París, ¿te animas?** we're going to Paris, do you fancy *o* feel like coming?; **~se a hacer algo: ¿alguien se anima a acompañarme?** does anyone feel like coming with me?; **hasta el abuelo se animó a bailar** even grandpa got up and had a dance; **nadie se anima a dar su opinión** nobody dares to give their opinion; **parece que no se anima a llover** it looks as if it's not going to rain after all

anime SM (*Caribe*) polyethylene

anímicamente ADV mentally

anímico ADJ mental; **estado ~** state of mind

animismo SM animism

animista Ⓐ ADJ animistic
Ⓑ SMF animist

animita SF (*Cono Sur*) roadside shrine

➤ LENGUA Y USO: **anhelo** 35.4

ánimo SM [1] (= *moral*) spirits *pl*; **tiene mejor ~** he is in better spirits; **hay que mantener el ~ arriba** you've got to keep your spirits up; **admiro su fortaleza de ~** I admire her strength of spirit; **apaciguar** *o* **aplacar los ~s** to calm things down; **estar bajo de ~** to be in low spirits; **caer(se) de ~** to lose heart, get disheartened; **calmar los ~s** to calm things down; **dar ~s a algn** to cheer sb up; **enardecer** *o* **encrespar los ~s** to rouse passions, inflame passions; **los ~s estaban muy encrespados** feelings were running high; **no consigo hacerme el ~ de levantarme temprano** I can't bring myself to get up early; **levantar el ~** to raise one's spirits; **recobrar el ~** to regain the strength; **estar sin ~** to be in low spirits; **no tengo el ~ para bromas** I'm not in the mood for jokes; *ver tb* **disposición**, **estado**
[2] (= *aliento*) encouragement; **un mensaje de ~** a message of encouragement; **¡ánimo!** (*para alegrar*) come on!, cheer up!; (*ante un reto*) come on!, go for it!; **dar** *o* **infundir ~(s) a algn** to give encouragement to sb, encourage sb
[3] (= *fuerza, coraje*) courage; **hay que afrontar el futuro con mucho ~** you have to face the future with great strength *o* courage; **no me encuentro con ~ de ir al cine** I don't feel up to going to the cinema
[4] (= *intención*) intention; **no he venido con ~ de pelea** I haven't come here to fight *o* with the intention of fighting; **no había ~ de venganza en lo que dijo** there was nothing vengeful in what he said; **no estaba en mi ~ decir nada ofensivo** I didn't mean to say anything offensive; **lo dijo sin ~ de ofenderte** he meant no offence, he didn't mean to offend you; **una empresa sin ~ de lucro** a non-profit-making company; *ver tb* **presencia**
[5] (= *pensamiento*) mind; **la idea estaba presente en el ~ de todos** the idea was uppermost in everyone's thoughts *o* minds; **el suceso dejó una huella profunda en mi ~** the incident marked me deeply
[6] (= *alma*) soul, spirit

animosamente ADV (= *con valor*) bravely; (= *con brío*) with spirit, in lively fashion

animosidad SF animosity, ill will

animoso ADJ (= *valiente*) brave; (= *brioso*) spirited, lively

aniñado ADJ [1] [*aspecto*] childlike; [*conducta*] childish, puerile
[2] (*Cono Sur*) (= *animoso*) spirited, lively
[3] (*Cono Sur*) (= *guapo*) handsome

aniñarse ▸conjug 1a◂ VPR to act childishly

aniquilación SF, **aniquilamiento** SM annihilation, destruction

aniquilador ADJ destructive

aniquilar ▸conjug 1a◂ Ⓐ VT [1] (= *destruir*) [+ *enemigo*] to annihilate, destroy; [+ *equipo rival*] to crush, annihilate
[2] (= *matar*) to kill
Ⓑ **aniquilarse** VPR [1] (*Mil etc*) to be annihilated, be wiped out
[2] (= *deteriorarse*) to deteriorate, decline; (*Med*) to waste away; [*riqueza*] to be frittered away

anís SM [1] (*Bot*) anise, aniseed
[2] (= *bebida*) anisette; ✦**MODISMOS estar hecho un ~** (*Andes**) to be dressed up to the nines; **llegar a los anises** (*Andes**) to turn up late
[3] (*Andes*) (= *energía*) strength, energy

anisado ADJ aniseed-flavoured, aniseed-flavored (*EEUU*)

aniseros* SMPL (*Andes*) ✦**MODISMOS entregar los ~** to kick the bucket*; **vaciar los ~ a algn** to bump sb off*

anisete SM anisette

anivelar ▸conjug 1a◂ VT = **nivelar**

aniversario SM [*de un suceso*] anniversary; (= *cumpleaños*) birthday

anjá EXCL [1] (*Caribe, Méx**) (= *¡claro!*) of course!; (= *¡eso es!*) that's it!
[2] (*Caribe*) (= *¡bravo!*) bravo!; (*reprobación*) come off it!*

Anjeo SM Anjou

Ankara SF Ankara

ano SM anus

anoche ADV yesterday evening, last night; **antes de ~** the night before last

anochecedor(a) SM/F late bird, *person who keeps late hours*

anochecer ▸conjug 2d◂ Ⓐ VI [1] (= *venir la noche*) to get dark
[2] **anochecimos en Toledo** we got to Toledo as night was falling
Ⓑ SM nightfall, dusk; **al ~** at nightfall, at dusk; **antes del ~** before nightfall, before it gets dark

anochecida SF nightfall, dusk

anodino Ⓐ ADJ [1] (*Med*) anodyne (*frm*); (= *inocuo*) anodyne, harmless, inoffensive
[2] [*persona*] dull
Ⓑ SM (*Med*) anodyne

ánodo SM anode

anomalía SF anomaly

anómalo ADJ anomalous

anona SF (*CAm, Méx*) scaly custard apple, sweetsop

anonadación SF, **anonadamiento** SM [1] (= *asombro*) amazement, astonishment
[2] (= *abatimiento*) discouragement; (= *humillación*) humiliation
[3] (= *destrucción*) annihilation, destruction; (= *derrota*) crushing

anonadado ADJ stunned; **me quedé ~ ante un paisaje tan bello** I was stunned *o* left speechless by the beauty of the countryside; **vuestras opiniones me tienen ~** your opinions leave me utterly perplexed

anonadador ADJ crushing, overwhelming

anonadar ▸conjug 1a◂ Ⓐ VT to stun; **me anonadó su descaro** I was stunned *o* left speechless by her cheek
Ⓑ **anonadarse** VPR [1] (= *ser derrotado*) to be crushed, be overwhelmed
[2] (= *abatirse*) to get discouraged

anónimamente ADV anonymously

anonimato SM, **anonimia** SF anonymity; **mantenerse en el ~** to remain anonymous

anónimo Ⓐ ADJ anonymous; *ver* **sociedad 3**
Ⓑ SM [1] (= *anonimato*) anonymity; **conservar** *o* **guardar el ~** to remain anonymous
[2] (= *persona*) anonymous person
[3] (= *carta*) anonymous letter; (= *carta maliciosa*) poison-pen letter; (= *documento*) anonymous document; (= *obra literaria*) unsigned literary work

anorak SM anorak

anorexia SF anorexia ► **anorexia nerviosa** anorexia nervosa

anoréxico/a Ⓐ ADJ anorexic
Ⓑ SM/F anorexic

anormal ADJ [1] (= *no normal*) abnormal
[2] (*) (= *imbécil*) silly, cretinous

anormalidad SF abnormality

anormalmente ADV abnormally, unusually

anotación SF [1] (= *nota*) (*por escrito*) note, annotation (*frm*); (*al hablar*) observation; **un manuscrito con anotaciones a mano de Cervantes** a manuscript with hand-written notes of Cervantes ► **anotación al margen** marginal note, note in the margin ► **anotación en cuenta** (*Com*) account entry
[2] (= *acto*) **era el encargado de la ~ de todos los resultados** he was in charge of noting down the results
[3] (*Baloncesto*) point

anotador(a) Ⓐ SM/F [1] (*Literat*) annotator
[2] (*Dep*) scorer
Ⓑ SM (*LAm*) scorecard

anotar ▸conjug 1a◂ Ⓐ VT [1] (= *apuntar*) [1·1] (*en cuaderno*) to make a note of, note down; (*en lista, tabla*) to enter, record; **anota la cifra total** make a note of *o* note down the total figure; **anotó la matrícula del coche** he took down the registration number of the car; **anota los resultados en las casillas** enter the results in the boxes; **se han olvidado de ~ los intereses** they have forgotten to record the interest rates
[1·2] (*Estadística*) [+ *velocidad, tiempo*] to log
[2] (*esp Cono Sur*) (= *inscribir*) enrol, enroll (*EEUU*); **¿me ~on en el registro?** have you written me down in the register?; **anótame para la excursión** put me down for the outing
[3] (*Literat*) [+ *texto, libro*] to annotate
[4] (*Dep*) [+ *punto*] to score
Ⓑ **anotarse** VPR [1] (*Dep*) [+ *punto, gol*] to score; **~se una victoria** to win a victory, gain a victory; ✦**MODISMO ¡anótate un tanto!*** give yourself a pat on the back!*
[2] (*Fin*) [+ *precio*] to fetch; [+ *operación, puntos*] to register; **la serigrafía de Warhol se anotó 440.000 dólares** the Warhol screen print fetched 440,000 dollars; **el mercado bursátil se anotó 279,65 puntos** the stock market registered 279.65 points
[3] (*esp Cono Sur*) (= *inscribirse*) to enrol, enroll (*EEUU*); **—estamos organizando un viaje —¡yo me anoto!** "we're organizing a trip" — "count me in! *o* I'll come too!"; **—Ana va a ayudarnos —nosotros también nos anotamos** "Ana is going to help us" — "we'll help too"

anovulatorio SM (= *inhibidor*) anovulant; (= *píldora*) contraceptive pill

ANPE SF ABR = **Asociación Nacional del Profesorado Estatal**

anquilosado ADJ [1] [*músculo, miembro*] stiff; (*Med*) ankylosed (*frm*)
[2] [*pensamiento, sociedad*] stagnant

anquilosamiento SM, **anquilosis** SF [1] [*de músculo, pierna*] stiffness; (*Med*) ankylosis
[2] [*de pensamiento, sociedad*] stagnation

anquilosar ▸conjug 1a◂ Ⓐ VT [1] [+ *músculo, pierna*] to get stiff; (*Med*) to ankylose (*frm*)
[2] (= *detener*) to paralyze
Ⓑ VI (*Aut, Mec*) to seize up
Ⓒ **anquilosarse** VPR to stagnate

anquilostoma SM hookworm

ánsar SM goose

ansarino SM gosling

Anselmo SM Anselm

ansia SF [1] (= *anhelo*) yearning, longing; **~ de libertad/amor** yearning *o* longing for freedom/love; **~ de poder/riqueza/conocimiento/aventura** thirst for power/wealth/knowledge/adventure; **el ~ de superación** the will to outdo oneself; **el ~ de vivir la ayudó a recuperarse** the will to live helped her to recover; **el ~ de placeres** the desire for pleasure; **tenía ~s de verla** he was yearning *o* longing to see her; **comer con ~** to eat ravenously; **beber con ~** to drink thirstily; **besarse con ~** to kiss hungrily; **mirar con ~ a algn** to look longingly at sb
[2] (= *ansiedad*) anxiety, worry; (= *angustia*) anguish
[3] **ansias** (= *náuseas*) nausea *sing*; **tener ~s** to feel sick *o* nauseous

ansiado ADJ longed-for; **el momento tan ~** the long-awaited moment

ansiar ▸conjug 1b◂ Ⓐ VT to long for, yearn for; **~ hacer algo** to long to do sth, yearn to do sth
Ⓑ VI **~ por algn** to be madly in love with sb

ansiedad SF [1] (= *preocupación*) anxiety, worry
[2] (*Med*) anxiety, nervous tension

ansina ADV (*LAm*) = **así**

ansiolítico Ⓐ ADJ sedative
Ⓑ SM sedative, tranquillizer

ansioso ADJ [1] (= *preocupado*) anxious, worried; (= *deseoso*) eager, solicitous; **esperábamos ~s** we waited anxiously; **~ de** *o* **por algo** greedy for sth
[2] (*Med*) (= *tenso*) anxious, suffering from nervous tension; (= *bascoso*) sick, queasy

anta SF [1] (= *ciervo*) elk, moose
[2] (*LAm*) (= *danta*) tapir

antagónico ADJ antagonistic; (= *opuesto*) opposing

antagonismo SM antagonism

antagonista SMF antagonist

antagonístico ADJ = **antagónico**

antagonizar ▸conjug 1f◂ VT to antagonize

antañazo††* ADV a long time ago

antaño (*liter*) ADV long ago, in years past, in years gone by

antañón†* ADJ ancient, very old, of long ago

antañoso ADJ (*Andes*) ancient, very old

antara SF (*Andes*) Indian flute

antarca ADV (*Andes, Cono Sur*) on one's back; **caerse ~** to fall flat on one's back

antártico Ⓐ ADJ Antarctic
Ⓑ SM **el Antártico** the Antarctic

Antártida SF Antarctica

ante¹ SM [1] (*Zool*) (= *ciervo*) elk, moose; (= *búfalo*) buffalo; (*Méx*) (= *tapir*) tapir
[2] (= *piel*) suede
[3] (*Méx*) (= *dulce*) macaroon

▼**ante**² PREP [1] (= *en presencia de*) [*persona*] before
[2] (= *enfrentado a*) [*peligro*] in the face of, faced with; [*dificultad, duda*] faced with; **~ esta posibilidad** in view of this possibility; **~ tantas posibilidades** faced with so many possibilities; **estamos ~ un gran porvenir** we have a great future before us
[3] **~ todo** above all; **~ todo hay que recordar que …** first of all let's remember that …

-ante *ver* **Aspects of Word Formation in Spanish 2**

ante… PREF ante…

anteado ADJ buff-coloured, buff-colored (*EEUU*), fawn

anteanoche ADV the night before last

anteayer ADV the day before yesterday

antebrazo SM forearm

anteburro SM (*LAm*) tapir

antecámara SF (*Arquit*) anteroom, antechamber; (= *sala de espera*) waiting room; (*en parlamento*) lobby

antecedente Ⓐ ADJ previous, preceding; **visto lo ~** in view of the foregoing
Ⓑ SM [1] (*Mat, Fil, Gram*) antecedent
[2] **antecedentes** (= *historial*) record *sing*, history *sing*; [*de enfermedad*] history *sing*; **tener buenos ~s** to have a good record; **no tener ~s** to have a clean record; **un hombre sin ~s** a man with a clean record; **en esta familia no hay ~s de esta dolencia** this family doesn't have a history of this complaint; **¿cuáles son sus ~s?** what's his background?; **estar en ~s** to be well informed; **poner a algn en ~s** to put sb in the picture ► **antecedentes delictivos, antecedentes penales, antecedentes policiales** criminal record

anteceder ▸conjug 2a◂ VT to precede, go before

antecesor(a) Ⓐ ADJ preceding, former
Ⓑ SM/F (*en cargo etc*) predecessor; (= *antepasado*) ancestor, forebear (*frm*)

antecocina SF scullery

antecomedor SM (*LAm*) *room adjoining the dining room*

antedatar ▸conjug 1a◂ VT to antedate

antedicho ADJ aforesaid, aforementioned

antediluviano ADJ antediluvian

anteiglesia SF (*Rel*) porch

antejuela SF (*CAm*) = **lentejuela**

antelación SF **con ~** in advance, beforehand; **con mucha ~** long in advance, long beforehand

antelina SF suede

antellevar ▸conjug 1a◂ VT (*Méx*) to run over, knock down

antellevón SM (*Méx*) accident

antemano: **de ~** ADV in advance, beforehand

antena SF [1] (*Zool*) feeler, antenna; **tener ~ para** (= *intuición*) to have a feeling for, have a nose for
[2] (*Náut*) lateen yard
[3] (*Radio, TV, Telec*) aerial, antenna; **estar en ~** to be on the air; **permanecer en ~** to stay on the air; **salir en ~** to go out on the air, be broadcast; **el programa es el sexto en duración en ~** the programme is the sixth longest-running on TV ► **antena colectiva** communal aerial ► **antena de televisión** television aerial ► **antena direccional, antena dirigida** directional aerial ► **antena emisora** transmitting aerial ► **antena encerrada** built-in aerial ► **antena interior** indoor aerial ► **antena parabólica** satellite dish, dish antenna (*EEUU*) ► **antena receptora** receiving aerial
[4] **antenas*** (= *oídos*) ears

antenatal ADJ antenatal, prenatal

antenombre SM title

anteojera SF [1] (†) spectacle case
[2] **anteojeras** [*de caballo*] blinkers, blinders (*EEUU*)

anteojero/a† SM/F spectacle maker, optician

anteojo SM [1] (= *lente*) spyglass, telescope, small telescope ► **anteojo de larga vista** telescope
[2] **anteojos** (*esp LAm*) (= *gafas*) glasses, spectacles, eyeglasses (*EEUU*); (*Aut, Téc etc*) goggles; (= *prismáticos*) binoculars; (*para la ópera*) opera glasses; [*de caballo*] blinkers, blinders (*EEUU*) ► **anteojos ahumados** smoked glasses ► **anteojos de concha** horn-rimmed spectacles ► **anteojos de sol, anteojos para el sol** sunglasses

antepagar ▸conjug 1h◂ VT to prepay

antepasado/a Ⓐ ADJ previous, before last
Ⓑ SM/F ancestor, forbear (*frm*); **~s** ancestors

antepatio SM forecourt

antepecho SM [*de puente*] rail, parapet; [*de ventana*] ledge, sill; (*Mil*) parapet, breastwork

antepenúltimo ADJ last but two, antepenultimate (*frm*)

anteponer ▸conjug 2q◂ Ⓐ VT [1] (*lit*) to place in front (**a** of)
[2] (*fig*) (= *preferir*) to prefer (**a** to)
Ⓑ **anteponerse** VPR to be in front (**a** of)

anteportal SM porch

anteproyecto SM preliminary plan ► **anteproyecto de ley** draft bill

antepuerto SM outer harbour *o* (*EEUU*) harbor

antepuesto ADJ preceding, coming before

antequerano/a Ⓐ ADJ of/from Antequera
Ⓑ SM/F native/inhabitant of Antequera; **los ~s** the people of Antequera

antera SF anther

anterior ADJ [1] (*en el espacio*) [*parte*] front; **el motor está en la parte ~ del coche** the engine is in the front (part) of the car; **las patas ~es** the forelegs
[2] (*en una sucesión*) [*página, párrafo*] previous, preceding; **el capítulo ~** the previous *o* preceding chapter; **el capítulo ~ a éste** the chapter before this one; **se subió en la parada ~** he got on at the stop before *o* at the previous stop; **retiro lo ~** I take back what I just said
[3] (*en el tiempo*) previous; **en ~es ocasiones** on previous occasions; **el día ~** the day before; **un texto ~ a 1140** a text dating from before 1140; **las horas ~es a la operación** the hours before the operation; **la discusión ~ al asesinato** the discussion prior to the killing; **los enfrentamientos ~es a la guerra** the clashes leading up to *o* preceding the war; **eso fue muy ~ a tu llegada** that was a long time before you arrived
[4] (*Ling*) anterior

anterioridad SF priority; **con ~** previously, beforehand; **con ~ a esto** prior to this, before this

anteriormente ADV previously, before; **~, lo hacíamos así** we used to do it like this

antes Ⓐ ADJ before; **llame el día ~ para pedir cita** call the day before for an appointment; **ocurrió unos momentos ~** it happened a few moments earlier *o* before; **el tren ha llegado una hora ~** the train has arrived an hour early *o* before

➤ LENGUA Y USO: **ante² 3** 53.5

Ⓑ ADV [1] *(en el tiempo)* [1·1] *(con relación a otro acontecimiento)* **yo llegué ~** I arrived first; **el edificio que habían comenzado dos años ~** the building that had been started two years before *o* previously; **no te vayas sin ~ consultarle** don't go without *o* before consulting her first, don't go without consulting her beforehand, don't go until you've consulted her; **lo vio ~ que yo** he saw it first *o* before I did *o* before me; **~ de algo** before sth; **~ de 1900** before 1900; **la cena estará lista para ~ de las nueve** dinner will be ready by *o* before nine; **una semana ~ de la firma del contrato** a week before *o* prior to *(más frm)* signing the contract; **~ de anoche** the night before last; **~ de ayer** the day before yesterday; **~ de terminado el discurso** before the speech was over; **~ de una semana no vamos a saber nada** we won't know anything for a week; **el año 27 ~ de Cristo** 27 BC, 27 before Christ; **~ de hacer algo** before doing sth; **~ de salir del coche, asegúrese de que están las ventanillas cerradas** before you get *o* before getting out of the car, make sure that the windows are closed; **mucho ~ de algo** long before sth; **mucho ~ de conocerte** a long time before I met you *o* meeting you, long before I met you *o* meeting you *(más frm)*; **~ de *o* que nada** *(en el tiempo)* first of all; *(indicando preferencia)* above all; **~ de nada dejad que me presente** first of all, allow me to introduce myself; **~ que nada, hay que mantener la calma** above all, we must keep calm; **somos, ~ que nada, demócratas** we are first and foremost democrats; **poco ~ de algo** just *o* shortly before sth; **~ de que** (+ *SUBJUN*) before; **~ de que te vayas** before you go; **esperamos lograrlo ~ de que termine la década** we hope to achieve this before the end of the decade

[1·2] *(en el pasado)* **~ fumaba un paquete de tabaco al día** before, I smoked a packet of cigarettes a day, I used to smoke a packet of cigarettes a day; **~ no pasaban estas cosas** these things didn't use to happen before *o* in the past; **de ~: nuestra casa de ~** our old house, our previous house; **ya no tienen la alegría de ~** they don't have the joie de vivre they used to have; **ya no soy el mismo de ~** I'm not the same person I was *o* I used to be; **fue una boda de las de ~** it was an old-style wedding; **ya no se hacen películas como las de ~** they don't make films like they used to *o* like they did in the old days

[1·3] (= *hasta ahora*) before, before now; **nunca ~ he tenido problemas** I've never had any problems before

[1·4] (= *más temprano*) earlier; **no he podido venir ~** I couldn't come any earlier; **los viernes salimos un poco ~** on Fridays we leave a little earlier; **no te he podido llamar ~** I couldn't call you sooner *o* earlier; **cuanto ~** as soon as possible; **cuanto ~ mejor** the sooner the better; **lo ~ posible** as soon as possible

[1·5] (= *más joven*) at a younger age, at an earlier age; **cada vez se casan los hijos ~** kids get married at a younger *o* an earlier age these days

[2] *(en el espacio)* before; **tres páginas ~** three pages before; **~ de algo** before sth; **la calle que hay ~ del semáforo** the street before the traffic lights

Ⓒ CONJ *(indicando preferencia)* sooner, rather; **preferimos ir en tren ~ que en avión** we prefer to go by train rather than by plane; **no cederemos: ~ gastamos todo nuestro dinero** we shall never give up: we would rather *o* sooner spend all our money; **~ bien** ◊ **~ al contrario** but rather; **~ no** *(Chile, Méx)* just as well, luckily; **vi lo furiosa que estaba, ~ no te pegó** I saw how angry she was, just as well *o* luckily she didn't hit you; **~ que hacer algo** rather than doing sth; **~ que irme a la India, preferiría viajar por Europa** rather than going to India, I'd prefer to travel around Europe

antesala SF (= *habitación*) anteroom, antechamber; **en la ~ de** (= *al borde de*) on the verge of, on the threshold of; ✦***MODISMO* hacer ~** (= *esperar*) to wait to go in (*to see sb/do sth*); (= *pasar el tiempo*) to cool one's heels

antesalazo SM *(Méx)* long wait (*before admission*)

antetítulo SM introductory heading, prefatory heading

anteúltimo ADJ *(Cono Sur)* penultimate

anti... PREF anti...

antiabortista Ⓐ ADJ **campaña ~** anti-abortion campaign

Ⓑ SMF anti-abortionist

antiaborto ADJ INV anti-abortion, pro-life

antiácido ADJ, SM antacid

antiadherencia SF non-stick properties *pl*; **prueba ~** non-stick test

antiadherente ADJ non-stick

antiaéreo Ⓐ ADJ anti-aircraft

Ⓑ SM *(LAm)* anti-aircraft gun

antialcohólico/a Ⓐ ADJ *(Med)* **centro ~** detoxification unit; **grupo ~** alcoholics anonymous

Ⓑ SM/F teetotaller

antialérgico ADJ anti-allergic

antiamericano ADJ anti-American

antiapartheid ADJ anti-apartheid

antiarrugas ADJ INV anti-wrinkle, wrinkle *antes de s*

antiatómico ADJ **refugio ~** fall-out shelter

antiatraco ADJ INV, **antiatracos** ADJ INV **dispositivo ~** anti-theft device, security device

antibacteriano ADJ, SM antibacterial

antibalas ADJ INV bullet-proof

antibalístico ADJ antiballistic

antibelicista Ⓐ ADJ anti-war pacifist

Ⓑ SMF pacifist

antibiótico ADJ, SM antibiotic

antibloqueo SM **sistema de ~ de frenos** ABS braking system, anti-lock braking system

antibombas ADJ INV **refugio ~** bomb shelter

anticalcáreo ADJ **dispositivo ~** anti-scaling device

anticanceroso ADJ anti-cancer, cancer *antes de s*; **tratamiento ~** cancer treatment

anticarro ADJ INV anti-tank

anticaspa ADJ INV dandruff *antes de s*, anti-dandruff

anticelulítico ADJ anti-cellulite, cellulite *antes de s*

antichoque ADJ INV, **antichoques** ADJ INV **panel ~** shock-resistant panel

anticiclón SM anticyclone

anticiclonal ADJ, **anticiclónico** ADJ anticyclonic

anticipación SF (= *adelanto*) **hacer algo con ~** to do sth in good time; **llegar con ~** to arrive early, arrive in good time; **llegar con diez minutos de ~** to come ten minutes early; **reservar con ~** to book in advance, book early

anticipadamente ADV in advance, beforehand; **le doy las gracias ~** I thank you in advance

anticipado ADJ (= *con antelación*) early; **pago ~** advance payment; **gracias anticipadas** thanks in advance; **por ~** in advance, beforehand

anticipar ▸conjug 1a◂ Ⓐ VT [1] [+ *fecha, acontecimiento*] to bring forward; **~on las vacaciones** they took their holiday early; **no anticipemos los acontecimientos** let's not cross our bridges before we come to them, let's not get ahead of ourselves

[2] [+ *factura etc*] to pay in advance; [+ *dinero*] to advance, lend, loan

[3] **~ algo con placer** (= *esperar*) to look forward to sth; **~ las gracias a algn** (= *adelantar*) to thank sb in advance

[4] (= *prever*) to anticipate, foresee; **~ que ...** to anticipate that ...

Ⓑ **anticiparse** VPR [1] [*acontecimiento*] to take place early

[2] **~se a un acontecimiento** to anticipate an event; **~se a algn** to beat sb to it; **usted se ha anticipado a mis deseos** you have anticipated my wishes; **~se a hacer algo** to do sth ahead of time, do sth before the proper time; **~se a una época** to be ahead of one's time

anticipo SM [1] [*de dinero*] advance; **pedir un ~** to ask for an advance

[2] **ser el ~ de algo** to be a foretaste of sth; **esto es sólo un ~** this is just a foretaste, this is just a taste of what's to come

[3] *(Jur)* retaining fee

anticlerical ADJ, SMF anticlerical

anticlericalismo SM anticlericalism

anticlímax SM INV anticlimax

anticlinal SM [1] *(Geol)* anticline

[2] *(LAm)* watershed

anticoagulante ADJ, SM anticoagulant

anticoba SF brutal frankness, outspokenness

anticolesterol ADJ cholesterol-free, low in cholesterol

anticomunista ADJ, SMF anti-communist

anticoncepción SF contraception, birth-control

anticoncepcional ADJ birth-control *antes de s*, contraceptive

anticoncepcionismo SM contraception, birth control

anticonceptivo Ⓐ ADJ birth-control *antes de s*, contraceptive; **métodos ~s** methods of birth control; **píldora anticonceptiva** contraceptive pill

Ⓑ SM contraceptive

anticongelante ADJ, SM antifreeze

anticonstitucional ADJ unconstitutional

anticonstitucionalidad SF unconstitutionality

anticontaminante ADJ anti-pollution

anticorrosivo ADJ anticorrosive, antirust

anticristo SM Antichrist

anticuado ADJ [*maquinaria, infraestructura, tecnología*] antiquated; [*moda*] old-fashioned, out-of-date; [*técnica*] obsolete; **quedarse ~** to go out of date

anticuario/a Ⓐ ADJ antiquarian Ⓑ SM/F (= *comerciante*) antique dealer; (= *coleccionista*) antiquarian, antiquary

anticuarse ▸conjug 1d◂ VPR (*Ling etc*) to become antiquated, go out of date; [*técnica*] to become obsolete

anticucho SM (*Perú, Chile*) kebab

anticuerpo SM antibody

antidemocráticamente ADV undemocratically

antidemocrático ADJ undemocratic

antideportivo ADJ unsporting, unsportsmanlike

antidepresivo Ⓐ ADJ antidepressant Ⓑ SM antidepressant, antidepressant drug

antiderrapante ADJ non-skid

antideslizante Ⓐ ADJ (*Aut*) non-skid; [*piso*] non-slip Ⓑ SM non-skid tyre, non-skid tire (*EEUU*)

antideslumbrante ADJ anti-glare

antidetonante ADJ anti-knock

antidisturbios Ⓐ ADJ INV **policía ~** riot police, riot control police Ⓑ SMF member of riot police

antidóping ADJ INV, **antidopaje** ADJ INV **control ~** drugs test, check for drugs

antídoto SM antidote (**contra** for, to)

antidroga ADJ INV **brigada ~** drug squad; **campaña ~** anti-drug campaign; **tratamiento ~** treatment for drug addiction

antidúmping ADJ INV **medidas ~** anti-dumping measures

antiecológico ADJ **producto ~** product damaging to the environment, environmentally unsafe product

antieconómico ADJ uneconomic, uneconomical

antienvejecimiento ADJ INV anti-ageing

antier ADV (*LAm*) = **anteayer**

antiestático ADJ antistatic

antiestético ADJ unsightly, ugly

antiestrés ADJ INV anti-stress, stress *antes de s*

antifascismo SM anti-fascism

antifascista ADJ, SMF anti-fascist

antifatiga ADJ INV **píldora ~** anti-fatigue pill, pep pill*

antifaz SM [1] (= *máscara*) mask [2] (‡) (= *preservativo*) condom, johnny*, rubber (*EEUU**)

antifeminismo SM anti-feminism

antifeminista ADJ, SMF anti-feminist

antífona SF antiphony

antifranquismo SM opposition to Franco

antifranquista Ⓐ ADJ anti-Franco Ⓑ SMF opponent of Franco, person opposed to Franco

antifraude ADJ INV **acción ~** action to combat fraud

antifriccional ADJ antifriction

antifrís SM (*LAm*) antifreeze

antifuego ADJ INV [*puerta, barrera*] fire *antes de s*, fireproof; **lucha ~** firefighting

antigás ADJ **careta ~** gas mask

antígeno SM antigen

antiglobalización SF anti-globalization; **grupo ~** anti-globalization group

antiglobalizador(a) ADJ anti-globalization *antes de s*

antigolpes ADJ INV shockproof

Antígona SF Antigone

antigripal ADJ INV **vacuna ~** flu vaccine

antigualla SF (= *objeto*) old thing, relic; (= *cuento*) old story; (= *individuo*) has-been; **~s** old junk *sing*

antiguamente ADV in the past, in the old days; **~ las cosas eran de otra manera** things were different in the past *o* in the old days; **pongo en duda lo que ~ creía** now I'm questioning what I once thought

antigüedad SF [1] (= *época*) antiquity; **los artistas de la ~** the artists of antiquity, the artists of the ancient world; **alta ~** ◊ **remota ~** high antiquity; **de toda ~** from time immemorial [2] (= *edad*) antiquity, age; (*en empleo*) seniority; **la fábrica tiene una ~ de 200 años** the factory has been going *o* in existence for 200 years [3] (= *objeto*) antique; **~es** antiques; **tienda de ~es** antique shop

antiguerra ADJ INV anti-war

antiguo/a Ⓐ ADJ [1] (= *viejo*) [*ciudad, costumbre*] old; [*coche*] vintage; [*mueble, objeto, libro*] antique; **las antiguas tradiciones** old traditions; **el Antiguo Testamento** the Old Testament; **rallies de coches ~s** vintage car rallies; **a la antigua (usanza)** in the old-fashioned way; **cocinan a la antigua usanza** they cook in the old style *o* in the old-fashioned way; **de** *o* **desde ~** from time immemorial; **una medicina usada desde muy ~** a medicine that has been used from time immemorial; **nuestra amistad viene de ~** our friendship dates back a long way; **en lo ~** in olden days (*liter*), in ancient times; *ver tb* **chapado, música** [2] (*Hist*) [*civilización, restos*] ancient; **la antigua Grecia** ancient Greece; **el palacio árabe más ~** the oldest Arab palace, the most ancient Arab palace; **Antiguo Régimen** ancien régime; *ver tb* **edad 2** [3] (= *anterior*) old, former; **la antigua capilla, ahora sala de exposiciones** the old *o* former chapel, now an exhibition hall; **un ~ novio** an old boyfriend, an ex-boyfriend; **mi ~ jefe** my former boss, my ex-boss; **la antigua Yugoslavia** the former Yugoslavia; **más ~** [*cliente, socio*] longest-standing; [*empleado, prisionero*] longest-serving; **el socio más ~** the most senior member, the longest-standing member, the oldest member; **es más ~ que yo en el club** he has been in the club longer than me; *ver tb* **alumno** [4] (= *anticuado*) [*traje, estilo, persona*] old-fashioned; [*mentalidad*] outdated; **lleva un peinado muy ~** she has a very old-fashioned hair style Ⓑ SM/F [1] (= *anticuado*) **tu madre es una antigua** your mother is really old-fashioned, your mother is a real fuddy-duddy* [2] (= *veterano*) **el más ~** the oldest one; **los más ~s tienen derecho a votar primero** the oldest are entitled to vote first [3] (*Hist*) **los ~s** the ancients

antihéroe SM antihero

antihigiénico ADJ unhygienic, insanitary

antihistamínico ADJ, SM antihistamine

antihumano ADJ inhuman

antiimperialismo SM anti-imperialism

antiimperialista ADJ, SMF anti-imperialist

antiincendios ADJ INV **equipo ~** fire-fighting team; **servicio ~** fire-fighting services

antiinflacionista ADJ anti-inflationary

antiinflamatorio ADJ, SM anti-inflammatory

antillanismo SM *word or phrase peculiar to the Antilles*

antillano/a Ⓐ ADJ of/from the Antilles, West Indian Ⓑ SM/F native/inhabitant of the Antilles, West Indian; **los ~s** the people of the Antilles, the West Indians

Antillas SFPL Antilles, West Indies; **el mar de las ~** the Caribbean, the Caribbean Sea

antilogaritmo SM antilogarithm

antilógico ADJ illogical

antílope SM antelope

antimacasar SM antimacassar

antimanchas ADJ INV **superficie ~** stain-resistant surface

antimateria SF antimatter

antimilitarismo SM antimilitarism

antimilitarista ADJ, SMF antimilitarist

antimisil Ⓐ ADJ antimissile; **misil ~** antimissile missile Ⓑ SM antimissile

antimonio SM antimony

antimonopolio ADJ INV, **antimonopolios** ADJ INV **ley ~** anti-trust law

antimosquitos ADJ INV mosquito *antes de s*; **red ~** mosquito net

antinacional ADJ unpatriotic

antinatural ADJ unnatural

antiniebla ADJ INV **faros ~** fog lamps

antinomia SF antinomy (*frm*), conflict of authority

antinuclear ADJ antinuclear

Antioquía SF Antioch

antioxidante Ⓐ ADJ antioxidant, anti-rust Ⓑ SM antioxidant

antipalúdico ADJ antimalarial

antipara SF screen

antiparabólico* ADJ (*Caribe*) wild, over the top

antiparasitario Ⓐ ADJ antiparasitic Ⓑ SM antiparasitic drug

antiparras* SFPL glasses, eyeglasses (*EEUU*), specs*

antipatía SF (= *sentimiento*) antipathy (**hacia** towards; **entre** between), dislike (**hacia** for); (= *actitud*) unfriendliness (**hacia** towards)

antipático ADJ unpleasant, disagreeable; **es un chico de lo más ~** he's a horrible *o* a thoroughly unpleasant boy; **me es muy ~** I don't like him at all; **en un ambiente ~** in an unfriendly environment, in an uncongenial atmosphere

antipatizar ▸conjug 1f◂ VI (*LAm*) to feel unfriendly; **~ con algn** to dislike sb

antipatriótico ADJ unpatriotic

antiperras SFPL (*Andes*) half-moon glasses, half-moon spectacles

antípodas SFPL antipodes

antipolilla ADJ INV mothproof

antiproteccionista ADJ anti-protectionist, free-trade *antes de s*

antiproyectil ADJ INV antimissile

antiquísimo ADJ ancient

antiquista (*Méx*) Ⓐ ADJ antiquarian
Ⓑ SMF antiquarian, antique dealer

antirrábico ADJ **vacuna antirrábica** anti-rabies vaccine

antirracista ADJ, SMF anti-racist

antirreflectante ADJ anti-glare

antirreglamentario ADJ (= *ilegal*) unlawful, illegal; (*Dep*) foul

antirresbaladizo ADJ non-skid

antirretroviral Ⓐ ADJ anti-retroviral
Ⓑ SM anti-retroviral drug

antirrino SM antirrhinum

antirrobo Ⓐ ADJ INV **sistema ~** anti-theft system
Ⓑ SM (*tb* **dispositivo ~**) anti-theft device

antirruido ADJ INV **sistema ~** noise-reduction system; **comisión ~** noise-abatement committee; **ley ~** noise-pollution law

antisemita Ⓐ ADJ anti-Semitic
Ⓑ SMF anti-Semite

antisemítico ADJ anti-Semitic

antisemitismo SM anti-Semitism

antiséptico ADJ, SM antiseptic

antisocial ADJ antisocial

antisudoral (*LAm*) ADJ, SM deodorant

antitabaco ADJ INV **campaña ~** anti-smoking campaign

antitabaquismo SM anti-smoking attitudes *pl*

antitabaquista ADJ anti-smoking

antitanque ADJ anti-tank

antitaurino ADJ anti-bullfighting

antiterrorista ADJ **medidas ~s** measures against terrorism; **Ley Antiterrorista** ≈ Prevention of Terrorism Act

▼**antítesis** SF INV antithesis

antitetánica SF anti-tetanus injection

antitético ADJ antithetic, antithetical

antitranspirante ADJ, SM anti-perspirant

antivaho ADJ INV **dispositivo ~** demister, demisting device

antivirus SM INV antivirus

antiviviseccionista SMF antivivisectionist

antivuelco ADJ INV **barra ~** anti-roll bar

antofagastino/a (*Cono Sur*) Ⓐ ADJ of/from Antofagasta
Ⓑ SM/F native/inhabitant of Antofagasta; **los ~s** the people of Antofagasta

antojadizo ADJ [1] (= *caprichoso*) **es muy ~** he's always taking a fancy to something or other
[2] (= *poco fiable*) unpredictable

antojado ADJ **~ con** *o* **por** (= *con capricho de*) taken by, hankering after; [*mujer embarazada*] craving for

antojarse ▸conjug 1a◂ VPR [1] (= *apetecer*) **antojársele a algn algo** to take a fancy to sth, want sth; **se me antoja una cervecita** I could go for a nice beer; **antojársele a algn hacer algo** to have a mind to do sth; **se le antojó ir al cine** he took it into his head to go to the cinema; **no se le antojó decir otra cosa** it didn't occur to him to say anything else; **no se me antoja ir** I don't feel like going
[2] (= *parecer*) **~ que** to imagine that; **se me antoja que no estará** I have the feeling that he won't be in; **¿cómo se le antoja esto?** how does this seem to you?

antojitos* SMPL (*Cono Sur*) (= *caramelos*) sweets, candy (*EEUU*); (*Méx*) (= *tapas*) snacks, nibbles

antojo SM [1] (= *capricho*) whim; **hacer a su ~** to do as one pleases; **cada uno a su ~** each to his own; **¿cuál es su ~?** what's your idea?; ✦***MODISMO*** **no morirse de ~** (*Cono Sur*) to satisfy a whim
[2] [*de embarazada*] craving; **tener ~s** to have cravings (*during pregnancy*)
[3] (*Anat*) birthmark

antología SF (= *colección*) anthology; (*Arte*) retrospective; **un gol de ~** a goal for the history books, a goal that will go down in history

antológica SF (*Arte*) retrospective

antológico ADJ [1] (*Arte*) **exposición antológica** retrospective
[2] (= *destacado*) memorable; **un gol ~** a goal for the history books, a goal that will go down in history

antónimo SM antonym

Antonio SM Anthony

antonomasia SF antonomasia; **por ~** par excellence

antorcha SF [1] (= *tea*) torch
[2] (= *guía*) mentor

antracita SF anthracite

ántrax SM anthrax

antro SM (= *cueva*) cavern; (* *pey*) (= *local*) dive* ► **antro de corrupción** den of iniquity

antropofagia SF cannibalism

antropófago/a Ⓐ ADJ man-eating *antes de s*, cannibalistic
Ⓑ SM/F cannibal; **~s** anthropophagi (*frm*), cannibals

antropoide ADJ, SMF anthropoid

antropoideo SM anthropoid

antropología SF anthropology ► **antropología social** social anthropology

antropológico ADJ anthropological

antropólogo/a SM/F anthropologist

antropomorfismo SM anthropomorphism

antruejo SM carnival (*three days before Lent*)

antucá SM (*Cono Sur*) sunshade, parasol

antuviada SF sudden blow, bump

antuvión* SM sudden blow, bump; **de ~** suddenly, unexpectedly

anual ADJ [*reunión, periodicidad*] yearly, annual; [*planta*] annual; **la cuota es de 100 euros ~es** the yearly *o* annual fee is 100 euros

anualidad SF [1] (*Fin*) annual payment ► **anualidad vitalicia** life annuity
[2] (= *suceso*) annual occurrence

anualizado ADJ (*Fin*) annual

anualmente ADV annually, yearly

anuario SM (= *libro*) yearbook, annual; (= *guía*) directory ► **anuario militar** military list ► **anuario telefónico** telephone directory

anubarrado ADJ cloudy, overcast

anublar ▸conjug 1a◂ Ⓐ VT [1] [+ *cielo*] to cloud, cloud over; [+ *luz*] to obscure
[2] [+ *planta*] to wither, dry up
Ⓑ **anublarse** VPR [1] [*cielo*] to cloud over, become overcast
[2] [*planta*] to wither, dry up
[3] (= *desvanecerse*) to fade away

anudar ▸conjug 1a◂ Ⓐ VT [1] (= *atar*) to knot, tie
[2] [+ *cuento*] to resume, take up again
[3] [+ *voz*] to choke, strangle
Ⓑ **anudarse** VPR [1] [*cinta*] to get into knots
[2] [*planta*] to remain stunted
[3] **se me anudó la voz (en la garganta)** I got a lump in my throat

anuencia SF consent

anuente ADJ consenting, consentient

anulación SF [*de contrato*] annulment, cancellation; [*de ley*] repeal

▼**anular¹** ▸conjug 1a◂ Ⓐ VT [1] [+ *contrato*] to cancel, rescind; [+ *ley*] to repeal; [+ *decisión*] to override; [+ *matrimonio*] to annul
[2] [+ *elecciones, resultado*] to declare null and void; [+ *gol, tanto*] to disallow; **han anulado la votación por irregularidad** they have declared the vote null and void because of irregularities
[3] [+ *cita, viaje, evento*] to cancel; **~on el partido por causa de la lluvia** they cancelled the match because of the rain
[4] [+ *cheque*] to cancel
[5] [+ *efecto*] to cancel out, destroy
[6] (*Mat*) to cancel out
[7] [+ *persona*] to overshadow; **su potente carácter anula a sus amigos** her strong personality overshadows her friends
[8] (*frm*) (= *incapacitar*) to deprive of authority, remove from office
Ⓑ **anularse** VPR [1] (= *amilanarse*) to fade into the background; **se anula ante su padre** he fades into the background when his father is there
[2] (= *neutralizarse*) **los dos campos magnéticos se anulan** the two magnetic fields cancel each other out; **las dos sustancias se anulan mutuamente** the two substances neutralize each other

anular² Ⓐ ADJ ring-shaped, annular; **dedo ~** ring finger
Ⓑ SM ring finger

anunciación SF announcement; **Anunciación** (*Rel*) Annunciation

anunciador(a) SM/F (*Méx Radio, TV*) announcer; (*Teat*) compere

anunciante SMF advertiser

▼**anunciar** ▸conjug 1b◂ Ⓐ VT [1] (= *hacer público*) to announce; **han anunciado la devaluación del euro** they have announced the devaluation of the euro; **el ministro anunció su dimisión** the minister announced that he was resigning; **la princesa anunció que se casaba** the princess announced that she was getting married; **anunciamos nuestra oposición a las privatizaciones** we declared our opposition to privatization
[2] (= *convocar*) to call; **han anunciado una rueda de prensa para hoy** they have called a press conference for today; **el gobierno ~á hoy la convocatoria de elecciones** the government will call elections today
[3] (*Com*) to advertise
[4] (= *augurar*) **no nos anuncia nada bueno** it is not a good sign, it bodes ill for us; **este viento anuncia tormenta** this wind means there is a storm coming; **el pronóstico del tiempo anuncia nevadas** they're forecasting snow, the weather forecast says there will be snow
[5] (*frm*) (*a una visita*) to announce; **el mayordomo anunció a la Duquesa de Villahermosa** the butler announced the Duchess of

➤ LENGUA Y USO: **antítesis** 53.3 **anular¹ A3** 47.4, 48.4 **anunciar A1** 51.1, 51.2

Villahermosa; **¿a quién debo ~?** who shall I say it is?, what name should I say?
Ⓑ **anunciarse** VPR [1] (*Com*) to advertise
[2] (= *augurarse*) **el festival se anuncia animado** it promises to be *o* looks like being a lively festival; **¿cómo se anuncia la cosecha este año?** how's the harvest looking this year?

▼**anuncio** SM [1] (*Com*) (*en un periódico*) advertisement, advert, ad*; (*en TV, radio*) advertisement, advert, commercial; (= *cartel*) poster; **poner un ~ en un periódico** to put an advertisement *o* advert *o* ad* in a newspaper; **"prohibido fijar** *o* **pegar anuncios"** "post *o* stick no bills"; **hombre ~** sandwich-board man ► **anuncio publicitario** advertisement, advert, commercial ► **anuncios clasificados** classified ads*, classified advertisements, classifieds ► **anuncios de relax** personal services ads ► **anuncios por palabras** classified ads, small ads*; *ver tb* **tablón**
[2] (= *notificación*) announcement; **el ~ de su muerte causó mucha tristeza** the announcement of her death caused great sadness; **hoy se hará el ~ de su boda** their wedding will be announced today; **un ~ de bomba** a bomb warning
[3] (= *presagio*) omen, sign; **fue un ~ de las desgracias futuras** it was an omen *o* a sign of the misfortunes to come; **es ~ de un futuro mejor** it heralds a better future; **esos nubarrones son ~ de tormenta** those black clouds mean there is a storm coming

anuo ADJ (*frm*) annual

anverso SM obverse

anzuelo SM (*para pescar*) fish hook; (= *aliciente*) bait, lure; **echar el ~** to offer a bait, offer an inducement; ✦***MODISMOS*** **picar en el ~** ◊ **tragarse el ~** to swallow the bait

añada SF [1] (= *año*) year, season
[2] (= *trozo de campo*) piece of field, strip

añadido Ⓐ ADJ (= *que se agrega*) added; (= *adicional*) additional, extra; **lo ~** what is added
Ⓑ SM [1] (*Tip*) addition
[2] (= *pelo*) hairpiece

añadidura SF (= *lo que se agrega*) addition; (*Com*) extra; **dar algo de ~** to give sth extra; **con algo de ~** with sth into the bargain; **por ~** in addition, on top of that

▼**añadir** ▸conjug 3a◂ VT [1] (= *agregar*) to add (**a** to)
[2] [+ *encanto, interés*] to add, lend

añagaza SF (*Caza*) lure, decoy; (= *ardid*) ruse

añal Ⓐ ADJ [1] [*suceso*] yearly, annual
[2] (*Agr*) year-old
Ⓑ SM yearling

añangá SM (*Cono Sur*) the devil

añango (*Andes*) Ⓐ ADJ [*niño*] sickly
Ⓑ SM small portion

añañay* EXCL (*Cono Sur*) great!*, super!*

añapar ▸conjug 1a◂ VT (*LAm*) to smash to bits

añar SM (*LAm*) **hace ~es que ...** it's ages since ...

añascar ▸conjug 1g◂ VT to scrape together, get together bit by bit

añaz SM (*Andes*) skunk

añeja* SF (*Caribe*) old lady*, mum*

añejar ▸conjug 1a◂ Ⓐ VT to age
Ⓑ **añejarse** VPR [*vino*] to mature, age; (= *ranciarse*) to get stale, go musty

añejo ADJ [1] (*Culin*) [*vino, queso*] mature; [*jamón*] well-cured
[2] (*pey*) (= *rancio*) stale, musty
[3] [*noticia, historia*] old, stale

añicos SMPL pieces, fragments; **hacer un vaso ~** to smash a glass to bits *o* to smithereens; **hacer un papel ~** to tear a piece of paper into little *o* tiny bits; **hacerse ~** to shatter; **estar hecho ~** (= *cansado*) to be worn out, be shattered*

añil Ⓐ SM (*Bot*) indigo; (= *color*) indigo; (*para lavado*) blue, bluing
Ⓑ ADJ INV indigo

añilar ▸conjug 1a◂ VT (= *teñir*) to dye indigo; [+ *ropa*] to blue

añinos SMPL lamb's wool *sing*

año SM [1] (= *periodo de tiempo*) year; **el ~ pasado** last year; **el ~ próximo** ◊ **el ~ que viene** next year; **el ~ entrante** the coming year; **el ~ antepasado** the year before last; **esperamos ~s y ~s** we waited years and years; **cinco toneladas al ~** five tons a year; **al ~ de casado** a year after his marriage, after he had been married a year; **el ~ 66 después de Cristo** 66 A.D.; **en el ~ 1980** in 1980; **en los ~s 60** in the sixties; **en estos últimos ~s** in recent years; **hace ~s** ◊ **~s ha** years ago; **los 40 ~s** ◊ **los ~s difíciles** *o* **negros** (*Esp*) the Franco years (*1936-75*); ✦***MODISMOS*** **estar de buen ~** to look well-fed; **en el ~ de la nana** *o* **pera** *o* **polca** in the year dot, way back; **una lavadora del ~ de la nana** *o* **de la pera** a washing machine from the year dot; **el ~ verde** (*LAm*) never; ✦***REFRÁN*** **dentro de cien ~s, todos calvos** we all die in the end ► **año bisiesto** leap year ► **año civil**, **año común** calendar year ► **año de gracia** year of grace ► **año de nuestra salud** year of Our Lord ► **año económico** financial year ► **año escolar** school year ► **año fiscal** tax year ► **año lectivo** academic year ► **año luz** light-year; **100 ~s luz** 100 light-years; **los nórdicos están a ~s luz** the Scandinavians are light-years ahead (of the rest of us); **el resto de corredores está a ~s luz de los dos campeones** the other runners are light-years behind the two champions ► **año natural** calendar year ► **Año Nuevo** New Year; **día de Año Nuevo** New Year's Day; **¡feliz ~ nuevo!** happy New Year!; **felicitar el ~ (nuevo) a algn** to wish sb (a) Happy New Year ► **año presupuestario**: **el ~ presupuestario va de noviembre a octubre** the budget covers the period from *o* runs from November to October ► **año sabático** sabbatical (year) ► **año santo** Holy Year
[2] [*de edad*] **¿cuántos ~s tienes?** how old are you?; **tengo nueve ~s** I'm nine (years old); **una niña de tres ~s** a three-year-old girl, a girl of three; **niños menores de un ~** children under (the age of) one; **(nunca) en los ~s que tengo** never in all my life; **a mis ~s** at my age; **a sus ~s se mueve como una quinceañera** at *o* despite her age she still moves like a teenager; **cumplir ~s** to have one's birthday; **cumplir (los) 21 ~s** to have *o* celebrate one's 21st (birthday); **entrado en ~s** elderly; **llevar diez ~s a algn** to be ten years older than sb; **¡por muchos ~s!** (*en cumpleaños*) many happy returns!; (*en brindis*) your *o* good health!; (†) (*en presentación*) how do you do?; **de pocos ~s** young; **quitarse ~s** (= *mentir*) to lie about one's age; **con ese lifting te has quitado diez ~s de encima** you look ten years younger after that face-lift; **sacar ~s a algn** to be older than sb; **le saca muchos ~s a su amiga** she is much older than her friend; → KILOS, METROS, AÑOS

año-hombre SM (*pl* **años-hombre**) man-year

añojal SM fallow land

añojo/a SM/F yearling

añorante ADJ yearning, longing

añoranza SF (= *recuerdos*) nostalgia, yearning, longing (**de** for); (*por pérdida*) sense of loss

añorar ▸conjug 1a◂ Ⓐ VT [+ *país*] to yearn for, miss, be homesick for; [+ *difunto, pérdida*] to mourn
Ⓑ VI to pine, grieve

añoso ADJ aged, full of years

añublar ▸conjug 1a◂ VI = **anublar**

añublo SM blight, mildew

añudar ▸conjug 1a◂ = **anudar**

añusgar ▸conjug 1h◂ Ⓐ VI (= *atragantarse*) to choke; (= *enfadarse*) to get angry
Ⓑ **añusgarse** VPR to get cross

aojada SF (*Andes*) skylight

aojar ▸conjug 1a◂ VT to put the evil eye on

aojo SM evil eye

aoristo SM aorist

aorta SF aorta

aovado ADJ oval, egg-shaped

aovar ▸conjug 1a◂ VI to lay eggs

aovillarse ▸conjug 1a◂ VPR to roll o.s. into a ball, curl up

AP SF ABR (*Esp Hist, Pol*) = **Alianza Popular**

Ap. ABR (= **apartado postal** *o* **de correos**) PO Box

APA SF ABR (= **Asociación de Padres de Alumnos**) ≈ PTA

apa¹ EXCL [1] (*Méx*) (= *¡Dios Santo!*) goodness me!, good gracious!
[2] (= *ánimo*) cheer up!; (= *levántate*) get up!, up you get!; (= *recógelo*) pick it up!; (= *basta*) that's enough!

apa²: **al ~** ADV (*Cono Sur*) on one's back

apabullante ADJ shattering, crushing, overwhelming

apabullar ▸conjug 1a◂ Ⓐ VT [+ *rival*] to crush; **se le ve algo apabullado por las circunstancias** he was rather overwhelmed by the situation
Ⓑ **apabullarse** VPR to panic

apacentadero SM pasture

apacentar ▸conjug 1j◂ Ⓐ VT [1] (*Agr*) [+ *ganado*] to graze, feed
[2] [+ *discípulos*] to teach; [+ *deseos, pasión*] to gratify
Ⓑ **apacentarse** VPR [1] (*Agr*) [*ganado*] to graze, feed
[2] (= *alimentarse*) to feed (**con, de** on)

apachar ▸conjug 1a◂ VT (*Perú*) to steal

apache SM/F [1] (= *indio*) Apache, Apache Indian
[2] (= *bandido*) crook, bandit

apacheta SF [1] (*Andes, Cono Sur Rel*) cairn, wayside shrine
[2] (= *montón*) pile, heap
[3] (*Pol*) clique; (= *confabulación*) ring, gang
[4] (*Com*) ill-gotten gains *pl*; ✦***MODISMO*** **hacer la ~*** to make one's pile*

apachico SM (*LAm*) bundle

➤ LENGUA Y USO: **anuncio 1** 46.1 **añadir 1** 53.5

apachurrar ▸conjug 1a◂ VT (*esp LAm*) (= *aplastar*) to crush, squash; (= *romper*) to smash

apacibilidad SF (= *mansedumbre*) gentleness; [*de tiempo*] calmness

apacible ADJ (= *manso*) [*animal, persona*] gentle, mild; [*temperamento*] gentle, even; [*tiempo*] calm; [*viento*] gentle; [*tarde, noche*] pleasant; **es un tío muy ~** he's a very even-tempered *o* placid *o* mild-mannered guy

apaciblemente ADV gently, mildly

apaciguador ADJ pacifying, calming, soothing

apaciguamiento SM (= *tranquilidad*) calming down; (*Pol*) appeasement

apaciguar ▸conjug 1i◂ Ⓐ VT (= *tranquilizar*) to calm down; [+ *manifestantes*] to pacify, appease, mollify; (*Pol*) to appease
Ⓑ **apaciguarse** VPR to calm down, quieten down

apadrinamiento SM [1] [*de artista*] sponsorship, patronage
[2] (= *apoyo*) backing, support

apadrinar ▸conjug 1a◂ VT [1] (*Rel*) [+ *niño*] to act as godfather to; [+ *novio*] to be best man for
[2] [+ *artista*] to sponsor, be a patron to
[3] (= *apoyar*) to back, support
[4] [+ *duelista*] to act as second to

apadronarse ▸conjug 1a◂ VPR to register (as a resident)

apagadizo ADJ slow to burn, difficult to ignite

apagado Ⓐ ADJ [1] [*volcán*] extinct; [*cal*] slaked; **estar ~** [*fuego*] to be out; [*luz, radio*] to be off
[2] [*sonido*] muted, muffled; [*voz*] quiet
[3] [*color*] dull
[4] [*persona, temperamento*] listless, spiritless; [*mirada*] lifeless, dull
Ⓑ SM switching-off; **botón de ~** off button, off switch

apagador SM [1] (= *extintor*) extinguisher
[2] (*Mec*) silencer, muffler (*EEUU*); (*Mús*) damper
[3] (*Cono Sur, Méx*) (= *interruptor*) switch

apagafuegos Ⓐ ADJ INV **avión ~** fire-fighting plane
Ⓑ SM (= *avión*) fire-fighting plane
Ⓒ SMF (= *persona*) troubleshooter

apagar ▸conjug 1h◂ Ⓐ VT [1] [+ *fuego, vela, cerilla*] to put out; (*soplando*) to blow out; **apagó el cigarrillo en el cenicero** he put out *o* stubbed out his cigarette in the ashtray; **"por favor, apaguen sus cigarrillos"** "please extinguish all cigarettes"; ✦**MODISMO** **(entonces) apaga y vámonos** let's forget it (then)
[2] (*Elec*) to turn off, switch off; **apaga la luz/tele** turn *o* switch the light/TV off; **apagó el motor y salió del coche** she switched off the engine and got out of the car; **~ el sistema** (*Inform*) to close *o* shut down the system
[3] [+ *sed*] to quench
[4] [+ *ira*] to calm; [+ *rencor*] to pacify
[5] [+ *dolor*] to take away, soothe
[6] [+ *sonido*] to muffle, deaden; (*Mús*) to mute
[7] [+ *color*] to tone down, soften
[8] [+ *cal*] to slake
[9] (*Andes, Caribe*) [+ *arma de fuego*] to empty, discharge
Ⓑ **apagarse** VPR [1] [*fuego, vela*] to go out; (*con el viento*) to blow out; [*volcán*] to become extinct
[2] [*luz*] to go out; [*aparato*] (*automáticamente*) to switch off, go off; (*por avería*) to stop working; **el motor se apaga en caso de incendio** the engine switches off if there is a fire; **la tele se me apagó durante el partido** the TV stopped working during the match
[3] [*ira, rencor*] to subside, die away; **su entusiasmo se apagó con los años** his enthusiasm died away *o* subsided over the years
[4] [*sonido*] to die away
[5] [*persona*] to fade (away); **su vida se apaga** his life is coming to an end *o* ebbing away; **su mirada se apagó con los años** the light went out of her eyes over the years

apagavelas SM INV candle snuffer

apagón SM power cut ▶ **apagón informativo, apagón de noticias** news blackout

apagoso ADJ (*LAm*) = **apagadizo**

apaisado ADJ oblong

apajarado ADJ (*Cono Sur*) daft, scatterbrained

apalabrar ▸conjug 1a◂ Ⓐ VT [1] (= *convenir en*) to agree to; **estar apalabrado a una cosa** to be committed to sth
[2] (= *encargar*) to bespeak; (= *contratar*) to engage
Ⓑ **apalabrarse** VPR to come to an agreement (**con** with)

apalabrear ▸conjug 1a◂ (*LAm*) = **apalabrar**

Apalaches SMPL **Montes ~** Appalachians

apalancado* ADJ [1] (= *apoltronado*) settled
[2] (= *apoyado*) propped (up)
[3] (= *estancado*) vegetating

apalancamiento SM leverage

apalancar ▸conjug 1g◂ Ⓐ VT [1] (= *para levantar*) to lever up
[2] (= *para abrir*) to prise *o* (*EEUU*) prize off, lever off
[3] (*Cono Sur**) **~ a algn** to wangle a job for sb*
Ⓑ **apalancarse** VPR [1] (= *apoltronarse*) to settle down; **se apalanca en el sofá y no se mueve en toda la tarde** he settles down on the sofa and doesn't budge all afternoon
[2] (= *apoyarse*) to prop o.s. (up); **se apalancó en la barra del bar y acabó borracho** he propped himself (up) on the bar and ended up drunk
[3] (= *instalarse*) to settle in; **no quiero que se apalanque en mi piso** I don't want him taking up residence in my flat
[4] (= *estancarse*) to vegetate, go to seed; **se mudó al pueblo y se apalancó** she moved to the village and just vegetated *o* went to seed

apalé EXCL (*Méx*) [1] (*sorpresa*) goodness me!
[2] (*aviso*) look out!, watch it!

apaleada SF (*Cono Sur, Méx*) winnowing

apaleamiento SM beating, thrashing

apalear ▸conjug 1a◂ VT [1] (= *zurrar*) to beat, thrash; [+ *moqueta*] to beat; **~ oro** ◊ **~ plata** to be rolling in money
[2] (*Agr*) to winnow

apaleo SM (= *paliza*) beating; (*Agr*) winnowing

apalizar* ▸conjug 1f◂ VT to beat up*

apallar ▸conjug 1a◂ VT (*Andes*) to harvest

apamparse ▸conjug 1a◂ VPR (*Cono Sur*) to become bewildered

apanado Ⓐ ADJ (*LAm*) breaded, cooked in breadcrumbs
Ⓑ SM (*Andes*) beating

apanalado ADJ honeycombed

apanar ▸conjug 1a◂ VT (*LAm*) to coat in breadcrumbs

apancle SM (*Méx*) irrigation ditch

apandar‡ ▸conjug 1a◂ VT to rip off‡, knock off‡

apandillar ▸conjug 1a◂ Ⓐ VT to form into a gang
Ⓑ **apandillarse** VPR to gang up, band together

apando SM (*Méx*) punishment cell

apandorgarse ▸conjug 1h◂ VPR (*Perú*) to become lazy

apani(a)guarse ▸conjug 1i◂ VPR (*Andes, Caribe*) to gang up

apanicar* ▸conjug 1g◂ VT (*Cono Sur*) to cause panic in, frighten

apantallado ADJ (*Méx*) (= *impresionado*) impressed, overwhelmed; (= *achatado*) overwhelmed, crushed; **quedar ~** (= *boquiabierto*) to be left open-mouthed

apantallar[1] ▸conjug 1a◂ VT to screen, shield

apantallar[2] ▸conjug 1a◂ VT (*Méx*) (= *impresionar*) to impress; (= *achatar*) to crush, overwhelm; (= *dejar boquiabierto*) to fill with wonder

apantanar ▸conjug 1a◂ VT to flood

apañado ADJ [1] (= *práctico*) [*persona*] clever; [*objeto*] handy
[2] (= *ordenado*) neat, tidy
[3] (*) **¡estás ~!** you've had it!; **estar ~ para hacer algo** to have difficulty in doing sth, have trouble doing sth; **estoy ~ si lo hago** I'll be in trouble if I do it; **~s estaríamos si confiáramos en eso** we'd be fools if we relied on that
[4] (*económicamente*) **los hijos quedarán bien ~s** the children will be well provided for

apañador(a) SM/F [1] (*Dep*) catcher
[2] (*) (= *amañador*) fixer*

apañar ▸conjug 1a◂ Ⓐ VT [1] (= *arreglar*) to fix; **¿me puedes ~ esta radio rota?** can you fix this broken radio for me?
[2] (*) (= *preparar*) to get ready; **apañó una cena con pocos ingredientes** he put together a dinner with just a few ingredients; **apañó la mesa antes de que llegaran los comensales** she got the table ready before the guests arrived; **apaña al niño que nos vamos pronto** get the child ready, we'll be going soon
[3] (= *amañar*) [+ *elecciones*] to rig*, fix*
[4] (*Méx*) (= *perdonar*) to forgive, let off
[5] (*Cono Sur*) (= *encubrir*) [+ *crimen*] to cover up; [+ *criminal*] to harbour, harbor (*EEUU*), hide
Ⓑ **apañarse** VPR [1] (*tb* **apañárselas**) to manage, get by; **yo me (las) apaño muy bien solo** I manage *o* get by very well on my own; **yo me (las) apaño con poco dinero** I get by *o* manage without much money; **ya me (las) ~é por mi cuenta** I'll manage *o* get by on my own; **apáñate(las) como puedas** you'll have to manage as best you can; **apáñate(las) con lo que tengas** make do with what you've got; **ya me (las) ~é para llegar a Sevilla** I'll find a way of getting to Seville somehow
[2] (*esp Cono Sur*) **~se algo** to get one's hands on sth, get hold of sth

apaño SM [1] (= *de algo roto*) **me hizo un ~ en el lavabo** he fixed up the washbasin for me; **esta radio no tiene ~** this radio can't be fixed; **el problema del fraude no tiene ~** there's no answer to the problem of fraud
[2] (= *chanchullo*) fix*; **el resultado del partido fue un ~** the match was a fix*, the match was fixed *o* rigged*; **hicieron un ~ para ga-**

nar las elecciones the election was fixed *o* rigged*

3 (= *componenda*) deal; **un ~ entre los partidos evitó su dimisión** a deal between the parties avoided him having to resign

4 (**) **estar para un ~** to be a gorgeous piece of ass**

5 (†) (= *amorío*) affair; (= *amante*) lover

apañuscar* ▸conjug 1g◂ VT 1 (= *ajar*) to rumple; (= *aplastar*) to crush

2 (= *robar*) to pinch*, steal

apapachar* ▸conjug 1a◂ (*Méx*) VT (= *mimar*) to spoil; (= *abrazar*) to cuddle, hug

apapachos* SMPL (*Méx*) (= *abrazos*) cuddles, hugs; (= *caricias*) caresses

aparador SM (= *mueble*) sideboard; (= *vitrina*) showcase; (*esp LAm*) (= *escaparate*) shop window; ✦*MODISMO* **estar de ~** to be dressed up to receive visitors

aparadorista SMF (*Méx*) window dresser

aparar† ▸conjug 1a◂ VT 1 (= *disponer*) to arrange, prepare

2 [+ *manos*] to stretch out (*to catch sth*)

3 (*Agr*) to weed, clean

aparatarse ▸conjug 1a◂ VPR (*Andes, Cono Sur*) **se aparata** it's brewing up for a storm, there's a storm coming

aparatejo* SM gadget

aparato SM 1 (*Téc*) machine; **uno de esos ~s para hacer café** one of those coffee machines *o* coffee-making things*; **un ~ para medir el nivel de contaminación** a device to measure pollution levels ► **aparato antirrobo** anti-theft device ► **aparato de escucha** listening device ► **aparato de medición** measuring instrument ► **aparato de relojería** clockwork mechanism ► **aparato fotográfico** photographic instrument, camera ► **aparato lector de microfilmes** microfilm reader ► **aparatos de mando** (*Aer*) controls ► **aparatos periféricos** (*Inform*) peripherals ► **aparatos sanitarios** bathroom fittings

2 (*Elec*) (= *electrodoméstico*) appliance; (= *televisor, radio*) set; **~ de uso doméstico** domestic appliance ► **aparato de radio** radio ► **aparato de televisión** television set ► **aparato eléctrico** electrical appliance

3 (*Telec*) phone, telephone; **al ~: —¿puedo hablar con Pilar Ruiz? —al ~** "can I speak to Pilar Ruiz?" — "speaking"; **¡Gerardo, al ~!** Gerardo, telephone!; **colgar el ~** to put down the phone, hang up; **ponerse al ~** to come to the phone; **tener a algn al ~** to have sb on the line

4 (*Med*) **ya respira sin ayuda del ~** she can now breath without the apparatus *o* device ► **aparato auditivo** hearing aid ► **aparato circulatorio** circulatory system ► **aparato dental, aparato de ortodoncia** brace, braces *pl* (*EEUU*) ► **aparato digestivo** digestive system ► **aparato genital femenino** female genitalia ► **aparato genital masculino** male genitalia ► **aparato ortopédico** surgical appliance, orthopedic aid ► **aparato para sordos** hearing aid ► **aparato respiratorio** respiratory system

5 (*Gimnasia*) (= *máquina*) exercise machine, fitness machine; (= *anillas, barras*) piece of apparatus; **fallaron en casi todos los ~s** they failed on almost all the apparatus

6 (*Aer*) aircraft, airplane (*EEUU*)

7 (= *formalismo, artificio*) **todo el ~ con el que viaja un rey** all the pomp and ceremony which accompanies a king when he travels; **el festival llevaba un gran ~ de protocolo** the festival was accompanied by a great show of protocol; **viaja sin ~ ceremonial** he travels without any ceremonial escort; **nos lo contó con gran ~ de misterio** she told us all about it with a great air of mystery

8 (*Pol*) (= *estructura*) [*de base*] machine; [*de control*] machinery; **el ~ del partido** the party machine, the party apparatus; **un fuerte ~ publicitario** a powerful publicity machine; **ven a la Iglesia como un ~ de poder** they see the Church as a power structure ► **aparato electoral** electoral machine; ► **aparato estatal** state system, government machinery

9 (*Met*) **una tormenta con gran ~ eléctrico** a storm with a great deal of thunder and lightning

10 (= *indicios*) signs *pl*, symptoms *pl*; (*Med*) symptoms *pl*; (*Psic*) syndrome

11 (*Literat*) ► **aparato crítico** critical apparatus

12 (*) (= *pene*) equipment*; (= *vagina*) pussy**

aparatosamente ADV spectacularly; **el torero fue volteado ~ en el aire** the bullfighter was tossed up in the air spectacularly; **se marcharon ~ de la reunión** they marched out of the meeting in a dramatic way

aparatosidad SF 1 (= *exageración*) showiness, ostentation

2 [*de accidente, caída*] spectacular nature

aparatoso ADJ 1 (= *exagerado*) [*persona, gestos*] showy, ostentatious; [*objeto, ropa*] flamboyant; **la boda fue muy aparatosa** the wedding was very extravagant *o* over the top*; **¡qué ~ eres al hablar!** you've got such a showy *o* flamboyant way of speaking

2 [*accidente, caída*] spectacular, dramatic

aparcacoches SMF INV car park attendant

aparcadero SM car park, parking lot (*EEUU*)

aparcamiento SM, **aparcamento** SM (*CAm, Caribe*) 1 (= *acción*) parking ► **aparcamiento en doble fila** double parking

2 (= *lugar*) car park, parking lot (*EEUU*) ► **aparcamiento subterráneo** underground car park

3 (= *apartadero*) lay-by

aparcar ▸conjug 1g◂ Ⓐ VT 1 [+ *vehículo*] to park

2 (*) (= *aplazar*) [+ *proyecto de ley*] to shelve; [+ *idea*] to put on the back burner

Ⓑ VI to park

aparcería SF 1 (*Com*) partnership; (*Agr*) share-cropping

2 (*Cono Sur*) (= *compañerismo*) comradeship, friendship

aparcero/a SM/F 1 (*Com*) co-owner, partner; (*Agr*) sharecropper

2 (*Cono Sur*) (= *compañero*) comrade, friend

apareamiento SM 1 [*de animales*] mating

2 [*de objetos*] matching, pairing

aparear ▸conjug 1a◂ Ⓐ VT 1 [+ *animales*] to mate

2 [+ *objetos*] to pair, match

Ⓑ **aparearse** VPR [*animales*] to mate

aparecer ▸conjug 2d◂ Ⓐ VI 1 (= *presentarse*) to appear, turn up*; **apareció en casa sin avisar** he appeared *o* turned up* at the house without warning; **apareció borracho** he turned up drunk

2 [*algo oculto*] to appear, turn up*; **aparecieron dos nuevos cadáveres en la fosa** two more bodies appeared *o* turned up* in the trench

3 [*algo perdido*] to reappear, turn up*; **ya ha aparecido mi paraguas** my umbrella has finally reappeared *o* turned up*

4 (= *surgir*) to appear; **han aparecido los primeros síntomas** the first symptoms have appeared; **han aparecido pintadas en la fachada del ayuntamiento** some graffiti has appeared on the front of the town hall

5 (= *editarse*) [*libro, disco*] to come out

6 (= *figurar*) [*dato, nombre*] to appear; **mi nombre no aparece en el censo electoral** my name does not appear on the electoral register, my name is not on the electoral register; **aparece brevemente en una película reciente** he appears briefly in a recent film

Ⓑ **aparecerse** VPR [*fantasma, espíritu*] to appear; **Nuestra Señora se apareció a Bernadette** Our Lady appeared to Bernadette

aparecido/a SM/F ghost

aparejado ADJ 1 (= *apto*) fit, suitable; (= *listo*) ready (**para** for)

2 (*fig*) **ir ~ con** (= *ser inseparables*) to go hand in hand with; **llevar** *o* **traer algo ~** (= *traer consigo*) to entail sth

aparejador(a) SM/F 1 (*en una obra*) (= *capataz*) clerk of works; (*Arquit*) master builder; (= *encargado de la administración*) quantity surveyor

2 (*Náut*) rigger

aparejar ▸conjug 1a◂ Ⓐ VT (= *preparar*) to prepare, get ready; [+ *caballo*] to saddle, harness; (*Náut*) to fit out, rig out; [+ *lienzo*] to size, prime

Ⓑ **aparejarse** VPR 1 (= *prepararse*) to get ready; (= *equiparse*) to equip o.s.

2 (*CAm, Caribe*) to mate, pair

aparejo SM 1 (= *acto*) preparation

2 (= *herramientas*) gear, equipment

3 [*de caballería*] (= *arreos*) harness; (*CAm, Méx*) (= *silla*) saddle; (*Andes*) (= *silla de mujer*) woman's saddle

4 (*Pesca*) ► **aparejo de anzuelos** set of hooks ► **aparejos de pesca** fishing tackle

5 (= *poleas*) lifting gear, block and tackle

6 (*Náut*) rigging

7 (*Arquit*) bond, bonding

8 (*Arte*) sizing, priming

aparellaje SM control gear

aparencial ADJ apparent

aparentar ▸conjug 1a◂ Ⓐ VT 1 (= *parecer*) to look; **no aparenta su edad** *o* **sus años** she doesn't look her age; **aparenta menos años de los que tiene** he looks younger than he is; **aparenta ser más joven de lo que es** he looks younger than he is

2 (= *fingir*) [+ *interés, sorpresa, indiferencia*] to feign; **aparentó ignorancia de su obra** (*frm*) she feigned ignorance of his work, she pretended not to know his work; **aparenta estar estudiando** he pretends to be studying; **tendrás que ~ que te encanta** you'll have to pretend you love it

Ⓑ VI to show off; **le gusta mucho ~** he really likes showing off

aparente ADJ 1 (= *no real*) apparent; **su interés es sólo ~** he just pretends to be interested, he just feigns interest

2 (= *patente*) apparent; **no hubo lesión ~** there was no apparent injury; **sin motivo ~** for no apparent reason; **ganó la carrera sin esfuerzo ~** she won the race with no apparent effort

3 (*) (= *atractivo*) attractive, smart; **tiene un novio muy ~** she has a very good-looking boyfriend; **esta figurilla está aquí muy ~** this figurine looks very good *o* goes very well here

aparentemente ADV 1 (= *según parece*) seemingly

2 (= *evidentemente*) visibly, outwardly

aparición SF 1 (= *acto*) appearance; (= *publicación*) publication; **un libro de próxima ~** a forthcoming book ► **aparición en público** public appearance

2 (= *aparecido*) apparition, spectre

apariencia SF (= *aspecto*) appearance; **tiene la misma ~ que el planeta Tierra** it has the same appearance as planet Earth; **la misma ~ del resto de los estudiantes** the same appearance as the rest of the students; **bajo su ~ despistada hay un genio** behind his absent-minded appearance he is a genius; **con ~ de**: **una chica con ~ de alemana** a German-looking girl; **un jarabe con ~ de miel** a syrup that looks like honey; **de ~**: **una herida de sospechosa ~** a suspicious-looking wound; **es rico sólo de ~** he only appears to be rich; **en ~**: **José, en ~ rudo, es muy cortés** although José may seem *o* appear rude on the surface, he is very polite; **en ~, el coche estaba perfecto** to all appearances, the car was in perfect condition; **guardar** *o* **salvar las ~s** to keep up appearances; ✦*MODISMO* **las ~s engañan** appearances can be deceptive; *ver tb* **fiar C1**

aparragado/a (*Cono Sur*) Ⓐ ADJ stunted, dwarfish

Ⓑ SM/F dwarf

aparragarse ▸conjug 1h◂ VPR 1 (*CAm*) (= *hacerse un ovillo*) to roll up, curl up

2 (*Cono Sur*) (= *agacharse*) to squat, crouch down

3 (*CAm, Cono Sur, Méx*) (= *no crecer*) to remain stunted, stay small; (= *encogerse*) to shrink, grow small

apartadero SM (*Aut*) lay-by; (*Ferro*) siding

apartadijo SM 1 (= *porción*) small portion, bit

2 = **apartadizo B**

apartadizo Ⓐ ADJ (= *huraño*) unsociable

Ⓑ SM recess, alcove, nook

apartado Ⓐ ADJ 1 (= *lejano*) remote, isolated; **un pueblo muy ~** a very remote *o* isolated village; **su casa está un poco apartada** her house is a bit out-of-the-way; **~ de** [*lugar*] far from; [*persona*] isolated from; **donde vivía, estaba ~ de todos nosotros** where he lived he was isolated from us all; **ha conseguido mantenerse ~ de los problemas** she's managed to keep out of the problems

2 (= *solitario*) [*vida, persona*] solitary

Ⓑ SM 1 (*Correos*) (*tb* **~ de correos**) (*tb* **~ postal**) Post Office box, P.O. Box, box number; **~ de correos 325** P.O. Box 325

2 (= *sección*) (*Literat*) section; (*Jur*) section, sub-section; **vamos a empezar por el ~ dedicado a la economía** let's begin with the section on the economy; **en el ~ de sanidad han aumentado los gastos** in the area of health, costs have increased

3 (= *sala*) spare room, side room ► **apartado de localidades** ticket agency

4 (*Metal*) extraction

apartahotel SM aparthotel

apartamento SM apartment, flat ► **apartamentos turísticos** holiday apartments

apartamiento SM 1 (= *separación*) separation

2 (= *aislamiento*) seclusion, isolation

3 (= *lugar*) secluded spot, remote area

apartar ▸conjug 1a◂ Ⓐ VT 1 (= *alejar*) **aparta las piezas blancas de las negras** separate the white pieces from the black ones; **aparta la sartén del fuego** take the pan off the heat; **lograron ~ la discusión de ese punto** they managed to turn the discussion away from that point; **no podía ~ mi pensamiento de ella** I couldn't get her out of my head; **~ la mirada/los ojos de algo** to look away from sth, avert one's gaze/one's eyes from sth (*liter*); **apartó la mirada de la larga fila de casas** she looked away from *o* (*liter*) averted her gaze from the long row of houses; **no aparta los ojos de la comida** he can't keep his eyes off the food

2 (= *quitar de en medio*) **tuvo que ~ los papeles de la mesa para colocar allí sus libros** he had to push aside the papers on the table to place his books there; **apartó el micrófono a un lado** she put the microphone aside *o* to one side; **apartó la cortina y miró a la calle** he drew *o* pulled back the curtain and looked out into the street; **le apartó los cabellos de la frente** she brushed her hair off her forehead; **avanzaban apartando la maleza** they made their way through the undergrowth, pushing *o* brushing it aside as they went

3 [+ *persona*] 3·1 (*de lugar*) **lo apartó un poco para hacerle algunas preguntas** she took him to one side to ask him a few questions; **los guardaespaldas apartaban a las fans** the bodyguards pushed the fans aside *o* away; **aparta al niño de la ventana** move the child away from the window

3·2 (*de otra persona*) (*lit*) to separate; (*fig*) to drift apart; **si no los apartamos se matarán** if we don't separate them they'll kill each other; **el tiempo los ha ido apartando** they have grown *o* drifted apart with time

3·3 (*de actividad, puesto*) to remove; **el ministro lo apartó de su puesto** the minister removed him from his post; **su enfermedad la apartó de la política activa** her illness kept her away from playing an active role in politics; **si yo fuera el entrenador, lo ~ía del equipo** if I was the coach I would remove him from the team; **lo ~on de su intención de vender la casa** they dissuaded him from selling the house

4 (= *reservar*) to put aside, set aside; **si le interesa este vestido se lo puedo ~** if you like this dress I can put *o* set it aside for you; **"se apartan muebles"** "a deposit secures any piece of furniture"; **hemos apartado un poco de comida para él** we've put *o* set aside a little food for him; **picar las verduras y ~las a un lado** chop the vegetables and put them to one side

5 (*Correos*) to sort

6 (*Ferro*) to shunt, switch (*EEUU*)

7 (*Agr*) [+ *ganado*] to separate, cut out

8 (*Jur*) to set aside, waive

9 (*Min*) to extract

Ⓑ **apartarse** VPR 1 (= *quitarse de en medio*) to move out of the way; **¿puedes ~te un poco?** can you move out of the way a bit?; **se apartó a tiempo para evitar el puñetazo** he moved aside *o* moved out of the way to avoid the punch; **se ~on para dejarla pasar** they moved aside to let her through; **¡apártense! ¡que está herido!** out of the way *o* stand clear! he's wounded!; **se apartó unos pasos** she moved *o* walked away a few paces; **~se de** [+ *persona, lugar, teoría*] to move away from; [+ *camino, ruta*] to stray from, wander off; [+ *actividad, creencia*] to abandon; **nos apartamos unos metros del vehículo** we moved a few metres away from the vehicle; **apártate del fuego** get *o* move away from the fire; **nunca se aparta de mi lado** she never leaves my side; **nunca se apartó de esta regla** he never strayed from this rule; **se apartó de la política** she left *o* abandoned politics; **no se aparta del teléfono por si suena** she's always sitting by the phone in case it rings; **consiguió ~se de la bebida** he managed to give up drinking; **¡apártate de mi vista!** get out of my sight!; ✦*MODISMO* **~se del buen camino** to go off the straight and narrow

2 (= *distanciarse*) [*dos personas*] to part, separate; [*dos objetos*] to become separated; **con el tiempo se han ido apartando** they have drifted *o* grown apart with time; **las cifras se apartan de las predicciones** the figures are far off the predictions; **esta novela se aparta del estilo del resto de su obra** this novel is a far cry from the style of the rest of his work; **el libro se aparta del realismo sentimentalista** the book diverges *o* strays from sentimentalist realism

3 (*Jur*) to withdraw from a suit

aparte Ⓐ ADJ INV separate; **guárdalo en un cajón ~** keep it in a different *o* separate drawer; **lo tuyo es un caso ~** you're a special case; **capítulo ~ merece la corrupción política** another question altogether is political corruption; **mantenerse ~** to keep away

Ⓑ ADV 1 (= *a un lado*) **se la llevó ~ para contarle sus confidencias** he took her aside to confide in her; **bromas ~, ¿qué os parece que me vaya a vivir a El Cairo?** joking aside *o* seriously though, what do you think of me going to live in Cairo?; **diferencias ideológicas ~, perseguimos el mismo fin** ideological differences aside, we're after the same thing; **dejando ~ el norte, este país no es muy montañoso** leaving aside the north, this country is not very mountainous; **hacerle a algn ~** to exclude sb; **poner algo ~** to put sth aside; **la ropa sucia ponla ~** put the dirty clothes to one side, put aside the dirty clothes; **ser algo ~** to be something superior; *ver tb* **modestia**

2 (= *por separado*) separately; **tendremos que considerar eso ~** we'll have to consider that separately; **deberías lavar las toallas ~** you should wash the towels separately

3 (= *además*) besides; **~, yo ya soy mayorcita para que me manden** besides, I'm too old to be bossed about like that; **—¿y no paga el alquiler? —sí, eso ~** "and he doesn't pay the rent?" — "yes, that as well"; **300 euros, ~ impuestos** 300 euros, taxes aside; **~ hay un examen práctico** there is also a practical

exam

Ⓒ PREP ~ **de** apart from; **~ del mal tiempo, las vacaciones fueron estupendas** apart from the bad weather, the holidays were great; **~ de que** apart from the fact that

Ⓓ SM 1 (*Teat*) aside; **hacer un ~ con algn** to take sb to one side

2 (*Tip*) paragraph, new paragraph; **punto y ~** new paragraph

apartheid SM apartheid

aparthotel SM aparthotel

apartidismo SM non-political nature, non-party character

apartidista ADJ apolitical, non-party *antes de s*

apasionadamente ADV 1 (= *con pasión*) passionately

2 (*pey*) (= *con parcialidad*) in a biased way, in a prejudiced way

apasionado/a Ⓐ ADJ 1 (= *con pasión*) [*persona*] passionate; [*discurso*] impassioned; **~ por algo** passionate about sth

2 (= *parcial*) biased, prejudiced

Ⓑ SM/F admirer, devotee; **los ~s de Góngora** devotees of Góngora, Góngora enthusiasts

apasionamiento SM (= *entusiasmo*) passion, enthusiasm; (= *fervor*) vehemence, intensity; **hacer algo con ~** to do sth with passion

apasionante ADJ exciting, thrilling

apasionar ▸conjug 1a◂ Ⓐ VT 1 (= *entusiasmar*) **le apasiona el teatro de Shakespeare** he loves Shakespeare's plays; **le apasionan los ordenadores** he's mad about computers; **el grupo que apasiona a las quinceañeras** the group the teenagers are mad about; **a mí el fútbol no me apasiona** I'm not exactly passionate about football

2 (*frm*) (= *afligir*) to afflict, torment

Ⓑ **apasionarse** VPR to get excited; **cuando habla de literatura se apasiona** she gets very excited when she talks about literature; **~se con algo** to get excited about sth; **~se por algo**: **se apasionó por la idea de una Europa única** he became very excited by the idea of a United Europe; **~se por algn** to fall madly in love with sb

apaste SM (*CAm*), **apaxte** SM (*CAm*) clay pot, clay jug

apatía SF (= *abulia*) apathy; (*Med*) listlessness

apático ADJ (= *abúlico*) apathetic; (*Med*) listless

apátrida Ⓐ ADJ 1 (= *sin nacionalidad*) stateless

2 (*Cono Sur*) (= *sin patriotismo*) unpatriotic

Ⓑ SMF (*Cono Sur*) unpatriotic person

apatronarse ▸conjug 1a◂ VPR (*Andes, Cono Sur*) **~ de algn** (= *amancebarse*) to find a protector in sb; (= *buscar empleo*) to seek a domestic post with sb; (*Andes*) (= *encargarse*) to take charge of sb

apatusco SM 1 (= *adornos*) frills *pl*, adornments *pl*

2 (*Caribe*) (= *enredo*) trick; (= *fingimiento*) pretence, pretense (*EEUU*); (= *intrigas*) intrigue

APD SF ABR (*Esp*) = **Asociación para el Progreso de la Dirección**

Apdo. ABR, **apdo.** ABR (= **apartado postal** *o* **de correos**) P.O. Box

apeadero SM 1 (*para montar*) mounting block, step

2 (*Ferro*) halt, stopping place

3 (= *alojamiento*) temporary lodging, pied-à-terre

apear ▸conjug 1a◂ Ⓐ VT 1 (= *ayudar a bajar*) to help down, help to alight (**de** from); [+ *objeto*] to take down, get down (**de** from); [+ *árbol*] to fell

2 [+ *caballo*] to hobble; [+ *rueda*] to chock

3 (*Arquit*) to prop up

4 [+ *problema*] to solve, work out; [+ *dificultad*] to overcome

5 (= *disuadir*) **~ a algn de su opinión** to persuade sb that his opinion is wrong

6 **~ el tratamiento a algn** (= *suprimir el tratamiento*) to drop sb's title

7 (*) (= *despedir*) to give the boot*, sack*; **~ a algn de su cargo** to remove sb from his post

8 (*Andes*) (= *matar*) to kill

9 (*CAm*) (= *reprender*) to dress down*, tell off*

Ⓑ **apearse** VPR 1 (= *bajarse*) (*de caballo, mula*) to dismount; (*de tren, autobús*) to get off, alight (*frm*); **yo me apeo en la próxima parada** I'm getting off at the next stop; ✦*MODISMO* **no ~se del burro** to refuse to climb *o* back down

2 **~se en** (*LAm*) to stay at, put up at

3 **~se de algo** (*Andes*) (= *librarse*) to get rid of sth

4 **no apeársela** (*CAm*) (= *estar borracho*) to be drunk all the time

apechugar* ▸conjug 1h◂ Ⓐ VI 1 (= *empujar*) to push, shove; **¡apechuga!** (= *ánimo*) buck up!, come on!

2 **~ con** (= *aguantar*) to put up with, swallow; [+ *cometido*] (= *cargar con*) to take on; **~ con las consecuencias** to take the consequences

Ⓑ VT 1 (*Cono Sur, Caribe*) (= *agarrar*) to grab, grab hold of, seize

2 (*Andes*) (= *sacudir*) to shake violently

Ⓒ **apechugarse** VPR **~se con algo** to face up to sth, take the consequences of sth

apedazar ▸conjug 1f◂ VT 1 (= *remendar*) to mend, patch

2 (= *despedazar*) to tear to pieces, cut into pieces

apedrear ▸conjug 1a◂ Ⓐ VT (*como castigo*) to stone; (*en pelea*) to throw stones at

Ⓑ VI 1 (= *granizar*) to hail

2 (*Méx‡*) (= *apestar*) to stink, reek

Ⓒ **apedrearse** VPR (*Bot*) to be damaged by hail

apedreo SM 1 (= *acto*) stoning

2 (= *granizo*) hail

3 (*Bot*) damage by hail

apegadamente ADV devotedly

apegado ADJ attached, devoted (**a** to)

apegarse ▸conjug 1h◂ VPR **~ a** to become attached to, become devoted to

apego SM attachment (**a** to), devotion (**a** to)

apelable ADJ (*Jur*) appealable, that can be appealed against, subject to appeal

apelación SF 1 (*Jur*) appeal; **sin ~** without appeal, final; **interponer ~** to appeal, lodge an appeal; **presentar su ~** to present one's appeal; **ver una ~** to consider an appeal

2 (= *remedio*) help, remedy; **no hay ~** ◊ **esto no tiene ~** it's a hopeless case

apelante SMF appellant

apelar ▸conjug 1a◂ Ⓐ VI 1 (*Jur*) to appeal; **~ contra algo** to appeal (against) sth

2 **~ a** 2·1 (= *invocar*) to appeal to; **apeló al sentido común para resolver el problema** he appealed to people's common sense to solve the problem; **apelamos al presidente a que cumpla sus compromisos** we appeal to the president to keep his promises

2·2 (= *recurrir a*) to resort to; **tuvo que ~ a sus encantos personales** she had to resort to charm, she had to make use of her charm

Ⓑ VT (*Jur*) to appeal (against); **han apelado la sentencia** they have appealed (against) the sentence

apelativo SM (*Ling*) appellative; (= *apellido*) surname

apeldar‡ ▸conjug 1a◂ VT **~las** to beat it*

apellidar ▸conjug 1a◂ Ⓐ VT 1 (= *llamar*) to call

2 (††) (= *aclamar*) **~ a algn por rey** to proclaim sb king

Ⓑ **apellidarse** VPR to be called; **¿cómo se apellida usted?** what's your surname?

apellido SM 1 (= *nombre de familia*) surname, family name ► **apellido de soltera** maiden name

2 (= *apodo*) nickname

> **APELLIDO**
>
> *In the Spanish-speaking world most people use two* **apellidos**, *the first being their father's first surname, and the second their mother's first surname: e.g. the surname of the children of Juan* **García López**, *married to Carmen* **Pérez Rodríguez** *would be* **García Pérez**. *Married women normally retain their own surnames but in exceptional cases they add their husband's first surname to their first surname: e.g. Carmen Pérez de García. In such cases she could also be referred to as* **(la) señora de García**. *In Latin America it is usual for the second surname to be shortened to an initial in correspondence: e.g. Juan García L.*

apelmazado ADJ 1 [*masa*] compact, solid; [*salsa, líquido*] thick, lumpy; [*pelo*] matted

2 [*estilo*] clumsy

apelmazar ▸conjug 1f◂ Ⓐ VT to compress

Ⓑ **apelmazarse** VPR to get lumpy

apelotonar ▸conjug 1a◂ Ⓐ VT to roll into a ball

Ⓑ **apelotonarse** VPR [*colchón*] to become lumpy; [*animal*] to curl up, curl up into a ball; [*gente*] to mass, crowd together

apenado ADJ 1 (= *triste*) sorry

2 (*LAm*) (= *avergonzado*) ashamed, embarrassed; (= *tímido*) shy, timid

apenar ▸conjug 1a◂ Ⓐ VT 1 (= *afligir*) to grieve, cause pain to

2 (*LAm*) (= *avergonzar*) to shame

Ⓑ **apenarse** VPR 1 (= *afligirse*) to grieve, distress o.s.; **~se de** *o* **por algo** to grieve about sth, distress o.s. on account of sth

2 (*LAm*) (= *avergonzarse*) to be ashamed; (= *ser triste*) to be sorry, be sad; (= *ser tímido*) to be shy; (= *sonrojarse*) to blush; **no se apene, no tiene importancia** (*Méx*) don't worry, it doesn't matter

▼ **apenas** Ⓐ ADV 1 (= *casi no*) hardly, scarcely (*más frm*); **~ consigo dormir** I can hardly *o* scarcely *o* barely sleep; **—¿has leído mucho últimamente? —apenas** "have you been reading much lately?" — "hardly anything"; **cocinan sin ~ aceite** they cook with hardly any oil; **siguió trabajando durante horas, sin ~ acusar el cansancio** he went on

➤ LENGUA Y USO: apenas A1 43.2

working for hours, without hardly showing signs of tiredness; **~ nada** hardly anything; **no recuerdo ~ nada** I don't remember hardly anything; **no sé ~ nada de ese tema** I don't know hardly anything about that subject, I know almost nothing *o* next to nothing about that subject; **~ nadie** hardly anybody; **~ sí: ~ si nos habló durante toda la cena** he hardly *o* barely *o* scarcely said a word to us throughout the whole dinner; **~ si nos queda dinero** we have hardly any money left
[2] (= *casi nunca*) hardly ever; **ahora ~ voy** I hardly ever go now
[3] (= *escasamente*) only; **faltan ~ cinco minutos** there's only five minutes to go; **hace ~ un año que nos conocimos** it's only a year ago that we met; **había muy pocos alumnos, ~ diez o doce** there were very few students, only *o* barely ten or twelve; **yo ~ tenía catorce años** I was barely fourteen, I was only just fourteen
[4] (= *solamente*) only; **~ voy por la página cinco** I'm only on page five; **~ entonces me di cuenta de lo que pasaba** it was only then that I realized what was happening
Ⓑ CONJ (*esp LAm*) (= *en cuanto*) as soon as; **abandonaron la ciudad ~ amanecido** they left the city as soon as it got light; **~ llegue, te llamo** I'll phone you as soon as I arrive; **~ había cumplido quince años cuando ...** he'd only just turned fifteen when ...

APENAS

El adverbio **apenas** tiene dos traducciones principales en inglés: **hardly** y **scarcely**, este último usado en lenguaje más formal.

- Estos adverbios se colocan normalmente detrás de los verbos auxiliares y modales y delante de los demás verbos:

  Apenas podía hablar después del accidente
  He could hardly** o **scarcely speak after the accident
  Apenas nos conocemos
  We hardly** o **scarcely know each other

- Sin embargo, en oraciones temporales, podemos colocar **hardly** y **scarcely** al principio de la oración si queremos reforzar la inmediatez de algo, o como recurso estilístico en cuentos y relatos. En este caso los adverbios van siempre seguidos de un verbo auxiliar, con lo que se invierte el orden normal del sujeto y el verbo en inglés, quedando la estructura **hardly/ scarcely** + **had** + **SUJETO** + **PARTICIPIO** + **when** ... :

  Apenas me había acostado cuando oí un ruido extraño
  Hardly** o **Scarcely had I gone to bed when I heard a strange noise

NOTA: En este sentido se suele utilizar también **no sooner** + **had** + **SUJETO** + **PARTICIPIO** + **than** ... :

  No sooner had I gone to bed than I heard a strange noise

Para otros usos y ejemplos ver la entrada.

apencar* ▸conjug 1g◂ VI to slog away*, slave away*

apendectomía SF appendectomy

apendejarse ▸conjug 1a◂ VPR (*Caribe*) (= *hacer el tonto*) to get silly, act the fool; (= *acobardarse*) to lose one's nerve

apéndice SM [1] (*Anat, Literat*) appendix; (*Jur*) schedule
[2] (*fig*) (= *satélite*) appendage

apendicitis SF INV appendicitis

Apeninos SMPL Apennines

apenitas ADV (*Andes, Cono Sur*) = **apenas**

apensionado ADJ (*Andes, Cono Sur, Méx*) sad, depressed

apensionar ▸conjug 1a◂ Ⓐ VT (*Andes, Cono Sur, Méx*) to sadden, grieve
Ⓑ **apensionarse** VPR to become sad, get depressed

apeñuscarse ▸conjug 1g◂ VPR (*Cono Sur*) to crowd together

apeo SM [1] (*Jur*) surveying
[2] (*Arquit*) (= *soporte*) prop, support; (= *andamio*) scaffolding
[3] (*Agr*) felling

apeorar ▸conjug 1a◂ VI to get worse

aperado ADJ (*Cono Sur*) well-equipped

aperar ▸conjug 1a◂ Ⓐ VT [1] [+ *aparejo*] to repair
[2] [+ *caballo*] to harness
[3] (= *abastecer*) **~ a algn de herramientas** to provide *o* equip sb with tools
Ⓑ **aperarse** VPR **~se de algo** to equip o.s. with sth, provide o.s. with sth; **estar bien aperado para** to be well equipped for

apercancarse ▸conjug 1g◂ VPR (*Cono Sur*) to go mouldy, go moldy (*EEUU*)

aperchar ▸conjug 1a◂ VT (*CAm, Cono Sur*) to pile up, stack up

apercibimiento SM [1] (= *preparación*) preparation
[2] (= *aviso*) warning
[3] (*Jur*) caution

apercibir ▸conjug 3a◂ Ⓐ VT [1] (= *preparar*) to prepare; (= *proveer*) to furnish; **con los fusiles apercibidos** with rifles at the ready
[2] (= *avisar*) to warn, advise
[3] (*Jur*) to caution
[4] (= *ver*) to notice, see
[5] [+ *error etc*] = **percibir**
Ⓑ **apercibirse** VPR to prepare, prepare o.s., get ready (**para** for); **~se de** (= *proveerse*) to provide *o* equip o.s. with; (= *percibir*) to notice

apercollar ▸conjug 1l◂ VT [1] (= *agarrar*) to seize by the neck
[2] (= *matar*) to fell, kill (*with a blow on the neck*)
[3] (‡) (= *detener*) to knock off‡, nick‡

apergaminado ADJ [*papel*] parchment-like; [*piel*] dried up, wrinkled; [*cara*] wizened

apergaminarse ▸conjug 1a◂ VPR [*papel*] to become like parchment; [*piel*] to dry up, get yellow and wrinkled

apergollar ▸conjug 1a◂ VT (*LAm*) (= *agarrar*) to grab by the throat; (= *engañar*) to trap, ensnare

aperital SM (*Cono Sur*) = **aperitivo**

aperitivo SM (= *comida*) appetizer; (= *bebida*) aperitif

apero SM [1] (*Agr*) (= *instrumento*) implement; (= *animales*) ploughing team, plowing team (*EEUU*)
[2] (*LAm*) (= *arneses*) harness, trappings *pl*; (*LAm*) (= *silla*) saddle
[3] **aperos** (*Agr*) (= *equipo*) farm equipment *sing*

aperrarse* ▸conjug 1a◂ VPR (*Cono Sur*) to dig one's heels in

aperreado* ADJ wretched, lousy*; **llevar una vida aperreada** to lead a wretched *o* lousy* life

aperreador* ADJ bothersome, tiresome

aperrear ▸conjug 1a◂ Ⓐ VT [1] (= *azuzar perros contra*) to set the dogs on
[2] (*) (= *acosar*) to plague; (= *cansar*) to wear out, tire out
Ⓑ **aperrearse** VPR (*) [1] (= *ser acosado*) to get harassed; (= *trabajar demasiado*) to slave away*, overwork
[2] (*LAm*) (= *insistir*) to insist

aperreo* SM [1] (= *trabajo duro*) overwork; (= *problema*) harassment, worry
[2] (*LAm*) (= *molestia*) nuisance; (= *ira*) rage; **¡qué ~ de vida!** it's a dog's life!, what a life!

apersogar ▸conjug 1h◂ VT [+ *animal*] to tether, tie up; (*Caribe*) (= *atar cosas juntas*) to string together

apersonado ADJ **bien ~** presentable, nice-looking; **mal ~** unprepossessing

apersonarse ▸conjug 1a◂ VPR (*Jur*) to appear in person; (*Com*) to have a business interview

apertura SF [1] (= *acción*) opening; **la ~ de la caja torácica es una operación delicada** the opening of the rib cage is a delicate operation, opening the rib cage is a delicate operation; **la ~ del cajón activó la bomba** opening the box set off the bomb; **la ~ de la cuenta bancaria requiere tiempo** opening a bank account takes time; **la ~ de las puertas es automática** the doors open automatically
[2] (= *comienzo*) start, beginning; **hoy se celebra la ~ del curso académico** today is the start *o* beginning of the new academic year; **la ~ del plazo de matrícula se ha aplazado** the starting date for enrolment has been postponed; **la ~ del juicio se realiza hoy** the trial opens today; **ceremonia de ~** opening ceremony; **sesión de ~** opening session
[3] (*Fot*) aperture
[4] (*Pol*) (= *liberalización*) opening-up; **la ~ política tras la muerte de Franco** the political opening-up after Franco's death
[5] (*Jur*) [*de testamento*] reading; **~ de un juicio hipotecario** foreclosure
[6] (*Ajedrez*) opening

aperturar ▸conjug 1a◂ VT to open

aperturismo SM (= *liberalización*) liberalization, relaxation; (*Pol*) (= *política*) policy of liberalization

APERTURISMO

In the final years of the Franco régime and after Franco's death in 1975, politicians who wanted to liberalize and democratize the political system were known as **aperturistas** *while die-hard right-wingers who wanted the régime or something very similar to continue were known as* **inmovilistas***.*

⇨ *See also* TRANSICIÓN A LA DEMOCRACIA

aperturista Ⓐ ADJ [*tendencia etc*] liberalizing, liberal
Ⓑ SMF liberalizer, liberal

apesadumbrado ADJ sad, distressed

apesadumbrar ▸conjug 1a◂ Ⓐ VT to grieve, sadden
Ⓑ **apesadumbrarse** VPR to be grieved, distress o.s. (**con, de** about, at)

apesarar(se) ▸conjug 1a◂ = **apesadumbrar**

apescollar ▸conjug 1l◂ VT (*Cono Sur*) to seize by the neck

apesgar ▸conjug 1h◂ VT to weigh down

apestado ADJ [1] (= *maloliente*) stinking, reeking; (*Med*) plague-ridden
[2] **estar ~ de** (= *repleto*) to be infested with

apestar ▸conjug 1a◂ Ⓐ VT [1] (*Med*) to infect (*with the plague*)
[2] (*con olor*) to stink out
[3] (*fig*) (= *corromper*) to corrupt, spoil, vitiate (*frm*); (= *molestar*) to plague, harass; (= *repugnar*) to sicken, nauseate
Ⓑ VI to stink, reek (**a** of)
Ⓒ **apestarse** VPR [1] (*Med*) (*con la peste*) to catch the plague; (*Andes, Cono Sur*) (= *resfriarse*) to catch a cold
[2] (*Bot*) to be blighted

apestillar ▸conjug 1a◂ VT (*Cono Sur*) [1] (= *agarrar*) to catch, grab hold of
[2] (= *regañar*) to tell off, reprimand

apestoso ADJ [1] (= *hediondo*) stinking, reeking; [*olor*] awful, putrid
[2] (= *asqueroso*) sickening, nauseating; (= *molesto*) annoying, pestilential

apetachar ▸conjug 1a◂ VT to patch, mend

▼**apetecer** ▸conjug 2d◂ Ⓐ VT [1] (= *desear*) to crave, long for
[2] (= *atraer*) **me apetece un helado** I feel like *o* I fancy an ice cream; **¿te apetece?** how about it?, would you like to?
Ⓑ VI **la idea no apetece** the idea has no appeal *o* is not very attractive; **un vaso de jerez siempre apetece** a glass of sherry is always welcome

apetecible ADJ attractive, tempting

apetencia SF hunger (**de** for)

apetente ADJ hungry

APETI SF ABR = **Asociación Profesional Española de Traductores e Intérpretes**

apetite† SM [1] (= *condimento*) seasoning (*to whet one's appetite*)
[2] (= *estímulo*) incentive

apetito SM [1] (= *gana de comer*) appetite (**de** for); **abrir el ~** to whet one's appetite; **ese olor me está abriendo el ~** that smell is making me hungry; **comer con ~** to eat heartily *o* with appetite; **siempre tiene muy buen ~** he's always got a good *o* hearty appetite; **¿tienes ~?** are you hungry?
[2] (= *deseo*) desire, relish (**de** for); **me quitó el ~ de hacerlo** it destroyed my appetite for doing it ▸ **apetito sexual** sexual appetite

apetitoso ADJ [1] (= *gustoso*) appetizing; (= *sabroso*) tasty; (= *tentador*) tempting, attractive
[2] (= *comilón*) fond of good food

api SM [1] (*Andes*) *non-alcoholic maize drink*
[2] (*Andes, Cono Sur*) (= *añicos*) **el vaso se hizo ~** the glass was smashed to pieces

apiadar ▸conjug 1a◂ Ⓐ VT to move to pity
Ⓑ **apiadarse** VPR **~se de** to pity, take pity on

apiado SM (*Cono Sur*) celery liqueur

apicarado ADJ roguish, mischievous

apicararse ▸conjug 1a◂ VPR to go off the rails*

ápice SM [1] (= *punta*) apex, top
[2] [*de problema*] crux; **estar en los ~s de** to be well up in, know all about
[3] (*fig*) (= *jota*) **ni ~** not a whit; **no ceder un ~** not to yield an inch; **no importa un ~** it doesn't matter a bit

apichicarse ▸conjug 1g◂ VPR (*Cono Sur*) to squat, crouch

apicultor(a) SM/F beekeeper, apiarist (*frm*)

apicultura SF beekeeping, apiculture (*frm*)

apilado SM piling, heaping

apiladora SF stacker

apilar ▸conjug 1a◂ Ⓐ VT to pile up, heap up
Ⓑ **apilarse** VPR to pile up, mount

apilonar ▸conjug 1a◂ VT (*LAm*) = **apilar**

apimplado* ADJ sloshed*, pissed**, trashed (*EEUU**)

apiñado ADJ [1] (= *apretado*) crammed, packed (**de** with)
[2] [*forma*] cone-shaped, pyramidal (*frm*)

apiñadura SF, **apiñamiento** SM crowding, congestion

apiñar ▸conjug 1a◂ Ⓐ VT (= *agrupar*) to crowd together, bunch together; (= *apretar*) to pack in; [+ *espacio*] to overcrowd, congest
Ⓑ **apiñarse** VPR to crowd together, press together; **la multitud se apiñaba alrededor de él** the crowd pressed round him

apio SM [1] (= *planta*) celery ▸ **apio nabo** celeriac
[2] (*Esp**) (= *afeminado*) queer*, poof*, fag (*EEUU**)

apiolar* ▸conjug 1a◂ VT [1] (= *detener*) to nab*, nick*
[2] (= *matar*) to do in*, bump off*

apiparse* ▸conjug 1a◂ VPR to stuff o.s.*

apir SM (*LAm*), **apiri** SM (*LAm*) mine worker

apirularse ▸conjug 1a◂ VPR (*Cono Sur*) to get dressed up to the nines

apisonadora SF (*con rodillo*) steamroller, road roller; (= *pisón*) tamp hammer

apisonar ▸conjug 1a◂ VT (*con rodillo*) to roll, roll flat; (*con pisón*) to tamp down, ram down

apitiquarse ▸conjug 1a◂ VPR (*Andes*) to get depressed

apitonar ▸conjug 1a◂ Ⓐ VT [+ *cáscara*] to pierce, break through
Ⓑ VI [*cuernos*] to sprout; [*animal*] to begin to grow horns
Ⓒ **apitonarse** VPR (*) (= *enfadarse*) to go into a huff*; [*dos personas*] (= *pelearse*) to have a slanging match*

apizarrado ADJ slate-coloured, slate-colored (*EEUU*)

aplacar ▸conjug 1g◂ Ⓐ VT (= *apaciguar*) [+ *persona*] to appease, placate; [+ *hambre*] to satisfy; [+ *sed*] to quench, satisfy; **intenté ~ los ánimos de todos** I tried to calm everyone down
Ⓑ **aplacarse** VPR [*tormenta*] to die down; **al final se ~on los ánimos** people finally calmed down

aplanacalles* SM INV (*LAm*) idler, layabout*

aplanado ADJ [1] [*superficie*] levelled, leveled (*EEUU*)
[2] (*) [*persona*] **la noticia lo dejó ~** he was stunned by the news; **quedar ~** to be stunned

aplanador SM ▸ **aplanador de calles** idler, layabout

aplanamiento SM (= *nivelación*) levelling, leveling (*EEUU*), flattening; (= *derrumbe*) collapse

aplanar ▸conjug 1a◂ Ⓐ VT [1] (= *nivelar*) to level, make even; ✦**MODISMO ~ calles** (*LAm**) to loaf about
[2] (*Andes*) [+ *ropa*] to iron, press
[3] (*) (= *asombrar*) to bowl over
Ⓑ **aplanarse** VPR [1] (*Arquit*) to collapse, cave in
[2] (= *desanimarse*) to get discouraged; (= *aletargarse*) to become lethargic, sink into lethargy

aplanchar ▸conjug 1a◂ VT (*LAm*) = **planchar A**

aplastamiento SM crushing

aplastante ADJ overwhelming, crushing

aplastar ▸conjug 1a◂ Ⓐ VT [1] [+ *insecto etc*] to squash, crush
[2] (*fig*) (= *vencer*) to crush, overwhelm; (*con argumentos*) to floor
Ⓑ **aplastarse** VPR [1] (= *quedarse plano*) to be squashed; [*coche*] to crash, smash (**contra** on, against)
[2] (= *espachurrarse*) to flatten o.s.; **se aplastó contra la pared** he flattened himself against the wall
[3] (*Cono Sur*) (= *desanimarse*) to get discouraged, lose heart; (= *atemorizarse*) to get scared, take fright; (= *agotarse*) to wear o.s. out, tire o.s. out

aplatanado* ADJ [1] (= *soso*) lumpish, lacking all ambition; (= *aletargado*) weary, lethargic
[2] **está ~** (*Caribe*) (= *acriollado*) he has gone native

aplatanarse* ▸conjug 1a◂ VPR [1] (= *abandonarse*) to become lethargic, sink into lethargy
[2] (*Caribe*) (= *acriollarse*) to go native

aplatarse ▸conjug 1a◂ VPR (*Caribe*) to get rich

aplaudir ▸conjug 3a◂ Ⓐ VT [1] [+ *actuación*] to applaud
[2] (= *aprobar*) to welcome, approve
Ⓑ VI (= *dar palmadas*) to applaud, clap

▼**aplauso** SM [1] (= *palmadas*) applause; **un ~ cerrado** a warm round of applause; **~s** applause *sing*, clapping *sing*
[2] (= *aprobación*) approval, acclaim

aplazamiento SM [*de acto*] postponement; (*Fin*) deferment

aplazar ▸conjug 1f◂ Ⓐ VT (= *posponer*) [+ *reunión, juicio*] (*antes de iniciarse*) to postpone, put back; (*ya iniciado*) to adjourn; [+ *pago*] to defer; **han aplazado el examen al martes** they have postponed the exam until Tuesday, they have put the exam back until Tuesday; **ha aplazado su decisión hasta su regreso** he has postponed *o* put off the decision until his return
Ⓑ VI (*CAm*) (= *suspender*) to fail

aplebeyado ADJ coarse, coarsened

aplebeyar ▸conjug 1a◂ Ⓐ VT to coarsen, degrade
Ⓑ **aplebeyarse** VPR to become coarse

aplicabilidad SF [1] [*de decisión, teoría*] applicability (**a** to); **la ~ de los principios de Mendel al hombre** the applicability of Mendel's principles to man; **una norma de ~ inmediata** a norm that will be made applicable immediately
[2] (*Téc*) applicability

aplicable ADJ [1] [*crema, pomada*] applicable; **"no es ~ a los niños"** "not to be used on children"
[2] [*interés, método*] applicable; **un ejemplo ~ en la mayoría de los casos** an example applicable *o* that can be applied to the majority of cases; **~ a algn/algo** applicable to sb/sth; **el 3% de comisión ~ a los empresarios** the 3% charge applicable to businessmen; **una oferta ~ a mayores de 60 años** an offer applicable to over-60s

➤ LENGUA Y USO: **apetecer A2** 28.1 **aplauso 2** 40.4

aplicación SF 1 (= *uso externo*) (*tb Med*) use, application (*frm*); **recomiendan la ~ de compresas frías** they recommend the use *o* application (*frm*) of cold compresses; **una o dos aplicaciones diarias** to be applied once or twice daily; **"sólo de ~ externa"** "for external use only"; **tras la ~ de la primera capa de pintura** after applying the first coat of paint; **~ tópica** external use
2 (= *puesta en práctica*) [*de acuerdo, impuesto, medida*] implementation, application; [*de método*] implementation; [*de sanción, castigo*] imposition; **la ~ de las nuevas tecnologías en la industria** the implementation of new technologies in industry; **en ~ de la ley 9/1968** in accordance with law 9/1968; **una brigada encargada de vigilar la ~ de las sanciones** a brigade in charge of overseeing the imposition of sanctions
3 (= *dedicación*) application; **le falta ~ en el estudio** he doesn't apply himself enough to his studies, le lacks application in his studies (*frm*)
4 (= *aplique*) (*Cos*) appliqué; **una puerta con hermosas aplicaciones de metal** (*Téc*) a door with beautiful metalwork overlay
5 **aplicaciones** (= *usos*) (*Téc*) uses, applications; (*Com, Inform*) applications; **un producto con múltiples aplicaciones en la industria** a product with multiple uses in industry; **aplicaciones comerciales** business applications; **aplicaciones de gestión** management applications
6 (*Bol, Col, Ven*) (= *solicitud*) application; **enviar una ~** to send an application

aplicado ADJ 1 [*ciencia*] applied
2 (= *estudioso*) conscientious, diligent; **un niño muy ~** a very conscientious *o* diligent child; **es muy ~ en matemáticas** he works very hard at mathematics

aplicador Ⓐ ADJ applicator *antes de s*
Ⓑ SM applicator

aplicar ▸conjug 1g◂ Ⓐ VT 1 (= *poner*) 1·1 (*Med*) [+ *crema, pomada*] to apply; [+ *inyección, tratamiento*] to give, administer (*frm*) (**a** to); **~ suavemente sobre la piel** apply lightly over the skin; **se debe ~ quimioterapia** it needs to be treated with chemotherapy
1·2 (*frm*) [+ *pintura, pegamento*] to apply (*frm*)
2 (= *poner en práctica*) [+ *teoría*] to put into practice; [+ *técnica*] to use; [+ *principio*] to apply; [+ *descuento*] to give; [+ *sanción, castigo*] to impose, apply; **ahora tienes que ~ lo que has aprendido** now you have to put into practice what you have learnt; **su objetivo es ~ los acuerdos de paz** her aim is to put the peace agreements into practice *o* effect; **no se puede ~ la ley a su caso** the law cannot be applied to their case; **le ~on la legislación antiterrorista en el interrogatorio** he was questioned under anti-terrorist laws; **medidas que serán aplicadas progresivamente** measures that will be implemented step by step; **van a ~ una política de austeridad** they are going to impose a policy of austerity; **durante el verano aplicamos descuentos especiales** during the summer we offer *o* give special discounts
3 (= *dedicar*) **~ a algo** [+ *esfuerzos, tiempo*] to devote to sth; [+ *recursos*] to apply to sth; **aplica tus esfuerzos a conseguir tus objetivos** devote your efforts to achieving your aims
Ⓑ VI (*Bol, Col, Ven*) to apply; **~ a algo** to apply for sth
Ⓒ **aplicarse** VPR 1 [+ *crema, pomada*] to apply (**a, en** to); **aplíquese la pomada en la quemadura** apply the cream to the burn
2 (= *esforzarse*) **si no te aplicas más, vas a suspender** if you don't work harder *o* if you don't apply yourself to your studies, you are going to fail; **~se en algo** to work hard at sth; *ver tb* **cuento**[1] **1**

aplique SM (= *lámpara*) wall lamp; (*Teat*) piece of stage décor; (*Cos*) appliqué

aplomado ADJ self-confident

aplomar ▸conjug 1a◂ Ⓐ VT 1 (*Arquit*) to plumb
2 (*Chile*) (= *dar vergüenza*) to embarrass
Ⓑ **aplomarse** VPR 1 (*Arquit*) to collapse, cave in
2 (*Chile*) (= *avergonzarse*) to get embarrassed
3 (= *ganar aplomo*) to become self-assured, gain confidence

aplomo SM (= *serenidad*) assurance, self-possession; (= *gravedad*) gravity, seriousness; (*pey*) (= *frescura*) nerve, cheek; **dijo con el mayor ~** he said with the utmost assurance; **perder el ~** to get worried, get rattled*; **¡qué ~!** what a nerve!, what a cheek!

apocado ADJ (= *tímido*) timid; (= *humilde*) lowly; (= *falto de voluntad*) spiritless, spineless

apocalipsis SM INV apocalypse; **el Apocalipsis** (*Biblia*) Revelations

apocalíptico ADJ (= *del Apocalipsis, espantoso*) apocalyptic; [*estilo*] obscure, enigmatic

apocamiento SM 1 (= *timidez*) timidity; (= *humildad*) lowliness; (= *falta de voluntad*) spinelessness
2 (= *depresión*) depression, depressed state

apocar ▸conjug 1g◂ Ⓐ VT 1 (= *reducir*) to make smaller, reduce
2 (= *humillar*) to belittle, humiliate; (= *intimidar*) to intimidate; **nada me apoca** nothing scares me
Ⓑ **apocarse** VPR (= *intimidarse*) to shy away; (= *rebajarse*) to sell o.s. short, run o.s. down

apochongarse ▸conjug 1h◂ VPR (*Cono Sur*) to get scared, be frightened

apocopar ▸conjug 1a◂ VT to apocopate (*frm*), shorten

apócope SF apocope, apocopation; **"san" es ~ de "santo"** "san" is an apocopated form of "santo"

apócrifo ADJ apocryphal

apodar ▸conjug 1a◂ VT to nickname, dub

apoderado/a SM/F agent, representative; (*Jur*) proxy, attorney; (*Mús, Dep*) manager

apoderar ▸conjug 1a◂ Ⓐ VT 1 (= *autorizar*) to authorize, empower
2 (*Jur*) to grant power of attorney to
Ⓑ **apoderarse** VPR **~se de** to seize, take possession of

apodíctico ADJ apodictic, necessarily true

apodo SM (= *mote*) nickname; (*Jur*) false name, alias

apódosis SF INV apodosis

apogeo SM (*Astron*) apogee; (= *punto culminante*) peak, height; **estar en el ~ de su fama** to be at the height of one's fame; **estar en todo su ~** to be on top form

apolillado ADJ moth-eaten

apolilladura SF moth hole

apolillar ▸conjug 1a◂ Ⓐ VT (*Cono Sur**) **estarla apolillando** to be snoozing*
Ⓑ **apolillarse** VPR (*por la polilla*) to get moth-eaten; (= *hacerse viejo*) to get old

apolíneo ADJ (*Mit*) Apollonian; (*Literat*) classically handsome

apolismado ADJ (*Andes*) (= *enclenque*) sickly, weak; (*CAm*) (= *vago*) lazy; (*Méx, Caribe*) (= *deprimido*) gloomy, depressed; (*Caribe*) (= *estúpido*) stupid

apolismar ▸conjug 1a◂ Ⓐ VT (*LAm*) to ruin, destroy
Ⓑ VI (*CAm*) to laze about, idle
Ⓒ **apolismarse** VPR (*LAm*) (= *enfermar*) to grow weak, weaken; (= *deprimirse*) to get worried, get depressed; (= *desanimarse*) to lose heart

apoliticismo SM apolitical nature, non-political nature

apolítico ADJ (= *neutral*) apolitical; (*de interés general*) non-political

apoliyar ▸conjug 1a◂ VT = **apolillar**

Apolo SM Apollo

apologética SF apologetics *sing*

apologético ADJ apologetic

apología SF (= *defensa*) defence, defense (*EEUU*); (= *elogio*) eulogy; **una ~ del terrorismo** a statement in support *o* in defence of terrorism

apologista SMF apologist

apoltronado ADJ lazy, idle

apoltronarse ▸conjug 1a◂ VPR **se apoltronó en el sofá** she settled down on the sofa; **desde que se jubiló se ha apoltronado y no hace nada** he has taken it very easy since he retired and never does anything much

apolvillarse ▸conjug 1a◂ VPR (*Cono Sur*) to be blighted

apoplejía SF apoplexy, stroke

apoplético ADJ apoplectic

apoquinar* ▸conjug 1a◂ VT to fork out*, cough up*

aporcar ▸conjug 1g◂ VT to earth up

aporrar* ▸conjug 1a◂ Ⓐ VI to dry up*, get stuck (*in a speech etc*)
Ⓑ **aporrarse** VPR to become a bore, become a nuisance

aporreado Ⓐ ADJ [*vida*] wretched, miserable; [*persona*] rascally
Ⓑ SM (*Caribe*) meat stew, chili stew

aporreamiento SM beating

aporrear ▸conjug 1a◂ Ⓐ VT 1 (= *pegar*) to beat, club; (= *dar una paliza a*) to beat up
2 (*con el puño*) to thump, pound; **~ el piano** to hammer away at the piano
3 (*LAm*) (= *vencer*) to beat, defeat
4 (= *acosar*) to bother, pester
Ⓑ **aporrearse** VPR (= *pelearse*) to lay into each other; (= *trabajar*) to slave away*, slog*

aporreo SM 1 (= *paliza*) beating
2 (= *ruido*) thumping, pounding
3 (= *molestia*) bother, nuisance

aportación SF contribution; **aportaciones de la mujer** dowry *sing*

aportar ▸conjug 1a◂ Ⓐ VT 1 [+ *bienes, dinero*] to contribute; **aportó sus conocimientos de física nuclear** he contributed his knowledge of nuclear physics; **~ ideas** to contribute ideas; **su estudio no aporta nada nuevo** his study contributes nothing new; **aporta el**

25% del calcio necesario it provides 25% of the calcium requirement; **el viaje me aportó nuevas sensaciones** the journey brought me new experiences
[2] [+ *pruebas*] to provide
Ⓑ VI (*Náut*) to reach port
Ⓒ **aportarse** VPR (*Chile*) (= *aparecer*) to show up

aporte SM (*LAm*) contribution

aportillar ▸conjug 1a◂ Ⓐ VT (= *romper*) to break down, break open; [+ *muro*] to breach
Ⓑ **aportillarse** VPR (= *desplomarse*) to collapse, tumble down

aposentar ▸conjug 1a◂ Ⓐ VT to lodge, put up
Ⓑ **aposentarse** VPR to lodge, put up (**en** at)

aposento SM (= *cuarto*) room; (= *hospedaje*) lodging

aposesionarse ▸conjug 1a◂ VPR **~ de** to take possession of

aposición SF apposition; **en ~** in apposition

apositivo ADJ appositional

apósito SM dressing

aposta ADV on purpose, deliberately

apostadero SM (*Mil*) posting; (*Náut*) naval station

apostador(a) SM/F better, punter; **~(a) profesional** bookmaker

apostar[1] ▸conjug 1a◂ Ⓐ VT (*Mil*) to station, position; **había soldados apostados en todas las esquinas** there were soldiers stationed *o* positioned at every corner
Ⓑ **apostarse** VPR **~se en un lugar** to position o.s. in *o* at a place

apostar[2] ▸conjug 1l◂ Ⓐ VT to bet (**a, en** on); **he apostado diez euros en la quiniela** I've bet ten euros on the football pools; **~ algo a algo** to bet sth on sth; **aposté diez libras al ganador** I bet ten pounds on the winner; **ha apostado su futuro político a la victoria en las elecciones** he has staked his political future on the election victory; **~ algo a que** (+ *INDIC*) to bet sth that; **apuesto lo que sea a que es mentira** I'll bet you anything that it's a lie; **he apostado treinta euros con él a que no gana** I've bet him thirty euros that he won't win
Ⓑ VI to bet (**a, por** on); **no me gusta ~ a los caballos** I don't like to bet *o* gamble on the horses; **~ por algo**: **apostó por la calidad en vez de la cantidad** he opted *o* went for quality not quantity; **no todo el mundo apostaba por su éxito** not everyone believed in his success; **creía en el proyecto y apostó por nosotros** he believed in the project and was behind us all the way *o* backed us all the way; **han apostado por una política de neutralidad** they have committed themselves to a policy of neutrality; **~ a que** to bet that; **apuesto a que no lo encontráis** I bet that you don't find it; **—no creo que él sea culpable —pues yo apuesto a que sí** "I don't think he's guilty" — "I bet he is"
Ⓒ **apostarse** VPR to bet; **me apuesto cualquier cosa a que no vienen** I bet you anything they don't come; **¿qué te apuestas a que gano yo?** what do you bet that I'll win?; **apostárselas a *o* con algn** to compete with sb

apostasía SF apostasy

apóstata SMF apostate

apostatar ▸conjug 1a◂ VI [1] (*Rel*) to apostatize (**de** from)
[2] (= *cambiar de bando*) to change sides

apostema SF abscess

a posteriori ADV [1] (= *después*) (*gen*) at a later stage; [*comprender*] with (the benefit of) hindsight
[2] (*Lógica, Jur*) a posteriori

apostilla SF footnote

apostillar ▸conjug 1a◂ VT [1] (= *poner apostillas a*) to add notes to, annotate
[2] (= *agregar*) to add, chime in with; [+ *observación*] to echo; **—sí, apostilló una voz** "yes," a voice added

apóstol Ⓐ SM (*Rel*) apostle
Ⓑ SMF [*de ideas, movimientos*] advocate

apostolado SM apostolate ► **apostolado seglar** lay ministry

apostólico ADJ apostolic

apostrofar ▸conjug 1a◂ VT [1] (= *dirigirse a*) to apostrophize (*frm*), address
[2] (= *injuriar*) to insult

apóstrofe SM [1] (*en retórica*) apostrophe
[2] (= *injuria*) insult; (= *reprensión*) rebuke, reprimand

apóstrofo SM apostrophe

apostura SF (= *esmero*) neatness; (= *elegancia*) elegance; (= *belleza*) good looks *pl*

apotegma SM apothegm, maxim

apoteósico ADJ huge, tremendous

apoteosis SF INV apotheosis

apoyabrazos SM INV armrest

apoyacabezas SM INV headrest

apoyador(a) Ⓐ SM (= *soporte*) support, bracket
Ⓑ SM/F (*Pol*) seconder

apoyalibros SM INV book end

apoyapié(s) SM INV footrest

▼ **apoyar** ▸conjug 1a◂ Ⓐ VT [1] (= *reclinar*) to rest, lean; **apoya la cabeza en mi hombro** rest *o* lean your head on my shoulder; **no apoyes los codos en la mesa** don't put *o* lean your elbows on the table; **apoya la bicicleta contra la pared** lean the bicycle against the wall
[2] (= *ayudar*) to support; **no me apoyan en nada de lo que hago** they don't support me in anything I do; **no ~emos más al gobierno** we will no longer support the government; **los nuevos datos apoyan mi teoría** the new information supports my theory
[3] (= *basar*) to base; **apoya su argumento en los siguientes hechos** he bases his argument on the following facts
[4] (= *secundar*) [+ *propuesta, idea*] to support
[5] (*Arquit, Téc*) to support
Ⓑ **apoyarse** VPR [1] (= *reclinarse*) to lean; **apóyate aquí** lean on this; **~se en algo/algn** to lean on sth/sb; **apóyate en mi hombro para pasar el arroyo** lean on my shoulder while we cross the stream; **~se contra algo** to lean against sth; **me apoyé contra la pared** I leaned against the wall; **la cúpula se apoya en tres pilares** the dome is supported by three pillars
[2] (= *basarse*) **~se en algo** to be based on sth; **¿en qué se apoya usted para decir eso?** on what do you base that statement?
[3] (= *confiar*) **~se en algn** to rely on sb; **se apoyó en sus amigos para pasar la crisis** she relied on her friends to get through the crisis

apoyatura SF [1] (= *apoyo*) support
[2] (*Mús*) appoggiatura

▼ **apoyo** SM [1] (= *ayuda*) support; **siempre cuento con el ~ de mis padres** I can always rely on my parents' support; **han retirado su ~ parlamentario** they've withdrawn their support in parliament; **~ económico** financial support; **~ psicológico** counselling, counseling (*EEUU*)
[2] (*a una propuesta, idea*) support, backing
[3] (= *apoyatura*) support; **el paraguas también me sirve de ~** my umbrella is also a support

apozarse ▸conjug 1f◂ VPR (*Andes, Cono Sur*) to form a pool

APRA SF ABR (*Perú Pol*) = **Alianza Popular Revolucionaria Americana**

apreciable ADJ [1] (= *perceptible*) appreciable, substantial; [*cantidad*] considerable; **~ al oído** audible
[2] [*persona*] (= *digno de aprecio*) worthy, esteemed; **los ~s esposos** the esteemed couple

apreciación SF [1] (= *evaluación*) appreciation, appraisal; (*Com, Fin*) valuation, appraisal (*EEUU*); **según nuestra ~** according to our estimation ► **apreciación del trabajo** job evaluation
[2] (= *subida*) appreciation

apreciado ADJ worthy, esteemed; **"Apreciado Sr. ..."** "Dear Sir ..."

apreciar ▸conjug 1b◂ Ⓐ VT [1] (= *tener cariño a*) to be fond of, like; **aprecio mucho a tu padre** I'm very fond of your father
[2] (= *valorar*) to value; **~ algo (en) mucho** to value sth highly; **~ algo (en) poco** to attach little value to sth, set little value on sth
[3] (= *percibir*) [+ *comida, música*] to appreciate; **no sabe ~ un buen vino** he doesn't know how to appreciate a good wine
[4] (*Fin*) [+ *moneda*] to revalue
[5] (= *agradecer*) to appreciate; **aprecio mucho lo que han hecho por mí** I really appreciate what they've done for me
[6] (= *detectar*) to notice, detect; **no apreció el sarcasmo en sus palabras** he didn't notice *o* detect the sarcasm in her words; **~on una fractura en el hueso** they detected *o* found a bone fracture; **este barómetro no aprecia cambios mínimos** this barometer doesn't detect *o* register very small changes
[7] (*LAm*) (= *realzar*) to add value to, enhance, improve
Ⓑ **apreciarse** VPR [1] (= *percibirse*) **se aprecia la diferencia** you can tell *o* appreciate the difference; **como se aprecia en la radiografía ...** as you can see in the X-ray ...; **se ~á un aumento de las temperaturas** there will be a rise in temperature
[2] [*moneda*] to appreciate, rise (in value); [*valor*] to appreciate, rise

apreciativo ADJ appreciative; **una mirada apreciativa** an appraising look, a look of appraisal

apreciatorio ADJ **presión apreciatoria** upward pressure; **tendencia apreciatoria** upward tendency, tendency to rise

aprecio SM [1] (*Com, Fin*) valuation, appraisal (*EEUU*)
[2] (= *estima*) appreciation; **no hacerle ~ algo** to pay no heed to sth; **tener a algn en gran ~** to hold sb in high regard; **en señal de**

➤ LENGUA Y USO: **apoyar A2** 38.2, 39.1, 39.3, 40.2 **apoyo 2** 38.1, 38.2, 40.2

mi ~ as a token of my esteem
[3] (= *caso*) **no hacer ~ de algo** (*Méx*) to pay no attention to sth, take no notice of sth

aprehender ▸conjug 2a◂ VT [1] [+ *individuo*] to apprehend, detain; [+ *bienes*] to seize
[2] (*Fil*) to understand; (= *concebir*) to conceive, think; (= *concretar*) to pin down

aprehensible ADJ (= *comprensible*) understandable; (= *concebible*) conceivable; **una idea difícilmente ~** an idea which is difficult to pin down, an idea not readily understood

aprehensión SF [1] [*de individuo*] apprehension, capture; [*de bienes*] seizure
[2] (*Fil*) (= *comprensión*) understanding; (= *percepción*) conception, perception

apremiador ADJ, **apremiante** ADJ urgent, pressing

apremiar ▸conjug 1b◂ Ⓐ VT [1] (= *apurar*) to urge, urge on, press; (= *obligar*) to force; **~ a algn a hacer algo** ◊ **~ a algn para que haga algo** to press sb to do sth
[2] (= *dar prisa a*) to hurry, hurry along
[3] (= *oprimir*) to oppress; (= *acosar*) to harass
Ⓑ VI to be urgent; **apremiaba repararlo** it was an urgent task to repair it, it was urgent to get it repaired; **el tiempo apremia** time is pressing

apremio SM [1] (= *urgencia*) urgency, pressure; (= *obligación*) compulsion; **por ~ de trabajo/tiempo** because of pressure of work/time; **procedimiento de ~** compulsory procedure
► **apremio de pago** demand note
[2] (*Jur*) writ, judgment
[3] (= *opresión*) oppression; (= *acoso*) harassment

aprender ▸conjug 2a◂ Ⓐ VT to learn; **~ algo de memoria** to learn sth (off) by heart, memorize sth; **~ a hacer algo** to learn to do sth
Ⓑ VI to learn
Ⓒ **aprenderse** VPR = **A**

aprendiz(a) SM/F [1] [*de oficio*] apprentice; (*Com etc*) trainee, intern (*EEUU*); **estar de ~ con algn** to be apprenticed to sb; ✦MODISMO **~ de todo y oficial de nada** jack of all trades and master of none ► **aprendiz de brujo** sorcerer's apprentice ► **aprendiz(a) de comercio** business trainee
[2] (= *novato*) beginner, novice; (*Dep*) novice, junior

aprendizaje SM [1] (*industrial etc*) apprenticeship; (*Com etc*) training period, internship (*EEUU*); **hacer su ~** to serve one's apprenticeship; **pagar su ~*** to learn the hard way
[2] (= *el aprender*) learning; **dificultades de ~** learning difficulties

aprensar ▸conjug 1a◂ VT [1] (*Téc*) to press, crush
[2] (*fig*) (= *oprimir*) to oppress, crush; (= *afligir*) to distress

aprensión SF [1] (= *miedo*) apprehension, fear; (= *capricho*) odd idea; (= *hipocondría*) hypochondria, fear of being ill
[2] (= *reparo*) misgiving; (= *escrúpulos*) squeamishness

aprensivo ADJ (= *preocupado*) apprehensive, worried; (= *escrupuloso*) squeamish

apresador(a) SM/F captor

apresamiento SM capture

apresar ▸conjug 1a◂ VT [1] (= *coger*) to catch; [+ *criminal*] to capture, catch; [+ *buque*] to take
[2] [*animal*] to seize
[3] (*Jur*) to seize

aprestado ADJ ready; **estar ~ para** (+ *INFIN*) to be ready to + *infin*

aprestar ▸conjug 1a◂ Ⓐ VT (= *preparar*) to prepare, get ready; (*Arte*) to prime, size; [+ *tejido*] to size
Ⓑ **aprestarse** VPR to prepare, get ready; **~se a** *o* **para hacer algo** to prepare *o* get ready to do sth

apresto SM [1] (= *tratamiento*) stiffening, starching
[2] (= *sustancia*) size

apresuradamente ADV hurriedly, hastily

apresurado ADJ (= *hecho con prisa*) hurried, hasty; [*paso*] quick

apresuramiento SM hurry, haste

apresurar ▸conjug 1a◂ Ⓐ VT (= *dar prisa a*) to hurry, hurry along; (= *acelerar*) to speed up; [+ *paso*] to quicken
Ⓑ **apresurarse** VPR to hurry, make haste; **~se a** *o* **por hacer algo** to hurry to do sth; **me apresuré a sugerir que ...** I hastily suggested that ..., I hastened to suggest that ...

apretadamente ADV tightly

apretadera SF [1] (= *correa, cuerda*) strap, rope
[2] **apretaderas*** pressure *sing*, insistence *sing*

apretado ADJ [1] [*tapa, tornillo, ropa*] tight; **no hagas el nudo tan ~** don't make the knot so tight; **el jersey te queda demasiado ~** the jumper is too tight on you; **le puso la venda bien apretadita en la pierna** she put the bandage tightly around his leg, she tightened the bandage around his leg
[2] (= *difícil*) difficult; **hemos pasado por épocas muy apretadas** we have been through some quite difficult *o* hard times; **andamos muy ~s de dinero** we are very short of money; **una victoria muy apretada** a very close victory
[3] (= *ocupado*) [*agenda, mañana*] busy; **un ~ programa de actividades** a very full *o* busy programme of activities
[4] (= *apretujado*) (*en asiento, vehículo*) squashed, cramped; **si te sientas ahí, vamos a estar muy ~s** if you sit there we're going to be really squashed *o* cramped; **pusieron a los hinchas ~s contra las vallas** they shoved *o* pushed the fans against the barriers
[5] (*) (= *tacaño*) tight-fisted*, tight*
[6] (*) (= *tozudo*) pig-headed*
[7] [*escritura*] cramped
[8] (*Méx*) (= *presumido*) conceited
[9] (*Caribe*) (*sin dinero*) broke*, flat (*EEUU**)
[10] (*Ven*) (= *aprovechado*) **usa el teléfono sin pedir permiso ¡qué ~ es!** he uses the phone without asking permission, he's got a real cheek*

apretar ▸conjug 1j◂ Ⓐ VT [1] [+ *tapa, tornillo, nudo*] to tighten
[2] (= *pulsar*) [+ *interruptor, pedal, tecla*] to press; [+ *gatillo*] to squeeze, pull; **aprieta el botón derecho del ratón** press the right-hand button on the mouse; **~ el acelerador** to put one's foot down (on the accelerator), depress the accelerator (*frm*)
[3] (= *apretujar*) [3·1] [+ *objeto*] to squeeze, grip; (*para que no caiga*) to clutch; **apretó bien los papeles en la cartera** he packed *o* squeezed the papers into the briefcase; **apretaba entre sus manos un ramo de flores** he was clutching a bunch of flowers in his hands; **con un puro apretado entre los dientes** with a cigar between his teeth; **hay que ~ el compost con los dedos** you have to press the compost down with your fingers; **~ los dientes** to grit one's teeth, clench one's teeth; **~ la mano a algn** to shake sb's hand; **~ el puño** to clench one's fist
[3·2] [+ *persona*] (*contra pared, suelo*) to pin, press; (*con los brazos*) to clasp, clutch; **me apretaba con todo su cuerpo contra la pared** he pinned *o* pressed me against the wall with his whole body; **la apretó con fuerza entre sus brazos** he clasped *o* clutched her tightly in his arms
[4] (= *presionar*) **~ a algn** to put pressure on sb; **nos aprieta mucho para que estudiemos** he puts a lot of pressure on us to study, he pushes us to study hard; ✦MODISMO **~ las clavijas** *o* **las tuercas a algn** to put *o* tighten the screws on sb
[5] **~ el paso** to quicken one's pace
[6] **aprieta mucho la letra cuando escribe** he bunches up the words when he writes
[7] (*Mil*) [+ *asedio*] to step up, intensify; [+ *bloqueo*] to tighten
Ⓑ VI [1] (= *oprimir*) [*zapatos*] to be too tight, pinch one's feet; [*ropa*] to be too tight; **estos zapatos aprietan** these shoes are too tight, these shoes pinch my feet; **este vestido me aprieta en la cintura** this dress is too tight for me around the waist; *ver tb* **zapato**
[2] (= *aumentar*) [*dolor, frío*] to get worse; [*viento*] to intensify; **es media mañana y el hambre aprieta** it's half way through the morning and I'm beginning to feel hungry; **cuando el frío aprieta** when the cold gets worse, when it gets really cold; **donde más aprieta el calor** where the heat is at its worst
[3] (= *presionar*) to put on the pressure, pile on the pressure*; **la oposición aprieta cada vez más** the opposition are putting on more and more pressure; **si le aprietan un poco más, confesará** if they put a bit more pressure on him, he'll confess; **~ con el enemigo** to close with the enemy; *ver tb* **Dios 3**
[4] (= *esforzarse*) **si apretáis un poco al final, aprobaréis** if you make an extra effort at the end, you'll pass
[5] **~ a hacer algo**: **si aprieta a llover** if it starts to rain heavily; **apretamos a correr** we broke into a run
[6] **¡aprieta!** nonsense!, good grief!
[7] (*Chile*) (= *irse con prisa*) **apretemos que viene la profesora** let's run for it, the teacher's coming; **fueron los primeros en salir apretando después del golpe** they were the first ones to make a getaway after the coup
[8] (‡) (*al defecar*) to push
Ⓒ **apretarse** VPR [1] (= *arrimarse*) (*en asiento*) to squeeze up; (*para abrigarse*) to huddle together; **¿os podéis ~ un poco para hacerme sitio?** could you squeeze up a bit to make room for me?; **los diez sospechosos se apretaban en dos bancos** the ten suspects were squeezed together on two benches; **se aprietan unos contra otros en busca de calor** they huddle together for warmth
[2] **~se el cinturón** to tighten one's belt

apretón SM [1] (= *presión*) squeeze; **con un ~ en el brazo me indicó que me callase** he squeezed my arm *o* he gave my arm a squeeze to tell me to be quiet; **los apretones y empujones del metro** the pushing and shoving on the underground ► **apretón financiero** financial squeeze

2 (= *abrazo*) hug; **dar un ~ a algn** to give sb a hug ► **apretón de manos** handshake; **se dieron un ~ de manos** they shook hands

3 (= *apuro*) = **aprieto 1**

4 (= *esfuerzo*) push; **con un ~ más al final habría aprobado** with an extra effort at the end, he would have passed

5 (*en una carrera*) dash, sprint

6 (*euf*) [*de vientre*] urgent call of nature (*euf*)

apretujar ▸conjug 1a◂ VT (= *apretar*) to press hard, squeeze hard; (= *abrazar*) to hug, give a bear hug; (= *estrujar*) to crush, crumple; **estar apretujado entre dos personas** to be sandwiched *o* squashed between two people

apretujón SM 1 (= *apretón*) hard squeeze; (= *abrazo*) big hug, bear hug

2 (= *agolpamiento*) press, crush, jam

apretura SF 1 = **apretón 1, 3**; = **apretujón 2**

2 (= *pobreza*) poverty

aprieto SM 1 (= *apuro*) predicament; **estar** *o* **verse en un ~** to be in a predicament, be in a tight spot, be in an awkward situation; **poner a algn en un ~** to put sb in a predicament, put sb in an awkward situation; **la derrota puso en un ~ su continuidad como entrenador** the defeat put his continuation as trainer in jeopardy; **ayudar a algn a salir de un ~** to help sb out of trouble *o* out of a tight spot

2 (= *presión*) = **apretón 1**

a priori ADV 1 (= *antes*) (*gen*) beforehand; [*juzgar*] in advance

2 (*Lógica, Jur*) a priori

apriorismo SM *tendency to resolve matters quickly*

apriorístico ADJ 1 (= *deductivo*) a priori, deductive

2 (= *precipitado*) hasty, premature

aprisa ADV quickly, hurriedly

aprisco SM sheepfold

aprisionar ▸conjug 1a◂ VT (= *encarcelar*) to imprison, put in prison; (= *atar*) to bind, tie; (= *atrapar*) to trap; (= *aherrojar*) (*tb fig*) to shackle

aprismo SM (*Andes*) *doctrine of APRA*

aprista Ⓐ ADJ pertaining to APRA, supporting APRA

Ⓑ SMF supporter of APRA

▼**aprobación** SF 1 (*Pol*) [*de una ley*] passing; **la ~ parlamentaria de la ley** the passing of the law by parliament; **esta ley requiere la ~ por referéndum** this law has to be ratified by a referendum; **el gobierno ha dado su ~ al tratado** the government has ratified the treaty

2 [*de informe, plan, acuerdo*] approval, endorsement; **necesito tu ~ para realizar la venta** I need your approval *o* endorsement to go ahead with the sale; **mis padres nunca me dieron su ~ para casarme** my parents never gave my marriage their approval

aprobado Ⓐ ADJ approved

Ⓑ SM pass, passing grade (*EEUU*)

▼**aprobar** ▸conjug 1l◂ Ⓐ VT 1 [+ *ley, proyecto de ley*] to pass; [+ *informe, plan, acuerdo*] to approve, endorse; **el parlamento aprobó el tratado** the treaty was approved *o* endorsed by Parliament

2 [+ *alumno, asignatura*] to pass; **¿aprobaste el examen?** did you pass the exam?; **no he aprobado las matemáticas** I haven't passed mathematics; **no me han aprobado la literatura** I didn't get a pass in literature

3 [+ *decisión, actitud*] to approve of; **no apruebo tu amistad con esa chica** I don't approve of your friendship with that girl; **mi familia aprobó mi decisión de casarme** my family approved of my decision to get married

Ⓑ VI to pass; **aprobé en francés** I passed (in) French

aprobatorio ADJ **una mirada aprobatoria** an approving look

aproches SMPL 1 (*Mil*) approaches

2 (*LAm*) (= *vecindario*) neighbourhood *sing*, neighborhood *sing* (*EEUU*), district *sing*

aprontamiento SM quick delivery, rapid service

aprontar ▸conjug 1a◂ Ⓐ VT (= *preparar*) to prepare without delay; (= *entregar*) to deliver at once

Ⓑ VI (= *pagar*) to pay in advance

apronte SM (*Cono Sur*) 1 (*Dep*) heat, preliminary race

2 **~s** preparations; **irse en los ~s** to waste one's energy on unnecessary preliminaries

apropiación SF appropriation ► **apropiación ilícita** illegal seizure, misappropriation ► **apropiación indebida de fondos** misappropriation of funds, embezzlement

apropiadamente ADV appropriately, fittingly

apropiado ADJ appropriate (**para** for), suitable (**para** for)

apropiar ▸conjug 1b◂ Ⓐ VT 1 (= *adecuar*) to adapt (**a** to), fit (**a** to)

2 **~ algo a algn** (= *dar*) to give sth to sb; (*LAm*) (= *asignar*) to assign sth to sb; (= *otorgar*) to award sth to sb

Ⓑ **apropiarse** VPR **~se (de) algo** to appropriate sth

apropincuarse ▸conjug 1d◂ VPR (*hum*) to approach

aprovechable ADJ **unos cuantos consejos ~s** some useful pieces of advice; **estas tablas son ~s para hacer cajas** those boards can be used to make boxes; **esa camisa es ~ todavía** you can still wear that shirt, that shirt is still wearable

aprovechadamente ADV profitably

aprovechado/a Ⓐ ADJ 1 (= *usado*) **terrenos muy poco ~s** lands that have not been made the best of; **bien ~** [*dinero, tiempo*] well-spent; [*espacio, recursos*] well-exploited; [*oportunidad*] well-taken, well-used; **el espacio está muy bien ~ en este apartamento** good use has been made of the space in this flat, the space in this flat has been really well exploited; **mal ~** [*dinero, tiempo, oportunidad*] wasted; [*espacio, recursos*] badly-exploited

2 (= *oportunista*) selfish, self-seeking; **no seas tan ~** don't be so selfish *o* self-seeking; **ese vendedor es muy ~** that salesman is a real opportunist

3 (= *ahorrador*) thrifty; **un contable muy ~** a very thrifty accountant

4 (= *aplicado*) [*trabajador*] industrious, hardworking; [*alumno*] resourceful

Ⓑ SM/F (= *oportunista*) **es un ~** he's such a scrounger*, he's such an opportunist

aprovechamiento SM 1 (= *utilización*) use; **un mejor ~ del espacio** a better use of space; **carbón destinado a su ~ como combustible** coal intended to be used as fuel; **un sistema de ~ del suelo** a system of soil exploitation

2 (= *provecho*) **sigue las asignaturas con ~** he is progressing in his studies; **conseguir** *o* **sacar el máximo ~ de algo** to get the maximum use *o* advantage out of sth, make the most of sth

aprovechar ▸conjug 1a◂ Ⓐ VT 1 (= *utilizar*) use; **algunas algas son aprovechadas en medicina** some algae are used in medicine; **un intento de ~ los recursos naturales de la zona** an attempt to take advantage of *o* use the area's natural resources; **ha sabido ~ la ocasión y hacer un buen negocio** he managed to take advantage *o* use the opportunity to make a profitable deal; **no quiso ~ su oferta** he chose not to take up their offer; **~ algo para hacer algo** to use sth to do sth, take advantage of sth to do sth; **aprovechó el descanso para tomarse un café** she used *o* took advantage of the break to have a coffee; **vamos a ~ este espacio para hacer un armario** we are going to use this space for a wardrobe; **aproveché que tenía la tarde libre para ir de compras** I took the opportunity of having an afternoon off to go shopping; **quiero ~ esta oportunidad para agradecerles a todos su apoyo** I want to take this opportunity to thank everyone for their support

2 (= *sacar el máximo provecho de*) [+ *tiempo, espacio, ocasión*] to make the most of; [+ *conocimientos, experiencia*] to make use of, make good use of; **hay que organizarse y saber ~ el tiempo** you have to be organized and know how to make the most of *o* get the most out of your time; **hemos movido los muebles para ~ mejor el espacio** we moved the furniture to make better use of the space; **sabe ~ muy bien su atractivo** he knows how to make the most of his good looks; **Sánchez aprovechó el cansancio de su rival** Sánchez capitalized on *o* took advantage of her opponent's tiredness

Ⓑ VI 1 (= *obtener provecho*) **tú que eres soltera, aprovecha y disfruta** make the most of the fact that you're single and enjoy yourself; **su estrategia no le aprovechó para nada** his strategy did not prove to be of any use *o* advantage to him at all; **~ para hacer algo** to take the opportunity to do sth; **salió a pasear y aprovechó para hacer unas compras** he went out for a walk and took the opportunity to do some shopping; **aprovecha para pedirles el dinero que te deben** take the opportunity to ask them for the money they owe you; **¡que aproveche!** (*al comer*) enjoy your meal!, bon appétit!, enjoy! (*EEUU*)

2 (= *progresar*) to progress; **en ese curso no aprovechamos nada** we didn't get anywhere with that course

Ⓒ **aprovecharse** VPR 1 (= *abusar*) to take advantage; **lo puedes usar, pero sin ~te** you can use it but don't take advantage; **todos se aprovechan de mí** everybody takes advantage of me

2 (*Esp*) (= *sacar provecho de*) to make the most of; **aprovechaos ahora que tenéis tiempo** make the most of it now that you have time; **la mayoría no se aprovecha de estos beneficios** most people don't take ad-

➤ LENGUA Y USO: **aprobación 2** 40.2 **aprobar A3** 38.2, 40.3

vantage of these benefits; **hay que ~se de que tenemos tiempo libre** we have to make the most of the fact that we have free time
[3] (*en sentido sexual*) **~se de** [+ *adulto*] to take advantage of; [+ *niño*] to abuse

aprovechón/ona* Ⓐ ADJ opportunistic
Ⓑ SM/F opportunist

aprovisionador(a) SM/F supplier

aprovisionamiento SM [1] (= *provisiones*) supply
[2] (= *acto*) purchasing, buying

aprovisionar ▸conjug 1a◂ VT to supply

aprox. ABR (= **aproximadamente**) approx

aproximación SF [1] (*Mat*) approximation (**a** to)
[2] (= *proximidad*) nearness, closeness; **no parece ni por ~ que vaya a ceder** he seems to be nowhere near giving up, he doesn't look remotely like giving up
[3] (= *acercamiento*) approach (**a** to); (*Pol*) rapprochement
[4] (*en lotería*) consolation prize

aproximadamente ADV approximately

aproximado ADJ (= *que se aproxima*) approximate; [*cálculo etc*] rough

aproximamiento SM = **aproximación**

aproximar ▸conjug 1a◂ Ⓐ VT to bring near, bring nearer (**a** to); **~ una silla** to bring a chair over, draw up a chair
Ⓑ **aproximarse** VPR [1] (= *arrimarse*) to come near, come closer; **~se a** (= *acercarse*) to near, approach; **el tren se aproximaba a su destino** the train was nearing *o* approaching its destination
[2] **~se a** [+ *cierta edad*] to be nearly, be getting on for
[3] **~se a** (= *intentar reconciliarse*) to approach, approximate to

aproximativo ADJ (= *que se aproxima*) approximate; [*cálculo etc*] rough

Aptdo. ABR, **aptdo.** ABR (= **apartado postal** *o* **de correos**) P.O. Box

aptitud SF [1] (= *conveniencia*) suitability, fitness (**para** for)
[2] (= *capacidad*) aptitude, ability; **carece de ~** he hasn't got the talent; **demostrar tener ~es** to show promise ► **aptitud para los negocios** business sense

apto ADJ [1] (= *idóneo*) suitable (**para** for, to), fit (**para** for, to); **~ para desarrollar** suitable for developing; **~ (para menores)** (*Cine*) suitable for children; **no ~ (para menores)** (*Cine*) unsuitable for children; **~ para el servicio** (*Mil*) fit for military service
[2] (= *hábil*) competent, capable; **ser ~ para aprender** to be quick to learn
[3] (*Escol*) pass *antes de s*

Apto. ABR (= **apartamento**) Apt

apuesta SF [1] (*en juego*) bet; **la ~ era de 10.000 pesetas** the bet was 10,000 pesetas, it was a 10,000 peseta bet; **hagan sus ~s, señores** place your bets, ladies and gentlemen; **¿cuántas ~s has hecho esta semana en la quiniela?** how much did you bet on the pools this week?
[2] (= *desafío*) **te hago una ~ a que …** I bet you that …
[3] (= *opción*) **nuestra ~ por la modernización supondrá un aumento gradual de los gastos** our commitment to modernization will lead to a gradual increase in expenditure; **ésa es una ~ de futuro** that is a future hope, that is a hope for the future
[4] (*Bridge*) bid

apuesto ADJ [1] (= *guapo*) handsome, nice-looking
[2] (= *pulcro*) neat, elegant; (*hum*) (= *peripuesto*) dapper, natty

Apuleyo SM Apuleius

apunamiento SM (*Andes, Cono Sur*) altitude sickness, mountain sickness

apunarse ▸conjug 1a◂ VPR (*Andes, Cono Sur*) to get altitude *o* mountain sickness

apuntación SF (= *nota*) note; (*Mús*) notation

apuntado ADJ [1] (= *con punta*) [*ventana, sombrero*] pointed; [*arco*] lancet
[2] (= *escrito*) **lo tengo ~ en alguna parte** I have it written down somewhere
[3] (*Cono Sur**) (= *borracho*) merry*, tight*

apuntador(a) SM/F [1] (*Teat*) prompter; ✦**MODISMO no se salvó ni el ~*** no-one was spared
[2] (*Méx Dep*) scorer

apuntalamiento SM propping-up, underpinning

apuntalar ▸conjug 1a◂ Ⓐ VT [1] (*Min, Arquit*) to prop up, shore up; (*Mec*) to strut
[2] (= *respaldar*) to support, back
Ⓑ **apuntalarse** VPR (*Costa Rica*) to have a snack

apuntamiento SM [1] [*de arma*] aiming
[2] (= *anotación*) **yo realicé el ~ de la mercancía** I noted down the merchandise
[3] (*Jur*) judicial report
[4] [*de arco, curva*] pointedness
[5] [*de viga, muro*] support

apuntar ▸conjug 1a◂ Ⓐ VT [1] (= *dirigir*) [+ *cámara, pistola, misil*] to aim (**a** at), train (**a** on)
[2] (= *sugerir*) to point out; **apuntó la necesidad de una huelga** he pointed out the need for a strike; **apuntó la posibilidad de que no hubiera sido un suicidio** she suggested the possibility that it had not been a suicide, she pointed out that it might not have been a suicide
[3] (= *anotar*) [3·1] (*en cuaderno*) make a note of, note down; (*en lista, tabla*) to enter, record; **apuntó la dirección en su agenda** she made a note of the address in her diary, she noted down the address in her diary; **apuntó la temperatura en un gráfico** she recorded *o* wrote down the temperature on a graph; **apúntalo en mi cuenta** put it on my account; **~ una cantidad a cuenta de algn** to charge a sum to sb's account
[3·2] (*Estadística*) [+ *velocidad, tiempo*] to log
[4] (= *inscribir*) (*en lista*) to put down; (*en colegio, curso*) to enrol, enroll (*EEUU*); (*en concurso, competición*) to enter, put down; **¿me puedes ~ para la cena de Navidad?** could you put me down for the Christmas dinner?; **lo han apuntado en un colegio privado** they have enrolled him at a private school
[5] (= *decir en voz baja*) (*a actor*) to prompt; **~ la respuesta a algn** to whisper the answer to sb
[6] (= *afilar*) to sharpen, put a point on
[7] (= *apostar*) [+ *dinero*] to bet
[8] (*Cos*) to fasten
Ⓑ VI [1] (= *señalar*) (*con arma*) to aim; (*con dedo, objeto*) to point at; **no apuntes hacia ninguna persona** (*con arma*) don't aim at anybody *o* don't point your gun at anybody; (*con dedo*) don't point at anybody; **¡apunten! ¡disparen!** take aim! fire!; **~ con: todos le apuntaban con el dedo** everyone pointed their fingers at her; **no apuntes con la botella hacia la ventana** don't point the bottle at the window; **~ a algn con un arma** to aim at sb, point a gun at sb; **me apuntó al pecho con un fusil** he aimed *o* pointed the gun at my chest; **apuntó con su pistola al cajero y se llevó todo el dinero** he held up the cashier with his gun and took all the money; ✦**MODISMO ~ y no dar** to fail to keep one's word
[2] (= *dirigirse*) to point; **la proa apuntaba hacia el sur** the prow was pointing south; **sus declaraciones apuntaban en la dirección opuesta** his statements pointed in the opposite direction; **ese chico apunta demasiado alto** that kid sets his sights too high
[3] (= *anotar*) to note down; **¿tienes dónde ~?** have you got something to note this down on?; **apunta, dos kilos de patatas y uno de uvas** note this down *o* make a note, two kilos of potatoes and a kilo of grapes
[4] (= *surgir*) [*barba*] to sprout; **ya empezaba a ~ el día** the day was dawning; **una tendencia que ya comenzaba a ~ a finales del siglo** a tendency that had already begun to emerge at the end of the century; **el maíz apunta bien este año** (*LAm*) the corn is coming on nicely this year
[5] **~ a algo** to point to sth; **una hipótesis apunta al origen romano del yacimiento** one hypothesis suggests that the site is of Roman origin; **todo apunta a que van a ganar las elecciones** there is every indication *o* sign that they will win the elections, everything points to them winning the election; **todo parece ~ a que …** everything seems to indicate that …
[6] (*LAm*) (= *apostar*) to bet, place bets
Ⓒ **apuntarse** VPR [1] (= *inscribirse*) (*en lista*) to put one's name down; (*en colegio, curso*) to enrol, enroll (*EEUU*), register; (*en partido, asociación*) to join; (*en concurso, competición*) to enter, put one's name down; **como el viaje es tan barato nos hemos apuntado** as the trip is so cheap we've put our names down to go; **he ido a ~me al paro** I went to sign on the dole; **nos hemos apuntado a un plan de pensiones** we have taken out *o* joined a pension plan; **me he apuntado a un curso de inglés** I've signed up for an English course, I've enrolled on an English course; **~se a una moda** to follow a fashion
[2] (*) **¿te apuntas a un café?** do you fancy a coffee?; **nos vamos de vacaciones a Cuba, ¿alguien se apunta?** we are going on holiday to Cuba, anyone interested? *o* does anyone fancy coming?; **si vais al cine el domingo, llamadme, que yo me apunto** if you're going to the cinema on Sunday, call me, I'll be up for it*; ✦**MODISMO ~se a un bombardeo** (*Esp*) to be game for anything, be up for anything*
[3] (= *obtener*) **~se un tanto** (*Dep*) to score a point; (*fig*) to chalk up a point, score a point, stay one up; **~se una victoria** to score a win, chalk up a win
[4] (= *vislumbrarse*) **a lo lejos se apuntaba la luz del faro** you could make out the lighthouse in the distance; **han seguido la dirección que ya se apuntaba al principio** they have continued in the direction that was evi-

dent from the start
[5] [*vino*] to turn sour
[6] (*Cono Sur**) (= *emborracharse*) to get tight*

apunte SM [1] **apuntes** (= *notas*) notes; **¿me puedes pasar los ~s de la última clase?** could you give me the notes from the last class?; **ahora unos breves ~s sobre la actualidad** now for some short news items; **sacar ~s** (*Educ*) to take notes; (*Arte*) to make sketches; **tomar ~s** to take notes; ✦*MODISMO* **llevar al ~ a algn** (*Cono Sur*) (= *hacer caso*) to take notice of sb; (= *vigilar*) to keep tabs on sb* ► **apuntes de campo** nature notes
[2] (*Com*) (= *anotación*) entry; (*Cono Sur*) (= *listado*) list of debts, note of money owing
[3] (*Arte*) sketch
[4] (*Literat*) outline
[5] (= *amago*) hint; **con un ~ de sonrisa en los labios** with the hint of a smile on his lips
[6] (*Teat*) (= *persona*) prompter; (= *texto*) prompt book
[7] (*Naipes*) (= *jugador*) punter; (= *apuesta*) bet

apuntillar ▸conjug 1a◂ VT [1] [+ *toro*] to finish off
[2] (*fig*) (= *rematar*) to round off

apuñadura SF knob, handle

apuñalar ▸conjug 1a◂ VT to stab, knife; **~ a algn por la espalda** (*lit, fig*) to stab sb in the back; **~ a algn con la mirada** to look daggers at sb

apuñar ▸conjug 1a◂ VT [1] (= *asir*) to seize, seize in one's fist
[2] (*Cono Sur*) (= *amasar, heñir*) to knead, knead with the fists

apuñear ▸conjug 1a◂ VT, **apuñetear** ▸conjug 1a◂ VT to punch, strike

apurada* SF (*LAm*) **¿por qué no te echas** *o* **pegas una ~?** why don't you get a move on* *o* hurry up?; ✦*MODISMO* **a las ~s** (*Arg, Uru*) in a rush; **todo lo hace a las ~s** she rushes everything, she does everything in a rush; **andaba a las ~s** she was in a rush

apuradamente ADV [1] (= *con dificultad*) with great difficulty; **logramos salir ~ de aquel agujero** we managed to get out of that hole with great difficulty; **consiguieron la victoria ~** they gained a hard-fought victory, they gained victory with great difficulty
[2] (= *con precisión*) precisely, exactly
[3] (*LAm*) (= *de prisa*) hurriedly, in a rush

apurado Ⓐ ADJ [1] (= *falto*) (*de dinero*) hard up; (*de tiempo*) in a hurry, in a rush; **a final de mes siempre ando algo ~** I'm always a bit hard up at the end of the month; **siempre voy muy ~ de tiempo** I'm always in a hurry *o* rush; **tú vives ~** you're always stressed out; ✦*MODISMO* **casarse ~** (*LAm*) to have a shotgun wedding
[2] (= *difícil*) [*situación*] critical; [*triunfo, victoria*] hard-fought; **en tan ~ trance, decidieron entregarse** being in such a critical state, they decided to give in; **un ~ triunfo frente el Cáceres** a hard-fought victory against Cáceres
[3] (= *avergonzado*) **nunca te había visto tan apurada** I had never seen you so embarrassed; **estaba muy ~ porque iba a llegar tarde** I was really worried because I was going to be late
[4] (*Esp*) (= *preciso*) [*limpieza, frenada*] precise, exact; [*afeitado*] close, smooth
Ⓑ SM (= *afeitado*) close shave; **la cuchilla que le proporciona el máximo nivel de ~** the razor that gives you the closest shave

apuramiento SM [1] (= *agotamiento*) exhaustion
[2] (= *aclaración*) verification
[3] (*Téc*) purification, refinement

apurar ▸conjug 1a◂ Ⓐ VT [1] (= *agotar*) [+ *bebida*] to drink up; [+ *comida*] to eat up; [+ *provisión, medios*] to use up, exhaust, finish off; **apuró hasta la última gota de agua** he drank up the last drop of water; **apura tu copa, que nos vamos** drink up, we're going; **apuró la copa hasta el final** he drained the glass; **tenemos que ~ todos los medios para conseguir nuestro objetivo** we have to exhaust all our means to achieve our aim; **apuró hasta el último momento de sus vacaciones** he stretched out his holiday until the last moment
[2] (= *agobiar*) to put pressure on, pressurize; **deja que haga lo que pueda sin ~lo** let him do what he can without pressurizing him *o* putting him under pressure; **no dejes que el trabajo te apure** don't let your work get on top of you; **si se me apura, yo diría que es la mejor playa de España** if pushed, I would say that it is the best beach in Spain
[3] (= *avergonzar*) to embarrass; **me apuraba oírla hablar de esa manera** it really embarrassed me to hear her speak like that
[4] (= *comprobar*) [+ *detalles*] to check on; [+ *cuestión*] to study minutely; [+ *misterio*] to clear up, get to the bottom of
[5] (*esp LAm*) (= *meter prisa*) to rush, hurry; **¡no me apures!** don't rush *o* hurry me!
[6] (*Téc*) to purify, refine
Ⓑ VI (*Chile*) to be urgent; **este trabajo le apura mucho** this job is very urgent; **me apura ver al doctor** I have to see the doctor urgently
Ⓒ **apurarse** VPR [1] (= *agobiarse*) to get upset, worry (**por** about, over); **se apura por poca cosa** she gets upset *o* worries about the slightest thing; **¡no te apures, que todo se arreglará!** don't worry, everything will be all right!
[2] (= *esforzarse*) to make an effort, go hard at it; **~se por hacer algo** to strive to do sth
[3] (*esp LAm*) (= *apresurarse*) to hurry, hurry up; **¡apúrate!** get a move on!; **no te apures** there's no hurry
[4] **~se la barba** (*Esp*) to have a close shave

apuro SM [1] (= *aprieto*) predicament; **en caso de auténtico ~, siempre puedes vender las joyas** if you're in real difficulty *o* in a real predicament you can always sell the jewels; **pueden servir para un caso de ~** they might be useful in an emergency; **vencieron con ~s, por 90-87** they won 90-87, not without a struggle; **vivimos sin ~s gracias a esa pensión** we have no financial worries thanks to that pension; **en ~s: ayudan a empresas en ~s** they help companies in difficulty; **arriesgó su vida para socorrer a un anciano en ~s** he risked his life to help an old man in distress; **llámame si te ves en ~s** call me if you are in trouble; **se vieron en ~s para hacer el hojaldre** they found it difficult to make *o* had trouble making the puff pastry; **pasar ~s** [*de dinero*] to suffer hardship; (*al hacer algo*) to have difficulties; **antes de hacerse famoso pasó muchos ~s** before he became famous he suffered great hardship; **pasaron algunos ~s para llegar a la final** they had a bit of a struggle to reach the final; **poner a algn en ~s** to put sb in an awkward situation, make things awkward for sb; **sacar a algn de un ~** to get sb out of a mess; **me ha sacado de más de un ~** he has got me out of more than one mess; **gracias por sacarme del ~ delante de todos** thanks for getting me off the hook in front of everyone; **salir de un ~** to get out of a tight spot
[2] (= *vergüenza*) embarrassment; **se desnudó sin ningún ~** he took off his clothes without any embarrassment; **en mi vida he pasado más ~** I've never been so embarrassed in all my life; **¡qué ~!** how embarrassing!; **me da ~** it embarrasses me, I'm embarrassed; **me da ~ hasta mirarla** I feel embarrassed just looking at her; **sigue dándome ~ entrar sola en los bares** I'm still too embarrassed to go into bars on my own
[3] (*LAm*) (= *prisa*) rush; **tener ~** [*persona*] to be in a hurry, be in a rush; [*actividad*] to be urgent; **tenemos mucho ~ en llegar** we need to be there as soon as possible; ✦*MODISMO* **casarse de ~** to have a shotgun wedding

apurón SM (*LAm*) (= *prisa*) great haste, great hurry; (*Cono Sur*) (= *impaciencia*) impatience; **andar a los apurones** (*Cono Sur*) to do things in a rush *o* hurry

apurruñar ▸conjug 1a◂ VT (*Caribe*) (= *maltratar*) to maltreat, handle roughly; (= *manosear*) to mess up, rumple

aquejar ▸conjug 1a◂ VT [1] (= *afligir*) to bother, trouble; (= *importunar*) to worry, harass; (= *cansar*) to weary, tire out; **¿qué le aqueja?** what's up with him?
[2] (*Med*) to afflict; **le aqueja una grave enfermedad** he suffers from a serious disease

aquel(la) Ⓐ ADJ DEM that; **~los/as** those
Ⓑ SM (*Esp**) (= *gracia*) charm; (= *atractivo*) sex appeal; **tiene mucho ~** she's got it*, she certainly has sex appeal

aquél(la) PRON DEM that, that one; **~los/as** those, those ones; **éstos son negros mientras ~los son blancos** these ones are black, whereas those ones are white; **~ que está en el escaparate** the one that's in the window; **todo ~ que ...** anyone who ...; **como ~ que dice** so to speak

aquelarre SM [1] (= *reunión de brujas*) witches' coven
[2] (= *barahúnda*) uproar, din

aquello PRON DEM INDEF that; **~ no tuvo importancia** that wasn't important; **~ no me gusta** I don't like that; **~ que te conté de mi hermano** that business about my brother I told you about; **~ de que no iba a venir fue mentira** when they said he wasn't coming it was a lie; **¡no se te olvide ~!** see you don't forget what I told you about *o* what I told you to do *etc*!; **~ fue de miedo*** that was awful, wasn't that awful?

aquerenciado ADJ (*Cono Sur, Méx*) in love, loving

aquerenciarse ▸conjug 1b◂ VPR [1] **~ a un lugar** [*animal*] to become attached to a place
[2] (*Cono Sur, Méx*) (= *enamorarse*) to fall in love

aqueridarse ▸conjug 1a◂ VPR (*Caribe*) to set up house together, move in together

aquí ADV [1] (*en el espacio*) here; **~ dentro** in here; **~ mismo** right here; **ven ~** come here;

soy de ~ I'm from (round) here; **la gente de ~** (the) people here; **a 2km de ~** 2km from here; **~ Pepe, ~ Manolo** this is Pepe and this is Manolo; **andar de ~ para allá** to walk up and down *o* to and fro; **hasta ~** so far, thus far (*frm*), as far as here; **por ~** round here; **por ~ cerca** round here somewhere; **venga por ~** come this way; **no pasó por ~** he didn't come this way; **he ~ la razón** (*frm*) herein lies the reason (*frm*); ✦***MODISMOS*** **ni de ~ a Lima** *o* **la Luna** there's no comparison; **y ~ no ha pasado nada** and we'll say no more about it; **hubo un lío de ~ te espero*** there was a tremendous fuss

2 (*en el tiempo*) **de ~ en adelante** from now on; **de ~ a un mes** a month from now; **de ~ a nada** in next to no time; **hasta ~** up till now

3 **de ~ que** and so, that's why

aquiescencia SF acquiescence

aquiescente ADJ acquiescent

aquietar ▸conjug 1a◂ Ⓐ VT (= *sosegar*) to quieten down, calm down; [+ *temor*] to allay

Ⓑ **aquietarse** VPR to calm, calm down

aquijotado ADJ quixotic

aquilatar ▸conjug 1a◂ Ⓐ VT 1 [+ *metal*] to assay; [+ *joya*] to value, grade

2 (*fig*) (= *evaluar*) to size up, weigh up

Ⓑ **aquilatarse** VPR (*Cono Sur*) to improve

Aquiles SM Achilles

aquilón SM (*poét*) (= *viento*) north wind; (= *norte*) north

Aquisgrán SM Aachen, Aix-la-Chapelle

aquisito* ADV (*LAm*) = **aquí**

aquistar†† ▸conjug 1a◂ VT to win, gain

Aquitania SF Aquitaine

A.R. ABR = **Alteza Real**

ara[1] SF (= *altar*) altar; (= *piedra*) altar stone; **en ~s de** in honour *o* (*EEUU*) honor of; **en ~s de la exactitud** in the interests of precision

ara[2] SM (*LAm*) (= *pájaro*) parrot

árabe Ⓐ ADJ Arab; **lengua ~** Arabic; **palabra ~** Arabic word; **estilo ~** (*Arquit*) Mauresque

Ⓑ SMF 1 (= *de Arabia*) Arab

2 (*Méx*) (= *vendedor ambulante*) hawker, street vendor

Ⓒ SM (*Ling*) Arabic

arabesco ADJ, SM arabesque

Arabia SF Arabia ► **Arabia Saudí, Arabia Saudita** Saudi Arabia

arábigo Ⓐ ADJ [*número*] Arabic

Ⓑ SM (*Ling*) Arabic; **está en ~*** it's Greek to me; **hablar en ~*** to talk double Dutch*

arábigoandaluz ADJ of Al-Andalus, *of Muslim (southern) Spain*

arabismo SM arabism

arabista SMF Arabist

arabizar ▸conjug 1f◂ VT to arabize

arable ADJ (*esp LAm*) arable

arácnido SM arachnid

arada SF 1 (*Agr*) (= *acción*) ploughing, plowing (*EEUU*)

2 (= *tierra*) ploughed land, plowed land (*EEUU*)

3 (= *jornada*) day's ploughing, day's plowing (*EEUU*)

arado SM 1 plough, plow (*EEUU*)

2 (= *reja*) ploughshare, plowshare (*EEUU*)

3 (*Andes*) (= *tierra*) ploughland, plowed land (*EEUU*), tilled land; (= *huerto*) orchard

arador SM ploughman, plowman (*EEUU*)

Aragón SM Aragon

aragonés/esa Ⓐ ADJ, SM/F Aragonese

Ⓑ SM (*Ling*) Aragonese

aragonesismo SM aragonesism, *word or phrase etc peculiar to Aragon*

araguato Ⓐ ADJ (*Caribe*) dark, tawny-coloured, tawny-colored (*EEUU*)

Ⓑ SM (*Andes, Caribe, Méx*) howler monkey

arambel SM 1 (*Cos*) patchwork hangings *pl*, patchwork quilt

2 (= *triza*) rag, shred, tatter

arana SF (= *trampa*) trick, swindle; (= *mentira*) lie

araná SM (*Caribe*) straw hat

arancel SM tariff, duty ► **arancel protector** protective tariff

arancelario ADJ tariff *antes de s*, customs *antes de s*; **barrera arancelaria** tariff barrier; **protección arancelaria** tariff protection

arándano SM bilberry, blueberry ► **arándano agrio, arándano colorado, arándano encarnado** cranberry

arandela SF 1 (*Téc*) washer

2 [*de vela*] drip collar

3 (*Andes*) (= *chorrera*) frill, flounce

4 **arandelas** (*Col*) (= *pastelitos*) teacakes, buns

araña SF 1 (*Zool*) spider; **tela de ~** spider's web; ✦***MODISMO*** **matar la ~** (= *comer*) to take the edge off one's appetite; (= *perder el tiempo*) to waste time

2 (= *candelabro colgante*) chandelier ► **araña de mesa** candelabrum

arañar ▸conjug 1a◂ VT 1 (= *herir*) to scratch

2 (= *recoger*) to scrape together; **pasó los exámenes arañando** (*Arg*) he just scraped through the exams

3 (*) [+ *beneficios*] to rake off, cream off

arañazo SM, **arañón** SM scratch

arañonero SM spider plant

arao SM guillemot

arar ▸conjug 1a◂ VT 1 (*Agr*) to plough, plow (*EEUU*), till

2 (*fig*) (= *hacer surcos en*) to mark, wrinkle

arara SM (*LAm*) parrot

arate‡ SM blood

araucano/a ADJ, SM/F Araucanian

> **ARAUCANO**
>
> *The* **Araucanos** *from the south-east of Latin America fiercely resisted both Inca and Spanish attempts to colonize them and are known for their independence and indomitable spirit. Their exploits are celebrated in* **La Araucana**, *an epic poem by Alonso de Ercilla (1533-94). The* **Araucano** *language, also known as* **Mapuche**, *is today spoken by over 300,000 people in Chile and Argentina, and many words of Araucanian origin are used in Chilean and Argentinian Spanish. The name* **Chile** *is Araucanian for "Land's End".*

araucaria SF araucaria, monkey-puzzle tree

arbitrador(a) SM/F arbiter, arbitrator

arbitraje SM 1 (= *juicio*) arbitration ► **arbitraje industrial** industrial arbitration ► **arbitraje laboral** industrial arbitration

2 (*Com*) arbitrage

3 (*Dep*) refereeing

arbitrajista SMF arbitrageur

arbitral ADJ of a referee, of an umpire; **una decisión ~** a referee's ruling; **el equipo ~** the referee and his linesmen *o* assistant referees

arbitrar ▸conjug 1a◂ Ⓐ VT 1 [+ *disputa*] to arbitrate in; (*Tenis*) to umpire; (*Boxeo, Ftbl*) to referee

2 [+ *recursos*] to bring together; [+ *fondos*] to raise

Ⓑ VI 1 (= *actuar como árbitro*) to arbitrate; (*Dep*) to umpire, referee; **~ en una disputa** to arbitrate in a dispute; **~ entre A y B** to arbitrate between A and B

2 (*Fil*) to act freely, judge freely

Ⓒ **arbitrarse** VPR to get along, manage

arbitrariamente ADV arbitrarily

arbitrariedad SF 1 (= *cualidad*) arbitrariness

2 (= *acto*) arbitrary act; (= *ultraje*) outrage

arbitrario ADJ arbitrary

arbitrio SM 1 (= *libre albedrío*) free will

2 (= *medio*) means

3 (*Jur*) decision, judgment; **al ~ de** at the discretion of; **dejar al ~ de algn** to leave to sb's discretion

4 (= *impuesto*) excise tax ► **arbitrio municipal de plusvalía** municipal capital gains tax

arbitrismo SM arbitrariness, arbitrary nature

arbitrista SMF promoter of crackpot *o* utopian schemes

árbitro/a SM/F (*Jur*) arbiter, arbitrator; (*Tenis*) umpire; (*Boxeo, Ftbl*) referee

árbol SM 1 (*Bot*) tree; ✦***MODISMOS*** **los ~es no dejan ver el bosque** you can't see the wood for the trees; **estar en el ~** (*Andes*) to be in a powerful position ► **árbol de la ciencia** tree of knowledge, tree of knowledge of good and evil ► **árbol de Navidad** Christmas tree ► **árbol de Pascua** (*Cono Sur*) Christmas tree ► **árbol frutal** fruit tree ► **árbol genealógico** family tree

2 (*Mec*) shaft ► **árbol del cigüeñal** crankshaft ► **árbol de levas** camshaft ► **árbol de transmisión** transmission shaft ► **árbol motor** driving shaft

3 (*Náut*) mast ► **árbol mayor** mainmast

4 (*Inform*) tree

arbolado Ⓐ ADJ 1 [*tierra*] wooded, tree-covered; [*calle*] tree-lined, lined with trees

2 [*mar*] heavy

Ⓑ SM woodland

arboladura SF rigging

arbolar ▸conjug 1a◂ Ⓐ VT [+ *bandera*] to hoist, raise; [+ *buque*] to fit with masts; (= *esgrimir*) to brandish

Ⓑ **arbolarse** VPR [*caballo*] to rear up

arboleda SF grove, coppice

arboledo SM woodland

arbolejo SM small tree

arbóreo ADJ 1 (*Zool*) arboreal, tree *antes de s*

2 (*forma*) tree-like, tree-shaped

arborícola ADJ arboreal, tree-dwelling

arboricultor(a) SM/F forester

arboricultura SF forestry

arborización SF replanting, replanting of trees, reafforestation

arborizar ▸conjug 1f◂ VI to plant trees, replant trees

arbotante SM 1 (*Arquit*) flying buttress

2 (*Méx*) (= *lámpara*) wall lamp

arbustivo ADJ bushy

arbusto SM shrub, bush

arca SF [1] (= *cofre*) chest; (= *caja fuerte*) safe; **ser un ~ cerrada** [*persona*] to be inscrutable ► **arca de hierro** strongbox ► **arcas públicas** public funds
[2] (*Rel*) ► **Arca de la Alianza** Ark of the Covenant ► **Arca de Noé** Noah's Ark
[3] (= *depósito*) tank, reservoir ► **arca de agua** water tower
[4] (*Anat*) flank, side

arcabucero SM arquebusier, harquebusier

arcabuco SM thick forest, impenetrable vegetation

arcabuz SM arquebus, harquebus

arcada SF [1] (= *serie de arcos*) arcade
[2] [*de puente*] arch, span; **de una sola ~** single-span
[3] **arcadas** (*Med*) retching *sing*; **sentir ~s** to retch; **sentía ~s pensando aquello** the very thought of it made him feel sick

árcade ADJ, SMF Arcadian

Arcadia SF Arcady

arcádico ADJ, **arcadio** ADJ Arcadian

arcaduz SM [1] (= *caño*) pipe, conduit; [*de noria*] bucket [2] (*fig*) (= *medio*) channel, way, means

arcaico ADJ archaic

arcaísmo SM archaism

arcaizante ADJ [*estilo*] old-fashioned; [*tono*] nostalgic; [*persona*] fond of archaisms

arcángel SM archangel

arcano Ⓐ ADJ arcane, recondite
Ⓑ SM secret, mystery

arcar ►conjug 1g◄ = **arquear**

arce SM maple, maple tree

arcediano SM archdeacon

arcén SM [1] [*de autopista*] hard shoulder; [*de carretera*] verge, berm (*EEUU*) ► **arcén de servicio** service area
[2] (= *borde*) border, edge, brim; [*de muro*] curb, curbstone

archi... PREF arch...; (*en palabras compuestas, p.ej.*) **~conservador** ultra-conservative; **~fresco** as fresh as one can get; **~popular** extremely popular; **un niño ~malo** a terribly naughty child; **un hombre ~estúpido** an utterly stupid man

archiconocido ADJ extremely well-known, famous

archidiácono SM archdeacon

archidiócesis SF INV archdiocese

archiduque SM archduke

archiduquesa SF archduchess

archienemigo/a SM/F arch enemy

archimillonario/a SM/F multimillionaire

archipámpano* SM big shot*; **el ~ de Sevilla** the Great Panjandrum

archipiélago SM [1] [*de islas*] archipelago
[2] [*de problemas*] mass (of troubles), sea (of difficulties)

archirrepetido ADJ hackneyed, trite, over-used

archisabido ADJ extremely well-known; **un hecho ~** common knowledge

architonto/a Ⓐ ADJ utterly silly
Ⓑ SM/F utter fool, complete idiot

archivado Ⓐ ADJ (*LAm*) out-of-date, old-fashioned Ⓑ SM filing

archivador(a) Ⓐ SM/F (*en archivo*) archivist; (*en oficina*) filing clerk
Ⓑ SM (= *mueble*) filing cabinet; (= *carpeta*) file

archivar ►conjug 1a◄ VT [1] (= *guardar en un archivo*) to file, store away; (*Inform*) to archive
[2] (*fig*) [+ *plan*] to shelve, put on the back burner; (= *memorizar*) to put to the back of one's mind
[3] (*LAm*) (= *retirar*) to take out of circulation
[4] (*Cono Sur*) (= *encarcelar*) to jail

archivero/a SM/F [*de oficina*] filing clerk; (= *bibliotecario*) archivist; **~ público** registrar

archivista SMF (*LAm*) archivist

archivo SM [1] (= *sitio*) archive, archives *pl*; **fotos de ~** library photos; **imágenes de ~** library pictures ► **Archivo Nacional** Public Record Office
[2] (= *documentos*) **~s** files; **buscaremos en los ~s** we'll look in the files ► **archivos policiales** police files, police records ► **archivo sonoro** sound archive
[3] (*Inform*) file; **nombre de ~** file name ► **archivo adjunto** attachment ► **archivo comprimido** zip file ► **archivo de seguridad** backup file ► **archivo de transacciones** transactions file ► **archivo fuente** source file ► **archivo maestro** master file
[4] **de ~*** (= *viejo*) ancient, out of the ark
[5] (*Andes*) (= *oficina*) office
[6] (*Cono Sur, Méx*) (= *cárcel*) jail, prison

arcilla SF clay ► **arcilla cocida** baked clay ► **arcilla de alfarería, arcilla figulina** potter's clay ► **arcilla refractaria** fire clay

arcilloso ADJ clayey

arcipreste SM archpriest

arco SM [1] (*Anat, Arquit, Geom*) arch ► **arco de herradura** horseshoe arch, Moorish arch ► **arco detector de metales** metal detector ► **arco ojival** pointed arch ► **arco redondo** round arch ► **arco triunfal** triumphal arch
[2] (= *arma*) bow ► **arcos y flechas** bows and arrows
[3] (*Mús*) bow ► **arco de violín** violin bow
[4] (*Pol*) (*fig*) ► **arco constitucional, arco parlamentario** *range of democratic parties represented in parliament* ► **arco político** political spectrum
[5] (*Mat, Elec*) arc ► **arco iris** rainbow ► **arco voltaico** arc lamp
[6] (*LAm Dep*) goal

arcón SM large chest

ardedor ADJ (*Caribe, Méx*) quick-burning, easy to light

Ardenas SFPL Ardennes

ardentía SF (*Med*) heartburn; (*Náut*) phosphorescence

arder ►conjug 2a◄ Ⓐ VT [1] (= *quemar*) to burn
[2] (*esp LAm**) [*herida*] to sting, make smart
Ⓑ VI [1] (= *quemarse*) to burn; **~ sin llama** to smoulder, smolder (*EEUU*)
[2] [*abono*] to ferment; [*trigo etc*] to heat up
[3] (*poét*) (= *resplandecer*) to glow, shine, blaze; (= *relampaguear*) to flash
[4] (*fig*) (= *consumirse*) to burn, seethe; **~ de** *o* **en amor** to burn with love; **~ de** *o* **en ira** to seethe with anger; **~ en guerra** to be ablaze with war; ✦*MODISMO* **la cosa está que arde** things are coming to a head
Ⓒ **arderse** VPR to burn away, burn up; [*cosecha etc*] to parch, burn up

ardid SM ruse; **~es** tricks, wiles

ardido ADJ [1] (= *valiente*) brave, bold, daring
[2] (*LAm*) (= *enojado*) cross, angry

ardiente ADJ [1] (= *que quema*) burning; (= *que brilla*) [*color*] blazing; [*flor*] bright red
[2] [*deseo, interés*] burning; [*amor*] ardent, passionate; [*aficionado*] passionate; [*partidario*] fervent, ardent

ardientemente ADV ardently, fervently, passionately

ardilla Ⓐ SF [1] (*Zool*) squirrel; **andar como una ~** to be always on the go ► **ardilla de tierra** gopher ► **ardilla listada** chipmunk
[2] (*LAm**) clever businessman/businesswoman, shrewd businessman/businesswoman; (*pey*) (= *trapichero*) wheeler-dealer*
Ⓑ ADJ INV (*) sharp, clever

ardiloso ADJ [1] (*Andes, Cono Sur*) (= *mañoso*) crafty, wily
[2] (*Cono Sur*) (= *soplón*) loose-tongued

ardimiento[1] SM (= *acto*) burning

ardimiento[2] SM (= *bizarría*) courage, dash

ardita SF (*Andes, Caribe, Cono Sur*) = **ardilla**

ardite SM **(no) me importa un ~** I don't give a damn; **no vale un ~** it's not worth a brass farthing

ardor SM [1] (= *calor*) heat
[2] (*Med*) ► **ardor de estómago** heartburn
[3] (= *fervor*) ardour, ardor (*EEUU*), eagerness; (= *bizarría*) courage, dash; [*de argumento*] heat, warmth; **en el ~ de la batalla** in the heat of battle

ardoroso ADJ [1] (= *caliente*) hot, burning; **en lo más ~ del estío** in the hottest part of the summer
[2] (= *ferviente*) ardent, fervent

arduamente ADV arduously

arduidad SF arduousness

arduo ADJ arduous, hard

área SF [1] (= *zona, superficie*) area ► **área de castigo** (*Dep*) penalty area ► **área de descanso** (*Aut*) rest area ► **área de gol, área de meta** goal area ► **área de penalty** (*Dep*) penalty area ► **área de servicio** (*Aut*) service area
[2] (*Inform*) ► **área de excedentes** overflow area
[3] (= *campo*) **en el ~ de los impuestos** in the field of taxation
[4] (= *medida*) area (*100 square metres*)
[5] ► **área metropolitana** metropolitan area, urban district ► **área verde** (*Caribe*) green area, park area

arena SF [1] (*Geol*) sand; ✦*MODISMO* **sembrar en ~** to labour *o* (*EEUU*) labor in vain ► **arenas de oro** (*fig*) gold dust *sing* ► **arenas movedizas** quicksands
[2] (*Med*) **arenas** stones
[3] (*Dep*) arena

arenal SM [1] (= *terreno arenoso*) sandy spot
[2] (*Golf*) bunker, sand trap (*EEUU*)
[3] (*Náut*) sands *pl*, quicksand

arenar ►conjug 1a◄ VT [1] (= *restregar con arena*) to sand, sprinkle with sand
[2] (*Téc*) to sand, polish with sand, rub with sand

arenga SF [1] (= *discurso*) harangue*, sermon*
[2] (*Chile*) (= *discusión*) argument, quarrel

arengar ►conjug 1h◄ VT to harangue

arenguear ►conjug 1a◄ VI (*Cono Sur*) to argue, quarrel

arenillas SFPL (*Med*) stones

arenisca SF sandstone

arenisco ADJ sandy

arenoso ADJ sandy

arenque SM herring ► **arenque ahumado** kipper

areómetro SM hydrometer

arepa SF (*LAm*) corn pancake; **hacer ~s**** to make love (*lesbians*)

arepera SF (*LAm*) 1 (= *vendedora de arepas*) "arepa" seller
2 (**) (= *tortillera*) lesbian

arepero SM (*Caribe*) poor wretch

arequipa SF (*Andes*) rice pudding

arequipeño/a Ⓐ ADJ of/from Arequipa
Ⓑ SM/F native/inhabitant of Arequipa; **los ~s** the people of Arequipa

arete SM earring; ✦*MODISMO* **ir** *o* **estar de ~** (*Caribe*) to be a hanger-on

argamandijo* SM set of tools, tackle

argamasa SF mortar

argamasar ▸conjug 1a◂ Ⓐ VT to mortar
Ⓑ VI to mix mortar

árgana SF crane

árganas SFPL (*esp Cono Sur*) wicker baskets, panniers (*carried by horse*)

Argel SM Algiers

Argelia SF Algeria

argelino/a ADJ, SM/F Algerian

argén SM argent

argentado ADJ (*Téc*) silver-plated; [*voz*] silvery

argentar ▸conjug 1a◂ VT to silver-plate

argénteo ADJ = **argentino**[1]

argentería SF [*de plata*] silver embroidery; [*de oro*] gold embroidery

Argentina SF (*tb* **la ~**) the Argentine, Argentina

argentinismo SM argentinism, *word or phrase etc peculiar to Argentina*

argentino[1] ADJ (*poét*) silver, silvery

argentino[2]**/a** ADJ, SM/F Argentinian, Argentine

argento SM (*poét*) silver ► **argento vivo** quicksilver

argo SM argon

argolla SF 1 (= *anilla*) ring; (*para caballo*) hitching ring; (= *aldaba*) door knocker; (= *gargantilla*) choker; [*de servilleta*] serviette ring; (*LAm*) (= *anillo*) [*de boda*] wedding ring; [*de novios*] engagement ring; **cambio de ~s** (*Cono Sur*) engagement
2 (*Dep*) *a game like croquet*

argollar ▸conjug 1a◂ Ⓐ VT 1 (*Andes*) [+ *cerdo*] to ring; (*Méx*) (= *enganchar*) to hitch to a ring
2 **~ a algn** (*Méx*) to have a hold over sb (*because of a service rendered*)
Ⓑ **argollarse** VPR (*Andes*) to get engaged

argón SM argon

argonauta SM Argonaut

Argos SM Argus

argot [ar'go] SM (*pl* **argots**) slang ► **argot pasota** dropout slang

argótico ADJ slang *antes de s*

argucia SF sophistry (*frm*), hair-splitting; **~s** nit-picking* *sing*

argüende SM (*LAm*) argument

argüir ▸conjug 3g◂ Ⓐ VT 1 (= *razonar*) to argue, contend; (= *indicar*) to indicate, point to; (= *inferir*) to deduce; (= *probar*) to prove, show; **esto arguye su poco cuidado** this shows his lack of care; **de ahí arguyo su buena calidad** that tells me it's good quality
2 (= *argumentar, justificarse*) to argue, claim; **arguyó que no era culpa suya** he claimed it wasn't his fault
3 (= *reprochar*) to reproach; **me argüían con vehemencia** they vehemently reproached me; **~ a algn (de) su crueldad** to reproach sb for their cruelty
Ⓑ VI to argue (**contra** against, with)

argumentable ADJ arguable

argumentación SF (= *acción*) arguing; (= *razonamiento*) argument, reasoning

argumentador ADJ argumentative

argumental ADJ (*Literat*) plot *antes de s*; **línea ~** line of the plot, storyline

argumentar ▸conjug 1a◂ VT, VI to argue; **~ que …** to argue that …, contend that …

argumentista SMF scriptwriter

▼ **argumento** SM 1 [*de razonamiento*] argument (*tb Jur*); **no me convencen tus ~s** I'm not convinced by your arguments *o* reasoning
2 (*Literat, Teat*) plot; (*TV etc*) storyline ► **argumento de la obra** plot summary, outline
3 (*LAm*) (= *discusión*) argument, discussion, quarrel

aria SF aria

aridecer ▸conjug 2d◂ Ⓐ VT to dry up, make arid
Ⓑ VI, **aridecerse** VPR to dry up, become arid

aridez SF aridity, dryness

árido Ⓐ ADJ arid, dry
Ⓑ SM 1 **áridos** (*Com*) dry goods; **medida para ~s** dry measure
2 (= *hormigón*) sand and cement

Aries SM Aries

ariete SM 1 (*Mil*) battering ram
2 (*Dep*) striker

arigua SF (*Caribe*) wild bee

arillo SM earring

ario/a ADJ, SM/F Aryan

ariqueño/a Ⓐ ADJ of/from Arica
Ⓑ SM/F native/inhabitant of Arica; **los ~s** the people of Arica

ariscar ▸conjug 1g◂ Ⓐ VT (*CAm, Caribe*) [+ *animal*] to pacify, control; [+ *persona*] to make suspicious
Ⓑ **ariscarse** VPR (*CAm, Caribe*) to run away

arisco ADJ [*animal*] unfriendly; [*persona*] unsociable, standoffish, surly

arista SF (*Bot*) beard; (*Geom*) edge; (*Alpinismo*) arête; (*Arquit*) arris

aristocracia SF aristocracy

aristócrata SMF aristocrat

aristocrático ADJ aristocratic

Aristófanes SM Aristophanes

aristón SM mechanical organ

Aristóteles SM Aristotle

aristotélico ADJ Aristotelian

aritmética SF arithmetic

aritmético/a Ⓐ ADJ arithmetical
Ⓑ SM/F arithmetician

Arlequín SM Harlequin

arlequín SM 1 (= *persona cómica*) buffoon
2 (= *helado*) Neapolitan ice cream

arlequinada SF (*Hist*) harlequinade; (= *bufonada*) buffoonery, piece of buffoonery

arlequinesco ADJ grotesque, ridiculous

Arlés SF Arles

arma SF 1 (*Mil*) weapon; **los guerrilleros entregaron las ~s** the guerrillas handed over their weapons; **un fabricante de ~s** an arms manufacturer; **nos apuntaba con un ~** he pointed a gun at us; **¡a las ~s!** to arms!; **¡~s al hombro!** shoulder arms!; **alzarse en ~s** to rise up in arms; **¡descansen ~s!** order arms!; **¡presenten ~s!** present arms!; **rendir las ~s** to lay down one's arms; **estar sobre las ~s** to be under arms; **tocar (al) ~** to sound the call to arms; **tomar las ~s** to take up arms; ✦*MODISMOS* **de ~s tomar**: **es una mujer de ~s tomar** she's not someone you mess around with; **limpiar el ~**†** to have a screw**; **pasar a algn por las ~s** (= *ejecutar*) to execute sb; **volver el ~ contra algn** to turn the tables on sb ► **arma arrojadiza** missile ► **arma atómica** atomic weapon ► **arma biológica** biological weapon ► **arma blanca** cold steel ► **arma convencional** conventional weapon ► **arma de combate** assault weapon ► **arma de doble filo** double-edged sword ► **arma de fuego** firearm ► **arma larga** shotgun ► **arma negra** fencing foil ► **arma química** chemical weapon ► **arma reglamentaria** service weapon, regulation weapon ► **armas cortas** small arms ► **armas de destrucción masiva** weapons of mass destruction
2 (= *medio*) weapon; **la movilización popular es su ~ más fuerte** popular mobilization is its most powerful weapon; **su sarcasmo es sólo un ~ defensiva** her sarcasm is just self-defence
3 (*Mil*) (= *cuerpo*) arm ► **arma de infantería** infantry arm
4 (*Mil*) **las ~s** (= *profesión*) the military, the armed services
5 **armas** [*de escudo*] arms

armada SF 1 (*nacional*) navy; (*escuadra*) fleet; **la Armada Británica** the British Navy; **la Armada Invencible** the Spanish Armada; **un oficial de la ~** a naval officer
2 (*Cono Sur*) (= *lazo*) lasso

armadía SF = **almadía**

armadijo SM trap, snare

armadillo SM armadillo

armado ADJ 1 [*persona, lucha*] armed (**con, de** with); **ir ~** to go armed, be armed; ✦*MODISMO* **~ hasta los dientes** armed to the teeth
2 (= *montado*) mounted, assembled
3 [*hormigón*] reinforced
4 [*tela*] toughened
5 (*LAm*) (= *testarudo*) stubborn

armador(a) Ⓐ SM/F 1 (*Náut*) shipowner; (*Hist*) privateer
2 (*Mec*) fitter, assembler
Ⓑ SM 1 (= *vestido*) jerkin
2 (*LAm*) (= *chaleco*) waistcoat, vest (*EEUU*); (= *percha*) coat hanger

armadura SF 1 (*Mil, Hist*) armour, armor (*EEUU*); **una ~** a suit of armour
2 (*Téc*) (= *armazón*) framework; (*en hormigón*) reinforcing bars; [*de gafas*] frame; (*Anat*) skeleton; (*Elec*) armature ► **armadura de la cama** bedstead
3 (*Mús*) key signature

armaduría SF (*LAm*) car assembly plant

Armagedón SM Armageddon

armamentismo SM arms build-up

armamentista ADJ arms *antes de s*; **carrera ~** arms race

armamento SM 1 (*Mil*) armament; **~s** armaments, arms; *ver tb* **carrera 2**

➤ LENGUA Y USO: **argumento 1** 53.2, 53.3

2 (*Náut*) fitting-out
3 (*Téc*) framework

armar ▸conjug 1a◂ Ⓐ VT 1 [+ *persona, ejército*] to arm (**con, de** with); **un arsenal suficiente para ~ a un comando** enough weapons to arm a commando group; **vino armado de brocha y pintura** he came armed with a brush and paint; **se desconoce quién ha armado a los terroristas** it is not known who provided *o* supplied the terrorists with arms; *ver tb* **caballero**
2 (= *montar*) [+ *mueble, ventana, juguete*] to assemble, put together; [+ *tienda de campaña*] to pitch, put up; [+ *trampa*] to set; (*LAm*) [+ *rompecabezas*] to piece together, put together; [+ *cigarrillo*] to roll; **tuvimos que desarmar la cama y volverla a ~** we had to take the bed apart and reassemble it *o* put it back together again
3 (*) (= *organizar*) **~ una bronca** *o* **un escándalo** to kick up a fuss; **~on un follón tremendo con lo del cambio de horario** they kicked up a real fuss about the timetable change; **amenacé con marcharme armando un escándalo y cedieron** I threatened to leave and create a scene, so they gave in; **el cuadro que ha armado tanta polémica** the painting which has caused such controversy; **por favor, id entrando despacio, sin ~ jaleo** go in slowly please, without making a racket; **armarla** to stir up trouble; **buena la armó con esa declaración** he really stirred up trouble with that statement; **pienso ~la hasta que consiga lo que quiero** I'm going to make a real fuss until I get what I want
4 [+ *hormigón*] to reinforce
5 (*Mil*) [+ *bayoneta*] to fix; [+ *rifle, cañón*] to load; [+ *arco*] to bend
6 (*Náut*) to fit out, commission
7 (*Cos*) [+ *chaqueta, solapa*] to stiffen; **una chaqueta sin ~** a loose jacket
8 **~ un pleito** (*LAm**) to kick up a fuss*, get ready
Ⓑ **armarse** VPR 1 [*soldado, atracador*] to arm o.s. (**con, de** with); ✦*MODISMO* **~se hasta los dientes** to be armed to the teeth
2 (= *proveerse*) **~se de algo** to arm o.s. with sth; **los periodistas, armados de prismáticos y teleobjetivos** the journalists, armed with binoculars and telephoto lenses; **con este tráfico hay que ~se de paciencia** you need a lot of patience in traffic like this; **~se de valor** to pluck up courage
3 (*) (= *organizarse*) **¡que follón se armó!** there was a big fuss; **¡menudo escándalo se armó con lo de esa boda!** what a commotion there was with that wedding!*; **se está armando una crisis** a crisis is brewing; *ver tb* **Dios 3**
4 **~se un lío***: **me armé un lío tremendo con todas las direcciones que me diste** I got into a real muddle* *o* mess with all the addresses you gave me
5 (*CAm*) to balk, shy
6 (*CAm, Caribe*) (= *obstinarse*) to become obstinate; (= *negarse*) to refuse point blank; (*Ven*) [*caballo*] to come to a halt
7 (*Méx**) (= *enriquecerse*) to make a packet*
8 **~se con algo** (*Ven*) to run off with sth

armario SM [*de cocina*] cupboard, closet (*EEUU*); [*de ropa*] wardrobe, closet (*EEUU*) ► **armario botiquín** medicine chest *o* cabinet ► **armario empotrado** built-in cupboard ► **armario ropero** wardrobe, closet (*EEUU*)

armatoste SM 1 (= *objeto*) monstrosity; (*Mec*) contraption; (*Aut*) old crock*, jalopy*, old banger* 2 (= *persona*) bungling great fool*

armazón SM *o* SF 1 (= *armadura*) frame; (*fig*) (= *esqueleto*) framework; (*Aer, Aut*) body, chassis; [*de mueble*] frame
2 (*LAm*) (= *estantes*) shelving

armella SF eyebolt

Armenia SF Armenia

armenio/a ADJ, SM/F Armenian

armería SF 1 (= *museo*) military museum
2 (= *tienda*) gunsmith's, gunsmith's shop
3 (= *oficio*) gunmaking
4 (*Heráldica*) heraldry

armero SM 1 (= *artesano*) gunsmith; (= *fabricante*) arms manufacturer
2 (= *armario*) gun rack

armiño SM 1 (*Zool*) stoat
2 (= *piel*) ermine
3 (*Heráldica*) ermine

armisticio SM armistice

armón SM (*tb* **~ de artillería**) gun carriage, limber

armonía SF harmony; **en ~** in harmony (**con** with)

armónica SF harmonica, mouth organ; *ver tb* **armónico**

armónicamente ADV harmoniously

armonicista SMF harmonica player, mouth organist

armónico Ⓐ ADJ harmonic
Ⓑ SM (*Mús*) harmonic; *ver tb* **armónica**

armonio SM harmonium

armoniosamente ADV harmoniously

armonioso ADJ harmonious

armonizable ADJ **ser ~** to be reconcilable (**con** with)

armonización SF (*Mús*) harmonization; (= *conciliación*) reconciliation; **ley de ~** coordinating law

armonizador ADJ **ley ~a** coordinating law

armonizar ▸conjug 1f◂ Ⓐ VT (*Mús*) to harmonize; [+ *diferencias*] to reconcile
Ⓑ VI (*Mús*) to harmonize (**con** with); **~ con** (= *avenirse*) to harmonize *o* be in keeping with; [*colores*] to tone in with

ARN SM ABR (= **ácido ribonucleico**) RNA

arnaco SM (*Andes*) useless object, piece of lumber

arnero SM (*LAm*) sieve

arnés SM 1 (*Mil, Hist*) armour, armor (*EEUU*)
2 (*en montañismo, paracaidismo*) harness ► **arnés de seguridad** safety harness
3 **arneses** (= *arreos*) harness *sing*, trappings; (= *avíos*) gear *sing*, tackle *sing*

árnica SF 1 (= *planta, tintura*) arnica
2 (*Dep*) **pedir ~** to throw in the towel

aro[1] SM [*de tonel*] ring, hoop; [*de rueda*] rim; (= *servilletero*) napkin ring; (*Andes, Cono Sur*) (= *arete*) earring; **aros** (= *juego*) quoits; ✦*MODISMOS* **hacer un ~** (*Cono Sur*) to have a break; **pasar por el ~** to fall into line ► **aro de émbolo** piston ring ► **aro de rueda** wheel rim

aro[2] SM (*Bot*) lords-and-ladies

aroma SM (= *perfume*) aroma, scent; [*de vino*] bouquet

aromaterapia SF aromatherapy

aromático ADJ aromatic, sweet-scented

aromatizador SM air-freshener

aromatizante SM flavouring, flavoring (*EEUU*), aromatic spice

aromatizar ▸conjug 1f◂ VT (= *perfumar*) to scent; [+ *aire*] to freshen; (*Culin*) to spice, flavour with herbs, flavor with herbs (*EEUU*)

arpa SF harp; ✦*MODISMO* **tocar el ~*** to be a thief, live by thieving

arpado ADJ serrated

arpar[1] ▸conjug 1a◂ VT (= *arañar*) to scratch, claw, claw at; (= *hacer pedazos*) to tear, tear to pieces

arpar[2]* ▸conjug 1a◂ VT (*LAm*) (= *robar*) to pinch*, nick*

arpegio SM arpeggio

arpeo SM grappling iron

arpero/a SM/F (*Méx*) (= *ladrón*) thief, burglar; (= *arpista*) harpist

arpía SF (*Mit*) harpy; (= *mujer*) old bag*

arpicordio SM harpsichord

arpillar ▸conjug 1a◂ VT (*CAm*) to pile up

arpillera SF sacking, sackcloth

> **ARPILLERA**
>
> ***Arpilleras** is the term used for the colourful pictures made in many parts of Latin America by appliquéing scraps of fabric onto a hessian backing. During the Pinochet dictatorship in Chile they became politically significant since working-class women used them to depict the reality of life under military rule. As these **arpilleras** escaped the scrutiny of the male-dominated regime, they provided women with a means of recording events as well as obtaining income from abroad.*

arpir SM (*Andes, Cono Sur*) mine worker

arpista SMF (*Mús*) harpist; (*Cono Sur*) (= *ladrón*) thief, burglar

arpón SM harpoon

arponar ▸conjug 1a◂ VT, **arponear** ▸conjug 1a◂ VT to harpoon

arponero ADJ **navío ~** whaler, whaling vessel

arquear ▸conjug 1a◂ Ⓐ VT 1 (= *doblar*) to arch, bend
2 [+ *lana*] to beat
3 (*Náut*) to gauge; (*LAm Com*) to tot up
Ⓑ VI (*Med*) to retch
Ⓒ **arquearse** VPR (= *doblarse*) to arch, bend; [*superficie*] to camber

arqueo SM 1 (*Arquit*) arching
2 (*Náut*) capacity; (*Com*) [*de caja*] filling up, cashing up ► **arqueo bruto** gross tonnage

arqueolítico ADJ Stone-Age *antes de s*

arqueología SF archaeology, archeology (*EEUU*) ► **arqueología industrial** industrial archaeology ► **arqueología submarina** underwater archaeology

arqueológico ADJ archaeological, archeological (*EEUU*); **investigación arqueológica** dig, excavation

arqueólogo/a SM/F archaeologist, archeologist (*EEUU*)

arquería SF arcade, series of arches

arquero/a SM/F 1 (*Mil*) bowman, archer

[2] (*Com*) cashier
[3] (*LAm Dep*) goalkeeper

arqueta SF chest

arquetípico ADJ archetypal, archetypical

arquetipo SM archetype

Arquímedes SM Archimedes

arquimesa SF desk, escritoire

arquitecto/a SM/F architect ► **arquitecto/a de jardines, arquitecto/a paisajista** landscape gardener ► **arquitecto/a técnico/a** quantity surveyor

arquitectónico ADJ architectural

arquitectura SF architecture ► **arquitectura de jardines, arquitectura paisajista** landscape gardening

arquitrabe SM architrave

arrabal SM [1] (= *barrio de las afueras*) suburb; **~es** (= *afueras*) outskirts
[2] (*LAm*) (= *barrio bajo*) slums *pl*, slum quarter

arrabalero/a Ⓐ ADJ [1] (= *de las afueras*) suburban; (*pey*) (= *de barrio bajo*) of/from the poorer areas [2] (= *basto*) common, coarse
Ⓑ SM/F [1] (= *de las afueras*) suburbanite; (*pey*) (= *de barrio bajo*) person from the poorer areas
[2] (= *persona basta*) common sort, coarse person

arrabio SM cast iron

arracacha SF (*Andes*) idiocy, silliness

arracacho SM (*Andes*) idiot

arracada SF pendant earring

arracimado ADJ clustered, in a cluster

arracimarse ▸conjug 1a◂ VPR to cluster together

arraigadamente ADV firmly, securely

arraigado ADJ [*costumbre*] deep-rooted; [*creencia*] deep-seated; [*persona*] property-owning

arraigar ▸conjug 1h◂ Ⓐ VT [1] (*fig*) (= *establecer*) to establish
[2] (*LAm Jur*) to place under a restriction order
Ⓑ VI [*planta*] to take root
Ⓒ **arraigarse** VPR [1] [*planta*] to take root
[2] [*costumbre*] to take root, establish itself, take a hold; [*persona*] to settle, establish o.s.

arraigo SM [1] (*Bot*) rooting; **de fácil ~** easily rooted
[2] (= *bienes*) land, real estate; **hombre de ~** man of property
[3] [*de creencia etc*] deep-seatedness; **de mucho** *o* **viejo ~** deep-rooted
[4] (= *influencia*) hold, influence; **tener ~** to have influence
[5] **orden de ~** (*Cono Sur, Méx*) restriction order

arralar ▸conjug 1a◂ VT (*Méx*) to thin out

arramblar ▸conjug 1a◂ VI **~ con*** to make off with, pinch*

arrancaclavos SM INV claw hammer

arrancada SF (= *arranque*) sudden start; (= *aceleración*) sudden acceleration; (= *sacudida*) jerk, jolt; (*esp LAm*) (= *fuga*) sudden dash, escape attempt

arrancadero SM starting point

arrancado Ⓐ ADJ (*) (= *arruinado*) broke*, penniless
Ⓑ SM (*Aut*) starting, ignition

arrancador SM starter

arrancamiento SM [*de diente, pelo*] pulling out; [*de planta, árbol*] uprooting; [*de carteles*] tearing down; [*de bolso, arma*] snatching; **una campaña de ~ de carteles electorales** a campaign to tear down election posters

arrancar ▸conjug 1g◂ Ⓐ VT [1] (= *sacar de raíz*)
[1·1] [+ *planta, pelo*] to pull up; [+ *clavo, diente*] to pull out; [+ *pluma*] to pluck; [+ *ojos*] to gouge out; [+ *botón, esparadrapo, etiqueta*] to pull off, tear off; [+ *página*] to tear out, rip out; [+ *cartel*] to pull down, tear down; **he estado arrancando las malas hierbas del jardín** I've been pulling up the weeds in the garden; **le arrancó la oreja de un mordisco** he bit off his ear; **azulejos arrancados de las paredes de una iglesia** tiles that have been pulled off the walls of a church
[1·2] [*explosión, viento*] to blow off; **una explosión le arrancó las dos piernas** an explosion blew both his legs off; **el vendaval ha arrancado varios árboles** the gale has uprooted several trees; **el golpe le arrancó dos dientes** the blow knocked two of his teeth out; *ver tb* **cuajo, raíz**
[1·3] (*Med*) [+ *flema*] to bring up
[2] (= *arrebatar*) to snatch (**a, de** from); (*con violencia*) to wrench (**a, de** from); **le arrancó al niño de los brazos** she snatched the baby from his arms; **no podían ~le el cuchillo** they were unable to get the knife off him, they were unable to wrest *o* wrench the knife from him; **el viento me lo arrancó de las manos** the wind blew it out of my hands, the wind snatched it from my hands (*más frm*)
[3] (= *provocar*) [+ *aplausos*] to draw; [+ *risas*] to provoke, cause; **el tenor arrancó una gran ovación** the tenor received a great ovation; **hemos conseguido ~le una sonrisa** we managed to get a smile out of him; **el beso arrancó algunos suspiros entre el público** when they kissed part of the audience let out a sigh; **~ las lágrimas a algn** to bring tears to sb's eyes
[4] (= *separar*) **~ a algn de** [+ *lugar*] to drag sb away from; [+ *éxtasis, trance*] to drag sb out of; [+ *vicio*] to wean sb off a bad habit; **no había forma de ~la del teléfono** there was no way I could drag her away from the phone
[5] (= *obtener*) [+ *apoyo*] to gain, win; [+ *victoria*] to snatch; [+ *confesión, promesa*] to extract; [+ *sonido, nota*] to produce; **no hubo forma de ~le una palabra** we couldn't get a word out of him; **~ información a algn** to extract information from sb, get information out of sb
[6] (*Aut*) [+ *vehículo, motor*] to start; **un motor de los que se arrancan con manivela** an engine that you crank up
[7] (*Inform*) [+ *ordenador*] to boot, boot up, start up; **tengo problemas para ~ el ordenador** I have problems starting up *o* booting the computer
Ⓑ VI [1] [*vehículo, motor*] to start; **el coche no arranca** the car won't start *o* isn't starting; **esperé hasta que arrancó el tren** I waited until the train left
[2] (= *moverse*) to get going, get moving; **¡venga, arranca!*** come on, get going *o* get moving!, come on, get a move on!*
[3] (= *comenzar*) to start; **¿desde dónde arranca el camino?** where does the road start?; **el momento donde arrancó nuestra relación** the moment when our relationship started; **~ a hacer algo** to start doing sth, start to do sth; **arrancó a hablar a los dos años** she started talking *o* to talk when she was two; **arrancó a cantar/llorar** he broke *o* burst into song/tears; **~ de** to go back to, date back to; **esta celebración arranca del siglo XV** this celebration dates *o* goes back to the 15th century; **problemas que arrancan de muy antiguo** problems that go back a long way
[4] (*Náut*) to set sail
[5] (*Arquit*) [*arco*] to spring (**de** from)
[6] (*Chile**) (= *escapar*) **salieron arrancado** they ran away; **arranquemos de aquí** let's get away from here; **tuvieron que ~ del país** they had to get out of the country; ✦**MODISMO ~ a perderse** to make a dash for it*
Ⓒ **arrancarse** VPR [1] (= *quitarse*) [+ *pelo*] to pull out; [+ *botón*] to pull off; **he ido al dentista a ~me un diente** I went to the dentist to have a tooth pulled out *o* extracted
[2] (= *empezar*) **se ~on a cantar** they burst into song; **en mitad del paseo se arrancó a recitar un poema** in the middle of the walk she started to recite a poem; **~se por seguiriyas** to break into a seguidilla
[3] (*Chile**) (= *escaparse*) **se me arrancó el perro** my dog got away; **me arranqué de la oficina más temprano** I left the office earlier; **se ~on de la cárcel** they escaped from prison
[4] (*Chile**) (= *aumentar*) to shoot up*; **hay que evitar que se arranque la inflación** we have to prevent inflation from shooting up*
[5] (*Chile, Méx*) [*caballo*] to shy

arranchar ▸conjug 1a◂ Ⓐ VT [1] (*Náut*) [+ *velas*] to brace; [+ *costa*] to skirt, sail close to
[2] (*Andes*) (= *arrebatar*) to snatch away (**a** from)
Ⓑ **arrancharse** VPR [1] (= *reunirse*) to gather together; (= *comer*) to eat together
[2] (*Caribe, Méx*) (= *acomodarse*) to settle in, make o.s. comfortable; (*Caribe*) (= *adaptarse*) to make the best of it

arrancón SM (*Méx*) = **arrancada**

arranque SM [1] (*Mec*) starting mechanism; **el motor tiene algunos problemas de ~** the engine has problems getting started; ✦**MODISMO ni para el ~** (*Méx**) **¡10.000 pesos!, con eso ni para el ~** 10,000 pesos! that's nowhere near enough*; **no tengo ni para el ~** I haven't got nowhere near enough ► **arranque automático** starter motor ► **arranque en frío** cold start ► **arranque manual** crank start; *ver tb* **motor**
[2] (= *comienzo*) beginning; **el ~ de esta tradición se remonta al siglo XVIII** the beginning of this tradition dates back to the 18th century; **el ~ de la historia es muy original** the beginning of the story is very original; *ver tb* **punto**
[3] (= *impulso*) **me falta ~ para embarcarme en esta empresa** I'm not bold enough to embark on this venture; **aprovechando este ~ de la economía** taking advantage of this burst in the economy; **necesita un poco más de ~ para ganar el partido** he needs a little more drive to win the match
[4] (= *arrebato*) [*de generosidad, franqueza*] outburst; [*de ira, violencia*] fit; [*de energía*] burst; **en un ~ de generosidad** in an outburst of generosity; **en un ~ de celos** in a fit of jealousy
[5] (= *ocurrencia*) witty remark; **tiene muy buenos ~s** he makes some very witty remarks
[6] (= *base*) [*de columna, arco*] base; [*de escalera*] foot

arranquera* SF (*Andes, CAm, Caribe*), **arranquitis*** SF (*Andes, CAm, Caribe*) ✦**MODISMO** **estar en la ~** to be completely broke*

arrapiezo SM [1] (= *harapo*) rag, tatter
[2] (= *mocoso*) whippersnapper

arras SFPL [1] (*Fin, Com*) pledge *sing*, security *sing*
[2] (*Hist*) *13 coins given by bridegroom to bride*

arrasador ADJ = **arrollador**

arrasamiento SM (= *nivelación*) levelling, leveling (*EEUU*); [*de un edificio*] demolishing; [*de un territorio*] devastation; **bombardeo de ~** carpet bombing

arrasar ▸conjug 1a◂ Ⓐ VT [1] (= *nivelar*) to level; [+ *edificio*] to demolish; (*esp en guerra*) to raze to the ground; [*ciclón, terremoto*] to devastate
[2] (= *colmar*) to fill to the brim
Ⓑ VI [1] (*Meteo*) to clear
[2] (= *triunfar*) to triumph, achieve a great success; (*Pol etc*) to sweep the board
Ⓒ **arrasarse** VPR (*Meteo*) to clear; **se le ~on los ojos de** o **en lágrimas** her eyes filled with tears

arrastracueros SM INV (*Caribe*) crook, shyster (*EEUU*)

arrastrada* SF whore, hooker (*EEUU**); *ver tb* **arrastrado**

arrastradizo ADJ dangling, trailing

arrastrado/a Ⓐ ADJ [1] **llevar algo ~** to drag sth along
[2] (= *pobre*) poor, miserable; **andar ~** to have a wretched life
[3] (= *pícaro*) wily, rascally
[4] (*LAm*) (= *servil*) cringing, servile
Ⓑ SM/F (= *pícaro*) rogue, rascal; (*Méx*) (= *necesitado*) down-and-out; *ver tb* **arrastrada**

arrastradora SF (*Perú*) prostitute

arrastrar ▸conjug 1a◂ Ⓐ VT [1] [+ *objeto pesado*] to drag; [+ *carro*] to pull; [+ *caravana*] to tow; [+ *vestido, capa*] to trail (along the ground); **no arrastres la silla por el suelo** don't drag that chair (along the ground); **~ los pies** to drag one's feet, shuffle along; **~ las palabras** to slur one's words
[2] (= *transportar*) [*río, viento*] to sweep away o along; **la corriente arrastró las ramas** the current swept the branches away o along
[3] (= *atraer*) to draw, attract; **su última película ha arrastrado mucho público** his latest film has drawn o attracted large audiences; **no te dejes ~ por esa idea** don't get carried away by that idea; **~ a algn a hacer algo** to sweep sb into doing sth
[4] (= *soportar*) **este país arrastra desde hace décadas el problema del paro** this country's been dogged by unemployment for decades; **arrastra un complejo de inferioridad desde la adolescencia** he's had an inferiority complex ever since he was a youth
[5] (= *provocar*) [+ *dificultad, problema*] to bring with it; **su dimisión arrastró varias crisis financieras** his resignation brought with it several financial crises
[6] (*Bridge*) [+ *triunfos*] to draw
Ⓑ VI [1] [*vestido, capa*] to trail (along the ground), drag; **te arrastra el vestido** your dress is trailing (along the ground) o dragging
[2] (*Bot*) to trail
Ⓒ **arrastrarse** VPR [1] (= *reptar*) [*bebé, serpiente*] to crawl; [*herido*] to drag o.s.; **la oruga se arrastraba lentamente por el suelo** the caterpillar crawled along the ground; **la víctima se arrastró hasta la puerta** the victim dragged himself to the door
[2] (= *humillarse*) to grovel; **se arrastró ante el profesor para conseguir el aprobado** he grovelled to the teacher so as to get a pass mark

arrastre SM [1] (= *acción*) dragging, pulling; (*Aer*) drag; (*Pesca*) trawling; **flota de ~** trawling fleet, fleet of trawlers ► **arrastre por correa** belt-drive
[2] (*Méx, CAm*) (= *influencia*) influence; **tener mucho ~** to have friends in high places
[3] (*Taur*) removal of dead animal; **estar para el ~*** to be knackered*
[4] (*Inform*) ► **arrastre de dientes** tractor ► **arrastre de papel por fricción** friction feed ► **arrastre de papel por tracción** tractor feed

arrastrero Ⓐ ADJ trawler *antes de s*; **flota arrastrera** trawling fleet, fleet of trawlers
Ⓑ SM trawler

array SM (*Inform*) array ► **array empaquetado** packed array

arrayán SM myrtle

arre EXCL (= *voz de arriero*) gee up!; (*LAm*) (*metiendo prisa*) hurry up!, get a move on!

arreada SF (*Cono Sur, Méx Agr*) round-up; (*Jur*) cattle-rustling; (*Mil*) press-ganging

arreado ADJ (*Andes, Cono Sur, Méx*) sluggish, ponderous

arreador SM [1] (= *arriero*) muleteer; (*Andes*) (= *capataz*) foreman
[2] (*LAm*) (= *látigo*) long whip

arrear ▸conjug 1a◂ Ⓐ VT [1] (= *estimular*) [+ *ganado etc*] to drive
[2] (= *poner arreos a*) to harness
[3] (*CAm, Cono Sur, Méx*) [+ *ganado*] to rustle
[4] (*) [+ *golpe*] to give
Ⓑ VI to hurry along; **¡arrea!** (= *muévete*) get moving!; (*repulsa*) get away!; (*Esp*) (*asombro*) Christ!, well I'm damned!; (*admiración*) look at that!

arrebañaduras SFPL leftovers

arrebañar ▸conjug 1a◂ VT (= *juntar*) to scrape together; [+ *comida*] to eat up, clear up

arrebatadamente ADV (= *apresuradamente*) suddenly, violently; (= *impetuosamente*) headlong, rashly; **hablar ~** to speak in a rush

arrebatadizo ADJ excitable, hot-tempered

arrebatado ADJ [1] (= *apresurado*) hasty, sudden, violent
[2] (= *impetuoso*) rash, impetuous
[3] (= *absorto*) rapt, bemused
[4] (= *extático*) ecstatic
[5] [*cara*] flushed

arrebatamiento SM [1] (= *acción*) snatching away, seizure
[2] (= *abstracción*) captivation; (= *éxtasis*) ecstasy, rapture; (= *emoción*) excitement; (= *ira*) anger

arrebatar ▸conjug 1a◂ Ⓐ VT [1] (= *quitar violentamente*) to snatch away, wrench (**a** from); [+ *vida*] to take; [*viento etc*] to carry off, carry away; [+ *persona*] to carry away, carry off, abduct (*frm*); **le arrebató el revólver** he snatched the pistol from him; **le ~on la victoria** they snatched victory from under his very nose; **~ la vida a algn** to take sb's life
[2] (= *conmover*) to stir; (= *cautivar*) to captivate; (= *alegrar*) to exhilarate; **se dejó ~ por su entusiasmo** he got carried away by his enthusiasm
[3] (*Agr*) to parch
Ⓑ **arrebatarse** VPR [1] (= *excitarse*) to get carried away, get excited; **~se de cólera** to be overcome with anger
[2] (*Culin*) to burn, overcook

arrebatiña SF scramble, scramble to pick sth up; **coger algo a la ~** to snatch sth up

arrebato SM (= *ira*) rage; (= *éxtasis*) ecstasy, rapture; **en un ~ de cólera** in an outburst of anger; **en un ~ de entusiasmo** in a sudden fit of enthusiasm

arrebiatarse ▸conjug 1a◂ VPR (*CAm*) (= *unirse*) to join up, join together; (*Méx*) (= *decir amén a todo*) to follow the crowd, agree automatically, agree automatically with everything

arrebol SM (= *colorete*) rouge; [*de cielo*] red glow; **arreboles** (= *nubes*) red clouds

arrebolar ▸conjug 1a◂ Ⓐ VT to redden
Ⓑ **arrebolarse** VPR [1] (= *pintarse*) to apply rouge
[2] (= *enrojecer*) to blush
[3] (*Caribe*) (= *vestirse*) to dress up

arrebozar ▸conjug 1f◂ Ⓐ VT [1] (= *embozar*) to cover, cover with a cloak; (= *disimular*) to conceal
[2] (*Culin*) to cover, coat; [+ *taza*] to fill right up
Ⓑ **arrebozarse** VPR [1] (= *embozarse*) to cover one's face
[2] (*Entomología*) to swarm

arrebujar ▸conjug 1a◂ Ⓐ VT [1] [+ *objetos*] to jumble together, jumble up
[2] [+ *niño*] to wrap up, cover
Ⓑ **arrebujarse** VPR to wrap o.s. up (**con** in, with)

arrechada SF (*CAm, Méx*) = **arrechera**

arrechar ▸conjug 1a◂ Ⓐ VT (*LAm**) to arouse, excite
Ⓑ VI [1] (*CAm*) (= *animarse*) to show energy, begin to make an effort
[2] (*LAm**) (= *estar cachondo*) to feel randy*
Ⓒ **arrecharse** VPR (*LAm**) [1] (= *ponerse cachondo*) to get aroused, get excited
[2] (= *enfadarse*) to get angry

arrechera SF [1] (*LAm*) (= *celo*) [*de animal*] heat, mating urge; (*) [*de persona*] arousal
[2] (*Méx*) (= *capricho*) whim, fancy
[3] (*Caribe*) (= *mal humor*) bad mood

arrecho Ⓐ ADJ [1] (*LAm**) (*sexualmente*) **estar ~** [*persona*] to be in the mood, feel randy*; [*animal*] to be on heat
[2] (*LAm**) (= *furioso*) angry, furious
[3] (*CAm, Méx*) (= *vigoroso*) vigorous; (= *enérgico*) energetic; (= *valiente*) brave
[4] (*Caribe*) **¡qué ~!** what fun!
Ⓑ SM [1] **en ~** (*CAm, Méx*) [*animal*] on heat
[2] **es un ~** (*CAm**‡*) (= *fastidio*) he's a bloody nuisance‡, he's a pain in the ass‡

arrechucho* SM [1] (= *impulso*) sudden impulse; [*de cólera*] fit, outburst; (= *dificultad*) unforeseen difficulty, new problem
[2] (*Med*) turn

arreciar ▸conjug 1b◂ Ⓐ VI [*tormenta*] to get worse, intensify; [*viento*] to get stronger; [*demanda*] to intensify
Ⓑ **arreciarse** VPR [1] = **A**
[2] (*Med*) to get stronger, pick up

arrecife SM reef ► **arrecife coralino**, **arrecife de coral** coral reef

arrecirse ▸conjug 3b◂ VPR (*LAm*) to be frozen stiff

arredo* EXCL **¡~ vaya!** (*CAm, Méx*) get lost!*

arredomado ADJ (*LAm*) sly, artful

arredrar ▸conjug 1a◂ Ⓐ VT [1] (= *asustar*) to scare, frighten
[2] (= *hacer retirarse*) to drive back; (= *apartar*) to remove, separate
Ⓑ **arredrarse** VPR [1] (= *intimidarse*) to be scared, be frightened; **~se ante algo** to shrink away from sth; **sin ~se** unmoved, undaunted
[2] (= *retirarse*) to draw back, move away (**de** from)

arregazado ADJ [*falda*] tucked up; [*nariz*] snub

arregazar ▸conjug 1f◂ VT to tuck up

arregionado/a Ⓐ ADJ [1] (*Andes, Méx*) (= *de mal genio*) ill-tempered, sharp; (*Andes*) (= *irreflexivo*) impulsive; (*Andes*) (= *mohino*) sulky; (*Andes*) cross, angry
[2] (*Caribe*) (= *estimado*) highly regarded
Ⓑ SM/F (*Caribe*) highly respected person

arreglada SF ► **arreglada de bigotes** (*Cono Sur**) dirty deal, shady business

arregladamente ADV in an orderly way

arreglado ADJ [1] (= *ordenado*) [*habitación, casa*] neat and tidy; [*conducta*] orderly
[2] (= *acicalado*) smart, smartly dressed; **¿dónde irá tan arreglada?** where would she go looking so smart *o* so smartly dressed?
[3] [*asunto, pelea*] (= *resuelto*) sorted out; (= *amañado*) arranged; **un matrimonio ~** an arranged marriage; **un precio ~** a reasonable price
[4] ✦*MODISMO* **estar ~: ¡pues estamos ~s!** that's done it!*, we've really had it now!*; **estaría yo ~ si ahora tuviera que pagarlo todo** I would be in a fine mess now if I had to pay for it all myself*; **está arreglada si espera que yo la llame** if she expects me to call her, she's got another think coming*; **estamos ~s con tantos invitados** we are in a fine mess with so many guests coming*; **¡pues estamos ~s contigo!** you're nothing but trouble, you are!*
[5] **~ a algo** in accordance with sth; **un código ~ a la ley** a code in accordance with the law
[6] (*LAm*) (= *esterilizado*) sterilized

arreglador(a) SM/F arranger

Arreglalotodo* SM **el Señor ~** Mr Fixit*

arreglar ▸conjug 1a◂ Ⓐ VT [1] (= *reparar*) [+ *electrodoméstico, reloj*] to repair, fix, mend; [+ *coche*] to repair, fix; [+ *zapatos, vestido*] to mend, repair; [+ *casa*] to do up; **¿cuánto te ha costado ~ el coche?** how much did it cost you to have your car repaired *o* fixed?; **tengo que llevar estos zapatos a ~** I have to take these shoes to the mender's *o* to be mended; **quiero que le arreglen las mangas** I want to have the sleeves altered; **están arreglando la carretera de la costa** they are repairing the coast road; **vendrá un hombre a ~ el jardín** a man is coming to do the garden
[2] (= *acicalar*) to get ready; **arregló a los niños para ir de paseo** she got the children ready for their stroll; **voy a que me arreglen el pelo** I'm going to have my hair done; **sólo quiero que me arregle las patillas** I only want you to tidy up the sideburns; **¡a ti te voy a ~ yo!** (*iró*) I'll show you!*
[3] (= *resolver*) [+ *asunto*] to sort out; [+ *conflicto, disputa*] to settle; [+ *problema*] to solve, sort out; **consiguió ~ lo del préstamo** he managed to sort out the loan; **no te preocupes por el dinero, yo lo ~é** don't worry about the money, I'll sort it out *o* I'll take care of that; **intentaron ~ el conflicto de forma diplomática** they tried to sort out *o* settle the conflict by diplomatic means; **tuvimos que ~ varios números en las cuentas** we had to correct some figures in the accounts; **pegándole no vas a ~ nada** you're not going to solve anything by hitting him; **este dinero les ~á la vida** this money will help sort their lives out; **si te crees que vas a ~ el mundo, vas listo** (*iró*) if you think you're going to put the world to rights, you've got another think coming*; **~ cuentas con algn** to settle accounts with sb
[4] (= *ordenar*) [+ *casa, habitación*] to tidy, tidy up; **los sábados arreglo mi cuarto** I tidy my room on Saturdays; **estoy arreglando la mesa para la cena** I'm arranging the table for dinner
[5] (= *organizar*) to arrange; **ya lo tenemos todo arreglado para la mudanza** we have got everything ready *o* arranged for the move; **lo arregló todo para que la entrevista fuera el lunes** he fixed up *o* arranged everything so the interview could be on Monday
[6] (= *acordar*) [+ *detalles*] to settle; [+ *cita*] to arrange, fix up; **dime lo que habéis arreglado** tell me what you've arranged; **ya hemos arreglado el precio** we have already agreed (on) the price; **hemos arreglado que si yo no puedo hacerlo lo hará él** we have arranged that if I can't do it, he will
[7] (*Mús*) to arrange
[8] (*Culin*) [+ *ensalada*] to dress
[9] (*LAm*) (= *amañar*) to arrange
[10] (*LAm*) [+ *deuda*] to pay, repay; **le trabajé un mes y todavía no me arregla** (*Chile*) I worked for him for a month and still haven't been paid
[11] (*LAm*) (= *esterilizar*) [+ *macho*] to castrate; [+ *hembra*] to spay
[12] (*Chile*) [+ *registro, documento*] to update
Ⓑ **arreglarse** VPR [1] (= *acicalarse*) to get o.s. ready; [+ *pelo, manos*] to do; **yo tardo poco en ~me** I won't take a moment to get myself ready; **se arregla mucho para ir a trabajar** she gets really dressed up to go to work; **~se la boca** to get one's teeth seen to; **~se la corbata** to adjust one's tie; **~se el pelo** [*uno mismo*] to fix one's hair; (*en peluquería*) to have one's hair done
[2] (= *ponerse de acuerdo*) to come to an agreement; **no consiguieron ~se en el precio** they didn't manage to come to an agreement about the price; **~se a algo** to conform to sth; **las leyes deben ~se a los principios fundamentales** laws should conform to fundamental principles; **~se con algn: me he arreglado con ella para cambiar los turnos** I've arranged to swap shifts with her
[3] [*novios*] (= *reconciliarse*) to make up; (†) (= *empezar a salir*) to start courting†; **estuvieron un tiempo peleados, pero ya se han arreglado** they fell out for a while, but now they made (it) up
[4] (= *mejorarse*) to improve; **si las cosas no se arreglan la empresa tendrá que cerrar** if things don't improve the firm will have to close down; **si el tiempo se arregla, iremos a la playa** if the weather improves we'll go to the beach; **los problemas no se arreglan solos** problems don't sort themselves out
[5] (= *apañarse*) to manage; **con este dinero me arreglo** I can get by *o* I can manage on this money; **~se con/sin algo** to manage with/without sth; **¿cómo os arregláis sin el coche?** how do you manage without the car?; **para comer me arreglo con un bocadillo** at lunch, I make do with a sandwich, I manage on a sandwich for lunch; ✦*MODISMO* **arreglárselas*** to manage; **¿cómo te las arreglas para trabajar tanto y no cansarte?** how do you manage to work so hard and not get tired?; **sabe arreglárselas muy bien solito** he manages perfectly well on his own; **arreglárselas para hacer algo** to manage to do sth; **no sé cómo se las arregla para salir adelante con ese sueldo** I don't know how he manages to get by on that salary; **ya me las ~é para convencerlo** I'll find a way of convincing him

arreglista SMF arranger

arreglo SM [1] (= *reparación*) repair; **la cocina necesita unos pequeños ~s** the kitchen needs a few repairs; **"se hacen ~s"** [*de ropa*] "alterations"; [*de electrodomésticos*] "repairs done"; **el ~ del televisor son 75 euros** it's 75 euros to repair *o* mend *o* fix the TV; **el horno no tiene ~** the oven is beyond repair; **ese problema tiene fácil ~** that problem is easy to sort out *o* solve; **mi marido no tiene ~*** my husband is a hopeless case*
[2] (= *aseo*) [*de persona*] appearance; [*de pelo, barba*] trim; **cuida mucho su ~ personal** he takes great care over his appearance; **un ~ de barba** a beard trim
[3] (= *orden*) order; **vivir con ~** to live an orderly life
[4] (= *acuerdo*) agreement; **tenemos un arreglillo con el jefe** we have made a little arrangement with the boss; **con ~ a** [+ *norma, ley*] in accordance with; [+ *circunstancias, criterio*] according to; **con ~ a lo dispuesto en el artículo 47** in accordance with the provisions of Article 47; **los han ordenado con ~ a su tamaño** they have been arranged according to size; **llegar a un ~** to reach a compromise ► **arreglo de cuentas** settling of old scores
[5] [*de amantes*] affair
[6] (*Mús*) [*de obra original*] arrangement; (*a partir de texto literario*) setting
[7] (*Inform*) array
[8] ► **arreglo floral** flower arrangement; **clases de ~ floral** flower arranging classes

arregostarse ▸conjug 1a◂ VPR **~ a** to take a fancy to

arregosto SM fancy, taste (**de** for)

arrejarse ▸conjug 1a◂ VPR (*Cono Sur*) (= *arriesgarse*) to take a risk

arrejuntado/a* SM/F live-in lover; **los ~s** the couple living together

arrejuntarse* ▸conjug 1a◂ VPR to set up house together, shack up together*; **vivir arrejuntados** to live together

arrejunte* SM cohabitation, living together

arrellanarse ▸conjug 1a◂ VPR, **arrellenarse** ▸conjug 1a◂ VPR [1] (= *ponerse cómodo*) to lounge, sprawl; **~ en el asiento** to lie back in one's chair
[2] (*en un trabajo*) to be happy in one's work

arremangado ADJ (= *vuelto hacia arriba*) turned up, tucked up; [*nariz*] turned up, snub

arremangar ▸conjug 1h◂ Ⓐ VT [+ *mangas, pantalones*] to roll up; [+ *falda*] to tuck up
Ⓑ **arremangarse** VPR (= *subirse las mangas*) to roll up one's sleeves; (= *subirse los pantalones*) to roll up one's trousers; (= *subirse la falda*) to tuck up one's skirt

arrematar* ▸conjug 1a◂ VT to finish, complete

arremeter ▸conjug 2a◂ Ⓐ VT [+ *caballo*] to spur on, spur forward
Ⓑ VI 1 (= *atacar*) to rush forward, attack; ~ **a** o **contra algn** to attack sb, launch o.s. at sb; **el coche arremetió contra la pared** the car smashed into the wall
2 (*fig*) (= *chocar*) to offend good taste, shock the eye

arremetida SF 1 (= *ataque*) attack, assault; (= *empujón*) shove, push; (= *ímpetu*) onrush
2 [*de caballo*] sudden start

arremolinarse ▸conjug 1a◂ VPR [*gente*] to crowd around, mill around; [*corriente*] to swirl, eddy; [*bailadores, polvo*] to swirl, whirl

arrempujar* ▸conjug 1a◂ VT = **empujar**

arrendable ADJ **casa ~** house to let, house available for letting

arrendador(a) SM/F 1 (= *propietario*) landlord/landlady; (*Jur*) lessor; (*Com*) franchisor
2 (= *inquilino*) tenant; (*Jur*) lessee; (*Com*) franchisee

arrendajo SM 1 (*Orn*) jay
2 (= *imitador*) mimic

arrendamiento SM 1 [*de casa, piso*] renting; [*de tierras*] leasing; [*de máquinas, servicios*] hiring; **tomar una casa en ~** to rent a house ► **arrendamiento financiero** leasing
2 (= *precio*) rent, rental
3 (= *contrato*) contract, agreement; (*Com*) (= *concesión*) franchise

arrendar¹ ▸conjug 1j◂ VT 1 [*propietario*] [+ *inmuebles*] to let, lease; [+ *máquinas*] to hire out
2 [*usuario*] [+ *inmuebles*] to rent, lease; [+ *máquinas*] to hire

arrendar² ▸conjug 1j◂ VT [+ *caballo*] to tie, tether (*by the reins*)

arrendatario/a SM/F 1 [*de vivienda*] (= *inquilino*) tenant; (*Jur*) lessee, leaseholder
2 [*de coche*] hirer

arrendero/a SM/F (*Cono Sur, Méx*) = **arrendatario**

arreo SM 1 (= *adorno*) adornment
2 **arreos** [*de caballo*] harness *sing*, trappings; (= *avíos*) gear *sing*
3 (*LAm*) (= *animales*) drove, drove of cattle; (= *acto*) roundup

arrepentidamente ADV regretfully, repentantly

arrepentido/a Ⓐ ADJ (= *pesaroso*) sorry; (*Rel*) repentant; **terrorista ~** reformed terrorist; **estar ~ de algo** to regret sth, be sorry about sth; **se mostró muy ~** he was very sorry
Ⓑ SM/F (*Rel*) penitent; (= *terrorista*) reformed terrorist

arrepentimiento SM 1 (= *pesar*) regret; (*Rel*) repentance; [*de terrorista etc*] reformation
2 (*Arte*) (= *enmienda*) change (*made by the artist to a picture*)

arrepentirse ▸conjug 3i◂ VPR to repent, be repentant; **~ de algo** to regret sth; **~ de haber hecho algo** to regret doing sth, regret having done sth; **no ~ de nada** to have no regrets, not be sorry for anything

arrequín SM (*LAm*) 1 (= *ayudante*) helper, assistant
2 (*Agr*) leading animal, leading animal of a mule train

arrequives SMPL 1 (= *ropa*) finery *sing*, best clothes; (= *adornos*) frills, trimmings
2 (= *circunstancias*) circumstances

arrestado ADJ bold, daring

arrestar ▸conjug 1a◂ Ⓐ VT (= *detener*) to arrest, detain; (= *encarcelar*) to imprison, put in prison; **~ en el cuartel** (*Mil*) to confine to barracks
Ⓑ **arrestarse** VPR **~se a algo** to rush boldly into sth; **~se a todo** to be afraid of nothing

arresto SM 1 (*Jur*) (= *acción*) arrest; (= *detención*) remand; (*Mil*) detention, confinement; **estar bajo ~** to be under arrest ► **arresto domiciliario** house arrest ► **arresto mayor** (*Esp*) *imprisonment for from one month and a day to six months* ► **arresto menor** (*Esp*) *imprisonment for from one day to thirty days* ► **arresto preventivo** preventive detention
2 **arrestos** (= *arrojo*) daring *sing*; **tener ~s** to be bold, be daring

arrevesado ADJ (*LAm*) = **enrevesado**

arria SF (*LAm*) mule train, train of pack animals

arriada SF flood

arriado ADJ (*LAm*) = **arreado**

arrianismo SM Arianism

arriano/a ADJ, SM/F Arian

arriar ▸conjug 1c◂ Ⓐ VT 1 [+ *bandera*] to lower, strike; [+ *vela*] to haul down; [+ *cable*] to loosen
2 (= *inundar*) to flood
Ⓑ **arriarse** VPR to flood, become flooded

arriate SM 1 (*Bot*) (= *era*) bed, border
2 (= *camino*) road

arriba Ⓐ ADV 1 (*indicando situación*) above; **los platos y las tazas están ~** the cups and saucers are above; **allí ~** up there; **aquí ~** up here; **de ~**: **el botón de ~** the top button; **los dientes de ~** my top o upper row of teeth; **la parte de ~** the top; **la parte de ~ del biquini** the bikini top; **los de ~** those above; (= *los que mandan*) the people o those at the top; **estos azulejos hacen juego con los de ~** these tiles match those above; **órdenes (que vienen) de ~** orders from above; **desde ~** from above; **visto desde ~ parece más pequeño** seen from above it looks smaller; **está más ~** it's higher o further up; **pon esos libros ~ del todo** put those books right at the top
2 (*indicando dirección*) **escaparon (por la) calle ~** they escaped up the street; **de ~ abajo** from top to bottom, from head to foot; **rasgó el cuadro de ~ abajo** he slashed the painting from top to bottom; **me dio un masaje de ~ abajo** he massaged me from head to foot; **vestida de negro de ~ abajo** dressed completely in black, dressed in black from head to foot; **esa ley debe cambiar de ~ abajo** this act must be completely revised; **se puede mirar el catálogo de ~ abajo** you can read the catalogue through from beginning to end; **mirar a algn de ~ abajo** to look sb up and down; **andar para ~ y para abajo** ◊ **ir de ~ para abajo** to run back and forth; **hacia ~** up(wards); **mire hacia ~** look up; **hasta ~**: **subí hasta ~** I climbed to the top; **llenar la copa hasta ~** to fill the glass to the brim; **el estadio está lleno hasta ~** the stadium is chock-a-block; **está hasta ~ de trabajo*** he's up to his eyes in work*; **llegar ~** to get to the top; **"este lado para ~"** "this side up"; **de la cintura para ~** from the waist up; **un juego para niños de ocho años para ~** a game for children of eight and over; **de diez dólares para ~** from ten dollars upwards; *ver tb* **agua, cuesta, patas**
3 (*en casa*) upstairs; **~ están los dormitorios** the bedrooms are upstairs; **los vecinos de ~** our upstairs neighbours; **grité de tal manera que los de ~ lo oyeron** I shouted so loud that the people upstairs heard me
4 (*en texto*) above; **lo escrito ~** what has been written above; **como hemos dicho más ~** as has been said above; **la persona ~ mencionada** the abovementioned o aforementioned person
5 **~ de** (*esp LAm*) (= *encima de*) on top of; (= *por encima de*) above, over; (= *más alto que*) higher than, further up than; (= *más de*) more than; **lo dejé ~ del refrigerador** I left it on top of the fridge; **viven en el departamento ~ del mío** they live in the flat above mine; **el río ~ de la ciudad** the river above the town; **~ mío** (*esp Cono Sur*) over me, above me, on top of me
Ⓑ EXCL (= *a levantarse*) up you get!; **¡~ ese ánimo!** cheer o chin up!; **¡manos ~!** hands up!; **¡~ el telón!** raise the curtain!; **¡~ el Depor!** (*Dep*) up (with) Depor !; **¡~ el socialismo!** long live socialism!

arribada SF (*Náut*) arrival, entry into harbour o (*EEUU*) harbor; **entrar de ~** to put into port ► **arribada forzosa** unscheduled stop

arribaje SM (*Náut*) arrival, entry into harbour, entry into harbor (*EEUU*)

arribano ADJ (*Cono Sur*) upper, higher

arribar ▸conjug 1a◂ VI 1 (*esp LAm*) (= *llegar*) to arrive; (*Náut*) (= *llegar a puerto*) to put into port; (= *ir a la deriva*) to drift; **~ a** to reach
2 (*Med, Fin*) (= *convalecer*) to recover, improve

arribazón SF (= *abundancia de peces*) coastal abundance of fish, off-shore shoal; [*de dinero*] bonanza

arribeño/a SM/F 1 (*LAm*) (= *serrano*) highlander, inlander
2 (*Cono Sur*) (= *forastero*) stranger

arribismo SM social climbing

arribista SMF upstart, arriviste (*frm*)

arribo SM (*esp LAm*) arrival; **hacer su ~** to arrive

arriendo SM = **arrendamiento**

arriero SM muleteer

arriesgadamente ADV (= *peligrosamente*) riskily, dangerously; (= *intrépidamente*) daringly, boldly

arriesgado ADJ 1 [*acto*] risky, hazardous; **unas ideas arriesgadas** some dangerous ideas; **me parece ~ prometerlo** I would be rash to promise it
2 [*individuo*] (= *intrépido*) bold, daring; (*pey*) (= *impetuoso*) rash, foolhardy

arriesgar ▸conjug 1h◂ Ⓐ VT (= *poner en riesgo*) to risk, hazard; [+ *oportunidad*] to endanger, put at risk; [+ *conjetura*] to hazard, venture; [+ *dinero*] to stake

Ⓑ **arriesgarse** VPR to take a risk, expose o.s. to danger; **~se a hacer algo** to risk doing sth; **~se a una multa** to risk a fine; **~se en una empresa** to venture upon an enterprise

arrimadero SM (= *arrimo*) support; (= *apeadero*) mounting block, step

arrimadillo SM matting (*used as wainscot*)

arrimadizo/a Ⓐ ADJ (*fig*) parasitic
Ⓑ SM/F parasite, hanger-on

arrimado/a Ⓐ ADJ [1] [*imitación*] close
[2] (*Col, Méx, Ven**) (= *aprovechado*) **viven ~s con los suegros** they scrounge off their in-laws
[3] (*Méx**) (= *juntos*) **—¿son marido y mujer? —no, están ~s nomás** "are they married?" — "no, they're just living together"
Ⓑ SM/F [1] (*Col, Méx, Ven**) (= *aprovechado*) scrounger*
[2] (*Caribe*) (= *intruso*) unwelcome guest
[3] (*Andes*) (= *amante*) lover
[4] (*Cono Sur**) (= *mantenido*) kept man/woman (*pey*)

arrimar ▸conjug 1a◂ Ⓐ VT [1] (= *acercar*) to move nearer, move closer (**a** to), to bring nearer, bring closer (**a** to); **arrima tu silla a la mía** bring your chair nearer to mine; **~on el coche al bordillo a empujones** they pushed the car nearer to the kerb; **se saludan sólo arrimando la cara** they just touch cheeks when they greet each other; **arrima el sofá contra la pared** move *o* push the sofa against the wall; **~ las espuelas a un caballo** to dig one's spurs into a horse; **~ un golpe a algn** (*Méx**) to hit sb, strike sb; **~ el oído a la puerta** to put one's ear to the door; **vivir arrimado a algn** (*gen*) to live with sb; (*con dependencia económica*) to live off sb; (*sexualmente*) to shack up; *ver tb* **ascua, hombro**
[2] (= *ignorar*) [+ *persona*] to ignore; [+ *proyecto*] to shelve; **el plan quedó arrimado** the plan was shelved; ✦**MODISMO ~ los libros** to give up studying, drop out*
[3] (*Náut*) [+ *carga*] to stow
Ⓑ **arrimarse** VPR [1] (*a un lugar*) to come nearer, come closer (**a** to); **arrímate un poco más a la pared** get a little nearer to the wall; **no te arrimes mucho al precipicio** don't get too close to the precipice; **se arrimó mucha gente a mirar** many people gathered round to look; **me arrimé a la pared para que no me vieran** I flattened myself against the wall so that they wouldn't see me; **se arrimó a la lumbre** she huddled closer to the fire
[2] **~se a algn** (*gen*) to come closer to sb; (*para pedir algo*) to come up to sb; (*buscando calor*) to snuggle up to sb; (*para sacar dinero*) to scrounge off sb*; **arrímate para que te vea mejor** come closer so I can see you better; **paraban la música si alguien se arrimaba demasiado a su pareja** they stopped the music if anyone got too close to their partner; **bailaban muy arrimados** they were dancing cheek-to-cheek, they were dancing very close; **se me fue arrimando hasta que se sentó a mi lado** he edged closer until he was sitting right next to me; **se nos arrimó a preguntar la hora** he came up to us to ask the time; **se arriman a los que están en el poder** they ingratiate themselves with those in power; **se ~on a la casa de la madre del marido** at home they scrounged off their mother in law*; **arrímate a mí** cuddle up to me, snuggle up to me; *ver tb* **sol**
[3] (*Taur*) to fight close to the bull
[4] (*Méx**) (= *vivir juntos*) to live together

arrimo SM [1] (= *ayuda*) protection; **al ~ de algn/algo** with the support of sb/with the help of sth; **prosperó al ~ de su tío** he prospered with his uncle's support; **nos resguardamos al ~ de un árbol** we sheltered under a tree
[2] (= *apego*) attachment; **no siente ~ por nadie** he doesn't feel attached to anybody, he doesn't feel any attachment to anybody
[3] (*) (= *amorío*) affair
[4] (*Constr*) partition
[5] (*Chile*) (= *consola*) (*tb* **mesa de ~**) console table

arrimón SM (= *holgazán*) loafer, idler; (= *gorrón*) sponger*; **estar de ~** to hang about, loaf around

arrinconado ADJ (= *olvidado*) forgotten, neglected; (= *marginado*) out in the cold*; (= *remoto*) remote; (= *abandonado*) abandoned

arrinconar ▸conjug 1a◂ Ⓐ VT [1] [+ *objeto*] to put in a corner; [+ *enemigo*] to corner
[2] (= *abandonar*) to lay aside, discard; (= *dar carpetazo a*) to shelve, put on the back burner; (= *apartar*) to push aside; (= *marginar*) to leave out in the cold*
Ⓑ **arrinconarse** VPR to become a recluse

arriñonado ADJ kidney-shaped

arriñonar* ▸conjug 1a◂ VT to wear out, exhaust; **estar arriñonado** to be knackered*

arriscadamente ADV boldly, resolutely

arriscado ADJ [1] (*Geog*) craggy
[2] [*persona*] (= *resuelto*) bold, resolute; (= *animoso*) spirited; (= *ágil*) brisk, agile

arriscamiento SM boldness, resolution

arriscar¹ ▸conjug 1g◂ Ⓐ VT to risk
Ⓑ **arriscarse** VPR to take a risk

arriscar² ▸conjug 1g◂ Ⓐ VT (*Andes, Cono Sur, Méx*) (= *doblar*) to turn up, fold up, tuck up; (= *encrespar*) to stiffen; [+ *nariz*] to wrinkle
Ⓑ VI [1] (*Andes*) (= *enderezarse*) to draw o.s. up, straighten up
[2] **~ a** (*LAm*) to amount to
Ⓒ **arriscarse** VPR [1] (= *engreírse*) to get conceited
[2] (*Andes, CAm*) (= *vestir con elegancia*) to dress up to the nines

arriscocho ADJ (*Andes*) restless

arrivista = **arribista**

arrizar ▸conjug 1f◂ VT (*Náut*) [+ *vela*] to reef; (= *asegurar*) to fasten, lash down

arroba SF [1] (= *medida de peso*) 25 pounds; (= *medida de líquidos*) *a variable liquid measure*; ✦**MODISMO por ~s*** tons*, loads*; **tiene talento por ~s** he has loads of talent, he oozes talent*
[2] (*Internet*) (*en dirección electrónica*) at

arrobador ADJ entrancing, enchanting

arrobamiento SM (= *éxtasis*) ecstasy, rapture; (*Rel*) trance; **salir de su ~** to emerge from one's state of bliss, come back to earth*

arrobar ▸conjug 1a◂ Ⓐ VT to entrance, enchant
Ⓑ **arrobarse** VPR (= *embelesarse*) to go into ecstasies, be enraptured; [*místico etc*] to go into a trance

arrobo SM = **arrobamiento**

arrocero/a Ⓐ ADJ rice *antes de s*; **cultivo ~** rice cultivation; **industria arrocera** rice industry
Ⓑ SM/F (*Caribe*) gatecrasher

arrochelarse ▸conjug 1a◂ VPR (*Andes*) [*ganado*] to take a liking to a place; [*perro*] to refuse to go out; [*caballo*] to balk, shy

arrodajarse ▸conjug 1a◂ VPR (*CAm*) to sit cross-legged

arrodillarse ▸conjug 1a◂ VPR to kneel, kneel down, go down on one's knees; **estar arrodillado** to be kneeling, be kneeling down, be on one's knees

arrogancia SF (= *altanería*) arrogance, haughtiness; (= *orgullo*) pride

arrogante ADJ (= *altanero*) arrogant, haughty; (= *orgulloso*) proud

arrogantemente ADV (= *con altanería*) arrogantly, haughtily; (= *con orgullo*) proudly

arrogarse ▸conjug 1h◂ VPR **~ algo** to assume sth, take sth on o.s.

arrojadamente ADV boldly

arrojadizo ADJ **arma arrojadiza** missile, projectile

arrojado ADJ (= *valiente*) daring, dashing; (= *temerario*) reckless

arrojallamas SM INV flamethrower

arrojar ▸conjug 1a◂ Ⓐ VT [1] (= *lanzar*) to throw; (*con fuerza*) to hurl; **la niña arrojaba piedras al río** the girl was throwing stones into the river; **los hinchas ~on piedras contra la policía** the fans threw *o* hurled stones at the police; **arroja el papel al cubo de la basura** throw the paper into the wastepaper basket; **"no arrojar basura"** "no tipping"
[2] [+ *humo, lava*] to send out
[3] [+ *resultados, datos*] to produce; **la investigación ha arrojado datos muy negativos** the investigation has produced some very negative data; **la transacción arrojó un balance positivo** the transaction yielded a profit; **este estudio arroja (alguna) luz sobre el tema** this study sheds some light on the subject; **el accidente arrojó 80 muertos** (*LAm*) the accident left 80 dead
[4] (= *expulsar*) to throw out; **lo arrojó de casa por su comportamiento** she threw him out of the house because of his behaviour
[5] (*LAm*) (= *vomitar*) to bring up, vomit
Ⓑ **arrojarse** VPR (= *lanzarse*) to throw o.s.; (*con fuerza*) hurl o.s.; **se arrojó a mis brazos y lloró** he threw *o* flung himself into my arms and wept; **el ladrón se arrojó desde el quinto piso** the thief threw *o* hurled himself from the fifth floor; **el asesino se arrojó sobre su víctima** the killer threw *o* hurled himself on his victim

arrojo SM daring, fearlessness; **con ~** boldly, fearlessly

arrollado SM (*Cono Sur*) rolled pork

arrollador ADJ **un ataque ~** a crushing attack; **por una mayoría ~a** by an overwhelming majority; **es una pasión ~a** it is a consuming passion; **tenía una personalidad ~a** she had an overwhelming *o* overpowering personality

arrollar¹ ▸conjug 1a◂ VT [1] (= *enrollar*) (*gen*) to roll up; [+ *cable, cuerda, hilo*] to coil, wind
[2] (= *arrastrar*) [*río*] to sweep away, wash away; [+ *enemigo*] to rout; [+ *adversario*] to crush; [+ *peatón*] to run over, knock down; **~on a sus rivales** they crushed their rivals
[3] [+ *persona*] (*en debate*) to crush; (= *asombrar*) to dumbfound, leave speechless

arrollar² ▸conjug 1a◂ VT = **arrullar A**

arromar ▸conjug 1a◂ VT to blunt, dull

arropar ▸conjug 1a◂ Ⓐ VT [1] (= *vestir*) to wrap up, wrap up with clothes; (*en cama*) to tuck up, tuck up in bed
[2] (*fig*) (= *proteger*) to protect
Ⓑ **arroparse** VPR to wrap o.s. up; **¡arrópate bien!** wrap up warm!

arrope SM (= *jarabe*) syrup; [*de mosto*] grape syrup; [*de miel*] honey syrup

arrorró SM (*LAm*) lullaby

arrostrado ADJ **bien ~** nice-looking; **mal ~** ugly

arrostrar ▸conjug 1a◂ Ⓐ VT [+ *consecuencias*] to face, face up to; [+ *peligro*] to brave, face
Ⓑ VI [1] **~ a algo** to show a liking for sth
[2] **~ con** = **A**
Ⓒ **arrostrarse** VPR **~se con algn** to face up to sb

arroyada SF [1] (= *barranco*) gully, stream bed
[2] (= *inundación*) flood, flooding

arroyo SM [1] (= *riachuelo*) stream, brook; (= *cauce*) watercourse; (*LAm*) (= *río*) river; (*Méx*) (= *barranco*) gully, ravine
[2] (= *cuneta*) gutter; **poner a algn en el ~** to turn sb onto the streets; **sacar a algn del ~** to drag sb from the gutter; **ser del ~** to be an orphan

arroyuelo SM small stream, brook

arroz SM rice; ✦**MODISMO** **hubo ~ y gallo muerto** (*Esp, Caribe**) it was a slap-up do* ► **arroz a la cubana** *rice with banana, tomato sauce and fried egg* ► **arroz blanco** white rice ► **arroz hervido** boiled rice ► **arroz hinchado** puffed rice ► **arroz con leche** rice pudding ► **arroz integral** brown rice

arrozal SM rice field, paddy field

arrufarse ▸conjug 1a◂ VPR (*Caribe*) to get annoyed, get angry

arruga SF [1] (*en piel*) wrinkle, line; (*en ropa*) crease
[2] (*Andes**) (= *estafa*) swindle, con*; (= *deuda*) debt; **hacer una ~** (*Andes*) to cheat

arrugado ADJ [*cara etc*] wrinkled, lined; [*papel etc*] creased; [*vestido*] crumpled, creased up

arrugar ▸conjug 1h◂ Ⓐ VT [+ *cara*] to wrinkle, line; [+ *ceño*] to knit; [+ *papel*] to crumple, screw up; [+ *ropa*] to ruck up, crumple; **~ la cara** to screw up one's face; **~ el entrecejo** to knit one's brow, frown
Ⓑ **arrugarse** VPR [1] [*cara*] to wrinkle, wrinkle up, get wrinkled; [*ropa*] to crease, get creased; [*planta*] to shrivel up
[2] (*Méx**) (= *asustarse*) to get scared, get frightened

arrugue SM (*Caribe*) = **arruga**

arruinado ADJ [1] [*persona, reputación, vida*] ruined
[2] (*Cono Sur, Méx*) (= *enclenque*) sickly, stunted; (*Cono Sur*) (= *miserable*) wretched, down and out

arruinamiento SM ruin, ruination

arruinar ▸conjug 1a◂ Ⓐ VT [1] (= *empobrecer*) to ruin
[2] (= *destruir*) to wreck, destroy
[3] (*LAm*) (= *desvirgar*) to deflower
Ⓑ **arruinarse** VPR [*compañía*] to be ruined; [*edificio*] to fall into ruins, fall down, collapse

arrullar ▸conjug 1a◂ Ⓐ VT [+ *niño*] to lull to sleep, sing to sleep; [+ *amante*] to say sweet nothings to
Ⓑ VI to coo
Ⓒ **arrullarse** VPR to bill and coo

arrullo SM (*Orn*) cooing; [*de amantes*] billing and cooing; [*de agua, olas*] murmur; (= *canción*) lullaby

arrumaco SM [1] (= *caricia*) caress
[2] (= *halago*) piece of flattery; **andar con ~** to flatter
[3] (= *vestido etc*) *eccentric item of dress or adornment*
[4] **arrumacos** (= *cariñitos*) show of affection *sing*, endearments

arrumaje SM stowage

arrumar ▸conjug 1a◂ Ⓐ VT [1] (*Náut*) to stow
[2] (= *amontonar*) to pile up
Ⓑ **arrumarse** VPR to become overcast

arrumbar¹ ▸conjug 1a◂ VT [1] [+ *objeto*] (= *apartar*) to put aside, discard; (= *olvidar*) to neglect, forget
[2] [+ *individuo*] (*en discusión*) to silence, floor; (= *apartar*) to remove

arrumbar² ▸conjug 1a◂ (*Náut*) Ⓐ VI to set course (**hacia** for)
Ⓑ **arrumbarse** VPR to take one's bearings

arrume SM (*Andes, Caribe*) pile, heap

arruncharse ▸conjug 1a◂ VPR (*Andes*) to curl up, roll up

arrurruz SM arrowroot

arrutanado ADJ (*Andes*) plump

arrutinarse ▸conjug 1a◂ VPR to get into a routine, get set in one's ways

arsenal SM [1] (*Náut*) naval dockyard; (*Mil*) arsenal; **el ~ nuclear** the nuclear arsenal
[2] (= *conjunto numeroso*) storehouse, mine

arsenalera SF (*Cono Sur*) surgeon's assistant, theatre auxiliary

arsénico SM arsenic

arte SM o SF (*gen m en sing, f en pl*) [1] (= *pintura, música*) art; **~s** (*Univ*) arts; **~s y oficios** arts and crafts; **bellas ~s** fine arts; **~ de vivir** art of living; **el séptimo ~** the cinema, film; **~ de los trucos** conjuring; **por ~ de magia** by magic, as if by magic; ✦**MODISMO** **no tener ~ ni parte en algo** to have nothing whatsoever to do with sth ► **arte abstracto** abstract art ► **artes decorativas** decorative arts ► **artes gráficas** graphic arts ► **artes marciales** martial arts ► **arte poética** poetics *sing* ► **arte pop** pop art ► **artes plásticas** plastic arts; *ver tb* **amor 1**
[2] (= *habilidad*) skill; (= *astucia*) craftiness; **malas ~s** trickery *sing*; **por malas ~s** by trickery
[3] (= *artificio*) workmanship, artistry; **sin ~** (*como adj*) clumsy; (*como adv*) clumsily
[4] (*Literat*) ► **arte mayor** *Spanish verse of eight lines each of twelve syllables dating from the 15th century* ► **arte menor** *Spanish verse usually of four lines each of six or eight syllables*
[5] (*Pesca*) **~ de pesca** (= *red*) fishing net; (= *caña etc*) fishing tackle

artefacto SM [1] (*Téc*) device, appliance ► **artefacto explosivo** bomb, explosive device ► **artefacto incendiario** incendiary device ► **artefacto infernal** bomb, explosive device ► **artefacto nuclear** nuclear device ► **artefactos de alumbrado** light fittings, light fixtures
[2] (*Arqueología*) artefact, artifact (*EEUU*)
[3] (*Aut**) old crock, jalopy*, old banger*

artejo SM knuckle

arteramente ADV cunningly, artfully

arteria SF [1] (*Med*) artery
[2] (= *calle*) artery; **la ~ principal de una ciudad** the main thoroughfare of a town

artería SF cunning, artfulness

arterial ADJ arterial

arterioesclerosis SF INV, **arteriosclerosis** SF INV arteriosclerosis

artero ADJ cunning, artful, crafty

artesa SF trough

artesanal ADJ craft *antes de s*, handicraft *antes de s*; **industria ~** craft industry, handicraft industry; **productos ~es** crafts, handicrafts

artesanía SF (= *arte*) craftmanship; (= *productos*) crafts *pl*, handicrafts *pl*; (= *artes y oficios*) arts and crafts; **obra de ~** piece of craftsmanship; **zapatos de ~** craft shoes, hand-made shoes

artesano/a Ⓐ ADJ home-made, home-produced
Ⓑ SM/F craftsman/craftswoman, artisan

artesiano ADJ **pozo ~** artesian well

artesón SM [1] [*de cocina*] kitchen tub
[2] (*Arquit*) coffer, caisson; (= *adorno*) moulding, molding (*EEUU*)
[3] (*Andes, Méx*) (= *bóveda*) vault; (= *arcos*) arcade, series of arches; (= *terraza*) flat roof, terrace

artesonado SM coffered ceiling

artesonar ▸conjug 1a◂ VT [1] (= *poner paneles a*) to coffer
[2] (= *estucar*) to stucco, mould, mold (*EEUU*)

ártico Ⓐ ADJ Arctic
Ⓑ SM **el Ártico** the Arctic

articulación SF [1] (*Anat*) articulation (*frm*), joint
[2] (*Mec*) joint ► **articulación esférica** ball-and-socket joint ► **articulación universal** universal joint
[3] (*Ling*) articulation

articuladamente ADV distinctly, articulately

articulado Ⓐ ADJ [1] [*persona*] articulate
[2] (*Anat, Mec*) articulated, jointed; (*Aut*) [*volante*] collapsible
Ⓑ SM [*de ley, reglamento*] article

articular ▸conjug 1a◂ Ⓐ VT [1] (*Ling*) to articulate
[2] (*Mec*) to articulate, join together
[3] (*Jur*) to article
[4] (*Andes, Cono Sur**) (= *regañar*) to tell off*, dress down*
Ⓑ VI (*Cono Sur*) (= *reñir*) to quarrel, squabble; (= *quejarse*) to grumble, moan*

articulista SMF columnist, contributor (*to a paper*)

artículo SM [1] (*Com*) article, item; **~s** commodities, goods ► **artículos alimenticios** foodstuffs ► **artículos de consumo** consumer goods ► **artículos de escritorio** stationery ► **artículos de marca** branded goods; (*Com*) proprietary goods ► **artículos de plata** silverware *sing* ► **artículos de primera necesidad** basic commodities, essentials ► **artículos de tocador** toiletries
[2] (*escrito*) article; (*TV*) feature, report; (*en revista erudita*) article, paper; (*en libro de referencia*) entry, article ► **artículo de fondo** leader, editorial ► **artículo de portada** cover story, front-page article
[3] (*Ling*) article ► **artículo definido** definite article ► **artículo indefinido** indefinite arti-

cle
[4] [*de ley, documento*] article, section, item

artífice SMF (*Arte*) artist, craftsman/craftswoman; (= *hacedor*) maker; (= *inventor*) inventor; **el ~ de la victoria** the architect of victory

artificial ADJ [*flor, luz, inseminación*] artificial; [*material*] artificial, man-made; **fuegos ~es** fireworks

artificialidad SF artificiality

artificializar ▸conjug 1f◂ VT to make artificial, give an air of artificiality to

artificialmente ADV artificially

artificiero/a SM/F explosives expert, bomb-disposal officer

artificio SM [1] (= *arte*) art, craft; (= *truco*) artifice; (= *astucia*) cunning, sly trick
[2] (= *aparato*) device, appliance
[3] (= *hechura*) workmanship, craftsmanship

artificiosamente ADV (= *ingeniosamente*) skilfully, skillfully (*EEUU*), ingeniously; (= *astutamente*) cunningly, artfully

artificioso ADJ (= *ingenioso*) skilful, skillful (*EEUU*), ingenious; (= *astuto*) cunning, artful, sly

artillería SF [1] (*Mil*) artillery ► **artillería antiaérea** anti-aircraft guns *pl* ► **artillería de campaña** field guns *pl* ► **artillería pesada** heavy artillery
[2] (*Dep**) forward line

artillero SM [1] (*Mil*) artilleryman; (*Aer, Náut*) gunner; (*Min*) explosives expert
[2] (*Dep**) forward

artilugio SM [1] (= *aparato*) gadget, contraption
[2] (= *truco*) gimmick, stunt
[3] (= *chisme*) thingummy*, gizmo (*EEUU**), whatsit*

artimaña SF [1] (*Caza*) trap, snare
[2] (= *ingenio*) cunning

artista SMF [1] (*Arte*) artist
[2] (*Teat, Cine*) artist, artiste ► **artista de cine** film actor/film actress ► **artista de teatro** actor/actress ► **artista de variedades** variety artist *o* artiste ► **artista invitado/a** guest artist *o* artiste
[3] (*) (= *persona hábil*) **es un ~ haciendo paella** he's an expert at making paella

artísticamente ADV artistically

artístico ADJ artistic

artrítico ADJ arthritic

artritis SF INV arthritis ► **artritis reumatoide** rheumatoid arthritis

artrópodo SM arthropod; **artrópodos** SMPL (*como clase*) arthropoda

artrosis SF INV osteoarthritis

Arturo SM Arthur

Artús SM **el Rey ~** King Arthur

aruñón SM [1] (*Andes*) (= *ladrón*) thief, pickpocket [2] = **arañazo**

arveja SF [1] (*Bot*) vetch
[2] (*LAm*) (= *guisante*) pea

Arz. ABR, **Arzbpo.** ABR (= **arzobispo**) Abp

arzobispado SM archbishopric

arzobispal ADJ archiepiscopal; **palacio ~** archbishop's palace

arzobispo SM archbishop

arzón SM saddle tree ► **arzón delantero** saddlebow

as SM [1] (*Naipes*) ace; (*dominó*) one ► **as de espadas** ace of spades; ✦*MODISMO* **guardarse un as en la manga** to have an ace up one's sleeve
[2] (*) (= *campeón*) ace; **es un as** he's a star* ► **as del fútbol** star player ► **as del volante** champion driver, crack driver*
[3] (*Tenis*) ace

asa[1] SF [1] (= *agarradero*) handle
[2] (= *pretexto*) lever, pretext; ✦*MODISMO* **ser muy del ~*** to be well in

asa[2] SF (*Bot*) (= *jugo*) juice

asadera SF (*Cono Sur*) baking tin

asadero Ⓐ ADJ roasting, for roasting
Ⓑ SM [1] (*Elec*) spit roaster; (= *lugar caluroso*) oven
[2] (*Méx*) (= *queso blando*) cottage cheese

asado Ⓐ ADJ [1] (*Culin*) roast *antes de s*, roasted; **carne asada** roast meat; **~ al horno** baked; **~ a la parrilla** grilled, broiled (*EEUU*); **bien ~** well done; **poco ~** rare
[2] (*LAm*) (= *enfadado*) cross, angry
[3] (*) **estar ~** (*Caribe*) to be broke*
Ⓑ SM [1] (*Culin*) roast, joint
[2] (*Cono Sur*) (= *comida*) barbecue; (= *carne asada*) barbecued meat

asador SM [1] (= *varilla*) spit; (= *aparato*) spit roaster ► **asador a rotación, asador rotatorio** rotary spit
[2] (= *restaurante*) carvery

asadura Ⓐ SF [1] (*Anat*) **asaduras** entrails, offal *sing*; (*Culin*) chitterlings; ✦*MODISMO* **echar las ~s** to bust a gut*
[2] (= *pachorra*) sluggishness, laziness; **tiene ~s** he's terribly lazy
Ⓑ SMF (*) stolid person, dull sort*

asaetear ▸conjug 1a◂ VT [1] to shoot, hit (*with an arrow*)
[2] (*fig*) (= *acosar*) to bother, pester

asalariado/a Ⓐ ADJ wage-earning
Ⓑ SM/F [1] (= *empleado*) wage earner
[2] (*pey*) (= *mercenario*) hireling; **es ~ de la Mafia** he's in the pay of the Mafia

asalariar ▸conjug 1b◂ VT to employ

asalmonado ADJ salmon coloured, salmon colored (*EEUU*)

asaltabancos SMF INV bank robber

asaltador(a) SM/F, **asaltante** SMF [*de persona*] attacker, assailant; [*de banco, tienda*] raider

asaltar ▸conjug 1a◂ VT [1] [+ *persona*] to attack, assault; (*Mil*) to storm; [+ *banco, tienda etc*] to break into, raid; (*en disturbios etc*) to loot, sack; **lo ~on cuatro bandidos** he was held up by four bandits; **anoche fue asaltada la joyería** the jeweller's was raided last night, last night there was a break-in at the jeweller's
[2] [*dudas*] to assail; [*idea*] to cross one's mind; **le asaltó una idea** he was struck by an idea, an idea crossed his mind
[3] [*desastre, muerte*] to fall upon, surprise, overtake

asalto SM [1] (= *atraco*) robbery; **~ a un banco** bank raid, bank robbery
[2] (*Mil*) attack, assault; **el ~ al Parlamento** the attack *o* assault on parliament, the storming of parliament; **tomar por ~** to take by storm; *ver tb* **tropa 1**
[3] (*Boxeo*) round
[4] (*Esgrima*) ► **asalto de armas** fencing bout
[5] (= *acoso*) hounding, harassment; **el continuo ~ de los paparazzi** the constant hounding *o* harassment by the paparazzi
[6] (*Caribe, Méx*) (= *fiesta sorpresa*) surprise party

asamblea SF [1] (= *reunión*) meeting; [*de trabajadores*] mass meeting; **llamar a ~** (*Mil, Hist*) to assemble, muster
[2] (= *congreso*) congress, assembly ► **asamblea general** general assembly ► **Asamblea Nacional** National Assembly

asambleario ADJ **las decisiones asamblearias** the assembly's decisions; **los representantes ~s** the representatives to the assembly

asambleísta SMF member of the assembly

asapán SM (*Méx*) flying squirrel

asar ▸conjug 1a◂ Ⓐ VT [1] (*Culin*) to roast; **~ al horno** to bake; **~ a la parrilla** to grill, broil (*EEUU*)
[2] (*fig*) (= *acosar*) to pester, plague (**con, a** with)
Ⓑ **asarse** VPR (*fig*) to be terribly hot, roast; **me aso de calor** I'm roasting, I'm boiling; **aquí se asa uno vivo** it's boiling hot here

asascuarse* ▸conjug 1d◂ VPR (*Méx*) to roll up into a ball

asaz ADV (*Literat*) very, exceedingly; **una tarea ~ difícil** an exceedingly difficult task

asbesto SM asbestos

ascendencia SF [1] (= *linaje*) ancestry; (= *origen*) origin; **de remota ~ normanda** of remote Norman ancestry
[2] (= *dominio*) ascendancy; (= *influencia*) hold, influence

ascendente Ⓐ ADJ [*movimiento*] ascending; [*tendencia*] rising, increasing; **en una curva ~** in an upward curve; **la carrera ~ del pistón** the upstroke of the piston; **el tren ~** the up train
Ⓑ SM (*Astrol*) ascendant

ascender ▸conjug 2g◂ Ⓐ VI [1] (= *subir*) [*persona*] (*en montaña*) to climb up; (*en el aire*) to rise, ascend (*frm*); **ascendieron hasta 3.500 metros** they climbed to 3,500 metres; **ascendieron por el otro lado del monte** they made their ascent on the other side of the mountain, they climbed up the other side of the mountain; **el globo ascendió por los aires** the balloon rose *o* ascended (*frm*) into the air; **ascendía por las escaleras** (*liter*) she ascended (*liter*) *o* climbed the steps
[2] [*temperatura, presión*] to go up, rise
[3] **~ a** [3·1] [*empleado, equipo, militar*] to be promoted to; **ascendió al cargo de presidente de la compañía** he was promoted to company president, he rose to the position of company president; **el Málaga ha ascendido a primera división** Málaga have gone up to the first division, Málaga have been promoted to the first division; **~ al trono** to ascend the throne
[3·2] [*cantidad*] to amount to, come to; **los beneficios ascendieron a miles de libras** the profits amounted *o* came to thousands of pounds; **el número de heridos asciende ya a 20** the number of wounded has now risen to *o* has now reached 20; **¿a cuánto ascendió la factura?** how much did the bill come to?
Ⓑ VT [+ *empleado, militar*] to promote; **lo ascendieron a teniente** he rose *o* was promoted to the rank of lieutenant

ascendiente Ⓐ ADJ = **ascendente A**
Ⓑ SMF (= *persona*) ancestor, forebear (*frm*)
Ⓒ SM (= *influencia*) ascendancy (*frm*), (powerful) influence (**sobre** over)

ascensión SF 1 (= *subida*) (*a montaña*) ascent; (*al poder*) rise; **la ~ al Mont Blanc** the ascent of Mont Blanc; **la ~ del comunismo** the rise of communism; **desde su ~ al trono** (*frm*) since his accession to the throne (*frm*)
2 [*de empleado, militar, equipo*] promotion (**a** to); **su ~ a teniente** his promotion to lieutenant; **la ~ del Chelsea en la liga ha sido vertiginosa** Chelsea's rise in the league has been dramatic
3 (*Rel*) **la Ascensión** the Ascension; **Día de la Ascensión** Ascension Day

ascensional ADJ [*curva, movimiento etc*] upward; (*Astron*) ascendant, rising

ascensionista SMF 1 (= *escalador*) mountain climber, mountaineer
2 (*en globo*) balloonist

ascenso SM 1 (= *subida*) (*a montaña*) ascent; (*al poder*) rise; **en el ~ al Everest** on the ascent of Everest; **se produjo el ~ de la burguesía al poder** the bourgeoisie rose to power
2 (= *aumento*) [*de temperatura, precio, popularidad*] rise; [*de beneficios, impuestos*] increase; **habrá un ~ general de las temperaturas** temperatures will go up *o* rise everywhere, there will be a rise in temperatures everywhere; **temperaturas en ~** rising temperatures, temperatures on the rise; **la Bolsa experimentó un ~ de 4,5 puntos** shares on the Stock Exchange rose by 4.5 points; **se quejan del ~ de los impuestos** they are complaining about the increase in taxes
3 (= *mejora*) rise; **preocupa el ~ electoral de los neofascistas** the increased popularity *o* the rise in popularity of the neo-fascists is giving cause for concern
4 [*de empleado, militar, equipo*] promotion (**a** to); **soldados con posibilidades de ~** soldiers with promotion prospects; **su ~ a general** his promotion to the rank of general; **su ~ en la empresa ha sido impresionante** his rise within the company has been extraordinary; **acaban de conseguir el ~ a primera división** they have just managed to gain promotion to the first division

ascensor SM lift, elevator (*EEUU*); (*Téc*) elevator

ascensorista SMF lift attendant, elevator operator (*EEUU*)

ascesis SF asceticism

asceta SMF ascetic

ascético ADJ ascetic

ascetismo SM asceticism

asco SM 1 (= *sensación*) disgust, revulsion; **¡qué ~!** how disgusting!, how revolting!; **¡qué ~ de gente!** what awful *o* ghastly* people!; **coger ~ a algo** to get sick of sth; **dar ~ a algn** to sicken sb, disgust sb; **me das ~** you disgust me; **me dan ~ las aceitunas** I loathe olives; **hacer ~s a algo** to turn up one's nose at sth; **poner cara de ~** to look disgusted, pull a face; **morirse de ~** (*Esp**) to be bored to tears *o* to death
2 (= *objeto*) **es un ~** it's disgusting; **estar hecho un ~** to be filthy; **poner a algn de ~** (*Méx**) to call sb all sorts of names

ascua SF live coal, ember; **¡~s!** ouch!;
✦*MODISMOS* **arrimar el ~ a su sardina** to look after number one; **estar como ~ de oro** to be shining bright; **estar en ~s** to be on tenterhooks; **pasar por algo como sobre ~s** to rush through sth; **tener a algn sobre ~s** to keep sb on tenterhooks; **sacar el ~ con la mano del gato** ◊ **sacar el ~ con mano ajena** to get sb else to do the dirty work

aseadamente ADV (= *con limpieza*) cleanly; (= *con arreglo*) neatly, tidily

aseado ADJ (= *limpio*) clean; (= *arreglado*) neat, tidy

aseador(a) SM/F (*Chile*) cleaner

asear ▸conjug 1a◂ Ⓐ VT 1 (= *lavar*) to wash; (= *limpiar*) to clean up; (= *pulir*) to smarten up
2 (= *adornar*) to adorn, embellish (*frm*)
Ⓑ **asearse** VPR to tidy o.s. up, smarten o.s. up

asechanza SF trap, snare

asechar ▸conjug 1a◂ VT to set a trap for

asediador SM besieger

asediar ▸conjug 1b◂ VT 1 (*Mil*) to besiege; (*Náut*) to blockade
2 (= *molestar*) to bother, pester; [+ *amante*] to chase, lay siege to (*frm*)

asedio SM 1 (*Mil*) siege; (*Náut*) blockade
2 (*Fin*) run ► **asedio de un banco** run on a bank

según* ADV, PREP (*LAm*) = **según**

asegurable ADV insurable

aseguración SF insurance

asegurado/a Ⓐ ADJ 1 (= *con seguro*) insured (**de, contra** against; **en** for); **la casa está asegurada contra incendios** the house is insured against fire; **sólo estaba ~ contra daños a terceros** he was only insured for third party liability; **el coche no estaba ~** the car was uninsured *o* was not insured; **¿está ~ su coche a todo riesgo?** is your car fully insured?
2 (= *cierto*) **el éxito de la huelga está ~** the success of the strike is assured; **tenemos el éxito ~** we are bound to be successful
Ⓑ SM/F **el ~** (= *tomador*) the policyholder; (= *beneficiario*) the insured (*frm*)

asegurador(a) Ⓐ ADJ insurance *antes de s*
Ⓑ SM/F insurer; **~ indirecto** underwriter

aseguradora SF insurance company

▼ **asegurar** ▸conjug 1a◂ Ⓐ VT 1 (= *sujetar*) to secure; **unos cables aseguran la carpa** the marquee is held in place *o* secured by cables; **hay que ~ mejor el cuadro a la pared** the painting needs to be more firmly fixed *o* secured to the wall; **~ algo con algo** to secure sth with sth; **aseguró con cola las patas del armario** he secured the legs of the wardrobe with glue; **~on los fardos con cuerdas** they fastened *o* secured the bundles with rope
2 (= *proteger*) [+ *zona, edificio*] to make secure (**contra** against)
3 (= *garantizar*) [+ *derecho*] to guarantee; **eso asegura el cumplimiento de los acuerdos** that ensures *o* guarantees that the agreements will be fulfilled; **si quieres ~te el aprobado, tienes que estudiar más** if you want to be certain of passing, you'll have to study more; **es posible, pero no lo aseguro** it's possible, but I can't tell you for sure; **es verdad, se lo aseguro** it's true, take my word for it *o* I assure you; **~ a algn que** to assure sb that; **nos ~on que no habría retrasos** they assured us that there would not be any delays
4 (= *declarar*) to maintain; **asegura que no salió de casa** he maintains that he didn't leave the house; **asegura no saber nada del asunto** he maintains *o* affirms that he knew nothing about the matter; **asegura estar dispuesto a ayudarnos** he says that he is willing to help us
5 (*Com, Fin*) [+ *vehículo, vivienda*] to insure (**de, contra** against; **en** for); **han asegurado los cuadros en más de seis mil millones** the paintings have been insured for more than six thousand million; **deberías ~ el coche a todo riesgo** you should have your car fully insured, you should take out a comprehensive insurance policy
Ⓑ **asegurarse** VPR 1 (= *cerciorarse*) to make sure; **para ~nos del todo** in order to make quite sure; **ya me aseguro yo de que llegue a tiempo** I'll make sure that it arrives on time
2 (= *garantizarse*) to make sure of, assure o.s. of; **tuvo que luchar para ~se la victoria** he had a struggle to make sure of victory *o* to assure himself of victory; **han conseguido ~se su presencia en la final** they have made sure of their presence in the final
3 (*Com, Fin*) to insure o.s., take out an insurance policy

ASELE SF ABR = **Asociación para la Enseñanza del Español como Lengua Extranjera**

asemejar ▸conjug 1a◂ Ⓐ VT 1 (= *hacer parecido*) to make look alike, make similar; (= *copiar*) to copy
2 (= *comparar*) to liken, compare (**a** to)
Ⓑ **asemejarse** VPR (= *parecerse*) (*de carácter*) to be alike, be similar; (*de aspecto*) to look alike; (= *compararse*) to compare (**a** to); **~se a** to be like, resemble

asendereado ADJ 1 [*camino*] beaten, well-trodden
2 [*vida*] wretched, miserable

asenderear ▸conjug 1a◂ VT **~ a algn** to chase sb relentlessly, hound sb

asenso SM 1 (= *consentimiento*) assent; **dar su ~** to assent
2 (= *acto de creer*) credence; **dar ~ a** to give credence to

asentada SF sitting; **de una ~** at one sitting

asentaderas* SFPL behind* *sing*, bottom *sing*, seat *sing*

asentado ADJ 1 (= *instalado*) [*persona*] settled; [*tropas*] located, positioned; [*ciudad, campamento*] situated, located; **los israelíes ~s en Cisjordania** Israelis settled on the West Bank; **no está ~ del todo en su trabajo** he's still not totally settled in his job; **un escritor argentino ~ en Madrid** an Argentinian writer living in Madrid; **un campamento ~ a orillas del río** a camp situated *o* located on the riverbanks; **la iglesia estaba asentada sobre terreno arcilloso** the church was built on clay soil; **la mesa no está bien asentada** the table is wobbly
2 (= *establecido*) [*costumbre, tradición*] well-established; [*creencia*] deep-rooted, deeply-rooted, firmly held; **marcas firmemente asentadas en el mercado europeo** brands that are well-established in the European market; **una empresa asentada en España desde hace años** a company that has been established in Spain for many years; **la mafia está asentada aquí desde hace tiempo** the mafia has existed here for years; **sus argumentos están ~s en suposiciones** his argu-

➤ LENGUA Y USO: **asegurar A3** 42.1 **B1** 29.2, 42.1

ments are based on suppositions
3 [*persona*] **ser ~** to be well-balanced

asentador SM 1 [*de navajas*] razor strop
2 (*Com*) dealer, middleman

asentamiento SM 1 (= *acción*) [*de personas, partículas*] settlement
2 (= *lugar*) [*de personas*] settlement, establishment; [*de animales*] colony; **un ~ fenicio** a Phoenician settlement
3 (= *pueblo*) shanty town, township
4 (*Med*) settling

asentar ▸conjug 1j◂ Ⓐ VT 1 (= *colocar*) [+ *objeto*] to place, fix; [+ *tienda de campaña*] to pitch; [+ *campamento*] to set up, pitch
2 (= *establecer*) [+ *principio*] to lay down; [+ *opinión*] to state; **el documento en el que se asientan las bases de la paz** the document in which the foundations for peace are laid out *o* laid down; **como se asienta en las actas** as stated in the minutes
3 (= *sentar*) to seat, sit down; **lo ~on en el trono** they seated him on the throne; ✦**MODISMOS ~ la cabeza** ◊ **~ el juicio** to settle down
4 (= *aplanar*) [+ *tierra*] to firm down; [+ *costura*] to flatten
5 (= *afilar*) [+ *filo*] to sharpen; [+ *cuchillo*] to sharpen, hone
6 [+ *golpe*] to deal
7 (*Com*) [+ *pedido*] to enter, book; [+ *libro mayor*] to enter up; **~ algo al debe de algn** to debit sth to sb; **~ algo al haber de algn** to credit sth to sb
8 (*Constr*) [+ *cimientos*] to lay down
9 (*Téc*) [+ *válvula*] to seat
10 (*Méx frm*) to state; **asentó que la economía estaba en vías de recuperación** he stated that the economy was recovering
Ⓑ VI to be suitable, suit
Ⓒ **asentarse** VPR 1 (= *estar situado*) [*ciudad*] to stand, be situated; **se asentaba sobre unos terrenos pantanosos** it stood *o* was situated on marshland
2 (= *posarse*) [*líquido, polvo*] to settle; [*ave*] to alight
3 (= *sentarse*) [*persona*] to sit down, seat o.s.
4 (= *consolidarse*) to settle; **parece que se asienta la moda de los vinos blancos jóvenes** young white wines seem to be becoming fashionable; **se ha asentado muy bien en ese papel** she has settled into that role very nicely
5 (= *basarse*) **~se en** *o* **sobre algo** to be based on sth
6 (*Arquit*) to subside
7 (*LAm*) (= *adquirir madurez*) to settle down

asentimiento SM assent, consent

asentir ▸conjug 3i◂ VI 1 (= *mostrarse conforme*) to assent, agree; **~ con la cabeza** to nod, nod one's head in agreement
2 **~ a** (= *consentir en*) to agree to, consent to; [+ *pedido*] to grant; [+ *convenio*] to accept; **~ a la verdad de algo** to recognize the truth of sth

asentista SMF contractor, supplier

aseñorado ADJ gentlemanly/ladylike

aseo SM 1 (= *acto*) washing, toilet (*frm*); (= *higiene*) cleanliness
2 **aseos** (= *retrete*) toilet *sing*, rest room *sing* (*EEUU*)

Asepeyo SF ABR (= **Asistencia Sanitaria Económica para Empleados y Obreros**) *job-related health insurance scheme*

aséptico ADJ aseptic

asequible ADJ (= *alcanzable*) attainable; [*plan*] feasible; [*precio*] reasonable, within reach

aserción SF assertion

aserradero SM sawmill

aserrador(a) SM/F sawyer

aserradora SF power saw, chain saw

aserradura SF (= *corte de sierra*) saw cut; **aserraduras** (= *serrín*) sawdust *sing*

aserrar ▸conjug 1j◂ VT to saw, saw through

aserrín SM sawdust

aserruchar ▸conjug 1a◂ VT (*LAm*) = **aserrar**

asertar ▸conjug 1a◂ VT to assert, affirm

asertividad SF assertiveness

asertivo ADJ assertive

aserto SM assertion

asesinado/a SM/F murder victim, murdered person

asesinar ▸conjug 1a◂ VT 1 (= *matar*) to murder; (*Pol*) to assassinate
2 (= *molestar*) to pester, plague to death, pester the life out of*

asesinato SM (= *acto*) murder, homicide (*EEUU*); (*Pol*) assassination ► **asesinato en primer grado** murder in the first degree, first-degree murder (*EEUU*) ► **asesinato en segundo grado** murder in the second degree, second degree murder (*EEUU*) ► **asesinato frustrado** attempted murder ► **asesinato legal** judicial murder ► **asesinato moral** character assassination ► **asesinatos en serie** serial killings

asesino/a Ⓐ ADJ murderous
Ⓑ SM/F murder/murderess, killer; (*Pol*) assassin ► **asesino/a en serie, asesino/a múltiple** serial killer ► **asesino/a profesional** hired killer

asesor(a) Ⓐ ADJ advisory
Ⓑ SM/F adviser, consultant ► **asesor(a) administrativo/a** management consultant ► **asesor(a) de cuentas** tax accountant ► **asesor(a) de imagen** public relations adviser ► **asesora del hogar** (*Cono Sur*) maid ► **asesor(a) financiero/a** financial adviser ► **asesor(a) fiscal** tax accountant ► **asesor(a) jurídico/a** legal adviser ► **asesor(a) técnico/a** technical adviser *o* consultant

asesoramiento SM advice

asesorar ▸conjug 1a◂ Ⓐ VT 1 (*Jur*) to advise, give legal advice to, give professional advice to
2 (*Com*) to act as consultant to
Ⓑ **asesorarse** VPR 1 **~se con** to take advice from, consult
2 **~se de una situación** to take stock of a situation

asesorato SM (*LAm*) 1 (= *acto*) advising
2 (= *oficina*) consultant's office

asesoría SF 1 (= *acto*) advising; (= *cargo*) consultancy ► **asesoría jurídica** legal advice ► **asesoría técnica** technical consultancy
2 (= *honorario*) adviser's fee
3 (= *oficina*) consultant's office

asestar ▸conjug 1a◂ VT 1 [+ *arma*] to aim (**a** at, in the direction of); [+ *tiro*] to fire
2 [+ *golpe*] to deal; **~ una puñalada a algn** to stab sb

aseveración SF assertion, contention

aseveradamente ADV positively

aseverar ▸conjug 1a◂ VT to assert

asexuado ADJ sexless

asexual ADJ asexual

asfaltado Ⓐ ADJ asphalt *antes de s*, asphalted
Ⓑ SM 1 (= *proceso*) asphalting
2 (= *superficie*) asphalt surface; (*Aer*) tarmac

asfaltar ▸conjug 1a◂ VT to asphalt

asfáltico ADJ asphalt *antes de s*, blacktop (*EEUU*)

asfalto SM asphalt, blacktop (*EEUU*); (*Aer*) tarmac; ✦**MODISMO regar el ~‡** to kick the bucket‡

asfixia SF (= *agobio*) suffocation, asphyxiation; (*Med*) asphyxia

asfixiador ADJ, **asfixiante** ADJ suffocating; (*Med, Jur*) asphyxiating; **calor asfixiante** suffocating heat, stifling heat; **gas asfixiante** poison gas; **una política asfixiante para el comercio** a policy that stifles *o* strangles trade

asfixiar ▸conjug 1b◂ Ⓐ VT 1 (= *ahogar*) to suffocate; (*Med, Jur*) to asphyxiate; **asfixió a la víctima con un cojín** he suffocated the victim with a cushion; **se confirma que la víctima fue asfixiada** it has been confirmed that the victim was suffocated *o* asphyxiated; **este humo nos asfixia** this smoke is asphyxiating *o* suffocating us; **este calor seco me asfixia** this dry heat is suffocating; **los ~on con gas tóxico** they gassed them (to death); **la asfixió bajo el agua** he drowned her
2 (= *agobiar*) **el pequeño pueblo la asfixiaba** village life was suffocating *o* stifling her; **tanto trabajo lo asfixia** all this work is getting on top of him *o* getting to him *o* getting him down; **los impuestos han asfixiado el comercio** taxation has suffocated trade
Ⓑ **asfixiarse** VPR 1 (= *ahogarse*) to suffocate, asphyxiate; **me asfixio con tanto humo** all this smoke is suffocating me; **murieron asfixiados en el incendio** they suffocated (to death) *o* asphyxiated in the fire
2 (= *agobiarse*) to suffocate, feel stifled; **estar asfixiado** (= *sin dinero*) to be broke*; (= *en aprieto*) to be up the creek‡; **estoy asfixiado con tantos exámenes** all these exams are getting on top of me
3 [*negocio, economía, empresario*] to be strangled; **este país se asfixia a causa del embargo** this country is being strangled by the embargo

asgo *ver* **asir**

▼**así** Ⓐ ADV 1 (= *de este modo*) 1·1 (*con ser*) **—te engañaron, ¿no es ~? —sí, ~ es** "they deceived you, didn't they?" — "yes, they did", "they deceived you, isn't that so?" —"yes, it is"; **usted es periodista ¿no es ~?** you're a journalist, aren't you?; **yo soy ~** that's the way I am; **perdona, pero creo que eso no es ~** excuse me, but I think that's not true; **~ es como lo detuvieron** that's how *o* this is how they arrested him; ✦**MODISMO ¡(que) ~ sea!**: **—sólo les falta ganar la copa —que ~ sea** "all they have to do is win the cup" — "let's hope they do"; **—que el Señor esté con vosotros —~ sea** "(may) God be with you" — "Amen"
1·2 (*con otros verbos*) like that, like this; **lo hizo ~** he did it like that *o* like this; **esto no puede seguir ~** things can't go on this way, this can't go on like this; **se iniciaba ~ una nueva etapa** thus *o* so a new phase began; **¡~**

➤ LENGUA Y USO: así B2 44.1

se habla! that's what I like to hear!; **~ ocurrió el accidente** that's how *o* this is how the accident happened; **~ me agradecen lo que hice por ellos** this is the thanks I get for what I did for them; **~ están las cosas** that's the way things are; **puede leer el contrato si ~ lo desea** you can read the contract if you wish; **¿por qué te pones ~? no es más que un niño** why do you get worked up like that? he's only a child; **—salúdelos de mi parte —~ lo haré** "give them my best wishes" — "I will"; **dijo que llamaría y ~ lo hizo** he said he would call and he did

2 (*acompañando a un sustantivo*) like that; **un hombre ~** a man like that, such a man (*más frm*); **¿por una cosa ~ se han enfadado?** they got angry over a thing like that?

3 **~ de** 3·1 (+ *SUSTANTIVO*) **tuvieron ~ de ocasiones de ganar y no las aprovecharon** they had so *o* this many chances to win but didn't take them

3·2 (+ *ADJ, ADV*) **un baúl ~ de grande** a trunk as big as this, a trunk this big; **él todo lo hace ~ de rápido** he does everything that fast, that's how fast he does everything; **no para de comer y luego ~ está de gordita** she never stops eating, that's why she's so plump; **no creo que puedas hacerlo ~ de bien** I can't believe that you can do it that well; **~ de feo era que ...** (*LAm*) he was so ugly that ...

4 **~ como** 4·1 (= *lo mismo que*) the same way as; **~ como tú te portes conmigo, me portaré yo** I'll behave the same way as you do to me; **~ en la Tierra como en el Cielo** on Earth as it is in Heaven

4·2 (= *mientras que*) whereas, while; **~ como uno de sus hijos es muy listo, el otro no estudia nada** whereas *o* while one of their children is very clever, the other doesn't study at all

4·3 (= *además de*) as well as; **se necesita el original ~ como una copia** you need the original as well as a copy

5 (*otras locuciones*) **~ las cosas** with things as they are; **por ~ decirlo** so to speak; **no ~** unlike; **los gastos fueron espectaculares, no ~ los resultados** the expenditure was astonishing, unlike the results; **¡~ no más!** (*Méx**) (= *sin cuidado*) anyhow; (= *sin motivo*) just like that; **es un tema muy importante para tratarlo ~ no más** it's a very important issue, you can't just treat it any old how; **a mí me cuesta tanto y él lo hace ~ no más** I find it really hard, but he does it easily *o* just like that; **se fue ~ no más, sin decir nada** he left just like that, without saying anything; **lo echaron del trabajo ~ no más** they gave him the sack just like that*; **o ~** about, or so; **20 dólares o ~** about 20 dollars, 20 dollars or so; **llegarán el jueves o ~** they'll arrive around Thursday, they'll arrive on Thursday or thereabouts; **~ sin más** just like that; **y ~ sucesivamente** and so on and so forth; **~ y todo** even so; ✦*MODISMOS* **así así** so-so; —**¿cómo te encuentras hoy? —así así** "how do you feel today?" — "so-so"; **~ o asá*** ◊ **~ o asao*** ◊ **~ que asá*** it makes no odds, one way or another; **~ como ~** ◊ **~ que ~** just like that; **no gastan el dinero ~ como ~** they don't spend money willy-nilly; **no se hace ~ como ~** it's not as easy as all that; **~ porque sí** just for the sake of it, just for the hell of it*; **y empezó a insultarme ~ porque sí** and he began to insult me just for the sake *o* hell of it*; **no hemos conseguido el éxito ~ porque sí** it's no accident that we've become successful; **~ es la vida** such is life, that's life

Ⓑ CONJ 1 (= *aunque*) even if; **~ tenga que recorrer el mundo entero, la encontraré** even if I have to travel the whole world, I'll find her

2 (= *consecuentemente*) so; **se gastó todo el dinero y ~ no pudo ir de vacaciones** he spent all the money, so he couldn't go on holiday; **esperan lograr un acuerdo, evitando ~ la huelga** they are hoping to reach an agreement and so avoid a strike, they are hoping to reach an agreement, thereby *o* thus avoiding a strike (*frm*); **~ pues** so; **ha conseguido una beca, ~ pues, podrá seguir estudiando** he got a grant, so he can carry on studying; **~ (es) que** so; **estábamos cansados, ~ que no fuimos** we were tired so we didn't go

3 (= *ojalá*) **¡~ te mueras!** I hope you drop dead!*

4 (= *en cuanto*) **~ que** (+ *SUBJUN*) as soon as; **~ que te enteres, comunícamelo** as soon as you find out, let me know; **~ que pasen unos años todo se olvidará** in a few years everything will be forgotten

Asia SF Asia ► **Asia Menor** Asia Minor

asiático/a Ⓐ ADJ Asian, Asiatic
Ⓑ SM/F Asian

asidero SM 1 (= *asa*) handle
2 (= *agarro*) hold, grasp
3 (= *pretexto*) pretext; (= *base*) basis; **eso no tiene ~** there is no basis for that, that is unfounded

asiduamente ADV (= *con persistencia*) assiduously; (= *con regularidad*) frequently, regularly

asiduidad SF 1 (= *persistencia*) assiduousness
2 (= *regularidad*) regularity
3 **~es** attentions, kindnesses

asiduo/a Ⓐ ADJ (= *persistente*) assiduous; (= *frecuente*) frequent, regular; [*admirador*] devoted; **parroquiano ~** regular (customer); **como ~ lector de su periódico** as a regular reader of your newspaper
Ⓑ SM/F regular, regular customer; **era un ~ del café** he was one of the café's regulars *o* regular customers; **es un ~ del museo** he is a frequent visitor to the museum

asiento SM 1 (= *mueble*) seat, chair; (= *lugar*) place; [*de bicicleta*] saddle; **no ha calentado el ~** he hasn't stayed long; **tomar ~** to take a seat ► **asiento de atrás** [*de coche*] rear seat; [*de moto*] pillion seat ► **asiento delantero** front seat ► **asiento expulsor, asiento lanzable, asiento proyectable** (*Aer*) ejector seat ► **asiento reservado** reserved seat ► **asiento trasero** = **asiento de atrás**
2 (= *sitio*) site, location
3 (= *fondo*) [*de jarrón, silla*] bottom; (*) (= *nalgas*) bottom, seat
4 (*Mec*) seating ► **asiento de válvula** valve seating
5 (= *poso*) sediment
6 (*Arquit*) settling; **hacer ~** to settle, sink
7 (*Náut*) trim
8 (= *arraigo*) settling, establishment; **estar de ~** to be settled; **vivir de ~ con algn** to live in sin with sb
9 (*LAm*) (*tb* **~ minero**) (= *población minera*) mining town
10 (*Com*) (= *contrato*) contract; (*en libro*) entry ► **asiento contable** book-keeping entry ► **asiento de cierre** closing entry
11 (*Pol*) treaty, peace treaty
12 (= *estabilidad*) stability; (= *juicio*) good sense, judgment; **hombre de ~** sensible man

asignable ADJ **~ a** assignable to, which can be assigned to

asignación SF 1 (= *acto*) assignment, allocation; (= *cita*) appointment
2 (*Fin*) allowance ► **asignación de presupuesto** budget appropriation ► **asignación económica** allowance ► **asignación por kilometraje** ≈ mileage allowance ► **asignación presupuestaria** (*Caribe*) budget ► **asignación semanal** weekly allowance

asignado SM (*Andes*) wages paid in kind

asignar ▸conjug 1a◂ VT (= *adjudicar*) to assign; [+ *recursos etc*] to allocate, apportion; [+ *labor*] to set; (*Inform*) to allocate; [+ *persona*] to appoint; [+ *causas*] to determine

asignatario/a SM/F (*LAm*) heir/heiress, legatee

asignatura SF subject, course; **aprobar una ~** to pass a subject, pass in a subject ► **asignatura pendiente** (*Educ*) failed subject, resit subject; (= *asunto pendiente*) matter pending

asigunas* SFPL **según ~** (*Caribe*) it all depends

asilado/a SM/F (*en institución*) inmate; (*Pol*) refugee, political refugee

asilar ▸conjug 1a◂ Ⓐ VT 1 (= *internar*) to put into a home, put into an institution
2 (= *albergar*) to take in, give shelter to; (*LAm*) (= *dar asilo político a*) to give political asylum to
Ⓑ **asilarse** VPR 1 (= *refugiarse*) to take refuge (**en** in); (*Pol*) to seek political asylum
2 [*anciano etc*] to enter a home, enter an institution

asilo SM 1 (= *institución*) home, institution ► **asilo de ancianos** old people's home ► **asilo de huérfanos**† orphanage, children's home ► **asilo de locos** lunatic asylum ► **asilo de niños expósitos**† orphanage, children's home ► **asilo de pobres** poorhouse
2 (*Pol etc*) asylum; (*fig*) (= *abrigo*) shelter, refuge; **derecho de ~** right of sanctuary; **pedir (el) ~ político** to ask for political asylum

asilvestrarse ▸conjug 1a◂ VPR [*tierra*] to become wooded, revert to woodland; [*planta*] to establish itself in the wild

asimetría SF (= *falta de simetría*) asymmetry; (= *desequilibrio*) imbalance

asimétrico ADJ asymmetric, asymmetrical

asimiento SM 1 (= *acción*) seizing, grasping
2 (= *apego*) attachment

asimilable ADJ **fácilmente ~** readily assimilated, easy to assimilate

asimilación SF assimilation

asimilado Ⓐ ADJ similar, related; **establecimientos hoteleros y ~s** hotels and the like
Ⓑ SM (*LAm*) professional, person attached to the army

asimilar ▸conjug 1a◂ Ⓐ VT to assimilate
Ⓑ **asimilarse** VPR 1 (= *establecerse*) to become assimilated
2 **~se a** (= *parecerse*) to resemble

asimismo ADV (= *igualmente*) likewise, in the same way; (= *también*) also

asín* ADV = **así**

asíncrono ADJ asynchronous
asintomático ADJ asymptomatic
asir ▸conjug 3a; tiempo presente como **salir**◂ Ⓐ VT to grasp, take hold of (**con** with; **de** by); **ir asidos del brazo** to walk along arm-in-arm
Ⓑ VI (*Bot*) to take root
Ⓒ **asirse** VPR to take hold; **~se a** *o* **de** (= *agarrarse*) to seize; **~se de** (*fig*) (= *aprovecharse*) to avail o.s. of (*frm*), take advantage of; **~se con algn** to grapple with sb
Asiria SF Assyria
asirio/a ADJ, SM/F Assyrian
asisito ADV (*Andes etc*) = **así**
asísmico ADJ (*LAm*) **construcción asísmica** earthquake-resistant building; **medidas asísmicas** anti-earthquake measures
asistencia SF [1] (*Escol etc*) attendance (**a** at); (*Teat*) audience; **¿había mucha ~?** were there many people there?
[2] (= *ayuda*) help, assistance; (*Med*) care, nursing; (*en casa*) domestic help ► **asistencia intensiva** intensive care ► **asistencia letrada** legal aid ► **asistencia médica** medical care ► **asistencia pública** (*Cono Sur*) public health authority ► **asistencia sanitaria** health care ► **asistencia social** welfare work, social work
[3] (*Méx*) (= *habitación*) spare room, guest room, den (*EEUU*)
[4] **asistencias** (*Fin*) allowance *sing*
asistencial ADJ social security *antes de s*, welfare *antes de s* (*EEUU*)
asistenta SF charwoman, daily help ► **asistenta social** social worker
asistente SMF [1] (= *ayudante*) assistant; (*Mil*) orderly; (*Andes*) (= *criado*) servant ► **asistente social** social worker
[2] **los ~s** (= *presentes*) those present
asistido/a Ⓐ ADJ **~ por ordenador** computer-aided
Ⓑ SM/F (*Andes, Méx*) boarder, lodger, resident
asistir ▸conjug 3a◂ Ⓐ VI [1] (= *acudir*) to attend, go; **no se sabe cuántas personas ~án** it's not known how many people will attend *o* go; **¿va usted a ~?** will you be attending *o* going?; **~ a algo** to attend sth, go to sth; **no asistió a mi clase** he did not attend my lesson, he did not come to my lesson; **asiste a misa todos los domingos** he attends Mass every Sunday, he goes/comes to Mass every Sunday
[2] (*Naipes*) to follow suit
Ⓑ VT [1] (= *ayudar*) **~ a algn** to help sb, assist sb (*frm*); **una institución que asiste a los inmigrantes** an organization that helps immigrants
[2] (*Med*) **~ a** [+ *paciente, enfermo*] to care for, look after; [+ *herido, accidentado*] to look after, help; **~ un parto** to deliver a baby
[3] (= *presenciar*) **~ a algo** to witness sth; **estamos asistiendo a una nueva revolución tecnológica** we are witnessing a new technological revolution
[4] (*Jur*) **su abogado le asistió en la declaración** his lawyer was present when he gave his statement
[5] (*frm*) (= *respaldar*) **le asiste el derecho a recurrir la sentencia** you have the right to appeal (against) the sentence; **le asiste la razón** he has right on his side
[6] (*frm*) (= *atender*) to serve, wait on; **asistió a los invitados en el hotel** he served *o* waited on the hotel guests
askenazi ADJ, SMF Ashkenazi
asma SF asthma ► **asma bronquial** bronchial asthma
asmático/a ADJ, SM/F asthmatic
asnada* SF silly thing
asnal* ADJ asinine, silly
asnar ADJ **ganado ~** donkeys
asnear* ▸conjug 1a◂ VI (*LAm*) (= *hacer tonterías*) to act the fool, do sth silly; (= *ser patoso*) to be clumsy
asnería* SF silly thing
asno/a SM/F [1] (*Zool*) donkey, ass
[2] (= *tosco*) ass, fathead*; **¡soy un ~!** I'm an ass!*
asociación SF (= *acción*) association; (= *sociedad*) society, association; (*Com, Fin*) partnership; **por ~ de ideas** by association of ideas ► **asociación aduanera** customs union ► **asociación de padres de alumnos** parent-teacher association ► **asociación de vecinos** residents' association ► **asociación libre** free association ► **asociación obrera** trade union ► **asociación para el delito** criminal conspiracy
asociado/a Ⓐ ADJ associated; [*miembro etc*] associate
Ⓑ SM/F associate, member; (*Com, Fin*) partner
asocial Ⓐ ADJ asocial
Ⓑ SMF social misfit, socially maladjusted person
asociar ▸conjug 1b◂ Ⓐ VT [1] (= *relacionar*) to associate, connect; **se trata de ~ imágenes y números** it's all about associating *o* connecting images and numbers; **di con la solución asociando ideas** I came up with the solution by making (logical) connections; **~ algo con algo** to associate sth with sth, connect sth with sth; **asocio el azahar con Andalucía** I associate *o* connect orange blossom with Andalusia; **no quiero que me asocien con él** I don't want to be associated with him; **me suena, pero no puedo ~lo con nada** I know him, but I don't know where from *o* but I can't place him; **~ algo a algo** to link sth with *o* to sth; **asocian este gen al cáncer de mama** this gene is linked with *o* to breast cancer
[2] (*Com, Fin*) to take into partnership
[3] (= *unir*) [+ *recursos*] to pool, put together
Ⓑ **asociarse** VPR [1] **~se (con)** to join together (with), join forces (with); **los sindicatos de izquierda se ~on** the left-wing trade unions joined together *o* joined forces
[2] (*Com, Fin*) **~se (con)** to go into partnership (with)
[3] **~se a algo** to join sth, become a member of sth; **Grecia buscaba ~se a la UE** Greece was seeking to join *o* become a member of the EU
[4] [*circunstancias, hechos*] to combine
asocio SM (*LAm*) **en ~** in association (**de** with)
asolación SF destruction, devastation
asolador ADJ devastating
asolanar ▸conjug 1a◂ Ⓐ VT to dry up, parch
Ⓑ **asolanarse** VPR to dry up, be ruined
asolar[1] ▸conjug 1a◂ = **asolanar**
asolar[2] ▸conjug 1a◂ Ⓐ VT to raze, raze to the ground, destroy
Ⓑ **asolarse** VPR [*líquidos*] to settle
asoleada SF (*LAm*) sunstroke
asoleado ADJ (*CAm*) [1] [*persona*] stupid
[2] [*animal*] tired out
asoleadura SF (*Cono Sur*) sunstroke
asolear ▸conjug 1a◂ Ⓐ VT to put in the sun
Ⓑ **asolearse** VPR [1] (= *tomar el sol*) to sunbathe
[2] (*LAm*) (= *coger insolación*) to get sunstroke
[3] (*CAm*) (= *atontarse*) to get stupid
asoleo SM (*Méx*) sunstroke
asomada SF [1] (= *aparición*) brief appearance
[2] (= *vislumbre*) glimpse, sudden view
asomadero SM (*Andes*) viewing point, vantage point
asomar ▸conjug 1a◂ Ⓐ VT [1] [+ *cabeza, hocico*] (*hacia arriba*) to lift; (*hacia fuera*) to poke out; **el animal asoma el hocico y husmea el aire** the animal lifts its snout and sniffs the air; **abrió la puerta y asomó la cabeza** she opened the door and poked her head round it; **asomó la cabeza por encima de la valla para mirar** he peeped over the fence; **asomó la cabeza por el hueco de la escalera** he leaned over the stairwell; **"prohibido asomar la cabeza por la ventanilla"** "do not lean out of the window"; **¿desde cuándo no asomas la cabeza por aquí?*** when was the last time you came round here?*
[2] (*Taur*) **~ el pañuelo** to raise the flag
Ⓑ VI [1] (= *verse*) [*sol, luna*] (*al salir*) to come up; (*entre las nubes*) to come out; **el sol empezó a ~ en el horizonte/por entre las nubes** the sun began to come up on the horizon/come out from behind the clouds; **en la ventana asoma el cañón de un fusil** the barrel of a gun appears at the window; **Jerusalén asoma entre los montes** Jerusalem comes into sight between the hills; **le asomaba la cartera por el bolsillo del pantalón** his wallet was sticking out of his trouser pocket; **el vestido le asomaba por debajo del abrigo** her dress was showing below her coat; **de pronto asomó un buque entre la niebla** a ship suddenly loomed up out of the fog
[2] (*) [*persona*] **hace tiempo que no asoma por aquí** it's been a while since he came round here*; **se casó con el primero que asomó por la puerta** she married the first who poked *o* stuck his head round the door*
[3] (= *salir*) [*planta*] to come up; [*arruga, cana*] to appear; [*diente*] to cut; **ya empiezan a ~ los narcisos** the daffodils are beginning to come up now; **por la tarde le asomaba ya la barba** he already had five o'clock shadow*, by the afternoon his stubble was beginning to show; **ya le empiezan a ~ algunas canas** he has already got some grey hairs coming through *o* appearing; **ya le han asomado varios dientes** she has already cut several teeth
[4] (= *comenzar*) **nació apenas asomado el año** he was born at the very start of the new year, he was born when the new year had barely got underway
Ⓒ **asomarse** VPR [1] [*persona*] **algunos vecinos se ~on a mirar** some neighbours came out to look; **"prohibido asomarse"** "do not lean out of the window"; **~se a** *o* **por** [+ *precipicio, barandilla*] to lean over; [+ *ventana*] (*para mirar*) to look out of; (*sacando el cuerpo*) to lean out of; **me asomé a la ventana y vi que no estaba el coche** I looked out of the window and saw that the car wasn't there; **la vie-**

ron asomada a la ventana, regando las macetas they saw her leaning out of the window, watering her plants; **asomaos a la terraza para ver la vista** come out on to the terrace to see the view; **¡ven, asómate a la puerta!** come on, come to the door!; **vamos a ~nos a las calles esta mañana** (*Radio, TV*) let's take a look at what's happening on the streets this morning; **si nos asomamos al panorama de la economía actual** if we take a brief look at the current economic situation
[2] (= *mostrarse*) **el ciprés se asomaba por encima de la tapia** the cypress showed above the wall, the cypress protruded over the top of the wall
[3] (*) (= *emborracharse*) to get tight*, get tipsy
[4] (*Andes*) (= *acercarse*) to approach, come close, come close to

asombradizo ADJ easily alarmed

asombrador ADJ amazing, astonishing

asombrar ▸conjug 1a◂ Ⓐ VT [1] (= *extrañar*) to amaze, astonish; **nos asombra ese repentino cambio** we are amazed *o* astonished at this sudden change; **me asombra verte trabajar tanto** I'm amazed *o* astonished to see you working so hard; **este chico no deja de ~me** that boy never ceases to amaze me; **a mí ya nada me asombra** nothing surprises me any more
[2] (*frm*) (= *hacer sombra*) to shade
[3] (*frm*) (= *oscurecer*) [+ *color*] to darken
[4] (*frm*) (*asustar*) to frighten
Ⓑ **asombrarse** VPR [1] (= *extrañarse*) to be amazed, be astonished; **me asombré con** *o* **de su extraña reacción** I was amazed *o* astonished by his strange reaction; **se asombró (de) que lo supieras** she was amazed *o* astonished that you knew; **no me asombro por** *o* **de nada** nothing surprises me
[2] (*frm*) (= *asustarse*) to take fright
[3] (*CAm*) (= *desmayarse*) to faint

asombro SM [1] (= *sorpresa*) amazement, astonishment; **lo miró con ~** he looked at it with amazement *o* astonishment; **para ~ de todos** ◊ **ante el ~ de todo el mundo** to everyone's amazement *o* astonishment; **tener cara** *o* **mirada de ~** to look amazed *o* astonished; **no salgo de mi ~** I can't get over it
[2] (*frm*) (= *susto*) fear, fright

asombrosamente ADV amazingly, astonishingly

asombroso ADJ amazing, astonishing

asomo SM [1] (= *aparición*) appearance
[2] (= *indicio*) sign, indication; **ante cualquier ~ de discrepancia** at the slightest hint of disagreement; **sin ~ de violencia** without a trace of violence; **ni por ~** (= *de ningún modo*) by no means; **¡ni por ~!** (= *¡ni en broma!*) no chance!, no way!

asonada SF [1] (= *personas*) mob, rabble
[2] (= *motín*) riot, disturbance

asonancia SF [1] (*Literat*) assonance
[2] (*fig*) (= *correspondencia*) correspondence, connection; **no tener ~ con** to bear no relation to

asonantar ▸conjug 1a◂ VT, VI to assonate (**con** with)

asonante Ⓐ ADJ assonant
Ⓑ SF assonant, assonant rhyme

asonar ▸conjug 1l◂ VI to assonate

asordar ▸conjug 1a◂ VT to deafen

➤ LENGUA Y USO: **aspecto 2** 53.2

asorocharse ▸conjug 1a◂ VPR (*LAm*) to get mountain sickness

asosegar ▸conjug 1h y 1j◂ = **sosegar**

aspa SF [1] (*Arquit*) crosspiece; [*de molino*] sail, arm; [*de ventilador*] blade; **en ~** X-shaped; **ventilador de ~** rotary fan
[2] (*Mat*) multiplication sign
[3] (*Téc*) reel, winding frame
[4] (*Cono Sur*) (= *asta*) horn

aspadera SF reel, winder

aspado ADJ (*de forma*) X-shaped; [*persona*] with arms outstretched; **estar ~ en algo** to be all trussed up in sth

aspador SM reel, winder

aspamentero *etc* ADJ (*Cono Sur, Méx*) = **aspaventero** *etc*

aspar ▸conjug 1a◂ Ⓐ VT [1] (*Téc*) to reel, wind
[2] (*) (= *fastidiar*) to vex, annoy; **¡que te aspen!** get lost!*; **¡que me aspen si lo sé!** I'm buggered if I know!**, I'm blowed if I know!*; **lo hago aunque me aspen** wild horses wouldn't stop me doing it, I'll do it if it's the last thing I do
[3] (*Rel*) to crucify
Ⓑ **asparse** VPR [1] (= *retorcerse*) to writhe
[2] (= *esforzarse*) to do one's utmost, go all out (**por algo** to get sth)

aspaventero/a Ⓐ ADJ excitable
Ⓑ SM/F excitable person

aspaviento SM exaggerated display of feeling; **hacer ~s** to make a great fuss

▼ **aspecto** SM [1] (= *apariencia*) look; **no lo conozco, pero no me gusta su ~** I don't know him, but I don't like the look of him; **un señor con ~ de ejecutivo** a man who looks/looked like an executive; **un hombre de ~ saludable** a healthy-looking man; **tener ~ simpático** to look friendly; **¿qué ~ tenía?** what did he look like?; **el debate iba tomando un ~ desagradable** the discussion was starting to turn ugly; **tener buen ~** to look well; **tener mal ~**: **Juan tiene muy mal ~** Juan isn't looking good *o* well at all; **esa herida tiene mal ~** that wound looks nasty
► **aspecto exterior** outward appearance
[2] (= *punto*) aspect; **los ~s a tener en cuenta para el análisis** aspects to bear in mind when analysing the problem; **estudiar todos los ~s de una cuestión** to study all aspects of an issue; **en algunos ~s me parece una obra genial** in some respects I think it is a work of genius; **el ~ más destacado de la teoría** the strong(est) point of the theory; **bajo ese ~** from that point of view
[3] (*Geog*) aspect
[4] (*Arquit*) aspect
[5] (*Ling*) aspect
[6] **al primer ~**† at first sight

aspectual ADJ aspectual

ásperamente ADV **contestó ~** he answered gruffly; **criticar ~** to criticize bitterly

aspereza SF [*de terreno*] roughness, ruggedness; (= *acidez*) sourness, tartness; [*de carácter*] surliness; **contestar con ~** to answer harshly; ✦*MODISMO* **limar ~s** to smooth things over

asperges SM INV [1] (= *aspersión*) sprinkling
[2] (*Rel*) aspergillum

asperillo SM slight sour taste, slight bitter taste

asperjar ▸conjug 1a◂ VT (= *rociar*) to sprinkle; (*Rel*) to sprinkle with holy water

áspero ADJ [1] (*al tacto*) rough; [*terreno*] rough, rugged; [*filo*] uneven, jagged, rough
[2] (*al gusto*) sour, tart
[3] [*clima*] harsh; [*trato*] rough
[4] [*voz*] rough, rasping; [*tono*] surly, gruff; [*temperamento*] sour; [*disputa etc*] bad-tempered

asperón SM sandstone

aspersión SF [*de agua etc*] sprinkling; (*Agr*) spraying; **riego por ~** watering by spray, watering by sprinklers

aspersor SM sprinkler

áspid SM, **áspide** SM asp

aspidistra SF aspidistra

aspillera SF loophole

aspiración SF [1] (*Zool, Med*) breathing in, inhalation; (*Ling*) aspiration; (*Mús*) short pause
[2] (*Mec*) air intake
[3] (= *anhelo*) aspiration; **aspiraciones** aspirations, ambition *sing*; **es un hombre sin aspiraciones** he's not an ambitious man, he's a man with no aspirations

aspirada SF aspirate

aspirado ADJ aspirate

aspirador Ⓐ ADJ **bomba ~a** suction pump
Ⓑ SM (*tb* **~ de polvo**) vacuum cleaner, hoover®; **pasar el ~** to vacuum, hoover

aspiradora SF vacuum cleaner, hoover®; **pasar la ~** to vacuum, hoover

aspirante Ⓐ ADJ [1] [*persona*] aspiring
[2] (= *aspirador*) **bomba ~** suction pump
Ⓑ SMF candidate, applicant (**a** for); **~ de marina** naval cadet

aspirar ▸conjug 1a◂ Ⓐ VT [1] [+ *aire*] to breathe in, inhale; [+ *líquido*] to suck in, take in; [+ *droga*] to sniff
[2] (*Ling*) to aspirate
Ⓑ VI **~ a algo** to aspire to sth; **no aspiro a tanto** I do not aim so high; **~ a hacer algo** to aspire to do sth, aim to do sth; **el que no sepa eso que no aspire a aprobar** whoever doesn't know that can have no hope of passing

aspirina SF aspirin

aspudo ADJ (*Cono Sur*) big-horned

asqueante ADJ nauseating, disgusting

asquear ▸conjug 1a◂ Ⓐ VT to disgust; **me asquean las ratas** I loathe rats, rats disgust me
Ⓑ **asquearse** VPR to be nauseated, feel disgusted

asquerosamente ADV disgustingly, revoltingly

asquerosidad SF [1] (= *suciedad*) filth; **estar hecho** *o* **ser una ~** to be filthy; **hacer ~es** to make a mess
[2] (= *dicho*) obscenity; (= *truco*) dirty trick; **¡qué ~ acaba de decir!** what an obscene *o* a disgusting thing to say!

asqueroso ADJ [1] (= *repugnante*) disgusting, revolting; [*condición*] squalid; (= *sucio*) filthy
[2] (= *de gusto delicado*) squeamish

asquiento ADJ (*Andes*) [1] (= *quisquilloso*) fussy
[2] = **asqueroso**

asta SF [1] (= *arma*) lance, spear; (= *palo*) shaft; [*de banderas*] flagpole; [*de brocha*] handle; **a media ~** at half mast
[2] (*Zool*) horn, antler; **dejar a algn en las ~s del toro** to leave sb in a jam *o* in a pickle*

astabandera SF (*LAm*) flagstaff, flagpole

ástaco SM crayfish

astado Ⓐ ADJ horned
Ⓑ SM bull

astear ▸conjug 1a◂ VT (*Cono Sur*) to gore

aster SF aster

asterisco SM asterisk; **señalar con un ~** ◊ **poner ~ a** to asterisk, mark with an asterisk

asteroide SM asteroid

astigmático ADJ astigmatic

astigmatismo SM astigmatism

astil SM [*de herramienta*] handle, haft; [*de flecha*] shaft; [*de balanza*] beam

astilla SF [1] (= *fragmento*) splinter, chip; **astillas** (*para fuego*) kindling *sing*; **hacer algo ~s** to smash sth into little *o* tiny pieces; **hacerse ~s** to shatter into little *o* tiny pieces; *ver* **palo 1**
[2] (*Esp**) (= *soborno*) small bribe, sweetener*; **dar ~ a algn** to give sb a cut*; **ese tío no da ~** he's a tight-fisted so-and-so*

astillar ▸conjug 1a◂ Ⓐ VT (= *hacer astillas*) to splinter, chip; (= *hacer pedazos*) to shatter, smash to pieces
Ⓑ **astillarse** VPR (= *levantarse astillas en*) to splinter; (= *hacerse pedazos*) to shatter, smash to pieces

astillero SM shipyard, dockyard

astracán SM astrakhan

astracanada* SF silly thing, silly thing to do

astrágalo SM (*Arquit, Mil*) astragal; (*Anat*) ankle bone, astragalus

astral ADJ astral

astreñir ▸conjug 3h y 3i◂ = **astringir**

astrilla SF (*Cono Sur*) = **astilla**

astringente Ⓐ ADJ astringent (*frm*), binding
Ⓑ SM astringent

astringir ▸conjug 3e◂ VT [1] (*Anat*) to constrict, contract; (*Med*) to bind
[2] (= *constreñir*) to bind, compel

astro SM [1] (*Astron*) star, heavenly body; **el ~ Rey** the sun
[2] (*Cine*) star

astrofísica SF astrophysics *sing*

astrofísico/a SM/F astrophysicist

astrolabio SM astrolab

astrología SF astrology

astrológico ADJ astrological

astrólogo/a SM/F astrologer

astronauta SMF astronaut

astronáutica SF astronautics *sing*

astronave SF spaceship

astronometría SF astrometry

astronomía SF astronomy

astronómico ADJ astronomical

astrónomo/a SM/F astronomer

astroso ADJ [1] (= *sucio*) dirty; (= *desaliñado*) untidy, shabby
[2] (= *malhadado*) ill-fated, ill-starred
[3] (= *vil*) contemptible

astucia SF [1] (= *sagacidad*) astuteness, cleverness; (= *maña*) guile, cunning; **actuar con ~** to act cunningly, be crafty
[2] **una ~** a clever trick

astur ADJ, SMF Asturian

asturiano/a Ⓐ ADJ, SM/F Asturian
Ⓑ SM (*Ling*) Asturian

Asturias SF (*tb* **el Principado de ~**) Asturias ► **príncipe de Asturias** crown prince, ≈ Prince of Wales

asturleonés ADJ of/from Asturias and León

astutamente ADV (= *con sagacidad*) cleverly, smartly; (= *con maña*) craftily, cunningly

astuto ADJ (= *sagaz*) astute, clever; (= *mañoso*) crafty, sly

asueto SM time off, break; **día de ~** day off; **tomarse una tarde de ~** to take an afternoon off

asumible ADJ [*responsabilidad, riesgo*] acceptable, permissible; [*cambio, error*] acceptable

asumidamente ADV supposedly

asumir ▸conjug 3a◂ Ⓐ VT [1] (= *responsabilizarse de*) [+ *reto, tarea*] to take on; [+ *cargo*] to take up; [+ *mando*] to take over, assume (*más frm*); **no han sido capaces de ~ la tarea de gobernar** they have been incapable of taking on the task of government; **el alcalde debería ~ sus responsabilidades por el accidente** the mayor should take *o* assume responsibilities for the accident; **el gobierno asumió el compromiso de crear empleo** the government committed itself *o* undertook the commitment (*más frm*) to creating employment; **ha asumido la cartera de Sanidad** he has been appointed Health Minister; **asumió la presidencia en 1999** he took up *o* assumed (*más frm*) the presidency in 1999; **ha asumido la dirección de la empresa en un momento muy difícil** he has taken control of *o* has taken over the company at a very difficult time; **los socialistas asumieron el poder en 1982** the socialists came to power in 1982
[2] (= *aceptar*) [+ *consecuencias*] to take, accept; [+ *crítica*] to accept; [+ *problema, enfermedad, derrota*] to come to terms with, accept; **un empresario debe invertir y ~ el riesgo** a businessman must invest and take the risk; **lo hice asumiendo el riesgo de ser castigado** I did it in the knowledge that I risked being punished; **estoy dispuesto a ~ todas las críticas** I am willing to accept all the criticism; **ya he asumido que no podré volver a esquiar** I've already come to terms with *o* accepted the fact that I won't be able to ski again; **la familia ha asumido su muerte con serenidad** the family has taken her death calmly
[3] (= *adoptar*) to adopt, take; **asumieron una actitud crítica** they adopted *o* took a critical stance; **la población había asumido una actitud contraria a la presencia militar** people had come out against the military presence; **asumió el papel de víctima** he took on the role of victim
[4] (= *adquirir*) to assume; **la cuestión del paro ha asumido una dimensión distinta** the question of unemployment has taken on *o* assumed a different dimension; **el fuego asumió enormes proporciones** the fire took on major proportions
[5] (= *suponer*) **~ que** to assume that; **asumieron que era cierto** they assumed that it was true
Ⓑ VI (*Pol*) to take office, take up office

asunceño/a Ⓐ ADJ of/from Asunción
Ⓑ SM/F native/inhabitant of Asunción; **los ~s** the people of Asunción

Asunción SF (*Geog*) Asunción

asunción SF assumption; **la Asunción** (*Rel*) the Assumption

asunto SM [1] (= *cuestión*) matter; **un ~ familiar grave** an urgent family matter; **vine a discutir unos ~s** I came to discuss several matters *o* issues; **no sé nada de ese ~** I don't know anything about it *o* the matter; **el ~ de los impuestos divide al gobierno** the government is divided on the matter *o* question *o* issue of taxes; **hemos tratado el ~ de nuestro divorcio** we've talked about the subject of our divorce; **~s a tratar** agenda; **no te metas en mis ~s** mind your own business; **¡esto es ~ mío!** that's my business *o* affair!; **¡~ concluido!** that's an end to the matter!; **—me ha llamado el jefe a su despacho —mal ~** "the boss has called me to his office" — "doesn't look good"; **ir al ~** to get down to business; **el ~ es que ...** the thing is (that) ... ► **asunto de honor** question of honour *o* (*EEUU*) honor
[2] (*Jur*) case; **estuvo implicado en un ~ de desfalco** he was involved in a case of embezzlement
[3] (*Pol*) **el ~ Rumasa** the Rumasa affair; **Ministerio de Asuntos Exteriores** Foreign Ministry, Foreign Office, State Department (*EEUU*) ► **asuntos exteriores** foreign affairs
[4] (= *aventura amorosa*) affair; **es ~ de faldas** there's a woman involved in this somewhere along the line ► **asunto de alcoba** bedroom intrigue
[5] (*Cono Sur*) **¿a ~ de qué lo hiciste?** why did you do it?
[6] (*Caribe*) **poner ~** to pay attention
[7] (*Literat†*) (= *tema*) subject

asurar ▸conjug 1a◂ VT [1] (*Culin etc*) to burn; (*Agr*) to burn up, parch
[2] (= *inquietar*) to worry

asurcar ▸conjug 1g◂ VT = **surcar**

asustadizo ADJ [1] [*persona*] (= *que se asusta mucho*) easily frightened; (= *nervioso*) nervy, jumpy
[2] [*animal*] shy, skittish

asustar ▸conjug 1a◂ Ⓐ VT (= *causar miedo a*) to frighten, scare; (= *espantar*) to alarm, startle
Ⓑ **asustarse** VPR to be frightened, get scared; **~se de algo** to be frightened by sth, get alarmed about sth; **¡no te asustes!** don't be alarmed!; **~se de hacer algo** to be afraid *o* scared *o* frightened to do sth

asusto SM (*Andes*) = **susto**

A.T. ABR (= **Antiguo Testamento**) OT

-ata *ver* **Aspects of Word Formation in Spanish 2**

atabacado ADJ [1] [*color*] tobacco-coloured, tobacco-colored (*EEUU*)
[2] **con aliento ~** (*Cono Sur*) with breath smelling of tobacco

atabal SM kettledrum

atabalear ▸conjug 1a◂ VI [*caballo*] to stamp; (*con dedos*) to drum

atacable ADJ attackable, assailable

atacado ADJ [1] (= *pusilánime*) fainthearted; (= *vacilante*) dithery, irresolute
[2] (= *tacaño*) mean, stingy

atacador(a) Ⓐ SM (*Mil*) ramrod
Ⓑ SM/F attacker, assailant

atacadura SF fastener, fastening

atacante SMF attacker, assailant

atacar ▸conjug 1g◂ Ⓐ VT [1] [+ *enemigo, ciudad, fortaleza*] to attack
[2] (*Med, Quím*) [*enfermedad, plaga, sustancia*]

to attack; **ataca al hígado** it attacks the liver; **la gripe me ataca todos los inviernos** I get struck down by the flu every winter; **me estaba atacando el sueño** I was succumbing to sleep; **este niño me ataca los nervios*** that child gets on my nerves*
[3] (= *criticar*) [+ *teoría, planteamiento, propuesta*] to attack; **~on despiadadamente su enfoque marxista** they mercilessly attacked her Marxist approach
[4] (= *combatir*) [+ *problema*] to tackle, combat; **se pretende ~ el desempleo** the aim is to tackle *o* combat unemployment; **pretenden ~ la epidemia de meningitis** they aim to tackle *o* combat the meningitis epidemic
[5] (= *abordar*) **el gobierno debe ~ la reforma laboral** the government should get moving on labour reform*; **tengo que ~ a las matemáticas*** I'll have to get stuck into my maths*; **la orquesta atacó la novena de Beethoven** the band launched into Beethoven's Ninth; **¿puedo ~ al pastel?*** can I get stuck into the cake?*
(B) VI to attack
(C) **atacarse** VPR (*LAm**) to stuff o.s.*

atachable ADJ (*Méx*) compatible (**a** with)

atachar ▸conjug 1a◂ VT (*Méx*) to plug in

ataché SM (*CAm, Caribe*) paper clip

ataderas* SFPL garters

atadero SM (= *cuerda*) rope, fastening; (= *cierre*) fastening; (= *sitio*) place for tying; (*Méx*) (= *liga*) garter; **eso no tiene ~** you can't make head or tail of it, there's nothing to latch on to

atadijo SM loose bundle

atado (A) ADJ [1] (= *amarrado*) tied
[2] (= *tímido*) shy, inhibited; (= *indeciso*) irresolute
(B) SM bundle; **~ de cigarrillos** (*Cono Sur*) packet of cigarettes

atadora SF binder

atadura SF [1] (= *acción*) tying, fastening
[2] (= *cuerda*) string, rope; (*Agr*) tether
[3] (= *enlace*) bond
[4] (= *limitación*) limitation, restriction

atafagar ▸conjug 1h◂ VT [1] [+ *olor*] to stifle, suffocate
[2] (= *molestar*) to pester the life out of

ataguía SF cofferdam, caisson

atajar ▸conjug 1a◂ (A) VT [1] (= *interceptar*) to stop, intercept; [+ *ruta de fuga*] to cut off; (*Arquit*) to partition off; (*Dep*) to tackle; (*LAm*) (= *coger*) to catch, catch in flight; **~ un golpe** to parry a blow; **~ a algn** (*LAm*) to hold sb back (*to stop a fight*); **me quiso ~ al almuerzo** (*LAm*) she wanted me to stay for lunch
[2] [+ *debate*] to cut short; [+ *discurso etc*] to interrupt; [+ *proceso*] to end, stop, call a halt to; [+ *abuso*] to put a stop to; **este mal hay que ~lo** we must put an end to this evil
(B) VI (= *tomar un atajo*) to take a short cut (**por** by way of, across); (*Aut*) to cut corners
(C) **atajarse** VPR [1] (= *detenerse*) to stop short
[2] (= *avergonzarse*) to feel ashamed of o.s.; (= *aturdirse*) to be overcome by confusion, be all of a dither
[3] (*Cono Sur*) (= *controlarse*) to keep one's temper, control o.s.

atajo SM [1] (*en camino*) short cut; ✦***MODISMO*** **echar por el ~** to seek a quick solution; ✦***REFRÁN*** **no hay ~ sin trabajo** short cuts don't help in the long run
[2] (*Dep*) tackle

atalaje SM = **atelaje**

atalaya (A) SF [1] (= *torre*) watchtower, observation post
[2] (= *posición estratégica*) vantage point
(B) SM lookout, observer

atalayador(a) SM/F lookout; (= *fisgón*) snooper, spy

atalayar ▸conjug 1a◂ VT (= *observar*) to observe; (= *vigilar*) to watch over, guard; (= *espiar*) to spy on

atañer ▸conjug 2f; defectivo◂ VI **~ a** to concern, have to do with; **en lo que atañe a eso** with regard to that, concerning that; **eso no me atañe** it's no concern of mine, it has nothing to do with me

atapuzar ▸conjug 1f◂ (*Caribe*) (A) VT to fill, stop up
(B) **atapuzarse** VPR to stuff o.s.

ataque SM [1] (*Mil*) attack; **se dejó expuesto al ~** he left himself open to attack; **un ~ a** *o* **contra algo/algn** an attack on sth/sb; **lanzar un ~** to launch an attack; **volver al ~** to return to the attack; **pasar al ~** to go on the offensive; **¡al ~!** charge! ► **ataque aéreo** air raid, air strike ► **ataque a superficie** ground attack, ground strike ► **ataque fingido** sham attack ► **ataque frontal** frontal attack ► **ataque por sorpresa** surprise attack ► **ataque preventivo** pre-emptive strike
[2] (*Med*) attack; **le dio un ~ de tos** he had a coughing fit *o* a fit of coughing ► **ataque al corazón, ataque cardíaco** heart attack ► **ataque cerebral** brain haemorrhage *o* (*EEUU*) hemorrhage ► **ataque de nervios** nervous breakdown ► **ataque epiléptico** epileptic fit ► **ataque fulminante** stroke
[3] (= *arranque*) fit; **me entró** *o* **dio un ~ de risa** I got a fit of the giggles; **cuando se entere le da un ~*** she'll have a fit when she finds out* ► **ataque de celos** fit of jealousy ► **ataque de ira** fit of anger
[4] (= *crítica*) attack; **~ a** *o* **contra algo/algn** attack on sth/sb; **un duro ~ a** *o* **contra la ley electoral** a fierce attack on the electoral law
[5] (*Dep*) attack

atar ▸conjug 1a◂ (A) VT [1] (= *amarrar*) to tie, tie up; [+ *cautivo*] to bind, tie up; (= *abrochar*) to fasten; [+ *animal*] to tether; [+ *gavilla*] to bind; **zapatos de ~** lace-up shoes; **está de ~** he's raving mad; ✦***MODISMO*** **dejar algo atado y bien atado** to leave no loose ends, leave everything properly tied up
[2] (= *impedir el movimiento a*) to stop, paralyze; ✦***MODISMOS*** **~ corto a algn** to keep sb on a close rein; **~ la lengua a algn** to silence sb; **~ las manos a algn** to tie sb's hands; **verse atado de pies y manos** to be tied hand and foot
(B) VI **ni ata ni desata** this is getting us nowhere
(C) **atarse** VPR [1] (= *liarse*) to get into a muddle; **~se en una dificultad** to get tied up in a difficulty
[2] (= *sentirse violento*) to be embarrassed, get embarrassed
[3] (= *ceñirse*) **~se a la letra** to stick to the literal meaning; **~se a una opinión** to stick to one's opinion, not budge from one's opinion

ataracea SF = **taracea**

atarantado ADJ (*Cono Sur*) impetuous

atarantar ▸conjug 1a◂ (A) VT [1] (= *aturdir*) to stun, daze; **quedó atarantado** he was stunned, he was unconscious
[2] (= *dejar atónito*) to stun, dumbfound
(B) **atarantarse** VPR [1] to be stunned, be dumbfounded
[2] (*Chile*) (= *darse prisa*) to hurry
[3] (*Méx*) (*comiendo*) to stuff o.s.
[4] (*CAm*) (*bebiendo*) to get drunk

atarazana SF dockyard

atardecer ▸conjug 2d◂ (A) VI to get dark; **atardecía** night was falling
(B) SM dusk, evening; **al ~** at dusk

atardecida SF dusk, nightfall

atareado ADJ busy, rushed; **andar muy ~** to be very busy

atarear ▸conjug 1a◂ (A) VT to assign a task to
(B) **atarearse** VPR to work hard, keep busy; **~se con algo** to be busy doing sth

atarjea SF (= *conducto*) sewage pipe, drain; (*Andes*) (= *presa de agua*) reservoir

atarragarse ▸conjug 1h◂ VPR (*LAm*) to stuff o.s., overeat

atarugar ▸conjug 1h◂ (A) VT [1] (= *llenar*) to stuff, cram
[2] (= *asegurar*) to fasten
[3] [+ *agujero*] to plug, stop, bung up
[4] (*) **~ a algn** (= *hacer callar*) to shut sb up
(B) **atarugarse** VPR [1] (= *atragantarse*) to swallow the wrong way
[2] (= *embrollarse*) to get confused, be in a daze
[3] (*) (= *atiborrarse*) to stuff o.s., overeat

atasajar ▸conjug 1a◂ VT to jerk

atascadero SM [1] (= *lodazal*) mire, bog
[2] (= *obstáculo*) stumbling block

atascar ▸conjug 1g◂ (A) VT [+ *agujero etc*] to plug, bung up; [+ *cañería*] to clog up; [+ *fuga*] to stop; [+ *proceso*] to hinder
(B) **atascarse** VPR [1] (*en lodazal*) to get stuck; (*Aut*) to get into a jam; [*motor*] to stall; **se quedó atascado a mitad de la cuesta** he got stuck halfway up the climb
[2] (*fig*) (= *no poder seguir*) to get bogged down; (*en discurso*) to dry up*
[3] [*cañería*] to get clogged up
[4] (*LAm Med*) to have an internal blockage

atasco SM (= *obstrucción*) obstruction, blockage; (*Aut*) traffic jam

ataúd SM coffin, casket (*EEUU*)

ataujía SF [1] (*Téc*) damascene, damascene work
[2] (*CAm*) (= *desagüe*) conduit, drain

ataviar ▸conjug 1c◂ (A) VT [1] (= *vestir*) to dress up, get up (**con, de** in)
[2] (*LAm*) (= *adaptar*) to adapt, adjust, accommodate
(B) **ataviarse** VPR to dress up, get o.s. up (**con, de** in)

atávico ADJ atavistic

atavío SM (= *atuendo*) getup; **~s** finery *sing*

atavismo SM atavism

ate SM (*Méx*) quince jelly

atecomate SM (*Méx*) tumbler

atediante ADJ boring, wearisome

atediar ▸conjug 1b◂ (A) VT to bore, weary
(B) **atediarse** VPR to get bored

ateísmo SM atheism

ateísta ADJ atheistic

atejonarse ▸conjug 1a◂ VPR (*Méx*) to hide

atelaje SM [1] (= *caballos*) team, team of horses

2 (= *arreos*) harness; (= *equipo*) equipment; (*) (= *ajuar*) trousseau

atembado ADJ (*Andes*) silly, stupid

atemorizar ▸conjug 1f◂ Ⓐ VT to frighten, scare

Ⓑ **atemorizarse** VPR to get frightened, get scared (**de, por** at, by)

atempar* ▸conjug 1a◂ VI (*CAm*) to wait, hang around

atemperar ▸conjug 1a◂ VT 1 (= *moderar*) to temper, moderate

2 (= *ajustar*) to adjust, accommodate (**a** to); **~ los gastos a los ingresos** (*Com*) to balance outgoings with income

atemporal ADJ timeless

atemporalado ADJ stormy

atemporalidad SF timelessness

Atenas SF Athens

atenazar ▸conjug 1f◂ VT (*fig*) to grip; [+ *duda etc*] to torment, beset; **~ los dientes** to grit one's teeth; **el miedo me atenazaba** I was gripped by fear

atención SF 1 (= *interés*) attention; **la novela mantiene la ~ del lector** the novel keeps the reader's attention; **esta emisora dedica especial ~ a la música** this station places particular emphasis on music *o* devotes particular attention to music; **¡~, por favor!** attention, please!; **siguen con ~ las explicaciones** they follow the explanations attentively; **garantizarán los derechos de todos, con especial ~ a las minorías** they will guarantee everybody's rights, particularly those of minorities; **en ~ a algo** (*frm*) in view of sth; **en ~ a los intereses de los clientes** in view of the clients' interests; **el premio le fue concedido en ~ a sus méritos** she was awarded the prize on merit; **llamar la ~ a algn** (= *atraer*) to attract sb's attention; (= *reprender*) to tell sb off; **siempre va llamando la ~ por como viste** the way he dresses always catches the eye *o* attracts attention; **me llamó la ~ no verte por allí** I was surprised not to see you there; **a mí el chocolate no me llama mucho la ~** I'm not too fond of *o* keen on chocolate; **nos llamó la ~ sobre el peligro que corrían los refugiados** he drew our attention to the danger that the refugees were in; **me llamaron la ~ por llegar tarde** they told me off for arriving late; **prestar ~** to pay attention (**a** to); **léelo detenidamente, prestando especial ~ a la letra pequeña** read it carefully, paying particular attention to the small print; **prestad mucha ~ a lo que voy a decir** pay close attention to what I am going to say; **los niños necesitan que les presten mucha ~** children need to be given a lot of attention

2 (= *precaución*) care; **necesitas poner más ~ en lo que haces** you need to take greater care over what you do; **cuando vayas de vacaciones, ~ a los precios** when you go on holiday, watch out for the prices; **"¡atención! — frenos potentes"** "beware!: powerful brakes"; **¡atención!** look out!, careful!; (*Mil*) attention!; *ver tb* **toque**

3 (= *cortesía*) **no tuvo ni la ~ de enviarle unas flores** he didn't even have the kindness *o* thought to send her flowers; **le agradezco la ~** that's very thoughtful of you; **ha tenido una bonita ~ regalándome el libro** it was a really nice thought of hers to buy me that book; **me colmó de atenciones** he showered me with attention

4 (= *asistencia*) **vive rodeada de todas las atenciones necesarias** she has all the care and attention that she needs; **han descuidado la ~ al público** they have neglected the customers; **horario de ~ al público** (*en oficina*) "hours of business"; (*en tienda*) "opening hours" ► **atención al cliente** customer service; **departamento de ~ al cliente** customer service department; **el personal de ~ al cliente** the staff who serve customers ► **atención médica** medical attention ► **atención personalizada** personalized service ► **atención primaria** primary health care ► **atención psicológica** counselling ► **atención psiquiátrica** psychiatric treatment; **centro de ~ psiquiátrica** psychiatric clinic ► **atención sanitaria** medical attention

5 **atenciones** (= *obligaciones*) duties, responsibilities

6 (*Correspondencia*) **a la ~ de** for the attention of; (*en sobre*) attention

atencioso ADJ (*LAm*) = **atento**

atender ▸conjug 2g◂ Ⓐ VT 1 (= *ocuparse de*) 1·1 [+ *asunto*] to deal with; **atiende primero lo más urgente** deal with the most urgent things first; **para ~ los gastos de las vacaciones** to meet the holiday expenses

1·2 [+ *paciente*] to look after; **en el hospital es donde mejor atendido está** you'll be better looked after in hospital; **están atendiendo a los animales heridos** they are looking after *o* seeing to *o* caring for the injured animals; **sólo atienden los casos urgentes** they only deal with urgent cases; **necesitamos a alguien que atienda a la abuela** we need someone to look after *o* care for grandma

2 (= *recibir*) to see; **el propio presidente atendió al delegado** the president himself saw the delegate; **el doctor la ~á en un momento** the doctor will see you now

3 (*Com*) 3·1 [+ *cliente*] (*en tienda*) to serve; (*en oficina*) to see; **¿lo atienden, señor?** are you being served, sir?; **siéntese, enseguida la ~án** take a seat, they'll see you in a minute

3·2 [+ *consulta, negocio, oficina*] (*como encargado*) to run; (*como trabajador*) to work in; **yo atiendo el negocio personalmente** I run the business myself; **atiendo la recepción cuando la secretaria no está** I work in reception *o* I man the reception desk when the secretary is not there; **el servicio de habitaciones está mal atendido** the room service is very sloppy

4 (= *prestar atención a*) [+ *ruego, petición*] to respond to, comply with (*frm*); [+ *necesidades, demanda*] to meet; [+ *compromiso, obligación*] to fulfill; [+ *reclamaciones, protesta, queja*] to deal with; [+ *aviso, consejo*] to heed; **deben ~ las demandas de la población** they should respond to the people's demands; **no atendieron la petición de extraditarlos a España** they did not comply with the request to extradite them to Spain (*frm*); **los 25 autobuses son insuficientes para ~ la demanda** the 25 buses are not enough to meet the demand; **Señor, atiende nuestras súplicas** (*Rel*) Lord, heed our prayers

5 (*Telec*) [+ *teléfono, llamada*] to answer; **no había nadie para ~ el teléfono** there was nobody to answer the phone

6 (*Mec*) [+ *máquina*] to supervise

7 (*LAm*) (= *asistir a*) to attend, be present at

Ⓑ VI 1 (= *prestar atención*) to pay attention; **ahora, a ver si atendéis, que esto es importante** now, pay attention, this is important; **~ a algo/algn** to listen to sth/sb; **atended a lo que voy a decir** listen to what I'm going to say; **ahora atendedme un momento** pay attention to what I'm about to say; **¡tú atiende a lo tuyo!** mind your own business!; **atendiendo a** [+ *criterio, datos*] according to; [+ *situación, circunstancias*] bearing in mind, considering; **se han clasificado en distintos grupos atendiendo a su origen** they have been put into different groups according to their origin; **atendiendo a las circunstancias, lo recibiré personalmente** given the circumstances, I will see him in person, bearing in mind *o* considering the circumstances, I will see him in person; *ver tb* **razón 3**

2 (= *ocuparse de*) **~ a** [+ *detalles*] to take care of; [+ *necesidades, demanda*] to meet; **lo primero que hace es ~ al desayuno de los niños** the first thing she does is to see to the kids' breakfast; **no quiso ~ a sus amenazas** he didn't heed their warnings; **~ a un giro** to honour *o* (*EEUU*) honor a draft; **~ a una orden o pedido** (*Com*) to attend to an order

3 (*Com*) (= *servir*) to serve; **¿quién atiende aquí?** who's serving here?

4 **~ por** to answer to the name of; **extraviado caniche blanco; atiende por Linda** lost: white poodle; answers to the name of Linda

5 (*Telec*) [*teléfono, llamada*] to answer; **nadie atendió a nuestra llamada de socorro** nobody answered our distress call

6 (*Mec*) [*máquina*] to supervise

atendible ADJ [*petición, reivindicación*] worthy of consideration; **esa objeción no es ~** that is not a valid objection, that objection is not worthy of consideration

ateneo SM cultural association, cultural centre, cultural center (*EEUU*)

atenerse ▸conjug 2k◂ VPR **~ a** 1 (= *ceñirse a*) **aténgase a lo que se le pregunta** confine yourself to answering the question

2 (= *cumplir*) **~ a la ley** to abide by *o* obey the law; **aténgase a lo que se le ordena** follow the orders; **debes atenerte a lo acordado** you must stick to what has been agreed

3 (= *remitirse a*) **me atengo a mis declaraciones previas** I stand by my previous statements; **simplemente nos atenemos a lo que has dicho** we are simply taking into account *o* bearing in mind what you said; **contigo nunca sé a qué atenerme** I never know what to expect with you; **si lo haces atente a las consecuencias** if you do it, you'll have to take the consequences

4 (= *adaptarse a*) to keep within; **atente a tus ingresos y no gastes tanto** keep within your income and don't spend so much; **viven ateniéndose a sus posibilidades** they live within their means

ateniense ADJ, SMF Athenian

atentado Ⓐ ADJ (= *prudente*) prudent, cautious; (= *moderado*) moderate

Ⓑ SM (= *ofensa*) offence, felony (*EEUU*); (= *crimen*) outrage, crime; (= *ataque*) assault, attack; (*Pol*) attempt; **~ a o contra la vida de algn** attempt on sb's life; ► **atentado contra el pudor, atentado contra la honra** indecent assault ► **atentado golpista** attempted coup ► **atentado suicida** suicide bombing, suicide attack ► **atentado terrorista** terrorist attack

atentamente ADV [1] (= *con atención*) [*escuchar, observar*] attentively; [*leer*] carefully; **debes seguir ~ todos sus consejos** you should follow all his advice carefully
[2] (= *cortésmente*) **se dirigió a mí muy ~** she spoke to me very kindly; **lo saludó muy ~** she greeted him very warmly; **le saluda ~** (*en cartas formales*) yours faithfully, yours sincerely, sincerely yours (*EEUU*)

> **ATENTAMENTE**
>
> Para traducir **atentamente** o **le saluda atentamente** al inglés británico hay que tener en cuenta la diferencia de uso entre **Yours sincerely** y **Yours faithfully**:
>
> • Se traduce por **Yours sincerely** cuando hemos empezado la carta con **Dear Mr/Mrs Brown**, es decir, conocemos al destinatario y le queremos dar un tratamiento más cordial.
>
> • Se traduce por **Yours faithfully** cuando no conocemos al destinatario de la carta y hemos empezado escribiendo **Dear Sir**, **Dear Sirs** o **Dear Sir or Madam**.
>
> • En inglés americano se usa **Sincerely yours** en ambos casos.
>
> *Para otros usos y ejemplos ver la entrada.*

atentar ▸conjug 1a◂ Ⓐ VI **~ a** *o* **contra** to commit an outrage against; **~ contra la honra de algn** to indecently assault sb; **~ contra la ley** to break the law; **~ contra la vida de algn** to make an attempt on sb's life
Ⓑ VT [+ *crimen etc*] to attempt, try to commit

atentatorio ADJ illegal, criminal; **un acto ~ a ...** an act which poses a threat to ..., an act which undermines ...

atento ADJ [1] (= *pendiente*) [*persona*] attentive; [*mirada*] watchful; **tenéis que estar ~s en clase** you have to be attentive in class, you have to pay attention in class; **estáte ~ y avísanos si lo ves** stay alert *o* keep a look out and let us know if you see him; **ante la mirada atenta del árbitro** under the referee's watchful eye; **estar ~ a** [+ *explicación*] to pay attention to; [+ *peligro*] to be on the alert for, be on the lookout for; [+ *movimiento, ruido*] to listen out for; **estuvo muy ~ a todo lo que le decíamos** he paid full attention to everything we told him; **hay que estar ~ a cualquier error** you have to watch *o* listen out for the slightest mistake; **está siempre ~ a las nuevas tendencias** he always keeps an eye out for the latest trends
[2] (= *cortés*) attentive; **últimamente está muy ~ con ella** he has been very attentive to her recently; **fue muy ~ de tu parte** that was very thoughtful of you; **un dependiente muy ~** a very helpful *o* attentive sales assistant; **como indicaba en su atenta carta** (*frm*) as indicated in your kind letter (*frm*); **su ~ y seguro servidor** (*frm*) yours truly
[3] **~ a algo** in view of sth, in consideration of sth (*frm*); **~ a que** considering that, in view of the fact that

atenuación SF (= *aminoración*) attenuation; (*Ling*) understatement; [*de efectos etc*] lessening; (*Jur*) extenuation

atenuante Ⓐ ADJ extenuating; **circunstancias ~s** extenuating circumstances, mitigating circumstances
Ⓑ SM *o* F extenuating circumstance, mitigating circumstance

atenuar ▸conjug 1e◂ Ⓐ VT (= *aminorar*) to attenuate; (*Jur*) [+ *crimen etc*] to extenuate; [+ *importancia*] to minimize; [+ *impresión etc*] to tone down; [+ *impacto*] to cushion, lessen
Ⓑ **atenuarse** VPR to weaken

ateo/a Ⓐ ADJ atheistic
Ⓑ SM/F atheist

ateperetarse ▸conjug 1a◂ VPR (*CAm, Méx*) to get confused, get bewildered

atepocate SM (*Méx*) tadpole

aterciopelado ADJ velvety

aterido ADJ stiff with cold

aterirse ▸conjug 3a; imperfecto; úsase sólo en infin y pp◂ VPR to get stiff with cold

aterrada SF landfall

aterrador ADJ terrifying

aterraje SM (*Aer*) landing; (*Náut*) landfall

aterrar¹ ▸conjug 1a◂ Ⓐ VT to terrify
Ⓑ **aterrarse** VPR to be terrified (**de** by)

aterrar² ▸conjug 1j◂ Ⓐ VT [1] (= *derribar*) to pull down, demolish, destroy
[2] (= *cubrir*) to cover with earth; (*Agr*) to earth up
[3] (*CAm*) (= *obstruir*) to choke, obstruct
Ⓑ VI (*Aer*) to land; (*Náut*) to reach land
Ⓒ **aterrarse** VPR (*Náut*) to stand inshore; **navegar aterrado** to sail inshore

aterrazamiento SM terracing

aterrazar ▸conjug 1f◂ VT to terrace

aterrizaje SM (*Aer*) landing ► **aterrizaje a vientre** pancake landing ► **aterrizaje de emergencia** emergency landing, forced landing ► **aterrizaje de panza** pancake landing ► **aterrizaje de urgencia** emergency landing, forced landing ► **aterrizaje duro** hard landing ► **aterrizaje forzoso** emergency landing, forced landing ► **aterrizaje suave** soft landing ► **aterrizaje violento** crash landing

aterrizar ▸conjug 1f◂ VI to touch down, land

aterronar ▸conjug 1a◂ Ⓐ VT to cake, harden
Ⓑ **aterronarse** VPR to get lumpy

aterrorizador ADJ terrifying

aterrorizar ▸conjug 1f◂ VT (= *aterrar*) to terrify; (*Mil, Pol*) to terrorize

atersar ▸conjug 1a◂ VT to smooth

atesar ▸conjug 1j◂ VT (*LAm*) = **atiesar**

atesoramiento SM hoarding, accumulation

atesorar ▸conjug 1a◂ VT [+ *dinero, riquezas*] to hoard, accumulate; [+ *virtudes*] to possess

atestación SF (*Jur*) attestation; (*Pol*) deposition

atestado¹ SM (*Jur*) affidavit, statement ► **atestado policial** police statement

atestado² ADJ [1] (= *lleno*) packed; **~ de** packed with, crammed with, full of
[2] (= *testarudo*) obstinate, stubborn

atestar¹ ▸conjug 1a◂ VT (*Jur*) to attest, testify to; (= *dar prueba de*) to vouch for; **una palabra no atestada** an unattested word, an unrecorded word

atestar² ▸conjug 1j◂ Ⓐ VT (= *llenar*) to pack, stuff (**de** with); **~ a algn de frutas*** to stuff sb with fruit
Ⓑ **atestarse** VPR to stuff o.s. (**de** with)

atestiguación SF [1] (= *acción*) attestation
[2] (*Jur*) deposition, testimony

atestiguar ▸conjug 1i◂ VT (*Jur*) to testify to, give evidence of; (= *dar prueba de*) to attest, vouch for

atezado ADJ [1] (= *bronceado*) tanned
[2] (= *negro*) black

atezar ▸conjug 1f◂ Ⓐ VT [1] (*al sol*) to tan, burn [2] (= *ennegrecer*) to blacken, turn black
Ⓑ **atezarse** VPR to get tanned

atiborrado ADJ **~ de** full of, stuffed with, crammed with

atiborrar ▸conjug 1a◂ Ⓐ VT to fill, stuff (**de** with); **~ a un niño de dulces*** to stuff a child with sweets
Ⓑ **atiborrarse** VPR to stuff o.s. (**de** with)

ático SM (= *desván*) attic; (= *apartamento*) penthouse

atiesar ▸conjug 1a◂ Ⓐ VT to tighten, tighten up
Ⓑ **atiesarse** VPR (= *ponerse tieso*) to tighten; (*en la construcción*) to bind

atigrado ADJ (= *con manchas*) striped, marked like a tiger; [*gato*] tabby

atigronarse ▸conjug 1a◂ VPR (*Caribe*) to get strong

Atila SM Attila

atildado ADJ elegant, stylish

atildar ▸conjug 1a◂ Ⓐ VT [1] (*Tip*) to put a tilde over
[2] (= *acicalar*) to tidy, clean, clean up
[3] (= *criticar*) to criticize, find fault with
Ⓑ **atildarse** VPR to spruce o.s. up

atilincar ▸conjug 1g◂ VT (*CAm*) to tighten, stretch

atinadamente ADV (= *correctamente*) correctly; (= *sensatamente*) sensibly; (= *pertinentemente*) pertinently; **según dijo ~** as he rightly said

atinado ADJ (= *correcto*) accurate, correct; (= *sensato*) wise, sensible; (= *pertinente*) pertinent; (= *agudo*) penetrating; **unas observaciones atinadas** some pertinent remarks; **una decisión poco atinada** a rather unwise decision

atinar ▸conjug 1a◂ Ⓐ VI [1] (= *acertar*) to be right; **siempre atina** he always gets it right, he always hits the nail on the head; **el médico no le atina** the doctor doesn't know what's wrong with him, the doctor can't find out what's wrong with him; **~ a** *o* **con** *o* **en** to hit upon, find; **~ al blanco** to hit the mark
[2] (= *conseguir*) **~ a hacer algo** to succeed in doing sth
Ⓑ VT [+ *solución*] to hit upon, find; (= *acertar*) to guess right; (= *encontrar*) to succeed in finding

atingencia SF (*LAm*) [1] (= *relación*) connection, relationship
[2] (= *obligación*) obligation
[3] (= *reserva*) qualification; (= *aclaración*) clarification; (= *observación*) remark, comment

atingido ADJ [1] (*Andes, Cono Sur*) depressed, down-in-the-mouth; (= *débil*) feeble, weak; (= *tímido*) timid
[2] (*Andes*) (= *sin dinero*) penniless
[3] (*Méx*) (= *taimado*) sly, cunning

atingir ▸conjug 3c◂ VT [1] (*LAm*) to concern, relate to [2] (*Andes*) (= *oprimir*) to oppress

atiparse* ▸conjug 1a◂ VPR to stuff o.s.*

atípicamente ADV atypically, untypically

atipicidad SF atypical nature

atípico ADJ atypical, exceptional

atiplado ADJ high-pitched

atiplar ▸conjug 1a◂ Ⓐ VT [+ *voz*] to raise the pitch of
Ⓑ **atiplarse** VPR [*voz*] to go higher, become shrill; [*persona*] to talk in a high voice, talk in a squeaky voice

atipujarse ▸conjug 1a◂ VPR (*CAm, Méx*) to stuff o.s.

atirantar ▸conjug 1a◂ Ⓐ VT [1] (*= poner tirante*) to tighten, tauten; **estar atirantado entre dos decisiones** to be torn between two decisions
[2] (*Andes, Cono Sur*) (*= estirar*) to stretch out on the ground
Ⓑ **atirantarse** VPR (*Méx**) (*= estirar la pata*) to kick the bucket*

atisba SM (*Andes*) (*= vigilante*) watchman, look-out; (*= espía*) spy

atisbadero SM peephole

atisbador(a) SM/F (*= guardia*) watcher; (*= espía*) spy

atisbar ▸conjug 1a◂ VT [1] (*= espiar*) to spy on, watch; (*= mirar*) to peep at; **~ a algn a través de una grieta** to peep at sb through a crack
[2] (*= lograr ver*) to see, make out, discern (*frm*); **atisbamos un rayo de esperanza** we can just see a glimmer of hope

atisbo SM [1] (*= acción*) spying, watching
[2] (*= indicio*) inkling, indication

atizadero SM [1] (*para el fuego*) poker
[2] (*= estímulo*) spark, stimulus

atizador SM [1] (*para el fuego*) poker
[2] (*fig*) ► **atizador de la guerra** warmonger

atizar ▸conjug 1f◂ Ⓐ VT [1] [+ *fuego*] to poke, stir; [+ *horno*] to stoke; [+ *vela*] to snuff, trim
[2] [+ *discordia*] to stir up; [+ *pasión*] to fan, rouse
[3] (*) [+ *golpe*] to give
Ⓑ VI **¡atiza!*** gosh!
Ⓒ **atizarse** VPR (*) [1] (*= fumar marihuana*) to smoke marijuana
[2] (*= beberse*) **se atizó el vaso** he knocked back the whole glass*

atizonar ▸conjug 1a◂ VT to blight, smut

Atlante SM Atlas

atlántico Ⓐ ADJ Atlantic
Ⓑ SM **el (Océano) Atlántico** the Atlantic, the Atlantic Ocean

Atlántida SF Atlantis

atlantista Ⓐ ADJ NATO *antes de s*
Ⓑ SMF NATO supporter

atlas SM INV atlas

atleta SMF athlete

atlético ADJ athletic

atletismo SM athletics *sing*; **copa del mundo de ~** athletics world cup ► **atletismo en pista cubierta, atletismo en sala** indoor athletics

atmósfera SF [1] (*Fís, Meteo*) atmosphere; **mala ~** (*Radio*) atmospherics *pl*
[2] (*en sitio cerrado*) atmosphere
[3] (*fig*) (*= ambiente*) atmosphere
[4] (*fig*) (*= campo*) sphere, sphere of influence; **Juan tiene buena ~** (*LAm*) Juan enjoys considerable social standing, Juan stands well with everybody

atmosférico ADJ atmospheric

atoar ▸conjug 1a◂ VT to tow

atoc SM (*Andes*) fox

atocar ▸conjug 1g◂ VT (*LAm*) = **tocar A**

atocha SF esparto

atochal SM esparto field

atochamiento SM (*Cono Sur*) traffic jam

atochar SM = **atochal**

atocinado* ADJ fat, tubby*

atocinar ▸conjug 1a◂ Ⓐ VT [1] (*Agr*) [+ *cerdo*] to cut up; [+ *carne*] to cure
[2] (†*) (*= asesinar*) to do in*, bump off*
Ⓑ **atocinarse** VPR (†*) [1] (*= sulfurarse*) to fly off the handle
[2] (*= enamorarse*) to fall madly in love

atocle SM (*Méx*) *sandy soil rich in humus*

atol SM (*LAm*) cornflour drink

atolada SM (*CAm*) party

atole SM (*LAm*) cornflour drink

atoleada SF (*CAm*) party

atolería SF (*LAm*) *stall etc where "atol" is sold*

atolladero SM [1] (*= lodazal*) mire, morass
[2] (*= aprieto*) jam*, fix*; **estar en un ~** to be in a jam *o* a fix*; **salir del ~** to get out of a jam *o* a fix*; **sacar a algn del ~** to get sb out of a jam *o* a fix*

atollar ▸conjug 1a◂ VI, **atollarse** VPR [1] (*= atascarse*) to get stuck in the mud, get bogged down
[2] (*= meterse en un lío*) to get into a jam *o* a fix*

atolón SM atoll

atolondrado ADJ [1] (*= aturdido*) bewildered, stunned
[2] (*= irreflexivo*) thoughtless, reckless; (*= casquivano*) scatterbrained; (*= tonto*) silly

atolondramiento SM [1] (*= aturdimiento*) bewilderment
[2] (*= irreflexión*) thoughtlessness, recklessness

atolondrar ▸conjug 1a◂ Ⓐ VT (*= aturdir*) to bewilder; (*= pasmar*) amaze
Ⓑ **atolondrarse** VPR (*= aturdirse*) to be bewildered; (*= quedarse pasmado*) to be amazed

atomía SF (*LAm*) [1] (*= acto*) evil deed, savage act
[2] **decir ~s** to shoot one's mouth off* (**a** to)

atómico ADJ atomic

atomista Ⓐ ADJ atomistic
Ⓑ SMF atomist

atomización SF (*con atomizador*) spraying; (*Pol*) atomization

atomizador SM atomizer, spray

atomizar ▸conjug 1f◂ Ⓐ VT [1] (*con atomizador*) to spray
[2] (*Pol*) to atomize
Ⓑ **atomizarse** VPR to break up (**en** into), fragment

átomo SM atom; **ni un ~ de** not a trace of ► **átomo de vida** spark of life

atonal ADJ atonal

atonía SF lethargy, apathy

atónito ADJ amazed, astounded; **me miró ~** he looked at me in amazement *o* astonishment

átono ADJ atonic, unstressed

atontadamente ADV (*= aturdidamente*) in a bewildered way; (*= como tonto*) stupidly, foolishly

atontado ADJ [1] (*= aturdido*) bewildered, stunned
[2] (*= tonto*) stupid, thick*

atontar ▸conjug 1a◂ Ⓐ VT [1] (*Med*) to stupefy
[2] (*= aturdir*) to bewilder, stun
Ⓑ **atontarse** VPR to get bewildered, get confused

atontolinamiento SM bewilderment

atontolinar ▸conjug 1a◂ VT (*= pasmar*) to daze; (*= aturdir*) to stun; **quedar atontolinado** to be in a daze

atorafo ADJ (*Caribe*) anxious

atorar ▸conjug 1a◂ Ⓐ VT [1] (*= obstruir*) to stop up, obstruct; (*= inmovilizar*) to stop, immobilize
[2] (*esp LAm*) to stop, hold up
Ⓑ **atorarse** VPR [1] (*esp LAm*) (*= atragantarse*) to choke, swallow the wrong way; (*= trabarse la lengua*) to get tongue-tied
[2] (*Cono Sur*) (*= ponerse salvaje*) to get wild, get fierce

atormentador(a) Ⓐ ADJ tormenting
Ⓑ SM/F torturer

atormentar ▸conjug 1a◂ Ⓐ VT [1] (*Mil etc*) to torture
[2] (*= causar aflicción*) to torment; (*= acosar*) to plague, harass; (*= tentar*) to tantalize
Ⓑ **atormentarse** VPR to torment o.s.

atornillador SM screwdriver

atornillar ▸conjug 1a◂ VT [1] (*Téc*) to screw down
[2] (*Méx**) (*= molestar*) to bother, annoy, pester*

atoro SM (*LAm*) [1] (*= destrucción*) destruction
[2] (*= aprieto*) difficulty, fix*, jam*

atorón SM (*LAm*) traffic jam

atorozarse ▸conjug 1f◂ VPR (*CAm*) to choke, swallow the wrong way

atorrante (*Andes, Cono Sur*) Ⓐ ADJ lazy
Ⓑ SMF tramp, bum (*EEUU**)

atorrantear ▸conjug 1a◂ VI (*Cono Sur*) to live like a tramp, be on the bum (*EEUU*)

atortolado ADJ **están ~s** they're like two turtle-doves

atortolar ▸conjug 1a◂ VT (*= asustar*) to rattle, scare; (*= pasmar*) to shatter, flabbergast

atortujar ▸conjug 1a◂ Ⓐ VT to squeeze flat
Ⓑ **atortujarse** VPR (*CAm*) to be shattered, be flabbergasted

atorunado ADJ (*Cono Sur*) stocky, bull-necked

atosigador ADJ [1] (*= venenoso*) poisonous
[2] (*= que importuna*) pestering, worrisome; (*= que presiona*) pressing

atosigante ADJ = **atosigador 2**

atosigar ▸conjug 1h◂ Ⓐ VT [1] (*= envenenar*) to poison
[2] (*= importunar*) to harass, plague, pester*; (*= presionar*) to rush, put pressure on, pressurize
Ⓑ **atosigarse** VPR to slog away*, slave away*

atóxico ADJ non-poisonous

atrabancar ▸conjug 1g◂ Ⓐ VT to rush, hurry over
Ⓑ **atrabancarse** VPR to be in a fix*, get into a jam*

atrabiliario ADJ bad-tempered, irascible (*frm*)

atrabilis SF INV bad temper

atracadero SM pier

atracado ADJ (*CAm*) mean, stingy

atracador(a) Ⓐ SM/F (*en la calle*) mugger; (*en tienda, banco*) armed robber, raider ► **atracador(a) armado/a** armed robber ► **atracador(a) de bancos** bank robber
Ⓑ SM (†) [*de diligencias*] highwayman

atracar ▸conjug 1g◂ Ⓐ VT [1] (= *robar*) [+ *banco*] to hold up; [+ *individuo*] to mug; [+ *avión*] to hijack
[2] (*Náut*) to bring alongside; [+ *astronave*] to dock (**a** with)
[3] (= *atiborrar*) to stuff, cram
[4] (*LAm*) (= *molestar*) to harass, pester; (= *zurrar*) to thrash, beat
[5] (*Caribe Aut*) to park
Ⓑ VI (*Náut*) **~ al** *o* **en el muelle** to berth at the quay
Ⓒ **atracarse** VPR [1] (= *atiborrarse*) to stuff o.s. (**de** with)
[2] (*CAm, Méx*) (= *pelearse*) to brawl, fight
[3] (*Caribe*) (= *acercarse*) to approach, come up; **~se a** to approach, come up to

atracción SF [1] (*Fís*) attraction ► **atracción gravitatoria** gravity, gravitational pull
[2] (= *acción*) attraction; [*de persona*] attractiveness, appeal, charm ► **atracción sexual** sexual attraction
[3] (*tb* **~ de feria**) attraction, fairground attraction; **parque de atracciones** funfair; **atracciones** (*Teat*) (= *espectáculos*) attractions

atraco SM [*de banco etc*] holdup, robbery; [*de paseante*] mugging; [*de avión*] hijack, hijacking ► **atraco a mano armada** armed robbery; **¡es un ~!** (*fig*) it's daylight robbery!

atracón* SM blow-out*, chow-down (*EEUU*✱); **darse un ~** to stuff o.s. (**de** with), to pig out* (**de** on)

atractivamente ADV attractively

atractividad SF attractiveness

atractivo Ⓐ ADJ attractive
Ⓑ SM attractiveness, appeal

atraer ▸conjug 2o◂ Ⓐ VT [1] (*Fís*) to attract
[2] (= *hacer acudir a sí*) to draw, lure; [+ *apoyo etc*] to win, draw; [+ *atención*] to attract, engage; [+ *imaginación*] to appeal to; **dejarse ~ por** to allow o.s. to be drawn towards; **sabe ~(se) a la juventud** he knows how to win young people over
Ⓑ **atraerse** VPR **se atrajo las simpatías de todos** he won everyone's affection, everyone liked him; **se atrajo el rencor del jefe** the boss began to resent him

atragantarse ▸conjug 1a◂ VPR [1] (*al comer*) to choke (**con** on), swallow the wrong way; **me atragantè con una espina** I choked on a fish bone, I got a fish bone stuck in my throat; **se me atragantó una miga de pan** a crumb went down the wrong way
[2] (*al hablar*) to lose the thread of what one is saying
[3] (*) (= *caer mal*) **el tío ese se me atraganta** that guy gets up my nose*, I can't stomach that guy*

atrague SM **¡qué ~!** (*Caribe*) what an idiot!

atraillar ▸conjug 1a◂ VT to put on a leash

atramparse ▸conjug 1a◂ VPR [1] [*persona*] (= *caer en una trampa*) to fall into a trap; (= *meterse en un aprieto*) to get stuck, get o.s. into a jam*
[2] [*tubo*] to clog, get blocked up; (= *atascarse*) to stick, catch, jam

atrancar ▸conjug 1g◂ Ⓐ VT [1] [+ *puerta*] to bar, bolt; [+ *cañería*] to clog, block up; (*fig*) [+ *escotillas*] to batten down
[2] (*Cono Sur*) (= *estreñir*) to constipate
Ⓑ VI (*al andar*) to stride along, take big steps; (*al leer*) to skim
Ⓒ **atrancarse** VPR [1] (= *atascarse*) to get bogged down (**en** in); (*Mec*) to jam; (*haciendo algo*) to get stuck
[2] (*Méx**) (= *porfiarse*) to dig one's heels in, be stubborn
[3] (*Cono Sur**) (= *estreñirse*) to get constipated

atranco SM = **atascadero**

atrapada SF save

atrapamaridos* Ⓐ ADJ INV **mujer ~** = **B**
Ⓑ SF *woman on the look-out for a husband*

atrapamoscas SM INV flypaper

atrapar ▸conjug 1a◂ VT [1] (*en trampa*) to trap; (= *apresar*) to capture; [+ *resfriado etc*] to catch; **quedaron atrapados en la montaña** they were trapped on the mountainside; **~ un empleo** to land a job
[2] (= *engañar*) to take in, deceive

atraque SM [1] (*Náut*) mooring place, berth
[2] [*de astronave*] link-up, docking

atrás Ⓐ ADV [1] (*posición*) [1·1] (= *a la espalda*) behind; **la pelota le vino de ~** the ball came from behind; **la tienda está ahí ~** the shop is back there; **~ mío** (*esp Cono Sur*) behind me; **quedarse ~** to fall behind, get left behind
[1·2] (= *al final*) at the back; **los alumnos de ~ estaban fumando** the pupils at the back were smoking; **más ~ se ve mejor la pantalla** you can see the screen better if you sit further back; **ese capítulo está más ~** that chapter is further back; **la parte de ~** the back, the rear; **está muy ~ en la fila** he is a long way down the queue; **las patas de ~** the back legs; **la rueda de ~** the back *o* rear wheel; *ver tb* **asiento**
[2] (*dirección*) backwards; **dar un paso ~** to take a step back(wards); **ir hacia** *o* **para ~** to go back(wards); **échense ~, por favor** move back please; **lo has prometido y no puedes echarte ~** you can't back out now, you promised; *ver tb* **marcha 5**
[3] (*en sentido temporal*) **días ~** days ago; **cuatro meses ~** four months back; **este odio viene de ~** this hatred goes (a long) way back; **desde muy ~** for a very long time; **dejaron ~ sus rencores** they put aside their bitterness; **mirar ~** ◊ **volver la vista ~** to look back
[4] **~ de** (*LAm*) = **detrás 3**
Ⓑ EXCL **¡atrás!** back!, get back!

atrasado Ⓐ ADJ [1] (= *con retraso*) late, behind, behind time; [*pago*] overdue; [*número de revista etc*] back *antes de s*; **andar** *o* **estar ~** [*reloj*] to be slow; **estar un poco ~** [*persona*] to be a bit behind; **estar ~ en los pagos** to be in arrears; **estar ~ de medios** to be short of resources; **estar ~ de noticias** lack up-to-date information
[2] **estar ~** (*CAm**) (= *sin dinero*) to be broke*
[3] [*país*] backward; [*alumno etc*] slow, backward
Ⓑ SM **es un ~** he's behind the times

atrasar ▸conjug 1a◂ Ⓐ VT [+ *progreso*] to slow down; [+ *salida etc*] to delay; [+ *reloj*] to put back
Ⓑ VI [*reloj*] to lose time, be slow; **mi reloj atrasa ocho minutos** my watch is eight minutes slow
Ⓒ **atrasarse** VPR [1] (= *quedarse atrás*) to stay back, remain behind; [*tren etc*] to be late; [*reloj*] to be slow; **~se en los pagos** to be in arrears
[2] (*LAm*) [*proyecto etc*] to suffer a setback; (*Cono Sur*) (= *lastimarse*) to hurt o.s. (**de** in); [*mujer*] to be pregnant

atraso SM [1] (= *retraso*) delay, time lag; [*de reloj*] slowness; [*de país etc*] backwardness; **el tren lleva ~** the train is late; **salir del ~** to catch up, make up lost time; **llegar con 20 minutos de ~** to arrive 20 minutes late; **¡esto es un ~!** this is just holding things up!
[2] **atrasos** (*Com, Fin*) arrears; [*de pedidos etc*] backlog *sing*, quantity pending *sing*; **cobrar ~s** to collect arrears
[3] (*Andes*) (= *revés*) setback
[4] **tener un ~** (*LAm Med*) to have a period

atravesada SF (*LAm*) crossing, passage

atravesado ADJ [1] (= *de través*) **la farola quedó atravesada en la calle** the lamppost fell across the street; ✦*MODISMO* **tener ~***: **lo tengo ~** I can't stand him; **tengo ~ este programa de tele** I can't stand this TV programme
[2] (= *malintencionado*) treacherous
[3] (= *bizco*) squinting, cross-eyed
[4] (*Zool*) mongrel, cross-bred

atravesar ▸conjug 1j◂ Ⓐ VT [1] (= *colocar a través*) to put across; **atravesamos un tronco en el camino** we put a tree trunk across the road
[2] (= *cruzar*) [+ *calle, puente, frontera*] to cross; **~on España en tren** they crossed *o* travelled across Spain by train; **esta avenida atraviesa la capital** this road passes through *o* crosses the capital; **el túnel atraviesa la montaña** the tunnel goes *o* passes under the mountain
[3] (= *sufrir*) [+ *período, situación, crisis*] to go through; **mi familia atraviesa momentos difíciles** my family is going through a difficult time
[4] (= *perforar*) [+ *cuerpo, órgano*] to go through; **la bala le atravesó el cráneo** the bullet went through his skull; **~ a algn con una espada** to run sb through with a sword
Ⓑ **atravesarse** VPR [1] (= *colocarse a través*) **un camión se nos atravesó en la carretera** a lorry came out into the road in front of us; **se me ha atravesado una raspa en la garganta** I've got a fishbone stuck in my throat; **~se en una conversación** to butt into a conversation
[2] (*) (= *hacerse insoportable*) **se me ha atravesado Antonio** I've had all I can take of Antonio*

atrayente ADJ attractive

atrechar ▸conjug 1a◂ VI (*Caribe*) to take a short cut

atrecho SM (*Caribe*) short cut

atreguar ▸conjug 1i◂ Ⓐ VT to grant a truce to
Ⓑ **atreguarse** VPR to agree to a truce

atrenzo SM (*LAm*) (= *apuro*) trouble, difficulty; **estar en un ~** to be in trouble, have a problem

atreverse ▸conjug 2a◂ VPR [1] (= *osar*) to dare; **~ a hacer algo** to dare to do sth; **no me atrevo** ◊ **no me atrevería** I wouldn't dare; **¿te atreves?** are you game?, will you?; **¡atrévete!** (= *amenaza*) just you dare!; **~ a una empresa** to undertake a task; **~ con un rival** to take on a rival; **se atreve con todo** he'll tackle anything; **me atrevo con una tarta** I could manage a cake
[2] **~ con algn** ◊ **~ contra algn** (= *probar suerte*) to try one's luck with sb*; (= *insolentarse*) to be insolent to sb

atrevidamente ADV [1] (= *con audacia*) daringly, boldly
[2] (= *con insolencia*) cheekily

atrevido/a Ⓐ ADJ [1] [*persona*] (= *audaz*) daring, bold; (= *insolente*) cheeky, sassy (*EEUU*); **el periodista le hizo preguntas muy atrevidas** the reporter asked him some very daring *o* bold questions; **no seas tan ~ con el jefe** don't be so cheeky to the boss
[2] [*chiste*] daring, risqué; **un escote muy ~** a very daring neckline
Ⓑ SM/F cheeky person

atrevimiento SM [1] (= *audacia*) daring, boldness
[2] (= *insolencia*) insolence, cheek; (= *osadía*) forwardness

atrevismo SM ostentatiousness

atrezzo SM = **attrezzo**

atribución SF [1] (*Literat etc*) attribution
[2] **atribuciones** (*Pol*) powers *pl*, functions *pl*

atribuible ADJ attributable (**a** to); **obras ~s a Góngora** works which are attributed to Góngora

▼**atribuir** ▸conjug 3g◂ Ⓐ VT [1] **~ a algn/algo** to attribute to sb/sth; [+ *excusa*] to put down to sb/sth; (*Jur*) to impute to sb/sth
[2] (*Pol*) **las funciones atribuidas a mi cargo** the powers conferred on me by my post
Ⓑ **atribuirse** VPR **~se algo** to claim sth for o.s.; **~se la responsabilidad de un atentado** to claim responsibility for an attack

atribulación SF affliction, tribulation

atribulado Ⓐ ADJ afflicted, suffering
Ⓑ SM **los ~s** the afflicted, the suffering, the sufferers

atribular ▸conjug 1a◂ Ⓐ VT to grieve, afflict
Ⓑ **atribularse** VPR to grieve, be distressed

atributivo ADJ attributive

atributo SM [1] (= *cualidad*) attribute
[2] (= *emblema*) emblem, sign of authority
[3] (*Ling*) predicate

atril SM (*para libro*) bookrest, reading desk; (*Mús*) music stand; (*Rel*) lectern

atrincar ▸conjug 1g◂ Ⓐ VT (*LAm*) to tie up tightly
Ⓑ **atrincarse** VPR (*Méx*) to be stubborn, dig one's heels in

atrincheramiento SM entrenchment

atrincherar ▸conjug 1a◂ Ⓐ VT to fortify with trenches
Ⓑ **atrincherarse** VPR [1] (*Mil*) to entrench o.s., dig in; **están muy fuertemente atrincherados** (*fig*) they are very strongly entrenched
[2] **~se en** (= *adoptar una postura*) to take one's stand on; (= *protegerse*) to take refuge in

atrio SM (*Hist*) atrium, inner courtyard; (*Rel*) vestibule, porch; [*de garaje*] forecourt

atrochar ▸conjug 1a◂ VI to take a short cut

atrocidad SF [1] (*Mil etc*) atrocity, outrage
[2] (*) (= *tontería*) foolish thing, silly thing; **decir ~es** to talk nonsense
[3] (*) (= *exageración*) **¡qué ~!** how dreadful!, how awful!; **la comedia es una ~** the play is awful; **me gustan los helados una ~** I'm extremely fond of ice cream

atrofia SF atrophy ► **atrofia muscular** muscular atrophy

atrofiar ▸conjug 1b◂ Ⓐ VT to atrophy
Ⓑ **atrofiarse** VPR to atrophy, be atrophied

atrojarse ▸conjug 1a◂ VPR (*Méx*) to be stumped (for an answer), be stuck (for an answer)

atrompetado ADJ bell-shaped; **nariz atrompetada** flared nostrils *pl*

atronadamente ADV recklessly, thoughtlessly

atronado ADJ reckless, thoughtless

atronador ADJ (= *ensordecedor*) deafening; [*aplausos*] thunderous

atronamiento SM bewilderment, stunned state

atronar ▸conjug 1l◂ VT [1] (= *ensordecer*) to deafen
[2] (= *aturdir*) to bewilder, stun
[3] (*Taur*) (= *acogotar*) to fell with a blow on the neck

atropellada SF (*Cono Sur*) attack, onrush

atropelladamente ADV **correr ~** to run helter-skelter; **hablar ~** to gabble; **decidir algo ~** to rush into a decision about sth

atropellado ADJ [*acto*] hasty, precipitate; [*estilo*] brusque, abrupt; [*ritmo*] violent

atropellador/a SM/F hooligan

atropellaplatos* SMF INV clumsy servant

atropellar ▸conjug 1a◂ Ⓐ VT [1] (= *arrollar*) to knock down, run over; **la atropelló un taxi** she was knocked down *o* run over by a taxi; **una multitud de gente me atropelló mientras paseaba** a crowd of people barged into me as I was out walking
[2] (= *humillar*) **no te dejes ~ por nadie** don't let anyone walk (all) over you
[3] (= *infringir*) [+ *derecho, constitución, estatuto*] to sweep aside, ride roughshod over
Ⓑ VI (*) (= *empujar*) to push; **oye, por favor, no atropelles** hey, stop pushing (and shoving), please
Ⓒ **atropellarse** VPR [1] (= *empujarse*) **entraron de uno en uno sin ~se** they went in one by one without pushing and shoving
[2] (= *precipitarse*) to rush; **el actor se atropelló al recitar** the actor gabbled his recitation; **no te atropelles y hazlo con tranquilidad** don't rush — take your time

atropello SM [1] (*Aut*) accident; (= *empujón*) shove, push; (= *codeo*) jostling
[2] (= *abuso*) abuse (**de** of), disregard (**de** for); **los ~s del dictador** the crimes of the dictator

atroz ADJ [1] (= *terrible*) atrocious; (= *cruel*) cruel, inhuman; (= *escandaloso*) outrageous
[2] (*) (= *enorme*) huge, terrific; (= *malísimo*) dreadful, awful

atrozmente ADV [1] (= *terriblemente*) atrociously; (= *con crueldad*) cruelly; (= *escandalosamente*) outrageously
[2] (*) (= *muchísimo*) dreadfully, awfully

ATS SMF ABR (*Esp*) (= **ayudante técnico sanitario**) Registered Nurse

attaché SM attaché case

atto. ABR = **atento**

attrezzo SM (*Teat*) properties *pl*; (= *equipo*) kit, gear

ATUDEM SF ABR (*Esp*) = **Asociación Turística de Estaciones de Esquí y Montaña**

atuendo SM [1] (= *vestido*) attire
[2] (= *boato*) pomp, show

atufado* ADJ [1] (= *enojado*) cross, angry; (*Andes*) dazed
[2] (*CAm, Caribe*) (= *vanidoso*) proud, stuck-up*

atufamiento* SM irritation, vexation

atufar* ▸conjug 1a◂ Ⓐ VT [1] [*olor*] to overcome, overpower
[2] (= *molestar*) to irritate, vex
Ⓑ **atufarse** VPR [1] [*vino*] to turn sour
[2] [*persona*] to be overcome (*by smell or fumes*)
[3] (= *enojarse*) to get cross, get angry (**con, de, por** at, with)
[4] (*Andes*) (= *aturdirse*) to get bewildered, become confused; (*CAm, Caribe*) (= *engreírse*) to be proud, become vain

atufo* SM irritation, vexation

atulipanado ADJ tulip-shaped

atún SM [1] (= *pez*) tuna (fish); ✦**MODISMO** **querer ir por ~ y ver al duque** to want to have it both ways, want to have one's cake and eat it too
[2] (*) (= *imbécil*) nitwit*

atunero Ⓐ ADJ tuna *antes de s*
Ⓑ SM [1] (= *pescador*) tuna fisherman
[2] (= *barco*) tuna fishing boat

aturar ▸conjug 1a◂ VT to close up tight

aturdidamente ADV [1] (= *atolondradamente*) in a bewildered way
[2] (= *sin reflexionar*) thoughtlessly, recklessly

aturdido ADJ [1] (= *atolondrado*) bewildered, dazed
[2] (= *irreflexivo*) thoughtless, reckless

aturdimiento SM, **aturdidura** SF (*Cono Sur*)
[1] (= *atolondramiento*) bewilderment
[2] (= *irreflexión*) thoughtlessness, recklessness

aturdir ▸conjug 3a◂ Ⓐ VT [1] (*físicamente*) (*con golpe*) to stun, daze; [*ruido*] to deafen; [*droga, movimiento, vino*] to make giddy, make one's head spin
[2] (= *atolondrar*) to stun, dumbfound; (= *dejar perplejo*) to bewilder; **la noticia nos aturdió** the news stunned us, we were stunned by the news
Ⓑ **aturdirse** VPR (= *atolondrarse*) to be stunned; (= *quedarse perplejo*) to be bewildered

aturrullado* ADJ bewildered, perplexed

aturrullar* ▸conjug 1a◂ Ⓐ VT to bewilder, perplex
Ⓑ **aturrullarse** VPR to get flustered; **no te aturrulles cuando surja una dificultad** don't get flustered when a problem comes up

atusamiento SM smartness, elegance

atusar ▸conjug 1a◂ Ⓐ VT [+ *pelo*] (= *cortar*) to trim; (= *alisar*) to smooth, smooth down
Ⓑ **atusarse** VPR to dress up to the nines; **~se el bigote** to stroke one's moustache

audacia SF (= *atrevimiento*) boldness, audacity; (= *descaro*) cheek, nerve

audaz ADJ bold, audacious

audazmente ADV boldly, audaciously

audibilidad SF audibility

audible ADJ audible

audición SF [1] (*Med*) hearing
[2] (*Teat*) audition; **dar ~ a algn** to audition sb, give sb an audition; **le hicieron una ~ para el papel** they gave him an audition for the part
[3] (*Mús*) concert ► **audición radiofónica** radio concert
[4] (*LAm Com, Fin*) audit

audiencia SF [1] (= *acto*) audience; (= *entrevista*) formal interview; **recibir a algn en ~** to grant sb an audience
[2] (*Jur*) (= *tribunal*) court; (= *palacio*) assizes *pl*; (= *sala*) audience chamber ► **audiencia**

➤ LENGUA Y USO: **atribuir A1** 44.2

pública (*Pol*) public hearing
[3] (= *personas*) audience; [*de periódico*] readership; (*Radio, TV*) audience; **índice de ~** ratings *pl*, audience ratings *pl*

audífono SM [1] [*de sordo*] hearing aid
[2] (*LAm*) (= *auricular*) receiver; **audífonos** (= *cascos*) headphones

audímetro SM audience meter

audio SM audio

audiofrecuencia SF audio frequency

audiolibro SM audio book

audiómetro SM audiometer

audiovisual Ⓐ ADJ audiovisual
Ⓑ SM audiovisual presentation

auditar ▸conjug 1a◂ VT to audit

auditivo Ⓐ ADJ auditory (*frm*), hearing *antes de s*
Ⓑ SM receiver

audito SM audit, auditing

auditor(a) SM/F [1] (*Jur*) (*tb* **~(a) de guerra**) judge advocate
[2] (*Fin*) auditor ► **auditor(a) de cuentas** auditor ► **auditor(a) externo/a** external auditor
[3] (*Méx Ferro*) ticket inspector

auditora SF firm of auditors, auditors *pl*

auditoría SF (*Com, Fin*) audit, auditing ► **auditoría administrativa** management audit ► **auditoría de gestión** management audit ► **auditoría externa** external audit ► **auditoría financiera** financial audit ► **auditoría general** general audit ► **auditoría interna** internal audit ► **auditoría operativa** management audit

auditorio SM [1] (= *público*) audience
[2] (= *local*) auditorium, hall

auge SM [1] (= *apogeo*) peak; **el agroturismo aún no ha alcanzado su ~** rural tourism has not yet reached its peak; **Internet conocerá su ~ en la próxima década** the Internet will reach its peak in the next decade; **está en el ~ de su popularidad** he is at the peak *o* height of his popularity; **ya ha pasado el ~ del tecno** the heyday of techno is over
[2] (= *ascendencia*) **el rápido ~ del fundamentalismo** the rapid rise of fundamentalism; **un momento de ~ de la industria** a time of industrial growth; **una moda en ~** an increasingly popular fashion; **el feminismo está en ~** feminism is increasingly successful *o* influential, feminism is on the up and up*; **el sector turístico está en pleno ~** tourism is booming *o* experiencing a boom; **una empresa en pleno ~** a firm in full expansion
[3] (*Astron*) apogee

Augias SM **establos de ~** Augean Stables

augurar ▸conjug 1a◂ VT [*cosa*] to augur; [*individuo*] to predict, foresee; **~ que ...** to predict that ...

augurio SM [1] (= *presagio*) omen; (= *profecía*) prediction; **consultar los ~s** to take the auguries
[2] **augurios** (= *deseos*) best wishes (**para** for); **con nuestros ~s para ...** with our best wishes for ...; **mensaje de buenos ~s** goodwill message

augustal ADJ Augustan

Augusto SM Augustus

augusto ADJ august

aula SF (*Escol*) classroom; (*Univ*) lecture room ► **aula magna** assembly hall, main hall

aulaga SF furze, gorse

aulario SM lecture room building

áulico/a Ⓐ ADJ court *antes de s*, palace *antes de s*
Ⓑ SM/F courtier

aullar ▸conjug 1a◂ VI to howl, yell

aullido SM howl, yell; **dar ~s** to howl, yell

aumentador SM booster

aumentar ▸conjug 1a◂ Ⓐ VT [1] [+ *tamaño*] to increase; (*Fot*) to enlarge; (*Ópt*) to magnify
[2] [+ *cantidad*] to increase; [+ *precio*] to increase, put up; [+ *producción*] to increase, step up; **me van a ~ el sueldo** they are going to increase *o* raise my salary; **no aumentes la velocidad todavía** don't speed up yet; **esto aumentó el número de parados** this swelled the numbers of the unemployed
[3] [+ *intensidad*] to increase; **su dimisión ha aumentado la tensión política** his resignation has increased political tension; **estas pastillas pueden ~ las molestias** these tablets can make the problem worse
[4] (*Elec, Radio*) to amplify
Ⓑ VI [1] [*tamaño*] to increase
[2] [*cantidad, precio, producción*] to increase, go up; **las temperaturas ~án mañana** temperatures will rise tomorrow; **el número de asesinatos ha aumentado en 200** the number of killings has increased *o* gone up by 200; **este semestre aumentó la inflación en un 2%** inflation has increased *o* gone up by 2% over the last 6 months
[3] [*intensidad*] to increase; **el calor aumenta por la tarde** the heat increases in the afternoon; **su popularidad ha aumentado** his popularity has increased *o* risen; **la crispación política aumenta por momentos** political tension is increasing *o* rising by the moment
[4] **~ de** to increase in; **~ de peso** [*objeto*] to increase in weight; [*persona*] to put on *o* gain weight; **~ de tamaño** to increase in size

aumentativo ADJ, SM augmentative

aumento SM [1] [*de tamaño*] increase; (*Fot*) enlargement; (*Ópt*) magnification
[2] [*de cantidad, producción, velocidad, intensidad*] increase; [*de precio*] increase, rise; **un ~ del número de turistas** an increase in the number of tourists; **se registró un ~ de temperatura** an increase *o* rise in temperature was recorded; **un ~ del calor** a rise in temperature ► **aumento de peso** (*en objeto*) increase in weight; (*en persona*) weight gain ► **aumento de población** population increase ► **aumento de precio** rise in price ► **aumento de sueldo, aumento salarial** (pay) rise
[3] (*Elec, Radio*) amplification
[4] **ir en ~** to be on the increase
[5] (*Ópt*) magnification; **una lente de 30 ~s** a lens of 30x magnification; **unas gafas de mucho ~** glasses with very strong lenses
[6] (*Méx*) (= *posdata*) postscript

aun ADV [1] (= *incluso*) even; **yo pagaría mil y ~ dos mil** I'd pay a thousand, even two thousand; **~ siendo tan joven es muy responsable** even though he's so young he's very responsible; **~ los ricos sufrirán la crisis** (*frm*) even the rich will suffer the effects of the crisis
[2] **~ así: ~ así, no creo que fuera** even so, I don't think I'd go; **es muy rica y ~ así trabaja** she's very rich but she still works
[3] **~ cuando: ~ cuando me lo rogara, no se lo daría** even if he begged me I wouldn't give it to him; **va en camisa ~ cuando hace frío** he goes around in a shirt even when it's cold
[4] **ni ~** not even; **no lo aceptaría ni ~ regalado** I wouldn't accept it even as a present; **ni ~ pagándome haría yo eso** I wouldn't do that (even) if you paid me; **y ni ~ así lo haría** and I wouldn't do it even then

aún ADV [1] (= *todavía*) (*temporal*) still, yet; **~ está aquí** he's still here; **~ no lo sabemos** we still don't know, we don't know yet; **¿no ha venido ~?** hasn't he come yet?; → TODAVÍA
[2] (= *incluso*) even; **y ~ se permite el lujo de sermonearme** and he even goes so far as to lecture me; **más ~** even more; **la comida italiana me gusta más ~** I like Italian food even more *o* better; **si vienes lo pasaremos ~ mejor** if you come we'll enjoy ourselves even more
[3] (*) (= *quizás*) perhaps, maybe; **—¿lo comprarás? —si lo rebajan, ~** "will you buy it?" — "if they reduce it, perhaps."

aunar ▸conjug 1a◂ Ⓐ VT to join, unite
Ⓑ **aunarse** VPR to unite

aunque CONJ although, though, even though; **~ estaba cansado vino con nosotros** although he was tired he came with us; **~ no me creas** even though you may not believe me; **~ llueva vendremos** we'll come even if it rains; **es guapa ~ algo bajita** she's pretty but rather short, she's pretty even if she is on the short side; **~ más ...** however much ..., no matter how much ...

AUNQUE

Aunque se puede traducir al inglés por **although, though, even though** o **even if**.

• Por regla general, cuando la cláusula introducida por **aunque** indica un hecho (**aunque** + INDICATIVO), en inglés coloquial se traduce por **though** y en lenguaje más formal por **although**:

Aunque había un montón de gente, al final pude encontrar a Carlos
Though there were a lot of people there, I managed to find Carlos
No esperaba eso de él, aunque entiendo por qué lo hizo
I did not expect that from him, although I can understand why he did it

• **Even though** introduce la oración subordinada, enfatizando con más fuerza el contraste con la principal, cuando **aunque** va seguido de un hecho concreto, no una hipótesis, y equivale a **a pesar de que**:

Llevaba un abrigo de piel, aunque era un día muy caluroso
She wore a fur coat, even though it was a very hot day

• Si **aunque** tiene el sentido de **incluso si** (**aunque** + SUBJUNTIVO), se traduce por **even if**:

Debes ir, aunque no quieras
You must go, even if you don't want to
Me dijo que no me lo diría, aunque lo supiera
He said he wouldn't tell me even if he knew

Para otros usos y ejemplos ver la entrada.

aúpa Ⓐ EXCL (*al levantar a un niño*) up!, upsadaisy!; (*para animar*) up!, come on!; **¡~ Toboso!** up Toboso!
Ⓑ ADJ (*) **una función de ~** a slap-up do*; **una paliza de ~** a good thrashing*; **una tormenta de ~** a hell of a storm*; **es de ~** it's absolutely awful

au pair SMF au pair

aupar ▸conjug 1a◂ VT (= *levantar*) to help up; [+ *pantalón etc*] to hitch up; (= *ensalzar*) to praise; **sus discos la han aupado al primer puesto** her records have lifted her *o* shot her up to top spot; **~ a algn al poder** to raise sb to power

aura SF [1] (= *brisa*) gentle breeze, sweet breeze
[2] (= *popularidad*) popularity, popular favour, popular favor (*EEUU*)
[3] (*LAm*) (= *pájaro*) vulture, buzzard (*EEUU*)

áureo ADJ [1] (*liter*) (= *de oro*) golden
[2] (*Esp Hist*) **nuestra literatura áurea** our literature of the Golden Age

aureola SF, **auréola** SF (*Rel*) halo, aureole (*frm*); (= *gloria*) fame

aureolar†† ▸conjug 1a◂ VT (*esp LAm*) [+ *persona*] to praise, extol the virtues of; [+ *reputación etc*] to enhance, add lustre to

aurícula SF auricle

auricular Ⓐ ADJ aural, of the ear; **el pabellón ~** the outer ear
Ⓑ SM [1] (= *dedo*) little finger
[2] [*de teléfono*] receiver, handset; **auriculares** (= *cascos*) headphones, earphones

auriculoterapia SF auriculotherapy

aurífero ADJ gold-bearing

aurora SF (*lit, fig*) dawn ► **aurora boreal, aurora borealis** northern lights *pl*

auscultación SF sounding, auscultation (*frm*)

auscultar ▸conjug 1a◂ VT to sound, auscultate (*frm*)

ausencia SF absence; **condenar a algn en su ~** to sentence sb in his absence; **hacer buenas ~s de algn**† to speak kindly of sb in their absence, remember sb with affection; **tener buenas ~s**† to have a good reputation; ✦***MODISMO*** **en ~ del gato se divierten los ratones** when the cat's away the mice will play; *ver* **brillar 2**

ausentarse ▸conjug 1a◂ VPR (= *marcharse*) to absent o.s. (**de** from); (= *no acudir*) to stay away (**de** from)

ausente Ⓐ ADJ [1] (*físicamente*) absent (**de** from); **estar ~ de** to be absent from, be missing from; **estar ~ de su casa** to be away from home
[2] (*mentalmente*) daydreaming
Ⓑ SMF (*Escol etc*) absentee; (*Jur*) missing person

auspiciado ADJ sponsored, backed

auspiciador(a) Ⓐ ADJ **firma ~a** sponsoring firm
Ⓑ SM/F sponsor

auspiciar ▸conjug 1b◂ VT [1] (= *patrocinar*) to back, sponsor
[2] (*LAm*) (= *desear éxito a*) to wish good luck to

auspicios SMPL [1] (= *patrocinio*) auspices, sponsorship *sing*; **bajo los ~ de** under the auspices of, sponsored by
[2] (= *augurio*) omen; **buenos ~** good omen; **malos ~** bad omen

auspicioso ADJ auspicious

austeramente ADV (= *con frugalidad*) austerely; (= *con severidad*) sternly, severely

austeridad SF (= *frugalidad*) austerity; (= *severidad*) severity ► **austeridad económica** economic austerity

austero ADJ (= *frugal*) austere; (= *severo*) severe

austral Ⓐ ADJ [1] (= *del sur*) southern; **el Hemisferio Austral** the Southern Hemisphere
[2] (*Cono Sur*) (= *del sur de Chile*) of/from southern Chile
Ⓑ SM (*Arg*) *monetary unit from 1985-1991*

Australia SF Australia

australiano/a ADJ, SM/F Australian

australopiteco/a SM/F, **australopitecus** SMF Australopithecus

Austria SF Austria

austríaco/a ADJ, SM/F, **austriaco/a** ADJ, SM/F Austrian

austro SM (*liter*) (= *sur*) south; (= *viento*) south wind

austro-húngaro ADJ Austro-Hungarian

autarquía SF [1] (*Pol*) autarchy (*frm*), self-government
[2] (*Econ*) autarky (*frm*), national self-sufficiency

autazo SM (*LAm*) theft of a car

auténtica SF (*Jur*) (= *certificación*) certification; (= *copia*) authorized copy

auténticamente ADV authentically, genuinely

autenticar ▸conjug 1g◂ VT to authenticate

autenticidad SF authenticity

auténtico ADJ [1] (= *legítimo*) authentic; [*persona*] genuine; **un ~ espíritu de servicio** a true spirit of service; **es un ~ campeón** he's a real champion; **éste es copia y no el ~** this one is a copy and not the real one; **días de ~ calor** days of real heat, really hot days
[2] (*) (= *estupendo*) great*, brilliant*

autentificar ▸conjug 1g◂ VT to authenticate

autería SF (*Cono Sur*) (= *presagio*) evil omen, bad sign; (= *brujería*) witchcraft

autero/a[1] SM/F (*LAm*) (= *ladrón*) car thief

autero/a[2] SM/F (*Cono Sur*) [1] (= *pesimista*) pessimist, defeatist [2] (= *gafe*) jinx*

autillo SM tawny owl

autismo SM autism

autista Ⓐ ADJ autistic
Ⓑ SMF autistic, autistic person; **es un ~** he's autistic

autístico ADJ autistic

auto[1] SM (*esp Cono Sur*) car, automobile (*EEUU*) ► **auto de choque** bumper car, dodgem

auto[2] SM [1] (*Jur*) edict, judicial decree ► **auto de comparecencia** summons, subpoena (*EEUU*) ► **auto de ejecución** writ of execution ► **auto de prisión** warrant for arrest ► **auto de procesamiento** charge, indictment
[2] **autos** (= *documentos*) proceedings, court record *sing*; **estar en ~s** to be in the know; **poner a algn en ~s** to put sb in the picture
[3] (*Rel, Teat*) mystery play, religious play ► **auto del nacimiento** nativity play ► **auto sacramental** eucharistic play
[4] (*Hist*) ► **auto de fe** auto-da-fé; **hacer un ~ de fe de algo**† (*fig*) to burn sth

auto... PREF auto..., self-...

autoabastecerse ▸conjug 2d◂ VPR (= *autoproveerse*) to supply o.s. (**de** with); (= *ser autosuficiente*) to be self-sufficient

autoabastecimiento SM self-sufficiency

autoacusación SF self-accusation

autoacusarse ▸conjug 1a◂ VPR to accuse o.s.

autoadherente ADJ self-adhesive

autoadhesivo ADJ self-adhesive

autoadministrarse ▸conjug 1a◂ VPR [1] **~ una droga** to take a drug
[2] (*Pol*) to govern o.s., be self-governing

autoadulación SF self-praise

autoafirmación SF assertiveness

autoaislarse ▸conjug 1a◂ VPR to isolate o.s.

autoalarma SF car alarm

autoalimentación SF (*Inform*) ► **autoalimentación de hojas** automatic paper feed

autoanálisis SM INV self-analysis

autoanalizador SM analyser, auto-analyser

autoanalizarse ▸conjug 1f◂ VPR to analyze o.s., do self-analysis

autoaprendizaje SM self-study; **curso de ~** self-study course; **programa de ~** self-study programme, self-study program (*EEUU*)

autoaprovisionamiento SM self-sufficiency

autoayuda SF self-help

autobiografía SF autobiography

autobiográfico ADJ autobiographic, autobiographical

autobomba SF fire engine

autobombearse ▸conjug 1a◂ VPR to blow one's own trumpet

autobombo SM self-praise, self-glorification; **hacerse el ~** to blow one's own trumpet

autobronceador SM self-tanning lotion

autobús SM bus; (*LAm*) [*de distancia*] coach, bus (*EEUU*) ► **autobús de dos pisos** double-decker, double-decker bus ► **autobús de línea** long-distance coach ► **autobús escolar** school bus

autobusero/a Ⓐ ADJ bus *antes de s*
Ⓑ SM/F bus driver

autocalificarse ▸conjug 1g◂ VPR **~ de** to describe o.s. as

autocar SM coach, bus (*EEUU*) ► **autocar de línea** long-distance coach, inter-city coach ► **autocar de línea regular** scheduled coach

autocaravana SF camper, motor home (*EEUU*), camping vehicle

autocargador ADJ **camión ~** self-loading truck

autocarril SM (*LAm*) railway car

autocartera SF holding of its own shares (*by a company*)

autocensura SF self-censorship

auto-choque SM bumper car, dodgem

autocine SM drive-in cinema

autoclave SM (*Med*) autoclave

autocompasión SF self-pity

autocomplaciente ADJ self-satisfied

autocomprobación SF self-test

autoconcederse ▸conjug 2a◂ VPR **~ un título** to grant o.s. a title

autoconfesado ADJ self-confessed

autoconfesarse ▸conjug 1a◂ VPR to confess o.s.

autoconfesión SF self-confession

autoconfianza SF self-confidence

autoconservación SF self-preservation

autoconsumo SM [*de alimentos*] personal consumption; [*de bienes*] personal use

autocontrol SM [1] (= *autodominio*) self-control, self-restraint
[2] (*Téc*) self-monitoring
autoconvencerse ▸conjug 2d◂ VPR to convince o.s.
autocracia SF autocracy
autócrata SMF autocrat
autocrático ADJ autocratic
autocremarse ▸conjug 1a◂ VPR to set fire to o.s., burn o.s. (to death)
autocrítica SF self-criticism
autocrítico ADJ self-critical
autocross SM INV autocross
autóctono ADJ indigenous, native
autocue SM autocue
autodefensa SF self-defence, self-defense (*EEUU*)
autodefinirse ▸conjug 3a◂ VPR to define o.s., state one's position
autodegradación SF self-abasement
autodenominarse ▸conjug 1a◂ VPR to call o.s.
autodestrucción SF self-destruction
autodestructible ADJ, **autodestructivo** ADJ self-destructive, self-destructing
autodestruirse ▸conjug 3g◂ VPR to self-destruct
autodeterminación SF self-determination
autodidacta Ⓐ ADJ [*persona*] self-taught; [*formación, método*] autodidactic (*frm*)
Ⓑ SMF autodidact, self-taught person
autodidacto/a ADJ, SM/F = **autodidacta**
autodisciplina SF self-discipline
autodisciplinado ADJ self-disciplined
autodisparador SM self-timer
autodominio SM self-control
autódromo SM racetrack, racing circuit
autoedición SF desktop publishing
autoelevador SM, **autoelevadora** SF (*Cono Sur*) forklift truck
autoempleo SM self-employment
autoengaño SM self-deception, self-delusion
autoerótico ADJ autoerotic
autoescuela SF driving school
autoestima SF self-esteem
autoestop SM = **autostop**
autoestopista SMF = **autostopista**
autoevaluación SF self-assessment
autoexcluirse ▸conjug 3g◂ VPR to exclude o.s.
autoexploración SF self-examination
autoexpresión SF self-expression
autofecundación SF self-fertilization
autofelicitación SF self-congratulation
autofinanciable ADJ, **autofinanciado** ADJ self-financing
autofinanciarse ▸conjug 1b◂ VPR to finance o.s.
autógena SF welding
autógeno ADJ autogenous
autogestión SF self-management
autogiro SM autogiro
autogobernarse ▸conjug 1j◂ VPR to govern o.s., be self-governing
autogobierno SM self-government
autogol SM own goal
autogolpe SM *coup organized by the government itself to allow it to take extra powers*
autógrafo SM autograph
autohipnosis SF INV autohypnosis, self-hypnosis
autoimpuesto ADJ self-imposed
autoincluirse ▸conjug 3g◂ VPR to include o.s.
autoinculpación SF [1] (= *autoacusación*) self-incrimination
[2] (*Jur*) plea of guilty
autoinculparse ▸conjug 1a◂ VPR to incriminate o.s.
autoinducido ADJ self-induced
autoinfligido ADJ self-inflicted
autoinmune ADJ autoimmune
autoinmunidad SF autoimmunity
autoinmunitario ADJ, **autoinmunológico** ADJ autoimmune
autolavado SM car-wash
autolesionarse ▸conjug 1a◂ VPR to inflict injury on o.s., injure o.s.
autolimpiable ADJ self-cleaning
autollamarse ▸conjug 1a◂ VPR to call o.s.
automación SF automation
automarginación SF dropping-out
automarginado/a Ⓐ ADJ **persona automarginada** drop-out
Ⓑ SM/F drop-out
automarginarse ▸conjug 1a◂ VPR to drop out; **~ de** to drop out of
autómata SM automaton, robot ► **autómata industrial** industrial robot
automática SF [1] (= *ciencia*) automation
[2] (= *lavadora*) washing machine
[3] (*Mil*) automatic
automáticamente ADV automatically
automaticidad SF automaticity
automático Ⓐ ADJ automatic; **lavadora automática** (automatic) washing machine
Ⓑ SM [1] (*Cono Sur*) (= *restaurante*) self-service restaurant, automat (*EEUU*)
[2] (= *cierre*) press stud, popper, snap (fastener) (*EEUU*)
automatismo SM automatism
automatización SF automation ► **automatización de fábricas** factory automation ► **automatización de oficinas** office automation
automatizado ADJ automated
automatizar ▸conjug 1f◂ VT to automate
automedicarse ▸conjug 1g◂ VPR to treat o.s.
automedonte SM (*LAm hum*) coachman
automercado SM (*Caribe*) supermarket
automoción SF [1] (= *transporte*) transport, road transport
[2] (= *automóvil*) **la industria de la ~** the car industry, the automobile industry (*EEUU*); **gasóleo de ~** diesel for automobiles
automodelismo SM model car racing
automodelista SMF model car enthusiast
automontable ADJ self-assembly
automotor Ⓐ ADJ [1] (= *autopropulsado*) self-propelled
[2] (*LAm*) car *antes de s*, automobile *antes de s* (*EEUU*)
Ⓑ SM [1] (*Ferro*) diesel train
[2] (*LAm*) (= *vehículo*) motor vehicle
automóvil Ⓐ ADJ [1] (= *autopropulsado*) self-propelled
[2] car *antes de s*, automobile *antes de s* (*EEUU*)
Ⓑ SM car, automobile (*EEUU*); **ir en ~** to drive, go by car, travel by car ► **automóvil de alquiler** hire car ► **automóvil de carreras** racing car ► **automóvil de choque** bumper car, dodgem ► **automóvil de importación** imported car, foreign car
automovilismo SM motoring ► **automovilismo deportivo** motor racing
automovilista SMF motorist, driver
automovilístico ADJ car *antes de s*, auto *antes de s* (*EEUU*); **accidente ~** car accident; **industria automovilística** car industry
automutilación SF self-mutilation
automutilarse ▸conjug 1a◂ VPR to mutilate o.s.
autonomía SF [1] (= *independencia*) autonomy; (= *autogobierno*) self-government; **Estatuto de Autonomía** (*Esp*) Devolution Statute
[2] (= *territorio*) autonomous region, autonomy
[3] (*Aer, Náut*) range; **el avión tiene una ~ de 5.000km** the aircraft has a range of 5,000km; **de gran ~** long range ► **autonomía de vuelo** range
[4] [*de pila, batería*] battery range
autonómico ADJ (*Pol*) autonomous, self-governing; **elecciones autonómicas** elections for the autonomous regions; **política autonómica** policy concerning the autonomies; **el proceso ~** the process leading to autonomy; **región autonómica** autonomous region
autonomismo SM separatism, movement towards autonomy
autónomo/a Ⓐ ADJ [1] (*Pol*) autonomous, self-governing
[2] (*Inform*) stand-alone, off-line
[3] [*persona*] self-employed; **trabajo ~** self-employment
Ⓑ SM/F self-employed person
autopatrulla SM (*Méx*) patrol car
autopegado ADJ self-sealing
autopiano SM (*Caribe*) pianola
autopista SF motorway, freeway (*EEUU*) ► **autopista de la información** information superhighway ► **autopista de peaje** toll road, turnpike (*EEUU*) ► **autopista perimetral** ring road, bypass
autopolinización SF self-pollination
autopreservación SF self-preservation
autoproclamado ADJ self-proclaimed
autoproclamarse ▸conjug 1a◂ VPR to proclaim o.s.
autoprofesor SM teaching machine
autoprogramable ADJ **ordenador ~** intelligent computer
autopropulsado ADJ self-propelled
autopropulsión SF self-propulsion
autopropulsor ADJ self-propelling
autoprotegerse ▸conjug 2c◂ VPR to protect o.s.
autopsia SF post mortem, autopsy; **hacer** o **practicar la ~ a algn** to carry out an autopsy on sb
autopublicidad SF self-advertisement; **hacer ~** to indulge in self-advertisement
autor(a) SM/F [1] [*de obra*] author, writer; [*de idea*] creator, originator, inventor; **el ~ de la novela** the author of the novel; **el ~ del cuadro** the painter; **el ~ de mis días** my father
[2] [*de delito*] perpetrator; **los presuntos ~es del crimen** the suspected killers; **el ~ intelectual** the mastermind; **el ~ material** *the person directly responsible (for the crime)*

autoría SF authorship; **la ~ del atentado** the responsibility for the attack

autoridad SF 1 (= *potestad*) authority; **las ~es** the authorities; **~es aduaneras** customs authorities; **¡abran a la ~!** open up in the name of the law!; **entregarse a la ~** to give o.s. up (*to the police*) ► **autoridad de sanidad** health authorities *pl* ► **autoridad local** local authority
2 (= *persona*) authority
3 (= *boato*) pomp, show

autoritario/a ADJ, SM/F authoritarian

autoritarismo SM authoritarianism

autoritativo ADJ authoritative

autorización SF authorization, permission; **~ para hacer algo** authorization *o* permission to do sth

autorizadamente ADV officially, authoritatively

▼**autorizado** ADJ 1 (= *oficial*) authorized, official
2 (= *fiable*) authoritative
3 (*Com*) approved; **la persona autorizada** the officially designated person, the approved person

▼**autorizar** ▸conjug 1f◂ VT 1 (= *dar facultad a*) to authorize, empower; (= *permitir*) to approve, license; **~ a algn para** (+ *INFIN*) to authorize sb to + *infin*, empower sb to + *infin*; **el futuro no autoriza optimismo alguno** the future does not warrant *o* justify the slightest optimism
2 (*Jur*) to legalize

autorradio SF car radio

autorrealización SF self-fulfilment

autorrealizado ADJ self-fulfilled

autorrealizarse ▸conjug 1f◂ VPR to feel fulfilled

autorregulable ADJ self-adjusting

autorregulación SF self-regulation

autorretrato SM self-portrait

autoservicio SM 1 (= *tienda*) self-service store, self-service shop
2 (= *restaurante*) self-service restaurant

autosostenerse ▸conjug 2k◂ VPR to pay one's own way, be self-supporting

autostop SM hitch-hiking; **hacer ~** to hitch-hike, thumb lifts; **viajar en ~** to hitch-hike; **fuimos haciendo ~ de Irún a Burgos** we hitch-hiked from Irún to Burgos, we got a lift from Irún to Burgos

autostopismo SM hitch-hiking

autostopista SMF hitch-hiker

autosuficiencia SF 1 (*Econ*) self-sufficiency
2 (*pey*) (= *petulancia*) smugness

autosuficiente ADJ 1 (*Econ*) self-sufficient
2 (*pey*) (= *petulante*) smug

autosugestión SF autosuggestion

autotanque SM tanker, tank truck (*EEUU*)

autotitularse ▸conjug 1a◂ VPR to title o.s., call o.s.

autoventa ADJ INV **vendedor ~** travelling salesman, representative who travels by car

autovía SF main road, trunk road, state highway (*EEUU*) ► **autovía de circunvalación** bypass, ring road

autovivienda SF caravan, trailer

Auvernia SF Auvergne

auxiliar[1] (A) ADJ 1 (*Univ*) assistant *antes de s*
2 (*Ling*) auxiliary
3 [*plantilla*] ancillary
(B) SMF 1 (= *subordinado*) assistant ► **auxiliar administrativo** administrative assistant ► **auxiliar de cabina** steward/stewardess ► **auxiliar de clínica, auxiliar de enfermería** auxiliary nurse, nursing auxiliary, nurse's aide (*EEUU*) ► **auxiliar de laboratorio** lab assistant, laboratory assistant ► **auxiliar de vuelo** steward/stewardess ► **auxiliar domiciliario** domestic, home help, home helper (*EEUU*) ► **auxiliar sanitario** health worker ► **auxiliar técnico sanitario** nurse
2 (*Univ*) ► **auxiliar de conversación** conversation assistant ► **auxiliar de lengua inglesa** English language assistant
3 (*Dep*) linesman, assistant referee ► **auxiliar técnico** (*LAm Dep*) coach, trainer

auxiliar[2] ▸conjug 1b◂ VT 1 (= *ayudar*) to help, assist; [+ *agonizante*] to attend
2 (*Pol etc*) to aid, give aid to

auxilio SM help, assistance (*más frm*); **primeros ~s** (*Med*) first aid; **acudir en ~ de algn** to come to sb's aid; **pedir ~** to ask for help *o* assistance; **prestar ~** to give help *o* assistance ► **auxilio espiritual** (*Rel*) consolations of religion *pl*; (= *sacramentos*) last rites *pl* ► **auxilio social** welfare service

Av. ABR (= **Avenida**) Av., Ave

a/v ABR (*Com*) = **a vista**

avada‡ SM (*Caribe*) queer‡, fag (*EEUU*‡)

avahar ▸conjug 1a◂ (A) VT to blow on, warm with one's breath
(B) VI, **avaharse** VPR to steam, give off steam *o* vapour

aval SM 1 (*Com*) endorsement; [*de firma*] guarantee; **dar su ~ a** [+ *fiador*] to be a guarantor for; (*Fin*) to underwrite ► **aval bancario** banker's reference
2 (*Pol*) backing, support

avalancha SF 1 [*de nieve*] avalanche
2 (*fig*) **una ~ de gente** a flood *o* torrent of people; **una ~ de cartas** an avalanche of letters

avalar ▸conjug 1a◂ VT 1 (*Fin*) to underwrite; [+ *individuo*] to act as guarantor for
2 (*Com*) to endorse, guarantee; [+ *persona*] (= *responder de*) to answer for

avalentado ADJ, **avalentonado** ADJ boastful, arrogant

avalista SMF (*Fin*) guarantor; (*Com*) endorser

avalorar ▸conjug 1a◂ VT 1 (*Com*) to appraise
2 (= *animar*) to encourage

avaluación SF (*LAm*), **avaluada** (*LAm*) SF valuation, appraisal

avaluar ▸conjug 1e◂ VT to value, appraise (**en** at)

avalúo SM valuation, appraisal

avancarga SF ► **cañón de avancarga** muzzle loader

avance SM 1 (= *movimiento*) advance; **el ~ de las tropas** the advance of the troops; **el ~ del feminismo** the advance of feminism
2 (= *progreso*) advance; **grandes ~s en el terreno de la genética** major advances in the field of genetics; **Pedro ha hecho grandes ~s en matemáticas** Pedro has made great progress in mathematics; **la reunión concluyó sin ~s** no progress had been made by the end of the meeting
3 (*Fin*) advance (payment)
4 (*Cine*) (= *tráiler*) trailer; **un ~ de la programación matinal** (*TV*) a look ahead at the morning's programmes ► **avance informativo** news headlines, advance news summary
5 (*Com*) (= *balance*) balance; (= *cálculo*) estimate
6 (*Elec*) lead
7 (*Mec*) feed
8 (*Cono Sur*) (= *ataque*) attack, raid
9 (*Cono Sur*) (= *regalo*) tempting offer, inducement (*made to secure sb's goodwill*)
10 (*CAm*) (= *robo*) theft

avante ADV (*esp LAm*) (= *adelante*) forward; (*Náut*) forward, ahead; **todo ~** (*Náut*) full steam ahead; **¡avante!** forward!; **salir ~** to get ahead, get on in the world

avanzada SF (*Mil*) (= *soldados*) advance party, advance guard; (= *puesto*) outpost

avanzadilla SF (= *patrulla*) scout, patrol; (= *avanzada*) advance party

avanzado ADJ (= *adelantado*) advanced; [*pómulo*] prominent; [*diseño*] advanced; [*ideas, tendencia*] advanced, avant-garde, progressive; **de edad avanzada** ◊ **~ de edad** advanced in years; **a una hora avanzada** at a late hour

avanzar ▸conjug 1f◂ (A) VT 1 (= *mover*) to move forward, advance; **avanzó la ficha cuatro casillas** he moved the counter forward four spaces, he advanced the counter four spaces; **avanza un poco tu silla** move your chair forward a bit
2 [+ *dinero*] to advance
3 [+ *opinión, propuesta*] to put forward
4 [+ *resultado*] to predict; [+ *predicción*] to make
5 (*Caribe*) (= *vomitar*) to vomit
(B) VI 1 (= *ir hacia adelante*) to advance, move forward; **el ejército avanzó de madrugada** the army advanced *o* moved forward at dawn; **no me esperéis, seguid avanzando** don't wait for me, carry on
2 (= *progresar*) to make progress; **estudio mucho pero no avanzo** I work hard but I don't make any progress *o* headway; **ha avanzado mucho en química** she has made great progress in chemistry; **las conversaciones de paz no parecen ~** the peace talks do not seem to be progressing *o* making (any) progress; **la genética avanza a ritmo vertiginoso** genetics is progressing *o* advancing at a dizzy speed
3 [*noche, invierno*] to draw on, approach
(C) **avanzarse** VPR **~se algo** (*CAm, Méx*) to steal sth

avanzo SM (*Com*) (= *balance*) balance sheet; (= *cálculo*) estimate

avaricia SF avarice, greed, greediness

avariciosamente ADV avariciously, greedily

avaricioso ADJ, **avariento** ADJ avaricious, greedy

avariosis SF INV (*LAm*) syphilis

avaro/a (A) ADJ miserly, mean; **ser ~ de** *o* **en alabanzas** to be sparing in one's praise; **ser ~ de palabras** to be a person of few words
(B) SM/F miser

avasallador ADJ overwhelming

avasallamiento SM subjugation

avasallar ▸conjug 1a◂ (A) VT 1 (= *subyugar*) to subjugate
2 **~ a algn** (= *obligar*) to steamroller sb (*into*

➤ LENGUA Y USO: **autorizado 1** 36.2 **autorizar 1** 36.3

agreement or compliance)
Ⓑ **avasallarse** VPR to submit, yield

avatar SM [1] (= *encarnación*) incarnation; (= *transformación*) change, transformation; **~es** (= *vicisitudes*) ups and downs
[2] (= *etapa*) phase; (= *ola*) wave ► **avatar destructivo** wave of destruction

Avda. ABR (= **Avenida**) Av., Ave

AVE SM ABR (= **Alta Velocidad Española**) *high speed train*

ave SF (= *pájaro*) bird; (*esp LAm*) (= *pollo*) chicken ► **ave acuática, ave acuátil** water bird ► **ave canora, ave cantora** songbird ► **ave de corral** chicken, fowl ► **ave del paraíso** bird of paradise ► **ave de paso** bird of passage ► **ave de presa, ave de rapiña** bird of prey ► **ave marina** sea bird ► **ave negra** (*Cono Sur*) crooked lawyer ► **ave nocturna** night bird (*tb fig*) ► **aves de corral** poultry *sing* ► **ave zancuda** wader, wading bird

avechuco* SM ragamuffin, ne'er-do-well

avecinarse ▸conjug 1a◂ VPR to approach, come near

avecindarse ▸conjug 1a◂ VPR to take up one's residence, settle

avefría SF lapwing

avejentado ADJ [*piel, rostro*] old; **le encontré ~ para su edad** I thought he looked old for his age

avejentar ▸conjug 1a◂ Ⓐ VT **el pelo blanco te avejentaba mucho** your grey hair made you look much older *o* put years on you
Ⓑ VI, **avejentarse** VPR to age

avejigar ▸conjug 1h◂ Ⓐ VT to blister
Ⓑ **avejigarse** VPR to blister

avellana SF [1] (*Bot*) hazelnut
[2] (*Perú*) firecracker

avellanado ADJ [1] [*color*] nutbrown
[2] [*piel*] wrinkled, wizened
[3] [*sabor*] nutty

avellanal SM hazel wood

avellanar[1] SM hazel wood

avellanar[2] ▸conjug 1a◂ Ⓐ VT (*Téc*) to countersink
Ⓑ **avellanarse** VPR to become wrinkled

avellanedo SM hazel wood

avellano SM hazel nut tree

avemaría SF [1] (*Rel*) (= *cuenta*) rosary bead; (= *oración*) Ave Maria, Hail Mary
[2] **al ~** at dusk; **en un ~** in a twinkling, in a jiffy*; **saber algo como el ~*** to know sth inside out

avena SF oats *pl* ► **avena loca, avena morisca, avena silvestre** wild oats *pl*

avenado ADJ half-crazy, touched*, nuts*

avenal SM oatfield

avenamiento SM drainage

avenar ▸conjug 1a◂ VT to drain

avenencia SF (= *acuerdo*) agreement; (*Com*) deal

avenida SF [1] (= *calle*) avenue
[2] [*de río*] flood, spate

avenido ADJ **están muy bien ~s** [*personas*] they get on well; [*pareja*] they're well matched; **están muy mal ~s** [*personas*] they get on badly; [*pareja*] they're badly matched

avenimiento SM agreement, compromise

avenir ▸conjug 3a◂ Ⓐ VT to reconcile, bring together
Ⓑ VI to come to pass
Ⓒ **avenirse** VPR [1] (*Com etc*) to come to an agreement; [*hermanos etc*] to get on well together; **no se avienen** they don't get on
[2] **~se con algo** (= *estar de acuerdo*) to be in agreement with sth; (= *resignarse*) to resign o.s. to sth; **~se con algn** to reach an agreement with sb; **¡allá te las avengas!*** that's your look-out!*, that's up to you!
[3] **~se a hacer algo** to agree to do sth

aventado ADJ (*LAm*) daring

aventador SM (*para fuego*) fan, blower; (*Agr*) winnowing fork

aventadora SF winnowing machine

aventajadamente ADV outstandingly, extremely well

aventajado ADJ outstanding; **~ de estatura** exceptionally tall

▼ **aventajar** ▸conjug 1a◂ Ⓐ VT [1] (= *superar*) to surpass, excel (**en** in); (*en carrera*) to outstrip; (*CAm Aut*) to overtake; **~ con mucho a algn** to beat sb easily, be far better than sb, leave sb standing*; **Juan aventaja a Pablo por cuatro puntos** Juan leads Pablo by four points
[2] (= *mejorar*) to improve, better
[3] (= *preferir*) to prefer
Ⓑ **aventajarse** VPR (= *adelantarse*) to get ahead; **~se a** to surpass, excel

aventar ▸conjug 1j◂ Ⓐ VT [1] [+ *fuego*] to fan, blow; (*Agr*) to winnow
[2] (= *expulsar*) to chuck out*, throw out; (*LAm*) (= *arrojar*) to throw
[3] (= *lanzar al aire*) to cast to the winds; [*viento*] to blow away; (*Caribe Agr*) to dry in the wind
Ⓑ **aventarse** VPR [1] [*vela etc*] to fill with air, swell up
[2] (✱) (= *largarse*) to beat it*
[3] (= *atacar*) to attack
[4] (*LAm*) (= *tirarse*) to throw o.s.; (= *arriesgarse*) to take risks

aventón* SM (*Méx*) (= *empujón*) push, shove; **pedir ~** to hitch a lift, hitch a ride (*EEUU*)

aventura SF [1] (= *suceso*) adventure; **nos contó las ~s de su viaje** he told us of the adventures he had had on his journey; **una película de ~s** an adventure film
[2] (= *riesgo*) **invertir ahora es una ~** investing at this time is a gamble; **se fue a América a buscar trabajo a la ~** he went to America and took a chance on *o* gambled on finding work, he went to America on the off-chance of finding work; **se lanzaron a la ~ de montar un negocio** they embarked on the venture of setting up a business
[3] (*) (= *amorío*) fling*, brief affair; **tuvo una ~ con un estudiante** she had a fling* *o* a brief affair with a student
[4] (*frm*) (= *contingencia*) chance, contingency

aventurado ADJ risky, hazardous; **es ~ suponer ...** it's a bit too much to suppose that ...

aventurar ▸conjug 1a◂ Ⓐ VT (= *arriesgar*) to venture, risk; [+ *opinión etc*] to hazard; [+ *capital*] to risk, stake
Ⓑ **aventurarse** VPR to dare, take a chance; **~se a hacer algo** to venture to do sth, risk doing sth; ✦**REFRÁN el que no se aventura no pasa la mar** nothing ventured, nothing gained

aventurero/a Ⓐ ADJ adventurous, enterprising
Ⓑ SM/F adventurer/adventuress
Ⓒ SM (*Mil*) mercenary, soldier of fortune; (*pey*) (= *arribista*) social climber

avergonzado ADJ **estar ~** to be ashamed (**de, por** about, at)

avergonzar ▸conjug 1f, 1l◂ Ⓐ VT (= *hacer pasar vergüenza*) to shame, put to shame; (= *poner en un aprieto*) to embarrass
Ⓑ **avergonzarse** VPR [1] (= *sentir vergüenza*) to be ashamed (**de, por** about, at, of); **~se de hacer algo** to be ashamed to do sth; **se avergonzó de haberlo dicho** he was ashamed at having said it
[2] (= *sentirse violento*) to be embarrassed

avería[1] SF [1] (*Com etc*) damage; (*Mec*) breakdown; **en caso de ~ llame al 3474** in the event of a breakdown call 3474; **el coche tiene una ~** there's something wrong with the car
[2] (*Cono Sur*) (= *matón*) tough guy*, thug; (= *criminal*) dangerous criminal; **ser de ~** to be dangerous

avería[2] SF (*Orn*) (= *pajarera*) aviary; (= *aves*) flock of birds

avería[3] SF (*Com, Náut*) average ► **avería gruesa** general average

averiado ADJ [1] (*Mec*) broken down, faulty; **los faros están ~s** the lights have failed, there's something wrong with the lights; **"Averiado"** "Out of order"
[2] [*fruto etc*] damaged, spoiled

averiar ▸conjug 1c◂ Ⓐ VT (*Mec*) to cause a breakdown in, cause a failure in; (= *estropear*) to damage
Ⓑ **averiarse** VPR [1] (*Mec*) to have a breakdown; (= *estropearse*) to get damaged; **debe de haberse averiado** [*coche*] it must have broken down; [*ascensor*] it must be out of order; **se averió el arranque** the starter failed, the starter went wrong
[2] (*Méx*) (= *perder la virginidad*) to lose one's virginity

averiguable ADJ verifiable

averiguación SF [1] (= *comprobación*) verification; (= *investigación*) inquiry, investigation
[2] (*CAm, Méx*) (= *riña*) quarrel, argument

averiguadamente ADV certainly

averiguado ADJ certain, established; **es un hecho ~** it is an established fact

averiguador(a) SM/F investigator

averiguar ▸conjug 1i◂ Ⓐ VT to find out, establish (*frm*); **debemos ~ cuándo llega el tren** we must find out when the train arrives; **averigua cuál es su hermano** find out who the brother is; **nunca ~on quién era el asesino** they never found out *o* (*frm*) established *o* discovered who the killer was; **~ la solución** to find out the answer; **ya han averiguado la identidad del padre** they have found out *o* (*frm*) established *o* discovered the identity of the father; **~ las causas de un problema** to find out *o* (*frm*) establish the causes of a problem; **un estudio para ~ el alcance de la tragedia** a study to find out *o* (*frm*) establish the extent of the tragedy; **han averiguado que el presidente malversaba fondos** it has been established *o* discovered that the president was embezzling funds; **—¿quién ha roto el vaso? —¡averigua!** "who broke the glass?" — "who knows!"
Ⓑ VI (*CAm, Méx**) (= *pelear*) to quarrel
Ⓒ **averiguarse** VPR (*tb* **averiguárselas**) (*esp Méx*) to manage, get by; **yo me (las) averiguo**

➤ LENGUA Y USO: **aventajar A1** 32.2

muy bien solo I manage *o* get by very well on my own; **yo me (las) averiguo con poco dinero** I get by *o* manage without much money; **ya me (las) ~é por mi cuenta** I'll manage *o* get by on my own; **averíguate(las) como puedas** you'll have to manage as best you can; **averíguate(las) con lo que tengas** make do with what you've got; **ya me las ~é para llegar a Barcelona** I'll find a way of getting to Barcelona somehow; **~se** *o* **averiguárselas con algn: tú olvídate, ya me (las) ~é yo con él** don't worry about it I'll sort it out with him; **~se** *o* **averiguárselas bien con algn** to get on (well) with sb; **ellos dos se las averiguan bien** the two of them get on well (together)

averiguata SF (*Méx*) argument, fight

averigüetas* SMF INV (*Andes*) snooper, busybody

averrugado ADJ warty

▼**aversión** SF (= *repulsión*) aversion; (= *aborrecimiento*) disgust, loathing; **~ hacia** *o* **por algo** aversion to sth; **~ a algn** aversion for sb; **cobrar ~ a algn/algo** to take a strong dislike to sb/sth

avestruz SM [1] (= *ave*) ostrich ► **avestruz de la pampa** rhea
[2] (*LAm**) (= *imbécil*) dimwit*, idiot

avetado ADJ veined, streaked

avetoro SM bittern

avezado ADJ accustomed, inured; **los ya ~s en estos menesteres** those already experienced in such activities

avezar ▸conjug 1f◂ Ⓐ VT to accustom, inure (**a** to)
Ⓑ **avezarse** VPR to become accustomed; **~se a algo** to get used to sth, get hardened to sth, get inured to sth (*frm*)

aviación SF [1] (= *locomoción*) aviation
[2] (*Mil*) air force; **la ~ francesa** the French air force

AVIACO SF ABR (*Esp*) (= **Aviación y Comercio S.A.**) *airline*

aviado ADJ [1] **estar ~** (*Arg*) to be well off, have all one needs
[2] **estar ~** (*en un lío*) to be in a mess; **¡~s estamos!** what a mess we're in!, we're in a right mess!

aviador(a)[1] SM/F [1] (*Aer*) (= *piloto*) pilot, airman; (= *tripulante*) crew member; (*Mil*) member of the air force
[2] (*Méx**) phantom employee

aviador(a)[2] SM/F (*Andes, Caribe*) (= *financiador*) mining speculator, mining financier; (= *prestamista*) moneylender, loan shark*

aviar ▸conjug 1c◂ Ⓐ VT [1] (= *preparar*) to get ready, prepare; (= *ordenar*) to tidy up; (= *proveer*) to supply (**de** with)
[2] (*LAm*) (= *prestar dinero a*) to advance money to
[3] **~ a algn** (= *dar prisa a*) to hurry sb up, gee sb up*; **¡vamos aviando!** let's get a move on!
Ⓑ **aviarse** VPR to get ready; **~se para hacer algo** to get ready to do sth

aviario SM aviary

aviatorio ADJ (*LAm*) **accidente ~** air crash, plane crash

avícola ADJ poultry *antes de s*; **granja ~** poultry farm

avicultor(a) SM/F poultry farmer

avicultura SF poultry farming

ávidamente ADV (= *con entusiasmo*) avidly, eagerly; (= *con codicia*) greedily

avidez SF (= *entusiasmo*) avidity, eagerness (**de** for); (= *codicia*) greed, greediness (**de** for); **con ~** (= *con entusiasmo*) avidly, eagerly; (= *con codicia*) greedily

ávido ADJ (= *entusiasta*) avid, eager (**de** for); (= *codicioso*) greedy (**de** for); **~ de sangre** bloodthirsty

aviejarse ▸conjug 1a◂ VPR to age before one's time

avieso Ⓐ ADJ [1] (= *torcido*) distorted, crooked
[2] (= *perverso*) perverse, wicked; (= *siniestro*) sinister; (= *rencoroso*) spiteful
Ⓑ SM (*Andes*) abortion

avifauna SF birds *pl*, bird life

avilantarse ▸conjug 1a◂ VPR to be insolent

avilantez SF insolence

avilés/esa Ⓐ ADJ of/from Ávila
Ⓑ SM/F native/inhabitant of Ávila; **los avileses** the people of Ávila

avilesino/a Ⓐ ADJ of/from Avilés
Ⓑ SM/F native/inhabitant of Avilés; **los ~s** the people of Avilés

avillanado ADJ boorish, uncouth

avinagrado ADJ [*sabor*] sour, acid; [*individuo*] sour, jaundiced

avinagrar ▸conjug 1a◂ Ⓐ VT to sour
Ⓑ **avinagrarse** VPR [*individuo*] to be crotchety; [*vino etc*] to turn sour

Aviñón SM Avignon

avío SM [1] (= *prevención*) preparation, provision; [*de pastor*] provisions for a journey
[2] (*LAm Agr*) loan
[3] **hacer su ~*** (= *enriquecerse*) to make one's pile*; (*iró*) (= *armarla*) to make a mess of things
[4] **¡al ~!** (= *¡en marcha!*) get cracking!, get on with it!
[5] **avíos** (= *equipo*) gear *sing*

avión SM [1] (*Aer*) aeroplane, plane, aircraft, airplane (EEUU); **por ~** (*Correos*) by airmail; **enviar artículos por ~** to send goods by plane; **ir en ~** to go by plane, go by air ► **avión a chorro** jet plane ► **avión ambulancia** air ambulance ► **avión a reacción** jet plane ► **avión de carga** freight plane, cargo plane ► **avión de caza** fighter, pursuit plane ► **avión de chorro** jet plane ► **avión de combate** fighter, pursuit plane ► **avión de despegue vertical** vertical take-off plane ► **avión de papel** paper dart ► **avión de pasajeros** passenger aircraft ► **avión de reacción** jet plane ► **avión de transporte** transport plane ► **avión espía** spy plane ► **avión sanitario** air ambulance
[2] (*Orn*) martin
[3] **hacer el ~ a algn*** (= *hacer daño*) to do sb down, cause sb harm; (*esp Andes*) (= *estafar*) to cheat sb
[4] (*CAm*) (= *juego*) hopscotch

avionazo (*esp Méx*) SM plane crash, accident to an aircraft

avioncito SM ► **avioncito de papel** paper dart

avionero SM (*Andes, Cono Sur*) airman

avioneta SF light aircraft

aviónica SF aviation, avionics *sing*

avionístico ADJ aeroplane *antes de s*, flying *antes de s*; **miedo ~** fear of flying

avisadamente ADV sensibly, wisely

avisado ADJ sensible, wise; **mal ~** rash, ill-advised

avisador(a) Ⓐ SM (= *timbre*) electric bell; (*Culin*) timer ► **avisador de incendios** fire alarm
Ⓑ SM/F [1] (= *informante*) informant; (= *mensajero*) messenger; (= *denunciador*) informer
[2] (*Cine, Teat*) programme seller

▼**avisar** ▸conjug 1a◂ VT [1] (= *informar*) to tell, notify (*frm*); **¿por qué no me avisaste?** why didn't you tell me?; **avísale cuando acabes** tell him *o* let him know when you finish; **la policía ya ha avisado a los familiares** the police have now told *o* (*frm*) notified *o* (*frm*) informed the family; **me avisó (de) que no comería en casa** she told me she wouldn't be eating at home; **nos avisó (de) que se casaba** he told us he was getting married; **lo hizo sin ~** he did it without telling anyone; **se presentó en casa sin ~** he turned up at home without telling anyone *o* without warning; **me ~on con una semana de antelación** they gave me a week's notice
[2] (= *llamar*) to call; **~ un taxi** to call a taxi; **~ al médico** to call the doctor, send for the doctor; **"avisamos grúa"** (*Esp*) "cars parked here will be towed away"
[3] (= *advertir*) to warn; **te aviso (de) que te denunciaré si no pagas** I warn you I shall report you if you don't pay; **un dispositivo que avisa (de) que la línea está interceptada** a device that warns you that the line is bugged

aviso SM [1] (= *notificación*) notice; **recibimos un ~ por escrito** we received written notice *o* notice in writing; **"Aviso: cerrado el lunes"** "Notice: closed Mondays"; **hasta nuevo ~** until further notice; **sin previo ~** without warning *o* notice; **salvo ~ contrario** unless otherwise informed; **dar ~ a algn de algo** to notify *o* inform sb of sth; **mandar ~** to send word ► **aviso de bomba** bomb alert
[2] (= *advertencia*) warning; **el bombardeo fue un ~ a los rebeldes** the bombing was a warning to the rebels; **poner a algn sobre ~** to warn sb; **ya está usted sobre ~** you have been warned
[3] (*Com, Fin*) demand note; **según (su) ~** as per order, as ordered ► **aviso de envío** dispatch note ► **aviso de mercancías** advice note
[4] (*Inform*) prompt
[5] (*esp LAm Com*) advertisement ► **aviso económico** classified advertisement ► **aviso mural** poster, wall poster

avispa SF [1] (= *insecto*) wasp
[2] (= *persona*) sharp person, clever person

avispado ADJ [1] (= *astuto*) sharp, clever; (*pey*) (= *taimado*) sly, wily
[2] (*LAm*) (= *nervioso*) jumpy*, nervous

avispar ▸conjug 1a◂ Ⓐ VT [+ *caballo*] to spur on; (= *despabilar*) to prod
Ⓑ **avisparse** VPR (= *despabilarse*) to liven up; (= *preocuparse*) to fret, worry; (*LAm*) (= *alarmarse*) to become alarmed

avispero SM [1] (= *nido*) wasps' nest
[2] (*Med*) carbuncle
[3] (*) (= *enredo*) hornet's nest, mess; **meterse en un ~** to get o.s. into a jam*

avispón SM hornet

avistamiento SM sighting

➤ LENGUA Y USO: **aversión** 34.3 **avisar 1** 30

avistar ▸conjug 1a◂ Ⓐ VT to sight, catch sight of
Ⓑ **avistarse** VPR to have an interview (**con** with)

avitaminosis SF INV vitamin deficiency

avituallamiento SM provisioning, supplying

avituallar ▸conjug 1a◂ Ⓐ VT to provision, supply with food
Ⓑ **avituallarse** VPR to provision o.s.

avivado/a* (*Cono Sur*) Ⓐ ADJ forewarned, alerted
Ⓑ SM/F smart alec*, wise guy (*EEUU**)

avivar ▸conjug 1a◂ Ⓐ VT [+ *fuego*] to stoke, stoke up; [+ *color*] to brighten; [+ *dolor*] to intensify; [+ *pasión*] to excite, arouse; [+ *disputa*] to add fuel to; [+ *interés*] to stimulate; [+ *esfuerzo*] to revive; [+ *efecto*] to enhance, heighten; [+ *combatientes*] to urge on
Ⓑ **avivarse** VPR (= *cobrar vida*) to revive, take on new life; (= *animarse*) to cheer up, become brighter; **¡avívate!** look alive!, snap out of it!

avizor Ⓐ ADJ **estar ojo ~** to be on the alert, be vigilant
Ⓑ SM watcher

avizorar ▸conjug 1a◂ VT to watch, spy on

avocastro SM (*Cono Sur*) = **abocastro**

avorazado ADJ (*Méx*) greedy, grasping

avutarda SF great bustard

axial ADJ axial

axila SF armpit

axiológico ADJ axiological

axioma SM axiom

axiomático ADJ axiomatic

axis SM INV axis

ay Ⓐ EXCL [1] (*dolor*) ow!, ouch!
[2] (*pena*) oh!, oh dear!; **¡ay de mí!** whatever shall I do?; **¡ay del que lo haga!** woe betide the man who does it!
[3] (*sorpresa*) oh!, goodness!
Ⓑ SM (= *gemido*) moan, groan; (= *suspiro*) sigh; (= *grito*) cry; **un ay desgarrador** a heartrending cry

aya SF governess

ayatolá SM, **ayatollah** SM ayatollah

Ayax SM Ajax

ayer Ⓐ ADV yesterday; **repitieron el capítulo de ~** yesterday's episode was repeated; **~ por la mañana** yesterday morning; **antes de ~** the day before yesterday; **~ eran terroristas, hoy en día comparten el gobierno** yesterday they were terrorists, today they are part of the government; **~ mismo** (*Esp*) ◊ **~ mismamente** o (*LAm*) **no más** only yesterday; **parece que fue ~** it seems like (only) yesterday; **no es (cosa) de ~** it's nothing new; ✦**MODISMO no nací ~** I wasn't born yesterday
Ⓑ SM **el ~** (*liter*) yesteryear (*liter*); **las canciones del ~** the songs of yesteryear (*liter*); **el Madrid del ~** the Madrid of yesteryear (*liter*), old Madrid

ayllu SM (*Andes*) Indian commune

aymara ADJ, SMF, **aymará** ADJ, SMF Aymara

ayo SM tutor

ayote SM (*Méx, CAm*) (= *calabaza*) pumpkin; (*hum*) (= *cabeza*) nut‡, noggin (*EEUU*‡), bonce‡; **dar ~s a algn** to jilt sb, give sb the elbow; **la fiesta fue un ~** (*Méx*) the party was a disaster

ayotoste SM armadillo

ayte. ABR (= **ayudante**) asst

Ayto ABR = **Ayuntamiento**

ayuda Ⓐ SF [1] (= *asistencia*) help, assistance (*más frm*) ▸ **ayuda a domicilio** home help, home helper (*EEUU*) ▸ **ayudas a la navegación** aids to navigation, navigational aids ▸ **ayuda compensatoria** ≈ income support, welfare (*EEUU*) ▸ **ayuda económica** economic aid ▸ **ayuda humanitaria** humanitarian aid ▸ **ayuda visual** visual aid ▸ **ayudas audiovisuales** audiovisual aids ▸ **ayudas familiares** family allowances
[2] (*Med*) (= *enema*) enema; (*LAm*) (= *laxante*) laxative
Ⓑ SM (= *paje*) page ▸ **ayuda de cámara** valet

ayudado SM (*Taur*) *two-handed pass with the cape*

ayudador(a) SM/F helper

ayudanta SF helper, assistant

ayudante SMF (= *que ayuda*) helper, assistant; (*Mil*) adjutant; (*Téc*) technician; (*Golf*) caddie; (*Escol, Univ*) assistant ▸ **ayudante de dirección** (*Teat etc*) production assistant ▸ **ayudante de laboratorio** lab(oratory) assistant, lab(oratory) technician ▸ **ayudante del electricista** electrician's assistant, electrician's helper (*EEUU*) ▸ **ayudante de realización** (*TV*) production assistant ▸ **ayudante ejecutivo** executive assistant ▸ **ayudante técnico sanitario** Registered Nurse

ayudantía SF (= *cargo*) assistantship; (*Mil*) adjutancy; (*Téc*) post of technician

ayudar ▸conjug 1a◂ Ⓐ VT (= *asistir*) to help, assist, aid; **~ a algn a hacer algo** to help sb to do sth; **¿me puedes ~ con la limpieza esta tarde?** can you help me out with the cleaning this afternoon?; **me ayudó a bajar del autobús** he helped me off the bus; **me ayuda muchísimo** he's a great help to me, he helps me a lot
Ⓑ **ayudarse** VPR (*mutuamente*) to help each other; (= *valerse de*) to make use of, use; ✦**REFRÁN ayúdate y Dios te ~á** God helps those who help themselves

> **AYUDAR**
>
> **Ayudar** se puede traducir por **help**, **assist** y **aid**.
>
> • La manera más frecuente de traducir **ayudar** es por **help**. Si **help** va seguido de un verbo, éste puede ir en infinitivo *con* o *sin* **to**:
>
> ¿Puedes ayudarnos?
> ***Can you help (us)?***
> Siempre le ayuda con la tarea
> ***He always helps her with her homework***
> ¿Me puedes ayudar a preparar la cena?
> ***Can you help me (to) get dinner ready?***
>
> • **Ayudar** se traduce por **assist** en un registro bastante más formal y se construye frecuentemente en la estructura **to assist somebody with something**:
>
> La comadrona ayudó al médico con el parto
> ***The midwife assisted the doctor with the delivery***
>
> • **Ayudar** se traduce por **aid** en inglés formal en el contexto de asesorar o prestar ayuda a un grupo de personas necesitadas:
>
> ...los intentos de Estados Unidos de ayudar a los refugiados kurdos…
> ***...attempts by the United States to aid Kurdish refugees...***
>
> *Para otros usos y ejemplos ver la entrada.*

ayudista SMF (*Cono Sur*) supporter

ayudita* SF small contribution

ayunar ▸conjug 1a◂ VI (= *no comer*) to fast; **~ de algo** (*fig*) (= *privarse*) to go without sth

ayunas SFPL **salir en ~** to go out without any breakfast; **estar** o **quedarse en ~** (= *ser ignorante*) to be completely in the dark; (= *no caer*) to miss the point

ayuno Ⓐ SM fast, fasting; **guardar ~** to fast; **día de ~** fast day
Ⓑ ADJ [1] (*Rel etc*) fasting
[2] (= *privado*) deprived; **estar ~ de algo** to know nothing about sth

ayuntamiento SM [1] (= *corporación*) district council, town council, city council
[2] (= *Casa Consistorial*) town hall, city hall
[3] (= *cópula*) sexual intercourse; **tener ~ con algn** to have intercourse with sb

ayuntar ▸conjug 1a◂ VT [1] (*Náut*) to splice
[2] (*Andes Agr*) to yoke, yoke together

ayuya SF (*Cono Sur*) flat roll, scone

azabachado ADJ jet-black

azabache SM (*Min*) jet; **~s** jet trinkets

azacán/ana SM/F drudge, slave; **estar hecho un ~** to be worked to death

azacanarse ▸conjug 1a◂ VPR to drudge, slave away

azada SF hoe

azadón SM large hoe, mattock, pickax (*EEUU*)

azadonar ▸conjug 1a◂ VT to hoe

azafata SF [1] (*Aer*) air hostess, stewardess, flight attendant (*EEUU*); (*TV*) hostess; (*Náut*) stewardess; (= *compañera*) escort (*supplied by escort agency*) ▸ **azafata de congresos** conference hostess ▸ **azafata de vuelo** air hostess
[2] (*Cono Sur*) = **azafate**
[3] (*Hist*) lady-in-waiting

azafate SM flat basket, tray

azafrán SM saffron

azafranado ADJ [*color*] saffron-coloured, saffron-colored (*EEUU*); [*sabor*] saffron-flavoured, saffron-flavored (*EEUU*)

azafranar ▸conjug 1a◂ VT (*Culin*) (= *dar color a*) to colour with saffron, color with saffron (*EEUU*); (= *sazonar*) to flavour with saffron, flavor with saffron (*EEUU*)

azagaya SF assegai, javelin

azahar SM orange blossom

azalea SF azalea

azar SM [1] (= *suerte*) chance, fate; **al ~** at random; **por ~** accidentally, by chance; **juego de ~** game of chance; **los ~es de la vida** life's ups and downs; **no es un ~ que ...** it is no mere accident that ..., it is not a matter of chance that ...; **decir al ~** to say to nobody in particular
[2] (= *desgracia*) accident, piece of bad luck

azararse¹ ▸conjug 1a◂ VPR [1] (= *malograrse*) to go wrong, go awry
[2] = **azorar B**

azararse² ▸conjug 1a◂ VPR (= *ruborizarse*) to blush, redden

azarear ▸conjug 1a◂ VT, **azarearse** VPR = **azorar**

azarosamente ADV (= *con riesgo*) hazardously; (= *con percances*) eventfully

azaroso ADJ [1] (= *arriesgado*) risky, hazardous; [*vida*] eventful
[2] (= *malhadado*) unlucky

Azerbaiyán SM Azerbaijan

azerbaiyaní ADJ, SMF Azerbaijani

azerbaiyano/a ADJ, SM/F Azerbaijani

azerí Ⓐ ADJ Azeri
Ⓑ SMF (= *persona*) Azeri
Ⓒ SM (*Ling*) Azeri

ázimo ADJ unleavened

aznarismo SM *policies and following of José María Aznar - Spanish Prime Minister from 1996 to 2004*

aznarista Ⓐ ADJ *related to José María Aznar or his policies*, Aznar *antes de s*; [*intelectual, círculos*] pro-Aznar
Ⓑ SMF Aznar supporter

-azo, -aza *ver* **Aspects of Word Formation in Spanish 2**

azocar ▸conjug 1g◂ VT (*Caribe*) to pack tightly

azófar SM brass

azogado Ⓐ ADJ restless, fidgety; **temblar como un ~** to shake like a leaf, tremble all over
Ⓑ SM silvering

azogar ▸conjug 1h◂ Ⓐ VT (= *cubrir con azogue*) to coat with quicksilver; [+ *espejo*] to silver
Ⓑ **azogarse** VPR to be restless, be fidgety

azogue SM mercury, quicksilver; **ser un ~** to be always on the go; **tener ~** to be restless, be fidgety

azolve SM (*Méx*) sediment, deposit

azonzado ADJ (*Cono Sur*) silly, stupid

azor SM goshawk

azora SF (*LAm*) = **azoramiento**

azorado ADJ [1] (= *alarmado*) alarmed, upset
[2] (= *turbado*) embarrassed, flustered
[3] (= *emocionado*) excited

azoramiento SM [1] (= *alarma*) alarm
[2] (= *turbación*) embarrassment, fluster
[3] (= *emoción*) excitement

azorar ▸conjug 1a◂ Ⓐ VT [1] (= *alarmar*) to alarm
[2] (= *turbar*) to embarrass, fluster
[3] (= *emocionar*) to excite; (= *animar*) to urge on, egg on
Ⓑ **azorarse** VPR [1] (= *alarmarse*) to get alarmed, get rattled*
[2] (= *sentirse violento*) to be embarrassed, get flustered

Azores SFPL Azores

azoro SM [1] (*esp LAm*) = **azoramiento**
[2] (*CAm*) (= *fantasma*) ghost

azorrillarse ▸conjug 1a◂ VPR (*Méx*) to hide away, keep out of sight

azotacalles SMF INV idler, loafer

azotaina SF beating, spanking; **¡te voy a dar una ~!** I'm going to give you a good hiding!*

azotamiento SM whipping, flogging

azotar ▸conjug 1a◂ Ⓐ VT [1] (= *latigar*) to whip, flog; (= *zurrar*) to thrash, spank; (*Agr*) to beat; [*lluvia, olas*] to lash; **un viento huracanado azota la costa** a hurricane is lashing the coast
[2] ✦*MODISMO* **~ las calles** to loaf around the streets
Ⓑ **azotarse** VPR (*Méx*) (= *darse aires*) to put on airs, fancy o.s.

azotazo SM [*de látigo*] stroke, lash; [*de mano*] spank

azote SM [1] (= *látigo*) whip, scourge
[2] (= *golpe*) [*de látigo*] stroke, lash; [*de mano*] spanking; **ser condenado a 100 ~s** to be sentenced to 100 lashes ► **azotes y galeras** the same old stuff
[3] (= *calamidad*) scourge; **Atila, el ~ de Dios** Attila, the Scourge of God

azotea SF [1] (*Arquit*) (= *terraza*) flat roof, terrace roof; (*Andes, Cono Sur*) (= *casa*) flat-roofed adobe house
[2] (‡) (= *cabeza*) bonce‡, head; **estar mal de la ~** to be round the bend *o* twist‡, be off one's head

azotera SF (*LAm*) (= *acto*) beating, thrashing; (= *látigo*) cat-o'-nine-tails

AZT SM ABR (= **azidotimidina**) AZT

azteca ADJ, SMF Aztec

azúcar SM *o* SF (*en LAm gen SF*) sugar ► **azúcar blanca/o** white sugar ► **azúcar blanquilla/o** white sugar ► **azúcar cande, azúcar candi** sugar candy, rock candy ► **azúcar de caña** cane sugar ► **azúcar de cortadillo** lump sugar ► **azúcar Demerara** demerara sugar, brown sugar ► **azúcar en polvo** (*Col*) icing sugar, confectioner's sugar (*EEUU*) ► **azúcar en terrón** lump sugar ► **azúcar extrafina/o, azúcar fina/o** caster sugar ► **azúcar flor** (*Chile*) icing sugar, confectioners' sugar (*EEUU*) ► **azúcar impalpable** (*Arg*) icing sugar, confectioners' sugar (*EEUU*) ► **azúcar lustre** caster sugar ► **azúcar mascabada/o** cane sugar ► **azúcar morena/o, azúcar negra/o** brown sugar

azucarado ADJ sugary, sweet

azucarar ▸conjug 1a◂ VT [1] (= *agregar azúcar a*) to sugar, add sugar to; (= *bañar con azúcar*) to ice with sugar, coat with sugar
[2] (*fig*) (= *suavizar*) to soften, mitigate; (= *endulzar*) to sweeten

azucarera SF sugar refinery

azucarería SF (*Caribe, Méx*) sugar shop

azucarero Ⓐ ADJ sugar *antes de s*; [*zona*] sugar-producing, sugar-growing
Ⓑ SM sugar bowl

azucena SF white lily, Madonna lily ► **azucena rosa** belladonna lily ► **azucena tigrina** tiger lily

azud SM, **azuda** SF (= *noria*) waterwheel; (= *presa*) dam, irrigation dam, mill dam

azuela SF adze

azufre SM (*Quím*) sulphur, sulfur (*EEUU*); (*Rel etc*) brimstone

azufroso ADJ sulphurous, sulfurous (*EEUU*)

azul Ⓐ ADJ blue; **sangre ~** noble blood, blue blood
Ⓑ SM (= *color*) blue; (= *grado*) blueness ► **azul celeste** sky blue ► **azul claro** light blue ► **azul de cobalto** cobalt blue ► **azul de mar** navy blue ► **azul de ultramar** ultramarine ► **azul eléctrico** electric blue ► **azul marino** navy blue ► **azul de Prusia** Prussian blue ► **azul pavo** peacock blue ► **azul turquesa** turquoise

azulado ADJ blue, bluish

azular ▸conjug 1a◂ Ⓐ VT to colour blue, color blue (*EEUU*), dye blue
Ⓑ **azularse** VPR to turn blue

azulear ▸conjug 1a◂ VI [1] (= *volverse azul*) to go blue, turn blue
[2] (= *tirar a azul*) to be bluish; (= *mostrarse azul*) to show blue, look blue

azulejar ▸conjug 1a◂ VT to tile

azulejería SF [1] (= *azulejos*) tiling
[2] (= *industria*) tile industry

azulejista SMF tiler

azulejo SM [1] (= *ladrillo vidriado*) glazed tile; (*en el suelo*) floor tile
[2] (*Caribe*‡) (= *policía*) cop*
[3] (*Méx*) (= *color*) bluish colour, bluish color (*EEUU*)
[4] (*Méx*) (= *pez*) *sardine-like fish*

azulenco ADJ bluish

azulete SM blue (*for washing*)

azulgrana Ⓐ ADJ INV [1] [*color*] blue and scarlet
[2] (*Dep*) of Barcelona Football Club
Ⓑ SMPL INV **los Azulgrana** the Barcelona club, the Barcelona team

azulina SF cornflower

azulino ADJ bluish

azulón ADJ, SM deep blue

azuloso ADJ (*LAm*) bluish

azumagarse ▸conjug 1h◂ VPR (*Cono Sur*) to rust, get rusty

azumbrado* ADJ tight*

azumbre SM *liquid measure (= 2.016 litres)*

azur SM azure

azurumbado ADJ (*CAm, Méx*) (= *tonto*) silly, stupid; (= *borracho*) drunk

azuzar ▸conjug 1f◂ VT [1] **~ a los perros a algn** to set the dogs on sb, urge the dogs to attack sb
[2] (*fig*) [+ *persona*] to egg on, urge on, incite; [+ *emoción*] to stir up, fan

B b

B, b [be] SF (= *letra*) B, b; **se escribe con B de Barcelona** it's written with a B

B. ABR (*Rel*) = **Beato/a**

baba SF **1** (= *saliva*) [*de adulto*] spittle, saliva; [*de niño*] dribble; [*de perro*] slobber; **echar ~** to drool, slobber; [*niño*] to dribble; **mala ~*** (= *malhumor*) bad temper; (= *mal genio*) nasty character; ✦***MODISMO* se le caía la ~** he was thrilled to bits *o* pieces
2 (= *mucosidad*) (*en nariz*) mucus; [*de caracol*] slime, secretion
3 (*Col, Ven*) small crocodile

babador SM bib

babalao* SM (*Cuba*) quack

babasfrías SM INV (*Andes, Méx*) fool

babaza SF **1** (= *mucosidad*) [*de caracol*] slime; [*de nariz*] mucus
2 (*Zool*) slug

babear ▸conjug 1a◂ Ⓐ VI **1** (= *echar saliva*) [*adulto*] to slobber, drool; [*niño*] to dribble
2 (= *quedarse admirado*) to drool (**por** over)
Ⓑ **babearse** VPR **1** (*Méx**) **~se por algo** to yearn for sth, drool at the thought of sth
2 (*Cono Sur*) to feel flattered, glow with satisfaction

Babel SM Babel; **Torre de ~** Tower of Babel

babel SM *o* SF bedlam

babeo SM [*de adulto*] slobbering, drooling; [*de niño*] dribbling; [*de perro*] slobbering

babero SM **1** [*de bebé*] (*para el pecho*) bib; (*más grande*) apron
2 (*para el colegio*) smock

babi* SM **1** [*de bebé*] bib
2 (*para el colegio*) smock

Babia SF ✦***MODISMO* estar en ~** to be daydreaming, be in the clouds

babieca Ⓐ ADJ simple-minded, stupid
Ⓑ SMF dolt

babilla SF (*Vet*) stifle

Babilonia SF (= *ciudad*) Babylon; (= *reino*) Babylonia

babilonia SF bedlam; *ver tb* **babilonio**

babilónico ADJ Babylonian

babilonio/a ADJ, SM/F Babylonian; *ver tb* **babilonia**

bable SM *Asturian dialect*

babor SM port, port side; **a ~** to port, on the port side; **poner el timón a ~** ◊ **virar a ~** to turn to port, port the helm; **¡tierra a ~!** land to port!; **de ~** port *antes de s*

babosa SF slug; *ver tb* **baboso**

babosada* SF **1** (*CAm, Méx*) (= *disparate*) piece of stupidity; **¡~s!** rubbish!; **decir ~s** to talk nonsense *o* rubbish
2 (*LAm*) (= *persona inútil*) dead loss*, useless thing*

babosear ▸conjug 1a◂ Ⓐ VT **1** [*perro*] to slobber over
2 (= *halagar*) to drool over
3 (*Méx**) (= *manosear*) to manhandle
4 (*CAm, Méx**) (= *tratar de bobo*) to take for a fool, treat like a fool
5 (= *tratar superficialmente*) **muchos han baboseado este problema** lots of people have taken a superficial look at this problem
6 (*CAm*) to insult
Ⓑ VI **1** (= *echar saliva*) [*adulto*] to slobber, drool; [*niño*] to dribble; [*perro*] to slobber
2 (*Méx*) (= *holgazanear*) to mess about

baboseo SM **1** (= *saliva*) [*de adulto*] drooling, slobbering; [*de niño*] dribbling; [*de perro*] slobbering
2 (= *halago excesivo*) infatuation, drooling

baboso/a Ⓐ ADJ **1** (= *con baba*) [*adulto*] drooling, slobbering; [*niño*] dribbling; [*perro*] slobbering; [*caracol*] slimy
2 [*persona*] (= *sentimental*) slushy; (= *sensiblero*) mushy, foolishly sentimental; (= *adulador*) fawning, snivelling; (= *sucio*) dirty
3 (*LAm*) (= *tonto*) silly
4 (*CAm**) rotten*, caddish*
Ⓑ SM/F (*Méx, CAm*) fool, idiot; (*pey*) drip*; *ver tb* **babosa**

babucha SF **1** (= *zapatilla*) slipper; ✦***MODISMO* llevar algo a ~** (*Cono Sur*) to carry sth on one's back
2 (= *prenda*) (*Caribe*) child's bodice; (*LAm*) loose blouse, smock
3 **babuchas** (*Caribe*) rompers; (*Méx*) high-heeled boots

babuino SM baboon

babujal SM (*Caribe*) witch, sorcerer

baby SM **1** (*LAm*) (= *bebé*) baby; (*Aut*) small car, mini; **~ fútbol** table football
2 = **babi**

baca SF **1** (= *portaequipajes*) luggage rack, roof rack
2 (= *techo*) [*de autocar*] top; (*contra la lluvia*) rainproof cover

bacal SM (*Méx*) corncob

bacalada‡ SF sweetener*, backhander*, payola (*EEUU*)

bacaladero ADJ cod *antes de s*; **flota bacaladera** cod fleet

bacaladilla SF blue whiting

bacalao SM **1** (= *pez*) cod, codfish; ✦***MODISMOS* cortar el ~*** to be the boss, have the final say, run the show; **¡te conozco, ~!*** I've rumbled you!*; **ser un ~*** to be as thin as a rake
2 (*Cono Sur*) miser, scrooge*
3 (*Esp***) cunt**

bacán* Ⓐ ADJ posh*, classy*
Ⓑ SM (= *rico*) wealthy man; (= *protector*) sugar daddy*; (= *señorito*) playboy; (= *elegante*) toff*, dude (*EEUU*)

bacanal Ⓐ ADJ bacchanalian
Ⓑ **bacanales** SFPL orgy *sing*

bacanalear ▸conjug 1a◂ VI (*CAm*) to have a wild time

bacane SM (*Caribe*) driving licence, driver's license (*EEUU*)

bacanería* SF (*Cono Sur*) (= *elegancia*) sharp dressing, nattiness; (= *ostentación*) vulgar display, ostentation

bacante SF **1** (*Mit*) bacchante
2 (= *mujer ebria*) drunken and noisy woman

bacará SM, **bacarrá** SM baccarat

baceador* SM (*Caribe*) con man

bacelar ▸conjug 1a◂ VT (*Caribe*) to con, trick

bacenica SF (*LAm*) = **bacinica**

baceta SF (*Naipes*) pack, stock

bacha SF (*Caribe*) spree, merry outing

bachata SF (*Caribe*) spree

bachatear ▸conjug 1a◂ VI (*Caribe*) to go on a spree, go out for a good time

bachatero SM (*Caribe*) reveller, carouser

bache SM **1** (*Aut*) hole, pothole ► **bache de aire** (*Aer*) air pocket
2 (= *mal momento*) bad patch, rough patch; **atravesar un ~** to go through a bad *o* rough patch; **remontar el** *o* **salir del ~** to get through the bad *o* rough patch, pull through; **salvar el ~** to get the worst over, be over the worst ► **bache económico** slump, depression

bacheado ADJ [*carretera*] pot-holed

bachicha SF **1** (*Cono Sur pey*) (= *italiano*) dago**, wop**, guinea (*EEUU***)
2 (*Méx*) (= *restos*) leftovers *pl*; (= *colilla*) cigarette end, cigar stub; [*de bebida*] dregs *pl*
3 (*Méx Fin*) nest egg, secret hoard

bachiche SM (*Andes pey*) = **bachicha 1**

bachiller Ⓐ ADJ (††) garrulous, talkative
Ⓑ SMF (*Escol*) secondary school graduate, high school graduate (*EEUU*)
Ⓒ SM **1** (*Escol*††) *ver* **bachillerato**
2 (†† *hum*) (= *charlatán*) windbag*

bachillera†† SF (= *erudita*) bluestocking; (= *gárrula*) chatterbox*; (= *astuta*) cunning woman, scheming woman

bachillerato SM [1] (*Escol*) *higher secondary-education course* ► **bachillerato comercial** certificate in business studies ► **bachillerato del magisterio** certificate for students going on to do teacher training ► **bachillerato elemental** lower examination, ≈ GCSE ► **bachillerato laboral** certificate in agricultural *o* technical studies ► **bachillerato superior** higher certificate, ≈ A level; → ESO
[2] (*Univ, Hist*) bachelor's degree

bachillerear†† ▸conjug 1a◂ VI to talk a lot, prattle away

bachillería†† SF [1] (= *cotorreo*) talk, prattle
[2] (= *disparate*) piece of nonsense

bacía SF (= *recipiente*) (*gen*) basin; [*de afeitar*] barber's bowl, shaving bowl

bacilar ADJ bacillary

bacilarse ▸conjug 1a◂ VPR (*Andes*) to have a good time

bacilo SM bacillus, germ

bacilón* Ⓐ ADJ brilliant, great
Ⓑ SM (*Andes*) fun, good time; *ver tb* **vacilón**

bacín SM [1] (= *recipiente*) (*para orinar*) chamber pot; [*de mendigo*] beggar's bowl
[2] (= *cepo*) poor box
[3] (= *persona miserable*) wretch, cur

bacinete SM (*LAm*) lavatory pan

bacinica SF small chamber pot

Baco SM Bacchus

bacón SM bacon

bacteria SF bacterium, germ; **bacterias** bacteria, germs ► **bacteria asesina** killer bacteria *pl*

bacterial ADJ, **bacteriano** ADJ bacterial

bactericida Ⓐ ADJ antibacterial, bactericidal, germicidal
Ⓑ SM bactericide, germicide

bactérico ADJ bacterial

bacteriología SF bacteriology

bacteriológico ADJ bacteriological

bacteriólogo/a SM/F bacteriologist

bacteriosis SF INV bacteriosis

báculo SM [1] (= *bastón*) stick, staff ► **báculo pastoral** crozier, bishop's staff
[2] (= *apoyo*) prop, support; **ser el ~ de la vejez de algn** to be sb's comfort in old age

badajada SF, **badajazo** SM [1] [*de campana*] stroke, chime
[2] (= *cotilleo*) piece of gossip
[3] (= *tontería*) rubbish, garbage

badajear ▸conjug 1a◂ VI to swing to and fro

badajo SM [1] [*de campana*] clapper
[2] (*) (= *charlatán*) chatterbox

badajocense, badajoceño/a Ⓐ ADJ of/from Badajoz
Ⓑ SM/F native/inhabitant of Badajoz; **los ~s** the people of Badajoz

badana SF sheepskin; ✦***MODISMO*** **sobarle** *o* **zurrarle la ~ a algn*** to give sb a good hiding*

badaza SF (*Caribe*) strap (*for standing passenger*)

badén SM (*Aut*) (= *bache*) dip; (*para agua*) gutter

badil SM, **badila** SF fire shovel

badilejo SM (*Andes*) trowel, builder's trowel

bádminton SM badminton

badulaque SM [1] (= *idiota*) idiot, nincompoop
[2] (*Cono Sur**) rogue

badulaquear ▸conjug 1a◂ VI [1] (= *ser idiota*) to be an idiot, act like an idiot
[2] (*Cono Sur**) to be a rogue, be dishonest

bafle SM, **baffle** SM speaker, loudspeaker

bagaje SM [1] (= *conocimientos*) experience, background ► **bagaje cultural** cultural background
[2] (*Mil*) (= *equipaje*) baggage, equipment
[3] (= *mula*) pack mule

bagatela SF [1] (= *objeto*) trinket, knick-knack
[2] (= *nimiedad*) trifle; **una ~** a mere trifle; **son ~s** they're not worth worrying about
[3] (*Mús*) bagatelle

bagayo/a⁑ (*Cono Sur*) Ⓐ SM/F (= *persona inútil*) useless lump, berk⁑
Ⓑ SM (= *lío*) bundle, tramp's bundle; (= *carga*) heavy *o* awkward burden; (= *cosas robadas*) loot; (= *contrabando*) contraband goods *pl*
Ⓒ SF (= *mujer fea*) old hag*

bagazo SM [1] (= *residuo*) chaff, husks *pl*; [*del azúcar*] sugar cane pulp, sugar cane mash
[2] (*LAm*) (= *persona inútil*) dead loss*

bagre Ⓐ ADJ [1] (*LAm*) vulgar, coarse
[2] (*CAm*) clever, sharp
Ⓑ SMF (*LAm*⁑) (= *persona astuta*) sly person; (= *fea*) ugly mug⁑
Ⓒ SM (*LAm*) (= *pez*) catfish; ✦***MODISMO*** **pica el ~** (*Cono Sur**) I'm starving

bagrero ADJ (*Andes*) fond of ugly women

bagual (*Cono Sur*) Ⓐ ADJ [1] [*caballo*] wild, untamed
[2] (= *huraño*) unsociable
Ⓑ SM [1] (= *caballo salvaje*) wild horse, untamed horse; ✦***MODISMO*** **ganar los ~es** (*Hist*) to escape, get to safety
[2] (= *huraño*) unsociable person

bagualada SF (*Cono Sur*) [1] [*de caballos*] herd of wild horses
[2] (= *torpeza*) stupid thing, stupid thing to do

bagualón ADJ (*Cono Sur*) half-tamed

baguío SM hurricane, typhoon

bah EXCL (*indicando desdén*) bah!, pooh!, phooey (*EEUU**); (*indicando incredulidad*) never!

Bahamas SFPL **las ~, las Islas ~** the Bahamas

bahareque SM = **bajareque**

baharí SM sparrowhawk

bahía SF bay

baho SM (*CAm Culin*) *dish of meat and yucca*

bahorrina SF [1] (= *suciedad*) dirt, filth
[2] (= *gentuza*) riffraff, scum

bahreiní ADJ, SMF Bahreini

bailable Ⓐ ADJ **música ~** music that you can dance to
Ⓑ SM (†) dance number

bailada SF (*LAm*) dance

bailadero SM (= *sala*) dance hall; (= *pista*) dance floor

bailador(a) Ⓐ ADJ dancing
Ⓑ SM/F dancer

bailaor(a) SM/F flamenco dancer

bailar ▸conjug 1a◂ Ⓐ VI [1] (= *danzar*) to dance; **sacar a algn a ~** to ask sb to dance, ask sb for a dance; **le bailaban los ojos de alegría** her eyes sparkled with happiness; ✦***MODISMOS*** **éste es otro que bien baila** here's another one (of the same kind); **¡que me quiten lo bailado** *o* **bailao!*** nobody can take away the good times I've had!; **~ con la más fea**: **siempre me toca ~ con la más fea** I always draw the short straw; **~ al son que tocan**: **los políticos bailan al son que le tocan los militares** the politicians toe the line given them by the military
[2] [*peonza*] to spin (round)
[3] [*mueble*] to be wobbly, be unsteady
[4] (*) [*ropa, calzado*] to be miles too big*; **he adelgazado y me bailan los pantalones** I've lost weight and my trousers are miles too big for me*
Ⓑ VT [1] (= *danzar*) to dance; **~ flamenco** to dance flamenco; **~ el vals** to waltz, dance the waltz; **~ un vals** to dance a waltz
[2] [+ *peonza*] to spin
[3] (*LAm**) (= *timar*) **le ~on la herencia** they cheated her out of her inheritance
Ⓒ **bailarse** VPR **~se a algn** (*Méx**) to thrash sb

bailarín/ina Ⓐ ADJ dancing
Ⓑ SM/F dancer; (*tb* **~/ina de ballet**) (= *hombre*) ballet dancer; (= *mujer*) ballet dancer, ballerina; **primera bailarina** prima ballerina ► **bailarina del vientre** belly dancer ► **bailarín/ina de claqué** tap dancer

bailata⁑ SF = **baile**

baile SM [1] (= *acción*) dancing; **lo mío no es el ~** dancing is not my thing*; *ver tb* **academia 1, pareja 3, pista 3**
[2] (= *pieza*) dance; **¿me concede este ~?** (*frm*) may I have this dance? (*frm*) ► **baile agarrado** slow dance
[3] (= *arte*) dance; **la sardana, el ~ típico de Cataluña** the sardana, the traditional dance of Catalonia ► **baile clásico** ballet ► **baile de salón** ballroom dancing ► **baile flamenco** flamenco dancing ► **baile folklórico, baile popular** folk dancing
[4] (= *fiesta*) dance; (*formal*) ball; **me han invitado a un ~** I have been invited to a dance ► **baile de candil** (*LAm*) village dance ► **baile de contribución** (*CAm, Caribe*) public dance ► **baile de disfraces** fancy-dress ball ► **baile de etiqueta** (formal) ball ► **baile de fantasía, baile de máscaras** (*LAm*) masked ball ► **baile de medio pelo** (*LAm*) village dance
[5] (*Med*) ► **baile de San Vito** St Vitus' dance
[6] (*Fbtl*) **hacer el ~*** *to dribble the ball aimlessly, playing for time*
[7] (= *confusión*) **hubo un ~ de cifras antes del anuncio de la victoria** the figures went first one way and then the other before the final victory was announced

bailecito SM (*LAm*) folk dance

bailón ADJ **es muy ~** he loves dancing

bailongo ADJ dance *antes de s*; **música bailonga** music for dancing, music you can dance to

bailotear ▸conjug 1a◂ VI to dance about, jump about

bailoteo* SM dancing; **estuvieron toda la noche de ~** they were out all night dancing

baivel SM bevel

baja SF [1] (= *descenso*) fall, drop; **se produjo una ~ continuada de las temperaturas** there was a continued fall *o* drop in temperatures; **una ~ repentina de los beneficios** a sudden fall *o* drop in profits; **sigue la ~ en la cotización de la lira** the lira continues to fall; **el gobierno anunció una ~ de los tipos de interés** the government announced a cut in interest rates; **a la ~** [*evolución, tendencia*] downward; **se ha producido una orientación del mercado a la ~** the market has started on a downward trend; **el precio del algodón sigue a la ~** the price of cotton continues to fall; **la patronal está presionando los salarios a la ~** employers are forcing wages down; **abrir a la ~** (*Bolsa*) to open down; **cerrar a la ~** (*Bolsa*) to close down; **la Bolsa cerró a la ~ en el día de ayer** the Stock Exchange closed down *o* was down at the close of trading yesterday; **corregir algo a la ~** to adjust sth downwards; **cotizarse a la ~** (*Bolsa*) to trade low; **estar en ~** to be in decline; **su reputación estuvo en ~ en los últimos meses** his reputation was on the *o* in decline over the last few months; **la Bolsa está en ~** there is a downward trend in the Stock Exchange, the Stock Exchange is in decline

[2] (= *cese*) (*en organización, subscripción, trabajo*) **hubo tantas ~s que el club tuvo que cerrar** so many people left that the club had to close down; **la ~ de dos de los países miembros** the departure of two member countries; **el nuevo estilo de la revista ha causado numerosas ~s** the new style of the magazine has led many people to cancel their subscription; **dar de ~** [+ *socio*] to expel; [+ *abogado, médico*] to strike off; [+ *militar*] to discharge; [+ *empleado*] to dismiss, fire; [+ *empresa, sociedad*] to dissolve; [+ *coche*] to take out of circulation; [+ *avión, tren*] to decommission; [+ *teléfono, luz*] to have disconnected; **la dieron de ~ del club por no pagar la suscripción** her membership of the club was cancelled because she had failed to pay her subscription; **la dirección decidió dar de ~ al nuevo profesor** the board decided to dismiss the new teacher; **hemos dado de ~ la luz** we had the electricity disconnected; **darse de ~** [*de club, institución, partido*] to leave; [*de revista, periódico*] to cancel one's subscription; **numerosos suscriptores han decidido darse de ~ de la revista** many readers have decided to cancel their subscription to the magazine; **nos dimos de ~ del teléfono** we had the telephone disconnected; **pedir la ~** to hand in one's resignation ► **baja incentivada** voluntary redundancy ► **baja por incentivo** voluntary redundancy ► **baja por jubilación** retirement ► **baja por jubilación anticipada** early retirement ► **baja voluntaria** (*por dimisión*) voluntary redundancy; (*por jubilación*) early retirement

[3] (= *ausencia laboral*) **dar de ~**: **se le dará de ~ a partir del día de la operación** she will be on sick leave from the day of the operation; **estar de ~** to be on sick leave, be off sick; **pedir la ~** to ask for *o* apply for sick leave ► **baja laboral** leave ► **baja maternal** maternity leave ► **baja médica** sick leave ► **baja permanente** indefinite sick leave ► **baja por enfermedad** sick leave; **el número de ~s por enfermedad** the number of people taking sick leave ► **baja por maternidad** maternity leave ► **baja por paternidad** paternity leave ► **baja retribuida** paid leave

[4] (*Dep*) (*por descalificación*) suspension; (*por lesión*) injury; **el equipo sufrió dos ~s por sendas tarjetas rojas** the team lost two players for red card offences; **el partido registró varias ~s en ambos equipos** there were several injuries for both teams during the match

[5] (*Esp Med*) (= *certificado*) medical certificate, sick note*

[6] (*Mil*) (= *víctima*) casualty; **hasta la fecha no ha habido ninguna ~** there have been no casualties to date

bajá SM pasha

bajacaliforniano/a Ⓐ ADJ of/from Baja California

Ⓑ SM/F native/inhabitant of Baja California; **los ~s** the people of Baja California

bajada SF [1] (= *camino*) **la ~ hasta el río** (= *sendero*) the path down to the river; (= *carretera*) the road down to the river; **una ~ muy difícil para un esquiador sin experiencia** a very difficult slope for an inexperienced skier

[2] (= *acción*) descent; **en la ~ alcanzamos los 150km/h** on the way down *o* descent we got up to 150km/h; **salimos antes de la ~ del telón** we left the theatre before the curtain went down; ✦***MODISMO*** **ser una ~ de pantalones** (*LAm**) to be a shameful action ► **bajada de aguas** gutter ► **bajada de bandera** minimum (taxi) fare

[3] (= *disminución*) fall, drop; **una drástica ~ de las temperaturas** a dramatic fall *o* drop in temperature; **sufrió una ~ de azúcar** his sugar level fell *o* dropped

[4] (*Esp‡*) [*de drogas*] **cuando le da la ~ del éxtasis** when he's coming down from ecstasy

bajamar SF low tide, low water

bajante SF *o* SM drainpipe, downspout (*EEUU*)

BAJAR

De vehículos

• **Bajar(se) de** un vehículo privado o de un taxi se traduce por **get out of**, mientras que **bajar(se) de** un vehículo público (tren, autobús, avión, *etc*) se traduce por **get off**:

Bajó del coche y nos saludó

She got out of the car and said hello

No baje del tren en marcha

Don't get off the train while it is still moving

• Debe emplearse **get off** cuando nos referimos a bicicletas, motos y animales de montura:

Se bajó de la bicicleta

He got off his bicycle

Otros verbos de movimiento

• **Bajar la escalera/la cuesta** *etc*, por regla general, se suele traducir por **come down** o por **go down**, según la dirección del movimiento (hacia o en sentido contrario del hablante), pero **come** y **go** se pueden substituir por otros verbos de movimiento si la oración española especifica la forma en que se baja mediante el uso de adverbios o construcciones adverbiales:

Bajó las escaleras deprisa y corriendo

She rushed down the stairs

Bajó la cuesta tranquilamente

He ambled down the hill

Para otros usos y ejemplos ver la entrada.

bajar ►conjug 1a◄ Ⓐ VT [1] (= *llevar abajo*) to take down; (= *traer abajo*) to bring down; **¿has bajado la basura?** have you taken the rubbish down?; **¿me bajas el abrigo?, hace frío aquí fuera** could you bring my coat down? it's cold out here; **te he bajado la maleta del armario** I got your suitcase down from the wardrobe; **la bajó del caballo** he helped her down off the horse; **¿me baja a la Plaza Mayor?** (*en taxi*) could you take me to the Plaza Mayor?

[2] (= *mover hacia abajo*) [+ *bandera, ventanilla*] to lower; [+ *persiana*] to put down, lower; **~ el telón** to lower the curtain; **dimos un paseo para ~ la comida** we had a walk to help us digest our meal

[3] (*con partes del cuerpo*) [+ *brazos*] to drop, lower; **bajó la vista** *o* **los ojos** he looked down; **bajó la cabeza** she bowed *o* lowered her head

[4] (= *reducir*) [+ *precio*] to lower, put down; [+ *fiebre, tensión, voz*] to lower; **los comercios han bajado los precios** businesses have put their prices down *o* lowered their prices

[5] [+ *radio, televisión, gas*] to turn down; **baja la radio que no oigo nada** turn the radio down, I can't hear a thing; **¡baja la voz, que no estoy sordo!** keep your voice down, I'm not deaf!

[6] **~ la escalera** (*visto desde arriba*) to go down the stairs; (*visto desde abajo*) to come down the stairs

[7] (= *perder*) to lose; **bajé seis kilos** I lost six kilos

[8] (*Inform*) to download

[9] (= *humillar*) to humble, humiliate

[10] (*Caribe‡*) (= *pagar*) to cough up*, fork out*

[11] (*Andes‡*) (= *matar*) to do in‡

Ⓑ VI [1] (= *descender*) (*visto desde arriba*) to go down; (*visto desde abajo*) to come down; **baja y ayúdame** come down and help me; **¡ahora bajo!** I'll be right down!

[2] (= *apearse*) (*de autobús, avión, tren, moto, bici, caballo*) to get off; (*de coche*) to get out; **~ de** [+ *autobús, avión, tren, moto, bici, caballo*] to get off; [+ *coche*] to get out of

[3] (= *reducirse*) [*temperatura, fiebre, tensión arterial*] to go down, fall, drop; [*hinchazón, calidad*] to go down; **han bajado los precios** prices have fallen *o* come *o* gone down; **el dólar bajó frente al euro** the dollar fell against the euro; **los coches han bajado de precio** cars have come down in price; **el partido bajó de cinco diputados a dos** the party went down from five deputies to two

[4] **~ de** (= *perder*): **el avión empezó a ~ de altura** the plane started to lose height; **el ejercicio te hará ~ de peso** exercise will help you to lose weight

[5] **no ~ de** (= *no ser menos de*): **el regalo no ~á de 15 euros** you won't pay less than 15 euros for the present; **la venta no ha bajado nunca de mil** sales have never fallen below a thousand; **los termómetros no han bajado de 30 grados** temperatures haven't dropped below 30 degrees

[6] [*regla*] to start; **me acaba de ~ la regla** my period has just started

Ⓒ **bajarse** VPR [1] (*de árbol, escalera, silla*) to get down (**de** from); **¡bájate de ahí!** get down from there!

[2] (*de autobús, tren, avión, moto, bici*) to get off; (*de coche*) to get out; **~se de** [+ *autobús, tren, avión, moto, bici*] to get off; [+ *coche*] to get out of; **se bajó del autobús antes que yo** he got off the bus before me

[3] **~se algo de Internet** to download sth from the Internet

[4] **~se del vicio*** to kick the habit*

[5] (= *inclinarse*) to bend down; **~se a recoger algo** to bend down to pick sth up

[6] (= *rebajarse*) to lower o.s.; **~se a hacer algo vil** to lower o.s. to do sth mean
[7] (*Cono Sur*) (= *alojarse*) to stay, put up; **~se en** to stay at; *ver tb* **pantalón 1**

bajareque SM [1] (*LAm*) (= *tapia*) mud wall
[2] (*Caribe*) (= *cabaña*) hovel, shack
[3] (*CAm*) (= *llovizna*) fine drizzle
[4] (*CAm*) (= *caña*) bamboo

bajativo SM (*Cono Sur*) digestif

bajel SM (*liter*) (= *barco*) vessel, ship

bajera SF [1] (*Arquit*) lower ground floor, basement
[2] (*Andes, CAm, Caribe*) (= *hojas*) *lower leaves of the tobacco plant*; (= *tabaco*) rough tobacco, inferior tobacco
[3] (*Andes, CAm, Caribe*) (= *persona sin importancia*) insignificant person, nobody
[4] (*Cono Sur*) horse blanket

bajero ADJ [1] (= *de abajo*) lower, under-; **falda bajera** underskirt; **sábana bajera** bottom sheet
[2] (*CAm*) (*en cuesta, bajada*) downhill, descending

bajetón ADJ (*LAm*) short, small

bajeza SF [1] (= *maldad*) vileness, baseness
[2] (= *acto malvado*) mean deed, vile deed

bajial SM (*LAm*) (= *terreno bajo*) lowland; (= *terreno inundado*) flood plain

bajini*, **bajinis***: **por lo ~(s)** ADV [*decir*] very quietly, in an undertone

bajío SM [1] (*Náut*) shoal, sandbank
[2] (*LAm*) lowland; **el Bajío** (*Méx*) *the fertile plateau of northern Mexico*
[3] **bajíos** (*Méx*) *flat arable land on a high plateau*

bajista Ⓐ ADJ downward; **tendencia ~** downward *o* bearish trend
Ⓑ SMF (*Mús*) bassist
Ⓒ SM (*Fin*) bear

bajo Ⓐ ADJ [1] (= *de poca altura*) [*objeto*] low; [*persona*] short; [*parte*] lower, bottom; [*tierra*] low-lying; [*agua*] shallow; **una silla muy baja** a very low chair; **mi hermano es muy ~** my brother is very short; **en la parte baja de la ciudad** in the lower part of the town; **planta baja** ground floor, first floor (*EEUU*); **los ~s fondos** the underworld *sing*
[2] (= *inclinado*) **contestó con la cabeza baja** she answered with her head bowed; **con los ojos ~s** with downcast eyes
[3] (= *reducido, inferior*) [*precios, temperaturas, frecuencia*] low; [*calidad*] low, poor; **de baja calidad** low-quality, poor-quality; **de ~ contenido en grasas** low-fat; **~ en calorías** low-calorie; **la temporada baja** the low season; **estar ~ de algo**: **estar ~ de ánimo** *o* **de moral** to be in low spirits; **estar ~ de forma (física)** to be unfit, be out of shape
[4] [*sonido*] faint, soft; [*voz, tono*] low; **hablar en voz baja** to speak quietly *o* in a low voice; **decir algo por lo ~** to say sth under one's breath; **hacer algo por lo ~** to do sth secretly
[5] [*etapa*] **en la baja Edad Media** in the late Middle Ages; **~ latín** Low Latin
[6] [*oro, plata*] *with a high level of impurities*
[7] [*color*] (= *apagado*) dull; (= *pálido*) pale
[8] (= *humilde*) low, humble; [*clase*] lower; [*condición*] lowly; [*barrio*] poor; [*tarea*] menial
[9] (*pey*) (= *vulgar*) common, ordinary; (= *mezquino*) base, mean
[10] **por lo ~** (= *a lo menos*) at (the) least
Ⓑ SM [1] (*Cos*) [*de vestido*] hem; [*de pantalones*] turn-up, cuff (*EEUU*)
[2] [*de edificio*] (= *piso*) ground floor, first floor (*EEUU*); **vivo en un ~** I live on the ground floor ► **bajo comercial** ground-floor *o* (*EEUU*) first-floor business premises
[3] (*Mús*) (= *instrumento*) bass; (= *voz*) bass; (= *guitarrista*) bass (guitar) player, bassist; **Elena toca el ~ en un grupo** Elena plays bass (guitar) in a group ► **bajo profundo** basso profundo
[4] **bajos** [*de edificio*] ground floor *sing*, first floor *sing* (*EEUU*); [*de coche*] underside; (*euf*) [*del cuerpo*] private parts
[5] (= *hondonada*) hollow
[6] (*Náut*) = **bajío 1**
Ⓒ ADV [*volar*] low; [*tocar, cantar*] quietly, softly; **el avión volaba muy ~** the plane was flying very low; **hablar ~** (= *en voz baja*) to speak quietly, speak softly; (= *tener una voz suave*) to be softly spoken, be soft spoken; **¡más ~, por favor!** quieter, please!
Ⓓ PREP [1] (= *debajo de*) under; **Juan llevaba un libro ~ el brazo** Juan was carrying a book under his arm; **~ cero** below zero; **estamos a dos grados ~ cero** it's two degrees below zero; **~ la lluvia** in the rain; **~ tierra** underground; **toda la familia está ya ~ tierra** the whole family are dead and buried
[2] (= *dependiente de, sometido a*) under; **~ Napoleón** under Napoleon; **~ los efectos de la droga** under the influence of drugs; **~ el título de ...** under the title of ...; **~ mi punto de vista** from my point of view; **~ el reinado de** in the reign of; **está ~ la tutela de su tío** her uncle is her legal guardian; *ver tb* **fianza 1**, **juramento 1**, **llave 1**

bajón SM [1] (= *descenso*) [*de presión, temperatura*] fall, drop; [*de salud*] decline, worsening; (*Com, Fin*) sharp fall; **dar** *o* **pegar un ~** [*persona, salud*] to go downhill; [*precios*] to fall away sharply; [*mercado*] to slump ► **bajón de moral** slump in morale
[2] (*Mús*) bassoon
[3] (‡) withdrawal symptoms *pl* (*after drug use*)

bajorrelieve SM bas-relief

bajuno ADJ [*truco*] base, underhand

bajura SF [1] **pesca de ~** shallow-water fishing, coastal fishing
[2] (*de poca altura*) lowness
[3] (*de tamaño pequeño*) smallness, small size
[4] (*Caribe Geog*) lowland

bakaladero/a* Ⓐ ADJ rave *antes de s*
Ⓑ SM/F raver

bakalao* Ⓐ ADJ INV rave *antes de s*
Ⓑ SM rave, rave music; **la ruta del ~** *weekend-long tour of a series of rave parties*

bala Ⓐ SF [1] (= *proyectil*) bullet; **una ~ perdida lo alcanzó en el hombro** he was hit in the shoulder by a stray bullet; **sonaron dos disparos de ~** two gunshots rang out; **disparar una ~** to fire a bullet; **a prueba de ~s** bullet-proof; **un chaleco a prueba de ~s** a bullet-proof vest; ✦***MODISMOS*** **como una ~** like a shot; **entró como una ~** he came shooting in, he came in like a shot; **el tren pasó como una ~** the train shot *o* flew past; **comió como una ~ y se fue** he bolted his food down and left; **no le entran ~s** (*Chile*) he's as hard as nails*; **ni a ~** (*Méx, Col**) no way*; **estar** *o* **quedar con la ~ pasada** (*Chile*) to be seething; **ser una ~** (*Caribe**) to be a pain in the neck*; **tirar con ~** not to pull one's punches ► **bala de cañón** cannonball ► **bala de fogueo** blank (cartridge) ► **bala de goma** plastic bullet, rubber bullet ► **bala de salva** blank round ► **bala fría** spent bullet ► **bala trazadora** tracer bullet
[2] (= *fardo*) bale; **una ~ de heno** a bale of hay
[3] (*Tip*) ► **bala de entintar** ink(ing) ball
[4] (*LAm Dep*) shot; **lanzamiento de ~** shot put
Ⓑ SMF (*) (= *juerguista*) ✦***MODISMO*** **ser un ~ perdida** to be a good-for-nothing

balaca SF [1] (*LAm*) (= *baladronada*) boast, brag
[2] (*Andes*) (= *boato*) show, pomp

balacada SF (*Cono Sur*) = **balaca**

balacear ▸conjug 1a◂ VT (*CAm, Méx*) to shoot, shoot at

balacera SF (*CAm, Méx*) (= *tiroteo*) shooting, exchange of shots; (= *balas*) hail of bullets; (= *enfrentamiento armado*) shoot-out

balada SF (*Mús*) ballad, ballade; (*Literat*) ballad

baladí ADJ trivial, paltry

baladista SMF (= *compositor*) writer of ballads; (= *cantante*) ballad singer

baladrar ▸conjug 1a◂ VI to scream, howl

baladre SM oleander, rosebay

baladrero ADJ loud, noisy

baladro SM scream, howl

baladrón/ona Ⓐ ADJ boastful
Ⓑ SM/F braggart, bully

baladronada SF (= *dicho*) boast, brag; (= *hecho*) piece of bravado

baladronear ▸conjug 1a◂ VI (= *decir*) to boast, brag; (= *hacer*) to indulge in bravado

bálago SM [1] (= *paja*) straw, long straw
[2] (= *jabón*) soapsuds *pl*, lather

balance SM [1] (*Fin*) [*de una cuenta*] balance; (= *documento*) balance (sheet); (*Com*) [*de existencias*] stocktaking, inventory (*EEUU*); **hacer ~** [*de una cuenta*] to draw up a balance; [*de existencias*] to take stock, do the stocktaking ► **balance consolidado** consolidated balance sheet ► **balance de comprobación** trial balance ► **balance de pagos** balance of payments ► **balance de situación** balance sheet
[2] (= *resultado*) **el ~ de víctimas mortales en el accidente** the death toll in the accident, the number of dead in the accident; **el equipo tiene un ~ de dos victorias y tres derrotas** so far the team have had two wins and three defeats; **un abogado con un buen ~ de casos ganados** a lawyer who has won a good proportion of his cases
[3] (= *evaluación*) [*de hecho, situación*] assessment, evaluation; **los puntos negros en el ~ del año académico** the black spots in the assessment *o* evaluation of the academic year; **hizo ~ de los cinco años de su gobierno** he assessed *o* evaluated *o* took stock of the five years of his government
[4] (= *balanceo*) to-and-fro motion; [*de un barco*] roll, rolling
[5] (= *indecisión*) vacillation
[6] (*Caribe*) (= *mecedora*) rocking chair

balanceado SM (*Boxeo*) swing

balancear ▸conjug 1a◂ Ⓐ VT to balance
Ⓑ **balancearse** VPR [1] (= *oscilar*) [*persona*] (*al andar*) to move to and fro; (*en mecedora, columpio*) to rock; [*péndulo*] to swing; [*barco, avión*] to roll
[2] (= *vacilar*) to hesitate, waver, vacillate (*frm*)

balanceo SM [1] (= *vaivén*) (*al andar*) to-and-fro motion; (*al mecerse*) rocking; [*de barco, avión*] roll, rolling
[2] (*LAm Aut*) (*tb* ~ **de ruedas**) wheel balancing

balancín SM [1] (= *barra*) [*de balanza*] balance beam; [*de equilibrista*] balancing pole; (*para llevar cargas*) yoke
[2] (*para mecerse*) (= *columpio*) seesaw, teeter-totter (EEUU); (= *mecedora*) rocking chair; (= *juguete*) child's rocking toy
[3] (*Mec*) (*en motor*) rocker, rocker arm; [*de carro*] swingletree; [*de máquina*] beam
[4] (*Náut*) outrigger

balandra SF yacht, sloop

balandrán SM cassock

balandrismo SM yachting

balandrista SMF yachtsman/yachtswoman

balandro SM yacht, sloop

balanza SF [1] (= *instrumento*) scales *pl*; (*Quím*) balance; ✦*MODISMO* **estar en la ~** to be in the balance ► **balanza de cocina** kitchen scales *pl* ► **balanza de cruz** grocer's scales *pl* ► **balanza de laboratorio** precision scales *pl* ► **balanza de muelle** spring balance ► **balanza de precisión** precision scales *pl* ► **balanza romana** steelyard
[2] (*Com, Pol*) balance ► **balanza comercial, balanza de pagos** balance of payments ► **balanza de poder, balanza política** balance of power ► **balanza por cuenta corriente** balance on current account
[3] (*frm*) (= *sensatez*) judgment

balaquear ▸conjug 1a◂ VI to boast

balar ▸conjug 1a◂ VI to bleat, baa

balasto[1] SM (*Ferro*) sleeper, tie (EEUU)

balasto[2] SM (*Cono Sur, Méx*) (*gen*) ballast; (*Téc*) aggregate

balastro SM = **balasto**[2]

balata SF (*LAm Aut*) brake lining

balaustrada SF balustrade

balaustre SM baluster

balay SM (*LAm*) wicker basket

balazo SM (= *tiro*) shot; (= *herida*) bullet wound; **matar a algn de un ~** to shoot sb dead

balboa SF *Panamanian currency unit*

balbucear ▸conjug 1a◂ VT, VI [*adulto*] to stammer, stutter; [*niño*] to babble

balbuceo SM [*de adulto*] stammering, stuttering; [*de niño*] babbling

balbuciente ADJ [*persona, voz*] stammering, stuttering; [*niño*] babbling

balbucir ▸conjug 3f◂ VT, VI (*se usan únicamente las formas que tienen* **i** *en la desinencia*) = **balbucear**

Balcanes SMPL **los ~** the Balkans; **los Montes ~** the Balkan Mountains; **la Península de los ~** the Balkan Peninsula

balcánico ADJ Balkan

balcanización SF Balkanization

balcarrias SFPL, **balcarrotas** SFPL (*Andes*) sideburns

balcón SM [1] (= *terraza pequeña*) balcony
[2] (= *mirador*) vantage point

balconada SF row of balconies

balconeador(a) SM/F (*Cono Sur*) onlooker, observer

balconear ▸conjug 1a◂ Ⓐ VT (*Cono Sur*) to watch closely (*from a balcony*); (*en juego*) to sneak a look at
Ⓑ VI (*CAm*) [*amantes*] to talk at the window

balconero SM cat burglar

balda SF shelf

baldada SF (*Cono Sur*) bucketful

baldado/a Ⓐ PP *de* **baldar**
Ⓑ ADJ [1] (= *lisiado*) crippled
[2] (*) (= *agotado*) **estar ~** to be knackered*
Ⓒ SM/F cripple, disabled person

baldaquín SM, **baldaquino** SM canopy

baldar ▸conjug 1a◂ VT [1] (= *lisiar*) to cripple
[2] (*) (= *agotar*) to shatter
[3] (*Naipes*) to trump

balde[1] SM (= *cubo*) bucket, pail ► **balde de la basura** (*LAm*) trash can

balde[2] SM [1] **de ~** (= *gratis*) (for) free, for nothing; **obtener algo de ~** to get sth (for) free, get sth for nothing; **vender algo medio de ~** to sell sth for a song
[2] **estar de ~** (= *ser superfluo*) to be unwanted; (= *estorbar*) to be in the way
[3] **en ~** in vain; **los años no pasan en ~** the years don't go by in vain; **por lo menos el viaje no ha sido en ~** at least the journey wasn't in vain; **¡ni en ~!** (*LAm*) no way!*, not on your life!
[4] **¡no de ~!** (*CAm*) goodness!, I never noticed!

baldear ▸conjug 1a◂ VT [1] (= *limpiar*) (*con cubos de agua*) to wash (down), swill with water; (*con manguera*) to hose down
[2] (*Náut*) to bale out, bail out (EEUU)

baldeo SM [1] (= *limpieza*) (*con cubos de agua*) washing-down; (*con manguera*) hosing down
[2] (‡) (= *navaja*) chiv‡, knife

baldío Ⓐ ADJ [1] (= *sin cultivos*) [*campo*] fallow, uncultivated; [*terreno*] waste
[2] (= *inútil*) vain, useless
[3] (= *ocioso*) lazy, idle
Ⓑ SM (*Agr*) (= *campo sin cultivos*) uncultivated land, fallow land; (= *solar*) wasteland

baldón SM (= *afrenta*) affront, insult; (= *deshonra*) blot, stain

baldonar ▸conjug 1a◂ VT (= *insultar*) to insult; (= *deshonrar*) to blot, disgrace

baldosa SF [1] (*para el suelo*) floor tile
[2] (*LAm*) (= *lápida*) tombstone

baldosado SM (= *suelo*) (*en casa*) tiled floor, tiling; (*en el exterior*) paving

baldosar ▸conjug 1a◂ VT [+ *suelo*] to tile; [+ *camino*] to pave (*with flagstones*)

baldoseta SF small tile

baldosín SM tile

balduque SM red tape

baleado/a SM/F (*CAm, Méx*) shooting victim, person who has been shot

balear[1] ▸conjug 1a◂ (*CAm, Méx*) Ⓐ VT (= *disparar contra*) to shoot, shoot at; (= *matar*) to shoot down, shoot dead; **morir baleado** to be shot dead
Ⓑ **balearse** VPR (*esp LAm*) to exchange shots, shoot at each other

balear[2] Ⓐ ADJ Balearic
Ⓑ SMF native/inhabitant of the Balearic Isles; **los ~es** the people of the Balearic Islands

Baleares SFPL (*tb* **Islas** ~) Balearics, Balearic Islands

baleárico ADJ Balearic

baleo SM [1] (*CAm, Méx*) (= *tiroteo*) shooting
[2] (*Méx*) (= *abanico*) fan

balero SM [1] (*LAm*) (= *juguete*) cup-and-ball toy
[2] (*Méx Mec*) ball bearing
[3] (*Cono Sur*‡) head, nut‡, noggin (EEUU‡)

balido SM bleat, baa

balín SM pellet; **balines** buckshot *sing*

balinera SF (*Andes*) ball bearing, ball bearings *pl*

balística SF ballistics *sing*

balístico ADJ ballistic

balita SF [1] (= *balín*) pellet
[2] (*Cono Sur*) (= *canica*) marble

baliza SF [1] (= *boya*) (*Náut*) buoy, marker; (*Aer*) beacon, marker
[2] **balizas** (*LAm Aut*) sidelights, parking lights

balizaje SM, **balizamiento** SM ► **balizaje de pista** (*Aer*) runway lighting, runway beacons *pl*

balizar ▸conjug 1f◂ VT (*Náut*) to mark with buoys; (*Aer*) to light *o* mark with beacons

ballena SF [1] (*Zool*) (= *animal*) whale; (= *hueso*) whalebone; **parece una ~*** she's like a beached whale* ► **ballena azul** blue whale
[2] (*Cos*) [*de corsé*] bone, stay

ballenato SM whale calf

ballenear ▸conjug 1a◂ VI to whale, hunt whales

ballenera SF whaler, whaling ship

ballenero Ⓐ ADJ whaling; **industria ballenera** whaling industry
Ⓑ SM [1] (= *pescador*) whaler
[2] (= *barco*) whaler, whaling ship

ballesta SF [1] (*Hist*) crossbow
[2] (*Mec*) spring; **las ~s** the springs, the suspension *sing*

ballestero SM (*Hist*) crossbowman

ballestrinque SM clove hitch

ballet [ba'le] SM (*pl* **ballets** [ba'les]) (= *disciplina, espectáculo*) ballet; (= *grupo de bailarines*) troupe of dancers, dance troupe ► **ballet acuático** synchronized swimming

balletístico ADJ ballet *antes de s*

balneario Ⓐ ADJ **estación balnearia** spa
Ⓑ SM [1] (*Med*) spa, health resort
[2] (*LAm*) seaside resort

balneoterapia SF balneotherapy

balompédico ADJ soccer *antes de s*, football *antes de s*

balompié SM soccer, football

balón SM [1] (*Dep*) ball; ✦*MODISMOS* **achicar balones*** ◊ **echar balones fuera*** to dodge the issue ► **balón de boxeo** boxing ball, punchball ► **balón de playa** beach ball ► **balón de reglamento** regulation ball ► **balón suelto** loose ball
[2] (= *recipiente*) (*Quím*) bag (*for gas*); (*Meteo*) balloon; (*Arg*) (= *vaso*) balloon glass; (*Andes, Cono Sur*) (= *bombona*) drum, canister ► **balón de oxígeno** oxygen cylinder; **la noticia fue un ~ de oxígeno para la economía** the news gave the economy a real boost
[3] (*Com*) bale

balonazo SM **me dio un ~** he thumped me with the ball

baloncestista SMF basketball player

baloncestístico ADJ basketball *antes de s*

baloncesto SM basketball

balonmanear ▸conjug 1a◂ VI (*Dep*) to handle, handle the ball

balonmanista SMF handball player

balonmano SM handball

balonvolea SM volleyball

balota SF (*Perú*) ballot

balotaje SM (*Méx*) (= *votación*) balloting, voting; (= *recuento*) counting of votes

balotar ▸conjug 1a◂ VI (*Perú*) to ballot, vote

balsa[1] SF 1 (*Náut*) (= *embarcación*) raft ► **balsa de salvamento, balsa salvavidas** life raft ► **balsa neumática** rubber dinghy
2 (*Bot*) balsa, balsa wood

balsa[2] SF 1 (= *charca*) pool, pond; **el pueblo es una ~ de aceite** the village is as quiet as the grave
2 (*Méx*) (= *pantano*) swamp, marshy place

balsadera SF, **balsadero** SM ferry, ferry station

balsámico ADJ 1 (*de bálsamo*) balmy
2 (= *relajante*) soothing

bálsamo SM 1 (= *sustancia*) balsam, balm
2 (= *consuelo*) balm, comfort
3 (*Cono Sur*) [*de pelo*] hair conditioner

balsar SM (*Andes, Caribe*) overgrown marshy place

balsear ▸conjug 1a◂ VT 1 [+ *río*] to cross by ferry, cross on a raft
2 [+ *personas, mercancías*] to ferry across

balsero/a SM/F 1 (= *conductor de balsa*) ferryman/ferrywoman
2 **balseros** boat people (*especially Cuban, seeking refuge in the USA*)

balsón[1] SM (*Méx*) (= *pantano*) swamp, bog; (= *agua estancada*) stagnant pool

balsón[2] ADJ (*Andes*) fat, flabby

balsoso ADJ (*Andes*) soft, spongy

Baltasar SM Balthazar; (*Biblia*) Belshazzar

báltico ADJ Baltic; **los estados ~s** the Baltic states; **el Mar Báltico** the Baltic, the Baltic Sea

baluarte SM bastion

balumba SF 1 (= *masa*) (great) bulk, mass
2 (= *montón*) pile, heap
3 (*LAm*) (= *alboroto*) noise, uproar

balumbo SM bulky thing, cumbersome object

balumoso ADJ (*LAm*) bulky, cumbersome

baluquero SM (*Fin*) forger

balurdo Ⓐ ADJ (*LAm*) flashy
Ⓑ SM (*Cono Sur**) crooked deal*

bamba[1] SMF (*Caribe*) black man/black woman

bamba[2] SF 1 (*Esp*) (= *zapatilla*) plimsoll, sneaker (*EEUU*)
2 (*CAm, Ven*) (= *moneda*) silver coin
3 (*Andes Bot*) bole, swelling (*on tree trunk*)
4 (*Andes*) (= *gordura*) fat, flabbiness

bamba[3]† SF (*Esp*) fuzz‡, police

bambalear ▸conjug 1a◂ VI = **bambolear**

bambalina SF (*Teat*) drop, drop scene; **entre ~s** behind the scenes

bambalúa SM (*LAm*) clumsy fellow, lout

bambarria* SMF idiot, fool

bamboleante ADJ 1 (= *inestable*) [*persona, mesa*] wobbly; [*paso*] unsteady
2 [*pantalones*] baggy

bambolear ▸conjug 1a◂ VI, **bambolearse** ▸conjug 1a◂ VPR (*al andar*) to sway; [*péndulo, lámpara*] to swing, sway; [*silla, mesa*] to wobble; [*tren*] to sway

bamboleo SM [*de péndulo, lámpara*] swinging, swaying; [*de silla, mesa*] wobbling, unsteadiness; [*de tren*] rolling

bambolla* SF (= *ostentación*) show, ostentation; (= *farsa*) sham

bambollero* ADJ showy, flashy

bambú SM bamboo

bambudal SM (*Andes*) bamboo grove

banal ADJ (= *poco importante*) [*comentario, tema*] banal; [*persona*] ordinary, commonplace

banalidad SF 1 (= *cualidad*) [*de comentario, tema*] banality; [*de persona*] ordinariness
2 **banalidades** small talk *sing*, trivialities; **intercambiar ~es con algn** to swap small talk with sb, exchange trivialities with sb

banalizar ▸conjug 1f◂ VT to trivialize

banana SF (*esp LAm*) (= *fruta*) banana; (= *árbol*) banana tree

bananal SM (*LAm*), **bananera** SF (*LAm*) banana plantation

bananero Ⓐ ADJ 1 (*LAm*) (= *de bananas*) banana *antes de s*; **compañía bananera** banana company; **plantación bananera** banana plantation
2 (*Pol*) third-world *antes de s*, backward; **república bananera** banana republic
3 (*) vulgar, coarse
Ⓑ SM banana tree

banano SM 1 (= *árbol*) banana tree
2 (*LAm*) (= *fruta*) banana

banas SFPL (*Méx Rel*) banns

banasta SF large basket, hamper

banasto SM large round basket

banca SF 1 (*Com, Fin*) banking; **horas de ~** banking hours; **la Banca** the banking community, the banks *pl* ► **banca comercial** commercial banking ► **banca industrial** merchant banking, investment banking ► **banca telefónica** telephone banking
2 (*en juegos*) bank; **hacer saltar la ~** to break the bank; **tener la ~** to be banker, hold the bank
3 (= *puesto*) stand, stall
4 (*LAm*) (= *asiento*) bench
5 (*Cono Sur*) (= *influencia*) pull, influence; **tener (gran) ~** to have (lots of) pull *o* influence

bancada SF 1 (= *banco*) stone bench
2 (*Mec*) bed, bedplate
3 (*Náut*) thwart, (oarsman's) seat ► **bancada corrediza** [*de remo*] sliding seat

bancal SM 1 (*Agr*) (= *terraza*) terrace; (= *terreno cultivado*) patch, plot
2 (*Mec*) runner, bench cover

bancar ▸conjug 1g◂ (*Cono Sur*) Ⓐ VT 1 (= *pagar*) to pay for
2 (= *aguantar*) to put up with
Ⓑ **bancarse** VPR **~se algo/a algn** to put up with sth/sb

bancario/a Ⓐ ADJ bank *antes de s*, banking; **giro ~** bank draft
Ⓑ SM/F bank clerk, bank employee

bancarrota SF 1 (*Fin*) bankruptcy; **declararse en** *o* **hacer ~** to go bankrupt
2 (= *fracaso*) failure

bancazo SM (*Méx*) bank robbery

banco SM 1 (= *asiento*) (*al aire libre*) bench, seat; (*en iglesia*) pew; [*de carpintero*] bench ► **banco azul** (*Pol*) ministerial benches *pl* ► **banco de pruebas** (*lit*) test bed; (*fig*) testing ground
2 (*Com, Fin*) bank ► **banco central** central bank ► **banco comercial** commercial bank ► **banco de ahorros** savings bank ► **banco de crédito** credit bank ► **banco de inversiones** investment bank ► **banco de liquidación** clearing house ► **banco ejidal** (*Méx*) cooperative bank ► **banco emisor** issuing bank ► **banco en casa** home banking ► **banco fiduciario** trust company ► **banco mercantil** merchant bank ► **Banco Mundial** World Bank ► **banco por acciones** joint-stock bank
3 (= *reserva*) [*de información, órganos*] bank ► **banco de datos** data bank ► **banco de esperma** sperm bank ► **banco de memoria** memory bank ► **banco de sangre** blood bank
4 (*Geog*) (*en el mar*) bank, shoal; (= *estrato*) stratum, layer; (*Andes*) (= *suelo aluvial*) deposit (*of alluvial soil*); (*Caribe*) (= *tierra elevada*) raised ground ► **banco de arena** sandbank ► **banco de hielo** ice field, ice floe ► **banco de niebla** fog bank ► **banco de nieve** snowdrift
5 [*de peces*] shoal, school

banda SF 1 (= *grupo*) [*de música*] band; [*de delincuentes, amigos*] gang; [*de guerrilleros*] band; [*de partidarios*] party, group; [*de aves*] flock; **negociaciones a tres ~s** three-party talks, trilateral negotiations; ✦*MODISMO* **cerrarse en ~** to stand firm, be adamant ► **banda armada** armed gang ► **banda terrorista** terrorist group
2 (= *cinta*) (*en la ropa*) band, strip; [*de gala*] sash ► **banda magnética** magnetic strip ► **banda transportadora** conveyor belt
3 (= *franja*) [*de tierra*] strip, ribbon; [*de carretera, pista de atletismo*] lane ► **banda ancha** broadband ► **banda de frecuencia** band, waveband ► **la banda de Gaza** the Gaza Strip ► **banda de rodaje, banda de rodamiento** (*Aut*) tread ► **banda de sonido** sound track ► **la Banda Oriental** (*esp Cono Sur*) Uruguay ► **banda salarial** wage scale ► **banda sonora** [*de película*] soundtrack; (*en carretera*) rumble strip
4 (= *lado*) [*de río*] side, bank; [*de monte*] side, edge; [*de barco*] side; **de la ~ de acá** on this side; **dar un barco a la ~** to careen a ship; **irse a la ~** to list; ✦*MODISMO* **coger a algn por ~**: **¡como te coja por ~!** I'll get even with you!
5 (*Dep*) sideline, touchline; **fuera de ~** out of play, in touch; **sacar de ~** to take a throw-in, throw the ball in ► **línea de banda** sideline, touchline
6 (*Billar*) cushion

bandada SF 1 (*Zool*) [*de aves*] flock; [*de peces*] shoal 2 (*LAm*) = **banda 1**

bandazo SM 1 (= *sacudida*) (*al andar*) lurch, jolt; (*Náut*) heavy roll; (*LAm Aer*) air pocket, sudden drop; **dar ~s: el coche iba dando ~s** the car swerved from side to side; **caminaba dando ~s** he stumbled along, he reeled from side to side
2 (= *cambio repentino*) marked shift

bandear ▸conjug 1a◂ Ⓐ VT 1 (*CAm*) (= *perseguir*) to pursue, chase; (= *pretender*) to court
2 (*CAm*) (= *herir*) to wound severely; (*Cono Sur*) (*con comentario*) to hurt

[3] (*Cono Sur*) (= *cruzar*) to cross, go right across

Ⓑ **bandearse** VPR [1] (= *ir de un lado a otro*) to move to and fro; (*Méx Náut*) to move to the other side of a boat

[2] (*Cono Sur Pol*) to change parties

[3] (*Méx*) (= *vacilar*) to vacillate; (= *cambiar de dirección*) to go one way and then another

[4] (*Esp**) (= *arreglárselas*) to shift for o.s., get by on one's own

bandeja SF [1] (*para llevar a la mesa, en nevera*) tray; ✦*MODISMO* **poner** *o* **servir algo en ~ (de plata) a algn** to hand sth to sb on a plate; **te lo han puesto en ~** they've made it very easy for you ► **bandeja de alimentación de papel** (*Inform*) paper-feed tray ► **bandeja de entrada** in-tray ► **bandeja de quesos** cheeseboard ► **bandeja de salida** out-tray ► **bandeja para horno** oven tray

[2] (*Cono Sur*) (*en carretera*) central reservation, median strip (*EEUU*)

bandera SF [1] [*de país, ciudad*] flag; [*de regimiento*] colours, colors *pl* (*EEUU*); **la ~ está a media asta** the flag is (flying) at half mast; **arriar la ~** to lower *o* strike the colours; **izar la ~** to raise *o* hoist the flag; **jurar ~** to swear allegiance to the flag; ✦*MODISMO* **estar hasta la ~*** to be packed out ► **bandera a cuadros, bandera ajedrezada** chequered flag, checkered flag (*EEUU*) ► **Bandera Azul** Blue Flag ► **bandera blanca** white flag ► **bandera de conveniencia** flag of convenience ► **bandera de esquina** corner flag ► **bandera de la paz** white flag ► **bandera de parlamento** (*Hist*) flag of truce, white flag ► **bandera de popa** ensign ► **bandera de proa** jack ► **bandera negra, bandera pirata** Jolly Roger, skull and crossbones ► **bandera roja** red flag ► **la bandera roja y gualda** the Spanish flag

[2] (= *idea*) banner; **bajo la ~ de la renovación** under the banner of change and renewal

[3] [*de taxi*] **bajar la ~** to pick up a fare

[4] ✦*MODISMO* **de ~** (*Esp†*) fantastic; **se ha comprado un coche de ~** she's bought a fantastic car; **es una mujer de ~** she's one hell of a woman*

[5] (*Inform*) marker, flag

banderazo SM **el ~ de llegada** the chequered flag, the checkered flag (*EEUU*); **el ~ de salida** the starting signal; **dar el ~ de salida** to signal the start, give the starting signal

bandería SF (= *bando*) faction; (= *parcialidad*) bias, partiality

banderilla SF [1] (*Taur*) banderilla; ✦*MODISMOS* **clavar ~s a algn** to goad sb; **poner un par de ~s a algn** to taunt sb, provoke sb ► **banderilla de fuego** banderilla with attached firecracker

[2] (*Culin*) savoury appetizer, savory appetizer (*EEUU*)

[3] (*LAm*) scrounging

banderillear ▸conjug 1a◂ VT (*Taur*) *to stick the banderillas into the neck of the bull*

banderillero SM (*Taur*) banderillero, *bullfighter who uses the banderillas*

banderín SM (*para adornar*) small flag, pennant; (*Ferro*) signal flag ► **banderín de enganche** recruiting centre, recruiting post ► **banderín de esquina** corner flag

banderita SF (= *bandera pequeña*) little flag; [*de caridad*] flag (*sold for charity*); **día de la ~** flag day

banderizo ADJ [1] (= *faccioso*) factional, factionalist [2] (= *alterado*) fiery, excitable

banderola SF [1] (= *bandera pequeña*) banderole; (*Mil*) pennant ► **banderola de esquina** corner flag

[2] (*Cono Sur*) (= *travesaño*) transom

bandidaje SM, **bandidismo** SM banditry

bandido SM [1] (= *delincuente*) bandit, outlaw

[2] (*) **¡bandido!** you rogue!, you beast!

bando SM [1] (= *edicto*) edict, proclamation

[2] **bandos** (*Rel*) banns

[3] (= *facción*) (*Pol*) faction, party; (*Dep*) side; **uno del otro ~*** one of them*; **pasarse al otro ~** to change sides

bandola SF [1] (*Mús*) mandolin

[2] (*Andes*) (= *capa*) bullfighter's cape

[3] (*Caribe*) (= *fuete*) knotted whip

bandolera SF bandoleer; **llevar algo en ~** to wear sth across one's chest; *ver tb* **bandolero**

bandolerismo SM brigandage, banditry

bandolero/a Ⓐ SM/F bandit

Ⓑ SM (*Hist*) highwayman; *ver tb* **bandolera**

bandolina SF mandolin

bandoneón SM (*Cono Sur*) *large accordion*

bandullo‡ SM belly, guts* *pl*; **llenarse el ~** to stuff o.s.*

bandurria SF bandurria (*lute-type Spanish instrument*)

Banesto SM ABR = **Banco Español de Crédito**

bangaña SF (*LAm*), **bangaño** SM (*LAm*) [1] (*Bot*) calabash, gourd, squash (*EEUU*)

[2] (= *vasija*) vessel made from a gourd

Bangladesh SM Bangladesh

bangladesí ADJ, SMF Bangladeshi

banjo SM banjo

banner ['baner] SM (*pl* **banners**) (*Internet*) banner ad

banquear ▸conjug 1a◂ VT [1] (*Aer*) to bank

[2] (*LAm*) to level, flatten out

banqueo SM [1] terraces *pl*, terracing

[2] (*Aer*) bank, banking

banquero/a SM/F banker

banqueta SF [1] (= *taburete*) stool; (= *banquillo*) low bench; (*Aut*) bench seat ► **banqueta de piano** piano stool

[2] (*CAm, Méx*) (= *acera*) pavement (*Brit*), sidewalk (*EEUU*)

banquetazo* SM spread*, blow-out*

banquete SM banquet, feast ► **banquete anual** annual dinner ► **banquete de boda(s)** wedding reception ► **banquete de gala** state banquet

banquetear ▸conjug 1a◂ VI to banquet, feast

banquillo SM (= *asiento*) bench; (*Dep*) bench, team bench; (*Jur*) dock; **el portero tuvo que quedarse en el ~** the goalkeeper had to stay *o* remain on the bench ► **banquillo de los acusados** dock

banquina SF (*Arg, Uru*) hard shoulder, berm (*EEUU*)

banquisa SF ice field, ice floe

banquito SM (*Arg*) stool

bantam SF [1] (*tb* **gallina de ~**) bantam

[2] (*LAm*) (= *persona*) small restless person

bántam SM (*esp LAm Dep*) bantamweight

bantú ADJ, SMF Bantu

banyo SM (*LAm*) banjo

bañada SF (*LAm*) [1] (= *baño*) (*en bañera*) bath; (*en mar, río*) swim, dip

[2] [*de pintura*] coat

bañadera SF [1] (*LAm*) bathtub, bath

[2] (*Arg*) open-top bus

bañado SM [1] (*LAm*) (= *pantano*) swamp, marshland [2] (*Andes*) (= *charco*) rain pool [3] (*Téc*) bath

bañador(a) Ⓐ SM/F bather, swimmer

Ⓑ SM [1] (= *prenda*) [*de mujer*] bathing costume, swimsuit, bathing suit; [*de hombre*] (swimming) trunks *pl*

[2] (*Téc*) tub, trough

bañar ▸conjug 1a◂ Ⓐ VT [1] **~ a algn** to bath sb, bathe sb (*EEUU*), give sb a bath; **bañé al bebé esta mañana** I bathed the baby this morning, I gave the baby a bath this morning

[2] (*Culin*) **una galleta bañada en coñac** a biscuit dipped *o* soaked in brandy; **he bañado el pastel de** *o* **con chocolate** I've covered the cake with chocolate icing, I've iced the cake with chocolate

[3] (= *dar una capa de*) to plate; **esta pulsera está bañada en oro** this bracelet is gold-plated

[4] (= *cubrir*) **bañado en sangre/sudor** [*persona*] bathed *o* drenched in blood/sweat; [*ropa*] drenched in blood/sweat; **tenía la cara bañada en lágrimas** her face was bathed in *o* wet with tears

[5] [*mar, lago*] to wash (*liter*); **el Mediterráneo baña las costas catalanas** the Catalan coast is washed by the Mediterranean; **la capital está bañada por el Guadalquivir** the Guadalquivir runs through the capital

[6] [*luz, sol*] to flood, bathe; **el sol bañaba de luz su cuarto** the sun flooded his room with light, the sun bathed his room in light

Ⓑ **bañarse** VPR [1] (*en bañera*) to have a bath, take a bath; (*en mar, piscina*) to swim; **siempre me baño por la mañana** I always have *o* take a bath in the morning; **en verano vamos a ~nos al río** in the summer we go swimming in the river; **"prohibido bañarse"** "no bathing"

[2] **¡anda a ~te!** (*Cono Sur**) get lost!*, go to hell!‡

bañata* SM (*Esp*) swimsuit, bathing costume

bañera SF bath, bathtub ► **bañera de hidromasaje** whirlpool bath

bañero/a SM/F (*Cono Sur*) lifeguard

bañista SMF [1] (*en mar, río*) bather

[2] (*Med*) (*en balneario*) patient

baño SM [1] (= *bañera*) bath, bathtub; **cuarto de ~** bathroom; (= *aseo*) toilet, bathroom (*esp EEUU*)

[2] (= *acción*) (*en bañera*) bath; (*en el mar, piscina*) swim; **darse** *o* **tomar un ~** (*en bañera*) to have *o* take a bath; (*en mar, piscina*) to have a swim, go for a swim; **playas aptas para el ~** beaches suitable for bathing ► **baño de asiento** hip bath ► **baño de burbujas** foam bath, bubble bath ► **baño de ducha** showerbath ► **baño de espuma** foam bath, bubble bath ► **baño de fuego** baptism of fire ► **baño de masas, baño de multitudes** walkabout; **darse un ~ de masas** *o* **multitudes** to go on a walkabout, mingle with the crowd ► **baño de pies** foot bath ► **baño de sangre** bloodbath ► **baño de sol**: **darse** *o* **tomar un ~ de sol** to sunbathe ► **baño de vapor** steam bath ► **baño ocular** eyebath

► **baño ruso** (*Cono Sur*) steam bath ► **baño turco** Turkish bath

3 (*Culin*) **le dio un ~ de licor a las galletas** she soaked the biscuits in liqueur; **le he dado un ~ de chocolate al pastel** I've covered the cake with chocolate icing, I've iced the cake with chocolate ► **baño María** bain-marie

4 [*de oro, plata*] plating; [*de pintura*] coat; **el pendiente tiene un ~ de plata** the earring is silver-plated ► **baño de revelado** developing bath

5 (*Arte*) wash

6 **baños** (*Med*) spa *sing*; **ir a ~s†** to take the waters†, bathe at a spa (*EEUU*) ► **baños termales** thermal baths

7 (= *paliza*) **darle un ~ a algn*** to thrash sb*, wipe the floor with sb*

8 (*Caribe*) (= *lugar*) cool place

bao SM (*Náut*) beam

baobab SM baobab

baptismo SM **el ~** the Baptist faith

baptista ADJ, SMF Baptist

baptisterio SM baptistery

baque SM bang, thump

baqueano/a ADJ, SM/F = **baquiano**

baquelita SF bakelite

baqueta SF 1 (*Mil*) ramrod; ✦**MODISMOS correr ~s** ◊ **pasar por ~s** to run the gauntlet; **mandar a ~** to rule tyrannically; **tratar a algn a (la) ~** to treat sb harshly

2 (*Mús*) [*de tambor*] drumstick; (*CAm, Méx*) [*de marimba*] hammer

baquetazo SM **tratar a algn a ~ limpio*** to give sb a hard time

baqueteado ADJ [*persona*] experienced; [*mueble*] worse for wear, battered

baquetear ▸conjug 1a◂ VT 1 (= *fastidiar*) to annoy, bother

2 (= *maltratar*) to treat harshly; **ha sido baqueteado por la vida** life's been hard on him

baqueteo SM annoyance, bother; **es un ~** it's an imposition, it's an awful bind*

baquetudo ADJ (*Caribe*) sluggish, slow

baquía SF (*LAm*) 1 (= *conocimientos locales*) local expertise

2 (†) (= *habilidad*) expertise, skill

baquiano/a Ⓐ ADJ 1 (*LAm*) (= *que conoce una región*) familiar with a region

2 (*esp LAm*) (= *experto*) expert, skilful, skillful (*EEUU*); ✦**REFRÁN para hacerse ~ hay que perderse alguna vez** one learns the hard way

Ⓑ SM/F 1 (*LAm*) (= *guía*) guide, scout; (*Náut*) pilot

2 (*esp LAm*) (= *experto*) expert; (= *experto local*) local expert, *person with an intimate knowledge of a region*

báquico ADJ (*liter*) Bacchic (*liter*)

báquiro SM (*Col, Ven*) peccary

bar SM bar ► **bar de alterne, bar de citas** singles bar ► **bar de copas** nightclub

baraca SF *charismatic gift of bringing good luck blessing*

barahúnda SF (= *alboroto*) uproar

baraja SF 1 (= *juego de cartas*) pack of cards; (*Méx*) cards; **jugar ~** (*LAm*) to play cards; ✦**MODISMOS jugar a** *o* **con dos ~s** to play a double game, double deal; **romper la ~** to break off the engagement, end the conflict

2 **barajas** (= *pelea*) fight *sing*, set-to* *sing*

> **BARAJA ESPAÑOLA**
>
> *The Spanish deck of cards differs from its British and American counterpart, known in Spain as the* **baraja francesa**. *The four Spanish suits,* **oros, copas, espadas** *and* **bastos** *("golden coins", "goblets", "swords" and "clubs") each contain 9 numbered cards, although for certain games only 7 are used, and 3 picture cards:* **sota, caballo** *and* **rey** *(jack, queen, king).*

barajadura SF shuffle, shuffling

barajar ▸conjug 1a◂ Ⓐ VT 1 [+ *cartas*] to shuffle

2 (= *considerar*) [+ *nombres, candidatos*] to consider, weigh up; **se baraja la posibilidad de que ...** the possibility that ... is being weighed up *o* considered, there is discussion about the possibility that ...; **las cifras que se barajan ahora** the figures now being put *o* bandied about

3 (= *mezclar*) to jumble up, mix up

4 (*Cono Sur, Méx*) [+ *asunto*] (= *confundir*) to confuse; (= *demorar*) to delay

5 (*Cono Sur*) (= *ofrecer*) to pass round, hand round

6 (*Cono Sur*) (= *agarrar*) to catch (*in the air*); ✦**MODISMO ~ algo en el aire** to see the point of sth

Ⓑ VI to quarrel, squabble

Ⓒ **barajarse** VPR 1 (*esp LAm*) (= *pelear*) to fight, brawl

2 (= *mezclarse*) to get jumbled up, get mixed up

barajo Ⓐ EXCL (*LAm euf*) = **carajo**

Ⓑ SM (*Andes*) (= *pretexto*) pretext, excuse; (= *salida*) loophole

barajuste SM (*Caribe*) stampede, rush

baranda¹ SF 1 [*de balcón*] rail, railing; [*de escalera*] handrail

2 (*Billar*) cushion

baranda²‡ SM chief, boss

barandal SM (= *pasamanos*) handrail; (= *soporte de pasamanos*) base, support; (= *balaustrada*) balustrade

barandilla SF [*de balcón*] rail, railing; [*de escalera*] banisters *pl*, bannisters *pl*; (*Andes*) altar rail

barata SF 1 (*Méx*) (= *venta*) sale, bargain sale; (= *mercado*) street market

2 (*Andes*) (= *sección de gangas*) bargain counter; (= *tienda*) cut-price store; ✦**MODISMO a la ~*** (= *sin orden*) any old how*; **tratar a algn a la ~** to treat sb with scorn

3 (*Chile*) (= *cucaracha*) cockroach, roach (*EEUU*)

baratear ▸conjug 1a◂ VT (= *vender barato*) to sell cheaply; (= *vender perdiendo dinero*) to sell at a loss

baratejo* ADJ cheap and nasty, trashy

baratero/a Ⓐ ADJ 1 (*esp LAm*) (= *barato*) cheap; [*tendero*] cut-price *antes de s*, discount *antes de s*; **tienda baratera** shop offering bargains, cut-price store, discount store

2 (*Cono Sur*) [*regateo*] haggling

Ⓑ SM/F 1 (*en el juego*) *person who extracts money from winning gamblers*

2 (*LAm*) (= *tendero*) cut-price shopkeeper, discount storekeeper

3 (*Cono Sur*) (= *persona que regatea*) haggler

baratez SF (*Caribe*), **baratía** SF (*Andes*) cheapness

baratija SF 1 (= *objeto*) trinket; (= *cosa insignificante*) trifle

2 **baratijas** (*Com*) cheap goods; (*pey*) trash *sing*, junk *sing*

baratillero SM seller of cheap goods

baratillo SM 1 (= *artículos usados*) secondhand goods *pl*; (= *artículos baratos*) cheap goods *pl*

2 (= *tienda*) secondhand shop, junk shop; (= *sección de gangas*) bargain counter

3 (= *saldo*) bargain sale; **cosa de ~** trash, junk

4 (= *mercadillo*) street market

barato Ⓐ ADJ 1 (= *económico*) cheap; **este vestido es muy ~** this dress is very cheap; **el café sale más ~ a granel** coffee is cheaper if you buy it in bulk; ✦**REFRÁN lo ~ sale caro** buying cheap things is false economy, cheap things turn out expensive in the end

2 (= *de mala calidad*) [*música, imitación*] cheap; [*novela*] trashy

3 (= *indigno*) [*demagogia, electoralismo*] cheap; **esa actitud es patriotismo ~** that attitude is just cheap patriotism

Ⓑ ADV cheap, cheaply; **el coche nos costó ~** the car was cheap; **en este restaurante se come muy ~** you can eat very cheaply in this restaurant; **vivo muy ~** I live very cheaply

Ⓒ SM (= *mercadillo*) street market

baratón Ⓐ ADJ (*Andes, CAm, Méx*) [*argumento*] weak, feeble; [*comentario*] well-worn, trite

Ⓑ SM (*CAm*) (= *ganga*) bargain; (= *saldo*) sale

baratura SF low price, cheapness

baraúnda SF = **barahúnda**

barba Ⓐ SF 1 (= *pelo*) beard; **llevar** *o* **tener ~** to have a beard; **lleva** *o* **tiene ~ de tres días** he's got three days' stubble, he's got three days' growth of beard; **tiene la ~ cerrada** *o* **muy poblada** he's got a very thick beard, his beard grows thickly; **arreglarse** *o* **hacerse** *o* **recortarse la ~** to trim one's beard; **dejarse ~: me estoy dejando ~** I'm growing a beard; **por ~: dos naranjas por ~** two oranges apiece *o* per head; ✦**MODISMOS colgar ~s al santo** to give sb his due; **hacer algo en las ~s de algn** to do sth right under sb's nose; **hacerle la ~ a algn** (*Méx*) (= *adular*) to fawn on sb, flatter sb; **llevar a algn de la ~** to lead sb by the nose; **mentir por la ~** to lie through one's teeth; **tener pocas ~s** to be inexperienced; **a ~ regalada** abundantly; **subirse a las ~s de algn** to be cheeky to sb; **tirarse de las ~s** to be tearing one's hair (out); **un hombre con toda la ~** a real man, a regular guy (*EEUU**); ✦**REFRÁN cuando las ~s de tu vecino veas pelar pon las tuyas a remojar** you should learn from other people's mistakes ► **barba de chivo** goatee (beard) ► **barba honrada** distinguished personage

2 (= *mentón*) chin

3 [*de ave*] wattle; [*de mejillón, cabra*] beard ► **barba de ballena** whalebone

4 (*Bot*) [*de raíz*] beard

Ⓑ SM (*Teat†*) (= *papel*) old man's part; (= *actor*) *performer of old men's roles*; (= *villano*) villain

Barba Azul SM Bluebeard

barbacana SF [*de defensa*] barbican; (= *tronera*) loophole, embrasure

barbacoa SF [1] (= *asadero*) barbecue
[2] (*CAm, Méx, Ven*) (= *carne*) barbecued meat
[3] (*LAm*) (= *cama*) bed (*made with a hurdle supported on sticks*)
[4] (*Andes*) (= *estante*) rack (*for kitchen utensils*)
[5] (*Andes*) (= *desván*) loft, attic
[6] (*Andes*) tap dance

Barbada SF **la ~** Barbados

barbado Ⓐ ADJ bearded, with a beard
Ⓑ SM [1] (= *hombre con barba*) man with a beard; (= *hombre adulto*) full-grown man
[2] (*Bot*) cutting (*with roots*); **plantar de ~** to transplant, plant out

Barbados SM Barbados

barbar ▸conjug 1a◂ VI [1] (= *dejarse barba*) to grow a beard
[2] (*Bot*) to strike root

Bárbara SF Barbara

bárbaramente ADV [1] (= *cruelmente*) cruelly, savagely
[2] (*) (= *estupendamente*) tremendously*; **pasarlo ~** to have a tremendous time*

barbáricamente ADV barbarically

barbárico ADJ barbaric

barbaridad SF [1] (= *desatino*) **es una ~ conducir con esta niebla** it's madness to drive in this fog; **es capaz de hacer cualquier ~** he's capable of anything, he will stop at nothing; **decir ~es** (= *tonterías*) to talk nonsense; **¡qué ~!**: **¡qué ~! ¿cómo puedes comer tanto?** that's incredible *o* amazing! how can you eat so much?; **¡qué ~! ¡consentirle que hable así a sus padres!** that's awful! letting him talk to his parents like that!; **¡qué ~! ¡qué bien hablas el inglés!** that's incredible *o* amazing! your English is really good!
[2] (= *brutalidad*) atrocity; **las ~es que se cometieron en la guerra** the atrocities committed during the war; **las pruebas con animales son una ~** it is horrible to experiment on animals
[3] (= *palabrota*) **cuando se enfada dice** *o* **suelta muchas ~es** he says some terrible things when he gets angry
[4] **una ~*** (= *mucho*) (*como adv*) **comimos una ~** we ate loads *o* tons *o* masses*, we stuffed ourselves*; **cuesta una ~** it costs a fortune; **nos divertimos una ~** we had a great *o* fantastic time*; **nos gustó una ~** we thought it was great *o* fantastic*; **habló una ~** he talked his head off*; **se nota una ~** it sticks out a mile*; **me quiere una ~** he loves me to death*; **había una ~ de gente** there were loads *o* tons *o* masses of people*

barbarie SF [1] (= *atraso*) barbarism
[2] (= *crueldad*) barbarity, cruelty

barbarismo SM [1] (*Ling*) barbarism
[2] = **barbarie**

bárbaro/a Ⓐ ADJ [1] (*Hist*) barbarian
[2] (= *cruel*) barbarous, cruel; (= *espantoso*) awful, frightful
[3] (= *grosero*) rough, uncouth; (= *inculto*) ignorant
[4] (*) (= *increíble*) tremendous*, smashing*; **un éxito ~** a tremendous *o* smashing success*; **es un tío ~** he's a great *o* fantastic guy*; **hace un frío ~** it's freezing; **¡qué ~!** (= *estupendo*) great!, terrific!; (= *horrible*) how awful!
Ⓑ ADV (*) (= *estupendamente*) brilliantly; **lo pasamos ~** we had a tremendous time*; **canta ~** she signs brilliantly, she's a terrific singer
Ⓒ EXCL (*Cono Sur**) fine!, OK!*
Ⓓ SM/F [1] (*Hist*) barbarian
[2] (= *bruto*) uncouth person; **conduce como un ~** he drives like a madman; **gritó como un ~** he gave a tremendous shout, he shouted like mad

barbarote* SM brute, savage

barbas* SM INV beardie*, bearded guy*

barbear ▸conjug 1a◂ Ⓐ VT [1] (*LAm*) to shave
[2] (*CAm, Méx*) (= *lisonjear*) to fawn on, flatter
[3] (*Méx*) [+ *ganado*] to throw, fell
[4] (*esp LAm*) (= *alcanzar*) to come up to, be as tall as
[5] (*CAm*) (= *fastidiar*) to annoy, bore
[6] (*) (= *ver*) to see, spot
[7] (*CAm**) (= *regañar*) to tell off
Ⓑ VI [1] **~ con** = **A4**
[2] (*CAm**) (= *entrometerse*) to stick one's nose in, poke one's nose in

barbechar ▸conjug 1a◂ VT [1] (= *dejar en barbecho*) to leave fallow
[2] (= *arar*) to plough for sowing, plow for sowing (*EEUU*)

barbechera SF fallow, fallow land

barbecho SM [1] (= *terreno*) fallow, fallow land; **estar en ~** (*Agr*) to be left fallow; (*fig*) to be in preparation; ✦**MODISMO firmar como en un ~** to sign without reading
[2] (= *tierra arada*) ploughed land ready for sowing
[3] (= *preparación*) preparation for sowing

barbería SF [1] (= *peluquería*) barber's, barber's shop
[2] (= *arte*) hairdressing

barbero Ⓐ ADJ (*CAm, Méx**) (= *adulador*) grovelling; [*niño*] affectionate, cuddly
Ⓑ SM [1] (= *peluquero*) barber; **"El ~ de Sevilla"** "The Barber of Seville"
[2] (*Guat, Méx**) flatterer

barbeta* SMF (*Cono Sur*) fool

barbetear ▸conjug 1a◂ VT (*Méx*) [+ *ganado*] to throw (to the ground) *o* fell (*by twisting the head of*)

barbicano ADJ grey-bearded, white-bearded

barbihecho ADJ freshly shaven

barbijo SM (*Andes, Cono Sur*) [1] (= *correa*) chinstrap
[2] (= *chirlo*) slash, scar
[3] (= *pañuelo*) headscarf (*knotted under the chin*)

barbilampiño Ⓐ ADJ [1] (= *sin barba*) beardless, clean-shaven
[2] (= *de cara de niño*) baby-faced
[3] (= *inexperto*) inexperienced
Ⓑ SM (= *novato*) novice, greenhorn

barbilindo ADJ (= *pulcro*) dapper, spruce; (*pey*) dandified, foppish

barbilla SF chin, tip of the chin

barbiponiente ADJ [1] (= *con barba incipiente*) beginning to grow a beard, with a youthful beard
[2] (= *inexperto*) inexperienced, green

barbiquejo SM [1] = **barbijo 1, 3**
[2] (*Caribe*) (= *bocal*) bit

barbiturato SM barbiturate

barbitúrico ADJ, SM barbiturate

barbo SM barbel ► **barbo de mar** red mullet, goatfish (*EEUU*)

barbón SM [1] (= *hombre con barba*) bearded man, man with a (big) beard; (= *anciano*) greybeard, old hand
[2] (*Zool*) billy goat

barbotear ▸conjug 1a◂ VT, **barbotar** ▸conjug 1a◂ VT to mutter, mumble

barboteo SM muttering, mumbling

barbudo Ⓐ ADJ bearded
Ⓑ SM (*a veces pey*) bearded man

barbulla SF hullabaloo

barbullar ▸conjug 1a◂ VI to jabber away, talk noisily

Barça SM **el ~** (*Esp**) Barcelona Football Club

barca SF boat, small boat ► **barca de pasaje** ferry ► **barca de pesca, barca pesquera** fishing boat

barcada SF [1] (= *carga*) boat load
[2] (= *viaje*) boat trip; (= *travesía*) ferry crossing

barcaje SM toll

barcarola SF barcarole

barcaza SF barge ► **barcaza de desembarco** (*Mil*) landing craft

Barcelona SF Barcelona

barcelonés/esa Ⓐ ADJ of/from Barcelona
Ⓑ SM/F native/inhabitant of Barcelona; **los barceloneses** the people of Barcelona

barchilón/ona SM/F [1] (*Andes*) (= *enfermero*) nurse
[2] (*Andes, Cono Sur*) (= *curandero*) quack doctor

barcia SF chaff

barcino ADJ reddish-grey

barco SM (= *embarcación*) boat; [*de gran tamaño*] ship, vessel (*frm*); **en ~** by boat, by ship; ✦**MODISMO como ~ sin timón** irresolutely, lacking a firm purpose ► **barco almirante** flagship ► **barco cablero** cable ship ► **barco carbonero** collier ► **barco cisterna** tanker ► **barco contenedor** container ship ► **barco de apoyo** support ship ► **barco de carga** cargo boat ► **barco de guerra** warship ► **barco de vapor** steamer ► **barco de vela** sailing boat, sailboat (*EEUU*) ► **barco meteorológico** weather ship ► **barco minero** collier ► **barco náufrago** wreck ► **barco nodriza** supply ship ► **barco patrullero** patrol boat ► **barco vivienda** houseboat; *ver tb* **abandonar A1**

barco-madre SM (*pl* **barcos-madre**) mother ship

barda SF [1] protective covering on a wall; (*Méx*) high hedge, fence, wall
[2] **bardas** top *sing* of a wall, walls
[3] (*) jacket

bardal SM wall topped with brushwood

bardana SF burdock

bardar ▸conjug 1a◂ VT to thatch

bardo SM bard

baremar ▸conjug 1a◂ VT to assess

baremo SM [1] (= *escala de valores*) scale
[2] (= *criterio*) yardstick, gauge, gage (*EEUU*)
[3] (*Mat*) ready reckoner

bareo* SM **ir de ~** to go drinking, go pub-crawling*

barillero SM (*Méx*) hawker, street vendor

bario SM barium

barítono SM baritone

barjuleta SF knapsack

barloventear ▸conjug 1a◂ VI [1] (*Náut*) to beat to windward
[2] (= *vagar*) to wander about

Barlovento: **Islas de ~** SFPL Windward Isles

barlovento SM windward; **a ~** to windward; **de ~** windward *antes de s*; **ganar el ~ a** to get to windward of

barman SM (*pl* **barmans**) barman, bartender

Barna. ABR = **Barcelona**

barniz SM [1] (= *sustancia*) (*para dar brillo*) varnish; (*para cerámica*) glaze; (*en metal*) gloss, polish; **dar (de) ~ a algo** to varnish sth ► **barniz de uñas** nail varnish
[2] (= *cualidad superficial*) veneer
[3] (*Aer*) dope

barnizado SM varnishing

barnizar ▸conjug 1f◂ VT [1] (= *cubrir con barniz*) [+ *madera, mueble*] to varnish; [+ *cerámica*] to glaze [2] (= *encubrir*) to put a gloss on

barométrico ADJ barometric

barómetro SM barometer ► **barómetro aneroide** aneroid barometer

barón SM [1] (= *título*) baron; (*Pol*) chief, big wig*
[2] (*Caribe**) pal*, buddy (*EEUU*)

baronesa SF baroness

baronía SF barony

baronial ADJ baronial

barquero/a SM/F [*de barcaza, barca*] boatman/boatwoman; [*de embarcadero*] ferryman/ferrywoman

barquía SF skiff, rowing boat, rowboat (*EEUU*)

barquilla SF [1] (*Aer*) [*de globo*] basket; [*de dirigible*] gondola, car
[2] (*Náut*) log
[3] (*LAm*) = **barquillo**

barquillo SM (*Culin*) rolled wafer; (= *helado*) cornet, cone

barquinazo SM [1] (= *caída*) tumble, hard fall
[2] (= *movimiento brusco*) (*Aut*) bump, jolt; (*Andes*) sudden start

barra SF [1] (= *pieza alargada*) bar; [*de metal*] bar, ingot; (*en armario*) rail; (*en un bar*) bar, counter; (*en autoservicio*) counter; (*Mec*) rod; [*de bicicleta*] crossbar; **beber en la ~** to drink at the bar; **la bandera de las ~s y estrellas** the Stars and Stripes; ✦*MODISMOS* **a ~s derechas** honestly; **no pararse en ~s** to stick at nothing ► **barra americana** singles bar ► **barra antivuelco** anti-roll bar ► **barra de carmín** lipstick ► **barra de cereales** cereal bar ► **barra de chocolate** (*Cono Sur*) bar of chocolate, chocolate bar, candy bar (*EEUU*) ► **barra de cortina** curtain rod ► **barra de equilibrio(s)** beam ► **barra de espaciado** space bar ► **barra de herramientas** (*Inform*) toolbar ► **barra de labios** lipstick ► **barra de pan** French stick, French loaf ► **barra espaciadora** space bar ► **barra estabilizadora** anti-roll bar ► **barra fija** horizontal bar, fixed bar ► **barra libre** free bar ► **barras asimétricas** asymmetric bars ► **barras paralelas** parallel bars
[2] (*Tip*) (*tb* **~ oblicua**) oblique stroke, slash ► **barra inversa** backslash
[3] (*Heráldica*) stripe, bar
[4] (*Náut*) bar, sandbank
[5] (*Jur*) (= *banquillo*) dock; **llevar a algn a la ~** to bring sb to justice; **la Barra** (*Méx*) the Bar, the legal profession, the Bar Association (*EEUU*)
[6] (*Mús*) bar
[7] (*Cono Sur*) (= *público*) (*en concierto, espectáculo*) audience, spectators *pl*; (*Dep*) fans *pl*, supporters *pl*; **había mucha ~** there was a big audience
[8] (*Cono Sur*) (= *pandilla*) gang; (= *camarilla*) clique, coterie
[9] (*Caribe*) river mouth, estuary

Barrabás SM Barrabas; ✦*MODISMO* **ser un ~** [*adulto*] to be wicked; [*niño*] to be mischievous, be naughty

barrabasada SF mischief, piece of mischief

barraca[1] SF [1] (= *cabaña*) hut, cabin; [*de obreros*] workmen's hut; (*en Valencia*) small farmhouse
[2] (= *chabola*) shanty, hovel; **una zona de ~s** an area of shantytown
[3] (*en feria*) stall, booth ► **una barraca de feria** a fairground stall *o* booth ► **barraca de tiro al blanco** shooting gallery ► **barraca persa** (*Cono Sur*) cut-price store
[4] (*Andes*) (= *depósito*) large storage shed; (*en mercado*) market stall
[5] ✦*MODISMO* **creerse algo a la ~** to believe sth implicitly

barraca[2] SF (*LAm Mil*) barracks

barracón SM [1] (= *cabaña*) big hut; (*Caribe Agr*) farmworkers' living quarters
[2] (*en feria*) (= *caseta*) large booth, stall; (= *espectáculo*) sideshow ► **barracón de espejos, barracón de la risa** hall of mirrors

barracuda SF barracuda

barragana SF (= *concubina*) concubine; (††) morganatic wife

barrajes SMPL (*Andes*) shanty town *sing*

barranca SF gully, ravine

barrancal SM place full of ravines

barranco SM [1] (= *hondonada*) gully, ravine
[2] (= *precipicio*) cliff; [*de río*] steep riverbank
[3] (= *obstáculo*) difficulty, obstacle

barraquismo SM problem of the slums, shanty town problem

barrar ▸conjug 1a◂ VT to daub, smear (**de** with)

barreal SM (*Cono Sur*) (= *tierra*) heavy clay land; (*CAm*) (= *pantano*) bog

barrear ▸conjug 1a◂ VT (= *poner barricadas*) to barricade, fortify; (= *bloquear con una barra*) to bar, fasten with a bar

barredera SF [1] (= *vehículo*) street sweeper, road sweeper ► **barredera de alfombras, barredera mecánica** carpet sweeper
[2] (= *persona*) street sweeper, road sweeper

barredor SM (*tb* **~ de frecuencia**) frequency sweeper

barredura SF [1] (= *acción*) sweep, sweeping
[2] **barreduras** (= *restos*) sweepings; (= *basura*) rubbish *sing*, refuse *sing*, garbage (*EEUU*)

barreminas SM INV minesweeper

barrena SF [1] (= *taladro*) (*para pared*) drill; (*para asfalto*) pneumatic drill; (*Min*) rock drill, mining drill ► **barrena de guía** centre *o* (*EEUU*) center bit ► **barrena de mano, barrena pequeña** gimlet
[2] (*Aer*) **entrar en ~** to go into a spin

barrenado* ADJ **estar ~** to be dotty*

barrenar ▸conjug 1a◂ VT [1] (= *taladrar*) [+ *madera, metal*] to drill, bore; [+ *roca*] to blast; [+ *barco*] to scuttle
[2] (= *volar*) to blast
[3] (= *frustrar*) to foil, frustrate
[4] (*Jur*) to violate, infringe

barrendero/a SM/F street sweeper, road sweeper

barrenillo SM [1] (*Zool*) borer
[2] (*Caribe*) (= *empeño*) foolish persistence; (*Cono Sur, Méx*) (= *preocupación*) constant worry; (= *manía*) pet idea

barreno SM (= *perforación*) borehole; (*Min*) blasthole; **dar ~ a un barco** to scuttle a ship

barreño SM washing bowl, washbowl

barrer ▸conjug 2a◂ Ⓐ VT [1] (*con escoba*) to sweep; [+ *suelo*] to sweep, sweep clean; [+ *habitación*] to sweep (out); [+ *objeto*] to sweep aside, sweep away
[2] (*Mil, Náut*) to sweep *o* rake (*with gunfire*)
[3] (= *eliminar*) [+ *obstáculo*] to sweep aside, sweep away; [+ *rival*] to sweep aside, overwhelm; [+ *dudas*] to sweep aside, dispel; **los candidatos del partido barrieron a sus adversarios** the party's candidates swept their rivals aside; ✦*MODISMO* **~ con todo** to make a clean sweep
Ⓑ VI [1] (= *con escoba*) to sweep up
[2] (= *llevarse*) ✦*MODISMOS* **~ para** *o* **hacia dentro** to look after number one; **comprar algo al ~** (*Cono Sur*) to buy sth in a job lot
Ⓒ **barrerse** VPR [1] (*Méx*) [*caballo*] to shy, start
[2] (*Méx**) (= *humillarse*) to grovel

barrera SF [1] (= *obstáculo*) barrier; **levantó la ~ para dejarnos pasar** he lifted the barrier to let us through; **crema ~** barrier cream; **contraconcepción anticonceptivo de ~** barrier contraception; **método anticonceptivo de ~** barrier method; **ya ha traspasado la ~ de los treinta** he has passed the 30-year-old mark ► **barrera aduanera, barrera arancelaria** tariff barrier ► **barrera comercial** trade barrier ► **barrera coralina** coral reef ► **barrera de color** colour *o* (*EEUU*) color bar ► **barrera de contención** containing wall ► **barrera del sonido** sound barrier; **este avión supera** *o* **traspasa** *o* **rompe la ~ del sonido** this plane can break the sound barrier ► **barrera de seguridad** safety barrier ► **barrera generacional** generation gap ► **barrera protectora** safety barrier ► **barrera racial** colour *o* (*EEUU*) color bar
[2] (*en carretera*) roadblock ► **barrera de peaje, barrera de portazgo** toll gate, turnpike
[3] (*Ferro*) crossing gate
[4] (*Taur*) (= *valla*) barrier; (= *primera fila*) first row; *ver tb* **toro 3**
[5] (*Dep*) [*de jugadores*] wall
[6] (*Mil*) (= *barricada*) barricade; (= *parapeto*) parapet ► **barrera de fuego** barrage ► **barrera de fuego móvil** creeping barrage
[7] (= *impedimento*) barrier, obstacle; **poner ~s a algo** to hinder sth, obstruct sth

barrero Ⓐ ADJ (*Cono Sur*) [*caballo*] that likes heavy going
Ⓑ SM (= *tierra fangosa*) muddy ground; (*Andes, Cono Sur*) (= *saladar*) salt soil

bar-restaurante SM bar-cum-restaurant

barretina SF *Catalan cap*

barriada SF (= *barrio*) quarter, district; (*LAm*) (= *chabolas*) slum, shanty town

barrial SM [1] (*Méx*) (= *tierra*) heavy clay land
[2] (*LAm*) (= *pantano*) bog

barrica SF large barrel, cask

barricada SF barricade

barrida SF (*con escoba*) sweep, sweeping; [*de policía*] sweep, raid; (*en elecciones*) landslide

barrido SM (*con escoba*) sweep, sweeping; (*Elec*) scan, sweep; ✦**MODISMO vale tanto para un ~ como para un fregado** he can turn his hand to anything

barriga SF [1] (*Anat*) belly; (= *panza*) paunch; **echar ~** to get middle-age spread; **estás echando ~** you're getting a bit of a belly*; **con la cerveza echas ~** beer makes you fat; **me duele la ~** I have a sore stomach; **hacer una ~ a una chica*** to get a girl in the family way; **llenarse la ~** to stuff o.s.; **tener ~*** (= *estar encinta*) to be in the family way*; (= *ser gordo*) to be fat; ✦**MODISMO rascarse** *o* **tocarse la ~*** to do damn-all*
[2] (= *parte abultada*) [*de jarra*] belly, rounded part; [*de muro*] bulge

barrigón/ona, barrigudo/a Ⓐ ADJ potbellied
Ⓑ SM/F (*Andes, Caribe**) child, kid*

barriguera SF girth, horse's girth

barril SM [1] (= *tonel*) (*gen*) barrel; [*de madera*] cask; [*de metal*] keg; **cerveza de ~** draught *o* (*EEUU*) draft beer, beer on draught; ✦**MODISMOS comer del ~** (*Andes*) to eat poor-quality food; **ser un ~ de pólvora** to be a powder keg ► **barril de petróleo** barrel of oil
[2] (*LAm*) (= *cometa hexagonal*) hexagonal kite

barrila* SF row; **dar la ~** to kick up a fuss

barrilería SF [1] (= *almacén*) barrel store
[2] (= *tienda, taller*) cooper's shop
[3] (= *arte*) cooperage

barrilero/a SM/F cooper

barrilete Ⓐ SM [1] (= *barril*) [*de metal*] keg; [*de madera*] cask
[2] [*de revólver*] chamber
[3] (*Téc*) clamp
[4] (*Méx Jur*) junior barrister
[5] (*Cono Sur*) (= *cometa de juguete*) kite
Ⓑ SF (*Cono Sur*) restless woman

barrilla SF (*Bot, Quím*) barilla, saltwort

barrillo SM (= *grano*) pimple; (*con la cabeza negra*) blackhead

barrio SM [1] (= *distrito*) area, district, neighborhood (*EEUU*); **una casa en un ~ residencial** a house in a residential area *o* district *o* (*EEUU*) neighborhood; **el ~ de Gracia** Gracia district; **mi ~** my part of town, my neighborhood (*EEUU*); **un piso en un ~ céntrico** a flat in the centre of town; **vive en el ~ judío de Córdoba** he lives in the Jewish quarter of Cordova; **los ~s de la periferia** the outlying suburbs *o* areas, the outskirts; **tiendas de ~** local shops, corner shops, neighborhood stores (*EEUU*); **cine de ~** local cinema; ✦**MODISMOS el otro ~*** the next world; **irse al otro ~*** to snuff it*; **mandar a algn al otro ~*** to do sb in* ► **barrio bruja** (*Andes*) shanty town ► **barrio chino** [*de mayoría china*] Chinatown, Chinese quarter; [*de prostitución*] (*Esp*) red-light district ► **barrio comercial** [*de negocios*] business quarter, commercial district; [*de tiendas*] shopping area, shopping district ► **barrio de chabolas** shanty town ► **barrio de tolerancia** (*Andes*) red-light district ► **barrio dormitorio** commuter suburb, dormitory suburb ► **barrio exterior** outer suburb ► **Barrio Gótico** *historic district with principally Gothic architecture* ► **barrio latino** Latin quarter ► **barrio miseria**† shanty town ► **barrio obrero** working-class area, working-class district, working-class neighborhood (*EEUU*) ► **barrios bajos** poorer areas (of town) ► **barrios marginales** poorer areas (of town)
[2] (*LAm*) shanty town

barriobajero ADJ [1] [*zona, vida*] slum *antes de s*
[2] (= *vulgar*) vulgar, common

barrisco: **a ~** ADV jumbled together, in confusion, indiscriminately

barritar ▸conjug 1a◂ VI [*elefante*] to trumpet

barrito SM trumpeting

barrizal SM mire

barro SM [1] (= *lodo*) mud; **me llené de ~** I got covered in mud
[2] (*Arte*) (= *arcilla*) potter's clay; **~ cocido** baked clay; **una vasija de ~** a clay pot
[3] (= *loza*) earthenware; **un cacharro de ~** an earthenware dish; **barros** earthenware *sing*, crockery *sing*
[4] (‡) (= *dinero*) dough‡, brass*; **tener ~ a mano** to be in the money
[5] (*Cono Sur**) (= *desacierto*) **hacer un ~** to drop a clanger*
[6] (*Anat*) pimple
[7] ► **barros jarpa** (*Chile*), **barros luca** (*Chile*) *toasted ham and cheese sandwich*

barroco Ⓐ ADJ [1] [*estilo, período*] baroque
[2] (= *recargado*) elaborate
Ⓑ SM (= *estilo*) baroque, baroque style; (= *período*) baroque period

barroquismo SM [1] (= *estilo barroco*) baroque, baroque style
[2] (= *adorno excesivo*) excess

barroso ADJ [1] (= *con barro*) muddy
[2] [*color*] mud-coloured, mud-colored (*EEUU*); [*ganado*] reddish; (*CAm*) (= *blancuzco*) off-white
[3] (*Anat*) pimply

barrote SM [1] [*de celda*] bar; **los ~s de la ventana** the bars on the window
[2] [*de silla*] rung

barruntar ▸conjug 1a◂ VT (= *adivinar*) to guess, conjecture; (= *sospechar*) to suspect

barrunte SM sign, indication

barrunto SM [1] (= *adivinanza*) guess, conjecture; (= *indicio*) sign, indication; (= *sospecha*) suspicion; (= *presentimiento*) foreboding
[2] (*Caribe, Méx Meteo*) *north wind which brings rain*

Barsa SM = **Barça**

bartola SF ✦**MODISMO echarse** *o* **tenderse a la ~*** to be lazy, take it easy*

bartolear ▸conjug 1a◂ VI (*Cono Sur*) to be lazy, take it easy*

bartolina SF (*CAm, Méx*) dark cell, dungeon

Bartolo SM (*forma familiar*) *de* **Bartolomé**

bartolo* ADJ (*Méx*) thick*, stupid

Bartolomé SM Bartholomew

bartulear ▸conjug 1a◂ VI (*Cono Sur*) to think hard, rack one's brains

bártulos* SMPL things, belongings; (*Téc*) tools; **liar los ~** to pack up one's things *o* belongings

barucho* SM (*pey*) seedy bar

barullento ADJ (*Cono Sur*) noisy, rowdy

barullo SM [1] (= *alboroto*) racket; (= *confusión*) confusion; **armar ~** to make a racket; **esta habitación está hecha un ~** this room is a mess
[2] **a ~** in abundance, in great quantities

barzón SM saunter, stroll; **dar barzones** to saunter around, stroll around

barzonear ▸conjug 1a◂ VI to saunter around, stroll around

basa SF [1] (*Arquit*) base (*of a column*)
[2] (= *fundamento*) basis, foundation

basalto SM basalt

basamentar ▸conjug 1a◂ VT = **basar**

basamento SM (*Arquit*) base

➤ **basar** ▸conjug 1a◂ Ⓐ VT [+ *teoría, argumento*] to base; **basó su teoría en los más modernos descubrimientos** he based his theory on the very latest discoveries
Ⓑ **basarse** VPR [1] (= *tener como base*) **~se en algo** to be based on sth; **la película está basada en hechos reales** the film is based on actual events
[2] (= *usar como base*) **para la novela me basé en la vida de mi abuela** the novel was inspired by the life of my grandmother, I based the novel on the life of my grandmother; **¿en qué te basas para decir eso?** what basis *o* grounds have you got for saying that?

basca SF [1] (*) (= *grupo*) crowd; (= *pandilla*) gang, pals *pl*
[2] (= *impulso*) **le dio la ~** he had a sudden urge
[3] (= *rabieta*) fit of rage, tantrum
[4] **bascas** (*esp LAm Med*) nausea *sing*, sick feeling *sing*; **le entraron ~s** he felt nauseated, he felt sick; **dar ~s a algn** to turn sb's stomach

bascosidad SF [1] (= *porquería*) filth, dirt
[2] (*Andes*) (= *obscenidad*) obscenity

bascoso ADJ [1] (= *delicado*) squeamish, easily upset; (*Med*) queasy
[2] (*LAm*) (= *nauseabundo*) nauseating, sick-making*
[3] (*Andes*) (= *obsceno*) obscene

báscula SF (= *con plato*) scales *pl*, weighing machine; (*romana*) steelyard; (*para camiones*) weighbridge ► **báscula biestable** flip-flop, toggle ► **báscula de(l) baño** bathroom scales *pl* ► **báscula de cocina** kitchen scales *pl* ► **báscula de puente** weighbridge

basculable ADJ (*Aut*) [*luz*] directional, with swinging beam

basculante SM tipper, dumper, dump truck (*EEUU*)

báscula-puente SF weighbridge

bascular ▸conjug 1a◂ VI [1] (= *inclinarse*) to tilt, tip up; (= *columpiarse*) to seesaw; (= *mecerse*) to rock to and fro
[2] (*Pol*) to swing
[3] (*Inform*) to toggle

base Ⓐ SF [1] (= *parte inferior*) base; **la ~ de la columna** the base of the pillar; **este jarrón tiene muy poca ~** this vase has a very narrow base; **la fecha de caducidad viene en la ~ del paquete** the use-by date is on the base *o* the bottom of the pack; **la ~ del cráneo** the base of the skull
[2] (= *fondo*) [*de pintura*] background; [*de maquillaje*] foundation; **sobre una ~ de amarillo** on a yellow background; **primero se coloca una ~ de tomate** start by laying a tomato base
[3] (= *fundamento*) basis; **ese artículo no tie-**

➤ LENGUA Y USO: **basar** B2 44.1

ne ~ científica alguna that article has no scientific basis at all; **la ~ del éxito está en el trabajo** the key to success is hard work; **carecer de ~** [*acusación*] to lack foundation, be unfounded; [*argumento*] to lack justification, be unjustified; **de ~** [*error, dato*] basic, fundamental; [*activista, apoyo*] grass-roots *antes de s*; **en ~ a** (*uso periodístico*) **un programa elaborado en ~ a criterios subjetivos** a programme based on subjective criteria; **en ~ a lo que acabamos de ver** based on what we have just seen; **en ~ a que: no publicaron la carta en ~ a que era demasiado larga** they didn't publish the letter because it was too long; **partir de una ~: un juez tiene que partir de una ~ de neutralidad absoluta** a judge must start out from a position of absolute neutrality; **partiendo de esta ~, nos planteamos la necesidad ...** on this assumption, we think it necessary ...; **partir de la ~ de que ...** to take as one's starting point that ...; **sentar las ~s de algo** to lay the foundations of sth; **Chomsky sentó las ~s de la gramática generativa** Chomsky laid the foundations of generative grammar; **su visita sentó las ~s para una futura cooperación** her visit paved the way for *o* laid the foundations of future cooperation; **sobre la ~ de algo** on the basis of sth; **hay que negociar sobre la ~ de resoluciones previas** we must negotiate on the basis of previous resolutions; ✦*MODISMO* **coger a algn fuera de ~** (*CAm, Caribe*) to catch sb out ► **base de poder** power base

[4] (= *componente principal*) **la leche es la ~ de su alimentación** his diet is milk-based; **la ~ de este jabón es la soda** this soap is soda-based; **a ~ de algo: una dieta a ~ de arroz** a rice-based diet, a diet based on rice; **un plato a ~ de verduras** a vegetable-based dish, a dish based on vegetables; **este aparato funciona a ~ de ultrasonidos** this machine works with ultrasound; **sólo conseguirás salir adelante a ~ de mucho esfuerzo** you will only get ahead by working hard; **a ~ de hacer algo** by doing sth; **así, a ~ de no hacer nada, poco vas a conseguir** you won't achieve much by doing nothing; **a ~ de insistir, la convenció para comprar la casa** by *o* through his insistence, he persuaded her to buy the house; ✦*MODISMO* **a ~ de bien** (*Esp**) **hoy hemos trabajado a ~ de bien** we've done loads of work today*; **nos divertimos a ~ de bien** we had a whale of a time*; **cenamos a ~ de bien** we had a really good meal ► **base imponible** (*Econ*) taxable income

[5] (= *conocimientos básicos*) grounding; **le falta un poco de ~** he doesn't have the proper grounding; **este manual le aportará una buena ~ de química** this handbook will give you a good grounding in chemistry

[6] (*Mil*) base ► **base aérea** air base ► **base aeronaval** naval air base ► **base avanzada** forward base ► **base de lanzamiento** launch site ► **base de operaciones** operations base ► **base espacial** space station ► **base naval** naval base

[7] **bases** [7·1] (= *condiciones*) [*de concurso*] conditions, rules; [*de convocatoria*] requirements

[7·2] (*Pol*) **las ~s** the rank and file

[8] (*Inform*) ► **base de datos** database ► **base de datos documental** documentary database ► **base de datos relacional** relational database

[9] (*Mat*) (*en una potencia*) base

[10] (*Quím*) base

[11] (*Téc*) base, mounting

[12] (*Agrimensura*) base, base line

[13] (*Ling*) (*tb* **~ derivativa**) base form

[14] (*Béisbol*) base

[15] (‡) (= *droga*) base

Ⓑ SMF (*Baloncesto*) guard

Ⓒ ADJ INV [1] (= *de partida*) [*campamento, campo*] base *antes de s*; [*puerto*] home *antes de s*; **dejamos el campamento ~ por la mañana** we left base camp in the morning

[2] (= *básico*) [*idea*] basic; [*documento, texto*] provisional, draft; **han aprobado el texto ~ para el nuevo convenio** they have approved the provisional *o* draft text of the new agreement; **alimento ~** staple (food); **color ~** base colour *o* (*EEUU*) color; *ver tb* **salario, sueldo**

baseballista SMF (*LAm*) baseball player

basebolero/a Ⓐ ADJ (*Caribe*) baseball *antes de s*

Ⓑ SM/F (*Caribe*) baseball player

básica SF = **EGB**

▼**básico** ADJ basic

Basilea SF Basle, Basel

basílica SF basilica

basilisco SM (*Mit*) basilisk; (*Méx*) iguana; ✦*MODISMOS* **estar hecho un ~** to be furious; **ponerse como un ~** to get terribly angry

básket SM basketball

basoto ADJ of/from Lesotho

basquear ▸conjug 1a◂ (*LAm*) VI (= *sentir náuseas*) to be nauseated, feel sick; **hacer ~ a algn** to make sb feel sick, turn sb's stomach

básquet SM (*tb* **pelota ~**) basketball

basquetbolero/a Ⓐ ADJ (*LAm*) basketball *antes de s*

Ⓑ SM/F (*LAm*) basketball player

basquetbolista SMF (*LAm*) basketball player

basquetbolístico ADJ (*LAm*) basketball *antes de s*

basquiña SF skirt

basta SF tacking stitch, basting stitch

bastante Ⓐ ADJ [1] (= *suficiente*) enough (**para** for); **hay ~ sitio para todos** there is enough room for everyone; **¿no tienes ya ~s?** haven't you got enough?; **no había ~ público** there wasn't a big enough audience

[2] (= *mucho*) quite a lot of, a fair amount of; **han dejado ~ comida** they've left quite a lot of *o* a fair amount of food; **hace ~ frío** it's quite cold; **se marchó hace ~ rato** he left quite some time ago; **la calidad deja ~ que desear** the quality leaves much to be desired

[3] (= *muchos*) quite a lot of, quite a few; **había ~s invitados en la recepción** there were quite a lot of *o* quite a few guests at the reception; **—¿tienes muchos cuadros? —bastantes** "do you have many paintings?" — "quite a few"

[4] (*Méx*) (= *demasiado*) too much

Ⓑ ADV [1] (= *suficiente*) enough; **ya has comido ~** you've eaten enough; **no tenemos ~ para ir de vacaciones** we haven't enough to go on holiday; **ya tienen ~ como para que vayamos también nosotros con nuestros problemas** they've got enough on their plate already without us taking our problems along; **es lo ~ alto como para alcanzarlo** he's tall enough to reach it

[2] (= *de forma considerable*) (*con verbos*) quite a lot; (*con adjetivos, adverbios*) quite; **los niños han cambiado ~** the children have changed a fair amount *o* quite a lot; **lo he visto ~ últimamente** I've seen a fair amount of him *o* quite a lot of him recently; **me gusta ~** I quite like it, I like it quite a lot; **el libro está ~ bien** it's a fairly good book, it's quite a good book; **estoy ~ cansado** I'm rather *o* quite tired; **habla inglés ~ bien** she speaks quite good English, her English is quite good; **vivo ~ lejos** I live quite a long way away

bastantemente ADV sufficiently

bastar ▸conjug 1a◂ Ⓐ VI [1] (= *ser suficiente*) to be enough; **eso me basta** that's enough for me; **esta información debería ~ al juez** this information should be enough for the judge; **baste decir que ...** suffice it to say that ...; **como ejemplo, baste decir que los beneficios han aumentado en un 20%** by way of example, suffice it to say that profits have risen by 20%; **~ para hacer algo** to be enough to do sth; **suele ~ una esponja para absorber el agua** a sponge is usually enough *o* all it takes to soak up the water; **me bastó una foto para reconocerlo** one look at a photo was enough to recognize him, one look at a photo was all it took for me to recognize him; **una mirada bastó para hacerme callar** one look was enough to make me shut up, one look was all it took to make me shut up; **me bastó leer el primer párrafo para saber que era un genio** I only had to read the first paragraph to know that he was a genius; **basta que ... para que ...: basta que queramos llegar pronto a casa, para que haya un atasco** just when we want to get home quickly, there's a traffic jam; **basta saber que ...** it is enough to know that ...

[2] (*terciopersonal*) **con eso basta** that's enough; **me basta con tu palabra** your word's good enough for me; **con la intención basta** it's the thought that counts; **basta con dar una vuelta por la ciudad para ...** you only need to take a walk round the city to ...; **no basta con ...** it's not enough to ...; **no basta con decir que uno no es culpable, hay que demostrarlo** it's not enough to say you're not guilty, you have to prove it

[3] (*exclamación*) **¡basta!** ◊ **¡basta ya!** that will do!, that's enough!; **¡basta de charla!** that's enough chatter!; **¡basta de tonterías!** that's enough nonsense!; **¡basta ya de llorar!** that's enough crying!

[4] ✦*MODISMOS* **hasta decir basta: nevó hasta decir basta** it snowed like there was no tomorrow; **bailamos hasta decir basta** we danced till we dropped; **es honrado hasta decir basta** he's as honest as the day is long; **~ y sobrar** to be more than enough; **con esa comida basta y sobra para un mes** that food is more than enough for a month; **no hablamos alemán, nos basta y sobra con el inglés** we don't speak German, English is all we need

Ⓑ **bastarse** VPR **yo sola me basto para cuidarlo** I'm well capable of looking after him on my own; **se bastan y se sobran para llevar ellos el negocio** they're more than capable of running the business themselves; **~se a sí mismo** to be self-sufficient

➤ LENGUA Y USO: **básico** 53.2

bastardear ▸conjug 1a◂ Ⓐ VT to bastardize
Ⓑ VI [1] (*Bot*) to degenerate
[2] (= *degenerar*) to degenerate, fall away

bastardía SF [1] (= *cualidad*) bastardy
[2] (= *bajeza*) meanness, baseness
[3] (= *acción vil*) wicked thing

bastardilla SF (*Tip*) (*tb* **letra ~**) italic type, italics *pl*; **en ~** in italics; **poner en ~** to italicize

bastardo/a Ⓐ ADJ [1] (= *ilegítimo*) bastard
[2] (= *mezquino*) mean, base
[3] (*Bot*) (= *híbrido*) hybrid, mixed
Ⓑ SM/F bastard

bastear ▸conjug 1a◂ VT to tack, stitch loosely

bastedad SF, **basteza** SF coarseness, vulgarity

bastero/a SM/F (*Méx*) pickpocket

bastes‡ SMPL (*Esp*) fingers

bastez SF coarseness, vulgarity

bastidor SM [1] (= *armazón*) (*Téc, Cos*) frame, framework; [*de ventana*] frame; [*de lienzo*] stretcher; [*de vehículo*] chassis
[2] (*Teat*) wing; **entre ~es** behind the scenes; **estar entre ~es** to be offstage; **dirigir entre ~es** to pull the strings
[3] (*Andes, Cono Sur*) (= *celosía*) lattice window
[4] (*Caribe*) (= *catre*) metal bedstead
[5] (*Caribe, Méx*) (= *colchón*) interior sprung mattress

bastilla SF hem

bastillar ▸conjug 1a◂ VT to hem

bastimentar ▸conjug 1a◂ VT to supply, provision

bastimento SM [1] (= *provisiones*) supply
[2] (*Náut*) vessel

bastión SM bastion

basto Ⓐ ADJ [1] [*superficie, piel*] coarse
[2] [*persona, comportamiento*] rude, vulgar
Ⓑ SM [1] (*Naipes*) ace of clubs; **bastos** clubs (*one of the suits in the Spanish card deck*); ✦MODISMO **pintan ~s** things are getting tough, the going's getting tough; → BARAJA ESPAÑOLA
[2] (= *albarda*) packsaddle
[3] (*LAm*) **bastos** soft leather pad (*used under the saddle*)

bastón SM [1] (*para andar*) (walking) stick; **necesita llevar ~ para andar** he needs a stick for walking ▸ **bastón alpino, bastón de alpinista** alpenstock ▸ **bastón de esquí** ski stick ▸ **bastón de estoque** swordstick ▸ **bastón de montaña** alpenstock
[2] [*de policía*] truncheon, billy (club) (*EEUU*); [*de militar*] baton; ✦MODISMOS **empuñar el ~** to take command; **meter el ~** to intervene ▸ **bastón de mando** baton, sign of authority
[3] (*Heráldica*) vertical bar, pallet

bastonazo SM (= *golpe*) blow (*with a stick*)

bastoncillo SM [1] (*para los oídos*) cotton bud, Q-tip® (*EEUU*)
[2] (*Anat*) rod, retinal rod

bastoncito SM [1] [*de pan*] bread stick
[2] (*para los oídos*) cotton bud, Q-tip® (*EEUU*)

bastonear ▸conjug 1a◂ VT to beat (*with a stick*), hit (*with a stick*)

bastonera SF umbrella stand

bastonero/a SM/F [1] [*de bailes*] master of ceremonies (*at a dance*), compere, emcee (*EEUU*)
[2] (*Caribe*) scoundrel, tough nut*

bastón-taburete SM shooting stick

basuco* SM cocaine base, unpurified cocaine

basura SF [1] (= *desechos*) (*en casa*) rubbish, garbage (*EEUU*); (*por el suelo*) litter; **hay mucha ~ en la calle** there's a lot of litter in the street; **"prohibido arrojar basuras (y escombros)"** "no dumping", "no tipping" ▸ **basura espacial** space junk ▸ **basura radiactiva** radioactive waste
[2] (= *contenedor*) (*en casa*) dustbin, trash can (*EEUU*); (*en la calle*) litter bin, trash can (*EEUU*); **tirar algo a la ~** to put o throw sth in the bin
[3] (= *persona o cosa despreciable*) trash, rubbish; **es una ~*** he's a shocker*, he's a rotter*; **la novela es una ~** the novel is rubbish

basural SM (*LAm*) rubbish dump

basurear ▸conjug 1a◂ VT **~ a algn** (*Cono Sur*) (= *empujar*) to push sb along; (= *humillar*) to humiliate sb; (= *insultar*) to be rude to sb, rubbish sb*

basurero/a Ⓐ SM/F (= *persona*) dustman/dustwoman, garbage collector (*EEUU*)
Ⓑ SM [1] (= *vertedero*) rubbish dump; (*Agr*) dung heap
[2] (*LAm*) (= *cubo*) litter bin, trash can (*EEUU*)

basuriento ADJ (*Andes, Cono Sur*) full of rubbish

Basutolandia SF (*Hist*) Basutoland

bata[1] SF [1] (*para levantarse de la cama*) dressing gown; (*encima de la ropa*) housecoat; [*de playa*] wrap
[2] [*de médico*] white coat; [*de científico*] laboratory coat, lab coat ▸ **bata blanca** white coat
[3] (= *guardapolvo*) overall, smock

bata[2‡] SF mother

batacazo SM [1] (= *porrazo*) thump
[2] (*LAm*) (= *golpe de suerte*) stroke of luck, fluke

bataclán SM (*LAm*) striptease show, burlesque show (*EEUU*)

bataclana SF (*LAm*) striptease girl, stripper

batahola* SF (= *ruido*) din, hullabaloo*; (= *jaleo*) rumpus*

bataholear ▸conjug 1a◂ VI, **batajolear** ▸conjug 1a◂ VI (*Andes*) (= *pelear*) to brawl; (= *ser travieso*) to be mischievous, play pranks

batalla SF [1] (= *lucha*) battle; **librar** o **trabar ~** to do battle ▸ **batalla campal** pitched battle
[2] (= *sufrimiento*) fight, struggle; **ropa de ~** everyday clothes *pl*
[3] (*Aut*) wheelbase

batallador(a) Ⓐ ADJ battling, fighting
Ⓑ SM/F (= *luchador*) battler, fighter; (*Dep*) fencer

batallar ▸conjug 1a◂ VI (= *luchar*) to battle, fight

batallita SF **contar ~s*** to go over old times

batallón Ⓐ ADJ **cuestión batallona** vexed question
Ⓑ SM battalion ▸ **batallón de castigo, batallón disciplinario** punishment squad

batán SM [1] (= *lugar*) fulling mill; (= *herramienta*) fulling hammer
[2] (*Cono Sur*) (= *tintorería*) dry cleaner's
[3] (*Andes*) (= *espesura de tela*) thickness (*of cloth*)

batanar ▸conjug 1a◂ VT [1] (*Téc*) to full
[2] (*) to beat, thrash

batanear ▸conjug 1a◂ VT = **batanar 2**

batanero/a SM/F fuller

bataola SF = **batahola**

batasuno/a Ⓐ ADJ of Herri Batasuna
Ⓑ SM/F member/supporter of Herri Batasuna

batata Ⓐ ADJ [1] (*Cono Sur*) (= *tímido*) bashful, shy
[2] (*Caribe, Cono Sur*) (= *simple*) simple, gullible
[3] (*Caribe*) (= *llenito*) chubby, plump; (= *rechoncho*) squat
Ⓑ SF [1] (*Bot*) sweet potato, yam
[2] (*Cono Sur*) (= *timidez*) bashfulness, embarrassment
[3] (*Andes, Caribe*) (= *pantorrilla*) calf (*of the leg*)
[4] (*Cono Sur**) (= *coche*) car, auto(mobile) (*EEUU*)

batatar SM (*LAm*) sweet potato field

batatazo* SM (*esp LAm*) (= *golpe de suerte*) stroke of luck, fluke

batayola SF (*Náut*) rail

bate SM (*esp LAm*) bat, baseball bat; ✦MODISMO **estar al ~ de algo** (*CAm, Caribe*) to be in charge of sth ▸ **bate de béisbol** baseball bat ▸ **bate de polo** polo stick

batea SF [1] (= *bandeja*) tray
[2] (*LAm*) (= *artesa para lavar*) washing trough
[3] (*Min*) washing pan
[4] (*Ferro*) flat car, low waggon
[5] (*Náut*) flat-bottomed boat, punt

bateador(a) SM/F batter

batear ▸conjug 1a◂ Ⓐ VT to hit
Ⓑ VI [1] (*esp LAm Dep*) to bat
[2] (*Caribe**) (= *tragar*) to overeat

batel SM small boat, skiff

batelero/a SM/F boatman/boatwoman

batelón SM (*LAm*) canoe

batería Ⓐ SF [1] (*Elec*) battery; **se ha agotado la ~** the battery is flat; ✦MODISMO **(re)cargar las ~s** to recharge one's batteries ▸ **batería de arranque** starter battery ▸ **batería seca** dry battery
[2] (= *fila*) [*de luces*] bank, battery; (*en teatro*) footlights *pl*; (*para gallinas*) battery; [*de soldados*] battery; **aparcar en ~** to park at an angle to the kerb
[3] (*Mús*) (= *instrumento*) drums *pl*; [*de orquesta*] percussion instruments *pl*; **¿tocas la ~?** do you play the drums?
[4] (*Culin*) ▸ **una batería de cocina** a set of kitchen equipment
[5] (*LAm Béisbol*) hit, stroke
[6] (*Andes*) (= *ronda de bebidas*) round
[7] (*Méx*) **dar ~** to raise a rumpus; **dar ~ a algn*** to make trouble for sb, make a lot of work for sb
Ⓑ SMF (= *persona*) (*en grupo*) drummer

baterista SMF (*LAm*) drummer

batey SM (*Caribe*) outbuildings *pl* (*of sugar refinery*)

batiburrillo SM hotchpotch, hodgepodge (*EEUU*)

baticola SF [1] [*de montura*] crupper
[2] (*Andes*) (= *taparrabos*) loincloth
[3] (*Cono Sur*) (= *pañal*) nappy, diaper (*EEUU*)

batida SF [1] (= *búsqueda*) [1·1] (*Caza*) beating
[1·2] [*de policía, ejército*] (*buscando algo*) search; (*haciendo detenciones*) raid; **por las noches salíamos a hacer una ~** we used to comb o search the area at night; **dieron una ~ por el centro de la ciudad** they carried out a raid in the city centre
[2] (= *acuñación*) minting

[3] (*Andes*) (= *persecución*) chase
[4] (*Andes, Caribe*) (= *paliza*) beating, thrashing

batido Ⓐ PP *de* **batir**
Ⓑ ADJ [1] [*camino*] well-trodden, beaten
[2] [*seda*] shot
Ⓒ SM [1] (= *bebida*) milk shake, shake (*esp EEUU*); **un ~ de frutas** a fruit shake
[2] (= *golpe*) beat, beating; **se oía un ~ de tambores** you could hear drums beating *o* the beat of drums
[3] (*Culin*) (= *rebozo*) batter

batidor(a) Ⓐ SM/F [1] (*Caza*) beater; (*Mil*) scout
[2] (*Orfebrería*) ► **batidor(a) de oro** gold beater
[3] (*Arg*) (= *delator*) informer
Ⓑ SM [1] (*Culin*) whisk ► **batidor mecánico** egg beater, egg whisk
[2] (= *peine*) wide-toothed comb
[3] (*CAm*) (= *vasija*) wooden bowl, mixing bowl

batidora SF [1] (*eléctrica*) (food) mixer, blender ► **batidora de brazo** hand blender
[2] (*manual*) whisk

batiente Ⓐ ADJ *ver* **mandíbula**
Ⓑ SM [1] (= *marco de puerta*) jamb; (= *marco de ventana*) frame, case; (= *hoja de puerta*) leaf, panel
[2] (*Náut*) open coastline
[3] (*Mús*) damper

batifondo SM (*Cono Sur*) uproar, tumult

batín SM [1] (= *bata de hombre*) [*de casa*] dressing gown; [*de playa*] beach-wrap
[2] (= *chaqueta*) smoking jacket

batintín SM gong

batir ▸conjug 3a◂ Ⓐ VT [1] (= *vencer, superar*) [+ *adversario, enemigo*] to beat; [+ *récord*] to break, beat; **batieron al Osasuna por 4 a 1** they beat Osasuna 4-1; **el cáncer ha sido batido en muchos frentes** cancer has been beaten on many fronts; **batió el récord mundial de 400 metros vallas** she broke *o* beat the world 400 metres hurdles record; **las ventas han batido todos los récords este año** sales have broken *o* beaten all records this year
[2] (*Culin*) [+ *huevos*] to beat, whisk; [+ *nata, crema*] to whip; [+ *mantequilla, margarina*] to cream; [+ *leche*] (*para hacer mantequilla*) to churn; **se bate el queso con el huevo** beat the cheese with the egg
[3] (= *recorrer*) (*Mil*) to comb, search; (*Caza*) to beat; **la policía batió la zona pero no encontró nada** the police combed *o* searched the area but found nothing
[4] (= *agitar*) [+ *alas*] to flap; [+ *pestañas*] to flutter; [+ *brazos*] to flap, wave; **~ palmas** to clap one's hands; **~ el vuelo** to fly off, take flight
[5] (= *golpear*) [5·1] [+ *tambor, metal*] to beat; **el ~ de los martillos contra el metal** the sound of hammers beating the metal, the clang of hammers on metal
[5·2] [*lluvia, olas, viento*] to beat on *o* against; [*sol*] to beat down on; **las olas batían la orilla de la playa** the waves were beating on *o* against the shore; **el viento batía con fuerza las ventanas** the wind was pounding on *o* against the windows
[5·3] [+ *moneda*] to mint; *ver tb* **cobre 1**
[6] (= *derribar*) [+ *edificio*] to knock down, demolish; [+ *privilegio*] to do away with
[7] (*Mil*) [+ *muro*] to batter, pound; **los cañones batieron las murallas de la ciudad** the cannons battered *o* pounded the city walls
[8] (= *cardar*) [+ *lana*] to comb out, card; [+ *pelo*] to backcomb
[9] (*Andes*) (= *enjuagar*) [+ *ropa*] to rinse (out)
[10] (*Arg*) (= *denunciar*) to inform on
Ⓑ VI [1] [*lluvia, olas, viento*] to beat; **el viento batía con fuerza contra los cristales** the wind pounded on *o* against the windows
[2] [*puerta, persiana*] **se oía el ~ de una puerta** you could hear a door banging; **baten las persianas con el viento** the blinds rattle in the wind
[3] [*tambor*] to ring out, sound
Ⓒ **batirse** VPR [1] (= *luchar*) to fight; **se batió contra la enfermedad con todas sus fuerzas** she fought the illness with all her strength; **~se con algn** to fight sb, have a fight with sb; **~se en duelo** to fight a duel
[2] **~se en retirada** to beat a retreat

batiscafo SM bathyscaph, bathyscaphe

batista SF cambric, batiste

bato[1] SM simpleton

bato[2]* SM father

batonista SF drum majorette

batracio SM batrachian

Batuecas SFPL **las ~** ✦MODISMO **estar en las batuecas** to be daydreaming, be in a world of one's own

batueco* ADJ stupid, silly

batuque* SM (*Cono Sur*) uproar

batuquear* ▸conjug 1a◂ VT (*Andes, Méx*) (= *batir*) to shake, shake up

baturrillo SM hotchpotch, hodgepodge (*EEUU*)

baturro/a Ⓐ ADJ (= *rudo*) uncouth, rough
Ⓑ SM/F Aragonese peasant

batusino/a SM/F idiot, fool

batuta SF (*Mús*) baton; ✦MODISMO **llevar la ~** to be the boss, be firmly in command

batzoki SM political party bar/headquarters

baudio SM (*Inform*) baud

baúl SM [1] (= *arca*) trunk; ✦MODISMO **el ~ de los recuerdos** the back of the mind ► **baúl armario** wardrobe trunk ► **baúl camarote** cabin trunk ► **baúl de viaje** portmanteau ► **baúl mundo** large trunk, Saratoga trunk ► **baúl ropero** wardrobe trunk
[2] (*LAm Aut*) boot, trunk (*EEUU*)
[3] (*) (= *vientre*) belly

bauprés SM bowsprit

bausa SF (*Andes, Méx*) (= *pereza*) laziness, idleness

bausán SM, **bausana** SF [1] (= *figura*) dummy; (*fig*) simpleton
[2] (*Andes*) (= *holgazán*) good-for-nothing

bausano SM (*CAm*) idler, lazy person

bauseador SM (*Andes*) idler, lazy person

bautismal ADJ baptismal

bautismo SM baptism, christening; ✦MODISMO **romper el ~ a algn*** to knock sb's block off* ► **bautismo de fuego** baptism of fire ► **bautismo del aire** maiden flight

Bautista Ⓐ ADJ Baptist; **Iglesia ~** Baptist Church; **San Juan ~** St John the Baptist
Ⓑ SMF Baptist; **el ~** the Baptist

bautizar ▸conjug 1f◂ VT [1] (*Rel*) to baptize, christen; **la ~on con el nombre de Teresa** she was christened Teresa
[2] (= *nombrar*) [+ *objeto, barco*] to christen, name
[3] (= *poner apodo*) to nickname, dub
[4] (= *diluir*) [+ *vino*] to water, dilute; [+ *persona*] to drench, soak

bautizo SM [1] (= *acto*) baptism, christening
[2] (= *celebración*) christening party

bauxita SF bauxite

bávaro/a ADJ, SM/F Bavarian

Baviera SF Bavaria

baya SF berry

bayajá SM (*Caribe*) headscarf

báyer* SF (*Cono Sur*) dope*, pot*

bayeta SF [1] (= *trapo de cocina*) (cleaning) cloth; **¿has pasado la ~ por la mesa?** have you wiped the table?
[2] (= *tejido*) flannel
[3] (*Billar*) baize
[4] (*Andes*) (= *pañal*) nappy, diaper (*EEUU*)

bayetón SM [1] (= *trapo*) bearskin, thick woollen cloth
[2] (*Andes*) (= *poncho largo*) long poncho

bayo Ⓐ ADJ bay
Ⓑ SM [1] (= *caballo*) bay, bay horse
[2] (*Méx*) bean

Bayona SF Bayonne

bayoneta SF bayonet ► **bayonetas caladas** fixed bayonets; **luchar a ~s caladas** to fight with fixed bayonets

bayonetazo SM (= *arremetida*) bayonet thrust; (= *herida*) bayonet wound

bayonetear ▸conjug 1a◂ VT (*LAm*) to bayonet

bayoya SM (*Caribe*) row, uproar; **es un ~ aquí** it's pandemonium here

bayunca SF (*CAm*) bar, saloon

bayunco/a Ⓐ ADJ (*CAm*) (= *tonto*) silly, stupid; (= *tímido*) shy; (= *grosero*) crude, vulgar
Ⓑ SM/F (*CAm*) uncouth peasant (*name applied by Guatemalans to other Central Americans*)

baza SF [1] (*Naipes*) trick; **hacer una ~** to make *o* win a trick ► **baza de honor** honours trick
[2] (*en asunto, negocio*) (= *recurso*) weapon; (= *oportunidad*) chance; **han usado el miedo como ~ electoral** they have used fear as an electoral weapon; **Carlos es una de las principales ~s del equipo** Carlos is one of the team's main weapons; **el equipo supo aprovechar sus ~s** the team made the most of its chances; **jugar una ~: si juega bien su ~, conseguirá el trabajo** if he plays his cards right, he'll get the job; **no es el momento de jugar su principal ~** this is not the time to play their trump card; **están jugando su última ~** they are playing their last hand; **Alemania juega una ~ muy firme para el Mundial** Germany has a good chance of winning the World Cup; ✦MODISMOS **meter ~*** to butt in; **le encanta meter ~ aunque no tenga ni idea del tema** she loves butting in even though she has no idea about the subject; **cuando habla no deja meter ~ a nadie** when he's speaking he doesn't let anybody get a word in edgeways; **sacar ~ de algo** (*Esp*) to turn sth to one's (own) advantage; **es de los que siempre sacan ~ de todo** he's one of those people who always turns everything to their own advantage

bazar SM [1] (= *mercado*) bazaar
[2] (= *tienda*) (= *grandes almacenes*) large retail store; (= *juguetería*) toy shop; (*LAm*) bazaar, charity fair; (*Méx*) second-hand shop; (*Cono

Sur) (= *ferretería*) ironmonger's, ironmonger's shop

bazo Ⓐ ADJ yellowish brown
Ⓑ SM (*Anat*) spleen

bazofia SF [1] (= *sobras*) leftovers *pl*, scraps *pl* of food; (*para cerdos*) pigswill
[2] (= *producto de mala calidad*) pigswill, hogwash (*EEUU*)

bazooka SF, **bazuca** SF bazooka

bazucar ▸conjug 1g◂ VT, **bazuquear** ▸conjug 1a◂ VT (= *agitar*) to stir; (= *sacudir*) to shake, jolt

bazuqueo SM (= *agitación*) stirring; (= *sacudida*) shaking, jolting ► **bazuqueo gástrico** rumblings *pl* in the stomach

BCE SM ABR (= **Banco Central Europeo**) ECB

BCG SM ABR (= **Bacilo Calmette-Guérin**) BCG

Bco. ABR (= **Banco**) bk

be[1] SF *name of the letter B*; ✦*MODISMOS* **be por be** in detail; **esto tiene las tres bes** (*"bueno, bonito y barato"*) this is really very nice, this is just perfect ► **be chica** (*Méx*) V ► **be larga** (*LAm*), **be grande** (*Méx*) B

be[2] SM baa

beata⁑ SF (*Fin*) one peseta; *ver tb* **beato**

beatería SF (= *santidad*) affected piety; (= *hipocresía*) cant, sanctimoniousness

beaterío* SM goody-goodies* *pl*, sanctimonious people *pl*

beatificación SF beatification

beatificar ▸conjug 1g◂ VT to beatify

beatífico ADJ beatific

beatitud SF (= *santidad*) beatitude; (= *bendición*) blessedness; **su Beatitud** His Holiness

beatnik ['bitnik] SMF (*pl* **beatniks** ['bitnik]) beatnik

beato/a Ⓐ ADJ [1] (*Rel*) (= *beatificado*) blessed
[2] (= *piadoso*) devout, pious; (= *santurrón*) sanctimonious
[3] (*frm, hum*) (= *feliz*) happy
Ⓑ SM/F [1] (*Rel*) lay brother/sister
[2] (= *devoto*) devout man/woman
[3] (*pey*) (= *hombre*) holy Joe*; (= *mujer*) excessively pious woman, sanctimonious woman; *ver tb* **beata**

Beatriz SF Beatrice

bebe/a SM/F (*Cono Sur*) baby

bebé SM baby; **~ foca** baby seal; **dos ~s panda** two baby pandas ► **bebé de diseño** designer baby; *ver tb* **bebé-probeta**

bebecina SF (*Andes*) (= *embriaguez*) drunkenness; (= *juerga*) drinking spree

bebedera SF [1] (*Andes*) (= *embriaguez*) habitual drunkenness
[2] (*CAm, Méx*) (= *juerga*) drinking bout, drunken spree

bebedero Ⓐ ADJ drinkable, good to drink
Ⓑ SM [1] (*para aves*) water bowl; (*en jaula*) water dispenser
[2] (*para ganado*) drinking trough
[3] [*de botijo, jarro*] spout
[4] (*Chile, Méx*) drinking fountain
[5] (*Andes Com*) *establishment selling alcoholic drinks*

bebedizo Ⓐ ADJ drinkable
Ⓑ SM (*medicinal*) potion; (*mágico*) love potion, philtre, philter (*EEUU*)

bebedor(a) Ⓐ ADJ hard-drinking
Ⓑ SM/F drinker; (*pey*) heavy drinker ► **bebedor(a) empedernido/a** hardened drinker

bebendurria SF [1] (= *juerga*) drinking spree
[2] (*Andes, Méx*) (= *borrachera*) drunkenness
[3] (*Cono Sur*) (= *fiesta*) drinking party

bebé-probeta SMF (*pl* **bebés-probeta**) test-tube baby

beber ▸conjug 2a◂ Ⓐ VT [1] [+ *agua, leche, cerveza*] to drink; **¿qué quieres (de) ~?** what would you like to drink?; **no bebe alcohol** he doesn't drink; **~ algo con la lengua** to lap sth up; **~ algo a sorbos** to sip sth; **~ algo a tragos** to gulp sth, gulp sth down
[2] (*frm*) (= *absorber*) to drink in; **bebían las palabras del orador** they were drinking in the speaker's words; **toda su filosofía la bebió de Platón** all his philosophy comes from Plato
Ⓑ VI [1] (*gen*) to drink; **no debes ~ y comer a la vez** you shouldn't eat and drink at the same time; **bebió de la botella** he drank straight from the bottle
[2] (= *beber alcohol*) to drink; **—¿quieres vino? —no, gracias, no bebo** "would you like some wine?" — "no thanks, I don't drink"; **su padre bebe muchísimo** his father drinks a lot, his father is a heavy drinker; **si bebes, no conduzcas** don't drink and drive; ✦*MODISMO* **~ como un cosaco** to drink like a fish
[3] (= *brindar*) **~ por algo/algn** to drink to sth/sb; **bebimos por mi nuevo hijo** we drank to my new son; *ver tb* **salud 3**
Ⓒ **beberse** VPR to drink; **bébetelo que nos vamos** drink up, we're going; **se lo bebió todo** he drank it all (up)
Ⓓ SM drinking; **disfruto con el buen ~** I like a (good) drink

beberaje SM (*Cono Sur*) drink (*esp alcoholic*)

bebercio* SM booze*

bebereca* SF (*Andes*) booze*

beberecua* SF (*Andes*) [1] (= *juerga*) boozing*
[2] = **bebereca**

beberrón/ona ADJ, SM/F = **bebedor**

bebestible Ⓐ ADJ (*LAm*) drinkable
Ⓑ **bebestibles** SMPL drinks

bebezón SF (*Caribe*) [1] (= *bebida*) drink, booze*
[2] (= *embriaguez*) drunkenness; (= *juerga*) drinking spree

bebezona* SF booze-up*

bebible ADJ drinkable; **no ~** undrinkable

bebida SF [1] (= *líquido*) drink, beverage ► **bebida no alcohólica** soft drink, non-alcoholic drink ► **bebida refrescante** soft drink
[2] (*tb* **~ alcohólica**) drink, alcoholic drink; **dado a la ~** hard-drinking; **darse** *o* **entregarse a la ~** to take to drink; **tener mala ~** to get violent with drink

bebido Ⓐ PP *de* **beber**
Ⓑ ADJ **estar ~** to be drunk

bebistrajo* SM nasty drink, filthy drink

bebito/a SM/F (*Cono Sur*) little baby

BEBS ABR (*Inform*) (= **basura entra, basura sale**) GIGO

beca SF [1] (= *ayuda*) (*por méritos o en concurso*) scholarship; (*ayuda económica general*) grant
[2] (= *vestido*) sash, hood

becacina SF snipe

becada SF (*Orn*) woodcock

becado/a Ⓐ ADJ [*estudiante*] who holds a scholarship; [*investigador*] who holds an award; **está aquí ~** he's here on a grant
Ⓑ SM/F (*por méritos o en concurso*) scholarship holder; (*por ayuda económica general*) grant holder

becar ▸conjug 1g◂ VT to award a scholarship/grant to

becario/a SM/F [1] (= *con beca*) = **becado**
[2] (= *estudioso*) scholar, fellow

becerrada SF (*Taur*) fight with young bulls

becerrillo SM calfskin

becerro SM [1] (= *animal*) yearling calf, bullock ► **becerro de oro** golden calf
[2] (= *piel*) calfskin
[3] (*Rel, Hist*) cartulary, register

bechamel SF béchamel sauce

becuadro SM (*Mús*) natural sign

Beda SM Bede

bedel(a) SM/F [*de facultad*] ≈ head porter; [*de colegio*] ≈ janitor; [*de edificio oficial, museo*] caretaker

bedoya SM (*Andes*) idiot

beduino/a ADJ, SM/F Bedouin; (*pey*) savage

befa SF jeer, taunt

befar ▸conjug 1a◂ VT, **befarse** VPR **~(se) de** to scoff *o* jeer at, taunt

befo Ⓐ ADJ [1] (= *de labios gruesos*) thick-lipped
[2] (= *zambo*) knock-kneed
Ⓑ SM (= *labio*) lip

begonia SF begonia

behaviorismo SM behaviourism, behaviorism (*EEUU*)

behaviorista ADJ, SMF behaviourist, behaviorist (*EEUU*)

BEI SM ABR (= **Banco Europeo de Inversiones**) EIB

beibi⁑ SF girlfriend, bird⁑, chick (*EEUU*⁑)

beicon SM bacon

beige [beis] ADJ, SM beige

Beirut SM Beirut

béisbol SM baseball

beisbolero/a Ⓐ ADJ (*LAm*) baseball *antes de s*
Ⓑ SM/F (*esp LAm*) (= *jugador*) baseball player; (= *aficionado*) baseball fan

beisbolista SM (*esp LAm*) baseball player

beisbolístico ADJ baseball *antes de s*

bejuco SM (*LAm*) (= *caña*) reed, liana; ✦*MODISMO* **no sacar ~** (*Caribe**) to miss the boat

bejuquear ▸conjug 1a◂ VT (*LAm*) (= *zurrar*) to beat, thrash

bejuquero SM (*Andes*) confused situation, mess

bejuquillo SM [1] (*Caribe, Méx Bot*) *variety of liana*
[2] (*Andes*) (= *vainilla*) vanilla

bejuquiza SF (*Andes*) beating, thrashing

Belcebú SM Beelzebub

beldad SF (*liter*) [1] (= *cualidad*) beauty
[2] (= *persona*) beauty, belle

beldar ▸conjug 1j◂ VT to winnow (*with a fork*)

belduque SM (*CAm, Méx*) pointed sword

Belén SM Bethlehem

belén SM [1] [*de Navidad*] nativity scene, crib, crèche (*EEUU*) ► **belén viviente** *representation*

of the Nativity by real people
[2] (= *confusión*) bedlam; (= *lugar*) madhouse; ✦MODISMO **meterse en belenes** to get into a mess, get into trouble

belenista SMF maker of nativity scenes

beleño SM henbane

belfo ADJ, SM = **befo**

belga ADJ, SMF Belgian

Bélgica SF Belgium

bélgico ADJ Belgian

Belgrado SM Belgrade

Belice SM Belize

beliceño/a ADJ, SM/F Belizean

belicismo SM warmongering, militarism

belicista Ⓐ ADJ warmongering, militaristic
Ⓑ SMF warmonger

bélico ADJ [1] [*actitud*] warlike
[2] [*material, juguete*] war *antes de s*

belicosidad SF (= *actitud*) warlike spirit; (= *agresividad*) belligerence, aggressiveness

belicoso ADJ (= *guerrero*) warlike; (= *agresivo*) bellicose, aggressive

beligerancia SF belligerency

beligerante ADJ belligerent; **no ~** non-belligerent

belinún/una SM/F (*Cono Sur*) simpleton, blockhead*

belitre SMF [1] (= *granuja*) rogue, scoundrel
[2] (*Andes, CAm*) [*niño*] (= *astuto*) shrewd child; (= *inquieto*) restless child

bellaco/a Ⓐ ADJ [1] [*persona*] (= *malvado*) wicked; (= *astuto*) cunning, sly; (= *pícaro*) rascally
[2] (*Cono Sur, Méx*) [*caballo*] vicious, hard-to-control; (*Andes, CAm*) brave
Ⓑ SM/F (= *bribón*) scoundrel, rogue
Ⓒ SM (*Cono Sur, Méx*) (= *caballo*) difficult horse

belladona SF deadly nightshade

bellamente ADV (= *hermosamente*) beautifully; (= *con gran elegancia*) finely

bellaqueada SF (*Cono Sur*) bucking, rearing

bellaquear ▸conjug 1a◂ VI [1] (= *engañar*) to cheat, be crooked*
[2] (*Andes, Cono Sur*) (= *encabritarse*) to shy; (= *ser terco*) to dig one's heels in

bellaquería SF [1] (= *acto*) dirty trick
[2] (= *cualidad*) (= *maldad*) wickedness; (= *astucia*) cunning, slyness

belleza SF [1] (= *cualidad*) beauty, loveliness
[2] (= *persona bella*) beauty; **es una ~ (de mujer)** she's a beautiful woman; **Juan es una ~ (de hombre)** Juan is a very handsome man
[3] (= *cosa bella*) beauty; **las ~s de Mallorca** the beauties of Majorca
[4] **de ~** beauty *antes de s*

bello ADJ [1] (= *hermoso*) beautiful, lovely; **es una bella persona** he's a lovely person; **Bellas Artes** Fine Art
[2] (= *elegante*) fine

bellota SF [1] [*de encina*] acorn
[2] [*de clavel*] bud
[3] (*Anat**) Adam's apple
[4] (*para perfumes*) perfume box, pomander
[5] ► **bellota de mar, bellota marina** sea urchin

bemba‡ SF (*LAm*) lip

bembo (*LAm*), **bembudo** (*LAm*) ADJ thick-lipped
Ⓑ SM thick lip

bemol SM [1] (*Mús*) flat
[2] **bemoles*** (*euf*) ✦MODISMOS **esto tiene muchos** *o* **tres ~es** this is a tough one; **¡tiene ~es la cosa!** (*iró*) that's just bloody great!*

bencedrina® SF Benzedrine®

benceno SM benzene

bencina SF [1] (*Quím*) benzine
[2] (*Chile*) petrol, gas(oline) (*EEUU*)

bencinera SF (*Chile*) (= *estación de servicio*) petrol *o* (*EEUU*) gas station; (= *bomba*) petrol *o* (*EEUU*) gas pump

bencinero/a SM/F (*Cono Sur*) petrol station attendant, gas station attendant (*EEUU*)

bendecir ▸conjug 3o◂ VT [1] [+ *persona, agua, casa, vino, pan*] to bless; **~ la comida** *o* **la mesa** to say grace
[2] (= *loar*) to praise

bendición SF [1] [*de persona, agua*] blessing, benediction; **echar la ~** to give one's blessing (**a** to); ✦MODISMO **echar la ~ a algo**: **será mejor echarle la ~*** it will be best to have nothing more to do with it ► **bendición de la mesa** grace (*before meals*) ► **bendiciones nupciales** wedding ceremony *sing*
[2] ✦MODISMO **... que es una ~**: **lo hace que es una ~** he does it splendidly; **llovió que era una ~ de Dios** there was such a lovely lot of rain

bendiga *etc*, **bendije** *etc ver* **bendecir**

bendito/a Ⓐ ADJ [1] [*persona, casa*] blessed; [*santo*] saintly; [*agua*] holy; **¡~s los ojos que te ven!** you're a sight for sore eyes!; **¡bendita la madre que te parió!** what a daughter for a mother to have!; **¡~ sea Dios!** thank goodness!; ✦MODISMO **venderse como pan ~** to sell like hot cakes
[2] (*iró*) (= *maldito*) blessed
[3] (= *dichoso*) happy; (= *afortunado*) lucky
[4] (= *de pocas luces*) simple, simple-minded
Ⓑ SM/F [1] (= *santo*) saint
[2] (= *bobo*) simpleton, simple soul; **es un ~** he's so sweet; ✦MODISMO **dormir como un ~** to sleep like a log
Ⓒ SM (*Cono Sur*) [1] (= *oración*) prayer
[2] (= *hornacina*) wayside shrine
[3] (= *cabaña*) native hut

benedícite SM grace

benedictino ADJ Ⓐ ADJ Benedictine
Ⓑ SM Benedictine; ✦MODISMO **es obra de ~s** it's a monumental task

Benedicto SM Benedict

benefactor(a) Ⓐ ADJ beneficent; *ver tb* **estado 4**
Ⓑ SM/F benefactor

beneficencia SF [1] (= *virtud*) doing good
[2] (*tb* **asociación de ~**) charity, charitable organization; **vivir de la ~** to live on charity ► **beneficencia social** social welfare

beneficiado/a Ⓐ SM/F **el único ~ ha sido el intermediario** the only one to benefit was the middleman
Ⓑ SM (*Rel*) incumbent, beneficiary

beneficial ADJ *relating to ecclesiastical benefices*; **terreno ~** glebe, glebe land

beneficiar ▸conjug 1b◂ Ⓐ VT [1] (= *favorecer*) to benefit; **el acuerdo sólo beneficia a las economías más desarrolladas** the agreement only benefits the more developed economies; **la empresa más beneficiada por esta ayuda** the company which benefitted most from this aid; **esta huelga no beneficia a nadie** this strike is of no benefit to anyone; **esa conducta no te va a ~** such behaviour will do you no favours *o* won't do you any good; **el ex director beneficiaba a sus amigos mediante las adjudicaciones de obras** the ex-director favoured his friends by awarding them work contracts; **la lluvia beneficia al campo** rain is good for the countryside
[2] (*Com*) to sell at a discount
[3] (*Min*) (= *extraer*) to extract; (= *tratar*) to process
[4] (*LAm*) [+ *animal*] (= *descuartizar*) to butcher; (= *matar*) to slaughter
[5] (*CAm*) [+ *persona*] to shoot, kill
Ⓑ VI to be of benefit; **de momento ninguna de estas técnicas ~á** for the moment none of these techniques will be of any benefit
Ⓒ **beneficiarse** VPR [1] (= *obtener provecho*) to benefit; **los bancos son los que más se benefician** it's the banks that profit *o* benefit most; **el campo es el que más se beneficia con la lluvia** it's the countryside that gets most benefit from the rain, it's the countryside that benefits most from the rain; **~se de algo** to benefit from sth; **los suscriptores se ~án de esta oferta** subscribers will benefit from this offer
[2] **~se a algn** (*Esp*‡) (*sexualmente*) to lay sb‡; (*CAm*) (= *matar*) to shoot sb

beneficiario/a SM/F [*de herencia, póliza*] beneficiary; [*de beca, subsidio*] recipient; [*de cheque*] beneficiary, payee; **sus hijos son los principales ~s de su éxito** his children are the main beneficiaries of his success

beneficiencia SF (*Méx*) welfare

▼**beneficio** SM [1] (= *ventaja*) benefit; **los manipulan para su ~** they manipulate them to their own advantage *o* for their own benefit; **concederle a algn el ~ de la duda** to give sb the benefit of the doubt; **a ~ de algn** in aid of sb; **un recital a ~ de los niños de Somalia** a recital in aid of the children of Somalia; **en ~ de algn**: **aprovechó las cualidades literarias de su mujer en ~ propio** he exploited his wife's literary talent to his own advantage *o* for his own benefit; **estaría dispuesto a retirarse en ~ de otro aspirante** he would be prepared to withdraw in favour of another candidate; **en** *o* **por tu propio ~, es mejor que no vengas** for your own good *o* benefit *o* in your own interests, it's best if you don't come ► **beneficio de justicia gratuita** legal aid; *ver tb* **oficio 1**
[2] (*Com, Fin*) profit; **estos bonos han producido enormes ~s** these bonds have yielded enormous profits; **obtener** *o* **tener ~s** to make a profit; **obtuvieron 1.500 millones de ~ el año pasado** they made a profit of 1,500 million last year ► **beneficio bruto** gross profit ► **beneficio de explotación** operating profit, trading profit ► **beneficio distribuible** distributable profit ► **beneficio económico** financial gain ► **beneficios excesivos** excess profits ► **beneficio líquido** (*en un balance*) net profit; (*en una transacción*) net profit, clear profit ► **beneficio neto** = **beneficio líquido** ► **beneficio no realizado** unrealized profit ► **beneficio operativo** operating profit, trading profit ► **beneficio por acción** earnings per share *pl* ► **beneficios antes de impuestos** pre-tax profits, profits before tax ► **beneficios im-**

➤ LENGUA Y USO: **beneficio 1** 53.4

previstos windfall profits ► **beneficios marginales** fringe benefits ► **beneficios postimpositivos** after-tax profits, profits after tax ► **beneficios preimpositivos** pre-tax profits ► **beneficios previstos** anticipated profits ► **beneficios retenidos** retained profits; *ver tb* **margen A4**
[3] (= *función benéfica*) benefit (performance)
[4] (= *donación*) donation
[5] (*Rel*) living, benefice
[6] (*Min*) [*de mina*] exploitation, working; [*de mineral*] (= *extracción*) extraction; (= *tratamiento*) processing, treatment
[7] (*LAm*) (= *descuartizamiento*) butchering; (= *matanza*) slaughter
[8] (*CAm*) [*de café*] coffee processing plant

beneficiosamente ADV **influir ~ en algo** to have a beneficial effect on sth, be beneficial to sth

beneficioso ADJ [1] (= *provechoso*) beneficial; **una solución beneficiosa para todos** a beneficial solution for everyone; **el ejercicio es ~ para la salud** exercise is beneficial to health
[2] (*Com*) profitable

benéfico ADJ [1] (= *acción, influencia*) beneficial
[2] (= *caritativo*) charitable; **concierto ~** charity concert; **función benéfica** charity performance; **obra benéfica** charity; **organización** *o* **sociedad benéfica** charity, charitable organization

Benemérita SF **la ~** (= *la Guardia Civil*) the Civil Guard; → GUARDIA CIVIL

benemérito/a Ⓐ ADJ [1] (= *merecedor*) worthy, meritorious
[2] (= *destacado*) distinguished; **el ~ hispanista** the distinguished hispanist
Ⓑ SM/F **un ~ de la patria** a national hero

beneplácito SM approval, consent; **dar su ~** to give one's blessing *o* consent

benevolencia SF (= *bondad*) benevolence, kindness; (= *jovialidad*) geniality

benevolente ADJ, **benévolo** ADJ [1] (= *bondadoso*) benevolent, kind; **estar ~ con algn** to be well-disposed towards sb, be kind to sb
[2] (= *jovial*) genial

Bengala SF Bengal; **el Golfo de ~** the Bay of Bengal

bengala SF [1] (= *luz de aviso*) flare; (= *fuego*) Bengal light
[2] (*Bot*) rattan

bengalí Ⓐ ADJ Bengali
Ⓑ SMF (= *persona*) Bengali
Ⓒ SM (*Ling*) Bengali

Bengasi SM Bengazi

benignamente ADV [1] (= *amablemente*) kindly, benignly; (= *con gentileza*) graciously, gently
[2] (= *ligeramente*) mildly

benignidad SF [1] [*de persona*] kindness
[2] (*Meteo, Med*) mildness

benigno ADJ [1] [*persona*] kind, benevolent
[2] [*clima*] mild
[3] (*Med*) [*tumor*] benign, non-malignant; [*ataque, caso*] mild

Benito SM Benedict

benito ADJ, SM = **benedictino**

Benjamín SM Benjamin

benjamín/ina Ⓐ SM/F [1] (*más joven*) baby of the family, youngest child
[2] (*Dep*) young player
Ⓑ SM (= *botella*) half bottle

benjasmín (*Cono Sur*) = **benjamín A**

benzina SF (*Cono Sur*) = **bencina**

beo** SM cunt**

beocio* ADJ stupid

beodez SF drunkenness

beodo/a Ⓐ ADJ drunk
Ⓑ SM/F drunk, drunkard

beorí SM American tapir

beque (*CAm*) Ⓐ ADJ stammering
Ⓑ SMF stammerer

bequista SMF (*CAm, Caribe*) = **becario**

berbecí SMF (*Méx*) quick-tempered person

berbén SM (*Méx*) scurvy

berberecho SM cockle

berberí ADJ, SMF = **bereber**

Berbería SF Barbary

berberisco ADJ Berber

berbiquí SM carpenter's brace ► **berbiquí y barrena** brace and bit

BERD SM ABR (= **Banco Europeo para la Reconstrucción y el Desarrollo**) EBRD

berdel SM mackerel

bereber ADJ, SMF, **beréber** ADJ, SMF, **berebere** ADJ, SMF Berber

berengo/a (*Méx*) Ⓐ ADJ foolish, stupid
Ⓑ SM/F idiot

berenjena SF [1] aubergine, eggplant (*EEUU*)
[2] (*Caribe**) nuisance, bother

berenjenal SM [1] aubergine field, eggplant field (*EEUU*)
[2] (= *lío*) mess, trouble; **en buen ~ nos hemos metido** we've got ourselves into a fine mess

bereque ADJ (*CAm*) cross-eyed

bergante SM scoundrel, rascal

bergantín SM brig

Beri S ✦**MODISMO andar** *o* **ir con las de ~** (= *tener genio*) to have a violent temper; (= *tener malas intenciones*) to have evil intentions

beriberi SM (*Med*) beriberi (fever)

berilio SM beryllium

berilo SM (*Min*) beryl

berkelio SM berkelium

Berlín SM Berlin ► **Berlín Oeste** (*Hist*) West Berlin

berlina SF [1] (*Aut*) saloon car, sedan (*EEUU*)
[2] (*Cono Sur*) doughnut, donut (*EEUU*)

berlinés/esa Ⓐ ADJ Berlin *antes de s*
Ⓑ SM/F Berliner

berma SF (*Chile Aut*) hard shoulder, berm (*EEUU*), emergency lane

bermejo ADJ [1] (= *rojizo*) [*color*] reddish, ginger; [*gato*] ginger; (*Cuba, Méx*) [*toro, vaca*] light brown
[2] (*Caribe*) (= *único*) matchless, unsurpassed

bermellón SM vermilion

bermuda SF (*LAm*) meadow grass

Bermudas SFPL (*tb* **Islas ~**) Bermuda

bermudas SMPL Bermuda shorts; **unas ~** a pair of Bermuda shorts

Berna SF Berne

bernardina* SF yarn, tall story

Bernardo SM Bernard

bernés/esa Ⓐ ADJ of/from Berne
Ⓑ SM/F native/inhabitant of Berne; **los berneses** the people of Berne

berraco* SM noisy brat

berrear ▸conjug 1a◂ Ⓐ VI [1] (= *gritar*) [*animal*] to bellow; [*niño*] to howl, bawl
[2] (*Mús hum*) to bawl
Ⓑ **berrearse** VPR to squeal*, grass*

berrenchín SM = **berrinche**

berreo* SM howling, bawling

berreta* ADJ (*Cono Sur*) cheap, flashy

berretín* SM (*Cono Sur*) (= *obsesión*) obsession, mania; (= *terquedad*) pigheadedness

berrido SM [1] (= *grito*) [*de animal*] lowing; [*de niño*] howl
[2] **berridos** bawling *sing*

berrinche* SM [1] (= *rabieta*) rage, tantrum; **coger** *o* **llevarse un ~** to fly into a rage
[2] (*LAm**) (= *hedor*) pong*, stink

berrinchudo* ADJ [1] [*persona*] cross, bad-tempered
[2] (*Méx*) [*animal*] on heat

berro SM [1] (*Bot*) watercress
[2] (*Caribe*) (= *enojo*) rage, anger

berza Ⓐ SF cabbage; ✦**MODISMO mezclar ~s con capachos*** to get things in a shocking mess ► **berza lombarda** red cabbage
Ⓑ **berzas*** SMF INV = **berzotas**

berzal SM cabbage patch

berzotas* SMF INV twit*, chump*

besamanos SM INV (*Hist*) (= *recepción*) royal audience; (= *saludo*) forelock touching

besamel SF white sauce, bechamel sauce

besana SF *land to be ploughed*

besar ▸conjug 1a◂ Ⓐ VT [1] (*con los labios*) to kiss; ✦**MODISMO ~ la mano a algn** to pay one's humble respects (**a** to)
[2] (= *tocar con suavidad*) to graze, touch
Ⓑ **besarse** VPR [1] (*con los labios*) to kiss, kiss one another
[2] (*) (= *chocar con la cabeza*) to bump heads

▼**beso** SM [1] (= *con los labios*) kiss; **dar un ~ a algn** to kiss sb, give sb a kiss; **echar** *o* **tirar un ~ a algn** ◊ **dar un ~ volado a algn** to blow sb a kiss ► **beso de la muerte** kiss of death ► **beso de tornillo, beso lingual** French kiss
[2] (= *choque*) bump, collision

besograma SM kissagram

besotear ▸conjug 1a◂ VT (*Méx*) = **besuquear**

bestia Ⓐ ADJ (*) [1] (= *bruto*) **ese tío ~ le ha vuelto a pegar a su mujer** that brute *o* animal* has been beating his wife again; **no lo vayas a asustar ¡no seas ~!** you're not going to frighten him, are you? don't be such such a brute *o* such an animal!*; **los hinchas llegaron en plan ~** (*Esp*) the supporters came looking for trouble; ✦**MODISMO poner a algn ~** (*Esp***) **esa tía me pone ~** I've really got the hots for her*
[2] **a lo ~: un deporte parecido a la lucha libre pero más a lo ~** a sport that's similar to wrestling but more rough; **lo tuyo son mentiras a lo ~** your lies are real whoppers*; **todo lo haces a lo ~** you make a mess of everything you do; **hoy hemos entrenado a lo ~** we trained really hard today; **comimos a lo ~** we really stuffed ourselves*, we pigged out*; **conducen a lo ~** they drive like idiots; **bebe a lo ~** he drinks like a fish
[3] (= *ignorante*) thick*; **es tan ~ que no sabe ni sumar** he's so thick he can't even add up*; **¡anda, no seas ~! ¡eso no puede ser verdad!** don't be an idiot! that can't be true!

➤ LENGUA Y USO: **beso 1** 48.2

[4] (*con admiración, asombro*) **¡qué ~! ¡ha ganado todos los partidos!** she's amazing *o* incredible! she's won all the matches!; **¡qué ~! ¡se come cuatro huevos diarios!** it's amazing! she eats four eggs a day!; **¡qué ~ eres, le has ganado al campeón!** what a star! you beat the champion!

Ⓑ SMF (*) (= *bruto*) **¡eres un ~!** you're a brute!, you're an animal!*; **el muy ~ se ha bebido media botella de whisky él solo** that animal drank half a bottle of whisky on his own*; **es un ~ con el trabajo** he works like a dog*

Ⓒ SF (*Zool*) beast; ✦*MODISMO* **ser una mala ~** to be a nasty piece of work* ► **bestia de arrastre** draught animal, draft animal (*EEUU*) ► **bestia de carga** beast of burden, pack animal ► **bestia de tiro** draught animal, draft animal (*EEUU*) ► **bestia feroz, bestia salvaje** wild animal, wild beast ► **bestia negra, bestia parda** bête noire

bestiada* SF **una ~ de algo** masses of sth, tons of sth*; ✦*MODISMO* **disfrutar ~s** to enjoy o.s. hugely

bestial ADJ [1] (= *violento*) beastly, bestial; **instintos ~es** beastly *o* bestial instincts; **fue un crimen ~** it was a beastly *o* brutal crime

[2] (*) (= *enorme*) terrific*, tremendous*; **la máquina hacía un ruido ~** the machine made a terrific *o* tremendous noise*; **tengo un sueño ~** I'm incredibly tired; **tengo unas ganas ~es de irme de vacaciones** I'm just dying to go on holiday*

[3] (*Esp**) (= *estupendo*) smashing*, super*; **¡es un tío ~!** he's a smashing *o* super guy!*; **pasamos un rato ~** we had a smashing *o* super time*, we had a whale of a time*

bestialidad SF [1] (= *cualidad*) beastliness, bestiality

[2] (= *acción brutal*) act of brutality; **en las guerras se cometen muchas ~es** in wars many acts of brutality are committed

[3] (*) (= *disparate*) **comer tanto es una ~** eating so much is just gross*; **no dice más que ~es** he's so coarse

[4] (*) (= *cantidad excesiva*) **la cena nos costó una ~** the meal cost us a fortune *o* packet*; **los precios han subido una ~** prices have rocketed*; **he dormido una ~** I slept for absolutely ages*; **una ~ de** a mass of*, tons of*; **había una ~ de gente** there were masses of people*, there were tons of people*

[5] (*en sentido sexual*) bestiality

bestialismo SM bestiality

bestialmente ADV [1] (= *violentamente*) savagely; **fue ~ asesinado** he was savagely murdered

[2] (*) (= *enormemente*) **era ~ rico** he was filthy rich*

[3] (*Esp**) (= *estupendamente*) **lo pasamos ~** we had a great *o* super time*, we had a whale of a time*

bestiario SM bestiary

best-seller SM (*pl* **best-sellers**) bestseller

besucar* ▸conjug 1g◂ VT = **besuquear**

besucón/ona* Ⓐ ADJ **es muy ~** he's always dishing out kisses*

Ⓑ SM/F **es un ~** he's always dishing out kisses*

besugo Ⓐ SM sea bream; **ojos de ~** bulging eyes

Ⓑ SMF (*) idiot

besuguera SF [1] (*Culin*) fish pan

[2] (*Náut*) fishing boat

[3] (*Galicia*) (= *pez*) bream

besuquear* ▸conjug 1a◂ Ⓐ VT to cover with kisses

Ⓑ **besuquearse** VPR (= *besarse*) to kiss (each other) a lot; (= *magrearse*) to neck*, smooch*

besuqueo* SM (*con besos*) kissing; (*con arrumacos*) necking*, smooching*

beta SF beta

betabel (*Méx*) Ⓐ ADJ old, ancient

Ⓑ SM beetroot, beet (*EEUU*)

betabloqueador SM betablocker

betarraga SF (*LAm*), **betarrata** SF beetroot, beet (*EEUU*)

betel SM betel

Bética SF (*Literat*) Andalusia; (*Hist*) Baetica

bético ADJ [1] (*Literat*) Andalusian

[2] (= *del Betis*) of Real Betis F.C.

betonera SF (*Cono Sur*) concrete mixer

betún SM [1] (*para zapatos*) shoe polish; **dar (de) ~ a algo** to polish sth; ✦*MODISMO* **darse ~*** to show off

[2] (*Quím*) (*tb* **~ asfáltico**) bitumen ► **betún de Judea, betún judaico** asphalt; *ver tb* **altura 3**

betunero/a SM/F shoeblack, bootblack

bezo SM (= *labio*) thick lip; (*Med*) proud flesh

bezudo ADJ thick-lipped

bi... PREF bi...

biaba* SF (*Cono Sur*) punch; **dar la ~ a algn** (= *golpear*) to beat sb up; (= *derrotar*) to defeat sb, crush sb

bianual ADJ, SM (*Bot*) biannual

bianualmente ADV biannually

biatlón SM biathlon

Bib. ABR (= **Biblioteca**) Lib

biberón SM feeding bottle, baby's bottle; **voy a dar el ~ al niño** I'm going to give the baby his bottle

Biblia SF Bible; **la Santa ~** the Holy Bible; ✦*MODISMOS* **es la ~ (en verso)*** it's the tops*; **saber la ~ en verso** to know everything

bíblico ADJ biblical

biblio... PREF biblio...

bibliobús SM mobile library, bookmobile (*EEUU*)

bibliofilia SF bibliophily, love of books

bibliófilo/a SM/F bibliophile, book lover

bibliografía SF bibliography

bibliográfico ADJ bibliographic(al)

bibliógrafo/a SM/F bibliographer

bibliomanía SF bibliomania

bibliometría SF bibliometry

bibliométrico ADJ bibliometric

bibliorato SM (*Cono Sur*) box file

biblioteca SF [1] (= *edificio*) library ► **biblioteca ambulante** mobile library, bookmobile (*EEUU*) ► **biblioteca circulante** [*de préstamo*] lending library; (*ambulante*) circulating library ► **biblioteca de consulta** reference library ► **biblioteca de préstamo** lending library ► **biblioteca pública** public library ► **biblioteca universitaria** university library

[2] (= *mueble*) bookcase, bookshelves *pl*

bibliotecario/a Ⓐ ADJ library *antes de s*; **servicios ~s** library services

Ⓑ SM/F librarian

bibliotecnia SF, **bibliotecología** SF, **biblioteconomía** SF library science, librarianship

biblioteconomista SMF librarian

bicameral ADJ (*Pol*) two-chamber, bicameral

bicameralismo SM *system of two-chamber government*

bicampeón/ona SM/F two-times champion, twice champion

bicarbonatado ADJ bicarbonated, fizzy

bicarbonato SM bicarbonate ► **bicarbonato sódico, bicarbonato de soda** (*Quím*) bicarbonate of soda; (*Culin*) baking soda

bicentenario ADJ, SM bicentenary

bíceps SM INV biceps

bicha SF [1] (*) (= *serpiente*) snake; ✦*MODISMO* **mentar la ~** to bring up an unpleasant subject ► **bicha negra** bête noire, pet aversion

[2] (*CAm*) (= *niña*) child, little girl

[3] (*Andes*) (= *olla*) large cooking pot

bichadero SM (*Cono Sur*) watchtower, observation tower

bichará SM (*Cono Sur*) poncho (*with black and white stripes*)

bicharraco/a* SM/F [1] (*Zool*) (= *animal*) creature; (= *insecto*) creepy-crawly*

[2] (*iró*) (= *niño*) little monster

biche Ⓐ ADJ [1] (*LAm*) (= *no maduro*) unripe, immature

[2] (*Cono Sur*) (= *débil*) weak; (= *de mal color*) pale, off-colour

[3] (*Méx**) (= *fofo*) soppy*, empty-headed

Ⓑ SM (*Andes*) large cooking pot

bicheadero SM (*Cono Sur*) = **bichadero**

bichear ▸conjug 1a◂ VT (*esp Cono Sur*) (= *mirar*) to observe; (= *espiar*) to spy on

bichería SM (*LAm*) (= *insectos*) insects *pl*, bugs *pl*, creepy-crawlies* *pl*

bichero SM [1] (*en barca*) boat hook

[2] (*Pesca*) gaff

bichi‡ ADJ (*Méx*) naked, starkers‡

bichicori* ADJ (*Méx*) skinny

bichito SM [1] small creature, little insect

[2] (‡) (= *ácido*) LSD tablet

bicho SM [1] (*Zool*) (*gen*) small animal; (= *insecto*) bug, creepy-crawly*; (*Taur*) bull; (*Cuba, Cono Sur*) (= *gusano*) maggot, grub; (*Andes*) (= *serpiente*) snake; (*LAm*) (= *animal extraño*) odd-looking creature; ✦*MODISMOS* **de puro ~** (*LAm*) out of sheer pig-headedness; **matar el ~** to quench one's thirst; **tener ~** to be dying of thirst; ✦*REFRÁN* **~ malo nunca muere** the devil looks after his own

[2] **bichos** vermin *sing*, pests

[3] (*) (= *persona*) oddball*; **mal ~** rogue, villain; **es un mal ~** he's a nasty piece of work, he's a rotter*; **todo ~ viviente** every living soul, every man-jack of them ► **bicho raro** weirdo*

[4] (* *pey*) (= *niño*) brat*; **sí, bichito** yes, my love

[5] (*CAm*) (= *niño*) child, little boy

[6] (*Andes*) (= *peste aviar*) fowl pest

[7] (*Mil*) squaddie*, recruit

[8] (*Caribe*) (= *chisme*) what's-it*, thingummy*

[9] (*CAm, Méx***) (= *pene*) prick**

bichoco ADJ (*Cono Sur*) (= *inútil*) useless; (*para el trabajo*) unfit to work

bici* SF bike*

bicicleta SF bicycle, cycle; **andar** *o* **ir en ~** to cycle; **montar en ~** to ride a bike ► **bicicleta de carreras** racing bicycle ► **bicicleta de ejercicio, bicicleta de gimnasio** exercise bike ► **bicicleta de montaña** mountain bike ► **bicicleta estática, bicicleta fija, bicicleta gimnástica** exercise bike

bicicletero/a* Ⓐ ADJ bicycle *antes de s*
Ⓑ SM/F cyclist

biciclo†† SM velocipede††

bicicross SM INV cyclo-cross

bicilíndrico ADJ two-cylinder *antes de s*, twin-cylinder *antes de s*

bicimoto SM (*CAm*) moped

bicoca SF [1] (*Esp**) (= *trabajo fácil*) cushy job*; (= *ganga*) bargain
[2] (*LAm Rel*) (= *solideo*) skullcap, calotte
[3] (*Andes, Cono Sur*) (= *golpe*) slap, smack; (*con los dedos*) snap of the fingers

bicolor ADJ two-colour, two-color (*EEUU*); (*Aut*) two-tone

bicultural ADJ bicultural

bicúspide Ⓐ ADJ bicuspid
Ⓑ SM bicuspid

BID SM ABR (= **Banco Interamericano de Desarrollo**) IDB

bidé SM, **bidet** [bi'de] SM (*pl* **bidés** *o* **bidets**) bidet

bidel SM (*LAm*) bidet

bidimensional ADJ two-dimensional

bidireccional ADJ bidirectional; **~ simultáneo** full duplex

bidón SM (= *barril*) (*grande*) drum; (*pequeño*) can ► **bidón de aceite** oil drum ► **bidón de basura** rubbish bin, trash can (*EEUU*)

biela SF (*Téc*) connecting rod

bielástico ADJ with two-way stretch

bielda SF winnowing fork

bieldar ▸conjug 1a◂ VT to winnow (*with a fork*)

bieldo SM winnowing rake

Bielorrusia SF Belorussia

bielorruso/a ADJ, SM/F Belorussian

bien Ⓐ ADV [1] (= *satisfactoriamente*) well; **hablas ~ el español** you speak good Spanish, you speak Spanish well; **el libro se ha vendido ~** the book has sold well; **no veo muy ~** I can't see very well; **lo sé muy ~** I know that perfectly well; **viven ~** they live well; **me gusta la carne ~ hecha** I like my meat well-done; **~ gracias, ¿y usted?** fine thanks, and you?; **¡muy ~!** very good!; (*aprobando un discurso*) hear, hear!; **¡qué ~!** great!, excellent!; **oler ~** to smell good; **saber ~** to taste good
[2] (= *correctamente*) **¿has puesto ~ la rueda?** have you put the wheel on properly?; **si no cierras la tapa ~, se saldrá el líquido** if you don't screw the top on properly, the liquid will leak out; **se limpia ~ el pescado** clean the fish thoroughly *o* well; **¡~ hecho!** well done!; **has contestado ~** you gave the right answer, you answered correctly; **no consigo hacerlo ~** I can't seem to do it right; **haces ~** you're (quite) right; **hacer ~ en: hiciste ~ en decírselo** you were right to tell him, you did the right thing in telling him
[3] **estar ~: ¿estás ~?** are you all right?, are you OK?; **aquí se está ~** it's nice here; **¡está ~!, lo haré** O.K. *o* all right, I'll do it!; **¡pues sí que estamos ~!** this is a fine mess we're in!; **ese libro está muy ~** that book's very good, that's a very good book; **estás muy ~ con ese sombrero** you look really nice with that hat; **la casa está muy ~** the house is really nice; **está muy ~ que ahorres dinero** it's very good that you're saving; **que esté(s) ~** (*Col**) bye*; **¡eso no está ~!** (*a un niño*) that's not very nice!; **te está ~ la falda** the skirt fits you fine; **¡ya está ~!** that's enough!; **ya está ~ de quejas** that's (quite) enough complaining; **estar ~ de algo: estar ~ de salud** to be well, be in good health; **estar ~ de dinero** to be well off; **no está ~ de la cabeza** he isn't right in the head
[4] (= *de acuerdo*) **¡bien!** all right!, O.K.!; — **¿quieres que vayamos al cine? —bien** "shall we go to the cinema?" — "O.K. *o* all right"; **si a ustedes les parece ~** if it's all right with *o* by you
[5] (= *muy*) **un café ~ caliente** a nice hot coffee; **un coche ~ caro** a pretty expensive car; **~ temprano** pretty early; **estoy ~ seguro** I am pretty certain; **eso es ~ tonto** that's pretty silly; **esperamos hasta ~ entrada la noche** we waited until very late at night, we waited until well into the night
[6] **~ de** (= *muchos*): **~ de veces** lots of times; **¡te han dado ~ de regalos!** you got a lot of presents!; **bebe ~ de café** he drinks a lot of coffee
[7] (= *de buena gana*) **yo ~ iría, pero ...** I'd gladly go, but ..., I'd be happy to go, but ...; **~ me tomaría ahora un café** I'd love a coffee now
[8] (= *fácilmente*) easily; **~ se ve que ...** it is easy to see that ...; **¡~ podía habérmelo dicho!** he could have told me!
[9] (*locuciones*) **estar a ~ con algn** to be on good terms with sb; **de ~ en ~** *o* **mejor** better and better; **~ que mal** one way or another, by hook or by crook; **más ~** rather; **más ~ bajo** on the short side, rather short; **más ~ creo que ...** I actually think ...; **pues ~** well; **tener a ~ hacer algo** to see fit to do sth; **sus padres tienen a ~ que se vaya a vivir con su tía** her parents have seen fit to send her to live with her aunt; **le ruego tenga a ~ inscribirme en la lista** please be so kind as to include me on the list, I would be grateful if you would include me on the list; **le ruego tenga a ~ comunicarlo a sus lectores** please be kind enough to inform your readers; **~ es verdad que ...** it is of course true that ...; **¿y ~?** well?
Ⓑ CONJ [1] **si ~** although; **si ~ es cierto que ...** although it's true that ...
[2] **no ~** ◊ **ni ~** (*Cono Sur*): **no ~ llegó, empezó a llover** no sooner had he arrived than it started to rain, as soon as he arrived it started to rain
[3] (*en alternancia*) **~ por avión, ~ en tren** either by air or by train; **~ se levantó, ~ se sentó** whether he stood up or sat down
Ⓒ ADJ [*persona*] well-to-do; [*restaurante, barrio*] posh*; **son gente ~** they're well-to-do; **son de casa ~** they come from a good home
Ⓓ SM [1] (= *bondad*) good; **el ~ y el mal** good and evil; **hacer el ~** to do good; **hombre de ~** good man
[2] (= *provecho*) good; **el ~ común** *o* **público** the common good; **en ~ de** for the good of; **hacer algo para el ~ de** to do sth for the good of; **es por tu ~** it's for your own good
[3] (*apelativo*) **mi ~** my dear, my darling
[4] **bienes** (= *géneros*) goods; (= *propiedad*) property *sing*, possessions; (= *riqueza*) riches, wealth *sing* ► **bienes activos** active assets ► **bienes de capital** capital goods ► **bienes de consumo** consumer goods ► **bienes de consumo duraderos** consumer durables ► **bienes de equipo** capital goods ► **bienes de inversión** capital goods ► **bienes de la tierra** agricultural produce *sing* ► **bienes de producción** industrial goods ► **bienes de servicio** services ► **bienes dotales** dowry *sing* ► **bienes duraderos** durables ► **bienes fungibles** perishables ► **bienes gananciales** shared possessions ► **bienes inmuebles** real estate *sing* ► **bienes mostrencos** unclaimed property *sing* ► **bienes muebles** personal property *sing*, goods and chattels ► **bienes públicos** government property *sing* ► **bienes raíces** real estate *sing*, realty *sing* (*EEUU*) ► **bienes relictos** estate *sing*, inheritance *sing* ► **bienes semovientes** livestock *sing* ► **bienes terrestres** worldly goods

bienal Ⓐ ADJ biennial
Ⓑ SF biennial exhibition, biennial show

bienamado ADJ beloved

bienandante ADJ (= *feliz*) happy; (= *próspero*) prosperous

bienandanza SF (= *felicidad*) happiness; (= *prosperidad*) prosperity

bienaventuradamente ADV happily

bienaventurado ADJ [1] (*Rel*) blessed
[2] (= *feliz*) happy, fortunate
[3] (= *ingenuo*) naïve

bienaventuranza SF [1] (*Rel*) (= *vida eterna*) bliss, eternal bliss
[2] **las Bienaventuranzas** the Beatitudes
[3] (= *felicidad*) happiness; (= *bienestar*) well-being, prosperity

bienestar SM (= *satisfacción*) well-being, welfare; (= *comodidad*) comfort ► **bienestar social** social welfare; **estado de ~ social** welfare state

bienhablado ADJ well-spoken

bienhadado ADJ lucky

bienhechor(a) Ⓐ ADJ beneficent, generous
Ⓑ SM/F benefactor/benefactress

bienhechuría SF (*Caribe*) improvement (*to property*)

bienintencionado ADJ well-meaning

bienio SM two-year period

bienoliente ADJ sweet-smelling, fragrant

bienpensante Ⓐ ADJ sanctimonious, goody-goody*
Ⓑ SMF do-gooder*, goody-goody*

bienquerencia SF (= *afecto*) affection; (= *buena voluntad*) goodwill

bienquerer ▸conjug 2t◂ Ⓐ VT to like, be fond of
Ⓑ SM (= *afecto*) affection; (= *buena voluntad*) goodwill

bienquistar ▸conjug 1a◂ Ⓐ VT to bring together, reconcile
Ⓑ **bienquistarse** VPR to become reconciled; **~se con algn** to gain sb's esteem

bienquisto ADJ well-liked, well-thought-of (**con, de, por** by)

bienudo* ADJ (*Cono Sur*) well-off

bienvenida SF [1] (*a un lugar*) welcome; **dar la ~ a algn** to welcome sb; **calurosa ~** warm

welcome; **fiesta de ~** welcome party
[2] (= *saludo*) greeting

bienvenido ADJ, EXCL **¡bienvenido!** welcome!; **¡bienvenidos a bordo!** welcome on board!; **siempre serás ~ aquí** you will always be welcome here

bienvivir ▸conjug 3a◂ VI (= *vivir con comodidad*) to live in comfort; (*de acuerdo con las reglas*) to live decently, lead a decent life

bies SM **al ~** (*Cos*) on the cross

bifásico ADJ (*Elec*) two-phase

bife SM (*Cono Sur*) [1] (= *filete*) steak, beefsteak
[2] (= *bofetada*) slap

bífido ADJ [*lengua*] forked; *ver tb* **espina 3**

bifidus SM INV, **bífidus** SM INV **yogur con ~ activo** yoghurt with live *o* active bifidus

bifocal Ⓐ ADJ bifocal; **gafas ~es** bifocals
Ⓑ **bifocales** SMPL *o* SFPL bifocals

bifronte ADJ two-faced

biftec SM steak, beefsteak

bifurcación SF (= *división*) [*de calle*] fork; (*Elec*) junction; (*Inform, Ferro*) branch

bifurcado ADJ forked

bifurcarse ▸conjug 1g◂ VPR [*camino*] to fork, branch off; [*vía*] to diverge

bigamia SF bigamy

bígamo/a Ⓐ ADJ bigamous Ⓑ SM/F bigamist

bigardear* ▸conjug 1a◂ VI to loaf around, laze around

bigardo/a Ⓐ ADJ (= *vago*) lazy, idle; (= *libertino*) licentious
Ⓑ SM/F (= *vago*) idler; (= *libertino*) libertine

bígaro SM, **bigarro** SM winkle

bignonia SF ► **bignonia del Cabo** Cape honeysuckle

bigornia SF (double-headed) anvil

bigotazo SM huge moustache, huge mustache (*EEUU*)

bigote SM [1] (*tb* **~s**) moustache, mustache (*EEUU*); **~ de cepillo** toothbrush moustache; ✦***MODISMOS*** **chuparse los ~s** (*Cono Sur*) to lick one's lips; **de ~*** terrific*, marvellous; (*pey*) awful; **menear el ~*** to eat, scoff*
[2] (*Zool*) whiskers *pl* ► **bigotes de morsa** walrus moustache

bigotudo ADJ with a big moustache *o* (*EEUU*) mustache

bigudí SM curler, hair curler

bijirita SF (*Caribe*) [1] (= *cometa*) kite
[2] ✦***MODISMO*** **empinar la ~*** (= *beber*) to booze*, drink a lot; (= *enriquecerse*) to make money by dubious methods

bikini SM (SF *en Arg*) bikini

bilateral ADJ bilateral

bilbaíno/a Ⓐ ADJ of/from Bilbao
Ⓑ SM/F native/inhabitant of Bilbao; **los ~s** the people of Bilbao

Bilbao SM Bilbao

bilbilitano/a Ⓐ ADJ of/from Calatayud
Ⓑ SM/F native/inhabitant of Calatayud; **los ~s** the people of Calatayud

Bilbo SM = **Bilbao**

biliar ADJ bile *antes de s*, gall *antes de s*; **cálculo ~** gallstone

bilingüe ADJ bilingual

bilingüismo SM bilingualism

bilioso ADJ [1] (*Med*) bilious
[2] (= *irritable*) bilious, peevish

bilis SF INV (*Med*) bile; ✦***MODISMOS*** **descargar la ~ en** *o* **contra algn** to vent one's spleen on sb; **se le exalta la ~** he gets very cross; **eso me revuelve la ~** it makes my blood boil; **tragar ~** to put up with it

billar SM [1] (= *juego*) billiards; (*con 22 bolas*) snooker; **mesa de ~** billiard/snooker table ► **billar americano** pool ► **billar automático**, **billar romano** pin table [2] (= *mesa*) billiard/snooker table [3] **billares** [*de billar*] billiard/snooker/pool hall; [*de otros juegos*] amusement arcade

billete SM [1] (*Fin*) note, bill (*EEUU*); **un ~ de cinco libras** a five-pound note; **un ~ de 100 dólares** a 100-dollar bill; ✦***MODISMO*** **tener ~ largo** (*Cono Sur**) to be rolling in it* ► **billete de banco** banknote
[2] [*de transporte*] ticket; **¿puedes comprarme** *o* **sacarme el ~?** can you buy me a ticket?; **medio ~** half fare; **un ~ de libre circulación** a travel-card ► **billete azul** *ticket for off-peak travel* ► **billete de avión** plane ticket ► **billete de ida** single *o* (*EEUU*) one-way ticket ► **billete de ida y vuelta** return *o* (*EEUU*) round-trip ticket ► **billete electrónico** e-ticket ► **billete kilométrico** *concessionary ticket allowing free travel for a certain number of kilometres* ► **billete sencillo** single *o* (*EEUU*) one-way ticket
[3] (*esp LAm*) [*de cine, espectáculo*] ticket; **ya están los ~s a la venta** tickets are now on sale ► **billete de abono** season ticket ► **billete de favor** complimentary ticket
[4] [*de lotería*] ticket
[5] (†) (= *carta*) note, short letter ► **billete amoroso** love letter, billet-doux

billetera SF, **billetero** SM wallet, billfold (*EEUU*)

billón SM billion, trillion (*EEUU*)

billonario/a SM/F billionaire

bilobulado ADJ bilobate

bilongo SM (*Cuba*) (= *mal de ojo*) evil eye; **echar ~ en** to put the evil eye on, cast a spell on; **tener ~** to bristle with difficulties

bilonguear ▸conjug 1a◂ VT (*Caribe*) to cast a spell on, put the evil eye on

bimba[1]* SF top hat, topper*

bimba[2]* SF (*Méx*) (= *embriaguez*) drunkenness; (= *borrachera*) drunken spree, binge

bimba[3]‡ SF wallet, billfold (*EEUU*)

bimbalete SM (*Méx*) (= *columpio*) swing; (*basculante*) seesaw, teeter-totter (*EEUU*)

bimbollo SM (*Méx*) bun

bimensual ADJ [1] (= *cada dos meses*) bimonthly, two-monthly [2] (= *dos veces al mes*) fortnightly, semimonthly (*EEUU*)

bimensuario Ⓐ ADJ bimonthly, two-monthly
Ⓑ SM bimonthly publication

bimestral ADJ bimonthly, two-monthly

bimestralmente ADV bimonthly, every two months

bimestre Ⓐ ADJ bimonthly, two-monthly
Ⓑ SM [1] (= *período*) two-month period
[2] (= *pago*) bimonthly payment, two-monthly payment

bimilenario Ⓐ ADJ bimillenary Ⓑ SM bimillenary, two-thousandth anniversary

bimotor Ⓐ ADJ twin-engined
Ⓑ SM twin-engined plane

binadera SF, **binador** SM weeding hoe

binar ▸conjug 1a◂ VT to hoe, dig over

binario ADJ [1] (*Mat, Inform*) binary
[2] (*Mús*) two-four

bincha SF (*Andes, Cono Sur*) hairband

bingo SM [1] (= *juego*) bingo; **hacer ~** (*lit*) to get a (full) house; (*fig*) to hit the target, turn up trumps [2] (= *sala*) bingo hall

binguero/a SM/F bingo hall attendant

binoculares SMPL [1] (= *prismáticos*) binoculars; (*Teat*) opera glasses
[2] (= *quevedos*) pince-nez *sing*

binóculo SM pince-nez

binomio SM [1] (*Mat*) binomial
[2] (= *pareja*) **el ~ ejército-gobierno** the government-army pairing

bio... PREF bio...

bioactivo ADJ bioactive

bioagricultura SF organic farming

biocarburante SM biofuel

biociencia SF bioscience

biodegradable ADJ biodegradable

biodegradación SF biodegradation

biodegradar ▸conjug 1a◂ Ⓐ VT to biodegrade
Ⓑ **biodegradarse** VPR to biodegrade

biodetergente SM biodegradable detergent

biodiversidad SF biodiversity

bioestadística SF biostatistics *pl*, vital statistics *pl*

bioética SF bioethics *sing*

bioético/a Ⓐ ADJ bioethical
Ⓑ SM/F bioethicist, expert in bioethics

biofísica SF biophysics *sing*

biogás SM biogas

biogénesis SF biogenesis

biogenética SF genetic engineering

biografía SF biography

biografiado/a SM/F subject of a biography, biographee

biografiar ▸conjug 1c◂ VT to write the biography of

biográfico ADJ biographical

biógrafo/a Ⓐ SM/F biographer Ⓑ SM (*LAm*†) (= *cine*) cinema, movie theater (*EEUU*)

bioingeniería SF bioengineering

biología SF biology ► **biología aplicada** applied biology ► **biología celular** cell biology ► **biología marina** marine biology ► **biología molecular** molecular biology ► **biología vegetal** plant biology

biológico ADJ [*ciclo, origen, padre*] biological; [*alimento*] organic; **cultivo ~** organically-grown produce; **guerra biológica** biological warfare

biólogo/a SM/F biologist

biomagnetismo SM biomagnetism

biomasa SF biomass

biombo SM folding screen

biomédico ADJ biomedical

biometría SF biometry, biometrics *sing*

biométrico ADJ [*datos, tecnología, mecanismo*] biometric

biónico ADJ bionic

bioorgánico ADJ bio-organic

biopiratería SF biopiracy

bioprospección SF bioprospecting

bioprospector ADJ [*empresa*] bioprospecting *antes de s*

biopsia SF biopsy

bioquímica SF biochemistry

bioquímico/a Ⓐ ADJ biochemical
Ⓑ SM/F biochemist
biorritmo SM biorhythm
bioscopia SF bioscopy
bioseguridad SF biosafety
biosensor SM biosensor
biosfera SF biosphere
biosíntesis SF INV biosynthesis
biosintético ADJ biosynthetic
biotecnología SF biotechnology
biotecnológico ADJ biotechnological
biotecnólogo/a SM/F biotechnologist
bioterrorismo SM bioterrorism
bioterrorista Ⓐ SMF bioterrorist
Ⓑ ADJ bioterrorist *antes de s*
biótico ADJ biotic
biotipo SM biotype
biotopo SM biotope
biotransformación SF biotransformation
bióxido SM dioxide ► **bióxido de carbono** carbon dioxide
BIP SM ABR (= **Banco Internacional de Pagos**) BIS
bip SM pip, beep
bipartidismo SM two-party system
bipartidista ADJ two-party *antes de s*
bipartido ADJ bipartite, two-party *antes de s*
bipartito ADJ = **bipartido**
bípedo SM biped
biplano SM biplane
biplaza Ⓐ ADJ INV two-seater *antes de s*
Ⓑ SM (*Aer*) two-seater
bipolaridad SF bipolarity
biquini SM (SF *en Arg*) bikini
BIRD SM ABR (= **Banco Internacional para la Reconstrucción y el Desarrollo**) IBRD
birdie SM (*Golf*) birdie
BIRF SM ABR = **Banco Internacional de Reconstrucción y Fomento**
birimbao SM Jew's harp
birlar* ▸conjug 1a◂ VT (= *quitar*) to pinch*, nick*; **me han birlado la bici** my bike's been nicked o pinched*; **le birló la novia** he pinched his girl*; **le ~on el empleo** he was done out of the job*
birlibirloque SM ✦**MODISMO por arte de ~** as if by magic
birlocha SF [1] (= *cometa*) kite
[2] (*Méx*⁑) (= *auto*) old banger⁑, jalopy
birlonga SF ✦**MODISMO hacer algo a la ~** to do sth carelessly, do sth sloppily
Birmania SF Burma
birmano/a ADJ, SM/F Burmese
birome SF (*Cono Sur*) (= *bolígrafo*) ballpoint pen, Biro®; (= *lápiz*) propelling pencil
birra* SF beer
birreactor Ⓐ ADJ twin-jet *antes de s*
Ⓑ SM twin jet, twin-jet plane
birreta SF (*Rel*) biretta, cardinal's hat
birrete SM [1] (= *gorro*) (*Univ*) mortarboard; (*Jur*) judge's cap [2] (*Rel*) = **birreta**
birrí SM (*Andes*) snake
birria SF [1] (*esp Esp*) (= *cosa fea*) monstrosity; (= *cosa inútil*) useless object; **la novela es una ~*** the novel is rubbish o trash; **entre tanta ~** among so much trash
[2] (*Andes**) (= *obsesión*) set idea
[3] (*Cono Sur, Méx*) (= *bebida*) tasteless drink; (*Méx*) (= *guiso*) stew
[4] ✦**MODISMO jugar de ~** (*LAm*) to play half-heartedly
[5] (*CAm**) (= *cerveza*) beer
birriondo ADJ (*LAm*) [1] (*) (= *asustadizo*) jumpy, highly strung [2] (⁑) (= *cachondo*) randy*, horny*
birrioso* ADJ awful
biruji SM (*esp Cono Sur*) chilly wind
birutilla SF (*Cono Sur*) pot scourer
birutillar ▸conjug 1a◂ VT (*Cono Sur*) to polish
bis Ⓐ ADV (= *dos veces*) twice; (*en una calle*) **vive en el 24 ~** he lives at 24B
Ⓑ SM (*Teat*) encore; **la banda hizo dos ~es** the band played two encores; **¡bis!** encore!
bisabuelo/a SM/F great-grandfather/great-grandmother; **~s** great-grandparents
bisagra SF Ⓐ ADJ **acontecimiento ~** decisive event, event that marks a watershed; **partido ~** *party that holds the balance of power*
Ⓑ SF [1] (*Téc*) hinge
[2] (*) [*de caderas*] waggle, wiggle
bisar ▸conjug 1a◂ Ⓐ VT [1] to give as an encore, repeat
[2] (*Cono Sur*) to encore, demand as an encore
Ⓑ VI to give an encore
bisbisar ▸conjug 1a◂ VT to mutter, mumble
bisbisear ▸conjug 1a◂ VT (= *murmurar*) to mutter, mumble; (*Cono Sur*) to whisper
bisbiseo SM muttering, mumbling
bisbita SF pipit
biscote SM rusk, melba toast (*EEUU*)
biscúter SM (*Aut*) three-wheeler
bisecar ▸conjug 1g◂ VT to bisect
bisel SM [1] (*Téc*) bevel, bevel edge
[2] (*Mús*) finger hole, keyhole
biselado ADJ bevel *antes de s*, bevelled
biselar ▸conjug 1a◂ VT to bevel
bisemanal ADJ twice-weekly
bisemanalmente ADV twice-weekly
bisexuado ADJ hermaphrodite, twin-sex
bisexual ADJ, SMF bisexual
bisexualidad SF bisexuality
bisgra⁑ SF (*Caribe*) armpit
bisiesto ADJ **año ~** leap year
bisilábico ADJ, **bisílabo** ADJ two-syllabled
bismuto SM bismuth
bisnieto/a SM/F great-grandson/great-granddaughter; **~s** great-grandchildren
bisnis⁑ SM INV (= *clientela*) (prostitute's) clients, clientèle
bisojo ADJ = **bizco A**
bisonte SM bison
bisoñada SF (= *comentario*) naïve remark; (= *acto*) naïve thing to do
bisoñé SM toupée
bisoñez SF inexperience
bisoño Ⓐ ADJ (= *principiante*) green, inexperienced; (*Mil*) raw
Ⓑ SM (= *principiante*) greenhorn; (*Mil*) raw recruit, rookie*
bisté SM, **bistec** SM (*pl* **bistés** o **bistecs**) [1] (= *filete*) steak, beefsteak
[2] (⁑) tongue; ✦**MODISMO achantar el ~** to shut one's trap⁑
bistongo ADJ (*CAm, Caribe, Méx*) spoiled, indulged
bisturí SM scalpel
bisunto ADJ greasy, grubby
bisutería SF costume jewellery o (*EEUU*) jewelry, imitation jewellery o (*EEUU*) jewelry
bit SM (*Inform*) bit ► **bit de parada** stop bit ► **bit de paridad** parity bit
bitácora SF (*Náut*) binnacle
bitensional ADJ (*Elec*) *equipped to work on two different voltages*
bíter SM bitters
bitio SM bit
bitoque SM [1] [*de barril*] bung, spigot
[2] (*CAm*) (= *desagüe*) drain
[3] (*LAm*) (= *cánula*) short tube, injection tube (*of a syringe*)
[4] (*Cono Sur*) (= *canilla*) tap, faucet (*EEUU*)
[5] (*Cono Sur*) (= *bulto*) bump, swelling
bituminoso ADJ bituminous
bivalvo ADJ, SM bivalve
bivio SM (*LAm*) road junction
Bizancio SM Byzantium
bizantino/a Ⓐ ADJ [1] (*Hist*) Byzantine
[2] (= *baldío*) idle, pointless; (= *irreal*) over-subtle, unreal; **discusión bizantina** pointless argument
[3] (*fig*) (= *decadente*) decadent
Ⓑ SM/F Byzantine
bizarramente ADV [1] (= *valientemente*) gallantly, bravely
[2] (= *generosamente*) generously, splendidly
bizarría SF [1] (= *valor*) gallantry, bravery
[2] (= *generosidad*) generosity
bizarro ADJ [1] (= *valiente*) gallant, brave
[2] (= *generoso*) generous
bizbirindo ADJ (*Méx*) lively, bright
bizcar ▸conjug 1g◂ Ⓐ VT [+ *ojo*] to wink
Ⓑ VI to squint, be cross-eyed
bizco/a Ⓐ ADJ cross-eyed, squinting; **mirada bizca** squint, cross-eyed look; **ponerse ~** to squint, look cross-eyed; ✦**MODISMOS dejar a algn ~** to leave sb open-mouthed; **quedarse ~** to be flabbergasted
Ⓑ SM/F cross-eyed person, someone with a squint
Ⓒ ADV **mirar ~** to squint, look cross-eyed
bizcochera SF biscuit barrel, biscuit tin
bizcochería SF (*Méx*) pastry shop
bizcocho SM [1] (*Culin*) (= *pastel*) sponge cake; (*más pequeño*) sponge finger, lady finger (*EEUU*); ✦**MODISMO embarcarse con poco ~** to set out unprepared ► **bizcocho borracho** *sponge soaked in wine and syrup*
[2] (*Náut*) hardtack
[3] (= *cerámica*) biscuit ware
[4] (*Méx*) (= *galleta*) biscuit
[5] (*Méx*⁑⁑) (= *órgano sexual*) cunt⁑⁑
bizcorneado ADJ (*Caribe*) = **bizco A**
bizcornear ▸conjug 1a◂ VI (*Caribe*) to squint
bizcorneto ADJ (*Andes, Méx*) = **bizco A**
Bizkaia SF Biscay (*Basque province*)
bizma SF poultice
bizmar ▸conjug 1a◂ VT to poultice
biznieto/a SM = **bisnieto**
bizquear ▸conjug 1a◂ VI to squint
bizquera* SF (*esp LAm*) squint
bla-bla-bla SM claptrap, hot air
blanca SF [1] (*Hist*) *old Spanish copper coin*; ✦**MODISMOS estar sin ~*** ◊ **no tener ~*** to be broke*, be skint*
[2] (*Mús*) minim, half note (*EEUU*)

[3] (*Ajedrez*) white piece; **yo llevo las ~s** I'll be white
[4] (*Dominó*) blank ► **blanca doble** double blank
[5] (*) (= *cocaína*) coke*; (= *heroína*) smack*; *ver tb* **blanco**

Blancanieves SF Snow White

blanco/a Ⓐ ADJ [1] (= *de color blanco*) white; **el pantalón ha quedado blanquísimo** the trousers have come out really white; **se te está poniendo el pelo ~** your hair is going white; **un vino ~** a white wine; **es de color ~** it's white; ✦***MODISMO*** **~ como la nieve** as white as snow
[2] [*raza*] white; **una mujer blanca** a white woman
[3] (= *pálido*) [*cara, cutis*] fair; **soy muy ~ de piel** I'm very fair-skinned; **estar ~** [*cara*] to be pale; [*cuerpo*] to be white; **tenía la cara muy blanca** his face was very pale; **el más ~ de toda la playa** the whitest person on the beach; ✦***MODISMO*** **~ como la cera** *o* **como el papel** *o* **como la pared** as white as a sheet
[4] (*Literat*) [*verso*] blank
Ⓑ SM/F (= *persona*) white man/woman; **el ladrón era un ~, fuerte, de 1,80** the thief was white, heavily built, 6ft tall; **llegó acompañado de dos ~s** he arrived with two white people; **los ~s** white people; *ver tb* **trata**
Ⓒ SM [1] (= *color*) white; **me gusta el ~ para vestir** I like wearing white; **calentar algo al ~** to heat sth till it is white-hot; **de ~: casarse de ~** to get married in white, have a white wedding; **pintar algo de ~** to paint sth white; **vestirse de ~** to wear white; **en ~ y negro** black and white; **imágenes en ~ y negro** black and white pictures; ✦***MODISMOS*** **decir que lo ~ es negro** to swear that black is white; **no distinguir lo ~ de lo negro** to be unable to tell right from wrong; **poner los ojos en ~** to roll one's eyes; **verlo todo ~ o negro** to see everything in black and white ► **blanco de España** whiting ► **blanco de plomo** white lead ► **blanco y negro** (*Culin*) *iced coffee with cream*; *ver tb* **carpintero 1**, **punta A2**
[2] (= *parte blanca*) ► **blanco de la uña** half-moon ► **blanco del huevo** white of the egg, egg white ► **blanco del ojo** white of the eye; ✦***MODISMO*** **no parecerse a algn ni en el ~ de los ojos** to look nothing like sb
[3] (= *blancura*) whiteness
[4] (= *objetivo*) target; **el puente era un ~ fácil** the bridge was an easy target; **apunta al ~** aim for the target; **dar en el ~** (*lit*) to hit the target; **tus críticas han dado en el ~** your criticisms were right on target *o* were spot on; **has dado en el ~ escogiendo esta carrera** you did exactly the right thing in choosing that degree course; **ese comentario tuyo dio en el ~, por eso dolió tanto** that remark of yours hit home, that's why it hurt so much; **hacer ~** to hit the target; **hacer ~ en algo** to hit sth; **la patrullera hizo ~ en dos lanchas** the patrol boat hit two launches; **la prensa la hizo ~ de sus críticas** the press singled her out for criticism, she was the target of attacks by the press; **lo hicieron ~ de sus sátiras** they held him up to ridicule; **ser (el) ~ de** [+ *crítica*] to be the target of; [+ *burla*] to be the butt of; **se convirtió en el ~ de sus críticas** he became the target of their criticism; **la modelo fue el ~ de todas las miradas** the model was the centre of attention, all eyes were on the model ► **blanco móvil** moving target; *ver tb* **tiro 1**
[5] (= *espacio sin escribir*) blank, blank (space); **un ~ entre las dos palabras** a blank (space) between the two words
[6] **en ~** blank; **una página en ~** a blank page; **un cheque en ~** a blank cheque; **rellene los espacios en ~** fill in the blanks; **dejar algo en ~** to leave sth blank; **he dejado el examen en ~** I left the exam paper blank, I didn't write anything on the exam paper; **dejé varias preguntas en ~ en el examen** there were several questions I didn't answer in the exam; **votar en ~** to return a blank ballot paper; ✦***MODISMOS*** **pasar la noche en ~** not to sleep a wink*, have a sleepless night; **quedarse en ~: el concursante se quedó en ~** the contestant's mind went blank; **no pude contestar porque se me quedó la mente en ~** I couldn't answer because my mind went blank
[7] (= *pausa*) gap, break; **hay varios ~s entre las clases** there are several gaps *o* breaks between classes
[8] (= *mancha blanca*) (*pequeña*) white spot; (*más grande*) white patch
[9] (*Puerto Rico*) (= *formulario*) blank, blank form
[10] **los Blancos** (*Uru Pol*) *political party*; *ver tb* **blanca**

blancón ADJ (*Andes*) white-skinned

blancor SM whiteness

blancote Ⓐ ADJ [1] sickly white, unhealthily white
[2] (*) (= *cobarde*) yellow*, cowardly
Ⓑ SM (*) yellow belly*, coward

blancura SF whiteness

blancuzco ADJ (= *parecido al blanco*) whitish; (= *blanco sucio*) dirty-white, off-white

blandamente ADV [1] (*al tacto*) (= *sin aspereza*) mildly, gently; (= *mullido*) tenderly
[2] (*en el trato*) indulgently

blandear[1] ▸conjug 1a◂ VT = **blandir**

blandear[2] ▸conjug 1a◂ Ⓐ VT (= *convencer*) to convince, persuade
Ⓑ VI, **blandearse** VPR (= *ceder*) to soften, yield, give way; **~ con algn** to humour sb, humor sb (*EEUU*)

blandengue* Ⓐ ADJ soft, weak
Ⓑ SMF softie*

blandenguería* SF softness, weakness

blandiporno* ADJ INV **película ~** soft-porn film

blandir ▸conjug 3a; defectivo; no utilizado en presente◂ Ⓐ VT to brandish, flourish
Ⓑ **blandirse** VPR to wave to and fro, swing

blando/a Ⓐ ADJ [1] (= *tierno*) [*madera, droga, agua*] soft; [*pasta*] smooth; [*carne*] tender; (*pey*) flabby; **~ de boca** [*caballo*] tender-mouthed; **~ de carnes** flabby; **~ al tacto** soft to the touch
[2] (= *indulgente*) [*persona*] soft, indulgent; [*carácter*] soft, delicate; [*política*] soft, wet; **~ de corazón** soft-hearted, sentimental; **ser ~ con el crimen** to be soft on crime; **llevar una vida blanda** to live an easy life
[3] (= *cobarde*) cowardly
Ⓑ SM/F (*Pol*) soft-liner, moderate; (*Mil*) dove

blandón SM (*Rel*) (= *vela delgada*) wax taper; (= *candelabro*) large candlestick

blandorro/a* Ⓐ ADJ [*sabor*] tasteless, insipid; [*sonrisa*] weak, sheepish
Ⓑ SM/F [1] (= *pusilánime*) weakling, wimp*
[2] (= *cobarde*) coward

blanducho ADJ (*pey*) [*madera, superficie*] soft; [*carne*] flabby (*pey*)

blandujo ADJ softish

blandura SF [1] (= *suavidad*) [*de madera, cama*] softness; [*de carne*] tenderness; [*de agua, pasta*] softness
[2] (= *templanza*) [*de clima*] mildness
[3] (= *dulzura*) gentleness, tenderness
[4] **blanduras** endearments, sweet nothings

blanduzco ADJ softish

blanqueada SF [1] (*LAm*) (= *blanqueo*) [*de ropa*] bleaching; [*de pared, casa*] whitewashing
[2] (*Méx Dep**) whitewash

blanqueado Ⓐ ADJ [*pared, casa*] whitewashed
Ⓑ SM = **blanqueo**

blanqueador(a) SM/F bleacher

blanquear ▸conjug 1a◂ Ⓐ VT [1] (= *poner blanco*) [+ *dientes*] to whiten; [+ *ropa*] to bleach; [+ *pared, fachada*] to whitewash; [+ *oro, plata*] to blanch; **la nieve blanqueaba el paisaje** the snow turned the landscape white, the snow whitened the landscape
[2] (*Esp**) [+ *dinero*] to launder*; [+ *falta, persona culpable*] to whitewash
Ⓑ VI to turn white, go white; **el pelo le blanqueó con los años** his hair went *o* turned white over the years; **ya blanquea la nieve en las montañas** the mountains are now covered in white (snow)

blanquecer ▸conjug 2d◂ VT = **blanquear A1, B**

blanquecino ADJ off-white, whitish

blanqueo SM [*de dientes*] whitening; [*de pared, casa*] whitewashing; [*de ropa*] bleaching ► **blanqueo de dinero** money laundering

blanquiazul Ⓐ ADJ [1] blue and white
[2] (*Dep*) of Espanyol football club
Ⓑ SMF Espanyol player/supporter *etc*; **los ~es** Espanyol football club/team *etc*

blanquillo Ⓐ ADJ whitish; **azúcar ~** white sugar; **trigo ~** white wheat
Ⓑ SM [1] (*CAm, Méx*) (= *huevo*) egg
[2] (*Chile, Perú*) (= *durazno*) white peach
[3] (*Caribe, Cono Sur*) (= *pez*) whitefish

blanquimiento SM bleach, bleaching solution

blanquín SM ► **blanquín de gallina** (*Caribe euf*) hen's egg

blanquinegro ADJ black-and-white

blanquita* SF (*Caribe*) cocaine

blasfemador(a) Ⓐ ADJ blasphemous
Ⓑ SM/F blasphemer

blasfemamente ADV blasphemously

blasfemar ▸conjug 1a◂ VI [1] (*Rel*) to blaspheme (**contra** against)
[2] (= *decir tacos*) to curse, swear

blasfemia SF [1] (*Rel*) blasphemy
[2] (= *taco*) swearword, curse

blasfemo/a ADJ, SM/F = **blasfemador**

blasón SM [1] (*Heráldica*) (= *escudo*) coat of arms; (= *ciencia*) heraldry
[2] (= *honor*) honour, honor (*EEUU*), glory

blasonar ▸conjug 1a◂ Ⓐ VT [1] [+ *escudo*] to emblazon
[2] (= *encomiar*) [+ *persona*] to praise, extol
Ⓑ VI to boast, boast about

blazer SM blazer

bleck SM (*Cono Sur*) pitch, tar; ✦*MODISMO* **dar una mano de ~ a algn** to discredit sb, blacken sb's name

bledo SM *ver* **importar² A2.1**

bleque SM (*Cono Sur*) = **bleck**

blindado Ⓐ ADJ [*vehículo*] armour-plated, armor-plated (*EEUU*); [*chaleco*] bullet-proof; [*cable*] shielded; **carro ~** armoured *o* (*EEUU*) armored car; **puerta blindada** reinforced door
Ⓑ SM armoured *o* (*EEUU*) armored vehicle

blindaje SM [*de vehículo*] armour-plating, armor-plating (*EEUU*); [*de cable*] shield

blindar ▸conjug 1a◂ VT [+ *vehículo*] to armour-plate, armor-plate (*EEUU*); [+ *cable*] to shield

b.l.m. ABR (= **besa la mano**) *courtesy formula*

bloc SM (*pl* **blocs**) (*para notas*) pad, writing pad ▸ **bloc de dibujos** sketch pad ▸ **bloc de ejercicios** jotter, exercise book ▸ **bloc de notas** [*de estudiante*] notepad; [*de periodista*] reporter's notebook ▸ **bloc de taquigrafía** shorthand book

blocaje SM (= *bloqueo*) (*Dep*) tackle, stop; (*Mil*) blockade; (*Mec*) gripping, locking

blocao SM (*Mil*) blockhouse

blocar ▸conjug 1g◂ VT (*Dep*) [+ *jugador*] to tackle; [+ *balón*] to stop, trap

blof SM (*LAm*) bluff; **hacer un ~ a algn** to bluff sb

blofear ▸conjug 1a◂ (*LAm*) VI to boast, brag

blofero ADJ (*LAm*) boastful, bragging

blofista SMF (*LAm*) boaster, braggart

blog [bloɣ] SM (*pl* **blogs**) blog

blogger ['bloɣer] SMF (*pl* **bloggers**) blogger

blonda SF 1 (= *encaje*) blond lace
2 (*Cono Sur*) (= *rizo*) curl

blondo ADJ 1 (*liter*) (= *rubio*) blond, fair, flaxen (*liter*)
2 (*LAm*) (= *liso*) soft, smooth, silken
3 (*CAm*) (= *lacio*) lank
4 (*Cono Sur, Méx*) (= *rizado*) curly

bloque SM 1 (= *trozo*) [*de piedra, mármol*] block; [*de helado*] brick ▸ **bloque de casas** block, block of houses ▸ **bloque de cilindros** cylinder block ▸ **bloque de hormigón** block of concrete ▸ **bloque de papel** = **bloc** ▸ **bloque de sellos** block of stamps ▸ **bloque de viviendas** block of flats ▸ **bloque publicitario** commercial break
2 (= *bloqueo*) (*en tubo, salida*) block, blockage, obstruction 3 (*Pol*) bloc; **el ~ comunista** the communist bloc; **en ~** en bloc 4 (*Inform*) block

bloqueante Ⓐ ADJ paralysing, inhibiting
Ⓑ SM (= *droga*) inhibitor, anticatalyst

bloquear ▸conjug 1a◂ Ⓐ VT 1 (= *obstaculizar*) [+ *entrada, salida*] to block (off); [+ *camino, proyecto, proceso*] to block; **un tractor bloqueaba la carretera** the road was blocked by a tractor, a tractor was blocking the road; **~on la puerta con un sillón** they blocked *o* barricaded the door with an armchair; **los manifestantes ~on la calle en protesta** the demonstrators blocked the street as a protest; **la oposición bloqueó la ley en la cámara** the opposition blocked the bill in parliament; **la policía nos bloqueó el paso** the police barred our way
2 (= *atascar*) [+ *mecanismo*] to jam (up), block; [+ *cerradura, línea telefónica*] to jam; [+ *volante*] to lock; **los oyentes ~on la centralita de la emisora** listeners jammed the radio station's switchboard
3 (= *aislar*) to cut off; **quedaron bloqueados por la nieve** they were cut off by the snow
4 (*Mil*) to blockade
5 (*Com, Fin*) to freeze; **fondos bloqueados** frozen assets
6 (*Dep*) [+ *jugador*] to tackle; [+ *balón*] to stop, trap
Ⓑ **bloquearse** VPR 1 (= *paralizarse*) [*persona*] **me bloqueé en el examen** my mind went blank in the exam, I had a (mental) blank in the exam; **cuando me habla me bloqueo** when he speaks to me I get completely tongue-tied; **me quedé bloqueado ante tanta información** I was overwhelmed by the amount of information; **siempre me bloqueo ante el peligro** I always freeze in the face of danger
2 (= *atascarse*) [*mecanismo*] to jam (up); [*cerradura, línea telefónica, centralita*] to jam; [*frenos, volante*] to lock

bloqueo SM 1 (*Mil*) blockade; **burlar** *o* **forzar el ~** to run the blockade 2 (*Com, Fin*) ▸ **bloqueo de fondos** freezing of assets ▸ **bloqueo informativo** news blackout 3 ▸ **bloqueo mental** mental block

b.l.p. ABR (= **besa los pies**) *courtesy formula*

bluejean SM INV (*LAm*) jeans *pl*, denims *pl*

Bluetooth® SF Bluetooth®; **tecnología ~** Bluetooth technology

blufar *etc* ▸conjug 1a◂ VI = **blofear** *etc*

bluff SM bluff

blumes SMPL ✦*MODISMO* **tener ~** (*Caribe**) to be fussy, be finicky

blusa SF 1 (= *camisa*) blouse 2 (= *mono*) overall 3 (= *bata*) smock

blusero/a Ⓐ ADJ blues *antes de s*, rhythm and blues *antes de s*
Ⓑ SM/F blues fan, rhythm and blues fan

blusón SM (= *camisa grande*) long shirt, loose shirt; [*de pintor*] smock

Blvr. ABR (= **Bulevar**) Blvd

BM SM ABR (= **Banco Mundial**) WB

BN Ⓐ ABR (*Esp*) = **Biblioteca Nacional**
Ⓑ SM ABR (*Perú*) = **Banco de la Nación**

b/n ABR (= **blanco y negro**) b/w

B.º ABR 1 (*Fin*) (= **Banco**) bk
2 (*Com*) = **beneficiario**

boa SF boa

boardilla SF = **buhardilla**

boatiné SF **bata de ~** padded dressing-gown

boato SM show, ostentation

bob SM bobsleigh

bobada SF silly thing, stupid thing; **esto es una ~** this is nonsense; **este programa es una ~** this programme is stupid; **decir ~s** to say silly things, talk nonsense; **¡no digas ~s!** come off it!, don't talk nonsense!; **hacer ~s** to do stupid things; **cuando está borracho no para de hacer ~s** when he's drunk he's always doing stupid things

bobales* SMF INV nitwit*, dolt

bobalicón/ona Ⓐ ADJ utterly stupid
Ⓑ SM/F nitwit, clot*, dumbbell (*EEUU**)

bobamente ADV (= *tontamente*) stupidly; (= *inocentemente*) naïvely

bobático* ADJ silly, half-witted

bobear ▸conjug 1a◂ VI (= *hacer tonterías*) to fool about, do silly things; (= *decir tonterías*) to talk nonsense, say silly things

bobelas* SMF INV idiot, chump*

bobera SF = **bobería**

boberá SMF (*Caribe*) fool

bobería SF 1 (= *cualidad*) silliness, idiocy
2 = **bobada**

bobeta Ⓐ ADJ (*Cono Sur*) silly, stupid
Ⓑ SMF (*Cono Sur*), **bobetas** SMF INV (*Andes*) fool, idiot

bobicomio SM (*Andes*) lunatic asylum

bóbilis ADV ✦*MODISMO* **de ~** (= *gratis*) free, for nothing; (= *sin esfuerzo*) without lifting a finger

bobina SF (= *carrete*) (*Cos*) reel; (*Téc, Pesca*) spool; (*Fot*) spool, reel; (*Aut, Elec*) coil ▸ **bobina de encendido** ignition coil

bobinado SM (*Elec*) winding

bobinadora SF winder, winding machine

bobinar ▸conjug 1a◂ VT to wind

bobo/a Ⓐ ADJ (= *tonto*) silly, stupid; (= *ingenuo*) simple, naïve; ✦*MODISMO* **estar** *o* **andar ~ con algo** to be crazy about sth
Ⓑ SM/F (= *tonto*) idiot, fool; (*Teat*) clown, funny man; ✦*MODISMOS* **entre ~s anda el juego** (*iro*) they're well matched, one's as bad as the other; **a los ~s se les aparece la madre de Dios** fortune favours fools
Ⓒ SM/F 1 (*Caribe**) (= *reloj*) watch
2 (*Cono Sur*) (= *corazón*) heart, ticker*

boboliche SMF (*Andes*) fool

bobsleigh ['bobslei] SM bobsleigh

boca Ⓐ SF 1 (*Anat*) mouth; **no debes hablar con la ~ llena** you shouldn't talk with your mouth full; **tengo que arreglarme la ~** I must get my teeth seen to; **aceituna de ~** eating olive; **(respiración) ~ a ~** mouth-to-mouth resuscitation; **¡cállate la ~!*** shut up!*, shut your mouth!*; **~ abajo** face down; **estar tumbado ~ abajo** to be lying face down; **se cuelgan los manojos ~ abajo** hang the bunches upside down; **~ arriba** face up; **poner a algn ~ arriba** to turn sb on his back ▸ **boca de escorpión** wicked tongue ▸ **boca de mar** (*Culin*) crab stick
2 **en ~ de**: **suena extraño en ~ de un socialista** it sounds odd coming from a socialist; **está en ~ de todos** it's on everybody's lips; **puso esa frase en ~ de un personaje suyo** he gave that phrase to one of his characters; **por ~ de** through; **hablan por ~ del negociador** they speak through the negotiator; **lo sabemos por ~ de los propios autores del delito** we know so from the people responsible for the crime
3 ✦*MODISMOS* **no abrió la ~ en toda la tarde** he didn't open his mouth *o* he didn't say a word all afternoon; **buscar la ~ a algn** (= *hacer hablar*) to try to draw sb out; (= *provocar*) to provoke sb; **coserse la ~*** to keep quiet, keep mum*; **dar ~*** to gab*, chat; **de ~ en ~**: **la cosa anda de ~ en ~** the story is doing the rounds; **ella anda de ~ en ~** everyone is talking about her; **de ~ para afuera**: **apoyó la idea de ~ para afuera** he paid lip-service to the idea; **eso lo dice de ~ para afuera** he's just saying that, that's what he says (but he doesn't mean it); **decir algo con la ~ chica** *o* **pequeña** to say sth without really meaning it; **sin decir esta ~ es mía** without a word to anybody; **hablar por ~ de ganso** to parrot other people's opinions; **hacer ~**

to whet sb's appetite; **se me hace la ~ agua** my mouth is watering; **irse la ~ a algn**: **se me fue la ~** it just slipped out; **llenársele la ~ a algn**: **esa Europa con la que se les llena la ~** this Europe that they're always talking about; **se le llena la ~ del coche** all he can talk about is the car; **meter a algn en la ~ del lobo** to put sb on the spot; **meterse en la ~ del lobo** to put one's head in the lion's mouth; **(oscuro) como ~ de lobo** pitch black; **partir la ~ a algn*** to smash sb's face in*; **a pedir de ~**: **todo salió a pedir de ~** it all turned out perfectly; **quedarse con la ~ abierta** to be dumbfounded; **me lo has quitado de la ~** you took the words right out of my mouth; **¡que tu ~ sea santa!** (*Caribe*) I hope you're right!; **tapar la ~ a algn** to keep sb quiet, shut sb up*; **torcer la ~** (= *hacer un gesto*) to make a wry face; (= *burlarse*) to sneer; ✦***REFRANES*** **en ~ cerrada no entran moscas** silence is golden; **el que tiene ~ se equivoca** we all make mistakes, to err is human; **por la ~ muere el pez** silence is golden, it's best to keep one's own counsel; *ver tb* **sabor**

[4] (= *abertura, entrada*) [*de túnel, cueva, vasija*] mouth; [*de tonel*] bunghole; [*de puerto*] entrance; [*de arma*] muzzle; ✦***MODISMO*** **a ~ de jarro**: **beber a ~ de jarro** to drink to excess; **disparar a ~ de jarro** to shoot point-blank, shoot at close range ► **boca de incendios** hydrant ► **boca del estómago** pit of the stomach ► **boca de metro** underground *o* (*EEUU*) subway entrance ► **boca de mina** pithead, mine entrance ► **boca de riego** hydrant ► **boca de río** river mouth, estuary

[5] [*de vino*] flavour, flavor (*EEUU*); **tener buena ~** to have a good flavour

[6] [*de crustáceo*] pincer

[7] [*de herramienta*] cutting edge

[8] ► **boca de dragón** (*Bot*) snapdragon

[9] (*Inform*) slot

[10] **bocas** (= *personas*) mouths; **son seis ~s las que tengo que alimentar** I have six mouths to feed

Ⓑ SM [1] ► **boca a boca**: **aplicar** *o* **hacer** *o* **practicar el ~ a ~ a algn** to give sb mouth-to-mouth resuscitation, give sb the kiss of life

[2] (‡) [*de cárcel*] screw‡, warder

bocabajear ▸conjug 1a◂ VT (*LAm*) to put down, crush

bocabajo SM (*Caribe*) beating

bocacalle SF side street; **la primera ~ a la derecha** the first turning *o* road on the right

bocacha SF [1] (‡) bigmouth‡

[2] (*Mil, Hist*) blunderbuss

bocacho ADJ (*Cono Sur**) big-mouthed

Bocacio SM Boccaccio

bocadear ▸conjug 1a◂ VT to cut up (*for eating*)

bocadillería SF (*Esp*) snack bar, sandwich bar

bocadillo SM [1] (*Esp*) sandwich (*made with French bread*); **un ~ de queso** a cheese baguette

[2] (*en historietas*) balloon, bubble

bocadito SM [1] (= *mordisco*) morsel, bit

[2] **bocaditos** (*Andes*) snack *sing*, appetizer *sing*; ✦***MODISMO*** **a ~s** piecemeal

[3] (*Caribe*) (= *cigarrillo*) *cigarette wrapped in tobacco leaf*

bocado SM [1] (= *de comida*) mouthful; (= *aperitivo*) snack; **~ exquisito** titbit; **no he probado ~ en todo el día** I've not had a bite to eat all day; **intentaba hablar entre ~ y ~** I was trying to talk between mouthfuls; **tomar un ~** to have a bite to eat; ✦***MODISMOS*** **no hay para un ~** that's not nearly enough; **el ~ del león** the lion's share; **~ sin hueso** sinecure, soft job

[2] (= *mordisco*) bite; **le arrancó la oreja de un ~** he bit his ear off; **pegar un ~ a algo/algn** to bite sth/sb; **le he dado sólo un ~ a tu tortilla** I've only had a bite out of your omelette

[3] (*para caballo*) bit

[4] ► **bocado de Adán** Adam's apple

[5] (*) (= *astilla*) sweetener*, backhander*, payola (*EEUU*)

[6] (*Andes*) (= *veneno*) poison, animal poison

bocajarro ADV **a ~** [*disparar*] at point-blank range; **decir algo a ~** to say sth bluntly, say sth without mincing one's words

bocal SM [1] (= *jarro*) pitcher, jar

[2] (*Mús*†) mouthpiece

bocallave SF keyhole

bocamanga SF [1] (*Cos*) cuff, wristband

[2] (*Méx*) (= *agujero*) hole for the head (*in a cape*)

bocamina SF (*Min*) pithead, mine entrance

bocana SF estuary

bocanada SF [1] (= *ráfaga*) [*de humo*] puff; [*de viento, aliento*] gust, blast; ✦***MODISMO*** **echar ~s** to boast, brag

[2] [*de vino*] mouthful, swallow

[3] ► **bocanada de gente** crush of people

bocaracá SM (*CAm*) snake

bocarada SF (*LAm*) = **bocanada**

bocarte SM anchovy

bocata* SM sandwich

bocatería* SF ≈ sandwich bar

bocatero/a SM/F (*Caribe*) loudmouth*, braggart

bocatoma SF (*LAm*) water intake, inlet pipe

bocazas* SMF INV bigmouth*

bocera SF smear on the lips

boceras* SMF INV loudmouth*

bocetista SMF sketcher

boceto SM (= *esquema*) sketch, outline; (= *diseño*) design; (= *maqueta*) model, mock-up

bocha SF [1] (= *bola*) bowl; **juego de las ~s** bowls

[2] (*Cono Sur*‡) (= *cabeza*) nut*, noggin (*EEUU*‡)

bochar ▸conjug 1a◂ VT [1] (*LAm*) (= *rechazar*) to rebuff, reject; **~ a algn** to give sb a dressing down

[2] (*Arg**) (= *suspender*) to fail, flunk*

boche SM [1] (*Chile*) husks *pl*, chaff

[2] (*LAm*) (= *rechazo*) snub; **dar ~ a algn** to snub sb

[3] (*Andes, Cono Sur*) row, fuss

bochinche SM [1] (= *jaleo*) uproar, commotion

[2] (*Andes, Caribe*) (= *chisme*) piece of gossip

[3] (*Méx*) (= *baile*) rave-up*; (= *fiesta*) wild party

[4] (*Méx*) (= *bar*) seedy bar, dive*

[5] (*Méx*) (= *tienda*) local store

[6] (*Caribe*) muddle, mess

bochinchear ▸conjug 1a◂ VI (*LAm*) to make a commotion

bochinchero/a (*esp LAm*) Ⓐ ADJ rowdy, brawling

Ⓑ SM/F (*LAm*) brawler

bochinchoso ADJ [1] (*LAm*) (= *chismoso*) gossiping, gossipy

[2] (*Andes*) (= *agresivo*) rowdy, noisy

[3] (= *quisquilloso*) fussy, finicky

bocho SM **ser un ~** (*Cono Sur*) to be brainy, be clever

bochorno SM [1] (= *calor*) sultry weather, stuffy weather*

[2] (*Med*) hot flush

[3] (= *vergüenza*) embarrassment, shame; **¡qué ~!** how embarrassing!

bochornoso ADJ [1] [*tiempo, día*] close*, stuffy*

[2] (= *vergonzoso*) degrading, shameful; **es un espectáculo ~** it is a degrading spectacle, it is a shameful sight

bocina SF [1] (*Mús, Aut*) horn; **tocar la ~** (*Aut*) to sound one's horn, blow one's horn ► **bocina de niebla** foghorn

[2] (= *megáfono*) megaphone

[3] (*LAm*) (= *trompetilla*) ear trumpet

[4] (*Méx Telec*) mouthpiece

[5] (*Cono Sur*) (= *soplón*) grass‡, informer, fink (*EEUU*‡)

bocinar ▸conjug 1a◂ VI (*Aut*) to sound one's horn, blow the horn, hoot

bocinazo SM (*Aut*) toot, blast (*of the horn*); ✦***MODISMO*** **dar el ~‡** to grass‡

bocinero/a SM/F horn player

bocio SM goitre, goiter (*EEUU*)

bock [bok] SM (*pl* **bocks** [bok]) beer glass, tankard

bocón/ona Ⓐ ADJ [1] (= *jactancioso*) boastful, big-mouthed‡

[2] (*Caribe, Cono Sur*) (= *gritón*) loud-mouthed; (= *chismoso*) backbiting, gossipy

[3] (*Méx*) (= *poco discreto*) indiscreet

Ⓑ SM/F bigmouth‡

bocoy SM hogshead, large cask

boda SF [1] (= *ceremonia*) wedding, marriage; (= *convite*) reception, wedding reception

[2] (= *aniversario*) ► **bodas de diamante** [*de pareja*] diamond wedding *sing*, diamond wedding anniversary *sing*; [*de asociación*] diamond jubilee ► **bodas de oro** [*de pareja*] golden wedding *sing*, golden wedding anniversary *sing*; [*de asociación*] golden jubilee ► **bodas de plata** [*de pareja*] silver wedding *sing*, silver wedding anniversary *sing*; [*de asociación*] silver jubilee

bodega SF [1] (= *depósito*) [*de alimentos*] storeroom; [*de vinos*] wine cellar; [*de una casa*] cellar

[2] (*tb* **~ de carga**) (*Aer, Náut*) hold

[3] (= *tienda*) [*de vinos, licores*] wine shop; (*LAm*) [*de comestibles*] grocer's shop, grocery store (*EEUU*)

[4] (*esp LAm*) (= *bar*) bar

bodegaje SM (*Chile*) storage

bodegón SM [1] (= *restaurante*) cheap restaurant

[2] (*Arte*) still life

bodegonista SMF still-life painter

bodeguero/a Ⓐ ADJ (*Caribe*) coarse, common

Ⓑ SM/F [1] [*de vino*] (= *productor*) wine producer; (= *encargado*) cellarman/cellarwoman; (= *dueño*) owner of a bodega

[2] (*Andes, Caribe*) (= *tendero*) grocer

bodijo* SM (= *boda*) quiet wedding; (*pey*) misalliance

bodolle SM (*Cono Sur*) billhook

➤ LENGUA Y USO: **boda 1** 51.3

bodoque SM 1 [*de ballesta*] small ball, pellet
2 (*CAm, Méx Med*) (= *bulto*) lump, swelling; (= *bolita*) lump, ball
3 (*Méx*) (= *tonto*) dimwit*
4 (*CAm*) (= *manojo*) bunch
5 (*Méx*) (= *cosa mal hecha*) badly-made thing

bodorrio SM 1 (= *boda*) (*pey*) poor wedding
2 (*Méx*) (= *fiesta*) rowdy party

bodrio SM 1 (*) (= *porquería*) rubbish, garbage (*EEUU*), trash; **la película era un ~** the film was rubbish *o* a load of tosh*; **un ~ de sitio** an awful place
2 (*esp LAm*) (= *confusión*) mess

body SM (*pl* **bodies**) body stocking

BOE SM ABR (*Esp*) (= **Boletín Oficial del Estado**) ≈ Hansard, ≈ The Congressional Record (*EEUU*)

> **BOE**
>
> *The* **Boletín Oficial del Estado** *is a daily Spanish-government publication in which new laws, directives and executive decisions are published together with advertisements for public-sector posts and contracts. It is provided free of charge to all government agencies and state organizations including schools, embassies and public libraries.*

bóer Ⓐ ADJ Boer
Ⓑ SMF (*pl* **bóers**) Boer

bofe SM (*Zool*) lung; ✦*MODISMOS* **echar los ~s*** to slog one's guts out; **echar los ~s por algo*** to go all out for sth

bofetada SF (= *tortazo*) slap in the face; (= *puñetazo*) punch, punch in the face; **dar de ~s a algn** to hit *o* punch *o* slap sb; **darse de ~s** [*personas*] to come to blows; [*colores*] to clash

bofetón SM punch, punch in the face

bofia‡ Ⓐ SF **la ~** the pigs‡ *pl*
Ⓑ SMF pig‡, cop*

boga[1] SF (= *moda*) fashion, vogue; **la ~ de la minifalda** the fashion for the miniskirt; **estar en ~** to be in fashion, be in vogue; **poner algo en ~** to establish a fashion for sth

boga[2] SF (*Ferro*) bogey

boga[3] Ⓐ SMF (= *remador*) rower, oarsman/oarswoman
Ⓑ SF rowing

bogada SF stroke (*of an oar*)

bogador(a) SM/F, **bogante** SMF rower, oarsman/oarswoman

bogar ▸conjug 1h◂ VI to row

bogavante SM 1 (*Náut*) stroke, first rower
2 (*Zool*) lobster

bogotano/a Ⓐ ADJ of/from Bogotá
Ⓑ SM/F native/inhabitant of Bogotá; **los ~s** the people of Bogotá

bogotazo SM 1 (*LAm*) *Bogotá rising of 1948*
2 (*Andes*) ruin, destruction, pillage

bohardilla SF = **buhardilla**

Bohemia SF Bohemia

bohémico ADJ (*Geog*) Bohemian

bohemio/a ADJ, SM/F 1 (*Geog*) Bohemian
2 (= *poco convencional*) bohemian

bohío SM (*LAm*) (= *choza*) hut, shack

boicot SM (*pl* **boicots**) boycott; **hacer el ~ a algo** to boycott sth

boicotear ▸conjug 1a◂ VT to boycott

boicoteo SM boycott, boycotting

boicotero SM (*LAm*) boycott

boina Ⓐ SF beret
Ⓑ SMF ► **boina verde** commando

boite [bwat] SF, **boîte** [bwat] SF nightclub

boj SM (= *planta*) box; (= *madera*) boxwood

boje ADJ (*Méx*) silly, stupid

bojote SM 1 (*LAm*) (= *paquete*) bundle, package
2 **un ~ de** a lot of, a load of*
3 (*CAm*) (= *trozo*) lump, chunk
4 (*Caribe*) (= *alboroto*) fuss, row

bol SM 1 (= *cuenco*) bowl; (*para ponche*) punchbowl
2 (*LAm*) (= *lavafrutas*) finger bowl
3 (*Dep*) ninepin
4 (*Pesca*) dragnet

bola SF 1 (= *cuerpo esférico*) ball; [*de helado*] scoop; (= *canica*) marble; **van a sacar la ~ premiada** they're going to pick the winning ball; **del susto se me ha hecho una ~ en el estómago** my stomach knotted up with fright; ✦*MODISMO* **estar hecho una ~** (= *gordo*) to be round as a barrel, be chubby*; (= *acurrucado*) to be curled up (in a ball) ► **bola de alcanfor** mothball ► **bola de contar** abacus bead ► **bola de cristal** crystal ball ► **bola de fuego** (*Mil*) fireball; (*Meteo*) ball lightning ► **bola del mundo** globe ► **bola de naftalina** mothball ► **bola de nieve** snowball ► **bola de tempestad, bola de tormenta** storm signal ► **bola negra** black ball; *ver tb* **pie 2, queso 1**
2 (*Dep*) ball; [*de petanca*] boule; ✦*MODISMOS* **andar como ~ huacha** (*Chile*) ◊ **andar como ~ sin manija** (*Arg, Uru*) to be at a loose end; **dar ~** (*Cono Sur**) to take notice; **se lo he dicho mil veces pero no me da ~** I've told him a thousand times but he doesn't take any notice *o* a blind bit of notice; **¡dale ~!** what, again!; **dar la ~** (*Esp†‡*) to be released (from jail); **dejar que ruede la ~** to let things take their course; **escurrir la ~** to take French leave; **ir a su ~** (*Esp**) to do one's own thing*; **aquí cada uno va a su ~** everyone does their own thing here*; **tú (ve) a tu ~** just do your own thing*; **parar ~(s)** (*Col, Ven*) to pay attention; **no me paró ~s** he didn't take any notice, he didn't pay attention; **pasar la ~*** to pass the buck*; **pasarse de la ~** (*Caribe**) to go too far; **no rascar ~** (*Esp‡*) not to lift a finger* ► **bola de billar** billiard ball, snooker ball; ✦*MODISMO* **tener la cabeza como una ~ de billar** to be as bald as a coot ► **bola de partido** (*Esp Tenis*) match ball ► **bola de set** (*Esp Tenis*) set point
3 (*en lana, algodón*) bobble; **para que no le salgan ~s es mejor lavarlo a mano** it's best to wash it by hand to stop bobbles; **hacerse ~s** [*jersey, abrigo*] to get bobbly; (*Méx**) [*persona*] to get o.s. tied up in knots
4 (*Esp*) (= *músculo*) [*del brazo*] biceps; [*de la pantorrilla*] calf muscle; **sacar ~** to flex one's muscles
5 (‡) (= *cabeza*) nut*, noggin (*EEUU‡*); **tú estás mal de la ~** you're nuts*; ✦*MODISMO* **cambiar la ~** (*Caribe**) to change one's mind
6 **bolas**** (= *testículos*) balls**; ✦*MODISMOS* **en ~s‡** (= *desnudo*) naked; **tíos en ~s** naked men; **aquí todo el mundo va** *o* **está en ~s** everyone goes round naked *o* in the nude here; **en esta cala está permitido ponerse en ~s** they allow nude bathing on this beach; **tras el incendio nos quedamos en ~s** the fire completely cleaned us out*; **hasta las ~s**** pissed off**; **estoy hasta las ~s de él** I'm pissed off with him**; **me tiene hasta las ~s con sus tonterías** I'm pissed off with his fooling around**, I've had it up to here ith his fooling around*; **pillar a algn en ~s‡** to catch sb on the hop*; **¡qué ~s!** (*Caribe, Cono Sur**) what a nerve!*
7 (*) (= *mentira*) fib; **¡vaya ~ que nos metiste!** what a fib you told us!; **este niño nos quiere meter una ~** that boy's trying to put one past us*; **¡qué ~ más grande!** what a whopper!*; **¿no te habrás tragado esa ~?** you didn't swallow that one, did you?*, you didn't fall for it, did you?*
8 (= *rumor*) **correr la ~** to spread the word; **¿quién ha corrido la ~ de que se van a vivir al extranjero?** who's been spreading the word that they're going to move abroad?
9 (*Méx*) **dar ~** to polish shoes
10 (*Naipes*) (grand) slam; **media ~** small slam
11 (*Náut*) signal (with discs)
12 (*Tip*) golf ball
13 (*Mec*) ball bearing
14 (*Méx*) (= *jaleo*) row, hubbub; (= *pelea*) brawl; ✦*MODISMO* **se armó la ~** all hell broke loose*

bolacear ▸conjug 1a◂ VI (*Cono Sur*) to talk rubbish

bolaco SM (*Cono Sur*) ruse, device

bolada SF 1 (= *lanzamiento*) (*Ftbl*) throw; (*Atletismo*) putt; (*Billar*) stroke
2 (*LAm*) (= *suerte*) stroke of luck, lucky break; (= *ganga*) bargain, good deal
3 (*Cono Sur*) ► **bolada de aficionado** (*Cono Sur*) intervention (*by a third party*)
4 (*LAm*) (= *mentira*) fib, lie
5 (*Méx*) (= *chiste*) joke, witty comment; (= *engaño*) trick, con*
6 (*Cono Sur*) (= *golosina*) titbit, treat

bolado SM 1 (*LAm**) (= *asunto*) deal, affair; **esta noche tengo un ~** I've got something on tonight
2 (*Méx*) (= *amorío*) love affair, flirtation
3 (*CAm*) clever stroke
4 (*CAm*) (= *cuento*) fib, tale; (= *chisme*) rumour, piece of gossip
5 (*LAm**) (= *favor*) **¡hazme un ~!** do me a favour!*

bolamen** SM balls** *pl*

bolardo SM bollard

bolata SM ex-con‡, old lag‡

bolate SM (*Andes*) = **volate**

bolazo SM 1 (*Cono Sur*) (= *tontería*) silly remark, piece of nonsense; (= *noticia falsa*) false news; (= *mentira*) fib, lie; (= *error*) mistake, error; ✦*MODISMO* **mandarse un ~** to put one's foot in it
2 (*Méx*) ✦*MODISMO* **al** *o* **de ~** at random

bolchevique ADJ, SMF Bolshevik

bolchevismo SM Bolshevism

bolea SF (*Dep*) volley

boleada[1] SF (*Méx*) shoeshine

boleada[2] SF (*Cono Sur**) hunt, hunting expedition (*with bolas*)

boleado[1] (*Cono Sur*) ADJ **estar ~** to have lost one's touch

boleado[2] SM (*Méx*) shoeshine

boleador(a) SM/F (*Méx*) (= *limpiabotas*) shoeshine boy/girl

boleadoras SFPL (*Cono Sur*) bolas; → GAUCHO

bolear ▸conjug 1a◂ Ⓐ VT 1 (= *lanzar*) [+ *pelota*] to throw; **has boleado esa pelota demasiado baja** you threw that ball too low
2 (*LAm*) (= *cazar*) *to catch with bolas*
3 (*LAm*) (= *vencer*) to floor, flummox*
4 (*LAm*) [+ *candidato*] to reject, blackball; (*) [+ *obrero*] to sack*, fire*
5 (*Méx*) [+ *zapatos*] to polish, shine
Ⓑ VI (*Billar*) to play for fun, knock the balls about
Ⓒ **bolearse** VPR 1 (*Cono Sur*) (= *darse la vuelta*) [*caballo*] to rear and fall; [*coche*] to overturn
2 (*Cono Sur*) (= *avergonzarse*) to be shamefaced

boleco ADJ (*CAm*) drunk

bolera SF bowling alley, skittle alley

bolería SF (*Méx*) shoeshine shop

bolero[1] ADJ truant

bolero[2] SM (*Mús*) bolero

bolero[3] SM (*Méx*) bootblack, shoeshine boy

boleta SF 1 (*LAm*) (= *billete*) ticket; (= *recibo*) receipt
2 (*LAm*) [*de voto*] ballot paper, voting paper; (*Cono Sur Jur*) draft
3 (*Cono Sur**) ✦*MODISMOS* **hacer la ~ a algn** to bump sb off*; **ser ~** to be condemned to death

boletería SF (*LAm*) 1 (= *agencia*) ticket agency; (*en estación*) ticket office, booking office; (*Teat*) box office
2 (*Dep*) (= *recaudación*) gate, takings *pl*

boletero/a SM/F (*LAm*) ticket clerk, ticket seller

boletín SM 1 (= *publicación informativa*) bulletin; (*Univ*) journal, review; (*Escol*) report ► **boletín de inscripción** registration form ► **boletín de noticias** news bulletin ► **boletín de pedido** order form ► **boletín de precios** price list ► **boletín de prensa** press release ► **boletín de suscripción** subscription form ► **boletín facultativo** medical report ► **boletín informativo** news bulletin, news sheet ► **boletín meteorológico** weather report *o* forecast ► **boletín naviero** shipping register ► **Boletín Oficial del Estado** (*Esp*) ≈ Hansard, ≈ The Congressional Record (*EEUU*); → BOE
2 (= *billete*) ticket
3 (*Mil*) pay warrant

boleto SM 1 [*de quiniela*] coupon ► **boleto de apuestas** betting slip ► **boleto de lotería** lottery ticket ► **boleto de quinielas** pools coupon
2 (*LAm*) (= *billete*) ticket ► **boleto de ida y vuelta** return *o* (*EEUU*) round-trip ticket ► **boleto electrónico** e-ticket
3 ✦*MODISMO* **de ~** (*LAm*) at once

boli* SM pen, Biro®, ballpoint pen

bolichada SF lucky break, stroke of luck; ✦*MODISMO* **de una ~** at one go

boliche[1] SM 1 (= *juego*) bowls *sing*, bowling
2 (= *bola*) jack
3 (= *bolos*) skittles *sing*
4 (= *bolera*) bowling alley
5 (= *juguete*) cup-and-ball toy
6 (= *red*) small dragnet
7 (= *horno*) small furnace, smelting furnace

boliche[2] SM 1 (*LAm*) (= *tenducha*) small grocery store; (*Cono Sur*) (= *café*) cheap snack bar
2 (*Andes*) (= *tahona*) cheap bakery
3 (*Cono Sur*) (= *garita*) gambling den

boliche[3]* SM (*LAm*) Bolivian

bolichera SF (*Perú*) fishing boat

bolichero/a SM/F (*LAm*) grocer, shopkeeper

bólido SM 1 (*Aut*) racing car; **iba como un ~*** he was really shifting*
2 (*Náut*) powerboat, speedboat
3 (*Astron*) meteorite

bolígrafo SM pen, ballpoint pen, Biro®

bolilla SF 1 (*Cono Sur*) (= *canica*) marble
2 (*Cono Sur Univ*) (piece of paper bearing) examination question; **dar ~ a algo** to take notice of sth

bolillo SM 1 (*Cos*) bobbin (*for lacemaking*)
2 (*LAm Mús*) drumstick
3 (*Méx*) (= *panecillo*) bread roll

bolina SF 1 (= *cabo*) bowline; (= *sonda*) lead, sounding line; **de ~** close-hauled; **navegar de ~** to sail close to the wind
2 (*) (= *jaleo*) racket, row

bolinga‡ Ⓐ ADJ **estar ~** to be canned*
Ⓑ SF **estar de ~** to be on the booze*; **ir de ~** to go on the booze*

bolita SF 1 (= *bola pequeña*) (*hueca*) small ball; (*maciza*) pellet; (*Cono Sur*) (= *canica*) marble
2 (*Cono Sur Pol*) ballot paper

bolívar SM *Venezuelan currency unit*; ✦*MODISMO* **no verle la cara a Bolívar*** to be broke*

Bolivia SF Bolivia

bolivianismo SM bolivianism, *word/phrase etc peculiar to Bolivia*

boliviano/a ADJ, SM/F Bolivian

bollera‡ SF dyke**; *ver tb* **bollero**

bollería SF (= *dulces*) pastries *pl;* (= *establecimiento*) baker's (shop), pastry shop

bollero/a SM/F baker, pastry cook *o* chef; *ver tb* **bollera**

bollo SM 1 (*Culin*) [*de pan*] bread roll; (*dulce*) scone, bun; ✦*MODISMOS* **perdonar el ~ por el coscorrón** to realize that it's more trouble than it's worth; **no pela ~** (*Caribe*) he never gets it wrong
2 (*en el coche*) dent; **tengo el coche lleno de ~s** my car is full of dents
3 (*Med*) bump, lump
4 (*Cos*) puff
5 (= *confusión*) confusion, mix-up; ✦*MODISMOS* **armar un ~** to make a fuss; **meter a algn en un ~** to get sb into trouble
6 **bollos** (*Andes*) (= *problemas*) troubles
7 (*CAm, Caribe***) cunt**

bollón SM 1 (= *tachón*) stud, ornamental stud
2 (= *pendiente*) button earring

bolo[1] SM 1 (= *cilindro*) skittle, ninepin (*EEUU*); ✦*MODISMOS* **andar en ~** (*Andes*) to be naked; **ir en ~** (*Caribe*) to run off, run away; **tumbar ~** (*Andes*) to do well, bring it off
2 **bolos** (= *juego*) skittles *sing*, ninepins (*EEUU*) *sing*; ✦*MODISMO* **echar a rodar los ~s** to stir up trouble, make mischief
3 (*Med*) large pill
4 (*Naipes*) slam
5 (= *moneda*) (*Caribe*) one-peso coin; (*Ven*) one-bolívar coin
6 (*Méx*) (= *regalo*) christening present (*from godparents*)
7 (**) (= *pene*) prick**

bolo[2] (*CAm, Cuba, Méx*) Ⓐ ADJ drunk
Ⓑ SM drunk

bolo[3]‡ SM (*Mús*) gig, concert

bolón SM 1 (*Cono Sur*) (= *piedra*) quarry stone
2 (*Cuba, Méx*) (= *muchedumbre*) mob

Bolonia SF Bologna

bolonio/a* SM/F dunce, ignoramus

boloñesa SF bolognese sauce, meat sauce

bolsa SF 1 (*para llevar algo*) bag; **una ~ de caramelos** a bag of sweets; **una ~ de patatas** *o* (*LAm*) **papas fritas** a packet *o* bag of crisps; **una ~ de papel** a paper bag; **una ~ de plástico** a plastic bag; ✦*MODISMO* **hacer algo ~** (*Cono Sur**) to ruin sth; **le pegaron hasta dejarlo hecho ~** they beat him to a pulp ► **bolsa de agua caliente** hot-water bottle ► **bolsa de asar** roasting bag ► **bolsa de asas** carrier bag ► **bolsa de aseo** toilet bag ► **bolsa de basura** (*para cubo grande*) rubbish bag, bin bag, garbage bag (*EEUU*); (*para cubo pequeño*) bin liner ► **bolsa de cultivo** growbag ► **bolsa de deportes** sports bag ► **bolsa de hielo** ice-pack ► **bolsa de la compra** shopping bag ► **bolsa de mano** overnight bag, travelling bag ► **bolsa de palos** (*Golf*) golf bag ► **bolsa de playa** beach bag ► **bolsa de tabaco** tobacco pouch ► **bolsa para el mareo** sickbag
2 (*Méx*) [*de mujer*] handbag
3 (= *bolsillo*) pocket
4 (*Zool*) [*de canguro*] pouch; [*de calamar*] sac
5 (*Anat*) [*de sangre, pus*] build-up; **una pequeña ~ de pus** a small build-up of pus; **tenía unas ~s enormes en los ojos** she had huge bags under her eyes ► **bolsa de aguas** amniotic sac; **ya ha roto la ~ de aguas** her waters have broken ► **bolsa escrotal** scrotum ► **bolsa lacrimal** tear duct
6 (= *acumulación*) [*de gas, personas*] pocket; **muchos votos procedían de la ~ de indecisos** many of their votes came from those who were undecided; **una enorme ~ de desempleo** a huge number of unemployed, very high levels of unemployment ► **bolsa de agua** pocket of water ► **bolsa de aire** air pocket ► **bolsa de gas** pocket of gas ► **bolsa de petróleo** pocket of oil ► **bolsa de pobreza** pocket of poverty
7 (= *arruga*) (*en papel pintado*) bubble; **esa blusa te hace ~s** that blouse goes all baggy *o* doesn't hang right on you
8 (*Fin*) (= *mercado*) **la Bolsa** the Stock Exchange, the Stock Market; **perdieron casi todo jugando a la ~** they lost almost everything playing the market; **las empresas que cotizan en ~** quoted *o* listed companies; **sacar una emisión a ~** to float an issue on the stock market *o* exchange ► **bolsa de cereales** corn exchange ► **bolsa de divisas** currency market, foreign exchange market ► **bolsa de empleo** employment office ► **bolsa de granos** corn exchange ► **bolsa de la propiedad** property section, property page(s) ► **bolsa de trabajo** employment exchange ► **bolsa negra** (*Chile*) black market
9 [*de dinero*] **sólo busca engordar la ~** all he's trying to do is line his pockets*; **¡la ~ o la vida!** your money or your life!; ✦*MODISMOS* **no abrir la ~** to be tight with one's money; **hacer algo a la ~** (*Chile*) to do sth at somebody else's expense ► **bolsa de estudios** (study) grant ► **bolsa de viaje**

travel grant
[10] (*Boxeo*) purse

bolsear ▸conjug 1a◂ Ⓐ VT **la ~on** she had her handbag stolen; **~ a algn** (*CAm, Méx*) to pick sb's pocket
Ⓑ VI [1] (*CAm, Méx*) (= *robar*) to pick pockets
[2] (*CAm, Cono Sur, Méx*) (= *estafar*) to cheat, swindle

bolsicón SM (*Andes*) thick flannel skirt

bolsicona SF (*Andes*) peasant woman

bolsillo SM [1] [*de chaqueta, pantalón*] pocket; **lo pagué de mi ~** I paid it out of my own pocket; **guardar algo en el ~** to put sth in one's pocket; ✦*MODISMOS* **doler a algn en el ~** to hurt sb's pocket; **meterse a algn en el ~** to have sb eating out of one's hand; (*Pol**) to buy sb off; **rascarse el ~*** to pay up, fork out*; **tener a algn en el ~** to have sb eating out of one's hand, have sb in one's pocket; **tentarse el ~** to consider one's financial circumstances
[2] **de ~** pocket *antes de s*, pocket-size; **acorazado de ~** pocket battleship; **edición de ~** pocket edition

bolsín SM kerb market (*in stocks and shares*)

bolsiquear ▸conjug 1a◂ VT (*Cono Sur*) **~ a algn** (= *registrar*) to search sb's pockets, go through sb's pockets; (= *robar*) to pick sb's pockets

bolsista SMF [1] (*Fin*) stockbroker
[2] (*CAm, Méx*) (= *ratero*) pickpocket

bolsita SF (*tb* **~ de té**) tea bag

bolso SM [1] [*de mano*] bag, handbag, purse (*EEUU*) ► **bolso de aseo** toilet bag ► **bolso de bandolera** shoulder bag ► **bolso de viaje** travelling bag, traveling bag (*EEUU*)
[2] (= *monedero*) purse, moneybag, pocketbook
[3] (*Náut*) **hacer ~** [*vela*] to fill, belly out

bolsón Ⓐ ADJ [1] (*Andes*) (= *tonto*) silly, foolish
[2] (*Caribe*) (= *perezoso*) lazy
Ⓑ SM [1] (*Perú*) (= *bolso*) bag, handbag, purse (*EEUU*)
[2] (*Bol Min*) lump of ore
[3] (*LAm*) [*de escuela*] satchel, schoolbag
[4] (*Méx*) (= *lago*) lagoon
[5] (*Andes*) (= *tonto*) fool

bolsonada SF (*Andes, Cono Sur*) silly thing to do

boludear⁑ ▸conjug 1a◂ VI (*Cono Sur*) to piss about**

boludez⁑ SF (*Cono Sur*) [1] (= *cosa fácil*) piece of cake*
[2] (= *acto*) stupid thing to do
[3] **boludeces** shit** *sing*, crap** *sing*

boludo/a⁑ (*Cono Sur*) Ⓐ ADJ thick*, stupid
Ⓑ SM/F arsehole**, asshole (*EEUU***), jerk (*EEUU**)

bomba Ⓐ SF [1] (*Mil*) bomb; **arrojar** *o* **lanzar una ~** (*desde un avión*) to drop a bomb; (*desde el suelo*) to throw a bomb; **poner una ~** to plant a bomb; **a prueba de ~(s)** bomb-proof; **un muro de hormigón a prueba de ~s** a bomb-proof concrete wall; **tiene un estómago a prueba de ~** he's got a cast-iron stomach; **es de una honestidad a prueba de ~** he is as honest as the day is long; ✦*MODISMO* **caer** *o* **sentar como una ~** [*noticia*] to come as a bombshell, be a bombshell; **la cena me cayó como una ~** dinner did not agree with me at all; **las especias me sientan como una ~ en el estómago** spices really upset my stomach ► **bomba atómica** atomic bomb ► **bomba cazabobos** booby-trap bomb ► **bomba de acción retardada** time bomb ► **bomba de dispersión** cluster bomb ► **bomba de efecto retardado** time bomb ► **bomba de fósforo** incendiary bomb ► **bomba de fragmentación** fragmentation bomb ► **bomba de hidrógeno** hydrogen bomb ► **bomba de humo** (*lit*) smoke bomb; (*fig*) smokescreen; **es una ~ de humo para encubrir otras cosas** it is a smokescreen to cover up other things ► **bomba de implosión** suction bomb ► **bomba de mano** (hand) grenade ► **bomba de mortero** mortar bomb, mortar shell ► **bomba de neutrones** neutron bomb ► **bomba de profundidad** depth charge ► **bomba de racimo** (*Cono Sur*) cluster bomb ► **bomba de relojería** time bomb ► **bomba fétida** stink bomb ► **bomba fosfórica** incendiary bomb ► **bomba H** H-bomb ► **bomba incendiaria** incendiary bomb ► **bomba lacrimógena** tear-gas canister, tear-gas bomb ► **bomba lapa** limpet mine ► **bomba nuclear** nuclear bomb ► **bomba sucia** dirty bomb ► **bomba volante** flying bomb
[2] (*Téc*) [*de agua, de aire*] pump; **la ~ de la bicicleta** the bicycle pump; **dar a la ~** to pump, work the pump ► **bomba aspirante** suction pump ► **bomba bencinera** (*Chile*) petrol station, gas station (*EEUU*) ► **bomba de aire** (air) pump ► **bomba de alimentación** feed pump ► **bomba de cobalto** (*Med*) cobalt bomb ► **bomba corazón-pulmón** (*Med*) heart-lung machine ► **bomba de engrase** grease gun ► **bomba de gasolina** (*en motor*) fuel pump; (*en gasolinera*) petrol *o* (*EEUU*) gas(oline) pump ► **bomba de inyección (de combustible)** (fuel) injection pump ► **bomba de pie** foot pump ► **bomba de succión** suction pump ► **bomba impelente** force pump ► **bomba impulsora** force pump
[3] (*Periodismo*) [3·1] (= *notición*) bombshell; **la dimisión del presidente fue una auténtica ~** the president's resignation was a real bombshell; **esta boda ha sido la ~ del año** this wedding has been the big news of the year; **noticia ~** bombshell
[3·2] (*) (= *éxito*) smash hit*; **este disco será una ~** this record will be a smash hit*
[4] (*Mús*) slide
[5] [*de lámpara*] glass, globe
[6] (*Andes, Caribe*) (= *burbuja*) bubble; (= *pompa de jabón*) soap bubble
[7] (*Col, Ven*) (*tb* **~ gasolinera**) petrol station, gas station (*EEUU*)
[8] (*Chile*) [*de bomberos*] (= *vehículo*) fire engine; (= *estación*) fire station; (= *cuerpo*) fire brigade
[9] (*Andes, Ven*) (= *globo*) balloon; (*Caribe*) (= *cometa*) round kite
[10] (*Caribe*) (= *tambor*) big drum; (= *baile*) *dance accompanied by a drum*
[11] (*CAm, Perú*) (= *borrachera*) drunkenness; **estar en ~** to be drunk
[12] (*LAm*) (= *rumor*) false rumour; (= *mentira*) lie; (*Caribe*) (= *noticia falsa*) hoax
Ⓑ ADJ INV (*Esp*†*) (= *estupendo*) **estar ~** [*persona*] to be gorgeous*; **esa tía está ~** that girl is gorgeous*; **éxito ~*** phenomenal success; **el grupo está teniendo un éxito ~ en su gira** the group is having a phenomenally successful tour
Ⓒ ADV (*Esp**) **pasarlo ~** to have a whale of a time*, have a super time*

bombachas SFPL [1] (*Andes, Cono Sur*) (= *pantalón*) baggy trousers
[2] (*Cono Sur*) (= *bragas*) panties

bombacho Ⓐ ADJ baggy, loose-fitting
Ⓑ **bombachos** SMPL (= *pantalones*) baggy trousers; [*de golf*] plus-fours

bomba-lapa SF (*pl* **bombas-lapa**) limpet mine

bombardear ▸conjug 1a◂ VT [1] (= *lanzar bombas*) (*desde el aire*) to bomb; (*desde tierra*) to bombard, shell [2] (= *lanzar preguntas*) to bombard (**a, con** with); **~ a algn a preguntas** to bombard sb with questions

bombardeo SM [1] (*Mil*) (*desde el aire*) bombing; (*con artillería*) bombardment, shelling ► **bombardeo aéreo** (*contable*) air raid, air attack; (*incontable*) air bombardment (**contra, sobre** on); ► **bombardeo de saturación** saturation bombing ► **bombardeo en picado** dive bombing; *ver tb* **apuntar C2**
[2] [*de preguntas*] bombardment

bombardero Ⓐ ADJ bombing
Ⓑ SM (*Aer*) bomber

bombardino SM (*Mús*) tuba, bass saxhorn

bombasí SM fustian

bombástico ADJ (= *grandilocuente*) bombastic; (*Caribe*) (= *elogioso*) complimentary, eulogistic

bomba-trampa SF (*pl* **bombas-trampa**) booby-trap bomb

bombazo SM [1] (= *explosión*) explosion
[2] (*) (= *notición*) bombshell
[3] (*) (= *éxito*) smash hit*; **esa película puede ser un ~** that film could be a smash hit*

bombeador SM [1] (*Cono Sur Aer*) bomber
[2] (*Cono Sur*) (= *explorador*) scout; (= *espía*) spy

bombear ▸conjug 1a◂ Ⓐ VT [1] (*Téc*) [+ *agua, sangre*] to pump
[2] (*Ftbl*) to lob; **un balón bombeado** a high ball
[3] (*Mil*) to shell
[4] (*Cos*) to pad
[5] (= *alabar*) to praise up, inflate the reputation of
[6] (*Cono Sur*⁑) (= *espiar*) to spy on, observe closely
[7] (*Andes, Ven*) (= *despedir*) to sack*, fire*
[8] (*CAm*) (= *robar*) to steal
Ⓑ VI (*Caribe*) (= *emborracharse*) to get drunk
Ⓒ **bombearse** VPR [*techo, pared*] to bulge; [*madera*] to warp

bombeo SM [1] (= *acción*) pumping; **estación de ~** pumping station
[2] (= *convexidad*) [*de superficie*] bulge; [*de madera*] warp

bombero/a SM/F [1] (*de incendios*) firefighter, fireman; **cuerpo de ~s** fire brigade; **llamar a los ~s** to call the fire brigade
[2] (= *persona problemática*) troublemaker; *ver tb* **idea 2**
[3] (*Arg Mil*) (= *explorador*) spy, scout
[4] (*LAm Aut*) petrol-pump attendant, gas station attendant (*EEUU*)

bombilla SF [1] (*Elec*) bulb, light bulb; ✦*MODISMO* **se le encendió la ~** (= *se dio cuenta*) the penny dropped; (= *tuvo una idea genial*) he had a brilliant idea ► **bombilla de flash**, **bombilla fusible** flash bulb
[2] (*Náut*) ship's lantern

[3] (*Cono Sur*) (= *tubito*) *tube for drinking maté*; (= *pajita*) drinking straw
[4] (*Méx*) (= *cuchara*) ladle

bombillo SM [1] (*LAm Elec*) light bulb
[2] (*Téc*) U-bend, trap

bombín SM [1] (= *sombrero*) bowler hat, derby (*EEUU*)
[2] (*Cono Sur*) [*de aire*] pump

bombita SF (*Cono Sur*) light bulb

bombo Ⓐ ADJ [1] (= *aturdido*) dumbfounded, stunned
[2] (*LAm*) (= *tibio*) lukewarm
[3] (*Cuba*) (= *comida*) tasteless, insipid; [*persona*] stupid, thick*
[4] (*Méx*) [*carne*] bad, off
Ⓑ SM [1] (*Mús*) bass drum; **tengo la cabeza como un ~** my head's throbbing *o* buzzing; ✦***MODISMOS*** **estar con ~*** to be in the family way*; **hacer un ~ a una chica*** to put a girl in the family way*; **anunciar algo a ~ y platillo** to announce sth amid a lot of hype, go in for a lot of publicity about sth; **poner a algn ~** (*Méx**) (= *insultar*) to hurl insults at sb; (= *golpear*) to hit sb
[2] (*en sorteos*) drum
[3] (*) (= *elogio exagerado*) exaggerated praise; (*Teat, Cine*) hype*; **dar ~ a algn** to praise sb to the skies; **darse ~** to blow one's own trumpet*
[4] (*Cono Sur*) ✦***MODISMOS*** **mandar a algn al ~‡** to knock sb off‡; **irse al ~** to come to grief, fail
[5] (*Náut*) barge, lighter
[6] (*Caribe*) (= *sombrero*) bowler hat, derby (*EEUU*)

bombón SM [1] [*de chocolate*] chocolate
[2] (*) (= *objeto*) beauty, gem; (= *chica*) peach*, smasher*
[3] (*) (= *chollo*) gift*, cinch‡

bombona SF [1] ► **bombona de butano** gas cylinder
[2] (= *garrafón*) carboy

bombonera SF [1] (= *caja*) sweet box; (= *lata*) sweet tin, sweet box
[2] (*) (= *lugar*) cosy little place

bombonería SF sweetshop, confectioner's, confectioner's shop, candy store (*EEUU*)

bómper SM (*CAm, Caribe*) bumper, fender (*EEUU*)

Bón. ABR (= **Batallón**) Battn

bonachón ADJ (= *de buenas intenciones*) good-natured, easy-going; (*pey*) simple, naïve

bonachonamente ADV (= *con buenas intenciones*) good-naturedly, in an easy-going way; (*pey*) naïvely

bonaerense Ⓐ ADJ of/from Buenos Aires
Ⓑ SMF native/inhabitant of Buenos Aires; **los ~s** the people of Buenos Aires

bonancible ADJ [*viento*] light

bonanza SF [1] (*Náut*) fair weather, calm conditions; **ir en ~** (*Náut*) to have fair weather; (= *prosperar*) to go well, prosper
[2] (*Min*) bonanza
[3] (= *prosperidad*) prosperity, boom; **estar en ~** (*Com*) to be booming; **ir en ~** go well, prosper

bonazo ADJ = **buenazo**

bonchar* ▸conjug 1a◂ VI (*Caribe*) (= *hacer una fiesta*) to have a party; (= *pasarlo bien*) to have a good time

bonche¹ SM (*LAm*) (= *montón*) load, bunch

bonche²* SM (*Caribe*) [1] (= *fiesta*) party
[2] (= *cosa divertida*) amusing thing; (= *persona divertida*) amusing person

bonche³* SM petting*, necking*

bonchón SM, **bonchona** SF fun-loving person

bondad SF (= *cualidad*) goodness; (= *amabilidad*) kindness; **tener la ~ de hacer algo** to be so kind as to do sth, be good enough to do sth; **tenga la ~ de pasar** please go in; **tenga la ~ de no fumar** please refrain from smoking

bondadosamente ADV [1] (= *amablemente*) kindly
[2] (= *con buenas intenciones*) good-naturedly

bondadoso ADJ (= *amable*) kind-hearted; (= *de buenas intenciones*) good-natured

bondi SM (*Cono Sur*) tram

bonete SM (*Rel*) biretta; (*Univ*) mortarboard; **¡bonete!** (*CAm**) not on your life!, no way!*; ✦***MODISMO*** **a tente ~** doggedly, insistently

bonetería SF (*esp Méx*) haberdasher's (shop), notions store (*EEUU*)

bóngalo SM, **bongaló** SM bungalow

bongo SM (*Náut*) (*LAm*) large canoe; (*Andes*) small punt

bongó SM (*Caribe*) bongo, bongo drum

boni‡ SM = **boniato**

boniata Ⓐ ADJ (*LAm*) edible, non-poisonous
Ⓑ SF (*Caribe*) edible yucca, cassava

boniato SM sweet potato, yam

bonificación SF [1] (= *pago*) bonus; (*esp Agr*) betterment, improvement (*in value*)
[2] (*Com*) (= *descuento*) allowance, discount
[3] (*Dep*) allowance of points

bonificar ▸conjug 1g◂ Ⓐ VT [1] (*Agr*) to improve
[2] (*Com*) to allow, discount
Ⓑ **bonificarse** VPR to improve

bonísimo (*frm*) ADJ SUPERL *de* **bueno**

bonitamente ADV (= *con delicadeza*) nicely, neatly; (= *con maña*) craftily

bonitero Ⓐ ADJ bonito *antes de s*
Ⓑ SM [1] (= *pescador*) bonito fisherman
[2] (= *barco*) bonito fishing boat

bonito¹ Ⓐ ADJ [1] (= *bello*) pretty; **María es un ~ nombre** María is a pretty name; **Amelia tiene una cara bonita** Amelia has a pretty face; **el pueblo más ~ de Andalucía** the prettiest village in Andalusia; **es un bebé muy ~** he's a very pretty baby, he's a lovely baby; **un hombre ~** (*Cono Sur*) a handsome man; **¡qué ~! ¡contestarle así a tu padre!** (*iró*) that's nice, answering your father back like that!; **¡~ follón se armó!*** (*iró*) there was certainly a bit of a row!; **lo ~**: **lo ~ sería que no hubiera guerras** it would be nice if there were no wars; **quedar ~**: **ese cuadro queda ahí muy ~** that picture looks very nice there; **el vendedor me lo pintó todo muy ~** the salesman painted me a very pretty picture of it; ✦***MODISMO*** **~ como un sol** as pretty as a picture
[2] (= *considerable*) **una bonita cantidad** *o* **suma** a tidy little sum*, a pretty penny*
Ⓑ ADV (*LAm**) nicely; **ella canta ~** she sings nicely; **se te ve ~** it looks good on you

bonito² SM (= *pez*) tuna, bonito

bonitura SF (*LAm*) beauty, attractiveness

bono SM [1] (= *vale*) voucher, certificate ► **bono de metro** underground pass
[2] (*Fin*) bond ► **bono de caja** debenture bond ► **bono del estado** government bond ► **bono del Tesoro** Treasury bond ► **bono de tesorería** debenture bond

bono-bus SM (*pl* **bono-buses**) (*Esp*), **bonobús** SM (*pl* **bonobuses**) (*Esp*) bus pass

bono-loto SF, **bonoloto** SF *state-run weekly lottery*; → LOTERÍA

bono-metro SM underground pass

bonsai SM bonsai

bonzo SM bonze; **quemarse a lo ~** to set o.s. alight

boñiga SF, **boñigo** SM [*de vaca*] cow pat; [*de caballo*] horse dung

boom [bum] SM boom; **dar ~ a un problema** to exaggerate a problem, make a meal of a problem ► **boom inmobiliario** property boom

boomerang [bumeran] SM (*pl* **boomerangs**) boomerang

boqueada SF gasp; **dar la última ~** to breathe one's last

boquear ▸conjug 1a◂ Ⓐ VT to say, utter, pronounce
Ⓑ VI [1] (= *quedar boquiabierto*) to gape, gasp
[2] (= *estar expirando*) to be at one's last gasp
[3] (= *terminar*) to be in its final stages

boquera Ⓐ SF [1] (*Agr*) sluice
[2] (*Med*) lip sore
Ⓑ **boqueras‡** SMF INV screw‡, warder

boqueriento ADJ [1] (*Med*) suffering from lip sores
[2] (*Cono Sur*) (= *miserable*) wretched, miserable

boquerón SM [1] (= *pez*) fresh anchovy
[2] (= *abertura*) wide opening, big hole
[3] (*) (= *persona*) = **malagueño**

boquete SM [1] (= *agujero*) hole; **abrieron un ~ en el muro** they made a hole in the wall
[2] (= *abertura*) gap, opening

boqui‡ SMF screw‡, warder

boquiabierto ADJ open-mouthed; **quedarse ~** to be dumbstruck

boquiancho ADJ wide-mouthed

boquiblando ADJ [*caballo*] tender-mouthed

boquifresco* ADJ (= *descarado*) outspoken, cheeky*, sassy (*EEUU**)

boquilla SF [1] (*Mús*) mouthpiece
[2] (= *extremo*) [*de manga*] nozzle; [*de cocina*] burner; [*de biberón*] teat, nipple (*EEUU*); [*de pipa*] stem; (*para fumar*) cigarette holder; **cigarros con ~** tipped cigarettes
[3] ✦***MODISMO*** **de ~**: **apoyó la idea de ~** he paid lip-service to the idea; **eso lo dice de ~** he's just saying that, that's what he says (but he doesn't mean it); **promesa de ~** insincere promise, promise not meant to be kept
[4] (*Andes*) (= *chisme*) rumour, piece of gossip

boquillazo SM (*Andes*) rumour, talk

boquillero ADJ (*Caribe*) smooth-talking, sweet-talking

boquirroto ADJ talkative, garrulous

boquirrubio Ⓐ ADJ [1] (= *gárrulo*) talkative; (= *de mucha labia*) glib; (= *indiscreto*) indiscreet, loose-tongued
[2] (= *simple*) simple, naïve
Ⓑ SM fop, dandy

boquita SF **~ de piñón** pursed lips *pl*

boquitinguero ADJ (*Cono Sur*) gossipy
boquituerto ADJ wry-mouthed
boquiverde* ADJ foul-mouthed
boraciar ▸conjug 1b◂ VI (*Cono Sur*) to boast, brag
bórax SM borax
borbollar ▸conjug 1a◂ VI, **borbollear** ▸conjug 1a◂ VI [1] (= *burbujear*) to bubble, boil up [2] (= *chisporrotear*) to splutter
borbollón SM = **borbotón**
borbollonear ▸conjug 1a◂ VI = **borbollar**
Borbón SM Bourbon
borbónico ADJ Bourbon *antes de s*
borbotar ▸conjug 1a◂ [1] VI (= *hacer burbujas*) to bubble; (*al hervir*) to boil, boil up, boil over [2] (= *nacer*) to gush forth, well up
borbotón SM (= *de agua, líquido*) bubbling, boiling; **salir a borbotones** [*agua, sangre*] to gush out; **hablar a borbotones** to talk nineteen to the dozen
borceguí SM (= *botín*) high shoe, laced boot; [*de bebé*] bootee
borda SF (*Náut*) [1] gunwale, rail; **motor de fuera ~** outboard motor; ✦***MODISMO*** **echar** *o* **tirar algo por la ~** to throw sth overboard [2] (= *vela*) mainsail [3] (= *choza*) hut
bordada SF (*Náut*) tack; **dar ~s** (*lit*) to tack; (*fig*) to pace to and fro
bordado SM embroidery, needlework
bordadora SF needlewoman
bordadura SF embroidery, needlework
bordalesa* SF (*Cono Sur*) *wine barrel holding 225 litres*
bordante SMF (*Caribe, Méx*) lodger, roomer (*EEUU*)
bordar ▸conjug 1a◂ [1] VT (*Cos*) to embroider; **bordado a mano** hand-embroidered [2] (= *hacer perfectamente*) to do supremely well; **ha bordado su papel** she was excellent in her part
borde[1] SM [1] [*de asiento, andén, pañuelo*] edge; [*de plato*] rim, lip; [*de vaso, sombrero*] brim; [*de carretera, camino*] side; [*de ventana*] ledge; [*de río*] edge, bank; **se sentó en el ~ del sofá** she sat down on the edge of the sofa; **fotos con los ~s en blanco** photos with white borders *o* edges; **sembró semillas en los ~s del césped** he sowed some seeds at the sides *o* edges of the lawn; **iba andando por el ~ de la carretera** she was walking by the roadside *o* by the side of the road; **en el ~ del Sena** on the banks of the Seine ► **borde de ataque** (*Aer*) leading edge ► **borde de la acera** kerb, curb (*EEUU*) ► **borde de salida** (*Aer*) trailing edge [2] **al ~ de** [+ *precipicio, lago, cráter*] at *o* on the edge of; [+ *quiebra, histeria, crisis*] on the verge of; **el régimen está al ~ del colapso** the regime is on the verge of collapse *o* on the point of collapsing; **estamos al mismo ~ del desastre** we are on the very brink of disaster; **su carrera política está al ~ del abismo** her political career is teetering on the edge of the abyss; **están al ~ de los cuarenta años** they're close to forty, they're hitting *o* pushing forty*; **al ~ del mar** beside the sea; **al ~ de la muerte** at death's door; **estuvo al ~ de la muerte por congelación** she nearly froze to death
borde[2] (*Esp*) (A) ADJ [1] (‡) (= *antipático*) nasty; **estuviste muy ~ con él** you were very nasty to him; **estuvo toda la mañana en plan ~** he was in a strop‡ *o* in a foul mood* all morning; **ponerse ~ (con algn)** to get stroppy (with sb)*, get nasty (with sb) [2] [*planta, árbol*] wild [3] (††) [*niño*] illegitimate (B) SMF (‡) **¡eres un ~!** you're a nasty piece of work!*
bordear ▸conjug 1a◂ (A) VT [1] (= *rodear*) to skirt (round); **tuvimos que ~ la montaña** we had to skirt round the mountain; **navegamos bordeando la costa** we sailed along the edge of the coast [2] [*calle, árboles*] (= *estar alrededor de*) to border, border on; (= *flanquear*) to line; **la calle que bordeaba el parque** the street bordering (on) the park; **un paseo que bordea el mar** a promenade running along the sea; **un camino bordeado de cipreses** a road lined with cypress trees [3] (= *acercarse a*) [+ *edad*] to be approaching, be close to; [+ *genialidad, obsesión*] to border on; **bordea los sesenta años** he's approaching sixty, he's close to sixty; **su comportamiento bordea la estupidez** his behaviour borders on stupidity [4] (*Cono Sur*) (= *evitar*) **~ un asunto** to skirt round *o* avoid a (tricky) subject (B) VI (*Náut*) to tack
bordejada SF (*Caribe Náut*) tack
bordejar ▸conjug 1a◂ VI (*Caribe*), **bordejear** ▸conjug 1a◂ VI (*Caribe Náut*) to tack
bordelés/esa (A) ADJ of/from Bordeaux (B) SM/F native/inhabitant of Bordeaux; **los bordeleses** the people of Bordeaux
bordería* SF stroppiness*; **decir ~s** to be rude
bordillo SM kerb, curb (*EEUU*)
bordin SM (*Andes, Caribe, Méx*) boarding house
bordinguero/a SM/F (*Andes, Caribe, Méx*) landlord/landlady
bordo SM [1] (*Náut*) **a ~** aboard, on board; **"bienvenidos a ~"** "welcome aboard"; **estar a ~ del barco** to be on board the ship; **con ordenador de a ~** with on-board computer; **ir a ~** (*Náut*) to go on board; (*Aer*) to board; **de alto ~**: **buque de alto ~** big ship, seagoing vessel; **personaje de alto ~** distinguished person, influential person [2] (= *bordada*) tack; **dar ~s** to tack [3] (*Méx Agr*) roughly-built dam [4] (*Cono Sur*) (= *dique*) raised furrow [5] (*CAm*) [*de montaña*] peak, summit
bordó (*Arg*) ADJ INV, SM maroon
bordón SM [1] (= *bastón*) [*de peregrino*] staff; [*de ciego*] stick [2] (= *ayuda*) helping hand [3] (*Mús*) (= *cuerda*) bass string; (= *registro*) bass stop, bourdon [4] (*Literat*) refrain [5] (*Andes, CAm*) (= *hijo menor*) youngest son
bordona SF (*Cono Sur*) *sixth string of the guitar*; **bordonas** bass strings of the guitar
bordoncillo SM pet word, pet phrase
bordonear ▸conjug 1a◂ (A) VT (*Mús*) to strum (B) VI (*Andes*) (= *zumbar*) to hum
bordoneo SM (*Mús*) strumming
boreal ADJ northern; **el hemisferio ~** the northern hemisphere
borgesiano ADJ, **borgiano** ADJ Borgesian, characteristic of J L Borges
Borgoña SF Burgundy
borgoña SM (*tb* **vino de ~**) Burgundy
bórico ADJ boric
boricua ADJ, SM/F, **borinqueño/a** ADJ, SM/F Puerto Rican
Borja SM (= *familia italiana*) Borgia
borla SF [*de cortina*] tassel; [*de gorro*] pompom; (*Univ*) tassel; **tomar la ~** (*Univ*) to take one's master's degree *o* doctorate ► **borla de empolvarse** powder puff
borlete SM (*Méx*), **borlote** SM (*Méx*) row, uproar
borne SM (*Elec*) terminal
borneadizo ADJ easily warped, flexible
bornear ▸conjug 1a◂ (A) VT [1] (= *torcer*) to twist, bend [2] (*Arquit*) to put in place, align [3] (*Méx*) [+ *pelota*] spin (B) **bornearse** VPR to warp, bulge
borneco ADJ (*Cono Sur*) small, short
borneo SM [1] (= *torcimiento*) twisting, bending [2] (*Arquit*) alignment [3] (*Náut*) swinging at anchor
boro SM (*Quím*) boron
borona SF [1] (= *maíz*) maize, corn (*EEUU*) [2] (= *mijo*) millet [3] (*CAm*) (= *migaja*) crumb
borra SF [1] (= *relleno*) (*para colchones*) flock; (*para cojines*) stuffing [2] (= *pelusa*) [*de polvo*] fluff; (*Bot*) down ► **borra de algodón** cotton waste ► **borra de seda** floss silk [3] (*Zool*) yearling ewe [4] (= *sedimento*) sediment, lees [5] (*) (= *charla insustancial*) empty talk; (= *tonterías*) trash, rubbish
borrachear* ▸conjug 1a◂ VI to booze*, get drunk habitually
borrachera SF [1] (= *estado*) drunkenness; **coger** *o* **pillar** *o* **agarrar** *o* (*Méx*) **ponerse una ~** to get drunk; **quitarse la ~** to sober up [2] (= *juerga*) spree, binge
borrachez SF drunkenness, drunken state
borrachín SM boozer*
borracho/a (A) ADJ [1] [*persona*] **está ~** he's drunk; **es muy ~** he's a drunkard, he's a heavy drinker; ✦***MODISMO*** **estar ~ como una cuba** to be plastered*, be blind drunk* [2] (= *poseído*) drunk, blind (**de** with) [3] (*Culin*) [*bizcocho*] tipsy (*soaked in liqueur o spirit*); [*fruta*] marinated [4] (*de color*) violet (B) SM/F drunkard, drunk
borrado SM erasure
borrador SM [1] (= *versión*) [*de texto*] first draft, rough copy; [*de pintura, dibujo*] rough sketch; **hacer un nuevo ~** to do a redraft [2] (= *cuaderno*) scribbling pad, scratch pad (*EEUU*); (*Com*) daybook [3] (*para pizarra*) rubber, duster, eraser (*EEUU*)
borradura SF erasure, crossing out
borraja SF borage; *ver tb* **agua 1**
borrajear ▸conjug 1a◂ VT, VI to scribble, scrawl
borrar ▸conjug 1a◂ (A) VT [1] (= *hacer desaparecer*) [1·1] [+ *palabra, dibujo*] (*con goma*) to rub out, erase; (*con borrador*) to rub off, clean off; **la fecha había sido cuidadosamente borrada** the date had been carefully

rubbed out o erased; **borra lo que has puesto en la pizarra** rub off o clean off what you've put on the blackboard; **bórralo con Tippex** white it out with Tipp-Ex®, tippex it out; ✦*MODISMO* **~ a algn/algo del mapa** to wipe sb/sth off the map

1·2 [+ *señal, mancha*] to remove; [+ *pintada*] to clean off; [+ *huellas*] to wipe off, rub off

1·3 [+ *mensaje, fichero*] to delete, erase; [+ *canción, película*] to tape over, erase; **he borrado todos los mensajes del contestador** I've erased o deleted all the messages on the answering machine; **¿no habrás borrado el partido de fútbol?** you haven't taped over o erased the football match, have you?

1·4 [+ *impresión*] to wipe away, erase; **he borrado de mi mente aquellas imágenes** I have wiped away o erased those images from my mind; **consiguió ~ aquellos malos recuerdos** he managed to wipe away o erase all those painful memories; **era como si se hubieran borrado 40 años de la historia** it was as if 40 years of history had been wiped clean o erased; **no podía ~ de su cara las huellas del cansancio** he was unable to wipe away the signs of fatigue from his face

2 (= *limpiar*) [+ *disquete, cinta*] to erase; [+ *pantalla*] to clear; **~ la pizarra** to clean the blackboard

3 (= *dar de baja a*) **~ a algn de** [+ *clase, actividad*] to take sb out of, remove sb from; [+ *lista, curso*] to take sb off, remove sb from; **borró a los niños de la clase de natación** she took the children out of the swimming class, she removed the children from the swimming class; **bórranos de la excursión del sábado** take us off the list for Saturday's outing, count us out of Saturday's outing*

4 (*Fot*) (= *poner borroso*) to blur

5 (*Pol*) **~ a algn** (*euf*) to deal with sb, dispose of sb

Ⓑ **borrarse** VPR 1 (= *darse de baja*) **~se de** [+ *club, asociación*] to cancel one's membership of, resign from; [+ *curso*] to drop out of; **se borró de la biblioteca** she cancelled her library membership; **siempre hay alguien que se borra del curso al principio** there's always somebody who drops out of the course at the beginning

2 (= *desaparecer*) [*señal, marca*] to fade away; [*imagen, recuerdo*] to fade; [*duda, sospecha, temor*] to disappear, be dispelled; [*sonrisa*] to vanish; **se había borrado el código** the code number had faded away; **eso se borra con agua** that comes off o washes off with water; **lo que pasó aquel día se me ha borrado con el tiempo** the memory of what happened that day has faded with time; **no se han borrado las sospechas entre la pareja** the suspicion between the two of them has not disappeared o been dispelled

3 (*Fot*) to fade

borrasca SF 1 area of low pressure, depression; **viene una ~ por el Atlántico** there's low pressure o a low approaching from the Atlantic

2 (= *tormenta*) (*en tierra*) storm; (*en el mar*) squall

3 (= *peligro*) peril, hazard; (= *mala racha*) setback

4 (*) (= *juerga*) orgy, spree

borrascoso ADJ 1 [*tiempo*] stormy; [*viento*] squally, gusty

2 (= *problemático*) stormy, tempestuous

borrasquero ADJ riotous, wild

borregada* SF student rag*, prank

borregaje SM (*Cono Sur*) flock of lambs

borrego/a Ⓐ SM/F 1 (*Zool*) (= *oveja joven*) lamb, yearling lamb; (= *oveja adulta*) sheep

2 (= *persona*) **le siguieron como ~s** they followed him like sheep

Ⓑ SM 1 (*Cuba, Méx**) hoax

2 **borregos** (= *nubes*) fleecy clouds; (*Náut*) foamy crests of waves, white horses, white caps (*EEUU*)

borreguil ADJ meek, like a lamb

borreguillo SM fleece ► **forro de borreguillo** fleece lining

borricada SF silly thing, piece of nonsense

borrico/a Ⓐ SM/F 1 (*Zool*) donkey/she-donkey

2 (= *persona*) fool

Ⓑ SM (*Téc*) sawhorse, sawbuck (*EEUU*)

borricón* SM, **borricote*** SM (= *hombre paciente*) long-suffering person

borriquete SM (*Arte*) easel; (*Téc*) sawhorse, sawbuck (*EEUU*)

borrón SM 1 (= *mancha*) blot, stain; ✦*MODISMO* **hacer ~ y cuenta nueva** (= *olvidar el pasado*) to let bygones be bygones; (= *empezar de nuevo*) to wipe the slate clean

2 (= *vergüenza*) blemish

3 (*Literat*) rough draft; (*Arte*) preliminary sketch; **estos borrones** (*iró*) these humble jottings

borronear ▸conjug 1a◂ VT 1 (= *garabatear*) to scribble, scrawl

2 (= *hacer borrador de*) to make a rough draft of

borroso ADJ 1 (= *indistinguible*) [*foto, imagen*] blurred, indistinct; [*escrito*] smudgy; **lo veo todo ~** everything is blurred

2 [*idea, recuerdo*] vague, hazy

boruca* SF row, din

borujo SM lump, pressed mass, packed mass

borujón SM 1 (*Med*) bump, lump

2 (= *lío*) bundle

boruquear ▸conjug 1a◂ VT (*Méx*) (= *revolver*) to mix up, mess up; (= *inmiscuirse*) to stir up

boscaje SM 1 (= *bosque*) thicket, grove

2 (*Arte*) woodland scene

Bosco SM **el ~** Hieronymus Bosch

boscoso ADJ wooded

Bósforo SM **el (Estrecho del) ~** the Bosp(h)orus

Bosnia SF Bosnia ► **Bosnia Herzegovina** Bosnia Herzegovina

bosnio/a ADJ, SM/F Bosnian

bosorola SF (*CAm, Méx*) sediment, dregs *pl*

bosque SM 1 (= *terreno con árboles*) wood; (*más denso*) forest

2 (*LAm**) (= *selva*) jungle, rainforest ► **bosque pluvial** rainforest

bosquecillo SM copse, small wood

bosquejar ▸conjug 1a◂ VT 1 (*Arte*) to sketch

2 (= *dar forma a*) [+ *idea*] to sketch, outline; [+ *plan*] to draft

bosquejo SM 1 (*Arte*) sketch

2 (= *forma provisional*) [*de idea*] sketch, outline; [*de plan*] draft

bosquete SM copse, small wood

bosquimán(a) SM/F, **bosquimano/a** SM/F African bushman/bushwoman

bosta SF (= *excremento*) dung, droppings *pl*; (*para estiércol*) manure

bostezar ▸conjug 1f◂ VI to yawn

bostezo SM yawn

bota SF 1 (= *calzado*) boot; ✦*MODISMOS* **morir con las ~s puestas** to die with one's boots on; **ponerse las ~s*** (= *enriquecerse*) to strike it rich; (= *comer mucho*) to have a blow-out* ► **botas camperas** cowboy boots ► **botas de agua** wellingtons, gumboots ► **botas de campaña** cowboy boots ► **botas de esquí** ski boots ► **botas de fútbol** football boots ► **botas de goma** gumboots ► **botas de media caña** ankle boots ► **botas de montaña** mountain boots ► **botas de montar** riding boots

2 ► **bota de vino** *wineskin bottle*

3 (= *tonel*) large barrel

4 (= *medida*) 516 litres

botada SF (*LAm*) (= *tirada*) [*de objeto, pelota*] throw, throwing; [*de basura*] throwing away; (*) [*de trabajador*] sacking*

botadero SM 1 (*LAm*) (= *vertedero*) rubbish dump

2 (*Andes*) (= *vado*) ford

botado/a Ⓐ ADJ 1 (= *descarado*) cheeky, sassy (*EEUU**)

2 (*Méx**) (= *barato*) dirt cheap

3 (*CAm*) (= *despilfarrador*) spendthrift

4 (*Andes*) (= *resignado*) resigned; (= *dispuesto para todo*) ready for anything, resolute

5 (*CAm, Méx*) (= *borracho*) blind drunk

Ⓑ SM/F 1 (*LAm*) (*tb* **niño ~**) foundling

2 (*Andes*) (= *vago*) good-for-nothing, bum (*EEUU**)

botador(a) Ⓐ SM/F (*LAm*) (= *despilfarrador*) spendthrift

Ⓑ SM 1 (*Náut*) pole, punt pole

2 (= *sacaclavos*) nail-puller, claw-hammer

botadura SF 1 (*Náut*) launching

2 (*LAm*) = **botada**

botafuego SM (††) linstock; (*) quick-tempered person

botalodo SM (*Andes, Caribe*) mudguard, fender (*EEUU*)

botalón SM 1 (*Náut*) outrigger ► **botalón de foque** jib-boom

2 (*Andes, Cono Sur*) (= *viga*) beam, prop

3 (*Andes*) (= *poste*) post, stake; [*de atar*] hitching post

botana SF (*Méx*) snack, appetizer

botanearse* ▸conjug 1a◂ VPR **~ a algn** (*LAm*) to speak ill of sb, drag sb's name through the dirt

botaneo* SM (*LAm*) gossip, malicious gossip, slander

botánica SF botany

botánico/a Ⓐ ADJ botanical

Ⓑ SM/F botanist

botanista SMF botanist

botar ▸conjug 1a◂ Ⓐ VT 1 (*Dep*) [+ *pelota*] to bounce

2 (*Náut*) [+ *barco*] to launch; [+ *timón*] to put over

3 (*LAm*) (= *tirar*) to throw away, throw out, chuck out*; (= *despedir*) to fire*, sack*; **~ un saque de esquina** to take a corner kick; **lo ~on de su trabajo** he was fired o sacked*

4 (*LAm*) (= *derrochar*) to fritter away,

squander
5 (Chile, Col, Ven) (= derramar) to spill
6 (Chile, Col, Ven) (= derribar) [+ florero, persona] to knock over; [+ árbol] to knock down
Ⓑ VI 1 (Esp) [pelota] to bounce; [coche] to bump, jolt; [caballo] to rear up
2 (Esp) [persona] to jump; **estaba botando de alegría** she was jumping for joy; ✦MODISMO **está que bota*** he's hopping mad*

botaratada SF wild scheme, nonsensical idea

botarate SM/F 1 (= loco) madcap
2 (= imbécil) idiot
3 (LAm) (= despilfarrador) spendthrift

botarel SM buttress

botarga SF motley, clown's outfit

botavara SF 1 (Náut) boom
2 (Caribe) [de carro] pole, shaft

bote[1] SM 1 [de pelota] bounce; **dar un ~** to bounce
2 (Esp) (= salto) [de persona, caballo] jump; **se levantó de un ~** he jumped up, he leapt to his feet; **dar** o **pegar un ~** [persona] to jump; [coche] to bump, jolt; ✦MODISMOS **a ~ pronto*** (just) off the top of one's head*; **dar el ~ a algn*** to chuck sb out*, give sb the boot*, give sb the push*; **darse el ~** (Esp*) to beat it*; **de ~ y voleo** instantly
3 (= arremetida) (con un arma) thrust; (con el cuerpo) lunge

bote[2] SM 1 (= recipiente) [de vidrio] jar; [de plástico] container; [de metal] (para conservas, pintura) can, tin; (para bebidas) can; **un ~ de colonia** a bottle of cologne; **de ~** canned, tinned; **esta sopa es de ~** this is canned o tinned soup; **es rubia de ~*** she's a fake blonde; ✦MODISMOS **chupar del ~** (Esp*) to line one's own pocket*, feather one's own nest*; **estar de ~ en ~*** to be packed, be jam-packed*; **estar en el ~** (Esp*) [título, premio] to be in the bag*, be all sewn up*; **meterse a algn en el ~** (Esp*) to talk sb round, sweet-talk sb*; **pegarse el ~ con algn** to get on with sb like a house on fire*; **tener algo en el ~** (Esp*) to have sth in the bag*, have sth all sewn up*; **tener a algn (metido) en el ~** (Esp*) to have sb in one's pocket*
► **bote de basura** (Méx) dustbin, trash can (EEUU) ► **bote de cerveza** (Esp) (lleno) can of beer; (vacío) beer can ► **bote de cuestación** collecting tin ► **bote de humo** smoke canister
2 (como propina) **hoy hemos sacado un ~ de 40 euros** we got 40 euros in tips today; **un euro para el ~** a euro for the tips box; **"bote"** "tips"
3 (= fondo común) kitty; **poner un ~** to have a kitty; **pusimos un ~ de diez libras cada uno** we each put ten pounds into the kitty
4 (en lotería, quiniela) jackpot; **hay un ~ de 300 millones** the jackpot is 300 million
5 (CAm, Méx, Ven*) (= cárcel) jail, nick*, can (EEUU*)

bote[3] SM (= barca) [de pesca] boat; (deportivo) skiff ► **bote de a ocho** racing eight ► **bote de carrera** skiff ► **bote de paseo** rowing boat, rowboat (EEUU) ► **bote de paso** ferryboat ► **bote de remos** rowing boat, rowboat (EEUU) ► **bote de salvamento** lifeboat ► **bote hinchable** inflatable dinghy ► **bote neumático** rubber dinghy ► **bote patrullero** patrol boat ► **bote salvavidas** lifeboat

botella SF 1 (= envase) bottle; **de** o **en ~** bottled; **cerveza de ~** bottled beer; **media ~** half bottle; **~ de vino** (= contenido) bottle of wine; (= envase) wine bottle ► **botella de Leiden** Leyden jar 2 (Caribe) (= prebenda) sinecure, soft job (in government)

botellazo SM blow with a bottle

botellería SF (Cono Sur) wine shop

botellero SM wine rack

botellín SM small bottle, half bottle

botellón* SM (Esp) open-air drinking session (involving groups of young people)

botepronto SM (Dep) half-volley; ver tb **bote**[1] **1**

botería SF (Cono Sur) shoe shop

bote-vivienda SM (pl **botes-vivienda**) houseboat

botica SF 1 (= establecimiento) chemist's, chemist's shop, pharmacy (EEUU), drugstore; ✦MODISMO **de todo como en ~** everything under the sun
2 (*) (= cremallera) trouser fly, flies pl

boticario/a SM/F chemist, druggist (EEUU)

botija Ⓐ SF 1 (= vasija) earthenware jug; ✦MODISMOS **estar como una ~** to be as round as a barrel; **poner a algn como ~ verde** (CAm) to insult sb
2 (CAm) (= tesoro) buried treasure
Ⓑ SMF (Uru*) (= chaval) kid*

botijo SM 1 (= recipiente) *earthenware drinking jug with spout and handle*
2 (*) [de policía] water cannon

botijón* ADJ (Méx) pot-bellied

botijuela SF (LAm) 1 (= jarro) earthenware jug 2 (= tesoro) buried treasure

botillería SF (Chile) off-licence, liquor store (EEUU)

botillero SM (Méx) shoemaker, cobbler

botín[1] SM [de guerra] booty, plunder; [de ladrón] loot

botín[2] SM 1 (= calzado) ankle boot
2 (= polaina) legging, spat
3 (Chile) (= borceguí) bootee
4 (Cono Sur) (= calcetín) sock

botina SF (= calzado) high shoe; [de bebé] bootee

botiquín SM 1 (= armario) medicine cabinet; (= conjunto de medicinas) first-aid kit ► **botiquín de emergencia, botiquín de primeros auxilios** first-aid kit
2 (= enfermería) first-aid post, first-aid station (EEUU), sick bay
3 (Caribe hum) (para bebidas) drinks cupboard

boto Ⓐ ADJ 1 [punta] blunt
2 (= torpe) dull, dim
Ⓑ SM *wineskin bottle*

botón SM 1 (Cos, Téc) button; **apretar** o **pulsar el ~** to press the button; ✦MODISMO **¡ni un ~!*** not a sausage!* ► **botón de alarma** alarm, alarm button ► **botón de arranque** starter, starter switch ► **botón de contacto** push-button ► **botón de destrucción** destruct button ► **botón de muestra** sample, illustration ► **botón de presión** push-button
2 (Bot) bud ► **botón de oro** buttercup

botonadura SF buttons pl, set of buttons

botonar ▸conjug 1a◂ (LAm) Ⓐ VT to button, button up
Ⓑ VI to bud, sprout

botones SM INV bellboy, bellhop (EEUU)

Botsuana SF Botswana

botulismo SM botulism

boutique [buˈtik] SF boutique ► **boutique del pan** *fashionable bakery specializing in foreign and wholefood bread*

bóveda SF 1 (Arquit) vault ► **bóveda celeste** vault of heaven ► **bóveda craneal** cranial cavity ► **bóveda de cañón** barrel vault
2 (= cueva) cave, cavern

bovedillas* SFPL ✦MODISMO **subirse a las ~** to go up the wall*

bovino Ⓐ ADJ bovine; **carne bovina** beef; **ganado ~** cattle
Ⓑ SM bovine; **ovinos y ~s** sheep and cattle; **carne de ~** beef

box SM 1 (Aut) pit; **entrar en ~es** to go into the pits, make a pit stop
2 (Equitación) stall
3 (LAm) (= boxeo) boxing

boxeador(a) SM/F boxer

boxear ▸conjug 1a◂ VI to box

boxeo SM boxing

bóxer SMF boxer, boxer dog

boxístico ADJ, **boxeril** ADJ (Cono Sur) boxing *antes de s*

boya SF (Náut) buoy; (Pesca) float ► **boya de campana** bell buoy

boyada SF drove of oxen

boyante ADJ 1 (Náut) buoyant
2 (= próspero) [persona] buoyant; [negocio] prosperous

boyar ▸conjug 1a◂ VI to float

boyazo SM (CAm, Cono Sur) punch

boyé SM (Cono Sur) snake

boyera SF, **boyeriza** SF cattle shed

boyero/a Ⓐ SM/F (= persona) oxherd, drover
Ⓑ SM 1 (= perro) cattle dog
2 (Andes) (= aguijada) goad, spike

bozada SF (Andes) halter

bozal Ⓐ SM 1 [de perro] muzzle
2 (LAm) [de caballo] halter
Ⓑ ADJ 1 (= nuevo) [recluta] new, raw; [animal] wild, untamed
2 (= tonto) stupid
3 (LAm) [negro] pure
4 (LAm) *speaking broken Spanish*

bozo SM 1 [de adolescente] fuzz
2 (= boca) mouth, lips pl
3 (= cabestro) halter, headstall

bracamonte SM (Andes) ghost

bracear ▸conjug 1a◂ Ⓐ VT 1 (Náut) to measure in fathoms
2 [+ horno] to tap
Ⓑ VI 1 (= mover los brazos) to swing one's arms; (al nadar) to swim
2 (= luchar) to wrestle, struggle

bracero SM 1 (Agr) (= jornalero) farmhand, farm labourer o (EEUU) laborer
2 (= peón) labourer, laborer (EEUU), navvy
3 **ir de ~** to walk arm-in-arm

bracete SM **ir del ~** to walk arm-in-arm

bracmán SM Brahman, Brahmin

braco Ⓐ ADJ pug-nosed
Ⓑ SM (tb **perro ~**) setter

braga SF 1 **bragas** [*de mujer*] knickers, panties; ✦*MODISMOS* **dejar a algn en ~s*** to leave sb empty-handed; **estar en ~s*** to be broke*, be skint*; **estar hecho una ~*** to be knackered*; **pillar a algn en ~s*** to catch sb with his pants down*
2 [*de niño*] nappy, diaper (*EEUU*)
3 (*Náut, Téc*) sling, rope (*for hoisting*)

bragado ADJ gritty

bragadura SF (*Cos*) crotch

braga-faja SF panty girdle

bragapañal SM disposable nappy, disposable diaper (*EEUU*)

bragazas* SM INV henpecked husband

braguero SM (*Med*) truss

bragueta SF (*Cos*) fly, flies *pl*, zipper (*EEUU*); ✦*MODISMOS* **estar como ~ de fraile** (*Cono Sur*) to be very solemn; **oír por la ~*** (= *estar sordo*) to be stone-deaf; (= *entender mal*) to misunderstand; (= *ser torpe*) to be pretty thick*; **ser hombre de ~** to be a real man

braguetazo* SM marriage for money; **dar el ~** to marry for money

braguetero Ⓐ ADJ 1 (= *lascivo*) lecherous, randy
2 (*LAm*) (*al casarse*) *who marries for money*; (*Andes, Caribe*) (= *vividor*) *who lives on a woman's earnings*; **todos saben que es ~** everyone knows he married for money Ⓑ SM lecher, womanizer

braguillas SM INV brat

braguitas SFPL panties

brahmán SM Brahman, Brahmin

braille ['braile] SM Braille

brainstorming [breɪnstɔrmɪn] SM (*pl* **brainstormings**) (= *actividad*) brainstorming; **una sesión de ~** a brainstorming session; **hacer un ~** to have a brainstorming session

brama SF (*Zool*) rut, rutting season

bramadero SM (*LAm*) tethering post

bramante SM twine, string

bramar ▸conjug 1a◂ VI 1 (*Zool*) [*toro, elefante*] to bellow; [*león*] to roar
2 [*persona*] **están que braman con el alcalde*** they're hopping mad with the mayor
3 (*Meteo*) [*viento*] to howl, roar; [*mar*] to thunder

bramido SM [*de toro, elefante*] bellow, bellowing; [*de león*] roar, roaring

brandy SM brandy

branquia SF gill; **~s** gills

brasa SF live coal, hot coal; **carne a la ~** grilled meat, barbecued meat; ✦*MODISMOS* **atizar la ~** to stir things up, add fuel to the flames; **estar en ~s** to be on tenterhooks; **estar hecho una ~** to be very flushed

brasear ▸conjug 1a◂ VT to braise

brasería SF grill

brasero SM 1 (= *como calefacción*) [*de carbón*] brazier; (*eléctrico*) heater
2 (*Méx*) fireplace
3 (*Andes*) (= *hoguera*) large bonfire
4 (*Méx*) (= *hornillo*) small stove

Brasil SM Brazil

brasileño/a ADJ, SM/F, **brasilero/a** ADJ, SM/F Brazilian

brava SF 1 (*Méx*) (= *disputa*) row, fight; ✦*MODISMO* **a la ~** like it or not; **a la ~ tendrás que ir** you'll have to go whether you like it or not
2 (*Caribe*) ✦*MODISMO* **dar una ~ a algn** to lean on sb*, intimidate sb

bravata SF 1 (= *amenaza*) threat
2 (= *fanfarronada*) boast, brag; **echar ~s** to boast, talk big*

braveador(a) Ⓐ ADJ blustering, bullying
Ⓑ SM/F bully

bravear ▸conjug 1a◂ VI 1 (= *jactarse*) to boast, talk big 2 (= *bravuconear*) to bluster

bravera SF vent, window (*in an oven*)

bravero/a (*Caribe*) Ⓐ ADJ bullying
Ⓑ SM/F bully

braveza SF 1 (= *ferocidad*) [*de animal*] ferocity, savageness; [*del viento*] fury
2 (= *valor*) bravery

bravío Ⓐ ADJ 1 (*Zool*) (= *feroz*) ferocious, savage; (= *indómito*) wild, untamed 2 (*Bot*) wild 3 (= *rudo*) uncouth, coarse Ⓑ SM ferocity

bravo Ⓐ ADJ 1 [*animal*] fierce, ferocious; *ver tb* **toro 1**
2 [*persona*] (= *malhumorado*) bad-tempered; (= *jactancioso*) boastful, swaggering; (= *valentón*) boastful, swaggering; **ponerse ~ con algn** to get angry with sb
3 [*mar*] rough, stormy; [*paisaje*] rugged; *ver tb* **costa² 1**
4 (= *excelente*) fine, excellent
5 (*LAm Culin*) hot, spicy
Ⓑ EXCL bravo!, well done!
Ⓒ SM thug

bravucón/ona Ⓐ ADJ swaggering
Ⓑ SM/F braggart

bravuconada SF boast

bravura SF 1 (= *ferocidad*) ferocity
2 (= *valor*) bravery
3 = **bravata**

braza SF 1 (*Natación*) breaststroke; **nadar a ~** to swim breaststroke ► **braza de espalda** back stroke ► **braza de mariposa** butterfly stroke 2 (*Náut*) ≈ fathom

brazada SF 1 (= *movimiento*) movement of the arms
2 (*Remo*) stroke
3 (*Natación*) stroke, style
4 (= *cantidad*) armful
5 (*LAm Náut*) (= *braza*) ≈ fathom

brazado SM armful

brazal SM 1 (= *banda de tela*) armband
2 (*Agr*) irrigation channel

brazalete SM 1 (= *joya*) bracelet
2 (= *banda de tela*) armband

brazo SM 1 [*de persona*] arm; [*de animal*] foreleg; **se echó a los ~s de su madre** he threw himself into his mother's arms; **dar el ~ a algn** to give sb one's arm; **le dio el ~ al bajar del autobús** he gave her his arm as they got off the bus; **coger a algn del ~** to take sb by the arm; **cogió a su hermano del ~** she took her brother by the arm; **iban (cogidos) del ~** they were walking arm in arm; **llevar a algn en ~s** to carry sb in one's arms; ✦*MODISMOS* **con los ~s abiertos** with open arms; **dar el ~ a torcer** to give way, give in; **luchar a ~ partido** to fight tooth and nail; **ser el ~ derecho de algn** to be sb's right-hand man/woman ► **brazo de gitano** (*Culin*) swiss roll ► **brazo de reina** (*Cono Sur Culin*) swiss roll; *ver tb* **huelga 1**, **cruzado A1**
2 [*de sillón, tocadiscos, grúa, cruz*] arm ► **brazo de lámpara** lamp bracket ► **brazo de lámpara de gas** gas bracket ► **brazo de lectura** pick-up arm ► **brazo lector** pick-up arm
3 (= *sección*) ► **brazo armado** military wing ► **brazo político** political wing ► **brazo secular** secular arm
4 (*Geog*) ► **brazo de mar** inlet, arm of the sea, sound; ✦*MODISMO* **estar** *o* **ir hecho un ~ de mar** to be dressed up to the nines* ► **brazo de río** channel, branch of river
5 [*de árbol*] branch, limb
6 (*liter*) (= *fuerza*) arm; **el ~ de la ley** the long arm of the law
7 **brazos** (= *trabajadores*) hands, men

brazuelo SM (*Zool*) shoulder

brea SF 1 (= *alquitrán*) tar, pitch
2 (= *cubierta*) tarpaulin, tarp (*EEUU*)

break [brek] SM (*Mús*) break dancing

brear ▸conjug 1a◂ VT 1 (= *maltratar*) to abuse, ill-treat; **~ a algn a golpes** *o* **palos** to beat sb up
2 (= *embromar*) to make fun of, tease

brebaje SM potion; (*hum*) brew, concoction

brecha SF 1 (= *abertura*) breach, opening; **abrir ~ en una muralla** to breach a wall; **batir en ~** (*Mil*) to breach; (*fig*) to get the better of; ✦*MODISMOS* **estar en la ~** to be in the thick of things; **hacer ~ en algn** to make an impression on sb; **seguir en la ~** to go on with one's work, keep at it
2 (*entre personas*) rift; (*entre opiniones*) gap
3 (*Med*) gash, wound

brecina SF (*Bot*) heath

breck SM (*Cono Sur*) = **breque 2**

brécol SM broccoli

brega SF 1 (= *lucha*) struggle; **andar a la ~** to slog away
2 (= *riña*) quarrel, row
3 (= *broma*) trick, practical joke; **dar ~ a algn** to play a trick on sb

bregar ▸conjug 1h◂ VI 1 (= *luchar*) to struggle, fight (**con** against, with)
2 (= *reñir*) to quarrel
3 (= *trabajar mucho*) to slog away; **tendremos que hacerlo bregando** we shall have to do it by sheer hard work

breguetear ▸conjug 1a◂ VI (*Andes*) to argue

breje‡ SM (*Esp*) **¿cuántos ~s tienes?** how old are you?

brejetero ADJ (*Caribe*) trouble-making, mischief-making

breke SM (*CAm Aut*) brake

bren SM bran

breña SF, **breñal** SM scrub, rough ground

breñoso ADJ (= *con maleza*) rough, scrubby; (= *con zarzas*) brambly

breque SM (*LAm*) 1 (= *carroza*) brake
2 (*Ferro*) guard's van, baggage car (*EEUU*)
3 (*Mec*) brake

brequear ▸conjug 1a◂ VT, VI (*LAm*) to brake

brequero SM (*Andes, CAm, Méx*) brakeman

Bretaña SF Brittany

brete SM 1 (= *cepo*) shackles *pl*
2 (= *apuro*) predicament; **estar en un ~** to be in a jam*; **poner a algn en un ~** to put sb on the spot
3 (*Caribe*‡) screw‡, lay‡

breteles SMPL (*LAm*) straps (*on garment*)

bretón/ona Ⓐ ADJ, SM/F Breton

Ⓑ SM [1] (*Ling*) Breton
[2] **bretones** (= *coles*) Brussels sprouts

breva SF [1] (*Bot*) early fig; ✦*MODISMOS* **¡no caerá esa ~!** no such luck!; **pelar la ~** (*Cono Sur*) to steal; **poner a algn como una ~** to beat sb black and blue
[2] (= *puro*) flat cigar; (*Caribe*) [*de calidad*] good-quality cigar
[3] (*LAm*) (= *tabaco*) chewing tobacco
[4] (*) (= *puesto*) plum, plum job; (= *gaje*) perk*
[5] (= *cosa fácil*) **es una ~** it's a cinch*, it's a pushover*; **para él es una ~** it's chickenfeed to him*

breve Ⓐ ADJ [1] (= *corto*) short, brief; **una ~ rueda de prensa** a short *o* brief press conference; **continuaremos tras un ~ descanso** we shall continue after a short break *o* a brief pause; **un brevísimo periodo de tiempo** a very short period of time; **enviaron una nota muy ~, sólo dos líneas** they sent a very short note, just two lines long; **seré muy ~** I shall be very brief; **dimos un ~ repaso a la lección** we briefly went over the lesson; **expuso el problema en ~s palabras** he briefly explained the problem; **en ~s palabras, se negó a dimitir** in short, he refused to resign; **en ~** (= *pronto*) shortly, before long
[2] [*vocal*] short
Ⓑ SM [1] (*Prensa*) short news item
[2] (*Rel*) papal brief
Ⓒ SF (*Mús*) breve

brevedad SF [*de mensaje*] shortness; [*de texto*] brevity; [*de estilo*] conciseness; **con** *o* **a la mayor ~ (posible)** as soon as possible; **bueno, para mayor ~ ...** well, to be brief ...; **llamado por ~ ...** called for short ...

brevemente ADV briefly, concisely

brevería SF (*Tip*) note, short news item; (*en conversación*) snippet; **"Breverías"** (= *sección de periódico*) "News in Brief"

brevete SM [1] (= *nota*) note, memorandum
[2] (*LAm Aut*) driving licence *o* (*EEUU*) license

breviario SM (*Rel*) breviary; (= *compendio*) compendium

brezal SM moor, heath

brezar ▸conjug 1f◂ VT to rock, lull (*in a cradle*)

brezo SM [1] (*Bot*) heather
[2] [*de pipa*] briar

briaga SF (*Méx*) drunkenness

briago ADJ (*Méx*) drunk

briba SF vagabond's life, idle life; **andar** *o* **vivir a la ~** to loaf around, be on the bum (*EEUU*)

bribón/ona Ⓐ ADJ [1] (= *vago*) lazy
[2] (= *criminal*) dishonest, rascally
Ⓑ SM/F [1] (= *vagabundo*) vagabond, vagrant
[2] (= *holgazán*) loafer
[3] (= *granuja*) rascal, rogue

bribonada SF dirty trick, piece of mischief

bribonear ▸conjug 1a◂ VI [1] (= *gandulear*) to idle, loaf around
[2] [*ser granuja*] to be a rogue, play dirty tricks

bribonería SF [1] (= *briba*) vagabond's life, idle life
[2] (= *picardía*) roguery

bribonesco ADJ rascally, knavish

bricbarca SF *large sailing ship*

bricolador(a) SM/F do-it-yourself enthusiast, DIY enthusiast

bricolage SM do-it-yourself, DIY

bricolagista SMF do-it-yourself enthusiast, DIY enthusiast

bricolaje SM do-it-yourself, DIY

bricolajista SMF, **bricolero/a** SM/F do-it-yourself enthusiast, DIY enthusiast

brida SF [1] [*de caballo*] bridle; **ir a toda ~** to go at top speed; ✦*MODISMO* **tener a algn a ~ corta** to keep sb on a tight rein, keep sb under strict control
[2] (*Téc*) (= *abrazadera*) clamp; [*de tubería*] flange
[3] (*Ferro*) fishplate
[4] (*Med*) adhesion

bridge [briʒ, britʃ] SM (*Naipes*) bridge

bridgista [bri'ʒista] SMF bridge player

bridgístico [bri'ʒistiko] ADJ bridge *antes de s*; **el mundo ~** the bridge world

bridón SM [*de caballo*] snaffle; (*Mil*) bridoon

briega SF [1] (= *pelea*) fight, brawl
[2] (= *trabajo duro*) slog

brigada Ⓐ SF [1] (*Mil*) brigade
[2] (= *grupo*) [*de obreros*] gang; [*de policía*] squad ► **brigada antidisturbios** riot squad ► **brigada antidrogas** drug squad ► **brigada de bombas** bomb-disposal unit ► **brigada de delitos monetarios** fraud squad ► **brigada de estupefacientes** drug squad ► **brigada fluvial** river police ► **brigada móvil** flying squad ► **brigada sanitaria** sanitation department ► **Brigadas Internacionales** International Brigades
Ⓑ SMF (*Mil*) sergeant major

brigadier SM brigadier, brigadier-general (*EEUU*)

brigadilla SF squad, detachment

brigadista SMF **~ internacional** member of the International Brigade

brigán SM (*CAm, Caribe Hist*) brigand, bandit

brigandaje SM (*Caribe Hist*) brigandage, banditry

brigantino/a Ⓐ ADJ of/from La Corunna
Ⓑ SM/F native/inhabitant of La Corunna; **los ~s** the people of La Corunna

Brígida SF Bridget

Briján SM ✦*MODISMO* **saber más que ~** to be very smart, know the lot

brik SM (*pl* **briks**) carton

brillante Ⓐ ADJ [1] (= *reluciente*) [*luz, sol, color*] (*gen*) bright; (*muy fuerte*) brilliant; [*superficie pulida*] shiny; [*pelo*] glossy, shiny; [*joyas, lentejuelas*] sparkling, glittering; **un estampado amarillo ~** a bright *o* brilliant yellow pattern; **los focos eran demasiado ~s** the floodlights were too bright; **un vestido de satén ~** a shiny satin dress; **¡qué ~ ha quedado el suelo!** the floor is really shiny now!; **frota los zapatos hasta que estén bien ~s** polish the shoes until they are nice and shiny; **tenía los ojos ~s por la emoción** her eyes sparkled with excitement
[2] (= *excelente*) brilliant; **al final de su ~ carrera deportiva** at the end of her brilliant sporting career; **su actuación fue absolutamente ~** her performance was absolutely outstanding *o* brilliant; **su ~ conversación** her sparkling conversation
Ⓑ SM diamond, brilliant; **un anillo de ~s** a diamond ring

brillantemente ADV [1] (= *extraordinariamente*) brilliantly; **respondió ~ a sus preguntas** he answered her questions brilliantly; **la orquesta ha despedido ~ la temporada** the orchestra bid a brilliant farewell to the season
[2] (= *con brillo*) brightly

brillantez SF [1] (= *brillo*) (*gen*) brightness; (*más fuerte*) brilliance
[2] (= *excelencia*) brilliance; **ahí está la ~ de la novela** that is the brilliance of the novel; **con ~** brilliantly; **hemos cumplido nuestro objetivo con ~** we have achieved our aim brilliantly; **ganaron el partido con ~** they won the match in brilliant style; **dar ~ a algo** to add a bit of sparkle to sth
[3] (= *boato*) splendour, splendor (*EEUU*)

brillantina SF brilliantine, hair cream

brillar ▸conjug 1a◂ VI [1] (= *relucir*) [*luz, sol*] to shine; [*estrella, ojos*] to shine, sparkle; [*metal, superficie, pelo*] (*gen*) to shine; (*por estar mojado, grasiento*) to glisten; [*joyas, lentejuelas*] to sparkle, glitter; **la luz de la vela brillaba en la oscuridad** the light of the candle shone in the dark; **le brillaban los ojos de alegría** her eyes shone *o* sparkled with happiness; **¡cómo te brillan los zapatos!** what shiny shoes!; **el mar brillaba a la luz de la luna** the sea glistened in the moonlight; **le brillaba la cara por el sudor** his face glistened with sweat
[2] (= *sobresalir*) to shine; **Argentina brilló en la segunda mitad** Argentina shone in the second half; ✦*MODISMOS* **~ con luz propia** to stand out on one's own; **~ por su ausencia**: **el ingenio ha brillado por su ausencia** there has a been a distinct lack of ingenuity; **en la cena las bebidas ~on por su ausencia** there was a distinct lack of drinks at dinner

brillazón SF (*Cono Sur*) mirage

brillo SM [1] (= *resplandor*) [*de luz, sol, estrella*] (*gen*) brightness; (*más fuerte*) brilliance; [*de pantalla*] brightness; [*de tela, pelo, zapatos, superficie*] shine, sheen; [*de papel, foto*] glossiness; [*de joyas, lentejuelas*] sparkle, glitter; **estas luces emiten demasiado ~** these lights are too bright; **el ~ de la luna sobre el agua** the moonlight shining on the water; **lo noté en el ~ de sus ojos** I noticed it in her sparkling eyes; **el ~ de la navaja lo asustó** he was frightened by the gleam of the knife; **estos zapatos no tienen ~** these shoes have no shine; **¿le revelamos las fotos con ~?** would you like gloss photos?, would you like a gloss finish to the photos?; **se puede ajustar el ~** the brightness can be adjusted; **dar** *o* **sacar ~ a** [+ *suelo, plata, zapatos*] to polish, shine; [+ *muebles*] to polish; **este producto da mucho ~ a la madera** this product gives wood an excellent shine ► **brillo de labios** lip gloss ► **brillo de uñas** clear nail polish, clear nail varnish
[2] (= *esplendor*) brilliance, splendour, splendor (*EEUU*); **fueron cautivados por el ~ de la profesión** they were captivated by the splendour of the profession; **la ausencia de varios jugadores importantes ha restado ~ al torneo** the absence of several important players has taken the shine off the tournament

brilloso ADJ (*LAm*) shiny

brin SM fine canvas, duck

brincar ▸conjug 1g◂ Ⓐ VT [+ *pasaje*] (*en lectura*) to skip, miss out
Ⓑ VI [1] (*esp LAm*) (= *saltar*) [*niño*] to jump (up

and down); (*con un solo pie*) to hop; [*cordero*] to skip about, gambol; ✦*MODISMOS* **está que brinca** he's hopping mad; **~ de cólera** to fly into a rage
[2] (= *rebotar*) to bounce
Ⓒ **brincarse** VPR **~se a algn** (*Andes**) to bump sb off*

brinco SM (= *salto*) (*gen*) jump, leap; (*al correr*) skip; **de** *o* **en un ~** at one bound; **dar ~s** to hop (about), jump (about); **pegar un ~** to jump, give a start; ✦*MODISMOS* **a ~s** by fits and starts; **¿para qué son tantos ~s estando el suelo parejo?** (*CAm, Méx*) what's all the fuss about?; **quitar los ~s a algn** to take sb down a peg

brindar ▸conjug 1a◂ Ⓐ VT [1] (= *ofrecer*) to offer, afford; **los árboles brindaban sombra** the trees afforded shade; **~ a algn (con) algo** to offer sth to sb; **le brinda la ocasión** it gives *o* affords him the opportunity; **bríndame un cigarro** (*hum*) give me a cigarette; **me brindó una copa** he bought me a drink
[2] (= *dedicar*) to dedicate (**a** to)
Ⓑ VI **~ por algn/algo** to drink to sb/sth, toast sb/sth; **~on por los novios** they drank a toast to the newly-weds; **¡brindemos por la unidad!** here's to unity!
Ⓒ **brindarse** VPR **~se a hacer algo** to offer to do sth; **se brindó a ayudarme** he offered to help me

brindis SM INV [1] (*para celebrar algo*) toast; **hacer un ~ por algn/algo** to toast sb/sth, drink a toast to sb/sth
[2] (= *dedicatoria*) dedication, ceremony of dedication
[3] (*Andes, Caribe*) (= *recepción*) official reception; (= *fiesta*) cocktail party

brío SM [1] (= *ánimo*) spirit, verve; **es hombre de ~s** he's a man of spirit, he's a man of mettle
[2] (= *decisión*) determination; **cortar los ~s a algn** to clip sb's wings
[3] (= *elegancia*) elegance

briosamente ADV [1] (= *con ánimo*) with spirit, dashingly, with verve
[2] (= *con decisión*) resolutely
[3] (= *elegantemente*) elegantly

brioso ADJ [1] (= *animoso*) spirited, full of verve
[2] (= *decidido*) determined
[3] (= *elegante*) elegant

briqueta SF briquette

brisa SF breeze

brisca SF *Spanish card game similar to whist but in which it is not necessary to follow suit*

brisera SF (*LAm*), **brisero** SM (*LAm*) windshield (*for a lamp*)

brisita SF **tener** *o* **pasar una ~** to be hungry, have an empty stomach

británico/a Ⓐ ADJ British
Ⓑ SM/F British person, Briton, Britisher (*EEUU*); **los ~s** the British

britano/a (*Hist, Literat*) Ⓐ ADJ British
Ⓑ SM/F Briton

brizna SF [1] (= *hebra*) [*de hierba*] blade; [*de judía*] string
[2] (= *trozo*) piece, fragment; (*muy pequeño*) scrap; **no me queda ni una ~** I haven't a scrap left
[3] (*LAm*) drizzle

briznar ▸conjug 1a◂ VI (*LAm*) to drizzle

broca SF [1] (*Cos*) reel, bobbin
[2] (*Mec*) (drill) bit
[3] [*de zapato*] tack

brocado SM brocade

brocal SM [1] (= *borde*) rim, mouth
[2] [*de pozo*] curb, parapet
[3] (*Méx*) kerb, curb (*EEUU*)

brocha Ⓐ SF [1] (= *para pintar*) paintbrush, large paintbrush; **pintor de ~ gorda** (*lit*) painter and decorator; (*fig*) bad painter
[2] ► **brocha de afeitar** shaving brush
[3] (*Cono Sur*) skewer, spit
[4] (*CAm**) (= *zalamero*) creep*
Ⓑ ADJ (*CAm*) meddling, creeping*, servile; ✦*MODISMO* **hacerse ~** (*CAm*) to play the fool

brochada SF, **brochazo** SM brushstroke

broche SM [1] (*Cos*) clasp, fastener
[2] (= *joya*) brooch; ✦*MODISMOS* **el ~ final** ◊ **el ~ de oro** the finishing touch
[3] (*LAm*) (*para papel*) paperclip; (*Cono Sur*) (*para ropa*) clothes peg, clothespin (*EEUU*)

brocheta SF skewer

brochón Ⓐ ADJ (*Caribe*) flattering
Ⓑ SM whitewash brush

bróculi SM, **broculí** SM broccoli

bróder* SM (*pl* **bróders**) (*CAm*) lad, fellow*

broker SM (*pl* **brokers**) (*Cono Sur Fin*) broker

brollero ADJ (*Caribe*) troublemaking, mischief-making

broma SF [1] (= *cachondeo*) **ni en ~** never, not on any account; **lo decía en ~** I was only joking, I was only kidding*; **estar de ~** to be in a joking mood; **tomar algo a ~** to take sth as a joke
[2] (= *chiste*) joke; **no es ninguna ~** it's no joke, this is serious; **la ~ me costó caro** the affair cost me dear; **no hay ~s con la autoridad** you can't play games with the authorities; **~s aparte …** joking aside …; **¡déjate de ~s!** quit fooling!, joke over!; **gastar ~s** to tell jokes; **gastar una ~ a algn** to play a joke on sb; **estar para ~s**: **¡para ~s estoy!** (*iró*) a fine time for joking!; **no está para ~s** he's in no mood for jokes; **entre ~s y veras** half-joking(ly) ► **broma pesada** practical joke, hoax
[3] (*Caribe, Cono Sur*) (= *decepción*) disappointment; (= *molestia*) vexation, annoyance
[4] (*Zool*) shipworm

bromato SM bromate

bromazo SM unpleasant joke, stupid practical joke

bromear ▸conjug 1a◂ VI to joke, crack jokes*; **creía que bromeaba** I thought he was joking

bromista Ⓐ ADJ **es muy ~** he's full of jokes, he's a great one for jokes
Ⓑ SMF (= *chistoso*) joker; (= *gracioso*) practical joker, leg-puller*; **lo ha hecho algún ~** some joker did this

bromuro SM bromide

bronca* SF [1] (= *follón*) row; **armar una ~** to kick up a fuss; **se armó una ~ tremenda** there was an almighty row*; **buscar ~** to be looking for a fight, be spoiling for a fight; **dar una ~ a algn** (*Teat, Taur*) to give sb the bird*
[2] (= *regañina*) ticking off*; **nos echó una ~ fenomenal** he came down on us like a ton of bricks*
[3] (= *ruido*) racket*
[4] (*Cono Sur*) (= *rabia*) anger, fury; **me da ~** it makes me mad*

broncamente ADV (= *con dureza*) roughly, harshly; (= *con malos modos*) rudely

bronce SM [1] (= *aleación*) bronze; **una medalla de ~** a bronze medal; ✦*MODISMOS* **ligar ~** (*Esp**) to get a suntan; **ser de ~** to be inflexible, be deaf to all appeals ► **bronce de campana** bell metal ► **bronce de cañon** gunmetal ► **bronce dorado** ormolu
[2] (= *latón*) brass
[3] (*Mús*) brass instruments
[4] (*Arte*) bronze, bronze statue
[5] (= *moneda*) copper coin
[6] (*LAm*) (= *campana*) bell

bronceado Ⓐ ADJ [1] [*persona, piel*] tanned, brown
[2] (*color*) bronze, bronze coloured *o* (*EEUU*) colored
Ⓑ SM [1] [*de piel*] tan, suntan
[2] (*Téc*) bronze finish

bronceador SM suntan lotion

broncear ▸conjug 1a◂ Ⓐ VT [1] [+ *piel*] to tan, bronze
[2] (*Téc*) to bronze
Ⓑ **broncearse** VPR to get a tan, get a suntan

broncería SF (*Cono Sur*) ironmonger's (shop), ironmongery, hardware store (*EEUU*)

bronco ADJ [1] [*superficie*] rough, coarse
[2] [*metal*] brittle
[3] [*voz*] gruff, hoarse; (*Mús*) rasping, harsh
[4] [*actitud, porte*] gruff, rude
[5] [*caballo*] unbroken

broncodilatador SM bronchodilator

bronconeumonía SF bronchopneumonia

broncopulmonar ADJ broncho-pulmonary

bronquedad SF [1] [*de superficie*] roughness
[2] [*de metal*] brittleness
[3] [*de voz*] gruffness, harshness

bronquial ADJ bronchial

bronquina* SF = **bronca 1**

bronquinoso* ADJ (*Caribe*) quarrelsome, brawling

bronquios SMPL bronchial tubes; **estaba malo de los ~** he had a bad chest

bronquítico/a Ⓐ ADJ bronchitic
Ⓑ SM/F bronchitis sufferer

bronquitis SF INV bronchitis ► **bronquitis crónica** chronic bronchitis

broquel SM shield

broquelarse ▸conjug 1a◂ VPR to shield o.s.

broquero SM (*Méx*) brace

broqueta SF skewer

brota SF bud, shoot

brotar ▸conjug 1a◂ VI [1] (*Bot*) [*planta, semilla*] to sprout, bud; [*hoja*] to sprout, come out; [*flor*] to come out
[2] [*agua*] to spring up; [*río*] to rise; [*lágrimas, sangre*] to well (up)
[3] (= *aparecer*) to spring up; **han brotado sectas por todos sitios** sects have sprung up all over the place; **las protestas populares ~on de la crisis económica** popular protest sprang from the recession; **como princesa brotada de un cuento de hadas** (*liter*) like a princess out of a fairy tale
[4] (*Med*) (= *epidemia*) to break out; (= *erupción, grano, espinilla*) to appear; **le ~on granos por toda la cara** spots appeared all over his face, he came out in spots all over his face

brote SM [1] (*Bot*) shoot ► **brotes de soja** bean sprouts, bean shoots

2 (= aparición) [de rebelión] outbreak; [de enfermedad] outbreak; **un ~ de violencia** an outbreak of violence; **un ~ de sarampión** an outbreak of measles
3 (= erupción cutánea) rash

broza SF 1 (Bot) dead leaves, brushwood
2 (en discurso) rubbish, trash, garbage (EEUU)
3 (= brocha) hard brush
4 (Tip) printer's brush

brucelosis SF INV brucellosis

bruces ADV **de ~** face down; **caer de ~** to fall flat on one's face; **estar de ~** to lie face downwards, lie flat on one's stomach

bruja Ⓐ ADJ **estar ~** (Caribe, Méx‡) to be broke*, be flat (EEUU*); **ando bien ~‡** I'm skint‡
Ⓑ SF 1 (= hechicera) witch
2 (*) (= arpía) old hag*; (Méx) woman
3 (Caribe, Cono Sur) (= fantasma) spook*, ghost; (= puta) whore
4 (Orn) barn owl

Brujas SF Bruges

brujear ▸conjug 1a◂ Ⓐ VT (Caribe) (tb fig) to stalk, pursue
Ⓑ VI 1 (= hacer brujería) to practise witchcraft
2 (Caribe, Méx) (= ir de juerga) to go on a spree

brujería SF 1 (= hechizos) witchcraft, sorcery, (black) magic
2 (Caribe) (= pobreza) poverty

brujeril ADJ witch-like

brujo Ⓐ ADJ enchanting
Ⓑ SM 1 (= hechicero) wizard, sorcerer
2 (LAm) shaman, medicine man*

brújula SF 1 (Náut) compass; ✦MODISMO **perder la ~** to lose one's bearings ▸ **brújula de bolsillo** pocket compass
2 (= mira) guide, norm

brujulear ▸conjug 1a◂ Ⓐ VT 1 [+ cartas] to uncover (gradually)
2 (*) (= adivinar) to guess
3 (= tratar de conseguir) to intrigue for, try to wangle
Ⓑ VI (*) 1 to manage, get along, keep going
2 (Andes, Caribe) to go on the booze*, go on a bender‡

brulote SM 1 (Chile) rude word, dirty word
2 (Cono Sur) (= escrito) obscene letter

bruma SF (= niebla) mist, fog; (en el mar) sea mist ▸ **bruma del alba** morning mist

brumoso ADJ misty, foggy

bruno ADJ dark brown

bruñido Ⓐ ADJ polished, burnished
Ⓑ SM 1 (= acto) polish, polishing ▸ **bruñido de zapato** shoeshine
2 (= brillo) shine, gloss

bruñidor(a) SM/F polisher, burnisher

bruñir ▸conjug 3h◂ Ⓐ VT 1 (= sacar brillo a) [+ metal, mármol] to polish, burnish
2 (= maquillar) to make up (with cosmetics)
3 (CAm) (= molestar) to pester
Ⓑ **bruñirse** VPR to make up, make o.s. up

bruscamente ADV 1 (= repentinamente) suddenly, brusquely, sharply
2 (= rudamente) sharply, abruptly

brusco Ⓐ ADJ 1 (= repentino) [descenso, curva, declive] sharp; [movimiento] sudden; [cambio] abrupt, sudden
2 (= grosero) [actitud, porte] curt, brusque; [comentario] rude
Ⓑ SM (Bot) butcher's broom

Bruselas SF Brussels

bruselas SFPL tweezers; **unas ~** a pair of tweezers

bruselense Ⓐ ADJ of/from Brussels
Ⓑ SMF native/inhabitant of Brussels; **los ~s** the people of Brussels

brusquedad SF 1 (= cambio repentino) suddenness
2 (= rudeza) brusqueness, abruptness; **hablar con ~** to speak sharply

brutal ADJ 1 (= salvaje) brutal
2 (*) (= genial) terrific*
3 (CAm) (= asombroso) incredible, amazing

brutalidad SF 1 (= cualidad) brutality
2 (= acción) **una ~** an act of brutality
3 (= estupidez) stupidity
4 (*) **me gusta una ~** I think it's great, I love it

brutalizar ▸conjug 1f◂ Ⓐ VT (= tratar mal) [+ persona, animal] to brutalize, treat brutally; [+ mujer] to rape
Ⓑ **brutalizarse** VPR to become brutalized

brutalmente ADV brutally

bruteza SF 1 (= brutalidad) brutality
2 (= tosquedad) coarseness, roughness

Bruto SM Brutus

bruto/a Ⓐ ADJ 1 (= salvaje) brutish; **¡no seas ~!** don't be so rough!
2 (= estúpido) stupid, ignorant; **¡no seas ~!** don't be an idiot!; **es muy ~** he's pretty thick*
3 (= inculto) uncouth
4 (= sin alterar) [materias] raw; [medidas] gross; **en ~** [superficie, terreno] rough; [diamantes] uncut; **hierro en ~** crude iron, pig iron; **peso ~** gross weight; **petróleo ~** crude oil; **producto ~** gross product; **salario ~** gross salary; **a lo ~** roughly, crudely; ✦MODISMO **más ~ que un adoquín** as dumb as an ox
5 **pegar a algn en ~** (Caribe) to beat sb mercilessly
6 (Cono Sur) (= de mala calidad) poor-quality, inferior
Ⓑ SM (animal) brute, beast
Ⓒ SM/F 1 (= salvaje) brute, boor; **¡bruto!** you beast!
2 (= idiota) idiot

bruza SF 1 (= cepillo) coarse brush; (para caballos) horse brush
2 (Tip) printer's brush

Bs.As. ABR (= **Buenos Aires**) BA

Bto./a. ABR (Rel) = **Beato/a**

bto. ABR (= **bruto**) gr

bu* SM bogeyman; **hacer el bu a algn** to scare sb

búa SF pimple

buba SF, **bubón** SM (= inflamación) bubo

bubónico ADJ **peste bubónica** bubonic plague

bubute SM (Caribe) beetle

bucal ADJ [higiene] oral; **por vía ~** orally, by mouth

bucanero SM buccaneer

bucarán SM buckram

búcaro SM 1 (= jarrón) vase
2 (= arcilla) clay, fragrant clay

buccino SM whelk

buceador(a) SM/F diver

bucear ▸conjug 1a◂ VI 1 (= nadar bajo el agua) to swim under water; (= sumergirse) to dive
2 (= investigar) to explore, look below the surface

buceo SM diving ▸ **buceo de saturación** saturation diving

buchaca SF (CAm, Caribe) (= bolso) saddlebag; (Billar) pocket

buchada SF mouthful (of liquid)

buchante‡ SM shot

buche SM 1 (= estómago) (Orn) crop; (Zool) maw; (liter) belly; ✦MODISMOS **guardar algo en el ~** to keep sth very quiet; **llenar el ~*** to fill one's belly; **sacar el ~*** to show off; **sacar el ~ a algn*** to make sb talk
2 (= trago) mouthful; (Andes) shot, slug (EEUU) (of drink); **hacer ~s con algo** to rinse one's mouth out with sth
3 (Cos) (= bolsa) bag; (= arruga) wrinkle, pucker; **hacer ~** to be baggy, wrinkle up
4 (LAm Med) (= bocio) goitre, goiter (EEUU); (= paperas) mumps
5 (Andes) (= chistera) top hat
6 (Caribe) (= tonto) fool, idiot

buchí SM (CAm) rustic, peasant

buchinche SM (Caribe) (= casa) hovel; (= tienda) pokey little shop

bucle SM 1 [de pelo] curl, ringlet
2 (= curva) curve, bend; (Aer, Inform) loop ▸ **bucles anidados** nested loops

bucodental ADJ [salud, higiene] oral; [tratamiento, clínica] dental

bucólica SF 1 (Literat) bucolic poem, pastoral poem
2 (*) meal

bucólico ADJ bucolic, pastoral

Buda SM Buddha

budín SM 1 (= dulce) pudding; (LAm) (= pastel) cake; **~ de pescado** fish pie
2 (*) (= persona) **esa chica es un ~** that girl's a peach o a smasher*

budismo SM Buddhism

budista ADJ, SMF Buddhist

budleia SF buddleia

buen ADJ ver **bueno**

buenamente ADV 1 (= fácilmente) easily, without difficulty
2 (= de buena gana) willingly

buenamoza SF (Andes euf) jaundice

buenaventura SF 1 (= suerte) good luck, good fortune
2 (= adivinación) fortune; **decir** o **echar la ~ a algn** to tell sb's fortune

buenazo/a Ⓐ ADJ (= buena persona) kindly, good-natured; (= sufrido) long-suffering
Ⓑ SM/F good-natured person; **el ~ de Marcos** good old Marcos; **ser un ~** to be kindhearted, be soft (pey)

buenmozo ADJ (Cono Sur) good-looking, handsome

bueno/a Ⓐ ADJ (before sm sing **buen**) 1 (gen) good; [tiempo] fine, good, fair; **es un buen libro** it's a good book; **está muy ~ este bizcocho** this sponge cake is lovely o really good; **tiene buena voz** she has a good voice; **les gusta la buena vida** they like the good life; **es buen traductor** he's a good translator; **hace buen tiempo** the weather's fine o good o fair; **los ~s tiempos** the good old days; **la mano buena** (hum) the right hand;

¡~ está! (*LAm*) that's enough!; **¡qué ~!** (*esp LAm*) excellent!, great!; **lo ~ es que ...** the best thing is that ..., the best part is that ...; **lo ~ fue que ni siquiera quiso venir** the best thing *o* part was that he didn't even want to come; ✦*REFRÁN* **lo ~, si breve, dos veces ~** brevity is the soul of wit

2 (= *bondadoso*) [*persona*] kind, good; **fue muy ~ conmigo** he was very kind *o* good to me; **es usted muy ~** you are very kind; **sé ~** be good; **es buena persona** he's a nice person, he's a good sort; ✦*MODISMO* **es más ~ que el pan** he's a good soul

3 (= *apropiado*) good; **éste es un buen momento para comprar** this is a good time to buy; **no es ~ que esté solo** it's not good for him to be alone; **ser ~ para** to be good for; **esta bebida es buena para la salud** this drink is good for your health

4 (*de salud*) **estar ~** to be well; **ponerse ~** to get better

5 (*) (= *atractivo*) **está muy ~** he's a bit of all right*, he's gorgeous*

6 (= *considerable*) good, large; **un buen número de ...** a good *o* large number of ...; **una buena cantidad de dinero** a large amount of money; **un buen trozo de ...** a nice big piece of ...; **le eché un buen rapapolvo** I gave him a good telling-off; **le di un buen susto** I gave him a real fright; **ganó ~s duros** she earned a good deal of money

7 (*iró*) **¡buen conductor!** a fine driver you are!, some driver you are!; **¡ésa sí que es buena!** that's a good one!; **¡buena la has liado** *o* **hecho!** you've really gone and done it now!; **¡en buen lío me he metido!** I've got myself into a fine mess!; **¡estaría ~!*** I should hope not!; **estaría ~ que ...** it would be just great if ...; **luego verás lo que es ~*** then you'll see; **le pusieron ~*** (= *lo pegaron*) they beat the living daylights out of him*; (= *lo criticaron*) they slagged him off*; **le dio un tortazo de los ~s** he gave him a hell of a thump*

8 (*en saludos*) **¡buenas!** hello!; **~s días** good morning; **buenas tardes** (*a primera hora*) good afternoon; (*más tarde*) good evening; **¿qué hay de ~?** what's new?

9 ✦*MODISMOS* **estar de buenas** to be in a good mood; **estar en la buena** (*Andes*) (*de buen humor*) to be in a good mood; (= *tener suerte*) to be in luck; **hacer algo a la buena de Dios** to do sth any-old-how; **por las buenas**: **resolver algo por las buenas** to settle sth amicably; **irás por las buenas o por las malas** you'll go whether you like it or not; **si no me obedeces por las buenas, tendrás que hacerlo por las malas** you can either do as I say willingly, or I'll have to force you to do it; **de buenas a primeras** suddenly, without warning; **decir una noticia a algn de buenas a primeras** to spring a piece of news on sb

Ⓑ ADV **¡bueno!** all right!, O.K.!; (*Méx Telec*) hello!; **~, pues ...** well ...; **~, resulta que ...** well, it so happens that ...; **~, ¿y qué?** well, so what?, well?; **¡pero ~, cómo puedes ser tan bruto!** honestly, how can you be so stupid!; **pero ~, no nos vamos a meter en historias** but anyway, let's not go into this

Ⓒ SM/F 1 **el ~** [*de la película*] the goody*, the good guy*

2 **el ~ de Manolo** good old Manolo

buenón* ADJ nice-looking, good-looking

Buenos Aires SM Buenos Aires

buey SM 1 (*Zool*) ox ► **buey almizclado** musk ox ► **buey corneta** (*Andes, Cono Sur*) one-horned ox; (*fig*) (= *entrometido*) busybody, nosey-parker*; ✦*MODISMO* **nunca falta un ~ corneta** (*Andes, Cono Sur*) there's always someone who can't keep his mouth shut ► **buey de Francia** crab ► **buey de mar** *variety of crab or crawfish* ► **buey marino** manatee ► **buey muerto** (*Caribe*) bargain

2 ✦*MODISMOS* **como ~es** enormous; **chinches como ~es** bedbugs the size of elephants, enormous bedbugs; **cuando vuelen los ~es** when pigs fly; **hablar de ~es perdidos** (*Cono Sur*) to waste one's breath; **pegar ~es** (*CAm*) to go to sleep; **poner los ~es antes que el carro** to put the cart before the horse; **saber con los ~es que ara** (*Caribe*) to know who your friends are; **sacar el ~ de la barranca** (*Méx*) to bring it off; **ser un ~ para algo**: **es un ~ para el trabajo** he's a tremendous worker; **~ suelto** free agent; (= *soltero*) bachelor

3 (*LAm*) (= *cornudo*) cuckold

4 (*Caribe*) (= *dineral*) big sum of money

bueyada SF (*LAm*) drove of oxen

bufa* Ⓐ ADJ (*Caribe, Méx*) tight*, drunk

Ⓑ SF 1 (= *broma*) joke, piece of clowning

2 (*Caribe*) (= *embriaguez*) drunkenness

búfalo Ⓐ ADJ (*Caribe**) great*, fantastic*

Ⓑ SM buffalo

bufanda SF 1 (= *prenda*) scarf

2 (‡) (= *soborno*) sweetener*, back-hander*

3 (= *gaje*) perk*

bufar ▸conjug 1a◂ Ⓐ VI [*toro*] to snort; [*gato*] to spit; **está que bufa** he's furious; **~ de ira** to snort with rage

Ⓑ **bufarse** VPR (*Méx*) [*pared*] to bulge

bufarrón* SM (*Cono Sur*) pederast, child molester

bufé SM (*pl* **bufés**) = **bufet**

bufeo SM (*CAm, Caribe, Méx*) (= *atún*) tunny; (= *delfín*) dolphin

bufet [bu'fe] SM (*pl* **bufets**) 1 (= *comida*) (= *cena*) buffet supper, cold supper; (= *almuerzo*) buffet lunch ► **bufet libre** fixed buffet, set-price buffet; **"bufet libre: 10 euros"** "eat as much as you like for 10 euros"

2 (= *comedor*) [*de hotel*] dining room

3 (= *restorán*) restaurant

4 (= *mueble*) sideboard

bufete SM 1 (= *mesa*) desk

2 [*de abogado*] (= *oficina*) lawyer's office; (= *negocio*) legal practice; **establecer su ~** to set up in legal practice

3 (*Culin*) = **bufet 1**

buffer SM (*Inform*) buffer

buffet [bu'fe] SM (*pl* **buffets**) = **bufet 1**

bufido SM snort

bufo Ⓐ ADJ 1 (= *cómico*) comic, farcical; **ópera bufa** comic opera

2 (*Caribe*) spongy

Ⓑ SM 1 (= *payaso*) clown, funny man; (*Mús*) buffo

2 (*Cono Sur*‡) (= *homosexual*) queer (‡), fag (*EEUU*‡)

bufón Ⓐ ADJ funny, comical

Ⓑ SM 1 (= *payaso*) clown

2 (*Hist*) jester

bufonada SF 1 (= *comentario*) jest; (= *acto*) piece of buffoonery

2 (*Teat*) farce

bufonear ▸conjug 1a◂ VI, **bufonearse** VPR 1 (= *bromear*) to joke, jest

2 (= *payasear*) to clown, play the fool

bufonesco ADJ 1 (= *gracioso*) funny, comical

2 (= *de payaso*) clownish

bufoso* SM (*Arg*) gun, shooter*

buga* SM 1 (*Aut*) car, wheels* *pl*

2 (= *persona*) straight person*, heterosexual

buganvilla SF bougainvillea

bugle SM bugle

bugui-bugui SM boogie-woogie

buhardilla SF, **buharda** SF 1 (= *desván*) loft

2 (= *ventana*) dormer window, dormer (*EEUU*)

búho SM 1 (*Orn*) owl, long-eared owl ► **búho real** eagle owl

2 (= *persona*) unsociable person, recluse

buhonería SF 1 (= *acto*) peddling, hawking

2 (= *mercancías*) pedlar's wares *pl*, hawker's wares *pl*

buhonero SM pedlar, ped(d)ler (*EEUU*), hawker

buido ADJ 1 (= *puntiagudo*) sharp, pointed

2 (= *estriado*) fluted, grooved

buitre Ⓐ SM (*Orn*) vulture ► **buitre alimoche** Egyptian vulture ► **buitre leonado** Griffon vulture

Ⓑ SMF (*) (= *persona gorrona*) scrounger*

buitrear ▸conjug 1a◂ Ⓐ VT 1 (*) (= *gorronear*) to scrounge*

2 (*LAm*) (= *matar*) to kill

3 (*Andes, Cono Sur**) (= *vomitar*) to throw up, vomit

Ⓑ VI (*Andes, Cono Sur*) to be sick, vomit

buitrón SM fish trap

buja SF (*Méx Aut*) axle box

bujarra‡ SM, **bujarrón‡** SM queer‡, fag (*EEUU*‡)

buje SM axle box, bushing

bujería SF trinket, knick-knack

bujero‡ SM hole

bujía SF 1 (*Aut*) spark plug

2 (*Elec*) candle power

3 (†) (= *vela*) candle; (= *candelero*) candlestick

4 (*CAm*) (= *bombilla*) light bulb

bula SF (*Rel*) bull; ✦*MODISMOS* **no poder con la ~*** to have no strength left for anything; **no me vale la ~ de Meco** I'm done for

bulbiforme ADJ bulbiform

bulbo SM 1 (*Anat, Bot, Med*) bulb

2 (*Méx*) valve, tube (*EEUU*)

3 (*Cono Sur Elec*) bulb

bulboso ADJ bulbous

buldog [bul'dog] SM (*pl* **buldogs**) bulldog

bule SM (*Méx Bot*) gourd, squash (*EEUU*); (= *cántaro*) water pitcher; ✦*MODISMO* **llenarse hasta los ~s** to stuff o.s.*; ✦*REFRÁN* **el que nace para ~ hasta jícara no para** you can't escape your destiny

bulerías SFPL *Andalusian song accompanied with clapping and dancing*

bulevar SM boulevard, avenue

Bulgaria SF Bulgaria

búlgaro/a Ⓐ ADJ, SM/F Bulgarian

Ⓑ SM (*Ling*) Bulgarian

bulimia SF bulimia, binge-eating syndrome (*EEUU*)

bulín SM (*Cono Sur*) 1 [*de soltero*] bachelor flat
2 (= *burdel*) room (*used for sexual encounters*)

bulla SF 1 (= *bullicio*) row, racket; **armar** *o* **meter ~** to make a row, make a racket*
2 (= *bronca*) quarrel, brawl; **meter algo a ~** to throw sth into confusion
3 (= *prisa*) hurry; **tengo mucha ~** I'm in a real hurry; **métele ~** hurry him up along
4 (= *muchedumbre*) crowd, mob
5 **ser el hombre de la ~** (*Caribe*) to be the man of the moment

bullabesa SF fish soup, bouillabaisse

bullaje SM noisy crowd, mob

bullanga SF disturbance, riot

bullanguero/a Ⓐ ADJ riotous, rowdy
Ⓑ SM/F 1 (= *persona ruidosa*) noisy person
2 (= *alborotador*) troublemaker

bullaranga SF (*LAm*) 1 (= *bullicio*) noise, row
2 (= *disturbio*) riot

bullarengue: SM bottom, woman's bottom

bulldog SM (*Zool*) bulldog

bulldozer [bul'doθer] SM (*pl* **bulldozers** [bul'doθer]) bulldozer

bullebulle* SMF (= *entrometido*) busybody; (= *intranquilo*) fusspot, fussbudget (*EEUU**)

bullero ADJ (*LAm*) = **bullicioso**

bullicio SM 1 (= *ruido*) din, hubbub
2 (= *actividad*) activity, bustle
3 (= *confusión*) confusion
4 (= *disturbio*) disturbance

bulliciosamente ADV 1 (= *ruidosamente*) [*protestar*] noisily; [*jugar*] boisterously
2 (= *con gran actividad*) busily

bullicioso ADJ 1 (= *ruidoso*) [*lugar*] noisy; [*niño*] boisterous
2 (= *con actividad*) busy, bustling

bullir ▸conjug 3h◂ Ⓐ VI 1 [*agua*] (= *hervir*) to boil; (= *agitarse*) to bubble (up); **el agua bullía ligeramente** the water bubbled gently; *ver tb* **sangre A2**
2 (= *moverse*) to move, stir; **no bullía** he didn't move, he never stirred; **Londres está que bulle de juventud** London is bursting with young people; **la ciudad bullía de actividad** the town was humming with activity; **bullía de indignación** he was seething with indignation
3 [*insectos*] to swarm
Ⓑ VT to move, stir; **no bulló pie ni mano** he did not lift a finger
Ⓒ **bullirse** VPR to move, stir

bulo SM hoax

bulón SM bolt

bulto SM 1 (= *abultamiento*) bulge; **se le notaba un ~ debajo de la chaqueta** you could see a shape *o* bulge under his jacket; ✦**MODISMOS buscar el ~ a algn*** to provoke *o* push sb; **menear el ~ a algn*** to thrash sb
2 (= *silueta*) shape; **vimos un ~ moviéndose entre los árboles** we saw a shape moving in the trees; **sin gafas sólo distingo los ~s** without glasses I can only make out shapes; **ir al ~** (*Taur*) to go for the body; (*Ftbl*) to go for the man
3 (= *volumen*) space, room; **no ocupa** *o* **hace ~** it doesn't take up any space *o* room; **he comprado regalos que ocupen poco ~** I've bought presents that won't take up much space *o* that are not too bulky; **error de ~** glaring error; **de mucho ~** (*lit*) bulky; (*fig*) important; **de poco ~** (*lit*) small; (*fig*) unimportant; **llevaba dos bolsas de poco ~** she carried two small bags; **no discutamos por cosas de poco ~** let's not argue about unimportant things; ✦**MODISMOS a ~** at a rough guess; **así, a ~, debe de haber unas mil botellas** at a rough guess there must be about a thousand bottles; **calcular algo a ~** to work sth out roughly, make a rough estimate of sth; **decir algo a ~**: **di algo a ~** just have a guess; **escurrir el ~*** (= *desaparecer*) to duck out*; (= *cambiar de tema*) to dodge the issue*; **ir de ~** ◊ **hacer ~** to swell the number(s), make up the number(s); **allí sólo estábamos para hacer ~** we were only there to make up *o* swell the numbers; **no hay que hacer nada, sólo ir de ~** we don't have to do anything, we just have to be there *o* to go along
4 (= *paquete*) [*de compra*] bag; [*de ropa, papel*] bundle; [*de equipaje*] piece of luggage *o* (*EEUU*) baggage; **vino cargado de ~s del supermercado** he arrived laden with bags from the supermarket; **el camión trajo todos los ~s pesados** the truck brought all the heavy loads; **pon los ~s en el maletero** put the luggage in the boot, put the baggage in the trunk (*EEUU*) ► **bulto de mano** item of hand luggage
5 (*Med*) (= *quiste*) lump; (= *chichón*) bump; **le salió un ~ en el cuello** he got a lump on his neck; **del golpe me salió un ~ en la frente** I got a bump on my forehead when I hit myself
6 (= *estatua*) statue
7 (*Mil*‡) squaddie*, recruit
8 (*Ven*) [*de escolar*] satchel, bag

bululú* SM (*Ven*) excitement, fuss

bumerán SM boomerang

bumerang [bume'ran] SM (*pl* **bumerangs** [bume'ran]) boomerang

bunga SF (*Caribe*) lie

bungalow ['boŋgalo, buŋga'lo] SM (*pl* **bungalows** ['boŋgalo, buŋga'lo]) bungalow

bungee ['banji] SM bungee jumping

bungo SM (*CAm*) = **bongo**

buniato SM = **boniato**

bunjo SM **hacer ~** (*Caribe*) to hit the jackpot

búnker ['buŋker] SM (*pl* **búnkers** ['buŋker]) 1 (*Mil*) bunker
2 (*Golf*) bunker, sand trap (*EEUU*)
3 (*Pol*) reactionary clique, reactionary core

búnquer SM = **búnker**

buñolería SF 1 (= *panadería*) *bakery where "buñuelos" are made*
2 (= *tienda*) *shop where "buñuelos" are sold*

buñuelo SM 1 (*Culin*) fritter, ≈ doughnut, ≈ donut (*EEUU*)
2 (*) (= *chapuza*) botched job, mess

BUP SM ABR (*Esp Escol*) (= **Bachillerato Unificado y Polivalente**) *former secondary-school certificate and course for 14-17 age group*

buque SM 1 (= *barco*) ship, boat; **ir en ~** to go by ship, go by sea ► **buque almirante** flagship ► **buque anfibio** amphibious craft ► **buque carguero** freighter ► **buque cisterna** tanker ► **buque correo** mailboat ► **buque costero** coaster ► **buque de abastecimiento** supply ship ► **buque de carga** freighter ► **buque de desembarco** landing craft ► **buque de guerra** warship; (*Hist*) man-of-war ► **buque de línea** liner; (*Hist*) ship of the line ► **buque de pasajeros** passenger ship ► **buque de ruedas** paddle-steamer ► **buque de vapor** steamer, steamship ► **buque de vela** sailing ship ► **buque escolta** escort vessel ► **buque escuela** training ship ► **buque espía** spy ship ► **buque factoría** factory ship ► **buque fanal**, **buque faro** lightship ► **buque granelero** bulk-carrier ► **buque hospital** hospital ship ► **buque insignia** flagship ► **buque mercante** merchantman, merchant ship ► **buque minador** minelayer ► **buque nodriza** mother ship ► **buque portacontenedores** container ship ► **buque portatrén** train ferry ► **buque velero** sailing ship
2 (= *cabida*) capacity
3 (= *casco*) hull

buqué SM bouquet (*of wine*)

buraco SM (*Cono Sur*) hole

burata: SF (*Caribe*) cash, dough:

burbuja SF bubble; **un refresco sin ~s** a still drink; **un refresco con ~s** a fizzy drink; **hacer ~s** [*persona*] to blow bubbles; [*gaseosa*] to fizz

burbujeante ADJ bubbly, fizzy

burbujear ▸conjug 1a◂ VI [*agua hirviendo*] to bubble; [*champán, gaseosa*] to fizz

burbujeo SM bubbling

burda: SF door

burdégano SM hinny

burdel SM brothel

Burdeos SM Bordeaux

burdeos Ⓐ ADJ INV maroon, dark red
Ⓑ SM INV (*tb* **vino de ~**) claret, Bordeaux, Bordeaux wine

burdo ADJ 1 [*persona*] coarse, rough
2 [*excusa, mentira*] clumsy

burear* ▸conjug 1a◂ (*Andes*) Ⓐ VT to con*, trick Ⓑ VI to go out on the town*

bureo* SM 1 (= *diversión*) entertainment, amusement; **ir de ~** to go out on the town*
2 (= *paseo*) stroll; **darse un ~** to go for a stroll

bureta SF burette

burgalés/esa Ⓐ ADJ of/from Burgos
Ⓑ SM/F native/inhabitant of Burgos; **los burgaleses** the people of Burgos

burgo SM hamlet

burgomaestre SM burgomaster

burgués/esa Ⓐ ADJ 1 (= *de clase media*) middle-class; **pequeño ~** lower middle-class
2 (*Pol pey*) bourgeois
3 (= *de la ciudad*) town *antes de s*
Ⓑ SM/F 1 (*de clase media*) middle-class person; (*Pol pey*) bourgeois; **pequeño ~** lower middle-class person; (*Pol pey*) petit bourgeois
2 (= *ciudadano*) townsman/townswoman

burguesía SF middle-class, bourgeoisie; **alta ~** upper middle class; **pequeña ~** lower middle class; (*Pol pey*) petit bourgeoisie

buril SM burin, engraver's chisel

burilar ▸conjug 1a◂ VT to engrave

burka SM (*a veces* SF) burqa

burla SF 1 (= *mofa*) gibe, taunt; **hacer ~ de algn** to make fun of sb, mock sb; **hace ~ de todo** he makes fun of *o* mocks everything
2 (= *broma*) joke; **fue una ~ cruel** it was a cruel trick
3 **burlas** joking *sing*, fun *sing*; **de ~s** in fun, tongue in cheek; **gastar ~s con algn** to make fun of sb; **entre ~s y veras** half-joking(ly)

burladero SM [1] (*Taur*) covert (*barrier behind which the bullfighter protects himself from the bull*)
[2] (*Aut*) traffic island; (*en túnel*) recess
burlador(a) Ⓐ ADJ mocking
Ⓑ SM/F [1] (= *cínico*) mocker
[2] (= *bromista*) practical joker
Ⓒ SM (†) Don Juan
burlar ▸conjug 1a◂ Ⓐ VT [1] (= *engañar*) [+ *persona*] to deceive, trick; [+ *enemigo*] to outwit; [+ *vigilancia*] to defeat; [+ *bloqueo*] to run
[2] (= *frustrar*) [+ *ambición, plan*] to thwart, frustrate; [+ *esperanzas*] to ruin, frustrate
[3] (= *seducir*) to seduce
[4] (*) (= *saber usar*) to know how to use, be able to handle; **ya burla la moto** she can handle the bike now*
Ⓑ **burlarse** VPR [1] (= *bromear*) to joke, banter; **yo no me burlo** I'm serious, I'm not joking
[2] **~se de algn** to mock sb, make fun of sb
burlería SF [1] (= *mofa*) mockery
[2] (= *engaño*) trick, deceit
[3] (= *cuento*) tall story, fairy tale
[4] (= *bromas*) fun
burlesco ADJ [1] (= *cómico*) funny, comic
[2] (*Literat*) burlesque
burlete SM draught excluder, weather strip (*EEUU*)
burlisto ADJ (*Cono Sur, CAm, Méx*) = **burlón A**
burlón/ona Ⓐ ADJ (= *bromista*) [*persona*] mocking, teasing; [*risa, voz*] sardonic; **dijo ~** he said teasingly
Ⓑ SM/F [1] (= *bromista*) joker
[2] (= *mofador*) mocker, scoffer
Ⓒ SM (*Méx**) mockingbird
buró SM [1] (= *escritorio*) bureau, (roll-top) desk
[2] ► **buró político** (*Pol*) executive committee [3] (*Méx*) (= *mesita de noche*) bedside table, night stand *o* table (*EEUU*)
burocracia SF bureaucracy
burócrata SMF [1] (*pey*) bureaucrat
[2] (= *funcionario*) civil servant, administrative official, public official
burocrático ADJ [1] (*pey*) bureaucratic
[2] (= *de los funcionarios*) official, civil service *antes de s*
burocratizar ▸conjug 1f◂ VT to bureaucratize
buromática SF, **burótica** SF office automation, office computerization
burqa SM (*a veces* SF) burqa
burra SF [1] (*Zool*) donkey, she-donkey; *ver tb* **burro B3**
[2] (*Esp**) (= *bicicleta*) bike
burrada SF [1] (= *tontería*) stupid thing; **decir ~s** to talk nonsense; **hacer ~s** to do stupid things; **no hagas ~s con el coche** don't do anything stupid with the car
[2] (*) (= *mucho*) **me gusta una ~** I like it a lot; **sabe una ~** he knows a hell of a lot*; **una ~ de cosas** a whole heap of things, loads of things*
burrajo ADJ (*Méx*) vulgar, rude
burrear‡ ▸conjug 1a◂ VT [1] (= *robar*) to rip off‡
[2] (= *engañar*) to con*
burrero/a Ⓐ ADJ (*Cono Sur hum*) horse-loving, race-going
Ⓑ SM/F [1] (*Méx*) mule driver, donkey driver
[2] (*Caribe*) (= *malhablado*) coarse person, foul-mouthed person
[3] (*Cono Sur hum*) horse-lover
Ⓒ SM (*CAm*) (= *burros*) *large herd of donkeys*
burricie* SF stupidity
burro Ⓐ ADJ [1] (*) (= *estúpido*) stupid; **¡qué ~! ¡no sabe la capital de Italia!** what a fool *o* moron*, he doesn't know the capital of Italy!
[2] (= *bruto*) **¡deja de empujar, no seas ~!** stop pushing, you great oaf *o* you big brute!*; **¡el muy ~ se comió el pastel entero!** he ate the whole cake, the pig!*
[3] (= *obstinado*) pig-headed*; **ponerse ~** to dig one's heels in, be pigheaded*
Ⓑ SM [1] (*Zool*) donkey; (*Cono Sur hum*) racehorse; (= *perdedor en carrera*) also-ran; **salto de ~** (*Méx*) leapfrog; ✦***MODISMOS*** **apearse** *o* **bajar(se) del ~*** to back down; **a pesar de las críticas, el gobierno no se apea** *o* **baja del ~** in spite of the criticism, the government refuses to back down; **¡el niño no se apea** *o* **baja del ~!** this kid doesn't know when he's beaten!; **bajar del ~ a algn** to take sb down a peg (or two)*, put sb in his/her place*; **caer ~s aparejados** (*Caribe**) to rain cats and dogs; **caerse del ~*** to admit defeat; **es un ~ cargado de letras** he's a pompous ass*; **comer ~**: **esto comió ~** (*Cono Sur**) it got lost, it vanished; **el ~ grande, ande o no ande*** never mind the quality, feel the width*; **no ver tres en un ~***: **sin gafas no veo tres en un ~** without my glasses I'm as blind as a bat*; **en el bosque no se veía tres en un ~** in the wood you couldn't see your hand in front of your face*; **poner a algn a caer de un ~*** to savage sb, tear sb to shreds; **ver ~s negros** (*Cono Sur**) to see stars; **si los ~s volaran** pigs might fly; **si los ~s volaran, todos nos haríamos ricos con ese negocio** this business could make us rich, and pigs might fly ► **burro de agua** (*Caribe, Méx*) big wave ► **burro de carga**: **trata a su empleados como ~s de carga** he treats his workers like slaves
[2] (*) (= *estúpido*) fool, moron*; **¡burro!, tres y dos son cinco** you fool *o* moron*, three plus two makes five!
[3] (*) (= *bruto*) **eres un ~, lo has roto** you're so rough you've gone and broken it; **el ~ de Juan seguía pegándole** that brute Juan kept on hitting him; **el ~ de Antonio se comió su plato y el mío** that pig Antonio ate all his own dinner and mine too*; ✦***MODISMO*** **trabaja como un burro** he works like a slave, he works all the hours God sends*
[4] (= *obstinado*) stubborn fool; **es un ~ y no lo vas a convencer** he's so pig-headed* *o* stubborn you'll never persuade him
[5] (*Naipes*) ≈ old maid
[6] (*Téc*) sawhorse, sawbuck (*EEUU*)
[7] (*Méx*) (= *escalera*) stepladder
[8] (*Andes, Caribe*) (= *columpio*) swing
burrumazo* SM (*Caribe*) blow, thump
bursátil ADJ stock-exchange *antes de s*, stock-market *antes de s*; **crisis ~** stock-market crisis; **desplome ~** stock-market crash
bursitis SF INV bursitis
burucuyá SF (*Arg, Par*) passionflower
burujaca SF (*LAm*) saddlebag
burujo SM = **borujo**
burundanga SF (*Cuba*) [1] (= *objeto sin valor*) piece of junk; **es ~** it's just a piece of junk; **de ~** worthless
[2] (= *lío*) mess, mix-up
burusca SF (*CAm*) kindling
bus SM [1] (= *autobús*) bus, coach
[2] (*Inform*) bus ► **bus de expansión** expansion bus ► **bus de memoria** memory bus
busa‡ SF **tener ~** (*Esp*) to feel hungry
busaca SF [1] (*Andes, Caribe*) saddlebag
[2] (*Caribe*) satchel
busca Ⓐ SF search; **la niebla dificultaba la ~** the search was hampered by fog; **están analizando la muestra a la ~ de impurezas** they are analyzing the sample in search of impurities *o* to search for impurities; **en ~ de** in search of; **salieron en ~ del niño desaparecido** they set off in search of the missing child; **empezó a llamar por teléfono a todas partes en mi ~** he began phoning around everywhere to try and find me; **se marcharon en ~ de fortuna** they went off to seek their fortune ► **busca y captura**: **el juez dictó orden de ~ y captura del fugitivo** the judge ordered the fugitive's (immediate) capture; **estar en ~ y captura** to be wanted, be on the run*
Ⓑ SM (*Esp*) (= *mensáfono*) bleeper*, pager
buscabullas* SMF (*Caribe, Méx*) troublemaker
buscada SF = **busca A**
buscador(a) Ⓐ SM/F (= *persona*) ► **buscador(a) de agua** water-diviner ► **buscador(a) de diamantes** diamond prospector ► **buscador(a) de fortuna** fortune-seeker ► **buscador(a) de oro** gold prospector ► **buscador(a) de setas** mushroom-gatherer ► **buscador(a) de talentos** talent spotter, talent scout ► **buscador(a) de tesoros** treasure hunter
Ⓑ SM [1] (*Internet*) search engine
[2] (= *mecanismo*) scanner
buscaniguas SM INV (*Andes, CAm*) squib, cracker
buscapersonas SM INV = **busca B**
buscapié SM hint
buscapiés SM INV jumping jack, firecracker (*EEUU*)
buscapleitos SMF INV (*LAm*) troublemaker
buscar ▸conjug 1g◂ Ⓐ VT [1] (= *tratar de encontrar*) [1·1] [+ *persona, objeto perdido, trabajo*] to look for; **estuvieron buscando a los montañeros** they were searching for *o* looking for the mountaineers; **llevo meses buscando trabajo** I've been job-hunting for months, I've been looking for a job for months; **el ejército busca a un comando enemigo** the army is searching for *o* looking for an enemy commando unit; **el terrorista más buscado del país** the most wanted terrorist in the country; **"se busca piso"** "flat wanted"; **"chico busca chica"** "boy seeks girl"; **el acomodador me buscó un asiento al fondo** the usher found me a seat at the back; **las plantas buscan la luz** plants grow towards the light; ✦***MODISMO*** **~le tres pies al gato** (= *buscar complicaciones*) to complicate matters, make things difficult; (= *buscar defectos*) to split hairs, nitpick*; ✦***REFRÁN*** **busca y encontrarás** seek and you shall find
[1·2] (*en diccionario, enciclopedia*) to look up; **busca el número en la guía** look up the number in the directory
[1·3] (*con la vista*) to try to spot, look for; **lo busqué entre el público pero no lo vi** I tried to spot him *o* looked for him in the crowd but I didn't see him

[2] (= *tratar de conseguir*) [+ *solución*] to try to find; **no sé lo que buscas con esa actitud** I don't know what you're aiming to *o* trying to achieve with that attitude; **con esta novela se busca la creación de un estilo diferente** this novel attempts to *o* aims to create a different style; **yo no busco la fama** I'm not looking for fame; **sólo buscaba su dinero** he was only out for *o* after her money; **como tienen una niña ahora van buscando la parejita** as they've got a girl they're trying for a boy now; **~ excusas** to make excuses; **~ hacer algo** to seek to do sth, try to do sth; **siempre buscaba hacerlo lo mejor posible** she always sought *o* tried to do the best possible thing; **ir a ~ algo/a algn: ha ido a ~ una servilleta** she's gone to fetch *o* get a napkin; **ve a ~ a tu madre** go and fetch *o* get your mother; **voy a ~ tabaco** I'll go and get some cigarettes; ✦*MODISMOS* **~la ◊ ~ pelea** to be looking for a fight, be looking for trouble; **vino buscando pelea** he was looking for trouble *o* a fight, he was spoiling for a fight*; **~ la ruina a algn** to be the ruin of sb; **este hijo mío me va a ~ la ruina** this son of mine will be the ruin of me

[3] (= *recoger*) to pick up, fetch; **¿vais a ir a ~me a la estación?** are you going to pick me up *o* fetch me from the station?; **vino a ~ sus plantas** she came to pick up *o* fetch her plants

[4] (*Inform*) to search

[5] (= *preguntar por*) to ask for; **¿quién me busca?** who is asking for me?

Ⓑ VI to look; **ya puedes dejar de ~, aquí tienes las llaves** you can stop looking, here are the keys; **¿has buscado bien?** have you looked properly?; **busca en la página 45** look on page 45; **¡busca!** (*al perro*) fetch!

Ⓒ **buscarse** VPR [1] [+ *marido, trabajo*] to find (o.s.); [+ *ayuda, patrocinador*] to get, find; **deberías ~te un ayudante** you should find yourself an assistant; **ya tendrías que ~te trabajo** you should find yourself a job *o* start looking for a job; ✦*MODISMO* **~se la vida*** (= *ganar dinero*) to try to earn *o* make a living; (= *arreglárselas solo*) to manage on one's own, get by on one's own; **yo me busco la vida como puedo** I (try to) earn *o* make a living as best as I can; **no me vengas con historias, búscate la vida** stop bothering me, sort it out for yourself

[2] [+ *problemas*] **no te busques más problemas** don't bring more problems on yourself, don't make more trouble for yourself; **él se lo buscó** he brought it on himself, he asked for it*; ✦*MODISMO* **buscársela*** to ask for trouble, ask for it*; **te la estás buscando** you're asking for it, you're asking for trouble; **él se la buscó** he asked for it*

buscarruidos SM INV rowdy, troublemaker

buscas* SFPL (*LAm*) perks*, profits on the side

buscatesoros SMF INV treasure hunter, treasure seeker

buscavidas SMF INV [1] (= *persona ambiciosa*) go-getter

[2] (= *fisgón*) snooper, nosey-parker*

buscón/ona Ⓐ ADJ (= *deshonesto*) thieving, crooked

Ⓑ SM/F (††) (= *ladronzuelo*) petty thief, rogue

buscona SF (*pey*) whore

buseca SF [1] (*Andes, Caribe*) small bus, minibus

[2] (*Cono Sur*) thick stew

busilis* SM INV difficulty, snag; **ahí está el ~** that's the problem; **dar en el ~ del asunto** to reach the crux of the matter

búsqueda SF search (**de** for); **continúa la ~ de los desaparecidos** the search for the missing people continues; **hacer una ~** to do a search; **a *o* en ~ de algo** in search of sth; **estamos trabajando en la ~ de una vacuna** we're working on finding a vaccine ► **búsqueda del tesoro** treasure hunt ► **búsqueda de votos** canvassing ► **búsqueda y sustitución** (*Inform*) find and replace

busto SM [1] (= *escultura*) bust ► **busto parlante** talking head

[2] (*Anat*) chest

butaca SF [1] (= *sillón*) armchair, easy chair ► **butaca orejera** wing-chair

[2] (*Teat*) seat ► **butaca de platea, butaca de patio** seat in the stalls *o* (*EEUU*) orchestra

butacón SM large armchair

butanero SM gas-bottle delivery man

butano SM (*tb* **gas ~**) butane, butane gas; **bombona de ~** large Calor®, *large butane gas cylinder*; **color ~** orange

butaque SM (*LAm*) small armchair

buten ADV **de ~*** terrific*, tremendous*

butifarra SF [1] (= *embutido*) *Catalan sausage*; ✦*MODISMO* **hacer (la) ~ a algn*** ≈ to give sb the two-fingers sign, make an obscene gesture to sb

[2] (*) (= *media*) *badly-fitting stocking*

[3] (*Perú*) *meat and salad roll*

[4] ✦*MODISMO* **tomar a algn para la ~** (*Cono Sur**) to make a laughing stock of sb

butiondo ADJ lewd, lustful

butrón* SM [1] (= *agujero*) *hole made to effect a break-in*

[2] (= *robo*) burglary, break-in

butronero* SM burglar

butuco ADJ (*CAm*) short, squat

buz SM respectful kiss, formal kiss; **hacer el ~** to bow and scrape

buzamiento SM (*Geol*) dip

buzar ▸conjug 1f◂ VI (*Geol*) to dip

buzo[1] SM diver

buzo[2] SM (*Andes, Cono Sur*) (= *chándal*) track-suit; (= *mono*) jumpsuit

buzón SM [1] (*Correos*) (*en casa*) letterbox, mailbox (*EEUU*); (*en calle*) postbox, letterbox, mailbox (*EEUU*); **echar una carta al ~** to post a letter; ✦*MODISMOS* **cerrar el ~‡** to keep one's trap shut*; **vender un ~ a algn** (*Cono Sur**) to sell sb a dummy, pull the wool over sb's eyes ► **buzón de alcance** late-collection postbox ► **buzón de sugerencias** suggestions box ► **buzón de voz** voice mail

[2] (*Inform*) mailbox

[3] (= *tapón*) plug

[4] (= *compuerta*) sluice

[5] (*Pol*) *courier in secret organization*

buzonear ▸conjug 1a◂ VT to deliver door-to-door

buzonero/a SM/F (*LAm*) postal employee (*who collects from letterboxes*)

byte SM (*Inform*) byte

Cc

C¹, c [θe] (*esp LAm*) [se] SF (= *letra*) C, c

C² ABR (= **centígrado**) C

C. ABR (= **Compañía**) Co

c. ABR 1 (= **capítulo**) ch, c., chap
2 (= **cuenta**) a/c, acc., acct.

c³ ABR (= **centímetros cúbicos**) cc

C-14 ABR (= **carbono 14**) C.14; **datación por C-14** C.14 dating

C/ ABR (= **Calle**) St

c/ ABR 1 (= **cuenta**) a/c, acc., acct.
2 (= **capítulo**) ch, c., chap
3 (= **carretera**) Rd

Cª ABR (= **compañía**) Co.

ca EXCL not a bit of it!, never!

C.A. ABR 1 (*Elec*) (= **corriente alterna**) AC
2 (*Esp Pol*) = **Comunidad Autónoma**
3 (*Dep*) (= **Club Atlético**) AC

cabal Ⓐ ADJ 1 (= *exacto*) **llegó a las doce ~es** he arrived at exactly twelve o'clock, he arrived at twelve o'clock precisely; **5 euros ~es** exactly 5 euros
2 (*frm*) (= *completo*) **una ~ formación humanística** a thorough classical education; **esto nos proporciona una idea ~ del asunto** this provides us with a clearer and fuller picture of the matter
3 (= *sensato*) upright
Ⓑ **cabales** SMPL **no está en sus ~es** she isn't in her right mind; **perdió sus ~es por ella** he lost his mind over her
Ⓒ EXCL (†) **¡cabal!** perfectly correct!, right!

cábala SF 1 (*Rel*) cab(b)ala
2 (= *intriga*) cabal, intrigue
3 **cábalas** (= *conjeturas*) **hacer ~s** to speculate, conjecture

cabalgada SF (*Hist*) (= *tropa*) troop of riders; (= *incursión*) cavalry raid

cabalgador SM rider, horseman

cabalgadura SF [*de montar*] mount, horse; [*de carga*] beast of burden

cabalgar ▸conjug 1h◂ Ⓐ VT 1 [*jinete*] to ride
2 [*semental*] to cover, serve
Ⓑ VI to ride, go riding; **~ en mula** to ride (on) a mule; **~ sin montura** ◊ **~ a pelo** to ride bareback

cabalgata SF 1 (= *desfile*) mounted procession, cavalcade ► **cabalgata de Reyes** Twelfth Night procession
2 [*de jinete*] ride

> **CABALGATA DE REYES**
>
> *The* **cabalgata de Reyes** *is a float parade held on 5 January, the eve of Epiphany, in most Spanish towns and cities. It celebrates the coming of the Three Kings with their gifts for the infant Jesus. In the course of the* **cabalgatas**, *the Three Kings throw sweets into the crowd.*
>
> ⇨ *See also* DÍA DE REYES

cabalidad SF **a ~** perfectly, adequately

cabalista SMF schemer, intriguer

cabalístico ADJ (= *de la cábala*) cabalistic; (= *misterioso*) occult, mysterious

caballa SF (Atlantic) mackerel

caballada SF 1 (*Zool*) drove of horses
2 (*LAm*) (= *animalada*) stupid thing to do; **has hecho una ~** that was a stupid thing to do

caballaje SM horsepower

caballar ADJ horse *antes de s*, equine; **ganado ~** horses *pl*; **cara ~** horse-face

caballazo SM (*LAm*) collision between two horsemen, accident involving a horse

caballejo SM 1 (= *poney*) pony
2 (= *rocín*) old horse, nag*

caballerango SM (*Méx*) groom

caballerear ▸conjug 1a◂ VI to play the gentleman

caballeresco ADJ 1 (*Hist*) knightly, chivalric; **literatura caballeresca** chivalresque literature, books of chivalry; **orden caballeresca** order of chivalry
2 [*sentimiento*] fine, noble; [*carácter*] gentlemanly, noble; [*conducta*] chivalrous

caballerete SM 1 (= *jovenzuelo*) young man
2 (= *presumido*) cocky youngster, Jack-the-lad*

caballería SF 1 (= *montura*) mount, steed (*liter*); (= *caballo*) horse; (= *mula*) mule ► **caballería de carga** beast of burden
2 (*Mil*) cavalry ► **caballería ligera** light cavalry, light horse
3 (*Hist*) chivalry; (= *orden*) order of chivalry; **libros de ~s** books of chivalry ► **caballería andante** knight errantry
4 **andarse en ~s** to overdo the compliments
5 (*CAm, Caribe, Cono Sur, Méx Agr*) *a land measurement of varying size (usually 42 hectares)*

caballericero SM (*CAm, Caribe*) groom

caballeriza SF 1 (= *cuadra*) stable; [*de cría*] stud, horse-breeding establishment ► **caballeriza de alquiler** livery stable
2 (= *empleados*) stable hands *pl*, grooms *pl*

caballerizo SM groom, stableman ► **caballerizo del rey** equerry ► **caballerizo mayor del rey** master of the king's horse

caballero SM 1 (= *hombre educado*) gentleman; **es todo un ~** he is a real gentleman; *ver tb* **pacto**
2 (*fórmula de cortesía*) **¿qué desea tomar, ~?** what would you like to drink, sir?; **señoras y ~s** ladies and gentlemen
3 (= *hombre*) **camisa de ~** man's shirt; **peluquería de ~s** gents' hairdresser's; **servicio de ~s** gents, men's toilets, men's; **ropa de ~** menswear; **"caballeros"** (= *servicios*) "gents", "gentlemen"
4 (*Hist*) knight; **los ~s de la Tabla Redonda** the Knights of the Round Table; **armar ~ a algn** to knight sb; **el Caballero de la Triste Figura** the Knight of the Doleful Countenance, Don Quixote; **~ de Santiago** Knight of (the Order of) Santiago ► **caballero andante** knight errant

caballerosamente ADV (= *con cortesía*) like a gentleman, in a gentlemanly fashion; (= *con nobleza*) chivalrously

caballerosidad SF (= *cortesía*) gentlemanliness; (= *nobleza*) chivalry

caballeroso ADJ (= *cortés*) gentlemanly; (= *noble*) chivalrous; **poco ~** ungentlemanly

caballerote SM (*pey*) so-called gentleman, gentleman unworthy of the name

caballete SM (*Arte*) easel; (*Téc*) trestle; [*de tejado, de tierra labrada*] ridge; [*de chimenea*] cowl; (*Anat*) bridge (of the nose) ► **caballete de pintor** painter's easel ► **caballete de serrar** sawhorse, sawbuck (*EEUU*) ► **caballete para bicicleta** bicycle clamp, bicycle rest

caballista SMF (= *jinete*) horseman/woman; (= *experto*) expert on horses

caballito SM 1 (= *caballo*) little horse, pony; ✦***MODISMO*** **llevar a algn a ~** to give sb a piggy-back ► **caballito del diablo** dragonfly ► **caballito de mar** sea horse ► **caballito de niño** (*para mecerse*) rocking horse; (*con palo (y rueda)*) hobby-horse ► **caballito marino** sea horse
2 (*Méx*) (= *compresa*) sanitary towel, sanitary napkin (*EEUU*)
3 **caballitos** [*de feria*] merry-go-round *sing*, carousel *sing* (*esp EEUU*)

caballo SM 1 (= *animal*) horse; **a ~: una mujer a ~** a woman on horseback o riding a horse; **vino a ~** he came on horseback, he rode here; **me gusta montar a ~** I like (to go) horse riding; **paseo a ~** (horse) ride; **tropas de a ~** mounted troops; ✦***MODISMOS*** **de ~:**

huge, massive; **una dosis de ~** a huge dose, a massive dose; **una depresión de ~** a terrible depression, a really deep depression; **a ~ entre**: **Andalucía, a ~ entre oriente y occidente** Andalusia, halfway between the east and the west; **vivo a ~ entre Madrid y Barcelona** I spend my time between Madrid and Barcelona, I spend half my time in Madrid, half in Barcelona; **como ~ desbocado** rashly, hastily; **ir a mata ~*** to go at breakneck speed, go like the clappers*; ✦*REFRÁN* **a ~ regalado no le mires el diente** don't look a gift horse in the mouth ► **caballo blanco**† white knight ► **caballo de batalla**: **han convertido el asunto en su ~ de batalla personal** the issue has become their hobbyhorse; **esto se convirtió en el ~ de batalla de la reunión** this became the bone of contention in the meeting ► **caballo de carga** packhorse ► **caballo de carreras** racehorse ► **caballo de caza** hunter ► **caballo de guerra** warhorse, charger ► **caballo de manta**, **caballo de silla** saddle horse ► **caballo de tiro** carthorse, plough horse, plow horse (*EEUU*) ► **Caballo de Troya** Trojan horse

2 (*Ajedrez*) knight; (*Naipes*) *equivalent of queen in the Spanish pack of cards*

3 (*Mec*) (*tb* **~ de fuerza, ~ de vapor**) horsepower; **un motor de 100 ~s** a 100 horsepower engine; **¿cuántos ~s tiene este coche?** what horsepower is this car?, what's this car's horsepower?; **un dos ~s** a 2CV ► **caballo de vapor decimal** metric horsepower

4 (*Dep*) ► **caballo con arcos** pommel horse, side horse ► **caballo de saltos** vaulting horse, long horse

5 [*de carpintero*] sawhorse, sawbuck (*EEUU*)

6 (‡) (= *heroína*) smack‡, sugar‡

caballón SM (*Agr*) ridge

caballuno ADJ horse-like, horsy

cabalmente ADV (= *exactamente*) exactly; (= *bien*) properly; (= *completamente*) completely, fully; (= *a conciencia*) thoroughly

cabanga SF (*CAm*) nostalgia, blues*, homesickness; **estar de ~** to be homesick

cabaña SF 1 (= *choza*) hut, cabin; (*pobre*) hovel, shack ► **cabaña de madera** log cabin

2 (*Billar*) baulk

3 (*Agr*) (= *rebaño*) (large) flock; (= *ganado*) livestock

4 (*Cono Sur*) (= *estancia*) cattle-breeding ranch

cabañero SM herdsman

cabañuelas SFPL (*LAm*) folk weather predictions, *weather predictions made by country people, based on weather variations in the first few days of January and August*; (*Andes*) (= *lluvias*) first summer rains; (*Méx*) (= *periodo*) first twelve days of January (*used to predict the weather*)

cabaré SM, **cabaret** [kaβa're] SM (*pl* **cabarés** *o* **cabarets**) (= *espectáculo*) cabaret, floor show; (= *boîte*) cabaret, nightclub

cabaretera SF (= *bailarina*) cabaret entertainer, cabaret dancer, showgirl; (= *chica de alterne*) night-club hostess

cabaretero ADJ of a nightclub; **con ambiente ~** with a nightclub atmosphere

cabás SM schoolbag, satchel

cabe¹ PREP (*liter*) close to, near to

cabe² SM (*Dep*) header

cabe³ SM (= *golpe*) **dar un ~ a algo** to harm sth, do harm to sth; **dar un ~ al bolsillo** to make a hole in one's pocket ► **cabe de pala** windfall, lucky break

cabeceada SF (*LAm*) nod (of the head), shake of the head; **dar ~s** to nod off; **echarse una ~** to have a nap

cabecear ▸conjug 1a◂ Ⓐ VT 1 [+ *balón*] to head

2 [+ *vino*] to strengthen; [+ *vinos*] to blend

3 (*Cos*) to bind (the edge of)

Ⓑ VI 1 (*al dormir*) to nod off; (= *negar*) to shake one's head; [*caballo*] to toss its head

2 [*barco*] to pitch; [*carruaje*] to lurch, sway; [*carga*] to shift, slip

cabeceo SM 1 (*al dormir*) nod; (= *negativa*) shake of the head; [*de caballo*] toss of the head

2 [*de un barco*] pitching; [*de un carruaje*] lurching, lurch; [*de una carga*] shifting, slipping

cabecera SF 1 [*de página*] top; [*de artículo*] heading; [*de carta*] opening; (*Inform*) title-page; **la noticia apareció en la ~ de todos los periódicos** the news made the headlines in all the newspapers; **ha ocupado la ~ de todos los telediarios** it has been headline news on every news programme ► **cabecera de cartel** main attraction

2 [*de río*] headwaters *pl*

3 [*de manifestación*] head, front

4 [*de cama*] headboard; **tenía una bandera a la ~ de la cama** he had a flag at the head of the bed; *ver tb* **libro 1**, **médico B**

5 [*de mesa*] head; **se sentaron en la ~ de la mesa** they sat at the head of the table

6 [*de organización, ministerio*] top (level); **desde la ~ del ministerio** from top ministerial level

cabecero SM headboard, bedhead

cabeciduro ADJ (*Andes, Caribe*) stubborn, pigheaded

cabecilla SMF ringleader

cabellera SF 1 (= *pelo*) hair, head of hair; (= *postizo*) switch, hairpiece; ✦*MODISMO* **soltarse la ~*** to let one's hair down

2 (*Astron*) tail

cabello SM hair; **analizaremos sólo un ~** we shall analyse just a single hair; **llevaba el ~ recogido atrás** she had *o* wore her hair tied back; **te deja los ~s brillantes** it leaves your hair shiny ► **cabello de ángel** *confectionery and pastry filling made of pumpkin and syrup*

cabelludo ADJ (= *peludo*) hairy, shaggy; (*Bot*) fibrous

caber ▸conjug 2l◂ VI 1 (= *haber espacio para*) to fit (**en** into); **tu guitarra no cabe en mi armario** your guitar won't fit in my cupboard; **en este baúl no cabe** it won't fit in *o* go into this trunk, there's no room for it in this trunk; **en mi coche caben dos maletas más** there's room for two more suitcases in my car; **¿cabe alguien más?** is there room for anyone else?; **¿cabemos todos?** is there room for us all?; **no cabe nadie más** there's no room for anyone else; **en este baúl ya no cabe más** there's no more room (for anything) in this trunk; ✦*MODISMOS* **¡no me cabe en la cabeza!** I can't understand it!; **no ~ en sí** (= *estar feliz*) to be beside o.s.; (= *ser engreído*) to be big-headed*, to be full of o.s.; **no cabe en sí de contento** *o* **gozo** he's beside himself with joy, he's over the moon

2 (= *tener cabida*) **en la bandeja de papel caben 100 hojas** the paper tray will hold 100 sheets; **en este depósito caben 20 litros** this tank holds 20 litres; **un sofá donde caben dos** a two-seater sofa

3 **~ por** to go through; **eso no cabe por esta puerta** that won't go through this door

4 (*Mat*) **veinte entre cinco cabe a cuatro** five into twenty goes four (times)

5 [*ser posible*] 5.1 [+ *explicación*] to be possible; **sólo caben dos explicaciones** there are only two possible explanations; **la única explicación que cabe es que …** the only possible explanation is that …; **todo cabe en ese chico** that boy is capable of anything, nothing would surprise me from that boy; **no cabe en él hacerlo** he doesn't have it in him to do it; **ya no caben más lamentaciones** it's no use complaining; **no cabe perdón** it's inexcusable

5.2 (+ *INFIN*) **cabe imaginar distintas posibilidades** different possibilities can be imagined; **la persona más generosa que cabe imaginar** the most generous person you could imagine, the most generous person imaginable; **cabe intentar otro sistema** it would be worth trying another system; **cabe preguntar si …** one might *o* could ask whether …

5.3 **dentro de lo que cabe** under the circumstances; **se trata al animal lo mejor posible dentro de lo que cabe** the animal is treated as well as possible under the circumstances; **nos llevamos bastante bien, dentro de lo que cabe** we get on quite well, under the circumstances *o* considering; **no cabe duda de que …** there is *o* can be no doubt that …, the only thing for it is to …, there's nothing for it but to …; **no cabe más que**: **no cabe más que esperar a ver lo que pasa** we can only wait *o* all we can do is wait *o* the only thing for it is to wait and see what happens; **no cabe más que obedecer** there's no option but to obey; **cabe la posibilidad de que …**: **¿no cabe la posibilidad de que usted haya sido utilizada?** is it not possible that you might have been used?; **cabe la posibilidad que en unos días nos comuniquen algo** (there is a chance that) we may hear from them in a few days; **el flash no resulta aconsejable, puesto que cabe la posibilidad de asustar a los animales** it's best not to use a flash as it is liable to frighten the animals; **si cabe**: **a mí me parece que es aún mejor, si cabe** I think it's even better, if that's possible; **ahora está más amable, si cabe** she's even friendlier now; **mejoraremos, si cabe, el servicio posventa** we will improve our after-sales service, wherever possible

6 (= *corresponder*) **me cabe el honor/la satisfacción de presentarles (a) …** I have the honour/it gives me great pleasure to introduce …; **me cupo el privilegio de …** I had the privilege of …; **me cupo la responsabilidad de dirigir el país** the responsibility of running the country fell to me; **le cupieron 120 dólares** his share was 120 dollars, he got 120 dollars (as his share); *ver tb* **suerte 1**

cabestrar ▸conjug 1a◂ VT to halter, put a halter on

cabestrillo SM sling; **con el brazo en ~** with one's arm in a sling

➤ LENGUA Y USO: caber 5 53.2

cabestro SM 1 (= *brida*) halter; ✦*MODISMO* **llevar a algn del ~** to lead sb by the nose
2 (= *buey*) leading ox, bell-ox
3 (*) (= *cornudo*) cuckold; (= *lerdo*) thickie*

cabeza Ⓐ SF 1 [*de persona*] head; **se rascó la ~** he scratched his head; **me duele la ~** I've got a headache, my head aches; **los aviones pasan por encima de nuestras ~s** the planes are flying overhead; **afirmar con la ~** to nod (one's head); **agarrarse la ~** to hold one's head in one's hands; **asentir con la ~** to nod (one's head); **caer de ~** to fall headfirst *o* headlong; **se tiró al agua de ~** he dived headfirst into the water; **marcar de ~** (*Dep*) to score with a header; **lavarse la ~** to wash one's hair; **levantar la ~** (= *mirar*) to look up; **negar con la ~** to shake one's head; **por ~: cinco dólares por ~** five dollars a head, five dollars per person; **se me va la ~** I feel giddy; **volver la ~** to look round, turn one's head; **al oírlos volví la ~** when I heard them I looked round *o* turned my head; **me da vueltas la ~** my head's spinning
2 ✦*MODISMOS* **andar** *o* **ir de ~*** to be snowed under; **andar en ~** (*LAm*) to go bareheaded; **no estar bien de la ~*** = **estar mal de la cabeza**; **cortar ~s: será necesario cortar ~s** heads will have to roll; **esconder la ~** to keep one's head down; **írsele a algn de la ~: se me fue de la ~** it went right out of my mind; **jugarse la ~** to risk one's neck; **lanzarse de ~ a** (= *atacar*) to rush headlong at; (= *precipitarse*) rush headlong into; **levantar ~** to get back on one's feet again; **el Sporting sigue sin levantar ~** Sporting still haven't managed to end their poor run of form, Sporting haven't managed to turn the corner; **el país no termina de levantar ~** the country still hasn't managed to turn the corner; **hay sectores como la construcción que empiezan a levantar ~** some sectors, such as construction, are starting to pick up; **estar mal de la ~***: **hace falta estar mal de la ~ para hacer eso** you'd have to be out of your mind to do that; **no quiero acabar mal de la ~** I don't want to go off my head; **mantener la ~ fuera del agua** to keep one's head above water; **meter la ~ en la arena** to bury one's head in the sand; **meter algo en la ~ a algn: por fin le metimos en la ~ que ...** we finally got it into his head that ...; **metérsele a algn en la ~: se le ha metido en la ~ hacerlo solo** he's taken *o* got it into his head to do it alone; **esa melodía la tengo metida en la ~** I can't get that tune out of my head; **pasársele a algn por la ~: jamás se me pasó por la ~** it never entered my head; **perder la ~ por** to lose one's head over; **es ~ de pescado** (*Cono Sur**) it's sheer nonsense; **hablar ~s de pescado** (*Cono Sur**) to talk drivel, talk through the back of one's head*; **tener ~ de pollo** (*Cono Sur**) to have a memory like a sieve; **quitar algo de la ~ a algn** to get sth out of sb's head; **romper la ~ a algn** to smash sb's face in; **romperse la ~** to rack one's brains; **sacarse una idea de la ~** to get an idea out of one's head; **sentar ~** to settle down; **subirse a la ~: el vino se me subió a la ~** the wine went to my head; **tener ~** to be bright; **tengo la ~ como un bombo** my head is ringing; **tener la ~ dura** to be stubborn; **tener la ~ sobre los hombros** to have one's head screwed on (the right way); **tener mala ~** (= *tener mala memoria*) to have a bad memory; (= *ser despistado*) to be absent-minded; **estar tocado de la ~** to be soft in the head; **traer de ~ a algn** to drive sb mad; **vestirse por la ~**† (= *ser mujer*) to be female; (= *ser sacerdote*) to be a cleric; *ver tb* **calentar A1**
3 (= *frente*) **a la ~ de: a la ~ de la manifestación** at the head *o* front of the demonstration; **con Pérez a la ~ del gobierno** with Pérez at the head of the government; **ir en ~** to be in the lead; **ir en ~ de la lista** to be at the top of the list, head the list
4 (= *distancia*) head; **ganar por una ~ (escasa)** to win by a (short) head; **le saca una ~ a su hermano** he is a head taller than his brother
5 (*de montaña*) top, summit
6 (= *objeto*) ► **cabeza atómica** atomic warhead ► **cabeza buscadora** homing head, homing device ► **cabeza de ajo** bulb of garlic ► **cabeza de biela** (*Mec*) big end ► **cabeza de dragón** (*Bot*) snapdragon ► **cabeza de escritura** (*Tip*) golf ball ► **cabeza de guerra** warhead ► **cabeza de impresión** (*Inform*) head, printhead ► **cabeza de partido** administrative centre ► **cabeza de plátanos** (*LAm*) bunch of bananas ► **cabeza de playa** beachhead ► **cabeza de puente** bridgehead ► **cabeza explosiva** warhead ► **cabeza grabadora** recording head ► **cabeza impresora** (*Inform*) head, printhead ► **cabeza nuclear** nuclear warhead ► **cabeza sonora** recording head
Ⓑ SMF 1 (= *líder*) head, leader; **es ~ de las fuerzas armadas** he's head *o* the leader of the armed forces; **es ~ del grupo rebelde** he's the leader of the rebel group
2 ► **cabeza caliente** extremist ► **cabeza cuadrada*** bigot ► **cabeza de chorlito*** scatterbrain ► **cabeza de familia** head of the household ► **cabeza de serie** (*Dep*) seed ► **cabeza de serrín*** airhead* ► **cabeza de turco** scapegoat ► **cabeza dura** stubborn person; **es un ~ dura** he's as stubborn as a mule ► **cabeza hueca** idiot ► **cabeza pelada** (*Hist*) Roundhead ► **cabeza rapada** skinhead ► **cabeza sin seso** idiot ► **cabeza visible** head, leader

cabezada SF 1 (= *cabezazo*) head butt, butt; (= *porrazo*) blow on the head; ✦*MODISMO* **darse de ~s** to rack one's brains
2 (= *cabeceo*) shake of the head, nod; **dar ~s** to nod (sleepily), doze; **dar** *o* **echar una ~** have a nap
3 (*Náut*) pitch, pitching; **dar ~s** to pitch
4 (= *parte de arreos*) head stall; [*de bota*] instep; [*de zapato*] vamp
5 (*Andes, Cono Sur*) saddle tree
6 (*Caribe, Cono Sur*) [*de río*] headwaters

cabezadita SF **echar una ~*** to have a snooze*, doze

cabezal SM 1 (= *almohada*) pillow, bolster; [*de dentista etc*] headrest; (*Med*) pad, compress
2 (*Inform*) head; [*de vídeo, cassette*] head
3 **~ de enganche** (*Aut*) towbar

cabezazo SM (*gen*) head butt, butt; (= *porrazo*) bump on the head; (*Dep*) header

cabezo SM (*Geog*) hillock, small hill; (*Náut*) reef

cabezón Ⓐ ADJ 1 (*) (= *cabezudo*) bigheaded, with a big head; (= *terco*) pigheaded
2 [*vino*] heady
Ⓑ SM 1 (*) (= *cabeza*) big head
2 (*Cos*) hole for the head
3 (= *cuello*) collar band; **llevar a algn de los cabezones** to drag sb along against his will
4 **cabezones** (*en un río*) white water *sing*

cabezonada* SF pig-headed thing to do

cabezonería* SF pig-headedness

cabezota* Ⓐ ADJ pig-headed
Ⓑ SMF pig-headed person

cabezudo Ⓐ ADJ (*) = **cabezón A**
Ⓑ SM *carnival figure with an enormous head*

cabezuela SF (*Bot*) head (of a flower); (= *capullo*) rosebud

cabida SF 1 (= *capacidad*) (*en depósito, caja*) capacity; (*en vehículo*) space, room; **necesitamos un depósito de mayor ~** we need a tank with a greater capacity; **en este autobús no hay ~ para 20 personas** this bus can't hold *o* take 20 people, there isn't space *o* room in this bus for 20 people; **dar ~ a: el auditorio puede dar ~ a más de mil espectadores** the concert hall can accommodate more than a thousand people, the concert hall has a capacity of more than a thousand; **los hoteles no podrán dar ~ a tantos turistas** the hotels will not be able to accommodate so many tourists; **con el nuevo tratado se da ~ a los países del Este** the new treaty opens the way for *o* embraces the Eastern bloc countries; **tener ~: el teatro tiene ~ para 600 personas** the theatre holds 600 people, the theatre has a capacity of 600; **la impresora tiene ~ para 200 hojas** the printer can hold *o* take up to 200 sheets
2 (= *aceptación*) **no hay ~ para la superstición** there is no place *o* room for superstition; **dar ~ a: en este periódico no se da ~ a las ideas de vanguardia** there's no place *o* room for avant-garde ideas in this newspaper; **ya no le vamos a dar más ~ en esta casa** he will no longer be welcome in this house; **tener ~: personajes de ese tipo no tienen ~ en nuestro programa** there is no place *o* room in our programme for characters like that
3 (*Náut*) capacity
4 (= *terreno*) area

cabildear ▸conjug 1a◂ VI (= *presionar*) to lobby; (= *conspirar*) to intrigue

cabildeo SM (= *presión*) lobbying; (= *intrigas*) intriguing, intrigues *pl*

cabildero/a SM/F lobbyist, member of a pressure group; (*pey*) intriguer

cabildo SM 1 (*Rel*) (= *personas*) chapter; (= *junta*) chapter meeting
2 (*Pol*) (= *ayuntamiento*) town council; (*Parl*) lobby ► **cabildo insular** (*en Canarias*) inter-island council
3 (*Caribe*) [*de negros*] gathering of black people; (= *reunión desordenada*) riotous assembly

cabilla** SF **dar ~ a algn** to fuck sb**, screw sb**

cabillo SM end; (*Bot*) stalk, stem

cabina SF 1 [*de discjockey, intérprete*] booth; (*tb* **~ telefónica, ~ de teléfono(s)**) telephone booth, telephone box; **no te pude llamar porque no había ninguna ~** I couldn't call you because there was no phone box ► **cabina de grabación** recording booth ► **cabina de prensa** press box ► **cabina de proyección** projection room ► **cabina electoral** voting booth

2 [*de tren, camión*] cab
3 (*Aer*) [*de pasajeros*] cabin; [*de pilotos*] cockpit ► **cabina a presión** pressurized cabin ► **cabina de mando** (*Aer*) flight deck, cockpit
4 (*Náut*) bridge

cabinada SF cabin cruiser

cabinero/a SM/F (*Col*) (= *hombre*) steward, flight attendant (*EEUU*); (= *mujer*) air hostess, stewardess, flight attendant (*EEUU*)

cabinista SMF projectionist

cabio SM (= *viga*) beam, joist; [*del techo*] rafter; (*en puerta, ventana*) lintel, transom

cabizbajo ADJ dejected, downcast, crestfallen

cabla SF (*LAm*) trick

cable SM 1 (*Elec*) (= *hilo*) wire; (*con cubierta aislante*) cable; **tiene varios ~s sueltos** there are several loose wires; **el ~ del micrófono/amplificador** the microphone/amplifier cable *o* lead; ✦*MODISMOS* **se le cruzaron los ~s*** he totally flipped*; **se le pelaron los ~s** (*CAm**) he got all mixed up ► **cable de alta tensión** high-voltage cable ► **cable de cobre** copper wire
2 (*Mec*) [*de acero*] cable; ✦*MODISMO* **echar un ~ a algn*** to give sb a helping hand ► **cable de remolque** towline, towrope
3 (*Telec*) cable, wire; **televisión por ~** cable television, cable TV ► **cable coaxial** coaxial cable ► **cable de fibra óptica** fibreoptic cable, optical fibre, optical fiber (*EEUU*) ► **cable óptico** optical cable
4 (= *cablegrama*) cable; **enviar un ~ a algn** to cable sb

cableado SM wiring

cablear ▸conjug 1a◂ VT to wire up

cablegrafiar ▸conjug 1c◂ VI to cable, wire

cablegráfico ADJ cable *antes de s*; **transferencia cablegráfica** cable transfer

cablegrama SM cable, cablegram

cablero SM cable ship

cablevisión SF cable television, cable TV

cablista ADJ (*LAm*) sly, cunning

cabo SM 1 (= *trozo pequeño*) [*de cuerda, hilo*] thread; [*de vela, lápiz*] stub; **falta cortar los cabitos de hilo** the loose threads just need cutting off; **iluminamos la habitación con un ~ de vela** we used the stub *o* end of a candle to light the room with; **escribía con un cabito** he was writing with a pencil stub ► **cabo de vela** (*Náut*) rope, cable
2 (*locuciones*) **al ~** (*frm*) (= *al final*) in the end; (= *después de todo*) at the end of the day; **al ~, su dedicación a la música ha rendido sus frutos** in the end, his dedication to music has borne fruit, his dedication to music has finally borne fruit; **al ~, su gran satisfacción era oír los aplausos** at the end of the day, his greatest satisfaction was to hear the applause; **al ~ de** after; **al ~ de tres meses** after three months, three months later; **llevar a ~** [+ *acción, investigación, tarea*] to carry out; [+ *viaje*] to make; **estamos llevando a ~ un proyecto en colaboración con la universidad** we are carrying out a joint project with the university; **ya hemos llevado a ~ la recogida de firmas** we have already collected the signatures; **en esta piscina se llevarán a ~ las pruebas de natación** the swimming events will take place in this pool; ✦*MODISMOS* **atar ~s**: **atando ~s, me di cuenta de que ...** I put two and two together and realized that ...; **de ~ a ~** ◊ **de ~ a rabo** from beginning to end, from start to finish; **me leí el libro de ~ a rabo en un día** I read the book from beginning to end *o* from start to finish in a day; **me recorrí el pueblo de ~ a rabo y no encontré ningún restaurante** I went all through the village and didn't find a single restaurant; **estar al ~ de la calle de algo** (*Esp*) to be fully aware of sth; **no dejar ningún ~ suelto** (*preparando algo*) to leave nothing to chance; (*investigando algo*) to tie up all the loose ends; *ver tb* **fin 3.1**
3 (= *graduación*) [*de militar*] corporal; [*de policía*] sergeant ► **cabo de escuadra** corporal ► **cabo de mar** petty officer ► **cabo primero** first officer
4 (*Geog*) cape ► **Cabo Cañaveral** Cape Canaveral ► **Cabo de Buena Esperanza** Cape of Good Hope ► **Cabo de Hornos** Cape Horn ► **Cabo Verde** Cape Verde
5 (*Remo*) stroke

cabotaje SM cabotage, coasting trade, coastal traffic

caboverdiano/a ADJ, SM/F Cape Verdean

cabra SF 1 (*Zool*) goat; (= *hembra*) nanny goat, she-goat; (= *almizclero*) musk deer; ✦*MODISMO* **estar como una ~** to be crazy; ✦*REFRÁN* **la ~ siempre tira al monte** a leopard does not change its spots, what's bred in the bone will out in the flesh ► **cabra montés** Spanish ibex
2 (*LAm*) (= *truco*) trick, swindle; (= *dado*) loaded dice
3 (*Cono Sur*) (= *carro*) light carriage; [*de carpintero*] sawhorse, sawbuck (*EEUU*)
4 (*Cono Sur**) (= *niña*) little girl
5 (= *moto*) motorbike; *ver tb* **cabro**

cabracho SM large-scaled scorpion fish

cabrahígo SM wild fig

cabrales SM INV *strong cheese from Asturias*

cabré *etc ver* **caber**

cabreado‡ ADJ pissed off**

cabreante‡ ADJ infuriating, maddening

cabrear‡ ▸conjug 1a◂ Ⓐ VT to piss off**
Ⓑ **cabrearse** VPR 1 (= *enfadarse*) to get pissed off**
2 (= *sospechar*) to get suspicious
3 (*Cono Sur*) (= *aburrirse*) to get bored

cabreo‡ SM **¡menudo ~ lleva!** she's really pissed off!**; **coger un ~** to fly off the handle*, fly into a rage

cabreriza SF goat shed, goat house

cabrerizo/a Ⓐ SM/F goatherd
Ⓑ ADJ (= *de las cabras*) goat *antes de s*

cabrero/a Ⓐ ADJ (*Cono Sur**) bad-tempered; **ponerse ~** to fly off the handle*
Ⓑ SM/F goatherd

cabrestante SM capstan, winch

cabria SF hoist, derrick ► **cabria de perforación** drilling rig

cabrio SM rafter

cabrío Ⓐ ADJ goatish; **macho ~** billy goat, he-goat
Ⓑ SM (= *rebaño*) herd of goats

cabriola 1 SF gambol, skip; **hacer ~s** [*persona*] to caper about; [*caballo*] to buck, prance around; [*cordero*] to gambol
2 (*Caribe*) (= *travesura*) prank, piece of mischief

cabriolar ▸conjug 1a◂ VI [*persona*] to caper (about), prance (around); [*caballo*] to buck; [*cordero*] to gambol

cabriolé SM cabriolet

cabriolear ▸conjug 1a◂ VI = **cabriolar**

cabritada* SF dirty trick

cabritas SFPL (*Chile*) popcorn *sing*

cabritilla SF kid, kidskin

cabrito SM 1 (*Zool*) kid; **a ~** astride
2 (*) (= *cabrón*) swine*; (= *cornudo*) cuckold; [*de prostituta*] client; **¡cabrito!** you swine!*
3 **cabritos** (*Chile*) (= *palomitas*) popcorn *sing*

cabro/a Ⓐ SM (*LAm Zool*) (= *macho*) he-goat, billy goat
Ⓑ SM/F (*Cono Sur**) 1 (= *niño*) small child, kid; (= *amante*) lover, sweetheart
2 (‡) (= *homosexual*) queer‡, fag (*EEUU‡*); *ver tb* **cabra**

cabrón/ona** Ⓐ SM (= *cornudo*) cuckold
Ⓑ SM/F 1 **¡cabrón!** you bastard!**; **es un ~** he's a bastard**; **el muy ~ le robó el coche** the bastard stole his car**; **el tío ~ ese** that bastard**
2 (*LAm*) [*de burdel*] brothel keeper; (*Andes, Cono Sur*) (= *chulo*) pimp; (*CAm, Cono Sur*) (= *traidor*) traitor; (*Andes*) (= *maricón*) queer‡, fag (*EEUU‡*); **¡cabrón!** (= *idiota*) you stupid berk!‡

cabronada** SF 1 (= *mala pasada*) dirty trick; **hacer una ~ a algn** to play a dirty trick on sb
2 (= *lata*) fag*, bugger**

cabronazo** SM bastard**, bugger**; **¡jo, ~!** (*hum*) hey, you old bastard!**

cabroncete* SM little twerp*

cabruno ADJ goat *antes de s*

cábula SF (*LAm*) 1 (= *complot*) intrigue, cabal
2 (= *trampa*) trick, stratagem
3 (= *amuleto*) amulet

cabulear ▸conjug 1a◂ VI (*Andes, CAm, Caribe*) to scheme

cabulero (*Andes, CAm, Caribe*) Ⓐ ADJ tricky, cunning, scheming
Ⓑ SM trickster, schemer

cabuya SF (*LAm Bot*) pita, agave; (= *fibra*) pita fibre; (*Náut*) (= *cuerda*) rope, cord, *especially one made from pita fibre*; ✦*MODISMOS* **dar ~** (*Caribe*) to put things off; **ponerse en la ~*** to cotton on*; **vérsele a algn las ~s** to see what sb is up to, see what sb's (little) game is

caca* SF 1 (*lenguaje infantil*) poo*, poop (*EEUU**), number two*; **¿quieres hacer ~?** do you want to do a poo?*; **el niño tiene** *o* **se ha hecho ~** the child has pooed himself*; **¡caca!** (= *no toques*) dirty!
2 (= *birria*) rubbish, crap**; **tenemos un ejército que es una ~** our army is rubbish, our army is crap**; **estoy hecha una ~** I feel like shit**

caca-can* SM pooper-scooper*

cacaguatal SM (*CAm*) cocoa field

cacahual SM (*LAm*) cacao plantation

cacahuete SM, **cacahuate** (*Méx*) SM peanut, monkey nut; (= *groundnut*) (= *planta*) groundnut; **aceite de ~** peanut oil

cacao SM 1 (*Bot*) cacao; (= *bebida*) cocoa; **~ en polvo** cocoa powder; ✦*MODISMOS* **pedir ~** (*LAm*) to give in, beg for mercy; **ser gran ~** to have influence; **no valer un ~** (*LAm*) to be worthless
2 (*) (= *jaleo*) fuss, to-do; ✦*MODISMOS* **armar** *o* **montar un ~** to cause havoc; **se armó un buen ~** all hell broke loose*; **tener un ~ en**

la cabeza* to be all mixed up ► **cacao mental*** mental confusion

cacaotal SM cocoa plantation

cacaraña SF [1] (= *señal*) pockmark
[2] (*CAm*) (= *garabato*) scribble

cacarañado ADJ pitted, pockmarked

cacarañar ▸conjug 1a◂ VT [1] [*viruelas*] to pit, scar, pockmark
[2] (*Méx*) (= *arañar*) to scratch; (= *pellizcar*) pinch

cacarear ▸conjug 1a◂ Ⓐ VT to boast about, make much of; **ese triunfo tan cacareado** that much-trumpeted victory
Ⓑ VI [*gallina*] to cluck; [*gallo*] to crow

cacareo SM [*de gallo*] crowing; [*de gallina*] clucking; (*fig*) boasting, crowing

cacarico ADJ (*CAm*) numb

cacarizo ADJ (*Méx*) pitted, pockmarked

cacastle SM (*CAm, Méx*) (= *esqueleto*) skeleton; (= *canasta*) large wicker basket; (= *armazón*) wicker carrying frame

cacatúa SF [1] (*Orn*) cockatoo
[2] (*) (= *vieja*) old bat*, old bag*, old cow*

cacaxtle SM (*CAm, Méx*) = **cacastle**

cacera SF ditch, irrigation channel

cacereño/a Ⓐ ADJ of/from Cáceres
Ⓑ SM/F native/inhabitant of Cáceres; **los ~s** the people of Cáceres

cacería SF [1] (= *actividad*) hunting, shooting; **ir de ~** to go hunting, go shooting
[2] (= *partida*) hunt, shoot, shooting party; **organizar una ~** to organize a hunt ► **cacería de brujas** witch-hunt ► **cacería de zorros** fox hunt
[3] (= *animales cazados*) bag, total of animals etc bagged
[4] (*Arte*) hunting scene

cacerola SF pan, saucepan

cacerolazo SM (*Cono Sur*) banging on pots and pans (*as political protest*)

cacha SF [1] [*de arma*] butt
[2] (⁑) (*Anat*) (= *muslo*) thigh; **cachas** (= *muslos*) thighs; (= *culo*) bottom *sing*; ✦***MODISMOS*** **estar ~s** (= *ser musculoso*) to have plenty of muscles, be well set-up; (= *ser atractivo*) to be dishy*; [*mujer*] to be hot stuff*; **hasta las ~s** up to the hilt, completely
[3] (*Andes*) (= *cuerno*) horn
[4] (*Andes*) [*de gallo*] *metal spur attached to the leg of a fighting cock*
[5] (*Andes*) (= *arca*) large chest
[6] (*Chile**) (= *burla*) **sacar ~(s) a** *o* **de algn** to make fun of sb
[7] (*LAm*) (= *cachete*) cheek
[8] (*CAm**) (= *apaño*) crooked deal*
[9] (*CAm*) (= *oportunidad*) opportunity
[10] ✦***MODISMOS*** **estar a medias ~s** (*Méx**) to be tipsy; **estar fuera de ~** to be out of danger; **hacer la ~** (*CAm**) to put one's back into it; **hacer ~s** (*CAm**) to try hard; **¡qué ~!** (*CAm**) what a nuisance!

cachaciento ADJ (*CAm, Cono Sur*) = **cachazudo A**

cachaco* SM [1] (*Perú*) (= *policía*) copper*, cop*
[2] (*Andes, Caribe*) (= *petimetre*) fop, dandy; (= *desaliñado*) scruff*
[3] (*Caribe**) (= *entrometido*) busybody, nosey-parker*
[4] (*Col*) (= *bogotano*) person from Bogotá

cachada SF [1] (*LAm*) (= *embestida*) butt, thrust; (*Taur*) goring
[2] (*Cono Sur*) (= *broma*) joke, leg-pull*

cachador* (*Cono Sur*) Ⓐ ADJ fond of practical jokes Ⓑ SM practical joker

cachafaz* ADJ (*LAm*) (= *pillo*) rascally; (= *taimado*) crafty; (= *fresco*) cheeky*, sassy (*EEUU**)

cachalote SM sperm whale

cachancha SF (*Caribe*) patience; **estar de ~ con algn*** to suck up to sb*

cachaña SF (*Chile*) [1] (*Orn*) small parrot
[2] (= *broma*) hoax, leg-pull*; (= *mofas*) mockery, derision
[3] (= *arrogancia*) arrogance
[4] (= *estupidez*) stupidity
[5] (= *arrebatiña*) rush, scramble (for sth)

cachañar ▸conjug 1a◂ VT (*Chile*) **~ a algn** to pull sb's leg; (*Cono Sur*) = **cachar[1]**

cachar[1] ▸conjug 1a◂ VT [1] (*Andes, CAm*) (= *cornear*) to butt, gore
[2] (*Cono Sur*) (= *ridiculizar*) to make fun of, ridicule; (= *fastidiar*) to annoy, irritate
[3] (*Andes, Cono Sur*⁑) (= *follar*) to screw⁑
[4] (*Méx**) (= *registrar*) to search
[5] (= *romper*) to smash, break, break in pieces; [+ *madera*] to split; (*Agr*) to plough up

cachar[2] ▸conjug 1a◂ VT [1] (*Cono Sur*) [+ *bus etc*] to catch
[2] (*CAm*) (= *obtener*) to get, obtain; (*CAm, Cono Sur*) (= *robar*) to steal
[3] (*Cono Sur, Méx*) [+ *delincuente*] to surprise, catch in the act
[4] (*Cono Sur*) [+ *sentido etc*] to penetrate; [+ *persona, razón*] to understand; **sí, te cacho** sure, I get it*
[5] (*Andes, CAm, Caribe Dep*) [+ *pelota*] to catch

cacharpari SM (*Perú*) farewell banquet

cacharpas SFPL (*LAm*) (= *trastos*) useless objects, lumber *sing*, junk *sing*; (= *cosas sueltas*) odds and ends

cacharpaya SF (*Andes, Cono Sur*) (= *fiesta*) send-off, farewell party; (*Cono Sur*) (= *despedida*) farewell; (= *festividad*) minor festivity

cacharpearse ▸conjug 1a◂ VPR (*LAm*) to dress up

cacharra⁑ SF gun, pistol, rod (*EEUU**)

cacharrazo* SM bash*, bang; **darse** *o* **pegarse un ~** (*Aut*) to prang the car*

cacharrear ▸conjug 1a◂ VT (*CAm, Caribe*) to throw into jail, jail

cacharrería SF [1] (= *tienda*) crockery shop; **como un elefante en una ~** like a bull in a china shop
[2] (= *cacharros*) crockery, pots *pl*
[3] (*Andes*) (= *ferretería*) ironmongery

cacharro SM [1] [*de cocina*] pot, dish; **fregar los ~s** to do *o* wash the dishes ► **cacharros de cocina** pots and pans
[2] (*) (= *trasto*) useless object, piece of junk; (*Aut*) old crock, jalop(p)y; (*Andes*) trinket
[3] (*) (= *aparato*) gadget
[4] (⁑) (= *pistola*) rod⁑, pistol
[5] (*CAm, Caribe*) (= *cárcel*) jail

cachativa SF **tener ~** (*Cono Sur*) to be quick on the uptake

cachaza SF [1] (= *lentitud*) **lo hace todo con mucha ~** he does everything very slowly; **¡menuda ~, llegaremos tarde por su culpa!** he's so slow, we're going to be late because of him!
[2] (= *licor*) ≈ rum

cachazo SM (*LAm*) (= *golpe*) butt (*with the horns*); (= *herida*) goring

cachazudo/a Ⓐ ADJ (= *lento*) slow; (= *flemático*) calm, easy-going
Ⓑ SM/F (= *lento*) slowcoach*, slowpoke (*EEUU**); (= *tranquilo*) phlegmatic person

cache[1]* ADJ (*Arg*) tacky, kitsch

cache[2] SM *o* SF (*Inform*) cache, cache memory

caché Ⓐ SM = **cachet**
Ⓑ ADJ (*Inform*) cached

cachear ▸conjug 1a◂ VT [1] (= *registrar*) to search, frisk (for weapons)
[2] (*LAm Taur*) to butt, gore
[3] (*LAm*) (= *pegar*) to punch, slap
[4] (= *abrir*) to split, cut open

cachejo* SM (*Esp*) **un ~ (de) pan** a little bit of bread; **aquel ~ de partido** that awful game

cachemir SM, **cachemira** SF cashmere

Cachemira SF Kashmir

cacheo SM searching, frisking (for weapons)

cachería SF [1] (*Andes, CAm Com*) small business, sideline
[2] (*Cono Sur**) (= *falta de gusto*) bad taste; (= *desaseo*) slovenliness

cachero Ⓐ ADJ [1] (*CAm, Caribe*) (= *embustero*) deceitful
[2] (*CAm*) (= *trabajador*) hard-working, diligent
Ⓑ SM (*LAm*) sodomite

cachet [ka'tʃe] SM (*pl* **cachets** [ka'tʃes]) [1] (= *sello distintivo*) cachet; (= *carácter*) character, temperament
[2] [*de artista*] fee

cachetada SF (*LAm*) (= *golpe*) slap, clip on the ear; (= *paliza*) beating

cachetazo SM [1] (*LAm*) (= *bofetada*) slap, punch; (*fig*) snub
[2] (*LAm*) (= *trago*) swig*, slug (*EEUU**)
[3] (*CAm, Caribe**) (= *favor*) favour, favor (*EEUU*); **¡hazme un ~!** do me a favour!

cachete SM [1] (= *golpe*) slap, punch in the face; **darse de ~s con algn** to fight with sb
[2] (= *arma*) dagger
[3] (= *mejilla*) (fat) cheek; (*Med*) swollen cheek
[4] (*CAm*) (= *favor*) favour, favor (*EEUU*)
[5] **cachetes** (*Cono Sur**) (= *culo*) bottom *sing*

cacheteada SF (*Cono Sur*) slap, box on the ear

cachetear ▸conjug 1a◂ Ⓐ VT (*LAm*) (= *pegar*) to slap *o* smack in the face
Ⓑ VI (*Cono Sur*) (= *comer*) to eat well

cachetero SM [1] (= *puñal*) dagger
[2] (*Taur*) *bullfighter who finishes the bull off with a dagger*

cachetina* SF fist fight, punch-up*

cachetón ADJ (*) [1] (*LAm*) (= *de cara rechoncha*) plump-cheeked, fat-faced
[2] (*Méx*) (= *descarado*) impudent, barefaced; (*Cono Sur*) (= *orgulloso*) proud, haughty
[3] (*CAm*) (= *atractivo*) attractive, congenial

cachicamo SM (*Andes, Caribe*) armadillo

cachicán† Ⓐ ADJ sly, crafty
Ⓑ SM [1] (*Agr*) foreman
[2] (*) (= *hombre astuto*) sly character

cachicuerno ADJ [*arma*] with a horn handle

cachifo/a* SM/F [1] (*Col*) (= *jovenzuelo*) kid*
[2] (*Ven*) (= *criado*) servant

cachila* SF (*Cono Sur*) old heap*, old banger*

cachimba Ⓐ SF [1] (= *pipa*) pipe
[2] (*CAm*) (= *cartucho*) empty cartridge
[3] (*Cono Sur*) (= *pozo*) *shallow well or water hole*
[4] (*Cuba*‡) (= *prostituta*) tart‡, slut‡
[5] ✦*MODISMO* **fregar la ~ a algn*** to get on sb's nerves
Ⓑ ADJ (*) fantastic*, great*; *ver tb* **cachimbo**

cachimbazo* SM (*CAm*) [1] (= *golpe*) thump, blow
[2] (= *trago*) shot, slug (*EEUU**)

cachimbo/a Ⓐ SM/F [1] (*Caribe*) (= *pobre*) poor man/woman
[2] (*Perú Univ*) fresher, freshman; *ver tb* **cachimba**
Ⓑ SM [1] (*LAm*) (= *pipa*) pipe; **chupar ~** (*Ven*) to smoke a pipe; (*hum*) [*niño*] to suck one's thumb
[2] (*Caribe*) (= *ingenio*) small sugar mill
[3] (*CAm**) (= *montón*) pile, heap
[4] (*Andes Mil*) soldier, squaddie*

cachimbón* ADJ (*CAm*) smart, sharp

cachipolla SF mayfly

cachiporra SF [1] (= *porra*) truncheon, cosh, (billy) club (*EEUU*)
[2] (*Cono Sur**) (= *jactancioso*) braggart

cachiporrazo* SM blow with a truncheon *etc*

cachiporrear* ▸conjug 1a◂ Ⓐ VT (*Mús etc*) to bash*, pound
Ⓑ **cachiporrearse** VPR (*Cono Sur*) to brag, boast

cachito SM [1] (= *trocito*) a bit, a little; **a ~s** bit by bit
[2] (*LAm**) (= *poquito*) **espera un ~** just a minute, hang on a sec*; **un ~ de café** a drop of coffee
[3] (*Andes*) (= *juego de dados*) dice game; (= *cubilete*) dice cup

cachivache SM [1] (= *vasija*) pot
[2] **cachivaches** (= *trastos*) trash *sing*, junk *sing*

cacho¹ SM [1] (*) (= *miga*) crumb; (= *trozo*) bit, small piece; **¡~ de gloria!** my precious!; **¡~ de ladrón!** you thief!; **es un ~ de pan*** he's really kind, he's got a heart of gold; **a ~s** bit by bit; **caerse a ~s** to fall apart, be falling to pieces
[2] (*LAm*) (= *cuerno*) horn; (*Cono Sur*) (*para beber*) cup (made of horn)
[3] (*Andes, Cono Sur*) (= *dados*) dice, set of dice; (= *cubilete*) dice cup; **jugar al ~** to play dice
[4] (*Cono Sur*) [*de plátanos*] bunch
[5] (*Cono Sur*) (= *géneros*) unsaleable *o* unsold goods *pl*; (= *objeto*) useless thing
[6] (*LAm*) (= *chiste*) funny story, joke; (= *broma*) prank, practical joke; (*Caribe*) (= *mofa*) mockery, derision
[7] (*Caribe*‡) (= *marijuana*) joint‡, spliff‡
[8] (*Caribe*‡‡) (= *pene*) prick‡‡
[9] (*Cono Sur*) (= *problema*) problem; (= *apuro*) jam*, tricky situation
[10] ✦*MODISMOS* **¡~s para arriba!** (*Cono Sur**) that's marvellous!, splendid!; **echar ~ a algn** (*Andes**) to outshine sb, go one better than sb; **empinar el ~** (*LAm**) (= *beber*) to drink; **estar fuera de ~** to be in safe keeping, be out of danger; **pegar los ~s a algn** (*CAm**) to cheat on sb, be unfaithful to sb; **raspar el ~ a algn** (*Cono Sur**) to tell sb off*

cacho² SM (= *pez*) [*de río*] chub; [*de mar*] (red) surmullet

cachón SM (= *ola*) wave, breaker; (= *cascada*) small waterfall

cachondear* ▸conjug 1a◂ (*CAm, Méx*) Ⓐ VI (= *acariciar*) to pet*, make out (*EEUU*‡); (= *besarse*) to snog‡, smooch*
Ⓑ **cachondearse** VPR [1] to take things as a joke; **~se de algn** to take the mickey out of sb‡, make fun of sb
[2] (*LAm**) to get turned on*

cachondeo* SM [1] (= *bromas*) joking; (= *guasa*) laugh*, messing about; (= *burla*) teasing, nagging; **estar de ~** to be in the mood for a laugh; **hacer algo en plan de ~** to do sth for a lark *o* a laugh; **tomar a ~** to treat as a joke; **para ella la vida es un ~ continuo** life for her is just one big joke
[2] (= *juerga*) **estar de ~** to live it up, have a great time
[3] (= *jaleo*) trouble; **armar un ~** to make a fuss
[4] (= *desastre*) farce, mess; **¡esto es un ~!** what a farce this is!, what a mess!

cachondez* SF [1] [*de animal*] heat
[2] [*de persona*] randiness*

cachondo* ADJ [1] [*animal*] on heat
[2] (= *persona*) randy*, horny*; **ser ~** to be sexy; **estar ~** to feel randy *o* horny*
[3] (= *juerguista*) fun-loving, riotous
[4] (= *gracioso*) funny, amusing, jokey; **~ mental** crazy but likable

cachorro/a SM/F [1] (*Zool*) (*gen*) cub; (= *perro*) puppy, pup
[2] (*LAm*) (= *persona*) uncouth person; **¡cachorro!** (*Caribe**) you brute!, you rat!*

cachuca‡ SF (*Andes*) nick‡, can (*EEUU**), prison

cachucha‡ SF (*Col, Méx*) cap

cachucho SM [1] (= *pez*) sea bream
[2] (= *alfiletero*) pin box
[3] (*Andes*) (= *sustento*) daily bread; **ganarse el ~** to make a living

cachudo Ⓐ ADJ [1] (*Méx*) (= *con cuernos*) horned
[2] (*Col*) (= *rico*) wealthy
[3] (*Cono Sur*) suspicious, distrustful; (= *taimado*) cunning
[4] (*Méx*) (= *triste*) long-faced, miserable
Ⓑ SM **el ~** the devil, the horned one

cachuela SF [1] (*Culin*) *stew made from pig or rabbit offal*
[2] (*LAm*) (*en un río*) rapids *pl*

cachupín/ina SM/F (*CAm, Méx Hist pey*) Spanish settler

cachureo SM (*Cono Sur*) bric-a-brac, junk, bits and pieces *pl*

cachuzo* ADJ (*Arg*) worn-out, old

cacica SF (*LAm*) (= *jefe*) woman chief; (= *esposa*) chief's wife; (*Pol*) wife of a local boss *etc*

cacicada SF (= *arbitrariedad*) despotic act, high-handed act; (= *abuso*) abuse of authority

cacillo SM ladle

cacimba SF [1] (*Andes, Caribe, Cono Sur*) beach well; (*Caribe*) [*de árbol*] *hollow of tree where rain water is collected*; (*Andes*) (= *wáter*) outdoor privy
[2] (*Caribe, Méx*) (= *casucha*) hovel, slum

cacique SM [1] (*LAm Hist*) chief, headman; (*Pol*) local party boss; (*fig*) petty tyrant, despot
[2] (*Cono Sur*) (= *vago*) *person who lives idly in luxury*
[3] (*Andes, CAm, Méx*) (= *ave*) oriole

caciquil ADJ despotic, tyrannical

caciquismo SM (*Pol*) (system of) dominance by the local party boss; (*fig*) petty tyranny, despotism

cacle SM (*Méx*) rough leather sandal

caco* SM [1] (= *ladrón*) thief; (= *carterista*) pickpocket; (= *criminal*) crook*
[2] (= *cobarde*) coward

cacofonía SF cacophony

cacofónico ADJ cacophonous

cactus SM INV, **cacto** SM cactus

cacumen* SM (= *inteligencia*) brains *pl*; (= *agudeza*) nous* *sing*

> **CADA**
>
> • **Cada** se traduce por **each** cuando queremos individualizar, cuando se conocen o se le quiere dar importancia a los elementos dentro del grupo:
>
> A cada miembro del personal se le asignó una tarea específica
> ***Each member of staff was allocated a specific task***
> Quiero tener una charla con cada uno de vosotros
> ***I want to have a chat with each of you***
>
> • Se traduce por **every** cuando el número de elementos del grupo no se conoce o no importa, cuando se está generalizando:
>
> Cada empresa funciona de una manera distinta
> ***Every company works differently***
> Cada día me dice una cosa
> ***Every day he tells me something different***
> Cada vez que viene nos trae un regalo
> ***Every time he comes he brings us a present***
>
> NOTA: En expresiones como **cada dos meses/cada tres años**/*etc*, **cada** se traduce por **every**:
>
> Se hace una revisión cada tres meses
> ***He has a check-up every three months***
>
> • Cuando hablamos sólo de dos cosas o personas, **cada** solamente se puede traducir por **each**:
>
> Es importante que cada gemelo desarrolle su propia personalidad
> ***It is important that each twin develops his own personality***
>
> NOTA: Cuando **each** o **every** forman parte del sujeto, el verbo va en singular.
>
> *Para otros usos y ejemplos ver la entrada.*

cada ADJ INV [1] (*uso distributivo*) (*con elementos individuales*) each; (*con números, tiempo*) every; **~ uno de los jugadores dispone de cuatro fichas** each player has four counters; **habrá una mesa por ~ ocho invitados** there will one table for every eight guests; **han aumentado los beneficios en todos y ~ uno de los sectores** profits have risen in each and every sector; **~ cual busca la felicidad como quiere** we all seek *o* each one of us seeks happiness in our own way
[2] (*indicando frecuencia*) every; **juega al fútbol ~ domingo** he plays football every Sunday; **~ cierto tiempo** every so often, every now and then; **~ dos días** every couple of days, every other day; **los problemas de ~ día** everyday problems; **cinco de ~ diez** five out of every ten; **¿~ cuánto tiempo?** how often?; **~ que** (*Méx*) whenever, every time (that); **~ vez que** whenever, every time (that); **~ vez que voy al extranjero** whenever *o*

every time (that) I go abroad; ✦*MODISMO* ~ **dos por tres** every other minute, all the time; **~ dos por tres sonaba el teléfono** the phone rang every other minute *o* all the time

3 (*indicando progresión*) **~ vez más** more and more; **te necesito ~ vez más** I need you more and more; **encontrar trabajo es ~ vez más difícil** finding a job is increasingly difficult *o* is (getting) more and more difficult; **me siento ~ vez más viejo** I feel (I'm getting) older and older; **~ vez mejor** better and better; **~ vez menos** less and less; **~ vez peor** worse and worse

4 (*uso enfático*) **¡tienes ~ cosa!** the things you come out with!; **¡oye una ~ historia!** the things you hear nowadays!; **¡se compra ~ coche!** you should see the cars he buys!

cadalso SM (*Jur*) (= *patíbulo*) scaffold; (*Téc*) stand, platform

cadarzo SM floss, floss silk

cadáver SM [*de persona*] (dead) body, corpse; [*de animal*] body, carcass; **¡sobre mi ~!** ◊ **¡por encima de mi ~!** over my dead body!; **ingresó ~** he was dead on arrival (at hospital) ► **cadáver en el armario** (*fig*) skeleton in the cupboard

cadavérico ADJ cadaverous, ghastly; (= *pálido*) deathly pale

caddie SMF, **caddy** ['kadi] SMF (*Golf*) caddie

cadena SF 1 [*de eslabones, de joyería*] chain; **se me salió la ~ de la bici** the chain came off my bike, my bike chain came off; **la ~ del perro** the dog chain; **la ~ del reloj** the watch chain; **tirar de la ~ (del wáter)** to flush the toilet, pull the chain; **no echó la ~ de la puerta** he didn't put the door-chain on ► **cadena (antirrobo)** chain ► **cadena de distribución** distribution chain ► **cadena de oruga** caterpillar track

2 (*Radio, TV*) (= *canal*) channel ► **cadena de televisión** TV channel

3 (*Audio*) ► **cadena de sonido** sound system ► **cadena musical** music centre, sound system

4 (*Com*) [*de hoteles, tiendas, restaurantes*] chain ► **cadena comercial** retail chain

5 ► **cadena montañosa** mountain range

6 (= *sucesión*) [*de acontecimientos, átomos*] chain; [*de atentados*] string, series; **en ~: colisión en ~** multiple collision, (multiple) pile-up; **efecto en ~** knock-on effect; **reacción en ~** chain reaction; **trabajo en ~** assembly-line work ► **cadena alimenticia** food chain ► **cadena de caracteres** (*Inform*) character string ► **cadena de ensamblaje** assembly line ► **cadena de fabricación** production line ► **cadena de montaje** assembly line ► **cadena de producción** production line

7 ► **cadena perpetua** (*Jur*) life imprisonment, life; **el juez lo condenó a ~ perpetua** the judge sentenced him to life (imprisonment)

8 **cadenas** (*Aut*) tyre *o* (*EEUU*) tire chains; **es obligatorio el uso de ~s** the use of tyre chains is compulsory

cadencia SF 1 (= *ritmo*) cadence, rhythm

2 (*Mús*) (*en frase musical*) cadence; [*de solista*] cadenza

3 (= *frecuencia*) **a una ~ de 1.000 unidades diarias** at the rate of 1,000 units per day

cadencioso ADJ [*voz*] melodious; [*música*] rhythmic(al); [*andares*] swinging

cadeneta SF (*Cos*) chain stitch ► **cadeneta de papel** paper chain

cadenilla SF, **cadenita** SF small chain; (= *collar*) necklace

cadera SF hip; **ponerse una prótesis de ~** to have a hip replacement

caderamen* SM big hips *pl*, massive hips *pl*

cadetada SF thoughtless action, irresponsible act

cadete SM (*Mil etc*) cadet; (*Dep*) junior; (*LAm*) (= *aprendiz*) apprentice; (*en oficina*) office boy

cadí SM (*Hist*) cadi

Cádiz SM Cadiz

cadmio SM cadmium

caducar ▸conjug 1g◂ VI 1 (*Com, Jur*) to expire, lapse; [*permiso, plazo*] to run out; [*costumbre*] to fall into disuse; **esta oferta caduca el 31 de mayo** valid until May 31, this offer runs until May 31; **el abono ha caducado** the season ticket has expired

2 [*comida*] to be *o* go past its sell-by date

caducidad SF expiry, expiration (*EEUU*); **fecha de ~** (*gen*) expiry date; [*de alimentos*] sell-by date, best-before date

caduco ADJ 1 (*Bot*) deciduous; **árbol de hoja caduca** deciduous tree

2 [*persona*] senile, decrepit

3 [*ideas etc*] outdated, outmoded

4 [*belleza*] faded

5 [*placer etc*] fleeting

6 (*Com, Jur*) lapsed, expired, invalid; **quedar ~** to lapse, be out of date, have expired

caduquez SF senility, decrepitude

C.A.E. ABR (*Com*) (= **cóbrese al entregar**) COD

caedizo Ⓐ ADJ (= *inestable*) unsteady; (= *débil*) weak; (*Bot*) deciduous

Ⓑ SM (*Andes*) (= *edificio*) shed; (= *techo*) sloping roof

caer

▸conjug 2n◂
A VERBO INTRANSITIVO B VERBO PRONOMINAL
Para las expresiones ***caer en la cuenta, caer en desuso, caer en el olvido, caer enfermo, caer redondo, caerse de risa****, ver la otra entrada.*

Ⓐ VERBO INTRANSITIVO

1 **persona, objeto** 1·1 (*desde la posición vertical*) to fall; **me hice daño al ~** I fell and hurt myself; **cayó al suelo y se dio un golpe en la cabeza** he fell to the ground and hit his head; **tropezó y cayó de espaldas** she stumbled and fell on her back; **cayó muerto de un tiro** he was shot dead; **hacer ~ algo** to knock sth over; **al pasar hizo ~ la lámpara** he knocked the lamp over as he brushed past

1·2 (*desde una altura*) to fall; **cayó de un tercer piso** he fell from the third floor; **el niño cayó al río** the child fell into the river; **cayó una bomba en el mercado** a bomb fell on the market; **el avión cayó al mar** the plane came down in the sea; **el coche cayó por un barranco** the car went over a cliff; **dejar ~** [+ *objeto*] to drop; [+ *comentario*] to slip in; **se sobresaltó y dejó ~ la bandeja** she gave a start and dropped the tray; **dejó ~ que estaba buscando otro trabajo** he let slip that he was looking for another job; **dejarse ~** (*sobre sofá, cama*) to fall; (= *visitar*) to drop in, drop by; **se dejó ~ sobre la cama** he fell onto the bed; **suele dejarse ~ por aquí** he usually drops in *o* by; **~ sobre algo/algn** to fall on sth/sb; **una gran piedra cayó sobre el tejado** a large stone fell on the roof; **cayeron sobre nosotros rocas enormes** huge boulders fell on us; **los presos cayeron sobre el guarda** the prisoners fell on the warder; **los fotógrafos cayeron sobre ella** the photographers pounced on her; **queremos que caiga sobre él todo el peso de la Ley** we want the full weight of the law to be brought to bear on him; ✦*MODISMO* **estar al ~** to be imminent; **su excarcelación está al ~** his release is imminent *o* is expected any day; **el jefe está al ~** the boss will be here any moment

2 **lluvia, helada** **la lluvia caía incesantemente sobre Madrid** the rain was falling continuously on Madrid; **cayó un chaparrón** there was a heavy shower; **¡qué nevada ha caído!** what a heavy snowfall!, what a heavy fall of snow!; **cayó un rayo en la torre** the tower was struck by lightning

3 **= colgar** to hang, fall; **es una tela que cae mucho** it's a fabric which hangs *o* falls nicely; **le caía un mechón sobre la frente** a lock of hair fell across his forehead

4 **= bajar** [*precio, temperatura*] to fall, drop; **~á la temperatura por debajo de los veinte grados** the temperature will fall *o* drop below twenty degrees; **el dólar cayó más de cinco centavos** the dollar fell over five cents; **la bolsa de Nueva York ha vuelto a ~** the New York stock exchange has fallen again; *ver tb* **picado B2**

5 **= ser derrotado** [*soldados, ejército*] to be defeated; [*deportista, equipo*] to be beaten; [*ciudad, plaza*] to fall, be captured; [*criminal*] to be arrested; **cayó en la final ante su rival polaco** he was beaten in the final by his Polish rival; **ha caído el gobierno** the government has fallen

6 **= morir** to fall, die; **muchos cayeron en el campo de batalla** many fell *o* died on the field of battle; **cayó como un valiente** he died a hero; **cayeron abatidos por las balas** they were killed by the gunfire; ✦*MODISMOS* **~ como chinches** ◊ **~ como moscas** to drop like flies

7 **~ en** (= *incurrir*): **~ en un engaño** to be tricked; **no debemos ~ en el triunfalismo** we mustn't give way to triumphalism *o* to crowing over our triumphs; **~ en el error de hacer algo** to make the mistake of doing sth; **~ en la tentación** to give in *o* yield to temptation; **y no nos dejes ~ en la tentación** (*Biblia*) and lead us not into temptation; ✦*MODISMO* **~ bajo**: **¡qué bajo has caído!** (*moralmente*) how low can you get!, how can you sink so low?; (*socialmente*) you've certainly come down in the world!; *ver tb* **trampa 2**

8 **= darse cuenta** **no caigo** I don't get it*, I don't understand; **ya caigo** I see, now I understand, now I get it*; **~ en que** to realize that

9 **fecha** to fall, be; **su cumpleaños cae en viernes** her birthday falls *o* is on a Friday; **¿en qué cae el día de Navidad?** what day is Christmas Day?, what day does Christmas fall on?

10 **= tocar** **el premio gordo ha caído en Madrid** the first prize (in the lottery) *o* the jackpot went to Madrid; **~le a algn: le pueden ~ muchos años de condena** he could

get a very long sentence; le puede ~ una multa de 50 dólares he could get a 50 dollar fine; ✦MODISMO ¡la que nos ha caído encima! that's just what we needed!; ver tb suerte 3

[11] [= estar situado] to be; ¿por dónde cae eso? whereabouts is that?; eso cae más hacia el este that lies o is further to the east

[12] ~ dentro de (= estar comprendido en): no cae dentro de mis atribuciones it is not within my powers; esta cuestión no cae dentro del ámbito de este trabajo that falls outside the scope of this study; eso cae dentro de la responsabilidad de los ayuntamientos that falls within the remit of town councils

[13] [= causar impresión] no les caí (CAm) I didn't hit it off with them, I didn't get on well with them, they didn't take to me; ~ bien a algn: me cae (muy) bien I (really) like him, I like him (very much); no me cae nada bien I don't like him at all; Pedro no le cayó bien a mi padre Pedro didn't make a very good impression on my father, my father didn't really take to Pedro; ~ gordo o fatal a algn*: me cae gordo o fatal el tío ése I can't stand that guy; ~ mal a algn: me cae mal I don't like him

[14] [= sentar] [14·1] [información, comentario] me cayó fatal lo que me dijiste I was very upset by what you said, what you said really upset me; la noticia cayó como un mazazo the news was a blow

[14·2] [ropa] ~le bien a algn to suit sb; ~le mal a algn not to suit sb

[15] [= terminar] al ~ la noche at nightfall; al ~ la tarde at dusk

Ⓑ caerse VERBO PRONOMINAL

[1] [persona, objeto] [1·1] (desde la posición vertical) [persona, objeto] to fall over; [edificio] to collapse, fall (down); ¿te has caído? did you fall over?; ¡cuidado, no te caigas! watch out or you'll fall over!; tropecé y estuve a punto de ~me I tripped and nearly fell (over); se cayó y se torció el tobillo she fell (over) and twisted her ankle; se ha caído el perchero the coat stand has fallen over; el edificio se está cayendo the building is falling down; ~se al suelo to fall to the ground

[1·2] (desde una altura) to fall; se cayó al agua she fell into the water; se cayó por la ventana he fell out of the window; ~se de algo to fall off sth; se cayó del caballo he fell off his horse; los libros se cayeron del estante the books fell off the shelf; el niño se cayó de la cama the child fell out of bed

[1·3] caérsele algo a algn: se me cayeron las monedas I dropped the coins; se me ha caído el guante I've dropped my glove; sin el botón se te van a ~ los pantalones without the button your trousers will fall down

[2] [= desprenderse] [hoja] to fall off; [diente] to fall out; se me está cayendo el pelo my hair is falling out; se me ha caído un botón de la chaqueta a button has come off my jacket

[3] ~se de: se cae de cansancio he's so tired he could drop; me caigo de sueño I'm so sleepy I could drop, I'm asleep on my feet; el edificio se cae de viejo the building is so old it's falling to bits o it's on the point of collapsing

café SM [1] (Bot) (= bebida) coffee; ~ ~ real coffee, coffee that really is coffee ► café americano large black coffee ► café cerrero (Andes) strong black coffee ► café completo (Cono Sur) continental breakfast ► café con leche white coffee, coffee with milk, coffee with cream (EEUU); (‡) (= homosexual) queer‡, fag (EEUU‡) ► café cortado coffee with a dash of milk ► café descafeinado decaffeinated coffee ► café en grano coffee beans pl ► café exprés expresso coffee ► café helado iced coffee ► café instantáneo instant coffee ► café irlandés Irish coffee ► café molido ground coffee ► café negro (small) black coffee ► café pintado (Andes), café quemado (Caribe) coffee with a drop of milk ► café solo black coffee ► café soluble instant coffee ► café tinto (LAm) black coffee ► café torrefacto roasted coffee ► café tostado roasted coffee

[2] (= cafetería) café, coffee shop ► café cantante café with entertainment

[3] (Cono Sur*) (= reprimenda) ticking-off*

[4] ✦MODISMO mal ~*: estar de mal ~ to be in a bad mood; (CAm) to be out of sorts; tener mal ~ (= genio) to have a nasty temper; (= intenciones) to have evil intentions

[5] color ~ brown; ~ avellana (como adj) nut-brown

cafecito SM (LAm) black coffee

café-concierto SM café which provides musical entertainment

cafeína SF caffein(e)

cafetal SM [1] (= plantío) coffee plantation

[2] (CAm) (= árbol) coffee tree

cafetalero/a (LAm) Ⓐ ADJ coffee antes de s, coffee-growing; industria cafetalera coffee industry

Ⓑ SM/F coffee grower

cafetalista SMF (LAm) coffee grower

cafetear* ▸conjug 1a◂ VT (Cono Sur) to tick off*, tell off*

café-teatro SM (= lugar) café with live theatre; (= espectáculo) live entertainment; (= comedia) stand-up comedy

cafetera SF [1] (= aparato) coffee maker, coffee machine; (= jarra) coffee pot; ✦MODISMO estar como una ~* to be off one's head o rocker* ► cafetera automática coffee machine ► cafetera de filtro filter coffee maker ► cafetera exprés espresso coffee maker

[2] (Aut*) old banger*, jalop(p)y*; [de policía] police car; ver tb cafetero

cafetería SF [1] (gen) café, coffee shop; (= autoservicio) cafeteria; (Ferro) buffet, refreshment car (EEUU)

[2] (LAm) (= tienda) retail coffee shop

cafetero/a Ⓐ ADJ [1] [finca, sector] coffee antes de s; [país] coffee producing; industria cafetera coffee industry

[2] (= aficionado al café) soy muy ~ I really like (my) coffee

[3] (= aficionado a los cafés) fond of going to cafés; es muy ~ he spends a lot of time in cafés

Ⓑ SM/F (*) (= dueño) café proprietor, café owner; (= cultivador) coffee grower; (= comerciante) coffee merchant; ver tb cafetera

cafetín SM small café

cafeto SM coffee tree

cafetucho SM seedy little café

cafiche‡ SM (Cono Sur) pimp, ponce‡

cafichear‡ ▸conjug 1a◂ VI (Cono Sur) to live off sb else, ponce‡

cafiche‡ SM (Cono Sur) pimp, ponce‡

caficultor(a) SM/F (CAm) coffee grower

caficultura SF (CAm) coffee growing

cáfila SF group, flock (esp on the march); una ~ de disparates a string of nonsense

cafiolo‡ SM (Cono Sur) pimp, ponce‡

cafre Ⓐ SMF [1] [de África] Kaffir

[2] (= bruto) savage; como ~s like savages, like beasts

Ⓑ ADJ [1] (de África) Kaffir

[2] (= brutal) uncouth, boorish

caftán SM caftan, kaftan

cagaaceite SM missel thrush, mistle thrush

cagada⁑ SF [1] (= excremento) shit⁑, crap⁑; ~s de perro dog shit⁑ sing

[2] (= error) cock-up⁑, fuck-up⁑, screw-up (EEUU⁑)

[3] (= tonterías) crap⁑, balls⁑ pl; decir una ~ to talk a load of crap⁑

[4] (= porquería) crap⁑; el discurso fue una ~ the speech was total crap⁑

cagadera⁑ SF (LAm) tener ~ to have the shits⁑ o trots* o runs*

cagadero⁑ SM bog‡, john (EEUU‡)

cagado⁑ ADJ shit-scared⁑; no se atreve a salir, está ~ de miedo he daren't go out, he's shit-scared⁑; no seas tan ~ don't be such a gutless coward

cagajón* SM horse-dung, mule-dung

cagalera⁑ SF tener ~ to have the shits⁑ o trots* o runs*; ¡menuda ~! what a mess!

cagar⁑ ▸conjug 1h◂ Ⓐ VI (= defecar) to shit⁑, have a shit⁑, take a shit (EEUU⁑); ✦MODISMO ¡está que no caga! he's on cloud nine!

Ⓑ VT [1] [+ ropa] to dirty, soil

[2] ✦MODISMOS ~la to blow it*, balls up⁑; ¡la hemos cagado! we've ballsed up!⁑, we've blown it!‡; ir cagando leches to bomb along*; irse cagando leches to leg it*, scarper*

[3] (Arg) (= dañar) to harm

[4] (Arg) (= defraudar) to rip off*

Ⓒ cagarse VPR [1] to shit o.s.⁑; se cagó en los pantalones he shat himself⁑, he messed his pants

[2] ✦MODISMOS ~se de miedo to shit o.s.⁑; ~se de risa to piss o.s. (laughing)⁑; me cago de risa con los chistes de tu hermano your brother's jokes really crack me up*; ~se en algn/algo not to give a toss‡ o a shit⁑ o a fuck⁑ about sb/sth; ¡me cago en diez o en la mar o en la leche! bloody hell!⁑, shit!⁑; ¡cada vez que bebía se cagaba en la madre de todo el mundo! whenever he drank he'd start effing and blinding at everything and everyone o telling everyone to go to hell*; ¡me cago en la puta o en la hostia! fucking hell!⁑; ¡me cago en la leche que mamaron! screw them!⁑; ¡me cago en el gobierno! to hell with o sod the government!*; ... y se caga la perra ... (Esp) and you never saw anything like it; ~se patas abajo: tenía tanto miedo que se cagó patas abajo he was so frightened, he shat himself⁑

[3] ✦MODISMO que te cagas (como adj) damn‡, bloody‡; ¡en la sierra hace un frío que te cagas! it's bloody freezing in the

mountains!‡; **el jefe tiene una cara que te cagas** the boss has got a bloody nerve‡; **la película estaba que te cagabas** the film was bloody brilliant‡; **la tía estaba que te cagas** she was drop dead gorgeous*

cagarruta SF [1] [*de animal*] pellet, dropping
[2] **es una ~ de su padre** (*Esp*‡) he's the spitting image of his father

cagatintas* SMF INV [1] (= *oficinista*) pen-pusher, pencil pusher (*EEUU*)
[2] (*Andes*) (= *avaro*) miser

cagón/ona‡‡ Ⓐ ADJ [1] = **cagado**
[2] [*bebé*] **ser ~** to keep dirtying one's nappies
Ⓑ SM/F [1] (= *cobarde*) wimp*
[2] (= *bebé*) **ser un ~** to keep dirtying one's nappies

caguama SF (*Méx*) large turtle

cague‡‡ SM **le entró un ~ de mucho cuidado** he was scared shitless‡‡

cagüen‡‡ = **cago en**; *ver* **cagar C2**

cagueruelas‡ SFPL the runs‡, the trots‡

cagueta‡ SMF, **caguetas**‡ SMF INV, **caguica**‡ SMF INV chicken

caguitis‡ SF INV **entrarle ~ a algn** to get the wind up*

Cahispa SF ABR = **Caja Hispana de Previsión**

cahuín SM (*Chile*) [1] (= *borrachera*) drunkenness
[2] (‡) (= *lío*) cock-up‡, screw-up (*EEUU*‡‡)
[3] (= *reunión*) rowdy gathering

caída SF [1] (= *accidente*) fall; [*de caballo*] fall, tumble; **tuvo una aparatosa ~ de la moto** he had a spectacular fall from his motorbike; **sufrir una ~** to have a fall, take a tumble; **durante un campeonato regional, sufrió una grave ~ del caballo** during a regional championship, he had a bad fall *o* tumble off his horse ► **caída de agua** waterfall ► **caída de cabeza**: **sufrir una ~ de cabeza** to fall headfirst, header* ► **caída en barrena** spiral fall
[2] [*de gobierno, imperio*] fall, collapse; [*de un gobernante*] downfall; **la ~ del Muro de Berlín** the collapse *o* fall of the Berlin Wall; **la crisis ocasionó la ~ del gobierno** the crisis brought down the government; **la ~ del Imperio Romano** the fall of the Roman Empire; **la ~ de Napoleón se produjo en Waterloo** Waterloo was Napoleon's downfall
[3] (= *pérdida*) [*de cabello, dientes*] loss; **un champú contra la ~ del cabello** a shampoo that helps prevent hair loss
[4] (*Dep*) ► **caída al vacío**, **caída libre** free fall
[5] (= *descenso*) [*de precios, ventas*] fall, drop; [*de divisa*] fall; **la espectacular ~ de precios afectó con gran dureza a numerosas economías** many economies were hard hit by the dramatic fall *o* drop in prices; **el gobierno está decidido a frenar la ~ de la libra** the government is determined to curb the fall of the pound; **~ de la temperatura** drop in temperature; **~ de tensión** (*Med*) drop in blood pressure; (*Elec*) drop in voltage; **~ de la actividad económica** downturn in the economy; **~ en picado** sharp fall; **el banco intervino para evitar la ~ en picado del dólar** the bank intervened to stop the dollar taking a nose-dive *o* plummeting
[6] **a la ~ del sol** *o* **de la tarde** at sunset
[7] (= *desprendimiento*) fall; **había una continua ~ de piedras desde la cima de la montaña** rocks fell continuously from the top of the mountain
[8] (= *inclinación*) [*de terreno*] slope; (*brusco*) drop
[9] [*de tela, ropa*] hang; **esta chaqueta tiene buena ~** this jacket hangs well ► **caída de hombros** slope of the shoulders ► **caída de ojos**: **tenía una ~ de ojos entre coqueta y malvada** the way she lowered her eyes was somewhere between coquettish and wicked
[10] (*Rel*) **la Caída** the Fall
[11] ► **caída radiactiva** radioactive fallout
[12] **caídas** [12·1] (*) (= *golpes*) witty remarks; **¡qué ~s tiene!** isn't he witty?
[12·2] (= *lana*) low-grade wool *sing*

caído Ⓐ ADJ (*gen*) fallen; [*cabeza*] hanging; [*hombros*] drooping; [*cuello*] turndown; [*flor etc*] limp, drooping; **estar ~ de sueño** to be dead tired
Ⓑ SM [1] (= *muerto*) **los ~s** the fallen; **los ~s por España** (*en el bando franquista*) those who died for Spain; **monumento a los ~s** war memorial, monument to the fallen
[2] (*Méx*) (= *soborno*) backhander*, sweetener*

caifán* SM (*Méx*) pimp*, ponce*

caigo *etc ver* **caer**

caimacán SM (*Andes*) (= *persona importante*) important person, big shot*; (= *estrella*) ace, star, expert

caimán SM [1] (= *cocodrilo*) caiman, alligator
[2] (*Andes*) (= *iguana*) iguana
[3] (*LAm*) (= *estafador*) con man, swindler
[4] (*Méx Téc*) chain wrench
[5] (*Andes*) (= *gandul*) lazybones*

caimanear ▸conjug 1a◂ (*LAm*) Ⓐ VT (= *estafar*) to swindle, cheat
Ⓑ VI (= *cazar*) to hunt caiman *o* alligators

caimiento SM [1] (= *acto*) fall, falling; (*Med*) decline
[2] (= *desfallecimiento*) dejection

Caín SM Cain; ✦**MODISMOS** **pasar las de ~*** to go through hell*; **venir con las de ~*** to have evil intentions

cainismo SM fratricidal violence, fratricidal treachery

cainita ADJ (*frm*) **odio ~** brotherly hatred; **un país ~** a country where brother hates brother

cairel SM (= *peluca*) wig; (*Cos*) fringe

cairelear ▸conjug 1a◂ VT to trim, fringe

Cairo SM **el ~** Cairo

caita (*Cono Sur*) Ⓐ ADJ INV (= *montaraz*) wild, untamed; (= *huraño*) unsociable, withdrawn
Ⓑ SM (= *trabajador*) migratory agricultural worker

caite SM (*CAm*) rough sandal

caitearse ▸conjug 1a◂ VPR **caiteárselas** (*CAm*) to run away, beat it*

caja SF [1] (= *recipiente*) box; [*de cervezas, refrescos*] crate; **una ~ de cartón** a cardboard box; **la ~ tonta*** (= *tele*) the box*, the goggle-box*, the idiot box (*EEUU**) ► **caja china** Chinese box ► **caja de cerillas** (*llena*) box of matches; (*vacía*) matchbox ► **caja de colores** box of crayons ► **caja de herramientas** toolbox ► **caja de Pandora** Pandora's box ► **caja de sorpresas** (= *juego*) jack-in-the-box; **ser una ~ de sorpresas** to be full of surprises ► **caja de zapatos** shoebox ► **caja negra** [*de avión*] black box
[2] (*Com*) (*en supermercado*) checkout; (*en tienda*) till, cash desk; (*en banco*) window, cash desk; **robaron todo el dinero que había en la ~** they stole all the money in the till; **para pagar, pase por ~** please pay at the cash desk *o* till *o* checkout; **entrar en ~**: **ha entrado muy poco dinero en ~** takings have been low; **hacer ~** to cash up; **después de cerrar hacen ~** after closing they cash up; **hicieron una ~ de 5.000 euros** they took (in) 5,000 euros; **ingresar en ~**: **hemos ingresado 5.000 euros en ~** we have taken (in) 5,000 euros ► **caja B** B account, secret account *o* fund, slush fund ► **caja de ahorros** savings bank ► **caja de caudales** safe, strongbox ► **caja de pensiones** pension fund ► **caja de resistencia** emergency fund, contingency fund ► **caja fuerte** safe, strongbox ► **Caja Postal de Ahorros** ≈ Post Office Savings Bank ► **caja registradora** cash register, cash till
[3] [*de reloj*] case, casing; [*de radio, TV*] casing, housing; [*de fusil*] stock ► **caja de cambios** (*Mec*) gearbox ► **caja de empalmes** junction box ► **caja de fusibles** fuse box ► **caja del cigüeñal** crankcase ► **caja de registro** manhole, inspection hole
[4] (*Mús*) (= *tambor*) drum; [*de piano*] case; [*de violín*] soundbox; ✦**MODISMO** **despedir** *o* **echar a algn con ~s destempladas** to send sb packing*, throw *o* kick sb out ► **caja de música** music box ► **caja de resonancia** [*de un instrumento*] soundbox; **sirve de ~ de resonancia a los terroristas** it's a sounding board for terrorists ► **caja de ritmos** drum machine, beatbox*
[5] (*Anat*) ► **caja craneana** skull, cranial cap ► **caja de dientes*** set of choppers* ► **caja torácica** thoracic cavity
[6] (*) (= *ataúd*) box*, coffin ► **caja de muerto** coffin, casket (*EEUU*)
[7] (*Bot*) seed case, capsule
[8] (*Tip*) case ► **caja alta** upper case ► **caja baja** lower case
[9] (*Mil*) **entrar en ~** to join up, enlist ► **caja de reclutamiento**, **caja de reclutas** recruiting office
[10] (*Cono Sur*) (= *lecho de río*) (dried up) riverbed

cajear* ▸conjug 1a◂ VT (*Andes, CAm*) to beat up*

cajero/a Ⓐ SM/F (*gen*) cashier; (*en banco*) cashier, (bank) teller; (*en supermercado etc*) checkout operator
Ⓑ SM ► **cajero automático** cash dispenser, automated *o* automatic teller machine (*frm*)

cajeta SF [1] (*LAm*) (= *dulce de leche*) fudge, soft toffee; (*Méx*) (= *dulce de jalea*) jelly; (*CAm, Méx*) (= *caramelo*) sweet, candy (*EEUU*)
[2] (*CAm, Méx*) (*para dulces*) round sweet box
[3] (*Andes, CAm*) [*de animal*] lip
[4] ✦**MODISMO** **de ~** (*CAm, Méx*) (*iró*) first-class, super
[5] (*Méx**) (= *cobarde*) coward; (= *enclenque*) wimp*
[6] (*Cono Sur*‡‡) (= *vagina*) cunt‡‡

cajete SM (*Méx*) [1] (= *cazuela*) earthenware pot *o* bowl
[2] (*) (= *wáter*) toilet, loo*, john (*EEUU*‡)
[3] (‡) (= *culo*) bum‡, ass (*EEUU*‡)

cajetilla Ⓐ SF [1] (= *paquete*) packet, pack (*EEUU*) ► **cajetilla de cigarrillos**, **cajetilla de tabaco** packet *o* (*EEUU*) pack of cigarettes
[2] (*Caribe*) (= *dientes*) teeth *pl*
Ⓑ SM (*Cono Sur**) (= *petimetre*) dude*, toff*; (= *urbanita*) city slicker (*EEUU*); (= *afeminado*) poof‡, queen‡, fag (*EEUU*‡)

cajista SMF compositor, typesetter

cajón SM [1] [*de mueble*] drawer ► **cajón de sastre**: **esta palabra es un ~ de sastre** this is a catch-all term; **esta sección es un ~ de sastre** this section is a bit of a ragbag *o* mixed bag
[2] (= *caja*) big box, crate ► **cajón de embalaje** crate, packing case ► **cajón de suspensión**, **cajón hidráulico** caisson
[3] (*Méx*) (= *puesto*) stall ► **cajón de ropa** draper's (shop), dry-goods store (*EEUU*)
[4] (*Dep*) ► **cajón de salida** starting gate
[5] ✦***MODISMO*** **de ~***: **eso es de ~** that goes without saying
[6] (*Andes, Cono Sur*) (= *ataúd*) coffin, casket (*EEUU*)
[7] (*LAm Geog*) ravine

caju SM cashew (nut)

cajuela SF (*Méx Aut*) boot, trunk (*EEUU*)

cal SF lime; ✦***MODISMOS*** **cerrar algo a ~ y canto** to shut sth firmly *o* securely; **de ~ y canto** firm, strong; **dar una de ~ y otra de arena** to apply a policy of carrot and stick ► **cal apagada**, **cal muerta** slaked lime ► **cal viva** quicklime

cala[1] SF [1] (*Geog*) (= *ensenada*) cove
[2] (*Náut*) hold
[3] (*Pesca*) fishing ground

cala[2] SF [1] (*Culin*) [*de fruta*] sample slice; **hacer ~ y cata** to test for quality
[2] (*Med*) (= *supositorio*) suppository; (= *sonda*) probe
[3] (*Aut*) dipstick

cala[3]* SF (*Esp*) peseta

cala[4]‡ SM (*Mil*) glasshouse‡, prison

calabacear* ▸conjug 1a◂ VT (*Univ*) [+ *candidato*] to fail; [+ *amante*] to jilt

calabacera SF pumpkin (plant)

calabacín SM [1] (*Bot*) courgette, zucchini (*EEUU*)
[2] (= *idiota*) dolt

calabacita SF (*Esp*) courgette, zucchini (*EEUU*)

calabaza SF [1] (*Bot*) pumpkin; (= *recipiente*) gourd, calabash
[2] (= *idiota*) dolt
[3] (*) (= *cabeza*) bonce‡, nut*, noggin (*EEUU*‡)
[4] **dar ~s a** [+ *candidato, estudiante*] to fail; [+ *amante*] to jilt; (= *ofender*) to snub, offend; **llevarse** *o* **recibir ~s** [*estudiante*] to fail; [*amante*] to be jilted; **salir ~** to be a flop*, prove a miserable failure

calabazada SF (= *cabezada*) head butt; (= *golpe en la cabeza*) blow on the head

calabazazo SM bump on the head

calabazo SM [1] (*Bot*) pumpkin, gourd, squash (*EEUU*)
[2] (*Caribe Mús*) drum

calabobos* SM INV drizzle

calabozo SM (= *prisión*) prison; (= *celda*) prison cell; (*Mil*) military prison; (*esp Hist*) dungeon

calabrote SM (*Náut*) cable-laid rope, cable rope

calache* SM (*CAm*) thing, thingummyjig*, thingamajig (*EEUU**); **reúne tus ~s** get your things, get your bits and pieces

calada SF [1] (= *mojada*) soaking
[2] [*de red*] lowering
[3] [*de ave*] swoop, dive
[4] [*de tabaco*] puff, drag*
[5] (*) (= *regañada*) ticking-off*; **dar una ~ a algn** to tick sb off*, haul sb over the coals

caladero SM fishing ground

calado Ⓐ ADJ [1] (= *mojado*) soaked; **estar ~ (hasta los huesos)** to be soaked (to the skin)
[2] (*Cos*) openwork *antes de s*
[3] [*gorro etc*] **con la boina calada hasta las orejas** with his beret pulled down over his ears
[4] [*bayoneta*] fixed
Ⓑ SM [1] (*Téc*) fretwork; (*Cos*) openwork
[2] (*Náut*) depth of water; [*de barco*] draught, draft (*EEUU*); **en iguales ~s** on an even keel
[3] (*fig*) depth; (= *alcance*) scope; (= *importancia*) importance; **una razón de mayor ~** a more convincing reason; **un descubrimiento de gran ~** a very important discovery
[4] (*Mec*) stall, stalling

calafate SM caulker, shipwright

calafatear ▸conjug 1a◂ VT to caulk, plug up

calaguasca SF (*LAm*) rum

calagurritano/a Ⓐ ADJ of Calahorra
Ⓑ SM/F native/inhabitant of Calahorra; **los ~s** the people of Calahorra

calamaco SM (*Méx Culin*) kidney bean

calamar SM squid ► **calamares a la romana** squid rings fried in batter

calambrazo* SM attack of cramp

calambre SM [1] (*muscular*) **me dan ~s** I get cramp ► **calambre de escribiente** writer's cramp
[2] (*Elec*) shock; **un cable que da ~** a live wire

calambur SM (*LAm*) pun

calamidad SF (= *desastre*) calamity, disaster; (= *persona*) **es una ~** he's a dead loss*; **estar hecho una ~** to be in a very bad way; **¡vaya ~!** what terrible luck!

calamina SF [1] (*Med, Min*) calamine
[2] (*Chile, Bol, Perú*) (= *chapa*) corrugated iron

calaminado ADJ (*LAm*) bumpy, uneven

calamita SF lodestone; (= *aguja*) magnetic needle

calamitosamente ADV calamitously, disastrously

calamitoso ADJ calamitous, disastrous

cálamo SM (*Bot*) stem, stalk; (*Mús*) reed; (*Mús Hist*) flute; (= *pluma*) pen; **empuñar el ~** to take up one's pen; **menear ~** to wield a pen

calamocano* ADJ [1] (= *borracho*) merry*, tipsy
[2] (= *cariñoso*) doting

calamoco SM icicle

calamorra* SF head, nut‡

calamorrada* SF (= *cabezada*) head butt; (= *golpe en la cabeza*) bump on the head

calandraco ADJ (*Andes, Cono Sur*) (= *fastidioso*) annoying, tedious; (= *casquivano*) scatter-brained

calandria[1] SF (*Orn*) calandra lark

calandria[2] Ⓐ SF [1] (*Téc*) calender
[2] (*Fin*‡) one peseta
[3] (= *argot*) underworld slang, argot
Ⓑ SMF (*) (= *persona*) malingerer

calaña SF sort; **gente de esa ~** people of that ilk *o* sort

calañés SM (*Andalucía*) *hat with a turned-up brim*

calar[1] Ⓐ ADJ calcareous (*frm*), lime *antes de s*
Ⓑ SM limestone quarry

calar[2] ▸conjug 1a◂ Ⓐ VT [1] [*líquido, lluvia, humedad*] to soak (through); **la lluvia me caló la ropa** the rain soaked *o* drenched my clothes; **~ a algn (hasta) los huesos** to cut sb through to the bone; **un frío y una humedad que calan los huesos** cold and damp that cut through to the bone
[2] (*) (= *percatar*) to suss (out)*; **lo calé nada más conocerlo** I had him sussed as soon as I'd met him*; **¡nos ha calado!** he's sussed *o* rumbled us!*, we've been sussed *o* rumbled!*
[3] (*Téc*) [+ *metal, madera*] to fret; **sierra de ~** fret saw
[4] [+ *bayoneta*] to fix
[5] [+ *mástil*] to fix, fit; [+ *vela*] to lower; [+ *red*] to cast; **el buque cala 12 metros** the ship draws 12 metres, the ship has a draught of 12 metres
[6] (*Andes*) (= *aplastar*) to crush, flatten; (= *humillar*) to humiliate
Ⓑ VI (= *penetrar*) **esa moda no caló en España** that fashion did not take on *o* catch on in Spain; **su defensa caló en el jurado** the arguments in his defence got through to the jury; **una ideología que está calando en la sociedad** an ideology that is catching on in society; **esta opinión ha calado entre la población** this opinion has taken deep root among the public; **su mensaje caló hondo en nuestra generación** her message had a deep effect *o* made a deep impression on our generation
Ⓒ **calarse** VPR [1] (= *mojarse*) to get soaked, get drenched; **me calé hasta los huesos** I got soaked to the skin
[2] [*material, ropa*] to let water in, get wet; [*zapatos*] to let water in; **esos zapatos se calan** those shoes will let water in as soon as it rains
[3] [*motor, vehículo*] to stall; **se le caló el coche** his car stalled
[4] [+ *sombrero, gorra*] to pull down; [+ *gafas, careta*] to put on; **se caló el sombrero hasta la frente** he pulled his hat down over his forehead

calarredes SM INV trawler

calatear ▸conjug 1a◂ VT (*Perú*) to undress

calato ADJ (*Perú*) (= *desnudo*) naked; (*fig*) penniless, broke*

calavera Ⓐ SF [1] (*Anat*) skull
[2] (*Méx Aut*) tail-light, rear light
[3] (*Entomología*) death's-head moth
Ⓑ SM (= *juerguista*) reveller; (= *locuelo*) madcap; (= *libertino*) rake, roué; (= *canalla*) rotter†, cad†, heel†

calaverada SF madcap escapade

calaverear ▸conjug 1a◂ VI to live it up*; (*pey*) to lead a wild life, live recklessly

calca SF [1] (*Perú*) (= *granero*) barn, granary
[2] (*LAm*) (= *copia*) copy

calcado Ⓐ ADJ (= *idéntico*) **ser ~ a algo** to be just like sth; **ese bolso es ~ al mío** that bag is just like mine; **ser ~ a algn** to be the spitting image of sb; **es ~ a su padre** he's the spitting image of his father
Ⓑ SM (*Téc*) tracing

calcañal SM, **calcañar** SM, **calcaño** SM heel

calcar ▸conjug 1g◂ VT [1] (*Téc*) to trace, make a tracing of
[2] (= *plagiar*) to copy, imitate; **~ A en B** (= *copiar*) to model A on B, base A on B

calcáreo ADJ calcareous, lime *antes de s*

calce SM [1] (*Mec*) (= *llanta*) (steel) tyre; (=

cuña) wedge, shim; (= *punta*) iron tip
2 (*Andes*) (= *empaste*) filling (*of a tooth*)
3 (*Méx Tip*) [*de documento*] foot (of a document), lower margin; (= *firma*) signature; **firmar al ~** to sign at the foot *o* bottom of the page
4 (*Cono Sur*) (= *oportunidad*) chance, opportunity

cal. cen. ABR (= **calefacción central**) c.h.

calcés SM masthead

calceta SF 1 **hacer ~** to knit
2 (= *media*) (knee-length) stocking
3 (= *hierro*) fetter, shackle

calcetería SF 1 (= *oficio*) hosiery
2 (= *tienda*) hosier's (shop)

calcetero/a SM/F hosier

calcetín SM sock; ✦*MODISMO* **darle la vuelta al ~** to turn things upside-down ► **calcetín de viaje**‡ French letter, rubber (*esp EEUU*‡)

calcha SF (*Cono Sur*) 1 (= *ropa*) clothing; [*de cama*] bedding; (= *arreos*) harness
2 (= *cerneja*) fetlock
3 (= *flequillo*) fringe (of hair)
4 (= *harapos*) tatters *pl*, strands *pl*

calchona SF (*Cono Sur*) ghost, bogey; (*fig*) hag

calchudo ADJ (*Cono Sur*) shrewd, cunning

calcícola Ⓐ ADJ calcicolous
Ⓑ SF calcicole

calcificación SF calcification

calcificante ADJ calcifying

calcificar ▸conjug 1g◂ VT, **calcificarse** VPR to calcify

calcífugo ADJ calcifugous

calcina SF concrete

calcinación SF calcination

calcinar ▸conjug 1a◂ Ⓐ VT 1 (= *quemar*) to burn, reduce to ashes, blacken; **las ruinas calcinadas del edificio** the charred remains of the building; **cuerpos calcinados** charred bodies; **murió calcinado** he burned to death
2 (*) (*fastidiar*) to bother, annoy
Ⓑ **calcinarse** VPR to calcine

calcio SM calcium

calco SM 1 (*Téc*) tracing
2 (*Ling*) calque (**de** on), loan translation (**de** from)
3 (= *imitación*) copy, imitation; **ser un ~ de algn** to be the spitting image of sb
4 **calcos**‡ (= *pies*) plates‡, feet; (= *zapatos*) shoes

calcomanía SF transfer, decal (*EEUU*)

calculable ADJ calculable

calculador ADJ 1 (*gen*) calculating
2 (*LAm*) (= *egoísta*) selfish, mercenary

calculadora SF calculator; (*Hist*) calculating machine ► **calculadora de bolsillo** pocket calculator

calcular ▸conjug 1a◂ VT 1 (*Mat*) (*exactamente*) to calculate, work out; **debes ~ la cantidad exacta** you must calculate *o* work out the exact number; **~ la distancia entre dos puntos** to calculate *o* work out the distance between two points; **calculé mal la distancia y me caí** I misjudged the distance and fell
2 (*estimativamente*) **~ que** to reckon (that); **calculo que debe de tener unos cuarenta años** I reckon *o* (*esp EEUU*) figure he must be about 40 (years old); **¿cuánto calculas que puede costar?** how much do you reckon it might cost?; **se calcula que habrá unos diez heridos** about ten people are estimated to have been wounded; **calculo que llegará mañana** I reckon *o* (*esp EEUU*) figure he'll come tomorrow
3 (= *planear*) to work out, figure out; **lo calculó todo hasta el más mínimo detalle** he worked *o* figured it all out down to the last detail
4 (*) (= *imaginar*) **—¿tienes ganas de ir? —¡calcula!** "are you looking forward to going?" — "what do you think? *o* you bet (I am)!"*
5 (*Arquit*) [+ *puente, bóveda*] to design, plan

cálculo SM 1 (*gen*) calculation, reckoning; (= *conjetura*) estimate, conjecture; (*Mat*) calculus; **según mis ~s** by my reckoning, by my calculations; **obrar con mucho ~** to act cautiously; **hoja de ~** spreadsheet; **libro de ~s hechos** ready reckoner ► **cálculo de costo** costing, pricing (*EEUU*) ► **cálculo de probabilidades** theory of probability ► **cálculo diferencial** differential calculus ► **cálculo mental** mental arithmetic
2 (*Med*) stone ► **cálculo biliar** gallstone

Calcuta SF Calcutta

calda SF 1 (= *calentamiento*) (*gen*) heating; (*en hornos de fundición*) stoking
2 **caldas** (= *baños*) hot springs, hot mineral baths

caldeado ADJ lively; **ambiente ~** (= *animado*) lively atmosphere; (= *tenso*) heated atmosphere; **los ánimos estaban ~s** feelings were running high, an argument broke out and the atmosphere grew very tense *o* heated

caldeamiento SM warming, heating

caldear ▸conjug 1a◂ Ⓐ VT (= *calentar*) to warm (up), heat (up); (*Téc*) to weld; **~ los ánimos de la gente** to work people up
Ⓑ **caldearse** VPR [*local*] to get hot; [*ambiente*] to get tense *o* heated

caldeo SM warming, heating; (*Téc*) welding

caldera SF (*Téc*) boiler; (= *caldero*) cauldron; (*Cono Sur*) (= *cacerola*) pot; (= *tetera*) teapot; (= *pava*) kettle; (*Andes*) crater; ✦*MODISMO* **las ~s de Pe(d)ro Botero** hell

calderero SM boilermaker ► **calderero remendón** tinker

caldereta SF 1 (*Culin*) [*de pescado*] fish stew; [*de cordero*] lamb stew
2 (= *caldera pequeña*) small boiler; (= *cacerola*) stewpan
3 (*Rel*) holy water vessel
4 (*Caribe*) (= *viento*) warm wind from the sea

calderilla SF 1 (*Fin*) small change; **en ~** in small change
2 (*Rel*) holy water vessel

caldero SM cauldron, copper

calderón SM 1 (*Mús*) pause (sign)
2 (= *caldera grande*) large boiler, cauldron
3 (*Tip*) paragraph sign, section mark

calderoniano ADJ relating to Calderón; **héroe ~** Calderonian hero; **estudios ~s** Calderón studies

caldo SM 1 (= *sopa*) soup, broth; (= *consomé*) (clear) soup; **con un caldito te sentirás mejor** you'll feel better with some nice hot soup *o* broth inside you
2 [*de guiso*] juice; **tómate el ~ del estofado** have some of the juice from the stew; **la salsa se hace con el ~ de la carne** the sauce is made from the stock *o* juice of the meat; **hierva las verduras/los huesos para hacer el ~** boil the vegetables/the bones to make a stock; **cubitos de ~** stock cubes
3 ► **caldo de cultivo** (*Biol*) culture medium; (*fig*) breeding ground; **el ~ de cultivo del fascismo** the breeding ground of fascism
4 ✦*MODISMOS* **cambiar el ~ a las aceitunas**‡ to have a leak‡; **hacer el ~ gordo a algn*** to make things easy for sb, make it easy for sb; **se le hacía ~ la cabeza** (*Cono Sur*) he worried a lot about it; **poner a algn a ~*** (= *regañar*) to tell sb off, give sb a ticking off*; ✦*REFRÁN* **si no quieres ~, taza y media** *o* **dos tazas** it never rains but it pours
5 (= *vino*) wine; **los ~s jerezanos** the wines of Jerez
6 (= *aceite*) oil
7 (*Méx*) sugar cane juice

caldoso ADJ [*sopa*] watery, thin; [*arroz*] soggy

calducho SM (*Cono Sur*) day off

cale SM slap, smack

calé Ⓐ ADJ gipsy *antes de s*, gypsy *antes de s*
Ⓑ SMF gipsy, gypsy

calefacción SF heating; **sistema de ~** heating (system) ► **calefacción central** central heating

calefaccionable ADJ **espejo exterior ~** heated wing mirror

calefaccionar ▸conjug 1a◂ VT (*Cono Sur*) to heat (up)

calefactor Ⓐ ADJ heating *antes de s*; **sistema ~** heating system
Ⓑ SM heater

calefón SM (*Cono Sur*) water heater, boiler ► **calefón a gas** gas-fired water heater *o* boiler

caleidoscópico ADJ kaleidoscopic

caleidoscopio SM kaleidoscope

calendar ▸conjug 1a◂ VT to schedule, programme, program (*EEUU*)

calendario SM calendar; [*de reforma etc*] timetable; [*de trabajo etc*] schedule; ✦*MODISMO* **hacer ~s** to muse, dream ► **calendario de pared** wall calendar ► **calendario de taco** tear-off calendar

caléndula SF marigold

calentador SM heater ► **calentador de agua** water heater ► **calentador de cama** (*Hist*) bedwarmer, warming pan ► **calentador de gas** gas-fired boiler *o* water heater ► **calentador de inmersión** immersion heater ► **calentador eléctrico** electric fire ► **calentadores de piernas** legwarmers

calentamiento SM 1 (= *acción*) (*a temperatura alta*) heating; (*a temperatura media*) warming; **a consecuencia de un ~ excesivo** as a result of overheating ► **calentamiento de la atmósfera, calentamiento del planeta, calentamiento global** global warming
2 (*Dep*) warm-up

calentar ▸conjug 1j◂ Ⓐ VT 1 [+ *líquido, metal, mineral, comida*] (*a temperatura alta*) to heat (up); (*a temperatura media*) to warm (up); **¿caliento un poco más la sopa?** shall I heat (up) the soup a bit more?; **tómate este café, que te caliente un poco el estómago** have this coffee, it will warm you up inside; **¿dónde puedo ~ la voz?** where can I warm up?; **estaban calentando piernas antes del partido** they were doing leg warm-up exercises before the match; **~ motores** (*lit*) to warm up

the engines; (*fig*) to gather momentum; **los coches ya están calentando motores** the cars are already warming up their engines; **ya calentaba motores la huelga general** the general strike was already gathering momentum; ✦*MODISMO* **~ la cabeza** *o* **los cascos a algn*** (= *marear*) to pester sb; (= *empujar*) to egg sb on; **tras ~le mucho la cabeza han conseguido convencerlo** after endlessly pestering him they finally convinced him; **le ~on los cascos hasta que se metió en la pelea** they egged him on until he finally joined in the fight; *ver tb* **rojo B1**
2 [+ *ambiente, ánimos*] **no fueron capaces de ~ los ánimos de los asistentes** they couldn't get the audience fired up; **el torero inició la faena de rodillas para ~ al público** the bullfighter began with kneeling passes to get the spectators warmed up
3 (*) (*sexualmente*) to turn on*
4 (*esp LAm**) (= *enojar*) to make cross, make mad (*esp EEUU**)
5 (*) (= *zurrar*) **~ bien a algn** to give sb a good hiding
6 (*Chile**) [+ *examen, materia*] to cram for*
Ⓑ VI 1 (= *dar calor*) [*sol*] to get hot; [*estufa, radiador, fuego*] to give off heat, give out heat; **cuando caliente más el sol** when the sun gets hotter; **el radiador apenas calienta** the radiator hardly gives off *o* gives out any heat
2 (*Dep*) to warm up, limber up
Ⓒ **calentarse** VPR 1 (= *caldearse*) [*persona*] to warm o.s. up; [*plancha, sartén*] to heat up, get hot; [*habitación*] to warm up; [*motor, coche*] (*al encenderse*) to warm up; (*en exceso*) to overheat; **nos calentamos a la lumbre** we warmed ourselves up by the fire; ✦*MODISMO* **~se la cabeza** *o* **los cascos (por algo)*** to agonize (about sth), fret (over sth)
2 (*) (= *animarse*) **se calentaban con los aplausos del público** they got a buzz from the audience's applause*; **los ánimos se ~on y acabaron a golpes** feelings began to run high *o* things got heated and it ended in a punch-up
3 (*) (*sexualmente*) to get turned on*
4 (*LAm**) (= *enojarse*) to get cross, get mad (*esp EEUU**)
5 (*Cono Sur**) (= *disgustarse*) to get upset

calentón‡ Ⓐ ADJ randy*, horny*
Ⓑ SM 1 (*Andes, Cono Sur**) randy devil*, horny devil*
2 **darse el ~** ◊ **tener un ~** to feel randy *o* horny*

calentorro/a‡ SM/F randy *o* horny devil*

calentura SF 1 (*Med*) fever, (high) temperature; **estar con** *o* **tener ~** to be feverish, have a temperature; ✦*MODISMO* **tener ~ de pollo** (*hum*) to pretend to be ill
2 (*en labios*) cold sore
3 (*Chile*) tuberculosis
4 (*Andes, Cono Sur*) (= *cachondez*) (*) randiness*, horniness*
5 (*LAm*) (= *furia*) anger

calenturiento ADJ 1 (*Med*) feverish
2 (= *impúdico*) dirty, prurient; (= *exaltado*) rash, impulsive; **las mentes calenturientas** (*Pol etc*) the hotheads
3 (*Cono Sur*) (= *tísico*) consumptive, tubercular

calenturón* SM high fever

calenturoso ADJ feverish

calera SF (= *cantera*) limestone quarry; (= *horno*) limekiln

calero Ⓐ ADJ lime *antes de s*
Ⓑ SM limekiln

calés‡ SMPL bread‡ *sing*, money *sing*

calesa SF chaise, calash, buggy

calesera SF *Andalusian jacket*

calesín SM gig, fly

calesita SF (*Andes, Cono Sur*) merry-go-round, carousel (*EEUU*)

caleta SF 1 (*Geog*) cove, small bay, inlet
2 (*Andes*) (= *barco*) coasting vessel, coaster
3 (*Andes*) (= *escondite*) cache

caletero/a Ⓐ SM/F 1 (*Caribe*) (= *estibador*) docker, port worker
2 (*Caribe*) (*en tienda*) shop assistant, salesclerk (*EEUU*)
Ⓑ SM (*LAm Ferro*) milk train

caletre* SM gumption*, brains *pl*; **no le cabe en el ~** he can't get it into his thick head*

calibración SF calibration

calibrado ADJ calibrated

calibrador SM (*gen*) gauge, gage (*EEUU*); [*de mordazas*] calliper(s) ► **calibrador de alambre** wire gauge

calibraje SM calibration

calibrar ▸conjug 1a◂ VT (*Téc*) to calibrate; (*fig*) (= *evaluar*) to gauge, gage (*EEUU*), measure

calibre SM 1 (= *diámetro*) [*de bala, proyectil, casquillo*] calibre, caliber (*EEUU*); [*de pistola, rifle, cañón*] calibre, bore; [*de tubo, conducto, tornillo*] calibre; **de alto** *o* **gran** *o* **grueso ~** large-bore; **de bajo** *o* **pequeño ~** small-bore; **casquillos del ~ 9 parabellum** .9 Parabellum cases; **nunca he visto un coche de tal ~** I've never seen such a massive car
2 (= *importancia*) calibre; **no tenemos un poeta del ~ de Lorca** we do not have a poet of the calibre of Lorca; **tienen problemas de gran ~** they have problems of a serious nature
3 (*Cono Sur*) **palabras de grueso ~** rude words, crude language *sing*; **un chiste de grueso ~** a crude joke

calicanto SM (*Caribe, Cono Sur*) (= *muro*) stone wall; (= *muelle*) jetty

calicatas‡ SFPL (= *culo*) backside* *pl*

caliche SM 1 (*LAm*) saltpetre bed, caliche; (= *terreno*) nitrate-bearing ground
2 (*Cono Sur*) (= *jalbegue*) *crust of whitewash which flakes from a wall*
3 **echar un ~**‡ to have a screw‡

calicó SM calico

calidad SF 1 [*de objeto, material, producto*] quality; [*de servicio*] quality, standard; **la ~ del agua ha empeorado** the quality of the water has worsened; **han mejorado la ~ de la enseñanza** they have improved the quality *o* standard of education, they have raised standards in education; **de (buena) ~** good-quality, quality *antes de s*; **fruta de (buena) ~** good-quality fruit, quality fruit; **turismo de ~** quality tourism; **vinos de ~** quality wines; **de mala ~** low-quality, poor-quality ► **calidad de vida** quality of life
2 (= *condición*) position, status; **su ~ de presidente se lo prohíbe** his position *o* status as president prohibits him from doing so; **en ~ de: te lo digo en ~ de amigo** I'm telling you as a friend
3 (*Inform*) ► **calidad de borrador** draft quality, draft ► **calidad de carta**, **calidad de correspondencia** letter quality ► **calidad de texto** text quality

cálido ADJ (*gen*) hot; [*color, sonrisa*] warm; [*aplausos*] enthusiastic

calidoscópico ADJ kaleidoscopic

calidoscopio SM kaleidoscope

calienta *etc ver* **calentar**

calientabiberones SM INV bottle warmer

calientabraguetas‡ SF INV prick-teaser‡, prick-tease‡, cock-teaser‡

calientacamas SM INV electric blanket

calientafuentes SM INV hotplate, plate warmer

calientapiernas SMPL legwarmers

calientapiés SM INV (*gen*) foot warmer; [*de agua caliente*] hot-water bottle

calientaplatos SM INV hotplate, plate warmer

calientapollas‡ SF INV (*Esp*) prick-teaser‡, pricktease‡, cock-teaser‡

CALIENTE

A la hora de traducir el adjetivo **caliente**, hay que tener en cuenta la diferencia en inglés entre los adjetivos **warm** y **hot**.

- Se utiliza **warm** cuando nos referimos a algo que está templado, que no quema o que no está suficientemente frío:

  El biberón del niño ya está caliente
  The baby's bottle is warm now
  ¡Esta cerveza está caliente!
  This beer is warm!

- Se emplea **hot** cuando estamos hablando de una temperatura alta, que puede quemar:

  No toques la sartén, está muy caliente
  Don't touch the frying pan, it's very hot
  Me apetece un café calentito
  I fancy a nice hot cup of coffee

Para otros usos y ejemplos ver la entrada.

caliente ADJ 1 (= *que quema*) hot; **no toques la plancha, que está ~** don't touch the iron, it's hot; **un café bien ~** a piping hot coffee; **dieron la noticia cuando todavía estaba ~** the news was released hot off the press; **comer ~** to have a hot meal, have some hot food; **servir algo ~** to serve sth hot; ✦*MODISMOS* **en ~: tuvo que responderle en ~** he had to answer him there and then *o* on the spur of the moment; **así, en ~, no sé qué decirle** offhand, I don't know what to say; **agarrar a algn en ~** (*Méx**) to catch sb red-handed
2 (= *no frío*) warm; **esta cerveza está ~** this beer is warm; **si te abrigas con la manta estarás más calentito** if you wrap the blanket around you, you'll feel warmer; **el cuerpo estaba todavía ~ cuando lo tocaron** the body was still warm to the touch; **me gusta el pan calentito** I like my bread nice and warm; ✦*REFRÁN* **ande yo ~ y ríase la gente** (*en el vestir*) I dress for comfort, not for show; (*en el comportamiento*) I do my own thing and don't care what people say
3 (= *violento*) [*época, lugar*] turbulent; [*discusión*] heated; [*batalla*] raging; (*LAm*) [*persona*] angry, mad*; **los sindicatos anunciaron un otoño ~** trade unions warned of a turbulent autumn ahead; **~ de cascos** hot-headed
4 (*en juegos*) warm; **¡caliente, caliente!** warm!, getting warmer!

[5] (*) (*en sentido sexual*) **estar ~** to feel horny‡; **poner ~ a algn** to turn sb on*, make sb horny‡; **ponerse ~** to get turned on*, get horny‡

califa SM caliph

califal ADJ caliphal; **la Córdoba ~** Cordova under the Caliphs, the Cordova of the Caliphs

califato SM caliphate

calificación SF [1] (*Escol etc*) grade, mark
[2] [*de una película*] rating, certificate; **la película recibió la ~ X** the film was awarded an X certificate, the film was X-rated
[3] (= *descripción*) description
[4] (= *posición*) rating, standing

calificado ADJ [1] (= *competente*) qualified, competent; [*obrero*] skilled
[2] (= *conocido*) well-known, eminent
[3] (*Der*) [*prueba*] undisputed; [*robo*] proven
[4] (*Méx Jur*) qualified, conditional

calificar ▸conjug 1g◂ Ⓐ VT [1] **~ algo/a algn como** *o* **de algo** to describe sth/sb as sth, call sb/sth sth; **calificó su política como** *o* **de racismo encubierto** he called their policy covert racism, he described their policy as covert racism; **el párroco lo calificó de impertinente** the parish priest described him as *o* called him impertinent; **documentos calificados como alto secreto** documents classified as top secret
[2] (*Escol*) [+ *examen*] to mark, grade (*EEUU*); [+ *alumno*] to give a mark to, give a grade to (*EEUU*)
[3] (*frm*) (= *ennoblecer*) to distinguish
Ⓑ **calificarse** VPR (*LAm Pol*) to register as a voter

calificativo Ⓐ ADJ qualifying
Ⓑ SM **sólo merece el ~ de ...** it can only be described as ...; **lo que han hecho estos gamberros no tiene ~s** what these hooligans have done beggars belief

California SF California

california SF (*Cono Sur*) [1] (= *carrera*) horse-race
[2] (*Téc*) wire stretcher

californiano/a ADJ, SM/F Californian

calígine (*poét*) SF (= *neblina*) mist; (= *oscuridad*) gloom

caliginoso ADJ (*poét*) (*con neblina*) misty; (= *oscuro*) gloomy

caligrafía SF (= *arte*) calligraphy; (= *letra*) handwriting

caligrafiar ▸conjug 1c◂ VT to write in a stylish hand

caligráfico ADJ calligraphic

calilla SF (*LAm*) [1] (= *persona*) bore
[2] (= *molestia*) nuisance
[3] (= *engaño*) hoax; (= *broma*) tired *o* old joke

calima SF = **calina**

calimocho SM wine and cola

calina SF haze, mist

calinoso ADJ hazy, misty

calipso SM calypso

caliqueño SM [1] (= *cigarro*) type of cheap cigar
[2] (‡*) prick‡*; **echar un ~** to have a screw‡*

calistenia SF callisthenics *sing*, calisthenics *sing* (*EEUU*)

cáliz SM [1] (*Rel*) chalice, communion cup; (= *copa*) goblet, cup ► **cáliz de amargura** bitter cup, cup of sorrow
[2] (*Bot*) calyx

caliza SF limestone

calizo ADJ **piedra caliza** limestone; **tierra caliza** limy soil

callada SF **a la** *o* **de ~** on the quiet, secretly; **dar la ~ por respuesta** to say nothing in reply

calladamente ADV (= *silenciosamente*) quietly, silently; (= *en secreto*) secretly

callado ADJ [1] [*carácter*] quiet, reserved
[2] (= *silencioso*) quiet; **todo estaba muy ~** everything was very quiet; **tener algo ~** to keep quiet about sth, keep sth secret; **¡qué ~ te lo tenías!** you kept pretty quiet about it!; **más ~ que un muerto** as quiet as a mouse*; **pagar para tener ~ a algn** to pay to keep sb quiet, pay for sb's silence; **nunca te quedas ~** you always have an answer for everything

callampa SF (*Chile*) [1] (= *hongo*) mushroom; (= *paraguas*) umbrella, brolly*
[2] **callampas** (= *suburbios*) shanty town *sing*

callana SF [1] (*LAm Culin*) flat earthenware pan
[2] (*Cono Sur hum*) (= *reloj*) pocket watch

callandito* ADV, **callandico*** ADV (= *sin ruido*) softly, very quietly; (= *furtivamente*) stealthily

callar ▸conjug 1a◂ Ⓐ VI [1] (= *dejar de hablar*) to be quiet; **¡calla, que no puedo oír la radio!** be *o* keep quiet, I can't hear the radio!, shut up *o* (*EEUU*) hush up, I can't hear the radio!*; **su madre le mandó ~** his mother ordered him to be quiet, his mother told him to shut up; **—Ernesto se casa —¡calla! ¡eso no puede ser!** "Ernesto is getting married" — "you're joking! that can't be true!"
[2] (= *no hablar*) to say nothing, keep quiet; **al principio optó por ~** initially he decided to say nothing *o* keep quiet; ✦**REFRÁN quien calla, otorga** silence is *o* gives *o* implies consent
Ⓑ VT [1] (= *hacer callar*) **calló a los niños con un cuento** he got the children to be *o* keep quiet by reading them a story; **reparten dinero para ~ las protestas** they're giving out money to silence *o* quell complaints; **¡calla** *o* **cállate la boca!*** shut your mouth!‡, shut your face!‡
[2] (= *ocultar*) to keep to o.s., keep quiet; **será mejor ~ este asunto** it's best to keep this matter to ourselves o keep this matter quiet
Ⓒ **callarse** VPR [1] (= *dejar de hablar*) to stop talking, go quiet; **al entrar el profesor todos se ~on** when the teacher came in, everyone stopped talking *o* went quiet; **¡cállense, por favor!** please be quiet!; **si empieza a hablar, ya no se calla** once he starts talking, he doesn't stop
[2] (= *no decir nada*) to say nothing, keep quiet; **en esas circunstancias es mejor ~se** in those circumstances, it would be best to say nothing *o* keep quiet

calle SF [1] (= *vía pública*) street; (*con más tráfico*) road; **una ~ muy céntrica** a street right in the centre of town; **~ abajo** down the street; **~ arriba** up the street; ✦**MODISMOS abrir ~** to make way, clear the way; **echar por la ~ de en medio** to push on, press on regardless; **se los lleva a todos de ~*** they just can't stay away from her, they find her irresistible; **llevar** *o* **traer a algn por la ~ de la amargura*** to make sb's life a misery* ► **calle cerrada** (*Ven, Col, Méx*), **calle ciega** (*Ven, Col*), **calle cortada** (*Cono Sur*) dead end, dead-end street, cul-de-sac ► **calle de doble sentido** two-way street ► **calle de sentido único**, **calle de una mano** (*Cono Sur*), **calle de una sola vía** (*Col*), **calle de un solo sentido** (*Chile*) one-way street ► **calle peatonal** pedestrianized street, pedestrian street ► **calle principal** main street ► **calle residencial** residential street (*with low speed limit and priority for pedestrians*) ► **calle sin salida** cul-de-sac, dead end, dead end street; *ver tb* **aplanar A1**, **cabo 2**
[2] (= *no casa*) [2.1] **la ~: he estado todo el día en la ~** I've been out all day; **se sentaba en la ~ a ver pasar a la gente** he used to sit out in the street *o* outside watching the people go by; **a los dos días de su detención ya estaba otra vez en la ~** two days after his arrest he was back on the streets again; **el grupo tiene ya tres discos en la ~** the group already have three records out; **irse a la ~** to go out, go outside; **¡iros a la ~ a jugar!** go and play outside!; **salir a la ~** (= *persona*) to go outside; (= *disco, publicación*) to come out; **llevo varios días sin salir a la ~** I haven't been out of the house *o* outside for several days; **el periódico salió ayer a la ~ por última vez** the paper came out yesterday for the last time; ✦**MODISMOS coger la ~*** to up and leave*; **dejar a algn en la ~** to put sb out of a job; **echar a algn a la ~** to throw sb out on the street; **echarse a la ~** to take to the streets; **hacer la ~** (*euf*) to walk the streets; **poner a algn (de patitas) en la ~*** to kick sb out; **quedarse en la ~** (= *sin trabajo*) to be out of a job; (= *sin vivienda*) to be homeless; **tomar la ~** to take to the streets; *ver tb* **hombre A1**
[2.2] **de ~: ropa de ~** (= *no de estar en casa*) *clothes for wearing outside the house*; (= *no de gala*) everyday clothes *pl*; **iba vestido de ~** (*Mil*) he was wearing civilian clothes, he was wearing civvies*
[3] **la ~** (= *gente*) the public; **vamos a oír ahora la opinión de la ~** we're now going to hear what members of the public think; **la presión de la ~** the pressure of public opinion
[4] (*Natación, Atletismo*) lane; (*Golf*) fairway
[5] (*Aer*) ► **calle de rodadura**, **calle de rodaje** taxiway

calleja SF = **callejuela**

callejear ▸conjug 1a◂ VI to wander (about) the streets, stroll around; (*pey*) to loaf around, hang about

callejera SF street-walker

callejero Ⓐ ADJ [1] (*gen*) street *antes de s*; **accidente ~** street accident; **disturbios ~s** street riots; **mercado ~** street market
[2] [*persona*] **son muy ~s** they are always out and about; *ver tb* **perro A1**
Ⓑ SM [1] (*guía*) street directory, street plan
[2] (*Aut*) runabout

callejón SM (= *calleja*) alley, passage; (*Andes*) (= *calle*) main street; (*Taur*) space between inner and outer barriers; (*Geog*) narrow pass ► **callejón sin salida** cul-de-sac, dead end; (*fig*) blind alley; **las negociaciones están en un ~ sin salida** the negotiations are at an impasse, the negotiations are stalemated; **gente de ~** (*Andes*) low-class people

callejuela SF [1] (= *calle*) side street, small street; (= *pasaje*) alley, passage

[2] (= *subterfugio*) subterfuge; (*fig*) way out (of the difficulty)

callicida SM corn cure

callista SMF chiropodist, podiatrist (*EEUU*)

callo SM [1] (*Med*) [*de pie*] corn; [*de mano*] callus, callosity (*frm*); ✦*MODISMOS* **criar ~s** to become inured, become hardened; **dar el ~** (*Esp**) to slog, work hard, slave away*
[2] (*) (= *persona fea*) **María/Juan es un ~** María/Juan is as ugly as sin
[3] **callos** (*Culin*) tripe *sing*

callosidad SF callosity (*frm*), hard patch (*on hand etc*)

calloso ADJ calloused, rough

calma SF [1] (= *tranquilidad*) calm; **la ~ ha vuelto al equipo** calm has been restored to the team; **en la ~ de la noche** in the calm of the night; **¡calma!** (*en una discusión*) calm down!; (*ante un peligro*) keep calm!; **cuando llegaron los niños se acabó la ~** when the children arrived, the peace and quiet ended; **pasó la noche en ~** he had a peaceful night; **hubo un periodo de ~ entre las elecciones municipales y las legislativas** there was a lull between the local and the general elections; **con ~** calmly; **conservar** *o* **mantener la ~** to keep calm, stay calm; **perder la ~** to lose one's cool*; **tomárselo con ~** to take it easy*
[2] (= *relajo excesivo*) **me atendieron con una ~ increíble** they served me in a very relaxed fashion
[3] (*Náut, Meteo*) calm; **navegamos con la mar en ~** we sailed in a calm sea ► **calma chicha** dead calm

calmadamente ADV calmly

calmado ADJ calm; **estar ~** to be calm; **sería mejor esperar a que las cosas estén más calmadas** it would be better to wait until things have calmed down *o* are calmer

calmante Ⓐ ADJ soothing, sedative
Ⓑ SM sedative, tranquillizer

calmar ▸conjug 1a◂ Ⓐ VT [1] (= *relajar*) [+ *persona*] to calm (down); [+ *ánimos*] to calm; [+ *nervios*] to calm, steady; **intenté ~la pero seguía llorando** I tried to calm her down but she kept crying; **estas pastillas le ayudarán a ~ la ansiedad** these pills will help reduce *o* relieve your anxiety; **esta medida ~á la tensión en el país** this measure will reduce tension in the country
[2] (= *aliviar*) [+ *dolor, picor*] to relieve; [+ *tos*] to soothe; [+ *sed*] to quench
Ⓑ **calmarse** VPR [1] [*persona*] to calm down; **¡cálmese!** calm down!
[2] (*Meteo*) [*viento*] to drop; [*olas*] to calm down; ✦*MODISMO* **~se las aguas**: **las aguas se ~án tras las elecciones** things will quieten down after the elections
[3] (*Fin*) [*mercado*] to settle down

calmazo SM dead calm

calmécac SM (*Méx Hist*) *Aztec school for priests*

calmo¹ ADJ [*aguas, mar, persona*] calm; [*ambiente*] peaceful

calmo² ADJ (*esp LAm*) [*tierra*] barren

calmosamente ADV [1] (= *con tranquilidad*) calmly
[2] (= *lentamente*) slowly, sluggishly

calmosidad SF [1] (= *tranquilidad*) calm, calmness
[2] (= *lentitud*) slowness, sluggishness

calmoso ADJ [1] (= *tranquilo*) calm
[2] (= *lento*) slow, sluggish

caló SM gipsy dialect, gypsy dialect

calofriarse ▸conjug 1c◂ VPR = **escalofriarse**

calofrío SM = **escalofrío**

calor SM (*a veces* SF) [1] (= *alta temperatura*) heat; **no puedo dormir con este ~** I can't sleep in this heat; **no soporto los ~es del verano** I can't cope with the heat in summer; **un material resistente al ~** a heat-resistant material; **¡qué ~!** it's really hot!; **nos sentamos al ~ de la chimenea** we sat by the heat of the fire, we sat by the warm fireside; **dar ~**: **el fuego da un ~cito muy agradable** the fire gives off a very pleasant heat; **esta camiseta me da demasiado ~** this shirt is too hot *o* warm; **entrar en ~** to get warm; **un café para entrar en ~** a coffee to warm you/us up; **hacer ~** to be hot; **hace muchísimo ~** it's very hot; **mañana hará mucho ~** it will be very hot tomorrow; **pasar ~** to be hot; **nunca he pasado tanto ~ como hoy** I've never been *o* felt as hot as today; **tener ~** to be hot; **tengo mucho ~** I'm very hot; *ver tb* **asar B**
[2] (= *afecto*) warmth and affection; **un niño falto de ~** a child deprived of warmth and affection ► **calor humano** human warmth
[3] **calores** [*de la menopausia*] hot flushes, hot flashes (*EEUU*)

caloría SF calorie

calórico ADJ caloric

calorífero Ⓐ ADJ heat-producing, heat-giving
Ⓑ SM (= *sistema*) heating system; (= *estufa*) furnace, stove; (= *radiador*) heater, radiator ► **calorífero mural** wall radiator

calorífico ADJ calorific; **potencia calorífica** calorific value

calorifugar ▸conjug 1h◂ VT [+ *caldera, tubo*] to lag

calorífugo ADJ (= *resistente*) heat-resistant, non-conducting; (= *incombustible*) fireproof

calorro/a* SM/F gipsy, gypsy

calostro SM colostrum

calote* SM (*Cono Sur*) swindle, trick, con*; **dar ~** to skip payments, leave without paying

calotear* ▸conjug 1a◂ VT (*Cono Sur*) to swindle, con*

calta SF (*tb* **~ palustre**) marsh marigold

caluga SF (*Cono Sur*) toffee

caluma SF (*Perú*) gap, pass (*in the Andes*)

calumnia SF (= *difamación*) slander, calumny (*frm*); (*Jur*) (*oral*) slander (**de** of); (*escrita*) libel (**de** on)

calumniador(a) SM/F (= *difamador*) slanderer; (*en prensa etc*) libeller

calumniar ▸conjug 1b◂ VT (= *difamar*) to slander; (*en prensa etc*) to libel; ✦*REFRÁN* **calumnia, que algo queda** if you throw enough mud, some sticks

calumnioso ADJ (= *difamatorio*) slanderous; (*en prensa etc*) libellous, libelous (*EEUU*)

calurosamente ADV warmly, enthusiastically

caluroso ADJ [*día, tiempo*] warm, hot; [*recibimiento*] warm, enthusiastic; [*aplausos*] enthusiastic

calva SF (= *cabeza*) bald head; (= *parte sin pelo*) bald patch; (*en alfombra, piel, tela*) bare patch, worn place; [*de bosque etc*] clearing

Calvados SM Calvados

calvario SM [1] (= *via crucis*) Stations of the Cross *pl* ► **el Calvario** (*Biblia*) Calvary
[2] (= *martirio*) torment; **su matrimonio fue un ~** her marriage was a torment (to her); **pasar un ~** to suffer agonies

calvatrueno†* SM [1] (= *calvo*) bald pate
[2] (= *tarambana*) madcap

calvero SM [1] [*de bosque*] glade, clearing
[2] (= *cantera*) clay pit

calvicie SF baldness ► **calvicie precoz** premature baldness

calvinismo SM Calvinism

calvinista Ⓐ ADJ Calvinist, Calvinistic
Ⓑ SMF Calvinist

calvo Ⓐ ADJ [1] [*persona*] bald; [*piel*] bald, hairless; **un señor ~ con gafas** a bald man with glasses; **quedarse ~** to go bald; ✦*MODISMO* **más ~ que una bola de billar** as bald as a coot; *ver tb* **tanto C2**
[2] [*terreno*] bare, barren
Ⓑ SM bald man

calza SF [1] (*Mec*) wedge, chock; **poner ~ a** to wedge, chock, scotch
[2] (*) (= *media*) stocking
[3] (*Col Med*) (= *empaste de dientes*) filling
[4] **calzas**† (= *medias*) hose *pl*; (= *pantalón*) breeches; ✦*MODISMO* **estar en ~s prietas** to be in a fix

calzada SF (= *carretera*) road; [*de casa*] drive; (*LAm*) (= *avenida*) avenue; (*Caribe*) (= *acera*) pavement, sidewalk (*EEUU*); **el coche se salió de la ~** the car went off *o* left the road ► **calzada romana** Roman road

calzado Ⓐ ADJ **conviene ir ~** it's better to wear shoes, one has to wear something on one's feet; **~ con** wearing; **iba calzada con unos zapatos rojos** she was wearing red shoes
Ⓑ SM footwear; **vendemos todo tipo de ~** we sell all types of footwear *o* shoes; **fábrica de ~** shoe factory

calzador SM shoehorn; (*Andes, Cono Sur*) penholder

calzar ▸conjug 1f◂ Ⓐ VT [1] [+ *zapatos etc*] (= *llevar*) to wear; (= *ponerse*) to put on; **calzaba zapatos verdes** she was wearing green shoes; **¿qué número calza usted?** what size shoes do you wear *o* take?, what size do you take?; ✦*MODISMO* **el que primero llega se la calza** first come first served
[2] [+ *niño etc*] to put shoes on; (= *proveer de calzado*) to provide with footwear, supply with shoes; **me ayudó a ~me las botas** he helped me to put my boots on
[3] (*Mil etc*) [+ *armas*] to bear
[4] (*Téc*) [+ *rueda etc*] to scotch, chock; (*con cuña*) to put a wedge (under); (= *bloquear*) to block; (= *asegurar*) to secure
[5] (*Col*) [+ *diente*] to fill
[6] (= *poner punta a*) to tip, put an iron tip on
Ⓑ VI [1] **calza bien** he wears good shoes
[2] (*) ✦*MODISMOS* **calza poco** ◊ **no calza mucho** he's pretty dim*
Ⓒ **calzarse** VPR [1] **~se los zapatos** to put one's shoes on
[2] (*) **~se un empleo** to get a job; **~se a algn** to keep sb under one's thumb
[3] **~se a algn**** to screw sb**

calzo SM [1] (*gen*) wedge; (*Mec*) shoe, brakeshoe; (*Náut*) skid, chock
[2] (*Ftbl*) professional foul (*euf*)

calzón SM 1 (*Esp*) (= *pantalón corto*) shorts *pl*; ✦**MODISMOS amarrarse los calzones** to act resolutely; **hablar a ~ quitado** (= *hablar claro*) to call a spade a spade, speak openly *o* frankly; (*sin parar*) to talk without stopping; **ponerse los calzones** to wear the trousers; **tener (muchos) calzones** (*Méx*) to be tough ► **calzón de baño**† bathing trunks *pl*
2 (*LAm*) (= *ropa interior*) [*de mujer*] pants *pl*, knickers *pl*, panties *pl* (*esp EEUU*); [*de hombre*] underpants, pants, shorts (*EEUU*)
3 (*LAm*) [*de bebé*] ► **calzón desechable** disposable nappy ► **calzón de vinilo** plastic pants
4 **calzones rotos** (*Cono Sur Culin*) doughnuts, donuts (*EEUU*)

calzonarias SFPL (*Andes, Col*), **calzonarios** SMPL (*Pan*) pants, knickers, panties (*esp EEUU*)

calzonazos* SM INV (= *marido*) henpecked husband; (= *tonto*) stupid twit*; (= *débil*) wimp*

calzoncillos SMPL underpants, pants, shorts (*EEUU*) ► **calzoncillos del nueve largo***, **calzoncillos marianos*** long johns*

calzoneras SFPL (*Méx*) trousers buttoned down the sides

calzoneta SF (*CAm, Méx*) swimming trunks *pl*

calzonudo ADJ (*Andes, CAm, Cono Sur*) (= *estúpido*) stupid; (= *débil*) weak-willed, timid; (*Méx*) (= *enérgico*) energetic; (= *audaz*) bold, brave

CAM SF ABR = **Comunidad Autónoma de Madrid**

cama SF 1 bed; **una ~ para los invitados** a spare bed; **una habitación con dos ~s** a twin-bedded room; **está en la ~ durmiendo** he's asleep in bed, he's in bed sleeping; **caer en ~** to fall ill; **estar en ~** to be in bed; **guardar ~** to stay in bed; **hacer la ~** to make the bed; **irse a la ~** to go to bed; **llevarse a algn a la ~** to get sb into bed; **meterse en la ~** to go to bed; **mojar la ~** to wet the bed, wet one's bed ► **cama camera** three-quarter bed ► **cama de agua** water bed ► **cama de campaña** camp bed ► **cama de matrimonio** double bed ► **cama de tijera** folding bed ► **cama doble** double bed ► **cama elástica** trampoline ► **cama individual** single bed ► **cama litera** bunk bed ► **cama nido** truckle bed, trundle bed (*EEUU*) ► **cama plegable** folding bed ► **cama redonda** group sex ► **cama solar** sunbed ► **cama turca** divan bed; ✦**REFRÁN quien mala ~ hace en ella yace** you've made your bed and now you must lie in it
2 [*de carro*] floor
3 (*Geol*) layer

camachuelo SM bullfinch

camada SF 1 (*Zool*) litter, brood; (= *pandilla*) gang, band; **son lobos de una ~** they're birds of a feather
2 (*Geol*) layer; (*Arquit*) course (of bricks); [*de huevos, frutas*] layer

camafeo SM cameo

camagua SF (*CAm*) ripening maize, ripening corn (*EEUU*); (*Méx*) unripened maize

camal SM 1 (= *cabestro*) halter
2 (= *palo*) pole (*from which dead pigs are hung*); (*Andes*) (= *matadero*) slaughterhouse, abattoir

camaleón SM chameleon

camaleónico ADJ chameleon-like

camalote SM camalote (*aquatic plant*)

camama* SF (= *mentira*) lie; (= *engaño*) trick

camamila SF camomile

camanance SM (*CAm*) dimple

camanchaca* SF (*Cono Sur*) thick fog, peasouper*

camándula SF 1 (= *rosario*) rosary
2 (= *astucia*) **tener muchas ~s*** to be full of tricks, be a sly sort

camandulear ▸conjug 1a◂ VI to be sanctimonious, be falsely devout; (*LAm*) (= *intrigar*) to intrigue, scheme; (= *vacilar*) to bumble, avoid taking decisions

camandulería SF sanctimoniousness, false devotion

camandulero/a Ⓐ ADJ (= *beato*) sanctimonious, falsely devout; (= *taimado*) sly, tricky; (*LAm*) (= *enredador*) intriguing, scheming; (= *zalamero*) fawning, bootlicking*
Ⓑ SM/F (= *gazmoño*) prude, prig; (= *hipócrita*) hypocrite; (= *vividor*) sly sort, tricky person; (*LAm*) (= *intrigante*) intriguer, schemer

cámara Ⓐ SF 1 [*de fotos, televisión*] camera; **a ~ lenta** in slow motion; **a ~ rápida** in fast-forward ► **cámara de cine** film camera ► **cámara de fotos** camera ► **cámara de seguridad** security camera ► **cámara de vídeo** video camera ► **cámara digital** digital camera ► **cámara fotográfica** camera ► **cámara oculta** hidden camera ► **cámara oscura** camera obscura; *ver tb* **chupar A1**
2 (†) (= *habitación*) chamber ► **cámara acorazada** [*de archivo*] strongroom, vaults *pl*; [*de banco*] vaults *pl* ► **cámara ardiente** funeral chamber ► **cámara de aislamiento** isolation room ► **cámara de descompresión** decompression chamber ► **cámara de gas** [*de ejecución*] gas chamber ► **cámara de tortura** torture chamber ► **cámara frigorífica** cold-storage room, refrigerated container ► **cámara mortuoria** funeral chamber ► **cámara nupcial** bridal chamber
3 (*Pol*) house, chamber ► **Cámara Alta** Upper House, Upper Chamber ► **Cámara Baja** Lower House, Lower Chamber ► **Cámara de Comercio** Chamber of Commerce ► **Cámara de los Comunes** House of Commons ► **Cámara de los Lores** House of Lords ► **Cámara de Representantes** House of Representatives ► **cámara legislativa** legislative chamber ► **Cámara Regional** regional parliament
4 (*Hist*) [*de palacio*] royal chamber; **médico de ~** royal doctor; **gentilhombre de ~** gentleman-in-waiting; *ver tb* **ayuda B**
5 (*Náut*) (= *camarote*) cabin; [*de oficiales*] wardroom ► **cámara de cartas** chart house ► **cámara de motores** engine room
6 [*de neumático*] (inner) tube; **cubierta sin ~** tubeless tyre, tubeless tire (*EEUU*)
7 (*Mec*) ► **cámara de combustión** combustion chamber ► **cámara de compresión** compression chamber ► **cámara de oxígeno** oxygen tent
8 (*Anat*) cavity
9 **cámaras** (*Med*†) diarrhoea *sing*, diarrhea *sing* (*EEUU*); ✦**MODISMO tener ~s en la lengua** to tell tales (out of school)
Ⓑ SMF camera operator, cameraman/camerawoman

camarada SMF 1 (*en partido político*) comrade
2 (*en el trabajo*) colleague; (*en el colegio*) school friend
3 (= *amigo*) pal*, mate*, buddy (*EEUU**)

camaradería SF (*en partido político*) comradeship; (*entre amigos*) camaraderie, matiness*; (*en deportes*) camaraderie, team spirit

camarata‡ SM waiter

camarera SF (*en hotel*) maid, chambermaid; (*en casa*) parlourmaid

camarero/a Ⓐ SM/F 1 (*en restaurante*) waiter/waitress ► **camarero/a principal** head waiter, maître (d'hôtel) (*EEUU*)
2 (*Náut*) steward/stewardess; (*Aer*) steward/stewardess, flight attendant (*EEUU*)
Ⓑ SM (*Hist*) chamberlain ► **camarero mayor** (*Hist*) royal chamberlain

camareta SF (*Náut*) cabin ► **camareta alta** deckhouse

camarico SM (*Cono Sur*) 1 (= *lugar*) favourite place 2 (= *amor*) love affair

camarilla SF 1 [*de presidente etc*] entourage; (*pey*) clique, coterie
2 (*en organización*) faction; (*en partido*) (party) caucus; (*en cuerpo legislativo*) lobby, pressure group
3 (= *cuarto*) small room

camarín SM 1 (*Teat*) dressing room; (= *tocador*) boudoir; (= *cuarto pequeño*) side room
2 (*Rel*) (*para imagen*) chapel; (*para joyas*) *room where jewels etc belonging to an image are kept*
3 (*LAm*) [*de tren*] sleeping compartment; [*de barco*] cabin; [*de ascensor*] lift car, elevator car (*EEUU*)

camarista SMF (*Arg*) member of Court of Appeal

camarógrafo/a SM/F cameraman/camerawoman

camarón SM 1 (*Zool*) shrimp
2 (*CAm*) (= *propina*) tip, gratuity
3 (*Andes**) (= *traidor*) turncoat; **hacer ~** to change sides, go over to the other side *o* camp
4 (*CAm**) (= *trabajo*) casual *o* occasional work
5 (*Cono Sur*) (= *litera*) bunk (bed)

camaronear ▸conjug 1a◂ VI 1 (*Méx*) (= *pescar camarones*) to go shrimping
2 (*Andes Pol*) to change sides

camaronero SM (*Andes*) kingfisher

camarote SM (*Náut*) cabin ► **camarote de lujo** first-class cabin, stateroom

camarotero SM (*LAm*) steward, cabin servant

camaruta* SF bar girl

camastro SM rickety old bed

camastrón Ⓐ ADJ (*) sly, untrustworthy
Ⓑ SM (*CAm*) (= *cama*) large bed, double bed

camayo SM (*Perú Agr*) foreman, overseer (*of a country estate*)

cambado ADJ (*Andes, Caribe, Cono Sur*) bow-legged

cambalache SM 1 (= *trueque*) swap, exchange
2 (*LAm*) (= *tienda*) secondhand shop, junk shop

cambalachear ▸conjug 1a◂ VT to swap, exchange

cambar ▸conjug 1a◂ VT (*Caribe, Cono Sur*) = **combar**

cámbaro SM crayfish

cambiable ADJ [1] (= *modificable*) changeable
[2] (= *intercambiable*) exchangeable (**por** for)

cambiadiscos SM INV record-changer

cambiadizo ADJ changeable

cambiado ADJ [1] (= *diferente*) **estás muy cambiada desde la última vez que te vi** you've really changed since the last time I saw you
[2] (= *intercambiado*) reversed; **sus padres tenían los papeles ~s** the parents' roles were reversed

cambiador SM [*de dinero*] moneychanger; [*de productos*] barterer; (*LAm Ferro*) pointsman, switchman (*EEUU*)

cambiante Ⓐ ADJ (= *variable*) [*situación*] changing; [*tiempo, viento*] changeable; [*persona, carácter*] moody; **vivimos en un mundo ~** we live in an ever-changing world
Ⓑ SMF (= *cambista*) moneychanger
Ⓒ SM [1] (= *tela*) iridescent fabric
[2] **cambiantes** (*en nácar, tela*) changing colours, iridescence *sing*

cambiar ▸conjug 1b◂ Ⓐ VT [1] (= *modificar*) to change; **tendremos que ~ el color de nuestro logotipo** we'll need to change the colour of our logo; **eso no cambia mucho las cosas** that doesn't change things much
[2] (= *intercambiar*) to exchange, swap*; **te cambio el rotulador verde por el rojo** I'll exchange my green pen for that red one, I'll swap you the green pen for the red one*; **¿me cambias el sitio?** can we change places?, can we swap places?*
[3] (= *reemplazar*) to change; **¿les has cambiado el agua a los peces?** have you changed the water in the fish tank?; **ha ido a ~le los pañales al niño** she's gone to change the baby's nappy; **¿me lo puede ~ por otra talla?** could I change *o* exchange this for another size?
[4] (= *trasladar*) to move; **van a ~ la oficina al piso de arriba** they are going to move the office up a floor; **nos van a ~ de aula** they are moving us to another classroom
[5] (*Fin, Com*) to change; **tengo que ~ 800 euros en** *o* (*LAm*) **a libras** I have to change 800 euros into pounds; **¿tienes para ~me 50 euros?** have you got change for a 50-euro note?
Ⓑ VI [1] (= *volverse diferente*) [*persona, situación*] to change; [*voz*] to break; **desde que te fuiste nada ha cambiado** nothing has changed since you left; **nada lo hará ~** nothing will make him change; **si es así, la cosa cambia** if it's true, that changes things, well that's a different story then; **con doce años ya le había cambiado la voz** his voice had already broken at the age of twelve
[2] **~ de** [+ *actitud, canal, dirección*] to change; [+ *casa*] to move; **cuando no le interesa algo, cambia de tema** whenever he isn't interested in something, he changes the subject; **su vida cambió de rumbo 180 grados** the course of her life changed completely; **tú lo que necesitas es ~ de aires** what you need is a change of scene; **~ de dueño** to change hands; **~ de idea** *u* **opinión** to change one's mind; **~ para mejor/peor** to change for the better/worse; *ver tb* **camisa 1**, **tercio 2**
[3] (*Transporte*) to change; **tienes que ~ en King's Cross** you have to change at King's Cross
[4] (*Radio*) **¡cambio!** over!; **¡cambio y corto!** ◊ **¡cambio y fuera!** over and out!
Ⓒ **cambiarse** VPR [1] [*persona*] to change, get changed; **me cambio y estoy lista** I'll just change *o* I'll just get changed and then I'll be ready
[2] [+ *peinado, ropa, camisa*] to change; **¿te has cambiado el peinado?** have you changed your hairstyle?
[3] **~se de algo** to change sth; **llovió tanto que tuve que ~me de chaqueta** it rained so much that I had to change jackets; **para ~se de médico hay que rellenar este formulario** to change doctors you need to fill in this form; **~se de casa** to move house
[4] (= *intercambiarse*) to exchange, swap*; **¿nos cambiamos las camisetas?** shall we exchange *o* swap* T-shirts?; **siempre están cambiándose la ropa** they are always borrowing each other's clothes; **~se por algn** to change places with sb, swap places with sb*; **no me ~ía por ella** I wouldn't want to swap* *o* change places with her

➤ LENGUA Y USO: cambio 4 44.1

cambiario ADJ (*Fin*) exchange *antes de s*; **estabilidad cambiaria** stability of *o* in the exchange rate; **liberalización cambiaria** freeing of exchange controls *o* rates *etc*

cambiavía SM (*Caribe, Méx Ferro*) [1] (= *persona*) pointsman, switchman (*EEUU*)
[2] (= *agujas*) points *pl*, switch (*EEUU*)

cambiazo* SM (*Com*) switch; **dar el ~** to switch the goods; **dar el ~ a algn** to switch the goods on sb

▼**cambio** SM [1] (= *variación*) change; **ha habido un ~ de planes** there has been a change of plan; **el matrimonio supuso un ~ radical en mi vida** marriage meant a complete change in my life; **el entrenador ha hecho ya tres ~s en lo que va de partido** the coach has already made three substitutions *o* changes so far in the match; **estamos en la época de ~ entre el otoño y el invierno** we are in the changeover period between autumn and winter; **necesito un ~ de aires** I need a change of scene; **siempre nos veíamos durante el ~ de clase** we always used to meet in the break between classes; **un ~ para mejor/peor** a change for the better/worse ► **cambio climático** climatic change ► **cambio de agujas** (*Ferro*) points junction, switch junction (*EEUU*) ► **cambio de domicilio** change of address ► **cambio de gobierno** (*completo*) change of government; (*parcial*) reshuffle ► **cambio de guardia** changing of the guard ► **cambio de impresiones** exchange of views ► **cambio de la marea** turn of the tide ► **cambio de línea** (*Inform*) line feed ► **cambio de marchas** (= *acción*) gear change; (= *mecanismo*) gear stick, gearshift (*EEUU*); **hacer el ~ de marchas** to change gear; **un coche con ~ automático de marchas** a car with an automatic gearbox ► **cambio de opinión** change of opinion, turn in opinion ► **cambio de página** (*Inform*) form feed ► **cambio de pareja** change of partners (*in dancing*) ► **cambio de rasante**: **prohibido adelantar en un ~ de rasante** no overtaking on the brow of a hill ► **cambio de sentido** change of direction ► **cambio de sexo** sex change ► **cambio de tercio** (*Taur*) change of stage (*in a bullfight*); **se produjo un ~ de tercio en la conversación** the conversation changed direction *o* subject ► **cambio de velocidades** = **cambio de marchas** ► **cambio de vía** (*Ferro*) points *pl*, switches *pl* (*EEUU*); **hacer el ~ de vía** to go through the points *o* switches ► **cambio genético** genetic change
[2] (= *intercambio*) exchange, swap*; **hicimos un ~ de coche** we exchanged cars, we swapped cars*; **salimos ganando con el ~** the exchange worked out in our favour
[3] (*Fin*) [3·1] (= *dinero suelto*) change; **no tengo ~ para el teléfono** I don't have any change for the phone; **¿tienes ~ de 50 euros?** do you have change for 50 euros?, can you change 50 euros?; **quédese con el ~** keep the change; **te han dado mal el ~** they've given you the wrong change
[3·2] [*de moneda extranjera*] (= *tipo*) exchange rate; **son 40 dólares al ~** that is 40 dollars at the current exchange rate; **al ~ del mes de febrero** at the February exchange rate; **"Cambio"** "Bureau de Change", "Change" ► **cambio a término** forward exchange ► **cambio de divisas** foreign exchange
[4] **a ~** in return, in exchange; **lo ganó todo sin ceder nada a ~** he won it all without giving anything in return; **"admitimos su coche usado a ~"** "cars taken in part exchange", "trade-ins accepted"; **a ~ de** in return for, in exchange for; **reclamaba dinero a ~ de su silencio** he demanded money in return *o* exchange for keeping quiet (about it)
[5] **en ~** whereas; **yo nunca llego a tiempo, en ~ ella es muy puntual** I never arrive on time, whereas she is very punctual; **¿pero qué ha sucedido en ~?** but instead, what has happened?

cambista SMF money changer

Camboya SF Cambodia, Kampuchea

camboyano/a ADJ, SM/F Cambodian, Kampuchean

cambray SM cambric

cambrón SM (= *espino*) buckthorn; (= *zarza*) bramble

cambrona* SF (*Cono Sur*) tough cotton cloth

cambucho SM (*Cono Sur*) (= *cono*) paper cone; (= *cesta*) straw basket for waste paper *o* dirty clothes; (= *tapa*) straw cover (*for a bottle*); (= *cuartucho*) miserable little room

cambujo/a (*CAm, Méx*) Ⓐ ADJ [*animal*] black; [*persona*] dark, swarthy
Ⓑ SM/F mestizo

cambullón* SM (*LAm*) (= *estafa*) swindle; (= *compló*) plot, intrigue; (= *cambio*) swap, exchange

cambur SM (*Ven*) [1] (= *plátano*) banana; (= *árbol*) banana tree
[2] (*) (= *prebenda*) government post, soft job, cushy number*; (= *dinero*) windfall
[3] (= *funcionario*) public servant, state employee

cambuto ADJ (*Perú*) (= *pequeño*) small, squat; (= *gordito*) chubby

camelar ▸conjug 1a◂ VT [1] (= *persuadir*) to cajole, win over; **tener camelado a algn** to have sb wrapped round one's little finger
[2] [+ *mujer*] (= *flirtear*) to flirt with, make up to*; (= *conquistar*) to attract
[3] (*Méx*) (= *mirar*) to look into, look towards *etc*; (= *espiar*) to spy on; (= *perseguir*) to pursue, hound

camelia SF camellia

camelista SMF [1] (= *cuentista*) joker
[2] (= *halagador*) flatterer, bootlicker*

camellar* ▸conjug 1a◂ VI (*Caribe*) to work (hard)

camellear: ▸conjug 1a◂ VI to push drugs, be a pusher

camelleo: SM drug-pushing

camellero SM camel driver

camello SM [1] (*Zool*) camel ► **camello bactriano** Bactrian camel
[2] (‡) (= *traficante*) dealer*, pusher*
[3] (*Náut*) camel

camellón SM [1] (*Méx Aut*) central reserve *o* reservation, median strip (*EEUU*)
[2] (= *bebedero*) drinking trough
[3] (*Agr*) ridge (*between furrows*)

camelo* SM [1] (= *timo*) swindle; **¡esto es un ~!** it's all a swindle!; **me huele a ~** it smells fishy*, there's something funny going on here
[2] (= *mentira*) humbug; **dar ~ a algn** (= *reírse*) to make fun of sb; (= *engañar*) to put one over on sb; **a mí me da que es un ~** I don't believe a word of it*
[3] (= *flirteo*) flirtation; (= *coba*) blarney

camerino SM (*Teat*) dressing room; (*Méx Ferro*) roomette

camero ADJ [1] [*colcha, sábana*] for a three-quarter bed; **cama camera** three-quarter bed
[2] (*Caribe*) (= *grande*) big

Camerún SM Cameroon

camilla SF (*Med*) stretcher; (= *sofá*) couch, sofa; (= *cuna*) cot; (= *mesa*) table with a heater underneath

camillero/a SM/F stretcher-bearer

camilucho SM (*Cono Sur, Méx*) Indian day labourer

caminante SMF (= *viajero*) traveller, traveler (*EEUU*), wayfarer (*liter*); (*a pie*) walker

caminar ▸conjug 1a◂ Ⓐ VI [1] (= *andar*) to walk; **iban caminando por el parque** they were walking in the park; **fuimos caminando a casa de María** we walked to María's house; **hemos venido caminando** we walked (here), we came on foot; **salen a ~ después de comer** they go (out) for a walk after lunch; **~ sin rumbo** to walk *o* wander about aimlessly
[2] (= *progresar*) to move; **el cortejo caminaba en silencio** the funeral procession was moving silently; **caminamos hacia una sociedad sin clases** we are moving towards a classless society
[3] (*LAm*) (= *funcionar*) to work; **esto no camina** this doesn't work
Ⓑ VT to walk; **caminamos cuatro kilómetros** we walked four kilometres

caminata SF (= *paseo largo*) long walk; (*campestre*) hike, ramble

caminero Ⓐ ADJ **peón ~** navvy, road labourer, road laborer (*EEUU*)
Ⓑ SM (*LAm*) road builder

caminito SM ► **caminito de rosas** (*fig*) primrose path

camino SM [1] (*sin asfaltar*) track; (= *sendero*) path; (= *carretera*) road; **un ~ de montaña** a mountain path; **~ de tierra** dirt track; **~ sin firme** unsurfaced road; ✦*MODISMO* **todos los ~s conducen a Roma** all roads lead to Rome ► **Caminos, Canales y Puertos** (*Univ*) Civil Engineering ► **camino de acceso** access road ► **camino de Damasco** road to Damascus ► **camino de entrada** access road ► **camino de herradura** bridle path ► **camino de ingresos, camino de peaje** toll road ► **camino de rosas**: **la vida no es ningún ~ de rosas** life's no bed of roses ► **Camino de Santiago** *pilgrims' route to Santiago de Compostela*, Way of St James ► **camino de sirga** towpath ► **camino forestal** forest track; (*para paseos*) forest trail ► **camino francés** (*Hist*) = **Camino de Santiago** ► **camino real** highroad (*also fig*) ► **camino trillado**: **~s turísticos no trillados** tourist routes that are off the beaten track; **experimentan con nuevas técnicas, huyen de los ~s trillados** they are experimenting with new techniques and avoiding conventional approaches *o* the well-trodden paths; **este escritor ha recorrido los ~s trillados de sus antecesores** this writer has been down the well-trodden paths followed by his predecessors ► **camino vecinal** minor road
[2] (= *ruta*) [2·1] (*lit*) way, route; (= *viaje*) journey; **volvimos por el ~ más corto** we took the shortest way *o* route back; **¿sabes el ~ a su casa?** do you know the way to his house?; **es mucho ~** it's a long way; **está a varios días de ~** it's several days' journey away; **después de tres horas de ~** after travelling for three hours; **nos quedan 20 kms de ~** we still have 20 kms to go; **¿cuánto ~ hay de aquí a San José?** how far is it from here to San José?; **~ de Lima** on the way to Lima; **iba ~ de Nueva York** I was on my way to New York; __abrirse__ **~ entre la multitud** to make one's way through the crowd; __de__ **~ a**: **lo puedo recoger de ~ al trabajo** I can collect it on my way to work; **la farmacia me queda de ~** the chemist's is on my way; __echar__ **~ adelante** to strike out; __en__ **el ~** on the way, en route; **nos encontramos en el ~ a Zaragoza** we met on the way to Zaragoza; **tienen dos niños, y otro en ~** they have two children, and another on the way; **ponerse en ~** to set out *o* off; **a** __medio__ **~** halfway (there); **a medio ~ paramos para comer** halfway there, we stopped to eat; **se quedaron a** __mitad__ **de ~** they only got halfway (there); **a mitad de ~ entre Dublín y la frontera** halfway between Dublin and the border; **la verdad está a mitad de ~ entre las dos posturas** the truth is somewhere between the two views
[2·2] (*fig*) (= *medio*) path, course; **es el ~ a la fama** it's the path to fame; **es el ~ al desastre** it's the road to ruin; **el ~ a** __seguir__: **yo te explico el ~ a seguir** I'll tell you the way *o* route; **me indicaron el ~ a seguir para resolver el problema** they showed me what needed to be done to solve the problem; **censurar estos programas no es el ~ a seguir** censoring these programmes isn't the solution *o* the right thing to do; ✦*MODISMOS* **abrirse ~ en la vida** to get ahead (in life); **allanar el ~**: **eso sería allanar el ~ a sus adversarios** that would make things easy for their rivals; **los nervios de su rival le allanaron el ~** her opponent's nerves made it easy for her; **errar el ~** to lose one's way; **estar en ~** to be on the way; **estamos en ~ de solucionar el problema** we're on the way to solving the problem; **está en ~ de desaparecer** it's on its way out; **ir ~ de**: **va ~ de convertirse en un gran centro financiero** it is on its way to becoming a major financial centre; **vamos ~ del desastre** we are heading for disaster; **ir por buen ~** to be on the right track; **traer a algn por buen ~** (= *orientar*) to put sb on the right track *o* road; (= *desengañar*) to set sb straight; **ir por mal ~** to be on the wrong track; **las cosas van por buen ~** things are going well; **llevar a algn por mal ~** to lead sb astray; **quedarse en el ~**: **varios corredores se quedaron en el ~** several runners didn't make it to the end; **un 70% sacó el diploma y el resto se quedó en el ~** 70 per cent of them got the diploma, the rest didn't make it; **ir por su ~** to go one's own sweet way; **en vez de seguir las normas él fue por su ~** instead of following the rules he just went his own sweet way *o* did his own thing; **no me fijo en mis rivales, yo sigo por mi ~** I don't take any notice of what my rivals are doing, I just do my own thing; **tirar por el ~ de en medio** to take the middle way
[3] (*Inform*) path
[4] (*Andes, Cono Sur*) (= *alfombra, tapete*) runner, strip of carpet *o* matting ► **camino de mesa** table runner

CAMINO DE SANTIAGO

The **Camino de Santiago** *is a medieval pilgrim route stretching from the Pyrenees to Santiago de Compostela in northwest Spain, where tradition has it that the body of Saint James the Apostle (Spain's patron saint) is buried. At one time Santiago de Compostela came next only to Jerusalem and Rome as the most popular destination for Christian pilgrims from all over Europe. Those who had made the long, dangerous journey returned proudly wearing on their hat or cloak the* **venera** *or* **concha** *(scallop shell) traditionally associated with this pilgrimage — Saint James' body had reportedly been found covered in scallops. Today this symbolic shell can still be seen all along the* **Camino de Santiago**, *carved on ancient buildings and painted on modern-day road signs marking the historic route for the benefit of tourists and pilgrims.*
In astronomy the **Camino de Santiago** *is another name for the* **Vía Láctea** *(Milky Way), hence the title of Buñuel's famous satirical film about the route to Compostela.*

camión SM (*Aut*) lorry, truck (*esp EEUU*); [*de reparto*] van; [*de caballos*] heavy wagon, dray; (*Méx*) bus; (= *carga*) lorryload, truckload (*esp EEUU*); **dos camiones de alimentos** two lorryloads of food; **estar como un ~*** to be a smasher*, be gorgeous ► **camión articulado** articulated lorry, trailer truck (*EEUU*) ► **camión blindado** armoured truck, armored truck (*EEUU*) ► **camión bomba** lorry bomb, truck bomb ► **camión cisterna** tanker, tank wagon ► **camión de agua** water cart, water wagon ► **camión de bomberos** fire engine ► **camión de caja a bajo nivel** low loader ► **camión de carga** haulage truck ► **camión de la basura** dustcart, refuse lorry, garbage truck (*EEUU*) ► **camión de mudanzas** removal van, moving van (*EEUU*) ► **camión de reparto** delivery van ► **camión de riego** water cart, water wagon ► **camión de volteo** (*Méx*) dump truck ► **camión frigorífico** refrigerator lorry, refrigerated truck ► **camión ganadero** cattle truck ► **camión vivienda** camper van ► **camión volquete** dump truck, tipper truck

camionaje SM haulage, trucking (*EEUU*)

camionero/a SM/F 1 lorry driver, truck driver (*EEUU*)
2 (*Méx*) (*en autobús*) bus driver

camioneta SF (= *camión*) van, light truck; (= *coche*) estate car, station wagon (*EEUU*); (*CAm*) (= *autobús*) bus; (*Caribe*) minibus ► **camioneta de reparto** delivery van ► **camioneta detectora** detector van ► **camioneta de tina** (*CAm*) pick-up (truck)

camión-grúa SM (*pl* **camiones-grúa**) tow truck, towing vehicle

camionista SM = **camionero**

camión-tanque SM (*pl* **camiones-tanque**) tanker

camisa SF 1 (= *prenda*) shirt; ✦*MODISMOS* **cambiar de ~** to change sides; **jugarse hasta la ~** to put one's shirt on it*, bet one's last penny; **no llegarle a algn la ~ al cuerpo**: **no le llegaba la ~ al cuerpo** he was simply terrified; **meterse en ~ de once varas** to get into it way over one's head; **perder hasta la ~** to lose everything, lose the shirt off one's back ► **camisa de dormir** nightdress ► **camisa de fuerza** straitjacket; *ver tb* **manga 1**
2 (*LAm*) garment, article of clothing
3 (= *piel*) [*de serpiente*] slough; [*de guisante, trigo*] skin
4 (*Mec*) case, casing ► **camisa de agua** water jacket ► **camisa de gas** gas mantle
5 [*de libro*] dust jacket

camisería SF (= *tienda*) outfitter's; (= *taller*) shirtmaker's

camisero Ⓐ ADJ [*blusa, vestido*] shirt *antes de s*
Ⓑ SM (*que confecciona*) shirt maker; (= *vendedor*) outfitter

camiseta SF 1 (*interior*) vest, singlet, undershirt (*EEUU*); (*exterior*) T-shirt; **una ~ de algodón** a cotton vest; **una ~ sin mangas** a sleeveless vest; **una ~ de tirantes** a vest; ✦*MODISMO* **ponerse la ~** (*Cono Sur**) to roll up one's sleeves, put one's back into it
2 (*Dep*) shirt, jersey, strip; **la ~ de la selección nacional** the national team shirt *o* jersey; ✦*MODISMO* **sudar la ~*** to sweat blood ► **camiseta de deporte** sports shirt, sports jersey
3 (*LAm*) nightdress

camisilla SF (*Caribe, Cono Sur*) = **camiseta**

camisola SF (*Méx*) sports shirt

camisolín SM stiff shirt front, dickey

camisón SM [*de mujer*] nightdress, nightgown; [*de hombre*] nightshirt

camita[1] ADJ, **camítico** ADJ (*de Cam*) Hamitic

camita[2] SF (= *cama*) small bed, cot

camomila SF camomile

camón SM (= *cama grande*) big bed; (*Arquit*) oriel window ► **camón de vidrios** glass partition

camorra SF fight, row, set-to*; **armar ~** to kick up a row; **buscar ~** to go looking for trouble

camorrear* ▸conjug 1a◂ VI (*CAm, Cono Sur*) to have a row

camorrero/a ADJ, SM/F = **camorrista**

camorrista Ⓐ ADJ rowdy, troublemaking
Ⓑ SMF rowdy, hooligan

camotal SM (*LAm*) sweet potato field *o* plot

camote SM 1 (*LAm*) (= *batata*) sweet potato; (*Méx*) (= *bulbo*) tuber, bulb
2 (*CAm, Cono Sur Med*) bump, swelling
3 (*Cono Sur*) (= *piedra*) large stone
4 (*Cono Sur*) (= *persona*) bore
5 (*CAm*) [*de pierna*] calf
6 (*CAm**) (= *molestia*) nuisance, bother
7 (*LAm*) (= *amor*) love; (= *enamoramiento*) crush*; **tener un ~ con algn** to have a crush on sb*
8 (*Andes, Cono Sur**) (= *amante*) lover, sweetheart
9 (*Cono Sur*) (= *mentirilla*) fib
10 (*Andes, Cono Sur*) (= *tonto*) fool
11 (*LAm**) **poner a algn como ~** to give sb a telling off*; ✦*MODISMO* **tragar ~** (= *tener miedo*) to have one's heart in one's mouth; (= *balbucir*) to stammer

camotear ▸conjug 1a◂ Ⓐ VI 1 (*Méx*) (= *vagar*) to wander about aimlessly
2 (*CAm*) (= *molestar*) to be a nuisance, cause trouble
Ⓑ VT 1 (*Cono Sur*) (= *estafar*) to rob, fleece*; (= *engañar*) to take for a ride*
2 (*CAm*) (= *molestar*) to annoy

campa Ⓐ SF open field, open space
Ⓑ ADJ INV **tierra ~** treeless land

campal ADJ **batalla ~** pitched battle

campamentista SMF camper

campamento SM camp, encampment; **~ para prisioneros** prison camp; **~ de refugiados** refugee camp ► **campamento de base** base camp ► **campamento de trabajo** labour *o* (*EEUU*) labor camp ► **campamento de verano** holiday camp

campana Ⓐ SF 1 [*de iglesia, puerta*] bell; [*de orquesta*] bell, chime; **a ~ tañida** ◊ **a toque de ~** to the sound of bells; ✦*MODISMOS* **echar** *o* **lanzar las ~s a vuelo** to celebrate; **aún es pronto para echar las ~s al vuelo** it's still too early to celebrate *o* to start spreading the good news; **estar ~** (*Caribe**) to be fine; **hacer ~(s)*** to play truant; **oír ~s (y no saber de dónde vienen)** not to have a clue
2 (*Téc*) [*de la chimenea*] hood ► **campana de humos**, **campana extractora** extractor hood
3 (*Buceo*) ► **campana de buzo**, **campana de inmersión** diving bell
4 (*Cono Sur*) (= *campo*) country(side)
Ⓑ SMF (*LAm**) (= *vigilante*) look-out; **hacer de ~** to keep watch

campanada SF 1 [*de campana*] stroke, peal
2 (= *escándalo*) scandal, sensation; **detener al Ministro sería una ~ tremenda** arresting the Minister would cause a tremendous scandal *o* stir; **dar la ~** to cause (quite) a stir

campanario SM 1 [*de iglesia etc*] belfry, bell tower, church tower
2 (*pey*) **de ~** mean, narrow-minded; **espíritu de ~** parochial *o* parish-pump attitude

campanazo SM 1 = **campanada 2**
2 (*Andes*) (= *advertencia*) warning

campaneado ADJ much talked-of

campanear ▸conjug 1a◂ VI 1 (*Mús*) to ring the bells
2 (*LAm**) [*ladrón*] to keep watch

campaneo SM pealing, chiming

campanero SM (*Téc*) bell founder; (*Mús*) bell ringer

campaniforme ADJ bell-shaped

campanilla SF 1 (= *campana*) small bell, handbell; (*eléctrica*) bell; **de (muchas) ~s** high-class, grand
2 (= *burbuja*) bubble
3 (*Anat*) uvula
4 (*Cos*) tassel
5 (*Bot*) bellflower, campanula ► **campanilla blanca**, **campanilla de febrero** snowdrop

campanillazo SM loud ring, sudden ring

campanillear ▸conjug 1a◂ VI to ring, tinkle

campanilleo SM ringing, tinkling

campanología SF campanology, bell-ringing

campanólogo/a SM/F campanologist, bell-ringer

campante ADJ 1 (= *despreocupado*) **siguió tan ~** he went on as if nothing had happened *o* without batting an eyelid; **allí estaba tan ~** there he sat as cool as a cucumber
2 (= *destacado*) outstanding

campanudo ADJ 1 [*objeto*] bell-shaped; [*falda*] wide, flared
2 [*estilo*] high-flown, bombastic, windy*; [*orador*] pompous; **dijo ~** he said pompously

campánula SF bellflower, campanula ► **campánula azul** bluebell

campaña SF 1 (*Pol, Com*) campaign; **una ~ antidroga** an anti-drugs campaign, a campaign against drugs; **una ~ de recogida de firmas** a petition; **hacer ~** to campaign ► **campaña de descrédito**, **campaña de desprestigio** smear campaign ► **campaña de imagen** image campaign ► **campaña de protesta** protest campaign ► **campaña de publicidad** advertising campaign ► **campaña de ventas** sales campaign ► **campaña electoral** election campaign ► **campaña publicitaria** advertising campaign
2 (*Mil*) campaign; **la ~ de Rusia** the Russian campaign; *ver tb* **hospital**, **tienda 2**, **traje**[2]
3 (= *campo*) countryside; (= *llano*) plain

campañol SM vole

campar ▸conjug 1a◂ VI 1 (*Mil etc*) to camp
2 (= *sobresalir*) to stand out, excel; **~ por sus respetos** to please o.s.

campear ▸conjug 1a◂ VI 1 (*Agr*) [*ganado*] to go to graze, go out to pasture; [*persona*] to work in the fields
2 (*Bot*) to show green
3 (*Mil*) to reconnoitre; (*LAm*) to scour the countryside
4 **ir campeando*** to carry on, keep going
5 (*LAm*) (= *ir de camping*) to camp, go camping
6 (*Andes*) (= *atravesar*) to make one's way through
7 (*Andes*) (= *fardar*) to bluster

campechana SF 1 (*Caribe, Méx*) (= *bebida*) cocktail
2 (*Méx*) [*de mariscos*] seafood cocktail

campechanería SF, **campechanía** SF (= *cordialidad*) good nature, cheerfulness; (= *franqueza*) frankness, openness; (= *generosidad*) generosity

campechano ADJ 1 (= *cordial*) good-natured, cheerful, genial; (= *franco*) frank, open; (= *generoso*) generous; (= *amigable*) comradely
2 (*Caribe**) (= *campesino*) peasant *antes de s*

campeón/ona SM/F champion ► **campeón/ona de venta** best seller

campeonar ▸conjug 1a◂ VI to win the championship, emerge as champion

campeonato SM [1] (*Dep*) championship; **el ~ de Liga** the League championship; **los ~s de pista cubierta** the indoor championships
[2] (*Esp**) **de ~: se armó una bronca de ~** there was one hell of an argument*; **se agarra unas borracheras de ~** he gets incredibly *o* unbelievably drunk, he gets blind drunk*

campeonísimo/a SM/F undisputed champion

campera SF (*Arg*) windcheater, bomber jacket* ► **campera de duvet** (*Cono Sur*) quilted jacket

campero Ⓐ ADJ [1] (= *al descubierto*) unsheltered, (out) in the open; **fiesta campera** open-air party; **ganado ~** stock that sleeps out in the open
[2] (*LAm*) [*persona*] knowledgeable about the countryside; (= *experto en agricultura*) expert in farming matters
[3] [*animal*] trained to travel in difficult country, sure-footed
Ⓑ SM (*Col*) (= *vehículo*) four-wheel drive (vehicle)

camperuso/a* (*Caribe*) Ⓐ ADJ [1] (= *rural*) rural, rustic
[2] (= *huraño*) reserved, stand-offish
Ⓑ SM/F (= *campesino*) peasant

campesinado SM peasantry, peasants *pl*

campesino/a Ⓐ ADJ [*población*] rural; [*familia, revuelta*] peasant *antes de s*; **una organización campesina** an organization representing peasant farmers; **siempre ocultó su origen ~** she always concealed her rustic *o* peasant origins; **la vida campesina** country life, rural life
Ⓑ SM/F [1] (= *persona del campo*) country person
[2] (= *labrador*) farmer; (= *labrador pobre*) peasant
[3] (*Andes*) (= *indio*) Indian

campestre ADJ [1] country *antes de s*, rural
[2] (*Bot*) wild

camping ['kampin] SM (*pl* **campings** ['kampin]) [1] (= *actividad*) camping; **estar** *o* **ir de ~** to go camping; **hacer ~** to go camping
[2] (= *lugar*) campsite, campground (*EEUU*)

campiña SF (= *campo*) countryside, open country; (*cultivado*) flat stretch of farmland, large area of cultivated land

campirano/a SM/F (*LAm*) [1] (= *campesino*) peasant; (*pey*) rustic, country bumpkin, hick (*EEUU**)
[2] (*Agr*) (= *perito*) expert in farming matters; (= *guía*) guide, pathfinder; (= *jinete*) skilled horseman; (= *ganadero*) stockbreeding expert

campiruso/a ADJ, SM/F (*Caribe*) = **camperuso**

campista[1] SMF camper

campista[2] Ⓐ ADJ [1] (*CAm, Caribe*) rural, country *antes de s*
[2] (*LAm*) = **campero A2**
Ⓑ SM (*CAm*) herdsman, cattleman, herder (*EEUU*)

campisto Ⓐ ADJ (*CAm*) rural, country *antes de s*
Ⓑ SM [1] (*CAm*) (= *campesino*) peasant
[2] (*CAm Agr*) (= *veterinario*) amateur vet

campo SM [1] (= *terreno no urbano*) country; **viven en el ~** they live in the country *o* countryside; **los domingos salimos al ~** on Sundays we go out to the country; **el ~ está precioso** the countryside looks beautiful; **la gente del ~** country people *o* folk; **a ~ raso** out in the open ► **campo a través** cross-country; **campeonato de ~ a través** cross-country championship; **los tres prisioneros huyeron ~ a través** the three prisoners fled cross-country
[2] (*Agr*) (*para cultivar*) **un ~ de trigo** a wheat field; **~s de amapolas** poppy fields; **los obreros del ~** farm workers, agricultural workers; **los productos del ~** farm produce, country produce; **trabajar en el ~** to work the land ► **campo de cultivo** (*lit*) farm land; (*fig*) breeding ground
[3] (*Dep*) (= *estadio*) ground; (= *cancha*) pitch, field (*EEUU*); **jugaron en el ~ del Barcelona** they played at Barcelona's ground; **el portero tuvo que abandonar el ~** the goalkeeper had to leave the pitch *o* field; **el equipo perdió en su ~** the team lost at home ► **campo de deportes** sports ground ► **campo de fútbol** football pitch ► **campo de golf** golf course ► **campo de juego** playing field
[4] (= *espacio delimitado*) ► **campo de aterrizaje** landing field ► **Campo de Gibraltar** *Spanish territory around the border with Gibraltar* ► **campo de minas** minefield ► **campo de tiro** firing range; **estar dentro del ~ de tiro de algn** to be in sb's firing range ► **campo petrolífero** oilfield ► **campo santo** cemetery, churchyard ► **Campos Elíseos** (*en París*) Champs Elysées; (*Mit*) Elysian Fields
[5] (*Mil*) (= *campamento*) camp; **levantar el ~** (*Mil*) to break camp, strike camp; (= *irse*) to make tracks*; ✦**MODISMO dejar el ~ libre** to leave the field open ► **campo de aviación** airfield, airdrome (*EEUU*) ► **campo de batalla** battlefield; **quedar en el ~ de batalla** to fall in battle ► **campo de concentración** concentration camp ► **campo de ejercicios** exercise ground ► **campo de entrenamiento** training camp ► **campo de exterminio** extermination camp ► **campo de maniobras** training camp ► **campo de pruebas** testing ground ► **campo de refugiados** refugee camp ► **campo de trabajo** [*de castigo*] labour *o* (*EEUU*) labor camp; [*de vacaciones*] work camp
[6] (= *grupo*) field ► **campo alfanumérico** alphanumeric field ► **campo léxico** lexical field ► **campo numérico** numeric field ► **campo semántico** semantic field
[7] (= *ámbito*) field; **el ~ de las ciencias** the field of science; **investigación de ~** field investigation ► **campo de acción, campo de actuación** scope, room for manoeuvre *o* (*EEUU*) maneuver ► **campo de investigación** field of investigation ► **campo gravitatorio** gravity field, field of gravity ► **campo magnético** magnetic field ► **campo visual** field of vision, visual field; *ver tb* **trabajo 1**
[8] (*Arte*) background
[9] (*Heráldica*) field
[10] (*Andes*) (= *estancia*) farm, ranch; (*Cono Sur*) (= *tierra pobre*) barren land; (*Andes, Cono Sur Min*) mining concession
[11] (*LAm*) (= *espacio*) space, room; **no hay ~** there's no room *o* space

camposantero SM cemetery official

camposanto SM churchyard, graveyard, cemetery

Campsa SF ABR (*Esp*) = **Compañía Arrendataria de Monopolio de Petróleos, S.A.**

campus SM INV (*Univ*) campus

campusano SM, **campus(i)o** SM (*CAm*) peasant

camuesa SF pippin, dessert apple

camueso SM [1] (*Bot*) apple tree
[2] (*) (= *tonto*) dolt, blockhead*, clod (*EEUU**)

camuflado ADJ camouflaged; [*coche policial*] unmarked

camuflaje SM camouflage

camuflar ▸conjug 1a◂ VT to camouflage

can SM [1] (*hum*) (= *perro*) dog, mutt*, pooch*
[2] (*Mil*) trigger
[3] (*Arquit*) corbel

cana[1] SF (*tb* **~s**) white *o* grey *o* (*EEUU*) gray hair; ✦**MODISMOS echar una ~ al aire*** to let one's hair down; **faltar a las ~s** to show a lack of respect for one's elders; **peinar ~s** to be getting on

cana[2] (*LAm**) Ⓐ SF [1] (= *cárcel*) jail; (= *celda*) prison cell; **caer en ~** to land in jail
[2] (= *policía*) police
Ⓑ SM (= *policía*) policeman

canabis SM cannabis

canaca SMF [1] (*Andes, Cono Sur***) (= *chino*) Chink**, Chinese
[2] (*Cono Sur*) (= *dueño*) brothel-keeper; (= *burdel*) brothel

Canadá SM **el ~** Canada

canadiense Ⓐ ADJ, SMF Canadian
Ⓑ SM (*tb* **chaqueta ~**) lumber jacket

canal Ⓐ SM [1] (*Náut, Geog*) (*natural*) channel; (*artificial*) canal; **Canal de la Mancha** English Channel; **Canal de Panamá** Panama Canal ► **Canal de Suez** Suez Canal
[2] (*Agr, Ing*) (= *conducto*) channel ► **canal de desagüe** drain ► **canal de drenaje** drainage channel ► **canal de riego** irrigation channel
[3] (*Anat*) canal, tract ► **canal del parto** birth canal ► **canal digestivo** digestive tract
[4] (*TV*) channel; **no cambies de ~** don't change *o* switch channels ► **canal autonómico** *television channel of an autonomous region* ► **canal de pago** pay channel, subscription channel ► **canal de televentas** shopping channel ► **canal de televisión** television channel ► **canal por cable** cable channel ► **canal vía satélite** satellite channel
[5] (= *medio*) channel; **el problema se resolvió por los ~es habituales** the problem was resolved through the usual channels ► **canal de distribución** distribution channel ► **canales de comunicación** channels of communication, communication channels
[6] (*Caribe Aut*) lane
Ⓑ SF [1] (*Téc*) pipe, conduit ► **canal maestra** main pipe
[2] (*Arquit*) [*de columna*] groove; **~es** fluting *sing*
[3] (*Agr*) dressed carcass; **peso en ~** dressed weight

canaladura SF = **acanaladura**

canaleta SF (*Cono Sur*) (= *canalón*) gutter (*on roof*); (= *tubería*) pipe, conduit

canalete SM paddle

canalización SF [1] [*de un río*] canalization
[2] [*de inversiones etc*] channelling, channeling (*EEUU*)
[3] (*Téc*) piping; (*Elec*) wiring; [*de gas etc*] mains *pl*; (*LAm*) [*de cloacas*] sewerage system, drains

canalizar ▸conjug 1f◂ VT [1] [+ *río*] to canalize; [+ *agua*] to harness; (*por tubería*) to pipe; [+ *aguas de riego*] to channel

2 [+ *inversiones etc*] to channel, direct
3 (*Elec*) [+ *impulso, mensaje*] to carry

canalizo SM navigable channel

canalla* Ⓐ SMF swine*; **¡canalla!** you swine!
Ⓑ SF rabble, riffraff; **la ~ periodística** o **de la prensa** the press mob*

canallada SF (= *hecho*) dirty trick; (= *dicho*) nasty remark, vile thing to say

canallesco ADJ mean, despicable; **diversión canallesca** low form of amusement

canalón SM 1 (= *cañería*) (*en el tejado*) gutter, guttering; (= *bajante*) drainpipe
2 **canalones** (*Culin*) cannelloni

canana SF 1 (*Mil*) cartridge belt
2 (*LAm Med*) goitre
3 (*Caribe*) (= *mala pasada*) mean trick, dirty trick
4 **cananas** (*LAm*) (= *esposas*) handcuffs

canapé SM 1 (= *sofá*) sofa, couch
2 (*Culin*) canapé

Canarias SFPL (*tb* **las Islas ~**) the Canaries, the Canary Islands

canario[1]/a Ⓐ ADJ from/of the Canary Islands
Ⓑ SM/F Canary Islander, native/inhabitant of the Canary Isles; **los ~s** the people of the Canary Islands

canario[2] Ⓐ SM 1 (*Orn*) canary
2 (‡) prick**
3 (*LAm*) (= *amarillo*) canary yellow
Ⓑ EXCL (*) well I'm blowed!*

canarión/ona SM/F native/inhabitant of Gran Canaria

canasta SF 1 (= *cesta*) (round) basket; (*para comida*) hamper; (*Com*) crate ► **canasta para papeles** wastepaper basket
2 (*Baloncesto*) basket ► **canasta triple** three-point shot
3 (*Naipes*) canasta
4 (*Méx, Col Aut*) luggage rack

canastero/a SM/F basket maker, basketweaver

canastilla SF 1 [*de bebé*] (baby's) layette
2 (*Andes, Caribe, Cono Sur*) [*de novia*] trousseau; (*hum*) bottom drawer, hope chest (*EEUU*)
3 (= *cestita*) small basket; (*Méx*) (= *papelera*) wastepaper basket ► **canastilla de la costura** sewing basket

canastillo SM 1 (= *bandeja*) wicker tray, small basket
2 [*de bebé*] (baby's) layette

canasto SM 1 (= *cesto*) large basket; [*de comida*] hamper; (*Com*) crate
2 (*Col*) (= *criado*) servant
3 **¡canastos!** good heavens!

cáncamo SM (*Náut*) eyebolt ► **cáncamo de argolla** ringbolt

cancamurria* SF = **murria**

cancamusa* SF trick; **armar una ~ a algn** to throw sand in sb's eyes

cancán SM 1 (= *baile*) cancan
2 (= *enagua*) stiff, flounced petticoat
3 **cancanes** (*Cono Sur*) (= *pantimedias*) tights, pantyhose *sing* (*EEUU*)

cáncana SF (*Cono Sur*) [*de asar*] spit; [*de vela*] candlestick; (*Andes*) (= *persona*) thin person

cancanco* SM (*Caribe Aut*) breakdown

cancanear ▸conjug 1a◂ VI 1 (= *gandulear*) to loiter, loaf about
2 (*Cono Sur*) (= *bailar*) to dance the cancan
3 (*Andes, CAm, Méx*) (= *tartamudear*) to stammer; (= *expresarse mal*) to express o.s. with difficulty; (= *leer mal*) to read haltingly

cancaneo SM (*Andes, CAm, Méx*) (*al leer*) faltering; (= *tartamudeo*) stammering

cáncano SM louse; ✦**MODISMO andar como ~ loco** to go round in circles

cancel SM 1 (= *contrapuerta*) storm door, windproof door
2 (= *tabique*) partition, thin wall; (*Méx*) (= *mampara*) folding screen

cancela SF wrought-iron gate

cancelación SF cancellation; (*Inform*) deletion

cancelar ▸conjug 1a◂ VT 1 [+ *pedido, suscripción, tarjeta*] to cancel; [+ *cuenta bancaria*] to close
2 [+ *reunión, concierto, viaje, proyecto*] to cancel; **~on el vuelo a causa de la nieve** they cancelled the flight because of the snow
3 [+ *deuda*] to pay off; **tendré que ahorrar para ~ el crédito** I'll have to save up to pay off my debt
4 (*LAm*) (= *pagar*) to pay, settle

cancelaría SF papal chancery

cáncer SM 1 (*Med*) cancer ► **cáncer cervical, cáncer de cuello uterino** cervical cancer, cancer of the cervix ► **cáncer de los huesos** bone cancer ► **cáncer de mama** breast cancer ► **cáncer de ovario** ovarian cancer ► **cáncer de pulmón** lung cancer
2 **Cáncer** (*Astron*) Cancer

cancerado ADJ (*Med*) cancerous; (*fig*) corrupt

cancerarse ▸conjug 1a◂ VPR 1 (*Med*) [*tumor*] to become cancerous; [*persona*] to get cancer
2 (*fig*) to become corrupt

cancerbero SM 1 (= *guardameta*) goalkeeper
2 (*Mit*) **el Cancerbero** Cerberus

cancerígeno ADJ carcinogenic

cancerología SF (= *estudio*) study of cancer, cancer research; (= *tratamiento*) cancer treatment

cancerólogo/a SM/F cancer specialist

canceroso/a Ⓐ ADJ cancerous
Ⓑ SM/F cancer patient, cancer sufferer

cancha SF 1 (*Dep*) (= *de tenis, baloncesto*) court; [*de fútbol*] ground ► **cancha de bolos** (*LAm*) bowling alley ► **cancha de golf** (*LAm*) golf course
2 (*Cono Sur*) (= *espacio*) room; **abrir ~** to make way, make room; ✦**MODISMOS estar en su ~** to be in one's element; **dar ~ a algn: hay que dar ~ a los jóvenes escritores** we have to give a chance to young writers; **medios de difusión que dan mucha ~ a los terroristas** media that give a lot of coverage o exposure to terrorists
3 (*en aeropuerto*) ► **cancha de aterrizaje** (*Cono Sur*) landing strip, runway
4 (*LAm*) (= *experiencia*) experience; **tener ~** to be experienced
5 (*LAm*) (= *hipódromo*) racecourse, racetrack (*EEUU*); ✦**MODISMO en la ~ se ven los pingos** o **gallos** actions speak louder than words
6 (*LAm*) (= *maíz*) toasted corn
7 (*Andes**) (= *tajada*) cut

canchar ▸conjug 1a◂ VT (*Andes, Cono Sur*) to toast

canche ADJ 1 (*CAm*) (= *rubio*) blond(e)
2 (*Andes*) [*comida*] poorly seasoned, tasteless

canchero/a Ⓐ ADJ (*Cono Sur Dep*) experienced
Ⓑ SM/F 1 (*LAm Dep*) (= *cuidador*) groundsman/groundswoman; (= *jugador*) experienced player
2 (= *experto*) experienced person
3 (*Cono Sur*) (= *vago*) layabout, loafer

canchón SM (*Andes*) enclosed field

cancilla SF gate

canciller SMF 1 (= *presidente*) chancellor; **el ~ Kohl** Chancellor Kohl
2 (*LAm Pol*) (= *ministro*) ≈ Foreign Secretary, ≈ Secretary of State (*EEUU*), Minister for Foreign Affairs

cancilleresco ADJ chancellery *antes de s*, chancery *antes de s*; (= *diplomático*) diplomatic

cancillería SF (*en embajada*) chancery, chancellery; (*LAm*) (= *ministerio*) ministry of foreign affairs, foreign ministry

canción SF 1 (*Mús*) song ► **canción de amor** love song ► **canción de cuna** lullaby ► **canción infantil** nursery rhyme ► **canción protesta** protest song
2 (*Literat*) ballad ► **canción de gesta** chanson de geste, epic poem

cancionero SM (*Mús*) song book; (*Literat*) anthology, collection of verse

cancionista† SMF 1 (= *compositor*) songwriter
2 (= *cantante*) singer, vocalist; [*de baladas*] ballad singer

canco SM 1 (*Cono Sur*) (= *jarro*) earthenware jug; (= *tiesto*) flowerpot; (= *orinal*) chamberpot
2 **cancos** (*Andes, Cono Sur*) (= *nalgas*) buttocks; (= *caderas*) hips

cancro SM (*Bot*) canker; (*Med*) cancer

candado SM 1 (*gen*) padlock; [*de libro*] clasp, hasp; **cerrar algo con ~** to padlock sth; **poner algo bajo siete ~s** to lock sth safely away ► **candado digital** combination lock
2 (*Andes*) (= *barba*) goatee beard

candanga SM (*Méx*) **el ~** the devil

candar ▸conjug 1a◂ VT to lock

cande ADJ **azúcar ~** sugar candy, rock candy

candeal Ⓐ ADJ **pan ~** white bread; **trigo ~** bread wheat
Ⓑ SM (*Cono Sur Culin*) egg flip

candela SF 1 (= *vela*) candle; (= *candelero*) candlestick; (*Fís*) candle power; **en ~** (*Náut*) vertical; ✦**MODISMOS acabársele la ~ a algn‡: se le acabó la ~** he snuffed it‡; **arrimar ~ a algn*** to give sb a tanning*; **estar con la ~ en la mano** to be at death's door
2 (*esp LAm*) (= *fuego*) fire; (*para cigarro*) light; **pegar** o **prender ~ a** to set fire to, set alight; ✦**MODISMOS dar ~*** to be a nuisance; **dar ~ a algn*** to rough sb up*
3 (*Bot*) blossom

candelabro SM candelabra

Candelaria SF Candlemas

candelaria SF (*Bot*) mullein

candelejón* ADJ (*Andes*) simple, slow

candelero SM 1 (= *candelabro*) candlestick; (= *lámpara*) oil lamp; ✦**MODISMO en (el) ~: estar en el ~** [*persona*] to be in the spotlight o limelight; [*tema*] to be in the news; **poner algo en ~** to bring sth into the limelight; **tema en ~** hot topic, subject of great current interest
2 (*Náut*) stanchion

candelilla SF 1 (= *vela*) small candle
2 (*Bot*) catkin
3 (*LAm*) (= *luciérnaga*) glow worm; (*Cono Sur*) (= *libélula*) dragonfly; (*Andes*) (= *niño*) lively

child
4 (*Caribe, Cono Sur Cos*) hem, border

candelizo SM icicle

candelo ADJ (*Andes*) reddish-blond(e)

candencia SF white heat

candente ADJ 1 [*metal*] (= *rojo*) red-hot; (= *blanco*) white-hot
2 [*cuestión*] burning; **un tema de ~ actualidad** a red-hot issue, a subject that everyone is talking about

candi ADJ **azúcar ~** sugar candy, rock candy

candidatizar ▸conjug 1f◂ VT to propose, nominate

candidato/a SM/F 1 (= *aspirante*) candidate (**a** for); (*para puesto*) applicant (**a** for)
2 (*Cono Sur*‡) sucker‡

candidatura SF 1 (*a un cargo*) candidature, candidacy; **presentar su ~** to put o.s. forward for a post, stand for a post
2 (= *lista*) list of candidates; (= *papeleta*) ballot paper

candidez SF 1 (= *simpleza*) simplicity, ingenuousness; (= *inocencia*) naïveté; (= *estupidez*) stupidity
2 (= *comentario*) silly remark

cándido ADJ 1 (= *simple*) simple, ingenuous; (= *inocente*) naïve; (= *estúpido*) stupid
2 (*poét*) snow-white

candil SM 1 (= *lámpara*) oil lamp; (*Méx*) (*tb* **~ de prisma**) chandelier; ✦*MODISMO* **(poder) arder en un ~** [*vino*] to pack a powerful punch, be very strong; [*tema etc*] to be pretty strong stuff
2 (*Zool*) tine, small horn

candileja SF 1 (= *depósito*) oil reservoir of a lamp; (= *lámpara*) small oil lamp
2 **candilejas** (*Teat*) footlights

candinga¹ SF (*Cono Sur*) impertinence, insistence

candinga² SM (*Méx*) **el ~** the devil

candiota SF wine cask

candiotero SM cooper

candombe SM (*LAm*) African dance

candomblé SM candomblé

candonga SF 1 (*) (= *lisonjas*) blarney, flattery; (= *truco*) trick; (= *broma*) playful trick, hoax, practical joke; (= *guasa*) teasing; **dar ~ a algn** to tease sb, kid sb*
2 **candongas** (*Andes*) (= *pendientes*) earrings
3 (‡) (= *moneda*) one peseta
4 (‡) (*Anat*) scrotum
5 (‡) (= *mujer*) whore, tart‡, slut‡

candongo* Ⓐ ADJ (= *zalamero*) smooth, oily; (= *taimado*) sly, crafty; (= *vago*) lazy
Ⓑ SM (= *cobista*) creep‡, toady*, flatterer; (= *taimado*) sly sort; (= *vago*) shirker, idler, lazy blighter‡

candonguear* ▸conjug 1a◂ Ⓐ VT (= *bromear*) to tease, kid*
Ⓑ VI (= *vaguear*) to shirk, dodge work

candonguero* ADJ = **candongo A**

candor SM 1 (= *inocencia*) innocence, lack of guile; (= *candidez*) frankness, candidness
2 (*poét*) pure whiteness

candorosamente ADV (= *con inocencia*) innocently, guilelessly, simply; (= *con franqueza*) frankly, candidly

candoroso ADJ (= *inocente*) innocent, guileless; (= *franco*) frank, candid

candungo SM (*Perú*) idiot

canear* ▸conjug 1a◂ VT to bash*, hit

caneca SF 1 (*Méx*) (= *vasija*) glazed earthenware pot; (*Cono Sur*) (= *balde*) wooden bucket; (*Col*) (*para basura*) rubbish bin, garbage can (*EEUU*); (*Caribe*) (= *bolsa de agua*) hot water bottle; (*Andes*) (= *lata*) can, tin; [*de petróleo etc*] drum; (= *porrón*) wine bottle (with a spout)
2 (*Cuba*) (= *medida*) liquid measure of 19 ltrs

caneco ADJ (*Andes*) tipsy

canela Ⓐ SF 1 (*Bot, Culin*) cinnamon; ✦*MODISMO* **ser ~ fina** *o* **en rama**: **Ana es ~ fina** *o* **en rama** Ana is wonderful; **este torero es ~ fina** he's a brilliant bullfighter; **prueba estas gambas, son ~ fina** try these prawns, they're exquisite ► **canela en polvo** ground cinnamon ► **canela en rama** stick cinnamon; *ver tb* **flor A3**
2 (*Caribe*) (= *mulata*) mulatto girl
Ⓑ EXCL (*euf*) good gracious!

canelero SM cinnamon tree

canelo Ⓐ ADJ cinnamon(-coloured *o* (*EEUU*) -colored)
Ⓑ SM cinnamon tree; ✦*MODISMO* **hacer el ~*** to act *o* play the fool

canelón SM 1 = **canalón 2**
2 (= *carámbano*) icicle
3 (*CAm*) (= *rizo*) corkscrew curl
4 **canelones** (*Culin*) cannelloni

canesú SM 1 (= *parte superior*) yoke
2 (= *prenda*) underbodice, camisole

caney SM 1 (*Ven*) (= *cabaña*) log cabin, hut; (*Caribe*) [*de jefe*] chief's house; (*Andes, Caribe*) (= *cobertizo*) large shed
2 (*LAm*) [*de río*] river bend

canfín SM (*CAm, Caribe*) petrol, gasoline (*EEUU*)

cangalla* SMF (*LAm*) coward

cangallar* ▸conjug 1a◂ VT (*Andes, Cono Sur*) to pinch*, swipe‡

cangilón SM 1 (= *jarro*) pitcher; [*de metal*] metal tankard; [*de noria*] bucket, scoop
2 (*LAm*) (= *carril*) cart track, rut

cangrejo SM 1 [*de mar*] crab; [*de río*] crayfish; **está más rojo que un ~** (*por el sol*) he is as pink *o* red as a lobster; ✦*MODISMO* **avanzar como los ~s** to make little headway
2 (*Náut*) gaff
3 (*Andes*) (= *idiota*) idiot; (= *granuja*) rogue, crafty person
4 (*LAm*) (= *misterio*) mystery, enigma
5 (‡) (= *moneda*) 25 peseta coin

cangri‡ SM 1 (= *cárcel*) nick‡, can (*EEUU*‡), prison
2 (*Rel*) church
3 (= *moneda*) 25-peseta coin

cangro SM (*Andes, CAm, Méx*) cancer

canguelo* SM, **canguis*** SM **le entró el ~ justo antes de entrar** he got the jitters just before he went in*; **tener ~** to have the jitters*

canguro Ⓐ SM 1 (*Zool*) kangaroo
2 (= *impermeable*) cagoule
3 (*Náut*) ferry
Ⓑ SMF (*) [*de niños*] baby-sitter; **esta noche hago de ~** I'm baby-sitting tonight; **—¿a qué te dedicas? —trabajo de ~** "what do you do for a living?" — "I do some baby-sitting"

caníbal Ⓐ ADJ 1 (= *antropófago*) cannibal(istic), man-eating
2 (= *feroz*) fierce, savage
Ⓑ SMF cannibal

canibalesco ADJ cannibalistic

canibalismo SM 1 (= *antropofagia*) cannibalism
2 (= *ferocidad*) fierceness, savageness

canibalizar ▸conjug 1f◂ VT to cannibalize

canica SF 1 (= *bola*) marble
2 **canicas** (= *juego*) marbles; (⁑) (= *testículos*) balls⁑

caniche SMF poodle

canicie SF greyness, grayness (*EEUU*), whiteness (*of hair*)

canícula SF 1 (= *verano*) dog days *pl*; (= *calor*) midsummer heat
2 (= *mediodía*) midday sun
3 **Canícula** Dog Star, Sirius

canicular Ⓐ ADJ **calores ~es** midsummer heat
Ⓑ **caniculares** SMPL dog days

canicultura SF dog breeding

canijo* ADJ 1 (= *pequeño*) puny; (= *endeble*) weak, sickly
2 (*Méx*) (= *astuto*) sly

canilla SF 1 (= *espinilla*) (*tb* **~ de la pierna**) shinbone, shin; (*esp LAm*) (= *pierna*) shank, thin leg
2 (= *cúbito*) (*tb* **~ del brazo**) armbone, ulna
3 (*Orn*) wing bone
4 (*Téc*) bobbin, reel
5 (*esp LAm*) (= *grifo*) tap, faucet (*EEUU*); [*de tonel*] spigot, tap; **irse como una ~*** ◊ **irse de ~*** to have the trots‡
6 [*de tela*] rib
7 (*Méx*) **a ~** by hook or by crook; **tener ~** to be very strong
8 (*Caribe*) (= *cobardía*) cowardice

canillento ADJ (*Andes*) long-legged

canillera SF 1 (*Dep*) shin guard
2 (*LAm*) (= *miedo*) fear; (= *cobardía*) cowardice

canillita SM (*Andes, Cono Sur*) newsboy

canillón ADJ, **canilludo** ADJ (*LAm*) long-legged

canina SF dog dirt

caninez SF ravenous hunger

canino Ⓐ ADJ canine, dog *antes de s*; **exposición canina** dog show; **hambre canina** ravenous hunger; **tener un hambre canina** to be ravenous
Ⓑ SM canine (tooth)

canje SM exchange

canjeable ADJ (*gen*) exchangeable; (*Fin*) exchangeable for cash, cashable

canjear ▸conjug 1a◂ VT [+ *prisioneros*] to exchange; [+ *cupón*] to cash in

cannabis SM cannabis

cano ADJ 1 [*pelo, barba*] (= *gris*) grey, gray (*EEUU*); (= *blanco*) white; **una mujer de pelo ~** a grey-haired *o* (*EEUU*) gray-haired *o* white-haired woman
2 [*persona*] (= *con pelo gris*) grey-haired, gray-haired (*EEUU*); (= *con pelo blanco*) white-haired

canoa SF 1 (*gen*) canoe ► **canoa automóvil** motor boat, launch ► **canoa fuera borda** outboard motorboat
2 (*) (= *porro*) joint*
3 (*LAm*) (= *conducto*) conduit, pipe; (= *comedero*) feeding trough; [*de gallinas*] chicken coop; [*de palomas*] dovecot

canódromo SM dog track

canoero/a SM/F (*LAm*), **canoísta** SMF canoeist

canólogo/a SM/F expert on dogs

canon SM (*pl* **cánones**) 1 (= *modelo*) canon (*frm*); **una novela que sigue los cánones tradicionales** a novel which follows the traditional norms *o* canons; **el ~ de belleza** the model of beauty
2 (*Rel*) canon; ✦*MODISMO* **como mandan los cánones**: **se niega a dimitir, como mandan los cánones de la dignidad política** he is refusing to resign, as the norms of political dignity require; **primero tomamos un vinito, como mandan los cánones** (*hum*) first let's have our requisite glass of wine
3 (= *impuesto*) tax, levy ► **canon de arrendamiento** rate of rental ► **canon del agua** water charge, water rate ► **canon de traspaso** (*Dep*) transfer fee
4 (*Mús*) canon

canonical ADJ of a canon *o* prebendary, canonical

canonicato SM (*Rel*) canonry; (*) sinecure, cushy job*

canónico ADJ canonical; **derecho ~** canon law

canóniga SF nap before lunch; ✦*MODISMO* **coger una ~*** to have one too many

canónigo SM canon

canonista SM canon lawyer, expert in canon law

canonización SF canonization

canonizar ▸conjug 1f◂ VT (*Rel*) to canonize; (*fig*) to applaud, show approval of

canonjía SF (*Rel*) canonry; (*) sinecure, cushy job*

canoro ADJ melodious, sweet, tuneful; **ave canora** songbird

canoso ADJ 1 [*persona*] (= *con pelo gris*) grey-haired, gray-haired (*EEUU*); (= *con pelo blanco*) white-haired
2 [*pelo, barba*] (= *gris*) grey, gray (*EEUU*); (= *blanco*) white

canotaje SM boating

canotier SM, **canotié** SM straw hat, boater

cansadamente ADV 1 (= *fatigadamente*) wearily, in a tired way
2 (= *de forma aburrida*) tediously, boringly

CANSADO

¿"Tired" o "tiring"?

Hay que tener en cuenta la diferencia entre **tired** y **tiring** a la hora de traducir **cansado**.

• Lo traducimos por **tired** cuando queremos indicar que *estamos* o que nos sentimos cansados:

Se sintió cansado y se marchó
He felt tired and left
Estoy cansado de trabajar
I'm tired of working
Estábamos cansados del viaje
We were tired after the journey

• Lo traducimos por **tiring** cuando queremos indicar que algo *es* **cansado**, es decir, que nos produce cansancio:

Conducir 140 kms. todos los días es muy cansado
Driving 140 kms every day is very tiring

Para otros usos y ejemplos ver la entrada.

cansado ADJ 1 (= *fatigado*) [*persona*] tired (**de** from); [*aspecto, apariencia*] weary, tired; [*ojos*] tired, strained; **lo noto ~ últimamente** he's been looking tired lately; **es que nació cansada** (*iró*) she was born lazy; **con voz cansada** with a weary voice; *ver tb* **vista A1**
2 (= *harto*) **estar ~ de algo** to be tired of sth; **estoy ~ de que me hagan siempre la misma pregunta** I'm tired of always being asked the same question; **estamos más que ~s de tanta corrupción** we are sick and tired of all this corruption; **¡ya estoy ~ de vuestras tonterías!** I've had enough of this nonsense of yours!; **estar ~ de hacer algo** to be tired of doing sth; **estoy ~ de tanto viajar** I'm tired of so much travelling; **sus amigos, ~s de esperarlo, se habían ido** tired of waiting, his friends had left
3 (= *pesado*) tiring; **debe de ser ~ corregir tantos exámenes** it must be tiring marking *o* to mark so many exams, marking so many exams must be tiring
4 ✦*MODISMO* **a las cansadas** (*Cono Sur*) at long last

cansador ADJ (*Cono Sur*) tiring

cansancio SM 1 (= *fatiga*) tiredness; **ante los primeros síntomas de ~** at the first signs of tiredness *o* weariness; **ya empezaban a acusar el ~** they were already beginning to feel tired *o* weary; **estar muerto de ~** to be dead tired
2 (= *hastío*) boredom; **ha dejado el trabajo por ~** he left his job out of boredom; ✦*MODISMO* **hasta el ~** endlessly; **lo hemos discutido hasta el ~** we've discussed it endlessly

cansar ▸conjug 1a◂ Ⓐ VT 1 (= *fatigar*) to tire, tire out; **no canse más a la paciente con sus preguntas** don't tire the patient (out) with your questions; **me cansa mucho trabajar en el jardín** I get really tired working in the garden, working in the garden really tires me out, I find working in the garden really tiring; **~ la vista** to strain one's eyes, make one's eyes tired
2 (= *aburrir*) **no quiero ~os con tanta gramática** I don't want to bore you with too much grammar; **me cansa ir siempre a los mismos bares** I get tired of *o* bored with always going to the same old bars, it's boring always going to the same old bars
3 (*Agr*) [+ *tierra*] to exhaust
Ⓑ VI 1 (= *fatigar*) to be tiring; **conducir cansa mucho** driving is very tiring
2 (= *hartar*) **los niños cansan a veces** children can sometimes be tiresome *o* trying
Ⓒ **cansarse** VPR 1 (= *fatigarse*) to get tired; **me canso mucho subiendo las escaleras** I get very tired going up stairs; **se cansa con nada** the slightest effort makes him tired, he gets tired at the slightest effort; **cuando ando mucho se me cansan las piernas** when I walk a lot my legs get very tired; **se me cansan los ojos con la televisión** television strains my eyes, my eyes get tired watching television
2 (= *hartarse*) to get bored; **~se de algo** to get tired of sth, get bored with sth; **se cansó de él y lo dejó** she got tired of him *o* got bored with and left him; **~se de hacer algo** to get tired of doing sth; **me cansé de esperar y me fui** I got tired of waiting and left; **no me canso de repetirle que deje de fumar** I'm always telling him to stop smoking

cansera* SF bother; (*LAm*) wasted effort

cansinamente ADV (= *con cansancio*) wearily; (= *sin vida*) lifelessly

cansino ADJ 1 (= *lento*) weary; **andaba con paso ~** he walked wearily, he walked with a weary step
2 (= *pesado*) tiring

cantable Ⓐ ADJ suitable for singing, to be sung; (*Mús*) cantabile, melodious
Ⓑ SM *sung part of a "zarzuela"*

Cantabria SF (*gen*) Cantabria; (*frec*) Santander

cantábrico ADJ Cantabrian; **Mar Cantábrico** Bay of Biscay; **los (Montes) ~s** the Cantabrian Mountains

cántabro/a ADJ, SM/F Cantabrian

cantada* SF (*Méx*) squealing*, grassing*, ratting (*EEUU**)

cantadera SF (*LAm*) loud singing, prolonged singing

cantado ADJ ✦*MODISMO* **estar ~** to be totally predictable

cantador(a) SM/F folksinger, singer of popular songs

cantal SM 1 (= *piedra*) boulder; (= *bloque*) stone block
2 (= *pedregal*) stony ground

cantaleta SF (*LAm*) (= *repetición*) boring repetition *o* chorus, tedious refrain; (= *quejas*) constant nagging

cantaletear ▸conjug 1a◂ VT (*LAm*) 1 (= *repetir*) to repeat ad nauseam, say over and over
2 (= *embromar*) to laugh at, make fun of

cantalupo SM, **cantalupa** (*CAm*) SF cantaloupe

cantamañanas* SMF INV bullshitter**

cantante Ⓐ SMF singer; **es ~ de un grupo de rock** he's a singer in a rock band ► **cantante de ópera** opera singer
Ⓑ ADJ singing; *ver tb* **voz 2.2**

cantaor(a) SM/F Flamenco singer

cantar ▸conjug 1a◂ Ⓐ VI 1 (*Mús*) to sing; **cantas muy bien** you sing very well; **en esa región hablan cantando** (*fig*) they talk in a singsong way in that region; **los monjes cantaban en la abadía** the monks chanted *o* sang in the abbey; *ver tb* **voz 2.2**
2 [*pájaro*] to sing; [*gallo*] to crow; [*cigarra, grillo*] to chirp
3 (*liter*) (= *alabar*) to sing of, sing the praises of; **los poetas que le cantan a la mar** the poets who sing of *o* sing the praises of the sea
4 (*) (= *revelar*) to spill the beans*; (*a la policía*) to squeal*; ✦*MODISMOS* **~ de plano** to tell all, make a full confession; **los hechos cantan por sí solos** the facts speak for themselves
5 (*) (= *oler mal*) to stink*, reek; **te cantan los pies** your feet really stink* *o* reek
Ⓑ VT 1 [+ *canción*] to sing; [+ *mantra, canto gregoriano*] to chant; [+ *misa*] to sing, say; [+ *número de lotería*] to call out; ✦*MODISMOS* **~las claras*** to call a spade a spade; **~ a algn las cuarenta*** to give sb a piece of one's mind*; **su madre le cantó las cuarenta cuando llegó a casa** his mother gave him a piece of her mind when he got home*; **~ victoria**: **es muy pronto para ~ victoria, la crisis política continúa** it is too early to claim victory, the political crisis continues; **—creo que ya está solucionado —no cantes victoria** "I think it's sorted out" — "don't speak too soon" *o* "don't count your chickens (before they're hatched)"

[2] (*liter*) [+ *mérito, belleza*] to praise, eulogize
[3] (= *revelar*) to confess; **cantó todo lo que sabía** he confessed all that he knew
Ⓒ SM [1] (= *canción*) song; (*Rel*) chant
[2] (*Literat*) **el Cantar de los Cantares** the Song of Songs; ✦*MODISMO* **eso es otro ~** that's another story ► **cantar de gesta** chanson de geste, epic poem; *ver tb* **gallo¹ 1**

cántara SF [1] (= *recipiente*) large pitcher
[2] (= *medida*) *liquid measure = 16.13 litres*

cantarería SF [1] (= *tienda*) pottery shop, earthenware shop
[2] (= *cerámica*) pottery

cantarero SM potter, dealer in earthenware

cantárida SF (= *insecto*) Spanish fly; (*Med*) cantharides

cantarín/ina Ⓐ ADJ [*persona*] fond of singing; [*arroyo*] tinkling, babbling; [*voz*] singsong, lilting
Ⓑ SM/F singer

cántaro SM [1] (= *vasija*) pitcher, jug; (= *cantidad*) jugful; **a ~s** in plenty; ✦*MODISMO* **llover a ~s** to rain cats and dogs, rain buckets
[2] **cántaros**‡ (= *pechos*) tits**‡

cantata¹ SF (*Mús*) cantata

cantata²‡ SF (= *soplo*) tip-off

cantautor(a) SM/F singer-songwriter

cante SM [1] (*Mús*) ► **cante flamenco, cante jondo** Andalusian gipsy singing, Flamenco singing
[2] (= *extravagancia*) **dar el ~*** to make a fool of o.s.; **con ese peinado vas a dar el ~** you'll look really silly with that haircut; **ser un ~*** to be ridiculous; **no puedes salir con ese sombrero, es un ~** you can't go out wearing that hat, it looks ridiculous
[3] (‡) (= *soplo*) tip-off (to the police)

cantegril SM (*Uru*) shanty town, slum

cantera SF [1] (*Min*) quarry, pit ► **cantera de arena** sandpit ► **cantera de piedra** stone quarry
[2] [*de artistas etc*] source; (*Dep*) reserve of young players; **Escocia es una ~ de grandes futbolistas** Scotland produces many talented footballers

canterano/a Ⓐ ADJ reserve *antes de s*
Ⓑ SM/F reserve player

cantería SF [1] (*Min*) quarrying, stone cutting
[2] (*Arquit*) masonry, stonework
[3] (= *piedra*) piece of masonry, stone, ashlar

cantero SM [1] (*Min*) quarryman; (*Arquit*) stonemason
[2] (= *cabo*) end, extremity ► **cantero de pan** crust of bread
[3] (*Cono Sur*) [*de plantas*] bed, plot; [*de flores*] flowerbed; (*Andes, Méx*) [*de caña*] plot of sugar cane

cántico SM (*Rel*) canticle; (*fig*) song

cantidad Ⓐ SF [1] (= *medida*) amount, quantity; **hay que poner la misma ~ de azúcar que de harina** you have to add the same amount *o* quantity of sugar as of flour; **según la ~ de trabajo que tengas** depending on the amount of work you have; **hay que sumar ambas ~es** you have to add the two amounts together; **en ~: hemos recibido mercancía en ~** we have received huge amounts *o* quantities of stock; ✦*MODISMO* **en ~es industriales** (*hum*): **bebo café en ~es industriales** I drink coffee by the bucketful *o* by the gallon ► **cantidad de movimiento** (*Fís*) momentum
[2] [*de personas, animales, cosas*] number; **había gran ~ de gente** there was a large number of people; **¿has visto la ~ de discos que tienes?** do you realize just how many records you've got?
[3] (*) (= *gran cantidad*) [3·1] **~ de** loads of*; **tengo ~ de trabajo** I've got loads of work*; **vino a verme ~ de gente** loads of people came to see me*; **tengo ~ de cosas que hacer** I've loads to do*
[3·2] (*LAm*) **cualquier ~*** loads*; **—¿había mucha gente? —¡cualquier ~!** "were there many people?" — "loads!"*; **cualquier ~ de errores** loads of mistakes*
[4] [*de dinero*] sum, amount; **por una pequeña ~ se lo enviamos a su domicilio** for a small sum *o* amount we'll deliver it to your house; **hay que abonar una ~ a cuenta** a payment must be made on account; **pagaron ~es millonarias por los derechos de la película** they paid millions for the film rights ► **cantidad alzada** flat rate ► **cantidad a pagar** amount to pay ► **cantidad bruta** gross amount ► **cantidad neta** net amount ► **cantidad simbólica** nominal fee
[5] [*de sílaba*] quantity
Ⓑ ADV (*esp Esp*‡) **sabe ~ de eso** he knows loads about that*; **le va el alcohol ~** he's into drinking in a big way‡; **me gustas ~** I like you a lot, I think you're really cool‡; **ese asunto es ~ de chungo** the whole thing's really dodgy*; **ese tío está ~ de bueno** that guy's really hunky*

cantiga SF, **cántiga** SF song, poem

cantil SM (*en roca*) shelf, ledge; [*de costa*] coastal shelf; (= *risco*) cliff

cantilena SF [1] (= *canción*) ballad, song
[2] = **cantinela**

cantillos SMPL (= *juego*) jacks

cantimplora SF (*para agua*) water bottle, canteen; (*para licores*) hip flask; (*Téc*) syphon; (*Andes*) powder flask; **¡cantimplora!** (*Andes**) not on your life!

cantina SF [1] (*Ferro*) buffet, refreshment car; (*Mil etc*) canteen, cafeteria (*EEUU*); (= *café-bar*) snack bar; (*LAm*) bar, saloon; (*Cono Sur*) (= *restaurante*) cheap restaurant
[2] (= *bodega*) wine cellar
[3] (= *para llevar comida*) hamper; (*Andes*) [*de leche*] milk churn
[4] **cantinas** (*Méx*) (= *alforjas*) saddlebags

cantinela SF **la misma ~** the same old story; **y toda esa ~*** and all that jazz*

cantinero/a SM/F (= *bárman*) barman/barmaid, bartender; (= *dueño*) publican

cantinflismo SM (*Méx*) babble, empty chatter

cantío SM (*Caribe*) folksong, popular song

cantiral SM stony ground, stony place

canto¹ SM [1] (*Mús*) (= *arte*) singing; (= *canción*) song; (*Rel*) chant; **estudió ~ en Barcelona** she studied singing in Barcelona; **clases de ~** singing lessons; **se oían los ~s alegres de los niños** you could hear the joyful songs of the children ► **canto de sirena** siren call, siren song ► **canto gregoriano** Gregorian chant, (Gregorian) plainsong ► **canto llano** plainsong
[2] [*de pájaro*] song; [*de gallo*] crow; [*de grillo, chicharra*] chirp ► **canto del cisne** swan song
[3] (*liter*) song, hymn; **un ~ a la libertad** a hymn *o* song to freedom

CANTIDAD

Cantidad, como sustantivo, se puede traducir al inglés por **amount**, **number**, **sum**, **quantity** y **figure**.

• Cuando **cantidad** expresa cuánto tenemos, necesitamos u obtenemos de algo se traduce por **amount**, palabra que se usa en el contexto de nombres incontables:

Le preocupaba la cantidad de trabajo que tenía que hacer
He was worried about the amount of work he had to do

! Se puede decir **a large amount** y **a small amount**, pero es incorrecto decir **a big amount** o **a little amount**:

• Cuando hablamos de una **cantidad** de personas, animales o cosas, (nombres en plural), **cantidad** se traduce por **number**. Con la expresión **the number of** el verbo va en singular y con **a number of** en plural:

En los últimos 30 años la cantidad de consumidores de electricidad ha aumentado en un 50 por ciento
In the last 30 years, the number of electricity consumers has risen by 50 per cent
Me esperaban una gran cantidad de recibos sin pagar
A large number of bills were waiting for me

! Hay que tener en cuenta que con **number** también podemos utilizar **large** y **small**, pero no **big** ni **little**.

• Hablando de dinero, **cantidad** se traduce por **sum**. Puede aparecer con **large**, **small** o **huge**:

Los fabricantes gastan enormes cantidades de dinero en anunciar sus productos
Manufacturers spend huge sums of money on advertising their products

• Una **cantidad** que se puede medir o contar se puede traducir por **quantity**. Puede ir acompañado de **large** o **small**:

Quiero un kilo de patatas y la misma cantidad de manzanas
I'd like a kilo of potatoes and the same quantity of apples
Sólo necesitas una cantidad muy pequeña
You only need a very small quantity

NOTA: **Amount** también es posible en el contexto de sustancias incontables:
You only need a very small amount

• Una **cantidad** específica, expresada numéricamente, se traduce por **figure**, que puede aparecer con los adjetivos **high** y **low**:

Al final se decidieron por una cantidad de veinte mil libras
Finally, they decided on a figure of twenty thousand pounds

Para otros usos y ejemplos ver la entrada.

canto² SM [1] (= *borde*) [*de mesa, libro*] edge; **de ~: el libro cayó de ~** the book fell on its side; **pon el libro de ~** stand the book on end *o* on its side; ✦*MODISMOS* **al ~*: cada vez que se veían, pelea al ~** every time they saw each other there was inevitably an argument, every time they saw each other an argument was the order of the day; **faltar el ~ de un duro: ha faltado el ~ de un duro para que se caiga** he was *o* came this close to falling ► **canto de pan** heel of bread, crust (of bread)

[2] (= *piedra*) pebble; ✦*MODISMO* **darse con un ~ en los dientes*** to think o.s. lucky, count o.s. lucky; **si no llega a los 10 euros nos podemos dar con un ~ en los dientes** we can think *o* count ourselves lucky if it comes to less than 10 euros ► **canto rodado** pebble

cantón¹ SM [1] (*Pol*) canton
[2] (*Mil*) cantonment
[3] (= *esquina*) corner

cantón² SM (*Cos*) cotton material

cantonada SF **dar ~ a algn** to dodge sb, shake sb off

cantonal ADJ cantonal

cantonear ▸conjug 1a◂ VI to loaf around

cantonera SF [1] (= *anaquel*) corner shelf; (= *escuadra*) corner bracket, angle iron; (= *mesita*) corner table; (= *armario*) corner cupboard; [*de libro, mueble etc*] corner piece
[2] (*) (= *prostituta*) streetwalker, hustler (*EEUU**)

cantonero SM loafer, idler, good-for-nothing

cantonés/esa (A) ADJ, SM/F Cantonese
(B) SM (*Ling*) Cantonese

cantor(a) (A) ADJ singing, that sings; **ave ~a** songbird
(B) SM/F (= *persona*) singer; (*Orn*) songbird

Cantórbery SM Canterbury

cantorral SM stony ground, stony place

cantuariense ADJ of/from Canterbury

cantuja SF (*Perú*) underworld slang

cantúo‡ ADJ **una mujer cantúa** a woman with a smashing figure*

canturía SF (= *canto*) singing, vocal music; (= *ejercicio*) singing exercise; (*pey*) monotonous singing, droning

canturrear ▸conjug 1a◂ VT, VI to sing softly, croon; (*con la boca cerrada*) to hum

canturreo SM soft singing, crooning; (*con la boca cerrada*) humming

canutazo‡ SM telephone call

canutero SM (*LAm*) barrel (*of pen*)

canuto (A) SM [1] (= *tubo*) small tube, small container
[2] (*) (= *porro*) joint*
[3] (*Bot*) internode
[4] (*) (= *persona*) telltale, tattletale (*EEUU*)
[5] (*) (= *teléfono*) phone, blower*
[6] (*Cos*) needle case
(B) ADJ (*) [1] super*, smashing*
[2] ✦*MODISMO* **pasarlas canutas** to have a rough time of it

canzonetista SF vocalist, crooner

caña SF [1] (= *junco*) reed; (= *tallo*) stem, stalk; **un techo de ~** a roof of reed thatch; **azúcar de ~** cane sugar; **ron de ~** cane rum; ✦*MODISMOS* **dar** *o* **meter ~**‡: **la policía le dio ~ a los manifestantes** the police laid into the demonstrators*; **la prensa le ha dado ~ al gobierno** the press has really laid into the government, the press has really given the government some stick*; **le han metido ~ al jefe para que nos aumente el sueldo** they've been going on at my boss to give us a pay rise; **tendrás que darle** *o* **meterle ~ si quieres acabarlo pronto** you'll have to get stuck into it if you want to finish it soon; **le mete mucha ~ al coche** he really steps on the gas; **las ~s se vuelven lanzas** a joke can easily turn into something unpleasant ► **caña de azúcar** sugar cane ► **caña de bambú** cane ► **caña dulce**, **caña melar** sugar cane; *ver tb* **miel**
[2] (*tb* **~ de pescar**) fishing rod
[3] (= *vaso*) **una ~ (de cerveza)** a small glass of beer; **¡dos ~s!** two beers please; **una ~ de vino** a tall wineglass, a long glass
[4] (*Anat*) [*de la pierna*] shinbone; [*de caballo*] shank
[5] [*de bota*] leg; **botas de media ~** calf-length boots
[6] [*de columna*] shaft
[7] (*esp LAm*) (= *aguardiente*) cane liquor; **estar con la ~ mala** (*Cono Sur**) to have a hangover*
[8] (*Min*) gallery
[9] (*Náut*) [*de ancla*] shank; [*de timón*] tiller, helm
[10] (*Caribe**) (= *trago*) swig*, drink
[11] (*Andes, Caribe*) (= *bulo*) false rumour; (= *bravata*) bluff, bluster
[12] (*LAm*) (= *pajita*) (drinking) straw
[13] (†**) (= *pene*) prick**

cañabrava SF (*LAm*) reed

cañada SF [1] (= *barranco*) gully, ravine; (= *valle*) glen
[2] (*Agr*) (= *camino*) cattle track, drover's road
[3] (*LAm*) (= *arroyo*) stream; (= *terreno*) low-lying wet place

cañadón SM (*Cono Sur*) *low-lying part of a field flooded in wet weather*

cañamar SM hemp field

cañamazo SM embroidery canvas

cañamelar SM sugar-cane plantation

cañameno ADJ hempen

cañamero ADJ hemp *antes de s*

cañamiel SF sugar cane

cáñamo SM (*Bot*) hemp; (= *tela*) hemp cloth; (*CAm, Caribe, Cono Sur*) (= *cuerda*) hemp rope ► **cáñamo agramado** dressed hemp ► **cáñamo índico** (*CAm*), **cáñamo indio** Indian hemp, marijuana plant

cañamón SM hemp seed; (*para pájaros*) birdseed

cañata‡ SF (glass of) beer

cañavera SF reed grass

cañaveral SM [1] (*Bot*) reedbed
[2] (*Col Agr*) sugar-cane plantation

cañazo SM (*Andes*) cane liquor; ✦*MODISMO* **dar ~ a algn** to play a trick on sb

cañear* ▸conjug 1a◂ VI to drink, carouse

cañengo ADJ (*Andes, Caribe*), **cañengue** ADJ (*Andes, Caribe*) (= *débil*) weak, sickly; (= *flaco*) skinny

cañeo* SM drinking, carousal

cañería SF [1] (= *tubo*) pipe; (= *sistema*) pipes *pl*, piping; (= *desaguadero*) drain
[2] (*Mús*) organ pipes
[3] (‡) (= *vena*) main line‡

cañero (A) ADJ [1] (*LAm*) sugar-cane *antes de s*; **machete ~** sugar-cane knife
[2] (*Andes, Caribe*) (= *mentiroso*) lying; (= *fanfarrón*) boastful
(B) SM [1] (*Téc*) pipe fitter
[2] (*LAm Agr*) owner *o* manager of a sugar-cane plantation
[3] (*Andes, Caribe*) (= *mentiroso*) bluffer; (= *fanfarrón*) boaster

cañete SM small pipe

cañí ADJ, SMF = **calé**

cañita SF (*Andes*) (drinking) straw

cañiza SF coarse linen

cañizal SM, **cañizar** SM (*natural*) reedbed; (*Agr*) sugar-cane plantation

cañizo SM wattle

caño SM [1] (= *tubo*) tube, pipe; (*Mús*) pipe; [*de fuente*] jet, spout; (*Arquit*) gutter; (= *alcantarilla*) drain, (open) sewer; (*Andes*) (= *grifo*) tap, faucet (*EEUU*)
[2] (*Min*) gallery
[3] (= *bodega*) wine cellar
[4] (*Náut*) navigation channel, deep channel; (*Andes, Caribe*) (= *río*) narrow navigable river

cañón (A) SM [1] [*de artillería*] cannon; **el castillo estaba defendido por 30 cañones** the castle was defended by 30 cannons ► **cañón antiaéreo** anti-aircraft gun ► **cañón antitanque** anti-tank gun ► **cañón de agua** water cannon ► **cañón de avancarga** muzzle loader ► **cañón de campaña** field gun ► **cañón de nieve (artificial)** snow cannon
[2] [*de escopeta*] barrel; ✦*MODISMO* **ni a ~** *o* **cañones** (*Chile, Perú*) not at all ► **cañón arponero** harpoon ► **cañón de ánima rayada**, **cañón rayado** rifled barrel, rifled bore; *ver tb* **escopeta 1**
[3] [*de pipa*] stem; [*de pluma*] quill, calamus
[4] (= *valle*) canyon, gorge; **el Gran Cañón del Colorado** the Grand Canyon
[5] (*Andes*) (= *puerto de montaña*) pass; (= *vereda*) mountain path
[6] (*Mús*) (organ) pipe
[7] (*Arquit*) [*de ascensor*] shaft
[8] (*Téc*) [*de televisor*] (electron) gun ► **cañón de luz** spot(light) ► **cañón láser** laser gun
[9] (*Andes Bot*) trunk
(B) ADJ INV (†) (= *estupendo*) fabulous*, marvellous, marvelous (*EEUU**); **una mujer ~** one hell of a woman‡
(C) ADV (†) ✦*MODISMO* **pasarlo ~** to have a whale of a time*

cañonazo SM [1] (*Mil*) cannon shot; **cañonazos** (= *fuego*) cannon fire *sing*; **salva de 21 ~s** 21-gun salute ► **cañonazo de advertencia** (*Náut*) warning shot, shot across the bows
[2] (*Ftbl*) shot, volley, fierce shot

cañonear ▸conjug 1a◂ (A) VT to shell, bombard
(B) **cañonearse** VPR (*Cono Sur**) to get tight*

cañoneo SM shelling, bombardment

cañonera SF [1] (*Náut*) (*tb* **lancha ~**) gunboat
[2] (*LAm*) (= *pistolera*) holster
[3] (*Mil, Hist*) embrasure

cañonero/a (A) SM/F (*LAm Dep*) striker
(B) SM (*Mil*) gunboat

cañusero/a SM/F (*Andes*) owner of a sugar-cane plantation

cañutero SM pincushion

cañuto SM = **canuto**

caoba SF mahogany

caolín SM kaolin

caos SM INV chaos; **su mesa de trabajo era un ~ total** his desk was complete chaos, his desk was a complete mess; **esta ciudad es un auténtico ~** this city is a complete shambles* ► **caos circulatorio** traffic chaos

caótico ADJ chaotic

caotizar ▸conjug 1f◂ VT to throw into disarray, cause chaos in

C.A.P. SM ABR (= **Certificado de Aptitud Pedagógica**) ≈ PGCE

cap. ABR, **cap.º** ABR (= **capítulo**) ch, c., chap

capa SF [1] (= *prenda*) cloak, cape; **una comedia de ~ y espada** a cloak-and-dagger play; ✦*MODISMOS* **andar** *o* **estar de ~ caída** (= *estar triste*) to look *o* be crestfallen, be down in the mouth; (= *estar en decadencia*) to be in *o* on the decline; **defender algo a ~ y espada** to fight tooth and nail for sth; **hace de su ~ un sayo** he does as he pleases ► **capa de agua** (= *chubasquero*) raincape ► **capa torera** bullfighter's cape
[2] (= *estrato*) layer; **la ~ atmosférica** the atmosphere; **las ~s de la atmósfera** the layers *o* strata of the atmosphere; **la ~ de ozono** the ozone layer; **amplias ~s sociales** *o* **de la población** broad strata of society; **un corte de pelo a ~s** a layered cut; **madera de tres ~s** three-ply wood ► **capa freática** aquifer, phreatic stratum
[3] (= *recubrimiento*) **una ~ de hielo** a sheet of ice; **una ~ de nieve** a blanket of snow; **los muebles tenían una densa ~ de polvo** the furniture had a thick layer of dust; **una fina ~ de grasa** a film of grease; **le di dos ~s de pintura** I gave it two coats of paint; **el pastel tiene dos ~s de chocolate** the cake has two layers of chocolate
[4] (*Náut*) **estar** *o* **ponerse a la ~** to lie to
[5] (*frm*) **so** *o* **bajo ~ de** (= *bajo la apariencia de*) in *o* under the guise of; (= *con el pretexto de*) on *o* under the pretext of, as a pretext for; **so** *o* **bajo ~ ética, predican un puritanismo extremo** in *o* under the guise of ethics, they are preaching extreme puritanism; **so** *o* **bajo ~ de modernizar la empresa han reducido la plantilla** on *o* under the pretext of modernizing the company they have cut back the staff

capaburro SM (*LAm*) pirana

capacha* SF [1] (*Cono Sur*) (= *cárcel*) nick*, slammer*, can (*EEUU**); **caer en la ~** to fall into the trap
[2] (= *espuerta*) basket

capacheca SF (*Andes, Cono Sur*) street vendor's barrow *o* stall

capacho SM [1] (= *cesto*) wicker basket, big basket; (*Téc*) hod; (*LAm*) (= *alforja*) saddlebag
[2] (*Andes, Cono Sur*) (= *sombrero*) old hat

capacidad SF [1] [*de vehículo, teatro, depósito*] capacity; **una sala con ~ para 900 personas** a hall with a capacity of 900 people; **un disquete con ~ de 1.44 MB** a diskette with a capacity of 1.44 MB; **"capacidad: 40 viajeros sentados"** "seating capacity: 40"; **un avión con ~ para 155 pasajeros** a 155-seater aircraft, an aircraft that can carry 155 passengers ► **capacidad de almacenamiento** storage capacity ► **capacidad de carga** carrying capacity, freight capacity ► **capacidad útil** effective capacity; *ver tb* **medida 1**
[2] (= *habilidad*) ability; **necesitamos una persona con ~ para afrontar desafíos** we require a person with the ability to face challenges; **esas bacterias tienen una mayor ~ de reproducción** those bacteria have a greater capacity for reproduction; **su ~ para manejar el balón era asombrosa** his ball skills were amazing; **no tiene ~ para los negocios** he has no business sense *o* business acumen ► **capacidad adquisitiva** (*Com*) purchasing power, buying power ► **capacidad de aprendizaje** learning ability ► **capacidad de convocatoria** [*de orador*] pulling power; [*de huelga, manifestación*] appeal, popular appeal ► **capacidad de decisión** decision-making ability ► **capacidad de ganancia** (*Com*) earning power, earning capacity ► **capacidad de trabajo**: **tiene una enorme ~ de trabajo** she can get through a tremendous amount of work, she has an enormous capacity for hard work ► **capacidad financiera** financial standing ► **capacidad física** physical capacity ► **capacidad intelectual** intellectual ability ► **capacidad mental** mental ability
[3] (= *autoridad*) authority; **no tenemos ~ para modificar las decisiones del gobierno** we do not have the authority to alter government decisions
[4] (*Jur*) capacity ► **capacidad civil** civil capacity ► **capacidad legal** legal capacity

capacitación SF [1] (*Educ*) **conseguir la ~ de piloto** to qualify as a pilot
[2] (*Jur*) capacitation

capacitado ADJ **el candidato más ~** the best-qualified candidate; **estar ~ para hacer algo** to be qualified to do sth; **los únicos ~s para alcanzar los cuartos de final** the only ones capable of reaching the quarter-finals

capacitar ▸conjug 1a◂ Ⓐ VT [1] (= *preparar*) to prepare; **una formación que no capacita a los jóvenes para incorporarse en el mercado laboral** training which fails to give young people the skills they need to enter the job market, training which fails to prepare young people for the job market
[2] (= *habilitar*) to qualify; **este título me capacita para ejercer como abogado** this qualification qualifies *o* entitles me to work as a lawyer
Ⓑ **capacitarse** VPR **~se para algo** to qualify for sth

capacitor SM capacitor

capadura SF castration

capar ▸conjug 1a◂ VT [1] [+ *animal*] to castrate, geld
[2] (*fig*) to reduce, cut down, curtail
[3] (*Caribe, Méx Agr*) to cut back, prune
[4] (*Andes, Caribe*) [+ *comida*] to start on

caparazón SM [1] (= *concha*) shell; **encerrarse en su ~** to withdraw into one's shell; **salir de su ~** to come out of one's shell
[2] (*para caballo*) (*con comida*) nosebag; (= *manta*) caparison

caparrón SM bud

caparrosa SF copperas, vitriol ► **caparrosa azul** copper sulphate

capataz SMF foreman/forewoman, overseer

➤ **capaz** ADJ [1] (= *competente*) capable, able; **es una persona muy ~** he is a very capable *o* able person; **~ de hacer algo** capable of doing sth; **antibióticos capaces de curar la infección** antibiotics capable of curing the infection; **no han sido capaces de localizar las joyas** they were unable to find the jewels; **una película ~ de hacerme llorar** a film that can make me cry; **no es ~ ni de freír un huevo** he can't even fry an egg; **¡es ~ de no venir!** he's quite capable of not coming!; **es ~ de cualquier tontería** he can do some really stupid things, he's capable of the stupidest things; **ser ~ para algo** to be capable of sth; **~ para testar** (*Jur*) competent to make a will
[2] (= *que se atreve*) **¿no me crees ~?** do you think I won't?; **ser ~** to dare; **¿a que no eres ~?** you wouldn't dare!, I bet you wouldn't!; **si eres ~, dime eso otra vez** just say that again, if you dare!; **ser ~ de hacer algo**: **si soy ~ de hacerlo** if I can bring myself to do it; **no fue ~ de tirarse a la piscina** he just couldn't bring himself to dive into the pool; **fui ~ de decirle lo que pensaba** I managed to tell him what I thought
[3] (= *con capacidad*) **un auditorio ~ para 1.200 personas** an auditorium with a capacity of 1,200 people, an auditorium that holds 1,200 people
[4] (*LAm**) **~ que**: **~ que llueva** it might rain; **~ que se perdió** he might have got lost; **es ~ que venga mañana** he might come tomorrow

capazo SM (= *cesto*) large basket; (*para niño*) Moses basket, (wicker) carrycot

capcioso ADJ cunning, deceitful; **pregunta capciosa** trick question

capea SF *bullfight with young bulls*

capeador SM *bullfighter who uses the cape*

capear ▸conjug 1a◂ Ⓐ VT [1] (*Taur*) wave the cape at; (*fig*) to take in, deceive
[2] (*Náut*) **~ el temporal** (*lit, fig*) to ride out *o* weather the storm
[3] (= *esquivar*) to dodge
[4] (*Culin*) to top, cover (**con** with)
Ⓑ VI (*Náut*) to ride out the storm

capellada SF (= *puntera*) toecap; (= *remiendo*) patch

capellán SM chaplain ► **capellán castrense**, **capellán de ejército** military chaplain, padre*

capellanía SF chaplaincy

capelo SM [1] (*Rel*) (= *sombrero*) cardinal's hat; (= *dignidad*) cardinalate
[2] (*Cono Sur, Méx*) (= *tapa*) bell glass, glass cover
[3] (*LAm Univ*) ► **capelo de doctor** doctor's gown

capero SM hallstand, hatstand

Caperucita Roja SF (Little) Red Riding Hood

caperuza SF [*de tela*] (pointed) hood; (*Mec*) hood, cowling; [*de bolígrafo*] cap, top ► **caperuza de chimenea** chimney cowl

Cap. Fed. ABR (*Arg*) = **Capital Federal**

capi[1]* SM = **capitán**

capi[2] SF (*Andes, Cono Sur*) (= *harina*) white maize flour; (= *maíz*) maize, corn (*EEUU*); (= *vaina*) unripe pod

capi[3]* SF (*esp LAm*) capital (city)

capia SF (*Andes, Cono Sur*) white maize flour

capiango SM (*Cono Sur*) clever thief

capicúa Ⓐ ADJ palindromic (*frm*)
Ⓑ SM palindrome (*frm*), symmetrical number (*e.g. 12321*)

capigorra SM, **capigorrón** SM idler, loafer

capilar Ⓐ ADJ hair *antes de s*, capillary; **loción ~** hair lotion; **tubo ~** capillary
Ⓑ SM capillary

capilaridad SF capillarity

capilla SF [1] (*Rel*) chapel ► **capilla ardiente** funeral chapel ► **capilla de la Virgen** Lady Chapel ► **capilla mayor** choir, chancel
[2] **estar en (la) ~** [*condenado a muerte*] to be awaiting execution; (= *estar en peligro*) to be in great danger; (= *estar sobre ascuas*) to be on tenterhooks
[3] (*Mús*) choir
[4] (*Tip*) proof sheet; **estar en ~s** to be at the proof stage, be in proof

➤ LENGUA Y USO: **capaz 1** 43.4

[5] (= *camarilla*) group of supporters, following
[6] (= *caperuza*) cowl; (*Téc*) hood, cowl

capiller(o) SM churchwarden, sexton

capillo SM [1] [*de bebé*] baby's bonnet; [*de halcón*] hood
[2] (*Bot, Zool*) = **capullo**

capirotazo SM flip, flick

capirote SM [1] (*Univ, Orn*) hood
[2] (= *golpe*) flip, flick
[3] **tonto de ~** dunce, complete idiot
[4] (*Culin*) cloth strainer (*for coffee etc*)

capirucho SM hood

capiruchu SM (*CAm*) *child's toy consisting of wooden cup and ball*

capisayo SM (*Andes*) vest, undershirt (*EEUU*)

capitación SF poll tax, capitation

capital Ⓐ ADJ [1] (= *clave*) [*nombre, personaje*] key; [*rasgo*] main; **una figura ~ de la democracia española** a key figure in Spanish democracy; **su obra ~ es el Quijote** his supreme work is Don Quixote; **esta pregunta es de importancia ~** this question is of paramount *o* cardinal *o* capital importance; **esto tuvo una importancia ~ en su vida** this was of paramount *o* cardinal importance in his life; **los puntos ~es de su discurso** the cardinal *o* main points of her speech; **la ciudad ~** the capital city
[2] (= *mortal*) **pecado ~** mortal sin; **la pena ~** capital punishment
[3] (*LAm*) **letra ~** capital letter
Ⓑ SM (*Fin*) [*de empresa*] capital; [*de persona*] capital, money; **la empresa ha ampliado el ~** the company has increased its capital ▸ **capital activo** working capital ▸ **capital en acciones** share capital, equity capital ▸ **capital extranjero**: **la entrada de ~ extranjero** the inflow of foreign capital; **han vendido la empresa al ~ extranjero** they have sold the company to foreign capital *o* investors ▸ **capital fijo** fixed capital ▸ **capital flotante** floating capital ▸ **capital humano** human resources *pl* ▸ **capital privado** private capital ▸ **capital riesgo** risk capital, venture capital
Ⓒ SF [1] [*de país*] capital (city); [*de provincia*] main city, provincial capital; **soy de Málaga ~** I am from the city of Málaga (*as opposed to the province*); **Praga, la ~ europea de la cerveza** Prague, the beer capital of Europe
[2] (*Tip*) decorated initial capital

capitalidad SF capital status, status as capital

capitalino/a (*LAm*) Ⓐ ADJ of/from the capital
Ⓑ SM/F [1] native/inhabitant of the capital; **los ~s** those that live in the capital
[2] (*) city slicker*

capitalismo SM capitalism ▸ **capitalismo de Estado** state capitalism ▸ **capitalismo monopolista** monopoly capitalism ▸ **capitalismo salvaje** ruthless capitalism

capitalista ADJ, SMF capitalist

capitalización SF capitalization; [*de interés*] compounding

capitalizar ▸conjug 1f◂ VT [1] to capitalize; [+ *interés*] to compound
[2] (*fig*) to capitalize on, turn to one's advantage

capitán SM (*gen*) captain; (*fig*) leader, chief; (*Méx*) (*en hotel*) maître d'(hôtel) ▸ **capitán de corbeta** lieutenant commander ▸ **capitán de fragata** commander ▸ **capitán del puerto** harbour *o* (*EEUU*) harbor master ▸ **capitán de navío** captain ▸ **capitán general** [*de ejército*] ≈ field marshal; [*de armada*] chief of naval operations

capitana SF [1] (*Dep, Mil*) (woman) captain; (*Hist*) captain's wife
[2] (*Náut*) flagship

capitanear ▸conjug 1a◂ VT [+ *equipo*] to captain; [+ *rebeldes*] to lead, command

capitanía SF [1] (*Mil*) (= *rango*) captaincy; (= *edificio*) headquarters *pl* ▸ **capitanía del puerto** harbour master's office ▸ **capitanía general** (= *puesto*) *command of a military district*; (= *edificio*) *headquarters of a military district*
[2] (*Náut*) (= *derechos*) harbour dues *pl*, harbor dues *pl* (*EEUU*)

capitel SM (*Arquit*) capital

capitolio SM (= *edificio grande*) large edifice, imposing building; (= *acrópolis*) acropolis; **el Capitolio** the Capitol

capitoné SM [1] [*de mudanzas*] removal van, moving van (*EEUU*), furniture van
[2] (*Cono Sur*) quilt, quilted blanket

capitonear ▸conjug 1a◂ VT (*Cono Sur*) to quilt

capitoste* SM (= *jefe*) bigwig*, boss; (= *tirano*) petty tyrant

capitulación SF [1] (*Mil*) capitulation, surrender ▸ **capitulación sin condiciones** unconditional surrender
[2] (= *convenio*) agreement, pact; **capitulaciones (de boda** *o* **matrimoniales)** marriage contract *sing*, marriage settlement *sing*

capitular[1] ▸conjug 1a◂ Ⓐ VT [1] [+ *condiciones*] to agree to, agree on
[2] (*Jur*) to charge (**de** with), impeach
Ⓑ VI [1] (*Mil*) (= *rendirse*) to capitulate, surrender
[2] (= *pactar*) to come to terms, make an agreement (**con** with)

capitular[2] ADJ (*Rel*) chapter *antes de s*; **sala ~** chapter house, meeting room

capitulear ▸conjug 1a◂ VI (*Andes, Cono Sur Parl*) to lobby

capituleo SM (*Andes, Cono Sur Parl*) lobbying

capítulo SM [1] [*de libro*] chapter; [*de ley*] section; **eso es ~ aparte** that's another question altogether; **esto merece ~ aparte** this deserves separate treatment
[2] (= *reprensión*) reproof, reprimand ▸ **capítulo de culpas** charge, impeachment
[3] (= *tema*) subject, matter; **en el ~ de las pensiones ...** on the subject of pensions ...; **ganar ~** to make one's point
[4] (= *contrato*) ▸ **capítulos matrimoniales** marriage contract *sing*, marriage settlement *sing*
[5] (= *junta*) meeting (*of a council*); (*Rel*) chapter; ✦**MODISMO llamar a algn a ~** to call sb to account, take sb to task
[6] (*Rel*) chapter house

capo Ⓐ SM (= *jefe*) boss; (= *persona influyente*) bigwig*; (= *perito*) expert; [*de la mafia*] capo; (*esp Col*) drug baron; **es un ~** (*en arte, profesión*) he's a real pro*, he's brilliant
Ⓑ ADJ INV great*, fabulous*

capó SM (*Aut*) bonnet, hood (*EEUU*); (*Aer*) cowling

capoc SM kapok

capón[1]* SM rap on the head

capón[2] Ⓐ ADJ castrated
Ⓑ SM [1] (= *pollo*) capon; (*) (= *hombre*) eunuch
[2] (*Cono Sur*) (= *cordero*) castrated sheep, wether; (= *carne*) mutton
[3] (*Cono Sur**) (= *novato*) novice, greenhorn

caponera SF [1] (*Agr*) chicken coop, fattening pen; (*fig*) place of easy living, open house
[2] (‡) (= *cárcel*) clink‡

caporal SM (*Mil*) corporal; (= *jefe*) chief, leader; (*esp LAm*) (= *capataz*) foreman (*on cattle ranch*)

capot [ka'po] SM (*Aut*) bonnet, hood (*EEUU*)

capota SF [1] (= *prenda*) bonnet
[2] [*de carruaje, cochecito*] hood; (*Aut*) hood, top (*EEUU*); (*Aer*) cowling ▸ **capota plegable** folding hood, folding top (*EEUU*)

capotar ▸conjug 1a◂ VI (*Aut*) to turn over, overturn; (*Aer*) to nose-dive; (*fig*) to fall down, collapse

capote SM [1] (= *capa*) cloak; (*Mil*) cape, capote; ✦**MODISMOS de ~** (*Méx*) on the sly, in an underhand way; **darse ~** (*Méx*) to give up one's job; **dijo algo para su ~** he said sth to himself; **echar un ~ a algn** to give *o* lend sb a helping hand; **hacer ~** (*Arg**) to be very successful
[2] (*Taur*) (bullfighter's) cape ▸ **capote de brega** *cape used in the first part of the bullfight* ▸ **capote de paseo** *bullfighter's ceremonial capelet*

capotear ▸conjug 1a◂ VT [1] (*Taur*) to play with the cape
[2] (= *engañar*) to deceive, bamboozle
[3] (= *esquivar*) to dodge, duck
[4] (*Cono Sur Naipes*) to win all the tricks against, whitewash*

capotera SF [1] (*LAm*) (= *colgador*) clothes hanger
[2] (*Cono Sur*) (= *azotaina*) beating
[3] (*CAm*) (= *lona*) tarpaulin, tarp (*EEUU*)

capotudo ADJ frowning, scowling

capricho SM [1] (= *antojo*) whim, (passing) fancy, caprice (*liter*); **tiene sus ~s** he has his little whims; **es un ~ nada más** it's just a passing fancy; **por puro ~** just to please o.s.; **entra y sale a su ~** he comes and goes as he pleases; **hacer algo a ~** to do sth any old how
[2] (= *cualidad*) whimsicality, fancifulness
[3] (*) (*amante*) plaything*
[4] (*Mús*) caprice, capriccio; (*Arte*) caprice

caprichosamente ADV capriciously

caprichoso ADJ [1] [*persona*] capricious
[2] [*idea, novela, etc*] whimsical, fanciful

caprichudo ADJ stubborn, obstinate, unyielding (*about one's odd ideas*)

Capricornio SM Capricorn

cápsula SF (*Med, Aer*) capsule; [*de botella*] cap; [*de tocadiscos*] pick-up; [*de cartucho*] case; (*Caribe*) cartridge ▸ **cápsula de mando** command module ▸ **cápsula espacial** space capsule ▸ **cápsula fulminante** percussion cap

capsular ADJ capsular; **en forma ~** in capsule form

captación SF ▸ **captación de capital** (*Fin*) capital raising ▸ **captación de clientes**: **es la encargada de la ~ de clientes** she's in charge of attracting new customers ▸ **captación de datos** data capture ▸ **captación de fondos** fundraising ▸ **captación de votos** vote-winning

captador SM (*Téc*) sensor

captafaros SM INV (*tb* **placa de ~**) reflector

captar ▸conjug 1a◂ VT 1 (= *atraer*) [+ *dinero, capital*] to raise; [+ *votos*] to win; [+ *clientes, audiencia*] to attract; **con la campaña ~on miles de nuevos votantes** through the publicity campaign they won thousands of new voters; **intentaron ~ nuevos clientes** they tried to attract new clients; **esto no logró ~ el interés del público** this failed to capture public interest; **llora para ~ la atención de sus padres** he cries to get his parents' attention
2 [+ *emisora, señal*] to pick up; **no capto BBC1** I don't *o* can't pick up BBC1; **un aparato que capta las señales acústicas** a device that picks up *o* captures sound signals; **esta antena no capta bien las imágenes** you don't get a good picture with this aerial, this aerial doesn't give a good picture; **un videoaficionado captó esta escena** this scene was caught on amateur video
3 (= *comprender*) [+ *sentido, esencia*] to get, grasp; **supo ~ la importancia política del asunto** she managed to grasp the political significance of the matter; **no ha sabido ~ el mensaje del electorado** she has failed to pick up on *o* get *o* understand the message from the electorate; **no captó la indirecta** he didn't get *o* take the hint
4 [+ *aguas*] to collect; **el pantano capta las aguas de lluvia** the reservoir collects rainwater

captor(a) SM/F captor

captura SF [*de prisionero, animal*] capture; [*de droga*] seizure; [*de pesca*] catch ► **captura de datos** data capture

capturar ▸conjug 1a◂ VT [+ *prisionero, animal*] to capture; [+ *droga*] to seize

capturista SMF (*Méx*) typist; (*en computadora*) computer operator, keyboarder

capucha SF 1 [*de prenda*] hood; (*Rel*) hood, cowl ► **capucha antihumo** smoke hood
2 (= *acento*) circumflex accent

capuchina SF 1 (*Bot*) nasturtium
2 (*Rel*) Capuchin sister

capuchino SM 1 (*Rel*) Capuchin
2 (*LAm Zool*) Capuchin monkey
3 (= *café*) cappuccino (coffee)

capucho SM cowl, hood

capuchón SM 1 [*de pluma*] top, cap
2 [*de prenda*] hood
3 (*Fot*) hood
4 ► **capuchón de válvula** (*Aut*) valve cap
5 (= *prenda*) capuchin, lady's hooded cloak

capujar ▸conjug 1a◂ VT (*Cono Sur*) 1 (= *atrapar*) to catch in the air, snatch out of the air; (= *arrebatar*) to snatch
2 (= *anticiparse*) to say what sb was about to say

capullada** SF daft thing to do/say

capullo[1] SM 1 (= *flor*) bud ► **capullo de rosa** rosebud
2 (*Zool*) cocoon
3 (**) (*del pene*) head; ✦*MODISMO* **porque no me sale del ~** because I don't want to
4 [*de bellota*] cup
5 (*tela*) coarse silk cloth

capullo[2]**/a**** SM/F (= *imbécil*) twit*; **¡eres un ~!** you're a daft sod!**

caqui SM khaki, olive drab (*EEUU*); ✦*MODISMO* **marcar el ~** to do one's military service

caquino SM (*Méx*) **reírse a ~s** ◊ **reírse a ~ suelto** to laugh uproariously, cackle

cara SF 1 (= *rostro*) face; **tiene la ~ alargada** he has a long face; **en la fiesta me encontré con varias ~s conocidas** I saw several familiar faces at the party; **se los tiré a la ~** I threw them in his face; **los banqueros sin ~** the faceless bankers; **conocido como "~ cortada"** known as "scarface"; **~ a ~**: **se encontraron ~ a ~** they met face to face; **un encuentro ~ a ~** a face-to-face encounter; **asomar la ~** to show one's face; **de ~**: **corrimos con el viento de ~** we ran into the wind; **el sol les daba de ~** the sun was shining in their eyes; **el viento me pegaba de ~** the wind was blowing into my face; **de ~ a**: **nos sentamos de ~ al sol** we sat facing the sun; **de ~ al norte** facing north; **reformas de ~ a las próximas elecciones** reforms with an eye on the next elections *o* for the next elections; **no soy nada optimista de ~ al futuro** I'm not at all optimistic about the future; **hay que estar prevenidos de ~ a afrontar los cambios** we have to be prepared for the changes; **volver la ~ hacia algn** to turn one's face towards sb; **no vuelvas la ~ atrás** don't look back; **no se puede volver la ~ ante la corrupción** you cannot turn a blind eye to corruption; ✦*MODISMOS* **caérsele a algn la ~ de vergüenza**: **se le tendría que caer la ~ de vergüenza** she ought to be ashamed of herself; **se le caía la ~ de vergüenza** he blushed with embarrassment; **cruzar la ~ a algn** to slap sb in the face; **dar la ~** to face the consequences; **dar la ~ por algn** to come to sb's defence; **a ~ descubierta** openly; **decir algo en la ~ de algn** to say sth to sb's face; **a dos ~s**: **actuar a dos ~s** to engage in double-dealing; **echar algo a la ~***: **lo mejor que te puedes echar a la ~** the very best you could wish for; **echar algo en ~ a algn** to reproach sb for sth; **echaron en ~ a los estudiantes su escasa participación** they reproached the students for not joining in enough; **le echan en ~ haber abandonado su país** they accuse him of having abandoned his country; **hacer ~ a** [+ *dificultades*] to face up to; [+ *enemigo*] to stand up to; **huir la ~ a algn** to avoid sb; **lavar la ~ a algo** to make sth look presentable; **le lavó la ~ al piso** she made the flat look presentable; **querían lavar la ~ al partido** they wanted to make the party look better; **mirar a algn a la ~** to look sb in the face; **partir la ~ a algn** to smash sb's face in; **cuidado con lo que dices o te parto la ~** just watch it or I'll smash your face in; **partirse la ~ con algn** to have a fight with sb; **partirse la ~ por algo** to fight for sth; **plantar ~ a** [+ *persona, críticas*] to stand up to; [+ *problema*] to face up to, confront; **por la ~***: **entrar por la ~ en una fiesta** to gatecrash a party; **es alcalde por la ~** he's only mayor because of his connections; **está viviendo con sus padres y cobrando el paro por la ~** he's living with his parents and getting away with claiming dole money at the same time; **no me lo van a dar por mi ~ bonita** they're not going to hand it to me on a plate; **romper la ~ a algn** to smash sb's face in; **sacar la ~ por algn** to stick up for sb; **nos veremos las ~s** you haven't seen the last of me
2 (= *expresión*) **poner mala ~** to grimace, make a (wry) face; **no pongas esa ~** don't look like that; **puso ~ de alegría** his face lit up; **tener ~ de**: **tenía ~ de querer pegarme** he looked as if he wanted to hit me; **tener ~ de estar aburrido** to look bored; **tener buena ~** [*enfermo*] to be looking well; [*comida*] to look appetizing; **tener mala ~** [*enfermo*] to look ill; [*comida*] to look bad; ✦*MODISMOS* **poner ~ de circunstancias** to look serious; **tener ~ de acelga** (*por enfado*) to have a face a mile long; (*por enfermedad*) to look pale, look washed out; **tener ~ de aleluya** to look overjoyed, be beaming with joy; **tener ~ de chiste** to be wearing a ridiculous expression; **tener ~ de corcho** to be a cheeky devil*; **tener ~ de estatua** to have a wooden expression; **tener ~ de hereje** to be as ugly as sin; **tener ~ de (justo) juez** to look stern; **tener ~ de monja boba** to look all innocent; **tener ~ de palo** to have a wooden expression; **tener ~ de pascua(s)** to be grinning from ear to ear; **tener ~ de pocos amigos** to look very unfriendly; **tener ~ de vinagre** to have a sour face
3 (*) (= *descaro*) cheek*, nerve*; (= *valor*) nerve*; **¡qué ~ más dura!*** what a cheek *o* nerve!*; **¡qué ~ tienes!** what a cheek you've got!*, you've got a nerve!*; **¿con qué ~ le voy a pedir eso?** how do you expect me to have the nerve to ask her for that?*; **tener ~ para hacer algo** to have the nerve to do sth*; ✦*MODISMOS* **tener más ~ que espalda** ◊ **tener más ~ que un elefante con paperas** to be a cheeky devil*
4 (= *lado*) [*de moneda, montaña, figura geométrica*] face; [*de disco, planeta, papel*] side; [*de tela*] face, right side; (*Arquit*) face, front; **escribir por ambas ~s** to write on both sides; **intentaron ascender por la ~ norte** they tried to climb the north face; **~ A** (*en disco*) A side; **~ adelante** facing forwards; **~ atrás** facing backwards; **~ o cruz** ◊ **~ o ceca** (*Arg*) heads or tails; **echar** *o* **jugar** *o* **sortear algo a ~ o cruz** to toss for sth; **lo echamos a ~ o cruz** we tossed for it; **~ y cruz**: **~ y cruz de una cuestión** both sides of a question

caraba‡ SF **es la ~** it's the absolute tops‡; (*pey*) it's the last straw

carabao SM Philippine buffalo

cárabe SM amber

carabela SF caravel

carabina SF 1 (*Mil*) carbine, rifle; ✦*MODISMO* **ser la ~ de Ambrosio*** to be a dead loss* ► **carabina de aire comprimido** airgun
2 (= *persona*) chaperone; **hacer** *o* **ir de ~** to go as chaperone, play gooseberry*

carabinero SM 1 (*Mil*) rifleman, carabineer; [*de frontera*] border guard; (*LAm*) policeman
2 (*Zool*) prawn

cárabo SM tawny owl

caracha* SF (*LAm*) mange, itch

carachento* ADJ (*LAm*), **carachoso*** ADJ (*LAm*) mangy, scabby

caracho Ⓐ ADJ violet-coloured
Ⓑ EXCL **¡caracho!** (*Andes**) sugar!*, shoot!*, I'll be darned! (*EEUU**)

caracol SM 1 (*Zool*) snail; (*esp LAm*) (= *concha*) (sea) shell, snail shell ► **caracol comestible** edible snail ► **caracol de mar** winkle
2 (= *rizo*) curl

3 (*Arquit*) spiral; (*Cono Sur*) *circular shopping centre*; **escalera de ~** spiral staircase, winding staircase; **subir en ~** [*humo*] to spiral up, corkscrew up; **hacer ~es** [*persona*] to weave about, zigzag; (*pey*) to reel, stagger; [*caballo*] to prance about
4 **¡~es!** (*euf*, *) (*sorpresa*) good heavens!; (*ira*) damn it!

caracola SF (*Zool*) large shell

caracoleante ADJ winding, spiral

caracolear ▸conjug 1a◂ VI [*caballo*] to prance about, caracole

caracolillo SM kiss-curl

carácter SM (*pl* **caracteres**) 1 [*de persona*] character; **tiene un ~ muy fuerte** he has a strong personality; **no tiene ~** he lacks character, he's a weak character; **tener el ~ abierto** to be open, have an open nature; **tener buen ~** to be good-natured; **persona de ~** person of *o* with character; **una persona de mucho ~** person with a strong character *o* a lot of personality; **de ~ duro** hard-natured; **imprimir ~** to be character-building, build up character; **pasé un año en el ejército y eso imprime ~** I spent a year in the army, and that builds up character; **tener mal ~** to be ill-tempered; **tener el ~ reservado** to be of a quiet *o* reserved disposition
2 [*de edificio, estilo*] character; **una casa con mucho ~** a house with a lot of character
3 (= *índole*) nature; **algunos datos de ~ biográfico** some biographical data; **problemas de ~ general** problems of a general nature; **una visita con ~ oficial/privado** an official/private visit; **información de ~ reservado** information of a confidential nature; **la despenalización tiene ~ retroactivo** the decriminalization will be applied retrospectively; **un aumento de sueldo con ~ retroactivo** a backdated pay rise; **la estación se utilizará para trenes de ~ urbano** the station will be used by trains serving the city; **con ~ de urgencia** as a matter of urgency
4 (*Biol*) trait, characteristic ► **carácter adquirido** acquired characteristic ► **carácter dominante** dominant trait, dominant characteristic ► **carácter hereditario** hereditary trait ► **carácter recesivo** recessive trait
5 (*Tip*) character; **una pintada con caracteres árabes** (a piece of) graffiti written in Arabic; **está escrito con caracteres góticos** it is written in Gothic (script) ► **caracteres de imprenta** block letters ► **carácter de letra** handwriting
6 (*Inform*) character ► **carácter alfanumérico** alphanumeric character ► **carácter comodín** wild character ► **carácter de cambio de página** form feed character ► **carácter de petición** prompt ► **carácter libre** wildcard character
7 (*LAm Literat, Teat*) character

caracteriológico ADJ character *antes de s*; **cambio ~** character change, change of character

característica SF characteristic, feature

característicamente ADV characteristically

▼**característico/a** Ⓐ ADJ characteristic (**de** of)
Ⓑ SM/F (*Teat*) character actor/actress

caracterizable ADJ (that can be) characterized

caracterización SF characterization

➤ LENGUA Y USO: **característico A** 53.1

caracterizado ADJ (= *distinguido*) distinguished, of note; (= *especial*) special, peculiar, having special characteristics; (= *típico*) typical

caracterizar ▸conjug 1f◂ Ⓐ VT 1 (*gen*) to characterize; (= *distinguir*) to distinguish, set apart; (= *tipificar*) to typify
2 (*Teat*) [+ *papel*] to play with great effect
3 (= *honrar*) to confer (a) distinction on, confer an honour on
Ⓑ **caracterizarse** VPR 1 **~se por algo** to be characterized by sth
2 (*Teat*) to make up, dress for the part

caracú SM (*LAm*) bone marrow

caradura Ⓐ SMF cheeky person, sassy person (*EEUU*); **¡caradura!** you've got a cheek *o* a nerve!*
Ⓑ SF cheek*, nerve*

carajear ▸conjug 1a◂ VT (*Cono Sur*) to insult, swear at

carajiento ADJ (*Andes*) foul-mouthed

carajillo SM *coffee with a dash of brandy, anis etc*

carajito* SM (*LAm*) kid*, small child

carajo** Ⓐ SM 1 (*con valor enfático*) **—me debes dinero —¡qué dinero ni qué ~!** "you owe me some money" — "I don't owe you a damn *o* bloody thing!" *o* "like hell I do!"‡; **¡qué ~, si no quiere venir que se quede!** if he doesn't want to come he can damn well *o* bloody well stay!‡
2 **un ~**: **no entendí un ~** I didn't understand a damn *o* bloody thing‡; **me importa un ~** I couldn't give a damn* *o* toss‡; **no vale un ~** it isn't worth a thing *o* penny; **—llévame a mi casa —¡y un ~!** "take me home" — "like hell I will!"*
3 **al ~**: **¡al ~ con los libros!** to hell with the books!*; **irse al ~: ¡vete al ~!, estoy harto de ti** go to hell! I'm sick of you‡; **¿que te ha tocado la lotería? ¡vete al ~!** you've won the lottery? like hell (you have)!*; **todo el trabajo se fue al ~** all the work went down the tubes*; **mandar al ~: si te molesta, mándalo al ~** if he bothers you, tell him to piss off**
4 **del ~**: **hace un frío del ~** it's bloody freezing*; **una bronca del ~** a hell of a row; **¡esta paella está del ~!** this is a damn good paella!, this paella is bloody brilliant‡
5 (= *pene*) prick**, dick**; ✦**MODISMO en el quinto ~** in the back of beyond*
Ⓑ EXCL **¡carajo!** damn (it)!*; **¡cállate ya, ~!** shut up, damn it!*; **¡~, qué viento!** this damn *o* bloody wind!‡; **¡~ con el coche!** this damn *o* bloody car!‡, damn this car!‡

caramanchel SM 1 (*LAm*) (= *cabaña*) hut, shack
2 (*Andes*) (= *puesto*) street vendor's stall

caramba EXCL (*indicando sorpresa*) good gracious!; (*indicando extrañeza*) how strange!; (*indicando protesta*) for crying out loud!

carámbano SM icicle

carambola SF (*Billar*) (= *juego*) billiards *sing*; (= *golpe*) cannon, carom (*EEUU*); **¡carambolas!** (*LAm euf**) hell!*, wow!*; ✦**MODISMO por ~** by fluke

caramel SM sardine

caramelear* ▸conjug 1a◂ VT (*Andes*) (= *engañar*) to con*, deceive; (= *engatusar*) to suck up to*, flatter

caramelizado ADJ caramelized

caramelo SM 1 (= *golosina*) sweet, piece of candy (*EEUU*)
2 (*Culin*) caramel; **un jersey color ~** a caramel-coloured *o* (*EEUU*) caramel-colored jersey; **a punto de ~** [*azúcar*] caramelized; ✦**MODISMO estar a punto de ~** [*proyecto*] to be ripe for implementation; **el acuerdo está ya a punto de ~** the agreement is on the verge of success; **—¿se ha convencido? —no, pero está a punto de ~** "is he persuaded?" — "no, but he's not far off it"; **un par de horas en la cárcel te ponen a punto de ~** a couple of hours in jail soon soften you up
3 (= *incentivo*) sweetener; **es sólo un ~ para evitar protestas** it's just a sweetener to stop us protesting; **agitan el ~ de los subsidios para ganar votos** they're waving the carrot of subsidies to attract votes; **su apoyo es un ~ envenenado** his support is a sugar-coated pill

caramillo SM 1 (*Mús*) flageolet
2 (= *montón*) untidy heap
3 (= *chisme*) piece of gossip; **armar un ~** to make mischief, start a gossip campaign
4 (= *jaleo*) fuss, trouble

caramilloso† ADJ fussy

caranchear ▸conjug 1a◂ VT (*Cono Sur*) to irritate, annoy

carancho SM 1 (*Perú*) (= *búho*) owl
2 (*Cono Sur*) (= *buitre*) vulture, turkey buzzard (*EEUU*)

caranga SF (*Andes, CAm*), **carángano** SM (*LAm*) louse

carantamaula† SF 1 (= *careta*) grotesque mask
2 (‡) (= *cara*) ugly mug‡; (= *persona*) ugly person

carantoña SF 1 (= *caricia*) caress; (= *zalamería*) sweet talk; **no me vengas con ~s** don't give me any of your sweet talk; **hacer ~s a algn** (= *acariciar*) to caress sb; (= *halagar*) to sweet-talk sb, butter sb up
2 (= *careta*) grotesque mask; ✦**MODISMO es una ~*** she's mutton dressed up as lamb*
3 (‡) (= *cara*) ugly mug‡

caraota SF (*Ven*) bean

carapacho SM shell, carapace; **meterse en su ~** to go into one's shell

carapintada Ⓐ ADJ ultra right-wing
Ⓑ SMF rebel, right-wing ultranationalist

caraqueño/a Ⓐ ADJ of/from Caracas
Ⓑ SM/F native/inhabitant of Caracas; **los ~s** the people of Caracas

caráspita EXCL (*Cono Sur*) damn!

carátula SF 1 (= *portada*) [*de vídeo*] case; [*de disco*] sleeve
2 (= *careta*) mask; **la ~** (*Teat*) the stage, the theatre
3 (*Méx*) (= *muestra de reloj*) face, dial

caratular ▸conjug 1a◂ VT (*Cono Sur*) to entitle, call

caravana SF 1 (*Aut*) [*de camiones, coches*] convoy; (= *atasco*) tailback, line of traffic (*EEUU*); **ir en ~** to go in convoy; **las ~s que se forman en el camino de la playa** the tailbacks of traffic heading for the beach
2 (= *remolque*) caravan, trailer (*EEUU*)
3 (*Hist*) caravan
4 (*Caribe*) (= *trampa*) bird trap
5 (*Méx*) (= *cortesía*) flattering remark, com-

pliment; **bailar** *o* **correr** *o* **hacer la ~ a algn** to overdo the compliments with sb
6 **caravanas** (*Cono Sur*) (= *pendientes*) large earrings

caravanera SF, **caravansera** SF, **caravasar** SM caravanserai

caravaning [kara'βanin] SM caravanning, RV *o* camper vacationing (*EEUU*)

caravanismo SM caravanning, RV *o* camper vacationing (*EEUU*)

caravanista SMF caravaner

caray EXCL = **caramba**

carbohidrato SM carbohydrate

carbólico ADJ carbolic

carbón SM 1 (*Min*) coal ► **carbón bituminoso** soft coal, bituminous coal ► **carbón de leña** charcoal ► **carbón de piedra** coal ► **carbón menudo** small coal, slack ► **carbón pardo** brown coal ► **carbón térmico** steam coal ► **carbón vegetal** charcoal; ✦***MODISMO*** **¡se acabó el ~!** that's that, then!
2 (*Tip*) (*tb* **papel ~**) carbon paper; **copia al ~** carbon copy
3 (*Arte*) charcoal; **dibujo al ~** charcoal drawing
4 (*Elec*) carbon
5 (*Agr*) smut

carbonada SF 1 (= *cantidad de carbón*) large load of coal
2 (*Andes, Cono Sur*) (= *guiso*) meat stew; (= *carne*) chop, steak
3 (*Cono Sur*) (= *sopa*) thick soup, broth; (= *picadillo*) mince, ground meat (*EEUU*)

carbonatado ADJ carbonated

carbonato SM carbonate ► **carbonato de calcio** calcium carbonate ► **carbonato sódico** sodium carbonate

carboncillo SM charcoal; **un retrato al ~** a portrait in charcoal

carbonear ▸conjug 1a◂ VT 1 (= *convertir en carbón*) to make charcoal of
2 (*Cono Sur*) (= *incitar*) to push, egg on

carbonera SF 1 (= *mina*) coalmine
2 (*en casa*) coal bunker
3 (*Téc*) charcoal kiln; *ver tb* **carbonero**

carbonería SF coalyard

carbonero/a Ⓐ ADJ coal *antes de s*; **barco ~** collier; **estación carbonera** coaling station
Ⓑ SM/F (= *vendedor*) coal merchant, coalman; *ver tb* **fe 1**
Ⓒ SM 1 (*Náut*) collier
2 (*Orn*) coal tit; *ver tb* **carbonera**

carbónico Ⓐ ADJ carbonic
Ⓑ SM (*Cono Sur*) (*tb* **papel ~**) carbon, carbon paper

carbonífero ADJ carboniferous; **la industria carbonífera** the coal industry

carbonilla SF 1 (*Min*) coal dust
2 (*Aut*) carbon, carbon deposit
3 (*LAm Arte*) charcoal

carbonización SF (*Quím*) carbonization

carbonizar ▸conjug 1f◂ Ⓐ VT 1 (*Quím*) to carbonize
2 [+ *madera*] to make charcoal of; **quedar carbonizado** (= *quemado*) to be charred, be burnt to a cinder; (= *electrocutado*) to be electrocuted
Ⓑ **carbonizarse** VPR (*Quím*) to carbonize

carbono SM carbon ► **carbono 14** carbon 14

carbonoso ADJ carbonaceous

carborundo SM carborundum

carbunclo SM 1 (*Min*) carbuncle
2 (*Med*) anthrax

carbunco SM (*Med*) anthrax

carburador SM carburettor, carburetor (*EEUU*)

carburante SM fuel

carburar ▸conjug 1a◂ VI 1 (*Aut*) to carburet
2 (*) (= *dar buen rendimiento*) **esta lavadora no carbura** this washing machine is not working very well; **no he dormido bien y hoy no carburo** I haven't slept well and I can't think straight today *o* I'm not very with it today*

carburo SM carbide ► **carburo de silicio** silicon carbide

carca* ADJ, SMF INV 1 (= *reaccionario*) reactionary
2 (= *anticuado*) square*; **¡qué tío más ~!** what a square!

carcacha* SF (*Méx Aut*) old crock

carcaj SM 1 (= *para flechas*) quiver
2 (*Méx*) rifle case

carcajada SF loud laugh, guffaw; **reírse a ~s** to roar with laughter; **soltar una ~** to burst out laughing

carcajeante ADJ [*conducta*] riotous; [*abrazo*] hearty; [*decisión*] ridiculous, laughable

carcajear ▸conjug 1a◂ VI, **carcajearse** VPR to roar with laughter

carcamal* SM old crock*

carcamán[1] SM 1 (*Náut*) tub, hulk
2 (*Andes, Caribe**) old crock*, wreck

carcamán[2]**/ana** SM/F 1 (*Caribe**) (= *persona*) low-class person
2 (*Andes, Caribe**) (= *inmigrante*) poor immigrant
3 (*Cono Sur Pol*) diehard, reactionary

carcancha SF (*Méx*) bus

carcasa SF 1 (= *armazón*) casing
2 (*Aut*) [*de motor*] chassis; [*de neumático*] carcass
3 [*de móvil*] fascia

carcayú SM wolverine

cárcel SF 1 (= *prisión*) prison, jail; **poner** *o* **meter a algn en la ~** to jail sb, send sb to jail ► **cárcel de régimen abierto** open prison ► **cárcel del pueblo** people's prison ► **cárcel modelo** model prison
2 (*Téc*) clamp

carcelario ADJ prison *antes de s*

carcelería SF imprisonment, detention

carcelero Ⓐ ADJ prison *antes de s*
Ⓑ SM warder, jailer, guard (*EEUU*)

carcinogén SM carcinogen

carcinogénesis SF INV carcinogenesis

carcinogénico ADJ carcinogenic

carcinógeno SM carcinogen

carcinoma SM carcinoma

carcocha SF (*Andes*) = **carcacha**

carcoma SF 1 (= *insecto*) woodworm
2 (= *preocupación*) anxiety, perpetual worry

carcomer ▸conjug 2a◂ Ⓐ VT 1 [+ *madera*] to eat into, eat away
2 [+ *salud*] to undermine
Ⓑ **carcomerse** VPR 1 (*Arquit*) to be worm-eaten
2 (*Med*) to waste away

carcomido ADJ 1 [*madera*] infested with woodworm
2 (= *podrido*) rotten, decayed

CÁRCEL

Uso del artículo

A la hora de traducir expresiones como **a la cárcel**, **en la cárcel**, **desde la cárcel**, *etc*, hemos de tener en cuenta el motivo por el que alguien acude al recinto o está allí.

- Se traduce **a la cárcel** por **to jail** *o* **to prison**, **en la cárcel** por **in jail** *o* **in prison**, **desde la cárcel** por **from jail** *o* **from prison** *etc*, cuando alguien va o está allí en calidad de preso:

¿Cuánto tiempo estuvo en la cárcel?
How long was he in jail *o* ***prison?***
No sabemos por qué los metieron en la cárcel
We don't know why they were sent to jail *o* ***prison***

- Se traduce **a la cárcel** por **to the jail** *o* **to the prison**, **en la cárcel** por **in the jail** *o* **in the prison**, **desde la cárcel** por **from the jail** *o* **from the prison** *etc*, cuando alguien va o está allí por otros motivos:

Fueron a la cárcel a inspeccionar el edificio
They went to the jail *o* ***prison to inspect the building***
Las visitas no pueden estar en la cárcel más de media hora
Visitors may only stay at the jail *o* ***prison for half an hour***

Para otros usos y ejemplos ver la entrada.

carcoso ADJ (*Andes*) dirty, mucky

carda SF 1 (*Bot*) teasel
2 (*Téc*) teasel, card
3 (= *acto*) carding
4 (*) (= *reprimenda*) reprimand; **dar una ~ a algn** to rap sb's knuckles

cardamomo SM cardamom

cardán SM universal joint

cardar ▸conjug 1a◂ VT 1 (*Textiles*) to card, comb; ✦***MODISMO*** **~ la lana a algn*** to tell sb off, rap sb's knuckles
2 [+ *pelo*] to backcomb
3 (**) (= *copular*) to screw**, fuck**

cardenal SM 1 (*Rel*) cardinal
2 (*Med*) bruise
3 (*Orn*) cardinal, cardinal bird
4 (*Chile Bot*) geranium

cardenalato SM cardinalate

cardenalicio ADJ **capelo ~** cardinal's hat

cardencha SF (*Bot, Téc*) teasel

cardenillo SM verdigris

cárdeno ADJ [*color*] purple, violet; [*agua*] opalescent

cardiaco/a, **cardíaco/a** Ⓐ ADJ 1 cardiac, heart *antes de s*; **ataque ~** heart attack
2 (*) **estar ~ con algo** to be delighted with sth
Ⓑ SM/F sufferer from a heart complaint

cardinal ADJ cardinal

cardio... PREF cardio...

cardiocirujano/a SM/F heart surgeon

cardiograma SM cardiogram

cardiología SF cardiology

cardiológico ADJ cardiological

cardiólogo/a SM/F cardiologist

cardiorrespiratorio ADJ cardiorespiratory

cardiosaludable ADJ good for the heart

cardiovascular ADJ cardiovascular

cardo SM thistle; **✦MODISMO es un ~*** (= *insociable*) he's a prickly customer*; (= *feo*) he's as ugly as sin*

cardón SM (*Cono Sur*) *species of giant cactus*

cardumen SM, **cardume** SM [1] (*Pesca*) shoal
[2] (*Andes, Cono Sur**) (= *muchos*) mass; **un ~ de gente** a mass of people, a load of people*

carea SM sheepdog

carear ▸conjug 1a◂ Ⓐ VT [+ *personas*] to bring face to face; [+ *textos*] to compare
Ⓑ **carearse** VPR to come face to face

▼carecer ▸conjug 2d◂ VI [1] **~ de** to lack; **carece de talento** he lacks talent, he has no talent; **no carecemos de dinero** we don't lack for money, we're not short of money; **eso carece de sentido** that doesn't make sense
[2] (*Cono Sur*) (= *hacer falta*) **carece hacerlo** we/you have to do it, it is necessary to do it; **carece no dejarla** we must not let her

carecimiento SM lack, need

carel SM side, edge

carena SF [1] (*Náut*) careening; **dar ~ a algo** to careen sth
[2] (†*) ragging*, teasing, hazing (*EEUU**); **dar ~ a algn** to rag sb*, tease sb, haze sb (*EEUU**)

carenar ▸conjug 1a◂ VT to careen

carencia SF [1] (= *ausencia*) lack; (= *escasez*) lack, shortage, scarcity (*frm*); **una ~ absoluta de recursos económicos** a total lack of economic resources; **la ~ de agua y alimentos empieza a ser preocupante** the lack *o* shortage *o* scarcity of water is starting to become worrying; **para compensar las ~s vitamínicas** to make up for vitamin deficiencies; **sufrió graves ~s emocionales y materiales** he suffered extreme emotional and material deprivation
[2] (*Econ*) (= *periodo*) *period free of interest payments and debt repayments*

carencial ADJ **estado ~** state of want; **enfermedad ~** deficiency disease

carente ADJ **~ de** lacking in, devoid of (*frm*)

carentón ADJ (*Cono Sur*) large-faced

careo SM (*Jur*) confrontation, face-to-face meeting; **someter a los sospechosos a un ~** to bring the suspects face to face

carero* ADJ [*tienda*] expensive, dear, pricey*

carestía SF [1] (= *escasez*) scarcity, shortage; **época de ~** period of shortage
[2] (*Com*) high price, high cost ► **carestía de la vida** high cost of living

careta SF mask; **quitar la ~ a algn** to unmask sb ► **careta antigás** gas mask ► **careta de esgrima** fencing mask ► **careta de oxígeno** oxygen mask

careto‡ SM ugly mug‡; **¡vaya ~ que tiene!** what an ugly mug!‡

carey SM [1] (= *material*) tortoiseshell
[2] (*Zool*) turtle

carga SF [1] (= *cargamento*) [1·1] [*de camión, lavadora*] load; [*de barco*] cargo; [*de tren*] freight; **el camión volcó con toda la ~** the lorry overturned with a full load; **la lavadora admite cinco kilos de ~** the washing machine has a maximum load of five kilos
[1·2] (= *acto*) loading; **"zona reservada para carga y descarga"** "loading and unloading only"; **andén de ~** loading platform; **de ~ frontal** front-loading *antes de s*; **de ~ superior** top-loading *antes de s*
[1·3] (= *peso*) load; **no puedo con tanta ~** I can't take *o* manage such a heavy load; **la ~ que aguantaba la columna** the weight supported by the column
► **carga aérea** air cargo ► **carga de fractura** breaking load ► **carga de pago** payload ► **carga de rotura** breaking load ► **carga fija, carga muerta** dead load ► **carga útil** payload; *ver tb* **bestia C**, **buque 1**
[2] (= *responsabilidad*) burden; **no quiero ser una ~ para mis hijos** I don't want to be a burden to my children; **la ~ de la prueba** (*Jur*) the burden of proof; **yo soy quien lleva la ~ de esta casa** I'm the one who takes responsibility for everything in this house; **no sabes la ~ que me quitas de encima** you can't imagine what a weight off my mind that is ► **carga de trabajo** workload ► **carga financiera** (*por gastos*) financial burden; (*por intereses*) financial expense, financing cost ► **carga fiscal**, **carga impositiva** tax burden ► **carga lectiva** *hours of attendance at lectures or seminars* ► **cargas familiares** dependants, dependents (*EEUU*) ► **cargas sociales** social security contributions ► **carga tributaria** tax burden
[3] (= *contenido*) **el discurso tenía una fuerte ~ emocional** the speech was charged with great emotion; **se caracteriza por un exceso de ~ ideológica** it is characterized by its excessive ideological content
[4] (*en armas*) charge; **una ~ de tres kilos de explosivo** three kilos of explosives ► **carga de pólvora** (*Min*) gunpowder charge ► **carga de profundidad** depth charge ► **carga explosiva** explosive charge
[5] (= *recambio*) [*de pluma*] cartridge; [*de bolígrafo*] refill; **se le ha acabado la ~ al mechero** the lighter has run out of fuel
[6] (= *ataque*) (*Mil, Dep*) charge; **¡a la ~!** charge!; **✦MODISMO volver a la ~: a los pocos minutos el equipo volvió a la ~** a few minutes later the team returned to the attack; **el grupo vuelve a la ~ con un nuevo disco** the group are back with a new record ► **carga de caballería** cavalry charge ► **carga policial** police charge
[7] (*Elec*) [*de un cuerpo*] charge; [*de generador, circuito*] load ► **carga eléctrica** electrical charge, electric charge ► **carga estática** static

cargada SF [1] (*Méx*) **✦MODISMO ir a la ~** to jump on the bandwagon
[2] (*Cono Sur**) nasty practical joke

cargaderas SFPL (*Andes*) braces, suspenders (*EEUU*)

cargadero SM [1] (*Min*) (*en estación*) loading platform, goods platform; (*en puerto*) loading bay
[2] (*Arquit*) lintel

cargado Ⓐ PP *de* **cargar**
Ⓑ ADJ [1] (= *con cargamento*) loaded; **el ascensor iba demasiado ~** the lift was overloaded; **la furgoneta iba cargada hasta los topes** the van was packed full; **déjame que te ayude, que vas muy cargada** let me help you, you've got such a lot to carry; **~ de algo**: **los árboles estaban ya ~s de fruta** the trees were already weighed down *o* loaded down with fruit; **se presentó ~ de regalos** he arrived weighed down *o* loaded down with presents; **viajaba cargada de maletas** she was travelling with a ton of luggage, she was travelling loaded down with *o* weighed down with luggage; **iba cargada de joyas** she was dripping with jewels; **estamos muy ~s de trabajo** we're snowed under (with work), we're overloaded with work; **un país ~ de deudas** a country burdened *o* weighed down with debt; **la dejó cargada de hijos** he left her a brood of children to look after; **estar ~ de años** to be weighed down with age; **fue un partido ~ de tensión** it was a match fraught with tension; **ser ~ de espaldas** *o* **hombros** to be round-shouldered; **estar ~ de razón** to be totally in the right
[2] (= *fuerte*) [*café, bebida alcohólica*] strong; **este gin tonic está muy ~** this gin and tonic is too strong
[3] [*ambiente*] (= *no respirable*) stuffy; (= *lleno de humo*) smoky; (= *tenso*) fraught, tense; **abre la ventana que esto está muy ~** open the window, it's very stuffy in here; **el ambiente de la reunión estaba cada vez más ~** the atmosphere in the meeting became increasingly fraught *o* tense
[4] (*Meteo*) (= *bochornoso*) close, overcast
[5] (*Mil*) [*arma*] loaded; [*bomba, mina*] live
[6] (*Elec*) [*batería, pila*] charged; [*cable*] live
[7] [*dados*] loaded
[8] [*ojos*] heavy; **tener los ojos ~s de sueño** to have one's eyes heavy with sleep
[9] (*) (= *borracho*) tanked up‡; **salimos bien ~s del bar** when we left the bar we were really tanked up‡

cargador(a) Ⓐ SM/F (= *persona*) [*de camión*] loader; [*de barco*] docker; [*de horno*] stoker; (*Méx*) porter ► **cargador(a) de muelles** docker
Ⓑ SM [1] (*Téc*) [*de pistola, metralleta*] magazine; [*de cañón*] chamber; [*de bolígrafo*] filler; [*de pluma*] cartridge ► **cargador de acumuladores, cargador de baterías** battery charger ► **cargador de discos** (*Inform*) disk pack ► **cargador de pilas** battery charger
[2] (*Mil, Hist*) ramrod
[3] **cargadores** (*Col*) (= *tirantes*) braces, suspenders (*EEUU*)

cargadora SF (*Andes, Caribe*) nursemaid

cargamento SM [1] [*de barco, avión*] (= *mercancías*) cargo; (= *remesa*) shipment; **el ~ del buque** the ship's cargo; **el último ~ de cigarrillos** the last shipment of cigarettes; **se han incautado de un ~ de armas** they have seized an arms shipment ► **cargamento de retorno** return cargo
[2] [*de camión, tren*] load

cargante* ADJ [*discurso, personaje*] annoying; [*tarea*] irksome; [*persona*] trying; **¡qué tío más ~!** what a pain that bloke is!*

cargar ▸conjug 1h◂ Ⓐ VT [1] [+ *peso*] (= *echar*) to load; (= *llevar*) to carry; **~on los sacos en dos camiones** they loaded the sacks onto two lorries; **iba cargando la pesada cruz** he was carrying the heavy cross; **iba cargando al niño sobre los hombros** he was carrying the child on his shoulders; **cargó a sus espaldas una enorme mochila** he swung a huge rucksack up onto his back; **cuando cargaba el peso sobre la pierna mala** when he shifted the weight onto his bad leg
[2] (= *llenar*) [2·1] [+ *vehículo, pistola, lavadora, cámara*] to load; **han terminado de ~ el avión** they've finished loading the plane; **~on el coche hasta arriba de maletas** they loaded the car up with suitcases

➤ LENGUA Y USO: **carecer 1** 53.6

2·2 (= *llenar de combustible*) [+ *mechero, pluma*] to fill; [+ *batería, pilas*] to charge; [+ *horno*] to stoke

2·3 (*en exceso*) **has cargado la sopa de sal** you've overdone the salt *o* put too much salt in the soup; **tratamos de no ~ a los alumnos con demasiadas horas de clase** we try not to overburden the students with too many teaching hours; ✦*MODISMOS* **~ la mano** ◊ **~ las tintas** to exaggerate

2·4 [+ *imaginación, mente*] to fill; **le cargó la cabeza de ideas disparatadas** she filled his head with wild ideas

2·5 (*Inform*) to load

3 (= *cobrar*) **3·1** (*en cuenta*) to charge; **~ una cantidad en cuenta a algn** to charge an amount to sb's account; **me lo pueden ~ en mi cuenta** you can charge it to my account; **~ una factura con un porcentaje por servicio** to add a service charge to a bill

3·2 [+ *contribución*] to charge for; [+ *impuesto*] to levy

4 (= *hacer recaer*) **~ las culpas (de algo) a algn** to blame sb (for sth), put the blame (for sth) on sb; **buscan a alguien a quien ~ la culpa** they are looking for somebody to blame *o* to put the blame on; **~ la culpabilidad en** *o* **sobre algn** to hold sb responsible, put the blame on sb

5 (= *agobiar*) **~ a algn de algo: el ser campeones nos carga de responsabilidad** being champions places a lot of responsibility on our shoulders; **~ a algn de nuevas obligaciones** to burden sb with new duties; **~ a algn de deudas** to encumber sb with debts

6 (= *acusar*) to charge, accuse; **~ algo a algn** ◊ **~ a algn con algo** to charge sb with sth, accuse sb of sth; **~ a algn de poco escrupuloso** to accuse sb of being unscrupulous, charge sb with being unscrupulous

7 (= *soportar*) [+ *culpa*] to take; [+ *responsabilidad*] to accept; [+ *carga*] to shoulder; **cargó toda la responsabilidad del fracaso** he accepted full responsibility for the disaster

8 (*) (= *fastidiar*) **esto me carga** this gets on my nerves*, this bugs me*; **deja de ~me** stop being such a pain*

9 (*) (= *suspender*) to fail

10 (*Mil*) (= *atacar*) to charge, attack

11 (*Náut*) [+ *vela*] to take in

12 [+ *dados*] to load

13 (*LAm*) (= *llevar*) **¿cargas dinero?** have you got any money on you?; **~ anteojos** to wear glasses; **~ revólver** to carry a gun

14 (*Andes, Cono Sur*) [*perro*] to attack, go for

Ⓑ VI **1** (= *echar carga*) (*Aut*) to load up; (*Náut*) to take on cargo

2 **~ con** **2·1** [+ *objeto*] (= *levantar*) to pick up; (= *llevar*) to carry

2·2 [+ *culpa, responsabilidad*] to take; [+ *consecuencias*] to suffer; **la empresa ~á con los gastos del viaje** the company will bear the travel expenses

3 (= *atacar*) **la policía cargó contra los manifestantes** the police charged the demonstrators; **el presidente cargó contra la prensa** the president attacked the press; **~ sobre algn** (= *presionar*) to urge sb, press sb; (= *molestar*) to pester sb

4 (= *apoyarse*) **~ en** *o* **sobre algo** [*persona*] to lean on *o* against sth; [*muro, bóveda*] to rest on sth, be supported by sth

5 (*Ling*) [*acento*] to fall (**en, sobre** on)

6 (*Meteo*) to turn, veer (**a** to; **hacia** towards)

Ⓒ **cargarse** VPR **1** (= *llenarse*) **~se de** [+ *fruta, dinero*] to be full of, loaded with; [+ *culpa, responsabilidad*] to take; **mis pulmones se ~on de humo** my lungs filled with smoke; **el árbol se había cargado de manzanas** the tree was heavy laden with apples; **~se de hijos** to have lots of children; **~se de paciencia** to summon up one's patience

2 (*) (= *destruir*) [+ *jarrón, juguete*] to smash, break; [+ *esperanzas, vida*] to ruin; **¡te lo has cargado!*** you've gone and knackered it*

3 [*aire, ambiente*] **la atmósfera se cargó antes de la tormenta** the atmosphere became oppressive before the storm; **el ambiente se cargó de humo** the air became filled with smoke

4 [*cielo*] to become overcast

5 (*Elec*) to become charged

6 (*) (= *hartarse*) **me he cargado ya de tantas lamentaciones tuyas** I've had enough of your moaning

7 (*) (= *enfadarse*) to get annoyed

8 (*Esp**) **~se a algn** (= *suspender*) to fail sb; (= *matar*) to bump sb off*, do sb in‡; (= *eliminar*) to get rid of sb, remove sb

9 **cargársela*** to get into hot water*, get it in the neck*; **te la vas a ~** you're in for it*, you've had it*

cargazón SF **1** (= *carga*) load; (*Náut*) cargo, shipment

2 (*Med*) heaviness ► **cargazón de espaldas** stoop

3 (*Meteo*) bank of heavy cloud

4 (*Cono Sur*) heavy crop of fruit (*on tree*)

cargo SM **1** (= *puesto*) post; **ocupa el ~ de comisario europeo desde hace tres años** he has held the office *o* post of European Commissioner for three years; **dejó el ~ de embajador en 1992** he left his post as ambassador in 1992; **alto ~** (= *persona*) top official, senior official; (= *puesto*) high-ranking position, top post; **ha dimitido un alto ~ directivo** a top *o* senior official has resigned; **han quedado vacantes tres altos ~s** three high-ranking positions *o* top posts have become vacant; **desempeñar un ~** to hold a position; **jurar el ~** to be sworn in; **poner el ~ a disposición de algn** (*euf*) to offer up one's post to sb ► **cargo público** (= *puesto*) public office; (= *persona*) person in public office

2 **a ~ de** **2·1** (= *responsable de*) in charge of, responsible for; **las tropas a ~ de los refugiados** the troops in charge of *o* responsible for the refugees; **los detectives a ~ de la investigación** the detectives in charge of *o* heading the investigation

2·2 (= *bajo la responsabilidad de*) **la presentación del programa estuvo a ~ de una actriz desconocida** the programme was presented by an unknown actress; **"formación a ~ de la empresa"** "training will be provided"; **la clausura del festival estará a ~ de Plácido Domingo** Plácido Domingo will be the main attraction of the festival's closing ceremony; **un concierto a ~ de la orquesta de cámara de la ciudad** a concert performed by the city's chamber orchestra; **la llamada irá a mi ~** I'll pay for the phone call; **las reparaciones correrán a ~ del dueño** the cost of repairs will be met by the owner, repairs will be paid for by the owner; **tener algo a su ~** to be in charge of sth, be responsible for sth; **20 policías tenían a su ~ la seguridad del monarca** 20 policemen were in charge of *o* responsible for the king's security; **los niños que tengo a mi ~** the children in my care *o* charge (*frm*)

3 **hacerse ~ de** (= *encargarse*) to take charge of; (= *pagar*) to pay for; (= *entender*) to realize; **cuando él murió, su hijo se hizo ~ del negocio** when he died, his son took charge of *o* took over the business; **el ejército se hizo ~ del poder** the army took over power *o* took control; **el abuelo se hizo ~ del niño** the boy's grandfather took care of him; **deben hacerse ~ de los daños causados a los muebles** they should pay for breakages to the furniture; **la empresa no quiso hacerse ~ de la reparación** the company refused to meet the costs of repair; **me hago ~ de la importancia de estas conversaciones** I am aware of *o* realize how important these talks are; **—estamos pasando unos momentos difíciles —sí, ya me hago ~** "we're going through difficult times" — "yes, I understand *o* realize"

4 (*Com*) charge; **podrá recibir información sin ~ alguno** you can receive information free of charge; **paga siempre con ~ a su cuenta corriente** he always charges payments directly to his current account

5 (*Jur*) charge; **el fiscal retiró los ~s contra el acusado** the prosecution dropped all the charges against the defendant; **fue puesto en libertad sin ~s** he was released without charge ► **cargo de conciencia**: **tengo ~ de conciencia por el tiempo perdido** I feel guilty about all that wasted time; *ver tb* **pliego**, **testigo A1**

6 (*Chile, Perú*) (= *certificación*) date stamp (*providing proof of when a document was submitted*)

cargosear* ▸conjug 1a◂ VT (*LAm*) to pester, annoy

cargoso* ADJ (*LAm*) annoying

carguera SF (*Andes, Caribe*) nursemaid

carguero SM **1** (= *vehículo*) (*Náut*) cargo boat; (*Aer*) freight plane ► **carguero militar** military transport craft

2 (*Andes, Cono Sur*) (= *bestia de carga*) beast of burden

carguío SM load

cari ADJ (*Cono Sur*) grey, gray (*EEUU*)

cariacontecido ADJ crestfallen, down in the mouth

cariado ADJ [*muela*] decayed

cariadura SF caries, decay

cariancho ADJ broad-faced

cariar ▸conjug 1b◂ Ⓐ VT to cause to decay, cause decay in

Ⓑ **cariarse** VPR to decay, become decayed

cariátide SF caryatid

caribe Ⓐ ADJ **1** (*Geog*) Caribbean; **Mar Caribe** Caribbean, Caribbean Sea

2 (*LAm*) (= *caníbal*) cannibalistic

Ⓑ SM/F Carib

caribeño/a Ⓐ ADJ Caribbean

Ⓑ SM/F Carib

caribú SM caribou

caricato SM (*Cono Sur, Méx*) = **caricatura**

caricatura SF **1** [*de persona*] caricature

2 (*en periódico, dibujos animados*) cartoon

caricaturesco ADJ absurd, ridiculous

caricaturista SMF [1] (= *dibujante*) caricaturist [2] [*de periódico, dibujos animados*] cartoonist

caricaturización SF caricaturization, caricaturing

caricaturizar ▸conjug 1f◂ VT to caricature

caricia SF (*a persona*) caress; (*a animal*) pat, stroke; **hacer ~s a** to caress, stroke

caricioso ADJ caressing, affectionate

CARICOM SM ABR (= **Caribbean Community and Common Market**) CARICOM

caridad SF charity; **vive de la ~ de las gentes del barrio** she lives on *o* off the charity of the local people; **obra de ~** act of charity; **condonarle la deuda es una obra de ~** writing off his debt is an act of charity; **hizo muchas obras de ~** she did many charitable deeds; **dinero destinado a obras de ~** money given to charity, charity money; **¡una limosna, por ~!** could you spare some change *o* a little money (out of charity), please?; ✦**REFRÁN la ~ empieza por uno mismo** charity begins at home

caries SF INV [1] (*Med*) tooth decay, caries; **está recomendado contra la ~** it's recommended for the prevention of tooth decay; **tengo una ~ en la muela del juicio** I've got some decay in my wisdom tooth [2] (*Agr*) blight

carigordo* ADJ fat-faced

carilampiño ADJ [1] (= *afeitado*) clean-shaven [2] (= *joven*) smooth-faced, beardless

carilargo* ADJ [1] (= *de cara larga*) long-faced [2] (= *enfadado*) annoyed

carilla SF [1] [*de folio, página*] side [2] (= *careta*) bee veil

carilleno* ADJ round-faced, full-faced

carillo* ADJ a bit expensive, on the dear side

carillón SM carillon

carimbo SM (*LAm*) branding iron

▼ **cariño** SM [1] (= *afecto*) love, affection; **demostró mucho ~ por sus hijas** he showed great love *o* affection for his daughters; **falta de ~** lack of affection; **palabras de ~** affectionate words; **coger ~ a algn/algo** to grow *o* become fond of sb/sth, become attached to sb/sth; **con ~: trata a sus plantas con mucho ~** she takes loving care of her plants; **lo recuerdo con ~** I have fond memories of it, I remember it with great affection; **con ~, Luis** (*en carta*) love (from) Luis; **dar ~ a algn** to be affectionate to sb; **sentir ~ por algn** to be fond of sb, like sb; **tener ~ a algn/algo** to be fond of sb/sth, like sb/sth; **tomar ~ a algn/algo** to grow *o* become fond of sb/sth, become attached to sb/sth [2] (*apelativo*) darling, honey*; **ven aquí, ~** come here darling [3] (= *caricia*) **dar** *o* **hacer (un) ~ a algn** to caress sb, stroke sb [4] (*LAm*) (= *regalo*) gift, token (of affection) [5] **cariños** (= *saludos*) love; **Rosa te manda muchos ~s** Rosa sends her love

cariñosamente ADV affectionately, lovingly, fondly

cariñoso ADJ affectionate, loving

carioca Ⓐ ADJ of/from Rio de Janeiro Ⓑ SMF native/inhabitant of Rio de Janeiro; **los ~s** the people of Rio de Janeiro

cariparejo* ADJ poker-faced, inscrutable

carirraído* ADJ brazen, shameless

➤ LENGUA Y USO: cariño 1 50.3

carirredondo* ADJ round-faced

carisellazo SM (*Andes*) toss of a coin; **echar un ~** to toss a coin, spin a coin

carisma SM charisma

carismático ADJ charismatic

carita SF (= *cara pequeña*) little face; ✦**MODISMOS de ~** (*Andes*) first-class; **dar** *o* **hacer ~** (*Méx*) [*mujer*] to return a smile, flirt, flirt back; **hacer ~s** (*Andes*) to make faces

caritativamente ADV charitably

caritativo ADJ charitable (**con, para** to)

cariz SM [1] (= *aspecto*) look; **este asunto está tomando mal ~** this is beginning to look bad, I don't like the look of this; **en vista del ~ que toman las cosas** in view of the way things are going [2] (*Meteo*) outlook

carlanca SF [1] (= *collar*) spiked dog-collar [2] (*Andes, CAm*) (= *grillo*) shackle, fetter [3] (*CAm, Cono Sur*) (= *persona*) bore, pest, drag; (= *aburrimiento*) boredom, tedium; (= *enojo*) annoyance, irritation [4] **carlancas** (= *picardía*) tricks, cunning *sing*; **tener muchas ~s** to be full of tricks

carlinga SF cockpit, cabin

carlismo SM Carlism

> **CARLISMO**
>
> *The controversial change which Ferdinand VII of Spain made to the law in order to allow his daughter Isabella to succeed him instead of his brother, Carlos María Isidro de Borbón, gave rise to Carlism, a movement supporting Carlos's claim to the throne. It also sparked off a series of armed conflicts. The First Carlist War (1833-1839) was declared by Carlos when Isabella came to the throne, the Second (1860) was started by his son of the same name, and the Third (1872-76) by a grandson, another Don Carlos. The last Carlist pretender, Alfonso, died in 1936 without descendants, although that did not prevent the* **Falange Española** *from later backing the Carlist cause in an attempt to prevent the current king, Juan Carlos, being designated Franco's successor. To this day there is still a Carlist party in Spain.*
>
> ⇨ *See also* FALANGE ESPAÑOLA

carlista ADJ, SMF Carlist

carlistada SF Carlist attack, Carlist uprising

Carlitos SM (*forma familiar*) *de* **Carlos** Charlie

Carlomagno SM Charlemagne

Carlos SM Charles

Carlota SF Charlotte

carlota SF (*Culin*) charlotte

carmelita Ⓐ ADJ [1] (*Rel*) Carmelite [2] (*LAm*) light brown, tan Ⓑ SMF Carmelite; **~ descalzo** discalced Carmelite

carmelitano ADJ Carmelite

carmelito ADJ (*LAm*) light brown, tan

Carmelo SM Carmelite convent

Carmen SM (*Rel*) Carmelite Order

carmen[1] SM (*en Granada*) villa with a garden

carmen[2] SM (*liter*) song, poem

carmenar* ▸conjug 1a◂ VT [1] (= *cardar*) [+ *lana*] to card, teasel; [+ *seda*] to unravel; [+ *pelo*] to disentangle; **~ a algn*** to pull sb's hair [2] (*) (= *estafar*) to fleece, swindle

carmesí ADJ, SM crimson

carmín SM [1] (= *color*) carmine [2] (= *pintalabios*) lipstick [3] (*Bot*) dog rose

carminativo ADJ carminative

carmíneo ADJ carmine, crimson

carnada SF bait

carnal Ⓐ ADJ [1] (*Rel*) carnal, of the flesh [2] [*pariente*] full, blood *antes de s*; **hermano ~** full brother; **primo ~** first cousin; **tío ~** real uncle Ⓑ SM (*Méx**) pal*, buddy (*EEUU**)

carnalidad SF lust, carnality

carnaval SM [1] (= *fiesta*) carnival [2] (*Rel*) Shrovetide; **martes de ~** Shrove Tuesday

> **CARNAVAL**
>
> **Carnaval** *is the traditional period of fun, feasting and partying that precedes the start of Lent (***Cuaresma***). The most important day is probably Shrove Tuesday (***Martes de Carnaval***), but throughout* **Carnaval** *there are fancy-dress parties, parades and firework displays. In some places in Spain, the changeover from* **Carnaval** *to Lent on Ash Wednesday is marked by the* **Entierro de la Sardina**. *This is a grotesque funeral parade in which the symbolic cardboard figure of a sardine is marched through the streets and finally ceremonially burnt or buried. Although banned under Franco, partly because of the irreverent nature of the activities and partly because of the dangers posed by people wandering around freely in disguise,* **Carnaval** *has recently enjoyed a revival in Spain, with Cádiz and Tenerife being particularly well known for their celebrations.*

carnavalero ADJ, **carnavalesco** ADJ carnival *antes de s*

carnavalito SM (*Andes, Chile*) folk song and dance

carnaza SF [1] (= *cebo*) (*para peces*) groundbait; (*para leones*) scraps *pl* of meat [2] [*de escándalo, suceso*] **dar ~ a la gente** to feed people (with) juicy titbits

carne Ⓐ SF [1] (*Culin*) meat; ✦**MODISMOS poner toda la ~ en el asador** to pull out all the stops, give it one's all; **no ser ~ ni pescado** to be neither fish nor fowl, be neither one thing nor the other; **ser ~ de algo***: **son ~ de cañón** they are cannon-fodder; **son ~ de prestamista** they are prime targets for moneylenders; **eran ~ de prisión** they were prime candidates to end up in prison ► **carne adobada** marinated meat ► **carne asada** roast meat ► **carne blanca** white meat ► **carne bovina, carne de bovino** beef ► **carne congelada** frozen meat ► **carne cruda** raw meat ► **carne de carnero** mutton ► **carne de cerdo, carne de chancho** (*LAm*) pork ► **carne de cordero** lamb ► **carne de res** (*LAm*) beef ► **carne deshilachada** (*CAm, Méx*) stewed meat ► **carne de ternera** veal ► **carne de vaca** beef ► **carne de venado** venison ► **carne magra, carne mollar** lean meat ► **carne marinada** (*LAm*) salt meat ► **carne molida** (*LAm*), **carne picada** mince, ground meat (*esp EEUU*) ► **carne porcina** pork ► **carne roja** red meat ► **carne salvaji-**

na game ► **carnes blandas** (*Cono Sur*) white meat *sing* ► **carne tapada** stewed meat, stew
2 (*Anat*) flesh; ✦**MODISMOS de ~ y hueso**: **las marionetas parecían actores de ~ y hueso** the puppets were just like real-life actors; **ser de ~ y hueso** to be only human; **me enamoro como cualquier chica de mi edad, soy de ~ y hueso** I fall in love like any girl of my age, I'm only human; **en ~ y hueso** in the flesh; **en ~ viva**: **tenía las rodillas en ~ viva** his knees were raw; **un programa que muestra el horror en ~ viva** a programme that shows the full horror ► **carne de gallina** gooseflesh, goose pimples *pl*, goose bumps *pl* (*EEUU*); **me pone la ~ de gallina** [*de frío, emoción*] it gives me goose pimples *o* (*EEUU*) goose bumps; [*de miedo*] it gives me the creeps, it makes my flesh crawl
3 **carnes** [*de persona*] **de abundantes ~s** amply proportioned; **criar** *o* **echar ~s** to put on weight; **entrado** *o* **metido en ~s** plump, overweight; **algo metidita en ~s** somewhat plump; **de pocas ~s** thin, skinny
4 (*Rel*) flesh; **la ~ es débil** the flesh is weak; **el Verbo se hizo ~** the Word was made flesh; **los pecados de la ~** sins of the flesh
5 (*Bot*) flesh, pulp; (*LAm*) [*de árbol*] heart(wood) ► **carne de membrillo** quince jelly
Ⓑ ADJ **color ~** flesh-coloured, flesh-colored (*EEUU*); **medias de color ~** flesh-coloured tights

carné SM = **carnet**

carneada SF (*Cono Sur*) slaughter, slaughtering

carnear ▸conjug 1a◂ VT 1 (*Cono Sur*) [+ *ganado*] to slaughter; [+ *persona*] to murder, butcher 2 (*Chile*) to deceive, take in*

carnecería SF = **carnicería**

carnerada SF flock of sheep

carnerear ▸conjug 1a◂ VI (*Cono Sur*) to blackleg, be a strikebreaker

carnerero SM shepherd

carnero SM 1 (*Zool*) sheep, ram; ✦**MODISMOS no hay tales ~s** there's no such thing; **cantar para el ~**‡ to kick the bucket‡, peg out‡ ► **carnero de la sierra** (*LAm*), **carnero de la tierra** (*LAm*) llama, alpaca, vicuña ► **carnero de simiente** breeding ram ► **carnero marino** seal
2 (*Culin*) mutton
3 (= *piel*) sheepskin
4 (*Cono Sur*) (= *esquirol*) blackleg, scab*
5 ✦**MODISMO botarse** *o* **echarse al ~** (*Cono Sur*) to chuck it all up*, throw in the towel

carnestolendas SFPL Shrovetide *sing*

carnet [kar'ne] SM (*pl* **carnets** [kar'nes]) **tiene ~ del partido socialista** he has a membership card for the Socialist party; **un miembro con ~** a card-carrying member; **una fotografía tamaño ~** a passport-sized photo ► **carnet de conducir** driving licence, driver's license (*EEUU*); **sacarse el ~ de conducir** to get one's driving licence ► **carnet de estudiante** student card ► **carnet de identidad** identity card; → DNI ► **carnet de prensa** press pass ► **carnet de socio** membership card ► **carnet por puntos** penalty-points driving licence, *type of driving licence in which drivers start out with a certain number of points that can be reduced or lost if they commit driving offences, potentially culminating in the loss of the licence*

carnicería SF 1 (*Com*) butcher's, butcher's shop 2 (= *matanza*) slaughter, carnage; **ha sido una ~ de inocentes** it was a slaughter of the innocent 3 (*Andes*) slaughterhouse

carnicero/a Ⓐ ADJ 1 (= *carnívoro*) carnivorous, meat-eating
2 (= *cruel*) cruel, bloodthirsty
Ⓑ SM/F 1 (= *persona*) butcher
2 (= *carnívoro*) carnivore, meat-eater

cárnico ADJ meat *antes de s*; **industria cárnica** meat industry

carnitas SFPL (*Méx*) barbecued pork *sing*

carnívoro Ⓐ ADJ carnivorous, meat-eating
Ⓑ SM carnivore, meat-eater

carnosidad SF 1 (= *masa carnosa*) fleshy part
2 (= *gordura*) corpulence, fleshiness
3 (*Med*) proud flesh

carnoso ADJ meaty

carnudo ADJ fleshy

caro Ⓐ ADJ 1 (= *costoso*) expensive, dear; **un coche carísimo** a very expensive car; **costar ~** to be expensive, cost a lot; **el abrigo me costó muy ~** my coat was very expensive, my coat cost a lot; **le costó ~ tal atrevimiento** his daring cost him dear; **pagar ~ algo** to pay dearly for sth; **pagó cara su insolencia** he paid dearly for his insolence; **salir ~**: **un piso amueblado sale más ~** a furnished flat is more expensive; **en total el viaje nos salió muy ~** altogether the trip was *o* proved very expensive
2 (= *querido*) (*liter*) dear, beloved; **las cosas que nos son tan caras** the things which are so dear to us; **¡mi ~ amigo!** my dear *o* beloved friend!
Ⓑ ADV **vender ~**: **esa tienda vende ~** that shop is expensive

carocas†* SFPL 1 (= *lisonjas*) flattery *sing*
2 (= *caricias*) caresses

carocha* SF (*Méx*) old banger*, jalopy*

caroleno SM (*Méx*) backslang

Carolina[1] SF Caroline

Carolina[2] SF (*Geog*) ► **Carolina del Norte** North Carolina ► **Carolina del Sur** South Carolina

carolingio ADJ Carolingian

carón (*LAm*) Ⓐ ADJ broad-faced
Ⓑ SM (‡) mug‡, face

carona SF 1 (*Equitación*) (= *paño*) saddlecloth; (= *parte del caballo*) saddle; ✦**MODISMO andar con las ~s ladeadas** (*Cono Sur*) to have problems 2 (*Cono Sur*) bed

carota* SMF cool customer*

carótida SF carotid, carotid artery

carozo SM 1 cob of maize, corncob (*EEUU*)
2 (*LAm*) [*de fruta*] stone, pit (*EEUU*)

carpa[1] SF (= *pez*) carp ► **carpa dorada** goldfish

carpa[2] SF 1 [*de circo*] big top
2 (= *toldo*) awning
3 (*esp LAm*) (= *tienda de campaña*) tent
4 (*Méx*) travelling show

CARPA

In Mexico a **carpa** *is a travelling show held under a big top. Originating in the nationalistic aftermath of the Mexican revolution,* **carpas** *toured agricultural communities and mining towns offering a menu of satire, slapstick humour, dramatic sketches and humorous monologues, as well as acrobatics, tightrope walking and other circus entertainments. It was in the* **carpa** *that the Mexican comic character, Cantinflas, started life.*

⇨ *See also* PELADO

carpanta SF 1 (*) (= *hambre*) ravenous hunger
2 (*Méx*) gang

Cárpatos ADJ **Montes ~** Carpathians

carpeta SF 1 (*para papeles, documentos*) folder, file; ✦**MODISMO cerrar la ~** to close the file (*in an investigation*) ► **carpeta de anillas** ring binder ► **carpeta de información** information folder, briefing kit
2 (= *cartera*) briefcase
3 [*de mesa*] table cover
4 (*LAm*) (= *pupitre*) table, desk

carpetazo SM ✦**MODISMO dar ~ a algo** to shelve sth, do nothing about sth

carpetovetónico ADJ terribly Spanish, Spanish to the core

carpidor SM (*LAm*), **carpidora** SF (*LAm*) weeding hoe

carpincho SM (*Cono Sur*) capybara

carpintear ▸conjug 1a◂ VI 1 (*como profesional*) to carpenter 2 (*como aficionado*) to do woodwork (*as a hobby*)

carpintería SF 1 (= *arte, oficio*) carpentry, joinery
2 (= *afición*) woodwork
3 (= *taller*) carpenter's shop

carpintero SM 1 (*Téc*) carpenter ► **carpintero de blanco** joiner ► **carpintero de buque** ship's carpenter, shipwright ► **carpintero de carretas, carpintero de prieto** cartwright, wheelwright ► **carpintero de ribera** = **carpintero de buque**
2 (*Orn*) woodpecker

carpir ▸conjug 3a◂ VT (*LAm*) to weed, hoe

carraca SF 1 (*Mús, Dep*) rattle
2 (= *vehículo viejo*) (= *coche*) old banger, jalopy*; (= *barco*) tub
3 (*Téc*) ratchet brace
4 ✦**MODISMO echar ~** (*Andes*) to lie

carraco Ⓐ ADJ feeble, decrepit
Ⓑ SM (*) (= *coche*) old banger*, jalopy*

carrada SF (*Cono Sur*) = **carretada**

carral SM barrel, vat

carralero SM cooper

carrasca SF kermes oak; ✦**MODISMO ser de ~*** to be absolutely awful

carrascoloso‡ ADJ (*LAm*) grumpy*, touchy, irritable

carraspear ▸conjug 1a◂ VI (*al hablar*) to be hoarse, have a frog in one's throat; (*al aclararse*) to clear one's throat

carraspeo SM **es incómodo oír en el cine los continuos ~s** it's unpleasant hearing people continuously clearing their throats in the cinema

carraspera SF hoarseness

carrasposo ADJ 1 (*Med*) hoarse, with a sore throat
2 (*LAm*) rough, harsh

carrera SF 1 (= *acción*) (*tb Béisbol*) run; **tuvimos que pegarnos una ~ para no perder el tren** we had to run for it so as not to miss the train; **emprendí una loca ~ en dirección a la salida** I made a mad dash *o* rush for the exit; **¿nos echamos una ~ hasta el muro?** race you to the wall?; **nos fuimos de una ~ y llegamos en cinco minutos** we ran for it *o* rushed over and got there in five minutes; ✦*MODISMOS* **a la ~** at (full) speed, hurriedly; **consiguieron escapar a la ~** they managed to make a quick getaway; **siento tener que dar explicaciones tan a la ~** I'm sorry to have to explain in such a rush; **tuvo que hacer el trabajo a la ~** he had to rush through the job *o* do the job in a rush; **a ~ tendida** at full speed, flat out* ► **carrera de aterrizaje** landing run ► **carrera de despegue** take-off run ► **carrera del oro** gold rush

2 (= *competición*) race; **las ~s de Fórmula 1** Formula 1 races ► **carrera armamentista, carrera armamentística** arms race ► **carrera campo a través** cross country race ► **carrera ciclista** (bi)cycle race ► **carrera contrarreloj** (*lit*) time trial; (*fig*) race against time ► **carrera corta** dash, sprint ► **carrera de armamentos** arms race ► **carrera de caballos** horse race ► **carrera de coches** motor race ► **carrera de ensacados** (*Cono Sur*) sack race ► **carrera de fondo** long-distance race ► **carrera de galgos** greyhound race ► **la Carrera de Indias** (*Hist*) the Indies run ► **carrera de medio fondo** middle-distance race ► **carrera de obstáculos** (*Atletismo, Equitación*) steeplechase; (*para niños*) obstacle race ► **carrera de relevos** relay, relay race ► **carrera de resistencia** long-distance race ► **carrera de sacos** sack race ► **carrera de vallas** (*Atletismo*) hurdles; (*Equitación*) steeplechase ► **carrera espacial** space race ► **carrera pedestre** walking race ► **carrera popular** fun run

3 (*tb* **~ universitaria**) (university) course; **no sabe qué hará cuando termine la ~** he doesn't know what he'll do after university *o* when he finishes his course; **está en primero de ~** she's in her first year (at university); **quiere que sus hijos estudien una ~** she wants her children to go to university; **había comenzado a estudiar la ~ de Medicina** she had started studying medicine; **dar ~ a algn** to pay sb through college; **hacer una ~: estoy haciendo la ~ de Económicas** I'm doing a degree in economics; **tener ~** to have a (university) degree ► **carrera de ciencias** science degree ► **carrera de letras** arts degree

4 (*tb* **~ profesional**) career; **tuvo una brillante ~ como actriz** she had an outstanding career as an actress; **se encuentra en uno de los momentos más difíciles de su ~ política** this is one of the most difficult moments of her political career; **diplomático de ~** career diplomat; **militar de ~** career officer; **hacer ~** to advance one's career, pursue a career; **quiso hacer ~ en el partido** he tried to pursue a career *o* advance his career in the party; **muchos prefieren hacer ~ en el extranjero** many prefer to pursue careers abroad; ✦*MODISMOS* **hacer ~ de** *o* **con algn** to make headway with sb; **no hago ~ con este niño** I can't make any headway *o* I'm getting nowhere with this child; **hacer la ~*** to be on the game* ► **carrera artística** [*de actor*] career as an actor; [*de pintor, escultor*] artistic career ► **carrera cinematográfica** film career ► **carrera literaria** literary career, career as a writer ► **carrera militar** career as a soldier, military career ► **carrera política** political career, career as a politician

5 (*en medias*) run, ladder

6 (= *recorrido*) [*de desfile*] route; [*de taxi*] ride, journey; [*de barco*] run, route; [*de estrella, planeta*] course; **la ~ del sol** the course of the sun

7 (= *avenida*) avenue

8 (*Mec*) [*de émbolo*] stroke; [*de válvula*] lift ► **carrera ascendente** upstroke ► **carrera descendente** downstroke

9 (= *hilera*) row, line; [*de ladrillos*] course

10 (= *viga*) beam, rafter

11 (*Mús*) run

carrerilla SF **a ~** non-stop, continuously; **de ~** on the trot, in succession; **lo dijo de ~** he reeled it off in one go; **tomar ~** to take a run up

carrerista Ⓐ ADJ fond of racing
Ⓑ SMF 1 (= *aficionado a carreras de caballos*) racing man/woman, racegoer, professional punter
2 (= *ciclista*) racing cyclist
3 (*Pol*) careerist, career politician
Ⓒ SF (*) streetwalker, hustler (*EEUU**)

carrero SM carter, cart driver

carreta SF 1 (= *carro*) (*cubierta*) waggon, wagon; (*sin cubrir*) cart; ✦*MODISMO* **tener la ~ llena** (*Caribe*) to be weighed down by problems ► **carreta de bueyes** oxcart ► **carreta de mano** = **carretilla 1**
2 (*Col, Ven*) wheelbarrow

carretada SF waggonload, wagonload, cart load; ✦*MODISMO* **a ~s: había pan a ~s** there was loads of bread; **llegaron a ~s** they came by the waggonload

carretaje SM cartage, haulage

carrete SM 1 (*Fot*) film
2 (*Cos*) reel, bobbin; ✦*MODISMOS* **dar ~ a algn*** to keep sb amused *o* entertained; **tiene ~ para rato*** she could gab all day*
3 (*Elec*) coil ► **carrete de encendido** (*Aut*) ignition coil ► **carrete de inducción** induction coil
4 (*Pesca*) reel

carretear ▸conjug 1a◂ VT 1 [+ *carga*] to cart, haul
2 [+ *carro*] to drive
3 (*Aer*) to taxi

carretel SM 1 (*Pesca*) reel, fishing reel
2 (*Náut*) log reel

carretela SF 1 (*Hist*) coach, carriage
2 (*CAm*) (= *carro*) cart

carretera SF road, highway (*esp EEUU*); **la ~ entre Barcelona y Sitges** the Barcelona-Sitges road, the road between Barcelona and Sitges; **de ~: bar de ~** roadside bar; **accidente de ~** road accident, traffic accident; **control de ~** roadblock; **por ~: un viaje por ~** a road journey, a journey by road; **transporte por ~** road transport; **circulación por ~** (road) traffic; **hemos venido por ~** we drove here ► **carretera comarcal** local road, ≈ B road ► **carretera de acceso** approach road ► **carretera de circunvalación** bypass, ring road, beltway (*EEUU*) ► **carretera general** main road ► **carretera nacional** ≈ A road, ≈ state highway (*EEUU*) ► **carretera radial** arterial road

carretero Ⓐ ADJ **camino ~** vehicular road
Ⓑ SM 1 (= *transportista*) cartwright, wheelwright; ✦*MODISMOS* **fumar como un ~** to smoke like a chimney; **jurar como un ~** to swear like a trooper
2 (*LAm*) road

carretilla SF 1 (*tb* **~ de mano**) handcart, barrow ► **carretilla de horquilla, carretilla elevadora** fork-lift truck
2 (*Hort*) wheelbarrow
3 (*en tienda*) trolley, cart (*EEUU*)
4 (= *buscapiés*) squib, cracker
5 (*Cono Sur*) (= *quijada*) jaw, jawbone
6 (*Col*) (= *serie*) lot, series
7 ✦*MODISMO* **de ~: saber algo de ~** to know sth by heart; **aprender algo de ~** to learn sth parrot fashion *o* by rote

carretón SM small cart ► **carretón de remolque** trailer

carricero SM ► **carricero común** reed warbler

carricoche SM covered wagon, caravan, gipsy caravan

carricuba SF water cart

carriel SM (*Andes, CAm*) leather case

carril SM 1 (*en carretera*) lane; **el camión invadió el ~ izquierdo** the truck wandered into the left lane ► **carril bici** cycle lane, bikeway (EEUU) ► **carril bus** bus lane ► **carril de acceso** slip road ► **carril de aceleración** acceleration lane ► **carril de adelantamiento** overtaking lane, fast lane
2 (*Ferro*) (= *vía*) rail; (*Caribe, Cono Sur*) (= *tren*) train
3 (= *camino*) track, lane
4 (*Agr*) [*del arado*] furrow
5 (*LAm Dep*) (= *calle*) lane

carrilano (*Chile*) Ⓐ ADJ railway *antes de s*, railroad *antes de s* (*EEUU*)
Ⓑ SM railway labourer, railroad laborer (*EEUU*)

carril-bici SM (*pl* **carriles-bici**), cycle lane, bikeway (*EEUU*)

carril-bus SM (*pl* **carriles-bus**), bus lane

carrilera SF 1 (= *rodera*) rut, track
2 (*Caribe Ferro*) siding

carrilero SM 1 (*Andes Ferro*) railwayman, railroad man (*EEUU*)
2 (*Cono Sur*‡) (= *embaucador*) con man*

carrillera SF 1 (*Zool*) jaw
2 [*de casco*] chinstrap

carrillo SM 1 (*Anat*) cheek, jowl; ✦*MODISMO* **comer a dos ~s** to stuff o.s.*, stuff one's face*
2 (*Téc*) pulley

carrindanga* SF (*Cono Sur*) old banger*, jalopy*

carriola SF truckle bed

carrito SM 1 (*para llevar cosas*) (*en supermercado*) trolley, cart (*EEUU*); (*en hotel*) tea trolley, serving trolley ► **carrito de bebidas** drinks trolley ► **carrito de golf** golf trolley ► **carrito de postres** dessert trolley
2 (*Caribe*) (= *taxi*) taxi

carrizal SM reedbed

carrizo SM 1 (*Bot*) reed
2 **carrizos** (*Andes, Méx*) (= *piernas*) thin *o* spindly legs, pins‡, gams (*EEUU**)
3 ✦*MODISMO* **no nos ayudan un ~** (*Ven*) they do nothing at all to help us

carro SM 1 (= *carreta*) cart, waggon, wagon; ✦*MODISMOS* **aguantar ~s y carretas** to put up with anything; **apearse** *o* **bajarse del ~*** to leave off, give it a rest*; **¡para el ~!*** hold your horses!; **pararle el ~ a algn*** to tell sb to stop; **poner el ~ delante de las mulas** *o* **los bueyes** to put the cart before the horse; **subirse al ~** to climb *o* jump on the bandwagon;

tirar del ~ to do all the donkey work; **untar el ~ a algn** to grease sb's palm ► **carro alegórico** float ► **carro aljibe** water cart ► **carro de golf** golf buggy ► **carro de guerra** (*Hist*) chariot ► **carro de la compra** shopping trolley, shopping cart (*EEUU*)
2 (*Mil*) tank ► **carro blindado** armoured car, armored car (*EEUU*), armour-plated car, armor-plated car (*EEUU*) ► **carro de asalto, carro de combate** tank
3 (*LAm*) (= *coche*) car; (= *taxi*) cab, taxi; (= *vagón*) carriage, car (*esp EEUU*); (= *autobús*) bus, coach ► **carro comedor** (*Méx*) dining car, restaurant car ► **carro correo** mail van ► **carro cuba** tank truck ► **carro de mudanzas** removal van, moving van (*EEUU*) ► **carro dormitorio** (*Méx*) sleeping car ► **carro fúnebre** hearse ► **carro tranvía, carro urbano** tramcar, streetcar (*EEUU*)
4 [*de máquina de escribir*] carriage
5 (= *carga*) cartload; **un ~ de problemas** a whole load of problems

carrocería SF 1 (*Aut*) bodywork
2 (= *taller*) coachbuilder's, body shop

carrocero/a SM/F coachbuilder, car-body maker

carrocha SF eggs *pl* (*of insect*)

carromato SM covered wagon, caravan, gypsy caravan

carroña SF carrion

carroñero ADJ 1 [*persona*] vile, foul
2 **animal ~** animal which feeds on carrion

carroño ADJ 1 (= *putrefacto*) rotten, putrid, foul
2 (*Andes*) (= *cobarde*) cowardly

carroza Ⓐ SF 1 (= *vehículo*) [*de caballos*] coach, carriage; [*de carnaval*] float ► **carroza fúnebre** hearse
2 (*Náut*) awning
Ⓑ SMF 1 (= *viejo*) old boy*, old geezer‡; (= *vieja*) old girl*
2 (= *carca*) old fogey*
Ⓒ ADJ INV (*) 1 (= *viejo*) old
2 (= *carca*) **es muy ~** he's an old fogey*

carruaje SM carriage

carrujo‡ SM (*LAm*) joint‡, reefer‡

carrusel SM 1 [*de verbena*] merry-go-round, roundabout, carousel (*EEUU*)
2 (*Fot*) carrousel, circular slide tray
3 [*de regalos*] revolving display

carry-all SM (*Cono Sur*) estate car, station wagon (*EEUU*)

▼**carta** SF 1 (*Correos*) letter; **echar una ~ (al correo)** to post a letter; ✦***MODISMOS*** **a ~ cabal** thoroughly, in every respect; **era honrado a ~ cabal** he was totally honest; **es un caballero a ~ cabal** a true *o* real gentleman; **tomar ~s en el asunto** to step in ► **carta abierta** open letter ► **carta adjunta** covering letter ► **carta certificada** registered letter ► **carta de acuse de recibo** letter of acknowledgement ► **carta de amor** love letter ► **carta de asignación** letter of allotment ► **carta de aviso** letter of advice ► **carta de despido** letter of dismissal, pink slip (*EEUU**) ► **carta de dimisión** letter of resignation ► **carta de pésame** letter of condolence ► **carta de presentación** letter of introduction; **esta exposición es la mejor ~ de presentación del pintor** this exhibition is the best introduction to the painter ► **carta de recomendación** (*para un trabajo*) letter of recommendation; (*como presentación*) letter of introduction ► **carta de solicitud** (letter of) application ► **carta pastoral** pastoral letter ► **carta postal** (*LAm*) postcard ► **carta urgente** special-delivery letter
2 (*Jur, Com*) (= *documento*) ► **carta blanca** carte blanche; **dar ~ blanca a algn** to give sb carte blanche; **tener ~ blanca** to have a free hand, have carte blanche ► **carta de ciudadanía** naturalization papers *pl* ► **carta de crédito** letter of credit; **~ de crédito documentaria** documentary letter of credit; **~ de crédito irrevocable** irrevocable letter of credit ► **carta de emplazamiento** summons ► **carta de hidalguía** letters patent of nobility *pl* ► **carta de intenciones** letter of intent ► **carta de naturaleza** naturalization papers *pl*; ✦***MODISMO*** **adquirir** *o* **tomar ~ de naturaleza** to come to be like one of the natives, be thoroughly accepted ► **carta de pago** receipt, discharge in full ► **carta de pedido** (*Com*) order ► **carta de portes** bill of lading ► **carta de venta** bill of sale ► **carta ejecutoria** letters patent of nobility *pl* ► **carta verde** (*Aut*) green card, certificate of insurance (*EEUU*) ► **cartas credenciales** credentials
3 (= *estatuto*) charter; **la Carta de las Naciones Unidas** the United Nations Charter ► **Carta de Derechos** Bill of Rights ► **Carta Magna** (= *constitución*) constitution; (*Brit Hist*) Magna Carta ► **Carta Social (Europea)** (European) Social Charter
4 (*Naipes*) card; **una baraja de ~s españolas** a pack of Spanish (playing) cards; **echar las ~s a algn** to tell sb's fortune (*with cards*); **fui a una pitonisa a que me echara las ~s** I went to a fortune-teller to have my fortune told with cards; **jugar a las ~s** to play cards; ✦***MODISMOS*** **¡~ canta!** there it is in black and white!; **enseñar las ~s** to show one's hand; **poner las ~s boca arriba** *o* **sobre la mesa** to put *o* lay one's cards on the table; **no saber a qué ~ quedarse** not to know what to think, be undecided; **a ~s vistas** openly, honestly ► **carta de figura** picture card
5 (*Culin*) menu; **a la ~** à la carte ► **carta de vinos** wine list
6 (= *mapa*) (*Geog*) map; (*Náut*) chart ► **carta acotada** contour map ► **carta astral** star chart ► **carta bomba** letter-bomb ► **carta de flujo** flowchart ► **carta de marear** chart ► **carta de navegación, carta de viaje, carta de vuelo** flight plan ► **carta geográfica, carta marítima** chart ► **carta meteorológica** weather chart, weather map ► **carta náutica, carta naval** chart
7 (*TV*) ► **carta de ajuste** test card

carta-bomba SF (*pl* **cartas-bomba**) letter-bomb

cartabón SM 1 (= *instrumento*) [*de dibujante*] set square, triangle (*EEUU*); [*de carpintero*] square, set square
2 (*Mil*) quadrant

cartagenero/a Ⓐ ADJ of/from Cartagena
Ⓑ SM/F native/inhabitant of Cartagena; **los ~s** the people of Cartagena

cartaginés/esa ADJ, SM/F Carthaginian

Cartago SF Carthage

cartapacio SM 1 (= *cuaderno*) notebook
2 (= *carpeta*) folder

carta-tarjeta SF (*pl* **cartas-tarjeta**) letter card

cartear ▸conjug 1a◂ Ⓐ VI (*Naipes*) to play low
Ⓑ **cartearse** VPR to correspond (**con** with); **se ~on durante dos años** they wrote to each other for two years

cartel SM 1 (= *póster*) poster; **el ~ del Festival** the poster for the Festival; **"se prohíbe fijar carteles"** "stick no bills", "post no bills"; **ser cabeza de ~** to be top of the bill; **en ~: esa película ya no está en ~** that film is not showing yet, that film is not on yet; **"Cats" lleva años en ~** "Cats" has been running for years
2 (= *letrero*) sign; **no vi el ~ de "prohibido fumar"** I didn't see the no smoking sign
3 (= *fama*) **tener ~** to be well known; **un torero de ~** a star bullfighter

cártel SM cartel, trust

cartela SF 1 (= *papel*) slip of paper, bit of card
2 (*Arquit*) console

cartelera SF [*de cine*] hoarding, billboard; (*en periódico*) entertainments *pl*, what's on section*; **se mantuvo en la ~ durante tres años** it ran for three years

cartelero SM billsticker, billposter

cartelista SMF poster artist, poster designer

cartelón SM large notice

carteo SM correspondence, exchange of letters

cárter SM (*Mec*) housing, case ► **cárter de cigüeñal** crankcase

cartera SF 1 (= *monedero*) [*de hombre*] wallet, billfold (*EEUU*); [*de mujer*] purse, billfold (*EEUU*)
2 (*LAm*) (= *bolso*) handbag, purse (*EEUU*)
3 [*de colegial*] satchel, schoolbag
4 (*para documentos*) briefcase; ✦***MODISMO*** **en ~** in the pipeline; **tenemos en ~ varios proyectos** we have several projects in the pipeline ► **cartera de mano** briefcase
5 (*Pol*) **renunció a la ~ de Cultura** he turned down the post of Minister of Culture; **el actual titular de la ~ de Interior** the present Minister of the Interior; **ministro sin ~** minister without portfolio
6 (*Com, Fin*) ► **cartera de acciones** stock portfolio, share portfolio ► **cartera de pedidos** order book ► **cartera de valores** securities portfolio
7 (*Cos*) (*en bolsillo*) pocket flap; *ver tb* **cartero**

carterero/a SM/F (*Cono Sur*) pickpocket

carterista SMF pickpocket

carterita SF ► **carterita de fósforos** (*esp LAm*) book of matches

cartero/a SM/F postman/postwoman, mailman/mailwoman (*EEUU*); *ver tb* **cartera**

cartesiano/a ADJ, SM/F Cartesian

cartilaginoso ADJ cartilaginous

cartílago SM cartilage

cartilla SF 1 (*Escol*) primer, first reader; ✦***MODISMOS*** **cantar** *o* **leer la ~ a algn** to take sb to task, give sb a severe ticking off; **no saber (ni) la ~** not to know a single thing
2 (= *documento*) ► **cartilla de ahorros** bank book ► **cartilla de identidad** identity card ► **cartilla del paro** unemployment card ► **cartilla de racionamiento** ration book ► **cartilla de seguridad, cartilla de seguro** social security card
3 (*Rel*) certificate of ordination
4 (*Mil*) record

cartografía SF cartography, mapmaking

cartografiado SM mapping

➤ LENGUA Y USO: carta 1 48.1

cartográfico ADJ cartographic, cartographical

cartógrafo/a SM/F cartographer, mapmaker

cartomancia SF fortune-telling (*with cards*)

cartomante SMF fortune-teller (*who uses cards*)

cartón SM [1] (= *material*) cardboard ► **cartón acanalado** corrugated cardboard ► **cartón alquitranado** tar paper ► **cartón de embalaje** wrapping paper ► **cartón de encuadernar** millboard ► **cartón piedra** papier mâché
[2] (= *caja*) ► **cartón de huevos** (*lleno*) box of eggs; (*vacío*) egg box ► **cartón de leche** (*lleno*) carton of milk; (*vacío*) milk carton ► **cartón de tabaco** pack of cigarettes
[3] (*Arte*) cartoon
[4] [*de bingo*] card

cartoné SM **en ~** [*libro*] in boards, bound in boards

cartón-madera SM hardboard

cartuchera SF [1] (*para pistola*) cartridge belt
[2] (*) (*en muslos*) *excess fat on the upper thighs*

cartuchería SF cartridges *pl*, ammunition

cartucho SM [1] (*Mil*) cartridge ► **cartucho en blanco** blank cartridge [2] (= *bolsita*) paper cone; [*de monedas*] roll [3] ► **cartucho de datos** (*Inform*) data cartridge

Cartuja SF (*Rel*) Carthusian order

cartuja SF Carthusian monastery

cartujano ADJ, SM Carthusian

cartujo SM Carthusian

cartulaje‡ SM pack of cards

cartulario SM cartulary

cartulina SF card; **una ~** a piece of card ► **cartulina amarilla** (*Ftbl*) yellow card ► **cartulina roja** (*Ftbl*) red card

carura SF [1] (*Andes, CAm, Cono Sur*) (= *lo costoso*) high price, dearness
[2] (*Andes, CAm, Cono Sur*) (= *objeto*) expensive thing; **en esta tienda sólo hay ~s** everything in this shop is dear
[3] (*Cono Sur*) (= *carestía*) lack, shortage

CASA SF ABR (*Esp*) = **Construcciones Aeronáuticas, S.A.**

casa SF [1] (= *vivienda*) house; **una ~ en el campo** a house in the country, a country house; **ir de ~ en ~ vendiendo** to sell things from door to door ► **casa adosada** *terraced villa* ► **Casa Blanca**: **la Casa Blanca** the White House ► **casa consistorial** town hall ► **casa cuartel** *Civil Guard police station including living quarters for families of policemen* ► **casa cuna** (*Hist*) foundling home; (*moderna*) day-nursery, crèche ► **casa de acogida** (*para enfermos, menores*) hostel; (*para mujeres maltratadas*) refuge ► **casa de alquiler**: **vivo en una ~ de alquiler** I live in rented accommodation ► **casa de asistencia** boarding house ► **casa de azotea** penthouse ► **casa de baños** public bathhouse ► **casa de bebidas**† drinking house ► **casa de beneficencia**† poor-house ► **casa de bombas** pumphouse ► **casa de campaña** (*LAm*) tent ► **casa de campo** country house ► **casa de citas** brothel ► **casa de comidas** *cheap restaurant* ► **casa de corrección**† young offenders institution, reformatory (*EEUU*) ► **casa de correos** post office ► **casa de cultura** *municipal arts centre* ► **casa de Dios** house of God ► **casa de ejercicios** retreat house ► **casa de fieras** zoo ► **casa de guarda** lodge ► **casa de huéspedes** boarding house ► **casa de juego** gambling house ► **casa de labor**, **casa de labranza** farmhouse ► **la Casa de la Moneda** *Chilean presidential palace* ► **casa de locos** (= *manicomio*) madhouse, asylum; (= *lugar caótico*) madhouse ► **casa de maternidad** maternity hospital ► **casa de muñecas** doll's house ► **casa de pisos** block of flats, apartment block ► **casa de putas*** brothel ► **casa de seguridad** (*Cono Sur Pol*) safe house ► **casa de socorro** first-aid post ► **casa de tolerancia**† house of ill repute ► **casa de vecindad** tenement block ► **casa de vicio**† brothel ► **casa encantada** haunted house ► **casa mortuoria** house of the deceased ► **casa pareada** semi-detached house ► **casa parroquial** parish house ► **casa religiosa** [*de monjes*] monastery; [*de monjas*] convent ► **casa rodante** caravan, trailer ► **la Casa Rosada** *Argentinian presidential palace* ► **casa rural** (*de alquiler*) holiday cottage; (= *pensión*) rural B & B ► **casa solariega** (*habitada*) family seat, ancestral home; (*usada como museo*) stately home
[2] (= *hogar*) home; **estábamos en ~** we were at home; **se fue a ~** she went home; **estábamos en ~ de Juan** we were at Juan's (place); **¿dónde tiene usted su ~?** where is your home?; **está usted en su ~** make yourself at home; **es una ~ con alegría** it's a happy home, it's a happy household; **la ~ de Lorca en Fuentevaqueros** Lorca's former home in Fuentevaqueros; **abandonar la ~** to leave home; **de ~**: **un animal de ~** a pet, a family pet; **ropa de ~** clothes for wearing around the house; **estoy vestido de ~** I'm in the clothes I wear around the house; **en ~** at home; **debes dejar claro quién manda en ~** you should make it quite clear who's in charge at home; **¿está la señora en (la) ~?** is the lady of the house in?, is the lady of the house at home?; **me he dejado los libros en (mi) ~** I've left my books at home; **está fuera de ~** she's out, she's not at home; **ir a ~** to go home; **ir hacia ~** to head for home; **ir a ~ de Juan** to go to Juan's (place); **llevar la ~** to run the household; **poner ~** to set up house; **poner ~ a una mujer** to set a woman up in a little place; **estar por la ~** to be about the house; **salir de ~** to leave home; **sentirse como en su ~** to feel at home; **siéntase como en su ~** make yourself at home; **ser de la ~** to be like one of the family ► **casa paterna** parents' home ► **casa y comida** board and lodging
[3] ✦**MODISMOS** **de andar por ~**: **zapatos de andar por ~** shoes for wearing around the house; **una explicación de andar por ~** a rough-and-ready explanation; **psicoanálisis de andar por ~** homespun psychoanalysis; **como una ~***: **una rata como una ~** a massive great rat; **una mentira como una ~** a whopper*; **un penalti como una ~** a clear-cut penalty; **está en ~ Dios*** it's miles away*; **echar la ~ por la ventana** to spare no expense; **echaron la ~ por la ventana comprándonos regalos para la boda** they really went to town on buying us presents for our wedding*; **empezar la ~ por el tejado** to put the cart before the horse; **franquear la ~ a algn** to open one's house to sb; **hacer ~** to get rich; **poner a algn en ~** to do sb a great favour; **poner su ~ en orden** to put one's own house in order; **no tener ~ ni hogar** to be homeless; **esto es la ~ de Tócame Roque** everyone just does as they like in this house, it's utter chaos in this house
[4] (= *asociación*) ► **casa de España** *club for expatriate Spaniards* ► **casa de Galicia** *Club for expatriate Galicians* ► **Casa del Pueblo** (*Pol*) *social club run by Spanish socialist party*
[5] (*Dep*) home ground; **la ~ del Real Madrid** Real Madrid's (home) ground; **equipo de ~** home team; **jugar en ~** to play at home; **jugar fuera de ~** to play away (from home); **perdieron en ~ ante el Betis** they lost at home to Betis
[6] (*en juegos*) home; **si sacas tres seguidos, te vuelves a tu ~** if you get three in a row you go back to the beginning *o* go back to home
[7] (*en bar, restaurante*) **un postre de la ~** one of our own special desserts; **una botella de vino de la ~** a bottle of house wine; **hoy invita la ~** it's on the house today
[8] (= *empresa*) firm, company ► **casa armadora** shipping company ► **casa bancaria** banking house ► **casa central** head office ► **casa de banca** banking house ► **casa de discos** record company ► **casa de empeños** pawnshop ► **casa de (la) moneda** mint ► **casa de modas** fashion house ► **casa de préstamos** pawnshop ► **casa discográfica** record company ► **casa editorial** publishing house ► **casa matriz** (= *oficina*) head office; (= *empresa*) parent company
[9] (= *linaje*) house; **la Casa de Saboya** the House of Savoy; **la Casa de Austria** the Hapsburgs ► **casa real** royal household

> **CASA**
>
> **Uso de la preposición "to" con "home"**
>
> A la hora de traducir expresiones como **ir a casa**, **volver a casa**, **venir a casa**, hay que tener en cuenta que **home** sigue directamente al verbo (*sin* **to**):
>
> Quiero irme a casa
> ***I want to go home***
> No puede volver a casa
> ***He can't go back home***
>
> **NOTA:** Sin embargo, **to** sí se pone cuando **home** viene calificado:
>
> Quiere volver a su antigua casa
> ***She wants to return to her former home***
>
> *Para otros usos y ejemplos ver la entrada.*

> **CASA DE CONTRATACIÓN**
>
> *The* **Casa de Contratación** *was responsible for the regulation of Spain's trade with her Latin American colonies. Founded in 1503 by the Crown, the* **Casa de Contratación** *supervised all transatlantic ships operating between certain ports in Spain and Latin America, notably between Cádiz in Spain and Veracruz in Mexico. The* **Casa** *also collected the levy (known as the* **quinto***) of a fifth of all colonial gold and silver, and regulated the African slave trade with Cartagena de Indias, Colombia. As the volume of trade increased, the* **Casa** *operated armed fleets to protect shipments from piracy.*

casabe SM cassava

casa-bote SF (*pl* **casas-bote**) houseboat

casaca SF [1] (= *prenda*) dress coat; (*Andes, Cono Sur*) blouson, zip jacket; ✦**MODISMO**

cambiar de ~ to be a turncoat ► **casaca de montar** riding coat
[2] (*) (= *boda*) wedding, marriage
casación SF cassation, annulment
casacón SM greatcoat
casa-cuartel SF (*pl* **casas-cuarteles**) residential barracks (*for Civil Guard*)
casadero ADJ marriageable, old enough to get married; **una muchacha en edad casadera** a girl of marriageable age, a girl old enough to get married
casado/a (A) ADJ married; **¿está** *o* (*LAm*) **es usted casada?** are you married?; **está ~ con mi prima** he's married to my cousin; **todas sus hijas están muy bien casadas** all her daughters have married well
(B) SM/F married man/woman; **estuvo saliendo con un ~** she was going out with a married man; **Pierce es su apellido de casada** Pierce is her married name; **no está contenta con su vida de casada** she is dissatisfied with married life; **los ~s** (= *hombres*) married men; (= *hombres y mujeres*) married people; **los recién ~s** the newlyweds
(C) SM [1] (*Tip*) imposition
[2] (*LAm Culin*) *two separate varieties of food eaten together*
casal SM [1] (*en el campo*) (= *casa*) country house; (= *granja*) farmhouse; (= *solar*) ancestral home
[2] (*Cono Sur*) (= *pareja*) [*de esposos*] married couple; [*de animales*] pair
casamata SF casemate
casamentero/a SM/F matchmaker
casamiento SM (= *unión*) marriage; (= *ceremonia*) wedding, wedding ceremony ► **casamiento a la fuerza** shotgun wedding ► **casamiento de conveniencia** marriage of convenience ► **casamiento por amor** love match
casampolga SF (*CAm Zool*) black widow spider
Casandra SF Cassandra
casapuerta SF entrance hall, vestibule
▼**casar** ▸conjug 1a◂ (A) VT [1] (= *unir en matrimonio*) to marry; **los casó el cura del pueblo** they were married by the village priest
[2] (= *dar en matrimonio*) to marry off; **ya ha casado a todas sus hijas** she's married off all her daughters
[3] (= *hacer coincidir*) to match up; **casa los estampados antes de coser las telas** match up the patterns before sewing the pieces together
[4] (*Tip*) to impose
(B) VI [1] (= *armonizar*) **estas dos piezas casan perfectamente** these two pieces go together *o* fit together perfectly; **hay una serie de datos que no casan** there are a number of details that don't tally *o* match up; **sus dos declaraciones no casan** her two statements do not match up *o* tally; **~ con algo**: **el color de la alfombra no casa con el del sofá** the colour of the carpet doesn't go with that of the sofa; **mis noticias no casan con las tuyas** the news I have doesn't tally with *o* match yours; **tanta modestia no casa con sus ansias de poder** such modesty doesn't go with *o* tally with his craving for power
[2] (*frm*) (= *contraer matrimonio*) **casó con una chica del pueblo** he married *o* he got married to a girl from the town
(C) **casarse** VPR to marry, get married; **¿cuándo te casas?** when are you getting married?; **se casó con una italiana** he married an Italian woman, he got married to an Italian woman; ✦**MODISMO no ~se con nadie**: **respeta a todo el mundo, pero no se casa con nadie** he respects everyone but doesn't side with any of them; *ver tb* **civil A2**, **iglesia**, **nupcias**, **penalti**
casa-refugio SF (*pl* **casas-refugio**) refuge for battered wives
casatienda SF shop with dwelling accommodation, shop with flat over it
casba SF, **casbah** SF kasbah
casca SF [1] (= *corteza*) bark (*for tanning*)
[2] (= *uvas*) marc (*of grapes*)
[3] ► **cascas almibaradas** candied peel
cascabel (A) SM little bell; ✦**MODISMOS de ~ gordo** pretentious; **ser un ~** to be a scatterbrain; **echar** *o* **soltar el ~** to drop a hint; **poner el ~ al gato** to bell the cat; *ver tb* **serpiente**
(B) SF (*LAm*) rattlesnake, rattler (*EEUU**)
cascabela SF (*LAm*) rattlesnake, rattler (*EEUU**)
cascabelear ▸conjug 1a◂ (A) VT to take in*, beguile
(B) VI [1] (*LAm*) (= *tintinear*) to jingle, tinkle
[2] (= *ser atolondrado*) to be a scatterbrain
[3] (*Cono Sur*) (= *refunfuñar*) to moan, grumble
cascabeleo SM jingling, tinkling
cascabelero/a* (A) ADJ scatterbrained
(B) SM/F scatterbrain
cascabillo SM [1] (= *campanilla*) little bell
[2] (*Bot*) husk, shuck (*EEUU*)
cascada SF waterfall, cascade
cascado ADJ [1] [*objeto*] broken, broken down
[2] [*persona*] worn out
[3] (*Mús*) [*voz*] cracked; [*piano*] tinny
cascajo SM [1] (= *grava*) gravel, piece of gravel
[2] [*de vasija*] fragments *pl*, shards *pl*
[3] (= *trasto*) junk, rubbish, garbage (*EEUU*); ✦**MODISMO estar hecho un ~*** to be a wreck*
cascajoso ADJ gritty, gravelly
cascanueces SM INV nutcracker; **un ~** a pair of nutcrackers
cascar ▸conjug 1g◂ (A) VT [1] (= *romper*) [+ *nuez*] to crack; [+ *huevo*] to break, crack; [+ *taza, plato*] to chip
[2] (*) (= *pegar*) **cuando se entere tu padre, te casca** when your father finds out, he'll thump you *o* give you a bashing*; **cuando se pelea con sus amigos, siempre le cascan** when he fights with his friends they always give him a bashing*
[3] (*) (= *poner*) **me ~on una multa por aparcar mal** I was landed with *o* slapped with a fine for parking in the wrong place*
[4] (= *chivar*) to squeal*, tell*
[5] ✦**MODISMO ~la**‡ (= *morirse*) to kick the bucket*; **la cascó la semana pasada** he kicked the bucket last week*
(B) VI (*) (= *charlar*) to chatter, natter*
(C) **cascarse** VPR [1] (= *romperse*) [*nuez*] to crack; [*huevo*] to break, crack; [*taza, plato*] to chip; **se le ha cascado la voz** his voice has gone
[2] ✦**MODISMO cascársela**** to wank**, jerk off**
cáscara SF [1] (= *cubierta*) [*de huevo, nuez*] shell; [*de grano*] husk, shuck (*EEUU*); [*de fruta*] peel, rind, skin; **patatas cocidas con ~** potatoes in their jackets; ✦**MODISMOS ser de la ~ amarga*** to be wild, be a troublemaker; (*Pol*) have radical ideas; (*sexualmente*) to be the other sort; **dar ~s de novillo a algn** (*LAm*) to thrash sb ► **cáscara de huevo** eggshell ► **cáscara de limón** lemon peel ► **cáscara de plátano** banana skin ► **cáscara sagrada** (*Farm*) cascara
[2] (* *euf*) **¡cáscaras!** well I'm blowed!*; ✦**MODISMO no hay más ~s** there's no other way out*
[3] **cáscaras** (*Andes*‡) (= *ropa*) clothes, togs*, threads (*EEUU**)
[4] ✦**MODISMO tener ~** (*CAm**) to have a cheek*
cascarazo* SM [1] (*Andes, Caribe*) (= *puñetazo*) punch
[2] (*Andes*) (= *azote*) lash
[3] (*Caribe*) (= *trago*) swig*, slug (*EEUU**)
cascarear* ▸conjug 1a◂ (A) VT (*Andes, CAm*) to belt*, smack
(B) VI (*Méx**) to scrape a living
cascarilla (A) ADJ (*Caribe, Cono Sur*) (= *enojadizo*) touchy, quick-tempered
(B) SF [1] (*Caribe, Cono Sur*) quick-tempered person
[2] (*Andes, Cono Sur Med*) medicinal herb
cascarón SM eggshell, broken eggshell; ✦**MODISMOS meterse en su ~** to go into one's shell; **está recién salido del ~** he's a bit wet behind the ears
cascarrabias SMF INV grouch*
cascarria SF (*Cono Sur*) [1] (*) (= *mugre*) filth, muck
[2] (*Agr*) sheep droppings *pl*
cascarriento* ADJ (*Cono Sur*) filthy, greasy, mucky*
cascarrón* ADJ gruff, abrupt, rough
cascarudo (A) ADJ thick-shelled, having a thick skin
(B) SM (*Cono Sur*) beetles (*collectively*)
casco SM [1] [*de soldado*] helmet; [*de obrero*] protective helmet, safety helmet, hard hat; [*de motorista, ciclista*] (crash) helmet; **los ~s azules (de la ONU)** the UN blue berets; ► **casco de acero** steel helmet
[2] [*de ciudad*] ► **casco antiguo**: **el ~ antiguo de la ciudad** the old quarter *o* part of the city ► **casco histórico**: **el ~ histórico de la ciudad** the historic city centre *o* (*EEUU*) center ► **casco urbano** built-up area ► **casco viejo**: **el ~ viejo de la ciudad** the old quarter *o* part of the city
[3] (= *envase*) empty bottle; **te dan 50 céntimos al devolver el ~** they give you 50 cents back on the empty (bottle); **había ~s (de botellas) por todo el parque** there were empty bottles *o* empties all over the park
[4] **cascos** [*de walkman*] headphones
[5] **cascos*** (= *cabeza*) nut* *sing*; ✦**MODISMOS alegre** *o* **ligero de ~s** (= *irreflexivo*) reckless, foolhardy; (= *frívolo*) flighty; **sentar los ~s** to settle down; *ver tb* **calentar A1**
[6] (= *pezuña*) hoof
[7] (= *trozo*) [*de fruta*] segment, piece; [*de cebolla*] slice; [*de vasija*] fragment, shard
[8] (*Náut*) [*de barco*] hull
[9] (*Mec*) [*de cableado*] casing
[10] (*LAm*) (= *edificio vacío*) empty building

➤ LENGUA Y USO: **casar C** 51.3

11 (*LAm Agr*) ranch house, ranch and outbuildings; (*Cono Sur*) [*de hacienda*] part, section

12 [*de sombrero*] crown

cascorros* SMPL (*Méx*) shoes

cascorvo* ADJ (*CAm*) bow-legged

cascote SM piece of rubble; **~s** rubble *sing*

cascundear ▸conjug 1a◂ VT (*CAm*) to beat, thrash

cáseo SM curd

caseoso ADJ cheesy, like cheese

casería SF 1 (= *casa*) country house

2 (*LAm*†) (= *clientela*) customers *pl*, clientèle

caserío SM country house

caserna SF (*LAm*) barracks *pl*

casero/a Ⓐ ADJ 1 (= *hecho en casa*) [*comida, sopa, artefacto*] homemade; [*remedio*] household, home *antes de s*; **cocina casera** home cooking; **un vídeo ~** a home video; **eso es filosofía casera** that is homespun philosophy; **tareas caseras** housework *sing*, domestic chores; **de fabricación casera** homemade; **sufrió un pequeño accidente ~** she had a minor domestic accident, she had a small accident at home

2 (= *hogareño*) **soy muy ~** I'm the home-loving sort, I'm the stay-at-home type; **llevan una vida muy casera** they're always at home

3 (*Dep*) **una victoria casera** a home win, a win for the home side; **un árbitro ~** *a referee biased in favour of the home team*

Ⓑ SM/F 1 (= *propietario*) landlord/landlady

2 (*en casa de campo*) caretaker

3 (= *inquilino*) tenant, occupier

4 (= *persona hogareña*) home bird*, homebody (*EEUU*)

5 (*LAm*) (= *cliente*) customer, client

6 (*Caribe*) (= *repartidor*) delivery man/woman

caserón SM large house, ramshackle house

caseta SF 1 (= *lugar cerrado*) [*de bañista*] changing room; (*en exposición*) stand; (*en mercado*) stall ▸ **caseta del timón** (*Náut*) wheelhouse ▸ **caseta de perro** kennel, doghouse (*EEUU*)

2 [*de feria*] stall

3 (*Ftbl*) dugout; **mandar a algn a la ~** to send sb for an early bath, send sb off

casete [ka'set] Ⓐ SF (= *cinta*) cassette

Ⓑ SM (= *aparato*) cassette player

casetera SF (*LAm*) cassette deck

cash [katʃ] SM (*pl* **cash**) (*tb* **~ and carry**) cash-and-carry store

casi ADV 1 (= *indicando aproximación*) almost, nearly; **está ~ terminado** it's almost *o* nearly finished; **son ya ~ las tres** it's almost *o* nearly three o'clock; **¡huy!, ~ me caigo** oops! I almost *o* nearly fell over; **hace ~ un año que empezó la guerra** it's almost a year since war broke out; **nada ha cambiado en los ~ dos años transcurridos** nothing has changed in what is almost two years; **despidieron a la ~ totalidad de la plantilla** they sacked virtually *o* practically the entire staff; **estaba congelado, o ~** it was frozen, or very near it; **ocurre lo mismo en ~ todos los países** the same thing happens in virtually *o* practically all countries; **—¿habéis terminado? —casi, casi** "have you finished?" — "just about *o* very nearly"; **~ nada** almost *o* virtually nothing, hardly anything; **no sabemos ~ nada de lo que está ocurriendo** we know almost *o* virtually nothing about what's going on, we know hardly anything about what's going on; **100 dólares ..., ¡~ nada!** (*iró*) 100 dollars, a mere trifle!; **~ nunca** hardly ever, almost never; **~ nunca hay sitio en la biblioteca** there is hardly ever any room in the library; **~ siempre** almost always

2 (*indicando indecisión*) almost; **no sé, ~ prefiero no ir** I don't know, I think I'd rather not go; **~ sería mejor empezar otra vez** it might be better to start again

> **CASI**
>
> Las dos traducciones principales de **casi** en inglés son **almost** y **nearly**:
>
> Estoy casi lista
> ***I'm almost** o **nearly ready***
> Eran casi las cuatro cuando sonó el teléfono
> ***It was almost** o **nearly four o'clock when the telephone rang***
> Nos vemos casi todos los días
> ***We meet almost** o **nearly every day***
>
> • Cuando **almost** y **nearly** acompañan a un verbo, se colocan detrás de éste si se trata de un verbo auxiliar o modal y delante en el caso de los demás verbos:
>
> Casi me rompo la muñeca
> ***I almost** o **nearly broke my wrist***
> Mi hijo ya casi habla
> ***My son can almost** o **nearly talk***
>
> Sin embargo, hay algunos casos en los que no podemos utilizar **nearly**:
>
> • delante de adverbios que terminan en **-ly**
>
> "¿Qué estáis haciendo aquí?", nos preguntó casi con enfado
> ***"What are you doing here?" he asked almost angrily***
>
> • delante de **like**:
>
> Se comporta casi como un niño
> ***He behaves almost like a child***
>
> • acompañando a adjetivos o sustantivos que, normalmente, no pueden ser modificados:
>
> El mono tenía una expresión casi humana
> ***The monkey had an almost human expression***
> Me pareció casi un alivio
> ***I found it almost a relief***
>
> • delante de palabras de sentido negativo, como **never**, **no**, **none**, **no-one**, **nothing** y **nowhere**; en estos casos, muchas veces se traduce también por **practically**:
>
> No dijo casi nada
> ***She said almost** o **practically nothing***
> No había casi nadie en la fiesta
> ***There was almost** o **practically no-one at the party***
>
> **NOTA:** En estos casos también se puede usar la construcción **hardly** + **ever/any/anything/** *etc*:
>
> ***She said hardly anything*** ◇ ***There was hardly anyone at the party***
>
> *Para otros usos y ejemplos ver la entrada.*

casilla SF 1 (= *caseta*) [*de jardín*] hut, shed; (*en parque, jardín zoológico*) keeper's lodge; (*en mercado*) stall; [*de guardagujas*] pointsman's *o* (*EEUU*) switchman's hut ▸ **casilla electoral** (*Méx*) polling-station

2 (= *compartimento*) (*para cartas*) pigeonhole, mail box (*EEUU*); [*de caja*] compartment; [*de formulario*] box; [*de papel*] ruled column, section ▸ **casilla de correos, casilla postal** post office box (number), P.O. Box

3 (*en ajedrez, damas*) square; ✦***MODISMOS*** **sacar a algn de sus ~s** to infuriate sb, drive sb up the wall*; **salirse de sus ~s** to fly off the handle*

4 (= *cabina*) (*en tren, camión*) cab

5 (*Teat*) box office

6 (*Andes*) (= *retrete*) lavatory, bathroom (*EEUU*)

7 (*Caribe*) (= *trampa*) bird trap

casillero SM 1 (*para cartas*) (*en oficina*) pigeonholes *pl*, set of pigeonholes; (*en oficina de correos*) sorting rack

2 (*para equipaje*) luggage locker

3 (*Ftbl**) scorer

casimba SF (*LAm*) = **cacimba**

casimir SM cashmere

casimiro ADJ (*LAm hum*) cross-eyed

casinista SM clubman, member of a casino

casino SM 1 [*de juego*] casino

2 (*club social*) club

3 (*Cono Sur*) (= *comedor*) canteen

Casio SM Cassius

casis SF INV (*tb* **~ de negro**) blackcurrant (bush) ▸ **casis de rojo** redcurrant (bush)

casita SF small house, cottage; **los niños están jugando a las ~s** the children are playing houses

▼**caso** SM 1 (= *circunstancia*) 1·1 (*gen*) case; **ahí tienes el ~ de Pedro** take Pedro's case; **en esos ~s la policía corta la circulación** in such cases the police block the road off; **en el ~ de Francia** in France's case, in the case of France; **me creía en el ~ de informarles** I felt obliged to inform you

1·2 **en ~ afirmativo** if so; **en (el) ~ contrario** if not, otherwise; **en cualquier ~** in any case; **en ~ de** in the event of; **esto protege al conductor en ~ de accidente** this protects the driver in the event of an accident; **en ~ de necesidad** if necessary; **en ~ de no ser posible** should it not be possible; **en (el) ~ de que venga** if he comes, should he come; **en ~ de que llueva, iremos en autobús** if it rains, we'll go by bus; **en ese ~** in that case; **en el mejor de los ~s** at best; **en ~ necesario** if necessary; **en ~ negativo** if not, otherwise; **en el peor de los ~s** at worst; **en su ~** where appropriate; **su finalidad es el cuidado y, en su ~, educación de los niños** their aim is to care for and, where appropriate, educate the children; **en tal ~** in such a case; **en todo ~** in any case; **en último ~** as a last resort, in the last resort; **en uno u otro ~** one way or the other; *ver tb* **extremo**[1] **1**

1·3 **darse el ~**: **todavía no se ha dado el ~** such a situation hasn't yet arisen; **dado el ~ que tuvieras que irte, ¿a dónde irías?** in the event that you did have to go, where would you go?; **el ~ es que ...**: **el ~ es que se me olvidó su nombre** the thing is I forgot her name; **el ~ es que tiene razón** the fact is (that) she's right; **el ~ es que no me gustó** basically I didn't like it; **el ~ es que me entiendan** the main thing is to make myself understood; **hablar al ~** to keep to the point; **hacer al ~** to be relevant; **pongamos por ~ que ...** let us suppose that ...; **pongamos por ~ a Luis** let's take Luis as an example; **ponte en mi ~** put yourself in my position; **según el ~** as the case may be; **necesitan una o dos sesiones de rayos, según el ~**

➤ LENGUA Y USO: **caso 4** 29.2

they need either one or two X-ray treatment sessions, as the case may be *o* depending on the circumstances; **sustitúyase, según el ~, por una frase u otra** replace with one or other of the phrases, as appropriate; **según lo requiera el ~** as the case may require, depending on the requirements of the case in question; **este ejemplo debería servir para el ~** this example should serve our purpose *o* should do; **no tiene ~** (*Méx*) there's no point (in it); **¡vamos al ~!** let's get down to business!; **vaya por ~ …** to give an example …; **venir al ~** to be relevant; **no venir al ~** to be beside the point; **verse en el ~ de hacer algo** to be obliged to do sth

2 (*Med*) case; **ha habido tres ~s de meningitis** there have been three cases of meningitis ► **caso clínico** clinical case

3 (= *asunto*) affair; (*Jur*) case; **el ~ Hess** the Hess affair; **la juez encargada del ~** the judge hearing the case; **es un ~ perdido** [*situación*] it's a hopeless case; [*persona*] he's a dead loss, he's hopeless ► **caso de autos** case in hand ► **caso de conciencia** question of conscience ► **caso fortuito** (*Jur*) act of God; (= *suceso imprevisto*) unforeseen circumstance ► **caso límite** extreme case

4 **hacer ~ a** *o* **de algo** to take notice of sth, pay attention to sth; **no me hacen ~** they take no notice of me, they pay no attention to me; **no le hagas ~** don't take any notice of him; **¡no haga usted ~!** take no notice!; **hazle ~, que ella tiene más experiencia** listen to her, she has more experience; **maldito el ~ que me hace*** a fat lot of notice he takes of me*; **ni ~: tú a todo lo que te diga ¡ni ~!*** take no notice of what he says!; **se lo dije, pero ni ~** I told him, but he took absolutely no notice; **hacer ~ omiso de algo** to ignore sth

5 (*Ling*) case

casona SF large house

casorio* SM 1 (= *matrimonio precipitado*) hasty marriage, unwise marriage

2 (*Méx*) (= *boda*) wedding, marriage

caspa SF dandruff

Caspio ADJ **Mar ~** Caspian Sea

caspiroleta SF (*Andes, Caribe, Cono Sur*) egg-nog, egg flip

cáspita EXCL my goodness!

casposo ADJ covered in dandruff

casquería SF tripe and offal shop

casquero/a SM/F seller of tripe and offal

casquete SM 1 (= *casco*) (*Mil*) helmet; (*Mec*) cap ► **casquete de hielo** icecap ► **casquete de nieve** snowcap ► **casquete polar** polar icecap

2 (= *gorra*) skullcap

3 **echar un ~**** to have a screw**

casquijo SM gravel

casquillo SM 1 (= *cápsula*) (*Téc*) ferrule, tip; (*Mil*) cartridge case ► **casquillo de bala** bullet shell

2 (*LAm*) horseshoe

casquinona SF (*Andes*) (= *botella*) beer bottle; (= *cerveza*) beer

casquivano/a Ⓐ ADJ scatterbrained

Ⓑ SM/F scatterbrain

casta SF 1 (= *clan*) caste; **el sistema de ~s de la India** the Indian caste system

2 (= *estirpe*) stock; **es de ~ de aristócratas** she is of aristocratic stock; **eso me viene de ~** it's in my blood; ✦***REFRÁN*** **de ~ le viene al galgo** it's in the blood *o* genes

3 (= *grupo social*) class; **la ~ militar** the military class

4 (= *calidad*) class; **el equipo jugó con ~** the team played with class; **un toro de ~** a thoroughbred bull; **un torero de ~** a top class bullfighter

5 (*Méx Tip*) font

castamente ADV chastely, purely

castaña SF 1 (= *fruto*) chestnut ✦***MODISMOS*** **conducir a toda ~*** to drive flat out; **sacar a algn las ~s del fuego** to get sb off the hook; **ser una ~*** to be a drag*; **¡toma ~!*** (*indicando disfrute*) take that!; (*indicando sorpresa*) just imagine! ► **castaña de agua** water chestnut ► **castaña de Indias** horse chestnut ► **castaña del Brasil** Brazil nut ► **castaña de Pará** Brazil nut

2 (*) (= *golpe*) punch; **darse una ~** to give o.s. a knock

3 (*) (= *borrachera*) **cogerse una ~** to get pissed**

4 [*de pelo*] bun, chignon

5 (= *vasija*) demijohn

6 (*) (= *año*) **tiene 71 ~s** he's 71 (years old)

castañar SM chestnut grove

castañazo* SM (= *puñetazo*) punch, thump; (= *choque*) bump

castañero/a SM/F chestnut seller

castañeta SF 1 (*con dedos*) snap (*of the fingers*)

2 **castañetas** (*Mús*) castanets

castañetazo SM snap, crack, click

castañetear ▸conjug 1a◂ Ⓐ VT 1 [+ *dedos*] to snap

2 (*Mús*) to play on the castanets

Ⓑ VI 1 (= *sonar*) [*dedos*] to snap, click; [*dientes*] to chatter; [*huesos*] to crack; **~ con los dedos** to snap one's fingers

2 (*Mús*) to play the castanets

castañeteo SM 1 (= *sonido*) [*de dedos*] snapping; [*de dientes*] chattering; [*de huesos*] cracking

2 (*Mús*) sound of the castanets

castaño Ⓐ ADJ [*pelo*] chestnut, chestnut-coloured, chestnut-colored (*EEUU*); [*ojos*] brown; ✦***MODISMO*** **esto pasa de ~ oscuro** this is beyond a joke

Ⓑ SM (*Bot*) chestnut tree; ✦***MODISMO*** **pelar el ~** (*Caribe**) to hoof it* ► **castaño de Indias** horse chestnut tree

castañuela SF castanet; ✦***MODISMO*** **estar como** *o* **hecho unas ~s** to be very merry, be in high spirits

castañuelo ADJ [*caballo*] chestnut-coloured, chestnut-colored (*EEUU*), brown

castellanizar ▸conjug 1f◂ VT to hispanicize, give a Spanish form to

castellano/a Ⓐ ADJ (*Pol*) Castilian; (*Ling*) Spanish

Ⓑ SM/F Castilian

Ⓒ SM (*Ling*) Castilian, Spanish

CASTELLANO

In the Spanish-speaking world **castellano** *rather than* **español** *is a very common term for the Spanish language. Under the Spanish Constitution* **castellano** *is Spain's official language, but in some of the* **Comunidades Autónomas** *it shares official status with another language. Use of one or other term in Spain will depend on where the speaker is from, and where they place themselves in the linguistic debate, while in general the Latin Americans tend to favour the term* **castellano**.

⇨ See also LENGUAS COOFICIALES, COMUNIDAD AUTÓNOMA

castellanohablante, castellanoparlante Ⓐ ADJ Castilian-speaking, Spanish-speaking

Ⓑ SMF Castilian speaker, Spanish speaker

castellonense ADJ, SMF = **castellonés**

castellonés/esa Ⓐ ADJ of/from Castellón

Ⓑ SM/F native/inhabitant of Castellón; **los castelloneses** the people of Castellón

casticidad SF, **casticismo** SM 1 (*Ling*) purity, correctness

2 [*de costumbres*] traditional character, authenticity

casticista ADJ, SMF purist

castidad SF chastity, purity

castigador(a) SM/F ladykiller/seductress

castigar ▸conjug 1h◂ VT 1 (*por delito, falta*)

1·1 [+ *delincuente, pecador, culpable*] to punish (**por** for); [+ *niño*] (*gen*) to punish; (*sin salir*) to ground, keep in; **es un delito que puede ser castigado con 15 años de prisión** it is a crime punishable by 15 years' imprisonment; **la profesora me dejó castigado al terminar las clases** the teacher kept me in *o* made me stay behind after school; **la ~on por decir mentiras** she was punished for telling lies; **lo ~on sin postre** he was not allowed any dessert as punishment; **~ la carne** (*Rel*) to mortify the flesh

1·2 (*Dep*) to penalize (**por** for); **lo ~on con tarjeta amarilla** he was given a yellow card; **el árbitro los castigó con un penalti** the referee awarded a penalty against them

1·3 (*Com, Pol*) to punish; **Cuba fue castigada con sanciones comerciales** Cuba was punished with economic sanctions; **el socialismo salió muy castigado de las urnas** socialism suffered heavy losses in the elections

2 (= *perjudicar*) [*guerra, crisis*] to afflict, affect; [*calor*] to beat down on; [*frío*] to bite into; **el sol castigó con dureza a los tenistas** the sun beat down mercilessly on the tennis players; **la ciudad más castigada por los bombardeos** the city worst hit by the bombing

3 (*físicamente*) (= *maltratar*) to damage, harm; **castigamos a nuestro cuerpo con los excesos en la bebida** we harm our bodies with excessive drinking; **~ el hígado** (*iró*) to damage one's liver

4 [+ *caballo*] to ride hard; **~ mucho a un caballo** to ride a horse very hard

5 (= *corregir*) [+ *estilo*] to refine; [+ *texto*] to correct, revise

6 (= *enamorar*) to seduce

7 (*Com*) [+ *gastos*] to reduce

8 (*Méx*) (= *apretar*) [+ *tornillo, cuerda*] to tighten (up)

castigo SM 1 (*por delito, falta*) punishment; **celda de ~** punishment cell; **una cosa así no puede quedarse sin ~** such an act cannot go unpunished; **el gobierno ha sufrido un duro ~ en las urnas** the government has suffered heavy losses in the elections ► **castigo corporal** corporal punishment ► **castigo divino** divine retribution

2 (*Dep*) penalty; **área de ~** penalty area, penalty box; **golpe de ~** (*Rugby*) penalty, penalty kick
3 (= *tormento*) **ese cantante es un ~ que no nos merecemos** we don't deserve to have a singer like that inflicted upon us; **el partido fue un ~ para los aficionados** the match was purgatory for the fans; **la artillería sometió durante horas a la ciudad a un duro ~** the artillery pounded the city for hours on end
4 (*Literat*) correction

Castilla SF Castile ► **Castilla la Nueva** New Castile ► **Castilla la Vieja** Old Castile; ✦*MODISMO* **¡ancha es ~!** it takes all sorts!

castilla SF (*Cono Sur, Méx*) 1 (*Ling*) Castilian, Spanish; ✦*MODISMO* **hablar la ~** to speak Spanish
2 ✦*MODISMO* **de ~** (*Hist*) Spanish, from the old country

Castilla-León SM Castile and León

castillejo SM 1 (*Arquit*) scaffolding
2 [*de niño*] babywalker

castillo SM castle ► **castillo de arena** sandcastle ► **castillo de fuego** firework set piece ► **castillo de naipes** house of cards ► **castillo de popa** aftercastle ► **castillo de proa** forecastle; ✦*MODISMO* **~s en el aire** castles in the air

casting ['kastin] SM (*Cine*) casting

castizo ADJ 1 (= *tradicional*) traditional
2 (= *auténtico*) pure, authentic; **es un tipo ~** he's one of the best; **un aragonés ~** a true-blue Aragonese, an Aragonese through and through
3 (*Ling*) pure, correct

casto ADJ chaste, pure

castor SM beaver

castoreño SM 1 (= *sombrero*) beaver
2 (*Taur*) picador's hat

castóreo SM (*Farm*) castor

castra SF 1 (*Bot*) (= *acto*) pruning
2 (= *época*) pruning season

castración SF 1 (*Zool*) castration, gelding
2 (*Bot*) pruning
3 (*Agr*) extraction of honeycombs

castrado Ⓐ ADJ castrated
Ⓑ SM eunuch

castrar ▸conjug 1a◂ VT 1 (*Zool*) [+ *toro*] to castrate; [+ *caballo*] to geld; [+ *gato*] to doctor
2 (*Bot*) to prune, cut back
3 (= *debilitar*) to impair, weaken

castrense ADJ army *antes de s*, military

castro SM 1 (= *fortaleza*) hill-fort
2 (*Hist*) Iron-Age settlement

casual Ⓐ ADJ 1 (= *fortuito*) chance *antes de s*; **un encuentro ~** a chance encounter; **es un hecho ~ y aislado** it's an isolated, chance happening; **su éxito no es ~, sino fruto del trabajo** his success cannot be put down to chance but is the product of hard work; **el descubrimiento de la obra fue ~** the work was discovered by chance; **nada es ~** nothing happens by chance; **de forma** *o* **manera ~** by chance; **no es ~ que ...** it's no coincidence that ...
2 (*Ling*) case *antes de s*; **desinencia ~** case ending
Ⓑ SM **por un ~*** by any chance

casualidad SF 1 (= *azar*) chance; (= *coincidencia*) coincidence; **¿cree en el destino o en la ~?** do you believe in destiny or in chance?; **sería mucha ~** *o* **ya sería ~ que os pusieseis enfermos los dos al mismo tiempo** it would be too much of a coincidence if you both fell ill at the same time; **nuestra victoria no ha sido fruto de la ~** our victory was no fluke; **da la ~ de que ...** it (just) so happens that ...; **dio la ~ de que ...** it just so happened that ...; **ese día dio la ~ de que decidí salir a dar una vuelta** that day I happened to decide to go out for a walk, as luck would have it I decided to go out for a walk that day; **de** *o* **por ~** by chance; **tuve muchísima suerte en el accidente: estoy vivo de ~** I was really lucky in the accident: it's purely by chance *o* pure chance that I'm still alive; **un día entró de ~** he dropped in *o* by one day; **nos enteramos casi por ~** we found out almost by accident; **¿no tendrás un pañuelo, por ~?** you wouldn't happen to have a handkerchief, would you?; **no meten un gol ni por ~** they've got no chance *o* hope of scoring a goal; **no toca un libro ni por ~** he would never think of picking up a book; **¡qué ~!** what a coincidence!; **¡qué ~ verle aquí!** what a coincidence meeting you here!, fancy meeting you here!
2 (= *suceso casual*) coincidence; **fue una pura ~** it was sheer coincidence; **mi carrera profesional es una suma de ~es** my career has been a series of coincidences; **por una de esas ~es de la vida** by one of life's little coincidences
3 **casualidades** (*CAm*) (= *víctimas*) casualties

casualmente ADV by chance, fortuitously (*frm*); **~ lo vi ayer** I happened to see him yesterday

casuario SM cassowary

casuca SF, **casucha** SF hovel

casuista SMF casuist

casuística SF casuistry

casulla SF chasuble

cata¹ SM *o* SF 1 (= *acto*) tasting, sampling ► **cata de vino** wine tasting
2 (= *porción*) sample
3 (*LAm Min*) trial excavation, test bore
4 ✦*MODISMO* **ir en ~ de algo*** to go looking for sth

cata² SF (*LAm*) (= *loro*) parrot

catabre SM (*Andes, Caribe*) gourd

catacaldos† SM INV 1 (= *persona inconstante*) rolling stone
2 (= *entrometido*) busybody, meddler
3 (*Arte*) dilettante

cataclismismo SM doomwatching

cataclismista SMF doomwatcher

cataclismo SM cataclysm

catacumbas SFPL catacombs

catador SM 1 [*de comida*] taster, sampler
2 [*de vinos*] taster

catadura SF 1 (= *acto*) tasting, sampling
2 (= *aspecto*) looks *pl*, appearance; **de mala ~** nasty-looking

catafalco SM catafalque

catafotos SMPL (*Aut*) cat's-eyes

catajarria SF (*Caribe*) string, series

catalán/ana Ⓐ ADJ, SM/F Catalan, Catalonian
Ⓑ SM (*Ling*) Catalan

> **CATALÁN**
>
> *Catalan is a romance language whose earliest literature dates back to the 12th century. In the Middle Ages Catalan military expansion spread the use of the language beyond modern Catalonia, but following the unification of Castile and Aragon the language lost ground to Castilian. During the Franco régime the use of Catalan and other minority national languages was prohibited in the media and in public institutions. This, together with the influx of Castilian-speaking immigrants, posed a threat to the survival of the language. Since 1979, when Catalonia's autonomous government, the* **Generalitat**, *was reestablished and Catalan gained* **lengua cooficial** *status, the language has returned to public life in Catalonia and is flourishing. Indeed, many Catalan authors publish first in Catalan and only later in Castilian. Outside Catalonia, Catalan is also spoken by large numbers of people in the Balearic Islands and Andorra.* **Valenciano**, *a language spoken in the Valencia region, is closely related.*
>
> ⇨ *See also* LENGUAS COOFICIALES

catalanismo SM 1 (*Ling*) catalanism, *word or phrase etc peculiar to Catalonia*
2 (= *tendencia*) *sense of the differentness of Catalonia*; (*Pol*) doctrine of Catalan autonomy, belief in Catalan autonomy

catalanista Ⓐ ADJ that supports *etc* Catalan autonomy; **el movimiento ~** the movement for Catalan autonomy; **la familia es muy ~** the family strongly supports Catalan autonomy
Ⓑ SMF supporter *etc* of Catalan autonomy

catalanizar ▸conjug 1f◂ VT to make Catalan, make a Catalan version of

catalejo SM spyglass, telescope

catalepsia SF catalepsy

cataléptico/a ADJ, SM/F cataleptic

Catalina SF Catherine

catálisis SF INV catalysis

catalítico ADJ catalytic

catalizador SM 1 (*Quím*) catalyst
2 (*Aut*) catalytic converter

catalizar ▸conjug 1f◂ VT to catalyse

catalogable ADJ classifiable

catalogación SF cataloguing, cataloging (*EEUU*)

catalogar ▸conjug 1h◂ VT 1 (*en catálogo*) to catalogue, catalog (*EEUU*)
2 (= *clasificar*) to classify (**de** as); **una zona catalogada de interés artístico** an area classified *o* designated as "of artistic interest"

catálogo SM catalogue, catalog (*EEUU*); **el libro está fuera de ~** the book is out of print ► **catálogo colectivo** union catalogue ► **catálogo de materias** subject index ► **catálogo de viajes** travel brochure

Cataluña SF Catalonia

catamarán SM catamaran

cataplasma SF 1 (*Med*) poultice
2 (*) (= *persona*) bore

cataplines* SMPL goolies**

cataplum EXCL bang!, crash!

catapulta SF catapult, slingshot (*EEUU*)

catapultar ▸conjug 1a◂ VT to catapult

catapum EXCL bang!, crash!

catapún* ADJ **una cosa del año ~** an ancient old thing*; **películas del año ~** films from the year dot

catar ▸conjug 1a◂ VT [1] (*Culin*) to taste, sample
[2] (= *examinar*) to examine, inspect
[3] (= *mirar*) to look at; **¡cata!** ◊ **¡cátale!** just look at him!
[4] [+ *colmenas*] to extract honeycombs from

catarata SF [1] (*Geog*) waterfall, cataract ► **Cataratas de Niágara** Niagara Falls
[2] (*Med*) cataract

catarral ADJ catarrhal

catarriento ADJ (*LAm*) = **catarroso**

catarro SM (*Med*) (= *resfriado*) cold; (= *mucosidad*) catarrh; **pescarse** *o* **pillarse un ~** to catch a cold ► **catarro crónico del pecho** chest trouble

catarroso ADJ with a cold; (*Med*) catarrhal

catarsis SF INV catharsis

catártico ADJ cathartic

catasalsas† SM INV = **catacaldos**

catastral ADJ relating to the property register; **valores ~es** property values, land values

catastro SM property register, land registry

catástrofe SF catastrophe, disaster; **esta guerra ha supuesto una ~ para el país** this war has been a catastrophe *o* a disaster for the country; **~ aérea/ferroviaria** air/rail disaster; **la fiesta fue una ~** the party was a disaster ► **catástrofe natural** natural disaster

catastrófico ADJ catastrophic, disastrous

catastrofismo SM alarmism

catastrofista Ⓐ ADJ alarmist
Ⓑ SMF alarmist

catatán SM (*Cono Sur*) punishment

catatar ▸conjug 1a◂ VT (*Andes*) to ill-treat

catauro SM (*Caribe*) basket

catavinos SM INV [1] (= *enólogo*) wine taster
[2] (= *copa*) wine taster's glass
[3] (*) (= *bebedor*) boozer*

cate SM [1] (= *golpe*) punch, bash*
[2] (*) (= *suspenso*) **dar un ~ a algn** to fail sb, flunk sb (*EEUU**)

catear ▸conjug 1a◂ VT [1] (= *buscar*) to search
[2] (= *probar*) to test, try
[3] (*) [+ *candidato, estudiante, examen*] to fail, flunk (*EEUU**)
[4] (*LAm Min*) to prospect
[5] (*Méx*) [*policía*] to raid

catecismo SM catechism

catecúmeno/a SM/F catechumen

cátedra Ⓐ SF [1] (*en universidad*) chair, professorship; **ostentar una ~** to hold a chair (**de** in); **hablar ex ~** (*Rel*) to speak ex cathedra; (*fig*) to speak with authority; **hacer oposiciones** *u* **opositar para una ~** to compete for a chair *etc* by public competitive examination; **sentar ~ sobre algo** to pontificate about sth
[2] (*en enseñanza secundaria*) post of head of department
[3] (= *aula*) seminar room
[4] (*Caribe**) wonder, marvel; **es ~** ◊ **está la ~** it's marvellous
Ⓑ ADJ (*Caribe*) wonderful, marvellous, excellent

catedral SF cathedral; ✦**MODISMO como una ~*** enormous, gigantic

catedralicio ADJ cathedral *antes de s*

catedrático/a SM/F [1] [*de universidad*] professor ► **catedrático/a de inglés** professor of English
[2] (*en enseñanza secundaria*) head of department ► **catedrático/a de inglés** head of English, head of the English department

cátedro* SM = **catedrático**

categoría SF [1] (*en clasificación*) category; **existen tres ~s diferentes** there are three different categories; **obtuvo la ~ de cinturón amarillo** he got his yellow belt; **hoteles de máxima ~** top-class *o* top-flight hotels; **de primera ~** [*hotel, servicio*] first-class *antes de s* ► **categoría gramatical** part of speech ► **categoría laboral** work category ► **categoría profesional** professional status ► **categoría social** social group
[2] (= *calidad*) quality; **fue un espectáculo de ~** it was a top-quality show; **telenovelas de ínfima ~** soap operas of the very worst kind; **han confirmado su reconocida ~ artística** they have confirmed their recognized status *o* standing as artists; **no hay hoy ningún maestro de su ~** nowadays there are no maestros of his calibre *o* in his class; **es hombre de cierta ~** he is a man of some standing; **productos de baja ~** poor quality products; **de ~** [*deportista, artista*] top-class *antes de s*; **es una orquesta de ~** it is a top-class orchestra
[3] (= *apartado*) (*en premio*) category; (*en deporte*) event; **en la ~ de ensayo** in the essay section *o* category; **en la ~ femenina** in the women's event
[4] (= *rango profesional*) grade; (*Mil*) rank; **fue ascendido a la ~ de director general** he was promoted (to the position of) director general; **oficial de baja ~** low-ranking officer

categóricamente ADV categorically

categórico ADJ [*respuesta*] categorical; [*mentira*] outright, downright; [*orden*] express

categorización SF categorization

categorizar ▸conjug 1f◂ VT to categorize

catenaria SF (*Elec, Ferro*) overhead power cable

cateo SM (*Méx*) search, raid

catequesis SF INV (*Rel*) catechesis

catequista SMF (*Rel*) catechist

catequizar ▸conjug 1f◂ VT [1] (*Rel*) to catechize, instruct in Christian doctrine
[2] (*) (= *convencer*) to win over, talk round

catering ['katerin] SM INV catering ► **empresa de catering** caterer's, catering firm

caterva SF throng, crowd; **venir en ~** to come in a throng, come thronging

catetada* SF piece of nonsense

catéter SM catheter

catetismo* SM slow-wittedness, boorishness, stupidity

cateto/a* SM/F yokel*, hick (*EEUU**)

catimbao SM (*Andes, Cono Sur*) clown, carnival clown

catinga SF [1] (*Andes, Cono Sur*) (= *olor corporal*) [*de persona*] body odour; [*de animales*] strong smell
[2] (*Cono Sur*) (= *soldado*) soldier

catingoso ADJ (*Andes, Cono Sur*), **catingudo** ADJ (*Andes, Cono Sur*) stinking, foul-smelling

catire/a (*Caribe, Col*) Ⓐ ADJ (= *de pelo rubio*) fair, fair-haired; (= *de piel blanca*) fair-skinned
Ⓑ SM/F [*de pelo rubio*] fair-haired person; [*de piel blanca*] fair-skinned person

catisumba SF (*CAm*), **catisumbada** SF (*CAm*) **una ~ de algo** lots of sth, loads of sth

catita SF (*LAm*) parrot

catitear ▸conjug 1a◂ VI (*Cono Sur*) to dodder, shake (*with old age*)

catiusca Ⓐ ADJ (*Esp*) **botas ~s** wellington boots
Ⓑ SF wellington boot, welly*

catoche SM (*Méx*) bad mood, bad temper

catódico ADJ cathodic, cathode *antes de s*

cátodo SM cathode

catolicidad SF catholicity

catolicismo SM Catholicism, Roman Catholicism

católico/a Ⓐ ADJ (*Rel*) Catholic, Roman Catholic; **no ~** non-Catholic; ✦**MODISMO no estar muy ~*** to be under the weather
Ⓑ SM/F Catholic

Catón SM Cato

catón SM [1] (= *crítico*) severe critic
[2] (= *libro*) primer, first reading book; **eso está en el ~** that is absolutely elementary

catorce Ⓐ ADJ INV, PRON (*gen*) fourteen; (*ordinal, en la fecha*) fourteenth; **le escribí el día ~** I wrote to him on the fourteenth
Ⓑ SM (= *número*) fourteen; (= *fecha*) fourteenth; *ver tb* **seis**

catorceavo Ⓐ SM fourteenth part
Ⓑ ADJ fourteenth; *ver tb* **sexto**

catorrazo SM (*Méx*), **catorro** SM (*Méx*) punch, blow

catracho/a* (*CAm pey*) Ⓐ ADJ of/from El Salvador, Salvadorean
Ⓑ SM/F native/inhabitant of El Salvador, Salvadorean; **los ~s** the people of El Salvador

catre SM [1] (= *litera*) cot; ✦**MODISMO cambiar el ~** to change the subject ► **catre de tijera**, **catre de viento** campbed, folding bed
[2] (*) (= *cama*) bed
[3] ► **catre de balsa** (*Cono Sur*) (= *barquito*) raft

catrecillo SM folding seat

catrera* SF (*Cono Sur*) bunk, bed

catrín† SM (*CAm, Méx*) toff*, dude (*EEUU**)

catsup SM ketchup, catsup (*EEUU*)

Catulo SM Catullus

caucarse ▸conjug 1g◂ (*Cono Sur*) VPR [1] [*persona*] to get old
[2] [*comida*] to go stale

caucasiano/a ADJ, SM/F Caucasian

caucásico/a ADJ, SM/F Caucasian

Cáucaso SM Caucasus

cauce SM [1] (= *lecho*) [*de río, arroyo*] riverbed; [*de canal*] bed; (= *curso*) course; **el ~ del río se seca en verano** the riverbed dries up in the summer; **desviaron el ~ del río** they changed *o* diverted the course of the river; **tras las riadas, las aguas han vuelto a su ~** the river has returned to its normal level after the floods
[2] (= *medio*) channel, means; **por ~s legales** through legal channels *o* means; **han actuado fuera de los ~s oficiales** they have acted outside the official channels; **tras el encuentro, las negociaciones volvieron a su ~** following that encounter, negotiations returned to their normal course; ✦**MODISMO dar ~ a algo**: **este juego da ~ a la imaginación de los niños** this game provides a channel *o* outlet for children's imagination
[3] (*Agr*) irrigation channel

cauch SM (*CAm, Caribe*) couch

cauchal SM rubber plantation

cauchar Ⓐ SM (*Andes*) rubber plantation
Ⓑ VI ▸conjug 1a◂ (*Andes*) to tap, tap trees for rubber

cauchera SF **1** (*Bot*) rubber plant, rubber tree
2 (*Andes*) (= *cauchal*) rubber plantation

cauchero/a Ⓐ ADJ rubber *antes de s*; **industria cauchera** rubber industry
Ⓑ SM/F (*LAm*) worker in a rubber plantation

caucho[1] SM **1** (= *material*) rubber ► **caucho en bruto** natural rubber ► **caucho esponjoso** foam rubber ► **caucho natural** natural rubber ► **caucho sintético** synthetic rubber
2 (*LAm Aut*) tyre, tire (*EEUU*)
3 (*LAm*) (= *impermeable*) raincoat, mac
4 (*Andes*) (= *manta*) waterproof blanket; (= *zapato*) rubber shoe

caucho[2] SM (*Caribe*) couch

cauchutado ADJ rubberized

cauchutar ▸conjug 1a◂ VT to rubberize

caución SF **1** (= *cautela*) caution, wariness
2 (*Jur*) security, bond; **admitir a algn a ~** to grant sb bail

caucionar ▸conjug 1a◂ VT **1** (= *prevenir*) to prevent, guard against
2 (*Jur*) to bail, go bail for

caudal SM **1** [*de río*] volume (of water); **el ~ del río es el normal para esta época del año** the volume of water in the river is normal for this time of year; **el ~ del río desciende en verano** the level of the river goes down in the summer; **la ciudad se abastece del ~ del Guadalquivir** the city draws its water supply from the Guadalquivir
2 (= *fortuna*) fortune, wealth; **malgastó todo su ~** he squandered his entire fortune *o* all his wealth ► **caudal público, caudales públicos** public funds; *ver tb* **caja 2**
3 [*de información, datos, ideas*] wealth, volume

caudaloso ADJ **1** [*río*] wide, fast-flowing; (*liter*) mighty
2 (= *abundante*) copious, abundant

caudillaje SF **1** (= *jefatura*) leadership; **bajo el ~ de algn** under the leadership of sb
2 (*LAm Pol pey*) tyranny, rule by political bosses

caudillismo SM autocratic government

caudillo SM **1** (*Mil*) leader, chief; **el Caudillo** (*Esp*) the Caudillo, Franco
2 (*Pol*) boss*
3 (*LAm*) (= *tirano*) tyrant; (= *líder*) political boss, leader

caula SF (*CAm, Cono Sur*) plot, intrigue

cauri SM cowrie

causa[1] SF **1** (= *motivo*) cause; **la niebla pudo haber sido la ~ del accidente** the accident could have been caused by fog, the fog could have been the cause of *o* reason for the accident; **algunos protestaron sin ~ justificada** some protested for no good reason *o* without true cause; **por ~s ajenas a nuestra voluntad** for reasons beyond our control; **el fuego se inició por ~s desconocidas** it is not known how the fire was started; **veamos cuál es la ~ de todo esto** let us see what the reason for this is; **relación ~-efecto** cause and effect relationship ► **causa final** final cause ► **causa primera** first cause; *ver tb* **conocimiento 2**, **doctor A**
2 a *o* **por ~ de** because of; **el concierto fue aplazado a ~ de la lluvia** the concert was postponed because of rain; **dos personas han muerto a ~ de una explosión** two people have died in an explosion; **no quiero que sufras por mí ~** I don't want you to suffer for my sake *o* on my account
3 (= *ideal*) cause; **la ~ palestina** the Palestinian cause; **es por una buena ~** it's for a good cause; **hacer ~ común con algn** to make common cause with sb ► **causa perdida** lost cause
4 (*Jur*) (*tb* **~ judicial**) lawsuit, case ► **causa criminal** criminal prosecution

causa[2] SF **1** (*Cono Sur*) (= *tentempié*) snack, light meal
2 (*Perú*) (= *plato*) *fish and potato pie, served cold*

causal Ⓐ ADJ **1** [*factor, relación*] causal
2 (*Ling*) **oración ~** clause of reason
Ⓑ SF reason, grounds *pl*

causalidad SF causality

causante Ⓐ ADJ **la explosión ~ del incendio** the explosion that caused the fire
Ⓑ SMF **1** (= *origen*) cause; **el mal tiempo fue el ~ del retraso** the delay was caused by bad weather; **eres el ~ de todas mis desgracias** you are the cause of all my misfortunes
2 (*Méx*) taxpayer
3 (*Jur*) [*de sucesión*] **el ~** the deceased

causar ▸conjug 1a◂ VT [+ *problema, consecuencia, víctima*] to cause; [+ *impresión*] to make; **su mal carácter le causa muchos problemas** his temper causes him a lot of problems; **el tobillo aún le causa algún problema** his ankle is still giving him trouble; **la explosión causó heridas a dos personas** the explosion injured two people, the explosion left two people injured; **la noticia ha causado gran preocupación** the news has caused enormous concern; **sus declaraciones han causado el efecto esperado** her statements have produced *o* had the desired effect; **el poema le causó una honda impresión** the poem made a great impression on him; **su frialdad me causa un profundo dolor** I find his coolness very hurtful; **~ asombro a algn** to amaze sb; **~ emoción a algn** to move sb; **~ extrañeza a algn** to puzzle sb; **~ risa a algn** to make sb laugh

causativo ADJ causative

causear ▸conjug 1a◂ VI (*Chile*) to have a snack

causeo SM (*Cono Sur*) = **causa**[2]

cáustica SF caustic

cáustico ADJ caustic

cautamente ADV cautiously, warily, carefully

cautela SF **1** (= *cuidado*) caution, wariness; **con mucha ~** very cautiously; **tener la ~ de hacer algo** to take the precaution of doing sth
2 (*pey*) (= *astucia*) cunning

cautelar[1] ADJ precautionary; **prisión ~** preventive detention

cautelar[2] ▸conjug 1a◂ Ⓐ VT **1** (= *prevenir*) to prevent, guard against
2 (*LAm*) (= *defender*) to protect, defend
Ⓑ **cautelarse** VPR to be on one's guard (**de** against)

cautelosamente ADV **1** (= *con cautela*) cautiously, warily, carefully
2 (*pey*) (= *astutamente*) cunningly, craftily

cauteloso ADJ **1** (= *cuidadoso*) cautious, wary, careful
2 (*pey*) (= *astuto*) cunning, crafty

cauterio SM **1** (*Med*) cautery, cauterization
2 (= *remedio*) drastic remedy

cauterizador Ⓐ ADJ cauterizing
Ⓑ SM cautery, cauterant

cauterizar ▸conjug 1f◂ VT **1** (*Med*) to cauterize
2 (= *atajar*) to eradicate

cautivador ADJ, **cautivante** ADJ captivating

cautivar ▸conjug 1a◂ VT **1** (= *hacer prisionero a*) (*Mil*) to capture, take prisoner
2 (= *hechizar*) to captivate; **su belleza me cautivó** her beauty captivated me

cautiverio SM, **cautividad** SF **1** [*de prisionero*] captivity
2 [*de siervo*] bondage, serfdom

cautivo/a ADJ, SM/F captive

cauto ADJ cautious, wary, careful

cava[1] SM cava

> **CAVA**
>
> *A sparkling white or occasionally rosé Spanish wine,* **cava** *is produced mainly in the* **Penedès** *region using the traditional techniques developed in Champagne, France. To maintain the constant temperature important to the process, the wine is stored and fermented in cellars or* **cavas**, *hence the name. Varieties of* **cava** *include: medium (***semiseco***), dry (***seco***), very dry (***brut***) and the extra dry variety especially recommended by connoisseurs called* **brut nature**.

cava[2] SF **1** (= *lugar*) (= *para el vino*) wine cellar; [*de garaje*] pit
2 (*Caribe*) (= *nevera*) icebox

cava[3] SF (= *acción*) digging

cavador(a) SM/F digger ► **cavador(a) de oro** gold digger

cavadura SF digging, excavation

cavar ▸conjug 1a◂ Ⓐ VT (*en el suelo*) [+ *fosa, hoyo*] to dig; [+ *pozo*] to sink; (*Agr*) [+ *tierra*] to dig over; [+ *cepas*] to dig round
Ⓑ VI **1** (*en el suelo*) to dig
2 (= *investigar*) to delve (**en** into), go deeply (**en** into)
3 (= *meditar*) to meditate profoundly (**en** on)

cavazón SF digging, excavation

caverna SF cave, cavern

cavernícola Ⓐ ADJ **1** (= *de caverna*) cave-dwelling, cave *antes de s*; **hombre ~** caveman
2 (*Pol**) reactionary
Ⓑ SMF **1** (= *habitante de caverna*) cave dweller
2 (*Pol**) reactionary, backwoodsman

cavernoso ADJ **1** (= *hueco*) [*lugar*] cavernous; [*montaña*] full of caves, honeycombed with caves
2 [*voz*] resounding, deep

caviar SM caviar, caviare

cavidad SF cavity ► **cavidad bucal** oral cavity ► **cavidad nasal** nasal cavity ► **cavidad oral** oral cavity

cavilación SF **1** (= *meditación*) deep thought, rumination
2 (= *sospecha*) suspicion

cavilar ▸conjug 1a◂ VI to think deeply, ponder

➤ LENGUA Y USO: causa[1] 2 44.1

cavilosear ▸conjug 1a◂ VI [1] (*Caribe*) (= *ilusionarse*) to harbour illusions; (= *vacilar*) to vacillate, hesitate
[2] (*CAm*) (= *chismear*) to gossip

cavilosidad SF suspicion

caviloso ADJ [1] (= *obsesionado*) brooding, suspicious
[2] (*CAm*) (= *chismoso*) gossipy, backbiting
[3] (*Andes*) (= *agresivo*) quarrelsome, touchy; (= *quisquilloso*) fussy, finicky

cayado SM [1] (*Agr*) crook
[2] (*Rel*) crozier

cayena SF cayenne pepper

cayendo *etc ver* **caer**

cayo SM (*Ant*) islet, key ► **Cayo Hueso** Key West

cayubro ADJ (*Andes*) reddish-blond, red-haired

cayuca‡ SF (*Caribe*) head, bean*

cayuco SM (*LAm*) *small Indian canoe*

caz SM [1] [*de riego*] irrigation channel
[2] [*de molino*] millrace

caza Ⓐ SF [1] (= *acción*) hunting; (*con fusil*) shooting; **la ~ del jabalí** boar hunting; **la ~ del zorro** foxhunting; **la ~ de la perdiz** partridge shooting; **~ con hurón** ferreting; **a la ~ de algo**: **los periodistas andan siempre a la ~ de noticias** journalists are always on the hunt for *o* out in pursuit of news; **van a la ~ de nuevos talentos** they are on the hunt for new talent; **dar ~ a** (= *perseguir*) to give chase to, pursue; (= *alcanzar*) to hunt down; **dieron ~ al ciervo** they gave chase to *o* pursued the deer; **dieron orden de dar ~ al fugitivo** they ordered the fugitive to be hunted down; **los corredores consiguieron dar ~ al escapado** the runners managed to catch (up with) the breakaway leader; **ir de ~** to go hunting; (*con fusil*) to go (out) shooting; ✦*MODISMO* **levantar la ~** to put up the game ► **caza de brujas** witchhunt ► **caza de control** culling ► **caza del hombre** manhunt ► **caza furtiva** poaching ► **caza mayor** game hunting ► **caza menor** small game hunting; (*con fusil*) small game shooting ► **caza submarina** underwater fishing ► **caza y captura**: **estar a la ~ y captura de la noticia** to be on the hunt for news; **operación de ~ y captura de criminales** operation to track down and catch criminals; *ver tb* **coto**[1] **1**
[2] (= *animal cazado*) game; (*Culin*) game ► **caza mayor** big game ► **caza menor** small game
Ⓑ SM (*Aer*) fighter (plane) ► **caza de escolta** escort fighter

cazaautógrafos SMF INV autograph hunter

cazabe SM (*LAm Culin*) cassava bread, cassava flour

caza-bombardero SM fighter-bomber

cazaclavos SM INV nail puller

cazadero SM hunting ground

cazador(a) SM/F (*gen*) hunter; (*a caballo*) huntsman/huntswoman ► **cazador(a) de alforja**, **cazador(a) de pieles** trapper ► **cazador(a) furtivo/a** poacher

cazadora SF jacket ► **cazadora de cuero**, **cazadora de piel** leather jacket ► **cazadora tejana** denim jacket

cazador-recolector SM (*pl* **cazadores-recolectores**) hunter-gatherer

cazadotes SM INV fortune-hunter

cazaejecutivos SMF INV (*Com*) headhunter

cazafortunas SMF INV fortune hunter, gold digger

cazagenios SMF INV [1] (*Univ*) talent scout, talent spotter
[2] (*Com*) headhunter

cazamariposas SM INV butterfly net

cazaminas SM INV minesweeper

cazamoscas SM INV flycatcher

cazanazis SMF INV Nazi-hunter

cazar ▸conjug 1f◂ Ⓐ VT [1] [+ *animales*] to hunt; (*con fusil*) to shoot
[2] [+ *ladrón, fugitivo*] to hunt down
[3] [+ *corredor, ciclista*] to catch (up with)
[4] [+ *votos*] to capture; [+ *electores, votantes*] to win (over)
[5] (*) (= *atrapar*) to land*; **al final cazó un magnífico empleo** in the end he landed an excellent job*; **su aspiración es ~ un hombre para casarse** her ambition is to land herself a husband*
[6] (*) (= *sorprender*) to catch; **los cazó robando** he caught them stealing
[7] (*) (= *comprender*) to understand; **es el mejor alumno, lo caza todo enseguida** he's the best pupil, he understands *o* gets* everything at once; *ver tb* **vuelo**[2] **1**
Ⓑ VI to hunt; **salir a ~** to go (out) hunting; (*con fusil*) to go (out) shooting

cazarrecompensas SMF INV bounty hunter

cazasubmarinos SM INV [1] (*Náut*) (= *en superficie*) destroyer; (*sumergible*) hunter-killer
[2] (*Aer*) anti-submarine craft

cazatalentos SMF INV talent scout, talent spotter

cazatanques SM INV **avión ~** anti-tank aircraft

cazatesoros SMF INV treasure hunter

cazaturistas ADJ INV **lugar ~** tourist trap, touristy place

cazcalear†* ▸conjug 1a◂ VI to fuss around, buzz about

cazcarrias SFPL splashes of mud (*on one's clothes*)

cazcarriento ADJ splashed with mud, mudstained

cazo SM [1] (= *cacerola*) saucepan ► **cazo de cola** gluepot
[2] (= *cucharón*) ladle
[3] (‡) (= *chulo*) pimp

cazolero SM milksop

cazoleta SF [1] [*de cocina*] pan, small pan
[2] [*de pipa*] bowl
[3] [*de sostén*] cup
[4] [*de espada*] guard
[5] [*de escudo*] boss
[6] (*Mec*) housing

cazón SM dogfish

cazonete SM (*Náut*) toggle

cazuela SF [1] (= *recipiente*) [*de metal*] pan; [*de barro*] casserole (dish)
[2] (= *guiso*) stew, casserole
[3] (*Teat*) gods *pl*

cazurro ADJ [1] (= *huraño*) surly, sullen
[2] (= *testarudo*) stubborn

cazuz SM ivy

CC Ⓐ SF ABR (*Esp Pol*) = **Coalición Canaria**
Ⓑ ABR [1] (*Aut*) = **Código de la Circulación**
[2] (*Pol*) = **Comité Central**
[3] = **Cuerpo Consular**

C.C. ABR (*Elec*) (= **corriente continua**) DC

c.c. ABR (= **centímetros cúbicos**) cc

c/c ABR (= **cuenta corriente**) C/A, a/c (*EEUU*)

CCAA SFPL ABR (*Esp Pol*) = **Comunidades Autónomas**

CCI SF ABR (= **Cámara de Comercio Internacional**) ICC

CCOO SFPL ABR (*Esp*) (= **Comisiones Obreras**) *Communist trades union*

> **CCOO**
>
> ***Comisiones Obreras*** *is the Spanish communist trade union federation. Banned under the dictatorship of General Franco, it was relegalized following Franco's death and is nowadays one of Spain's two largest trades unions, together with* **UGT**.

CD SM ABR (= **compact disc**) CD

C.D. ABR [1] (= **Cuerpo Diplomático**) CD
[2] = **Club Deportivo**

c/d ABR [1] (= **en casa de**) c/o
[2] (*Com*) = **con descuento**

C. de J. ABR (= **Compañía de Jesús**) S.J.

CD-I [θeðe'i] SM ABR (= **Compact Disc Interactive**) CD-I

C.D.N. SM ABR (*Esp*) (= **Centro Dramático Nacional**) ≈ RADA

CD-ROM [θeðe'rom] SM ABR (= **Compact Disc Read-Only Memory**) CD-ROM

CDS SM ABR (*Esp Pol*) = **Centro Democrático y Social**

Cdte. ABR (= **comandante**) Cdr, Cmdr

CDU SF ABR = **Clasificación Decimal Universal**

CE Ⓐ SF ABR (= **Comunidad Europea**) EC
Ⓑ SM ABR = **Consejo de Europa**

ce SF the name of the letter *c*, C; ✦*MODISMOS* **ce por be** down to the tiniest detail; **por ce o por be** somehow or other

ceba SF [1] (*Agr*) fattening
[2] [*de arma*] priming
[3] [*de horno*] stoking

cebada SF barley ► **cebada perlada** pearl barley

cebadal SM barley field

cebadera SF [1] (*Agr*) nosebag
[2] (*Téc*) hopper

cebadero SM [1] (= *comerciante*) barley dealer
[2] (= *mula*) leading mule (*of a team*)
[3] (= *sitio*) feeding place
[4] (*Téc*) *mouth for charging a furnace*

cebado Ⓐ ADJ (*LAm*) [*animal*] man-eating
Ⓑ SM [1] (*Agr*) fattening
[2] [*arma de fuego*] priming

cebador SM (*Cono Sur Aut*) choke

cebadura SF = **ceba 1**

cebar ▸conjug 1a◂ Ⓐ VT [1] [+ *animal*] to fatten (up); **ceban a los pavos con piensos artificiales** they fatten up the turkeys on artificial feeds; **cuando voy a casa mi madre me ceba*** when I go home my mother feeds me up
[2] [+ *anzuelo, cepo, trampa*] to bait
[3] [+ *fuego, horno*] to feed, stoke (up); [+ *arma*] to prime
[4] (*frm*) [+ *pasión, odio*] to feed, nourish; [+ *cólera*] to feed
[5] (*Cono Sur*) [+ *maté*] to brew
Ⓑ VI [*tuerca, tornillo*] to catch, grip; [*clavo*] to go in
Ⓒ **cebarse** VPR **~se con *o* en algn: la oposi-**

ción se cebó con *o* **en el presidente** the opposition launched a savage *o* furious attack on the president; **el paro se ceba especialmente en los jóvenes** unemployment hits young people particularly hard; **estaba enfadada y se cebó conmigo** she was angry and took it out on me *o* vented her anger on me

cebeísmo SM enthusiasm for CB radio

cebeísta SMF CB radio enthusiast

cebellina SF (*Zool*) sable

cebiche SM (*Cono Sur Culin*) *raw fish or shellfish dish*

cebo SM [1] (*Pesca*) bait
[2] (*Agr*) feed, fodder
[3] (*Téc*) fuel
[4] [*de arma*] charge, primer

cebolla SF [1] (*Bot*) (= *hortaliza*) onion; [*de tulipán*] bulb ► **cebolla escalonia** shallot
[2] (*) (= *cabeza*) nut*

cebollado ADJ (*LAm*) cooked with onions

cebollana SF chive

cebolleta SF [1] (*Bot*) (= *cebolla*) spring onion, green onion (*EEUU*); (= *cebollana*) chive
[2] (**) (= *pene*) prick**

cebollina SF, **cebollino** SM [1] (= *cebolleta*) spring onion, green onion (*EEUU*)
[2] (= *semilla*) onion seed
[3] (= *cebollana*) chive

cebollita SF (*LAm Bot*) (*tb* ~ **china**) spring onion

cebollón SM [1] (*Cono Sur pey*) old bachelor
[2] (*) (= *borrachera*) **llevaba un ~ enorme cuando salió del bar** he was plastered when he left the bar*

cebollona SF (*Cono Sur pey*) old maid*, spinster

cebolludo ADJ [1] (*Bot*) bulbous
[2] (*) [*persona*] vulgar

cebón Ⓐ ADJ fat, fattened
Ⓑ SM fattened animal

ceboruco SM [1] (*Caribe*) (= *arrecife*) reef
[2] (*Méx*) (= *terreno quebrado*) rough rocky place
[3] (*Caribe*) (= *maleza*) brush, scrub, scrubland

cebra SF zebra

cebú SM zebu

CECA SF ABR [1] (= **Comunidad Europea del Carbón y del Acero**) ECSC
[2] = **Confederación Española de Cajas de Ahorro**

Ceca SF **andar** *o* **ir de la ~ a la Meca** to go hither and thither, chase about all over the place

ceca SF (*Fin*) mint

CECE SF ABR = **Confederación Española de Centros de la Enseñanza**

cecear ▸conjug 1a◂ VI (*por defecto*) to lisp; (*Ling*) to pronounce "s" as "th"

ceceo SM (*por defecto*) lisp; (*Ling*) pronunciation of "s" as "th"

ceceoso ADJ lisping, with a lisp

Cecilia SF Cecily

Cecilio SM Cecil

cecina SF [1] (= *carne seca*) cured meat, smoked meat
[2] (*Cono Sur*) jerked meat, jerked beef

CEDA SF ABR (*Esp Hist*) = **Confederación Española de Derechas Autónomas**

ceda SM ► **ceda el paso** (*Aut*) priority, right of way

cedazo SM sieve

cedente SMF (*Jur*) assignor

ceder ▸conjug 2a◂ Ⓐ VT [1] [+ *propiedad*] to transfer; [+ *territorio*] to cede (*frm*), hand over; **me cedió el asiento** she let me have her seat, she gave up her seat (for me); **cedió los derechos de autor a su familia** she gave up *o* over the authorial rights to her family; **el director ha cedido el puesto a su colaborador** the director has decided to hand over the post to his colleague; ~ **la palabra a algn** to give the floor to sb (*frm*), call upon sb to speak; **"ceda el paso"** "give way", "yield" (*EEUU*); ~ **terreno a algn/algo** to give ground to sb/sth
[2] (*Dep*) [+ *balón*] to pass
Ⓑ VI [1] (= *transigir*) to give in, yield (*frm*); **los negociadores tendrán que ~** the negotiators will have to give way *o* yield; ~ **a algo** to give in to sth, yield to sth; ~ **al chantaje** to give in *o* yield to blackmail; ~ **ante algn/algo** to give in to sb/sth, yield to sb/sth; **no ~emos a** *o* **ante sus amenazas** we will not give in to *o* yield to his threats; ~ **en algo**: **no ceden en su empeño de ganar la liga** they're not giving in *o* up in their endeavour to win the league
[2] (= *disminuir*) [*viento*] to drop, die down; [*lluvia*] to ease up; [*frío*] to abate, ease up; [*fiebre*] to go down; [*dolor*] to lessen
[3] [*suelo, viga*] to give way, give; **el techo cedió y se derrumbó** the roof gave (way) and collapsed
[4] (= *dar de sí*) [*zapatos, prenda, elástico*] to stretch, give; **el tejido ha cedido y me queda ancho** the material has stretched *o* given and now it's too big for me

cedible ADJ transferable

cedilla SF cedilla

cedizo ADJ [*carne*] high, tainted

cedro SM cedar

cedrón SM (*Cono Sur Culin*) lemon verbena

cédula SF [1] (= *documento*) document; **dar ~ a algn** to license sb ► **cédula de aduana** customs permit ► **cédula de cambio** bill of exchange ► **cédula de identidad** (*LAm*) identity card, ID ► **cédula en blanco** blank cheque, blank check (*EEUU*) ► **cédula hipotecaria** mortgage bond ► **cédula personal** identity card ► **cédula real** royal letters patent
[2] (= *ficha*) index card
[3] (*Com*) warrant

cedulista SMF (*Fin*) holder (*of a certificate, etc*)

CEE SF ABR (= **Comunidad Económica Europea**) EEC

cefalea SF migraine

cefálico ADJ cephalic

céfiro SM zephyr

cegador ADJ blinding; **brillo ~** blinding glare

cegajoso ADJ weepy, bleary-eyed

cegamiento SM [*de tubería*] blockage

cegar ▸conjug 1h, 1j◂ Ⓐ VT [1] (= *deslumbrar*) to blind; **el camión me cegó con las luces** the lights of the lorry blinded me
[2] (= *ofuscar*) [+ *persona*] to blind; **le ciega la pasión** he is blinded by passion
[3] (= *obstruir*) [+ *tubería, agujero*] to block up, stop up; [+ *pozo*] to block up; [+ *puerta, ventana*] to wall up
Ⓑ VI to go blind, become blind
Ⓒ **cegarse** VPR [1] (= *ofuscarse*) to be blinded (**de** by); **se cegó de furia** he was blinded by anger
[2] (= *obstruirse*) to block

cegato* ADJ, **cegatón*** ADJ half blind*

cegatoso ADJ = **cegajoso**

cegué *ver* **cegar**

ceguera SF, **ceguedad** SF [1] (= *pérdida de visión*) blindness ► **ceguera nocturna** night blindness
[2] (= *obcecación*) blindness (to reason)

CEI SF ABR (= **Comunidad de Estados Independientes**) CIS

ceiba SF (*LAm Bot*) ceiba tree, kapok tree

Ceilán SM (*Hist*) Ceylon

ceilanés/esa ADJ, SM/F (*Hist*) Ceylonese

ceja SF [1] (*Anat*) eyebrow; **~s pobladas** bushy eyebrows, thick eyebrows; **arquear las ~s** to raise one's eyebrows; **fruncir las ~s** to knit one's brows, frown; ✦*MODISMOS* **estar endeudado hasta las ~s*** to be up to one's eyes in debt; **meterse algo entre ~ y ~*** to get sth firmly into one's head; **tener a algn entre ~ y ~*** to have no time for sb; **quemarse las ~s*** to burn the midnight oil
[2] (*Téc*) rim, flange
[3] (*Cos*) edging
[4] (*Arquit*) projection
[5] (*Geog*) brow, crown
[6] (*Mús*) bridge

cejar ▸conjug 1a◂ VI [1] (= *retroceder*) to move back, go back; (*en discusión*) to back down; **no ~** to keep it up, keep going; **no ~ en sus esfuerzos** to keep at it; **no ~ en su trabajo** to keep up the work; **sin ~** unflinchingly
[2] (= *ceder*) to give way, back down

cejijunto ADJ with eyebrows very close together

cejilla SF (*Mús*) bridge

cejudo ADJ with bushy eyebrows

celacanto SM coelacanth

celada SF [1] (= *emboscada*) ambush, trap; **caer en la ~** to fall into the trap
[2] (*Hist*) helmet

celador(a) SM/F (= *vigilante*) [*de edificio*] guard; [*de cárcel*] warder, guard (*EEUU*); [*de centro escolar*] porter; [*de museo*] attendant, warder; [*de hospital*] hospital porter; [*de aparcamiento*] parking attendant

celaje SM [1] (= *nubes*) (*Meteo*) sky with coloured *o* (*EEUU*) colored clouds; (*Náut*) clouds *pl*; **~s** sunset clouds
[2] (*Arte*) cloud effect
[3] (*Arquit*) skylight
[4] (= *presagio*) sign, promising sign, token
[5] (*Andes, Caribe*) (= *fantasma*) ghost; ✦*MODISMO* **como un ~** in a flash

celar[1] ▸conjug 1a◂ Ⓐ VT (= *vigilar*) [+ *paciente, seguridad*] to watch over; (*en un examen*) to invigilate; ~ **la justicia** to see that justice is done
Ⓑ VI **~ por** *o* **sobre algo** to watch over sth

celar[2] ▸conjug 1a◂ VT (= *ocultar*) to conceal, hide

celda SF cell ► **celda de castigo** solitary confinement cell

celdilla SF [1] [*de colmena*] cell
[2] (*Arquit*) niche

cele ADJ (*CAm*) [1] [*color*] light green
[2] [*fruta*] unripe

celebérrimo ADJ SUPERL *de* **célebre**

celebración SF [1] (= *realización*) **tras la ~ de las elecciones** after the elections were held; **durante la ~ del pleno municipal** during the council meeting
[2] (= *fiesta*) celebration; **una ~ familiar** a family celebration; **un año de grandes celebraciones** a year of great celebrations
[3] (*Rel*) [*de misa, festividad*] celebration; **coincidiendo con la ~ del Ramadán** coinciding with the celebration of Ramadan
[4] (= *alabanza*) celebration

celebrante SM (*Rel*) celebrant, officiating priest

▼ **celebrar** ▸conjug 1a◂ Ⓐ VT [1] (= *festejar*) [+ *aniversario, acontecimiento*] to celebrate; **siempre celebramos la Navidad en familia** we always celebrate Christmas as a family; **estamos celebrando que hemos aprobado los exámenes** we're celebrating passing our exams; **en mayo se celebra el día de los trabajadores** Labour Day is in May; **el día 22 se celebra la fiesta de santa Cecilia** the 22nd is the feast day of Saint Cecilia; **tu santo se celebra el día 19 de marzo** your saint's day is on the 19th of March
[2] (= *llevar a cabo*) [+ *congreso, juicio, elecciones, fiesta*] to hold; [+ *acuerdo, contrato*] to sign; **la reunión se ~á el viernes por la tarde** the meeting will take place *o* will be held on Friday afternoon; **el partido no pudo ~se a causa de la lluvia** the match could not be played because of rain
[3] (*frm*) (= *alegrarse de*) **lo celebro** I'm delighted; **lo celebro por él** I'm very pleased for him; **celebro comprobar que conserva su sentido del humor** I'm delighted *o* very pleased to see that he's still got his sense of humour; **celebro que hayas aceptado ese trabajo** I'm delighted *o* very pleased that you've accepted that job; **celebro que no sea nada grave** I'm glad it's nothing serious
[4] (= *alabar*) [+ *valor, belleza*] to celebrate, praise; [+ *ventajas*] to preach, dwell on; [+ *bromas, gracias*] to laugh at
[5] (*Rel*) [+ *boda, ceremonia*] to perform; **~ una misa** to celebrate mass, say mass
Ⓑ VI [*sacerdote*] to celebrate mass, say mass

célebre ADJ famous, celebrated, noted (**por** for)

celebridad SF [1] (= *fama*) celebrity, fame
[2] (= *persona famosa*) celebrity

celeque ADJ (*CAm*) green, unripe

célere ADJ (*liter*) rapid, swift

celeridad SF speed, swiftness; **con ~** quickly, promptly

celeste ADJ [1] (= *del cielo*) heavenly
[2] [*color*] sky blue

celestial ADJ [1] (*Rel*) celestial
[2] (= *delicioso*) heavenly

celestina SF procuress

celestinazgo SM procuring

celibato SM celibacy

célibe ADJ, SMF celibate

célico ADJ (*liter*) heavenly, celestial

celidonia SF celandine

celinda SF (*Bot*) mock orange

cellisca SF sleet

cellisquear ▸conjug 1a◂ VI to sleet

cello[1] SM (*Mús*) cello

cello[2] SM = **celo**[2]

celo[1] SM [1] (= *diligencia*) zeal; **hacer algo con ~** to do sth zealously *o* with zeal ► **celo profesional** professional commitment, commitment to one's job; *ver tb* **huelga 1**
[2] (*Rel*) zeal
[3] (*Zool*) [*de hembra*] oestrus, estrus (*EEUU*); [*de macho*] rut; **una hembra en ~** a female on heat *o* in season; **estar en ~** to be on heat, be in season
[4] **celos** jealousy *sing*; **los ~s la consumen** she's eaten up with jealousy; **dar ~s a algn** to make sb jealous; **tener ~s de algn** to be jealous of sb

celo[2]® SM (= *cinta adhesiva*) Sellotape®, Scotchtape® (*EEUU*), sticky tape

celo[3] SM (*Mús*) cello

celofán SM cellophane

celosamente ADV [1] (= *con fervor*) zealously
[2] (*pey*) (= *sin confianza*) suspiciously, distrustfully
[3] (= *con celos*) jealously

celosía SF [1] (= *enrejado*) lattice, lattice window
[2] (= *contraventana*) slatted shutter
[3] (= *celos*) jealousy

celoso ADJ [1] [*marido, hermano*] jealous (**de** of)
[2] (= *ferviente*) zealous; (*en el trabajo*) conscientious
[3] (= *desconfiado*) suspicious, distrustful
[4] (*LAm Mec*) highly sensitive
[5] (*Andes*) [*barca*] unsteady, easily upset
[6] (*LAm*) [*arma*] delicate, liable to go off; **éste es un fusil ~** this gun is quite liable to go off

celta Ⓐ ADJ Celtic Ⓑ SMF Celt Ⓒ SM (*Ling*) Celtic

Celtiberia SF Celtiberia

celtibérico/a ADJ, SM/F Celtiberian

celtíbero/a ADJ, SM/F Celtiberian

céltico ADJ Celtic

célula SF [1] (*Biol, Elec*) cell ► **célula de silicio** silicon chip ► **célula fotoeléctrica** photoelectric cell ► **célula fotovoltaica** photovoltaic cell ► **célula germen** germ cell ► **célula grasa** fat cell ► **célula madre** stem cell; **investigación con ~s madre** stem cell research ► **célula nerviosa** nerve cell ► **célula sanguínea** blood cell
[2] (*Pol*) cell ► **célula terrorista** terrorist cell
[3] (*Aer*) airframe

celular ADJ cellular, cell *antes de s*; **tejido ~** cell tissue; *ver tb* **coche**[1] **1**

celulítico ADJ [*célula, proceso*] cellulite *antes de s*; [*persona*] with cellulite

celulitis SF INV cellulitis

celuloide SM celluloid; **llevar algo al ~** to make a film of sth

celulosa SF cellulose

CEM SM ABR (*Esp*) = **Centro de Estudios para la Mujer**

cementación SF (*Téc*) case-hardening, cementation

cementar ▸conjug 1a◂ VT (*Téc*) to case-harden, cement

cementera SF cement works

cementerio SM (*municipal*) cemetery; (*en iglesia*) graveyard ► **cementerio de coches** used-car dump, junkyard (*EEUU*) ► **cementerio nuclear** nuclear waste dump

cementero ADJ cement *antes de s*

cementista SM cement worker

cemento SM [1] [*de construcción*] cement ► **cemento armado** reinforced concrete ► **cemento Portland** Portland cement ► **cemento reforzado** reinforced concrete
[2] (*LAm*) (= *pegamento*) glue
[3] [*de diente*] cement

cemita SF (*LAm*) white bread roll

CEN SM ABR (*Esp*) = **Consejo de Economía Nacional**

cena SF (*a última hora*) supper; (*como comida principal*) dinner; **nos invitó a una ~ en el restaurante** he invited us to dinner at a restaurant; **la Última Cena** the Last Supper ► **Cena de Baltasar** Belshazzar's Feast ► **cena de gala** dinner function, formal dinner; (*Pol*) state banquet ► **cena de negocios** business dinner ► **cena de trabajo** working dinner

cena-bufete SF (*pl* **cenas-bufete**) buffet-supper

cenáculo SM group, coterie

cenador SM arbour, arbor (*EEUU*)

cenaduría SF (*Méx*) eating house, restaurant

cena-espectáculo SF (*pl* **cenas-espectáculo**) dinner show, dinner with a floor show

cenagal SM [1] (= *pantano*) bog, quagmire
[2] (= *desorden*) mess, nasty business

cenagoso ADJ muddy

cena-homenaje SF (*pl* **cenas-homenaje**) formal dinner, celebratory dinner; **ofrecer una ~ a algn** to hold a dinner for sb

cenar ▸conjug 1a◂ Ⓐ VI (*a última hora*) to have supper; (*como comida principal*) to have dinner; (*en ocasión formal*) to dine (*frm*); **cenamos a las diez de la noche** we have supper at ten o'clock; **los británicos cenan a las seis** the British have dinner at six o'clock; **el rey cenó en la embajada de Alemania** the king had dinner at *o* (*frm*) dined at the German Embassy; **vengo cenado** I've had dinner *o* supper already, I've had (my) dinner, I've already eaten; **me han invitado a ~** they've asked me to dinner; **salir a ~** to go out to dinner, dine out (*frm*)
Ⓑ VT (*a última hora*) to have for supper; (*como comida principal*) to have for dinner; **siempre ceno algo muy ligero** I always have a very light supper

cenceño ADJ thin, skinny; *ver tb* **pan 1**

cencerrada SF *noise made with cowbells, pots and pans etc, on festive occasions or in mockery*

cencerrear ▸conjug 1a◂ VI [1] [*campanillas*] to jingle [2] [*motor*] to rattle [3] (*Mús*) to make a dreadful noise

cencerreo SM [1] [*de campanillas*] jangle
[2] [*de motor*] rattle, clatter
[3] (*Mús*) dreadful noise

cencerro SM cowbell; ✦*MODISMOS* **a ~s tapados** stealthily, on the sly; **estar como un ~*** to be round the bend*

cendal SM [1] (= *gasa*) gauze
[2] (= *tela fina*) fine silk stuff, sendal

Cenebad SM ABR (*Esp Escol*) = **Centro Nacional de Educación Básica a Distancia**

cenefa SF [1] (*Cos*) edging, border
[2] (*Arquit*) border

➤ LENGUA Y USO: **celebrar A4** 38.1

cenetista Ⓐ ADJ **política ~** policy of the CNT
Ⓑ SMF member of the CNT

cenicero SM ashtray

cenicienta SF **soy la ~ de la casa** I'm the dogsbody round here; **la Cenicienta** Cinderella

ceniciento ADJ ashen (*liter*), ash-coloured, ash-colored (*EEUU*)

cénit SM, **cenit** SM zenith

ceniza SF [1] (= *polvo*) ash; **reducir algo a ~s** to reduce sth to ashes; **✦MODISMO huir de las ~s y dar en las brasas** to jump out of the frying pan into the fire
[2] **cenizas** [*de persona*] ashes, mortal remains

cenizo Ⓐ ADJ [1] [*color*] ashen (*liter*), ash-coloured, ash-colored (*EEUU*)
[2] (*) (= *de mala suerte*) **es un avión ~** it's a plane with a jinx on it*
Ⓑ SM [1] (*) (= *mala suerte*) jinx*; **tener el ~** to have a jinx on one*; **✦MODISMO entrar el ~ en casa** to have a spell of bad luck
[2] (= *persona*) jinx*
[3] (*Bot*) goosefoot

cenobio SM monastery

cenobita SMF c(o)enobite

cenojil SM garter

cenorrio* (*hum*) SM posh dinner*, slap-up do*

cenotafio SM cenotaph

cenote SM (*CAm, Méx*) natural well

censado SM census-taking

censal ADJ = **censual**

censar ▸conjug 1a◂ VT to take a census of

censista SMF census official, census taker

censo SM [1] (= *lista*) census; **elaborar** *o* **hacer un ~** to take a census ► **censo de población** population census ► **censo electoral** electoral roll, list of registered voters (*EEUU*)
[2] (*Hist, Fin*) (= *tributo*) tax; (= *alquiler*) (annual) ground rent

censor SM [1] (*Pol*) censor
[2] (*Com, Fin*) ► **censor(a) de cuentas** auditor ► **censor(a) jurado/a de cuentas** chartered accountant, certified public accountant (*EEUU*)
[3] (= *crítico*) critic

censual ADJ [1] [*demografía*] census *antes de s*, relating to a census
[2] (*Fin*) mortgage *antes de s*
[3] (= *de elecciones*) electoral, relating to the electoral roll

censura SF [1] (= *supresión*) censorship; **la ~ de prensa** press censorship; **sometieron todos sus libros a la ~** they censored all his books
[2] (= *institución*) censors *pl*; **el autor tuvo problemas con la ~** the author had problems with the censors
[3] (= *condena*) censure (*frm*), criticism; **lanzó palabras de ~ contra los políticos** he spoke words of censure (*frm*) *o* criticism against the politicians; **digno de ~** reprehensible; *ver tb* **moción 1**, **voto 1**
[4] (*Com, Fin*) ► **censura de cuentas** auditing

censurable ADJ reprehensible

censurar ▸conjug 1a◂ VT [1] (*Pol*) to censor
[2] [+ *obra, película*] to censor
[3] (= *criticar*) to censure (*frm*), criticize

censurista Ⓐ ADJ censorious
Ⓑ SMF critic, faultfinder

➤ LENGUA Y USO: centrar C1 53.2, 53.6

cént ABR (= **céntimo**) c

centaura SF centaury

centauro SM centaur

centavo SM [1] (*partitivo*) hundredth, hundredth part
[2] (*Fin*) cent

centella SF [1] (= *chispa*) spark
[2] (= *rayo*) flash of lightning; **salió como una ~ del cuarto** he was out of the room as quick as a flash *o* in a flash

centelleante ADJ [*luz, diamante*] sparkling; [*estrella*] twinkling; [*metal*] gleaming, glinting; [*fuego*] flickering

centellear ▸conjug 1a◂ VI [*luz, diamante*] to sparkle; [*estrella*] to twinkle; [*metal*] to gleam, glint; [*fuego*] to flicker

centelleo SM [*de luz, diamante*] sparkle; [*de estrella*] twinkle; [*de metal*] glint

centena SF, **centenada** SF hundred

centenal SM [1] (*Agr*) rye field
[2] (= *centena*) hundred

centenar[1] SM hundred; **a ~es** by the hundred, in hundreds, in their hundreds

centenar[2] SM (*Agr*) rye field

centenario/a Ⓐ ADJ centenary
Ⓑ SM/F centenarian, hundred-year-old person
Ⓒ SM centenary, centennial

centeno SM rye

centésima SF hundredth, hundredth part

centesimal ADJ centesimal

centésimo Ⓐ ADJ hundredth; **centésima parte** hundredth
Ⓑ SM [1] (*partitivo*) hundredth, hundredth part; *ver tb* **sexto**
[2] (*LAm*) (= *moneda*) centésimo, *one-hundredth part of a balboa etc*

centígrado ADJ centigrade

centigramo SM centigram

centilitro SM centilitre, centiliter (*EEUU*)

centímetro SM centimetre, centimeter (*EEUU*); → KILOS, METROS, AÑOS

céntimo SM [1] hundredth part
[2] [*de euro*] cent; **no vale un ~** it's worthless

centinela SMF (*Mil*) sentry, guard; **estar de ~** to be on guard; **hacer ~** to keep watch, be on the look-out

centiplicado ADJ hundredfold

centolla SF, **centollo** SM spider crab

centón SM [1] (*Cos*) patchwork quilt
[2] (*Literat*) cento

central Ⓐ ADJ [1] (= *principal*) [1·1] [*personaje, idea*] central, main; **el personaje ~ de la novela** the central *o* main character in the novel; **el tema ~ de la reunión** the main subject of the meeting
[1·2] [*oficina*] head *antes de s*; [*banco*] central; [*ordenador*] mainframe *antes de s*; **la oficina ~ del banco** the head office of the bank; **la empresa tiene su sede ~ en Nueva York** the company's headquarters is in New York; *ver tb* **calefacción**
[2] (= *del medio*) [*región, zona*] central; **en la zona ~ de la imagen** in the centre of the image; **la parte ~ de la plaza** the centre of the square
[3] (= *no regional*) [*gobierno, administración*] central
Ⓑ SF [1] (*tb* **oficina ~**) [*de empresa*] head office; (*a nivel internacional*) headquarters; **la ~ de la OMS en Ginebra** the headquarters of the WHO in Geneva ► **central de abasto** (*Méx*) market ► **central de correos** main post office, general post office ► **central de teléfonos** telephone exchange ► **central obrera**, **central sindical** trade union confederation ► **central telefónica** telephone exchange
[2] (= *factoría*) plant, station; (*tb* **~ nuclear**) nuclear power station; **la ~ de Chernobyl** Chernobyl nuclear power station ► **central azucarera** (*Cuba, Perú*) sugar mill ► **central de bombeo** pumping-station ► **central de energía** power station ► **central depuradora** sewage works *pl* ► **central eléctrica** power station ► **central hidroeléctrica** hydroelectric power station ► **central lechera** dairy ► **central térmica** power station; **~ térmica de fuel-oil/de gas** oil-fired/gas-fired power station
Ⓒ SMF (*Ftbl*) central defender

centralidad SF centrality, central importance

centralismo SM centralism

centralista[1] ADJ, SMF centralist

centralista[2] SM (*Caribe*) sugar-mill owner

centralita SF (*Telec*) switchboard

centralización SF centralization

centralizado Ⓐ ADJ centralized; **cierre ~** central locking
Ⓑ SM centralization

centralizar ▸conjug 1f◂ VT to centralize

▼ **centrar** ▸conjug 1a◂ Ⓐ VT [1] (= *colocar*) [+ *imagen, texto*] to centre, center (*EEUU*); **la foto no está bien centrada** the photo is not centred correctly; **el cuadro no está centrado** the picture isn't straight; **~ el balón** to knock the ball into the centre
[2] (= *concentrar*) [+ *investigación*] to focus, centre, center (*EEUU*); [+ *esfuerzos*] to concentrate; [+ *atención*] to focus; **la policía centró las investigaciones en torno a dos jóvenes delincuentes** the police investigation focused *o* centred on two young criminals, the police focused *o* centred their investigation on two young criminals; **he centrado mi nueva obra en sólo dos personajes** my new play focuses on *o* centres on only two characters; **los cuadros de Goya ~on el interés del público** Goya's paintings captured the interest of the public
Ⓑ VI (*Dep*) to centre, center (*EEUU*)
Ⓒ **centrarse** VPR [1] **~se en** [*estudio, investigación, debate, programa*] to be focused on, centre on, center on (*EEUU*); [*obra, película, exposición*] to be focused on; **la atención internacional se centraba en El Salvador** international attention focused on *o* centred on El Salvador; **sus investigaciones se centran en la Europa medieval** her research focuses on *o* centres on medieval Europe; **un mercado centrado exclusivamente en los jóvenes** a market aimed exclusively at *o* geared exclusively toward young people
[2] (= *equilibrarse*) to settle down; **tuvo una época muy loca pero después se centró** he went through a very wild period but then he settled down
[3] (= *acomodarse*) to settle in, find one's feet

céntrico ADJ central; **está muy ~** it's very central; **un restaurante ~** a restaurant in the centre of town, a downtown restaurant (*EEUU*)

centrífuga SF centrifuge

centrifugadora SF [1] (*para ropa*) spin-dryer
[2] (*Téc*) centrifuge

centrifugar ▸conjug 1h◂ VT [1] [+ *ropa*] to spin-dry
[2] (*Téc*) to centrifuge

centrífugo ADJ centrifugal

centrípeto ADJ centripetal

centrismo SM centrism, *political doctrine of the centre*

centrista Ⓐ ADJ centrist
Ⓑ SMF centrist, *member of a centrist party*

centro Ⓐ SM [1] (= *medio*) centre, center (*EEUU*); **las regiones del ~ del país** the central areas of the country, the areas in the centre of the country; **pon el jarrón en el ~ de la mesa** put the vase in the middle *o* centre of the table; **el balón se hallaba en el ~ del campo** the ball was in midfield; ✦*MODISMO* **estar en su ~** to be in one's element ► **centro de gravedad** centre of gravity ► **centro de mesa** centrepiece ► **centro neurálgico** nerve centre
[2] [*de ciudad*] centre, center (*EEUU*); **no se puede aparcar en el ~** you can't park in the centre (of town), you can't park downtown (*EEUU*); **un edificio del ~ de Madrid** a building in the centre of Madrid *o* in Madrid town centre *o* (*EEUU*) in downtown Madrid; **"centro ciudad"** "city centre", "town centre"; **ir al ~** to go into town, go downtown (*EEUU*)
[3] (*Pol*) centre, center (*EEUU*); **ser de ~** [*persona*] to be a moderate; [*partido*] to be in the centre; **los partidos de ~ izquierda** the parties of the centre-left, the centre-left parties
[4] (= *foco*) [*de huracán*] centre, center (*EEUU*); [*de incendio*] seat; **ha sido el ~ de varias polémicas últimamente** he has been at the centre *o* heart of various controversies lately; **el gobierno se ha convertido en el ~ de las críticas** the government has become the target of criticism; **ser el ~ de atención** *o* **atracción** *o* **interés** to be the focus *o* centre of attention; **Zaire fue el ~ del interés internacional** Zaire was the focus of *o* was at the centre of international attention; **ser un ~ de intrigas** to be a hotbed of intrigue; **ser el ~ de las miradas: Roma es estos días el ~ de todas las miradas** all eyes are on Rome at the moment
[5] (= *establecimiento*) centre; **dos alumnos han sido expulsados del ~** two students have been expelled from the school *o* centre; **~s con más de 500 trabajadores** companies with over 500 workers ► **centro cívico** community centre ► **centro comercial** shopping centre, shopping mall ► **centro cultural** (*en un barrio, institución*) (local) arts centre; [*de otro país*] cultural centre ► **centro de abasto** (*Méx*) market ► **centro de acogida**: **~ de acogida de menores** children's home; **~ de acogida para mujeres maltratadas** refuge for battered women; **~ de acogida de refugiados** refugee reception centre ► **centro de atención de día** day-care centre ► **centro de atención primaria** primary care centre ► **centro de beneficios** profit centre ► **centro de cálculo** computer centre ► **centro de coordinación** [*de la policía*] operations room ► **centro de datos** data processing centre ► **centro de decisión** decision-making centre ► **centro de detención** detention centre ► **centro (de determinación) de costos** (*Com*) cost centre ► **centro de día** day centre ► **centro de distribución** distribution centre ► **centro de enseñanza** (*gen*) educational institution; (= *colegio*) school ► **centro de enseñanza media**, **centro de enseñanza secundaria** secondary school ► **centro de enseñanza superior** higher education institution ► **centro de jardinería** garden centre, garden center (*EEUU*) ► **centro de llamadas** call centre ► **centro de planificación familiar** family planning clinic ► **centro de proceso de datos** data processing centre ► **centro de protección de menores** child protection centre ► **centro de rastreo** (*Astron*) tracking centre ► **centro de salud** health centre ► **centro de trabajo** workplace; **en los ~s de trabajo** in the workplace ► **centro docente** educational institution ► **centro escolar** school ► **centro espacial** space centre ► **centro médico** (*gen*) medical establishment; (= *hospital*) hospital ► **centro penitenciario** prison, penitentiary (*EEUU*) ► **centro recreacional** (*Cuba, Ven*) sports centre, leisure centre ► **centro sanitario** = **centro médico** ► **centro universitario** (= *facultad*) faculty; (= *universidad*) university
[6] (= *población*) ► **centro de población** population centre ► **centro turístico** (= *lugar muy visitado*) tourist centre; (*diseñado para turistas*) tourist resort ► **centro urbano** urban area, city
[7] (= *ropa*) (*CAm*) (= *juego*) trousers and waistcoat, pants and vest (*EEUU*); (*Andes, Caribe*) (= *enaguas*) underskirt; (*Andes*) (= *falda*) thick flannel skirt
Ⓑ SMF (*Ftbl*) centre; **delantero ~** centre-forward; **medio ~** centre-half

centroafricano/a Ⓐ ADJ Central African
Ⓑ SM/F native *o* inhabitant of the Central African Republic

Centroamérica SF Central America

centroamericano/a ADJ, SM/F Central American

centrocampismo SM midfield play

centrocampista SMF (*Dep*) midfielder; **los ~s** the midfield

centrocampo SM midfield

centroderecha SM centre-right

Centroeuropa SF Central Europe

centroeuropeo/a ADJ, SM/F Central European

centroizquierda SM centre-left

cénts ABR (= **céntimos**) c

centuplicar ▸conjug 1g◂ VT to increase a hundredfold, centuplicate (*frm*)

céntuplo Ⓐ ADJ hundredfold, centuple
Ⓑ SM centuple

centuria SF century

centurión SM centurion

cenutrio* SM twit*, twerp*

cénzalo SM mosquito

cenzontle SM (*CAm, Méx*) mockingbird

ceñido ADJ [1] [*vestido*] figure-hugging; [*traje*] tight-fitting; [*vaqueros*] skintight
[2] (= *reducido*) **una novela ceñida a las normas clásicas** a novel that sticks close to classical principles; **~ y corto** brief and to the point
[3] [*curva*] tight

ceñidor SM sash, girdle

ceñir ▸conjug 3h, 3k◂ Ⓐ VT [1] (= *ajustar*) **el vestido le ceñía el cuerpo** the dress clung to *o* hugged her body, the dress was really tight-fitting; **la faja le ceñía el talle** the sash fitted tightly around her waist
[2] (*Cos*) to take in; **habrá que ~ más el talle** the waist will need to be taken in more
[3] (*liter*) (= *rodear*) to surround, encircle; **la muralla que ciñe la ciudad** the wall that surrounds *o* encircles the city; **un lazo de terciopelo le ceñía la cintura** she had a velvet ribbon around her waist, a velvet ribbon encircled *o* (*liter*) girdled her waist; **ceñí su cuerpo con mis brazos** I wrapped my arms around his body
[4] (*liter*) (= *llevar puesto*) **la corona que ciñó nuestro rey** the crown that our king wore, the crown that rested on the head of our king
Ⓑ **ceñirse** VPR [1] (= *reducirse*) **~se a algo: esta biografía se ciñe a la vida personal del autor** this biography limits itself *o* restricts itself to the author's personal life; **me voy a ~ a algunos detalles significativos** I am going to limit *o* restrict myself to certain relevant details
[2] (= *atenerse*) **~se a algo: no se ciñeron a lo acordado** they did not keep to *o* stick to the agreement; **será difícil ~se al presupuesto** it will be difficult to keep to *o* keep within *o* stay within the budget; **por favor, cíñase a las preguntas del fiscal** please keep to the questions of the public prosecutor, please limit yourself to answering the questions of the public prosecutor
[3] (*frm*) (= *ponerse*) to put on; **quiso ~se de nuevo el traje de novia** she wanted to put on her wedding dress again; **se ciñó la correa alrededor de la cintura** she put the belt around her waist; **se ciñó la gorra y se marchó** he put *o* pulled his hat on and left; **~se la corona** to be crowned, take the crown (*liter*); **~se la espada**†† to put on one's sword, gird one's sword (*liter*)

ceño SM [1] (= *expresión*) frown, scowl; **arrugar** *o* **fruncir el ~** to frown, knit one's brows; **mirar con ~ a algn** to frown at sb, scowl at sb, give black looks to sb
[2] [*de las nubes, del mar*] threatening appearance

ceñudo ADJ frowning, scowling

CEOE SF ABR (= **Confederación Española de Organizaciones Empresariales**) ≈ CBI

CEP SM ABR (*Esp*) (= **Centro de Educación de Profesores**) *teacher training centre*

cepa SF [1] (= *tronco*) [*de árbol*] stump; [*de vid*] stock
[2] [*de persona*] stock; **es de buena ~ castellana** he's of good Castilian stock; **es un inglés de pura ~** he's English through and through, he's every inch an Englishman
[3] (*Arquit*) pier
[4] (*Biol*) strain
[5] (*Méx*) (= *hoyo*) pit, trench

CEPAL SF ABR (= **Comisión Económica para América Latina y el Caribe**) ECLAC

cepero SM trapper

cepillado SM [1] [*de ropa, dientes, pelo*] brushing; **se elimina con un suave ~** you can get rid of it with a gentle brushing
[2] [*de madera*] planing

cepilladura SF = **cepillado**

cepillar ▸conjug 1a◂ Ⓐ VT [1] [+ *ropa, dientes, pelo*] to brush
[2] [+ *madera*] to plane, plane down

[3] (*) (= *suspender*) to fail, flunk (*esp EEUU**)
[4] (*) (= *adular*) to flatter, butter up
[5] (*) (= *robar*) to rip off*
[6] (*) (= *ganar*) to win, take (**a** from)
Ⓑ **cepillarse** VPR [1] [+ *dientes, pelo*] to brush
[2] **~se a algn*** (= *matar*) to bump sb off*; (**) (= *copular con*) to screw sb**
[3] (*) (= *robar*) **~se algo** to rip sth off*

cepillo SM [1] (*para ropa, dientes, pelo*) brush; **lleva el pelo cortado al ~** he has a crew cut ► **cepillo de baño** toilet brush ► **cepillo de dientes** toothbrush ► **cepillo de púas (metálicas)** wire brush ► **cepillo para el pelo** hairbrush ► **cepillo para la ropa** clothes brush ► **cepillo para las uñas** nailbrush
[2] (*para barrer*) brush ► **cepillo para el suelo** scrubbing brush
[3] (*para madera*) plane
[4] (*Rel*) poorbox, alms box
[5] (*LAm*) (= *adulador*) flatterer, bootlicker*

cepillón/ona: Ⓐ ADJ soapy*
Ⓑ SM/F creep**

cepo SM [1] (*Caza*) trap, snare ► **cepo conejero** snare ► **cepo lobero** wolf-trap
[2] (*Aut*) (wheel) clamp
[3] [*de yunque, ancla*] stock
[4] (*Bot*) branch, bough
[5] (*Rel*) poorbox, alms box

ceporrez* SF idiocy

ceporro* SM [1] (= *idiota*) twit*, idiot
[2] (= *gordo*) **estar como un ~** to be very fat

Cepsa SF ABR (*Com*) = **Compañía Española de Petróleos, Sociedad Anónima**

CEPYME SF ABR = **Confederación Española de la Pequeña y Mediana Empresa**

cequión SM (*Cono Sur*) *large irrigation channel*

cera SF [1] wax; **depilarse a la ~** ◊ **hacerse la ~** to wax one's legs o arms *etc*; ✦*MODISMO* **ser como una ~** to be as gentle as a lamb ► **cera de abejas** beeswax ► **cera de los oídos** earwax ► **cera de lustrar** wax polish ► **cera de para suelos** floor polish
[2] **ceras** [*de colmena*] honeycomb *sing*
[3] (*Andes, Méx*) (= *vela*) candle

cerafolio SM chervil

cerámica SF [1] (*Arte*) ceramics *sing*, pottery
[2] (= *conjunto de objetos*) ceramics *pl*, pottery

cerámico ADJ ceramic

ceramista SMF potter

cerbatana SF [1] (*Mil*) blowpipe
[2] (= *juguete*) peashooter
[3] (*Med*) ear trumpet

cerca¹ SF (= *valla*) [*de madera, alambre*] fence; [*de piedra, ladrillo*] wall ► **cerca eléctrica** electrified fence, electric fence ► **cerca viva** hedge

cerca² Ⓐ ADV [1] (*indicando proximidad*) (*de aquí o allí*) near, nearby; (*entre objetos, personas*) close; **no había un hospital ~** there wasn't a hospital near there o nearby; **está aquí ~** it's very o just near here; **¿está ~ la estación?** is the station near here o nearby?; **está tan ~ que puedo ir andando** it's so near here o so close I can just walk; **las casas están tan ~ que se pueden oír las conversaciones de los vecinos** the houses are so close (to each other) that you can hear what the neighbours are saying; **quería tener más ~ a los amigos** he wanted to be nearer (to) o closer to his friends; **las vacaciones están ya ~** the holidays are nearly here, the holidays are not far off now; **~ de** near (to), close to; **viven ~ de la playa** they live near (to) o close to the beach; **estaba sentada ~ de mí** she was sitting near me; **se sentía muy ~ de su familia** she felt very close to her family
[2] **de ~** [2·1] (= *a poca distancia*) [*ver*] close up; [*seguir, observar, vigilar*] closely; **no veo bien de ~** I can't see things close up, I'm long-sighted; **visto de ~, parece mayor** when you see him close up o at close quarters, he seems older; **pudo ver de ~ la pobreza** she got to see poverty close at hand o at close quarters; **el coche iba a gran velocidad, seguido de ~ por su escolta** the car was travelling at a high speed, followed closely by its escort; **seguí de ~ la guerra a través de los periódicos** I followed the war closely in the newspapers
[2·2] (= *en persona*) in person; **para todos aquellos que no puedan ver la exposición de ~** for all those unable to see the exhibition in person; **he tenido la oportunidad de conocer de ~ a muchos famosos** I have had the opportunity of meeting many famous people personally o in person; **los que lo conocen de ~ hablan muy bien de él** those who know him well speak very highly of him; **la crisis me ha afectado muy de ~** the crisis has affected me personally; **no conoce de ~ los problemas de la población** he does not have first-hand o personal knowledge of the people's problems
[3] **~ de** (= *casi*) nearly; **hay ~ de ocho toneladas** there are nearly eight tons of it; **~ de 2.500 personas** nearly 2,500 people; **son ~ de las seis** it's nearly six o'clock; **estar ~ de hacer algo** to come close to doing sth; **he estado ~ de tirar el libro por la ventana** I've come close to throwing that book out of the window; **estuvimos tan ~ de conseguir la victoria ...** we were so close to obtaining victory ...
[4] (*esp Cono Sur*) **~ nuestro/mío** near us/me
Ⓑ SM (†) [1] (= *aspecto*) **tiene buen ~** it looks all right close up
[2] **cercas** (*Arte*) foreground *sing*

cercado SM [1] (= *recinto*) enclosure; (= *huerto*) enclosed garden, orchard
[2] (= *valla*) fence, wall ► **cercado eléctrico** electrified fence
[3] (*Andes*) (= *ejido*) communal lands
[4] (*Andes Hist*) *state capital and surrounding towns*

cercanía SF [1] (= *proximidad*) nearness, proximity
[2] **cercanías** (= *alrededores*) neighbourhood *sing*, neighborhood (*EEUU*) *sing*, vicinity *sing*; (= *suburbios*) outskirts, suburbs; **tren de ~s** suburban train, commuter train

cercano ADJ [1] [*lugar*] nearby; **entraron en un bar ~** they went to a nearby bar; **acudió a la comisaría más cercana** he went to the nearest police station; **sentía la presencia cercana de su madre** he felt the presence of his mother nearby; **~ a** close to, near, near to; **un hotel ~ al aeropuerto** a hotel close to o near (to) the airport; **una cifra cercana a los tres millones de dólares** a figure close to three million dollars
[2] [*amigo, pariente*] close; **su colaborador más ~** his closest collaborator; **~ a** close to; **según fuentes cercanas al ministerio** according to sources close to the ministry; **personas cercanas a la organización terrorista** people closely linked to the terrorist organization
[3] (*en el tiempo*) **en el futuro ~** in the near future; **cree cercana la firma del acuerdo** he believes that they are close to signing the agreement; **ahora, cuando está ~ el primer aniversario de su muerte** now, as the first anniversary of her death approaches

Cercano Oriente SM Near East

cercar ▸conjug 1g◂ VT [1] [+ *campo, terreno*] to enclose; (*con vallas*) to fence in, wall in
[2] [+ *persona*] to surround, ring
[3] (*Mil*) [+ *pueblo, ciudad*] to surround, besiege; [+ *tropas*] to cut off, surround

cercén ADV **cortar a ~** to sever; **cortar un brazo a ~** to sever an arm

cercenar ▸conjug 1a◂ VT [1] (= *recortar*) to cut o trim the edges of
[2] [+ *brazo, pierna*] to sever
[3] (= *reducir*) [+ *gastos*] to cut down, reduce; [+ *texto*] to shorten, cut down

cerceta SF teal, garganey

cerciorar ▸conjug 1a◂ Ⓐ VT **~ a algn de algo** to convince sb of sth
Ⓑ **cerciorarse** VPR **~se de algo** make sure o certain of sth; **cerciórense de que las luces están apagadas** make sure o certain that the lights are switched off

cerco SM [1] (*Agr*) (= *recinto*) enclosure
[2] (*LAm*) (= *valla*) fence, hedge; ✦*MODISMO* **saltar el ~** (*Cono Sur*) to jump on the bandwagon
[3] (*Téc*) [*de rueda*] rim; [*de tonel*] hoop
[4] (= *borde externo*) [*de estrella*] halo; [*de mancha*] ring
[5] (= *corrillo*) social group, circle
[6] (*Mil*) siege; **alzar** o **levantar el ~** to raise the siege; **poner ~ a algo** to lay siege to sth, besiege sth
[7] (*Arquit*) casing, frame

cercón ADV (*LAm*) rather close

cerda SF [1] (*Zool*) sow; *ver tb* **cerdo**
[2] (= *pelo*) [*de cepillo, jabalí, tejón*] bristle; [*de caballo*] horsehair
[3] (**) (= *puta*) slut

cerdada SF dirty trick

cerdear ▸conjug 1a◂ VI [1] (*Mús*) to rasp, screech
[2] (*) (= *aplazar*) to put things off

Cerdeña SF Sardinia

cerdito/a SM/F piglet

cerdo¹ SM [1] (*Zool*) pig, hog (*EEUU*); **todos los políticos son unos ~s** all politicians are bastards o swine*; ✦*MODISMO* **comer como un ~** (= *mucho*) to stuff o.s; (= *sin modales*) to eat like a pig; ✦*REFRÁN* **a todos los ~s les llega su San Martín** everyone gets their just deserts sooner or later, everyone gets their comeuppance in the end ► **cerdo ibérico** Iberian pig ► **cerdo marino** porpoise; *ver tb* **cerda**
[2] (*Culin*) pork; **carne de ~** pork

cerdo²/a* Ⓐ ADJ [1] (= *sucio*) filthy, dirty
[2] (= *malhablado*) **no digas palabrotas, no seas tan ~** don't swear o curse, don't be so foul-mouthed o crude
[3] (= *maleducado*) **no eructes en público, no seas ~** don't belch in public, don't be such a pig o don't be so gross!
[4] (= *canalla*) rotten*

Ⓑ SM/F [1] (= *sucio*) slob*; **¡mira cómo tienes la habitación! ¡eres un ~!** look at the state of your room! you're a real slob! *o* you're filthy!*
[2] (= *malhablado*) foul-mouthed pig
[3] (= *maleducado*) **es un ~, siempre habla con la boca llena** he's such a pig *o* so gross eating with his mouth full all the time*
[4] (= *canalla*) swine*/cow*; *ver tb* **cerda**

cerdoso ADJ bristly

cereal Ⓐ ADJ cereal, grain *antes de s*
Ⓑ SM [1] (= *grano*) cereal, grain ► **cereal forrajero** fodder grain
[2] **cereales** [*de desayuno*] cereal *sing*, cereals; **he tomado ~es para desayunar** I've had cereal for breakfast

cerealista Ⓐ ADJ grain-producing *antes de s*
Ⓑ SMF cereal farmer; (*Com*) grain dealer

cerealístico ADJ grain *antes de s*, cereal *antes de s*

cereal-pienso SM (*pl* **cereales-pienso**) fodder grain

cerebelo SM cerebellum

cerebral ADJ [1] (= *del cerebro*) cerebral, brain *antes de s*
[2] (*pey*) (= *calculador*) scheming, calculating

cerebralismo SM intellectualism, cerebralism

cerebro SM [1] (*Anat*) brain; ✦***MODISMOS* estrujarse el ~*** to rack one's brains; **ser un ~*** to be brilliant, be really brainy ► **cerebro electrónico** electronic brain ► **cerebro gris** éminence grise
[2] (= *dirigente*) brains *pl*; **es el ~ del equipo** he's the brains of the team

ceremonia SF [1] (= *acto*) ceremony ► **ceremonia de apertura** opening ceremony ► **ceremonia de clausura** closing ceremony ► **ceremonia inaugural** inaugural ceremony ► **ceremonia religiosa** religious ceremony, (religious) service
[2] (= *afectación*) formality, ceremoniousness; **es muy llano y le molesta tanta ~** he's very straightforward and all this formality annoys him; **¡déjate de ~s!** don't stand on ceremony!; **sin ~: el rey nos habló sin ~s** the king spoke to us plainly *o* without any ceremony; **se despidió sin ~s** he said goodbye without a fuss

ceremonial ADJ, SM ceremonial

ceremoniosamente ADV ceremoniously

ceremonioso ADJ [*reunión, saludo, visita*] formal; [*ambiente*] ceremonious

céreo ADJ (*liter*) waxen (*liter*)

cerería SF wax-chandler's shop, chandlery

cerero SM wax chandler

cereza SF [1] (= *fruta*) cherry; **un jersey rojo ~** a cherry-red jumper ► **cereza silvestre** wild cherry
[2] (*LAm*) (= *cáscara*) husk of coffee bean

cerezal SM cherry orchard

cerezo SM cherry tree

cerilla SF [1] (= *fósforo*) match
[2] (*Anat*) earwax
[3] (*Rel*) wax taper

cerillazo* SM **pegar un ~ a algo** to set a match to sth

cerillero/a SM/F match seller

cerillo SM (*LAm*) match

cernedor SM sieve

cerneja SF fetlock

cerner ▸conjug 2g◂ Ⓐ VT [1] (*filtrar*) [+ *harina*] to sift, sieve; [+ *tierra*] to sieve
[2] (= *observar*) to scan, watch
Ⓑ VI [1] (*Bot*) to bud, blossom
[2] (*Meteo*) to drizzle
Ⓒ **cernerse** VPR [1] [*ave*] to hover; [*avión*] to circle
[2] [*amenaza*] **~se sobre algo/algn** to hang over sth/sb
[3] (*al andar*) to waddle

cernícalo SM [1] (*Orn*) kestrel
[2] (*) (= *persona torpe*) lout, dolt
[3] **coger un ~*** to get tight*
[4] (*Andes Orn*) hawk, falcon

cernidillo† SM [1] (= *modo de andar*) swagger, rolling gait
[2] (*Meteo*) drizzle

cernido SM [1] (= *acto*) sifting
[2] (= *harina*) sifted flour
[3] (*Andes Meteo*) drizzle

cernidor SM sieve

cernidura SF sifting

cero SM [1] (*Fís, Mat*) zero; **ocho grados bajo ~** eight degrees below zero; **desde las ~ horas** from twelve o'clock midnight; ✦***MODISMOS* estoy a ~ de dinero** I'm broke*; **empezar** *o* **partir de ~** to start from scratch; **tendremos que partir nuevamente de ~** we'll have to start from scratch again; **ser un ~ a la izquierda** to be useless ► **cero absoluto** absolute zero
[2] (*Ftbl, Rugby*) nil, zero (*EEUU*); **ganaron por tres goles a ~** they won by three goals to nil, they won three nil; **empataron a ~** they drew nil-nil, it was a no-score draw; **estamos 40 a ~** (*Tenis*) it's 40-love
[3] (*Educ*) nought; **me han puesto un ~** I got nought out of ten
[4] (*) (= *coche-patrulla*) police car

ceroso ADJ waxen (*liter*), waxy

cerote SM [1] (*Téc*) wax, shoemaker's wax
[2] (*) (= *miedo*) panic
[3] (*CAm, Méx*) (= *excremento*) piece of human excrement, stool; ✦***MODISMOS* estar hecho un ~** (*Andes*) ◊ **tener ~** (*Cono Sur, Méx*) to be covered in muck

cerotear ▸conjug 1a◂ VT [+ *hilo*] to wax

cerquillo SM [1] (*LAm*) (= *flequillo*) fringe, bangs *pl* (*EEUU*)
[2] [*de monje*] *fringe of hair round the tonsure*
[3] (*Téc*) seam, welt

cerquita* ADV quite near, close by

cerradero Ⓐ ADJ (= *dispositivo*) locking, fastening; **caja cerradera** box that can be locked, box with a lock
Ⓑ SM (= *mecanismo de cierre*) locking device; (*en cerradura*) strike, keeper; [*de monedero*] purse strings

cerrado ADJ [1] (= *no abierto*) [*puerta, ventana, boca*] closed; [*puño*] clenched; [*curva*] sharp, tight; **escuchaban música con los ojos ~s** they were listening to music with their eyes closed; **respira con la boca cerrada** breathe with your mouth closed; **"cerrado"** "closed"; **"cerrado por vacaciones"** "closed for holidays", "closed for vacation" (*EEUU*); **"cerrado por reformas"** "closed for refurbishment"; **la puerta no estaba cerrada con llave** the door was not locked; **se lo dio en un sobre ~** he gave it to her in a sealed envelope; **¿está el grifo bien ~?** is the tap turned off properly?; **esa fábrica lleva varios años cerrada** that factory has been closed for years; **el caso está ~** the case is closed; **el mitin se celebró en un recinto ~** the rally was held indoors; **huele a ~** it smells stuffy in here; **~ a** closed to; **los jardines están ~s al público** the gardens are closed to the public; **el aeropuerto permanece ~ al tráfico aéreo** the airport remains closed to all air traffic; *ver tb* **puerta 3**
[2] (= *apretado*) [*barba*] thick, full; [*bosque*] dense, thick; [*ambiente, atmósfera*] stuffy; **el candidato fue recibido con una cerrada ovación** the presidential candidate was given a rapturous welcome; *ver tb* **descarga 3**
[3] [*cielo*] cloudy, overcast; [*noche*] dark, black; **era ya noche cerrada cuando llegamos a casa** it was completely dark by the time we got home
[4] (*Ling*) [*acento*] broad, strong; [*vocal*] closed; **tiene un acento muy ~** she has a very broad *o* strong accent; **hablaba con ~ acento gallego** he spoke with a broad *o* strong *o* thick Galician accent
[5] [*persona*] [5·1] (= *intransigente*) **la gente de este pueblo es muy cerrada** the people in this village don't much like strangers; **no está ~ a ningún tipo de sugerencias** he is open to all suggestions
[5·2] (= *torpe*) (*tb* **~ de mollera**) dense, thick*
[5·3] (= *reservado*) reserved
[6] (*Com*) [*precio*] fixed; **a precio ~** at a fixed price

cerradura SF (*Mec*) lock ► **cerradura de combinación** combination lock ► **cerradura de golpe, cerradura de muelle** spring lock ► **cerradura de seguridad** safety lock

cerraja SF [1] (*Mec*) lock
[2] (*Bot*) sow thistle

cerrajería SF [1] (= *oficio*) locksmith's craft, locksmith's trade
[2] (*Com*) locksmith's, locksmith's shop

cerrajero/a SM/F locksmith

cerrar ▸conjug 1j◂ Ⓐ VT [1] (*hablando de un objeto abierto*) [+ *puerta, ventana, boca*] to close, shut; [+ *cremallera*] to do up; [+ *camisa*] to button, do up; [+ *cortina*] to draw; [+ *paraguas, válvula*] to close; [+ *carta*] to seal; [+ *costura, herida*] to sew up; **no puedo ~ esta maleta** I can't close *o* shut this suitcase; **cierra los ojos** close *o* shut your eyes; **~ algo de golpe** to slam sth shut; **cerró el libro de golpe** she banged *o* slammed the book shut; **los colegios ~on sus puertas a causa de la huelga** the schools closed because of the strike; **cerré la puerta con llave** I locked the door; **cierra el pico*** shut your trap‡; **~ el puño** to clench one's fist; *ver tb* **fila 3.2**
[2] (= *desconectar*) [+ *gas, grifo, radiador*] to turn off
[3] (= *bloquear*) [+ *agujero, brecha, tubo*] to block (up); [+ *frontera, puerto*] to close; **una roca cerraba la entrada a la cueva** a rock was obstructing the entrance to the cave; **han cerrado la frontera** they have closed the border; **~ el paso a algn** to block sb's way; **trató de entrar, pero le ~on el paso** he tried to get in, but they blocked *o* barred his way
[4] [+ *tienda, negocio*] (*al final de la jornada*) to close, shut; (*para siempre*) to close, close down
[5] [+ *jardín, terreno*] (*con cerca*) to fence in; (*con muro*) to wall in
[6] (= *poner fin a*) [6·1] [+ *debate, narración, programa*] to close, end; **~ el sistema** (*Inform*) to shut down the system

6·2 [+ *desfile*] to bring up the rear of; **los manifestantes que cerraban la marcha** the demonstrators bringing up the rear *o* at the rear; **cierra la cabalgata la carroza de Santa Claus** the last float in the procession is the one with Santa Claus
7 **~ un trato** to seal a deal
Ⓑ VI 1 (*hablando de un objeto abierto*) [*puerta, ventana*] to close, shut; [*bragueta*] to do up; [*paraguas, válvula*] to close; [*herida*] to close up; **la puerta cierra mal** the door won't close *o* shut properly; **un estuche que cierra con llave** a jewellery box with a lock
2 [*persona*] **cierra, que se va a escapar el gato** close *o* shut the door or the cat will get out; **te dejo las llaves para que cierres** I am leaving you the keys so you can lock up
3 [*tienda, negocio*] to close, shut; **¿a qué hora cierran las tiendas el sábado?** what time do the shops close *o* shut on Saturday?; **cerramos a las nueve** we close at nine; **las discotecas no cierran en toda la noche** the discos stay open all night
4 (*Fin*) (*en la Bolsa*) to close
5 (*en dominó*) to block; (*en Scrabble*) to use one's tiles up; **¡cierro!** I'm out!
6 (= *atacar*) **~ con** *o* **contra algn** to grapple with sb; **~ con el enemigo** to engage the enemy at close quarters
Ⓒ **cerrarse** VPR 1 [*puerta, ventana*] to close, shut; [*bragueta*] to do up; [*paraguas, válvula*] to close; [*herida*] to close up; **la puerta se cerró detrás de mí** the door closed *o* shut behind me; **la ventana se cerró de golpe** the window slammed shut; **este sofá-cama se cierra con gran facilidad** this sofa-bed is very easy to fold away; **se me cierran los ojos** I can't keep my eyes open
2 [*persona*] **ciérrate bien el abrigo** do your coat up properly; **~se la cremallera** to do one's zip up
3 (*Com*) to close, shut; **la tienda se cierra a las nueve** the shop closes *o* shuts at nine; **el museo se cerró por obras** the museum closed for refurbishment
4 (= *obcecarse*) **~se a algo**: **no hay que ~se a nada sin probarlo primero** you should never dismiss anything without trying it first; **no puedes ~te a la evidencia** you can't ignore the evidence; **~se en algo**: **se ~on en una actitud beligerante** they persisted with a belligerent attitude; **~se en hacer algo** to persist in doing sth; ✦***MODISMO*** **~se en banda** (= *mostrarse inflexible*) to refuse to budge; (= *unirse*) to close ranks
5 (= *terminar*) to close, end; **el trimestre se cerró con un aumento del desempleo** the quarter closed *o* ended with a rise in unemployment; **se ha cerrado el plazo para las votaciones** the period for voting has closed *o* is over
6 [*cielo*] to cloud over, become overcast; [*invierno, noche*] to close in
7 (*Mil*) to close ranks

cerrazón SF 1 (= *obstinación*) bloody-mindedness
2 (= *torpeza*) dimwittedness
3 [*del cielo*] threatening sky, storm clouds *pl*

cerrero ADJ 1 [*animal*] wild
2 [*persona*] rough, uncouth
3 (*LAm*) (= *sin azúcar*) unsweetened, bitter

cerril ADJ 1 [*terreno*] rough, mountainous
2 [*animal*] untamed, unbroken
3 [*persona*] (= *brusca*) rough, uncouth; (= *de miras estrechas*) small-minded

cerrilismo SM 1 (= *brusquedad*) roughness, uncouthness
2 (= *estrechez de miras*) small-mindedness

cerrillar ▸conjug 1a◂ VT [+ *moneda*] to mill

cerro SM 1 (*Geog*) hill; ✦***MODISMO*** **andar** *o* **echarse** *o* **ir por los ~s de Úbeda** to wander off the point, go off at a tangent
2 (*Zool*) back; ✦***MODISMO*** **ir en ~** to ride bareback
3 (*Téc*) *bunch of cleaned hemp or flax*
4 (*Andes*) (= *montón*) heap, load; **un ~ de algo** a heap of sth, a load of sth

cerrojazo SM slamming; **dar un ~** (*lit*) to slam the bolt; (*fig*) to end unexpectedly

cerrojo SM 1 (= *mecanismo*) bolt, latch; **echar el ~** to bolt the door
2 (*Dep*) (*tb* **táctica de ~**) defensive play, negative play

certamen SM competition, contest ▸ **certamen de belleza** beauty contest

certeramente ADV accurately

certero ADJ 1 (= *correcto*) [*respuesta*] accurate; [*decisión*] correct, right; [*acto*] sure
2 [*tiro*] well-aimed; **es un cazador ~** he's a crack shot

▼**certeza** SF 1 (= *seguridad*) certainty; **tener la ~ de que ...** to know for certain that ..., be sure that ...; **¿lo sabes con ~?** do you know (that) for certain?
2 (= *precisión*) accuracy

certidumbre SF 1 (= *seguridad*) certainty
2 (= *confianza*) conviction

certificable ADJ certifiable

certificación SF 1 (= *acción*) certification
2 (*Correos*) registration
3 (*Jur*) affidavit

certificado Ⓐ ADJ 1 (*Correos*) [*carta, paquete*] registered; **envié la carta por correo ~** I sent the letter by registered mail *o* post
2 (= *aprobado*) certified; **el avión estaba ~ para volar** the plane was certified to fly
Ⓑ SM 1 (= *documento*) certificate ▸ **certificado de acciones** (*Com*) share *o* stock certificate ▸ **certificado de aptitud** certificate of attainment ▸ **certificado de autenticidad** certificate of authenticity ▸ **certificado de ciudadanía** naturalization papers *pl* ▸ **certificado de defunción** death certificate ▸ **certificado de depósito** certificate of deposit ▸ **certificado de escolaridad** *completion certificate for compulsory education* ▸ **certificado de estudios** school-leaving certificate ▸ **certificado de garantía** certificate of guarantee ▸ **certificado de nacimiento** birth certificate ▸ **certificado de origen** certificate of origin ▸ **certificado de penales** good-conduct certificate ▸ **certificado de vacuna** vaccination certificate ▸ **certificado escolar** = **certificado de escolaridad** ▸ **certificado médico** medical certificate
2 (*Correos*) registered item

certificar ▸conjug 1g◂ VT 1 (*Jur*) to certify; **~ que ...** to certify that ...
2 (*Correos*) to register

certitud SF certainty

cerúleo ADJ (*liter*) cerulean (*liter*), sky blue

cerumen SM earwax

cerval ADJ deer *antes de s*, deer-like

cervantino ADJ Cervantine; **estilo ~** Cervantine style, style of Cervantes; **estudios ~s** Cervantes studies, studies of Cervantes

cervantista SMF Cervantes scholar, specialist in Cervantes

cervatillo SM fawn

cervato SM fawn

cervecera SF brewery

cervecería SF (= *bar*) bar, public house, beer hall (*EEUU*)

cervecero/a Ⓐ ADJ beer *antes de s*; **la industria cervecera** the brewing industry
Ⓑ SM/F brewer

cerveza SF beer; **una caña de ~** a glass of beer *o* lager ▸ **cerveza de barril** draught beer, draft beer (*EEUU*) ▸ **cerveza de malta** malt beer ▸ **cerveza de sifón** (*CAm*) = **cerveza de barril** ▸ **cerveza embotellada** bottled beer ▸ **cerveza negra** stout ▸ **cerveza rubia** lager

cervical ADJ 1 (= *del cuello*) neck *antes de s*, cervical
2 (= *del útero*) cervical

Cervino SM **el Monte ~** Mont Cervin, the Matterhorn

cerviz SF 1 (= *nuca*) nape (of the neck); ✦***MODISMOS*** **bajar** *o* **doblar la ~** to submit, bow down; **de dura ~** stubborn, headstrong
2 (= *útero*) cervix

cervuno ADJ deer-like

cesación SF cessation, suspension ▸ **cesación del fuego** ceasefire ▸ **cesación de pagos** suspension of payments

cesante Ⓐ ADJ 1 [*empleado*] redundant, laid-off; (*esp LAm*) unemployed
2 [*funcionario*] suspended; **el ministro ~** the outgoing minister
3 [*embajador*] recalled
Ⓑ SMF redundant worker, laid-off worker (*EEUU*)

cesantear ▸conjug 1a◂ VT (*Cono Sur*) to dismiss, sack*

cesantía SF (*esp LAm*) (= *desempleo*) unemployment; (= *paga*) redundancy money, redundancy payment; [*de funcionario*] suspension

cesar ▸conjug 1a◂ Ⓐ VI 1 (= *parar*) to stop; **un ruido que no cesa** an incessant noise; **no ~ de hacer algo**: **el paro no cesa de aumentar** unemployment is constantly increasing; **no cesaba de repetirlo** he kept repeating it; **no cesa de hablar** he never stops talking; **sin ~** incessantly, nonstop; **repetía sin ~ que siempre estaríamos juntos** she kept saying that we would always be together
2 (= *dimitir*) to leave, quit (*EEUU*); **acaba de ~ como presidente de la empresa** he has just left his job as company director; **~ en su cargo** [*empleado*] to resign, leave one's job; [*alto cargo*] to leave office
Ⓑ VT 1 (= *despedir*) to dismiss; **ha sido cesado de su cargo en el ministerio** he has been dismissed from his post at the ministry
2 (= *parar*) [+ *ataque*] to stop

César SM Caesar; ✦***REFRÁN*** **dar al ~ lo que es del ~ y a Dios lo que es de Dios** to render unto Caesar that which is Caesar's and unto God that which is God's

cesaraugustano/a ADJ, SM/F = **zaragozano**

cesárea SF (*Med*) Caesarean, Caesarean sec-

➤ LENGUA Y USO: **certeza 1** 43.1

tion; **le han tenido que hacer una ~** she had to have a Caesarean (section)

cesáreo ADJ [1] Caesarean
[2] (*Med*) **operación cesárea** Caesarean section

cese SM [1] (= *parada*) cessation; **un acuerdo sobre el ~ de la violencia** an agreement on the cessation of violence; **un ~ temporal de los bombardeos** a temporary halt *o* cessation to the bombing; **el ~ de (las) hostilidades** the cessation of hostilities ► **cese de alarma** (*Mil*) all-clear signal ► **cese de pagos** suspension of payments ► **cese el fuego** ceasefire
[2] (= *despido*) dismissal; **dar el ~ a algn** to dismiss sb
[3] (= *dimisión*) resignation; **entregué mi ~ al jefe** I handed in my resignation *o* gave in my notice to the boss

CESEDEN SM ABR (*Esp*) = **Centro Superior de Estudios de la Defensa Nacional**

CESID SM ABR, **Cesid** SM ABR (*Esp*) (= **Centro Superior de Información de la Defensa**) *military intelligence service*

cesio SM caesium, cesium (*EEUU*)

cesión SF [1] [*de territorio*] cession (*frm*), giving up
[2] (*Jur*) granting, transfer ► **cesión de bienes** surrender of property

cesionario/a SM/F grantee, assignee

cesionista SMF grantor, assignor

césped SM [1] (= *planta*) grass ► **césped artificial** artificial turf, Astroturf®
[2] (= *terreno plantado*) lawn
[3] (*Dep*) pitch

cesta SF [1] (= *canasta*) basket; ✦*MODISMO* **llevar la ~*** to play gooseberry, be a third wheel (*EEUU*) ► **cesta de costura** sewing basket ► **cesta de la compra** shopping basket; (*Econ*) *cost of a week's shopping* ► **cesta de Navidad** Christmas box, Christmas hamper ► **cesta de picnic** picnic hamper
[2] (*en baloncesto, pelota vasca*) basket

cestada SF basketful

cestería SF [1] (= *arte*) basketmaking
[2] (= *conjunto de cestas*) wickerwork, basketwork; **silla de ~** wicker chair, wicker-work chair
[3] (= *tienda*) basketwork shop

cestero/a SM/F basketmaker

cestillo SM [1] (= *cesto pequeño*) small basket
[2] [*de globo*] basket

cesto SM [1] (= *canasta*) basket, hamper ► **cesto de la colada** linen basket, clothes basket
[2] ✦*MODISMO* **estar hecho un ~*** to be very drowsy
[3] (*) (= *gamberro*) lout

cesura SF caesura

cetáceo ADJ, SM cetacean

cetárea SF, **cetaria** SF shellfish farm

cetme SM rifle

cetorrino SM basking shark

cetrería SF falconry, hawking

cetrero SM [1] (*Caza*) falconer
[2] (*Rel*) verger

cetrino ADJ [*tez*] sallow; [*persona, temperamento*] melancholy

cetro SM [1] (= *bastón de mando*) sceptre, scepter (*EEUU*); ✦*MODISMO* **empuñar el ~** to ascend the throne
[2] (= *poder*) sway, dominion
[3] (*LAm Dep*) crown, championship

CEU SM ABR (*Esp*) (= **Centro de Estudios Universitarios**) *private university*

Ceuta SF Ceuta

ceutí Ⓐ ADJ from *o* of Ceuta
Ⓑ SMF native *o* inhabitant of Ceuta; **los ~es** the people of Ceuta

C.F. ABR (= **Club de Fútbol**) FC

cf. ABR (= **compárese**) cf

CFC SM ABR (= **clorofluorocarbono**) CFC

cfr. ABR (= **confróntese**) cf

CG SF ABR (*Esp Pol*) = **Coalición Galega**

cg ABR (= **centígramo(s)**) cg

CGC-L SM ABR (*Esp*) = **Consejo General de Castilla y León**

CGPJ SM ABR (*Esp*) (= **Consejo General del Poder Judicial**) *government body which oversees legal profession*

CGS SF ABR (*Guat, El Salvador*) = **Confederación General de Sindicatos**

CGT SF ABR [1] (*Méx, Perú, Esp*) = **Confederación General de Trabajadores**
[2] (*Arg*) = **Confederación General del Trabajo**

Ch, ch [tʃe] SF *combination of consonants formerly considered a separate letter of the Spanish alphabet*

ch. ABR (= **cheque**) ch

cha SM Shah

chabacanear ►conjug 1a◄ VI (*LAm*) to say *o* do coarse things

chabacanería SF [1] (= *mal gusto*) vulgarity, bad taste
[2] (= *comentario grosero*) **una ~** a coarse *o* vulgar remark

chabacanizar ►conjug 1f◄ VT to trivialize

chabacano[1] ADJ [*chiste*] vulgar, coarse, in bad taste; [*objeto*] cheap; [*trabajo*] shoddy

chabacano[2] SM (*Méx*) apricot, apricot tree

chabola SF shack; **~s** shanty town

chabolismo SM *problem of shanty towns*

chabolista Ⓐ ADJ slum *antes de s*, shanty-town *antes de s*
Ⓑ SMF slum dweller, shanty-town dweller

chabón/a* Ⓐ ADJ daft, stupid
Ⓑ SM/F twit*

chaca* SF ✦*MODISMO* **estar en la ~** (*Caribe*) to be flat broke*

chacal SM jackal

chacalín/ina (*CAm*) SM/F [1] (= *niño*) kid*, child
[2] (= *camarón*) shrimp

chacanear ►conjug 1a◄ VT [1] (*Cono Sur*) [+ *caballo*] to spur violently
[2] (*Cono Sur*) (= *fastidiar*) to pester, annoy
[3] (*Andes*) (= *usar*) to use daily

chacaneo SM ✦*MODISMO* **para el ~** (*Andes*) for daily use, ordinary

chácara[1] SF [1] (*LAm*) sore, ulcer
[2] (*CAm*) large bag (*made of leather*)

chácara[2] SF (*LAm*) = **chacra**

chacarera SF *Argentinian folk dance*; *ver tb* **chacarero**

chacarería SF [1] (*LAm Agr*) market gardens *pl*, truck farms *pl* (*EEUU*)
[2] (*Andes, Cono Sur*) (= *industria*) horticulture, market gardening, truck farming (*EEUU*)

chacarero/a Ⓐ SM/F (*LAm*) (= *granjero*) small farmer, market gardener, truck farmer (*EEUU*); *ver tb* **chacarera**
Ⓑ SM (*Chile*) (*tb* **sandwich ~**) sandwich
Ⓒ ADJ (*LAm*) small farm *antes de s*

chacha* SF [1] (= *criada*) maid, housemaid
[2] (†) (= *niñera*) nanny, nursemaid

chachacaste SM (*CAm*) liquor, brandy

chachachá SM, **cha-cha-cha** SM [1] (= *baile*) cha-cha-cha, cha-cha
[2] (= *juego*) solitaire

chachal SM (*CAm*) charm necklace

chachalaca* (*CAm, Méx*) Ⓐ ADJ chatty
Ⓑ SF chatterbox

chachar ►conjug 1a◄ VT (*LAm*) [+ *coca*] to chew

cháchara SF [1] chatter, chit-chat*; **estar de ~*** to chatter, gab*
[2] **cháchras** (*Méx*) (= *trastos*) junk *sing*
[3] (*Andes*) (= *chiste*) joke

chacharachas SFPL (*Cono Sur*) useless ornaments

chacharear ►conjug 1a◄ Ⓐ VT (*Méx*) to deal in
Ⓑ VI to chatter, gab*

chacharería SF (*Cono Sur, Méx*) trinkets *pl*

chacharero/a Ⓐ ADJ chattering
Ⓑ SM/F [1] (*) (= *parlanchín*) chatterbox
[2] (*Méx*) (= *vendedor*) rag-and-bone man

chachi* Ⓐ ADJ great*, brill*; **¡qué ~!** that's great!, that's brill!*; **¡estás ~!** you look great!*
Ⓑ ADV great*, brill*; **nos lo pasamos ~** we had a great* time

chachipén ADJ, ADV = **chachi**

chacho* SM [1] (= *chico*) boy, lad
[2] (*CAm*) (= *gemelo*) twin
[3] (*Méx*) (= *criado*) servant

chachos SMPL (*CAm*) Siamese twins

chacina SF [1] (= *carne para embutidos*) pork
[2] (= *embutidos*) cold meats *pl*, cold cuts *pl* (*EEUU*)
[3] (= *cecina*) dried meat

chacinería SF pork butcher's, pork butcher's shop

chacinero ADJ pork *antes de s*; **industria chacinera** pigmeat industry

chacó SM shako

chacolí SM *sharp-tasting Basque wine*

chacolotear ►conjug 1a◄ VI to clatter

chacoloteo SM clatter, clattering

chacón SM Philippine lizard

chacota* SF **estar de ~** to be in a joking mood; **echar** *o* **tomar algo a ~** to make fun of sth

chacotear ►conjug 1a◄ Ⓐ VI to have fun
Ⓑ **chacotearse** VPR **~se de algo** to make fun of sth

chacoteo SM (*Cono Sur*) = **chacota**

chacotería SF (*Cono Sur*) = **chacota**

chacotero ADJ, **chacotón** ADJ (*Cono Sur*) fond of a joke

chacra SF (*Andes, Cono Sur*) small farm

chacuaco Ⓐ ADJ (*LAm*) coarse, rough
Ⓑ SM [1] (*CAm*) (= *cigarro*) roughly-made cigar
[2] (*CAm, Méx*) (= *colilla*) cigar stub

Chad SM Chad

chadiano/a ADJ, SM/F Chadian

chador SM chador

chafa* ADJ (*Méx*) useless

chafallar ►conjug 1a◄ VT to botch, botch up

chafallo SM botched job

chafalonía SF (*Andes*) *worn-out gold jewellery*

chafalote Ⓐ ADJ (*Cono Sur*) (= *ordinario*) common, vulgar
Ⓑ SM 1 = **chafarote**
2 (*LAm*‡) (= *pene*) prick‡

chafar ▸conjug 1a◂ VT 1 (= *aplastar*) [+ *pelo*] to flatten; [+ *ropa*] to crumple, crease; [+ *patatas*] to mash
2 [+ *persona*] **~** *o* **dejar chafado a algn** to crush sb, take the wind out of sb's sails*; **quedó chafado** he was speechless
3 (= *estropear*) to ruin, spoil; **~ las vacaciones a algn** to ruin sb's holidays; **le ~on el negocio** they messed up the deal for him
4 (*Cono Sur*) (= *engañar*) to hoax, deceive

chafardear ▸conjug 1a◂ VI to gossip

chafardeo SM gossip

chafardero/a Ⓐ ADJ **es muy ~** he's a terrible gossip
Ⓑ SM/F gossip

chafarote SM 1 (= *alfanje*) cutlass
2 (*) (= *espada*) sword
3 (*LAm*) machete
4 (*CAm*‡) (= *policía*) cop*

chafarrinada SF spot, stain

chafarrinar ▸conjug 1a◂ VT to blot, stain

chafarrinón SM spot, stain; ✦*MODISMO* **echar un ~ a algn**† to smear *o* slander sb

chafiro SM (*CAm, Méx*), **chafirro** SM (*CAm, Méx*) knife

chaflán SM 1 (= *inclinación*) bevel; **la casa que hace ~** the house on the corner
2 (= *casa*) corner house

chaflanar ▸conjug 1a◂ VT to bevel, chamfer

chaflar* ▸conjug 1a◂ VT (*Chile*) to expel, fire*

chagra Ⓐ SF (*Ecu*) = **chacra**
Ⓑ SM (*Andes*) peasant farmer

chagrín SM shagreen

chagua SF (*Andes*) gang

chaguar ▸conjug 1i◂ VT (*Cono Sur*) [+ *ropa*] to wring, wring out; [+ *vaca*] to milk

cháguar SM (*LAm*) (= *fibra*) agave fibre, hemp

cháguara SF (*Cono Sur*) = **cháguar**

chagüe SM (*CAm*) swamp, bog

chagüite SM (*CAm, Méx*) (= *pantano*) swamp; (= *campo*) flooded field; (= *bananal*) banana plantation

chagüitear* ▸conjug 1a◂ VI (*CAm, Méx*) to chat, natter*

chah SM Shah

chai‡ SF bird*, chick (*EEUU*‡)

chaine SM (*Andes, CAm*) shoeshine

chainear ▸conjug 1a◂ VT (*CAm*) to shine, polish

chaira SF 1 [*de afilar*] sharpening steel
2 [*de zapatero*] shoemaker's knife

chairar ▸conjug 1a◂ VT (*Cono Sur*) to sharpen

chal SM shawl ► **chal de noche** evening wrap

chala SF 1 (*Andes, Cono Sur*) [*de maíz*] maize leaf, maize husk
2 (*Cono Sur**) money, dough*; ✦*MODISMO* **pelar la ~ a algn** to fleece sb*
3 (*Cono Sur*) (= *zapato*) sandal

chalado* ADJ crazy*; **¡estás ~!** you're crazy!*; **¡ven acá, ~!** come here, you idiot!; **estar ~ por algo/algn** to be crazy about sth/sb*

chaladura* SF crankiness*

chalán SM 1 [*de caballos*] dealer, horse dealer
2 (= *estafador*) shady businessman, shark
3 (*LAm*) horse breaker

chalana SF barge, lighter

chalanear ▸conjug 1a◂ Ⓐ VT 1 (= *tratar con maña*) [+ *persona*] to beat down; [+ *negocio*] to bring off
2 (*LAm*) (= *adiestrar*) to break in, tame
3 (*Cono Sur**) (= *acosar*) to pester
4 (*CAm*) (= *burlarse de*) to make fun of
Ⓑ VI to bargain shrewdly

chalaneo SM, **chalanería** SF 1 (= *trato*) hard bargaining, horse trading
2 (= *trampas*) trickery, deception

chalaquear* ▸conjug 1a◂ (*CAm*) Ⓐ VT to trick, con*
Ⓑ VI to chatter away, rabbit on*

chalar* ▸conjug 1a◂ Ⓐ VT to drive crazy *o* round the bend*
Ⓑ **chalarse** VPR to go crazy*, go off one's rocker*; **se ha chalado por ella** he's crazy *o* nuts about her; **se chaló por su vecina** he fell madly in love with his neighbour; **se ha chalado por las motos** he's crazy about motorbikes

chalchihuite SM (*Méx*) jade

chale‡ SMF (*Méx pey*) Chink*

chalé SM = **chalet**

chaleco SM [*de traje*] waistcoat, vest (*EEUU*); [*de lana*] sleeveless pullover; ✦*MODISMOS* **a ~** (*CAm, Méx*) by hook or by crook; **quedar como ~ de mono** (*Cono Sur*) to lose one's credibility ► **chaleco antibalas** bulletproof vest ► **chaleco de fuerza** (*LAm*) straitjacket ► **chaleco de seguridad** (*Aut*) reflective safety vest ► **chaleco salvavidas** life jacket, life preserver (*EEUU*)

chalecón Ⓐ ADJ (*Méx*) tricky, deceitful
Ⓑ SM con man*

chalequear ▸conjug 1a◂ VT (*Cono Sur, Méx*) (= *estafar*) to trick; (= *robar*) to steal

chalet [tʃa'le] SM (*pl* **chalets** [tʃa'les]) 1 (= *casa con jardín*) (*independiente*) detached house; (*en hilera*) terraced house; [*de campo*] villa, cottage; [*de una sola planta*] bungalow; [*de montaña*] chalet ► **chalet adosado** terraced house ► **chalet pareado** semi-detached house, duplex (*EEUU*)
2 (*Dep*) clubhouse

chalina SF 1 (= *corbata ancha*) cravat
2 (*LAm*) scarf

chalón SM (*LAm*) shawl, wrap

chalona SF (*LAm*) dried meat, dried mutton

chalote SM shallot

chalupa[1] SF 1 (= *embarcación*) launch, boat ► **chalupa salvavidas** lifeboat
2 (*Méx*) small canoe

chalupa[2] SF (*Méx Culin*) stuffed tortilla

chalupa[3]* ADJ crazy; **volver ~ a algn** to drive sb crazy

chamaco/a SM/F (*esp Méx*) 1 (= *niño*) kid
2 (= *novio*) boyfriend/girlfriend

chamada SF 1 (= *leña*) brushwood
2 (= *incendio*) brushwood fire
3 (*) (= *humo*) smoke

chamagoso* ADJ (*Méx*) (= *mugriento*) filthy; (= *chabacano*) crude, rough

chamal SM (*Andes, Cono Sur*) blanket (*worn by Indian women as tunic, men as trousers*)

chamanto SM (*Chile*) ruana dress, poncho

chamar* ▸conjug 1a◂ VT, VI to smoke

chámara SF, **chamarasca** SF 1 (= *leña*) kindling, brushwood
2 (= *incendio*) brush fire, blaze

chamarilero/a SM/F, **chamarillero/a** SM/F secondhand dealer

chamarra SF 1 (= *chaqueta*) sheepskin jacket, leather jacket
2 (*CAm, Méx*) (= *manta*) rough blanket, poncho
3 (*CAm**) (= *engaño*) con*, swindle

chamarrear* ▸conjug 1a◂ VT (*CAm*) to con*, swindle

chamarrero SM (*Caribe*) quack doctor

chamarro SM (*LAm*) 1 (= *manta*) coarse woollen *o* (*EEUU*) woolen blanket
2 (= *serape*) poncho, woollen *o* (*EEUU*) woolen cape

chamba[1] SF 1 (*Andes*) (= *tierra*) turf, sod; (= *charca*) pond, pool; (= *zanja*) ditch
2 (*Méx**) (= *trabajo*) work, business; (= *sueldo*) wages *pl*, pay; (= *sueldo bajo*) low pay; (= *chollo*) soft job*
3 (*Caribe, Méx**) dough‡, bread (*EEUU*‡)

chamba[2]* SF luck; **por ~** by a fluke; **¡vaya ~ que has tenido!** you lucky thing!

chambeador(a)* (*Méx*) Ⓐ ADJ hard-working
Ⓑ SM/F hard worker, slogger*

chambear* ▸conjug 1a◂ (*Méx*) VI to earn one's living

chambelán SM chamberlain

chamberga* SF coat

chambergo SM 1 (= *sombrero*) [*de ala ancha*] broad-brimmed soft hat; (*Hist*) cocked hat
2 (*) (= *chaquetón*) coat

chambero SM (*Méx*) draughtsman, draftsman (*EEUU*)

chambón/ona* Ⓐ ADJ 1 (= *patoso*) clumsy
2 (= *afortunado*) lucky
3 (= *desaseado*) slovenly
Ⓑ SM/F fluky player; ✦*MODISMO* **hacer algo a la chambona** (*Andes*) to do sth in a rush

chambonada* SF 1 (= *torpeza*) awkwardness, clumsiness
2 (= *suerte*) luck
3 (= *error*) blunder

chambonear* ▸conjug 1a◂ VI 1 [*ser torpe*] to botch up
2 (= *tener suerte*) to have a stroke of luck, win by a fluke

chamborote ADJ (*Andes, CAm*) long-nosed

chambra[1] SF 1 (= *bata*) housecoat 2 (= *blusa*) blouse 3 (= *chaqueta*) loose jacket

chambra[2] SF (*Caribe*) (= *alboroto*) din, hubbub

chambra[3] SF (*Caribe*) (= *machete*) machete, broad knife

chambrana SF (*Andes, Caribe*) row, uproar

chambre‡ SM (*CAm*) tittle-tattle, gossip

chambroso‡ ADJ (*CAm*) gossipy

chamburgo SM (*Andes*) pool, stagnant water

chamelicos* SMPL (*Andes, Cono Sur*) (= *trastos*) lumber *sing*, junk *sing*; (= *ropa*) old clothes

chamiza SF 1 [*de techo*] thatch, thatch palm
2 (= *leña*) brushwood

chamizo SM 1 (= *cabaña*) thatched hut
2 (= *chabola*) shack
3 (= *mina*) illegal coalmine
4 (= *leño*) half-burned log; (= *árbol*) half-burned tree

chamo/a* SM/F (*LAm*) kid*, child

chamorro Ⓐ ADJ [*cabeza*] shorn, close-cropped
Ⓑ SM ► **chamorro de cerdo** (*Méx*) leg of pork

champa SF [1] (*Andes, Chile*) (= *tierra*) sod, turf
[2] (*Andes, Chile*) [*de pelo*] (= *greña*) mop of hair; (= *maraña*) tangled mass
[3] (*CAm*) (= *cobertizo*) shed; (= *tienda de campaña*) tent

champán SM champagne

champanero ADJ champagne *antes de s*

champanizar ▸conjug 1f◂ VT [+ *vino*] to add a sparkle to

Champaña SF Champagne

champaña SM champagne

champañazo SM (*Cono Sur*) champagne party

champañero ADJ champagne *antes de s*

champi* SM = **champiñón**

champiñón SM mushroom

champú SM shampoo ► **champú acondicionador** conditioning shampoo ► **champú anticaspa** anti-dandruff shampoo

champudo ADJ (*LAm*) [*pelo*] dishevelled, messy; [*persona*] long-haired

champurrado SM (*LAm*) [1] [*de bebidas*] mixture of alcoholic drinks, cocktail
[2] (*) (= *lío*) mess
[3] (*Méx*) [*de chocolate*] *thick chocolate drink*

champurrar ▸conjug 1a◂ VT (*esp LAm*) [+ *bebidas*] to mix, make a cocktail of

champurreado SM (*Cono Sur*) [1] (*Culin*) hastily-prepared dish
[2] (= *prisa*) hash, botch
[3] = **champurrado**

champurrear ▸conjug 1a◂ VT (*Caribe*) [1] [+ *bebidas*] to mix, make a cocktail of
[2] = **chapurrear**

chamuchina* SF (*LAm*) [1] (= *turba*) rabble, mob
[2] (= *niños*) crowd of small children, mob of kids*
[3] (*Andes, Caribe*) (= *jaleo*) row, shindy*; (= *riña*) row, quarrel

chamullar‡ ▸conjug 1a◂ Ⓐ VT to speak, talk; **yo también chamullo el caló** I can talk slang too; **¿qué chamullas tú?** what are you burbling about?
Ⓑ VI [1] (= *hablar*) to speak, talk; **chamullaban en árabe** they were jabbering away in Arabic
[2] (*Cono Sur*) to cook up a story

chamuscar ▸conjug 1g◂ Ⓐ VT [1] (= *quemar*) to scorch, singe
[2] (*Méx*) (= *vender barato*) to sell cheap
Ⓑ **chamuscarse** VPR [1] (= *quemarse*) to get scorched, singe
[2] (*Andes**) to fly off the handle*

chamusquina SF [1] (= *quemadura*) singeing, scorching
[2] (= *riña*) row, quarrel; ✦**MODISMO esto huele a ~** there's trouble brewing
[3] (*Andes, CAm*) (= *niños*) bunch of kids*

chan SM (*CAm*) local guide

chanada* SF trick, swindle

chanar‡ ▸conjug 1a◂ VT (*tb* **~ de algo**) to understand sth

chanca SF (*Andes, Cono Sur*) [1] (= *molienda*) grinding, crushing
[2] (= *paliza*) beating

chancaca SF [1] (*CAm*) [*de maíz*] maize cake, wheat cake
[2] (*LAm*) (= *azúcar*) dark brown sugar
[3] (*Andes Med*) sore, ulcer

chancadora SF (*Chile*) grinder, crusher

chancar ▸conjug 1g◂ VT (*LAm*) [1] (= *moler*) to grind, crush
[2] (= *pegar*) to beat, ill-treat
[3] (*Andes, Cono Sur*) (= *estropear*) to botch, bungle

chance Ⓐ SM (*a veces* SF) (*LAm*) [1] (= *oportunidad*) chance; **dale ~** let him have a go
[2] (= *suerte*) good luck
Ⓑ CONJ (*Méx*) maybe, perhaps

chancear ▸conjug 1a◂ VI, **chancearse** VPR [1] (= *bromear*) to joke, make jokes (**de** about); **~se de algn** to make fun of sb
[2] (= *jugar*) to fool about, play around (**con** with)

chancero ADJ fond of a joke

chancha SF [1] (*LAm Zool*) sow
[2] (*Cono Sur*) (= *carro*) small wooden cart; (*) (= *bicicleta*) bike*
[3] (*Andes*) ✦**MODISMO hacer la ~*** to play truant, play hooky (*EEUU*)

chanchada* SF (*LAm*) dirty trick

chánchamo SM (*Méx Culin*) tamale

cháncharas SFPL ✦**MODISMO andar en ~ máncharas** to beat about the bush

chanchería SF (*LAm*) pork-butcher's, pork-butcher's shop

chanchero SM (*LAm*) pork butcher

chanchi* ADJ, ADV = **chachi**

chanchito* SM (*LAm*) **mi ~** my darling

chancho (*LAm*) Ⓐ ADJ dirty, filthy
Ⓑ SM [1] (= *cerdo*) pig, hog (*EEUU*); (= *carne*) pork; ✦**MODISMOS son como ~s** they're as thick as thieves; **hacerse el ~ rengo** to pretend not to notice; **quedar como ~** to come off badly ► **chancho salvaje** wild boar
[2] (*Ajedrez*) blocked piece
[3] (*Cono Sur*) = **chancadora**
[4] (*Cono Sur*) [*de suelos*] floor polisher

chanchono* SM lie

chanchullero/a* Ⓐ ADJ crooked, bent*
Ⓑ SM/F crook

chanchullo* SM fiddle*, wangle*; **andar en ~s** to be on the fiddle*, be mixed up in something shady

chanciller SM = **canciller**

chancillería SF chancery

chancla SF [1] (= *zapatilla*) flip-flop, thong (*EEUU*)
[2] (= *zapato viejo*) old shoe

chancleta Ⓐ SF [1] flip-flop, thong (*EEUU*); **ir en ~s** to wear flip-flops; ✦**MODISMOS estar hecho una ~*** to be a wreck*; **tirar la ~** (*Cono Sur*) to have a good time
[2] (*LAm*) baby girl
[3] (*Caribe*) accelerator
Ⓑ SMF (*) good-for-nothing

chancletero ADJ (*LAm*), **chancletudo** ADJ (*LAm*) [1] (= *ordinario*) common, low-class
[2] (= *desaseado*) scruffy

chanclo SM [1] (= *zueco*) clog
[2] [*de goma*] overshoe, galosh

chancón/ona* SM/F (*Andes*) swot*, grind (*EEUU**)

chancro SM chancre

chandal SM (*pl* **chandals**), **chándal** SM (*pl* **chándals**) tracksuit

chanelar* ▸conjug 1a◂ VT to catch on to, twig*

chanfaina SF [1] (*Culin*) cheap stew
[2] (*Andes, CAm*) (= *enredo*) mess; (= *suerte*) lucky break

chanfle SM [1] (*Cono Sur**) cop*
[2] (*LAm*) = **chaflán**

chanflón ADJ [1] (= *deforme*) misshapen
[2] (= *basto*) crude, coarse

changa SF [1] (*Andes, Cono Sur*) (= *chapuza*) odd job
[2] (*Andes*) (= *propina*) tip (*to a porter*)
[3] (*Caribe*) (= *broma*) joke; *ver tb* **chango**

changador SM (*Andes, Cono Sur*) (= *mozo de cordel*) porter; (= *trabajo*) odd job

changango SM (*Cono Sur*) (= *guitarra*) small guitar

changarín* SM (*Arg*) casual labourer, casual laborer (*EEUU*)

changarro SM (*Méx*) small shop

changarse‡ ▸conjug 1h◂ VPR to break, break down, go wrong

chango/a Ⓐ ADJ [1] (*Méx*) (= *listo*) quick, sharp; **¡ponte ~!** wake up!
[2] (*Chile*) (= *tonto*) silly
[3] (*Caribe, Méx*) (= *juguetón*) mischievous, playful
[4] (*Cono Sur*) (= *molesto*) annoying
[5] **la gente está changa** (*Méx*) there are lots of people
Ⓑ SM/F [1] (*Méx*) small monkey
[2] (*Cono Sur, Méx*) (= *niño*) kid; (= *criado*) young servant; *ver tb* **changa**

changuear ▸conjug 1a◂ VI (*Andes, Caribe, Méx*) = **chancear**

changüí†* SM [1] (= *chiste*) joke
[2] (= *engaño*) trick; **dar changüi a algn** (= *engañar*) to trick sb; (= *tomar el pelo*) to tease sb

changurro SM crab

chanquetes SMPL whitebait *pl*

chanta‡ SMF (*Cono Sur*) (= *fanfarrón*) loudmouth*; (= *informal*) fraud

chantaje SM blackmail; **hacer ~ a algn** to blackmail sb ► **chantaje emocional** emotional blackmail

chantajear ▸conjug 1a◂ VT to blackmail

chantajista SMF blackmailer

chantar ▸conjug 1a◂ VT [1] **~ algo a algn** to tell sb sth to his face
[2] (*Perú, Chile**) (= *arrojar*) to throw, chuck; **~ a algn en la cárcel** to throw sb in jail, put sb in jail; **~ a algn en la calle** to throw sb out
[3] (*Cono Sur*) (= *abandonar*) to leave in the lurch; (= *engañar*) to deceive, trick
[4] (*Andes, Cono Sur*) [+ *golpe*] to give

chantre SM (*Rel*) precentor

chanza SF [1] (= *chiste*) joke; **de** *o* **en ~** in fun, as a joke; **estar de ~** to be joking
[2] **chanzas** (= *diversión*) fun *sing*

chañaca SF (*Cono Sur*) [1] (*Med*) itch, rash
[2] (= *mala reputación*) bad reputation

chao* EXCL bye*, cheerio*, so long (*esp EEUU**), see ya (*esp EEUU**)

chapa SF [1] (= *material*) sheet metal; **la escultura incorpora ~ y madera** the sculpture includes sheet metal and wood
[2] (= *lámina*) **una ~ de metal** a metal sheet, a sheet of metal; **una ~ de madera** a wooden

panel; **una ~ de acero** a steel plate; **la ~ del coche** the panel of the car; **una mesa revestida con ~ de nogal** a table covered with a walnut veneer ► **chapa acanalada**, **chapa ondulada** corrugated iron (sheet)
3 [*de policía*] badge; [*de adorno*] badge; **lleva la cazadora llena de ~s** he has badges all over his jacket
4 [*de botella*] cap, top
5 (*Cono Sur*) [*de matrícula*] ► **chapa de patente** licence *o* (EEUU) license plate
6 **chapas** (= *juego*) *game of throwing bottle tops*
7 (*Esp*‡) *one-hundred-peseta coin*; ✦MODISMO **estar sin ~**† not to have a farthing *o* cent
8 ✦MODISMO **hacer ~s**‡ (= *prostituirse*) to turn tricks‡
9 (*LAm*) (= *cerradura*) lock; (= *tirador*) (door) handle
10 **hombre de ~**† sensible man

chapado ADJ [*metal*] plated; [*muebles*] veneered, finished; **~ de roble** with an oak veneer, with an oak finish; **~ de oro** gold-plated; ✦MODISMO **~ a la antigua** old-fashioned, of the old school

chapalear ▸conjug 1a◂ VI = **chapotear**

chapaleo SM = **chapoteo**

chapapote SM (*Méx*) (= *pez*) tar, pitch; (= *asfalto*) asphalt

chapar ▸conjug 1a◂ Ⓐ VT 1 (= *cubrir*) [+ *metal*] to plate; [+ *muebles*] to veneer, finish; [+ *pared*] to tile
2 [+ *frase, observación*] to come out with; **le chapó un "no" como una casa** he gave him a flat "no"
3 (‡) (= *cerrar*) [+ *local, negocio*] to shut, close
4 (*Perú*) (= *asir*) to seize; (= *atrapar*) to catch; (= *espiar*) to spy on
Ⓑ VI 1 (‡) (= *estudiar*) to swot*, cram*
2 (‡) (= *dormir*) to kip*, sleep

chaparra SF 1 (= *árbol*) kermes oak
2 (= *maleza*) brush, scrub

chaparrada SF = **chaparrón**

chaparral SM thicket (*of kermes oaks*), chaparral

chaparrear ▸conjug 1a◂ VI (= *llover*) to pour down

chaparreras SFPL (*Méx*) leather chaps

chaparro/a Ⓐ ADJ 1 (= *rechoncho*) squat
2 (*esp LAm*) (= *bajito*) short
Ⓑ SM dwarf oak, kermes oak
Ⓒ SM/F 1 (= *persona*) short chubby person
2 (*Méx*) child, kid*

chaparrón SM 1 (*Meteo*) downpour, cloudburst; ✦MODISMO **aguantar el ~** to face the music*
2 [*de insultos*] barrage; [*de cartas*] flood

chapatal SM muddy place

chape SM (*Andes, Cono Sur*) tress, pigtail

chapear ▸conjug 1a◂ Ⓐ VT 1 = **chapar A1**
2 (*LAm Agr*) to weed
3 (= *sonar*) to rattle
4 **~ a algn** (*Caribe*) to cut sb's throat
Ⓑ VI (*LAm*) to clear the ground

chapeau [tʃa'po] Ⓐ EXCL bravo!, well done!
Ⓑ SM 1 ✦MODISMO **hacer ~** to take off one's hat (**ante** to)
2 (= *felicitación*) congratulations

chapeo‡ SM hat

chapero‡ SM 1 (= *prostituto*) rent boy*
2 (= *homosexual*) queer**, poof**, fag (EEUU‡)

chapeta SF flush (*on the cheeks*)

chapetón Ⓐ ADJ (*LAm**) (= *novato*) inexperienced, green*; (= *torpe*) clumsy, awkward
Ⓑ SM 1 (*LAm**) *European greenhorn in Latin America*
2 (*Méx*) horse brass
3 (= *lluvia*) downpour

chapetonada SF 1 (*Andes**) *illness suffered by Europeans on arrival in Latin America*
2 (*Ecu*) (= *novatada*) blunder
3 (*Andes, Cono Sur*) (= *torpeza*) awkwardness, clumsiness
4 (*Caribe*) (= *aguacero*) sudden downpour

chapín Ⓐ ADJ (*LAm*) bowlegged, with crooked feet
Ⓑ SM 1 (= *zueco*) clog
2 (*CAm*) Guatemalan

chapinada SF (*CAm hum*) *action typical of a Guatemalan*, dirty trick

chapiri‡ SM hat

chápiro* SM **¡por vida del ~!** ◊ **¡voto al ~!** damn it!

chapisca SF (*CAm*) maize harvest

chapista SM 1 (*Téc*) tinsmith
2 (*Aut*) panel beater

chapistería SF body shop

chapita* SF (*Andes*) cop*

chapitel SM (*Arquit*) [*de columna*] capital; [*de torre*] spire

chapo[1] ADJ (*Méx*) stunted, dwarf *antes de s*

chapo[2] SM (*Méx Culin*) maize porridge

chapó Ⓐ EXCL bravo!, well done!
Ⓑ SM ✦MODISMO **hacer ~** to take one's hat off (**ante** to)

chapodar ▸conjug 1a◂ VT 1 [+ *árbol*] to prune
2 (= *reducir*) to cut down, reduce

chapola SF (*Andes*) butterfly

chapolín SM (= *juego*) pool

chapopote SM (*Méx*) = **chapapote**

chapote SM (*CAm, Caribe, Méx*) (= *pez*) pitch, tar; (= *asfalto*) asphalt

chapotear ▸conjug 1a◂ VI (*en el agua*) to splash about; **~ en el barro** to splash around in the mud

chapoteo SM splashing

chaptalizar ▸conjug 1f◂ VT to chaptalize, add sugar to

chapucear ▸conjug 1a◂ VT 1 [+ *trabajo*] to botch, make a mess of
2 (*Méx*) (= *estafar*) to swindle

chapuceramente ADV shoddily

chapucería SF 1 (= *cualidad*) shoddiness
2 (= *chapuza*) botched job, shoddy piece of work

chapucero/a Ⓐ ADJ 1 [*trabajo*] shoddy, slapdash
2 [*persona*] sloppy, slapdash
Ⓑ SM/F bungler

chapulín SM 1 (*Méx*) large grasshopper
2 (*CAm**) child, kid*

chapupa* SF ✦MODISMO **me salió de pura ~** (*CAm*) it was pure luck, it was sheer fluke

chapuro SM (*CAm*) asphalt

chapurrear* ▸conjug 1a◂ VT, **chapurrar*** ▸conjug 1a◂ VT **chapurrea el italiano** he speaks broken *o* bad Italian

chapuz SM 1 = **chapuza**
2 (= *chapuzón*) ducking

chapuza SF 1 (= *trabajo mal hecho*) botched job, shoddy piece of work
2 (= *trabajo ocasional*) odd job; **siempre está haciendo ~s en la casa** he's always doing odd jobs around the house
3 (*Méx*) trick, swindle

chapuzar ▸conjug 1f◂ Ⓐ VT to duck
Ⓑ VI, **chapuzarse** VPR to dive, dive in

chapuzas* SMF INV botcher*

chapuzón SM 1 (= *zambullida*) dip, swim; **darse un ~** to go for a dip, go for a swim
2 [*de cápsula*] splashdown
3 (*LAm**) cloudburst, downpour

chaqué SM morning coat

chaquet [tʃa'ke] SM (*pl* **chaquets** [tʃa'kes]) = **chaqué**

chaqueta SF jacket; ✦MODISMOS **cambiar de ~** to change sides; **volarse la ~** (*CAm***) to toss off** ► **chaqueta de cuero** leather jacket ► **chaqueta de punto** cardigan

chaquetar ▸conjug 1a◂ VT, VI (*Méx*) = **chaquetear**

chaquete SM backgammon

chaquetear* ▸conjug 1a◂ Ⓐ VT to slag off‡, criticize
Ⓑ VI 1 (= *cambiar de política*) to change sides, be a turncoat, turn traitor
2 (= *acobardarse*) to go back on one's word, chicken out*, rat*

chaquetero/a* SM/F turncoat

chaquetón SM three-quarter coat

charada SF charade

charadrio SM plover

charal SM (*Méx*) small fish; ✦MODISMO **estar como ~*** to be as thin as a rake

charaludo* ADJ (*Méx*) thin

charamusca SF 1 (*LAm*) (*tb* **~s**) firewood, kindling
2 (*Cono Sur, Méx*) (= *dulce*) candy twist
3 (*Caribe*) (= *alboroto*) noise, row

charanga SF 1 (*Mús, Mil*) brass band; *ver tb* **España**
2 (*) (= *jaleo*) hullabaloo*, racket*
3 (*LAm*) (= *baile*) informal dance, hop*

charango SM (*LAm*) small guitar

charanguero ADJ = **chapucero A**

charape SM (*Méx*) *type of "pulque"*

charca SF pond, pool

charchina* SF (*LAm*) old crock, old banger‡, jalopy

charco SM pool, puddle; ✦MODISMO **cruzar** *o* **pasar el ~** to cross the water; (*esp*) to cross the Pond (*the Atlantic*)

charcón[1] ADJ (*Andes, Cono Sur*) thin, skinny

charcón[2] SM pool (*in a river*)

charcutería SF 1 (= *productos*) cooked pork products *pl*
2 (= *tienda*) pork butcher's, pork butcher's shop

charcutero/a SM/F pork butcher

charla SF 1 (= *conversación*) chat; ✦MODISMO **es de ~ común** it's common knowledge
2 (= *chismes*) gossip
3 (= *conferencia*) talk ► **charla literaria** literary talk, informal literary lecture ► **charla radiofónica** radio talk

charla-coloquio SF (*pl* **charlas-coloquio**) talk (*followed by debate*)

charlado* SM **echar un ~** to have a chat

charlador ADJ talkative

charladuría SF (*tb* **~s**) prattle

charlar ▸conjug 1a◂ VI [1] (= *conversar*) to chat (**de** about)
[2] (= *chismear*) to gossip

charlatán/ana Ⓐ ADJ [1] (= *hablador*) talkative
[2] (= *chismoso*) gossipy
Ⓑ SM/F [1] (= *hablador*) chatterbox
[2] (= *chismoso*) gossip
[3] (= *estafador*) trickster, confidence trickster, con man*
[4] (= *vendedor aprovechado*) smooth-tongued salesman

charlatanear ▸conjug 1a◂ VI to chatter away

charlatanería SF [1] (= *locuacidad*) talkativeness; (*pey*) hot air
[2] (= *chismorreo*) gossip
[3] (= *engaños*) quackery, charlatanism
[4] [*de vendedor*] sales talk, patter

charlatanismo SM = **charlatanería 1**

charlestón SM charleston

charleta SMF (*Cono Sur*) [1] (= *hablador*) chatterbox
[2] (= *chismoso*) gossip

charli⁑ SM 1,000-peseta note

charlista SMF speaker, lecturer

Charlot SM Charlie Chaplin

charlota SF *type of frozen cream cake*

charlotada SF [1] (*Teat*) gag
[2] (*Taur*) mock bullfight

charlotear ▸conjug 1a◂ VI to chatter, talk a lot

charloteo SM chatter

charnego/a SM/F (*pey*) *Southern Spanish immigrant who has settled in Catalonia*

charnela SF, **charneta** SF hinge

charol SM [1] (= *barniz*) varnish; ✦**MODISMO darse ~** to brag
[2] (= *cuero*) patent leather
[3] (*LAm*) (= *bandeja*) tray

charola SF [1] (*LAm*) (= *bandeja*) tray
[2] **charolas** (*CAm*) (= *ojos*) eyes

charolado ADJ polished, shiny

charolar ▸conjug 1a◂ VT to varnish

charolés ADJ, SM Charolais

charpa SF (*CAm*) [1] (*Mil*) pistol belt, sword belt
[2] (*Med*) sling

charquear ▸conjug 1a◂ VT (*LAm*) [1] [+ *carne*] to dry, jerk
[2] [+ *persona*] to slash, cut to pieces

charquecillo SM (*Andes Culin*) dried salted fish

charqui SM [1] (*LAm*) (= *carne*) jerked beef, jerky (*EEUU*)
[2] (*Cono Sur*) (= *frutas*) dried fruit; (= *legumbres*) dried vegetables *pl*; ✦**MODISMO hacer ~ a algn** = **charquear 2**

charquicán SM (*Cono Sur Culin*) *dish of dried meat and vegetables*

charra SF [1] (*Salamanca*) (= *campesina*) peasant woman; (= *mujer de clase baja*) low-class woman, coarse woman
[2] (*CAm*) (= *sombrero*) broad-brimmed hat
[3] (*Andes*) (= *grano*) itch, pimple
[4] (*CAm*⁑) (= *pene*) prick⁑, tool⁑; *ver tb* **charro**

charrada SF [1] (= *adorno*) flashy ornament
[2] (= *torpeza*) coarseness
[3] (*Mús*) country dance

charral SM (*CAm*) scrub, scrubland

charramasca SF (*CAm*) firewood, kindling

charrán[1] SM (*Orn*) tern

charrán[2] SM rascal, villain

charranada* SF dirty trick

charrar⁑ ▸conjug 1a◂ VI [1] (= *hablar*) to talk, burble [2] (= *soplar*) to blab

charrasca SF [1] (*LAm*) knife
[2] (††) trailing sword

charrasquear* ▸conjug 1a◂ VT [1] (*Méx*) (= *apuñalar*) to knife, stab
[2] (*Andes, CAm, Caribe*) (= *rasguear*) to strum

charré SM trap, dog-cart

charreada SF (*Méx*) public fiesta

charrería SF (*Méx*) horsemanship

charretera SF [1] (*Mil*) epaulette
[2] (*Cos*) shoulder pad

charro Ⓐ ADJ [1] [*gente*] rustic
[2] (= *de mal gusto*) [*ropa*] loud, gaudy; [*objeto*] flashy, showy
[3] (= *salmantino*) Salamancan
[4] (*Méx*) [*costumbres*] traditional, picturesque; → CONJUNTO, MARIACHI
Ⓑ SM [1] (= *pueblerino*) rustic
[2] (*Méx*) (= *vaquero*) typical Mexican
[3] (*Méx*) (= *sombrero*) wide-brimmed hat
[4] (*Méx**) corrupt union boss
[5] (*Salamanca*) peasant; *ver tb* **charra**

charrúa ADJ, SMF (*Cono Sur*) Uruguayan

chart (*pl* **charts**) (*Bolsa*) Ⓐ SM (= *gráfico*) market forecast, stock market forecast
Ⓑ SMF (= *analista*) market analyst

chárter Ⓐ ADJ INV **vuelo ~** charter, charter flight
Ⓑ SM (*pl* **chárters** ['tʃarter]) charter, charter flight

chartista Ⓐ ADJ market *antes de s*, stock market *antes de s*
Ⓑ SMF market analyst

chasca SF [1] (= *leña*) brushwood (*from pruning trees*)
[2] (*Andes, Cono Sur*) (= *greña*) mop of hair, tangled hair

chascar ▸conjug 1g◂ Ⓐ VT [1] (= *hacer sonar*) [+ *lengua*] to click; [+ *dedos*] to snap; [+ *látigo*] to crack; [+ *grava*] to crunch
[2] [+ *comida*] to swallow
Ⓑ VI [*leña*] to crackle

chascarrillo SM funny story

chasco SM [1] (= *desilusión*) disappointment; **dar un ~ a algn** to disappoint sb; **llevarse un ~** to be disappointed, be let down; **¡vaya ~ que me llevé!** I was just sick about that!, I felt really let down
[2] (= *broma*) trick, joke; **dar un ~ a algn** to play a trick on sb

chascón ADJ (*Chile*) (= *greñudo*) with a tangled mop of hair

chasis SM INV, **chasís** SM INV (*LAm*) [1] (*Aut*) chassis; ✦**MODISMO quedarse en el ~*** to get terribly thin
[2] (*Fot*) plateholder

chasque SM (*LAm*) = **chasqui**

chasquear[1] ▸conjug 1a◂ VT [1] (= *decepcionar*) to disappoint, let down
[2] (= *engañar*) to play a trick on, fool
[3] [+ *promesa*] to break

chasquear[2] ▸conjug 1a◂ Ⓐ VT, VI = **chascar**
Ⓑ **chasquearse** VPR (*Andes**) to make a mess of things, mess things up*

chasqui SM (*LAm Hist*) messenger, courier

chasquido SM (= *ruido seco*) [*de lengua*] click; [*de dedos*] snap; [*de madera*] crack

chasquilla SF (*Andes, Cono Sur*), **chasquillas** SFPL (*Andes, Cono Sur*) (= *flequillo*) fringe, bangs *pl* (*EEUU*)

chat SM (*Internet*) chat room

chata SF [1] (*Med*) bedpan
[2] (*Náut*) barge
[3] (*Cono Sur Ferro*) flatcar
[4] (*) (= *escopeta*) sawn-off shotgun

chatarra SF scrap, scrap iron; **vender para ~** to sell for scrap ► **chatarra espacial** space junk

chatarrería SF scrapyard, scrap merchant's, junkyard (*EEUU*)

chatarrero/a SM/F scrap dealer, scrap merchant

chatear* ▸conjug 1a◂ VI [1] (*Internet*) to chat
[2] (*en bar*) to have a few glasses of wine

chateo* SM [1] (*Internet*) chatting [2] drinking; **ir de ~** to go out for a few glasses of wine

chatero/a Ⓐ ADJ chat *antes de s*
Ⓑ SM/F chat room user

chati* SMF love, darling

chato Ⓐ ADJ [1] [*nariz*] snub
[2] (= *plano*) [*objeto*] flattened, blunt; [*barco*] flat
[3] (*Arquit*) low, squat
[4] (*Andes, Chile*) [*persona*] short
[5] (*Méx*) (= *pobre*) poor, wretched; ✦**MODISMO quedarse ~*** to be disappointed (**con** at)
Ⓑ SM tumbler, wine tumbler

chatón SM large mounted stone

chatre ADJ (*Andes, Cono Sur*) smartly-dressed; ✦**MODISMO está hecho un ~** he's looking very smart

chatungo* ADJ = **chato A1**

chau EXCL = **chao**

chaucha Ⓐ ADJ INV (*LAm*) [1] (*Agr*) early
[2] (*Med*) [*nacimiento*] premature; [*mujer*] who gives birth prematurely
[3] (*Cono Sur*) (= *malo*) poor-quality; (= *soso*) insipid, tasteless, characterless; (= *de mal gusto*) in poor taste
Ⓑ SF [1] (*LAm*) (= *patata*) early potato
[2] (*Cono Sur*) (= *judía verde*) string bean
[3] (*Perú*) (= *comida*) food; ✦**MODISMO pelar la ~** (*Andes, Cono Sur*) to brandish *o* use one's knife
[4] (*Chile, Perú**) (= *dinero*) dough*; **le cayó la ~** the penny dropped
[5] **chauchas** (*Cono Sur**) peanuts*, trifles

chauchau SM (*Chile, Perú*) stew, chow*

chauchera SF (*Andes, Cono Sur*) purse, coin purse (*EEUU*)

chauchero SM (*Cono Sur*) [1] (= *recadero*) errand boy
[2] (= *trabajador*) poorly-paid worker

chaufa SF (*LAm*) Chinese fried rice

chauvinismo SM chauvinism

chauvinista ADJ, SMF chauvinist

chava⁑ SMF (*CAm, Méx*) = **chaval**

chaval(a)* SM/F lad/lass, boy/girl, kid*; **es todavía un ~** he's only a kid still

chavalada* SF = **chavalería**

chavalería* SF young people, kids* *pl*

chavalo* SM (*Nic*) lad, kid*

chavalongo SM (*Cono Sur*) [1] (= *fiebre*) fever

[2] (= *insolación*) sunstroke
[3] (= *modorra*) drowsiness, drowsy feeling

chavea* SMF lad, kid*

chaveta Ⓐ SF [1] (*Téc*) cotter, cotter pin; ✦***MODISMOS*** **perder la ~*** to go off one's rocker*; **perder la ~ por algn** to lose one's head over sb
[2] (*LAm*) (= *navaja*) broad-bladed knife
Ⓑ ADJ INV **estar ~‡** to be nuts*

chavetear ▸conjug 1a◂ VT (*Andes, Caribe*) to knife

chavo/a Ⓐ SM **no tener** *o* **estar sin un ~** to be skint*, be stony broke*
Ⓑ SM/F (*Méx, CAm**) guy*/girl

chavó* SM lad, kid*

chayote SM chayote, vegetable pear (*EEUU*)

chayotera SF chayote, chayote plant

che[1] SF the (name of the) letter ch

che[2] EXCL (*Cono Sur*) hey!; (*en conversación*) man, boy, friend

che[3]* SM (*Chile*) Argentinian

checa SF [1] (= *policía*) secret police
[2] (= *comisaría*) secret police headquarters; (‡) (= *cárcel*) nick‡, jail

checar ▸conjug 1g◂ VT (*esp Méx*) = **chequear**

cheche SM (*Caribe*) bully, braggart

chechear ▸conjug 1a◂ VT (*Cono Sur*) = **vosear**

chécheres SMPL (*Andes, CAm*) (= *cosas*) things, gear *sing*; (= *cachivaches*) junk *sing*, lumber *sing*

chechón ADJ (*Méx*) spoilt, pampered

checo/a Ⓐ ADJ, SM/F Czech
Ⓑ SM (*Ling*) Czech

checoslovaco/a ADJ, SM/F Czechoslovakian

Checoslovaquia SF Czechoslovakia

chef SM (*pl* **chefs**) chef

cheira SF = **chaira**

Chejov SM Chekhov

chele ADJ (*CAm*) fair, blond/blonde

chelear ▸conjug 1a◂ VT (*CAm*) to whiten, whitewash

cheli* SM [1] bloke*, guy*; **ven acá, ~** come here, man
[2] (*Ling*) Madrid slang

chelín SM shilling

chelista SMF cellist

chelo[1] ADJ (*Méx*) fair, blond/blonde

chelo[2] SM (*Mús*) (= *instrumento*) cello; (= *músico*) cellist

chepa Ⓐ SF hump
Ⓑ SMF hunchback

cheposo/a Ⓐ ADJ hunchbacked
Ⓑ SM/F hunchback

▼ **cheque** SM cheque, check (*EEUU*); **un ~ por 400 euros** a cheque for 400 euros; **cobrar un ~** to cash a cheque; **extender un ~** to make out *o* write a cheque; **pagar con ~** to pay by cheque ▸ **cheque abierto** open cheque ▸ **cheque abierto cruzado** crossed cheque ▸ **cheque al portador** cheque payable to bearer ▸ **cheque bancario** banker's cheque ▸ **cheque caducado** out-of-date cheque ▸ **cheque conformado** certified cheque ▸ **cheque de compensación** clearing cheque ▸ **cheque de viaje, cheque de viajero** traveller's cheque ▸ **cheque en blanco** blank cheque ▸ **cheque nominativo** order cheque; **un ~ nominativo a favor de Luis González** a cheque made out to *o* made payable to Luis González ▸ **cheque regalo** gift voucher ▸ **cheque sin fondos** bounced cheque

➤ LENGUA Y USO: **cheque** 47.5

chequear ▸conjug 1a◂ VT [1] (*esp LAm*) (= *comprobar*) [+ *cuenta, documento, salud*] to check; [+ *persona*] to check on, check up on
[2] (*LAm*) [+ *equipaje*] to check in
[3] (*LAm*) [+ *cheque*] to make out, write
[4] (*Méx Aut*) to service

chequeo SM [1] (*Med*) check-up
[2] (*Aut*) service

chequera SF (*LAm*) cheque book, checkbook (*EEUU*)

cherife SM (*LAm*) sheriff

cherna SF wreckfish

chero* SM (*CAm*) pal*, mate*, buddy (*EEUU**)

cheruto SM cheroot

cherva SF castor oil plant

cheurón SM chevron

chévere* Ⓐ ADJ (*Col, Ven*) great*, fabulous*
Ⓑ SM (*Caribe*) bully, braggart

chevió SM, **cheviot** SM cheviot

chibola SF (*CAm*) [1] (= *refresco*) fizzy drink, pop*, soda (*EEUU*)
[2] = **chibolo**
[3] (= *canica*) marble

chibolo SM (*Andes, CAm*) bump, swelling

chic Ⓐ ADJ INV chic, smart
Ⓑ SM elegance

chica SF [1] (= *criada*) maid, servant
[2] ▸ **chica de alterne** bar-girl, bar-room hostess ▸ **chica de conjunto** chorus girl; *ver tb* **chico**

chicana SF (*Méx*) chicanery

chicanear ▸conjug 1a◂ VI (*Méx*) to use trickery, be cunning

chicanería SF (*LAm*) chicanery

chicanero ADJ [1] (*Méx*) tricky, crafty
[2] (*Andes*) (= *tacaño*) mean

chicano/a Ⓐ ADJ Chicano, Mexican-American
Ⓑ SM/F Chicano, Mexican immigrant in the USA

chicar* ▸conjug 1g◂ VI (*Andes*) to booze*, drink

chicarrón/ona Ⓐ ADJ strapping, sturdy
Ⓑ SM/F strapping lad/sturdy lass

chicato* ADJ (*Cono Sur*) short-sighted, near-sighted (*EEUU*)

chicha[1] SF [1] (*LAm*) (= *bebida*) maize liquor, corn liquor (*EEUU*); ✦***MODISMOS*** **ni ~ ni limonada** *o* **limoná*** neither fish nor fowl, neither one thing nor the other; **estas cosas están como ~** (*Andes**) there are hundreds *o* any number of these things; **sacar la ~ a algo/algn** (*Cono Sur**) to milk sth/sb dry ▸ **chicha de uva** unfermented grape juice
[2] (*Andes, CAm**) (= *berrinche*) rage, bad temper; **estar de ~** to be in a bad mood

> **CHICHA**
>
> ***Chicha*** *is a strong alcoholic drink made from fermented maize and produced in Peru, where it is associated with ceremonial and ritual occasions. It is now an element of what is known as* ***chicha*** *culture, a dynamic blend of traditional Indian and modern imported styles and fashions created out of the migration of the rural poor to major cities.* ***Chicha*** *music has become the most popular music in Peru. It combines the traditional Andean* ***huayno*** *with tropical, Afro-Hispanic music and electronic instruments.*

chicha[2]* SF meat; ✦***MODISMOS*** **tiene poca(s) ~(s)** she's as thin as a rake*; **de ~ y nabo** insignificant

chicha[3] ADJ **calma ~** (*Náut*) dead calm

chícharo (*LAm*) SM [1] (= *guisante*) pea
[2] (= *garbanzo*) chickpea

chicharra SF [1] (*Entomología*) harvest bug, cicada; ✦***MODISMOS*** **es como ~ en verano** it's nasty, it's unpleasant; **canta la ~** it's terribly hot, it's roasting*
[2] (= *persona habladora*) chatterbox
[3] (*Elec*) (= *timbre*) bell, buzzer; (*Telec*) bug*, bugging device
[4] (*CAm, Caribe*) (= *chicharrón*) crackling (*of pork*)
[5] (‡) (= *droga*) reefer*
[6] (‡) (= *monedero*) purse, coin purse (*EEUU*)

chicharrero[1] SM [1] (= *horno*) oven, hothouse
[2] (*) (= *lugar muy caliente*) oven, furnace

chicharrero[2]**/a** Ⓐ ADJ of/from Tenerife
Ⓑ SM/F native/inhabitant of Tenerife; **los ~s** the people of Tenerife

chicharro SM horse-mackerel

chicharrón SM [1] (*Culin*) **chicharrones (de cerdo)** pork scratchings, pork cracklings (*EEUU*); ✦***MODISMO*** **estar hecho un ~*** [*carne*] to be burnt to a cinder; [*persona*] to be as red as a lobster*
[2] (*por el sol*) lobster*
[3] (*Caribe*) (= *adulador*) flatterer

chiche Ⓐ ADJ (*CAm*) easy, simple; **está ~** it's a cinch*
Ⓑ ADV (*CAm*) easily
Ⓒ SM [1] (*CAm, Méx**) (= *pecho*) breast, tit‡
[2] (*Cono Sur*) (= *joya*) trinket; (= *juguete*) small toy
Ⓓ SF (*Méx*) nursemaid

chichear ▸conjug 1a◂ VT, VI to hiss

chicheo SM hiss, hissing

chichera‡ SF (*CAm*) jail, clink‡, can (*EEUU**)

chichería SF (*Andes*) [1] (= *bar*) chicha bar
[2] (= *fábrica*) chicha brewery

chichero SM [1] (= *vendedor*) chicha seller
[2] (= *fabricante*) chicha maker

chichi* SF [1] (= *vulva*) fanny**, beaver (*EEUU***)
[2] (*Méx*) (= *teta*) tit**
[3] (*Méx*) (= *niñera*) nursemaid

chichicaste SM (*CAm*) [1] (*Bot*) nettle
[2] (*Med*) nettle rash

chichigua SF [1] (*CAm, Méx*) (= *niñera*) nursemaid
[2] (*Caribe*) (= *cometa*) kite
[3] (*Méx*) (= *animal manso*) tame animal; (= *hembra*) nursing animal
[4] (*Méx**) pimp

chicho SM [1] (= *bucle*) curl, ringlet
[2] (= *bigudí*) curler, roller

chichón[1]* ADJ [1] (*Cono Sur*) (= *jovial*) merry, jovial
[2] (*CAm*) (= *fácil*) easy, straightforward; **está ~** it's a piece of cake*

chichón[2] SM (= *bulto*) lump, swelling

chichonear ▸conjug 1a◂ VI (*Cono Sur*) to joke

chichonera SF helmet

chichus SM (*CAm*) flea

chicle SM chewing gum ▸ **chicle de globo** bubble gum ▸ **chicle sin azúcar** sugar-free chewing gum

chiclear ▸conjug 1a◂ VI (*CAm, Méx*) 1 (= *cosechar*) to extract gum
2 (= *masticar chicle*) to chew gum

chiclero SM (*Méx, CAm*) gum collector

chico/a Ⓐ ADJ 1 (= *pequeño*) small, little; ✦*MODISMOS* **dejar ~ a algn** to put sb in the shade; **quedarse ~** to be humiliated; *ver tb* **patria, perra 2**
2 (= *joven*) young; **yo era muy ~, pero me acuerdo de ella** I was very young but I remember her; **de ~ no me gustaban las verduras** I didn't like vegetables when I was little, as a child, I didn't like vegetables
Ⓑ SM/F 1 (= *joven*) boy/girl; **me gusta un ~ de Barcelona** there's a guy* *o* boy from Barcelona I like; **es un buen ~** he's a good lad; **el entrenador tiene bien preparados a sus ~s** the trainer has his lads well prepared; **las chicas de la oficina** the girls at the office
2 (= *niño*) boy/girl; **los ~s de la clase** the boys in the class ► **chico de la calle** street kid* ► **chico de los recados** office boy, messenger boy
3 (= *hijo*) boy/girl; **no nos hemos divorciado aún por los ~s** we haven't got divorced yet because of the kids* *o* children
4 (= *novio*) boyfriend/girlfriend; **¿sales con algún ~?** are you going out with anyone?, have you got a boyfriend?
5 (*apelativo*) 5·1 (*a un adulto*) **mira, ~, déjalo** OK, just leave it, will you?; **chica, ¡qué cambiada estás!** hey! *o* you know, you look so different!; **¡hola, ~s! ¿qué tal?** hi, guys! how're you doing?*; **hola chicas ¡ya estoy aquí!** hi, girls, here I am!
5·2 (*a un niño*) **¡oye, ~! ¿quieres ganarte un poco de dinero?** hey! do you want to earn yourself a bit of money?; **chica, ¡no corras!** don't run, dear!; *ver tb* **chica**
Ⓒ SM (*LAm Naipes*) game, round; (*Billar*) game; (*Snooker*) frame

chicolear* ▸conjug 1a◂ Ⓐ VI 1 (*Méx*) (= *flirtear*) to flirt, say nice things
2 (*Andes*) (= *divertirse*) to amuse o.s., have a good time
Ⓑ **chicolearse** VPR (*Andes*) to amuse o.s.

chicoleo SM (*Méx*) 1 (= *piropo*) compliment
2 (*) (= *flirteo*) flirting
3 (*Andes*) (= *cosa infantil*) childish thing; **no andemos con ~s** let's be serious

chicolero ADJ flirtatious

chicoria SF chicory

chicota SF (*pey*) big girl

chicotazo SM (*LAm*) lash

chicote SM 1 (*) (= *chico*) big chap*, fine lad
2 (*Náut*) piece of rope, rope end
3 (*LAm*) whip, lash
4 (*) (= *puro*) cigar; (= *colilla*) cigar stub

chicotear ▸conjug 1a◂ (*LAm*) Ⓐ VT 1 (= *azotar*) to whip, lash
2 (= *pegar*) to beat up
3 (*Andes*) (= *matar*) to kill
Ⓑ VI [*cola*] to lash about

chifa SM (*Chile, Perú*) Chinese restaurant

chifla SF (*Dep*) 1 (= *sonido*) hissing, whistling
2 (= *silbato*) whistle

chifladera* SF (*CAm, Méx*) crazy idea

chiflado/a* Ⓐ ADJ crazy*, barmy*; **esa chica le tiene ~** he's crazy about that girl; **estar ~ con** *o* **por algo/algn** to be crazy about sth/sb
Ⓑ SM/F nutter*, nutcase*

chifladura SF 1 = **chifla**
2 (*) (= *locura*) craziness; **una ~** a crazy idea, a wild scheme; **su ~ es el ajedrez** he is crazy *o* mad about chess; **ese amor no es más que una ~** what he calls love is just a foolish infatuation

chiflar[1] ▸conjug 1a◂ Ⓐ VT 1 [+ *silbato*] to blow
2 (*Teat*) to hiss, boo, whistle at
3 (*) (= *beber*) to drink, knock back*
4 (*) (= *encantar*) to entrance, captivate; (= *volver loco*) to drive crazy; **esa chica le chifla** he's crazy about that girl; **me chiflan los helados** I just adore ice cream; **me chifla ese grupo** I think that group is fantastic*
Ⓑ VI 1 (*esp LAm*) to whistle, hiss
2 (*CAm, Méx*) [*ave, pájaro*] to sing
Ⓒ **chiflarse** VPR (*) 1 **~se con** *o* **por algo/algn** to go crazy about sth/sb
2 ✦*MODISMO* **chiflárselas** (*CAm*) to snuff it*

chiflar[2] ▸conjug 1a◂ VT (*Téc*) [+ *cuero*] to pare, pare down

chiflato SM whistle

chifle SM 1 (= *silbido*) whistle
2 [*de ave*] call, bird call
3 (*CAm, Caribe Hist*) powder horn, powder flask

chiflete SM whistle

chiflido SM (*esp LAm*) 1 (= *silbido*) whistle
2 (= *siseo*) hiss

chiflón SM 1 (*LAm*) (= *viento*) (sudden) draught *o* (*EEUU*) draft (*of air*)
2 (*CAm, Caribe, Cono Sur*) [*de río*] rapids *pl*, very strong current; (*CAm*) waterfall
3 (*Méx*) (= *caz*) flume, race
4 (*Méx*) (= *tobera*) nozzle

chigüín/ina* SM/F (*CAm*) kid*

chihuahua SM Chihuahua

chiíta ADJ, SMF, **chiita** ADJ, SMF Shiite, Shi'ite

chilaba SF jellaba(h)

chilacayote SM (*LAm*) gourd

chilango/a (*Méx*) Ⓐ ADJ of/from Mexico City
Ⓑ SM/F native/inhabitant of Mexico City; **los ~s** the people of/from Mexico City

chilaquiles SMPL (*Méx*) *tortilla fried in thick chili or green tomato*

chilco SM (*Chile*) wild fuchsia

Chile SM Chile

chile SM 1 (*Bot, Culin*) chili, chili pepper ► **chile con carne** chili con carne
2 (*CAm**) (*tb* **~s**) (= *broma*) joke

chilear* ▸conjug 1a◂ VI (*CAm*) to tell jokes

chilena SF overhead kick, scissors kick

chilenismo SM chilenism, *word or phrase peculiar to Chile*

chileno/a ADJ, SM/F Chilean

chilicote SM (*Andes, Cono Sur Entomología*) cricket

chilindrón SM **al ~** cooked with tomatoes and peppers

chilla[1] SF (= *tabla*) thin board, weatherboard, clapboard (*EEUU*)

chilla[2] SF (*Chile*) (= *zorro*) small fox

chilla[3] SF (*Méx*) 1 (= *pobreza*) poverty; **estar en la ~** to be very poor
2 (*Teat*) gods, gallery

chillador ADJ howling, screeching, screaming

chillante ADJ 1 (= *que chilla*) howling, screeching
2 = **chillón**

chillar ▸conjug 1a◂ Ⓐ VI 1 (= *gritar*) [*persona*] to shriek, scream; [*gato, animal salvaje*] to screech, yowl; [*ratón*] to squeak; [*cerdo*] to squeal; [*ave*] to screech, squawk; [*radio*] to blare; ✦*MODISMOS* **el cochino chilló** (*Caribe, Méx*) he let the cat out of the bag*, he squealed*; **no ~** (*LAm*) to keep one's mouth shut, not say a word
2 (*Mec*) [*frenos*] to screech, squeal
3 [*colores*] to scream, jar, be loud
4 (*LAm*) (= *llorar*) to bawl
Ⓑ **chillarse** VPR 1 (*LAm*) (= *quejarse*) to complain (**con** to), protest (**con** to)
2 (*Andes, Caribe, Méx**) (= *enojarse*) to get cross; (= *ofenderse*) to take offence, get into a huff
3 (*CAm*) (= *sofocarse*) to get embarrassed

chillería SF row, hubbub

chillido SM [*de persona*] shriek, scream; [*de gato, animal salvaje*] screech, yowling; [*de ratón*] squeak; [*de cerdo*] squeal; [*de ave*] screech, squawk

chillo SM 1 (*CAm*) (= *deuda*) debt
2 (*Caribe*) (= *muchedumbre*) rabble, mob
3 (*Andes*) (= *ira*) anger; (= *protesta*) loud protest

chillón[1]**/ona*** Ⓐ ADJ 1 [*persona*] loud, shrill, noisy
2 [*sonido, tono*] shrill
3 [*color*] loud, garish, lurid; **un naranja ~** a loud *o* garish *o* lurid orange colour
4 (*LAm*) (= *quejumbroso*) moaning, whingeing*
Ⓑ SM/F (*LAm*) 1 (= *quejón*) moaner, whinger
2 (= *gritón*) loudmouth*

chillón[2] SM (*Téc*) small nail, panel pin, finishing nail (*EEUU*)

chillonamente ADV [*hablar, quejarse*] loudly, shrilly; [*vestir*] loudly

chilpayate* SM (*Méx*) kid*

chilposo ADJ (*Cono Sur*) ragged, tattered

chimal SM (*Méx*) dishevelled hair, mop of hair

chimar ▸conjug 1a◂ VT 1 (*CAm, Méx*) (= *molestar*) to annoy, bother
2 (*CAm*) (= *arañar*) to scratch
3 (*CAm***) (= *copular*) to fuck**, screw**

chimba[1] SF 1 (*Andes, Cono Sur*) (= *orilla*) opposite bank (of a river); (= *barrio*) suburb
2 (*Andes*) (= *vado*) ford

chimba[2] SF (*Andes*) (= *trenza*) pigtail

chimbar ▸conjug 1a◂ VT (*Andes, Cono Sur*) to ford

chimbero ADJ (*Cono Sur*) 1 (*de chimba*) slum *antes de s*
2 (= *grosero*) coarse, rough

chimbo Ⓐ ADJ (*) 1 (*Col, Ven*) (= *gastado*) worn-out, wasted, old
2 (*Col*) (= *falso*) fake; [*cheque*] dud*
Ⓑ SM (*Andes*) piece of meat

chimenea SF 1 (*en el tejado*) chimney; [*de fábrica*] smokestack, chimney ► **chimenea de aire** air shaft ► **chimenea refrigeradora** cooling tower
2 (*dentro de casa*) fireplace, hearth; **encender la ~** to light the fire ► **chimenea francesa** fireplace
3 [*de barco*] funnel
4 (*Min*) shaft
5 (*) (= *cabeza*) nut*, noggin (*EEUU**), head; ✦*MODISMO* **estar mal de la ~** to be wrong in the head*

chimichurri SM (*Cono Sur*) strong barbecue sauce

chimiscolear ▸conjug 1a◂ VI (*Méx*) 1 (= *chismear*) to go around looking for gossip
2 (= *curiosear*) to poke one's nose in*

chimiscolero/a SM/F (*Méx*) gossip, busybody

chimpancé SMF chimpanzee

chimpín SM (*Andes*) brandy, liquor

chimuelo ADJ (*LAm*) toothless

china[1] SF 1 (= *porcelana*) china, chinaware
2 (= *piedra*) pebble; ✦MODISMOS **poner ~s** to put obstacles in the way; **tocarle a algn la ~***: **nos tocó la ~ de ser niños en los cincuenta** we had the misfortune *o* bad luck to be children in the fifties; **te ha tocado la ~ de cuidar de los niños** you drew the short straw, you've got to look after the children
3 (‡) [*de droga*] lump, piece
4 (= *seda*) China silk
5 **chinas** (= *juego*) *game played with pebbles*
6 (*Andes*) (= *trompo*) spinning-top
7 (= *abanico*) fan, blower
8 (*Caribe, Méx*) (= *naranja*) orange; *ver tb* **chino**

china[2] SF (*Andes, Cono Sur*) (= *niñera*) nursemaid; *ver tb* **chino**

China SF China

chinaca‡ SF **la ~** (*Méx*) the plebs*, the proles

chinado‡ ADJ crazy

chinaloa‡ SF (*Méx*) heroin, smack‡

chinampa SF (*Méx*) man-made island (*for cultivation on lakes*)

chinar‡ ▸conjug 1a◂ VT to carve up*, slash

chinarro SM large pebble, stone

chinazo SM blow from a stone; ✦MODISMO **le tocó el ~*** he had bad luck

chinchada SF (*Cono Sur*) tug-of-war

chinchal SM (*Caribe*) [*de tabaco*] tobacco stall; (= *tienda*) small shop

chinchar* ▸conjug 1a◂ Ⓐ VT to pester, annoy; **me chincha tener que hacerlo** it annoys *o* bugs* me having to do it
Ⓑ **chincharse** VPR to get annoyed, get cross; **¡para que te chinches!** so there!; **¡y que se chinchen los demás!** and the others can go jump in the lake!* *o* can get stuffed!‡

chincharrero SM (*Andes*) small fishing boat

chinche Ⓐ SM *o* SF 1 bedbug; ✦MODISMO **caer** *o* **morir como ~s** to die like flies
2 (= *chincheta*) drawing pin, thumbtack (*EEUU*)
3 (= *molestia*) nuisance
4 (*Cono Sur**) (= *rabieta*) pique, irritation
Ⓑ SMF (= *persona molesta*) nuisance; (*Andes, CAm*) naughty child

chincheta SF drawing pin, thumbtack (*EEUU*)

chinchetear ▸conjug 1a◂ VT to pin up

chinchibí SM (*Andes, CAm, Cono Sur*), **chinchibirra** SF (*Cono Sur*) ginger beer

chinchilla SF chinchilla

chinchín[1] SM 1 (= *música*) street music
2 (*Cono Sur*) (= *sonajero*) baby's rattle

chinchín[2] SM (*Caribe*) drizzle

chin-chin EXCL chin-chin, cheers

chinchón SM *aniseed spirit from the town of Chinchón*

chinchona SF quinine

chinchorrería SF 1 (= *pesadez*) fussiness
2 (= *chisme*) piece of gossip

chinchorrero ADJ 1 (= *quisquilloso*) fussy (*about details*)
2 (= *chismoso*) gossipy

chinchorro SM 1 (= *red*) dragnet
2 (= *chalupa*) rowing boat, rowboat (*EEUU*)
3 (*LAm*) (= *hamaca*) hammock; (= *vivienda*) poor tenement
4 (*Caribe*) (= *tienda*) little shop

chinchoso ADJ 1 full of bugs
2 = **chinchorrero**
3 (= *pesado*) tiresome

chinchudo* ADJ (*Cono Sur*) **estar ~** to be in a grumpy mood

chinchulines SMPL (*Cono Sur Culin*) chitterlings, chitlins

chindar‡ ▸conjug 1a◂ VT to chuck out*

chinear ▸conjug 1a◂ Ⓐ VT (*CAm*) 1 (= *llevar en brazos*) to carry in one's arms
2 (= *mimar*) to spoil
Ⓑ VI (*Cono Sur*) *to have an affair with someone of mixed race*

chinel‡ SM guard

chinela SF 1 (= *zapatilla*) slipper
2 (= *chanclo*) clog

chinero[1] SM china cupboard

chinero[2] ADJ (*Andes, Cono Sur*) *fond of mixed-race girls*

chinesco ADJ Chinese; *ver tb* **sombra 1**

chinetero ADJ (*Cono Sur*) = **chinero**[2]

chinga* SF (*CAm*) 1 (= *colilla*) fag end, cigar stub
2 (= *posos*) dregs *pl*
3 (*CAm, Caribe*) (= *pequeña cantidad*) drop, small amount; **una ~ de agua** a drop of water
4 (*Caribe*) (= *borrachera*) drunkenness
5 (*Méx**) (= *paliza*) beating-up

chingada** SF (*CAm, Méx*) 1 (= *acto sexual*) fuck**, screw**; **hijo de la ~** bastard**, son of a bitch (*EEUU***)
2 (= *molestia*) bloody nuisance**

chingadazo* SM (*CAm, Méx*) bash*, punch

chingado** ADJ (*CAm, Méx*) lousy**, bloody**; **estar ~** to be cross, be upset

chingadura SF (*Cono Sur*) failure

chingana SF 1 (*Andes, Cono Sur*) dive*, tavern; [*de baile*] cheap dance hall
2 (*Cono Sur*) (= *fiesta*) wild party

chinganear ▸conjug 1a◂ VI (*Andes, Cono Sur*) to go out on the town, live it up*

chinganero/a (*Andes, Cono Sur*) Ⓐ ADJ fond of living it up*, wildly social
Ⓑ SM/F owner of a "chingana"

chingar ▸conjug 1h◂ Ⓐ VT 1 (= *beber con exceso*) to knock back*
2 (**) (= *copular*) to fuck**, screw**; ✦MODISMOS **no chingues** (*Méx*) don't mess me around*; **¡chinga tu madre!** (*Méx*) fuck off!**
3 (*CAm*) [+ *cola*] to dock, cut off
Ⓑ VI 1 to get pissed**
2 (*CAm, Méx**) to lark about*
Ⓒ **chingarse** VPR (*) 1 (= *emborracharse*) to get pissed*
2 (*CAm, Méx*) to fail; **la fiesta se chingó** the party was a disaster*

chingo Ⓐ ADJ 1 (*CAm*) [*vestido*] short; [*cuchillo*] blunt; [*animal*] tailless
2 (*CAm*) (= *desnudo*) naked, half-naked
3 (*Ven*) (= *pequeño*) small
4 (*Ven**) [*persona*] snub-nosed; [*nariz*] snub
5 (*Ven**) (= *loco*) **estar ~ por algo** to be crazy about sth
Ⓑ SM 1 (*Andes*) (= *caballo*) colt
2 (*Andes, CAm*) (= *barca*) small boat
3 **chingos** (*CAm*) underclothes
4 (*Méx**) **un ~ de algo** loads of sth*

chingón* SM (*Méx*) big shot*, boss

chingue SM (*Chile*) skunk

chinguear *etc* ▸conjug 1a◂ VT (*CAm*) = **chingar**

chinguirito SM 1 (*Caribe, Méx*) (= *licor*) rough liquor, firewater
2 (*Andes, Caribe*) (= *trago*) swig*

chinita SF (*Andes, Cono Sur Zool*) (= *mariquita*) ladybird, ladybug (*EEUU*)

chinito/a SM/F 1 (*Cono Sur*) (= *criado*) servant/maid
2 (*LAm*) (*apelativo*) dear, dearest
3 (*Andes, Caribe, Cono Sur*) (= *indio*) Indian boy/Indian girl

chino[1]**/a** Ⓐ ADJ Chinese; **barrio ~** red-light district
Ⓑ SM/F 1 (= *persona*) Chinese man/woman; ✦MODISMOS **quedar como un ~** (*Cono Sur**) to come off badly; **trabajar como un ~** (*esp Cono Sur**) to work like a dog; **es trabajo de ~s*** it's slave labour *o* (*EEUU*) labor
2 (*LAm*) (= *mestizo*) mestizo, person of mixed race (*of Amerindian and European parentage*); (= *indio*) Indian, Amerindian
3 (*LAm*) (= *criado*) servant/maid
Ⓒ SM 1 (*Ling*) Chinese; ✦MODISMOS **hablar en ~*** to talk gobbledygook; **ni que hablara en ~** it was all Greek to me; **me suena a ~*** [*idioma*] it sounds like double Dutch to me; [*tema*] it's all Greek to me
2 (*Culin*) conical strainer
3 (*Andes, CAm*) (= *cerdo*) pig, hog (*EEUU*)
4 **chinos** (*Méx*) (= *rizos*) curls
5 (*Arg, CAm*) (= *rabia*) anger; **le salió el ~** he lost his temper; **tener un ~** to be angry; *ver tb* **china**

chino[2] SM (*Geol*) pebble, stone

chinólogo/a SM/F expert in Chinese affairs, Sinologist; (*hum*) China watcher

chinorri‡ SF bird*, chick (*EEUU‡*)

chip SM 1 (*Inform*) chip; ✦MODISMO **cambiarse el ~*** to get up to date, get with it ► **chip de memoria** memory chip ► **chip de silicio** silicon chip
2 (*Culin*) crisp, chip (*EEUU*)
3 (*Golf*) chip, chip shot

chipe* Ⓐ ADJ (*CAm*) 1 (= *enfermizo*) weak, sickly
2 (= *llorón*) whining, snivelling
Ⓑ SMF (*Andes, CAm, Méx*) baby of the family

chipear ▸conjug 1a◂ Ⓐ VT (*CAm*) to bother, pester
Ⓑ VI (*Andes, CAm*) to moan, whine

chipén†‡ Ⓐ ADJ ✦MODISMO **de ~** super*, smashing*
Ⓑ ADV marvellously, really well; **comer de ~** to have a super meal*
Ⓒ SF **la ~** the truth

chipi ADJ, SMF = **chipe**

chipiar* ▸conjug 1a◂ VT (*CAm*) to bother, pester

chipichipi* SM (*CAm, Méx*) continuous drizzle

chipichusca* SF whore, hooker (*EEUU‡*)

chipil* ADJ (*Méx*) sad, gloomy

chipión* SM (*CAm*) telling-off*

chipirón SM baby squid

chipotear ▸conjug 1a◂ VT (*CAm*) to slap

Chipre SF Cyprus

chipriota ADJ, SMF Cypriot

chiquear ▸conjug 1a◂ Ⓐ VT (*Méx*) 1 (= *mimar*) to spoil, indulge
2 (= *dar coba a*) to flatter, suck up to*
Ⓑ **chiquearse** VPR 1 (*Méx*) (= *mimarse*) to be pampered
2 (*CAm*) (= *contonearse*) to swagger along, sway one's hips

chiqueo SM 1 (*Caribe, Méx*) (= *caricia*) caress
2 (*CAm*) (= *contoneo*) swagger

chiquero Ⓐ SM 1 (= *pocilga*) pigsty, pigpen (*EEUU*)
2 (*Taur*) bull pen
3 (*Cono Sur*) hen run
Ⓑ ADJ [*persona*] fond of kids

chiquilicuatro* SM, **chiquilicuatre*** SM nobody, insignificant person; **es un ~** he's a nobody

chiquilín* SM (*CAm, Cono Sur, Méx*) tiny tot, small boy

chiquillada SF 1 childish prank; **esos son ~s** that's kid's stuff*
2 (*esp LAm**) (= *niños*) kids* *pl*, group of children

chiquillería SF kids* *pl*

chiquillo/a SM/F kid*, child

chiquirín SM (*CAm Entomología*) cricket

chiquirritín* ADJ, **chiquirrito*** ADJ small, tiny

chiquitear ▸conjug 1a◂ VI 1 (= *jugar*) to play like a child
2 (*) (= *beber*) to tipple

chiquitín/ina* Ⓐ ADJ tiny
Ⓑ SM/F tiny tot

chiquito/a Ⓐ ADJ (*esp LAm**) small; ✦***MODISMO*** **es ~ pero matón** he may be small but he's tough
Ⓑ SM/F (*) kid*; ✦***MODISMO*** **no andarse con chiquitas** not to beat about the bush
Ⓒ SM 1 (= *vaso*) small glass of wine
2 (*Cono Sur**) (= *pedacito*) **un ~** a bit, a little

chiquitura SF 1 (*CAm*) (= *nimiedad*) small thing
2 (*CAm*) = **chiquillada**

chira SF 1 (*Andes*) (= *andrajo*) rag, tatter
2 (*CAm*) (= *llaga*) wound, sore

chirajos SMPL 1 (*CAm*) (= *trastos*) lumber, junk
2 (*Andes*) (= *andrajos*) rags, tatters

chirajoso ADJ (*CAm*) ragged, tattered

chircal SM (*Andes*) brickworks *pl*, tileworks *pl*

chiri‡ SM joint‡

chiribita SF 1 (= *chispa*) spark; ✦***MODISMO*** **estar que echa ~s*** to be hopping mad
2 **chiribitas*** (= *destellos*) spots before the eyes; ✦***MODISMO*** **los ojos le hacían ~s** her eyes sparkled, her eyes lit up
3 (*Bot*) daisy

chiribitil SM 1 (= *desván*) attic, garret
2 (= *cuchitril*) cubbyhole

chiribito SM poker

chirigota SF 1 (*) (= *broma*) joke; **fue motivo de ~** it got a laugh, it caused some amusement; **estar de ~** to be joking; **tomarse algo a ~** to take sth as a joke *o* in good heart; (*pey*) to treat sth too lightly
2 (*en carnaval*) *group that sings humorous and satirical songs during Carnival*

chirigotero ADJ full of jokes, facetious

chirimbolo* SM 1 (= *trasto*) thingummyjig*, thingamajig (*EEUU**)
2 **chirimbolos** (= *bártulos*) things, gear* *sing*

chirimía SF shawm

chirimiri SM drizzle

chirimoya SF 1 (= *fruta*) custard apple, cherimoya (*EEUU*)
2 (‡) (= *cabeza*) nut*, noggin (*EEUU**), head

chirimoyo SM 1 (= *planta*) custard apple tree, cherimoya tree (*EEUU*)
2 (*Cono Sur**) dud cheque*

chirinada SF 1 (*Cono Sur*) (= *fracaso*) failure, disaster
2 = **chirinola**

chiringuito SM refreshment stall, refreshment stand

chirinola SF 1 (= *discusión*) heated discussion
2 (= *nimiedad*) trifle, bagatelle
3 (= *juego*) skittles *pl*

chiripa SF 1 (*) (= *casualidad*) fluke, stroke of luck; **de** *o* **por ~** by a fluke, by chance
2 (*Billar*) lucky break

chiripá SM (*Cono Sur*) Amerindian breeches *pl*, *kind of blanket worn as trousers*; **gente de ~** country people, peasants

chiripero Ⓐ ADJ lucky, fluky
Ⓑ SM lucky sort

chirís* SMF (*CAm*) kid*, child

chirivía SF 1 (*Bot*) parsnip
2 (*Orn*) wagtail

chirivisco SM (*CAm*) firewood, kindling

chirla[1] SF mussel, clam

chirla[2]‡ SF armed hold-up

chirlata* SF whore, hooker (*EEUU*‡)

chirle ADJ 1 [*sopa*] insipid
2 (= *aburrido*) flat, dull, wishy-washy*; **poeta ~** mere versifier, third-rate poet

chirlo SM 1 (= *corte*) gash, slash (*in the face*)
2 (= *cicatriz*) scar, long scar
3 (*Arg**) (= *cachete*) slap

chirola* SF 1 (*CAm, Caribe*) (= *cárcel*) nick*, jail, can (*EEUU**)
2 (*Arg*) **chirolas** (= *monedas*) **unas pocas ~s** a few pennies

chirona‡ SF nick*, jail, can (*EEUU**); **estar en ~** to be in the nick*; **lo metieron en ~** he was banged up‡

chiros SMPL (*Andes*) rags, tatters

chiroso ADJ (*Andes, CAm*) ragged, tattered

chirota SF (*CAm*) tough woman

chirote* ADJ (*Andes*) daft*

chirri‡ SM joint‡

chirriado ADJ (*Andes*) (= *gracioso*) witty; (= *alegre*) merry, jovial

chirriar ▸conjug 1b◂ VI 1 (*Zool*) [*grillo*] to chirp, sing; [*ave*] to screech, squawk
2 [*bisagra, puerta*] to creak, squeak
3 [*frenos*] to screech, squeal
4 (*Andes*) (= *tiritar*) (*de frío*) to shiver

chirrido SM 1 (*Zool*) [*de grillo*] chirp, chirping; [*de ave*] screech, screeching, squeak, squeaking
2 [*de bisagra, puerta*] creak, creaking, squeak, squeaking
3 [*de frenos*] screeching, squealing

chirrión SM 1 (= *carro*) tumbrel
2 (*Andes, CAm, Méx*) (= *látigo*) whip
3 (*CAm*) (= *sarta*) string, line
4 (*CAm*) (= *charla*) chat, conversation (*esp between lovers*)

chirrionar ▸conjug 1a◂ VT (*Méx*) to whip, lash

chirrisco ADJ 1 (*CAm, Caribe*) (= *diminuto*) very small, tiny; **viejo ~** dirty old man
2 (*Méx**) [*mujer*] flirtatious

chirucas SFPL *canvas mountain boots*

chirumen* SM nous*, savvy*

chirusa* SF (*Cono Sur*) (= *niña*) girl, kid*; (= *mujer*) poor woman

chis EXCL (*pidiendo silencio*) sh!; (*llamando a alguien*) hey!, psst!

chischís SM (*Andes, CAm, Caribe*) drizzle

chiscón SM hovel

chisgarabís* SM meddler, nosey-parker*

chisguete* SM swig*, drink

chisme SM 1 (*) (= *cosa*) thing; **¿y este ~ para qué sirve?** and what's this thing for?; **tiene la cartera llena de ~s** her bag is full of all sorts of things *o* bits and pieces; **un ~ para cortar metal** a thing *o* whatnot* *o* thingummyjig* for cutting metal with
2 (= *cotilleo*) **se sabe todos los ~s** he knows all the gossip; **me contó un ~ sobre Juan** she told me the gossip about Juan

chismear ▸conjug 1a◂ VI to gossip, spread scandal

chismería SF, **chismerío** SM (*Cono Sur*) gossip, scandal

chismero/a ADJ, SM/F = **chismoso**

chismografía SF gossip

chismorrear ▸conjug 1a◂ VI = **chismear**

chismorreo SM = **chismería**

chismoso/a Ⓐ ADJ gossiping, scandalmongering
Ⓑ SM/F gossip

chispa Ⓐ SF 1 [*de luz, fuego*] spark; ✦***MODISMOS*** **echar ~s: está que echa ~s*** he's hopping mad*; **perder ~** to lose one's/its sparkle
2 (= *gota de lluvia*) drop; **caen ~s** it's just spitting
3 (= *pizca*) bit, tiny amount; **una ~ de café** a tiny drop of coffee; **una ~ de sal** a pinch of salt; **ni ~** not the least bit; **eso no tiene ni ~ de gracia** that's not in the least bit funny; **si tuviera una ~ de inteligencia** if he had an ounce of intelligence
4 (= *ingenio*) wit; **la historia tiene ~** the story's quite amusing; **Juan tiene ~** John's quite witty; ✦***MODISMO*** **es de ~ retardada*** he's slow on the uptake
5 (*) (= *borrachera*) drunkenness; **coger** *o* **pillar una ~** to get sloshed*; **estar con** *o* **tener la ~** to be tight*
6 (*CAm, Méx*) **dar ~** to work, be successful, yield results
7 (*Andes*) (= *rumor*) rumour, rumor (*EEUU*)
8 (*Andes*) (= *arma*) gun, weapon
Ⓑ ADJ INV 1 (= *borracho*) **estar ~*** to be sloshed*
2 (*Méx*) (= *divertido*) funny, amusing
Ⓒ SM (*) (*tb* **~s**) electrician

chisparse* ▸conjug 1a◂ VPR 1 (*Andes*) (= *emborracharse*) to get tight*
2 (*CAm, Méx*) (= *huir*) to run away, slip off

chispazo SM 1 spark; ✦***MODISMO*** **primeros ~s** first signs
2 = **chisme 2**

chispeante ADJ sparkling, scintillating

chispear ▸conjug 1a◂ VI 1 [*leña, fuego*] to throw out sparks

2 (= *destellar*) to sparkle, scintillate
3 (*Meteo*) to drizzle

chispero[1] Ⓐ ADJ (*Andes, Caribe*) gossiping, scandalmongering
Ⓑ SM (*CAm*) 1 (††) (= *encendedor*) lighter
2 (*Aut*) spark plug, sparking plug

chispero[2]**/a*** Ⓐ ADJ of low-class Madrid
Ⓑ SM/F low-class inhabitant of Madrid

chispita* SF **una ~ de vino** a drop of wine

chisporrotear ▸conjug 1a◂ VI [*aceite*] to spit; [*carne*] to sizzle; [*leña*] to crackle; [*fuego*] to throw out sparks

chisporroteo SM [*de aceite*] spitting, spluttering; [*de carne*] sizzling; [*de leña*] sparking, crackling

chisquero SM pocket lighter

chist EXCL = **chis**

chistada SF bad joke

chistar* ▸conjug 1a◂ VI **nadie chistó** nobody said a word; **a ése no le chista nadie** you don't dare answer him back; **no ~** not to say a word; **sin ~** without a word

chiste SM joke; **caer en el ~** to get the joke, get it; **dar en el ~** to guess right; **hacer ~ de algo** ◊ **tomar algo a ~** to take sth as a joke; **tiene ~** it's funny; **no veo el ~** I don't get it
► **chiste verde** blue joke, dirty joke

chistera SF 1 (= *sombrero*) top hat ► **chistera de mago** magician's hat
2 (*Pesca*) fish basket
3 (*Dep*) *variety of pelota racket*

chistosamente ADV funnily, amusingly

chistoso/a Ⓐ ADJ funny, amusing
Ⓑ SM/F wit, funny person

chistu SM = **txistu**

chistulari SM = **txistulari**

chita[1] SF ✦**MODISMO a la ~ callando** (= *sin molestar*) unobtrusively; (= *con disimulo*) on the quiet, on the sly

chita[2] SF 1 (*Anat*) anklebone; ✦**MODISMOS dar en la ~*** to hit the nail on the head; **no se me da una ~*** ◊ **(no) me importa una ~*** I don't care two hoots (**de** about)
2 (= *juego*) *boys' game played with an anklebone*
3 (*Méx*) (= *saco*) net bag; (= *dinero*) money; (= *ahorros*) small amount of money saved, nest egg

chita[3]* EXCL (*Chile*) (= *caramba*) damn!*, Jesus!*; **¡por la ~!** damn it!*

chiticalla* SMF quiet sort

chiticallando ADV = **chita**[1]

chitón EXCL sh!

chiva Ⓐ SF 1 (*Zool*) kid; (= *cabra*) nanny goat; ✦**MODISMO estar como una ~*** to be crazy
2 (*LAm*) (= *barba*) goatee, goatee beard
3 (*CAm*) (= *manta*) blanket, bedcover; **~s** bedclothes
4 (*Andes, CAm*) (= *autobús*) bus; (= *coche*) car
5 (*Caribe, Cono Sur*) (= *niña*) naughty little girl; (*CAm, Cono Sur*) (= *marimacho*) mannish woman; (*Andes, Caribe, Cono Sur*) (= *vividora*) immoral woman
6 (*CAm, Cono Sur*) (= *rabieta*) rage, tantrum
7 (*Caribe*) (= *mochila*) knapsack
8 **chivas** (*Méx**) (= *trastos*) junk *sing*
9 (*Cono Sur**) fib, tall story; ✦**MODISMO meter una ~** to cook up a story
10 (*Caribe**) (= *delator*) grass‡, informer
Ⓑ ADJ (*CAm**) (= *despabilado*) alert, sharp
Ⓒ EXCL (*CAm**) look out!, careful!

chivar* ▸conjug 1a◂ Ⓐ VT (*LAm*) (= *fastidiar*) to annoy, upset
Ⓑ **chivarse** VPR 1 (= *dar un chivatazo*) to squeal* (**a, con** on), grass* (**a, de** on); **se chivó a la policía** he squealed *o* grassed to the police*; **~se a la maestra** to tell the teacher
2 (*LAm*) to get annoyed

chivata‡ SF 1 (= *linterna*) torch
2 (= *pluma*) fountain-pen

chivatazo* SM tip-off; **dar el ~** to inform, give a tip-off

chivatear ▸conjug 1a◂ Ⓐ VI 1 = **chivar B1**
2 (*Cono Sur*) to shout
3 (*Andes, Cono Sur*) (= *saltar*) to jump about; (= *retozar*) to indulge in horse-play, have a noisy free-for-all
4 (*Caribe*) (= *impresionar*) to create a big impression
Ⓑ **chivatearse** VPR (*Caribe*) to get scared

chivato SM 1 (*) (= *soplón*) informer
2 (*Zool*) kid
3 (*Ven**) prominent person
4 (*LAm*) (= *niño*) child, kid*
5 (*Andes*) (= *pillo*) rascal, villain
6 (*Andes*) (= *aprendiz*) apprentice, mate
7 (*Cono Sur*) (= *aguardiente*) cheap liquor, firewater
8 (*Aut*) indicator, indicator light
9 (= *busca*) pager, beeper

chivearse* ▸conjug 1a◂ VPR (*CAm*) to get embarrassed

chivera SF (*Andes, CAm*) goatee, goatee beard

chivero SM 1 (*Andes*) (= *conductor*) bus driver
2 (*Andes*) (= *matón*) brawler
3 (*Caribe*) (= *intrigante*) intriguer

chiviroso* ADJ (*CAm*) outgoing, extrovert

chivitería SF (*Uru*) steakburger stall

chivito SM (*Uru*) steakburger ► **chivito canadiense** *meat, egg and salad sandwich*

chivo Ⓐ SM 1 (*Zool*) billy goat; ✦**MODISMO esto huele a ~** (*Caribe, Cono Sur**) this smells fishy, there's something fishy about this*
► **chivo expiatorio** scapegoat
2 (*Cono Sur*) (= *rabia*) fit of anger; ✦**MODISMOS comer ~** (*Andes, Caribe**) ◊ **ponerse como ~** (*CAm, Caribe**) to be furious
3 (*CAm*) (= *dados*) dice; (= *juego*) game of dice
4 (*Caribe*) (= *estafa*) fraud; (= *intriga*) plot, intrigue; (= *acto de contrabando*) smuggling; (= *géneros*) contraband, smuggled goods *pl*
5 (*Méx*) (= *jornal*) day's wages; (= *anticipo*) advance; (= *soborno*) backhander*, sweetener*
6 (*Caribe*) (= *golpe*) punch, blow
7 (*Andes, CAm*) (= *niño*) naughty boy, scamp
8 (*CAm**) (= *guatemalteco*) Guatemalan
9 (*CAm‡*) (= *chulo*) pimp
10 (‡) (= *maricón*) poofter‡
Ⓑ ADJ (*CAm**) 1 (= *guatemalteco*) Guatemalan
2 **andas bien ~** you're looking very smart

chivón/ona (*Caribe*) Ⓐ ADJ annoying, irritating
Ⓑ SM/F bore

chocante ADJ 1 (= *sorprendente*) startling, striking
2 (= *raro*) odd, strange; **lo ~ es que** the odd thing about it is that
3 (= *escandaloso*) shocking, scandalous
4 (*esp LAm*) (= *pesado*) tiresome; (= *desagradable*) offensive, unpleasant

chocantería SF (*LAm*) 1 (= *descaro*) impertinence
2 (= *chiste*) coarse joke

chocar ▸conjug 1g◂ Ⓐ VI 1 (= *colisionar*) [*coches, trenes*] to collide, crash; [*barcos*] to collide; **los dos coches ~on de frente** the two cars crashed head on *o* were in a head-on collision; **~ con** *o* **contra** [+ *vehículo*] to collide with, crash into; [+ *objeto*] to bang into; [+ *persona*] to bump into; **para no ~ contra el avión** to avoid crashing into *o* colliding with the plane; **el buque chocó con una mina** the ship struck a mine; **el balón chocó contra el poste** the ball hit the post; **chocaban unos contra otros por los pasillos** people bumped into each other in the corridors
2 (= *enfrentarse*) [*opiniones, personalidades*] to clash; **~ con** [+ *ideas, intereses*] to run counter to, be at odds with; [+ *obstáculos, dificultades*] to come up against, run into; [+ *personas*] to clash with; **esa propuesta choca con los intereses de EEUU** that proposal runs counter to *o* is at odds with American interests; **no choca con ninguna idea religiosa** it does not clash with any religion; **ésa sería una de las mayores dificultades con las que ~ían en este proyecto** that would be one of the biggest problems they would come up against in this project; **por su carácter chocaba a menudo con sus compañeros de trabajo** he often clashed with his colleagues because of his confrontational nature
Ⓑ VT 1 (= *sorprender*) to shock; **¿no te choca la situación actual?** don't you find the current situation shocking?; **me chocó muchísimo lo que dijo** I was really shocked by what he said, what he said really shocked me; **me choca que no lo hayan hecho** I am surprised that they haven't done it; **no me choca que haya dimitido** I'm not surprised that he's resigned
2 (= *hacer chocar*) [+ *vasos*] to clink; [+ *manos*] to shake; **¡chócala!*** ◊ **¡choca esos cinco!*** put it there!*; **~ la mano de algn** to shake hands with sb
3 (*Méx*) (= *asquear*) to disgust; **me choca su actitud** I find his attitude offensive
Ⓒ **chocarse** VPR (*Méx Aut*) to have a crash

chocarrear ▸conjug 1a◂ VI 1 (= *tontear*) to clown, act the fool
2 (= *contar chistes*) to tell rude jokes

chocarrería SF 1 (= *cualidad*) coarseness, vulgarity
2 **una ~** a dirty joke

chocarrero ADJ coarse, vulgar

chocha SF (*tb* **~ perdiz**) woodcock; *ver tb* **chocho**[3]

chochada* SF (*CAm*) (= *nimiedad*) triviality; **~s** bits and pieces

chochaperdiz SF woodcock

chochear ▸conjug 1a◂ VI 1 (*por la edad*) to dodder, be senile
2 (*por el cariño*) to be soft

chochecientos* ADJ umpteen*

chochera SF 1 (= *cualidad*) senility
2 (= *acción*) sentimental act
3 (= *adoración*) **tener ~ por algn** to dote on sb, be crazy about sb
4 (*Andes, Cono Sur*) (= *preferido*) favourite, favorite (*EEUU*), pet

chochez SF = **chochera 1, 2, 3**

chochín SM [1] (*Orn*) wren

[2] (*) (= *novia*) bird*, chick (*EEUU**)

chochita SF wren

chocho[1] (A) ADJ [1] (= *senil*) doddering, senile

[2] (= *embelesado*) soft, doting, sentimental; **estar ~ por algn** to dote on sb, be soft on sb

[3] (*Cono Sur*) (= *contento*) delighted, pleased

(B) EXCL (*CAm**) no kidding!*, really?

chocho[2] SM [1] (= *caramelo*) candy stick; **chochos** (= *golosinas*) sweets, candy *sing* (*EEUU*) ► **chochos de vieja** *lupin seeds sold at street stalls, fairs etc for eating*

[2] (**) (= *vulva*) pussy**

[3] (*) (= *lío*) rumpus*, shindy*

chocho[3]**/a*** (A) ADJ (*CAm*) (= *nicaragüense*) Nicaraguan

(B) SM/F [1] (= *drogadicto*) drug addict

[2] (*CAm*) (= *nicaragüense*) Nicaraguan; *ver tb* **chocha**

chochoca* SF (*CAm*) nut*, noggin (*EEUU**), head

chocholear ▸conjug 1a◂ VT (*Andes*) to spoil, pamper

chock SM (*Andes, Caribe Aut*) choke

choclo[1] SM [1] (= *zueco*) clog; ✦**MODISMO meter el ~** (*Méx**) to put one's foot in it

[2] (*Méx*) low-heeled shoe

choclo[2] SM [1] (*LAm Agr*) (= *planta*) maize, corn (*EEUU*); (= *mazorca*) corncob; (= *granos*) sweetcorn

[2] **choclos** (*Cono Sur*) [*de niño*] (= *brazos*) children's arms; (= *piernas*) children's legs

[3] (*Andes*) **un ~ de algo** a group of sth, a lot of sth

[4] (*Cono Sur*) (= *dificultad*) difficulty, trouble; (= *molestia*) annoyance; (= *carga*) burden, task

choclón SM (*Chile*) crowd

choco[1] (*Chile*) SM poodle

choco[2] ADJ (*Andes, Cono Sur*) (= *rojo*) dark red; (= *chocolate*) chocolate-coloured, chocolate-colored (*EEUU*); (= *moreno*) swarthy, dark

choco[3] (A) ADJ (*Chile*) [1] (= *manco*) one-armed

[2] (= *cojo*) one-legged

[3] (= *tuerto*) one-eyed

(B) SM [1] (*Cono Sur*) (= *tocón*) stump (*of tree*)

[2] (*Andes*) (= *sombrero*) top hat

[3] (*Méx***) (= *vulva*) cunt**

choco[4] SM (*Zool*) cuttlefish

choco[5]* SM (= *droga*) = **chocolate B2**

chocolatada SF *party or gathering at which one drinks hot chocolate*

chocolate (A) ADJ (*LAm*) chocolate-coloured, chocolate-colored (*EEUU*)

(B) SM [1] (*para comer*) chocolate; (*para beber*) drinking chocolate, cocoa ► **chocolate blanco** white chocolate ► **chocolate con leche** milk chocolate ► **chocolate negro** plain chocolate

[2] (*) (= *hachís*) hash*, pot*; **darle al ~** to be hooked on drugs

[3] (*LAm hum*) blood; ✦**MODISMOS dar a algn agua de su propio ~** (*Méx**) to give sb a taste of his own medicine; **sacar el ~ a algn** to make sb's nose bleed, give sb a bloody nose

chocolatera SF [1] chocolate pot

[2] (*) piece of junk

chocolatería SF [1] (= *fábrica*) chocolate factory

[2] (= *tienda*) chocolate shop

chocolatero (A) ADJ (= *de chocolate*) chocolate *antes de s*; **no soy muy ~** I'm not very fond of o keen on chocolate, I'm not a great one for chocolate o a great chocolate eater*

(B) SM [1] (*Andes*) (*para chocolate*) chocolate pot

[2] (*Caribe, Méx*) (= *viento*) strong northerly wind

chocolatina SF chocolate bar

chocolear ▸conjug 1a◂ (*Andes*) (A) VT to dock, cut off the tail of

(B) VI to get depressed

chófer SMF, **chofer** SMF (*LAm*) [1] [*de coche*] driver

[2] [*de autobús*] bus driver

cholada SF (*Andes pey*) *action typical of a "cholo"*

cholar* ▸conjug 1a◂ VT to nick*, pinch*

cholería SF (*Andes*), **cholerío** SM (*Andes*) *group of "cholos"*

cholga SF (*Cono Sur*) mussel

cholla* SF [1] (= *cabeza*) nut*, noggin (*EEUU**), head

[2] (= *cerebro*) brains *pl*

[3] (*CAm*) (= *herida*) wound, sore

[4] (*Andes, CAm*) laziness, slowness

chollo* SM [1] (= *buena oportunidad*) snip*, bargain; **el piso es un ~ por ese precio** the apartment is a snip* o a bargain at that price; **¡qué ~ de trabajo!** what a cushy job!*

[2] (= *amorío*) love affair

cholludo ADJ (*Andes, CAm*) lazy, slow

cholo/a (A) ADJ [1] (*LAm*) half-breed*, mestizo

[2] (*Chile*) (= *miedoso*) cowardly

(B) SM/F [1] (*Andes, Cono Sur*) (= *mestizo*) dark-skinned person

[2] (*CAm*) (= *indio*) half-civilized Indian

[3] (*Cono Sur*) (= *indio*) Indian

[4] (*LAm*) (= *peruano*) Peruvian

[5] (*Cono Sur*) (= *cobarde*) coward

[6] (*Andes*) (*apelativo*) darling, honey (*EEUU*)

chomba SF (*Chile*), **chompa** SF (*Andes, Cono Sur*) sweater, jumper

chompipe SM (*CAm*) turkey

chonchón SM (*Chile*) lamp

chonco (*CAm*) (A) ADJ = **choco**[3]

(B) SM stump

chongo SM [1] (*Méx*) (= *moño*) bun

[2] (*Cono Sur*) (= *cuchillo*) blunt knife, worn-out knife

[3] (*Caribe*) (= *caballo*) old horse

[4] (*CAm, Méx*) **chongos** (= *trenzas*) pigtails

chonta SF (*Andes*) palm shoots *pl*

chontal (A) ADJ [1] (*CAm*) (= *salvaje*) wild, uncivilized; (= *rebelde*) rebellious; (= *revoltoso*) unruly

[2] (*Andes, CAm, Caribe*) (= *inculto*) uncivilized; (= *grosero*) rough, coarse

[3] (*Caribe*) (= *de habla inculta*) rough-spoken

(B) SM (*Andes*) peach palm

chop SM (*Chile*) [1] (= *vaso*) large beer glass

[2] (= *cerveza*) draught beer, draft beer (*EEUU*)

chopa* SF jacket

chopazo* SM (*Cono Sur*), **chope** SM (*Cono Sur*) punch, bash*

chopera SF poplar grove

chopería SF (*Chile*) bar, beer bar

chopito SM baby squid

chopo SM [1] (*Bot*) black poplar ► **chopo de Italia, chopo lombardo** Lombardy poplar

[2] (*Mil**) gun; ✦**MODISMO cargar con el ~** to join up

chopp SM (*Chile*) = **chop**

choque SM [1] [*de vehículos*] crash, collision ► **choque frontal** head-on collision ► **choque múltiple** multiple crash, pile-up; *ver tb* **coche**[1] **1**

[2] (= *desavenencia*) clash; **hubo un ~ entre ambos ministros** there was a clash between the two ministers; **un ~ de personalidades** a personality clash; **un ~ de culturas** a clash of cultures

[3] (= *lucha*) clash; **hubo varios ~s entre la población civil** there were several clashes between civilians; *ver tb* **fuerza 8**, **tropa 1**

[4] (*Dep*) (= *partido*) encounter, clash

[5] (= *conmoción*) **su muerte fue un ~ para ella** his death was a shock for her; **sufrí un ~ cultural al llegar a este país** I had a culture shock when I came to this country

[6] (*Med*) shock

choquezuela SF kneecap

chorar* ▸conjug 1a◂ VT [1] [+ *casa*] to burgle, burglarize (*EEUU*)

[2] [+ *objeto*] to rip off*

chorbo/a* SM/F [1] (= *novio*) boyfriend; (= *novia*) girlfriend, bird*, chick (*EEUU**)

[2] (= *tío*) bloke*, guy*; (= *tía*) bird*, chick (*esp EEUU**)

chorcha SF [1] (*Méx*) (= *fiesta*) noisy party; **una ~ de amigos** a group of friends (*out for a good time*)

[2] (*CAm Orn*) crest, comb

[3] (*CAm Med*) goitre

[4] (*CAm***) (= *clítoris*) clit*, clitoris

chorchero ADJ (*Méx*) party-loving

chorchi* SM soldier

chorear* ▸conjug 1a◂ (A) VI (*Chile*) (*refunfuñar*) to grumble, complain; **estar choreado** to be miffed*, be upset

(B) VT [1] (*Chile*) (= *hartar*) **me chorea** it gets up my nose*

[2] (*Cono Sur, Perú*) (= *robar*) to pinch*, nick*

choreo SM (*Chile*) complaint

chori* SM [1] (= *cuchillo*) chiv*, knife

[2] = **chorizo 3**

choricear* ▸conjug 1a◂ VT to rip off*, lift*

choricería* SF crookedness*, corruption

choricero* SM = **chorizo 3**

chorizada* SF [1] (= *engaño*) swindle, con*

[2] (= *robo*) theft

chorizar* ▸conjug 1f◂ VT (= *robar*) to nick*; **me han chorizado la bici** they've nicked my bike*

chorizo SM [1] (*Culin*) *hard pork sausage*

[2] (*en circo*) balancing pole

[3] (*) (= *ratero*) small-time crook*; (= *maleante*) criminal; (= *carterista*) pickpocket

[4] (*Andes, Cono Sur Culin*) **bife de ~** rump steak

[5] (*Andes, Cono Sur Arquit*) *mixture of clay and straw used in plastering*

[6] (*Andes**) (= *idiota*) idiot

[7] (*Caribe*) (= *mulato*) mulatto

chorlito SM, **chorlitejo** SM (*Orn*) plover; *ver tb* **cabeza B2**

chorlo/a SM/F (*Andes, CAm, Caribe*) great-great-grandchild

choro[1]* SM [1] (= *persona*) thief, burglar

[2] (*Ling*) thieves' slang

choro[2] SM (*Andes, Cono Sur Zool*) mussel

chorote SM [1] (= *bebida*) (*Méx, Ven*) drinking chocolate (*with brown sugar*); (*Andes*) thick

drinking chocolate
[2] (*Caribe*) (= *bebida espesa*) *any thick drink*; (= *bebida aguada*) watery drink; (= *café*) coffee
[3] (*Andes*) (= *chocolatera*) unglazed chocolate pot

chorra Ⓐ SF [1] (‡) (= *suerte*) luck; **¡qué ~ tiene!** how jammy can you get!*; **de ~** by chance
[2] (*Cono Sur*) underworld slang
[3] (**) (= *pene*) prick**
Ⓑ SMF (‡) (= *idiota*) fool, idiot

chorrada SF [1] [*de líquido*] extra drop; ✦*MODISMO* **dar algo con ~** to give sth and a bit extra
[2] (*) (= *objeto insignificante*) knick-knack; **le regalaremos cualquier ~** we'll give her some little thing
[3] (*) (= *tontería*) **la película es una ~** the film is nonsense*; **no digas ~s** stop talking drivel
[4] (‡) [*de orina*] **echar la ~** to have a piss**

chorrar‡ ▸conjug 1a◂ VT = **chorar**

chorrear ▸conjug 1a◂ Ⓐ VI [1] (= *salir a chorros*) to gush (out), spout; **la sangre le chorreaba por la frente** blood was gushing (out) *o* spouting from his forehead; **estar chorreando de sudor** to be dripping with sweat
[2] (= *gotear*) to drip; **la ropa chorrea todavía** the clothes are still dripping water *o* wringing wet
[3] [*dinero*] to trickle in, come in in dribs and drabs; **chorrean todavía las solicitudes** applications are still trickling in *o* coming in in dribs and drabs
Ⓑ VT [1] (*Mil**) (= *regañar*) to tick off*, dress down*
[2] (= *verter*) to pour
[3] (*Cono Sur*) (= *robar*) to pinch*
[4] (*Andes*) (= *mojar*) to soak
Ⓒ **chorrearse** VPR **~se algo*** to pinch sth

chorreo SM [1] (= *flujo*) gushing, spouting
[2] (= *goteo*) dripping
[3] [*de dinero*] trickle (**de** on)
[4] (*) (= *reprimenda*) ticking-off*, dressing-down*
[5] ► **chorreo mental‡** nonsense, rubbish, garbage (*EEUU*)

chorreón SM [1] (= *cascada*) cascade
[2] (= *de aceite, vinagre*) *ver tb* **chorretón**

chorrera SF [1] (= *pitorro*) spout
[2] **chorreras** (*Cos*) frill *sing*; *ver tb* **jamón A1**
[3] (*Méx*) (= *montón*) stream, string; **una ~ de algo** a stream *o* string of sth
[4] (*Caribe**) (= *regañina*) ticking-off*, dressing-down*

chorrero‡ ADJ jammy‡, lucky

chorretada SF [1] (= *chorro*) squirt, jet
[2] = **chorrada 1**

chorretón SM [1] (= *chorro*) **echa un buen ~ de aceite** put plenty of oil on it; **un ~ de agua de colonia** a splash of cologne
[2] (= *mancha*) dribble

chorrillo SM steady trickle

chorro SM [1] [*de líquido*] jet, stream; **salía un buen ~ de agua del grifo** there was a strong flow of water from the tap; **se añade un chorrito de leche** add a drop of milk; **beber a ~** to drink without touching the bottle
[2] (*Téc*) jet, blast; **un avión con propulsión a ~** jet-propelled plane; **motor a ~** jet engine ► **chorro de arena** sandblast ► **chorro de vapor** steam jet
[3] (= *montón*) stream, string; **un ~ de insultos** a stream *o* string of insults; **un ~ de palabras** a torrent of words; **un ~ de voz** a verbal blast, a really loud voice; ✦*MODISMO* **a ~s** in plenty, in abundance; **llover a ~s** to pour (down); **salir a ~s** to gush forth, come spurting out; **hablar a ~s** to talk nineteen to the dozen
[4] (‡) (= *suerte*) jam‡, luck; **¡qué ~ tiene!** he's so jammy!‡
[5] (*Cono Sur**) (= *ladrón*) thief, pickpocket
[6] (*Andes*) [*de látigo*] lash
[7] (*CAm*) (= *grifo*) tap, faucet (*EEUU*)
[8] (*Caribe**) (= *reprimenda*) ticking-off*, dressing-down*

chorvo/a‡ SM/F = **chorbo**

chota SF ✦*MODISMO* **estar como una ~*** to be hopping mad*

chotacabras SM INV nightjar, goatsucker (*EEUU*)

chotear* ▸conjug 1a◂ Ⓐ VT [1] (*LAm*) (= *burlarse de*) to make fun of
[2] (*Andes*) (= *mimar*) to spoil, pamper
[3] (*CAm*) [+ *sospechoso*] to shadow, tail
Ⓑ **chotearse** VPR [1] (= *bromear*) to joke (**de** about)
[2] (= *confesar*) to cough‡, inform

choteo* SM kidding*, joking; **estar de ~** to be kidding*

chotis SM INV *traditional dance of Madrid*; ✦*MODISMO* **ser más agarrado que un ~*** to be tight-fisted

choto Ⓐ ADJ [1] (*CAm*) (= *abundante*) abundant, plentiful
[2] (= *de poco valor*) crummy‡
[3] (= *viejo*) clapped-out*
Ⓑ SM [1] (*Zool*) (= *cabrito*) kid; (= *ternero*) calf; ✦*MODISMO* **ser un viejo ~** to be a stupid old twit*
[2] (*Cono Sur‡*) (= *pene*) prick**

chotuno ADJ [*cabrito, ternero*] sucking, very young; [*cordero*] weakly; ✦*MODISMO* **oler a ~** to smell bad

chova SF crow, rook ► **chova piquirroja** chough

chovinismo *etc* SM = **chauvinismo** *etc*

chow-chow ['tʃautʃau] SM (*pl* **chow-chow**) chow

choza SF hut, shack

chozno/a SM/F great-great-great-grandchild

christmas ['krismas] SF, **chrisma** ['krisma] SM (*pl* **christmas** ['krismas]) Christmas card

chubasco SM [1] (*Meteo*) heavy shower ► **chubasco de nieve** brief snowstorm
[2] (= *contratiempo*) setback; **aguantar el ~** to weather the storm

chubascoso ADJ squally, stormy

chubasquero SM [1] (= *impermeable*) cagoule, foul-weather gear (*EEUU*)
[2] (‡ *hum*) French letter

chucán ADJ (*CAm*) [1] (= *gracioso*) buffoonish
[2] (= *grosero*) coarse, rude

chúcaro ADJ (*LAm*) [1] (= *salvaje*) wild, untamed
[2] (= *tímido*) shy

chucear ▸conjug 1a◂ VT (*LAm*) to prick, goad

chucha SF [1] (*Zool*) bitch
[2] (*) (*apelativo*) sweetheart
[3] (*Andes Zool*) opossum
[4] (*Andes*) (= *olor*) B.O.
[5] (*Andes*) (= *juego*) hide-and-seek
[6] (*Andes, Cono Sur*) (= *vulva*) cunt**
[7] (†) (= *peseta*) peseta

chuchada SF (*CAm*) trick, swindle

chuchear[1] ▸conjug 1a◂ VI to hunt, trap, fowl

chuchear[2] ▸conjug 1a◂ VI = **cuchichear**

chuchería SF [1] (= *golosina*) sweet, candy (*EEUU*)
[2] (= *bocada*) titbit
[3] (= *adorno*) trinket

chuchito SM = **chucho B10**

chucho Ⓐ ADJ [1] (*CAm**) (= *tacaño*) mean, stingy*
[2] (*Andes*) [*fruta*] soft, watery; [*persona*] wrinkled
[3] (*Méx*) (*chismoso*) gossipy
Ⓑ SM [1] (= *perro callejero*) mongrel; **¡chucho!** down boy!
[2] (= *pastel*) *custard-filled doughnut*
[3] (*) (= *novio*) sweetheart
[4] (*Caribe Ferro*) switch
[5] (*Caribe*) (= *látigo*) rawhide whip
[6] (*Cono Sur*) (= *cárcel*) jail
[7] (*LAm*) (= *escalofrío*) shakes *pl*, shivers *pl*; (= *fiebre*) fever; **entrarle a algn el ~*** to get the jitters*
[8] (*CAm**) (= *persona ostentosa*) spiv*
[9] (*LAm‡*) (= *canuto*) joint*, reefer*
[10] (*Andes, CAm, Méx Culin*) tamale

chuchoca* SF (*Cono Sur*) ✦*MODISMO* **estar en la ~** to be in the thick of it, be where the action is

chuchumeca* SF (*Andes, Cono Sur*) whore, tart*, hooker (*EEUU**)

chuchumeco* SM [1] (*Méx*) (= *enano*) dwarf, runt
[2] (= *tacaño*) mean person, skinflint
[3] (*Cono Sur*) (= *enfermizo*) sickly person; (= *derrochador*) wastrel
[4] (*Andes*) (= *viejo*) old dodderer
[5] (*Andes, Caribe**) (= *encopetado*) toff*, dude (*EEUU**)
[6] (*Caribe**) (= *idiota*) idiot

chuchurrío* ADJ [1] [*flor, planta*] wilted
[2] [*persona*] down

chuco ADJ [1] (*Andes, CAm, Méx*) [*pescado*] high, off
[2] (*CAm*) (= *asqueroso*) disgusting, filthy

chucrú SM, **chucrut** SM, **chucruta** SF sauerkraut

chueca SF [1] (*Bot*) stump
[2] (*Anat*) *round head of a bone*
[3] (= *broma*) practical joke, prank; **gastar una ~ a algn** to play a joke on sb

chueco ADJ (*LAm*) [1] (= *torcido*) crooked, bent; **un negocio ~** a crooked deal*
[2] (= *patizambo*) bandy-legged
[3] (*Andes, Cono Sur*) (= *patituerto*) pigeon-toed
[4] (*Méx*) (= *manco*) one-armed; (= *con una sola pierna*) one-legged
[5] (*Méx*) (= *de mala vida*) loose-living; (= *sospechoso*) suspicious

chufa SF [1] (= *tubérculo*) tiger nut; **horchata de ~** *drink made from tiger nuts*
[2] (*) (= *puñetazo*) bash*, punch
[3] (†*) (= *peseta*) peseta

chufeta SF = **chufleta**

chufla SF joke, merry quip; **a ~** jokingly; **tomar algo a ~** to take sth as a joke

chuflarse ▸conjug 1a◂ VPR to joke, make jokes

chuflay SM (*Cono Sur*) (= *bebida*) punch

chufleta SF [1] (= *broma*) joke
[2] (= *mofa*) taunt

chufletear ▸conjug 1a◂ VI [1] (= *bromear*) to joke
[2] (= *mofarse*) to jeer

chuico SM (*Chile*) demijohn

chula SF [1] (= *madrileña*) woman from the back streets (*of Madrid*), low-class woman, coarse woman
[2] (= *charra*) loud wench, flashy female, brassy girl
[3] (*LAm*) (= *novia*) girlfriend

chulada SF [1] (= *grosería*) coarse thing
[2] (= *truco*) mean trick
[3] (*) **¡qué ~ de moto!** wow! what a fantastic bike!*
[4] (*) = **chulería 4**

chulángano†‡ SM roughneck‡, tough*

chulapa SF *Madrid girl in traditional dress*

chulear* ▸conjug 1a◂ VT [1] (= *reírse de*) to make fun of
[2] (= *afanar*) to pinch*, swipe*
[3] [+ *prostitutas*] to live off

chulería SF [1] (= *encanto*) natural charm, winning ways
[2] (= *vulgaridad*) commonness, vulgarity
[3] (= *bravuconada*) **déjate de ~s conmigo** don't get all cocky with me*
[4] (*) (= *cosa bonita*) **esa moto es una ~** that bike is really nice; **me he comprado una ~ de camiseta** I've bought a really nice *o* gorgeous T-shirt

chulesco ADJ = **chulo 1**

chuleta Ⓐ SF [1] [*de carne*] chop, cutlet ▸ **chuleta de cerdo** pork chop ▸ **chuleta de cordero** lamb chop ▸ **chuleta de ternera** veal chop, veal cutlet
[2] (*Cos*) insert
[3] (*Téc*) filling
[4] (*) (= *golpe*) punch, bash*
[5] (*Escol**) crib*, trot (*EEUU*)
[6] **chuletas*** (= *patillas*) sideburns, sideboards
[7] (*Golf**) divot
Ⓑ SM (*) (= *fanfarrón*) show-off*; (= *persona agresiva*) pushy person*; (= *fresco*) cheeky individual*; = **chulo D**
Ⓒ ADJ INV cheeky*, smart (*EEUU**), sassy (*EEUU**)

chuletada SF barbecue, cookout (*EEUU*) (*mainly consisting of chops*)

chuletón SM large steak, T-bone steak

chulillo SM (*Andes*) tradesman's assistant

chulleco ADJ (*Cono Sur*) twisted, crooked

chullo SM (*Perú*) woollen cap

chulo Ⓐ ADJ (*) [1] (= *arrogante*) cocky*; **vino uno muy ~ y me insultó** this guy comes up to me all cocky *o* bold as brass and insulted me*; **una mujer se abanicaba, muy chula ella, en la ventana** a woman was fanning herself in the window, bold as brass *o* as brazen as you like; **ponerse ~: se puso en plan ~** he got all cocky*; **no te pongas ~ conmigo** don't get cocky with me*
[2] (= *bonito*) **¡qué vestido más ~!** what a lovely dress!; **¡qué ~ me ha quedado el dibujo!** my drawing looks great!; **chica, estás chulísima** (*LAm*) you look gorgeous
Ⓑ ADV (*CAm, Méx**) well; **jugar ~** to play well
Ⓒ SMF (*Hist*) *typical working-class person from Madrid*
Ⓓ SM [1] (*) (*tb* **~ putas**) pimp
[2] (*Col**) (= *buitre*) vulture, buzzard (*EEUU*)
[3] (*Taur*) *bullfighter's assistant*

chulón ADJ (*CAm*) naked

chuma SF (*Andes, Cono Sur*) drunkenness

chumacera SF [1] (*Mec*) ball bearing
[2] (*Náut*) rowlock, oarlock (*EEUU*)

chumado* ADJ (*Arg*) drunk, tight*

chumarse* ▸conjug 1a◂ VPR (*Arg*) to get drunk

chumbar ▸conjug 1a◂ VT [1] (*Cono Sur*) [*perro*] to attack, go for; **¡chúmbale!** at him, boy!
[2] (*Andes*) (= *fusilar*) to shoot
[3] (*Andes*) [+ *bebé*] to swaddle

chumbe SM (*LAm*) sash

chumbera SF prickly pear

chumbo SM [1] (*Bot*) prickly pear
[2] (*Andes***) (= *pene*) prick**

chumeco SM (*CAm*) apprentice

chuminada* SF [1] (= *tontería*) silly thing, piece of nonsense
[2] (= *detalle*) petty detail

chumino** SM cunt**

chumpa SF (*CAm*) jacket

chumpi SM (*Andes*) = **chumbe**

chumpipe SM (*CAm*) turkey

chumpipear ▸conjug 1a◂ VI (*CAm*) to wander about

chunche* SM (*CAm*) whatsit*, thingumabob*

chuncho/a (*Perú pey*) Ⓐ ADJ [1] (= *salvaje*) savage, rustic
[2] (= *inculto*) uncivilized
[3] (= *tímido*) bashful, shy
Ⓑ SM/F savage Indian

chunco ADJ (*Andes, CAm*) = **choco**[3]

chuneco/a* (*CAm*) ADJ, SM/F Jamaican

chunga* SF fun; **contar ~s** to crack jokes*; **decir algo de ~** to say sth jokingly *o* in fun; **estar de ~** to be in a joking mood; **en plan de ~** for a laugh

chungarse* ▸conjug 1h◂ VPR = **chunguearse**

chungo‡ ADJ [1] [*lavadora, televisor*] bust*; [*fruta*] rotten
[2] (= *desagradable*) nasty
[3] (= *feo*) ugly, hideous
[4] (= *con mala pinta*) dodgy*, dicey*
[5] (= *enfermo*) **he estado un poco ~** I've been feeling a bit rop(e)y *o* dodgy*

chungón/ona* SM/F joker, tease

chunguearse* ▸conjug 1a◂ VPR to crack jokes*; **~ de algn** to make fun of sb

chuño SM (*LAm*) potato starch

chupa[1] SF ✦**MODISMO poner a algn como ~ de dómine** to give sb a real ticking off*; **en la prensa le pusieron como ~ de dómine** they gave him a tremendous pasting in the press*

chupa[2]* SF (= *chaqueta*) leather jacket

chupa[3] SF (*LAm*) (= *borrachera*) drunkenness; (= *reunión*) drinking session

chupachupa‡ SMF sucker‡

chupacirios* SMF INV holy Willie*

chupada SF [1] [*de biberón, caramelo*] suck
[2] (*en pipa*) pull, puff; **dar ~s a la pipa** to puff away at one's pipe; ✦**MODISMO se cree la última ~ del mate** (*Cono Sur**) he thinks he's the cat's pyjamas *o* the bees knees*

chupadero* SM (*Arg*) (*1975-81*) *secret military prison*

chupado/a Ⓐ ADJ [1] (= *flaco*) gaunt, skinny*; **está ~ de cara** his face looks *o* he looks very gaunt, he looks very hollow-cheeked
[2] [*falda*] tight
[3] **estar ~ de frío** to be pinched with cold
[4] **estar ~*** (= *borracho*) to be drunk
[5] **está ~*** (= *fácil*) it's dead easy*
Ⓑ SM/F (*Cono Sur**) (= *desaparecido*) missing person

chupador SM [1] teething ring
[2] (*LAm**) (= *borracho*) drunkard

chupaflor SM (*LAm*) hummingbird

chupagasolina* Ⓐ ADJ INV gas-guzzling*, heavy on petrol
Ⓑ SM INV gas-guzzler*

chupalla SF (*Cono Sur, Méx*) straw hat

chupamangas‡ SM INV (*Andes, Cono Sur*), **chupamedias**‡ SM INV (*Andes, Cono Sur*) creep‡, bootlicker*, brown-nose (*EEUU*‡)

chupamirto SM (*Caribe, Méx*) hummingbird

chupandina* SF (*Cono Sur*) boozy party*

chupar ▸conjug 1a◂ Ⓐ VT [1] (= *succionar*) [+ *biberón, caramelo, bolígrafo*] to suck; [+ *pipa*] to puff at, puff on; **el trabajo le está chupando la salud** his work is undermining his health; **chupó lo que pudo mientras estuvo en la organización** he milked the organization for all he could while he was there; **le chupan el dinero** they're milking him dry; ✦**MODISMOS ~ cámara*** to get as much (media) exposure as possible; **~ el balón*** (*Ftbl*) to hog the ball; **~ la sangre a algn** to bleed sb dry, take sb for everything they've got
[2] (*) (= *aguantar*) to put up with, take; ✦**MODISMO ~ banquillo** (*Ftbl*) to sit on the substitutes' bench
[3] [*planta*] [+ *agua*] to absorb, take in, take up
[4] (*) (= *beber*) to drink, knock back*
[5] **chupársela a algn**** to suck sb off**
Ⓑ VI to suck; ✦**MODISMO ~ del bote*** to line one's pocket
Ⓒ **chuparse** VPR [1] (= *succionar*) **~se el dedo** (*lit*) to suck one's finger; **¿tú te crees que me chupo el dedo?** (*fig*) do you think I was born yesterday?, do you take me for a mug?*; ✦**MODISMO ~se los dedos***: **la paella estaba para ~se los dedos** the paella was absolutely delicious; **hacen unas hamburguesas para ~se los dedos** their hamburgers are to die for *o* are finger-licking good (*hum*)
[2] (*) (= *aguantar*) **nos chupamos toda la conferencia de pie** we had to go through the whole of the lecture standing; **tuve que ~me cuatro horas de tren** I had to sit in a train for four hours; **~se un insulto** (*LAm*) to swallow an insult; ✦**MODISMO ¡chúpate esa!** put that in your pipe and smoke it!*
[3] (*Med*) to waste away

chupasangres* SM INV (*Cono Sur pey*) bloodsucker

chupatintas* SM INV (*pey*) penpusher, pencil pusher (*EEUU*)

chupe SM [1] (*Andes, Cono Sur Culin*) (= *guiso*) stew
[2] (*Cono Sur*) (= *tapa*) snack

chupeta SF (*Náut*) roundhouse

chupete SM [1] [*de niño*] dummy, pacifier (*EEUU*)

[2] (LAm) (= pirulí) lollipop
[3] (LAm) (= chupada) suck
[4] ✦MODISMO de ~ delicious
chupetear ▸conjug 1a◂ Ⓐ VT [+ polo] to suck; [+ helado] to lick
Ⓑ VI to suck, suck slowly
chupeteo SM sucking
chupetón* SM lovebite, hickey (EEUU*)
chupi* Ⓐ ADJ super*, brilliant*
Ⓑ ADV pasarlo ~ to have a great time*
chupín SM (Arg) fish and potato stew
chupinazo SM [1] (= disparo) loud bang
[2] (Dep) hard kick, fierce shot
chupinudo* ADJ = chupi
chupito* SM [de bebida alcohólica] shot*
chupo SM [1] (LAm Med) boil
[2] (Andes) (= biberón) baby's bottle
chupón/ona Ⓐ SM/F (*) (= parásito) sponger*
Ⓑ SM [1] (Bot) sucker
[2] (= piruleta) lollipop ► chupón de caramelo toffee apple
[3] (LAm) (= chupete) dummy, pacifier (EEUU); (= biberón) baby's bottle
[4] (Méx) teat
[5] (Andes, Caribe) [de pipa] puff, pull
[6] (Andes) boil
chupóptero* SM bloodsucker
churdón SM (= fruta) raspberry; (= planta) raspberry cane; (= jarabe) raspberry syrup, raspberry purée
churi‡ SM chiv‡, knife
churo[1] ADJ (Andes, Cono Sur) handsome, attractive
churo[2] SM [1] (Andes Mús) coiled wind instrument
[2] (Andes) (= escalera) spiral staircase
[3] (Andes) (= rizo) curl
[4] (Andes) (= cárcel) nick‡, jail, can (EEUU*)
churra[1] SF (Andes, Cono Sur) girl
churra[2]* SF (= suerte) luck, jam‡
churrasco SM [1] (= filete a la parrilla) barbecued meat
[2] (Cono Sur) (= filete) steak
churrasquear ▸conjug 1a◂ VI (Cono Sur) to eat steak
churrasquería SF barbecue stall
churre[1] SF thick grease, grime
churre[2] SM (Andes) bloke‡, guy*
churrería SF shop or stall selling churros
churrero/a Ⓐ ADJ (‡) lucky, jammy‡
Ⓑ SM/F person who makes and sells "churros"
churrete SM dirty mark (esp on a child's face)
churretear ▸conjug 1a◂ VT (LAm) to stain, dirty
churretón SM dirty mark, esp on a child's face
churria SF [1] (Méx, Col) stain
[2] churrias (Andes, CAm, Caribe*) (= diarrea) runs*, trots*
churriento ADJ [1] (= sucio) filthy
[2] (LAm) (= suelto) loose
churrigueresco ADJ [1] (Arquit) churrigueresque
[2] (= excesivamente adornado) excessively ornate
churro Ⓐ ADJ [lana] coarse
Ⓑ SM [1] (Culin) flour fritter eaten with coffee or hot chocolate; ✦MODISMO venderse como ~s to sell like hot cakes
[2] (*) (= chapuza) botch, mess; el dibujo ha salido hecho un ~ the sketch came out all wrong
[3] (*) (= suerte) fluke
[4] (Andes, Cono Sur*) attractive person, dish*
[5] (‡) (= pene) prick‡
[6] (Méx*) bad film

> **CHURROS**
>
> *Churros, long fritters made with flour and water, are popular in much of Spain and are often eaten with thick hot chocolate either for breakfast or as a snack. In Madrid, they eat a thicker variety of churro called a porra.*

churrullero ADJ talkative, gossipy
churruscar ▸conjug 1g◂ Ⓐ VT to fry till crisp
Ⓑ VI to sizzle
Ⓒ churruscarse VPR to burn
churrusco[1] SM burnt toast
churrusco[2] ADJ (Andes, CAm) [pelo] kinky, curly
churumbel* SM [1] (= niño) kid*
[2] (= tipo) bloke*, guy*
churumbela SF [1] (Mús) flageolet
[2] (CAm) maté cup
[3] (Andes) (= pipa) short-stemmed pipe
[4] (Andes) (= preocupación) worry, care
churumen* SM nous*, savvy*
chus EXCL ✦MODISMO no decir ~ ni mus* not to say a word
chuscada SF witty remark, joke
chusco[1] ADJ [1] (= gracioso) funny, droll
[2] (Andes) [perro] mongrel; [caballo] ordinary; [persona] coarse, ill-mannered
chusco[2] SM un ~ de pan a hunk of bread
chuse SM (Andes) blanket
chusma SF rabble, riffraff
chusmaje SM (LAm) = chusma
chuspa SF (LAm) bag, pouch
chusquero* SM (Mil) ranker
chut SM [1] (Dep) shot (at goal)
[2] (‡) (= de droga) shot*, fix‡
chuta[1]‡ SF [1] (= jeringuilla) needle [2] = chut 2
chuta[2]‡ EXCL ¡chuta! (Cono Sur) good God!, good heavens!
chutador(a) SM/F (Dep) shooter
chutar ▸conjug 1a◂ Ⓐ VI [1] (Dep) to shoot (at goal)
[2] está que chuta* [persona] he's hopping mad*; [comida] it's scalding hot
[3] (*) (= ir bien) to go well; dale diez euros y va que chuta give him ten euros and he'll be more than happy
Ⓑ chutarse VPR (*) [+ heroína] to shoot up*
chutazo* SM fierce drive, fierce shot (at goal)
chute SM [1] (Dep) shot (at goal)
[2] (*) [de droga] shot*, fix*
chuzar ▸conjug 1f◂ VT (Andes) to prick
chuzo Ⓐ SM [1] (= bastón) spiked stick
[2] (= aguijón) prick, goad; (CAm) [de alacrán] sting; ✦MODISMOS caer ~s de punta* to rain cats and dogs, pelt down*; echar ~s* to brag
[3] (Mil, Hist) pike
[4] (Andes) shoe
[5] (Cono Sur) (= zapapico) pickaxe, pickax (EEUU)
[6] (Caribe, Cono Sur) (= látigo) whip
[7] (CAm) (= pico) beak
[8] (‡) (= pene) prick‡
Ⓑ ADJ (CAm*) [pelo] lank
chuzón ADJ [1] (= astuto) wily
[2] (= ingenioso) witty, amusing
chuzonada SF piece of tomfoolery, piece of buffoonery
CI Ⓐ SM ABR (= coeficiente de inteligencia o intelectual) IQ
Ⓑ SF ABR (LAm) (= cédula de identidad) ID
CIA SF ABR (EEUU) (= Central Intelligence Agency) CIA
cía SF hip bone
Cía. ABR (= Compañía) Co
cianhídrico ADJ hydrocyanic
cianotipia SF, cianotipo SM blueprint
cianuro SM cyanide ► cianuro potásico potassium cyanide
ciar ▸conjug 1c◂ VI [1] (= ir hacia atrás) to go backwards, back up; (Náut) to go astern
[2] (= cambiar de opinión) to back down
ciática SF sciatica
ciático ADJ sciatic
cibercafé SM cybercafe
ciberespacial ADJ cyberspace antes de s
ciberespacio SM cyberspace
cibernauta SMF cybernaut
cibernética SF cybernetics sing
cibernético ADJ cybernetic
ciberpunk SM cyberpunk
cibersexo SM cybersex
ciberterrorismo SM cyberterrorism
ciberterrorista SMF cyberterrorist
cicatear ▸conjug 1a◂ VI to be stingy, be mean
cicatería SF stinginess, meanness
cicatero/a Ⓐ ADJ stingy, mean
Ⓑ SM/F miser, skinflint
cicatriz SF [1] [de herida] scar
[2] (= mal recuerdo) scar
cicatrización SF healing, cicatrization (frm)
cicatrizar ▸conjug 1f◂ Ⓐ VT to heal
Ⓑ cicatrizarse VPR to heal, heal up, form a scar
Cicerón SM Cicero
cicerone SMF guide, cicerone
ciceroniano ADJ Ciceronian
ciclamato SM cyclamate
ciclamen SM, ciclamino SM cyclamen
cíclico ADJ cyclic, cyclical
ciclismo SM cycling ► ciclismo de montaña mountain biking ► ciclismo en ruta road racing
ciclista Ⓐ ADJ cycle antes de s; vuelta ~ cycle race
Ⓑ SMF cyclist
ciclo SM [1] (en hechos repetidos) cycle; un ~ reproductor de corta duración a short reproductive cycle; empieza un nuevo ~ económico a new economic cycle is beginning ► ciclo circadiano circadian cycle ► ciclo de instrucción instruction cycle ► ciclo del nitrógeno nitrogen cycle ► ciclo de vida life cycle ► ciclo menstrual menstrual cycle ► ciclo vital life cycle
[2] [de conferencias] series; [de cine, conciertos] season
[3] (Escol) el segundo ~ de primaria the second stage of primary school
[4] (Literat) cycle; las historias del ~ artúrico the stories of the Arthurian cycle
ciclo-cross SM INV cyclo-cross

ciclomotor SM moped

ciclón SM cyclone; ✦**MODISMO como un ~**: **entró como un ~ en la cocina** he burst into the kitchen; **salió como un ~ del despacho** she dashed out of the office ► **ciclón tropical** tropical cyclone

cíclope SM Cyclops

ciclópeo ADJ gigantic, colossal

ciclorama SM cyclorama

ciclostil SM cyclostyle

ciclostilado ADJ cyclostyled

ciclostilar ▸conjug 1a◂ VT to cyclostyle

ciclostilo SM = **ciclostil**

ciclotrón SM cyclotron

cicloturismo SM touring by bicycle

cicloturista SMF touring cyclist

-cico -cica; (*a veces tb* **-ecico, -ecica**) *ver* **Aspects of Word Formation in Spanish 2**

CICR SM ABR (= **Comité Internacional de la Cruz Roja**) ICRC

cicuta SF hemlock

cidiano ADJ relating to the Cid; **estudios ~s** Cid studies

cidra SF citron

cidracayote SM (*LAm*) gourd, calabash

cidro SM citron, citron tree

ciego/a Ⓐ ADJ 1 (= *invidente*) blind; **es ~ de nacimiento** he has been blind from *o* since birth, he was born blind; **la justicia es ciega** justice is blind; **dejar ~ a algn** to blind sb; **las luces me dejaron ~ por un momento** the lights blinded me for a moment; **el accidente la dejó ciega** she was blinded in the accident; **estar ~** to be blind; **pero ¿estás ~? ¿no ves que el semáforo está en rojo?** are you blind or what? can't you see the lights are red?; **quedarse ~** to go blind; **se quedó ~ después del accidente** he was blinded in the accident, he went blind as a result of the accident; ✦**MODISMO más ~ que un topo** as blind as a bat
2 (*por ofuscación*) 2·1 [*persona*] blind; **~ a** blind to; **~ a las necesidades del resto del mundo** blind to the needs of the rest of the world; **~ de celos** blind with jealousy; **~ de dolor** in absolute agony; **~ de ira** *o* **rabia** blind with rage
2·2 [*violencia*] mindless, senseless; [*fanatismo*] mindless
3 (= *total*) [*confianza, fe*] unquestioning, blind (*pey*); **tenían una confianza ciega en su líder** they had unquestioning *o* (*pey*) blind faith in their leader; **exijo de todos mis hombres una obediencia ciega** I demand unquestioning obedience from all my men
4 (= *bloqueado*) [*arco, entrada*] blind; [*conducto, tubo*] blocked
5 (‡) (= *borracho*) blind drunk*, pissed‡; (*con drogas duras*) high*; (*con drogas blandas*) stoned‡; **ponerse ~ a** *o* **de algo** (= *borracho*) to get pissed on sth‡, get trashed on sth (*EEUU*‡); (*con drogas duras*) to get high on sth*; (*con drogas blandas*) to get stoned on sth‡; (*comiendo*) to stuff o.s. with sth*
6 **a ciegas** 6·1 (= *sin ver*) **andar** *o* **caminar a ciegas** to grope one's way; **avanzamos a ciegas hasta encontrar el interruptor** we groped our way to the light switch; **buscó a ciegas la puerta** he searched blindly for the door, he groped about searching for the door; **volar a ciegas** to fly blind
6·2 (= *sin pensar*) [*actuar, decidir*] in the dark; [*obedecer*] unquestioningly, blindly (*pey*); **creíamos a ciegas todo lo que decía el partido** we unquestioningly *o* (*pey*) blindly believed everything the party said, we believed everything the party said without question; *ver tb* **cita 1.2**
Ⓑ SM/F (= *invidente*) blind man/blind woman; **una organización de ~s** an organization for the blind, a blind people's organization
Ⓒ SM 1 (*Esp*‡) **¡qué ~ llevaba!** [*de alcohol*] he was blind drunk* *o* pissed!‡; [*de drogas duras*] he was high as a kite*; [*de drogas blandas*] he was stoned out of his mind‡
2 (*Anat*) caecum, cecum (*EEUU*)
3 (*Caribe*) (= *claro*) forest clearing

cielito SM 1 (*Mús*) *Argentinian folk dance*
2 (= *apelativo cariñoso*) my love, sweetheart

cielo SM 1 (*Astron, Meteo*) sky; **el ~ está cubierto** the sky is overcast *o* cloudy; **el ~ estaba despejado** it was a cloudless *o* clear day; **a ~ abierto** [*mina, explotación*] opencast, open cut (*EEUU*); **a ~ descubierto** in the open; ✦**MODISMOS cambiar del ~ a la tierra** (*Chile*) to change out of all recognition; **llegar** *o* **venir (como) caído** *o* **llovido del ~** (*inesperado*) to come (totally) out of the blue; (*muy oportuno*) to be a godsend; **irse al ~ con todo y zapatos** (*Méx*): **tú te vas al ~ con todo y zapatos** you'll be blessed in heaven; **juntársele a algn el ~ con la tierra** (*LAm*): **se le juntó el ~ con la tierra** he lost his nerve; **poner a algn por los ~s** to praise sb to the skies; **remover ~ y tierra** to move heaven and earth; **tocar el ~ con las manos** (*Cono Sur, Perú, Col*): **conseguir que me ayude es tocar el ~ con las manos** getting him to help me would be virtually impossible; **si me lo ganara sería como tocar el ~ con las manos** if I won it, it would be like a dream come true; **venírsele a algn el ~ abajo**: **se le vino el ~ abajo** the heavens opened
2 (*Rel*) heaven; **Padre Nuestro que estás en los ~s** Our Father who art in heaven; **¡cielos!** good heavens!; **ganar el ~** to win salvation; **ir al ~** to go to heaven; ✦**MODISMOS clamar al ~**: **es una injusticia que clama al ~** it is a gross injustice; **¡esto clama al ~!** it's an outrage!, it's outrageous!; **estar en el séptimo ~** to be in seventh heaven; **ganar el ~ con rosario ajeno** to cash in on other people's hard work; **ver el ~ abierto**: **cuando me ofrecieron el trabajo vi el ~ abierto** when I was offered the job I saw my chance; **vimos el ~ abierto cuando dijo que podíamos quedarnos en su casa** it was a great relief when he said we could stay in his house
3 (*) (*uso afectivo*) **¡mi ~!** ◊ **¡~ mío!** my love, sweetheart; **el jefe es un ~** the boss is a real sweetie*; **¡has fregado los platos! eres un ~** you've washed the dishes! you're a real angel
4 (= *parte superior*) [*de la boca*] roof; [*de una cama*] canopy; (*CAm*) [*de un coche*] roof ► **cielo máximo** (*Aer*) ceiling
5 (*Arquit*) (*tb* **~ raso**) ceiling

ciempiés SM INV centipede

cien[1] ADJ, PRON (*antes de s, apócope de* **ciento**) a hundred, one hundred; **~ mil** a hundred thousand; **las últimas ~ páginas** the last hundred pages; **diez por ~** ten per cent; **es de lana ~ por ~** it's pure wool, it's a hundred per cent wool; **es español ~ por ~** he's Spanish through and through; **lo apoyo al ~ por ~** I support it wholeheartedly; ✦**MODISMOS estar hasta el ~** (*Andes*) to be on one's last legs; **me pone a ~*** (= *enfadar*) it drives me up the wall*; (= *calentar sexualmente*) it makes me feel horny *o* randy*; *ver tb* **seis**

> **CIEN, CIENTO**
>
> • La traducción de **cien(to)** puede ser **a hundred** o **one hundred**:
>
> Tengo que escribir cien páginas
> ***I've got to write a** o **one hundred pages***
> Murió a la edad de ciento veinte años
> ***He died at the age of a** o **one hundred and twenty***
> Sin embargo, hay que utilizar siempre **one hundred**
>
> • cuando **cien(to)** va detrás de otra cifra:
>
> El curso cuesta dos mil ciento noventa libras
> ***The course costs two thousand one hundred and ninety pounds***
>
> • cuando se quiere precisar que se trata de **cien(to)** y no de doscientos, *etc*:
>
> ***I said "one hundred" not "two hundred"***
>
> *Para otros usos y ejemplos ver las entradas* ***cien y ciento.***

cien[2]‡ SM bog‡, lavatory, john (*EEUU**)

ciénaga SF marsh, swamp

ciencia SF 1 (= *conocimiento*) science; **los avances de la ~** the advances of science; ✦**MODISMOS saber algo a ~ cierta** to know sth for certain *o* for a fact; **no tener mucha ~**: **esto no tiene mucha ~** there's nothing difficult about it ► **ciencia ficción** science fiction ► **ciencia infusa**: **lo sabe por ~ infusa** (*iró*) he has God-given intelligence
2 (= *doctrina*) science, sciences *pl*; **un hombre de ~** a man of science ► **ciencias naturales** natural science *sing* ► **ciencias ocultas** occultism *sing* ► **ciencias sociales** social science, social sciences *pl*
3 **ciencias** (*Educ*) science *sing*, sciences; **estudia una carrera de ~s** she's doing a science degree ► **Ciencias de la Educación** Education *sing* ► **Ciencias de la Información** Media Studies ► **Ciencias Económicas** Economics *sing* ► **Ciencias Empresariales** Business Studies ► **Ciencias Exactas** Exact Sciences ► **Ciencias Físicas** Physical Science *sing* ► **Ciencias Políticas** Political Science *sing*

ciencia-ficción SF science fiction

Cienciología SF Scientology

cieno SM 1 (= *lodo*) mud
2 (= *depósito fluvial*) silt

cienoso ADJ muddy, miry

científicamente ADV scientifically

cientificidad SF scientific nature

científico/a Ⓐ ADJ scientific
Ⓑ SM/F scientist ► **científico/a social** social scientist

cientifismo SM scientific spirit

cientista SMF (*LAm*) scientist; **~ social** social scientist

ciento Ⓐ ADJ, PRON a hundred, one hundred; **~ veinte** one hundred and twenty, a hundred and twenty
Ⓑ SM 1 a hundred, one hundred; **~s de personas** hundreds of people; **te lo he dicho ~s de veces** I've told you hundreds of

times; **varios ~s de profesores** several hundred teachers; **a** *o* **por ~s: casos como éste se producen a** *o* **por ~s** there are cases like this by the hundred, there are hundreds of cases like this; **las víctimas se cuentan a** *o* **por ~s** the death toll runs into hundreds; ✦***MODISMOS*** **dar ~ y raya a algn** to be more than a match for sb; **~ y la madre*: ¡allí había ~ y la madre!** the world and his wife were there*, there were loads of people there*; → CIEN, CIENTO

[2] **por ~** per cent; **el cuarenta y dos por ~ de los estudiantes** forty-two per cent of the students; **hay un cinco por ~ de descuento** there is a five per cent discount; **el ~ por ~** a *o* one hundred per cent; **el ~ por ~ de las participantes son mujeres** a *o* one hundred per cent of the participants are women; **los hoteles están al ~ por ~ de su capacidad** the hotels are full to capacity, the hotels have a hundred per cent occupancy

cierne SM blossoming, budding; **en ~(s)** (*Bot*) in blossom; (*fig*) in its infancy; **es un ajedrecista en ~s** he's a budding chess champion

cierra *etc ver* **cerrar**

cierre SM [1] (= *acto*) [*de verja, puerta*] (*gen*) closing, shutting; (*con llave*) locking; (*automático*) central locking; [*de edificio, establecimiento, frontera*] closing; **un dispositivo especial controla el ~ de la puerta** the door is closed *o* shut by a special device; **se está incumpliendo el horario de ~ de los bares** bars are not observing closing time; **cuatro horas después del ~ de los colegios electorales** four hours after the polling stations closed; **el mal tiempo obligó al ~ del aeropuerto** the airport was forced to close due to the bad weather ► **cierre empresarial, cierre patronal** lockout

[2] (= *fin*) [*de una emisión*] closedown; [*de campaña electoral*] end, close; [*de la Bolsa*] close; [*de año fiscal*] end; **el mitin de ~ de la campaña electoral** the final rally of the electoral campaign; **al ~: al ~ de esta edición de noticias** at the end of this news bulletin; **al ~ de impresión** at the time of going to press; **al ~ de la sesión de ayer** at the close of trading yesterday; **precio de ~** closing price

[3] [*de negocio, carretera, instalaciones*] closure; **los vecinos piden el ~ de la factoría** local residents are demanding the closure of the factory; **muchos comerciantes se verán obligados al ~ de sus comercios** many traders will find themselves having to close down their businesses

[4] (= *mecanismo*) [*de maleta, puerta*] catch; [*de collar, pulsera, libro*] clasp; [*de vestido*] fastener, snap fastener ► **cierre antirrobo** anti-theft lock ► **cierre centralizado** (*Aut*) central locking ► **cierre de dirección** (*Aut*) steering lock ► **cierre eclair** (*Chile*) zip, zip fastener, zipper (*esp EEUU*) ► **cierre hermético** airtight seal ► **cierre metálico** (= *persiana*) metal shutter; (= *cremallera*) metal zip ► **cierre relámpago** (*Cono Sur, Perú*) zip, zip fastener, zipper (*esp EEUU*)

[5] **echar el ~** [5·1] (*a un local, comercio*) (*temporalmente*) to close; (*definitivamente*) to close down; **estaba echando el ~ a la tienda** he was locking the shop up *o* locking up the shop

[5·2] (*Esp**) (= *callar*) **¡echa el ~!** give it a rest!; **echar el ~ a algn** to shut sb up

cierrecler SM (*Chile*) zip, zip fastener, zipper (*esp EEUU*)

cierro SM (*Chile*) fence

ciertamente ADV certainly; **no era ~ uno de los más inteligentes** he was certainly not one of the brightest

cierto ADJ [1] (= *verdadero*) true; **los rumores resultaron ser ~s** the rumours turned out to be true; **¿es ~ eso?** is that really so?, is that true?; **ha mejorado mucho, ¿no es ~?** it has improved a lot, don't you think?; **es ~, es mejor que nos vayamos** yes *o* you're right, I think we'd better go; **~, es un problema grave** it's certainly a serious problem; **estar en lo ~** to be right; **lo ~ es que** the fact is that, the truth of the matter is that; **nadie habló sobre ello pero lo ~ es que todos estaban preocupados** nobody talked about it but the fact is *o* the truth of the matter is that everyone was worried; **es ~ que** it's true that; **no es ~ que mi mujer me haya abandonado** it is not true that my wife has walked out on me

[2] (= *seguro*) certain, sure; **les espera una muerte cierta** they are heading for certain death; **hay indicios ~s de mejoría** there are clear signs of improvement; **lo único ~ es que ...** the only sure thing is that ...; **saber algo de ~** to know sth for certain

[3] (*uso indefinido*) [3·1] (*en sing*) a certain; **cierta persona que yo conozco** a certain person I know; **no me gusta ~ tipo de literatura** there's a certain type of literature which I don't like; **ocurre con cierta frecuencia** it happens fairly frequently; **en todos sus movimientos había un ~ aire de misterio** everything he did had a certain air of mystery about it; **me alejé de allí con una cierta sensación de preocupación** I left there feeling a little anxious, I left there with a certain feeling of anxiety; **~ día de mayo** one day in May; **en cierta ocasión** on one occasion, once; **durante ~ tiempo** for a while; **estuvieron buscándolo durante ~ tiempo** they looked for it for a while; **las monedas nacionales se mantendrían en uso durante un ~ tiempo** national currencies would continue to be used for a (certain) time; *ver tb* **edad 1, manera 2, modo 2, punto 8, sentido B6**

[3·2] (*en pl*) some, certain; **es mejor no hablar de ciertas cosas** some *o* certain things are better not discussed

[4] **por ~** by the way, incidentally; **por ~, ¿qué es de tu hermano?** by the way, *o* incidentally, what's your brother doing now?; **un libro que, por ~, recomiendo totalmente** a book which, by the way, *o* incidentally, I would thoroughly recommend

cierva SF hind

ciervo SM (*Zool*) (*gen*) deer; (*macho*) stag, buck; (*Culin*) venison ► **ciervo común** red deer ► **ciervo volante** stag beetle

cierzo SM north wind

CIF SM ABR (= **Cédula de Identificación Fiscal**) company or personal tax code

cifosis SF INV (*Med*) kyphosis

cifra SF [1] (= *dígito*) figure; **las ~s dadas por el Ministerio** the figures provided by the Ministry; **un número de seis ~s** a six-figure number ► **cifras de ventas** sales figures

[2] (= *cantidad*) number; **piensa una ~** think of a number; **la ~ de parados es preocupante** the number of unemployed people is worrying; **la ~ oficial de muertos** the official death toll; **ganan ~s astronómicas** they earn astronomical sums

[3] **en ~** (= *codificado*) coded, in code

cifradamente ADV [1] (= *en clave*) in code

[2] (= *resumiendo*) in brief, in a shortened form

cifrado (A) ADJ [*mensaje*] coded, in code

(B) SM (en)coding, ciphering

cifrar ▸conjug 1a◂ (A) VT [1] [+ *mensaje*] to code, write in code; (*Ling*) to encode

[2] [+ *esperanzas, ilusiones*] to pin, place (**en** on)

[3] [+ *ganancias, pérdidas*] to calculate; **cifran las pérdidas por el terremoto en miles de millones** losses caused by the earthquake have been calculated at billions

[4] [+ *discurso, explicación*] (= *compendiar*) to summarize; (= *abreviar*) to abbreviate

(B) **cifrarse** VPR **todas las esperanzas se cifran en él** all hopes are centred on him

cigala SF Dublin Bay prawn

cigarra SF cicada

cigarral SM (*Toledo*) *country house on the banks of the Tagus*

cigarrera SF [1] (= *estuche*) cigar case

[2] (= *obrera*) cigar maker; (= *vendedora*) cigar seller

cigarrería SF (*LAm*) (= *tienda*) tobacconist's (shop), tobacco *o* smoke shop (*EEUU*); (= *fábrica*) tobacco factory

cigarrero SM (= *obrero*) cigar maker; (= *vendedor*) cigar seller

cigarrillo SM cigarette; **cajetilla** *o* **paquete de ~s** pack(et) of cigarettes; **cartón de ~s** box of cigarettes; **liar un ~** to roll a cigarette

cigarro SM [1] (= *cigarrillo*) cigarette

[2] (*tb* **~ puro**) cigar ► **cigarro habano** Havana cigar

cigoto SM zygote

ciguato ADJ [1] (*Caribe, Méx*) (= *simple*) simple, stupid

[2] (*Caribe, Méx*) (= *pálido*) pale, anaemic, anemic (*EEUU*)

cigüeña SF [1] (*Orn*) stork

[2] (*Mec*) crank, handle; (*Náut*) winch, capstan

[3] (*CAm Mús*) barrel organ

[4] (*Caribe Ferro*) bogie, bogy

cigüeñal SM crankshaft

CIJ SF ABR (= **Corte Internacional de Justicia**) ICJ

cija SF (= *cuadra*) sheep shed; (= *pajar*) hayloft

cilampa SF (*CAm*) drizzle

cilampear ▸conjug 1a◂ VI (*CAm*) to drizzle

cilantro SM (*Bot, Culin*) coriander

cilicio SM (= *vestidura áspera*) hair shirt; (= *con pinchos*) *spiked belt or chain etc worn by penitents*

cilindrada SF cylinder capacity

cilindradora SF steamroller, road roller

cilindraje SM cylinder capacity

cilindrar ▸conjug 1a◂ VT to roll, roll flat

cilíndrico ADJ cylindrical

cilindrín‡ SM cigarette, fag*; **incinerar el ~** to light up

cilindro SM [1] (*Mat, Téc*) cylinder; (*en máquina de escribir*) roller ► **cilindro compresor, cilindro de caminos** steamroller, road roller

➤ LENGUA Y USO: **cierto 1** 53.3, 53.4 **2** 53.6

2 (*Méx*) (= *organillo*) barrel organ
3 (*) (= *sombrero de copa*) top hat

cilla SF 1 (= *granero*) tithe barn, granary
2 (= *diezmo*) tithe

cima SF 1 [*de montaña*] top, summit; **la ~ del Aconcagua** the top *o* summit of Aconcagua; **dieron ~ a la montaña** they reached *o* got to the summit *o* top of the mountain; **las ~s más altas de los Alpes** the highest peaks in the Alps
2 (= *cúspide*) **está en la ~ de su carrera** she is at the peak *o* height of her career; **llegó a la ~ del éxito profesional** she achieved the pinnacle of success in her profession; **conoció las más altas ~s del poder** he knew *o* experienced the very heights of power; **han dado ~ a las negociaciones** they brought the negotiations to a successful conclusion
3 [*de árbol*] top

cimarra SF **hacer ~** (*Cono Sur*) to play truant

cimarrón/ona Ⓐ ADJ 1 (*LAm Bot, Zool*) wild, untamed
2 (*LAm*) [*persona*] (= *inculto*) rough, uncouth; (= *vago*) lazy; **negro ~** (*Hist*) runaway slave, fugitive slave
3 (*Cono Sur*) [*mate*] bitter, unsweetened
Ⓑ SM/F (*Hist*) runaway slave, maroon
Ⓒ SM (*Cono Sur*) unsweetened mate

cimarronear ▸conjug 1a◂ VI (*LAm*) to run away

cimba SF 1 (*Andes*) (= *cuerda*) plaited rope of hard leather
2 (*Andes*) (= *trenza*) pigtail
3 (*Andes*) (= *escala*) rope ladder

címbalo SM cymbal

cimbel SM 1 (= *señuelo*) decoy (*also fig*)
2 (‡) [*de hombre*] prick‡

cimborio SM, **cimborrio** SM 1 (*Arquit*) (= *cúpula*) dome; (= *base*) base of a dome
2 (*Min*) roof

cimbrar ▸conjug 1a◂ VT 1 (= *agitar*) to shake, swish, swing; (= *curvar*) to bend
2 **~ a algn*** to clout sb (with a stick); **le cimbró de un porrazo** he clouted him with his stick

cimbreante ADJ swaying

cimbrear ▸conjug 1a◂ Ⓐ VT (= *hacer oscilar*) to swish, swing; (= *curvar*) to bend; (= *agitar*) to shake
Ⓑ VI to swing round
Ⓒ **cimbrearse** VPR 1 (= *balancearse*) to sway; (= *curvarse*) to bend; (= *agitarse*) to shake; **~se al viento** to sway in the wind
2 (= *andar con garbo*) to walk gracefully

cimbreño ADJ [*vara*] pliant, flexible; [*talle*] willowy, lithe

cimbreo SM (= *balanceo*) swaying; (= *agitación*) shaking; (= *curvado*) bending

cimbrón SM 1 (*Andes, CAm, Cono Sur*) (= *sacudida*) shudder
2 (*LAm*) [*de lazo*] crack
3 (= *tirón*) jerk, yank*, tug
4 (*Cono Sur, Méx*) (= *espadazo*) *blow with the flat of a sword*
5 (*Andes*) (= *dolor*) sharp pain

cimbronada SF, **cimbronazo** SM 1 (*Andes, Cono Sur, Méx*) = **cimbrón**
2 (*Caribe*) earthquake

cimentación SF 1 (= *cimientos*) foundation
2 (= *acción*) laying of foundations

cimentar ▸conjug 1j◂ VT 1 (*Arquit*) to lay the foundations of *o* for
2 (= *fundar*) to found, establish
3 (= *reforzar*) [+ *relaciones, cooperación*] to strengthen, cement
4 [+ *oro*] to refine

cimera SF crest (*tb Heráldica*)

cimero ADJ (= *superior*) [*pico*] highest, topmost; [*puesto*] highest; [*proyecto, figura*] crowning, finest

cimiento SM (*Arquit*) foundation; [*de amistad, sociedad*] foundation; **abrir los ~s** to dig the foundations; **echar los ~s de algo** to lay the foundations for sth

cimitarra SF scimitar

cimpa SF (*Andes*) = **cimba**

cinabrio SM cinnabar

cinc SM zinc

cincel SM chisel

cincelado SM (= *labrado*) chiselling; (= *grabado*) engraving

cincelador SM 1 (= *persona*) (*en metal*) engraver; (*en piedra*) stone cutter
2 (= *herramienta*) (chipping) chisel, chipping hammer

cincelar ▸conjug 1a◂ VT 1 [+ *piedra, mármol*] to chisel, carve, cut; [+ *metal*] engrave
2 [+ *proyecto*] to fine-tune; [+ *memorias*] to be specific about

cincha SF 1 [*de caballo*] girth, saddle strap; ✦***MODISMO*** **a revienta ~s** (= *apresuradamente*) at breakneck speed, hurriedly; (*LAm*) (= *con renuencia*) reluctantly
2 (*para sillas*) webbing
3 (*Andes*) **tener ~** to have some black/Indian blood in one

cinchada SF (*Cono Sur, Méx*) tug-of-war

cinchar ▸conjug 1a◂ Ⓐ VT [+ *caballo*] to girth, secure the girth of; (*Téc*) to band, hoop, secure with hoops
Ⓑ VI (*Cono Sur**) (= *trabajar*) to work hard; **~ por** (= *apoyar*) to root for

cincho SM (*gen*) belt, girdle; (= *aro*) iron hoop, metal band; (*CAm, Caribe, Méx*) = **cincha 1**

cinchona SF (*LAm*) quinine bark

cinco Ⓐ ADJ INV, PRON (*gen*) five; (*ordinal, en la fecha*) fifth; **las ~** five o'clock; **le escribí el día ~** I wrote to him on the fifth; ✦***MODISMOS*** **estar sin ~*** ◊ **no tener ni ~*** to be broke*; **le dije cuántas son ~** I told him a thing or two; **no estar en sus ~*** to be off one's rocker*; **saber cuántas son ~** to know what's what; **tener los ~ muy listos*** to be light-fingered; **¡vengan esos ~!*** shake on it!*
Ⓑ SM 1 (= *número*) five; (= *fecha*) fifth; (*Educ*) five (*the pass mark*); **sacar un ~ pelado** to scrape through*
2 (*Ven*) (= *guitarra*) five-stringed guitar
3 (*Méx**) (= *trasero*) bottom, backside*
4 (*CAm, Méx*) (= *moneda*) five-peso piece; *ver tb* **seis**

cincuenta ADJ INV, PRON, SM (*gen*) fifty; (*ordinal*) fiftieth; **los (años) ~** the fifties; ✦***MODISMO*** **cantar las ~ a algn** to haul sb over the coals; *ver tb* **seis**

cincuentañero/a Ⓐ ADJ fiftyish, about fifty
Ⓑ SM/F *person of about fifty, person in his/her fifties*

cincuentavo SM fiftieth part; *ver tb* **sexto B**

cincuentena SF fifty, about fifty; **una ~ de** fifty-odd, fifty or so

cincuentenario SM 50th anniversary

cincuenteno ADJ fiftieth; *ver tb* **sexto A**

cincuentón/ona Ⓐ ADJ fifty-year old, fiftyish
Ⓑ SM/F *person in his/her fifties*

cine SM 1 (= *arte*) cinema; **el ~ español** Spanish cinema; **hacer ~** to make films *o* movies (*esp EEUU*); **de ~: actor de ~** film actor, movie actor (*EEUU*); **festival de ~** film festival; **era una casa de ~*** it was a fairytale house, the house was like something out of a film; **me lo pasé de ~*** I had a fantastic *o* brilliant time, I had a whale of a time* ► **cine de acción** action films *pl*, action movies *pl* (*EEUU*) ► **cine de animación** animated films *pl* ► **cine de arte y ensayo** art cinema ► **cine de autor** auteur cinema ► **cine de aventuras** adventure films *pl*, adventure movies *pl* (*esp EEUU*) ► **cine de terror** horror films *pl*, horror movies *pl* (*esp EEUU*) ► **cine mudo** silent films *pl*, silent movies *pl* ► **cine negro** film noir ► **cine sonoro** talking films *pl*, talkies* *pl*
2 (= *local*) cinema, movie theater (*EEUU*); **¿quieres ir al ~?** do you want to go to the cinema *o* (*esp EEUU*) the movies? ► **cine de barrio** local cinema, local (movie) theater (*EEUU*) ► **cine de verano** open-air cinema, open-air movie theater (*EEUU*)

cine... PREF cine...

cineasta SMF film maker, moviemaker (*EEUU*)

cine-club SM (*pl* **cine-clubs, cine-clubes**) film club

cinefilia SF love of the cinema

cinéfilo/a SM/F (= *aficionado*) film fan, movie fan (*EEUU*); (= *especialista*) film buff*, movie buff (*EEUU*)

cinegética SF hunting, the chase

cinegético ADJ hunting *antes de s*, of the chase

cinema SM cinema, movie theater (*EEUU*)

cinemateca SF film library, film archive

cinemático ADJ cinematic

cinematografía SF cinematography, films, film making, movie making (*EEUU*)

cinematografiar ▸conjug 1a◂ VT to film

cinematográfico ADJ film *antes de s*, cinematographic (*frm*)

cinematógrafo SM 1 (= *cine*) cinema, movie theater (*EEUU*)
2 (= *aparato*) (film) projector

cineración SF incineration

cinerama SM cinerama

cinerario ADJ 1 [*urna*] cinerary
2 = **ceniciento**

cinéreo ADJ ash-grey, ash-gray (*EEUU*), ashen (*liter*)

cineteca SF (*LAm*) film archive

cinética SF kinetics *sing*

cinético ADJ kinetic

cingalés/esa Ⓐ ADJ Sinhalese
Ⓑ SM/F Sinhalese; **los cingaleses** the Sinhalese
Ⓒ SM (*Ling*) Sinhalese

cíngaro/a Ⓐ ADJ gipsy
Ⓑ SM/F gipsy (*esp Hungarian*)

cinguería SF (*Cono Sur*) (= *obra*) sheet-metal work; (= *taller*) sheet-metal shop

cinguero SM (*Cono Sur*) sheet-metal worker

cínicamente ADV cynically

cínico/a Ⓐ ADJ cynical
Ⓑ SM/F cynic

cinismo SM cynicism; **¡qué ~!** how cynical!, what a nerve!*

cinofilia SF [1] (*gen*) dog-fancying, dog-breeding
[2] (= *personas*) dog-fanciers, dog-breeders

cinólogo/a SM/F canine expert

cinta SF [1] (= *tira*) ribbon; **se recogió el pelo con una ~** she tied her hair back with a ribbon ► **cinta adhesiva** adhesive tape ► **cinta aislante, cinta de aislar** (*CAm, Méx*) insulating tape ► **cinta elástica** elastic ► **cinta métrica** tape measure
[2] [*de vídeo, sonido*] tape ► **cinta de audio** audio tape ► **cinta de casete** cassette tape ► **cinta de vídeo** video tape ► **cinta limpiadora** head cleaner, head-cleaning tape ► **cinta magnética** magnetic tape ► **cinta magnetofónica** audio tape ► **cinta virgen** blank tape
[3] (*Cine*) film
[4] (*Téc*) ► **cinta de equipajes** baggage *o* luggage carousel ► **cinta transportadora** conveyor belt
[5] (*Culin*) ► **cinta de cerdo, cinta de lomo** loin of pork
[6] (*Bot*) spider plant

cinteado ADJ beribboned

cintero SM [1] [*de mujer*] girdle
[2] (= *cuerda*) rope

cintillo SM [1] [*de sombrero*] hatband; (*LAm*) (*para pelo*) hairband
[2] (= *anillo*) small ring with jewels
[3] (*Tip*) heading, collective heading
[4] (*Caribe*) (= *bordillo*) kerb, curb (*EEUU*)

cinto SM (= *cinturón*) belt; [*de traje típico, militar*] girdle, sash; **armas de ~** side arms ► **cinto negro** black belt

cintura SF [1] (*Anat*) waist; **me rodeó la ~ con los brazos** she put her arms around my waist; **tiene poca ~** she has a slim waist; **tengo 76cm de ~** my waist (measurement) is 76cm; **de ~ para abajo** from the waist down; **con la dieta redujo unos centímetros de ~** with his diet he reduced his waistline by a few centimetres, with his diet he took a few centimetres off his waistline ► **cintura de avispa** wasp waist
[2] [*de falda, pantalón*] waist; **un pantalón ancho de ~** a pair of trousers that are loose-fitting around the waist; **un vestido alto de ~** a high-waisted dress; ✦*MODISMO* **meter a algn en ~** to bring sb into line, make sb toe the line

cinturilla SF waistband

cinturón SM [1] (*gen*) belt; [*de traje típico, militar*] girdle, sash; (†) [*de espada*] sword belt; ✦*MODISMO* **apretarse** *o* **ajustarse el ~** to tighten one's belt ► **cinturón de castidad** chastity belt ► **cinturón de salvamento** lifebelt, life preserver (*EEUU*) ► **cinturón de seguridad** safety belt ► **cinturón salvavidas** lifebelt, life preserver (*EEUU*)
[2] (= *zona*) belt, zone; **el ~ industrial de Madrid** the Madrid industrial belt ► **cinturón de miseria** slum area; (*Méx*) [*de chabolas*] shanty town ► **cinturón verde** green belt
[3] (*Dep*) belt
[4] (= *carretera*) ► **cinturón de circunvalación, cinturón de ronda** ring road, bypass, beltway (*EEUU*)

ciña, ciñendo *etc ver* **ceñir**

CIP SM ABR [1] (*Esp*) = **Club Internacional de Prensa**
[2] (*Esp*) = **Centro de Investigación para la Paz**
[3] (*Perú*) = **Centro Internacional de la Papa**

cipayo SM [1] (*Brit Mil, Hist*) sepoy
[2] (*Cono Sur Pol*) *politician in the service of foreign commerce*

cipe SM (*LAm*) sickly baby

cipo SM (= *monumento*) memorial stone; (= *mojón*) milestone, signpost

cipote Ⓐ ADJ [1] (*Andes, Caribe*) (= *estúpido*) stupid, thick*
[2] (*CAm*) (= *rechoncho*) plump, chubby
Ⓑ SM [1] (*CAm, Caribe*) (= *chico*) lad, youngster
[2] (*Esp***) (= *pene*) prick**
[3] (*CAm*) (= *maza*) Indian club
[4] (*) (= *idiota*) chump*, blockhead*, clod (*EEUU**)
[5] (*Andes**) **~ de chica** smashing girl*; **~ de película** great film*
[6] (*) (= *barriga*) belly, guts*

cipotear** ▸conjug 1a◂ VT (*Esp*) to screw**

ciprés SM cypress (tree)

cipresal SM cypress grove

CIR SM ABR (*Esp Mil*) = **Centro de Instrucción de Reclutas**

circadiano ADJ circadian

circense ADJ circus *antes de s*, of the circus

circo SM [1] (= *espectáculo*) circus ► **circo ambulante** travelling circus, traveling circus (*EEUU*) ► **circo romano** Roman circus
[2] (*Geol*) cirque ► **circo glaciar** glacier cirque, glacial cirque

circonio SM zirconium

circuir ▸conjug 3g◂ VT to encircle, surround

circuitería SF circuitry

circuito SM [1] (= *pista*) circuit, track; **un ~ de fórmula-1** a formula-1 circuit ► **circuito de carreras** racetrack, racecourse (*esp EEUU*), (motor) racing circuit ► **circuito urbano** city circuit, town circuit
[2] (= *círculo*) circuit; **el mejor tenista del ~ profesional** the best tennis player on the professional circuit; **sus películas forman parte del ~ comercial** his films are mainstream commercial films
[3] (*Elec*) circuit; **corto ~** short circuit
[4] (*Telec*) ► **circuito cerrado (de televisión)** closed-circuit (television)
[5] (= *gira*) tour; **un ~ en autobús por Andalucía** a bus tour around Andalusia

circulación SF [1] (*Aut*) traffic; **calle de gran ~** busy street; **en el continente la ~ es por la derecha** on the Continent they drive on the right ► **circulación prohibida** no traffic ► **circulación rodada** vehicular traffic; **"cerrado a la circulación rodada"** "closed to vehicular traffic *o* vehicles" ► **circulación única** (*Méx*) one way (traffic)
[2] (*Med*) circulation ► **circulación de la sangre, circulación sanguínea** circulation of the blood
[3] (*Fin*) circulation; **estar fuera de ~** to be out of circulation, be no longer current; **poner algo en ~** to issue sth, put sth into circulation ► **circulación fiduciaria** paper money, paper currency

circulante ADJ [1] (*gen*) circulating; [*biblioteca*] mobile
[2] (*Fin*) [*capital*] working

circular ▸conjug 1a◂ Ⓐ VI [1] [*vehículo*] to run; **el metro no circula los domingos** the underground does not run on Sundays, there is no underground service on Sundays; **este tren circula a muy alta velocidad** this train goes *o* travels *o* runs at very high speeds; **mañana ~án muchos vehículos por las carreteras** there will be many vehicles on the roads tomorrow; **circule por la izquierda** drive on the left
[2] [*peatón*] to walk; **por favor, circulen por la acera** please walk on the pavement; **¡circulen!** move along!
[3] [*ciudadano, mercancía*] to move around; **los españoles pueden ~ libremente por la UE** Spaniards can move around freely *o* have free movement within the EU
[4] [*moneda*] to be in circulation
[5] [*sangre*] to circulate; [*agua*] to flow
[6] [*rumor*] to go round, circulate
Ⓑ VT to circulate
Ⓒ ADJ (= *redondo*) circular; **un edificio ~** a circular building; **un salón con** *o* **de forma ~** a circular *o* round hall; **el autobús tiene un recorrido ~** the bus follows *o* has a circular route; **una carta ~** a circular
Ⓓ SF (= *carta*) circular

circularidad SF circularity

circulatorio ADJ [1] (*gen*) circulatory
[2] (*Aut*) traffic *antes de s*; **colapso ~** traffic jam, traffic stoppage

círculo SM [1] (= *circunferencia*) circle; **las sillas estaban puestas en ~** the chairs were set out in a circle ► **círculo de giro, círculo de viraje** turning circle ► **círculo máximo** great circle ► **círculo polar antártico** Antarctic Circle ► **círculo polar ártico** Arctic Circle ► **círculo vicioso** vicious circle
[2] (= *grupo*) circle; **los ~s íntimos del ministro confirmaron su dimisión** sources close to the minister confirmed his resignation
[3] (= *club*) club
[4] (= *campo*) scope, compass, extent

circun... PREF circum...

circuncidar ▸conjug 1a◂ VT [1] (*Med*) to circumcise
[2] (= *restringir*) to curtail; (= *moderar*) to moderate

circuncisión SF circumcision

circunciso/a Ⓐ ADJ (*Med*) circumcised
Ⓑ SM/F (*gen*) circumcised man/woman; (*Hist*) *term used in the past to refer to either a Jew or a Moor*

circundante ADJ surrounding

circundar ▸conjug 1a◂ VT to surround

circunferencia SF circumference

circunferir ▸conjug 3i◂ VT to circumscribe, limit

circunflejo SM circumflex

circunlocución SF, **circunloquio** SM circumlocution, roundabout expression

circunnavegación SF circumnavigation

circunnavegar ▸conjug 1a◂ VT to sail round, circumnavigate

circunscribible ADJ circumscribable

circunscribir ▸conjug 3a◂ (*pp* **circunscrito**)
Ⓐ VT to circumscribe (**a** to)
Ⓑ **circunscribirse** VPR (= *limitarse*) to be limited, be confined (**a** to)

circunscripción SF (*gen*) circumscription; (*Mil*) district; (*Pol*) constituency, electoral district

circunspección SF circumspection, prudence

circunspecto ADJ [*persona*] circumspect; [*palabras*] carefully chosen, guarded

circunstancia SF circumstance; **dadas las ~s** in *o* under the circumstances; **estar a la altura de las ~s** to rise to the occasion; **en las ~s actuales** under present circumstances, the way things are at the moment ▸ **circunstancias agravantes** aggravating circumstances ▸ **circunstancias atenuantes** extenuating *o* mitigating circumstances

circunstanciado ADJ detailed

circunstancial ADJ [1] (*gen*) circumstantial; [*caso*] incidental; **mi estancia en Lima era ~** I just happened to be in Lima
[2] (= *temporal*) [*arreglo, acuerdo*] makeshift, temporary

circunstante Ⓐ ADJ [1] (= *que rodea*) surrounding
[2] (= *presente*) present
Ⓑ SMF **los ~s** those present

circunvalación SF **carretera de ~** ring road, bypass, beltway (*EEUU*)

circunvecino ADJ adjacent, neighbouring, neighboring (*EEUU*), surrounding

cirial SM processional candlestick

cirílico ADJ, SM Cyrillic

cirio SM [1] (*Rel*) (wax) candle
[2] (*) (= *jaleo*) squabble; **montar un ~** to kick up a row

cirquero SM (= *empresario*) circus impresario; (*Méx*) (= *trabajador*) acrobat

cirro SM cirrus

cirrocúmulo SM cirrocumulus

cirrosis SF INV cirrhosis ▸ **cirrosis hepática** cirrhosis of the liver

cirrostrato SM cirrostratus

ciruela SF plum ▸ **ciruela claudia** greengage ▸ **ciruela damascena** damson ▸ **ciruela pasa**, **ciruela seca** prune ▸ **ciruela verdal** greengage

ciruelo SM [1] (*Bot*) plum tree
[2] (**) (= *pene*) prick**
[3] (*) (= *necio*) dolt, idiot

cirugía SF surgery ▸ **cirugía estética** cosmetic surgery ▸ **cirugía plástica** plastic surgery

ciruja SMF (*Cono Sur*) scavenger (*on rubbish dumps*)

cirujano/a SM/F surgeon ▸ **cirujano/a plástico/a** plastic surgeon

ciscar ▸conjug 1g◂ Ⓐ VT [1] (= *ensuciar*) to dirty *o* soil *o* mess up (*frm*)
[2] (*Cuba, Méx**) (= *avergonzar*) to put to shame
[3] (*Caribe, Méx*) (= *meterse con*) to provoke, needle*
Ⓑ **ciscarse** VPR [1] (*euf*) (= *hacerse de vientre*) to do one's business*; (*encima*) to mess oneself; **los que se ciscan en las teorías** those who thumb their noses at theories; **¡me cisco en todo!*** blast it!*
[2] (*Cuba, Méx**) (= *avergonzarse*) to feel ashamed
[3] (*Caribe, Méx*) (= *ofenderse*) to get upset, take offence

cisco SM [1] (*Min*) coaldust, dross; ✦***MODISMOS*** **estar hecho (un) ~*** to be a wreck, be all in; **hacer algo ~** to tear sth to bits, smash sth to smithereens
[2] (*) (= *riña*) row, shindy*; **armar un ~** ◊ **meter ~** to kick up a row, make trouble
[3] (*Méx*) (= *miedo*) fear, fright

ciscón ADJ (*Caribe, Méx*) touchy

Cisjordania SF the West Bank

cisjordano/a Ⓐ ADJ of/from the West Bank
Ⓑ SM/F native/inhabitant of the West Bank; **los ~s** the people of the West Bank

cisma SM [1] (*Rel*) schism; (*Pol*) split; (= *desacuerdo*) discord, disagreement
[2] (*Andes*) (= *remilgo*) prudery
[3] (*Andes*) (= *chismes*) gossip

cismático ADJ [1] (*Rel*) schismatic(al); (*fig*) troublemaking, dissident
[2] (*Andes*) (= *remilgado*) prudish
[3] (*Andes*) (= *chismoso*) gossipy

cisne SM [1] (*Orn*) swan
[2] (*Cono Sur*) (= *borla de empolvarse*) powder puff

Cister SM, **Císter** SM Cistercian Order

cisterciense ADJ, SM Cistercian

cisterna SF cistern, tank; **buque ~** tanker

cistitis SF INV cystitis

cita SF [1] (= *encuentro*) [1·1] (*con médico, profesional*) appointment; **tengo ~ con el dentista** I have a dental appointment, I have an appointment at the dentist's; **concertar una ~** to make an appointment, arrange an appointment; **pedir ~** to make an appointment
[1·2] [*de novios*] date; **tener una ~** to have a date
▸ **cita a ciegas** blind date
[2] (= *reunión*) meeting; **tengo una ~ con la junta directiva** I have a meeting with the board of directors; **los ciudadanos tienen una ~ con las urnas el domingo** the country goes to the polls on Sunday; **acudir a una ~** to attend a meeting; **darse ~** (= *quedar citado*) to arrange to meet; (= *encontrarse*) to gather; **los mejores atletas del mundo se han dado ~ aquí hoy** the world's top athletes have gathered here today; **lugar de ~** meeting place; **este café es lugar de ~ de escritores famosos** this café is a meeting place for famous writers; *ver tb* **casa 1**
[3] (= *punto de encuentro*) event; **los Juegos Olímpicos son la ~ más importante del deporte mundial** the Olympic Games are the most important sporting event in the world; **ser ~ obligada**: **este festival es ~ obligada para los amantes de la danza** this festival is a must for lovers of dance; **estos días París se convierte en ~ obligada para los diseñadores de moda** for these few days, Paris becomes the only place to be for fashion designers
[4] (= *mención literal*) [*de escrito, libro*] quotation; [*de parte de discurso, declaraciones*] quote; **una ~ de Quevedo** a quotation from Quevedo; **varias ~s del presidente** several quotes from the president; **la ~ más famosa de Groucho Marx** Groucho Marx's most famous quote; **un diccionario de ~s** a dictionary of quotations ▸ **cita textual** direct quote; **se escribe así cuando se trata de una ~ textual** it's written like this when it's a direct quote; **"es intolerable" (~ textual de un compañero de la oficina)** "it's intolerable", as a colleague from work said, in the words of a colleague from work, "it's intolerable"

citable ADJ quotable

citación SF [1] [*de un libro*] quotation
[2] (*Jur*) summons, citation ▸ **citación a licitadores** invitation to tender ▸ **citación judicial** summons, subpoena

citadino/a* (*LAm*) Ⓐ ADJ urban
Ⓑ SM/F urban *o* city dweller

citado ADJ aforementioned; **en el ~ país** in the aforementioned country

citar ▸conjug 1a◂ Ⓐ VT [1] (= *mencionar*) [1·1] [+ *ejemplo, caso*] to quote, cite; **el informe cita a Francia, Italia e Irlanda** the report quotes *o* cites France, Italy and Ireland; **todo tipo de plásticos, entre los que podemos ~ el nilón** all kinds of plastics, such as nylon for example
[1·2] [+ *frase, autor, fuentes*] to quote; **cita a Platón en su libro** he quotes Plato in his book; **las fuentes citadas por el periódico** the sources quoted by the newspaper; **~ textualmente** to quote word for word, quote verbatim; **~on textualmente varios párrafos** they quoted several paragraphs word for word *o* verbatim; **no quería que ningún "imbécil" —cito textualmente— le quitara el puesto** he wasn't having any "idiot" — and I quote — taking the job away from him
[2] (= *convocar*) **la ~on a las nueve de la mañana** she was given an appointment for nine in the morning; **¿está usted citado?** do you have an appointment?; **la cité para ultimar unos detalles** I arranged to see her to go over some details
[3] (*Jur*) [*juez*] to summon; [*abogado, defensa, fiscal*] to call; **~ a algn a declarar** to summon sb to give evidence; **tiene facultades para ~ testigos** he has the power to call witnesses
[4] (*Taur*) to incite, provoke
Ⓑ **citarse** VPR [1] [*varias personas*] to arrange to meet; **nos citamos a las cuatro** we arranged to meet at four; **quedamos citados para el día siguiente** we made a date for the following day; **~se con algn** to arrange to meet sb
[2] [*novios*] to make a date

cítara SF zither

-cito, -cita (*a veces tb* **-ecito, -ecita**) *ver* **Aspects of Word Formation in Spanish 2**

citófono SM (*Andes*) buzzer

citología SF [1] (= *análisis*) smear test
[2] (*Biol*) cytology

citotóxico ADJ cytotoxic

citrato SM citrate

cítrico Ⓐ ADJ citric
Ⓑ **cítricos** SMPL citrus fruits

citrícola ADJ citrus *antes de s*

citrón SM lemon

CiU ABR (*Esp Pol*) (= **Convergència i Unió**) *Catalan political coalition*

ciudad SF [1] (*de gran tamaño*) city; (*más pequeña*) town; **se levanta temprano para ir a la ~** he gets up early to go into the city *o* into town; **la ~ de Granada** (the city of) Granada; **la Ciudad Condal** *name for the city of Barcelona*; **la Ciudad del Turia** *name for the city of Valencia* ▸ **Ciudad del Cabo** Cape Town ▸ **Ciudad del Vaticano** Vatican City ▸ **Ciudad de México** Mexico City ▸ **ciudad dormitorio** dormitory town, bedroom com-

munity (*EEUU*) ► **ciudad natal** home town, native city, native town ► **ciudad perdida** (*Méx*) shanty town
2 (= *instalaciones*) ► **ciudad deportiva** sports complex ► **ciudad sanitaria** hospital complex ► **ciudad universitaria** university campus

ciudadanía SF 1 (= *habitantes*) citizens *pl*, citizenry (*frm*); (*Hist*)
2 (= *status*) citizenship; **derechos de ~** rights of citizenship ► **ciudadanía de honor** freedom of the city

ciudadano/a Ⓐ ADJ civic, city *antes de s*; **el orgullo ~** civic pride
Ⓑ SM/F citizen; **el ~ de a pie** the man in the street; **~ de honor** freeman of the city; **~ del mundo** citizen of the world; **~s de segunda clase** second-class citizens

ciudadela SF 1 (*Mil*) citadel, fortress
2 (*LAm*) (= *casa pobre*) tenement block

ciudad-estado SF (*pl* **ciudades-estado**) city-state

ciudadrealeño/a Ⓐ ADJ of/from Ciudad Real
Ⓑ SM/F native/inhabitant of Ciudad Real; **los ~s** the people of Ciudad Real

civeta SF civet cat

civeto SM civet

cívico Ⓐ ADJ [*deber*] civic; [*persona*] public-spirited, civic-minded
Ⓑ SM 1 (*Arg*) (= *vaso de cerveza*) large glass of beer
2 (*LAm*) (= *policía*) policeman

civil Ⓐ ADJ 1 (= *no militar*) [*autoridad, aviación*] civil; [*vida, víctima, población*] civilian; **guerra ~** civil war; **va vestido de ~** he's wearing civilian clothes, he's in civilian clothes; **la sociedad ~** civil society
2 (= *no religioso*) civil; **matrimonio ~** civil wedding, registry office wedding; **contrajo matrimonio ~** he got married in a registry office (wedding); **casarse por lo ~** to have a civil wedding, have a registry office wedding, be married in a civil ceremony
3 (*Jur*) [*responsabilidad, desobediencia*] civil; *ver tb* **código 1**, **derecho C1**, **gobernador B**, **guardia A**, **protección**, **registro 5**
Ⓑ SMF 1 (= *persona no militar*) civilian
2 (= *guardia*) civil guard

civilidad SF civility, courtesy, politeness

civilización SF civilization

civilizado ADJ civilized

civilizador ADJ civilizing

civilizar ▸conjug 1f◂ Ⓐ VT to civilize
Ⓑ **civilizarse** VPR to become civilized

civilizatorio ADJ civilizing

civismo SM sense of civic responsibility, public-spiritedness

cizalla SF, **cizallas** SFPL 1 (= *tijeras*) wire cutters, metal shears; (= *guillotina*) guillotine
2 (= *fragmento*) shavings, metal clippings

cizaña SF 1 (*Bot*) darnel; (*Biblia*) tares
2 (= *discordia*) discord; **meter** *o* **sembrar ~** to sow discord (**entre** among), create a rift (**entre** between)
3 (= *vicio*) vice, corruption, harmful influence

cizañar ▸conjug 1a◂ VT, **cizañear** VT to sow discord among

cizañero/a SM/F troublemaker, mischief-maker

cl ABR (= **centilitro(s)**) cl

clac Ⓐ SM (*pl* **claques**) opera hat, cocked hat
Ⓑ SF claque

clamar ▸conjug 1a◂ Ⓐ VT [+ *justicia, venganza*] to clamour for, clamor for (*EEUU*), cry out for; [+ *inocencia*] to proclaim
Ⓑ VI (= *protestar*) to protest; **~ contra** to protest against, cry out against; **~ por** to clamour for, clamor for (*EEUU*), to cry out for; ✦**MODISMO** **~ al cielo** *o* **a Dios** to be an absolute outrage; **una injusticia que clama al cielo** an absolutely outrageous injustice

clamidia SF chlamydia

clamor SM 1 (= *griterío*) clamour, clamor (*EEUU*), roar; **el ~ de los espectadores** the clamour *o* roar of the spectators
2 (= *protesta*) outcry; **un gran ~ contra la corrupción** a great outcry against corruption; **este poema es un ~ contra la violencia** this poem is a protest against death
3 [*de campana*] toll

clamorear ▸conjug 1a◂ Ⓐ VT = **clamar A**
Ⓑ VI [*campana*] to toll

clamoreo SM 1 (= *griterío*) clamour(ing), clamor(ing) (*EEUU*), prolonged shouting
2 (= *ruegos*) beseeching, pleading
3 (= *protestas*) sustained outcry, vociferous protests ► **clamoreos de protesta** vociferous protests

clamorosamente ADV clamorously

clamoroso ADJ 1 [*éxito*] resounding, enormous; [*acogida, recibimiento*] rapturous
2 (= *vociferante*) clamorous

clan SM (*Hist*) clan; [*de gángsters*] family, mob*

clandestinamente ADV clandestinely

clandestinidad SF secrecy, clandestinity, secret nature; **en la ~** in secrecy; **movimiento en la ~** (*Pol*) underground movement; **pasar a la ~** to go into hiding, go underground

clandestinista SM (*LAm*) bootlegger

clandestino/a Ⓐ ADJ 1 [*reunión, cita*] secret, clandestine; [*boda*] secret; [*pasos*] stealthy
2 (*Pol*) [*actividad, movimiento*] clandestine, underground; [*agente*] secret, undercover; [*inmigrante*] illegal; **andar ~** (*LAm Pol*) to be underground
Ⓑ SM/F illegal immigrant
Ⓒ **clandestinos** SMPL (*Andes*) shacks

clánico ADJ clannish, clan *antes de s*

claque SF claque

claqué SM tap dancing

claqueta SF clapperboard

clara SF 1 [*de huevo*] egg white; **bata las ~s a punto de nieve** whisk the egg whites until they form peaks; **una ~ de huevo** the white of an egg, an egg white
2 (*Esp*) (= *cerveza con gaseosa*) shandy, lager shandy
3 (= *calva*) bald patch

claraboya SF skylight

claramente ADV clearly; **es una medida ~ inadecuada** this measure is clearly inadequate

clarea SF *white wine with cinnamon, sugar and spices added*

clarear ▸conjug 1a◂ Ⓐ VI 1 (*Meteo*) (= *despejarse*) to clear up
2 (*al amanecer*) [*día*] to dawn, break; [*cielo*] to grow light; **ya empieza a ~** it's starting to get light now
3 (= *escasear*) **con la altura el monte ya clarea** as you go up the vegetation becomes more sparse; **ya le empieza a ~ el pelo** he's beginning to lose his hair
4 (= *transparentarse*) [*tela*] to be transparent; **ya empiezan a ~le las sienes** he's beginning to go grey at the temples
Ⓑ VT (= *iluminar*) to light up; (= *aclarar*) to make lighter
Ⓒ **clarearse** VPR 1 [*tela*] to be transparent
2 (*) (= *delatarse*) to give the game away

clareo‡ SM **darse un ~** (= *pasear*) to take a stroll; (= *irse*) to hoof it*

clarete SM (= *tinto claro*) light red wine; [*de Burdeos*] claret

claridad SF 1 (= *luminosidad*) light; **me despierta la ~** the light wakes me; **en la ~ de la mañana** in the light of the morning, in the brightness of the morning light (*liter*); **este cuarto tiene mucha ~** this room is very light
2 [*de explicación*] clarity; **explicar/expresar algo con ~** to explain sth clearly
3 (= *nitidez*) [*de sonido, voz*] clarity; [*de imagen*] sharpness, clarity; **oír/ver algo con ~** to hear/see sth clearly
4 (= *sinceridad*) frankness; **hablar con ~** to speak frankly

claridoso ADJ (*CAm, Méx*) blunt, plain-spoken

clarificación SF 1 (= *aclaración*) clarification
2 [*de vino, licor*] clarification
3 (= *iluminación*) illumination, lighting (up)

clarificador ADJ = **clarificante A**

clarificante Ⓐ ADJ [*experiencia, charla*] illuminating, enlightening; [*notas, teoría*] explanatory
Ⓑ SM clarifier, clarifying agent

clarificar ▸conjug 1g◂ VT 1 [+ *asunto, problema*] to clarify
2 [+ *líquidos*] to clarify
3 (= *iluminar*) to illuminate, light (up)

clarín Ⓐ SM 1 (*Mús*) (= *instrumento*) bugle, trumpet; [*de órgano*] clarion
2 (*Chile Bot*) sweet pea
Ⓑ SMF (= *instrumentista*) bugler

clarinada* SF uncalled-for remark

clarinazo SM warning signal

clarinero SM bugler

clarinete Ⓐ SM (= *instrumento*) clarinet
Ⓑ SMF (= *persona*) clarinettist

clarinetista SMF clarinettist

clarión SM chalk, white crayon

clarisa Ⓐ ADJ **monja ~** = **B**
Ⓑ SF nun of the Order of St Clare

clarividencia SF 1 (= *adivinación*) clairvoyance
2 (= *previsión*) farsightedness; (= *discernimiento*) discernment; (= *intuición*) intuition

clarividente Ⓐ ADJ 1 (= *que adivina el futuro*) clairvoyant
2 (= *previsor*) far-sighted; (= *discerniente*) discerning; (= *intuitivo*) intuitive
Ⓑ SMF clairvoyant

▼**claro** Ⓐ ADJ 1 (= *no oscuro*) [*piel*] fair; [*color*] light, pale; **un vestido verde ~** a light *o* pale green dress; **pelo castaño ~** light brown hair; **una alemana de ojos ~s** a blue-eyed German girl
2 (= *evidente*) 2·1 (*con sustantivos*) [*ejemplo, prueba, ventaja*] clear; [*inconveniente*] obvious; [*desastre*] total, absolute; **esto es un ~ reflejo de que el sistema no funciona** this is a clear indication that the system does not work; **España ganó por un ~ 15-6** Spain won a decisive 15-6 victory, Spain were clear

➤ LENGUA Y USO: **claro A2** 42.1, 53.2, 53.6

winners by 15-6; **... aseguró, en clara referencia a sus superiores** ... he asserted, clearly referring *o* in an obvious reference to his superiors

2·2 (*con verbos*) **dejar algo ~** to make sth clear; **ha dejado bien ~ que no quiere vernos más** he has made it quite clear he does not want to see us again; **dejar las cosas claras** *o* **en ~** to get things clear, get things straight*; **estar ~** to be clear; **el futuro del equipo no está muy ~** the future of the team is not very clear; **¿está ~?** is that clear?; **estar ~ que** to be clear that, be obvious that; **está ~ que así no vamos a ninguna parte** it's clear *o* obvious that we'll get nowhere like this; **no está nada ~ que nuestro partido vaya a ganar las elecciones** it's not at all clear that our party will win the election; **quedar ~** to be clear; **si te lees la bibliografía, te quedará todo más ~** if you read the books on the reading list, it'll all be clearer to you *o* you'll have a better idea of things; **así quedarán claras nuestras intenciones** this way our intentions will be (quite) clear; **tener algo ~** to be sure of sth, be clear about sth; **ni siquiera tengo ~ lo que me espera mañana** I'm not even sure *o* clear what's in store for me tomorrow; **es importante tener nuestro objetivo bien ~** it is important to be sure of our objective; **no lo tengo nada ~** I'm not at all sure, I don't really know

2·3 ✦*MODISMOS* **a las claras**: **prefiero decírselo a las claras** I prefer to tell him straight (out); **su triunfo deja bien a las claras el buen momento que atraviesa** his victory is a clear indication *o* sign that he is on excellent form; **ser más ~ que el agua** ◊ **ser ~ como la luz del día** to be crystal-clear; **las cuentas claras**: **me gustan las cuentas claras** I like to have *o* keep things clear; **el ministro ha presentado las cuentas claras al Parlamento** the minister has been quite straightforward with Parliament; **llevarlo** (*Esp*) *o* **tenerlo ~** (*iró*): **lo tienes ~** things won't be easy for you; **sacar algo en ~ (de algo)**: **sólo hemos sacado en ~ que no pretende dimitir** all that we can safely *o* definitely say is that he has no intention of resigning; **lo único que la policía consiguió sacar en ~ durante el interrogatorio** the only definite thing the police got from the interview; **no he sacado nada en ~ de esa conferencia** I'm still none the wiser after that lecture; **ver algo ~**: **no ven ~ cómo van a poder terminar a tiempo** they can't really see how they are going to finish on time; **el ministro ve ~ que se puede lograr un acuerdo** the minister is optimistic about reaching an agreement; **lo vi ~ en cuanto oí la noticia** it became clear to me when I heard the news; **sus padres no veían muy ~ el tema** his parents weren't too sure about the matter

3 (= *poco espeso*) [*té, café*] weak; [*caldo*] thin

4 (= *luminoso*) [*día, mañana*] bright; [*habitación, casa*] light, bright

5 (= *transparente*) [*agua*] clear; [*tejido*] transparent

6 (= *nítido*) [*sonido, voz*] clear; [*imagen*] sharp, clear

7 (= *escaso*) [*pelo*] thin; [*bosque*] light, sparse

8 (= *preciso*) [*idea*] clear; **tiene las ideas muy claras** he really knows what he wants from life; **una mente clara** (*lit*) a clear mind; (*fig*) a clear thinker

9 (= *sincero*) frank; **ser ~** to be frank

Ⓑ ADV 1 (= *con precisión*) [*oír, ver, hablar*] clearly

2 (= *sinceramente*) frankly; **hablar ~** to speak frankly, be frank; ✦*MODISMO* **~ y raspado** (*Ven*) frankly and to the point

3 (*tras invitaciones, peticiones*) sure; **—¿puedo usar tu coche mañana? —¡claro!** "can I use your car tomorrow?" — "sure!"; **—¿queréis venir a cenar? —¡claro!** "would you like to come to dinner?" — "sure!"

4 (*uso enfático*) **¡claro! por eso estaba ayer tan rara** of course! that's why she was acting so funny yesterday; **a menos que, ~ está, él también la conozca** unless of course he knows her too; **—¿por qué no te disfrazas tú? —¡~, para que os riáis de mí todos!** "why don't you dress up?" — "oh sure, so you can all laugh at me!"; **~ que**: **~ que nadie se imaginaba lo que vendría después** of course nobody could imagine what would happen afterwards; **¡~ que no!** of course not!; **~ que no es verdad** of course it isn't true; **¡~ que sí!** yes, of course!

Ⓒ SM 1 (*Meteo*) bright spell, sunny interval; **habrá nubes y ~s** it will be cloudy with bright spells *o* sunny intervals; **un pequeño ~ entre las nubes** a slight break in the clouds ► **claro de luna** moonlight

2 [*de tiempo*] lull; **aprovechamos un clarillo para salir a comprar** we took advantage of a little lull to go and do some shopping; ✦*MODISMO* **velar de ~ en ~** to lie awake all night

3 (= *espacio despejado*) (*entre personas*) space; (*entre árboles*) clearing; [*de pelo*] bald patch; **se pueden ver algunos ~s en la sala** there are a few (empty) spaces in the hall

4 (*en un texto*) gap, space; (*en discurso*) pause

5 (*Arquit*) (= *claraboya*) skylight; (= *abertura*) window (opening)

6 (*Caribe Culin*) guava jelly

7 (*Caribe*) (= *bebida*) sugar-cane brandy

claroscuro SM chiaroscuro

clase Ⓐ SF 1 (*Escol*) 1·1 (= *lección*) lesson, class; **una ~ de historia** a history lesson *o* class; **~ de música** music lesson; **~ de conducir** driving lesson; **dar** *o* (*Chile*) **hacer ~(s)** [*profesor*] to teach; (*Esp*) [*alumno*] to have lessons; ✦*MODISMO* **fumarse** *o* **saltarse** *o* **soplarse la ~*** to skip class*, skive off*

1·2 (= *instrucción*) school; **hoy no tengo ~** I don't have school today; **los viernes salgo de ~ a las cuatro** on Fridays I finish school at four; **faltar a ~** to miss school, be absent

1·3 (= *aula*) classroom

1·4 (= *grupo de alumnos*) class; **es el primero de la ~** he is top of the class; **la gente de mi ~** my classmates, my class; **compañero de ~** classmate

► **clase nocturna** evening class ► **clase particular** private lesson; **doy clases particulares de francés** I teach private lessons in French; **"se dan clases particulares"** "private tuition offered"

2 (*Univ*) 2·1 (*práctica*) (= *lección, instrucción*) class; (= *aula*) classroom; **hoy no tengo ~** I don't have any classes today; **dar** *o* (*LAm frm*) **dictar ~** [*profesor*] to teach; [*alumno*] (*Esp*) to have classes

2·2 (= *lección*) lecture; **hoy no voy a ~** I'm not going to any lectures today, I'm not going to University today; **dar ~** [*profesor*] to teach, lecture; [*alumno*] to have lectures; **doy ~ de Derecho Civil** I teach civil law

2·3 (= *aula*) lecture room

► **clase magistral** master class

3 (= *tipo*) kind, sort; **gente de todas ~s** all kinds *o* sorts of people, people of all kinds; **les deseo toda ~ de felicidad** I wish you every happiness; **con toda ~ de detalles** in great detail, down to the last detail

4 (= *calidad*) quality; **productos de primera ~** top-quality products

5 (*en viajes*) class; **primera ~** first class; **viajar en primera ~** to travel first class; **segunda ~** second class, standard class; **un billete de segunda ~** a second class ticket ► **clase económica** economy class ► **clase preferente** club class ► **clase turista** tourist class

6 (= *elegancia*) class; **una persona con ~** someone with class; **tener ~** to have class; **tu hermana tiene mucha ~** your sister has a lot of class, your sister's very classy

7 (*Sociol*) class; **la lucha de ~s** the class struggle; **las ~s acomodadas** the well-to-do, the moneyed classes; **la ~ dirigente** *o* **dominante** the ruling class; **la ~ médica** the medical profession; **la ~ política** politicians *pl*, the political establishment (*Sociol*); **las ~s privilegiadas** the privileged classes ► **clase alta** upper class; **una joven de ~ alta** an upper-class girl ► **clase baja** lower class; **un chico de ~ baja** a lower-class boy ► **clase media** middle class; **una familia de ~ media** a middle-class family ► **clase media-alta** upper-middle class ► **clase media-baja** lower-middle class ► **clase obrera** working class; **la mentalidad de la ~ obrera** the working-class mentality ► **clase social** social class

8 (*Biol, Bot*) class

9 (*Mil*) ► **clases de tropa** non-commissioned officers

Ⓑ ADJ (*Andes**) first-rate, classy*

CLÁSICO

¿"Classic" o "classical"?

Hay que tener en cuenta que el adjetivo **clásico** se puede traducir por **classic** o por **classical**:

- Se traduce por **classic** cuando el sustantivo al que acompaña reúne todas las características propias de su especie o cuando nos referimos a películas, libros, etc de una calidad extraordinaria:

  Es el clásico ejemplo de niño mimado

  He's a classic example of a spoilt child

  ...una de las historias de detectives clásicas de esa época...

  ...one of the classic detective stories of that time...

- Se traduce por **classical** cuando **clásico** hace referencia a la música clásica o a asuntos relacionados con las civilizaciones griega y romana:

  Cuanta más música clásica escucho más me gusta

  The more classical music I listen to the more I enjoy it

  El Partenón es uno de los ejemplos más significativos de la arquitectura clásica

  The Parthenon is one of the most significant examples of classical architecture

Para otros usos y ejemplos ver la entrada.

clásicas SFPL (*Univ*) classics

clasicismo SM classicism
clásico Ⓐ ADJ 1 (*Arte, Mús*) classical
2 (= *característico*) classic; **el ~ error de los estudiantes ingleses** the classic mistake of students of English; **es la clásica plazuela española** it is a typical Spanish square
3 (= *de época*) [*coche*] vintage
4 [*costumbre*] time-honoured; **le dio el ~ saludo** he gave him the time-honoured greeting
5 (= *destacado*) outstanding, remarkable
Ⓑ SM 1 (= *obra, película*) classic
2 (= *artista, escritor*) outstanding figure, big name*
clasificable ADJ classifiable
clasificación SF 1 (= *categorización*) classification
2 (= *ordenación*) [*de documentos*] classification; (*Inform, Correos*) sorting
3 (*Náut*) rating
4 (*en torneo*) qualification
5 (= *lista*) table, league
clasificado Ⓐ ADJ [*anuncios*] classified; [*película*] rated
Ⓑ **clasificados** SMPL (*LAm*) classifieds
clasificador SM 1 (= *mueble*) filing cabinet ► **clasificador de cartas** letter file
2 (= *aparato*) collator
3 (= *persona*) classifier
clasificar ▸conjug 1g◂ Ⓐ VT 1 (= *categorizar*) to classify; **lo ~on bajo la letra B** they classified it under letter B
2 (= *ordenar*) [+ *documentos*] to classify; (*Correos, Inform*) to sort
Ⓑ **clasificarse** VPR (*Dep*) **mi equipo se clasificó en segundo lugar** my team came *o* was placed second; **no se clasificó el equipo para la final** the team did not qualify for the final
clasificatoria SF (= *ronda*) qualifying round; (*Atletismo*) heat
clasificatorio ADJ [*fase, prueba*] qualifying; **tabla clasificatoria** league table
clasismo SM 1 (= *actitud discriminatoria*) classism
2 (= *estructura social*) class structure
clasista Ⓐ ADJ 1 [*actitud*] class-conscious, classist; (*pey*) snobbish; **Gran Bretaña es aún una sociedad muy ~** Britain is still a very class-conscious society; **un análisis ~** a classist analysis
2 (= *de clases*) class *antes de s*
Ⓑ SMF class-conscious person; (*pey*) snob
claudia SF greengage
claudicación SF giving way, abandonment of one's principles, backing down ► **claudicación moral** failure in one's moral duty
claudicar ▸conjug 1g◂ VI 1 (= *rendirse*) to give in; **no claudicó ante el chantaje** he did not give in to the blackmail
2 (= *renunciar*) **~ de algo** to renounce sth; **no podemos ~ de nuestras convicciones** we cannot renounce our convictions
3 (†) (= *cojear*) to limp
4 (†) (= *engañar*) to act deceitfully
5 (†) (= *vacilar*) to waver, stall
Claudio SM Claudius
claustral SMF (*Univ*) member of the Senate
claustro SM 1 (*Rel*) cloister
2 (*Univ*) staff, faculty (*EEUU*); (= *junta*) senate; (= *asamblea*) staff meeting
3 (*Anat*) ► **claustro materno** womb
claustrofobia SF claustrophobia
claustrofóbico ADJ claustrophobic
cláusula SF clause ► **cláusula de exclusión** (*Com*) exclusion clause ► **cláusula de reajuste de los precios** escalation clause ► **cláusula de rescisión** cancellation clause ► **cláusula de revisión** trigger clause
clausura SF 1 [*de local, edificio*] closure
2 [*de olimpiada, congreso*] closing ceremony; [*de tribunal*] closing session; **discurso de ~** closing speech
3 (*Rel*) (= *recinto*) cloister; (= *reclusión religiosa*) cloister, religious seclusion; **convento de ~** enclosed convent, enclosed monastery
4 (*Méx Jur*) [*de negocio*] closing down
clausurar ▸conjug 1a◂ VT 1 [+ *debate, curso*] to close, bring to a close
2 [+ *negocio, edificio*] to close, close down
3 (*LAm*) [+ *casa*] to close (up)
clava SF club, cudgel
clavada SF 1 (= *salto*) dive
2 (*) **pegar una ~ a algn** to rip sb off*, overcharge sb
clavadista SMF (*CAm, Méx Dep*) diver
clavado Ⓐ ADJ 1 (= *fijo*) (*con clavos, puntas*) nailed
2 (= *decorado*) [*mueble*] studded with nails
3 [*ropa*] just right
4 **dejar a algn ~** to leave sb speechless; **quedó ~** he was speechless *o* dumbfounded
5 **a las cinco clavadas** at five sharp *o* on the dot
6 (= *idéntico*) **es Pedro ~** he's the spitting image of Pedro; **es** *o* (*LAm*) **está ~ a su padre** he's the spitting image of his father
7 **¡clavado!** exactly!, precisely!
Ⓑ SM (= *salto*) dive; **dar un ~** to dive, take a dive
clavar ▸conjug 1a◂ Ⓐ VT 1 (= *hincar*) [+ *clavo*] to hammer in; **le clavó un cuchillo en el cuello** he stuck a knife in his throat; **me clavé un alfiler mientras cosía** I stuck a needle in(to) my finger while I was sewing; **le clavó las uñas en la cara** she dug her nails into his face; **~ banderillas** (*Taur*) *to thrust banderillas into the bull's neck*
2 (= *fijar*) (*con clavos*) to nail; **ha clavado unas tablas en la puerta** he has nailed some panels onto the door; **clavó con chinchetas un póster de su equipo** he pinned up a poster of his team; ✦*MODISMO* **~ la mirada** *o* **los ojos en algn/algo** to fix one's gaze *o* one's eyes on sb/sth
3 [+ *joya*] to set, mount
4 (*Ftbl*) [+ *pelota*] to hammer, drive; **el delantero clavó el balón en la red** the forward hammered *o* drove the ball into the net
5 (*) (= *cobrar de más*) to rip off*; **me ~on 350 euros por una cena** I got ripped off to the tune of 350 euros for a meal; **—pagué cuarenta euros —pues, te han clavado** "I paid forty euros" — "you were ripped off"
6 (*) (= *hacer perfecto*) **—¿cómo has hecho el examen? —lo he clavado** "how did the exam go?" — "it was spot on"*
7 (*Méx*)(*) (= *robar*) to swipe*, nick*, pinch*
Ⓑ **clavarse** VPR 1 [*espina, astilla*] **se me ha clavado una astilla en la mano** I've got a splinter in my hand; **se me clavó una raspa en la garganta** a fishbone got stuck in my throat
2 (*reflexivo*) **se clavó la espada** he stabbed himself with his sword
3 (*CAm, Méx Dep*) to dive
clave Ⓐ SF 1 (= *código*) code; **la ~ de la caja fuerte** the code of *o* to the safe; **la ~ secreta** the secret code; **en ~** in code; **hablan en ~** they speak in code; **mensaje en ~** coded message, message in code ► **clave de acceso** (*Inform*) password ► **clave de búsqueda** (*Inform*) search key ► **clave de clasificación** (*Inform*) sort key
2 (= *quid*) key; **la ~ del problema** the key to the problem; **una de las ~s para entender el tema** one of the keys to understanding the subject
3 (*Mús*) clef ► **clave de fa** bass clef ► **clave de sol** treble clef
4 (= *sentido*) **una interpretación en ~ económica** an economic interpretation, an interpretation from an economic viewpoint *o* perspective; **una novela escrita en ~ de humor** a novel written in a humorous style *o* tone
5 (*Arquit*) keystone
Ⓑ SM (*Mús*) harpsichord
Ⓒ ADJ (= *esencial*) [*tema, punto, factor, personaje*] key *antes de s*; **una figura ~ en la política catalana** a key figure in Catalan politics; **cuestión ~** key question; **palabra ~** keyword
clavecín SM spinet
clavel SM carnation; ✦*MODISMO* **no tener un ~*** to be broke*
clavellina SF pink
clavelón SM marigold, African marigold
clavero[1] SM (*Bot*) clove tree
clavero[2] SM (= *llavero*) key-holder
claveteado SM studding, studs
clavetear ▸conjug 1a◂ VT 1 (= *adornar*) [+ *puerta, mueble*] to stud, decorate with nails
2 [+ *cordón*] to put a metal tip on, tag
3 [+ *trato*] to clinch, close
clavicémbalo SM harpsichord, clavicembalo
clavicordio SM clavichord
clavícula SF collar bone, clavicle
clavidista SMF (*Méx Dep*) diver
clavija SF (*Carpintería*) peg, dowel, pin; (*Mús*) peg; (*Elec*) plug; ✦*MODISMO* **apretar las ~s a algn** to put the screws on sb* ► **clavija de dos patas, clavija hendida** cotter pin, split pin
clavijero SM 1 (*Mús*) pegbox
2 (= *percha*) clothes rack
clavillo SM, **clavito** SM 1 (*Téc*) pivot, pin ► **clavillo de tijeras** pin, rivet
2 (*Bot*) clove
clavo SM 1 [*de carpintero*] nail; [*de adorno*] stud; ✦*MODISMOS* **agarrarse a un ~ ardiendo**: **estoy tan desesperado que me agarraría a un ~ ardiendo** I'm so desperate I'd do anything *o* I'm capable of anything; **los estudiantes se agarran a esta ley como a un ~ ardiendo** the students are pinning their hopes on this law as their last hope; **como un ~**: **llegó a las dos en punto, como un ~** she arrived at two o'clock on the dot; **a las doce, como un ~, llamaba a la puerta** at twelve o'clock, as regular as clockwork, he would call at the door; **dar en el ~** to hit the nail on the head; **dar una en el ~ y ciento en la he-**

rradura to be more often wrong than right; **entrar de ~** to squeeze in; **¡por los ~s de Cristo!** for heaven's sake!; **remachar el ~** (= *empeorar*) to make matters worse; **meter algo de ~** to slip sth in; **ser una verdad de ~ pasado** to be patently obvious; ✦*REFRÁN* **un ~ saca a otro ~** a new worry helps to take the pain away *o* take your mind off the old one ► **clavo romano** brass-headed nail ► **clavo sin cabeza** panel pin
2 [*de botas de fútbol*] stud; [*de zapatillas de correr*] spike
3 [*de montañismo*] piton
4 (*Bot*) (*tb* **~ de olor**) clove
5 (= *callo*) corn
6 (*Med*) (= *pieza metálica*) (metal) pin, (metal) rod
7 (*CAm, Méx Min*) *rich vein of ore*
8 (*Andes, Cono Sur*) (= *cosa desagradable*) **es un ~ tener que levantarse temprano** it's a real pain *o* bind having to get up so early; **¡vaya ~ que te han vendido!** they've sold you a dud!*
9 (*CAm, Méx*) (= *problema*) problem, snag

claxon SM (*pl* **claxons** *o* **cláxones**) horn; **tocar el ~** to sound *o* blow one's horn, hoot, honk

claxonar ▸conjug 1a◂ VI to sound *o* blow one's horn, hoot, honk

claxonazo SM hoot, toot (on the horn), honk

clemátide SF clematis

clemencia SF (= *misericordia*) mercy, clemency; (*Jur*) leniency

clemente ADJ (= *misericordioso*) merciful, clement; (*Jur*) lenient

clementina SF clementine, tangerine

Cleopatra SF Cleopatra

cleptomanía SF kleptomania

cleptómano/a ADJ, SM/F kleptomaniac

clerecía SF 1 (= *oficio*) priesthood
2 (= *grupo*) clergy

clergyman [klerxi'man] ADJ INV **traje ~** *modernized form of priest's attire (adopted in Spain 1962)*

clerical Ⓐ ADJ clerical
Ⓑ SM (*CAm, Caribe*) clergyman, minister

clericalismo SM clericalism

clericato SM, **clericatura** SF priesthood

clericó SM (*Cono Sur*) mulled wine

clérigo SM (*católico*) priest; (*anglicano*) clergyman, priest

clero SM clergy

clic SM click; **hacer ~ en algo** (*Inform*) to click on sth; **hacer doble ~ en algo** to double-click on sth

clicar ▸conjug 1g◂ VI (*Inform*) to click; **clica en el icono** click on the icon; **~ dos veces** to double-click

cliché SM 1 (*Tip*) stencil 2 (= *tópico*) cliché
3 (*Fot*) negative

click SM = **clic**

cliente SMF [*de tienda, bar, restaurante, banco*] customer; [*de empresa*] customer, client; [*de hotel*] guest, customer; **el ~ siempre tiene la razón** the customer is always right ► **cliente fijo**, **cliente habitual** regular customer

clientela SF (*Com*) clientele, customers *pl*; (*Med*) practice, patients *pl*

clientelismo SM patronage system

clima SM (*Meteo*) climate; [*de reunión*] atmosphere; [*de situación*] climate ► **clima artificial** (*LAm*) air conditioning ► **clima de opinión** climate of public opinion

climatérico ADJ climacteric

climático ADJ climatic

climatización SF air conditioning

climatizado ADJ air-conditioned

climatizador SM air-conditioner

climatología SF (= *ciencia*) climatology; (= *tiempo*) weather

climatológico ADJ climatological; **estudios ~s** studies in climate *o* climatic change

climatólogo/a SM/F climatologist

clímax ['klimas] SM INV climax

clinch [klinʃ] SM (*LAm*), **clincha** SF (*LAm*) clinch

clínica SF 1 (= *hospital*) clinic; [*de formación*] teaching hospital ► **clínica ambulatoria** outpatients' department ► **clínica de reposo** convalescent home, rest home
2 (*Univ*) clinical training; *ver tb* **clínico**

clínicamente ADV clinically; **~ muerto** clinically dead

clínico/a Ⓐ ADJ [*asistencia, análisis*] clinical; **hospital ~** teaching hospital
Ⓑ SM/F (= *médico*) consultant; *ver tb* **clínica**

clip SM (*pl* **clips** [klis]) 1 [*de sujección*] (*para papeles*) paper clip; [*de collar, pulsera*] fastener; [*de pantalón*] trouser-clip
2 (*LAm*) (= *pendiente*) clip-on earring
3 [*de vídeo*] videoclip

clipe SM = **clip**

clíper SM clipper

cliqueable ADJ clickable

cliquear ▸conjug 1a◂ VI to click; **cliquea en el icono** click on the icon

clisar ▸conjug 1a◂ VT to stereotype, stencil

clisé SM 1 (*Tip*) cliché, stereotype plate; (*Fot*) negative 2 (= *tópico*) cliché

clisos‡ SMPL peepers‡, eyes

clitoridectomía SF clitoridectomy

clítoris SM INV clitoris

clo SM cluck (= **hacer clo**) to cluck

cloaca SF sewer, drain

cloacal ADJ 1 [*sistema*] sewage *antes de s*
2 (*hum*) [*chiste*] lavatorial

cloch(e) SM (*CAm, Méx*) clutch

clon SM clone

clonación SF, **clonaje** SM cloning

clonar ▸conjug 1a◂ VT to clone

clónico Ⓐ ADJ clonal, cloned
Ⓑ SM (*Inform*) clone

cloquear ▸conjug 1a◂ VI to cluck

cloqueo SM clucking

cloración SF chlorination

clorador SM chlorinator

cloral SM chloral

clorar ▸conjug 1a◂ VT to chlorinate

clorhídrico ADJ hydrochloric

clorinar ▸conjug 1a◂ VT to chlorinate

clorinda SF (*Cono Sur*) bleach

cloro SM chlorine

clorofila SF chlorophyl(l)

clorofluorocarbono SM chlorofluorocarbon

cloroformar ▸conjug 1a◂ VT (*LAm*), **cloroformizar** ▸conjug 1f◂ VT to chloroform

cloroformo SM chloroform

cloruro SM chloride ► **cloruro de cal** chloride of lime ► **cloruro cálcico** calcium chloride ► **cloruro de hidrógeno** hydrogen chloride ► **cloruro de polivinilo** polyvinyl chloride ► **cloruro sódico** sodium chloride

closet SM, **clóset** SM (*LAm*) (*gen*) (built-in) cupboard; (*para ropa*) (built-in) wardrobe, closet (*EEUU*)

clown [klawn] SM (*pl* **clowns** [klawn]) clown

clownesco ADJ clownish

club SM (*pl* **clubs** *o* **clubes**) 1 (= *sociedad*) club ► **club de fans** fan club ► **club de fútbol** football club ► **club de golf** golf club ► **club deportivo** sports club ► **club de tiro** shooting club, rifle club ► **club náutico** yacht club 2 (= *bar*) club ► **club de alterne** hostess club ► **club de carretera** roadside brothel ► **club nocturno** night club

clubista SMF club member

clueca SF broody hen

clueco ADJ 1 [*gallina*] broody
2 (*Cono Sur*) (= *enfermizo*) sickly, weak
3 (*Caribe**) (= *engreído*) stuck-up*

cluniacense ADJ, SM Cluniac

clutch SM (*Méx*) clutch

cm ABR (= **centímetro(s)**) cm

cm² ABR (= **centímetros cuadrados**) sq. cm

cm³ ABR (= **centímetros cúbicos**) cc

CN SF ABR (= **carretera nacional**) ≈ "A" road

CNA SM ABR (= **Congreso Nacional Africano**) ANC

CNC SM ABR (*Col*) = **Consejo Nacional del Café**

CNEA SF ABR (*Arg*) = **Comisión Nacional de Energía Atómica**

Cnel. ABR (= **Coronel**) Col

CNI SF ABR (*Chile*) (= **Central Nacional de Informaciones**) *Chilean secret police*

CNMV SF ABR = **Comisión Nacional del Mercado de Valores**

CNT SF ABR 1 (*Esp*) (= **Confederación Nacional del Trabajo**) *anarchist trade union*
2 (*Cono Sur, Méx*) (= **Confederación Nacional de Trabajadores**) *trade union*

co... PREF co...

coa SF 1 (*CAm, Caribe, Méx Agr*) (*para cavar*) long-handled narrow spade; (*para sembrar*) pointed stick for sowing seed
2 (*Cono Sur*) (= *argot*) underworld slang

coacción SF coercion, compulsion; **con ~** under duress

coaccionador ADJ constraining, compelling

coaccionar ▸conjug 1a◂ VT to coerce, pressure

coactivo ADJ coercive

coacusado/a SM/F co-defendant

coadjutor(a) SM/F assistant, coadjutor (*frm*)

coadyuvar ▸conjug 1a◂ VI **coadjuvar a** to contribute to

coagulación SF [*de sangre*] coagulation, clotting; [*de leche*] curdling

coagulante SM coagulant

coagular ▸conjug 1a◂ Ⓐ VT [+ *sangre*] to coagulate, clot, congeal; [+ *leche*] to curdle
Ⓑ **coagularse** VPR to coagulate; [*sangre*] to coagulate, clot, congeal; [*leche*] to curdle

coágulo SM clot, coagulum (*frm*) ► **coágulo de sangre**, **coágulo sanguíneo** blood clot

coalescente ADJ coalescent

coalición SF coalition; **gobierno de ~** coalition government

coalicionarse ▸conjug 1a◂ VPR to form a coalition

coaligado/a Ⓐ ADJ **estar ~s** to be allied Ⓑ SM/F ally

coaligarse ▸conjug 1h◂ VPR to make common cause (**con** with)

coartada SF alibi; **alegar una ~** to produce an alibi

coartar ▸conjug 1a◂ VT to limit, restrict

coaseguro SM coinsurance

coatí SM (*LAm*) coati

coautor(a) SM/F joint author, co-author

coaxial ADJ coaxial

coba SF [1] (= *adulación*) soft soap*, cajolery; **dar ~ a algn** to suck up to sb, play up to sb [2] (= *mentirilla*) fib; (= *truco*) neat trick

cobalto SM cobalt

cobarde Ⓐ ADJ (*en lucha, aventura*) cowardly; (*ante sangre, alturas*) faint-hearted; (= *tímido*) timid Ⓑ SMF coward

cobardear ▸conjug 1a◂ VI to be a coward, show cowardice, act in a cowardly way

cobardía SF (= *miedo*) cowardice, cowardliness; (= *timidez*) faint-heartedness, timidity

cobardón SM shameful coward, great coward

cobaya SF guinea pig

cobayismo SM *use of animals or humans in medical experiments*

cobayo SM guinea pig

cobertera SF [1] (= *tapadera*) lid, cover; [*de reloj*] watchcase [2] (*Bot*) white water lily [3] (†) (= *alcahueta*) procuress

cobertizo SM [1] (*para animales, útiles*) shed [2] (= *refugio*) shelter ► **cobertizo de aviación** hangar ► **cobertizo de coche** carport [3] (= *tejadillo*) lean-to

cobertor SM bedspread, coverlet

cobertura SF [1] (*Radio, TV*) [*de noticia, acontecimiento*] coverage; **la ceremonia recibió amplia ~ informativa** the ceremony was widely covered, the ceremony received wide news coverage [2] (*Radio, TV, Telec*) (= *ámbito*) range; **este teléfono sólo tiene ~ nacional** this phone only has a range within this country; **no hay ~** (*al interlocutor*) you're breaking up; (*al acompañante*) I can't get a signal; (*dicho por la empresa de telefonía*) there's no network coverage; **una emisora de ~ regional** a regional radio station [3] [*de un crédito*] cover ► **cobertura de desempleo** unemployment benefit, unemployment insurance (*EEUU*) ► **cobertura de dividendo** dividend cover ► **cobertura del seguro** insurance cover ► **cobertura sanitaria** health care ► **cobertura social** welfare (services) *pl* [4] (= *cubierta*) **el fuego ha dañado la ~ vegetal** the fire has damaged the vegetation

cobija SF [1] (*Arquit*) ridge tile [2] (*LAm*) (= *manta*) blanket; [*de vestir*] poncho; **las ~s** the bedclothes; ✦*MODISMO* **pegársele a algn las ~s** to oversleep [3] (*Caribe*) (= *techo*) roof (of palm leaves)

cobijar ▸conjug 1a◂ Ⓐ VT [1] (= *proteger*) to protect, shelter; (= *hospedar*) to take in, give shelter to; (*Pol, Jur*) to harbour, harbor (*EEUU*) [2] (*Andes, Caribe*) (= *techar*) to thatch, roof with palms Ⓑ **cobijarse** VPR to (take) shelter

cobijo SM (= *protección, hospedaje*) shelter

cobista* Ⓐ ADJ greasy*, smarmy* Ⓑ SMF bootlicker*, toady*

cobo SM (*Caribe*) [1] (*Zool*) sea snail [2] (= *persona*) unsociable person, shy person; **ser un ~** to be shy, be withdrawn

cobra¹ SF (*Zool*) cobra

cobra² SF (*Caza*) retrieval

cobrable ADJ, **cobradero** ADJ [*cheque*] cashable; [*precio*] chargeable; [*suma*] recoverable

cobrador(a) SM/F [1] (*Com*) collector ► **cobrador del frac**® debt collector (*working for company* ***Cobrador del Frac***®*, whose livery includes a tailcoat*) [2] (*en bus, tren*) conductor/conductress

cobranza SF [1] = **cobro** [2] (*Caza*) retrieval

cobrar ▸conjug 1a◂ Ⓐ VT [1] (= *pedir como pago*) to charge; **cobran 200 dólares por arreglarlo** they charge 200 dollars to repair it; **¿qué me va usted a ~?** what are you going to charge me?; **¿cuánto os cobra de alquiler?** how much rent does she charge you?; **me han cobrado demasiado** they've charged me too much, they've overcharged me; **¿me cobra, por favor?** how much do I owe you?, can I have the bill, please?; **¿me cobra los cafés?** how much do I owe you for the coffees? [2] (= *recibir*) **no han cobrado el dinero prometido** they haven't been paid *o* received the money they were promised; **no hemos cobrado los dividendos** we haven't received any dividends; **cobran un sueldo anual de nueve millones** they get *o* earn *o* receive an annual salary of nine million; **¿cuánto cobras al año?** how much do you get *o* earn a year?; **nuestro vecino está cobrando el paro** our neighbour is on unemployment benefit; **cantidades a** *o* **por ~** amounts payable, amounts due; **cuentas a** *o* **por ~** accounts receivable; ✦*MODISMO* **~ palos** (= *paliza*) to get a beating; (= *crítica*) to get *o* receive a lot of criticism [3] (= *recoger dinero de*) [+ *deuda, alquiler, impuesto*] to collect; [+ *cheque*] to cash; [+ *subsidio, pensión*] to draw; **voy a ir a ~ el desempleo** I'm going to draw my unemployment benefit; **tienen problemas para ~ las multas** they have problems collecting the fines [4] (= *adquirir*) **los ordenadores han cobrado una gran importancia** computers have become very important; **~ actualidad** to become topical; **~ cariño a algn** to grow fond of sb; **~ fama** to become famous; **~ fama de inteligente/ladrón** to acquire a reputation for being intelligent/a thief; **~ fuerzas** to gather one's strength; **~ vida** [*personaje, juego*] to come alive; **el campo reverdece y cobra vida** the field turns green again and is infused with new life; **en la película todo cobra vida propia** the film takes on a life of its own [5] (= *recuperar*) [+ *pieza de caza*] to retrieve, fetch; [+ *cuerda*] to pull in, take in [6] (*LAm*) **~ a algn** to press sb for payment Ⓑ VI [1] (= *recibir dinero*) [1·1] (*como sueldo*) to be paid; **cobra los viernes** he gets paid on Fridays; **te pagaré en cuanto cobre** I'll pay you as soon as I get my wages; **el lechero vino a ~** the milkman came for his money, the milkman came to be paid; **los atletas cobran por participar en la carrera** the athletes get paid *o* receive a fee for taking part in the race [1·2] (*por servicio*) to charge; **ahora cobran por renovar la tarjeta** they have introduced a charge for renewing your card; **no cobramos por llevarlo a domicilio** we don't charge for delivery; **~ por los servicios prestados** to charge for services rendered [2] (*) (= *recibir golpes*) **¡vas a ~!** you're (in) for it! Ⓒ **cobrarse** VPR [1] (= *recibir dinero*) **¡cóbrese, por favor!** can I pay, please?; **¡se cobra aquí, por favor!** pay over here, please! [2] **~se un favor** to call in a favour; **~se (la) venganza** to take one's revenge [3] [+ *muertos, víctimas*] to claim; **el accidente se cobró la vida de tres personas** the accident claimed the lives of three people [4] **~se de una pérdida** to make up for a loss [5] (*Med*) (= *volver en sí*) to come to

cobre SM [1] (*Min*) copper; (*LAm**) (= *céntimo*) cent; **no tengo un ~** I haven't a cent/penny; ✦*MODISMOS* **batir(se) el ~** (= *trabajar mucho*) to work with a will, work hard, hustle (*EEUU*); (*en discusión*) to get worked up; **batirse el ~ por** (+ *INFIN*) to go all out to + *infin* [2] (*Culin*) copper pans *pl* [3] (*Mús*) brass [4] (*LAm*) ✦*MODISMO* **enseñar el ~** to show one's true colours

cobreado ADJ copperplated

cobreño ADJ (= *de cobre*) copper *antes de s*; (= *parecido al cobre*) coppery

cobrero SM coppersmith

cobrizo ADJ coppery, copper-coloured, copper-colored (*EEUU*)

cobro SM [1] (= *recaudación*) [*de cheque*] cashing, encashment (*frm*); [*de salario, subsidio*] receipt, collection; [*de pensión*] collection, drawing; [*de factura, deuda*] collection; **endurecerán los requisitos para el ~ de pensiones** they will tighten up the requirements for drawing *o* collecting pensions; **protestó por el ~ de 50 euros por el servicio** he complained about the 50-euro charge for the service; **cargo** *o* **comisión por ~** collection charge ► **cobro revertido**: **llamada a ~ revertido** reverse charge call, collect call (*EEUU*); **llamar a ~ revertido** to reverse the charges, call collect (*EEUU*), call toll-free (*EEUU*) [2] (= *pago*) **nos comprometemos a garantizar el ~ de las pensiones** we make a guarantee that the pensions will be paid [3] (†) **poner algo en ~** to put sth in a safe place, put sth out of harm's way; **ponerse en ~** to take refuge

coca¹ SF [1] (*Bot*) coca; (= *droga*) coke* [2] (*Méx**) ✦*MODISMO* **de ~** free

COCA

In Peru, Colombia and Bolivia, the leaves of the Erythroxylon coca plant have traditionally been chewed as a mild stimulant and for a variety of medicinal purposes. As such, they are sold quite legally in street markets. Since **coca** *is also the raw material for cocaine, peasant farmers in remote areas grow it to sell to the illegal drugs trade. Cartels in Cali and Medellín control most of the processing, shipment and distribution of cocaine and retain most of the profits. The cocaine industry brings few benefits to the vast majority of Latin Americans and the power struggle between the drug barons and government is responsible for widespread violence.*

coca² SF [1] (*) (= *cabeza*) head, nut*, noggin (*EEUU**)
[2] (‡) (= *golpe*) rap on the nut‡
[3] [*de pelo*] bun, coil
[4] (*en cuerda*) kink

coca³* SF Coke®, Coca-Cola®

cocacho SM (*Andes, Cono Sur*) tap on the head

cocacolo/a SM/F (*Andes*) frivolous teenager

cocacolonización SF (*hum*) Americanization

cocada SF [1] (*CAm Culin*) coconut sweet
[2] (= *viaje*) length of a journey
[3] (*Andes Aut*) tyre *o* (*EEUU*) tire grip
[4] (*Bol, Perú*) coca plug

cocaína SF cocaine

cocaínico ADJ cocaine *antes de s*

cocainomanía SF cocaine addiction

cocainómano/a SM/F cocaine addict

cocal SM coca plantation

cocalero/a Ⓐ ADJ coca *antes de s*
Ⓑ SM/F coca grower

cocción SF [1] (*Culin*) (*gen*) cooking; (= *hervor*) boiling; (= *duración*) cooking time; **el agua de ~** cooking liquid ► **cocción al horno** baking ► **cocción al vapor** steaming
[2] (*Téc*) firing, baking

cóccix SM INV coccyx

cocear ▸conjug 1a◂ VT, VI to kick (**contra** against)

cocer ▸conjug 2b, 2h◂ Ⓐ VT [1] (*Culin*) (= *hervir*) to boil; **cocemos la leche antes de tomarla** we boil the milk before drinking it; *ver tb* **haba 1**
[2] (*Culin*) (= *guisar*) to cook; **cueza el pescado a fuego suave** cook the fish over a gentle heat; **~ al vapor** to steam; **~ al horno** to bake
[3] (*Téc*) [+ *ladrillos, cerámica*] to fire
Ⓑ VI [*vino*] to ferment
Ⓒ **cocerse** VPR [1] (= *hervir*) to boil
[2] (= *guisarse*) to cook; (*al vapor*) to steam; (*al horno*) to bake; **la carne tarda más en ~se que el pescado** meat takes longer to cook than fish
[3] (*) (= *tramarse*) **algo raro se está cociendo en el comité** something strange is brewing in the committee; **voy a ver qué se cuece por aquí** I'm going to see what's going on here
[4] (*) (= *pasar calor*) to bake*, roast*, boil*; **en este piso se cuece uno en verano** this apartment is baking *o* roasting *o* boiling in summer*
[5] (‡) (= *emborracharse*) to get plastered‡, get smashed‡

cocha SF (*Andes, Cono Sur*) (= *charca*) pool; (= *pantano*) swamp; (= *laguna*) lagoon; *ver tb* **cocho**

cochambre SF (= *mugre*) filth, muck; **esa silla es una ~** that chair is filthy *o* disgusting; ✦**MODISMO caer en la ~** to sink very low

cochambroso ADJ filthy

cochayuyo SM (*LAm*) edible seaweed

cochazo* SM whacking great car*

coche¹ SM [1] (= *automóvil*) car, automobile (*EEUU*); (*frm*) **fuimos a Almería en ~** we drove to Almeria, we went to Almeria by car; **una exposición de ~s antiguos** a vintage car show ► **coche blindado** armoured car, armored car (*EEUU*) ► **coche bomba** car bomb ► **coche celular** police van, patrol wagon (*EEUU*) ► **coche de alquiler** hire car ► **coche de bomberos** fire engine ► **coche de caballos** coach, carriage ► **coche de carreras** racing car ► **coche de choque** bumper car, dodgem car ► **coche de cortesía** courtesy car ► **coche de época** vintage car ► **coche de línea** coach, long distance bus (*esp EEUU*) ► **coche de muertos** hearse ► **coche de ocasión** used car, second-hand car ► **coche deportivo** sports car ► **coche de punto**† taxi ► **coche de turismo** private car ► **coche escoba** (*Ciclismo*) sag wagon ► **coche fúnebre** hearse ► **coche K** unmarked police-car ► **coche mortuorio** hearse ► **coche patrulla** patrol car ► **coche radio-patrulla** radio patrol car ► **coche usado** used car, second-hand car ► **coche Z**, **coche zeta** police car, patrol car; ✦**MODISMO en el ~ de San Fernando** on Shanks's pony, on Shanks's mare (*EEUU*)
[2] (*Ferro*) coach, car (*esp EEUU*), carriage ► **coche cama** sleeping car, sleeper, Pullman (*EEUU*) ► **coche comedor** dining car, restaurant car ► **coche de correos** mail van ► **coche de equipajes** luggage van, baggage car (*EEUU*) ► **coche de literas** couchette car ► **coche de viajeros** passenger coach ► **coche directo** through carriage
[3] [*de bebé*] pram, baby carriage (*EEUU*)
[4] (*Méx*) (= *taxi*) taxi, cab

coche² SM (*CAm, Méx*) (= *animal*) pig, hog (*esp EEUU*); (= *carne*) pork ► **coche de monte** wild pig *o* boar

coche-bomba SM (*pl* **coches-bomba**) car bomb

coche-cabina SM (*pl* **coches-cabina**) bubble-car

coche-cama SM (*pl* **coches-cama**) sleeping car, sleeper, Pullman (*EEUU*)

cochecillo SM small carriage *etc* ► **cochecillo de inválido** invalid carriage

cochecito SM [1] (= *juguete*) toy car ► **cochecito de niño** toy car
[2] (*para bebé*) pram, baby carriage (*EEUU*); (*para niño*) pushchair, (baby) buggy, stroller (*EEUU*)
[3] (*Med*) wheelchair

coche-comedor SM (*pl* **coches-comedor**) dining-car, restaurant car

coche-correo SM (*pl* **coches-correo**) (*Ferro*) mail-van, mobile sorting-office

coche-cuba SM (*pl* **coches-cuba**) tank lorry, water wagon

coche-habitación SM (*pl* **coches-habitación**) caravan, trailer (*EEUU*)

cochemonte SM (*CAm*) wild pig, wild boar

coche-patrulla SM (*pl* **coches-patrulla**) patrol car

cochera SF [*de coches*] carport; [*de autobuses*] depot; [*de trenes*] engine shed; [*de tranvías*] tram shed, tram depot; [*de carruajes*] coach house ► **cochera de alquiler** livery stable

cocherada SF (*Méx*) coarse *o* vulgar expression

coche-restaurante SM (*pl* **coches-restaurante**) dining car, restaurant car

cochería SF (*Arg*) undertaker's

cochero Ⓐ ADJ **puerta cochera** carriage entrance
Ⓑ SM coachman; ✦**MODISMO hablar (en) ~** (*Méx*) to use coarse language ► **cochero de punto**† cabman, cabby*

cocherón SM (*Ferro*) engine-shed, locomotive depot

coche-salón SM (*pl* **coches-salón**) (*Ferro*) saloon coach

cochina SF sow; *ver tb* **cochino**

cochinada SF [1] (= *suciedad*) filth, filthiness
[2] (= *comentario*) filthy remark
[3] (= *cosa*) filthy object, dirty thing
[4] (= *canallada*) dirty trick; **hacer una ~ a algn** to play a dirty trick on sb

Cochinchina SF Cochin China; *ver tb* **Conchinchina**

cochinear* ▸conjug 1a◂ VI to talk dirty

cochinería SF = **cochinada**

cochinilla SF [1] (*Zool*) woodlouse
[2] (*Culin*) cochineal
[3] **de ~** (*Cuba, Méx*) trivial, unimportant

cochinillo SM (= *animal*) piglet; (= *carne*) suck(l)ing pig

cochino/a Ⓐ ADJ [1] (= *sucio*) filthy, dirty
[2] [*trabajo, sueldo, vacaciones*] rotten*, lousy*; [*mentira*] filthy*, rotten*; [*tiempo*] rotten*, lousy*, filthy*; **esta vida cochina** this rotten *o* miserable life*
Ⓑ SM/F [1] (= *animal*) pig, hog (*esp EEUU*) ► **cochino de leche** sucking pig, suckling pig
[2] (= *mala persona*) swine*
[3] (= *guarro*) filthy pig*; *ver tb* **cochina**

cochiquera SF, **cochitril** SM pigsty (*tb fig*)

cocho/a* (*LAm*) Ⓐ ADJ old
Ⓑ SM/F old man/old woman; *ver tb* **cocha**

cochón SM (*Hond*) poof‡, queer‡, fag (*EEUU*‡)

cochoso ADJ (*Andes*) filthy

cochura† SF [1] (= *acto*) = **cocción**
[2] (= *hornada*) batch of (loaves, cakes, bricks *etc*)

cocido Ⓐ ADJ [1] (*Culin*) boiled, cooked; **bien ~** well done
[2] (= *borracho*) **estar ~*** to be sloshed*
[3] (= *acalorado*) **estar ~*** to be roasting*
[4] **estar ~ en algo*** to be well versed in sth, be expert at sth
Ⓑ SM (*Esp*) stew (*of meat, bacon, chickpeas etc*); ✦**MODISMO ganarse el ~** to earn one's living

cociente SM (*Mat*) quotient; (*Dep*) [*de goles*] goal average ► **cociente intelectual** intelligence quotient, IQ

cocina SF [1] (= *habitación*) kitchen; **muebles de ~** kitchen units; ✦**MODISMO llegar hasta la ~** (*Dep*) to slice *o* burst through the defence ► **cocina amueblada** fitted kitchen; *ver tb* **batería A4, cuchillo 1**
[2] (= *aparato*) stove, cooker ► **cocina de gas** gas cooker, gas stove ► **cocina de petróleo** (*LAm*) oil stove ► **cocina económica** range ► **cocina eléctrica** electric cooker, electric stove (*esp EEUU*)
[3] (= *actividad*) cooking, cookery; (= *arte*) cuisine, cookery; **no me gusta nada la ~** I don't like cookery *o* cooking at all; **libro de ~** cookery book, cookbook (*EEUU*); **la ~ valenciana** Valencian cuisine, Valencian cookery; **alta ~** haute cuisine ► **cocina casera** home cooking

cocinada SF (*LAm*) (period of) cooking, cooking time

cocinado SM cooking

cocinar ▸conjug 1a◂ Ⓐ VT to cook
Ⓑ VI [1] (= *guisar*) to cook
[2] (= *tramar*) to plot, cook up*; **deben estar cocinando algo** they must be plotting something, they must be up to something

cocinero/a SM/F cook

cocineta SF (*LAm*) 1 (= *cuarto*) kitchenette, small kitchen
2 (= *aparato*) small cooker, small stove

cocinilla SF 1 (= *cuarto*) kitchenette, small kitchen
2 (= *aparato*) (*cocina pequeña*) small cooker, small stove; [*de alcohol*] spirit stove, alcohol stove (*EEUU*); (= *escalfador*) chafing dish

cocker ['koker] SM cocker spaniel, cocker

coco[1] SM 1 (*Bot*) (= *fruto*) coconut; (= *árbol*) coconut palm
2 (*) (= *cabeza*) nut*, noggin (*EEUU**), head; **se ha dado un golpe en el ~** he banged his head, he banged himself on the nut*; **no anda muy bien del ~** she's not right in the head*; **tuve que romperme el ~ para resolver el problema** I had to rack my brains to come up with an answer to the problem; ✦***MODISMOS*** **comer el ~ a algn**: **la tele les ha comido el ~** the TV has got them brainwashed; **mira, tío, no me comas el ~** hey, stop going on about it; **comerse el ~** to worry (one's head); *ver tb* **comedura**
3 (= *prodigio*) whizz*; **mi hermano es un ~ para las matemáticas** my brother is a whizz at maths*

coco[2] SM 1 (= *fantasma*) bogeyman, boogeyman (*EEUU**); **¡que viene el ~!** the bogeyman's coming!
2 (= *persona fea*) **es un ~** he's an ugly devil, he's ugly as sin*
3 **hacer ~s a algn** (= *carantoñas*) to make eyes at sb; (= *halagos*) to coax sb, wheedle sb

coco[3] SM 1 (= *bacteria*) coccus
2 (= *insecto*) weevil

cococha SF *in cod and hake, fleshy part of the jaw, considered a delicacy*

cocodrilo SM crocodile

cocol SM (*Méx*) sesame seed bun

cocoliche SM (*Cono Sur Ling*) *hybrid Spanish of Italian immigrants*

cócona SF (*Caribe*) tip

coconote SM (*Méx*) 1 (= *niño*) chubby child
2 (= *adulto*) squat person

cocoroco ADJ (*Cono Sur**) (= *engreído*) stuck-up*; (= *descarado*) insolent, cheeky*, sassy (*EEUU**)

cocorota SF nut*, noggin (*EEUU**), head

cocoso ADJ worm-eaten

cocotal SM coconut plantation, coconut grove

cocotero SM coconut palm

cóctel ['koktel, 'kotel] SM (*pl* **cóctels** *o* **cócteles**) 1 (= *bebida*) cocktail
2 (= *snack, entrante*) cocktail ► **cóctel de frutas** fruit cocktail ► **cóctel de gambas** prawn cocktail ► **cóctel de mariscos** seafood cocktail
3 (= *reunión*) cocktail party; **ofrecer un ~ en honor de algn** to hold a cocktail party in sb's honour
4 ► **cóctel (Molotov)** petrol bomb, Molotov cocktail

coctelera SF cocktail shaker

cocuyo SM (*LAm*) 1 (= *insecto*) firefly, glowfly (*EEUU*)
2 (*Aut*) rear light

cod. ABR = **código**

coda SF 1 (*Mús*) coda
2 (*Téc*) wedge

codal SM 1 (*Bot*) layered vine shoot
2 (*Arquit*) strut, prop

codaste SM stern post

codazo SM 1 (= *golpe*) **darle un ~ a algn** (*disimuladamente*) to give sb a nudge, nudge sb; (*con fuerza*) to elbow sb; **abrirse paso a ~s** to elbow one's way through
2 (*Méx*) ✦***MODISMO*** **dar ~ a algn** to tip sb off, warn sb

codear ▸conjug 1a◂ Ⓐ VT 1 (= *empujar con el codo*) to elbow, jostle, nudge
2 (*Andes, Cono Sur*) (= *insistir*) **~ a algn** to keep on at sb, pester sb
Ⓑ VI 1 (= *empujar con el codo*) (*disimuladamente*) to nudge; (*con fuerza*) to elbow, jostle; **abrirse paso codeando** to elbow one's way through
2 (*Andes, Cono Sur**) to sponge*, live by sponging*
Ⓒ **codearse** VPR (= *alternar*) **~se con** to hobnob with, rub shoulders with

codeína SF codeine

CODELCO SF ABR (*Chile*) = **Corporación del Cobre**

codeo* (*LAm*) SM 1 (= *sablazo*) sponging*
2 (= *insistencia*) pestering

codera SF (= *parche*) elbow patch; [*de protección*] elbow guard

codeso SM laburnum

códice SM codex

codicia SF (= *avaricia*) greed; (*por lo ajeno*) covetousness

codiciable ADJ desirable, covetable

codiciado ADJ [*medalla, trofeo*] coveted; [*zona, casa*] sought-after; **obtuvo el ~ título** he won the coveted title

codiciar ▸conjug 1b◂ VT [+ *dinero, bienes*] to desire; [+ *lo ajeno*] to covet

codicilo SM codicil

codiciosamente ADV greedily, covetously

codicioso ADJ covetous, greedy

codificación SF 1 (*Jur*) codification
2 [*de mensajes, textos*] encoding ► **codificación de barras** bar coding

codificado SM **el programa se emitirá en ~** the programme will be encrypted

codificador SM encoder

codificar ▸conjug 1g◂ VT 1 (*Jur*) to codify
2 [+ *mensaje, información*] to encode, code; (*TV*) to encrypt, scramble

código SM 1 (= *reglamento*) code ► **código civil** civil code ► **código de conducta** code of conduct ► **Código de Derecho Canónico** Canon Law Code ► **código de la circulación** highway code ► **código de leyes** statute book ► **código deontológico** code of practice, ethics (*esp EEUU*) ► **código ético** code of ethics ► **código militar** military law ► **código penal** penal code
2 [*de signos, números*] code; **teclee su ~ secreto** key in your password ► **código binario** binary code ► **código de acceso** access code ► **código de barras** bar code ► **código de colores** colour code, color code (*EEUU*) ► **código de máquina** (*Inform*) machine code ► **código de operación** (*Inform*) operational code ► **código de señales** signal code ► **código genético** genetic code ► **código hexadecimal** hexadecimal code ► **código legible por máquina** machine-readable code ► **código máquina** (*Inform*) machine code ► **código postal** postcode, zip code (*EEUU*)

codillo SM 1 (*Zool*) (= *articulación*) elbow; (= *pata*) upper foreleg; [*de cerdo*] knuckle ► **codillo de cerdo** (*Méx Culin*) pig's trotter
2 (*Téc*) elbow (joint), bend
3 (*Bot*) stump (of a branch)

codirigir ▸conjug 3c◂ VT to co-direct

codo[1] SM 1 (*Anat*) elbow; [*de caballo*] knee; ✦***MODISMOS*** **a base de ~s**: **sacó la oposición a base de ~s** he won the post by sheer hard work *o* through sheer hard graft; **comerse los ~s de hambre** to be utterly destitute; **dar con el ~** *o* **de ~ a algn** (*CAm*) to nudge sb; **empinar el ~*** to have a few*, bend the elbow*; **hablar por los ~s** to talk nineteen to the dozen, talk a blue streak (*EEUU*); **hacer ~s** ◊ **hincar los ~s** to swot*; **morderse un ~** (*Méx, Cono Sur*) to restrain o.s.; **partirse** *o* **romperse los ~s** to slog*; **ser del ~** ◊ **ser duro de ~** (*CAm*) to be mean ► **codo de tenista** tennis elbow
2 **codo a codo**: **hubo un ~ a ~ por el segundo puesto** there was a close battle for second place, it was neck and neck for second place; **las elecciones serán un ~ a ~ entre socialistas y nacionalistas** the elections are going to be a close-run thing *o* a neck and neck affair between the Socialists and Nationalists; **fue un combate ~ a ~** it was a neck and neck fight
3 **codo con codo** (*como adverbio*): **enemigos políticos se sentaron ~ con ~ en el funeral** political foes sat down together *o* sat side by side with each other at the funeral, political foes rubbed shoulders with each other at the funeral; **en las elecciones quedaron ~ con ~ con los socialistas** in the elections they were neck and neck with the Socialists; **luchar ~ con ~** to fight shoulder to shoulder, fight side by side; **trabajar ~ con ~** to work side by side *o* closely together
4 [*de camisa, chaqueta*] elbow
5 [*de tubería*] elbow, bend
6 (= *medida*) cubit

codo[2]* ADJ (*Méx*) (= *tacaño*) mean, stingy

codorniz SF quail

COE SM ABR = **Comité Olímpico Español**

coedición SF [*de libro*] joint publication; (= *acto*) joint publishing

coeditar ▸conjug 1a◂ VT to publish jointly

coeducación SF coeducation

coeducacional ADJ coeducational

coeficiente SM (*Mat*) coefficient; (*Econ*) rate; (*Med*) degree ► **coeficiente aerodinámico** drag factor ► **coeficiente de caja** cash deposit requirement ► **coeficiente de incremento** rate of increase ► **coeficiente de inteligencia** intelligence quotient, IQ ► **coeficiente de penetración aerodinámica** drag factor ► **coeficiente intelectual, coeficiente mental** intelligence quotient, IQ

coercer ▸conjug 2b◂ VT to constrain (*frm*)

coerción SF coercion (*frm*)

coercitivamente ADV coercively

coercitivo ADJ coercive

coestrella SMF co-star

coetáneo/a ADJ, SM/F contemporary (**con** with); **es famoso entre sus ~s** he is famous among his peers *o* contemporaries

coevo ADJ coeval

coexistencia SF coexistence ► **coexistencia pacífica** peaceful coexistence

coexistente ADJ coexistent

coexistir ▸conjug 3a◂ VI to coexist (**con** with)

cofa SF top ► **cofa mayor** maintop

cofabricar ▸conjug 1g◂ VT to manufacture jointly

cofia SF [*de enfermera, criada, monja*] cap; (††) coif; (†) (= *redecilla*) hair net

cofinanciación SF joint financing

cofinanciar ▸conjug 1b◂ VT to finance jointly

cofrade SM member (of a brotherhood), brother

cofradía SF (*Rel*) brotherhood, fraternity; (= *gremio*) guild, association; [*de ladrones etc*] gang; → SEMANA SANTA

cofre SM (= *caja*) chest; (*para joyas*) casket, jewellery *o* (*EEUU*) jewelry box, jewel case; (*Méx Aut*) bonnet, hood (*EEUU*)

cofrecito SM casket

cofundador(a) SM/F co-founder

cogedero Ⓐ ADJ [*fruto*] ripe for picking
Ⓑ SM handle

cogedor SM [*de polvo, basura*] dustpan; [*de ceniza*] (small) shovel

coger

▸conjug 2c◂
A VERBO TRANSITIVO
B VERBO INTRANSITIVO
C VERBO PRONOMINAL

Para las expresiones ***coger desprevenido, coger in fraganti****, ver la otra entrada.*

Ⓐ VERBO TRANSITIVO

1 = *con la mano* 1·1 (= *tomar*) to take; **¿puedo ~ éste?** can I take this one?; **~ un libro de un estante** to take a book from a shelf; **coge un poco más de queso** have a bit more cheese; **~ a algn de la mano** to take sb by the hand; **ir cogidos de la mano** to walk along holding hands *o* hand in hand

1·2 (= *levantar*) to pick up; **cogió la guitarra y se puso a tocar** he picked up the guitar and started to play; **coge al niño, que está llorando** pick up the baby, he's crying; **cogió el bolso y salió de casa** she picked up her handbag and went out

1·3 (*con fuerza*) to grasp; **la cogió por la muñeca y no la soltó** he grabbed her by the wrist and wouldn't let go

1·4 (= *sostener*) to hold; **coge bien el bolígrafo** hold the biro properly; **no ha cogido un fusil en la vida** he's never held a gun in his life

2 = *escoger* to pick; **cogió el azul** she picked the blue one; **coge el que más te guste** take *o* pick the one you like best; **has cogido un mal momento** you've picked a bad time

3 + *flor, fruta* to pick

4 = *quitar* (*gen*) to take; (= *pedir prestado*) to borrow; **me coge siempre las cerillas** he's always taking my matches; **¿quién ha cogido el periódico?** who's taken the newspaper?; **¿te puedo ~ el bolígrafo?** can I borrow your pen?; **te he cogido la regla** I've borrowed your ruler, I've pinched your ruler*

5 = *apuntar* to take (down); **cogió la dirección del cliente** she took (down) the customer's address; **~ apuntes** to take notes

6 *esp Esp* = *conseguir* to get; **¿nos coges dos entradas?** would you get us two tickets?; **cógeme un buen sitio** get me a good place; **he cogido un billete de avión** I've bought an air ticket; **~ hora para el dentista/en la peluquería** to make an appointment to see *o* with the dentist/at the hairdresser's

7 = *adquirir* 7·1 [+ *enfermedad*] to catch; **~ un resfriado** to catch a cold; **el niño cogió sarampión** the child got *o* caught measles; **~ frío** to get cold; **ha cogido una insolación** she's got sunstroke

7·2 [+ *costumbre, hábito*] to get into; [+ *acento*] to pick up; **ha cogido la costumbre de morderse las uñas** she has got into the habit of biting her nails; **ha cogido la manía de las quinielas** he's caught the pools craze; **cogieron acento irlandés** they picked up an Irish accent

7·3 [+ *fuerzas*] to gather; [+ *velocidad*] to gather, pick up

8 = *atrapar* 8·1 (*esp Esp*) [+ *persona, pez, balón*] to catch; **¡coge la pelota!** catch the ball!; **¡por fin te he cogido!** caught you at last!; **les cogieron con varios kilos de heroína** they were caught with several kilos of heroin

8·2 (*esp Esp*) [*toro*] (= *cornear*) to gore; (= *voltear*) to toss

8·3 (*esp Esp*) [*coche*] (= *atropellar*) to knock down, run over

8·4 (*Mil*) to take prisoner, capture; **han cogido a quince soldados** fifteen soldiers have been taken prisoner *o* have been captured

9 *esp Esp* = *sorprender* to catch; **la cogieron robando** they caught her stealing; **~ a algn en una mentira** to catch sb lying, catch sb in a lie; **la guerra nos cogió en Francia** the war found *o* caught us in France; **la noche nos cogió todavía en el mar** the night caught us still at sea; **antes que nos coja la noche** before night overtakes us *o* comes down on us; ✦***MODISMOS*** **~ a algn detrás de la puerta** ◊ **~ a algn en la hora tonta** to catch sb at a disadvantage; **~ de nuevas a algn** to take sb by surprise

10 = *empezar a sentir* **~ aversión a algo** to take a strong dislike to sth; **~ cariño a algn** to grow *o* become fond of sb, become attached to sb; **~ celos de algn** to become jealous of sb

11 = *tomarse* to take; **no sé si podré ~ vacaciones** I don't know if I'll be able to take any holidays; **¿vas a ~ fiesta mañana?** are you going to take tomorrow off?, are you going to take the day off tomorrow?

12 = *entender* [+ *sentido, giro*] to get; **¿no has cogido el chiste?** don't you get the joke?

13 *esp Esp* = *aceptar* [+ *empleados, trabajo*] to take on; [+ *alumnos*] to take in; [+ *pacientes*] (*en hospital*) to take in; (*en consultorio*) to take on; **acabo de ~ una secretaria nueva** I've just taken on a new secretary

14 = *alquilar* to take, rent; **cogimos un apartamento** we took *o* rented an apartment

15 = *viajar en* [+ *tren, avión, autobús*] to take; **vamos a ~ el tren** let's take *o* get the train; **quiero ~ el tren de las tres** I want to catch the three o'clock train

16 = *ir por* to take; **coja la primera calle a la derecha** take the first street on the right; **no cojas las curvas tan rápido** don't take the bends so fast

17 = *recibir* [+ *emisora, canal*] to pick up, get; **con esta radio cogemos Radio Praga** we can pick up *o* get Radio Prague on this set

18 = *retener* [+ *polvo*] to gather, collect; **esta moqueta coge mucho polvo** this carpet gathers *o* collects a lot of dust; **los perros cogen pulgas** dogs get *o* catch fleas

19 = *aprender* to pick up; **los niños lo cogen todo enseguida** children pick things up very quickly

20 = *incorporarse a* **cogí la conferencia a la mitad** I joined the discussion halfway through; **cogí la obra casi al final** the play was almost over when I got there

21 *Méx, Arg, Ven***: *sexualmente* to fuck**, screw**

Ⓑ VERBO INTRANSITIVO

1 = *estar* to be; **¿coge muy lejos de aquí?** is it very far from here?; **el cine coge bastante cerca** the cinema is quite near here; **el banco me coge de camino** the bank's on my way

2 = *ir* **~ por**: **cogió por esta calle** he went down this street

3 *Esp** = *caber* to fit; **aquí no coge** there's no room for it here, it doesn't fit (in) here

4 *planta* to take

5 *Méx, Arg, Ven***: *sexualmente* to fuck**, screw**

6 ✦***MODISMO*** **cogió y se fue*** he just upped and left *o* offed*

Ⓒ **cogerse** VERBO PRONOMINAL

1 = *sujetarse* **~se a** *o* **de algo** to hold on to sth; **se cogió a** *o* **de las rejas** he held on to the bars; **cógete a** *o* **de la cuerda** hold on to the rope; **~se a algn** to hold on to sb; **cógete a mí, que aquí resbala** hold on to me, it's slippery here

2 *enfático* 2·1 (= *pillarse*) [+ *catarro, gripe*] to catch; **~se los dedos en la puerta** to catch one's fingers in the door; **~se una borrachera** to get drunk

2·2 (= *tomarse*) [+ *vacaciones*] to take; **hace tiempo que no me cojo unas vacaciones** it's a long time since I took a holiday

2·3 (= *agarrar*) [+ *objeto*] to grab; **cógete una silla** grab a chair

cogestión SF joint management

cogida SF 1 (*Taur*) (= *cornada*) goring; **sufrir una ~** to be gored
2 (*Agr*) (= *cosecha*) harvest; (*Pesca*) catch; (= *acto*) [*de moras, fresas*] picking, gathering; [*de cereales*] harvesting
3 (*LAm***) screw**, fuck**

cogido SM (*Cos*) fold, gather, tuck

cogienda SF 1 (*Andes, Caribe*) = **cogida 2**
2 (*Méx***) fucking**, screwing**

cognado ADJ, SM cognate

cognición SF, **cognitividad** SF cognition

cognitivo ADJ, **cognoscitivo** ADJ cognitive

cogollo SM 1 (*Bot*) [*de lechuga, col*] heart; [*de árbol*] top; (*LAm*) [*de caña de azúcar*] sugarcane top; (= *brote*) shoot, sprout
2 (= *lo mejor*) best part, cream; **el ~ de la sociedad** the cream of society
3 [*de asunto, problema*] heart, crux; [*de ciudad*] centre, center (*EEUU*)
4 (*Caribe*) (= *sombrero*) straw hat

cogorza* SF **pescar una ~** to get plastered*

cogotazo SM (= *golpe*) blow on the back of the neck; (*Boxeo*) rabbit punch

cogote SM 1 (*Anat*) back of the neck, nape; **coger a algn por el ~** to take sb o grab sb o pick sb up by the scruff of the neck; ✦*MODISMOS* **estar hasta el ~** to have had it up to here; **ponérselas en el ~** (*CAm*‡) to beat it*
2 **de ~** (*Cono Sur*) [*animal*] fat; **carne de ~** (*Cono Sur*) rubbish, trash, garbage (*EEUU*)

cogotudo‡ Ⓐ ADJ (*Andes, Cono Sur*) well-heeled*, filthy rich*; (*Caribe*) powerful
Ⓑ SM (*LAm*) (= *nuevo rico*) self-made man, parvenu; **es un ~** he's got friends in high places

coguionista SMF co-scriptwriter

cogujada SF woodlark

cogulla SF cowl

cohabitación SF (= *vida en común*) cohabitation (*frm*); (*Pol*) coexistence

cohabitar ▸conjug 1a◂ VI (= *vivir juntos*) to live together, cohabit (*frm*); (*Pol*) to coexist

cohechar ▸conjug 1a◂ VT to bribe, offer a bribe to

cohecho SM bribery

coheredero/a SM/F coheir/coheiress, joint heir/joint heiress

coherencia SF 1 [*de ideas, razonamiento, exposición*] coherence
2 [*de acciones, proyecto, política*] consistency
3 (*Fís*) cohesion

coherente ADJ 1 [*texto, idea, exposición, argumentación*] coherent; **no sería ~ cumplir con sus órdenes** it wouldn't make sense to follow his orders
2 [*proyecto, política*] consistent; **~ con** in line with, in tune with

coherentemente ADV 1 (= *razonar, exponer, pensar*) coherently
2 (= *actuar*) consistently

cohesión SF cohesion

cohesionado ADJ united, unified

cohesionador ADJ **elemento ~** unifying force

cohesionar ▸conjug 1a◂ VT to unite, draw together

cohesivo ADJ cohesive

cohete Ⓐ SM 1 (*gen*) rocket ► **cohete de señales** flare, distress rocket ► **cohete espacial** (space) rocket ► **cohete luminoso** flare, distress rocket
2 (*Méx**) (= *pistola*) piece*, pistol
3 (*Cono Sur*) **al ~** to no effect
4 (*Méx*) (= *mecha*) blasting fuse
Ⓑ ADJ (*CAm, Méx**) (= *borracho*) drunk, tight*

cohetería SF 1 (= *fábrica*) fireworks factory; (= *tienda*) fireworks shop
2 (= *ciencia*) rocketry

cohibición SF 1 (*Jur*) restraint
2 (*Med*) inhibition

cohibido ADJ 1 (= *tímido*) shy, timid, self-conscious; (= *incómodo*) awkward, ill-at-ease; **sentirse ~** to feel awkward o ill-at-ease
2 (*Jur*) restrained, restricted
3 (*Med*) inhibited

cohibir ▸conjug 3a◂ Ⓐ VT 1 (= *incomodar*) to make awkward o ill-at-ease; (= *avergonzar*) to make shy, embarrass
2 (*Jur*) to restrain, restrict
3 (*Med*) to inhibit
Ⓑ **cohibirse** VPR 1 (= *incomodarse*) to feel awkward o ill-at-ease; (= *avergonzarse*) to feel embarrassed, become shy
2 (*Med*) to feel inhibited

cohombro SM cucumber

cohonestar ▸conjug 1a◂ (*frm*) VT 1 [+ *acto*] to cover up
2 [+ *diferencias*] to reconcile

cohorte SF cohort

COI SM ABR (= **Comité Olímpico Internacional**) IOC

coima SF 1 (*LAm**) (= *soborno*) backhander*, sweetener*, bribe; (= *acto*) bribing, bribery
2 (‡) (*en el juego*) rake-off*
3 (††) (= *concubina*) concubine; (= *puta*) whore

coimacracia* SF (*Perú*) rule of graft

Coimbra SF Coimbra

coime SM 1 (*Andes*) (= *camarero*) waiter
2 (†) (= *chulo*) pimp, ponce
3 (†) (*en el juego*) gambling operator

coimear ▸conjug 1a◂ VT (*Andes, Cono Sur*) (= *sobornar*) to bribe; (= *aceptar sobornos*) to take bribes from

coimero/a (*Andes, Cono Sur*) Ⓐ ADJ easily bribed, bent‡
Ⓑ SM/F bribe-taker; **son unos ~s** they are all bent‡

coincidencia SF 1 (= *casualidad*) coincidence; **es pura ~** it's just a coincidence, it's pure coincidence; **dio la ~ de que yo también estaba allí** it was a coincidence that I was also there
2 (= *acuerdo*) agreement; **en ~ con** in agreement with

coincidente ADJ coincident; **ser ~ con algn/algo** to be coincident with sb/sth

coincidentemente ADV coincidentally

▼**coincidir** ▸conjug 3a◂ VI 1 (*en el tiempo*) to happen at the same time, occur simultaneously (*frm*), to coincide; **para que se produzca una explosión han de ~ varias circunstancias** for an explosion to occur several circumstances must happen at the same time; **~ con algo** to coincide with sth; **la exposición coincide con el 50 aniversario de su muerte** the exhibition coincides with the 50th anniversary of his death; **mis vacaciones nunca coinciden con las de los niños** my holidays are never at the same time as my children's; **no puedo ir al concierto porque coincide con el examen** I can't go to the concert because it clashes with the exam
2 (*en un lugar*) to happen to meet; **coincidimos en el teatro** we happened to meet at the theatre; **he coincidido con él en varias fiestas pero nunca nos han presentado** I've coincided with him at some parties but we've never been introduced; **el punto en que las dos líneas coinciden** the point at which both lines meet
3 (= *estar de acuerdo*) 3·1 **~ con algn** to agree with sb; **coincido plenamente contigo en este punto** I fully agree with you on this point; **~ en algo**: **todos coinciden en que ésta es su mejor película** everyone agrees that this is his best film; **los observadores internacionales coinciden en afirmar que ...** international observers all agree that ...
3·2 [*informes, versiones, resultados*] to coincide; **las conclusiones de ambos estudios coinciden** the conclusions of the two studies coincide; **ambos ensayos coinciden en sus conclusiones** both essays reach the same conclusion; **~ con algo** to agree with sth, coincide with sth; **los hechos no coinciden exactamente con las declaraciones del testigo** the facts don't exactly agree with the witness's statement
4 (= *ajustarse*) [*huellas, formas*] to match, match up; **~ con algo** to match (up with) sth; **sus huellas dactilares no coinciden exactamente con las del asesino** his fingerprints don't match the murderer's exactly o don't match up exactly with the murderer's

cointérprete SMF fellow actor

coinversión SF joint investment

coipo SM, **coipu** SM (*LAm*) coypu

coirón SM (*Andes*) thatch

coito SM intercourse, coitus (*frm*) ► **coito anal** anal intercourse, anal sex

cojan *etc ver* **coger**

cojear ▸conjug 1a◂ VI 1 [*persona*] (= *estar cojo*) to limp, hobble (along); (= *ser cojo*) to be lame; **cojea de la pierna izquierda** (*temporalmente*) she's limping on her left leg; (*permanentemente*) she's lame in her left leg, she has a limp in her left leg; ✦*MODISMOS* **cojean del mismo pie** they're two of a kind; **sabemos de qué pie cojea** we know his weak points o weaknesses
2 [*mueble*] to wobble, be wobbly

cojera SF (= *estado*) lameness; (*al andar*) limp

cojijo† SM 1 (*Entomología*) bug, small insect
2 (= *queja*) peeve*, grudge, grumble

cojijoso† ADJ peevish, grumpy

cojín SM 1 (= *almohadilla*) cushion
2 (‡ *euf*) = **cojón**

cojinete SM 1 (= *almohadilla*) small cushion
2 (*Mec*) bearing ► **cojinete a bolas, cojinete de bolas** ball bearing ► **cojinete de rodillos** roller bearing
3 (*Ferro*) chair
4 **cojinetes** (*Andes, Caribe, Méx*) saddlebags

cojinillos SMPL (*CAm, Méx*) saddlebags

cojo[1]/a Ⓐ ADJ 1 (= *de andar defectuoso*) lame; **está un poco ~ por la caída** he's a bit lame from the fall; **~ de un pie** lame in one foot; **salió ~ del campo de juego** he left the ground limping; *ver tb* **pata A2**
2 (= *con una sola pierna, pata*) one-legged; **el típico pirata ~** the typical one-legged pirate; **se quedó ~ en la guerra** he lost a leg in the war
3 [*mueble, objeto*] wobbly
4 (= *incompleto*) [*equipo, organización*] weak, lame; **su expulsión dejó ~ al equipo** his sending-off left the team weak
Ⓑ SM/F 1 [*de andar defectuoso*] lame person
2 (*con una sola pierna*) one-legged person; ✦*REFRÁN* **el ~ echa la culpa al empedrado** a bad workman blames his tools

cojo[2] *ver* **coger**

cojón** SM 1 (= *testículo*) ball‡; ✦*MODISMOS* **con cojones**: **es un tío con cojones** he's got balls** o guts*; **echar cojones a algo** to brave sth out; **estar hasta los cojones**: **estoy hasta los cojones de este trabajo** I'm really pissed off with this job‡, I'm fed up to the back teeth with this job*; **ya estoy hasta los cojones de que me insulte** I'm totally pissed off (with) being insulted‡; **hago lo que me sale de los cojones** I do what I

➤ LENGUA Y USO: coincidir 3 53.6

damn well like *o* bloody well like‡; **¡olé sus cojones!** good for him!; **pasarse algo por (el forro de) los cojones**: **me lo paso por los cojones** I don't give a fuck‡‡ *o* toss‡ about it; **tener cojones**: **no tienes cojones de decírmelo a la cara** you haven't got the balls to tell me to my face‡‡; **tocar los cojones a algn**: **este tío me está tocando los cojones** this guy is pissing me off‡; **tocarse los cojones**: **se pasa el día tocándose los cojones** he spends all day doing fuck all‡‡ *o* sod all‡

2 (*como exclamación*) **callaos ya, ¡cojones!** shut up, for fuck's sake!‡‡; **¡los cojones!** ◊ **¡y un ~!**: **—dame el dinero —¡(y) un ~** *o* **los cojones!** "give me the money" — "go fuck yourself!"‡‡

3 (*como intensificador*) **¿qué cojones haces aquí?** what the fuck are you doing here!‡‡; **pero, ¿quién cojones se han creído que son?** who the fuck do they think they are?‡‡; **de cojones**: **¡hace un frío de cojones!** it's fucking freezing!‡‡; **con dos sueldos viven de cojones** with two salaries they have a fucking great life‡‡; **de los cojones**: **no aguanto al periodista ese de los cojones** I can't stand that fucking journalist‡‡; **por cojones**: **tienes que hacerlo por cojones** you fucking well have to do it‡‡

4 **un ~** (*como adverbio*): **cuesta un ~** it's worth a fucking fortune‡‡; **no me importa un ~ lo que tú digas** I don't give a fuck what you think‡‡; **ese tío sabe un ~** he knows fucking loads‡‡

cojonudamente‡ ADV brilliantly, awesomely (*EEUU**)

cojonudo‡ ADJ 1 (*Esp*) (= *estupendo*) brilliant*, awesome (*EEUU**); **un tío ~** a great bloke‡ *o* guy*; **¡qué ~!** great stuff!*

2 (= *grande*) huge, colossal; (= *muy importante*) very important; (= *destacado*) outstanding

3 (= *gracioso*) really funny

4 (*LAm*) (= *holgazán*) lazy, slow; (= *tonto*) stupid

cojudear‡ ▸conjug 1a◂ (*LAm*) Ⓐ VT to con*, swindle

Ⓑ VI to mess about

cojudez‡‡ SF (*Andes, Cono Sur*) nonsense, stupidity; **¡déjate de cojudeces!** stop pissing around!‡‡

cojudo/a Ⓐ ADJ 1 [*animal*] (= *sin castrar*) entire, not castrated; (= *semental*) used for stud purposes

2 (*Cono Sur*‡‡) (= *estúpido*) stupid

Ⓑ SM/F cretin*, stupid prick‡‡

cok [kok] SM, **coke** ['koke] SM (*LAm Min*) coke

col SF cabbage ► **col china** Chinese leaves *pl*, bok choy (*EEUU*) ► **col de bruselas** (Brussels) sprout ► **col de Saboya** savoy (cabbage) ► **col lombarda** red cabbage ► **col rizada** curly kale ► **col roja** red cabbage; ✦***REFRÁN*** **entre ~ y ~, lechuga** variety is the spice of life

col. ABR 1 (= **columna**) col

2 = **colaboradores**; **y ~** et al.

col.ª ABR (= **columna**) col

cola¹ SF 1 [*de animal, avión, cometa*] tail; ✦***MODISMOS*** **tener ~ de paja** (*Uru**) to feel guilty; **traer ~**: **la decisión del árbitro va a traer ~** this is not the last we will hear of the referee's decision ► **cola de caballo** (= *en el pelo*) pony tail; (= *planta*) horsetail ► **cola de milano**, **cola de pato** (*Téc*) dovetail ► **cola de rata** (*Pesca*) fly line

2 [*de frac*] tail; [*de vestido*] train

3 (= *hilera*) queue, line (*EEUU*); **hay una ~ enorme en la taquilla del cine** there's a huge queue at the box office; **se formó una ~ de dos kilómetros debido al accidente** a two-kilometre tailback formed because of the accident; **¡a la ~!** get in the queue!, get in line! (*EEUU*); **hacer ~** to queue (up), line up (*EEUU*); **ponerse a la ~** to join *o* get into the queue, join *o* get into the line (*EEUU*)

4 (= *parte final*) [*de manifestación*] tail end, back; [*de carrera*] back; **el ciclista estaba en** *o* **a la ~ del pelotón** the cyclist was at the back of *o* at the tail end of the pack; **los equipos en la ~ de la tabla** the teams at the foot *o* bottom of the table; **estamos a la ~ de las sociedades civilizadas** we are at the bottom of the league of civilized societies; **el equipo está en el tercer puesto por la ~** the team is sitting third place from (the) bottom

5 (*) (= *pene*) willy*, weenie (*EEUU**)

6 (*Ven Aut*) **pedir ~** to ask for a lift *o* ride (*EEUU*)

7 (*Cono Sur**) (= *trasero*) bum‡, bottom, ass (*EEUU**); (= *cóccix*) coccyx

cola² SF (= *pegamento*) glue, gum; (*para decorar*) size; **pintura a la ~** distemper; (*Arte*) tempera; ✦***MODISMOS*** **comer ~** (*Cono Sur*) to be let down, be disappointed; **no pegar ni con ~**: **esas cortinas no pegan ni con ~** those curtains just don't go with the rest; **el final de la película no pega ni con ~** the ending of the film is totally unconvincing; **el verde y el azul no pegan ni con ~** green and blue just don't go together ► **cola de carpintero** wood glue ► **cola de contacto** contact adhesive ► **cola de impacto** impact adhesive ► **cola de pescado** fish glue ► **cola de retal** size

cola³ SF 1 (= *planta*) cola, kola

2 (= *bebida*) cola, Coke®

3 (*Andes*) (= *refresco*) fizzy drink ► **cola de naranja** orangeade

cola⁴* SM (*Chile*) poof‡, queer‡

colaboración SF 1 (= *cooperación*) collaboration; **escrito en ~ con mi tutor** written in collaboration with my tutor ► **colaboracíon ciudadana** help from the public

2 (*en periódico*) (*gen*) contribution; (= *artículo*) article

3 [*de congreso*] paper

4 (= *donativo*) contribution

colaboracionismo SM collaboration

colaboracionista SMF collaborator, collaborationist

colaborador(a) SM/F 1 (*en trabajo, misión*) collaborator, co-worker

2 (*en periódico, revista*) contributor

3 (*en congreso*) contributor

4 (*con dinero*) contributor

colaborar ▸conjug 1a◂ VI to collaborate; **ambas organizaciones ~on estrechamente** the two organizations collaborated closely *o* worked closely together; **te necesitamos ¡colabora!** we need you, come and join us!; **~ a algo** to contribute to sth; **colaboró a la resolución del problema** he contributed to solving the problem; **~ con algn** to collaborate with sb; **~ con algo**: **colaboramos con los movimientos pacifistas** we are collaborating with the peace groups; **colaboró con cien euros** he contributed a hundred euros; **~ en algo**: **nuestra empresa ~á en el proyecto** our company is to collaborate on the project; **el viento colaboró en la propagación del incendio** the wind contributed to the spread of the fire; **~ en un periódico** to contribute to a newspaper, write for a newspaper

colaborativo ADJ collaborative

colación SF 1 (= *mención*) **sacar** *o* **traer a ~** to mention, bring up

2 (= *refrigerio*) light meal, collation (*frm*)

3 (= *comparación*) collation, comparison

4 (*LAm*) (= *dulce*) box of sweets

5 (*Univ*) conferral

colacionar ▸conjug 1a◂ VT to collate, compare

colada SF 1 (= *lavado*) washing; **hacer la ~** to do the washing; **día de ~** washday; **tender la ~** to hang out the washing; **todo saldrá en la ~** it will all come out in the wash

2 (= *lejía*) bleach, lye

3 (*Geol*) outflow

4 (*Agr*) sheep run, cattle run; *ver tb* **colado**

coladera SF 1 (*Culin*) strainer

2 (*Méx*) (= *alcantarilla*) sewer

coladero SM (*para té, infusión*) strainer; (*con agujeros*) colander; [*de malla*] sieve; ✦***MODISMO*** **dejar como un ~** to riddle with bullets

coladicto/a SM/F glue-sniffer‡

colado/a Ⓐ ADJ 1 [*metal*] cast

2 ✦***MODISMO*** **estar ~ por algn*** to be madly in love with sb

3 **aire ~** draught, draft (*EEUU*)

Ⓑ SM/F (= *intruso*) intruder; (*en fiesta, recepción*) gatecrasher; *ver tb* **colada**

colador SM (*para té, infusión*) strainer; (*con agujeros*) colander; [*de malla*] sieve; ✦***MODISMO*** **dejar como un ~** to riddle with bullets

coladura SF 1 (= *filtración*) straining

2 (*) (= *metedura de pata*) clanger*, blunder

3 **coladuras** grounds, dregs

colágeno SM collagen

colapsar ▸conjug 1a◂ Ⓐ VT 1 (= *derribar*) to cause to collapse 2 [+ *tráfico, circulación*] to bring to a halt *o* standstill; [+ *puerta*] to jam, block; [+ *entrada*] to block

Ⓑ VI, **colapsarse** VPR (= *derrumbarse*) to collapse, go to pieces

colapso SM 1 (*Med*) **el boxeador sufrió un ~** the boxer collapsed ► **colapso cardíaco** heart failure ► **colapso cardiovascular** circulatory collapse ► **colapso respiratorio** respiratory failure

2 [*de régimen, imperio, empresa*] collapse; **el país está al borde del ~ económico** the country is on the verge of economic collapse

3 (= *paralización*) **el accidente provocó el ~ del tráfico** the accident caused traffic to come to a standstill *o* to grind to a halt

colar ▸conjug 1l◂ Ⓐ VT 1 [+ *leche, infusión, verduras, caldo*] to strain

2 (*) (*furtivamente*) 2·1 [*objetos*] to sneak; **consiguió ~lo por la aduana** he managed to sneak it through customs; **le coló un gol al portero** he sneaked a goal past the keeper

2·2 **~ algo a algn** (= *dar algo malo*) to palm sth off on sb, palm sb off with sth; (= *hacer creer algo*) to spin sb a yarn about sth*; **quiso**

~nos varias monedas falsas he tried to palm off some forged coins on us *o* palm us off with some forged coins; **me coló una peras podridas** he palmed off some rotten pears on me, he slipped me some rotten pears; **el ladrón intentó ~les que era el revisor de la luz** the burglar tried to pass himself off as the electricity man, the burglar tried to spin them a yarn about being the electricity man; **¡a mí no me la cuelas!** don't give me any of that!*

2·3 **~ a algn** (*en espectáculo, cine*) to sneak sb in

3 [+ *metal*] to cast

4 (= *blanquear*) [+ *ropa*] to bleach

Ⓑ VI 1 (*) (= *ser creído*) **diles que estás enfermo, igual cuela** say you're ill, they might swallow it*; **me parece que tu historia no va a ~** I don't think your story will wash*, I don't think they'll swallow your story*; **tienes que copiar muy bien la firma para que cuele el cheque** you'll need to copy the signature very well if you want the cheque to go through

2 (*) (= *beber*) to booze*, tipple

Ⓒ **colarse** VPR 1 (= *filtrarse*) **el agua se cuela por las rendijas** the water seeps (in) through *o* gets in through the cracks; **se le coló el balón** the ball slipped past him; **la moto se iba colando entre la fila de coches** the motorbike slipped through the line of cars

2 [*personas*] (*sin pagar*) to get in without paying; (*en lugar prohibido*) to sneak in; (*en fiesta*) to gatecrash; **intentaron ~se en el concierto** they tried to get into the concert without paying; **se coló silenciosamente en la habitación** he sneaked quietly into the room; **un equipo de segunda división se había colado en las semifinales** a second division team had slipped through to the semifinals

3 [*error*] **se le ~on varias faltas al revisar el texto** he overlooked several mistakes when revising the text

4 (*en una cola*) to jump the queue, cut in line (*EEUU*); **se me intentó ~** he tried to jump the queue in front of me; **¡oiga, no se cuele!** excuse me, there's a queue!

5 (*Esp**) (= *equivocarse*) to get it wrong*; **¡huy! ¡me colé!** oops! I got it wrong!*; **ahí te has colado porque yo no dije nada de eso** you got it wrong there, because I didn't say anything about that

6 (*Esp*) (= *enamorarse*) **~se por algn** to fall for sb

colateral ADJ collateral

colca SF (*Andes*) (= *troje*) barn, granary; (= *almacén*) storeroom; (= *ático*) attic store, loft

colcha SF bedspread, counterpane

colchón SM 1 (*gen*) mattress; ✦*MODISMO* **servir de ~ a** to act as a buffer for ► **colchón de aire** airbed; (*Téc*) air cushion ► **colchón de muelles** spring mattress, interior sprung mattress ► **colchón de plumas** feather bed ► **colchón neumático** airbed

2 (= *precio*) floor price, reserve price; (= *fondos*) reserve fund

colchoneta SF mat

colcrén SM cold cream

cole* SM = **colegio 1**

colear ▸conjug 1a◂ Ⓐ VT 1 [+ *toro*] to hold on to the tail of

2 (*LAm**) (= *regañar*) to nag, give a hard time*

3 (*CAm*) (= *seguir*) to tail, follow

Ⓑ VI 1 [*perro*] to wag its tail; [*caballo*] to swish its tail; [*pez*] to wriggle

2 (*fig*) **el asunto todavía colea** the affair is still not settled; ✦*MODISMO* **estar vivito y coleando** to be alive and kicking

3 (*CAm, Caribe*) (*en edad*) **colea en los 50** he's close on 50, he's knocking on 50*

Ⓒ **colearse** VPR (*Caribe*) 1 (*Aut*) to skid (out of control)

2 [*huésped*] to arrive unexpectedly *o* uninvited

colección SF collection; **es de ~** (*Méx*) it's a collector's item

coleccionable Ⓐ ADJ collectable

Ⓑ SM (= *objeto*) collectable; (*Prensa*) pull-out section

coleccionador(a) SM/F collector

coleccionar ▸conjug 1a◂ VT, VI to collect

coleccionismo SM collecting

coleccionista SMF collector

colecta SF 1 (= *recaudación*) collection (for charity)

2 (*Rel*) collect

colectar ▸conjug 1a◂ VT to collect

colecticio ADJ 1 (*Mil*) raw, untrained

2 **tomo ~** omnibus edition, collected works

colectivamente ADV collectively

colectivero SM (*LAm*) (mini-)bus driver, *driver of a "colectivo"*

colectividad SF (*gen*) collectivity; (= *grupo*) group, community; **en ~** collectively

colectivización SF collectivization

colectivizar ▸conjug 1f◂ VT to collectivize

colectivo Ⓐ ADJ 1 [*responsabilidad, esfuerzo*] collective; [*obra, proyecto*] collective, group *antes de s*; **el transporte ~** collective transport; **acción colectiva** joint action; *ver tb* **convenio, inconsciente B, negociación**

2 (*Ling*) collective

Ⓑ SM 1 (= *grupo*) group; **el ~ más desfavorecido de la sociedad** the least favoured group in society

2 (*LAm*) (= *autobús*) bus; (= *taxi*) taxi

colector SM 1 (*Elec*) collector; (*Mec*) sump, trap; **~ de aguas residuales** main sewer ► **colector solar** solar panel

2 (†) (= *recaudador*) collector

colega SMF 1 [*de trabajo*] colleague

2 (= *amigo*) (*) mate*, pal*, buddy (*EEUU**); (*en oración directa*) man*

colegiado/a Ⓐ ADJ 1 [*médico, profesor, ingeniero*] member of a professional body; **has de estar ~ para ejercer de profesor** you have to be a member of the professional association of teachers to work as a teacher; **decisión colegiada** decision voted on by members; **tribunal ~** bench of judges

2 (*LAm*) (= *cualificado*) qualified

Ⓑ SM/F (*Dep*) referee; (*Med*) doctor

colegial(a) Ⓐ ADJ 1 (*Escol*) school *antes de s*

2 (*Rel*) collegiate

3 (*Méx*) (= *inexperto*) raw, green*, inexperienced

Ⓑ SM/F schoolboy/schoolgirl

colegialidad SF 1 (= *cuerpo*) college; [*asociación, institución*] collegiate, membership

2 (= *cualidad*) collegiality, corporate feeling

colegiarse ▸conjug 1a◂ VPR to become a member of a professional body

colegiata SF collegiate church

colegiatura(s) SF(PL) (*Méx*) school fees, university fees

colegio SM 1 (*Escol*) school; **mañana no hay ~** there's no school tomorrow; **ir al ~** to go to school; **los niños están en el ~** the children are at school; **estudió en este ~** he went to this school ► **colegio de curas** Catholic boys school (*run by priests*) ► **colegio de monjas** convent school ► **colegio de pago** fee-paying school ► **colegio mayor** (*Univ*) hall of residence; (*Hist*) college ► **colegio privado** private school ► **colegio público** state school, public school (*EEUU*) ► **Colegio Universitario** university college

2 (= *corporación*) ► **colegio cardenalicio** College of Cardinals ► **colegio de abogados** bar (association) ► **colegio de arquitectos** architects' association ► **Colegio de cardenales** College of Cardinals ► **colegio de médicos** medical association

3 (*Pol*) ► **colegio electoral** (= *lugar*) polling station; (= *electores*) electoral college

COLEGIO

Uso del artículo

A la hora de traducir expresiones como **al colegio/a la escuela** o **en el colegio/en la escuela, desde el colegio/desde la escuela** *etc*, hemos de tener en cuenta el motivo por el que alguien acude al recinto o está allí:

- Se traduce **al colegio/a la escuela** por **to school**, **en el colegio** o **en la escuela** por **at school** y **desde el colegio** o **desde la escuela** por **from school** cuando alguien va o está allí en calidad de alumno:

  El primer día que fui al colegio me pasé toda la mañana llorando

  The first day I went to school I spent the whole morning crying

  Juan todavía está en el colegio. Lo han castigado

  Juan's still at school. He's been given a detention

- Se traduce **al colegio/a la escuela** por **to the school**, **en el colegio/en la escuela** por **at the school** y **desde el colegio/desde la escuela** por **from the school** cuando alguien va o está en el centro por otros motivos:

  Ayer fueron mis padres al colegio para hablar con el director

  Yesterday my parents went to the school to talk to the headmaster

  Podemos quedar en el colegio y luego ir a tomar algo

  We can meet at the school and then go for a drink

Para otros usos y ejemplos ver la entrada.

colegir ▸conjug 3c, 3k◂ (*frm*) VT 1 (= *juntar*) to collect, gather

2 (= *inferir*) to infer (**de** from); **de lo cual colijo que ...** from which I deduce *o* gather that ...

coleóptero SM coleopteran, coleopteron

cólera Ⓐ SF 1 (= *ira*) anger, rage; **descargar la ~ en** to vent one's anger on; **montar en ~** to fly into a rage

2 (*Anat*) bile

Ⓑ SM (*Med*) cholera

colérico ADJ (= *furioso*) angry, furious; (= *malhumorado*) irritable, bad-tempered

colero SM (*Chile*) top hat

colesterol SM cholesterol

coleta SF [1] [*de pelo*] ponytail; (*Taur*) pigtail; **gente de ~** bullfighters; ✦**MODISMO cortarse la ~** to quit, retire, hang up one's spurs*; **me cortaré la ~ si ...*** I'll eat my hat if ...
[2] (= *adición*) postscript, afterthought

coletazo SM [1] [*de animal*] *blow or thrash or swipe with the tail*
[2] (*Aut*) swaying movement; **dar ~s** to sway about; ✦**MODISMO está dando los últimos ~s** [*régimen, sistema*] it's in its death throes; [*moda*] it's had its day; [*huracán*] it's petering out

coletero SM scrunchy

coletilla SF (*en carta, discurso*) postscript, afterthought; (*en frase*) tag

coleto SM [1] (*) ✦**MODISMOS decir para su ~** to say to o.s.; **echarse algo al ~** (= *comer*) to put sth away; (= *beber*) to drink sth down; **echarse un libro al ~** to get through *o* polish off a book*
[2] (*Caribe*) (= *fregasuelos*) mop
[3] (*Hist*) doublet, jerkin

colgadero SM (= *gancho*) peg; (= *percha*) hanger

colgadizo Ⓐ ADJ hanging, loose
Ⓑ SM (= *tejadillo*) piece of roofing; (*Caribe*) (= *techo*) flat roof

colgado Ⓐ PP *de* **colgar**
Ⓑ ADJ [1] (= *pendiente*) **la bombilla colgada del techo** the light bulb hanging from the ceiling; **este cuadro estuvo ~ muchos años en el museo de la ciudad** this picture hung for many years in the city museum; **me dejaron ~ del teléfono** I was left hanging on the phone; **está ~ del teléfono todo el día** he's on the phone all day long; *ver tb* **colgar B**
[2] (= *ahorcado*) hanged, hung
[3] (*) [*asignatura*] **tengo la física colgada** I have to resit *o* retake physics; **me han dejado el inglés ~** I've failed English
[4] **dejar ~ a algn*** (*en una situación difícil*) to leave sb in the lurch*; (*en una cita*) to stand sb up*; **se fue del país y me dejó ~ con todas las facturas del negocio** he's left the country and left me in the lurch with all the company invoices to sort out*; **vendrás ¿no?, espero que no me dejes ~** you'll be there, won't you? I hope you're not going to stand me up*
[5] (‡) (= *drogado*) spaced out‡; (= *chiflado*) nuts*; (= *sin dinero*) broke*, short of money; **estoy ~ de deudas** I'm up to my neck in debts*
[6] (‡) (= *enviciado*) **~ de algo** hooked on sth*; **estar ~ del bingo** to be hooked on bingo*; **estar ~ de las emociones fuertes** to be hooked on big thrills*; **estar ~ de la tele** to be glued to the TV*
[7] (‡) (= *enamorado*) **estoy muy ~ de ella** I'm crazy about her*
[8] (*Chile**) (= *ignorante*) clueless*; **salí muy ~ de la clase** I left the class completely clueless*; **estoy muy ~ en geografía** I haven't got a clue about geography*, I'm clueless in geography*
Ⓒ SMF (‡) [1] (= *drogadicto*) druggie*
[2] (= *chiflado*) nutter*

colgadura SF (*tb* **~s**) hangings *pl*, drapes *pl*; (= *tapiz*) tapestry ► **colgaduras de cama** bed hangings *o* curtains

colgajo SM [1] (= *trapo*) strip, shred
[2] (*Bot*) bunch (*of grapes hung to dry*)
[3] (*Med*) flap of skin

colgante Ⓐ ADJ hanging; **jardín ~** hanging garden; *ver tb* **puente A1**
Ⓑ SM [1] (= *joya*) pendant
[2] (*Arquit*) festoon
[3] (*Caribe*) [*de reloj*] watch chain

colgar ▸conjug 1h, 1l◂ Ⓐ VT [1] (= *colocar pendiendo*) [+ *cuadro, diploma*] to hang, put up; [+ *colada, banderines*] to hang out; [+ *cartel, letrero, lámpara, cortina*] to put up; [+ *ropa*] (*en armario*) to hang up; (*para secar*) to hang out; **cuelga el abrigo en la percha** hang your coat on the hook; **cada día cuelgan el cartel de "no hay billetes"** every day the "sold out" sign goes up; **le colgó un collar al** *o* **del cuello** he put *o* hung a necklace around her neck; ✦**MODISMOS ~ las botas** to hang up one's boots; **~ los estudios** to give up one's studies; **~ los hábitos** to leave the priesthood; **~ los libros** to give up one's studies; **~ la raqueta** to hang up one's racket; **~ el uniforme** to hang up one's uniform
[2] (= *ahorcar*) to hang; **¡que lo cuelguen!** hang him!, string him up!*
[3] [+ *teléfono*] to put down; **~ a algn** to hang up on sb, put the phone down on sb; **colgó el teléfono** he hung up; **dejar el teléfono mal colgado** to leave the phone off the hook
[4] (= *atribuir*) [+ *apodo, mote*] to give; **le ~on el mote de "el lobo"** they nicknamed him "el lobo"; **enseguida te cuelgan la etiqueta de envidioso** they label you as jealous straight away; **~ la culpa a algn** to pin the blame on sb; *ver tb* **sambenito 1**
Ⓑ VI [1] [*cuadro, lámpara*] to hang; **~ de** [+ *techo*] to hang from; [+ *pared*] to hang on; **hay telarañas colgando del techo** there are cobwebs hanging from the ceiling; **lo encontraron con la jeringuilla aún colgando del brazo** he was found with the syringe still hanging from his arm; **de la pared colgaba un espejo** there was a mirror hanging on the wall; **llevar algo colgado a** *o* **del cuello** to wear sth round one's neck
[2] (= *caer suelto*) [*rizos, tirabuzones*] to hang down; **le colgaban dos ricitos sobre la frente** she had two little curls hanging down over her forehead; **la ropa le colgaba por todas partes** his clothes were hanging off him
[3] (*al teléfono*) to hang up; **han colgado** they've hung up, they've put the phone down; **no cuelgue, por favor** please, hold the line
Ⓒ **colgarse** VPR [1] (= *estar suspendido*) **~se de** to hang from; **se colgó de una grúa durante varias horas** he hung from a crane for several hours; **~se del brazo de algn** to take hold of sb's arm, take sb by the arm; **~se del cuello de algn** to throw one's arms around sb's neck; **~se del teléfono**: **se colgó del teléfono durante más de una hora** she was on the phone for over an hour
[2] (= *ahorcarse*) to hang o.s.
[3] (= *ponerse*) to put on; **se colgó el bolso del** *o* **al hombro** she put her bag on her shoulder
[4] (*Esp*‡) (= *con drogas*) to flip*, blow one's head‡
[5] (*Chile, Méx*) *to plug illegally into the mains*

> **COLGAR**
>
> **¿"Hanged" o "hung"?**
>
> • Cuando **colgar** significa **ahorcar**, **hang** es un verbo regular y **hanged** es tanto el pasado como el participio:
>
> Le colgaron al amanecer
> ***He was hanged at dawn***
>
> • En el resto de los casos **hang** es irregular, y **hung** es la forma tanto de pasado como de participio:
>
> He colgado el cuadro en mi habitación
> ***I've hung the picture in my room***
>
> *Para otros usos y ejemplos ver la entrada.*

colibrí SM hummingbird

cólico SM colic

colicuar ▸conjug 1d◂ Ⓐ VT (= *derretir*) to melt; (= *disolver*) to dissolve
Ⓑ **colicuarse** VPR (= *derretir*) to melt; (= *disolver*) to dissolve; [*gas*] to liquefy

colifato* (*Cono Sur*) Ⓐ ADJ nuts‡, crazy
Ⓑ SM madman, nutcase‡

coliflor SF cauliflower

coligado Ⓐ ADJ allied, coalition *antes de s*; **estar ~s** to be allied, be in league
Ⓑ SM ally

coligarse ▸conjug 1h◂ VPR to unite, join together, make common cause (**con** with)

coliguacho SM (*Cono Sur*) horsefly

coligüe SM (*Arg, Chile*) bamboo

colilla SF cigarette butt, cigarette end, fag end‡; ✦**MODISMO ser una ~*** to be past it, be all washed up*

colimba* (*Arg*) Ⓐ SM recruit, conscript, draftee (*EEUU*)
Ⓑ SF military service; **hacer la ~** to do one's military service

colimbo[1] SM (*Orn*) diver, loon (*EEUU*)

colimbo[2] SM (*Arg*) recruit, conscript, draftee (*EEUU*)

colín SM (*Caribe*) cane knife

colina SF hill

colinabo SM kohlrabi

colindante ADJ adjacent, adjoining, neighbouring, neighboring (*EEUU*)

colindar ▸conjug 1a◂ VI to adjoin, be adjacent; **~ con** [*país*] to have a border with; [*casa, finca*] to adjoin

colirio SM eye drops *pl*

colirrojo SM redstart

colís SM (*Andes*) cane knife

Coliseo SM Coliseum

colisión SF [1] [*de vehículos*] collision, crash ► **colisión de frente** head-on collision ► **colisión en cadena** multiple collision, multiple pile-up ► **colisión frontal** head-on collision ► **colisión múltiple** multiple collision, multiple pile-up
[2] (*entre personas, intereses, ideas*) clash

colisionar ▸conjug 1a◂ VI to collide; **~ con** *o* **contra** [*tren, autobús, coche*] to collide with; [*persona, ideas*] to clash with, conflict with

colista Ⓐ SM (*Dep*) bottom team (in the league)
Ⓑ SMF person standing in a queue, person standing in a line (*EEUU*)

colita[1] SF (*Ven Aut*) lift; **hacer ~** to hitchhike, thumb a lift
colita[2]* SF [*de niño*] willy*, weenie (*EEUU**)
colitis SF INV colitis
colla SMF (*Bol, Perú*) Indian from the altiplano
collado SM [1] (= *colina*) hill; (*más pequeña*) hillock
[2] (= *puerto*) mountain pass
collage [ko'la:ʒ] SM collage
collalba SF (*Orn*) wheatear
collar SM [1] (= *adorno*) necklace; (= *insignia*) chain (of office) ► **collar de perlas** pearl necklace
[2] [*de perro*] (dog) collar; (*Zool*) collar, ruff
[3] (*Mec*) collar, ring
[4] ► **collar de fuerza** stranglehold
collarín SM surgical collar ► **collarín ortopédico** orthopaedic collar
colleja SF [1] (*planta*) campion
[2] (*) (*golpe*) slap on the back of the neck
collera SF [1] (*Agr*) horse collar
[2] **colleras** (*Cono Sur*) (= *gemelos*) cufflinks
collie ['koli] SM collie
collín SM (*CAm*), **collines** SM (*Andes*) cane knife, machete
colmado Ⓐ ADJ [*vaso*] full to the brim (**de** with), full (**de** of); [*río*] overflowing (**de** with); [*plato, cuchara*] heaped (**de** with); **una cucharada colmada** a heaped tablespoonful; **una carrera colmada de incidentes** an eventful race
Ⓑ SM (= *tienda*) grocer's shop, grocery store (*EEUU*); (*Andalucía*) (= *bodega*) retail wine shop; (= *restaurante*) cheap seafood restaurant
colmar ▸conjug 1a◂ VT [1] (= *llenar*) [+ *vaso, recipiente*] to fill to the brim, fill to overflowing, fill right up (**de** with); [+ *cuchara, plato*] to heap (**de** with)
[2] [+ *ambición, esperanzas*] to fulfil, fulfill (*EEUU*), realize
[3] **~ a algn de algo: ~ a algn de honores** to shower sb with honours *o* (*EEUU*) honors; **~ a algn de improperios** to heap insults *o* abuse on sb, shower sb with insults *o* abuse; **~ a algn de alabanzas** to heap praise on sb
colmatación SF silting
colmena SF [1] [*de abejas*] beehive, hive; **este edificio/barrio es una ~** this building is a warren
[2] (*Méx*) (= *abeja*) bee; (= *conjunto*) bees
colmenar SM apiary
colmenero/a SM/F beekeeper
colmillo SM (*Anat*) eye tooth, canine (tooth); (*Zool*) fang; [*de elefante, morsa, jabalí*] tusk; **enseñar los ~s** to show one's teeth, bare one's teeth; ✦**MODISMOS escupir por el ~** to talk big*, brag; **tener ~s** (*Méx*) to be long in the tooth*; **tener el ~ torcido** to be an old fox; **¡ya tengo ~s!** (*Méx*) you can't fool me!
colmillón SM (*LAm*) greed
colmilludo ADJ [1] (= *dentudo*) with big teeth *o* fangs *o* tusks
[2] (*) (= *sagaz*) sharp, alert
colmo SM **¡eres el ~! ¡deja ya de quejarte!** you really take the biscuit! just stop complaining!; **¡esto es el ~! ¡ya no lo aguanto más!** this is the last straw! I can't stand it any longer!; **tu hermano es el ~, no paro de reírme con él** your brother is hilarious *o* is something else*, he makes me laugh so much; **el ~ de la elegancia** the height of elegance; **para ~** to top it all, to cap it all; **y, para ~, se le rompió el ordenador** and to top *o* cap it all his computer broke; **para ~ de desgracias** *o* **de males** to make matters worse; ✦**MODISMO ser el ~ de los ~s**: **que la mismísima policía le robe es ya el ~ de los ~s** to be robbed by the police themselves really is the limit
colocación SF [1] (= *acto*) (*gen*) placing; [*de bomba*] planting; [*de baldosa, moqueta, primera piedra*] laying; [*de cuadro*] hanging; **la simple ~ de un espejo frente a otro da sensación de espacio** simply placing one mirror opposite another creates an impression of space; **una fuga de gas producida por la incorrecta ~ del regulador** a gas leak caused by the incorrect installation of the regulator *o* by installing the regulator incorrectly; **la campaña consistirá en la ~ de carteles en lugares públicos** the campaign will consist of putting up posters in public places
[2] (= *empleo*) job; **no encuentro ~** I can't find a job; **agencia de colocaciones** employment agency
[3] (= *situación*) positioning; **el balón no entró gracias a la buena ~ del portero** thanks to the good positioning of the goalkeeper, the ball did not go in; **he cambiado la ~ de los muebles** I've rearranged the furniture
[4] (*Com*) [*de acciones*] placing, placement
colocado ADJ [1] (*en trabajo*) **estar ~** to be in work, have a job; **mi hija está muy bien colocada** my daughter has a very good job
[2] (*Esp*‡) (= *drogado*) high*; (= *borracho*) smashed*, plastered*, trashed (*EEUU*‡)
[3] **apostar para ~** to back (a horse) for a place
[4] (*Chile**) **estar ~** to be well in*; **estar ~ con algn** to be well in with sb*
colocar ▸conjug 1g◂ Ⓐ VT [1] (= *situar*) (*gen*) to place; [+ *cartel*] to put up; [+ *bomba*] to plant, place; [+ *tropas*] to position, place; [+ *baldosa, moqueta, primera piedra*] to lay; [+ *cuadro*] to hang; (*Náut*) [+ *quilla*] to lay down; **coloca en cada plato una bola de helado** place a scoop of ice cream on each plate; **colocamos la estatua en el centro** we placed the statue in the centre; **de un solo pase colocó la pelota en la portería** he put *o* placed the ball in the net with just one touch; **coloca las tazas en su sitio** put the cups away; **~on carteles en el colegio** they put posters up around the school; **~ un producto en el mercado** to place a product on the market
[2] (= *ordenar*) [+ *muebles, objetos, libros*] to arrange; **tenemos que ~ los muebles de otro modo** we need to arrange the furniture differently; **he colocado las revistas por orden alfabético** I've arranged the magazines in alphabetical order; **colocó a los niños en fila** he lined the children up
[3] (= *dar trabajo*) **~ a algn** [*agencia*] to get sb a job; [*empresario, jefe*] to give sb a job; **ha colocado a su hermano como camarero en su bar** he got his brother a job as a waiter in his bar
[4] (*Fin*) [+ *acciones, dinero*] to place
[5] (†) (= *casar*) to marry off; **tiene a todas sus hijas bien colocadas** she has all her daughters nicely married off
[6] (*) (= *endilgar*) **~ algo a algn** to palm sth off on sb, palm sb off with sth; **nos han colocado un vídeo que no funciona** they've palmed us off with a video that doesn't work; **no sé a quién ~ estas enciclopedias** I don't know who to palm these encyclopaedias off on; **otra vez quería ~nos el mismo rollo** he tried to fob us off with the same old story again*
Ⓑ VI (*Esp*‡) [*drogas, alcohol*] **este vino coloca** this wine is pretty strong stuff
Ⓒ **colocarse** VPR [1] (*en un lugar*) (*de pie*) to stand; (*sentado*) to sit; **colócate aquí** stand here; **siempre se coloca en el mismo asiento** she always sits in the same seat; **me coloqué en primera fila** I took my place in the front row
[2] (*en una clasificación*) **se acaban de ~ en quinto lugar** they have just moved into fifth place; **el programa se ha colocado en el primer lugar de la lista de audiencia** the programme is now top of the ratings *o* has reached the top of the ratings
[3] (*en un trabajo*) to get a job; **se ha colocado como** *o* **de enfermera** she's got a job as a nurse
[4] (*Esp*‡) (= *emborracharse*) to get pissed‡, get trashed (*EEUU*‡) (**con** on); (= *drogarse*) to get high* (**con** on)
colocata‡ SMF (= *borracho*) drunk*; (= *drogado*) junkie*
colocho (*CAm*) Ⓐ ADJ (= *rizo*) curly(-haired)
Ⓑ **colochos** SMPL [1] (= *rizos*) curls
[2] (= *virutas*) wood shavings
colocolo SM (*Chile*) [1] (= *gato montés*) codcod, *type of wildcat*
[2] (= *monstruo*) mythical monster
colocón‡ SM **cogerse un ~** to get high‡
colodrillo SM back of the neck
colofón SM [1] (*Tip*) colophon
[2] (*) (= *culminación*) culmination
colofonia SF rosin, colophony
Colombia SF Colombia
colombianismo SM *word/phrase etc peculiar to Colombia*
colombiano/a Ⓐ ADJ of/from Colombia
Ⓑ SM/F native/inhabitant of Colombia; **los ~s** the Colombians, the people of Colombia
colombicultor(a) SM/F pigeon-breeder
colombicultura SF pigeon-breeding
colombino ADJ of Columbus, relating to Columbus
colombofilia SF pigeon breeding, pigeon-fancying
colombófilo/a SM/F pigeon-fancier
colon SM (*Anat*) colon
Colón SM Columbus
colón SM monetary unit of Costa Rica and El Salvador
Colonia SF Cologne
colonia[1] SF [1] (= *territorio*) colony; **las antiguas ~s españolas** the former Spanish colonies
[2] (= *comunidad*) [*de personas*] community; [*de animales, células*] colony; **la ~ norteamericana en Madrid** the American community in Madrid ► **colonia bacteriana** bacterial colony
[3] (= *grupo de edificios*) ► **colonia obrera** working-class housing scheme ► **colonia penal** penal colony
[4] (= *campamento*) summer camp; **irse de ~s** to go (off) to summer camp ► **colonia de va-**

caciones holiday camp ► **colonia de verano** summer camp

5 (*Méx*) residential suburb, residential area; **Colonia Quintanilla del D.F.** the Quintanilla area of the capital ► **colonia proletaria** shanty town

6 (= *cinta*) silk ribbon

colonia² SF (*tb* **agua de ~**) cologne, eau de Cologne

coloniaje SM (*LAm*) (= *época*) colonial period; (= *sistema*) colonial government; (*pey*) (= *esclavitud*) slavery

colonial ADJ [*época*] colonial; [*alimentos, productos*] overseas *antes de s*, imported (*originally referring to imports from Spanish colonies*)

colonialismo SM colonialism

colonialista ADJ, SMF colonialist

colonización SF [*de país, territorio*] colonization

colonizador(a) Ⓐ ADJ [*proceso, país, lengua*] colonizing

Ⓑ SM/F [*de país, territorio*] colonist, colonizer

colonizar ▸conjug 1f◂ VT 1 [+ *país, territorio*] to colonize

2 (*Biol*) to colonize

colono/a SM/F 1 [*de país, territorio*] colonist; (= *nativo de una colonia*) colonial

2 (*Agr*) tenant farmer

3 (*Caribe*) [*de azúcar*] sugar planter

4 (*Andes Hist*) (= *indio*) Indian bound to an estate

coloqueta⁑ SF 1 (= *detención*) arrest; **dar una ~ a** to nick⁑, arrest

2 (= *redada*) police sweep

3 = **colocata**

coloquial ADJ colloquial

coloquiante SMF (= *hablante*) speaker; (*en charla, debate*) person taking part in a discussion; **mi ~** the person I was (*etc*) talking to

coloquiar ▸conjug 1b◂ VI to talk, discuss

coloquio SM 1 (= *debate*) discussion; **un ~ sobre el aborto** a discussion about abortion; **charla-~** ◊ **conferencia-~** talk followed by a discussion

2 (= *congreso*) conference, symposium; **un ~ internacional sobre el comercio** an international trade conference *o* symposium

3 (*frm*) (= *diálogo*) dialogue, dialog (*EEUU*), colloquy (*frm*)

color SM (a veces SF) 1 (= *coloración*) colour, color (*EEUU*); **los ~es del arco iris** the colours of the rainbow; **el ~ azul** blue; **¿de qué ~ es?** what colour is it?; **¿de qué ~ tiene los ojos?** what colour are her eyes?, what colour eyes does she have?; **es de ~ verde** it's green; **una falda (de) ~ rojo** a red skirt; **un traje (de) ~ canela** a cinnamon-coloured suit; **lo quisiera en ~ verde** I'd like it in green; **a ~** colour *antes de s*, color *antes de s* (*EEUU*); **fotocopias a ~** colour photocopying; **a todo ~** full-colour; **coger ~** = **tomar color**; **dar ~ a algo** to colour sth in; **le dio ~ al dibujo** he coloured in the drawing; **de ~**: **ropa de ~** coloured *o* (*EEUU*) colored clothes; **viste de ~** she wears coloured clothes; **en ~** colour *antes de s*; **película en ~** colour film; **televisión en ~** colour television; **tomar ~**: **esa tela no ha tomado bien el ~** that material has not dyed at all well; **cuando la cebolla haya tomado ~** when the onion has gone *o* turned golden brown; **el proyecto empieza a tomar ~** the project is starting to take shape ► **color apagado** subdued colour ► **color pastel** pastel colour ► **color primario** primary colour

2 [*de la cara*] colour, color (*EEUU*); **tener buen ~** to have good colour; **tener mal ~** to look off colour; ✦**MODISMOS ponerse de mil ~es** to go bright red; **sacar los ~es a algn** to make sb blush; **le salieron los ~es** she blushed, she flushed red

3 (= *raza*) colour, color (*EEUU*); **sin distinción de sexo o ~** regardless of sex or colour; **persona de ~** coloured person

4 (= *tipismo*) **la feria ha perdido el ~ de antaño** the festival has lost the flavour *o* (*EEUU*) flavor *o* feel it used to have ► **color local** local colour

5 ✦**MODISMOS de ~ de rosa**: **lo describió todo de ~ de rosa** she described it all in very rosy terms; **verlo todo de ~ de rosa** to see everything through rose-tinted *o* rose-coloured spectacles; **la vida no es de ~ de rosa** life isn't all roses; **no hay ~*** there's no comparison; **subido de ~** [*chiste*] risqué; [*discusión*] heated

6 **colores** (*tb* **lápices de ~es**) coloured pencils, crayons; **una caja de ~es** a box of coloured pencils *o* crayons

7 **colores** (*Dep*) colours; **una bufanda con los ~es del Barcelona** a scarf with the Barcelona colours; **los ~es nacionales** the national colours

8 (= *cosmético*) blusher, rouge; **ponerse ~** to put on blusher *o* rouge

9 (= *interés*) colour; **el partido no tuvo ~** the game lacked colour

10 (††) **so ~ de** under pretext of

coloración SF (*gen*) coloration, colouring, coloring (*EEUU*); (*Zool*) coloration

colorado Ⓐ ADJ 1 (= *rojo*) red; ✦**MODISMOS ~ como un tomate** as red as a beetroot *o* (*EEUU*) beet; **poner ~ a algn** to make sb blush; **ponerse ~** to blush

2 (*LAm*) [*chiste*] blue

Ⓑ SM 1 (= *color*) red

2 (*Caribe*) (= *escarlatina*) scarlet fever

3 **los Colorados** *Uruguayan political party*

colorante Ⓐ ADJ colouring, coloring (*EEUU*)

Ⓑ SM colouring (matter)

colorar ▸conjug 1a◂ VT (= *pintar*) to colour, color (*EEUU*); (= *teñir*) to dye, tint; **~ algo de amarillo** to colour/dye sth yellow

coloratura SF coloratura

coloreado Ⓐ ADJ (= *pintado*) coloured, colored (*EEUU*); (= *teñido*) tinted

Ⓑ SM (= *pintado*) colouring, coloring (*EEUU*); (= *teñido*) tinting

colorear ▸conjug 1a◂ Ⓐ VT 1 = **colorar**

2 (= *justificar*) to justify, put in a favourable light; (= *quitar importancia a*) to whitewash, gloss over

Ⓑ VI 1 [*frutos*] to ripen

2 (= *tirar a rojo*) to be reddish

3 (= *ponerse colorado*) to redden

colorete SM rouge, blusher

colorido SM colour(ing), color(ing) (*EEUU*) ► **colorido local** local colour

colorín Ⓐ ADJ (*Cono Sur*) strawberry *o* reddish blond(e)

Ⓑ SM 1 (= *color*) bright colour, bright color (*EEUU*); **con muchos colorines** all bright and colourful; **¡qué colorines tiene el niño!** what rosy cheeks the little fellow has!; **y ~, colorado, este cuento se ha acabado** and they all lived happily ever after, and that is the end of the story

2 (*Orn*) goldfinch

3 (*Med*) measles

colorinche* (*Arg, Perú*) Ⓐ ADJ loud*

Ⓑ SM loud colour*, loud color (*EEUU**)

colorir ▸conjug 3a; defectivo◂ Ⓐ VT 1 (= *pintar*) to colour, color (*EEUU*)

2 (*fig*) = **colorear A2**

Ⓑ VI to take on a colour, take on a color (*EEUU*), colour up, color up (*EEUU*)

colorista Ⓐ ADJ colouristic, coloristic (*EEUU*)

Ⓑ SMF colourist

colosal ADJ [*edificio, montaña*] colossal; [*comida, fiesta*] amazing*, fantastic*

coloso SM 1 (= *titán*) colossus; **el ~ del norte** (*esp LAm*) *the United States*

2 (*Cono Sur Aut*) trailer

coludo ADJ (*Cono Sur*) long-tailed

columbario SM columbarium

Columbina SF Columbine

columbrar ▸conjug 1a◂ (*liter*) VT 1 (= *divisar*) to make out, glimpse

2 (= *conjeturar*) to guess

3 [+ *solución*] to begin to see

columna SF 1 (*Arquit*) column

2 (*Tip*) [*de periódico*] column; **~ periodística** newspaper column; **un documento escrito a dos ~s** a document in two-columns, a two-column document

3 [*de soldados, tanques*] column; **~ blindada** armoured *o* (*EEUU*) armored column; *ver tb* **quinto A**

4 (*Anat*) (*tb* **~ vertebral**) spine, spinal column, backbone; **son la ~ vertebral del equipo** they form the backbone of the team; **la más firme ~ de la democracia** the steadiest pillar of democracy

5 (*Aut*) ► **columna de dirección** steering column

6 (*Téc*) [*de mercurio*] column

columnata SF colonnade

columnista SMF columnist

columpiar ▸conjug 1b◂ Ⓐ VT **~ a algn** (*en columpio*) to push sb; (*en mecedora*) to rock sb

Ⓑ **columpiarse** VPR 1 (*en columpio*) to swing; (*en mecedora*) to rock

2 (*) (= *meter la pata*) to drop a clanger*

3 (†) (*fig*) to swing to and fro, seesaw

columpio SM 1 [*de niños*] swing ► **columpio basculante, columpio de tabla** seesaw, teeter-totter (*EEUU*)

2 (*LAm*) (= *mecedora*) rocking chair

colusión SF collusion

colza SF (*Bot*) rape, colza; **aceite de ~** rapeseed oil

coma¹ SM (*Med*) coma; **en ~** in a coma; **entrar en (estado de) ~** to go into a coma; **salir del (estado de) ~** to come out of the coma ► **coma diabético** diabetic coma ► **coma profundo** deep coma

coma² SF 1 (*Tip*) comma; ✦**MODISMO sin faltar** *o* **sin saltarse una ~**: **recitó todo el poema sin saltarse una ~** he recited the whole poem word perfect *o* without leaving out a single word; *ver tb* **punto 2**

2 (*Mat*) ≈ point (*Spanish uses a comma in place of a point*); **doce ~ cinco** twelve point five ► **coma decimal** decimal point ► **coma**

flotante floating point
[3] (*Mús*) comma

comadre SF [1] (= *chismosa*) gossip
[2] (= *vecina*) neighbour, neighbor (*EEUU*); (= *amiga*) friend
[3] (= *madrina*) godmother
[4] (*Med*) (= *partera*) midwife
[5] (= *alcahueta*) go-between, procuress
[6] (‡) (= *maricón*) pansy‡

comadrear ▸conjug 1a◂ VI to gossip

comadreja SF weasel

comadreo SM, **comadrería** SF chatting, nattering*

comadrona SF midwife

comal SM (*CAm, Méx*) (clay) griddle

comanche ADJ, SMF Comanche

comandancia SF [1] (= *función*) command
[2] (= *grado*) rank of major
[3] (= *central*) headquarters *pl*
[4] (= *zona*) area under a commander's jurisdiction
[5] (*Méx*) police station

comandanta SF [1] (*gen*) commander; (*Mil*) major; (*Hist*) major's wife
[2] (*Náut*) flagship

comandante SMF [1] (= *jefe*) commander, commandant; (*Aer*) (*tb* **~ de vuelo**) captain; **segundo ~** copilot, second pilot; (*tb* **~ de policía**) (*Méx*) chief of police, chief superintendent ► **comandante en jefe** commander-in-chief
[2] (= *grado*) major

comandar ▸conjug 1a◂ VT to command

comandita SF limited partnership, silent partnership (*EEUU*); **en ~*** all together, as a team; **fuimos todos en ~ a hablar con el jefe** we all went together to talk to the boss

comanditario ADJ **socio ~** sleeping partner, silent partner (*EEUU*)

comando SM [1] (*Mil*) (= *grupo*) commando unit, commando group ► **comando de acción** active service unit ► **comando de información** intelligence unit ► **comando suicida** suicide squad ► **comando terrorista** terrorist cell, terrorist squad
[2] (*Mil*) (= *soldado*) commando
[3] (*Mil*) (= *mando*) command
[4] (*Téc*) control; (*Inform*) command ► **comando a distancia** remote control ► **comando vocal** voice command
[5] (= *prenda*) duffle coat

comarca SF *administrative division comprising a number of municipalities*

comarcal ADJ [*carretera*] local; [*emisora*] regional

comarcano ADJ neighbouring, neighboring (*EEUU*), bordering

comarcar ▸conjug 1g◂ VI to border (**con** on), be adjacent (**con** to)

comatoso ADJ comatose

comba SF [1] (= *curvatura*) bend; (*en viga*) warp, sag
[2] (= *cuerda*) skipping rope, jump rope (*EEUU*); **saltar a la ~** to skip, jump rope (*EEUU*); **dar a la ~** to turn the skipping rope
[3] (= *juego*) skipping, jumping rope (*EEUU*)
[4] ✦*MODISMO* **no pierde ~** he doesn't miss a trick

combadura SF [1] = **comba 1**
[2] (*Aut*) camber

combar ▸conjug 1a◂ Ⓐ VT (= *curvar*) to bend, curve
Ⓑ **combarse** VPR (= *hacer curva*) to bend, curve; (= *alabearse*) to bulge, warp; [*techo*] to sag

combate SM (*Mil*) combat; (*Boxeo*) contest, fight; [*de ideas, sentimientos*] conflict; **estar fuera de ~** (*lit, fig*) to be out of action; (*Boxeo*) to be knocked out; **dejar** *o* **poner a algn fuera de ~** (*lit, fig*) to put sb out of action; (*Boxeo*) to knock sb out; **ganar por fuera de ~** to win by a knockout ► **combate a muerte** fight to the death ► **combate naval** naval battle, sea battle ► **combate singular** single combat

combatiente SMF combatant; **no ~** noncombatant

combatir ▸conjug 3a◂ Ⓐ VI [*ejército, soldado*] to fight; **su padre combatió en la Guerra** his father fought in the War; **ha combatido por conseguir un acuerdo** she has fought to achieve an agreement
Ⓑ VT [+ *fraude, desempleo, injusticia, enfermedad*] to combat, fight; [+ *frío*] to fight (off); **dedicó todo su esfuerzo a ~ al enemigo** he put all his effort into fighting *o* combatting the enemy; **combatió las tesis capitalistas** he fought against *o* combatted capitalist theses; **un buen libro para ~ el aburrimiento** a good book to fight off *o* combat boredom; **medidas para ~ el fuego** firefighting measures

combatividad SF fighting spirit

combativo ADJ combative, spirited

combazo SM (*Cono Sur*) punch

combés SM waist

combi[1]* SF [1] (= *prenda*) slip
[2] (= *ardid*) fiddle*, wangle*

combi[2]* SF, **combinable** SF [1] (= *furgoneta*) combi (van)
[2] (*Méx*) (= *bus*) minibus

combinación SF [1] [*de elementos, factores*] combination; **una elegante ~ de colores** an elegant combination of colours
[2] [*de números*] combination; **sabía la ~ de la caja fuerte** he knew the combination of the safe; **la ~ ganadora del sorteo** the winning combination (of the draw)
[3] (*Quím*) compound
[4] [*de transportes*] connection; **hay muy buena ~ de autobuses** there is a very good bus connection
[5] (= *prenda*) slip
[6] (*Literat*) ► **combinación métrica** stanza form, rhyme scheme

combinacional ADJ combinatory, combinational

combinadamente ADV jointly, in combination with (**con** with)

combinado SM [1] [*de bebidas*] cocktail
[2] (*Cono Sur*) radiogram
[3] (= *equipo*) selection, team

combinar ▸conjug 1a◂ Ⓐ VT [1] [+ *esfuerzos, movimientos*] to combine; [+ *colores*] to match, mix
[2] [+ *plan, proyecto*] to devise, work out
Ⓑ **combinarse** VPR [1] [*personas*] to get together, join together; **~se para hacer algo** to get *o* join together to do sth
[2] (*Méx*) (= *alternarse*) to take it in turns

combinatoria SF (*Mat*) combinatorial analysis

combinatorio ADJ combinatorial, combinative; **análisis ~** (*Mat*) combinatorial analysis

combo Ⓐ ADJ (= *combado*) bent; (= *arqueado*) bulging; (= *torcido*) warped
Ⓑ SM [1] (*LAm*) (= *martillo*) sledgehammer
[2] (*Andes, Cono Sur*) (= *golpe*) slap; (= *puñetazo*) punch
[3] (*Col**) (= *pandilla*) gang

combustible Ⓐ ADJ combustible
Ⓑ SM (= *carburante*) fuel ► **combustible fósil** fossil fuel ► **combustible líquido** liquid fuel

combustión SF combustion ► **combustión espontánea** spontaneous combustion

comebolas* SM INV (*Caribe*) sucker*, mug*

comecocos* Ⓐ SM INV [1] (= *obsesión*) obsession, hang-up*; (= *pasatiempo*) brainteaser, idle pastime, absorbing but pointless activity; (= *lavacerebros*) brainwashing exercise
[2] (= *preocupación*) nagging worry
[3] (= *videojuego*) Pacman®
Ⓑ SMF INV [1] (= *preocupación*) worry
[2] (= *persona*) **es todo un ~ y los tiene a todos haciendo lo que él quiere** he brainwashes everyone into doing what he wants

COMECON SM ABR (= **Council for Mutual Economic Assitance**) Comecon

comedero Ⓐ SM [1] (*Agr*) feeding trough, trough; (*Orn*) feeding box, feeder
[2] (= *comedor*) dining room; [*de animal*] feeding place
[3] (*Caribe*) (= *prostíbulo*) brothel
[4] (*Andes*) (= *sitio favorito*) haunt, hang-out*
Ⓑ ADJ (†) (= *comestible*) eatable, edible

comedia SF [1] (*Teat*) (= *obra cómica*) comedy; **alta ~** high comedy; **La divina ~** The Divine Comedy ► **comedia de costumbres** comedy of manners ► **comedia de enredo** comedy of intrigue ► **Comedia del Arte** commedia dell'arte ► **comedia musical** musical ► **comedia negra** black comedy
[2] (*Teat*) (= *obra dramática*) play; **una ~ en un acto** a one-act play ► **comedia de capa y espada** cloak-and-dagger play
[3] (*TV*) ► **comedia de situación** situation comedy, sitcom*
[4] (= *fingimiento*) play-acting; **¡déjate ya de tanta ~!** stop your play-acting!; **hacer ~** to play-act; **¡deja de hacer ~ y di la verdad!** stop play-acting *o* pretending and tell the truth!

COMEDIA

The Spanish **comedias** *written by dramatists of the Golden Age, or* **Edad de Oro**, *were five-act plays performed in open-air theatres. They involved stock characters similar to those of the Italian Commedia dell'Arte: a beautiful lady, her suitor, servants and go-betweens. In these* **comedias**, *which were not always comical in nature, action and a moral theme took precedence over character. Cloak and dagger episodes were built around plots involving disguises and mistaken identity. They dealt primarily with affairs of the nobility, while peasants were there to provide comic relief or to enhance particular pastoral themes. One of the most prolific* **comedia** *writers was Lope de Vega, who wrote on religious, historical and social themes. Other major* **comedia** *writers were Pedro Calderón de la Barca and Tirso de Molina, from whose pen came the figure of the* *archetypal seducer, Don Juan, in* **El Burlador de Sevilla y Convidado de Piedra** *(1630).*

comediante/a SM/F 1 (*Teat*) (= *actor*) actor/actress
2 (= *humorista*) (= *hombre, mujer*) comedian; (*sólo mujer*) comedienne
3 (= *farsante*) play-actor

comedidamente ADV (= *moderadamente*) moderately; (= *cortésmente*) courteously

comedido ADJ 1 (= *moderado*) moderate, restrained
2 (*esp LAm*) (= *solícito*) obliging

comedieta SF light comedy

comedimiento SM 1 (= *moderación*) moderation, restraint
2 (*esp LAm*) (= *solicitud*) helpfulness

comedio† SM 1 [*de territorio, lugar*] middle
2 (= *intervalo*) interval

comediógrafo/a SM/F playwright

comedirse ▸conjug 3k◂ VPR 1 (*en conducta*) (= *mostrar moderación*) to show restraint; **~ en las palabras** to choose one's words carefully
2 **~ a** (*LAm*) + INFIN to offer to + *infin*, volunteer to + *infin*

comedón SM blackhead

comedor Ⓐ SM 1 (*en casa*) dining room; (*en barco, tren*) restaurant; (*en colegio, facultad*) dining hall, lunch room (*EEUU*); (*en trabajo*) canteen; *ver tb* **salón 1**
2 (= *mobiliario*) dining-room suite
Ⓑ ADJ **Juan es muy buen ~** Juan's a big eater, Juan likes his food

comedura SF **~ de coco** *o* **de tarro*** = **comecocos A1**

comefuegos SMF INV fire-eater

comegente‡ SM (*Andes, Caribe*) glutton

comehostias* SMF INV goody-goody*

comején SM 1 (= *insecto*) termite, white ant
2 (*Andes*) (= *glotón*) glutton
3 (*Andes*) (= *preocupación*) nagging worry, gnawing anxiety

comelitona SF (*Méx*) = **comilona**

comelón/ona ADJ, SM/F (*LAm*) = **comilón**

comelona SF (*LAm*) = **comilona**

comemierdas‡ SMF INV shit‡

comendador SM knight commander (*of a military order*)

comendatorio ADJ **carta comendatoria** letter of recommendation

comensal SMF 1 (= *compañero de mesa*) fellow diner (*frm*); **habrá 13 ~es** there will be 13 for dinner, there will be 13 people dining (*frm*); **mis ~es** my fellow diners (*frm*)
2 (*Andes*) (*en hotel*) guest

comensurabilidad SF commensurability

comentador(a) SM/F commentator

comentar ▸conjug 1a◂ Ⓐ VT 1 (= *explicar*) [+ *poema, texto*] to comment on
2 (= *hablar de*) [+ *noticia, hecho*] to discuss; **no pude ~ la situación con nadie** I couldn't discuss the situation with anyone; **antes prefiero ~lo con mi mujer** I'd like to discuss it with my wife first; **es un secreto, no lo comentes** it's a secret, don't tell anyone (about it) *o* don't mention it to anyone
3 (= *decir*) **le estaba comentando que estás muy cambiada** I was saying to *o* telling him that you've changed a lot; **me han comentado que se casa** I've heard *o* I gather he's getting married; **me han comentado que es un buen libro** I've heard that it's a good book
4 (*TV, Radio*) [+ *partido*] to commentate on
Ⓑ VI 1 (= *opinar*) **no quiso ~ al respecto** she didn't want to comment on it; **~ sobre algo** to comment on sth
2 (*) (= *charlar*) to chat; **comentando con los amigos, se le escapó el secreto** he let slip the secret while chatting to *o* talking to friends

comentario SM 1 (= *observación*) comment; **hizo varios ~s irónicos sobre mi familia** he made some sarcastic comments *o* remarks about my family; **esto merece ~ aparte** this deserves separate comment; **"sin ~s"** "no comment"; **el tema no merece ~** the matter does not deserve mention; **sin más ~, pasemos a ver la película** without further ado, let's watch the film; **hacer un ~: le hizo un ~ al oído** she said something in his ear; **no hizo ~ alguno al respecto** he made no comment on the matter
2 (= *redacción*) essay; **un ~ sobre "El Quijote"** an essay on Don Quixote ► **comentario de texto** (*literario*) (literary) commentary; (*lingüístico*) textual analysis
3 **comentarios** (= *cotilleo*) gossip *sing*; **dar lugar a ~s** to lead to gossip

comentarista SMF commentator; **~ deportivo** sports commentator

comento (*frm*) SM 1 (= *observación*) comment
2 (*de un texto*) commentary
3 (= *embuste*) lie

comenzar ▸conjug 1f, 1j◂ Ⓐ VT to begin, start, commence (*frm*); **comenzamos el rodaje ayer** we began *o* started *o* commenced (*frm*) filming yesterday; **comenzó la charla con un agradecimiento** she began *o* started the talk with a word of thanks; **comenzó su carrera literaria hace dos décadas** she began her literary career two decades ago; **la empresa comienza la construcción hoy** the company starts the construction work today; **hemos comenzado mal el año** we started the year badly; **comenzamos el recorrido en la iglesia** we start our trip at the church
Ⓑ VI [*proyecto, campaña, historia, proceso*] to begin, start; **¿puedo ~?** may I start *o* begin?, can I start *o* begin?; **el partido comienza a las ocho** the match starts *o* begins at eight; **comenzó diciendo que estaba de acuerdo conmigo** she began by saying that she agreed with me; **comenzó a los diez años haciendo recados** he began *o* started at the age of ten as a messenger boy; **al ~ el año** at the start *o* beginning of the year; **~ a hacer algo** to start *o* begin doing sth, start *o* begin to do sth; **la nieve comenzó a caer de nuevo** the snow started falling again, the snow began to fall again; **comencé a trabajar a los dieciocho años** I started *o* began working at eighteen; **podéis ~ a comer** you can start eating; **los invitados ya han comenzado a llegar** the guests have started arriving *o* to arrive; **aquel día comenzó a tener problemas con el oído** that day she began having trouble with her hearing; **~ con algo: la película comienza con una pelea** the film starts *o* begins with a fight; **para ~** to start with; **para ~, una sopa de verduras** to start with, vegetable soup; **~ por: no sé por dónde ~** I don't know where to start *o* begin; **la reforma ha comenzado por la educación** reform has started *o* begun with education; **comenzó por agradecernos nuestra presencia** she started *o* began by thanking us for coming; **para sentirte mejor, comienza por comer bien** in order to feel better, start by eating well; **su nombre comienza por m** his name begins with m; **todos sois culpables, comenzando por ti** you're all guilty, starting with you

comer ▸conjug 2a◂ Ⓐ VT 1 [+ *comida*] to eat; **¿quieres ~ algo?** would you like something to eat?; **no tienen qué ~** they have nothing to eat; ✦*MODISMO* **sin ~lo ni beberlo: sin ~lo ni beberlo, me vi envuelto en un caso de contrabando de drogas** without really knowing how, I found myself involved in a drug smuggling case; **ha recibido una herencia sin ~lo ni beberlo** he's come into an inheritance without having done anything to deserve it; *ver tb* **coco**[1] **2, tarro 2**
2 (= *almorzar*) to have for lunch, eat for lunch; **los domingos suelo ~ paella** on Sundays I usually have paella for lunch
3 (= *hacer desaparecer*) **el pelo te come la cara** your hair's covering half your face; **esto come las existencias** this devours the stocks; **poco a poco el polvo fue comiendo la casa** dust gradually took over the house; **~ terreno: la derecha les está comiendo terreno** the right is gaining ground on them; **el equipo se dejó ~ el terreno** the team conceded a lot of ground
4 (= *destruir, consumir*) **un ácido que come la plata** an acid that corrodes silver; **el agua comió la piedra** the water wore down the stone; **eso les come la moral** that's eating away at their morale; **le come la envidia por dentro** she is eaten up *o* consumed with envy
5 (= *escocer*) **el picor me come la pierna** my leg's stinging
6 (*Ajedrez*) to take
Ⓑ VI 1 (= *ingerir alimento*) to eat; **¿qué hay para ~?** what have we got to eat?, what is there to eat?; **los leones tienen que cazar para ~** lions have to hunt to eat; **¡come y calla!** shut up and eat your food!*; **~ de algo** (= *tomar comida*) to eat sth; (= *vivir*) to live off sth; **come de los platos de los demás** she eats other people's food; **no todos podemos ~ de lo que cultivamos** not all of us can live off what we grow ourselves; **~ fuera** to eat out; ✦*MODISMOS* **~ con los ojos: siempre comes con** *o* **por los ojos** your eyes are bigger than your stomach; **~ como una vaca** *o* **fiera** to eat like a horse; **no ~ ni dejar ~** to be a dog in the manger; **el mismo que come y viste** the very same
2 (= *tomar la comida principal*) (*esp Esp*) (*a mediodía*) to have lunch; (*LAm*) (*por la noche*) to have dinner; **comemos a la una** we have lunch at one; **me gusta ~ fuerte y cenar poco** I like to have a big lunch and a light evening meal
3 **dar de ~** to feed; **estaba dando de ~ al niño** she was feeding her child; **dar de ~ a las gallinas** to feed the hens; **ni siquiera nos dio de ~** she didn't even give us anything to eat
4 (*Andes*‡) **~ a algn** to screw sb‡
Ⓒ **comerse** VPR 1 [+ *comida*] to eat; **sólo me he comido un bocadillo** all I've had to

➤ LENGUA Y USO: **comenzar B** 53.1, 53.2

eat is a sandwich; **¿quién se ha comido mi queso?** who's eaten my cheese?; **se lo comió todo** he ate it all (up); **~se las uñas** to bite one's nails; **✦MODISMOS ~se a algn a besos** to smother sb in kisses; **~se a algn con los ojos** *o* **la vista** to devour sb with one's eyes; **¿cómo se come eso?** what on earth is that?; **está para comérsela*** she's really gorgeous *o* tasty*; **~se el mundo** to conquer the world; **~se a algn por pies** to take sb in completely; *ver tb* **coco[1] 2, rosca 2, tarro 2, vista A2.2**

[2] (= *destruir*) **el sol se ha ido comiendo los colores de la alfombra** the sun has bleached the carpet, the sun has caused the colours of the carpet to fade; **el ácido se ha comido el metal** the acid has eaten the metal away; **✦MODISMO se comen unos a otros** they're at daggers drawn

[3] [+ *capital, recursos*] to eat up; **en un mes se comió toda la herencia** he blew his entire inheritance within a month

[4] (= *saltarse*) [+ *párrafo*] to miss out; [+ *consonante*] to swallow; **se come las palabras** he swallows his words

Ⓓ SM **tan necesario como el ~** as necessary as eating; **era muy parco en el ~** he didn't eat much, he wasn't a big eater; **el buen ~** good food; **Fernando es de buen ~** Fernando enjoys his food

comerciabilidad SF marketability, saleability

comerciable ADJ [1] (*Com*) marketable, saleable; **valores ~s** marketable securities

[2] (†) (= *sociable*) sociable

comercial Ⓐ ADJ [1] (= *de tiendas*) [*área, recinto*] shopping *antes de s*; **un centro ~** a shopping centre

[2] (= *financiero*) [*carta, operación*] business *antes de s*; [*balanza, déficit, guerra, embargo*] trade *antes de s*; [*intercambio, estrategia*] commercial; **el interés ~ de la empresa** the commercial *o* trading interests of the company; **su novela alcanzó un gran éxito ~** his novel was very successful commercially, his novel achieved great commercial success; **han reanudado las relaciones ~es** they have resumed trading relations; *ver tb* **agente A, local B1**

[3] [*aviación, avión, piloto*] civil

[4] [*cine, teatro, literatura*] commercial; **una película muy ~** a very commercial film

Ⓑ SMF (= *vendedor*) salesperson

comercializable ADJ marketable, saleable

comercialización SF (= *explotación comercial*) commercialization; (= *puesta en mercado*) marketing

comercializar ▸conjug 1f◂ VT (= *explotar comercialmente*) to commercialize; (= *lanzar al mercado*) to market

comercialmente ADV commercially

comerciante SMF [1] (*gen*) trader, dealer; (*a gran escala*) merchant; (= *tendero*) shopkeeper, storekeeper (*EEUU*) ► **comerciante al por mayor** wholesaler ► **comerciante al por menor** retailer ► **comerciante exclusivo** sole trader

[2] (= *interesado*) **es un ~** he's very money-minded

comerciar ▸conjug 1b◂ VI [*dos empresas*] to do business (together); [*naciones*] to trade; **~ con** [+ *empresa*] to do business with, have dealings with; [+ *país*] to trade with; [+ *mercancías*] to deal in, trade in, handle

comercio SM [1] (= *actividad*) trade, commerce; **medidas para favorecer el ~ con Francia** measures to promote trade *o* commerce with France; **defensores del libre ~** champions of free trade; **el ~ de textiles** the textile trade ► **comercio de exportación** export trade ► **comercio de importación** import trade ► **comercio E, comercio electrónico** e-commerce ► **comercio exterior** foreign trade ► **comercio interior** domestic trade ► **comercio internacional** international trade ► **comercio justo** fair trade ► **comercio minorista** retail trade; *ver tb* **cámara A3**

[2] (= *tienda*) shop, store (*EEUU*); **¿a qué hora cierran hoy los ~s?** what time do the shops *o* stores close today?; **ha comenzado la huelga del ~** the shopkeepers' *o* (*EEUU*) storekeepers' strike has started

[3] (= *intercambio*) ► **comercio carnal** sexual intercourse ► **comercio social** social intercourse

comestible Ⓐ ADJ (= *digerible*) edible

Ⓑ **comestibles** SMPL [1] (= *alimentos*) food *sing*; (*Com*) foodstuffs; (*en tienda, supermercado*) groceries; **tienda de ~s** grocer's (shop), grocery (*EEUU*)

[2] (= *provisiones*) provisions

cometa[1] SM (*Astron*) comet

cometa[2] SF kite ► **cometa delta** (*Andes*), **cometa voladora** (*Andes*) hang glider

cometer ▸conjug 2a◂ VT [+ *crimen, delito, pecado*] to commit; [+ *atentado*] to carry out; [+ *error*] to make; **ha cometido una falta de ortografía** she made a spelling mistake; **el tenista cometió dos dobles faltas** the tennis player made two double faults; **no ~ás actos impuros** thou shalt not commit impure acts

cometido SM task, mission; **tiene un ~ difícil en este viaje** she has a difficult task *o* mission on this trip; **el detective cumplió con su ~** the detective fulfilled his task *o* mission; **el ~ del Metro es el transporte de viajeros** the task of the Metro is to transport passengers

comezón SF [1] (= *picor*) itch, itching; [*de calor*] tingle, tingling sensation; **siento ~ en el brazo** my arm itches, my arm is tingling

[2] (= *inquietud*) itch (**por** for); **sentir ~ de hacer algo** to feel an itch to do sth

comi* SF = **comisaría 1**

comible ADJ eatable

Comibol SF ABR (*Bol*) = **Corporación Minera de Bolivia**

cómic ['komik] SM (*pl* **cómics** ['komik]) comic

comicastro/a SM/F ham (actor/actress)*

comicidad SF funniness, comicalness

comicios SMPL elections, voting *sing*

cómico/a Ⓐ ADJ [1] (= *gracioso*) comic(al), funny

[2] (*Teat*) comedy *antes de s*; **autor ~** playwright

Ⓑ SM/F [1] (*Teat*) (comic) actor/actress

[2] (= *humorista*) comedian/comedienne

comida SF [1] (= *alimento*) food; **le echas mucha sal a la ~** you put too much salt on your food; **sirvió la ~ en cuencos** she served the food in bowls; **nos hemos quedado sin ~** we've got no food left; **no me gusta la ~ india** I don't like Indian food; **mamá está haciendo** *o* **preparando la ~** mum is making lunch; **no sirven ~ después de las tres** they don't serve food *o* meals after three o'clock; **acábate la ~** finish your meal, eat up your meal ► **comida a domicilio** meals on wheels *pl* ► **comida basura** junk food ► **comida casera** home cooking ► **comida infantil** baby food ► **comida para gatos** cat food ► **comida para perros** dog food ► **comida precocinada, comida preparada** ready meals *pl*, pre-cooked meals *pl* ► **comida rápida** fast food

[2] (= *acto de comer*) meal; **ganamos una ~ para dos personas** we won a meal for two; **tómese una pastilla después de cada ~** take one tablet after meals; **hacemos la ~ fuerte al mediodía** we have our main meal at midday ► **comida de negocios** business lunch ► **comida de trabajo** working lunch

[3] (*esp Esp*) (= *almuerzo*) lunch; **la hora de la ~** lunch time

[4] (*LAm*) (= *cena*) dinner, evening meal

[5] (‡) ► **comida de coco, comida de tarro**: **en la mili le han hecho una ~ de coco** *o* **tarro** they brainwashed him when he was in the army; **este libro es una ~ de coco** *o* **tarro** this book is pretty heavy stuff*

> **CÓMICO**
>
> **¿"Comic" o "comical"?**
>
> El adjetivo **cómico** se puede traducir por **comic** y **comical**, pero éstos no son intercambiables.
>
> **Comic**
>
> • Algo que es **cómico** porque se hace o se dice con la intención de hacer reír a la gente se traduce al inglés por **comic**:
>
> El efecto cómico se consigue poniéndose ropa que te queda grande
>
> ***Comic effect is achieved by wearing clothes that are too big***
>
> • **Cómico** también se traduce por **comic** para describir algo perteneciente o relativo a la comedia:
>
> ...un actor cómico...
>
> ***...a comic actor...***
>
> **NOTA:** Hay que tener en cuenta que en este caso **comic** nunca funciona como atributo.
>
> **Comical**
>
> • **Cómico** se traduce por **comical** para describir algo o a alguien que resulta gracioso o absurdo (a menudo porque es raro o inesperado):
>
> Su gesto rozaba lo cómico
>
> ***Her expression was almost comical***
>
> Hay algo en él ligeramente cómico
>
> ***There is something slightly comical about him***
>
> *Para otros usos y ejemplos ver la entrada.*

comidilla SF [1] **ser la ~ del barrio** to be the talk of the town

[2] (= *pasatiempo*) hobby, special interest

comido ADJ [1] **estar ~** to have had lunch *etc*; **vengo ~** I've had lunch (before coming)

[2] **✦MODISMO es lo ~ por lo servido** it doesn't pay, it's not worth while

comience SM (*Andes*) = **comienzo**

comienzo SM [1] (= *principio*) [*de película, historia, partido*] beginning, start; [*de proyecto, plan*] beginning; [*de enfermedad*] onset; **desde el ~ supe que el asesino era el mayordomo** I knew the butler was the murderer from the beginning *o* the start; **ese fue el ~ de una**

serie de desastres that was the first in a series of disasters; **al ~: al ~ no entendía nada** at first I didn't understand anything; **al ~ de la primavera** in early Spring, at the start of Spring; **los ~s: en los ~s de este siglo** at the beginning of this century; **en los ~s del proceso democrático** in the early *o* initial stages of the democratic process; **una etapa muy difícil en sus ~s** a very difficult stage, initially

2 **dar ~** [*acto, curso*] to start, begin, commence (*frm*); **la ceremonia dio ~ a las cinco de la tarde** the ceremony started *o* began *o* (*frm*) commenced at five o'clock

3 **dar ~ a** [+ *acto, ceremonia*] to begin, start; [+ *carrera*] to start; [+ *etapa*] to mark the beginning of; **su último libro daba ~ a una nueva etapa** his last book marked the beginning of a new phase; **el director dio ~ al curso académico** the headmaster inaugurated the academic year

comillas SFPL quotation marks, quotes (*EEUU*); **entre ~** in inverted commas, in quotes (*EEUU*)

comilón/ona Ⓐ ADJ greedy

Ⓑ SM/F (= *buen comedor*) big eater; (= *glotón*) glutton, pig*

comilona* SF feast, blowout*

cominero/a Ⓐ ADJ fussy

Ⓑ SM/F fusspot*, fussbudget (*EEUU*), fussy person

comino SM cumin, cumin seed; ✦***MODISMOS*** **no vale un ~** it's not worth tuppence; **(no) me importa un ~** ◊ **no se me da un ~** I couldn't give a toss‡, I couldn't care less (**de** about)

Comintern SF ABR (= **Communist International**) Comintern

comiquero ADJ comic

comisaría SF 1 [*de policía*] police station, precinct (*EEUU*)

2 (*Mil*) administrative office; (*Náut*) purser's office

comisariado SM 1 (= *delegación*) commission

2 (*Pol*) commissary

comisariato SM administrative office

comisario/a SM/F 1 (= *delegado*) commissioner; **alto ~** high commissioner ► **comisario/a europeo/a** European commissioner

2 [*de policía*] superintendent, captain (*EEUU*)

3 (*Pol*) commissar

4 (*Mil*) administrative officer, service corps officer

5 [*de exposición*] organizer

6 (*Náut*) purser

7 [*de hipódromo*] steward ► **comisario/a de carreras** course steward

comiscar ▸conjug 1g◂ VT to nibble (at)

comisión SF 1 (= *encargo*) assignment, task, commission (*frm*); (= *misión*) mission, assignment

2 (*Pol*) commission; (= *junta*) committee ► **comisión de seguimiento** watchdog committee ► **Comisión Europea** European Commission ► **comisión investigadora** investigating committee, board of enquiry, board of inquiry (*EEUU*) ► **Comisiones Obreras** Communist trade union ► **comisión mixta** joint committee ► **comisión parlamentaria** parliamentary committee ► **comisión permanente** standing committee ► **comisión planificadora** planning board

3 (*Fin*) board

4 (*Com*) (= *pago*) commission; **a ~** on a commission basis ► **comisión porcentual** percentage commission (**sobre** on); ► **comisión sobre las ventas** sales commission

5 (= *ejecución*) commission; [*de ultraje*] perpetration; **pecado de ~** sin of commission

6 ► **comisión de servicio(s)** (= *destino provisional*) secondment, temporary transfer; (= *permiso de ausencia*) leave of absence

comisionado/a SM/F 1 (= *delegado*) commissioner

2 (= *miembro*) (*Pol*) committee member; (*Com, Fin*) board member

comisionar ▸conjug 1a◂ VT to commission

comisionista SMF commission agent, person working on a commission basis

comiso SM (*Jur*) 1 (= *acto*) seizure, confiscation

2 (= *géneros*) confiscated goods

comisquear ▸conjug 1a◂ VT = **comiscar**

comistrajo SM bad meal, awful food

comisura SF corner, angle, commissure (*frm*) ► **comisura de los labios** corner of the mouth

comité SM committee ► **comité de apelación** committee *o* board of appeal ► **comité de dirección** steering committee ► **comité de empresa** works committee, shop stewards' committee ► **Comité de No Intervención** Non-Intervention Committee ► **comité de redacción** (*gen*) drafting committee; (*Prensa*) editorial committee ► **Comité Directivo** (*Dep*) board (of management) ► **comité ejecutivo** executive board

comitiva SF (= *cortejo*) retinue; **la ~ del rey** the King's retinue; **la ~ de fotógrafos que sigue todos sus pasos** (*fig, hum*) the retinue of photographers who follow his every move ► **comitiva fúnebre** cortège, funeral procession

como Ⓐ ADV 1 (*indicando semejanza*) like; **tienen un perro ~ el nuestro** they've got a dog like ours; **se portó ~ un imbécil** he behaved like an idiot; **es ~ un pez** it's like a fish; **juega ~ yo** he plays like me *o* like I do; **~ éste hay pocos** there are few like this *o* him; **sabe ~ a queso** it tastes a bit like cheese; **blanco ~ la nieve** as white as snow; **tuvo resultados ~ no se habían conocido antes** it had results such as had never been known before

2 (*introduciendo ejemplo*) such as; **hay peces, ~ truchas y salmones** there are fish, such as trout and salmon; **tiene ventajas, ~ son la resistencia y durabilidad** it has advantages, such as *o* like strength and durability

3 (*indicando modo*) 3·1 (+ *INDIC*) **lo hice ~ me habían enseñado** I did it as I had been taught; **hazlo ~ te dijo ella** do it like* *o* the way she told you; **toca ~ canta** she plays like* *o* the same way as she sings; **no es ~ me lo imaginaba** it isn't as *o* like* I imagined it; **prefiero ~ lo haces tú** I prefer it the way you do it; **la manera ~ sucedió** the way (in which) it happened; **fue así ~ comenzó** that was how it began; **lo levanté ~ pude** I lifted it as best I could; **tal ~: tal ~ lo había planeado** just as *o* the way I had planned it

3·2 (+ *SUBJUN*) **hazlo ~ quieras** do it however you want *o* like; **hazlo ~ puedas** do your best, do the best you can; **~ sea** at all costs; **tratan de mantenerse en el poder ~ sea** they will do whatever it takes to stay in power; **está decidido a salvar ~ sea la vida del niño** he's determined to do whatever it takes to save the child's life; **sea ~ sea** in any case; **hay que evitar que nos eliminen sea ~ sea** we must avoid getting knocked out at all costs

4 (= *en calidad de*) as; **lo usé ~ cuchara** I used it as a spoon; **asistió ~ espectador** he attended as a spectator; **lo dice ~ juez** he says it speaking as a judge; **vale más ~ poeta** he is better as a poet

5 (= *más o menos*) about, around; **había ~ cincuenta** there were about *o* around fifty; **vino ~ a las dos** he came at about *o* around two; **sentía ~ tristeza** she felt a sort *o* kind of sadness

6 (*con valor causal*) **libre ~ estaba** free as he was

Ⓑ CONJ 1 (+ *INDIC*) (= *ya que*) as, since; **~ no tenía dinero** as *o* since I had no money

2 (+ *INDIC*) (= *según*) as; **~ dice mi profesor** as my teacher says; **~ se ve en el gráfico** as you can see from the diagram; **tal (y) ~ están las cosas** the way things are, as things stand; **tal ~ están los precios de las motos …** with motorbike prices as they are at the moment …

3 (+ *INDIC*) (= *cuando*) as soon as; **así ~ nos vio lanzó un grito** as soon as he saw us he shouted

4 (+ *INDIC*) (= *que*) **verás ~ les ganamos** we'll beat them, you'll see; **ya verás ~ no vienen** I bet they won't come; **de tanto ~: tienen las manos doloridas de tanto ~ aplaudieron** they clapped so much their hands hurt; **de tanto ~ odio a los dos, no sé a quien odio más** I hate them both so much, I don't know which I hate the most

5 (+ *SUBJUN*) (= *si*) if; **~ vengas tarde, no comes** if you're late you'll get nothing to eat; **~ sea cierto, ¡estamos perdidos!** if it's true, we're done for!; **¡~ lo pierdas!** you'd better not lose it!, don't you lose it!; **~ no: ~ no lo haga en seguida …** if he doesn't do it at once …, unless he does it at once …; **no salimos, ~ no sea para ir al cine** we only go out if it's to go to the cinema, we don't go out unless it's to go to the cinema

6 **~ que** as if; **¡~ que yo soy tonto y me creo esas mentiras!** as if I was stupid enough to believe lies like that!; **¡~ que te van a pagar!** don't tell me they're going to pay you!; **hizo ~ que no nos veía** he pretended not to see us; **al tragar nota ~ que le molesta** he shows discomfort when swallowing

7 **~ si** as if, as though; **siguió leyendo, ~ si no hubiera oído nada** he kept on reading, as if *o* as though he hadn't heard; **sentí ~ si fuera a caerme** I felt as if *o* as though I was about to fall; **~ si no hubiera pasado nada** as if *o* as though nothing had happened; **se comporta ~ si me odiara** he behaves as if *o* as though he hated me; **~ si fuera a llover** as if *o* as though it was going to rain

8 **~ para: ¡es ~ para denunciarlos!** it's enough to make you want to report them to the police!; **tampoco es ~ para enfadarse tanto** there's no need to get so angry about it

9 (*CAm, Méx*) **a ~ dé** *o* **diera lugar** at any cost; *ver tb* **así A5, pronto A4, querer B1, B3, C**

cómo Ⓐ ADV [1] (*interrogativo*) [1·1] (= *de qué modo*) how?; **¿~ se hace?** how do you do it?; **¿~ se escribe?** how do you spell it?; **¿~ están tus nietos?** how are your grandchildren?; **¿~ está usted?** how are you?; **¿~ te llamas?** what's your name?; **¿~ te va?** how are you doing?; **¿~ lo has pasado en la fiesta?** how was the party?; **¿y eso tú ~ lo sabes?** but, how do you know?; **no sé ~ hacerlo** I don't know how to do it; **—¿~ va el Barcelona? —el primero** "how's Barcelona doing" — "they're first"; **¿~ soportas a ese idiota?** how do you put up with that idiot?; **¿~ se te ocurrió llamarlo tan tarde?** what(ever) were you thinking of, ringing him so late?; **no me digas ~ tengo que comportarme** don't you tell me how to behave; **fue así ~ comenzó todo** that was how it all began; **no había ~ seguir su ritmo** there was no way of keeping up with him
[1·2] (*en descripciones*) **¿~ es tu casa?** what's your house like?; **¿~ es tu hermano?** what's your brother like?; **¿~ es de alto el armario?** how tall is the cupboard?, what height is the cupboard?; **¿~ está de alto tu niño?** how tall is your child?
[1·3] (= *¿por qué?*) why?; **¿~ es que no viniste?** why didn't you come?; **—no fui a la fiesta —¿~ no?** "I didn't go to the party" — "why not *o* how come?"; **—¿me dejas este libro? —¡~ no!** "can I borrow this book?" — "of course!"
[1·4] (*indicando extrañeza*) what?; **¿cómo? ¿que tú no lo sabías?** what? you mean you didn't know?; **¿y ~ es eso?** how come?, how can that be?; **¿~ que Mónica no vino a la boda?** what do you mean, Monica didn't come to the wedding?; **¿~ te atreves?** how dare you!; **—pues no lo haré —¿~ que no?** "I won't do it" — "what do you mean, you won't do it?"; **¿~ que no sabes nada? no me lo creo** what do you mean, you don't know anything about it? I don't believe you
[1·5] (= *¿perdón?*) sorry?, what's that?; **¿~ dice?** I beg your pardon?
[1·6] **¿a ~?: ¿a ~ están** *o* **son las peras?** how much are the pears?; **¿a ~ estamos hoy?** what's the date today?
[2] (*exclamativo*) **¡~ llueve!** look at the rain!; **¡~ corre!** he can certainly run!; **¡hay que ver ~ está el tiempo!** what terrible weather!; **¡~ me gusta ir a la playa!** I love going to the beach!; **—toma, un regalito —¡~ eres!** "here's a small present" — "you shouldn't have!"; **—no quiero prestarte dinero —¡~ eres!** "I won't lend you any money" — "you mean thing!"; **¡~ te has puesto de harina!** you're covered in flour!; **está lloviendo ¡y ~!** just look at the rain!
Ⓑ EXCL **¡cómo! ¿sólo cuatro libros?** what do you mean, four books!; **¡pero ~! ¿todavía no has acabado?** what are you doing! haven't you finished yet?
Ⓒ SM **el ~ y el por qué de las cosas** the whys and wherefores; **aclaró el ~ y el dónde podremos pescar** he explained the conditions for us to be allowed to fish

cómoda SF chest of drawers

cómodamente ADV (= *confortablemente*) comfortably; (= *convenientemente*) conveniently

comodidad SF [1] (= *confort*) comfort; **vivir con ~** to live in comfort
[2] (= *conveniencia*) convenience; **pensar en su propia ~** to consider one's own interest; **venga a su ~** come at your convenience
[3] **comodidades** (= *servicios*) comforts, amenities; (*LAm Com*) commodities, goods ► **comodidades de la vida** good things of life, life's comforts

comodín Ⓐ SM [1] (*Naipes*) joker
[2] (= *excusa*) pretext, stock excuse
[3] (*Ling*) catch-all, all-purpose word
[4] (*Inform*) wildcard
[5] (*Mec*) useful gadget
Ⓑ ADJ (*Andes, Caribe, Méx*) = **comodón**

cómodo ADJ [1] (= *confortable*) [*cama, silla, habitación*] comfortable; [*trabajo, tarea*] agreeable
[2] (= *conveniente*) [*instrumento, objeto*] handy; [*arreglo, horario*] convenient
[3] (= *descansado*) comfortable; **así estarás más ~** you'll be more comfortable this way; **ponerse ~** to make o.s. comfortable
[4] [*persona*] (= *perezoso*) lazy; (= *tranquilo*) laid-back*

comodón/a Ⓐ ADJ (= *regalón*) comfort-loving; (= *pasivo*) easy-going, liking a quiet life; (= *perezoso*) lazy
Ⓑ SM/F (= *perezoso*) lazybones*; **es un ~** he likes his home comforts

comodonería SF love of comfort

comodoro SM commodore

comoquiera CONJ [1] **~ que** + *INDIC* since, in view of the fact that
[2] **~ que** + *SUBJUN* in whatever way; **~ que sea eso** however that may be

comp. ABR (= **compárese**) cp

compa* SMF [1] (*CAm, Méx*) (= *compañero*) pal*, buddy (*EEUU**)
[2] (*Nic Hist*) Nicaraguan freedom fighter

compacidad SF compactness

compact SM (*pl* **compacts**) (*tb* **~ disc**) compact disc

compactación SF compacting, compression

compactadora SF compacter

compactar ▸conjug 1a◂ VT to compact, compress

compacto Ⓐ ADJ compact; **disco ~** compact disc
Ⓑ SM (*Mús*) compact hi-fi system

compadecer ▸conjug 2d◂ Ⓐ VT (= *apiadarse de*) to pity, be sorry for; (= *comprender*) to sympathize with
Ⓑ **compadecerse** VPR [1] **~se de** = A
[2] (†) **~se con** to fit with

compadrada SF (*Cono Sur*) cheek, insolence

compadrazgo SM [1] (= *parentesco*) *status of godfather*
[2] (*LAm*) (= *amistad*) close friendship

compadre SM [1] (= *padrino*) godfather
[2] (*esp LAm**) (= *amigo*) friend, pal*, buddy (*esp EEUU**); (*en oración directa*) friend
[3] (*Cono Sur*) (= *jactancioso*) braggart, loudmouth; (= *engreído*) show-off*; (= *matón*) bully

compadrear ▸conjug 1a◂ VI [1] (*esp LAm**) [*amigos*] to be mates*, be buddies (*EEUU**)
[2] (*Cono Sur*) (= *jactarse*) to brag, show off; (= *presumir*) to put on airs; (= *amenazar*) to give threatening looks

compadreo SM (*esp LAm*) companionship, close contact

compadrito SM (*Cono Sur*) = **compadre 3**

compaginable ADJ compatible; **motivos difícilmente ~s** motives that are hard to reconcile

compaginación SF (= *armonización*) arrangement, combination; [*de papeles impresos*] putting in order, collation; (*Tip*) makeup

compaginar ▸conjug 1a◂ Ⓐ VT [1] (= *armonizar*) to combine; **~ el trabajo con la familia** to combine work and having a family
[2] (= *ordenar*) to put together, put in order
[3] (*Tip*) to make up
Ⓑ **compaginarse** VPR (= *concordar*) to agree, tally; **~se con** (*gen*) to tally with; [+ *colores*] to blend with; **esa conducta no se compagina con su carácter** this behaviour is out of character for him

compañerismo SM (= *camaradería*) comradeship, friendship; (*Dep etc*) team spirit

compañero/a SM/F [1] (*gen*) companion; (*Dep, Naipes*) partner; (*Dep*) [*de equipo*] team-mate ► **compañero/a de armas** comrade-in-arms ► **compañero/a de baile** dancing partner ► **compañero/a de cama** bedfellow ► **compañero/a de candidatura** running mate ► **compañero/a de clase** schoolmate, classmate ► **compañero/a de cuarto** roommate ► **compañero/a de infortunio** companion in misfortune ► **compañero/a de juego** playmate ► **compañero/a de piso** flatmate, roommate (*EEUU*) ► **compañero/a de rancho** messmate ► **compañero/a de trabajo** (*en fábrica*) workmate, fellow worker; (*en oficina*) colleague ► **compañero/a de viaje** fellow traveller, fellow traveler (*EEUU*) ► **compañero/a sentimental** partner
[2] **dos calcetines que no son ~s** two odd socks, two socks which do not match; **¿dónde está el ~ de éste?** where is the one that goes with this?, where is the other one (of the pair)?
[3] (*Pol*) brother/sister; **¡compañeros!** comrades!

compañía SF [1] (*gen*) company; **en ~ de** with, accompanied by, in the company of; **pasé la tarde en ~ de unos amigos** I spent the afternoon with *o* (*frm*) in the company of some friends; **hacer ~ a algn** to keep sb company; **andar en malas ~s** ◊ **frecuentar malas ~s** to keep bad company
[2] (*Com, Teat, Rel*) company; **Pérez y Compañía** Pérez and Company ► **compañía afiliada** associated company ► **compañía concesionadora** franchiser ► **compañía de bandera** national company ► **Compañía de Jesús** Society of Jesus ► **compañía de seguros** insurance company ► **compañía inversionista** investment trust ► **compañía naviera** shipping company ► **compañía (no) cotizable** (un)listed company ► **compañía pública** public company ► **compañía tenedora** holding company
[3] (*Mil*) company

comparabilidad SF comparability

comparable ADJ comparable (**a** to; **con** with)

▼**comparación** SF [1] (= *cotejo*) comparison; **en ~ con** in comparison with, beside; **es sin ~** it is beyond compare
[2] (*Literat*) simile

▼**comparado** ADJ [1] [*estudio, proyecto*] comparative
[2] **~ con** compared with *o* to

➤ LENGUA Y USO: **comparación 1** 32.1, 32.3, 32.5, 53.5 **comparado 2** 32.1, 53.5

comparar ▸conjug 1a◂ Ⓐ VT to compare (**a** to; **con** with, to); **~ dos archivos** (*Inform*) to compare two files; **he estado comparando los precios** I've been comparing prices; **por favor, no compares, esta casa es mucho mejor que la que tenías antes** there's no comparison, this house is much better than the one you had before

Ⓑ **compararse** VPR **~se a** *o* **con** to compare with *o* to; **él no puede ~se a ti** *o* **contigo** he doesn't stand *o* bear comparison with you, he comes nowhere near you*

comparativo ADJ, SM comparative

comparecencia SF (*Jur*) appearance (in court); **su no ~** his non-appearance; **orden de ~** summons, subpoena (*EEUU*)

comparecer ▸conjug 2d◂ VI (*Jur*) to appear (in court); **~ ante un juez** to appear before a judge

comparecimiento SM = **comparecencia**

comparencia SF (*Cono Sur*) = **comparecencia**

comparendo SM (*Jur*) (= *orden*) summons; (= *documento*) subpoena

comparsa Ⓐ SF **1** [*de carnaval*] group

2 (*Teat*) **la ~** the extras *pl*

3 (= *persona subordinada*) puppet

Ⓑ SMF **1** (*Teat*) extra

2 (*Caribe*) (= *bailadores*) dance troupe

comparsería SF extras, supernumeraries

compartible ADJ **1** (= *que se puede compartir*) which can be shared

2 (= *aceptable*) [*opinión*] acceptable, readily shared

compartimentación SF compartmentalization

compartimentado ADJ compartmentalized

compartimento SM, **compartimiento** SM **1** (= *acción*) division, sharing; (= *distribución*) distribution

2 (*Transportes*) compartment ► **compartimento de equipajes** luggage compartment, baggage compartment (*esp EEUU*) ► **compartimento estanco** watertight compartment

3 (*Aer*) ► **compartimento de bombas** bomb bay ► **compartimento de carga** hold

compartir ▸conjug 3a◂ VT **1** [+ *casa, cuarto, comida, ropa*] to share; **~ algo con algn** to share sth with sb; **comparto habitación con otro estudiante** I share a room with another student

2 [+ *ganancias*] to share (out), divide (up); [+ *gastos*] to share; **compartimos las ganancias a medias** we shared (out) *o* divided (up) the profits between us; **comparten los gastos del viaje** they are sharing the costs of the trip

3 [+ *opinión*] to share; [+ *objetivos*] to agree with; [+ *sentimientos*] to share; **no comparto ese criterio** I do not share that view

compás SM **1** (*Mús*) time; (= *ritmo*) beat, rhythm; (= *división*) bar, measure (*EEUU*); **a ~** in time; **al ~ de la música** in time to the music; **fuera de ~** off beat, not in time; **martillar a ~** to hammer rhythmically; **llevar el ~** to keep time; **perder el ~** to lose the beat; **entraron a los compases de un vals** they came in to the strains of a waltz; **mantenemos el ~ de espera** we are still waiting ► **compás de 2 por 4** 2/4 time ► **compás de vals** waltz time

2 (*Mat*) (*tb* **~ de puntas**) compass, pair of compasses

3 (*Náut*) compass

compasado ADJ measured, moderate

compasar ▸conjug 1a◂ VT **1** (*Mat*) to measure (with a compass)

2 [+ *gastos, tiempo*] to adjust

3 (*Mús*) to divide into bars

compasión SF (= *pena*) compassion, sympathy; (= *piedad*) pity; **no siento ~ por ella** I have no sympathy for her; **¡por ~!** for pity's sake!; **tener ~ de** to take pity on, feel sorry for; **mover a algn a ~** to move sb to pity; **tener pronta ~** be easily moved to pity

compasivamente ADV (*gen*) compassionately, pityingly; (= *comprensivamente*) sympathetically

compasividad SF = **compasión**

compasivo ADJ compassionate

compatibilidad SF compatibility

compatibilización SF harmonization

compatibilizar ▸conjug 1f◂ VT to harmonize, reconcile, bring into line, make compatible (**con** with)

compatible ADJ (*Inform*) compatible (**con** with)

compatriota SMF compatriot, fellow countryman/countrywoman

compeler ▸conjug 2a◂ VT to compel; **~ a algn a** (+ *INFIN*) to compel sb to + *infin*

compendiar ▸conjug 1b◂ VT to abridge, condense, summarize

compendio SM (= *tratado breve*) compendium; (*Univ, Téc*) summary; **en ~** briefly, in short

compendiosamente ADV briefly, succinctly

compendioso ADJ [*libro, discurso*] (= *abreviado*) condensed, abridged; (= *sucinto*) brief, succinct

compenetración SF mutual understanding, fellow feeling, natural sympathy

compenetrarse ▸conjug 1a◂ VPR **1** (= *entenderse*) to understand one another; **~ con algo/algn** to identify with sth/sb; **estamos muy compenetrados** we understand each other very well

2 (*Quím*) to interpenetrate, fuse

compensación SF **1** (= *pago*) compensation; **como** *o* **en ~** as compensation; **le ofreció 100.000 dólares como ~** he offered him 100,000 dollars' compensation ► **compensación económica** financial compensation ► **compensación por daños y perjuicios** damages *pl* ► **compensación por despido** severance pay, redundancy payment

2 (= *recompensa*) **no espero ninguna ~ por mis desvelos** I don't expect any reward for my efforts; **este trabajo me ofrece muy pocas compensaciones** this job is very unrewarding; **en ~: tendrán que devolver sus tierras, pero en ~, ...** they will have to give up their land, but in return *o* in exchange, ...; **en ~ por lo mal que se portó ayer** to make up for his (bad) behaviour yesterday

3 (= *equilibrio*) **medidas de ~** compensatory measures; **un mecanismo de ~ de precios** a compensatory price mechanism

4 (*Jur*) [*de deudas*] compensation, redress

5 (*Fin*) clearing; **cámara de ~** clearing house

compensador ADJ compensating, compensatory

compensar ▸conjug 1a◂ Ⓐ VT **1** (= *indemnizar*) to compensate (**por** for); **~ económicamente a algn** to compensate sb financially; **lo ~on con 100 dólares por los cristales rotos** he received 100 dollars' compensation for the broken windows; **¿cómo puedo ~te por lo que has hecho por mí?** how can I repay you for what you have done for me?

2 (= *equilibrar*) [+ *pérdida, falta*] to compensate for, make up for; [+ *efecto, bajada*] to compensate for, offset; [+ *gastos*] to repay, reimburse; [+ *error*] to make amends for; **le ponen luz artificial para ~ la falta de sol** they put in artificial lighting to compensate for *o* make up for the lack of sunlight; **espero que el resultado le compense la molestia** I hope the result makes it worth your trouble

3 (*Mec*) [+ *ruedas*] to balance

4 (*Fin*) [+ *cheque*] to clear

Ⓑ VI **no compensa** it's not worth it, it's not worthwhile; **te compensa hacerlo** it's worth you doing it, it's worth your while doing it *o* to do it; **compensa gastarse más dinero ahora y ahorrarlo después** it pays to spend more now and save money later, it's worth spending more now to save money later on; **el esfuerzo no compensa** it's not worth the effort; **no me compensa el tiempo que he invertido** it isn't worth the time I've spent on it

compensatoriamente ADV by way of compensation

compensatorio ADJ [*indemnización*] compensatory; [*educación*] remedial

competencia SF **1** (= *rivalidad*) competition; **nos enfrentamos a la ~ de los productos norteamericanos** we are faced by competition from American products; **existe una fuerte ~ entre las dos empresas por el control del mercado externo** the two companies are vying for control of the foreign market, there is fierce competition between the two companies for control of the foreign market; **~ desleal** unfair competition; **~ despiadada** ruthless competition; **en ~ con algn/algo** in competition with sb/sth; **en ~ directa con el sector privado** in direct competition with the private sector; **actúan en ~ con el estado** they are in competition with the state; **hacer la ~ a algn/algo** to compete with sb/sth; **dos compañías nos hacen la ~** we have two companies to compete with; **¿me quieres hacer la ~?** are you trying to compete with me?; **libre ~** free competition

2 (= *rival*) competition; **han conseguido hundir a la ~** they have managed to beat the competition; **ahora trabaja para la ~** she's working for the competition now; **la ~ tiene mejores ofertas** our competitors have better offers, the competition has better offers

3 (= *capacidad*) competence, ability; **no dudo de tu ~ como abogado** I am not questioning your competence *o* ability as a lawyer ► **competencia lingüística** linguistic competence, linguistic ability

4 (= *responsabilidad*) **ese tema no es de mi ~** that matter is outside my jurisdiction *o* my competence; **esta decisión es ~ exclusiva del gobierno** this decision is the exclusive jurisdiction of the government, only the government is competent to deal with this decision; **las ~s legales del Consejo de Administración** the jurisdiction *o* areas of competence of the Administrative Council

5 **competencias** (*Pol*) powers; **~s transfe-**

➤ LENGUA Y USO: **comparar B** 32.1, 32.4, 32.5, 53.5 **compartir 3** 38.1

ridas a las comunidades autónomas powers devolved *o* transferred to the autonomous regions
[6] (*LAm Dep*) competition

competente ADJ [1] (= *responsable*) competent (*frm*); **la autoridad ~** the proper *o* (*frm*) competent authority; **esto se elevará al ministerio ~** this will be sent to the appropriate ministry *o* to the ministry concerned; **de fuente ~** from a reliable source; **ser ~ para hacer algo** to be competent to do sth (*frm*)
[2] (= *capaz*) competent; **necesitamos gente ~** we need competent people; **es muy ~ en su especialidad** he is very competent in his field

competentemente ADV competently

competer ▸conjug 2a◂ VI **~ a algn** to be the responsibility of sb; **un tema que compete al Ministerio del Exterior** a matter that comes under the jurisdiction of *o* that is the responsibility of the Foreign Office; **es al gobierno a quien compete mantener la seguridad** it falls to the government to maintain law and order, it is the government that is responsible for maintaining law and order; **este tema compete exclusivamente al director** this subject is the exclusive concern *o* responsibility of the director

competición SF [1] (= *enfrentamiento*) competition; **deporte de ~** competitive sport
[2] (= *concurso*) competition, contest; **mañana comenzará la ~ de tiro con arco** the archery competition starts tomorrow; **acaba de comenzar la ~ electoral** the electoral race has begun

competido ADJ [*carrera*] hard-fought, close-run

competidor(a) Ⓐ ADJ (*gen*) competing, rival
Ⓑ SM/F [1] (*gen*) competitor; (*Com*) rival (**a** for)
[2] (*en concurso*) contestant

competir ▸conjug 3k◂ VI [1] (= *enfrentarse*) to compete; **~ con** *o* **contra algo/algn** to compete with *o* against sth/sb; **son incapaces de ~ con** *o* **contra gente más joven** they are incapable of competing with *o* against younger people; **~ en algo** to compete in sth; **los equipos que ~án en este campeonato** the teams competing in this championship; **~ en el mercado** (*Com*) to compete in the market; **~ por algo** to compete for sth; **cuatro películas compiten por el Oscar** four films are competing for the Oscar
[2] (= *compararse*) **~ con algo**: **no hay nada que pueda ~ con un buen vino** you can't beat a good wine, nothing can compare with a good wine; **es el único modelo que compite en precio con sus rivales** it's the only model which can compete *o* compare with its rivals in terms of price; **en cuanto a resistencia Miguel no puede ~ con Andrés** when it comes to stamina Miguel is no match for Andrés

competitivamente ADV competitively

competitividad SF competitiveness

competitivo ADJ competitive

compilación SF compilation; **tiempo de ~** (*Inform*) compile time

compilador(a) Ⓐ SM/F (= *persona*) compiler
Ⓑ SM (*Inform*) compiler ► **compilador incremental** incremental compiler

compilar ▸conjug 1a◂ VT to compile

➤ LENGUA Y USO: **complacer** **A** 46.5, 51.2 **B** 51.1

compincharse ▸conjug 1a◂ VPR to band together, team up; **estar compinchados*** to be in cahoots* (**con** with)

compinche* SMF [1] (= *amigo*) pal*, mate*, buddy (*EEUU**)
[2] (= *cómplice*) partner in crime, accomplice

compita* SMF (*Nic Hist*) comrade*, Nicaraguan freedom fighter

complacencia SF [1] (= *placer*) pleasure, satisfaction
[2] (= *agrado*) willingness; **lo hizo con ~** he did it gladly
[3] (= *indulgencia*) indulgence; **tiene excesivas ~s con los empleados** he is too indulgent towards his employees
[4] (*LAm*) (= *autosatisfacción*) complacency

▼ **complacer** ▸conjug 2w◂ Ⓐ VT [1] (*gen*) to please; [+ *cliente*] to help, oblige; [+ *jefe*] to humour; **nos complace anunciarles ...** we are pleased to announce ...; **¿en qué puedo ~le?** (*Com frm*) can I help you?, what can I do for you?
[2] [+ *deseo*] to indulge, gratify
Ⓑ **complacerse** VPR **~se en hacer algo** to take pleasure in doing sth; **el Banco se complace en comunicar a su clientela que ...** the bank is pleased to inform its customers that ...

complacido ADJ pleased, satisfied; **me miró ~** he gave me a pleased look; **quedamos ~s de la visita** we were pleased with our visit

complaciente ADJ [1] (= *indulgente*) indulgent; [*marido*] complaisant
[2] (= *solícito*) obliging, helpful

complejidad SF complexity

complejo Ⓐ ADJ (*gen*) complex
Ⓑ SM [1] (*Psic*) complex ► **complejo de culpa, complejo de culpabilidad** guilt complex ► **complejo de Edipo** Oedipus complex ► **complejo de Electra** Electra complex ► **complejo de inferioridad** inferiority complex ► **complejo de superioridad** superiority complex ► **complejo persecutorio** persecution complex
[2] (= *instalaciones*) complex ► **complejo deportivo** sports complex, sports centre *o* (*EEUU*) center ► **complejo industrial** industrial complex ► **complejo petroquímico** petrochemical complex ► **complejo recreativo** leisure complex, leisure centre *o* (*EEUU*) center ► **complejo residencial** housing development ► **complejo turístico** tourist development
[3] (*Quím*) complex ► **complejo vitamínico** vitamin complex

complementar ▸conjug 1a◂ Ⓐ VT to complement
Ⓑ **complementarse** VPR to complement each other

complementariamente ADV in addition (**a** to), additionally

complementariedad SF complementarity

complementario Ⓐ ADJ (*gen*) complementary; **visita complementaria** follow-up visit
Ⓑ SM (*en lotería*) bonus number

complemento Ⓐ SM [1] (*Mat*) complement
[2] (*Ling*) complement, object ► **complemento directo** direct object ► **complemento circunstancial** adverbial ► **complemento indirecto** indirect object ► **complemento preposicional** prepositional complement
[3] (= *parte*) **el vino es un ~ de la buena comida** wine is the ideal complement to good food; **sería el ~ de su felicidad** it would complete her happiness
[4] **oficial de ~** (*Mil*) reserve officer
[5] (= *pago*) ► **complemento de destino** extra allowance (attached to a post) ► **complemento de productividad** performance-related bonus ► **complemento de sueldo** bonus, extra pay ► **complemento por peligrosidad** danger money ► **complemento salarial** bonus, extra pay
[6] (*Cine*) short, supporting feature
Ⓑ **complementos** SMPL (*Aut*) [*de moda*] accessories

completa SF (*Caribe*) full (cheap) meal

completamente ADV completely

completar ▸conjug 1a◂ VT [1] (= *terminar*) to complete, finish; (= *perfeccionar*) to finish off, round off; (*Méx*) to match; **me falta un sello para ~ la serie** I need one stamp to complete the series; **completó su formación en varias universidades norteamericanas** she finished off her education at a number of American universities
[2] [+ *pérdida*] to make good

completas SFPL compline

completez SF completeness

completo Ⓐ ADJ [1] (= *entero*) [*dieta*] balanced; [*colección*] complete; [*texto, informe*] full, complete; [*felicidad*] complete, total; [*panorama*] full; **tomamos una comida ligera pero completa** we had a light but full meal; **un coche con equipamiento ~** a car with a full range of fittings; **un laboratorio de idiomas con equipamiento ~** a fully-equipped language lab; **las poesías completas de San Juan de la Cruz** the complete poems of San Juan de la Cruz; **trabajar a tiempo ~** to work full time; *ver tb* **jornada 1**, **obra 2.2**, **pensión 3**
[2] (= *lleno*) full; [*hotel*] full, fully booked; **"completo"** (*en pensión, hostal*) "no vacancies"; (*en taquilla*) "sold out"; **al ~: el tren está al ~** the train is full; **el hotel estaba al ~** the hotel was fully booked *o* full; **asistió el ayuntamiento al ~** the entire council was present
[3] (= *total*) [*éxito, fracaso*] complete, total; **la película fue un ~ fracaso** the film was a complete *o* total flop; **por ~** [*desaparecer, desconocer*] completely; **ha quedado destruido por ~** it was completely destroyed; **se me olvidó por ~** I completely forgot; **la niebla cubrió por ~ el paisaje** the fog completely covered the countryside; **está dedicado por ~ a su trabajo** he is totally dedicated to his work; **su partido apoyaba por ~ la iniciativa** his party fully supported the initiative, his party gave its full support to the initiative; **el problema quedará resuelto por ~** the problem will be solved once and for all
[4] (= *terminado*) **la novela está ya casi completa** the novel is almost finished
[5] (= *bien hecho*) **ha entregado un trabajo muy ~** he's handed in a very thorough piece of work; **este libro es pequeño, pero bastante ~** this book is small, but quite comprehensive
[6] (= *polifacético*) [*actor, deportista*] all-round; **un atleta muy ~** an all-round athlete
Ⓑ SM (*Chile*) hot dog (*with salad*)

complexión SF 1 (*Anat*) build, constitution; **un hombre de ~ fuerte** a well-built man, a man with a strong constitution
2 (*LAm*) (= *tez*) complexion

complexionado ADJ **bien ~** strong, tough, robust; **mal ~** weak, frail

complexional ADJ constitutional

complicación SF 1 (= *problema*) complication; **han surgido complicaciones** complications have arisen; **una persona sin complicaciones** an uncomplicated person
2 (= *cualidad*) complexity; **no captó la ~ del asunto** he did not grasp the complexity of the matter

complicado ADJ (= *complejo*) complicated, complex; (*Med*) [*fractura*] compound; [*estilo*] elaborate; [*persona*] complex; [*método*] complicated, involved; (*Jur*) involved, implicated

complicar ▸conjug 1g◂ Ⓐ VT 1 (*gen*) to complicate
2 (*Jur*) to involve, implicate (**en** in)
Ⓑ **complicarse** VPR 1 (*gen*) to get complicated; **~se la vida** to make life difficult for o.s.
2 **~se en algo** to get involved *o* mixed up in sth

cómplice SMF accomplice

complicidad SF complicity, involvement (**en** in)

compló SM, **complot** SM (*pl* **complots**) plot, conspiracy, intrigue

complotado/a SM/F plotter, conspirator

complotar ▸conjug 1a◂ VI to plot, conspire

complutense ADJ of Alcalá de Henares

componedor(a) SM/F **~ de huesos** bonesetter

componenda SF 1 (= *arreglo temporal*) temporary arrangement
2 (= *acuerdo sucio*) shady deal

componente Ⓐ ADJ (*gen*) component, constituent
Ⓑ SM 1 (= *miembro*) member
2 (= *parte*) (*Quím*) component; (*Mec*) part, component; (*Culin*) ingredient ► **componentes lógicos** (*Inform*) software
3 (*Meteo*) **un viento de ~ norte** a northerly wind

componer ▸conjug 2q◂ (*pp* **compuesto**) Ⓐ VT
1 (= *constituir*) [+ *comité, jurado, organización*] to make up; **los doce miembros que componen la junta** the twelve members who make up the board; **componen el jurado once personas** the jury is made up of eleven people; **los cuadros que componen esta exposición** the pictures that make up this exhibition, the pictures in this exhibition
2 (= *escribir*) [+ *poesía, sinfonía, canción*] to compose, write; [+ *poema, tratado, redacción*] to write; **compuso la música de varios ballets** he composed *o* wrote the music for several ballets
3 (= *arreglar*) [+ *objeto roto*] to mend, repair, fix; (*Med*) [+ *hueso*] to set; **a éste no hay quien le componga*** he's a hopeless case
4 (= *curar*) [+ *estómago*] to settle; [+ *espíritu*] to soothe; [+ *abuso*] to set to rights, correct
5 (*Tip*) [+ *texto*] to typeset, set, compose
6 (*Culin*) to prepare
Ⓑ **componerse** VPR 1 **~se de** to consist of; **se compone de seis partes** it consists of six parts; **la cena se compone de dos platos y postre** dinner consists of two courses and dessert
2 (= *arreglarse*) to dress up; **le gusta ~se para salir** she likes to dress up to go out
3 [*tiempo atmosférico*] to improve, clear up
4 (*Méx*) [*persona*] to recover, get better
5 **componérselas*** to manage; **me las compuse cómo pude y salí adelante** I managed as best I could and carried on; **siempre se las compone para salirse con la suya** he always manages to get his own way; ✦MODISMO **¡allá** *o* **que se las componga (como pueda)!*** that's his problem, that's his funeral*

componible ADJ 1 [*objeto roto*] repairable, worth mending 2 (= *que se puede conciliar*) reconcilable, capable of settlement

comportable ADJ bearable

comportamental ADJ behavioural, behavioral (*EEUU*)

comportamiento SM 1 behaviour, behavior (*EEUU*); **un premio al buen ~** a prize for good behaviour ► **comportamiento sexual** sexual behaviour, sexual behavior (*EEUU*) ► **comportamiento social** social behaviour, social behavior (*EEUU*)
2 [*de mercado, automóvil*] performance; **el ~ de la Bolsa** the performance of the stock market ► **comportamiento en carretera** road performance

comportar ▸conjug 1a◂ Ⓐ VT 1 (= *significar*) to involve; **no comporta obligación alguna** it carries no obligation, you are under no obligation
2 (= *aguantar*) to bear, endure, put up with
3 (*Andes, Cono Sur*) (= *causar*) to entail, bring with it
Ⓑ **comportarse** VPR to behave; **~se como es debido** to behave properly, conduct o.s. in a proper fashion (*frm*); **~se mal** to misbehave, behave badly

comporte SM 1 = **comportamiento**
2 (= *porte*) bearing, carriage

composición SF 1 (*Mús, Quím, Arte*) composition
2 (*Educ*) essay
3 ► **composición de lugar** stocktaking, inventory; **hacerse una ~ de lugar** to take stock (of one's situation)
4 (*Tip*) typesetting ► **composición por ordenador** computer typesetting
5 [*de desacuerdo*] settlement; [*de personas*] reconciliation ► **composición procesal** (*Jur*) out-of-court settlement
6 (= *arreglo*) arrangement

compositor(a) SM/F 1 (*Mús*) composer
2 (*Tip*) compositor
3 (*Cono Sur*) (= *curandero*) quack doctor, bonesetter

compost ['kompos] SM compost

compostación SF, **compostaje** SM composting

compostelano/a Ⓐ ADJ of/from Santiago de Compostela
Ⓑ SM/F native/inhabitant of Santiago de Compostela; **los ~s** the people of Santiago de Compostela

compostura SF 1 (= *dignidad*) composure; **perder la ~** to lose one's composure
2 (= *arreglo*) mending, repair; **estar en ~** to be under repair
3 (= *constitución*) composition, make-up; (= *estructura*) structure
4 (†) (= *condimento*) condiment, seasoning
5 (†) (= *aseo*) neatness; (= *adorno*) adornment
6 (†) (= *acuerdo*) arrangement, agreement, settlement

compota SF compote, preserve ► **compota de manzanas** stewed apples

compotera SF dessert dish

compra SF 1 (= *proceso*) purchase, purchasing, buying; **hacer la ~** to do the shopping; **tengo que ir a la ~** I've got to do the shopping, I've got to go shopping; **ir de ~s** to go shopping; **prueba de ~** proof of purchase; **ticket de ~** receipt ► **compra a crédito** buying on credit ► **compra a granel** (*Com*) bulk buying ► **compra al contado** cash purchase ► **compra a plazos** hire purchase, installment plan (*EEUU*) ► **compra por catálogo** mail order ► **compra proteccionista** (*Com*) support buying ► **compra y venta** buying and selling
2 (= *artículo*) purchase; **es una buena ~** it's a good buy

comprador(a) SM/F (*Com*) buyer, purchaser; (*en tienda*) shopper, customer ► **comprador(a) principal** head buyer

comprar ▸conjug 1a◂ Ⓐ VT 1 (= *adquirir*) [+ *casa, comida, regalo*] to buy, purchase (*frm*); **¿te has comprado por fin la bici?** did you buy the bike in the end?; **~ algo a algn** (*para algn*) to buy sth for sb, buy sb sth; (*de algn*) to buy sth from sb; **le compré un vestido a mi hija** I bought a dress for my daughter, I bought my daughter a dress; **siempre le compro la carne a este carnicero** I always buy my meat from this butcher; **si decides vender el coche, yo te lo compro** if you decide to sell the car, I'll buy it from *o* off you; **~ algo al contado** to pay cash (for sth), pay sth in cash; **~ algo al detalle** to buy sth retail; **~ algo a plazos** to buy sth on hire purchase; **~ algo al por mayor** to buy sth wholesale; **~ algo al por menor** to buy sth retail; **~ deudas** to factor
2 (= *sobornar*) to bribe, buy off*; **intentaron ~ al juez** they tried to bribe *o* buy off* the judge; **el árbitro está comprado** they've bribed the referee
Ⓑ VI (= *hacer la compra*) to buy, shop; **nunca compro en grandes almacenes** I never buy *o* shop in department stores

compraventa SF 1 (*gen*) buying and selling, dealing; **negocio de ~** second-hand shop
2 (*Jur*) contract of sale

comprender ▸conjug 2a◂ Ⓐ VT 1 (= *entender*) to understand; **espero que comprendan nuestras razones** I hope that they understand our reasons; **compréndeme, no me quedaba más remedio** you have to understand, I had no choice; **te comprendo perfectamente** I understand perfectly; **no acabo de ~ qué es lo que pasa** I still don't understand what's going on; **no comprendo cómo ha podido pasar esto** I don't see *o* understand how this could have happened; **hacer ~ algo a algn**: **esto bastó para hacernos ~ su posición** this was all we needed to understand his position; **hacerse ~** to make o.s. understood
2 (= *darse cuenta*) to realize; **al final comprendió que yo no iba a ayudarle** he finally realized I wasn't going to help him; **comprendemos perfectamente que haya gente a**

quien le molesta el tabaco we fully understand *o* appreciate that some people are bothered by smoking
3 (= *incluir*) to comprise (*frm*); **la colección comprende cien discos y cuarenta libros** the collection consists of *o* (*frm*) comprises a hundred records and forty books; **el primer tomo comprende las letras de la A a la G** the first volume covers *o* (*frm*) comprises letters A to G; **está todo comprendido en el precio** the price is all-inclusive; **el período comprendido entre 1936 y 1939** the period from 1936 to 1939 *o* between 1936 and 1939; *ver tb* **edad 1**
Ⓑ VI 1 (= *entender*) to understand; **¿comprendes?** do you understand?; **no hay forma de hacerle ~** there is no way to make him understand
2 (= *darse cuenta*) **¡ya comprendo!** now I see!, I get it (now)!*; **como tú ~ás, no soy yo quién para juzgarlo** as you will appreciate *o* understand, I'm not the best person to judge him

▼**comprensible** ADJ 1 (= *justificable*) understandable; **es ~ que haya actuado así** it's understandable that he behaved in that way; **no es ~ que no haya dicho nada** it's hard to understand why he hasn't said anything
2 (= *inteligible*) **eso no le resulta ~ a nadie** nobody can understand that; **un arte ~** an accessible art

comprensiblemente ADV understandably

comprensión SF 1 (= *entendimiento*) understanding; **los dibujos nos ayudan a la ~ del texto** the drawings help us to understand the text *o* help our understanding of the text; **un ejercicio de ~ auditiva** a listening comprehension test
2 (= *actitud comprensiva*) understanding; **ha mostrado una gran ~ con nuestros problemas** he has shown great understanding of our problems

comprensivo ADJ understanding

compresa SF 1 (*para mujer*) sanitary towel, sanitary napkin (*EEUU*)
2 (*Med*) compress

compresibilidad SF compressibility

compresible ADJ compressible

compresión SF compression

compresor SM compressor

comprimible ADJ compressible

comprimido Ⓐ ADJ (*gen*) compressed
Ⓑ SM (*Med*) pill, tablet ► **comprimido para dormir** sleeping pill

comprimir ▸conjug 3a◂ Ⓐ VT 1 (*Téc*) to compress (**en** into); (= *prensar*) to press (down), squeeze down; (*Inform*) to zip; (= *condensar*) to condense
2 (= *controlar*) to control; [+ *lágrimas*] to hold back
Ⓑ **comprimirse** VPR (*gen*) to get compressed; [*personas*] to squeeze *o* squash together

comprobable ADJ verifiable, capable of being checked; **un alegato fácilmente ~** an allegation which is easy to prove

comprobación SF (= *proceso*) checking, verification; (= *datos*) proof; **de difícil ~** hard to prove; **en ~ de ello** as proof of what I say ► **comprobación general de cuentas** (*Com*) general audit

comprobador SM tester ► **comprobador de lámparas** valve tester

comprobante Ⓐ ADJ **documento ~** supporting document
Ⓑ SM (= *documento*) proof, supporting document; (*Com*) receipt, voucher

comprobar ▸conjug 1l◂ VT 1 (= *examinar*) [+ *billete, documento, frenos*] to check; **compruebe el aceite antes de salir de viaje** check your oil before setting out; **compruebe el cambio antes de salir de la tienda** check your change before leaving the shop; **comprobó la hora y decidió marcharse** he checked the time and decided to leave; **tendré que ~ si se han cumplido los objetivos** I shall have to see *o* check whether the objectives have been met; **necesito algún documento para ~ su identidad** I need some document that proves your identity, I need some proof of identity; **compruebe nuestros productos usted mismo** try our products for yourself
2 (= *confirmar*) [+ *teoría, existencia*] to prove; [+ *eficacia, veracidad*] to verify, confirm; **pudimos ~ que era verdad** we were able to verify *o* confirm *o* establish that it was true; **comprobó sus ideas experimentalmente** he proved his arguments through experiments
3 (*frm*) (= *darse cuenta*) to realize; **~on que el candidato era demasiado joven** they realized that the candidate was too young

comprometedor ADJ compromising

comprometer ▸conjug 2a◂ Ⓐ VT 1 (= *poner en evidencia*) to compromise; **aquellas cartas lo comprometían** those letters compromised him
2 (= *implicar*) **~ a algn en algo** (*futuro*) to involve sb in sth; (*pasado*) to implicate sb in sth
3 (= *obligar*) **~ a algn a algo** to commit sb to sth; **esta firma no le compromete a nada** this signature does not commit you to anything
4 (= *arriesgar*) [+ *conversaciones, éxito, reputación, paz*] to jeopardize; **han comprometido la neutralidad del país** they have jeopardized the neutrality of the country; **su rebelión comprometió la vida de los rehenes** his rebellion endangered *o* jeopardized the hostages' lives
5 (= *apalabrar*) [+ *habitación, entrada*] to reserve, book; **ya he comprometido la casa** I've already promised the house to someone
6 (= *invertir*) to invest, tie up; **ha comprometido todo su capital en esta empresa** he has invested all his capital in this company, all his capital is tied up in this company
7 (*frm*) (= *afectar*) **la bala le comprometió el pulmón** the bullet damaged his lung; **la gangrena le ha comprometido la rodilla** the gangrene has spread to *o* affected his knee
Ⓑ **comprometerse** VPR 1 (= *contraer un compromiso*) to commit o.s.; **no te comprometas demasiado pronto** don't commit yourself too soon; **~se a algo** to commit o.s. to sth; **la compañía se compromete a una subida de 250 euros mensuales** the company is committed to a pay rise of 250 euros a month; **se compromete con él a cosas que luego no cumple** he makes him promises he then doesn't keep; **~se en algo** to commit o.s. to sth; **~se a hacer algo** to commit o.s. to doing sth, undertake to do sth; **se han comprometido a reducir el paro** they have committed themselves to reducing unemployment, they have undertaken to reduce unemployment; **me comprometí a ayudarte y lo haré** I promised to help you and I will, I said I'd help you and I will; **me comprometo a terminar el trabajo para el viernes** I promise to finish the work by Friday
2 (= *implicarse socialmente*) to commit o.s., make a commitment; **~se políticamente (con algo)** commit o.s. politically (to sth), to make a political commitment (to sth)
3 (= *citarse*) **ya me he comprometido para el sábado** I've arranged to do something else on Saturday; **~se con algn** to arrange to see sb
4 [*novios*] to get engaged; **se han comprometido y se casarán pronto** they have got engaged and will be getting married soon; **~se con algn** to get engaged to sb

comprometido ADJ 1 (= *difícil*) awkward, embarrassing; **nos vimos en una situación muy comprometida** we found ourselves in a very awkward *o* embarrassing situation
2 (*socialmente*) [*escritor, artista*] politically committed, engagé; [*arte*] politically committed; **un artista no ~** art which is not politically committed, art without any political commitment; **estar ~ con algo** to be committed to sth; **está ~ con la causa** he's committed to the cause
3 (*por cita, trabajo*) **ya están ~s para jugar el sábado** they've already arranged to play on Saturday, they've booked to play on Saturday; **ya estaba ~ con otro proyecto** he was already committed to another project; **estar ~ a hacer algo** to be committed to doing sth
4 (*antes del matrimonio*) engaged; **estar ~ con algn** to be engaged to sb

compromisario/a SM/F convention delegate

▼**compromiso** SM 1 (= *obligación*) 1·1 (*por acuerdo, ideología*) commitment; **el gobierno reiteró su ~ con el plan de paz** the government reiterated its commitment to the peace plan; **nuestro ~ con la cultura** our commitment to cultural projects; **esperamos que cumplan con su ~ de bajar los impuestos** we hope they will honour their commitment to lowering taxes; **sin ~** without obligation; **pida presupuesto sin ~** ask for an estimate without obligation
1·2 (*por convenciones sociales*) **aunque no tenemos ~ con ellos, los vamos a invitar** we're going to invite them even though we're under no obligation to; **si le regalas ahora algo, la pondrás en el ~ de invitarte a cenar** if you give her a present now, you'll make her feel obliged to take you out to dinner; **por ~** out of a sense of duty; **fui a la boda por ~** I felt obliged to go to the wedding, I went to the wedding out of a sense of duty; **por ~ no lo hagas** don't feel obliged to do it; **verse en el ~** to feel obliged; **me vi en el ~ de tener que invitarlos a cenar** I felt obliged to invite them to dinner
► **compromiso político** political commitment ► **compromiso público** public commitment ► **compromiso social** social commitment
2 (= *aprieto*) **poner a algn en un ~** to put sb in an awkward position
3 (= *acuerdo*) agreement; (*con concesiones mutuas*) compromise; **aceptar un ~** to accept a compromise; **una fórmula de ~** a compro-

➤ LENGUA Y USO: **comprensible 1** 53.6 **compromiso 5** 51.2, 52.2

mise, a compromise formula; **una solución de ~** a compromise solution ► **compromiso histórico** historic agreement ► **compromiso verbal** unwritten agreement

4 (= *cita*) 4·1 (*con otras personas*) engagement; **ahora, si me disculpan, tengo que atender otros ~s** now, if you will excuse me, I have other engagements; **mañana no puede ser, tengo un ~** tomorrow is impossible, I'm otherwise engaged; **¿tienes algún ~ para esta noche?** do you have anything arranged for tonight?

4·2 (*Dep*) match; **en su próximo ~ frente al Zaragoza** in their next match against Zaragoza

5 [*de matrimonio*] engagement; **han roto su ~** they have broken off their engagement; **soltero y sin ~** single and unattached ► **compromiso matrimonial** engagement, engagement to marry

6 (*Med*) **una afección cardíaca con ~ hepático** a heart condition affecting the liver

compuerta SF 1 (*en canal*) sluice, floodgate; (*en puerta*) hatch

2 (*Inform*) gate

compuesto Ⓐ PP *de* **componer**; **estar ~ de** to be composed of, consist of; **un caldo ~ de apio y cebolla** a soup (made) of celery and onion; **un grupo ~ por 15 personas** a group of 15 people

Ⓑ ADJ 1 (*Mat, Fin, Ling, Quím*) compound; (*Bot*) composite

2 (= *elegante*) dressed up, smart; ✦*MODISMO* **compuesta y sin novio** all dressed up and nowhere to go

3 (= *tranquilo*) composed

Ⓒ SM 1 (*Quím*) compound ► **compuesto químico** chemical compound

2 (*Ling*) compound, compound word

3 (*Med, Odontología*) compound

compulsa SF 1 (= *cotejo*) checking, comparison

2 (*Der, Admin*) certified true copy, attested copy

compulsar ▸conjug 1a◂ VT 1 (= *comparar*) to collate, compare

2 (*Der, Admin*) to make an attested copy of

compulsión SF compulsion

compulsivamente ADV compulsively

compulsivo ADJ 1 [*deseo, hambre*] compulsive

2 (= *obligatorio*) compulsory

compulsorio ADJ (*LAm*) compulsory

compunción SF (*liter*) (= *arrepentimiento*) compunction, remorse; (= *tristeza*) sorrow

compungido ADJ (= *arrepentido*) remorseful, contrite; (= *triste*) sad, sorrowful

compungir ▸conjug 3c◂ Ⓐ VT (= *arrepentir*) to make remorseful, arouse feelings of remorse in

Ⓑ **compungirse** VPR (= *arrepentirse*) to feel remorseful (**por** about, because of), feel sorry (**por** for); (= *entristecerse*) to feel sad, be sorrowful

compurgar ▸conjug 1h◂ VT (*Andes, Cono Sur, Méx*) [+ *ofensa*] to purge; (*Méx Jur*) [+ *pena*] to serve out

computación SF (*esp LAm*) 1 (= *cálculo*) calculation

2 (*esp LAm Inform*) computing; **cursos de ~** computer courses

computacional ADJ (*esp LAm*) computational, computer *antes de s*

computador SM (*esp LAm*), **computadora** SF (*esp LAm*) computer ► **computador central** mainframe computer ► **computador de (sobre) mesa** desktop computer ► **computador digital** digital computer

computadorización SF computerization

computadorizado ADJ computerized

computadorizar ▸conjug 1f◂ VT to computerize

computar ▸conjug 1a◂ VT to calculate, compute (**en** at)

computarización SF computerization

computarizado ADJ computerized

computarizar ▸conjug 1f◂ VT to computerize

computerización SF computerization

computerizado ADJ computerized

computerizar ▸conjug 1f◂ VT to computerize

computista SMF computer user

cómputo SM (= *cálculo*) calculation, computation; (*Méx*) (= *suma*) total; **según nuestros ~s** according to our calculations

COMSAT SM ABR (= **satélite de comunicaciones**) Comsat, COMSAT

comulgante SMF communicant

comulgar ▸conjug 1h◂ Ⓐ VT (*Rel*) to administer communion to

Ⓑ VI 1 (*Rel*) to take communion, receive communion

2 **~ con** (*gen*) to like, accept, agree with; [+ *ideas*] to share; [+ *personas*] to sympathize with; **hay varias cosas con las que ella no comulga** there are several things that she doesn't agree with; *ver tb* **rueda 1**

comulgatorio SM communion rail, altar rail

común Ⓐ ADJ 1 (= *compartido*) [*afición, intereses*] common; [*amigo*] mutual; **tienen una serie de características comunes** they share a series of features, they have a series of common features *o* features in common; **a través de un amigo ~** through a mutual friend; **~ a algn/algo** common to sb/sth; **una situación ~ a todos los países europeos** a situation common to all European countries; **lo ~ a todas las democracias** what all democracies share in common, a feature common to all democracies

2 (= *colectivo*) [*causa, frente, espacio*] common; [*gastos*] communal; **tener algo en ~** to have sth in common; **su pasión por el fútbol es lo único que tienen en ~** their passion for football is all they have in common; **no tenemos nada en ~** we have nothing in common; **la pareja tuvo dos hijos en ~** the couple had two children together; **hacer algo en ~** to do sth together; **poner en ~** [+ *iniciativas, problemas*] to share; *ver tb* **acuerdo 1**, **bien D2**, **denominador**, **fosa**, **lugar 1**, **mercado**, **sentido B1.2**

3 (= *frecuente*) [*enfermedad, opinión*] common, widespread; [*costumbre*] widespread; [*cualidad*] common, ordinary; **el consumo de alcohol es una práctica ~** alcohol consumption is very common *o* widespread; **el concierto fue más largo de lo ~** the concert was longer than usual; **~ y corriente** perfectly ordinary; **fuera de lo ~** exceptional, extraordinary; **tiene una voz única, algo fuera de lo ~** she has a unique voice, quite exceptional *o* extraordinary; **por lo ~** as a rule; **~ y silvestre** (*LAm*) = **común y corriente** *ver tb* **delincuente**, **nombre 2**

4 (*Esp Educ*) [*asignatura*] core

Ⓑ SM 1 **el ~ de los mortales** ordinary mortals, any ordinary person; **el ~ de las gentes** the common man; **bienes del ~** public property

2 (*) (= *retrete*) toilet, bathroom

3 (*Pol*) (*en el Reino Unido*) **los Comunes** the Commons; **la Cámara de los Comunes** the House of Commons

comuna SF 1 (= *comunidad*) commune

2 (*LAm*) (= *municipio*) municipality, county (*EEUU*)

comunacho/a SM/F (*Cono Sur pey*) commie*

comunal ADJ communal, community *antes de s*

comunalmente ADV communally, as a community

comunicable ADJ 1 [*opinión, conocimiento*] **una emoción difícilmente ~** an emotion difficult to communicate *o* convey

2 [*persona*] sociable

comunicación SF 1 (= *conexión*) communication; **¿tenemos otra vez ~ con el estadio?** has communication with the stadium been restored?; **no existe ~ entre los dos pueblos** there is no way of getting from one town to the other, there is no means of communication between the two towns; **entre nosotros falla la ~** we just don't communicate well, we have poor communication ► **comunicación de masas** mass communication ► **comunicación no verbal** non-verbal communication; *ver tb* **medio C4**

2 (= *contacto*) contact; **no hemos tenido más ~ con él** we have had no further contact with him; **establecer ~ con algn** to establish contact with sb; **estar en ~ con algn** to be in contact *o* touch with sb; **ponerse en ~ con algn** to get in contact *o* touch with sb, contact sb

3 (*por teléfono*) **cortar la ~** to hang up; **dijo su nombre y se cortó la ~** he said his name and the line went dead *o* we were cut off

4 **comunicaciones** (= *conjunto de medios*) communications; **se han interrumpido las comunicaciones a causa del temporal** communications have been interrupted due to bad weather; **el satélite facilitará las comunicaciones** the satellite will facilitate communications

5 (= *escrito*) (= *mensaje*) message; (= *informe*) report; (*Pol*) communiqué

6 (*Univ*) (*en congreso*) paper; **presentar una ~ (sobre algo)** to give *o* present a paper (on sth)

7 (*Literat*) rhetorical question

comunicacional ADJ communication *antes de s*

comunicado Ⓐ ADJ 1 [*habitaciones*] connected; **las dos habitaciones están comunicadas** the two rooms are connected

2 [*pueblo, zona*] **la urbanización está muy mal comunicada** the housing estate has poor transport connections *o* is not easily accessible; **el pueblo está bien ~ por tren** the town has good train connections, the town is easily accessible by train

Ⓑ SM (= *notificación*) statement, press release, communiqué (*frm*); **han hecho público un ~ con la lista de los candidatos** they have issued a statement *o* press release *o* (*frm*) communiqué with the list of candidates ► **comunicado conjunto** joint statement, joint communiqué (*frm*) ► **comunicado de prensa** press release ► **comunicado oficial** official statement

comunicador(a) SM/F communicator; **un buen ~** a good communicator

comunicante SMF 1 (= *informador*) informant; **según ~ anónimo** according to an anonymous *o* unnamed source
2 (*en congreso*) speaker; *ver tb* **vaso 3**

▼**comunicar** ▸conjug 1g◂ Ⓐ VT 1 (= *decir*) 1·1 [+ *decisión, resultado*] to announce; **ha comunicado su decisión de abandonar la orquesta** he has announced his decision to leave the orchestra; **ha sido el encargado de ~ la noticia** he was given the task of announcing the news; **no pudo ~ la situación exacta del velero** he was unable to give *o* state the yacht's exact position; **según ~on fuentes del gobierno** according to government sources
1·2 **~ algo a algn** to inform sb of sth; **una vez comunicado el hallazgo a la policía** once the police had been informed of the discovery; **le ~on su despido por carta** they informed her of her dismissal by letter; **cuando le ~on la noticia** when they told her the news; **~ a algn que** to inform sb that; **comunicamos a los señores pasajeros que ...** we would like to inform passengers that ...; **nos comunican desde Lisboa que ...** we have heard from Lisbon that ...
2 (*al teléfono*) **¿me comunica con la dirección, por favor?** could I speak to the manager, please?, could you put me through to the manager, please?
3 (= *transmitir*) [+ *sensación, entusiasmo*] to convey, communicate, transmit; (*Fís*) [+ *movimiento, fuerza*] to transmit; **nos comunicó su miedo** his fear spread to us *o* communicated itself to us
4 (= *unir*) to connect; **el pasillo comunica ambas oficinas** the offices are connected by a corridor; **han comunicado el comedor con la cocina** the dining-room and the kitchen have been knocked together
Ⓑ VI 1 (*Esp*) [*teléfono*] to be engaged; **su teléfono comunicaba todo el tiempo** her telephone was engaged all the time; **está comunicando** ◊ **comunica** it's engaged; *ver tb* **señal 8**
2 [*cuarto, habitación*] to connect; **la cocina comunica con el comedor** the kitchen connects with the dining-room
3 (*Esp*) [*persona*] **sabe ~ con la gente** she's a good communicator
Ⓒ **comunicarse** VPR 1 (= *establecer comunicación*) 1·1 (*uso recíproco*) to communicate; **se comunican en inglés/por fax** they communicate in English/by fax, they use English/fax (to communicate); **aunque no nos vemos, nos comunicamos a menudo** although we don't see each other, we're often in touch *o* in contact
1·2 (*uso transitivo*) **nos comunicamos nuestras impresiones** we exchanged impressions
1·3 **~se con algn** to communicate with sb; **necesitan una emisora con la que ~se con nosotros** they need a radio to communicate with us; **se comunicó telefónicamente con su esposa** he spoke to his wife on the phone; **en mi trabajo tengo que ~me con gente de muchos paises** my work brings me into contact with people from many different countries
2 (= *entenderse*) **~se bien con algn** to connect well with sb; **hay gente con la que me comunico muy bien** there are some people I connect with really well; **se comunica mal con sus empleados** he can't communicate with his employees
3 (= *transmitirse*) **el entusiasmo del capitán se comunicó a toda la tripulación** the captain's enthusiasm spread to *o* communicated itself to the whole crew
4 (= *unirse*) to be connected (**con** to); **sus habitaciones se comunicaban** they had adjoining rooms, their rooms were connected; **el salón se comunica con la cocina a través de un pasillo** the living room is connected to the kitchen by a corridor

➤ LENGUA Y USO: comunicar A1 51.4

comunicatividad SF communicativeness, powers of communication

comunicativo ADJ [*método, función, persona*] communicative; **tiene una gran capacidad comunicativa** he is a great communicator, he has great communicative skills; **es muy poco ~** he's very uncommunicative

comunicología SF communication theory

comunicólogo/a SM/F communication theorist

comunidad SF 1 (*gen*) community; (= *sociedad*) society, association; (*Rel*) community; (*Andes*) commune (*of free Indians*); **de** *o* **en ~** (*Jur*) jointly ► **comunidad autónoma** (*Esp*) autonomous region ► **Comunidad Británica de Naciones** British Commonwealth ► **Comunidad de Estados Independientes** Commonwealth of Independent States ► **comunidad de vecinos** residents' association ► **Comunidad (Económica) Europea** European (Economic) Community ► **Comunidad Europea del Carbón y del Acero** European Coal and Steel Community ► **comunidad lingüística** speech community
2 (= *pago*) [*de piso*] service charge, charge for communal services

> **COMUNIDAD AUTÓNOMA**
>
> *In Spain the* **comunidades autónomas** *are any of the 19 administrative regions consisting of one or more provinces and having political powers devolved from Madrid, as stipulated by the 1978 Constitution. They have their own democratically elected parliaments, form their own cabinets and legislate and execute policies in certain areas such as housing, infrastructure, environment, health and education, though Madrid still retains jurisdiction for all matters affecting the country as a whole, such as defence, foreign affairs and justice. The* **Comunidades Autónomas** *are: Andalucía, Aragón, Asturias, Islas Baleares, Canarias, Cantabria, Castilla y León, Castilla-La Mancha, Cataluña, Extremadura, Galicia, Madrid, Murcia, Navarra, País Vasco, La Rioja, Comunidad Valenciana, Ceuta, and Melilla.*
>
> *The term* **Comunidades Históricas** *refers to Galicia, Catalonia and the Basque Country, which for reasons of history and language consider themselves to some extent separate from the rest of Spain. They were given a measure of independence by the Second Republic (1931-1936), only to have it revoked by Franco in 1939. With the transition to democracy, these groups were the most vociferous and successful in their demand for home rule, partly because they already had experience of federalism and had established a precedent with autonomous institutions like the Catalan* **Generalitat**.

comunión SF communion; **Primera Comunión** First Communion; **hacer la Primera Comunión** to take one's First Communion

comunismo SM communism

comunista Ⓐ ADJ communist
Ⓑ SMF communist; **~ libertario** libertarian communist

comunitariamente ADV communally

comunitario Ⓐ ADJ 1 [*centro, servicios, cooperación*] community *antes de s*; [*jardín, pasillos*] communal
2 (= *de la comunidad europea*) Community *antes de s*
Ⓑ SM (= *país*) EC member state

comunizar ▸conjug 1f◂ VT to communize

comúnmente ADV commonly; **como ~ se cree** as is commonly believed; **lo que ~ se llama mal de amores** what is commonly called love sickness

con PREP 1 (*indicando compañía, instrumento, medio*) with; **vivo ~ mis padres** I live with my parents; **¿~ quién vas a ir?** who are you going with?; **atado ~ cuerda** tied with string; **lo tomo ~ limón** I take it with lemon; **~ su ayuda** with his help; **ducharse ~ agua fría** to have a cold shower; **lo he escrito ~ bolígrafo** I wrote it in pen; **andar ~ muletas** to walk on *o* with crutches; **~ este sol no hay quien salga** no one can go out in this sun; **~ el tiempo** in the course of time, with time
2 (*indicando características, estado*) **un hombre ~ principios** a man of principle; **llegó ~ aspecto relajado** she arrived looking relaxed; **un amigo ~ aspecto de jugador de rugby** a friend who is built like a rugby player; **gente joven ~ ganas de divertirse** young people out for a good time; **murió ~ 60 años** she died at the age of 60
3 (*indicando combinación*) and; **pan ~ mantequilla** bread and butter; **vodka ~ naranja** vodka and orange; **café ~ leche** white coffee; **arroz ~ leche** rice pudding
4 (*indicando contenido*) **una cazuela ~ agua caliente** a pan of hot water; **un maletín ~ dinero** a briefcase full of money; **encontraron una maleta ~ 800.000 dólares** they found a suitcase containing 800,000 dollars *o* with 800,000 dollars in it
5 (*indicando modo*) **se levantó ~ rapidez** he got up quickly; **ábrelo ~ cuidado** open it carefully; **anda ~ dificultad** she walks with difficulty; **desayunamos ~ apetito** we ate our breakfast with relish; **estar ~ algo**: **estar ~ dolor de muelas/la pierna escayolada** to have toothache/one's leg in plaster; **está ~ la gripe** he's got flu; **~ mucho gusto** certainly, by all means
6 (*como complemento personal de algunos verbos*) to; **¿~ quién hablas?** who are you speaking to?; **voy a hablar ~ Luis** I'll talk to Luis; **se ha casado ~ Jesús** she's married Jesús, she's got married to Jesús; **estoy emparentado ~ la duquesa** I am related to the duchess; **no sabemos lo que va a pasar ~**

nosotros we don't know what's going to happen to us; **me escribo ~ ella** she and I write to each other

[7] (*tras adjetivos*) to, towards; **amable ~ todos** kind to *o* towards everybody; **ser insolente ~ el jefe** to be disrespectful to *o* towards the boss

[8] (*con decimales*) **once ~ siete** (*11,7*) eleven point seven (*11.7*); **un dólar ~ cincuenta centavos** one dollar fifty cents

[9] (= *pese a*) in spite of; **~ tantas dificultades, no se descorazonó** in spite of all *o* for all the difficulties he didn't lose heart; **~ ser su madre, le odia** even though she is his mother she hates him; **~ todo (y ~ eso), la gente se lo pasó bien** in spite of everything, people had a good time

[10] (*en exclamaciones*) **¡vaya ~ el niño!*** the cheeky monkey!*; **¡~ lo bien que se está aquí!** and it's so nice here too!; **no me dejó ni un trocito, ~ lo que me gustan esos caramelos** he didn't even let me have a tiny piece, and he knows how much I like those sweets

[11] (*indicando una condición*) [11·1] (+ *INFIN*) **~ estudiar un poco apruebas** with a bit of studying you should pass; **cree que ~ confesarlo se librará del castigo** he thinks that by owning up he'll escape punishment; **~ decirle que no voy, se arreglará todo** when I tell him I'm not going, everything will be fine; **~ llegar a las seis estará bien** if you come by six it will be fine; **~ llegar tan tarde nos perderemos la comida** by arriving so late we're going to miss the meal

[11·2] **~ que** + *SUBJUN*: **~ que me digas tu teléfono basta** if you just give me your phone number that'll be enough; **~ que me invite, me conformo** as long as *o* provided that she invites me, I don't mind; **basta ~ que nos remita la tarjeta cumplimentada** all you have to do is send us the completed card; *ver tb* **tal C4**

Conacyt SM ABR (*Méx*) = **Consejo Nacional de Ciencia y Tecnología**

CONADEP SF ABR (*Arg Pol*) = **Comisión Nacional sobre la Desaparición de Personas**

Conasupo SF ABR (*Méx*) (= **Compañía Nacional de Subsistencias Populares**) *government buying and selling organization for subsidized food, clothes and furniture*

conato SM [1] (= *intento*) attempt; **hizo un ~ de entrar** he made an attempt to get in ► **conato de robo** attempted robbery

[2] (*frm*) (= *esfuerzo*) **poner ~ en algo** to put an effort into sth

concatenación SF linking, concatenation (*frm*) ► **concatenación de circunstancias** chain *o* series of circumstances

concatenar ▸conjug 1a◂ VT to link together

concavidad SF concavity, hollow, cavity

cóncavo Ⓐ ADJ concave

Ⓑ SM hollow, cavity

concebible ADJ conceivable, thinkable; **no es ~ que …** it is unthinkable that …

concebir ▸conjug 3k◂ Ⓐ VT [1] (= *crear*) [+ *plan, proyecto*] to conceive, devise; [+ *personaje*] to create; [+ *historia*] to think up, invent

[2] (= *imaginar*) to conceive of, imagine; **no concibo una tarde de verano sin una siesta** I can't conceive of *o* imagine a summer afternoon without a siesta

[3] (= *entender*) **una forma diferente de ~ las cosas** a different way of seeing things; **eso es amor concebido sólo como pasión** this is love viewed only as passion; **concebía el Estado como su propiedad personal** he thought *o* considered the State his personal property; **no concibe que haya gente con ideas mejores que las suyas** he can't comprehend that there are people with better ideas than his

[4] (= *engendrar*) [+ *hijo*] to conceive; **el gol nos hizo ~ esperanzas de victoria** the goal brought *o* gave us hopes of victory; **esto le hizo ~ la sospecha de que pasaba algo** this planted the suspicion in his mind *o* made him suspect that something was wrong

Ⓑ VI (= *quedar encinta*) to conceive, become pregnant; **concibió a una avanzada edad** she conceived *o* became pregnant at a late age

conceder ▸conjug 2a◂ VT [1] (= *dar*) [+ *beca, premio*] to award, grant; [+ *crédito, permiso, deseo, entrevista*] to grant; **su mujer no quería ~le el divorcio** his wife didn't want to grant *o* give him a divorce; **el juez les concedió el divorcio** the judge granted them a divorce; **sólo concedió unos minutos para unas preguntas** he only allowed a few minutes for some questions; **el árbitro les concedió el gol** the referee awarded them the goal; **le concedieron el honor de presidir el congreso** they conferred on him the honour of presiding over the conference; **¿me concede el honor de este baile?** may I have the pleasure of this dance?

[2] (*frm*) (= *admitir*) to concede, admit; **concedo que el error fue mío** I concede *o* admit it was my mistake

concejal(a) SM/F town *o* city councillor, town *o* city councilman/councilwoman (*EEUU*)

concejalía SF post of town *o* city councillor, post of town councilman (*EEUU*), seat on the town *o* city council

concejil ADJ (= *del concejo*) council *antes de s*; (= *municipal*) municipal, public

concejo SM council; **~ municipal** town council, city council

concelebrar ▸conjug 1a◂ VT to concelebrate

concentración SF [1] (= *centralización*) concentration, centralization; **contra la ~ de poder en Madrid** against the concentration *o* centralization of power in Madrid

[2] (*mental*) concentration

[3] (= *mitin*) gathering, meeting, rally; (*Dep*) [*de equipo*] base; **una ~ en pro de los derechos humanos** a gathering in support of human rights; **una ~ de motos** a motorcycling rally

[4] (*Educ*) ► **concentración escolar** *rural school at centre of a catchment area*

[5] (*LAm Com*) merger

concentrado Ⓐ ADJ concentrated

Ⓑ SM [1] (*Culin*) extract, concentrate ► **concentrado de carne** meat extract

[2] (*Pol*) demonstrator

concentrar ▸conjug 1a◂ Ⓐ VT to concentrate

Ⓑ **concentrarse** VPR [1] (= *reunirse*) to gather (together), assemble; **se ~on cientos de personas** hundreds of people gathered (together)

[2] (*mentalmente*) to concentrate (**en** on); **concéntrate en lo que estás haciendo** concentrate on what you're doing

[3] (= *estar concentrado*) to concentrate, be concentrated; **el interés se concentra en esta lucha** interest is centred on this fight

concéntrico ADJ concentric

concepción SF [1] (*Biol*) conception; **la Inmaculada Concepción** the Immaculate Conception

[2] (= *idea*) conception, idea

[3] (= *facultad*) understanding

conceptismo SM conceptism, *witty, allusive and involved style of esp 17th century*; → CULTERANISMO, CONCEPTISMO

conceptista Ⓐ ADJ [*estilo, novela*] witty, allusive and involved

Ⓑ SMF (= *escritor*) writer in the style of conceptism

▼ **concepto** SM [1] (= *idea*) concept, notion; **formarse un ~ de algo** to get an idea of sth; **un ~ grandioso** a bold conception, a bold plan

[2] (= *opinión*) view, judgment; **en mi ~** in my view; **formarse un ~ de algn** to form an opinion of sb; **¿qué ~ has formado de él?** what do you think of him?; **tener buen ~ de algn, tener en buen ~ a algn** to think highly of sb

[3] (= *condición*) heading, section; **bajo ningún ~** in no way, under no circumstances; **bajo todos los ~s** from every point of view, in every way, in every respect; **en** *o* **por ~ de** as, by way of; **se le pagó esa cantidad en** *o* **por ~ de derechos** he was paid that amount as royalties; **deducciones en** *o* **por ~ de seguro** deductions for social security; **por dicho ~** for this reason; **por ningún ~** in no way

[4] (*Literat*) conceit

conceptual ADJ conceptual

conceptualización SF conceptualization

conceptualizar ▸conjug 1f◂ VT to conceptualize

conceptuar ▸conjug 1e◂ VT to judge, deem (*frm*); **le conceptúo poco apto para eso** I think *o* consider him unsuited for that; **~ a algn de** *o* **como …** to regard sb as …, deem sb to be (*frm*)

conceptuosamente ADV (= *con ingenio*) wittily; (*pey*) over-elaborately, in a mannered way

conceptuoso ADJ (= *ingenioso*) witty, full of conceits; (*pey*) overelaborate, mannered

concerniente ADJ **~ a** concerning, relating to; **en lo ~ a** with regard to, concerning

▼ **concernir** ▸conjug 3i; defectivo◂ VI **~ a** to concern; **eso a mi no me concierne** that does not concern me, that is of no concern to me, that is not of my concern; **por lo que a mi concierne** as far as I am concerned; **en lo que concierne a …** with regard to …, concerning …

concertación SF [1] (= *acto*) harmonizing; (= *coordinación*) coordination; (= *reconciliación*) reconciliation; **política de ~** consensus politics *pl* ► **concertación social** social harmony

[2] (= *pacto*) agreement, pact

concertadamente ADV (= *metódicamente*) methodically, systematically; (= *ordenadamente*) in an orderly fashion; (= *armoniosamente*) harmoniously

concertado ADJ [1] (= *metódico*) systematic, concerted; (= *ordenado*) ordered; (= *armonioso*) harmonious

➤ LENGUA Y USO: **concepto 1** 53.1 **2** 40.4 **concernir** 53.2

[2] [*centro, colegio, hospital*] officially approved, state assisted

concertar ▸conjug 1j◂ Ⓐ VT [1] (*frm*) [+ *entrevista*] to arrange, set up; **~ una cita** to arrange *o* make an appointment
[2] [+ *salario, precio*] to agree (on); [+ *póliza, seguro*] to take out; **~ un acuerdo** to reach an agreement; **han concertado una estrategia** they have agreed (on) a strategy; **hemos concertado suprimir dos puntos del acuerdo** we have agreed to delete two points from the agreement; **le ~on matrimonio cuando tenía diez años** they arranged her marriage when she was ten years old
[3] (*Mús*) (= *armonizar*) [+ *voces*] to harmonize; [+ *instrumentos*] to tune (up)
Ⓑ VI [1] (*frm*) [*cifras, datos*] to agree, match (up)
[2] (*Ling*) to agree
[3] (*Mús*) [*voces*] to harmonize; [*instrumentos*] to be in tune
Ⓒ **concertarse** VPR **~se para hacer algo** (*frm*) to agree to do sth

concertina SF (= *instrumento*) concertina

concertino/a SM/F leader of the orchestra, concertmaster (*EEUU*)

concertista SMF soloist, solo performer; **~ de guitarra** concert guitarist; **~ de piano** concert pianist

concesión SF [1] (*en acuerdo, negociación*) concession, granting
[2] (*Jur, Pol*) [*de nacionalidad, libertad*] granting
[3] [*de un premio*] award
[4] (*Com*) [*de fabricación*] licence, license (*EEUU*); [*de venta*] franchise; [*de transporte*] concession, contract

concesionario/a SM/F (*Com*) (*gen*) licence holder, license holder (*EEUU*), licensee; [*de venta*] franchisee, authorized dealer; [*de transportes*] contractor ► **concesionario/a exclusivo/a** sole agency, exclusive dealership

concesivo ADJ concessive

Concha SF (*forma familiar*) *de* **María de la Concepción**

concha SF [1] (*Zool*) shell; ✦***MODISMOS*** **meterse en su ~** to retire into one's shell; **tener muchas ~s** to be very sharp, be a sly one; **tiene más ~s que un galápago** he's as slippery as an eel ► **concha de perla** (*Andes*) mother-of-pearl; → CAMINO DE SANTIAGO
[2] (= *carey*) tortoiseshell
[3] [*de porcelana*] flake, chip
[4] (*Teat*) prompt box
[5] (*Andes, Caribe*) (= *descaro*) nerve, cheek*; **¡qué ~ la tuya!** you've got a nerve!, you've got a cheek!*
[6] (*Andes*) (= *pereza*) sloth, sluggishness
[7] (*LAm euf*) = **coño;** ✦***MODISMO*** **¡~(s) de tu madre!** bastard!‡, son of a bitch! (*EEUU*‡)
[8] (*Caribe*) (= *cartucho*) cartridge case
[9] (*Caribe*) (= *piel*) peel; (= *corteza*) bark

conchabado/a SM/F (*LAm*) servant

conchabar ▸conjug 1a◂ Ⓐ VT [1] (*LAm*) [+ *persona*] to hire for work, engage, employ
[2] (= *mezclar*) to mix, blend
[3] (*Andes, Cono Sur*) (= *trocar*) to barter
Ⓑ **conchabarse** VPR [1] (= *confabularse*) to gang up (**contra** on), conspire, plot (**contra** against); **los dos estaban conchabados** the two were in cahoots*
[2] (*LAm*) (= *colocarse, esp como criado*) to hire o.s. out, get a job (as a servant)

conchabo SM [1] (*LAm*) (= *contratación*) hiring, engagement; **oficina de ~** (*Cono Sur*) employment agency for domestics
[2] (*Cono Sur*) (= *permuta*) barter(ing)

cónchale EXCL (*Caribe*) **¡cónchale!** well!, goodness!, jeez (*EEUU**)

Conchinchina* SF ✦***MODISMO*** **estar en la ~** to be miles away, be on the other side of the world

Conchita SF = **Concha**

conchito SM (*Andes, Cono Sur*) youngest child, baby of the family

concho[1] SM [1] (*LAm*) (= *poso*) dregs *pl*, sediment; (= *residuo*) residue; ✦***MODISMOS*** **hasta el ~** to the very end; **irse al ~** (*Cono Sur*) to go down, go under, sink
[2] **conchos** (= *sobras*) left-overs

concho[2]* EXCL (*euf*) sugar!*

concho[3] SM (*Caribe*) (= *taxi*) taxi

concho[4] (*CAm*) Ⓐ ADJ crude, vulgar
Ⓑ SM (= *campesino*) peasant; (*pey*) (= *paleto*) rustic, country bumpkin, hick (*EEUU*)

concho[5] SM (*Andes, Cono Sur*) = **conchito**

conchudo/a* Ⓐ ADJ (*Andes, Cono Sur*) sluggish, slow
Ⓑ SM/F [1] (*Andes, Cono Sur*) (= *idiota*) bloody idiot‡, jerk (*EEUU**)
[2] (*Puerto Rico*) (= *persona terca*) stubborn person, pigheaded person

conciencia SF [1] (= *moralidad*) conscience; **pesará sobre su ~** it will weigh on his conscience; **no tienes ~, tratar así a tu pobre madre** you have no conscience, treating your poor mother like that; **en ~** in all conscience; **en ~ no podemos permitir que se produzca esa situación** in all conscience, we cannot allow that situation to arise; **actuar** *u* **obrar en ~** to act in good conscience; **votar en ~** to vote according to one's conscience; **libertad de ~** freedom of conscience; **tener la ~ limpia** to have a clear conscience; **tener mala ~** to have a guilty *o* bad conscience; **remorder a algn la ~**: **me remuerde la ~ por haberle mentido** I've got a guilty *o* bad conscience about lying to him; **tener la ~ tranquila** to have a clear conscience ► **conciencia de culpa** guilty conscience; *ver tb* **ancho A4, anchura 3, cargo 5, gusanillo 4, objetor, preso B**
[2] **a ~** (= *con dedicación*) conscientiously; (= *con mala intención*) on purpose; **trabaja a ~** she works conscientiously; **me tuve que preparar a ~ para el examen** I had to prepare very thoroughly for the exam; **una casa construida a ~** a solidly *o* well built house; **lo has hecho a ~ para fastidiarme** you deliberately did it to annoy me, you did it on purpose to annoy me
[3] (= *capacidad de juicio*) awareness; **debería haber una mayor ~ sobre los riesgos del alcohol** people should be more aware of the risks of alcohol, there should be greater awareness of the risks of alcohol; **lo ha hecho con plena ~ del daño que podía causar** he did it in full knowledge of the damage he might cause, he was fully aware of the damage he might cause when he did it; **a ~ de que ...** fully aware that ..., in the certain knowledge that ...; **despertar la ~ de algn** to raise sb's consciousness *o* awareness; **tener ~ de algo**: **no tienen ~ de nación** they have no sense of national identity; **tenían plena ~ de lo que hacían** they were fully aware of what they were doing; **tomar ~ de algo** to become aware of sth; **tomar ~ de que ...** to become aware that ... ► **conciencia crítica** critical awareness ► **conciencia de clase** class consciousness ► **conciencia social** social conscience
[4] (*Med*) consciousness; **perder la ~** to lose consciousness

concienciación SF (*Esp*) **una campaña de ~ ciudadana** a campaign to raise public awareness

concienciado ADJ (*Esp*) socially aware

concienciar ▸conjug 1b◂ (*Esp*) Ⓐ VT (= *sensibilizar*) **~ a algn de un problema** to raise sb's awareness of an issue; **un anuncio para ~ a los conductores de que no beban** an advert to raise drivers' awareness about drink-driving
Ⓑ **concienciarse** VPR **~se de algo** to become aware of sth

concientización SF (*LAm*) = **concienciación**

concientizado ADJ (*LAm*) = **concienciado**

concientizar ▸conjug 1f◂ VT (*LAm*) = **concienciar**

concienzar ▸conjug 1f◂ VT = **concienciar**

concienzudamente ADV conscientiously; **trabaja ~** she works conscientiously; **un informe realizado ~** a painstaking report

concienzudo ADJ [1] [*estudiante, trabajador*] conscientious
[2] [*estudio, esfuerzo*] painstaking, thorough

concierto SM [1] (*Mús*) (= *función*) concert; (= *obra*) concerto ► **concierto de arias** song recital ► **concierto de cámara** chamber concert ► **concierto sinfónico** symphony concert
[2] (*frm*) (= *acuerdo*) agreement; **de ~ con** in agreement with; **quedar de ~ acerca de** to be in agreement with regard to; **los fabricantes, en ~ con los vendedores, se han negado a la exportación de los vehículos** the manufacturers, together with the retailers, have refused to export the vehicles
[3] (*Pol*) (= *orden*) order; **la incorporación de España al ~ europeo** Spain's admission into Europe; *ver tb* **orden A1.2**

conciliable ADJ reconcilable; **dos opiniones no fácilmente ~s** two opinions which it is not easy to reconcile

conciliábulo SM secret meeting, secret discussion

conciliación SF [1] (*entre personas*) conciliation, reconciliation
[2] (= *afinidad*) affinity, similarity

conciliador(a) Ⓐ ADJ conciliatory
Ⓑ SM/F conciliator

conciliar[1] ▸conjug 1b◂ Ⓐ VT [1] [+ *enemigos*] to reconcile; [+ *ideas*] to harmonize, bring into line
[2] **~ el sueño** to get to sleep
[3] [+ *respeto, antipatía*] to win, gain
Ⓑ **conciliarse** VPR = **A3**

conciliar[2] Ⓐ ADJ (*Rel*) of a council, council *antes de s*
Ⓑ SM council member

conciliatorio ADJ conciliatory

concilio SM council; **el Segundo Concilio Vaticano** the Second Vatican Council

concisamente ADV concisely, briefly

concisión SF conciseness, brevity

conciso ADJ concise, brief

concitar ▸conjug 1a◂ VT [1] (= *provocar*) to stir up, incite (**contra** against)
[2] (= *reunir*) to gather, assemble, bring together

conciudadano/a SM/F fellow citizen

conclave SM, **cónclave** SM conclave

▼**concluir** ▸conjug 3g◂ Ⓐ VT [1] (= *finalizar*) [+ *estudios, trabajo*] to finish, complete, conclude (*frm*); **~emos las obras en 2004** work will finish in 2004, the work will be completed in 2004; **regresó a España tras ~ su visita oficial a China** he returned to Spain after concluding *o* ending his official visit to China
[2] (= *alcanzar*) [+ *acuerdo, pacto*] to reach
[3] (= *deducir*) to conclude; **el informe concluye que ese no es el factor más importante** the report concludes that this is not the most important factor; **~ algo de algo** to deduce sth from sth
Ⓑ VI (*frm*) (= *finalizar*) [*acto, proceso, evento*] to conclude, finish, end; [*era, etapa*] to end, come to an end; [*plazo*] to expire; **el acto concluyó con un brindis** the ceremony concluded *o* finished *o* ended with a toast; **las negociaciones concluyeron en un tratado de paz** the talks ended in a peace treaty; **cuando la investigación concluya** when investigations are complete *o* have been completed; **y para ~ ...** and finally ...
Ⓒ **concluirse** VPR to end; **así se concluye un nuevo capítulo de esta serie** so ends *o* so we conclude another chapter in this series

▼**conclusión** SF conclusion; **en ~** in conclusion, finally; **llegar a la ~ de que ...** to come to the conclusion that ...; **extraiga usted las conclusiones oportunas** draw your own conclusions

concluyente ADJ conclusive, decisive

concluyentemente ADV conclusively, decisively

concolón SM (*LAm*) scrapings

concomerse ▸conjug 2a◂ VPR ✦*MODISMO* **~ de impaciencia*** to be itching with impatience

concomitante ADJ concomitant

cononete SM (*Méx*) child, little one

concordancia SF [1] (= *acuerdo*) agreement; (= *armonía*) harmony
[2] (*Ling*) concord, agreement
[3] (*Mús*) harmony
[4] **concordancias** (*Literat*) concordance *sing*

concordante ADJ concordant

concordar ▸conjug 1l◂ Ⓐ VT [1] (= *armonizar*) to reconcile, bring into line
[2] (*Ling*) to make agree
Ⓑ VI [1] (= *armonizar*) to agree (**con** with), tally (**con** with), correspond (**con** to); **esto no concuerda con los hechos** this does not square with *o* fit in with the facts; **los dos concuerdan en sus gustos** the two have the same tastes
[2] (*Ling*) to agree

concordato SM concordat

concorde ADJ **estar ~s** to be agreed, be in agreement; **estar ~ en hacer algo** to agree to do sth; **poner a dos personas ~s** to bring about agreement between two people

concordia SF [1] (= *armonía*) concord, harmony; (= *conformidad*) conformity
[2] (= *anillo*) double finger-ring
[3] **Línea de la Concordia** (*Cono Sur*) frontier between Chile and Peru

concreción SF [1] (= *precisión*) precision; **le falta ~ al expresarse** she lacks precision in expressing herself; **intenta responder a las preguntas con mayor ~** try to be more precise when you reply to the questions
[2] (= *materialización*) realization; **llegó el momento de la ~ de sus deseos** the time for realizing her dreams arrived; **su falta de ~ a la hora de marcar goles** their failure to make an impression when it came to scoring
[3] (*Fís*) concretion
[4] (*Med*) stone

concretamente ADV [1] (= *específicamente*) specifically; **se refirió ~ a dos** he specifically mentioned two; **estoy buscando esta película ~** I'm looking for this film in particular, I'm specifically looking for this film; **estuvimos en Inglaterra, ~ en Manchester** we were in England, in Manchester to be exact *o* precise
[2] (= *exactamente*) exactly; **¿qué dijo ~?** what exactly did he say?

concretar ▸conjug 1a◂ Ⓐ VT [1] (= *precisar*) to specify; (= *concertar*) to settle; **los expertos prepararán un documento que ~á los términos del acuerdo** experts are to draw up a document which will specify the terms of the agreement; **el portavoz no quiso ~ más datos** the spokesman declined to go into details *o* to be more specific; **en la reunión no concretamos nada** we didn't settle (on) anything specific at the meeting, nothing specific came out of the meeting; **pusieron una fecha tope para ~ los acuerdos** they gave a deadline for the details of the agreement to be settled; **llámame para ~ los detalles** call me to fix *o* settle the details
[2] (= *resumir*) to sum up; **has concretado mi pensamiento en unas pocas palabras** you've summed up my thoughts in a few words
[3] (= *materializar*) [3·1] (*LAm*) [+ *sueños, esperanzas*] **la publicación de sus poemas vino a ~ uno de sus grandes deseos** the publication of his poems was the realization of one of his dearest wishes
[3·2] (*Chile*) [+ *oferta, donación*] to materialize
[4] (*Chile Constr*) to concrete
Ⓑ VI [1] (= *puntualizar*) **concretemos** let's be more specific
[2] (*Ftbl*) (= *marcar*) **no lograron ~ ante puerta** they were unable to make any impression in front of goal
Ⓒ **concretarse** VPR [1] (= *materializarse*) [1·1] [*ley, prohibición*] to come into force; [*esperanzas*] to be fulfilled; [*sueños*] to come true; **queda por ver cómo se concretan en la práctica los puntos del acuerdo** it remains to be seen how the points contained in the agreement work out in practice; **nunca llegó a ~se su proyecto** his project never came to anything, nothing came of his project; **su ayuda nunca llegó a ~se** their help never materialized *o* was never forthcoming
[1·2] **~se en algo**: **un avance de la derecha que se concretó en su triunfo electoral** an advance by the right which resulted in its electoral win; **el proyecto se concretaba en tres objetivos principales** in essence the project had three main objectives
[2] (= *limitarse*) **~se a algo** to limit o.s. to sth, confine o.s. to sth; **el profesor se concretó al siglo XVIII** the teacher limited *o* confined himself to the 18th century; **~se a hacer algo** to limit *o* confine o.s. to doing sth

concretizar ▸conjug 1f◂ VT = **concretar**

▼**concreto** Ⓐ ADJ [1] (= *específico*) [*medida, propuesta*] specific, concrete; [*hecho, resultado*] specific; [*fecha, hora*] definite, particular; **una forma concreta de llevarlo a la práctica** a specific way of putting it into practice; **voy a poner algunos ejemplos ~s** I'm going to give a few specific examples; **en un plazo breve tendremos datos más ~s** we will have more specific *o* precise information shortly; **no me dijo ninguna hora concreta** he didn't tell me any definite *o* particular time; **en este caso ~** in this particular case; **lo importante son los hechos ~s** the most important thing is the actual facts
[2] (= *no abstracto*) concrete; **un nombre ~** a concrete noun
[3] **en ~** [3·1] (*con verbos*) **nos referimos, en ~, al abuso del alcohol** we are referring specifically to alcohol abuse; **he viajado mucho por Africa, en ~, por Kenia y Tanzania** I've travelled a lot in Africa, specifically in Kenya and Tanzania *o* in Kenya and Tanzania to be precise; **¿qué dijo en ~?** what exactly did he say?
[3·2] (*con sustantivos*) **¿busca algún libro en ~?** are you looking for a particular *o* specific book?, are you looking for any book in particular?; **no se ha decidido nada en ~** nothing definite *o* specific has been decided
Ⓑ SM (*LAm*) (= *hormigón*) concrete
► **concreto armado** reinforced concrete

concubina SF concubine

concubinato SM concubinage

concúbito SM copulation

conculcación SF (*gen*) infringement; [*de ley*] violation

conculcar ▸conjug 1g◂ VT (*gen*) to infringe (on); [+ *ley*] to break, violate

concupiscencia SF [1] (= *lujuria*) lustfulness, concupiscence (*frm*)
[2] (= *codicia*) greed, avarice

concupiscente ADJ [1] (= *lujurioso*) lustful, lewd, concupiscent (*frm*)
[2] (= *avaro*) greedy, avaricious

concurrencia SF [1] (= *coincidencia*) concurrence; (= *simultaneidad*) simultaneity, coincidence
[2] (= *público*) (*Dep*) spectators *pl*; (*Cine, Teat*) audience
[3] (= *asistencia*) attendance, turnout; **había una numerosa ~** there was a big attendance *o* turnout
[4] (*Com*) competition

concurrente Ⓐ ADJ [1] [*suceso*] concurrent
[2] (*Com*) competing
Ⓑ SMF [1] (= *asistente*) person present, person attending; **los ~s** those present, the audience
[2] (*en carrera, competición*) entrant; **este año ha aumentado el número de ~s en la maratón** the number of people entering the marathon has gone up this year

concurrido ADJ [*local*] crowded, much frequented; [*calle*] busy, crowded; (*Teat etc*) popular, well-attended, full (of people)

concurrir ▸conjug 3a◂ VI [1] (= *acudir*) **~ a algo** to attend sth; **cien personas concurrieron a la subasta** a hundred people attended the

➤ LENGUA Y USO: concluir A3 53.4 conclusión 53.4 concreto A3 53.1

auction; **diez millones de votantes ~án a las urnas** ten million voters will go to the polls
[2] (= *participar*) to take part; **al certamen podrá ~ el que lo desee** anyone who wishes may take part in the competition; **tres bailarinas concurren al premio** three dancers are competing for the prize; **todos los partidos que concurren a las elecciones** all parties taking part in the election; **concurre como candidato a la presidencia** he's running as a candidate for the presidency
[3] (*frm*) (= *combinarse*) **concurrieron los factores necesarios para la desertificación** the necessary factors for desertification were present; **si concurren las circunstancias siguientes** given *o* in the following circumstances; **en ella concurren las mejores cualidades** she combines the best qualities; **~ en algo: numerosos factores concurren en el éxito de esta empresa** many factors combine to make this company a success; **~ a algo: las circunstancias que concurrieron a la ruina del campo** the circumstances that combined to bring about the demise of the countryside, the circumstances that contributed to the demise of the countryside
[4] (= *confluir*) [*ríos, calles*] to meet, converge

concursado/a SM/F insolvent debtor, bankrupt

concursante SMF [1] (*para un empleo*) candidate
[2] (*en juego, concurso*) contestant; (*Dep*) competitor

concursar ▸conjug 1a◂ Ⓐ VI [1] (*por un empleo*) to compete; **va a ~ por la vacante** he is going to apply *o* compete for the vacancy
[2] (*en un concurso*) to take part
Ⓑ VT (*Jur*) to declare insolvent, declare bankrupt

concurso Ⓐ SM [1] (*Com*) tender; **presentar algo a ~** to open sth up to tender, put sth out to tender
[2] (= *competición*) competition, contest; (*TV, Radio*) quiz, game show; **un ~ de poesía** a poetry competition; **queda ya fuera de ~** he's out of the running now ► **concurso de belleza** beauty contest ► **concurso de ideas** (*Arquit*) design competition ► **concurso de pastoreo** sheepdog trials *pl* ► **concurso de redacción** essay competition ► **concurso de saltos** show-jumping contest *o* competition ► **concurso hípico** horse show, show-jumping contest *o* competition ► **concurso radiofónico** radio quiz show
[3] (= *examen*) examination, open competition; **ganar un puesto por ~** to win a post in open competition ► **concurso de méritos** competition for posts ► **concurso oposición** public competition
[4] ► **concurso de acreedores** (*Jur*) meeting of creditors
[5] (= *coincidencia*) coincidence, concurrence
[6] (= *ayuda*) cooperation, help; **con el ~ de** with the help of; **prestar su ~** to help, collaborate
Ⓑ ADJ **corrida ~** bullfighting competition; **programa ~** TV game show; **cata ~** wine-tasting competition

concurso-subasta SM (*pl* **concursos-subasta**) competitive tendering

concusión SF [1] (*Med*) concussion
[2] (*Fin*) extortion

concusionario/a SM/F extortioner

condado SM (= *demarcación territorial*) county; (*Hist*) earldom

condal ADJ **Ciudad Condal** Barcelona

conde SM earl, count; **el Conde Fernán González** Count Fernán González

condecoración SF (= *acción*) decoration; (= *insignia*) decoration, medal; (= *divisa*) badge

condecorar ▸conjug 1a◂ VT to decorate (**con** with)

condena SF [1] (= *pronunciamiento*) sentence, conviction; (= *período*) term (of imprisonment); **cumplir una ~** to serve a sentence; **el año pasado hubo diez ~s por embriaguez** last year there were ten convictions for drunkenness; ✦***MODISMO*** **ser algn la ~ de otra** (*Méx*) to be the bane of sb's life ► **condena a perpetuidad, condena de reclusión perpetua** life sentence, sentence of life imprisonment
[2] (= *desaprobación*) condemnation

condenable ADJ reprehensible

condenación SF [1] (*gen*) condemnation; (*Rel*) damnation; (= *censura*) disapproval, censure; (*Jur*) = **condena 1**
[2] **¡condenación!** damn!, damnation!

condenadamente* ADV **es un trabajo ~ duro** it's bloody hard work‡; **una mujer ~ lista** a damn *o* darned clever woman*

condenado/a Ⓐ ADJ [1] (*Jur*) condemned, convicted; (*Rel*) damned
[2] (= *destinado*) [*cambio, reforma, ley*] doomed; **la reforma estaba condenada al fracaso** the reform was doomed to failure; **~ al olvido** destined for oblivion; **el buque ~** the doomed *o* fated vessel; **una especie condenada a la extinción** a species doomed to extinction; **instituciones condenadas a desaparecer** institutions doomed to disappear
[3] (*) (= *maldito*) damn*, flaming* (*euf*); **¡aquel ~ teléfono!** that damn *o* flaming *o* wretched phone!*, that bloody phone!‡
[4] (*) [*niño*] mischievous, naughty
[5] (*Cono Sur*) (= *listo*) clever; (= *astuto*) sharp
Ⓑ SM/F [1] (*Jur*) prisoner; **el ~ a muerte** the condemned man; ✦***MODISMO*** **trabaja como un ~** he works like a Trojan
[2] (*Rel*) damned soul
[3] **el ~ de mi tío*** that wretched *o* damned uncle of mine*

▼**condenar** ▸conjug 1a◂ Ⓐ VT [1] (= *desaprobar, criticar*) to condemn
[2] (*Jur*) to convict, find guilty, sentence; (*a pena capital*) to condemn; **~ a algn a tres meses de cárcel** to sentence sb to three-months in jail, give sb a three month prison sentence; **le ~on por ladrón** they found him guilty of robbery; **~ a algn a una multa** to sentence sb to pay a fine
[3] (*Rel*) to damn
[4] (*Arquit*) to wall up, block up
[5] (†*) (= *fastidiar*) to vex, annoy
Ⓑ **condenarse** VPR [1] (*Jur*) to confess, own up; (= *reprocharse*) to blame o.s.
[2] (*Rel*) to be damned
[3] (†*) (= *enfadarse*) to get cross, get irate

condenatorio ADJ condemnatory; **declaración condenatoria** statement of condemnation

condensación SF condensation

condensado ADJ condensed

condensador SM condenser

condensar ▸conjug 1a◂ Ⓐ VT to condense
Ⓑ **condensarse** VPR to condense, become condensed

condesa SF countess

condescendencia SF [1] (= *deferencia*) obligingness; (= *indulgencia*) affability; **aceptar algo por ~** to accept sth so as not to hurt feelings
[2] (*pey*) **tratar a algn con ~** to patronize sb

condescender ▸conjug 2g◂ VI to acquiesce, comply, agree; **~ a** to consent to, say yes to; **~ a los ruegos de algn** to agree to sb's requests; **~ en hacer algo** to agree to do sth

condescendiente ADJ [1] (= *deferente*) obliging; (= *afable*) affable; (= *conforme*) acquiescent
[2] (*pey*) **ser ~ con algn** to patronize sb

condición SF [1] (= *requisito*) condition; **lo haré con una ~** I'll do it on one condition; **ha puesto como ~ el que se respeten los derechos humanos** he has made it a condition that human rights be respected; **están negociando las condiciones de la entrega de los rehenes** they are negotiating the conditions for the release of the hostages; **las condiciones del contrato** the terms *o* conditions of the contract; **a ~ de que ...** ◊ **con la ~ de que ...** on condition that ...; **te dejaré salir con la ~ de que no vuelvas tarde** I'll let you go out provided (that) *o* on condition (that) you don't come back late; **acepté a ~ de que no dijera nada a nadie** I agreed on condition that he didn't say anything to anyone; **~ indispensable** essential condition; **~ previa** precondition; **entregarse** *o* **rendirse sin condiciones** to surrender unconditionally; **rendición sin condiciones** unconditional surrender; **~ sine qua non** essential condition, sine qua non ► **condiciones de favor** concessionary terms ► **condiciones de pago** terms of payment, payment terms ► **condiciones de uso** instructions for use ► **condiciones de venta** terms of sale, conditions of sale ► **condiciones económicas** [*de contrato*] financial terms; [*de profesional*] fees; *ver tb* **pliego**
[2] **condiciones** [2·1] (= *situación*) conditions; **las condiciones de luz eran muy buenas** the light conditions were very good; **si se dan las condiciones adecuadas, ganaremos las elecciones** if the conditions are right, we will win the election; **viven en condiciones infrahumanas** they live in subhuman conditions; **en condiciones normales** under normal conditions *o* circumstances; **estar en (buenas) condiciones** [*lugar, máquina*] to be in good condition; [*alimentos*] to be fresh; [*deportista*] to be fit; **el terreno de juego está en perfectas condiciones** the pitch is in perfect condition; **el coche se encuentra en excelentes condiciones** the car is in excellent condition; **esa leche no está en buenas condiciones** that milk is not fresh; **estar en condiciones de** *o* **para hacer algo** [*enfermo*] to be well *o* fit enough to do sth; [*deportista*] to be fit (enough) to do sth; **la industria automovilística no está en condiciones de enfrentarse a la competencia** the car industry is not in a condition to face up to competition; **estar en malas condiciones** [*coche, libro, campo de juego*] to be in bad condition; **me devolvieron el libro en pésimas condi-**

➤ LENGUA Y USO: condenar A1 41

ciones they returned the book to me in a terrible state *o* condition; **el queso estaba en malas condiciones** the cheese had gone bad, the cheese was off

2·2 **en condiciones** (= *decente*) proper; **no tengo tiempo de echarme una siesta en condiciones** I don't have time for a proper siesta; **antes de irnos lo dejaremos todo en condiciones** we'll leave everything in order before we go

2·3 (= *cualidades*) **no tiene condiciones para la pintura** she is not cut out to be a painter; **no reúne las condiciones necesarias para este trabajo** he doesn't fulfil the requirements for this job; **el edificio no reúne condiciones para museo** the building is not suitable for use as a museum

► **condiciones de trabajo** working conditions ► **condiciones de vida** living conditions ► **condiciones físicas** physical condition *sing*; **el equipo se encuentra en excelentes condiciones físicas** the team is in excellent physical condition; **no está en condiciones físicas de boxear** he is not physically fit (enough) to box ► **condiciones laborales** working conditions ► **condiciones sanitarias** [*de bar, restaurante*] health requirements; [*de hospital*] sanitary conditions; *ver tb* **igualdad 1**, **inferioridad**

3 (= *naturaleza*) condition; **la ~ humana** the human condition; **el derecho a no ser discriminada por su ~ de mujer** the right not to be discriminated against on the grounds of being *o* because one is a woman; **tiene muy buena ~** he's very good-natured

4 (= *clase social*) social background; **personas de distinta ~** people of different social backgrounds; **personas de humilde ~** people from a humble background

5 (= *posición*) position; **su ~ de artista no lo autoriza a hacer eso** his position as an artist does not allow him to do this; **les pidieron algún documento acreditativo de su ~ de pasajeros** they were asked for some documentary evidence proving that they were passengers; **en su ~ de presidente** in his capacity as president

condicionado ADJ conditional; **la oferta está condicionada a la demanda** the offer is conditional on demand; **prestó su apoyo ~ a una serie de ayudas económicas** he gave his support, conditional on a financial aid package

condicional ADJ (*tb Ling*) conditional; **hizo una oferta ~** she made a conditional offer; **nos prestó su ayuda de forma ~** he gave us his help on a conditional basis *o* subject to certain conditions; *ver tb* **libertad 1**

condicionalmente ADV conditionally

condicionamiento SM conditioning

condicionante Ⓐ ADJ determining

Ⓑ SM *o* SF determining factor, determinant

condicionar ▸conjug 1a◂ VT 1 (= *influir*) to condition, determine; **¿en qué medida condiciona el clima su forma de vida?** to what extent does the climate condition *o* determine your way of life?

2 (= *supeditar*) **~ algo a algo** to make sth conditional on sth; **condicionó su apoyo a la retirada del otro candidato** he made his support conditional on the withdrawal of the other candidate

condigno ADJ proper, corresponding

condimentación SF seasoning

condimentar ▸conjug 1a◂ VT (*gen*) to flavour, flavor (*EEUU*), season; (*con especias*) to spice

condimento SM (*gen*) seasoning, flavouring, flavoring (*EEUU*); (= *aliño*) dressing

condiscípulo/a SM/F fellow student, fellow pupil

condolencia SF condolence, sympathy

condolerse ▸conjug 2h◂ VPR **~ de** *o* **por** to sympathize with, feel sorry for

condominio SM 1 (*Jur*) joint ownership; (*Pol*) condominium

2 (*LAm*) (= *piso*) condominium, condo*, apartment (*owned by the occupant*)

condón SM condom ► **condón femenino** female condom

condonación SF 1 [*de pena*] remission, reprieve

2 [*de deuda*] cancellation

condonar ▸conjug 1a◂ VT 1 (*Jur*) **~ una pena** to lift a sentence

2 (*Fin*) [+ *deuda*] to cancel, forgive

cóndor SM condor

conducción SF 1 (*Com*) management; [*de líquidos*] piping; (*por cable*) wiring; (*Fís*) conduction

2 (*Aut*) driving; **coche de ~ interior** saloon car ► **conducción descuidada**, **conducción imprudente**, **conducción negligente** careless driving ► **conducción por la derecha** right-hand drive ► **conducción temeraria** reckless driving

3 (*Téc*) (= *tubo*) pipe; (= *cable*) cabling ► **conducción de agua** water pipe ► **conducción principal de agua** water main ► **conducción principal de gas** gas main

4 (*TV, Radio*) presentation

conducente ADJ **~ a** conducive to, leading to

conducir ▸conjug 3n◂ Ⓐ VT 1 (*Aut*) to drive

2 (= *llevar*) to take, lead; **este pasillo conduce a los pasajeros al avión** this corridor leads *o* takes passengers to the plane; **el general condujo al ejército a la victoria** the general led the army to victory; **la secretaria nos condujo hasta la salida** the secretary showed us out

3 [+ *electricidad, calor*] to conduct; [+ *agua, gas*] to convey

4 (*frm*) (= *estar a cargo de*) [+ *negocio, empresa*] to manage; [+ *equipo*] to lead; [+ *debate*] to chair, lead

5 (*TV, Radio*) to present

Ⓑ VI 1 (*Aut*) to drive; **¿sabes ~?** can you drive?, do you know how to drive?; **si bebes, no conduzcas** don't drink and drive

2 (= *llevar*) **~ a algo** to lead to sth; **esta carretera conduce al aeropuerto** this road leads to the airport, this road takes you to the airport; **un infarto que le condujo a la muerte** a heart attack which led to his death; **¿esa actitud a qué conduce?** where will that attitude get you?; **esto no nos conduce a ninguna parte** *o* **a nada** this is getting us nowhere

Ⓒ **conducirse** VPR (*frm*) (= *comportarse*) to behave, conduct o.s. (*frm*), bear o.s. (*liter*)

conducta SF 1 (= *comportamiento*) conduct, behaviour, behavior (*EEUU*); **le dieron un permiso de tres días por buena ~** he was allowed home for three days because of his good conduct *o* behaviour; **una persona de ~ irreprochable** a person whose conduct has been beyond reproach; **la ~ sexual de los españoles** the sexual habits *o* behaviour of Spaniards; **mala ~** misconduct, misbehaviour; **cambiar de ~** to mend one's ways ► **conducta compulsiva** compulsive behaviour

2 (*Com*) direction, management

conductibilidad SF conductivity

conductismo SM behaviourism, behaviorism (*EEUU*)

conductista ADJ, SMF behaviourist, behaviorist (*EEUU*)

conductividad SF = **conductibilidad**

conductivo ADJ conductive

conducto SM 1 [*de agua, gas*] pipe, conduit; (*Anat*) duct, canal; (*Elec*) lead, cable; **~s** (*Aut*) leads ► **conducto alimenticio** alimentary canal ► **conducto biliar** bile duct ► **conducto de desagüe** drain ► **conducto de humo** flue ► **conducto lacrimal** tear duct

2 (= *medio*) channel; (= *persona*) agent, intermediary; **por ~ de** through, by means of; **por los ~s normales** through the usual channels

conductor(a) Ⓐ ADJ (*Fís*) **un material ~** a conductive material; **el agua salada es mejor ~ que el agua dulce** salt water is much more conductive than fresh water; **un material ~ de la electricidad** a material that conducts electricity

Ⓑ SM/F 1 [*de coche, camión, autobús*] driver; [*de moto*] rider; **este impuesto afectará a todos los ~es de vehículos** this tax will affect all motorists

2 (*TV, Radio*) presenter

3 (*LAm Mús*) conductor

4 (*frm*) (= *dirigente*) leader

Ⓒ SM (*Fís*) conductor; **no ~** non-conductor

conductual ADJ behavioural, behavioral (*EEUU*)

condueño/a SM/F joint owner, part owner, co-owner

conduje *etc ver* **conducir**

condumio* SM grub‡, chow (*EEUU*‡), food

conectable ADJ connectable (**a** to)

conectado ADJ connected; **estar ~** [*aparato*] to be on; [*cable*] to be live

conectar ▸conjug 1a◂ Ⓐ VT 1 [+ *cables, tubos*] to connect (up); **he conectado el ordenador a Internet** I've connected the computer to the Internet; **todavía no hemos conectado la luz en el piso nuevo** we still haven't had the electricity connected in the new flat; **conecta el televisor para ver las noticias** switch on the television to watch the news; **~ un aparato eléctrico a tierra** to earth *o* (*EEUU*) ground an electrical appliance; *ver tb* **masa² 6**

2 (= *enlazar*) **~ algo con algo** to link sth to sth; **esta autovía ~á Granada con Almería** this dual carriageway will link Granada and *o* to Almería; **la secretaria no me quiso ~ con el jefe** the secretary wouldn't put me through to the boss; **una oración que me conecta con Dios** a prayer which puts me in touch with God

3 (= *relacionar*) **no logro ~ una cosa con la otra** I can't see how one thing connects with another, I can't see how everything ties in together; **conectó todos los datos y resolvió el problema** he put all the facts together and solved the problem

Ⓑ VI [1] (*) (= *congeniar*) **Ana y Eugenia conectan bien** Ana and Eugenia have a lot in common; **un autor que ha sabido ~ con el público** an author who knows how to get through to *o* reach the public; **no hemos logrado ~ con el electorado** we didn't manage to get through to the electorate
[2] (= *enlazar*) **esta carretera ~á con la autopista** this road will link up to *o* provide a link to the motorway; **este tren conecta con el de Málaga** this train connects (up) with the Malaga train; **la obra conecta con la tradición poética española** the work ties in with Spanish poetic tradition
[3] (*TV, Radio*) **conectamos con nuestro corresponsal en Londres** and now it's over to our correspondent in London, and now we're going over to our correspondent in London
Ⓒ **conectarse** VPR (*Inform*) **~se a Internet** to get connected to the Internet

conectividad SF connectivity

conectivo ADJ connective

conector SM connector

coneja SF doe (rabbit)

conejar SM (rabbit) hutch

conejera SF [1] (= *madriguera*) warren, burrow; (= *jaula*) rabbit hutch
[2] (‡) (= *tasca*) den, dive‡

conejillo SM ► **conejillo de Indias** guinea pig

conejita* SF bunny girl

conejo Ⓐ SM [1] (*Zool*) rabbit ► **conejo casero** (*gen*) tame rabbit; (= *mascota*) pet rabbit ► **conejo de monte**, **conejo silvestre** wild rabbit
[2] (*Anat***) (= *órgano sexual*) pussy**
[3] (*CAm*) (= *detective*) detective, sleuth*; **andar de ~** (*LAm*) to be (operating) under cover
[4] (*Mil*) recruit*, squaddie*
Ⓑ ADJ (*CAm*) (= *soso*) flat, unsweetened; (= *amargo*) bitter, sour

conejuna SF rabbit fur, coney

conexión SF [1] (= *relación*) connection; **no encuentro la ~ entre los dos hechos** I don't see the connection between the two facts; **no existe ~ entre lo que declaró y lo que sucedió** what he said bears no relation to what happened; **pretenden establecer ~ con nuestro partido** their aim is to establish links with our party; **gritaba cosas sin ~ ninguna** he was shouting incoherently
[2] (*Elec*) connection; **en caso de mala ~, apague el aparato** if there is a bad connection, switch off the machine; **hemos solicitado la ~ a la red eléctrica** we have applied to have the electricity connected; **~ a tierra** earth, ground (*EEUU*)
[3] (*TV, Radio, Telec*) **tenemos ~ con nuestro corresponsal en Londres** we are going over to our London correspondent; **seguimos en ~ telefónica con el presidente** we still have a telephone link with the president ► **conexión en directo** live link-up
[4] (*Inform*) interface ► **conexión en paralelo** parallel interface
[5] **conexiones** (= *contactos*) contacts; **tenía conexiones en el Ministerio** he had contacts at the Ministry; **conexiones familiares** family connections

conexionarse ▸conjug 1a◂ VPR (= *ponerse en contacto*) to get in touch; (= *hacer contactos*) to make connections, establish contacts

conexo ADJ connected, related

confabulación SF [1] (= *complot*) plot, conspiracy; (= *intriga*) intrigue
[2] (*Com*) ring

confabularse ▸conjug 1a◂ VPR [1] (= *conchabarse*) to plot, conspire, scheme
[2] (*Com*) to form a ring

confección SF [1] (= *preparación*) making-up, preparation
[2] (*Cos*) dressmaking; **industria de la ~** clothing industry; **traje de ~** ready-to-wear suit; **es una ~ Pérez** it's a Pérez creation ► **"confección de caballero"** menswear
[3] (*Farm*) concoction, preparation

confeccionado ADJ **~ a la medida** made to measure

confeccionador SM (*Prensa*) layout man

confeccionar ▸conjug 1a◂ VT [1] [+ *lista*] to make out, write; [+ *informe*] to prepare, write up
[2] (*Cos*) to make (up)
[3] (*Culin*) to make, bake
[4] (*Farm*) to concoct, make up

confeccionista SMF clothing manufacturer

confederación SF confederation

confederado/a ADJ, SM/F confederate

confederal ADJ federal

confederarse ▸conjug 1a◂ VPR to confederate, form a confederation

conferencia SF [1] (*Pol*) (= *congreso*) conference, meeting ► **conferencia cumbre** summit, summit conference ► **conferencia de desarme** disarmament conference ► **conferencia de prensa** press conference ► **conferencia de ventas** sales conference ► **conferencia episcopal** synod
[2] (= *charla*) lecture; **dar una ~** to give a lecture
[3] (*Telec*) call; **facilidad de ~ múltiple** follow-on call facility ► **conferencia a cobro revertido** reverse charge *o* call, collect call (*EEUU*) ► **conferencia de persona a persona** personal call, person-to-person call (*EEUU*) ► **conferencia interurbana** long-distance call
[4] (*Inform*) conference, conferencing

conferenciante SMF lecturer

conferenciar ▸conjug 1b◂ VI to confer (**con** with), be in conference (**con** with)

conferencista SMF (*LAm*) lecturer

conferir ▸conjug 3i◂ (*frm*) VT [1] [+ *premio*] to award (**a** to); [+ *honor*] to confer (**a** on), bestow (**a** on)
[2] (= *proporcionar*) to lend, give; **los cuadros confieren un aire de dignidad a la sala** the paintings lend an air of dignity to the room
[3] (= *cotejar*) [+ *documentos*] to compare (**con** with)

confesante SM penitent

confesar ▸conjug 1j◂ Ⓐ VT [1] (= *admitir*) [+ *error*] to admit, acknowledge; [+ *crimen*] to confess to, own up to
[2] (*Rel*) [+ *pecados*] to confess; [*sacerdote*] to confess, hear the confession of
Ⓑ VI (= *admitir*) to confess, own up; ✦***MODISMO*** **~ de plano** to own up
Ⓒ **confesarse** VPR (*Rel*) to confess, make one's confession; **me confesé de mis pecados** I confessed my sins; **ayer me confesé** I made my confession yesterday; ✦***MODISMO*** **¡que Dios nos coja confesados!** God help us!, Lord have mercy!

confesión SF confession

confesional ADJ [1] (= *religioso*) confessional, denominational
[2] (*de la confesión*) confessional; **secreto ~** secrecy of confession

confesionario SM, **confesonario** SM confessional (box)

confeso/a Ⓐ ADJ [1] (*Jur*) self-confessed
[2] (*Hist*) (= *judío*) converted
Ⓑ SM/F (*Hist*) converted Jew
Ⓒ SM (*Rel*) lay brother

confesor SM confessor

confeti SM confetti

confiabilidad SF reliability, trustworthiness

confiable ADJ reliable, trustworthy

confiadamente ADV [1] (= *con seguridad*) confidently
[2] (= *ingenuamente*) trustingly

confiado ADJ [1] (= *seguro*) confident; **está muy ~** he's very confident; **se presentó muy ~ ante el juez** he seemed very confident when he appeared before the judge; **~ en algo** confident of sth; **se mostró ~ en que obtendría el puesto** he seemed confident that he would obtain the post; **~ en sí mismo** self-confident
[2] (= *ingenuo*) trusting
[3] (= *vanidoso*) vain, conceited

confianza SF [1] (= *credibilidad*) confidence; **ese abogado tuyo no me inspira ~** that lawyer of yours doesn't exactly fill me with confidence; **en un clima de ~** in an atmosphere of trust; **de ~** [*producto*] reliable; **una persona de ~** (= *competente*) a reliable person; (= *honrada*) a trustworthy person; **hable con alguien de su ~** speak to someone you trust; **un producto de mi entera ~** a product I have complete faith *o* confidence in; **defraudar la ~ de algn** to let sb down; **ganarse la ~ de algn** to win sb's confidence; **dar** *o* **conceder un margen de ~ a algn** to place one's trust in sb; **perder la ~ en algo/algn** to lose faith in sth/sb; **perder la ~ de algn** to lose sb's confidence; **poner su ~ en algn** to put *o* place one's trust in sb; **preso de ~** trusty; **puesto de ~** position of responsibility; **recuperar la ~ de** *o* **en algo** to regain one's faith *o* confidence in sth; **tener ~ en algn** to have faith *o* confidence in sb ► **confianza ciudadana** public confidence ► **confianza mutua** mutual trust; *ver tb* **hombre A1, moción 1**
[2] (= *seguridad*) confidence; **dar ~ a algn** to give sb confidence, make sb confident; **ya no le duele el pie y eso le da más ~ al andar** her foot no longer hurts so she's more confident walking; **infundir ~ a algn** to inspire confidence in sb; **tener ~ en algo** to be confident of sth; **tienen plena ~ en su victoria** they are fully confident of victory; **tener ~ en que …** to be confident that … ► **confianza en sí mismo** self-confidence; **necesitas tener más ~ en ti mismo** you need to have more confidence in yourself, you need more self-confidence
[3] (= *amistad*) **no te preocupes porque estemos nosotros delante, que hay ~** don't mind us, we're all friends here; **entre amigos debe haber ~** friends should trust each other; **con ~: te lo digo con toda ~** I'm being

completely open with you; **podéis tratarme con toda ~** you can treat me as one of yourselves; **de ~**: **puedes hablar delante de él, es de ~** you can speak freely in front of him, he's a friend; **un amigo de ~** a close friend, an intimate friend; **en ~**: **(dicho sea) en ~** *o* **hablando en ~, no me fío nada de él** between you and me, I don't trust him at all; **aquí estamos en ~** we're all friends here; **tener ~ con algn** to be on close terms with sb; **díselo tú, que tienes más ~ con ella** you tell her, you're closer to her

[4] **confianzas** (= *libertades*) **se toma demasiadas ~s contigo** he takes too many liberties with you, he's a bit too familiar with you; **detesto las ~s con los criados** I hate it when people are too familiar with their servants; **¿qué ~s son ésas?** don't be so familiar!

confianzudo ADJ [1] (= *demasiado familiar*) overfamiliar, fresh
[2] (*LAm*) (= *entrometido*) meddlesome

confiar ▸conjug 1c◂ Ⓐ VT **~ algo a algn** [+ *misión, tarea, cuidado, educación*] to entrust sb with; [+ *secreto, preocupaciones*] to confide to sb; [+ *voto*] to give sb; **le ~on una misión imposible** they entrusted him with an impossible mission; **la aplicación del acuerdo se ~á a la ONU** the UN will be entrusted with *o* will be responsible for implementing the agreement; **les ~on la gestión de la publicidad** they were put in charge of publicity; **confíenos sus ahorros** trust your savings to us; **confió a sus hijos al cuidado de sus abuelos** he left his children in the care of their grandparents; **le confié por qué no había ido aquella noche** I confided to him why I hadn't gone that night; **~ algo al azar** to leave sth to fate
Ⓑ VI **~ en algn/algo** to trust sb/sth; **confío en ti** I trust you; **confiemos en Dios** let us trust in God; **no deberías ~ en su palabra** you shouldn't trust his word *o* what he says; **confío plenamente en la justicia** I have complete faith *o* confidence in justice; **confían en él para que resuelva el problema** they trust him to solve the problem; **~ en hacer algo**: **confiamos en poder ganar la partida** we are confident that we can win the game, we are confident of winning the game; **~ en que** to hope that; **confiemos en que todo salga bien** let's hope that everything goes well; **confío en que podáis echarme una mano** I trust that you can give me a hand; **confían en que este libro sea un gran éxito** they are confident this book will be a success
Ⓒ **confiarse** VPR [1] (*con excesiva seguridad*) **no te confíes, te queda mucho por estudiar** you shouldn't be so over-confident *o* sure of yourself, you still have a lot more to study
[2] (= *sincerarse*) **~se a algn** to confide in sb
[3] (= *entregarse*) **~se a algo** to entrust o.s. to sth

confidencia SF (= *secreto*) confidence, secret; (*a policía*) tip-off; **hacer ~s a algn** to confide in sb, tell sb secrets

confidencial ADJ confidential

confidencialidad SF confidentiality; **en la más estricta ~** in the strictest confidence

confidencialmente ADV confidentially

confidente/a SM/F [1] (= *amigo*) confidant/ confidante, intimate friend
[2] (*Jur*) informer; (= *agente secreto*) secret agent ► **confidente policial** police informer

configurabilidad SF configurability

configuración SF [1] (*gen*) shape, configuration; **la ~ del terreno** the lie of the land; **la ~ del futuro** the shape of things to come
[2] (*Inform*) configuration ► **configuración de bits** bit configuration

configurar ▸conjug 1a◂ VT to shape, form

confín SM [1] (= *límite*) boundary
[2] (= *horizonte*) horizon
[3] **confines** [*de la tierra, atmósfera*] confines, limits; (= *parte exterior*) remote parts, outermost parts, edges

confinación SF, **confinamiento** SM confinement

confinar ▸conjug 1a◂ Ⓐ VT (*Jur*) to confine (**a, en** in); (*Pol*) to banish, exile (**a** to)
Ⓑ VI (= *limitar*) **~ con** to border on (*tb fig*)
Ⓒ **confinarse** VPR (= *encerrarse*) to shut o.s. away

▼ **confirmación** SF confirmation (*tb Rel*)

▼ **confirmar** ▸conjug 1a◂ Ⓐ VT [1] [+ *noticia, rumor, temor*] to confirm; **esto confirma mis peores sospechas** this confirms my worst suspicions; **según ~on fuentes policiales** as police sources confirmed, according to police sources; ✦***REFRÁN*** **la excepción confirma la regla** the exception proves the rule
[2] [+ *vuelo, cita*] to confirm; **el presidente confirmó su asistencia a la reunión** the president confirmed that he would be attending the meeting
[3] (= *reafirmar*) [+ *sentencia*] to confirm; **esta victoria le confirma como el mejor atleta mundial** this win confirms him as the best athlete in the world; **esto me confirma más en mi postura** this makes me more convinced that I'm right
[4] (*Rel*) to confirm
Ⓑ **confirmarse** VPR [1] (*Rel*) to be confirmed
[2] (= *reafirmarse*) **me confirmo en la creencia de que es culpable** I stand by my belief that he is guilty

confirmatorio ADJ confirmatory

confiscación SF confiscation

confiscar ▸conjug 1g◂ VT to confiscate

confisgado ADJ (*CAm*) mischievous, naughty

confitado ADJ **fruta confitada** crystallized fruit

confitar ▸conjug 1a◂ VT [1] (= *conservar*) (*en almíbar*) to preserve (in syrup); (*con azúcar*) to candy
[2] (= *endulzar*) (*tb fig*) to sweeten

confite SM sweet, candy (*EEUU*)

confitería SF [1] (= *arte*) confectionery
[2] (= *tienda*) confectioner's (*frm*), sweet shop, candy store (*EEUU*); (*Andes, Cono Sur*) (= *cafetería*) café and cake shop

confitero/a SM/F confectioner

confitura SF (= *mermelada*) preserve, jam; (= *fruta escarchada*) crystallized fruit

conflagración SF [1] (= *perturbación*) flare-up, outbreak ► **conflagración bélica** outbreak of war
[2] (= *incendio*) conflagration

conflictividad SF [1] (= *tensiones*) tensions and disputes *pl*; **la ~ laboral** industrial disputes, labour *o* (*EEUU*) labor troubles ► **conflictividad social** social unrest
[2] (= *cualidad*) controversial nature

conflictivo ADJ [*sociedad*] troubled; [*asunto*] controversial; [*sistema*] unstable; [*situación*] tense, troubled; **la edad conflictiva** the age of conflict; **punto ~** point at issue; **zona conflictiva** troubled region, trouble spot

conflicto SM [1] (= *enfrentamiento*) conflict; **esto provocó un ~ entre China y Taiwan** this caused a conflict between China and Taiwan; **el ~ vasco** the Basque conflict; **estar en ~** to be in conflict; **los intereses de las dos empresas están en ~** the interests of the two companies are in conflict; **sus ideas y las mías están en ~** we have conflicting ideas; **los agricultores españoles están en ~ con los franceses** Spanish farmers are in dispute with the French; **las partes en ~** (*Pol*) the warring parties *o* factions; (*Jur*) the parties in dispute; **entrar en ~ con algo/algn** to come into conflict with sth/sb ► **conflicto armado** armed conflict ► **conflicto bélico** military conflict ► **conflicto de intereses** conflict of interests, clash of interests ► **conflicto generacional** generation gap ► **conflicto laboral** labour dispute, labor dispute (*EEUU*)
[2] (= *dilema*) dilemma
[3] (*Psic*) conflict

conflictual ADJ = **conflictivo**

confluencia SF confluence

confluente Ⓐ ADJ confluent
Ⓑ SM confluence

confluir ▸conjug 3g◂ VI [1] [*ríos*] to meet, come together
[2] [*gente*] to gather

conformación SF [1] (= *forma*) structure, configuration
[2] (= *constitución*) **la ~ de la plantilla** the line-up of the team

conformado Ⓐ ADJ [1] (= *formado*) **los asientos son firmes y bien ~s** the seats are firm and well-shaped
[2] (= *resignado*) resigned
Ⓑ SM (*Téc*) moulding, molding (*EEUU*), shaping

conformar ▸conjug 1a◂ Ⓐ VT [1] (= *dar forma a*) [+ *proyecto, educación, escultura*] to shape; **¿tiene conformado ya su equipo?** has he chosen his team yet?
[2] (= *constituir*) to make up; **seis de los ocho cuentos que conforman este libro** six of the eight stories that make up this book; **un universo conformado por millones de estrellas** a universe composed of *o* made up of millions of stars; **una exposición conformada por 25 esculturas** an exhibition composed of *o* made up of 25 sculptures
[3] (= *adaptar*) **trataba de ~ su vida a ese ideal** he tried to make his life conform to that ideal, he tried to shape his life around that ideal; **el pueblo no debe ~ su voluntad a la de sus gobernantes** the people's will should not be subject to that of their governors
[4] (= *contentar*) [+ *persona*] to keep happy; **lo conforma con regalos** she keeps him happy with presents; **no me vas a ~ dándome dinero** you won't keep me quiet by giving me money
[5] [+ *cheque, talón*] to authorize, endorse
[6] [+ *enemigos*] to reconcile
Ⓑ VI **~ con algn** to agree with sb
Ⓒ **conformarse** VPR [1] (= *estar satisfecho*) **~se con algo** to be happy with sth; **yo me**

➤ LENGUA Y USO: confirmación 47.3 confirmar A1 38.1, 47.3

conformo con cualquier cosa para cenar I'm happy to have anything for dinner; **yo me conformo con lo que tengo** I'm happy *o* satisfied with what I have; **no se conforma con nada** he's never happy *o* satisfied; **tuvo que ~se con la medalla de plata** she had to settle for the silver medal, she had to be satisfied with the silver medal; **de momento me conformo con no perder dinero** at the moment I'm just happy not to be making a loss; **el hombre ya no se conforma con transformar la naturaleza** Man is no longer content *o* satisfied with transforming nature; **no hay que ~se con pensar, hay que actuar** thinking is not enough, we have to act

2 (= *corresponderse*) **~se con** [+ *reglas, política*] to comply with; **eso no se conforma con nuestra política de pagos** that does not comply with our pay policy; **no parece ~se con el original** it doesn't seem to correspond to the original

3 (= *tomar la forma*) **~se como** to take the form of; **la representación se conforma como un viaje existencial** the performance takes the form of an existential journey

conforme Ⓐ ADJ 1 (= *satisfecho*) **¿conforme?** (are we) agreed?; **¡conforme!** agreed!, all right!; **he revisado el contrato, está todo ~** I've gone over the contract, everything is in order; **estar ~ con algo/algn** to be happy *o* satisfied with sth/sb; **no está ~ con el precio** he's not happy *o* satisfied with the price; **estar ~ en que** to agree that; **todos se mostraron ~s en que había que buscar otra solución** everyone agreed *o* was agreed that another solution had to be found; **todos están ~s en apoyar esta propuesta** everyone agrees *o* is agreed that we should support this proposal; **quedarse ~: no se quedó ~ con la propina** he wasn't happy *o* satisfied with the tip; **parece que ha quedado algo más ~ después de la explicación** he seems a little happier after that explanation

2 **~ con** (= *correspondiente a*) consistent with; **el resultado ha estado ~ con nuestras esperanzas** the result is consistent with our expectations

3 **~ a** (= *según*) according to; **serán juzgados ~ a las leyes libanesas** they will tried under Lebanese law, they will tried according to Lebanese law; **todo marcha ~ a lo previsto** everything is going according to plan; **actuaron ~ a las instrucciones que les dieron** they acted in accordance with the instructions they received, they acted according to instructions; *ver tb* **derecho C1**

Ⓑ CONJ 1 (= *como*) as; **lo hice ~ me dijiste** I did it as you told me to; **todo quedó ~ estaba** everything remained as it was

2 (= *a medida que*) as; **~ entraban, se iban sentando** as they came in, they sat down; **~ avanza el verano aumenta el calor** as summer progresses, the heat increases; **~ subes la calle, a mano derecha** on the right as you go up the street

Ⓒ SM (= *aprobación*) approval, authorization; **dar** *o* **poner el ~** to authorize; **el juez dio su ~ a la liberación del prisionero** the judge authorized the prisoner's release; **necesito que me des tu ~ a esta factura** I need you to approve *o* authorize payment of this invoice

conformidad SF 1 (= *acuerdo*) agreement; **no hubo ~ con respecto a ese tema** there was no agreement on this subject

2 (= *consentimiento*) consent; **dar su ~ a algo** to give one's consent to sth; **hasta que no dé su ~** until he gives his consent

3 (*frm*) (= *resignación*) resignation, forbearance; **soportar algo con ~** to put up with sth with resignation; ✦*REFRÁN* **el tiempo da la ~** time heals all wounds, time is a great healer

4 **de** *o* **en ~ con algo** (*frm*) in accordance with sth (*frm*)

conformismo SM conformism, conventionality

conformista ADJ, SMF conformist

confort [kon'for(t)] SM (*pl* **conforts** [kon'for(t)]) 1 (= *comodidad*) comfort; **"todo confort"** "all mod cons"

2 (*Cono Sur euf*) (= *papel higiénico*) toilet paper

confortabilidad SF comfort

confortable Ⓐ ADJ comfortable

Ⓑ SM (*Andes*) sofa

confortablemente ADV comfortably

confortante ADJ 1 (= *consolador*) comforting

2 (*Med*) soothing

confortar ▸conjug 1a◂ VT 1 (= *consolar*) to comfort

2 (*Med*) to soothe

confortativo Ⓐ ADJ 1 (= *consolador*) comforting, consoling

2 (*Med*) soothing

Ⓑ SM 1 (= *consuelo*) comfort, consolation

2 (*Med*) tonic, restorative

confraternidad SF fraternity, brotherhood

confraternización SF fraternization

confraternizar ▸conjug 1f◂ VI to fraternize (**con** with)

confrontación SF 1 (= *enfrentamiento*) confrontation ► **confrontación nuclear** nuclear confrontation

2 (*Literat*) comparison

confrontar ▸conjug 1a◂ Ⓐ VT 1 [+ *peligro*] to confront, face, face up to

2 (= *carear*) to bring face to face; **~ a algn con otro** to confront sb with sb else

3 [+ *textos*] to compare, collate

Ⓑ VI to border (**con** on)

Ⓒ **confrontarse** VPR **~se con** to confront, face up to

Confucio SM Confucius

confundible ADJ **fácilmente ~ con** easily mistaken for, easily confused with

confundido ADJ 1 (= *equivocado*) **puede que esté ~, pero creo que te he visto antes** I could be mistaken *o* wrong, but I think I've seen you before

2 (= *confuso*) confused; **se quedó confundida después de tantas preguntas** she was confused after so many questions; **—algo falla aquí, dijeron ~s** "there's something wrong here," they said in some confusion

confundir ▸conjug 3a◂ Ⓐ VT 1 (= *equivocar*) to confuse; **en este planteamiento se están confundiendo causa y efecto** this approach confuses cause and effect; **no confundamos las cosas, por favor** let's not confuse things, please; **siempre os confundo por teléfono** I always get you mixed up on the phone; **confundimos el camino** we went the wrong way; **~ algo/a algn con algo/algn** to get sth/sb mixed up with sth/sb, mistake sth/sb for sth/sb; **la confundí con su hermana gemela** I got her mixed up with her twin sister, I mistook her for her twin sister; **no se debe ~ a Richard Strauss con Johann Strauss** Richard Strauss should not be confused with Johann Strauss; **su sabor no se puede ~ con nada** its taste is unmistakable; *ver tb* **culo 1, velocidad 1**

2 (= *mezclar*) [+ *papeles*] to mix up; **me confundieron todas las facturas** they mixed up all the bills

3 (= *desconcertar*) to confuse; **sus palabras nos confundieron a todos** we were all confused by what he said; **técnicas para ~ al adversario** techniques for confusing your opponent; **me confunde con tanta palabrería** he confuses me *o* gets me confused with all that talk of his, I find all that talk of his confusing

4 (= *turbar*) to overwhelm; **me confundía con tantas atenciones** her kindness was overwhelming, I was overwhelmed by all her kindness

Ⓑ **confundirse** VPR 1 (= *equivocarse*) to make a mistake; **me he confundido al mandar el mensaje** I made a mistake when I sent the message; **~se de: lo siento, se ha confundido de número** I'm sorry, you have the wrong number; **~se en: se confundió en un cero al hacer la multiplicación** he got a zero wrong *o* he made a mistake over a zero when doing the multiplication; **para no ~me en la espesa niebla** so as not to lose my way *o* get lost in the thick fog; **es bastante normal ~se en los aparcamientos** it's quite easy to get mixed up in car parks

2 (= *mezclarse*) **realidad y fantasía se confunden en la mente del protagonista** reality and fantasy become confused in the mind of the main character; **~se con algo: el mar se confundía con el cielo** the sea blended with the sky; **los policías se confundían con los manifestantes** the police mingled with the demonstrators; **se confundió con la multitud** he disappeared into the crowd

confusamente ADV **hablaba ~** his speech was muddled *o* confused; **lo recuerdo ~** I have a vague *o* hazy memory of it

confusión SF 1 (= *equivocación*) confusion; **lo que provocó la ~** what caused the confusion; **para evitar confusiones** to avoid confusion; **ha habido una ~ en los nombres** there was a mix-up with the names, there was some confusion with the names; **esta carta no es para mí, debe de tratarse de una ~** this letter is not for me, there must be some mistake; **por ~** by mistake

2 (= *desconcierto*) confusion; **el terremoto produjo una gran ~ en las calles** the earthquake caused great confusion in the streets; **tiene una gran ~ de ideas** his ideas are very confused; **la recuerdo con bastante ~** I have a hazy *o* vague memory of her

3 (= *turbación*) **sentí tal ~ que no pude ni dar las gracias** I was so overwhelmed that I couldn't even say thank-you; **tantas alabanzas me produjeron una gran ~** I found all that praise overwhelming

confusional ADJ **estado ~** confused state, state of confusion

confusionismo SM confusion, uncertainty; **sembrar el ~ y desconcierto** to spread alarm and despondency

confusionista Ⓐ ADJ muddle-headed
Ⓑ SMF muddle-headed person

confuso ADJ 1 (= *poco claro*) [*ideas, noticias*] confused; [*recuerdo*] hazy; [*ruido*] indistinct; [*imagen*] blurred; **tiene las ideas muy confusas** he has very confused ideas, his ideas are very mixed up; **llegaban noticias confusas** confused reports were coming in; **una situación muy confusa** a very confused situation
2 (= *desconcertado*) confused; **nunca lo había visto tan ~** I had never seen him so confused; **no sé qué decir, estoy ~** I don't know what to say, I'm overwhelmed

confutar ▸conjug 1a◂ VT to confute

conga SF conga

congal SM (*Méx*) brothel

congelación SF 1 [*de alimentos, líquidos*] freezing
2 (*Med*) frostbite
3 (*Fin*) freeze, freezing ► **congelación de créditos** credit freeze ► **congelación de salarios** wage freeze
4 ► **congelación de imagen** [*de vídeo*] freeze-frame

congelado ADJ 1 [*carne*] frozen, chilled; [*grasa*] congealed; **¡estoy ~!** I'm frozen *o* freezing!
2 (*Med*) frostbitten
3 (*Fin*) frozen, blocked

congelador SM 1 (= *electrodoméstico*) freezer, deep freeze ► **congelador horizontal** chest freezer ► **congelador vertical** cabinet freezer
2 (*Náut*) frozen-food vessel

congeladora SF deep freeze, freezer

congelar ▸conjug 1a◂ Ⓐ VT 1 [+ *carne, agua*] to freeze; [+ *sangre, grasa*] to congeal
2 (*Med*) to affect with frostbite
3 (*Fin*) to freeze, block; [+ *proceso*] to suspend, freeze
4 [+ *imagen de vídeo*] to freeze
Ⓑ **congelarse** VPR 1 [*carne, agua*] to freeze; [*sangre, grasa*] to congeal
2 (*Med*) to get frostbitten

congénere SM fellow, person *etc* of the same sort; **el criminal y sus ~s** the criminal and others like him

congeniar ▸conjug 1b◂ VI to get on (**con** with); **congeniamos con los dos hermanos** we hit it off with the two brothers

congenital ADJ (*LAm*) = **congénito**

congénitamente ADV congenitally

congénito ADJ congenital

congestión SF congestion

congestionado ADJ 1 [*circulación*] congested
2 (*Med*) [*pecho, pulmones, nariz*] congested; **tener el pecho ~** to be chesty
3 [*rostro*] flushed, red

congestionamiento SM (*Caribe*) traffic jam

congestionar ▸conjug 1a◂ Ⓐ VT to congest, produce congestion in
Ⓑ **congestionarse** VPR to become congested; **se le congestionó la cara** his face became flushed *o* turned read

conglomeración SF conglomeration

conglomerado SM 1 (*Geol, Téc*) conglomerate
2 (= *aglomeración*) conglomeration

conglomerar ▸conjug 1a◂ VT, **conglomerarse** VPR to conglomerate

Congo SM **el ~** the Congo; ✦**MODISMO ¡vete al ~!**‡ get lost!‡

congo/a SM/F (*LAm*) black man/woman, black person

congoja SF anguish, distress

congola SF (*Andes*) pipe

congoleño/a ADJ, SM/F Congolese

congolés/esa ADJ, SM/F = **congoleño**

congosto SM narrow pass, canyon

congraciador ADJ ingratiating

congraciamiento SM ingratiation

congraciante ADJ ingratiating

congraciar ▸conjug 1b◂ Ⓐ VT to win over
Ⓑ **congraciarse** VPR to ingratiate o.s. (**con** with)

congratulación SF congratulation; **congratulaciones** congratulations

congratular ▸conjug 1a◂ Ⓐ VT to congratulate (**por** on)
Ⓑ **congratularse** VPR to congratulate o.s., be pleased; **de eso nos congratulamos** we are glad about that

congregación SF 1 (= *asamblea*) gathering, assembly; (= *sociedad*) brotherhood, guild
2 (*Rel*) congregation; **la ~ de los fieles** the (Catholic) Church

congregacionalista Ⓐ ADJ congregational
Ⓑ SMF congregationalist

congregar ▸conjug 1h◂ Ⓐ VT to bring together
Ⓑ **congregarse** VPR to gather, congregate

congresal SMF (*LAm*) = **congresista**

congresional ADJ congressional

congresista SMF delegate, member (*of a congress*); (*en EEUU*) member of Congress

congreso SM 1 [*de científicos, profesionales, políticos*] conference; **un ~ médico** a medical conference ► **congreso anual** annual conference; *ver tb* **palacio**
2 (*Pol*) **Congreso** (*en Reino Unido*) ≈ Parliament; (*en EEUU*) ≈ Congress ► **Congreso de los Diputados** (*Esp Pol*) ≈ House of Commons, ≈ House of Representatives (*EEUU*)

CONGRESO DE LOS DIPUTADOS

The **Congreso de los Diputados**, *the lower house in the Spanish Parliament, has 350 seats. Members* (**diputados**) *are elected by proportional representation for a maximum term of four years. The house itself chooses the prime minister* (**Presidente del Gobierno**) *by majority vote and he/she is invited in turn by the King to form the government.*
⇨ *See also* CORTES GENERALES, SENADO

congresual ADJ parliamentary, congressional

congrio SM conger, conger eel

congruencia SF 1 (*Mat*) congruence
2 (= *coherencia*) suitability

congruente ADJ, **congruo** ADJ 1 (*Mat*) congruent, congruous (**con** with)
2 (= *coherente*) suitable

cónico ADJ [*forma*] conical; [*sección*] conic

conífera SF conifer

conífero ADJ coniferous

conimbricense Ⓐ ADJ of/from Coimbra
Ⓑ SMF native/inhabitant of Coimbra

conjetura SF conjecture, surmise; **por ~** by guesswork; **son meras ~s** it's just guesswork

conjeturable ADJ that can be guessed at; **es ~ que ...** one may conjecture that ...

conjetural ADJ conjectural

conjeturar ▸conjug 1a◂ VT to guess, guess at, surmise (**de, por** from; **que** that)

conjugación SF conjugation

conjugar ▸conjug 1h◂ Ⓐ VT 1 (*Ling*) to conjugate
2 (= *reunir*) to combine; **es difícil ~ los deseos de los dos** it is difficult to please them both; **la obra conjuga cualidades y defectos** the work has both good qualities and defects
Ⓑ **conjugarse** VPR 1 (*Ling*) to be conjugated
2 (= *unirse*) to fit together, blend

conjunción SF conjunction

conjuntado ADJ 1 (= *coordinado*) coordinated
2 (= *unido*) united, combined

conjuntamente ADV jointly, together; **~ con** together with

conjuntar ▸conjug 1a◂ Ⓐ VT 1 (= *coordinar*) to coordinate
2 (= *unir*) to unite, combine
Ⓑ VI **~ con** to go with, match

conjuntero/a* SM/F band member

conjuntivitis SF INV conjunctivitis

conjuntivo ADJ conjunctive

conjunto Ⓐ ADJ joint, combined; **operaciones conjuntas** (*Mil*) combined operations
Ⓑ SM 1 (= *totalidad*) whole; **formar un ~** to form a whole; **impresión de ~** overall impression; **vista de ~** all-embracing view; **en ~** as a whole, altogether; **hay que estudiar esos países en ~** you have to study these countries as a whole; **en su ~** in its entirety ► **conjunto monumental** *collection of historic buildings*
2 (= *ropa*) ensemble; **un ~ de falda y blusa** a matching skirt and blouse
3 (*Mús*) [*de cámara*] ensemble; (*pop*) group; **un ~ de música pop** a pop group
4 (*Teat*) chorus; **chica de ~** chorus girl
5 (*Dep*) (= *equipo*) team
6 [*de muebles*] suite ► **conjunto de baño** bathroom suite
7 (*Mat, Inform*) set ► **conjunto integrado de programas** integrated software suite
8 (*Mec*) unit, assembly

conjura SF, **conjuración** SF plot, conspiracy

conjurado/a SM/F plotter, conspirator

conjurar ▸conjug 1a◂ Ⓐ VT 1 (*Rel*) to exorcise, cast out
2 [+ *peligro*] to ward off; [+ *pensamiento*] to rid o.s. of
3 (= *rogar*) to entreat (*frm*), plead with
Ⓑ VI **~ contra algn** to plot *o* conspire against sb
Ⓒ **conjurarse** VPR to get together in a plot, plot together, conspire together

conjuro SM 1 (*Rel*) exorcism; (= *hechizo*) spell; **al ~ de sus palabras** under the spell of his words
2 (= *ruego*) entreaty (*frm*), plea

conllevar ▸conjug 1a◂ VT 1 [+ *sentido*] to convey, carry
2 (= *implicar*) to imply, involve
3 (= *aguantar*) to bear, put up with; **~ las penas de otro** to take sb else's troubles on one's shoulders

conmemoración SF commemoration

conmemorar ▸conjug 1a◂ VT to commemorate

conmemorativo ADJ commemorative

conmigo PRON with me; **¿por qué no vienes ~?** why don't you come with me?; **se portó muy bien ~** he was very good to me; **atento ~** kind to *o* towards me; **no estoy satisfecho ~ mismo** I'm not proud of myself

conmilitón SM fellow soldier

conminación SF 1 (= *amenaza*) threat
2 (*Méx Jur*) judgement

conminar ▸conjug 1a◂ VT 1 (= *amenazar*) to threaten (**con** with)
2 (= *avisar*) to warn officially
3 (*Méx*) (= *desafiar*) to challenge

conminatorio ADJ threatening, warning

conmiseración SF sympathy, commiseration

conmoción SF 1 (*Geol*) shock, tremor
2 (*Med*) ► **conmoción cerebral** concussion
3 (= *perturbación*) shock; **producir una ~ desagradable a algn** to give sb a nasty shock
4 (*Pol*) disturbance; **una ~ social** a social upheaval

conmocionado ADJ (*Med*) shocked, concussed

conmocionar ▸conjug 1a◂ VT 1 (= *conmover*) to move, affect deeply
2 (= *turbar*) to shake profoundly, cause an upheaval in
3 (*Med*) to put into shock, concuss

conmovedor ADJ moving, touching, poignant

conmovedoramente ADV touchingly, movingly

conmover ▸conjug 2h◂ Ⓐ VT 1 (*Geol*) to shake
2 (= *enternecer*) to move, touch
3 (= *turbar*) to upset
Ⓑ **conmoverse** VPR 1 (*Geol*) to shake, be shaken
2 (= *enternecerse*) to be moved *o* be touched

conmuta SF (*Andes, Cono Sur*) change, alteration

conmutación SF 1 [*de pago, pena*] commutation
2 (*Inform*) switching ► **conmutación de mensajes** message switching ► **conmutación de paquetes** packet switching

conmutador SM 1 (*Elec*) switch
2 (*LAm Telec*) (= *centralita*) switchboard

conmutar ▸conjug 1a◂ VT 1 (= *trocar*) to exchange (**con, por** for); (= *transformar*) to convert (**en** into)
2 (*Jur*) to commute (**en, por** to)

connatural ADJ innate, inherent (**a** in)

connaturalizarse ▸conjug 1f◂ VPR to become accustomed (**con** to), to become acclimatized, become acclimated (*EEUU*) (**con** to)

connivencia SF connivance; **estar en ~ con** to be in collusion with

connotación SF 1 (= *sentido*) connotation
2 (= *parentesco*) distant relationship

connotado ADJ (*LAm*) (= *famoso*) famous, renowned; (= *destacado*) outstanding

connotar ▸conjug 1a◂ VT to connote

cono SM cone

conocedor(a) Ⓐ ADJ expert (**de** in), knowledgeable (**de** about); **muy ~ de** very knowledgeable about
Ⓑ SM/F expert (**de** in), connoisseur (**de** of); **es buen ~ de ganado** he's a good judge of cattle

conocencia SF (*esp LAm*) girlfriend, sweetheart

conocer ▸conjug 2d◂ Ⓐ VT 1 [+ *persona*]
1·1 (= *saber quién es*) to know; **conozco a todos sus hermanos** I know all his brothers and sisters; **¿de qué lo conoces?** where do you know him from?; **la conozco de haber trabajado juntos** I know her from having worked with her; **¿conoces a Pedro?** have you met Pedro?, do you know Pedro?; **no me conoce de nada** he doesn't know me from Adam; **la conozco de oídas** I've heard of her, I know of her; **lo conozco de vista** I know him by sight
1·2 (= *ver por primera vez*) to meet; **la conocí en Sevilla** I met her in Seville
1·3 (= *saber cómo es*) to get to know; **cuando la conozcas mejor** when you get to know her better; **la única forma de ~lo es vivir con él** the only way to get to know him is to live with him; ✦***MODISMOS*** **la conozco como la palma de la mano** I know her like the back of my hand; **la conozco como si la hubiera parido** I know her inside out, I can read her like a book
1·4 (= *reconocer*) to recognize, know; **te he conocido por el modo de andar** I recognized *o* knew you from the way you walk
2 (= *tener conocimiento de*) [+ *método, resultado*] to know; [+ *noticia*] to hear; **conozco un camino más corto** I know a shorter way; **ella conoce una forma más fácil de hacerlo** she knows an easier way to do it; **el enfermo debe ~ la verdad** the patient must be told *o* must know the truth; **conozco las dificultades** I know (about) the difficulties; **no conocía tus dotes de pintor** I didn't know what a good painter you were; **conocía la existencia de los documentos** she knew of the documents' existence; **queremos ~ de cerca la situación** we want to get to know the situation at first hand; **investigaciones destinadas a ~ la verdad** investigations aimed at establishing the truth; ✦***REFRÁN*** **más vale lo malo conocido que lo bueno por ~** better the devil you know than the devil you don't
3 [+ *país, ciudad*] **me encantaría ~ China** I would love to go to China; **no conozco Buenos Aires** I've never been to Buenos Aires, I don't know Buenos Aires; **quiero ~ mundo** I want to see the world
4 (= *dominar*) to know; **conoce su oficio** he knows his job; **no conozco mucho el tema** I don't know much about the subject; **conoce cuatro idiomas** she speaks *o* knows four languages
5 (= *experimentar*) **ha conocido dos guerras mundiales** she has lived through two world wars; **los muchos terremotos que ha conocido Italia** the many earthquakes there have been in Italy; **todavía no ha conocido el amor** he's never known love
6 (= *distinguir*) to know, tell; **conoce cuáles son buenos y cuáles malos** he knows *o* can tell which are good and which are bad; **por tu cara se te conoce que estás sano** you can tell from your face that you are healthy
7 **dar a ~** [+ *información*] to announce; [+ *declaración, informe, cifras*] to release; **dio a ~ sus intenciones** she announced her intentions, she made her intentions known; **dieron a ~ el ganador del premio a través de la radio** the prize was announced on the radio; **no dieron a ~ su paradero por motivos de seguridad** they didn't reveal where they were staying for security reasons; **los hechos se dieron a ~ en enero** the facts came to light in January; **darse a ~** [*persona*] to become known, make a name for o.s.; **se dio a ~ en una película de Almodóvar** he made his name in an Almodóvar film; **darse a ~ a algn** to make o.s. known to sb
8 (*Jur*) [+ *causa*] to try
Ⓑ VI 1 (= *saber*) **~ de algo**: **¿alguien conoce de algún libro sobre el tema?** does anybody know (of) a book on the subject?
2 (*Jur*) **~ de** *o* **en una causa** to try a case
Ⓒ **conocerse** VPR 1 (*uso reflexivo*) **~se a sí mismo** to know o.s.
2 (*uso recíproco*) 2·1 (= *tener relación con*) to know each other, know one another; **¿os conocéis?** have you met?, do you know each other?; **ya nos conocemos, no hace falta que nos presentes** we've already met, there's no need to introduce us
2·2 (*por primera vez*) to meet; **¿dónde os conocisteis?** where did you (first) meet?; **se conocieron en un baile** they met at a dance
2·3 (= *familiarizarse*) to get to know each other, get to know one another; **Juan y yo nunca llegamos a ~nos bien** Juan and I never really got to know each other
3 (= *reconocerse*) [*uno mismo*] to recognize o.s.; [*dos personas*] to recognize each other; **no me conocía en la foto** I didn't recognize myself in the photo; **se miraron pero no se conocieron** they looked at each other but didn't recognize each other
4 (= *saber*) to know; **me lo conozco de memoria** I know it off by heart
5 (*uso impersonal*) **se conocen varios casos** several cases are known; **se conocen con el nombre de composites** they are known as composites; **a esta enfermedad no se le conoce cura** this illness has no known cure; **no se le conoce ninguna novia** he doesn't have a girlfriend as far as anyone knows; **se conoce que ...** apparently ..., it seems that ...; **se conoce que se lo han contado** apparently he's been told about it, it seems that he's been told about it; **se conoce que no le ha sentado bien** he's obviously not best pleased

CONOCER

• **Conocer**, aplicado a personas o cosas, se traduce generalmente por **know**:

No conozco muy bien a su familia
I don't know his family very well
Nos conocemos desde que éramos pequeños
We have known each other since we were little
Conoce Manchester como la palma de la mano
He knows Manchester like the back of his hand

• Sin embargo, cuando queremos indicar que se trata del primer encuentro, se debe utilizar **meet**:

La conocí en una fiesta
I (first) met her at a party
¿Conoces a Carmen? Ven que te la presento
Have you met Carmen? Come and I'll introduce you

Para otros usos y ejemplos ver la entrada.

conocible ADJ knowable

conocido/a Ⓐ ADJ 1 (= *público*) [*dato*] known; [*persona*] well-known; **un médico ~** a well-known doctor; **un hecho conocidísimo** a very well-known fact; **más ~ por Michel** better known as Michel
2 (= *familiar*) familiar; **su cara me es conocida** I recognize his face, his face is familiar
Ⓑ SM/F acquaintance

▼ **conocimiento** SM 1 (= *saber*) knowledge; **un ~ profundo del tema** a thorough knowledge of the subject; **conocimientos** (= *nociones*) knowledge *sing*; **tengo algunos ~s musicales** I have some knowledge of music; **mis pocos ~s de filosofía/cocina** my limited knowledge of philosophy/cookery; **tener ~s generales de algo** to have a general knowledge of sth
2 (= *información*) knowledge; **el encuentro tuvo lugar sin ~ público** the meeting took place without the public's knowledge; **dar ~ de algo**: **dimos ~ del robo a la policía** we informed the police about the robbery; **llegar a ~ de algn** to come to sb's attention *o* notice; **tener ~ de algo**: **aún no tenemos ~ de su detención** we still do not know that he has been arrested; **no tenemos ~ del accidente** we are unaware of the accident; **se les informó al tenerse ~ del suceso** they were informed as soon as it was known what had happened; **poner algo en ~ de algn** to bring sth to sb's attention; **desea ponerlo en ~ público** he wants it brought to the public's attention, he wishes it to be made public; **el Ministro ha puesto en ~ del rey su decisión** the minister has informed the king of his decision ► **conocimiento de causa**: **hacer algo con ~ de causa** to be fully aware of what one is doing; **hablar con ~ de causa** to know what one is talking about
3 (= *consciencia*) consciousness; **estuvo sin ~ durante unos minutos** he was unconscious for a few minutes; **perder el ~** to lose consciousness; **quedarse sin ~** to lose consciousness; **recobrar** *o* **recuperar el ~** to regain consciousness
4 (= *sentido común*) common sense; **los niños no tienen ~** children have no common sense
5 (*Jur*) cognizance (*frm*)
6 (*Com*) ► **conocimiento de embarque** bill of lading ► **conocimiento de embarque aéreo** air waybill

conorte SM (*LAm*) comfort

Cono Sur SM (*Pol*) Argentina, Chile and Uruguay, Southern Cone

conozca *etc ver* **conocer**

conque* Ⓐ CONJ so, so then; **¿~ te pillaron?** so they caught you then?
Ⓑ SM 1 (= *condición*) condition, reservation; **~s** ifs and buts
2 (*) (= *dinero*) wherewithal, means

conqué* SM (*LAm*) = **conque B2**

conquense Ⓐ ADJ of/from Cuenca
Ⓑ SMF native/inhabitant of Cuenca; **los ~s** the people of Cuenca

conquista SF conquest; **ir de ~** (*fig*) to be dressed to kill

conquistador(a) Ⓐ ADJ conquering
Ⓑ SM/F conqueror
Ⓒ SM 1 (*Hist*) conquistador
2 (*) (= *seductor*) ladykiller

conquistar ▸conjug 1a◂ VT 1 (*Mil*) to conquer (**a** from); **los países conquistados por los romanos** the countries conquered by the Romans
2 [+ *puesto, simpatía*] to win; [+ *adversario*] to win round, win over; (= *enamorar*) to win the heart of; **la conquistó con su sonrisa** he won her over with his smile; **~ el título de campeón** to win the championship title; **los escaladores no lograron ~ la montaña** the climbers failed to conquer the mountain

consabido ADJ 1 (= *conocido*) well-known; [*frase*] old, oft-repeated
2 (= *susodicho*) above-mentioned

consagración SF 1 (*Rel*) consecration, dedication
2 [*de costumbre*] establishment

consagrado ADJ 1 (*Rel*) consecrated (**a** to), dedicated (**a** to)
2 (= *tradicional*) hallowed, traditional; **según la expresión consagrada** in the time-honoured *o* (*EEUU*) -honored phrase; **principios ~s en la constitución** principles enshrined in the constitution; **un actor ~** an established actor

consagrar ▸conjug 1a◂ Ⓐ VT 1 (*Rel*) to consecrate, dedicate (**a** to); [+ *emperador*] to deify
2 [+ *esfuerzo, tiempo, vida*] to devote, dedicate (**a** to); [+ *monumento, placa*] to put up (**a** to)
3 [+ *fama*] to confirm; **este triunfo lo consagra como un cirujano excepcional** this success confirms him as a really exceptional surgeon
Ⓑ **consagrarse** VPR 1 (*por fama*) to establish o.s.
2 **~se a** to devote o.s. to

consanguíneo ADJ related by blood, consanguineous (*frm*)

consanguinidad SF blood relationship, consanguinity (*frm*)

consciencia SF = **conciencia**

consciente Ⓐ ADJ 1 **ser ~ de algo** to be conscious *o* aware of sth
2 (*Med*) **estar ~** to be conscious
3 (*Jur*) fully responsible
4 (= *sensato*) responsible
Ⓑ SM conscious, conscious mind

conscientemente ADV consciously

conscripción SF (*esp LAm*) conscription, draft (*EEUU*)

conscripto SM (*esp LAm*) conscript, draftee (*EEUU*)

consecución SF [*de resultado, visado, beca, permiso*] obtaining; [*de meta*] attainment, achievement; [*de premio, campeonato*] winning; **les ayudó en la ~ de trabajo** he helped them find work; **para la ~ de estos objetivos** in order to attain these goals (*frm*), to achieve these goals

▼ **consecuencia** SF 1 (= *resultado*) consequence; **esto es ~ de una mala gestión** this is the consequence *o* result of bad management; **una decisión de ~s imprevisibles** a decision with unforeseeable consequences; **a ~ de algo** as a result of sth; **falleció a ~ de las heridas** he died as a result of his injuries; **atenerse a las ~s** to take *o* accept the consequences; **hazlo, pero atente a las ~s** do it, but you'll have to take *o* accept the consequences; **como ~** as a result, in consequence (*frm*); **como ~, está al borde de la bancarrota** as a result *o* in consequence he is on the verge of bankruptcy; **ha muerto como ~ del frío** it died from *o* as a result of the cold; **esto tuvo** *o* **trajo como ~ el aumento del paro** this led to *o* resulted in an increase in unemployment; **en ~** (*frm*) consequently; **no se trata, en ~, de ningún principiante** so *o* therefore *o* consequently, this can't be a beginner we are talking about; **está enamorado y, en ~, feliz** he is in love, and therefore he is happy; **padecer las ~s** to suffer the consequences; **tener ~s**: **tuvo graves ~s para la economía** it had serious consequences for the economy; **el accidente no tuvo ~s graves** the accident was not serious; **últimas ~s**: **llevar algo hasta sus últimas ~s** to take sth to its logical conclusion ► **consecuencia directa** direct consequence, direct result
2 (= *conclusión*) conclusion; **sacar ~s de algo** to draw conclusions from sth ► **consecuencia lógica** logical conclusion
3 (= *coherencia*) **actuar** *u* **obrar en ~** to act accordingly; **se comportó en ~ con sus ideas** he acted in accordance with his beliefs
4 (= *importancia*) importance
5 (*esp LAm*) (= *honradez*) integrity

consecuente ADJ 1 (= *coherente*) consistent (**con** with); **una actuación ~ con su ideología** behaviour consistent with their ideology
2 (*Fil*) consequent
3 (= *importante*) important; **no demasiado ~** not very important
4 (*LAm*) (= *honrado*) **una persona ~** an honourable person, a person of integrity

consecuentemente ADV consistently

consecutivo ADJ consecutive

conseguible ADJ obtainable, attainable

conseguido ADJ successful

conseguir ▸conjug 3d, 3k◂ VT [+ *meta, objetivo*] to achieve; [+ *resultado*] to obtain, achieve; [+ *premio, campeonato*] to win; [+ *entradas, empleo, dinero*] to get; [+ *documento, visado, beca, permiso*] to get, obtain; [+ *acuerdo*] to reach; **siempre consigue lo que se propone** he always achieves what he sets out to do; **consiguieron la victoria por tres millones de votos** they won by three million votes; **consiguieron la mayoría absoluta** they won *o* gained an absolute majority; **si insistimos lo ~emos** if we keep trying we'll manage it; **ha conseguido un estilo muy personal** she has achieved a very individual style; **~ hacer algo** to manage to do sth; **he conseguido aprobar el examen** I managed to pass the exam; **no conseguí dar con la solución** I didn't manage to find the answer; **no consigo entender tu argumento** I just don't quite understand your argument; **~ que algn haga algo** to get sb to do sth; **al final conseguí que me devolvieran el dinero** I got them to give me my money back in the end, I got my money back from them in the end; **vas a ~ que papá se enfade** you'll make daddy cross

conseja SF old wives' tale

consejería SF 1 (*Esp Pol*) ministry in a regional government
2 (= *concejo*) council, commission

consejero/a SM/F 1 (= *asesor*) adviser
2 (*Téc*) consultant; (*Com*) director; (*en comisión*) member of a board *etc*; ► **consejero/a de publicidad** advertising

➤ LENGUA Y USO: conocimiento 1 46.2 consecuencia 1 44.1

consultant ► **consejero/a delegado** managing director, chief executive officer (*EEUU*) ► **consejero/a militar** military adviser
[3] [*de autonomía*] minister in a regional government

consejillo SM inner cabinet, kitchen cabinet

▼ **consejo** SM [1] (= *sugerencia*) advice; **un ~** a piece of advice; **~s** advice *sing*; **su ~** his advice; **¿quieres que te dé un ~?** would you like me to give you some advice?; **¿qué ~ me das?** what would you suggest?, how would you advise me?; **pedir ~ a algn** to ask sb for advice, ask sb's advice ► **consejo pericial** expert advice
[2] (= *organismo*) (*Pol*) council; (*Com*) board; (*Jur*) tribunal ► **consejo asesor** advisory board ► **consejo de administración** board of directors ► **consejo de disciplina** disciplinary board ► **Consejo de Europa** Council of Europe ► **consejo de guerra** court-martial ► **consejo de guerra sumarísimo** drumhead court-martial ► **consejo de ministros** (= *entidad*) cabinet; (= *reunión*) cabinet meeting ► **consejo de redacción** editorial board ► **Consejo de Seguridad** Security Council ► **Consejo General del Poder Judicial** (*Esp*) *governing body of the Spanish judiciary*

CONSEJO

• Para traducir la palabra **consejo** al inglés, hemos de tener en cuenta que el sustantivo **advice** es incontable y lleva el verbo en singular:
Te voy a dar un consejo
Let me give you some advice
Los consejos que me diste han sido muy útiles
The advice you gave me has been very useful
Actuó siguiendo los consejos de su abogado
He acted on his lawyer's advice
• Cuando queremos referirnos a un **consejo** en particular o a un número determinado de consejos, lo traducimos con la expresión **piece/pieces of advice** o a veces **bit/bits of advice**:
Te voy a dar un consejo
Let me give you a piece *o* ***a bit of advice***
Tengo dos buenos consejos para quien quiere vender su casa
I have two useful pieces of advice for anyone selling their house
Para otros usos y ejemplos ver la entrada.

consenso SM [1] (*esp Pol*) consensus
[2] (= *consentimiento*) consent

consensuado ADJ [*texto*] agreed; **llegaron a un acuerdo ~** they achieved a consensus; **es una solución consensuada** it's a solution that has been reached by consensus

consensual ADJ agreed; **unión ~** common-law marriage

consensuar ▸conjug 1e◂ VT to agree on, reach an agreement on, reach a consensus on

consentido/a Ⓐ ADJ [1] (= *mimado*) spoiled, spoilt
[2] [*marido*] complaisant
Ⓑ SM/F **es una consentida** she's totally spoiled

consentidor ADJ [*madre*] indulgent; [*marido*] complaisant

▼ **consentimiento** SM consent

consentir ▸conjug 3i◂ Ⓐ VT [1] (= *permitir*) to allow; (= *tolerar*) to tolerate; **¡eso no se puede ~!** we can't have *o* allow that!; **aquí no te consienten hablar** they don't let you speak here; **no te consiento que vayas** I can't allow you to go
[2] (= *soportar*) to stand, bear; **la plataforma no consiente más peso** the platform will not bear *o* take any more weight; **el abrigo consiente un arreglo más** the overcoat will bear repairing once more
[3] (= *mimar*) to spoil
Ⓑ VI to agree, consent, say yes; **~ en hacer algo** to agree to do sth
Ⓒ **consentirse** VPR to break, give, give way

conserje SMF [*de facultad*] ≈ head porter; [*de colegio*] ≈ janitor; [*de hotel*] hall porter; [*de edificio oficial, museo*] caretaker ► **conserje de noche** night porter

conserjería SF porter's office, porter's lodge

conserva SF [1] (= *proceso*) preserving
[2] (*Culin*) (= *alimentos*) preserve, preserves *pl*; (= *mermelada*) jam; (= *encurtido*) pickle; **no comemos muchas ~s** we don't eat much tinned *o* (*EEUU*) canned food; **en ~** tinned, canned (*EEUU*); **atún en ~** tinned *o* (*EEUU*) canned tuna; **~s de carne** tinned *o* (*EEUU*) canned meat ► **conservas alimenticias** tinned *o* (*EEUU*) canned food
[3] (*Náut*) convoy; **navegar en (la) ~** to sail in convoy

conservación SF [1] [*del medio ambiente*] conservation; **instinto de ~** instinct of self-preservation ► **conservación de la energía** energy conservation ► **conservación de la naturaleza** nature conservation ► **conservación de suelos** soil conservation
[2] (*Culin*) preservation ► **conservación refrigerada** cold storage
[3] (*Arquit*) maintenance, upkeep ► **gastos de conservación** maintenance costs

conservacionismo SM conservationism

conservacionista Ⓐ ADJ conservationist, conservation *antes de s*
Ⓑ SMF conservationist

conservado ADJ **estar muy bien ~** [*persona*] to look very well for one's age, be very well-preserved (*hum*); [*mueble*] to be in very good condition (*frm*)

conservador(a) Ⓐ ADJ [1] (*Pol*) conservative, Tory
[2] (*Culin*) preservative
Ⓑ SM/F [1] (*Pol*) conservative, Tory
[2] [*de museo*] curator, keeper; **~ adjunto** assistant keeper

conservadurismo SM conservatism

conservante SM preservative

conservar ▸conjug 1a◂ Ⓐ VT [1] (= *mantener*) [+ *calor*] to retain, conserve; [+ *tradición, costumbre*] to preserve; **el frío conserva los alimentos** the cold preserves food; **con este sistema de cierre se conserva más la energía** this lock system saves *o* conserves more energy; **todavía conservamos el piso de Madrid** we are still keeping on the flat in Madrid; **todavía conservo las amistades del colegio** I still keep up the friendships I had at school; **conserva intactas sus facultades mentales** she is still in full possession of her mental faculties; **conservo un recuerdo magnífico de esas vacaciones** I have wonderful memories of that holiday; **un producto para ~ la piel tersa** a product to keep the skin smooth; **conservaba un aspecto juvenil** she still looked youthful; **ante todo hay que ~ la calma** above all we must keep calm; *ver tb* **línea A10**
[2] (= *guardar*) [+ *secreto*] to keep; **conservo todas mis fotografías en un baúl** I keep all my photographs in a chest; **aún conservo varias cartas suyas** I still have several of his letters; **el museo conserva los mejores cuadros del pintor** the museum has *o* houses the artist's best paintings; **consérvese en lugar seco y fresco** store in a cool dry place
[3] (*Culin*) (= *poner en conserva*) to preserve
Ⓑ **conservarse** VPR [1] [*tradición, costumbre, ruinas*] to survive; **los alimentos se conservan mejor en la nevera** food keeps better in a fridge; **se han conservado intactos en el ámbar** they have been preserved intact in the amber; **aquel hecho todavía se conserva en la memoria británica** that fact is still fresh in the British memory *o* is still remembered in Britain
[2] [*persona*] **¡qué bien se conserva!** he looks very well for his age!, he's very well-preserved (*hum*); **se conserva muy joven para su edad** she keeps herself looking young; **se conserva en forma** he keeps himself fit *o* in shape

conservatismo SM conservatism

conservativo ADJ preservative

conservatorio SM [1] (*Mús*) conservatoire, conservatory
[2] (*LAm*) (= *invernáculo*) greenhouse
[3] (*Cono Sur*) (= *escuela*) private school

conservero ADJ canning *antes de s*; **la industria conservera** the canning industry

considerable ADJ considerable; **hubo un retraso ~** there was a considerable delay; **hemos tenido pérdidas ~s** we have suffered substantial *o* considerable losses

consideración SF [1] (= *deliberación*) consideration; **ese asunto merece la mayor ~** that matter deserves serious consideration; **en ~** under consideration; **dos elementos entran en ~ a la hora de decidir** two factors should be taken into consideration when making a decision; **someter algo a la ~ de algn** to put sth to sb for consideration; **tener** *o* **tomar algo en ~** to take sth into consideration
[2] (= *punto a considerar*) **hizo hincapié en la ~ de que …** he stressed the fact that …; **aquí pueden hacerse algunas consideraciones** a few points can be made here; **tales consideraciones no se ajustan a la realidad** such statements *o* views do not reflect reality; **sin querer entrar en consideraciones acerca de su propia actuación** without entering into a discussion of his actual performance
[3] (= *concepción*) conception; **la ~ del idioma como poder político** the conception of language as political power
[4] (= *importancia*) status; **tiene la ~ de lengua nacional** it has the status of a national language; **de ~** [*herida, daños*] serious; **daños de poca ~** minor damage; **sufrió quemaduras de diversa ~** he suffered burns of varying degrees of seriousness
[5] (= *atención*) consideration; **eso sería una falta de ~ hacia nuestros invitados** that would be showing a lack of consideration towards our guests; **nos trataron con gran ~** they were very considerate to us; **¡qué falta**

➤ LENGUA Y USO: **consejo 1** 28.1, 29.2 **consentimiento** 36.2

de ~! how inconsiderate!; **en ~ a algo/algn** out of consideration for sth/sb; **lo dejaron libre en ~ a sus circunstancias** he was released out of consideration for his circumstances; **le dieron un premio en ~ a su trabajo** they awarded her a prize in recognition of her work; **sin ~: tratar a algn sin ~** to show no consideration for sb; **sin ~ a la libertad de la persona** with no regard for personal freedom; **tener ~ a** *o* **con algn** to show consideration to sb; **no tuvieron ninguna ~ con las víctimas** they showed no consideration for the victims

6 (= *estima*) regard; **tengo una gran ~ por él** I have (a) great regard for him, I hold him in high regard

7 (*en cartas*) **le saludo con mi más distinguida ~** (*frm*) I remain yours faithfully (*frm*); **De mi (mayor) ~** (*LAm*) Dear Sir/Madam

consideradamente ADV considerately

considerado ADJ 1 (= *atento*) considerate; **ojalá todos fueran tan ~s como tú** if only everybody was as thoughtful *o* considerate as you; **ser ~ con algn** to be considerate to sb

2 (= *estimado*) **está ~ (como) el mejor corredor del mundo** he is considered (to be) the best runner in the world; **el robo está ~ un delito** robbery is regarded as *o* considered a crime; **estar bien ~** to be highly-regarded; **su profesión no está muy bien considerada** his profession is not very highly-regarded; **estar mal ~** (= *no aceptado*) to be frowned upon; (= *menospreciado*) to be undervalued

considerando SM (*Jur*) point, item, statement

▼**considerar** ▸conjug 1a◂ Ⓐ VT 1 (= *reflexionar sobre*) to consider; **considera las ventajas y los inconvenientes de tu decisión** think about *o* consider the advantages and disadvantages of your decision; **tengo que ~ el tema con detenimiento** I must give this matter some thought

2 (= *tener en cuenta*) **considerando lo que cuesta, la calidad podría ser mejor** considering what it costs, the quality could be better; **considera que ésta puede ser tu última oportunidad** bear in mind that this could be your last chance

3 (= *creer*) **~ algo/a algn (como)** + ADJ to consider sth/sb to be + *adj*; **lo considero imposible** I consider it (to be) impossible; **se le considera culpable del robo** he is believed to be *o* considered to be guilty of the robbery; **se le considera como uno de los grandes pintores de este siglo** he is considered (to be) *o* regarded as one of the great painters of this century; **lo considero hijo mío** I look on him *o* regard him as my own son; **~ que** to believe that, consider that; **considero que deberíamos hacer algo** I believe *o* consider that we should do something

4 (*Jur*) **considerando...** whereas ... (*word with which each item in a judgement begins*)

Ⓑ **considerarse** VPR to consider o.s.; **yo me considero bastante guapo** I consider myself quite good-looking; **me considero una persona normal** I consider myself (to be) a normal person

consigna SF 1 (= *orden*) order; **seguir** *o* **cumplir las ~s del Gobierno** to follow government orders ► **consignas de vuelo** operating instructions for a flight, operational orders for a flight

2 (= *eslogan*) slogan

3 [*de equipaje*] left-luggage office, checkroom (*EEUU*) ► **consigna automática** left-luggage locker

consignación SF 1 (*Com*) consignment, shipment

2 (*Fin*) allocation

3 (*Méx Jur*) remand

consignador SM consignor

consignar ▸conjug 1a◂ VT 1 (*Com*) to send, dispatch (**a** to)

2 (*Fin*) (= *asignar*) to assign (**para** to, for); [+ *créditos*] to allocate

3 (= *registrar*) to record, register; (= *escribir*) to set down, state; **olvidé ~ mi nombre** I forgot to write my name in, I forgot to state my name; **el hecho no quedó consignado en ningún libro** the fact was not recorded *o* set down in any book

4 (*CAm, Méx Jur*) to remand, hold for trial

consignatario/a SM/F 1 (*Com*) consignee; (*Náut*) broker, agent

2 (*Jur*) trustee

3 [*de carta*] recipient, addressee

consigo[1] *ver* **conseguir**

consigo[2] PRON 1 (= *con él*) with him; (= *con ella*) with her; (= *con uno mismo*) with you, with one; (= *con usted*) with you; (= *con ellas, ellos*) with them; **siempre lleva ~ un paraguas** he always carries an umbrella with him; **siempre hay que llevar un pañuelo ~** you *o* (*más frm*) one should always carry a handkerchief; **¿tienen su pasaporte ~?** do you have your passports with you?; **mis hermanas no llevaban dinero ~** my sisters didn't have any money with *o* on them; **llevar** *o* **traer algo ~: la separación llevó** *o* **trajo ~ terribles consecuencias** the separation had terrible consequences; **el acuerdo llevará** *o* **traerá ~ un incremento de las ventas** the agreement will result in increased sales; ✦***MODISMO*** **no tenerlas todas ~: lo preparó todo bien y aun así no las tenía todas ~** he prepared it all well enough but he still wasn't quite sure about it

2 **~ mismo** with himself; **estaba contento ~ mismo** he was pleased with himself; **vive en paz ~ misma** she is at peace with herself; **hablaba ~ misma** she was talking to herself; **no puede ser amable quien no está contento ~ mismo** you can't be nice to others when you are not happy with yourself; **no son sinceros ~ mismos** they are not being honest with themselves; **son muy exigentes ~ mismos** they ask a lot of themselves

consiguiente ADJ 1 (= *resultante*) consequent, resulting

2 **por ~** consequently

consiguientemente ADV consequently, therefore

consistencia SF consistence, consistency

consistente ADJ 1 [*materia*] (= *sólido*) solid, firm, tough; (= *espeso*) thick

2 [*argumento*] sound, valid

3 **~ en** consisting of

4 [*persona, conducta*] consistent

consistir ▸conjug 3a◂ VI 1 **~ en** (= *componerse de*) to consist of; **la decoración consiste en un cuadro y un jarrón** the decoration consisted of a picture and a vase; **este periódico consiste en varias secciones fijas** this newspaper is made up of various regular sections

2 **~ en** (= *ser*): **el juego consiste en adivinar palabras** the object of the game is to guess words; **su misión consiste en aclarar el problema** her task is to solve the problem; **su atractivo consiste en su timidez** her shyness is what makes her attractive; **el secreto** *o* **truco consiste en añadir un poco de vino** the secret lies in adding a little wine; **todo consiste en saber qué es lo importante** it's all a question of knowing what's important; **¿en qué consiste el trabajo?** what does the job involve *o* entail?; **¿en qué consiste para ti la democracia?** what does democracy mean for you?; **su política consiste en decir cosas impresionantes** his policy consists of saying things to impress

consistorial ADJ 1 (*Rel*) consistorial

2 **casa ~** town hall

consistorio SM 1 (*Rel*) consistory

2 (*Pol*) town council; (= *edificio*) town hall

consocio SMF fellow member; (*Com*) copartner, associate

consola SF 1 (= *mesa*) console table

2 (*Inform, Mús*) console ► **consola de mandos** control console ► **consola de videojuegos** games console

consolación SF consolation

consolador Ⓐ ADJ consoling, comforting

Ⓑ SM (*sexual*) dildo

consolar ▸conjug 1l◂ Ⓐ VT to console, comfort; **me consuela de no haber ido** it's one consolation for not having gone

Ⓑ **consolarse** VPR to console o.s. (**por** about)

consolatorio ADJ consolatory

consolidación SF consolidation

consolidar ▸conjug 1a◂ Ⓐ VT 1 (= *afianzar*) to consolidate, strengthen; **hemos consolidado nuestra amistad** we've strengthened our friendship; **una democracia consolidada** a consolidated democracy

2 (*Arquit*) to shore up; **~ la estructura del edificio** to shore up the structure of the building

3 (*Fin*) to fund

Ⓑ **consolidarse** VPR strengthen

consomé SM consommé, clear soup

consonancia SF 1 (= *conformidad*) **en ~ con** in accordance *o* harmony with

2 (*Mús*) harmony, consonance (*frm*)

3 (*Literat*) consonance, rhyme

consonante Ⓐ ADJ 1 (*Mús*) harmonious, consonant (*frm*)

2 (*Ling*) consonantal

3 (*Literat*) rhyming

Ⓑ SF (*Ling*) consonant

consonántico ADJ consonantal

consonar ▸conjug 1l◂ VI 1 (*Mús*) (*tb fig*) to be in harmony, harmonize

2 (*Literat*) to rhyme (**con** with)

consorciarse ▸conjug 1b◂ VPR to form a consortium *o* syndicate, go into partnership

consorcio SM 1 (*Com*) consortium, syndicate

2 (= *unión*) relationship

3 [*de circunstancias*] conjunction

consorte SMF 1 (= *esposo/a*) consort, spouse; **príncipe ~** prince consort

2 (= *compañero*) partner, companion

3 **consortes** (*Jur*) accomplices

conspicuo ADJ eminent, famous

conspiración SF conspiracy

conspirador(a) SM/F conspirator

➤ LENGUA Y USO: considerar A1 53.2

conspirar ▸conjug 1a◂ VI to conspire, plot (**con** with; **contra** against); **~ para hacer algo** to conspire to do sth

conspirativo ADJ conspiratorial

constancia SF [1] (= *perseverancia*) perseverance; **la ~ en los estudios le llevó al éxito** he achieved success through perseverance in *o* by persevering at his studies
[2] (= *evidencia*) **no existe ~ de ello** there is no record of it; **escribo para dar** *o* **dejar ~ de estos hechos** I am writing to put these facts on record; **quiso dejar ~ de su visita** she wanted to leave some token of her visit; **quiero que quede ~ de mi intervención** I want my contribution to be put *o* go on record; **tengo ~ de que todo es cierto** I have proof that it is all true
[3] (*LAm*) (= *comprobante*) documentary proof, written evidence

constante Ⓐ ADJ [1] (= *continuado*) constant; **la búsqueda ~ de la verdad** the constant search for truth; **un día de lluvia ~** a day of constant *o* persistent rain
[2] (= *frecuente*) constant; **recibía ~s advertencias de su jefe** she was getting constant warnings from her boss
[3] (= *perseverante*) [*persona*] persevering
[4] (*Fís*) [*velocidad, temperatura, presión*] constant
Ⓑ SF [1] (= *factor predominante*) **el mar es una ~ en su obra** the sea is a constant theme *o* an ever-present theme in his work; **el paro es una ~ en la economía española** unemployment is a permanent feature of the Spanish economy ► **constante histórica** historical constant
[2] (*Mat*) constant
[3] (*Med*) ► **constantes vitales** vital signs

constantemente ADV constantly

Constantino SM Constantine

Constantinopla SF Constantinople

Constanza SF Constance

constar ▸conjug 1a◂ VI [1] (= *ser evidente*) **consta que ...** it is a fact that ...; **me consta que ...** I have evidence that ...
[2] (= *aparecer, figurar*) **~ (en)** to appear (in), be given (in *o* on); **no consta en el catálogo** it isn't listed in the catalogue; **en el carnet no consta su edad** his age is not stated on the licence *o* (*EEUU*) license; **y para que así conste ...** and for the record ...; **que consten los hechos** let's put the record straight; **hacer ~** to put on record
[3] **que conste: que conste que no estoy de acuerdo** for the record, I disagree; **conste que yo no lo aprobé** let it be clearly understood that I did not approve; **que conste que lo hice por ti** believe me, I did it for your own good
[4] (= *componerse*) **~ de** to consist of, be composed of
[5] (*Literat*) to scan

constatable ADJ observable, evident; **es ~ que ...** it can be observed that ...

constatación SF confirmation, verification

constatar ▸conjug 1a◂ VT [1] (= *confirmar*) **estos datos constatan la existencia de vida en el planeta** this data proves the existence of life on the planet; **la autopsia constata que fue un ataque al corazón** the post mortem confirms that it was a heart attack; **pude ~ que era verdad** I was able to establish that it was true; **yo mismo pude ~ su calidad** I was able to see the quality of it for myself
[2] (= *afirmar*) to state; **—el presidente ha vuelto a ganar —constató el portavoz** "the president has won again," stated the spokesman

constelación SF constellation

constelado ADJ (*Meteo*) starry, full of stars; (*fig*) bespangled (**de** with)

consternación SF consternation, dismay

consternado ADJ **estar ~** to be dismayed; **dejar ~** = **consternar**

consternar ▸conjug 1a◂ Ⓐ VT to dismay
Ⓑ **consternarse** VPR to be dismayed (**con** by)

constipación SF = **constipado B**

constipado Ⓐ ADJ **estar ~** to have a cold
Ⓑ SM (*Med*) cold; **coger un ~** to catch a cold

constiparse ▸conjug 1a◂ VPR to catch a cold

constitución SF [1] (= *creación*) setting up; **vamos a proceder a la ~ de un comité de representantes** we are going to set up a committee of representatives
[2] (= *composición*) **a causa de la nueva ~ del gobierno** because of the make-up of the new cabinet; **la ~ del equipo hace pensar que el entrenador quiere un juego de ataque** the line-up suggests that the coach favours an attacking game
[3] (= *complexión*) constitution; **es de ~ débil** he has a weak constitution
[4] (*Pol*) constitution; **la Constitución** the Constitution; **jurar la Constitución** to swear allegiance to the Constitution

> **LA CONSTITUCIÓN ESPAÑOLA**
>
> *Since its first one of 1812, Spain has had no fewer than nine constitutions, including the current one, which brought stability to Spanish political life. Drawn up by the democratically elected* **UCD** *government, the* **Constitución de 1978** *symbolizes the spirit of reconciliation that prevailed during Spain's transition to democracy (1975-82), and has helped the country through a period of radical but peaceful change. The Constitution was ratified by Parliament on October 31, 1978 and approved by a referendum on December 6, finally receiving the royal assent on December 27, 1978. Apart from setting forth general principles on the nature of the Spanish state, it deals with such issues as the powers of the* **comunidades autónomas** *(regional governments), the role of the Crown in a parliamentary monarchy, and the status of Spain's different languages.*
>
> ⇨ *See also* COMUNIDAD AUTÓNOMA, LENGUAS COOFICIALES

constitucional ADJ constitutional

constitucionalidad SF constitutionality

constitucionalmente ADV constitutionally

constituir ▸conjug 3g◂ Ⓐ VT (*frm*) [1] (= *crear, fundar*) [+ *comité, asamblea*] to set up, constitute (*frm*); [+ *empresa*] to set up; **constituyeron una comisión de investigación** a committee of inquiry was set up *o* (*frm*) constituted; **constituyeron la empresa entre tres socios** the company was set up by three partners
[2] (= *estar formado por*) to make up, constitute; **el comité lo constituyen 12 miembros** the committee is made up *o* composed of 12 members, the committee comprises 12 members; **estar constituido por** to be made up of, be composed of, comprise
[3] (= *representar*) to constitute (*frm*); **la pesca constituye la principal riqueza de la región** fishing represents *o* (*frm*) constitutes the region's main source of wealth; **una llamada anónima no constituye delito** making an anonymous call does not constitute a crime (*frm*); **para mí constituye un gran honor** this represents a great honour for me; **eso no constituye ninguna molestia** that is no inconvenience at all; **los Beatles pronto llegaron a ~ una leyenda** the Beatles soon became a legend
[4] (= *nombrar*) **constituyeron la nación en república** the country was made a republic; **lo constituyó en heredero de su imperio** she designated him heir to her empire; **~ a algn en árbitro** to appoint sb as arbitrator
Ⓑ **constituirse** VPR [1] (= *formarse*) [*sociedad, empresa*] to be set up; [*estado*] to be constituted; **¿en qué fecha se constituyó la sociedad?** when was the company set up?
[2] (= *convertirse*) to become; **el pueblo se constituyó en un importante centro turístico** the town became a major tourist centre; **se han constituido en una amenaza para el proceso de paz** they have become a threat to the peace process; **~se como** *o* **en** (*Com, Pol*): **la factoría se ~á en empresa autónoma** the factory will be set up as *o* will become an independent company; **el país tiene derecho a ~se en estado independiente** the country has the right to constitute itself as *o* to become an independent state
[3] (*frm*) (= *personarse*) **~se en un lugar** to present o.s. at a place

constitutivo Ⓐ ADJ [*elemento*] constituent; **va contra los valores ~s del orden social** it goes against the fundamental values of social order; **ser ~ de delito** to constitute a crime
Ⓑ SM constituent element

constituyente Ⓐ ADJ [1] [*asamblea, congreso*] constituent
[2] [*elemento, sintagma*] constituent
Ⓑ SM [1] (= *elemento*) constituent; **uno de los ~s del sintagma nominal** one of the constituents *o* constituent parts of the noun phrase
[2] (*Pol*) constituent member

constreñir ▸conjug 3h, 3k◂ VT [1] (= *limitar*) to restrict
[2] (= *obligar*) **~ a algn a hacer algo** to compel *o* force *o* (*frm*) constrain sb to do sth
[3] (*Med*) to constrict

constricción SF constriction

construcción SF [1] (= *acción*) construction, building; **en (vía de) ~** under construction ► **construcción de buques** shipbuilding ► **construcción de carreteras** road building ► **construcción naval** shipbuilding
[2] (= *sector laboral*) construction industry
[3] (= *estructura*) structure
[4] (*Ling*) construction

constructivamente ADV constructively

constructivismo SM constructivism

constructivista ADJ, SMF constructivist

constructivo ADJ constructive

constructo SM construct

constructor(a) Ⓐ ADJ building, construction *antes de s*
Ⓑ SM/F builder ► **constructor(a) cinematográfico(a)** set designer, set builder ► **constructor(a) de buques** shipbuilder ► **constructor(a) naval** shipbuilder

constructora SF (*tb* **empresa ~**) construction company

construible ADJ suitable for building

construir ▸conjug 3g◂ Ⓐ VT 1 [+ *barco, carretera, hospital*] to build
2 (*Ling, Geom*) to construct
Ⓑ **construirse** VPR (*Ling*) **este verbo se construye con "en"** this verb takes "en"

consuegro/a SM/F father-in-law/mother-in-law of one's son/daughter

consuelda SF comfrey

consuelo SM solace, comfort; **llorar sin ~** to weep inconsolably; **premio de ~** consolation prize

consuetudinario ADJ 1 (= *usual*) habitual, customary; (*hum*) [*borracho*] hardened
2 **derecho ~** common law

cónsul SMF consul ► **cónsul general** consul general

consulado SM (= *cargo*) consulship; (= *sede*) consulate

consular ADJ consular; **Sección Consular** Consular Section

consulta SF 1 (= *pregunta*) enquiry; **para cualquier ~, llamen a partir de las cinco** if you have any enquiries, please call after five o'clock; **hice una ~ telefónica al banco** I telephoned the bank to make an enquiry; **¿le puedo hacer una ~?** can I ask you something?; **servicio de ~** enquiry service ► **consulta de saldo** statement request; *ver tb* **biblioteca 1**, **libro 1**, **obra 2.2**
2 (*Med*) (= *visita*) consultation; (= *local*) surgery, consulting room, office (*EEUU*); **horas de ~** *u* **horario de ~** surgery hours; **el pediatra pasa ~ a las tres** the paediatrician has a surgery *o* sees patients at three; **el doctor no pasa ~ a domicilio** the doctor does not make home visits
3 (*Pol*) (= *referéndum*) referendum ► **consulta electoral** elections *pl* ► **consulta popular** referendum, plebiscite
4 **consultas** (= *negociaciones*): **se llegó a un acuerdo tras intensas ~s** an agreement was reached after intense negotiations; **ronda** *o* **rueda de ~s** round of talks
5 (*Jur*) review
6 (*Inform*) enquiry

consultable ADJ **~ por todos** which can be consulted by anybody

consultación SF consultation

consultar ▸conjug 1a◂ Ⓐ VT 1 (= *pedir opinión*) to consult; **decidieron irse sin ~me** they decided to go without consulting me; **es mejor que consultes a un médico** you'd better go to *o* see a doctor; **~ algo con algn** to discuss sth with sb; **lo ~é con mi abogado** I'll discuss it with my lawyer; ✦**MODISMO** **~ algo con la almohada** to sleep on sth
2 [+ *diccionario, libro, base de datos, archivo*] to consult; **consulté las páginas web en gallego** I consulted the web pages in Galician; **consulta la palabra en el diccionario** look the word up in the dictionary; **consulté el saldo de mi cuenta** I checked my account balance
Ⓑ VI **~ con algn: no lo haré sin ~ antes contigo** I won't do it without discussing it with you first

consúlting [kon'sultin] SM (*pl* **consúltings** [kon'sultin]) business consultancy

consultivo ADJ consultative

consultor(a) Ⓐ SM/F consultant ► **consultor(a) en dirección de empresas** (*Com*) management consultant
Ⓑ SM (*Inform*) ► **consultor de ortografía** spellchecker

consultora SF consultancy, consultancy firm

consultoría SF consultancy, consultancy firm ► **consultoría de dirección**, **consultoría gerencial** management consultancy (firm)

consultorio SM 1 (*Med*) surgery, doctor's office (*EEUU*)
2 [*de abogado*] office
3 [*de revista*] (*tb* **~ sentimental**) problem page, agony column
4 (*Radio*) phone-in (*for listeners' queries*)

consumación SF 1 (*Jur*) commission, perpetration
2 [*de matrimonio*] consummation

consumado Ⓐ ADJ (= *perfecto*) consummate, perfect; (= *imbécil*) thorough, out-and-out
Ⓑ SM (‡) 1 (= *cosas robadas*) loot, swag*
2 (= *droga*) hash*

consumar ▸conjug 1a◂ VT 1 (= *acabar*) to complete; [+ *trato*] to close, complete
2 [+ *crimen*] to commit; [+ *asalto, robo*] to carry out
3 [+ *matrimonio*] to consummate
4 (*Jur*) [+ *sentencia*] to carry out
5 (*Andes, CAm*) (= *hundir*) to submerge

consumerismo SM = **consumismo**

consumible ADJ **bienes ~s** consumer goods

consumición SF 1 (= *acción*) consumption
2 (= *bebida*) drink; (= *comida*) food; **no pagó su ~** he did not pay for what he had (to eat/drink) ► **consumición mínima** cover charge

consumido ADJ 1 [*fruta*] shrivelled, shrunken
2 [*persona*] (= *flaco*) skinny
3 (= *tímido*) timid; (= *inquieto*) fretful, easily upset

consumidor(a) SM/F consumer; **productos al ~** consumer products ► **consumidor(a) de drogas** drug user, drug taker

consumir ▸conjug 3a◂ Ⓐ VT 1 [+ *comida, bebida, droga*] to consume (*frm*); **en este bar se consume más vino que cerveza** more wine than beer is drunk *o* (*frm*) consumed in this bar; **consúmase inmediatamente después de abierto** consume immediately after opening; **sólo consumo alimentos frescos** I only eat fresh food; **en casa no consumimos leche de cabra** we don't drink goat's milk at home; **no pueden sentarse aquí si no van a ~ nada** you can't sit here if you're not going to have anything to eat or drink; **consuma productos andaluces** buy Andalusian products; **~ preferentemente antes de …** best before …
2 [+ *energía, gasolina*] to use, consume (*frm*); **mi coche consume muy poco** my car uses very little fuel; **consume gran cantidad de gasolina en el despegue** it consumes vast quantities of fuel on take-off; **la moto consume cinco litros a los 100kms** the motorbike does 100kms to (every) five litres
3 [+ *tiempo*] to take up
4 (= *extinguir*) [+ *salud*] to destroy; **el cáncer lo está consumiendo** cancer is destroying him, he's being wasted away by cancer; **estos niños me están consumiendo la paciencia** these children are trying *o* taxing my patience, my patience is wearing thin with these children; **el tejado fue consumido por las llamas** the roof was consumed by the flames
5 (= *desesperar*) **los celos lo consumen** he is consumed *o* eaten up with jealousy; **su terquedad me consume** his stubbornness gets on my nerves
6 (*Andes, CAm*) (= *sumergir*) to submerge
Ⓑ VI 1 (= *comer*) to eat; (= *beber*) to drink; **por favor, váyase si no va a ~** please leave if you're not going to eat or drink
2 (= *gastar*) to consume; **el mercado nos impulsa a ~ sin parar** the market encourages us to consume constantly
Ⓒ **consumirse** VPR 1 [*líquido*] to boil away; [*salsa*] to reduce
2 [*vela, cigarro*] to burn down; **se le consumió el cigarro entre los dedos** the cigarette burned out between his fingers; **se le estaba consumiendo el cigarro mientras hablaba** his cigarette was burning down as he spoke
3 [*enfermo, anciano*] to waste away
4 [*tiempo*] to run out
5 (= *desesperarse*) **se consume de envidia al ver mis triunfos** he's green with envy at my success; **se consumía de pena tras la muerte de su hija** she was consumed with grief after the death of her daughter; **me consumía en deseos de abrazarlo** I had a burning desire to embrace him, I was consumed with a desire to embrace him (*liter*)

consumismo SM consumerism

consumista Ⓐ ADJ consumer *antes de s*, consumerist
Ⓑ SMF consumer

consumo SM 1 [*de productos*] consumption; **el ~ de bebidas alcohólicas** alcohol consumption; **una charla sobre el ~ de drogas** a talk on drug use; **ha aumentado nuestro ~ de gas** our gas consumption has gone up, we are using more gas; **ordenadores de bajo ~** low-energy computers; **bienes de ~** consumer goods; **fecha de ~ preferente** best-before date; **precios al ~** retail prices; **sociedad de ~** consumer society
2 **consumos** (*Fin*) municipal tax on food

consunción SF consumption

consuno: de ~ ADV with one accord

consustancial ADJ consubstantial; **ser ~ con** to be inseparable from, be all of a piece with

contabilidad SF (= *práctica*) accounting, book-keeping; (= *profesión*) accountancy; **yo llevo la ~** I keep the books; **libros de ~** account books; **"Contabilidad"** "Accounts", "Accounts Department" ► **contabilidad analítica** variable costing *o* (*EEUU*) pricing ► **contabilidad creativa** creative accountancy ► **contabilidad de costos** cost accounting ► **contabilidad de doble partida** double-entry book-keeping ► **contabilidad de gestión** management accounting ► **contabilidad de inflación** inflation accounting ► **contabilidad financiera** financial accounting ► **contabilidad por partida simple** single-entry book-keeping

contabilizable ADJ eligible for inclusion

contabilización SF accounting, accountancy

contabilizadora SF accounting machine, adding machine

contabilizar ▸conjug 1f◂ VT 1 (*Fin*) to enter in the accounts
2 (= *tener en cuenta*) to reckon with, take into account

contable Ⓐ ADJ countable
Ⓑ SMF (= *tenedor de libros*) book-keeper; (= *licenciado*) accountant

contactar ▸conjug 1a◂ VI ~ **con** to contact, get in touch with

contacto SM 1 (= *acto de tocar*) contact; **el ~ físico** physical contact; **entrar en ~ con algo** to come into contact with sth
2 (= *trato*) touch; **hace años que perdí ~ con ella** I lost touch with her years ago; **estar en ~ con algn** to be in touch with sb; **nos mantenemos en ~ por teléfono** we keep in touch by phone; **ponerse en ~ con algn** to get in touch with sb, contact sb
3 (*Aut*) ignition
4 (*Elec*) contact
5 (*Méx*) (= *enchufe*) plug
6 (= *encuentro*) meeting
7 (*Fot*) contact print
8 **contactos** (= *conocidos*) contacts; **sección de ~s** [*de un periódico*] contact section, contacts; **agencia de ~s** dating agency

contado Ⓐ ADJ (= *reducido*) **un ~ número de países** a small number of countries; **en contadas ocasiones** on rare occasions; **contadas veces** seldom, rarely; **son ~s los que ...** there are few who ...; **pero son contadísimos los que pueden** but those who can are very few and far between; ✦*MODISMO* **tiene los días ~s** his days are numbered
Ⓑ SM 1 (*Com*) **al ~** for cash, cash down; **lo pagué al ~** I paid cash for it; **pago al ~** cash payment; **precio al ~** cash price
2 **por de ~** (= *por supuesto*) naturally, of course; **tomar algo por de ~** to take sth for granted
3 (*Andes*) (= *plazo*) instalment, installment (*EEUU*)

contador(a) Ⓐ ADJ counting
Ⓑ SM/F 1 (*esp LAm Com*) book-keeper, accountant; (*Jur*) receiver
2 (*Andes*) (= *prestamista*) pawnbroker, moneylender
Ⓒ SM 1 (*Náut*) **~ (de navío)** purser
2 (*Téc*) meter ► **contador de agua** water meter ► **contador de aparcamiento** parking meter ► **contador de electricidad** electricity meter ► **contador de gas** gas meter ► **contador de revoluciones** tachometer ► **contador de taxi** taximeter ► **Contador Geiger** Geiger counter

contaduría SF 1 (= *profesión*) accountancy
2 (= *oficina*) accountant's office; (*Andes*) [*del prestamista*] pawnbroker's, pawnshop
3 (*Teat*) box office

contagiar ▸conjug 1b◂ Ⓐ VT 1 (*Med*) [+ *enfermedad*] to pass on, transmit (*frm*), give (**a** to); [+ *víctima*] to infect (**con** with); **no quiero ~te** I don't want to give it to you
2 (*fig*) (= *transmitir*) to infect (**con** with); **me ha contagiado su optimismo** his optimism has rubbed off on me
Ⓑ **contagiarse** VPR 1 (*Med*) [*enfermedad*] to be contagious, be catching; [*persona*] to become infected; **~se de algo** to become infected with sth, catch sth; **tiene la gripe y no quiere que los niños se contagien** he has (the) flu and doesn't want the children to catch it
2 (*fig*) (= *transmitirse*) to be contagious; **el mal ejemplo se contagia** a bad example is contagious *o* catching; **me contagié de alegría al verla tan contenta** I was overjoyed when I saw how happy she was

contagio SM 1 (*Med*) infection, contagion
2 (*fig*) contamination

contagioso ADJ 1 (*Med*) [*enfermedad*] contagious; [*enfermo*] infected, infectious
2 (*fig*) catching; [*risa*] infectious

contáiner SM container

contaje SM count, counting

contaminación SF 1 (*Meteo*) [*de aire, mar*] pollution; [*de alimentos, agua potable*] contamination ► **contaminación acústica** noise pollution ► **contaminación ambiental** environmental pollution ► **contaminación atmosférica** air pollution ► **contaminación del aire** air pollution
2 (*textual*) corruption; (*Literat*) influence

contaminador(a) SM/F polluter

contaminante SM pollutant

contaminar ▸conjug 1a◂ Ⓐ VT 1 [+ *aire, mar*] to pollute; [+ *alimentos, agua potable*] to contaminate; [+ *ropa*] to soil
2 [+ *texto*] to corrupt; (*Literat*) to influence, affect
3 (*Rel*) to profane
Ⓑ **contaminarse** VPR [*alimentos, agua potable*] to be contaminated, become contaminated (**con** with; **de** by); [*agua, aire*] to become polluted

contante ADJ **dinero ~ (y sonante)** cash

contar ▸conjug 1l◂ Ⓐ VT 1 (= *calcular*) [+ *objetos, números, puntos*] to count; [+ *dinero*] to count, count up; **estaba contando los minutos que quedaban para el final** I was counting the minutes till the end; **cuenta cuántos alumnos hay en la clase** count how many pupils there are in the class
2 (= *relatar*) to tell; **nos contó un cuento muy bonito** she told us a very nice story; **cuéntanos lo que ocurrió** tell us what happened; **¿qué les voy a ~ que ustedes no sepan?** what can I tell you that you don't already know?; **el paro está peor y la corrupción, ¿qué le voy a ~?** unemployment has got worse and as for corruption, what can I say?; **si pierdo el trabajo, ya me ~ás de qué vamos a vivir** you tell me what we'll live on if I lose my job; **¿y a mí qué me cuentas?** so what?; **¡a mi me lo vas a ~!** you're telling me!*, tell me about it!*; **se cuenta que ...** it is said that ...; ✦*MODISMO* **¡una obra que ni te cuento!*** one hell of a fine work*; *ver tb* **abuelo 1**
3 (= *tener la edad de*) **la Constitución española cuenta 20 años** the Spanish constitution is 20 years old; **María cuenta 32 años** María is 32 years of age
4 (= *incluir*) to count; **lo cuento entre mis amigos** I count him among my friends; **a mi ya me cuentan como adulto** I'm counted as an adult now; **seis en total, sin ~me a mí** six altogether, not counting me; **1.500 sin ~ las propinas** 1,500, excluding tips, 1,500, not counting tips; **se le cuenta entre los más ricos** he is reckoned among the richest
5 (= *tener en cuenta*) to remember, bear in mind; **cuenta que es más fuerte que tú** remember *o* don't forget he's stronger than you are
Ⓑ VI 1 (*Mat*) to count; **sabe ~ hasta 20** he can count (up) to 20; **~ con los dedos** to count on one's fingers; ✦*MODISMO* **parar de ~***: **hay dos sillas, una mesa y para ya de ~** there are two chairs, a table, and that's it
2 (= *relatar*) to tell; **luego te ~é** I'll tell you later; **ojalá tengas suerte con la entrevista de trabajo, ya me ~ás** I hope the job interview goes well, I look forward to hearing ali about it; **es muy largo de ~** it's a long story; ✦*MODISMO* **cuenta y no acaba (de hablar)** he never stops talking
3 (= *importar, valer*) to count; **aquí lo que cuenta es la ganancia final** what counts here is the final profit; **el último gol no cuenta** the last goal doesn't count; **este examen no cuenta para la nota final** this exam doesn't count towards the final mark; **~ por dos**: **los domingos una hora cuenta por dos** on Sundays one hour counts as two; **come tanto que cuenta por dos** he eats enough for two; ✦*MODISMO* **la intención es lo que cuenta** it's the thought that counts
4 **~ con** 4·1 (= *confiar en*) to count on; **cuenta conmigo** you can rely *o* count on me; **no cuentes con mi ayuda** don't count on my help; **cuento con que no llueva** I'm counting on it not raining
4·2 (= *tener presente*) **tienes que ~ con el mal estado de la carretera** you have to take into account *o* remember the bad state of the road; **lo calcularon sin ~ con nosotros** they worked it out without taking us into account; **cuenta con que es más fuerte que tú** bear in mind *o* remember he's stronger than you are; **no contábamos con eso** we hadn't bargained for that; **sin ~ con que ...** leaving aside the fact that ...
4·3 (= *incluir*) to count in; **cuenta conmigo para la cena** count me in for dinner; **lo siento, pero para eso no cuentes conmigo** I'm sorry but you can count me out of that; **no contéis con nosotros para el viernes, estaremos ocupados** don't expect us on Friday, we'll be busy
4·4 (= *tener*) to have; **el polideportivo cuenta con una piscina olímpica** the sports centre has *o* boasts an Olympic-size swimming pool; **cuenta con varias ventajas** it has a number of advantages; **una democracia que tan sólo cuenta con dieciséis años de existencia** a democracy that has only existed for sixteen years
Ⓒ **contarse** VPR 1 (*al saludar*) **¿qué te cuentas?*** how's things?*
2 **~se entre** (= *incluirse*): **me cuento entre sus admiradores** I count myself among his admirers, I consider myself one of his admirers; **su película se cuenta entre las nominadas al óscar** his film is amongst those nominated for an Oscar
3 **~se por** (= *calcularse*): **sus seguidores se cuentan por miles** he has thousands of supporters, his supporters number several thousand; **los muertos se cuentan por centenares** the dead number several hundred

contemplación SF 1 (= *observación*) (*gen*) contemplation
2 (= *meditación*) meditation
3 **contemplaciones** 3·1 (= *indulgencia*) in-

dulgence *sing*; **tener demasiadas contemplaciones con algn** to be too indulgent towards sb, be too soft on sb; **tratar a algn con contemplaciones** to treat sb leniently

3·2 (= *ceremonias*) **no andarse con contemplaciones** not to stand on ceremony; **sin contemplaciones** without ceremony; **no me vengas con contemplaciones** don't come to me with excuses

▼ **contemplar** ▸conjug 1a◂ Ⓐ VT 1 (= *observar*) [+ *paisaje, edificio, cuadro*] to gaze at, contemplate; **se pasa horas contemplando el mar** she spends hours gazing at *o* contemplating the sea; **contemplaba su imagen en el espejo** she gazed at *o* contemplated her reflection in the mirror; **contemplaba a Juan en silencio** she gazed at Juan in silence; **desde aquí se contempla el valle entero** from here you can see the whole valley; **desde aquí se contempla una vista espectacular** there is a spectacular view from here; **la exposición podrá ~se aquí en octubre** the exhibition can be seen here in October; **pude ~ la belleza de Elena** (*frm*) I was able to look on Elena's beauty

2 (= *analizar*) **debemos ~ su obra desde otra perspectiva** we must look at *o* consider his work from another perspective

3 (= *mimar*) to indulge; **no contemples tanto a tus hijos** don't indulge your children so much

4 (*frm*) (= *considerar*) [+ *idea, posibilidad*] to consider

5 [*ley, tratado*] to provide for; **el acuerdo contempla una subida del 3%** the agreement provides for an increase of 3%; **la ley contempla los casos siguientes** the law provides for the following cases

Ⓑ VI (*Rel*) to meditate

contemplativo ADJ 1 [*vida, persona*] contemplative

2 (= *indulgente*) indulgent (**con** towards)

contemporáneo/a ADJ, SM/F contemporary

contemporización SF (= *acomodación*) temporizing; (*Pol*) appeasement

contemporizador(a) Ⓐ ADJ excessively compliant

Ⓑ SM/F temporizer

contemporizar ▸conjug 1f◂ VI (= *acomodarse*) to be compliant, show o.s. ready to compromise; (*pey*) to temporize (**con** with); **~ con algn** to hedge with sb; (*Pol*) to appease sb

contención SF 1 (*Mil*) containing, containment; **muro de ~** retaining wall; **operación de ~** holding operation

2 (= *restricción*) restraint; **sin ~** freely, without restraint

3 (= *rivalidad*) contention

4 (*Jur*) suit

contencioso Ⓐ ADJ 1 (*Jur*) contentious

2 [*carácter*] captious; [*asunto*] contentious

Ⓑ SM (= *disputa*) dispute; (= *problema*) problem; (= *punto conflictivo*) point of disagreement

contender ▸conjug 2g◂ VI 1 (= *lidiar*) to contend (**con** with; **sobre** over); (= *competir*) to compete; **~ en unas oposiciones** to take part in a competitive examination

2 (*Mil*) to fight

contendiente Ⓐ ADJ contending

Ⓑ SMF contestant, contender

contenedor SM 1 (*gen*) container ▸ **contenedor de basura(s)** rubbish skip ▸ **contenedor de escombros** skip, builder's skip ▸ **contenedor de vidrio** bottlebank

2 (*Náut*) container ship

contener ▸conjug 2k◂ Ⓐ VT 1 (= *incluir*) to contain; **el maletín contenía explosivos** the suitcase contained explosives; **el libro contenía un capítulo dedicado a su vida** the book contained a chapter on her life; **"no contiene alcohol"** "alcohol-free", "does not contain alcohol"

2 (= *frenar*) [+ *gente, muchedumbre*] to contain, hold back; [+ *revuelta, epidemia, infección*] to contain; [+ *invasión, lágrimas, emoción*] to contain, hold back; [+ *aliento, respiración*] to hold; [+ *hemorragia*] to stop; [+ *bostezo*] to stifle; [+ *inflación*] to check, curb; [+ *precios, déficit, consumo*] to keep down; **para ~ la tendencia al alza de los precios** to check the tendency for prices to rise; **no pude ~ la risa** I couldn't help laughing

3 (*Cono Sur*) (= *significar*) to mean

Ⓑ **contenerse** VPR (= *controlarse*) to control o.s., restrain o.s.; **me contuve para no llorar** I controlled *o* restrained myself so as not to cry

contenerización SF containerization

contenerizar ▸conjug 1f◂ VT to containerize

contenido Ⓐ ADJ 1 [*persona*] restrained, controlled

2 [*risa, emoción*] suppressed

Ⓑ SM 1 [*de recipiente, paquete*] contents *pl*; **el ~ de la maleta** the contents of the suitcase; **alimentos con un alto ~ de proteínas** foods with a high protein content

2 [*de programa, proyecto*] content; **el ~ político de la campaña** the political content of the campaign

contenta SF 1 (*Com*) endorsement; (*Mil*) good-conduct certificate

2 (*LAm Jur*) release, acknowledgement

contentadizo ADJ (*tb* **bien ~**) easy to please; **mal ~** hard to please

contentamente ADV contentedly

contentamiento SM contentment

contentar ▸conjug 1a◂ Ⓐ VT 1 (= *complacer*) [+ *persona*] to please; (*frm*) [+ *deseo*] to satisfy; **decidió casarse para ~ a su familia** he decided to get married to please his family; **~ los deseos de todos** to satisfy everyone's wishes; **para ~ al cliente** to keep the customer happy

2 (*LAm*) (= *reconciliar*) **~ a dos personas** to reconcile two people

3 (*Com*) to endorse

Ⓑ **contentarse** VPR 1 **~se con algo: se contenta con cualquier cosa** he's happy with anything; **Israel no se contentó con esa enmienda** Israel was not satisfied with that amendment; **no quedaba vino, y me tuve que ~ con agua** there was no wine left so I had to make do with water; **el atleta se tuvo que ~ con un segundo puesto** the athlete had to be content with *o* had to settle for second place; **no se contenta con orientarme, sino que trata de controlarme** he's not content with just giving me guidance, he tries to control me; **me contento con saber que estás bien** I'm happy just knowing that you are all right; **me contento con que lo termines a tiempo** I'll be happy if you just finish it on time

2 (*LAm*) (= *reconciliarse*) **~se con algn** to become reconciled with sb

▼ **contento** Ⓐ ADJ 1 (= *alegre, feliz*) happy; **¿estás ~?** are you happy?; **estoy contenta de vivir aquí** I'm happy living here; **viven muy ~s en su casita del campo** they live very happily in their country cottage; **se pone muy ~ cuando viene la abuela** he's always pleased when his grandmother comes; **estar loco de ~** ◊ **no caber en sí de ~** (*frm*) to be overjoyed; ✦***MODISMO*** **estar más ~ que unas castañuelas** *o* **que unas pascuas** to be as happy as a sandboy

2 (= *satisfecho*) pleased; **no ~s con sus excusas, lo denunciaron** not satisfied with his excuses, they reported him; **estar ~ con algn/algo** to be pleased with sb/sth; **estoy contenta con mis hijos** I'm pleased with my children; **están muy ~s con el coche** they're very pleased with the car; **estar ~ de hacer algo** to be happy *o* pleased to do sth; **dejar a algn ~** to satisfy sb; **quedar ~ con algo** to be satisfied with sth; **no quedaron ~s con el trabajo** they were not satisfied with the work; **le das una golosina y se queda tan ~** he's perfectly happy if you give him a sweet; **lo escribió con b y se quedó tan ~** he wrote it with a b but didn't seem to let that bother him; **tener ~ a algn** to keep sb happy *o* satisfied; **contenta me tienes, hijo** (*iró*) oh, wonderful!, oh, great!*

3 (= *bebido*) merry; **no me emborraché, pero estaba ~** *o* **contentillo** I didn't get drunk but I was quite merry

Ⓑ SM (*frm*) (= *alegría*) happiness, joy; **el anuncio fue motivo de ~** the announcement gave cause for happiness *o* joy

contentura SF (*CAm, Caribe*) = **contento B**

conteo SM count, counting; (*Méx Dep*) count

contera SF 1 (*Téc*) tip, metal tip, ferrule

2 (= *remate*) little extra, small addition; **por ~** to crown *o* cap it all, as a final blow

contertuliano/a SM/F, **contertulio/a** SM/F fellow member (*of a social set*) ▸ **contertulianos/as de café** café companions

contesta SF (*LAm*) answer

contestable ADJ questionable, debatable

contestación SF 1 (= *respuesta*) answer, reply; **mala ~** sharp retort, piece of backchat; **dejar una carta sin ~** to leave a letter unanswered

2 ▸ **contestación a la demanda** (*Jur*) defence *o* (*EEUU*) defense plea

3 (*Pol*) protest; **movimiento de ~** protest movement

contestado ADJ contentious, controversial

contestador Ⓐ ADJ (*LAm*) cheeky, saucy, sassy (*EEUU**)

Ⓑ SM ▸ **contestador automático** answering machine, answerphone, Ansaphone®

contestar ▸conjug 1a◂ Ⓐ VT 1 (= *responder*) to answer, reply; [+ *saludo*] to return; **contesté todas las preguntas** I answered all the questions; **~ al teléfono** to answer the telephone; **~ una carta** to reply to a letter; **le pregunté que si vendría y contestó que sí** I asked him if he would come and he replied that he would

2 (= *replicar*) to answer back; **no le contestes así a tu madre** don't answer your mother back like that, don't talk back to your mother like that

➤ LENGUA Y USO: **contemplar A4** 35.3 **contento A2** 41

3 (*Jur*) to corroborate, confirm
Ⓑ VI 1 (= *responder*) to answer, reply; **abstenerse de ~** to make no reply; **no contestan** there's no reply *o* answer
2 (*Pol*) to protest

contestatario/a Ⓐ ADJ rebellious; **movimiento ~** protest movement
Ⓑ SM/F non-conformist

contesto SM (*Andes, Cono Sur, Méx††*) answer, reply

contestón* ADJ given to answering back, argumentative

contexto SM 1 (= *marco*) context; **sacar algo (fuera) de ~** to take sth out of context; **~ histórico** historical context
2 (*Téc*) web, tangle

contextualizar ▸conjug 1f◂ VT to provide a context for, set in a context

contextura SF 1 (*Téc*) contexture
2 (*Anat*) build, physique

contienda SF contest, struggle

contigo PRON with you; (*Rel*) with thee; **quiero ir ~** I want to go with you; **necesito hablar ~** I need to talk to you; **estamos ~** we're behind you, we're on your side

contigüidad SF contiguity

contiguo ADJ adjacent, contiguous (*frm*) (**a** to); **en un cuarto ~** in an adjoining room

continencia SF continence

continental ADJ continental

continentalidad SF continental nature

continente Ⓐ ADJ continent
Ⓑ SM 1 (*Geog*) continent; **el viejo ~** Europe, the Old World
2 (= *recipiente*) container
3 (= *aspecto*) bearing; **de ~ distinguido** with an air of distinction, with a distinguished air; **de ~ duro** harsh-looking

contingencia SF (*gen*) contingency; (= *posibilidad*) eventuality, possibility

contingentación SF quota system

contingentado ADJ subject to a quota system

contingentar ▸conjug 1a◂ VT to make subject to quotas

contingente Ⓐ ADJ contingent
Ⓑ SM 1 (*Mil*) contingent
2 (*Com*) quota ▸ **contingente de importación** import quota
3 = **contingencia**

continuación SF 1 [*de acto, proceso, calle*] continuation; **el instinto de supervivencia asegura la ~ de la especie** the survival instinct ensures the continuation of the species; **el mal tiempo impidió la ~ del desfile** the bad weather prevented the parade from continuing; **mañana veremos la ~ de la serie** the series will be continued tomorrow; **esta película es la ~ de Rocky** this film is the sequel to Rocky
2 **a ~** (*en conversación*) next; (*en texto*) below; **a ~ viene una canción dedicada a todos nuestros oyentes** coming up next, a song dedicated to all our listeners; **el fin, como veremos a ~, justifica los medios** the end, as we shall now see, justifies the means; **a ~ vamos a presentarles a Margarita Pracatán** and now I would like to welcome Margarita Pracatán; **el poeta habló a ~ de su nuevo libro** the poet went on to speak about his new book, next the poet spoke about his new book; **según se expone a ~** as stated below
3 **a ~ de** following, after; **a ~ del sorteo ofrecerán una rueda de prensa** following *o* after the draw, they will give a press conference; **se sentaron uno a ~ del otro** they sat down one after another

continuadamente ADV continually

continuado Ⓐ ADJ continual
Ⓑ SM (*Cono Sur*) *a cinema showing films in continuous performance*

continuamente ADV 1 (= *repetidamente*) constantly, continually; **el teléfono sonaba ~** the telephone was ringing constantly *o* continually
2 (= *sin interrupción*) constantly, continuously; **el prisionero ha de ser vigilado ~** the prisoner has to be watched constantly *o* continuously

continuar ▸conjug 1e◂ Ⓐ VT to continue; **el tren continuó su marcha** the train continued its journey; **continuó sus estudios en Barcelona** she continued her studies in Barcelona; **~emos la clase mañana** we will go on with *o* continue the lesson tomorrow; **continuó su vida como antes** he went on with *o* continued with his life as before
Ⓑ VI 1 [*historia, espectáculo, guerra*] to continue, go on; **la búsqueda continuó durante toda la noche** the search continued *o* went on all night; **continúe, por favor** please continue, please go on; **la serie continúa la semana que viene** the series continues next week; **"~á"** "to be continued"; **pase lo que pase, la vida continúa** come what may, life goes on
2 (*en una situación*) **la puerta continúa cerrada** the door is still shut, the door remains shut (*frm*); **continúa muy grave** she is still in a critical condition, she remains in a critical condition (*frm*); **continúa en el mismo puesto de trabajo** she is still in the same post, she remains in the same post (*frm*); **continuaba en Noruega** he was still in Norway; **~ con algo** to continue with sth, go on with sth; **continuó con su trabajo** he continued with *o* went on with his work; **Pablo continúa con Irene** Pablo is still (together) with Irene; **~ con salud** to be still in good health, remain in good health (*frm*); **~ haciendo algo**: **continuó leyendo** she continued to read *o* reading, she went on reading; **la policía ~á investigando el caso** the police are to continue *o* go on investigating the case; **a pesar de todo, continúa diciendo lo que piensa** in spite of everything, she continues to speak her mind *o* she still speaks her mind; **continúa lloviendo** it's still raining; **continuaba trabajando para ellos** he still worked for them; **en cualquier caso continúo siendo optimista** in any case, I remain optimistic *o* I am still optimistic
3 [*camino, carretera*] to continue, go on, carry on; **el camino continúa hasta la costa** the road continues *o* goes on *o* carries on (all the way) to the coast

continuidad SF 1 (= *permanencia*) continuity; **el nuevo presidente supondrá una cierta ~ política** the new president will represent a certain political continuity
2 (= *continuación*) continuation; **estas elecciones serán cruciales para la ~ del proceso de paz** these elections will be crucial for the continuation of the peace process; **su ~ en el equipo está fuera de dudas** his continuation in the team is beyond doubt, there is no doubt whatsoever that he will remain *o* stay in the team
3 (*Cine, TV*) continuity

continuismo SM (*Pol*) preservation of the status quo

continuista SMF *person who maintains the status quo*

continuo Ⓐ ADJ 1 (= *ininterrumpido*) [*línea, fila*] continuous; [*dolor, movimiento, crecimiento*] constant, continuous; [*pesadilla, molestia*] constant; **marque el número cuando oiga una señal continua** dial the number when you hear a continuous tone; **la presencia continua de los militares lo hacía todo más difícil** the constant *o* continuous presence of the soldiers made everything more difficult; *ver tb* **evaluación 2**, **sesión 3**
2 (= *frecuente, repetido*) [*llamadas, amenazas, críticas, cambios*] constant, continual; **no aguanto sus continuas quejas** I can't bear his constant *o* continual complaining
3 (*Fís*) [*movimiento*] perpetual
4 (*Elec*) [*corriente*] direct
5 (*Ling*) continuous
6 **de ~** = **continuamente**
Ⓑ SM (*Fís*) continuum

contonearse ▸conjug 1a◂ VPR [*hombre*] to swagger; [*mujer*] to swing one's hips, wiggle one's hips

contoneo SM [*de hombre*] swagger; [*de mujer*] hipswinging, wiggle

contorcerse ▸conjug 2b y 2h◂ VPR to writhe, twist

contorno SM 1 (= *perfil*) outline; (*Geog*) contour; [*de moneda*] edge
2 (= *medida*) girth; **el ~ de cintura es de 26 pulgadas** her waist measurement is 26 inches; **el ~ de un árbol** the girth of a tree
3 **contornos** neighbourhood *sing*, neighborhood *sing* (EEUU), surrounding area *sing*; **Caracas y sus ~s** Caracas and its environs; **en estos ~s** in these parts, hereabouts

contorsión SF contortion; **hacer contorsiones** to writhe

contorsionarse ▸conjug 1a◂ VPR to contort o.s.

contorsionista SMF contortionist

Contra SF **la ~** (*Nic Hist*) the Contras *pl*

contra Ⓐ PREP 1 (*indicando oposición*) against; **no tengo nada ~ ti** I have nothing against you; **son cinco ~ uno** it's five against one; **una campaña ~ la discriminación** a campaign against discrimination; **el Sevilla juega ~ el Betis** Seville are playing (against) Betis; **un ataque ~ objetivos militares** an attack on military targets; **unas pastillas ~ el mareo** some (anti-)travel sickness pills; **~ la opinión de la mayoría, yo me opongo** contrary to the opinion of the majority, I oppose it; **en ~**: **¿quién está en ~?** who is against?; **tres votos a favor y dos en ~** three votes in favour and two against; **lo tenemos todo en ~** the odds are stacked against us; **tengo a toda la familia en ~** the whole family is against me; **el Barcelona tenía el marcador en ~** the score was not in Barcelona's favour; **en ~ de algo** against sth; **estoy en ~ de la subida de los impuestos** I'm against an increase in taxes; **en ~ de lo que habíamos pensado** contrary to what we had thought; **por ~** on the other hand

➤ LENGUA Y USO: **continuación 2** 53.2 **contra A1** 39.2

[2] (*indicando posición*) against; **apoyó la bici ~ la pared** she leaned the bike against the wall; **me abrazó fuerte ~ su pecho** she hugged me tightly to her breast
[3] (*indicando dirección*) against; **fue muy cansado remar ~ la corriente** it was very tiring rowing against the current; **se chocó ~ la valla** he crashed into the fence
[4] (*Com, Fin*) **cobrará el dinero ~ entrega del boleto ganador** you will receive the money when you produce the winning ticket; *ver tb* **reembolso**
Ⓑ SF [1] (*) (= *contraria*) **hacer la ~ a algn: no me hagas más la ~** stop being so obstructive, stop taking the opposite line all the time; **llevar la ~ a algn** to contradict sb; **no le gusta que le lleven la ~** he doesn't like to be contradicted; **¿por qué siempre tienes que llevar la ~?** why do you always have to be so contrary?
[2] (*LAm Med*) antidote
[3] (*Bridge*) double
Ⓒ SM (= *inconveniente*) disadvantage, drawback; **la fama también tiene sus ~s** fame also has its disadvantages *o* drawbacks; *ver tb* **pro A1**
Ⓓ EXCL (*) damn it*; **¡ya me has confundido otra vez, ~!** now you've got me all mixed up again, damn it!*

contra... PREF counter-..., contra...; **~manifestación** counter-demonstration; **~propaganda** counter-propaganda

contraanálisis SM follow-up test, counter-test

contrabajista SMF [*de orquesta*] double-bass player; [*de rock*] bass guitarist

contrabajo Ⓐ SM [1] (= *instrumento*) double bass
[2] (= *cantante, voz*) low bass, contrabasso
Ⓑ SMF (= *músico*) double bass player, double bassist

contrabalancear ▸conjug 1a◂ VT to counterbalance

contrabalanza SF counterbalance

contrabandear ▸conjug 1a◂ VI to smuggle, live by smuggling

contrabandista SMF smuggler ► **contrabandista de armas** gunrunner

contrabando SM [1] (= *actividad*) smuggling; **introducir** *o* **pasar algo de ~** to smuggle sth in; **lo trajeron al país de ~** they smuggled it into the country; **géneros de ~** smuggled goods; **amores de ~** (*fig*) clandestine love affairs ► **contrabando de armas** gun-running ► **contrabando de drogas** drug smuggling
[2] (= *mercancías*) contraband, smuggled goods *pl*

contracampaña SF counter-campaign

contracargo SM counter-charge

contracarro ADJ INV **defensas ~** anti-tank defences, anti-tank defenses (*EEUU*)

contracción SF [1] [*de una enfermedad*] contraction
[2] [*de compromiso, deuda*] contracting; [*de matrimonio*] contraction (*frm*)
[3] [*de músculo, metal*] contraction
[4] (*Ling*) contraction

contracepción SF contraception ► **contracepción de barrera** barrier contraception ► **contracepción oral** oral contraception

contraceptivo ADJ, SM contraceptive

contrachapado Ⓐ ADJ **madera contrachapada** = **B**
Ⓑ SM plywood

contracifra SF key, key to a code

contracorriente SF cross-current; **ir a ~** (*lit*) to go against the current, go upstream; (*fig*) to go against the tide

contráctil ADJ contractile

contractual ADJ contractual

contractualmente ADV contractually

contractura SF muscular contraction

contracubierta SF back cover (*of book*)

contracultura SF counter-culture

contracultural ADJ alternative, of the counter-culture

contracurva SF second bend, bend the other way

contradecir ▸conjug 3o◂ Ⓐ VT to contradict
Ⓑ **contradecirse** VPR to contradict o.s.

contradicción SF contradiction; **espíritu de ~: había en él cierto espíritu de ~** there were certain contradictions in his nature; **eres el espíritu de la ~, ahora piensas una cosa y luego cambias de idea** you're so contrary, one minute you think one thing, the next minute you've changed your mind; **~ de** *o* **en los términos** contradiction in terms; **están en ~** they stand in contradiction to each other

contradictorio ADJ contradictory

contradique SM outer harbour *o* (*EEUU*) harbor wall

contradón SM reciprocal gift

contraefecto SM counter-effect

contraejemplo SM counter-example

contraempuje SM counter-thrust

contraer ▸conjug 2o◂ Ⓐ VT [1] [+ *enfermedad*] to contract (*frm*), catch
[2] [+ *compromiso*] to make, take on; [+ *obligación*] to take on, contract (*frm*); [+ *deuda, crédito*] to incur, contract (*frm*); **~ matrimonio (con algn)** to marry (sb); **contrajo parentesco con la familia real** (*frm*) she married into the royal family
[3] [+ *costumbre*] to get into, acquire (*frm*)
[4] [+ *músculo, nervio*] to contract; **tenía el rostro contraído por el dolor** his face was contorted *o* twisted with pain; **tanta pobreza le contrajo el corazón** such poverty made his heart bleed
[5] [+ *metal, objeto*] to cause to contract; **la humedad contrae las cuerdas** dampness causes the ropes to contract
Ⓑ **contraerse** VPR [1] [*músculo, nervio*] to contract; **se le quedó el músculo contraído** his muscle contracted o tightened
[2] [*objeto, material*] to contract
[3] (*Ling*) to contract

contraespionaje SM counter-espionage

contraetiqueta SF second label, label on the back

contrafallar ▸conjug 1a◂ VT to overtrump

contrafuerte SM [1] (*Arquit*) buttress; (*Geog*) spur; (*Mil*) outwork
[2] [*de calzado*] stiffener

contragambito SM counter-gambit

contragolpe SM [1] (= *reacción*) counter-blow
[2] (*Dep*) counter-attack

contragolpear ▸conjug 1a◂ VI to strike back

contrahacer ▸conjug 2r◂ VT [1] (= *copiar*) to copy, imitate
[2] [+ *moneda*] to counterfeit; [+ *documento, prueba*] to forge, fake; [+ *libro*] to pirate

contrahaz SM wrong side

contrahecho ADJ [1] (*Anat*) hunchbacked
[2] (= *falso*) [*moneda*] counterfeit; [*documento, prueba*] fake, faked, forged; [*libro*] spurious

contrahechura SF [*de moneda*] counterfeit; [*de documento, prueba*] forgery, fake; [*de libro*] pirated edition, spurious edition

contraído ADJ [1] (= *encogido*) contracted
[2] (*Andes*) (= *diligente*) diligent, industrious

contraimagen SF mirror image; (*pey*) negative image

contraincendios ADJ INV **aparato ~** fire-prevention apparatus, fire-alarm system

contraindicación SF counter-indication

contrainformación SF disinformation

contrainforme SM counter-report

contrainsurgencia SF counter-insurgency

contrainteligencia SF counter-intelligence

contrairritante SM counterirritant

contralmirante SM, **contraalmirante** SM rear admiral

contralor SM (*LAm*) comptroller

contraloría SF (*LAm*) treasury inspector's office

contralto Ⓐ ADJ contralto Ⓑ SMF (= *mujer*) contralto; (= *hombre*) counter tenor

contraluz SM view against the light; **a ~** against the light

contramaestre SMF (*Náut*) boatswain; (*Téc*) foreman/forewoman

contramandar ▸conjug 1a◂ VT to countermand

contramandato SM counter-order

contramanifestación SF counter-demonstration

contramano SM **ir a ~** to go the wrong way; **eso queda a ~** that's in the other direction

contramarcha SF [1] (*Mil*) countermarch
[2] (*Aut*) reverse; **dar ~ (a)** to reverse; (*fig*) to go into reverse

contramarchar ▸conjug 1a◂ VI to countermarch

contramatar ▸conjug 1a◂ Ⓐ VT **~ a algn** (*LAm*) to bang sb against the wall
Ⓑ **contramatarse** VPR [1] (*LAm*) (= *chocarse*) to crash into sth, collide with sth
[2] **~se de hacer algo** (*Méx*) to repent of having done sth, regret doing *o* having done sth

contramedida SF counter-measure

contramenaza SF, **contraamenaza** SF counter-threat

contranatural ADJ unnatural

contraofensiva SF counter-offensive

contraoferta SF counter-offer

contraorden SF countermand

contrapartida SF [1] (*Com, Fin*) balancing entry
[2] (= *compensación*) compensation; **pero como ~ añade que ...** but in contrast she adds that ...; **como ~ de** as *o* in compensation for, in return for; **dar algo de ~ de algo** to give sth in return for sth

contrapelo SM **a ~** the wrong way; **acariciar un gato a ~** to stroke a cat the wrong way; **todo lo hace a ~** he does everything the wrong way round; **intervino muy a ~** he spoke up in a most unfortunate way

contrapesar ▸conjug 1a◂ VT [1] (= *hacer contrapeso*) to counterbalance
[2] (= *compensar*) to offset, compensate for

contrapeso SM [1] (*Téc*) counterpoise, counterweight; (*Com*) makeweight
[2] [*de equilibrista*] balancing pole
[3] (*fig*) counterweight

contrapié: **a ~** ADV **mi oponente me cogió a ~** my opponent caught me off-balance, my opponent wrongfooted me; **me pillaron a ~ al llegar antes de lo esperado** I was caught off-balance when they arrived earlier than expected

contrapoder SM anti-establishment movement

contraponer ▸conjug 2q◂ VT [1] (= *cotejar*) to compare, set against each other
[2] (= *oponer*) to oppose; **~ A a B** to set up A against B; **a esta idea ellos contraponen su teoría de que ...** against this idea they set up their theory that ...

contraportada SF back cover

contraposición SF [1] (= *cotejo*) comparison
[2] (= *oposición*) contrast, clash; **en ~ a** in contrast to; **pero en ~, ...** but on the other hand, ...

contraprestación SF compensation

contraproducente ADJ counterproductive; **tener un resultado ~** to have a boomerang effect, boomerang

contraproductivo ADJ counterproductive

contraprogramación SF competitive programming

contraprogramar ▸conjug 1a◂ VI to set competitive schedules

contrapropuesta SF counter-proposal

contrapuerta SF storm door

contrapuesto ADJ conflicting, opposing

contrapuntear ▸conjug 1a◂ VI (*Andes*) to compete in a verse duel; (*fig*) to compete

contrapunteo SM [1] (*Andes, Caribe, Cono Sur*) (= *riña*) argument, quarrel
[2] (*Andes, Cono Sur Literat*) improvised verse duel
[3] (*Andes, Caribe, Cono Sur*) (= *debate*) debate; **en ~** (*Andes*) in competition

contrapuntístico ADJ (*Mús*) contrapuntal; (*fig*) contrasting

contrapunto SM [1] (*Mús*) (*tb fig*) counterpoint
[2] (*LAm*) (= *concurso de poesía*) poetic competition with improvised verses; **de ~** in competition

contrargumento SM, **contraargumento** SM counter-argument

contrariado ADJ upset, annoyed, put out

contrariamente ADV **~ a lo que habíamos pensado** contrary to what we had thought

contrariar ▸conjug 1c◂ VT [1] (= *contradecir*) to contradict
[2] (= *oponer*) to oppose, go against; (= *dificultar*) to impede, thwart; **sólo lo hace por ~nos** he only does it to be contrary *o* awkward *o* difficult
[3] (= *fastidiar*) to vex, annoy

contrariedad SF [1] (= *obstáculo*) obstacle; (= *contratiempo*) setback, trouble; (= *pega*) snag, trouble
[2] (= *disgusto*) vexation, annoyance; **producir ~ a algn** to annoy sb
[3] (= *oposición*) contrary nature

▼**contrario/a** Ⓐ ADJ [1] (= *rival*) [*partido, equipo*] opposing; **el abogado de la parte contraria** the opposing party's lawyer; **no llegaron nunca a la portería contraria** they never got near the other *o* opposing side's goal; **se pasó al bando ~** he went over to the other *o* opposing side
[2] (= *opuesto*) [*extremo, efecto, significado, sexo*] opposite; **tuvo el resultado ~ al deseado** it had the opposite of the desired effect; **mi opinión es contraria a la vuestra** I have the opposite opinion to you; **soy ~ al aborto** I am opposed to *o* against abortion; **se mostraron ~s al acuerdo** they came out against the agreement, they were opposed to the agreement; **su actitud es contraria a los intereses del país** his attitude is against *o* contrary to the nation's interests; **dirección contraria**: **tomamos la dirección contraria** we went in the opposite direction; **lo multaron por ir en dirección contraria** he was fined for travelling in the wrong direction; **intereses ~s** conflicting *o* opposing interests; **pie ~**: **se puso el zapato en el pie ~** she put her shoe on the wrong foot; **sentido ~**: **un coche que venía en sentido ~** a car coming in the opposite direction; **el portavoz se expresó en sentido ~** the spokesperson expressed the opposite view; **en sentido ~ a las agujas del reloj** anti-clockwise; **viento ~** headwind; *ver tb* **caso 1.2**
[3] (*en locuciones*) **al ~** on the contrary, quite the opposite; **no me disgusta la idea, al ~, me encanta** I don't dislike the idea, on the contrary *o* quite the opposite, I think it would be wonderful; **—¿te aburres? —¡que va, al ~!** "are you bored?" — "no way, quite the opposite!"; **se puso el jersey al ~** he put his jumper on inside out; **antes al ~** ◊ **muy al ~** (*frm*) on the contrary; **al ~ de**: **todo salió al ~ de lo previsto** everything turned out the opposite of what we expected; **al ~ de lo que creíamos, hizo muy buen tiempo** contrary to what we thought, the weather turned out very nice; **siempre va al ~ de todo el mundo** she always has to be different to everyone else, she always does the opposite to everyone else; **al ~ que** *o* **de ella, yo no estoy dispuesto a aguantar** unlike her, I'm not willing to put up with it; **lo ~**: **¿qué es lo ~ de alto?** what is the opposite of tall?; **nunca he dicho lo ~** I never said anything else *o* different; **soy inocente, hasta que no se demuestre lo ~** I am innocent until proven otherwise; **a mí me pasa lo ~ que a ti** for me it's different than for you; **de lo ~** otherwise, or else; **salga o, de lo ~, llamaré a la policía** please leave, otherwise *o* or else I'll call the police; **por el ~**: **los inviernos, por el ~, son muy fríos** the winters, on the other hand *o* on the contrary, are very cold; **parece ir todo bien, y por el ~, la situación es muy complicada** it all appears to be going well, when in fact the situation is rather difficult; **todo lo ~** quite the opposite, quite the reverse; **—¿es feo? —no, todo lo ~** "is he ugly?" — "no, quite the opposite *o* reverse"; **no hay descenso de precios, sino todo lo ~** prices are not going down, quite the opposite *o* reverse, in fact; **es todo lo ~ de su marido** she is the exact opposite of her husband; **ha sucedido todo lo ~ de lo que esperábamos** exactly the opposite of what we expected has happened
Ⓑ SM/F opponent
Ⓒ SM (= *opuesto*) opposite; **¿cuál es el ~ del negro?** what is the opposite of black?
Ⓓ SF ✦*MODISMO* **llevar la contraria**: **¿por qué siempre tienes que llevar la contraria?** why do you always have to be so contrary?; **siempre me lleva la contraria en todo** he always contradicts me about everything; **no le gusta que le lleven la contraria** he doesn't like to be contradicted

contrarreembolso SM cash on delivery

Contrarreforma SF Counter-Reformation

contrarreloj Ⓐ ADV against the clock
Ⓑ ADJ **prueba ~** = C
Ⓒ SF time trial

contrarréplica SF rejoinder

contrarreplicar ▸conjug 1g◂ VI to answer back

contrarrestar ▸conjug 1a◂ VT [1] (= *resistir*) to resist; (= *oponerse*) to oppose
[2] (= *compensar*) to counteract; **~ el efecto de una vacuna** to counteract the effect of a vaccine
[3] [+ *pelota*] to return

Contrarrevolución SF (*Nic Hist*) *armed opposition to the Sandinista government of the 1980s*

contrarrevolución SF counter-revolution

contrarrevolucionario/a ADJ, SM/F counterrevolutionary

contrasentido SM [1] (= *contradicción*) contradiction; **aquí hay un ~** there is a contradiction here
[2] (= *disparate*) piece of nonsense; (= *inconsecuencia*) inconsistency; **es un ~ que él actúe así** it doesn't make sense for him to act like that

contraseña SF [1] (= *seña*) countersign, secret mark
[2] (*Mil, Inform*) password
[3] (*Teat*) (*tb* **~ de salida**) pass-out ticket

contrastar ▸conjug 1a◂ Ⓐ VT [1] [+ *metal*] to assay; [+ *medidas*] to check; [+ *radio*] to monitor; [+ *hechos*] to check, confirm
[2] (= *resistir*) to resist
Ⓑ VI [1] (= *hacer contraste*) to contrast (**con** with)
[2] **~ a** *o* **con** *o* **contra** (= *resistir*) to resist; (= *hacer frente a*) to face up to

▼**contraste** SM [1] (= *oposición*) contrast; **en ~ con** in contrast to; **por ~** in contrast; **hacer ~ con** to contrast with ➤ **contraste de pareceres** difference of opinion
[2] (*TV*) contrast
[3] [*de pesos y medidas*] (*tb* **marca del ~**) (= *sello*) hallmark; (= *acción*) assay; (= *persona*) inspector of weights and measures; (= *oficina*) weights and measures office

contrastivo ADJ (*Ling*) contrastive

contrata SF contract

contratacar ▸conjug 1g◂ VT, VI, **contraatacar** ▸conjug 1g◂ VT, VI to counter-attack

contratación SF [1] [*de albañil, fontanero*] hiring; [*de abogado*] hiring, contracting (*frm*); [*de empleado*] recruitment; **se ha prohibido la ~ de jugadores extranjeros** the signing of foreign players has been banned; **este año ha habido diez mil nuevas contrataciones** this year there have been ten thousand new

➤ LENGUA Y USO: **contrario A3** 53.3 **contraste 1** 32.1

contracts
[2] [*de vehículo, servicio*] hiring, hire

contratante SMF (*Com*) contractor; (*Jur*) contracting party

contrataque SM, **contraataque** SM counter-attack

contratar ▸conjug 1a◂ VT [1] [+ *empleado*] to take on; [+ *albañil, abogado*] to hire; [+ *jugador, artista*] to sign (up); **le ~on por un año** they took her on for a year, they gave her a one-year contract; **contrató a dos fontaneros para arreglar las tuberías** he hired two plumbers to fix the pipes; **han contratado nuevo personal** they have taken on *o* recruited new staff; **me han contratado por horas** they have hired me by the hour
[2] (= *alquilar*) [+ *vehículo, servicio*] to hire
[3] [+ *obra*] to put out to contract

contratenor SM counter-tenor

contraterrorismo SM counter-terrorism

contraterrorista ADJ **medidas ~s** measures against terrorism, anti-terrorist measures

contratiempo SM [1] (= *revés*) setback, reverse; (= *accidente*) mishap, accident
[2] (*Mús*) **a ~** offbeat

contratista SMF contractor ► **contratista de obras** building contractor, builder

contrato SM contract (**de** for); **incumplimiento de ~** breach of contract; **renovación del ~** renewal of contract ► **contrato a precio fijo** fixed-price contract ► **contrato a término** forward contract ► **contrato basura** mickey-mouse contract ► **contrato bilateral** bilateral agreement ► **contrato de alquiler** [*de casa*] lease, leasing agreement; [*de coche*] rental contract, hire contract ► **contrato de arrendamiento** rental agreement ► **contrato de compraventa** contract of sale ► **contrato de mantenimiento** maintenance contract, service agreement ► **contrato de sociedad** deed of partnership ► **contrato de trabajo** contract of employment, contract of service ► **contrato verbal** verbal agreement

contratuerca SF locknut

contravalor SM exchange value

contravención SF contravention, violation

contraveneno SM antidote (**de** to)

contravenir ▸conjug 3r◂ Ⓐ VT to contravene, infringe
Ⓑ VI **~ a** to contravene, infringe

contraventana SF shutter

contrayendo *ver* **contraer**

contrayente SMF **los ~s** the bride and groom

contribución SF [1] (= *colaboración*) contribution; **su ~ a la victoria** his contribution to the victory, his part in the victory; **poner a ~** to make use of, put to use
[2] (*Fin*) tax; **contribuciones** taxes, taxation *sing*; **exento de contribuciones** tax-free, tax-exempt (EEUU); **pagar las contribuciones** to pay one's taxes ► **contribución directa** direct tax ► **contribución municipal** rates *pl* ► **contribución territorial urbana** rates *pl*

contribuidor(a) SM/F contributor

contribuir ▸conjug 3g◂ VI [1] (= *colaborar*) to contribute; **cada uno contribuyó con diez euros** each person contributed ten euros; **~ a hacer algo** to help to do sth; **~ al éxito de algo** to contribute to *o* help towards the success of sth
[2] (*Fin*) to pay, pay in taxes

contribuyente SMF taxpayer

contrición SF contrition

contrincante SMF opponent, rival

contristar ▸conjug 1a◂ (*frm*) Ⓐ VT to sadden
Ⓑ **contristarse** VPR to grow sad, grieve

contrito ADJ (*frm*) contrite

control SM [1] (= *dominio, vigilancia*) control; **nunca pierde el ~** he never loses control; **bajo ~** under control; **fuera de ~** out of control; **perder el ~** to lose control (of o.s.); **hacerse con el ~ de algo** to take control *o* charge of sth; **~ de** *o* **sobre sí mismo** self-control ► **control armamentista** arms control ► **control de alquileres** rent control ► **control de calidad** quality control ► **control de cambio** exchange control ► **control de costos** cost control ► **control de créditos** credit control ► **control de existencias** stock control ► **control de la circulación** traffic control ► **control de la demanda** demand management ► **control de la natalidad** birth control ► **control del tráfico** traffic control ► **control de natalidad** birth control ► **control de precios** price control ► **control nuclear** nuclear inspection ► **control presupuestario** budget control
[2] (= *inspección*) (*Jur*) inspection, check; (*Com, Fin*) audit, auditing
[3] (= *puesto*) (*tb* **~ de carretera**) roadblock; (*tb* **~ de frontera**) frontier checkpoint; **montar un ~** to set up a roadblock ► **control de pasaportes** passport inspection
[4] [*de un aparato*] control ► **control del volumen** volume control ► **control de tonalidad** tone control ► **control remoto** remote control
[5] (= *examen*) (*Educ*) test
[6] (*Med*) test ► **control antidopaje** drugs test, dope test ► **control antidoping** drug test, dope test ► **control de alcoholemia** Breathalyser® test

controlable ADJ controllable

controladamente ADV in a controlled way

controlador(a) SM/F [1] (*Aer*) (*tb* **~ aéreo**) air-traffic controller
[2] **~ de estacionamiento** traffic warden
[3] (*LAm Ferro*) inspector, ticket-collector

controlar ▸conjug 1a◂ Ⓐ VT [1] (= *dominar*) [+ *situación, emoción, balón, vehículo, inflación*] to control; **los rebeldes controlan ya todo el país** the rebels now control the whole country, the rebels are now in control of the whole country; **mis padres quieren ~me la vida** my parents want to control my life; **no pudo ~ el impulso de pegarle** he couldn't control the urge to hit him; **medidas para ~ la calidad** quality-control measures; **los bomberos consiguieron ~ el fuego** the firefighters managed to bring the fire under control; **no controlo muy bien ese tema*** I'm not very hot on that subject*
[2] (= *vigilar*) **inspectores para ~ el proceso electoral** observers to monitor the electoral process; **deberías ~ tu peso** you should watch your weight; **contrólame al niño mientras yo estoy fuera*** can you keep an eye on the child while I'm out; **estoy encargado de ~ que todo salga bien** I'm responsible for checking *o* seeing that everything goes well; **controla que no hierva el café*** make sure the coffee doesn't boil, see that the coffee doesn't boil
[3] (= *regular*) to control; **este termostato controla la temperatura** this thermostat controls the temperature
Ⓑ VI (*) **he bebido tanto que ya no controlo** I've drunk so much I can't see straight*
Ⓒ **controlarse** VPR (= *dominarse*) to control o.s.; **¡no te exaltes, contrólate!** don't get worked up, control yourself!; **no pude ~me y le dije todo lo que pensaba** I couldn't control *o* stop *o* help myself and told him exactly what I thought; **deberías ~te con el tabaco** you should watch how much you smoke, you should try and keep your smoking down

controversia SF controversy

controversial ADJ controversial

controvertible ADJ controversial

controvertido ADJ controversial

controvertir ▸conjug 3i◂ Ⓐ VT to dispute, question
Ⓑ VI to argue

contubernio SM [1] (= *confabulación*) conspiracy
[2] (= *cohabitación*) cohabitation

contumacia SF [1] (= *terquedad*) obstinacy, stubborn disobedience
[2] (*Jur*) contempt, contempt of court

contumaz ADJ [1] (= *terco*) obstinate, stubbornly disobedient
[2] [*bebedor*] inveterate, hardened, incorrigible
[3] (*Jur*) guilty of contempt, guilty of contempt of court
[4] (*Med*) disease-carrying, germ-laden

contumazmente ADV obstinately

contumelia SF contumely

contumerioso ADJ (*CAm*) finicky, fussy

contundencia SF [1] [*de instrumento*] bluntness
[2] [*de argumentación, razonamiento*] forcefulness, convincing nature; [*de prueba*] conclusiveness

contundente ADJ [1] [*arma*] offensive; [*instrumento*] blunt
[2] (= *aplastante*) [*argumento*] forceful, convincing; [*prueba*] conclusive; [*derrota, victoria*] crushing, overwhelming; [*tono*] forceful; [*efecto, método*] severe; [*arbitraje*] strict, severe; [*juego*] tough, hard, aggressive

contundir ▸conjug 3a◂ VT to bruise, contuse

conturbar ▸conjug 1a◂ Ⓐ VT to dismay, perturb
Ⓑ **conturbarse** VPR to be troubled, become uneasy

contusión SF bruise, contusion (*frm*)

contusionar ▸conjug 1a◂ VT (= *magullar*) to bruise; (= *dañar*) to hurt, damage

contuso ADJ bruised

conuco SM (*Ven*) smallholding

conuquero SM (*Ven*) smallholder, farmer

conurbación SF conurbation

convalecencia SF convalescence

convalecer ▸conjug 2d◂ VI to convalesce, recover (**de** from)

convaleciente ADJ, SMF convalescent

convalidable ADJ which can be validated

convalidación SF validation; **tengo que solicitar la ~ de mis títulos** I need to have my qualifications validated

convalidar ▸conjug 1a◂ VT to validate

convección SF convection

convecino/a SM/F neighbour, neighbor (*EEUU*)

convectivo ADJ convective

convector SM convector

▼ **convencer** ▸conjug 2b◂ Ⓐ VT [1] **~ a algn (de algo)** to convince sb (of sth), persuade sb (of sth); **me convencieron de su inocencia** they convinced *o* persuaded me he was innocent *o* of his innocence; **al final la convencí de que era verdad** I eventually convinced *o* persuaded her it was true; **no me ~éis de lo contrario** you won't convince *o* persuade me otherwise

[2] **~ a algn (de *o* para hacer algo)** to persuade sb (to do sth); **me han convencido de *o* para que los vote** they persuaded me to vote for them; **no iba a salir, pero al final me convencieron** I wasn't going to go out, but in the end they persuaded me (to)

[3] (= *satisfacer*) **no nos convence del todo la propuesta** we are not entirely convinced about the proposal, the proposal is not entirely convincing; **ninguno de los dos candidatos me convence** neither of the two candidates seems very convincing *o* good to me; **su último disco no me convence nada** I'm not very impressed with her latest record, her latest record doesn't do much for me; **el torero convenció a su afición** the bullfighter did not disappoint his fans; **parece buena gente, pero no me acaba de ~** he seems nice enough but I'm not too sure about him; **su intervención no convenció a los votantes** his speech failed to win over the voters

Ⓑ **convencerse** VPR **al final se convenció y dejó de intentarlo** he eventually thought better of it and stopped trying; **¡convéncete ya, esa enfermedad no tiene cura!** I wish you'd understand, there's no cure for this illness!; **~se de algo**: **se convencieron de mi inocencia** they were persuaded of my innocence; **¿te convences ahora de que decía la verdad?** do you believe now that I was telling the truth?; **me convencí de que lo mejor era callarse** I came to the conclusion that it would be better to keep quiet; **tuvo que volver a casa para ~se de que había apagado todas las luces** he had to go back home to reassure *o* convince himself that he had switched off all the lights

convencido ADJ [*pacifista, cristiano*] committed, convinced; **estar ~ de algo** to be convinced of sth, be certain of sth, be sure of sth

convencimiento SM [1] (= *creencia*) conviction, certainty; **llegar al ~ de algo** to become convinced of sth; **llevar algo al ~ de algn** to convince sb of sth; **tener el ~ de que** to be convinced that

[2] [*acto*] convincing, persuasion

convención SF convention ► **Convención de Ginebra** Geneva Convention

convencional ADJ conventional

convencionalismo SM conventionalism

convencionero ADJ (*Andes, Méx*) comfort-loving, self-indulgent

convencionista SMF (*Méx*) *follower of Convención movement led by Zapata and Villa (1914-15)*

convenible ADJ [1] (= *apropiado*) suitable, fitting

[2] [*precio*] fair, reasonable

[3] [*persona*] accommodating

conveniencia SF [1] (= *utilidad*) [*de una acción*] advisability; **insistió en la ~ de adelantar las elecciones** she insisted on the advisability of bringing forward the election; **ser de la ~ de algn** to be convenient to sb, suit sb

[2] (= *provecho propio*) **a su ~** at your (own) convenience; **por ~**: **lo hace por ~** he does it because it suits him *o* because it's in his own interests; **se ha casado por ~** she made a marriage of convenience; **te lo digo por tu ~** I'm telling you for your own sake *o* in your own interest(s); **cambios dictados por ~s partidistas** changes dictated by party interests ► **conveniencias sociales** social conventions; *ver tb* **bandera 1**, **matrimonio 1**, **pabellón 7**

[3] **conveniencias**† (= *propiedad*) property *sing*; (= *renta*) income *sing*; [*de criado*] perquisites

[4] (†) (= *acuerdo*) agreement

[5] (†) (= *puesto*) domestic post, job as a servant

conveniente ADJ [1] (= *aconsejable*) advisable; **el comité hará lo que considere *o* estime ~** the committee will do as it sees fit, the committee will do what it considers advisable; **ser ~ hacer algo** to be advisable to do sth; **es ~ no tomar grasas en exceso** it is advisable not to eat too much fat; **es ~ que**: **es ~ que consulte con su abogado** it is advisable to consult your lawyer; **sería ~ que habláramos sobre el tema** it would be advisable *o* desirable for us to talk about the matter; **sería ~ que nos levantásemos temprano** it might be a good idea for us to get up early *o* if we got up early

[2] (= *indicado*) suitable; **la clase de cultivo ~ a cada tierra** the kind of crop suitable for each type of soil

[3] (= *provechoso*) convenient; **a usted le resultaría más ~ un fondo de pensiones** you would find a pension fund more convenient; **para nosotros es ~ la existencia de la competencia** the existence of competition is good for us *o* is in our interest

[4] (= *correcto*) proper; **se sentó frente a ella, guardando la ~ distancia** he sat down opposite her, keeping a proper distance

convenientemente ADV [1] (= *como debe ser*) [*arreglar, reparar, comportarse*] properly; **está permitido fumar sólo en las zonas de espera si están ~ separadas** smoking is only permitted in waiting areas if they are properly separated

[2] (*para conveniencia de algn*) conveniently; **la información fue ~ censurada** the information was conveniently censored

convenio SM agreement ► **convenio colectivo** collective bargain, general wages agreement ► **convenio comercial** trade agreement ► **convenio de nivel crítico** threshold agreement ► **convenio laboral** trade agreement ► **convenio salarial** wages agreement

▼ **convenir** ▸conjug 3r◂ Ⓐ VI [1] (= *ser adecuado*) **~ hacer algo**: **conviene recordar que éste es un tema serio** it should be remembered that this is a serious matter; **conviene reservar asiento** reservation is advisable; **convendría hacer algo al respecto** it might be desirable *o* advisable *o* appropriate to do something about it; **necesitaban reunirse para reflexionar sobre lo que convenía hacer** they needed to get together to reflect on the most appropriate course of action; **~ que**: **no conviene que nos vean juntos** we shouldn't be seen together, it is not advisable that we are seen together; **convendría que perdiese unos kilos** it might be a good idea *o* advisable to lose a few kilos

[2] (= *ser de interés*) to suit; **elija las fechas que mejor le convengan** choose the dates that suit you best; **esa hora no me conviene** that time is not convenient for me, that time doesn't suit me; **esa amistad no te convenía nada** that friendship was not good *o* right for you; **lo que más le conviene es reposo absoluto** the best thing for him *o* what he needs is complete rest; **~ a algn hacer algo**: **me conviene quedarme aquí** the best thing for me is to stay here, it is best for me to stay here; **no te conviene fumar** it's not good for you to smoke, smoking isn't good for you; **te convendría olvidar ese asunto** you would be well advised to forget all about this business

[3] **~ en algo** to agree on sth; **conveníamos en la necesidad de un cambio** we agreed on the need for change; **~ en hacer algo** to agree to do sth; **convinimos en dejar de vernos** we agreed to stop seeing each other; **~ en que** to agree that; **todos convienen en que está loco** everyone agrees that he is mad; **convinieron en que el plazo fuese de dos años** they agreed that it would be for a period of two years

Ⓑ VT [+ *precio, hora*] to agree on, agree; **convinimos la hora y el lugar** we agreed (on) a time and a place; **nos vimos a la hora convenida** we saw each other at the agreed time; **eso es más de lo convenido** that is more than what was agreed (on); **"precio/sueldo a ~"** "price/salary to be agreed", "price/salary negotiable"; **~ hacer algo** to agree to do sth; **hemos convenido no trabajar los sábados** we have agreed not to work on Saturdays

conventilleo SM (*Andes, Cono Sur*) gossip

conventillero/a (*Andes, Cono Sur*) Ⓐ ADJ gossipy

Ⓑ SM/F scandalmonger, gossip

conventillo SM (*esp LAm*) tenement house

convento SM [*de monjes*] monastery; [*de monjas*] convent, nunnery

conventual ADJ conventual

convergencia SF [1] (*Mat, Fís, Econ*) convergence

[2] (= *tendencia común*) common tendency, common direction; **~ de izquierdas** (*Pol*) grouping *o* coming together of left-wing forces

convergente ADJ [1] (*Mat, Fís*) convergent, converging

[2] (= *concurrente*) having a common tendency, tending in the same direction

[3] (*Esp Pol*) *of the Catalan coalition Convergència i Unió*

convergentemente ADV **~ con** together with, jointly with

converger ▸conjug 2c◂ VI, **convergir** ▸conjug 3c◂ VI [1] (*Mat, Fís*) to converge (**en** on)

[2] (*fig*) to tend in the same direction (**con** as); **sus esfuerzos convergen en un fin común** their efforts are directed towards the same objective

[3] (*Pol*) to come together

➤ LENGUA Y USO: convencer A1 43.1 A3 39.2 B 53.6 convenir A1 28.1, 29.2 A2 28.1

conversa SF (*esp LAm*) (= *charla*) talk, chat; (= *lisonjas*) smooth talk; *ver tb* **converso**

conversación SF conversation, talk; **cambiar de ~** to change the subject; **trabar ~ con algn** to strike up a conversation with sb

conversacional ADJ [*tono*] conversational; [*estilo*] colloquial

conversada* SF (*LAm*) chat

conversador(a) Ⓐ ADJ talkative, chatty
Ⓑ SM/F [1] (= *persona locuaz*) conversationalist
[2] (*LAm*) (= *zalamero*) smooth talker

conversar ▸conjug 1a◂ Ⓐ VT [1] (*Andes, Cono Sur*) (= *contar*) to tell, relate; (= *informar*) to report
[2] (*Caribe*) (= *ligar*) to chat up*
Ⓑ VI [1] (= *charlar*) to talk, chat
[2] (*Mil*) to wheel

conversata SF (*Cono Sur*) talk, chat

conversión SF [1] (= *cambio*) conversion
[2] (*Mil*) wheel

converso/a Ⓐ ADJ converted
Ⓑ SM/F convert; (*Hist*) converted Jew/Jewess; *ver tb* **conversa**; → RECONQUISTA

conversón/ona (*Andes*) Ⓐ ADJ talkative, gossiping
Ⓑ SM/F talkative person, gossip

conversor SM converter

convertibilidad SF convertibility

convertible Ⓐ ADJ convertible
Ⓑ SM (*LAm Aut*) convertible

convertidor SM converter ► **convertidor catalítico** catalytic converter

convertir ▸conjug 3i◂ Ⓐ VT [1] **~ algo en algo** to turn sth into sth; **~ a algn en algo** to turn sb into sth; **convirtió el pañuelo en una paloma** he turned the handkerchief into a dove; **la victoria le convirtió en un héroe** the victory turned him into a hero, the victory made him a hero; **han convertido el corral en un invernadero** they've converted the yard into a greenhouse; **~ metros en centímetros** to convert metres to centimetres; **~ dólares en libras** to convert dollars to pounds
[2] (*a una religión, ideología*) to convert; **convirtió a su hijo al catolicismo** she converted her son to catholicism
[3] (*Dep*) [+ *penalti*] to convert, score; [+ *gol, tanto*] to score
Ⓑ **convertirse** VPR [1] **~se en algo** to turn into sth; **el riachuelo se convirtió en un torrente** the stream turned into *o* became a torrent; **la rana se convirtió en un príncipe** the frog turned into a prince; **con la empresa se convirtió en millonario** the company made him a millionaire; **todos sus deseos se convirtieron en realidad** all her wishes came true
[2] (*Rel*) to be converted, convert; **se convirtió al Islam** he converted to Islam

convexidad SF convexity

convexo ADJ convex

convicción SF conviction

convicto/a Ⓐ ADJ convicted
Ⓑ SM/F (*LAm*) convict

convidada SF round (*esp of drinks*); **dar** *o* **pagar una ~** to stand a round

convidado/a SM/F guest

convidar ▸conjug 1a◂ Ⓐ VT [1] (= *invitar*) to invite; **~ a algn a hacer algo** to invite sb to do sth; **~ a algn a una cerveza** to buy sb a beer
[2] (= *incitar*) **~ a** to stir to, move to; **el ambiente convida a la meditación** the atmosphere is conducive to meditation
Ⓑ **convidarse** VPR [1] (= *invitarse*) to invite o.s. along
[2] (= *ofrecerse*) to volunteer, offer one's services

▼**convincente** ADJ convincing

convincentemente ADV convincingly

convite SM [1] (= *invitación*) invitation
[2] (= *función*) banquet, feast ► **convite a escote** Dutch treat

convivencia SF [1] [*de personas*] cohabitation, living together; **~ en familia** living with a family
[2] (*fig*) (*Pol*) coexistence
[3] (*Rel*) **irse de ~s** to go on a retreat

convivencial ADJ social

conviviente SMF (*Chile*) partner

convivir ▸conjug 3a◂ VI [1] (= *vivir juntos*) to live together; **~ con algn** to live with sb
[2] (= *coexistir*) [*personas*] to live together, live together in harmony; [*ideologías, razas*] to coexist

convocación SF calling, convening

convocante SMF organizer

convocar ▸conjug 1g◂ VT [1] [+ *elecciones, referéndum, huelga*] to call; [+ *asamblea, reunión*] to call, convene; [+ *manifestación*] to call for; [+ *concurso, oposiciones*] to announce; **convocó una conferencia de prensa** he called a press conference; **han convocado un congreso extraordinario para el lunes** they have called *o* convened a special conference for Monday; **~ Cortes** (*Hist*) to convoke parliament
[2] **~ a algn: ~on a los periodistas a una rueda de prensa** they called journalists to a press conference; **~on a todos los presos en el patio** they summoned all the prisoners to the yard; **los españoles serán convocados a las urnas en abril** Spaniards will go to the polls in April; **los jugadores convocados por el entrenador** the players selected by the trainer

convocatoria SF [1] (= *anuncio*) [*de concurso, oposiciones*] official announcement; **se ha anunciado la ~ del congreso socialista** the socialist congress has been called *o* convened; **han anunciado la ~ de elecciones generales** they have announced the date for the general election; **~ (pública) de plazas docentes** public notice *o* announcement of selection for teaching places; **en la última ~ el premio fue declarado desierto** in the last competition the prize was not awarded; **~ de huelga** strike call
[2] (= *ronda*) **ha aprobado todo en la ~ de septiembre** she passed everything in September's exams; **en primera ~, el candidato precisa el 51% de los votos** in the first round the candidate needs 51% of the votes

convólvulo SM convolvulus

convoy SM [1] (*Mil, Náut*) convoy; (*Ferro*) train
[2] (*frm*) (= *séquito*) retinue
[3] (= *vinagrera*) cruet, cruet stand
[4] (*Caribe*) (= *ensalada*) salad

convoyar ▸conjug 1a◂ Ⓐ VT [1] (= *escoltar*) to escort
[2] (*Cono Sur*) (= *financiar*) to back, sponsor
Ⓑ **convoyarse** VPR (*Caribe*) to connive together, plot

convulsión SF [1] (*Med*) convulsion [2] (*Geol*) tremor [3] (*Pol*) upheaval

convulsionar ▸conjug 1a◂ VT to convulse

convulsivo ADJ convulsive

convulso ADJ convulsed (**de** with)

conyugal ADJ conjugal (*frm*), married; **vida ~** married life

conyugalidad SF married life

cónyuge SMF spouse, partner; **cónyuges** married couple *sing*, husband and wife

coña** SF piss-taking**; **estar de ~** to be taking the piss**; **¡esto es la ~!** this is a fucking joke!**; **tomar algo a ~** to take sth as a joke

coñá SM = **coñac**

coñac [ko'ɲa] SM (*pl* **coñacs** [ko'ɲas]) brandy, cognac

coñazo* SM pain*; **dar el ~** to be a real pain

coñe* EXCL = **coño C**

coñearse** ▸conjug 1a◂ VPR to take the piss**

coñete ADJ (*Chile, Perú*) mean

coño[1]** Ⓐ SM (= *sexo femenino*) cunt**; ✦***MODISMOS*** **ser el ~ de la Bernarda** to be a disgrace; **estar hasta el ~ de algn/algo** to have had it up to here with sb/sth; **el quinto ~** the arse end of nowhere**, the back of beyond*; **viven en el quinto ~** they live out in the arse end of nowhere**; **lo hice porque me salió del ~** I did it because I bloody well felt like it*
Ⓑ EXCL [1] (*como expresión de enfado*) hell!*, damn!*, shit!**; **¡vámonos ya, ~!** come on, let's get a bloody move on!*; **¡ni hablar, ~, ni hablar!** not on your bloody life!*; **¿cómo ~?** how the fuck?**; **¿dónde ~?** where the fuck?**; **¿por qué ~?** why the fuck?**; **¿qué ~?** what the fuck?**; **¿a ti qué ~ te importa?** what the fuck does it matter to you?**; **¿qué ~ quieres?** what the fuck do you want?**; **que lo haga él, ¡qué ~!** let him do it for Christ's sake!*; **¡qué libro ni qué ~!** what bloody book!*; **—no puedo salir esta noche, tengo un compromiso —¡qué compromiso ni qué ~! tú sales hoy porque lo digo yo** "I can't go out tonight, I'm busy" — "busy my arse! you're going out today because I'm telling you"**
[2] (*como expresión de alegría*) bugger me!**; **¡esto hay que celebrarlo, ~!** well bugger me! this calls for a celebration!**

coño[2]**/a*** SM/F (*LAm pey*) (= *español*) *nickname for Spaniard*

cooficial ADJ **dos lenguas ~es** two languages equally recognized as official

cooficialidad SF **la ~ de dos lenguas** the equal official status of two languages

cool* [kul] ADJ INV cool*

cooperación SF cooperation

cooperador(a) Ⓐ ADJ cooperative, collaborating, participating
Ⓑ SM/F collaborator, co-worker

cooperante SMF voluntary worker, overseas voluntary worker

cooperar ▸conjug 1a◂ VI to cooperate (**en** in; **con** with); **~ a hacer algo** to cooperate in doing sth; **~ a un mismo fin** to work for a common aim; **~ en** to collaborate in, work together on; **los factores que ~on al fracaso** the factors which together led to failure, the factors which contributed to the failure

➤ LENGUA Y USO: **convincente** 53.4

cooperativa SF cooperative, co-op* ► **cooperativa agrícola** agricultural co-operative ► **cooperativa de crédito** credit union ► **cooperativa industrial** industrial cooperative

cooperativismo SM cooperativism; (*como movimiento*) cooperative movement

cooperativista SMF member of a cooperative

cooperativización SF cooperativization

cooperativizar ▸conjug 1f◂ VT to cooperativize

cooperativo ADJ cooperative

cooptación SF cooption

cooptar ▸conjug 1a◂ VT to coopt (**a** on, to)

coordenada SF coordinate

coordinación SF coordination

coordinado Ⓐ ADJ (= *armonizado*) coordinated; (*Mil*) [*operación*] combined
Ⓑ SMPL **coordinados** (= *ropa*) separates

coordinador(a) Ⓐ ADJ coordinating
Ⓑ SM/F coordinator

coordinadora SF coordinating committee

coordinar ▸conjug 1a◂ Ⓐ VT (= *armonizar*) [+ *movimientos, actividades, equipo, esfuerzo, trabajo*] to coordinate; **se reunieron para ~ una respuesta al conflicto** they met to coordinate a response to the conflict; **tiene dificultades para ~ sus ideas** he has difficulties in organizing his thoughts
Ⓑ VI (*) **ha bebido tanto que ya no coordina** he's had so much to drink that his coordination has gone; **hasta que no me tomo un café por las mañanas no coordino** I can't think straight in the mornings until I've had a coffee

copa SF 1 (= *recipiente*) (*para bebidas*) glass; (*para postres*) dessert glass; **huevo a la ~** (*Andes, Cono Sur*) boiled egg ► **copa balón** balloon glass, brandy glass ► **copa de champán** champagne glass ► **copa de coñac** brandy glass ► **copa flauta** champagne flute
2 (= *contenido*) drink; **os invito a una ~** let me buy you a drink; **una ~ de coñac te quitará el frío** a glass of brandy will warm you up; **ir(se)** *o* **salir de ~s** to go out for a drink; **tomarse una ~** to have a drink; **se tomó una ~ de más** he had one too many
3 [*de árbol*] top, crown; ✦***MODISMO*** **como la ~ de un pino***: **es un artista como la ~ de un pino** he's a real star; **es una idiotez como la ~ de un pino** that's the stupidest thing I've ever heard
4 (*Dep*) (= *trofeo, competición*) cup ► **Copa de Europa** European Cup ► **Copa del Mundo** World Cup ► **Copa del Rey** (*Esp*) *Spanish FA Cup* ► **Copa Libertadores** (*LAm*) Latinamerican inter-national cup
5 **copas** (*Naipes*) *one of the suits in Spanish card deck, represented by a goblet*; → BARAJA ESPAÑOLA
6 [*de sombrero*] crown; *ver tb* **sombrero 1**
7 [*de sujetador*] cup
8 (*Andes Aut*) hubcap

copado ADJ thick, with dense foliage

copal SM 1 (*CAm, Méx*) (= *resina*) resin
2 (*Hist*) incense

copantes SMPL (*CAm, Méx*) stepping stones

copar ▸conjug 1a◂ VT 1 (*Mil*) to surround, cut off
2 (*Econ*) to corner; **~ el mercado** to corner the market
3 (*Pol*) **han copado todos los escaños** they've made a clean sweep of all the seats
4 (*Naipes*) (*tb* **~ la banca**) to win, win all the tricks
5 (*Méx*) (= *monopolizar*) to monopolize

coparticipación SF joint participation (**en** in)

copartícipe SMF 1 (= *socio*) partner; (= *colaborador*) collaborator (**en** in)
2 (*Dep*) fellow participant, fellow competitor

copazo* SM *mixed drink of e.g. rum and Coke*

COPE SF ABR (= **Cadena de Ondas Populares Españolas**) *radio network*

copear ▸conjug 1a◂ VI 1 (*) (= *beber*) to booze*, tipple*
2 (*Com*) to sell wine (*etc*) by the glass

Copei SM ABR (*Ven*) (= **Comité Organizador para Elecciones Independientes**) *Christian Democrat party*

Copenhague SM Copenhagen

copeo SM **ir de ~*** to go drinking

copera SF (*Cono Sur*) hostess

Copérnico SM Copernicus

copero Ⓐ ADJ cup *antes de s*
Ⓑ SM (*Cono Sur*) waiter

copete SM 1 [*de persona*] tuft (of hair), quiff; [*de caballo*] forelock; [*de pájaro*] tuft, crest; ✦***MODISMOS*** **estar hasta el ~** to be really fed up; **de alto ~** aristocratic, upper-crust*
2 (= *altanería*) arrogance; **tener mucho ~** to be haughty, be stuck-up*

copetín SM (*Cuba, Cono Sur*) drink, aperitif

copetón ADJ 1 (*LAm*) = **copetudo 1**
2 (*Andes**) **estar ~** to be tight*

copetudo ADJ 1 (*Zool*) tufted, crested
2 (= *engreído*) haughty, stuck-up*

copia SF 1 (= *reproducción*) [*de fotografía, documento*] copy; (*Fin*) duplicate ► **copia al carbón** carbon copy ► **copia carbónica** (*Cono Sur*) carbon copy ► **copia certificada** certified copy ► **copia de calco** (*Cono Sur*) carbon copy ► **copia de respaldo, copia de seguridad** (*Inform*) back-up copy; **hacer una ~ de seguridad** to back up, make a back-up copy ► **copia en color** colour *o* (*EEUU*) color copy ► **copia en limpio** fair copy ► **copia fotostática** photostat, photocopy ► **copia impresa** (*Inform*) hard copy
2 (= *imitación*) [*de obra de arte, edificio*] copy
3 (*liter*) (= *abundancia*) abundance, plenty

copiado SM copying

copiador(a) Ⓐ SM/F (= *persona*) copier, copyist
Ⓑ SM (*tb* **libro ~**) letter-book

copiadora SF photocopier, Xerox® machine

copiante SMF copyist

copiar ▸conjug 1b◂ Ⓐ VT 1 (= *reproducir*) to copy (**de** from); [+ *estilo*] to imitate
2 [+ *dictado*] to take down; **~ al pie de la letra** to copy word for word; **~ por las dos caras** (*Téc*) to make a double-sided copy
Ⓑ VI (*en un examen*) to cheat

copichuela* SF social drink

copihue SM (*Chile*) Chilean bell flower (*national symbol of Chile*)

copilotar ▸conjug 1a◂ VT (*Aut*) to be the co-driver of; (*Aer*) to copilot

copiloto SMF 1 (*Aut*) co-driver
2 (*Aer*) co-pilot

copión/ona* SM/F 1 (= *alumno*) cheat
2 (= *imitador*) copycat*

copiosamente ADV copiously, abundantly, plentifully

copioso ADJ (= *abundante*) copious, abundant; [*lluvia*] heavy

copista SMF copyist

copistería SF copy shop

copita SF glass, small glass; **una ~ de jerez** a little glass of sherry; **tomarse unas ~s** to have a drink or two, have a couple of drinks

copla SF 1 (*Literat*) verse (*esp of 4 lines*)
2 (*Mús*) popular song, ballad; **coplas** verses; **hacer ~s** to write verse; ✦***MODISMOS*** **andar en ~s** to be the talk of the town; **la misma ~*** the same old song*; **quedarse con la ~: ¿os vais quedando con la ~?** do you follow?, do you get my drift?; **no valen ~s** it's no use your arguing *o* apologizing ► **coplas de ciego** doggerel
3 (*LAm Téc*) pipe joint

copo SM 1 [*de lino*] small bundle ► **copo de algodón** cotton ball ► **copo de nieve** snowflake ► **copos de avena** oatmeal *sing*, rolled oats ► **copos de maíz** cornflakes
2 (*LAm*) [*de árbol*] tree top
3 (*Cono Sur*) (= *nubes*) piled-up clouds *pl*

copón SM (= *copa*) large cup; (*Rel*) pyx; **un susto del ~*** a tremendous fright, a hell of a fright‡; **y todo el ~*** and all that stuff*, and all that*

coprocesador SM co-processor

coproducción SF joint production

coproducir ▸conjug 3n◂ VT to co-produce, produce jointly

copropiedad SF co-ownership

copropietario/a SM/F co-owner, joint owner

copucha SF (*Cono Sur*) gossip

copuchar ▸conjug 1a◂ VI (*Cono Sur*) to gossip

copuchento ADJ (*Cono Sur*) lying

copudo ADJ bushy, thick

cópula SF 1 (*Biol*) copulation ► **cópula carnal** copulation, sexual intercourse
2 (*Ling*) conjunction

copulador ADJ copulatory

copular ▸conjug 1a◂ VI to copulate (**con** with)

copulativo ADJ copulative

coque SM coke

coquear ▸conjug 1a◂ VI (*Andes, Cono Sur*) to chew coca

coqueluche SF whooping cough

coquero/a SM/F cocaine addict

coqueta SF (= *mueble*) dressing table; *ver tb* **coqueto**

coquetear ▸conjug 1a◂ VI to flirt (**con** with)

coqueteo SM, **coquetería** SF (= *cualidad*) flirtatiousness, coquetry; (= *acto*) flirtation

coqueto/a Ⓐ ADJ 1 [*vestido*] smart, natty*, attractive
2 (= *juguetón*) flirtatious, flirty
3 (= *presumido*) **es muy ~** he's very fussy about his appearance, he's very clothes-conscious
Ⓑ SMF 1 (= *juguetón*) flirt
2 (= *presumido*) **es una coqueta** she's very fussy about her appearance, she's very clothes-conscious; *ver tb* **coqueta**

coquetón ADJ 1 [*objeto*] neat*
2 [*persona*] = **coqueto A2**

coquilla SF (*Cono Sur*) shell

coquitos SMPL **hacer ~** to make faces (**a** at)

Cor. ABR (= **Coronel**) Col

coracha SF leather bag

coraje SM 1 (= *valor*) courage; **debes tener ~ y enfrentarte a la realidad** you have to be brave *o* have courage and face up to reality; **no tuvo el ~ de admitir su fallo** she wasn't brave enough to admit her mistake
2 (*) (= *rabia*) **hemos perdido el autobús, ¡qué ~!** we've missed the bus, what a pain!*; **me da ~ que me mientas** it makes me mad* *o* it really annoys me when you lie to me; **me da ~ verlo pasear con mi novia** it makes me mad to see him walking around with my girlfriend*

corajina SF fit of rage

corajudo ADJ 1 (= *irascible*) quick-tempered
2 (= *valiente*) brave, gutsy*

coral[1] (*Mús*) Ⓐ ADJ choral
Ⓑ SM chorale
Ⓒ SF choir

coral[2] Ⓐ SM (*Zool*) coral
Ⓑ SF (= *serpiente*) coral snake

coralina SF coralline

coralino ADJ coral *antes de s*, coralline

corambre SF hides, skins

Corán SM Koran

corana SF (*Andes, Cono Sur*) sickle

coránico ADJ Koranic

coraza SF 1 (*Mil, Hist*) cuirass; (= *protección*) protection
2 (*Náut*) armour-plating, armor-plating (*EEUU*)
3 (*Zool*) shell
4 (*Aut*) radiator cover

corazón SM 1 (*Anat*) heart; **le falló el ~** his heart failed, he had heart failure; **estar enfermo** *o* **mal del ~** to have heart trouble *o* problems; **padecer** *o* **sufrir del ~** to have a weak heart, have heart trouble *o* problems; **ser operado a ~ abierto** to have open heart surgery; *ver tb* **ataque 2**
2 ✦*MODISMOS* **abrir el ~ a algn** to open one's heart to sb, pour one's heart out to sb; **no caberle a algn el ~ en el pecho**: **cuando me lo dijeron no me cabía el ~ en el pecho** when they told me I was over the moon*; **de ~** sincerely; **te lo digo de ~** I mean it sincerely; **de buen ~** kind-hearted; **de gran ~** big-hearted; **de todo ~**: **se lo agradezco de todo ~** I thank you with all my heart *o* from the bottom of my heart; **la quería con todo mi ~** I loved her with all my heart; **ser duro de ~** to be hard-hearted; **encoger a algn el ~**: **aquellas imágenes me encogieron el ~** those scenes made my heart bleed; **un grito en la noche me encogió el ~** a scream during the night made my heart miss a beat; **llegar al ~ de algn**: **sus palabras me llegaron al ~** I was deeply touched by her words, her words touched my heart; **con el ~ en la mano** with one's hand on one's heart; **partir** *o* **romper el ~ a algn** to break sb's heart; **tener el ~ en la boca** *o* **en un puño** to have one's heart in one's mouth, be on tenterhooks; **tener un ~ de oro** to have a heart of gold; **tener el ~ de piedra** to have a heart of stone; **no tener ~** to have no heart, be heartless; **una mujer sin ~** a heartless woman; **no tener ~ para hacer algo** not to have the heart to do sth; *ver tb* **vuelco 2**
3 (*Prensa*) **la prensa del ~** gossip magazines *pl*; **una revista del ~** a gossip magazine
4 (*apelativo*) **sí, ~** yes, sweetheart; **¡hijo de mi ~!** (my) darling!
5 (= *centro*) [*de ciudad, zona, alcachofa*] heart; [*de manzana*] core; **limpie las manzanas y quíteles el ~** wash and core the apples
6 **corazones** (*Naipes*) hearts

corazonada SF 1 (= *presentimiento*) hunch
2 (= *impulso*) impulsive act

corazoncito* SM **tener su ~** to have a heart

corbata SF tie, necktie (*EEUU*) ► **corbata de lazo** bow tie ► **corbata de smoking** black tie ► **corbata michi** (*Andes*) bow tie

corbatín SM bow tie

corbeta SF corvette

corca SF woodworm

Córcega SF Corsica

corcel SM steed, charger

corcha SF cork bark, piece of cork bark

corchea SF quaver, eighth (note) (*EEUU*)

corchero ADJ cork *antes de s*; **industria corchera** cork industry

corcheta SF eye (*of hook and eye*)

corchete SM 1 (*Cos*) (= *broche*) hook and eye; (= *macho*) hook
2 **corchetes** (*Tip*) square brackets ► **corchetes agudos** angled brackets
3 (*Chile*) (= *grapa*) staple

corchetear ▸conjug 1a◂ VT (*Cono Sur*) to staple, staple together

corchetera SF (*Chile*) stapler

corcho SM 1 [*de botella*] cork; **sacar el ~ de la botella** to uncork the bottle
2 (= *corteza*) cork bark; **de ~** cork *antes de s* ► **corcho bornizo, corcho virgen** virgin cork
3 (= *estera*) cork mat
4 (= *zueco*) cork-soled clog
5 (*Pesca*) float

corcholata SF (*Méx*) metal bottle top

córcholis* EXCL good Lord!, dear me!

corchoso ADJ corklike, corky

corcor SM (*CAm, Caribe*) gurgle; **beber ~*** to swig*, knock it back*

corcova SF 1 (*Med*) hump, hunch
2 (*Andes, Cono Sur*) (= *fiesta*) all-night party

corcovado/a Ⓐ ADJ hunchbacked
Ⓑ SM/F hunchback

corcovar ▸conjug 1a◂ VT to bend, bend over

corcovear ▸conjug 1a◂ VI 1 (= *brincar*) [*persona*] to prance about, cut capers; [*caballo*] to buck
2 (*Andes, Caribe, Cono Sur*) (= *quejarse*) to grumble, grouse*
3 (*Méx*) (= *tener miedo*) to be frightened, be afraid

corcovo SM 1 (= *brinco*) prance, caper; [*de caballo*] buck
2 (*) (= *torcimiento*) crookedness*

cordada SF roped team

cordaje SM (= *cuerdas*) cordage, ropes; [*de raqueta*] strings; (*Náut*) rigging

cordal SM hill range

cordel SM cord, line; **a ~** in a straight line

cordelería SF 1 (= *cuerdas*) cordage, ropes; (*Náut*) rigging
2 (= *oficio*) ropemaking
3 (= *fábrica*) ropeyard, ropeworks

cordelero/a SM/F cordmaker, ropemaker

cordería SF cordage, cords, ropes

corderillo SM lambskin

cordero/a Ⓐ SM/F (*Zool*) lamb; ✦*MODISMOS* **¡no hay tales ~s!** it's nothing of the sort!; **es (como) un ~** he wouldn't say "boo" to a goose, he's as quiet as a mouse ► **cordero asado** roast lamb ► **Cordero de Dios** Lamb of God ► **cordero lechal** young lamb
Ⓑ SM (= *piel*) lambskin

corderuna SF lambskin

cordial Ⓐ ADJ 1 (= *afectuoso*) warm, cordial
2 (*Med*) invigorating
Ⓑ SM cordial, tonic

cordialidad SF warmth, cordiality

cordialmente ADV warmly, cordially; (*en carta*) sincerely

cordillera SF mountain range, mountain chain

cordillerano ADJ (*Cono Sur*) Andean

cordita SF cordite

Córdoba SF (*Esp*) Cordova; (*Arg*) Cordoba

córdoba SM (*Nic*) *monetary unit of Nicaragua*

cordobán SM cordovan, cordovan leather

cordobana SF ✦*MODISMO* **andar a la ~** to go around stark naked

cordobés/esa ADJ, SM/F Cordovan

cordón SM 1 (= *cuerda*) cord, string; [*de zapato*] lace, shoelace; **lana de tres cordones** three-ply wool; **aparcar en ~** to park in a (straight) line
2 (*Náut*) strand; (*Mil*) braid; **cordones** (*Mil*) aiguillettes
3 (*Elec*) flex, wire (*EEUU*), cord (*EEUU*) ► **cordón detonante** (*Cono Sur*) fuse
4 (*Anat*) cord ► **cordón umbilical** umbilical cord
5 [*de policía*] cordon ► **cordón sanitario** cordon sanitaire
6 (*Arquit*) cordon
7 (*Cono Sur*) (= *bordillo*) kerb, curb (*EEUU*)
8 (*Geog*) ► **cordón de cerros** (*Andes, Caribe, Cono Sur*) chain of hills
9 (*Andes, Caribe*) (= *licor*) liquor, brandy

cordoncillo SM 1 [*de tela*] rib; (= *bordado*) braid, piping
2 [*de moneda*] milled edge

cordura SF 1 (*Med*) sanity
2 (= *sensatez*) good sense; **con ~** sensibly, wisely

Corea SF Korea ► **Corea del Norte** North Korea ► **Corea del Sur** South Korea

coreano/a ADJ, SM/F Korean

corear ▸conjug 1a◂ VT to chorus; [+ *eslogan*] shout in unison, chant; (*Mús*) to sing in chorus, sing together; **su opinión es coreada por ...** his opinion is echoed by ...

coreografía SF choreography

coreografiar ▸conjug 1c◂ VT to choreograph

coreográfico ADJ choreographic

coreógrafo/a SM/F choreographer

Corfú SM Corfu

coriana SF (*Andes*) blanket

corifeo SM 1 (*Hist*) coryphaeus
2 (= *portavoz*) leader, spokesman

corindón SM corundum

corintio ADJ Corinthian

Corinto SM Corinth

corinto Ⓐ ADJ INV maroon, purplish
Ⓑ SM maroon, purplish colour

corista Ⓐ SMF (*Rel, Mús*) chorister
Ⓑ SF (*Teat*) chorus girl

coritatis* ADV **estar en ~** to be in the buff*
cormorán SM cormorant
cornada SF butt, goring; **dar una ~ a** to gore
cornadura SF [*de toro*] horns *pl*; [*de ciervo*] antlers *pl*
cornalina SF cornelian, carnelian
cornamenta SF [1] [*de toro*] horns *pl*; [*de ciervo*] antlers *pl*
[2] (*hum*) [*de marido*] cuckold's horns; ✦*MODISMO* **poner la ~ a algn** to cuckold sb
cornamusa SF (= *gaita*) bagpipe; (= *cuerna*) hunting horn
córnea SF cornea
corneal ADJ corneal
cornear ▸conjug 1a◂ VT to butt, gore
corneja SF crow ► **corneja calva** rook ► **corneja negra** carrion crow
córneo ADJ horny, corneous (*frm*)
córner ['korner] SM (*pl* **córners** ['korne, 'kornes]) [1] (*Dep*) corner, corner kick; **¡córner!** (*excl*) corner!; **enviar a ~** to send (out) for a corner; **sacar un ~** to take a corner
[2] (*LAm Boxeo*) corner
cornerina SF cornelian, carnelian
corneta Ⓐ SF (= *instrumento*) bugle; (*Caribe Aut*) horn ► **corneta acústica** ear trumpet ► **corneta de llaves** cornet ► **corneta de monte** hunting horn
Ⓑ SMF bugler, cornet player
cornetear ▸conjug 1a◂ VI (*Caribe Aut*) to sound one's horn
cornetín/ina Ⓐ SM (= *instrumento*) cornet
Ⓑ SM/F (= *instrumentista*) cornet player
cornetista SMF bugler
corneto ADJ (*CAm*) bow-legged
cornezuelo SM ergot
cornflaques SMPL (*LAm*), **cornflés** SMPL (*LAm*) cornflakes
cornial ADJ horn-shaped
córnico Ⓐ ADJ Cornish
Ⓑ SM (*Ling*) Cornish
corniforme ADJ horn-shaped
cornisa SF cornice; **la Cornisa Cantábrica** the Cantabrian coast
cornisamento SM entablature
corno SM (*Mús*) horn ► **corno de caza** hunting horn ► **corno inglés** cor anglais, English horn (*EEUU*)
Cornualles SM Cornwall
cornucopia SF [1] (*Mit*) cornucopia, horn of plenty
[2] (= *espejo*) *small ornamental mirror*
cornudo Ⓐ ADJ [1] (*Zool*) horned
[2] [*marido*] cuckolded
Ⓑ SM cuckold
cornúpeta SM (*Taur*) bull; (*hum*) cuckold
coro SM [1] (= *agrupación*) choir; **canto en un ~** I sing in a choir; **niño de ~** choirboy
[2] (= *composición*) (*en obra musical, tragedia*) chorus; **una chica del ~** a girl from the chorus, a chorus girl; **un ~ de críticas** a chorus of criticism; **decir algo a ~** to say sth in a chorus *o* in unison; **hacer ~ de** *o* **a las palabras de algn** to echo sb's words; ✦*MODISMO* **hacer ~ a algn** to back sb up
[3] (*Arquit*) choir
[4] [*de ángeles*] choir ► **coro celestial** celestial choir, heavenly choir
corola SF corolla
corolario SM corollary
corona SF [1] [*de rey, reina*] crown; [*de santo*] halo; (*tb* **~ de flores**) (*para la cabeza*) garland ► **corona de espinas** crown of thorns ► **corona de laurel** (*lit*) laurel wreath
[2] [*de difuntos*] wreath ► **corona funeraria, corona mortuoria** funeral wreath; *ver tb* **ceñir A4, B3**
[3] **la Corona** (= *monarquía*) the Crown; (*Hist*) (= *reino*) the kingdom; **el heredero de la ~** the crown prince; **en la mayor parte de la Corona de Castilla** throughout most of the Kingdom of Castile
[4] [*de muela*] (*natural*) crown; (*artificial*) crown, artificial crown
[5] (*Mec*) [*de coche*] crown wheel; [*de bicicleta*] chain wheel; [*de reloj*] winder, crown
[6] (*Fin*) [*de Suecia, Islandia, Rep. Checa*] crown
[7] (*Astron*) corona; (*Meteo*) halo; **la ~ solar** the sun's corona
[8] [*de monje*] tonsure
coronación SF [1] [*de rey*] coronation
[2] (= *fin*) end, culmination
[3] (*Arquit*) = **coronamiento 2**
[4] (*Ajedrez*) queening
coronamiento SM [1] (= *fin*) end, culmination
[2] (*Arquit*) crown
coronar ▸conjug 1a◂ VT [1] [+ *persona*] to crown; **~ a algn rey** to crown sb king
[2] **~ la cima** to reach the summit
[3] (= *completar*) to crown, culminate, end; **coronó su trayectoria deportiva con una gran victoria en Wimbledon** he crowned *o* culminated *o* ended his sporting career with a great win at Wimbledon; **~ algo con éxito** to crown sth with success; **para ~lo** to crown it all
[4] (*Ajedrez, Damas*) to queen
[5] (*Andes, Caribe, Cono Sur*) (= *poner los cuernos a*) to cuckold, make a cuckold of
coronario ADJ coronary
coronel SM/F colonel ► **coronel de aviación** group captain, colonel (*EEUU*)
coronela SF (*Hist*) colonel's wife
▼**coronilla** SF crown, top of the head; **andar** *o* **bailar** *o* **ir de ~** to bend over backwards to please sb; **dar de ~** to bump one's head; **estar hasta la ~** to be utterly fed up (**de** with)
coronta SF (*Andes, Cono Sur*) deseeded corncob
corotear ▸conjug 1a◂ VI (*Andes*) to move house
coroto SM [1] (*Ven*) (= *poder*) power; **tomar el ~** to take power
[2] **corotos** (*Col, Ven**) (= *trastos*) odds and ends
corpacho* SM, **corpanchón*** SM, **corpazo*** SM carcass*
corpiño SM (= *almilla*) bodice; (*LAm*) (= *sostén*) bra
corporación SF corporation
corporal ADJ corporal, bodily; **castigo ~** corporal punishment; **ejercicio ~** physical exercise; **higiene ~** personal hygiene
corporativismo SM corporate spirit
corporativo ADJ corporate
corporeidad SF corporeal nature
corporeizar ▸conjug 1f◂ Ⓐ VT (= *encarnar*) to embody
Ⓑ VI (= *aparecer*) to materialize, turn up
Ⓒ **corporeizarse** VPR (= *tomar cuerpo*) to come about
corpóreo ADJ corporeal, bodily
corpulencia SF burliness, stoutness; **cayó con toda su ~** he fell with his full weight
corpulento ADJ [*persona*] burly, heavily-built; [*árbol*] stout, solid, massive
Corpus SM Corpus Christi
corpus SM INV corpus, body
corpúsculo SM corpuscle
corral SM [1] (*Agr*) (= *patio*) farmyard; [*de aves*] poultry yard; (= *redil*) pen, corral (*EEUU*); [*de pesca*] weir; ✦*MODISMO* **hacer ~es** to play truant ► **corral de abasto** (*Cono Sur*) slaughterhouse ► **corral de carbonera** coal dump, coalyard ► **corral de madera** timberyard ► **corral de vacas*** slum ► **corral de vecindad** tenement
[2] [*de niño*] playpen
corralillo SM, **corralito** SM playpen
corralón SM [1] (= *patio*) large yard; (= *maderería*) timberyard
[2] (*Perú*) (= *terreno*) vacant site *o* (*EEUU*) lot
correa SF [1] (= *cinturón*) belt; (= *tira*) strap; (= *ronzal*) tether; (*para afilar una navaja*) strop; **la ~ de mi reloj** my watchstrap, my watchband (*EEUU*); ✦*MODISMO* **besar la ~**†† to eat humble pie
[2] [*de perro*] leash, lead
[3] (*Mec*) ► **correa de seguridad** safety belt ► **correa de transmisión** driving belt, drive ► **correa de transporte** conveyor belt ► **correa de ventilador, correa del ventilador** (*Aut*) fan belt ► **correa sin fin** endless belt ► **correa transportadora** conveyor belt
[4] (= *aguante*) give, elasticity; ✦*MODISMO* **tener ~: por cualquier cosa se enfada, tiene muy poca ~** she gets angry at the slightest thing, she has a very short fuse
correaje SM (= *correas*) straps *pl*; (*Agr*) harness; (*Mil*) leathers *pl*; (*Téc*) belting
correalizador(a) SM/F co-director
correcalles SF INV streetwalker, hooker (*EEUU**)
correcaminata SF fun run
corrección SF [1] (= *arreglo*) correction ► **corrección de pruebas** (*Tip*) proofreading ► **corrección por líneas** (*Inform*) line editing
[2] (= *censura*) rebuke, reprimand; (= *castigo*) punishment
[3] (= *perfección*) correctness
[4] (= *cortesía*) courtesy, good manners
correccional SM reformatory
correcorre SM (*Caribe*) headlong rush, stampede
correctamente ADV [1] (= *exactamente*) correctly, accurately
[2] (= *decentemente*) correctly, politely
correctivo ADJ, SM corrective
▼**correcto** ADJ [1] [*respuesta*] correct, right; **¡correcto!** right!
[2] (= *educado*) [*persona*] correct; [*conducta, comportamiento*] courteous; [*vestido*] proper, fitting; **estuvo muy ~ conmigo** he was very polite to me
[3] [*rasgos*] regular, well-formed
corrector(a) Ⓐ SM/F ► **corrector(a) de estilo** (*Prensa*) copy editor ► **corrector(a) de pruebas** (*Tip*) proofreader
Ⓑ SM [1] (= *líquido*) correcting fluid
[2] ► **corrector ortográfico** (*Inform*) spell checker, spelling checker
[3] (*tb* **~ dental**) brace, tooth brace

➤ LENGUA Y USO: **coronilla** 41 **correcto 1** 38.2

corredera SF [1] (*Téc*) slide; (= *ranura*) track, rail, runner; **puerta de ~** sliding door
[2] (*Náut*) log
[3] [*de molino*] upper millstone
[4] (= *cucaracha*) cockroach
[5] (*Dep*) racetrack
[6] (*Cono Sur*) (= *rápidos*) rapids *pl*

corredero SM [1] (*Méx Dep*) racetrack
[2] (*Andes*) (= *lecho de río*) old riverbed

corredizo ADJ [*puerta*] sliding; [*nudo*] running, slip *antes de s*; [*grúa*] travelling, traveling (*EEUU*)

corredor(a) Ⓐ SM/F [1] (*Dep*) (= *atleta*) runner; [*de coches*] driver ► **corredor(a) automovilista** racing driver ► **corredor(a) ciclista** racing cyclist ► **corredor(a) de fondo, corredor(a) de larga distancia** long-distance runner ► **corredor(a) de pista** track athlete
[2] (= *agente*) agent, broker ► **corredor(a) de apuestas** bookmaker ► **corredor(a) de bienes raíces** estate agent, real estate agent *o* broker (*EEUU*) ► **corredor(a) de bodas**†† matchmaker ► **corredor(a) de bolsa** stockbroker ► **corredor(a) de casas** house agent ► **corredor(a) de comercio** business agent ► **corredor(a) de fincas** estate agent, real estate agent *o* broker (*EEUU*) ► **corredor(a) de fincas rurales** land agent ► **corredor(a) de oreja**†† gossip ► **corredor(a) de propiedades** (*Cono Sur*) estate agent, real estate agent *o* broker (*EEUU*) ► **corredor(a) de seguros** insurance broker
Ⓑ SM [1] (= *pasillo*) corridor, passage ► **corredor de la muerte** death row ► **corredor de popa** (*Náut*) stern gallery
[2] (*Geog, Mil*) corridor ► **corredor aéreo** corridor, air corridor
[3] (*Méx Caza*) beater
[4] (*Mil*††) raider

correduría SF brokerage

corregible ADJ rectifiable

corregidor SM (*Hist*) chief magistrate

corregidora SF (*Hist*) wife of the chief magistrate

corregimiento SM (*Col*) small town

corregir ▸conjug 3c, 3k◂ Ⓐ VT [1] (= *rectificar*) [+ *error, defecto, rumbo, pruebas de imprenta*] to correct; [+ *vicio*] to get rid of; [+ *comportamiento*] to improve; [+ *tendencia*] to correct, counteract; (*Econ*) [+ *déficit*] to counteract; **¡deja ya de ~me!** stop correcting me!; **me gusta que me corrijan cuando hablo en inglés** I like people to correct me when I speak English; **corrígeme si me equivoco, pero creo que aquí hemos estado ya** correct me if I'm wrong, but I think we've been here before
[2] (*Educ*) [+ *examen, dictado, tareas*] to mark, grade (*EEUU*)
Ⓑ **corregirse** VPR [1] [*persona*] to reform, mend one's ways
[2] [*defecto*] **nadando se te ~á la desviación de columna** swimming will help to correct the curvature of your spine; **la miopía no puede ~se sola** shortsightedness does not cure itself

correlación SF correlation

correlacionar ▸conjug 1a◂ VT to correlate

correlativo ADJ, SM correlative

correligionario/a SM/F [1] (*Rel*) co-religionist
[2] (*Pol*) **el presidente y sus ~s** the president and his fellow party members

correlón ADJ [1] (*LAm*) [*persona*] fast, good at running [2] (*Méx, Ven*) (= *cobarde*) cowardly

correntada SF (*Cono Sur*) rapids *pl*, strong current

correntón Ⓐ ADJ [1] (= *activo*) busy, active
[2] (= *bromista*) jokey, jolly, fond of a lark
Ⓑ SM (*Andes, Caribe*) strong current

correntoso ADJ (*LAm*) [*río*] strong-flowing, rapid; [*agua*] torrential

correo SM [1] (= *correspondencia*) post, mail; **¿ha llegado el ~?** has the post *o* mail come?
[2] (= *servicio*) post, mail; **echar algo al ~** ◊ **poner algo en el ~** to post sth, mail sth (*esp EEUU*); **llevar algo al ~** to take sth to the post; **por ~** by post, through the post; **a vuelta de ~** by return (of post) ► **correo aéreo** airmail ► **correo basura** (*por carta*) junk mail; (*por Internet*) spam, junk e-mail ► **correo certificado** registered post ► **correo electrónico** e-mail, electronic mail ► **correo urgente** special delivery ► **correo web** webmail
[3] (= *oficina*) **Correos** post office *sing*; **ir a ~s** to go to the post office; **Dirección General de Correos** General Post Office
[4] **el ~** (*Ferro*) the mail train, the slow train
[5] (= *mensajero*) courier; (*Mil*) dispatch rider ► **correo de gabinete** Queen's Messenger, diplomatic courier (*EEUU*)

correosidad SF [1] (*Culin*) toughness, leatheriness [2] (= *flexibilidad*) flexibility

correoso ADJ [1] (*Culin*) tough, leathery
[2] (= *flexible*) flexible
[3] [*asunto, situación*] difficult, tricky*

correr ▸conjug 2a◂ Ⓐ VI [1] (= *ir deprisa*) [*persona, animal*] to run; [*vehículo*] to go fast; **tuve que ~ para alcanzar el autobús** I had to run to catch the bus; **se me acercó corriendo** he ran up to me; **subió las escaleras corriendo** he ran up the stairs; **corrió a decírselo** he ran to tell him; **¡cómo corre este coche!** this car's really fast!, this car can really go some!; **no corras tanto, que hay hielo en la carretera** don't go so fast, the road's icy; **echar a ~** to start running, break into a run; **el ladrón echó a ~** the thief ran off; ✦**MODISMO ~ como un galgo** *o* **gamo** to run like a hare
[2] (= *darse prisa*) to hurry, rush; **¡corre!** hurry (up)!; **corre que llegamos tarde** hurry (up) or we'll be late; **no corras que te equivocarás** don't rush it or you'll make a mistake; **me voy corriendo, que sale el tren dentro de diez minutos** I must dash, the train leaves in ten minutes; **llega el jefe, más vale que te vayas corriendo** the boss is coming so you'd better get out of here; **hacer algo a todo ~** to do sth as fast as one can; **salieron a todo ~** they rushed out as fast as they could
[3] (= *fluir*) [*agua*] to run, flow; [*aire*] to flow; [*grifo, fuente*] to run; **el río corre muy crecido** the river is running very high; **corre mucho viento** there's a strong wind blowing, it's very windy; **voy a cerrar la ventana porque corre un poco de aire** I'm going to shut the window because there's a bit of a draught *o* draft (*EEUU*); **el camino corre por un paisaje pintoresco** the road runs *o* goes through picturesque countryside; **han corrido ríos de tinta sobre el asunto** reams and reams have been written on the subject; **por sus venas corre sangre china** he has Chinese blood; **~ paralelo a**: **una cadena montañosa que corre paralela a la costa** a chain of mountains that runs parallel to the coast; **la historia de los ordenadores corre paralela a los adelantos en materia de semiconductores** the history of computers runs parallel to advances in semiconductor technology; ✦**MODISMO dejar las cosas ~** to let matters take their course; *ver tb* **sangre A1, A2**
[4] [*tiempo*] **el tiempo corre** time is getting on *o* pressing; **¡cómo corre el tiempo!** time flies!; **el mes que corre** the current month, the present month; **corría el año 1965** it was 1965; **al** *o* **con el ~ del tiempo** over the years; **en estos** *o* **los tiempos que corren** nowadays, these days; **en los tiempos que corren es difícil encontrar personas tan honradas** it's hard to find people as honest as him these days *o* nowadays; **es un tipo demasiado sensible para los tiempos que corren** he's too sensitive for this day and age
[5] (= *moverse*) [*rumor*] to go round; [*creencia*] to be widespread; **el dinero corre con fluidez** money is constantly changing hands; **las noticias corren muy deprisa** news travels fast; **corre por ahí un documento muy interesante** there's a very interesting document going around; **la noticia corría de boca en boca** the news was on everyone's lips; **la noticia corrió como la pólvora** the news spread like wildfire
[6] (= *hacerse cargo*) **eso corre de mi cuenta** I'll take care of that; **~ a cargo de algn**: **eso corre a cargo de la empresa** the company will take care of that; **la entrega del premio corrió a cargo del ministro de Cultura** the prize was presented by the Minister for Culture; **la música corrió a cargo de la RPO** the music was provided by the RPO; **la traducción ha corrido a cargo de Cortázar** the translation is by Cortázar; **~ con algo**: **~ con los gastos** to meet *o* bear the expenses; **el inversor corre con los riesgos** the investor bears the risk; **~ con la casa** to run the house, manage the house
[7] (*Fin*) [*sueldo*] to be payable; [*moneda*] to be valid; **su sueldo ~á desde el primer día del mes** his salary will be payable from the first of the month
[8] **~ a** *o* **por** (= *venderse*) to sell at
Ⓑ VT [1] (*Dep*) [+ *distancia*] to run; [+ *prueba*] to compete in; **corre cinco kilómetros diarios** she runs five kilometres a day; **corrí 50 metros hasta alcanzar la carretera** I ran for 50 metres until I reached the road; **Carl Lewis ha decidido no ~ los 100 metros** Carl Lewis has decided not to run (in) *o* compete in the 100 metres; **corrió la Vuelta a España** he competed in the Tour of Spain; **ha corrido medio mundo** he's been round half the world
[2] (= *desplazar*) [+ *objeto*] to move along; [+ *silla*] to move; [+ *balanza*] to tip; [+ *nudo*] to adjust; [+ *vela*] to unfurl; **corre un poco la silla para allá** move the chair (along) that way a little; **corrió el pestillo** she bolted the door; **corre la cortina** draw the curtain; *ver tb* **velo 1**
[3] (= *hacer correr*) [+ *caballo*] to run, race; [+ *caza*] to chase, pursue; **~ un toro** *to run in front of and avoid being gored by a charging bull for sport*
[4] (= *tener*) [+ *riesgo*] to run; [+ *suerte*] to suf-

fer, undergo; **corren el riesgo de ser encarcelados** they run the risk of being sent to prison; **no quería ~ la misma suerte de su amigo** he didn't want to suffer *o* undergo the same fate as his friend; **no corréis peligro** you're not in (any) danger; **el acuerdo no parece ~ peligro** the agreement doesn't seem to be in danger; *ver tb* **prisa**

5 (= *extender*) **el agua corrió la pintura** the water made the paint run; **las lágrimas le corrieron el maquillaje** her tears made her make-up run; **has corrido la tinta por toda la página** you've smeared the ink across the page

6 (*Mil*) (= *invadir*) to raid; (= *destruir*) to lay waste

7 (*Com*) to auction

8 (= *abochornar*) to embarrass

9 (*esp LAm**) (= *expulsar*) to chuck out*; **lo corrieron de la casa con gritos y patadas** they chucked him kicking and screaming out of the house*

10 **~la*** (= *ir de juerga*) to live it up*

Ⓒ **correrse** VPR 1 (= *desplazarse*) [*objeto, persona*] to move; [*peso*] to shift; **el tablero se ha corrido unos centímetros** the board has moved a few centimetres; **córrete un poco** move over *o* up a bit; **córrete un poco hacia este lado** move this way a bit; **el dolor se me ha corrido hacia la pierna** the pain has moved to my leg; **~se de asiento** to move up a seat

2 (= *extenderse*) [*colores, maquillaje, tinta*] to run; **se me han corrido las medias** I've got a ladder *o* (*EEUU*) run in my tights

3 **~se la clase*** to skive off*, play hooky (*EEUU**)

4 (*) (= *avergonzarse*) to be embarrassed; (= *aturdirse*) to be disconcerted

5 (*CAm, Caribe, Méx*) (= *huir*) to take flight, run away; (= *acobardarse*) to get scared, take fright

6 (**) (= *tener un orgasmo*) to come**

7 (*Perú***) to screw**; *ver tb* **juerga**

correría SF 1 (*Mil*) raid, foray

2 (= *viaje*) trip, excursion; **correrías** travels

correspondencia SF 1 (= *cartas*) mail, post; **abrir la ~** to open the mail; **despachar la ~** to deal with *o* attend to the mail ► **correspondencia entrante** incoming mail ► **correspondencia privada** private correspondence

2 (= *relación por correo*) correspondence; **estar en ~ con algn** to be in correspondence with sb; **mantener ~ con algn** to correspond with sb; **un curso de dibujo por ~** a correspondence course in drawing; **jugar al ajedrez por ~** to play chess by correspondence

3 (*en el metro*) connection; **"~ con las líneas 3 y 5"** "change here for lines 3 and 5"

4 (= *relación recíproca*) correspondence

5 (*Mat*) correspondence

▼ **corresponder** ▸conjug 2a◂ Ⓐ VI 1 (= *tocar*)

1·1 (*en reparto*) **nos correspondieron diez euros a cada uno** each of us got ten euros as our share

1·2 (*como derecho*) **le corresponde un tercio de los beneficios** a third share of the profits goes to him; **me corresponde un día de vacaciones cada dos semanas** I am due one day's holiday every two weeks; **este hecho no ocupa el lugar que le corresponde en la historia de España** this event does not occupy the place it should in Spanish history, this event is not accorded the importance it deserves in Spanish history

1·3 (*en sorteo, competición*) [*honor, victoria*] to go to; **el honor de representar a su país correspondió a Juan Blanco** the honour of representing his country fell to *o* went to Juan Blanco; **la victoria final correspondió a Escartín** the final victory was Escartín's, the final victory went to Escartín; **al primer premio le correspondieron 30.000 euros** the winner of the first prize received 30,000 euros

2 (= *incumbir*) **~ a algn** [*responsabilidad*] to fall to sb; **esta decisión le corresponde al director** this decision is for the director (to take), this decision falls to the director; **le corresponde a ella decidir** it's up to her to decide; **nos corresponde a todos garantizar la calidad** it's everyone's job to ensure quality; **a mí no me corresponde criticarlo** it is not for me to criticize him, it is not my place to criticize him; **"a quien corresponda"** "to whom it may concern"

3 (= *deberse*) **~ a algo**: **de los 50 millones de ganancias, 40 corresponden a ventas en el extranjero** out of profits of 50 million, 40 million comes from overseas sales *o* overseas sales account for 40 million; **la mayor parte de nuestra deuda corresponde a préstamos norteamericanos** most of our debt is a result of American loans, American loans account for most of our debt

4 (*frm*) (= *ser adecuado*) **~ a**: **se vistió como correspondía a la ocasión** she dressed suitably for the occasion; **fue recibido como corresponde a una persona de su cargo** he was received in a manner befitting a person of his rank, he was received as befitted a person of his rank

5 (= *concordar*) **~ a** *o* **con** to match with, match up with; **su versión de los hechos no corresponde a la realidad** her version of the events does not match up with *o* correspond to *o* tally with the truth; **el presunto delincuente, cuyas iniciales corresponden a las siglas R.C.A.** the alleged perpetrator of the crime, whose initials are R.C.A.; **los dos cadáveres hallados corresponden a los dos secuestrados** the two bodies found are those of the two kidnap victims; **esa forma de actuar no corresponde con sus principios** such behaviour is not in keeping with his principles

6 (= *retribuir*) **~ a** [+ *cariño, amor*] to return; [+ *favor, generosidad*] to repay, return; **ella lo amaba, pero él no le correspondía** she loved him but he did not return her love *o* love her back *o* love her in return; **un amor no correspondido** unrequited love; **nunca podré ~ a tanta generosidad** I can never adequately repay *o* return such generosity; **pero ella le correspondió con desprecio** but she responded with contempt, but all she gave in return was contempt

7 (*Mat*) to correspond

8 (*Ferro*) **~ con algo** to connect with sth

Ⓑ **corresponderse** VPR 1 (= *ajustarse*) **~se con algo** to match sth; **esas muestras no se correspondían con las del laboratorio** these samples did not match (up with) the laboratory ones; **el éxito deportivo no siempre se ha correspondido con una buena organización** sporting success has not always been matched by good organization; **eso no se corresponde con su modo de actuar** that is not in keeping with his usual behaviour

2 (= *coordinarse*) [*colores, piezas*] to match, go together

3 (*por carta*) **~se con algn** to correspond with sb

correspondiente Ⓐ ADJ 1 (= *apropiado*) appropriate; **adjunto le envío fotocopia de toda la documentación ~** I enclose a photocopy of all the appropriate documentation

2 **~ a**: **los datos ~s al año anterior** the figures for the previous year; **facturas ~s a gastos de viajes** invoices for travel expenses; **en el número ~ al 15 de agosto pasado, la revista …** in its issue of 15 August, the magazine …; **el partido ~ a la décima jornada de la liga** the match of the tenth day of the league championship

3 (= *respectivo*) respective; **dos épocas distintas, con sus ~s conflictos ideológicos** two different eras, with their respective ideological conflicts; **cada regalo con su tarjeta ~** each present with its own card; **entregó el premio y su ~ banda a la ganadora** he awarded the prize and accompanying sash to the winner

Ⓑ SMF [*de academia*] corresponding member

corresponsabilidad SF joint responsibility

corresponsable ADJ jointly responsible (**de** for)

corresponsal SMF correspondent, newspaper correspondent ► **corresponsal de guerra** war correspondent

corretaje SM brokerage

corretear ▸conjug 1a◂ Ⓐ VT 1 (*LAm*) (= *acosar*) to harass

2 (*CAm*) (= *ahuyentar*) to scare off

3 (*Cono Sur*) [+ *trabajo*] to hurry along, push*

Ⓑ VI 1 (= *ir de prisa*) to run about

2 (= *vagar*) to loiter, hang about the streets

correteo SM **andar en ~s** (*CAm*) to rush about

corretero/a SM/F busy person, gadabout

correvedile SMF, **correveidile** SMF (= *acusica*) tell-tale; (= *chismoso*) gossip

corrida SF 1 (= *carrera*) run; **dar una ~** to make a dash; **decir algo de ~** to rattle off sth; **en una ~** in an instant

2 **~ (de toros)** (*Taur*) bullfight; ✦**MODISMO** **tener ~ de toros (en casa)** to have a big family row

3 (**) (= *orgasmo*) orgasm

4 (*Geol*) outcrop

5 (*Chile*) (= *fila*) row, line

6 (*Caribe, Cono Sur*) (= *fiesta*) party, rave-up*, hot party (*EEUU*)

7 (*Méx*) (= *recorrido*) run, journey

corrido Ⓐ ADJ 1 [*habitación, galería*] continuous

2 [*cortinas*] drawn

3 (= *avergonzado*) abashed, embarrassed; **~ de vergüenza** covered with shame

4 (= *experimentado*) worldly-wise, sharp; **es una mujer corrida** she's a woman who has been around

5 (*con expresiones temporales*) **tres noches corridas** three nights running; **hasta muy corrida la noche** far into the night

6 [*peso, medida*] extra, extra large; **un kilo ~** a good kilo, a kilo and a bit

7 [*estilo*] fluent, confident; **de ~** fluently; **decir algo de ~** to rattle sth off; **se sabía la**

➤ LENGUA Y USO: corresponder A1 32.4

lección de ~ he knew it all right through, he could say it all from memory
8 (*Méx*) **comida corrida** fixed price menu
Ⓑ SM 1 (*Méx*) (= *balada*) ballad
2 (*Perú*) (= *fugitivo*) fugitive from justice

CORRIDO

Corridos *are Mexican ballads, usually sung by a solo voice and accompanied on the guitar. Traditionally they were used to narrate important events to semi-literate communities, and favourite themes include the Mexican Revolution and Mexican migration to the USA. The* ***corrido*** *is similar in form to the Spanish* ***romance*** *from which it derives, but deals with the common people's struggle for justice, rather than the chivalrous deeds of the aristocracy.*

corriente Ⓐ ADJ 1 (= *frecuente*) [*error, apellido*] common; **las intoxicaciones son bastante ~s en verano** cases of food poisoning are fairly common in summer; **la cocaína era ~ en sus fiestas** cocaine was commonly used *o* was commonplace at their parties; **aquí es ~ que la policía te pida la documentación** here it's quite common for the police to ask you for identification; **una combinación de cualidades que no es ~ encontrar en una misma persona** a combination of qualities not commonly *o* often found in the same person; **un término de uso ~** a common term, a term in common use; **poco ~** unusual
2 (= *habitual*) usual, customary; **lo ~ es llamar antes de venir** the usual thing is to phone before coming, it's customary to phone before coming; **es ~ que la familia de la novia pague la boda** it's customary for the bride's family to pay for the wedding, the bride's family usually pays for the wedding
3 (= *no especial*) ordinary; **no es nada especial, es sólo un anillo ~** it's nothing special, it's just an ordinary ring; **fuera de lo ~** out of the ordinary; **normal y ~** perfectly ordinary; **salirse de lo ~** to be out of the ordinary; ✦***MODISMO*** **~ y moliente** (*Esp*) very ordinary; **tiene un trabajo ~ y moliente** he has a very ordinary job, he has a run-of-the-mill job
4 (*en curso*) [*déficit, mes, año*] current; **el día 2 del ~ mes de marzo** (on) the second of this month; *ver tb* **cuenta 4**, **gasto 2**, **moneda 2**
5 [*agua*] running
6 (†) (= *en regla*) in order; **tiene ~ la documentación** his papers are in order; **todo está ~ para nuestra partida** everything is ready *o* fixed up for our departure; **estar** *o* **ir ~ en algo** to be up to date with sth; **está ~ en los pagos** he is up to date with his payments
Ⓑ SM 1 **al ~** 1·1 (= *al día*) up to date; **estoy al ~ de mis pagos a Hacienda** I'm up to date with *o* on my tax payments; **poner algo al ~** to bring sth up to date
1·2 (= *informado*) **estar al ~ (de algo)** to know (about sth); **puedes hablar sin miedo, ya estoy al ~** you can talk freely, I know (all) about it; **¿estaba usted al ~?** did you know (about it)?; **mantener a algn al ~ (de algo)** to keep sb up to date (on sth), keep sb informed (about sth); **poner a algn al ~ (de algo)** to bring sb up to date (on sth), inform sb (about sth); **ponerse al ~ (de algo)** to get up to date (with sth), catch up (on sth); **tener a algn al ~ (de algo)** to keep sb up to date (on sth), keep sb informed (about sth)
2 (*en cartas*) **el día 9 del ~** *o* **de los ~s** the 9th of this month
Ⓒ SF 1 [*de fluido*] current; **la ~ lo arrastraba hacia el mar** the current was carrying him out to sea; ✦***MODISMOS*** **dejarse llevar por la ~** to follow the crowd *o* stream, go with the flow (*esp EEUU*); **ir** *o* **navegar** *o* **nadar contra (la) ~** to swim *o* go against the tide; **seguir la ~ a algn** to humour *o* (*EEUU*) humor sb; **cuando se pone a hablar así es mejor seguirle la ~** when he starts talking like that it's best to humour him ► **corriente de agua** stream of water ► **corriente de Humboldt** Humboldt Current ► **corriente de lava** lava flow, stream of lava ► **corriente del Golfo** Gulf Stream ► **corriente sanguínea** bloodstream ► **corriente submarina** undercurrent, underwater current
2 [*de aire*] draught, draft (*EEUU*); **hay mucha ~** it's very draughty ► **corriente de aire** (*gen*) draught, draft (*EEUU*); (*Téc*) air current, air stream ► **corriente en chorro** jet stream ► **corriente térmica** thermal
3 (*Elec*) current; **anoche se cortó la ~** there was a power cut last night; **el cable tiene ~** the wire is live; **dar ~: no toques ese cable que da ~** don't touch that wire, it's live; **me dio (la) ~** I got a shock, I got an electric shock ► **corriente alterna** alternating current ► **corriente continua** direct current ► **corriente difásica** two-phase current ► **corriente directa** direct current ► **corriente eléctrica** electric current ► **corriente trifásica** three-phase current
4 (= *tendencia*) (*ideológica*) tendency; (*artística*) trend; **una ~ más radical dentro del partido** a more radical tendency within the party; **la ~ renovadora de la derecha** the trend towards renewal on the Right; **las ~s modernas del arte** modern trends in art ► **corriente de opinión** current of opinion ► **corriente de pensamiento** school of thought

corrientemente ADV usually, normally

corrillero/a SM/F idler, person with time to gossip

corrillo SM (= *grupo*) huddle, small group; (*pey*) clique, coterie

corrimiento SM 1 (*Geol*) slip ► **corrimiento de tierras** landslide
2 (*Med*) (= *secreción*) discharge; (*Caribe, Cono Sur*) (= *reúma*) rheumatism; (*Andes*) (= *flemón*) tooth abscess
3 (= *vergüenza*) embarrassment
4 (*Inform*) scrolling

corrincho SM 1 (= *muchedumbre*) mob
2 (*Andes*) (= *jaleo*) uproar, row
3 (*Andes*) (= *emoción*) excitement; (= *prisa*) haste

corro SM 1 [*de gente*] ring, circle; **la gente hizo ~** the people formed a ring *o* circle
2 (= *baile*) ring-a-ring-a-roses; **los niños cantan esto en ~** the children sing this in a ring
3 (*Fin*) pit, ring (*in the stock exchange*)
4 (*Agr*) plot, small field, patch

corroboración SF corroboration

▼**corroborar** ▸conjug 1a◂ VT to corroborate

corroborativo ADJ corroborative

corroer ▸conjug 2a◂ Ⓐ VT 1 (*Téc*) to corrode
2 (*Geol*) to erode
3 (= *reconcomer*) to corrode, eat away; **le corroen los celos** he is eaten up with jealousy
Ⓑ **corroerse** VPR to corrode, become corroded

corromper ▸conjug 2a◂ Ⓐ VT 1 (= *pudrir*) [+ *madera*] to rot; [+ *alimentos*] to turn bad
2 (= *estropear*) [+ *costumbres, lengua, joven*] to corrupt; [+ *placeres*] to spoil
3 (= *sobornar*) to bribe
4 (*) (= *enojar*) to vex, annoy
Ⓑ VI (*) to smell bad, stink*
Ⓒ **corromperse** VPR 1 (= *pudrirse*) [*madera*] to rot; [*alimentos*] to go bad
2 [*personas*] to become corrupted

corrompido ADJ 1 [*cosas*] rotten, putrid
2 [*personas*] corrupt

corroncha SF (*Andes, CAm*) crust, scale

corroncho ADJ 1 (*Caribe*) (= *torpe*) slow, sluggish
2 (*Andes*) [*persona*] difficult, prickly

corronchoso ADJ (*Andes, CAm, Caribe*) (= *burdo*) rough, coarse; (= *escamoso*) crusty, scaly

corrongo ADJ (*CAm, Caribe*) (= *excelente*) first-rate, splendid; (= *encantador*) charming, attractive

corrosión SF (*Quím*) corrosion; (*Geol*) erosion

corrosivo Ⓐ ADJ [*sustancia*] corrosive; [*lenguaje, estilo*] caustic
Ⓑ SM corrosive

corrte. ABR (= **corriente, de los corrientes**) inst

corrugación SF contraction, shrinkage

corrupción SF 1 (= *pudrición*) rot, decay
2 (*moral*) corruption
3 (*Jur*) corruption, graft; (= *soborno*) graft, bribery; **en el gobierno existe mucha ~** there is a lot of corruption in the government ► **corrupción de menores** corruption of minors
4 [*de lengua, texto*] corruption

corruptela SF 1 (= *corrupción*) corruption
2 (= *abuso*) corrupt practice, corrupt practise (*EEUU*), abuse

corruptible ADJ 1 [*persona*] corruptible, bribable
2 [*alimentos*] perishable

corrupto ADJ corrupt

corruptor(a) Ⓐ ADJ corrupting
Ⓑ SM/F corrupter, perverter

corsario SM privateer, corsair

corsé SM corset; (*fig*) straitjacket

corso[1]/a ADJ, SM/F Corsican

corso[2] SM (*Náut, Hist*) privateering, piratical enterprise

corta SF felling, cutting

cortaalambres SM INV wire cutters

cortabolsas SM INV pickpocket

cortacésped SM lawnmower

cortacircuitos SM INV circuit breaker, trip switch

cortacorrientes SM INV circuit breaker, trip switch

cortacutícula SF cuticle scissors

cortada SF 1 (*LAm*) (= *corte*) cut; (= *atajo*) short cut
2 [*de pan*] slice
3 (*Tenis*) stroke giving backspin

➤ LENGUA Y USO: **corroborar** 38.1

cortadillo SM [1] (= *vaso*) small glass, small tumbler
[2] (= *azúcar*) lump of sugar
[3] (*) (= *ligue*) affair

cortado (A) ADJ [1] (= *recortado, partido*) cut; **la carne cortada en trozos grandes** meat cut into large chunks; **~ a pico** [*montaña, acantilado*] steep, sheer, precipitous
[2] (= *pasado*) [*leche, mayonesa*] off; **tener** *o* **sentir el cuerpo ~** to feel off colour
[3] [*piel, labios*] chapped
[4] [*calle, carretera*] closed; **"carretera cortada por obras"** "closed for roadworks"
[5] [*café*] coffee with a little milk
[6] [*estilo*] (*gen*) disjointed; (*al hablar*) clipped
[7] [*película*] cut
[8] (*) [*persona*] shy; **es un tío muy ~** he's a really shy bloke*; **está ~ porque no os conoce** he's shy because he doesn't know you; **dejar ~** to cut short; **me dejó ~ en mitad de lo que estaba diciendo** he cut me short in the middle of what I was saying; **quedarse ~**: **no te quedes ~, hombre, di algo** come on, don't be shy, say something; **me quedé ~ cuando entré en la habitación y los vi besándose** I was left speechless when I came into the room and found them kissing
[9] **estar ~** (*esp LAm**) (= *arruinado*) to be broke*
(B) SM [1] (= *café*) coffee with a little milk
[2] (*Ballet*) leap

cortador(a) (A) ADJ cutting
(B) SM/F cutter
(C) SM ► **cortador de cristal** glass cutter

cortadora SF cutter, cutting-machine ► **cortadora de césped** lawnmower

cortadura SF [1] (= *incisión*) cut; (*grande*) slash, slit
[2] (*Geog*) narrow pass, defile
[3] **cortaduras** (= *recortes*) cuttings, clippings

cortafrío SM cold chisel

cortafuego(s) SM (INV) fire-break, fire lane (*EEUU*); (*Internet*) firewall

cortahuevos SM INV egg-slicer

cortahumedades SM INV damp course

cortalápices SM INV pencil sharpener

cortante (A) ADJ [1] [*instrumento*] cutting, sharp
[2] [*viento*] cutting, biting; **hace un frío ~** it's bitterly cold
[3] [*respuesta*] sharp, cutting
(B) SM (= *trinchador*) cleaver, chopper

cortapapel SM (*LAm*), **cortapapeles** SM INV (*para cartas*) paper knife; (*Téc*) paper cutter, guillotine

cortapicos SM INV earwig

cortapisa SF [1] (= *restricción*) restriction, condition; **sin ~s** with no strings attached
[2] (= *traba*) snag, obstacle; **poner ~s a algo/algn** to restrict *o* hold back sth/sb; **se pone ~s para sí mismo** he makes obstacles for himself; **hablar sin ~s** to talk freely
[3] (= *gracia*) charm, wit

cortaplumas SM INV penknife

cortapuros SM INV cigar cutter

cortar ▸conjug 1a◂ (A) VT [1] (*con algo afilado*) (*gen*) to cut; (*en trozos*) to chop; (*en rebanadas*) to slice; **corta la manzana por la mitad** cut the apple in half; **¿quién te ha cortado el pelo?** who cut your hair?; **corta el apio en trozos** cut *o* chop the celery into pieces
[2] (= *partir*) [+ *árbol*] to cut down; [+ *madera*] to saw; **~ la cabeza a algn** to cut sb's head off
[3] (= *dividir*) to cut; **la línea corta el círculo en dos** the line cuts *o* divides the circle in two
[4] (= *interrumpir*) [4·1] [+ *comunicaciones, agua, corriente*] to cut off; [+ *carretera, puente*] (= *cerrar*) to close; (= *bloquear*) to block; **han cortado el gas** the gas has been cut off; **las tropas estan intentando ~ la carretera que conduce al aeropuerto** the troops are trying to cut off the road to the airport; **han cortado el tráfico durante unos minutos** they've closed the road to traffic for a few minutes; **"carretera cortada al tráfico"** "road closed"; **sus seguidores han cortado la calle** her followers have blocked off the road; **nos ~on la retirada** they cut off our retreat; **~ la hemorragia** to stop the bleeding
[4·2] [+ *relaciones*] to break off; [+ *discurso, conversación*] to cut short; **~ la comunicación** to hang up
[5] (= *suprimir*) to cut; **la censura cortó una de las escenas** the censors cut one of the scenes
[6] [*frío*] to chap, crack; **el frío me corta los labios** the cold is chapping *o* cracking my lips
[7] (*Dep*) [+ *balón*] to slice
[8] [+ *baraja*] to cut
[9] (*) [+ *droga*] to cut*
(B) VI [1] (= *estar afilado*) to cut; **estas tijeras no cortan** these scissors are blunt *o* don't cut; *ver tb* **sano 1**
[2] (*Inform*) **"~ y pegar"** "cut and paste"
[3] (*Meteo*) **hace un viento que corta** there's a bitter *o* biting wind
[4] (= *acortar*) **podemos ~ por el parque** we can take a shortcut through the park; **es mejor que cortéis por el atajo** it would be better if you took the shortcut
[5] **~ con** (= *terminar*): **~ con el pasado** to make a break with the past; **hay que ~ con este comportamiento** we must put a stop to this behaviour; **es absurdo ~ con tu tía por culpa de su marido** it's ridiculous to break off contact with your aunt because of her husband; **ha cortado con su novia** he's broken up with *o* finished with his girlfriend
[6] **¡corta!*** give us a break!*; *ver tb* **rollo A5**
[7] (*Naipes*) to cut
[8] (*Radio*) **¡corto!** over!; **¡corto y cierro!** over and out!
[9] (*LAm Telec*) to hang up; **cortó** he hung up
(C) **cortarse** VPR [1] (*con algo afilado*) [1·1] [*persona*] to cut o.s.; **te vas a ~** you're going to cut yourself
[1·2] **me corté el dedo con un cristal** I cut my finger on a piece of glass; **~se las uñas** to cut one's nails; **ha ido a ~se el pelo** she's gone to get her hair cut, she's gone to the hairdresser's, she's gone for a haircut; **se cortó las venas** she slashed her wrists; ✦**MODISMO** **cortársela**‡: **si no acepta, me la corto** I'll be bloody amazed if he doesn't accept it‡
[2] (= *rajarse*) [*manos, labios*] to get chapped; [*material*] to split, come apart
[3] (*Culin*) [*mayonesa, natillas*] to curdle; [*leche*] to go off, curdle
[4] (*) (= *cohibirse*) to get embarrassed; **no te cortes** don't be shy; **no se corta a la hora de decir lo que piensa** she doesn't hold back at all when it comes to saying what she thinks; ✦**MODISMO** **no ~se un pelo**: **el entrenador, que no se corta un pelo, ha culpado al árbitro de la derrota** the coach, never one to hold back, has blamed the referee for the defeat
[5] (= *interrumpirse*) [*luz*] to go off, go out; **se ha cortado la comunicación** the line's gone dead; **se cortó la llamada** I was cut off
[6] (*Cono Sur**) (= *separarse*) to become separated (from the others), get left behind; (= *irse*) to clear off*; (*en trato*) to get left out; **~se solo** to go off on one's own
[7] (*Cono Sur**) (= *morirse*) to die

cortauñas SM INV nail clippers

cortavidrios SM INV glass cutter

cortavientos SM INV windbreak

corte[1] SM [1] (= *incisión, herida*) cut; **le hizo un ~ a la madera** he made a cut in the wood; **tienes un pequeño ~ en la pierna** you have a small cut on your leg; **hacerse un ~** to cut o.s.; **me he hecho un ~ en el dedo** I've cut my finger ► **corte longitudinal** lengthwise section, longitudinal section ► **corte transversal** cross section
[2] (*tb* **~ de pelo**) cut, haircut ► **corte a navaja** razor cut ► **corte a tijera** scissor cut
[3] (*Cos*) (= *diseño*) cut; **un traje de ~ muy moderno** a suit with a very modern cut ► **corte y confección** dressmaking
[4] (= *interrupción*) cut; **persisten los ~s de agua** the water keeps being cut off; **la censura dejó la película sin ~s** the censor did not cut the film ► **corte de carretera** (*para obras, accidente*) road closure; (*como protesta*) roadblock ► **corte de corriente** power cut ► **corte de digestión** stomach cramp ► **corte de luz** power cut ► **corte publicitario** commercial break
[5] (= *estilo*) **literatura de ~ tradicional** traditional (type) literature; **un discurso de ~ fascista** a speech with fascist undertones; **un sistema fiscal de ~ occidental** a western-style taxation system
[6] (= *trozo*) ► **corte de carne** cut of meat ► **corte (de helado)** wafer, ice cream sandwich (*EEUU*)
[7] (*) (= *respuesta contundente*) **dar un ~ a algn: ¡vaya ~ que te dieron!** that was one in the eye for you, wasn't it!; **dale un buen ~ y no te molestará más** tell him where to go and he won't bother you any more* ► **corte de mangas** *rude gesture made with the arm and hand which is the equivalent of giving the V-sign or, in the US, the finger*; **le hizo un ~ de mangas a los fotógrafos** he made a *o* the V-sign at the photographers, he gave two fingers to the photographers, he gave the photographers the finger (*EEUU*); **sus declaraciones son un ~ de mangas a la Constitución** his statements are a two-fingered salute to the Constitution
[8] (*) (= *vergüenza*) **es un ~ que te vean tus padres fumando** it's embarrassing when your parents see you smoking; **¡qué ~, me besó delante de todos!** how embarrassing! he kissed me in front of everyone!; **me da ~ que me vean contigo** I'm embarrassed to be seen with you; **me da mucho ~ hablar en público** I get really embarrassed if I have to speak in public; **llevarse un ~: me llevé un buen ~ cuando supe que tenía novio** I felt really silly when I found out she had a boyfriend

9 (= *borde*) edge; **con ~s dorados** with gilt edges; **dar ~ a algo** to sharpen sth, put an edge on sth
10 [*de disco*] track
11 (*Min*) stint
12 (*Cono Sur*) (= *importancia*) **darse ~s** to put on airs

corte² SF 1 [*de un rey*] (= *residencia*) court; (= *séquito*) court, entourage, retinue; **los ciudadanos de la ~** the court dwellers ► **corte celestial** heavenly court; *ver tb* **villa 1**
2 **hacer la ~ a algn** (= *cortejar*) to pay court to sb; (= *halagar*) to win favour with sb, lick sb's boots*, suck up to sb*; **no deja de hacerme la ~ a ver si le presto dinero** he keeps licking my boots o sucking up to me so that I'll lend him some money
3 (*Jur*) law court ► **Corte de Justicia** Court of Justice ► **Corte Suprema** Supreme Court
4 (= *ciudad*) capital, capital city; **La Corte** Madrid
5 **lasCortes** (*Pol*) Spanish parliament; **el Presidente disolvió las Cortes** the President dissolved Parliament; **una manifestación frente a las Cortes** a demonstration outside the Parliament building ► **Cortes Constituyentes** constituent assembly ► **Cortes de Castilla-La Mancha** Regional Assembly of Castile and La Mancha ► **Cortes de Castilla y León** Regional Assembly of Castile and León ► **Cortes Generales** Parliament

CORTES GENERALES

The Spanish parliament consists of a lower house, the **Congreso de los Diputados**, *and an upper house, the* **Senado**. *Members of the lower house are called* **diputados** *and members of the* **Senado** *are* **senadores**.
⇨ *See also* CONGRESO DE LOS DIPUTADOS, SENADO

cortedad SF 1 [*de tiempo*] shortness, brevity; [*de espacio*] smallness; (*tb* **~ de alcances**) stupidity ► **cortedad de vista** shortsightedness
2 (= *escasez*) dearth, lack
3 (= *timidez*) shyness, bashfulness ► **cortedad de ánimo** diffidence

cortejar ▸conjug 1a◂ VT to court, woo

cortejo SM 1 (= *séquito*) entourage, retinue
2 (*Rel*) procession ► **cortejo fúnebre** funeral cortège, funeral procession ► **cortejo nupcial** wedding party
3 (= *acción*) wooing, courting

cortés ADJ 1 (= *atento*) courteous, polite
2 **amor ~** courtly love

cortesana SF courtesan

cortesanía SF politeness

cortesano Ⓐ ADJ of the court, courtly; **ceremonias cortesanas** court ceremony
Ⓑ SM courtier

cortesía SF 1 (= *conducta*) courtesy, politeness; **visita de ~** courtesy call; **entrada de ~** complimentary ticket; **días de ~** (*Com*) days of grace; **por ~** as a courtesy
2 (= *etiqueta*) social etiquette; **la ~ pide que ...** etiquette demands that ...
3 [*de carta*] formal ending
4 (= *reverencia*) [*de hombre*] bow; [*de mujer*] curtsy; **hacer una ~ a algn** [*hombre*] to bow to sb; [*mujer*] to curtsy to sb
5 (= *regalo*) present, gift

cortésmente ADV courteously, politely

córtex SM cortex

corteza SF 1 [*de árbol*] bark; [*de pan*] crust; [*de fruta*] peel, skin; [*de queso, tocino*] rind; **se añade una ~ de limón** add a bit of lemon peel ► **corteza cerebral** cerebral cortex ► **corteza de cerdo** pork rind ► **corteza terrestre** earth's crust
2 (= *exterior*) outside, outward appearance
3 (= *grosería*) roughness, coarseness

corticoide SM corticoid

cortijo SM farmhouse

cortina SF (*para ventana*) curtain, drape (*EEUU*); (*Téc*) retaining wall; (*fig*) screen; ✦***MODISMOS*** **correr la ~** to draw a veil over sth; **descorrer la ~** to draw back the veil ► **cortina de ducha** shower curtain ► **cortina de fuego** (*Mil*) barrage ► **cortina de hierro** (*Pol*) iron curtain ► **cortina de humo** smoke screen ► **cortina de tienda** tent flap ► **cortina musical** (*Cono Sur TV*) musical interlude

cortinado SM (*Cono Sur*) curtains *pl*

cortinilla SF lace curtain

cortisona SF cortisone

corto Ⓐ ADJ 1 [*longitud, distancia*] short; **llevaba el pelo muy ~** she had very short hair; **una camisa de manga corta** a short-sleeved shirt; **vinimos por el camino más ~** we came by the shortest route; **un relato ~** a short story; **el vestido se le ha quedado ~** the dress has got too short for her; **el tiro se quedó ~** the shot fell short; *ver tb* **pantalón 1**
2 [*periodo, visita, reunión*] short, brief; **en un ~ espacio de tiempo** in a short space of time; **los días se van haciendo más ~s** the days are getting shorter; **la película se me hizo muy corta** the film was over *o* went very quickly; *ver tb* **plazo 1**
3 (= *escaso*) [*ración*] small; **dos niñas de corta edad** two very young girls; **~ de algo**: **un café con leche, pero ~ de café** a coffee with plenty of milk, a milky coffee; **~ de oído** hard of hearing; **ando** *o* **voy ~ de dinero** I'm short of money; **ando** *o* **voy muy ~ de tiempo** I'm short of time, I'm pressed *o* pushed for time; **~ de vista** shortsighted, nearsighted (*EEUU*); **quedarse ~**: **costará unos tres millones, y seguro que me quedo ~** it will cost three million, and I'm probably underestimating; **le dijo lo que pensaba de él, pero se quedó ~** she told him what she thought of him, but it still wasn't enough; **nos quedamos ~s con la bebida en la fiesta** we didn't have enough drink for the party; **esta ley se queda corta en sus pretensiones** this law does not go far enough
4 (= *tímido*) shy; ✦***MODISMO*** **ni ~ ni perezoso** as bold as brass
5 (= *torpe*) dim*, thick*; ✦***MODISMO*** **es más ~ que las mangas de un chaleco*** he's as thick as two short planks*; *ver tb* **alcance 7.1**, **entendederas**
Ⓑ SM 1 (*Cine*) short, short film, short movie (*EEUU*)
2 [*de cerveza, vino*] small glass; [*de café*] black coffee
Ⓒ SF **a la corta o a la larga** sooner or later

cortocircuitar ▸conjug 1a◂ VT to short-circuit

cortocircuito SM short-circuit; **poner(se) en ~** to short-circuit

cortometraje SM short

cortón¹ SM (*Entomología*) mole cricket

cortón²* ADJ 1 (= *tímido*) bashful, timid
2 **es muy ~** (*CAm*) (= *que interrumpe*) he's always interrupting

cortopunzante ADJ (*Cono Sur*) sharp

Coruña SF **La ~** Corunna

coruñés/esa Ⓐ ADJ of/from Corunna
Ⓑ SM/F native/inhabitant of Corunna; **los coruñeses** the people of Corunna

corva SF back of the knee

corvadura SF (= *curvatura*) curvature; (*Arquit*) arch

corvejón SM [*de caballo*] hock; [*de gallo*] spur

corveta Ⓐ ADJ (*CAm*) bow-legged
Ⓑ SF curvet, prance

corvetear ▸conjug 1a◂ VI to curvet, prance

corvina SF sea bass, croaker

corvo ADJ (= *curvo*) curved, bent; [*nariz*] hooked

corza SF doe

corzo/a SM/F roe deer

cosa SF 1 (= *objeto*) thing; **¿qué es esa ~ redonda?** what's that round thing?; **cogí mis ~s y me fui** I picked up my things and left; **no es otra ~ que una bolsa de plástico** it's nothing more than a plastic bag, it's just a plastic bag; **para el dolor de cabeza no tengo otra ~ que aspirina** all I have for headaches is aspirin; **~s de comer** things to eat; **las ~s del jardín** the gardening things; ✦***MODISMOS*** **es ~ fina*** it's excellent stuff*; **es ~ de ver** it's well worth seeing, you have to see it
2 (*uso indefinido*) **¿alguna ~ más?** anything else?; **o ~ así**: **20 kilos o ~ así** 20 kilos or thereabouts; **y ~s así** and suchlike; **cualquier ~** anything; **haría cualquier ~ por ella** I'd do anything for her; **este vino no es cualquier ~** this isn't just any old wine; **gran ~**: **el coche no vale gran ~** the car isn't worth much; **no ha servido de gran ~** it hasn't been much use; **la película no fue gran ~** the film wasn't up to much; **como futbolista no es gran ~** he's not a great footballer, he's not much of a footballer; **poca ~**: **lo qué recibieron a cambio fue poca ~** they didn't get much in return, they got very little in return; **vive bien con poca ~** she lives well on very little; **no te preocupes por tan poca ~** don't worry about a little thing like that; **jugamos a las cartas, leemos y poca ~ más** we play cards, read and do little else *o* and that's about it; **la vida es tan corta y somos tan poca ~** life is so short and we're so insignificant; **la chica es muy poquita ~** there's not much of her; **una ~** something; **hay una ~ que no me gusta** there is one thing I don't like; **¿me puedes decir una ~?** can you tell me something?; **una ~, se me olvidaba preguntarte por el precio** by the way, I forgot to ask you about the price; **en general está muy bien, sólo una ~ ...** on the whole, it's very good, there's just one thing ...
3 (= *asunto*) **eso es ~ tuya** that's your affair; **es ~ fácil** it's easy; **¿has visto ~ igual?** did you ever see the like?; **¡qué ~ más extraña!** how strange!; **es ~ de nunca acabar** there's no end to it; **ésa es ~ vieja** so what's new?, that's ancient history; **¡vaya una ~!** well!, there's a thing!; **la ~ es que ...** the thing is (that) ...; **la ~ puede acabar mal** things could end badly; **la ~ no está tan clara** it's not that clear; **la ~ está en considerar el problema desde otro ángulo** the thing to

do *o* the trick is to consider the problem from another angle; **no es ~ de broma** *o* **risa** it's no laughing matter; **no es ~ de que lo dejes todo** there's no need for you to give it all up; **no sea ~ que** in case; **trae el paraguas, no sea ~ que llueva** bring your umbrella in case it rains; **otra ~: no se hablaba de otra ~** people talked about nothing else; **¿hay otra ~ que pueda hacer?** is there anything else I can do?; **eso es otra ~** that's another matter *o* thing (entirely); **otra ~ es que la ley imponga 40 horas semanales para todos** it's another matter entirely for the law to oblige everyone to work 40 hours a week; **otra ~ sería si …** it would be quite another matter if …; **~ rara: y, ~ rara, nadie lo vio** and, oddly *o* funnily enough, nobody saw it; ✦*MODISMOS* **a otra ~, mariposa** it's time to move on; **como quien no quiere la ~: lo miraba como quien no quiere la ~** she cast a casual glance at the boy; **se levantó y se fue como quien no quiere la ~** she got up and left as inconspicuously as possible; **como si tal ~: me devolvió el libro roto como si tal ~** he gave me back the damaged book as if nothing had happened; **le dije que había sido seleccionado para el trabajo y se quedó como si tal ~** I told him he had got the job and he barely reacted; **decir una ~ por otra** to lie

4 (= *nada*) **no hay ~ peor** there's nothing worse; **jamás he visto ~ semejante** I've never seen anything like it, I've never seen the like of it; **¡no hay tal ~!** nothing of the sort!; **nunca he dicho nada sobre ese tema ni ~ que se le parezca** I never said anything about that subject or anything like it; ✦*MODISMO* **no es ninguna ~ del otro jueves** *o* **mundo** it's nothing to write home about

5 **cosas** 5·1 (= *acciones, asuntos*) **¡son ~s de Juan!** that's Juan all over!, that's just like Juan!; **son ~s de la edad** it's just old age; **¡~s de niños!** boys will be boys!; **¡qué ~s dices!** you do say some silly things!; **¡tienes unas ~s!** the things you say!; **meterse en ~s de otros** to stick one's nose in other people's business; ✦*MODISMO* **decir cuatro ~s a algn** to give sb a piece of one's mind

5·2 **las ~s** (= *situación*) things; **las ~s van mejor** things are going better; **tal como están las ~s** as things stand; **así las ~s, se marchó de la reunión** at this point, she left the meeting; **¡lo que son las ~s!** just imagine!, fancy that!; ✦*MODISMO* **las ~s de palacio van despacio** it all takes time, the mills of God grind slowly

6 **~ de** (*indicando tiempo*) about; **es ~ de un par de semanas** it takes about a couple of weeks; **en ~ de diez minutos** in about ten minutes

7 (*) (*droga*) hash*

8 (*LAm*) (*como conj*) **~ que: camina lento, ~ que no te canses** walk slowly so (that) you don't get tired; **no le digas nada, ~ que no se ofenda** don't say anything to him, that way he won't get offended, don't say anything to him in case he gets offended

cosaco/a ADJ, SM/F 1 (= *soldado*) Cossack; ✦*MODISMO* **beber como un ~** to drink like a fish

2 (*Cono Sur*) (= *policía*) mounted policeman

coscacho SM (*Andes, Cono Sur*) rap on the head

coscarana SF cracknel

coscarse* ▸conjug 1g◂ VPR to catch on, get it*

coscoja SF kermes oak

coscolino ADJ 1 (*Méx*) (= *malhumorado*) peevish, touchy; [*niño*] naughty

2 (*moralmente*) of loose morals

coscorrón SM 1 (= *golpe*) bump on the head

2 (= *contratiempo*) setback, knock

coscurro SM hard crust, hard crust of bread

cosecha SF 1 (= *recogida*) harvest; (= *temporada*) harvest, harvest time; **la ~ de 1972** (= *vino*) the 1972 vintage; **una buena ~ de éxitos políticos** a whole crop of political successes; **la película recibió una ~ de premios** the film received a whole crop of prizes

2 (= *producto*) crop; **de ~ propia** home-grown, home-produced; ✦*MODISMO* **cosas de su propia ~** things of one's own invention; **no añadas nada de tu ~** don't add anything that you've made up

3 (= *producción*) yield

cosechado SM harvesting

cosechadora SF combine harvester, combine (*EEUU*)

cosechar ▸conjug 1a◂ VT 1 (= *recoger*) [+ *cereales*] to harvest, reap; [+ *frutas*] to harvest, pick

2 (= *cultivar*) to grow, cultivate; **aquí sólo cosechan patatas** the only thing they grow here is potatoes

3 (= *ganar*) [+ *admiración, premios*] to win; [+ *respeto*] to win, earn; [+ *fracasos , éxitos*] to achieve; [+ *enemigos*] to earn, make; **no cosechó sino disgustos** all he got was troubles

cosechero/a SM/F harvester

cosechón SM bumper crop

coseno SM cosine

coser ▸conjug 2a◂ Ⓐ VT 1 [+ *vestido*] to sew, sew up; [+ *botón*] to sew on, stitch on; **es cosa de ~ y cantar** it's easy as pie*, it's as simple as ABC*

2 (*Med*) to stitch, stitch up; (*Náut*) to lash; **~ con grapas** to staple

3 (= *unir*) to unite, join closely (**con** to)

4 ✦*MODISMOS* **~ a algn a balazos** to riddle sb with bullets; **~ a algn a puñaladas** to stab sb repeatedly, carve sb up*; **lo encontraron cosido a puñaladas** his body was found full of stab wounds

Ⓑ VI to sew

Ⓒ **coserse** VPR **~se con algn** to become closely attached to sb

cosher ADJ INV kosher

cosiaca SF (*LAm*) small thing

cosido SM sewing, needlework

cosificación SF treating as an object; **el capitalismo conduce a la ~ de los obreros** capitalism leads to the workers being treated as objects

cosificar ▸conjug 1g◂ VT to treat as an object

cosignatario/a SM/F cosignatory

cosijoso ADJ (*CAm, Méx*) 1 (= *molesto*) bothersome, annoying

2 (= *displicente*) peevish, irritable

cosmética SF cosmetics *pl*

cosmético ADJ, SM cosmetic

cosmetizar ▸conjug 1f◂ VT to make cosmetic improvements to

cosmetólogo/a SM/F cosmetician

cósmico ADJ cosmic

cosmódromo SM cosmodrome

cosmogonía SF cosmogony

cosmografía SF cosmography

cosmógrafo/a SM/F cosmographer

cosmología SF cosmology

cosmonauta SMF cosmonaut

cosmopolita ADJ, SMF cosmopolitan

cosmos SM INV cosmos

cosmovisión SF world view

coso[1] SM (= *recinto*) enclosure; (*esp Taur*) bullring

coso[2] SM (= *insecto*) woodworm

coso[3]* SM (*esp Cono Sur*) (= *cosa*) thingummy*, thingamajig (*EEUU**), what-d'you-call-it

cospel SM (*Arg*) telephone token

cosquillar ▸conjug 1a◂ VT to tickle

cosquillas SFPL tickling, tickling sensation; **buscar las ~ a algn** to tease sb; **me hace ~** it tickles; **hacer ~ a algn** to tickle sb; **siento ~ en el pie** my foot tickles; **tener ~** to be ticklish; ✦*MODISMO* **no sufre ~** ◊ **tiene malas ~** he's touchy, he can't take a joke

cosquillear ▸conjug 1a◂ VT to tickle; **me cosquillea la idea de …** I've a notion to …, I've half a mind to …

cosquilleo SM tickling, tickling sensation

cosquilloso ADJ 1 (= *que tiene cosquillas*) ticklish

2 (= *quisquilloso*) touchy, prickly*

costa[1] SF 1 **a ~ de algo/algn: nos estuvimos riendo a ~ suya** we had a laugh at his expense; **lo ha conseguido a ~ de muchos sacrificios** he has achieved it by making many sacrifices; **quiere quedarse en el poder a ~ de lo que sea** he wants to remain in power at all costs *o* no matter what *o* whatever happens; **a toda ~** at all costs; **hay que impedir a toda ~ que esto se repita** we must prevent this from happening again at all costs

2 **costas** (*Jur*) costs; **condenar a algn en ~s** to order sb to pay costs

costa[2] SF 1 (*Geog*) [*del mar*] coast; **pasamos las vacaciones en la ~** we spend our holidays on the coast; **la ~ mediterránea** the Mediterranean coast; **la ~ del Pacífico** the Pacific coast; **la ~ del Atlántico es muy accidentada** the Atlantic coastline is very rugged ► **la Costa Azul** the Côte d'Azur ► **la Costa Blanca** the Costa Blanca ► **la Costa Brava** the Costa Brava ► **la Costa del Sol** the Costa del Sol ► **la Costa de Oro** the Gold Coast

2 (*Náut*) shore; **fuimos bordeando la ~ hasta el puerto** we hugged the shore all the way to the port ► **costa afuera** offshore

3 (*Cono Sur*) [*de un río*] bank, riverbank; [*de un lago*] shore

costabravense ADJ of the Costa Brava

Costa de Marfil SF Ivory Coast

costado SM 1 [*de objeto*] side; **neumáticos de ~ blanco** white-walled tyres

2 (*Anat*) side; **de ~** [*tumbarse*] on one's side; [*moverse*] sideways; **español por los cuatro ~s** Spanish through and through

3 (*Náut*) side; (*Mil*) flank

4 (*Méx Ferro*) platform

costal SM sack, bag; ✦*MODISMO* **estar hecho un ~ de huesos** to be all skin and bone, be a bag of bones

costalada SF, **costalazo** SM (= *caída*) bad fall; **darse una ~** to fall on one's back

costalar ▸conjug 1a◂ VI (*Cono Sur*) to roll over

costanera SF 1 (= *costado*) side, flank
2 (= *cuesta*) slope
3 (*Cono Sur*) (= *paseo marítimo*) seaside promenade, seaside drive
4 (*Caribe*) (*alrededor de un pantano*) firm ground (*surrounding a swamp*)
5 **costaneras** (*Arquit*) rafters

costanero ADJ 1 (= *que está en cuesta*) sloping
2 (= *costero*) coastal

▼**costar** ▸conjug 1l◂ Ⓐ VT 1 (*en dinero*) to cost; **la lámpara cuesta 45 euros** the lamp is *o* costs 45 euros; **¿cuánto te ha costado el libro?** how much did you pay for the book?, how much did the book cost (you)?; **¿cuánto cuesta este libro?** how much is this book?, how much does this book cost?; **el porte no me ha costado nada** it didn't cost me anything to have it delivered, the delivery didn't cost me anything; **reparar el tejado me ha costado un dineral** it cost me a fortune to have the roof mended; ✦*MODISMO* **~ un ojo de la cara*** to cost an arm and a leg*
2 (*en esfuerzo, tiempo*) **me ha costado lo mío llegar adonde he llegado** it's taken a lot to get where I am; **cada traducción nos cuesta muchas horas de trabajo** each translation takes us many hours of work; **~ trabajo**: **cuesta poco trabajo ser amable** it doesn't take much to be pleasant, it's not so hard to be pleasant; **¿te ha costado trabajo encontrar la casa?** did you have trouble finding the house?; ✦*MODISMOS* **cueste lo que cueste** whatever it takes; **~ Dios y ayuda**: **me costó Dios y ayuda convencerla** I had a hard job *o* time persuading her; *ver tb* **sangre A2**
3 (*en consecuencias*) to cost; **ese error te ~á el puesto** that mistake will cost you your job *o* will lose you your job; **el accidente por poco le cuesta la vida** the accident nearly cost him his life; **la violación le costó doce años de cárcel** the rape earned him twelve years in prison, he got twelve years in prison for the rape
Ⓑ VI 1 (*en dinero*) **este abrigo me ha costado muy barato** this coat was very cheap
2 (*en dificultad*) to be hard, be difficult; **al principio cuesta, pero luego se hace más fácil** it's hard *o* difficult at first but then it gets easier; **cuesta reconocerlo, pero es verdad** it's hard *o* difficult to admit it, but it's true; **~ a algn**: **lo que más me cuesta es el inglés** the thing I find hardest *o* most difficult is English; **me cuesta creer que seas hermano suyo** I find it hard *o* difficult to believe that you are his brother; **¿por qué no me llamas? ¡si no te cuesta nada!** why don't you give me a call? it's not so hard *o* difficult!; **no me cuesta nada llevarte** it's no trouble to give you a lift
3 (*en consecuencias*) **~ caro a algn** to cost sb dear; **un error que le costó caro** a mistake that cost him dear; **eso que acabas de decir te va a ~ caro** you'll pay dearly for what you've just said

Costa Rica SF Costa Rica

costarricense ADJ, SMF Costa Rican

costarriqueñismo SM *word or phrase peculiar to Costa Rica*

costarriqueño/a ADJ, SM/F Costa Rican

costasoleño ADJ of the Costa del Sol

coste SM (*Esp*) cost; **el ~ global de la operación** the overall cost of the operation; **el ~ social de la guerra** the social cost of the war; **a precio de ~** at cost, at cost price ► **coste de compra** initial cost ► **coste de fabricación** manufacturing cost ► **coste de la vida** cost of living ► **coste de mantenimiento** upkeep, maintenance cost ► **coste de reemplazo** replacement cost ► **coste efectivo** actual cost ► **coste neto** net cost ► **coste real** real cost ► **costes salariales** wage costs ► **costes de explotación** operating costs ► **costes de producción** production costs ► **costes financieros** financial costs ► **coste, seguros y flete** cost, insurance and freight, C.I.F. ► **costes laborales unitarios** unitary labour *o* (*EEUU*) labor costs

costear[1] ▸conjug 1a◂ Ⓐ VT (= *financiar*) to pay for, finance (*más frm*); (*Com, Fin*) to finance; (*Radio, TV*) to back, sponsor; **costea los estudios a su sobrino** he is paying for his nephew's education, he is financing his nephew's studies; **no lo podemos ~** we can't afford it
Ⓑ **costearse** VPR **~se los estudios** to pay for one's studies; **~se los caprichos** to pay for one's little indulgences

costear[2] ▸conjug 1a◂ VT (*Náut*) to sail along the coast of; [+ *río*] to sail close to the banks of

costear[3] ▸conjug 1a◂ VT (*Cono Sur*) [+ *ganado*] to pasture

coste-eficacia SM cost-efficiency

costeño/a Ⓐ ADJ coastal
Ⓑ SM/F (*LAm*) coastal dweller

costera SF 1 [*de paquete*] side
2 (*Geog*) slope
3 (= *costa*) coast
4 (*Pesca*) fishing season

costero ADJ coastal; [*barco, comercio*] coasting

costilla SF 1 (*Anat*) rib
2 (*Culin*) sparerib ► **costilla de cerdo** pork chop, pork cutlet
3 (*) ✦*MODISMOS* **todo carga sobre mis ~s** everything falls on my shoulders; **medir las ~s a algn** to beat sb
4 (*) (= *mujer*) wife, better half*

costillar SM 1 (*Anat*) ribcage
2 (*Culin*) ribs *pl*

costilludo ADJ broad-shouldered, strapping

costipado ADJ, SM = **constipado**

costo SM 1 (*esp LAm Fin*) cost ► **costo de expedición** shipping charges *pl*; *ver tb* **coste**
2 (*LAm*) (= *esfuerzo*) trouble, effort
3 (*Esp*‡) (= *hachís*) dope‡

costosamente ADV expensively

costoso ADJ costly, expensive

costra SF 1 (= *corteza*) crust
2 (*Med*) scab
3 [*de vela*] snuff

costroso ADJ 1 (= *con corteza*) crusty
2 (*Med*) scabby

costumbre SF 1 (*tradicional*) custom; **costumbres** customs, ways; **las ~s de esta provincia** the customs of this province; **novela de ~s** novel of (local) customs and manners
2 [*de una persona*] habit; **persona de buenas ~s** respectable person, decent person; **he perdido la ~** I've got out of the habit; **tener la ~ de hacer algo** ◊ **tener por ~ hacer algo** to be in the habit of doing sth
3 **de ~** (*adj*) usual; (*adv*) usually; **como de ~** as usual; **más que de ~** more than usual

costumbrismo SM (*Literat*) *literature of local customs and manners*

> **COSTUMBRISMO**
>
> **Costumbrismo** *is a literary genre which emerged in Spain in the 1830s. It concentrated on a detailed depiction of social and regional traditions and customs and often contrasted them with the changes brought by industrial development. Among the most noted writers of this movement were Fernán Caballero, Pedro Antonio de Alarcón, Juan Valera and José María de Pereda.*

costumbrista Ⓐ ADJ (*Literat*) of local customs and manners
Ⓑ SMF *writer about local customs and manners*

costura SF 1 (= *puntadas*) seam; **sin ~** seamless; **sentar las ~s** to press the seams; ✦*MODISMO* **sentar las ~ a algn*** to give sb a hiding*
2 (= *labor*) sewing, needlework; (= *confección*) dressmaking; **alta ~** haute couture, high fashion; **la ~ italiana** Italian fashion
3 (*Náut*) seam

costurar ▸conjug 1a◂ VT, VI, **costurear** VT, VI (*LAm*) = **coser**

costurera SF dressmaker, seamstress

costurero SM (= *caja*) sewing box; (= *cuarto*) sewing room

cota[1] SF 1 (*Hist*) ► **cota de malla** coat of mail
2 (*Caribe*) (= *blusa*) blouse

cota[2] SF 1 (*Geog*) height above sea level; (= *altura*) height, level; **misil de baja ~** low-flying missile; **volar a baja ~** to fly low
2 (= *cifra*) number, figure ► **cota de popularidad** level of popularity

cotarro SM 1 (*) (= *grupo*) ✦*MODISMOS* **alborotar el ~** to stir up trouble; **dirigir el ~** to be the boss, rule the roost
2 (†) (= *albergue*) night shelter for tramps; ✦*MODISMO* **andar** *o* **ir de ~ en ~** to wander about, gad about
3 (*Cono Sur**) (= *colega*) mate*, pal*, buddy (*EEUU**)

coteja SF (*LAm*) equal, match

cotejar ▸conjug 1a◂ VT 1 (= *comparar*) to compare, collate
2 (*Andes, Caribe*) (= *arreglar*) to arrange

cotejo Ⓐ ADJ (*LAm*) similar, same
Ⓑ SM 1 (= *comparación*) comparison, collation
2 (*Dep*) match, game

cotelé SM (*Chile*) corduroy

cotense SM (*Andes, Cono Sur, Méx*), **cotensia** SF (*Andes, Cono Sur*), **cotensio** SM (*Cono Sur*) coarse hemp fabric

coterna SF (*Andes*) broad hat

coterráneo/a Ⓐ ADJ from the same country, from the same region
Ⓑ SM/F compatriot, fellow-countryman/-woman; **un ~ le dio trabajo a Reilly en Mé-**

➤ LENGUA Y USO: **costar A2** 53.6

xico a fellow-countryman gave Reilly work in Mexico

cotí SM ticking

cotidianeidad SF daily nature, routine character

cotidiano ADJ daily, everyday; **la vida cotidiana** daily life, everyday life

cotiledón SM cotyledon

cotilla* SMF gossip

cotillear* ▸conjug 1a◂ VI to gossip

cotilleo* SM gossip, gossiping

cotillero/a SM/F = **cotilla**

cotillón SM ≈ New Year's Eve party

cotín SM (*Dep*) backhand return

cotitular SMF joint owner

cotiza SF (*LAm*) rough sandal

cotización SF [1] (*Fin*) price ► **cotización de apertura** opening price ► **cotización de cierre**, **cotización de clausura** closing price
[2] [*de club*] dues *pl*, subscription; (*a la Seguridad Social*) (National Insurance) contributions *pl* ► **cotización empresarial** employer contribution
[3] (= *cambio*) exchange rate

cotizado ADJ (= *solicitado*) in demand, sought-after; (= *estimado*) valued, esteemed; **uno de los corredores más ~s del ciclismo español** one of the most highly regarded Spanish cyclists; **un fotógrafo italiano, ~ internacionalmente** an internationally esteemed *o* acclaimed Italian photographer

cotizante SMF contributor

cotizar ▸conjug 1f◂ Ⓐ VI [1] (= *contribuir*) to make contributions, pay contributions; **no tiene pensión porque nunca ha cotizado** he doesn't have a pension because he hasn't made *o* paid any contributions; **~ a la Seguridad Social** to pay National Insurance contributions
[2] (*Fin*) **nuestra empresa cotiza ahora en Bolsa** our company is now quoted on the Stock Exchange; **al cierre cotizó a 3,21 euros** it closed at 3.21 euros, at the close it stood at 3.21 euros
Ⓑ VT [1] (= *pagar*) [+ *cuota, recibo, impuesto*] to pay
[2] (*Caribe, Cono Sur*) (= *valorar*) to value (**en** at)
[3] (*Cono Sur*) (= *prorratear*) to share out proportionally
[4] (*Andes, Caribe*) (= *vender*) to sell
Ⓒ **cotizarse** VPR [1] (*Com, Fin*) [*acciones*] to stand at, be quoted at; [*divisa*] to stand at; **estas acciones se están cotizando a once dólares** these shares are standing *o* are (being) quoted at eleven dollars; **éste es el valor que más se cotiza** this is the most commonly quoted price; **el dólar se cotizó hoy a 102,32 yenes** the dollar stood at 102.32 yen today
[2] (= *valorarse*) to be valued; **esos vídeos se cotizan en el mercado negro a 100 dólares cada uno** those videos are worth 100 dollars each on the black market, those videos are valued on the black market at 100 dollars each; **los conocimientos de inglés se cotizan muy alto** knowledge of English is highly valued

coto¹ SM [1] (= *reserva*) reserve ► **coto cerrado** closed shop; **los académicos son un ~ cerrado** the academic world is a closed shop ► **coto de caza** game preserve ► **coto de pesca** fishing preserve ► **coto forestal** forest reserve, forest estate ► **coto privado** private reserve ► **coto redondo** large estate
[2] **poner ~ a algo** to put a stop to sth; **medidas para poner ~ a la violencia** measures to put a stop to the violence
[3] (= *mojón*) boundary stone
[4] (*Com*) (= *acuerdo*) price-fixing agreement
[5] (*Bridge*) rubber

coto² SM (*LAm Med*) goitre, goiter (*EEUU*)

cotón SM [1] (= *tela*) printed cotton, cotton fabric
[2] (*Méx*) (= *camisa*) shirt; (= *blusa*) blouse

cotona SF [1] (*LAm*) (= *camisa*) *tightly woven cotton shirt*
[2] (*Méx*) (= *cazadora*) leather jacket, suede jacket
[3] (*Caribe*) (= *camisón*) child's nightdress

cotonete SM (*Méx*) cotton bud, Q-tip® (*EEUU*)

cotorina SF (*Méx*) jerkin

cotorra SF [1] (*Orn*) (= *loro*) parrot; (= *urraca*) magpie
[2] (*) (= *persona*) chatterbox*, windbag* (*pey*)

cotorrear* ▸conjug 1a◂ VI to chatter

cotorreo* SM [1] (= *plática*) chatter
[2] (*Méx**) (= *diversión*) fun, good time

cotorrera SF female parrot; = **cotorra 2**

cotorro* ADJ (*Méx*) (= *platicón*) chatty, talkative; (= *alborotado*) loud, noisy

cototo SM (*Cono Sur*) bump, bruise, bruise on the head

cotudo ADJ [1] (*LAm*) suffering from goitre *o* goiter (*EEUU*)
[2] (*Andes*) (= *tonto*) stupid

cotufa SF [1] (*Bot*) Jerusalem artichoke
[2] **cotufas** (*LAm*) popcorn *sing*

coturno SM buskin; (*Hist*) cothurnus; ✦*MODISMO* **de alto ~** lofty, elevated

COU SM ABR (*Esp*) (= **Curso de Orientación Universitaria**) *formerly, preparatory one-year course for the university entrance examinations*

covacha SF [1] (= *cueva*) small cave
[2] (= *vivienda*) hovel
[3] (*LAm*) (= *trastera*) lumber room, storage space
[4] (*Andes*) (= *puesto*) vegetable stall
[5] (*Caribe*) (= *perrera*) kennel

covachuela SF hovel

covadera SF (*LAm*) guano deposit

cover* SM (*Prensa*) cover story; (*Mús*) cover version

covin SM (*Cono Sur*), **covín** SM (*Cono Sur*) popcorn

cowboy [kao'βoi] SM (*pl* **cowboys**) cowboy

coxcojilla SF, **coxcojita** SF hopscotch

coxis SM INV coccyx

coy SM [1] (*Náut*) hammock
[2] (*Andes, Caribe*) (= *cuna*) cradle

coyón* ADJ (*Méx*) cowardly

coyotaje* SM (*Méx*) fixing*

coyote SM [1] (*Zool*) coyote, prairie wolf
[2] (*Méx, CAm**) (= *intermediario*) fixer*; (= *sablista*) con man*; (= *guía*) *guide for would-be immigrants to US*
[3] (*Méx Com, Fin*) speculator, dealer in shares *etc*

coyotear ▸conjug 1a◂ (*Méx*) VI [1] (*Com, Fin*) to deal in shares, speculate in shares
[2] [= *ser intermediario*] to act as go-between; [= *ser sablista*] to be a con man*

coyunda SF [1] (*CAm*) (= *correa*) strap; (= *dogal*) halter; (= *tralla*) lash, *part of whip*
[2] (*hum*) (*conyugal*) yoke, yoke of marriage

coyuntura SF [1] (*Anat*) joint
[2] (= *momento*) juncture; **en esta ~** at this juncture, at this moment in time; **esperar una ~ favorable** to wait for a suitable moment ► **coyuntura crítica** critical moment, critical juncture, conjuncture (*frm*)
[3] (= *situación*) situation; **la ~ política** the political situation

coyuntural ADJ relating to the moment *o* situation *etc*, relating to the present moment *o* situation *etc*; **datos ~es** relevant data; **medidas ~es** immediately relevant measures; **solución ~** interim solution

coyunturalismo SM opportunism

coyunturalmente ADV responding to the demands of the moment

coz SF [1] (= *patada*) kick; **dar (de) coces a** to kick; **tirar coces** to lash out (*tb fig*); ✦*MODISMO* **dar coces contra el aguijón** to kick against the pricks
[2] [*de fusil*] (= *retroceso*) recoil, kick; (= *culata*) butt
[3] [*de agua*] backward flow
[4] (= *insulto*) insult, rude remark; **tratar a algn a coces** to treat sb like dirt

CP ABR [1] (*Esp*) = **Caja Postal**
[2] (*Esp Com*) (= **contestación pagada**) RP
[3] (*LAm*) (= **casilla postal**) PO Box

CP/M SM ABR (= **Central Program for Microprocessors**) CP/M

CPN ABR (*Esp*) = **Cuerpo de la Policía Nacional**

cps. ABR (= **caracteres por segundo**) cps

crac¹ SM (*Com, Fin*) crash; **el viernes del Crac** Black Friday; **el ~ del 29** the 1929 Stock Exchange crash ► **crac financiero** financial crash

crac² EXCL crack!, snap!; **hizo crac y se abrió** it went snap! *o* crack! and came open

crack SM [1] (*LAm Dep*) (= *persona*) top player, star player; (= *caballo*) champion horse
[2] (*) (= *droga*) crack‡

crampón SM crampon

cranearse* ▸conjug 1a◂ VPR (*Chile, Perú*) to dream up

cráneo SM skull, cranium (*frm*); ✦*MODISMOS* **ir de ~***: **voy de ~** it's all going wrong for me; **va a ir de ~ si hace eso*** he'll be in trouble if he does that; **ir de ~ con algn*** to be on bad terms with sb; **esto me lleva** *o* **trae de ~*** this is driving me crazy *o* nuts*

crápula Ⓐ SF (= *embriaguez*) drunkenness; (= *disipación*) dissipation
Ⓑ SM wastrel

crapuloso ADJ (= *borracho*) drunken; (= *disoluto*) dissolute, dissipated

craquear ▸conjug 1a◂ VT to crack

craqueo SM cracking

crasitud SF fatness

craso ADJ [1] (= *gordo*) [*persona*] fat; [*líquido*] greasy, thick
[2] [*error*] gross, crass
[3] (*Andes, Cono Sur*) (= *grosero*) coarse

cráter SM crater

crawl [krol] SM crawl, front crawl

crayón SM crayon, chalk

crayota SF (*Andes*) wax crayon

creación SF [1] (= *acción*) [1·1] [*de obra, objeto, empleo, ambiente*] creation; **para la ~ artística es necesaria la libertad de expresión** freedom of expression is necessary for artistic creation; **alterna la ~ literaria con la profesión periodística** she divides her time between literary work and journalism; **un empleo de nueva ~** a newly created position
[1·2] [*de empresa, asociación*] **incentivos para la ~ de empresas** incentives aimed at creating new businesses; **piden la ~ de una comisión de investigación** they are asking for a committee of inquiry to be set up; **empresas de nueva ~** newly-created businesses; **Canadá es miembro de la OTAN desde su ~** Canada has been a member of NATO since its creation *o* foundation
[2] (= *cosa creada*) creation; **presentará sus últimas creaciones en Milán** he will show his latest creations *o* designs in Milano; **su última ~ teatral** his latest work for the stage
[3] **la Creacción** (*Rel*) the Creation

creacionismo SM creationism

creacionista SMF creationist

creador(a) Ⓐ ADJ creative
Ⓑ SM/F [1] [*de movimiento, organización, personaje*] creator
[2] (= *artista*) artist; (= *diseñador*) designer; **los grandes ~es del Renacimiento** the great artists of the Renaissance; **los ~es de moda juvenil** designers of youth fashion
Ⓒ SM **el Creador** (*Rel*) the Creator

crear ▸conjug 1a◂ VT [1] (= *hacer, producir*) [+ *obra, objeto, empleo*] to create; **el hombre fue creado a imagen de Dios** man was created in the image of God; **~on una ciudad de la nada** they created a city out of nothing
[2] (= *establecer*) [+ *comisión, comité, fondo, negocio, sistema*] to set up; [+ *asociación, cooperativa*] to form, set up; [+ *cargo, puesto*] to create; [+ *movimiento, organización*] to create, establish, found; **¿qué se necesita para ~ una empresa?** what do you need in order to set up *o* start a business?; **esta organización se creó para defender los derechos humanos** this organization was created *o* established *o* founded to defend human rights; **aspiraban a ~ un estado independiente** they aimed to create *o* establish *o* found an independent state
[3] (= *dar lugar a*) [+ *condiciones, clima, ambiente*] to create; [+ *problemas*] to cause, create; [+ *expectativas*] to raise; **el bloqueo ha creado una situación insostenible** the blockade has created an untenable situation; **el vacío creado por su muerte** the gap left *o* created by her death; **la nicotina crea adicción** nicotine is addictive
[4] (*liter*) (= *nombrar*) to make, appoint; **fue creado papa** he was made pope

creatividad SF creativity

creativo/a Ⓐ ADJ creative
Ⓑ SM/F (*tb* **~ de publicidad**) copywriter

crece SM *o* SF (*Cono Sur*) = **crecida**

crecepelo SM hair-restorer

crecer ▸conjug 2d◂ Ⓐ VI [1] (= *desarrollarse*) [*animal, planta, objeto*] to grow; **el jazmín ha dejado de ~** the jasmine has stopped growing; **te ha crecido mucho el pelo** your hair's grown a lot; **me he dejado ~ la barba** I've grown a beard; **crecí en Sevilla** I grew up in Seville; **la princesa fue creciendo en belleza y sabiduría** the princess grew in beauty and wisdom
[2] (= *aumentar*) [*cantidad, producción, sentimiento*] to grow; [*gastos*] to increase, rise; [*inflación*] to rise; [*desempleo*] to increase, grow, rise; **el número de heridos seguía creciendo** the number of wounded continued to grow; **la economía española ~á un 4%** the Spanish economy will grow by 4%; **crece el temor de un conflicto armado** there are growing fears of an armed conflict; **el viento fue creciendo en intensidad** the wind increased *o* grew in intensity; **~ en importancia** to grow in importance
[3] (= *extenderse*) [*ciudad*] to grow; [*río, marea*] to rise; [*luna*] to wax
Ⓑ **crecerse** VPR [1] (= *tomar fuerza*) **pocos jugadores saben ~se ante la adversidad** there are few players who can stand up and be counted in the face of adversity
[2] (*) (= *engreírse*) to get full of o.s.; **con nada que le digas ya se crece** whatever you say to him he still gets all full of himself *o* his head still starts to swell
[3] (*Cos*) **en el cuello se le crece un punto** increase one stitch at the neck, add one stitch at the neck

creces SFPL [1] **con ~** amply, fully; **superó las expectativas con ~** she far exceeded *o* surpassed all expectations; **superó con ~ el récord** he beat the record by a long way *o* a long chalk, he smashed the record; **pagar con ~ un error** to pay dearly for a mistake; **pagó con ~ lo que debía** he paid back the full amount and more, he gave back everything he owed and more; **había cumplido su obligación con ~** he had amply carried out his obligation; **devolver un favor/el cariño con ~** to return a favour/sb's affection hundredfold
[2] (*Cos*) room to let out; **para los niños se hace la ropa con ~** children's clothes are made to be let out

crecida SF [*de río*] (= *aumento del cauce*) rise in level; (= *inundación*) flooding

crecido ADJ [1] [*persona*] **está muy ~ para su edad** he's very tall *o* big for his age; **está ya crecidita para saber lo que se hace** (*iró*) she's old enough to know what she's doing
[2] [*río*] high; **el río siempre viene ~ a la altura del puente** the level of the river is always higher where it goes under the bridge; **los ríos van ~s por los deshielos de la primavera** the rivers are swollen from the spring thaws, river levels are high from the spring thaws
[3] [*cantidad, número*] large
[4] [*pelo, barba*] **tienes el pelo mucho más ~ que cuando te vi la última vez** your hair is much longer than last time I saw you; **llevaba la barba crecida de un día** he had a day's growth (on his chin)
[5] (= *engreído*) vain, conceited

creciente Ⓐ ADJ [1] [*tendencia, demanda, volumen*] growing, increasing; **existe un ~ interés por las nuevas tecnologías** there is growing *o* increasing interest in new technology
[2] [*luna*] waxing; *ver tb* **cuarto B2**
Ⓑ SM (*Astron*) [*de la luna*] crescent ► **el Creciente Rojo** the Red Crescent
Ⓒ SF [*de río*] flood ► **creciente del mar** flood tide

crecientemente ADV increasingly

crecimiento SM [1] (*en seres vivos*) growth; **el deporte favorece el ~** sport is good for growth; **tiene problemas de ~** he has growth problems
[2] (= *aumento*) growth; **bajo ~** low growth rate; **modelos de ~ económico** models of economic growth; **el ~ del gasto público** the growth *o* increase in public spending; **una población en ~** a growing population ► **crecimiento cero** (*Fin*) zero growth ► **crecimiento demográfico** population growth ► **crecimiento negativo** (*Fin*) negative growth ► **crecimiento sostenido** sustained growth ► **crecimiento vegetativo** (*Sociol*) natural increase

credencial Ⓐ ADJ accrediting; *ver tb* **carta 2**
Ⓑ SF [1] (= *documento*) document confirming appointment
[2] **credenciales** credentials

▼**credibilidad** SF credibility

crediticio ADJ credit *antes de s*

crédito SM [1] (= *fe*) credit; **dar ~ a algo** to believe sth, credit sth; **no podía dar ~ a sus oídos/ojos** he could hardly believe his ears/eyes
[2] (= *fama*) standing, reputation; **persona (digna) de ~** reliable person; **tiene ~ de muy escrupuloso** he has the reputation of being thoroughly honest
[3] (*Com, Fin*) credit; **a ~** on credit; **abrir ~ a** to give credit to ► **crédito a corto plazo** short-term credit ► **crédito a la exportación** export credit ► **crédito a largo plazo** long-term credit ► **crédito al consumidor** consumer credit ► **crédito bancario** bank credit ► **crédito de aceptación** acceptance credit ► **crédito de vivienda** mortgage ► **crédito diferido** deferred credit ► **crédito hipotecario** mortgage loan ► **crédito personal** personal credit ► **crédito puente** bridging loan, bridge loan (*EEUU*) ► **crédito renovable**, **crédito rotativo** revolving credit
[4] (*Univ*) credit
[5] (*Cine, TV*) **~s** credits

credo SM (*Rel*) creed; **el Credo** the Creed

credulidad SF credulity

crédulo/a Ⓐ ADJ gullible, credulous
Ⓑ SM/F **es tan ~** he's so gullible

creederas SFPL **tiene buenas ~** he's very gullible

creencia SF belief (**en** in); **en la ~ de que …** in the belief that …

creencial ADJ relating to belief

▼**creer** ▸conjug 2e◂ Ⓐ VI [1] (= *pensar*) **es de Madrid, según creo** I believe she's from Madrid; **no creo** I don't think so; **es difícil, no creas** it's hard enough, I can tell you
[2] **~ en** to believe in; **creen en Dios** they believe in God; **creo en la igualdad** I believe in equality; **¿crees en los fantasmas?** do you believe in ghosts?
Ⓑ VT [1] (= *considerar cierto*) to believe; **nadie me cree** nobody believes me; **créame** believe me, take my word for it; **no creo lo que dijo** I don't believe what she said; **¡ya lo creo!**: **—¿quieres un café? —¡ya lo creo!** "do you want some coffee?" — "you bet!"*; **¡ya lo creo que está roto!** you bet it's broken!, it

➤ LENGUA Y USO: **credibilidad** 53.6 **creer B2** 33.2, 53.5

certainly is broken!; **¿que yo voy a ir andando hasta el faro? ¡ya lo creo!** (*iró*) you think I'm going to walk all the way to the lighthouse? you must be joking!*; **¿que tú no sabías lo del examen? ¡sí, sí, ya lo creo!** (*iró*) you didn't know about the exam? oh, sure you didn't!*
2 (= *pensar*) to think; **creen haber descubierto el motivo** they think (that) they've discovered the reason; **~ que** to think (that); **no creo que pueda ir** I don't think I'll be able to go; **creo que es sincera** I think she's sincere, I believe her to be sincere; **creo que sí** I think so; **creo que no** I don't think so; **no puedo ~ que esto esté pasando** I can't believe this is happening; **no se vaya usted a ~ que …** don't go thinking that …, I wouldn't want you to think that …
3 (= *considerar*) to think; **no lo creía capaz de hacerlo** I didn't think him capable of doing it; **lo creo mi deber** I think *o* consider it (to be) my duty
Ⓒ **creerse** VPR 1 (= *considerar cierto*) to believe; **no me lo creo** I don't believe it; **eso no se lo ~á nadie** no one will believe that; **se cree todo lo que le dicen** he believes everything he's told; **hace falta que yo me lo crea** I remain to be convinced; **¡que te crees tú eso!*** you must be joking!*; **¡no te lo crees ni tú!*** come off it!*
2 (= *pensar*) to think; **¿de dónde te crees que sacan el dinero?** where do you think they get the money?; **¿pero tú qué te crees, que soy millonario?** what do you think I am, a millionaire or something?
3 (= *considerarse*) to think; **se cree muy listo** he thinks he's pretty clever; **¿quién te crees que eres?** who do you think you are?; **se cree alguien** he thinks he's somebody; **¿qué se ha creído?** who does he think he is?

creíble ADJ believable, credible; **¿es ~ que …?** is it conceivable that …?

creíblemente ADV credibly

creído/a Ⓐ ADJ 1 (= *engreído*) conceited
2 (= *crédulo*) credulous, trusting
Ⓑ SM/F **es un ~** he's very full of himself

crema Ⓐ SF 1 (*en cosmética, de zapatos*) cream ► **crema antiarrugas** anti-wrinkle cream ► **crema base** foundation cream ► **crema bronceadora** suntan lotion, suntan cream ► **crema de afeitar** shaving cream ► **crema de belleza** beauty cream ► **crema de día** day cream ► **crema de manos** hand cream ► **crema de noche** night cream ► **crema depilatoria** hair removing cream, depilatory cream ► **crema de protección solar** sun protection cream ► **crema de zapatos** shoe cream ► **crema hidratante** moisturizer, moisturizing cream ► **crema nutritiva** nourishing cream
2 (= *licor*) cream liqueur, crème
3 (*Culin*) (*tb* **~ de leche**) cream; **~ líquida** single cream, pouring cream; **una ~ de champiñones** cream of mushroom (soup) ► **crema agria** sour cream, soured cream ► **crema batida** whipped cream ► **crema catalana** *dessert similar to crème brûlée* ► **crema de cacahuete** peanut butter ► **crema de cacao, crema de chocolate** chocolate filling ► **crema inglesa** custard ► **crema pastelera** confectioner's cream, custard, crème pâtissière
4 **la ~** (= *lo mejor*) the cream; **la ~ de la sociedad** the cream of society
5 (*Tip*) (= *diéresis*) diaeresis, dieresis (*EEUU*)
6 (*Cono Sur*) ✦**MODISMO dejar la ~*** to make a hash of things*, put one's foot in it
Ⓑ ADJ INV [*color*] cream, cream-coloured, cream-colored (*EEUU*); **una chaqueta ~ claro** a light cream *o* cream-coloured jacket; **un coche color ~** a cream(-coloured) car

cremación SF cremation

cremallera SF 1 (*en material*) zip, zipper (*EEUU*); **cerrar la ~** do the zip *o* zipper up; **cierre de ~** zip, zip fastener, zipper (*EEUU*); ✦**MODISMO echar la ~*** to shut up*, button up*
2 (*Téc*) rack ► **cremallera y piñón** rack and pinion

cremar ▸conjug 1a◂ VT (*Méx*) to cremate

crematístico ADJ financial, economic

crematorio Ⓐ ADJ **horno ~ = B**
Ⓑ SM crematorium

crémor SM (*tb* **~ tártaro**) cream of tartar

cremosidad SF creaminess

cremoso ADJ creamy

crencha SF parting, part (*EEUU*)

creosota SF creosote

crep[1] SM (= *tela*) crêpe, crepe, crape; (= *caucho*) crêpe (rubber), crepe (rubber)

crep[2] SM, **crepa** SF (*LAm Culin*) pancake, crêpe

crepar‡ ▸conjug 1a◂ VI (*Cono Sur*) to peg out‡, kick the bucket‡

crepe SM *o* SF = **crep**[2]

crepé SM 1 = **crep**[1]
2 (*Méx*) (= *peluca*) wig

crepería SF pancake restaurant, crêperie

crepitación SF [*de leño*] crackling; [*de bacon*] sizzling

crepitar ▸conjug 1a◂ VI [*leño*] to crackle; [*bacon*] to sizzle

crepuscular ADJ twilight *antes de s*, crepuscular (*liter, frm*); **luz ~** twilight

crepúsculo SM twilight, dusk

cresa SF 1 (= *larva*) larva
2 [*de abeja*] eggs of the queen bee

crescendo SM crescendo; **ir en ~** to increase, get louder *o* greater *etc*

Creso SM Croesus

crespo Ⓐ ADJ 1 (= *rizado*) [*pelo*] curly; [*hoja*] curled
2 [*estilo*] involved, tortuous
3 [*persona*] cross, angry
Ⓑ SM (*esp Caribe*) (= *rizo*) curl, ringlet

crespón SM crêpe, crepe, crape

cresta SF 1 (*Orn*) (*gen*) crest; [*de gallo*] comb
2 (*Geog*) crest
3 [*de ola*] crest; ✦**MODISMO en la ~ de la ola** on the crest of a wave
4 (= *peluca*) wig, toupée

crestería SF (*Arquit*) (= *coronamiento*) cresting; (= *almenas*) crenellations *pl*

crestomatía SF anthology, collection of texts

crestón SM 1 [*de celada*] crest
2 (*Min*) outcrop

Creta SF Crete

creta SF chalk

cretáceo ADJ cretaceous

cretense ADJ, SMF Cretan

cretinada SF silly thing to do *o* say *etc*, stupid thing to do *o* say *etc*

cretinez SF stupidity

cretinismo SM cretinism

cretino/a Ⓐ ADJ cretinous
Ⓑ SM/F cretin

cretona SF cretonne

cretoso ADJ chalky

creyendo *etc ver* **creer**

creyente SMF believer; **no ~** non-believer, unbeliever

cría SF 1 (*Agr*) (= *actividad*) rearing; (*para la reproducción*) breeding; **hembra de ~** breeding female ► **cría caballar** horse breeding ► **cría de ganado** cattle breeding, stockbreeding ► **cría de peces** fish farming
2 (*Zool*) (= *camada*) litter; (= *individuo*) baby animal; **una ~ de ballena** a baby whale; **una ~ de león** a lion cub

criadero SM 1 (*Bot*) nursery
2 (*Zool*) breeding place, breeding ground ► **criadero de ostras** oyster bed ► **criadero de peces** fish hatchery, fish farm
3 (*Geol*) vein, seam

criadilla SF 1 (*Culin*) testicle ► **criadillas de tierra** truffles
2 (= *pan*) small loaf, roll
3 (= *patata*) potato, tuber

criado/a Ⓐ ADJ reared, brought up; **bien ~** well-bred; **mal ~** *ver* **malcriado**
Ⓑ SM/F 1 (= *sirviente*) (= *hombre*) servant; (= *mujer*) servant, maid ► **criado/a para todo** servant with general duties ► **criado/a por horas** (= *hombre*) *servant paid by the hour*; (= *mujer*) daily, *maid paid by the hour*
2 (*Naipes*) jack, knave

criador(a) Ⓐ SM/F breeder
Ⓑ SM **el Criador** (*Rel*) the Creator

criajo/a* SM/F wretched child, urchin

criandera SF (*LAm*) nursemaid, wet nurse

crianza SF 1 (*Agr*) (= *actividad*) rearing; (*para la reproducción*) breeding
2 (*Med*) lactation
3 [*de vinos*] vintage ► **vinos de crianza** vintage wines
4 (= *educación*) breeding; **mala ~** lack of breeding; **sin ~** ill-bred

> **CRIANZA**
> *Quality Spanish wine is often graded* **Crianza, Reserva** *or* **Gran Reserva** *according to the length of bottle-ageing and barrel-ageing it has undergone.* **Crianza** *wines are in their third year, reds having spent at least twelve months in cask and whites six.*
> ⇨ *See also* RESERVA

criar ▸conjug 1c◂ Ⓐ VT 1 (= *educar*) [+ *niño*] to bring up, raise (*esp EEUU*); **los crió su abuela hasta los diez años** they were brought up *o* raised by their grandmother till they were ten; ✦**REFRÁN Dios los cría y ellos se juntan** birds of a feather flock together
2 (= *amamantar*) to nurse, suckle, feed; **al niño lo crió su tía** the baby was nursed *o* suckled *o* fed by his aunt; **~ con biberón** to bottle-feed; **~ con el pecho** to breast-feed
3 [+ *ganado*] to rear, raise; [+ *aves de corral*] to breed; (*para competición*) to breed; ✦**REFRÁN cría cuervos (que te sacarán los ojos): qué mala suerte tuvo con sus hijos; ya sabes, cría cuervos …** she's been so unlucky with her children, after all she's done for them

they've repaid her with nothing but ingratitude

4 [+ *hortalizas*] to grow; ✦*MODISMO* **~ malvas**: **ya está criando malvas** he's pushing up the daisies*

5 (= *producir*) **los perros crían pulgas** dogs get fleas; **~ barriga** to get a belly*; **~ carnes** to put on weight; **esta tierra no cría malas hierbas** this soil doesn't produce any weeds; **~ polvo** to gather dust

Ⓑ VI 1 (= *tener crías*) to breed; **la gaviota suele ~ en las rocas** seagulls usually breed on rocks

2 (= *madurar*) [*vino*] to age, mature

Ⓒ **criarse** VPR to grow up; **se ~on juntos** they grew up together; **se ha criado con sus abuelos** he was brought up *o* raised by his grandparents; ✦*MODISMO* **~se en buena cuna** *o* **en buenos pañales** to be born with a silver spoon in one's mouth

criatura SF 1 (= *ser creado*) creature; **las ~s de Dios** God's creatures

2 (= *niño pequeño*) child; **todavía es una ~** he's only *o* still a child

3 (*dicho cariñosamente*) **la criaturita estaba asustada** the poor little thing *o* the poor creature was frightened; **¡pobre ~!** poor little thing!; **pero ~, ¿cómo no te has dado cuenta antes?** you silly thing, how come you didn't realize before?

criba SF 1 (= *instrumento*) sieve

2 (= *acto*) sifting, selection; ✦*MODISMOS* **hacer una ~** to sort out the sheep from the goats; **superar la ~** to slip through the net

cribar ▸conjug 1a◂ VT to sieve, sift

cric SM jack

Crimea SF Crimea

crimen SM 1 (= *asesinato*) murder; (= *delito grave*) crime ► **crimen contra la humanidad** crime against humanity ► **crimen de guerra** war crime ► **crimen de sangre** violent crime ► **crimen organizado** organized crime ► **crimen pasional** crime of passion, crime passionnel (*frm*)

2 (*) (= *barbaridad*) **es un ~ dejar aquí al niño** it's criminal to leave the child here

criminal Ⓐ ADJ [*comportamiento, acto*] criminal; **es ~ desperdiciar tanta comida** it's criminal *o* a crime to waste so much food

Ⓑ SMF (= *asesino*) murderer, killer; **un ~ sin escrúpulos** a ruthless murderer *o* killer ► **criminal de guerra** war criminal

criminalidad SF 1 (= *cualidad*) criminality

2 (= *índice*) crime rate

criminalista SMF 1 (*Univ*) criminologist

2 (*Jur*) criminal lawyer

criminalística SF criminology

criminalizar ▸conjug 1f◂ VT to criminalize; **~ un acto** to make an act a criminal offence

criminógeno ADJ conducive to crime, encouraging criminal tendencies

criminología SF criminology

criminólogo/a SM/F criminologist

crin SF (*Zool*) mane; (*Téc*) horsehair

crinolina SF crinoline

crinudo ADJ (*LAm*) long-maned

crío/a SM/F kid*, child; (*pey*) little brat*; **¡no seas ~!** grow up!, don't be such a baby!

criogénico ADJ cryogenic

criogenizar ▸conjug 1f◂ VT to freeze cryogenically

criollaje SM (*LAm*) Creoles *pl*

criollismo SM (*Chile*) local saying

criollo/a Ⓐ ADJ 1 (*Hist*) Creole; (= *de origen español*) of Spanish extraction

2 (*LAm*) (= *no extranjero*) native, native to America

Ⓑ SM/F 1 (*Hist*) Creole

2 (*LAm*) Peruvian/Colombian/Ecuadorean, etc, *native of a particular Latin American country, as opposed to a foreigner*; **un español y dos ~s** a Spaniard and two natives

3 (*Andes*) (= *cobarde*) coward

Ⓒ SM (*Ling*) Creole; **como dicen en ~** as they say in Latin America/Peru *etc*

criosfera SF cryosphere

cripta SF crypt

críptico ADJ cryptic

cripto... PREF crypto...

criptocomunista SMF crypto-communist

criptografía SF cryptography

criptográfico ADJ cryptographic, cryptographical

criptógrafo/a SM/F cryptographer

criptograma SM cryptogram

criptología SF cryptology

críquet SM cricket

crisálida SF chrysalis

crisalidar ▸conjug 1a◂ VI to pupate

crisantemo SM chrysanthemum

crisis SF INV 1 (*Econ, Pol, Sociol*) crisis; **la situación económica está pasando por una nueva ~** the economy is undergoing *o* going through a new crisis; **lo que está en ~ es el propio sistema** the system itself is in crisis; **nuestro matrimonio está en ~** our marriage is in crisis *o* going through a crisis; **hacer ~** to reach crisis point, come to a head ► **crisis de fe** crisis of faith ► **crisis de gobierno** government crisis ► **crisis de identidad** identity crisis ► **crisis de la vivienda** housing crisis ► **crisis de los cuarenta** midlife crisis ► **crisis económica** economic crisis ► **crisis energética** energy crisis ► **crisis ministerial** cabinet reshuffle

2 (*Med*) **alguien a quien recurrir en momentos de ~** someone to turn to in moments of crisis ► **crisis cardíaca** cardiac arrest, heart failure ► **crisis de ansiedad** anxiety attack ► **crisis epiléptica** epileptic fit, epileptic attack ► **crisis nerviosa** nervous breakdown ► **crisis respiratoria** respiratory failure

crisma[1] SF 1 (*Rel*) chrism

2 (‡) (= *cabeza*) nut‡, noggin (*EEUU*‡), head; **romper la ~ a algn** to knock sb's block off‡; **romperse la ~** to split one's head open

crisma[2] Ⓐ SM (*a veces* SF, *tb* **~s**) (*Esp*) Christmas card

Ⓑ SF (*Méx*) Christmas present

crismón SM *monogram of Christ*

crisol SM (*Téc*) crucible; (*fig*) melting pot

crispación SF tension, nervousness

crispado ADJ tense, on edge

crispante ADJ infuriating

crispar ▸conjug 1a◂ Ⓐ VT 1 [+ *músculo*] to cause to twitch, cause to contract; **con el rostro crispado por la ira** with his face contorted with anger; **eso me crispa (los nervios)** that gets on my nerves*; **tengo los nervios crispados** my nerves are all on edge

2 (= *enfadar*) **~ a algn*** to annoy sb intensely, really get on sb's nerves*

Ⓑ **crisparse** VPR [*músculo*] to twitch, contract; [*cara*] to contort; [*nervios*] to get all on edge; [*situación*] to become tense, get tenser

crispetas SFPL (*Andes*) popcorn *sing*

cristal SM 1 (= *vidrio normal*) glass; (= *vidrio fino*) crystal; **una puerta de ~** a glass door; **un vaso de ~** a glass; **una estatuilla de ~** a crystal statuette ► **cristal ahumado** smoked glass ► **cristal antibalas** bullet-proof glass ► **cristal blindado** reinforced glass ► **cristal cilindrado** plate glass ► **cristal de Bohemia** Bohemian glass ► **cristal de Murano** Venetian glass ► **cristal de patente** (*Náut*) bull's-eye ► **cristal de seguridad** safety glass ► **cristal esmerilado** frosted glass ► **cristal inastillable** shatterproof glass ► **cristal soplado** blown glass ► **cristal tallado** cut glass

2 (= *trozo de cristal*) piece of glass; **me he cortado con un ~** I've cut myself on a piece of glass; **hay ~es en el suelo** there's broken glass *o* there are pieces of broken glass on the floor; **se ha roto el ~ de la mesa** the glass table top has got cracked ► **cristales emplomados** leaded lights

3 [*de ventana*] window pane; [*de coche*] window; [*de gafas*] lens; **¿puedes subir un poco el ~?** can you wind the window up a bit? ► **cristal bifocal** bifocal lens ► **cristal de aumento** lens, magnifying glass

4 (*Min*) crystal ► **cristal de cuarzo** quartz crystal ► **cristal de roca** rock crystal ► **cristal de sílice** silica crystal ► **cristal líquido** liquid crystal

5 (= *espejo*) glass, mirror

cristalera SF 1 (= *ventana*) (*fija*) window; (*corredera*) French windows *pl*

2 (= *aparador*) display cabinet

cristalería SF 1 (= *arte*) glassmaking

2 (= *fábrica*) glassworks; (= *tienda*) glassware shop

3 (= *vasos*) glassware; (= *juego*) set of glasses

cristalero SM (*Cono Sur*) glass cabinet

cristalinamente ADV transparently

cristalino Ⓐ ADJ (*Fís*) crystalline; [*agua, explicación*] crystal-clear

Ⓑ SM crystalline lens

cristalizar ▸conjug 1f◂ Ⓐ VT to crystallize

Ⓑ VI 1 (*Fís*) to crystallize

2 [*proyecto, idea*] to crystallize, take shape

Ⓒ **cristalizarse** VPR 1 (*Fís*) to crystallize

2 [*proyecto, idea*] to crystallize, take shape

cristalografía SF crystallography

cristalógrafo/a SM/F crystallographer

cristero/a SM/F (*Méx*) *Catholic militant*

cristianamente ADV in a Christian way; **morir ~** to die in a state of grace

cristianar ▸conjug 1a◂ VT 1 (= *bautizar*) to christen, baptize

2 [+ *vino*] to water

cristiandad SF Christendom

cristianismo SM Christianity

cristianizar ▸conjug 1f◂ VT to Christianize

cristiano/a Ⓐ ADJ 1 (*Rel*) Christian

2 **vino ~** unwatered wine

Ⓑ SM/F (*Rel*) Christian ► **cristiano nuevo** (*Hist*) *converted Jew or Moor* ► **cristiano viejo** (*Hist*) *Christian with no Jewish or Moorish blood*

Ⓒ SM 1 (= *persona*) person; **eso lo sabe cualquier ~** anyone knows that; **eso no hay ~ que lo entienda** that is beyond anyone's comprehension; **no hay ~ que lo sepa** no one knows that; **este ~*** yours truly*

2 **hablar en ~** (= *claramente*) to talk sense; (= *en español*) to speak Spanish

Cristo SM (*Rel*) 1 (= *Jesucristo*) Christ; **en el año 41 antes de ~** in 41 B.C.; **en el año 80 después de ~** in 80 A.D.; ***✦MODISMOS*** **donde ~ dio las tres voces*** ◊ **donde ~ perdió la sandalia*** in the back of beyond*

2 (= *imagen*) figure of Christ; **un ~ barroco** a Baroque figure of Christ

cristo SM 1 (= *crucifijo*) crucifix; ***✦MODISMOS*** **poner a algn como un ~*** (= *criticar*) to tear sb to shreds, call sb every name under the sun; (= *pegar*) to give sb a real thumping*; **hecho un ~*** in a terrible mess; **volvió hecho un ~ de la pelea** he returned from the fight in a terrible mess *o* looking a terrible sight; **ni ~*: eso no lo entiende ni ~** no one on earth can understand that, absolutely no one can understand that; **no había ni (un) ~ en la manifestación** there wasn't a soul at the demonstration; **todo ~*: eso lo sabe ya todo ~** everyone knows that, every Tom, Dick and Harry knows that*

2 (*) (= *pelea*) **¡vaya ~!** what a to-do!*; **armar** *o* **montar un ~** to raise hell, make an almighty fuss*

Cristóbal SM Christopher ► **Cristóbal Colón** Christopher Columbus

criterio SM 1 (= *método*) criterion; **este es el ~ de selección que hemos seguido** this is the selection criterion that we have followed; **tenemos que unificar ~s** we have to agree on our criteria; **con ese mismo ~ también podríamos afirmar lo contrario** by the same token *o* criterion one could also state the opposite

2 (= *juicio*) judgement; **me impresiona su falta de ~** I'm struck by his lack of judgement *o* (*frm*) discernment; **tiene buen ~** he has good *o* sound judgement; **lo dejo a su ~** I leave it to your discretion *o* judgement

3 (= *punto de vista*) opinion, view; **no comparto ese ~** I do not share that opinion *o* view; **en mi ~** in my opinion *o* view; **diferencia de ~s** difference of opinion; **formarse un ~ sobre algo** to form an opinion of sth; **depende del ~ de cada uno** it depends on each person's *o* individual's viewpoint

criterioso* ADJ (*Cono Sur*) level-headed, sensible

crítica SF 1 (= *censura*) criticism; **recibir duras ~s** to be severely criticized, come in for severe criticism; **lanzó duras ~s contra el Gobierno** he levelled fierce criticism at the Government, he launched a fierce attack on the Government

2 (*en periódico, revista*) review; (= *ensayo, libro*) critique

3 **la ~** (= *los críticos*) the critics *pl*; **ser bien recibido por la ~** to be well received by the critics

4 (= *actividad*) criticism; (= *chismes*) gossip ► **crítica literaria** literary criticism ► **crítica teatral** dramatic criticism; *ver tb* **crítico**

criticable ADJ [*conducta, actitud*] reprehensible; **no es ~ que se te oponga** you can't blame him for standing against you

criticador(a) Ⓐ ADJ critical

Ⓑ SM/F critic

criticar ▸conjug 1g◂ Ⓐ VT 1 (= *censurar*) to criticize; **la actuación de la policía fue criticada por la oposición** the police behaviour was criticized by the opposition

2 (= *hablar mal*) **siempre está criticando a la gente** he's always criticizing people, he's always finding fault with people

3 (*Arte, Literat, Teat*) [+ *libro, obra*] to review

Ⓑ VI to gossip

criticastro/a SM/F hack critic, ignorant critic

criticidad SF critical nature; **fase de ~** critical phase

crítico/a Ⓐ ADJ critical; **encontrarse en un estado ~** (*Med*) to be in a critical condition

Ⓑ SM/F critic ► **crítico/a cinematográfico/a** film critic ► **crítico/a de arte** art critic ► **crítico/a de cine** film critic ► **crítico/a literario/a** literary critic ► **crítico/a musical** music critic; *ver tb* **crítica**

criticón/ona* Ⓐ ADJ hypercritical, critical, faultfinding; **es muy ~** he's always finding fault with people, he's hypercritical, he's so critical

Ⓑ SM/F faultfinder

critiquizar ▸conjug 1f◂ VT to be overcritical of, indulge in petty criticism of

CRM SM ABR = **certificado de regulación monetaria**

Croacia SF Croatia

croar ▸conjug 1a◂ VI to croak

croata ADJ, SMF Croat, Croatian; **los ~s** the Croats, the Croatians

croché SM crochet; **hacer ~** to crochet

crochet [kro'tʃe] SM 1 (*Cos*) crochet

2 (*Boxeo*) hook

crocitar ▸conjug 1a◂ VI to crow, caw

croissan [krwa'zan] SM, **croissant** [krwa'zan] SM croissant

croissantería [krwazante'ria] SF croissant shop

crol SM (*Natación*) crawl

cromado Ⓐ ADJ chromium-plated, chrome

Ⓑ SM chromium plating, chrome

cromático ADJ chromatic

cromatografía SF chromatography

cromatograma SM chromatogram

cromo SM 1 (*Quím*) chromium, chrome

2 (= *estampa*) picture card; (*Rel*) religious card; ***✦MODISMO*** **iba hecho un ~*** he was a sight*

3 (*Tip*) coloured print, colored print (*EEUU*)

cromosoma SM chromosome

cromosomático ADJ, **cromosómico** ADJ chromosomal

cromoterapia SF chromotherapy, colour therapy

crónica SF 1 [*de periódico*] feature, article; (*Radio, TV*) report; **"Crónica de sucesos"** "News in Brief" ► **crónica deportiva** sports page ► **crónica de sociedad** society column, gossip column ► **crónica literaria** literary page

2 (*Hist*) chronicle; (*fig*) account, chronicle

3 **Crónicas** (*Biblia*) Chronicles

crónico ADJ [*enfermedad, déficit, problema*] chronic; [*vicio*] ingrained

cronificación SF **en fase de ~** becoming chronic

cronificar ▸conjug 1g◂ Ⓐ VT (*Prensa*) to chronicle

Ⓑ VI (*Med*) to become chronic

Ⓒ **cronificarse** VPR (*Med*) to become chronic

cronista SMF 1 [*de periódico*] reporter, columnist ► **cronista de radio** radio commentator ► **cronista deportivo** sports writer ► **cronista de sucesos** accident and crime reporter ► **cronista social** society columnist

2 (*Hist*) chronicler

crono Ⓐ SM 1 (= *reloj*) stopwatch

2 (*tiempo*) time, recorded time; **ganó con un ~ de 6,59** she won with a time of 6.59; **hacer** *o* **marcar un ~ de** to do a time of, get a time of

Ⓑ SF time-trial

cronografista SMF (*Cono Sur*) timekeeper

cronograma SM (*Cono Sur*) timetable, schedule

cronología SF chronology

cronológicamente ADV chronologically, in chronological order

cronológico ADJ chronological; **en orden ~** in chronological order

cronometrada SF (*Dep*) time-trial

cronometrador(a) SM/F timekeeper

cronometraje SM timekeeping, timing; **~ electrónico** electronic timekeeping; **~ manual** manual timekeeping

cronometrar ▸conjug 1a◂ VT to time

cronómetro SM (*Téc*) chronometer; (*Dep*) stopwatch

croquet [kro'ke] SM croquet

croqueta SF croquette; **~ de pescado** fish croquette; **~ de pollo** chicken croquette

croquis SM INV sketch; **hacer un ~** to do *o* draw a sketch

cross [kros] SM INV 1 (*Atletismo*) (= *deporte*) cross-country running; (= *carrera*) cross-country race

2 (*Motociclismo*) (= *deporte*) moto(r)cross; (= *carrera*) moto(r)cross race

crostón SM crouton

crótalo SM 1 (*Zool*) rattlesnake, rattler (*EEUU**)

2 **crótalos** (*Mús*) castanets

croto* SM (*Cono Sur*) bum, layabout*

cruasán SM croissant

cruce SM 1 (*Aut*) [*de carreteras, autopistas*] junction, intersection; [*de cuatro esquinas*] crossroads; (*para peatones*) crossing, crosswalk (*EEUU*); **"cruce peligroso"** "dangerous junction" ► **cruce a nivel** level crossing, grade crossing (*EEUU*) ► **cruce de peatones**, **cruce peatonal** pedestrian crossing, crosswalk (*EEUU*)

2 **luces de ~** dipped headlights; **poner la luz** *o* **las luces de ~** to dip one's lights

3 (= *acto*) **hubo un ~ de acusaciones entre ellos** there was an exchange of accusations between them; **se produjo un ~ de miradas entre ellos** their eyes met; ***✦MODISMO*** **tener un ~ de cables*** to lose one's head* ► **cruce de aros** (*Ven*) engagement ceremony (*involving the exchange of rings*)

4 (*Telec*) crossed line; **hay un ~ en las líneas** the wires are crossed

5 (*Biol*) (= *proceso*) crossbreeding; (= *resultado*) cross; **ser un ~ de** *o* **entre un animal y otro** to be a cross *o* crossbreed between one animal and another

6 (*Mat*) intersection, point of intersection

7 (*Ling*) cross, mutual interference

crucerista SMF cruise passenger

crucero SM 1 (= *barco*) cruise ship, (cruise) liner; (*Mil*) cruiser ► **crucero de batalla** battle cruiser ► **crucero de lujo** luxury cruise ship, luxury (cruise) liner ► **crucero pesado** heavy cruiser
2 (= *viaje*) cruise; **hacer un ~** to go on a cruise; **velocidad de ~** cruising speed ► **crucero de placer, crucero de recreo** pleasure cruise
3 (*Arquit*) [*de templo*] transept
4 (= *viga*) crosspiece
5 (*Aut*) [*de carreteras*] crossroads; (*Ferro*) crossing
6 (= *persona*) crossbearer
7 (*Astron*) ► **Crucero (Austral)** Southern Cross
8 (= *misil*) cruise missile

cruceta SF 1 (= *viga*) crosspiece; (*Náut, Mec*) crosstree
2 (*Mec*) crosshead
3 (*Cono Sur*) (= *torniquete*) turnstile

crucial ADJ crucial

crucificar ▸conjug 1g◂ VT (*Rel*) to crucify; **si llega a perecer alguien, te crucifico** if anyone gets killed, I'll crucify you

crucifijo SM crucifix

crucifixión SF crucifixion

cruciforme ADJ cruciform

crucigrama SM crossword (puzzle)

crucigramista SMF crossword enthusiast

cruda* SF (*LAm*) (= *resaca*) hangover

crudelísimo ADJ, SUPERL *de* **cruel** (*liter*) most cruel, terribly cruel

crudeza SF 1 [*de imágenes, descripción*] coarseness, crudeness, crudity; **expresar algo con ~** to put sth crudely
2 [*del invierno*] harshness, bleakness
3 (*Culin*) [*de carne*] rawness; [*de frutas*] unripeness
4 [*de comida*] indigestibility
5 [*de agua*] hardness
6 (= *comida*) undigested food (in the stomach)

crudo Ⓐ ADJ 1 (*Culin*) 1·1 (= *sin cocinar*) [*carne*] raw; [*verduras*] raw, uncooked
1·2 (= *poco hecho*) underdone; **las patatas están crudas** the potatoes are underdone *o* are not properly cooked
2 **de color ~** natural; **un jersey de color ~** a natural-coloured *o* (*EEUU*) natural-colored jersey
3 (*Téc*) [*producto*] untreated; [*seda*] raw; [*lino*] unbleached
4 [*clima, invierno*] harsh, severe
5 [*descripción*] crude, coarse; [*imágenes*] harrowing; **la cruda realidad** the harsh reality
6 (*) (= *difícil*) **lo tienen ~ para encontrar un trabajo** they're having a hard *o* tough time finding a job; **lo tendrán ~ si piensan que ...** they'll have a tough time of it if they think that ...; **lo veo muy ~** it doesn't look (too) good
7 [*agua*] hard
Ⓑ SM 1 (= *petróleo*) crude (oil)
2 (*LAm**) (= *resaca*) hangover
3 (*Perú*) (= *arpillera*) sackcloth

cruel ADJ cruel; **fue una ~ ironía** it was a cruel irony; **el destino ~** cruel fate; **ser ~ con algn** to be cruel to sb

crueldad SF 1 (= *cualidad*) cruelty; **tratar a algn con ~** to treat sb cruelly
2 (= *acción*) cruelty; **¡es una ~!** that's so cruel!, it's such a cruel thing to do *o* say!

cruelmente ADV cruelly

cruento ADJ (*liter*) bloody, gory

crujía SF (*Arquit*) corridor, gallery; (*Med*) ward; (*Náut*) midship gangway; [*de cárcel*] wing; ✦*MODISMO* **pasar ~** to have a tough time of it

crujido SM 1 [*de papel, hojas, seda*] rustle, rustling; [*de madera, mueble, rama*] creak, creaking; [*de nieve, grava*] crunch, crunching; [*de leña ardiendo*] crackle, crackling
2 [*de articulaciones, huesos*] crack, cracking; [*de dientes*] grinding

crujiente ADJ [*galleta*] crunchy; [*pan*] crunchy, crusty; [*seda*] rustling; [*madera*] creaking

crujir ▸conjug 3a◂ VI 1 [*papel, seda, hojas*] to rustle; [*madera, mueble, rama*] to creak; [*leña ardiendo*] to crackle; [*galletas, nieve, grava*] to crunch
2 [*articulación, hueso*] to crack; [*dientes*] to grind; **le crujen los dientes** his teeth are grinding; **hacer ~ los nudillos** to crack one's knuckles

crupier SMF croupier

crustáceo SM crustacean

cruz SF 1 (= *figura*) cross; **en ~** cross-shaped; **coloque los dos palos en ~** put the two sticks in a cross-shape *o* in the shape of a cross; **con los brazos en ~** with one's arms outstretched; **firmar con una ~** to make one's mark; **hacerse cruces** to cross o.s.; **se hacía cruces cada vez que oía una palabrota** he crossed himself every time he heard a swearword; ✦*MODISMOS* **cargar la ~** (*Méx**) to have a hangover; **¡~ y raya!** that's quite enough!, no more!; **a partir de ahora, a los Pérez, ¡~ y raya!** that's it, I'm through with the Pérez family! *o* I've had it with the Pérez family!; **por éstas que son cruces** by all that is holy; **quedar en ~** to be in an agonizing situation ► **cruz de hierro** iron cross ► **Cruz del Sur** Southern Cross ► **cruz de Malta** Maltese Cross ► **cruz de mayo** (*LAm*), **cruz gamada** swastika ► **cruz griega** Greek cross ► **cruz latina** Latin cross ► **Cruz Roja** Red Cross
2 (= *suplicio*) **¡qué ~ tengo con estos hijos!** these kids of mine are a nightmare!*; **cada uno lleva su ~** each of us has his cross to bear
3 [*de espada*] hilt; [*de ancla*] crown; (*Tip*) dagger
4 [*de moneda*] tails; **¿cara o ~?** heads or tails?
5 (*Zool*) withers *pl*

cruza SF (*LAm*) 1 (*Biol*) cross, hybrid
2 (*Agr*) second ploughing *o* (*EEUU*) plowing

cruzada SF 1 (*Hist, fig*) crusade; **una ~ contra el terrorismo** a crusade against terrorism
2 **La Cruzada** *the Civil War of 1936-39 (in official Spanish usage up to 1975)*

cruzadilla SF (*CAm*) level crossing, grade crossing (*EEUU*)

cruzado Ⓐ ADJ 1 (= *atravesado*) **se sentó con las piernas cruzadas** he sat down with his legs crossed; **con los brazos ~s** with one's arms folded *o* crossed; **no podemos quedarnos con los brazos ~s** we can't sit back and do nothing, we can't just sit idly by and do nothing
2 [*chaqueta, americana*] double-breasted
3 [*cheque*] crossed
4 (*Zool*) crossbred
5 (*Andes**) hopping mad*, furious
Ⓑ SM 1 (*Hist*) crusader
2 (= *moneda*) cruzado (*Brazilian currency unit*)

cruzador(a)* SM/F (*Méx*) shoplifter

cruzamiento SM 1 (*Biol*) crossing
2 (*Ferro*) crossover

cruzar ▸conjug 1f◂ Ⓐ VT 1 [+ *calle, río, frontera, puente*] to cross; **han cruzado el Atlántico** they've crossed the Atlantic; **~ la (línea de) meta** to cross the finishing line; **al ~ la puerta** *o* **el umbral del palacio** when you set foot inside the palace; **~on el lago a nado** they swam across the lake
2 [*arrugas, líneas*] **profundas arrugas le cruzaban la cara** her face was covered in wrinkles; **una profunda cicatriz le cruzaba la mano** a deep scar ran across his hand; **el corte le cruzó la espalda de un lado a otro** the cut ran right across his back
3 (= *poner cruzado*) **~ un palo sobre otro** to place one stick across another; **~ la espada con algn** to cross swords with sb; **~ los dedos** (*lit, fig*) to cross one's fingers; **el equipo se juega la Copa —cruzo los dedos— mañana** the team is playing for the Cup tomorrow — (I'm keeping my) fingers crossed; **~ las piernas** to cross one's legs
4 [+ *palabras*] to exchange; **no ~on ni una palabra** they didn't exchange a (single) word
5 [+ *apuestas*] to place, make
6 (*Biol*) [+ *plantas, razas*] to cross
7 (*Náut*) to cruise
8 (*esp LAm Agr*) *to plough a second time in a criss-cross pattern*
9 (*Andes, Cono Sur*) (= *atacar*) to fight, attack
10 (*Ven*) **~ (los) aros** to celebrate the engagement ceremony (*involving the exchange of rings*)
Ⓑ VI [*peatón*] to cross; **cruza ahora, que no vienen coches** cross now, there are no cars coming; **~ por el puente** to cross over the bridge; **~ por el paso de peatones** to cross at the zebra crossing
Ⓒ **cruzarse** VPR 1 [*dos cosas, líneas*] to intersect, cross; [*caminos*] to cross; **nuestras cartas se ~on** our letters crossed in the post; **se ~on las miradas de los dos** their eyes met; ✦*MODISMO* **se le ~on los cables*** (*por enfado*) he just lost it*, he flipped*; (*por confusión*) he just lost track*
2 [*personas, vehículos*] 2·1 (= *encontrarse*) to pass each other; **iban tan deprisa que se ~on sin darse cuenta** they were in such a hurry that they passed each other without even noticing; **se cruzó con ella en la escalera** he passed her on the stairs; **hace tiempo que no me cruzo con él** I haven't seen him for a long time
2·2 (= *pasar por delante*) **se le cruzó otro coche y para evitarlo, se salió de la carretera** another car pulled out in front of him and he swerved off the road to avoid it; **dos hechos que se ~on en su camino cambiaron su vida** two things that happened to him changed his life
3 **~se con algn** (*Andes*) to fight sb, attack sb
4 (*Chile**) (= *ponerse bravucón*) **se le cruzó por un asunto de dinero** he took him on over money matters; **se cruza con cualquiera que lo contradiga** he'll stand up to anybody who contradicts him; **no te me cruces** don't get cocky with me*
5 (*Ven*) **~se (los) aros con algn** to exchange rings with sb

CSD SM ABR (*Esp*) (= **Consejo Superior de Deportes**) ≈ Sports Council

c.s.f. ABR (= **coste, seguro, y flete**) c.i.f.

CSIC [θe'sik] SM ABR (*Esp*) = **Consejo Superior de Investigaciones Científicas**

CSN SM ABR (*Esp*) = **Consejo de Seguridad Nuclear**

CSP SM ABR (*Esp*) = **Cuerpo Superior de Policía**

cta. ABR, **c.ta** ABR (= **cuenta**) a/c, acc., acct

cta. cte. ABR (= **cuenta corriente**) C/A, a/c (*EEUU*)

cta. cto. ABR (= **carta de crédito**) L/C

ctdad. ABR (= **cantidad**) qty

cte. ABR (= **corriente, de los corrientes**) inst

CTI SM ABR (= **Centro de Tratamiento Intensivo**) ICU

CTM SF ABR (*Méx*) = **Confederación de Trabajadores de México**

ctra. ABR (= **carretera**) Rd

CTV SF ABR (*Ven*) = **Confederación de Trabajadores de Venezuela**

cu SF Q, *name of the letter Q*

c/u ABR (= **cada uno**) ea

cuacar ▸conjug 1g◂ (*Andes, Caribe, Cono Sur*) VT **no me cuaca** (= *no quiero*) I don't want to; (= *no me cuadra*) it doesn't suit me

cuácara SF (*Andes*) (= *levita*) frock coat; (*Cono Sur*) (= *blusa*) workman's blouse

cuache (*CAm*) ADJ, SMF = **cuate**

cuaco SM [1] (*LAm*) (= *rocín*) nag
[2] (= *bolsista*) bag snatcher

cuaderna SF (*Náut*) (= *madera*) timber, lumber (*EEUU*); (= *costilla*) rib, frame

cuadernillo SM [1] (*gen*) booklet; **~ de sellos** book of stamps [2] (*Tip*) quinternion [3] (*Rel*) liturgical calendar

cuadernito SM notebook

cuaderno SM [1] (*para notas*) notebook; (*Escol*) jotter, exercise book, workbook (*EEUU*); **~ de espiral** spiral notebook, spiral-bound notebook ► **cuaderno de bitácora** (*Náut*) logbook ► **cuaderno de campo** field diary ► **Cuaderno de Cortes** (*Hist*) official parliamentary record ► **cuaderno de navegación** logbook ► **cuaderno de trabajo** logbook
[2] (*) (= *baraja*) pack of cards

cuadra SF [1] (*para caballos*) stable; **los mejores son los caballos de la ~ Martín** the best horses are from the Martín stable; **tienes la habitación que parece una ~*** your room looks like a pigsty*, your room is an absolute tip* ► **cuadra de carreras** racing stable
[2] (*LAm*) (= *manzana*) block; **vivo a dos ~s de aquí** I live two blocks from here
[3] [*de hospital*] ward
[4] (*Mil*) (= *barracón*) barracks *pl*
[5] (= *sala*) hall, large room; (*Andes*) reception room
[6] (*Andes*) (= *casa*) small rural property (*near a town*)
[7] (= *medida*) (*Cono Sur*) ≈ 125.50 metres; (*Andes, CAm, Caribe, Uru*) ≈ 83.5 metres

cuadrada SF (*Mús*) breve

cuadrado/a Ⓐ ADJ [1] (*Mat*) square; **dos metros ~s** two square metres; ✦***MODISMO*** **tenerlos ~s**** to have balls**
[2] [*objeto, superficie*] square
[3] (= *corpulento*) **estar ~** to be well-built, be hefty*
[4] (*Caribe, Cono Sur*) (= *grosero*) coarse, rude
[5] (*Andes*) (= *elegante*) graceful, elegant
[6] (*LAm**) (= *poco flexible*) **ser ~** to be narrow-minded
[7] (*Arg, Uru**) (= *poco inteligente*) dense, stupid
[8] (*Chile, Ven**) **estar ~ con algn** to side with sb; **el pueblo está ~ con el presidente** the people are siding with the president
Ⓑ SM/F (= *persona poco inteligente*) idiot
Ⓒ SM [1] (*Mat, Geom*) square; **cinco (elevado) al ~** five square(d), the square of five ► **cuadrado mágico** magic square
[2] (= *regla*) ruler, parallel ruler
[3] (*Téc*) die
[4] (*Cos*) gusset
[5] (*Tip*) quad, quadrat
[6] (*Caribe, Cono Sur**) (= *persona*) boor, oaf

Cuadragésima SF Quadragesima

cuadragésimo ADJ [1] (= *ordinal*) fortieth
[2] (= *partitivo*) **una cuadragésima parte** one fortieth; *ver tb* **sexto A**

cuadrangular ADJ quadrangular

cuadrángulo Ⓐ ADJ quadrangular
Ⓑ SM quadrangle

cuadrante SM [1] (*Mat, Náut*) quadrant; **el ~ noroccidental de la Península** the northwestern part *o* corner of the Peninsula
[2] [*de radio*] dial; [*de reloj*] face ► **cuadrante (solar)** sundial

cuadrar ▸conjug 1a◂ Ⓐ VI [1] [*cuentas, cifras*] to tally; **los números no cuadran** the numbers don't tally; **~ con algo** to square with sth, tally with sth
[2] [*misterio, historia*] to fit together; **todo parecía ~ perfectamente** everything seemed to fit together perfectly; **~ con algo** to fit in with sth; **su reacción no cuadraba con lo que me habían dicho de él** his reaction was at odds with *o* didn't fit in with what they had told me about him
[3] [*estilo, muebles*] to go, look right; **una silla Luis XIV no cuadra en esta habitación** a Louis XIV chair doesn't go in this room *o* doesn't look right in this room; **~ con algo** to go with sth
[4] **~ a algn** to suit sb; **los papeles dramáticos le cuadran muy bien a un actor como él** dramatic roles suit an actor like him very well; **ven mañana si te cuadra** come tomorrow if it suits you *o* if that's convenient
[5] **~ hacer algo** to be ready to do sth
[6] (*Ven**) (= *quedar*) to arrange to meet; **cuadramos para encontrarnos después del cine** we arranged to meet after the cinema; **¿a qué hora cuadraste con él?** what time did you arrange to meet him?
[7] (*Col**) (= *ennoviar*) **Juan y Ana se han cuadrado** Juan and Ana are going out; **~se con algn** to go out with sb
[8] (*Chile, Ven**) **~se con algn** to side with sb; **el pueblo se cuadró con el ministro** the people sided with the minister
[9] (*Chile**) **~se con algo** to donate sth
[10] (*Col, Ven, Perú*) (= *aparcar*) to park
[11] (*Perú, Ven**) **~se a algn** to take sb on; **se me cuadró y por poco me pega** he took me on and nearly hit me
Ⓑ VT [1] (*Mat*) to square
[2] (*Téc*) to square, square off
[3] (*Perú*) (= *aparcar*) [+ *carro*] to park
Ⓒ **cuadrarse** VPR [1] [*soldado*] to stand to attention
[2] (*en una actitud*) to dig one's heels in
[3] (*Caribe*) (= *enriquecerse*) to make one's pile*; (= *tener éxito*) to come out on top

cuadratín SM (*Tip*) quadrat, quad, space

cuadratura SF (*Mat*) quadrature; **la ~ del círculo** squaring the circle

cuadrícula SF (*Tip*) grid, ruled squares; [*de mapa*] grid

cuadriculado ADJ **papel ~** squared paper, graph paper; **mapa ~** grid map

cuadricular ▸conjug 1a◂ Ⓐ VT to draw squares on, draw a grid on
Ⓑ ADJ [*papel*] ruled in squares, squared; [*tela*] chequered, checkered (*EEUU*)

cuadrilátero Ⓐ ADJ quadrilateral, four-sided
Ⓑ SM (*Mat*) quadrilateral; (*Boxeo*) ring

cuadrilla SF [1] [*de amigos*] party, group; [*de obreros*] gang, team; **una ~ de chiquillos** a bunch of kids*; **¡menuda ~!** a fine bunch they are! ► **cuadrilla de demolición** demolition squad
[2] (*Taur*) *bullfighting team*
[3] (*Mil*) squad; (††) armed patrol ► **cuadrilla de noche** night shift, night squad

cuadrillazo SM (*Andes, Cono Sur*) gang attack

cuadrillero SM [1] (= *jefe*) [*de grupo*] group leader; [*de banda*] gang leader
[2] (*esp Andes, Cono Sur pey*) hooligan
[3] (= *trabajador*) worker (*in a team*)

cuadrilongo Ⓐ ADJ oblong
Ⓑ SM oblong

cuadringentésimo ADJ four hundredth

cuadripartido ADJ quadripartite

cuadrito SM (*Culin*) cube; **cortar en ~s** to dice

cuadrivio SM quadrivium

cuadro SM [1] (= *cuadrado*) square; **una camisa/un vestido a** *o* **de ~s** a checked *o* check shirt/dress; **~s escoceses** tartan (pattern); ✦***MODISMOS*** **quedarse a ~s*** to be flabbergasted*; **en ~**: **el equipo llegó en ~ al partido** they brought a drastically reduced side *o* team to the match; **hacerse la vida de ~s** *o* **cuadritos** (*Méx*) to make things complicated; **ser del otro ~** (*Uru**) to be gay
[2] (*Arte*) (= *pintura*) painting; (= *reproducción*) picture; **dos ~s de Velázquez** two paintings by Velázquez, two Velazquez paintings; **pintar un ~** to do a painting, paint a picture; ✦***MODISMO*** **ir hecho un ~** to be a (real) sight* ► **cuadro de honor** roll of honour, honor roll (*EEUU*)
[3] (= *escena*) (*Teat*) scene; (*fig*) scene, sight; **fue un ~ desgarrador** it was a heart-breaking scene *o* sight; **desde el avión los escaladores ofrecían un ~ impresionante** seen from the plane the climbers were an impressive sight; **llegaron calados hasta los huesos y llenos de barro ¡vaya ~!** they arrived soaked to the skin and covered in mud, what a sight (they were)! ► **cuadro viviente**, **cuadro vivo** tableau vivant
[4] (= *gráfico*) table, chart ► **cuadro de diálogo** dialog box ► **cuadro sinóptico** synoptic chart
[5] (= *tablero*) panel ► **cuadro de conmutadores**, **cuadro de distribución** (*Elec*) switchboard ► **cuadro de instrumentos** (*Aer*) instrument panel; (*Aut*) dashboard ► **cuadro de mandos** control panel
[6] (= *armazón*) [*de bicicleta, ventana*] frame
[7] **cuadros** (*tb* **~s de mando**) (*en empresa*) managerial staff; (*Admin, Pol*) officials; (*Mil*)

commanding officers ► **cuadros dirigentes** (*en empresa*) senior management; (*Admin, Pol*) senior officials; (*Mil*) senior officers ► **cuadros medios** (*en empresa*) middle management; (*Admin, Pol*) middle-ranking officials; (*Mil*) middle-ranking officers ► **cuadros superiores** = **cuadros dirigentes**

8 (*Med*) symptoms *pl*, set of symptoms; **el paciente presentaba un ~ vírico** the patient presented with viral symptoms (*frm*), the patient showed symptoms of a virus ► **cuadro clínico** symptoms *pl*, clinical symptoms *pl*

9 (= *descripción*) picture; **un verdadero ~ de la sociedad** a true picture of society ► **cuadro de costumbres** (*Literat*) *description of local customs*

10 (*en jardín, huerto*) bed, plot

11 (*Mil*) (= *formación*) square; ✦*MODISMO* **formar el ~** to close ranks

12 (*Dep*) team; **el ~ argentino** the Argentinian team

13 (*Cono Sur*) (= *matadero*) slaughterhouse, abattoir

14 (*Cono Sur*) (= *bragas*) knickers *pl*, panties *pl*

15 (*Andes*) (= *pizarra*) blackboard

cuadrúpedo SM quadruped, four-footed animal

cuádruple Ⓐ ADJ quadruple, fourfold

Ⓑ SM **yo he pagado el ~** I paid four times that; **el ~ del salario mínimo** four times the minimum salary

cuadruplicado ADJ quadruplicate; **por ~** in quadruplicate

cuadruplicar ▸conjug 1g◂ Ⓐ VT to quadruple; **hemos cuadruplicado nuestras ventas este año** we have quadrupled our sales this year; **las pérdidas cuadruplican las del año pasado** losses are four times last year's

Ⓑ **cuadruplicarse** VPR to quadruple, increase fourfold

cuádruplo Ⓐ ADJ fourfold, quadruple

Ⓑ SM = **cuádruple B**

cuajada SF [*de leche*] curd; (= *requesón*) curd cheese, cottage cheese; (*como postre*) junket

cuajado Ⓐ ADJ 1 [*leche*] curdled; [*sangre*] coagulated, congealed

2 (= *lleno*) **~ de** full of, filled with; **un cielo ~ de estrellas** a star-spangled sky, a star-studded sky, a sky studded with stars; **una corona cuajada de diamantes** a diamond-studded crown, a crown studded with diamonds; **una tapia cuajada de pintadas** a wall covered in graffiti; **una situación cuajada de peligros** a situation fraught with dangers; **un texto ~ de problemas** a text bristling with problems

3 (= *asombrado*) **estar ~** to be dumbfounded

4 (= *dormido*) **quedarse ~** to fall asleep

Ⓑ SM ► **cuajado de limón** lemon curd

cuajaleche SM 1 (*Culin*) cheese rennet

2 (*Bot*) bedstraw

cuajar ▸conjug 1a◂ Ⓐ VT 1 [+ *leche*] to curdle; [+ *gelatina*] to set; [+ *sangre*] to coagulate, clot; [+ *grasa*] to congeal

2 **~ algo de** (= *cubrir*) to cover sth with, adorn sth with; (= *llenar*) to fill sth with; **cuajó el tablero de cifras** he covered the board with figures

Ⓑ VI 1 [*nieve*] to lie; [*leche*] to curdle

2 [*moda, producto*] to catch on, take off; [*plan*] to take shape; [*idea, propuesta*] to be well received, be acceptable; [*truco*] to come off, work; **el acuerdo no cuajó** the agreement didn't come off *o* work out

3 (*Méx*) (= *charlar*) to chat

Ⓒ **cuajarse** VPR 1 [*leche*] to curdle; [*sangre*] to congeal, coagulate; [*gelatina*] to set

2 **~se de** to fill (up) with

3 (= *dormirse*) to fall fast asleep

cuajarón SM clot

cuajo SM 1 (*Zool, Culin*) rennet; **~ en polvo** powdered rennet

2 **arrancar algo de ~** to tear sth out by its roots; **arrancar una puerta de ~** to wrench a door out of its frame; **extirpar un vicio de ~** to eradicate a vice completely

3 (= *cachaza*) phlegm, calmness; **tiene mucho ~** he's very phlegmatic

4 **coger un ~*** to cry one's eyes out; *ver tb* **llorar B1**

5 (*Méx**) (= *charla*) chatter

6 (*Méx**) (= *mentirijilla*) fib

7 (*Méx**) (= *proyecto*) pipe dream

8 (*Méx Escol*) (= *recreo*) playtime, recess (*EEUU*)

9 (*Méx*) (= *látigo*) short whip

cual Ⓐ PRON 1 **el ~/la ~/ los ~es/las ~es**

1·1 (*aplicado a cosas*) which; **un balcón desde el ~ se puede ver toda la bahía** a balcony from which you can see the whole bay; **obtuvo una beca, gracias a la ~ pudo subsistir varios años** he got a grant, which gave him enough to live on for several years; **el estado al ~ se ha solicitado la extradición** the country from which extradition has been requested

1·2 (*aplicado a personas*) (*como sujeto*) who; (*como objeto*) who, whom; (*tras preposición*) whom; **se reunieron con el presidente, el ~ les informó del asunto** they had a meeting with the president, who briefed them on the affair; **tengo gran amistad con el director, al ~ conozco desde hace muchos años** the director, who *o* whom I have known for many years, is a great friend of mine; **había ocho chicos, tres de los ~es hablaban en inglés** there were eight boys, three of whom were speaking in English

2 **lo ~** which; **se rieron mucho, lo ~ me disgustó** they laughed a lot, which upset me; **con lo ~** with the result that; **se han construido dos escuelas más, con lo ~ contaremos con más de 2.000 plazas escolares** two more schools have been built, with the result that *o* which means that we will have more than 2,000 school places; **llegué tarde, con lo ~ no pude entrar** I arrived late, which meant I couldn't get in; **por lo ~** and therefore, consequently

3 **cada ~**: **miembros de distintas religiones, cada ~ con su libro sagrado** members of different religions, each (one) with their holy book; **cada ~ puede hacer lo que crea conveniente** everyone may do what they think fit; **depende del gusto de cada ~** it depends on individual taste, it depends on each individual's taste; **allá cada ~** everyone must look out for themselves; **allá cada ~ con su conciencia** that is a matter for each individual's conscience

4 **sea ~ sea** *o* **fuese** *o* **fuere** whatever; **nuestra postura no variará sea ~ sea el resultado de las elecciones** our position will not change whatever the outcome of the election (is *o* may be); **quiere entrar en un club de golf, sea ~ sea** he wants to join a golf club, and any one will do

Ⓑ ADV, CONJ (*liter*) like; **en la novela su amada se suicida ~ nueva Ofelia** in the novel his loved one commits suicide like a modern-day Ophelia; **frágil ~ mariposa** as delicate as a butterfly; **~ si** as if; **todos aplaudieron su sugerencia, ~ si de una idea genial se tratara** everyone applauded his suggestion, as if it were the most brilliant idea; *ver tb* **tal C1**

Ⓒ ADJ (*Jur*) said, aforementioned; **los ~es bienes** the said *o* aforementioned property

cuál Ⓐ PRON 1 (*interrogativo*) what, which (one); **¿~ quieres?** which (one) do you want?; **¿~ es su opinión sobre el tema?** what's your opinion on the subject?; **¿~ es el que dices?** which one are you talking about?; **ignora ~ será el resultado** he does not know what the outcome will be

2 **a ~ más**: **son a ~ más gandul** each *o* one is as lazy as the other; **una serie de coches a ~ más rápido** a series of cars each faster than the last; **gritaban a ~ más** one was shouting louder than the other; **~ más ~ menos** some more, some less

3 (*exclamativo*) **¡~ no sería mi asombro!** imagine the surprise I got!, imagine my surprise!; **¡~ gritan esos malditos!** (*frm*) how those wretched people shout!

Ⓑ ADJ (*esp Méx, Perú, Ven*) which?; **¿~ libro dices?** which book do you mean?; **¿~es carros?** which cars?; **tú ¿a ~ colegio vas?** which school do you go to?

cualidad SF 1 (= *virtud*) quality; (= *talento*) talent; **tiene buenas ~es** he has good qualities; **su principal ~ era la lealtad** loyalty was their main virtue, their foremost quality was loyalty; **defectos y ~es** faults and virtues; **hizo una demostración de sus ~es como actriz** she demonstrated her talent as an actress; **jóvenes que apuntan ~es** promising young people

2 (= *atributo*) attribute, characteristic

3 (*Fís, Fil*) property

cualificado ADJ 1 [*obrero*] skilled, qualified; **obrero no ~** unskilled worker

2 **estar ~ para hacer algo** to be qualified to do sth

3 = **calificado**

cualitativamente ADV qualitatively

cualitativo ADJ qualitative

cualquier(a)[1] (*pl* **cualesquier(a)**) ADJ INDEF 1 (*antes de s*) any; **como en ~ otro país europeo** as in any other European country; **~ día se presenta aquí** he could turn up here any day; **~ persona de por aquí te diría lo mismo** anyone from round here would tell you the same; **en ~ caso** in any case; **~ cosa** anything; **en un lugar como este puede ocurrir ~ cosa** in a place like this anything could happen; **en ~ lugar del mundo** anywhere in the world; **en ~ momento** at any time, (at) any moment; ✦*MODISMO* **~ tiempo pasado fue mejor** the grass is always greener (on the other side of the fence)

2 (*después de s*) any; **—¿cuál prefieres? —me da igual, uno ~a** "which one do you prefer?" — "it doesn't matter, any one (will do)"; **sucedió un día ~a** it happened on a day like any other day; **el presidente tendrá que ir a juicio, como un ciudadano ~a** the

president will have to go to court, like any ordinary citizen; **éste no es un coche ~a** this is not just any old car

[3] (*LAm*) (= *bastante*) **tienen ~ cantidad de juguetes** they have loads of toys*; **puede comer ~ cantidad y no se llena** he can eat loads and not get full*

cualquiera² (*pl* **cualesquiera**) Ⓐ PRON INDEF [1] (= *cualquier persona*) anyone, anybody; (= *cualquier cosa*) any one; **en un club como ése no admiten a ~** they don't accept just anyone *o* anybody into that club; **~ puede ser candidato a la presidencia** anyone *o* anybody can stand for president; **esos precios están al alcance de ~** those prices are within everyone's *o* everybody's means; **tal como gritaban los niños, ~ diría que los estaba torturando** the way the children were screaming anyone would think I was torturing them; **puedes coger ~** you can choose any one (you like); **es una costumbre como otra ~** it is a custom like any other

[2] **~ de** any, any of; **puede acudir a ~ de las sucursales del banco** you can go to any branch *o* any of the branches of the bank; **~ de mis alumnos podría realizar este proyecto** any *o* anyone of my pupils could do this project; **~ de los dos** either (one) of them, either of the two; **llama a Pedro o a Carlos, ~ de los dos** call Pedro or Carlos, either (one) of them *o* either of the two; **~ de los dos equipos** either team *o* either (one) of the two teams

[3] **~ que** (+ *SUBJUN*) [3·1] (*en general*) whatever; (*ante una elección*) whichever; **~ que sea el color de su piel** whatever the colour of their skin; **~ que sea tu problema** whatever your problem is, no matter what your problem is; **respetaremos el resultado de la votación, ~ que sea** we will respect the result of the vote, whatever that may be; **es caro, pero ~ que compres te va a costar una fortuna** it's expensive, but whichever (one) you buy it'll cost you a fortune

[3·2] (= *persona*) anyone who, anybody who; **~ que lo conozca te diría lo mismo** anyone *o* anybody who knows him *o* whoever knows him would tell you the same

[4] (*en exclamaciones*) **¡~ sabe!** who knows?; **¡~ le interrumpe ahora!** I wouldn't interrupt him at the minute!; **¡así ~!** it's all right for some!*

Ⓑ SM **un ~** a nobody; **yo no me caso con un ~** I'm not marrying just anybody

Ⓒ SF (*pey*) **una ~** a hussy*

cuan ADV (*liter*) **tan estúpidos ~ criminales** as stupid as they are criminal

cuán ADV how; **¡~ agradable fue todo eso!** how delightful it all was!

cuando Ⓐ CONJ [1] (*con valor temporal*) (*en un momento concreto*) when; (*en cualquier momento*) whenever; **~ llegué a su casa él ya se había ido** when I got to his house he had already left; **te lo diré ~ nos veamos** I'll tell you when I see you; **ven ~ quieras** come when(ever) you like; **~ iba allí lo veía** whenever I went there I saw him, I used to see him when(ever) I went there; **me acuerdo de ~ jugábamos en el patio** I remember when we used to play in the yard; **lo dejaremos para ~ estés mejor** we'll leave it until you're better

[2] (*con valor condicional, causal*) if; **~ él lo dice, será verdad** if he says so, it must be true; **~ no te ha dicho nada todavía, es que no piensa invitarte** if he hasn't said anything yet, that means he isn't thinking of inviting you

[3] (*con valor adversativo*) when; **yo lo hago todo, ~ es él quien debería hacerlo** I'm the one that does it all, when it should be him; *ver tb* **aun 3**

Ⓑ ADV [1] **fue entonces ~ comprendí la importancia del problema** it was then that *o* that was when I understood the seriousness of the problem; **en abril es ~ más casos hay** April is when there are most cases, it's in April that there are most cases; **de ~ en ~** ◊ **de vez en ~** from time to time, now and again, every so often

[2] **~ más** at (the) most; **tardaremos, ~ más, una semana** it will take us a week at (the) most *o* at the outside; **~ menos** at least; **esperamos llegar, ~ menos, a las semifinales** we are hoping to reach the semifinals, at least; **~ mucho** at (the) most; **~ no** if not; **docenas, ~ no cientos, de películas** dozens, if not hundreds, of films

Ⓒ PREP **eso fue ~ la guerra** that was during the war; **ocurrió ~ la boda** it happened at the time of the wedding; **~ niño yo era muy travieso** as a child *o* when I was a child I was very naughty

cuándo ADV [1] (*en oraciones interrogativas*) when; **¿~ te lo dijo?** when did he tell you?; **no sé ~ será** I don't know when it will be; **no me ha dicho aún desde ~ sabe la noticia** he hasn't told me yet how long he has known the news (for); **¿de ~ acá?** since when?; **¿desde ~?** since when?; **¿desde ~ os conocéis?** how long have you known each other?; **¿desde ~ trata uno así a su padre?** since when do you treat your father like that?; **¿hasta ~?** how long?; **¿hasta ~ vamos a aguantar esta injusticia?** how long are we going to put up with this injustice?; **¿hasta ~ ya no te veo?** when will I see you again *o* next?, how long will it be till I see you again?; **¿para ~ ...?** when ... by?; **¿para ~ estará listo el proyecto?** when will the project be ready (by)?; **¿para ~ una edición de sus obras completas?** when are we (ever) going to see an edition of his complete works?; **✦MODISMO no tener para ~** (*Chile**): **a este paso no tenemos para ~ terminar** we're never going to finish at this rate; **—¿esta lista ya? —¡no tiene para ~!** "is she ready yet?" — "she'll be a long time yet!"

[2] **¡~ no!** (*LAm*) just to make a change!; **se le perdieron las llaves ¡~ no!** he lost his keys, just to make a change!

cuandoquiera CONJ **~ que ...** whenever ...

cuantía SF [1] (= *cantidad*) [1·1] (= *importe*) quantity, amount; **¿cómo se calcula la ~ de la pensión?** how is the amount *o* level of pension calculated?; **el fraude supera la ~ de cinco millones** the fraud amounts to more than five million

[1·2] (= *alcance*) extent; **se ignora la ~ de las pérdidas** the extent of the losses is not known

[2] (= *importancia*) importance; **de mayor ~** more important, more significant; **de menor ~** ◊ **de poca ~** unimportant, of little account

cuántico ADJ **teoría cuántica** quantum theory

cuantificable ADJ quantifiable

cuantificación SF quantifying; **hacer una ~ de** to quantify

cuantificador SM quantifier

cuantificar ▸conjug 1g◂ VT [1] [+ *daños, pérdidas*] to quantify (*frm*), assess

[2] (*Fís*) to quantize

[3] (*Lógica*) to quantify

cuantimás* ADV **~ que** all the more so because

cuantioso ADJ [*suma, beneficios, daños*] substantial, considerable; [*pérdidas*] substantial, heavy; **el terremoto causó ~s daños materiales** the earthquake caused substantial *o* considerable material damage

cuantitativamente ADV quantitatively

cuantitativo ADJ quantitative

cuanto Ⓐ ADJ [1] (*indicando cantidad*) **daremos ~s créditos se precisen** we will give as many loans as (are) needed *o* whatever loans are needed; **~s hombres la ven se enamoran de ella** all the men that see her fall for her

[2] (*en correlación*) **~ más** the more; **~s más invitados vengan más comida habrá que preparar** the more guests come, the more food we'll have to prepare; **~ menos** the less; **~ menos dinero tiene la gente, menos gasta en salir a comer** the less money people have, the less they spend on eating out; **~s menos errores hagas mejor** the fewer mistakes you make, the better

[3] **unos ~s** (= *no muchos*) a few; (= *bastantes*) quite a few; **sólo unos ~s funcionarios permanecerán en el país** only a few officials will stay in the country; **he leído unos ~s libros suyos** I've read quite a few of his books

Ⓑ PRON [1] (*indicando cantidad*) all; **tiene todo ~ desea** he has everything *o* all (that) he wants; **tome ~ quiera** take as much as you want, take all you want

[2] (*en correlación*) **~s más** the more; **~s más mejor** the more the better; **~s menos** the fewer

[3] **unos ~s** (= *no muchos*) a few; (= *bastantes*) quite a few; **lo sabíamos unos ~s, pero la mayoría no** a few of us knew, but most people didn't; **hay unos ~s en clase que no hacen más que molestar** there are a few people in the class who do nothing but cause trouble; **—¿cuántos vinieron? —unos ~s** "how many people came?" — "quite a few"

Ⓒ ADV, CONJ [1] (*expresando correlación*) **~ antes mejor** the sooner the better; **~ más** the more; **~ más intentes convencerlo, menos caso te hará** the more you try to persuade him, the more he will ignore you; **~ más corto mejor** the shorter, the better; **~ menos** the less; **~ menos se hable sobre este asunto mejor** the less (that is) said about this issue, the better

[2] (*locuciones*) [2·1] **~ antes** as soon as possible; **tiene que estar terminado ~ antes** it has to be finished as soon as possible; **ven ~ antes** come as soon as you can *o* as soon as possible

[2·2] **en ~** (= *tan pronto como*) as soon as; (= *en calidad de*) as; **en ~ lo supe me fui** as soon as I heard I left; **iré en ~ pueda** I'll go as soon as I can; **el cuento infantil, en ~ género literario** children's stories, as a literary genre

[2·3] **en ~ a** as regards, as for; **en ~ a tu aumento de sueldo, lo discutiremos en diciembre** as regards *o* as for your pay rise, we'll discuss it in December; **el sistema tiene ventajas en ~ a seguridad y comodidad** as regards *o* with regard to safety and comfort, the system has advantages; **en ~ a mí** as for me

[2·4] **en ~ que** insofar as

[2·5] **~ más** especially; **siempre está nervioso, ~ más en época de exámenes** he's always nervous, all the more so *o* especially at exam time; **no escribe a nadie, ~ más a nosotros** he doesn't write to anyone, let alone us

[2·6] **~ menos** to say the least; **esta interpretación es, ~ menos, discutible** this interpretation is debatable to say the least

[2·7] **por ~** in that, inasmuch as (*frm*); **es un delito por ~ vulnera los derechos constitucionales** it is a crime in that *o* inasmuch as (*frm*) it violates constitutional rights; **llama la atención por ~ supone de innovación** it attracts attention because of its novelty value

cuánto Ⓐ ADJ [1] (*en oraciones interrogativas*) [1·1] (*en singular*) how much; **¿cuánta sal echo?** how much salt shall I add?; **¿~ tiempo ...?** how long ...?; **¿~ tiempo llevas viviendo en Perú?** how long have you been living in Peru (for)?

[1·2] (*en plural*) how many; **¿~s días libres tienes al año?** how many days off do you have a year?; **¿cuántas personas había?** how many people were there?; **no sabe ~s cuadros hay en su casa** he doesn't know how many paintings there are in his house

[2] (*en exclamaciones*) **¡cuánta gente!** what a lot of people!; **¡~ tiempo perdido!** think of all the time that's been wasted!; **¡cuántas viviendas han construido desde que me fui!** they've built so many houses since I left!; **¡~ borracho hay por las calles!*** the streets are full of drunks!

Ⓑ PRON [1] (*en preguntas, uso indirecto*) [1·1] (*tb ~ dinero*) how much; **¿~ has gastado?** how much have you spent?; **no sé ~ es** I don't know how much it is; **no me ha dicho ~ es** he hasn't told me how much it is; **¿a ~ están las peras?** how much are (the) pears?

[1·2] (*tb ~ tiempo*) how long; **¿~ durará esto?** how long will this last?; **¿cada ~?** how often?

[1·3] (*en plural*) how many; **¿~s de vosotros apoyaríais la huelga?** how many of you would support the strike?; **¿a ~s estamos?** what's the date today?, what date is it today?

[2] (*en exclamaciones*) **¡~ has gastado!** you've spent a fortune!; **¡~ has tardado!** you've been ages!, you took ages!; **¡~s has comprado!** you've bought so many!, you've bought loads!

[3] **no sé ~s**: **el señor no sé ~s** Mr So-and-So, Mr something-or-other; **el señor Anastasio no sé ~s** Mr Anastasio something-or-other

Ⓒ ADV [1] (*en preguntas, uso indirecto*) [1·1] (*de cantidad*) how much; **¿~ pesas?** how much do you weigh?; **no sé ~ quieres** I don't know how much you want

[1·2] (*de distancia*) how far; **¿~ hay de aquí a Bilbao?** how far is it from here to Bilbao?; **¿~ falta para llegar al pueblo?** how much further is the town?, how far is it to the town from here?

[2] (*en exclamaciones*) **¡~ has crecido!** how you've grown!; **¡~ trabajas!** how hard you work!; **¡~ me alegro!** I'm so glad!

> **CUÁNTO**
>
> **¿Cuánto tiempo?**
>
> • Cuando se habla de la duración de algo, **cuánto** se traduce al inglés por **how long** y se utiliza el pretérito perfecto cuando la acción comenzó en el pasado y continúa todavía:
>
> ¿Cuánto tiempo llevas esperando?
> ***How long have you been waiting?***
> ¿Cuánto hace que nos conocemos?
> ***How long have we known each other?***
>
> • En otros contextos, no debe utilizarse el pretérito perfecto:
>
> ¿Cuánto tardasteis en llegar a Barcelona?
> ***How long did it take you to get to Barcelona?***
> ¿Cuánto dura la película?
> ***How long is the film?***
>
> *Para otros usos y ejemplos ver la entrada.*

cuaquerismo SM Quakerism

cuáquero/a ADJ, SM/F Quaker

cuarcita SF quartzite

cuarenta ADJ INV, PRON, SM (*gen*) forty; (= *cuadragésimo*) fortieth; **los (años) ~** the forties; **los ~ rugientes** the Roaring Forties; **"Los ~ principales"** (*Radio, TV*) "the Top Forty" (*Spanish hit parade*); ✦***MODISMOS*** **cantar las ~** (*Naipes*) *to have the king and queen of trumps*; **cantar las ~ a algn** to tell sb a few home truths, tell sb a thing or two; **ésas son otras ~** (*Arg, Perú*) that's a different story; ✦***REFRÁN*** **hasta el ~ de mayo no te quites el sayo** ne'er cast a clout till May be out; *ver tb* **seis**

cuarentañero/a Ⓐ ADJ fortyish, about forty
Ⓑ SM/F person of about forty, person in his *o* her forties

cuarentavo Ⓐ ADJ [1] (= *ordinal*) fortieth
[2] (= *partitivo*) **la cuarentava parte** a fortieth
Ⓑ SM fortieth

cuarentena SF [1] (= *número*) about forty, forty-odd; **ambos rondan la ~** they're both around forty (years old); **una ~ de** some forty, forty or so
[2] (= *aislamiento*) quarantine; **poner a algn en ~** (*Med*) to put sb in quarantine, quarantine sb; (*fig*) to send sb to Coventry; **poner un asunto en ~** to suspend judgement on a matter
[3] (*Rel*) (= *cuaresma*) Lent

cuarentón/ona Ⓐ ADJ forty-something; **es ya ~** he's in his forties, he's forty-something
Ⓑ SM/F person in their forties

cuaresma SF Lent; → CARNAVAL

cuaresmal ADJ Lenten

cuark SM (*pl* **cuarks**) quark

cuarta SF [1] (*Mat*) quarter
[2] (= *palmo*) span
[3] (*Aut*) fourth gear, fourth; **meter la ~** to go into fourth (gear), put it *o* the car into fourth (gear)
[4] (*Náut*) point (*of the compass*)
[5] (*Méx*) (= *látigo*) *a short whip used for horse-riding*
[6] (*Cono Sur Agr*) extra pair of oxen
[7] ✦***MODISMOS*** **a la ~** short of money; **la situación económica nos trae a todos a la ~** the economic situation has left us all broke *o* short of money; **a fin de mes siempre andamos a la ~** at the end of the month we're always short of money; **es muy tacaño, nos tiene a todos a la ~** he's very mean, we're crying out for money; **andar de la ~ al pértigo** (*Cono Sur*) ◊ **vivir a la ~** (*Cono Sur, Méx*) to be on the bread line

cuartago SM pony

cuartazos* SM INV fat person, lump*

cuartear ▸conjug 1a◂ Ⓐ VT [1] [+ *res*] to cut up
[2] (*Mat*) to divide into four
[3] [+ *carretera*] to zigzag up
[4] (*Náut*) **~ la aguja** to box the compass
[5] (*Caribe, Méx*) (= *azotar*) to whip, beat
Ⓑ VI [1] (*Taur*) to dodge, step aside
[2] (*Naipes*) to make a fourth (player), make up a four
Ⓒ **cuartearse** VPR [1] (= *agrietarse*) to crack, split
[2] (*Taur*) to dodge, step aside
[3] (*Méx*) (= *desdecirse*) to go back on one's word

cuartel SM [1] (*Mil*) barracks; **vida de ~** army life, service life; **estar de ~**† to be on half-pay ► **cuarteles de invierno** (*Mil*) winter quarters; (*fig*) winter retreat *sing* ► **cuartel general** headquarters *pl*
[2] (= *tregua*) **no hubo ~ para los revoltosos** no mercy was shown to the rebels; **no dar ~** to give no quarter, show no mercy; **guerra sin ~** all-out war; **lucha sin ~** fight to the death
[3] (= *cuarta*) quarter
[4] (= *distrito*) quarter, district
[5] (*Heráldica*) quarter
[6] (*Hort*) bed

cuartelazo SM, **cuartelada** SF military uprising

cuartelero Ⓐ ADJ barracks *antes de s*; **utiliza un lenguaje ~** he swears like a trooper; **rancho ~** *food eaten by soldiers in barracks*
Ⓑ SM (*Andes*) waiter

cuartelillo SM [1] [*de policía*] police station; [*de bomberos*] fire station, fire *o* station house (*EEUU*)
[2] (‡) [*de droga*] dealer's share (*of drug deal*); **dar ~ a algn‡** to give sb their share

cuartería SF (*Caribe, Cono Sur*) bunkhouse (*on a ranch*)

cuarterón/ona Ⓐ SM [1] (= *peso*) quarter pound, quarter
[2] (*Arquit*) [*de ventana*] shutter; [*de puerta*] panel
Ⓑ SM/F (*LAm*) quadroon

cuarteta SF quatrain

cuarteto SM [1] (*Mús*) (= *conjunto, composición*) quartet, quartette ► **cuarteto de viento** wind quartet
[2] (*Literat*) quatrain

cuartil SM quartile

cuartilla SF [1] (= *hoja*) (*en general*) sheet (of paper); (= *medio folio*) A-5 sheet of paper; **un sobre tamaño ~** an A-5 envelope
[2] [*de caballo*] pastern
[3] (= *cuarta parte*) fourth part (*of a measure*)
[4] **cuartillas** (*Tip*) copy; (= *apuntes*) notes, jottings

cuarto Ⓐ ADJ (*ordinal*) fourth; **en ~ lugar** in fourth place; **la cuarta parte** a quarter; *ver tb* **sexto A**
Ⓑ SM [1] (= *habitación*) room; (= *dormitorio*) bedroom, room; **el ~ de los niños** the children's room; ✦***MODISMOS*** **echar su ~ a espaldas** to stick one's oar in; **hacer ~ a algn** (*Col*) to shelter sb ► **cuarto de aseo** toilet, cloakroom, bathroom (*EEUU*) ► **cuarto de baño** bathroom ► **cuarto de desahogo** lumber room ► **cuarto de estar** living room,

sitting room ► **cuarto de juego** playroom ► **cuarto frío** (*Culin*) cold store ► **cuarto intermedio** (*Arg, Uru*) **estar en ~ intermedio** to be in recess; **pasar a ~ intermedio** to adjourn the session ► **cuarto oscuro** (*Fot*) darkroom; (= *trastero*) broom cupboard; (*Arg, Uru*) voting booth ► **cuarto trastero** lumber room

2 (= *cuarta parte*) quarter; **un ~ de millón de dólares** a quarter of a million dollars; **un ~ (de) kilo** a quarter (of a) kilo; **(abrigo) tres ~s** three-quarter length coat; ✦***MODISMOS*** **de tres al ~** worthless, third-rate; **tres ~s de lo mismo**: **su amigo es un inútil, y él ... tres ~s de lo mismo** his friend is useless, and he's not much better; **en otros países ocurre tres ~s de lo mismo** it's the same story *o* it's more of the same in other countries ► **cuarto creciente** first quarter ► **cuarto de luna** quarter of the moon ► **cuarto menguante** last quarter ► **cuartos de final** quarter finals

3 (*en la hora*) quarter; **son las seis menos ~** ◊ **es un ~ para las seis** (*LAm*) it's a quarter to six; **a las seis y ~** at (a) quarter past six; ✦***MODISMO*** **tener algn/algo su ~ de hora** (*LAm*) to be all the rage; **tuvo su ~ de hora, ahora nadie lo lleva** it had its day *o* it was all the rage, now nobody wears it anymore ► **cuarto de hora** quarter of an hour; **tardó tres ~s de hora** it took him *o* he took three quarters of an hour

4 [*de animal, de cerdo, vaca*] joint; **un ~ de pollo** a chicken quarter, a quarter chicken; **cuartos** legs ► **cuartos delanteros** forequarters ► **cuartos traseros** hindquarters

5 (= *moneda*) *coin used in Spain in former times*; **cuartos*** (= *dinero*) dough* *sing*; **es hombre de muchos ~s** he's got pots of money*; ✦***MODISMOS*** **aflojar los ~s** to cough up*; **estar sin un ~** to be broke*; **dar ~s al pregonero** (*Esp*) to tell everyone one's private business; **por cinco ~s** (*Esp*) for a song; **¡qué coche ni qué ocho ~s!** car, my foot!; **no tener un ~** to be broke*

6 (*Tip*) quarto; **libro en ~** quarto volume

7 **estar de ~** (*Mil*) to be on watch

8 (††) (= *piso*) small flat; **poner ~** to set up house; **poner ~ a la querida** to set one's mistress up in a little place

9 (††) (= *servidumbre*) household, servants *pl*

cuartofinalista SMF quarter-finalist

cuartón SM dressed timber, beam, plank

cuartones SMPL dressed timber *sing*, beams, planks

cuartucho SM (= *habitación*) poky little room; (= *casucha*) hovel

cuarzo SM quartz ► **cuarzo hialino** rock crystal ► **cuarzo rosa**, **cuarzo rosado** rose quartz

cuás* SM (*Méx*) bosom pal*

cuásar SM quasar

cuasi ADV (*liter*) = **casi**

cuasi... PREF quasi-...

cuate (*CAm, Méx*) Ⓐ ADJ twin

Ⓑ SMF 1 (= *gemelo*) twin

2 (= *compadre*) mate*, pal*, buddy (*EEUU**)

3 (= *tipo*) guy*/girl

Ⓒ SM (= *escopeta*) double-barrelled gun

cuaternario Ⓐ ADJ quaternary; (*Geol*) Quaternary

Ⓑ SM **el ~** the Quaternary

cuatrear ▸conjug 1a◂, **cuatrerear** ▸conjug 1a◂ (*Cono Sur*) Ⓐ VT [+ *ganado*] to rustle, steal

Ⓑ VI to act treacherously

cuatrero/a Ⓐ SM/F [*de ganado*] rustler, stock thief; [*de caballos*] horse thief

Ⓑ ADJ (*CAm*) treacherous, disloyal

cuatrienal ADJ four-year *antes de s*, quadrennial (*frm*); **un plan ~** a four-year plan

cuatrifónico ADJ quadraphonic

cuatrillizo/a SM/F quadruplet

cuatrimestral ADJ 1 (= *de cada cuatro meses*) four-monthly, every four months; **son exámenes ~es** they are four-monthly exams, the exams are every four months

2 (= *de cuatro meses*) four-month(-long); **una asignatura ~** a four-month(-long) course, a course which lasts for four months

cuatrimestralmente ADV every four months

cuatrimestre SM four-month period

cuatrimotor Ⓐ ADJ four-engined

Ⓑ SM four-engined plane

cuatriplicado ADJ quadruplicate; **por ~** in quadruplicate

cuatro Ⓐ ADJ INV, PRON 1 (*gen*) four; (*ordinal, en la fecha*) fourth; **cada ~ días** every four days; **las ~** four o'clock; **le escribí el día ~** I wrote to him on the fourth

2 (= *pocos*) **sólo había ~ muebles** there were only a few sticks of furniture; **te escribo sólo ~ líneas para decirte que ...** I'm just dropping you a line to tell you that ...; **cayeron ~ gotas** a few drops fell; **más de ~ lo creen** quite a few people believe it; ✦***MODISMO*** **sólo había ~ gatos** the place was dead*, there was hardly a soul

Ⓑ SM 1 (*gen*) four; (= *fecha*) fourth; **el ~ de octubre** (on) the fourth of October, (on) October the fourth; *ver tb* **seis**

2 (*Méx*) (= *trampa*) trick, fraud; (= *error*) blunder

3 (*Ven Mús*) four-stringed guitar

4 (*Aut*) ► **cuatro latas*** Renault 4L ► **cuatro por cuatro** four-wheel drive vehicle

Ⓒ ► **cuatro ojos*** SMF INV four-eyes*

cuatrocientos/as ADJ, PRON, SMPL/SFPL four hundred; *ver tb* **seiscientos**

cuatrojos* SMF INV four-eyes*

cuba[1] SF 1 (= *tonel*) cask, barrel; (= *tina*) tub, vat; (*Ferro*) tank car; (*para el agua de lluvia*) rainwater butt; ✦***MODISMO*** **estar como una ~** to be as drunk as a lord ► **cuba de riego** water wagon, street sprinkler

2 (*) (= *panzudo*) pot-bellied person

cuba[2] SM (*Andes*) (= *hijo*) youngest child

Cuba SF Cuba; ✦***MODISMO*** **más se perdió en ~** it's not the end of the world

cubaje SM (*LAm*) volume, contents

cubalibre SM, **cuba-libre** SM (*pl* **cubas-libres** *o* **cuba-libres**) [*de ron*] (white) rum and Coke®; [*de ginebra*] gin and Coke®

cubanismo SM cubanism, *word or phrase etc peculiar to Cuba*

cubano/a ADJ, SM/F Cuban

cubata* SM = **cubalibre**

cubero SM cooper

cubertería SF cutlery, flatware (*EEUU*); **una ~ de plata** a set *o* canteen of silver cutlery, a silver flatware service (*EEUU*)

cubeta SF 1 (*Fot, Quím*) tray

2 [*de barómetro, termómetro*] bulb

3 (*para hielo*) ice tray

4 (= *tonel*) keg, small cask ► **cubeta de siembra** seed box

cubetera SF (*Cono Sur*) ice tray

cubicaje SM cubic capacity; (*Aut*) cylinder capacity

cubicar ▸conjug 1g◂ VT 1 (*Mat*) to cube

2 (*Fís*) to determine the volume of

cúbico ADJ cubic; **un objeto ~** a cubic *o* cube-shaped object; **metro ~** cubic metre; **raíz cúbica** cube root, cubic root

cubículo SM cubicle

cubierta SF 1 (= *cobertura*) cover(ing); [*de libro*] cover, jacket; [*de edificio*] roof; **~ de lona** tarpaulin

2 [*de rueda*] tyre, tire (*EEUU*); **~ sin cámara** tubeless tyre

3 (*Náut*) deck; **salir a ~** to go up *o* out on deck ► **cubierta de aterrizaje** flight deck ► **cubierta de botes** boat deck ► **cubierta de paseo** promenade deck ► **cubierta de popa** poop deck ► **cubierta de proa** foredeck ► **cubierta de vuelo** flight deck ► **cubierta principal** main deck

4 (*Méx*) (= *funda*) sheath

5 (= *pretexto*) cover, pretext

6 (= *sobre*) envelope; **bajo esta ~** under the same cover, enclosed herewith; **bajo ~ separada** under separate cover

cubierto Ⓐ PP *de* **cubrir**

Ⓑ ADJ 1 (*gen*) covered (**de** with, in); **un cheque no ~** a bad *o* unbacked cheque

2 [*cielo*] overcast

3 [*vacante*] filled; **la plaza está ya cubierta** the place has already been filled

4 (*Aut*) **poco ~** [*neumático*] threadbare, worn

5 (= *tocado*) [*persona*] with a hat

Ⓒ SM 1 (= *techumbre*) cover; **a** *o* **bajo ~** under cover; **estar a ~ de algo** to be safe from sth; **ponerse a ~** to take shelter, take cover; **ponerse a ~ de algo** to shelter from sth

2 (*para comer*) a piece of cutlery; **coge el ~ con la mano derecha** take the spoon/fork/knife with your right hand; **los ~s** the cutlery

3 (= *servicio de mesa*) place setting; **falta un ~, porque somos ocho** we're a place short, there are eight of us

4 (= *comida*) **pagaron 200 dólares por ~** they paid 200 dollars each *o* per head; **precio del ~** price per person *o* per head

cubil SM den, lair

cubilete SM 1 [*de dados*] cup

2 (= *cuenco*) basin, bowl; (= *copa*) goblet

3 (*Culin*) (= *molde*) mould, mold (*EEUU*); (= *bandeja*) pastry tray

4 (*LAm*) (= *intriga*) intrigue

5 (*LAm*) (= *chistera*) top hat; (= *hongo*) bowler hat

cubiletear ▸conjug 1a◂ VT 1 (*en el juego*) to shake the dice cup

2 (= *intrigar*) to intrigue, scheme

cubiletero/a SM/F conjurer

cubismo SM cubism

cubista ADJ, SMF cubist

cubitera SF ice-tray

cubito SM 1 (*tb* **~ de hielo**) ice cube

2 ► **cubito de caldo** stock cube

3 [*de niño*] bucket

cúbito SM ulna

cubo SM [1] (= *balde*) bucket, painful, pail; **~ para el carbón** coal scuttle ► **cubo de (la) basura** (*en casa*) dustbin, trash can (*EEUU*); (*en la calle*) litter bin, trash can (*EEUU*)
[2] (= *contenido*) bucketful, bucket, pailful, pail
[3] (*Mat*) cube; **cinco elevado al ~** five cubed
[4] (*Geom*) cube ► **cubo de Rubik** Rubik cube
[5] (*Mec*) barrel, drum
[6] [*de rueda*] hub
[7] [*de molino*] millpond
[8] (*Arquit*) round turret

cuboflash SM (*Fot*) flashcube

cubrebocas SM INV (*Med*) mask

cubrebotones SM INV button-cover

cubrecama SM coverlet, bedspread

cubrecorsé SM camisole

cubremesa SF table cover

cubreobjetos SM INV (*Biol*) slide cover

cubrerradiadores SM INV *cover for radiator*

cubrerrueda SF mudguard, fender (*EEUU*)

cubretetera SM tea cosy, tea cozy (*EEUU*)

cubrimiento SM [*de objeto*] covering; [*de noticia*] coverage

cubrir ►conjug 3a◄ (*pp* **cubierto**) (A) VT [1] (= *ocultar*) [1·1] [+ *superficie, objeto*] to cover; **un velo le cubría el rostro** a veil covered her face; **las nubes cubrían la cima de la montaña** the mountain top was covered by clouds; **habían cubierto el suelo de papeles** they had covered the floor with papers
[1·2] [*agua*] **lo cubrieron las aguas** the waters closed over it; **no te metas donde te cubra el agua** don't go out of your depth
[1·3] (= *poner techo a*) to roof, roof over; **queremos ~ parte del patio** we want to roof (over) part of the patio
[1·4] [+ *fuego*] to make up, bank up
[2] (= *llenar*) [+ *agujero*] to fill in; [+ *hueco*] to fill; **cubrieron el hoyo con la tierra del jardín** they filled in the hole with soil from the garden; **~ el hueco existente en el mercado** to fill the existing gap in the market; **~ a algn de alabanzas** to heap praises on sb; **~ a algn de atenciones** to lavish attention on sb; **~ a algn de besos** to smother sb with kisses; **~ a algn de improperios** to shower sb with insults; **~ a algn de oprobio** to bring shame on sb
[3] (= *proteger*) (*Dep, Mil*) to cover; **intenta llegar a las líneas enemigas: nosotros te ~emos** try to get to the enemy lines: we'll cover you; **~ su retirada** to cover one's retreat
[4] (= *recorrer*) [+ *ruta, distancia*] to cover; **cubrió 80 kms en una hora** he covered 80 km in an hour; **el autocar cubría el trayecto entre León y Madrid** the coach was travelling between León and Madrid
[5] (= *ocupar*) [+ *vacante, plaza*] to fill
[6] (= *pagar*) [+ *gastos, déficit, préstamo*] to cover; **esto apenas cubre los gastos** this scarcely covers the expenses
[7] (= *satisfacer*) [+ *necesidades, demanda*] to meet; **esto cubre todas nuestras necesidades** this meets all our needs
[8] (*Prensa*) [+ *suceso*] to cover; **todos los periódicos cubrieron la noticia** all the newspapers covered the event
[9] (*Zool*) (= *montar*) to cover
[10] (= *disimular*) [+ *emoción*] to cover up, conceal; **cubre su tristeza con una falsa alegría** she covers up *o* conceals her sadness with a false cheerfulness; ✦**MODISMO ~ las apariencias** *o* **las formas** to keep up appearances
(B) **cubrirse** VPR [1] [*persona*] [1·1] (= *ocultarse*) to cover o.s.; **~se la cabeza** to cover one's head; **~se el rostro** to cover one's face
[1·2] (= *ponerse el sombrero*) to put on one's hat
[2] (= *llenarse*) **~se de algo** to be covered with *o* in sth; **el campo se cubre de flores en primavera** the countryside is covered with flowers in spring; **~se de gloria** (*lit*) to cover o.s. with *o* in glory; (*iró*) to show o.s. up
[3] (= *protegerse*) to cover o.s.; **~se contra un riesgo** to cover *o* protect o.s. against a risk; ✦**MODISMO ~se las espaldas** to cover o.s., cover one's back
[4] (*Meteo*) [*cielo*] to become overcast

cuca SF [1] (*) (= *peseta*) peseta
[2] (**) [*de hombre*] prick**; (*CAm*) [*de mujer*] pussy**
[3] (= *cucaracha*) cockroach, roach*
[4] (= *jugador*) compulsive gambler
[5] **cucas** (= *dulces*) sweets, candy (*EEUU*)

cucambé SM (*Andes*) hide-and-seek

cucamente ADV (= *con astucia*) shrewdly; (= *taimadamente*) slyly, craftily

cucamonas* SFPL (= *palabras*) sweet nothings; (= *caricias*) caresses; (= *magreo*) fondling *sing*, petting* *sing*; **ella me hizo ~** she gave me a come-hither look

cucaña SF [1] (= *juego*) greasy pole
[2] (*) (= *chollo*) cinch*, piece of cake*; (= *prebenda*) plum job*, soft job*; (= *ganga*) bargain

cucañero/a* SM/F (= *astuto*) smart cookie*, shrewd person; (= *parásito*) hanger-on

cucar ►conjug 1g◄ VT [1] (= *guiñar*) to wink
[2] (= *burlarse de*) to deride, poke fun at
[3] (*LAm*) (= *instar*) to urge on, incite, provoke

cucaracha (A) SF [1] (*Zool*) cockroach
[2] (*Méx**) (= *coche*) old crock, old banger
[3] (‡) (= *droga*) roach‡
[4] (*Inform*) chip
(B) SM (*) priest

cucarachero SM [1] (*Andes, Caribe*) (= *parásito*) parasite, hanger-on
[2] (*Andes*) (= *adulador*) flatterer, creep‡

cucha SF (*Arg*) (= *cama*) bed; (= *caseta de perro*) kennel

cuchara (A) SF [1] (*para comer*) spoon; ✦**MODISMOS con la ~ grande** (*esp LAm*) **despacharse** *o* **servirse con la ~ grande** to look after number one*; **meter algo a algn con ~** to spoon-feed sb sth; **meter (la) ~** (*en conversación*) to butt in; (*en asunto*) to shove one's oar in; **soplar ~*** to eat; **soplar ~ caliente*** to eat well ► **cuchara de café** coffee spoon, ≈ teaspoon ► **cuchara de palo** wooden spoon ► **cuchara de postre** dessert spoon ► **cuchara de servir** serving spoon, tablespoon ► **cuchara de sopa** soup spoon
[2] (*Téc*) scoop, bucket
[3] (= *cucharón*) ladle
[4] (*LAm*) (= *llana*) flat trowel; **albañil de ~** skilled bricklayer
[5] (*CAm, Chile**) **hacer ~(s)** to pout
[6] **militar de ~*** officer who has risen from the ranks, ranker
(B) SMF (*Méx**) (= *carterista*) pickpocket

cucharada SF spoonful; **una ~ colmada** a heaped spoonful; **una ~ rasa** a level spoonful; **comer algo a ~s** to eat sth by the spoonful ► **cucharada de café** teaspoonful ► **cucharada de sopa**, **cucharada sopera** tablespoonful

cucharadita SF teaspoonful

cucharear ►conjug 1a◄ VT [1] (*Culin*) to spoon out, ladle out
[2] (*Agr*) to pitch, pitchfork

cucharetear ►conjug 1a◄ VI [1] (*con cuchara*) to stir (with a spoon)
[2] (= *entrometerse*) to meddle

cucharilla SF, **cucharita** SF [1] [*de café, té*] teaspoon
[2] (*Pesca*) spoon
[3] (*Golf*) wedge

cucharón SM [1] (*Culin*) ladle; ✦**MODISMO tener el ~ por el mango** to be the boss, be in control
[2] (*Téc*) scoop, bucket

cuche SM (*CAm*) pig, hog (*esp EEUU*)

cuché SM art paper

cuchi (*Perú*) (A) EXCL *call to a pig or hog*
(B) SM pig, hog (*esp EEUU*)

cuchichear ►conjug 1a◄ VI to whisper (**a** to)

cuchicheo SM whispering

cuchilear* ►conjug 1a◄ VT (*LAm*) to egg on

cuchilla SF [1] blade ► **cuchilla de afeitar** razor blade
[2] (= *cuchillo*) large kitchen knife; [*de carnicero*] chopper, cleaver
[3] [*de arado*] coulter, colter (*EEUU*)
[4] (*LAm*) (= *cortaplumas*) penknife
[5] (*Geog*) ridge, crest; (*Chile*) (= *colinas*) sharp ridge; (*Caribe*) (= *cumbre*) mountain top

cuchillada SF [1] (= *corte*) stab; (= *herida*) stab wound; **me di una ~ en el dedo** I cut my finger with a knife; **murió de una ~ en la garganta** she died from a knife wound *o* stab wound to the throat; **dar una ~ a algn** to stab sb; **matar a algn a ~s** to stab sb to death; **fue asesinado a ~s** he was stabbed to death; **hubo ~s** there was a serious fight; (*fig*) the knives really came out; **una ~ de cien reales**†† a long gash, a severe wound; ✦**MODISMO dar ~** (*Teat**) to make a hit
[2] (*Cos*) slash, slit

cuchillazo SM = **cuchillada 1**

cuchillería SF [1] (= *cubiertos*) cutlery, flatware (*EEUU*)
[2] (= *tienda*) cutler's (shop), flatware store (*EEUU*)

cuchillero (A) ADJ (*LAm*) quarrelsome, fond of brawling
(B) SM cutler

cuchillo SM [1] (*gen*) knife; ✦**MODISMOS pasar a ~** to put to the sword; **remover el ~ en la llaga** to turn the knife in the wound ► **cuchillo de carne** steak knife ► **cuchillo de caza** hunting knife ► **cuchillo de cocina** kitchen knife ► **cuchillo del pan** breadknife ► **cuchillo de trinchar** carving knife
[2] (*Arquit*) upright, support
[3] ► **cuchillo de aire** sharp draught, sharp draft (*EEUU*)
[4] (= *colmillo*) fang, tusk
[5] (*Cos*) gore

cuchipanda* SF blow-out*, chow-down (*EEUU*‡); **ir de ~** to go out on the town

cuchitril SM [1] (= *cuartucho*) hole*, hovel
[2] (*Agr*) (= *pocilga*) pigsty, pigpen (*EEUU*)

cucho[1] SM (*Andes*) = **cuchitril 1**

cucho[2]/a SM/F [1] (*CAm*) (= *jorobado*) hunchback [2] (*Méx*) (= *manco*) limbless person [3] (*Cono Sur*) (= *gato*) puss

cucho[3]* ADJ (*Méx*) (= *deprimido*) gloomy, depressed

cuchuche SM **ir a ~** (*CAm*) to ride piggyback

cuchuflé SM (*Caribe*) = **cuchuflí**

cuchufleta* SF [1] (= *broma*) joke, crack*
[2] (*Méx*) (= *baratija*) trinket, trifle

cuchuflí* SM (*Caribe*) uncomfortable place; (= *celda*) cell

cuchugos SMPL (*Andes, Caribe*) saddlebags

cuchumbo SM (*CAm*) (= *embudo*) funnel; (= *balde*) bucket, pail; [*de dados*] dice box; (= *juego*) game of dice

cuclillas SFPL **en ~** squatting, crouching; **ponerse en ~** to squat; **sentarse en ~** to sit on one's heels

cuclillo SM [1] (*Orn*) cuckoo
[2] (*) (= *cornudo*) cuckold

cuco/a Ⓐ ADJ [1] (= *persona*) (= *taimado*) sly, crafty; (= *astuto*) shrewd
[2] (= *bonito*) pretty, cute
Ⓑ SM/F (*) (= *persona*) wily bird*, sly one
Ⓒ SM [1] (*Orn*) cuckoo
[2] (= *oruga*) grub, caterpillar
[3] (*) (= *jugador*) gambler
[4] ✦*MODISMO* **hacer ~ a algn** (*Méx*) to poke fun at sb
[5] (*Cono Sur*) (= *sabelotodo*) smart guy*, wise guy*, know-all*
[6] (*Caribe***) (= *sexo femenino*) cunt**
[7] (*Andes, Cono Sur*) (= *fantasma*) bogeyman

cucú SM (= *canto*) cuckoo

cucuche (*CAm*) SM **ir a ~** to ride astride

cucufato/a* (*Andes, Cono Sur*) Ⓐ ADJ (= *hipócrita*) hypocritical, two-faced*; (= *mojigato*) prudish
Ⓑ SM/F (= *hipócrita*) hypocrite; (= *mojigato*) prude; (= *loco*) nut*

cuculí SM (*Andes, Cono Sur*) wood pigeon

cucurucho SM [1] [*de papel*] (paper) cone, (paper) twist, cornet; (*para helado*) cone, cornet
[2] (= *helado*) (ice-cream) cone
[3] (*Rel*) penitent's hood, pointed hat
[4] (*Aut*) cone
[5] (*Andes, CAm, Caribe*) (= *cumbre*) top, summit, apex
[6] (*Caribe*) (= *cuchitril*) hovel, shack

cucurucú SM, **cucurrucú** SM (*LAm*) cockadoodledoo

cueca SF (*Andes, Cono Sur*) *popular handkerchief dance*; (*Chile*) *Chilean national dance*

cuelga SF [1] (= *acto*) hanging (*of fruit etc to dry*); (= *racimo*) bunch (*of drying fruit etc*)
[2] (= *regalo*) birthday present
[3] (*Andes, Cono Sur Geog*) fall (*in the level of a stream etc*)

cuelgacapas SM INV (*en pared*) coat rack; (*de pie*) coat stand

cuelgue* SM [1] [*de drogas*] high*; **lleva un ~** he's completely high *o* spaced out*, he's really out of it *o* off his head*
[2] [*de vergüenza*] **¡qué ~!** how awful!, how embarrassing!

cuellicorto ADJ short-necked

cuellilargo ADJ long-necked

➤ LENGUA Y USO: **cuenta 3** 47.5

cuello SM [1] (*Anat*) neck; **cortar el ~ a algn** to cut sb's throat; ✦*MODISMOS* **apostar el ~***: **me apuesto el ~ a que no te atreves** I bet you anything you don't dare; **erguir el ~** to be stuck-up*; **jugarse el ~*** to stick one's neck out, put one's neck on the line; **levantar el ~** to get on one's feet again ► **cuello del útero, cuello uterino** cervix, neck of the womb
[2] [*de prenda*] collar; (= *talla*) (collar) size; ✦*MODISMO* **de ~ blanco** white-collar *antes de s* ► **cuello (a la) caja** crew neck ► **cuello alto** polo neck, turtle neck ► **cuello blando** soft collar ► **cuello (de) cisne** polo neck, turtleneck (*esp EEUU*) ► **cuello de pajarita** wing collar ► **cuello de pico** V-neck ► **cuello de quita y pon** detachable collar ► **cuello de recambio** spare collar ► **cuello postizo** detachable collar
[3] [*de botella*] neck ► **cuello de botella** (*Aut*) bottleneck

Cuenca SF Cuenca

cuenca SF [1] (*Geog*) bowl; (*fluvial*) basin; **la ~ del Ebro** the Ebro basin ► **cuenca hullera, cuenca minera** coalfield
[2] [*del ojo*] socket
[3] (*Hist*) (= *escudilla*) wooden bowl, begging bowl

cuenco SM [1] (= *recipiente*) earthenware bowl
[2] (= *concavidad*) hollow; [*de cuchara*] bowl ► **cuenco de la mano** hollow of the hand

▼**cuenta** SF [1] (*Mat*) (= *operación*) calculation, sum; **hacer una ~** to do a calculation; **echar** *o* **hacer ~s**: **vamos a hacer ~s de lo que ha costado la fiesta** let's work out how much the party cost; **no paraba de echar ~s con los dedos** she kept doing sums *o* adding things up on her fingers; ✦*MODISMOS* **hacer las ~s de la lechera** to indulge in wishful thinking, count one's chickens before they are hatched; **la ~ de la vieja**: **su hijo tiene 35, así que por la ~ de la vieja ella debe de tener 60** her son's 35, so I guess she must be 60; *ver tb* **claro A2.3**
[2] (= *cálculo*) count; **llevar la ~ (de algo)** to keep count (of sth); **perder la ~ (de algo)** to lose count (of sth); **salir a ~**: **sale más a ~** it works out cheaper; **no sale a ~** it isn't worth it; ✦*MODISMOS* **hacer algo con su ~ y razón** to be fully aware of what one is doing; **más de la ~**: **habla más de la ~** she talks too much; **ha bebido más de la ~** he's had one too many; **me cobraron más de la ~** they charged me over the odds; **pesa más de la ~** it weighs more than it should; **salirle las ~s a algn**: **al Estado no le salen las ~s** the State isn't able to balance its books; **le salieron mal las ~s** his plans went wrong ► **cuenta atrás** countdown; **ha empezado la ~ atrás para las próximas Olimpiadas** the countdown to the next Olympics has already begun
[3] (= *factura*) bill; [*de restaurante*] bill, check (*EEUU*); **¿nos puede traer la ~?** could we have *o* could you bring us the bill, please?; **pasar la ~ a algn** to send sb the bill; **pedir la ~** to ask for the bill; **vivir a ~ de algn** to live at sb's expense; ✦*MODISMO* **presentar las ~s del Gran Capitán** to make excessive demands
[4] (*Fin*) (*en banco*) account; **habían cargado los gastos en mi ~** they had charged the expenses to my account; **"únicamente en ~ del beneficiario"** "payee only"; **a ~** on account; **un dividendo a ~** an interim dividend; **retenciones a ~ del impuesto sobre la renta** income tax deducted at source; **le dieron una cantidad a ~ de lo que le debían** they paid him part of the money they owed him; **abonar una cantidad en ~ a algn** to credit a sum to sb's account; **abrir una ~** to open an account; **liquidar una ~** to settle an account ► **cuenta a plazo (fijo)** fixed-term deposit account ► **cuenta bancaria** bank account ► **cuenta corriente** current account, checking account (*EEUU*) ► **cuenta de ahorro(s)** deposit account, savings account ► **cuenta de amortización** depreciation account ► **cuenta de asignación** appropriation account ► **cuenta de caja** cash account ► **cuenta de capital** capital account ► **cuenta de crédito** credit account, loan account ► **cuenta de depósitos** deposit account ► **cuenta de diversos** sundries account ► **cuenta de gastos** expense account ► **cuenta de gastos e ingresos** income and expenditure account ► **cuenta de pérdidas y ganancias** profit and loss account ► **cuenta en participación** joint account ► **cuenta pendiente** unpaid bill, outstanding account ► **cuenta personal** personal account ► **cuenta por cobrar** account receivable ► **cuenta por pagar** account payable ► **cuenta presupuestaria** budget account ► **cuenta vivienda** mortgage account
[5] (*Internet*) account ► **cuenta de correo** e-mail account
[6] (*en disputa*) **ajustar ~s con algn** to settle one's scores with sb; **lo está buscando para ajustar ~s** he is searching for him because he has a few scores to settle with him; **voy a ajustarle las ~s** I'm going to have it out with him; **ajustar viejas ~s con algn** to settle an old score with sb; **arreglar las ~s a algn** (*Méx**) to punish sb; **tener ~s pendientes con algn** to have unfinished business with sb; **no querer ~s con algn** to want nothing to do with sb
[7] (= *explicación*) **dar ~ de algo** (= *informar*) to recount sth, report sth; (= *acabar*) to finish sth off; **tiene que darle ~ a ella de sus actos** he has to account to her for his actions; **no tiene que dar ~s a nadie** he's not answerable to anyone; **dar buena ~ de una botella** to finish off a bottle; **exigir** *o* **pedir ~s a algn** to call sb to account, bring sb to book; **rendir ~s a algn** to report to sb; **en resumidas ~s** in short, in a nutshell
[8] (= *consideración*) **caer en la ~ (de algo)** to catch on (to sth), see the point (of sth); **por fin cayó en la ~** he finally caught on, the penny finally dropped; **cuando cayó en la ~ de que lo engañaban** when he realized that they were deceiving him; **darse ~** (= *enterarse*) to realize; (= *ver*) to notice; **perdona, no me había dado ~ de que eras vegetariano** sorry, I didn't realize (that) you were a vegetarian; **¿te has dado ~ de que han cortado el árbol?** did you notice (that) they've cut down the tree?; **hay que darse ~ de que ...** one must not forget that ...; **¡date ~! ¿tú crees que es posible tener tanta cara?** just look at that, can you believe that anyone could have such a cheek!; **¿te das ~?** (*Arg*) can you believe it!; **habida ~ de eso** bearing that in mind; **haz ~ de que no voy** (*esp LAm*) just imagine I'm not going; **tener en ~** to take into account, bear in mind; **también hay que tener en ~ su edad** you must also take her

age into account, you must also bear in mind her age; **imponen sus ideas sin tener en ~ la opinión de la gente de la calle** they impose their ideas without taking ordinary people's opinions into consideration; **es otra cosa a tener en ~** that's another thing to remember *o* be borne in mind; **tomar algo en ~ a algn** to hold sth against sb; **está borracho y no sabe lo que dice, no se lo tomes en ~** he's drunk and doesn't know what he's saying, don't take any notice of him *o* don't hold it against him; **traer ~**: **no me trae ~ ir** it's not worth my while going; **trae ~ emplear a más gente** it's worth employing more people; **lo harán por la ~ que les trae** *o* **tiene** they'll do it if they know what's good for them
9 (= *responsabilidad*) **esta ronda corre de mi ~** this round's on me; **por mi ~** (= *solo*) on my own; **yo he de resolver esto por mi ~** I have to resolve this on my own; **trabajar por ~ ajena** to be an employee; **trabajar por ~ propia** to work for o.s., be self-employed; **por ~ y riesgo de algn** at one's own risk; **lo hizo por su ~ y riesgo, sin consultar a nadie** she did it off her own bat, without consulting anyone; *ver tb* **apañar B1**
10 (*en embarazo*) **está fuera de ~s** ◊ **ha salido de ~s** she's due
11 [*de rosario, collar*] bead; **~s de cristal** glass beads

cuentacorrentista SMF account holder, account holder of a current account

cuentacuentos SMF INV storyteller

cuentagotas SM INV dropper; ✦*MODISMO* **a** *o* **con ~** drop by drop, bit by bit

cuentakilómetros SM INV 1 [*de distancias*] mileometer, milometer, odometer (*esp EEUU*)
2 (= *velocímetro*) speedometer

cuentarrevoluciones SM INV rev counter, tachometer (*frm*)

cuente *etc ver* **contar**

cuentear ▸conjug 1a◂ Ⓐ VT 1 (*Andes*) (= *pretender*) to court; (= *felicitar*) to compliment
2 (*Méx**) (= *tomar el pelo*) to kid*, have on*
Ⓑ VI (*CAm*) to gossip

cuenterete SM (*CAm*) (= *chisme*) piece of gossip; (= *cuento*) tall story, tale

cuentero/a* SM/F (*Cono Sur*) 1 (= *mentiroso*) liar, fibber*
2 (= *estafador*) confidence trickster, con man*

cuentista SMF 1 (*Literat*) (= *escritor*) short-story writer; (= *narrador*) storyteller
2 (= *chismoso*) gossip; (= *soplón*) telltale
3 (= *mentiroso*) liar, fibber*
4 (*esp LAm**) (= *estafador*) confidence trickster, con man*

cuentística SF genre of the short story

cuento¹ SM 1 (= *historia corta*) short story; (*para niños*) story, tale; **el ~ de Blancanieves** the tale *o* story of Snow White; **contar un ~** to tell a story; **de ~**: **un héroe de ~** a storybook *o* fairytale hero; **una casita de ~** a fairytale house; **ir con el ~**: **en seguida le fue con el ~ a la maestra** he went straight off and told the teacher; ✦*MODISMOS* **aplicarse el ~** to take note; **el ~ de la lechera**: **eso es como el ~ de la lechera** it's a case of wishful thinking; **es el ~ de nunca acabar** it's a never-ending story ► **cuento corto** short story ► **cuento de hadas** a fairytale; **vive en un ~ de hadas** she lives in a fairytale world ► **cuento infantil** children's story
2 (*) (= *mentira*) **no le duele nada, no es nada más que ~** it doesn't hurt at all, he's just putting it on; **todo eso es puro ~ para no ir al colegio** he just made it all up because he doesn't want to go to school; **¡no me cuentes ~s!** ◊ **¡no me vengas con ~s!** ◊ **¡déjate de ~s!** don't give me that!*; **eso se me hace ~** (*Cono Sur**) I don't believe that for a minute, come off it!*; **tener ~**: **tu hermanito tiene mucho ~** your little brother is a big fibber*; ✦*MODISMOS* **tener más ~ que siete viejas** to have the gift of the gab*; **vivir del ~** to live by one's wits ► **cuento chino** tall story, cock-and-bull story*; **¡no me vengas con ~s chinos!** don't give me that (rubbish)!* ► **el cuento del tío** (*Andes, Cono Sur*) confidence trick, confidence game (*EEUU*) ► **cuento de viejas** old wives' tale
3 (*otras locuciones*) **¿a ~ de qué?**: **¿a ~ de qué sacas ese tema ahora?** what are you bringing that up for now?; **traer algo a ~** to bring sth up; **venir a ~**: **eso no viene a ~** that's irrelevant, that doesn't come into it, that has nothing to do with it; **todo esto viene a ~ de lo que acaba de pasar** this all has some bearing on what has just happened; **lo dijo sin venir a ~** she said it for no reason at all
4 (*frm*) (= *cómputo*) **sin ~** countless

cuento² SM [*de bastón*] point, tip

cuera SF 1 (*LAm*) (= *piel*) hide; (= *correa*) leather strap
2 (*Méx*) (= *chaqueta*) leather jacket
3 **cueras** (*CAm*) leggings (*for riding*)
4 (*Andes, CAm, Caribe*) (= *paliza*) flogging

cuerazo SM (*LAm*) lash

cuerda SF 1 (*gruesa*) rope; (*fina*) string, cord; (*para saltar*) skipping rope, jump rope (*EEUU*); **un metro de ~** a metre (length) of rope; **ató la caja con un trozo de ~** she tied up the box with a piece of string; **se ha roto la ~ de la persiana** the cord on the blind has broken; ✦*MODISMOS* **bajo ~**: **ha conseguido un visado bajo ~** she's got hold of a visa under the counter; **han llegado a un acuerdo bajo ~** they have reached an agreement in secret, they have made a secret agreement; **estirar la ~**: **estiraron la ~ para derrocar al gobierno** they put pressure on to bring the government down ► **cuerda de plomada** plumbline ► **cuerda de salvamento** lifeline ► **cuerda floja** tightrope; ✦*MODISMO* **caminar en la ~ floja** to walk a tightrope ► **cuerda salvavidas** lifeline
2 (*Mec*) [*de reloj*] winder; [*de juguete*] clockwork mechanism; **se me ha roto la ~ del reloj** the winder on my watch has broken; **un reloj de ~** a wind-up watch; **dale ~ al reloj** wind up the clock; **el juguete funciona con ~** it's a clockwork toy; ✦*MODISMOS* **dar ~ a algn***: **no para de hablar, parece que le han dado ~** he never stops talking, you'd think he'd been wound up; **quedarle ~ a algn***: **a ese viejo aún le queda mucha ~** the old boy's still got plenty of life *o* steam left in him*; **tener ~***: **después de dos años sin verse, estos tienen ~ para rato*** after two years apart, those two have got enough to keep them going for a while yet
3 (*Mús*) [*de instrumento*] string; **un cuarteto de ~** a string quartet; **sección de ~** string section, strings *pl*; ✦*MODISMO* **son de la misma ~** they're as bad as each other
4 (*Anat*) ► **cuerdas vocales** vocal cords
5 **cuerdas** (*Boxeo*) ropes; (*Hípica*) rails; ✦*MODISMO* **contra las ~s** on the ropes; **el escándalo puso al gobierno contra las ~s** the scandal put the government on the ropes
6 (*Mat, Arquit*) chord
7 (*Pesca*) *style of fishing with three or more flies mounted on struts tied to the main line*

cuerdamente ADV 1 (= *sensatamente*) sanely
2 (= *prudentemente*) wisely, sensibly

cuerdo ADJ 1 [*persona*] sane
2 [*acto*] sensible, wise

cuereada SF (*LAm*) beating, hiding*

cuerear ▸conjug 1a◂ VT 1 (*LAm*) [+ *animal*] to skin; [+ *persona*] to beat, whip, flay
2 **~ a algn** (*Caribe, Cono Sur*) to tear a strip off sb

cuerito SM **de ~ a ~** (*LAm*) from end to end

cueriza SF (*LAm*) beating, hiding*

cuerna SF 1 (*Zool*) horns *pl*; [*de ciervo*] antlers *pl*
2 (= *vaso*) drinking horn
3 (*Caza*) horn, hunting horn

cuerno SM 1 (*Zool*) horn; [*de ciervo*] antler; **el Cuerno de Africa** the Horn of Africa; **¡cuerno(s)!** gosh!*, blimey!‡; ✦*MODISMOS* **¡(y) un ~!** my foot!, you must be joking!; **coger al toro por los ~s** to take the bull by the horns; **estar en los ~s (del toro)** to be in a jam*; **irse al ~** [*negocio*] to fail, go to the wall*; [*proyecto*] to fall through; **¡que se vaya al ~!** he can go to hell!; **mandar a algn al ~** to tell sb to go to hell*; **mandar algo al ~** to consign sth to hell; **poner los ~s a algn** to cheat on sb, cuckold sb†; **romperse los ~s** to break one's back working, work one's butt off (*EEUU**); **¡así te rompas los ~s!** I hope you break your neck!; **saber a ~ quemado**: **esto me sabe a ~ quemado** it makes my blood boil ► **cuerno de la abundancia** horn of plenty
2 (*Culin*) roll, croissant
3 (*Mil*) wing
4 (*Mús*) horn ► **cuerno alpino** alpenhorn

cuero SM 1 (= *piel*) (*curtida*) leather; (*sin curtir*) skin, hide; [*de conejo*] pelt; **una chaqueta de ~** a leather jacket; ✦*MODISMOS* **andar en ~s** to go about stark naked; **dejar a algn en ~s** to clean sb out* ► **cuero adobado** tanned skin ► **cuero cabelludo** scalp ► **cuero charolado** patent leather
2 (= *odre*) wineskin
3 (‡) (= *borracho*) old soak‡; ✦*MODISMO* **estar hecho un ~** to be (as) drunk as a lord, be (as) drunk as a skunk (*esp EEUU**)
4 [*de grifo*] washer
5 (*LAm*) (= *látigo*) whip; ✦*MODISMO* **arrimar** *o* **dar el ~ a algn** to give sb a beating *o* thrashing
6 (*Dep*) (= *balón*) ball
7 (*Andes, Caribe pey*) (= *prostituta*) whore, hooker (*EEUU**); (*Andes*) (= *solterona*) old maid; (*Caribe‡*) (= *vieja*) old bag‡; (*Andes, Méx**) (= *amante*) mistress
8 (*CAm, Caribe**) (= *descaro*) cheek*, nerve*
9 (‡) (= *cartera*) wallet

cuerpada* SF (*Chile*) **tiene buena ~** she's got a good body

cuerpazo* SM 1 (= *cuerpo grande*) huge frame, mighty bulk
2 (= *cuerpo sexy*) bod*

cuerpear ▸conjug 1a◂ VI (*Cono Sur*) to dodge

cuerpo SM 1 (*Anat*) body; **me dolía todo el ~** my body was aching all over, I was aching all over; **se le metió el frío en el ~** he caught a chill; **nos sacó dos ~s de ventaja** she was two lengths ahead of us; **~ a ~**: **fue una lucha ~ a ~** it was hand-to-hand combat; **un ~ a ~ entre los dos políticos** a head-on *o* head-to-head confrontation between the two politicians; **de ~ entero** [*retrato, espejo*] full-length; **de medio ~** [*retrato, espejo*] half-length; **~ serrano** (*hum*) body to die for; **¡~ a tierra!** hit the ground!; **dar con el ~ en tierra** to fall down, fall to the ground; ✦**MODISMOS en ~ y alma** body and soul, wholeheartedly; **a ~ gentil**: **salió a ~ gentil** he went out without wrapping up properly; **un combate a ~ gentil** a hand-to-hand fight; **a ~ limpio** (= *sin ayuda*) unaided; **a ~ de rey**: **vive a ~ de rey** he lives like a king; **nos trataron a ~ de rey** they treated us like royalty; **hacer del ~** (*euf*) to defecate, have a bowel movement; **hurtar el ~** to sneak away, sneak off; **hurtó el ~ y eludió a sus vecinos** he sneaked off *o* away and avoided his neighbours; **pedirle a algn algo el ~**: **hice lo que en ese momento me pedía el ~** I did what my body was telling me to do at that moment
2 (= *cadáver*) body, corpse; **encontraron el ~ entre los matorrales** they found the body *o* corpse in the bushes; **de ~ presente**: **su marido aún estaba de ~ presente** her husband had not yet been buried; **funeral de ~ presente** funeral service, funeral
3 (= *grupo*) **el ~ social** society ► **cuerpo de baile** corps de ballet ► **cuerpo de bomberos** fire brigade, fire department (*EEUU*) ► **cuerpo de doctrina** body of teaching ► **cuerpo de leyes** body of laws ► **cuerpo de policía** police force ► **cuerpo de sanidad** medical corps ► **cuerpo diplomático** diplomatic corps ► **cuerpo electoral** electorate ► **cuerpo legislativo** legislative body
4 (= *parte*) [*de mueble*] section, part; [*de un vestido*] bodice; (= *parte principal*) main body; **un armario de dos ~s** a cupboard in two sections *o* parts
5 (= *objeto*) body, object ► **cuerpo celeste** heavenly body ► **cuerpo compuesto** compound ► **cuerpo del delito** corpus delicti ► **cuerpo extraño** foreign body ► **cuerpo geométrico** geometric shape ► **cuerpo simple** element
6 (= *consistencia*) [*de vino*] body; **un vino de mucho ~** a full-bodied wine; **dar ~ a algo**: **el suavizante que da ~ a su cabello** the conditioner that gives your hair body; **hay que darle un poco más ~ a la salsa** the sauce needs thickening a bit more; **sugirieron varios puntos para dar ~ al proyecto** they suggested several points to round out *o* give more substance to the project; **tomar ~** [*plan, proyecto, personaje, historia*] to take shape; **batió las claras hasta que tomaron ~** she beat the egg whites until they were fluffy *o* stiff; **el vino va tomando ~ con los años** aging gives the wine more body
7 (*Tip*) [*de letra*] point, point size; **negritas del ~ seis** six-point bold

cuerudo ADJ 1 (*LAm*) [*caballo*] slow, sluggish
2 (*LAm*) (= *incordiante*) annoying
3 (*Cono Sur*) (= *valiente*) brave, tough
4 (*CAm, Caribe*) (= *descarado*) impudent, cheeky*, sassy (*EEUU**)

cuervo SM 1 (= *ave*) raven; (*Cono Sur*) (= *buitre*) vulture, buzzard (*EEUU*) ► **cuervo marino** cormorant
2 (*) (= *cura*) priest

cuesco SM 1 (*Bot*) stone
2 (*) (= *pedo*) fart‡
3 (*Mec*) millstone (*of oil mill*)

cuesta SF 1 (= *pendiente*) hill, slope; **mi casa está al final de la ~** my house is at the top of the hill; **una ~ empinada** a steep slope; **bajamos la ~ corriendo** we ran down the hill; **~ abajo** downhill; **ir ~ abajo** to go downhill; **~ arriba** uphill; **me canso más cuando voy ~ arriba** I get more tired when I go uphill; **se me hace muy ~ arriba estudiar tan tarde** I find it a struggle to study so late at night; **la ~ de enero** *period of financial stringency following Christmas spending*
2 **a ~s** on one's back; **siempre va con su guitarra a ~s** he always goes around with his guitar on his back *o* slung over his shoulder; **llevé al niño a ~s a la cama** I carried the child up to bed on my back *o* shoulders; **se recorrieron Europa con la mochila a ~s** they went backpacking all around Europe; **se echa todas las responsabilidades a ~s** she takes all the responsibilities on her own shoulders

cuestación SF charity collection

cueste *etc ver* **costar**

▼**cuestión** SF 1 (= *asunto*) matter, question; **quedan algunas cuestiones por resolver** there are still a few matters *o* questions to be resolved; **eso es otra ~** that's another matter; **¡sigue gritando, la ~ es no dejarme tranquilo!*** (*iró*) carry on shouting, don't mind me!; **no sé por qué, pero la ~ es que ahora soy más pobre*** I don't know why, but the fact is that I'm poorer now than I was; **~ de**: **una ~ de honor** a matter of honour; **resolver el problema no es sólo ~ de dinero** the answer to the problem is not just a question of money; **su entrega a la policía es ~ de tiempo** it's only a matter of time before he gives himself up to the police; **todo es ~ de proponérselo** it's all a matter *o* question of telling yourself you can do it; **será ~ de irse ya a casa** it's time we were thinking of going home; **puedes beber, pero no es ~ de que te emborraches** you can have a drink or two, but there's no need to get drunk; **para solucionarlo tan sólo es ~ de que lo habléis** all you have to do to solve the problem is talk it over; **en ~** in question; **la persona en ~ resultó ser mi padre** the person in question turned out to be my father; **falleció en ~ de segundos** she died in a matter of seconds; **en ~ de política social hemos avanzado poco** we have made little progress in terms of social policy; *ver tb* **quid**, **vida 1**
2 (= *pregunta*) question; **el examen se compone de tres cuestiones** the exam is made up of three questions; **la ~ está en saber si ella estaba al corriente** the question is whether she knew ► **cuestión de confianza** vote of confidence
3 (= *duda*) **poner algo en ~** to call sth into question, raise doubts about sth

cuestionable ADJ questionable

cuestionador ADJ questioning

cuestionamiento SM questioning

cuestionar ▸conjug 1a◂ Ⓐ VT to question
Ⓑ VI to argue
Ⓒ **cuestionarse** VPR to ask o.s., question

cuestionario SM [*de sondeo*] questionnaire; (*Escol, Univ*) question paper

cuestor[1] SM (*Hist*) quaestor, questor (*EEUU*)

cuestor[2]**(a)** SM/F charity collector

cuete Ⓐ ADJ (*Méx**) drunk
Ⓑ SM 1 (*Andes, CAm, Méx*) (= *pistola*) pistol
2 (*CAm, Méx*) = **cohete**
3 (*Méx**) (= *embriaguez*) drunkenness
4 (*Méx Culin*) steak

cuetearse ▸conjug 1a◂ VPR (*Andes*) 1 (= *explotar*) to go off, explode
2 (‡) (= *morirse*) to kick the bucket‡

cueva SF 1 (*Geog*) cave ► **cueva de ladrones** den of thieves
2 (*para vino*) cellar, vault
3 (*Cono Sur***) (= *vagina*) pussy**
4 **tener ~** (*Cono Sur*‡) (= *suerte*) to be lucky

cuévano SM pannier, deep basket

cuezo SM ✦**MODISMO meter el ~*** to poke *o* stick one's nose in*

cui (*pl* **cuis**, **cuises**) SM (*LAm*) guinea pig

cuica SF (*Andes*) earthworm

cuico/a SM/F 1 (*Cono Sur*) (= *forastero*) foreigner, outsider
2 (*Andes, Cono Sur pey*) (= *boliviano*) Bolivian; (*Caribe*) (= *mejicano*) Mexican
3 (*Méx**) (= *policía*) pig**, cop*

cuidadero/a SM/F keeper

▼**cuidado** Ⓐ SM 1 (= *precaución*) 1·1 (*como advertencia directa*) **¡cuidado!** look out!, watch out!; **¡~ con el techo!** mind the ceiling!; **¡~ con los rateros!** watch out for pickpockets!; **"cuidado con el perro"** "beware of the dog"; **¡mucho ~ con lo que haces!** be very careful what you do!; **~ con hacer algo**: **cuidadito con abrir la boca** keep your mouth shut, remember!; **¡~ con perderlo!** mind you don't lose it!
1·2 **tener ~ (con algo)** to be careful (of sth); **¡ten ~!** careful!; **ten ~ con el paquete** careful with the parcel; **hay que tener ~ con los coches al cruzar la carretera** you must beware of cars when you cross the road; **tener ~ con algn** to watch out for sb, watch sb*, be careful of sb; **tener ~ de no hacer algo** to be careful *o* take care not to do sth; **debe tener ~ de no tomar mucho el sol** you should be careful *o* take care not to sunbathe too much
1·3 **andarse con ~** to tread carefully, tread warily; **¡ándate con ~!** watch how you go!, watch your step!
2 (= *atención*) care; **las prendas delicadas deben lavarse con ~** delicate garments should be washed with care; **analicemos con ~ el último de los ejemplos** let's analyse the last of the examples carefully; **poner/tener ~ en algo** to take care over sth; **pondremos especial ~ en la programación dedicada a los niños** we will take special care in planning children's programming; **han tenido sumo ~ en subrayar que no es su responsabilidad** they have taken the greatest care to stress that it is not their responsibility
3 [*de niño, enfermo, planta, edificio*] care; **recibió los ~s de varias enfermeras** she received medical care from a number of nurses; **los ~s regulares de manos y pies** regular hand and footcare; **¿es ése el pago que merecen nuestros ~s amorosos?** is that all the

➤ LENGUA Y USO: cuestión 1 53.1, 53.2 cuidado A1·1 34.5 A1·2 29.2, 29.3

reward we get for our tender loving care?; **estar al ~ de** (= *encargado de*) [+ *niños, familia, plantas*] to look after; [+ *proyecto*] to be in charge of; (= *cuidado por*) [*niños, jardín*] to be in the care of; [*departamento, sección*] to be run by; **antes la mujer tenía que quedarse al ~ de la casa** formerly women had to stay at home and look after the house; **una organización dedicada al ~ de minusválidos** an organization dedicated to caring for the disabled; **el monasterio está al ~ de la edición de miles de documentos** the monastery is in charge of editing thousands of documents; **dejó a su hija al ~ de una amiga** she left her daughter in the care of a friend; **la sección de publicidad está al ~ de M. Moyano** M. Moyano is in charge of the advertising department ► **cuidado personal** personal care ► **cuidados intensivos** intensive care *sing*; **unidad de ~s intensivos** intensive care unit ► **cuidados médicos** medical care *sing* ► **cuidados paliativos** palliative care *sing*

[4] (= *preocupación*) worry, concern; **pierda usted ~, ya me hago yo cargo de todo** don't worry about it, I'll take care of everything; **dar ~** to give cause for concern; **estar con ~** ◊ **sentir ~** to be anxious, be worried; ✦***MODISMOS*** **tener** *o* **traer sin ~**: **me tiene sin ~ lo que pase a partir de ahora** I don't care at all *o* I couldn't care less what happens from now on; **¡allá ~s!** let others worry about that!, that's their funeral!*

[5] **de ~*** [*chapuza, bromista*] real; **les echó una bronca de ~** he gave them a real telling-off*; **son unos racistas de ~** they're real racists; **es un tacaño de ~** he's really stingy; **está enfermo de ~** he is really *o* seriously ill; **traía una intoxicación de ~** she had bad food poisoning; **un enemigo de ~** a fearsome enemy

Ⓑ ADJ [*aspecto*] impeccable; [*trabajo, selección*] meticulous, careful; **una película con una ambientación muy cuidada** a film in which careful attention has been paid to the setting; **una cuidada edición de la obra** a beautifully-produced edition of the work; **el interior del coche está muy ~** the interior of the car is impeccable

cuidador/a SM/F [1] [*de niños*] childminder; [*de enfermos*] carer

[2] [*de caballos*] trainer; [*de zoo*] keeper, zookeeper; [*de terreno*] caretaker

[3] (*Boxeo*) second

cuidadosamente ADV carefully

cuidadoso ADJ [1] (= *atento*) [*persona, observación, estrategia*] careful; **es muy ~ con sus cosas** he's very careful with his things; **es muy ~ de su aseo personal** he takes a lot of care over his personal hygiene

[2] (= *prudente*) careful; **hay que ser ~ con gente así** you have to be careful with people like that

[3] (= *solícito*) attentive

cuidar ▸conjug 1a◂ Ⓐ VT [1] (= *atender*) [+ *familia, jardín, edificio*] to look after, take care of; [+ *rebaño*] to tend; **las personas que deciden quedarse en casa y ~ a sus hijos** people who decide to stay at home and look after their children; **se dedica a ~ niños por las noches** she does baby-sitting in the evenings; **una organización que cuida a los huérfanos de guerra** an organization caring for orphans of war

[2] (= *preocuparse por*) [+ *muebles, propiedades, entorno, salud*] to look after, take care of; **no cuidan nada la casa** they don't look after the house at all, they don't take any care of the house; **se preocupa mucho de ~ la línea** she watches her figure very carefully

[3] (= *poner atención en*) [+ *detalles, ortografía*] to pay attention to, take care over; **en ese restaurante cuidan mucho los detalles** they pay great attention to detail *o* take great care over the details in that restaurant; **el director cuidó al máximo la puesta en escena de la obra** the director took the greatest care over the production of the play; **cuida mucho su imagen liberal** she carefully cultivates her liberal image

Ⓑ VI [1] **~ de** to look after, take care of; **¿quién ~á de ti?** who will look after you?, who will take care of you?; **~ de hacer algo** to take care to do sth; **siempre cuidaba de mantener el termo lleno de agua caliente** he always took care to keep the thermos full of hot water; **cuide de no caer** careful you don't fall; **~ de que** to make sure that; **cuide de que no pase nadie** make sure nobody gets in; **cuidó de que todo saliera bien** he made sure that everything went smoothly

[2] **~ con**† to be careful of; **cuida con esa gente** be careful of those people

Ⓒ **cuidarse** VPR [1] [*persona*] to look after o.s., take care of o.s.; **desde que se quedó viudo ha dejado de ~se** since he lost his wife he hasn't been looking after himself properly *o* taking proper care of himself; **se cuida mucho** she takes good care of herself; **¡cómo te cuidas!** you do know how to look after yourself well!; **¡cuídate!** (*al despedirse*) take care!

[2] **~se de algo** (= *encargarse*) to take care of sth; (= *preocuparse*) to worry about sth; **los organizadores se cuidan del alojamiento y las comidas** the organizers take care of accommodation and meals; **no se cuida del qué dirán** she doesn't worry about what people think; **~se de hacer algo** to be careful to do sth, take care to do sth; **todos se cuidan de no ser los primeros en hacerlo** everyone is careful not to *o* takes care not to be the first to do it; **~se muy mucho de hacer algo** to take good *o* great care to do sth

cuido†† SM care; **en** *o* **para su ~** for your own good

cuita[1] SF (*liter*) (= *preocupación*) worry, trouble; (= *pena*) grief, affliction; (*civil, doméstico*) strife; **contar sus ~s a algn** to tell sb one's troubles

cuita[2] SF (*CAm, Méx*) (= *estiércol*) poultry manure; (= *excremento*) dung

cuitado ADJ (*liter*) [1] (= *preocupado*) worried, troubled

[2] (= *tímido*) timid

cuitlacoche SM (*Méx*) black mushroom (*that grows on corn*)

cuja SF [1] (= *cama*) bedstead

[2] (*CAm, Méx*) (= *sobre*) envelope

cujinillos SMPL (*Guat, Méx*) saddlebags

culada SF **darse una ~*** to drop a clanger*

culamen* SM bottom, bum*, butt (*esp EEUU**)

culandrón‡ SM queer‡, fag (*EEUU*‡)

culantrillo SM maidenhair

culantro SM coriander

culata SF [1] (*Mec*) [*de fusil*] butt; [*de cañón*] breech; [*de cilindro*] head

[2] (*Zool*) haunch, hindquarters

[3] (= *parte trasera*) rear, back

[4] (*Cono Sur*) (= *cobertizo*) hut, shelter

culatazo SM kick, recoil

culé* SMF *supporter of Barcelona Football Club*

culear ▸conjug 1a◂ Ⓐ VT (*Andes, Cono Sur, Méx***) to fuck**, screw**

Ⓑ VI [1] (*) (= *mover el culo*) to waggle one's bottom, waggle one's backside

[2] (*Andes, Cono Sur, Méx***) (= *fornicar*) to fuck**, screw**

culebra SF [1] (*Zool*) snake; **hacer ~** to zigzag ► **culebra de anteojos** cobra ► **culebra de cascabel** rattlesnake, rattler (*EEUU**)

[2] (*Mec*) worm (*of a still*)

[3] (*) (= *alboroto*) disturbance, disorder

[4] (*Andes*) (= *cuenta*) debt, bill

[5] (*Méx*) (= *manguera*) hosepipe

culebrear ▸conjug 1a◂ VI [*culebra*] to wriggle, wriggle along; [*carretera*] to zigzag, wind; [*río*] to wind, meander

culebreo SM [*de culebra*] wriggling; [*de carretera*] zigzag, winding; [*de río*] winding, meandering

culebrina SF [1] (*Meteo*) forked lightning

[2] (*Hist*) culverin

culebrón* SM soap opera, soap*

culeco ADJ [1] (*LAm*) [*gallina*] broody

[2] (*LAm*) [*persona*] home-loving

[3] (*Andes, Caribe, Cono Sur*) (= *enamorado*) **estar ~** to be head over heels in love

[4] **estar ~ con algo** (*Andes, CAm, Caribe, Méx**) (= *satisfecho*) to be very pleased about sth, be over the moon about sth; (= *orgulloso*) to be very proud of sth

culera SF seat (*of trousers*)

culeras* SMF INV coward, chicken*

culero/a Ⓐ ADJ lazy

Ⓑ SM [1] (= *pañal*) nappy, diaper (*EEUU*)

[2] (*CAm*‡) (= *maricón*) poof‡, queer‡, fag (*EEUU*‡)

Ⓒ SM/F (*) [1] [*de drogas*] drug courier, drug smuggler

[2] (*Méx*) (= *cobarde*) coward

culí SM coolie

culibajo* ADJ short, dumpy

culigordo* ADJ big-bottomed, broad in the beam*

culillo* SM [1] (*Andes, CAm, Caribe*) (= *miedo*) fear

[2] **tener ~** (*Caribe*) to be in a rush

culín SM (= *gota*) drop; **sólo queda un ~ de vino** there's only a tiny drop of wine left

culinario ADJ culinary, cooking *antes de s*

culipandear ▸conjug 1a◂ VI (*Caribe*) to stall, hedge

culmen Ⓐ SM [1] (= *colmo*) **el ~ de la ignorancia** the height of ignorance; (= *persona*) the epitome of ignorance

[2] (= *punto culminante*) **el ~ de su carrera** the crowning moment of his career; **llegar a su ~** to reach its height

Ⓑ ADJ **el momento ~ de su carrera** the crowning moment of her career; **el momento ~ de la campaña electoral** the culminating moment of the electoral campaign, the climax of the electoral campaign

culminación SF culmination

culminante ADJ [1] (*Geog*) highest, topmost

[2] [*momento*] culminating; **el momento ~ de la revolución** the culminating moment of the

revolution, the climax of the revolution; **este fue el momento ~ de su carrera** this was the crowning moment of his career; **en el momento ~ de la fiesta, se apagaron las luces** at the high point of the party, the lights went out; **el punto ~ de la novela** the climax of the novel

culminar ▸conjug 1a◂ Ⓐ VT [+ *objetivo*] to reach, attain; [+ *acuerdo*] to conclude; [+ *tarea, carrera*] to finish
Ⓑ VI to culminate (**en** in)

culo SM [1] (*) (= *nalgas*) backside*, bum*, arse**, ass (*EEUU**), butt (*EEUU**); (= *ano*) arsehole**, asshole (*EEUU***); **le dio un puntapié en el ~** he kicked him in the backside*; **le limpió el culito al niño** he wiped the baby's bottom; **caer de ~** to fall on one's backside*; **dar a algn por el ~**** (= *sexualmente*) to bugger sb; (= *fastidiar*) to piss sb off**; **me da por ~ tener que trabajar tan temprano** it really pisses me off having to go to work so early**; **¡que te den por (el) ~!**** fuck you!**, screw you!**; ✦**MODISMOS confunde el ~ con las témporas*** he can't tell his arse from his elbow**; **el ~ del mundo***: **está en el ~ del mundo** it's in the back of beyond; **es el ~ del mundo** it's the arsehole of the world**; **dejar a algn con el ~ al aire*** to leave sb stranded; **ir con el ~ a rastras*** to be in a fix *o* jam*; **ir de ~***: **con tanta llamada, esta mañana voy de ~** with all these calls this morning I'm way behind*; **si no apruebas esta asignatura vas de ~** if you don't pass this subject you've had it*; **en cuanto al paro, el país va de ~** the country's unemployment record is disastrous; **lamer el ~ a algn*** to lick sb's arse *o* (*EEUU*) ass*, kiss sb's arse *o* (*EEUU*) ass*; **meterse algo por el ~****: **¡métetelo por el ~!** stick it up your ass!**; **mojarse el ~***: **para conseguirlo tendrás que mojarte el ~** you won't achieve that without getting your feet wet*; **partirse el ~***: **me partí el ~ de risa con él** I laughed myself silly with him; **se parten el ~ por encontrar entradas** they're pulling their hair out trying to get tickets; **pasarse algo por el ~**** not to give a shit about sth**; **perder el ~ por algn/algo***: **pierde el ~ por ella** he's nuts about her*; **pierde el ~ por conocerlos** she's dying to be introduced to them; **ser un ~ de mal asiento**: **se mudó cinco veces en un año, es un ~ de mal asiento** she moved house five times in one year, she just can't stay in one place; **tomar por ~****: **¡vete a tomar por ~!**** screw you!**, fuck off!**, piss off!**; **¡que se vayan a tomar por ~!**** they can go screw themselves**, they can fuck *o* piss off**; **si nos pillan nos vamos todos a tomar por ~** if they catch us we'll all be fucked *o* screwed**; **el proyecto se fue a tomar por ~** the project went down the toilet*; **les mandó a tomar por ~** he told them to fuck off *o* piss off**; **un día se hartó y mandó el trabajo a tomar por ~** one day he got fed up with it and jacked his job in*; **su casa está a tomar por ~** her house is in the back of beyond; **~ que veo, ~ que deseo** if I see something I like then I have to have it
[2] (*) [*de vaso, botella*] bottom; **el vaso se rompió por el ~** the bottom of the glass broke; **—¿queda cerveza? —sí, un culillo** "is there any beer left in there?" — "yes, a drop"; **se bebió los ~s de todos los vasos** he drank the dregs of all the glasses; **gafas de ~ de vaso** pebble glasses

➤ LENGUA Y USO: culpa 1 45.2

culón ADJ = **culigordo**

culote SM, **culottes** SMPL [1] (*Dep*) cycling shorts *pl*
[2] (= *prenda íntima*) French knickers *pl*

▼**culpa** SF [1] (= *responsabilidad*) fault, blame; **es ~ suya** it's his fault, he's to blame; **la ~ fue de los frenos** the brakes were to blame; **no le alcanza ~** (*frm*) no blame attaches to him, he is blameless; **cargar con la ~ a algn** to pin *o* put the blame on sb; **echar la ~ a algn de algo** to blame sb for sth; **siempre me echan la ~ a mí** they're always blaming me *o* saying it's my fault; **por ~ del mal tiempo** because of the bad weather; **tener la ~ de algo** to be to blame for sth; **nadie tiene la ~** nobody is to blame, it's nobody's fault; **tú tienes la ~** you're to blame, it's your fault
[2] (*Jur*) guilt
[3] (= *pecado*) sin; **pagar las ~s ajenas** to pay for somebody else's sins

culpabilidad SF [1] (= *culpa*) guilt, culpability (*frm*); **admitió su ~ públicamente** he made a public admission of his guilt, he admitted his guilt publicly; **sentimiento de ~** guilt feelings *pl*, feelings of guilt *pl*; **complejo de ~** guilt complex
[2] (*Jur*) guilt; **veredicto de ~** verdict of guilty
[3] (= *responsabilidad*) responsibility

culpabilizar ▸conjug 1f◂ VT = **culpar**

culpable Ⓐ ADJ [1] [*persona*] guilty; **confesarse ~** to plead guilty; **declarar ~ a algn** to find sb guilty; **la persona ~** the person to blame *o* at fault, the culpable person (*frm*); (*Jur*) the guilty person, the culprit
[2] [*acto*] blameworthy; **con descuido ~** with culpable negligence (*frm*)
Ⓑ SMF [1] (= *responsable*) person to blame, person at fault
[2] (*Jur*) (= *responsable de un delito*) culprit; (= *condenado por un delito*) offender, guilty party

culpado/a Ⓐ ADJ guilty
Ⓑ SM/F culprit; (*Jur*) the accused

culpar ▸conjug 1a◂ VT (= *acusar*) to blame; **~ a algn de algo** to blame sb for sth

culposo ADJ (*esp LAm*) guilty, culpable

cultamente ADV (= *de manera culta*) in a cultured way; (*pey*) (= *con afectación*) affectedly, in an affected way

culteranismo SM (*Literat*) *latinized, precious and highly metaphorical style (esp 17th century)*

> **CULTERANISMO, CONCEPTISMO**
>
> ***Culteranismo** and **conceptismo** were opposing literary fashions which developed in the early 17th century in Spain. Luis de Góngora was the main exponent of **culteranismo**, also known as **gongorismo**. His poetry was very learned in style, full of metaphor, classical allusions, neologisms and deliberate syntactic playfulness. By contrast, **conceptismo**, as championed by Francisco de Quevedo, meant very precise, economic and rational language with complex ideas presented in a simple and succinct style. Góngora, who was much vilified in his time, and not only by Quevedo, found posthumous favour with generations of modern Spanish poets, most notably the **Generación del 27**.*
>
> ⇨ *See also* GENERACIÓN DEL 27/98

culterano/a (*Literat*) Ⓐ ADJ *latinized, precious and highly metaphorical*
Ⓑ SM/F writer in the style of "culteranismo"

cultismo SM learned word

cultista ADJ learned

cultivable ADJ cultivable, arable

cultivado ADJ [*campo, superficie*] cultivated; [*persona*] cultured, cultivated; [*perla*] cultured

cultivador[1] SM (*Agr*) cultivator

cultivador[2]**(a)** SM/F farmer, grower; **~ de vino** winegrower; **~ de café** coffee grower, coffee planter

cultivar ▸conjug 1a◂ VT [1] (*Agr*) [+ *tierra*] to farm, cultivate, till; [+ *cosecha*] to grow, raise
[2] (*Biol*) to culture
[3] [+ *amistad, arte, estudio*] to cultivate; [+ *talento*] to develop; [+ *memoria*] to develop, improve

cultivo SM [1] (= *acto*) cultivation, growing
[2] (= *cosecha*) crop; **el ~ principal de la región** the chief crop of the area; **rotación de ~s** crop rotation
[3] (*Biol*) culture; *ver tb* **caldo 3**

culto Ⓐ ADJ [1] [*persona*] cultured, educated; (*pey*) (= *afectado*) affected
[2] [*palabra, frase*] learned
Ⓑ SM [1] (*Rel*) (= *veneración*) worship; (= *ritual*) cult (**a** of); **libertad de ~** freedom of worship; **el ~ a Zeus** the cult of Zeus; **rendir ~ a** (*lit*) to worship; (*fig*) to pay homage *o* tribute to
[2] (= *admiración*) cult; **de ~** cult *antes de s*; **una película de ~** a cult movie ► **culto a la personalidad** personality cult

cultrún SM (*Cono Sur*) drum

cultura SF [1] (= *civilización*) culture; **la ~ griega** Greek culture; **la ~ clásica** Classical culture
[2] (= *saber*) **Juan tiene mucha ~** Juan is very knowledgeable *o* widely-read; **un hombre de gran ~** a very knowledgeable *o* cultured man
► **cultura de masas** popular culture
► **cultura general** general knowledge
► **cultura popular** popular culture
[3] (= *artes*) culture; **este gobierno no invierte en ~** this government is not investing in culture; **Ministerio de Cultura** Minister of Culture

cultural ADJ cultural; **tiene un bajo nivel ~** he's not very (well-)educated

culturalmente ADV culturally

culturismo SM body building

culturista SMF body builder

culturización SF education, enlightenment

culturizar ▸conjug 1f◂ Ⓐ VT to educate, enlighten
Ⓑ **culturizarse** VPR to educate o.s., improve one's mind

cuma SF [1] (*CAm*) (= *cuchillo*) curved machete, curved knife
[2] (*Andes*) (= *mujer*) woman (*of the village*); (= *comadre*) gossip

cumbancha SF (*Caribe*) spree, drinking bout

cumbia SF (= *música*) *Colombian dance music*; (= *baile*) *popular Colombian dance*

cúmbila SM (*Caribe*) pal*, buddy (*esp EEUU*)

cumbo SM [1] (*CAm*) (= *chistera*) top hat; (= *hongo*) bowler hat, derby (*EEUU*)
[2] (*CAm*) (= *taza*) narrow-mouthed cup

cumbre Ⓐ SF (*Geog*) summit, top; (*fig*) top, height; **conferencia en la ~** (*Pol*) summit, summit conference; **está en la ~ de su poderío** he is at the height of his power; **hacer ~** to make it to the top
Ⓑ ADJ INV **conferencia ~** summit conference; **momento ~** culminating point; **es su libro ~** it's his most important book

cume SM (*CAm*), **cumiche** SM (*CAm*) baby of the family

cumpa* SM (*LAm*) pal*, buddy (*esp EEUU*)

cumpleañero/a SM/F (*LAm*) birthday boy/ birthday girl

▼ **cumpleaños** SM INV birthday; **¡feliz ~!** happy birthday!, many happy returns!

cumplido Ⓐ ADJ 1 (= *perfecto*) complete, full; **un ~ caballero** a perfect gentlemen
2 (= *amplio*) [*ropa*] full; [*ración*] large, plentiful
3 (= *cortés*) courteous, correct; (= *formal*) formal
4 **tiene sesenta años ~s** he's sixty years old
Ⓑ SM 1 (= *alabanza*) compliment
2 (= *cortesía*) **visita de ~** courtesy call; **por ~** (= *por cortesía*) out of politeness, as a matter of courtesy; (= *por obligación*) out of a sense of duty; **¡sin ~s!** no ceremony, please!; **andarse con ~s** ◊ **usar ~s** to stand on ceremony, be formal; **cambiar los ~s de etiqueta** to exchange formal courtesies

cumplidor ADJ reliable, trustworthy

cumplimentar ▸conjug 1a◂ VT 1 [+ *formulario*] to complete, fill in
2 [+ *órdenes*] to carry out; [+ *deber*] to perform
3 (*frm*) [+ *superior, jefe*] to pay one's respects to (**por** on)

cumplimentero ADJ formal, ceremonious

cumplimiento SM 1 (= *satisfacción*) **el ~ de su promesa le reportará buena fama** fulfilling *o* keeping his promise will earn him a good reputation; **el ~ de sus obligaciones** keeping *o* fulfilling his obligations; **le felicitó por el ~ de todos los objetivos propuestos** he congratulated him on achieving all the proposed aims
2 [*de ley*] observance, compliance; **una ley de obligado ~ para los ciudadanos** a law that is binding on all citizens; **en ~ de lo estipulado por el acuerdo** in adherence to the terms stipulated in the agreement; **dar ~ a** to fulfil; **falta de ~** non-fulfilment
3 [*de condena*] **pasará tres años en prisión en ~ de la condena** he will spend three years in prison in order to complete his sentence
4 (*Com*) expiry, expiration (*EEUU*)

cumplir ▸conjug 3a◂ Ⓐ VT 1 (= *llevar a cabo*) [+ *amenaza*] to carry out; [+ *promesa*] to keep; [+ *objetivo, sueño*] to achieve; [+ *ambición*] to fulfil, fulfill (*EEUU*), achieve; [+ *papel*] to play; **los contratan para ~ las misiones más difíciles** they are hired to carry out *o* do the most difficult tasks; **la cárcel no cumple su función preventiva** prison is failing to fulfil its role as *o* to act as a deterrent; **los parques naturales cumplen la función de proteger nuestro patrimonio natural** nature reserves serve to protect our natural heritage; **cumplió su palabra de aumentarnos el sueldo** he kept his promise to give us a pay rise; **les ha acusado de no ~ su palabra** he has accused them of failing to keep *o* breaking their word
2 (= *obedecer*) [+ *ley, norma, sentencia*] to observe, obey; [+ *orden*] to carry out, obey; **sólo estoy cumpliendo órdenes** I'm only carrying out *o* obeying orders; **~ la voluntad del difunto** to carry out the wishes of the deceased; **hacer ~ la ley/un acuerdo** to enforce the law/an agreement
3 (= *alcanzar*) [+ *condición, requisito*] to comply with, fulfil, fulfill (*EEUU*), meet; **estos productos no cumplen las condiciones sanitarias exigidas** these products do not comply with *o* fulfil *o* meet the necessary health requirements; **cumplió su deseo de viajar a la India** he fulfilled his wish of travelling to India
4 (= *realizar*) [+ *condena, pena*] to serve; [+ *servicio militar*] to do, complete; **está cumpliendo 30 días de arresto** he is serving 30 days detention; **tiene el servicio militar cumplido** he has done *o* completed his military service
5 (*con periodos de tiempo*) 5·1 [+ *años*] **hoy cumple ocho años** she's eight today, it's her eighth birthday today; **el rey cumple hoy años** today is the King's birthday; **cumple 40 años en diciembre** she'll be 40 in December; **cuando cumplas los 21 años** when you're 21, when you reach the age of 21; **¿cuántos años va a ~?** how old is he going to be?; **¡que cumplas muchos más!** many happy returns!
5·2 [+ *aniversario, días*] **la democracia cumple su vigésimo aniversario** democracy is celebrating its twentieth anniversary; **el premio cumple su cincuentenario** the prize is currently in its fiftieth year; **el paro en el transporte cumple hoy su cuarto día** this is the fourth day of the transport strike
6 (*Naipes*) [+ *contrato*] to make
Ⓑ VI 1 (= *terminar*) [*plazo*] to end, expire; [*pago*] to fall due
2 (= *hacer lo correcto*) to do one's duty; **tengo la tranquilidad de haber cumplido** at least I can say that I did my duty *o* what was expected of me; **es muy profesional y siempre cumple** she is very professional — she never lets you down; **yo siempre cumplo en mi trabajo** I always do my job properly; **mi marido no cumple en la cama** (*hum*) my husband isn't performing (in bed); **prepárales una sopita y con eso cumples** just make them a bit of soup, that's as much as can be expected of you
3 **~ con** [+ *compromiso, acuerdo*] to honour, honor (*EEUU*); [+ *ley*] to observe, obey; [+ *condición, requisito, criterio*] to fulfil, fulfill (*EEUU*), comply with, meet; **estaba cumpliendo con su deber** he was doing his duty; **~ con los trámites de la aduana** to go through customs; **tendrá que ~ con lo estipulado en el acuerdo** he will have to comply with what was stipulated in the agreement; **tendrán que ~ con el calendario acordado** they will have to comply with the schedule we agreed on; **para ~ con los criterios de Maastricht** in order to comply with *o* meet the Maastricht criteria; **~ con la iglesia** to fulfil one's religious obligations
4 **~ por algn** to act on sb's behalf
5 (*frm*) (= *corresponder*) **lo he recibido dos veces, con la amabilidad que me cumple** I've received him twice, with the friendliness that is expected of me
6 (*Mil*) to finish one's military service
Ⓒ **cumplirse** VPR 1 (= *realizarse*) [*deseo, sueño, vaticinio*] to come true; [*plan, proyecto*] to be implemented
2 (= *acabarse*) [*plazo*] to expire; **se cumplió el plazo de dos años del visado** the two years of the visa expired; **el viernes se cumple el plazo para entregar las solicitudes** Friday is the deadline *o* last day for handing in applications; **la jornada se cumplió sin incidentes** the day passed off without incident; **hoy se cumple el 40 aniversario de su muerte** today is the 40th anniversary of her death; **ayer se cumplió un año desde que fui puesto en libertad** it was a year yesterday since I was released; **ayer se cumplió el quinto día de la campaña electoral** yesterday was the fifth day of the election campaign

cumquibus SM INV (*hum*) **el ~** the wherewithal (*hum*)

cumucho SM (*Cono Sur*) 1 (= *multitud*) gathering, mob, crowd
2 (= *cabaña*) hut, hovel

cumulativo ADJ cumulative

cúmulo SM 1 (= *montón*) heap, accumulation (*frm*); **un ~ de datos** a heap of facts; **un ~ de obstáculos** a whole series of obstacles; **es un ~ de virtudes** he's full of virtues, he's a paragon of virtue
2 (*Meteo*) cumulus

cumulonimbo SM cumulonimbus

cuna SF 1 [*de bebé*] cot, crib (*EEUU*); (*con balancines*) cradle; **canción de ~** lullaby; **casa ~** children's home ► **cuna portátil** carrycot
2 (= *lugar de nacimiento*) [*de persona*] birthplace; [*de tendencia, movimiento*] cradle; **Málaga, la ~ de Picasso** Málaga, the birthplace of Picasso; **Atenas, la ~ de las olimpiadas** Athens, the birthplace of the Olympics; **Escocia, la ~ del golf** Scotland, the home of golf
3 (= *linaje*) **de ~ humilde** of humble birth *o* stock *o* origin; **de noble ~** of noble birth; ✦*MODISMO* **criarse en buena ~** to be born with a silver spoon in one's mouth
4 **cunas** (= *juego*) cat's cradle *sing*

cundir ▸conjug 3a◂ VI 1 (= *rendir*) to produce a good quantity; **hoy no me ha cundido el trabajo** I didn't get very far with my work today, I didn't get much work done today; **no me cunde el tiempo** I'm not getting very far, I'm not getting a lot done, I'm not making very much headway
2 (= *extenderse*) to spread; **la noticia cundió** the news spread; **cunde el rumor que ...** there's a rumour going round that ...; **¡que no cunda el pánico!** there's no need for panic!, don't panic!
3 (= *multiplicarse*) to increase; **van cundiendo los efectos del paro** the effects of unemployment are multiplying
4 (= *hincharse*) [*arroz*] to swell

cunear ▸conjug 1a◂ Ⓐ VT to rock, cradle
Ⓑ **cunearse** VPR to rock, sway; (*al andar*) to swing along

cuneco/a SM/F (*Ven*) baby of the family

cuneiforme ADJ cuneiform

cuneta SF 1 [*de calle*] gutter; [*de carretera*] ditch; ✦*MODISMOS* **dejar a algn en la ~: Juan deja a Pedro en la ~** Juan leaves Pedro standing, Juan leaves Pedro way behind; **que-**

➤ LENGUA Y USO: cumpleaños 50.3

darse en la ~ to get left behind, miss the bus*
2 (*CAm, Méx*) [*de acera*] kerb, curb (*EEUU*)
cunicultura SF rabbit breeding
cuña SF 1 (*Téc*) wedge; [*de rueda*] chock
2 (*Tip*) quoin
3 **meter ~** to sow discord
4 (*) (= *pez gordo*) big shot*, fat cat*; **tener ~s** to have a lot of influence *o* pull
5 (*CAm, Caribe Aut*) two-seater car
6 (*Radio, TV*) spot, slot; (*Prensa*) space filler, brief item ► **cuña publicitaria** commercial
cuñadismo* SM nepotism, old boy network
cuñado/a SM/F brother-/sister-in-law
cuñete SM keg
cuño SM 1 (*Téc*) die-stamp; **de nuevo ~** [*palabra*] newly-coined; [*persona*] new-fledged
2 (= *sello*) stamp, mark
cuota SF 1 (= *parte proporcional*) share; **han aumentado sus ~s de poder en el gobierno** they've increased their share of power within the government ► **cuota de mercado** market share ► **cuota de pantalla** (*TV*) share of the viewing figures ► **cuota electoral** share of the vote
2 (= *parte asignada*) quota; **una reducción en la ~ española de producción de aceite** a reduction in Spain's oil production quota
3 (= *cantidad fija*) [*de club*] membership fee, membership fees *pl*; [*de sindicato*] dues *pl* ► **cuota de conexión** connection charge, connection fee ► **cuota de enganche** down payment ► **cuota de inscripción** (*a un curso*) enrolment fee, enrollment fee (*EEUU*); (*a una conferencia*) registration fee ► **cuota de instalación** installation charge, installation fee ► **cuota de socio** membership fee ► **cuota patronal** employer's contribution (*to national insurance*)
4 (*LAm*) (= *plazo*) **por ~s** by instalments *o* (*EEUU*) installments
cuotidiano (*frm*) ADJ = **cotidiano**
cupaje SM blending, blending of wines
cupe *etc ver* **caber**
cupé SM coupé
Cupido SM Cupid
cupiera *etc ver* **caber**
cuplé SM *type of light, sometimes risqué song originally sung in variety shows*
cupletista SF cabaret singer, singer of "cuplés"
cupo SM 1 (*Fin, Com*) quota ► **cupo de azúcar** sugar quota ► **cupo de importación** import quota
2 (*LAm*) capacity; **no hay ~** there's no room; **"no hay cupo"** (*Teat*) "house full", "sold out"
3 (*Mil*) draft; **excedente de ~** exempt from military service
cupolino SM hubcap
cupón SM (= *vale*) coupon; [*de lotería*] ticket; **~ de (los) ciegos** (*Esp*) *ticket for the lottery for the blind* ► **cupón de dividendos** dividend voucher ► **cupón de franqueo internacional** international reply coupon ► **cupón de interés** interest warrant ► **cupón de racionamiento** ration coupon ► **cupón de regalo** gift voucher, gift token, gift certificate (*EEUU*) ► **cupón de respuesta internacional** international reply coupon ► **cupón obsequio** gift voucher, gift token, gift certificate (*EEUU*)
cuponazo* SM special lottery prize
cuprero ADJ (*Chile*) copper *antes de s*

cúpula SF 1 (*Arquit*) dome, cupola
2 (*Náut*) turret
3 (*Bot*) husk, shell
4 (*Pol*) party leadership, leading members; (*Com, Fin*) top management
cuquería SF craftiness
cura¹ SM 1 (*Rel*) priest; **sí, señor ~** yes, father ► **cura obrero** worker priest ► **cura párroco** parish priest
2 (†) (= *yo mismo*) I, myself; **este ~** yours truly*; **no se ofrece este ~** this poor devil isn't volunteering
cura² SF 1 (*Med*) (= *curación*) cure; (= *tratamiento*) treatment; **no tiene ~** (*lit*) there is no cure for it; (*fig*) there's no remedy, it's quite hopeless; **tiene ~** it can be cured, it is curable; **primera ~** first aid ► **cura de choque** shock treatment ► **cura de reposo** rest therapy ► **cura de sueño** sleep therapy ► **cura de urgencia** emergency treatment, first aid
2 ► **cura de almas** (*Rel*) cure of souls
curable ADJ curable
curaca¹ SM (*Andes*) (= *cacique*) Indian chief, Indian native authority
curaca² SF (*Andes*) (= *ama*) priest's housekeeper
curación SF (*Med*) (= *proceso*) cure, healing; (= *tratamiento*) treatment; **primera ~** first aid
curadillo SM 1 (*Culin*) dried cod
2 (*Téc*) bleached linen
curado Ⓐ ADJ 1 (*Culin*) cured; [*pieles*] tanned, prepared
2 (*Andes, Cono Sur*) (= *borracho*) drunk
3 (= *endurecido*) hardened, inured; **estar ~ de espanto(s)** to have seen it all before
Ⓑ SM (*Culin*) curing
curador(a) SM/F 1 (*Jur*) (= *tutor*) guardian; (= *administrador*) executor
2 [*de museo*] curator
3 [*de enfermos*] healer ► **curador(a) por fe** faith-healer
curalotodo Ⓐ ADV INV cure-all
Ⓑ SM cure-all
curanderismo SM folk medicine; (*pey*) quack medicine, quackery
curandero/a SM/F quack, quack doctor
curar ▸conjug 1a◂ Ⓐ VT 1 (*Med*) (= *tratar*) to treat; (= *sanar*) to cure; **le están curando el resfriado con antibióticos** they're treating her cold with antibiotics; **este tratamiento me curó la bronquitis** this treatment cured my bronchitis; **le curó la herida con alcohol** she treated *o* dressed his wound with alcohol; **no le consiguió ~ la herida** he couldn't get his wound to heal; **para ~ los males de la sociedad** (*fig*) to cure all of society's ills; ✦***REFRÁN*** **el tiempo lo cura todo** time is a great healer
2 [+ *carne, pescado*] to cure; [+ *queso*] to mature; [+ *piel*] to tan; [+ *tela*] to bleach; [+ *madera*] to season
Ⓑ VI (*Med*) [*fármaco, medicamento*] to work; (*frm*) [*paciente*] to get better, recover
Ⓒ **curarse** VPR 1 (*Med*) [*paciente*] to get better, recover; [*herida*] to heal (up); **no se me ha curado la herida todavía** my wound still hasn't healed (up); **~se de algo: ya me he curado de la gripe** I've got over the flu now; **nunca se curó del mal de amores** he never got over his unrequited love; *ver tb* **salud 2**
2 (*frm*) (= *preocuparse*) **~se de algo: nunca se curó de agradar a sus súbditos** he never made any effort to please his subjects
3 (*Andes, Cono Sur**) (= *emborracharse*) to get drunk; (*Méx**) (*de resaca*) to have the hair of the dog*
curare SM curare, curari
curasao SM curaçao
curativo ADJ curative
curato SM curacy, parish
curazao SM curaçao
curca SF (*Andes, Cono Sur*) (= *joroba*) hump
curco/a (*Andes, Cono Sur*) Ⓐ ADJ hunchbacked
Ⓑ SM/F hunchback
curcuncho/a (*Andes, Chile*) Ⓐ SM (= *joroba*) hump
Ⓑ SM/F (= *jorobado*) hunchback
curda* Ⓐ ADJ sloshed*, pissed**, trashed (*EEUU**); **estar ~** to be sloshed*, be pissed**, be trashed (*EEUU**)
Ⓑ SF drunkenness; **agarrar una ~** to get sloshed*, get pissed**, get trashed (*EEUU**); **estar (con la) ~** ◊ **estar en ~** (*Cono Sur*) to be sloshed*, be pissed**, be trashed (*EEUU**); **tener una ~** to be sloshed*, be pissed**, be trashed (*EEUU**)
curdo/a Ⓐ ADJ Kurdish
Ⓑ SM/F Kurd
cureña SF gun carriage; **a ~ rasa** out in the open, exposed to the elements
curia SF 1 (*Rel*) (*tb* **~ romana**) papal Curia
2 (*Jur*) legal profession, the Bar, the Bar Association (*EEUU*)
curiana SF cockroach
curiara SF (*Ven*) dugout canoe
curiche* SM (*Cono Sur*) black man
curiosamente ADV 1 (= *extrañamente*) curiously, oddly
2 (= *pulcramente*) neatly, cleanly
curiosear ▸conjug 1a◂ Ⓐ VT 1 (= *husmear*) to nose out
2 (= *mirar*) (*en una tienda*) to look over, look round
Ⓑ VI 1 (= *husmear*) to snoop, pry
2 (= *mirar*) (*en una tienda*) to look round, wander round; (= *explorar*) to poke about; **~ por las tiendas** to wander round the shops; **~ por los escaparates** to go window-shopping
curiosidad SF 1 (= *interés*) curiosity; (= *indiscreción*) inquisitiveness; **despertar la ~ de algn** to arouse sb's curiosity; **estar muerto de ~** to be dying of curiosity; **tenemos ~ por saber si ...** we are curious to know if ...; **la ~ de noticias me llevó allí** the quest for news took me there
2 (= *objeto*) curiosity, curio
3 (= *aseo*) neatness, cleanliness
4 (= *esmero*) care, carefulness, conscientiousness
curioso/a Ⓐ ADJ 1 [*persona*] curious; (= *indiscreto*) inquisitive; **estar ~ por saber** to be curious to know; **~ de noticias** eager for news
2 (= *raro*) [*acto, objeto*] curious, odd; **¡qué ~!** how odd!, how curious!
3 (= *aseado*) neat, clean, tidy
4 (= *cuidadoso*) careful, conscientious
Ⓑ SM/F 1 (= *presente*) bystander, onlooker
2 (= *interesado*) **los ~s de la literatura** those interested in literature
3 (= *cotilla*) busybody

curiosón/ona SM/F busybody

curita SF (*LAm*) plaster, sticking plaster, Band-Aid® (*EEUU*)

currante* SMF worker

currar* ▸conjug 1a◂ VI, **currelar*** ▸conjug 1a◂ VI to work

curre* SM, **currelo*** SM work

curricular ADJ curriculum *antes de s*

currículo SM curriculum

▼**curriculum** SM, **currículum** SM (*tb* ~ **vitae**) curriculum vitae, résumé (*EEUU*)

currinche SM 1 (*Tip*) apprentice journalist, cub reporter
2 (*) (= *persona insignificante*) little man, non-entity

currito* SM working man, working bloke*

Curro SM (*forma familiar*) *de* **Francisco**

curro Ⓐ ADJ 1 (= *elegante*) smart; (= *ostentoso*) showy, flashy
2 (= *presumido*) cocky, brashly confident
Ⓑ SM 1 (*) = **curre**
2 (= *golpe*) bash*, punch; **dar un ~** to beat up
3 (*Arg**) (= *estafa*) rip-off‡

curroadicto/a* SM/F workaholic

currusco* SM hard crust (*at the end of French bread*)

currutaco/a Ⓐ ADJ 1 (= *ostentoso*) showy, loud
2 (*LAm*) (= *bajito*) short, squat
Ⓑ SM/F 1 (*LAm*) (= *persona bajita*) shortie*
2 (†) (= *petimetre*) toff*, dandy
3 **currutacos** (*CAm*) (= *diarrea*) diarrhoea *sing*, diarrhea *sing* (*EEUU*)

curry SM 1 (= *especia*) curry powder; **pollo al ~** curried chicken
2 (= *plato*) curry

cursante SMF (*LAm*) student

cursar ▸conjug 1a◂ Ⓐ VT 1 [+ *orden, mensaje*] to send, dispatch; [+ *solicitud*] to deal with
2 [+ *asignatura*] to study; [+ *curso*] to take, attend; **~ Matemáticas** to read Maths
3 (*frm*) [+ *sitio*] to frequent
Ⓑ VI **el mes que cursa** the present month

cursi Ⓐ ADJ 1 [*persona*] (= *amanerado*) affected; (= *remilgado*) prissy; (*en sus gustos*) twee
2 [*objeto*] twee
Ⓑ SMF **es una ~** (= *amanerada*) she's so affected; (= *niña remilgada*) she's so prissy; (*en sus gustos*) she's so twee

cursilada SF = **cursilería 2**

cursilería SF 1 (= *cualidad*) (= *amaneramiento*) (*gen*) affectation; [*de niña remilgada*] prissiness; (= *mal gusto*) tweeness
2 (= *acto*) **no soporto las ~s que dice** I can't stand her affected way of speaking; **hizo la ~ de cortarle el pelo al caniche** he was twee enough to get the poodle's hair cut

cursillista SMF member, member of a course

cursillo SM (= *curso*) short course; (= *conferencias*) short series of lectures

cursilón/ona SM/F = **cursi**

cursiva SF (*Tip*) italics *pl*; (= *escritura*) cursive writing

cursivo ADJ (*Tip*) italic; [*escritura*] cursive

curso SM 1 (*Escol, Univ*) (= *año escolar*) year; (= *clase*) year, class (*esp EEUU*); **este ~ empieza el dos de septiembre** this school year begins on the second of September; **los alumnos del segundo ~** second year pupils, the second years; **es el único chico de mi ~** he's the only boy in my year
2 (= *estudios*) course; **un ~ de informática** a course in computing; **apertura/clausura de ~** beginning/end of term ► **curso acelerado** crash course, intensive course ► **curso de actualización** refresher course ► **curso de formación** training course ► **Curso de Orientación Universitaria** = **COU** ► **curso de reciclaje** refresher course ► **curso intensivo** crash course, intensive course ► **curso lectivo** academic year ► **curso por correspondencia** correspondence course
3 [*de río*] course ► **curso de agua, curso fluvial** watercourse
4 (= *desarrollo*) course; **un nuevo tratamiento que retrasa el ~ de la enfermedad** a new treatment which delays the course of the illness; **deja que las cosas sigan su ~** let matters take their course; **seguimos por la tele el ~ de la carrera** we watched the progress *o* course of the race on TV; **la recuperación del enfermo sigue su ~ normal** the patient is recovering normally; **en ~**: **el proceso judicial está en ~** the case is under way *o* in progress; **el año en ~** the present year, the current year; **en el ~ de**: **en el ~ de la entrevista** during the interview, in *o* during the course of the interview; **en el ~ de la vida** in the course of a lifetime; **en el ~ de los años** over the years
5 (*frm*) **dar ~ a algo**: **dar ~ a una solicitud** to deal with an application; **estaba dando ~ a las instrucciones recibidas** she was carrying out the instructions she had received; **dio ~ a su indignación** she gave vent to her anger; **dar libre ~ a algo: dio libre ~ a sus pensamientos** he gave free rein to his thoughts; **dimos libre ~ a la imaginación** we let our imagination run wild
6 (*Com*) **moneda de ~ legal** legal tender

cursor SM 1 (*Téc*) slide
2 (*Inform*) cursor

curtido Ⓐ ADJ 1 [*cuero*] tanned
2 [*piel*] hardened, leathery; [*cara*] (*por sol*) tanned; (*por intemperie*) weather-beaten
3 (= *experimentado*) **estar ~ en** to be expert at, be skilled in
Ⓑ SM 1 (= *acto*) tanning
2 (= *cuero*) tanned leather, tanned hides *pl*

curtidor SM tanner

curtiduría SF, **curtiembre** SF (*LAm*) tannery

curtir ▸conjug 3a◂ Ⓐ VT 1 [+ *cuero*] to tan
2 [+ *piel*] to tan, bronze
3 (= *acostumbrar*) to harden, inure
Ⓑ **curtirse** VPR 1 (*por sol*) to become tanned; (*por intemperie*) to get weather-beaten
2 (= *acostumbrarse*) to become inured (**contra** to)
3 (*LAm*) (= *ensuciarse*) to get o.s. dirty

curul SF (*Col Pol*) seat (in parliament)

curva SF 1 [*de carretera, camino*] bend ► **curva en herradura** hairpin bend
2 (*Mat*) curve ► **curva de demanda** (*Com*) demand curve ► **curva de indiferencia** indifference curve ► **curva de la felicidad** (*hum*) paunch, beer-belly ► **curva de nivel** contour line ► **curva de rentabilidad** (*Com*) break-even chart
3 **curvas*** [*de mujer*] vital statistics; **¡tiene unas ~s!** what a body she's got!

curvar ▸conjug 1a◂ Ⓐ VT [+ *material*] to bend; [+ *labios*] to curl
Ⓑ **curvarse** VPR [*material*] to bow; [*estante*] to sag, bend; [*madera*] to warp

curvatura SF curvature ► **curvatura terrestre** Earth's curvature

curvilíneo ADJ curved, curvilinear

curvo ADJ 1 (= *curvado*) curved, bent
2 (*Andes*) (= *estevado*) bow-legged
3 (*Caribe*) (= *zurdo*) left-handed

cusca SF 1 **hacer la ~ a algn*** to play a dirty trick on sb
2 (*CAm*) (= *coqueta*) flirt
3 (*Méx*‡) (= *puta*) tart*, hooker (*EEUU*‡), whore

cuscha SF (*CAm*) liquor, rum

cuscurrante ADJ crunchy, crisp

cuscurro SM crouton

cuscús SM INV couscous

cusma SF (*Perú*) sleeveless shirt, tunic

cuspa SF (*Andes*) weeding

cuspar ▸conjug 1a◂ VT (*Andes*) to weed

cúspide SF 1 (*Anat*) cusp
2 (*Geog*) summit, peak; (*fig*) pinnacle, apex
3 (*Mat*) apex

cusqui SF **hacer la ~*** to bug*, annoy

custodia SF 1 (= *cuidado*) care, safekeeping, custody; **bajo la ~ de** in the care *o* custody of ► **custodia policial** police protection ► **custodia preventiva** protective custody
2 (= *escolta*) guard, escort
3 (*Rel*) monstrance

custodiar ▸conjug 1b◂ VT 1 (= *vigilar*) to guard, watch over
2 (= *cuidar de*) to take care of, look after
3 (= *proteger*) [+ *derechos, libertades*] to defend

custodio/a Ⓐ ADJ **ángel ~** guardian angel
Ⓑ SM/F (= *guardián*) custodian; (*Méx, Perú*) police officer

cususa SF (*CAm*) home-made liquor, home-made rum

CUT SF ABR (*Chile*) = **Central Unitaria de Trabajadores**

cutacha SF (*LAm*) = **cuma**

cutama SF 1 (*Chile*) (= *saco*) bag; (= *alforja*) saddlebag
2 (= *torpe*) clumsy person

cutáneo ADJ cutaneous, skin *antes de s*

cutaras SFPL (*CAm, Caribe, Méx*), **cutarras** SFPL (*CAm*) sandals, rough shoes

cúter SM cutter

cutí SM ticking

cutícula SF cuticle

cutis SM INV skin, complexion

cuto ADJ 1 (*Andes, CAm*) [*persona*] (= *tullido*) maimed, crippled; (= *desdentado*) toothless
2 (*Andes, CAm*) [*objeto*] damaged, spoiled
3 (*Andes*) (= *corto*) short

cutre* ADJ 1 [*persona*] (= *tacaño*) mean, stingy; (= *vulgar*) vulgar, coarse
2 [*lugar*] squalid, shabby; **un sitio ~** a dive*, a hole*
3 [*objeto*] tacky*

cutrería* SF 1 [*de persona*] (= *tacañería*) meanness, stinginess; (= *vulgaridad*) vulgarity, coarseness
2 [*de lugar*] (= *miseria*) squalidness, shabbiness; **su bar es una auténtica ~** his bar is a real dive *o* hole*

➤ LENGUA Y USO: **curriculum** 46.2

[3] [*de objeto*] **ese vestido me parece una ~** I think that dress is tacky*

cutter ['kuter] SM (*pl* **cutters**) [*de carpintero*] Stanley knife®, razor knife (*EEUU*); (*para papel*) artist's scalpel

cuya SF (*Caribe, Cono Sur*) gourd, drinking vessel

cuyano/a* ADJ, SM/F (*Chile*) Argentinian

cuy(e) (*pl* **cuis** *o* **cuyes**) SM (*LAm*) guinea pig

cuyo Ⓐ ADJ REL [1] (*de persona*) whose, of whom (*frm*); (*de cosa*) of which, whose; **la señora en cuya casa nos hospedábamos** the lady in whose house we were staying; **el asunto ~s detalles conoces** the matter of which you know the details
[2] **en ~ caso** in which case; **por cuya razón** and for this reason
Ⓑ SM (†*) (= *amante*) lover

cuz EXCL **¡cuz ~!** (*dicho a un perro*) here boy!

cuzqueño/a Ⓐ ADJ of/from Cuzco
Ⓑ SM/F native/inhabitant of Cuzco; **los ~s** the people of Cuzco

C.V. Ⓐ SM ABR (= **curriculum vitae**) CV
Ⓑ SMPL ABR (= **caballos de vapor**) HP, h.p.

C y F ABR (= **costo y flete**) CAF, c.a.f., C and F

czar SM = **zar**

Dd

D, d [de] SF (= *letra*) D, d

D. ABR 1 = **Don**; → DON/DOÑA
2 (*Fin*) = **debe**
3 (= **diciembre**) Dec

Da. ABR, **D.ª** ABR = **Doña**; → DON/DOÑA

dable ADJ possible, feasible; **en lo que sea ~** as far as possible; **no es ~ hacerlo** it is not possible *o* feasible to do it

dabuti‡ Ⓐ ADJ (= *estupendo*) super*, smashing*
Ⓑ ADV **pasarlo ~** to have a great time

DAC SM ABR (*LAm*) (= **diseño asistido por computador**) CAD

daca†† EXCL hand it over!; *ver tb* **toma B**

dacrón® SM Dacron®

dactilar ADJ **huellas ~es** fingerprints

dactílico ADJ dactylic

dáctilo SM dactyl

dactilografía SF typing, typewriting

dactilografiar ▸conjug 1c◂ VT to type

dactilógrafo/a SM/F typist

dactilograma SM (*Méx*) fingerprint

dadá SM, **dadaísmo** SM dadaism

dadista SMF (*Méx*) dice player

dadito SM (*Culin*) small cube; **cortar en ~s** to dice

dádiva SF 1 (= *regalo*) gift
2 (= *compensación*) sop

dadivosidad SF generosity, open-handedness

dadivoso ADJ generous, open-handed

dado[1] SM 1 (*en juegos*) die; **dados** dice; **echó** *o* **tiró los ~s** he threw the dice; **jugar a los ~s** to play dice
2 (*Arquit*) dado
3 (*Mec*) block

▼ **dado**[2] ADJ 1 (= *determinado*) **en un caso ~** in a given case; **dada su corta edad** in view of his youth; **dadas estas circunstancias** in view of *o* given these circumstances
2 **ser ~ a algo** to be given to sth; **es muy ~ a discutir** he is much given to arguing
3 ✦*MODISMO* **ir ~** (*): **si crees que te voy a pagar las vacaciones, vas ~** if you think I'm going to pay for your holidays, you've another think coming!
4 **~ que** + *SUBJUN* provided that, so long as; + *INDIC* given that

dador(a) SM/F 1 (*Com*) drawer
2 [*de carta*] bearer
3 (*Naipes*) dealer

Dafne SF Daphne

daga SF 1 (= *espada corta*) dagger
2 (*Caribe*) (= *machete*) machete

dagazo SM (*Caribe, Méx*) stab wound

daguerrotipo SM daguerreotype

daifa SF 1 (= *querida*) mistress, concubine
2 (= *prostituta*) prostitute

daiquiri SM, **daiquirí** SM daiquiri

dalia SF dahlia

Dalila SF Delilah

daliniano ADJ Daliesque

dallar ▸conjug 1a◂ VT to scythe, mow with a scythe

dalle SM scythe

Dalmacia SF Dalmatia

dálmata Ⓐ SMF 1 (= *persona*) Dalmatian
2 (= *perro*) dalmatian, dalmatian dog
Ⓑ ADJ Dalmatian

daltónico ADJ, **daltoniano** ADJ colour-blind, color-blind (*EEUU*)

daltonismo SM colour blindness, color blindness (*EEUU*)

dama SF 1 (= *señora*) lady; **~s y caballeros** ladies and gentlemen; **primera ~** (*Teat*) leading lady; (*Pol*) First Lady (*EEUU*) ► **dama de compañía** (*LAm*) lady companion ► **la Dama de Hierro** the Iron Lady ► **dama de honor** [*de reina*] lady-in-waiting; [*de novia*] bridesmaid ► **dama de noche** night jasmine ► **dama joven** (*Teat*) ingénue ► **dama regidora** carnival queen
2 (= *mujer noble*) lady
3 (= *amante*) lady, mistress; **el poeta y su ~** the poet and his lady *o* mistress
4 (= *pieza*) (*Ajedrez, Naipes*) queen; (*Damas*) king
5 **damas** (*juego*) draughts, checkers (*EEUU*)

damajuana SF, **damasana** (*LAm*) SF demijohn

Damasco SM Damascus

damasco SM 1 (= *tela*) damask
2 (= *ciruela*) damson
3 (*LAm*) (= *árbol*) apricot tree; (= *albaricoque*) apricot

damasquinado Ⓐ ADJ [*espada, metal*] damascene
Ⓑ SM damascene, damascene work

damasquinar ▸conjug 1a◂ VT to damascene, damask

damasquino ADJ 1 [*espada, metal*] damascene, damask
2 (*de Damasco*) Damascene

damero SM 1 (= *pasatiempo*) *type of crossword*
2 (= *tablero*) draughtboard, checkerboard (*EEUU*)

damesana SF (*LAm*) demijohn

damisela SF (*Hist*) damsel; (*pey*) courtesan, prostitute

damita SF (*CAm*) young lady

damnificado/a SM/F victim

damnificar ▸conjug 1g◂ VT [+ *persona*] to injure, harm; [+ *cosa*] to damage

Damocles SM Damocles

dandi, dandy Ⓐ SM dandy, fop
Ⓑ ADJ INV **estilo ~** dandy style

dandismo SM foppishness, foppish ways

danés/esa Ⓐ ADJ Danish
Ⓑ SM/F 1 (= *persona*) Dane
2 (= *perro*) (*tb* **gran ~**) Great Dane
Ⓒ SM (= *idioma*) Danish

Daniel SM Daniel

danta SF (*LAm*) 1 (= *tapir*) tapir
2 (= *anta*) elk, moose

dantesco ADJ 1 (*Literat*) of Dante, relating to Dante; **la obra dantesca** Dante's works
2 (= *horrible*) nightmarish; **un espectáculo ~** a nightmarish sight

dantzari [dan'sari] SMF *Basque folk-dancer*

Danubio SM Danube

danza SF 1 (= *arte*) dance ► **danza contemporánea** contemporary dance
2 (= *baile*) dance; ✦*MODISMO* **siempre está en ~** he's always on the go* ► **danza de apareamiento** courtship dance, mating display ► **danza de espadas** sword dance ► **danza de figuras** square dance ► **danza de la muerte** dance of death, danse macabre ► **danza de los siete velos** dance of the seven veils ► **danza del vientre** belly dance ► **danza de salón** ballroom dancing ► **danza guerrera** war dance ► **danza macabra** = **danza de la muerte**
3 (*) (= *negocio sucio*) shady affair; (= *lío*) mess; **meterse en la ~** to get caught up in a shady affair
4 (*) (*jaleo*) row, rumpus*; **armar una ~** to kick up a row *o* rumpus*; ✦*MODISMO* **no metas los perros en ~** let sleeping dogs lie

danzante/a SM/F 1 (= *bailarín*) dancer
2 (*) (= *persona activa*) live wire; (= *entrometido*) busybody; (= *zascandil*) scatterbrain, featherbrain (*EEUU*)

danzar ▸conjug 1f◂ Ⓐ VI 1 (= *bailar*) to dance; ✦*MODISMO* **llevo toda la mañana danzando*** I've been on the go all morning*
2 (*) (= *entrometerse*) to meddle
Ⓑ VT to dance

danzarín/ina Ⓐ ADJ (= *nervioso*) jumpy
Ⓑ SM/F 1 (= *bailarín*) dancer; **danzarina del**

➤ LENGUA Y USO: **dado**[2] **4** 44.1

vientre belly dancer
[2] = **danzante 2**

dañado ADJ [1] [*edificio, pelo, fruta*] damaged
[2] [*persona*] twisted, perverted

dañar ▸conjug 1a◂ Ⓐ VT [1] [+ *objeto, pelo, piel, salud*] to damage, harm; **el alcohol le ha dañado el hígado** alcohol has damaged his liver; **la recesión ha dañado el tejido social** the recession has damaged the social fabric; ✦*MODISMO* **~ la vista**: **es tan feo que daña la vista** it's an eyesore
[2] [+ *cosecha*] to damage, spoil
[3] [+ *reputación, carrera, proyecto*] to damage, harm; **es un intento de ~ su imagen pública** it's an attempt to damage *o* harm his public image
Ⓑ **dañarse** VPR [1] (= *hacerse daño*) to be hurt, be injured; **el ciclista se dañó al caer** the cyclist was hurt *o* injured when he fell off; **se dañó el brazo escalando** she hurt *o* injured her arm while climbing
[2] [*objeto*] to be damaged; **los cimientos no llegaron a ~se en el incendio** the foundations were not damaged in the fire
[3] [*cosecha*] to be damaged, be spoiled

dañinear ▸conjug 1a◂ (*Cono Sur*) VT [1] = **dañar**
[2] (= *robar*) to steal

dañino/a Ⓐ ADJ [1] (*para la salud*) harmful; **animales ~s** vermin *sing*, pests
[2] (*para el desarrollo de algo*) damaging (**para** to)
Ⓑ SM/F (*Cono Sur*) thief

daño SM [1] (*a algo*) damage, harm; **el granizo ha producido grandes ~s a los cultivos** the hail has caused extensive damage to crops; **estas medidas han ocasionado un gran ~ a la industria** these measures have caused a great deal of harm to the industry; **~s y perjuicios** damages ► **daños colaterales** collateral damage
[2] (*a alguien*) (*físico, emocional*) pain; (*económico*) harm; **¡ay, qué ~!** ow, that hurts!; **en ~ de** (*frm*) to the detriment of; **por mi ~** (*frm*) to my cost; **causar** *o* **hacer ~ a algn** to hurt sb; **¡suelta, que me haces ~!** let go, you're hurting me!; **el ajo me hace ~** garlic doesn't agree with me, garlic disagrees with me; **tanta comida picante hace ~ al estómago** all that spicy food is bad for the stomach; **hacerse ~** to hurt o.s.; **¿te has hecho ~?** have you hurt yourself?; **se hizo ~ en el pie** he hurt his foot ► **daños corporales** physical injury *sing*
[3] (*Med*) (= *mal*) problem, trouble; **los médicos no saben dónde está el ~** the doctors can't tell where the problem *o* trouble is
[4] (*LAm*) (= *maleficio*) spell, curse

dañoso ADJ harmful

DAO SM ABR (= **diseño asistido por ordenador**) CAD

dar

▸conjug 1q◂
Ⓐ VERBO TRANSITIVO
Ⓑ VERBO INTRANSITIVO
Ⓒ VERBO PRONOMINAL
Para las expresiones ***dar importancia, dar ejemplo, dar las gracias, dar clases, dar a conocer, dar a entender, darse prisa****, ver la otra entrada.*

Ⓐ VERBO TRANSITIVO
[1] = ***entregar, conceder*** [+ *objeto, mensaje, permiso*] to give; [+ *naipes*] to deal (out); [+ *noticias*] to give, tell; **le dio un bocadillo a su hijo** he gave his son a sandwich; **se lo di a Blanca** I gave it to Blanca; **me dieron un diploma por mi buen comportamiento** I was given a diploma for good conduct; **le dieron el primer premio** he was awarded *o* given first prize; **déme dos kilos** I'll have two kilos, two kilos, please; **ir dando cuerda** to pay out rope; **~ los buenos días a algn** to say good morning to sb, say hello to sb
[2] = ***realizar*** [+ *paliza*] to give; [+ *paso*] to take; **~ un alarido** to shriek; **~ una bofetada a algn** to slap sb; **~ un golpe a algn** to hit sb; **dio un golpe en la mesa** he banged on the table; **~ un grito** to let out a cry, give a cry; **~ un paseo** to go for a walk, take a walk; **~ un suspiro** to heave *o* give a sigh, sigh
[3] = ***celebrar*** [+ *fiesta*] to have, throw; **la embajada ~á una recepción** the embassy will hold a reception
[4] = ***encender*** [+ *luz*] to turn on; **¿has dado el gas?** have you turned on the gas?
[5] = ***presentar*** [+ *obra de teatro*] to perform, put on; [+ *película*] to show, screen; **dan una película de Almodóvar** there's an Almodóvar film on, they're showing *o* screening an Almodóvar film; **¿qué dan hoy en la tele?** what's on TV tonight?
[6] = ***hacer sonar*** [*reloj*] to strike; **el reloj dio las tres** the clock struck three; **ya han dado las ocho** it's past *o* gone eight o'clock
[7] = ***producir*** [+ *fruto*] to bear; [+ *ganancias, intereses*] to yield; **~ flores** to flower; **este negocio da mucho dinero** there's a lot of money in this business; **una inversión que da un 7% de interés** an investment that pays *o* yields 7% interest
[8] = ***tener como resultado*** **el cálculo dio 99** the sum worked out at 99; **el atleta dio positivo en el control antidoping** the athlete tested positive for drugs
[9] = ***hacer sentir*** [+ *placer*] to give; **me dio mucha alegría verla** I was very pleased to see her; **las babosas me dan asco** I find slugs disgusting *o* revolting; **este jersey me da demasiado calor** this jumper is too hot, I'm too hot in this jumper; **da gusto hablar con él** he's really nice to talk to; **tu padre me da miedo** I'm scared *o* frightened of your father; **me da pena tener que tirarlo** it's a pity to have to throw it away; **el vino me da sueño** wine makes me sleepy
[10] *** = fastidiar*** to ruin; **vinieron a visitarme y me dieron la tarde** they came to visit and ruined my afternoon; **¡me estás dando las vacaciones!** you're ruining the holiday for me!
[11]
◆ **dar por** (= *considerar*) to consider; **doy el asunto por concluido** I consider the matter settled, I regard the matter as settled; **le dieron por desaparecido** they gave him up for lost; **doy el dinero por bien empleado** I consider it money well spent; **lo daba por seguro** he was sure *o* certain of it; **lo podemos ~ por terminado** we can consider it finished
[12] ✦*MODISMOS* **¡y dale!** (= *¡otra vez!*) not again!; **estar/seguir dale que dale** *o* **dale que te pego** *o* (*LAm*) **dale y dale** to go/keep on and on; **la vecina está dale que dale al piano** our neighbour is pounding away at the piano; **estoy dale que dale a este problema** I've been bashing away at this problem*; **a mí no me la das*** you can't fool me; **¡ahí te las den todas!*** you just couldn't care less!; **por si vienen mal dadas** in case of emergency; (*ahorrar*) for a rainy day; **para ~ y tomar**: **tenemos botellas para ~ y tomar** we've got loads *o* stacks of bottles; **aquí hay basura para ~ y tomar** there's tons of rubbish here; **me da que ...** I have a feeling (that)...; **me da que no va a venir** I have a feeling (that) he's not going to come

Ⓑ VERBO INTRANSITIVO
[1] = ***entregar*** to give; **dame, yo te lo arreglo** give it here, I'll fix it for you; ✦*REFRÁN* **a quien dan no escoge** beggars can't be choosers
[2] = ***entrar*** **me dieron ganas de vomitar** I felt like being sick; **si te da un mareo siéntate** if you feel giddy, sit down; **le dio un fuerte dolor en el costado** he felt a sudden sharp pain in his side; **le dio un infarto** he had a heart attack
[3] = ***importar*** **¡qué más da! ◊ ¡da igual!** it doesn't matter!, never mind!; **¿qué más te da?** what does it matter to you?; **¿qué más da un sitio que otro?** surely one place is as good as another!, it doesn't make any difference which place we choose; **lo mismo da** it makes no difference *o* odds; **me da igual ◊ lo mismo me da ◊ tanto me da** it's all the same to me, I don't mind
[4] ***seguido de preposición***
◆ **dar a** (= *estar orientado*) [*cuarto, ventana*] to look out onto, overlook; [*fachada*] to face; **mi habitación da al jardín** my room looks out onto *o* overlooks the garden
◆ **darle a** (= *hacer funcionar*) [+ *botón*] to press; (= *golpear*) to hit; [+ *balón*] to kick; **dale a la tecla roja** hit *o* press the red key; **~le a la bomba** to pump, work the pump; **dale más fuerte a la bomba** pump harder; **¡dale!** hit him!; **no es capaz de ~le al balón de cabeza** he can't head the ball
◆ **dar con** (= *encontrar*) [+ *persona*] to find; [+ *idea, solución*] to hit on, come up with; **dimos con él dos horas más tarde** we found him two hours later; **al final di con la solución** I finally hit on the solution, I finally came up with the solution; **no doy con el nombre** I can't think of the name; **~ consigo en** to end up in; **dio consigo en la cárcel** he ended up in jail
◆ **dar contra** (= *golpear*) to hit; **el barco dio contra el puente** the ship hit the bridge
◆ **dar de**: **~ de palos a algn** to give sb a beating; **~ de puñetazos a algn** to punch sb; **~ de barniz a algo** to varnish sth; **~ de beber a algn** to give sb something to drink; **~ de comer a algn** to feed sb; **~ de sí** [*comida, bebida*] to go a long way; **lo que cada uno puede ~ de sí** what each person can contribute
◆ **dar en** [+ *blanco, suelo*] to hit; [+ *solución*] to hit on, come up with; **el sol me da en la cara** the sun is in my eyes; **~ en hacer algo** to take to doing sth; **han dado en llamarle Boko** they've taken to calling him Boko
◆ **darle a algn por hacer algo**: **le ha dado por no venir a clase** he has taken to cutting classes; **les dio por venir a vernos** they took it into their heads to come and see us; **últimamente le ha dado por el golf** he's taken up

➤ LENGUA Y USO: dar B3 34.5

golf lately; **al chico le daba por dormirse en la clase** the boy was always falling asleep in class; **la casa que a alguien le dio por llamar Miramar** the house that someone had the bright idea of calling Miramar

◆ **dar para** (= *ser suficiente*) to be enough for; **con eso da para cuatro personas** this is enough for four people; **mi pobre cabeza no da para más hoy** I don't think my poor head can take any more today

5

◆ **dar que hablar** to set people talking; **una película que da en qué pensar** a thought-provoking film, a film which gives you a lot to think about

Ⓒ **darse** VERBO PRONOMINAL

1 *= entregarse* to give in

2 *= golpearse* to hit o.s.; **¿dónde te has dado?** where did you hit yourself?; **~se con** *o* **contra** to bump into; **me he dado contra la esquina del armario** I bumped into the edge of the cupboard; *ver tb* **nariz 2**

3 *= ocurrir* [*suceso*] to happen; **si se da el caso** if that happens; **se han dado muchos casos** there have been a lot of cases; **se dio una situación extraña** a strange situation arose

4 *= crecer* to grow; **esa planta no se da en el sur** that plant doesn't grow in the south; **los pepinos se dan bien en esta tierra** cucumbers grow well on this land; **el cultivo se da bien este año** the crop is doing well this year

5 *seguido de preposición*

◆ **darse a** to take to; **~se a la bebida** to take to drink, start drinking

◆ **darse de sí** [*cuero, tela*] to give, stretch

◆ **dárselas de** to make o.s. out to be; **se las da de experto** he makes himself out to be an expert; **¡no te las des de listo!** stop acting clever!

◆ **darse por**: **no se dio por aludido** he didn't take the hint; **~se por ofendido** to take offence; **~se por perdido** to give o.s. up for lost; **con llegar me doy por satisfecho** I'll be quite happy if we just get there; **me doy por vencido** I give up, I give in

6

◆ **dársele bien a algn**: **se me dan bien las ciencias** I'm good at science; **se le dan muy bien las matemáticas** she's very good at maths

◆ **dársele mal a algn**: **se me dan muy mal los idiomas** I'm very bad at languages; **no se me da mal** I'm not doing too badly at it

7 ✦*MODISMOS* **no se me da un higo** *o* **bledo** *o* **rábano*** I don't care two hoots*; **dársela (con queso) a algn*** to fool sb, put one over on sb*

Dardanelos SMPL Dardanelles

dardo SM dart; **jugar a los ~s** to play darts

dares* SMPL **~ y tomares** arguments, bickering *sing*; **andar en ~ y tomares con algn** to bicker with sb, squabble with sb

Darío SM Darius

dársena SF 1 (*Náut*) dock ► **dársena de marea** tidal basin

2 (*Aut*) bus shelter

darviniano ADJ, **darwiniano** ADJ Darwinian

darvinismo SM, **darwinismo** SM Darwinism

darvinista ADJ, SMF, **darwinista** ADJ, SMF Darwinian

data SF 1 (= *fecha*) date and place (*on document*); **es de larga ~** it is long-established, it goes back a long way

2 (*Com*) item

datable ADJ datable, that can be dated

datación SF date, dating; **de difícil ~** hard to date ► **datación con carbono** carbon dating

datáfono SM dataphone

datar ▸conjug 1a◂ Ⓐ VT to date

Ⓑ VI **~ de** to date from, date back to; **esto data de muy atrás** this goes a long way back

datero* SM (*Cono Sur*) tipster

dátil SM 1 (*Bot*) date

2 (*Zool*) date mussel

3 **dátiles‡** (= *dedos*) fingers

datilera SF date palm

dativo SM (*Ling*) dative

dato SM 1 (= *información*) piece of information; **un ~ interesante** an interesting fact *o* piece of information; **no tenemos todos los ~s** we don't have all the facts; **otro ~ que tener en cuenta es ...** another thing to bear in mind is ... ► **datos de entrada** input data ► **datos de salida** output data ► **datos estadísticos** statistics ► **datos personales** personal details, particulars

2 (*Mat*) datum

David SM David

dB ABR (= **decibelio**) dB

d.C. ABR (= **después de Cristo**) AD

dcha. ABR (= **derecha**) R

d. de C. ABR (= **después de Cristo**) AD

DDT SM ABR (= **diclorodifeniltricloroetano**) DDT

de PREP

1 *relación* of; **las calles de Madrid** the streets of Madrid; **el alcalde de Valencia** the mayor of Valencia; **Cabo de Buena Esperanza** Cape of Good Hope; **la ciudad de Madrid** the city of Madrid; **en el mes de agosto** in the month of August; **un libro de consulta** a reference book; **un millón de euros** a million euros; **la carretera de Valencia** the Valencia road, the road to Valencia; **el interés del préstamo** the interest on the loan; **la llave de mi cuarto** the key to my room; **en el día de hoy** today; **tuvieron la desgracia de perder el partido** they were unlucky enough to lose the match; **ya era hora de que vinieses** it's about time you got here; **el hecho de que yo no supiera nada** the fact that I didn't know anything about it

2 *pertenencia* **la casa de Isabel** Isabel's house; **el coche de mi amigo** my friend's car; **un familiar de mi vecina** a relative of my neighbour's; **los coches de mis amigos** my friends' cars; **el vestuario de las actrices** the actresses's dressing room; **la señora de Pérez** Pérez' wife, Mrs Pérez; **es de ellos** it's theirs; **esa contestación es muy de ella** that answer is typical of her

3 *característica, material* **una cadena de oro** a gold chain; **no es de oro** it's not gold; **una puerta de cristal** a glass door; **una cocina de gas** a gas cooker; **este modelo es de electricidad** this model uses electricity, this is an electric model; **ropa de buena calidad** good-quality clothes; **un billete de primera clase** a first-class ticket; **la niña de pelo largo** the girl with the long hair; **ese tío del sombrero** that chap with *o* in the hat; **pintado de rojo** painted red; **lo tengo de varios colores distintos** I have it in several different colours

4 *contenido* **una caja de bombones** a box of chocolates; **una copa de vino** (*llena*) a glass of wine; (*vacía*) a wine glass; **una bolsita de té** a tea bag; **estaba hecha un saco de nervios** she was a bundle of nerves

5 *origen, distancia, espacio temporal* from; **soy de Galicia** I'm from Galicia; **Julia no es de aquí** Julia is not from round here; **los de Madrid son los mejores** the ones from Madrid are the best, the Madrid ones are the best; **es de buena familia** he's from a good family; **vuelo 507 (procedente) de Londres** flight 507 from London; **vive a 20km de Madrid** she lives 20km from Madrid; **aléjate del fuego** move away from the fire; **marcó un gol a dos minutos del final del partido** he scored two minutes from the end of the match; **el tren de Santiago** the Santiago train; **el avión pasó a muy poca altura del suelo** the plane flew by at very low altitude; **salir del cine** to come out of the cinema

◆ **de ... a ...**: **vivió de 1898 a 1937** he lived from 1898 to 1937; **de mi casa a la suya hay 5km** it is 5km from my house to his; **de mayo a julio** from May to July; **del 15 al 30** from the 15th to the 30th

6 *causa* **murió de viejo** he died from old age; **me dolían los pies de tanto andar** my feet were sore from all that walking; **de puro cansado** out of sheer tiredness; **no podía moverse de miedo** he was rigid with fear; **estar loco de alegría** to be wild with joy; **saltar de alegría** to jump for joy

7 *manera* **lo derribó de un solo puñetazo** he felled him with a single blow; **se puso a mi lado de un salto** he jumped to my side; **se lo bebió de un trago** he drank it all down in one go

◆ **de ... en ...**: **iban entrando de dos en dos** they came in two by two; **bajó la escalera de tres en tres** he came down the stairs three at a time; **de puerta en puerta** from door to door

8 *= respecto de* **estar mejor de salud** to be in better health, be better; **es fuerte de brazos** he has strong arms; **paralizado de las dos piernas** paralysed in both legs; **es muy estrecho de hombros** he doesn't have very broad shoulders

9 *tema* about; **un libro de biología** a biology book, a book on *o* about biology; **hablaba de política** he was talking about politics; **no sé nada de él** I don't know anything about him; **una clase de francés** a French class

10 *uso* **máquina de coser** sewing machine; **goma de mascar** chewing gum

11 *cantidad, medida, valor* **un chico de quince años** a fifteen-year-old boy; **un viaje de dos días** a two-day journey; **un embarazo de siete meses** a seven-month pregnancy; **una moneda de 5 pesos** a 5-peso coin; **tiene un metro de alto** it's a metre high

12 *con horas y fechas* **a las siete de la mañana** at seven o'clock in the morning, at seven a.m.; **son las dos de la tarde** it's two o'clock in the afternoon, it's two p.m.; **muy de mañana** very early in the morning; **el 3**

de mayo 3 May (*leído May the third o the third of May*)

13 *tiempo* **de día** during the day(time); **de noche** at night; **de niño** as a child; **de mayor voy a ser médico** when I grow up I'm going to be a doctor

14 *proporción* **tres de cada cuatro** three out of every four

15 *uso partitivo* of; **uno de nosotros** one of us; **comió un poco de pastel** she ate a bit of cake; **¡había una de gente!*** there were loads of people there!*

16 *autoría* by; **un libro de Cela** a book by Cela, a book of Cela's; **las películas de Almodóvar** Almodóvar's films

17 *como complemento agente* by; **fue amado de todos** he was loved by all; **el rey entró seguido de su séquito** the king entered, followed by his entourage; **tiene dos hijos de su primera mujer** he has two children by his first wife

18 *en aposición a sustantivos o adjetivos* **el bueno/pobre de Pedro** good/poor old Pedro; **el imbécil de Fernández** that idiot Fernández; **es un encanto de persona** he's a lovely person

19 *en comparaciones* than; **es más difícil de lo que creía** it's more difficult than I thought; **más/menos de siete** more/less than seven; **más de 500 personas** more than *o* over 500 people

20 *con superlativos* in; **el peor alumno de la clase** the worst pupil in the class; **el más caro de la tienda/mundo** the most expensive in the shop/world; **es el coche más caro del mercado** it's the dearest car on the market

21 (+ *INFIN*) **un problema fácil de resolver** an easily solved problem; **un libro agradable de leer** a nice book to read

◆ **ser de + *INFIN***: **es de admirar su lealtad** his loyalty is admirable; **es de esperar que recibamos una pronta respuesta** it is to be hoped that we receive a prompt reply; **sería de desear que actualizaran su información** it would be desirable for them to update their information

22 *dependiente de formas verbales* **la acusaban de hipócrita** they accused her of being a hypocrite; **colmar de elogios a algn** to shower praise on sb; **se dio cuenta de que lo sabía** she realized (that) she knew it; **de esto se deduce que ...** from this it can be deduced that ...; **disfrutar de la vida** to enjoy life; **¿qué esperabas de él?** what did you expect from him?; **limpiar algo de polvo** to dust sth; **llenar algo de algo** to fill sth with sth; **se sirvió de sus amigos para salir de un mal trago** he turned to his friends to help him through a difficult patch; **trabaja de camarero** he works as a waiter; **lo uso de despensa** I use it as a pantry; **vestido de azul** dressed in blue

23 *uso condicional* if; **de ser posible** if possible; **de haberlo sabido no habría venido** if I had known, I wouldn't have come; **de resultar esto así** if this turns out to be true; **de no ser así** if it were not so, were it not so; **de no** (*LAm*) (= *si no*) otherwise

dé *ver* **dar**

deambulador SM walking frame, Zimmer®

deambular ▸conjug 1a◂ VI to wander (about)

deambulatorio SM (*Rel*) ambulatory

deán SM (*Rel*) dean

debacle SF debacle, disaster

debajo ADV 1 (= *en la parte de abajo*) underneath; **antes de pintar la silla, pon un periódico ~** before you paint the chair, put some newspaper underneath; **el libro que está ~** the book underneath; **sólo lleva una camiseta (por) ~** he's only got a T-shirt on underneath; **ahí ~** down there; **ahí ~ hay un árbol** there's a tree down there; **de ~**: **la capa de ~ no se ve** you can't see the layer underneath *o* beneath; **el piso de ~** the flat below

2 **~ de** under; **~ de este árbol** under *o* beneath this tree; **vive en el piso ~ del nuestro** he lives in the flat below ours; **pasamos (por) ~ del puente** we went under *o* underneath the bridge; **me gusta nadar (por) ~ del agua** I like swimming underwater *o* under the water; **el Barcelona sigue por ~ del Atlético** Barcelona is still (trailing) behind Atlético; **el rango por ~ del de capitán** the rank below that of captain; **por ~ de la media** below average; **trabajan por ~ de sus posibilidades** they are working below their capabilities

▾ **debate** SM debate; **un ~ parlamentario** a parliamentary debate; **no entro en el ~ de si es bueno o malo** I won't enter into the debate about whether it is good or bad; **tuvimos un pequeño ~ sobre la película** we had a little discussion *o* debate about the film; **conceptos como el marxismo están a ~** concepts like Marxism are being re-evaluated; **poner o sacar un tema a ~** to raise an issue for discussion

▾ **debatir** ▸conjug 3a◂ Ⓐ VT 1 [+ *ley, presupuesto*] to debate

2 [+ *punto de vista, problema*] to discuss, debate

Ⓑ **debatirse** VPR 1 (= *luchar*) to struggle; **~se entre la vida y la muerte** to be fighting for one's life

2 (= *forcejear*) to writhe

debe SM (*en cuenta*) debit side; **asentar algo al ~ de algn** to debit sth to sb; **~ y haber** debit and credit

debelador(a) SM/F conqueror

debelar ▸conjug 1a◂ VT to conquer

▾ **deber** ▸conjug 2a◂ Ⓐ VT [+ *dinero, explicación, respeto*] to owe; **me debes cinco dólares** you owe me five dollars; **¿qué le debo?** (*en bares, tiendas*) how much (is it)?, how much do I owe you?; **me deben muchos favores** they owe me a lot of favours; **te debo una disculpa** I owe you an apology; **el teatro español debe mucho a Buero Vallejo** Spanish theatre owes a lot to Buero Vallejo; **todo lo que he conseguido se lo debo a mi padre** I have my father to thank for everything I have achieved, I owe everything I have achieved to my father

Ⓑ VI 1 (+ *INFIN*) (*obligación*) **debo intentar verla** I must try to see her; **no debes preocuparte** you mustn't worry; **no debes comer tanto** you shouldn't eat so much; **como debe ser** as it ought to *o* should be; **~ía cambiarse cada mes** it ought to *o* should be changed every month; **habrías debido traerlo** you ought to have *o* should have brought it; **no ~ías haberla dejado sola** you shouldn't have left her alone; **debíamos haber salido ayer** we were to have *o* should have left yesterday

2 (+ *INFIN*) (*suposición*) **debe (de) ser brasileño** he must be a Brazilian; **debe (de) hacer mucho frío allí** it must be very cold there; **debe (de) ser así** it must be like that, that's how it must be; **he debido (de) perderlo** I must have lost it; **no debe (de) ser muy caro** it can't be very dear; **no debe (de) tener mucho dinero** he can't have much money; **no debía (de) tener más de dieciocho años** she couldn't have been more than eighteen; **no debía (de) andar lejos de los 200.000 libros** it can't have been far off 200,000 books; **no debía (de) quedar ninguno vivo** it is unlikely that any survived

Ⓒ **deberse** VPR 1 **~se a algo** (= *tener por causa*) to be due to sth; **el retraso se debió a una huelga** the delay was due to a strike; **el accidente se debió al mal tiempo** the accident was caused by the bad weather; **se debe a que no hay carbón** it is because (of the fact that) there's no coal; **puede ~se a que ...** it may be because ...; **¿a qué se debe esto?** what is the reason for this?, why is this?; **¿a qué se debe el aumento?** what is the reason for the increase?; **no se sabe realmente a qué se debe la inestabilidad** we don't really know the reason for the instability

2 **~se a algn** (= *tener obligación hacia*) to have a duty to sb; **yo me debo a mis lectores** I have a duty to my readers; **se debe a su pueblo** he has a duty to his people

Ⓓ SM 1 (= *obligación*) duty; **mi ~ es advertir al Gobierno** it's my duty to warn the Government; **era mi ~ de hijo** it was my duty as a son; **es un ~ para con la comunidad** it's a duty to the community; **nunca hubiera faltado a su ~** he would never have failed in *o* to do his duty; **cumplir con un ~** to perform a duty, carry out a duty; **últimos ~es** last rites
► **deber ciudadano** civic duty

2 (= *deuda*) debt

3 **deberes** (*Escol*) homework *sing*; **~es de francés** French homework; **hacer los ~es del colegio** to do one's homework; **el profe me ha puesto unos ~es** the teacher has set me some homework

debidamente ADV [*ajustar, comer*] properly; [*cumplimentar*] duly; **si te comportas ~** if you behave properly; **un documento ~ redactado** a properly drawn up document

▾ **debido** ADJ 1 (= *adecuado*) due, proper; **a su ~ tiempo** in due course; **con el ~ respeto** with all due respect; **con las debidas precauciones** with all due *o* the necessary precautions; **en debida forma** duly; **como es ~** as is (only) right and proper; **no lo hizo como es ~** he didn't do it properly; **una fiesta como es ~** a proper *o* real party; **un padre como es ~ no haría eso** a true father would not do that; **más de lo ~** more than necessary

2 **~ a** owing to, because of; **~ a ello** owing to *o* because of this; **~ a la falta de agua** owing to *o* because of the water shortage; **~ a que** owing to *o* because of the fact that

débil Ⓐ ADJ 1 [*persona*] (*gen*) weak; (*extremadamente*) feeble; (*por mala salud o avanzada edad*) frail; **se encuentra un poco ~ de salud** his health is rather frail, he is in rather poor health

2 [*carácter*] weak; [*esfuerzo*] feeble, half-

hearted

3 (= *poco intenso*) [*voz, ruido*] faint; [*luz*] dim

Ⓑ SMF **es un ~ mental** he's a bit mentally deficient; *ver tb* **económicamente**

▼**debilidad** SF 1 (= *falta de fuerzas*) (*gen*) weakness; (*extrema*) feebleness; (*por mala salud o avanzada edad*) frailty ► **debilidad senil** senility

2 [*de carácter*] weakness; [*de esfuerzo*] feebleness, half-heartedness; **la ~ de su fuerza de voluntad** his lack of willpower

3 (= *poca intensidad*) [*de voz, ruido*] faintness; [*de luz*] dimness

4 (= *inclinación*) **los niños son mi ~** I love *o* adore children; **tengo ~ por el chocolate** I have a weakness for chocolate; **tener ~ por algn** to have a soft spot for sb

debilitación SF weakening, debilitation

debilitador ADJ, **debilitante** ADJ debilitating

debilitamiento SM = **debilitación**

debilitar ▸conjug 1a◂ Ⓐ VT 1 (*Med*) [+ *persona, sistema inmunológico*] to weaken, debilitate; [+ *salud*] to weaken

2 [+ *resistencia*] to weaken, impair

Ⓑ **debilitarse** VPR 1 [*persona*] to grow weaker, weaken

2 [*voz, luz*] to grow *o* become fainter

débilmente ADV [*sonreír, golpear, moverse*] weakly; [*protestar, quejarse*] half-heartedly; [*lucir, brillar*] dimly

debitar ▸conjug 1a◂ VT (*Com*) to debit

débito SM 1 (*Com*) (= *debe*) debit; (= *deuda*) debt ► **débitos varios** (*LAm*) [*de hotel*] sundries

2 ► **débito conyugal** conjugal duty, marital duty

debocar* ▸conjug 1g◂ VT, VI (*LAm*) to vomit, throw up

Débora SF Deborah

debú SM (*pl* **debús**), **debut** [de'βu] SM (*pl* **debuts**) début

debutante Ⓐ ADJ novice *antes de s*; **jugador ~** new player, new cap

Ⓑ SMF 1 (= *principiante*) beginner; (*en sociedad*) debutante

2 (*Dep*) new player; **el ~ marcó en el minuto 29** the new player scored in the 29th minute (of his first match)

debutar ▸conjug 1a◂ VI to make one's debut

década SF 1 (= *decenio*) decade; **la ~ de los noventa** the nineties

2 (= *serie*) set of ten, series of ten

decadencia SF (= *proceso*) decline, decay; (= *estado*) decadence; **estar en franca ~** to be in full decline; **caer en ~** to fall into decline

decadente ADJ [*moral, sociedad*] decadent; [*imperio, salud*] declining

decaer ▸conjug 2n◂ VI 1 [*imperio, país*] to decline; **desde que cerraron la fábrica el pueblo ha decaído** since they closed the factory the town has gone downhill

2 (= *disminuir*) [*entusiasmo, interés*] to wane, fade (away); [*esperanzas*] to fade; **su ánimo decayó tras la muerte de su padre** he lost heart after his father's death; **¡ánimo, que no decaiga!** bear up, don't lose heart!; **¡que no decaiga la fiesta!** come on, let's keep the party going!

3 (= *empeorar*) [*salud*] to fail, decline; [*enfermo*] to deteriorate, fail

4 (*Com*) [*demanda*] to fall off; [*calidad*] to decline, fall off

5 **~ en algo: ha decaído en belleza** her beauty has faded; **su fuerza dramática decae en intensidad al final** its dramatic force declines in intensity at the end

6 (*Náut*) to drift, drift off course

decagramo SM decagram

decaído ADJ down, low; **estar ~** to be down *o* low

decaimiento SM 1 (= *decadencia*) decline, decay

2 (= *empeoramiento*) [*de salud*] weakening; [*de ánimo*] discouragement

3 (*Com*) falling-off

decalaje SM shift of time, time lag

decalitro SM decalitre, decaliter (*EEUU*)

decálogo SM decalogue

decámetro SM decametre, decameter (*EEUU*)

decanato SM 1 (= *cargo*) deanship

2 (= *despacho*) dean's office

decano/a SM/F 1 (*Univ*) dean

2 [*de junta, grupo*] (= *de mayor edad*) senior member; (= *de más antigüedad*) doyen/doyenne

decantación SF 1 (*Téc*) decanting, decantation (*frm*)

2 (= *preferencia*) leaning (**hacia** towards)

decantamiento SM leaning

decantar[1] ▸conjug 1a◂ Ⓐ VT [+ *vino*] to decant; [+ *líquido*] to pour off

Ⓑ **decantarse** VPR **~se hacia algo** to move towards sth, evolve in the direction of sth; **~se por algo/algn** to opt for sth/sb, choose sth/sb; **~se por hacer algo** to opt to do sth, choose to do sth

decantar[2] ▸conjug 1a◂ VT to praise; **el tan decantado edificio** (*iró*) this much-vaunted building

decapado SM [*de pintura*] stripping

decapante SM [*de pintura*] paint stripper

decapar ▸conjug 1a◂ VT [+ *pintura, barniz*] to strip

decapitar ▸conjug 1a◂ VT to behead, decapitate

decasílabo Ⓐ ADJ decasyllabic, ten-syllable

Ⓑ SM decasyllable

decatlón SM decathlon

deceleración SF deceleration

decena SF 1 (= *diez*) **una ~ de barcos** (= *diez*) ten ships; (= *aproximadamente diez*) some *o* about ten ships; **~s de miles de manifestantes** tens of thousands of demonstrators

2 **decenas** (*Mat*) tens; **contar por ~s** to count in tens; **vender por ~s** to sell in tens

decenal ADJ decennial; **plan ~** ten-year plan

decencia SF 1 (= *pudor*) decency; (= *decoro*) decorum; (= *honestidad*) respectability; **faltar a la ~** to offend against decency *o* propriety

2 (= *aseo*) cleanliness, tidiness

decenio SM decade

decente ADJ 1 (= *pudoroso*) decent; (= *honesto*) respectable

2 (= *aceptable*) [*sueldo, empleo*] decent

3 (= *aseado*) clean, tidy

decentemente ADV 1 (= *con pudor*) [*comportarse*] respectably, decently; [*vestir*] respectably

2 (= *aseadamente*) tidily

decepción SF disappointment; **llevarse** *o* **sufrir una ~** to be disappointed

decepcionado ADJ disappointed; **estar ~ con algo** to be disappointed with sth

decepcionante ADJ disappointing

decepcionar ▸conjug 1a◂ VT to disappoint

decesado/a SM/F (*LAm*) deceased person

deceso SM (*LAm*) decease, passing

dechado SM 1 (= *modelo*) model; **no es ningún ~ de perfección** it isn't a model of perfection; **es un ~ de virtudes** she's a paragon of virtue

2 (*Cos*) sampler

decibel SM, **decibelio** SM decibel

decibélico ADJ loud, noisy

decible ADJ expressible; **eso no es ~** that cannot be expressed, there are no words to say it

decididamente ADV 1 (= *con decisión*) decisively; **tenemos que afrontar ~ el futuro** we have to face the future decisively; **entró ~ en la sala** he entered the room purposefully

2 (= *obviamente*) decidedly; **un poema ~ romántico** a decidedly romantic poem

3 (= *sin duda*) definitely; **~, vuelven a estar de moda los tacones** high heels are definitely back in fashion

▼**decidido** ADJ 1 (= *firme*) [*apoyo*] wholehearted; [*paso, gesto*] purposeful; [*esfuerzo, intento*] determined; [*defensor, partidario*] staunch, strong; [*actitud, persona*] resolute; **dio su apoyo ~ al proyecto** he gave his solid *o* wholehearted support to the project; **hubo un ~ apoyo a su propuesta entre la derecha** there was solid support for his proposal from the right; **andaba con paso ~** she walked purposefully *o* with a purposeful stride; **los más ~s saltaron al agua** the most resolute jumped into the water

2 **estar ~: voy a dejar el trabajo, ya estoy ~** I'm going to leave my job, I've made up my mind *o* I've decided; **estar ~ a hacer algo** to be resolved *o* determined to do sth; **estaba decidida a irse con él** she'd made up her mind to go with him, she was resolved *o* determined to go with him

▼**decidir** ▸conjug 3a◂ Ⓐ VT 1 (= *tomar una decisión*) to decide; **¿habéis decidido lo que vais a hacer?** have you decided what you are going to do?; **después de pensarlo mucho he decidido que sí** after giving it a lot of thought, I've decided to go ahead; **~ hacer algo** to decide to do sth; **decidieron no ir** they decided not to go

2 (= *determinar*) [+ *futuro, resultado*] to decide; [+ *asunto, disputa*] to settle, resolve; **el penalti decidió el partido** the penalty decided the match; **el resultado de los exámenes ~á su futuro** the exam results will decide her future

3 (= *convencer*) **¿qué fue lo que al final te decidió?** what finally made up your mind?, what finally decided you?, what finally made you decide?; **la huelga de trenes me decidió a ir en coche** the rail strike made me decide to take the car

Ⓑ VI to decide; **nadie va a ~ por ellos** no one will make the decision *o* decide for them; **tuvo que ~ entre varias opciones** she had to choose *o* decide from a number of options; **el juez decidió en nuestro favor** the judge ruled in our favour; **~ sobre algo** to decide on sth, make a decision on sth

Ⓒ **decidirse** VPR to decide, make up one's mind; **no me he decidido todavía** I haven't

➤ LENGUA Y USO: **debilidad 4** 34.2 **decidido 2** 35.2 **decidir A1** 35.2

decided *o* made up my mind yet; **¡decídete ya, que se hace tarde!** make up your mind! it's getting late; **~se a hacer algo** to decide to do sth, make up one's mind to do sth; **si me decido a marcharme de París ...** if I decide to *o* make up my mind to leave Paris ...; **ojalá se decida a visitarnos** I hope she decides to visit us; **parece que no se decide a llover** it looks as if it's not going to rain just yet; **~se por algo** to decide on sth; **se decidió por el más barato** she decided on the cheapest

decidor(a) Ⓐ ADJ [1] (= *gracioso*) witty, amusing
[2] (= *elocuente*) fluent, eloquent
Ⓑ SM/F [1] (= *chistoso*) wit, witty talker
[2] (= *narrador*) fluent speaker, eloquent speaker

decil SM decile

decilitro SM decilitre, deciliter (*EEUU*)

décima SF [1] [*de segundo, grado*] tenth; **tiene 37 y tres ~s** his temperature is 37.3 (degrees); **tiene sólo unas ~s (de fiebre)** he's only got a slight temperature
[2] (*Rel*) tithe
[3] (*Literat, Hist*) *a ten-line stanza*

decimación SF decimation

decimal Ⓐ ADJ decimal
Ⓑ SM decimal
Ⓒ SF ► **decimal periódica** recurring decimal

decimalización SF decimalization

decimalizar ▸conjug 1f◂ VT to decimalize

decímetro SM decimetre, decimeter (*EEUU*)

décimo Ⓐ ADJ tenth; *ver tb* **sexto**
Ⓑ SM [1] (*Mat*) tenth
[2] (*tb* **~ de lotería**) ≈ lottery ticket; → LOTERÍA, → EL GORDO

decimoctavo ADJ eighteenth; *ver tb* **sexto A**

decimocuarto ADJ fourteenth; *ver tb* **sexto A**

decimonónicamente ADV in the style of the 19th century

decimonónico ADJ nineteenth-century *antes de s*

decimonono ADJ, **decimonoveno** ADJ nineteenth; *ver tb* **sexto A**

decimoprimero ADJ eleventh; *ver tb* **sexto A**

decimoquinto ADJ fifteenth; *ver tb* **sexto A**

decimosegundo ADJ twelfth; *ver tb* **sexto A**

decimoséptimo ADJ seventeenth; *ver tb* **sexto A**

decimosexto ADJ sixteenth; *ver tb* **sexto A**

decimotercero ADJ, **decimotercio** ADJ thirteenth; *ver tb* **sexto A**

decir

▸conjug 3o◂
[A] VERBO TRANSITIVO
[B] VERBO INTRANSITIVO
[C] VERBO PRONOMINAL
[D] SUSTANTIVO MASCULINO

Para otras expresiones con el participio, ver ***dicho***.

Ⓐ VERBO TRANSITIVO

[1] [= ***afirmar***] to say; **ya sabe ~ varias palabras** she can already say several words, she already knows several words; **—tengo prisa —dijo** "I'm in a hurry," she said; **viene y dice: —estás despedido*** he goes "you're fired"*; **olvídalo, no he dicho nada** forget I said anything; **¿decía usted?** you were saying?; **como dicen los madrileños** as they say in Madrid; **como decía mi abuela** as my grandmother used to say; **como iba diciendo ...** as I was saying ...; **¿cómo ha dicho usted?** pardon?, what did you say?; **~ para** *o* **entre sí** to say to o.s.

◆ **decir que** to say (that); **mi amigo dice que eres muy guapa** my friend says (that) you're very pretty; **dicen que ...** they say (that) ..., people say (that) ...; **el cartel dice claramente que ...** the sign says clearly *o* clearly states that ...; **~ que sí/no** to say yes/no; **—¿viene? —dice que sí** "is she coming?" — "she says she is *o* she says so"; **la miré y me dijo que sí/no con la cabeza** I looked at her and she nodded/shook her head; *ver tb* **adiós B**

[2]

◆ **decir algo a algn** to tell sb sth; **¿quién te lo dijo?** who told you?; **se lo dije bien claro, pero no me hizo caso** I told her quite clearly, but she didn't take any notice of me; **tengo algo que ~te** there's something I want to tell you, I've got something to tell you; **hoy nos dicen las notas** they're telling *o* giving us our results today

◆ **decir a algn que** + *INDIC* to tell sb (that); **me dijo que no vendría** he told me (that) he wouldn't come; **ya te dije que no tiene ni idea** I told you he hasn't got a clue; **¿no te digo que no puedo ir?** I've already told you I can't go

◆ **decir a algn que** + *SUBJUN* (= *ordenar*) to tell sb to do sth; (= *pedir*) to ask sb to do sth; **la profesora me dijo que esperara fuera** the teacher told me to wait outside; **le dije que fuera más tarde** I told her to go later; **dile que venga a cenar mañana con nosotros** ask him to come and have supper with us tomorrow; **te digo que te calles** I said shut up

[3] [= ***contar***] [+ *mentiras, verdad, secreto*] to tell; **~ tonterías** to talk nonsense; *ver tb* **verdad 1**

[4] [= ***llamar***] to call; **¿cómo le dicen a esto en Perú?** what do they call this in Peru?; **se llama Francisco, pero le dicen Paco** his name is Francisco, but he's known as Paco; **le dicen "el torero"** he's known as "el torero"; **en México se le dice "recámara" al dormitorio** in Mexico they say "recámara" instead of "dormitorio"; **me dijo de todo** he called me all the names under the sun

[5] [= ***opinar***] to say; **podemos ir a Portugal, ¿tú qué dices?** we could go to Portugal, what do you say?; **¿tu familia qué dice de la boda?** what does your family say about the wedding?

[6] [***rectificando***] **había 8, digo 9** there were 8, I mean 9; **dirá usted aquel otro** you must mean that other one; **¡qué digo!** what am I saying?

[7] [***texto***] to say; **no puedo leer lo que dice** I can't read what it says; **no me dice nada este libro** this book leaves me cold; **como dice el refrán ...** as the saying goes...

[8] [+ ***misa***] to say

[9] [***locuciones en indicativo***] **digo ...** (*Méx*) well, er ...; **mis súbditos se presentarán ante mí ¡he dicho!** my subjects shall appear before me: I have spoken!; **y dice bien** and he is quite right; **como quien dice** (= *de alguna manera*) so to speak; (= *aproximadamente*) in a way, more or less; **aunque no es el director es, como quien dice, el que manda en la empresa** although he isn't the manager, he's the person in charge, so to speak, of the company; **está, como quien dice, aquí al lado** it's just round the corner, as they say; **como quien no dice nada** quite casually, as though it wasn't important; **lo mismo digo** likewise; **—gracias por todo —lo mismo digo** "thank you for everything" — "likewise!" *o* "thanks to you too!"; **pero dice mal** but he is wrong; **pues si esto te parece mucha gente, no te digo nada en verano** if you think this is a lot of people, you should see it in summer; **no lo digo por ti** I'm not referring to you, I'm not getting at you; **sí, porque tú lo digas** yes, sir, aye, aye, captain! (*iró*); **¿qué me dices?** (*sorpresa*) you don't say!, well I never!; (*incredulidad*) come off it!; **si tú lo dices** if you say so; **eso digo yo** that's (just) what I say; **deberías buscar trabajo, vamos, digo yo** you ought to look for a job, that's what I say, if you ask me, you ought to look for a job; **¡si te lo digo yo!** of course it's true!; **¡lo digo yo y basta!** you will do it because I say so!; **¡y que lo digas!** you can say that again!; ✦***MODISMOS*** **~ digo donde dijo Diego** to take back what one said earlier; **no dijo ni pío** ◊ **no dijo esta boca es mía** she never once opened her mouth; ✦***REFRÁN*** **dime con quien andas y te diré quien eres** a man is known by the company he keeps

[10] [***locuciones en infinitivo***] **dar que ~ (a la gente)** to make people talk, set tongues wagging; **es ~** that is (to say); **mi prima, es ~, la hija de Ana** my cousin, that is (to say) Ana's daughter; **ir a ~**: **¡a mí me lo vas a ~!** you're telling me!; **es mucho ~** that's saying something; **ni que ~ tiene que ...** it goes without saying that ...; **no hay más que ~** there's nothing more to say; **para ~lo con otras palabras** to put it another way, in other words; **~ por ~** to talk for talking's sake; **por así ~lo** so to speak; **querer ~** to mean; **¿qué quiere ~ "spatha"?** what does "spatha" mean?; **¿qué quiere usted ~ con eso?** what do you mean by that?; **¿querrás ~ un millón, no un billón?** do you mean a million rather than a billion?; **ya es ~** that's saying something; **les ha costado más cara que mi casa, y eso ya es ~** it cost them more than my house did, and that's saying something

[11] [***locuciones en subjuntivo, imperativo***] **no es que yo lo diga, pero ...** it's not because I say so, but ...; **es, digamos, un comerciante** he's a dealer, for want of a better word, he's a sort of dealer; **¡haberlo dicho!** ◊ **¡me lo hubieras dicho!** you could have told me *o* said!; **digámoslo así** so to speak, for want of a better word; **digan lo que digan** whatever they say; **y no digamos ...** not to mention ...; **y su madre, no digamos** not to mention his mother; **no es muy guapa que digamos** she's not what you'd call pretty, she's not exactly pretty; **no estuvo muy cortés, que digamos** he wasn't what you'd call polite, he wasn't exactly polite; **¡no me digas!** (*sorpresa*) you don't say!, well I never!; (*incredulidad*) come off it!; **¿qué quieres que te diga?** what can I say?

[12] [***locuciones en condicional***] **¿cómo (lo) diría yo?** how shall I put it?; **¿cómo diríamos?** how shall I put it?; **¡quién lo diría!** would you believe it!, who would have

thought it!

13

◆ **el qué dirán**: **pero no quiso por el qué dirán** but she didn't want to because of what people might say; **se preocupa mucho por el qué dirán** she's always worried about what people will say *o* think

Ⓑ VERBO INTRANSITIVO

1 *invitando a hablar* **—¿te puedo pedir un favor? —dime** "can I ask you a favour?" — "go ahead"; **¿diga?** ◊ **¿dígame?** (*al teléfono*) hello?; **usted dirá** (*invitando a hablar*) go ahead; (*sirviendo bebida*) say when; (*en tienda*) can I help you?; **—¿te gustaría cambiar de coche? —¡hombre, ya me dirás!** "would you like a new car?" — "you bet I would!"

2 *= indicar* **su nombre no me dice nada** her name doesn't mean anything to me; **su mirada lo dice todo** her expression says it all *o* speaks volumes; **eso dice mucho de su personalidad** that says a lot about her personality; **una situación que tan mal dice de nuestro gobierno** a situation which shows our government in such a bad light

Ⓒ **decirse** VERBO PRONOMINAL

1 *uso reflexivo* **yo sé lo que me digo** I know what I'm talking about *o* saying; **me dije que no volvería a hacerlo** I promised myself *o* told myself I wouldn't do it again; **él se lo dice todo** he seems to have all the answers; **al verlo me dije: —han pasado muchos años** when I saw him, I said *o* thought to myself "it's been a long time"

2 *uso impersonal* **se dice** it is said, they *o* people say; **no se diría eso ahora** you'd never say such a thing nowadays; **¿cómo se dice "cursi" en inglés?** what's the English for "cursi"?, how do you say "cursi" in English?; **se les ha dicho que ...** they have been told that ...; **y no se diga ...** not to mention ...; **no se diga que ...** never let it be said that ...; **se diría que no está** she doesn't seem to be here; **alto, lo que se dice alto, no es** he's not what you'd call tall, he's not exactly tall; **hablar portugués, lo que se dice hablar, no sé** I can't really speak Portuguese properly; **esto es lo que se dice un queso** now this is what I call a cheese; ✦*MODISMO* **eso se dice muy pronto** that's easier said than done

3 *= llamarse* to be called; **esta plaza se dice de la Revolución** this is called Revolution Square

Ⓓ SUSTANTIVO MASCULINO

1 *= dicho* saying; ✦*MODISMO* **es un ~** it's a manner of speaking; **pongamos, es un ~, que Picasso naciera en Madrid ...** let's suppose, just for the sake of argument, that Picasso had been born in Madrid...

2 **a ~ de** according to; **a ~ de la gente mayor** according to the older generation; **a ~ de todos** by all accounts

decisión SF 1 (*= determinación*) decision; (*Jur*) judgment; **forzar una ~** to force the issue; **tomar una ~** to make *o* take a decision ► **decisión por mayoría** majority decision

2 (*= firmeza*) decisiveness

3 (*= voluntad*) determination

decisivo ADJ [*resultado, factor, influencia, papel*] decisive; [*argumento*] winning; [*voto*] deciding; **una etapa decisiva de mi vida** a crucial *o* decisive stage in my life

DECIR

¿"Say" o "tell"?

• **Decir** se puede traducir por **say** o por **tell**. Por regla general, **say** simplemente *dice* y **tell** *informa* u *ordena hacer algo*.

• **Decir** generalmente se traduce por **say** en estilo directo. Normalmente no lleva un complemento de persona pero si se menciona a quién se está dirigiendo el hablante, el complemento de persona tiene que ir precedido por la preposición **to**:

"Ya son las tres", dije.
"It's already three o'clock," I said

"¡Qué tiempo más malo!" Eso fue lo único que me dijo
"What awful weather!" That's all he said to me

• En estilo indirecto, **decir** se puede traducir por **say** cuando simplemente se cuenta lo que alguien ha dicho. Si **say** lleva complemento de persona, éste se coloca después del complemento directo:

Dijo que se tenía que marchar
He said he had to leave

Me dijo algo que no entendí
He said something to me that I didn't understand

• **Decir** se traduce por **tell** cuando se *informa* o se *ordena hacer algo*. Suele llevar un objeto de persona sin la preposición **to**:

Me dijo que tenía una entrevista de trabajo
He told me he had a job interview

¡Te he dicho que no lo toques!
I told you not to touch it!

• Hay algunos usos idiomáticos en los que **decir** se traduce por **tell** aunque no lleva complemento de persona. Por ejemplo: **to tell the truth** (decir la verdad) y **to tell a lie** (decir una mentira).

Otros verbos

• Si **decir** va acompañado de un calificativo en español, a menudo se puede traducir al inglés por otros verbos que no sean **say** o **tell**:

"Lo he perdido todo", dijo entre sollozos
"I've lost everything," she sobbed

Dijo con voz ronca algo sobre necesitar un médico
He croaked something about needing a doctor

Para otros usos y ejemplos ver la entrada.

decisorio Ⓐ ADJ decision-making; **poderes ~s** decision-making powers; **proceso ~** decision-making process

Ⓑ SM (*Méx Jur*) judgment, verdict

declamación SF (*gen*) declamation; [*de poema*] recital, recitation

declamador(a) SM/F orator

declamar ▸conjug 1a◂ VT Ⓐ VT (*gen*) to declaim; [+ *versos, poema*] to recite

Ⓑ VI to declaim

declamatorio ADJ declamatory

declaración SF 1 (*= proclamación*) declaration ► **declaración de amor** declaration of love ► **declaración de derechos** (*Pol*) bill of rights ► **declaración de guerra** declaration of war ► **declaración de intenciones** declaration of intent ► **declaración de principios** declaration of principles ► **declaración de quiebra** declaration of bankruptcy

2 **declaraciones** (*a la prensa*) statement *sing*; **no quiso hacer declaraciones a los periodistas** he refused to talk to journalists, he refused to make a statement to journalists ► **declaraciones conjuntas** joint statement *sing*

3 (*a Hacienda*) tax return; **hacer la ~** to do one's tax return ► **declaración conjunta** joint tax return ► **declaración de aduana(s)** customs declaration ► **declaración de impuestos, declaración de ingresos, declaración de la renta** income tax return

4 (*Jur*) (*ante la policía, en juicio*) statement; **firmó una ~ falsa** he signed a false statement; **las declaraciones de los testigos son contradictorias** the evidence given by the witnesses is contradictory, the witnesses' statements are contradictory; **prestar ~** (*ante la policía*) to make a statement; (*en un juicio*) to give evidence, testify; **tomar la ~ a algn** to take a statement from sb ► **declaración de culpabilidad** plea of guilty, guilty plea ► **declaración de inocencia** plea of not guilty, not guilty plea ► **declaración inmediata** (*Méx*) verbal statement ► **declaración judicial** statement in court ► **declaración jurada** sworn statement, affidavit

5 [*de incendio, epidemia*] outbreak

6 (*Naipes*) bid

declaradamente ADV openly

declarado ADJ [*actitud, intención*] professed; **un ateo ~** a professed atheist

declarante SMF 1 (*Jur*) deponent

2 (*Naipes*) bidder

declarar ▸conjug 1a◂ Ⓐ VT 1 (*= proclamar*) [+ *guerra, independencia*] to declare; **Japón declaró la guerra a China** Japan declared war on China; **fue declarado el estado de sitio** a state of siege was declared; **el tribunal declaró la inconstitucionalidad de la ley** the court declared the law unconstitutional; **yo os declaro marido y mujer** I pronounce you man and wife; ✦*MODISMOS* **tener declarada la guerra a algo** to have declared war on sth; **tener declarada la guerra a algn** to have it in for sb*

2 (*= considerar*) to declare; **el tribunal médico lo declaró no apto para el servicio militar** the medical board declared him unfit for military service; **el bosque fue declarado zona protegida** the forest was declared a conservation area; **fue declarada abierta la competición** the competition was declared open; **el premio fue declarado desierto** the prize was not awarded; **este matrimonio podría ~se nulo** this marriage could be annulled; **~ culpable a algn** to find sb guilty; **~ inocente a algn** to find sb innocent

3 (*= manifestar*) (*en público, ante el juez*) to state; (*como anuncio, noticia*) to announce; **declaró su apoyo a la democracia** he stated his support for democracy; **el ministro declaró no saber nada del asunto** the minister stated that he knew nothing of the matter; **según declaró un portavoz del gobierno** as a government spokesperson announced

4 (*Com*) (*en la aduana, a Hacienda*) to declare; **¿(tiene) algo que ~?** (do you have) anything to declare?; **"nada que declarar"** "nothing to declare"

[5] (*Naipes*) to bid; **declaró dos picos** she bid two spades; **declaró menos de lo que tenía** he underbid
Ⓑ VI [1] (*Jur*) (= *testificar*) to give evidence, testify; **fue llamada a ~ por el juez** the judge called her to give evidence *o* to testify; **~ en falso** to commit perjury
[2] (= *declarar impuestos*) to submit one's tax return
[3] (*Naipes*) to bid
Ⓒ **declararse** VPR [1] (= *reconocerse*) to declare o.s.; **se han declarado objetores de conciencia** they have declared themselves conscientious objectors; **~se a favor de algo** to declare o.s. in favour of sth; **~se en bancarrota** *o* **quiebra** to declare o.s. bankrupt; **poco después de ~se abiertamente homosexual** shortly after coming out as a homosexual, shortly after announcing in public that he was a homosexual; **~se culpable** to plead guilty; **~se en huelga** to go on strike; **~se inocente** to plead not guilty; **~se en suspensión de pagos** to call in the receivers
[2] **~se a algn** to declare one's love to sb; **se le declaró en el jardín** he declared his love to her in the garden; **¿se te ha declarado ya?** has he told you he loves you yet?
[3] [*epidemia, guerra*] to break out; **se declaró un incendio en el almacén** a fire broke out in the warehouse; **el incendio se declaró en la cocina y se extendió por toda la casa** the fire started in the kitchen and spread throughout the house

declaratoria (*Jur*) Ⓐ ADJ declaratory
Ⓑ SF declaration

declinable ADJ declinable

declinación SF [1] (*Ling*) declension
[2] (*Astron, Náut*) declination
[3] (= *decaimiento*) decline, falling-off

▼ **declinar** ▸conjug 1a◂ Ⓐ VT [1] (= *rechazar*) [+ *honor, invitación*] to decline; (*Jur*) to reject; **declinamos cualquier responsabilidad** we cannot accept responsibility; **~ hacer algo** to decline to do sth
[2] (*Ling*) to decline
Ⓑ VI [1] (= *decaer*) to decline, decay
[2] (*liter*) [*día*] to draw to a close
[3] [*terreno*] to slope (away *o* down)
[4] (*Ling*) to decline

declive SM [1] [*de terreno, superficie*] incline, gradient; **un terreno en ~** sloping ground
[2] (= *decadencia*) decline; **en ~: es una ciudad en ~** it's a city in decline; **una ideología en ~** an ideology in decline *o* on the wane; **el consumo de alcohol está** *o* **va en ~** alcohol consumption is declining *o* is on the decline

decocción SF decoction

decodificador SM = **descodificador**

decodificar ▸conjug 1g◂ VT = **descodificar**

decolaje SM (*Andes, Chile*) take-off

decolar ▸conjug 1a◂ VI (*Andes, Chile*) to take off

decolorado ADJ [*pelo*] bleached; [*piel, ropa*] discoloured, discolored (*EEUU*)

decolorante SM bleaching agent

decolorar ▸conjug 1a◂ Ⓐ VT [+ *pelo*] to bleach; [+ *piel, ropa*] to discolour, discolor (*EEUU*)
Ⓑ **decolorarse** VPR [*pelo*] to get bleached; [*piel, ropa*] to get discoloured, become discolored (*EEUU*), fade; **el pelo se me ha decolorado con el sol** the sun has bleached my hair

➤ LENGUA Y USO: **declinar A1** 39.3

decomisar ▸conjug 1a◂ VT to seize, confiscate

decomiso SM seizure, confiscation

descongestionante SM decongestant

deconstrucción SF deconstruction

decoración SF [1] (= *adorno*) decoration ► **decoración de escaparates** window dressing ► **decoración de interiores, decoración del hogar** interior decorating
[2] (*Cine, Teat*) set, scenery

decorado SM (*Cine, Teat*) scenery, set

decorador(a) SM/F [1] [*de interiores*] decorator, interior decorator ► **decorador(a) de escaparates** window dresser
[2] (*Teat*) set designer

decorar¹ ▸conjug 1a◂ VT [+ *casa, habitación*] to decorate (**de** with)

decorar² ▸conjug 1a◂ VT [1] (= *aprender*) to learn, memorize
[2] (= *recitar*) to chorus

decorativo ADJ decorative

decoro SM [1] (= *decencia, dignidad*) decorum, decency ► **decoro virginal** maidenly modesty
[2] (= *honor*) honour, honor (*EEUU*), respect

decorosamente ADV decorously

decoroso ADJ [*conducta, lenguaje*] decorous; [*empleo, sueldo*] decent

decrecer ▸conjug 2d◂ VI [1] (= *disminuir*) [*importancia, interés*] to decrease; [*nivel de agua*] to subside, go down
[2] [*días*] to draw in

decreciente ADJ decreasing, diminishing

decrecimiento SM, **decremento** SM decrease

decrépito ADJ decrepit

decrepitud SF decrepitude

decretar ▸conjug 1a◂ Ⓐ VT [1] (= *ordenar*) to order; (*por decreto*) to decree; **~ que** to decree that
[2] [+ *premio*] to award (**a** to); **el árbitro ha decretado penalti** the referee has awarded a penalty
[3] (*Méx*) [+ *dividendo*] to declare
Ⓑ VI (*Jur*) to deliver a judgment

decretazo* SM *decree that comes into force without being agreed on by a majority*

decreto SM decree, order; (*Parl*) act; **real ~** royal decree; **por real ~** (*lit*) by royal decree; (*fig*) compulsorily, willy-nilly

decreto-ley SM (*pl* **decretos-leyes**) order in council, government decree

decúbito SM (*Med*) ► **decúbito prono** prone position ► **decúbito supino** supine position

decuplar ▸conjug 1a◂ VT, **decuplicar** ▸conjug 1g◂ VT to multiply tenfold, increase tenfold

décuplo Ⓐ ADJ tenfold
Ⓑ SM **es el ~ de lo que era** it is ten times what it was, it has increased tenfold

decurso SM (*liter*) **en el ~ de los años** over the years; **en el ~ del tiempo** in the course of time

dedada SF (= *cantidad*) (*lit*) thimbleful; (*fig*) very small quantity; **una ~ de mermelada** a spot *o* dab of jam; **una ~ de pimienta** a pinch of pepper; ✦**MODISMO dar una ~ de miel a algn** to give sb a crumb of comfort

dedal SM [1] (*Cos*) thimble
[2] (= *cantidad*) thimbleful

dedalera SF foxglove

dédalo SM [1] (= *laberinto*) labyrinth
[2] (= *lío*) tangle, mess

dedazo SM fingermark

dedicación SF [1] (= *entrega*) dedication (**a** to); **las profesiones de ~ humanitaria** the caring professions; **con ~ exclusiva** *o* **plena** full-time *antes de s*; **trabajar con ~ plena** to work full-time; **"dedicación plena"** "full-time"
[2] [*de discurso, libro*] dedication
[3] (*Rel*) consecration

dedicar ▸conjug 1g◂ Ⓐ VT [1] [+ *obra, canción*] to dedicate; **dedico este poema a mis padres** this poem is dedicated to my parents; **me dedicó una copia firmada de su última novela** she presented me with a signed copy of her latest novel; **quisiera ~ unas palabras de agradecimiento a …** I should like to address a few words of thanks to …; **el festival dedicó un homenaje al actor** the festival paid tribute to the actor
[2] [+ *tiempo, espacio, atención*] to devote, give; [+ *esfuerzo*] to devote; **dedico un día a la semana a ordenar mis papeles** I devote *o* give one day a week to organizing my paperwork; **ha dedicado toda su vida a los derechos humanos** she has dedicated *o* devoted her whole life to human rights; **dedica este terreno al cultivo del tulipán** he uses this land for growing tulips; **un programa dedicado a los deportes de invierno** a programme about *o* on winter sports
[3] (*Rel*) to dedicate, consecrate
Ⓑ **dedicarse** VPR [1] (*como profesión*) **~se a**: **se dedica a la enseñanza** he is a teacher, he's in teaching; **¿a qué se dedica usted?** what do you do (for a living)?; **se dedican a arreglar electrodomésticos** they repair domestic appliances
[2] (*como afición*) **~se a**: **se dedica a ver la tele todo el día** he spends the whole day watching TV; **en el verano se dedicó a la cerámica** he spent the summer doing *o* making pottery; **¡dedícate a lo tuyo!** mind your own business!
[3] (= *entregarse*) **~se a** to devote o.s. to; **se dedicó completamente a cuidar de sus padres** she devoted herself entirely to looking after her parents

dedicatoria SF dedication, inscription

dedicatorio ADJ dedicatory

dedil SM fingerstall

dedillo SM **conocer algo al ~** to know sth like the back of one's hand; **cumplir una orden al ~** to follow an order to the letter; **saber algo al ~** to have sth at one's fingertips

dedismo* SM arbitrary selection, arbitrary nomination

dedo SM [1] [*de mano, guante*] finger; [*de pie*] toe; **con la punta** *o* **la yema de los ~s** with one's fingertips; **apuntar** *o* **señalar algo/a algn con el ~** (*señalando*) to point at sth/sb; (*acusando*) to point the finger at sth/sb; **meterse el ~ en la nariz** to pick one's nose; ✦**MODISMOS a ~***: **vine a ~** I hitched here*; **he viajado por toda Alemania a ~** I hitched all round Germany*; **ha entrado a ~** he got the job because he knew somebody, he got the job through contacts; **han adjudicado a ~ todas las obras** they handed out all the building contracts to people they knew; **co-**

gerse los ~s (*Esp*) = **pillarse los dedos**; **contarse con los ~s** to count on one's fingers; **mis amigos se pueden contar con los ~s de una mano** I can count my friends on the fingers of one hand; **dale un ~ y se toma hasta el codo** give him an inch and he'll take a mile; **escaparse de entre los ~s** to slip through one's fingers; **hacer ~** (*Esp**) to hitch*; **hacer ~s** (*Mús*) to practise one's scales; **no levantar** *o* **mover un ~** not to lift a finger; **pillarse los ~s** (*Esp*) to get one's fingers burned; **poner el ~ en la llaga** (*de error*) to put one's finger on it; (*de tema delicado*) to touch a raw nerve; **poner el ~ en el renglón** (*Méx*) to put one's finger on it ► **dedo anular** ring finger ► **dedo auricular** little finger ► **dedo cordial**, **dedo (del) corazón**, **dedo (de en) medio** middle finger ► **dedo (en) martillo** hammer toe ► **dedo gordo** [*de la mano*] thumb; [*del pie*] big toe ► **dedo índice** index finger, forefinger ► **dedo meñique** [*de la mano*] little finger, pinkie (*EEUU, Escocia**); [*del pie*] little toe ► **dedo pulgar** thumb; *ver tb* **anillo**, **chupar**, **cruzar**, **ligero**

[2] (= *medida*) [*de altura, grosor*] *about an inch*; [*de cantidad*] drop; **cayeron cuatro ~s de nieve** about four inches of snow fell; **hay que meterle el bajo unos dos ~s** you'll have to turn up the trousers a couple of inches; **ponme un ~ de coñac** give me a drop of brandy; **dos deditos nada más** just a little drop; ✦***MODISMOS*** **estar a dos ~s de algo** to be *o* come within an inch *o* an ace of sth; **no tener dos ~s de frente*** to be as thick as two short planks*; **si tuvieras dos ~s de frente no te habrías metido en este lío** if you had any sense at all you wouldn't have got into this mess

dedocracia* SF *arbitrary exercise of power*

deducción SF [1] (*Fil*) (= *método*) deduction; (= *razonamiento*) inference
[2] (*Com*) deduction

deducible ADJ [1] (= *inferible, lógico*) deducible (**de** from); **según es fácilmente ~** as may readily be deduced
[2] (*en la declaración de la renta*) tax-deductible, deductible (*EEUU*)

▼**deducir** ▸conjug 3n◂ VT [1] (= *inferir*) [+ *razonamiento, conclusión*] to deduce, infer (**de** from); [+ *fórmula*] to derive (**de** from)
[2] (= *descontar*) to deduct; **deducidos los gastos** less charges

deductivo ADJ deductive

defalcar ▸conjug 1g◂ VT = **desfalcar**

defecación SF defecation

defecar ▸conjug 1g◂ VI to defecate

defección SF defection

defectible ADJ [1] (= *que puede fallar*) fallible, imperfect
[2] (= *defectuoso*) faulty

defectivo ADJ (*Ling*) defective

defecto SM [1] [*de persona*] (*físico*) defect; (*de personalidad*) fault, shortcoming; **un ~ congénito** a congenital defect; **el ~ que tiene es su mal genio** his one fault *o* shortcoming is his bad temper, the one flaw in his character is his bad temper; **su único ~ es que no sabe escribir a máquina** his only shortcoming is that he can't type ► **defecto de fonación**, **defecto del habla**, **defecto de pronunciación** speech defect, speech impediment ► **defecto de visión**: **tiene un ~ de visión** he has defective eyesight ► **defecto físico** physical defect
[2] [*de máquina, sistema*] fault; [*de tela, vestido, ornamento*] flaw, defect; **el ~ de tu teoría es su superficialidad** the flaw in your theory is its superficiality; **tiene un ~ de fábrica** *o* **fabricación** it has a manufacturing defect *o* fault, it's faulty *o* defective
[3] (*Jur*) ► **defecto de forma** technicality ► **defecto legal** legal defect
[4] **en su ~: Manolo, o en su ~, Gonzalo** Manolo, or failing him *o* failing that, Gonzalo; **por ~** (*Inform*) by default; ✦***MODISMO*** **pecar por ~**: **antes no paraba de hablar y ahora peca por ~** before, she never stopped talking, and now she's gone too far the other extreme *o* she's gone too far the other way; ✦***REFRÁN*** **más vale pecar por exceso que por ~** too much is better than too little

defectuosamente ADV defectively, faultily

defectuoso ADJ defective, faulty

defender ▸conjug 2g◂ Ⓐ VT (*Mil*) [+ *país, territorio, intereses*] to defend; [+ *causa, ideas*] to defend, champion; (*Jur*) to defend; **defiende sus opiniones con buenos argumentos** he defends his opinions with good arguments; **el Real Madrid defiende el título de campeón** Real Madrid are defending the championship title, Real Madrid are the defending champions; **nos defendió de los atracadores** he defended us against the muggers; **defiendo la tesis doctoral el mes que viene** I'm having a viva on *o* (*EEUU*) I'm defending my doctoral thesis next month
Ⓑ **defenderse** VPR [1] (= *protegerse*) **~se de** *o* **contra** [+ *calor, lluvia, sol*] to protect o.s. from; [+ *agresor, ataque*] to defend o.s. from *o* against; **se defendió del lobo con un palo** he defended himself from the wolf with a stick
[2] (= *desenvolverse*) to get by; **me defiendo en inglés** I can get by *o* along in English; **gana poco pero se defiende** she doesn't earn much but she gets by; **ya eres mayor, ya puedes ~te solo** you're old enough, you can get by *o* manage on your own now; **—¿sabes algo de ordenadores? —me defiendo** "do you know anything about computers?" — "I get by *o* I know a bit"; **se defendió muy bien en la entrevista** she performed very well in the interview; ✦***MODISMO*** **~se como un gato panza arriba** to fight tooth and nail (to defend o.s.)

defendible ADJ defensible

defendido/a SM/F (*Jur*) **mi ~** my client

defenestración SF (*hum*) abrupt dismissal, sudden removal

defenestrar ▸conjug 1a◂ VT (*hum*) to boot out (*hum*), oust, remove

defensa Ⓐ SF [1] (= *protección*) defence, defense (*EEUU*); **la ~ del territorio nacional** the defence of national territory; **la cueva nos sirvió de ~ contra la lluvia** the cave offered us protection from the rain; **en ~ de los derechos civiles** in defence of civil rights; **salió en ~ de su hermano** he came to his brother's defence; **en ~ propia** in self-defence; **(Ministerio de) Defensa** Ministry of Defence, Defense Department (*EEUU*) ► **defensa pasiva** civil defence ► **defensa personal** self-defence ► **defensas costeras** coastal defences
[2] (*Jur*) (= *abogado, argumentación*) defence, defense (*EEUU*)
[3] (*Dep*) **la ~** (= *jugadores*) the defence, the defense (*EEUU*)
[4] **defensas** (*Med*) defences, defenses (*EEUU*); **está bajo de ~s** his (body's) defences are low, his resistance is low
[5] **defensas** [*de toro*] horns; [*de elefante, jabalí*] tusks
[6] (*Náut*) fender
[7] (*Méx*) bumper, fender (*EEUU*)
Ⓑ SMF (*Dep*) defender ► **defensa escoba**, **defensa libre** sweeper

defensiva SF defensive; **estar a la ~** to be on the defensive

defensivo Ⓐ ADJ defensive; **política defensiva** defence policy, defense policy (*EEUU*)
Ⓑ SM defence, defense (*EEUU*), safeguard

defensor(a) Ⓐ SM/F [1] (= *protector*) [*de territorio, intereses*] defender; [*de causa, idea, derechos*] defender, champion; **mi pastor alemán es un ~ feroz** my Alsatian is a fierce guard dog ► **defensor(a) del pueblo** ombudsman
[2] (*Jur*) defence lawyer, defense attorney *o* lawyer (*EEUU*); **el ~ interrogó al testigo** counsel for the defence *o* defending counsel cross-examined the witness
[3] (*Dep*) [*de título*] defender
Ⓑ ADJ [1] (= *protector*) **una asociación ~a de los derechos de los marginados** an organization which defends *o* protects the rights of the underprivileged; **una organización ~a de los derechos civiles** a civil rights organization
[2] (*Jur*) **abogado ~** defence lawyer, defense attorney *o* lawyer (*EEUU*)

deferencia SF deference; **fue la única que nos trató con ~** she was the only one to treat us with deference *o* respect; **no tuvo la ~ de informarnos** he didn't have the courtesy to let us know; **en** *o* **por ~ a** *o* **hacia algn** out of *o* in deference to sb

deferente ADJ deferential

deferir ▸conjug 3k◂ Ⓐ VT (*Jur*) to refer, delegate
Ⓑ VI **~ a algo** to defer to sth

deficiencia SF [1] (= *defecto*) defect (**de** in, of)
[2] (= *falta*) deficiency ► **deficiencia auditiva** hearing impairment ► **deficiencia mental**, **deficiencia psíquica** mental deficiency, mental handicap ► **deficiencia visual** visual impairment

deficiente Ⓐ ADJ [1] (= *imperfecto*) [*mercancía, motor*] defective; [*sistema, estructura*] inadequate; **los ~s sistemas de seguridad** the inadequacy of the security systems
[2] (= *falto*) deficient (**en** in)
Ⓑ SMF ► **deficiente mental, deficiente psíquico** mentally handicapped person ► **deficiente visual** visually handicapped person

déficit SM (*pl* **déficits**) [1] (*Com, Fin*) deficit ► **déficit comercial**, **déficit exterior** trade deficit ► **déficit por cuenta corriente** current account deficit ► **déficit presupuestario** budget deficit
[2] (= *falta*) lack, shortage

deficitario ADJ [1] (*Fin*) [*empresa, operación*] loss-making; **financiación/reducción deficitaria** financing/reduction of the deficit; **tiene una cuenta deficitaria** his account is over-

➤ LENGUA Y USO: **deducir 1** 53.4

drawn
[2] **ser ~ en algo** to be short of sth, be lacking in sth

definible ADJ definable

definición SF [1] [*de palabra*] definition; **por ~** by definition
[2] (*Téc*) definition

definido ADJ [1] [*línea*] clearly defined; [*preferencia*] definite, clear; **bien ~** well defined, clearly defined; **~ por el usuario** (*Inform*) user-defined
[2] [*carácter*] tough, manly
[3] (*Ling*) definite

definir ▸conjug 3a◂ Ⓐ VT [1] [*+ concepto, palabra*] to define
[2] (= *calificar*) to describe; **definió el partido como aburrido** she described the match as boring
[3] (= *aclarar*) [*+ actitud, posición*] to define; [*+ contorno, silueta*] to define, make sharp
[4] (= *establecer*) [*+ poder, jurisdicción*] to define, establish; **esta ley define las competencias de cada administración** this law defines *o* establishes the powers of each authority
[5] (*Inform*) to define
Ⓑ **definirse** VPR [1] (= *calificarse*) to define o.s.; **se definió como liberal** he defined himself as a liberal
[2] (= *decidirse*) **la comisión aún no se ha definido con respecto al tema** the commission has not yet defined its position on the subject, the commission has not yet said where it stands on the subject; **el gobierno se definió a favor del pacto** the government came out in favour of the agreement

definitivamente ADV [1] (= *con seguridad*) definitely; **~ nos casamos el 14 de marzo** we are definitely getting married on 14th March
[2] (= *para siempre*) permanently; **se ha instalado ~ en la capital** he has settled permanently in the capital, he has settled in the capital for good; **eliminaron ~ el virus** they permanently eliminated the virus, they eliminated the virus for ever *o* for good *o* once and for all; **son teorías ~ superadas** these theories have now been permanently superseded
[3] (= *claramente*) definitely; **~, es la peor película del año** it's definitely the worst film of the year; **un autor ~ encasillable en el modernismo** an author who can definitely be classed as modernist

▼**definitivo** ADJ [1] (= *final*) definitive, final; **la clausura definitiva de la línea ferroviaria** the permanent closure of the railway line
[2] (= *inamovible*) [*proyecto, fecha, respuesta*] definite; **éste es el plan, pero no es ~** this is the plan, but it's not definite; **ya es ~ que las elecciones son en mayo** the election will now definitely be in May
[3] [*prueba*] definitive, conclusive
[4] **en definitiva: es, en definitiva, una pésima película** in short, it's a terrible film; **en definitiva, que no quieres venir** so you don't want to come then?; **éste es, en definitiva, el mejor pacto alcanzable** all in all *o* all things considered, this is the best deal we can expect to achieve

definitorio ADJ defining, distinctive

deflación SF deflation

deflacionar ▸conjug 1a◂ VT to deflate

➤ LENGUA Y USO: **definitivo 4** 53.4

deflacionario ADJ, **deflacionista** ADJ deflationary

deflactación SF (*Cono Sur*) deflation

deflactar ▸conjug 1a◂ VT (*Cono Sur*) to deflate

deflector SM (*Téc*) baffle, baffle plate

defoliación SF defoliation

defoliante SM defoliant

defoliar ▸conjug 1b◂ VT to defoliate

deforestar *etc* = **desforestar** *etc*

deformación SF [1] (= *alteración*) [*de manos, superficie*] deformation; [*de madera*] warping
[2] (*Radio*) distortion
[3] (*Mec*) strain
[4] ► **deformación profesional**: **—¡deja ya de hacer preguntas! —soy detective, es ~ profesional** "stop asking questions!" — "I'm a detective, it's a habit you pick up in this job"

deformante ADJ **espejo ~** distorting mirror

deformar ▸conjug 1a◂ Ⓐ VT [1] [*+ cuerpo*] to deform; **la artritis puede ~ los miembros** arthritis can deform limbs
[2] [*+ objeto*] to distort, deform; **el impacto deformó el chasis** the impact distorted *o* deformed the chassis; **si sigues tirando del jersey, lo ~ás** if you keep pulling at your sweater you'll pull it out of shape; **no te pongas mis zapatos que me los deformas** don't wear my shoes, you'll put them out of shape; **el calor deformó la madera** the heat warped the wood
[3] [*+ imagen, realidad*] to distort
Ⓑ **deformarse** VPR [1] [*cuerpo, miembro*] to become deformed
[2] [*madera, puerta*] to become warped, become twisted; **se le deformó el sombrero con la lluvia** her hat lost its shape in the rain, the rain made her hat lose its shape; **se le ~on los zapatos de tanto caminar** his shoes got out of shape from so much walking
[3] [*imagen*] to distort, become distorted

deforme ADJ [1] (= *de forma anormal*) [*espécimen, cuerpo*] deformed; [*cabeza, sombra*] misshapen
[2] (= *feo*) ugly

deformidad SF [1] (= *forma anormal*) deformity, malformation
[2] (= *defecto moral*) shortcoming

defraudación SF [1] (= *desfalco*) defrauding ► **defraudación de impuestos**, **defraudación fiscal** tax evasion
[2] (= *engaño*) deceit
[3] (= *decepción*) disappointment

defraudador(a) SM/F fraudster*

defraudar ▸conjug 1a◂ VT [1] (= *decepcionar*) [*+ persona*] to disappoint; [*+ esperanzas*] to dash, disappoint; [*+ amigos*] to let down; **este libro no te ~á** you won't be disappointed by this book
[2] (*Com*) [*+ acreedores*] to cheat, defraud; **~ impuestos** to evade one's taxes
[3] (*Fís*) to intercept, cut off

defraudatorio ADJ fraudulent

defuera ADV **por ~** outwardly, on the outside

defunción SF decease; **"cerrado por defunción"** "closed owing to bereavement"

defuncionar‡ ▸conjug 1a◂ VT to do in‡

DEG SMPL ABR (= **derechos especiales de giro**) SDR

degeneración SF [1] (= *proceso*) degeneration (**en** into)
[2] (= *estado*) degeneracy

degenerado/a Ⓐ ADJ degenerate
Ⓑ SM/F (*moralmente*) degenerate; (*sexualmente*) pervert

degenerar ▸conjug 1a◂ VI [1] (= *empeorar*) [*enfermedad*] to get worse; [*discusión, situación*] to degenerate (**en** into); **la manifestación degeneró en una sangrienta revuelta** the demonstration degenerated into a bloody riot
[2] (= *decaer*) to decline

degenerativo ADJ degenerative

deglución SF swallowing

deglutir ▸conjug 3a◂ VT, VI to swallow

degollación SF [1] [*de persona*] throat cutting; (*Jur*) beheading
[2] (= *masacre*) massacre ► **Degollación de los Inocentes** Slaughter of the Innocents

degolladero SM [1] (*Anat*) throat, neck
[2] (*Hist*) scaffold, block (*for executions*); ✦*MODISMO* **ir al ~** to expose o.s. to mortal danger; (*hum*) to put one's head in the lion's mouth
[3] (= *matadero*) slaughterhouse

degollador SM (*Hist*) executioner

degollar ▸conjug 1m◂ VT [1] (= *cortar la garganta de*) [*+ persona*] to cut the throat of, slit the throat of; [*+ animal*] to slaughter; **lo ~on** they cut *o* slit his throat
[2] (= *decapitar*) [*+ persona*] to behead; [*+ toro*] to kill badly, butcher
[3] (= *masacrar*) to massacre
[4] (= *arruinar*) [*+ comedia, papel*] to murder
[5] (*Cos*) to cut low in the neck

degradación SF [1] (= *deterioro*) [*de la salud*] deterioration; [*del litoral*] deterioration, degradation (*frm*); [*de calidad*] worsening, decline
[2] (= *bajeza*) degradation
[3] (*Mil*) demotion
[4] (*Geol*) impoverishment

degradante ADJ degrading

degradar ▸conjug 1a◂ Ⓐ VT [1] (= *deteriorar*) [*+ salud*] to cause to deteriorate; [*+ litoral*] to spoil; [*+ calidad*] to lower, make worse
[2] (*Mil*) to demote, downgrade
[3] (*Inform*) [*+ datos*] to corrupt
[4] (*Geol*) [*+ suelo*] to impoverish
Ⓑ **degradarse** VPR to demean o.s., degrade o.s.

degüello SM [1] [*de arma*] shaft
[2] **a ~**: **entrar a ~ en una ciudad** to put the people of a city to the sword; **tirarse a ~ contra algn** to lash out against sb

degustación SF tasting, sampling

degustar ▸conjug 1a◂ VT to taste, sample

dehesa SF [1] (= *pastos*) pasture, meadow
[2] (= *finca*) estate

deíctico ADJ, SM deictic

deidad SF [1] (= *dios*) deity ► **deidad pagana** pagan god, pagan deity
[2] (= *divinidad*) divinity

deificación SF deification

deificar ▸conjug 1g◂ VT [1] (*Rel*) to deify
[2] [*+ cantante, ídolo*] to deify, idolize
[3] [*+ persona, hijo*] to put on a pedestal

deísmo SM deism

deísta Ⓐ ADJ deistic, deistical
Ⓑ SMF deist

deixis SF INV deixis

dejación SF [1] (*Jur*) abandonment, relinquishment
[2] (*Andes, CAm*) (= *descuido*) carelessness

dejada SF (*Tenis*) let

dejadez SF [1] (*en el trabajo*) (= *falta de esfuerzo*) laziness; (= *falta de cuidado, atención*) carelessness
[2] (= *falta de aseo*) slovenliness

dejado ADJ [1] (= *desaliñado*) (*en las costumbres*) slovenly; (*en la apariencia*) scruffy; **es tan ~ que ni siquiera lava los platos** he's so slovenly he doesn't even bother to do the washing up; **va siempre muy ~** he's always very scruffy; **está muy dejada desde que vive en el campo** she's got very scruffy since she started living in the country; **con ese aspecto tan ~ nunca conseguirás trabajo** you'll never get a job looking so scruffy
[2] (= *negligente*) careless, sloppy; **comete esos errores porque es un ~** he makes those mistakes because he's so careless *o* sloppy; **eres muy ~ con tu familia** you don't bother much about *o* with your family; **no te escribe porque es una dejada** she doesn't write to you because she can't really be bothered; *ver tb* **Dios 3**

dejamiento SM = **dejadez**

DEJAR

Dejar en el sentido de prestar se puede traducir al inglés empleando **borrow** o **lend**. **Borrow** se usa cuando el sujeto es quien pide (significa tomar prestado) y **lend** cuando el sujeto es quien da (significa dejar prestado):

¿Me dejas tus botas de esquiar?
Can I borrow your ski boots? o ***Can you lend me your ski boots?***
¿Me podrías dejar tu reloj?
Could I borrow your watch? o ***Could you lend me your watch?***

! Borrow y **lend** no se utilizan normalmente con cosas que no pueden trasladarse de un sitio a otro:

¿Me dejas tu casa de campo este fin de semana?
Can I use your house in the country this weekend?

Para otros usos y ejemplos ver la entrada.

dejar

▸conjug 1a◂
[A] VERBO TRANSITIVO [C] VERBO PRONOMINAL
[B] VERBO INTRANSITIVO
Para las expresiones ***dejar caer, dejarse caer, dejar que desear, dejar dicho, dejarse llevar, dejar paso***, *ver la otra entrada.*

(A) VERBO TRANSITIVO

[1] ***= poner, soltar*** to leave; **he dejado las llaves en la mesa** I've left the keys on the table; **se lo dejo en la conserjería** I'll leave it for you at the porter's office; **dejé 1.500 euros de entrada** I put down 1,500 euros as a deposit; **podemos ~le los niños a mi madre si salimos** we can leave the children with my mother if we go out; **~ algo aparte** to leave sth aside; **~ atrás** [+ *corredor, vehículo adelantado, competidor*] to leave behind; **dejó atrás a los demás corredores** he left the other runners behind; **se vino de Holanda, dejando atrás a su familia** he came over from Holland, leaving his family behind; **~ a algn muy atrás** to leave sb a long way behind; **~ algo a un lado** to set sth aside

[2] ***al desaparecer, morir*** to leave; **el agua ha dejado una mancha en la pared** the water has left a stain on the wall; **te deja un sabor demasiado dulce después de comerlo** it leaves a sickly aftertaste in your mouth; **dejó todo su dinero a sus hijos** he left all his money to his children; **dejó dos niñas pequeñas** she left two small girls; **deja escritas tres novelas** he leaves three completed novels behind

[3] ***= guardar*** **¿me habéis dejado algo de tarta?** have you left *o* saved me some cake?; **deja algo de dinero para cuando lo necesites** put some money aside for when you need it

[4] ***= abandonar*** [4·1] [+ *actividad, empleo*] to give up; **dejó el esquí después del accidente** he gave up skiing after the accident; **ha dejado los estudios por el fútbol** he has given up his studies to pursue a career in football; **lo dejamos porque era muy difícil** we gave up because it was too hard; **lo dejamos por imposible** we gave it up as being impossible; **~ la bebida** to give up drink, stop drinking

[4·2] [+ *persona, lugar*] to leave; **~on al niño en la puerta de una iglesia** they left the child outside a church; **su novio la ha dejado** her boyfriend has left her; **dejé su casa al amanecer** I left his house at dawn

[4·3] (*en coche*) to drop off; **¿te dejo en tu casa?** shall I drop you off at your place?

[5] ***= no molestar*** **deja ya el ordenador, que lo vas a romper** leave the computer alone, you're going to break it; **déjame, quiero estar solo** leave me be, I want to be alone; **¡déjalo!** (= *¡no hagas eso!*) stop it!; (= *no te preocupes*) forget it!, don't worry about it!; **~ así las cosas** to leave things as they are; **dejémoslo así** let's leave it at that; **¡déjame en paz!** ◊ **déjame tranquilo** leave me alone!

[6] ***= posponer*** **~ algo para** to leave sth till; **~ algo para mañana** to leave sth till tomorrow; **~ algo para después** to leave sth till later; **he dejado el italiano para cuando tenga más tiempo** I've put off learning Italian till I have more time

[7] ***= prestar*** to lend; **le dejé mi libro de física** I lent him my physics book; **¿me dejas diez euros?** can you lend me ten euros?; **¿me dejas el coche?** can I borrow the car?, will you lend me the car?

[8] ***= permitir*** (+ *INFIN*) to let; **mis padres no me dejan salir de noche** my parents won't let me go out at night; **quiero pero no me dejan** I want to but they won't let me; **~ entrar a algn** to let sb in; **~ pasar a algn** to let sb through *o* past; **~ salir a algn** to let sb out

◆ **dejar que** + *SUBJUN*: **~ que las cosas vayan de mal en peor** to let things go *o* allow things to go from bad to worse

[9] ***indicando resultado*** (+ *ADJ*) **dejó la ventana abierta** she left the window open; **lo ha dejado muy triste** it has left him very sad; **me dejó confundido** she left me confused, she confused me; **nos dejó a todos asombrados** he stunned us all; **hay algo que quiero ~ bien claro** there is one thing I want to make perfectly clear; **~on el jardín tal como estaba** they left the garden as it was; **~ algo como nuevo**: **me han dejado el abrigo como nuevo** my coat was as good as new when it came back from them; **esa ducha me ha dejado como nueva** I feel like a different person after that shower

[10] ***= producir*** [+ *dinero*] **el negocio le deja lo justo para vivir** the business brings in just enough for him to live on; **ese fondo de inversión apenas me deja intereses** that investment fund barely pays any interest

[11]

◆ **dejar que** (= *esperar*): **deja que acabe de llover** wait for it to stop raining; **~on que pasara el temporal antes de zarpar** they waited for the storm to pass before setting sail; **deja que me toque la lotería y verás** just wait till I win the lottery, then you'll see

[12] ***= omitir*** to leave out, forget

(B) VERBO INTRANSITIVO

con una actividad **deja, ya lo hago yo** leave it, I'll do it; **deja, yo lo pago** no *o* it's all right, I'll pay for it

◆ **dejar de hacer algo** (*por un momento*) to stop doing sth; (*por una temporada*) to give up doing sth, stop doing sth; **cuando deje de llover** when it stops raining, when the rain stops; **¡déja de hacer eso!** stop that!; **yo dejé de ir hace muchos años** I gave up *o* stopped going years ago; **no puedo ~ de fumar** I can't give up *o* stop smoking; **cuando murió su padre dejó de comer** when her father died she stopped eating *o* she went off her food

◆ **no dejar de** + *INFIN*: **no deja de preguntarme por ti** he's always asking me about you; **eso no deja de tener gracia** it has its funny side; **no deja de ser raro que no haya venido** it's rather odd that she hasn't come; **no por eso deja de ser una tontería lo que has dicho** that doesn't change the fact that what you said was stupid; **no puedo ~ de asombrarme** I can't help being astonished; **no dejes de visitarlos** don't fail to visit them, make sure you visit them; **no dejes de comprar el billete** make sure you buy the ticket

(C) **dejarse** VERBO PRONOMINAL

[1] ***= abandonarse*** to let o.s. go; **empezó a ~se después de tener su primer hijo** she started to let herself go after she had her first child

[2] ***= olvidar*** to leave; **se dejó el bolso en un taxi** she left her bag in a taxi; **me he dejado el dinero en casa** I've left my money at home; **me he dejado la luz encendida** I've left the light on

[3] ***= dejar crecer*** to grow; **~se las uñas largas/el pelo largo** to grow long nails/hair; **~se barba** to grow a beard

[4] ***= permitir*** (+ *INFIN*) **~se convencer** to allow o.s. to be persuaded; **no se dejó engañar** he was not to be deceived; **el gato no se dejaba acariciar** the cat wouldn't let anyone stroke it; **—¿está bien la película? —se deja ver** "is the film any good?" — "it's watchable"; *ver tb* **vencer B1**

[5] ***= poderse*** (+ *INFIN*) **se dejó oír una débil voz** a weak voice could be heard; **ya se deja sentir el frío** it's starting to get colder

[6]

◆ **dejarse de** (= *terminar de*): **déjate de rollos y vamos al grano** stop messing around and let's get to the point; **déjate de bromas** stop

➤ LENGUA Y USO: dejar A7 36.1, 36.3 A8 36.1, 36.3

kidding around; **¡déjate de tonterías!** stop messing about *o* being silly!; **déjate de tanto hablar y estudia** stop talking all the time and do some studying; **¡déjate de andar y vamos a coger el coche!** forget about walking, let's get the car!

deje SM accent

dejo SM [1] (= *sabor*) aftertaste; **tiene un ~ raro** it has an odd aftertaste
[2] [*de arrogancia, laxitud*] touch
[3] (*Ling*) accent, trace of accent

del = **de + el**; *ver* **de**

Del. ABR = **Delegación**

delación SF denunciation

delantal SM [1] (*Culin*) apron; **~ de cuero** leather apron
[2] (*Escol*) pinafore

delante ADV [1] in front; **no hay ningún edificio ~** there are no buildings in front; **en el coche me gusta sentarme ~** I like to sit in the front of the car, when I'm in a car I like to sit in the front; **los más bajos que se pongan ~** can the shorter ones come to the front?; **no hables de Antonio con mis amigos ~** don't talk about Antonio in front of my friends; **no tengo el documento ~** I don't have the document in front of me; **entró al puerto (con) la popa ~** it entered the harbour stern first; de ~: **la parte de ~** the front part; **siempre se sentaba en el banco de ~** she always sat on the front bench; **el coche de ~** the car in front; hacia ~: **hizo un movimiento hacia ~** he moved forward(s); por ~: **yo iba por ~ con la linterna** I went in front with the torch; **un vestido que se abre por ~** a dress that opens at the front; **tenemos todavía cuatro horas por ~** we still have four hours in front of us; **todavía tiene mucha vida por ~** she still has her whole life ahead of her; **destruye al que se le pone por ~** he destroys anyone who gets in his way; **resuelve todos los problemas que se le pongan por ~** he solves any problem you put in front of him; *ver tb* **llevar C2**
[2] **~ de** in front of; **se colocó ~ de mí** he stood in front of me; **había un camión ~ del cine** there was a lorry in front of the cinema; **te espero ~ del cine** I'll meet you outside the cinema
[3] (*esp Cono Sur*) **~ mío/tuyo** in front of me/ you; **en tu ~** in front of you

delantera SF [1] [*de casa, vestido*] front
[2] (*Dep*) (= *línea de ataque*) forward line; **coger la ~ a algn** (*en carrera*) to take over the lead from sb; (*al contestar*) to beat sb to it; **llevar la ~** to be in the lead; **llevar la ~ a algn** to be ahead of sb; **sacar la ~ a algn** to steal a march on sb; **tomar la ~ a algn** = **coger la delantera a algn**
[3] (*Teat*) front row
[4] (*Anat*‡) knockers‡ *pl*, tits‡ *pl*
[5] **delanteras** (= *calzones*) chaps; (= *mono*) overalls

delantero/a Ⓐ ADJ [1] (= *de delante*) [*parte, fila, rueda*] front *antes de s*; [*patas de animal*] fore *antes de s*, front
[2] [*línea, posición*] (*Dep*) forward; (*en progreso*) first, foremost
Ⓑ SM/F (*Dep*) forward ► **delantero centro** centre-forward, center-forward (*EEUU*) ► **delantero extremo** outside forward, wing forward ► **delantero interior** inside forward

delatar ▸conjug 1a◂ VT [1] [*persona*] to denounce, inform against; **los delató a la policía** he reported them to the police
[2] [*actitud, mirada*] to betray, give away

delator(a) Ⓐ ADJ [*sonrisa, comentario*] revealing; [*mancha*] incriminating
Ⓑ SM/F informer

delco SM (*Aut*) distributor

delectación SF delectation

delegación SF [1] (= *acto*) delegation ► **delegación de poderes** (*Admin*) devolution
[2] (= *sucursal*) (*Com*) local office; [*del Estado*] *local office of a government department* ► **delegación del gobierno** *office of the government delegate to an autonomous community*
[3] (= *representantes*) delegation; **la ~ fue a cumplimentar al Ministro** the delegation went to pay its respects to the minister ► **delegación comercial** trade mission
[4] (*Méx*) (= *comisaría*) main police station; (= *municipio*) municipal district

delegado/a SM/F (= *representante*) delegate; (*Com*) representative, agent; (*Educ*) representative ► **delegado/a de alumnos**, **delegado/a de curso** student representative ► **delegado/a del Gobierno** (*Esp*) *government delegate to an autonomous community* ► **delegado/a sindical** shop steward

delegar ▸conjug 1h◂ VT to delegate; **~ algo en algn** to delegate sth to sb

deleitable ADJ delightful, delectable

deleitación SF, **deleitamiento** SM delectation

deleitar ▸conjug 1a◂ Ⓐ VT to delight, charm
Ⓑ **deleitarse** VPR to delight (**con, en** in); **~se en hacer algo** to delight in doing sth

deleite SM delight, pleasure; **los ~s de la carne** the pleasures of the flesh

deleitosamente ADV delightfully

deleitoso ADJ delightful, pleasing

deletéreo ADJ deleterious

deletrear ▸conjug 1a◂ VT [1] [+ *apellido, palabra*] to spell
[2] (= *descifrar*) to decipher, interpret
[3] (*Cono Sur*) (= *escudriñar*) to observe in great detail, look minutely at

deletreo SM [1] [*de apellido, palabra*] spelling, spelling-out
[2] (= *desciframiento*) decipherment, interpretation

deleznable ADJ [1] (= *despreciable*) atrocious
[2] [*arcilla, superficie*] crumbly
[3] [*argumento, construcción*] weak

délfico ADJ Delphic

delfín SM [1] (*Zool*) dolphin
[2] (*Pol*) designated successor, heir apparent
[3] (*Hist*) dauphin

delfinario SM dolphinarium

Delfos SM Delphi

delgadez SF [1] [*de persona*] (= *flaqueza*) thinness; (= *esbeltez*) slimness
[2] [*de tabla, muro*] thinness; [*de hilo*] fineness
[3] (†) (= *delicadeza*) delicateness
[4] (†) (= *agudeza*) sharpness

delgado Ⓐ ADJ [1] [*persona*] (= *esbelto*) slim; (= *flaco*) thin; **una jovencita muy delgada** a very slim young girl; **tienes los brazos demasiado ~s** your arms are too thin; **se ha quedado muy ~ con la enfermedad** he's got very thin from being ill; ✦**MODISMO** **~ como un fideo** as thin as a rake
[2] [*tabla, placa, muro, hebra*] thin; [*hilo*] fine
[3] (*Méx*) (= *aguado*) weak, thin
[4] (†) [*tierra*] poor
[5] (†) (= *delicado*) delicate
[6] (†) (= *agudo*) sharp, clever
Ⓑ ADV *ver* **hilar 2**

deliberación SF deliberation

deliberadamente ADV deliberately

deliberado ADJ deliberate

deliberar ▸conjug 1a◂ Ⓐ VT [1] (= *debatir*) to debate
[2] (= *decidir*) **~ hacer algo** to decide to do sth
Ⓑ VI to deliberate (**sobre** on), discuss (**si** whether); **el juez se retiró a ~** the judge retired to deliberate

deliberativo ADJ deliberative

delicadamente ADV delicately

delicadez SF [1] = **delicadeza**
[2] (= *debilidad física*) weakness
[3] (*frm*) (= *sensibilidad excesiva*) hypersensitivity

delicadeza SF [1] (= *suavidad*) [*de tejido, piel*] softness; [*de tela*] fineness; [*de color*] softness
[2] (= *cuidado*) gentleness; **la ~ con que transportó al enfermo** the gentleness with which she moved the patient; **con mucha ~** very gently
[3] (= *amabilidad*) **tuvo la ~ de ayudarme a bajar** he was kind enough to help me down, he did me the kindness of helping me down; **no tuvo la ~ de comunicárnoslo** he didn't have the decency to let us know
[4] (= *tacto*) tact, delicacy; **tuvo mucha ~ al presentar su queja** she made the complaint very tactfully *o* with great tact *o* with great delicacy; **tendrás que presentar la queja con mucha ~** you will have to make the complaint very tactfully *o* delicately; **falta de ~** tactlessness, indelicacy
[5] (= *dificultad*) delicacy, delicate nature; **no comprendió la ~ de la situación** he did not understand the delicacy *o* delicate nature of the situation
[6] (= *finura*) [*de rasgos*] delicacy; **la ~ con que ejecutó la pieza** the delicacy with which she performed the piece; **describió la ~ del ambiente de palacio** she described the refined atmosphere at the palace; **me enamoró la ~ de sus modales** I fell in love with his exquisite manners
[7] (= *sensibilidad excesiva*) hypersensitiveness

delicado ADJ [1] (= *suave*) [*tejido, piel*] delicate; [*tela*] fine; [*color*] soft
[2] (= *frágil*) [*máquina*] sensitive; [*salud*] delicate; **está ~ del estómago** he has a delicate stomach
[3] (= *fino*) [*rasgos*] delicate, fine; [*gusto*] delicate, subtle
[4] (= *difícil*) [*situación*] delicate, tricky; [*punto*] sore; [*tema*] delicate
[5] [*persona*] (= *difícil de contentar*) hard to please, fussy; (= *sensible*) hypersensitive; (= *discreto*) tactful; (= *atento*) considerate; **es muy ~ con la comida** he's very choosy about his food*

delicia SF delight; **tiene un jardín que es una ~** he has a delightful garden; **un libro que ha**

hecho las ~s de muchos niños a book which has delighted many children

deliciosamente ADV delightfully

delicioso ADJ [1] [*momento, sonido*] delightful
[2] [*comida, bebida*] delicious

delictivo ADJ criminal *antes de s*

Delilá SF Delilah

delimitación SF delimitation

delimitar ▸conjug 1a◂ VT to delimit

delincuencia SF crime; **las cifras de la ~** the incidence of crime ► **delincuencia de menores, delincuencia juvenil** juvenile delinquency ► **delincuencia informática** computer crime ► **delincuencia menor** petty crime

delincuencial ADJ criminal

delincuente Ⓐ ADJ delinquent
Ⓑ SMF (= *maleante*) criminal ► **delincuente común** common criminal ► **delincuente habitual** habitual offender ► **delincuente juvenil** juvenile delinquent

delineación SF, **delineamiento** SM delineation ► **delineación industrial** technical drawing

delineador SM eyeliner

delineante SMF draughtsman/draughtswoman, draftsman/draftswoman (*EEUU*)

delinear ▸conjug 1a◂ VT [1] [+ *contornos*] to outline
[2] [+ *plan, propuesta*] to delineate

delinquimiento SM delinquency

delinquir ▸conjug 3e◂ VI to commit an offence *o* (*EEUU*) offense

deliquio SM swoon, fainting fit

delirante ADJ [1] (*Med*) delirious, raving
[2] (= *disparatado*) [*idea*] crazy; [*chiste*] hilarious

delirantemente ADV deliriously

delirar ▸conjug 1a◂ VI [1] (*Med*) to be delirious
[2] (= *desatinar*) to rave, talk nonsense; **¡tú deliras!*** you must be mad!

delirio SM [1] (*Med*) delirium
[2] (= *frenesí*) **cuando acabó de hablar fue el ~** when he finished speaking the place went wild; **el chocolate me gusta con ~** I absolutely adore chocolate
[3] (= *manía*) ► **delirio de persecución** persecution mania ► **delirios de grandeza** delusions of grandeur
[4] **delirios** (= *disparate*) nonsense *sing*

delírium SM ► **delírium tremens** delirium tremens

delito SM [1] (*Jur*) (= *acción criminal*) crime; (= *infracción*) offence, offense (*EEUU*) ► **delito común** common crime ► **delito contra la propiedad** crime against property ► **delito de menor importancia** minor offence ► **delito de sangre** violent crime ► **delito fiscal** tax offence ► **delito menor** minor offence ► **delito político** political crime
[2] (= *fechoría*) (*lit*) felony; (*fig*) misdeed

delta Ⓐ SM (*Geog*) delta; *ver tb* **ala A2**
Ⓑ SF (= *letra*) delta

deltaplano SM [1] (= *aparato*) hang-glider
[2] (= *deporte*) hang-gliding

deltoideo ADJ, SM deltoid

deludir ▸conjug 3a◂ VT to delude

delusorio ADJ delusive

demacración SF emaciation

demacrado ADJ gaunt, haggard

demacrarse ▸conjug 1a◂ VPR to become emaciated

demagogia SF demagogy, demagoguery

demagógico ADJ demagogic

demagogismo SM demagogy, demagoguery

demagogo SM demagogue, demagog (*EEUU*)

demanda SF [1] (= *solicitud*) request (**de** for); (*exigiendo*) demand (**de** for); **escribir en ~ de ayuda** to write asking for help; **ir en ~ de algo** to go in search of sth, go looking for sth; ✦*MODISMO* **morir en la ~** to die in the attempt ► **demanda de extradición** extradition request ► **demanda del Santo Grial** quest for the Holy Grail ► **demanda de pago** demand for payment
[2] (*esp LAm*) (= *pregunta*) inquiry
[3] (*Com*) demand; **hay una gran ~ de profesores** teachers are in great demand; **tener ~** to be in demand; **ese producto no tiene ~** there is no demand for that product ► **demanda de mercado** market demand ► **demanda final** final demand ► **demanda indirecta** derived demand; *ver tb* **oferta 2**
[4] (*Teat*) call
[5] (*Elec*) load ► **demanda máxima** peak load
[6] (*Jur*) action, lawsuit; **entablar ~** to bring an action, sue; **presentar ~ de divorcio a algn** to sue sb for divorce ► **demanda civil** private prosecution ► **demanda judicial** legal action

demandado/a SM/F defendant; (*en divorcio*) respondent

demandante SMF [1] (*Jur*) plaintiff
[2] ► **demandante de empleo** job seeker

demandar ▸conjug 1a◂ VT [1] (= *exigir*) to demand
[2] (*Jur*) to sue, file a lawsuit against; **demandó al periódico por difamación** he sued the paper for libel; **~ a algn por daños y perjuicios** to sue sb for damages

demaquillador SM make-up remover

demarcación SF [1] [*de frontera, zona*] demarcation; **línea de ~** demarcation line
[2] (*Dep*) position

demarcar ▸conjug 1g◂ VT to demarcate

demarraje SM spurt, break, dash

demarrar ▸conjug 1a◂ VI to spurt, break away, make a dash

demás Ⓐ ADJ **los ~ libros** the other books, the rest of the books; **y ~ gente de ese tipo** and other people of that sort
Ⓑ PRON [1] **lo ~** the rest (of it); **los ~** the others, the rest (of them); **esto es lo importante y lo ~ se puede eliminar** this is the important thing, we can get rid of the rest; **todo lo ~** all the rest, everything else; **las ~ no tenían dinero** the others didn't have any money, the rest (of them) didn't have any money, no-one else had any money; **esta ropa es de Juan y lo ~ de Pedro** these clothes are Juan's and the others *o* the rest are Pedro's
[2] **por lo ~** otherwise, apart from that; **es muy larga, pero, por lo ~, es una buena novela** it's very long, but otherwise *o* apart from that it's a good novel
[3] **y ~** and so on, and so forth; **vimos la catedral, la muralla y ~** we saw the cathedral, the walls and so on *o* and so forth
[4] **por ~** (*frm*) [4·1] (= *a propósito*) **una característica que, por ~, no es exclusiva suya** a characteristic which, incidentally *o* by the way, is not unique to him; **ha escrito decenas de novelas, por ~ excelentes** he has written dozens of novels, which are excellent by the way, he has written dozens of novels, excellent ones at that
[4·2] (= *en vano*) **está por ~ presentar una queja** it is pointless to make a complaint; **nunca está por ~ solicitarlo** you have nothing to lose by asking for it, it is always worthwhile asking for it
[4·3] (= *demasiado*) excessively; **un informe extenso por ~** an excessively long report; **un político alabado por ~** a politician who has received excessive praise

demasía SF [1] (= *exceso*) excess; **con** *o* **en ~** too much, excessively; **habló en ~** he talked too much; **el maquillaje, en ~, es poco natural** too much make-up *o* an excess of make-up doesn't look very natural
[2] (= *insolencia*) insolence

demasiado Ⓐ ADJ [1] (= *excesivo*) too much; **eso es ~** that's too much; **hace ~ calor** it's too hot; **con ~ cuidado** with excessive care; **¡esto es ~!** that's the limit!; **no tengo ~ tiempo** I don't have much time; **¡qué ~!*** wow!*
[2] **demasiados** too many
Ⓑ ADV [1] (= *en exceso*) (*con adjetivos, adverbios*) too; (*con verbos*) too much; **es ~ pesado para levantarlo** it is too heavy to lift; **~ bien lo sé** I know it only too well; **comer ~** to eat too much
[2] (*LAm*) (= *mucho*) **lo siento ~** I'm very *o* really sorry; **es ~ sabio** he's very wise

DEMASIADO

¿"Too", "too much" o "too many"?

- **Demasiado** se traduce por **too** delante de *adjetivos y adverbios*:

  Hace demasiado calor
  It's too hot
  Hace un día demasiado bueno para quedarse trabajando en casa
  It's too nice a day to stay at home working
  Hablas demasiado deprisa
  You talk too quickly

- Se traduce por **too much** cuando **demasiado** describe o se refiere a nombres *incontables* y como complemento de verbos:

  Le he echado demasiada agua a las patatas
  I've put too much water in the potatoes
  Creo que he comido demasiado
  I think I've eaten too much
  Habla demasiado
  He talks too much

NOTA: Cuando acompaña a un verbo de tiempo **demasiado** suele traducirse como **too long**:

  Ha tardado demasiado en acabar la tesis
  He's taken too long to finish his thesis

Too many

- Se traduce por **too many** cuando **demasiado** precede a nombres *contables* en *plural*:

  Tiene demasiadas preocupaciones
  She has too many worries

Para otros usos y ejemplos ver la entrada.

demasié: Ⓐ ADJ, ADV **¡qué ~!** wow!*
Ⓑ SM **es un ~** it's way over the top

demediar▸conjug 1b◂ Ⓐ VT to divide in half
Ⓑ VI to be divided in half

demencia SF madness, insanity ► **demencia senil** senile dementia

demencial ADJ mad, demented

dementar▸conjug 1a◂ Ⓐ VT to drive mad
Ⓑ **dementarse** VPR to go mad, become demented

demente Ⓐ ADJ mad, demented
Ⓑ SMF lunatic; (*Med*) mental patient

demérito SM 1 (*frm*) (= *falta*) demerit (*frm*), fault; **es un ~ para nuestra familia** it brings discredit on *o* to our family; **va en ~ de todos** it brings discredit to everyone, it discredits everyone
2 (= *indignidad*) unworthiness
3 (*LAm*) (= *menosprecio*) contempt

demeritorio ADJ undeserving, unworthy

demo* Ⓐ SMF (*Chile*) Christian Democrat
Ⓑ SF (*Inform, Mús*) demo

democracia SF democracy ► **democracia parlamentaria** parliamentary democracy ► **democracia popular** people's democracy

demócrata Ⓐ ADJ 1 [*valores, país*] democratic
2 (*en Estados Unidos*) Democrat
Ⓑ SMF 1 (*gen*) democrat
2 (*en Estados Unidos*) Democrat

democratacristiano/a ADJ, SM/F Christian Democrat

democráticamente ADV democratically

democrático ADJ democratic

democratización SF democratization

democratizador ADJ democratizing

democratizar▸conjug 1f◂ VT to democratize

democristiano/a ADJ, SM/F Christian Democrat

demodé ADJ démodé, passé

demografía SF demography

demográficamente ADV demographically

demográfico ADJ demographic; **la explosión demográfica** the population explosion

demógrafo/a SM/F demographer

demoledor ADJ 1 [*ataque, efecto*] shattering
2 (= *destructivo*) [*argumento*] overwhelming; [*crítica*] devastating

demoledoramente ADV overwhelmingly

demoler▸conjug 2h◂ VT [+ *edificio*] to demolish, pull down; [+ *argumento, teoría*] to demolish

demolición SF demolition, disbanding

demonche SM (*euf*) = **demonio**

demoniaco ADJ, **demoníaco** ADJ demoniacal, demonic

demonio SM 1 (= *diablo*) devil; **ese ~ de niño** that demon *o* little devil of a child; **ser el mismísimo ~** to be a right little devil ► **demonio familiar** familiar spirit
2 (*) ✦**MODISMOS** **ir como el ~** to go like the devil, go hell for leather; **esto pesa como un ~** this is hellishly heavy; **¡vete al ~!** go to the devil *o* hell!; **¡que se lo lleve el ~!** to hell with it!; **un ruido de todos los** *o* **de mil ~s** a hell of a noise*; **esto sabe a ~s** this tastes awful; **tiene el ~ en el cuerpo** he can't sit still for five minutes
3 (*) (*frases de sentido exclamativo*) **¡qué ~s!** (*expresando ira*) hell!, damn it!; (*expresando sorpresa*) well, I'll be blowed!, what the devil?; **¡qué príncipe ni qué ~s!** prince my foot!*; **¿quién ~s será?** who the devil can that be?; **¿dónde ~s lo habré dejado?** where the devil can I have left it?

demonología SF demonology

demontre SM (*euf*) = **demonio**

demora SF 1 (= *retraso*) delay; **sin ~** without delay
2 (*Náut*) bearing

demorar ▸conjug 1a◂ Ⓐ VT [+ *viaje*] to delay; [+ *llegada, terminación*] to hold up
Ⓑ VI 1 (= *detenerse*) to stay on, linger on; **¡no demores!** don't be long!
2 (= *perder tiempo*) to waste time; **~ en hacer algo** (*LAm*) to take a long time to do sth, be slow in doing sth; **no demores mucho** don't be too long
Ⓒ **demorarse** VPR 1 = **B**
2 (= *tardar mucho*) to take a long time, be slow; **¿cuántos días se demora para ir allá?** (*LAm*) how many days does it take to get there?; **~se en hacer algo** to take a long time to do sth, be slow in doing sth

demorón ADJ (*LAm*) (= *lento*) slow; **ser ~ en hacer algo** to take a long time to do sth, be slow in doing sth

demoroso ADJ (*LAm*) 1 (= *moroso*) late, overdue
2 (= *lento*) slow; **ser ~ en hacer algo** to take a long time to do sth, be slow in doing sth

demos *ver* **dar**

demoscopia SF public opinion research

demoscópico ADJ **sondeo ~** public opinion survey, survey of public opinion

Demóstenes SM Demosthenes

demostrable ADJ demonstrable

demostración SF 1 (= *comprobación*) [*de ejemplo, producto*] demonstration; [*de teorema, teoría*] proof; **hicieron una ~ del funcionamiento** they gave a demonstration of how it worked ► **demostración comercial** commercial exhibition, trade exhibition
2 (= *manifestación externa*) [*de cariño, fuerza*] show; [*de amistad*] gesture; [*de cólera*] display

▼ **demostrar** ▸conjug 1l◂ VT 1 (= *probar*) to prove; **usted no puede ~ nada** you can't prove anything; **demostró que Galileo tenía razón** she proved Galileo right, she proved *o* showed that Galileo was right; **demostró lo mal que hablaba francés** it proved *o* showed how badly he spoke French; **ha demostrado ser muy buena amiga** she has shown herself to be a very good friend
2 (= *enseñar*) to show, demonstrate; **nos ~on cómo funcionaba el sistema eléctrico** they showed us *o* demonstrated to us how the electrical system worked
3 (= *mostrar*) [+ *emoción, sentimiento*] to show, display; **no demostró ningún interés en mis problemas** he showed *o* displayed no interest in my problems

demostrativo Ⓐ ADJ demonstrative
Ⓑ SM demonstrative

demótico ADJ demotic

demudación SF change, alteration (*of countenance*)

demudado ADJ [*rostro*] upset, distraught

demudar ▸conjug 1a◂ Ⓐ VT [+ *rostro*] to change, alter
Ⓑ **demudarse** VPR 1 [*expresión*] to change, alter
2 [*persona*] (= *perder color*) to turn pale; (= *alterarse*) to look upset; **se le demudó el rostro** the colour drained from her face; **continuó sin ~se** he went on without turning a hair

den *ver* **dar**

denante ADV (*LAm*), **denantes** ADV (*LAm*) (= *hace un rato*) earlier, a while ago; (= *antiguamente*) in past times

dendrocronología SF dendrochronology

dendrograma SM dendrogram, tree diagram

denegación SF [*de permiso, petición*] refusal; [*de derechos*] denial ► **denegación de auxilio** (*Jur*) failure to offer assistance (*though legally bound to do so*)

denegar ▸conjug 1h, 1j◂ VT 1 (= *rechazar*) [+ *permiso, petición*] to refuse; [+ *derechos*] to deny
2 (*Jur*) [+ *cargo*] to deny

dengoso ADJ (= *afectado*) affected; (= *coqueto*) coy

dengue SM 1 (= *remilgo*) prudery; **no me vengas con esos ~s** I don't want to hear your silly complaints
2 [*de persona*] (= *afectación*) affectation; (= *coquetería*) coyness
3 (*Med*) dengue fever, breakbone fever
4 (*Andes*) (= *contoneo*) wiggle

denguero ADJ = **dengoso**

denier SM denier

denigración SF denigration

denigrante ADJ 1 (= *difamante*) degrading
2 (= *injurioso*) insulting

denigrar ▸conjug 1a◂ VT (= *difamar*) to denigrate, run down; (= *injuriar*) to insult

denigratorio ADJ denigratory; **campaña denigratoria** campaign of denigration, smear campaign

denodadamente ADV boldly, dauntlessly, intrepidly; **luchar ~** to fight bravely

denodado ADJ bold, brave

denominación SF 1 (= *acto*) naming
2 (= *nombre*) name, designation ► **denominación social** (*Méx*) official company name
3 [*de billete*] denomination; **moneda de baja ~** (*LAm*) low value coin

> **DENOMINACIÓN DE ORIGEN**
>
> *The* **Denominación de Origen**, *abbreviated to* **D.O.**, *is a prestigious product classification which is awarded to food products such as wines, cheeses, sausages and hams that are produced in designated Spanish regions according to stringent production criteria.* **D.O.** *labels serve as a guarantee of quality.*

denominado ADJ named, called; **el ~ jet lag** so-called jet lag

denominador SM denominator ► **denominador común** (*Mat fig*) common denominator

denominar▸conjug 1a◂ VT to name, designate

denostar▸conjug 1l◂ VT (*frm*) to insult

denotación SF (*Ling, Fil*) denotation

denotar ▸conjug 1a◂ VT 1 (= *significar*) (*tb Ling*) to denote
2 (= *indicar*) to indicate, show; **eso denota un cambio en su política** that indicates a change in policy; **denotó nerviosismo en la entrevista** he showed a certain nervousness in the interview

➤ LENGUA Y USO: **demostrar 2** 53.3, 53.4

densamente ADV densely

densidad SF 1 (= *concentración*) [*de sustancia, tráfico*] density; [*de humo, vegetación*] thickness, denseness; [*de caracteres*] (*Inform*) pitch ► **densidad de grabación** recording density ► **densidad de población** population density
2 [*de discurso, relato*] denseness
3 (*Fís*) density

denso ADJ 1 (= *concentrado*) [*sustancia*] dense; [*tráfico*] heavy; [*humo, vegetación*] thick, dense
2 [*discurso, relato*] dense
3 (*Fís*) dense

dentado Ⓐ ADJ [*filo*] jagged; [*sello*] perforated; (*Bot*) dentate; **rueda dentada** cog
Ⓑ SM [*de sello*] perforation

dentadura SF teeth *pl*; **tener mala ~** to have bad teeth ► **dentadura artificial**, **dentadura postiza** false teeth *pl*, dentures *pl*

dental Ⓐ ADJ dental
Ⓑ SF (*Ling*) dental

dentamen* SM teeth *pl*

dentar ▸conjug 1j◂ Ⓐ VT [+ *filo*] to make jagged; [+ *superficie, sello*] to perforate; **sello sin ~** imperforate stamp, unperforated stamp
Ⓑ VI [*niño*] to teethe

dentellada SF 1 (= *mordisco*) bite, nip; **partir algo a ~s** to sever sth with one's teeth
2 (= *señal*) tooth mark

dentellar ▸conjug 1a◂ VI [*dientes*] to chatter; **estaba dentellando** his teeth were chattering; **el susto le hizo ~** the fright made his teeth chatter

dentellear ▸conjug 1a◂ VT to nibble

dentera SF 1 (= *grima*) **dar ~ a algn** to set sb's teeth on edge
2 (= *envidia*) envy, jealousy; **dar ~ a algn** to make sb jealous; **le da ~ que le hagan fiestas al niño** it makes him jealous when they make a fuss of the baby

dentición SF 1 (= *acto*) teething; **estar con la ~** to be teething
2 (= *dientes*) teeth *pl* ► **dentición de leche** milk teeth

dentífrico Ⓐ ADJ tooth *antes de s*; **pasta dentífrica** toothpaste
Ⓑ SM toothpaste

dentilargo ADJ long-toothed

dentina SF dentine, dentin (*EEUU*)

dentista SMF dentist

dentistería SF (*Col, Ven*) 1 (= *ciencia*) dentistry
2 (= *clínica*) dental clinic, dental surgery, dentist's office (*EEUU*)

dentística SF (*Chile*) dentistry

dentón ADJ toothy

dentradera SF (*Andes*), **dentrera** SF (*Andes*) housemaid

dentro ADV 1 inside; **María está ~** María is inside; **allí ~** in there; **vamos ~** let's go in(side); **comimos ~ porque estaba lloviendo** we ate inside *o* indoors because it was raining; **de** *o* **desde ~** from inside, from within (*frm*); **para ~**: **se fueron para ~** they went in(side); **mételo para ~ para que quepa en la funda** push it in so that it fits in the cover; **por ~** inside; **el edificio es precioso por ~** the building is beautiful inside; **la sandía es roja por ~** a watermelon is red on the inside; **el vestido lleva un forro por ~** the dress is lined *o* has a lining inside; **se siente muy desgraciado por ~** he feels very unhappy inside
2 **~ de** 2·1 (= *en el interior de*) in, inside; **~ de la casa** in(side) the house; **tenía un pañuelo ~ del bolso** she had a handkerchief in *o* inside her bag; **lo metió ~ del cajón** he put it in the drawer; **ascensos ~ de la empresa** promotions within the company
2·2 (= *después de*) in; **~ de tres meses** in three months, in three months' time; **llegará ~ de poco** he'll be here shortly
2·3 (= *en los límites de*) within; **esto no está ~ de mi competencia** this is not within my area of responsibility; **~ de lo posible** as far as possible; **su reacción estaba ~ de lo previsto** her reaction was what one might have expected; **~ de todo, me puedo considerar afortunado** all in all *o* all things considered, I can count myself lucky; *ver tb* **caber 5.3**

dentrodera SF (*Andes*) servant

denudación SF denudation

denudar ▸conjug 1a◂ VT to denude, lay bare

denuedo SM (*liter*) valour, valor (*EEUU*)

denuesto SM (*liter*) insult; **llenar a algn de ~s** to heap insults on sb

denuncia SF 1 [*de delito, infracción, accidente*] **hizo** *o* **presentó** *o* **puso una ~ en comisaría** he made a formal complaint *o* accusation to the police, he reported it to the police; **hice** *o* **presenté** *o* **puse una ~ por el** *o* **del robo del bolso** I reported the theft of the bag; **hacer** *o* **presentar** *o* **poner una ~ contra algn** to report sb, make *o* file a formal complaint against sb ► **denuncia falsa** false accusation
2 (= *crítica*) condemnation, denunciation; **el artículo es una ~ de las injusticias del sistema** the article is a condemnation *o* denunciation of the unfairness of the system

denunciable ADJ [*delito*] indictable, punishable

denunciación SF denunciation

denunciador(a) SM/F, **denunciante** SMF 1 [*de delito*] accuser; **el ~ del accidente** the person who reported the accident
2 (= *delator*) informer

denunciar ▸conjug 1b◂ VT 1 [+ *delito, accidente*] to report; **el accidente fue denunciado a la policía** the accident was reported to the police; **denuncié en comisaría el robo de mi bolso** I reported the theft of my handbag to the police; **han denunciado al director por malversación de fondos** the manager has been reported for embezzlement; **denunció a su alumno por insultarle** she reported the student for insulting her
2 (= *criticar*) to condemn, denounce; **denunció la política derechista del gobierno** he condemned *o* denounced the government's right-wing policies
3 (*frm*) (= *indicar*) to reveal, indicate; **el olor denunciaba la presencia del gas** the smell revealed *o* indicated the presence of gas
4 (†) (= *presagiar*) to foretell

denuncio SM = **denuncia 1**

deontología SF (= *ciencia*) deontology; (*profesional*) professional ethics *pl*

D.E.P. ABR (= **descanse en paz**) RIP

Dep. ABR 1 (= **Departamento**) Dept
2 (*Com*) = **Depósito**

deparar ▸conjug 1a◂ VT (= *proporcionar*) to provide with, afford (*frm*); **nos deparó la ocasión de conocer a su familia** it provided us with *o* (*frm*) afforded us the opportunity to meet his family; **los placeres que el viaje nos deparó** the pleasures which the trip afforded us (*frm*); **pero también nos deparó la solución** but it also furnished us with the solution; **lo que el destino nos depare** what fate has *o* holds in store for us; ✦**MODISMO** **¡Dios te la depare buena!** and the best of luck!

departamental ADJ departmental

departamento SM 1 [*de empresa, universidad*] department; **Departamento de Lingüística Aplicada** Department of Applied Linguistics ► **departamento de envíos** dispatch department ► **departamento de visados** visa section ► **departamento jurídico** legal department
2 [*de caja, tren*] compartment ► **departamento de fumadores** smoking compartment ► **departamento de no fumadores** non-smoking compartment ► **departamento de primera** first-class compartment
3 (*Náut*) ► **departamento de máquinas** engine room
4 (*LAm*) (= *piso*) flat, apartment (*EEUU*)
5 (*Andes, Chile*) (= *provincia*) province

departir ▸conjug 3a◂ VI (*frm*) converse (*frm*) (**con** with; **de** about)

depauperación SF 1 (= *empobrecimiento*) impoverishment
2 (*Med*) weakening

depauperar ▸conjug 1a◂ VT 1 (= *empobrecer*) to impoverish
2 (*Med*) to weaken

dependencia SF 1 (= *estado*) dependence (**de** on); ► **dependencia psicológica** psychological dependence, psychological dependency
2 (= *parentesco*) relationship
3 (*Arquit*) (= *habitación*) room ► **dependencia policial** police station; **permanecer en ~s policiales** to remain in police custody
4 (*Com*) (= *sección*) section, office; (= *sucursal*) branch office; (= *empleados*) personnel, employees *pl*
5 (*Pol*) dependency
6 **dependencias** (= *anexo*) [*de edificio, castillo*] outbuildings; [*de aparato*] accessories

depender ▸conjug 2a◂ VI 1 **—¿vas a ir? —depende** "are you going?" — "it depends"
2 **~ de algn/algo** to depend on sb/sth; **mi futuro depende de este examen** my future depends on this exam; **depende de lo que diga mi madre** it depends (on) what my mother says; **no te eches atrás ahora, que dependo de ti** don't back out now, I'm relying *o* depending on you; **sin coche, dependes de los demás** without a car you depend on *o* you're dependent on other people, without a car you have to rely on other people; **todavía depende económicamente de sus padres** he is still financially dependent on his parents; **depende completamente de las drogas** she is completely dependent on drugs
3 **~ de** [*empleado, institución*] to be accountable to, be answerable to; **esta oficina depende de la Generalitat** this office is accountable *o* answerable to the Generalitat
4 **~ de algn** (= *corresponder a*): **lo siento, su aceptación no depende de mí** I'm sorry, it's not up to me whether you are accepted or not

➤ LENGUA Y USO: **depender 2** 52.6

5 (*Pol*) **un territorio que depende de Gran Bretaña** a British dependency
dependiente[1] ADJ dependent (**de** on)
dependiente[2]**/a** SM/F (*en tienda*) shop assistant, sales assistant, salesclerk (*EEUU*)
depilación SF, **depilado** SM (*con crema, con depiladora*) hair removal, depilation; (*con cera*) waxing; (*con pinzas*) plucking
depilador Ⓐ ADJ **crema ~a** hair remover, depilatory cream
Ⓑ SM hair remover, depilatory
depiladora SF hair remover
depilar ▸conjug 1a◂ Ⓐ VT (*con crema, con depiladora*) to remove (unwanted) hair from; (*con cera*) to wax; (*con pinzas*) to pluck
Ⓑ **depilarse** VPR **~se las piernas** to wax one's legs; **~se las cejas** to pluck one's eyebrows
depilatorio Ⓐ ADJ depilatory
Ⓑ SM hair remover, depilatory
deplorable ADJ [*conducta*] deplorable; [*estado*] appalling; **vuestro comportamiento fue ~** your behaviour was deplorable
deplorar ▸conjug 1a◂ VT 1 (= *lamentar*) to deplore; **lo deploro mucho** I'm extremely sorry
2 (= *censurar*) to condemn
deponente Ⓐ ADJ 1 (*Ling*) deponent
2 (*Jur*) **persona ~** deponent, person making a statement
Ⓑ SMF (*Jur*) deponent
deponer ▸conjug 2q◂ Ⓐ VT 1 (= *dejar*) [+ *armas*] to lay down; [+ *actitud*] to change; **no conseguirás que deponga su actitud** you won't be able to persuade him to change his attitude
2 (= *quitar*) [+ *rey*] to depose; [+ *gobernante*] to oust, overthrow; [+ *ministro*] to remove from office
Ⓑ VI 1 (*Jur*) to give evidence
2 (*CAm, Méx*) (= *vomitar*) to vomit
deportación SF deportation
deportar ▸conjug 1a◂ VT to deport
deporte SM sport; **es muy aficionada al ~** she is very keen on sport; **el fútbol es mi ~ favorito** football is my favourite sport; **unas zapatillas de ~** a pair of sports shoes *o* trainers *o* (*EEUU*) sneakers ► **deporte blanco** winter sports *pl*; (*esp*) skiing ► **deporte de competición** competitive sport ► **deporte de exhibición** show event ► **deporte del remo** rowing ► **deporte de vela** sailing ► **deporte hípico** horse-riding ► **deporte náutico** (*con lancha*) water sports *pl* (*in which a boat is used*); (*con velero*) yachting ► **deportes acuáticos** water sports ► **deportes de invierno** winter sports
deportista Ⓐ ADJ sports *antes de s*, sporting; **el público ~** the sporting public; **es muy ~** she's very keen on sport(s), she's very sporty*
Ⓑ SMF sportsman/sportswoman
deportivamente ADV 1 (= *sin agresividad*) sportingly; **se tomó la derrota muy ~** she took the defeat very sportingly
2 (= *relacionado con el deporte*) **hablando ~** in sporting terms; **viste ~** she wears sports clothes
deportividad SF sportsmanship
deportivo Ⓐ ADJ 1 [*club, periódico, zapatillas*] sports *antes de s*; *ver tb* **puerto 1**
2 [*actitud*] sporting, sportsmanlike
3 [*ropa*] casual
Ⓑ SM 1 (*Aut*) sports car
2 **deportivos** (= *zapatos*) sports shoes, trainers, tennis shoes (*EEUU*)
3 (*Prensa*) sports paper
deposición SF 1 (= *derrocamiento*) [*de rey*] deposition; [*de gobernante*] overthrow, ousting; [*de ministro*] removal from office, sacking
2 (*Jur*) (= *testimonio*) deposition, evidence
3 (*euf*) (= *acto*) bowel movement; (= *excremento*) stool; **hacer una ~** to have a bowel movement
depositador(a) SM/F, **depositante** SMF (*Com, Fin*) depositor
depositar ▸conjug 1a◂ Ⓐ VT 1 (*frm*) (= *colocar*) [+ *flor, ofrenda*] to place (**en, sobre** on); [+ *mercancías*] to put away, store; **"depositen las bolsas en información"** "please leave your bags at the information desk"; **~ la confianza en algn** to place one's trust in sb
2 (*Fin*) [+ *dinero, joyas*] to deposit
Ⓑ **depositarse** VPR [*líquido, polvo*] to settle
depositaría SF (*Fin*) trust
depositario/a SM/F [*de dinero*] depository, trustee; [*de secreto*] repository ► **depositario/a judicial** official receiver
depósito SM 1 (= *contenedor*) (*gen*) tank ► **depósito de agua** (= *tanque*) water tank, cistern; (= *pantano*) reservoir ► **depósito de combustible** fuel tank ► **depósito de gasolina** petrol tank, gas tank (*EEUU*)
2 (= *almacén*) [*de mercancías*] warehouse, depot; [*de animales, coches*] pound; (*Mil*) depot; [*de desechos*] dump; **mercancías en ~** bonded goods ► **depósito afianzado** bonded warehouse ► **depósito de aduana** customs warehouse ► **depósito de alimentación** (*Inform*) feeder bin ► **depósito de basura** rubbish dump, tip ► **depósito de cadáveres** mortuary, morgue ► **depósito de carbono** coal tip ► **depósito de equipajes** left-luggage office, checkroom (*EEUU*) ► **depósito de libros** book stack ► **depósito de locomotoras** engine shed, roundhouse (*EEUU*) ► **depósito de maderas** timber yard, lumber yard (*EEUU*) ► **depósito de municiones** ammunition dump
3 (*Com, Fin*) deposit; **dejar una cantidad en ~** to leave a sum as a deposit ► **depósito a la vista** sight deposit ► **depósito a plazo (fijo)** fixed-term deposit ► **depósito bancario** bank deposit
4 (*Quím*) sediment, deposit
depravación SF 1 (= *cualidad*) depravity
2 (= *acto*) depraved act
depravado/a Ⓐ ADJ depraved, corrupt
Ⓑ SM/F degenerate
depravar ▸conjug 1a◂ Ⓐ VT to deprave, corrupt
Ⓑ **depravarse** VPR to become depraved
depre* Ⓐ SF (= *depresión*) **tiene la ~** she's feeling a bit low
Ⓑ ADJ **estar ~** to be feeling down
depreciación SF depreciation ► **depreciación acelerada** accelerated depreciation ► **depreciación normal** wear and tear
depreciar ▸conjug 1b◂ Ⓐ VT to depreciate, reduce the value of
Ⓑ **depreciarse** VPR to depreciate
depredación SF 1 (= *saqueo*) pillage
2 (*Zool*) predation
depredador Ⓐ ADJ [*animal, instinto*] predatory
Ⓑ SM (*Zool*) predator
depredar ▸conjug 1a◂ VT 1 (= *saquear*) to pillage
2 (*Zool*) to prey on
depresión SF 1 (*Med*) depression ► **depresión nerviosa** nervous breakdown ► **depresión posparto** postnatal depression
2 (= *hondonada*) (*en terreno*) depression; (*en horizonte, camino*) dip
3 (= *descenso*) [*de temperatura, presión*] drop, fall (**de** in); **~ del mercurio** fall in temperature
4 (*Econ*) depression, recession
5 (*Meteo*) depression
depresivo/a Ⓐ ADJ [*carácter, persona*] depressive; **es una persona depresiva** she's a depressive, she's always feeling depressed
Ⓑ SM/F depressive
deprimente Ⓐ ADJ depressing
Ⓑ SM depressant
deprimido ADJ depressed
deprimir ▸conjug 3a◂ Ⓐ VT 1 (*Psic*) to depress; **este tiempo me deprime** I find this weather depressing, this weather gets me down*; **la muerte de su marido la deprimió** the death of her husband sent her into a depression *o* made her depressed
2 (*Com*) [+ *mercado, economía*] to depress; [+ *consumo*] to slow (down)
3 (*Med*) [+ *sistema inmunológico*] to depress
Ⓑ **deprimirse** VPR to get depressed, become depressed
deprisa ADV *ver* **prisa**
depuración SF 1 (= *purificación*) [*de agua*] treatment, purification; [*de aguas residuales*] treatment; [*de estilo*] refinement
2 (*Pol*) purge
3 (*Inform*) debugging
depurado ADJ [*estilo*] pure, refined
depurador SM purifier
depuradora SF [*de agua*] water-treatment plant; (*en piscina*) filter system ► **depuradora de aguas residuales** sewage plant *o* farm
depurar ▸conjug 1a◂ VT 1 (= *purificar*) [+ *agua*] to treat, purify; [+ *aguas residuales*] to treat; [+ *sangre*] to cleanse
2 (*Pol*) to purge
3 (*Inform*) to debug
4 (*Caribe**) [+ *empleado*] to fire*
depurativo SM blood tonic
dequeísmo SM *tendency to use "de que" in place of "que" (eg "pienso de que")*
der. ABR, **der.º** ABR (= **derecho**) r
derbi SM (*pl* **derbis**), **derby** SM (*pl* **derbys**) (local) derby
derecha SF 1 (= *lado derecho*) **la ~** the right; **está prohibido adelantar por la ~** you're not allowed to overtake on the right; **se sentó a la ~ del embajador** he sat on the right *o* to the right of the ambassador; **toma el desvío de la ~** take the turning on the right; **seguir por la ~** to keep (to the) right; **torcer a la ~** to turn right; ✦***MODISMO*** **no dar** *o* **hacer nada a ~s** (*Esp*) not to do *o* get anything right; *ver tb* **conducción 2**
2 (*Anat*) (*tb* **mano ~**) right hand; (*tb* **pierna ~**) right leg; **escribe con la ~** he writes with his right hand
3 (*Esp Pol*) **la ~** the Right; **ser de ~s** to be right-wing; *ver tb* **extremo B**

derechamente ADV 1 (= *en línea recta*) straight, directly
2 (= *correctamente*) properly, rightly

derechazo SM 1 (*Boxeo*) right
2 (*Tenis*) forehand drive
3 (*Taur*) *pass with the cape*

derechismo SM right-wing outlook *o* tendencies *etc*

derechista Ⓐ ADJ right-wing
Ⓑ SMF right-winger

derechización SF drift towards the right

derechizar ▸conjug 1f◂ Ⓐ VT [+ *partido*] to lead towards the right
Ⓑ **derechizarse** VPR to move to the right, become right-wing

derecho Ⓐ ADJ 1 [*línea, dirección*] (= *recto*) straight; (= *vertical*) upright, straight; **traza las líneas derechas** draw the lines straight; **siéntate ~** sit upright *o* straight; **anda derecha** walk upright, stand straight when you walk; **poner algo ~** (= *no torcido*) to put sth straight, straighten sth; (= *no caído*) to stand sth upright; ✦**MODISMO tener a algn más ~ que una vela** to have sb under one's thumb
2 (= *del lado derecho*) [*brazo, pierna, oreja*] right; [*lado, cajón*] right-hand; **tiene toda la parte derecha del cuerpo paralizada** he's paralysed down the right side of his body; **entre por la puerta derecha** go through the right-hand door; *ver tb* **brazo 1**, **ojo 1**
3 (= *honrado*) honest, straight
4 (*CAm*) (= *afortunado*) lucky
Ⓑ ADV 1 (= *en línea recta*) **seguir ~** to carry *o* go straight on; **siga todo ~** carry *o* go straight on
2 (= *directamente*) straight; **después del cine, derechito para casa** after the cinema, straight home; **fui ~ a Londres** I went straight to London
Ⓒ SM 1 (*Jur*) (= *estudios, legislación*) law; (= *justicia*) justice; **estudiante de Derecho** law student; **Facultad de Derecho** Faculty of Law; **lo que manda el ~ en este caso** what justice demands in this case; **conforme a ~** in accordance with the law; **no actuó conforme a ~** he acted unlawfully; **propietario en ~** legal owner; **por ~** in law, legally; **lo que me corresponde por ~** what is legally mine, what is mine by law; **por ~ propio** in one's own right ▸ **derecho administrativo** administrative law ▸ **derecho canónico** canon law ▸ **derecho civil** civil law ▸ **derecho comunitario** Community law ▸ **derecho consuetudinario** common law ▸ **derecho de compañías** company law ▸ **derecho de familia** family law ▸ **derecho del trabajo** labour *o* (*EEUU*) labor law ▸ **derecho de sociedades** company law ▸ **derecho escrito** statute law ▸ **derecho fiscal** tax law ▸ **derecho foral** *legislation pertaining to those Spanish regions which have charters called "fueros"* ▸ **derecho internacional** international law ▸ **derecho laboral** labour law, labor law (*EEUU*) ▸ **derecho marítimo** maritime law ▸ **derecho mercantil** commercial law ▸ **derecho penal** criminal law ▸ **derecho político** constitutional law ▸ **derecho positivo** statute law ▸ **derecho privado** private law ▸ **derecho procesal** procedural law ▸ **derecho público** public law ▸ **derecho romano** Roman law ▸ **derecho tributario** tax law
2 [*de persona, entidad*] right; **"se reserva el derecho de admisión"** "the management reserve(s) the right to refuse admission"; **¿con qué ~ me hablas así?** what right have you to talk to me that way?; **es miembro de pleno ~** he's a full member; **¡no hay ~!** it's not fair!; **~ a la educación** right to education; **el ~ a la libertad** the right to be free; **~ a la intimidad** right to *o* of privacy; **lo único que nos queda es el ~ al pataleo** (*hum*) the only thing we can do is kick up a fuss*; **~ al voto** ◊ **~ a votar** (*gen*) right to vote; (*como derecho civil*) franchise, right to vote; **con ~ a algo** entitled to sth; **declaraciones de la renta con ~ a devolución** tax returns entitled to a rebate; **entrada con ~ a consumición** *entrance ticket including one free drink*; **dar ~ a hacer algo** to give the right to do sth; **eso no te da ~ a hablarme así** that doesn't give you the right to talk to me that way; **estar en su ~** to be within one's rights; **claro, estás en tu ~ de decir lo que quieras** of course, you are perfectly entitled to say whatever you like; **tener ~ a algo** to be entitled to sth; **no tenemos ~ a vacaciones** we are not entitled to holidays; **tener ~ a hacer algo** to have a *o* the right to do sth; **no tienes ningún ~ a insultarme** you have no right to insult me ▸ **derecho de asilo** right of asylum ▸ **derecho de huelga** right to strike ▸ **derecho de paso** right of way, easement (*EEUU*) ▸ **derecho de pernada** (*Hist*) droit du seigneur ▸ **derecho de réplica** right of reply ▸ **derecho de retención** (*Com*) lien ▸ **derecho de reunión** right of assembly ▸ **derecho de tránsito** right of passage ▸ **derecho de veto** right of veto ▸ **derecho de visita** right of access ▸ **derecho divino** divine right ▸ **derecho preferente** preferential right ▸ **derechos civiles** civil rights ▸ **derechos de la mujer** women's rights
3 **derechos** (*Com*) rights; **"reservados todos los ~s"** "all rights reserved"; **tienen los ~s exclusivos para la venta del disco** they have the exclusive rights to sales of the record ▸ **derechos cinematográficos** film rights ▸ **derechos de antena** broadcasting rights ▸ **derechos de autor** copyright *sing* ▸ **derechos de edición** publishing rights ▸ **derechos de emisión** (*TV, Radio*) broadcasting rights ▸ **derechos de patente** patent rights ▸ **derechos editoriales** publishing rights ▸ **derechos humanos** human rights; **Declaración de los Derechos Humanos** Declaration of Human Rights
4 **derechos** (= *honorarios*) [*de arquitecto, notario*] fee(s); (= *impuestos*) duty *sing*; **franco de ~s** duty-free; **sujeto a ~s** subject to duty, dutiable ▸ **derechos aduaneros**, **derechos arancelarios**, **derechos de aduana** customs duty ▸ **derechos de asesoría**, **derechos de consulta** consulting fees, consultancy fees ▸ **derechos de autor** royalties ▸ **derechos de enganche** (*Telec*) connection charges ▸ **derechos de entrada** import duties ▸ **derechos de exportación** export duties ▸ **derechos de importación** import duties ▸ **derechos de matrícula** registration fee *sing* ▸ **derechos de muelle** dock dues, docking fees (*EEUU*) ▸ **derechos de peaje** (*Aut*) toll *sing* ▸ **derechos portuarios** harbour dues, harbor dues (*EEUU*) ▸ **derechos reales** *tax paid after the completion of an official transaction*
5 (*tb* **lado ~**) [*de tela, papel*] right side; [*de calcetín, chaqueta*] outside; **¿cuál es el ~ de esta tela?** which is the right side of this fabric?; **puedes planchar la falda por el ~** you can iron the skirt on the outside; **poner algo al** *o* **del ~** to put sth the right side *o* way up; **pon el mantel del ~** put the tablecloth the right side *o* way up; **ponte la camiseta al ~** put your T-shirt on the right way round

derechohabiente SMF rightful claimant

derechura SF 1 (= *honestidad*) straightness; **hablar en ~** to speak plainly, talk straight; **hacer algo en ~** to do sth right away
2 (= *franqueza*) directness
3 (= *justicia*) rightness, justice
4 (*LAm*) (= *suerte*) luck, good luck

deriva SF (*Náut*) drift; **buque a la ~** ship adrift, drifting ship; **ir** *o* **estar a la ~** to drift; **el país va a la ~** the country has lost direction ▸ **deriva continental**, **deriva de los continentes** continental drift

derivación SF 1 (= *procedencia*) derivation
2 (*Elec*) shunt; **hacer una ~ en un alambre** to tap a wire; **en ~** shunt *antes de s*
3 (*Ling*) (= *etimología*) etymology, derivation; (= *composición*) word formation ▸ **derivación regresiva** back-formation
4 [*de río*] diversion

derivado Ⓐ ADJ derived
Ⓑ SM 1 (*Ling*) derivative
2 (*Industria, Quím*) by-product ▸ **derivado cárnico** meat product ▸ **derivado del petróleo** oil product ▸ **derivado lácteo** milk product; **~s lácteos** dairy products

derivar[1] ▸conjug 1a◂ Ⓐ VI 1 **~ de algo** (= *provenir de*) to derive from sth; **esta palabra deriva del griego** this word derives from *o* is derived from the Greek; **esta crisis deriva de una mala política financiera** this crisis stems from *o* springs from bad financial policy; **de estos datos se deriva que ...** from this it follows that ...
2 **~ en algo** (= *tener como resultado*) to lead to sth, result in sth; **esto derivó en la pérdida de las colonias** this led to *o* resulted in the loss of the colonies; **derivó en tragedia** it ended in tragedy
3 **~ hacia algo** to turn to sth; **la conversación derivó hacia otros temas** the conversation moved on to *o* turned to different topics; **en su vejez su interés derivó hacia la literatura** in his old age his interest turned to literature
4 (*Náut*) to drift
Ⓑ VT 1 [+ *carretera, río*] to divert
2 [+ *conversación, charla*] to divert, steer; **derivó el debate hacia temas menos controvertidos** he diverted *o* steered the discussion towards less controversial subjects
3 (*Mat*) to derive
4 (*Elec*) to shunt
Ⓒ **derivarse** VPR **~se de algo** [*palabra, término*] to derive from sth, be derived from sth

derivar[2] ▸conjug 1a◂ VI (*Náut*) to drift

derivativo ADJ, SM derivative

dermatología SF dermatology

dermatólogo/a SM/F dermatologist

dérmico ADJ skin *antes de s*; **enfermedad dérmica** skin disease

dermohidratante SM skin moisturizer

dermoprotector Ⓐ ADJ skin *antes de s*
Ⓑ SM skin protector

derogación SF [*de ley*] repeal; [*de contrato*] revocation

derogar ▸conjug 1h◂ VT [+ *ley*] to repeal; [+ *contrato*] to revoke

derrabar ▸conjug 1a◂ VT to dock, cut off the tail of

derrabe SM [*de monte*] rock-fall; [*de techo*] cave-in

derrama SF 1 (= *reparto*) apportionment of (local) tax
2 (= *sobretasa*) special levy
3 (= *tasación*) valuation, rating
4 (= *vale*) credit voucher
5 (= *dividendo*) interim dividend payment

derramadero SM spillway ► **derramadero de basura** rubbish dump

derramamiento SM 1 [*de líquido*] spilling; (*al rebosar*) overflowing ► **derramamiento de sangre** bloodshed
2 [*de vidas, recursos*] squandering
3 (= *esparcimiento*) scattering

derramar ▸conjug 1a◂ Ⓐ VT 1 (*fuera de recipiente*) [+ *líquido*] to spill; [+ *sangre, lágrimas, luz*] to shed; **~ una taza de café** to spill a cup of coffee
2 (= *desaprovechar*) [+ *talento, dinero*] to squander, waste
3 (= *esparcir*) [+ *favores*] to lavish, pour out; [+ *chismes, noticias*] to spread
4 [+ *impuestos*] to apportion
Ⓑ **derramarse** VPR 1 (= *salirse*) [*líquido*] to spill; [*harina*] to pour out, spill out; **llenar una taza hasta ~se** to fill a cup to overflowing
2 (= *esparcirse*) to scatter; **la multitud se derramó por todos lados** the crowd scattered in all directions

derrame SM 1 (= *acto*) = **derramamiento 1**
2 (*Med*) **tiene un ~ en el ojo** he's got a burst blood vessel in his eye ► **derrame cerebral** brain haemorrhage *o* (EEUU) hemorrhage ► **derrame sinovial** synovitis
3 (= *salida*) (*por encima del recipiente*) overflow; (*en pluma, recipiente*) leakage

derrapada SF, **derrapamiento** SM skid, skidding

derrapante ADJ **"camino derrapante"** (*Méx*) "slippery road"

derrapar ▸conjug 1a◂ Ⓐ VI (*Aut*) to skid
Ⓑ **derraparse** VPR (*Méx*) 1 (= *patinar*) to slip
2 **~se por algn*** to be mad about sb*

derrape SM 1 (*Aut*) skid
2 (*Caribe*‡) (= *alboroto*) uproar, shindy*

derredor SM **al** *o* **en ~ (de)** around, about; **en su ~** round about him

derrelicto SM (*Náut*) derelict

derrengado ADJ 1 (= *torcido*) bent, twisted
2 (= *cojo*) crippled, lame
3 (= *cansado*) **estar ~** to ache all over; **dejar ~ a algn** to wear sb out

derrengante ADJ exhausting, crippling

derrengar ▸conjug 1h◂ Ⓐ VT 1 (= *torcer*) to bend, twist
2 **~ a algn** (= *deslomar*) to break sb's back; (= *agotar*) to wear sb out
Ⓑ **derrengarse** VPR (*) to collapse; **~se de risa** to collapse with laughter, fall about laughing

derrepente SM (*CAm*) **de** *o* **en un ~** *ver* **repente 2**

derretido ADJ 1 (= *fundido*) [*mantequilla, helado*] melted; [*metal*] molten; [*nieve*] thawed
2 **estar ~ por algn** to be crazy about sb

derretimiento SM 1 (= *fundido*) [*de mantequilla, helado*] melting; [*de nieve*] thawing; **se produjo el ~ del metal en el horno** the metal was melted (down) in the furnace
2 (= *derroche*) squandering

derretir ▸conjug 3k◂ Ⓐ VT (= *fundir*) [+ *mantequilla, helado*] to melt; [+ *metal*] to melt, melt down; [+ *nieve*] to melt, thaw
Ⓑ **derretirse** VPR 1 (= *fundirse*) [*mantequilla, helado, metal*] to melt; [*nieve*] to thaw, melt
2 (*) (= *sulfurarse*) to get worked up
3 (*) (= *mostrarse sensible*) to come over all sentimental; **te derrites cada vez que te habla** whenever she speaks to you, you go all soppy *o* come over all sentimental

derribar ▸conjug 1a◂ Ⓐ VT 1 (= *derrumbar*) [+ *edificio*] to knock down, pull down; [+ *puerta*] to batter down; [+ *barrera*] to tear down; **van a ~ la fábrica** they are going to knock down *o* pull down the factory; **el huracán derribó varias casas** the hurricane blew down *o* brought down a number of houses
2 [+ *persona*] to knock down; (*Boxeo*) to floor
3 (*Aer*) to shoot down, bring down; **fue derribado sobre el lago** he was shot down over the lake
4 (*Caza*) to shoot, bag
5 [+ *gobierno*] to bring down, topple
6 [+ *pasión*] to subdue
Ⓑ **derribarse** VPR 1 (= *caer al suelo*) to fall down, collapse
2 (= *tirarse al suelo*) to throw o.s. down

derribo SM 1 [*de edificio*] knocking down, demolition
2 (*Lucha*) throw, take-down (EEUU)
3 (*Aer*) shooting down
4 (*Pol*) overthrow
5 **derribos** (= *escombros*) rubble *sing*, debris *sing*

derrisco SM (*Caribe*) gorge, ravine

derrocadero SM cliff, precipice, steep place

derrocamiento SM 1 [*de gobierno*] overthrow
2 [*de edificio*] demolition

derrocar ▸conjug 1g◂ Ⓐ VT 1 (*Pol*) [+ *gobierno*] to overthrow, topple; [+ *ministro*] to oust
2 [+ *edificio*] to knock down, demolish
3 (= *despeñar*) to hurl down
Ⓑ **derrocarse** VPR **~se por un precipicio** to throw o.s. over a cliff

derrochador(a) ADJ, SM/F spendthrift

derrochar ▸conjug 1a◂ VT 1 [+ *dinero, recursos*] to squander, waste
2 (= *tener*) [+ *energía, salud*] to be bursting with, be full of; **~ mal genio** to be excessively bad-tempered

derroche SM 1 (= *despilfarro*) waste, squandering; **regar todos los días es un ~ de agua** it's a waste of water watering the plants every day; **con un imperdonable ~ de recursos** with an unforgivable squandering of resources; **no se puede tolerar tal ~** such extravagance *o* wastefulness cannot be tolerated
2 (= *abundancia*) abundance, excess; **con un ~ de buen gusto** with a fine display of good taste

derrochón/ona ADJ, SM/F = **derrochador**

derrota[1] SF 1 (= *camino, vereda*) route, track
2 (*Náut*) course

derrota[2] SF (*Dep, Mil*) defeat; **sufrir una grave ~** (*en batalla, partido*) to suffer a heavy defeat; (*en proyecto*) to suffer a grave setback

derrotado ADJ 1 (= *vencido*) [*ejército*] defeated; [*equipo*] losing, defeated
2 [*vestidos, persona*] shabby; **un actor ~** a down-and-out actor

derrotar ▸conjug 1a◂ Ⓐ VT 1 (= *vencer*) [+ *ejército*] to defeat; [+ *equipo*] to defeat, beat
2 (= *estropear*) [+ *ropa*] to tear, ruin; (*fig*) [+ *salud*] to ruin
Ⓑ **derrotarse** VPR (‡) [*delincuente*] to cough‡, sing‡; **~se de algn** to grass on sb‡

derrotero SM 1 (*Náut*) course; ✦***MODISMO*** **tomar otro(s) ~(s)** to adopt a different course
2 (*Caribe*) (= *tesoro*) hidden treasure

derrotismo SM defeatism

derrotista ADJ, SMF defeatist

derruir ▸conjug 3g◂ VT to demolish, tear down

derrumbadero SM 1 (= *precipicio*) cliff, precipice, steep place
2 (= *peligro*) danger, hazard

derrumbamiento SM 1 [*de edificio*] (= *desplome*) collapse; (= *demolición*) demolition ► **derrumbamiento de piedras** rockfall ► **derrumbamiento de tierra** landslide
2 [*del techo*] collapse, cave-in
3 (= *descenso brusco*) [*de pacto, sistema*] collapse; [*de precios*] sharp fall

derrumbar ▸conjug 1a◂ Ⓐ VT 1 [+ *edificio*] to knock down, demolish
2 (= *despeñar*) to fling down, hurl down
3 (= *volcar*) to upset, overturn
Ⓑ **derrumbarse** VPR 1 (= *hundirse*) [*edificio*] to collapse, fall down; [*techo*] to fall in, cave in
2 (= *precipitarse*) [*persona*] to fling o.s., hurl o.s. (**por** down, over)
3 [*esperanzas*] to collapse; **se han derrumbado los precios** prices have tumbled

derrumbe SM 1 = **derrumbamiento**
2 (= *precipicio*) cliff, precipice, steep place
3 (= *peligro*) danger, hazard

derviche SMF dervish

des... PREF de..., des..., un..., dis...; **~colonización** decolonization; **~militarizado** demilitarized; **~empleo** unemployment; **~favorable** unfavourable; **~gana** unwillingness; **~alentador** discouraging

desabastecer ▸conjug 2d◂ VT to leave short

desabastecido ADJ **estar ~ de algo** to be out of sth; **nos cogió ~s de gasolina** it caught us out of *o* without petrol

desabastecimiento SM shortage, scarcity

desabillé SM deshabille

desabolladura SF (*esp LAm Aut*) panel beating

desabollar ▸conjug 1a◂ VT to knock the dents out of

desabonarse ▸conjug 1a◂ VPR to stop subscribing, cancel one's subscription

desabono SM 1 (= *acto*) cancellation of one's subscription
2 (= *descrédito*) discredit; **hablar en ~ de algn** to say damaging things about sb, speak ill of sb

desaborido/a Ⓐ ADJ [*comida*] insipid, tasteless; [*persona*] dull
Ⓑ SM/F **es un ~** he's so dull, he's such a bore

desabotonar ▸conjug 1a◂ Ⓐ VT to unbutton, undo
Ⓑ VI (*Bot*) to blossom
Ⓒ **desabotonarse** VPR [*camisa, pantalón*] to come undone; **él se desabotonó la camisa** he unbuttoned *o* undid his shirt

desabrido ADJ 1 (= *poco amable*) [*persona*] surly; [*tono*] harsh; [*respuesta*] sharp; [*debate*] bitter, acrimonious
2 [*comida*] tasteless, insipid
3 [*tiempo*] unpleasant

desabrigado ADJ 1 [*persona*] **no deberías salir ~ a la calle** you shouldn't go out without warm clothes on
2 [*lugar*] exposed

desabrigar ▸conjug 1h◂ Ⓐ VT 1 (= *quitar ropa a*) to remove the clothing of; **desabrígalo un poco, que hace mucho calor** take some *o* a layer of his clothes off, it's very hot
2 (= *desproteger*) to deprive of protection
Ⓑ **desabrigarse** VPR (*quitándose ropa*) to take off one's clothes; (*en la cama*) to throw off the bedcovers, kick off the bedcovers; **no te desabrigues cuando salgas** stay well wrapped up when you're outside

desabrigo SM 1 (= *acto*) uncovering
2 (= *falta de protección*) lack of protection

desabrimiento SM 1 (= *falta de amabilidad*) [*de persona*] surliness, rudeness; [*de tono*] harshness; [*de respuesta*] sharpness; [*de debate*] acrimony; **contestar con ~** to answer sharply
2 (*en comida*) tastelessness, insipidness
3 (= *disgusto*) unpleasantness
4 (= *depresión*) depression, lowness of spirits

desabrir ▸conjug 3a◂ VT 1 [+ *comida*] to give a nasty taste to
2 [+ *persona*] (= *amargar*) to embitter; (= *atormentar*) to torment

desabrochar ▸conjug 1a◂ Ⓐ VT 1 [+ *camisa, zapatos*] to undo; [+ *cremallera, bragueta*] to unfasten; **¿me puedes ~ el collar?** can you undo *o* unfasten my necklace?
2 [+ *secreto, misterio*] to penetrate
Ⓑ **desabrocharse** VPR 1 [*ropa*] to come undone; **¿me ayudas a ~me el vestido?** would you help me undo my dress?
2 (= *desahogarse*) to unburden o.s.

desaburrirse ▸conjug 3a◂ VPR (*LAm*) to enjoy o.s., have a good time

desacatador ADJ disrespectful, insulting

desacatar ▸conjug 1a◂ VT [+ *ley*] to disobey; [+ *norma*] to fail to comply with; [+ *persona*] to be disrespectful to

desacato SM 1 (= *desobediencia*) (*a la norma*) failure to comply (**a** with); (*a la autoridad*) disrespect (**a** for)
2 (*Jur*) contempt, act of contempt ▸ **desacato a la autoridad, desacato a la justicia, desacato al tribunal** contempt of court

desaceleración SF 1 (*Aut*) deceleration, slowing down
2 (*Econ*) downturn

desacelerar ▸conjug 1a◂ Ⓐ VT (*Aut*) to slow down
Ⓑ VI 1 (*Aut*) to decelerate, slow down
2 (*Econ*) to slow down, decline

desacertadamente ADV [*diagnosticar, opinar*] mistakenly, erroneously, wrongly; [*actuar*] unwisely, injudiciously

desacertado ADJ [*diagnóstico, opinión*] mistaken; [*medida*] unwise

desacertar ▸conjug 1j◂ VI (*al diganosticar, opinar*) to be mistaken, be wrong; (*al actuar*) to act unwisely

desachavar* ▸conjug 1a◂ VI (*Cono Sur*) to spill the beans*

desacierto SM (= *error*) mistake; (*al opinar*) unfortunate remark; **ha sido un ~ elegir este sitio** it was a mistake to choose this place; **fue uno de muchos ~s suyos** it was one of his many mistakes *o* errors

desacomedido ADJ (*Andes*) unhelpful, obstructive

desacomodado ADJ 1 (*euf*) (= *pobre*) badly off, hard up
2 (= *incómodo*) awkward, inconvenient
3 (= *parado*) unemployed, out of a job

desacomodar ▸conjug 1a◂ Ⓐ VT 1 (= *incomodar*) to put out, inconvenience
2 [+ *criado*] to discharge
Ⓑ **desacomodarse** VPR to lose one's post

desacompasado ADJ = **descompasado**

desaconsejable ADJ inadvisable

desaconsejado ADJ **tengo ~ hacer ejercicio** I've been advised not to do any exercise, I've been advised against doing any exercise

desaconsejar ▸conjug 1a◂ VT [+ *persona*] to dissuade, advise against; [+ *proyecto*] to advise against; **los rigores del viaje ~on esa decisión** the rigours of the journey made that decision inadvisable

desacoplable ADJ detachable, removable

desacoplar ▸conjug 1a◂ Ⓐ VT (*Elec*) to disconnect; (*Mec*) to uncouple
Ⓑ **desacoplarse** VPR to come off

desacordar ▸conjug 1l◂ Ⓐ VT to put out of tune
Ⓑ **desacordarse** VPR 1 (*Mús*) to get out of tune
2 (= *olvidar*) to be forgetful; **~se de algo** to forget sth

desacorde ADJ 1 (*Mús*) discordant
2 (= *diverso*) [*opiniones*] conflicting; [*colores*] clashing

desacostumbradamente ADV unusually

desacostumbrado ADJ 1 **estar ~ a algo: estamos ~s al frío** we're not used to the cold, we're unused to the cold
2 (= *insólito*) unusual

desacostumbrar ▸conjug 1a◂ Ⓐ VT **~ a algn de algo** to get sb out of the habit of sth
Ⓑ **desacostumbrarse** VPR **~se de algo** to get out of the habit of sth

desacralizar ▸conjug 1f◂ VT to demystify

desacreditado ADJ discredited

desacreditar ▸conjug 1a◂ Ⓐ VT [+ *político, gobierno*] to discredit
Ⓑ **desacreditarse** VPR to be discredited

desactivación SF defusing, making safe ▸ **desactivación de bombas, desactivación de explosivos** bomb disposal

desactivador SM bomb-disposal officer

desactivar ▸conjug 1a◂ Ⓐ VT [+ *bomba*] to defuse, deactivate; [+ *alarma*] to deactivate, neutralize
Ⓑ **desactivarse** VPR (*Inform*) to be disabled

desactualizado ADJ out of date

▼**desacuerdo** SM 1 (= *discrepancia*) disagreement, discord; **en ~** out of keeping (**con** with), at variance (**con** with); **la corbata estaba en ~ con la camisa** the tie didn't go with the shirt ▸ **desacuerdo amistoso** agreement to differ
2 (= *error*) error, blunder
3 (= *falta de memoria*) forgetfulness

desadaptación SF maladjustment

desadaptado/a ADJ, SM/F = **inadaptado**

desadeudarse ▸conjug 1a◂ VPR to get out of debt

desadorno SM bareness

desadvertido ADJ careless

desadvertir ▸conjug 3i◂ VT 1 (= *no ver*) to fail to notice
2 (= *desatender*) to disregard

desafecto Ⓐ ADJ disaffected; **~ a algo** hostile to sth; **elementos ~s al régimen** those hostile to the régime
Ⓑ SM disaffection

desaferrar ▸conjug 1a *o* 1j◂ Ⓐ VT 1 (= *soltar*) to loosen, unfasten; (*Náut*) [+ *ancla*] to weigh
2 (= *disuadir*) to dissuade
Ⓑ VI to weigh anchor

desafiador(a) Ⓐ ADJ 1 [*actitud, voz*] defiant
2 [*decisión, experiencia*] challenging
Ⓑ SM/F challenger

desafiante ADJ 1 [*actitud, voz*] defiant
2 [*decisión, experiencia*] challenging

desafiar ▸conjug 1c◂ VT 1 to challenge, dare; **~ a algn a hacer algo** to challenge *o* dare sb to do sth
2 [+ *peligro*] to defy
3 (= *competir*) to challenge, compete with
4 (*Méx*) (= *pelear*) to fight

desaficionarse ▸conjug 1a◂ VPR **~ de algo** to come to dislike sth

desafilado ADJ blunt

desafilar ▸conjug 1a◂ Ⓐ VT to blunt, dull
Ⓑ **desafilarse** VPR to get blunt

desafiliarse ▸conjug 1b◂ VPR to disaffiliate (**de** from)

desafinadamente ADV [*cantar, tocar*] out of tune, off key

desafinado ADJ out of tune

desafinar ▸conjug 1a◂ VI 1 (*Mús*) [*instrumento*] to be out of tune; [*cantante*] to sing out of tune; [*músico*] to play out of tune, be out of tune
2 (= *hablar inoportunamente*) to speak out of turn

desafío SM 1 (= *reto*) challenge; **es un ~ a todos nosotros** it is a challenge to us all
2 (= *combate*) duel
3 (*a peligro, muerte*) defiance

desaforadamente ADV [*comportarse*] outrageously; **gritar ~** to shout one's head off

desaforado ADJ [*comportamiento*] outrageous; [*persona*] lawless, disorderly; [*grito*] earsplitting; **es un ~** he's a violent sort, he's dangerously excitable

desaforarse ▸conjug 1l◂ VPR to behave in an outrageous way, act violently

desafortunadamente ADV unfortunately

desafortunado ADJ 1 (= *desgraciado*) unfortunate, unlucky
2 (= *no oportuno*) [*comentario, anuncio*] inopportune, unfortunate; [*decisión, medida*] unfortunate

desafuero SM outrage, excess

desagotar ▸conjug 1a◂ VT (*Arg*) to drain

➤ LENGUA Y USO: **desacuerdo 1** 53.6

desagraciado ADJ graceless, unattractive

desagradable ADJ unpleasant, disagreeable (*más frm*); **ser ~ con algn** to be unpleasant to sb

desagradablemente ADV unpleasantly

▼**desagradar** ▸conjug 1a◂ Ⓐ VT **me desagrada ese olor** I don't like that smell; **ese estilo no me desagrada en absoluto** I don't dislike that style at all; **me desagrada tener que hacerlo** I dislike having to do it
Ⓑ VI to be unpleasant

desagradecido/a Ⓐ ADJ [1] [*persona*] ungrateful
[2] [*trabajo*] thankless
Ⓑ SM/F **eres un ~** you're so ungrateful

desagradecimiento SM ingratitude

desagrado SM [1] (= *disgusto*) displeasure; **hacer algo con ~** to do sth unwillingly
[2] (= *descontento*) dissatisfaction

desagraviar ▸conjug 1b◂ Ⓐ VT [1] [+ *persona*] (*gen*) to make amends to (**de** for); (*con dinero*) to indemnify; (*con disculpas*) to apologize to
[2] [+ *agravio, ofensa*] to make amends for
Ⓑ **desagraviarse** VPR (= *vengarse*) to get one's own back

desagravio SM apology; **hacer algo en ~ de algo** to make amends for sth by doing sth

desagregación SF disintegration

desagregar ▸conjug 1h◂ Ⓐ VT to disintegrate
Ⓑ **desagregarse** VPR to disintegrate

desaguadero SM [1] [*de agua*] drain
[2] (*Méx**) loo*, john (*EEUU**)

desaguar ▸conjug 1i◂ Ⓐ VT [1] (= *vaciar*) [+ *líquido*] to drain; [+ *recipiente, bañera*] to empty, drain
[2] [+ *dinero, fortuna*] to squander
[3] (*Andes*) (= *enjuagar*) to rinse (out)
Ⓑ VI [1] [*líquido*] to drain away, drain off
[2] [*río*] **~ en algo** to flow into sth

desagüe SM [1] (= *acto*) drainage, draining
[2] (= *conducto*) [*de bañera, lavadora*] wastepipe, drainpipe; [*de azotea*] drain; [*de río, pantano*] drainage channel; **tubo de ~** drainpipe, wastepipe

desaguisado Ⓐ ADJ illegal
Ⓑ SM (= *lío*) mess; (= *acto ilegal*) crime

desahogadamente ADV comfortably

desahogado/a Ⓐ ADJ [1] (= *amplio*) [*habitación, casa, apartamento*] spacious; [*vestido*] loose-fitting; [*espacio*] clear, free
[2] [*vida, situación*] comfortable; **ahora andamos algo más ~s de tiempo** we're less pressed for time now
[3] (= *con dinero*) comfortably off
[4] (= *descarado*) brazen; **él, tan ~, se lo comió todo** he was brazen enough to eat it all up
Ⓑ SM/F brazen person

desahogar ▸conjug 1h◂ Ⓐ VT [1] (= *manifestar*) [+ *ira*] to vent (**en** on); **desahogó sus penas** she unburdened herself of her woes
[2] [+ *persona*] to console
Ⓑ **desahogarse** VPR [1] (= *desfogarse*) to let off steam*; **me desahogué diciéndole todo lo que pensaba** I got it out of my system by telling him everything I thought
[2] (= *confesarse*) to get it off one's chest*; **~se con algn** to pour one's heart out to sb
[3] (= *librarse*) (*de deuda*) to get out of; **~se de un problema** to get out of a difficulty

➤ LENGUA Y USO: desagradar A 34.3

desahogo SM [1] (= *alivio*) relief; **es un ~ de tantas cosas malas** it's an outlet for so many unpleasant things
[2] (= *comodidad*) comfort, ease; **vivir con ~** to be comfortably off
[3] (= *libertad*) freedom; **expresarse con cierto ~** to express o.s. with a degree of freedom
[4] (*) (= *descaro*) brazenness; **le habló con mucho ~** he spoke to her very cheekily *o* (*EEUU*) freshly

desahuciado ADJ [*caso*] hopeless; **estar ~** to be beyond recovery, be hopelessly ill

desahuciar ▸conjug 1b◂ Ⓐ VT [1] [+ *inquilino*] to evict
[2] (= *quitar esperanza a*) (*gen*) to deprive of hope; [+ *enfermo*] to declare beyond recovery; [+ *plan*] to give up as a lost cause; **con esa decisión le ~on definitivamente** with that decision they finally put an end to his hopes
[3] (*Chile*) [+ *empleado*] to dismiss
Ⓑ **desahuciarse** VPR to lose all hope

desahucio SM [1] [*de inquilino*] eviction
[2] (*Chile*) [*de empleado*] dismissal

desairado ADJ [1] (= *menospreciado*) disregarded; **quedar ~** to come off badly
[2] (= *desgarbado*) unattractive

desairar ▸conjug 1a◂ Ⓐ VT [1] [+ *persona*] to slight, snub; [+ *cosa*] to disregard
[2] (*Com*) to default on
Ⓑ VI **lo haré por no ~** I'll do it rather than cause offence *o* (*EEUU*) offense

desaire SM [1] (= *menosprecio*) slight, snub; **fue un ~ sin precedentes** it was an unprecedented slight *o* snub; **no lo tomes como un ~** don't be offended; **dar** *o* **hacer un ~ a algn** (= *rechazar*) to slight sb, snub sb; (= *ofender*) to offend sb; **¿no me va usted a hacer ese ~?** I won't take no for an answer!; **sufrir un ~** to suffer a rebuff
[2] (= *falta de garbo*) unattractiveness, gracelessness

desajustado ADJ ill-adjusted, poorly adjusted

desajustar ▸conjug 1a◂ Ⓐ VT [1] (= *desarreglar*) [+ *brillo, color*] to disarrange; [+ *máquina*] to put out of order
[2] [+ *planes*] to upset
Ⓑ **desajustarse** VPR [1] (= *estropearse*) [*máquina*] to break down; [*clavija, tornillo*] to come loose
[2] [*persona*] (= *estar en desacuerdo*) to disagree, fall out; (= *desdecirse*) to break one's word

desajuste SM [1] (= *desarreglo*) [*de hormonas, presupuesto*] imbalance; [*de máquina*] breakdown; **el ~ entre los países ricos y pobres** the disparity *o* imbalance between rich and poor countries
[2] (= *desacuerdo*) (*gen*) disagreement; [*de planes*] upsetting

desalación SF desalination

desalado[1] ADJ (= *apresurado*) hasty

desalado[2] ADJ desalted; [*agua salada*] desalinated

desaladora SF desalination plant

desalar[1] ▸conjug 1a◂ Ⓐ VT to clip the wings of
Ⓑ **desalarse** VPR [1] (= *apresurarse*) to rush; **~se por hacer algo** to rush to do sth
[2] (= *anhelar*) to long, yearn; **~se por hacer algo** to long *o* yearn to do sth

desalar[2] ▸conjug 1a◂ VT [+ *pescado*] to desalt; [+ *agua salada*] to desalinate

desalentador ADJ discouraging

desalentar ▸conjug 1j◂ Ⓐ VT [1] (= *desanimar*) to discourage
[2] (= *agotar*) to make breathless
Ⓑ **desalentarse** VPR to get discouraged, lose heart

desaliento SM [1] (= *desánimo*) discouragement
[2] (= *abatimiento*) dismay, dejection

desalinización SF desalination

desalinizador ADJ **planta ~a** desalination plant

desalinizar ▸conjug 1f◂ VT, **desalinar** ▸conjug 1a◂ VT to desalinate

desaliñado ADJ [1] (= *descuidado*) slovenly
[2] (= *desordenado*) untidy, dishevelled, disheveled (*EEUU*)
[3] (= *negligente*) careless, slovenly

desaliño SM [1] (= *descuido*) slovenliness
[2] (= *desorden*) untidiness
[3] (= *negligencia*) carelessness

desalmado ADJ cruel, heartless

desalmarse ▸conjug 1a◂ VPR **~ por algo** to long for sth, crave sth

desalojamiento SM [1] [*de inquilino*] eviction, ejection
[2] (= *desocupación*) [*de edificio*] evacuation; [*de barco*] abandonment

desalojar ▸conjug 1a◂ Ⓐ VT [1] [+ *inquilino*] to evict, eject
[2] (= *desocupar*) [+ *edificio*] to evacuate; [+ *barco*] to abandon; **las tropas han desalojado el pueblo** the troops have evacuated the village; **la policía desalojó el local** the police cleared the premises; **~ un tribunal de público** to clear a court
[3] [+ *contenido, gas*] to dislodge, remove
[4] (*Mil*) to dislodge, oust
[5] (*Náut*) to displace
Ⓑ VI to move out

desalojo SM [1] [*de inquilino*] eviction, ejection
[2] (= *desocupación*) [*de edificio*] evacuation; [*de barco*] abandonment

desalquilado ADJ vacant, untenanted

desalquilar ▸conjug 1a◂ Ⓐ VT to vacate, move out of
Ⓑ **desalquilarse** VPR to become vacant

desalterar ▸conjug 1a◂ Ⓐ VT to assuage, calm to quieten down
Ⓑ **desalterarse** VPR to calm down, quieten down

desamar ▸conjug 1a◂ VT to cease to love

desamarrar ▸conjug 1a◂ VT to untie; (*Náut*) to cast off

desamarre SM untying; (*Náut*) casting-off

desambiguar ▸conjug 1i◂ VT to disambiguate

desamor SM coldness, indifference

desamorado ADJ cold-hearted

desamortización SF [1] (*Jur*) disentailment
[2] (*Esp Hist*) *sale of Church lands*

desamortizar ▸conjug 1f◂ VT to disentail

desamparado ADJ [1] (= *sin protección*) helpless, defenceless, defenseless (*EEUU*); **los niños ~s de la ciudad** the city's waifs and strays; **sentirse ~** to feel defenceless *o* helpless
[2] [*lugar*] (= *expuesto*) exposed; (= *desierto*) deserted

desamparar ▸conjug 1a◂ VT **1** [+ *persona*] (= *abandonar*) to desert, abandon; (= *dejar indefenso*) to leave defenceless *o* (*EEUU*) defenseless
2 [+ *lugar*] to leave, abandon
3 [+ *actividad*] to cease, abandon

desamparo SM **1** (= *acto*) desertion, abandonment
2 (= *estado*) helplessness
3 (= *cese*) cessation

desamueblado ADJ unfurnished

desamueblar ▸conjug 1a◂ VT to remove the furniture from, clear the furniture out of

desandar ▸conjug 1p◂ VT **~ lo andado** ◊ **~ el camino** to retrace one's steps; **no se puede ~ lo andado** what's done can't be undone

desangelado ADJ **1** [*lugar*] soulless
2 [*persona*] charmless, dull, unattractive

desangramiento SM bleeding; **morir de ~** to bleed to death

desangrar ▸conjug 1a◂ Ⓐ VT **1** [+ *persona*] to bleed
2 [+ *lago*] to drain
3 (= *quitar dinero a*) to bleed white
Ⓑ **desangrarse** VPR (= *perder sangre*) to lose a lot of blood; (= *morir*) to bleed to death

desangre SM (*LAm*) bleeding, loss of blood

desanidar ▸conjug 1a◂ Ⓐ VT to oust, dislodge
Ⓑ VI to fly, begin to fly, leave the nest

desanimado/a Ⓐ ADJ **1** [*persona*] downhearted, dejected
2 [*espectáculo, fiesta*] dull, lifeless; **fue una fiesta de lo más ~** it was a terribly dull party
Ⓑ SM/F dropout (*from the labour market*)

desanimante ADJ discouraging

desanimar ▸conjug 1a◂ Ⓐ VT **1** (= *desalentar*) to discourage
2 (= *deprimir*) to depress, sadden
Ⓑ **desanimarse** VPR to get discouraged, lose heart; **no hay que ~se** we must not lose heart, we must keep our spirits up

desánimo SM **1** [*de persona*] (= *desaliento*) despondency; (= *abatimiento*) dejection
2 [*de lugar, fiesta*] dullness

desanudar ▸conjug 1a◂ VT [+ *nudo, lazo*] to untie, undo; [+ *misterio*] to unravel; **~ la voz** to find one's voice

desapacible ADJ [*tiempo*] unpleasant; [*sabor, carácter*] surly; [*tono*] harsh; [*sonido*] sharp, jangling; [*discusión*] bitter, bad-tempered; [*persona*] unpleasant

desaparcar ▸conjug 1g◂ VI to drive off

desaparecer ▸conjug 2d◂ Ⓐ VI **1** [*persona, objeto*] to disappear, go missing; **han desaparecido dos niños en el bosque** two children have disappeared *o* gone missing in the wood; **me han desaparecido diez euros** ten euros of mine have disappeared *o* gone missing; **con él desapareció toda una ideología** a whole ideology died with him; **el mago hizo ~ una paloma** the magician made a dove disappear; **¡desaparece de mi vista!** get out of my sight!; *ver tb* **mapa**
2 [*mancha, olor, síntoma*] to disappear, go (away)
3 (*euf*) (= *morir*) to pass away
Ⓑ VT (*LAm Pol*) to disappear; **desaparecieron a los disidentes** they disappeared the dissidents, the dissidents were disappeared

desaparecido/a Ⓐ ADJ [*persona, objeto*] missing; [*especie*] extinct; (*LAm Pol*) missing; **el libro ~** the missing book; **tres continúan ~s** three are still missing; **uno de los animales ~s** one of the extinct animals; **~ en combate** missing in action, MIA
Ⓑ SM/F (*LAm Pol*) missing person; **los ~s** missing persons *pl*; **número de muertos, heridos y ~s** number of dead, wounded and missing

LOS DESAPARECIDOS

Los desaparecidos *is the name given to those who disappeared during the military dictatorships in Argentina, Chile, Uruguay and Brazil in the 1970s. Thousands of people were taken from their homes, schools and places of work and never seen again. Few of "the disappeared" were ever found alive, although a certain number of bodies were recovered in mass graves. Families of the victims joined forces to form pressure groups like Argentina's* **Madres y Abuelas de la Plaza de Mayo**, *but although some managed to identify and recover the bodies of their relatives, the perpetrators were rarely brought to justice.*

desaparejar ▸conjug 1a◂ VT **1** [+ *caballo*] to unharness, unhitch
2 (*Náut*) to unrig

desaparición SF **1** [*de persona, objeto*] disappearance
2 [*de especie*] extinction

desapasionadamente ADV dispassionately, impartially

desapasionado ADJ dispassionate, impartial

desapego SM **1** (= *frialdad*) coolness, indifference (**hacia** towards)
2 (= *ecuanimidad*) detachment

desapercibido ADJ **1** (= *no visto*) unnoticed; **marcharse ~** to slip away unnoticed; **pasar ~** to go unnoticed
2 (= *desprevenido*) unprepared

desaplicación SF slackness, laziness

desaplicado ADJ slack, lazy

desapoderado ADJ [*acción, movimiento*] headlong, precipitate; [*pasión*] wild, violent, uncontrollable; [*avidez*] excessive; [*orgullo*] overweening

desapoderar ▸conjug 1a◂ VT (= *quitar autoridad a*) to deprive of authority; (= *quitar posesiones a*) to dispossess

desapolillarse ▸conjug 1a◂ VPR (*fig*) to get rid of the cobwebs

desaprender ▸conjug 2a◂ VT **1** [+ *lección*] to unlearn
2 (= *olvidar*) to forget

desaprensión SF unscrupulousness

desaprensivamente ADV unscrupulously

desaprensivo/a Ⓐ ADJ unscrupulous
Ⓑ SM/F **es un ~** he's an unscrupulous individual

desapretar ▸conjug 1j◂ VT to loosen

desaprobación SF [*de actitud, conducta, acción*] disapproval; [*de solicitud*] rejection

▼ **desaprobar** ▸conjug 1l◂ VT **1** (= *no aprobar*) to disapprove of
2 (= *condenar*) to condemn
3 [+ *solicitud*] to reject, dismiss

desaprobatorio ADJ disapproving

desapropiarse ▸conjug 1b◂ VPR **~ de algo** to divest o.s. of sth, surrender sth

desaprovechado ADJ **1** [*oportunidad, tiempo*] wasted
2 [*alumno, estudiante*] slack
3 [*terreno*] underused, unproductive

desaprovechamiento SM waste

desaprovechar ▸conjug 1a◂ Ⓐ VT [+ *ocasión, oportunidad*] to waste, miss; [+ *talento*] not to use to the full
Ⓑ VI (= *perder terreno*) to lose ground, slip back

desarbolado ADJ [*paisaje*] treeless

desarbolar ▸conjug 1a◂ VT to dismast

desarmable ADJ **mesa ~** foldaway table

desarmador SM **1** [*de fusil*] hammer
2 (*Méx*) (= *destornillador*) screwdriver

desarmante ADJ disarming

desarmar ▸conjug 1a◂ Ⓐ VT **1** (*Mil*) to disarm
2 (= *desmontar*) [+ *juguete*] to take apart, take to pieces; [+ *rompecabezas*] to break up; [+ *tienda de campaña*] to take down; [+ *estantería, mueble*] to dismantle, take apart; [+ *remos*] to ship; [+ *barco*] to lay up; [+ *barrera*] to remove, take down
3 (= *dejar sin argumentos*) [+ *persona*] to disarm; [+ *ira*] to calm
Ⓑ VI to disarm

desarme SM disarmament ▸ **desarme arancelario**, **desarme industrial** removal of tariff barriers ▸ **desarme unilateral** unilateral disarmament

desarraigado ADJ [*persona*] rootless, without roots

desarraigar ▸conjug 1h◂ VT **1** [+ *árbol*] to uproot
2 (= *separar*) [+ *pueblo, persona*] to uproot
3 [+ *costumbre*] to root out, eradicate

desarraigo SM [*de árbol, persona*] uprooting; [*de vicio*] eradication

desarrajar* ▸conjug 1a◂ VT (*LAm*) = **descerrajar 1**

desarrapado ADJ, SM/F = **desharrapado**

desarrebujar ▸conjug 1a◂ VT **1** (= *desenredar*) to untangle
2 (= *descubrir*) [+ *objeto oculto*] to uncover; [+ *misterio*] to clarify, elucidate

desarreglado ADJ **1** (= *desordenado*) untidy
2 (= *descuidado*) [*aspecto*] slovenly; [*comportamiento*] disorderly; [*hábitos*] disorganized, chaotic; (*al comer*) immoderate
3 (*Mec*) out of order

desarreglar ▸conjug 1a◂ Ⓐ VT **1** (= *desordenar*) [+ *cama, habitación*] to mess up; [+ *planes*] to upset; **los niños ~on el cuarto** the children messed up the room; **el viento le desarregló el peinado** the wind messed up her hair
2 (*Mec*) to put out of order
Ⓑ **desarreglarse** VPR **1** (= *desordenarse*) [*persona*] to get untidy; [*pelo*] to get messed up
2 (*Mec*) to break down

desarreglo SM **1** (= *desorden*) (*gen*) disorder, confusion; [*de habitación*] mess; [*de ropa*] untidiness; **viven en el mayor ~** they live in complete chaos
2 (*Mec*) trouble
3 (*Med*) **para evitar los ~s estomacales** in order to avoid stomach upsets

desarrimado* SM loner, lone wolf

desarrimar ▸conjug 1a◂ VT **1** (*de un lugar*) to

➤ LENGUA Y USO: **desaprobar 1** 41

move away, separate
2 (= *disuadir*) to dissuade

desarrollado ADJ developed; **bien ~** well-developed

desarrollar ▸conjug 1a◂ Ⓐ VT 1 [+ *economía, industria, mercado*] to develop
2 (= *explicar*) [+ *teoría, tema, punto*] to develop
3 (= *realizar*) [+ *trabajo, proyecto*] to carry out; [+ *técnica, método*] to develop; **aquí desarrollan un trabajo muy importante** they carry out very important work here; **han desarrollado nuevas técnicas de reciclaje de residuos** they have developed new techniques for waste recycling
4 [+ *capacidad, músculos, memoria*] to develop
5 (*Mec*) **el motor desarrolla 200 caballos** the engine develops 200hp
6 (*Mat*) [+ *ecuación, función*] to expand; **desarolló bien el problema pero no llegó a la solución** he applied the correct method *o* working but failed to find the solution, he worked through the problem correctly but failed to find the solution
7 (= *desenrollar*) [+ *algo enrollado*] to unroll; [+ *algo plegado*] to unfold, open (out)
Ⓑ **desarrollarse** VPR 1 (= *madurar*) [*adolescente*] to develop, reach puberty; [*planta, animal*] to develop, reach maturity; [*país*] to develop
2 (= *ocurrir*) [*suceso, reunión*] to take place; [*trama*] to unfold, develop; **la acción de la película se desarrolla en Roma** the action in the film takes place in Rome; **la manifestación se desarrolló sin incidentes** the demonstration passed off without incident
3 (= *desenrollarse*) [*algo enrollado*] to unroll; [*algo plegado*] to unfold, open (out)

desarrollismo SM policy of economic development

desarrollo SM 1 [*de economía, industria, mercado*] development; **la industria está en pleno ~** industry is developing rapidly; **un país en vías de ~** a developing country
► **desarrollo sostenible** sustainable development
2 [*de teoría, tema, punto*] development
3 (= *realización*) [*de proyecto, plan*] carrying out; [*de técnica, método*] development
4 [*de capacidad, memoria, músculos*] development
5 (*Mat*) [*de ecuación, función*] expansion; [*de problema*] working; **hizo bien el ~ del problema** he did the working correctly
6 [*de persona, animal, planta*] development; **es bueno para el ~ emocional del niño** it is good for the child's emotional development; **está en la edad del ~** she's reaching puberty, she's beginning to develop
► **desarrollo infantil** child development
7 [*de historia, acontecimiento*] development; **el ~ de la trama** the unfolding *o* development of the plot; **ocurrió durante el ~ del partido** it happened in the course of the match
8 [*de bicicleta*] gear ratio

desarropado ADJ **estar ~** (*en la cama*) to have lost the covers; (= *sin defensa*) to be exposed

desarropar ▸conjug 1a◂ Ⓐ VT to take the covers off
Ⓑ **desarroparse** VPR to throw the covers off; **todavía no hace tiempo como para ~se** it's not yet the weather for leaving off any layers of clothing

desarrugar ▸conjug 1h◂ VT (= *alisar*) [+ *mantel, sábana*] to smooth out; [+ *ropa*] to remove the creases from, remove the wrinkles from (*EEUU*)

desarticulación SF 1 (= *desmembración*) [*de máquina, reloj*] dismantling, taking to pieces; [*de comando, pandilla*] breaking up
2 [*de codo, rodilla*] dislocation

desarticulado ADJ disjointed

desarticular ▸conjug 1a◂ VT 1 (= *desarmar*) [+ *máquina, reloj*] to take apart, take to pieces; [+ *pandilla*] to break up; **~ un grupo terrorista** to force a terrorist group out of action
2 [+ *codo, rodilla*] to dislocate

desarzonar ▸conjug 1a◂ VT [+ *jinete*] to throw, unsaddle

desaseado ADJ [*persona*] dirty, grubby; [*aspecto, pelo*] untidy, unkempt

desasear ▸conjug 1a◂ VT to dirty, soil

desaseo SM [*de persona*] dirtiness, grubbiness; [*de aspecto*] untidiness

desasimiento SM 1 (= *acto*) (*al soltarse uno*) undoing; (*al ser soltado*) release
2 (= *desapego*) detachment (**de** from)

desasir ▸conjug 3a; presente como salir◂ Ⓐ VT (= *soltar*) to undo
Ⓑ **desasirse** VPR 1 (= *soltarse*) to extricate *o* free o.s. (**de** from)
2 **~se de algo** (= *ceder*) to let sth go, give sth up; (= *deshacerse de algo*) to rid o.s. of sth

desasistir ▸conjug 3a◂ VT (= *abandonar*) to desert, abandon; (= *desatender*) to neglect

desasnar ▸conjug 1a◂ VT (= *civilizar*) to civilize; (= *instruir*) to make less stupid

desasosegado ADJ uneasy, anxious

desasosegador ADJ, **desasosegante** ADJ disturbing, upsetting

desasosegar ▸conjug 1h, 1j◂ Ⓐ VT to make uneasy, make anxious
Ⓑ **desasosegarse** VPR to become uneasy, become anxious

desasosiego SM (= *inquietud*) uneasiness, anxiety; (= *intranquilidad*) restlessness; (*Pol*) unrest

desastrado ADJ 1 [*persona, aspecto*] (= *sucio*) scruffy, untidy; (= *harapiento*) shabby, ragged
2 (= *desgraciado*) unlucky

desastre SM disaster; **¡qué ~!** how awful!; **la función fue un ~** the show was a shambles; **como pintor es un ~** he's a totally useless painter; **llegó a la fiesta hecha un ~** she arrived at the party looking a terrible sight; **soy un ~ dibujando** I'm terrible *o* hopeless at drawing; **es un ~ de hombre*** he's a dead loss*

desastroso ADJ disastrous, calamitous

desatado ADJ (= *descontrolado*) uncontrolled; **está ~** he's gone absolutely wild*

desatar ▸conjug 1a◂ Ⓐ VT 1 [+ *nudo, cuerda, cordones*] to untie, undo; **desátate los zapatos** untie *o* undo your shoelaces; **desata el paquete y saca el regalo** untie *o* undo the parcel and take out the present; **no consiguió ~ al prisionero** he couldn't manage to untie the prisoner; **la bebida le desató la lengua** the drink loosened his tongue
2 (= *desencadenar*) [+ *guerra, crisis*] to trigger, spark (off); [+ *sentimiento, pasión*] to unleash; **las nuevas medidas han desatado una ola de atentados** the new measures have triggered *o* sparked (off) a wave of attacks; **sus palabras ~on una intensa polémica** his words sparked (off) *o* unleashed a storm of controversy
3 (= *disolver*) to dissolve
4 (†) **~ un compromiso** to break an agreement
Ⓑ **desatarse** VPR 1 (= *soltarse*) [*nudo, cuerda, cordones*] to come undone *o* untied; [*perro*] to break loose; **se le ~on los zapatos** his shoelaces came untied *o* undone; **el prisionero consiguió ~se** the prisoner managed to untie himself
2 (= *desencadenarse*) [*incendio, guerra, motín*] to break out; [*crisis, polémica*] to flare up; [*tormenta, escándalo*] to break; [*desastre*] to strike; **con el gol se desató el entusiasmo de la afición** the crowd's enthusiasm spilled over at the goal; **se desató en injurias contra el ministro** (*frm*) he unleashed a torrent of abuse against the minister

desatascador SM plunger, plumber's helper (*EEUU*)

desatascar ▸conjug 1g◂ VT 1 [+ *cañería*] to clear, unblock
2 [+ *carro*] to pull out of the mud; ✦*MODISMO* **~ a algn** to get sb out of a jam

desatención SF 1 (= *descuido*) inattention
2 (= *distracción*) inattentiveness
3 (= *descortesía*) discourtesy

desatender ▸conjug 2g◂ VT 1 (= *descuidar*) [+ *consejo, deseos*] to disregard, ignore; [+ *obligación*] to neglect
2 [+ *persona*] to neglect

desatentado ADJ 1 (= *irreflexivo*) thoughtless, rash
2 (= *desmesurado*) excessive, extreme

desatento ADJ 1 (= *descuidado*) heedless, careless
2 (= *distraído*) inattentive
3 (= *descortés*) discourteous (**con** to)

desatierre SM (*LAm*) slag heap

desatinadamente ADV foolishly

desatinado ADJ foolish

desatinar ▸conjug 1a◂ Ⓐ VT to perplex, bewilder
Ⓑ VI 1 (= *equivocarse*) (*al actuar*) to act foolishly; (*al hablar*) to talk nonsense
2 (= *ponerse nervioso*) to begin to act wildly

desatino SM 1 (= *cualidad*) (= *falta de cordura*) foolishness; (= *falta de tacto*) tactlessness
2 (= *error*) blunder, mistake; (*al actuar*) foolish act; **¡qué ~!** what rubbish!; **cometer un ~** to make a blunder
3 **desatinos** (= *disparates*) nonsense *sing*; **un libro lleno de ~s** a book stuffed with nonsense

desatochar ▸conjug 1a◂ VT (*Cono Sur*) [+ *tráfico*] to clear

desatornillador SM (*LAm*) screwdriver

desatornillar ▸conjug 1a◂ VT to unscrew

desatracar ▸conjug 1g◂ VI (*Náut*) to cast off

desatraillar ▸conjug 1a◂ VT to unleash, let off the lead

desatrancar ▸conjug 1g◂ VT 1 [+ *puerta*] to force open 2 [+ *cañería*] to unblock; [+ *pozo*] to clean out

desatraque SM casting-off

desatufarse ▸conjug 1a◂ VPR 1 (*quitarse el mal olor*) to get some fresh air
2 (= *calmarse*) to calm down

desautorización SF denial

desautorizado ADJ [1] (= *no aprobado*) (*gen*) unauthorized; [*informe*] repudiated
[2] (= *no oficial*) unofficial
[3] (= *no justificado*) unwarranted

desautorizar ▸conjug 1f◂ VT [1] (= *quitar autoridad a*) [+ *oficial*] to deprive of authority; [+ *palabras, declaración*] to discredit
[2] [+ *noticia*] to deny

desavenencia SF (= *desacuerdo*) disagreement; (= *riña*) quarrel

desavenido ADJ [1] (= *opuesto*) contrary
[2] (= *incompatible*) incompatible; **ellos están ~s** they have fallen out

desavenir ▸conjug 3r◂ Ⓐ VT (= *enemistar*) to make trouble between
Ⓑ **desavenirse** VPR to fall out (**con** with)

desaventajado ADJ disadvantageous

desavisado ADJ (= *desprevenido*) unwary; (= *desinformado*) uninformed

desayunado ADJ **vengo ~** I've had breakfast; **estar ~** to have had breakfast

desayunar ▸conjug 1a◂ Ⓐ VT to have for breakfast
Ⓑ VI, **desayunarse** VPR to have breakfast [1] (= *tomar el desayuno*) **~ con café** to have coffee for breakfast
[2] (= *enterarse*) **ahora me desayuno de ello** this is the first I've heard of it; **~ con algo** to get the first news of sth

desayuno SM breakfast ► **desayuno a la inglesa, desayuno británico** English breakfast ► **desayuno buffet** buffet breakfast ► **desayuno continental** continental breakfast ► **desayuno de trabajo** working breakfast

desazón SF [1] (= *desasosiego*) uneasiness
[2] (= *falta de sabor*) tastelessness
[3] (*Med*) discomfort

desazonante ADJ annoying, upsetting

desazonar ▸conjug 1a◂ Ⓐ VT [1] (= *desasosegar*) to make uneasy
[2] [+ *comida*] to make tasteless
Ⓑ **desazonarse** VPR [1] (*Med*) to be out of sorts
[2] (= *irritarse*) to be annoyed
[3] (= *preocuparse*) to worry

desbancar ▸conjug 1g◂ Ⓐ VT [1] (*de un puesto*) (= *quitar el puesto a*) to oust; (= *suplantar a*) to supplant (*in sb's affections*); **el corredor fue desbancado por el pelotón a cinco km de la meta** the pack overtook the leader five km from the finish
[2] (*en juegos*) [+ *banca*] to bust*; [+ *persona*] to take the bank from
Ⓑ VI (*Naipes*) to go bust*

desbandada SF rush (*to get away*); **hubo una ~ general de turistas** there was a mass exodus of tourists; **cuando empezó a llover hubo una ~ general** when it started to rain everyone rushed for shelter; **a la ~** in disorder; **retirarse a la ~** to retreat in disorder; **salir en ~** to run off *o* scatter in all directions

desbandar* ▸conjug 1a◂ VT (*Caribe*) [+ *empleado*] to fire*

desbandarse ▸conjug 1a◂ VPR [1] (*Mil*) to disband
[2] (= *huir*) to run off *o* scatter in all directions

desbande* SM (*Cono Sur*) rush (*to get away*)

desbarajustar ▸conjug 1a◂ VT [1] (= *causar confusión*) to throw into confusion
[2] (= *desordenar*) to mess up

desbarajuste SM confusion, chaos; **¡qué ~!** what a mess!

desbaratamiento SM [1] (= *descomposición*) [*de planes*] thwarting; [*de teoría*] destruction; [*de empresa, grupo*] ruin; **los culpan del ~ de nuestra región** they blame them for ruining our region
[2] (*Mil*) rout
[3] (*Med*) ► **desbaratamiento de vientre** bowel upset
[4] (= *derroche*) squandering

desbaratar ▸conjug 1a◂ Ⓐ VT [1] (= *descomponer*) [+ *plan*] to spoil, thwart; [+ *empresa, grupo*] to ruin; [+ *teoría*] to destroy; [+ *sistema*] to disrupt, cause chaos in
[2] (*Mil*) to rout
[3] [+ *fortuna*] to squander
[4] (*Mec*) to take to pieces
Ⓑ VI to talk nonsense
Ⓒ **desbaratarse** VPR [1] (*Mec*) to break down
[2] [*persona*] (= *descontrolarse*) to fly off the handle*; (= *desestabilizarse*) to become unbalanced

desbarbar* ▸conjug 1a◂ Ⓐ VT [+ *persona*] to shave; [+ *papel*] to trim, trim the edges of; [+ *planta*] to cut back, trim
Ⓑ **desbarbarse** VPR to shave

desbarrancadero SM (*LAm*) precipice

desbarrancar ▸conjug 1g◂ Ⓐ VT [1] (*LAm*) to fling over a precipice
[2] (*Andes, Caribe*) (= *arruinar*) to ruin
[3] (*Andes**) (= *aplastar*) to crush
Ⓑ **desbarrancarse** VPR [1] (*LAm*) to fall over a precipice
[2] (*) to come down in the world

desbarrar ▸conjug 1a◂ VI [1] (*al hablar*) to talk rubbish
[2] (= *hacer tonterías*) to act the fool

desbastación SF = **desbaste**

desbastado ADJ planed

desbastar ▸conjug 1a◂ Ⓐ VT [1] (*Téc*) [+ *madera*] to plane down; [+ *piedra*] to smooth down
[2] [+ *recluta, aprendiz*] to knock the corners off, lick into shape
Ⓑ **desbastarse** VPR [*persona*] to acquire some polish

desbaste SM [1] (*Téc*) [*de madera*] planing; [*de piedra*] smoothing
[2] [*de persona*] polishing

desbeber** ▸conjug 2a◂ VI to piss**

desbloquear ▸conjug 1a◂ VT [1] (= *quitar un obstáculo de*) [+ *caño*] to unblock; [+ *tráfico*] to free, get moving; [+ *negociación*] to break the stalemate in
[2] (*Com, Fin*) to unfreeze
[3] (*Mil*) to break the blockade of

desbloqueo SM [*de negociación*] breaking of the deadlock; [*de cuenta*] unfreezing, unblocking, freeing

desbocado ADJ [1] [*caballo*] runaway
[2] [*herramienta*] worn
[3] [*vestido, jersey*] baggy
[4] [*persona*] (= *malhablado*) foulmouthed; (= *descarado*) cheeky, sassy (*EEUU*)
[5] [*cañón*] wide-mouthed
[6] (*LAm*) [*líquido*] overflowing

desbocar ▸conjug 1g◂ Ⓐ VT [+ *vasija, taza*] to break the rim of
Ⓑ VI = **desembocar**
Ⓒ **desbocarse** VPR [1] (= *descontrolarse*) [*caballo*] to bolt; [*multitud*] to run riot, get out of control
[2] [*vestido, jersey*] to go baggy
[3] [*persona*] (= *insultar*) to let out a stream of insults

desbolado** ADJ (*Cono Sur*) disorganized

desbole** SM (*Cono Sur*) (= *desorden*) mess, mix-up; (= *alboroto*) row, racket

desbordamiento SM [1] [*de lago, río*] overflowing; **tras el ~ del río** after the river burst its banks *o* overflowed; **el ~ de los gastos** overspending
[2] (= *manifestación*) [*de cólera, fanatismo*] outburst; [*de alegría*] overflowing; [*de energía*] surge; **mi aguante está al borde del ~** my temper is about to boil over, my temper is at boiling point
[3] (*Inform*) overflow

desbordante ADJ [1] (= *que rebosa*) **una copa ~ de champán** a glass full to the brim with champagne; **la sala estaba ~ de gente** the room was full to bursting
[2] (= *abundante*) [*alegría, entusiasmo, actividad*] overwhelming; [*humor, imaginación*] unbounded, boundless
[3] **~ de** [+ *salud, entusiasmo, energía*] brimming (over) with; **una carta ~ de felicidad** a letter brimming (over) with happiness

desbordar ▸conjug 1a◂ Ⓐ VT [1] (= *rebosar*) **la lluvia ha desbordado el río** the rain has caused the river to burst its banks *o* to overflow; **la leche estuvo a punto de ~ el cazo** the milk nearly boiled over; **han desbordado la centralita con tantas llamadas** the switchboard has been inundated *o* overwhelmed with calls
[2] (= *exceder*) [+ *límite, previsiones*] to exceed; [+ *persona, tolerancia*] to be beyond, be too much for; **los beneficios han desbordado todas nuestras previsiones** profits have exceeded all our forecasts; **su fama ha desbordado las fronteras de este país** her fame has spread far beyond this country; **el trabajo me desborda** the work is just too much for me
[3] [+ *energía, entusiasmo*] to be brimming (over) with; **desborda alegría y buen humor** he's brimming (over) with happiness and good humour
[4] (*Mil*) [+ *enemigo, policía*] to break through; **~on las líneas enemigas** they broke through enemy lines
[5] (*Dep*) (= *aventajar*) to outplay; **~on por completo al equipo visitante** they totally outplayed the visiting team
Ⓑ **desbordarse** VPR [1] (= *rebosar*) [1·1] [*lavabo, río*] to overflow; [*líquido*] to overflow, spill (over); **con el deshielo se ha desbordado el cauce del río** with the thaw the river has burst its banks *o* overflowed; **se desbordó la espuma de la cerveza** the froth on the beer overflowed *o* spilled over; **~se de algo** to be overflowing with sth; **el cajón se desbordaba de cartas** the drawer was overflowing with letters
[1·2] **~se fuera de** [*epidemia, guerra*] to spread beyond; **la guerra se ha desbordado fuera de nuestras fronteras** the war has spread beyond our borders
[2] (= *desatarse*) [*ira*] to boil over; **la euforia se desbordó al final del partido** they were unable to contain their euphoria at the end of the match; **llegó un momento en que la**

emoción se desbordó it got to a point when emotions got out of hand *o* control
3 (= *excederse*) to get carried away; (*pey*) to lose control; **el público se desbordó en aplausos** the audience applauded ecstatically; **~se de alegría** to be brimming (over) with happiness

desborde SM (*Cono Sur*) = **desbordamiento**

desbraguetado* ADJ **estar ~** to be broke*

desbravador SM horse-breaker

desbravar ▸conjug 1a◂ Ⓐ VT (= *amansar*) [+ *caballo*] to break in; [+ *animal salvaje*] to tame
Ⓑ VI, **desbravarse** VPR 1 [*animal salvaje*] to become tamer
2 (= *perder fuerza*) [*corriente*] to lose its strength; [*viento*] to drop, become less wild; [*licor*] to lose its strength

desbrozadora SF weeding machine

desbrozar ▸conjug 1f◂ VT [+ *camino*] to clear (*of rubbish*); [+ *campo*] to clear of scrub; [+ *cosecha*] to weed

desburocratizar ▸conjug 1f◂ VT to make less bureaucratic

descabal ADJ, **descabalado** ADJ incomplete

descabalar ▸conjug 1a◂ VT [+ *juego*] to leave incomplete; [+ *medias*] to lose one of a pair of; [+ *planes*] to scupper

descabalgar ▸conjug 1h◂ Ⓐ VI to dismount
Ⓑ VT to unseat, remove from office

descabellado ADJ [*plan, idea*] crazy, wild, preposterous

descabellar ▸conjug 1a◂ VT 1 [+ *pelo*] to ruffle
2 (*Taur*) *to kill with a thrust to the neck*

descabello SM (*Taur*) final thrust, coup de grâce

descabezado ADJ 1 (= *sin cabeza*) headless
2 (= *insensato*) wild

descabezar ▸conjug 1f◂ Ⓐ VT 1 (= *quitar la cabeza de*) [+ *persona*] to behead; [+ *árbol*] to lop; [+ *planta*] to top
2 [+ *dificultad*] to surmount
Ⓑ **descabezarse** VPR 1 (*Bot*) to shed its grain
2 [*persona*] to rack one's brains

descachalandrado* ADJ (*Andes*) shabby, scruffy

descachalandrarse* ▸conjug 1a◂ VPR (*Andes*) to dress carelessly

descachar ▸conjug 1a◂ VT (*Andes, Caribe, Cono Sur*) to de-horn

descacharrado ADJ (*CAm*) dirty, slovenly

descacharrante* ADJ hilarious

descacharrar ▸conjug 1a◂ VT = **escacharrar**

descachimbarse* ▸conjug 1a◂ VI (*CAm*) to fall flat on one's face, come a cropper*

descafeinado Ⓐ ADJ 1 [*café*] decaffeinated
2 [*lenguaje, ideales*] diluted, watered-down
Ⓑ SM decaffeinated coffee

descafeinar ▸conjug 1a◂ VT 1 [+ *café*] to decaffeinate
2 [+ *lenguaje, ideales*] to dilute, water down

descalabrado ADJ **salir ~** to come out the loser (**de** in)

descalabrar ▸conjug 1a◂ Ⓐ VT 1 (= *golpear*) [+ *objeto*] to smash, damage; **~ a algn** to split sb's head open
2 (= *perjudicar*) to harm, damage
3 (*Náut*) to cripple, disable
Ⓑ **descalabrarse** VPR to hurt one's head

descalabro SM 1 (= *contratiempo*) blow, setback ► **descalabro electoral** disaster at the polls
2 (*Mil*) defeat

descalcificación SF (*Med*) lack of calcium, calcium deficiency

descalificación SF 1 (*Dep*) disqualification
2 (= *pérdida de crédito*) discrediting ► **descalificación global** widespread condemnation

descalificar ▸conjug 1g◂ VT 1 (*Dep*) to disqualify
2 (= *desacreditar*) to discredit

descalzar ▸conjug 1f◂ Ⓐ VT 1 **~ a algn** to take off sb's shoes
2 (= *quitar la cuña*) [+ *rueda*] to remove the chocks from; [+ *armario, mesa*] to remove the wedge(s) from
Ⓑ **descalzarse** VPR 1 to take off one's shoes; **~se los guantes** to take off one's gloves
2 [*caballo*] to cast a shoe

descalzo ADJ 1 (= *sin calzado*) barefoot, barefooted; **estar ~** ◊ **estar con los pies ~s** to be barefoot(ed); **ir ~** to go barefoot(ed)
2 (*Rel*) discalced
3 (= *indigente*) destitute; **su padre lo dejó ~** his father left him without a bean

descamarse ▸conjug 1a◂ VPR to flake off, scale off; (*Med*) to desquamate

descambiar* ▸conjug 1b◂ VT 1 (= *intercambiar*) to swap, change back
2 (*Com*) [+ *camisa, libro*] to change

descaminado ADJ [*proyecto*] misguided; **andar** *o* **ir ~** to be on the wrong track; **en eso no andas muy ~** you're not far wrong there; **andar ~ en algo** to be mistaken in *o* about sth

descaminar ▸conjug 1a◂ Ⓐ VT (= *hacer perderse*) (*lit*) to misdirect, put on the wrong road; (*fig*) to lead astray
Ⓑ **descaminarse** VPR (*en camino*) to go the wrong way; (*en proyecto, actividad*) to go astray

descamisado/a Ⓐ ADJ 1 (= *sin camisa*) shirtless
2 (= *con la camisa abierta*) open-shirted
3 (= *mal vestido*) ragged, shabby
Ⓑ SM/F 1 (= *desharrapado*) ragamuffin
2 (= *vagabundo*) down-and-out
3 (*Arg Hist, Pol*) Peronist

descamisar ▸conjug 1a◂ Ⓐ VT 1 [+ *persona*] (= *quitar la camisa*) to strip the shirt off; (= *arruinar*) to ruin; (*en el juego*) to fleece
2 [+ *fruta*] to peel
Ⓑ **descamisarse** VPR (*Cono Sur*) to take off one's shirt

descampado SM open space, area of empty ground; **comer al ~** to eat in the open air; **vivir en ~** to live in open country; **se fue a vivir en ~** he went off to live in the wilds

descansadero SM stopping place, resting place

descansado ADJ 1 [*persona*] rested, refreshed
2 [*lugar*] restful

descansapié SM pedal, footrest

descansar ▸conjug 1a◂ Ⓐ VI 1 (= *reposar*) to rest, have a rest; **siéntate aquí y descansa** sit down here and have a rest, sit down here and rest; **paramos en un bar a** *o* **para ~** we stopped at a bar for a rest *o* to have a rest; **necesito ~ para despejarme** I need (to have) a rest to clear my head; **no descansé en todo el día** I didn't have a moment's rest all day; **nadé diez largos sin ~** I swam ten lengths without a rest *o* break; **no ~á hasta conseguir que dimita el presidente** he will not rest until he gets the president to resign; **va al campo a ~ de las preocupaciones** she goes to the country to get away from *o* get a break from her worries
2 (= *dormir*) **a medianoche, se retiraron a ~** at midnight they retired (to bed); **¡hasta mañana! ¡que descanses!** see you in the morning! sleep well!
3 **~ sobre algo** [*cúpula, tejado*] to be supported by sth, rest on sth; [*argumento, tesis*] to be based on sth
4 (= *estar enterrado*) **aquí descansan los restos mortales de José Fernández** here lie the mortal remains of José Fernández; **tu tío, que en paz descanse** your uncle, may he rest in peace; **descanse en paz** rest in peace
5 (*Mil*) **¡descansen!** at ease!, stand at ease!
6 (*Agr*) [*terreno, parcela*] to rest, lie fallow
Ⓑ VT 1 (= *apoyar*) to rest; **dejé de leer para ~ la vista** I stopped reading to rest my eyes
2 (*Mil*) **¡descansen armas!** order arms!

descansillo SM (*en escalera*) landing

descanso SM 1 (= *reposo*) rest; **los niños no me dejan ni un minuto de ~** the children don't give me a moment's rest; **hoy es jornada de ~ en la competición** today is a rest day in the competition; **el silencio será bueno para el ~ del bebé** the quiet will be a good chance for the baby to get some rest *o* sleep; **tengo tres días de ~ a la semana** I get three days off every week
2 (= *pausa*) break; (*Dep*) half-time; (*Teat*) interval, intermission (*EEUU*); **hago un ~ cada dos horas** I have *o* take a break every two hours; **estudió sin ~ hasta aprobar** she studied constantly until she passed; **condujo toda la noche sin ~** he drove all night without a break
3 (= *alivio*) relief; **ya he aprobado, ¡qué ~!** I've passed! what a relief!; **es un ~ saber que estás tan cerca** it puts my mind at rest to know you are so close by
4 (*Rel*) **rogamos una oración por su eterno ~** we ask you to pray for her eternal rest
5 (*en escalera*) landing
6 (*Téc*) rest, support

descañonar ▸conjug 1a◂ VT 1 [+ *gallina*] to pluck
2 [+ *cara*] to shave against the grain
3 (*Naipes**) to fleece, clean out*

descapachar ▸conjug 1a◂ VT (*Andes*) [+ *maíz*] to husk

descapiruzar ▸conjug 1f◂ VT (*Andes*) to rumple the hair of

descapitalización SF 1 (= *pérdida*) **la empresa sufrió una ~ de 13.000 millones** the net worth of the company fell by 13,000 million
2 (*intencionada*) asset-stripping

descapitalizado ADJ undercapitalized

descapitalizar ▸conjug 1f◂ VT 1 (*no intencionadamente*) **~ una empresa** to reduce a company's net worth
2 (*intencionadamente*) to asset strip

descapotable ADJ, SM (*Aut*) convertible

descapsulador SM bottle-opener

descaradamente ADV 1 (= *sin vergüenza*)

shamelessly, brazenly
2 (= *con frescura*) cheekily, saucily

descarado Ⓐ ADJ 1 [*persona*] (= *desvergonzado*) shameless; (= *insolente*) cheeky, sassy (*EEUU*)
2 (= *evidente*) [*mentira*] barefaced; [*prejuicio*] blatant
Ⓑ ADV (*) **sí voy, ~** I'm going all right, you bet I'm going; **si supiera inglés, ~ que me iba a Londres** if I spoke English, you can bet your life I'd go to London

descararse ▸conjug 1a◂ VPR to behave impudently, be insolent, be cheeky (**con** to); **~ a pedir algo** to have the nerve to ask for sth

descarburar ▸conjug 1a◂ VT to decarbonize

descarga SF 1 [*de camión, mercancías*] unloading; **la ~ de residuos sólidos** the unloading of solid waste ► **descarga de aduana** customs clearance
2 [*de adrenalina, emociones*] release; **llorar es una buena ~ emocional** crying is a good way to release your emotions *o* a good form of release
3 (*Mil*) firing, discharge (*frm*); **recibió varias ~s en el pecho** he received several shots in his chest ► **descarga cerrada** volley
4 (*Elec*) discharge; **recibió una ~ eléctrica** he received an electric shock; ✦*MODISMO* **como una ~** suddenly, unexpectedly

descargadero SM wharf

descargado ADJ 1 [*arma*] unloaded
2 (*Elec*) [*pila*] run down; [*batería*] flat

descargador SM 1 (= *persona*) [*de camiones, mercancías*] unloader; [*de barcos*] docker, stevedore 2 (*Elec*) discharger

descargar ▸conjug 1h◂ Ⓐ VT 1 (= *quitar la carga de*) [+ *camión, contenedor, arma*] to unload; [+ *mercancías*] to unload; **están descargando los sacos del camión** they are unloading the sacks from the lorry
2 (= *disparar*) [+ *arma, tiro*] to fire
3 (= *soltar*) [+ *golpe*] to land; [+ *bomba*] to drop, release; **le descargó un puñetazo en la cara** he punched him in the face *o* landed a punch on his face; **empezó a ~ golpes sobre la mesa** he started banging (on) the table
4 (*Elec*) [+ *pila, batería*] to run down; [+ *corriente*] to discharge
5 (= *liberar*) [+ *tensión, agresividad*] to release; [+ *enfado, ira*] to vent; [+ *conciencia*] to ease; [+ *responsabilidad, sentimiento*] to offload; **siempre descarga su enfado con nosotros** he always vents his anger on us; **no descargues tu frustración sobre mí** don't take out *o* offload your frustration on me; **necesito a alguien en quien ~ mi corazón** I need to pour out my heart to somebody; **~ a algn de** [+ *obligación, responsabilidad*] to relieve sb of; [+ *deuda*] to discharge sb from; [+ *acusación*] to clear sb of, acquit sb of
6 (*euf*) [+ *vientre*] to evacuate, empty; [+ *vejiga*] to empty
7 (*Com*) [+ *letra*] to take up
8 (*Inform*) to download
Ⓑ VI 1 [*río*] to flow, run (**en** into)
2 [*tormenta*] to break; **la tempestad descargó sobre el barco** the storm broke over the ship; **una fuerte tromba de agua descargó sobre la ciudad** a torrential downpour fell on the city
3 (*Elec*) to discharge
Ⓒ **descargarse** VPR 1 (= *desahogarse*) to unburden o.s.; **se descargaba con sus amigos** she unburdened herself to her friends; **~se de** [+ *carga, problema*] to unburden o.s. of; [+ *responsabilidad*] to unload; **se descargó de todas sus responsabilidades sobre un colega** he unloaded all his responsibilities on to a colleague; **se descargó con él de todas sus penas** she poured out all her troubles to him
2 (*Elec*) [*batería*] to go flat; [*pila*] to run down; **a la cámara se le han descargado las pilas** the camera batteries have run out *o* run down
3 (*Jur*) to clear o.s. (**de** of)
4 (= *dimitir*) to resign
5 **~se algo de Internet** to download sth from the Internet

descargo SM 1 [*de camión, mercancías*] unloading
2 (= *disculpa*) **en ~ de su conciencia** to ease his conscience; **nota de ~** disclaimer
3 (*Jur*) **en ~ de algn** in defence *o* (*EEUU*) defense of sb; **quisiera decir algo en mi ~** I would like to say something in my defence; **pliego de ~** evidence; **testigo de ~** witness for the defence
4 (*Com*) (= *recibo*) receipt; [*de deuda*] discharge

descargue SM unloading

descarnado ADJ 1 [*cara, persona*] gaunt
2 [*estilo, descripción*] straightforward

descarnador SM [*de dientes*] dental scraper; [*de uñas*] cuticle remover

descarnar ▸conjug 1a◂ Ⓐ VT 1 [+ *hueso*] to remove the flesh from; [+ *piel*] to scrape the flesh from 2 (= *desgastar*) to eat away, corrode, wear down
Ⓑ **descarnarse** VPR to lose flesh, get thin

descaro SM (= *insolencia*) cheek*, nerve*; **tuvo el ~ de decirme que ...** he had the cheek *o* nerve to tell me that* ...; **¡qué ~!** what a cheek*!, what a nerve*!

descarozado ADJ (*Cono Sur*) [*fruta*] dried

descarriar ▸conjug 1c◂ Ⓐ VT 1 (*en camino*) [+ *persona*] to misdirect; [+ *animal*] to separate from the herd, single out
2 (*en proyecto, vida*) to lead astray
Ⓑ **descarriarse** VPR 1 (= *perder el camino*) [*persona*] to lose one's way; [*animal*] to stray; ✦*MODISMO* **ser una oveja descarriada** to be like a lost sheep
2 (= *desviarse de lo correcto*) to go astray

descarrilamiento SM derailment

descarrilar ▸conjug 1a◂ Ⓐ VI to be derailed
Ⓑ **descarrilarse** VPR 1 (*Ferro*) to be derailed
2 (*LAm*) [*persona*] to get off the track

descarrilo SM derailment

descartable ADJ 1 (= *desechable*) dispensable
2 (*Inform*) temporary

▼**descartar** ▸conjug 1a◂ Ⓐ VT 1 (= *eliminar*) [+ *candidato, plan, opción*] to reject, rule out; [+ *posibilidad, hipótesis*] to dismiss, discount; **no hay que ~ la existencia de agua en el planeta** we cannot dismiss *o* discount the possibility of water on the planet; **han descartado la convocatoria de elecciones anticipadas** they've ruled out (the possibility of) an early election; **ya puedes ~ lo de hacer una fiesta en casa** you can forget about having a party at home
2 (*Naipes*) to throw away, discard
Ⓑ **descartarse** VPR 1 (*Naipes*) **se descartó de un as** he threw away *o* discarded an ace
2 (= *excusarse*) **~se de algo** (*iró*) to excuse o.s. from sth

descarte SM 1 (= *rechazo*) rejection
2 (= *excusa*) excuse
3 (*Naipes*) discard

descasar ▸conjug 1a◂ VT 1 [+ *matrimonio, pareja*] to annul the marriage of
2 [+ *objetos*] (= *separar*) to separate; (= *desordenar*) to disarrange, upset the arrangement of

descascar ▸conjug 1g◂ Ⓐ VT [+ *nuez, huevo*] to shell; [+ *árbol*] to remove the bark from; [+ *fruta*] to peel
Ⓑ **descascarse** VPR 1 (= *romperse*) to smash to pieces, come apart
2 (*) (= *ponerse bravucón*) to bluster

descascarar ▸conjug 1a◂ Ⓐ VT 1 (= *quitar la corteza de*) [+ *naranja, limón*] to peel; [+ *nuez, huevo cocido, gamba*] to shell
2 (*Andes*) [+ *animal*] to flay, skin
3 (*Andes*) (= *deshonrar*) to dishonour, dishonor (*EEUU*)
Ⓑ **descascararse** VPR to peel, peel off

descascarillado SM [*de plato, vasija*] chipping; [*de pintura*] peeling, flaking; [*de pared*] peeling

descascarillar ▸conjug 1a◂ Ⓐ VT [+ *plato, vasija*] to chip; [+ *arroz*] to husk
Ⓑ **descascarillarse** VPR [*plato, vasija*] to get chipped; [*pintura*] to flake; **las paredes estaban descascarilladas** the paint had flaked off the walls

descastado Ⓐ ADJ 1 (= *indiferente*) cold, indifferent
2 [*persona*] untouchable
3 [*palabra*] improper
Ⓑ SM/F **es un ~** he's a cold fish

descaste SM culling

descatalogado ADJ [*libro*] out-of-print, unlisted; [*disco*] unlisted; [*producto*] discontinued

descaudalado ADJ penniless

descelerar VT ▸conjug 1a◂ = **desacelerar**

descendedero SM ramp

descendencia SF 1 (= *descendientes*) descendants *pl*; **morir sin dejar ~** to leave no children behind, die without issue (*frm*)
2 (= *origen*) descent

descendente ADJ 1 (= *hacia abajo*) [*dirección, trayectoria*] downward; [*orden, escala*] descending; [*cantidad*] diminishing; **tren ~** down train
2 (*Inform*) top-down

descender ▸conjug 2g◂ Ⓐ VT 1 [+ *escalera, colina*] to come down, go down, descend (*frm*); **descendió las escaleras y se nos acercó** he came down *o* (*frm*) descended the stairs and approached us
2 (= *llevar abajo*) **~ a algn** to lower sb; **~ algo** to lower sth; **descendieron al bombero al pozo** they lowered the fireman *o* let the fireman down into the well; **descendieron al gato del tejado** they brought *o* got the cat down from the roof; **un señor le ayudó a ~ el equipaje** a man helped her to get *o* reach her luggage down
3 (*en orden, jerarquía*) to downgrade, demote; **lo han descendido de categoría por ineficacia** he has been downgraded *o* demoted for inefficiency; **el single descendió tres puestos en las listas de éxitos** the single went down three places in the charts
Ⓑ VI 1 (= *disminuir*) [*fiebre*] to go down,

➤ LENGUA Y USO: **descartar A1** 42.3

abate; [*temperatura, precio, número, nivel*] to go down, fall, drop; [*ventas, demanda, producción*] to fall, drop (off); [*calidad*] to go down, decline; **el índice de paro descendió considerablemente** unemployment has fallen *o* gone down considerably
2 (*de un lugar a otro*) [*persona*] to come down, go down, descend (*frm*); [*avión*] to descend; **el río desciende limpio de la sierra** the river comes *o* runs down clean from the mountains
3 (*en orden, jerarquía*) to be downgraded, be demoted; (*Dep*) to be relegated; **ha descendido tras el reajuste de la plantilla** he has been downgraded *o* demoted in the staff reorganization; **el restaurante ha descendido de categoría** the restaurant has been downgraded; **su libro descendió al puesto cuarto** her book went down to fourth place
4 **~ de** (= *provenir de*): **esta palabra desciende del latín** this word comes from *o* derives from (the) Latin; **el hombre desciende del mono** man is descended from apes; **desciende de linaje de reyes** he is descended from *o* comes from a line of kings

descendiente SMF descendant; **murió sin ~s** he left no children behind, he died without issue (*frm*)

descendimiento SM descent; **el Descendimiento de la Cruz** the Descent from the Cross

descenso SM 1 [*de temperatura, nivel, precio, demanda*] fall, drop; **un ~ de la producción** a fall *o* drop in production; **un ~ en el número de escolares** a fall *o* drop in the number of pupils; **un ~ de la calidad del servicio** a decline in the quality of service ► **descenso térmico** fall *o* drop in temperature
2 (*de un lugar a otro*) descent; **inició el ~ 20 minutos antes de aterrizar** he began his descent 20 minutes before landing; **el ciclista se cayó en el ~** the cyclist fell off during the descent; **la prueba de ~** (*Dep*) the downhill event
3 (*en orden, jerarquía*) downgrading, demotion; (*Dep*) relegation; **el CD ha sufrido un ~ de tres puestos** the CD has gone down three places in the charts
4 (= *pendiente*) slope; **el ~ hacia el río** the slope down to the river

descentración SF maladjustment

descentrado ADJ 1 (*Téc*) [*pieza*] off-centre, off-center (*EEUU*); [*rueda*] out of true; **parece que el problema está ~** the problem seems to be out of focus, it seems that the question has not been properly stated
2 [*persona*] disorientated, disoriented (*esp EEUU*); **todavía está algo ~** he's still rather disorientated

descentralización SF decentralization

descentralizar ►conjug 1f◄ VT to decentralize

descentrar ►conjug 1a◄ VT to put off-centre*, to put off-center (*EEUU**), put off one's stroke

desceñir ►conjug 3h y 31◄ VT [+ *cinturón, ropa*] to loosen; [+ *nudo, corbata*] to undo, unfasten

descepar ►conjug 1a◄ VT 1 (*Agr*) to uproot, pull up by the roots
2 (= *eliminar*) to extirpate, eradicate

descercar ►conjug 1g◄ VT 1 (*Agr*) to remove the fence round, remove the wall round
2 (*Mil*) [+ *ciudad*] to relieve, raise the siege of

descerco SM (*Mil*) relief

descerebrado ADJ brainless, mindless

descerrajar ►conjug 1a◄ VT 1 [+ *cerradura, puerta*] to break open, force
2 [+ *tiro*] to let off, fire (**a** at)

descervigar ►conjug 1h◄ VT to break the neck of

deschachar* ►conjug 1a◄ VT (*CAm*) to sack*, fire*

deschalar ►conjug 1a◄ VT (*Andes, Cono Sur*) [+ *maíz*] to husk

deschapar ►conjug 1a◄ VT (*LAm*) [+ *cerradura*] to break

descifrable ADJ [*código*] decipherable; [*letra*] legible

descifrador(a) Ⓐ SM/F **el ~ del misterio** the man who solved the mystery
Ⓑ SM (= *instrumento*) decipherer

descifrar ►conjug 1a◄ VT 1 (= *descodificar*) [+ *escritura*] to decipher, make out; [+ *mensaje*] to decode; **está muy lejos y no puedo ~ lo que pone** it's too far away for me to decipher *o* make out what it says
2 (= *resolver*) [+ *problema*] to puzzle out; [+ *misterio*] to unravel

descinchar ►conjug 1a◄ VT [+ *caballo*] to loosen the girths of

desclasado/a Ⓐ ADJ *who has gone from one social class to another*
Ⓑ SM/F *person who has gone from one social class to another*

desclasificación SF (*Dep*) disqualification

desclasificar ►conjug 1g◄ VT (*Dep*) to disqualify

desclavar ►conjug 1a◄ VT to pull out the nails from, unnail

descobijar ►conjug 1a◄ VT to uncover, leave exposed

descocado ADJ 1 (= *descarado*) cheeky, sassy (*EEUU*)
2 (= *atrevido*) brazen

descocarse ►conjug 1g◄ VPR (= *descararse*) to be cheeky; (= *atreverse*) to be brazen

descochollado ADJ (*Cono Sur*) 1 (= *harapiento*) ragged, shabby
2 (= *malo*) wicked
3 (= *de mal genio*) ill-tempered

descoco SM 1 (= *descaro*) cheek, sass (*EEUU*)
2 (= *atrevimiento*) brazenness

descodificación SF decoding

descodificador SM decoder

descodificar ►conjug 1g◄ VT [+ *mensaje*] to decode

descoger ►conjug 2c◄ VT to spread out, unfold

descojonación** SF **¡es la ~!** it's the absolute bloody end!**

descojonado** ADJ (= *cansado*) knackered*, pooped (*EEUU**)

descojonante** ADJ 1 (= *gracioso*) bloody hilarious**
2 (= *impresionante*) bloody impressive**

descojonarse** ►conjug 1a◄ VPR 1 (= *reír*) to piss o.s. laughing**
2 (= *matarse*) to do o.s. in*

descojone** SM 1 (= *situación graciosa*) **¡qué ~!** what a bloody riot!**
2 (= *caos*) **¡esto es un ~!** what a bloody shambles!**

descolada SF (*Méx*) snub, rebuff

descolar ►conjug 1a◄ VT 1 [+ *animal*] to dock, cut the tail off
2 (*CAm*) (= *despedir*) to fire, sack
3 (*Méx*) (= *desairar*) to snub, slight

descolgado/a SM/F backslider

descolgar ►conjug 1h, 1l◄ Ⓐ VT 1 [+ *cuadro, cortina*] to take down, get down; **descuelga el abrigo de ahí** take the coat off there *o* down from there
2 [+ *teléfono*] to pick up; **dejó el teléfono descolgado** he left the phone off the hook
3 [+ *competidor, pelotón*] to pull away from; **quedar descolgado** to be left behind
Ⓑ **descolgarse** VPR 1 (= *bajar por una cuerda*) to let o.s. down, lower o.s.; **~se por** [+ *cuerda*] to slip down, slide down; [+ *pared*] to climb down; **~se por una montaña** (*escalando*) to climb down the face of a mountain; (*con cuerda*) to lower o.s. down the face of a mountain
2 (*) (= *aparecer inesperadamente*) [*persona*] to turn up unexpectedly; [*nube*] set in unexpectedly; [*sol*] to come out suddenly; **~se con una cifra** to come up with a figure; **~se con una estupidez** to come out with a silly remark, blurt out sth silly
3 (*Ciclismo*) **~se del pelotón** to be left behind the group

descollante ADJ outstanding

descollar ►conjug 1l◄ VI (= *sobresalir*) [*persona*] to stand out, be outstanding; [*montaña*] to tower; **descuella entre los demás** he stands out above the others; **la obra que más descuella de las suyas** his most outstanding work; **la iglesia descuella sobre los demás edificios** the church towers over the other buildings

descolocado ADJ [*objeto*] misplaced; [*lugar*] untidy; **sentirse ~** to feel out of place

descolocar ►conjug 1g◄ VT [+ *papeles, libros*] to misplace; [+ *cajón, habitación*] to mess up

descolón SM (*Méx*) snub, rebuff

descolonización SF decolonization

descolonizar ►conjug 1f◄ VT to decolonize

descoloramiento SM (*con tinte*) discoloration; (*con sol, desgaste*) fading

descolorar ►conjug 1a◄ VT = **decolorar 1**

descolorido ADJ 1 (= *sin color*) (*con tinte*) discoloured, discolored (*EEUU*); (*por el sol*) faded
2 [*persona*] pale

descombrar ►conjug 1a◄ VT to clear (*of obstacles*), disencumber

descomedidamente ADV 1 (= *excesivamente*) excessively
2 (= *groseramente*) rudely, insolently, disrespectfully

descomedido ADJ 1 [*tendencia, odio*] excessive, immoderate
2 [*persona*] rude, discourteous (**con** to, towards)

descomedimiento SM rudeness, discourtesy

descomedirse ►conjug 3k◄ VPR to be rude, be disrespectful (**con** to, towards)

descompaginar ►conjug 1a◄ VT to disarrange, disorganize, mess up

descompasadamente ADV excessively, disproportionately

descompasado ADJ 1 (= *excesivo*) excessive
2 (= *sin proporción*) out of all proportion; **de tamaño ~** disproportionately big; **a una hora descompasada** at an unearthly hour

descompasarse ▸conjug 1a◂ VPR = **descomedirse**

descompensar ▸conjug 1a◂ VT to unbalance

descompletar ▸conjug 1a◂ VT (*LAm*) (*gen*) to make incomplete; [+ *serie, conjunto*] to break, ruin

descomponer ▸conjug 2q◂ (*pp* **descompuesto**) (A) VT [1] (= *dividir*) [+ *palabra, frase*] to break down, break up; [+ *sustancia, molécula, número*] to break down; [+ *luz*] to break up, split up; **tienes que ~ el informe en partes** you have to break down the report into separate parts
[2] (= *pudrir*) [+ *alimento*] to rot; [+ *cadáver, cuerpo*] to decompose
[3] (*) (= *alterar*) **la mala noticia lo descompuso** the bad news really shook him; **me descompone tanto desorden** all this mess really gets to me* *o* irritates me; **las especias me descomponen el vientre** spicy food gives me diarrhoea *o* (*EEUU*) diarrhea
[4] (*) (= *romper*) to break
[5] (*frm*) [+ *peinado*] to disturb, disarrange; [+ *planes*] to upset, disrupt
(B) **descomponerse** VPR [1] (= *pudrirse*) to decompose, rot
[2] (*) (= *alterarse*) **me descompongo con tanto ruido** all this noise gets to me* *o* irritates me; **se le descompuso el cuerpo del frío** the cold made her feel unwell; **se me descompuso el vientre** I had an attack of diarrhoea *o* (*EEUU*) diarrhea; **se le descompuso la cara cuando se lo dije** her face fell when I told her
[3] (*Cono Sur*) (= *vomitar*) to be sick; (= *llorar*) to break down
[4] (*esp Méx*) (= *romperse*) to break down
[5] **~se el brazo** (*Andes*) to put one's arm out of joint

descomponible ADJ separable, detachable

descomposición SF [1] (= *putrefacción*) decomposition; **en avanzado estado de ~** in an advanced state of decomposition
[2] (= *separación*) [*de cifra*] breakdown ► **descomposición estadística** statistical breakdown
[3] (*Med*) ► **descomposición de vientre, descomposición intestinal** diarrhoea, diarrhea (*EEUU*)
[4] (*LAm Aut*) breakdown

descompostura SF [1] [*de cara*] discomposure
[2] (= *descaro*) brazenness
[3] (= *fallo*) (*LAm Téc*) breakdown, fault; (*Elec*) fault, failure
[4] (*esp Méx*) (= *desaliño*) untidiness
[5] (*Andes*) (= *dislocación*) dislocation

descompresión SF decompression

descomprimir ▸conjug 3a◂ VT (*Inform*) to unzip

descomprometido ADJ lacking in commitment, uncommitted

descompuesto (A) PP *de* **descomponer**
(B) ADJ [1] (= *estropeado*) (*esp Méx*) [*reloj*] broken; [*motor*] broken down; [*sistema*] disorganized, chaotic; [*cuarto*] untidy; [*aspecto*] slovenly; **el coche está ~** the car has broken down
[2] (*Med*) **estar ~** to have diarrhoea *o* (*EEUU*) diarrhea
[3] [*cifra*] decomposed
[4] [*roca*] loose
[5] (= *alterado*) [*rostro*] distorted
[6] [*persona*] (= *descarado*) brazen, forward; (= *furioso*) angry; **ponerse ~** to get angry, lose one's composure
[7] (*LAm**) (= *medio borracho*) tipsy

descomunal ADJ huge, enormous

desconcentración SF [1] (*Pol*) decentralization, breaking-up
[2] (= *defecto*) lack of concentration

desconcentrar ▸conjug 1a◂ (A) VT [1] [+ *industria*] to decentralize
[2] [+ *persona*] to distract
(B) **desconcentrarse** VPR to lose one's concentration, get distracted

desconceptuado ADJ discredited

desconceptuar ▸conjug 1e◂ VT to discredit

desconcertado ADJ disconcerted; **se quedó ~ sin saber qué decir** he was disconcerted and didn't know what to say; **el final de la película te deja ~** the end of the film leaves you rather puzzled *o* disconcerted

desconcertador ADJ, **desconcertante** ADJ disconcerting, upsetting

desconcertar ▸conjug 1j◂ (A) VT (= *desorientar*) to disconcert; **la pregunta me desconcertó** I was disconcerted by the question; **cambió de táctica para ~ al rival** she changed tactics to disconcert her opponent *o* to put her opponent off
(B) **desconcertarse** VPR (= *desorientarse*) to be disconcerted; **me desconcierto con sus extrañas ideas** I find his strange ideas disconcerting

desconchabar ▸conjug 1a◂ VT (*LAm*) to dislocate

desconchado SM (*en plato, vasija*) chip

desconchar ▸conjug 1a◂ (A) VT [+ *pared*] to strip off, peel off; [+ *loza*] to chip off; **las goteras han desconchado la pared** the leak has made some of the paint flake *o* peel off the wall
(B) **desconcharse** VPR [*plato, vasija*] to chip; **se ha desconchado la pared** the paint has flaked *o* peeled off the wall

desconcierto SM [1] (= *desorden*) disorder
[2] (= *desorientación*) uncertainty, confusion; **la inesperada medida ha creado un clima de ~** the unexpected measure has created a climate of uncertainty *o* confusion; **el cambio de táctica provocó ~ en el rival** his opponent was disconcerted by the change of tactics

desconectado ADJ [1] (*Inform*) offline
[2] [*persona*] **estar desconectado de algo** to have no contact with sth

desconectar ▸conjug 1a◂ (A) VT (*Elec*) [+ *gas, teléfono*] to disconnect; [+ *enchufe*] to unplug; [+ *radio, televisor*] to switch off, turn off; (*Inform*) to switch off
(B) VI (*durante una conversación*) to switch off

desconexión SF [1] (*Elec*) disconnection
[2] (*entre personas, capítulos*) lack of connection; **hay una ~ total entre las dos cosas** there is no connection at all between the two things; **su ~ con el manejo de la empresa** her own lack of involvement in the running of the firm

desconfiado ADJ distrustful, suspicious (**de** of)

desconfianza SF distrust, mistrust; **voto de ~** vote of no confidence

desconfiar ▸conjug 1c◂ VI [1] [*ser desconfiado*] to be distrustful *o* mistrustful; **~ de algn/algo** (= *no fiarse*) to distrust sb/sth, mistrust sb/sth; (= *no tener confianza*) to have no faith *o* confidence in sb/sth; **"desconfíe de las imitaciones"** "beware of imitations"; **desconfía de sus posibilidades** he has no faith in his chances; **desconfío de poder hacerlo** I don't think I can do it; **desconfío de que llegue a tiempo** I'm doubtful whether *o* I'm not confident that he will get here in time
[2] (= *sentirse inseguro*) to lack confidence

desconformar ▸conjug 1a◂ (A) VI (= *disentir*) to disagree, dissent
(B) **desconformarse** VPR **se desconforman** they do not get on well together

desconforme ADJ = **disconforme**

descongelación SF [1] [*de alimentos*] defrosting; **para la ~ de alimentos** for defrosting food
[2] [*de salarios*] freeing, unfreezing
[3] (*Aer*) de-icing

descongelado SM defrosting

descongelar ▸conjug 1a◂ (A) VT [1] (= *quitar el hielo de*) [+ *congelador*] to defrost; [+ *alimentos*] to defrost, thaw; [+ *coche*] to de-ice
[2] (*Econ, Fin*) [+ *créditos, salarios*] to unfreeze
(B) **descongelarse** VPR [*congelador*] to defrost; [*alimentos*] to defrost, thaw

descongestión SF [1] (= *alivio*) relief, relieving; **una política de ~** a policy of relieving population pressure in the cities
[2] [*de pulmones, nariz*] clearing, decongestion (*frm*)

descongestionante SM decongestant

descongestionar ▸conjug 1a◂ VT [1] (= *quitar el bullicio a*) [+ *calle, ciudad*] to relieve, ease congestion in; [+ *prisión*] to relieve overcrowding in; **una política de listas de espera que ~á los hospitales** a policy aimed at cutting hospital waiting lists
[2] (= *despejar*) [+ *pulmones, nariz*] to clear, decongest (*frm*); [+ *cabeza*] to clear

desconocer ▸conjug 2d◂ VT [1] (= *ignorar*) not to know, be ignorant of; **desconocen los principios fundamentales** they don't know the basic principles, they are ignorant of the basic principles; **no desconozco que …** I am not unaware that …
[2] (= *no reconocer*) [+ *persona*] not to recognize; [+ *obra*] to disown; **el poeta desconoció la obra** the poet disowned the work; **~ la autoridad del gobierno** to refuse to recognize the government's authority

desconocido/a (A) ADJ [1] (*gen*) unknown; **su apellido me es totalmente ~** his surname is completely unfamiliar to me; **una explosión de origen ~** an explosion of unknown origin; **por razones desconocidas** for reasons which are not known (to us *etc*); **el triunfo de un atleta ~** the success of an unknown athlete; **tiene miedo a lo ~** he's afraid of the unknown
[2] **estar ~: con ese traje estás ~** I'd hardly recognize you *o* you're unrecognizable in your new suit; **después del divorcio está ~** he's a changed person *o* he's like a different person since the divorce
(B) SM/F stranger; **un ~ llamó a la puerta** a stranger knocked on the door; **unos ~s le dispararon por la espalda** some unidentified attackers shot him in the back

desconocimiento SM [1] (= *falta de conocimientos*) ignorance
[2] (= *repudio*) disregard
[3] (= *ingratitud*) ingratitude

desconsideración SF thoughtlessness, inconsiderateness

desconsideradamente ADV inconsiderately, thoughtlessly

desconsiderado ADJ thoughtless, inconsiderate

desconsoladamente ADV [*llorar*] inconsolably; [*buscar*] disconsolately

desconsolado ADJ disconsolate

desconsolador ADJ distressing, grievous

desconsolar ▸conjug 1l◂ Ⓐ VT to distress
Ⓑ **desconsolarse** VPR to despair

desconstrucción SF deconstruction

desconsuelo SM (= *pena*) distress, grief; **con ~** sadly, despairingly

descontado ADJ **por ~** of course; **dar algo por ~** to take sth for granted; **por ~ que ...** (*como conj*) of course ...

descontaminación SF decontamination

descontaminar ▸conjug 1a◂ VT to decontaminate

descontar ▸conjug 1l◂ VT [1] (= *deducir*) to deduct, take off; **tienes que ~ diez euros del total** you have to deduct ten euros from the total, you have to take ten euros off the total; **me lo descuentan de mi nómina** it gets deducted from *o* taken off my wages, it comes off my wages
[2] (*Com*) (*al pagar*) **si pagas al contado te descuentan un 10%** they give you 10% off if you pay (in) cash, there is a discount of 10% *o* a 10% discount for cash; **me ~on 100 libras del total de la factura** they gave me £100 off the total bill, they gave me a discount of £100 on the total bill
[3] (= *excluir*) to exclude; **descontando los gastos de alojamiento** excluding *o* not including accommodation expenses; **son diez días si descuentas los días festivos** it's ten days excluding *o* not including public holidays; **sin ~ la hora y media de viaje** including *o* not excluding an hour and a half's travelling time; **descontándome a mí, todos están casados** apart from me, everyone is married

descontentadizo ADJ hard to please

descontentar ▸conjug 1a◂ VT to displease

descontento/a Ⓐ ADJ [1] (= *insatisfecho*) dissatisfied, discontented (**de** with)
[2] (= *disgustado*) disgruntled (**de** about, at)
Ⓑ SM/F (*Méx*) malcontent
Ⓒ SM [1] (= *insatisfacción*) dissatisfaction
[2] (= *disgusto*) disgruntlement
[3] (*Pol*) discontent, unrest; **hay mucho ~** there is a lot of unrest ▸ **descontento social** social unrest

descontextualización SF decontextualization

descontextualizar ▸conjug 1f◂ VT to decontextualize, take out of context

descontinuación SF discontinuation

descontinuar ▸conjug 1e◂ VT to discontinue

descontrol SM lack of control; **hay un ~ en la oficina** the office is in chaos; **esta organización es un ~** this organization is totally chaotic

descontroladamente ADV in an uncontrolled way

descontrolado ADJ [1] (= *sin control*) uncontrolled; **desarrollo ~** uncontrolled development; **elementos ~s** wild elements; (*Pol*) rebellious factions; **estar ~** to be out of control
[2] (*LAm*) (= *perturbado*) upset, irritated

descontrolarse ▸conjug 1a◂ VPR [1] (= *perder control*) to get out of control, go wild
[2] (*) (= *enojarse*) to blow one's top*, go up the wall*

desconvenir ▸conjug 3s◂ VI [1] [*personas*] to disagree (**con** with)
[2] [*no corresponder*] to be incongruous
[3] (= *diferir*) to differ (**con** from)
[4] (= *no convenir*) to be inconvenient

desconvocación SF calling-off, cancellation

desconvocar ▸conjug 1g◂ VT [+ *huelga, reunión*] to call off, cancel

desconvocatoria SF calling-off, cancellation

descoordinación SF lack of coordination

descoque SM = **descoco**

descorazonador ADJ discouraging, disheartening

descorazonamiento SM discouragement

descorazonar ▸conjug 1a◂ Ⓐ VT to discourage, dishearten
Ⓑ **descorazonarse** VPR to get discouraged, lose heart

descorbatado ADJ tieless

descorchador(a) Ⓐ SM/F bark stripper
Ⓑ SM corkscrew

descorchar ▸conjug 1a◂ VT [1] [+ *botella*] to uncork, open
[2] [+ *alcornoque*] to strip the bark from
[3] [+ *arca*] to force, break open

descorche SM uncorking, opening

descornar ▸conjug 1l◂ Ⓐ VT to de-horn, poll
Ⓑ **descornarse*** VPR [1] (= *trabajar*) to slog away*, work like a slave
[2] (= *pensar*) to rack one's brains
[3] (= *caer*) to break one's neck

descorrer ▸conjug 2a◂ VT [+ *cerrojo, cortina*] to draw back; [+ *velo*] to remove

descortés ADJ [*persona, comportamiento*] rude, impolite, discourteous (*frm*); **no quisiera ser ~, pero tenemos que marcharnos** I don't want to be *o* seem rude, but we really must be going

descortesía SF [1] (= *acto*) discourtesy
[2] (= *cualidad*) rudeness, impoliteness

descortésmente ADV discourteously, rudely, impolitely

descortezar ▸conjug 1f◂ VT [1] (= *quitar la corteza a*) [+ *árbol*] to strip the bark from; [+ *pan*] to cut the crust off; [+ *fruta*] to peel
[2] [+ *estilo, técnica*] to polish up, knock the corners off

descoser ▸conjug 2a◂ Ⓐ VT [1] (*Cos*) [+ *costura, puntos*] to unstitch, unpick
[2] (= *separar*) to separate, part; *ver tb* **labio**
Ⓑ **descoserse** VPR [1] (*Cos*) [*pantalón*] to come apart at the seam(s); [*costura, manga*] to come unstitched; **se me ha descosido el bajo de la falda** the hem of my skirt has come unstitched; **llevas un botón descosido** one of your buttons is loose *o* is coming off
[2] (*) **~se de risa** to split one's sides laughing
[3] (**) (= *ventosear*) to fart**

descosido/a Ⓐ ADJ [1] (*Cos*) unstitched, torn
[2] [*narración, historia*] disconnected, disjointed, chaotic
[3] [*persona*] (= *hablador*) talkative; (= *indiscreto*) big-mouthed*, indiscreet, blabbing
Ⓑ SM/F ✦MODISMOS **como un ~***: **beber como un ~** to drink an awful lot; **comer como un ~** to eat to excess, stuff o.s.; **gastar como un ~** to spend money wildly; **habla como un ~** he just rattles on and on*; **obrar como un ~** to act wildly
Ⓒ SM (*Cos*) open seam

descotado ADJ (*LAm*) = **escotado**

descoyuntado ADJ [1] (*Anat*) dislocated, out of joint
[2] [*narración, historia*] incoherent, disjointed, chaotic

descoyuntar ▸conjug 1a◂ Ⓐ VT [1] (*Anat*) to dislocate
[2] [+ *hechos*] to twist
Ⓑ **descoyuntarse** VPR [1] (*Anat*) **~se un hueso** to put a bone out of joint; **el hombro se me descoyuntó** I dislocated my shoulder
[2] (*) **~se de risa** to split one's sides laughing; **~se a cortesías** to overdo the courtesies, be over-polite

descrecer ▸conjug 2d◂ VI to decrease

descrédito SM (= *desprestigio*) discredit, disrepute; **caer en ~** to fall into disrepute; **ir en ~ de algn** to be to sb's discredit

descreencia SF unbelief

descreer ▸conjug 2e◂ Ⓐ VT to disbelieve, place no faith in
Ⓑ VI (*Rel*) to lose one's faith

descreído/a Ⓐ ADJ [1] (= *incrédulo*) unbelieving
[2] (= *ateo*) godless
Ⓑ SM/F unbeliever

descreimiento SM unbelief

descremado ADJ [*leche*] skimmed, low-fat

descremar ▸conjug 1a◂ VT [+ *leche*] to skim

describir ▸conjug 3a◂ (*pp* **descrito**) VT to describe

descripción SF description; **supera toda ~** it defies description

descriptible ADJ describable

descriptivo ADJ descriptive

descripto PP (*Cono Sur*) = **descrito**

descrismar* ▸conjug 1a◂ Ⓐ VT **~ a algn** to bash sb on the head*; **¡o eso o te descrismo!** either that or I'll bash you!*
Ⓑ **descrismarse** VPR [1] (= *romperse la cabeza*) (*con un golpe*) to split one's head open; (*al pensar*) to rack one's brains
[2] (= *trabajar*) to slave away
[3] (= *enojarse*) to blow one's top*

descrispar ▸conjug 1a◂ VT to take the tension out of

descrito PP *de* **describir**

descruzar ▸conjug 1f◂ VT [+ *piernas*] to uncross; [+ *brazos*] to unfold

descuadre SM imbalance

descuajar ▸conjug 1a◂ VT [1] [+ *masa, sólido*] to melt, dissolve
[2] (= *arrancar*) [+ *árbol, planta*] to uproot; [+ *diente*] to pull out
[3] (= *extirpar*) to eradicate, wipe out
[4] (= *desanimar*) to dishearten

descuajaringado* ADJ (= *destartalado*) broken-down; (= *desaliñado*) scruffy, shabby; **el libro estaba todo descuajeringado** the book was falling apart

descuajaringante* ADJ side-splitting

descuajaringar* ▸conjug 1h◂ Ⓐ VT (= *romper*) to break to bits *o* pieces

Ⓑ **descuajaringarse** VPR [1] (= *partirse*) [*brazo, pierna*] to come apart; **~se de risa** to split one's sides laughing; **es para ~se** it's enough to make you die laughing*
[2] (= *cansarse*) to tire o.s. out
[3] [*objeto*] to fall to bits

descuajeringar ▸conjug 1h◂ VT = **descuajaringar**

descuartizamiento SM [*de animal*] carving up, cutting up; [*de cuerpo, cadáver*] quartering

descuartizar ▸conjug 1f◂ VT [1] (= *despedazar*) [+ *animal*] to carve up, cut up; [+ *cuerpo, cadáver*] to quarter
[2] (= *hacer pedazos*) to tear apart; **ni que me descuarticen** not even if they tear me apart

descubierta SF [1] (*Mil*) reconnoitring, patrolling
[2] ✦*MODISMO* **a la ~** (= *sin disfraz*) openly; (= *sin protección*) in the open

descubierto Ⓐ PP *de* **descubrir**
Ⓑ ADJ [1] (= *sin cubrir*) [*cabeza, pecho*] bare; [*patio, piscina*] open-air; [*autobús, carroza*] open-top; [*cielo*] clear; **salió con el pecho ~** he went out bare-chested; **llevaba los hombros ~s** her shoulders were bare; **dame una carta boca abajo y dos descubiertas** give me one card face down and two face up
[2] (= *sin protección*) [*situación*] open, exposed; **una zona descubierta del bosque** an open area of the wood
[3] (= *sin sombrero*) bareheaded
[4] (*Com*) [*préstamo*] unbacked
Ⓒ SM [1] **al ~** (= *al aire libre*) outdoors, out in the open; (= *sin rodeos*) openly; (*Mil*) under fire; **pasamos la noche al ~** we spent the night outdoors *o* in the open; **dejar algo al ~** to expose sth (to view); **la humedad dejó al ~ varios murales antiguos** the damp brought some ancient murals to view, the damp exposed some ancient murals (to view); **la falda dejaba sus rodillas al ~** the skirt left her knees bare, the skirt exposed her knees; **poner algo al ~** to expose sth; **la operación policial que puso al ~ la estafa** the police operation that exposed the fraud; **quedar al ~** to be exposed; **quedaron al ~ sus malas intenciones** her bad intentions came to light *o* were exposed
[2] (*Com*) (*en cuenta corriente*) overdraft; (*en presupuesto*) shortage; **estar en ~** to be overdrawn, be in the red*; **girar al** *o* **en ~** to overdraw; **vender al ~** to sell short

descubretalentos SMF INV = **cazatalentos**

descubridero SM look-out post

descubridor(a) SM/F [1] [*de lugar, invento, deportista*] discoverer
[2] (*Mil*) scout

descubrimiento SM [1] (= *hallazgo*) [*de país, invento, deportista*] discovery; **la era de los grandes ~s** the age of great discoveries; **este restaurante ha sido todo un ~** this restaurant has been a real find *o* discovery
[2] [*de conspiración, estafa*] uncovering
[3] [*de secreto*] revelation
[4] [*de estatua, placa*] unveiling

descubrir ▸conjug 3a◂ (*pp* **descubierto**) Ⓐ VT
[1] (= *encontrar*) [+ *tesoro, tratamiento, persona oculta*] to discover, find; [+ *país, deportista*] to discover; **al revisar las cuentas ha descubierto numerosas irregularidades** when he went over the accounts he discovered *o* found numerous irregularities; **descubra Bruselas, corazón de Europa** discover Brussels, the heart of Europe; **he descubierto una tienda de ropa fantástica** I've discovered a fantastic clothes shop; **se dedica a ~ nuevos talentos** her job is to discover new talent; **los análisis han descubierto la presencia de un virus** the tests have revealed *o* shown up the presence of a virus; ✦*MODISMO* **~ América** to reinvent the wheel
[2] (= *averiguar*) [+ *verdad*] to find out, discover; **he descubierto la causa de su malhumor** I've found out *o* discovered why he's in such a bad mood; **descubrió que era alérgica a las gambas** she found out *o* discovered she was allergic to prawns
[3] (= *sacar a la luz*) [+ *conspiración, estafa*] to uncover; [+ *secreto, intenciones*] to reveal; **una red de narcotraficantes descubierta en Colombia** a drug-trafficking ring uncovered in Colombia; **nunca nos ~á sus secretos** he will never tell us his secrets, he will never reveal his secrets to us; **ha descubierto su verdadera identidad** he has revealed his true identity
[4] (= *delatar*) to give away; **fue la criada quien los descubrió a la policía** it was the maid who gave them away to the police; **lo descubrió su voz** his voice gave him away
[5] (= *destapar*) [+ *estatua, placa*] to unveil; [+ *cacerola*] to take the lid off; [+ *naipes*] to turn over, lay up; [+ *cara*] to uncover; **descubrió la cara y su contrincante le asestó un derechazo en la mandíbula** he uncovered his face and his opponent landed a right on his jaw; **le descubrió el tobillo para ver la cicatriz** she uncovered his ankle to look at the scar; ✦*MODISMO* **~ el juego a algn** to call sb's bluff; *ver tb* **pastel A3**
[6] (= *divisar*) to make out; **apenas se podía ~ al avión entre las nubes** you could just make out the plane among the clouds
[7] (*liter*) (= *transparentar*) to reveal; **la seda le descubría el escote** the silk revealed *o* exposed her cleavage
Ⓑ **descubrirse** VPR [1] (= *quitarse el sombrero*) to take one's hat off; (*para saludar*) to raise one's hat (in greeting); **~se ante algo/algn** to take one's hat off to sth/sb; **ante tal muestra de valor hay que ~se** you have to take your hat off to her for such bravery
[2] (= *dejar ver*) [+ *cara, rostro*] to uncover; [+ *cabeza*] to bare; **descúbrase el brazo, por favor** roll up your sleeve, please
[3] (= *delatarse*) to give o.s. away; **se descubrió con una falsa coartada** he gave himself away with a false alibi
[4] **~se a** *o* **con algn** to pour one's heart out to sb
[5] (= *mostrarse*) to reveal o.s.; **se descubre como un compositor de gran talento** he has revealed himself to be a composer of great talent

descuelgue SM [1] (*de algo colgado*) removal, taking out
[2] (*) (*de hacer algo*) opting out

descuento SM [1] (*Com*) discount; **un ~ del 3%** a discount of 3%, a 3% discount; **acciones a ~** shares below par; **con ~** at a discount; **hacer ~** to give a discount; **me hicieron un buen ~** they gave me a good discount; **¿me podría hacer un ~?** could I have a discount? ► **descuento por no declaración de siniestro** no claims bonus ► **descuento por pago al contado** cash discount ► **descuento por volumen de compras** volume discount
[2] (*Dep*) injury time, overtime (*EEUU*)

descuerar* ▸conjug 1a◂ VT [1] (*Chile*) to tell off*
[2] (*Cono Sur*) (= *desollar*) to flay, skin
[3] (*Cono Sur*) (= *infamar*) to defame

descuernar ▸conjug 1a◂ VT (*Andes, CAm, Caribe*) to de-horn

descueve* ADJ (*Cono Sur*) great*, fantastic*

descuidadamente ADV [1] (= *despreocupadamente*) carelessly
[2] (= *desaliñadamente*) untidily

descuidado ADJ [1] [*persona*] (= *despreocupado*) careless; (= *olvidadizo*) forgetful; (= *desprevenido*) unprepared; (= *tranquilo*) easy in one's mind; **coger** *o* **pillar a algn ~** to catch sb off his guard; **puedes estar ~** you needn't worry, you can relax
[2] (= *desaliñado*) [*aspecto*] untidy, slovenly; [*habitación*] untidy, messy
[3] (= *abandonado*) neglected; **con aspecto de niños ~s** with the look of neglected children

descuidar ▸conjug 1a◂ Ⓐ VT [1] (= *desatender*) [+ *deberes*] to neglect; [+ *consejo*] to disregard; **ha descuidado mucho su negocio** he has neglected his business a lot
[2] (= *olvidar*) to overlook
Ⓑ VI (= *no preocuparse*) not to worry; **¡descuida!** don't worry!, it's all right!; **descuida, que yo me encargo de esto** don't worry, I'll take care of this
Ⓒ **descuidarse** VPR [1] (= *no prestar atención*) to be careless; **~se de algo** not to bother about sth; **~se de hacer algo** not to bother to do sth, neglect to do sth
[2] (= *desprevenirse*) to drop one's guard; **si te descuidas** ◊ **como te descuides** if you don't watch out; **a poco que te descuides te cobran el doble** you've got to watch them all the time or they'll charge you double; **a poco que te descuides ya no está** before you know where you are it's gone; **en cuanto me descuidé me lo robaron** the moment I dropped my guard *o* stopped watching out they stole it from me
[3] (= *abandonarse*) to let o.s. go

descuidero/a SM/F sneak thief, pickpocket

descuido SM [1] (= *distracción*) **en un ~ le robaron el bolso** her bag was stolen when she wasn't looking *o* in a moment of inattention; **al menor ~ te puedes salir de la carretera** if your attention wanders *o* if you get distracted, even for a moment, the car can go off the road; **la colisión ocurrió por un ~ del maquinista** the crash was caused by a careless mistake on the part of the driver; **se me olvidó invitarla por ~** I carelessly forgot to invite her; **dejó caer el pañuelo como por ~** she dropped her handkerchief as if by accident
[2] (*frm*) (= *negligencia*) carelessness; **no toleran el ~ en el aspecto externo** they don't tolerate any carelessness in one's appearance; **con ~** carelessly

desculpabilizar ▸conjug 1f◂ VT to exonerate, free from blame

desculturización SF cultural impoverishment

desde PREP [1] (*indicando origen*) from; **lo llamaré ~ la oficina** I'll ring him from the office; **~ Burgos hay 30km** it's 30km from

Burgos; **~ Ávila hasta Madrid** from Ávila to Madrid; **~ abajo** from below; **~ arriba** from above; **~ lejos** from a long way off, from afar (*liter*)

2 (*con cantidades, categorías*) from; **camisetas ~ ocho euros** T-shirts from eight euros; **los platos van ~ la pasta hasta la paella** the dishes range from pasta to paella

3 (*en el tiempo*) **~ el martes** (= *el pasado*) since Tuesday; (= *el próximo*) after Tuesday; **~ el siglo XV en adelante** from the 15th century onward; **no existe ~ 1960** it ceased to exist in 1960; **~ ahora** from now on; **¿~ cuándo vives aquí?** how long have you been living here?; **¿~ cuándo ocurre esto?** how long has this been happening?; **~ entonces** since then; **~ hace tres años** for three years; **está lloviendo ~ hace tres días** it's been raining for three days; **~ el 4 hasta el 16** from the 4th until *o* to the 16th; **cerramos ~ las dos hasta las cuatro** we close from two until *o* to four; **~ niño** since childhood, since I was a child; **la conozco ~ niño** I've known her since I was a child; **~ siempre** always; **—¿~ cuándo eres comunista? —~ siempre** "since when have you been a communist?" — "I've always been one"

4 **~ luego** 4·1 (= *por supuesto*) of course; **—¿vendrás? —~ luego** "are you coming?" — "of course (I am)"; **eso, ~ luego, no es culpa mía** that, of course, is not my fault; **—¿quieres venir con nosotros? —~ luego que sí** "do you want to come with us?" — "of course I do"; **—¿no sabes nada de eso? —~ luego que no** "you don't know anything about it?" — "of course not"; **no era muy morena pero rubia ~ luego que no** she wasn't really dark-haired, but she certainly wasn't blonde

4·2 (*como coletilla*) **~ luego, vaya fama estamos cogiendo** we're certainly getting quite a reputation; **~ luego, ¿quién lo iba a pensar?** I ask you, who would have thought it?, well, who would have thought it?; **¡mira que olvidarte de llamar! ¡~ luego que eres despistado!** how could you forget to phone? you're so absent-minded!

5 **~ que** since; **~ que llegó el invierno** since winter arrived; **~ que llegó no ha salido** he hasn't been out since he arrived; **~ que se ha mudado está mejor** he's been better since he moved; **~ que se inventó la televisión** (ever) since television was invented; **escribo ~ que era pequeña** I've been writing since I was little; **~ que puedo recordar** ever since I can remember, as long as I can remember

desdecir ▸conjug 3o◂ Ⓐ VI 1 (= *desmerecer*) **~ de algo** to be unworthy of sth; **desdice de su patria** he is unworthy of his country; **esta novela no desdice de las otras** this novel is well up to the standard of the others

2 (= *no corresponder*) **~ de algo** to clash with sth; **la corbata desdice del traje** the tie clashes *o* doesn't go with the suit

Ⓑ **desdecirse** VPR to go back on what one has said; **~se de algo** to go back on sth; **~se de una promesa** to go back on a promise

desdén SM scorn, disdain; **al ~** disdainfully

desdentado ADJ toothless

desdeñable ADJ contemptible; **nada ~** far from negligible

desdeñar ▸conjug 1a◂ Ⓐ VT 1 (= *despreciar*) to scorn, disdain

2 (= *rechazar*) to turn up one's nose at

Ⓑ **desdeñarse** VPR **~se de hacer algo** to scorn to do sth, not deign to do sth

> **DESDE**
>
> **Expresiones temporales**
>
> En expresiones temporales, **desde** puede traducirse por **since**, **from** o, en combinación con **hace**/**hacía** por **for**.
>
> • **Desde** (**que**) se traduce por **since** siempre que se especifique a partir de cuándo comenzó una acción o un estado que sigue desarrollándose en el presente o en el momento en que se habla:
>
> Llevo aquí de vacaciones desde el viernes
> ***I have been here on holiday since Friday***
> No come mejillones desde que sufrió aquella intoxicación alimenticia
> ***He hasn't eaten mussels since he had that bout of food poisoning***
> Dijo que no la había visto desde la guerra
> ***He said he hadn't seen her since the war***
>
> ! Hay que tener en cuenta que en casos como éstos cuando se trata de algo que comienza en el pasado y sigue en el presente, el inglés hace uso del *pretérito perfecto* (en sus formas simple o progresiva).
>
> • Traducimos **desde** por **from** cuando **desde** simplemente indica el momento en el que empezó la acción cuando la oración indica el final de la acción o se implica, de algún modo, que ésta ya ha terminado:
>
> Y desde aquel día el rey no volvió a hablar del asunto
> ***And from that day on(wards), the king never spoke about the subject again***
>
> • La construcción **desde** ... **hasta** se traduce por **from** ... **until** o por **from** ... **to**:
>
> Trabajamos desde las nueve de la mañana hasta las cinco de la tarde
> ***We work from nine in the morning until** o **to five in the afternoon***
> Tendrás que pagar el alquiler desde julio hasta octubre
> ***You will have to pay rent from July until** o **to October***
>
> • **Desde hace** y **desde hacía** se traducen por **for** ya que van seguidos de una cantidad de tiempo:
>
> Estoy esperando desde hace más de una hora
> ***I have been waiting for over an hour***
> No se había sentido tan feliz desde hacía años
> ***He hadn't felt so happy for years***
>
> • En oraciones interrogativas, **desde cuándo** se traduce por **how long**. En este tipo de preguntas, el inglés utiliza el pretérito perfecto para referirse a algo que empezó en el pasado y continúa en el presente:
>
> ¿Desde cuándo os conocéis?
> ***How long have you known each other?***
>
> *Para otros usos y ejemplos ver la entrada.*

desdeñosamente ADV (= *con desprecio*) scornfully, disdainfully

desdeñoso ADJ scornful, disdainful

desdibujado ADJ 1 [*contorno*] blurred

2 (= *descolorado*) faded

desdibujar ▸conjug 1a◂ Ⓐ VT to blur, blur the outlines of

Ⓑ **desdibujarse** VPR to get blurred, fade; **el recuerdo se ha desdibujado** the memory has become blurred

desdicha SF 1 (= *infelicidad*) unhappiness

2 (= *contratiempo*) misfortune; **tuve la ~ de ser amigo suyo** I had the misfortune to be a friend of his, I was unlucky enough to be a friend of his; **para mi ~, mi suegra vive con nosotros** unfortunately for me, my mother-in-law lives with us

3 (*) (= *persona, cosa inútil*) dead loss*

desdichadamente ADV unhappily

desdichado/a Ⓐ ADJ 1 [*persona*] (= *infeliz*) unhappy; (= *desgraciado*) unlucky; **¡qué ~ soy!** how wretched I am!

2 [*día*] ill-fated; **fue un día ~** it was an ill-fated day

Ⓑ SM/F poor devil

desdicho PP *de* **desdecir**

desdinerar ▸conjug 1a◂ Ⓐ VT to impoverish

Ⓑ **desdinerarse** VPR (*) to cough up*, fork out‡

desdoblado ADJ 1 [*carretera*] two-lane

2 [*personalidad*] split

3 (*Escol*) **grupo ~** group which has been split into two

desdoblamiento SM 1 [*de carreteras*] widening

2 ► **desdoblamiento de la personalidad** split personality

3 (*Escol*) [*de grupos*] splitting into two

desdoblar ▸conjug 1a◂ Ⓐ VT 1 (= *desplegar*) [+ *pañuelo*] to unfold; [+ *mantel*] to spread out; [+ *alambre*] to untwist

2 (*Quím*) to break down (**en** into)

3 (= *duplicar*) to double; **~ un cargo** to split the functions of a post

4 [+ *carretera*] to widen

5 [+ *tema*] to expand upon, explain

Ⓑ **desdoblarse** VPR to divide, split in two

desdoble SM (*Fin*) reorganization of capital

desdorar ▸conjug 1a◂ VT to tarnish

desdoro SM (*en fama, reputación*) stigma, dishonour, dishonor (*EEUU*); **consideran un ~ trabajar** they think it dishonourable to work; **es un ~ para todos** it is a blot on us all; **hablar en ~ de algn** to speak disparagingly of sb, discredit sb by what one says

desdramatizar ▸conjug 1f◂ VT [+ *situación*] to take the drama out of; [+ *crisis*] to defuse

deseabilidad SF desirability

deseable ADJ 1 [*situación, solución*] desirable; **sería ~ un cambio** a change would be desirable; **no** *o* **poco ~** undesirable

2 [*cuerpo, persona*] desirable

▼ **desear** ▸conjug 1a◂ VT 1 (= *anhelar*) to want; **sólo deseo que me dejen en paz** I just want to be left in peace; **no deseo que le pase nada malo** I wouldn't want *o* wish anything bad to happen to him; **un embarazo no deseado** an unwanted pregnancy; **la vida que tanto había deseado** the life she had wanted so much *o* longed for; **dejar bastante** *o* **mucho que ~** to leave a lot to be desired; ✦***MODISMO*** **no se lo deseo a nadie** *o* **ni a mi peor enemigo** I wouldn't wish it on anyone *o* my worst enemy; **estar deseando algo**: **estaba deseando conocerte** I've been looking forward to meeting you; **estoy deseando que esto termine** I'm really looking forward to this finishing, I can't wait for this to finish; **estoy deseando que lleguen las vacaciones** I'm really looking forward to the holidays, I can't wait for *o* till the holidays; **ser de ~**: **sería de ~ que actualizaran**

➤ LENGUA Y USO: **desear 1, 3** 48.1, 48.2, 50.1, 50.2, 50.3, 50.4, 50.5, 51.3

su información it would be desirable for them to update their information; **es de ~ que mejoren nuestras relaciones** an improvement in our relations would be desirable; **no hemos avanzado tanto como sería de ~** we haven't made as much progress as we would have liked; *ver tb* **ver B9**
2 (*frm*) 2·1 (*en peticiones*) to wish; **~ía ver al director** I would like *o* I wish to see the manager; **el doctor desea hablar un momento con usted** the doctor wishes to speak to you for a moment; **todo se hará como tú desees** everything will be done as you wish
2·2 (*en preguntas, sugerencias*) **si lo desea se lo podemos enviar por correo** if you wish we can send it by post; **¿~ía el señor algún postre?** would Sir like a dessert?, do you wish a dessert?; **¿qué desean beber?** what would you like to drink?; **¿desea que le hagamos una factura?** do you wish us to make out an invoice?; **¿qué desea?** can I help you?
3 (*en fórmulas de cortesía*) [+ *éxito, suerte*] to wish; **os deseamos una Feliz Navidad** we wish you a Merry Christmas; **te deseo la mejor suerte del mundo** I wish you the best luck in the world; **le deseamos una pronta recuperación** we wish you a prompt recovery
4 (*sexualmente*) to want

desecación SF [*de terreno*] (*de forma artificial*) draining, drainage; (*por el sol*) drying, desiccation (*frm*)

desecado ADJ 1 [*fruta*] dried
2 [*lago, terreno*] (*de forma artificial*) drained; (*por el sol*) dried up

desecar ▸conjug 1g◂ Ⓐ VT 1 [+ *fruta*] to dry; [+ *coco*] to dessicate (*frm*)
2 (= *quitar la humedad*) [*persona*] to drain; **el sol ha desecado el lago** the sun has dried up the lake
Ⓑ **desecarse** VPR to dry up

desecha SF (*Andes*) = **desecho**

desechable ADJ 1 [*jeringuilla, pañal*] disposable; **envases ~s** non-returnable containers; **la oferta no es ~** the offer is not to be turned down lightly
2 [*variable*] temporary

desechar ▸conjug 1a◂ VT 1 (= *tirar*) [+ *basura*] to throw out; [+ *objeto inútil*] to scrap, get rid of
2 (= *rechazar*) [+ *consejo, miedo*] to cast aside; [+ *oferta*] to reject; [+ *plan*] to drop
3 (= *censurar*) to censure, reprove
4 [+ *llave*] to turn

desecho SM 1 (= *residuo*) **productos de ~** waste products; **ropa de ~** castoffs *pl*
► **desecho de hierro** scrap iron
2 **desechos** (= *desperdicios*) (*gen*) rubbish *sing*, garbage *sing* (*EEUU*); [*de la industria*] waste *sing*; [*de ropa*] castoffs; [*de animal*] offal *sing*
► **desechos radiactivos** radioactive waste
3 (*) (= *persona inútil*) dead loss*; **el ~ de la sociedad** the scum *o* dregs *pl* of society
4 (= *desprecio*) contempt, scorn
5 (*LAm*) (= *atajo*) short cut; (= *desvío*) detour; (= *sendero*) path, temporary road

desegregación SF desegregation

desegregar ▸conjug 1h◂ VT to desegregate

desellar ▸conjug 1a◂ VT to unseal, open

desembalaje SM unpacking

desembalar ▸conjug 1a◂ VT to unpack

desembanastar ▸conjug 1a◂ Ⓐ VT 1 (= *sacar*) to unpack
2 (*) [+ *espada*] to draw
3 [+ *secreto*] to blurt out
Ⓑ **desembanastarse** VPR 1 [*animal*] to break out
2 (= *bajar*) to alight

desembarazado ADJ 1 (= *desenvuelto*) free and easy; **~ de trabas** free, unrestrained
2 (= *libre*) clear, free
3 (= *sin carga*) unburdened, light

desembarazar ▸conjug 1f◂ Ⓐ VT 1 [+ *camino, cuarto*] to clear; **~ un cuarto de trastos** to clear a room of furniture
2 **~ a algn de algo** to rid sb of sth
3 (*Andes, Caribe, Cono Sur*††) (= *dar a luz a*) to give birth to
Ⓑ **desembarazarse** VPR **~se de algo** to get rid of sth

desembarazo SM 1 (= *acto*) [*de camino, cuarto*] clearing; [*de carga*] unburdening
2 (= *desenfado*) ease, naturalness; **hablar con ~** to talk easily, talk freely
3 (*LAm*) (= *parto*) birth

desembarcadero SM quay, landing stage

desembarcar ▸conjug 1g◂ Ⓐ VT [+ *personas*] to disembark; [+ *mercancías*] to unload
Ⓑ VI 1 (*de barco, avión*) [*pasajeros*] to disembark; [*tropas*] to land, disembark
2 (*esp LAm*) (*de tren*) to alight (*frm*) (**de** from), get out (**de** of)
3 **estar para ~*** to be about to give birth

desembarco SM [*de pasajeros*] disembarkation; [*de tropas*] landing, disembarkation; [*de mercancías*] unloading

desembargar ▸conjug 1h◂ VT (*Jur*) to lift the embargo on

desembargo SM lifting (*of an embargo*)

desembarque SM [*de pasajeros*] disembarkation; [*de mercancías*] unloading

desembarrancar ▸conjug 1g◂ VT [+ *barco*] to refloat

desembarrar ▸conjug 1a◂ VT to clear of mud, remove the silt from

desembaular ▸conjug 1a◂ VT 1 [+ *equipaje*] to unpack
2 (= *descargarse de*) to unburden o.s. of

desembocadero SM, **desembocadura** SF [*de río*] mouth; [*de alcantarilla*] outfall; [*de calle*] opening, end

desembocar ▸conjug 1g◂ VI 1 **~ en** [*río*] to flow into, run into; [*calle*] to join, lead into
2 **~ en** (= *terminar en*) to end in, result in; **esto desembocó en una tragedia** this ended in *o* led to tragedy

desembolsar ▸conjug 1a◂ VT 1 (= *pagar*) to pay out
2 (= *gastar*) to lay out

desembolso SM 1 (= *pago*) payment
► **desembolso de capital** capital outlay
► **desembolso inicial** deposit
2 (= *gastos*) outlay, expenditure; **cubrir ~s** to cover expenses

desembozar ▸conjug 1f◂ VT to unmask

desembragar ▸conjug 1h◂ Ⓐ VT (*Mec*) [+ *embrague*] to release, let out; [+ *marcha*] to disengage
Ⓑ VI (*Aut*) to declutch, let out the clutch

desembrague SM (*Aut*) (= *acto*) declutching; (= *mecanismo*) clutch release

desembravecer ▸conjug 2d◂ Ⓐ VT [+ *animal*] to tame; [+ *persona*] to calm, pacify
Ⓑ **desembravecerse** VPR to calm down

desembriagar ▸conjug 1h◂ Ⓐ VT to sober up
Ⓑ **desembriagarse** VPR to sober up

desembrollar ▸conjug 1a◂ VT 1 [+ *madeja*] to unravel
2 [+ *asunto, malentendido*] to sort out

desembuchar ▸conjug 1a◂ Ⓐ VT 1 [*ave*] to regurgitate
2 (*) [+ *conclusiones*] to come out with
Ⓑ VI (*) (= *confesar*) to spill the beans*; **¡desembucha!** out with it!, spit it out!
Ⓒ **desembucharse** VPR (*Chile*) to be sick

desemejante ADJ dissimilar; **su comportamiento es muy ~ al de su padre** his behaviour is very dissimilar to his father's

desemejanza SF dissimilarity

desemejar ▸conjug 1a◂ Ⓐ VT to alter, alter the appearance of, change (*for the worse*)
Ⓑ VI to be dissimilar, look different, not look alike

desempacar ▸conjug 1g◂ VT (*esp LAm*) to unpack

desempacharse ▸conjug 1a◂ VPR 1 (*Med*) **se desempachó** his stomach settled down
2 (= *perder la timidez*) to come out of one's shell

desempacho SM (= *soltura*) ease; (= *despreocupación*) unconcern; (= *desparpajo*) forwardness

desempadronarse‡ ▸conjug 1a◂ VPR (*Méx*) to do o.s. in‡, commit suicide

desempantanar ▸conjug 1a◂ VT [+ *asunto, problema*] to clear up, resolve

desempañador SM (*Aut*) demister

desempañar ▸conjug 1a◂ VT [+ *cristal*] (*con trapo*) to wipe clean; [*dispositivo antivaho*] to demist, defog (*EEUU*)

desempapelar ▸conjug 1a◂ VT [+ *pared*] to strip; [+ *paquete*] to unwrap

desempaquetar ▸conjug 1a◂ VT to unpack, unwrap

desempatar ▸conjug 1a◂ VI **van a jugar la prórroga para ver si desempatan** extra time will be played to try and break the deadlock *o* to get a result

desempate SM 1 (*Ftbl*) (= *partido*) **el ~ llegó con el gol de Roque** the breakthrough came with Roque's goal; **marcó el gol del ~ en el minuto 15** he put his side ahead *o* broke the deadlock in the 15th minute ► **desempate a penaltis** penalty shoot-out
2 (*Tenis*) tie break

desempedrar ▸conjug 1j◂ VT [+ *calle*] to take up the paving stones of; ✦**MODISMO** **ir desempedrando la calle** to dash along the street

desempeñar ▸conjug 1a◂ Ⓐ VT 1 [+ *propiedades, joyas*] to redeem, get out of pawn; **~ a algn** to get sb out of debt, pay sb's debts
2 (= *llevar a cabo*) [+ *deber, función*] to perform, carry out; [+ *papel*] (*tb Teat*) to play
3 (= *ocupar*) [+ *cargo*] to occupy, hold
Ⓑ **desempeñarse** VPR 1 (= *quitarse deudas*) to get out of debt
2 **~se como** (*LAm*) to act as

desempeño SM 1 [*de propiedades, joyas*] redeeming, redemption
2 [*de deber*] performance, carrying out; [*de cargo*] carrying out; **durante el ~ de sus funciones como presidente** in the course of

carrying out *o* performing his duties as president

[3] (*Teat*) performance; **un ~ meritorio** a worthy performance; **una mujer de mucho ~** a most active and able woman

desempleado/a Ⓐ ADJ unemployed, out of work

Ⓑ SM/F unemployed man/woman; **los ~s** the unemployed

desempleo SM [1] (= *falta de trabajo*) unemployment ► **desempleo de larga duración** long-term unemployment

[2] (= *subsidio*) unemployment benefit; **cobrar el ~** to draw unemployment benefit

desempolvar ▸conjug 1a◂ VT [1] [+ *libros, muebles*] to dust; [+ *objeto no usado*] to dust off

[2] [+ *recuerdos*] to revive

desencadenamiento SM [*de pasión, energía*] unleashing ► **desencadenamiento de hostilidades** outbreak of hostilities

desencadenante Ⓐ ADJ **los factores ~s del accidente** the factors which triggered (off) *o* caused the accident

Ⓑ SM cause, trigger

desencadenar ▸conjug 1a◂ Ⓐ VT [1] (= *quitar las cadenas de*) [+ *prisionero*] to unchain; [+ *perro*] to unleash

[2] (= *desatar*) [+ *ira*] to unleash; [+ *crisis*] to trigger, set off

Ⓑ **desencadenarse** VPR [1] (= *soltarse*) to break loose

[2] (= *estallar*) [*tormenta*] to burst; [*guerra*] to break out; **se desencadenó una violenta reacción** a violent reaction was unleashed; **se ~on los aplausos** applause broke out

desencajado ADJ [*cara*] twisted, contorted; [*mandíbula*] dislocated; [*ojos*] wild

desencajar ▸conjug 1a◂ Ⓐ VT [1] (*Anat*) [+ *hueso*] to throw out of joint; [+ *mandíbula*] to dislocate

[2] (*Mec*) to disconnect, disengage

Ⓑ **desencajarse** VPR [*cara*] to become distorted *o* contorted; [*ojos*] to look wild; **se le desencajó la mandíbula** he dislocated his jaw

desencajonar ▸conjug 1a◂ VT to unpack

desencallar ▸conjug 1a◂ VT [+ *barco*] to refloat

desencaminado ADJ (*lit*) headed in the wrong direction; (*fig*) misguided; **no vas muy ~** you're not far wrong there

desencantar ▸conjug 1a◂ VT [1] (= *quitar la ilusión a*) to disillusion, disenchant

[2] (= *quitar un encantamiento a*) to free from a spell

desencanto SM disillusion, disillusionment, disenchantment

desencapotarse ▸conjug 1a◂ VPR [*cielo*] to clear, clear up

desenchufar ▸conjug 1a◂ Ⓐ VT to disconnect, unplug

Ⓑ **desenchufarse** VPR (* *hum*) to unwind, switch off

desencoger ▸conjug 2c◂ Ⓐ VT [1] (= *extender*) to spread out

[2] (= *alisar*) to smooth out, straighten out

Ⓑ **desencogerse** VPR to lose one's timidity

desencolarse ▸conjug 1a◂ VPR to come unstuck

desenconar ▸conjug 1a◂ Ⓐ VT [1] [+ *cólera*] to calm down, soothe

[2] [+ *inflamación*] to soothe

Ⓑ **desenconarse** VPR [1] (= *calmarse*) [*odio*] to die down; [*persona*] to calm down

[2] [*inflamación*] to die down, go down

desencontrarse ▸conjug 1n◂ VPR (= *separarse*) to become separated, get split up; (= *no encontrarse*) to fail to meet up

desencorvar ▸conjug 1a◂ VT to unbend, straighten, straighten out

desencuadernar ▸conjug 1a◂ Ⓐ VT to unbind

Ⓑ **desencuadernarse** VPR to come unbound

desencuadrado ADJ (*Fot*) off centre

desencuentro SM [1] (= *falta de encuentro*) failure to meet up

[2] (= *falta de acuerdo*) mix-up

desendeudar ▸conjug 1a◂ Ⓐ VI (*LAm*) to pay one's debts, get out of the red

Ⓑ **desendeudarse** VPR (*LAm*) to pay one's debts, get out of the red

desenfadaderas SFPL **tener buenas ~** (= *no alterarse*) to be unflappable, be slow to anger; (*al salir de problemas*) to be good at getting out of jams

desenfadado ADJ [1] [*aire, carácter*] free, uninhibited

[2] [*persona*] (= *despreocupado*) free-and-easy, carefree; (= *desenvuelto*) self-confident; (= *descarado*) forward; (*en el vestir*) casual

[3] [*espacio*] free, unencumbered

desenfadar ▸conjug 1a◂ Ⓐ VT to pacify, calm down

Ⓑ **desenfadarse** VPR to calm down

desenfado SM [1] (= *despreocupación*) free-and-easy manner

[2] (= *libertad*) freedom, lack of inhibition

[3] (= *descaro*) forwardness

[4] (= *desenvoltura*) self-confidence

desenfocado ADJ (*por mal uso*) out of focus; (*de forma intencionada*) in soft focus

desenfocar ▸conjug 1g◂ Ⓐ VT [1] (*Fot*) to get out of focus

[2] [+ *asunto*] to read wrongly

Ⓑ **desenfocarse** VPR (*Fot*) to go out of focus

desenfoque SM (*por mal uso*) lack of focus, state of being out of focus; (*de forma intencionada*) soft focus

desenfrenadamente ADV wildly, in an uncontrolled way

desenfrenado ADJ [*persona*] wild, uncontrolled; [*apetito, pasiones*] unbridled

desenfrenarse ▸conjug 1a◂ VPR [1] (= *desmandarse*) [*persona*] to lose all self-control; [*multitud*] to run riot

[2] (*Meteo*) [*tempestad*] to burst; [*viento*] to rage

desenfreno SM [1] [*de pasiones*] unleashing

[2] (= *libertinaje*) licentiousness

desenfundar ▸conjug 1a◂ Ⓐ VT [+ *pistola*] to pull out, draw

Ⓑ VI (*) to flash*

desenganchar ▸conjug 1a◂ Ⓐ VT [1] (= *soltar*) [+ *cortinas*] to unhook; [+ *vagones*] to uncouple; [+ *caballo*] to unhitch

[2] (*Mec*) to disengage

Ⓑ **desengancharse** VPR (*) to kick the habit*; **~se de algo** to come off sth

desengañado ADJ [1] (= *decepcionado*) disillusioned

[2] (*Andes, Cono Sur*) (= *feo*) terribly ugly

desengañar ▸conjug 1a◂ Ⓐ VT [1] (= *desilusionar*) to disillusion; **es mejor no ~la** it is best not to take away her hopes *o* not to disillusion her

[2] (= *decepcionar*) to disappoint

[3] (= *abrir los ojos a*) to open the eyes of

Ⓑ **desengañarse** VPR [1] (= *desilusionarse*) to become disillusioned (**de** about)

[2] (= *decepcionarse*) to be disappointed

[3] (= *abrir los ojos*) to see the light, see things as they really are; **¡desengáñate!** wise up!*

desengaño SM [1] (= *desilusión*) disillusion, disillusionment; **los ~s te enseñarán** you'll learn the hard way

[2] (= *decepción*) disappointment; **sufrir un ~ amoroso** to be disappointed in love

desengranar ▸conjug 1a◂ VT to disengage

desengrasado ADJ [1] [*máquina*] rusty, needing oil

[2] (*Culin*) fat-free

desengrasar ▸conjug 1a◂ VT to degrease

desenhebrar ▸conjug 1j◂ VT to unthread

desenjaular ▸conjug 1a◂ VT [1] [+ *animal*] to take out of a cage

[2] (*) [+ *preso*] to let out of jail

desenlace SM [*de libro, película*] ending, dénouement (*frm*); [*de aventura*] outcome; **~ fatal** *o* **trágico** tragic ending; **el libro tiene un ~ feliz** the book has a happy ending

desenlatar ▸conjug 1a◂ VT (*LAm*) [+ *latas*] to open

desenlazar ▸conjug 1f◂ Ⓐ VT [1] (= *desatar*) to untie

[2] (= *resolver*) [+ *problema*] to solve; [+ *asunto*] to unravel

Ⓑ **desenlazarse** VPR [1] (= *desatarse*) to come undone

[2] [*libro, película*] to end, turn out

desenmarañar ▸conjug 1a◂ VT [1] [+ *cuerda, lana, pelo*] to untangle, disentangle

[2] [+ *misterio*] to unravel, clear up

desenmascarar ▸conjug 1a◂ VT (*lit*) to unmask; (*fig*) to unmask, expose

desenojar ▸conjug 1a◂ VT to soothe, appease, calm down

desenredar ▸conjug 1a◂ Ⓐ VT [1] [+ *pelo, lana*] to untangle, disentangle

[2] [+ *dificultad, problema*] to straighten out

Ⓑ **desenredarse** VPR (*de un problema*) to extricate o.s. (**de** from)

desenredo SM [1] (= *acto*) unravelling, disentanglement

[2] (*Literat*) dénouement

desenrollar ▸conjug 1a◂ Ⓐ VT [+ *alfombra*] to unroll; [+ *cable*] to unwind

Ⓑ **desenrollarse** VPR [*alfombra*] to unroll; [*cable*] to unwind

desenroscar ▸conjug 1g◂ VT [+ *tornillo*] to unscrew

desensibilizar ▸conjug 1f◂ VT to desensitize

desensillar ▸conjug 1a◂ VT to unsaddle

desentablar ▸conjug 1a◂ Ⓐ VT to break up

Ⓑ **desentablarse** VPR **se desentabló una discusión** a row broke out

desentenderse ▸conjug 2g◂ VPR [1] (= *simular ignorancia*) **~ de algo** to pretend not to know about sth

[2] (= *repudiar*) **~ de algo** to wash one's hands of sth, want nothing to do with sth; **se ha desentendido del asunto** he wants nothing to do with the matter

desentendido ADJ **hacerse el ~** to pretend not to notice; **se hizo el ~** he didn't take the hint; **no te hagas el ~** don't pretend you haven't heard

desentendimiento SM **su ~ sobre el asunto** his refusal to have anything to do with the matter

desenterrar ▸conjug 1j◂ VT [1] [+ *cadáver*] to disinter; [+ *tesoro*] to unearth
[2] [+ *recuerdo, odio*] to rake up

desentonado ADJ [1] (*Mús*) out of tune
[2] [*color*] clashing

desentonar ▸conjug 1a◂ Ⓐ VI [1] (= *no encajar*) [*persona, comentario*] to be out of place; [*colores*] to clash (**con** with); **para no ~** so as to do the right thing, so as to fall into line; **el edificio desentona con el entorno** the building doesn't fit in with the surroundings
[2] (*Mús*) to be out of tune
Ⓑ **desentonarse** VPR to raise one's voice angrily

desentono SM [1] (= *cualidad*) rudeness, disrespect
[2] (= *tono*) rude tone of voice

desentorpecer ▸conjug 2d◂ VT [1] [+ *miembro*] to stretch, loosen up
[2] (*) [+ *persona*] to polish up

desentramparse* ▸conjug 1a◂ VPR to get out of the red

desentrañar ▸conjug 1a◂ VT [1] (= *resolver*) [+ *misterio*] to get to the bottom of, unravel; [+ *significado*] to puzzle out
[2] (= *destripar*) to disembowel

desentrenado ADJ [*jugador*] out of training; [*soldado*] untrained

desentumecer ▸conjug 2d◂ Ⓐ VT [+ *miembro*] to stretch; [+ *músculos*] to loosen up
Ⓑ **desentumecerse** VPR to loosen up

desenvainar ▸conjug 1a◂ VT [1] (= *sacar de la vaina*) [+ *espada*] to draw, unsheathe; [+ *guisantes*] to shell; [+ *garras*] to show, put out
[2] (= *mostrar*) to reveal, expose

desenvoltura SF [1] (= *facilidad*) (*al moverse*) ease; (*al hablar*) fluency
[2] (= *falta de timidez*) confidence, self-confidence
[3] (*pey*) (= *desparpajo*) forwardness, brazenness

desenvolver ▸conjug 2h◂ (*pp* **desenvuelto**)
Ⓐ VT [1] (= *desliar*) [+ *paquete*] to unwrap; [+ *rollo*] to unwind, unroll; [+ *lana*] to disentangle, unravel
[2] [+ *teoría*] to develop
Ⓑ **desenvolverse** VPR [1] [*persona*] to manage, cope; **se desenvuelve muy bien en público** he comes across really well in public
[2] [*acción, suceso*] (= *suceder*) to go off; (= *desarrollarse*) to develop

desenvolvimiento SM development

desenvuelto Ⓐ PP *de* **desenvolver**
Ⓑ ADJ [1] (= *falto de timidez*) confident, self-confident
[2] (*al hablar*) fluent; (*pey*) forward, brazen

desenyugar ▸conjug 1h◂ VT (*LAm*), **desenyuntar** ▸conjug 1a◂ VT (*LAm*) to unyoke

▼ **deseo** SM [1] (= *anhelo*) desire, wish; **mi mayor ~ es encontrar un trabajo** my dearest wish *o* greatest desire is to find a job; **el ~ de poder** the lust for power; **un inacabable ~ de saber** an unquenchable thirst for knowledge; **llegó al poder con buenos ~s de mejorarlo todo** he came to power with every intention of improving things; **tengo ~s de verla** I yearn to see her, I'm longing to see her; **ardo en ~s de conocerla** (*liter*) I have a burning desire to meet her
[2] (= *cosa deseada*) wish; **pedir** *o* **formular un ~** to make a wish; **su último ~ fue que la incineraran** her dying wish was to be cremated; **nuestro ~ es que seas feliz** our wish is for you to be happy; **con mis mejores ~s para el Año Nuevo** with best wishes for the New Year; **tus ~s son órdenes** your wish is my command
[3] (*tb* **~ sexual**) desire

deseoso ADJ **estar ~ de hacer algo** to be anxious *o* eager to do sth

desequilibrado/a ADJ Ⓐ ADJ [*persona*] unbalanced; [*rueda*] out of balance, not properly balanced, out of true; [*distribución*] one-sided, lop-sided
Ⓑ SM/F unbalanced person; **es un ~ mental** he's mentally unbalanced

desequilibrador ADJ destabilizing

desequilibrar ▸conjug 1a◂ Ⓐ VT [1] [+ *barca, mueble*] to unbalance, make unbalanced
[2] [+ *persona*] (*físicamente*) to throw off balance; (*psicológicamente*) to unbalance
[3] **~ un país/régimen** to destabilize a country/regime
Ⓑ **desequilibrarse** VPR [*balanza*] to get out of balance; [*persona*] to become mentally unbalanced

desequilibrio SM [1] [*de mente*] unbalance
[2] (*entre cantidades*) imbalance
[3] (*Med*) unbalanced mental condition

deserción SF [1] (*Mil*) desertion
[2] (= *abandono*) (*de un partido a otro*) defection; (*de una actividad*) giving up

desertar ▸conjug 1a◂ VI to desert; **~ de** (*Mil*) to desert; **~ del hogar** to abandon one's home; **~ de sus deberes** to neglect one's duties; **~ de una tertulia** to stop going to a gathering

desértico ADJ [1] (= *del desierto*) desert *antes de s*
[2] (= *árido*) desert-like, barren
[3] (= *despoblado*) deserted

desertificar ▸conjug 1g◂ VT = **desertizar**

desertización SF [1] [*de terreno*] desertification
[2] (= *despoblación*) depopulation

desertizar ▸conjug 1f◂ VT [1] [+ *terreno*] to turn into a desert
[2] (= *despoblar*) to depopulate

desertor(a) SM/F (*Mil*) deserter; (*Pol*) defector

deservicio SM disservice

desescalada SF de-escalation

desescalar ▸conjug 1a◂ VT, VI to de-escalate

desescamar ▸conjug 1a◂ VT to descale, remove the fur from (*EEUU*)

desescarchador SM (*Mec*) defroster

desescolarización SF lack of schooling

desescolarizado ADJ **niños ~s** children deprived of schooling

desescombrar ▸conjug 1a◂ VT [1] [+ *lugar*] to clear up, clear of rubbish *o* debris *etc*, clean up
[2] [+ *cadáver*] to dig out, extract

desescombro SM clearing-up, clean-up

desespañolizar ▸conjug 1f◂ VT [+ *costumbre*] to weaken the Spanish nature of; [+ *persona*] to cause to become less Spanish, wean away from Spanish habits *etc*

desesperación SF [1] (= *pérdida de esperanza*) despair, desperation; **mirar a algn con ~** to look at sb despairingly; **nadar con ~** to swim desperately
[2] (= *resultado*) **es una ~** it's maddening; **es una ~ tener que ...** it's infuriating to have to ...

desesperada SF ✦*MODISMO* **hacer algo a la ~** to do sth as a last resort *o* in desperation

desesperadamente ADV desperately, despairingly

desesperado/a Ⓐ ADJ [1] (= *sin esperanza*) [*persona*] desperate; [*caso, situación*] hopeless; **estar ~ de algo** to have despaired of sth, have lost hope of sth
[2] [*esfuerzo*] furious, frenzied
Ⓑ SM/F **como un ~** like mad; **come como una desesperada** she eats as if she were half-starved

desesperante ADJ [*situación*] infuriating; [*persona*] infuriating, hopeless

desesperanza SF despair

desesperanzar ▸conjug 1f◂ Ⓐ VT to drive to despair
Ⓑ **desesperanzarse** VPR to lose hope, despair

desesperar ▸conjug 1a◂ Ⓐ VT [1] (= *exasperar*) **mi hermano me desespera** my brother drives me mad *o* crazy, my brother is infuriating *o* maddening; **me desespera que el tren llegue tarde** it's infuriating *o* maddening when the train is late
[2] (= *desalentar*) **no dejes que sus críticas te desesperen** don't let their criticism make you lose hope *o* heart, don't let their criticism get to you*; **tantos problemas la ~on y acabó dimitiendo** all these problems drove her to despair and in the end she resigned
Ⓑ VI (= *perder la esperanza*) to despair, lose hope; **sigue adelante, no desesperes** keep at it, don't despair *o* lose hope; **~ de hacer algo** (*frm*) to despair of doing sth, lose all hope of doing sth; ✦*REFRÁN* **el que espera, desespera** waiting gets you down
Ⓒ **desesperarse** VPR [1] (= *exasperarse*) **me desespero con tanto trabajo** all this work is driving me mad *o* crazy; **me estaba desesperando porque el taxi no llegaba** the taxi still hadn't come and I was going mad *o* crazy *o* getting desperate
[2] (= *desalentarse*) to despair, lose hope; **nunca se desespera aunque las cosas le vayan mal** she never loses hope *o* despairs even when things go badly for her; **no te desesperes si no apruebas a la primera** if you don't pass first time, don't despair *o* give up hope

desespero SM (*LAm*) despair, desperation

desespinar ▸conjug 1a◂ VT [+ *pescado*] to fillet, bone

desestabilización SF destabilization

desestabilizador ADJ [1] [*campaña, influencia*] destabilizing
[2] [*elemento, grupo*] subversive

desestabilizar ▸conjug 1f◂ VT [1] [+ *situación*] to destabilize
[2] [+ *confianza, orden moral*] to undermine

desestancar ▸conjug 1g◂ VT [+ *producto*] to remove the state monopoly from, allow a free market in

desestiba SF (*Náut*) unloading

➤ LENGUA Y USO: **deseo 1** 35.5

desestibar ▸conjug 1a◂ VT (*Náut*) to unload

desestimable ADJ insignificant

desestimar ▸conjug 1a◂ VT [1] (= *menospreciar*) to look down on
[2] (*Jur*) [+ *demanda, moción*] to reject

desestímulo SM disincentive

desestructurado ADJ badly structured; **familia desestructurada** broken home

desexilio SM (*LAm*) return from exile, return home

desfachatado* ADJ brazen, impudent, barefaced

desfachatez SF [1] (= *descaro*) brazenness, cheek
[2] **una ~** a cheeky remark*, a brazen remark

desfalcador(a) SM/F embezzler

desfalcar ▸conjug 1g◂ VT to embezzle

desfalco SM embezzlement

desfallecer ▸conjug 2d◂ VI [1] (= *perder las fuerzas*) to get weak; **~ de ánimo** to lose heart
[2] (= *desmayarse*) to faint

desfallecido ADJ (= *débil*) weak

desfallecimiento SM [1] (= *debilidad*) weakness
[2] (= *desmayo*) fainting fit

desfasado ADJ [1] (= *anticuado*) behind the times
[2] (*Téc*) out of phase
[3] **estar ~** (*Aer*) to be suffering from jetlag

desfasar ▸conjug 1a◂ VT [1] (= *dejar anticuado*) to phase out
[2] (*Elec*) to change the phase of

desfase SM (= *diferencia*) gap; **hay un ~ entre las dos generaciones** there's a generation gap ► **desfase horario** jet lag

desfavorable ADJ unfavourable, unfavorable (*EEUU*)

desfavorablemente ADV unfavourably, unfavorably (*EEUU*)

desfavorecer ▸conjug 2d◂ VT [1] [+ *persona, causa*] **estas medidas ~án a los pequeños agricultores** these measures will hurt small farmers *o* go against the interests of small farmers; **han desfavorecido las calles peatonales** they are opposed to the pedestrianization of the streets
[2] (= *sentar mal a*) [*ropa*] not to suit

desfavorecido ADJ [1] (= *discriminado*) disadvantaged
[2] (= *afeado*) **siempre salgo ~ en las fotos** I never look good in photos

desfibradora SF shredder, shredding machine

desfibrar ▸conjug 1a◂ VT [+ *papel*] to shred

desfibrilador SM defibrillator

desfiguración SF, **desfiguramiento** SM [1] (= *transformación*) [*de persona*] disfigurement; [*de monumento*] defacement; [*de la realidad*] distortion
[2] (*Fot*) blurring
[3] (*Radio*) distortion

desfigurado ADJ [*persona*] disfigured; [*sonido, voz, sentido, realidad*] distorted; [*foto*] blurred

desfigurar ▸conjug 1a◂ VT [1] (= *transformar*) [+ *cara*] to disfigure; [+ *cuerpo*] to deform; [+ *cuadro, monumento*] to deface; [+ *voz, sonido*] to distort, disguise; [+ *sentido*] to twist; [+ *suceso*] to misrepresent; **una cicatriz le desfigura la cara** his face is disfigured by a scar; **la niebla lo desfigura todo** the fog makes everything look strange
[2] (*Fot*) to blur

desfiladero SM defile, gorge

desfilar ▸conjug 1a◂ VI [1] (*Mil*) to parade; **~on ante el general** they marched past the general
[2] (= *pasar*) to come, pass by; **por su despacho han desfilado muchos acreedores** many creditors have passed through his office; **según acababan, iban desfilando por la puerta** as they finished, they filtered out of the door
[3] [*modelo*] to model; **nunca he desfilado con ropa de Armani** I've never modelled Armani clothes

desfile SM [1] (*Mil*) parade ► **desfile aéreo** flypast, flyover (*EEUU*) ► **desfile de la victoria** victory parade ► **desfile de promoción** passing-out parade ► **desfile naval** naval review
[2] [*de carrozas*] procession
[3] ► **desfile de modas, desfile de modelos** fashion show, fashion parade

desfiscalización SF exemption from tax

desfiscalizar ▸conjug 1f◂ VT to exempt from taxation

desfloración SF deflowering, defloration

desflorar ▸conjug 1a◂ VT [1] (= *aspecto, reputación*) to tarnish
[2] [+ *asunto*] to touch on
[3] (*liter*) [+ *mujer*] to deflower (*liter*)

desfogar ▸conjug 1h◂ Ⓐ VT [+ *cólera, frustración*] to vent (**con, en** on)
Ⓑ VI (*Náut*) [*tormenta*] to burst
Ⓒ **desfogarse** VPR [*persona*] to vent one's anger (**con, en** on); **tiene que hacer deporte para ~se** he needs to do sport to let off steam

desfogue SM venting

desfondado ADJ (*Fin*) bankrupt

desfondar ▸conjug 1a◂ Ⓐ VT [1] (= *romper el fondo*) to knock the bottom out of, stave in (*tb Náut*)
[2] (*Agr*) to plough deeply
Ⓑ **desfondarse** VPR to go to pieces, have the bottom fall out of one's life

desforestación SF deforestation

desforestar ▸conjug 1a◂ VT to deforest

desformatear ▸conjug 1a◂ VT to unformat

desgaire SM [1] (= *desaseo*) slovenliness, carelessness; **vestido al ~** dressed in a slovenly way
[2] (= *desdén*) scornful attitude, disdain; ✦MODISMOS **hacer algo al ~** to do sth with a scornful air; **mirar a algn al ~** to sneer at sb, look scornfully at sb

desgajado ADJ separated, unconnected

desgajar ▸conjug 1a◂ Ⓐ VT [1] (= *desprender*) [+ *rama*] to tear off; [+ *página, capítulo*] to tear out
[2] [+ *naranja*] to split into segments
[3] **~ a algn de un lugar** to tear sb away from somewhere
Ⓑ **desgajarse** VPR [1] [*rama*] to come off, break off
[2] **~se de algn** to tear o.s. away from sb

desgalichado ADJ [1] [*movimiento*] clumsy, awkward
[2] (= *poco cuidado*) [*vestido*] shabby, slovenly, sloppy; [*persona*] down-at-heel, unprepossessing

desgana SF [1] (= *falta de apetito*) lack of appetite
[2] (= *apatía*) unwillingness, reluctance; **su ~ para hacerlo** his unwillingness *o* reluctance to do it; **hacer algo a** *o* **con ~** to do sth unwillingly *o* reluctantly
[3] (*Med*) weakness, faintness

desganadamente ADV [1] [*comer*] in a desultory fashion
[2] [*decir, hacer*] without much interest, in a desultory fashion

desganado ADJ [1] (= *sin apetito*) not hungry; **estar** *o* **sentirse ~** to have no appetite
[2] (= *sin entusiasmo*) half-hearted; **estar ~** to be lethargic

desganarse ▸conjug 1a◂ VPR [1] (= *perder el apetito*) to lose one's appetite
[2] (= *perder el entusiasmo*) to lose interest (**de** in), get fed up (**de** with)

desgano SM = **desgana**

desgañitarse* ▸conjug 1a◂ VPR to shout one's head off*

desgarbado ADJ [*movimiento*] clumsy, ungainly; [*persona*] gawky

desgarbo SM [*de movimiento*] clumsiness; [*de persona*] gracelessness; [*de aspecto*] slovenliness

desgarrado ADJ [1] [*ropa*] (= *rasgado*) torn; (= *hecho trizas*) tattered, in tatters
[2] (= *descarado*) shameless, barefaced, brazen
[3] (= *vicioso*) licentious

desgarrador ADJ [*escena, noticia*] heartbreaking, heartrending; [*grito*] piercing; [*emoción*] heartrending

desgarramiento SM [1] [*de tela*] tearing, ripping
[2] [*de sociedad, país*] upheaval

desgarrar ▸conjug 1a◂ VT [1] [+ *vestido, papel*] to tear, rip
[2] [+ *corazón*] to break
[3] (*LAm*) [+ *flema*] to cough up

desgarro SM [1] (*en tela, papel*) tear, rip
[2] (*Med*) sprain
[3] (= *descaro*) brazenness
[4] (= *jactancia*) boastfulness
[5] (*LAm*) (= *expectoración*) expectoration; (= *flema*) phlegm

desgarrón SM [1] (*en tela, papel*) big tear
[2] (= *sentimiento*) agony

desgastar ▸conjug 1a◂ Ⓐ VT [1] [+ *ropa, zapatos, tejido, moqueta, neumático*] to wear out; [+ *tacones, suela*] to wear down; [+ *superficie*] to wear away; **las olas han desgastado las rocas** the waves have worn away the rocks; **la corrupción ha desgastado al gobierno** corruption has weakened the government
[2] [+ *rival, contrincante*] to wear down
Ⓑ VI (= *debilitar*) **veinte años de poder desgastan** after twenty years in power you get stale *o* run out of steam
Ⓒ **desgastarse** VPR [1] (= *gastarse*) [*ropa, zapatos, tejido, neumático*] to wear out; [*tacones, suela, grada*] to wear down; [*superficie, roca*] to wear away; **la cuerda se desgastó con el roce** friction wore away the rope
[2] (= *agotarse*) [*persona*] to wear o.s. out

desgaste SM [1] [*de ropa, zapatos, neumático*] wear; [*de superficie, roca*] wearing away, erosion
[2] (= *agotamiento*) **su larga enfermedad provocó un ~ en su organismo** her long ill-

ness exhausted her physically; **el poder produjo el ~ del gobierno** in power, the government grew stale *o* ran out of steam; **guerra de ~** war of attrition ► **desgaste físico** physical exhaustion

desglaciación SF thaw

desglobar ►conjug 1a◄ VT [+ *cantidades, cifras*] to break down, analyse, split up

desglosable ADJ 1 [*cifras*] which can be broken down
2 [*impreso*] separable, detachable

desglosar ►conjug 1a◄ VT 1 [+ *cantidades, cifras*] to break down
2 [+ *impreso*] to detach

desglose SM breakdown

desgobernado ADJ [*asunto*] uncontrollable, undisciplined; [*niño*] wild

desgobernar ►conjug 1j◄ VT 1 (*Pol*) to misgovern, misrule
2 [+ *asunto*] to handle badly
3 (*Anat*) to dislocate

desgobierno SM 1 (*Pol*) misgovernment, misrule
2 [*de empresa*] bad handling
3 (*Anat*) dislocation

desgolletar ►conjug 1a◄ VT [+ *botella*] to knock the neck off

desgoznar ►conjug 1a◄ Ⓐ VT 1 (= *sacar de los goznes*) [+ *puerta*] to take off its hinges, unhinge
2 (= *quitar goznes de*) to take the hinges off
Ⓑ **desgoznarse** VPR 1 [*persona*] to go wild, lose control
2 [*plan*] to be thrown out of gear

desgrabar ►conjug 1a◄ VT [+ *cinta*] to wipe, wipe clean

▼**desgracia** SF 1 (= *mala suerte*) misfortune; **tuve la ~ de encontrármelo en el cine** I had the misfortune to *o* I was unfortunate enough to run into him at the cinema; **por ~** unfortunately; **estar en ~** (*frm*) to have constant bad luck; **en la ~ se conoce a los amigos** a friend in need is a friend indeed
2 (= *revés*) misfortune; **la familia ha sufrido una serie de ~s** the family has suffered a series of misfortunes; **ha ocurrido una ~** something terrible has happened; **ha muerto, ¡qué ~!** she has died, what a terrible thing (to happen)!; **estos niños sólo me traen ~s** these children are nothing but trouble; ✦***MODISMO*** **las ~s nunca vienen solas** it never rains but it pours; *ver tb* **colmo**
3 ► **desgracias personales** (= *víctimas*) casualties; **no hay que lamentar ~s personales** there were no casualties
4 **caer en ~** to lose favour *o* (*EEUU*) favor, fall from favour *o* (*EEUU*) favor

▼**desgraciadamente** ADV unfortunately, unluckily

desgraciado/a Ⓐ ADJ 1 [*persona*] (= *sin suerte*) unlucky; (= *infeliz*) unhappy; **~ en (sus) amores** unlucky in love; **~ en el juego** unlucky at cards; **fue ~ en su matrimonio** he was unhappy in his marriage; **¡~ de ti si lo haces!** you'd better not do it!, it'll be the worse for you if you do!
2 [*vida, existencia*] **¡qué desgraciada existencia la mía!** how wretched I am!; **una vida desgraciada** a wretched life, a life of misery
3 [*accidente, situación*] unfortunate; **una desgraciada elección** an unfortunate choice; **ese día ~** that ill-fated day
4 (*LAm*) (= *asqueroso*) lousy*
Ⓑ SM/F 1 (= *infeliz*) poor wretch; **lo tiene aquel ~** that poor wretch has got it; **la hizo una desgraciada** (*pey*) he put her in the family way, he brought shame upon her (*euf*)
2 (= *miserable*) swine*

desgraciar ►conjug 1b◄ Ⓐ VT 1 (= *estropear*) to spoil
2 (= *ofender*) to displease
Ⓑ **desgraciarse** VPR 1 (= *estropearse*) [*máquina*] to be ruined; [*plan*] to fall through; **como te caigas te vas a ~** (*hum*) you'll do yourself a permanent injury if you fall; **se le desgració el niño antes de nacer** she had a miscarriage, she lost the baby
2 **~se con algn** to fall out with sb

desgranar ►conjug 1a◄ Ⓐ VT 1 [+ *trigo*] to thresh; [+ *guisantes*] to shell; **~ un racimo de uvas** to pick the grapes from a bunch; **~ las cuentas del rosario** to tell one's beads
2 [+ *sentido*] to spell out; **~ mentiras** to come out with a string of lies; **~ imprecaciones** to let fly with a string of curses
Ⓑ **desgranarse** VPR 1 (*Bot*) [*trigo*] to shed its grain; [*planta*] to drop its seeds
2 [*cuentas*] to come unstrung

desgrasado ADJ (*Culin*) fat-free

desgrasar ►conjug 1a◄ VT = **desengrasar**

desgravable ADJ tax-deductible

desgravación SF ► **desgravación de impuestos**, **desgravación fiscal** tax relief ► **desgravación personal** tax allowance

desgravar ►conjug 1a◄ Ⓐ VT 1 [+ *cantidad*] **puede ~ hasta 400 euros por cada hijo** you can claim tax relief of up to 400 euros for each child; **tener un plan de pensiones puede ~ un 10%** you can claim 10% tax relief if you have a pension plan
2 [+ *producto*] to eliminate tax on; **la ley les desgrava estas compras** the law allows them tax relief on these purchases
Ⓑ VI **esas inversiones desgravan** those investments are tax-deductible

desgreñado ADJ dishevelled, disheveled (*EEUU*)

desgreñar ►conjug 1a◄ VT to dishevel

desgreño* SM (*Andes, Cono Sur*) 1 (= *desorden*) untidiness
2 (= *desorganización*) disorder, disarray
3 (= *descuido*) carelessness

desguace SM 1 (= *despiece*) [*de barco*] breaking-up, scrapping; [*de coche*] scrapping
2 (= *lugar*) scrapyard, breaker's yard

desguarnecer ►conjug 2d◄ VT 1 (= *quitar los adornos de*) [+ *pared*] to strip bare; [+ *caballo*] to unharness; **~ un barco de las velas** to remove the sails from a boat
2 (*Téc*) to strip down
3 (*Mil*) [+ *pueblo*] to remove the garrison from; [+ *plaza fuerte*] to dismantle

desguarnecido ADJ 1 (= *sin adornos*) stripped, bare
2 (*Mil*) [*ciudad*] undefended, unprotected; [*flanco*] exposed

desguazar ►conjug 1f◄ VT 1 (= *desmantelar*) [+ *barco*] to break up, scrap; [+ *coche, avión*] to scrap
2 [+ *madera*] to dress, rough-hew

desgubernamentalizar ►conjug 1f◄ VT to remove from government control

deshabilitar ►conjug 1a◄ VT (*Inform*) to disable

deshabillé SM negligee

deshabitado ADJ [*edificio*] empty, vacant; [*zona, ciudad*] uninhabited

deshabitar ►conjug 1a◄ VT [+ *edificio*] to leave empty; [+ *zona, ciudad*] to depopulate

deshabituación SF 1 [*de costumbre*] losing the habit, breaking of the habit
2 (*Med*) treatment for drug dependency

deshabituar ►conjug 1e◄ Ⓐ VT **~ a algn de la droga** to get sb off drugs
Ⓑ **deshabituarse** VPR 1 (*de costumbre*) to lose the habit
2 **~se de la droga** to kick one's drug habit, conquer one's drug addiction

deshacer ►conjug 2r◄ (*pp* **deshecho**) Ⓐ VT 1 (= *separar*) [+ *nudo, lazo*] to untie, undo; [+ *costura*] to unpick; [+ *fila, corro*] to break up
2 (= *desarreglar*) [+ *maleta*] to unpack; [+ *rompecabezas*] to break up; [+ *paquete*] to undo, unwrap; [+ *cama*] (*al dormir*) to mess up; (*para cambiar las sábanas*) to strip; **deshacía una y otra vez su peinado** she kept redoing her hair; **era imposible ~ lo hecho** what had been done couldn't be undone; **puede hacer y ~ a su antojo** she is free to do as she wishes; **la cama estaba sin ~** the bed hadn't been slept in
3 (= *derretir*) [+ *nieve, helado*] to melt
4 (= *disolver*) [+ *pastilla, grumos*] to dissolve; (= *desmenuzar*) [+ *bizcocho, pastel, cubito de caldo*] to crumble; **~ algo en agua** to dissolve sth in water
5 (= *desgastar*) [+ *zapatos, ropa*] to wear out; [+ *metal*] to wear down, wear away
6 (= *estropear*) [+ *vista, proyecto, vida*] to ruin; **la marea deshizo los castillos de arena** the tide washed away *o* broke up our sandcastles; **este contratiempo nos ha deshecho los planes** this setback has ruined our plans
7 [+ *persona*] to shatter
8 [+ *contrato, alianza, acuerdo*] (= *romper*) to break; (= *cancelar*) to annul
9 (= *enmendar*) [+ *agravio*] to right, put right; [+ *equívoco, malentendido*] to resolve; ✦***MODISMO*** **~ el camino** to retrace one's steps
10 (= *dispersar*) [+ *manifestación*] to break up; [+ *enemigo*] to rout
11 (= *derrotar*) [+ *contrario*] to take apart, dismantle
Ⓑ **deshacerse** VPR 1 (= *separarse*) [*nudo*] to come undone, come untied; [*costura*] to come undone, split; [*moño, trenza*] to come undone
2 (= *romperse*) to smash, shatter; **el libro se le deshizo en las manos** the book came apart in his hands; **el jarrón se deshizo en sus manos** the vase just fell to pieces *o* came apart in his hands; **cuando lo levanté, se me deshizo todo** when I lifted it up it all fell to bits
3 (= *derretirse*) [*caramelo, hielo*] to melt; **se deshacen en la boca** they melt in your mouth; **el hielo se deshizo al subir la temperatura** the ice melted as the temperature rose
4 (= *desmembrarse*) [*organización, manifestación*] to break up; [*ejército*] to be routed; **cuando se deshizo la reunión** when the meeting broke up
5 (= *desaparecer*) to vanish; **se deshizo como el humo** it vanished into thin air
6 [*persona*] (= *afligirse*) to go to pieces; (= *impacientarse*) to be at one's wits' end; **se ha deshecho tras la tragedia** she has gone to

➤ LENGUA Y USO: **desgracia 1** 39.3, 52.5 **desgraciadamente** 47.4, 52.5

pieces since the tragedy

7 **~se de** (*queriendo*) to get rid of; (*sin querer*) to part with; (*Dep*) to dispose of; (*Com*) to dump; **logramos ~nos de él** we managed to get rid of him; **no quiero ~me de eso** I don't want to part with that

8 (= *esforzarse*) **se deshace trabajando** he works incredibly hard; **~se en**: **~se en cumplidos con algn** to be very complimentary towards sb, shower sb with compliments; **~se en elogios con algn** to be full of praise for sb, shower sb with praise; **~se en excusas** to apologize profusely; **~se en lágrimas** to burst *o* dissolve into tears; **se deshace por su familia** he bends over backwards for his family; **~se por hacer algo** to strive to do sth, do one's utmost to do sth; **~se por complacer a algn** to strive to please sb, do one's utmost to please sb

9 (*Med*) (= *debilitarse*) to get weak, grow feeble; (= *consumirse*) to waste away

desharrapado/a Ⓐ ADJ ragged
Ⓑ SM/F person dressed in rags; **los ~s de la sociedad** outcasts from society

deshebillar ▸conjug 1a◂ VT to unbuckle

deshebrar ▸conjug 1a◂ VT to unpick

deshechizar ▸conjug 1f◂ VT to remove the spell from, disenchant

deshecho Ⓐ PP *de* **deshacer**
Ⓑ ADJ 1 [*lazo, nudo*] undone
2 (= *roto*) [*objeto*] broken, smashed; **las camas están deshechas** the beds are unmade; **llegó con los nervios ~s** his nerves were shattered when he arrived; **tiene un brazo ~** he has a badly injured arm; **el pastel ha quedado ~** the cake is ruined; **estoy ~*** I'm shattered*
3 (*Med*) [*persona*] weak; [*salud*] broken
4 (*Cono Sur*) (= *desaliñado*) untidy
Ⓒ SM (*Andes, Caribe, Cono Sur*) short cut

deshelador SM (*Aer*) de-icer

deshelar ▸conjug 1j◂ Ⓐ VT [+ *tubería*] to thaw; [+ *congelador*] to defrost; [+ *avión, coche*] to de-ice
Ⓑ VI, **deshelarse** VPR [*nieve*] to thaw, melt; [*río, lago*] to thaw

desherbaje SM weeding

desherbar ▸conjug 1j◂ VT to weed

desheredado/a SM/F **los ~s** the dispossessed

desheredar ▸conjug 1a◂ VT to disinherit

desherrarse ▸conjug 1k◂ VPR [*caballo*] to cast a shoe

deshidratación SF dehydration

deshidratado ADJ dehydrated

deshidratar ▸conjug 1a◂ Ⓐ VT to dehydrate
Ⓑ **deshidratarse** VPR to become dehydrated

deshielo SM [*de nieve*] thaw; [*de congelador*] defrosting ► **deshielo diplomático** diplomatic thaw

deshierbe SM weeding

deshilachado ADJ frayed

deshilachar ▸conjug 1a◂ Ⓐ VT to fray
Ⓑ **deshilacharse** VPR to fray

deshilada SF **a la ~** 1 (*Mil*) in single file
2 (= *secretamente*) secretly, stealthily

deshilado SM (*Cos*) openwork

deshilar ▸conjug 1a◂ Ⓐ VT 1 (*Cos*) (= *desenmarañar*) to unravel; (= *deshilachar*) to fray
2 [+ *carne*] to shred
Ⓑ VI to get thin
Ⓒ **deshilarse** VPR to fray

deshilvanado ADJ [*historia, trama*] disjointed, incoherent

deshilvanar ▸conjug 1a◂ VT (*Cos*) to untack, take the stitches out of

deshinchar ▸conjug 1a◂ Ⓐ VT 1 [+ *neumático*] to let down
2 (*Med*) to reduce the swelling of
3 [+ *ira, furia*] to give vent to
Ⓑ **deshincharse** VPR 1 [*neumático*] to go flat
2 (*Med*) to go down
3 (= *perder el orgullo*) to get down off one's high horse

deshipotecar ▸conjug 1g◂ VT [+ *propiedad*] to pay off the mortgage on

deshojado ADJ [*rama*] leafless; [*flor*] stripped of its petals

deshojar ▸conjug 1a◂ Ⓐ VT 1 (*Bot*) [+ *árbol*] to strip the leaves off; [+ *flor*] to pull the petals off; *ver tb* **margarita 1**
2 [+ *libro*] to tear the pages out of
3 (*LAm*) [+ *maíz*] to husk; [+ *fruta*] to peel
4 (*Quím*) to defoliate
Ⓑ **deshojarse** VPR [*árbol*] to lose its leaves; [*flor*] to lose its petals

deshollejar ▸conjug 1a◂ VT [+ *uvas*] to peel, skin

deshollinador(a) SM/F chimney sweep

deshollinar ▸conjug 1a◂ VT 1 [+ *chimenea*] to sweep
2 (= *mirar con atención*) to take a close look at

deshonestamente ADV 1 (= *sin honradez*) dishonestly
2 (= *indecentemente*) indecently, lewdly

deshonestidad SF 1 (= *falta de honradez*) dishonesty
2 (= *indecencia*) indecency

deshonesto ADJ 1 (= *no honrado*) dishonest
2 (= *indecente*) indecent; *ver tb* **proposición 1**

deshonor SM 1 (= *pérdida del honor*) dishonour, dishonor (*EEUU*), disgrace
2 **un ~** an insult, an affront (**a** to); **no es ningún ~ trabajar** it is no disgrace to work

deshonorar ▸conjug 1a◂ VT 1 (= *deshonrar*) to dishonour, dishonor (*EEUU*), disgrace
2 (= *ser indigno de*) to be unworthy of
3 (= *despedir*) to dismiss, deprive of office *o* title *etc*

deshonra SF 1 (= *deshonor*) dishonour, dishonor (*EEUU*), disgrace; **no es ninguna ~ ser pobre** it is no dishonour *o* disgrace to be poor
2 (= *vergüenza*) shame; **lo tiene a ~** he thinks it beneath him; **tienen a ~ trabajar** they think it beneath them to work
3 (= *acto vergonzoso*) shameful act

deshonrabuenos SMF INV 1 (= *calumniador*) backbiter
2 (= *oveja negra*) black sheep (*of the family*)

deshonrar ▸conjug 1a◂ VT 1 [+ *familia, compañeros*] to dishonour, dishonor (*EEUU*), disgrace
2 (= *afrentar*) to insult
3 (*euf*) [+ *mujer*] to dishonour, dishonor (*EEUU*)

deshonroso ADJ dishonourable, dishonorable (*EEUU*), disgraceful

deshora SF **a ~** at an inconvenient time; **acostarse a ~** to go to bed at some unearthly hour; **comer a ~** to eat at odd times; **llegar a ~** to turn up unexpectedly

deshuesado ADJ [*carne*] boned; [*fruta*] stoned; [*aceituna*] pitted, stoned

deshuesar ▸conjug 1a◂ VT [+ *carne*] to bone; [+ *fruta*] to stone; [+ *aceituna*] to pit, stone

deshuevarse** ▸conjug 1a◂ VPR = **descojonarse**

deshumanización SF dehumanization

deshumanizador ADJ, **deshumanizante** ADJ dehumanizing

deshumanizar ▸conjug 1f◂ VT to dehumanize

deshumedecerse ▸conjug 2d◂ VPR to dry up, lose its moisture

desideologizado ADJ non-ideological, free of ideological considerations

desiderátum SM (*pl* **desiderátums** *o* **desiderata**) (*frm*) desideratum (*frm*), thing ideally required *o* desired

desidia SF 1 (= *pereza*) idleness
2 (*en el vestir*) slovenliness

desidioso ADJ 1 (= *perezoso*) idle
2 (= *desaseado*) slovenly

desierto Ⓐ ADJ 1 [*isla, región*] desert *antes de s*; [*paisaje*] bleak, desolate; [*calle, casa*] deserted; **la calle estaba desierta** the street was deserted
2 **declarar ~** [+ *oposiciones, premio*] to declare void
Ⓑ SM desert; ✦**MODISMOS arar en el ~** to plough *o* (*EEUU*) plow the sands; **clamar en el ~** to preach in the wilderness

designación SF 1 (*para un cargo*) appointment
2 (= *nombre*) designation

designar ▸conjug 1a◂ VT 1 (= *nombrar*) to appoint, designate; **el dictador designó a su sucesor** the dictator appointed *o* designated his successor; **la ~on para el puesto de supervisora** they appointed her (as) supervisor, she was appointed *o* designated (as) supervisor; **me han designado candidato** they have nominated me (as a candidate); **han designado a Sevilla sede del campeonato** Seville has been designated as the host city for the championship
2 (= *fijar*) [+ *fecha*] to fix, set
3 (*frm*) (= *denominar*) **la palabra "rosa" designa a una flor** the word "rose" denotes a flower; **~on el plan con el nombre de "Erasmus"** the plan was given the name of "Erasmus"

designio SM plan, design; **lo haré según sus ~s** I will act in accordance with his plans; **los ~s divinos** divine intentions

desigual ADJ 1 (= *diferente*) different; **dos hermanos muy ~es** two very different brothers; **las mangas de la chaqueta me han salido ~es** the sleeves of my jacket have come out different sizes; **los ciudadanos reciben un trato ~** people are treated differently, people are not treated equally *o* the same
2 [*lucha, batalla*] unequal
3 (= *irregular*) [*terreno, calidad*] uneven; [*letra*] erratic; **es una estudiante muy ~** she is a very erratic student; **los resultados del alumno son muy ~es** the pupil's marks vary widely *o* are not at all consistent

4 (= *variable*) [*tiempo*] changeable; [*carácter*] unpredictable

desigualar ▸conjug 1a◂ VT 1 (= *nivelar*) [+ *flequillo*] to make uneven; [+ *poderes, capacidades*] to unbalance
2 (*Dep*) to alter the balance of

desigualdad SF 1 (*Econ, Pol*) inequality
2 [*de carácter, tiempo*] unpredictability
3 (= *desnivel*) [*de terreno*] roughness; [*de escritura*] unevenness

desilusión SF 1 (= *decepción*) disappointment; **me llevé una gran ~ cuando lo vi** I was very disappointed when I saw him; **caer en la ~** to get disillusioned; **sufrir una ~** to suffer a disappointment
2 (= *pérdida de ilusiones*) disillusion, disillusionment

desilusionado ADJ disillusioned; **una visión desilusionada de la realidad** a disillusioned view of reality; **te veo muy ~ con la boda** you seem very disillusioned with *o* unexcited about the wedding

desilusionante ADJ disillusioning, disappointing

desilusionar ▸conjug 1a◂ Ⓐ VT 1 (= *decepcionar*) to disappoint
2 (= *hacer perder las ilusiones a*) to disillusion
Ⓑ **desilusionarse** VPR 1 (= *decepcionarse*) to be disappointed
2 (= *desengañarse*) to get disillusioned

desimantar ▸conjug 1a◂ VT to demagnetize

desincentivar ▸conjug 1a◂ VT to act as a disincentive to, discourage

desincentivo SM disincentive

desincrustante ADJ **agente ~** descaling agent; **producto ~** descaling product

desincrustar ▸conjug 1a◂ VT to descale, remove the fur from (*EEUU*)

desinencia SF (*Ling*) ending

desinfección SF, **desinfectado** SM disinfection

desinfectante ADJ, SM disinfectant

desinfectar ▸conjug 1a◂ VT to disinfect

desinfestar ▸conjug 1a◂ VT to decontaminate

desinflación SF (*Com*) disinflation

desinflado ADJ [*neumático*] flat

desinflar ▸conjug 1a◂ Ⓐ VT [+ *neumático*] to deflate, let the air out of
Ⓑ **desinflarse** VPR [*neumático*] to go down, go flat

desinformación SF 1 (= *información engañosa*) disinformation, misleading information, black propaganda
2 (= *ignorancia*) ignorance, lack of information

desinformado ADJ uninformed

desinformador(a) Ⓐ ADJ [*noticia*] false, calculated to deceive
Ⓑ SM/F spreader of disinformation

desinformar ▸conjug 1a◂ VT to misinform

desinformativo ADJ misleading, false

desinhibición SF lack of inhibition

desinhibido ADJ uninhibited

desinhibir ▸conjug 3a◂ Ⓐ VT to free from inhibitions
Ⓑ **desinhibirse** VPR to lose one's inhibitions

desinsectación SF protection against insect pests; **la ~ de un jardín** freeing a garden of insect pests

desinsectar ▸conjug 1a◂ VT to clear of insects

desintegrable ADJ fissile

desintegración SF 1 [*de estructura*] disintegration; [*de grupo*] break-up
2 [*de átomo*] splitting ▸ **desintegración nuclear** nuclear fission

desintegrar ▸conjug 1a◂ Ⓐ VT 1 [+ *grupo*] to break up
2 [+ *roca, cohete*] to disintegrate
3 [+ *átomo*] to split
Ⓑ **desintegrarse** VPR 1 [*grupo*] to break up
2 [*roca, cohete*] to disintegrate
3 [*átomo*] to split

desinterés SM 1 (= *falta de interés*) lack of interest
2 (= *altruismo*) unselfishness
3 (= *imparcialidad*) disinterestedness

desinteresado ADJ 1 (= *altruista*) unselfish
2 (= *imparcial*) disinterested

desinteresarse ▸conjug 1a◂ VPR 1 (= *perder interés*) to lose interest (**de, por** in)
2 (= *desentenderse*) **~ de algo** to take no interest in sth

desintoxicación SF detoxification, disintoxication; **centro de ~** detoxification centre, detoxification center (*EEUU*)

desintoxicar ▸conjug 1g◂ Ⓐ VT 1 (*Med*) to detoxify
2 (*de drogas*) to cure of drug addiction
Ⓑ **desintoxicarse** VPR (*de las drogas*) to undergo detoxification, undergo treatment for drug addiction; (*del alcohol*) to dry out

desinversión SF disinvestment

desinvertir ▸conjug 3i◂ VI to disinvest

desistimiento SM 1 (= *acción*) desisting
2 (*Jur*) waiver

desistir ▸conjug 3a◂ VI 1 (= *abandonar*) to cease, desist (*frm*); **no desistió en su empeño** she did not cease in *o* (*frm*) desist from her efforts; **~ de algo** to give up sth; **desistió de su intento de convencernos** he gave up trying to convince us; **~ de hacer algo** to desist from *o* give up doing sth
2 (*Jur*) **~ de un derecho** to waive a right

desjarretar ▸conjug 1a◂ VT 1 [+ *animal*] to hamstring
2 (*Med*) to weaken, debilitate

desjuntar ▸conjug 1a◂ VT 1 (= *separar*) to separate, take apart
2 (= *dividir*) to divide

deslavado ADJ 1 (= *medio lavado*) half-washed
2 = **deslavazado**

deslavar ▸conjug 1a◂ VT 1 (= *lavar a medias*) to half-wash, wash superficially
2 (= *desteñir*) to fade
3 (= *debilitar*) to weaken

deslavazado ADJ 1 (= *incoherente*) disjointed
2 [*tela, vestido*] (= *lacio*) limp; (= *desteñido*) faded; (= *aburrido*) colourless, colorless (*EEUU*)

deslave SM (*Méx*) landslide, rockfall

desleal ADJ 1 (= *infiel*) disloyal (**a, con** to)
2 (*Com*) [*competencia*] unfair

deslealmente ADV 1 (= *sin lealtad*) disloyally
2 (= *injustamente*) unfairly

deslealtad SF 1 (= *falta de lealtad*) (*gen*) disloyalty
2 (*Com*) unfairness

deslegalizar ▸conjug 1f◂ VT to outlaw, criminalize

deslegitimar ▸conjug 1a◂ VT to discredit, undermine

desleído ADJ 1 (= *disuelto*) dissolved
2 [*idea*] weak, woolly, wooly (*EEUU*)

desleír ▸conjug 3l◂ Ⓐ VT (= *disolver*) [+ *sustancia, materia*] to dissolve; [+ *líquido*] to dilute
Ⓑ **desleírse** VPR 1 (*en un líquido*) to dissolve
2 [*líquido*] to become diluted

deslenguado ADJ (= *malhablado*) foul-mouthed

deslenguarse ▸conjug 1i◂ VPR (= *hablar demasiado*) to shoot one's mouth off; (*groseramente*) to pour out obscenities

desliar ▸conjug 1c◂ Ⓐ VT (= *desatar*) [+ *nudo, lazo*] to untie, undo; [+ *paquete*] to open
Ⓑ **desliarse** VPR to come undone

desligado ADJ 1 (= *suelto*) loose, free
2 (= *separado*) separate, detached; **vive ~ de todo** he lives in a world of his own

desligamiento SM detachment (**de** from)

desligar ▸conjug 1h◂ Ⓐ VT 1 (= *desatar*) to untie, undo
2 (= *separar*) to detach; **~ el primer aspecto del segundo** to separate the first aspect from the second
3 (= *absolver*) to absolve, free (**de** from); **~ a algn de una promesa** to release sb from a promise
4 (= *aclarar*) to unravel, disentangle
Ⓑ **desligarse** VPR 1 [*nudo, lazo*] to come undone
2 [*persona*] to extricate o.s. (**de** from)

deslindable ADJ definable

deslindar ▸conjug 1a◂ VT 1 [+ *terreno*] to mark out, mark the limits *o* boundaries of
2 (= *definir*) to define

deslinde SM 1 (= *acto*) demarcation, fixing of limits *o* boundaries
2 (= *definición*) definition

desliz SM 1 (= *equivocación*) slip; **cometer un ~** to slip up; **los deslices de la juventud** the indiscretions of youth ▸ **desliz de lengua** slip of the tongue ▸ **desliz freudiano** Freudian slip
2 (*Aut*) skid

deslizadero SM 1 (= *tobogán*) slide
2 (= *sitio*) slippery spot
3 (*Téc*) chute, slide

deslizadizo ADJ slippery

deslizador SM 1 (= *patinete*) scooter
2 (*Náut*) small speedboat
3 (*Dep*) surfboard, aquaplane, water ski
4 [*de patín*] runner, skid

deslizamiento SM 1 (= *movimiento*) [*de cosas*] sliding; [*de persona*] slipping ▸ **deslizamiento de tierra** landslide
2 (*Aut*) skid
3 ▸ **deslizamiento salarial** (upward) drift of wages

deslizante ADJ sliding

deslizar ▸conjug 1f◂ Ⓐ VT 1 (*frm*) (= *pasar*) **deslicé la carta por debajo de la puerta** I slipped *o* slid the letter under the door; **deslizó el dedo por el armario y encontró polvo** she ran her finger along the cupboard and found it was dusty
2 (*frm*) (= *dar con disimulo*) to slip
3 (*frm*) (= *intercalar*) to slip in
Ⓑ **deslizarse** VPR 1 (= *resbalarse*) to slide; **el coche se deslizó unos metros** the car slid *o* slipped forward a few metres; **los niños se deslizaban por el pasamanos** the children were sliding down the banisters; **gotas de**

sudor se deslizaban por su frente beads of sweat ran *o* slid down his forehead; **el esquiador se desliza por la pista** the skier slips *o* skies down the slope; **la patinadora se deslizaba elegantemente** the skater was gliding along
2 (= *avanzar*) [*serpiente*] to slither; [*barco*] to glide, slip; **la anguila se deslizó entre mis manos** the eel slipped through my fingers; **el tren se desliza a 300km/h** the train glides along at 300km/h; **el agua se desliza mansamente** the water flows along gently
3 (*frm*) [*secreto*] to slip out; [*error*] to slip in, creep in

deslomar ▸conjug 1a◂ Ⓐ VT (= *romper el lomo de*) (*lit*) to break the back of; (*fig*) to wear out; **~ a algn a garrotazos** to club sb to a pulp
Ⓑ **deslomarse** VPR (*) to work one's guts out

deslucido ADJ 1 (= *sin brillo*) [*metal*] tarnished; [*mármol*] worn, faded
2 (= *aburrido*) [*actor*] dull, lacklustre; [*toro*] unimpressive; [*actuación*] undistinguished; **hizo un papel ~** he gave a lacklustre performance; **la fiesta resultó deslucida** the party was a flop; **el jugador estuvo muy ~** the player was far from his best; **quedar ~** to make a poor impression
3 (= *desgarbado*) graceless, inelegant

deslucimiento SM 1 [*de muebles, vestidos*] shabbiness
2 (= *falta de brillantez*) dullness
3 (= *falta de gracia*) gracelessness
4 (= *fracaso*) discrediting

deslucir ▸conjug 3f◂ Ⓐ VT 1 [+ *mármol*] to fade; [+ *metal*] to tarnish
2 (= *estropear*) to spoil, ruin; **la lluvia deslució el acto** the rain ruined the ceremony
3 [+ *persona*] to discredit
Ⓑ **deslucirse** VPR (= *fracasar*) to be discredited

deslumbrador ADJ, **deslumbrante** ADJ dazzling

deslumbramiento SM 1 (= *brillo*) glare, dazzle
2 (= *confusión*) confusion

deslumbrar ▸conjug 1a◂ VT 1 (*con la luz*) to dazzle
2 (= *impresionar*) to dazzle; **deslumbró a todos con su oratoria** he dazzled everyone with his oratory

deslustrado ADJ 1 (= *sin brillo*) [*vidrio*] frosted, ground; [*loza*] unglazed
2 [*actuación, papel*] dull, lacklustre, lackluster (*EEUU*)
3 [*reputación*] tarnished

deslustrar ▸conjug 1a◂ VT 1 (= *quitar lustre a*) [+ *vidrio*] to frost; [+ *loza*] to remove the glaze from
2 [+ *reputación*] to sully, tarnish

deslustre SM 1 (= *acto*) [*de vidrio*] frosting; [*de loza, paño*] removal of glaze; [*de muebles, adornos*] tarnishing
2 (*en reputación*) stigma, stain

deslustroso ADJ 1 (= *inadecuado*) unbecoming, unsuitable
2 (= *vergonzoso*) disgraceful

desmadejamiento SM enervation, weakness

desmadejar ▸conjug 1a◂ Ⓐ VT to enervate, weaken
Ⓑ **desmadejarse** VPR to weaken

desmadrado ADJ 1 (*) (= *desenfrenado*) **está muy ~ últimamente** he's been pretty wild recently*
2 (= *desinhibido*) uninhibited
3 (= *confuso*) confused

desmadrarse* ▸conjug 1a◂ VPR 1 (= *descontrolarse*) to get out of control, go wild; **~ por algn** to fall madly in love with sb
2 (= *divertirse*) to let one's hair down*
3 (= *excederse*) to go over the top; **los gastos se han desmadrado** costs have gone right over the top

desmadre* SM 1 (= *exceso*) excess; **¡es el ~!** this is just too much!; **esto va de ~ total** this is really getting out of hand
2 (= *confusión*) chaos
3 (= *juerga*) rave-up*, hot party (*EEUU*)

desmalezar ▸conjug 1f◂ VT (*LAm*) to weed

desmallar ▸conjug 1a◂ Ⓐ VT [+ *puntos*] to pull out; [+ *media*] to make a ladder in, make a run in
Ⓑ **desmallarse** VPR [*media*] to ladder, run (*EEUU*)

desmamar ▸conjug 1a◂ VT to wean

desmán[1] SM 1 (= *exceso*) excess
2 (= *ultraje*) outrage; **cometer un ~** to commit an outrage (**contra** on)

desmán[2] SM (*Zool*) muskrat

desmanchar ▸conjug 1a◂ Ⓐ VT (*LAm*) to clean, remove the spots *o* stains from
Ⓑ **desmancharse** VPR (*Andes, CAm**) 1 (= *salir de prisa*) to bolt out
2 (= *retirarse*) to withdraw
3 (*Agr*) to stray from the herd

desmandado ADJ 1 (= *desobediente*) unruly
2 [*caballo*] runaway

desmandarse ▸conjug 1a◂ VPR 1 (= *descontrolarse*) to get out of hand
2 [*caballo*] to bolt, run away

desmano: **a ~** ADV out of the way; **me pilla a ~** it's not on my way

desmanotado ADJ clumsy, awkward

desmantelación SF dismantling

desmantelamiento SM 1 (= *desmontaje*) [*de base, fábrica*] dismantling; [*de barcos*] unrigging
2 [*de organización*] disbanding

desmantelar ▸conjug 1a◂ Ⓐ VT 1 (= *desmontar*) [+ *base, fábrica*] to dismantle; [+ *máquina*] to strip down; [+ *andamio*] to take down; [+ *casa*] to strip of its contents
2 [+ *organización*] to disband; [+ *pandilla*] to break up
3 (*Náut*) to unrig
Ⓑ **desmantelarse** VPR [*casa*] to fall into disrepair

desmaña SF (= *torpeza*) (*al actuar*) clumsiness, awkwardness; (*al pensar, reaccionar*) slowness, helplessness

desmañado ADJ 1 (= *torpe*) clumsy
2 (= *lento*) slow

desmaquillador SM, **desmaquillante** SM make-up remover

desmaquillarse ▸conjug 1a◂ VPR to remove one's make-up

desmarcado ADJ (*Dep*) unmarked

desmarcar ▸conjug 1g◂ Ⓐ VT to disassociate (**de** from)
Ⓑ **desmarcarse** VPR 1 (*Dep*) to shake off one's attacker, get clear
2 (= *distanciarse*) to distance oneself (**de** from)

desmasificar ▸conjug 1g◂ VT [+ *cárceles, hospitales*] to reduce overcrowding in; **~ la universidad** to reduce student numbers

desmayado ADJ 1 (*Med*) unconscious
2 [*carácter*] dull, lacklustre, lackluster (*EEUU*)
3 [*color*] pale

desmayar ▸conjug 1a◂ Ⓐ VI [*persona*] to lose heart; [*esfuerzo*] to falter, flag
Ⓑ **desmayarse** VPR 1 (*Med*) to faint
2 [*planta*] to droop low, trail

desmayo SM 1 (*Med*) (= *acto*) faint, fainting fit; (= *estado*) unconsciousness; **le dio un ~** he fainted; **sufrir un ~** to have a fainting fit, faint
2 (= *languidez*) [*de voz*] faltering; [*del cuerpo*] languidness, limpness; **hablar con ~** to talk in a small voice, speak falteringly; **las ramas caen con ~** the branches are drooping low, the branches are trailing
3 (= *depresión*) dejection, depression

desmedido ADJ 1 [*tamaño, importancia*] (= *excesivo*) excessive; (= *desproporcionado*) out of all proportion
2 [*ambición*] boundless

desmedirse ▸conjug 3k◂ VPR to go too far

desmedrado ADJ 1 (= *estropeado*) impaired
2 (= *reducido*) reduced
3 (*Med*) puny, feeble

desmedrar ▸conjug 1a◂ Ⓐ VT 1 (= *perjudicar*) to impair
2 (= *estropear*) to spoil, ruin, affect badly
3 (= *reducir*) to reduce
Ⓑ VI, **desmedrarse** VPR 1 (= *decaer*) [*producción, interés*] to fall off, decline; [*conversación, país*] to go downhill
2 (= *deteriorarse*) to deteriorate
3 (*Med*) [*enfermo*] to get weak; [*niño*] to be sickly, waste away
4 (*Bot*) to grow poorly, do badly

desmedro SM 1 (= *perjuicio*) impairment
2 (= *reducción*) reduction
3 (= *decaimiento*) decline, deterioration
4 (*Med*) weakness, emaciation, thinness

desmejora SF deterioration

desmejorado ADJ **ha quedado muy desmejorada** she's lost her looks; **está muy desmejorada** (*Med*) she's not looking at all well

desmejoramiento SM deterioration

desmejorar ▸conjug 1a◂ Ⓐ VT 1 (= *dañar*) to spoil
2 (*Med*) to weaken
Ⓑ **desmejorarse** VPR 1 [*situación*] to deteriorate
2 [*persona*] (= *tener peor aspecto*) to lose one's looks; (*Med*) to get worse

desmelenado/a Ⓐ ADJ dishevelled, disheveled (*EEUU*)
Ⓑ SM/F long-haired lout

desmelenar ▸conjug 1a◂ Ⓐ VT [+ *peinado*] to dishevel
Ⓑ **desmelenarse** VPR (*) 1 (= *asearse*) to spruce o.s. up, pull one's socks up
2 (= *esforzarse*) to bend over backwards
3 (*) (= *ir de juerga*) to let one's hair down*

desmelene* SM excess; **¡es el ~!** it's sheer chaos!, it's way over the top!*

desmembración SF, **desmembramiento** SM 1 [*de cadáver, país*] dismemberment
2 [*de partido*] break-up

desmembrar ▸conjug 1j◂ Ⓐ VT 1 [+ *cadáver, país*] to dismember

2 [+ *partido*] to break up
B **desmembrarse** VPR 1 [*país*] to break up
2 [*partido*] to fall apart

desmemoria SF poor memory, forgetfulness

desmemoriado ADJ forgetful, absent-minded

desmemoriarse ▸conjug 1b◂ VPR to grow forgetful, become absent-minded

desmentida SF denial; **dar una ~ a algo** to deny sth

desmentido SM = **desmentida**

desmentimiento SM denial

desmentir ▸conjug 3i◂ A VT 1 (= *negar*) [+ *acusación*] to deny, refute; [+ *rumor*] to scotch, squelch (*EEUU*); [+ *teoría*] to refute; [+ *carácter, orígenes*] to belie; **~ rotundamente una acusación** to deny a charge flatly
2 (= *llevar la contraria*) [+ *persona*] to contradict
B VI to be out of line; **~ de algo** to belie sth
C **desmentirse** VPR 1 (= *contradecirse*) to contradict o.s.
2 (= *desdecirse*) to go back on one's word

desmenuzable ADJ crumbly

desmenuzar ▸conjug 1f◂ A VT 1 (*Culin*) [+ *pan*] to crumble; [+ *pescado, pollo*] to flake
2 (= *examinar*) to examine minutely
B **desmenuzarse** VPR to crumble

desmerecedor(a) A ADJ undeserving
B SM/F undeserving person

desmerecer ▸conjug 2d◂ A VT to be unworthy of
B VI 1 (= *deteriorarse*) to deteriorate
2 (= *perder valor*) to lose value
3 **~ de algo** to compare unfavourably o (*EEUU*) unfavorably with sth; **ésta no desmerece de sus otras películas** this is every bit as good as his earlier films

desmesura SF 1 (= *desproporción*) disproportion
2 (= *exceso*) excess, enormity
3 (= *falta de moderación*) lack of moderation

desmesuradamente ADV disproportionately, excessively; **abrir ~ la boca** to open one's mouth extra wide

desmesurado ADJ 1 (= *desproporcionado*) disproportionate
2 (= *enorme*) [*ambición*] boundless; [*dimensiones*] enormous
3 (= *descarado*) insolent

desmesurarse ▸conjug 1a◂ VPR to become insolent, forget o.s., lose all restraint

desmigajar ▸conjug 1a◂ A VT to crumble
B **desmigajarse** VPR to crumble

desmigar ▸conjug 1h◂ VT = **desmigajar**

desmilitarización SF demilitarization

desmilitarizado ADJ demilitarized

desmilitarizar ▸conjug 1f◂ VT to demilitarize

desmineralizado ADJ 1 [*actuación*] lifeless, lacklustre, lackluster (*EEUU*)
2 [*persona*] run down

desmineralizar ▸conjug 1f◂ VT to demineralize

desmirriado ADJ weedy

desmitificación SF demythologizing

desmitificador ADJ demythologizing

desmitificar ▸conjug 1g◂ VT to demythologize

desmochar ▸conjug 1a◂ VT 1 (= *cortar la parte superior de*) [+ *árbol*] to pollard, cut the top off; [+ *cuernos*] to blunt, file down
2 [+ *texto*] to cut

desmoche SM 1 [*de árbol*] pollarding
2 **hubo un ~ en el primer examen** there was a ruthless weeding out of candidates in the first exam

desmocho SM lopped branches, cuttings

desmodular ▸conjug 1a◂ VT (*Radio*) [+ *mensaje*] to scramble

desmolado ADJ toothless

desmoldar ▸conjug 1a◂ VT (*Culin*) to remove from its mould

desmonetizar ▸conjug 1f◂ VT 1 (*Fin*) to demonetize
2 (*Cono Sur*) (= *desvalorizar*) to devalue, devaluate (*EEUU*)

desmontable A ADJ 1 (= *desarmable*) [*mueble, estantería*] which can be taken apart; [*pieza*] detachable
2 (= *plegable*) collapsible
B SM tyre lever, tire lever (*EEUU*)

desmontaje SM dismantling, stripping down

desmontar ▸conjug 1a◂ A VT 1 (= *desarmar*) (*gen*) to dismantle; [+ *mueble, estantería*] to take apart; [+ *motor*] to strip down; [+ *máquina*] to take apart, take to pieces; [+ *tienda de campaña*] to take down; (*Náut*) [+ *vela*] to take down
2 [+ *terreno*] (= *nivelar*) to level; (= *quitar los árboles a*) to clear
3 [+ *jinete*] to throw, unseat; **~ a algn de un vehículo** to help sb down from a vehicle
4 (*Mil*) [+ *escopeta*] to uncock; [+ *artillería*] to knock out
B VI to dismount, alight (**de** from)

desmonte SM 1 (= *acto*) (*al allanar*) levelling, leveling (*EEUU*); (*al quitar los árboles*) clearing; **los trabajos exigirán el ~ de 200 metros cúbicos** the work will necessitate the removal of 200 cubic metres
2 (= *terreno*) levelled ground, leveled ground (*EEUU*)
3 (*Ferro*) cutting, cut (*EEUU*)
4 (= *madera*) felled timber

desmoralización SF demoralization

desmoralizado ADJ demoralized

desmoralizador ADJ demoralizing

desmoralizar ▸conjug 1f◂ A VT 1 [+ *ejército, persona*] to demoralize
2 [+ *costumbres*] to corrupt
B **desmoralizarse** VPR to lose heart, get demoralized

desmoronadizo ADJ 1 (= *que se desmigaja*) crumbling
2 (= *destartalado, maltrecho*) rickety

desmoronado ADJ [*casa, edificio*] tumbledown

desmoronamiento SM crumbling, collapse

desmoronar ▸conjug 1a◂ A VT 1 (= *desgastar*) to wear away
2 (= *erosionar*) to erode; **la erosión ha desmoronado loa muros** erosion has caused the walls to crumble
B **desmoronarse** VPR 1 (= *derrumbarse*) [*montaña, casa*] to crumble; [*ladrillos*] to fall, come down
2 (= *decaer*) to decay; **tras la muerte de su marido se desmoronó** after her husband's death she went to pieces

desmotivación SF lack of motivation

desmotivado ADJ unmotivated, lacking motivation

desmotivar ▸conjug 1a◂ VT to discourage

desmovilización SF demobilization

desmovilizar ▸conjug 1f◂ VT to demobilize

desmultiplicar ▸conjug 1g◂ VT (*Mec*) to gear down

desnacionalización SF denationalization

desnacionalizado ADJ 1 [*industria*] denationalized
2 [*persona*] stateless

desnacionalizar ▸conjug 1f◂ VT to denationalize

desnarigada SF (*hum*) **la ~** the skull

desnarigado ADJ flat-nosed

desnatado ADJ [*leche*] skimmed

desnatar ▸conjug 1a◂ VT 1 [+ *leche*] to skim; **leche sin ~** whole milk
2 (*Metal*) to remove the scum from

desnaturalizado ADJ 1 (*Quím*) denatured; **alcohol ~** methylated spirits *sing*
2 [*persona*] unnatural

desnaturalizar ▸conjug 1f◂ A VT 1 (*Quím*) to denature
2 (= *corromper*) [+ *persona*] to pervert; [+ *significado, sucesos*] to distort
B **desnaturalizarse** VPR (= *perder la nacionalidad*) to give up one's nationality

desnivel SM 1 [*de terreno*] (= *desigualdad*) drop; (= *tierra alta*) high ground; (= *tierra baja*) low ground
2 (= *diferencia*) difference (**entre** between)
3 (*Pol, Sociol*) inequality

desnivelado ADJ 1 [*terreno*] uneven
2 (= *desequilibrado*) unbalanced

desnivelar ▸conjug 1a◂ VT 1 [+ *terreno*] to make uneven
2 (= *desequilibrar*) [+ *calidad*] to make uneven; [+ *composición*] to upset, unbalance; [+ *balanza*] to tip

desnucar ▸conjug 1g◂ A VT to break the neck of
B **desnucarse** VPR to break one's neck

desnuclearización SF nuclear disarmament, denuclearization

desnuclearizado ADJ **región desnuclearizada** nuclear-free area

desnuclearizar ▸conjug 1f◂ VT to denuclearize

desnudar ▸conjug 1a◂ A VT 1 [+ *persona*] to undress; **él la desnudaba con la mirada** he was undressing her with his eyes
2 (*liter*) [+ *espada*] to unsheathe (*liter*)
3 (*Geol*) to denude
4 (*) [+ *jugador*] to fleece*
B **desnudarse** VPR 1 [*persona*] to undress, get undressed; **~se de cintura para arriba** to strip to the waist
2 **~se de algo** to get rid of sth; **el árbol se está desnudando de sus hojas** the tree is shedding o losing its leaves

desnudez SF 1 [*de persona*] nakedness, nudity
2 [*de paisaje*] bareness

desnudismo SM nudism

desnudista SMF nudist

desnudo A ADJ 1 (= *sin ropa*) [*persona*] naked; [*cuerpo*] naked, bare; **cavar con las manos desnudas** to dig with one's bare hands; **iba andando con los pies ~s** she was walking along barefoot
2 (= *sin adorno*) [*árbol*] bare; [*paisaje*] bare, featureless; **en las paredes desnudas** on the bare walls
3 (= *arruinado*) ruined, bankrupt; **quedarse**

~ to be ruined, be bankrupt; **~ de ideas** devoid of ideas
[4] (= *puro*) [*verdad*] plain, naked; [*estilo*] unadorned
Ⓑ SM [1] (*Arte*) nude; **la retrató al ~** he painted her in the nude; **llevaba los hombros al ~** her shoulders were bare ► **desnudo integral** full-frontal nudity
[2] **poner al ~** to lay bare

desnutrición SF malnutrition, undernourishment

desnutrido ADJ undernourished

desobedecer ▸conjug 2d◂ VT, VI to disobey

desobediencia SF disobedience ► **desobediencia civil** civil disobedience

desobediente ADJ disobedient

desobstruir ▸conjug 3g◂ VT to unblock, unstop, clear

desocupación SF [1] (*esp LAm*) (= *desempleo*) unemployment
[2] (= *ocio*) leisure
[3] [*de piso, fábrica*] clearance, clearing

desocupado ADJ [1] (= *libre*) [*asiento*] empty; [*casa, piso*] unoccupied; [*mesa en restaurante*] free
[2] [*tiempo*] spare, free
[3] [*persona*] (= *libre*) free, not busy; (= *sin empleo*) unemployed

desocupar ▸conjug 1a◂ Ⓐ VT [1] (= *vaciar*) [+ *casa, piso*] to vacate, move out of; [+ *recipiente*] to empty
[2] (= *desalojar*) [+ *fábrica, sala*] to clear, clear out
[3] [+ *contenido*] to remove, take out
Ⓑ VI (*) (= *defecar*) to go to the toilet
Ⓒ **desocuparse** VPR [1] (= *quedar libre*) to be free; **cuando me desocupe, te llamo** I'll call you when I'm free; **se ha desocupado aquella mesa** that table's free now
[2] **~se de un puesto** to give up a job
[3] (*Caribe, Cono Sur*) (= *dar a luz*) to give birth

desodorante SM deodorant

desodorizar ▸conjug 1f◂ VT to deodorize

desoír ▸conjug 3p◂ VT to ignore, disregard

desojarse ▸conjug 1a◂ VPR to strain one's eyes

desolación SF desolation

desolado ADJ [1] [*lugar*] desolate
[2] [*persona*] devastated; **estoy ~ por aquello** I'm devastated about that

desolador ADJ [1] (= *entristecedor*) [*imagen*] heartbreaking, heartrending; [*noticia*] devastating, distressing; [*paisaje*] bleak, cheerless
[2] [*epidemia*] devastating

desolar ▸conjug 1a◂ Ⓐ VT [1] [+ *ciudad, poblado*] to devastate, lay waste (to) (*liter*)
[2] [+ *persona*] to devastate
Ⓑ **desolarse** VPR to be devastated

desolidarizarse ▸conjug 1f◂ VPR **~ de algn/algo** to dissociate o.s. from sb/sth

desolladero SM slaughterhouse

desollado* ADJ brazen, barefaced

desollador(a) Ⓐ SM/F [1] [*de animal*] skinner
[2] (= *extorsionista*) extortioner, robber
Ⓑ SM (*Orn*) shrike

desolladura SF [1] (= *herida*) graze, abrasion (*frm*)
[2] (= *acto*) (*de despellejar*) skinning, flaying; (*de extorsionar*) extortion, piece of robbery

desollar ▸conjug 1l◂ Ⓐ VT [1] (= *quitar la piel a*) to skin, flay
[2] **~ vivo a algn** (= *hacer pagar*) to fleece sb; (= *criticar*) to tear sb to pieces
Ⓑ **desollarse** VPR **me he desollado la rodilla** I've grazed my knee

desopinar ▸conjug 1a◂ VT to denigrate

desorbitado ADJ [1] (= *excesivo*) [*precio*] exorbitant; [*pretensión*] exaggerated
[2] **con los ojos ~s** popeyed

desorbitante ADJ excessive, overwhelming

desorbitar ▸conjug 1a◂ Ⓐ VT [1] (= *exagerar*) to exaggerate
[2] (= *interpretar mal*) to get out of perspective
Ⓑ **desorbitarse** VPR [1] [*persona*] to lose one's sense of proportion
[2] [*asunto*] to get out of hand

desorden SM [1] (= *falta de orden*) [*de objetos, ideas*] chaos; [*de casa, habitación*] mess, untidiness; **no puedo encontrar nada entre tanto ~** I can't find anything amid all this chaos; **en ~** [*gente*] in confusion; [*objetos*] in a mess, in disorder (*más frm*); **la casa estaba en un ~ total** the house was in a complete mess; **poner las cosas en ~** to upset things
[2] (= *confusión*) confusion
[3] **desórdenes** (= *alborotos*) disturbances; (= *excesos*) excesses; (*Med*) disorders; **~es en las comidas** eating disorders

desordenadamente ADV [1] [*colocarse*] untidily
[2] [*entrar*] in a disorderly fashion
[3] [*escribir*] unmethodically

desordenado ADJ [1] (= *sin orden*) [*habitación, persona*] untidy, messy; [*objetos*] in a mess, jumbled
[2] (= *asocial*) [*vida*] chaotic; [*conducta*] disorderly; [*carácter*] unmethodical; [*niño*] wild, unruly
[3] [*país*] chaotic

desordenar ▸conjug 1a◂ Ⓐ VT [1] (= *poner en desorden*) [+ *cajón, armario*] to mess up; [+ *pelo*] to mess up, muss (up) (*EEUU**); [+ *habitación*] to make untidy, mess up; [+ *papeles*] to jumble up
[2] (= *causar confusión a*) to throw into confusion
[3] (*Mec*) to put out of order
Ⓑ **desordenarse** VPR [*casa*] to get untidy, get into a mess; [*papeles*] to get jumbled up

desorejado ADJ [1] (= *disoluto*) dissolute
[2] (*Andes, Caribe, Cono Sur*) (= *sin mangos*) without handles
[3] (*Andes*) (= *duro de oído*) hard of hearing; (*Mús*) tone deaf; ✦*MODISMO* **hacerse el ~*** to turn a deaf ear
[4] (*Caribe*) (= *pródigo*) lavish
[5] (*CAm*) (= *tonto*) silly

desorganización SF disorganization

desorganizar ▸conjug 1f◂ VT to disorganize

desorientado ADJ [1] (= *perdido*) **estoy algo ~** I've lost my bearings
[2] [*juventud*] disorientated, disoriented (*esp EEUU*)

desorientamiento SM, **desorientación** SF disorientation

desorientar ▸conjug 1a◂ Ⓐ VT [1] (= *extraviar*) **~ a algn** to disorientate sb, disorient sb (*esp EEUU*); **me desorientó el nuevo edificio de la esquina** the new building on the corner made me lose my bearings *o* disorientated me
[2] (= *despistar*) to lead astray
[3] (= *confundir*) to confuse
Ⓑ **desorientarse** VPR [1] (= *extraviarse*) to lose one's way, lose one's bearings
[2] (= *confundirse*) to get confused

desovar ▸conjug 1l◂ VI [*pez, anfibio*] to spawn; [*insecto*] to lay eggs

desove SM [*de pez, anfibio*] spawning; [*de insecto*] egg-laying

desovillar ▸conjug 1a◂ VT [1] [+ *lana*] to unravel, unwind
[2] [+ *misterio*] to unravel, clarify

desoxidar ▸conjug 1a◂ VT to deoxidize, de-rust

despabiladeras SFPL snuffers; **unas ~** a pair of snuffers

despabilado ADJ [1] (= *despierto*) wide awake
[2] (= *despejado*) sharp, quick

despabilar* ▸conjug 1a◂ Ⓐ VT [1] (= *despertar*) to wake up; **despabila a los niños, que es tarde** wake the children up *o* wake up the children, it's late; **el café me ha despabilado** the coffee's woken me up
[2] (= *avivar el ingenio de*) to buck up; **a ver si la despabilas un poco** maybe you can buck her up a bit*, maybe you can buck her ideas up a bit*
[3] [+ *vela*] to snuff (out)
Ⓑ VI [1] (= *despertar*) to wake up; **despabila, que son las ocho** wake up, it's eight o'clock
[2] (= *estar alerta*) to wake up, buck up*; **despabila o te engañarán siempre** wake up *o* buck up*, or you'll always end up being taken for a ride; **—ésta es mi última oportunidad —¡pues despabila!** "this is my last chance" — "better buck up then!* *o* better get your act together then!"*
[3] (= *apresurarse*) to hurry up, get a move on*; **despabila si no quieres llegar tarde** better hurry up *o* get a move on* or you'll be late
[4] (*Andes*) (= *pestañear*) to blink
Ⓒ **despabilarse** VPR [1] (= *despertarse*) to wake up; **despabílate que son ya las diez** wake up, it's ten o'clock already; **yo me despabilo con un café** one cup of coffee and I'm awake
[2] (= *estar alerta*) to wake up, buck up*; **despabílate si no quieres que te tomen por tonto** you'd better wake up *o* buck up* if you don't want people to take you for a fool
[3] (= *apresurarse*) to hurry up, get a move on*
[4] (*CAm, Caribe, Cono Sur*) (= *marcharse*) to vanish; (= *escaparse*) to slip away, slope off*

despachaderas SFPL [1] (= *respuesta*) surly retort *sing*, unfriendly answer *sing*
[2] (= *inteligencia*) resourcefulness *sing*, quickness of mind *sing*
[3] (= *sentido práctico*) business sense *sing*, practical know-how *sing*; **tener buenas ~** to be practical, be on the ball
[4] (= *descaro*) brazenness *sing*, insolence *sing*

despachado ADJ [1] (*Com*) **un kilo de patatas bien ~** a good kilo of potatoes; ✦*MODISMO* **ir ~** (*Esp**) **coge un pedazo y vas ~** take a piece and that's your lot*; **si se cree que me va a engañar, va ~** if he thinks he can fool me, he's got another think coming* *o* he'd better think again
[2] (*Esp*) (= *descarado*) brazen, insolent
[3] (*Esp*) (= *ingenioso*) resourceful

despachador(a) Ⓐ ADJ prompt, quick
Ⓑ SM/F [1] (= *empleado*) quick worker
[2] ► **despachador(a) de equipaje** baggage handler

despachante SMF (*Cono Sur*) [1] [*de oficina*] clerk
[2] (*tb* ~ **de aduanas**) customs agent

despachar ▸conjug 1a◂ Ⓐ VT [1] (= *atender*) [+ *problema, asunto*] to deal with; [+ *correspondencia*] to deal with, see to; **el consejo despachó todos los temas pendientes** the council dealt with all the outstanding issues; **quisiera dejar despachado este asunto hoy** I would like to get this matter settled *o* out of the way today
[2] (= *terminar*) [2·1] (*Com*) [+ *informe, negocio*] to finish
[2·2] (*) [+ *libro, tarea*] to knock off*; [+ *comida*] to dispose of*; [+ *bebida*] to knock back*; **ya llevo medio capítulo despachado** I've already knocked off half a chapter*; **despachamos el helado entre nosotros** between us we disposed of the ice cream*
[3] (= *vender*) [+ *fruta, entrada*] to sell
[4] (= *servir*) to serve; **¿le están despachando, señora?** are you being served, madam?; **en seguida le despacho** I'll be with you right away
[5] (= *enviar*) [+ *paquete, carta*] to send, mail (*EEUU*); [+ *mensajero*] to send; [+ *mercancías*] to ship, dispatch (**a** to)
[6] ~ **a algn*** (*de un lugar*) to send sb packing*; (*de un trabajo*) to sack sb*, fire sb*; (= *matar*) to get rid of sb, dispatch sb; **lo despaché de una patada** I kicked him out
Ⓑ VI [1] (*Com*) [*dependiente*] to serve; [*establecimiento*] to be open (for business); **a partir de las cinco no despachan** they are not open (for business) after five
[2] (*Esp*) (*en reunión*) ~ **con** (*gen*) to have a meeting with; [+ *asesor, abogado*] to consult (with); ~ **sobre algo** to discuss sth
[3] (*Esp**) (= *darse prisa*) to hurry up; **¡venga, despacha, que es tarde!** hurry up *o* come on, we're late!
Ⓒ **despacharse** VPR [1] (= *servirse*) to serve o.s.; **usted mismo puede ~se** you can serve yourself; ✦*MODISMO* **~se con el cucharón*** (*sirviendo comida*) to help o.s. to the biggest *o* best portion; (*fig*) to look after number one
[2] (*Esp**) (= *criticar*) **~se bien** *o* **a gusto con algn** (*delante de algn*) to give sb a piece of one's mind; (*a espaldas de algn*) to really lay into sb*; **se despachó bien con ella por llegar tarde** he gave her a piece of his mind for being late*; **se han despachado a gusto con el nuevo gobierno** they really laid into the new government*; **se despachó a gusto en su crítica a la película** he didn't pull his punches in his review of the film, he really laid into the film*
[3] (*) (= *terminar*) [+ *libro, tarea*] to knock off; [+ *comida*] to dispose of*; [+ *bebida*] to knock back*; **me despaché la conferencia en media hora** I knocked off my talk in half an hour*; **en un momento se ~on dos botellas de vino** they put away *o* knocked back two bottles of wine in no time*
[4] **~se de algo** to get rid of sth

despachero/a SM/F (*Chile*) shopkeeper, storekeeper (*EEUU*)

despacho SM [1] (= *oficina*) [1·1] [*de abogado, arquitecto*] office; (*en una casa*) study; **una mesa de ~** an office desk; **el Despacho Oval** the Oval Office
[1·2] (= *muebles*) office furniture
[2] (= *tienda*) shop; (*Chile*) grocer's shop ► **despacho de billetes**, **despacho de boletos** (*LAm*) booking office ► **despacho de localidades** box office ► **despacho de lotería** lottery ticket shop ► **despacho de pan** bread shop, bakery ► **despacho de telégrafos** telegraph office
[3] (= *mensaje*) (*Periodismo*) report; (*Mil*) dispatch; (*Pol*) communiqué ► **despacho de oficial** (*Mil*) commission ► **despacho telegráfico** telegram, wire (*EEUU*)
[4] (= *venta*) sale; **los domingos no hay ~ de billetes** there are no ticket sales on Sundays; **géneros sin ~** unsaleable goods; **tener buen ~** to find a ready sale, be in good demand
[5] (= *envío*) dispatch, sending (out) ► **despacho aduanal**, **despacho de aduanas** customs clearance
[6] (*Pol*) meeting, consultation
[7] (= *cualidad*) **tener buen ~** to be very efficient, be on top of one's job

despachurrar ▸conjug 1a◂ Ⓐ VT [1] [+ *fruta, pastel*] to crush, squash
[2] [+ *cuento*] to mangle
[3] [+ *persona*] to flatten
Ⓑ **despachurrarse** VPR [*fruta, pastel*] to get squashed, get crushed

despacio ADV [1] (= *lentamente*) slowly; **conduce muy ~** he drives very slowly; **¿puede hablar más ~?** can you speak more slowly?; *ver tb* **cosa 5.2**
[2] (= *silenciosamente*) **salí ~ para no molestar a nadie** I left quietly so as not to disturb anybody; **habla ~ que están durmiendo** speak quietly, they're asleep, keep your voice down, they're asleep
[3] (= *suavemente*) gently; **llamó ~ a la puerta** he knocked gently at the door

despaciosamente ADV (*LAm*) slowly

despacioso ADJ slow, deliberate

despacito* ADV [1] (= *lentamente*) slowly; **¡despacito!** slowly does it!; ✦*MODISMO* **~ y buena letra** easy does it
[2] (= *suavemente*) softly

despampanante* ADJ [*chica*] stunning

despampanar ▸conjug 1a◂ Ⓐ VT [1] [+ *vid*] to prune, trim
[2] (*) (= *asombrar*) to shatter, stun, bowl over
Ⓑ VI (*) (= *desconcertarse*) to blow one's top*; (= *desahogarse*) to give vent to one's feelings
Ⓒ **despampanarse** VPR (*) to give o.s. a nasty knock

despancar ▸conjug 1g◂ VT (*Andes*) [+ *maíz*] to husk

despanzurrar ▸conjug 1a◂ Ⓐ VT to crush, squash
Ⓑ **despanzurrarse** VPR [1] (= *despachurrar*) to get squashed, get crushed (**contra** against)
[2] (= *reventar*) to burst

desparasitar ▸conjug 1a◂ VT [1] (*de larvas*) to worm; (*de piojos*) to delouse
[2] [+ *lugar*] to disinfest

desparejado ADJ, **desparejo** ADJ odd; **están ~s** they're odd, they don't match

desparpajar ▸conjug 1a◂ (*CAm, Méx*) Ⓐ VT (= *desparramar*) to scatter
Ⓑ VI, **desparpajarse** VPR (= *despertarse*) to wake up

desparpajo SM [1] (= *desenvoltura*) self-confidence
[2] (= *descaro*) (*pey*) nerve*, cheek*
[3] (= *inteligencia*) savoir-faire
[4] (*CAm*) (= *confusión*) muddle
[5] (*Andes*) (= *comentario*) flippant remark

desparramado ADJ [*hojas, lentejas*] scattered; **la leche estaba desparramada por la mesa** the milk was spilled all over the table

desparramar ▸conjug 1a◂ Ⓐ VT [1] (= *esparcir*) [+ *hojas, lentejas*] to scatter (**por** over); [+ *líquido*] to spill
[2] (= *desperdiciar*) [+ *fortuna*] to squander; [+ *atención*] to spread too widely
Ⓑ **desparramarse** VPR [1] (= *esparcirse*) [*hojas, lentejas*] to scatter; [*líquido*] to spill, be spilt
[2] (*) (= *pasarlo bomba*) to have a whale of a time*

desparrame* SM confusion, disorder

desparramo SM [1] (*Caribe, Cono Sur*) (= *esparcimiento*) [*de objetos*] scattering, spreading; [*de líquido*] spilling
[2] (*Caribe, Cono Sur*) (= *fuga*) rush, stampede
[3] (*Cono Sur*) (= *desorden*) confusion, disorder

despatarrado ADJ **cayó al suelo ~** he fell over on the ground and was left sprawling; **no te sientes tan despatarrada** don't sit with your legs wide apart like that

despatarrante* ADJ side-splitting

despatarrar ▸conjug 1a◂ Ⓐ VT [1] (= *aturdir*) to amaze, dumbfound
[2] (= *asustar*) to scare to death
Ⓑ **despatarrarse** VPR [1] (= *abrir las piernas*) to open one's legs wide; (*en el suelo, al caer*) to do the splits
[2] (*) **~se de risa** to split one's sides laughing

despatriar ▸conjug 1b◂ VT (*Andes, Caribe*) to exile

despavorido ADJ terrified

despeado ADJ footsore, weary

despearse ▸conjug 1a◂ VPR to get footsore, get utterly weary

despechado ADJ spiteful

despechar ▸conjug 1a◂ Ⓐ VT [1] (= *provocar*) to anger, enrage
[2] (= *causar pena a*) to spite
[3] (= *hacer desesperar*) to drive to despair
[4] (*) [+ *niño*] to wean
Ⓑ **despecharse** VPR to get angry

despecho SM [1] (= *ojeriza*) spite; **por ~** out of sheer spite
[2] **a ~ de algo** in spite of sth, despite sth
[3] [*de niño*] weaning

despechugado* ADJ [*hombre*] bare-chested; [*mujer*] bare-breasted

despechugarse* ▸conjug 1h◂ VPR [*hombre*] to bare one's chest; [*mujer*] to bare one's breast

despectivamente ADV [1] (= *con desprecio*) contemptuously, scornfully
[2] (*Ling*) pejoratively

despectivo ADJ [1] (= *despreciativo*) contemptuous, scornful; **hablar de algn en términos ~s** to speak disparagingly of sb
[2] (*Ling*) pejorative

despedazar ▸conjug 1f◂ VT [1] (= *hacer pedazos*) [+ *objeto*] (*con la mano*) to tear apart, tear to pieces; (*con cuchillo*) to cut into pieces; [+ *presa*] to tear to pieces; [+ *víctima*] to chop (up) into pieces
[2] (= *criticar*) to tear to shreds, tear to pieces
[3] [+ *corazón*] to break

despedida SF [1] (*antes de irse*) goodbye, farewell; (*antes de viaje*) send-off; **cena/función de ~** farewell dinner/performance; **regalo de**

~ parting gift
2 (= *ceremonia*) farewell ceremony ► **despedida de soltera** hen party ► **despedida de soltero** stag party
3 (= *final*) (*en carta*) closing formula; (*Literat*) envoi; (*Mús*) final verse
4 (*Inform*) log off, log out

despedir ►conjug 3k◄ Ⓐ VT 1 (= *decir adiós a*) (*gen*) to say goodbye to; [+ *visita*] to see out; [+ *cliente*] to show out; **fuimos a ~lo a la estación** we went to see him off at the station; **¿cómo vais a ~ el año?** how are you going to see the new year in?
2 (= *librarse de*) [+ *empleado*] to dismiss, sack*; [+ *inquilino*] to evict; **~ algo de sí** to get rid of sth; **~ un pensamiento de sí** to put a thought out of one's mind
3 (= *lanzar*) [+ *objeto*] to hurl, fling; [+ *flecha*] to fire; [+ *jinete*] to throw; **salir despedido** to fly off*; ✦**MODISMO ~ el espíritu** to give up the ghost
4 (= *desprender*) [+ *olor, calor*] to give off
Ⓑ **despedirse** VPR 1 (= *decir adiós*) to say goodbye, take one's leave (*frm*); **se despidieron** they said goodbye to each other; **~se de algn** (*gen*) to say goodbye to sb, take one's leave of sb (*frm*); (*en estación, aeropuerto*) to see sb off; **¡ya puedes ~te de ese dinero!** you can say *o* kiss goodbye to that money!; **se despide atentamente** yours sincerely, sincerely yours (*EEUU*), yours faithfully
2 (= *dejar un empleo*) to give up one's job

despegado/a Ⓐ ADJ 1 (= *separado*) detached, loose; **el sobre está ~** the envelope has come unstuck; **el libro está ~** the book is falling apart
2 [*persona*] (= *indiferente*) cold, indifferent; **es muy ~** he isn't very close to his family
Ⓑ SM/F **es un ~ de la familia** he has cut himself off from his family

despegar ►conjug 1h◄ Ⓐ VT 1 (= *desprender*) [+ *cosas pegadas*] to unstick; [+ *sobre*] to open; **sin ~ los labios** without uttering a word
2 (= *separar*) to detach
Ⓑ VI (*Aer*) [*avión*] to take off; [*cohete*] to blast off
Ⓒ **despegarse** VPR 1 [*objeto*] to come unstuck; **se ha despegado el cartel** the poster's come unstuck
2 [*persona*] to become alienated (**de** from); **~se de los amigos** to break with one's friends; **~se del mundo** to renounce worldly things

despego SM = **desapego**

despegue SM 1 (*Aer*) [*de avión*] takeoff; [*de cohete*] blast-off ► **despegue corto** short take-off ► **despegue vertical** vertical takeoff
2 (= *crecimiento*) boom; **en los años sesenta hubo un ~ económico** in the sixties the economy took off, there was an economic boom in the sixties ► **despegue industrial** industrial boom

despeinado Ⓐ ADJ [*pelo*] ruffled, messed up; **estoy ~** my hair's a mess
Ⓑ SM tousled hairstyle

despeinar ►conjug 1a◄ Ⓐ VT [+ *pelo*] to ruffle; **¡me has despeinado!** look at the mess you've made of my hair!
Ⓑ **despeinarse** VPR to get one's hair in a mess

despejable ADJ explicable; **difícilmente ~** hard to explain

despejado ADJ 1 (= *sin obstáculos*) [*camino, mente*] clear; [*campo*] open; [*habitación, plaza*] spacious
2 [*cielo, día*] clear
3 (= *despierto*) awake, wide awake; (*Med*) free of fever
4 [*persona*] **ser ~** to be bright, be smart

despejar ►conjug 1a◄ Ⓐ VT 1 (*lugar*) to clear; **los bomberos ~on el teatro** the firemen cleared the theatre of people; **la policía obligó a ~ el tribunal** the police ordered the court to be cleared
2 (*Dep*) (*balón*) to clear
3 (= *resolver*) [+ *misterio*] to clear up; (*Mat*) [+ *incógnita*] to find
4 (*Inform*) [+ *pantalla*] to clear
5 (*Med*) [+ *nariz*] to unblock; [+ *cabeza*] to clear; [+ *persona*] to wake up
Ⓑ VI 1 (*de un lugar*) **¡despejen!** (*al moverse*) move along!; (*haciendo salir*) everybody out!
2 (*Dep*) to clear, clear the ball
3 (*Meteo*) to clear
Ⓒ **despejarse** VPR 1 (*Meteo*) [*cielo*] to clear; [*día*] to clear up; **se está despejando** the weather's clearing up
2 [*persona*] (= *despabilarse*) to brighten up; **me lavé la cara con agua fría para ~me** I washed my face with cold water to wake myself up; **voy a salir a ~me un poco** I'm going out to clear my head a bit
3 [*misterio*] to be cleared up

despeje SM 1 (*Dep*) clearance
2 [*de mente*] clarity, clearness of mind

despejo SM (*al pensar*) brightness; (*al actuar*) self-confidence, ease of manner; (*al hablar*) fluency

despellejar ►conjug 1a◄ VT 1 [+ *animal*] to skin
2 (= *criticar*) to tear to pieces
3 (*) (= *arruinar*) **~ a algn** to fleece sb

despelotado* ADJ 1 (= *desnudo*) half-naked, scantily clad
2 (= *desorganizado*) (*LAm*) disorganized

despelotar* ►conjug 1a◄ Ⓐ VT to strip, undress
Ⓑ **despelotarse** VPR 1 to strip, strip off
2 **~se de risa** to laugh fit to bust*

despelote* SM 1 (*) (= *desnudez*) stripping off
2 **¡vaya ~!** what a laugh!*; **se ha comprado un coche que es un ~** (*Cono Sur*) he's bought a fantastic car
3 (*LAm*) (= *lío*) mess
4 (*Caribe*) (= *juerga*) binge, great night

despeluchado ADJ dishevelled, disheveled (*EEUU*), tousled

despeluchar ►conjug 1a◄ VT to dishevel, tousle

despeluz(n)ar ►conjug 1f◄ Ⓐ VT 1 [+ *pelo*] to dishevel, tousle, rumple; **~ a algn** to horrify sb, make sb's hair stand on end
2 (*Caribe*) (= *arruinar*) to ruin, leave penniless
Ⓑ **despeluz(n)arse** VPR 1 [*pelo*] to stand on end
2 [*persona*] to be horrified

despenalización SF legalization, decriminalization

despenalizar ►conjug 1f◄ VT to legalize, decriminalize

despenar ►conjug 1a◄ VT 1 (= *consolar*) to console
2 (*) (= *matar*) to do in*, kill

despendedor ADJ extravagant

despendolado* ADJ uninhibited, wild*

despendole* SM lack of inhibitions, lack of restraint

despensa SF 1 (= *armario*) pantry, larder
2 (= *provisión de comestibles*) stock of food
3 (*Náut*) storeroom

despensero SM 1 (= *criado*) butler, steward
2 (*Náut*) storekeeper

despeñadero SM 1 (*Geog*) cliff, precipice
2 (= *riesgo*) risk, danger

despeñadizo ADJ dangerously steep, sheer, precipitous

despeñar ►conjug 1a◄ Ⓐ VT (= *arrojar*) to throw over a cliff
Ⓑ **despeñarse** VPR 1 (*por un barranco*) [*persona*] to throw o.s. over a cliff; [*coche*] to go over a cliff *o* off the side of the road
2 (= *caer*) to fall headlong

despeño SM 1 (= *caída*) fall, drop
2 (= *fracaso*) failure, collapse

despepitar ►conjug 1a◄ Ⓐ VT to remove the pips from
Ⓑ **despepitarse** VPR 1 (= *gritar*) to bawl, shriek
2 (= *obrar*) to rave, act wildly; **~se por algo** to long for sth, go overboard for sth*; **~se por hacer algo** to long to do sth; ✦**MODISMO salir despepitado*** to rush out, go rushing out

despercudir ►conjug 3a◄ VT 1 (= *limpiar*) to clean, wash
2 (*LAm*) [+ *persona*] to liven up, wake up, ginger up

desperdiciado ADJ wasteful

desperdiciador(a) ADJ, SM/F spendthrift

desperdiciar ►conjug 1b◄ VT [+ *comida, tiempo*] to waste; [+ *oportunidad*] to waste, throw away; [+ *fortuna*] to waste, squander

desperdicio SM 1 [*de tiempo*] waste; [*de dinero*] waste, squandering; **esta carne no tiene ~** all this meat can be eaten; **el libro no tiene ~** the book is excellent from beginning to end; **el muchacho no tiene ~** (*iró*) there's very little to be said in his favour
2 **desperdicios** [*de comida*] scraps; (*Biol, Téc*) waste products ► **desperdicios de algodón** cotton waste *sing* ► **desperdicios de cocina** kitchen scraps ► **desperdicios de hierro** scrap iron *sing*

desperdigado ADJ scattered, dotted

desperdigar ►conjug 1h◄ Ⓐ VT (= *esparcir*) [+ *rebaño, objetos*] to scatter; [+ *energía*] dissipate
Ⓑ **desperdigarse** VPR to scatter

desperezarse ►conjug 1f◄ VPR to stretch, stretch o.s.

desperezo SM stretch

desperfecto SM flaw, imperfection; **sufrió algunos ~s en el accidente** it suffered slight damage in the accident

despernado ADJ footsore, weary

despersonalizar ►conjug 1f◄ VT to depersonalize

despertador(a) Ⓐ SM/F (= *persona*) knocker-up
Ⓑ SM alarm clock ► **despertador de viaje** travelling clock, traveling clock (*EEUU*)

despertamiento SM 1 [*de persona*] awaken-

ing
[2] [*de cultura, civilización*] awakening, rebirth

despertar ▸conjug 1j◂ Ⓐ VT [1] (*del sueño*) to wake, wake up, awaken (*liter*)
[2] (= *recordar, incitar*) [+ *esperanzas*] to raise; [+ *recuerdo*] to revive; [+ *sentimiento*] to arouse; **me despertó el apetito** it whetted my appetite
Ⓑ VI, **despertarse** VPR to wake up, awaken; **siempre me despierto temprano** I always wake up early; **~ a la realidad** to wake up to reality
Ⓒ SM awakening; **el ~ religioso** the religious awakening; **el ~ de la primavera** the awakening of spring

despestañarse ▸conjug 1a◂ VPR (*Cono Sur*) [1] (= *desojarse*) to strain one's eyes
[2] (*) (= *estudiar*) to burn the midnight oil, swot*, grind (*EEUU**)

despiadadamente ADV mercilessly, relentlessly

despiadado ADJ [*persona*] heartless; [*ataque*] merciless

despicarse ▸conjug 1g◂ VPR to get even, get one's revenge

despichar ▸conjug 1a◂ Ⓐ VT (*Andes, Caribe, Cono Sur*) (= *aplastar*) (*lit*) to crush, flatten; (*fig*) to crush
Ⓑ VI (‡) to kick the bucket‡

despido SM [1] dismissal, sacking* ▸ **despido arbitrario** wrongful dismissal, unfair dismissal ▸ **despido colectivo** wholesale redundancies *pl* ▸ **despido disciplinario** dismissal on disciplinary grounds ▸ **despido forzoso** compulsory redundancy ▸ **despido improcedente** wrongful dismissal, unfair dismissal ▸ **despido incentivado** voluntary redundancy ▸ **despido injustificado** wrongful dismissal, unfair dismissal ▸ **despido injusto** wrongful dismissal, unfair dismissal ▸ **despido libre** right to hire and fire ▸ **despido voluntario** voluntary redundancy
[2] (= *pago*) severance pay, redundancy payment

despiece SM [1] [*de res*] quartering, carving-up
[2] (*Prensa*) comment, personal note

despierto ADJ [1] (= *no dormido*) awake
[2] (= *listo*) sharp
[3] (= *alerta*) alert

despiezar ▸conjug 1f◂ VT [1] [+ *res*] to quarter, carve up
[2] [+ *máquina, motor*] to break up

despilfarrado ADJ [1] (= *derrochador*) extravagant, wasteful
[2] (= *desaseado*) ragged, shabby

despilfarrador(a) Ⓐ ADJ (= *malgastador*) (*de dinero*) extravagant, wasteful; (*de recursos, esfuerzos*) wasteful
Ⓑ SM/F spendthrift

despilfarrar ▸conjug 1a◂ VT [+ *dinero*] to waste, squander; [+ *recursos, esfuerzos*] to waste

despilfarro SM [1] (= *derroche*) (= *acción*) waste, squandering; (= *cualidad*) extravagance, wastefulness
[2] (= *desaseo*) slovenliness

despintar ▸conjug 1a◂ Ⓐ VT [1] (= *quitar pintura a*) to take the paint off
[2] [+ *hechos*] to distort
[3] (*Chile**) **no ~ algo a algn** not to spare sb from sth
Ⓑ VI **éste no despinta de su casta** he is in no way different from the rest of his family
Ⓒ **despintarse** VPR [1] [*color*] to fade; (*con la lluvia*) to wash off
[2] **~se algo** to forget sth, wipe sth from one's mind; **no se me despinta que ...** I never forget that ..., I remember vividly that ...
[3] (*LAm*) [*maquillaje*] to run, get smudged
[4] (*Chile**) **no ~se de algn** *o* **algo** never to be without sb *o* sth

despiojar ▸conjug 1a◂ VT [1] (= *quitar los piojos a*) to delouse
[2] (*fig*) **~ a algn** to rescue sb from the gutter

despiole* SM (*Arg*) mess

despiporrante* ADJ killingly funny

despiporre* SM (= *caos*) mayhem; **¡fue el ~!** it was something out of this world!, it was just about the end!; **esto es el ~** this is the limit!

despique SM satisfaction, revenge

despistado/a Ⓐ ADJ [1] (= *distraído*) vague, absentminded
[2] (= *confuso*) confused, muddled; **ando muy ~ con todo esto** I'm terribly muddled about all this
Ⓑ SM/F (= *distraído*) scatterbrain, absent-minded person; **es un ~** he's very absent-minded; ✦*MODISMO* **hacerse el ~** (*para no entender*) to pretend not to understand; (*para no ver a algn*) to pretend not to be looking

despistaje SM (*Med*) early detection, early diagnosis

despistar ▸conjug 1a◂ Ⓐ VT [1] [+ *perro*] to throw off the scent; **lograron ~ a sus perseguidores** they managed to give the slip to *o* shake off their pursuers
[2] (= *confundir*) to mislead, fox; **esa pregunta está hecha para ~** that question is designed to mislead you
[3] (‡) (= *robar*) to nick‡; (= *timar*) rip off‡
[4] (*Med*) to detect early, diagnose at an early stage
Ⓑ **despistarse** VPR [1] (= *extraviarse*) to take the wrong route *o* road
[2] (= *confundirse*) to get confused
[3] (= *distraerse*) to get absent-minded; **no puedes ~te ni un momento** you can't let your attention wander for a moment

despiste SM [1] (= *error*) slip; **ha sido un ~** it was just a momentary lapse
[2] (= *distracción*) absent-mindedness; **¡qué ~ tienes!** you're so absent-minded!; **tiene un terrible ~** he's terribly absent-minded

desplacer ▸conjug 2w◂ Ⓐ VT to displease
Ⓑ SM displeasure

desplanchar ▸conjug 1a◂ Ⓐ VT [+ *ropa*] to crease, crumple
Ⓑ **desplancharse** VPR to crease, crumple

desplantador SM trowel

desplantar ▸conjug 1a◂ VT [1] [+ *planta*] to pull up, uproot, take up
[2] [+ *objeto*] to move out of vertical, tilt, put out of plumb

desplante SM [1] (= *dicho cortante*) rude remark; **dar** *o* **hacer un ~ a algn** to be short with sb
[2] **me hizo un ~** (*LAm**) she stood me up*
[3] (*en baile*) wrong stance
[4] (= *descaro*) insolence, lack of respect
[5] (*LAm**) (= *disparate*) crazy idea

desplazado/a Ⓐ ADJ [1] [*pieza*] wrongly placed
[2] **sentirse un poco ~** to feel rather out of place
Ⓑ SM/F (= *inadaptado*) misfit; (*Pol*) displaced person

desplazamiento SM [1] (= *movimiento*) [*de partículas*] displacement; [*de tropas*] movement ▸ **desplazamiento continental** continental drift ▸ **desplazamiento de tierras** landslide
[2] (= *viaje*) journey; **utiliza el tren para los ~s cortos** she uses the train for short journeys; **habrá más de diez millones de ~s en todo el país** over ten million journeys will be made throughout the country; **reside en Madrid aunque hace frecuentes ~s** she lives in Madrid but travels frequently
[3] [*de opinión, votos*] shift, swing ▸ **desplazamiento de la demanda** (*Com*) shift in demand
[4] (*Inform*) scrolling ▸ **desplazamiento hacia abajo** scrolling down ▸ **desplazamiento hacia arriba** scrolling up
[5] (*Náut*) displacement

desplazar ▸conjug 1f◂ Ⓐ VT [1] (= *mover*) [+ *objeto*] to move; [+ *tropas*] to transfer
[2] (= *suplantar*) to take the place of; **las cámaras digitales no han conseguido ~ a las convencionales** digital cameras have not taken the place of *o* superseded conventional ones; **lo ~on de su cargo** he was ousted from his position
[3] (*Fís, Náut, Téc*) to displace
[4] (*Inform*) to scroll
Ⓑ **desplazarse** VPR [1] [*objeto*] to move, shift
[2] [*persona, vehículo*] to go, travel; **tiene que ~se 25km todos los días** he has to travel 25km every day; **el avión se desplaza a más de 1500km/h** the aircraft travels at more than 1500km/h
[3] [*votos, opinión*] to shift, swing; **se ha desplazado un 4% de los votos** there has been a swing of 4% in the voting

desplegable Ⓐ ADJ **menú ~** pull-down menu
Ⓑ SM [1] (= *folleto*) folder, brochure
[2] (*Prensa*) centrefold

desplegar ▸conjug 1h, 1j◂ Ⓐ VT [1] (= *extender*) [+ *mapa, mantel*] to unfold; [+ *periódico*] to open, open out; [+ *alas*] to spread; [+ *bandera, velas*] to unfurl
[2] (*Mil*) [+ *misiles, tropas*] to deploy
[3] (= *utilizar*) [+ *energías*] to use; [+ *recursos*] to deploy
[4] [+ *misterio*] to clarify
Ⓑ **desplegarse** VPR [1] (= *extenderse*) [*flor*] to open, open out; [*alas*] to spread, spread out
[2] (*Mil*) to deploy

despliegue SM [1] (*Mil*) deployment
[2] [*de fuerzas*] display, show

desplomarse ▸conjug 1a◂ VPR [1] (= *derrumbarse*) [*persona, gobierno*] to collapse; [*edificio*] to topple over; (*al vacío*) to plummet down; **se ha desplomado el techo** the ceiling has fallen in; **caer desplomado** to collapse; **el avión se desplomó** the plane fell *o* dropped out of the sky
[2] (*Fin*) [*precios*] to slump, tumble

desplome SM [1] [*de edificio, sistema*] collapse; **de repente se produjo el ~ del edificio** the building suddenly collapsed
[2] (*Fin*) [*de cotización, divisa*] collapse, slump
[3] (*Aer*) pancake landing
[4] (*Alpinismo, Arquit, Geol*) overhang

desplumar ▸conjug 1a◂ Ⓐ VT [1] [+ *ave*] to pluck
[2] (*) (= *estafar*) to fleece*
Ⓑ **desplumarse** VPR to moult, molt (*EEUU*)

despoblación SF depopulation ▸ **despoblación del campo, despoblación rural** rural population drift

despoblado Ⓐ ADJ (= *con insuficientes habitantes*) underpopulated; (= *con pocos habitantes*) depopulated; (= *sin habitantes*) unpopulated
Ⓑ SM deserted spot

despoblar ▸conjug 1l◂ Ⓐ VT [1] (*de personas*) to depopulate
[2] (*de objetos*) to clear; **~ una zona de árboles** to clear an area of trees
Ⓑ **despoblarse** VPR to become depopulated, lose its population

despojar ▸conjug 1a◂ Ⓐ VT (*de bienes*) to strip; (*de honores, títulos*) to divest; (*Jur*) to dispossess; **habían despojado la casa de muebles** they had stripped the house of furniture; **verse despojado de su autoridad** to be stripped of one's authority
Ⓑ **despojarse** VPR [1] (= *desnudarse*) to undress
[2] **~se de** [+ *ropa*] to take off; [+ *hojas*] to shed; [+ *poderes*] to relinquish, give up; [+ *prejuicios*] to get rid of, free o.s. from

despojo SM [1] (= *saqueo*) plundering
[2] (*Mil*) (= *botín*) plunder, loot
[3] **despojos** [*de comida*] left-overs; [*de animal*] offal *sing*; [*de edificio*] rubble *sing*; [*de mineral*] debris *sing* ▸ **despojos de hierro** scrap iron *sing* ▸ **despojos mortales** mortal remains

despolitización SF depoliticization

despolitizar ▸conjug 1f◂ VT to depoliticize

despolvorear ▸conjug 1a◂ VT to dust

desportillado ADJ [1] [*taza, plato*] chipped
[2] (= *en malas condiciones*) [*coche*] battered; [*piso*] dingy

desportilladura SF chip

desportillar ▸conjug 1a◂ Ⓐ VT to chip
Ⓑ **desportillarse** VPR to get chipped

desposado ADJ recently married; **los ~s** the newly-weds

desposar ▸conjug 1a◂ Ⓐ VT [*sacerdote, novio*] to marry; **yo te desposo** I take you to be my lawful wedded wife/husband
Ⓑ **desposarse** VPR [1] (= *formalizar el noviazgo*) to get engaged (**con** to)
[2] (= *casarse*) to marry, get married

desposeer ▸conjug 2e◂ Ⓐ VT to dispossess (**de** of); **~ a algn de su autoridad** to strip sb of his authority
Ⓑ **desposeerse** VPR **~se de algo** to give sth up, relinquish sth

desposeído/a SM/F **los ~s** the have-nots, the dispossessed

desposeimiento SM (*frm*) dispossession

desposorios SMPL [1] (= *esponsales*) betrothal *sing*
[2] (= *ceremonia*) marriage *sing*, marriage ceremony *sing*

déspota SMF despot ▸ **déspota ilustrado/a** enlightened despot

despóticamente ADV despotically

despótico ADJ despotic

despotismo SM despotism ▸ **despotismo ilustrado** enlightened despotism

despotorrarse* ▸conjug 1a◂ VPR to laugh o.s. silly*

despotricar ▸conjug 1g◂ VI to rant and rave (**contra** about)

despreciable ADJ [1] [*persona*] despicable, contemptible
[2] (= *sin valor*) [*objeto*] worthless; [*cantidad*] negligible; **una suma nada ~** a not inconsiderable amount

despreciar ▸conjug 1b◂ Ⓐ VT [1] [+ *persona*] to despise, scorn; **desprecian a los extranjeros** they look down on foreigners
[2] (= *rechazar*) [+ *oferta, regalo*] to spurn, reject; **~ los peligros** to scorn the dangers; **no hay que ~ tal posibilidad** one should not discount such a possibility
Ⓑ **despreciarse** VPR **~se de hacer algo** to think it beneath o.s. to do sth, not deign to do sth

despreciativamente ADV scornfully, contemptuously

despreciativo ADJ [*observación, tono*] scornful, contemptuous; [*comentario*] derogatory

desprecintar ▸conjug 1a◂ VT to unseal

desprecio SM [1] (= *desdén*) scorn, contempt; **lo miró con ~** she looked at him contemptuously
[2] (= *desaire*) slight, snub; **le hicieron el ~ de no acudir** they snubbed him by not coming

desprender ▸conjug 2a◂ Ⓐ VT [1] (= *soltar*) [+ *gas, olor*] to give off; [+ *piel, pelo*] to shed
[2] (= *separar*) **el viento desprendió unas tejas del tejado** the wind detached some tiles from the roof; **desprendió el toallero de la pared** he took the towel rail down from the wall; **tuve que ~ el botón del abrigo** I had to take the button off my coat
Ⓑ **desprenderse** VPR [1] (= *soltarse*) [*pieza, botón*] to come off, become detached (*frm*); [*roca*] to come away; [*pintura, cal*] to peel, come off; **se te ha desprendido un botón del abrigo** one of the buttons has come off your coat; **se ha desprendido la cortina del salón** the living room curtain has come down
[2] [*gas, olor*] to issue; **se desprendía humo de la chimenea** smoke was issuing from the chimney; **en la reacción se desprende gas** gas is given off in the reaction; **se desprendían chispas del fuego** sparks were shooting out from the fire
[3] **~se de algo** (= *deshacerse*): **logramos ~nos de mi hermana pequeña** we managed to get rid of *o* shake off my little sister; **tuvimos que ~nos del coche** we had to part with *o* get rid of the car; **nunca se desprende de su muñequita** she never lets go of her little doll; **las serpientes se desprenden de la piel en esta época del año** snakes shed their skins at this time of year
[4] (= *concluirse*) **de esta declaración se desprende que ...** from this statement we can gather that ...

desprendido ADJ [1] (= *suelto*) [*pieza*] loose, detached; **uno de tus botones está ~** one of your buttons is coming off
[2] (= *generoso*) generous

desprendimiento SM [1] [*de pieza*] loosening ▸ **desprendimiento de matriz** prolapse ▸ **desprendimiento de retina** detachment of the retina; **ha sufrido un ~ de retina** he has a detached retina ▸ **desprendimiento de tierras** landslide
[2] (= *generosidad*) generosity

despreocupación SF [1] (= *falta de preocupación*) unconcern; (*al vestir*) sloppiness
[2] (= *tranquilidad*) nonchalance
[3] (= *indiferencia*) indifference

despreocupadamente ADV [*hablar, jugar*] nonchalantly; [*disfrutar*] in a carefree way; **se viste ~** she doesn't take much care about the way she dresses

despreocupado ADJ [1] (= *sin preocupación*) unworried, unconcerned; **vive ~ de todo** he has a carefree existence
[2] (*al hablar, jugar*) nonchalant
[3] (*en el vestir*) casual; (*pey*) careless, sloppy
[4] (= *imparcial*) unbias(s)ed, impartial
[5] (*Rel*) (= *indiferente*) indifferent, apathetic; (= *tolerante*) broad-minded
[6] (†) [*mujer*] loose

despreocupamiento SM lack of interest, apathy

despreocuparse ▸conjug 1a◂ VPR [1] (= *descuidarse*) **tú despreocúpate del coche, que ya me encargo yo** don't you worry about the car, I'll take care of it
[2] (= *ser indiferente*) to be unconcerned

despresar ▸conjug 1a◂ VT (*Cono Sur*) [+ *ave*] to cut up, carve up

desprestigiar ▸conjug 1b◂ Ⓐ VT [1] (= *criticar*) to disparage, run down
[2] (= *desacreditar*) to discredit; **tus meteduras de pata desprestigian a toda la profesión** your faux pas tarnish the reputation of our whole profession
Ⓑ **desprestigiarse** VPR to lose one's prestige

desprestigio SM [1] (= *denigración*) disparagement
[2] (= *descrédito*) discredit, loss of prestige; **campaña de ~** smear campaign; **esas cosas que van en ~ nuestro** those things which are to our discredit

desprevención SF unreadiness, unpreparedness

desprevenido ADJ (= *no preparado*) unready, unprepared; **coger** *o* **pillar** *o* (*LAm*) **agarrar a algn ~** to catch sb unawares, catch sb off his guard

desprivatizar ▸conjug 1f◂ VT to take into public ownership

desprogramar ▸conjug 1a◂ VT to deprogramme, deprogram (*EEUU*)

desprolijo* ADJ (*Arg*) untidy, sloppy*

desproporción SF disproportion, lack of proportion

desproporcionadamente ADV disproportionately

desproporcionado ADJ disproportionate

despropósito SM [1] (= *salida de tono*) inappropriate remark
[2] (= *disparate*) piece of nonsense

desprotección SF [1] (= *falta de protección*) vulnerability, defencelessness, defenselessness (*EEUU*)
[2] (*Jur*) lack of legal protection
[3] (*Inform*) deprotection

desprotegido ADJ unprotected, defenceless, defenseless (*EEUU*)

desproveer ▸conjug 2a◂ (*pp* **desprovisto** *y* **desproveído**) VT **~ a algn de algo** to deprive sb of sth

desprovisto ADJ **~ de algo** devoid of sth, without sth; **un libro no ~ de méritos** a book not without merit; **estar ~ de algo** to lack sth, be lacking in sth; **estar ~ de medios** to lack means

después ADV [1] (*con sentido temporal*) [1·1] (= *más tarde*) later, later on; (*tras un hecho concreto*) afterwards, after; **nos vemos ~** I'll see you later (on); **no me da tiempo antes de la cena, lo haré ~** I haven't got time before dinner, I'll do it after(wards); **poco ~** soon after(wards), not long after(wards); **lo vi en enero, pero ~ no lo he visto más** I saw him in January, but I haven't seen him since (then)

[1·2] (= *a continuación*) then, next; **¿qué pasó ~?** what happened then *o* next?

[2] (*con sentido espacial*) **primero está el bar y ~ mi casa** first there's the bar and then, next to it, my house; **gire a la derecha dos calles ~** take the second turning on the right after that

[3] (*en orden, jerarquía*) then; **primero está el director y ~ el subdirector** first there's the manager, and then the assistant manager

[4] **~ de** (*con sentido temporal*) after; **lo saludé ~ del funeral** I said hello to him after the funeral; **~ de aplicarse la mascarilla, relájese** after applying the mask, relax; **nadie llamó ~ de que te fueras** nobody called after you had gone; **no debería llegar ~ de las diez** I shouldn't be any later than ten; **llegó ~ de mí** he arrived after me; **no lo he vuelto a ver ~ de Navidad** I haven't seen him since Christmas; **~ de marcharse no hemos sabido nada de él** we haven't heard anything from him since he left; **en el año 300 ~ de Cristo** in (the year) 300 AD

[5] **~ de** (*en orden, jerarquía*) after, next to; **mi nombre está ~ del tuyo** my name comes next to *o* after yours

[6] **~ de todo** after all; **~ de todo, no parece tan antipático** he doesn't seem so unpleasant, after all

[7] **~ que*** after; **me ducharé ~ que tú** I'll have a shower after you

despuesito* ADV (*Méx*) right away, in just a moment

despulgar ▸conjug 1h◂ VT = **espulgar**

despuntado ADJ blunt

despuntar ▸conjug 1a◂ Ⓐ VT [+ *lápiz, cuchillo*] to blunt

Ⓑ VI [1] (*Bot*) [*plantas*] to sprout; [*flores*] to bud

[2] [*día*] to dawn; **al ~ el alba** at daybreak, at dawn

[3] [*persona*] (= *destacar*) to excel, stand out; **despunta en matemáticas** he shines *o* excels at maths; **despunta por su talento** she is outstandingly talented

desquiciado ADJ [*persona*] deranged, unhinged; **tiene los nervios ~s** his nerves are in tatters *o* shreds

desquiciamiento SM [1] [*de persona*] unhinging

[2] [*de orden, situación*] upsetting

desquiciante ADJ maddening

desquiciar ▸conjug 1b◂ Ⓐ VT [1] [+ *puerta*] to take off its hinges

[2] [+ *persona*] (= *turbar*) to drive mad; (= *volver loco a*) to unhinge, drive mad

[3] [+ *orden, situación*] to upset

Ⓑ **desquiciarse** VPR [*persona*] to go mad

desquicio SM (*CAm, Cono Sur*) confusion, disorder

desquitar ▸conjug 1a◂ Ⓐ VT [+ *pérdida*] to make good, make up

Ⓑ **desquitarse** VPR [1] (= *obtener satisfacción*) to obtain satisfaction; **~se de una pérdida** to make up for a loss, compensate o.s. for a loss

[2] (= *vengarse*) to get even (**con** with), get one's own back (**con** on); **~se de una mala pasada** to get one's own back for a dirty trick

[3] (*Com, Fin*) to recover a debt, get one's money back

desquite SM [1] (= *recompensa*) compensation

[2] (= *venganza*) revenge, retaliation; **tomarse el ~** to get one's own back; **tomarse el ~ de algo** to get one's own back for sth

[3] (*Dep*) (*tb* **partido de ~**) return match, return game

desratización SF **campaña de ~** anti-rat campaign

desratizador ADJ anti-rodent *antes de s*

desratizar ▸conjug 1f◂ VT to clear of rats

desrazonable ADJ unreasonable

desregulación SF deregulation

desregular ▸conjug 1a◂ VT to free, deregulate, remove controls from

desrielar ▸conjug 1a◂ (*LAm*) Ⓐ VI to derail

Ⓑ **desrielarse** VPR to be derailed

desriñonar ▸conjug 1a◂ VT = **deslomar**

desrizador SM, **desrizante** SM hair straightener

desrizar ▸conjug 1f◂ VT [+ *pelo*] to straighten

Dest. ABR = **destinatario**

destacadamente ADV notably, outstandingly

destacado ADJ [1] (= *distinguido*) (*gen*) outstanding; [*personaje*] distinguished; [*dato*] noteworthy

[2] (*Mil*) stationed; **los cascos azules ~s en la zona** the UN peacekeeping forces *o* blue helmets stationed in the area

destacamento SM (*Mil*) detachment ► **destacamento de desembarco** (*Náut*) landing party

destacar ▸conjug 1g◂ Ⓐ VT [1] (= *hacer resaltar*) to emphasize; **sirve para ~ su belleza** it serves to show off her beauty; **quiero ~ que …** I wish to emphasize that …

[2] (*Mil*) to detach, detail

[3] (*Inform*) to highlight

Ⓑ VI, **destacarse** VPR [1] (= *verse mejor*) to stand out; **~se contra** *o* **en** *o* **sobre algo** to stand out *o* be outlined against sth; **la torre se destaca contra el cielo** the tower is silhouetted against the sky

[2] [*persona*] to stand out (**por** because of)

destajar ▸conjug 1a◂ VT [1] [+ *trabajo*] to agree conditions for

[2] (*Naipes*) to cut

[3] (*LAm*) (= *despedazar*) [+ *reses*] to cut up

destajero/a SM/F, **destajista** SMF pieceworker

destajo SM [1] **a ~** (= *por pieza*) by the job; (= *con afán*) eagerly; (*Cono Sur**) by guesswork; **trabajar a ~** (*lit*) to do piecework; (*fig*) to work one's fingers to the bone; **trabajo a ~** piecework; **hablar a ~*** to talk nineteen to the dozen

[2] ► **destajo de esquí** ski-lift pass

destapado ADJ [1] (= *sin cubrir*) **la botella está destapada** somebody left the top off the bottle; **dejó la olla destapada** he left the saucepan uncovered

[2] (= *sin sábanas*) **hoy he dormido ~** I slept without any covers last night; **durmió ~** he slept with the covers off

[3] [*secreto, trama*] exposed, uncovered

destapador SM (*LAm*) bottle opener

destapamiento SM (*Méx Pol*) *announcement of official PRI presidential candidate*

destapar ▸conjug 1a◂ Ⓐ VT [1] (= *descubrir*) [+ *mueble*] to uncover; [+ *botella*] (*gen*) to open; (*con corcho*) to uncork; [+ *recipiente*] to take the lid off

[2] (*en la cama*) to take the bedclothes off; **lo destapó** she took the covers off him

[3] (= *hacer público*) [+ *secreto*] to reveal; [+ *escándalo*] to uncover

[4] (*LAm*) (= *desatascar*) to unblock

Ⓑ **destaparse** VPR [1] (= *descubrirse*) to get uncovered; **el niño se ha destapado** the bedclothes have fallen off the baby

[2] (= *revelarse*) to show one's true character; **se destapó metiéndose a monja** she astounded everyone by becoming a nun

[3] (= *desahogarse*) to open one's heart (**con** to)

[4] (= *perder los estribos*) to let fly, lose control

destape SM [1] [*de persona*] (= *estado*) nudity; (= *acto*) undressing, stripping off ► **destape integral** full-frontal nudity

[2] [*de costumbres*] permissiveness; (*Pol*) *process of liberalization*; **el ~ español** *the relaxation of sexual censorship (after Franco's death)*

destaponar ▸conjug 1a◂ VT [+ *conducto, tubería*] to unblock, clear

destartalado ADJ [1] [*casa*] (= *grande, mal dispuesta*) large and rambling; (= *ruinoso*) tumbledown

[2] [*coche*] rickety

destazar ▸conjug 1f◂ VT to cut up

destechar ▸conjug 1a◂ VT to unroof, take the roof off

destejar ▸conjug 1a◂ VT [1] [+ *techo*] to remove the tiles from

[2] (= *quitar la protección a*) to leave unprotected

destejer ▸conjug 2d◂ VT [1] (*Cos*) [+ *prenda de punto*] to undo; *ver tb* **tejer B1**

[2] (= *interferir*) to interfere with the progress of

destellante ADJ sparkling

destellar ▸conjug 1a◂ VI [*diamante, ojos*] to sparkle; [*metal*] to glint; [*estrella*] to twinkle

destello SM [1] (= *brillo*) [*de diamante, ojos*] sparkle; [*de metal*] glint; [*de estrella*] twinkling

[2] (*Téc*) signal light

[3] (= *pizca*) glimmer, hint; **tiene a veces ~s de inteligencia** he sometimes shows a glimmer of intelligence; **no tiene un ~ de verdad** there's not an atom of truth in it

destemplado ADJ [1] (*Mús*) out of tune

[2] (*Med*) (= *con fiebre*) feverish; **estar ~** to have a slight temperature *o* (*EEUU*) fever; **tienes el pulso ~** your pulse is a little irregular

[3] [*carácter*] (= *malhumorado*) ill-tempered; (= *áspero*) harsh

[4] (*Meteo*) unpleasant

destemplanza SF [1] (*Mús*) tunelessness

[2] (*Med*) (= *fiebre*) slight temperature, slight

fever (*EEUU*); (= *malestar*) indisposition
3 (= *falta de moderación*) intemperance, harshness
4 (*Meteo*) unpleasantness, inclemency

destemplar ▸conjug 1a◂ Ⓐ VT 1 (*Mús*) to put out of tune
2 (= *alterar*) to upset, disturb
Ⓑ **destemplarse** VPR 1 (*Mús*) to get out of tune
2 (*Med*) [*persona*] to have a slight temperature *o* (*EEUU*) fever; [*pulso*] to become irregular
3 [*máquina*] to break down
4 (*LAm*) (= *irritarse*) to get upset; **con eso me destemplo** that sets my teeth on edge

destemple SM 1 = **destemplanza**
2 [*de metal*] lack of temper, poorly-tempered nature

destensar ▸conjug 1a◂ VT to slacken, loosen

desteñido Ⓐ ADJ faded, discoloured, discolored (*EEUU*)
Ⓑ SM discolouring, discoloring (*EEUU*)

desteñir ▸conjug 3h, 3k◂ Ⓐ VT (= *quitar el color a*) to fade, discolour, discolor (*EEUU*)
Ⓑ VI, **desteñirse** VPR 1 (= *perder color*) to run; **se ha desteñido la camiseta** the T-shirt has run
2 (= *manchar*) to run; **esta tela no destiñe** this fabric won't run

desternillante* ADJ hilarious

desternillarse* ▸conjug 1a◂ VPR **~ de risa** to split one's sides laughing

desternille* SM laughter, hilarity

desterrado/a SM/F (= *exiliado*) exile

desterrar ▸conjug 1j◂ VT 1 (= *exiliar*) to exile, banish
2 (= *desechar*) to dismiss; **~ una sospecha** to banish a suspicion from one's mind; **~ el uso de las armas de fuego** to banish firearms, prohibit the use of firearms
3 (*Agr, Min*) to remove the soil from

destetar ▸conjug 1a◂ Ⓐ VT to wean
Ⓑ **destetarse** VPR 1 [*niño*] to be weaned; ✦**MODISMO** **~se con el vino** to have been brought up on wine
2 (‡) [*mujer*] to get her tits out‡

destete SM weaning

destiempo SM **a ~** at the wrong time

destierro SM 1 (= *exilio*) exile, banishment; **vivir en el ~** to live in exile
2 (= *lugar alejado*) remote spot

destilación SF distillation

destiladera SF 1 (= *alambique*) still
2 (*LAm*) (= *filtro*) filter

destilado SM distillation

destilador(a) Ⓐ SM (= *alambique*) still
Ⓑ SM/F distiller

destilar ▸conjug 1a◂ Ⓐ VT 1 (*goteando*) [+ *alcohol*] to distil; [+ *pus, sangre*] to ooze
2 (= *rebosar*) to exude; **la carta destilaba odio** the letter exuded hatred; **es una orden que destila crueldad** it is an order which is steeped in cruelty
Ⓑ VI 1 (= *gotear*) to drip
2 (= *rezumar*) to ooze, ooze out
3 (= *filtrarse*) to filter through

destilatorio SM 1 (= *aparato*) still
2 (= *fábrica*) distillery

destilería SF distillery ► **destilería de petróleo** oil refinery

destinado ADJ 1 (*Correos, Transportes*) **¿a quién va destinada la carta?** who is the letter addressed to?; **se perdieron todos los paquetes ~s a Madrid** all the parcels for *o* bound for Madrid were lost
2 (*en un trabajo*) **está ~ en Córdoba** [*empleado*] he's based in Córdoba; [*militar*] he's stationed in Córdoba
3 **~ a** *o* **para algo** [*dinero, fondos, material*] set aside for sth; **un camión ~ a** *o* **para el reparto** a lorry used for deliveries; **redujeron el espacio ~ al olivar** the area given over to olive trees has been reduced
4 **~ a algo** (= *predestinado*) destined for sth; **la obra estaba destinada al fracaso** the play was destined for failure *o* to fail; **estaba ~ a morir joven** he was destined to die young
5 **~ a algn/algo** (= *pensado para*) intended for sb/sth, aimed at sb/sth; **un libro ~ a los niños** a book intended for *o* aimed at children; **una nueva ley destinada a proteger al menor** a new law intended to protect minors, a new law aimed at protecting minors
6 **ir ~ a** (*Náut*) to be bound for

destinar ▸conjug 1a◂ VT 1 (= *dedicar*) [+ *fondos, espacio*] to allocate; [+ *tiempo*] to devote; **destinamos el 10% del presupuesto a educación** we allocate 10% of the budget to education; **~on tres salas a la exposición** they allocated three rooms to the exhibition; **~é este dinero a pagar el viaje** I'll use this money to pay for the trip; **~on mil euros para gastos imprevistos** they set aside *o* earmarked a thousand euros for contingencies; **destina su tiempo libre a hacer obras de caridad** she devotes her free time to charity work
2 (= *enviar*) [+ *empleado, funcionario*] to assign, post; [+ *militar*] to station, post; **le han destinado a Lima** he has been assigned *o* posted to Lima
3 (*frm*) (= *dirigir*) [+ *carta*] to address

destinatario/a SM/F [*de carta*] addressee; [*de giro*] payee; **los ~s de este proyecto** the project's target group

destino SM 1 (= *suerte*) destiny, fate; **es mi ~ no encontrarlo** I am fated not to find it; **el ~ lo quiso así** it was destined to happen; **rige los ~s del país** he rules the country's fate
2 [*de avión, viajero*] destination; **"a franquear en ~"** "postage will be paid by the addressee"; **van con ~ a Londres** they are going to London; (*Náut*) they are bound for London; **¿cuál es el ~ de este cuadro?** where is this picture going *o* for?; **salió con ~ al aeropuerto** she set off for the airport; **con ~ a Londres** [*avión, carta*] to London; [*pasajeros*] for London; [*barco*] bound for London
3 (= *puesto*) [*de empleado*] job, post; [*de militar*] posting; [*de funcionario*] placement; **¿qué ~ tienes?** where have you been placed?; **buscarse un ~ de sereno** to look for a job as a night watchman ► **destino público** public appointment
4 (= *uso*) use, purpose; **dar ~ a algo** to find a use for sth

destitución SF dismissal, removal

destituido ADJ **~ de algo** devoid of sth, bereft of sth

destituir ▸conjug 3g◂ VT 1 (= *despedir*) [+ *empleado*] to dismiss (**de** from); [+ *ministro, funcionario*] to remove from office; **ha sido destituido de su cargo** he has been removed from his post; **lo destituyeron por conducta inmoral** he was dismissed for immoral conduct
2 (= *privar*) **~ a algn de algo** to deprive sb of sth

destorcer ▸conjug 2b y 2h◂ Ⓐ VT [+ *cuerda*] to untwist, take the twists out of; [+ *alambre*] to straighten
Ⓑ **destorcerse** VPR (*Náut*) to get off course

destornillado* ADJ crazy, potty*

destornillador SM 1 (= *herramienta*) screwdriver ► **destornillador de estrella** Phillips screwdriver®
2 (*) (= *bebida*) screwdriver* (*cocktail of vodka and orange juice*)

destornillar ▸conjug 1a◂ Ⓐ VT to unscrew
Ⓑ **destornillarse** VPR 1 [*tornillo, tuerca*] to come unscrewed
2 (= *enloquecer*) to go round the bend*
3 (*LAm*) = **desternillarse**
4 (*Méx*) (= *rabiar*) to burble on, rave

destrabar ▸conjug 1a◂ VT 1 (= *desprender*) to loosen, detach
2 [+ *prisionero*] to unfetter, take the shackles off

destral SM small hatchet

destreza SF 1 (= *habilidad*) skill ► **destrezas lingüísticas** linguistic skills
2 (= *agilidad*) dexterity

destripacuentos SM INV interrupter, person who butts in

destripador SM (= *asesino*) murderer; **Jack el ~** Jack the Ripper

destripar ▸conjug 1a◂ VT 1 (= *quitar tripas a*) [+ *animal*] to gut; [+ *persona*] to disembowel
2 [+ *chiste, cuento*] to spoil

destripaterrones SM INV 1 (= *campesino*)
2 (*) clodhopper

destrocar* ▸conjug 1g y 1l◂ VT to swap, change back

destronamiento SM [*de rey*] dethronement; [*de gobierno*] overthrow

destronar ▸conjug 1a◂ VT [+ *rey*] to dethrone; [+ *gobierno*] to overthrow

destroncar ▸conjug 1g◂ VT 1 [+ *árbol*] to chop off, lop the top off
2 [+ *persona*] (= *mutilar*) to maim, mutilate; (= *agotar*) to tire out, exhaust
3 (= *estropear*) [+ *proyecto*] to ruin; [+ *desarrollo*] to harm, damage, dislocate; [+ *discurso*] to interrupt
4 [+ *caballo*] to wear out
5 (*LAm*) [+ *planta*] to uproot

destrozado ADJ 1 [*cristal, cerámica*] smashed, shattered; **quedó ~** [*traje, alfombra, zapato*] it was ruined; [*coche, jardín*] it was wrecked
2 [*persona*] (= *abatido*) shattered, devastated; (*) (= *cansado*) knackered*, pooped (*EEUU**), shattered*; [*corazón*] broken

destrozar ▸conjug 1f◂ VT 1 (= *romper*) [+ *cristal, cerámica*] to smash; [+ *edificio*] to destroy; [+ *ropa, zapatos*] to ruin; [+ *nervios*] to shatter; **ha destrozado el coche** he's wrecked the car; **encontraron los cuerpos destrozados** they found the mangled bodies
2 (= *dejar abatido a*) [+ *persona*] to shatter; [+ *corazón*] to break; [+ *ejército, enemigo*] to crush; **~ a algn en una discusión** to crush sb in an argument; **le ha destrozado el que no quisiera casarse con él** her refusal to marry him has devastated *o* shattered him
3 (= *arruinar*) [+ *persona, vida*] to ruin; **~ la armonía** to ruin the harmony

destrozo SM [1] (= *acción*) destruction
[2] **destrozos** (= *daños*) havoc *sing*; (= *pedazos*) debris *sing*; **causar** *o* **provocar ~s** to cause *o* wreak havoc (**en** in); **los ~s causados por las inundaciones** the destruction caused by the flooding, the havoc wrought by the floods; **los manifestantes provocaron numerosos ~s** the demonstrators caused extensive damage

destrozón ADJ **es muy ~** (*gen*) he's a terrible one for breaking things; (*con la ropa*) he's hard on his clothes

destrucción SF destruction ► **destrucción del empleo** job losses *pl*

destructible ADJ destructible

destructividad SF destructiveness

destructivo ADJ destructive

destructor Ⓐ ADJ destructive
Ⓑ SM (*Náut*) destroyer

destruible ADJ destructible

destruir ▸conjug 3g◂ Ⓐ VT [1] [+ *objeto, edificio*] to destroy; **el acusado había destruido todas las pruebas** the defendant had destroyed all the evidence; **el año pasado se destruyeron miles de empleos en la construcción** last year thousands of construction jobs were lost
[2] (= *estropear*) [+ *amistad, matrimonio, armonía*] to wreck, destroy; [+ *argumento, teoría*] to demolish; [+ *esperanza*] to dash, shatter; [+ *proyecto, plan*] to wreck, ruin
Ⓑ **destruirse** VPR (*Mat*) to cancel out, cancel each other out

desubicado ADJ [1] (= *mal situado*) badly positioned
[2] (*Cono Sur*) (= *falto de tacto*) tactless, silly

desubicar ▸conjug 1g◂ VT (*Cono Sur*) to disorientate

desudar ▸conjug 1a◂ VT to wipe the sweat off

desuellacaras SM INV [1] (= *barbero*) clumsy barber
[2] (= *bribón*) rogue, villain

desuello SM [1] (= *acto*) skinning, flaying
[2] (= *descaro*) brazenness, insolence
[3] (*) (= *robo*) extortion; **¡es un ~!** it's daylight robbery!

desuncir ▸conjug 3b◂ VT to unyoke

desunión SF [1] (= *separación*) separation
[2] (= *discordia*) disunity

desunir ▸conjug 3a◂ VT [1] (= *separar*) to separate
[2] (= *enemistar*) to cause a rift between; **el problema de la herencia ha desunido a la familia** the inheritance problem has split the family

desuñarse ▸conjug 1a◂ VPR [1] (= *trabajar*) to work one's fingers to the bone; **~ por hacer algo** to work one's fingers to the bone to do sth
[2] (= *hacer travesuras*) to be always up to mischief; **se desuña por el juego** he's an inveterate gambler

desurbanización SF relief of city overcrowding, dispersal of city population (*to satellite towns*)

desusado ADJ [1] (= *anticuado*) obsolete, antiquated; **esa palabra está desusada de los buenos escritores** that word is no longer in use among good writers
[2] (= *inusitado*) unusual

desusar ▸conjug 1a◂ Ⓐ VT to stop using, discontinue the use of, give up
Ⓑ **desusarse** VPR to go out of use, become obsolete

desuso SM disuse; **una expresión en ~** an obsolete expression; **caer en ~** to fall into disuse, become obsolete; **dejar algo en ~** to cease to use sth

desvaído ADJ [1] [*color*] pale, washed-out
[2] [*contorno*] vague, blurred
[3] [*persona*] characterless
[4] [*personalidad*] flat, dull

desvainar ▸conjug 1a◂ VT to shell

desvalido ADJ [1] (= *sin fuerzas*) helpless
[2] (= *desprotegido*) destitute; **niños ~s** waifs and strays; **los ~s** (*Pol*) the underprivileged

desvalijamiento SM robbing, robbery

desvalijar ▸conjug 1a◂ VT [+ *persona*] to rob; [+ *cajón, caja fuerte*] to rifle; [+ *casa, tienda*] to ransack

desvalimiento SM helplessness

desvalorar ▸conjug 1a◂ VT [+ *regalo, posesión*] to undervalue; [+ *moneda*] to devalue, devaluate (*EEUU*)

desvalorización SF [*de moneda*] devaluation

desvalorizar ▸conjug 1f◂ VT [+ *moneda*] to devalue, devaluate (*EEUU*); [+ *posesión*] to reduce the value of

desván SM loft, attic

desvanecer ▸conjug 2d◂ Ⓐ VT [1] (= *hacer desaparecer*) [+ *objeto*] to make disappear; [+ *duda*] to dispel; [+ *recuerdo, temor*] to banish
[2] (*Arte*) [+ *colores*] to tone down; [+ *contorno*] to blur
[3] (*Fot*) to mask
[4] (= *envanecer*) to make conceited; **el dinero lo ha desvanecido** the money has gone to his head
Ⓑ **desvanecerse** VPR [1] (= *desaparecer*) [*humo, niebla*] to clear, disperse; [*recuerdo, sonido*] to fade, fade away; [*duda*] to be dispelled
[2] (*Med*) to faint
[3] (*Quím*) to evaporate

desvanecido ADJ [1] (*Med*) **caer ~** to fall in a faint
[2] (= *engreído*) vain

desvanecimiento SM [1] (= *desaparición*) [*de colores, recuerdo, sonido*] fading; [*de contornos*] blurring; [*de dudas*] dispelling
[2] (*Med*) fainting fit, fainting spell (*EEUU*)
[3] (*Fot*) masking
[4] (*Radio*) fading
[5] (= *engreimiento*) vanity

desvarar ▸conjug 1a◂ VT to refloat

desvariar ▸conjug 1c◂ VI [1] (*Med*) to be delirious
[2] (*al hablar*) to rave, talk nonsense

desvarío SM [1] (*Med*) delirium
[2] (= *desatino*) absurdity
[3] **desvaríos** (= *disparates*) ravings

desvede SM *ending of the close season*

desvelado ADJ [1] (= *despierto*) sleepless, wakeful; **estar ~** to be awake, be unable to get to sleep
[2] (= *alerta*) watchful, vigilant

desvelar ▸conjug 1a◂ Ⓐ VT [1] (= *quitar el sueño*) to keep awake; **el café me desvela** coffee keeps me awake *o* stops me from getting to sleep
[2] (= *descubrir*) [+ *algo oculto*] to reveal, unveil; [+ *misterio*] to solve, explain
Ⓑ **desvelarse** VPR [1] (= *no poder dormir*) to be unable to get to sleep
[2] (= *vigilar*) to be watchful, keep one's eyes open; **~se por algo** to take great care over sth; **se desvela porque no nos falte de nada** she works hard so that we should not go short of anything; **~se por hacer algo** to do everything possible to do sth

desvelo SM [1] (= *falta de sueño*) lack of sleep, sleeplessness
[2] (= *vigilancia*) watchfulness
[3] **desvelos** (= *preocupaciones*) effort *sing*; **gracias a sus ~s** thanks to his efforts

desvencijado ADJ [*silla, mueble*] rickety; [*máquina*] broken-down

desvencijar ▸conjug 1a◂ Ⓐ VT [1] (= *romper*) to break
[2] (= *agotar*) [+ *persona*] to exhaust
Ⓑ **desvencijarse** VPR [1] (= *romperse*) to come apart, fall to pieces
[2] (*Med*) to rupture o.s.

desventaja SF [1] (= *perjuicio*) disadvantage; **estar en ~** to be at a disadvantage
[2] (= *inconveniente*) disadvantage, drawback

desventajado ADJ disadvantaged

desventajosamente ADV disadvantageously, unfavourably, unfavorably (*EEUU*)

desventajoso ADJ disadvantageous, unfavourable, unfavorable (*EEUU*)

desventura SF misfortune

desventuradamente ADV unfortunately

desventurado/a Ⓐ ADJ [1] (= *desgraciado*) [*persona*] unfortunate; [*viaje, encuentro*] ill-fated
[2] (= *tímido*) timid, shy
[3] (= *tacaño*) mean
Ⓑ SM/F wretch, unfortunate; **algún ~** some poor wretch *o* unfortunate

desvergonzado/a Ⓐ ADJ [1] (= *sin vergüenza*) shameless
[2] (= *descarado*) insolent
Ⓑ SM/F (= *no vergonzoso*) shameless person; (= *descarado*) insolent person

desvergonzarse ▸conjug 1f y 1l◂ VPR [1] (= *perder la vergüenza*) to lose all sense of shame
[2] (= *insolentarse*) to be impertinent, be insolent (**con** to), behave in a shameless way (**con** towards)
[3] **~ a pedir algo** to have the nerve to ask for sth, dare to ask for sth

desvergüenza SF [1] (= *mala conducta*) shamelessness
[2] (= *descaro*) effrontery, impudence; **esto es una ~** this is disgraceful, this is shameful; **¡qué ~!** what a nerve*!; **tener la ~ de hacer algo** to have the impudence *o* nerve* to do sth

desvertebración SF [1] (*Med*) dislocation
[2] (= *trastorno*) disruption

desvertebrado ADJ lacking cohesion, disorganized

desvertebrar ▸conjug 1a◂ VT [1] to dislocate
[2] (= *trastornar*) [+ *planes*] to disrupt, upset; [+ *pandilla*] to break up

desvestir ▸conjug 3k◂ Ⓐ VT to undress
Ⓑ **desvestirse** VPR to undress

desviación SF [1] (= *separación*) [*de trayectoria*] deviation (**de** from); [*de golpe, disparo*] deflection (**de** from); **es una ~ de sus principios** it is a deviation *o* departure from his principles

► **desviación de columna** abnormal curvature of the spine ► **desviación de fondos** diversion of funds ► **desviación normal** standard deviation
[2] (*Aut*) diversion ► **desviación de la circulación** traffic diversion

desviacionismo SM deviationism

desviacionista ADJ, SMF deviationist

desviadero SM (*Ferro*) siding

desviado ADJ [1] (= *apartado*) [*trayectoria*] oblique; [*bala*] deflected
[2] [*prácticas, conducta*] deviant
[3] [*lugar*] remote, off the beaten track; **~ de algo** remote from sth, away from sth

desviar ▸conjug 1c◂ Ⓐ VT [1] (= *apartar*) [+ *balón, flecha*] to deflect; [+ *golpe*] to parry; [+ *pregunta*] to evade; [+ *ojos*] to avert, turn away; [+ *tren*] to switch, switch into a siding; [+ *avión, circulación*] to divert (**por** through); **~ el cauce de un río** to alter the course of *o* divert a river; **~ la conversación** to change the subject; **~ el balón a córner** to send the ball out for a corner
[2] [+ *persona*] **lo ~on de su propósito** they dissuaded him from his intention; **~ a algn de su vocación** to turn sb from their vocation; **~ a algn de las malas compañías** to wean sb away from bad company; ✦**MODISMO** **~ a algn del buen camino** to lead sb astray
Ⓑ **desviarse** VPR [1] (*de camino*) [*persona*] to turn aside, turn away (**de** from); [*carretera*] to branch off; **~se de un tema** to stray off a subject; **tomamos la primera salida que se desviaba de la carretera de la costa** we took the first turning off the coastal road
[2] (*Náut*) to sail off course
[3] (*Aut*) to make a detour

desvincular ▸conjug 1a◂ Ⓐ VT to dissociate
Ⓑ **desvincularse** VPR [1] (= *aislarse*) to be cut off
[2] (= *alejarse*) to cut o.s. off (**de** from)

desvío SM [1] [*de trayectoria, orientación*] deflection (**de** from), deviation (**de** from)
[2] (*Aut*) (= *rodeo*) detour; (*por obras*) diversion
[3] (*Ferro*) siding

desvirgar ▸conjug 1h◂ VT [1] [+ *virgen*] to deflower (*liter*); **se casó con el hombre que la desvirgó** she married the man to whom she lost her virginity
[2] (*) = **estrenar**

desvirtuar ▸conjug 1e◂ Ⓐ VT [+ *argumento, razonamiento*] to detract from; [+ *efecto*] to counteract; [+ *sentido*] to distort; **la cláusula secreta desvirtuó el objetivo del tratado** the secret clause nullified the aim of the treaty
Ⓑ **desvirtuarse** VPR (= *estropearse*) to go off

desvitalizado ADJ dull, lifeless

desvitalizar ▸conjug 1f◂ Ⓐ VT [+ *nervio*] to numb
Ⓑ **desvitalizarse** VPR to flag

desvivirse ▸conjug 3a◂ VPR **~ por algo** (= *desear*) to crave sth, long for sth; (= *chiflarse por*) to be crazy about sth; **~ por los amigos** to do anything for one's friends; **~ por salir** to be dying to go out; **se desvivía por ayudarme** he used to go out of his way to help me

desyerba SF, **desyerbo** SM (*LAm*) weeding

desyerbar ▸conjug 1a◂ VT = **desherbar**

detal(l): **al ~** ADV retail

detalladamente ADV [1] (= *con detalles*) in detail
[2] (= *extensamente*) at great length

detallado ADJ [*informe, relato*] detailed; [*declaración*] circumstantial; [*conocimiento*] detailed, intimate

detallar ▸conjug 1a◂ VT [1] (= *contar con detalles*) to detail; (*en una lista, factura*) to itemize
[2] [+ *cuento*] to tell in detail
[3] (*Com*) to retail

detalle SM [1] (= *pormenor*) detail; **al ~** in detail; **con todo ~** ◊ **con todos los ~s** in full detail; **para más ~s vea ...** for further details see ...; **hasta en sus menores ~s** down to the last detail; **no pierde ~** he doesn't miss a trick; **me observaba sin perder ~** he watched my every move
[2] (= *atención*) nice gesture; **¡qué ~!** what a nice gesture, how thoughtful!; **tiene muchos ~s** he is very considerate *o* thoughtful; **lo que importa es el ~** it's the thought that counts; **es el primer ~ que te veo en mucho tiempo** it's the first sign of consideration I've had from you in a long time
[3] (= *regalo*) small gift
[4] (*Com*) **al ~** retail *antes de s*; **vender al ~** to retail; **comercio al ~** retail trade
[5] (*Fin*) (= *estado de cuenta*) statement; (= *factura*) bill

detallismo SM attention to detail, care for the details

detallista Ⓐ ADJ [1] (= *meticuloso*) meticulous
[2] (*Com*) retail *antes de s*; **comercio ~** retail trade
Ⓑ SMF [1] (= *meticuloso*) perfectionist
[2] (*Com*) retailer, retail trader

detalloso* ADJ kind, thoughtful

detección SF detection

detectable ADJ detectable

detectar ▸conjug 1a◂ VT to detect

detective SMF detective ► **detective privado/a** private detective

detectivesco ADJ detective *antes de s*; **dotes detectivescas** gifts as a detective

detector SM detector ► **detector de humo** smoke detector ► **detector de incendios** fire detector ► **detector de mentiras** lie detector ► **detector de metales** metal detector ► **detector de minas** mine detector

detención SF [1] (= *parada*) [*de una acción*] stoppage; (*con retraso*) holdup, delay; **una ~ de 15 minutos** a 15-minute delay ► **detención de juego** (*Dep*) stoppage
[2] (*Jur*) (= *arresto*) arrest; (= *prisión*) detention ► **detención cautelar** preventive detention ► **detención domiciliaria** house arrest ► **detención en masa** mass arrest ► **detención ilegal** unlawful detention ► **detención preventiva** police custody
[3] (= *cuidado*) care

detener ▸conjug 2k◂ Ⓐ VT [1] (= *parar*) to stop; **me detuvo en la calle** he stopped me in the street
[2] (= *retrasar*) to hold up, delay; **~ el progreso de algo** to hold up the progress of sth; **no quiero ~lo** I don't want to keep *o* delay you
[3] (= *retener*) [+ *objeto*] to keep
[4] (*Jur*) (= *arrestar*) to arrest; (= *encarcelar*) to detain
Ⓑ **detenerse** VPR [1] (= *pararse*) to stop; **¡no te detengas!** don't hang about!; **se detuvo a mirarlo** he stopped to look at it
[2] (= *demorarse*) to waste time (**en** on); **se detiene mucho en eso** he's taking a long time over that

detenidamente ADV [1] (= *minuciosamente*) carefully, thoroughly
[2] (= *extensamente*) at great length

detenido/a Ⓐ ADJ [1] (*Jur*) (*por poco tiempo*) arrested, under arrest; (*por más tiempo*) in custody
[2] (= *sin prisa*) [*narración, estudio*] detailed; [*análisis, examen*] thorough; [*visita*] unhurried, leisurely
[3] (= *tímido*) timid
[4] (= *tacaño*) mean, niggardly
Ⓑ SM/F (*en comisaría*) person under arrest; (*en cárcel*) prisoner

detenimiento SM care; **con ~** thoroughly

detentar ▸conjug 1a◂ VT [1] (*Dep*) [+ *récord*] to hold
[2] (= *poseer*) [+ *título*] to hold unlawfully; [+ *puesto*] to occupy unlawfully

detentor(a) SM/F (*Dep*) holder; **~(a) de marca** record holder; **~(a) de trofeo** cup holder, champion

detergente ADJ, SM detergent

deterger ▸conjug 2c◂ VT [+ *objeto*] to clean, clean of grease; [+ *herida*] to clean; [+ *plato*] to clean with detergent

deteriorado ADJ [1] [*edificio, mueble*] dilapidated
[2] [*ropa, alfombra*] worn

deteriorar ▸conjug 1a◂ Ⓐ VT [1] (= *estropear*) to damage; **la falta de medios puede ~ la calidad de la enseñanza** the lack of resources could harm *o* damage the quality of education
[2] (*Mec*) to cause wear and tear to
Ⓑ **deteriorarse** VPR [1] (= *estropearse*) to get damaged
[2] (= *empeorarse*) **su salud se está deteriorando** her health is getting worse *o* deteriorating; **las relaciones entre ambos países se han deteriorado** relations between the two countries have deteriorated
[3] (*Mec*) to wear, get worn

deterioro SM [1] (= *daño*) damage; **en caso de ~ de las mercancías** should the goods be damaged in any way; **sin ~ de sus derechos** without affecting his rights, without impinging on his rights (*más frm*)
[2] (= *empeoramiento*) deterioration
[3] (*Mec*) wear and tear

determinable ADJ determinable; **fácilmente ~** easy to determine

determinación SF [1] (= *decisión*) decision; **tomar una ~** to take a decision
[2] (= *valentía*) determination, resolution; **actuar con ~** to take determined action, act decisively
[3] [*de fecha, precio*] fixing

determinado ADJ [1] (= *preciso*) certain; **un día ~** on a certain *o* given day; **en momentos ~s** at certain times; **hay ~s límites** there are certain limits; **no hay ningún tema ~** there is no particular theme
[2] [*persona*] determined, resolute
[3] (*Ling*) [*artículo*] definite
[4] (*Mat*) determinate

determinante ADJ, SM determinant

determinar ▸conjug 1a◂ Ⓐ VT [1] (= *establecer*) to determine; **el gen que determi-**

na el color de los ojos the gene which determines eye colour; **~on un precio tras largas negociaciones** after lengthy negotiations they determined *o* fixed a price; **"precio por ~"** "price to be agreed"; **~ el rumbo** (*Aer, Náut*) to set a course; **el reglamento determina que …** the rule lays down *o* states that …
[2] (= *averiguar*) [+ *peso, volumen, causa*] to determine; [+ *daños*] to assess; **la policía logró ~ la verdad del asunto** the police succeeded in determining the truth of the matter
[3] (= *motivar*) to bring about, cause; **aquello determinó la caída del gobierno** that brought about *o* caused the fall of the government
[4] (= *decidir*) to decide; **~on asignarle más fondos al proyecto** they decided to allocate more funds to the project; **esto la determinó a continuar sus estudios** this decided her to continue with her studies
[5] (*Ling*) to determine
Ⓑ **determinarse** VPR (= *decidirse*) to decide, make up one's mind; **debe ~se por un médico u otro** you must decide on one doctor or another; **~se a hacer algo** to determine to do sth, decide to do sth

determinativo Ⓐ ADJ determinative
Ⓑ SM (*Ling*) determiner

determinismo SM determinism

determinista Ⓐ ADJ deterministic
Ⓑ SMF determinist

detersión SF cleansing

detestable ADJ [*persona*] hateful; [*costumbre*] detestable; [*sabor, tiempo*] foul

detestablemente ADV detestably

detestación SF detestation, hatred, loathing

➤ **detestar** ▸conjug 1a◂ VT to detest, loathe

detonación SF (= *acción*) detonation; (= *ruido*) explosion

detonador SM detonator

detonante Ⓐ ADJ explosive
Ⓑ SM [1] (= *explosivo*) explosive
[2] (= *causa*) trigger (**de** for); **eso fue el ~ de la crisis** that was what sparked off *o* triggered the crisis

detonar ▸conjug 1a◂ VI to detonate, explode

detracción SF disparagement

detractor(a) Ⓐ ADJ disparaging
Ⓑ SM/F detractor

detraer ▸conjug 2o◂ VT [1] (= *quitar*) to remove, separate, take away
[2] (= *desviar*) to turn aside
[3] (= *denigrar*) to disparage; (*Pol*) to knock*

detrás ADV [1] (= *en la parte posterior*) **el jardín está ~** the garden is at the back; **tiene una cremallera ~** it has a zip at the back; **en el coche me gusta sentarme ~** when I'm in the car I like to sit in the back; **los más altos que se pongan ~** can the tallest ones please stand at the back?; **yo estaba delante y él ~** I was in front and he was behind; **de ~**: **el asesino salió de ~** the murderer came out from behind; **los alumnos de ~ estaban fumando** the pupils at the back were smoking; **por ~**: **la atacaron por ~** she was attacked from behind; **siempre critica a sus amigos por ~** he's always criticizing his friends behind their backs; **la foto lleva una dedicatoria (por) ~** the photo has a dedication on the back
[2] (= *a continuación*) **primero el apellido y ~ el nombre** first the surname and then the forename; **paso yo delante y tú vienes ~** I'll go first and you follow; **entraron en el cuarto uno ~ de otro** they went into the room one after the other
[3] **~ de** behind; **~ del edificio** behind the building; **¿quién está ~ de este complot?** who's behind this plot?, who's behind all this?; **Susana anda ~ de Antonio** Susana's after Antonio; **por ~ de** behind; **dos puestos por ~ del Atlético** two places behind Atlético; **la carretera pasa por ~ del parque** the road goes behind the park
[4] **~ mío/tuyo** (*esp LAm**) behind me/you; **se colocó ~ nuestro** he stood behind us

detrasito* ADV (*LAm*) behind

detrimente ADJ detrimental

detrimento SM detriment; **lo hizo sin ~ de su dignidad** he did it without detriment to his dignity; **en ~ de algo** to the detriment of sth

detrito SM, **detritus** SM [1] (*Geol*) detritus
[2] (= *desechos*) debris

detuve *etc ver* **detener**

deuda SF [1] (= *obligación*) debt; **una ~ de gratitud** a debt of gratitude; **estar en ~ con algn** (= *estar agradecido*) to be indebted to sb
[2] (*Com*) debt; **contraer ~s** to get into debt; **estar lleno de ~s** to be heavily in debt; **estar en ~ con algn** (= *deber dinero*) to be in debt to sb ► **deuda a largo plazo** long-term debt ► **deuda exterior, deuda externa** foreign debt ► **deuda incobrable** bad debt ► **deuda morosa** bad debt ► **deuda pública** national debt, public borrowing ► **deudas activas** assets ► **deudas pasivas** liabilities
[3] (*Rel*) **perdónanos nuestras ~s** forgive us our trespasses *o* sins

deudo/a SM/F relative

deudor(a) Ⓐ ADJ [1] **saldo ~** debit balance
[2] **le soy muy ~** I am greatly indebted to you
Ⓑ SM/F debtor ► **deudor(a) hipotecario/a** mortgager ► **deudor(a) moroso/a** slow payer

deuterio SM (*Quím*) deuterium

devalar ▸conjug 1a◂ VI (*Náut*) to drift off course

devaluación SF devaluation

devaluar ▸conjug 1e◂ VT to devalue, devaluate (*EEUU*)

devaluatorio ADJ **tendencia devaluatoria** tendency to depreciate, tendency to lose value

devanadera SF (*Cos*) reel, spool

devanado SM (*Elec*) winding

devanador SM (= *carrete*) spool, bobbin

devanar ▸conjug 1a◂ Ⓐ VT [1] [+ *hilo*] to wind
[2] [*araña, gusano*] to spin
Ⓑ **devanarse** VPR [1] **~se los sesos** to rack one's brains
[2] (*Méx*) **~se de dolor** to double up with pain; **~se de risa** to double up with laughter

devanear ▸conjug 1a◂ VI to rave, talk nonsense

devaneo SM [1] (= *fruslería*) idle pursuit
[2] (= *amorío*) flirtation
[3] (*Med*) delirium

devastación SF devastation

devastador ADJ devastating

devastadoramente ADV devastatingly

devastar ▸conjug 1a◂ VT to devastate

devengado ADJ (*Fin*) [*intereses*] accrued; [*sueldo*] due, outstanding

devengar ▸conjug 1h◂ VT [1] [+ *intereses*] to yield, pay
[2] [+ *sueldo*] (= *ganar*) to earn; (= *tener que cobrar*) to be due

devengo SM [1] (= *beneficio*) amount earned
[2] **devengos** (= *ingresos*) income *sing*

devenir ▸conjug 3r◂ Ⓐ VI **~ en algo** to become sth, turn into sth
Ⓑ SM [1] (= *movimiento progresivo*) process of development; **una nación en perpetuo ~** a nation which is changing all the time, a nation in a constant process of development
[2] (= *transformación*) transformation

devoción SF [1] (*Rel*) devotion, devoutness; **la ~ a esta imagen** the veneration of this image; **con ~** devoutly; *ver* **santo B2**
[2] (= *admiración*) devotion (**a** to); **sienten ~ por su madre** they are devoted to their mother; **tener gran ~ a algn** to be absolutely devoted to sb; **tener por ~ hacer algo** to be in the habit of doing sth; ✦*MODISMO* **estar a la ~ de algn** to be completely under sb's thumb
[3] (= *práctica religiosa*) devotion, religious observance

devocional ADJ devotional

devocionario SM prayer book

devolución SF [1] [*de algo prestado, robado*] return; **nos pidió por escrito la ~ de los libros** he wrote asking for the books to be returned; **consiguieron la ~ de las joyas** they managed to get the jewels back
[2] (*Com*) [*de compra*] return; [*de dinero*] refund; **exigimos la ~ del dinero** we demand a refund; **"no se admiten devoluciones"** "no refunds will be given", "no goods returnable"; **sin ~** non-returnable ► **devolución de derechos** (*Fin*) drawback ► **devolución de impuestos** tax refund
[3] (*Jur, Pol*) [*de poder, territorio*] devolution
[4] [*de favor, visita*] return

devolver ▸conjug 2h◂ (*pp* **devuelto**) Ⓐ VT [1] (= *retornar*) [+ *algo prestado, robado*] to give back, return; [+ *carta, llamada, pelota, golpe*] to return; [+ *polizón, refugiado*] to return, send back; **¿cuándo tienes que ~ esos libros?** when do you have to take back *o* return those books?; **consiguió que le devolvieran las joyas** he managed to get the jewels back; **leyó la nota y se la devolvió** she read the note and handed *o* gave it back to him; **si nos devuelve el envase le descontamos 50 céntimos** if you bring back *o* return the container you'll get a 50-cent discount; **"devuélvase al remitente"** "return to sender"; **le devolvió la bofetada** she slapped him back; **devuelve el florero a su sitio** put the vase back in its place; ✦*MODISMOS* **~ la pelota a algn** to give sb tit for tat; **~ mal por bien** to return bad for good
[2] (*Com*) [2·1] (= *rechazar*) [+ *producto, mercancía*] (*en mano*) to take back, return; (*por correo*) to send back, return; **devolvió el abrigo a la tienda** he took the coat back to the shop, he returned the coat to the shop; **si a su hijo no le gusta lo puede ~** if your son doesn't like it you can return it *o* bring it back; **si desea ~lo, usted se hace cargo de los gastos del envío** if you choose to send it back *o* return it you have to pay the postage
[2·2] (= *reembolsar*) [+ *dinero*] (*de una compra*) to

➤ LENGUA Y USO: detestar 34.3

refund, give back; (*de un préstamo*) to pay back; **si no está satisfecho con la compra le devolvemos su dinero** if you are not satisfied with your purchase we will refund your money *o* give you your money back; **¿cuándo me vas a ~ el dinero que te presté?** when are you going to pay me back *o* give me back the money I lent you?; **la máquina me devolvía las monedas** the machine rejected my coins

2·3 [+ *cambio*] to give, give back; **me tiene que ~ cuatro euros** you have to give me back four euros, you owe me four euros; **estoy esperando que me devuelva el cambio** I'm waiting for my change; **"no devuelve cambio"** "no change given"

2·4 (*Fin*) [+ *cheque sin fondos*] to return

3 (= *corresponder*) [+ *cumplido, favor*] to return; **¿cuándo me vais a ~ la visita?** when are you going to pay a return visit *o* to return the visit?; **¿cómo podría ~te este favor?** how can I ever return this favour?

4 (= *restituir*) 4·1 [+ *salud, vista*] to restore, give back; **un sueñecito te ~á la energía** a nap will give you your energy back

4·2 (*a su estado original*) to restore; **el nuevo tratado ha devuelto la paz a la zona** the new treaty has restored peace to the area; **el sonido del teléfono me devolvió a la realidad** the sound of the telephone brought me back to reality

5 (*liter*) [+ *imagen*] to reflect; **el espejo nos devolvía una imagen distorsionada** the mirror reflected a distorted image of us

6 (= *vomitar*) to bring up

Ⓑ VI (= *vomitar*) to be sick; **creo que voy a ~** I think I'm going to be sick

Ⓒ **devolverse** VPR (*LAm*) (= *regresar*) to turn back

devorador ADJ [*pasión*] devouring; [*fuego*] all-consuming; [*hambre*] ravenous

devorar ▸conjug 1a◂ VT 1 (= *comer ávidamente*) [*animal*] to devour; [*persona*] to devour, wolf down*; **este coche devora los kilómetros** this car eats up the miles; **devora las novelas de amor** she laps up love stories; **la devoraba con la mirada** (*con cólera*) he looked at her as if he could kill her; (*con deseo*) he devoured her with his eyes

2 (= *destruir*) [+ *fortuna*] to run through; **todo lo devoró el fuego** the fire consumed everything; **lo devoran los celos** he is consumed with jealousy

devotamente ADV devoutly

devoto/a Ⓐ ADJ 1 (*Rel*) [*persona*] devout; [*obra*] devotional; **ser muy ~ de un santo** to have a special devotion to a saint; ✦**MODISMO ser ~ de la Virgen del puño** (*hum*) to be tight-fisted

2 (= *apegado, fiel*) devoted (**de** to); **su ~ amigo** your devoted friend; **su ~ servidor** (*frm*) your devoted servant; **es muy ~ de ese café** he is a big fan of that café

Ⓑ SM/F 1 (*Rel*) devout person; **los ~s** the faithful; (*en iglesia*) the congregation *sing*

2 (= *aficionado*) devotee; **la artista y sus ~s** the artist and her devotees *o* fans; **los ~s del ajedrez** devotees of chess

devuelto Ⓐ PP *de* **devolver**

Ⓑ SM (*) sick, vomit

dextrosa SF dextrose

deyección SF (*tb* **deyecciones**) 1 (*Med*) (= *acto*) motion; (= *heces*) excretion

2 (*Geol*) [*de avalancha*] debris; [*de erupción volcánica*] ejecta *pl*

deyectar ▸conjug 1a◂ VT (*Geol*) to deposit, leave, lay down

D.F. ABR (*Méx*) = **Distrito Federal**

Dg ABR = **decagramo(s)**

dg ABR (= **decigramo(s)**) dg

D.G. ABR 1 = **Dirección General**

2 (= **Director General**) DG

DGS SF ABR (*Esp*) 1 (= **Dirección General de Seguridad**) *national police headquarters*

2 (= **Dirección General de Sanidad**) ≈ Department of Health

DGT SF ABR 1 = **Dirección General de Tráfico**

2 = **Dirección General de Turismo**

dho. ABR (= **dicho**) aforesaid

di *etc ver* **dar, decir**

día SM 1 (= *período de 24 horas*) day; **pasaré un par de ~s en la playa** I'll spend a couple of days at the beach; **todos los ~s** every day; **pollitos de un ~** day-old chicks; **a los pocos ~s** within *o* after a few days, a few days later; **~ a ~** day in day out, day by day; **prefiero el ~ a ~** I prefer to do things from one day to the next *o* on a day-to-day basis; **el ~ a ~ en la gestión financiera de la empresa** the day-to-day running of the company's financial business; **siete veces al ~** seven times a day; **tres horas al ~** three hours a day; **al otro ~** the following day; **al ~ siguiente** the following day; **ese problema es ya de ~s** that's an old problem; **menú del ~** today's menu; **pan del ~** fresh bread; **de ~ en ~** from day to day; **~ (de) por medio** (*LAm*) every other day, on alternate days; **ocho ~s** a week; **quince ~s** a fortnight; **un ~ sí y otro no** every other day; **~ tras ~** day after day; ✦**MODISMOS a ~s** at times; **cuatro ~s** a couple of days, a few days; **todo el santo ~** the whole blessed day; **no tener más que el ~ y la noche** not to have two pennies to rub together ► **día azul** (*Ferro*) *cheap ticket day* ► **día de asueto** day off ► **día de ayuno** fast day ► **día de boda** wedding day ► **día de detención** quiet day ► **día de diario**, **día de entresemana** weekday ► **día de fiesta** holiday, public holiday ► **día de inactividad** quiet day ► **día de la banderita** flag day ► **Día de la Hispanidad** Columbus Day (*12 October*) ► **día de la Madre** Mother's Day ► **Día de la Raza** = **Día de la Hispanidad** ► **día del espectador** *day each week when cinema tickets are discounted* ► **día del Juicio (Final)** Judgment Day; **estaremos aquí hasta el ~ del Juicio** (*iró*) we'll be here till Kingdom come ► **Día de los Difuntos** All Souls' Day, Day of the Dead ► **día de los enamorados** St Valentine's Day ► **día de los inocentes** ≈ April Fools' Day (*1 April*) ► **Día de (los) Muertos** (*Méx*) All Souls' Day, Day of the Dead ► **día de paga** pay day ► **Día de Reyes** Epiphany (*6 January*) ► **día de trabajo** working day ► **día de tribunales** *day on which courts are open* ► **día de vigilia** day of abstinence ► **día feriado**, **día festivo** holiday, public holiday ► **día franco** (*Mil*) day's leave ► **día hábil** working day ► **día inhábil** non-working day ► **día laborable** working day ► **día lectivo** teaching day ► **día libre** day off ► **día malo**, **día nulo** off day ► **días de gracia** (*Com*) days of grace ► **día señalado** (*gen*) special day; (*en calendario*) red-letter day ► **día útil** working day, weekday;

→ DÍA DE LOS (SANTOS) INOCENTES, DÍA DE REYES

2 (= *no noche*) daytime; **durante el ~** during the day(time); **en pleno ~** in broad daylight; **hace buen ~** the weather's good today, it's a fine day; **¡buenos ~s!** ◊ **¡buen ~!** (*Cono Sur*) good morning!; **dar los buenos ~s a algn** to say good morning to sb; **de ~** by day, during the day; **duerme de ~ y trabaja de noche** he sleeps by day and works by night, he sleeps during the day and works at night; **ya es de ~** it's already light; **mientras sea de ~** while it's still light; **~ y noche** night and day

3 (= *fecha*) date; **¿qué ~ es hoy?** (*del mes*) what's the date today?; (*de la semana*) what day is it today?; **iré pronto, pero no puedo precisar el ~** I'll be going soon, but I can't give an exact date; **llegará el ~ dos de mayo** he'll arrive on the second of May; **hoy, ~ cinco de agosto** today, fifth August; **~ lunes/martes** *etc* (*LAm*) Monday/Tuesday *etc*; **el ~ de hoy** today; **el ~ de mañana** (*lit*) tomorrow; (*fig*) at some future date

4 (= *momento sin precisar*) **algún ~** some day; **un buen ~** one fine day; **cada ~ es peor** it's getting worse every day *o* by the day; **un ~ de éstos** one of these days; **el ~ menos pensado** when you least expect it; **en los ~s de la reina Victoria** in Queen Victoria's day, in Queen Victoria's times; **cualquier ~ (de estos)** one of these days; **cualquier ~ tendrá un accidente** he's going to have an accident one of these days *o* any day now; **¡cualquier ~!** (*iró*) not on your life!; **cualquier ~ viene** (*iró*) we'll be waiting till the cows come home for him to turn up; **¡cualquier ~ te voy a comprar una casa!** if you think I'm going to buy you a house you've got another think coming!; **en nuestros ~s** nowadays; **la prensa de nuestros ~s** today's press, the press these days; **uno de los principales problemas de nuestros ~s** one of the major problems of our day *o* our times; **ha durado hasta nuestros ~s** it has lasted to the present day; **otro ~** some other day, another day; **dejémoslo para otro ~** let's leave it for the moment *o* for another day; **¡hasta otro ~!** so long!; ✦**MODISMOS de un ~ para otro** any day now; **en ~s de Dios** *o* **del mundo** *o* **de la vida** never; **en su ~** (*referido al futuro*) in due course; (*referido al pasado*) in its/their *etc* day; **¡tal ~ hará un año!*** a fat lot I care!*; *ver tb* **hoy**

5 (= *actualidad*) **del ~** [*estilo*] fashionable, up-to-date; (= *fresco*) **pescado del ~** fresh fish; **estar al ~** (= *actualizado*) to be up to date; (= *de moda*) to be with it; **quien quiera estar al ~ en esta especialidad, que lea ...** anyone who wishes to keep up to date with this area of study, should read ...; **está al ~ vestir así** it's the thing to dress like that; **poner al ~** [+ *texto, contabilidad*] to bring up to date; [+ *base de datos*] to update; [+ *diario*] to write up; **ponerse al ~ (en algo)** to get up to date (with sth); **vivir al ~** to live from one day to the next

diabetes SF INV diabetes

diabético/a ADJ, SM/F diabetic

diabla SF, **diablesa** SF she-devil; ✦**MODISMO a la ~** carelessly, any old how*

diablillo* SM little devil, little monkey; **esta niña es un ~** this girl is a little imp

diablo SM [1] (= *demonio*) devil; **el ~ tentó a Jesús** the Devil tempted Jesus; **no le hagas caso, es un pobre ~** don't pay any attention to him, the poor devil; ✦*MODISMOS* **como un ~***: **esta mesa pesa como un ~** this table weighs a ton*; **del ~ o de mil ~s***: **hace un frío del ~ o de mil ~s** it's hellishly cold*, it's absolutely freezing; **¡~s! o ¡por todos los ~s!*** damn it!*, oh hell!*; **donde el ~ perdió el poncho** (*Cono Sur**) in some godforsaken spot*, in the back of beyond*; **irse al ~***: **el proyecto se fue al ~** the project was a miserable failure, the project failed miserably; **¡vete al ~!** get lost!*; **mandar al ~***: **no podía arreglarlo y lo mandé al ~** I couldn't fix it so I chucked it the hell away*; **se enfadó y nos mandó al ~** he got mad and told us to go to hell*; ✦*REFRÁN* **más sabe el ~ por viejo que por ~** there's no substitute for experience ► **diablos azules** (*LAm*) DTs*, pink elephants*; *ver tb* **demonio** *para otras frases*

[2] (*) (*como intensificador*) **¿cómo ~s se le ocurrió hacer tal cosa?** what on earth *o* what the hell made him do such a thing?*; **¿quién ~s te crees que eres?** who on earth *o* who the hell do you think you are?; **¡qué ~s! ¡yo también quiero ser rico!** damn it, I want to be rich too!*

[3] (*Cono Sur*) (= *carro*) heavy oxcart

diablura SF [1] (= *travesura*) prank

[2] **diabluras** (= *maldades*) mischief *sing*

diabólicamente ADV diabolically, fiendishly

diabólico ADJ [*palabras, rito*] diabolic, satanic; (= *malvado*) diabolical; (= *muy difícil*) fiendishly difficult; **tiene una escritura diabólica** his writing is fiendishly hard to understand

diábolo SM diabolo

diacho* SM (*euf*) = **diablo**

diaconato SM deaconry, diaconate

diaconía SF [1] (= *distrito*) deaconry

[2] (= *casa*) deacon's house

diaconisa SF deaconess

diácono SM deacon

diacrítico ADJ diacritic, diacritical; **signo ~** diacritic, diacritical mark

diacrónico ADJ diachronic

Diada SF *Catalan national day (11th September)*

> **DIADA NACIONAL DE CATALUNYA**
>
> *The* **Diada**, *or Catalonia's national day, is celebrated on 11 September to commemorate the fall of Barcelona to the Bourbon Philip V in 1714 at the end of the War of the Spanish Succession. Prior to this Catalonia had enjoyed a high degree of autonomy which it lost, along with its government, the* **Generalitat**. *For the* **Diada** *streets and balconies all over Catalonia are decked out with the Catalan flag with its four red stripes on a gold background.*

diadema SF [1] (*para el pelo*) diadem

[2] (= *de joyas*) tiara

diafanidad SF [*de cristal, agua*] transparency; [*de tejido*] filminess

diáfano ADJ [1] (= *translúcido*) [*agua*] crystal-clear, crystalline (*liter*); [*cristal*] translucent; [*tela*] diaphanous

[2] [*argumento, explicación*] crystal-clear; **es ~ que …** it is absolutely clear that …

[3] [*espacio*] open

diafragma SM [1] (*Anat*) diaphragm

[2] (= *anticonceptivo*) diaphragm, cap

[3] (*Fot*) diaphragm

diagnosis SF INV diagnosis

diagnóstica SF diagnostics *sing*

diagnosticar ▸conjug 1g◂ VT to diagnose

diagnóstico Ⓐ ADJ diagnostic

Ⓑ SM diagnosis ► **diagnóstico precoz** early diagnosis

diagonal ADJ, SF diagonal; **traza una ~** draw a diagonal line

diagonalmente ADV diagonally

diagrama SM diagram ► **diagrama circular** pie chart ► **diagrama de barras** bar chart ► **diagrama de bloques** block diagram ► **diagrama de dispersión** scatter diagram ► **diagrama de flujo** flow chart

dial SM (*Aut, Radio*) dial

dialectal ADJ dialectal, dialect *antes de s*

dialectalismo SM [1] (= *carácter*) dialectal nature, dialectalism; **un texto lleno de ~** a text containing a lot of dialect

[2] (= *palabra*) dialectalism, dialect word *o* phrase *etc*

dialéctica SF [1] (= *enfrentamiento*) dialectic

[2] (*Fil*) dialectics *pl*

dialéctico ADJ dialectical

dialecto SM dialect

dialectología SF dialectology

dialectólogo/a SM/F dialectologist

diálisis SF INV dialysis

dialogante Ⓐ ADJ open to dialogue *o* (*EEUU*) dialog, willing to discuss

Ⓑ SMF participant (*in a discussion*); **mi ~** the person I was talking to

dialogar ▸conjug 1h◂ Ⓐ VT to write in dialogue *o* (*EEUU*) dialog form

Ⓑ VI (= *conversar*) to have a conversation; **~ con algn** to engage in a dialogue *o* (*EEUU*) dialog with sb

diálogo SM [1] (= *conversación*) conversation; (*Pol*) dialogue; ✦*MODISMOS* **~ de sordos**: **fue un ~ de sordos** nobody listened to what anyone else had to say, it was a dialogue of the deaf; **ser un ~ para besugos** to be a fatuous exchange ► **diálogo norte-sur** North-South dialogue

[2] (*Literat*) dialogue, dialog (*EEUU*)

diamante SM [1] (= *joya*) diamond; **una pulsera de ~s** a diamond bracelet; ✦*MODISMO* **ser un ~ en bruto** to be a rough diamond ► **diamante de imitación** imitation diamond ► **diamante en bruto** uncut diamond ► **diamante falso** paste

[2] **diamantes** (*Naipes*) diamonds

diamantífero ADJ diamond-bearing

diamantino ADJ [1] (= *de diamante*) diamond-like, adamantine

[2] (= *reluciente*) glittering

diamantista SMF [1] (*Téc*) diamond cutter

[2] (*Com*) diamond merchant

diametral ADJ diametrical

diametralmente ADV diametrically; **~ opuesto a algo** diametrically opposed to sth

diámetro SM diameter; **faros de gran ~** wide-angle headlights ► **diámetro de giro** (*Aut*) turning circle

Diana SF Diana

diana SF [1] (= *centro de blanco*) bull's-eye; **dar en la ~ o hacer ~** (*lit*) to score a bull's-eye; (*fig*) to hit home

[2] [*de dardos*] dartboard

[3] (*Mil*) reveille; **tocar ~** to sound reveille

diantre SM **¡diantre!*** (*euf*) dash it!; **los había como un ~** (*Cono Sur*) there were the devil of a lot of them, there were loads of them

diapasón SM (*Mús*) [1] (= *tono*) (*al afinar*) diapason range; [*de voz*] tone; **bajar el ~** to lower one's voice; **subir el ~** to raise one's voice

[2] (= *instrumento*) (*para afinar*) tuning fork; (*de violín, guitarra*) fingerboard ► **diapasón normal** tuning fork

diapositiva SF [1] (*Fot*) slide ► **diapositiva en color** colour slide, color slide (*EEUU*)

[2] [*de vidrio*] lantern slide

diariamente ADV daily, every day

diariero SM (*Arg*) paperboy

diario Ⓐ ADJ [1] (= *todos los días*) daily; **tienen peleas diarias** they have arguments every day; **gastos ~s** everyday expenses

[2] (= *cada día*) a day; **cien dólares ~s** a hundred dollars a day

Ⓑ ADV (*LAm*) every day, daily

Ⓒ SM [1] (= *periódico*) newspaper, daily ► **diario de la mañana** morning paper ► **diario dominical** Sunday paper ► **diario hablado** (*Radio*) news, news bulletin ► **diario matinal** morning paper ► **diario vespertino** evening paper

[2] (= *libro*) diary ► **diario de a bordo** logbook ► **diario de entradas y salidas** (*Com*) daybook ► **diario de navegación** logbook ► **diario de sesiones** parliamentary report

[3] (*Fin*) daily expenses *pl*

[4] **a ~** daily; **de o para ~** everyday; **nuestro mantel de ~** our everyday tablecloth

diarismo SM (*LAm*) journalism

diarista SMF [1] [*de libro diario*] diarist

[2] (*LAm*) [*de periódico*] newspaper owner, newspaper publisher

diarrea SF diarrhoea, diarrhea (*EEUU*)

diarrucho* SM (*LAm*) rag*; **los ~s** the gutter press

diáspora SF (= *dispersión*) diaspora; **la ~** (*Hist*) the Diaspora

diatónico ADJ diatonic

diatriba SF diatribe, tirade

dibujante SMF [1] (*Arte*) (*gen*) draughtsman/draughtswoman, draftsman/draftswoman (*EEUU*); [*de cómics, dibujos animados*] cartoonist; [*de esbozos*] sketcher; [*de moda*] designer ► **dibujante de publicidad** commercial artist

[2] (*Téc*) draughtsman/draughtswoman, draftsman/draftswoman (*EEUU*)

dibujar ▸conjug 1a◂ Ⓐ VT [1] (*Arte*) to draw, sketch

[2] (*Téc*) to design

[3] (= *describir*) to sketch, describe

Ⓑ **dibujarse** VPR [1] (= *perfilarse*) to be outlined (**contra** against)

[2] [*emoción*] (*de forma permanente*) to show; (*de forma temporal*) to appear; **el sufrimiento se dibujaba en su cara** suffering showed in his face; **una sonrisa se dibujó en sus labios** a smile appeared on his lips

dibujo SM [1] (= *actividad*) drawing ► **dibujo lineal, dibujo técnico** technical drawing

[2] (= *representación gráfica*) (*Arte*) drawing;

(*Téc*) design; (*en periódico*) cartoon ► **dibujo al carbón** charcoal drawing ► **dibujo a pulso** freehand drawing ► **dibujo del natural** drawing from life ► **dibujos animados** cartoons

3 (*en papel, tela*) pattern; **con ~ a rayas** with a striped pattern ► **dibujo escocés** tartan, tartan design

4 (= *descripción*) description, depiction

dic. ABR, **dic.**e ABR (= **diciembre**) Dec

dicción SF 1 (= *pronunciación*) diction

2 (= *palabra*) word

diccionario SM dictionary ► **diccionario bilingüe** bilingual dictionary ► **diccionario de bolsillo** pocket dictionary ► **diccionario enciclopédico** encyclop(a)edic dictionary ► **diccionario geográfico** gazetteer

diccionarista SMF lexicographer, dictionary maker

dicha SF 1 (= *felicidad*) happiness; **para completar su ~** to complete her happiness; **es una ~ poder ...** it is a happy thing to be able to ...

2 (= *suerte*) good luck; **por ~** fortunately

dicharachería SF wittiness, raciness

dicharachero/a Ⓐ ADJ 1 (= *gracioso*) witty

2 (= *parlanchín*) talkative

Ⓑ SM/F 1 (= *gracioso*) wit

2 (= *parlanchín*) chatterbox

dicharacho SM coarse remark

dicho Ⓐ PP **o ~ de otro modo ...** or, putting it another way, ..., or, in other words ...; **con esto queda todo ~** that says it all; **bueno, lo ~** OK, then; **dejar algo ~**: **le dejó ~ lo que tenía que hacer antes de irse** she gave him instructions as to what he should do before leaving; **antes de morir dejó ~ que la casa era para su hijo** before dying he gave instructions for the house to go to his son; **~ y hecho** no sooner said than done; **o mejor ~** or rather; **~ sea de paso** incidentally, by the way; *ver tb* **propiamente 1**

Ⓑ ADJ (= *este*) this; **quieren reformar la ley y para ~ propósito ...** they wish to reform the law and to this end ...; **y en la cuarta de dichas cartas ...** and in the fourth of these letters ...; **vamos a hablar de Cáceres: dicha ciudad fue construida en ...** and now we come to Caceres: the city was built in ...; **dicha compañía fue disuelta en 1994** this *o* the said company was dissolved in 1994

Ⓒ SM 1 (= *máxima popular*) saying; **como dice el ~** as the saying goes; ✦*REFRÁN* **del ~ al hecho hay mucho trecho** saying is one thing, doing it is another

2 (= *comentario*) remark; **un ~ desafortunado** an unfortunate remark

3 **dichos** (*Rel*) *betrothal pledge*; **tomarse los ~s** to exchange promises of marriage

dichosamente ADV luckily, fortunately

dichoso ADJ 1 (= *feliz*) happy; **hacer ~ a algn** to make sb happy; **me siento ~ de hacer algo** I feel privileged to do sth

2 (= *afortunado*) lucky, fortunate; **¡~s los ojos!** how nice to see you!

3 (*) blessed; **¡aquel ~ coche!** that blessed car!

diciembre SM December; *ver tb* **septiembre**

dicotomía SF dichotomy

dictablanda SF (*hum*) kindly dictatorship, benevolent despotism

dictado SM 1 dictation; **escribir al ~** to take dictation; **escribir algo al ~** to take sth down (*as it is dictated*)

2 **dictados** (= *imperativos*) dictates; **los ~s de la conciencia** the dictates of (one's) conscience

3 (= *título*) honorific title

dictador(a) SM/F dictator

dictadura SF dictatorship

dictáfono SM Dictaphone®

dictamen SM 1 (= *informe*) report; **emitir un ~** to issue a report ► **dictamen contable** (*Méx*) auditor's report ► **dictamen facultativo** (*Med*) medical report ► **dictamen pericial** (*Jur*) expert (witness') report

2 (= *opinión*) opinion; (*Jur*) legal opinion; **tomar ~ de algn** to consult with sb

dictaminar ▸conjug 1a◂ Ⓐ VT [+ *juicio*] to pass; **aún no han dictaminado la hora de la muerte** they haven't yet established the time of death

Ⓑ VI to pass judgment, give an opinion (**en** on)

dictar ▸conjug 1a◂ Ⓐ VT 1 [+ *carta, texto*] to dictate (**a** to)

2 (*Jur*) [+ *sentencia*] to pass, pronounce; [+ *decreto*] to issue

3 (= *indicar*) to suggest, dictate; **lo que dicta el sentido común** what common sense suggests *o* dictates

4 (*LAm*) [+ *clase*] to give; [+ *conferencia*] to give, deliver; **~ las noticias** (*Radio, TV*) to read the news

Ⓑ VI to dictate; **~ a su secretaria** to dictate to one's secretary

dictatorial ADJ dictatorial

dicterio SM taunt

didáctica SF didactics *sing*; **departamento de ~** (*Univ*) education department

didacticismo SM didacticism

didáctico ADJ didactic

didactismo SM = **didacticismo**

Dido SF Dido

diecinueve ADJ INV, PRON, SM (*gen*) nineteen; (*ordinal, en la fecha*) nineteenth; **le escribí el día ~** I wrote to him on the nineteenth; *ver tb* **seis**

dieciochesco ADJ eighteenth-century *antes de s*

dieciocho ADJ INV, PRON, SM (*gen*) eighteen; (*ordinal, en la fecha*) eighteenth; **le escribí el día ~** I wrote to him on the eighteenth; *ver tb* **seis**

dieciochoañero/a ADJ, SM/F eighteen-year-old

dieciséis ADJ INV, PRON, SM (*gen*) sixteen; (*ordinal, en la fecha*) sixteenth; **a las ~ horas** at sixteen hundred hours; **le escribí el día ~** I wrote to him on the sixteenth; *ver tb* **seis**

diecisiete ADJ INV, PRON, SM (*gen*) seventeen; (*ordinal, en la fecha*) seventeenth; **le escribí el día diecisiés** I wrote to him on the seventeenth; *ver tb* **seis**

dieldrina SF dieldrin

diente SM 1 (*Anat*) [*de persona, caballo*] tooth; [*de elefante*] tusk; [*de reptil*] fang; **echar los ~s** to teethe; **lavarse** *o* **cepillarse los ~s** to clean *o* brush one's teeth; **le están saliendo los ~s** he's teething ► **diente canino** canine, canine tooth ► **diente cariado** decayed tooth, bad tooth ► **diente de leche** milk tooth ► **diente incisivo** incisor ► **diente molar** molar ► **dientes postizos** false teeth

2 ✦*MODISMOS* **estar a ~** to be ravenous; **decir algo para ~s afuera** to say one thing and mean another, say sth without meaning it; **enseñar los ~s** to show one's claws, turn nasty; **entre ~s**: **hablar entre ~s** to mumble, mutter; **se le oía maldecir entre ~s** you could hear him cursing under his breath; **hincar el ~ en** [+ *comida*] to bite into; [+ *asunto*] to get one's teeth into; **nunca pude hincarle el ~ a ese libro** I could never get my teeth into that book; **pelar el ~** (*LAm**) to smile affectedly; **poner a algn los ~s largos** to make sb green with envy; **se me ponen los ~s largos** I get green with envy; **tener buen ~** to be a hearty eater; ✦*REFRÁN* **más cerca están mis ~s que mis parientes** charity begins at home

3 (*Téc*) [*de máquina*] cog; [*de peine, sierra*] tooth; [*de hebilla*] tongue

4 (*Bot*) [*de ajo*] clove ► **diente de león** dandelion

diéresis SF INV diaeresis

diesel SM 1 (*tb* **motor ~**) diesel engine; **un (coche) ~** a diesel (car)

2 (= *combustible*) diesel

dieseleléctrico ADJ diesel-electric

diestra SF right hand; **siéntate a mi ~** sit on my right

diestramente ADV 1 (= *hábilmente*) skilfully, skillfully (*EEUU*), deftly

2 (= *astutamente*) shrewdly; (*pey*) cunningly

diestro Ⓐ ADJ 1 (= *derecho*) right; ✦*MODISMO* **a ~ y siniestro** left, right and centre; **repartir golpes a ~ y siniestro** to throw out punches left, right and centre

2 (= *hábil*) skilful, skillful (*EEUU*); (*con las manos*) handy

3 (= *astuto*) shrewd; (*pey*) sly

Ⓑ SM 1 (*Taur*) matador

2 (= *espadachín*) expert swordsman; (*en esgrima*) expert fencer

3 (= *correa*) bridle

4 (*Dep*) right-hander

dieta SF 1 (*Med*) diet; **la ~ mediterránea** the Mediterranean diet; **estar a ~** to be on a diet ► **dieta blanda** soft-food diet ► **dieta equilibrada** balanced diet ► **dieta láctea** milk diet

2 (*Pol*) diet, assembly

3 **dietas** (*de comida, viajes*) subsistence allowance *sing*, expenses

4 (*Andes*) (= *guiso*) stew

dietario SM engagement book

dietética SF dietetics *sing*

dietético/a Ⓐ ADJ dietetic, dietary; **restaurante ~** restaurant for people on a diet; **alimento ~** diet food

Ⓑ SM/F dietician

dietista SMF dietician

diez ADJ INV, PRON, SM ten; (*ordinal, en la fecha*) tenth; **las ~** ten o'clock; **un ~ para Pérez** ten out of ten for Pérez; **le escribí el día ~** I wrote to him on the tenth; **hacer las ~ de últimas** (*Naipes*) to sweep the board; (*fig*) to queer one's own pitch, damage one's own cause; *ver tb* **seis**

diezmar ▸conjug 1a◂ VT to decimate

diezmillo SM (*Méx*) sirloin steak

diezmo SM tithe

difamación SF 1 (*al hablar*) slander (**de** of)
2 (*por escrito*) libel (**de** on)

difamador(a) Ⓐ ADJ [*palabra*] slanderous; [*escrito*] libellous, libelous (*EEUU*)
Ⓑ SM/F (*al hablar*) slanderer; (*por escrito*) libeller, libeler (*EEUU*)

difamar ▸conjug 1a◂ VT 1 (*Jur*) (*al hablar*) to slander; (*por escrito*) to libel
2 (= *calumniar*) to slander, malign

difamatorio ADJ [*palabras, afirmación*] slanderous, defamatory; [*artículo, escrito*] libellous, libelous (*EEUU*), defamatory

▼**diferencia** SF 1 (= *distinción*) difference; **no veo ~ entre el original y la copia** I can't see any difference between the original and the copy; **va mucha ~ entre este libro y el anterior** there's a world of difference between this book and the previous one; **no debes hacer ~s entre tus hijos** you shouldn't discriminate between your children; **a ~ de** unlike; **a ~ de sus hermanas, ella es bajita** unlike her sisters, she's quite short; **con ~** by far; **Rosa es, con ~, la más guapa** Rosa is by far the prettiest, Rosa is the prettiest by a long way ▸ **diferencia salarial** (*Com*) wage differential, pay differential
2 (= *intervalo*) difference, gap; **hay una ~ de edad de diez años entre ellos** there's an age difference *o* age gap of ten years between them, there's ten years' difference in age between them; **llegaron con una ~ de diez minutos** they arrived ten minutes apart
3 (= *desacuerdo*) **ya han resuelto sus ~s** they've patched up their differences; **existen ~s en el partido con respecto al aborto** there are differences of opinion within the party on the issue of abortion; **partir la ~** (*frm*) to split the difference
4 (= *resto*) difference; **pagué la ~ en efectivo** I paid the difference in cash; **halla la ~ entre las dos cantidades** find the difference between the two amounts

diferenciable ADJ distinguishable

diferenciación SF differentiation

diferenciador ADJ distinguishing

diferencial Ⓐ ADJ [*rasgos*] distinguishing; [*ecuación*] differential; [*impuesto*] discriminatory
Ⓑ SM (*Aut*) differential
Ⓒ SF (*Mat*) differential

▼**diferenciar** ▸conjug 1b◂ Ⓐ VT 1 (= *hacer diferencias*) to distinguish, differentiate; **no sabe ~ entre uno y otro** she can't distinguish *o* differentiate between the two; **no sabe ~ entre el bien y el mal** he can't distinguish between good and evil
2 (= *hacer diferente*) to make different
3 (= *variar*) to vary the use of, alter the function of
4 (*Mat*) to differentiate
Ⓑ **diferenciarse** VPR 1 (= *ser diferente*) to differ, be different (**de** from); **no se diferencian en nada** they do not differ at all; **se diferencian en que …** they differ in that …
2 (= *destacarse*) to stand out; **este producto se diferencia por su calidad** this product stands out because of its quality

diferendo SM difference, disagreement

diferente ADJ 1 (= *distinto*) different; **dos personas completamente ~s** two completely different people; **ser ~ de** *o* **a algn/algo** to be different to *o* from sb/sth; **mi enfoque es ~ del** *o* **al tuyo** my approach is different to *o* from yours; **eso me da igual, ~ sería que no me invitaran a la fiesta** I don't mind about that, it would be different if they didn't invite me to the party
2 **~s** (= *varios*) various, several; **por aquí han pasado ~s personalidades** various *o* several celebrities have been here

diferentemente ADV differently

diferido ADJ **emisión en ~** (*Radio, TV*) recorded programme, recorded program (*EEUU*); **el partido se retransmitirá en ~ esta noche a las diez** a recording of the match will be broadcast at ten o'clock tonight

diferir (*frm*) ▸conjug 3i◂ Ⓐ VI 1 (= *discrepar*) to differ, disagree; **~ de algo** to disagree with sth; **difiero de todo lo que dijo** I disagree with everything he said; **~ de algn en algo** to differ with sb over sth; **difiero de mi tutor en el método a aplicar** I differ with my tutor over which method to apply
2 (= *ser diferente*) to be different, differ; **las dos declaraciones difieren en pequeños detalles** the two statements differ in some minor details, the two statements are different with regard to some minor details
Ⓑ VT 1 (= *aplazar*) to defer; **quieren ~ el pago hasta el año 2005** they want to defer payment until the year 2005
2 (= *enviar*) to refer; **han diferido el caso al Tribunal Supremo** the case was referred to the Supreme Court

▼**difícil** ADJ 1 (= *complicado*) [*problema*] difficult; [*tiempos, vida*] difficult, hard; [*situación*] difficult, delicate; **es ~ de hacer** it's difficult *o* hard to do; **es ~ que venga** he is unlikely to come; **me resulta muy ~ decidir** I find it very hard to decide, I have great difficulty in deciding; **creo que lo tiene ~** I think he's going to find it difficult
2 [*persona*] difficult; **es un hombre ~** he's a difficult man to get on with; **un niño ~** a difficult child
3 (*) [*cara*] ugly

difícilmente ADV 1 (= *con dificultad*) with difficulty
2 (= *apenas*) **~ se podrá hacer** we'll be hard-pressed to do it; **aquí ~ va a haber para todos** there's unlikely to be enough of this for everybody; **~ se alcanza eso** that is unlikely to be reached

dificultad SF 1 (= *obstáculo*) difficulty; **sin ~ alguna** without the least difficulty
2 (= *problema*) difficulty; **no hay ~ para aceptar que …** there is no difficulty about accepting that …; **tuvieron algunas ~es para llegar a casa** they had some trouble getting home; **ha tenido ~es con la policía** he's been in trouble with the police; **camina con ~** he has difficulty walking
3 (= *objeción*) objection; **poner ~es** to raise objections; **me pusieron ~es para darme el pasaporte** they made it difficult *o* awkward for me to get a passport

dificultar ▸conjug 1a◂ VT 1 (= *obstaculizar*) [+ *camino*] to obstruct; [+ *tráfico*] to hold up
2 (= *hacer difícil*) [+ *trabajo*] to make difficult; [+ *progreso*] to hinder, stand in the way of; [+ *movimientos*] to restrict; **las restricciones dificultan el comercio** the restrictions hinder trade *o* make trade difficult; **~ que suceda algo** to make it unlikely that sth will happen

dificultoso ADJ 1 (= *difícil*) difficult, hard
2 [*persona*] difficult, awkward
3 (*) [*cara*] ugly

difracción SF diffraction

difractar ▸conjug 1a◂ VT to diffract

difteria SF diphtheria

difuminadamente ADV sketchily

difuminado ADJ vague

difuminar ▸conjug 1a◂ Ⓐ VT [+ *dibujo, contorno*] to blur
Ⓑ **difuminarse** VPR 1 **~se en algo** to fade into sth
2 (= *disiparse*) to fade away

difumino SM stump

difundir ▸conjug 3a◂ Ⓐ VT 1 (= *extender*) [+ *calor, luz*] to diffuse; [+ *gas*] to give off
2 (= *propagar*) [+ *programa, imagen*] to broadcast, transmit; [+ *teoría, ideología*] to spread, disseminate; **~ una noticia** to spread a piece of news
Ⓑ **difundirse** VPR 1 [*calor, luz*] to become diffused
2 [*teoría*] to spread

difunto/a Ⓐ ADJ deceased; **el ~ ministro** the late minister
Ⓑ SM/F deceased, deceased person; **la familia del ~** the family of the deceased; *ver tb* **día 1**

difusión SF 1 [*de calor, luz*] diffusion
2 [*de noticia, teoría*] dissemination, spreading
3 (*Periodismo*) [*de programa*] broadcasting; [*de periódico*] circulation, readership figures *pl*; **los medios de ~** the media; **un diario de ~ nacional** a national newspaper

difuso ADJ 1 [*luz*] diffused
2 [*conocimientos*] vague, hazy
3 [*estilo, explicación*] wordy

difusor Ⓐ ADJ **el medio ~** (*Radio*) the broadcasting medium
Ⓑ SM [*de pelo*] blow-drier

digerible ADJ digestible

digerir ▸conjug 3i◂ VT 1 [+ *comida*] to digest; **no puedo ~ a ese tío*** I can't stomach that guy*
2 [+ *opinión, noticia*] to absorb, assimilate; **le ha costado ~ su fracaso** he's found it hard to take in his failure

digestible ADJ digestible

digestión SF digestion; **hacer la ~** to digest one's food, digest

digestivo 1 ADJ digestive
2 SM digestive

digesto SM (*Jur*) digest

digitación SF (*Mús*) fingering

digital Ⓐ ADJ 1 [*ordenador, reloj*] digital
2 (= *dactilar*) finger *antes de s*; **huellas ~es** fingerprints
Ⓑ SF 1 (*Bot*) foxglove
2 (= *droga*) digitalis

digitalizador SM (*Inform*) digitizer

digitalizar ▸conjug 1f◂ VT to digitize

digitalmente ADV digitally

dígito SM (*Mat, Inform*) digit ▸ **dígito binario** binary digit, bit ▸ **dígito de control** check digit

diglosia SF diglossia

dignación SF condescension

dignamente ADV 1 (= *con dignidad*) with dignity, in a dignified way
2 (= *apropiadamente*) fittingly, properly
3 (= *honradamente*) honourably, honorably

➤ LENGUA Y USO: **diferencia 1** 32.1, 32.4, 53.5 **diferenciar A1** 32.1 **difícil 1** 53.1, 53.6

(*EEUU*)
4 (= *decentemente*) decently

dignarse ▸conjug 1a◂ VPR 1 **~ a hacer algo** to deign to do sth, condescend to do sth
2 (*frm*) **dígnese venir a esta oficina** please be so kind as to come to this office

dignatario/a SM/F dignitary

dignidad SF 1 (= *cualidad*) dignity
2 (*de sí mismo*) self-respect; **herir la ~ de algn** to offend sb's self-respect
3 (= *rango*) rank; **tiene ~ de ministro** he has the rank of a minister

dignificar ▸conjug 1g◂ VT to dignify

digno ADJ 1 (= *merecedor*) **~ de elogio** praiseworthy; **~ de mención** worth mentioning; **~ de toda alabanza** thoroughly praiseworthy, highly commendable; **es ~ de nuestra admiración** it deserves our admiration; **es ~ de verse** it is worth seeing
2 [*persona*] (= *honesto*) honourable, honorable (*EEUU*); (= *circunspecto*) dignified
3 (= *decoroso*) decent; **viviendas dignas para los obreros** decent homes for the workers

digresión SF digression

dije[1] *ver* **decir**

dije[2] SM 1 (= *relicario*) locket
2 (= *amuleto*) charm

dije[3]* ADJ (*Cono Sur*) 1 (= *guapo*) good-looking
2 (= *encantador*) nice, sweet

dilación SF delay; **sin ~** without delay, immediately; **esto no admite ~** we cannot allow any delay in this matter, this matter is most urgent

dilapidación SF squandering, waste

dilapidar ▸conjug 1a◂ VT to squander, waste

dilatación SF 1 (*Med*) dilation
2 (*Fís*) expansion

dilatado ADJ 1 [*pupila*] dilated
2 (= *extenso*) [*conocimiento*] extensive; [*período*] long

dilatar ▸conjug 1a◂ Ⓐ VT 1 (= *extender*) [+ *pupila*] to dilate; [+ *metales*] to expand
2 [+ *fama*] to spread
3 (= *prolongar*) to protract, prolong
4 (= *retrasar*) to delay
Ⓑ **dilatarse** VPR 1 (= *extenderse*) [*pupila*] to dilate; [*cuerpo, metal*] to expand; **la llanura se dilata hasta el horizonte** the plain stretches right to the horizon; **el valle se dilata en aquella parte** the valley spreads out *o* widens at that point
2 (*al hablar*) to be long-winded
3 (*LAm*) (= *tardar*) **~se en hacer algo** to take a long time to do sth, be slow to do sth
4 (*CAm, Méx*) (= *retrasarse*) to be delayed, be late

dilatorias SFPL delaying tactics; **andar en ~ con algn** ◊ **traer a algn en ~** to use delaying tactics with sb, hedge with sb; **no me vengas con ~** don't hedge with me

dilatorio ADJ delaying; **andar con ~** to drag things out

dilección SF affection

dilema SM dilemma; **estar en un ~** to be in a dilemma

diletante SMF dilettante

diligencia SF 1 (= *cualidad*) (= *esmero*) diligence; (= *rapidez*) speed
2 (= *encargo*) errand; **hacer las ~s de costumbre** to take the usual steps; **practicar sus ~s para hacer algo** to make every possible effort to do sth, do one's utmost to do sth
3 (*Jur*) **diligencias** formalities ► **diligencias judiciales** judicial proceedings ► **diligencias policiales** police inquiries ► **diligencias previas** inquest *sing*
4 (= *carruaje*) stagecoach

diligenciado SM, **diligenciamiento** SM processing

diligenciar ▸conjug 1b◂ VT [+ *asunto*] to deal with; [+ *documento, solicitud*] to take steps to obtain

diligente ADJ 1 (= *esmerado*) diligent; **poco ~** slack
2 (= *rápido*) speedy

diligentemente ADV 1 (= *esmeradamente*) diligently
2 (= *con rápidez*) speedily

dilucidar ▸conjug 1a◂ VT 1 (= *aclarar*) [+ *asunto*] to elucidate, clarify; [+ *misterio*] to clear up
2 [+ *concurso*] to decide

dilución SF dilution

diluido ADJ [*líquido, sustancia*] diluted, dilute; [*café, té*] weak

diluir ▸conjug 3g◂ Ⓐ VT 1 [+ *líquido, sustancia*] to dilute
2 (= *aguar*) to water down
Ⓑ **diluirse** VPR to dissolve

diluvial ADJ torrential

diluviar ▸conjug 1b◂ VI to pour with rain

diluvio SM flood; **el Diluvio Universal** the Flood; **un ~ de cartas** a flood *o* deluge of letters; **¡fue el ~!** it was chaos!; **¡esto es el ~!** what a mess!

dimanar ▸conjug 1a◂ VI **~ de algo** to arise from sth, spring from sth

dimensión SF 1 (= *magnitud*) dimension; **la cuarta ~** the fourth dimension
2 **dimensiones** (= *tamaño*) size *sing*; **de grandes dimensiones** large; **tomar las dimensiones de algo** to take sth's measurements; **las dimensiones de la tragedia** the extent of the tragedy
3 (= *importancia*) stature, standing; **un matemático de ~ universal** a mathematician of international stature o standing

dimensionado SM measuring

dimensionar ▸conjug 1a◂ VT to measure

dimes SMPL **~ y diretes** (= *riñas*) bickering *sing*, squabbling *sing*; (= *chismes*) gossip *sing*; **andar en ~ y diretes con algn** to bicker with sb, squabble with sb

diminutivo ADJ, SM diminutive

diminuto ADJ tiny, diminutive

dimisión SF resignation; **presentar la ~** to hand in *o* submit one's resignation

dimisionar ▸conjug 1a◂ VI, VT = **dimitir**

dimisionario/a Ⓐ ADJ outgoing, resigning
Ⓑ SM/F person resigning, person who has resigned

dimitente Ⓐ ADJ resigning, outgoing, retiring; **el presidente ~** the outgoing chairman, the retiring chairman
Ⓑ SMF person resigning

dimitir ▸conjug 3a◂ Ⓐ VI to resign (**de** from); **~ de la jefatura del partido** to resign (from) the party leadership; **lo han obligado a ~** he has been forced to resign
Ⓑ VT to resign

din* SM dough*; **el ~ y el don** money and rank, dough and dukedom*

Dinamarca SF Denmark

dinamarqués/esa Ⓐ ADJ Danish
Ⓑ SM/F (= *persona*) Dane
Ⓒ SM (= *idioma*) Danish

dinámica SF 1 (*Fís*) dynamics *sing*
2 (= *funcionamiento*) dynamic; **la ~ de la sociedad** the dynamic of society ► **dinámica de grupo** group dynamics *pl*

dinamicidad SF dynamism

dinámico ADJ dynamic

dinamismo SM dynamism

dinamita SF dynamite

dinamitar ▸conjug 1a◂ VT to dynamite

dinamitazo SM dynamite explosion

dinamizador ADJ revitalizing

dinamizar ▸conjug 1f◂ VT to invigorate, put new energy into

dinamo SF, **dínamo** SF (SM *en LAm*) dynamo

dinastía SF dynasty

dinástico ADJ dynastic

dinerada SF, **dineral** SM fortune; **habrá costado un ~** it must have cost a bomb *o* fortune

dinerario ADJ money *antes de s*; **aportación no dineraria** non-cash contribution

dinerillo* SM small amount of money; **tiene su ~ ahorrado** she's got a bit of money put by

dinero SM money; **¿cuánto es en ~ finlandés?** how much is that in Finnish money?; **andar mal de ~** to be short of money; **el negocio no da ~** the business does not pay; **es hombre de ~** he is a man of means; **el ~ lo puede todo** money can do anything, money talks; **hacer ~** to make money; **tirar el ~** to throw money away; ✦***MODISMO*** **ganar ~ a espuertas** *o* **a porrillo** to make money hand over fist; ✦***REFRÁN*** **el ~ malo echa fuera al bueno** bad money drives out good ► **dinero barato** cheap money, easy money ► **dinero caro** dear money, expensive money (*EEUU*) ► **dinero contante** cash ► **dinero contante y sonante** hard cash ► **dinero de bolsillo** pocket money ► **dinero de curso legal** legal tender ► **dinero electrónico** e-money ► **dinero en caja** cash in hand ► **dinero en circulación** currency, money in circulation ► **dinero negro** undeclared money ► **dinero para gastos** pocket money ► **dinero sucio** dirty money, money from crime ► **dinero suelto** loose change

dingui SM dinghy

dinosaurio SM dinosaur

dintel SM lintel

diñar* ▸conjug 1a◂ VT **~la** to kick the bucket*; **diñársela a algn** to swindle sb

diocesano ADJ diocesan

diócesis SF INV diocese

diodo SM diode

dionisiaco ADJ, **dionisíaco** ADJ Dionysian

Dionisio SM Denis; (*Mit*) Dionysius

dioptría SF dioptre, diopter (*EEUU*); **¿cuántas ~s tienes?** what's your gradation *o* correction *o* prescription?

Dios SM 1 (*Rel*) God; **el ~ de los judíos** the Jewish God, the God of the Jews; **~ Hijo** God the Son; **~ Padre** God the Father; *ver tb* **bendición 2**, **temor**
2 (*en exclamaciones*) **¡Dios!** (*con sorpresa*)

God!; (*con fastidio*) for God's sake!; **¡~ mío!** ◊ **¡~ santo!** my God!, good God!; **¡alabado sea ~!** praise be to God!; **¡~ te bendiga!** ◊ **¡~ te lo pague!** God bless you!; **¡que ~ nos coja confesados!** God help us!; **¡con ~!** ◊ **¡vaya usted con ~!** (may) God be with you!††, Godspeed!††; **¡plegue a ~!** please God!; **¡válgame ~!** good God!; **¡vive ~!** by God!; **¡~ me librel!** God forbid!, Heaven forbid!; **¡líbreme ~ de que ...!** God *o* Heaven forbid that I ...!; **¡líbreme ~ de ese sufrimiento!** Heaven forbid that I should suffer so!; **¡por ~!** for heaven's sake!; **—¿puedo fumar? —¡claro, por ~!** "may I smoke?" — "of course! *o* please do!"; **una limosnita ¡por (el amor de) ~!** a few pennies, for the love of God!; **¡~ quiera que no llueva mañana!** let's hope it doesn't rain tomorrow; **¡no lo quiera ~!** God forbid!; **—ojalá te cures pronto —¡~ quiera!** "let's hope you get better soon!" — "I hope so too!"; **¡vaya por ~!** (*con compasión*) oh dear!; (*con fastidio*) oh blast!*; *ver tb* **bendito**

3 ✦*MODISMOS* **armar la de ~ (es Cristo)*** to raise hell, cause an almighty row; **a la buena de ~** (= *sin esmerarse*) any old how; (= *sin planificar*) just like that; **¡me cago en ~!**** for Christ's sake!*, for fuck's sake!**; **costar ~ y ayuda**: **costó ~ y ayuda convencerlo** it was a real job to persuade him; **dejado de la mano de ~**: **una casa dejada de la mano de ~** a godforsaken house; **estos pueblos están dejados de la mano de ~** these villages have been abandoned to their fate; **estás dejado de la mano de ~** there's no hope for you; **~ dirá** time will tell; **sin encomendarse a ~ ni al diablo** without thought for the consequences; **estar de ~** to be God's will; **estaba de ~ que pasara** it was God's will that it happened; **como ~ me dio a entender** as best as I could; **a ~ gracias** ◊ **gracias a ~** thank heaven, thank God; **como que hay (un) ~** (*esp Cono Sur*) you can bet on it; **como que hay ~ que ...** you can bet (your bottom dollar) that ...; **como ~ manda** (*con verbo*) properly; (*con sustantivo*) proper; **¡siéntate como ~ manda!** sit properly!; **a ver si te echas una novia como ~ manda** it's time you got yourself a proper girlfriend; **~ mediante** God willing; **~ mediante nos veremos en mayo otra vez** God willing, we'll see each other again in May; **como ~ lo echó** *o* **trajo al mundo*** stark naked, in one's birthday suit†; **un sitio donde ~ pasó de largo** (*hum*) a godforsaken spot; **que ~ me perdone, pero ...** may God forgive me, but ...; **poner a ~ por testigo** to swear by almighty God; **pongo a ~ por testigo que no sabía la verdad** as God is my witness *o* I swear by almighty God, I did not know the truth; **ponerse a bien con ~** to make one's peace with God; **si ~ quiere** God willing; **hasta mañana si ~ quiere** good night, God bless!; **que sea lo que ~ quiera**: **he decidido hacerlo, y que sea lo que ~ quiera** I've decided to do it, and worry about it later; **sabe ~** God knows; **sabe ~ dónde estará** God knows where he is; **sólo ~ sabe lo que he sufrido** God alone knows what I've suffered; **lo vino ~ a ver** he struck lucky, he had a stroke of luck; **que venga ~ y lo vea** may God strike me dead, I'll eat my hat; ✦*REFRANES* **~ aprieta pero no ahoga** *o* (*Cono Sur*) **ahorca** ◊ **~ castiga pero no a palos** (*Chile*) God shapes the back for the burden; **a ~ rogando y con el mazo dando** (*haciendo el bien*) God helps those who help themselves; (*si no se cumple lo que se dice*) practise what you preach; **~ da pan a quien no tiene dientes** it's a cruel world; **~ los cría y ellos se juntan** birds of a feather flock together; *ver tb* **clamar B**, **madrugar A1**

dios(a) SM/F god/goddess; **los ~es paganos** the pagan gods; **comimos como ~es** we ate like kings; ✦*MODISMOS* **no hay ~ que***: **no hay ~ que entienda eso** no-one on earth could understand that*; **ni ~*** no one; **en el accidente no se salvó ni ~** no one survived the accident; **todo ~*** everyone; **lo sabía todo ~** the world and his wife knew about it*, everyone knew about it; **tienes que pagar como todo ~** you have to pay like everyone else

dióxido SM dioxide ► **dióxido de carbono** carbon dioxide ► **dióxido de nitrógeno** nitrogen dioxide

dioxina SF dioxin

Dip. ABR = **Diputación**

diploma SM diploma

diplomacia SF diplomacy

diplomado/a Ⓐ ADJ qualified

Ⓑ SM/F 1 (= *con diploma*) holder of a diploma 2 (*Univ*) (= *con diplomatura*) graduate

diplomarse ▸conjug 1a◂ VPR (*esp LAm*) to graduate (*from college etc*)

diplomática SF 1 (*Hist, Jur*) diplomatics *sing*

2 (= *cuerpo*) diplomatic corps

3 (= *carrera*) diplomatic career, career in the foreign service; *ver tb* **diplomático**

diplomáticamente ADV diplomatically

diplomático/a Ⓐ ADJ 1 [*carrera, cuerpo*] diplomatic

2 (= *que tiene tacto*) diplomatic, tactful

Ⓑ SM/F diplomat; *ver tb* **diplomática**

diplomatura SF diploma course; → LICENCIATURA

dipsomanía SF dipsomania

dipsomaníaco/a SM/F, **dipsómano/a** SM/F dipsomaniac

díptero SM dipteran

díptico SM 1 (*Arte*) diptych

2 (*Com*) leaflet

diptongar ▸conjug 1h◂ VT, VI to diphthongize

diptongo SM diphthong

diputación SF 1 (= *delegación*) deputation

2 (*Pol*) ► **diputación permanente** standing committee ► **diputación provincial** (= *edificio*) ≈ county council offices *pl*, ≈ county commission offices *pl* (*EEUU*); (= *personas*) ≈ county council, ≈ county commission (*EEUU*); (= *edificio*) ≈ county council offices *pl*

diputado/a SM/F 1 (= *delegado*) delegate

2 (*Pol*) ≈ member of parliament, ≈ representative (*EEUU*); **el ~ por Guadalajara** the member for Guadalajara ► **diputado/a a Cortes** (*Esp*) member of the Spanish Cortes ► **diputado/a provincial** ≈ member of a county council, ≈ member of a county commission; → CONGRESO DE LOS DIPUTADOS

diputar ▸conjug 1a◂ VT to delegate, depute

dique SM 1 (= *muro de contención*) (*en río*) dyke, dike (*esp EEUU*); (*en puerto*) dock; **entrar en ~** ◊ **hacer ~** to dock ► **dique de contención** dam ► **dique flotante** floating dock ► **dique seco** dry dock

2 (= *rompeolas*) breakwater

3 (= *impedimento*) **poner un ~ a algo** to check sth, restrain sth; **es un ~ contra la expansión** it is a barrier to expansion

diquelar‡ ▸conjug 1a◂ VT 1 (= *ver*) to see

2 (= *vigilar*) to watch over, keep an eye on

3 (= *comprender*) to twig*, catch on to

Dir. ABR 1 = **dirección**

2 (= **director**) dir

dire* SMF = **director**

diré *etc ver* **decir**

dirección SF 1 (= *sentido*) direction; **la ~ del viento** the wind direction; **¿podría indicarme la ~ de la playa?** could you show me the way to the beach?; **"dirección prohibida"** "no entry"; **salir con ~ a** to leave for; **salió con ~ desconocida** he left for an unknown destination; **el tráfico con ~ a Barcelona** traffic for Barcelona; **trenes con ~ este** eastbound trains; **ir en ~ contraria** to go the other way; **de dos direcciones** (*Esp*): **calle de dos direcciones** two-way street; **conmutador de dos direcciones** two-way switch; **ir en ~ a** to go in the direction of, go towards, head for; **el taxi iba en ~ al aeropuerto** the taxi was going in the direction of *o* towards the airport, the taxi was heading for the airport; **el tráfico en ~ a Burgos** traffic for Burgos; **calle de ~ obligatoria** *o* **única** one-way street

2 (= *orientación*) way; **desconozco la ~ que están siguiendo los acontecimientos** I don't know which way events are going

3 (= *señas*) address; **su nombre y ~ completa** your full name and address; **la carta llevaba una ~ equivocada** the letter was wrongly addressed *o* had the wrong address; **poner la ~ a un sobre** to address an envelope ► **dirección absoluta** absolute address ► **dirección comercial** business address ► **dirección del remitente** return address ► **dirección electrónica** e-mail address ► **dirección IP** IP address ► **dirección particular** home address ► **dirección postal** postal address ► **dirección profesional** business address ► **dirección relativa** relative address

4 (= *control*) [*de empresa, hospital, centro de enseñanza*] running; [*de partido*] leadership; [*de película*] direction; **tomar la ~ de una empresa** to take over the running of a company; **le han confiado la ~ de la obra** he has been put in charge of the work; **se ha hecho cargo de la ~ de la orquesta** he's been appointed conductor of the orchestra; **con ~ de Polanski** directed by Polanski ► **dirección colectiva**, **dirección colegiada** (*Pol*) collective leadership ► **dirección de escena** stage management ► **dirección de orquesta** conducting ► **dirección empresarial** business management ► **dirección escénica** stage management

5 (= *personal directivo*) **la ~** [*de empresa, centro escolar*] the management; [*de partido*] the leadership; [*de periódico*] the editorial board; **"prohibido fumar en este local: la dirección"** "smoking is prohibited in this building: the management"; **habrá cambios en la ~ del partido** there will be changes in the party leadership

6 (= *cargo*) (*en colegio*) headship, principalship (*EEUU*); (*en periódico, revista*) editorship;

(*en partido*) leadership; [*de gerente*] post of manager; [*de alto cargo*] directorship
7 (= *despacho*) (*en colegio*) headteacher's office, principal's office (*EEUU*); (*en periódico, revista*) editor's office; [*de gerente*] manager's office; [*de alto cargo*] director's office
8 (= *oficina principal*) head office ► **Dirección General de Seguridad** State Security Office, State Security Service ► **Dirección General de Turismo** State Tourist Office ► **dirección provincial** *regional office of a government department*
9 (*Aut, Náut*) steering; **tiene la ~ averiada** the steering is faulty; **mecanismo de ~** steering (mechanism) ► **dirección asistida, dirección hidráulica** (*LAm*) power steering

direccional Ⓐ ADJ directional
Ⓑ **direccionales** SFPL (*Col, Méx Aut*) indicators, turn signals (*EEUU*)

direccionamiento SM (*Inform*) addressing

direccionar ►conjug 1a◄ VT 1 (*Inform*) to address
2 [+ *máquina, vehículo*] to operate

directa SF (*Aut*) top gear

directamente ADV directly; **fui ~ a casa** I went straight home

directiva SF 1 (= *dirección*) [*de empresa*] board of directors; [*de partido*] executive committee, leadership
2 (*Jur*) directive
3 **directivas** (= *instrucciones*) guidelines

directivo(a) Ⓐ ADJ [*junta*] managing; [*función*] managerial, administrative; [*clase*] executive
Ⓑ SM/F (*Com*) manager; **un congreso de los ~s de la industria** a conference for industry executives

directo Ⓐ ADJ 1 [*línea*] straight
2 [*pregunta, respuesta, lenguaje*] direct, straightforward; **es muy directa hablando** she's very direct
3 [*tren*] direct, through; [*vuelo*] direct, nonstop
4 **ir ~ a** to go straight to; **fui directa a la comisaría** I went straight *o* directly to the police station; **el balón fue ~ a portería** the ball went straight into the goal; **este tren va ~ a Granada** this is a through *o* direct train to Granada, this train goes direct to Granada
5 (= *sin intermediario*) direct; **recibo órdenes directas del sargento** I get my orders straight *o* direct from the sergeant
6 (*Ling*) [*complemento, traducción*] direct
7 (*Radio, TV*) **en ~** live; **una entrevista en ~** a live interview; **transmitir en ~** to broadcast live
Ⓑ SM (*Boxeo*) straight punch; (*Tenis*) forehand drive

director(a) Ⓐ ADJ [*consejo, junta*] governing; [*principio*] guiding
Ⓑ SM/F 1 (= *responsable*) [*de centro escolar*] headteacher, headmaster/headmistress, principal; [*de periódico, revista*] editor; (*Cine, TV*) director; [*de orquesta*] conductor; [*de hospital*] manager, administrator; [*de prisión*] governor, warden (*EEUU*) ► **director(a) artístico/a** artistic director ► **director(a) de cine** film director ► **director(a) de coro** choirmaster ► **director(a) de departamento** (*Univ*) head of department ► **director(a) de escena** stage manager ► **director(a) de funeraria** undertaker, funeral director, mortician (*EEUU*) ► **director(a) de interiores** (*TV*) studio director ► **director(a) de orquesta** orchestra conductor ► **director(a) de tesis** thesis supervisor, research supervisor
2 (*Com*) (= *gerente*) manager; (*de mayor responsabilidad*) director ► **director(a) adjunto/a** assistant manager ► **director(a) de empresa** company director ► **director(a) de exportación** export manager ► **director(a) de finanzas** financial director ► **director(a) de sucursal** branch manager ► **director(a) ejecutivo/a** executive director, managing director ► **director(a) general** general manager ► **director(a) gerente** managing director ► **director(a) técnico/a** technical manager
Ⓒ SM (*Rel*) ► **director espiritual** spiritual director

directorial ADJ (*Com*) managing, executive; **clase ~** managers *pl*, management class

directorio SM 1 (= *norma*) directive
2 (= *junta directiva*) directors *pl*, board of directors
3 (*Inform*) directory ► **directorio principal** root directory
4 ► **directorio de teléfonos, directorio telefónico** (*Méx*) telephone directory

directriz SF 1 (= *norma*) guideline
2 (*Mat*) directrix

dirigencia SF leadership

dirigente Ⓐ ADJ leading; **la clase ~** the ruling class
Ⓑ SMF (*Pol*) leader; **los ~s del partido** the party leaders ► **dirigente de la oposición** leader of the opposition

dirigible Ⓐ ADJ (*Aer, Náut*) steerable
Ⓑ SM dirigible, airship, blimp (*EEUU*)

dirigido ADJ [*misil*] guided; **~ a distancia** remote controlled

dirigir ►conjug 3c◄ Ⓐ VT 1 (= *orientar*) [+ *persona*] to direct; [+ *asunto*] to advise, guide; **lo dirigió con ayuda de un mapa** she showed him the way *o* directed him with the help of a map; **¿por qué no vas tú delante y nos diriges?** why don't you go first and lead the way?; **un asesor le dirige las finanzas** a consultant advises him on his finances; **estos principios dirigen nuestra política** these are the guiding principles behind our policy; **dirigían sus pasos hacia la iglesia** they made their way *o* walked towards the church; *ver tb* **palabra 2**
2 (= *apuntar*) [+ *arma, telescopio*] to aim, point (**a, hacia** at); [+ *manguera*] to turn (**a, hacia** on), point (**a, hacia** at); **dirigió los focos al escenario** he pointed *o* directed the lights towards the stage; **ordenó ~ el fuego hacia el enemigo** he ordered them to direct *o* aim their fire at the enemy
3 (= *destinar*) 3·1 [+ *carta, comentario, pregunta*] to address (**a** to); **la carta iba dirigida al director** the letter was addressed to the editor
3·2 [+ *libro, programa, producto*] to aim (**a** at); **una publicación dirigida al mercado infantil** a publication aimed at the children's market
3·3 [+ *acusación, críticas*] to make (**a, contra** against), level (**a, contra** at, against); [+ *ataques*] to make (**a, contra** against); **dirigieron graves acusaciones contra el ministro** serious accusations were made against the minister, serious accusations were levelled at *o* against the minister; **le dirigieron fuertes críticas** he was strongly criticized, he came in for some strong criticism
3·4 [+ *esfuerzos*] to direct (**a, hacia** to, towards); **hay que ~ todos nuestros esfuerzos hacia este fin** we must direct all our efforts to this end
4 (= *controlar*) [+ *empresa, hospital, centro de enseñanza*] to run; [+ *periódico, revista*] to edit, run; [+ *expedición, país, sublevación*] to lead; [+ *maniobra, operación, investigación*] to direct, be in charge of; [+ *debate*] to chair; [+ *proceso judicial*] to preside over; [+ *tesis*] to supervise; [+ *juego, partido*] to referee; **dirige el Departamento de Biología** he runs the Biology Department; **el Partido Comunista dirigió los destinos del país durante siete décadas** the Communist Party controlled the fate of the country for seven decades; **el equipo de jugadores que dirige Muñoz** the team of players led by Muñoz; **dirigió la investigación desde Madrid** he directed the investigation from Madrid; **dirigió mal las negociaciones** he handled the negotiations badly, he mismanaged the negotiations; *ver tb* **cotarro 1**
5 (*Cine, Teat*) to direct
6 (*Mús*) [+ *orquesta, concierto*] to conduct; [+ *coro*] to lead; **¿quién ~á el coro?** who will be the choirmaster?, who will lead the choir?
7 (= *conducir*) [+ *coche*] to drive; [+ *barco*] to steer; [+ *caballo*] to lead; **dirigió su coche hacia la izquierda** he steered *o* drove his car towards the left
Ⓑ **dirigirse** VPR 1 (= *ir*) **~se a** *o* **hacia** to head for; **se dirigía a la oficina cuando lo arrestaron** he was on his way to *o* heading for the office when he was arrested; **se dirigió en su coche al aeropuerto** he drove to the airport; **se dirigió hacia él y le dio una bofetada** she went over to him and slapped him
2 (= *ponerse en contacto*) **~se a algn** (*oralmente*) to speak to sb, address sb (*frm*); (*por escrito*) to contact sb; **el presidente se dirigió a la nación** the president spoke to *o* (*frm*) addressed the nation; **¿se dirige usted a mí?** are you speaking to me?; **"diríjase a ..."** "contact ..."; **me dirijo a usted para solicitarle su ayuda** I am writing (to you) to request your help
3 (= *estar destinado*) **~se a algo** to be aimed at sth; **el programa se dirige a los adultos** the programme is aimed at *o* geared towards adults; **toda sus esfuerzos van dirigidos a conseguir un nuevo récord** she is concentrating all her efforts on setting a new record

dirigismo SM control ► **dirigismo estatal** state control

dirigista ADJ, SMF interventionist

dirimente ADJ [*argumento*] decisive; [*voto*] casting; [*opinión, decisión*] final

dirimir ►conjug 3a◄ VT 1 [+ *contrato, matrimonio*] to dissolve, annul
2 [+ *disputa*] to settle

discada SF (*LAm*) collection of records

discado SM (*Andes, Cono Sur*) dialling, dialing (*EEUU*) ► **discado directo** direct dialling

discapacidad SF disability ► **discapacidad física** physical disability ► **discapacidad psíquica** mental disability

discapacitado/a Ⓐ ADJ incapacitated, disabled

Ⓑ SM/F disabled person ► **discapacitado/a psíquico/a** mentally disabled person

discapacitar ▸conjug 1a◂ VT to incapacitate, handicap

discar ▸conjug 1g◂ VT (*Andes, Cono Sur*) to dial

discernidor ADJ discerning, discriminating

discernimiento SM discernment

discernir ▸conjug 3k◂ Ⓐ VT 1 (= *distinguir*) to distinguish, discern; **~ una cosa de otra** to distinguish one thing from another
2 (*Jur*) [+ *tutor*] to appoint
3 (*esp LAm*) [+ *premio*] to award (**a** to)
Ⓑ VI to discern, distinguish (**entre** between)

disciplina SF 1 (= *normas*) discipline; **~ férrea** iron will ► **disciplina de partido, disciplina de voto** party discipline, party whip; **romper la ~ de voto** to defy the party whip ► **disciplina inglesa** bondage and discipline
2 (*Dep*) discipline; **ganó en la ~ de suelo** she came first in the floor exercises

disciplinante SMF (*Rel*) flagellant, penitent

disciplinar ▸conjug 1a◂ VT 1 (= *instruir*) [+ *persona, instintos*] to discipline; [+ *soldados*] to drill
2 (= *azotar*) to whip, scourge

disciplinario ADJ disciplinary

discipulado SM 1 (*Rel*) discipleship
2 (= *personas*) pupils *pl*, student body

discípulo/a SM/F 1 (*Rel, Fil*) disciple
2 (= *alumno*) pupil, student

discjockey [dis'jokei] SMF disc jockey

disco[1] SM 1 (*Mús*) record; **siempre está con el mismo ~ ◊ no cambia de ~*** he's like a cracked record* ► **disco compacto** compact disc ► **disco de larga duración** long-playing record ► **disco de oro** golden disc ► **disco de plata** silver disc ► **disco de platino** platinum disc ► **disco microsurco** long-playing record ► **disco sencillo** single
2 (*Inform*) disk ► **disco de arranque** startup disk, boot disk ► **disco de cabeza fija** fixed-head disk ► **disco duro, disco fijo** hard disk ► **disco flexible, disco floppy** floppy disk ► **disco magnético** magnetic disk ► **disco óptico** optical disk ► **disco rígido** hard disk ► **disco virtual** virtual disk
3 (*Dep*) discus
4 (= *señal*) (*Ferro*) signal ► **disco rojo** red light ► **disco verde** green light
5 ► **disco de freno** (*Aut*) brake disc
6 (*Telec*) dial
7 ► **disco volante** flying saucer

disco[2]* SF (= *discoteca*) disco

discóbolo/a SM/F discus thrower

discografía SF 1 (= *discos publicados*) records *pl*; **toda la ~ de los Beatles** the Beatles' entire back catalogue, all the records released by the Beatles
2 (= *colección*) record collection

discográfica SF record company, record label

discográfico ADJ record *antes de s*; **casa discográfica** record company, record label; **éxito ~** chart hit; **el momento ~ actual** the present state of the record industry

díscolo ADJ 1 (= *rebelde*) unruly
2 (= *travieso*) mischievous

disconforme ADJ [*opinión*] differing; **estar ~** to be in disagreement, disagree (**con** with)

disconformidad SF disagreement; **en ~ con el espíritu olímpico** contrary to the Olympic spirit

discontinuidad SF lack of continuity, discontinuity

discontinuo ADJ discontinuous; **línea discontinua** (*Aut*) broken line

discordancia SF discord; **eso está en ~ con lo que dijo antes** that contradicts what she said earlier

discordante ADJ 1 (*Mús*) discordant
2 [*opiniones*] clashing; **su traje fue la nota ~ en la reunión** his suit stuck out like a sore thumb in the meeting

discordar ▸conjug 1l◂ VI 1 (*Mús*) to be out of tune
2 (= *estar en desacuerdo*) [*personas*] to disagree (**de** with); [*colores, opiniones*] to clash

discorde ADJ 1 (*Mús*) [*sonido*] discordant; [*instrumento*] out of tune
2 [*opiniones*] clashing; **su actitud es ~ con la política del partido** his attitude is out of line with party policy
3 **estar ~** [*personas*] to disagree (**de** with), be in disagreement (**de** with)

discordia SF discord, disagreement; **sembrar la ~** to sow discord

discoteca SF 1 (= *lugar de baile*) disco, club, nightclub
2 (= *colección de discos*) record collection
3 (*LAm*) (= *tienda*) record shop

discotequero/a Ⓐ ADJ disco *antes de s*; **yo no soy muy ~*** I'm not into clubbing *o* going to discos
Ⓑ SM/F nightclubber

discreción SF 1 (= *prudencia*) discretion; **tenemos que actuar con ~** we must act discreetly; **me callé por ~** I tactfully kept quiet
2 **a ~**: **añadir azúcar a ~** add sugar to taste; **comer a ~** to eat as much as one likes; **con vino a ~** with as much wine as one wants; **¡a ~!** (*Mil*) stand easy!; **rendirse a ~** (*Mil*) to surrender unconditionally
3 **a ~ de algn** at sb's discretion

discrecional ADJ 1 [*poder*] discretionary
2 (= *facultativo*) optional; **parada ~** request stop, flag stop (*EEUU*); **servicio ~ de autobuses** private bus service

discrecionalidad SF discretional nature

discrepancia SF 1 (= *diferencia*) discrepancy
2 (= *desacuerdo*) disagreement

discrepante ADJ [*visión, opiniones*] divergent; **hubo varias voces ~s** there were some dissenting voices

discrepar ▸conjug 1a◂ VI 1 (= *estar en desacuerdo*) to disagree (**de** with); **discrepamos en varios puntos** we disagree on a number of points; **discrepo de esa opinión** I disagree with that view
2 (= *diferenciarse*) to differ (**de** from)

discretamente ADV 1 (= *sin notarse*) discreetly
2 (= *sobriamente*) soberly
3 (= *modestamente*) unobtrusively

discretear ▸conjug 1a◂ VI to try to be clever, be frightfully witty

discreto ADJ 1 (= *poco llamativo*) [*color, vestido*] sober; [*advertencia*] discreet
2 [*persona*] (= *prudente*) discreet; (= *listo*) shrewd
3 (= *mediano*) average, middling; **de inteligencia discreta** reasonably intelligent; **le daremos un plazo ~** we'll allow him a reasonable time; **unas ganancias discretas** modest profits
4 (*Fís*) discrete

discriminación SF discrimination (**contra** against); ► **discriminación laboral** discrimination in the workplace ► **discriminación positiva** positive discrimination, affirmative action (*EEUU*) ► **discriminación racial** racial discrimination ► **discriminación sexual** sex discrimination

discriminado ADJ **sentirse ~** to feel that one has been unfairly treated *o* has been discriminated against

discriminador SM discriminator

discriminar ▸conjug 1a◂ Ⓐ VT 1 [+ *persona, colectivo*] to discriminate against
2 [+ *colores, sabores*] to differentiate between
Ⓑ VI to discriminate (**entre** between)

discriminatoriamente ADV unfairly, in a biased way

discriminatorio ADJ discriminatory

▼ **disculpa** SF 1 (= *pretexto*) excuse
2 (= *perdón*) apology; **pedir ~s a algn por algo** to apologize to sb for sth

disculpable ADJ excusable, pardonable

▼ **disculpar** ▸conjug 1a◂ Ⓐ VT (= *perdonar*) to excuse, forgive; **disculpa que venga tarde** forgive me for coming late; **¡discúlpeme!** I'm sorry!; **le disculpan sus pocos años** his youth is an excuse, his youth provides an excuse; **te ruego me disculpes con el anfitrión** please make my apologies to the host
Ⓑ **disculparse** VPR to apologize (**con** to); **se disculpó por haber llegado tarde** he apologized for arriving late

disculpativo ADJ apologetic

discurrideras* SFPL wits, brains

discurrir ▸conjug 3a◂ Ⓐ VT (= *inventar*) to think up; **esos chicos no discurren nada bueno** these lads are up to no good
Ⓑ VI 1 (= *recorrer*) to roam, wander (**por** about, along)
2 [*río*] to flow
3 [*tiempo*] to pass; **la sesión discurrió sin novedad** the meeting went off quietly; **el verano discurrió sin grandes calores** the summer passed without great heat
4 (= *meditar*) to meditate (**en** about, on); **discurre menos que un mosquito** he just never thinks
5 (= *hablar*) to discourse (**sobre** about, on)

discursear ▸conjug 1a◂ VI to speechify

discursivo ADJ discursive

discurso SM 1 (= *alocución*) speech; **pronunciar un ~** to make a speech, give a speech; **otra vez me soltó el mismo discursito de siempre** he gave me the same old lecture as always ► **discurso de clausura** closing speech
2 (= *forma de hablar*) rhetoric; **su ~ nacionalista** his nationalist rhetoric
3 (= *habla*) speech, faculty of speech; **análisis del ~** discourse analysis
4 [*del tiempo*] **en el ~ del tiempo** with the passage of time; **en el ~ de cuatro generaciones** in the space of four generations

discusión SF 1 (= *riña*) argument; **eso no admite ~** there can be no argument about that; **tener una ~** to have an argument
2 (= *debate*) discussion; **estar en ~** to be un-

➤ LENGUA Y USO: **disculpa** 45.1 **disculpar A** 45.1

der discussion ► **discusión de grupo** group discussion

discutibilidad SF debatable nature

▼**discutible** ADJ debatable, arguable; **650 euros ~s** 650 euros o.n.o.; **es ~ si …** it is debatable *o* arguable whether …; **de mérito ~** of dubious worth

discutido ADJ [1] (= *hablado*) much-discussed
[2] (= *controvertido*) controversial; **su éxito fue discutidísimo** their success was highly controversial

discutidor ADJ argumentative, disputatious

▼**discutir** ▸conjug 3a◂ Ⓐ VT [1] (= *debatir*) [+ *plan, proyecto, idea*] to discuss; [+ *precio*] to argue about
[2] (= *contradecir*) to question, challenge; **~ a algn lo que está diciendo** to question *o* challenge what sb is saying
Ⓑ VI [1] (= *dialogar*) to discuss, talk
[2] (= *disputar*) to argue (**de, sobre** about, over); **¡no discutas!** don't argue!; **no le discutas porque él sabe más que tú del tema** don't argue with him because he knows more about the subject than you do; **~ de política** to argue about politics, talk politics

discutón* ADJ argumentative

disecar ▸conjug 1g◂ VT [1] (*Med*) to dissect
[2] (*para conservar*) [+ *animal*] to stuff; [+ *planta*] to preserve, mount

disección SF [1] (*Med*) dissection
[2] (= *de animal*) stuffing; (*de plantas*) preserving, mounting

diseccionar ▸conjug 1a◂ VT to dissect, analyse

diseminación SF [*de ideas*] dissemination; [*de semillas*] scattering ► **diseminación nuclear** spread of nuclear weapons

diseminar ▸conjug 1a◂ VT to spread, disseminate (*frm*)

disensión SF disagreement, dissension

disentería SF dysentery

disentimiento SM dissent, disagreement

disentir ▸conjug 3i◂ VI to dissent (**de** from), disagree (**de** with)

diseñador(a) SM/F designer ► **diseñador(a) de modas** fashion designer ► **diseñador(a) gráfico/a** graphic designer

diseñar ▸conjug 1a◂ VT [1] (*Téc*) to design
[2] (*Arte*) to draw, sketch
[3] (*con palabras*) to outline

diseño SM [1] (= *actividad*) design; **de ~ italiano** Italian-designed; **camisa de ~** designer shirt; **un asiento con ~ ergonómico** an ergonomically-designed seat ► **diseño asistido por ordenador, diseño asistido por computador** (*LAm*) computer-aided design ► **diseño de interiores** interior design ► **diseño de modas** fashion design ► **diseño gráfico** graphic design ► **diseño industrial** industrial design ► **diseño textil** textile design
[2] (= *dibujo*) (*Arte*) drawing, sketch; (*Cos*) pattern

disertación SF dissertation

disertar ▸conjug 1a◂ VI to discourse (**acerca de, sobre** upon); **~ largamente sobre algo** to speak at length about sth

disfavor SM disfavour, disfavor (*EEUU*)

disforme ADJ [1] (= *mal hecho*) ill-proportioned, badly-proportioned
[2] (= *monstruoso*) monstrous

disforzado* ADJ (*Andes*) [1] (= *santurrón*) prim, prudish
[2] (= *descarado*) cheeky*, sassy (*EEUU*)

disfraz SM [1] (= *traje*) (*para una fiesta*) fancy dress, costume (*EEUU*); (*para engañar a algn*) disguise; **yo fui a la fiesta con un ~ de pirata** I went to the party dressed as a pirate *o* in a pirate costume; **llevaba un ~ de hombre** she was disguised as a man; **baile de disfraces** fancy-dress ball
[2] (= *pretexto*) facade (**de** for); **bajo el ~ de algo** under the cloak of sth
[3] (*Mil*) camouflage

disfrazado ADJ disguised (**de** as); **ir ~ de algo** (*para ocultar algo*) to masquerade as sth; (*para fiesta*) to dress up as sth

disfrazar ▸conjug 1f◂ Ⓐ VT [1] [+ *persona*] to disguise (**de** as); **lo ~on de soldado** they disguised him as a soldier
[2] (= *ocultar*) [+ *sentimiento, verdad, intención*] to disguise, conceal; [+ *sabor*] to disguise
[3] (*Mil*) to camouflage
Ⓑ **disfrazarse** VPR [*persona*] (*para una fiesta*) to dress up (**de** as); (*para ocultarse de algo*) to disguise o.s. (**de** as)

▼**disfrutar** ▸conjug 1a◂ Ⓐ VT [1] (= *gozar de*) to enjoy; **espero que disfrutes tus vacaciones** I hope you enjoy your holiday
[2] (*frm*) (= *poseer*) to enjoy; **disfruta una posición inmejorable en el mercado** it enjoys an excellent market position
Ⓑ VI [1] (= *gozar*) to enjoy o.s.; **los niños disfrutan en la piscina** the children enjoy themselves in the swimming pool; **disfruté muchísimo hablando con ella** I very much enjoyed talking to her; **¡que disfrutes!** enjoy yourself!; **~ con algo** to enjoy sth; **Juan disfruta con el buen cine** Juan enjoys good films; **~ de algo** to enjoy sth; **tú sabes ~ de la vida** you know how to enjoy life
[2] **~ de algo** (= *poseer*) to enjoy sth; **disfruta de excelente salud** he enjoys excellent health; **disfrutan de una pensión del Estado** they enjoy *o* receive a state pension

disfrute SM enjoyment; **todos tenemos derecho al ~ de unas vacaciones** we all have the right to enjoy *o* have holidays

disfuerzo SM (*Andes*) [1] (= *descaro*) impudence, effrontery
[2] (= *remilgo*) prudishness
[3] **disfuerzos** (= *amenazas*) threats, bravado *sing*

disfunción SF malfunction

disfuncionalidad SF malfunction

disgregación SF [1] [*de grupo*] disintegration, breaking up
[2] [*de roca*] breaking up

disgregar ▸conjug 1h◂ Ⓐ VT [+ *grupo*] to break up; [+ *manifestantes*] to disperse
Ⓑ **disgregarse** VPR to disintegrate, break up (**en** into)

disgresión SF digression

disgustar ▸conjug 1a◂ Ⓐ VT to upset; **comprendí que le disgustaba mi presencia** I realized that my presence upset him; **me disgusta tener que repetirlo** I don't like having to repeat it; **es un olor que me disgusta** it's a smell I don't like; **estaba muy disgustado con el asunto** he was very displeased *o* upset about the matter
Ⓑ **disgustarse** VPR [1] (= *enfadarse*) to get upset
[2] (= *molestarse*) to be displeased, be offended (**con** about)
[3] [*amigos*] to fall out (**con** with)

disgusto SM [1] (= *pena*) **la noticia me causó un gran ~** I was very upset by the news; **eso te va a costar un ~** that is going to get you into trouble; **vas a darle un ~ a mamá con tan malas notas** Mum's going to be upset about those bad marks of yours; **nunca nos dio un ~** he never caused us any worry *o* trouble; **vas a matar a tu madre a ~s*** you'll be the death of your mother*, you'll send your mother to an early grave*; **—la han despedido —¡qué ~!** "they've fired her" — "that's terrible *o* awful!"
[2] (= *riña*) quarrel, row; **como sigas así, tú y yo tendremos un ~** if you carry on like that, we're going to fall out
[3] **a ~: hacer algo a ~** to do sth unwillingly; **estar** *o* **sentirse a ~** to be *o* feel ill at ease

disidencia SF [1] (*Pol*) dissidence
[2] (*Rel*) dissent

disidente Ⓐ ADJ (*Pol*) dissident
Ⓑ SMF [1] (*Pol*) dissident
[2] (*Rel*) dissenter, nonconformist

disidir ▸conjug 3a◂ VI to dissent

disílabo Ⓐ ADJ disyllabic
Ⓑ SM disyllable

disímil ADJ not alike, dissimilar

disimilación SF dissimilation

disimulación SF [1] (= *cualidad*) dissimulation
[2] [*de objeto, puerta*] concealment

disimuladamente ADV [1] (= *solapadamente*) furtively
[2] (= *astutamente*) cunningly, slyly
[3] (= *ocultamente*) covertly

disimulado ADJ [1] (= *solapado*) furtive, underhand
[2] (= *astuto*) sly
[3] (= *oculto*) covert; **estaba ~ entre unos papeles** it was hidden among some papers; ✦*MODISMO* **hacerse el ~** to pretend not to notice

disimular ▸conjug 1a◂ Ⓐ VT [1] [+ *emoción, alegría, tristeza*] to hide, conceal; **no pudo ~ lo que sentía** he couldn't hide *o* conceal what he felt
[2] [+ *defecto, roto*] to cover up, hide; [+ *sabor, olor*] to hide; **disimuló la mancha con un poco de pintura** she covered up *o* hid the mark with a bit of paint
[3] (†) (= *perdonar*) to excuse
Ⓑ VI (= *fingir*) to pretend; **lo sé todo, así que no disimules** I know everything so don't bother pretending; **has sido tú, no disimules** it was you, don't pretend it wasn't; **ahí está Juan: disimula** there's Juan: pretend you haven't seen him

disimulo SM [1] (= *fingimiento*) dissimulation; **con ~** cunningly, craftily
[2] (= *tolerancia*) tolerance

disimulón* ADJ furtive, shady

disipación SF [*de costumbres*] dissipation; [*de dinero*] squandering; [*de niebla*] lifting

disipado ADJ [1] (= *libertino*) dissipated
[2] (= *derrochador*) extravagant

disipador(a) SM/F spendthrift

disipar ▸conjug 1a◂ Ⓐ VT [1] (*Meteo*) [+ *niebla*] to drive away; [+ *nubes*] to disperse
[2] (= *hacer desaparecer*) [+ *duda, temor*] to dispel, remove; [+ *esperanza*] to destroy

➤ LENGUA Y USO: **discutible** 53.6 **discutir A** 53.6 **disfrutar B1** 34.2

3 [+ *dinero*] to squander, fritter away (**en** on)
Ⓑ **disiparse** VPR 1 (*Meteo*) [*niebla*] to lift; [*nubes*] to disperse
2 [*dudas*] to be dispelled

disjunto ADJ separate, discrete

diskette SM = **disqueta**

dislate SM 1 (= *absurdo*) absurdity; **eso es un ~** that's an absurd *o* ridiculous thing to do
2 **dislates** (= *disparates*) nonsense *sing*; **un texto cargado de ~s** a text full of nonsense *o* stupid comments

dislexia SF dyslexia

disléxico/a ADJ, SM/F dyslexic

dislocación SF 1 (*Med*) dislocation
2 [*de estado*] dismemberment

dislocado ADJ 1 (*Med*) dislocated
2 (= *alocado*) wild, unrestrained

dislocar ▸conjug 1g◂ Ⓐ VT (*Med*) to dislocate
Ⓑ **dislocarse** VPR (*Med*) **~se el tobillo** to dislocate one's ankle; **se le ha dislocado el hombro** he has dislocated his shoulder

disloque* SM 1 (= *locura*) **al llegar la medianoche aquello fue ya el ~** when midnight came it was utter madness; **es el ~** it's the last straw
2 (= *confusión*) confusion

disminución SF 1 (= *reducción*) [*de población, cantidad*] decrease, drop, fall; [*de precios, temperaturas*] drop, fall; [*de velocidad*] decrease, reduction; **una ~ en las importaciones** a drop *o* fall in imports; **la ~ de la capa de ozono** the depletion of the ozone layer; **uno de los síntomas es la ~ de la actividad política** one of the symptoms is a decrease in political activity; **continuar sin ~** to continue unchecked *o* unabated
2 (*Med*) [*de dolor*] reduction; [*de fiebre*] drop, fall
3 (*Cos*) [*de puntos*] decreasing

disminuido/a Ⓐ ADJ 1 (= *achicado*) inadequate; **no me siento ~ ante nadie** there's no one that makes me feel inadequate
2 (*Med*) handicapped
3 (*Econ*) [*intervalo, valor*] diminished
Ⓑ SM/F (*Med*) handicapped person; **un centro para ~s** a centre for the disabled *o* the handicapped ▸ **disminuido/a físico/a** physically-handicapped person ▸ **disminuido/a psíquico/a** mentally handicapped person ▸ **disminuido/a visual** visually handicapped person

disminuir ▸conjug 3g◂ Ⓐ VT 1 (= *reducir*) [+ *nivel, precio, gastos, intereses*] to reduce, bring down; [+ *riesgo, incidencia, dolor*] to reduce, lessen; [+ *temperatura*] to lower, bring down; [+ *prestigio, autoridad*] to diminish, lessen; [+ *fuerzas*] to sap; [+ *entusiasmo*] to dampen; **algunos bancos han disminuido en un 0,15% sus tipos de interés** some banks have reduced *o* brought down their interest rates by 0.15%; **hemos tenido que ~ la dosis** we've had to reduce the dose; **las vacunas disminuyen la resistencia a otros virus** vaccinations lower resistance to other germs; **disminuyó la velocidad para tomar la curva** she slowed down *o* reduced her speed to go round the bend; **durante el día disminuyen la vigilancia** security is not so strict during the day; **esta medicina me disminuye las fuerzas** this medicine is making me weaker *o* sapping my strength
2 (*Cos*) [+ *puntos*] to decrease
Ⓑ VI 1 (= *decrecer*) [*número, población*] to decrease, drop, fall; [*temperatura, precios*] to drop, fall; [*distancia, diferencia, velocidad, tensión*] to decrease; [*fuerzas, autoridad, poder*] to diminish; [*días*] to grow shorter; [*luz*] to fade; [*prestigio, entusiasmo*] to dwindle; **ha disminuido la tasa de natalidad** the birth rate has decreased *o* dropped *o* fallen; **el número de asistentes ha disminuido últimamente** attendance has decreased *o* dropped *o* fallen recently; **ya le está disminuyendo la fiebre** his temperature is dropping *o* falling now; **el paro disminuyó en un 0,3%** unemployment dropped *o* fell by 0.3%; **su poder disminuyó con el paso del tiempo** his power diminished as time went by; **con esta pastilla te ~á el dolor** this tablet will relieve *o* ease your pain
2 (= *empeorar*) [*memoria, vista*] to fail
3 (*Cos*) [*puntos*] to decrease

Disneylandia SF Disneyland

disociable ADJ separable

disociación SF dissociation

disociar ▸conjug 1b◂ Ⓐ VT to dissociate (**de** from)
Ⓑ **disociarse** VPR to dissociate o.s. (**de** from)

disoluble ADJ soluble

disolución SF 1 (= *acto*) dissolution
2 (*Quím*) solution ▸ **disolución de goma** rubber solution
3 (*Com*) liquidation
4 (*moral*) dissoluteness, dissipation

disoluto ADJ dissolute

disolvente SM solvent

disolver ▸conjug 2h◂ (*pp* **disuelto**) Ⓐ VT 1 [+ *azúcar, sal*] to dissolve
2 [+ *contrato, matrimonio, parlamento*] to dissolve
3 [+ *manifestación*] to break up; (*Mil*) to disband
Ⓑ **disolverse** VPR 1 [*azúcar, sal*] to dissolve
2 (*Com*) to go into liquidation
3 (= *deshacerse*) [*manifestación*] to break up; [*parlamento*] to dissolve

disonancia SF 1 (*Mús*) dissonance
2 (= *falta de armonía*) discord; **hacer ~ con algo** to be out of harmony with sth

disonante ADJ 1 (*Mús*) dissonant
2 (= *discordante*) discordant

disonar ▸conjug 1l◂ VI 1 (*Mús*) to be out of tune
2 (= *no armonizar*) to lack harmony; **~ con algo** to be out of keeping with sth, clash with sth

dísono ADJ discordant

dispar ADJ [*opiniones, aficiones*] different, disparate; [*rendimiento*] inconsistent

disparada SF (*LAm*) 1 (= *salida apresurada*) sudden departure; **ir a la ~** to go at full speed; **irse a la ~** to be off like a shot; **tomar la ~** (*Cono Sur**) to beat it*
2 (= *prisa*) rush

disparadero SM trigger, trigger mechanism; ✦**MODISMO poner a algn en el ~** to drive sb to distraction

disparado ADJ 1 (= *con prisa*) **entrar ~** to shoot in; **ir ~** to go like mad; **salir ~** to shoot out, be off like a shot
2 (*Caribe*‡) randy*, horny‡

disparador Ⓐ ADJ (*Méx**) lavish
Ⓑ SM 1 [*de arma*] trigger
2 (*Téc*) [*de cámara fotográfica*] release; [*de reloj*] escapement ▸ **disparador automático** delayed action release ▸ **disparador de bombas** bomb release

disparar ▸conjug 1a◂ Ⓐ VT 1 [+ *arma de fuego, proyectil, tiro*] to fire; [+ *flecha*] to shoot; [+ *gatillo*] to pull; **le ~on tres balazos** they fired three shots at him
2 (*Dep*) [+ *penalti, falta*] to take
3 (*Fot*) **para ~ la cámara, aprieta el botón** to take a photograph, press the button; **los paparazzi ~on sus cámaras al verla salir** the paparazzi clicked their cameras when they saw her come out; **dispara el flash, que está oscuro** use the flash, it's dark; **"prohibido disparar el flash"** "no flash photography"
4 [+ *consumo, precio*] **la subida del petróleo ha disparado la inflación** the rise in oil prices has caused inflation to shoot up
5 (= *hacer saltar*) [+ *alarma*] to trigger, set off; [+ *proceso, reacción*] to spark, spark off
Ⓑ VI 1 (*con un arma*) to shoot, fire; **¡quieto o disparo!** stop or I'll shoot *o* fire!; **los cazadores ~on al ciervo** the hunters shot *o* fired at the deer; **le ~on a la cabeza** they shot *o* fired at his head; **la policía disparó contra los manifestantes** the police fired on *o* shot at the demonstrators; **¡no dispares!** don't shoot!; **el asesino disparó a matar** the murderer shot to kill; **¡disparad!** fire!; **apuntó al blanco y disparó** he aimed at the target and fired
2 (*Dep*) to shoot; **el delantero disparó a puerta** the forward shot at *o* for goal
3 (*Fot*) to shoot; **¡enfoca y dispara!** focus the camera and shoot
4 (*Méx**) (= *gastar mucho*) to spend lavishly
5 = **disparatar**
Ⓒ **dispararse** VPR 1 [*arma de fuego*] to go off, fire
2 [*alarma*] to go off
3 [*consumo, precios, inflación*] to shoot up, rocket
4 [*pánico, violencia*] to take hold
5 (*al hablar*) to get carried away*
6 (*LAm*) (= *marcharse*) to rush off, shoot off*

disparatadamente ADV absurdly, nonsensically

disparatado ADJ crazy, nonsensical

disparatar ▸conjug 1a◂ VI 1 (= *decir disparates*) to talk nonsense
2 (= *hacer disparates*) to behave foolishly

disparate SM 1 (= *comentario*) foolish remark; **¡no digas ~s!** don't talk nonsense!; **¡qué ~!** what rubbish!, how absurd!
2 (= *acción*) **sacar el coche con esta niebla es un ~** taking the car out in this fog is just crazy *o* is a stupid thing to do; **está tan desesperado que es capaz de cualquier ~** he's so desperate he's capable of doing something really stupid
3 (= *error*) blunder; **hiciste un ~ protestando** it was foolish of you to complain
4 (*) **había un ~ de gente** there were absolutely loads of people; **costar un ~** to cost a ridiculous amount; **reírse un ~** to laugh o.s. silly
5 (*Arquit*) folly

disparejo ADJ 1 (= *diferente*) different
2 (= *desnivelado*) uneven; **los dos cuadros estaban ~s en la pared** the two pictures weren't level with each other on the wall

disparidad SF disparity

disparo SM 1 (= *tiro*) shot; **se oyeron varios ~s** some shooting was heard; **hacer ~s al aire** to fire into the air, shoot into the air ► **disparo de advertencia**, **disparo de intimidación** warning shot; (*Náut*) shot across the bows ► **disparo de salida** starting shot ► **disparo inicial** [*de cohete*] blast-off
2 (*Dep*) shot; **un buen ~ del delantero** a good shot by the striker
3 (*Mec*) release

dispendiador ADJ free-spending, big-spending

dispendio SM waste

dispendioso ADJ expensive

dispensa SF 1 (= *exención*) exemption (**de** from)
2 (*Rel*) dispensation

dispensabilidad SF dispensable nature

dispensable ADJ dispensable

dispensación SF dispensation

dispensador SM dispenser

dispensadora SF ► **dispensadora de monedas** change machine

dispensar ►conjug 1a◄ Ⓐ VT 1 (= *conceder*) [+ *ayuda*] to give; [+ *honores*] to grant; [+ *atención*] to pay; [+ *acogida*] to give, accord; [+ *receta*] to dispense
2 (= *perdonar*) to excuse; **¡dispénseme usted!** I beg your pardon!, sorry!; **~ que algn haga algo** to excuse sb for doing sth
3 (= *eximir*) to exempt (**de** from), excuse (**de** from); **~ a algn de una obligación** to excuse sb from an obligation; **me ~on del pago de la multa** they waived my fine, they excused me from payment of the fine; **~ a algn de hacer algo** to excuse sb from doing sth; **le han dispensado de hacer gimnasia** he's been excused from doing gymnastics; **así el cuerpo queda dispensado de ese esfuerzo** thus the body is freed from that effort *o* relieved of that effort
Ⓑ **dispensarse** VPR **no puedo ~me de esa obligación** I cannot escape that duty

dispensario SM 1 (= *clínica*) community clinic
2 (*en hospital*) outpatients' department

dispepsia SF dyspepsia

dispéptico ADJ dyspeptic

dispersar ►conjug 1a◄ Ⓐ VT [+ *multitud, grupo*] to disperse, scatter; [+ *manifestación*] to break up; [+ *enemigo*] to rout
Ⓑ **dispersarse** VPR [*multitud, grupo*] to disperse, scatter; [*manifestación*] to break up

dispersión SF 1 (= *acto*) [*de grupo, multitud*] dispersion; [*de manifestación*] breaking up; [*de energía, neutrones*] diffusion
2 (= *resultado*) dispersal

disperso ADJ 1 (= *diseminado*) scattered, dispersed; **~s en** *o* **por** scattered across *o* over
2 [*discurso, mente*] unfocussed, unfocused (*EEUU*)

displicencia SF 1 (= *mal humor*) peevishness
2 (= *desgana*) lack of enthusiasm; **trató a sus invitados con ~** he treated his guests in an offhand manner

displicente ADJ 1 (= *malhumorado*) peevish
2 (= *poco entusiasta*) unenthusiastic
3 (= *despreciativo*) offhand, disdainful

disponer ►conjug 2q◄ (*pp* **dispuesto**) Ⓐ VT 1 (= *colocar*) (*por orden*) to arrange; (*en fila*) to line up; (*de otro modo*) to set out; **dispuso los discos por orden alfabético** he arranged the records in alphabetical order; **dispuso a los niños de dos en dos** he lined up the children in twos; **dispuso los cubiertos sobre la mesa** he set out the cutlery on the table; **dispón las sillas en círculo** set out *o* arrange the chairs in a circle
2 (= *preparar*) to prepare, get ready; **dispuso la sala para el concierto** he prepared the hall *o* he got the hall ready for the concert; **~ la mesa** to lay the table
3 (= *mandar*) 3·1 [*persona, comisión*] to order; [*juez*] to rule, decree, order; **dispuso cerrar todas las puertas** he ordered all the doors to be shut; **el general dispuso que no saliera nadie** the general gave orders that *o* ordered that nobody was to go out; **el médico dispuso que guardara cama** the doctor ordered that she should stay in bed; **se dispuso que debía abandonar el país** it was decreed that he should leave the country; **mis padres lo han dispuesto así** my parents have decided that it should be that way; **el juez ha dispuesto que tenía que pagar la multa** the judge ruled *o* decreed *o* ordered that he must pay the fine
3·2 (*en código, testamento*) to lay down, stipulate; **el artículo 52 dispone que ...** Article 52 lays down *o* stipulates that ...; **dispuso que su patrimonio no fuera dividido** she laid down *o* stipulated that her estate should not be divided
Ⓑ VI 1 **~ de algo** (= *tener*) to have sth (at one's disposal); **no dispongo de dinero suficiente** I don't have enough money (at my disposal); **disponemos de muy poco tiempo** there is very little time available (to us), we have very little time (at our disposal); **los medios de que disponemos** the means available to us, the means at our disposal; **dispone de coche propio** he has his own car; **dispone de quince días para apelar** you have fifteen days to appeal
2 **~ de algo** (= *hacer uso de*) to make use of sth, use sth; **no puede ~ de esos bienes hasta que él muera** she cannot make use of *o* use those assets until his death; **puede ~ de mí para lo que necesites** I am at your disposal for whatever you might need
Ⓒ **disponerse** VPR 1 **~se a hacer algo** (= *estar a punto de*) to be about to do sth; (= *decidir*) to resolve to do sth; **en ese momento nos disponíamos a salir** at that moment we were about to go out; **me dispuse a cumplir con mi deber** I resolved to do my duty
2 (= *colocarse*) **~se para algo** to get into position for sth; **los coches se disponían para la salida** the cars were getting into position for the start

disponibilidad SF 1 [*de persona, producto*] availability; **empleado en ~** unposted employee, employee available for posting
2 **disponibilidades** (*Com*) resources, liquid assets; **~es líquidas** available liquid assets

disponible ADJ 1 (= *libre*) [*asiento, habitación, dinero*] available; [*tiempo*] spare; **quedan varias plazas ~s** there are various seats available; **no nos queda ninguna habitación ~** we don't have any vacancies *o* any rooms available; **este mes no tengo tiempo ~** I can't spare *o* I don't have the time this month
2 **estar ~** [*persona, habitación*] to be available, be free; **si me necesitas, por las tardes estoy ~** if you need me, I'm available *o* free in the afternoons; **¿a qué hora estará ~ la habitación?** what time will the room be available *o* free?; **la casa ya está ~ para que la ocupéis** the house is now ready for you to move in
3 [*militar*] available, available for duty

disposición SF 1 (= *colocación*) [*de muebles, capítulos*] arrangement; [*de casa, habitación*] layout; **la ~ del escenario** the layout of the stage
2 (= *disponibilidad*) disposal; **a ~ de algn** at sb's disposal; **un número de teléfono a ~ del público** a telephone number for public use *o* at the public's disposal; **estamos a tu ~ para lo que haga falta** we are at your disposal for whatever you may need; **puso su cargo a ~ de la asamblea** he offered his resignation to the assembly; **pasar a ~ judicial** to be taken into custody; **tener algo a su ~** to have sth at one's disposal, have sth available
3 (= *voluntad*) willingness; **han demostrado su ~ hacia el diálogo** they have shown their willingness to enter into a dialogue; **estar en ~ de hacer algo** (= *con ánimo de*) to be ready *o* willing to do sth; (= *en condiciones de*) to be in a position to do sth ► **disposición de ánimo** frame of mind
4 (= *aptitud*) aptitude, talent (**para** for); **no tenía ~ para la pintura** he had no aptitude *o* talent for painting
5 (*Jur*) (= *cláusula*) provision; (= *norma*) regulation; **según las disposiciones del código** according to the provisions of the statute; **una ~ ministerial** a ministerial order *o* regulation; **última ~** last will and testament
6 **disposiciones** (= *medidas*) arrangements; **adoptar** *o* **tomar las disposiciones para algo** to make arrangements for sth

dispositivo SM 1 (*Mec*) (= *aparato*) device; (= *mecanismo*) mechanism ► **dispositivo de alimentación** hopper ► **dispositivo de arranque** starting mechanism ► **dispositivo de seguridad** (= *mecanismo*) safety catch, safety (*EEUU*); (= *medidas*) security measures *pl* ► **dispositivo intrauterino** intrauterine device, coil ► **dispositivo periférico** peripheral device
2 **dispositivos** (*Mil*) forces ► **dispositivos de seguridad** security forces

dispuesto Ⓐ PP *de* **disponer**
Ⓑ ADJ 1 (= *preparado*) arranged, ready; **todo está ~ para las elecciones** everything is set *o* arranged *o* ready for the elections; **~ según ciertos principios** arranged according to certain principles; **los platos están ya ~s en la mesa** the plates are already laid out *o* set on the table; **¿estáis ~s para salir?** are you ready to leave?
2 (= *decidido*) willing; **es una persona muy dispuesta** she's always ready and willing; **estar ~ a**: **estábamos ~s al diálogo** we were willing *o* prepared to discuss the matter; **estoy ~ a ir a juicio si fuera necesario** I am quite prepared to go to court if necessary; **no estoy ~ a que me insulten** I refuse to be insulted; **bien ~** well-disposed; **estaba bien ~ hacia su oferta** he was well-disposed to their offer; **mal ~** ill-disposed; **poco ~** reluctant, unwilling; **parece poco dispuesta a colaborar** she seems reluctant *o* unwilling to cooperate

disputa SF [1] (= *discusión*) dispute, argument; **los asuntos en ~** the matters in dispute *o* at issue; **sin ~** undoubtedly, beyond dispute
[2] (= *controversia*) controversy

disputable ADJ disputable, debatable

disputado ADJ [*partido*] close, hard fought

disputador(a) Ⓐ ADJ disputatious, argumentative
Ⓑ SM/F (*Dep*) disputant

disputar ▸conjug 1a◂ Ⓐ VT [1] [+ *partido, encuentro*] to play, contest; [+ *campeonato, liga*] to play
[2] (*frm*) **~ algo a algn** to dispute sth with sb; **le disputamos a mi tío la casa** we disputed the ownership of the house with my uncle, we had a dispute with my uncle over the ownership of the house
Ⓑ VI **~ por algo** to compete for sth; **cinco candidatos disputan por el puesto** five candidates are competing for the job
Ⓒ **disputarse** VPR [1] (= *competir por*) **ocho escritores se disputan el premio** eight writers are contending *o* competing for the prize; **los hermanos se disputan la casa familiar** the brothers are disputing *o* in dispute over the family house
[2] (*Dep*) **el Mundial se disputó en Francia** the World Cup was played *o* contested in France; **el partido se suspendió cuando se disputaba el minuto cuatro** the match was suspended in the fourth minute of play

disque‡ SM **darse ~** (*Cono Sur*) to fancy o.s.*

disquería SF (*Caribe*) record shop

disquero ADJ record *antes de s*

disqueta SF (*LAm*), **disquete** SM (*Inform*) floppy disk, diskette ► **disquete de alta densidad** high density diskette

disquetera SF disk drive; **doble ~** dual floppy drive, double floppy drive ► **disquetera externa** external floppy drive

disquisición SF [1] (= *análisis*) disquisition
[2] **disquisiciones** (= *comentarios*) asides, digressions

Dist. ABR [1] (= **distancia**) dist
[2] (= **Distrito**) dist

distancia SF [1] (*en el espacio*) distance; **la ~ más corta entre dos puntos** the shortest distance between two points; **¿qué ~ hay entre Sevilla y Granada?** what's the distance between Seville and Granada?; **¿a qué ~ está Madrid de Barcelona?** how far (away) is Madrid from Barcelona?, how far is it from Madrid to Barcelona?; **la tienda está a 50 metros de ~** the shop is 50 metres away; **a tres metros de ~ del suelo** three metres from *o* off the ground; **a ~** from a distance; **el diseño se ve más claro a ~** you can see the design better from a distance; **el mando a ~** the remote control; **la Universidad a ~** ≈ the Open University; **una llamada a larga ~** a long-distance call; **acortar las ~s** to shorten the distance; **la nueva carretera acortará la ~** the new road will shorten the distance; **el Real Madrid ha acortado las ~s con el Barcelona** Real Madrid is closing in on Barcelona, Real Madrid is closing the gap with Barcelona; **ganar ~s** to get ahead, make progress; **guardar** *o* **mantener las ~s** ◊ **mantenerse a ~** to keep one's distance; **marcar ~s**: **el Atlético marcó ~s con el segundo clasificado** Atlético put some distance between itself and the second-placed team; **quieren marcar ~s con la dirección del partido** they want to distance themselves from *o* set themselves apart from the party leadership; **salvando las ~s**: **es, salvando las ~s, el Picasso de nuestros días** he's the Picasso of today, give or take some obvious differences ► **distancia de despegue** (*Aer*) length of takeoff ► **distancia de detención** stopping distance ► **distancia de frenado** braking distance ► **distancia de seguridad** (*Aut*) safe distance ► **distancia focal** focal length
[2] (*entre opiniones, creencias*) distance, gap; **hay una insalvable ~ entre los dos partidos** there's an unbridgeable distance *o* gap between the two parties

distanciado ADJ [1] (= *remoto*) remote (**de** from)
[2] (= *separado*) widely separated
[3] (*en relación afectiva*) **estamos algo ~s** we are not particularly close; **está distanciada de su familia** she has grown apart from her family; **estamos ~s en nuestras ideas** our ideas are a long way *o* poles apart

distanciador ADJ **efecto ~** distancing effect

distanciamiento SM [1] (= *acto*) spacing out
[2] (= *estado*) remoteness, isolation
[3] (= *distancia*) distance; **hay un ~ cada vez mayor entre ellos** they are growing further apart every day ► **distanciamiento generacional** generation gap
[4] (*Teat, Literat*) distancing effect

distanciar ▸conjug 1b◂ Ⓐ VT [1] [+ *objetos*] to space out, separate
[2] [+ *amigos, hermanos*] to cause a rift between
Ⓑ **distanciarse** VPR [1] [*dos personas*] to grow apart; **~se de la familia** to grow apart from one's family
[2] (*en carrera*) **consiguió ~se del otro corredor** he managed to put some distance between himself and the other runner

distante ADJ [1] [*lugar*] (= *lejano*) distant; (= *remoto*) far-off, remote; **~ 10km** 10km away
[2] [*persona, actitud*] distant

distar ▸conjug 1a◂ VI [1] (*en el espacio*) **dista cinco kilómetros de aquí** it is five kilometres from here; **¿dista mucho?** is it far?
[2] (= *diferir*) **dista mucho de la verdad** it's very far from the truth, it's a long way off the truth; **disto mucho de aprobarlo** I am far from approving of it

distender ▸conjug 2g◂ Ⓐ VT to distend, stretch; **~ las relaciones entre ambos países** to ease *o* steady relations between the two countries
Ⓑ **distenderse** VPR [*músculos*] to relax; [*relaciones*] to ease, steady

distendido ADJ [*ambiente, charla*] relaxed

distensión SF [1] (= *relajación*) **ambiente de ~** relaxed atmosphere
[2] (*Med*) strain ► **distensión muscular** muscle strain
[3] (*Pol*) détente

distensivo ADJ conciliatory

dístico SM distich

distinción SF [1] (= *diferencia*) distinction; **hacer una ~ entre ...** to make a distinction between ...; **a ~ de algo** unlike sth, in contrast to sth; **hacer una ~ con algn** to show special consideration to sb; **sin ~**: **todos serán tratados sin ~** everybody will be treated without distinction; **sin ~ de edad** irrespective *o* regardless of age; **sin ~ de raza** regardless of race, without distinction of race
[2] (= *privilegio*) distinction; **le acaban de otorgar una ~ al valor** he was honoured *o* (*EEUU*) honored for his bravery ► **distinción honorífica** honour, honor (*EEUU*)
[3] (= *elegancia*) elegance, refinement; **iba vestido con ~** he was elegantly dressed

distingo SM [1] (= *salvedad*) reservation; **hacer** *o* **poner ~s a algo** to raise reservations about sth
[2] (= *distinción*) subtle distinction

distinguible ADJ distinguishable

distinguido ADJ [1] (= *destacado*) [*figura*] distinguished; [*artista, escritor*] celebrated; [*alumno*] outstanding; **contamos con la distinguida presencia del premio Nobel de la Paz** we are honoured to have with us the Nobel Peace Prize winner
[2] (= *refinado*) [*modales, ropa*] elegant, refined; [*caballero, señora*] distinguished; **una distinguida forma de andar** an elegant *o* refined way of walking; **quisiera pedir a nuestro ~ público ...** I would like to ask our distinguished audience ...; **~ público, les vamos a presentar ...** ladies and gentlemen, allow me to present ...
[3] (*frm*) (*en cartas*) **"Distinguida Sra. Martínez"** "Dear Mrs Martinez"; **"Distinguido Señor"** (*LAm*) "Dear Sir"

distinguir ▸conjug 3d◂ Ⓐ VT [1] (= *diferenciar*)
[1·1] (= *ver la diferencia entre*) to distinguish; **no distingo bien los colores** I can't distinguish the colours very well; **no resulta fácil ~ a los mellizos** it is not easy to tell the twins apart, it's not easy to distinguish between the twins; **he puesto una etiqueta en la maleta para ~la** I've put a label on the suitcase to be able to tell it apart from *o* distinguish it from the others; **lo sabría ~ entre un millón** I would know it *o* recognize it anywhere; **¿sabes ~ un violín de una viola?** can you tell *o* distinguish a violin from a viola?; ✦**MODISMO no distingue lo blanco de lo negro** he doesn't know his right from his left
[1·2] (= *hacer diferente*) to set apart; **lo distingue su capacidad intelectual** his intellect sets him apart; **lo que nos distingue de los animales** what distinguishes us from the animals, what sets us apart from the animals
[1·3] (= *hacer una distinción entre*) to distinguish; **hay que ~ dos períodos** we need to distinguish two periods
[2] (= *ver*) [+ *objeto, sonido*] to make out; **no podía ~ la matrícula** I couldn't make out the number plate; **ya distingo la costa** I can see *o* make out the coast now
[3] (= *honrar*) [+ *amigo, alumno*] to honour, honor (*EEUU*); **me distingue con su amistad** I am honoured to have his friendship; **lo distinguieron con el Premio Nobel** he was honoured with the Nobel Prize
[4] (= *elegir*) to single out; **lo distinguieron para el ascenso** he was singled out for promotion
Ⓑ VI (= *ver la diferencia*) to tell the difference (**entre** between); (= *hacer una distinción*) to make a distinction (**entre** between); **lo mismo le da un vino malo que uno bueno, no distingue** it's all the same to him whether it's a bad wine or a good one, he can't tell the difference; **no era capaz de ~ entre lo bueno y lo malo** he couldn't tell the difference *o* dis-

tinguish between good and bad; **es un hombre que sabe ~** he is a discerning person; **en su discurso, distinguió entre el viejo y el nuevo liberalismo** in his speech he made a distinction between the old and the new liberalism

Ⓒ **distinguirse** VPR 1 (= *diferenciarse*) [*objeto*] to stand out; [*persona*] to distinguish o.s., make a name for o.s.; **nuestros productos se distinguen por su calidad** our products are distinguished by their quality, our products stand out for their quality; **se distinguió como importante investigador** he achieved renown *o* he made a name for himself as a leading researcher; **se distinguió por sus descubrimientos en física cuántica** he made a name for himself through his research into quantum physics; **no se distingue precisamente por su sutileza** subtlety is not exactly his strong point, he's not renowned for his subtlety; **nuestros muebles se distinguen del resto por calidad y diseño** our furniture stands out from the rest due to its superior quality and design

2 (= *reconocerse*) to be identified; **las cintas de cromo se distinguen por su envoltorio** chrome tapes can be identified by their packaging

distintivo Ⓐ ADJ [*rasgo, carácter*] distinctive; [*signo*] distinguishing

Ⓑ SM (= *insignia*) [*de policía*] badge, button (*EEUU*); [*de equipo*] emblem, badge; [*de empresa*] emblem, logo; **~ de minusválido** disabled sticker

distinto ADJ 1 (= *diferente*) different (**a, de** from); **son muy ~s** they are very different; **eso es ~** that's a different matter

2 (= *definido*) [*perfil, vista*] clear, distinct

3 **distintos** several, various; **hay distintas opiniones sobre eso** there are several *o* various opinions about that

distorsión SF 1 [*de sonido, imagen*] distortion

2 [*de los hechos*] distortion, twisting

3 (*Med*) twisting

distorsionador ADJ, **distorsionante** ADJ distorting

distorsionar ▸conjug 1a◂ VT to distort

distracción SF 1 (= *entretenimiento*) entertainment; **leer es mi ~ favorita** reading is my favourite pastime *o* form of entertainment; **no faltan distracciones para los niños** there is no lack of entertainment for the children; **colecciona sellos como ~** he collects stamps as a hobby

2 [*de preocupaciones, problemas*] distraction; **el trabajo me sirve de ~** my work is a distraction for me; **este libro te servirá de ~** this book will help you take your mind off things

3 (= *despiste*) **en un momento de ~ me robaron la cartera** my attention wandered *o* I got distracted for a moment and I had my wallet stolen; **la causa del accidente podría ser una ~ del conductor** the accident could have been caused by a lapse of concentration on the driver's part; **no te saludaría por ~** I must have been so distracted that I didn't say hello

4 (*Fin*) [*de dinero, fondos*] embezzlement

5 (= *libertinaje*) loose living, dissipation

distraer ▸conjug 2o◂ Ⓐ VT 1 (= *entretener*) to entertain, amuse; **distrajimos a los niños contándoles cuentos** we kept the children entertained *o* amused by telling them stories; **la música es lo que más me distrae** music is the thing I most enjoy; **necesito algo que me distraiga un poco** I need something to take my mind off things; **la cocina me distrae de mis problemas** cooking takes my mind off my problems; ✦***MODISMO*** **~ el hambre** to keep the wolf from the door

2 (= *despistar*) to distract (**de** from); **no haces más que ~me** all you do is distract me; **"prohibido distraer al conductor"** "do not distract the driver's attention"; **no me distraigas de mi trabajo** don't distract me from my work

3 (*Fin*) [+ *dinero, fondos*] to embezzle

4 (*moralmente*) to lead astray

Ⓑ VI (= *entretener*) [*pesca, ejercicio*] to be relaxing, take your mind off things; [*lectura, espectáculo*] to be entertaining, take your mind off things; **salir de compras distrae mucho** going shopping takes your mind off things

Ⓒ **distraerse** VPR 1 (= *entretenerse*) to keep o.s. entertained, keep o.s. amused; **me distraigo viendo la tele** I keep myself entertained *o* amused watching TV; **se distrae mucho con sus nietos** her grandchildren keep her entertained *o* amused; **deberías salir y ~te** you should get out and enjoy yourself

2 (= *despistarse*) to get distracted; **oye bien lo que digo y no te distraigas** listen carefully and don't let yourself get distracted; **se distrae mucho en clase** he gets very easily distracted in class; **me distraje un momento y se me quemó la comida** my attention wandered *o* I got distracted for a moment and the dinner got burnt; **se distrae con el vuelo de una mosca** he gets distracted by the slightest thing

distraídamente ADV absent-mindedly; **hojeaba ~ el periódico** she glanced absently *o* absent-mindedly through the newspaper; **se llevó ~ mis libros** she absent-mindedly took my books

distraído/a Ⓐ ADJ 1 (= *despistado*) 1·1 (*con estar*) **siempre está ~ en clase** he's always daydreaming in class, he never pays attention in class; **iba yo algo ~** I was walking along with my mind on other things; **me miró distraída** she glanced absently at me, she glanced at me absent-mindedly

1·2 (*con ser*) **soy muy ~** I'm very absent-minded

2 (= *entretenido*) entertained, amused; **la televisión me mantenía ~** the television kept me entertained *o* amused

3 (*Esp*) (= *divertido*) entertaining, amusing; **es un juego muy ~** it's a very entertaining *o* amusing game

4 (= *disoluto*) dissolute

Ⓑ SM/F **hacerse el ~** to pretend not to notice

distribución SF 1 (= *reparto*) [*de víveres, mercancías, película*] distribution; [*de correo*] delivery; [*de trabajo, tarea*] allocation; [*de folletos*] (*en buzones*) distribution; (*en mano*) handing out

2 (*Estadística*) distribution; **la ~ de los impuestos** the distribution of the tax burden

3 (*Arquit*) layout, ground plan

4 (*Aut, Téc*) distribution

5 (*Mec*) timing gears *pl*

distribuido ADJ **una casa bien distribuida** a well laid out house

distribuidor(a) Ⓐ ADJ (*Com*) **red ~a** distribution network; **casa ~a** distributor, distribution company

Ⓑ SM/F (= *persona*) [*de productos*] distributor; (*Correos*) sorter; (*Com*) dealer, stockist; **su ~ habitual** your regular dealer

Ⓒ SM 1 (= *máquina*) ► **distribuidor automático** vending machine

2 (*Aut*) distributor

3 (*LAm Aut*) motorway exit, highway exit (*EEUU*)

distribuidora SF (*Cine*) distributor

distribuir ▸conjug 3g◂ VT 1 (= *repartir*) [+ *víveres, mercancía, película*] to distribute; [+ *correo*] to deliver; [+ *trabajo, tarea*] to allocate; [+ *folletos*] (*en buzones*) to distribute; (*en mano*) to hand out

2 (= *entregar*) [+ *premios*] to give out; [+ *dividendos*] to pay

3 (*Téc*) [+ *carga*] to stow, arrange; [+ *peso*] to distribute equally

4 (*Arquit*) to plan, lay out

distributivo ADJ distributive

distrito SM 1 (*Admin*) district ► **distrito electoral** constituency, precinct (*EEUU*) ► **distrito postal** postal district

2 (*Jur*) circuit

distrofia SF (*Med*) dystrophy ► **distrofia muscular** muscular dystrophy

disturbio SM 1 (= *del orden*) (*de poca importancia*) disturbance; (*más grave*) riot; **los ~s causados por los hinchas** the disturbances caused by fans

2 (*Téc*) disturbance ► **disturbio aerodinámico** (*Aer*) wash, slipstream

disuadir ▸conjug 3a◂ VT to dissuade, deter; **~ a algn de hacer algo** to dissuade *o* deter sb from doing sth

disuasión SF 1 (= *convencimiento*) dissuasion; **le falta capacidad de ~** he doesn't have strong powers of persuasion

2 (*Mil*) deterrence ► **disuasión nuclear** nuclear deterrence; *ver tb* **fuerza 8**

disuasivo Ⓐ ADJ 1 [*palabras*] dissuasive

2 (*Mil*) **arma disuasiva** deterrent

Ⓑ SM deterrent

disuasorio ADJ (*Mil*) deterrent; *ver tb* **fuerza 8**

disuelto PP *de* **disolver**

disyuntiva SF 1 (= *opción*) alternative, choice

2 (= *dilema*) dilemma

disyuntivo ADJ disjunctive

disyuntor SM (*Elec*) circuit breaker

dita[1] SF 1 (= *garantía*) surety

2 (= *fianza*) security, bond

3 (*Andes*) (= *empréstito*) loan at a high rate of interest; (*LAm*) (= *deuda*) small debt

dita[2] SF (*Caribe*) dish, cup, pot

ditirambo SM dithyramb

DIU SM ABR (= **dispositivo intrauterino**) coil, IUD, IUCD

diurético ADJ, SM diuretic

diurno ADJ (*gen*) day *antes de s*, daytime *antes de s*; [*animal, planta*] diurnal

diva SF prima donna, diva; *ver tb* **divo**

divagación SF (= *disgresión*) digression; **divagaciones** wanderings, ramblings

divagador ADJ rambling, discursive

divagar ▸conjug 1h◂ VI 1 (= *salirse del tema*) to digress; **¡no divagues!** get on with it!, come

to the point!
2 (= *hablar vagamente*) to ramble

divagatorio ADJ digressive

diván SM 1 (= *asiento*) divan
2 [*de psiquiatra*] couch

diver* ADJ, **díver*** ADJ = **divertido**

divergencia SF divergence ► **divergencia de opiniones** difference of opinion

divergente ADJ divergent

divergir ▸conjug 3c◂ VI 1 [*líneas*] to diverge
2 [*opiniones*] to differ
3 [*personas*] to differ, disagree

diversidad SF diversity

diversificación SF diversification

diversificado ADJ diversified; **ciclo ~** (*Ven Educ*) upper secondary education

diversificador ADJ diversifying

diversificar ▸conjug 1g◂ Ⓐ VT to diversify
Ⓑ **diversificarse** VPR to diversify

diversión SF 1 (= *entretenimiento*) fun; **necesita un poco de ~** he needs a bit of fun
2 (= *pasatiempo*) hobby, pastime; **diversiones de salón** parlour games, indoor games
3 (*Mil*) diversion

diverso ADJ Ⓐ 1 (= *variado*) diverse, varied
2 (= *diferente*) different (**de** from)
3 **diversos** several, various; **está en ~s libros** it appears in several *o* various books
Ⓑ **diversos** SMPL (*Com*) sundries

divertido ADJ 1 (= *entretenido*) [*libro, película*] entertaining; [*chiste, persona*] funny, amusing; **la fiesta fue muy divertida** the party was great fun *o* very enjoyable; **el viaje fue muy ~** the trip was great fun; **¡qué ~! ¿ahora me dices que no puedes ir?** (*iró*) that's just great! now you tell me you can't go?
2 **estar ~** (*LAm**) to be tight*

DIVERTIDO

¿"Funny o fun"?

• **Divertido** sólo se puede traducir por **funny** si nos hace reír:

Acabo de ver una obra muy divertida
I've just seen a very funny play

• Cuando hablamos de una actividad o situación **divertida** (en el sentido de entretenida y agradable), a menudo se la puede describir en inglés como **fun**:

Me gusta jugar al escondite. Es muy divertido
I like playing hide and seek. It's great fun

! Fun es un sustantivo incontable y por lo tanto, al contrario que **funny**, no puede ir acompañado de adverbios como **very**. Se suele acompañar de **great**, **good** y **a lot of**.

Para otros usos y ejemplos ver la entrada.

divertimento SM (*Mús*) divertimento

divertimiento SM 1 (*Mil*) diversion
2 (*Mús*) divertissement

divertir ▸conjug 3i◂ Ⓐ VT 1 (= *hacer reír*) **sus imitaciones divierten mucho al público** the audience find his impressions very funny *o* amusing
2 (= *entretener*) to entertain, amuse; **divirtió a los niños con sus juegos de magia** he entertained the children with his magic tricks, he kept the children amused with his magic tricks
3 (*frm*) (= *distraer*) to distract
Ⓑ **divertirse** VPR 1 (= *pasarlo bien*) to have a good time, enjoy o.s.; **¡que te diviertas!** have a good time!, enjoy yourself!
2 (= *distraerse*) to amuse o.s.; **le compré este juego para que se divirtiera** I bought him this game to keep him amused; **cantamos sólo por** *o* **para ~nos** we sing just for fun

dividendo SM dividend ► **dividendo a cuenta** interim dividend ► **dividendo definitivo** final demand ► **dividendos por acción** earnings per share

dividir ▸conjug 3a◂ Ⓐ VT 1 (= *partir*) to divide; **los dividieron en tres grupos** they split them (up) *o* divided them into three groups; **las obras de Ibsen se pueden ~ en dos etapas** Ibsen's works can be divided into two periods; **dividía su tiempo entre el cargo y su familia** he divided his time between his job and his family; **la bodega del barco está dividida en cuatro secciones** the hold of the ship is divided into four sections
2 (*Mat*) to divide (**entre, por** by); **doce dividido entre** *o* **por cuatro son tres** twelve divided by four is three
3 (= *repartir*) [+ *ganancias, posesiones*] to split up, divide up; [+ *gastos*] to split; **hemos dividido el premio entre toda la familia** we have split up *o* divided up the prize among the whole family
4 (= *separar*) to divide; **los Pirineos dividen España y Francia** the Pyrenees divide France from Spain
5 (= *enemistar*) to divide; **utilizó el chantaje para ~nos** he used blackmail to divide us; **la guerra dividió al país** the war divided the country; ✦*REFRÁN* **divide y vencerás** divide and rule
Ⓑ VI (*Mat*) to divide (**entre, por** into); **se me ha olvidado ~** I've forgotten how to do division *o* how to divide
Ⓒ **dividirse** VPR 1 (= *partirse*) [*célula*] to divide; [*grupo, país*] to split; **el partido se dividió en dos tendencias** the party split into two factions; **me encantaría ayudarte, pero no puedo ~me** I'd love to help you, but I can't be in two places at once; **la Edad Media puede ~se en dos períodos** the Middle Ages can be divided *o* split into two periods; **la crítica estuvo muy dividida** the critics were very divided
2 (= *separarse*) [*personas*] to split up; [*camino, carretera*] to fork; **cuando llegamos al cruce nos dividimos** when we got to the crossroads, we split up; **los fundadores se dividieron porque sus ideas eran muy distintas** the founders split up because their ideas were so different; **la carretera se divide al llegar al km 28** the road forks at km 28
3 (= *repartirse*) [+ *trabajo, ganancias*] to split up, divide up; **es mucho más fácil si nos dividimos el trabajo** it is much easier if we split up *o* divide up the work

divierta* SF (*CAm*) village dance, hop*

divieso SM (*Med*) boil

divinamente ADV divinely; **lo pasamos ~** we had a wonderful time

divinidad SF 1 (= *dios*) **una ~** a deity; **la Divinidad** God, the Godhead ► **divinidad marina** sea god ► **divinidad pagana** pagan god/goddess
2 (= *esencia divina*) divinity
3 (= *preciosidad*) **¡qué ~!** ◊ **¡es una ~!** it's gorgeous!, it's lovely!

divinizar ▸conjug 1f◂ VT to deify

divino Ⓐ ADJ 1 (*Rel*) divine
2 (= *precioso*) divine, lovely; **la casa es divina** the house is lovely *o* divine
Ⓑ ADV (*) **pasarlo ~** to have a wonderful time

divirtiendo *etc ver* **divertir**

divisa SF 1 (= *distintivo*) emblem
2 (*Heráldica*) device, motto
3 (*tb* **~s**) (*Fin*) foreign currency; **control de ~s** exchange control ► **divisa de reserva** reserve currency

divisar ▸conjug 1a◂ VT to make out, distinguish

divisibilidad SF divisibility

divisible ADJ divisible

división SF 1 (= *separación*) [*de célula*] division; [*de átomo*] splitting; [*de gastos, ganancias*] division; **tras la ~ del país** after the country was divided; **hay ~ de opiniones** opinions are divided ► **división del trabajo** division of labour ► **división de poderes** division of powers
2 (*Mat*) division; **hacer una ~** to divide, do a division
3 (= *desunión*) [*de partido, familia*] division, split; **no existe ~ entre nosotros** there is no division *o* split between us
4 (*Dep*) division; **primera ~** first division; **segunda ~** second division ► **división de honor** top division; (*Ftbl*) premier division
5 (*Mil*) division; **general de ~** major general ► **división acorazada** tank division ► **la División Azul** the Blue Division
6 (*Com*) (= *sección*) division
7 (*Biol*) (= *categoría*) category
8 (= *zona*) ► **división administrativa, división territorial** administrative region

divisional ADJ divisional

divisionismo SM divisiveness

divisionista ADJ divisive

divisivo ADJ divisive

divismo SM 1 (= *sistema*) star system
2 (= *carácter*) artistic temperament, star temperament

divisor Ⓐ ADJ 1 [*panel, muro, línea*] dividing
2 [*cantidad, número*] dividing
Ⓑ SM (*Mat*) divisor; **máximo común ~** highest common factor, greatest common divisor

divisoria SF 1 (= *línea*) dividing line ► **divisoria de aguas** watershed
2 (*Geog*) divide ► **divisoria continental** continental divide

divisorio ADJ [*línea*] dividing; **línea divisoria de las aguas** watershed

divo/a SM/F star; *ver tb* **diva**

divorciado/a Ⓐ ADJ 1 [*persona, pareja*] divorced
2 [*opinión*] divided; **las opiniones están divorciadas** opinions are divided
Ⓑ SM/F divorcé/divorcée

divorciar ▸conjug 1b◂ Ⓐ VT 1 [+ *pareja*] to divorce
2 [+ *ideas, opiniones*] to divorce (**de** from), separate (**de** from)
Ⓑ **divorciarse** VPR to get divorced, get a divorce (**de** from)

divorcio SM 1 [*de una pareja*] divorce
2 (= *diferencia*) discrepancy; **existe un ~ entre los dos conceptos** the two ideas are divorced from each other

divorcista SMF pro-divorce campaigner

divulgación SF [1] [*de noticia, ideas*] spreading
[2] [*de descubrimiento, secreto*] disclosure; **revistas de ~ científica** popular science magazines

divulgar ▸conjug 1h◂ Ⓐ VT [1] [+ *noticia, ideas*] to spread
[2] [+ *secreto*] to divulge, disclose
Ⓑ **divulgarse** VPR [1] [*secreto*] to leak out
[2] [*rumor*] to get about

divulgativo ADJ, **divulgatorio** ADJ informative

dizque* ADV (*LAm*) (= *al parecer*) apparently; **~ vendrán hoy** they're supposed to be coming today

D.J.C. ABR = **después de Jesucristo**

dl ABR (= **decilitro(s)**) dl

Dls ABR, **dls** ABR (*LAm*) = **dólares**

DM ABR (= **Deutschmark**) DM, D-mark

Dm ABR [1] = **decimal**
[2] = **decámetro(s)**

dm ABR (= **decímetro(s)**) dm

D.m. ABR (= **Dios mediante**) DV

D.N. ABR = **Delegación Nacional**

DNI SM ABR (*Esp*) (= **documento nacional de identidad**) ID card

> **DNI**
>
> *The Spanish* **Documento Nacional de Identidad** *is a laminated plastic ID card which is renewable every 5 or 10 years, depending on the age of the holder. All Spanish nationals over the age of 14 are required to carry this card, which has their photo, fingerprints and personal details, at all times, and must be able to produce it to the police on request. As a legal document it is commonly used as proof of identity, for instance when opening a bank account, and it can be used instead of a passport for travelling around the EU. In Spain it is commonly known as the* **DNI**, *or else* **carnet (de identidad)**. *In Latin America a similar card is called the* **cédula (de identidad)**.

Dña. = **D.ª**; → DON/DOÑA

do SM (*Mús*) C ► **do de pecho** high C; ✦*MODISMO* **dar el do de pecho** to give one's all, do one's very best ► **do mayor** C major

D.O. SF ABR = **denominación de origen**; → DENOMINACIÓN DE ORIGEN

dóberman SM Doberman

dobladillar ▸conjug 1a◂ VT to hem

dobladillo SM [1] [*de vestido*] hem
[2] (= *vuelta*) [*de pantalón*] turn-up, cuff (*EEUU*)

doblado ADJ [1] [*carta, tela*] folded
[2] [*barra, rama*] bent, twisted
[3] [*persona*] bent over; **iba ~ por el dolor** he was bent over with the pain
[4] [*película*] dubbed

doblador[1]* SM (*CAm*) roll-your-own*, hand-rolled cigarette

doblador[2]**(a)** SM/F (*Cine*) dubber

dobladura SF fold

doblaje SM (*Cine*) dubbing

doblamiento SM folding

doblar ▸conjug 1a◂ Ⓐ VT [1] (= *plegar*) [+ *carta, tela, periódico*] to fold; [+ *alambre, pierna*] to bend; **dobló el mapa y se lo guardó** he folded up the map and put it away; **dóblales el bajo para afuera a tus pantalones** turn up (the hem of) your trousers; **no puedo ~ la rodilla del dolor** I can't bend my knee because of the pain
[2] (= *torcer*) [+ *esquina*] to turn, go round; [+ *cabo*] (*Náut*) to round
[3] (= *tener el doble de*) **su marido le dobla el sueldo** her husband earns twice as much as her, her husband earns double what she does; **te doblo la edad** I'm twice your age
[4] (= *duplicar*) [+ *cantidad, oferta*] to double; **doblen sus apuestas, señores** double your bets, gentlemen; **en verano nos doblan el trabajo** in summer our work doubles *o* is doubled
[5] (*Cine*) [5·1] (*en la voz*) [+ *película, actor*] to dub; **una película doblada al francés** a film dubbed into French
[5·2] (*en la acción*) [+ *actor*] to stand in for; **en las escenas de peligro lo dobla un especialista** a stunt man stands in for him in the dangerous scenes
[6] (*) [+ *persona*] **lo dobló de una patada** he kicked him and doubled him up from the pain; **~ a algn a palos** to beat sb up; **el sacrificio lo ha doblado** having to make this sacrifice has torn him apart
[7] (*Dep*) [+ *ciclista, corredor*] to lap; **ha conseguido ~ a los últimos corredores** he has managed to lap the last runners
[8] (*Teat*) **~ dos papeles** to take two parts
[9] (*Méx*) (= *matar*) to shoot down
Ⓑ VI [1] (= *girar*) [*persona, vehículo*] to turn; **~ a la derecha** to turn right; **~ a la izquierda** to turn left
[2] [*campana*] to toll; **~ a muerto** to sound the death knell
[3] (*Taur*) [*toro*] to collapse
[4] (‡) (= *morir*) to peg out‡
Ⓒ **doblarse** VPR [1] (= *plegarse*) [*papel, tela*] to fold (up); [*alambre, barra*] to bend; **se le ~on las rodillas** his knees buckled beneath him
[2] [*persona*] (= *encorvarse*) to bend; (= *retorcerse*) to double up; (= *doblegarse*) to give up, give in; **estaba doblándose de dolor** he was doubled up with pain; **no se doblaba ante los problemas** he didn't give up *o* in when faced by problems
[3] [*cantidad*] to double; **los precios se han doblado este año** prices have doubled this year; **el número de accidentes se ha doblado** the number of accidents has doubled

doble Ⓐ ADJ [1] [*puerta, tela, densidad, agente*] double; [*control, nacionalidad*] dual; [*ración, café*] large; [*cuerda*] extra strong; [*ventaja*] twofold; **un whisky ~** a double whisky; **no aparcar en ~ fila** no double-parking; **lo expulsaron por ~ amonestación** he was sent off after receiving a second yellow card; **una tela de ~ ancho** a double-width piece of fabric; **están trabajando a ~ turno** they are working double shifts; **tiene ~ motivo para quejarse** he has double reason to complain; **~ acristalamiento** (*Esp*) double glazing; **de ~ cara** [*disquete, hoja, espejo*] double-sided; [*abrigo, chaqueta*] reversible; **impresión a ~ cara** double-sided printing; **~ cristal** double glazing; **~ espacio** double-spacing; **diez páginas impresas a ~ espacio** ten pages printed in double-spacing; **~ falta** (*Baloncesto, Tenis*) double fault; **~ fondo** false bottom; **un maletín con ~ fondo** a case with a false bottom; **en todo lo que dice hay un ~ fondo** there's a double meaning in everything he says; **~ intención** double intention; **no iba con ~ intención** he did not have ulterior motives *o* double intentions; **~ juego** double-dealing; **hacer un ~ juego** to play a double game; **~ página** two-page spread, double-page spread; **una fotografía a ~ página** a two-page photograph; **~ personalidad** split personality; **de ~ sentido** [*calle*] two-way *antes de s*; [*chiste, palabra*] with a double meaning; **todo lo que dice tiene un ~ sentido** everything he says has a double meaning; **~ tracción** four-wheel drive; **visión ~** double vision; *ver tb* **imposición 3, moral**[2] **B1**
[2] (= *hipócrita*) [*persona*] two-faced
[3] (*Dominó*) [*ficha*] double; **el cuatro ~** the double four
Ⓑ ADV [*ver*] double; [*beber, comer*] twice as much; **con estas gafas veo ~** these glasses make me see double
Ⓒ SM [1] (= *cantidad*) **el ~**: **ahora gana el ~** now he earns twice as much, now he earns double; **su sueldo es el ~ del mío** his salary is twice as much as mine, his salary is double mine; **necesitamos una casa el ~ de grande** we need a house twice as big as this *o* double the size; **lleva el ~ de harina** it has twice the amount of flour, it has double the amount of flour; **¿cuál es el ~ de diez?** what's two times ten?; **apostar ~ contra sencillo** to bet two to one; **el ~ que** twice as much as; **gana el ~ que yo** he earns double what I do *o* twice as much as me; ✦*MODISMO* **~ o nada** double or quits
[2] (= *copia*) [*de documento*] duplicate copy; [*de llave*] duplicate key
[3] (*Cos*) (= *pliegue*) pleat
[4] [*de campanas*] toll(ing); **¿oyes el ~ de campanas?** can you hear the bells tolling?
[5] **dobles** (*Tenis*) doubles; **un partido de ~s** a doubles match ► **dobles (de) caballeros** men's doubles ► **dobles (de) damas**, **dobles femeninos** ladies' doubles ► **dobles masculinos** men's doubles ► **dobles mixtos** mixed doubles
[6] (*Bridge*) double ► **doble de castigo** penalty double ► **doble de llamada** asking double
[7] (‡) [*de cárcel*] prison governor, head warden (*EEUU*)
Ⓓ SMF [1] (*Cine*) double, stand-in
[2] (= *persona parecida*) (*gen*) double; [*de algún famoso*] lookalike; **me han dicho que tengo un ~** I've been told I have a double; **varios ~s de Elvis Presley** some Elvis Presley lookalikes
[3] (= *persona falsa*) double-dealer

doblegar ▸conjug 1h◂ Ⓐ VT [1] (= *vencer*) [+ *voluntad*] to break; [+ *enemigo, oponente*] to crush, vanquish (*liter*)
[2] (= *doblar*) to bend
[3] [+ *arma*] to brandish
Ⓑ **doblegarse** VPR to yield, give in

doblemente ADV [1] (= *por dos veces*) doubly
[2] (= *con hipocresía*) duplicitously

doblete SM **hacer ~** (*TV, Teat*) to double (**a** for)

doblez Ⓐ SM (*Cos*) (= *pliegue*) fold, hem; (= *dobladillo*) turnup, cuff (*EEUU*)
Ⓑ SF (= *falsedad*) duplicity

doblista SMF doubles player

doblón SM (*Hist*) doubloon ► **doblón de a ocho** piece of eight

doc. ABR [1] (= **docena**) doz
[2] (= **documento**) doc

doce Ⓐ ADJ INV, PRON (*gen*) twelve; (*ordinal, en la fecha*) twelfth; **las ~** twelve o'clock; **le escribí el día ~** I wrote to him on the twelfth
Ⓑ SM (= *número*) twelve; (= *fecha*) twelfth; *ver tb* **seis**

doceavo Ⓐ ADJ twelfth
Ⓑ SM [1] (*numeral*) twelfth
[2] (*Tip*) **en ~** in duodecimo

docena SF dozen; **media ~ de huevos** half a dozen eggs; **a** *o* **por ~s** by the dozen ▸ **docena del fraile** baker's dozen

docencia SF teaching

doceno ADJ twelfth

docente Ⓐ ADJ teaching *antes de s*; **centro ~** educational institution; **personal ~** teaching staff; **personal no ~** non-academic staff
Ⓑ SMF teacher

dócil ADJ [*animal*] docile; [*persona*] submissive, meek

docilidad SF [*de animal*] docility; [*de persona*] submissiveness, meekness

dócilmente ADV meekly

doctamente ADV learnedly

docto/a Ⓐ ADJ learned, erudite
Ⓑ SM/F scholar, learned person

doctor(a) Ⓐ SM/F (*Med, Univ*) doctor; **fue investido ~ honoris causa** he was made an honorary doctor; ✦**REFRÁN** **~es tiene la Iglesia** there are plenty of people well able to pass an opinion (on that) ▸ **doctor(a) en derecho** doctor of laws ▸ **doctor(a) en filosofía** Doctor of Philosophy
Ⓑ SM (*Rel*) father, saint

doctorado SM doctorate, PhD; **estudiante de ~** PhD student

doctoral ADJ [1] [*tesis, conferencia*] doctoral
[2] [*tono*] pedantic, pompous

doctorando/a SM/F PhD student

doctorar ▸conjug 1a◂ Ⓐ VT to confer a doctorate on
Ⓑ **doctorarse** VPR to receive *o* get one's PhD *o* doctorate

doctrina SF [1] (= *ideología*) doctrine
[2] (= *enseñanza*) teaching

doctrinal ADJ doctrinal

doctrinar ▸conjug 1a◂ VT to teach

doctrinario/a Ⓐ ADJ doctrinaire
Ⓑ SM/F doctrinarian

doctrinero SM (*LAm*) parish priest (*among Indians*)

docudrama SM docudrama, dramatized documentary

documentación SF [1] [*de vehículo*] documentation ▸ **documentación del barco** ship's papers *pl*
[2] [*de persona*] papers *pl*, documents *pl*; **la ~, por favor** your papers, please
[3] (*Prensa*) reference section

documentadamente ADV in a well-informed way

documentado ADJ [1] (= *informado*) **un libro bien ~** a well documented *o* researched book; **no estaba bien ~** I was not very well informed (about the subject)
[2] (= *con documentación*) **no voy ~** I don't have my papers with me

documental ADJ, SM documentary

documentalista SMF [1] (*TV*) documentary maker
[2] (*en biblioteca*) documentalist

documentar ▸conjug 1a◂ Ⓐ VT to document
Ⓑ **documentarse** VPR to do research, do one's homework

documento SM [1] (= *escrito*) document ▸ **documento adjunto** (*Inform*) attachment ▸ **documento justificativo** voucher, certificate ▸ **documento nacional de identidad** identity card; → DNI ▸ **documentos de envío** dispatch documents ▸ **documentos del coche** car documents
[2] (= *certificado*) certificate
[3] (= *testimonio*) document; **es un ~ vivo de aquella época** it is a living document of that period

dodecafónico ADJ dodecaphonic

dodecafonismo SM twelve-tone system, dodecaphonism

dodecágono SM dodecagon

dodo SM, **dodó** SM dodo

dodotis® SM INV nappy, diaper (*EEUU*)

dogal SM [1] (*para animal*) halter
[2] (*para ahorcar*) noose; **estar con el ~ al cuello** to be in a terrible fix *o* jam

dogma SM dogma

dogmáticamente ADV dogmatically

dogmático ADJ dogmatic

dogmatismo SM dogmatism

dogmatizador(a) SM/F dogmatist

dogmatizar ▸conjug 1f◂ VI to dogmatize

dogo SM bull mastiff ▸ **dogo alemán** Great Dane

dola* SF = **pídola**

dolamas SFPL, **dolames** SFPL [*de un caballo*] hidden defects; (*LAm**) chronic illness *sing*

dólar SM dollar; *ver tb* **montado 4**

dolencia SF ailment

doler ▸conjug 2h◂ Ⓐ VI [1] (*Med*) to hurt; **¿(te) duele?** does it hurt?; **la inyección no duele** the injection doesn't hurt; **me duele el brazo** my arm hurts; **me duele la cabeza** my head hurts; (*por migraña, resaca*) I've got a headache; **me duele el estómago** I've got (a) stomach ache; **me duelen las muelas** I've got toothache; **me duele la garganta** I've got a sore throat
[2] (= *afligir*) to hurt; **ese comentario me dolió** I was hurt by that comment, that comment hurt; **no me duele gastarme el dinero en esto** I don't mind spending money on this, spending money on this doesn't bother me; **me duele no poder prestártelo** I'm very sorry I can't lend it to you; **¡ahí le duele!** so THAT'S where the problem is!
Ⓑ **dolerse** VPR (*frm*) [1] (= *sufrir*) **me duelo por su ausencia** I miss him terribly; **¡duélete de mí!** pity me!
[2] (= *arrepentirse*) **~se de algo** to regret sth; **se duele de su pasado egoísta** she regrets her selfish past; **~se de los pecados** to repent of one's sins
[3] (= *quejarse*) to complain

dolido ADJ **estar ~ con algn** to be hurt by sb

doliente Ⓐ ADJ [1] (= *dolorido*) aching
[2] (= *enfermo*) ill
[3] (= *triste*) sorrowful; **la familia ~** the bereaved family
Ⓑ SMF [1] (*Med*) sick person
[2] (*en entierro*) mourner

dolmen SM dolmen

dolo SM fraud, deceit; **sin ~** openly, honestly

dolomía SF, **dolomita** SF dolomite

▼**dolor** SM [1] (*físico*) pain; **estar con ~es** (*antes del parto*) to feel one's labour pains beginning ▸ **dolor de cabeza** headache ▸ **dolor de espalda** backache ▸ **dolor de estómago** stomach ache ▸ **dolor de muelas** toothache ▸ **dolor de oídos** earache ▸ **dolores de parto** labour pains, labor pains (*EEUU*) ▸ **dolor sordo** dull ache
[2] (= *pesar*) grief, sorrow; **con ~ de mi corazón** with an ache in my heart; **le causa mucho ~** it causes him great distress

dolorido ADJ [1] (*Med*) sore; **la parte dolorida** the part which hurts
[2] [*persona*] distressed, upset
[3] [*tono*] pained

Dolorosa SF (*Rel*) **la ~** the Madonna, Our Lady of Sorrow

dolorosa SF (*hum*) bill, check (*EEUU*) (*in a restaurant*)

dolorosamente ADV [1] (*Med*) painfully
[2] (= *angustiosamente*) painfully, distressingly

doloroso ADJ [1] (*Med*) painful
[2] (= *angustioso*) painful, distressing

doloso ADJ fraudulent, deceitful

doma SF [*de caballo*] breaking-in; [*de animal salvaje*] taming

domable ADJ tamable

domador(a) SM/F [*de fieras*] tamer, trainer ▸ **domador(a) de caballos** horse-breaker

domadura SF = **doma**

domar ▸conjug 1a◂ VT [1] [+ *animal salvaje*] (= *amansar*) to tame; (= *adiestrar*) to train
[2] [+ *caballo*] to break in
[3] [+ *emoción*] to master, control

domeñar ▸conjug 1a◂ VT = **domar**

domesticación SF [1] (*en costumbres*) domestication [2] [*de animal salvaje*] taming

domesticado ADJ tame; **un tejón ~** a tame badger, a pet badger

domesticar ▸conjug 1g◂ Ⓐ VT to tame, domesticate
Ⓑ **domesticarse** VPR to become tame, become domesticated

domesticidad SF [1] (= *vida de hogar*) domesticity
[2] [*de animal*] captivity; **el lobo no vive bien en ~** the wolf does not take to living in captivity

doméstico/a Ⓐ ADJ [1] [*vida, servicio*] domestic *antes de s*; **animal ~** pet; **economía doméstica** home economy, housekeeping; **gastos ~s** household expenses; **las tareas domésticas** housework *sing*
[2] [*vuelo*] domestic
Ⓑ SM/F servant, domestic

Domiciano SM Domitian

domiciliación SF (*Fin*) direct debiting; **la ~ de los pagos** payment by direct debit

domiciliado ADJ **~ en Valencia** resident in Valencia

domiciliar ▸conjug 1b◂ Ⓐ VT [1] (*Fin*) **~ el pago de algo** to pay sth by direct debit; **pago domiciliado** direct debit, payment by direct debit; **~ su cuenta** to give the number of one's account, authorize direct debiting of one's account
[2] (*Méx*) [+ *carta*] to address
Ⓑ **domiciliarse** VPR to take up residence

➤ LENGUA Y USO: **dolor 2** 51.4

domiciliario ADJ **arresto ~** house arrest; **asistencia domiciliaria** home help

domicilio SM (= *hogar*) home, residence (*frm*); **servicio a ~** home delivery service; **ventas a ~** door-to-door selling; **sin ~ fijo** of no fixed abode ► **domicilio conyugal** conjugal home ► **domicilio particular** private residence ► **domicilio social** (*Com*) head office, registered office

dominación SF [1] (*Pol*) domination
[2] (*Mil*) commanding position

dominador ADJ [1] [*papel, persona*] dominating
[2] [*carácter*] domineering

dominante Ⓐ ADJ [1] (= *despótico*) domineering
[2] (= *predominante*) [*viento, tendencia, opinión, ideología*] dominant, prevailing; [*grupo, cultura, rasgo, tema, color*] dominant; [*papel, rol*] dominant, leading; **el consenso ha sido la nota ~ en las negociaciones** consensus has been the keynote *o* tenor of the negotiations; **el país ~ en ingeniería genética** the leading nation in genetic engineering
[3] (*Biol*) [*macho, gen*] dominant
[4] (*Mús*) dominant
Ⓑ SF (*Mús*) dominant

dominar ▸conjug 1a◂ Ⓐ VT [1] (= *controlar*) [+ *población, territorio*] to dominate; [+ *países*] to rule, rule over; [+ *adversario*] to overpower; [+ *caballo*] to control; **le domina la envidia** he is ruled by envy; **el tenista español dominó todo el set** the Spanish tennis player dominated the whole set
[2] (= *contener*) [+ *incendio, epidemia*] to check, bring under control; [+ *rebelión*] to put down, suppress; [+ *pasión*] to control, master; [+ *nervios, emoción*] to control; [+ *dolor*] to overcome
[3] [+ *técnica, tema*] to master; **domina bien la materia** she has a good grasp of the subject; **domina cuatro idiomas** he's fluent in four languages
[4] (= *estar por encima de*) **la catedral domina toda la ciudad** the cathedral dominates *o* towers above the whole town; **desde el castillo se domina toda la vega** from the castle you can look out over the whole plain
Ⓑ VI [1] [*edificio*] to tower
[2] (= *predominar*) [*color, rasgo*] to stand out; [*opinión, tendencia*] to predominate
Ⓒ **dominarse** VPR to control o.s.

dómine SM (*Hist*) schoolmaster

domingas* SFPL boobs*

Domingo SM Dominic

domingo SM Sunday; **el traje de los ~s** one's Sunday best; ✦***MODISMO*** **hacer ~** to take a day off ► **Domingo de la Pasión** Passion Sunday ► **Domingo de Ramos** Palm Sunday ► **Domingo de Resurrección** Easter Sunday; *ver tb* **sábado**

dominguejo SM (*Andes, Cono Sur*) scarecrow

dominguero/a Ⓐ ADJ Sunday *antes de s*; **pintor ~** Sunday painter; **el traje ~** one's Sunday best
Ⓑ SM/F [1] (= *excursionista*) Sunday excursionist
[2] (= *conductor*) Sunday driver

Dominica SF Dominica

dominical Ⓐ ADJ Sunday *antes de s*; **periódico ~** Sunday newspaper
Ⓑ SM Sunday supplement

dominicanismo SM *word or phrase peculiar to the Dominican Republic*

dominicano/a ADJ, SM/F (*Geog, Rel*) Dominican

dominico SM, **domínico** SM = **dominicano**

dominio SM [1] (= *control*) control; **tiene el ~ de la situación** he is in control of the situation ► **dominio de sí mismo, dominio sobre sí mismo** self-control
[2] (= *conocimiento*) command; **es impresionante su ~ del inglés** his command of *o* fluency in English is impressive; **¡qué ~ tiene!** isn't he good at it?; ✦***MODISMO*** **es del ~ público** it's common knowledge
[3] (= *autoridad*) authority (**sobre** over)
[4] (= *territorio*) dominion
[5] (*Educ*) field, domain
[6] (*Inform*) domain ► **nombre de dominio** domain name

dominó SM [1] (= *juego*) dominoes *pl*; (= *conjunto de fichas*) set of dominoes
[2] (= *pieza*) domino

dom.º ABR (= **domingo**) Sun

domo SM (*Méx*) skylight

domótica SF home automation

domótico ADJ automated, smart*

don¹ SM [1] (= *talento*) gift; **tiene un ~ especial para la música** she has a special gift for music; **tiene ~ con los niños** she has a way with children ► **don de gentes**: **tener ~ de gentes** to know how to handle people, be good with people ► **don de lenguas** gift for languages ► **don de mando** leadership qualities *pl*; (*Mil*) generalship ► **don de palabra** gift of the gab*, gift of gab (*EEUU**)
[2] (= *deseo*) wish; **el hada le concedió tres ~es** the fairy gave him three wishes
[3] (= *regalo*) gift

don² SM [1] (*tratamiento de cortesía*) **Don** (*en carta, sobre*) Esquire; **Sr. Don Fernando García** (*en correspondencia*) Mr F. García, Fernando García Esq.; **¿habéis visto a ~ Fernando?** have you seen Mr García?; **es ~ perfecto, él cree que nunca se equivoca** (*iró*) he thinks he's Mr Perfect and never makes a mistake; **el rey ~ Pedro** King Peter; *ver tb* **Juan**
[2] (*Arg, Col**) (*tratamiento popular*) mate*, buddy (*EEUU**)

> **DON/DOÑA**
>
> *A courtesy title,* **don/doña** *placed before the first name of an older or more senior man/woman is a way of showing them your respect when talking to them or about them. E.g.* **"¿Podría hablar con don César Roca?", "Buenos días doña Alicia. ¿Qué tal su viaje?"** *Although now becoming rarer, in Spain* **Don** *and* **Doña**, *often abbreviated to* **D.** *and* **Dña.**, *are commonly used before full names on official documents and contracts. In formal correspondence, they are used in combination with* **Sr., Sra.** *and* **Srta.**, *e.g.* **Sr. D. Bernardo Esplugas Martín, Sra. Dña. Ana Rodríguez.**

dona SF [1] (*Cono Sur*) gift
[2] **donas** (*Méx*) trousseau *sing*

donación SF [1] [*de bienes, órganos*] donation ► **donación de sangre** blood donation
[2] (*Jur*) gift

donado/a SM/F lay brother/lay sister

donador(a) SM/F donor

donaire SM [1] (*al hablar*) wit
[2] (*al moverse*) grace, elegance
[3] **un ~** a witticism; **dice muchos ~s** he's terribly witty

donante SMF donor ► **donante de órganos** organ donor ► **donante de sangre** blood donor

donar ▸conjug 1a◂ VT [+ *órganos*] to donate; [+ *sangre, propiedades, dinero*] to give, donate

donativo SM donation

doncel SM [1] (= *noble*) young nobleman, young squire [2] (*Hist*) page

doncella SF [1] (= *criada*) maidservant
[2] (= *virgen*) maiden, virgin
[3] (*Hist, Literat*) maid, maiden

doncellez SF [1] (= *virginidad*) virginity, maidenhood [2] (*Anat*) maidenhead

donde Ⓐ ADV [1] (+ *INDIC*) where; **la nota está ~ la dejaste** the note's where you left it; **la casa ~ nací** the house where I was born, the house I was born in; **el sitio ~ lo encontré** the place (where) I found it; **a ~**: **ahí es a ~ vamos nosotros** that's where we're going; **fue a ~ estaban ellos** he went to (the place) where they were; **de ~**: **el país de ~ vienen** the country they come from; **la caja de ~ lo sacó** the box he took it out of, the box from which he took it; **en ~**: **fui a la India, en ~ nos conocimos** I went to India, (which is) where we met; **el pueblo en ~ vive** the village where *o* in which he lives; **por ~**: **la escalera por ~ había salido** the empty staircase down which he had left; **la puerta por ~ se entra** the door you go in by; **la calle por ~ íbamos andando** the street we were walking along; **por ~ pasan lo destrozan todo** they destroy everything, wherever they go; **va siempre por ~ se le dice** she always goes wherever you tell her to
[2] (+ *SUBJUN*) wherever; **~ tú quieras** wherever you want; **quiero un trabajo ~ sea** I want a job anywhere *o* wherever; **estén ~ estén** wherever they may be; **vayas ~ vayas** wherever you go, everywhere you go; **vayas por ~ vayas** whichever way you go; ✦***REFRÁN*** **(allí) ~ fueres, haz lo que vieres** when in Rome, do as the Romans do
[3] (*Cono Sur*) (= *ya que*) as, since
Ⓑ PREP [1] (= *al lado de*) **es allí, ~ la catedral** it's over there by the cathedral; **lo guardamos ~ la ropa de cama** we keep it with the bed linen
[2] (= *en casa de*) **vamos ~ Ricardo** we're going to Ricardo's; **están cenando ~ mi madre** they are having dinner at my mother's

dónde INTERROG ADV [1] (*en cláusulas interrogativas*) where?; **¿~ lo dejaste?** where did you leave it?; **¿a ~ vás?** where are you going?; **¿de ~ eres?** where are you from?; **¿en ~?** where?; **¿por ~ se va al estadio?** how do I get to the stadium?; **¿por ~ queda la estación?** whereabouts is the station?
[2] (*en estilo indirecto*) where; **no sé ~ lo puse** I don't know where I put it; ✦***MODISMO*** **mira por ~***: **¡buscaban a un intérprete y mira por ~ me llamaron a mí!** they were looking for an interpreter and what do you know, they called me!; **¿así que tú has sido el vencedor? pues qué bien, mira por ~** (*iró*) so you won? well, stranger things have happened, I suppose (*iró*)
[3] (*LAm*) (= *¿cómo?*) how?

dondequiera Ⓐ ADV anywhere; **por ~** everywhere, all over the place

Ⓑ CONJ wherever; **~ que lo busques** wherever you look for it

donjuan SM, **donjuán** SM casanova, womanizer

donjuanismo SM womanizing

donosamente ADV (*liter*) wittily, amusingly

donoso ADJ (*liter*) witty, amusing; (*iró*) fine; **¡donosa idea!** (*iró*) highly amusing I'm sure!

Donosti(a) SF San Sebastián

donostiarra Ⓐ ADJ of/from San Sebastián
Ⓑ SMF native/inhabitant of San Sebastián; **los ~s** the people of San Sebastián

Don Quijote SM Don Quixote

donus SM INV, **donut** SM (*pl* **donuts**) ring doughnut, donut (*EEUU*)

doña SF **Doña Alicia Pérez** Mrs Alicia Pérez; **¿está ~ Alicia?** is Mrs Pérez in?; → DON/DOÑA

dopado Ⓐ ADJ [*caballo*] doped, doped-up*; [*persona*] on drugs; **un atleta ~** an athlete who has taken performance-enhancing drugs
Ⓑ SM [*de caballo*] doping; [*de deportista*] taking performance-enhancing drugs

dopaje SM = **dopado B**

dopar ▸conjug 1a◂ Ⓐ VT to dope, drug
Ⓑ **doparse** VPR to take performance-enhancing drugs

doping ['dopin] SM doping; **han intentado acusarlo de ~** they have tried to accuse him of having taken performance-enhancing drugs

dopingar ▸conjug 1h◂ VT to give performance-enhancing drugs to

doquier ADV **por ~** (*frm*) all over, everywhere, everyplace (*EEUU*)

doradito ADJ (*Culin*) golden brown

dorado Ⓐ ADJ 1 (= *parecido al oro*) gold *antes de s*, golden (*liter*); **los ~s sesenta** the golden sixties
2 (*Téc*) gilt, gilded
Ⓑ SM 1 (*Téc*) gilt, gilding
2 (= *pez*) dorado

doradura SF gilding

dorar ▸conjug 1a◂ Ⓐ VT 1 (*Téc*) to gild
2 (*Culin*) to brown; ✦*MODISMO* **~ la píldora** to sweeten the pill
Ⓑ **dorarse** VPR 1 [*cebolla, ajo*] to turn golden, brown; **rehogar la cebolla hasta que se dore** lightly fry the onion until golden brown
2 [*piel, persona*] to go brown, tan

dorífora SF Colorado beetle

dormida SF (*LAm*) 1 (= *sueño, descanso*) sleep
2 (*por una noche*) overnight stop

dormidera SF 1 (*Bot*) poppy, opium poppy
2 ✦*MODISMO* **tener buenas ~s** to get off to sleep easily

dormidero SM 1 [*de ganado*] sleeping place
2 [*de gallinas*] roost

dormido ADJ 1 [*persona*] **estar ~** (*durmiendo*) to be asleep; (*con sueño*) to be sleepy; **¿es que estás ~ o qué?** are you asleep or what?; **hablar ~** to talk in one's sleep; **andaba medio ~ por la calle** he walked down the street half asleep; **quedarse ~** to fall asleep; **me quedé dormida en el autocar** I fell asleep on the coach; **se está quedando ~** he's dropping off, he's falling asleep; **me quedé ~ y perdí la clase** I overslept and missed the class
2 [*pierna, brazo*] **tengo la mano dormida** my hand has gone to sleep; **todavía tengo la cara dormida por la anestesia** my face is still numb from the anaesthetic

dormilón/ona Ⓐ ADJ fond of sleeping
Ⓑ SM/F sleepyhead

dormilona SF 1 (= *silla*) reclining chair
2 (*Caribe*) (= *camisón*) nightdress, nightgown

dormir ▸conjug 3j◂ Ⓐ VI 1 (= *descansar*) to sleep; **no hagas ruido, que está durmiendo** don't make a noise, he's asleep; **sólo ha dormido cinco horas** she has only had five hours' sleep, she has only slept (for) five hours; **se fueron a ~ temprano** they went to bed early; **¡ahora, todos a ~!** come on, off to bed all of you *o* off to bed with you all; **la música no me dejaba ~** the music kept me awake; **es de poco ~** he doesn't need much sleep; **~ con algn** (*tb euf*) to sleep with sb; **~ de un tirón** to sleep right through (the night); **he dormido diez horas de un tirón** I've slept ten hours right through; ✦*MODISMOS* **~ como un bendito** *o* **un santo** to sleep like a baby; **~ como un lirón** *o* **un tronco** ◊ **~ a pierna suelta** to sleep like a log; *ver tb* **saco**[1] **1**
2 (= *pasar la noche*) to spend the night, stay the night; **dormimos en una pensión** we spent *o* stayed the night in a guesthouse; **llevo una semana sin ~ en casa** I haven't slept at home for a week; **~ al raso** to sleep out in the open, sleep rough
3 (= *estar olvidado*) to lie idle; **mi solicitud ha estado durmiendo en el fondo de un cajón** my application has been lying idle at the bottom of a drawer; **no deje ~ a sus ahorros** don't let your savings lie idle
Ⓑ VT 1 (= *adormecer*) [+ *niño*] to get (off) to sleep; [+ *adulto*] (*por aburrimiento*) to send to sleep; (*con anestesia*) to put to sleep; **no podía ~lo** I couldn't get him off to sleep; **ese programa me duerme** that programme sends me to sleep
2 **~ la siesta** to have a nap, have a siesta; ✦*MODISMOS* **~ el sueño de los justos** to sleep the sleep of the just; **~la*** ◊ **~ la mona*** to sleep it off*
3 (*euf*) (= *matar*) to put to sleep
Ⓒ **dormirse** VPR 1 [*persona*] 1·1 (= *quedarse dormido*) to fall asleep, go to sleep; **no te duermas** don't fall asleep, don't go to sleep; **se me durmió en los brazos** she fell asleep *o* went to sleep in my arms; **¡duérmete!** go to sleep!
1·2 (= *despertarse tarde*) to oversleep; **no llegué a la hora porque me dormí** I didn't arrive on time because I overslept
2 [*brazo, pierna*] to go to sleep; **se me ha dormido la mano** my leg has gone to sleep
3 (*) (= *descuidarse*) **si te duermes, te quedarás sin trabajo** if you don't stay on your toes, you'll lose your job; **duérmete y no conseguirás nada** if you waste time like this, you won't get anywhere; **no te duermas, respóndeme** wake up, give me an answer; ✦*MODISMO* **~se en los laureles** to rest on one's laurels

dormirela* SF nap, snooze

dormirlas SM hide-and-seek

dormitar ▸conjug 1a◂ VI to doze, snooze*

dormitorio SM 1 (= *habitación*) bedroom
► **dormitorio de servicio** room for domestic staff
2 (= *muebles*) bedroom suite
3 (*en internado, cuartel*) dormitory; *ver tb* **ciudad 1**

dornillo SM 1 (= *recipiente*) wooden bowl
2 (*Agr*) small trough

Dorotea SF Dorothy

dorsal Ⓐ ADJ dorsal
Ⓑ SM (*Dep*) number (*worn on player's back*)
Ⓒ SF ridge

dorsalmente ADV 1 (= *por el lado*) dorsally
2 [*flotar*] on one's back

dorso SM back; **escribir algo al ~** to write sth on the back; **"véase al ~"** "see overleaf", "please turn over"

> **DOS**
>
> **El uso de "both"**
>
> **Los dos** con el sentido de **ambos** se traduce por **both**, pero el lugar que ocupa en la oración y la construcción en la que se usa depende de varios factores:
>
> **Como sujeto de "be" o un verbo auxiliar/modal**
>
> - Con nombre solo:
>   Las dos hermanas son cantantes
>   ***Both (of the) sisters are singers* ◊ *The sisters are both singers***
>   Los dos castillos fueron construidos en el siglo XVIII
>   ***Both (of the) castles were built in the 18th century* ◊ *The castles were both built in the 18th century***
> - Con nombre y demostrativo/posesivo:
>   Estos dos niños son huérfanos
>   ***Both (of) these children are orphans* ◊ *These children are both orphans***
>   Mis dos hijos han emigrado
>   ***Both (of) my sons have emigrated* ◊ *My sons have both emigrated***
> - Sin nombre:
>   Los dos son jóvenes
>   ***Both of them are young* ◊ *They're both young***
>   Los dos sabemos esquiar
>   ***Both of us can ski* ◊ *We can both ski***
>
> **Como sujeto de otro verbo**
>
> - Con nombre solo:
>   Los dos chicos quieren estudiar medicina
>   ***Both (of the) boys want to study medicine* ◊ *The boys both want to study medicine***
> - Con nombre y demostrativo/posesivo:
>   Mis dos tíos viven solos
>   ***Both (of) my uncles live alone* ◊ *My uncles both live alone***
> - Sin nombre:
>   Los dos beben más de la cuenta
>   ***Both of them* o *They both drink too much***
>
> **Como objeto de un verbo o preposición**
>
> Los hemos invitado a los dos
> ***We've invited both of them* o *them both***
> Los dos me tenéis harta
> ***I'm fed up with both of you* o *you both***
>
> **NOTA:** Cuando **los dos** no puede substituirse por **ambos**, se traduce por **the two** + **NOMBRE EN PLURAL** o **the two of us/you/them**:
> ¿Tienes los dos libros que te dejé?
> ***Have you got the two books (that) I lent you?***
>
> *Para otros usos y ejemplos ver la entrada.*

dos Ⓐ ADJ INV, PRON 1 (*gen*) two; (*ordinal, en la fecha*) second; **~ a ~** two against two; **~ y ~ son cuatro** two and two are four; **~ por ~**

son cuatro two times two makes four; **de ~ en ~** in twos, two by two; **cortar algo en ~** to cut sth into two; **los ~ libros** both books; **le escribí el día ~** I wrote to him on the second; **~ piezas** two-piece; ✦*MODISMOS* **como ése no hay ~** they don't come any better than that; **como ~ y ~ son cuatro** as sure as sure can be, as sure as eggs are eggs; **cada ~ por tres** every five minutes; **no hay ~ sin tres** these things always come in threes

2 (= *dos personas*) **los ~** the two of them/us *etc*, both of them/us *etc*; **vosotros ~** you two; **es para los ~** it's for both of you/us *etc*

Ⓑ SM (= *número*) two; (= *fecha*) second; **estamos a ~** (*Tenis*) the score is deuce; ✦*MODISMO* **en un ~ por tres** in no time at all; *ver tb* **seis**

dos-caballos SM INV (*Aut*) deux-chevaux, 2 CV

doscientos/as ADJ, PRON, SM two hundred; *ver tb* **seiscientos A, B**

dosel SM canopy

doselera SF valance

dosificación SF dosage

dosificador SM dispenser

dosificar ▸conjug 1g◂ VT 1 (*Culin, Med, Quím*) to measure out

2 (= *no derrochar*) to be sparing with; **~ las fuerzas** to save one's strength; **el ministro ha dosificado sus apariciones** the minister has chosen his appearances carefully

dosis SF INV 1 (*Med*) dose

2 (*Quím*) proportion

3 (= *cantidad*) dose; **una buena ~ de paciencia** a great deal of patience; **con una buena ~ de vanidad** with a good measure of vanity; **en pequeñas ~** in small doses

dossier [dosi'er] SM (*pl* **dossiers** *o* **dossieres** [dosi'er]) dossier

dotación SF 1 (= *dinero*) endowment; **han aumentado la ~ del premio** the value of the prize has been increased, the prize money has been increased

2 (= *plantilla*) staff, personnel; (*Náut*) crew; **la ~ es insuficiente** we are understaffed; **una ~ del parque de bomberos** a team of firefighters

dotacional ADJ **suelo ~** non-residential land

dotado ADJ 1 [*persona*] gifted, exceptional (*EEUU*); **los niños excepcionalmente ~s** exceptionally gifted children; **un hombre muy bien ~*** a well-endowed man*; **~ de algo**: **María está dotada de talento musical** Maria is musically talented *o* gifted; **está ~ de una buena formación religiosa** he has received a good religious education; **~ para algo**: **Adela no está muy dotada para el deporte** Adela does not have great sporting ability *o* a great talent for sport

2 [*máquina, edificio*] **~ de algo: un hospital ~ de todos los adelantos técnicos** a hospital equipped with all the latest technology; **un coche ~ de cierre centralizado** a car fitted with central locking

3 [*premio, certamen*] **un premio ~ con un millón de euros** a prize worth a million euros

dotar ▸conjug 1a◂ VT 1 (= *equipar*) **~ (a) algo de** *o* **con algo** to provide sth with sth; **~on el teatro de una orquesta** the theatre was provided with an orchestra; **han dotado el laboratorio con los mejores instrumentos** the laboratory has been provided with the best equipment, the laboratory has been equipped with the best instruments; **han dotado el avión de toda la tecnología moderna** the plane has been equipped *o* fitted with all the latest technology; **intentan ~ al régimen de legitimidad** they are trying to legitimize the regime

2 **~ a algn de algo: dotó a su hija con un millón de rupias** he provided his daughter with a million rupees as a dowry; **la naturaleza lo dotó de buenas cualidades** he was endowed *o* blessed by nature with good qualities

dote SF 1 [*de novia*] dowry; **con un millón de ~** with a dowry of a million ► **dote nupcial** dowry

2 **dotes** (= *cualidades*) gifts, talents; **tiene excelentes ~s para la pintura** she has a great gift *o* talent for painting ► **dotes de adherencia** (*Aut*) road-holding qualities ► **dotes de mando** leadership qualities *pl*

dovela SF keystone, voussoir

doy *ver* **dar**

dozavo ADJ, SM = **doceavo**

dpdo. ABR (= **duplicado**) bis

Dpto. ABR (= **Departamento**) Dept

Dr. ABR (= **doctor(a)**) Dr

Dra. ABR (= **doctora**) Dr

dracma Ⓐ SM (= *moneda*) drachma

Ⓑ SF (*Farm*) drachm, dram

draconiano ADJ draconian

DRAE SM ABR = **Diccionario de la Real Academia Española**

draga SF 1 (= *máquina*) dredge

2 (= *barco*) dredger

dragado SM dredging

dragaminas SM INV minesweeper

dragar ▸conjug 1h◂ VT 1 [+ *río*] to dredge

2 [+ *minas*] to sweep for

drago SM dragon tree

dragomán SM dragoman

dragón SM 1 (*Mit*) dragon

2 (*Mil*) dragoon

3 (*Bot*) snapdragon

4 (*Méx**) (= *tragafuegos*) flame thrower

dragona SF 1 (*Mil*) shoulder knot, epaulette

2 (*Andes, Cono Sur, Méx*) [*de espada*] guard

3 (*Méx*) (= *capa*) hooded cloak

dragoncillo SM (*Bot*) tarragon

dragonear ▸conjug 1a◂ Ⓐ VI 1 (*LAm*) (= *presumir*) to boast, brag

2 (*Cono Sur*) (= *fingir ser*) **~ de algo** to pose as sth

Ⓑ VT (*Cono Sur*†) (= *cortejar*) to court, woo

drama SM 1 (= *género*) drama

2 (= *obra*) play; **menudo ~ montó con eso** she made a great drama out of it

dramática SF drama, dramatic art

dramáticamente ADV dramatically

dramaticidad SF dramatic quality

dramático Ⓐ ADJ dramatic; **no seas tan ~** don't make such a drama out of it, don't be such a drama-queen (*hum**)

Ⓑ SM (= *autor*) dramatist

dramatismo SM drama, dramatic quality

dramatizar ▸conjug 1f◂ VT to dramatize

dramaturgia SF (*al actuar*) drama, theatre art; (*al escribir*) play-writing

dramaturgo/a SM/F dramatist, playwright

dramón* SM (*hum*) strong drama, melodrama; **¡qué ~ montaste!** you made such a big scene, what a scene you made!

drapeado Ⓐ ADJ draped

Ⓑ SM drape

Draque SM Drake

drásticamente ADV drastically

drástico ADJ drastic

drenaje SM (*Agr, Med*) drainage

drenar ▸conjug 1a◂ VT 1 (*Agr, Med*) to drain

2 (*Fin*) to syphon off

Dresde SM Dresden

driblar ▸conjug 1a◂ = **driblear**

drible SM dribble

driblear ▸conjug 1a◂ Ⓐ VI (*Dep*) to dribble

Ⓑ VT **~ a algn** to dribble past sb

dril SM (= *tejido*) drill ► **dril de algodón** denim

drive SM (*Golf, Tenis*) drive

driver SM (*pl* **drivers**) (*Golf, Inform*) driver

driza SF halyard

droga SF 1 (*Med*) drug; **el problema de la ~** the problem of drugs; **cuando la ~ se convierte en adicción** when drug abuse becomes an addiction ► **droga blanda** soft drug ► **droga de diseño** designer drug ► **droga dura** hard drug ► **droga milagrosa** wonder drug

2 (*Dep*) dope

3 (*Com*) drug on the market, unsaleable article

4 (*LAm**) (*deuda*) debt; ✦*MODISMOS* **hacer ~** (*Méx**) to refuse to pay up; **mandar a algn a la ~** (*CAm, Caribe**) to tell sb to go to hell*

drogadicción SF drug addiction

drogadicto/a Ⓐ ADJ addicted to drugs; **su hijo ~** her drug addict son

Ⓑ SM/F drug addict

drogado SM [*de caballo*] doping

drogar ▸conjug 1h◂ Ⓐ VT 1 (*Med*) to drug

2 (*Dep*) to dope

Ⓑ **drogarse** VPR to take drugs

drogata‡ SMF druggy‡

drogodelincuencia SF drug-related crime

drogodelincuente SMF drug addict (*who finances his habit through petty crime*)

drogodependencia SF drug addiction

drogodependiente SMF drug addict, person dependent on drugs

drogota‡ SMF druggy‡

droguería SF *store that sells household goods, paint etc*

droguero/a SM/F 1 [*de tienda*] shopkeeper (*of a droguería*), storekeeper (*EEUU*)

2 (*LAm**) (= *tramposo*) cheat, crook, shyster (*EEUU*); (= *moroso*) slow payer

drogui* SM (*Cono Sur*) 1 (= *bebida*) liquor, alcohol

2 (= *borracho*) drunkard

droguista SMF = **droguero**

dromedario SM 1 (*Zool*) dromedary

2 (*Méx**) tailor

dromeo SM emu

dropar ▸conjug 1a◂ VT (*Golf*) to drop

druida SM druid

drupa SF drupe

DSE SF ABR (= **Dirección de la Seguridad del Estado**) *former national police headquarters*

Dto. ABR, **D.**^{to} ABR = **descuento**

dto. ABR (= **departamento**) dept, dpt

Dtor. ABR (= **Director**) Dir

Dtora. ABR (= **Directora**) Dir

dual ADJ, SM (*Ling*) dual

dualidad SF [1] [*de aspectos, personaje*] duality
[2] (*Cono Sur Pol*) tied vote, indecisive election

dualismo SM dualism

dubitativamente ADV doubtfully, hesitantly

dubitativo ADJ [*persona*] hesitant; [*actitud*] uncertain, hesitant

Dublín SM Dublin

dublinés/esa Ⓐ ADJ Dublin *antes de s*
Ⓑ SM/F Dubliner

ducado SM [1] (= *territorio*) duchy, dukedom
[2] (*Fin*) ducat

ducal ADJ ducal

ducentésimo ADJ two hundredth; *ver tb* **sexto**

ducha SF shower; **darse** *o* **tomarse** *o* **pegarse*** **una ~** to have a shower, take a shower (*esp EEUU*); ✦*MODISMO* **una ~ de agua fría**: **el rechazo de su propuesta fue una ~ de agua fría para él** the rejection of his proposal was a real shock to the system for him; **dar una ~ de agua fría a un proyecto** to pour cold water on a plan ► **ducha de teléfono** detachable-head shower, hand-held shower ► **ducha escocesa** alternately hot and cold shower ► **ducha vaginal** douche

duchar ▸conjug 1a◂ Ⓐ VT to give a shower to; (*Med*) to douche; **me has duchado con la manguera** you've drenched me with the hose
Ⓑ **ducharse** VPR to have a shower, take a shower (*esp EEUU*)

ducho ADJ **~ en algo** (= *experimentado*) experienced in sth; (= *hábil*) skilled at sth

duco SM lacquer; **pintar al ~** to lacquer

dúctil ADJ [1] [*metal*] ductile
[2] [*persona*] easily influenced

ductilidad SF ductility

▼**duda** SF [1] (= *incertidumbre*) doubt; **yo todavía tengo mis ~s sobre él** I still have my doubts about him; **tengo la ~ de si he apagado la luz o no** I'm not sure whether I turned off the light or not; **tengo enormes ~s religiosas** I have great religious doubts; **al principio tuve muchas ~s** I had a lot of misgivings *o* doubts at first; **queda la ~ en pie sobre ...** doubt remains about ...; **un hecho que no admite ~** an unquestionable fact; **ante la ~, no lo hagas** if in doubt, don't; **me asaltó la ~ de si ...** I was suddenly seized by a doubt as to whether ...; **no cabe ~ de que ...** there can be no doubt that ...; **no cabe ~ de que vendrá** he'll undoubtedly come; **no me cabe la menor ~ de que vamos a ganar** I have absolutely no doubt that we will win, there is absolutely no doubt in my mind that we will win; **no te quepa ~ de que se acordarán de ti** you can be sure that they will remember you; **en caso de ~** if in doubt; **"en caso de ~, consulte a su farmacéutico"** "if in doubt, consult your pharmacist"; **para desvanecer** *o* **disipar toda ~** in order to clear up any doubts, to banish all doubts; **estar en ~**: **aún está en ~ si él será el nuevo director** there's still some doubt as to *o* about whether he will be the new manager; **su profesionalismo no está en ~** his professionalism is not in doubt; **estoy en la ~ sobre si me iré de vacaciones o no** I'm undecided *o* in two minds about whether to go on holiday or not; **fuera de toda ~** beyond all doubt; **sin lugar a ~(s)** without doubt, undoubtedly; **dejar lugar a ~s** to leave no room for doubt; **poner algo en ~** to question sth, doubt sth; **nadie está poniendo en ~ su fidelidad** nobody is questioning *o* doubting his fidelity; **no pongo en ~ que sea verdad, pero ...** I don't doubt that it's true, but ...; **sacar a algn de ~s** *o* **de la ~** to clear things up for sb; **no me saca de ~s** I'm none the wiser; **salir de ~s**: **pregúntaselo a él, así saldremos de ~s** ask him, then we'll know; **pues no salimos de ~s** we're none the wiser, then; **sin ~** undoubtedly; **ésta es, sin ~ alguna, una de las mejores novelas que he leído** this is, without (any) doubt, one of the best novels I've read, this is undoubtedly one of the best novels I've read; **sin sombra de ~** without a shadow of a doubt; ✦*MODISMO* **la ~ ofende**: **¿cómo que si te lo voy a devolver?, por favor, la ~ ofende** what do you mean am I going to give it back to you?, how could you think otherwise?
[2] (= *pregunta*) question, query; **¿queda alguna ~?** are there any queries?; **me surge una ~** there's one point I'm not quite sure about

▼**dudar** ▸conjug 1a◂ Ⓐ VT [1] (= *no estar seguro de*) to doubt; **espero que venga, aunque lo dudo mucho** I hope she'll come, although I doubt very much (if) she will; **—yo te ayudaré —no lo dudo, pero ...** "I'll help you" — "I'm sure you will, but ..."; **es lo mejor para ti, no lo dudes** it's the best thing for you, believe me; **a no ~lo** undoubtedly; **~ que**: **dudo que sea verdad** I doubt (whether *o* if) it's true; **dudo que yo haya dicho eso** I doubt I said that; **no dudo que sea capaz de hacerlo** I don't doubt that he's capable of doing it; **~ si**: **dudaba si había echado la carta** I wasn't sure if I had posted the letter
[2] (= *vacilar sobre*) **lo dudé mucho y al final me decidí por el azul** I thought about it *o* dithered* a lot but in the end I decided on the blue one; **si yo fuera tú, no lo ~ía** if I were you, I wouldn't hesitate
Ⓑ VI [1] (= *desconfiar*) to doubt, have doubts; **~ de algo** to question sth, doubt sth; **los celos le hicieron ~ de su cariño** jealousy made her question *o* doubt his affection
[2] (= *vacilar*) **no sé qué hacer, estoy dudando** I don't know what to do, I'm in two minds *o* I'm undecided; **dudamos entre ir en autobús o en taxi** we were not sure whether to go by bus or taxi; **dudaba entre los dos** she couldn't decide between the two; **~ en hacer algo** to hesitate to do sth; **dudaba en comprarlo** he hesitated to buy it; **no dudes en llamarme** don't hesitate to call me

dudosamente ADV **un proyecto ~ legal** a scheme of dubious *o* questionable legality; **un sistema ~ eficaz** a less than effective system, a somewhat ineffective system; **un comentario ~ democrático** a somewhat anti-democratic comment

▼**dudoso/a** Ⓐ ADJ [1] (= *incierto*) [*diagnóstico, futuro*] doubtful, uncertain; [*resultado*] indecisive; **de origen ~** of doubtful *o* uncertain origin; **aún es dudosa su colaboración** it's still uncertain whether he will collaborate, his collaboration is still uncertain
[2] (= *vacilante*) [*persona*] hesitant; **estar ~** to be undecided, be in two minds
[3] (= *sospechoso*) [*actuación, dinero, reputación*] dubious; **el empleo de tácticas dudosas** the use of suspect *o* dubious tactics
Ⓑ SM/F **el voto de los ~s** the "undecided" vote

duela SF stave

duele *etc ver* **doler**

duelista SMF duellist

duelo[1] SM (*Mil*) duel; **batirse en ~** to fight a duel; **retar a algn a ~** to challenge sb to a duel ► **duelo a muerte** fight to the death, duel of death

duelo[2] SM [1] (= *luto*) mourning; **toda la familia está de ~** the whole family is in mourning; **se celebrarán tres días de ~** there will be three days of mourning; **la comitiva de ~** the funeral procession
[2] (= *velatorio*) wake
[3] (= *dolor*) grief, sorrow
[4] ✦*MODISMO* **sin ~** unrestrainedly; **gastar sin ~** to spend lavishly; **pegar a algn sin ~** to beat sb mercilessly

duende SM [1] (= *elfo*) goblin, elf ► **duende de imprenta** printer's devil
[2] (= *niño travieso*) imp
[3] (= *encanto*) magic; **tiene ~** it has a certain magic
[4] (*Inform*) gremlin

duendecillo SM pixie

dueña SF (= *encargada*) [*de casa*] housekeeper; [*de doncellas*] duenna

dueño/a SM/F [1] (= *propietario*) [*de casa, coche, perro*] owner; [*de negocio*] owner, proprietor/proprietress; [*de pensión, taberna*] landlord/landlady; **¿quién es el ~ del caballo?** who is the owner of the horse?, who owns the horse?; **cambiar de ~** to change hands
[2] **ser ~ de**: **ser ~ de la situación** to be the master of the situation, have the situation in hand; **la marina era dueña de los mares** the navy was mistress of the seas; **ser ~ de sí mismo** to have self-control; **eres ~ de hacer lo que te parezca** you can do as you please; **hacerse ~ de algo** to take over sth, take control of sth; **hacerse ~ de una situación** to take command of a situation

duerma *etc ver* **dormir**

duermevela SM *o* SF **pasé toda la noche en un ~** I tossed and turned all night

Duero SM Douro

dueto SM short duet

dula SF common land, common pasture

dulcamara SF nightshade

dulce Ⓐ ADJ [1] [*caramelo, galleta*] sweet; **este vino está muy ~** this wine is very sweet; **no me gusta lo ~** I don't like sweet things, I don't have a very sweet tooth; ✦*MODISMO* **más ~ que la miel** sweeter than honey; *ver tb* **agua 1**
[2] (= *suave*) [*metal, sonido, voz*] soft; [*carácter*] gentle; [*clima*] mild; [*música*] sweet; **un instrumento ~** a sweet-sounding instrument; **con el acento ~ del país** with the soft accent of the region
Ⓑ ADV softly; **habla muy ~** she speaks very softly
Ⓒ SM [1] (= *caramelo*) sweet, candy (*EEUU*); **a nadie le amarga un ~** something's better than nothing ► **dulce de almíbar** preserved fruit ► **dulce de leche** (*Arg*) caramelized condensed milk ► **dulce de membrillo**

➤ LENGUA Y USO: **duda 1** 42.1, 43.1, 53.6 **dudar A1** 43.1 **dudoso/a A1** 43.2, 53.6

quince jelly
2 **dulces** (*gen*) sweet things; (= *pasteles*) cakes and pastries; **le encantan los ~s** he loves sweet things
3 (*Andes, CAm, Caribe*) (= *azúcar*) sugar, brown sugar
4 (*Andes*) (= *paleta*) lollipop

dulcémele SM dulcimer

dulcemente ADV [*sonreír, cantar*] sweetly; [*acariciar*] gently; [*amar*] tenderly, fondly; [*contestar*] gently, softly

dulcería SF (*LAm*) confectioner's, sweetshop, candy store (*EEUU*)

dulcero ADJ **ser ~** to have a sweet tooth

dulcificante SM sweetener

dulcificar ▸conjug 1g◂ Ⓐ VT **1** (*Culin*) to sweeten
2 [+ *consecuencias, carácter, noticia*] to soften
Ⓑ **dulcificarse** VPR **1** [*carácter*] to mellow, become milder; [*consecuencias*] to become milder
2 [*clima*] to become milder

dulzón ADJ, **dulzarrón** ADJ **1** (= *demasiado dulce*) sickly-sweet
2 (*pey*) (= *empalagoso*) cloying

dulzonería SF **1** [*de caramelo, pastel*] sickly-sweetness
2 [*de persona*] cloying nature

dulzor SM, **dulzura** SF **1** [*de caramelo, pastel*] sweetness
2 [*de carácter*] sweetness, gentleness; **con ~** sweetly, softly

dumón* SF ✦*MODISMO* **vivir a la gran ~** to live the life of Riley

dúmper ['dumper] SM (*pl* **dúmpers**) dumper

dumping ['dumpin] SM (*Com*) dumping; **hacer ~** to dump goods

duna SF dune

dundeco* ADJ (*Andes, CAm*) silly, stupid

dundera* SF (*Andes, CAm*) silliness, stupidity

dundo* ADJ (*Andes, CAm*) = **dundeco**

Dunquerque SM Dunkirk

dúo SM **1** (= *composición*) duet, duo
2 [*de músicos, cantantes*] duo; **cantar a ~** to sing a duet; **me contestaron a ~** they answered me in unison

duodecimal ADJ duodecimal

duodécimo ADJ twelfth; *ver tb* **sexto**

duodenal ADJ duodenal

duodeno SM duodenum

dup. ABR, **dupdo.** ABR (= **duplicado**) bis

dupla SF (*Arg, Chile*) duo

dúplex SM INV **1** (= *piso*) duplex apartment, flat on two floors
2 (*Telec*) link-up
3 (*Inform*) duplex ▸ **dúplex integral** full duplex

duplicación SF duplication

duplicado Ⓐ ADJ duplicate; **número 14 ~** No. 14^A^
Ⓑ SM duplicate; **por ~** in duplicate

duplicar ▸conjug 1g◂ Ⓐ VT **1** [+ *documento*] to duplicate; [+ *llave*] to copy, duplicate
2 [+ *cantidad*] to double; **me duplica la edad** he's twice my age
Ⓑ **duplicarse** VPR [*cifra, ganancias*] to double

duplicidad SF duplicity, deceitfulness

duplo Ⓐ ADJ double
Ⓑ SM **doce es el ~ de seis** twelve is twice six

duque(sa) Ⓐ SM/F duke/duchess
Ⓑ SM (*Orn*) (*tb* **gran ~**) eagle owl

durabilidad SF durability

durable ADJ durable, lasting

duración SF **1** (= *extensión*) [*de conferencia, viaje*] length; [*de llamada*] time; **la ~ del disco** the length of the record; **¿cuál es la ~ del examen?** how long does the exam last?; **de larga ~** [*parado, paro*] long-term; [*enfermedad*] lengthy; **de poca ~** short ▸ **duración media de la vida** average life expectancy
2 [*de batería, pila*] life; **baterías de larga ~** long-life batteries

duradero ADJ [*ropa, tela*] hard-wearing; [*paz, efecto*] lasting; [*relación*] lasting, long-term *antes de s*

duralex® SM INV Duralex®

duramente ADV [*atacar*] fiercely; [*castigar, criticar*] harshly; [*entrenar, trabajar*] hard

> **DURANTE**
>
> Para traducir **durante** tenemos que diferenciar si hace referencia a cuándo ocurre la acción o a cuánto dura.
>
> **¿Cuándo ocurre la acción?**
>
> • Traducimos **durante** por **during** si nos referimos al intervalo de tiempo en que ocurre la acción, cuando la referencia temporal la indica un suceso o actividad determinados:
>
> Se conocieron durante la guerra
> ***They met during the war***
> Se puso enferma durante una visita a Madrid
> ***She became ill during a visit to Madrid***
> La bomba hizo explosión durante la entrega de premios
> ***The bomb went off during the prize-giving ceremony***
>
> • También se traduce por **during** cuando la referencia temporal viene indicada por un periodo de tiempo concreto:
>
> El tráfico es peor durante el verano
> ***The traffic is worse during the summer***
> Durante los años treinta la economía se hallaba en dificultades
> ***The economy was in difficulties during the 1930s***
>
> **NOTA:** Si se trata de una acción progresiva, o que continúa o que se repite durante todo el periodo de tiempo que se indica, es preferible traducir **durante** por **over**:
>
> La situación ha empeorado durante los últimos años
> ***The situation has worsened over the last few years***
> Durante el fin de semana el actor ha sido visto en varias ocasiones
> ***There have been several sightings of the actor over the weekend***
>
> **¿Cuánto dura la acción?**
>
> • Si nos referimos a la duración de la acción, **durante** se traduce generalmente por **for**:
>
> Llevo sufriendo dolores de cabeza durante más de treinta años
> ***I've been having headaches for more than 30 years***
> Fue periodista durante cuatro años
> ***He was a journalist for four years***
>
> *Para otros usos y ejemplos ver la entrada.*

durante PREP (*con espacio de tiempo*) during; (*expresando la duración*) for; **¿qué hiciste ~ las vacaciones?** what did you do in *o* during the holidays?; **¿ha llovido ~ el fin de semana?** did it rain at *o* over the weekend?; **habló ~ una hora** he spoke for an hour; **~ muchos años** for many years; **~ toda la noche** all through the night, all night long

durar ▸conjug 1a◂ VI **1** [*aventura, programa, enfermedad*] to last; **su matrimonio duró menos de dos años** their marriage lasted (for) less than two years; **¿cuánto dura la representación?** how long is the play?, how long does the play last?; **¿cuánto dura el trayecto?** how long is the journey?, how long does the journey take?; **la película duró cinco horas** the film was five hours long; **fue hermoso mientras duró** it was wonderful while it lasted *o* for as long as it lasted; **estuvo refugiado mientras duró la guerra** he was a refugee throughout the (whole length of the) war; **no duro ni un minuto más de pie** I can't stay standing (up) a minute longer; **aún duran los efectos del terremoto** the effects of the earthquake are still being felt; **mis esperanzas ~on poco** my hopes were short-lived; ✦*REFRÁN* **no hay mal ni bien que cien años dure** nothing lasts forever
2 [*comida, congelado, ropa*] to last; **a mí me duran mucho los zapatos** my shoes last me a long time; **esta camisa es mala, ~á poco** this shirt is poor quality, it won't last long; **aún me dura el aceite que traje** I've still got some of the oil that I brought back

duraznero SM (*esp LAm*) peach tree

durazno SM (*esp LAm*) (= *fruta*) peach; (= *árbol*) peach tree

Durero SM Dürer

durex® SM **1** (*Méx*) (= *cinta adhesiva*) Sellotape®, Scotch tape® (*EEUU*), sticky tape
2 (= *preservativo*) Durex®, sheath, condom

dureza SF **1** (= *resistencia*) [*de mineral, roca, agua*] hardness; [*de carne*] toughness; **la ~ de esta roca** the hardness of this rock; **el mineral de mayor ~** the hardest mineral
2 (= *agresividad*) [*de clima, régimen, crítica*] harshness, severity; [*de deporte, juego*] roughness; [*de ataque*] fierceness; [*de castigo, multa, sentencia*] severity, harshness; **la ~ extrema de la vida en la montaña** the extreme harshness of life in the mountains; **el rugby es un deporte de gran ~** rugby is a very rough sport; **la ~ negociadora del gobierno** the government's tough stance in the negotiations; **con ~**: **los delitos serán castigados con ~** any offence will be severely punished; **el ejército contraatacó con ~** the army counter-attacked fiercely; **arremetió con ~ contra el gobierno** he launched a fierce attack against the government
3 [*de tarea, prueba, examen*] hardness
4 (= *fortaleza*) hardiness, strength; **la ~ de las mujeres campesinas** the hardiness *o* strength of country women
5 (= *callo*) callus

durmiente Ⓐ ADJ sleeping; **la Bella Durmiente (del Bosque)** Sleeping Beauty
Ⓑ SMF (= *persona*) sleeper
Ⓒ SM (*Ferro*) sleeper, tie (*EEUU*)

duro/a Ⓐ ADJ **1** (= *resistente*) [*material, superficie, cama, agua*] hard; [*cable, alambre*] stiff;

[*pan*] hard, stale; [*carne*] tough; [*legumbres*] hard; [*articulación, mecanismo*] stiff; [*músculo*] firm, hard; **la cerradura está muy dura** the lock is very stiff; ✦*MODISMOS* **más ~ que una piedra** ◊ **más ~ que un mendrugo** as hard as nails, as tough as old boots; *ver tb* **huevo 1**

2 (= *agresivo*) [*clima, tiempo, crítica*] harsh, severe; [*deporte, juego*] rough; [*ataque*] fierce; [*castigo, sentencia*] severe, harsh; [*carácter, actitud*] tough; **fue un ~ golpe para el partido** it was a severe *o* heavy blow to the party; **una postura dura contra la droga** a tough stance *o* hard line against drugs; **el sector ~ del partido** the hardliners in the party; **es muy ~ con sus hijos** he's very strict *o* tough with his children; **hay que tener mano dura con los estudiantes** you have to be firm *o* strict with students, students need a firm hand; **rock ~** hard rock; ✦*MODISMO* **a las duras y a las maduras** through thick and thin, through good times and bad; *ver tb* **disco 2, núcleo, porno**

3 (= *difícil*) [*tarea, prueba, examen*] hard; **el slálom es una prueba muy dura** the slalom is a very hard *o* tough race; **este coche ha pasado las pruebas más duras** this car has passed the most stringent tests; **lo tienes ~ para aprobar*** it will be hard *o* difficult for you to pass; **¡qué dura es la vida!** it's a hard life!; ✦*MODISMO* **ser ~ de pelar** to be a hard nut to crack; *ver tb* **hueso 2**

4 (*) (= *torpe*) **es muy ~ para las matemáticas** he's hopeless *o* no good at maths*; **~ de mollera** dense*, dim*; **~ de oído** (= *medio sordo*) hard of hearing; (*Mús*) tone deaf

5 (*Méx**) (= *borracho*) **estar ~** to be drunk

Ⓑ ADV hard; **mi padre trabaja ~** my father works hard; **pégale** *o* **dale ~** hit him hard

Ⓒ SM (= *cinco pesetas*) five pesetas; (= *moneda*) five-peseta coin; **estar sin un ~*** to be broke*; ✦*MODISMOS* **¡lo que faltaba para el ~!*** it's the last straw!; **¡y que te den dos ~s!*** and you can get knotted!*; **vender ~s a tres pesetas**: **cree que en Estados Unidos venden ~s a tres pesetas** he thinks that in the States the streets are paved with gold

Ⓓ SM/F 1 (*en película, historia*) tough character; **se hizo el ~ para disimular su tristeza** he acted the tough guy *o* hard man in order to hide his sadness

2 (*Pol*) hard-liner

dux SM doge

DVD SM ABR (= **disco de vídeo digital**) DVD

DYA SF ABR (= **Detente y Ayuda**) *Spanish highway assistance organization*

E e

E¹, e [e] SF (*letra*) E, e

E² ABR (= **este**) E

e CONJ (*before words beginning with i and hi, but not hie*) and; *ver tb* **y**

-e *ver* **Aspects of Word Formation in Spanish 2**

e/ ABR (*Com*) (= **envío**) shpt

EA (*Esp*) Ⓐ ABR (*Mil*) = **Ejército del Aire**
Ⓑ SM ABR (*Pol*) (= **Eusko Alkartasuna**) *Basque political party*

ea EXCL (*llamando la atención*) hey!, say! (*EEUU*); (*dando ánimos*) come on!; **¡ea pues!** well then!; (= *veamos*) let's see!; **¡ea, andamos!** come on, let's go!

EAU SMPL ABR (= **Emiratos Árabes Unidos**) UAE

ebanista SMF cabinetmaker, carpenter

ebanistería SF 1 (= *oficio*) cabinetmaking
2 (= *obra*) woodwork, carpentry
3 (= *taller*) cabinetmaker's (work shop)

ébano SM ebony

ebonita SF ebonite

ebriedad SF intoxication (*frm*), drunkenness

ebrio ADJ 1 intoxicated (*frm*), drunk
2 (*fig*) blind (**de** with); **~ de alegría** beside o.s. with joy

Ebro SM Ebro

ebullición SF 1 [*de líquidos*] boiling; **entrar en ~** to begin to boil, come to the boil; **punto de ~** boiling point
2 (*fig*) (= *movimiento*) movement, activity; (= *estado cambiante*) state of flux; (= *alboroto*) turmoil; (= *emoción*) ferment; **la juventud está en ~** young people are boiling over (with excitement); **llevar un asunto a ~** to bring a matter to the boil

ebúrneo ADJ (*liter*) ivory, like ivory

eccehomo SM poor wretch; **estar hecho un ~** to be in a sorry state

eccema SM eczema

ECG SM ABR (= **electrocardiograma**) ECG

echacuervos SM INV 1 (= *chulo*) pimp
2 (= *tramposo*) cheat, impostor

echada SF 1 (= *acción*) throw, cast; [*de moneda*] toss
2 (*Méx*) (= *fanfarronada*) boast

echadizo/a Ⓐ ADJ 1 [*persona*] spying, sent to spy
2 [*propaganda*] secretly spread; [*carta*] circulated in a clandestine way
3 [*material*] waste
Ⓑ SM/F spy

echado ADJ, PP *de* **echar** 1 **estar ~** to lie, be lying (down)
2 (*CAm, Caribe*) (*económicamente*) well-placed, in a good position
3 (*CAm**) (= *perezoso*) lazy, idle
4 (*Andes**) (= *engreído*) stuck-up*, toffee-nosed*
5 ✦*MODISMOS* **es muy ~ pa'lante*** he's very pushy, he's very forward, he's not backward in coming forward*; **es muy ~ p'atrás*** (= *arrogante*) he's full of himself; (= *tímido*) he's very shy

echador(a) Ⓐ ADJ (*CAm, Méx*) boastful, bragging
Ⓑ SM/F 1 ► **echador(a) de cartas** fortune teller
2 (*CAm, Méx*) (= *presumido*) boaster, braggart

echao* ADJ = **echado 4, 5**

echar

▸conjug 1a◂

A VERBO TRANSITIVO — C VERBO PRONOMINAL
B VERBO INTRANSITIVO

*Para las expresiones **echar abajo, echar en cara, echar la culpa, echar en falta, echar de menos, echar a perder, echar raíces, echar a suertes**, ver la otra entrada.*

Ⓐ VERBO TRANSITIVO

1 *= tirar* [+ *pelota, piedra, dados*] to throw; [+ *basura*] to throw away; [+ *ancla, red*] to cast; [+ *moneda al aire*] to toss; [+ *mirada*] to cast, give; [+ *naipe*] to deal; **échame las llaves** throw me the keys; **échalo a la basura** throw it away; **¿qué te han echado los Reyes?** ≈ what did you get for Christmas?; ✦*MODISMO* **~las** (*Cono Sur**) to leg it*, scarper*; *ver tb* **cara 4**

2 *= poner* to put; **~ carbón a la lumbre** to put coal on the fire; **he echado otra manta en la cama** I've put another blanket on the bed; **¿te echo mantequilla en el pan?** shall I put some butter on your bread?; **échale un poco de azúcar a la mezcla** add a little sugar to the mixture; **tengo que ~ gasolina** I need to fill up (with petrol); *ver tb* **leña 1**

3 *= verter* to pour; **echó un poco de vino en un vaso** he poured some wine into a glass; **~ cera en un molde** to pour wax into a mould

4 *= servir* [+ *bebida*] to pour; [+ *comida*] to give; **échame agua** could you give *o* pour me some water?; **¿te echo más whisky?** shall I pour you some more whisky?; **no me eches tanto** don't give me so much; **tengo que ~ de comer a los animales** I have to feed the animals; ✦*MODISMO* **lo que le echen: resiste lo que le echen** she can take whatever they throw at her

5 *= dejar salir* **la chimenea echa humo** smoke is coming out of the chimney; **¡qué peste echan tus zapatos!*** your shoes stink to high heaven!*; *ver tb* **chispa A1, espuma 1, hostia 6, leche 9, peste 3, sangre A1**

6 *= expulsar* (*de casa, bar, tienda, club*) to throw out; (*del trabajo*) to fire*, sack*; (*de colegio*) to expel; **cuando protesté me ~on** when I protested they threw me out; **me echó de su casa** he threw me out of his house; **lo han echado del colegio** he's been expelled from school; **la ~on del trabajo** she's been fired *o* sacked*; **~ algo de sí** to get rid of sth, throw sth off

7 *= producir* [+ *dientes*] to cut; [+ *hojas*] to sprout; **está empezando a ~ barriga** he's starting to get a bit of a belly *o* paunch; **¡vaya mal genio que has echado últimamente!** you've become *o* got really bad-tempered recently!

8 *= cerrar* **~ la llave/el cerrojo** to lock/bolt the door; **~ el freno** to brake; **echa la persiana** can you draw the blinds?

9 *= mover* 9·1 [+ *parte del cuerpo*] **~ la cabeza a un lado** to tilt *o* cock one's head to one side; **~ el cuerpo hacia atrás** to lean back
9·2 (= *empujando*) to push; **~ a algn a un lado** to push sb aside; **~ atrás a la multitud** to push the crowd back

10 *= enviar* [+ *carta*] to post, mail (*EEUU*); **eché la carta en el buzón** I posted the letter; **¿dónde puedo ~ esta postal?** where can I post this postcard?

11 *= calcular* to reckon; **¿cuántos kilos le echas?** how much do you think *o* reckon she weighs?; **¿cuántos años le echas?** how old do you think *o* reckon he is?; **échale una hora andando** you can reckon on it taking you an hour if you walk

12 *= dar* [+ *discurso*] to give, make; **~ maldiciones** to curse; **~ una reprimenda a algn** to tick sb off, give sb a ticking-off; **he ido a que me echen las cartas** I've had my cards read

13 *con sustantivos que implican acciones* [+ *trago, partida*] to have; **¿echamos un café?** shall we have a coffee?; **salió al balcón a ~ un cigarrillo** he went out onto the balcony for a smoke *o* cigarette; **~ una multa a algn** to fine sb, give sb a fine; *ver tb* **polvo 5, vistazo**

14 *+ tiempo* **hay que ~le muchas horas** it

takes a long time; **de jóvenes nos echábamos nuestros buenos ratos de charla** we used to spend a lot of time talking when we were younger; **esta semana he echado cuatro horas extras** I did four hours overtime this week

[15] ** en cine, televisión* to show; **~on un programa sobre Einstein** there was a programme about Einstein on, they showed a programme about Einstein; **¿qué echan en el cine?** what's on at the cinema?

[16] *+ cimientos* to lay

[17] *Zool* (*para procrear*) **ha echado a su perra con un pastor alemán** he has mated his bitch with a German shepherd

[18] *Caribe, Cono Sur = azuzar* [+ *animal*] to urge on

Ⓑ VERBO INTRANSITIVO

= tirar **¡echa para adelante!** lead on!; **ahora tienes que ~ para adelante y olvidarte del pasado** you need to get on with your life and forget about the past; **es un olor que echa para atrás*** it's a smell that really knocks you back*; **echa para allá** move up; **~ por una calle** to go down a street; **echemos por aquí** let's go this way

◆ **echar a** + *INFIN*: **~ a correr** to break into a run, start running; **~ a reír** to burst out laughing, start laughing

Ⓒ **echarse** VERBO PRONOMINAL

[1] *= lanzarse* to throw o.s.; **~se en brazos de algn** to throw o.s. into sb's arms; **los niños se ~on al agua** the children jumped into the water; **~se sobre algn** (*gen*) to hurl o.s. at sb, rush at sb; (= *atacando*) to fall on sb

[2] *= acostarse* to lie down; **voy a ~me un rato** I'm going to lie down for a bit; **me eché en el sofá y me quedé dormido** I lay down *o* stretched out on the sofa and fell asleep; **se echó en el suelo** he lay down on the floor

[3] *= moverse* **échate un poco para la izquierda** move a bit to the left; **me tuve que ~ a la derecha para que adelantara** I had to pull over to the right to let him overtake; **~se atrás** (*lit*) to throw o.s. back(wards), move back(wards); (*fig*) to back out; **¡échense para atrás!** move back!

[4] *= ponerse* **se echó laca en el pelo** she put some hairspray on; **se echó una manta por las piernas** she put a blanket over her legs

◆ **echarse a** + *INFIN*: **se echó a correr** she broke into a run, she started running

[5] *uso enfático* **~se una novia** to get o.s. a girlfriend; **~se un pitillo** to have a cigarette *o* smoke; **~se una siestecita** to have a nap; **~se un trago** to have a drink; *ver tb* **A13**

[6] **echárselas de** to make o.s. out to be; **se las echa de experto** he makes himself out to be an expert

[7] *Méx* **~se algo encima** (= *asumir*) to take responsibility for sth; **~se a algn encima** to alienate sb, turn sb against one

[8] *Méx* = matar* **~se a algn** to bump sb off*

echarpe SM (*a veces* SF) (woman's) stole, scarf

echazón SF [1] (= *acto*) throwing

[2] (*Náut*) jetsam

echón/ona* SM/F (*Caribe, Méx*) braggart, swank*; **¡qué ~!** isn't he full of himself!*

echona SF (*Cono Sur*) small sickle, reaping hook

eclecticismo SM eclecticism

ecléctico/a ADJ, SM/F eclectic

eclesial ADJ ecclesiastic(al), church *antes de s*

eclesiástico Ⓐ ADJ (*gen*) ecclesiastic, ecclesiastical; [*autoridades*] church *antes de s*

Ⓑ SM clergyman, ecclesiastic

eclesiología SF ecclesiology

eclipsamiento SM eclipse

eclipsar ▸conjug 1a◂ VT (*Astron*) to eclipse; (*fig*) to eclipse, outshine

eclipse SM eclipse ► **eclipse lunar** eclipse of the moon, lunar eclipse ► **eclipse solar** eclipse of the sun, solar eclipse

eclíptica SF ecliptic

eclisa SF (*Ferro*) fishplate

eclosión SF [1] (= *aparición*) bloom, blooming; **hacer ~** [*huevos, larva*] to hatch; **el modernismo hizo ~ en Latinoamérica muy pronto** modernism burst onto the scene very early in Latin America

[2] (*Entomología*) hatching, emerging; **hacer ~** to hatch, emerge

eclosionar ▸conjug 1a◂ VI (*Entomología*) to hatch, emerge

eco SM [1] (= *sonido*) echo; **hacer ~** to echo

[2] (= *reacción*) echo; **despertar** *o* **encontrar ~** to produce a response (**en** from); **la llamada no encontró ~** the call produced no response, the call had no effect; **hacer ~** to make an impression; **hacerse ~ de una opinión** to echo an opinion; **tener ~** to catch on, arouse interest

eco... PREF eco...

ecoclimático ADJ ecoclimatic

ecoequilibrio SM ecobalance

ecografía SF (= *imagen*) ultrasound scan; (= *técnica*) ultrasound scanning

ecolalia SF (*Psic*) echolalia

ecolecuá EXCL (*LAm*) exactly!, that's it!

ecología SF ecology

ecológicamente ADV ecologically

ecológico ADJ [*desastre, zona, equilibrio*] ecological; [*producto*] environment-friendly; [*cultivo*] organic, organically-grown

ecologismo SM conservation(ism), environmentalism

ecologista Ⓐ ADJ conservation *antes de s*, environmental; **el partido ~** the Green party

Ⓑ SMF ecologist, environmentalist; **los ~s** the Greens

ecólogo/a SM/F ecologist, environmentalist

ecómetro SM echo sounder

economato SM (= *tienda*) cooperative store; [*de empresa*] company store; (*Mil*) ≈ NAAFI, ≈ PX (*EEUU*)

econometría SF econometrics *sing*

econométrico ADJ econometric

economía SF [1] (*gen*) economy ► **economía de empleo completo** full-employment economy ► **economía de guerra** war economy ► **economía de libre empresa**, **economía de libre mercado** free-market economy ► **economía de mercado** market economy ► **economía de pleno empleo** full-employment economy ► **economía de subsistencia** subsistence economy ► **economía dirigida** planned economy ► **economía doméstica** domestic service, home economics ► **economía mixta** mixed economy ► **economía negra** black economy ► **economía oculta** hidden economy ► **economía política** political economy ► **economías de escala** economies of scale ► **economía subterránea**, **economía sumergida** underground economy, black economy

[2] (= *estudio*) economics *sing*

[3] (= *ahorro*) economy, saving; **hacer ~s** to make economies, economize

[4] (*tb* **(Ministerio de) Economía (y Hacienda)**) Ministry of Finance, Treasury Department (*EEUU*)

económicamente ADV economically; **los ~ débiles** (*euf*) the poor; **los ~ fuertes** (*euf*) the well-off, the wealthy

economicidad SF [1] (*gen*) *economic nature or working etc*

[2] (= *rentabilidad*) economic viability, profitability

económico ADJ [1] (*gen*) economic; [*año*] fiscal, financial; **la situación económica** the economic situation

[2] (= *barato*) economical, inexpensive; **edición económica** cheap edition, popular edition

[3] (= *ahorrativo*) thrifty; (*pey*) miserly

> **ECONÓMICO**
>
> **¿"Economic" o "economical"?**
>
> • El adjetivo **económico** se traduce por **economic** cuando se refiere al comercio o las finanzas:
>
> China ha vivido cinco años de reformas económicas
>
> ***China has lived through five years of economic reforms***
>
> ...el ritmo del crecimiento económico...
>
> ***...the pace of economic growth...***
>
> • **Económico** se traduce por **economical** cuando se usa para describir algo que presenta una buena relación calidad-precio:
>
> Resulta más económico tener un coche de gasoil
>
> ***It is more economical to have a diesel-engined car***
>
> **NOTA: Economic** se puede usar en inglés para traducir **rentable**:
>
> Mantendremos las tarifas altas para que el servicio resulte rentable
>
> ***We shall keep the fares high to make the service economic***
>
> *Para otros usos y ejemplos ver la entrada.*

economista SMF economist

economizar ▸conjug 1f◂ Ⓐ VT to economize on; **~ tiempo** to save time

Ⓑ VI to economize

ecónomo/a SM/F (*gen*) trustee, guardian; (*Rel*) ecclesiastical administrator

ecosensible ADJ ecosensitive

ecosistema SM ecosystem

ecosonda SF, **ecosond(e)ador** SM echo sounder

ecotasa SF green tax, eco-tax

ecotipo SM ecotype

ectodermo SM ectoderm

ectópico ADJ ectopic

ectoplasma SM ectoplasm

ECU SF ABR (= **Unidad de Cuenta Europea**) ECU

ecu SM ecu

ecuación SF equation ► **ecuación cuadrática, ecuación de segundo grado** quadratic equation ► **ecuación diferencial** differential equation

Ecuador SM **el ~** Ecuador

ecuador SM 1 (*Geog*) equator
2 (= *punto medio*) mid point, half-way point, half-way mark; **estamos en el ~ de nuestra vida** we're at the mid-point in our lives

ecualizador SM equalizer

ecualizar ▸conjug 1f◂ VT to equalize, tie (*EEUU*)

ecuánime ADJ [*carácter*] level-headed; [*humor, ánimo*] calm; [*juicio*] impartial

ecuanimidad SF 1 (= *serenidad*) level-headedness, equanimity
2 (= *imparcialidad*) impartiality

ecuatoreñismo SM, **ecuatorianismo** SM *word o phrase etc peculiar to Ecuador*

ecuatorial ADJ equatorial

ecuatoriano/a ADJ, SM/F Ecuadoran

ecuestre ADJ equestrian

ecuménico ADJ ecumenical

ecumenismo SM ecumenicism

eczema SM eczema

ed. ABR 1 (= **edición**) ed
2 (= **editor**) ed
3 = **editorial**

edad SF 1 [*de persona, animal, árbol*] age; **¿qué ~ tiene?** how old is he?, what age is he?; **tenemos la misma ~** we're the same age; **a tu ~ yo ya sabía leer** I could read when I was your age; **jóvenes de ~es comprendidas entre los 18 y los 26 años** young people aged 18 to 26, young people between the age of 18 and 26; **no aparenta la ~ que tiene** she doesn't look her age; **su madre le dobla la ~** her mother is twice her age; **¿qué ~ le echas?** how old do you think he is?; **~ adulta** adulthood; **llegar a la ~ adulta** to become an adult, reach adulthood; **a la ~ de ocho años** at the age of eight; **murió a los 85 años de ~** she died when she was 85 *o* at the age of 85; **una mujer de ~ avanzada** a woman of advanced years; **se casó a una ~ avanzada** she married late in life; **un señor de cierta ~** a gentleman of a certain age; **a cierta ~ ya empiezan los dolores** at a certain age the aches and pains start; **un niño de corta ~** a young child; **una persona de ~** an elderly person; **en ~ escolar** of school age; **estar en (la) ~ de hacer algo** = **tener edad de hacer algo**; **~ de (la) jubilación** retirement age; **~ límite** age limit; **~ madura** middle age; **persona de ~ madura** middle-aged person; **mediana ~** = **edad madura**; **tener ~ de hacer algo** to be old enough to do sth; **ya tienes ~ de trabajar** you're old enough to work now; **no tener ~ para hacer algo** (= *ser muy joven*) not to be old enough to do sth, not to be of an age to do sth; (= *ser muy mayor*) to be too old to do sth; **ya no tengo ~ para ir a la discoteca** I'm too old now to go out clubbing; **tercera ~** (= *personas*) senior citizens *pl*, older people *pl*; (= *edad*) old age; **excursiones organizadas para la tercera ~** organized trips for senior citizens *o* older people; **llegar a la tercera ~ es traumático para muchas personas** for many people, reaching old age is traumatic; ✦***MODISMOS*** **estar en ~ de merecer**† to be of courting age†; **estar en la ~ del pavo** to be at that difficult *o* awkward age ► **edad mental** mental age ► **edad penal** age of legal responsibility, age of criminal responsibility ► **edad viril** manhood; *ver tb* **mayor A4, B1, mayoría 2, menor A1.4, B**
2 (*Hist*) age ► **Edad Antigua** *period from the beginning of history to the decline of the Roman Empire* ► **Edad Contemporánea** Modern Age, Modern Period ► **Edad de(l) Bronce** Bronze Age ► **Edad de(l) Hierro** Iron Age ► **Edad de Oro** (*Literat*) Golden Age (*of Spanish literature*) ► **Edad de Piedra** Stone Age ► **Edad Media** Middle Ages *pl* ► **Edad Moderna** *period from the Middle Ages to the French Revolution*

edafología SF pedology, study of soils

edecán SM 1 aide-de-camp
2 (*Méx*) assistant

edema SM oedema, edema (*EEUU*)

Edén SM Eden, Paradise; **es un ~** it's an earthly paradise, it's paradise on earth

ed. física ABR (= **educación física**) PE

edible ADJ (*LAm*) edible

edición SF 1 (= *acto*) publication, issue; (= *industria*) publishing; (*Inform*) editing; **el mundo de la ~** the publishing world; ✦***MODISMO*** **ser la segunda ~ de algn** to be the very image of sb, be the spitting image of sb* ► **edición de sobremesa** desktop publishing ► **edición electrónica** (= *creación*) electronic publishing; (= *texto*) electronic edition ► **edición en pantalla** on-line editing
2 [*de libro*] edition; **en ~ de** edited by; **"al cerrar la ~"** (*Tip*) "stop-press" ► **edición aérea** airmail edition ► **edición de bolsillo** pocket edition ► **edición de la mañana** morning edition ► **edición económica** cheap edition, popular edition ► **edición extraordinaria** special edition ► **edición numerada** numbered edition ► **edición príncipe** first edition ► **edición semanal** weekly edition ► **edición viva** edition in print, available edition
3 **ediciones** (= *editorial*): **Ediciones Ramírez** Ramirez Publications
4 (= *celebración*) **es la tercera ~ de este festival** this is the third occasion on which this festival has been held

edicto SM edict, proclamation

edificabilidad SF suitability for building

edificable ADJ **terreno ~** building land, land available for building

edificación SF 1 (*Arquit*) construction, building
2 (*moral*) edification

edificante ADJ edifying; **una escena poco ~** an unedifying spectacle

edificar ▸conjug 1g◂ VT 1 (*Arquit*) to build, construct
2 (*moralmente*) to edify

edificio SM 1 (*Arquit*) building, edifice (*frm*) ► **edificio de apartamentos** block of flats, apartment building *o* house (*EEUU*) ► **edificio de oficinas** office block ► **edificio inteligente** smart building, intelligent building
2 (*moral*) edification

edil SMF 1 (*Esp*) (= *concejal*) town councillor, councilman/councilwoman (*EEUU*); (= *dignatario*) civic dignitary
2 (*Hist*) aedile

Edimburgo SM Edinburgh

Edipo SM Oedipus

editaje SM editing

editar ▸conjug 1a◂ VT 1 (= *publicar*) to publish
2 (= *corregir*) (*tb Inform*) to edit

editor(a) Ⓐ ADJ publishing *antes de s*; **casa ~a** publishing house
Ⓑ SM/F 1 [*de libros, periódicos*] publisher
2 (= *redactor*) editor, compiler; (*TV*) editor
3 (*LAm*) [*de periódico*] editor
Ⓒ SM (*Inform*) ► **editor de pantalla** screen editor ► **editor de texto** text editor

editorial Ⓐ ADJ 1 [*industria, mundo*] publishing *antes de s*; **casa ~** publishing house
2 [*función, política*] editorial
Ⓑ SM leading article, editorial
Ⓒ SF publishing house

editorialista SMF leader writer

editorializar ▸conjug 1f◂ VI to write editorials; **el periódico editorializa contra ...** the paper argues editorially against ...; **el diario editorializa ...** the paper says in its editorial ...

Edo. ABR (*Méx*) = **Estado**

edredón SM eiderdown ► **edredón nórdico** duvet, comforter (*EEUU*)

ed. religiosa ABR (= **educación religiosa**) RE, RI

Eduardo SM Edward

educabilidad SF educability

educable ADJ educable (*frm*), teachable

educación SF 1 (*en el colegio*) education; **han aumentado el presupuesto de ~** they've increased the education budget; **(Ministerio de) Educación y Ciencia** Ministry of Education and Science ► **educación a distancia** distance learning ► **educación compensatoria** remedial education ► **educación de adultos** adult education ► **educación especial** special education ► **educación física** physical education ► **educación medioambiental** environmental education ► **educación preescolar** pre-school education, nursery education ► **educación primaria** primary education ► **educación privada** private education ► **educación sanitaria** health education ► **educación secundaria** secondary education ► **Educación Secundaria Obligatoria** (*Esp*) *secondary education, for 12- to 16-year-olds* ► **educación sexual** sex education
2 (*en familia*) upbringing; **Rosa recibió una ~ muy estricta** Rosa had a very strict upbringing, Rosa was very strictly brought up
3 (= *modales*) manners *pl*, good behavior (*EEUU*); **no tiene ~** she has no manners; **buena ~** good manners *pl*; **con ~**: **se lo pedí con ~** I asked her politely; **falta de ~**: **eso es una falta de ~** that's rude; **¡qué falta de ~!** how rude!; **mala ~** bad manners *pl*; **es de mala ~ comportarse así** it's bad manners *o* rude to behave like that
4 [*de voz, oído, animal*] training

educacional ADJ educational

educacionista SMF educationist, educationalist

educado ADJ (= *de buenos modales*) well-mannered, polite; (= *instruido*) cultivated; **mal ~** (= *de malos modales*) ill-mannered; (= *grosero*) rude

educador(a) SM/F educator, teacher

educando/a SM/F pupil

educar ▸conjug 1g◂ Ⓐ VT [1] (*Educ*) to educate; **la han educado en un colegio bilingüe** she was educated at a bilingual school
[2] (*en familia*) to bring up; **~on a sus hijos de una manera muy estricta** their children were brought up very strictly
[3] [+ *voz, oído*] to train
[4] [+ *animal*] to train
Ⓑ **educarse** VPR to be educated; **se educó en un colegio de pago** he was educated at a fee-paying school

educativo ADJ [1] (= *instructivo*) educational; **juguete ~** educational toy
[2] (= *pedagógico*) **política educativa** education policy; **sistema ~** education system; **reforma educativa** educational *o* school reform

edulcoración SF sweetening

edulcorante SM sweetener

edulcorar ▸conjug 1a◂ VT to sweeten

EE.UU. ABR (= **Estados Unidos**) US, USA

efe SF (name of the letter) F

efectismo SM sensationalism; **su obra rehúye todo ~** his work rejects all sensationalism; **la escena final de la película es de un gran ~** the final scene in the film is really dramatic

efectista ADJ, SMF sensationalist

efectivamente ADV [1] (= *verdaderamente*) really; **tengo que comprobar si ~ es así** I have to check if it really is like that
[2] (*confirmando algo*) indeed; **~, el robo fue llevado a cabo por dos personas** the theft was indeed carried out by two people; **—fue ese retraso lo que le salvó la vida —~, así es** "it was that delay that saved his life" — "yes, that's right *o* indeed it was"; **pensé que iba a llegar tarde, y, ~, así fue** I thought he would be late, and sure enough, he was

efectividad SF effectiveness; **exigieron que la policía actuara con una mayor ~** they demanded that the police act much more effectively

efectivo Ⓐ ADJ [1] (= *eficaz*) [*vacuna, táctica*] effective; **el tratamiento comenzará a ser ~ dentro de un mes** the treatment will begin to take effect *o* will become effective within a month
[2] (= *real*) **el poder ~ está en manos de la oposición** the real power is in the hands of the opposition; **la orden no será efectiva hasta mañana** the order will not take effect *o* become effective until tomorrow; **hacer ~** [+ *plan*] to put into effect; [+ *multa, pago*] to make payable; [+ *cheque*] to cash; **el gobierno hará efectiva la subida salarial antes de marzo** the government will put the pay rises into effect before March; **su dimisión, anunciada el martes, se hizo efectiva el jueves** his resignation, announced on Tuesday, took effect *o* became effective on Thursday
Ⓑ SM [1] (= *dinero*) cash; **en ~** in cash; **50 libras en ~** £50 (in) cash; **tres premios en ~** three cash prizes ▸ **efectivo en caja**, **efectivo en existencia** cash in hand
[2] **efectivos** (*Mil*) forces; **~s de la Policía** ◊ **~s policiales** police officers

efecto SM [1] (= *consecuencia*) effect; **los ~s devastadores de la crisis** the devastating effects of the crisis; **ya empiezo a notar los ~s de la anestesia** I'm starting to feel the effect of the anaesthetic now; **los cambios no produjeron ningún ~** the changes did not have *o* produce (*frm*) any effect; **la reforma tuvo por ~ el aumento de los ingresos** the reform had the effect of increasing revenue; **conducía bajo los ~s del alcohol** he was driving under the influence of alcohol; **causar ~** = **surtir** *o* **tener efecto**; **hacer ~** to take effect; **el calmante no le ha hecho ningún ~** the sedative has had no effect on him *o* has not taken effect; **por ~ de** (= *por acción de*) by; (= *a consecuencia de*) as a result of; **nos movíamos por ~ del viento** we were being driven by the wind; **la producción de vino se estancó por ~ de la crisis** wine production came to a halt as a result of the crisis; **de ~ retardado** [*bomba*] delayed-action *antes de s*; **es de ~s retardados** (*hum*) he's a bit slow on the uptake*; **surtir** *o* **tener ~** to have an effect; **el truco no surtió el ~ deseado** the trick did not have the desired effect; **las picaduras de avispas pueden tener ~s graves** wasp stings can have serious effects ▸ **efecto 2000** (*Inform*) millennium bug, Y2K ▸ **efecto bumerán** boomerang effect ▸ **efectos colaterales** collateral damage *sing* ▸ **efecto dominó** domino effect ▸ **efecto embudo** funnel effect ▸ **efecto invernadero** greenhouse effect ▸ **efecto óptico** optical illusion ▸ **efectos especiales** special effects ▸ **efectos secundarios** side effects ▸ **efectos sonoros** sound effects ▸ **efecto túnel** tunnel effect ▸ **efecto útil** (*Mec*) efficiency, output
[2] **en ~** indeed; **nos encontramos, en ~, ante un invento revolucionario** we are indeed faced with a revolutionary invention; **en ~, así es** yes, indeed *o* that's right; **y en ~, el libro estaba donde él dijo** sure enough, the book was where he had said it would be
[3] (= *vigencia*) [*de ley, reforma*] **una ley con ~ desde 1950** a law that has been in force since 1950; **~ retroactivo**: **esas medidas tendrán ~ retroactivo** those measures will be applied retroactively *o* retrospectively; **una subida con ~s retroactivos desde primeros de año** an increase backdated to the beginning of the year; **tener ~** to take effect, come into effect
[4] (*frm*) (= *objetivo*) purpose; **a ~s fiscales/prácticos** for tax/practical purposes; **a estos ~s se convocó una nueva reunión** a new meeting was called for this purpose; **a ~s legales** for legal purposes, in legal terms; **a ~s de contrato, los dos cónyuges son copropietarios** for the purposes of the contract, husband and wife are co-owners; **a ~s de máxima seguridad** in order to ensure the tightest security; **al ~** for the purpose; **una comisión designada al ~** a specially established commission, a commission set up for the purpose; **a ~s de hacer algo** in order to do sth; **a ~s de conseguir una rebaja de su condena** in order to achieve a reduction of his sentence; **llevar a ~** [+ *acción, cambio*] to carry out; [+ *acuerdo, pacto*] to put into practice; [+ *reunión, congreso*] to hold; **llevaron a ~ sus amenazas** they carried out their threats; **la reunión se llevará a ~ en Bruselas** the meeting is to be held in Brussels; **a tal ~** to this end, for this purpose; **a tal ~, han convocado un referéndum** to this end *o* for this purpose, a referendum has been called; **una habitación habilitada a tal ~** a room fitted out for this purpose; **a todos los ~s** to all intents and purposes; **lo reconoció como hijo suyo a todos los ~s** he recognized him to all intents and purposes as his son
[5] (= *impresión*) effect; **no sé qué ~ tendrán mis palabras** I don't know what effect *o* impact my words will have; **les has causado un ~ sorprendente a mis padres** you've made quite an impression on my parents; **ser de buen/mal ~** to create *o* give a good/bad impression; **es de mal ~ llegar tarde a una reunión** being late for a meeting creates *o* gives a bad impression
[6] (*Dep*) (*gen*) spin; (*Ftbl*) swerve; **sacó la pelota con ~** she put some spin on her service, she served with topspin; **dar ~ a la pelota** ◊ **lanzar la pelota con ~** (*Tenis*) to put spin on the ball; (*Ftbl*) to put a swerve on the ball
[7] **efectos** (*Com*) (= *bienes*) stock *sing*, goods; (= *documentos*) bills ▸ **efectos a cobrar** bills receivable ▸ **efectos a pagar** bills payable ▸ **efectos bancarios** bank bills ▸ **efectos de consumo** consumer goods ▸ **efectos de escritorio** writing materials ▸ **efectos descontados** bills discounted ▸ **efectos navales** chandlery *sing* ▸ **efectos personales** personal effects
[8] (*Numismática*) ▸ **efecto postal** postage stamp

efectuación SF accomplishment

efectuar ▸conjug 1e◂ VT [+ *acción, reparación, investigación*] to carry out; [+ *viaje, visita, declaración, pago*] to make; [+ *disparo*] to fire; [+ *censo*] to take; **la policía efectuó un registro en la vivienda** the police searched the house, the police carried out a search of the house; **los pagos serán efectuados en metálico** the payments will be made in cash; **el tren ~á parada en todas las estaciones** the train will stop at all stations

efedrina SF ephedrine

efeméride SF event (*remembered on its anniversary*); **"efemérides"** (*en periódico*) "list of the day's anniversaries"

efervescencia SF [1] [*de líquidos*] fizziness; **entrar** *o* **estar en ~** to effervesce
[2] (= *alboroto*) commotion; (= *ánimo*) high spirits *pl*

efervescente ADJ [1] (= *con burbujas*) [*pastilla, sustancia*] effervescent; [*bebida*] fizzy
[2] (= *animado*) high-spirited

eficacia SF [*de ley, remedio, producto, sanción*] effectiveness; [*de persona, método*] efficiency

eficaz ADJ [*ley, remedio, producto, sanción*] effective; [*persona, método, instrumento*] efficient

eficazmente ADV [1] (= *con efecto*) effectively
[2] (= *eficientemente*) efficiently

eficiencia SF efficiency

eficiente ADJ efficient

eficientemente ADV efficiently

efigie SF [1] (= *busto, escultura*) effigy
[2] (= *imagen pintada*) image; **tiene en su despacho una ~ de su abuelo** in his office he's got a portrait of his grandfather; **el euro tendrá la ~ del rey** the euro will carry a likeness of the king
[3] (*liter*) (= *personificación*) **es la ~ de la desesperación** she's despair personified

efímera SF mayfly

efímero ADJ ephemeral

eflorescente ADJ efflorescent

efluvio SM outpour, outflow; **un ~ de optimismo** a sudden burst of optimism

efugio SM subterfuge, evasion

efusión SF [1] (= *derramamiento*) [*de sentimientos*] outpouring; [*de sangre*] shedding ► **efusión de sangre** bloodshed, shedding of blood

[2] [*de persona*] (*gen*) effusion, outpouring; (*en el trato*) warmth, effusiveness; (*pey*) gushing manner; **con ~** effusively; **efusiones amorosas** amorous excesses

efusivamente ADV warmly, effusively; **me saludó muy ~** he gave me a very warm greeting, he greeted me very warmly; **me felicitó muy ~ por mi cumpleaños** he congratulated me very warmly *o* effusively on my birthday

efusividad SF effusiveness

efusivo ADJ [*persona, modales*] effusive; [*gracias*] effusive, warm; **mis más efusivas gracias** my warmest thanks

EGB SF ABR (*Esp*) (= **Educación General Básica**) *former primary school education*

Egeo SM **el Mar ~** the Aegean Sea

égida SF aegis, protection; **bajo la ~ de** under the aegis of

egipcio/a ADJ, SM/F Egyptian

Egipto SM Egypt

egiptología SF Egyptology

eglantina SF eglantine

eglefino SM haddock

égloga SF eclogue

ego SM ego

egocéntrico ADJ egocentric, egocentrical, self-centred, self-centered (*EEUU*)

egocentrismo SM egocentrism

egocentrista SMF egocentric, self-centred person, self-centered person (*EEUU*)

egoísmo SM egoism, selfishness

egoísta Ⓐ ADJ egoistical, selfish

Ⓑ SMF egoist, selfish person

egoístamente ADV egoistically, selfishly

egoistón* ADJ rather selfish

ególatra Ⓐ ADJ egomaniacal

Ⓑ SMF egomaniac

egolatría SF egomania

egotismo SM egotism

egotista Ⓐ ADJ egotistical, egotist

Ⓑ SMF egotist

egregio ADJ eminent, distinguished

egresado/a SM/F (*LAm*) (= *licenciado*) graduate

egresar ▸conjug 1a◂ VI (*LAm*) [1] (= *irse*) to go out, leave; **~ de** to go away from

[2] (*Univ*) to graduate

egreso SM (*LAm*) [1] (= *acto*) departure

[2] (= *salida*) exit

[3] (*Univ*) graduation

[4] (*Fin*) outgoings *pl*, expenditure

eh EXCL [1] (*llamando la atención*) hey!, say! (*EEUU*); **¡eh, ven aquí!** hey, come here!; **¡a mí no me repliques, eh!** hey, don't you answer me back!

[2] (*cuando no se ha entendido algo*) eh?; — **¿quieres venir con nosotros? —¿eh?** "do you want to come with us?" — "eh?"

eider SM eider duck

Eire SM Eire

ej. ABR (= **ejemplo**) ex

eje SM [1] (*Geog, Mat*) axis; ✦**MODISMO partir a algn por el ~***: **¿que no vienes?, pues me partes por el ~** so you're not coming? well, that really upsets up my plans; **me hizo una pregunta que me partió por el ~** he asked me a question which really stumped *o* floored me* ► **eje de abscisas** x-axis ► **eje de ordenadas** y-axis ► **eje de rotación** axis of rotation ► **eje de simetría** axis of symmetry

[2] [*de rueda*] axle ► **eje delantero** front axle ► **eje trasero** rear axle

[3] [*de máquina*] shaft, spindle; ✦**MODISMO untar el ~ a algn*** to grease sb's palm ► **eje de balancín** rocker shaft ► **eje de la hélice** propeller shaft ► **eje de impulsión, eje motor** drive shaft ► **eje del cigüeñal** crankshaft

[4] (= *centro*) **la economía fue el ~ de la conversación** the economy was the main topic of conversation, the conversation centred on the economy; **el ~ de la doctrina** the central point of the doctrine

[5] (*Hist*) **el Eje** the Axis

[6] ► **eje vial** (*Méx Aut*) urban motorway

ejecución SF [1] (= *ajusticiamiento*) execution ► **ejecución sumaria** summary execution

[2] (= *cumplimiento*) [*de orden*] carrying out, execution; [*de deseos*] fulfilment, fulfillment (*EEUU*); **poner en ~** to carry out

[3] (*Mús*) performance

[4] (*Jur*) attachment

ejecutable ADJ feasible, practicable; **legalmente ~** legally enforceable

ejecutante Ⓐ SMF (*Mús*) performer

Ⓑ SM (*Jur*) distrainer

ejecutar ▸conjug 1a◂ VT [1] (= *ajusticiar*) to execute

[2] (= *hacer cumplir*) [+ *orden, sentencia*] to carry out, execute; [+ *deseos*] to perform, fulfil, fulfill (*EEUU*)

[3] (*Mús*) to perform, play

[4] (*Inform*) to run

[5] (*Jur*) to attach, distrain on

ejecutiva SF (*Pol*) executive body, executive committee

ejecutivo/a Ⓐ ADJ [1] [*función, poder*] executive [2] (= *urgente*) [*petición*] pressing, insistent; [*respuesta*] prompt; [*negocio*] urgent, immediate

Ⓑ SM (*Pol*) executive; **el Ejecutivo** the Executive

Ⓒ SM/F (*Com*) executive ► **ejecutivo/a de cuentas** account executive ► **ejecutivo/a de ventas** sales executive

ejecutor(a) SM/F executor/executrix; **los ~es testamentarios** the executors of the will

ejecutoria SF [1] (= *título*) letters patent of nobility; (*fig*) pedigree

[2] (*Jur*) final judgment

ejem EXCL hem! (*cough*)

ejemplar Ⓐ ADJ exemplary, model

Ⓑ SM [1] (= *individuo*) (*gen*) example; (*Zool*) specimen, example; [*de libro*] copy; [*de revista*] number, issue ► **ejemplar de firma** specimen signature ► **ejemplar de regalo** complimentary copy ► **ejemplar gratuito** free copy ► **ejemplar obsequio** complimentary copy

[2] (= *precedente*) example, model, precedent; **sin ~** unprecedented

ejemplaridad SF exemplariness

ejemplarizador ADJ, **ejemplarizante** ADJ exemplary

ejemplarizar ▸conjug 1f◂ VT (*esp LAm*) (= *dar ejemplo*) to set an example to; (= *ilustrar*) to exemplify, illustrate

ejemplificar ▸conjug 1g◂ VT to exemplify, illustrate

▼**ejemplo** SM [1] (= *paradigma*) example; **¿puedes ponerme** *o* **darme un ~?** can you give me an example?; **por ~** for example, for instance; **poner como** *o* **de** *o* **por ~** to give as an example; **tomar algo por ~** to take sth as an example

[2] (= *modelo*) example; **dar ~ a algn** to set sb an example; **servir de** *o* **como ~** to serve as an example; ✦**MODISMOS predicar con el ~** to set a good example, lead by example; **ser el vivo ~ de algo** to be a model of sth; **es el vivo ~ de la cortesía** he's a model of politeness

ejercer ▸conjug 2b◂ Ⓐ VT [1] [+ *medicina, abogacía*] to practise, practice (*EEUU*); **es abogado pero no ejerce su profesión** he's a lawyer by training, but he doesn't practise

[2] (= *hacer efectivo*) [+ *influencia*] to exert, exercise; [+ *poder*] to exercise, wield; **ejerce mucha influencia sobre sus hermanos** he exerts *o* has a great deal of influence on his brothers

[3] [+ *derecho*] to exercise; **~ el derecho al voto** to exercise one's right to vote

Ⓑ VI [*profesional*] to practise, practice (*EEUU*) (**de** as); **es médico, pero ya no ejerce** he's a doctor, but he no longer practises

ejercicio SM [1] (*físico*) exercise; **la natación es un ~ muy completo** swimming is an all-round exercise; **hacer ~** to exercise ► **ejercicio de calentamiento** warm-up exercise ► **ejercicio de estiramiento** stretching exercise ► **ejercicio de mantenimiento** keep-fit exercise ► **ejercicios gimnásticos** gymnastic exercises

[2] (*Educ*) exercise; **la maestra nos puso varios ~s** the teacher gave us several exercises to do ► **ejercicio escrito** written exercise ► **ejercicio práctico** practical

[3] (*Mil*) exercise; **las tropas españolas participan en los ~s de la OTAN** Spanish troops are taking part in NATO exercises ► **ejercicio acrobático** (*Aer*) stunt ► **ejercicios de tiro** target practice *sing*

[4] [*de cargo*] **en el ~ de mi cargo** in the exercise of my duties; **abogado en ~** practising *o* (*EEUU*) practicing lawyer; **hicieron ~ de su derecho al voto** they exercised their right to vote

[5] (*Com, Fin*) financial year, fiscal year; **durante el ~ actual** during the current financial year ► **ejercicio contable** year of account, accounting year ► **ejercicio fiscal** fiscal year, tax year ► **ejercicio presupuestario** budget year

[6] (*Rel*) ► **ejercicios espirituales** retreat *sing*

ejerciente ADJ practising, practicing (*EEUU*)

ejercitar ▸conjug 1a◂ Ⓐ VT [+ *músculo, memoria*] to exercise; [+ *profesión*] to practise, practice (*EEUU*); [+ *ejército*] to drill, train; [+ *alumno*] to train, coach

Ⓑ **ejercitarse** VPR [+ *músculos, memoria*] to exercise; [+ *profesión*] to practise, practice (*EEUU*); (*Mil*) to drill, train

ejército SM [1] (*Mil*) army; **estar en el ~** to be in the army; **los tres ~s** the forces, the Services ► **ejército del aire** Air Force

➤ LENGUA Y USO: **ejemplo** 53.1, 53.5

► **ejército de ocupación** army of occupation ► **Ejército de Salvación** Salvation Army ► **ejército de tierra** Army ► **ejército permanente** standing army
[2] (= *multitud*) army; **un ~ de fotógrafos** an army of photographers
ejidatario/a SM/F (*esp Méx*) holder of a share in common lands
ejido SM common land
-ejo, **-eja** *ver* **Aspects of Word Formation in Spanish 2**
ejote SM (*CAm, Méx*) string bean
el, **la**, **los**, **las** ART DEF [1] (*con nombres de referente único o concreto*) the; **el sol** the sun; **perdí el autobús** I missed the bus; **¿está fría el agua?** is the water cold?; **¿ha llegado ya el abogado?** has the lawyer arrived yet?; **el tío ese*** that chap
[2] (*en algunos casos no se traduce*) [2·1] (*con nombres propios*) **La India** India; **en el México de hoy** in present-day Mexico; **el Real Madrid ganó la liga** Real Madrid won the league; **el General Prim** General Prim; **¿qué manda la señora?** what would madam like?; **ha llamado el Sr. Sendra** Mr. Sendra called; **dáselo a la Luisa*** give it to Luisa
[2·2] (*con nombres en sentido genérico*) **me gusta el baloncesto** I like basketball; **no me gusta el pescado** I don't like fish; **está en la cárcel** he's in jail
[2·3] (*con infinitivo*) **el hacerlo fue un error** doing it was a mistake, it was a mistake to do it
[2·4] (*con cifras, proporciones*) **la mitad de la población** half of the population; **ahora gano el 3% más** I now earn 3% more
[3] (*traducido por el posesivo*) **se lavó las manos** he washed his hands; **me he cortado el pelo** I've had my hair cut; **ayer me lavé la cabeza** I washed my hair yesterday; **me puse el abrigo** I put my coat on
[4] (*con expresiones temporales*) **a las ocho** at eight o'clock; **a los quince días** after a fortnight; **vendrá el lunes que viene** he's coming next Monday; **la reunión será el 15 de abril** the meeting's on 15 April; **en el mes de julio** in (the month of) July
[5] (= *uso distributivo*) **cuesta dos euros el kilo** it costs two euros a kilo
[6] (*en exclamaciones*) **¡el frío que hacía!** it was freezing!
[7] (*posesivo*) **el de**: **mi libro y el de usted** my book and yours; **este jugador y el de la camisa azul** this player and the one in the blue shirt; **el del sombrero rojo** the one with *o* in the red hat; **es un traje bonito, pero prefiero el de Ana** it's a nice suit, but I prefer Ana's; **y el de todos los demás** and that of everybody else, and everybody else's; **el idiota de Pedro no me contestó al teléfono** that idiot Pedro didn't answer the phone
[8] **el que** [8·1] (+ *INDIC*) **el que compramos no vale** the one we bought is no good; **a los que mencionamos añádase éste** add this one to the ones we mentioned; **yo fui el que lo encontró** I was the one who found it; **él es el que quiere** it's he who wants to, he's the one who wants to; **los que hacen eso son tontos** anyone who does that is a fool, those who do so are foolish
[8·2] (+ *SUBJUN*) whoever; **el que quiera, que lo haga** whoever wants to can do it

él PRON PERS MASC [1] (*sujeto*) (= *persona*) he; (= *cosa, animal*) it; **¡es él!** it's him!
[2] (*después de prep*) (= *persona*) him; (= *cosa, animal*) it; **esto es para él** this is for him; **vamos sin él** let's go without him
[3] (*uso posesivo*) **de él** (= *persona*) his; (= *cosa, animal*) its; **mis libros y los de él** my books and his; **todo eso es de él** all that is his, all that belongs to him
elaboración SF [1] (= *fabricación*) [*de producto*] production; [*de madera, metal*] working; **el proceso de ~ del vino** the wine-making process; **la ~ de nuestros quesos es artesanal** our cheeses are made by traditional methods
[2] (= *preparación*) [*de proyecto, presupuesto, lista, candidatura*] drawing up; [*de estrategia*] devising; **la ~ del plan pasó por diversas fases** the process of drawing up the plan went through various stages
[3] [*de documento, código*] writing, preparation
elaborar ▸conjug 1a◂ VT [1] (= *fabricar*) [+ *producto*] to produce, make; [+ *metal, madera*] to work; **elaboramos todos nuestros productos con ingredientes naturales** we make all our products from natural ingredients
[2] (= *preparar*) [+ *proyecto, plan*] to draw up, prepare; [+ *estrategia*] to devise; [+ *presupuesto, lista, candidatura*] to draw up; **cómo ~ un plan de emergencia** how to draw up *o* prepare an emergency plan
[3] [+ *documento, código*] to write, prepare
elación SF [1] (= *alegría*) elation
[2] (= *orgullo*) haughtiness, pride
[3] (= *pomposidad*) pomposity
[4] (*LAm*) (= *alegría*) elation
elasticidad SF [1] [*de material*] elasticity; [*de la madera*] spring
[2] (= *adaptabilidad*) elasticity
elástico Ⓐ ADJ [1] [*material*] elastic; [*principio*] flexible; [*superficie etc*] springy
[2] (= *adaptable*) (*gen*) elastic; (*moralmente*) resilient
Ⓑ SM (= *material*) elastic; (= *trozo*) piece of elastic; (= *goma*) elastic band
ELE ABR = **español como lengua extranjera**
ele SF (name of the letter) L
elección SF [1] (= *selección*) choice; **una ~ muy acertada** an excellent choice; **lo dejo a su ~** I'll leave the choice to you; **no tuve otra ~ que irme** I had no choice *o* alternative but to leave; **no queda otra ~** there is no choice *o* alternative; **su patria de ~** his chosen country ► **elección al azar** (*Mat*) random sampling
[2] (*Pol*) election (**a** for); ► **elecciones autonómicas** regional election *sing* ► **elecciones generales** general election *sing* ► **elecciones legislativas** parliamentary election *sing* ► **elecciones municipales** local elections ► **elecciones primarias** primaries
eleccionario ADJ (*LAm*) electoral, election *antes de s*
electivo ADJ elective
electo ADJ elect; **el presidente ~** the president-elect
elector(a) SM/F elector, voter
electorado SM electorate, voters *pl*
electoral ADJ electoral; **potencia ~** voting power

electoralismo SM electioneering
electoralista ADJ electioneering *antes de s*
electoralmente ADV electorally
electorero* ADJ electioneering *antes de s*
electorista ADJ election *antes de s*
eléctrica SF electricity company; *ver tb* **eléctrico**
electricidad SF electricity ► **electricidad estática** static electricity
electricista SMF electrician
eléctrico ADJ electric, electrical; *ver tb* **eléctrica**

ELÉCTRICO

¿"Electric" o "electrical"?

- El adjetivo **eléctrico** se traduce por **electric** cuando nos referimos a un aparato en particular o a la luz eléctrica:

Siempre duermo con una manta eléctrica
I always sleep with an electric blanket
...una estufa eléctrica...
...an electric heater...
...la invención de la luz eléctrica...
...the invention of electric light...

- En cambio, si hablamos de aparatos eléctricos en general o de la electricidad generada por un organismo vivo, se traduce por **electrical**:

...aparatos eléctricos...
...electrical appliances...
...componentes eléctricos...
...electrical components...
...la actividad eléctrica en el cerebro...
...electrical activity in the brain...
Eso ha ocurrido a consecuencia de un fallo eléctrico
That was caused by an electrical fault

electrificación SF electrification
electrificar ▸conjug 1g◂ VT to electrify
electrizante ADJ electrifying (*tb fig*)
electrizar ▸conjug 1f◂ VT, VT to electrify (*tb fig*); **su discurso electrizó al público** his speech electrified his listeners
electro... PREF electro...
electrocardiograma SM electrocardiogram
electrochapado ADJ electroplated
electrochoque SM electroshock
electroconvulsivo ADJ electroconvulsive
electrocución SF electrocution
electrocutar ▸conjug 1a◂ VT to electrocute
electrodinámica SF electrodynamics *sing*
electrodo SM, **eléctrodo** SM electrode
electrodoméstico Ⓐ ADJ **aparato ~** electrical household appliance
Ⓑ SM electrical household appliance ► **electrodomésticos de línea blanca** white goods, major appliances (*EEUU*)
electroencefalograma SM electroencephalogram
electroimán SM electromagnet
electrólisis SF INV electrolysis
electromagnético ADJ electromagnetic
electromagnetismo SM electromagnetism
electromotor SM electric motor
electrón SM electron
electrónica SF electronics ► **electrónica de consumo** consumer electronics ► **electrónica de precisión** precision electronics

electrónico ADJ [*juego, sistema, música*] electronic; [*microscopio*] electron *antes de s*; **proceso ~ de datos** (*Inform*) electronic data processing

electronuclear ADJ **central ~** nuclear power station; **programa ~** nuclear power programme

electrotecnia SF electrical engineering

electrotermo SM immersion heater, immersible heater (*EEUU*)

electrotren SM express electric train

elefante/a SM/F elephant; ✦*MODISMO* **como un ~ en una cacharrería** like a bull in a china shop ► **elefante blanco** white elephant

elefantino ADJ elephantine

elegancia SF [1] [*de persona*] (*en el hablar*) elegance; (*en los movimientos*) gracefulness; (*en el vestir*) stylishness, smartness
[2] [*de decoración*] tastefulness, elegance
[3] [*de estilo*] polish

elegante ADJ (*gen*) elegant; [*traje, fiesta, tienda*] fashionable, smart; [*sociedad*] fashionable, elegant; [*decoración*] tasteful; [*frase*] elegant, well-turned, polished

elegantemente ADV [*hablar*] elegantly; [*moverse*] gracefully; [*vestir*] stylishly, smartly; [*decorar*] tastefully, elegantly

elegantón ADJ, **elegantoso** ADJ (*LAm*) = **elegante**

elegía SF elegy

elegiaco ADJ, **elegíaco** ADJ elegiac

elegibilidad SF eligibility

elegible ADJ eligible

elegido ADJ [1] (= *escogido*) chosen, selected
[2] (*Pol*) elect, elected

elegir ▸conjug 3c, 3k◂ VT [1] (= *escoger*) to choose, select; **la eligieron por su profesionalidad** she was chosen *o* selected for her professionalism; **no sabía qué color ~** I didn't know which colour to choose; **a ~ entre cinco tipos** there are five sorts to choose *o* select from; **café con bizcochos a ~** coffee with a choice of cakes; **hablará en francés o italiano, a ~** he will speak in French or Italian as you prefer; **te dan a ~ entre dos modelos** you're given a choice of two models
[2] [+ *candidato*] to elect; **me eligieron delegado de curso** I was elected class representative

elementado ADJ (*Andes, Cono Sur*) (= *aturdido*) bewildered; (= *bobo*) silly, stupid

elemental ADJ [1] (= *básico, rudimentario*) elementary; **un curso de inglés ~** an elementary English course; **tiene nociones ~es de matemáticas** she's got a basic knowledge of maths; **eso va en contra de las reglas de cortesía más ~es** that's contrary to the most basic standards of politeness
[2] [*derecho, principio*] basic
[3] (= *necesario*) essential; **saber inglés es ~ para este trabajo** a knowledge of English is essential for this job
[4] (= *de los elementos*) elemental; **física ~** elemental *o* elementary physics

elementarse ▸conjug 1a◂ VPR (*Cono Sur*) to get bewildered

elemento SM [1] (= *parte*) element; **la integridad es un ~ importante de su carácter** integrity is an important element in his character; **los ~s de una máquina** the parts of a machine; **el ~ narrativo** the narrative element; **el ~ sorpresa** the element of surprise ► **elemento constituyente** constituent
[2] (*Fís, Quím*) element ► **elemento radioactivo** radioactive element
[3] (*Elec*) element; [*de pila*] cell
[4] (= *ambiente*) **estar en su ~** to be in one's element
[5] (= *persona*) **vino a verle un ~** (*LAm*) someone came to see you; **~s subversivos** subversive elements; **¡menudo ~ estás hecho, Pepe!** (*Esp**) you're a proper little terror Pepe!; **su marido es un ~ de cuidado** (*Esp**) her husband is a nasty piece of work*
[6] (*Andes, Caribe, Cono Sur*) (= *imbécil*) dimwit*
[7] (*Caribe*) (= *tipo raro*) odd person, eccentric
[8] **elementos** (= *nociones*) elements, basic principles; **~s de geometría** elements of geometry, basic geometry *sing*
[9] **elementos** (= *fuerzas naturales*) elements; **los cuatro ~s** the four elements; **quedó a merced de los ~s** (*liter*) she was left at the mercy of the elements
[10] ► **elementos de juicio** data *sing*, facts

Elena SF Helen

elenco SM [1] (= *lista*) catalogue, catalog (*EEUU*), list; (*Teat*) cast
[2] (*Andes, Cono Sur*) (= *personal*) staff, team
[3] (*LAm Dep*) (= *equipo*) team

elepé SM long-playing record, LP

elevación SF [1] [*de objeto, brazo*] raising
[2] (= *aumento*) [*de precios, tipos*] rise, increase; [*de nivel, temperatura*] rise; **la ~ del nivel del mar** the rise in the sea level
[3] (= *montículo*) hill, elevation (*frm*)
[4] (= *ascenso*) elevation; **su ~ al Papado** his elevation to the Papacy
[5] (*Jur*) presentation, submission; **la ~ de un recurso al Tribunal Supremo** the presentation *o* submission of an appeal to the High Court
[6] (= *sublimidad*) [*de estilo*] elevation, loftiness; [*de sentimientos*] nobility
[7] (*Rel*) (*en la misa*) elevation

elevadamente ADV loftily

elevado Ⓐ ADJ [1] (*en nivel*) [*precio, temperatura, cantidad*] high; [*velocidad*] high, great; [*ritmo*] great; **un porcentaje muy ~ de usuarios** a very high percentage of users; **debido al ~ número de accidentes** due to the large number of accidents
[2] (*en altura*) [*edificio*] tall; [*montaña, terreno*] high; *ver tb* **paso² A2**
[3] (= *sublime*) [*estilo*] elevated, lofty; [*pensamientos*] noble, lofty
[4] [*puesto, rango*] high, important
Ⓑ SM (*Cuba Ferro*) overhead railway; (*Aut*) flyover, overpass (*EEUU*)

elevador SM elevator, hoist; (*LAm*) lift, elevator (*EEUU*) ► **elevador de granos** elevator, grain elevator ► **elevador de tensión**, **elevador de voltaje** (*Elec*) booster

elevadorista SMF (*LAm*) lift operator, elevator operator (*EEUU*)

elevalunas SM INV ► **elevalunas eléctrico** electric windows

elevar ▸conjug 1a◂ Ⓐ VT [1] (= *levantar*) [+ *objeto, brazos*] to raise; **~on el coche con la grúa** they raised the car with the crane; **elevemos nuestro pensamiento a Dios** let us raise our thoughts to God; **una sinfonía que eleva el espíritu** a symphony that is spiritually uplifting *o* that uplifts the spirit
[2] (= *aumentar*) [2·1] [+ *precio, tipo, temperatura, calidad*] to raise; **el consumo de huevos eleva el nivel de colesterol** eating eggs increases *o* raises one's cholesterol level; **el juez le elevó la condena a dos años** the judge increased (the length of) his sentence to two years
[2·2] [+ *voz*] to raise; **~ el tono de la voz** to raise one's voice
[3] [+ *muro*] to raise, make higher
[4] **~ a algn a algo** to elevate sb to sth (*frm*); **lo ~on al pontificado** he was made Pope, he was elevated to the pontificate (*frm*); **~on a su ídolo a la categoría de dios** they raised *o* elevated (*frm*) their idol to the level of a god; **~ a algn a los altares** to canonize sb
[5] [+ *petición, solicitud*] to present, submit; **elevó una petición al Tribunal Supremo** he presented *o* submitted an appeal to the High Court, he appealed to the High Court
[6] (*Mat*) **~ al cuadrado** to square; **tres elevado al cuadrado** three squared; **~ al cubo** to cube; **~ un número a la cuarta potencia** to raise a number to the power of four
[7] (*Elec*) [+ *voltaje*] to boost
[8] (*Chile**) (= *reprender*) to tell off*
Ⓑ **elevarse** VPR [1] (= *erguirse*) [*montaña, edificio*] to rise; **la cordillera se eleva 2.500m sobre el nivel del mar** the mountain range rises to 2,500m above sea level; **el rascacielos se eleva por encima del parque** the skyscraper soars *o* rises above the park
[2] (= *estar situado*) to stand; **en la plaza se eleva la iglesia** the church stands in the square
[3] (= *ascender*) [*humo*] to rise; [*avión*] to climb; **el humo se elevaba hacia el cielo** the smoke rose into the sky; **el avión se elevó hasta 7.800 metros** the plane climbed to 7,800 metres; **el balón se elevó por encima de la portería** the ball went over the top of the goal
[4] (= *aumentar*) to rise, increase; **si se le eleva la fiebre** if his temperature rises *o* increases; **en el interior de la cámara la temperatura se eleva tres grados más** inside the chamber the temperature rises *o* increases by three degrees
[5] (= *alcanzar*) **~se a** [*cifra, cantidad*] to stand at, amount to; [*temperatura*] to be, reach; **la cifra de heridos se eleva ya a 300** the number of the injured now stands at 300 *o* is now 300; **la temperatura se elevó a 40 grados** the temperature reached 40 degrees
[6] (*en estilo*) **el tono de la obra se eleva al final** the tone of the work becomes loftier *o* more elevated at the end
[7] (= *enajenarse*) to go into raptures
[8] (= *envanecerse*) to get conceited

Elías SM Elijah

elidir ▸conjug 3a◂ Ⓐ VT to elide
Ⓑ **elidirse** VPR to elide, be elided

eliminable ADJ dispensable

eliminación SF [1] (= *de posibilidades*) elimination; **acertó la respuesta por ~** he got the right answer by (a) process of elimination
[2] [*de concursante, deportista*] elimination; **protestó por su ~ del concurso** she protested against her elimination from the competition
[3] (= *desaparición*) [*de mancha, obstáculo*] removal; [*de residuos*] disposal; **la ~ de la co-**

rrupción the rooting out of corruption
4 [*de incógnita*] elimination
5 (*Fisiol*) elimination

eliminar ▸conjug 1a◂ Ⓐ VT 1 (= *hacer desaparecer*) [+ *mancha, obstáculo*] to remove, get rid of; [+ *residuos*] to dispose of; [+ *pobreza*] to eliminate, eradicate; [+ *posibilidad*] to rule out; **un detergente que elimina las manchas** a washing powder that removes the stains; **debemos ~ la desigualdad entre los sexos** we must eliminate sexual inequality; **~ un directorio** (*Inform*) to remove *o* delete a directory
2 [+ *concursante, deportista*] to knock out, eliminate; **fueron eliminados de la competición** they were knocked out of *o* eliminated from the competition
3 (*euf*) (= *matar*) to eliminate, do away with*
4 [+ *incógnita*] to eliminate
5 (*Fisiol*) to eliminate
Ⓑ **eliminarse** VPR (*Méx*) to go away

eliminatoria SF (*Dep*) (= *partido*) qualifying round; (= *carrera*) heat; (= *competición*) qualifying competition

eliminatorio ADJ [*carrera, partido, examen*] qualifying; [*fase, ronda*] qualifying, preliminary

elipse SF ellipse

elipsis SF INV ellipsis

elíptico ADJ elliptical, elliptic

Elíseo¹ SM (*Biblia*) Elisha

Elíseo² SM (*clásico*) Elysium; **Los Campos ~s** the Champs Elysées

elisión SF elision

élite [ˈelite] SF, **elite** [eˈlite] SF elite

elitismo SM elitism

elitista ADJ, SMF elitist

elixir SM elixir ► **elixir bucal** mouthwash ► **elixir de la (eterna) juventud** elixir of life

ella PRON PERS FEM 1 (*sujeto*) (= *persona*) she; (= *cosa*) it
2 (*después de prep*) (= *persona*) her; (= *cosa*) it; **estuve con ~** I was with her; **no podemos sin ~** without her we can't
3 (*uso posesivo*) **de ~** (= *persona*) hers; (= *cosa*) its; **nada de esto es de ~** none of this is hers; **mi sombrero y el de ~** my hat and hers

ellas PRON PERS FPL *ver* **ellos**

elle SF (name of the letter) ll

ello PRON 1 it; **no tiene fuerzas para ~** he's not strong enough for it; **~ no es obstáculo para que venga** that shouldn't stop him coming; **~ es difícil** it's awkward; **~ no me gusta** I don't like it; **todo ~ se acabó** the whole thing is over and done with
2 (*locuciones*) **es por ~ por lo que ...** ◊ **es por ~ que ...** that is why ...; **por ~ no quiero** that's why I don't want to; **~ dirá** time will tell; **¡a por ~!** here goes!

ellos/as PRON PERS M/FPL 1 (*como sujeto*) they; **—¿quién lo sabe? —ellos** "who knows?" — "they do" *o* "them"; **ellas no lo saben** they don't know; **me dijiste que ~ no vendrían** you told me they wouldn't be coming; **ellas nunca llegan tarde, pero ellos sí** the girls never arrive late, but the boys do
2 (*después de prep*) them; **a ~: dáselo a ~** give it to them; **pregúntales a ellas** ask them; **no se lo digas a ~** don't tell them; **a ~ no les han robado** they didn't rob them; **estamos esperándolas a ellas** we're waiting for them; **con ~** with them; **entre ~** between them; **para ~** for them
3 (*en comparaciones*) **como ~** as them; **soy tan rica como ellas** I'm just as rich as them; **no puedo comportarme como ~** I can't behave like them; **que ~** than them; **tenemos más poder que ~** we're more powerful than them
4 (*como posesivo*) **de ~** theirs; **el libro es de ~** the book is theirs; **este dinero es de ellas** this money is theirs; **estuvimos en casa de ~** we were at their house; **fue culpa de ellas** it was their fault; *ver tb* **él**, **ella**

elocución SF elocution

elocuencia SF eloquence

elocuente ADJ eloquent; **un dato ~** a fact which speaks for itself

elocuentemente ADV eloquently

elogiable ADJ praiseworthy

elogiar ▸conjug 1b◂ VT to praise, eulogize (*liter*)

elogio SM (= *alabanza*) praise; (= *homenaje*) tribute; **queda por encima de todo ~** it's beyond praise; **hacer ~ de** to sing the praises of; **hizo un caluroso ~ del héroe** he paid a warm tribute to the hero

elogiosamente ADV with warm approval; **comentó ~ sus cualidades** he spoke very favourably *o* (*EEUU*) favorably of his qualities

elogioso ADJ highly favourable, highly favorable (*EEUU*); **en términos ~s** in highly favourable terms

elotada SF (*CAm, Méx Agr*) ears of maize *pl* (*collectively*)

elote SM (*CAm, Méx*) (= *mazorca*) corncob, corn on the cob; (= *maíz*) maize, corn (*EEUU*), sweet corn; ✦***MODISMOS*** **coger a algn asando ~s** to catch sb red-handed; **pagar los ~s*** to carry the can*

elotear ▸conjug 1a◂ VI (*CAm, Méx*) [*maíz*] to come into ear

El Salvador SM El Salvador

elucidación SF elucidation

elucidar ▸conjug 1a◂ VT to elucidate

elucubración SF lucubration

elucubrar ▸conjug 1a◂ VI to lucubrate

eludible ADJ avoidable

eludir ▸conjug 3a◂ VT 1 (= *evitar*) [+ *problema, responsabilidad*] to evade; [+ *control, vigilancia*] to dodge; [+ *pago, impuesto*] to avoid; **no eludas mis preguntas** don't evade *o* avoid my questions; **eludió pagar impuestos** he avoided paying tax; **~ el servicio militar** to avoid military service
2 [+ *persona*] to avoid; **siempre me estás eludiendo** you're always avoiding me; **logró ~ a sus perseguidores** she managed to evade her pursuers

elusivo ADJ elusive, evasive

E.M. ABR (= **Estado Mayor**) GS

Em.ª ABR = **Eminencia**

email [ˈimeil] SM (*pl* **emails**) (*gen*) e-mail; (= *dirección*) e-mail address; **mandar un ~ a algn** to e-mail sb, send sb an e-mail

emanación SF [*de gas, humo, luz*] (= *acto*) emission, emanation (*frm*); (= *olor*) smell; **emanaciones de gas** gas emissions; **emanaciones tóxicas** toxic emissions

emanar ▸conjug 1a◂ VI **~ de** to emanate from (*frm*), come from

emancipación SF emancipation

emancipado ADJ (= *liberado*) emancipated; (= *libre*) independent, free

emancipar ▸conjug 1a◂ Ⓐ VT to emancipate, free
Ⓑ **emanciparse** VPR to become emancipated, free o.s. (**de** from)

emascular ▸conjug 1a◂ VT to emasculate

embadurnar ▸conjug 1a◂ VT to daub, smear (**de** with)

embaidor†† SM cheat, swindler

embaimiento†† SM trick, swindle

embaír†† ▸conjug 3a; defectivo◂ VT to cheat, swindle

embajada SF 1 (= *edificio*) embassy
2 (= *cargo*) ambassadorship
3 (= *mensaje*) mission
4 (*pey*) unwelcome proposal, silly suggestion

embajador(a) SM/F ambassador (**en** in); **el ~ de España en Francia** the Spanish ambassador in France ► **embajador(a) itinerante** roving ambassador, ambassador at large ► **embajador(a) político/a** politically-appointed ambassador ► **embajador(a) volante** = **embajador itinerante**

embajadora SF (= *mujer de embajador*) ambassador's wife

embajatorio ADJ ambassadorial

embalado Ⓐ ADJ 1 (*) (= *rápido*) **el coche pasó ~** the car flew past
2 (*Caribe**) (= *drogado*) high‡
Ⓑ SM (= *embalaje*) packing, packaging

embalador(a) SM/F packer

embaladura SF (*LAm*), **embalaje** SM packing

embalar ▸conjug 1a◂ Ⓐ VT 1 (= *empaquetar*) [+ *mercancías*] to pack, parcel up, wrap; [+ *mercancías pesadas*] to crate
2 (*LAm Aut*) to race along
Ⓑ VI (*Caribe*) (= *huir*) to run off, escape
Ⓒ **embalarse** VPR (*) 1 (*Dep*) (= *acelerar*) to sprint, make a dash; (= *tomar velocidad*) to gather speed
2 (= *apresurarse*) **la profesora se embala hablando** the teacher gets carried away when she's speaking; **no te embales, que hay tiempo** don't rush yourself, there's time, take your time, there's no rush; **el orador se estaba embalando** the speaker was in full flow
3 (*LAm*) to run off, escape
4 (= *entusiasmarse*) to get carried away

embaldosado SM tiled floor

embaldosar ▸conjug 1a◂ VT to tile

embalsadero SM boggy place

embalsado SM (*Cono Sur*) mass of floating water weeds

embalsamar ▸conjug 1a◂ VT to embalm

embalsar ▸conjug 1a◂ Ⓐ VT 1 [+ *río*] to dam, dam up; [+ *agua*] to retain, collect; **este mes se han embalsado 1000 metros cúbicos** this month reservoir stocks have gone up by 1000 cubic metres
2 (*Náut*) to sling, hoist
Ⓑ VI (*Andes*) (= *cruzar*) to cross (*a river*)

embalse SM (= *presa*) dam; (= *lago*) reservoir

embanastar ▸conjug 1a◂ VT to put into a basket

embancarse ▸conjug 1g◂ VPR (*Andes, Cono Sur*) to silt up, become blocked by silt

embanderar ▸conjug 1a◂ VT to deck with flags

embanquetado SM (*LAm*) pavement(s), sidewalk(s) (*EEUU*)

embanquetar ▸conjug 1a◂ VT (*LAm*) to provide with pavements, provide with sidewalks (*EEUU*)

embarazada Ⓐ ADJ pregnant; **dejar ~ a una chica** to get a girl pregnant; **estar ~ de cuatro meses** to be four months pregnant
Ⓑ SF pregnant woman

embarazar ▸conjug 1f◂ VT [1] (= *estorbar*) to hamper, hinder
[2] [+ *mujer*] to make pregnant

embarazo SM [1] [*de mujer*] pregnancy; **durante el ~** during pregnancy; **interrumpir el ~** to terminate a pregnancy; **prueba del ~** pregnancy test ► **embarazo ectópico, embarazo extrauterino** ectopic pregnancy ► **embarazo involuntario** unwanted pregnancy ► **embarazo múltiple** multiple pregnancy ► **embarazo nervioso** phantom pregnancy ► **embarazo no deseado** unwanted pregnancy ► **embarazo psicológico** phantom pregnancy
[2] (= *turbación*) embarrassment; **nos miró con ~** she looked at us in embarrassment
[3] (= *estorbo*) obstacle, hindrance

embarazosamente ADV (= *molestamente*) awkwardly, inconveniently; (= *violentamente*) embarrassingly

embarazoso ADJ (= *molesto*) awkward, inconvenient; (= *violento*) embarrassing

embarcación SF [1] (= *barco*) boat, craft, (small) vessel ► **embarcación auxiliar** tender ► **embarcación de arrastre** trawler ► **embarcación de cabotaje** coasting vessel ► **embarcación de recreo** pleasure boat ► **embarcación de vela** sailing boat, sailboat (*EEUU*) ► **embarcación fueraborda** motorboat ► **embarcación pesquera** fishing boat
[2] (= *acto*) embarkation

embarcadero SM [1] (= *amarradero*) pier, jetty
[2] (*LAm Ferro*) *cattle loading yard of a station*

embarcar ▸conjug 1g◂ Ⓐ VT [1] (*en barco*) [+ *personas*] to embark, put on board; [+ *carga*] to ship, stow
[2] (= *implicar*) **~ a algn en una empresa** to launch sb on an enterprise
[3] (*LAm**) **~ a algn** to set sb up*
[4] (*Caribe*) (= *engañar*) to con*, trick
Ⓑ **embarcarse** VPR [1] (*en barco*) to embark, go on board; **~ para** to sail for
[2] (= *enrolarse*) [*marinero*] to sign on
[3] (= *implicarse*) **~se en un asunto** to get involved in a matter
[4] (*LAm*) (*en vehículo*) to get on, get in

embarco SM embarkation

embargar ▸conjug 1h◂ VT [1] (*Jur*) to seize, impound
[2] [+ *sentidos*] to overpower, overwhelm
[3] (= *estorbar*) to impede, hinder
[4] (= *frenar*) to restrain

▾**embargo** SM [1] (*Jur*) seizure, distraint
[2] (*Pol*) ► **embargo comercial** trade embargo
[3] **sin ~** still, however, nonetheless; **sin ~ de** despite the fact that
[4] (*Med*) indigestion

embarnizar ▸conjug 1f◂ VT to varnish

embarque SM [1] (*en barco*) [*de personas*] embarkation, boarding; [*de carga*] shipment, loading; **tarjeta de ~** boarding card
[2] (*Caribe**) (= *melodrama*) melodrama; (= *amorío*) emotional affair

➤ LENGUA Y USO: **embargo 3** 46.6, 53.3

embarrada* SF (*LAm*) blunder

embarrado ADJ [*calle etc*] muddy

embarradura SF smear, daub

embarrancamiento SM [*de barco*] running aground; [*de ballena*] beaching, stranding

embarrancar ▸conjug 1g◂ Ⓐ VT, VI [1] (*Náut*) to run aground
[2] (*Aut*) to run into a ditch
Ⓑ **embarrancarse** VPR [1] (*Náut*) to run aground; **quedarse embarrancado** to be beached, be stranded
[2] (*Aut*) to run into a ditch
[3] (*en un asunto*) to get bogged down

embarrar ▸conjug 1a◂ Ⓐ VT [1] (= *enfangar*) to splash with mud
[2] (*LAm*) [+ *pared*] (*con barro*) to cover with mud; (*con yeso*) to plaster
[3] **~ a algn** (*Caribe, Cono Sur*) to smear sb, damage sb's standing; (*CAm, Méx**) to set sb up*; **la embarré** (*Cono Sur**) I put my foot in it*, I spoiled things
Ⓑ VI (*Cono Sur*) to make a mess of things
Ⓒ **embarrarse** VPR [1] (*con barro*) to get covered in mud
[2] (*Caribe*) [*niño*] to dirty o.s.

embarrialarse ▸conjug 1a◂ VPR [1] (*CAm, Ven*) (= *enfangarse*) to get covered with mud
[2] (*CAm, Caribe**) (= *enredarse*) to get o.s. in a mess

embarullador ADJ bungling

embarullar ▸conjug 1a◂ VT to bungle, mess up

embastar ▸conjug 1a◂ VT to stitch, tack

embaste SM stitching, tacking

embate SM [1] (= *golpe*) [*de mar, viento*] beating, violence; [*de olas*] dashing, breaking, beating
[2] ► **embates de la fortuna** blows of fate
[3] (*Mil*) sudden attack

embaucador(a) SM/F (= *estafador*) trickster, swindler; (= *impostor*) impostor; (= *farsante*) humbug

embaucamiento SM swindle, swindling

embaucar ▸conjug 1g◂ VT to trick, fool, lead up the garden path*

embaular ▸conjug 1a◂ VT [1] to pack (*into a trunk*)
[2] (*) [+ *comida*] to tuck away*, stuff o.s. with; [+ *bebida*] to sink*, knock back*
[3] (*Caribe*) to clean out

embazar ▸conjug 1f◂ VT [1] (= *teñir*) to dye brown
[2] (= *pasmar*) to astound, amaze
[3] (= *estorbar*) to hinder

embebecer ▸conjug 2d◂ Ⓐ VT to fascinate
Ⓑ **embebecerse** VPR to be fascinated, be lost in wonder

embebecimiento SM [1] (= *fascinación*) absorption, fascination
[2] (= *encanto*) enchantment
[3] (= *asombro*) astonishment, wonderment

embeber ▸conjug 2a◂ Ⓐ VT [1] (= *absorber*) to absorb, soak up
[2] (*Cos*) to take in, gather
[3] (= *abstraer*) to absorb, distract
[4] (= *meter*) to insert, introduce (*frm*) (**en** into)
[5] (= *abarcar*) to contain, incorporate
Ⓑ VI (= *encoger*) to shrink
Ⓒ **embeberse** VPR [1] (= *abstraerse*) to be absorbed, become engrossed (**en** in)
[2] **~se de** to imbibe, become well versed in

embelecar ▸conjug 1g◂ VT to deceive, cheat

embeleco SM, **embelequería** (*LAm*) SF deceit, fraud

embelequero ADJ [1] (*LAm*) (= *aspaventero*) highly emotional, extremely fussy
[2] (*Andes, Caribe*) (= *tramposo*) shifty
[3] (*Caribe*) (= *frívolo*) frivolous, silly

embelesado ADJ spellbound, enraptured

embelesador ADJ enchanting, entrancing

embelesar ▸conjug 1a◂ Ⓐ VT to enchant, entrance
Ⓑ **embelesarse** VPR to be enchanted, be enraptured

embeleso SM enchantment, delight

embellecedor Ⓐ ADJ **productos ~es** beauty products
Ⓑ SM [1] (*Aut*) hub cap ► **embellecedores laterales** "go-faster" stripes
[2] (= *adorno*) trim

embellecer ▸conjug 2d◂ VT to embellish, beautify

embellecimiento SM embellishment

embestida SF (= *ataque*) (*gen*) attack; [*de olas, viento*] onslaught; [*de toro*] charge

embestir ▸conjug 3k◂ Ⓐ VT [1] (= *atacar*) to assault, attack
[2] (= *abalanzarse sobre*) to rush at, rush upon
[3] [*toro*] to charge
Ⓑ VI [1] (= *atacar*) to attack
[2] [*toro*] to rush, charge; **~ contra algn** to rush at sb; **el toro embistió contra la pared** the bull charged at the wall

embetunar ▸conjug 1a◂ VT [+ *zapatos*] to polish

embicar ▸conjug 1g◂ VT [1] (*Cono Sur Náut*) to head straight for land
[2] (*Caribe*) (= *insertar*) to insert
[3] (*Méx*) (= *invertir*) to turn upside down, upturn

embicharse ▸conjug 1a◂ VPR (*Cono Sur*) to become wormy, get maggoty

embiste SM (*Caribe*) = **embestida**

emblandecer ▸conjug 2d◂ Ⓐ VT [1] (= *poner blando*) to soften
[2] [+ *persona*] to mollify
Ⓑ **emblandecerse** VPR [1] (= *ponerse blando*) [*galletas, pan*] to go soggy; [*metal, plástico*] to soften, go soft
[2] [*persona*] (*temporalmente*) to relent; (*en carácter*) to become more soft-hearted

emblanquecer ▸conjug 2d◂ Ⓐ VT to whiten, bleach
Ⓑ **emblanquecerse** VPR to turn white, bleach

emblema SM emblem

emblemático ADJ emblematic

embobamiento SM (= *fascinación*) fascination; (= *perplejidad*) bewilderment

embobar ▸conjug 1a◂ Ⓐ VT to fascinate; **al niño le emboba la televisión** the child's fascinated by the television; **esa niña me emboba** that girl is driving me crazy
Ⓑ **embobarse** VPR to be amazed (**con, de, en** at), be fascinated (**con, de, en** by); **reírse embobado** to laugh like mad, laugh one's head off; **se quedó embobado mirando los pájaros** he was completely captivated *o* entranced by the birds

embobecer ▸conjug 2d◂ Ⓐ VT to make silly
Ⓑ **embobecerse** VPR to get silly

embocadura SF 1 (= *entrada*) [*de río*] mouth; (*Náut*) passage, narrows *pl*
2 (= *pieza*) [*de flauta, trompeta*] mouthpiece; [*de cigarrillo*] tip; [*de brida*] bit
3 [*de vino*] flavour, flavor (EEUU)
4 (*Teat*) proscenium arch

embocar ▸conjug 1g◂ Ⓐ VT 1 (= *insertar*) **~ algo** to put sth into sb's mouth; **~ la comida** to cram one's food, wolf one's food; **~ algo en un agujero** to insert sth into a hole; **~ la bola** (*Golf*) to hole the ball; (*Billar*) to pocket the ball, pot the ball
2 **~ un negocio** to undertake a piece of business
3 **~ algo a algn** (*fig*) to put one over on sb; **~ un túnel** to go into a tunnel, enter a tunnel
Ⓑ VI (*Golf*) to hole out

embochinchar ▸conjug 1a◂ VT (*LAm*) to throw into confusion, create chaos in

emboinado ADJ wearing a beret

embolado SM 1 (*Teat*) bit part, minor role
2 (*) (= *mentira*) fib*, lie
3 (*) (= *aprieto*) jam*, fix*; **meter a algn en un ~*** to put sb in a tight spot*
4 (= *toro*) bull with wooden balls on its horns

embolador(a) SM/F (*Andes*) shoeblack, bootblack (EEUU)

embolar ▸conjug 1a◂ VT 1 (*Taur*) [+ *cuernos*] to tip with wooden balls
2 (*Andes*) [+ *zapatos*] to black
3 (*CAm, Méx**) (= *emborrachar*) to make drunk

embolia SF (*Med*) embolism ► **embolia cerebral** brain embolism, blood clot on the brain

embolismar* ▸conjug 1a◂ VT to gossip about

embolismo SM 1 (= *lío*) muddle, mess, confusion
2 (= *cotilleo*) gossip, backbiting
3 (= *engaño*) hoax, trick

émbolo SM plunger; (*Mec*) piston

embolsar* ▸conjug 1a◂ VT, **embolsicar** ▸conjug 1g◂ VT 1 (*LAm*) (*en bolsillo*) to pocket, put into one's pocket
2 [+ *dinero, ganancias*] to collect, take in
3 (*Billar*) to pot, pocket

embolsillar ▸conjug 1a◂ VT **~ las manos** to put one's hands in one's pockets

embonar ▸conjug 1a◂ VT 1 (*Caribe, Cono Sur, Méx*) [+ *tierra*] to manure
2 (= *mejorar*) to improve
3 (*Náut*) to sheathe
4 (*Andes, Méx*) [+ *cuerda*] to join (the ends of)
5 (*Andes, Caribe, Méx*) **le embona el sombrero** the hat suits him

emboque* SM (= *engaño*) trick, hoax

emboquillado ADJ [*cigarrillo*] tipped

emboquillar ▸conjug 1a◂ VT 1 [+ *cigarrillo*] to tip
2 (*Cono Sur Arquit*) to point, repoint

emborrachar ▸conjug 1a◂ Ⓐ VT to make drunk
Ⓑ **emborracharse** VPR to get drunk (**con, de** on)

emborrar ▸conjug 1a◂ VT 1 (= *rellenar*) to stuff, pad, wad (**de** with)
2 (*) [+ *comida*] to cram, wolf

emborrascarse ▸conjug 1g◂ VPR 1 (*Meteo*) to get stormy
2 (= *irritarse*) to get cross, get angry
3 (*Com*) [*negocio*] to fail
4 (*Cono Sur, Méx*) [*mina*] to peter out

emborronar ▸conjug 1a◂ Ⓐ VT (= *manchar*) to blot, make blots on; (= *garabatear*) to scribble on
Ⓑ VI (= *manchar*) to make blots; (= *garabatear*) to scribble
Ⓒ **emborronarse** VPR to get smudged

emboscada SF ambush; **tender una ~ a** to lay an ambush for

emboscarse ▸conjug 1g◂ VPR to lie in ambush; **estaban emboscados cerca del camino** they were in ambush near the road

embotado ADJ (*lit, fig*) dull, blunt

embotamiento SM 1 (= *acción*) dulling, blunting (*tb fig*)
2 (= *estado*) dullness, bluntness (*tb fig*)

embotar ▸conjug 1a◂ VT 1 [+ *objeto*] to blunt
2 [+ *sentidos*] to dull, blunt; (= *debilitar*) to weaken, enervate

embotellado Ⓐ ADJ [*líquido, bebida*] bottled; [*discurso*] prepared, prepared beforehand
Ⓑ SM bottling

embotellador(a) Ⓐ ADJ **planta ~a** bottling plant; **compañía ~a** bottling company, bottler's
Ⓑ SM/F bottler

embotellamiento SM 1 (= *atasco*) traffic jam
2 (= *lugar*) bottleneck
3 [*de líquido*] bottling

embotellar ▸conjug 1a◂ Ⓐ VT 1 [+ *líquido*] to bottle
2 (*Mil*) to bottle up
3 (*Cono Sur, Caribe*) [+ *discurso*] to prepare beforehand, memorize
Ⓑ **embotellarse** VPR 1 (*Aut*) [*tráfico*] to get into a jam; [*vehículo*] to get caught in a traffic jam
2 (*Caribe*) to learn a speech off by heart

emboticarse ▸conjug 1g◂ VPR (*Cono Sur, Méx*) to stuff o.s. with medicines

embotijar ▸conjug 1a◂ Ⓐ VT (= *enfrascar*) to put into jars, keep in jars
Ⓑ **embotijarse** VPR 1 (= *hincharse*) to swell, swell up
2 (= *encolerizarse*) to fly into a passion

embovedar ▸conjug 1a◂ VT to arch, vault

embozadamente ADV covertly, stealthily

embozado ADJ 1 (= *cubierto*) muffled up (to the eyes)
2 (= *disimulado*) covert, stealthy

embozalar ▸conjug 1a◂ VT (*Cono Sur*) to muzzle

embozar ▸conjug 1f◂ Ⓐ VT 1 (= *cubrir*) to muffle, muffle up
2 (= *ocultar*) to cloak
Ⓑ **embozarse** VPR to muffle o.s. up (**con, de** in)

embozo SM 1 [*de la capa*] top of the cape, fold of the cape; ✦**MODISMO quitarse el ~** to drop the mask, end the play-acting
2 [*de sábana*] turnover
3 [*de persona*] (= *astucia*) cunning; (= *disimulo*) concealment; **sin ~** frankly, openly

embragar ▸conjug 1h◂ Ⓐ VT 1 (*Aut, Mec*) [+ *motor*] to engage; [+ *piezas*] to connect, couple
2 (*Náut*) to sling
Ⓑ VI (*Aut etc*) to put the clutch in

embrague SM clutch; ✦**MODISMO le patina el ~*** he's not right up top*, he's got a screw loose*

embravecer ▸conjug 2d◂ Ⓐ VT to enrage, infuriate
Ⓑ VI (*Bot*) to flourish
Ⓒ **embravecerse** VPR 1 [*mar*] to get rough, get choppy
2 [*persona*] to get furious

embravecido ADJ 1 [*mar*] rough, choppy; [*viento*] wild
2 [*persona*] furious, enraged

embravecimiento SM rage, fury

embrear ▸conjug 1a◂ VT to tar, cover with tar; **~ y emplumar a algn** to tar and feather sb

embretar ▸conjug 1a◂ Ⓐ VT (*LAm*) [+ *animales*] to pen, corral
Ⓑ VI (*Cono Sur*) (= *asfixiarse*) to suffocate; (= *ahogarse*) to drown

embriagador ADJ [*olor, perfume*] intoxicating; [*vino*] heady

embriagar ▸conjug 1h◂ Ⓐ VT 1 (= *emborrachar*) to make drunk
2 (= *fascinar*) to delight, enrapture
Ⓑ **embriagarse** VPR (= *emborracharse*) to get drunk

embriaguez SF 1 (= *borrachera*) drunkenness
2 (= *entusiasmo*) rapture, delight

embridar ▸conjug 1a◂ VT 1 [+ *caballo*] to bridle, put a bridle on
2 (= *contener*) to check, restrain

embriología SF embryology

embriólogo/a SM/F embryologist

embrión SM [*de ser vivo*] embryo; [*de proyecto, idea*] germ; **en ~** (*lit*) in embryo; (*fig*) in its infancy, in its early stages

embrionario ADJ embryonic

embrocación SF embrocation

embrocar ▸conjug 1g◂ Ⓐ VT 1 (*Cos*) [+ *hilo*] to wind (*on to a bobbin*); [+ *zapatos*] to tack
2 [+ *líquido*] to pour from one container into another
3 (= *volcar*) to turn upside down, invert
Ⓑ **embrocarse** VPR **~se un vestido** (*Méx*) to put a dress on over one's head

embrollante ADJ muddling, confusing

embrollar ▸conjug 1a◂ Ⓐ VT 1 (= *confundir*) to muddle, confuse
2 (= *involucrar*) to involve, embroil (*frm*)
Ⓑ **embrollarse** VPR to get into a muddle, get into a mess; **~se en un asunto** to get involved in a matter

embrollista SMF (*Andes, CAm, Cono Sur*) = **embrollón**

embrollo SM (= *confusión*) muddle, confusion; (= *aprieto*) fix*, jam*; (= *fraude*) fraud, trick; (= *mentira*) lie, falsehood

embrollón(a) SM/F troublemaker

embromado* ADJ 1 (*LAm*) tricky*, difficult
2 **estar ~** to be in a fix*; (*Med*) to be in a bad way; (*Fin*) to be in financial trouble o difficulties; (= *tener prisa*) to be in a hurry

embromar ▸conjug 1a◂ Ⓐ VT 1 (= *burlarse de*) to tease, make fun of
2 (= *engañar*) to hoodwink
3 (= *engatusar*) to wheedle, cajole
4 (*LAm**) (= *molestar*) to annoy; (= *perjudicar*) to harm, set back
5 (*Chile*) (= *atrasar*) to delay unnecessarily
Ⓑ **embromarse** VPR (*LAm*) (= *enojarse*) to get cross, get angry; (= *aburrirse*) to get bored

embroncarse ▸conjug 1g◂ VPR (*Cono Sur*) to get angry

embrujado ADJ [*persona*] bewitched; [*lugar*] haunted; **una casa embrujada** a haunted house

embrujar ▸conjug 1a◂ VT [+ *persona*] to bewitch, put a spell on; [+ *lugar*] to haunt; **la casa está embrujada** the house is haunted

embrujo SM 1 (= *acto*) bewitching
2 (= *maldición*) curse
3 (= *ensalmo*) spell, charm; **el ~ de la Alhambra** the enchantment *o* magic of the Alhambra

embrutecer ▸conjug 2d◂ Ⓐ VT to stupefy, dull the senses of
Ⓑ **embrutecerse** VPR to be stupefied

embuchacarse ▸conjug 1g◂ VPR (*CAm, Méx*) ~ **algo** to pocket sth

embuchado SM 1 (*Culin*) sausage
2 (*Pol*) electoral fraud
3 (*Teat*) gag

embuchar ▸conjug 1a◂ VT 1 (*Culin*) to stuff with minced meat
2 (*) [+ *comida*] to wolf, bolt; **estoy embuchado de cerveza*** I'm bloated with beer

embudar ▸conjug 1a◂ VT (*Téc*) to fit with a funnel, put a funnel into

embudo SM 1 (*para líquidos*) funnel; ✦**MODISMO la ley del ~** one law for one and another for another; **esto es como la ley del ~** there's one law for some people and another for the rest around here
2 [*de tráfico*] bottleneck

embullar ▸conjug 1a◂ (*LAm*) VT 1 (= *excitar*) to excite 2 [+ *enemigo*] to put to flight

embullo SM (*CAm*) (= *ruido*) excitement, revelry

emburujar ▸conjug 1a◂ Ⓐ VT 1 (= *mezclar*) to jumble together, jumble up; (= *amontonar*) to pile up; [+ *hilo*] to tangle up
2 (*Andes*) (= *desconcertar*) to bewilder
Ⓑ **emburujarse** VPR (*Andes, Caribe, Méx*) to wrap o.s. up

emburujo SM (*Caribe*) ruse, trick

embuste SM 1 (= *mentira*) lie
2 **embustes** (= *adornos*) trinkets

embustero/a Ⓐ ADJ 1 (= *mentiroso*) lying
2 **persona embustera** (*Cono Sur*) person who cannot spell properly
3 (*CAm*) (= *altanero*) haughty
Ⓑ SM/F (= *mentiroso*) liar

embute SM (*Méx*) bribe

embutido SM 1 (*Culin*) sausage
2 (*Téc*) inlay, inlaid work, marquetry
3 (*Cono Sur, Méx, Ven*) lace insert
4 (= *acción*) stuffing

embutir ▸conjug 3a◂ Ⓐ VT 1 (= *meter*) to stuff (**en** into); **ella estaba embutida en un vestido apretadísimo** she was squeezed into a terribly close-fitting dress
2 (*) (= *atiborrar*) to pack tight, stuff, cram (**de** with; **en** into)
3 (*Téc*) [+ *madera*] to inlay; [+ *metal*] to hammer, work
Ⓑ **embutirse** VPR (*) to stuff o.s. (**de** with)

eme SF 1 (name of the letter) M
2 (* *euf*) = **mierda**

emergencia SF 1 (= *urgencia*) emergency; **de ~** emergency *antes de s*
2 (= *acción*) emergence

emergente ADJ 1 [*nación, ideología, mercado*] emerging, emergent
2 (= *resultante*) resultant, consequent
3 (*Inform*) pop-up

emerger ▸conjug 2c◂ VI (= *aparecer*) to emerge; [*submarino*] to surface

emeritense Ⓐ ADJ of/from Mérida
Ⓑ SMF native/inhabitant of Mérida; **los ~s** the people of Mérida

emérito ADJ emeritus

emético ADJ, SM emetic

emigración SF [*de personas*] emigration; [*de aves*] migration

emigrado/a SM/F emigrant; (*Pol etc*) émigré(e)

emigrante ADJ, SMF emigrant

emigrar ▸conjug 1a◂ VI [*personas*] to emigrate; [*aves*] to migrate

Emilia SF Emily

emilianense ADJ of San Millán de la Cogolla

emilio* SM (*Inform hum*) e-mail; **mandar un ~ a algn** to e-mail sb

eminencia SF 1 (= *excelencia*) eminence
2 (*en títulos*) **Su Eminencia** His Eminence; **Vuestra Eminencia** Your Eminence
3 (*Geog*) height, eminence

eminente ADJ eminent, distinguished

eminentemente ADV eminently, especially

emir SM emir

emirato SM emirate

emisario/a SM/F emissary, envoy

emisión SF 1 (= *acción*) emission; (*Fin etc*) issue; (*Bolsa*) share issue ► **emisión de acciones, emisión de valores** flotation ► **emisión gratuita de acciones** rights issue
2 (*Radio, TV*) (= *difusión*) broadcasting; (= *programa*) broadcast, programme, program (*EEUU*) ► **emisión deportiva** sports programme ► **emisión publicitaria** commercial, advertising spot
3 (*Inform*) output

emisor Ⓐ ADJ **banco ~** issuing bank
Ⓑ SM 1 (*Radio, TV*) transmitter ► **emisor de radar** radar station
2 (*Fin*) issuing company

emisora SF radio station, broadcasting station ► **emisora comercial** commercial radio station ► **emisora de onda corta** shortwave radio station ► **emisora pirata** pirate radio station

emisor-receptor SM walkie-talkie

emitir ▸conjug 3a◂ VT 1 [+ *sonido, olor*] to emit, give off, give out
2 (*Fin*) [+ *dinero, sellos, bonos*] to issue; [+ *dinero falso*] to circulate; [+ *préstamo*] to grant, give
3 (= *expresar*) [+ *opinión*] to express; [+ *veredicto*] to return, issue, give; [+ *voto*] to cast
4 (*Radio, TV*) to broadcast; [+ *señal*] to send out

Emmo. ABR = **eminentísimo**

emoción SF 1 (= *sentimiento*) emotion; **llorar de ~** to be moved to tears; **sentir una honda ~** to feel a deep emotion; **nos comunica una ~ de nostalgia** it gives us a nostalgic feeling
2 (= *excitación*) excitement; **¡qué ~!** (*lit*) how exciting!; (*iró*) big deal!; **al abrirlo sentí gran ~** I felt very excited when I opened it; **con la ~ del momento no me di cuenta** in the heat of the moment I just didn't realise; **la ~ de la película no disminuye** the excitement *o* tension of the film does not flag

emocionado ADJ 1 (= *conmovido*) deeply moved, stirred 2 (= *entusiasmado*) excited

emocional ADJ emotional

emocionante ADJ 1 (= *conmovedor*) moving
2 (= *excitante*) exciting, thrilling

emocionar ▸conjug 1a◂ Ⓐ VT (= *excitar*) to excite, thrill; (= *conmover*) to move, touch
Ⓑ **emocionarse** VPR (= *entusiasmarse*) to get excited; (= *conmoverse*) to be moved, be touched; **¡no te emociones tanto!** don't get so worked up!; **me emociono con las películas románticas** I get all emotional when I watch romantic films; **cuando le gusta un tema se emociona y no para de hablar** when she's interested in a subject she gets carried away and doesn't stop talking

emoliente ADJ, SM emollient

emolumento SM emolument

emoticón SM, **emoticono** SM smiley, emoticon

emotividad SF emotive nature

emotivo ADJ [*persona*] emotional; [*escena*] moving, touching; [*palabras*] emotive, moving

empacada SF (*LAm*) 1 [*de caballo*] balk, shy
2 (= *terquedad*) obstinacy

empacadora SF 1 (*Agr*) baler
2 (*Méx*) packing company

empacar ▸conjug 1g◂ Ⓐ VT 1 (*esp LAm*) (*gen*) to pack; (*Andes, Méx*) (= *embalar*) to package
2 (*Agr*) to bale
Ⓑ VI (*Méx*) (= *hacer las maletas*) to pack
Ⓒ **empacarse** VPR 1 (= *enfadarse*) to get rattled*
2 (*LAm*) [*caballo*] to balk, shy
3 (*LAm*) (= *obstinarse*) to dig one's heels in

empachado ADJ 1 [*estómago*] upset; **estoy ~ de comer tanto chocolate** I've got indigestion from eating all that chocolate; **estoy ~ de tanto deporte en televisión** I'm fed up with all this sport on television
2 (= *avergonzado*) embarrassed

empachar ▸conjug 1a◂ Ⓐ VT 1 (= *causar indigestión*) to give indigestion to; **el chocolate empacha** chocolate gives you indigestion
2 (*fig*) (= *molestar*) to annoy; (= *aburrir*) to bore; **me empacha tanta música tecno** I get fed up with all this techno music
Ⓑ **empacharse** VPR 1 (*Med*) to get indigestion
2 (= *molestarse*) to get annoyed
3 (= *aburrirse*) to get bored, get fed up*
4 (= *avergonzarse*) to get embarrassed, feel awkward

empacho SM 1 (*Med*) indigestion; **darse** *o* **coger un ~ de algo** (*fig*) to get a bellyful of sth*
2 (= *timidez*) bashfulness; **sin ~** without ceremony; **no tener ~ en hacer algo** to have no objection to doing sth

empachoso ADJ 1 [*comida*] indigestible; **la nata me resulta empachosa** cream gives me indigestion
2 [*persona*] (= *empalagoso*) cloying, oversweet; (= *vergonzoso*) embarrassing

empadronamiento SM 1 (= *censo*) [*de habitantes*] census; [*de electores*] electoral register, list of registered voters (*EEUU*)
2 (= *acto*) [*de habitantes*] census taking; [*de electores*] registration

empadronar ▸conjug 1a◂ Ⓐ VT (= *censar*) (*como habitante*) to take a census of; (*como

elector) to register
Ⓑ **empadronarse** VPR to register

empajar ▸conjug 1a◂ VT to cover with straw, fill with straw

empalagar ▸conjug 1h◂ Ⓐ VT [1] [*comida*] to be too sweet for
[2] **su conversación me empalaga** I find his conversation too sickly-sweet
Ⓑ VI [*chocolate, tarta*] to be too sweet
Ⓒ **empalagarse** VPR to get sick (**de** of)

empalago SM [1] [*de comida*] cloying, palling
[2] [*de persona*] sickly-sweetness

empalagoso ADJ [1] (= *dulce*) cloying
[2] (= *pesado*) sickly-sweet

empalar ▸conjug 1a◂ Ⓐ VT to impale
Ⓑ **empalarse** VPR (*Andes, Cono Sur*) to dig one's heels in

empalidecer ▸conjug 2d◂ VI = **palidecer**

empalizada SF fence; (*Mil etc*) palisade, stockade

empalmar ▸conjug 1a◂ Ⓐ VT (= *juntar*) [+ *tuberías, cables*] to connect, join; [+ *cuerdas, películas*] to splice; **empalma los dos cables** connect the two cables; **fueron empalmando un tema de conversación tras otro** one subject led to another as they spoke
Ⓑ VI [1] (*Ferro*) [*trenes*] to connect; [*vías*] to join; **el cercanías empalma con el expreso de las nueve** the local train connects with the nine o'clock express
[2] [*carreteras, líneas*] to join; [*cables, piezas*] to connect (**con** with); **esta carretera empalma con la autopista** this road links up with *o* joins the motorway
[3] (= *sucederse*) to follow (on) (**con** from); **su programa empalma con las noticias** her programme follows (on from) the news
Ⓒ **empalmarse** VPR (**) to get a hard-on**

empalme SM [1] (*Téc*) joint, connection
[2] (= *conexión*) [*de vías, carreteras*] junction; [*de trenes*] connection
[3] (**) hard-on**, erection

empamparse ▸conjug 1a◂ VPR (*LAm*) [1] to get lost on the pampas; (= *desorientarse*) to lose one's way
[2] (= *asombrarse*) to be amazed

empanada SF [1] (*Culin*) meat pie, patty
[2] (= *fraude*) fraud, piece of shady business
[3] ▸ **empanada mental*** confusion

empanadilla SF patty, small pie

empanado ADJ [1] (*Culin*) *cooked or rolled in breadcrumbs or pastry*
[2] (= *atontado*) **estar ~** to be confused

empanar ▸conjug 1a◂ VT (*Culin*) (*con masa*) *to cover in a pastry case*; (*con pan rallado*) *to cook or roll in breadcrumbs or pastry*

empantanado ADJ flooded, swampy; (*fig*) [*proyecto*] bogged down

empantanar ▸conjug 1a◂ Ⓐ VT [1] (= *inundar*) to flood, swamp
[2] [+ *negociación, proyecto*] to bog down
Ⓑ **empantanarse** VPR [1] (= *inundarse*) to be flooded, get swamped
[2] [*asunto, negociación*] to get bogged down, get held up; **~se en un asunto** to get bogged down in a matter

empañado ADJ [*cristal, espejo*] misty, steamed-up; [*superficie*] tarnished; [*voz*] faint, unsteady; [*honra*] tarnished; **con los ojos ~s en lágrimas** with her eyes moist with tears

empañar ▸conjug 1a◂ Ⓐ VT [+ *cristal, espejo, gafas*] to steam up, mist over; [+ *superficie, honra*] to tarnish
Ⓑ **empañarse** VPR [1] [*cristales, gafas*] to get steamed up, mist over; [*voz*] to falter; **se le ~on los ojos de lágrimas** tears welled up in her eyes
[2] [*reputación*] to get tarnished

empañetar ▸conjug 1a◂ VT (*LAm*) (= *enyesar*) to plaster; (= *encalar*) to whitewash

empapar ▸conjug 1a◂ Ⓐ VT [1] (= *mojar*) to soak, drench; **cierra la ducha que me estás empapando** can you turn the shower off, you're soaking *o* drenching me; **estar empapado hasta los huesos** to be soaked to the skin
[2] (= *absorber*) to soak up; **empapó toda el agua con una bayeta** she soaked up all the water with a cloth
Ⓑ **empaparse** VPR [1] (= *mojarse*) to get soaked; **se me han empapado los zapatos** my shoes got soaked; **las patatas se ~on de aceite** the potatoes soaked up the oil
[2] (= *enterarse*) **~se de: se empapó de filosofía griega** he steeped himself in Greek philosophy; **se empapó de gramática antes del examen** he swotted up on grammar before the exam*; ✦*MODISMO* **¡para que te empapes!*** so there!; **yo he aprobado y tú no, ¡para que te empapes!** I passed and you didn't, so there!

empapelado SM (= *acción*) papering, paperhanging; (= *papel*) wallpaper

empapelador(a) SM/F paperhanger

empapelar ▸conjug 1a◂ VT [1] [+ *cuarto, pared*] to paper; [+ *caja*] to line with paper
[2] **~ a algn** (= *abrir expediente*) to throw the book at sb; (*) (= *matar*) to do sb in*

empapuzar ▸conjug 1f◂ VT to stuff with food

empaque SM [1] (*) (= *aspecto*) look, appearance
[2] (= *distinción*) presence
[3] (*LAm*) (= *descaro*) nerve, effrontery, cheek*

empaquetador(a) SM/F packer

empaquetadura SF packing; (*Mec*) gasket

empaquetar ▸conjug 1a◂ [1] VT to pack, parcel up; (*Com*) to package
[2] (= *conservar*) [+ *buque*] to mothball
[3] (*) [+ *soldado*] to punish

emparamarse ▸conjug 1a◂ VPR (*Andes, Caribe*)
[1] (= *entumecerse*) to go numb with cold
[2] (= *morir*) to die of cold
[3] (= *mojarse*) to get soaked

emparar* ▸conjug 1a◂ (*Andes*) Ⓐ VT to catch
Ⓑ **empararse** VPR [1] (= *sonrojarse*) to blush
[2] **~se de algo** to mock sth

emparedado SM sandwich

emparedar ▸conjug 1a◂ VT to confine

emparejamiento SM (*Biol*) pairing, mating; (*Psic*) pair bonding

emparejar ▸conjug 1a◂ Ⓐ VT [1] [+ *dos cosas, dos personas*] to pair, match
[2] (= *nivelar*) to level, make level
Ⓑ VI [1] (= *alcanzar*) to catch up (**con** with)
[2] (= *nivelarse*) to be even (**con** with)
Ⓒ **emparejarse** VPR to match

emparentado ADJ related by marriage (**con** to)

emparentar ▸conjug 1j◂ VI to become related by marriage (**con** to); **~ con una familia** to marry into a family

emparrado SM trained vine

emparrandarse ▸conjug 1a◂ VPR (*LAm*) to go on a binge*

empastado ADJ [1] (*Tip*) clothbound
[2] [*diente*] filled

empastar ▸conjug 1a◂ Ⓐ VT [1] [+ *diente*] to fill, stop
[2] (= *engomar*) to paste
[3] (*Tip*) to bind in stiff covers
[4] (*LAm*) to convert into pasture land
Ⓑ **empastarse** VPR (*Cono Sur*) [*ganado*] to get bloated

empaste SM [1] [*de diente*] filling
[2] (*Tip*) binding

empatar ▸conjug 1a◂ Ⓐ VT [1] (*Dep*) **han quedado vencedores tras ~ dos partidos** they eventually won after drawing two matches; **acaban de ~ el partido** they have just levelled the scores
[2] (*LAm*) (= *conectar*) to connect
[3] (*Caribe*) (= *acosar*) to bother, harass
[4] (*Cono Sur*) [+ *tiempo*] to waste
Ⓑ VI [1] (*Dep*) (*en partido*) to draw, tie (*EEUU*); (*en carreras*) to tie, have a dead heat; **los equipos ~on a dos** the teams drew two-all; **los tres equipos quedan empatados a puntos** the three teams are level on points
[2] (*en votación*) to tie

empate SM [1] (*en partido*) draw; **un ~ a cero** a nil-nil draw; **el gol del ~** the equalizer; **continúa el ~ en el marcador** the scores are still level
[2] (*en votación*) tie
[3] (*LAm*) (= *junta*) joint, connection

empatía SF empathy

empatizar ▸conjug 1f◂ VI (*tb* **~se**) to empathize (**con** with)

empavado* ADJ (*Caribe*) unlucky, jinxed*

empavar* ▸conjug 1a◂ VT (*Caribe*) to put a jinx on*, bring bad luck to

empavesado SM bunting

empavesar ▸conjug 1a◂ VT (= *adornar*) to deck, adorn; [+ *barco*] to dress

empavonar ▸conjug 1a◂ Ⓐ VT [1] (*Téc*) [+ *acero*] to blue
[2] (*LAm Mec*) to grease, cover with grease
Ⓑ **empavonarse** VPR (*CAm*) to dress up

empecatado* ADJ [1] (= *incorregible*) incorrigible
[2] (= *astuto*) wily
[3] (= *malhadado*) ill-fated
[4] (= *maldito*) damned, cursed

empecinadamente ADV stubbornly, pigheadedly

empecinado ADJ stubborn, pigheaded

empecinamiento SM stubbornness, pigheadedness

empecinarse ▸conjug 1a◂ VPR **~ en algo** to be stubborn about sth; **~ en hacer algo** to persist in doing sth

empedarse* ▸conjug 1a◂ VPR (*Méx, Cono Sur*) to get drunk, get sloshed*

empedernido ADJ [1] [*vicio*] hardened, inveterate; **un bebedor ~** a heavy drinker; **un fumador ~** a heavy smoker; **un pecador ~** an unregenerate sinner, a reprobate; **un soltero ~** a confirmed bachelor
[2] (= *cruel*) heartless, cruel

empedernir ▸conjug 3a: defectivo◂ Ⓐ VT to harden

Ⓑ **empedernirse** VPR (*fig*) to harden one's heart

empedrado Ⓐ ADJ [*superficie*] paved; [*cara*] pockmarked; [*cielo*] cloud-flecked
Ⓑ SM paving

empedrar ▸conjug 1j◂ VT to pave

empegado SM tarpaulin, tarp (*EEUU*)

empeine SM [1] [*de pie, zapato*] instep
[2] (= *vientre*) groin
[3] **empeines** (*Med*) impetigo *sing*
[4] (*Bot*) cotton flower

empella SF [1] [*de zapato*] upper; [*de zapatero*] vamp
[2] (*LAm*) lard

empellar ▸conjug 1a◂ VT to push, shove, jostle

empellón SM push, shove; **abrirse paso a ~es** to push roughly past; **dar empellones** to shove, jostle; **lo sacaron a empellones** they shoved *o* pushed him out of the door

empelotado* [1] ADJ (*LAm*) (= *desnudo*) naked, starkers*
[2] (*Méx*) (= *enamorado*) in love

empelotar ▸conjug 1a◂ Ⓐ VT [1] (*LAm*) (= *desvestir*) to undress, strip to the skin
[2] (*LAm Mec*) to strip down, dismantle, take to pieces
Ⓑ **empelotarse** VPR [1] (*) (= *emporrarse*) to get stoned*
[2] (*LAm**) to strip naked, strip off
[3] (*Caribe, Méx**) (= *enamorarse*) to fall head over heels in love

empelucado ADJ bewigged

empenachado ADJ [1] [*caballo*] plumed
[2] [*columna*] pretentious, extravagant

empenachar ▸conjug 1a◂ VT to adorn with plumes

empeñado ADJ [1] [*objeto de valor*] pawned; ✦**MODISMO estar ~ hasta los ojos** to be deeply in debt, be up to one's eyes in debt*
[2] (= *empecinado*) determined; **estar ~ en hacer algo** to be determined to do sth
[3] [*discusión*] bitter, heated

empeñar ▸conjug 1a◂ Ⓐ VT [1] [+ *objeto de valor*] to pawn, pledge
[2] (= *comprometer*) [+ *palabra*] to give; [+ *persona*] to engage, compel
[3] (= *comenzar*) to start
Ⓑ **empeñarse** VPR [1] (= *endeudarse*) to get into debt
[2] **~se en algo** to insist on sth; **~se en hacer algo** to be set on doing sth; **se empeñó en irse a trabajar al extranjero** he insisted on going to work abroad; **me empeñé en que estudiara inglés** I insisted that she should study English; **~se en una discusión** to get involved in a heated argument; **se empeña en que fue así** he insists that it was so
[3] **~se por algn** to intercede for sb

empeñero/a SM/F (*Méx*) pawnbroker, moneylender

empeño SM [1] (= *resolución*) determination; (= *insistencia*) insistence; **poner ~ en algo** to put a lot of effort into sth; **poner ~ en hacer algo** to strive to do sth; **tener ~ en hacer algo** to be bent on doing sth; **con ~** (= *con insistencia*) insistently; (= *con ahínco*) eagerly, keenly
[2] (= *tienda*) pawnshop
[3] (= *objeto*) pledge
[4] (= *empresa*) undertaking; **morir en el ~** to die in the attempt

empeñoso ADJ (*LAm*) persevering, diligent

empeoramiento SM deterioration, worsening

empeorar ▸conjug 1a◂ Ⓐ VT to make worse, worsen
Ⓑ VI, **empeorarse** VPR to get worse, worsen

empequeñecer ▸conjug 2d◂ Ⓐ VT [1] (= *achicar*) to dwarf, make (seem) smaller
[2] (= *menoscabar*) to minimize, belittle
Ⓑ VI **ha empequeñecido con los años** she has got smaller as she has got older

emperador SM [1] (= *gobernante*) emperor
[2] (= *pez*) swordfish

emperatriz SF empress

emperejilarse ▸conjug 1a◂ VPR to dress up, doll o.s. up*

empericarse* ▸conjug 1g◂ VPR [1] (*Andes*) (= *emborracharse*) to get drunk
[2] (*Caribe, Méx*) (= *ruborizarse*) to blush

emperifollar ▸conjug 1a◂ Ⓐ VT (*gen*) to adorn, deck; [+ *persona*] to doll up
Ⓑ **emperifollarse** VPR to dress up, doll o.s. up*

empernar ▸conjug 1j◂ VT to bolt, secure with a bolt

empero†† CONJ (*liter*) (= *pero*) but; (= *sin embargo*) yet, however; **estaba muy cansado, no se sentó ~** he was very tired, nonetheless he didn't sit down

emperramiento SM stubbornness, pigheadedness

emperrarse ▸conjug 1a◂ VPR to get stubborn, be obstinate; **~ en algo** to persist in sth

emperro SM (*esp Andes*) (= *terquedad*) stubbornness; (= *rabieta*) fit of temper

empertigar ▸conjug 1h◂ VT (*Chile*) [+ *caballo*] to hitch up

empezar ▸conjug 1f, 1j◂ Ⓐ VI [1] (= *comenzar*) (*gen*) to start, begin; (*en un puesto de trabajo*) to start; **el curso empieza en octubre** the course starts *o* begins in October; **el año ha empezado mal** the year got off to a bad start, the year started *o* began badly; **antes de ~, os recordaré que …** before we start *o* begin, I'd like to remind you that …; **al ~ el año** at the start *o* beginning of the year; **¿cuándo empieza el nuevo cocinero?** when does the new cook start?; **empecé de ayudante** I started as an assistant; **¡no empieces!*** don't you start!*; **para ~** to start with, begin with; **para ~ quisiera agradecerte tu presencia entre nosotros** I would like to start *o* begin by thanking you for being with us, to start *o* begin with, I would like to thank you for being with us; ✦**MODISMO todo es (cuestión de) ~** it's all a matter of getting started; *ver tb* **cero 1**
[2] **~ a hacer algo** (*gen*) to start *o* begin to do sth, start *o* begin doing sth; (*en un trabajo*) to start to do *o* doing sth; **empezó a llover** it started *o* began to rain, it started *o* began raining; **la película me está empezando a aburrir** the film is starting *o* beginning to bore me; **ya empiezo a entrar en calor** I'm starting *o* beginning to feel warm now; **empiezo a trabajar en octubre** I start work in October
[3] **~ haciendo algo** to begin *o* start by doing sth; **~emos pidiendo ayuda** we'll start *o* begin by asking for help; **la canción empieza diciendo que …** the song begins *o* starts by saying that …
[4] **~ con algo** [*película, curso, año*] to start *o* begin with sth; **la novela empieza con una referencia a Sartre** the novel starts *o* begins with a reference to Sartre; **empezamos con cerveza y acabamos con vino** we started on *o* began with beer and ended up on wine; **¿cuándo empezáis con las clases de inglés?** when do you start your English classes?; **¡no empieces otra vez con lo mismo!** don't start on that again!
[5] **~ por algo/algn** to start with sth/sb, begin with sth/sb; **~é por la cocina** I'll start *o* begin with the kitchen; **"huelga" empieza por hache** "huelga" starts *o* begins with (an) h; **no sé por dónde ~** I don't know where to start *o* begin; **la carcoma empezó por las patas del armario** the woodworm started in the legs of the wardrobe; **ya podías haber empezado por ahí** why couldn't you have said that at the beginning *o* at the start?; **~ por hacer algo** to start by doing sth, begin by doing sth
Ⓑ VT [+ *actividad, temporada*] to start, begin; [+ *botella, jamón*] to start; **hemos empezado mal la semana** the week got off to a bad start for us, the week started badly for us; **el queso está ya empezado** the cheese has already been started

empicotar ▸conjug 1a◂ VT to pillory

empiece* SM beginning, start

empiezo* SM (*LAm*) = **comienzo**

empilchar ▸conjug 1a◂ Ⓐ VT (*Cono Sur*) [+ *caballo*] to saddle; (*) [+ *persona*] to keep in clothes
Ⓑ **empilcharse** VPR (*Cono Sur**) to dress up, get dolled up*

empilonar ▸conjug 1a◂ VT (*LAm*) to pile up

empinada SF (*Aer*) steep climb

empinado ADJ [1] [*cuesta*] steep; [*edificio*] high, lofty
[2] (= *orgulloso*) proud

empinar ▸conjug 1a◂ Ⓐ VT (*gen*) to raise; [+ *botella*] to tip up; ✦**MODISMO ~ el codo** to booze*, prop up the bar*
Ⓑ VI (*) to drink, booze*
Ⓒ **empinarse** VPR [*persona*] to stand on tiptoe; [*caballo*] to rear up; (*Aer*) to zoom upwards

empingorotado* ADJ stuck-up*, toffee-nosed*

empipada* SF (*Andes, Cono Sur*) blow-out*, chow-down (*EEUU**)

empiparse ▸conjug 1a◂ VPR (*LAm*) [1] (= *comer*) to stuff o.s. with food
[2] (= *beber*) **se empipó una botella de vino él solito** he downed a bottle of wine all by himself

empírico/a Ⓐ ADJ empirical, empiric
Ⓑ SM/F empiricist

empirismo SM empiricism

empitonar ▸conjug 1a◂ VT (*Taur*) to gore, impale (on the horns of the bull)

empizarrado SM slate roof

empizarrar ▸conjug 1a◂ VT to roof with slates

emplantillar ▸conjug 1a◂ VT [1] (*Andes, Caribe, Cono Sur*) [+ *zapatos*] to put insoles into
[2] (*Andes, Cono Sur*) [+ *pared*] to fill with rubble

emplastar ▸conjug 1a◂ VT (*Med*) to put a plaster on, put a poultice on

emplasto SM [1] (*Med*) poultice

2 (= *arreglo*) makeshift arrangement
3 (= *persona*) sickly person

emplazamiento SM 1 (*Jur*) summons; (= *llamamiento*) summoning
2 (= *sitio*) location; (*Mil*) emplacement, gun emplacement
3 (*Com*) [*de producto*] product placement

emplazar ▸conjug 1f◂ VT 1 (= *convocar*) to summon, convene; (*Jur*) to summons
2 (= *ubicar*) (*gen*) to site, place; [+ *estatua*] to erect
3 **~ a algn a hacer algo** to call on sb to do sth

empleabilidad SF (*Econ, Pol*) employability

empleado/a SM/F (*gen*) employee; (= *oficinista*) clerk, office worker ► **empleada del hogar** servant, maid ► **empleado/a bancario/a, empleado/a de banco** bank clerk ► **empleado/a de correos** post-office worker ► **empleado/a de cuello y corbata** (*Cono Sur*) white-collar worker ► **empleado/a de finca urbana** porter, concierge ► **empleado/a de pompas fúnebres** undertaker's assistant, mortician's assistant (*EEUU*) ► **empleado/a de ventanilla** booking office clerk, counter clerk ► **empleado/a público/a** civil servant

empleador(a) SM/F employer

emplear ▸conjug 1a◂ Ⓐ VT 1 (= *usar*) to use; **puedes ~ cualquier jabón** you can use any soap (you like); **se emplea para abrillantar el suelo** it is used to polish the floor; **empleó todo tipo de artimañas para convencerla** he used all sorts of tricks to convince her; **siempre emplea una terminología muy rebuscada** he always uses *o* employs very affected language; **~ mal** to misuse; **ha empleado mal el término** she has misused the term; ✦*MODISMO* **¡le está bien empleado!** it serves him right!
2 [+ *trabajador*] to employ; **la fábrica emplea a veinte trabajadores** the factory employs twenty workers
3 [+ *tiempo, dinero*] to spend, use; **empleó toda la mañana para ordenar su despacho** he spent the whole morning tidying up his office; **ha empleado cuatro años en acabar la tesis** it's taken him four years to finish his thesis; **dinero bien empleado** money well spent; **~ mal el tiempo** to waste time
Ⓑ **emplearse** VPR (*frm*) **~se haciendo algo** to occupy o.s. doing sth, spend one's time doing sth; *ver tb* **fondo 6.2**

▼**empleo** SM 1 (= *uso*) use; [*de tiempo*] spending; (*Com*) investment; **"modo de empleo"** "instructions for use"; **el ~ de esa palabra es censurable** the use of that word is to be condemned
2 (= *trabajo*) employment, work; **pleno ~** full employment ► **empleo juvenil** youth employment ► **oficina de empleo** ≈ employment agency
3 (= *puesto*) job, post; **buscar un ~** to look for a job, seek employment; **estar sin ~** to be unemployed; **"solicitan empleo"** "situations wanted"; **suspender a algn de ~ y sueldo** to suspend sb without pay

emplomadura SF 1 (= *cubierta*) lead covering
2 (*Cono Sur*) [*de diente*] filling

emplomar ▸conjug 1a◂ VT 1 [+ *vidrieras*] to lead
2 (*con plomo*) (= *revestir*) to cover with lead, line with lead, weight with lead; (= *precintar*) to seal with lead
3 (*Arg, Uru*) [+ *diente*] to fill

emplumar ▸conjug 1a◂ Ⓐ VT 1 (= *cubrir*) to adorn with feathers
2 (= *castigar*) to tar and feather; **le ~on seis meses de cárcel*** they packed him off to prison for six months*
3 (*LAm**) (= *estafar*) to swindle
4 (*Hond**) (= *zurrar*) to beat up, thrash
5 (*Chile**) ✦*MODISMO* **~las** to run away, leg it*
Ⓑ VI 1 [*pájaro*] to grow feathers
2 (*LAm**) (= *huir*) to take to one's heels
Ⓒ **emplumarse** VPR ✦*MODISMO* **emplumárselas** (*Andes, Cono Sur**) (= *huir*) to run away, leg it*

emplumecer ▸conjug 2d◂ VI to grow feathers

empobrecer ▸conjug 2d◂ Ⓐ VT to impoverish
Ⓑ **empobrecerse** VPR to become poor

empobrecimiento SM impoverishment

empollar ▸conjug 1a◂ Ⓐ VT 1 (*Zool*) to incubate, sit on
2 (*) [+ *asignatura*] to swot up*
Ⓑ VI 1 [*gallina*] to sit, brood
2 [*abejas*] to breed
3 (*) [*estudiante*] to swot*, grind away (*EEUU*), cram

empolle* SM swotting*, cramming; **¡tiene un ~!** he's been working really hard, he really knows his stuff*

empollón/ona* SM/F (= *estudiante*) swot*, grind (*EEUU**)

empolvado ADJ [*sustancia*] powdery; [*superficie*] dusty

empolvar ▸conjug 1a◂ Ⓐ VT [+ *cara*] to powder; [+ *superficie*] to cover with dust
Ⓑ **empolvarse** VPR 1 [+ *cara*] to powder one's face
2 [*superficie*] to get dusty
3 (*CAm, Méx*) to get rusty, get out of practice
4 (*Caribe*) (= *huir*) to run away

emponchado ADJ 1 (*LAm*) (= *vestido de poncho*) wearing a poncho
2 (*Andes, Cono Sur*) (= *sospechoso*) suspicious

emponcharse ▸conjug 1a◂ VPR (*esp LAm*) to put on one's poncho

emponzoñamiento SM poisoning

emponzoñar ▸conjug 1a◂ VT to poison

emporcar ▸conjug 1g, 1l◂ VT to soil

emporio 1 SM emporium, trading centre, trading center (*EEUU*)
2 (*LAm*) large department store

emporrado: ADJ **estar ~** to be high (on drugs)‡

emporrarse* ▸conjug 1a◂ VPR to get stoned*

emporroso ADJ (*CAm, Caribe*) annoying

empotrable Ⓐ ADJ fitted, built-in
Ⓑ SM fitted unit, built-in unit

empotrado ADJ [*armario*] built-in; (*Mec*) fixed, integral

empotrar ▸conjug 1a◂ Ⓐ VT (*gen*) to embed, fix; [+ *armario*] to build in
Ⓑ **empotrarse** VPR **el coche se empotró en la tienda** the car embedded itself in the shop; **los vagones se ~on uno en otro** the carriages telescoped together

empotrerar ▸conjug 1a◂ VT 1 (*LAm*) [+ *ganado*] to pasture, put out to pasture
2 (*Caribe, Cono Sur*) [+ *tierra*] to enclose

empozarse ▸conjug 1f◂ VPR (*Méx*) to form pools

emprendedor ADJ enterprising, go-ahead

emprender ▸conjug 2a◂ VT 1 (= *empezar*) [+ *trabajo*] to undertake; [+ *viaje*] to embark on; **~ la marcha a** to set out for; **~ el regreso** to return; **~ la retirada** to retreat
2 **~la con algn** to take it out on sb; **la emprendieron a botellazos con el árbitro** they threw bottles at the referee

emprendimiento SM (*Cono Sur*) undertaking

empreñador* ADJ irksome, vexatious

empreñar ▸conjug 1a◂ Ⓐ VT 1 (= *dejar embarazada*) [+ *mujer*] to make pregnant; [+ *animal*] to impregnate, mate with
2 (*) (= *fastidiar*) to rile*, irk, vex
Ⓑ **empreñarse** VPR to become pregnant

empresa SF 1 (= *tarea*) enterprise ► **empresa libre** free enterprise ► **empresa privada** private enterprise
2 (*Com, Fin*) (= *compañía*) firm, company; **pequeñas y medianas ~s** small and medium-sized companies ► **empresa colectiva** joint venture ► **empresa de seguridad** security company ► **empresa de servicios públicos** public utility company ► **empresa de trabajo temporal** temp recruitment agency ► **empresa fantasma** dummy company ► **empresa filial** affiliated company ► **empresa fletadora** shipping company ► **empresa funeraria** undertaker's, mortician's (*EEUU*) ► **empresa matriz** parent company ► **empresa particular** private company ► **empresa pública** public sector company
3 (= *dirección*) management; **la ~ lamenta que ...** the management regrets that ...

empresariado SM (= *negocios*) business, business world; (= *gerentes*) managers *pl*, management

empresarial ADJ [*función, clase*] managerial; **estudios ~es** business studies; **sector ~** business sector

empresariales SFPL business studies

empresario/a SM/F 1 (*Com*) businessman/businesswoman; **pequeño ~** small businessman ► **empresario/a de pompas fúnebres** undertaker, mortician (*EEUU*) ► **empresario/a de transporte** shipping agent
2 [*de opera, teatro*] impresario
3 (*Boxeo*) promoter

empresología SF business consultancy

empresólogo/a SM/F business consultant

emprestar* ▸conjug 1a◂ VT (*LAm*) (= *dar prestado*) to lend

empréstito 1 SM loan, public loan ► **empréstito de guerra** war loan
2 (*Com*) (= *cantidad prestada*) loan capital

empufado* ADJ **estar ~** to be in debt, be in the red

empujada SF (*LAm*) push, shove

empujadora SF (*tb* **~ frontal**) bulldozer

empujadora-niveladora SF bulldozer

empujar ▸conjug 1a◂ VT (= *presionar*) (*gen*) to push; (*con fuerza*) to shove, thrust; (*Mec*) to drive; **"empujar"** (*en puertas*) "push"; **¡no empujen!** stop pushing!; **~ el botón a fondo** to press the button down hard

empujaterrones SM INV bulldozer

empujatierra SF bulldozer

empuje SM 1 (= *fuerza*) push, drive; **le falta ~** he lacks drive; **en un espíritu de ~** in a spirit of determination

➤ LENGUA Y USO: **empleo 3** 46.1

2 (= *empujón*) push, shove
3 (= *presión*) pressure; (*Mec, Fís*) thrust

empujón SM 1 (*con la mano*) push, shove; **abrirse paso a empujones** to push *o* shove one's way through; **avanzar a empujones** to go forward in fits and starts
2 (= *incitación*) push, drive; **dar un ~ a algo** to push sth through, push sth forward; **trabajar a empujones** to work intermittently

empulgueras SFPL thumbscrew

empuntar ▸conjug 1a◂ Ⓐ VT 1 to put a point on
2 ✦**MODISMO ~las** (*Andes*) to run away
Ⓑ **empuntarse** VPR (*Caribe*) (= *empecinarse*) to dig one's heels in; (= *caminar de puntillas*) to walk on tiptoe

empuñadura SF 1 [*de espada*] hilt; [*de herramienta*] handle
2 [*de cuento*] start, opening

empuñar ▸conjug 1a◂ VT 1 (= *coger*) to grasp, clutch; **~ las armas** to take up arms; ✦**MODISMO ~ el bastón** to take command
2 (*Cono Sur*) [+ *puño*] to clench
3 (*Andes*) (= *dar un puñetazo a*) to punch

empupar ▸conjug 1a◂ VI (*LAm*) to pupate

empurar* ▸conjug 1a◂ VT (*Mil*) to punish

empurrarse ▸conjug 1a◂ VPR (*CAm*) to get angry

E.M.T. SF ABR (*Esp*) = **Empresa Municipal de Transportes**

emú SM emu

emulación SF emulation

emulador(a) Ⓐ ADJ emulous (**de** of)
Ⓑ SM/F rival

emular ▸conjug 1a◂ VT to emulate

emulgente SM emulsifier

émulo/a Ⓐ ADJ emulous
Ⓑ SM/F rival, competitor

emulsión SF emulsion

emulsionante SM emulsifier

emulsionar ▸conjug 1a◂ VT to emulsify

en PREP 1 (*indicando lugar*) 1·1 (= *dentro de*) in; **está en el cajón/en el armario** it's in the drawer/in the wardrobe; **"curvas peligrosas en 2 kilómetros"** "dangerous bends 2 kilometres ahead"
1·2 (= *encima de*) on; **las llaves están en la mesa** the keys are on the table; **lo encontré tirado en el suelo** I found it lying on the floor; **la oficina está en el quinto piso** the office is on the fifth floor
1·3 (*con países, ciudades, calles*) **está en Argentina** it's in Argentina; **viven en Granada** they live in Granada; **está en algún lugar de Murcia** it's somewhere in Murcia; **la librería está en la calle Pelayo** the bookshop is on Pelayo street; **vivía en el número 17** she lived at number 17; **trabaja en una tienda** she works in a shop
1·4 (*con edificios*) **en casa** at home; **en el colegio** at school; **en la oficina** at the office; **te esperé en la estación** I waited for you at the station; **te veo en el cine** see you at the cinema
2 (*indicando movimiento*) into; **entré en el banco** I went into the bank; **me metí en la cama a las diez** I got into bed at ten o'clock; **meterse algo en el bolsillo** to put sth in(to) one's pocket; **entra en el coche** get in(to) the car; **no entra en el agujero** it won't go in(to) the hole; **ir de puerta en puerta** to go from door to door
3 (*indicando modo*) in; **en inglés** in English; **en pantalón corto** in shorts; **fotografías en color** colour photographs; **hablar en voz alta** to speak loudly; **una escultura en madera** a wooden sculpture; **una serie en diez capítulos** a ten-part series
4 (*indicando proporción*) by; **reducir algo en una tercera parte** to reduce sth by a third; **ha aumentado en un 20 por ciento** it has increased by 20 per cent
5 (*indicando tiempo*) **en 1605** in 1605; **en el siglo X** in the 10th century; **en invierno** in (the) winter; **en enero** in January; **lo hice en dos días** I did it in two days; **no he salido en todo el día** I haven't gone out all day; **en aquella ocasión** on that occasion; **mi cumpleaños cae en viernes** my birthday falls on a Friday; **en aquella época** at that time; **en ese momento** at that moment; **en Navidades** at Christmas; **ayer en la mañana** (*LAm*) yesterday morning; **en la mañana del accidente** (*LAm*) on the morning of the accident
6 (*indicando tema, ocupación*) **un experto en la materia** an expert on the subject; **es bueno en dibujo** he's good at drawing; **trabaja en la construcción** he works in the building industry; **Hugo en Segismundo** (*Cine, Teat*) Hugo as Segismundo, Hugo in the role of Segismundo
7 (*con medios de transporte*) by; **en avión** by plane; **en coche** by car; **en autobús** by bus
8 (*con cantidades*) at, for; **lo vendió en cinco dólares** he sold it at *o* for five dollars; **estimaron las ganancias en unos trescientos mil euros** they estimated the profits to be around three hundred thousand euros
9 (*con infinitivo*) **fue el último en hacerlo** he was the last to do it; **lo reconocí en el andar** I recognized him by his walk
10 (†) (*con gerundio*) **en viéndolo se lo dije** the moment I saw him I told him

en.° ABR (= **enero**) Jan

enaceitar ▸conjug 1a◂ VT to oil

Enagas SF ABR (*Esp*) = **Empresa Nacional del Gas**

enagua SF (*esp LAm*), **enaguas** SFPL petticoat

enaguazar ▸conjug 1f◂ VT to flood

enajenación SF, **enajenamiento** SM 1 (*Jur*) alienation ► **enajenación forzosa** expropriation
2 (*Psic*) alienation ► **enajenación mental** mental derangement
3 (= *distracción*) absentmindedness

enajenar ▸conjug 1a◂ Ⓐ VT 1 (*Jur*) [+ *propiedad*] to alienate, transfer; [+ *derechos*] to dispose of
2 (*Psic*) (*gen*) to alienate, estrange; (= *enloquecer*) to drive mad; (= *extasiar*) to enrapture, carry away
Ⓑ **enajenarse** VPR 1 **~se algo** to deprive o.s. of sth; **ha conseguido ~se la amistad de todos** he has managed to alienate himself from everybody
2 **~se de los amigos** to become estranged from one's friends
3 (= *extasiarse*) to be enraptured, be carried away

enaltecer ▸conjug 2d◂ VT to extol

enamoradizo ADJ who easily falls in love

enamorado/a Ⓐ ADJ 1 [*de persona*] in love (**de** with); **estar ~** to be in love; **estaban locamente ~s** they were madly in love; **estoy ~ de Ana** I'm in love with Ana
2 (*Caribe, Cono Sur*) = **enamoradizo**
Ⓑ SM/F 1 (= *amante*) lover; **el día de los ~s** St. Valentine's Day
2 (= *aficionado*) **es un ~ del fútbol** he's a real football fan, he really loves football

> **EN**
>
> Como preposición de lugar, **en** se traduce normalmente por **on**, **in** o **at**. La elección de una de estas tres preposiciones depende a menudo de cómo percibe el hablante la relación espacial. He aquí unas líneas generales:
>
> • Se traduce por **on** cuando **en** equivale a **encima de** o nos referimos a algo que se percibe como una superficie o una línea, por ejemplo una mesa, una carretera, *etc.*:
>
> "¿Has visto mi vestido?" — "Está en la tabla de planchar"
> ***"Have you seen my dress?" — "It's on the ironing-board"***
> Estaban tumbados en la playa
> ***They were lying on the beach***
> Está construyendo una casa en la colina
> ***He's building a house on the hill***
> ...un pueblo en la costa oeste...
> ***...a village on the west coast...***
> La gasolinera está en la carretera que va a Motril
> ***The petrol station is on the road to Motril***
> Dibujó un león en la hoja de papel
> ***He drew a lion on the piece of paper***
> Tiene un grano en la nariz
> ***He has a spot on his nose***
> Lo vi en la tele
> ***I saw him on TV***
>
> • Se usa **in** cuando equivale a **dentro de** o cuando nos referimos a un espacio que se percibe como limitado (calle, montañas, etc):
>
> Tus gafas están en mi bolso
> ***Your glasses are in my bag***
> Tienes una pestaña en el ojo
> ***You've got an eyelash in your eye***
> Lo leí en un libro
> ***I read it in a book***
> Se han comprado un chalet en la sierra
> ***They've bought a chalet in the mountains***
> Viven en la calle de Serrano
> ***They live in the Calle de Serrano***
>
> • Lo traducimos por **at** para referirnos a un edificio cuando hablamos de la actividad que normalmente se realiza en él o cuando **en** indica un lugar concreto. También se traduce por **at** cuando en la dirección incluimos el número o el nombre de la casa:
>
> ¿Por qué no comemos en el restaurante de tu hermano?
> ***Why don't we have lunch at your brother's restaurant?***
> Voy a pasar el día en el museo
> ***I'm going to spend the day at the museum***
> Te espero en la parada del autobús
> ***I'll meet you at the bus-stop***
> Vivimos en la calle Dale nº 12
> ***We live at 12 Dale Street***
>
> *Para otros usos y ejemplos ver la entrada.*

enamoramiento SM falling in love

enamorar ▸conjug 1a◂ Ⓐ VT 1 [+ *persona*] to win the love of

2 (= *encantar*) **me enamora este paisaje** I simply adore this scenery, I just love this scenery
Ⓑ **enamorarse** VPR to fall in love (**de** with)

enamoricarse* ▸conjug 1g◂ VPR, **enamoriscarse*** ▸conjug 1g◂ VPR to be infatuated (**de** with), get a crush* (**de** on)

enancar ▸conjug 1g◂ Ⓐ VT **~ a algn** (*LAm*) to put sb on the crupper (of one's horse)
Ⓑ VI (*Cono Sur*) (= *seguir*) to follow, be a consequence (**a** of)
Ⓒ **enancarse** VPR 1 (*LAm*) to get up on the crupper, ride behind
2 (*Méx*) [*caballo*] to rear up

enanez SF (*lit*) dwarfishness; (*fig*) stunted nature

enangostar ▸conjug 1a◂ Ⓐ VT to narrow
Ⓑ **enangostarse** VPR to narrow, get narrower

enanismo SM (*Med*) dwarfism

enanito/a SM/F dwarf

enano/a Ⓐ ADJ dwarf *antes de s*
Ⓑ SM/F dwarf, midget; (*pey*) runt; ✦*MODISMO* **disfrutar** o **pasárselo como un ~** to have a brilliant time

enantes ADV (*Andes*) = **denante(s)**

enarbolar ▸conjug 1a◂ Ⓐ VT [+ *bandera*] to hoist; [+ *espada*] to flourish
Ⓑ **enarbolarse** VPR 1 [*persona*] to get angry
2 [*caballo*] to rear up

enarcar ▸conjug 1g◂ VT 1 [+ *tonel*] to put a hoop on
2 (= *arquear*) [+ *cejas*] to raise; [+ *lomo*] to arch; [+ *pecho*] to throw out

enardecer ▸conjug 2d◂ Ⓐ VT 1 (= *dar fuerza a*) [+ *pasión*] to inflame; [+ *discusión*] to enliven, liven up
2 [+ *público*] (= *entusiasmar*) to fill with enthusiasm; (= *provocar*) to incite, inflame
Ⓑ **enardecerse** VPR 1 (*Med*) to become inflamed
2 (= *entusiasmarse*) to get excited (**por** about)

enarenar ▸conjug 1a◂ Ⓐ VT to cover with sand
Ⓑ **enarenarse** VPR (*Náut*) to run aground

enastado ADJ horned

encabalgamiento SM (*Literat*) enjambement

encabestrar ▸conjug 1a◂ Ⓐ VT 1 [+ *caballo*] to put a halter on
2 (= *convencer*) to induce
Ⓑ **encabestrarse** VPR (*LAm*) to dig one's heels in

encabezado Ⓐ ADJ [*vino*] fortified
Ⓑ SM 1 (*Méx Prensa, Tip*) (= *encabezamiento*) heading; (= *titular*) headline
2 (*Caribe*) (= *capataz*) foreman

encabezamiento SM 1 (= *en periódico*) headline, caption; (= *de carta*) heading; (= *preámbulo*) foreword, preface; (*Com*) bill head, letterhead
2 (= *registro*) roll, register

encabezar ▸conjug 1f◂ VT 1 [+ *movimiento, revolución, partido, delegación*] to lead; **dirigentes sindicalistas encabezaban la manifestación** union leaders led the demonstration
2 [+ *lista, liga*] to head, be at the top of; **el Betis encabeza la clasificación de la Liga** Betis are at the top of o heading the League; **el ciclista español encabeza la carrera** the Spanish cyclist is in the lead
3 [+ *carta, artículo*] to head; **la cita que encabeza el artículo** the quotation heading the article
4 [+ *vino*] to fortify
5 (††) [+ *población*] to register (*for tax purposes*)

encabrestarse ▸conjug 1a◂ VPR (*LAm*) = **emperrarse**

encabritamiento* SM fit of bad temper

encabritar ▸conjug 1a◂ Ⓐ VT (*) to rile*, make cross
Ⓑ **encabritarse** VPR 1 [*caballo*] to rear up
2 (*) (= *enfadarse*) to get riled*, get cross

encabronar* ▸conjug 1a◂ Ⓐ VT to make angry
Ⓑ **encabronarse** VPR to get riled*, get cross

encabuyar ▸conjug 1a◂ VT (*Andes, Caribe*) to tie up

encachado ADJ (*Cono Sur*) appealing, attractive

encachar ▸conjug 1a◂ Ⓐ VT 1 (*Taur*) [+ *cabeza*] to lower before charging
2 (*Chile**) to make nice
Ⓑ **encacharse** VPR (*Chile**) to spruce o.s. up

encachilarse* ▸conjug 1a◂ VPR (*Arg*) to get furious

encachimbado* ADJ **está ~** (*CAm*) he's livid, he's hopping mad*

encachimbarse* ▸conjug 1a◂ VPR (*CAm*) to fly off the handle*, lose one's temper

encachorrarse ▸conjug 1a◂ VPR (*Andes*) to get angry

encadenación SF, **encadenamiento** SM 1 [*de personas, objetos*] chaining, chaining together
2 [*de hechos, ideas*] linking, connection, concatenation (*frm*)

encadenado SM (*Cine*) fade, dissolve

encadenar ▸conjug 1a◂ Ⓐ VT 1 (= *atar con cadenas*) (*lit*) to chain, chain together; (*fig*) to tie down; **los negocios le encadenan al escritorio** business ties him to his desk
2 [+ *prisionero*] to fetter, shackle
3 [+ *de hechos, ideas*] to connect, link
4 (= *inmovilizar*) to shackle, paralyze, immobilize
Ⓑ VI (*Cine*) to fade in; **~ a** to fade to

encajable ADJ **500 piezas ~s una dentro de la otra** 500 pieces that fit together; **esa idea no es ~ en su concepción del mundo** that idea doesn't fit into the way he sees the world

encajadura SF 1 (= *acto*) insertion
2 (*para meter algo*) (= *hueco*) socket; (= *ranura*) groove; (= *armazón*) frame

encajar ▸conjug 1a◂ Ⓐ VT 1 (= *acoplar*) [+ *pieza, tapón*] to fit; [+ *partes*] to fit together; **no he podido ~ las dos partes** I haven't managed to fit the two parts together; **~ algo en algo** to fit sth into sth
2 (= *aceptar*) [+ *broma, crítica*] to take; [+ *desgracia, derrota*] to handle, cope with; **hay que ~ las críticas con sentido del humor** you have to be able to take criticism and not lose your sense of humour; **el equipo no supo ~ el resultado** the team couldn't handle o cope with the result; **no supo ~ el golpe** he couldn't handle it
3 (*) **~ algo a algn** (= *endilgar*) to lumber sb with sth*, dump sth on sb*; (= *timar*) to palm sth off on o onto sb*; **cada vez que se van me encajan a su gato** every time they go away they lumber me with their cat* o they dump their cat on me*; **le encajó un billete falso** he managed to palm a fake note off onto him*; **a mí no me encajas tú esa historia** I won't be taken in by a story like that
4 (= *dar, meter*) [+ *golpe, patada*] to give; **le encajó un buen bofetón** he gave him a good slap; **no le dejó ~ ni un solo comentario** she didn't let him get a word in edgeways
5 (= *dejarse meter*) to let in; **llevamos tres partidos sin ~ un gol** we've gone three matches without letting in a goal
Ⓑ VI 1 (= *ajustar*) [*puerta*] to fit; [*piezas*] to fit (together); **las dos partes ~on perfectamente** both parts fitted (together) perfectly; **~ en algo** to fit into sth
2 (= *coincidir*) [*teoría, coartada*] to fit; **aquí hay algo que no encaja** something here doesn't tally o fit; **ahora todo empieza a ~** it's all beginning to fall into place o fit together now; **~ con algo** to tie in with sth, tally with sth; **su versión no encaja con lo que he oído** his version does not tie in o tally with what I've heard
3 (= *integrarse*) **~ con algn** to fit in with sb; **los nuevos alumnos ~on bien con sus compañeros** the new students fitted in well with their classmates; **~ en** [+ *serie, papel*] to be right for; [+ *ambiente*] to fit in; **un espectáculo que puede ~ bien en Broadway** a show that could be just right for Broadway; **no creo que vayas a ~ en ese papel** I don't think you'll be right for o suit that role; **no le costó ~ en la oficina** he had no trouble fitting in in the office; **sus ideas encajan dentro de una mentalidad conservadora** her ideas are in keeping with a conservative mentality
Ⓒ **encajarse** VPR 1 (= *atrancarse*) **la puerta se quedó encajada** the door got jammed o stuck; **se me ha encajado el dedo en la botella** my finger's got stuck in the bottle; **el coche se encajó dentro del muro** the car jammed into the wall
2 (= *ponerse*) [+ *abrigo, sombrero*] to put on; **se encajó el sombrero hasta las orejas** he pulled his hat (on) down to his ears
3 (*Méx*) (= *aprovecharse*) to take advantage; **~se con algn** to take advantage of sb

encaje SM 1 (*Cos*) lace; **una blusa de ~** a lace blouse; **se le veían los ~s de las enaguas** you could see the lace of her petticoat ► **encaje de bolillos** (*lit*) bobbin lace; **tengo que hacer ~ de bolillos para que el sueldo me llegue a fin de mes** I have to juggle things around constantly to make ends meet
2 [*de piezas*] fitting
3 (= *cabida*) **una obra de difícil ~ en el concepto de teatro moderno** a work which does not fit easily into the concept of modern theatre
4 (*Téc*) (= *hueco*) socket; (= *ranura*) groove
5 (= *taracea*) inlay, mosaic ► **encaje de aplicación** appliqué, appliqué work
6 (*Fin*) reserve, stock ► **encaje de oro** gold reserve

encajero/a SM/F lacemaker

encajetillar ▸conjug 1a◂ VT to pack in boxes, box

encajonado SM cofferdam

encajonar ▸conjug 1a◂ Ⓐ VT 1 (= *guardar*) to box, box up, put in a box; (*Mec*) to box in
2 [+ *río*] to canalize
3 (= *meter en un sitio estrecho*) to squeeze in, squeeze through

Ⓑ **encajonarse** VPR [*río*] to run between steep banks

encajoso‡ SM (*LAm*) creep‡

encalabrinar* ▸conjug 1a◂ Ⓐ VT [1] (= *emborrachar*) to go to one's head
[2] **~ a algn** (= *enojar*) to get sb worked up; (= *atraer*) to attract sb
Ⓑ **encalabrinarse** VPR [1] **~se de algn** to become infatuated with sb, get a crush on sb
[2] (= *empeñarse*) to get an obsession, get the bit between one's teeth

encaladura SF [1] (= *blanqueo*) whitewash, whitewashing
[2] (*Agr*) liming

encalambrarse ▸conjug 1a◂ VPR (*LAm*) (= *acalambrarse*) to get cramp; (= *aterirse*) to grow stiff with cold

encalamocar ▸conjug 1g◂ Ⓐ VT (*Andes, Caribe*) [1] (= *emborrachar*) to make drunk
[2] (= *aturdir*) to confuse, bewilder
Ⓑ **encalamocarse** VPR (*Andes, Caribe*) [1] (= *emborracharse*) to get drunk
[2] (= *aturdirse*) to get confused, get bewildered

encalar ▸conjug 1a◂ VT [1] [+ *pared*] to whitewash
[2] (*Agr*) to lime

encalatarse ▸conjug 1a◂ VPR (*Andes*) [1] (= *desnudarse*) to strip naked
[2] (= *arruinarse*) to be ruined

encalladero SM shoal, sandbank

encalladura SF stranding, running aground

encallar ▸conjug 1a◂ Ⓐ VI [1] (*Náut*) to run aground, get stranded (**en** on)
[2] [*negociación*] (= *fracasar*) to fail; (= *estancarse*) to get bogged down
Ⓑ **encallarse** VPR [1] (*Náut*) to run aground, get stranded (**en** on)
[2] [*carne*] to go rubbery

encallecer ▸conjug 2d◂ VI, **encallecerse** VPR to harden, form corns

encallecido ADJ hardened

encalmada SF period of calm

encalmado ADJ [1] (*Náut*) becalmed
[2] (*Com, Fin*) quiet, slack

encalmarse ▸conjug 1a◂ VPR to calm down

encalomarse‡ ▸conjug 1a◂ VPR to hide

encalvecer ▸conjug 2d◂ VI to go bald

encamar ▸conjug 1a◂ Ⓐ VT [1] (*CAm, Méx*) (= *hospitalizar*) to take to hospital, hospitalize
[2] (*Caribe*) [+ *animal*] to litter, bed down; (*Méx*) [+ *niño*] to put to bed
Ⓑ **encamarse** VPR [1] [*persona*] to take to one's bed; **estar encamado** to be confined to bed; **~se con algn** (*Andes, Cono Sur*) to go to bed with sb, sleep with sb
[2] [*cosecha*] to be laid, be flattened
[3] [*animal*] to crouch, hide

encamburarse ▸conjug 1a◂ VPR (*Caribe*) (*gen*) to make good; (*como funcionario*) to achieve public office

encame SM den, lair

encamillado/a SM/F (*CAm, Méx*) stretcher case

encaminamiento SM (*Inform*) routing

encaminar ▸conjug 1a◂ Ⓐ VT [1] (= *orientar*) [+ *plan, esfuerzo*] to direct; [+ *alumno, hijo*] to guide, direct; **el proyecto está encaminado a ayudarles** the plan is designed to help them, the plan is aimed at helping them; **aquel maestro lo encaminó en sus estudios** that teacher guided *o* directed him in his studies
[2] (= *dirigir*) to direct; **una señora me encaminó hacia la autopista** a lady directed me towards the motorway; **encaminó sus pasos hacia el monasterio** (*liter*) he turned his steps towards the monastery (*liter*)
Ⓑ **encaminarse** VPR [1] **~se a** *o* **hacia** (= *dirigirse a*) to head for, set out for; **nos encaminamos hacia el pueblo** we headed *o* set out for the village
[2] **~se a** (= *tener como objetivo*) to be designed to, be aimed at; **nuestros esfuerzos se encaminan a la solución del conflicto** our efforts are designed to solve the conflict, our efforts are aimed at solving the conflict

encamotado* ADJ (*LAm*) **estar ~** to be in love (**de** with)

encamotarse* ▸conjug 1a◂ VPR (*LAm*) to fall in love (**de** with)

encampanado ADJ bell-shaped

encampanar ▸conjug 1a◂ Ⓐ VT [1] (= *elevar*) to raise
[2] (*Andes, Caribe*) (= *encumbrar*) to raise, raise on high
[3] (*Andes, Caribe, Méx**) (= *abandonar*) to leave in the lurch, leave in a jam*
[4] **~ a algn a** (*Caribe*) to send sb to
[5] (*Méx*) (= *agitar*) to excite, agitate
Ⓑ **encampanarse** VPR [1] (*LAm*) (= *encumbrarse*) to rise
[2] (*Col, Méx*) (= *enamorarse*) to fall in love
[3] (*Méx*) (= *meterse en un lío*) to get into a jam*
[4] (*Caribe*) to go off to a remote spot
[5] (*Andes**) (= *complicarse*) to become difficult, get complicated

encanado/a* SM/F (*Andes*) prisoner

encanalar ▸conjug 1a◂ VT, **encanalizar** ▸conjug 1f◂ VT to pipe

encanallarse ▸conjug 1a◂ VPR (= *envilecerse*) to become a bastard‡

encanar‡ ▸conjug 1a◂ VT (*Andes, Cono Sur*) to throw into jail

encandecer ▸conjug 2d◂ VT to make white-hot

encandelar ▸conjug 1a◂ VT (*Caribe*) to annoy, irritate

encandelillar ▸conjug 1a◂ VT (*LAm*) to dazzle

encandellar ▸conjug 1a◂ VT (*Andes*) [+ *fuego*] to fan

encandiladera† SF procuress†

encandilado ADJ [1] (*) (= *deslumbrado*) **estar ~ con algn** to be all taken with sb
[2] (= *tieso*) high, erect

encandiladora† SF procuress†

encandilar ▸conjug 1a◂ Ⓐ VT [1] (= *fascinar*) to daze, bewilder
[2] (= *deslumbrar*) to dazzle
[3] [+ *lumbre*] to stir, poke
[4] [+ *emoción*] to kindle, stimulate
Ⓑ **encandilarse** VPR [1] [*ojos*] to light up
[2] (= *quedar fascinado*) **se encandiló con la belleza de Laura** he was taken with *o* dazzled by Laura's beauty
[3] (*Andes, Caribe*) (= *asustarse*) to get scared

encanecer ▸conjug 2d◂ VI, **encanecerse** VPR [1] [*pelo*] to go grey, go gray (*EEUU*); [*persona*] to go grey
[2] (*con moho*) to go mouldy, go moldy (*EEUU*)

encanijado ADJ weak, puny

encanijarse ▸conjug 1a◂ VPR to grow weak, become emaciated

encanillar ▸conjug 1a◂ VT to wind (on to a spool)

▼**encantado** ADJ [1] (= *muy contento*) delighted; **si te encargas tú, yo por mí encantada** I'd be only too pleased *o* I'd be delighted if you'd take care of it; **estar ~ con algo/algn** to be delighted with sth/sb; **está encantada con el piso nuevo** she's delighted with the new flat; **estar ~ de algo: estoy ~ de tu éxito** I'm delighted at your success; **estoy encantada de poder ayudarte** I'm delighted to be able to help you
[2] (*en fórmulas de presentación*) **~ de conocerlo** (I'm) delighted to meet you; **—el Sr. Martínez —¡encantado!** "let me introduce you to Mr Martínez" — "how do you do!" *o* "pleased to meet you!"
[3] (= *embrujado*) enchanted
[4] (= *distraído*) **¡espabila, que parece que estés encantada!** wake up, you seem to be in a trance!

encantador(a) Ⓐ ADJ [*persona*] charming, delightful; [*lugar*] lovely
Ⓑ SM/F magician, enchanter/enchantress
► **encantador(a) de serpientes** snake charmer

encantadoramente ADV charmingly, delightfully

encantamiento SM enchantment

▼**encantar** ▸conjug 1a◂ Ⓐ VI (*con complemento personal*) to love; **me encanta tu casa** I love your house; **me encantan las flores** I adore *o* love flowers; **me ~ía que vinieras** I'd be delighted if you come, I'd love you to come
Ⓑ VT to cast a spell on *o* over, bewitch

encanto SM [1] (= *atractivo*) charm; **el pueblecito tiene mucho ~** the village has a lot of charm *o* is very charming; **no es guapa, pero tiene su ~** she isn't pretty, but she has charm; **se dejó seducir por sus ~s** he allowed himself to be seduced by her charms
[2] (= *maravilla*) **el niño es un ~** he's a charming *o* lovely *o* delightful little boy; **¡qué ~ de jardín!** what a lovely garden!
[3] (*uso apelativo*) darling; **¡oye, ~!** hello, gorgeous!*
[4] (= *encantamiento*) spell; **romper el ~** to break the spell; **el bolso desapareció como por ~** the bag disappeared as if by magic

encañada SF ravine

encañado SM pipe

encañar ▸conjug 1a◂ VT [1] [+ *agua*] to pipe
[2] [+ *planta*] to stake
[3] [+ *tierra*] to drain

encañizado SM wire netting fence

encañonar ▸conjug 1a◂ Ⓐ VT [1] [+ *agua*] to pipe
[2] (*) (= *asaltar con arma*) to stick up*, hold up; (= *amenazar*) to cover (with a gun)
Ⓑ VI [*ave*] to grow feathers

encapado ADJ cloaked, wearing a cloak

encapotado ADJ [1] [*cielo*] cloudy, overcast
[2] (*con capa*) wearing a cloak

encapotar ▸conjug 1a◂ Ⓐ VT to cover with a cloak
Ⓑ **encapotarse** VPR [1] [*cielo*] to become cloudy, cloud over, become overcast
[2] (= *ponerse la capa*) to put on one's cloak
[3] (= *enfurruñarse*) to frown

➤ LENGUA Y USO: **encantado 1** 38.3, 52.1 **encantar A** 52.2, 52.4, 52.5

encapricharse ▸conjug 1a◂ VPR to take a fancy (**con, por** to)

encapuchado/a Ⓐ ADJ hooded
Ⓑ SM/F masked man/woman

encapuchar ▸conjug 1a◂ VT **~ un pozo de petróleo** to cap an oil well

encarado ADJ **bien ~** nice-looking; **mal ~** evil-looking

encaramar ▸conjug 1a◂ Ⓐ VT [1] (= *subir*) to raise, lift up
[2] (= *alabar*) to praise, extol, extoll (*EEUU*)
Ⓑ **encaramarse** VPR (= *subirse*) to perch, sit up high; **~se a** [+ *árbol*] to climb up to, climb on to

encarapitarse ▸conjug 1a◂ VPR (*Andes, Caribe*) = **encaramar B**

encarar ▸conjug 1a◂ Ⓐ VT [1] [+ *problema*] to face, face up to, confront
[2] [+ *dos cosas*] to bring face to face
[3] [+ *arma*] to aim, point
Ⓑ VI (*Cono Sur*) to fall sick
Ⓒ **encararse** VPR **~se a** *o* **con algn** to confront sb

encarcelación SF, **encarcelamiento** SM imprisonment

encarcelar ▸conjug 1a◂ VT to imprison, jail

encarecer ▸conjug 2d◂ Ⓐ VT [1] (*Com*) to put up the price of
[2] (= *alabar*) to praise, extol, extoll (*EEUU*)
[3] **le encarezco que lo haga** I urge you to do it
Ⓑ VI, **encarecerse** VPR (*Com*) to get dearer

encarecidamente ADV insistently, earnestly

encarecimiento SM [1] [*de precio*] increase, rise
[2] (= *alabanza*) extolling
[3] (= *insistencia*) stressing, emphasizing; **con ~** insistently, strongly

encargado/a Ⓐ ADJ **estar ~ de algo** to be in charge of sth, be responsible for sth; **¿puedo hablar con la persona encargada de los impuestos?** can I speak to the person in charge of *o* responsible for taxes?; **la arteria encargada de conducir la sangre** the artery responsible for directing blood flow
Ⓑ SM/F (= *responsable*) [*de tarea, expedición*] person in charge; [*de tienda, restaurante*] manager; [*de parque, cementerio*] groundkeeper; **quisiera hablar con el ~ de las obras** I would like to speak to the person in charge of the building work; **él era el ~ de las bebidas** he was in charge of the drinks; **el ~ de la librería** the person in charge of the bookshop, the manager of the bookshop ► **encargado/a de campo** (*Dep*) groundsman/groundswoman ► **encargado/a de curso** student representative ► **encargado/a de la recepción** receptionist ► **encargado/a de mostrador** counter clerk ► **encargado/a de negocios** (*Pol*) chargé d'affaires ► **encargado/a de obra** site manager ► **encargado/a de prensa** press officer ► **encargado/a de relaciones públicas** public relations officer ► **encargado/a de seguridad** security officer ► **encargado/a de vestuario** (*Teat*) wardrobe manager; (*Cine, TV*) costume designer

▼**encargar** ▸conjug 1h◂ Ⓐ VT [1] [+ *tarea, misión*] to give; **encargó el cuidado de sus hijos a un familiar** he left his children in the care of a relative; **~ a algn de algo** to give sb the job of doing sth; **lo ~on de resolver el conflicto** he was given the job of resolving the conflict
[2] (*a profesional, empresa*) [+ *obra de arte, informe*] to commission; **nos ~on el diseño del folleto** they commissioned us to design the brochure
[3] (= *hacer un pedido de*) to order; **hemos encargado dos pizzas** we've ordered two pizzas; **encargué los libros por correo** I ordered the books by post; **le he encargado un traje al sastre** I've ordered a suit from my tailor; ✦*MODISMOS* **~ familia** to start a family; **~ un niño**: **¿habéis encargado otro niño?** are you having another child?, do you have another one on the way?*
[4] (= *pedir como favor*) **le encargué dos latas de caviar ruso** I asked him to bring *o* buy me two tins of Russian caviar; **me ha encargado varias cosas del supermercado** she's asked me to get her some things from the supermarket; **~ a algn que haga algo** to ask sb to do sth; **me encargó que le regara las plantas** he asked me to water his plants
[5] (= *aconsejar*) to advise; **le encargó varias veces que no dejara el tratamiento** he advised him several times not to stop the treatment
[6] (*Chile Der*) **~ reo a algn** to submit sb to trial
Ⓑ **encargarse** VPR **~se de** (= *ocuparse de*) to take care of; (= *ser responsable de*) to be in charge of; (= *tomar la responsabilidad de*) to take charge of; **¿qué empresa se va a ~ de la mudanza?** which firm is going to do *o* take care of the moving?; **ya me encargo yo de decírselo a todo el mundo** I'll make sure everyone knows, I'll take care of telling everyone; **de ése me encargo yo personalmente** (*hum*) I'll see to him myself!, I'll take care of him myself!; **yo me encargo de los asuntos culturales** I'm in charge of cultural affairs; **yo me encargo normalmente de cocinar** I normally do the cooking, I'm normally in charge of the cooking; **no irá, de eso me encargo yo** he won't go, I'll see to that *o* I'll make sure of that; **cuando ella murió, él se encargó del negocio** when she died, he took over the business *o* he took charge of the business

encargatoria SF (*Chile Der*) (*tb* **~ de reo**) committal for trial

encargo SM [1] (= *pedido*) order; **su ~ se perdió en el correo** your order got lost in the post; **de** *o* **por ~** [*traje, vestido*] tailor made, made to order; [*muebles*] made to order; **"se hacen tartas por ~"** "cakes made to order"; **ni hecho de ~ podrías ser más torpe** (*hum*) you couldn't be more clumsy if you tried
[2] (*profesional*) job, commission; **todavía no me ha salido ningún ~** I haven't been given any jobs *o* commissions yet; **una exposición realizada por ~ del Ayuntamiento** an exhibition commissioned by the Council
[3] (*para comprar algo*) errand; **ha salido a hacer un ~ a la tienda** he's gone to the shop on an errand; **le hice varios ~s de Nueva York** I asked him to buy a few things in New York, I asked him to bring back a few things from New York
[4] ✦*MODISMOS* **dejar a algn con ~** (*LAm**) to leave sb in the family way*; **traer a algn de ~** (*Méx**) to give sb a hard time*

encargue SM ✦*MODISMO* **estar de ~** (*Cono Sur**) to be expecting, be in the family way*

encariñado ADJ **estar ~ con** to be fond of

encariñarse ▸conjug 1a◂ VPR **~ con** to grow fond of, get attached to; (*Psic*) to bond

Encarna SF (*forma familiar*) *de* **Encarnación**

encarnación SF (*Rel*) incarnation; (= *personificación*) embodiment, personification

encarnadino ADJ blood-red

encarnado ADJ [1] (*Rel*) incarnate; **es la sencillez encarnada** it's simplicity itself
[2] (= *rojo*) [*color*] red; [*tez*] ruddy, florid (*pey*); **ponerse ~** to blush

encarnadura SF **tiene buena ~** his skin heals (up) well

encarnar ▸conjug 1a◂ Ⓐ VT [1] (= *personificar*) to personify; (*Teat*) [+ *papel*] to play, bring to life; **lago encarna el odio** Iago is hatred personified
[2] [+ *anzuelo*] to bait
Ⓑ VI [1] (*Rel*) to become incarnate
[2] (*Med*) to heal, heal up
[3] [*arma*] to enter the flesh, penetrate the body
Ⓒ **encarnarse** VPR (*Rel*) to become incarnate, be made flesh

encarnecer ▸conjug 2d◂ VI to put on flesh

encarnizadamente ADV bloodily, fiercely

encarnizado ADJ [1] [*batalla, lucha*] bloody, fierce
[2] (= *sangrante*) [*herida*] red, inflamed; [*ojo*] bloodshot

encarnizamiento SM [1] (= *ira*) rage, fury
[2] (= *crueldad*) bitterness, ferocity

encarnizar ▸conjug 1f◂ Ⓐ VT (= *volver cruel*) to make cruel; (= *enfadar*) to enrage
Ⓑ **encarnizarse** VPR to fight fiercely; **~se con algn** to attack sb viciously

encaro SM [1] (= *mirada*) stare, staring, gaze
[2] (= *puntería*) aim, aiming
[3] (*Hist*) blunderbuss

encarpetar ▸conjug 1a◂ VT [1] (= *guardar*) [+ *papeles*] to file away; [+ *proyecto*] to shelve, bury
[2] (*LAm*) [+ *moción*] to shelve, bury

encarrilamiento SM [*de conducta*] improvement; [*de niño*] guidance

encarrilar ▸conjug 1a◂ VT [1] [+ *tren*] to put back on the rails
[2] (= *dirigir*) to direct, guide; **no es fácil ~ a los niños en nuestros días** it's not easy to guide *o* provide guidance to one's children these days; **ir encarrilado** to be on the right lines; (*pey*) to be in a rut

encarrujar ▸conjug 1a◂ VT (*Cono Sur Cos*) to ruffle, frill

encartado/a SM/F (*Jur*) accused, defendant

encartar ▸conjug 1a◂ Ⓐ VT [1] (*Jur*) to summon
[2] (= *proscribir*) to outlaw
[3] (= *registrar*) to enrol, enroll (*EEUU*)
Ⓑ VI (*Naipes*) to lead
Ⓒ **encartarse** VPR (*Naipes*) *to take on one's opponent's suit*

encarte SM [1] (*Tip*) insert, inset
[2] (*Naipes*) lead

encartonar ▸conjug 1a◂ VT [1] (= *cubrir*) to cover with cardboard
[2] (*Tip*) to bind in boards

encartuchar ▸conjug 1a◂ VT (*LAm*) [+ *papel*] to roll up into a cone

➤ LENGUA Y USO: **encargar A3** 47.2

encasar ▸conjug 1a◂ VT [+ *hueso*] to set

encasillado Ⓐ ADJ [*actor*] typecast
Ⓑ SM pigeonholes *pl*, set of pigeonholes

encasillamiento SM 1 pigeonholing; **de difícil ~** difficult to categorize
2 (*Teat*) typecasting

encasillar ▸conjug 1a◂ VT 1 (= *poner en casillas*) to pigeonhole, categorize; (= *clasificar*) to classify; **no me gusta que me encasillen como escritor romántico** I don't like being pigeonholed *o* categorized as a romantic writer
2 (*Teat*) to typecast

encasquetar ▸conjug 1a◂ VT 1 [+ *sombrero*] to pull down tight
2 (*) **~ algo a algn** to foist sth on sb
3 (*) **~ una idea a algn** to put an idea into sb's head
4 (*Teat*) to typecast

encasquillador SM (*LAm*) blacksmith

encasquillar ▸conjug 1a◂ Ⓐ VT 1 (*LAm*) [+ *caballo*] to shoe
2 (*) (= *incriminar*) to frame*
Ⓑ **encasquillarse** VPR 1 [*bala, revólver*] to jam
2 (*Andes*) (*en discurso*) to get stuck, dry up*
3 (*Caribe*) (= *asustarse*) to get scared
4 (*Caribe**) (= *vacilar*) to waver

encastillado ADJ 1 (*Arquit*) castellated
2 [*persona*] (= *soberbio*) haughty; (= *obstinado*) stubborn

encastillar ▸conjug 1a◂ Ⓐ VT to fortify, defend with castles
Ⓑ **encastillarse** VPR 1 (*Mil*) to take to the hills
2 (*Hist*) to shut o.s. up in a castle
3 (= *obstinarse*) to refuse to yield; **~se en un principio** to stick to a principle, refuse to give up a principle

encatrado SM (*Cono Sur*) hurdle

encatrinarse ▸conjug 1a◂ VPR (*Méx*) to dress up

encauchado SM (*Andes, Caribe*) (= *tela*) rubberized cloth; (= *capa*) waterproof cape

encauchar ▸conjug 1a◂ VT to rubberize, waterproof

encausado/a SM/F (*Jur*) accused, defendant

encausar ▸conjug 1a◂ VT to prosecute, sue

encauzar ▸conjug 1f◂ VT 1 [+ *agua, río*] to channel
2 (= *dirigir*) to channel, direct; **las protestas se pueden ~ a fines positivos** the protests can be guided into useful channels

encefalitis SF INV encephalitis ▸ **encefalitis letárgica** sleeping sickness, encephalitis lethargica (*frm*)

encefalograma SM encephalogram

encefalomielitis SF INV ▸ **encefalomielitis miálgica** myalgic encephalomyelitis

encefalopatía SF ▸ **encefalopatía espongiforme bovina** bovine spongiform encephalopathy

enceguecer ▸conjug 2d◂ (*LAm*) Ⓐ VT to blind
Ⓑ VI, **enceguecerse** VPR to go blind

encelar ▸conjug 1a◂ Ⓐ VT to make jealous
Ⓑ **encelarse** VPR 1 [*persona*] to become jealous
2 (*Zool*) to rut, be on heat

encenagado ADJ 1 (= *enfangado*) muddy, mud-stained
2 (= *enviciado*) sunk in vice, depraved

encenagarse ▸conjug 1h◂ VPR 1 (= *enfangarse*) to get muddy
2 (= *enviciarse*) to become depraved

encendedor SM 1 (= *mechero*) lighter ▸ **encendedor de bolsillo** pocket lighter ▸ **encendedor de cigarrillos** cigarette lighter ▸ **encendedor de cocina** gas poker ▸ **encendedor de gas** gas lighter ▸ **encendedor del gas** gas poker
2 (= *persona*) lamplighter

encender ▸conjug 2g◂ Ⓐ VT 1 (= *prender*) [+ *fuego, cigarrillo*] to light; [+ *cerilla*] to strike; [+ *luz, radio*] to turn on, switch on, put on; [+ *gas*] to light, turn on; (*Inform*) to toggle on, switch on
2 (= *avivar*) [+ *pasiones*] to inflame; [+ *entusiasmo*] to arouse; [+ *celos, odio*] to awake; [+ *guerra*] to spark off
3 (*Caribe*) (= *azotar*) to beat; (= *castigar*) to punish
Ⓑ **encenderse** VPR 1 (= *prenderse*) to light; **¿cuándo se encienden las luces?** when is lighting-up time?
2 [*cara, ojos*] to light up
3 [*persona*] (= *exaltarse*) to get excited; (= *ruborizarse*) to blush; (= *estallar*) to break out; **~se de ira** to flare up with rage, fly into a temper

encendida* SF (*Caribe*) (= *paliza*) beating; (= *reprimenda*) telling-off*

encendidamente ADV passionately, ardently

encendido Ⓐ ADJ 1 (*gen*) alight; [*colilla, fuego*] lighted, lit; [*luz, radio*] on, switched on; [*hilo*] live; [*color*] glowing
2 (= *rojo vivo*) bright red; [*mejillas*] glowing; [*cara*] (*por el vino*) flushed; (*por la ira*) purple; [*mirada*] fiery, passionate
Ⓑ SM [*de faroles*] lighting; (*Aut*) ignition ▸ **encendido eléctrico** electric lighting

encendimiento SM (= *pasión*) passion, ardour, ardor (*EEUU*); (= *ansia*) eagerness; (= *intensidad*) intensity

encenizar ▸conjug 1f◂ VT to cover with ashes

encentar ▸conjug 1j◂ VT 1 (*para el uso*) to begin to use
2 [+ *pan*] to cut the first slice from

encerado Ⓐ ADJ 1 [*suelo*] waxed, polished
2 (= *de color cera*) wax-coloured, wax-colored (*EEUU*)
Ⓑ SM 1 (= *hule*) oilcloth
2 (*Escol*) blackboard
3 (*Náut*) tarpaulin, tarp (*EEUU*)

encerador(a) Ⓐ SM/F (= *persona*) polisher
Ⓑ SF polishing machine

encerar ▸conjug 1a◂ VT [+ *suelo*] to wax, polish

encercamiento SM (*LAm*) encirclement

encercar ▸conjug 1g◂ VT (*LAm*) = **cercar**

encerotar ▸conjug 1a◂ VT [+ *hilo*] to wax

encerradero SM fold, pen

encerrado ADJ **no soporto pasar todo el día encerrada** I can't stand being shut in all day; **el prisionero llevaba siete años encerrado** the prisoner had been locked up for seven years; **la puerta dio un portazo y me quedé encerrado** the door slammed shut and I was locked in

encerrar ▸conjug 1j◂ Ⓐ VT 1 (= *meter*) to shut (up); (*con llave*) to lock (up); **encerré el gato en la cocina** I shut the cat (up) in the kitchen; **lo ~on en su celda** they locked him in his cell; **la ~on en un psiquiátrico** they locked her up in a mental hospital; **~ una frase entre paréntesis** to put a phrase in brackets
2 (= *contener*) to contain; **el libro encierra profundas verdades** the book contains profound truths; **el plan encierra graves problemas** the plan has serious problems
3 (= *implicar*) to involve; **cualquier cambio encierra ciertos riesgos** any change involves certain risks
4 (*Ajedrez, Damas*) to block
Ⓑ **encerrarse** VPR 1 (= *meterse*) to shut o.s. (up); (*con llave*) to lock o.s. (up); **se encerró en su cuarto** she shut herself (up) in her room; **~se en sí mismo** to withdraw into o.s.; **~se en el silencio** to maintain a total silence
2 (*como protesta*) to hold a sit-in, stage a sit-in; **los manifestantes se ~on en el ayuntamiento** the demonstrators held *o* staged a sit-in in the town hall
3 (*Méx*) (= *ser hosco*) to be stand-offish

encerrona SF 1 (= *protesta*) sit-in
2 (= *trampa*) trap; **preparar a algn una ~** (*fig*) to lay *o* set a trap for sb

encespedar ▸conjug 1a◂ VT to turf

encestar ▸conjug 1a◂ VI (*Dep*) to score (a basket)

enceste SM (*Dep*) basket

enchalecar ▸conjug 1g◂ VT to place in a strait-jacket

enchapado SM [*de metal*] plating; [*de madera*] veneer

enchapar ▸conjug 1a◂ VT 1 (*Téc*) (*con metal*) to plate, overlay (*with metal*); (*con madera*) to veneer
2 (*Méx*) [+ *puerta*] to fit locks to

enchaquetarse ▸conjug 1a◂ VPR 1 (= *vestirse elegante*) to dress up
2 (*Andes, Caribe*) to put one's jacket on

encharcada SF pool, puddle

encharcado ADJ [*terreno*] swamped

encharcar ▸conjug 1g◂ Ⓐ VT 1 (= *formar charcos en*) to cover with puddles, turn into pools
2 (= *inundar*) to swamp, flood
Ⓑ **encharcarse** VPR 1 [*tierra*] to swamp, get flooded
2 [*agua*] (= *estancarse*) to become stagnant
3 (*Med*) [*pulmones*] to get clogged up
4 (*LAm*) (= *enfangarse*) to get muddy
5 (*Cono Sur*) (= *atascarse*) to get stuck in a puddle
6 **~se en los vicios** to wallow in vice

encharralarse ▸conjug 1a◂ VPR (*CAm*) to make an ambush, lie in ambush

enchastrar ▸conjug 1a◂ VT (*Cono Sur*) to dirty, make dirty

enchauchado* ADJ (*Cono Sur*) well-heeled

enchicharse* ▸conjug 1a◂ VPR 1 (*LAm*) (= *emborracharse*) to get drunk on chicha
2 (*Andes, CAm*) (= *enojarse*) to get angry, lose control

enchilada SF (*CAm, Méx*) stuffed tortilla

enchilado Ⓐ ADJ 1 (*CAm, Méx Culin*) seasoned with chili
2 (*Méx*) (= *rojo*) bright red
Ⓑ SM (*CAm, Méx*) stew with chili sauce

enchilar ▸conjug 1a◂ Ⓐ VT 1 (*LAm Culin*) to season with chili
2 (*Méx*) (= *molestar*) to annoy
Ⓑ VI (*Méx*) to sting, burn

Ⓒ **enchilarse** VPR (*Méx**) (= *enfadarse*) to get angry, get mad (*EEUU*); (*Méx*) (= *ruborizarse*) to go red in the face

enchiloso ADJ (*CAm, Méx*) [*sabor*] hot

enchilotarse* ▸conjug 1a◂ VPR (*Cono Sur*) to get cross

enchinar ▸conjug 1a◂ (*Méx*) Ⓐ VT [+ *pelo*] to curl, perm
Ⓑ **enchinarse** VPR **se le enchinó el cuerpo** he got goose pimples *o* goosebumps *o* (*EEUU*) gooseflesh

enchinchar ▸conjug 1a◂ Ⓐ VT 1 (*LAm*) (= *molestar*) to put out, bother
2 (*Méx*) [+ *persona*] to cause to waste time; [+ *asunto*] to delay
Ⓑ **enchincharse** VPR 1 (*LAm*) (= *infestarse*) to get infested with bugs
2 (*Arg, Méx*) (= *enfadarse*) to get bad-tempered

enchiquerar ▸conjug 1a◂ VT to pen, corral

enchironar* ▸conjug 1a◂ VT to jail, lock up, put away*

enchisparse* ▸conjug 1a◂ VPR (*LAm*) to get tight*

enchisterado ADJ top-hatted, with a top hat on

enchivarse* ▸conjug 1a◂ VPR (*Andes*) to fly into a rage

enchufable ADJ which plugs in, plug-in *antes de s*

enchufado/a* Ⓐ SM/F (*en escuela*) teacher's pet; (*en trabajo*) well-connected person, person with pull
Ⓑ ADJ **estar ~** to have connections

enchufar ▸conjug 1a◂ Ⓐ VT 1 (*Elec*) to plug in
2 (*Téc*) (*gen*) to join, fit together, fit in; [+ *dos tubos*] to telescope together
3 (*) (*en un trabajo*) **la han enchufado para el puesto de secretaria** they have set *o* lined her up for the secretary's job (*using contacts*), they pulled strings to get her the secretary's job
Ⓑ **enchufarse** VPR (*) 1 (*en el trabajo*) to wangle o.s. a job*, get a cushy job‡
2 (= *relacionarse bien*) to get in with the right people

enchufe SM 1 (*Elec*) (= *macho*) plug; (= *hembra*) socket; (*en la pared*) point, socket
▸ **enchufe múltiple** adaptor
2 (*Téc*) (= *conexión*) joint; (= *manguito*) sleeve, jacket (*EEUU*)
3 (*) (= *puesto laboral*) cushy job*
4 (*) (= *influencia*) useful contact; **lo consiguió por ~s** he pulled strings to do it; **tener ~s** to have connections

enchufismo* SM string-pulling*, wirepulling (*EEUU**)

enchufista* SM/F person who can pull strings, wirepuller (*EEUU**)

encía SF gum

encíclica SF encyclical

enciclopedia SF encyclopaedia, encyclopedia

enciclopédico ADJ encyclopaedic, encyclopedic

encielar ▸conjug 1a◂ VT (*CAm, Cono Sur*) to roof, put a roof on

encierra SF (*Cono Sur*) 1 (= *acto*) penning (*of cattle, for slaughter*)
2 (= *pasto*) winter pasture

encierre SM (*Caribe*) penning (*of cattle, for slaughter*)

encierro SM 1 (*de manifestantes*) sit-in; (*en fábrica*) sit-in, work-in
2 (= *reclusión*) **nunca sale de su habitación, no hay quien la saque de su ~** she never leaves her room, no one can persuade her to come out
3 (*Taur*) (= *fiesta*) *running of the bulls*; (= *toril*) bull pen; → SANFERMINES
4 (†) (= *cárcel*) prison

encima ADV 1 (*en el espacio*) **allí está el cerro y ~ el castillo** you can see the hill there and the castle on top; **le puse un libro ~** I put a book on top of it; **déjelo ahí ~** leave it up there; **el gato se me sentó ~** the cat sat on me; **me he echado el café ~** I've spilt the coffee on myself; **~ de** (*con contacto*) on top of; (*sin contacto*) above; **déjalo ~ de la mesa** leave it on top of the table; **colgó el cuadro ~ del sofá** he hung the painting above the sofa; **llevar** *o* **tener algo ~**: **no llevaba ~ la documentación** I didn't have the papers on me; **nunca tiene dinero ~** he never has any money on him; **creo que ya tienes bastante ~** I think you've got enough on your plate; **venirse ~ de algn** [*animal, vehículo*] to come (straight) at sb, bear down on sb; [*peso, mueble*] to fall on (top of) sb; **el armario se le vino ~** the wardrobe fell on top of me; **no sabía lo que se le venía ~ cuando llegara a casa** he didn't know what was going to hit him when he got home; ✦*MODISMOS* **echarse a algn ~** (*LAm*) to get on the wrong side of sb; **con su actitud se echó ~ a todos sus compañeros** he got on the wrong side of all his colleagues because of his attitude; **echársele ~ a algn** (= *atrapar*) to catch up with sb; (= *criticar*) to come down (hard) on sb; **el Parlamento se le echó ~** Parliament came down (hard) on him; **estar ~ de algn** (= *estar pendiente*) to stand over sb; (*pey*) to be on someone's back*; **tengo que estar siempre ~ de mis hijos para que estudien** I always have to stand over my children to make them work; **tengo a mi jefe siempre ~** my boss is always on my back*; **hacerse ~** (*LAm euf*) ◊ **hacérselo ~** (*Esp euf*) (= *orinarse*) to wet o.s.; (= *defecar*) to mess o.s.; **poner a algn el dedo** *o* **la mano ~** to lay a finger on sb; **quitarse algo/a algn de ~** to get rid of sth/sb; **nos hemos quitado un gran problema de ~** that's a great problem out of the way for us; *ver tb* **mundo 5**
2 (*en el tiempo*) upon; **ya tenemos el invierno ~ otra vez** winter is upon us again; **tenían ya la guerra ~** war was imminent *o* upon them; **se nos echó la noche ~** it grew dark, night fell; **se nos viene ~ la fecha de la boda** the wedding is nearly upon us, the wedding is just around the corner
3 **por ~** 3·1 (= *por lo alto*) over; **le eché una manta por ~** I put a blanket over her; **el avión les pasó por ~** the plane passed overhead; **por ~ tiene a su jefe y al director** there's his boss and the director above him; **por ~ de** over; **el avión pasó rozando por ~ de la catedral** the plane skimmed over the top of the cathedral; **ha nevado por ~ de los 2.500m** there is snow above *o* over 2,500 metres; **estar por ~ de algo** (*en cantidad, nivel*) to be above sth; (*en preferencia*) to come before sth; **la asistencia estuvo por ~ de lo habitual** there was above average attendance; **no hay nadie por ~ de ella** there's no one above her; **estoy por ~ de él en categoría** I'm higher in rank *o* level than him; **eso está por ~ de mis posibilidades** that's beyond my means; **la felicidad está por ~ del dinero** happiness comes before money; **estar por ~ del bien y del mal** to be above the law; **por ~ de todo** above all; **quiero hacerlo por ~ de todo** I want to do it above all else; **la seguridad por ~ de todo** safety first
3·2 (= *superficialmente*) **hoy hemos limpiado muy por ~** we've just done a quick clean today; **hicimos una revisión por ~ del texto** we had a quick check on the text; **hojear algo por ~** to leaf through sth
4 (= *además*) on top of that; **y ~ no me dio ni las gracias** and on top of that he didn't even thank me; **te lo envían a casa y ~ te regalan un libro** they send it to your house and you get a free book too *o* as well; **le toca la lotería y ~ se queja** she wins the lottery and even then she complains; **~ de** besides, as well as; **y luego, ~ de todo lo que dijo, se fue sin disculparse** and then, as well as *o* on top of saying all that, he left without apologizing
5 (*esp Cono Sur*) **~ mío/tuyo/***etc* above me/you/*etc*; **está siempre ~ mío vigilando lo que hago** he's always on top of me watching everything I do

encimar ▸conjug 1a◂ Ⓐ VT 1 (*LAm**) to add as a bonus
2 (*Dep*) to mark
Ⓑ VI (*Naipes*) to add a new stake

encime SM (*Andes*) bonus, extra

encimera SF worktop, work surface

encimero ADJ top, upper

encina SF ilex, holm oak

encinar SM holm-oak wood

encinta ADJ pregnant; (*Zool*) with young; **mujer ~** pregnant woman; **dejar a una chica ~** to get a girl pregnant

encintado SM kerb, curb (*EEUU*)

encizañar ▸conjug 1a◂ Ⓐ VT to sow discord among, create trouble among
Ⓑ VI to sow discord, cause trouble

enclaustrar ▸conjug 1a◂ Ⓐ VT 1 (*Rel*) to cloister
2 (= *ocultar*) to hide away
Ⓑ **enclaustrarse** VPR (= *encerrarse*) to shut o.s. away; **se enclaustró en su cuarto para preparse los exámenes** he shut himself away in his room to prepare for the exams

enclavado ADJ (= *situado*) **las ruinas están enclavadas en un valle** the ruins are set deep in a valley

enclavar ▸conjug 1a◂ VT 1 (= *situar*) to place
2 (*Téc*) (= *clavar*) to nail; (= *traspasar*) to pierce, transfix
3 (= *empotrar*) to embed, set
4 (*) (= *engañar*) to swindle, con*

enclave SM enclave

enclavijar ▸conjug 1a◂ VT to peg, pin

enclencle ADJ (*LAm*) terribly thin

enclenco ADJ (*Andes, Caribe*) = **enclenque**

enclenque ADJ weak, sickly

enclítica SF enclitic

enclítico ADJ enclitic

enclocar ▸conjug 1g y 1l◂ VI, **encloquecer** ▸conjug 2d◂ VI to go broody

encobar ▸conjug 1a◂ VI, **encobarse** VPR [*gallina*] to brood

encocorante* ADJ annoying, maddening

encocorar* ▸conjug 1a◂ Ⓐ VT to annoy, madden
Ⓑ **encocorarse** VPR [1] (= *enojarse*) to get cross, get mad
[2] (*Caribe*) (= *sospechar*) to get suspicious
[3] (*Cono Sur*) to put on airs

encofrado SM (*Téc*) form, plank mould

encofrar ▸conjug 1a◂ VT to plank, timber

encoger ▸conjug 2c◂ Ⓐ VT [1] [+ *tejidos*] to shrink
[2] (= *acobardar*) to intimidate
Ⓑ VI [*tela*] to shrink
Ⓒ **encogerse** VPR [1] to shrink
[2] **~se de hombros** to shrug one's shoulders
[3] [*persona*] (= *acobardarse*) to cringe; (= *desanimarse*) to get discouraged

encogidamente ADV shyly, bashfully

encogido ADJ [1] [*tejido*] shrunken
[2] (= *tacaño*) stingy*
[3] (= *tímido*) shy, bashful

encogimiento SM [1] [*de tejidos*] shrinking
[2] ► **encogimiento de hombros** shrug (*of the shoulders*)
[3] (= *timidez*) shyness, bashfulness

encogollado* ADJ (*Cono Sur*) stuck-up*, snobbish

encogollarse* ▸conjug 1a◂ VPR (*Cono Sur*) to get conceited, be haughty

encohetarse ▸conjug 1a◂ VPR (*Andes, CAm*) to get furious

encojar ▸conjug 1a◂ Ⓐ VT to lame, cripple
Ⓑ **encojarse** VPR [1] (= *cojear*) to go lame*
[2] (= *fingir enfermedad*) to pretend to be ill

encojonarse** ▸conjug 1a◂ VPR (*CAm*) to fly off the handle*, explode

encolar ▸conjug 1a◂ VT (= *engomar*) to glue, paste; (= *pegar*) to stick down, stick together; (= *aprestar*) to size

encolerizar ▸conjug 1f◂ Ⓐ VT to anger, provoke
Ⓑ **encolerizarse** VPR to get angry

encomendar ▸conjug 1j◂ Ⓐ VT to entrust, commend (**a** to, to the charge of)
Ⓑ **encomendarse** VPR **~se a** to entrust o.s. to

encomendería SF (*Perú*) grocery store, grocer's

encomendero SM [1] (*Perú*) grocer; (*Caribe*) wholesale meat supplier
[2] (*LAm Hist*) *holder of an encomienda*

encomiable ADJ laudable, praiseworthy

encomiar ▸conjug 1b◂ VT to praise, pay tribute to

encomienda SF [1] (= *encargo*) charge, mission
[2] (= *elogio*) praise
[3] (= *protección*) protection
[4] (= *patrocinio*) patronage
[5] (*LAm*) (= *almacén*) warehouse
[6] (*LAm*) (= *paquete postal*) parcel ► **encomienda contra reembolso** parcel sent cash on delivery
[7] **encomiendas**†† regards, respects
[8] (*Hist*) *colonial grant of land and native inhabitants to a settler*
[9] (*Hist, Mil*) command (*of a military order*)

> **ENCOMIENDA**
>
> *The* **encomienda** *was a repressive system fixing the Spanish conquistadors' entitlement to labour and tribute from Indian communities. Although the Indians theoretically remained free subjects of the Spanish Crown, in practice they were enslaved to the* **encomenderos** *(those having* **encomienda** *rights). One of its most celebrated opponents was the Dominican friar and former* **encomendero** *Fray Bartolomé de Las Casas (1474-1566). In 1542, in response to protests from the Church, and fearful of the growing power of the* **encomenderos**, *Charles V brought in laws aimed at phasing out the system. The Spanish settlers rebelled, but the Crown held fast to the central principle that* **encomienda** *rights should not be hereditary.*

encomio SM praise, eulogy

encomioso ADJ (*LAm*) laudatory, eulogistic

enconadamente ADV angrily, bitterly

enconado ADJ [1] [*discusión*] bitter
[2] (*Med*) (= *inflamado*) inflamed; (= *dolorido*) sore

enconamiento SM (*Med*) inflammation, soreness

enconar ▸conjug 1a◂ Ⓐ VT [1] (= *encolerizar*) to anger, irritate
[2] (= *enfervorecer*) [+ *disputa*] to inflame, embitter; [+ *odio, rencor*] to inflame
[3] (*Med*) (= *inflamar*) to inflame
Ⓑ **enconarse** VPR [1] (= *encolerizarse*) to get angry, get irritated
[2] (= *enfervorecerse*) [*agravio*] to fester, rankle; [*disputa*] to become inflamed, become bitter; [*odio, rencor*] to become inflamed
[3] (*Med*) to become inflamed

enconcharse ▸conjug 1a◂ VPR (*psicológicamente*) to go into one's shell; (*físicamente*) to retire into seclusion

encono SM [1] (= *rencor*) rancour, rancor (*EEUU*), spite, spitefulness
[2] (= *mala voluntad*) bad blood
[3] (*Col, Méx*) inflammation, soreness

enconoso ADJ [1] (= *malévolo*) malevolent
[2] (*Med*) sensitive
[3] (*LAm*) [*planta*] poisonous

encontradizo ADJ met by chance; **hacerse el ~** to contrive an apparently chance meeting, manage to bump into sb

encontrado ADJ [*situación*] conflicting; [*posiciones*] opposite; **las posiciones siguen encontradas** their positions are still poles apart; **tienen sentimientos ~s sobre el aborto** they have mixed feelings on abortion

encontrar ▸conjug 1l◂ Ⓐ VT [1] (= *hallar buscando*) to find; **al final encontré la casa** I finally found the house; **ha encontrado trabajo** he has found work *o* a job; **no encuentro las llaves** I can't find the keys; **no encontramos ningún sitio para alojarnos** we couldn't find anywhere to stay; **no encuentro mi nombre en la lista** I can't find *o* see my name on the list; **ya no vas a ~ entradas** you won't get any tickets now
[2] (*por casualidad*) [+ *objeto, dinero*] to find, come across; [+ *persona*] to meet, run into; **han encontrado unos restos romanos** they have found some Roman remains; **acabo de ~ 50 euros** I've just found 50 euros; **le ~on un tumor** they found him to have a tumour, he was found to have a tumour; **encontró la muerte en un accidente de tráfico** he met his death in a road accident; **~ a algn haciendo algo** to find sb doing sth; **la encontré llamando por teléfono** I found her making a phone call; **cuando llegué a casa lo encontré durmiendo** when I got home I found him asleep
[3] [+ *oposición*] to meet with, encounter; [+ *problema*] to find, encounter, come across; **hasta el momento sus actividades no han encontrado oposición** so far their activities haven't met with *o* encountered any opposition; **no encontré oposición alguna para acceder a su despacho** no one tried to stop me from getting into his office; **~ dificultades** to encounter difficulties, run into trouble; **no encontramos ninguna dificultad para llegar hasta allí** we didn't have any trouble getting there
[4] (= *percibir*) to see; **no le encuentro sentido a lo que dices** I can't see the sense in what you're saying; **no le encuentro ninguna lógica a esta situación** I can't make any sense of this situation; **no sé lo que le encuentran** I don't know what they see in her
[5] (= *considerar*) to find; **¿encuentras el libro fácil de leer?** do you find the book easy to read?; **yo la encuentro bastante atractiva** I find her quite attractive; **¿cómo encontraste a tus padres después del viaje?** how did you find your parents after the trip?; **encuentro muy correctos sus comentarios** I think his comments are absolutely right; **¿qué tal me encuentras?** how do I look?; **te encuentro estupendamente** you look fantastic
Ⓑ **encontrarse** VPR [1] (= *descubrir*) to find; **¿qué te has encontrado?** what have you found?; **se ~on la casa llena de gente** they found the house full of people; **me los encontré llorando a los dos** I found both of them crying; **~se con**: **al llegar nos encontramos con la puerta cerrada** when we arrived we found the door locked; **~se con algo de pura casualidad** to come across sth by pure *o* sheer chance; **~se con que**: **me encontré con que no tenía gasolina** I found (that) I was out of petrol; **~se a sí mismo** to find oneself
[2] (= *coincidir*) to meet; **se ~on en Lisboa** they met in Lisbon; **este es el punto en el que se encuentran las dos calles** this is the point where the two streets meet; **~se a algn** to run into sb, meet sb; **~se con** [+ *persona*] to run into, meet; [+ *obstáculo, dificultad*] to run into, encounter; **me encontré con Isabel en el supermercado** I ran into *o* met Isabel in the supermarket; **me lo encontré por la calle de casualidad** I ran into *o* bumped into him in the street by chance; **nos encontramos con muchos problemas en la escalada** we encountered *o* ran into *o* came up against a lot of problems during the ascent
[3] (= *quedar citados*) to meet; **¿nos encontramos en el aeropuerto?** shall we meet at the airport?; **nos encontramos en un bar** we met in a bar; **quedamos en ~nos a las siete** we arranged to meet at seven
[4] (= *chocar*) [*vehículos*] to crash, collide; [*opiniones*] to clash; **al tomar la curva se encontró de frente con el camión** he collided head-on with the lorry when he went round the bend

[5] (= *estar*) to be; **me dijeron que no se encontraba en casa** I was told that she wasn't at home; **no se encuentra aquí en este momento** he's not here at the moment; **los dos heridos se encuentran en coma** the two injured people are in a coma; **el museo se encontraba vacío** the museum was empty; **el ayuntamiento se encuentra en el centro de la ciudad** the city hall is situated *o* is in the town centre; **este cuadro se encuentra entre los más famosos de Goya** this picture is one of Goya's most famous ones, this picture is amongst Goya's most famous ones
[6] (*de salud*) (= *estar*) to be; (= *sentirse*) to feel; **su familia se encuentra perfectamente** his family are all very well; **se encuentra enferma** she is ill; **¿te encuentras mejor?** are you feeling better?; **~se bien** to be well; **ahora me encuentro bien** I'm well now; **hoy no me encuentro bien** I don't feel well today; **~se mal** to feel ill; **me encuentro mal** I feel ill, I don't feel very well

encontronazo SM, **encontrón** SM collision, crash, fender-bender (*EEUU**)

encoñado‡ ADJ **estar ~ con algn** to have the hots for sb*; **estar ~ con algo** to be mad keen on sth

encoñamiento‡ SM (= *enamoramiento*) infatuation; (= *capricho*) whim

encoñar‡ ▸conjug 1a◂ Ⓐ VT [1] (= *alentar*) to lead on, draw on, raise (false) hopes in
[2] (= *enojar*) to upset
Ⓑ **encoñarse** VPR **~se con algn** to get the hots for sb*

encopetado ADJ [1] (= *emperifollado*) dressed to the nines*
[2] (= *señorial*) posh*, grand
[3] (= *altanero*) haughty

encopetarse ▸conjug 1a◂ VPR [1] (= *acicalarse*) to dress to the nines*
[2] (= *engreírse*) to get conceited, give o.s. airs

encorajar ▸conjug 1a◂ Ⓐ VT [1] (= *inflamar*) to inflame
[2] (= *animar*) to encourage, put heart into
Ⓑ **encorajarse** VPR to fly into a rage

encorajinar ▸conjug 1a◂ Ⓐ VT [1] (*LAm*) = **encorajar**
[2] (= *enfadar*) to anger, irritate
Ⓑ **encorajinarse** VPR [1] (= *enfadarse*) to fly into a rage
[2] (*Cono Sur*) [*trato*] to fail, go awry

encorar ▸conjug 1l◂ VT to cover with leather

encorbatado ADJ wearing a tie

encorchado SM [1] [*de botella*] corking
[2] [*de abejas*] hiving

encorchar ▸conjug 1a◂ VT [1] [+ *botella*] to cork
[2] [+ *abejas*] to hive

encordado SM [1] (*Boxeo*) ring
[2] (*Cono Sur Mús*) (= *cuerdas*) strings *pl*; (= *guitarra*) guitar

encordar ▸conjug 1l◂ Ⓐ VT [1] (*Mús*) to fit strings to
[2] (= *atar*) to bind, tie (with ropes)
[3] [+ *espacio, zona*] to rope off
Ⓑ **encordarse** VPR [*alpinistas*] to rope themselves together

encordelar ▸conjug 1a◂ VT to tie (with string)

encornado ADJ **un toro bien ~** a bull with good horns

encornadura SF horns *pl*

encornar ▸conjug 1l◂ VT to gore

encornudar ▸conjug 1a◂ VT to cuckold

encorralar ▸conjug 1a◂ VT to pen, corral

encorsetar ▸conjug 1a◂ VT to confine, put into a straitjacket

encorvada SF stoop, bend; **hacer la ~*** to malinger, pretend to be ill

encorvado ADJ (= *doblado*) curved, bent; (= *inclinado*) stooping; (= *torcido*) crooked; **andar ~** to walk with a stoop

encorvadura SF (= *curva*) curve, curvature; (= *torcedura*) bend

encorvar ▸conjug 1a◂ Ⓐ VT (= *doblar*) to bend, curve; (= *inclinar*) to bend down, bend over; (= *torcer*) to make crooked
Ⓑ **encorvarse** VPR [1] [*persona*] (= *doblarse*) to stoop; (= *inclinarse*) to bend down, bend over, stoop; (= *torcerse*) to buckle
[2] (= *combarse*) to sag

encrespado ADJ [*pelo*] curly; [*mar*] choppy

encrespador SM curling tongs *pl*

encrespar ▸conjug 1a◂ Ⓐ VT [1] (= *rizar*) [+ *pelo*] to curl; [+ *plumas*] to ruffle; [+ *agua*] to ripple; [+ *mar*] to make rough
[2] (= *irritar*) to anger, irritate
Ⓑ **encresparse** VPR [1] (= *rizarse*) [*pelo*] to curl; [*agua*] to ripple; [*mar*] to get rough
[2] (= *irritarse*) to get cross, get irritated

encrestado ADJ haughty

encriptar ▸conjug 1a◂ VT (*Inform*) to encrypt

encrucijada SF (= *cruce*) crossroads; (= *empalme*) intersection; **poner a algn en la ~** to put sb on the spot; **estamos en la ~** we are at a crossroads

encuadernación SF [1] binding ► **encuadernación en cuero** leather binding ► **encuadernación en pasta** hardback (binding) ► **encuadernación en piel** cloth binding ► **encuadernación en tela** cloth binding
[2] (= *taller*) binder's

encuadernador(a) SM/F bookbinder

encuadernar ▸conjug 1a◂ VT to bind; **libro sin ~** unbound book

encuadrable ADJ **~ en** that can be placed in, that can be included in

encuadramiento SM [1] (= *acto*) framing
[2] (= *encuadre*) frame, framework

encuadrar ▸conjug 1a◂ Ⓐ VT [1] [+ *pintura*] to put in a frame, frame
[2] (= *clasificar*) to place, classify
[3] (= *abarcar*) to contain
[4] (*LAm*) (= *resumir*) to summarize, give a synthesis of
[5] (*Fot*) to frame; **la foto está mal encuadrada** the composition of the photo is poor
[6] (= *encajar*) to fit, insert (**en** into)
Ⓑ VI (*Cono Sur*) to fit, square (**con** with)

encuadre SM (*Fot*) setting, background, frame; (*fig*) setting

encuartar ▸conjug 1a◂ (*Méx*) Ⓐ VT [+ *ganado*] to tie up, rope
Ⓑ **encuartarse** VPR [1] [*animal*] to shy, balk
[2] (= *implicarse*) to get involved, get bogged down (**en** in)
[3] (= *interrumpir*) to butt in

encuartelar ▸conjug 1a◂ VT (*LAm*) to billet, put in barracks

encubierta SF fraud

encubierto Ⓐ PP *de* **encubrir**
Ⓑ ADJ (= *oculto*) hidden; (= *turbio*) underhand; (= *secreto*) undercover; [*crítica*] veiled

encubridor(a) Ⓐ ADJ concealing
Ⓑ SM/F [*de delito*] accessory (after the fact); [*de objeto robado*] receiver, fence*; **lo acusaron de ~ del homicidio** he was accused of helping to cover up the murder

encubrimiento SM [*de delito*] covering up; [*de objeto robado*] receiving; **se le acusó de ~** he was accused of being part of the cover-up operation, he was charged with being an accessory after the fact (*frm*)

encubrir ▸conjug 3a◂ (*pp* **encubierto**) VT [1] (*gen*) (= *ocultar*) to hide
[2] (*Jur*) [+ *delincuente*] to harbour, harbor (*EEUU*); [+ *delito*] to cover up
[3] (= *ayudar*) to be an accomplice in

encucurucharse* ▸conjug 1a◂ VPR (*Andes, CAm*) to get up on top, reach the top

encuentro SM [1] (= *reunión*) meeting; **un ~ fortuito** a chance meeting; **su primer ~ con la policía** his first encounter with the police ► **encuentro cumbre** summit meeting ► **encuentro de escritores** (small) congress of writers ► **encuentro en la cumbre** summit meeting
[2] **ir** *o* **salir al ~ de algn** to go to meet sb; **ir al ~ de lo desconocido** to go out to face the unknown
[3] (*Mil*) (= *enfrentamiento*) encounter; (= *escaramuza*) skirmish
[4] (*Dep*) (= *partido*) match ► **encuentro de ida** first leg ► **encuentro de vuelta** return leg
[5] (*Aut*) collision, crash
[6] [*de opiniones*] clash
[7] ✦***MODISMOS*** **llevarse a algn de ~** (*Caribe, Méx**) (= *arruinar*) to drag sb down, ruin sb; **llevarse todo de ~** (*Caribe**) to ride roughshod over everyone

encuerada* SF (*Caribe, Méx*) = **encuerista**

encuerado* ADJ (*Caribe, Méx*) (= *harapiento*) ragged; (= *desnudo*) nude, naked, starkers*

encuerar* ▸conjug 1a◂ Ⓐ VT (*LAm*) [1] (= *desnudar*) to strip, strip naked
[2] (= *dejar sin dinero*) to skin, fleece
Ⓑ **encuerarse** VPR [1] (*LAm*) (= *desnudarse*) to strip off, get undressed
[2] (*Caribe*) (= *vivir juntos*) to live together

encueratriz* SF (*Méx*) = **encuerista**

encuerista* SF (*Caribe, Méx*) striptease artiste, stripper

encuesta SF [1] (= *sondeo*) opinion poll, survey ► **encuesta de población activa** (*Esp*) *quarterly survey of the labour market, carried out by national statistics office* ► **Encuesta Gallup** Gallup Poll ► **encuesta por teléfono** telephone poll
[2] (= *pesquisa*) inquiry, investigation (**de** into); ► **encuesta judicial** post mortem

encuestador(a) SM/F pollster

encuestar ▸conjug 1a◂ VT to poll, take a poll of; **el 69 por 100 de los encuestados** 69% of those polled

encuetarse‡ ▸conjug 1a◂ VPR (*CAm*) to fly off the handle*, lose one's temper

encuitarse ▸conjug 1a◂ VPR [1] (*liter*) (= *afligirse*) to grieve
[2] (*Andes*) (= *endeudarse*) to get into debt

encujado SM (*Caribe*) framework, lattice

enculebrarse: ▸conjug 1a◂ VPR (*CAm*) to fly off the handle*, lose one's temper

enculecarse ▸conjug 1g◂ VPR (*LAm*) to go broody

encumbrado ADJ [1] [*persona*] exalted, haughty (*pey*) [2] [*edificio*] towering, high

encumbramiento SM [1] (= *acción*) raising, elevation
[2] (= *exaltación*) exaltation, eminence; (= *altanería*) haughtiness
[3] (= *altura*) height, loftiness

encumbrar ▸conjug 1a◂ Ⓐ VT [1] (= *alzar*) to raise, elevate
[2] (= *ensalzar*) to extol, exalt
Ⓑ **encumbrarse** VPR [1] [*edificio*] to rise, tower
[2] (= *engreírse*) to be proud, be haughty; **~se sobre algn** to be far superior to sb

encurdelarse: ▸conjug 1a◂ VPR (*Cono Sur*) to get sloshed*

encurrucarse* ▸conjug 1g◂ VPR (*LAm*) (*en cuclillas*) to squat, crouch; (*formando un ovillo*) to curl up (*in a ball*)

encurtidos SMPL pickles

encurtir ▸conjug 3a◂ VT to pickle

ende ADV **por ~** (*frm*) hence (*frm*), therefore

endeble ADJ [*persona*] feeble, weak; [*argumento, excusa*] feeble, flimsy

endeblez SF [*de persona*] weakness, frailty; [*de argumento, excusa*] flimsiness

endecasílabo Ⓐ ADJ hendecasyllabic
Ⓑ SM hendecasyllable

endecha SF lament, dirge

endecharse ▸conjug 1a◂ VPR to grieve, mourn

endémico ADJ [*enfermedad*] endemic; [*mal*] rife, chronic

endemoniado ADJ [1] (= *poseído*) possessed (of the devil)
[2] (= *travieso*) devilish, fiendish; (= *perverso*) perverse; (= *furioso*) furious, wild

endemoniar ▸conjug 1b◂ Ⓐ VT [1] (= *endiablar*) to bedevil
[2] (= *provocar*) to provoke
Ⓑ **endemoniarse** VPR (*) to get angry

endenantes* ADV (*LAm*) (= *hace algún tiempo*) a short time back; (= *antes*) earlier, before

endentar ▸conjug 1j◂ VT, VI (*Mec*) to engage, mesh (**con** with)

endentecer ▸conjug 2d◂ VI to teethe, cut one's teeth

enderezado ADJ (= *adecuado*) appropriate; (= *propicio*) favourable, favorable (*EEUU*)

enderezar ▸conjug 1f◂ Ⓐ VT [1] [+ *cable, alambre*] (= *poner derecho*) to straighten out, straighten up; (= *destorcer*) to unbend
[2] (= *poner vertical*) (*gen*) to set upright, stand vertically; (*Náut*) to right; [+ *vehículo*] to stand the right way up, put back on its wheels, straighten up
[3] (= *arreglar*) to put in order
[4] (= *dirigir*) to direct; **las medidas están enderezadas a** *o* **para corregirlo** the measures are designed to correct it
[5] (*en conducta*) **~ a algn** to correct sb's faults
Ⓑ **enderezarse** VPR [1] (= *ponerse recto*) to straighten up, draw o.s. up; (*Náut*) to right itself; (*Aer*) to flatten out
[2] **~se a un lugar** to set out for a place
[3] **~se a hacer algo** to take steps to do sth

Endesa SF ABR (*Esp*) = **Empresa Nacional de Electricidad, Sociedad Anónima**

endespués ADV (*Andes, Caribe*) = **después**

endeudamiento SM indebtedness, (extent of) debt

endeudarse ▸conjug 1a◂ VPR to get into debt (**con** with); **~ con algn** (*fig*) to become indebted to sb

endeveras ADV (*LAm*) = **veras 2**

endiabladamente ADV **~ difícil** devilish(ly) difficult

endiablado ADJ [1] (= *diabólico*) devilish, diabolical
[2] (= *travieso*) impish, mischievous
[3] (= *feo*) ugly
[4] (= *enfadado*) furious
[5] (= *difícil*) [*problema*] tricky; [*carretera*] difficult, dangerous

endiablar ▸conjug 1a◂ Ⓐ VT [1] (= *endemoniar*) to bedevil, bewitch
[2] (= *corromper*) to pervert, corrupt
Ⓑ **endiablarse** VPR to get furious

endibia SF endive, chicory (*EEUU*)

endija SF (*LAm*) = **rendija**

endilgar* ▸conjug 1h◂ VT **~ algo a algn: le endilgó una patada en el vientre** she kicked him in the stomach; **papá nos endilgó una insoportable disertación política** Dad gave us an unbearable lecture on politics; **siempre me endilgan los peores trabajos** I always get landed *o* saddled with the worst jobs*; **le han endilgado el sambenito de holgazán** they've labelled him as lazy

endiñar* ▸conjug 1a◂ VT [1] [+ *golpe*] **le endiñó un puñetazo** he thumped him one*; **le endiñó una patada en el culo** she booted him up the backside*
[2] = **endilgar**

endiosado ADJ stuck-up*, conceited

endiosamiento SM (= *engreimiento*) vanity, conceit; (= *altanería*) haughtiness

endiosar ▸conjug 1a◂ Ⓐ VT to deify; (*fig*) to make a god out of
Ⓑ **endiosarse** VPR [1] (= *engreírse*) to get conceited, give o.s. airs
[2] **~se en algo** to become absorbed in sth

enditarse ▸conjug 1a◂ VPR (*LAm*) to get into debt

endocrina SF (*tb* **glándula ~**) endocrine, endocrine gland

endocrino ADJ endocrine *antes de s*

endodoncia SF endodontics *sing*

endogamia SF inbreeding; **engendrado por ~** inbred

endógeno ADJ endogenous

endomingado ADJ in one's Sunday best

endomingarse ▸conjug 1h◂ VPR to put on one's Sunday best

endomorfo SM endomorph

endorfina SF endorphin

endorsar ▸conjug 1a◂ = **endosar**

endosante SMF endorser

endosar ▸conjug 1a◂ VT [1] [+ *cheque*] to endorse, back
[2] (= *confirmar*) to confirm
[3] (*) **~ algo a algn** to lumber sb with sth*

endosatario/a SM/F endorsee

endoso SM endorsement; **sin ~** unendorsed

endriago SM fabulous monster, dragon

endrina SF sloe

endrino SM blackthorn, sloe

endrogarse ▸conjug 1h◂ VPR (*Andes, Méx*) to get into debt

endulzante SM sweetener

endulzar ▸conjug 1f◂ VT to sweeten

endurecer ▸conjug 2d◂ Ⓐ VT [1] [+ *material, sustancia*] (= *poner duro*) to harden; (= *hacer más resistente*) to toughen; **un barniz que endurece las uñas** a varnish that hardens your nails; **el proceso de estiramiento endurece el metal** the drawing process toughens the metal; **ejercicios para ~ los músculos** exercises to strengthen the muscles
[2] [+ *persona*] (= *curtir*) to toughen up; (= *volver insensible*) to harden; **la vida del campo lo ~á** life in the country will toughen him up; **los años que pasó en la cárcel lo endurecieron** the years he spent in prison hardened him
[3] (*Jur*) [+ *ley*] to tighten, tighten up; [+ *pena, castigo*] to make more severe; **han endurecido la política antiterrorista** they've taken a tougher anti-terrorist line, they're toughening up on terrorism; **los sindicatos han endurecido su postura** the unions have taken a tougher stance; **proponen ~ las medidas contra el fraude** they're proposing to take tougher *o* firmer measures against fraud; **el gobierno ha endurecido los controles** the government has tightened (up) controls
Ⓑ **endurecerse** VPR [1] [*material, sustancia*] (= *ponerse duro*) to harden, get hard; (= *hacerse más resistente*) to toughen
[2] [*persona*] (= *curtirse*) to toughen up; (= *volverse insensible*) to harden, become hardened; **se le ha endurecido el corazón** he's become hardened *o* hard-hearted

endurecido ADJ [1] [*material, sustancia*] hardened, caked
[2] [*persona*] (= *curtido*) toughened; (= *insensible*) hardened

endurecimiento SM [1] (= *acto*) hardening; **el ~ de las arterias** the hardening of the arteries
[2] [*de persona*] (*por curtirse*) toughening up; (*por insensibilidad*) hardening

ENE ABR (= **estenordeste**) ENE

ene SF (name of the letter) N; **supongamos que hay ~ objetos** let us suppose there are X (number of) objects

ene. ABR (= **enero**) Jan

enea SF = **anea**

Eneas SM Aeneas

enebro SM juniper

Eneida SF Aeneid

enema SF enema

enemiga SF (= *enemistad*) enmity, hostility; (= *mala voluntad*) ill-will

enemigo/a Ⓐ ADJ enemy, hostile; (= *poco amistoso*) unfriendly; **ser ~ de algo** to be inimical to sth; **una actitud enemiga de todo progreso** an attitude inimical to all progress
Ⓑ SM/F (*gen*) enemy; (= *adversario*) foe, opponent; **pasarse al ~** to go over to the enemy
► **enemigo infiltrado, enemigo interior** enemy within

enemistad SF enmity

enemistar ▸conjug 1a◂ Ⓐ VT to make enemies of, cause a rift between
Ⓑ **enemistarse** VPR to become enemies; **~se**

con algn to fall out with sb, have a falling out with sb (*EEUU*)

energético ADJ [1] [*política*] energy *antes de s*; **la crisis energética** the energy crisis
[2] (= *vigorizante*) [*bebida, comida*] energy *antes de s*; [*componente*] energy-giving
[3] (= *vigoroso*) energetic
[4] (*LAm*) = **enérgico**

energía SF [1] (= *fuerza*) energy, drive; **obrar con ~** to act energetically; **reaccionar con ~** to react vigorously
[2] (*Téc*) power, energy ► **energía(s) alternativa(s)** alternative energy *sing* ► **energía atómica** atomic power ► **energía eléctrica** electric power, electricity ► **energía eólica** wind power ► **energía hidráulica** hydraulic power ► **energía nuclear** nuclear power ► **energía renovable** renewable energy ► **energía solar** solar power

enérgicamente ADV [*condenar, defender*] forcefully, vigorously; [*desmentir*] emphatically, vigorously; [*resistir*] strenuously; [*actuar*] boldly; **un proceso rentable energéticamente** an energy-efficient process

enérgico ADJ [*persona*] energetic, vigorous; [*gesto, habla, tono*] emphatic; [*esfuerzo*] determined; [*ejercicio*] strenuous; [*campaña*] vigorous, high-pressure; [*medida, golpe*] bold, drastic; [*ataque*] vigorous, strong; [*protesta*] forceful; **realizó su protesta de manera enérgica** he made his protest forcefully; **ponerse ~ con algn** to get tough with sb

energizar ▸conjug 1f◂ VT to energize

energúmeno/a SM/F [1] (= *loco*) madman/madwoman; **ponerse como un ~*** to get mad
[2] (= *gritón*) loud and irascible person
[3] (*Pol*) fanatic, extremist
[4] (= *poseso*) person possessed of the devil

enero SM January; *ver tb* **septiembre**

enervador ADJ, **enervante** ADJ enervating

enervar ▸conjug 1a◂ VT (= *debilitar*) to enervate, weaken; (= *poner nervioso a*) to get on sb's nerves

enésimo ADJ [1] (*Mat*) n^{th}; **elevado a la enésima potencia** (*lit*) raised to the nth power; (*fig*) to the nth degree
[2] (*fig*) **por enésima vez** for the umpteenth time, for the nth time

enfadadizo ADJ irritable, crotchety

enfadar ▸conjug 1a◂ Ⓐ VT [1] (= *irritar*) to anger, irritate
[2] (= *ofender*) to offend; **enfadé a mi madre porque no me gustó su comida** I offended my mother because I didn't like her cooking
[3] (*LAm*) (= *aburrir*) to bore
Ⓑ **enfadarse** VPR [1] (= *irritarse*) to get annoyed, get angry, get cross (**con** with; **por, de** about, at); **no te enfades con él, lo ha hecho sin intención** don't be cross *o* angry with him, he didn't mean to do it; **no te enfades, pero creo que lo has hecho mal** don't get offended, but I think you've done it wrong; **de nada sirve ~te** it's no good getting cross; **se enfadó con su novio** she fell out with her boyfriend; **se enfada por nada** he gets angry at the slightest thing
[2] (*LAm*) (= *aburrirse*) to be bored, get bored

enfado SM annoyance, anger

enfadoso ADJ (= *molesto*) annoying; (= *pesado*) tedious

enfajillar ▸conjug 1a◂ VT (*CAm, Méx Correos*) to put a wrapper on

enfangar ▸conjug 1h◂ Ⓐ VT to cover with mud
Ⓑ **enfangarse** VPR [1] (= *enlodarse*) to get muddy, get covered in mud
[2] (= *implicarse*) to dirty one's hands; **~se en el vicio** to wallow in vice

enfardado SM baling

enfardadora SF (*Agr*) baler, baling machine

enfardar ▸conjug 1a◂ VT to bale

énfasis SM [1] (*en la entonación*) emphasis; **hablar con ~** to speak emphatically; **poner el ~ en** to stress
[2] (= *insistencia*) stress

enfático ADJ emphatic; **dijo, ~** he said emphatically

enfatizar ▸conjug 1f◂ VT to emphasize, stress

enfebrecidamente ADV feverishly

enfebrecido ADJ feverish

enfermar ▸conjug 1a◂ Ⓐ VT (*Med*) to make ill; **su actitud me enferma** her attitude makes me sick
Ⓑ VI to fall ill, be taken ill (**de** with); **~ del corazón** to develop heart trouble **enfermarse** VPR (*esp LAm*) to fall ill, be taken ill (**de** with)

ENFERMEDAD

¿"Illness" o "disease"?

Enfermedad tiene dos traducciones principales en inglés: **illness** y **disease**.

• Lo traducimos por **illness** cuando no concretamos la enfermedad de la que se trata, y también cuando se refiere al tiempo que una persona está enferma:

Su enfermedad no le permite llevar una vida normal
Her illness prevents her from living a normal life

Adelgazó mucho durante su enfermedad
She lost a lot of weight during her illness

• Lo traducimos por **disease** cuando nos referimos a una enfermedad infecciosa, a una enfermedad en concreto o a un tipo específico de enfermedad:

Este tipo de enfermedad venérea es muy común
This type of venereal disease is very common

...mineros que sufren de enfermedades de pulmón...
...miners suffering from lung diseases...

Para otros usos y ejemplos ver la entrada.

enfermedad SF [1] (= *estado*) illness, sickness; **durante esta ~** during this illness; **ausentarse por ~** to be off sick; *ver tb* **baja 3**
[2] (*en concreto*) (*gen*) illness, disease; (= *mal*) complaint, malady; **una ~ muy peligrosa** a very dangerous disease; **pegar*** *o* **contagiar una ~ a algn** to give sb a disease ► **enfermedad contagiosa** contagious disease ► **enfermedad de Alzheimer** Alzheimer's (disease) ► **enfermedad de declaración obligatoria** notifiable disease ► **enfermedad degenerativa** degenerative disease ► **enfermedad de la descompresión** decompression sickness ► **enfermedad de la piel** skin disease ► **enfermedad del legionario** legionnaire's disease ► **enfermedad del sueño** sleeping sickness ► **enfermedad de transmisión sexual** sexually transmitted disease ► **enfermedad hereditaria** hereditary disease ► **enfermedad holandesa del olmo** Dutch elm disease ► **enfermedad profesional** occupational disease ► **enfermedad terminal** terminal illness ► **enfermedad transmisible** contagious disease ► **enfermedad transmitida por virus** viral infection ► **enfermedad venérea** venereal disease

enfermería SF [1] (= *hospital*) infirmary
[2] (= *estudios*) nursing
[3] (*en centro escolar*) sick bay

enfermero/a SM/F (*en hospital*) male nurse/nurse; (*Mil*) medical orderly; ► **enfermero/a ambulante** visiting nurse ► **enfermero/a jefe/a** head nurse

enfermizo ADJ [*persona*] sickly; [*mente*] morbid; [*pasión*] morbid, unhealthy

enfermo/a Ⓐ ADJ [1] ill, sick, unwell; **~ de amor** lovesick; **estar ~ de gravedad** *o* **peligro** to be seriously *o* dangerously ill; **caer** *o* **ponerse ~** to fall ill (**de** with); ✦***MODISMO*** **~ del chape** *o* **mate** (*Cono Sur*) crazy
[2] **estar ~** (= *encarcelado*) (*Cono Sur**) to be in jail
[3] (*Cono Sur**) **es ~ de malo** it's terribly bad; **es enferma de loca** she's clean crazy*
Ⓑ SM/F (*gen*) sick person; (*en hospital*) patient ► **enfermo/a terminal** terminal patient, terminally ill person

enfermoso ADJ (*LAm*) = **enfermizo**

enfervorizar ▸conjug 1f◂ VT to arouse, arouse fervour *o* (*EEUU*) fervor in

enfeudar ▸conjug 1a◂ VT (*Hist*) to enfeoff; **~ a algn de una propiedad** to grant sb (the freehold of) a property

enfiestarse ▸conjug 1a◂ VPR (*LAm*) to have a good time

enfilada SF enfilade

enfilar ▸conjug 1a◂ VT [1] (*Mil*) to rake with fire
[2] (= *colocar en fila*) to line up, put in a row
[3] (= *ensartar*) to thread
[4] [+ *calle*] to go straight along, go straight down; **el piloto trató de ~ la pista** the pilot tried to line up with the runway
[5] (= *apuntar*) [+ *pistola, cañón*] to aim, train on
[6] (*) (= *dirigir*) [+ *tema, asunto*] to direct; **el gobierno ya tiene enfilada la nueva ley de televisión digital** the government has already got the new act on digital TV ready
[7] (*) (= *coger manía a*) **tener enfilado a algn** to have it in for sb*

enfisema SM emphysema

enflaquecer ▸conjug 2d◂ Ⓐ VT (= *adelgazar*) to make thin; (= *debilitar*) to weaken, sap the strength of
Ⓑ VI, **enflaquecerse** VPR [1] (= *adelgazar*) to get thin, lose weight
[2] [*esfuerzo*] to flag
[3] (= *desanimarse*) to lose heart

enflaquecido ADJ thin

enflaquecimiento SM [1] (= *adelgazamiento*) loss of weight
[2] (= *debilitamiento*) weakening

enflatarse ▸conjug 1a◂ VPR [1] (*LAm*) (= *entristecerse*) to become depressed
[2] (*Caribe, Méx*) (= *enfadarse*) to become bad tempered

enflautada* SF (*Andes, CAm*) blunder

enflautado ADJ pompous

enflautar* ▸conjug 1a◂ VT (*LAm*) **~ algo a algn** to unload sth on to sb

enfocar ▸conjug 1g◂ Ⓐ VT [1] (*Fot*) to focus (**a, sobre** on)
[2] [+ *cuestión, problema*] to consider, look at; **podemos ~ este problema de tres maneras** we can approach this problem in three ways; **no me gusta su modo de ~ la cuestión** I don't like his approach to the question
Ⓑ VI, **enfocarse** VPR to focus (**a, sobre** on)

enfollonado* ADJ (= *confuso*) muddled, confused

enfollonarse* ▸conjug 1a◂ VPR to get muddled, get confused

enfoque SM [1] (*Fot*) (= *acción*) focusing; (= *resultado*) focus
[2] [*de tema*] approach
[3] **potencia de ~** magnifying power

enfoscar ▸conjug 1g◂ Ⓐ VT [+ *pared*] to fill with mortar
Ⓑ **enfoscarse** VPR [1] (= *malhumorarse*) to sulk, be sullen
[2] **~se en** to get absorbed in, get up to one's eyes in
[3] [*cielo*] to cloud over, become overcast

enfrascar ▸conjug 1g◂ Ⓐ VT to bottle
Ⓑ **enfrascarse** VPR **~se en un libro** to bury o.s. in a book; **~se en un problema** to get deeply involved in a problem; **se enfrascó en su laboratorio** he buried *o* hid himself away in his laboratory

enfrenar ▸conjug 1a◂ VT [1] (= *frenar*) [+ *caballo*] to bridle; (*Mec*) to brake
[2] (= *reprimir*) to curb, restrain

enfrentamiento SM (= *conflicto*) confrontation; (= *encuentro*) (face to face) encounter, (face to face) meeting; (*Dep*) encounter

enfrentar ▸conjug 1a◂ Ⓐ VT [1] (= *enemistar*) to set against; **la herencia enfrentó a los dos hermanos** the inheritance set the two brothers against each other *o* at loggerheads
[2] (= *afrontar*) [+ *dificultad*] to face (up to), confront; [+ *realidad*] to face (up to); **tienes que ~ el problema** you have to face (up to) *o* confront the problem
[3] (= *encarar*) **este partido ~á a los dos mejores tenistas** this match will bring together the two best tennis players, this match will bring the two best tennis players face to face
Ⓑ **enfrentarse** VPR [1] (= *pelear*) [*personas*] to have a confrontation; [*equipos*] to face each other; **Juan y su padre se ~on durante la comida** Juan and his father had a confrontation over lunch; **hoy se enfrentan el Madrid y el Barcelona** today Madrid and Barcelona are facing each other
[2] **~se a** *o* **con** [2·1] [+ *persona*] to confront; **se enfrentó a sus secuestradores** he confronted his kidnappers; **se ~on al enemigo** they faced *o* confronted the enemy; **la selección de España se enfrentó a la de Italia** the Spanish team came up against *o* faced the Italian team
[2·2] [+ *problema, dificultad*] to face (up to), confront; **se niega a ~se a la realidad** he refuses to face (up to) reality; **hay que ~se con el peligro** we have to face up to the danger

enfrente ADV [1] (= *en el lado opuesto*) opposite; **Luisa estaba sentada ~** Luisa was sitting opposite; **de ~** opposite; **la casa de ~** the house opposite, the house across the road; **~ de** opposite (to); **mi casa está ~ del colegio** my house is opposite the school, my house is across the road from the school; **se sentó ~ mío/tuyo** (*esp LAm**) he sat down opposite *o* facing me/you
[2] (= *delante*) in front; **te espero ~ del cine** I'll wait for you in front of the cinema

enfriadera SF cooling jar

enfriadero SM cold storage, cold room

enfriado SM cooling, chilling

enfriador SM cooler, cooling plant

enfriamiento SM [1] (= *acción*) [*de líquido*] (*gen*) cooling; (*en nevera*) refrigeration
[2] [*de pasión, entusiasmo, relaciones*] cooling
[3] (*Econ*) cooling-down
[4] (= *catarro*) cold, chill

enfriar ▸conjug 1c◂ Ⓐ VT [1] (= *refrescar*) [+ *vino, refresco*] to cool, chill; [+ *sopa, motor*] to cool down
[2] (= *quitar fuerza a*) [+ *pasión, economía*] to cool down; [+ *entusiasmo*] to dampen, cool
[3] (*LAm**) (= *matar*) to kill, bump off*
Ⓑ **enfriarse** VPR [1] (= *refrescarse*) [*alimentos*] (*lo suficiente*) to cool down, cool off; (*demasiado*) to get cold; **déjalo que se enfríe** leave it to cool (down); **se te va a ~ el café** your coffee's going to get cold
[2] (= *perder fuerza*) [*pasión*] to cool off; [*entusiasmo, relaciones*] to cool
[3] (*Med*) to catch a chill

enfrijolarse ▸conjug 1a◂ VPR (*Méx*) [*negocio*] to get messed up, fall through

enfullinarse ▸conjug 1a◂ VPR (*Cono Sur*) to get angry

enfundar ▸conjug 1a◂ Ⓐ VT [1] (= *guardar*) [+ *espada*] to sheathe; [+ *gafas, violín*] to put in its case; [+ *diente*] to cap
[2] (= *llenar*) to fill, stuff (**de** with)
[3] (*) [+ *comida*] to scoff*, wolf*
Ⓑ **enfundarse** VPR **se enfundó la capa** he wrapped himself (up) in his cape; **una señora enfundada en visón** a lady swathed in mink

enfurecer ▸conjug 2d◂ Ⓐ VT to enrage, madden
Ⓑ **enfurecerse** VPR [1] [*persona*] to get furious, fly into a rage
[2] [*mar*] to get rough

enfurruñarse* ▸conjug 1a◂ VPR [1] (= *enfadarse*) to get angry, get cross
[2] (= *ponerse mohino*) to sulk
[3] [*cielo*] to cloud over

engaitar* ▸conjug 1a◂ VT **~ a algn** to talk sb round

engajado ADJ (*Andes*) curly

engalanar ▸conjug 1a◂ Ⓐ VT to adorn, deck (**de** with)
Ⓑ **engalanarse** VPR to adorn o.s., dress up

engallado ADJ (= *arrogante*) arrogant, haughty; (= *confiado*) confident; (= *jactancioso*) boastful

engallinar ▸conjug 1a◂ VT (*LAm*) to cow, intimidate

enganchado* ADJ **estar ~ a la droga** to be hooked on drugs*

enganchar ▸conjug 1a◂ Ⓐ VT [1] (= *conectar con gancho*) (*gen*) to hook; [+ *caballo*] to harness; [+ *carro, remolque*] to hitch up; (*Mec*) to couple, connect; [+ *dos vagones*] to couple up
[2] (*) (= *atrapar*) to nab*; **lo enganchó la policía robando en la joyería** the police nabbed him robbing the jeweller's*
[3] (*) (= *atraer*) [+ *persona*] to rope in; [+ *marido*] to land; **a mi no me enganchan para cuidar a los niños** they're not going to rope me into looking after the children; **los programas que más enganchan** the programmes which get most people hooked
[4] (*Mil*) to recruit
[5] (*Méx*) [+ *trabajadores*] to contract
Ⓑ **engancharse** VPR [1] (= *quedarse prendido*) to get hooked up, catch (**en** on); (*Mec*) to engage (**en** with); **el vestido se enganchó en un clavo** the dress got caught on a nail; **~se a la droga*** to get hooked on drugs*, become addicted to drugs
[2] (*Mil*) to enlist, join up

enganche SM [1] (= *acto*) (*gen*) hooking, hooking up; [*de remolque*] hitching; (*Mec*) coupling, connection; (*Ferro*) coupling
[2] (= *mecanismo*) hook
[3] (*Mil*) (= *reclutamiento*) recruitment, enlistment; (= *pago*) bounty
[4] (*Méx Com*) (= *depósito*) deposit, initial payment
[5] (*Telec*) connection
[6] (*Caribe*) (= *trabajo*) job

enganchón SM tear

engañabobos Ⓐ SMF INV (= *persona*) trickster
Ⓑ SM (= *trampa*) trick, trap

engañadizo ADJ gullible

engañador(a) Ⓐ ADJ [*persona*] deceiving, cheating; [*cosa*] deceptive
Ⓑ SM/F (= *impostor*) impostor

engañapichanga* SF (*Arg*) swindle, hoax, fraud

engañar ▸conjug 1a◂ Ⓐ VT [1] [+ *persona*] (= *embaucar*) to deceive, trick; (= *despistar*) to mislead; (*con promesas, esperanzas*) to delude; (= *estafar*) to cheat, swindle; **engaña a su mujer** he's unfaithful to his wife, he's cheating on his wife; **a mí no me engaña nadie** you can't fool me; **no te dejes ~** don't let yourself be taken in; **logró ~ al inspector** he managed to trick the inspector
[2] **necesito picar algo para ~ el hambre** I need to nibble at sth to stop me feeling hungry; **~ el tiempo** to kill time
Ⓑ VI to be deceptive; ✦**REFRÁN las apariencias engañan** appearances are misleading
Ⓒ **engañarse** VPR [1] (= *equivocarse*) to be wrong, be mistaken; **en eso te engañas** you're wrong there
[2] (= *ocultarse la verdad*) to delude o.s., fool o.s.; **no te engañes** don't kid yourself

engañifa* SF trick, swindle

engañito SM (*Cono Sur*) small gift, token

engaño SM [1] (= *acto*) (*gen*) deception; (= *ilusión*) delusion; **todo es ~** it's all a sham; **llamarse a ~** to protest that one has been cheated; **que nadie se llame a ~** let nobody say he wasn't warned; **aquí no hay ~** there is no attempt to deceive anybody here, it's all on the level*
[2] (= *trampa*) trick, swindle
[3] (= *malentendido*) mistake, misunderstanding; **padecer ~** to labour under a misunderstanding, labor under a misunderstanding (*EEUU*); **no haya ~** let there be no mistake about it
[4] **engaños** (= *astucia*) wiles, tricks
[5] [*de pesca*] lure
[6] (*Cono Sur*) (= *regalo*) small gift, token

engañosamente ADV [1] [*comportarse*] deceitfully, dishonestly
[2] (= *en apariencia*) deceptively

engañoso ADJ (= *persona*) deceitful, dishonest; (= *apariencia*) deceptive; (= *consejo*) misleading

engarabitarse ▸conjug 1a◂ VPR [1] (= *subir*) to climb, shin up
[2] (= *padecer frío*) to get stiff with cold
[3] (*Andes*) (= *debilitarse*) to grow weak, get thin

engaratusar ▸conjug 1a◂ VT (*Andes, CAm, Méx*) = **engatusar**

engarce SM [1] [*de piedra, joyas*] setting, mount
[2] (= *inserción*) linking, connection
[3] (*Andes**) (= *jaleo*) row, shindy*

engaripolarse* ▸conjug 1a◂ VPR (*Caribe*) to doll o.s. up*

engarrotarse ▸conjug 1a◂ VPR [*miembros*] to get stiff

engarruñarse* ▸conjug 1a◂ VPR (*Andes, CAm, Méx*) = **engurruñarse**

engarzar ▸conjug 1f◂ Ⓐ VT [1] [+ *joya*] to set, mount; [+ *cuentas*] to thread
[2] [+ *ideas, tendencias*] to link, connect
[3] [+ *pelo*] to curl
Ⓑ **engarzarse** VPR (*Cono Sur*) to get tangled, get stuck

engastar ▸conjug 1a◂ VT [+ *joya*] to set, mount

engaste SM setting, mount

engatado ADJ thievish

engatusar ▸conjug 1a◂ VT to coax, wheedle; **~ a algn para que haga algo** to coax sb into doing sth; **no me vas a ~** you're not going to get round me

engendrar ▸conjug 1a◂ VT [1] (*Biol*) to beget, breed
[2] (*Mat*) to generate
[3] [+ *problemas, situación*] to cause

engendro SM [1] (*) (= *ser deforme*) freak; **¡mal ~!** ◊ **¡~ del diablo!** little monster!
[2] (= *feto*) foetus, fetus (*EEUU*)
[3] (= *invención*) idiotic scheme, impossible plan; **el proyecto es el ~ del ministro** the plan is the brainchild of the minister

engerido* ADJ (*Andes*) (= *alicaído*) down, glum

engerirse* ▸conjug 3k◂ VPR (*Andes*) to grow sad

engestarse* ▸conjug 1a◂ VPR (*Méx*) to scowl

englobar ▸conjug 1a◂ VT to include, comprise

engodo SM (*Caribe*) bait

engolado ADJ (*fig*) haughty

engolfarse ▸conjug 1a◂ VPR [1] (*Náut*) to sail out to sea
[2] **~ en** [+ *política*] to get deeply involved in; [+ *estudio*] to bury o.s. in

engolletarse ▸conjug 1a◂ VPR to give o.s. airs

engolondrinarse ▸conjug 1a◂ VPR [1] (= *envanecerse*) to get conceited
[2] (= *enamoriscarse*) to become infatuated

engolosinar ▸conjug 1a◂ Ⓐ VT to tempt, entice
Ⓑ **engolosinarse** VPR (= *encariñarse*) to grow fond (**con** of)

engomado ADJ gummed

engomar ▸conjug 1a◂ VT to gum, glue

engominar ▸conjug 1a◂ VT [+ *pelo*] to put hair cream on; **iba todo engominado** his hair was all smarmed down

engorda SF [1] (*LAm*) (= *cebadura*) fattening (up)
[2] (*Cono Sur*) (= *ganado*) fattened animals *pl*

engordante ADJ fattening

engordar ▸conjug 1a◂ Ⓐ VT [1] [+ *animal, persona*] to fatten (up)
[2] [+ *número*] to swell, increase
Ⓑ VI [1] (= *ponerse gordo*) to get fat; (= *aumentar de peso*) to put on weight; (*Agr*) to fatten
[2] [*comida*] to be fattening
[3] (*) (= *enriquecerse*) to get rich

engorde SM fattening (up)

engorrar ▸conjug 1a◂ VT (*LAm*) to annoy

engorro* SM hassle*, bother, nuisance

engorroso ADJ [*asunto*] bothersome, trying; [*situación, problema*] awkward

engrampador SM (*LAm*) stapler

engrampar ▸conjug 1a◂ VT (*LAm*) to clip together, staple

engranaje SM [1] (*Mec*) (= *rueda dentada*) [*de reloj*] cogs *pl*; [*de máquina*] gear teeth *pl*; (= *conjunto de engranajes*) gears *pl*, gear assembly; **el ~ transmite la fuerza a la muela** the gearwheels convey the power to the grindstone ► **engranaje cónico** bevel gears *pl* ► **engranaje de distribución** timing gear ► **engranaje de inversión de marcha** reverse gear assembly ► **engranaje diferencial** differential gear assembly ► **engranaje helicoidal** helicoidal gear assembly
[2] (= *sistema*) mechanism; **el delicado ~ de la justicia** the delicate mechanism of the judicial system; **el ~ de la dictadura** the machinery of the dictatorship; **una pieza básica del ~ de poder comunista** a fundamental part of the apparatus of communist power

engranar ▸conjug 1a◂ Ⓐ VT [1] (*Téc*) to gear; **~ algo con algo** to engage sth with sth
[2] [+ *ideas*] to link together, link up
Ⓑ VI to interlock; (*Mec*) to engage (**con** with); **A engrana con B** A is in gear with B; **A y B están engranados** A and B are in mesh
Ⓒ **engranarse** VPR (*Cono Sur, Méx Mec*) to seize up, get locked, jam

engrandecer ▸conjug 2d◂ VT [1] (= *aumentar*) to enlarge, magnify
[2] (= *ensalzar*) to speak highly of
[3] (= *exagerar*) to exaggerate

engrandecimiento SM [1] (= *aumento*) enlargement
[2] (= *exaltación*) exaltation
[3] (= *exageración*) exaggeration

engrane SM [1] (*Mec*) mesh, meshing
[2] (*Cono Sur, Méx Mec*) seizing, jamming

engrasación SF, **engrasado** SM greasing, lubrication

engrasador SM [1] (= *recipiente*) grease cup ► **engrasador de compresión**, **engrasador de pistón** grease gun
[2] (= *punto de engrase*) grease point; (*Aut*) grease nipple

engrasamiento SM greasing, lubrication

engrasar ▸conjug 1a◂ VT [1] (*Mec*) to grease, oil
[2] (= *manchar*) to stain with grease
[3] (*Agr*) to manure
[4] (*Méx Med*) to contract
[5] (*) (= *sobornar*) to bribe

engrase SM [1] (*Mec*) greasing, lubrication
[2] (*) (= *soborno*) bribe, sweetener (*EEUU*)

engreído/a Ⓐ ADJ [1] (= *vanidoso*) vain, stuck-up*
[2] (*LAm*) (= *afectuoso*) affectionate; (= *mimado*) spoiled, spoilt
Ⓑ SM/F bighead*, spoiled brat

engreimiento SM (= *vanidad*) vanity, conceit

engreír ▸conjug 3k◂ Ⓐ VT [1] (= *envanecer*) to make vain, make conceited
[2] (*LAm*) [+ *niño*] to spoil, pamper
Ⓑ **engreírse** VPR [1] (= *envanecerse*) to get conceited
[2] (*LAm*) (= *encariñarse*) to grow fond (**a, con** of)
[3] (*LAm*) [*niño*] to get spoiled, be pampered

engrifarse* ▸conjug 1a◂ VPR [1] (*Andes*) to get haughty
[2] (*Méx*) to get cross, get angry
[3] (‡) (= *colocarse*) to get high on drugs, get wasted‡

engrillar ▸conjug 1a◂ Ⓐ VT [1] (= *poner grilletes a*) to shackle
[2] (*Andes, Caribe*) to trick
Ⓑ **engrillarse** VPR [1] (*Caribe*) [*caballo*] to lower its head
[2] (*Caribe*) (= *engreírse*) to get conceited
[3] (*Andes, CAm*) (= *endeudarse*) to get into debt

engringolarse ▸conjug 1a◂ VPR (*Caribe*) to doll o.s. up

engriparse ▸conjug 1a◂ VPR to catch the flu

engrosar ▸conjug 1l◂ Ⓐ VT [1] [+ *cantidad*] to increase
[2] (= *espesar*) to thicken
Ⓑ VI (= *engordar*) to get fat
Ⓒ **engrosarse** VPR (= *aumentar*) to increase, swell

engrudar ▸conjug 1a◂ VT to paste

engrudo SM paste

engrupido/a* (*Cono Sur*) Ⓐ ADJ [1] (= *engreído*) stuck-up*, conceited
[2] (= *zalamero*) smooth-talking
Ⓑ SM/F (= *zalamero*) smooth talker; (= *embustero*) con*

engrupir* ▸conjug 3a◂ (*Cono Sur*) Ⓐ VT (= *engañar*) to con*
Ⓑ VI to blarney one's way in
Ⓒ **engrupirse** VPR (= *engañarse*) to be conned*; (= *engreírse*) to get conceited, put on airs

enguacharse ▸conjug 1a◂ VPR (*Andes*) to coarsen, get coarse

enguadar ▸conjug 1a◂ VT (*Caribe*) = **engatusar**

engualichar ▸conjug 1a◂ VT (*Cono Sur*) [1] (= *embrujar*) to bewitch (with a potion)
[2] [+ *amante*] to rule, tyrannize

enguandos* SMPL (*Andes*) knick-knacks

enguantado ADJ [*mano*] gloved

enguantarse ▸conjug 1a◂ VPR to put one's gloves on

enguaracarse ▸conjug 1g◂ VPR (*CAm*) to hide o.s. away

enguaraparse ▸conjug 1a◂ VPR (*CAm*) to ferment

enguasimar ▸conjug 1a◂ VT (*Caribe*) to hang

enguayabado* ADJ **está ~** (*Andes, Caribe*) he's got a hangover*, he's hung over*

enguijarrado SM cobbles *pl*

enguijarrar ▸conjug 1a◂ VT to cobble

enguirnaldar ▸conjug 1a◂ VT to garland, wreathe (**de, con** with)

engullir ▸conjug 3a, 3h◂ VT to gobble, gulp, gulp down

engurrioso* ADJ jealous, envious

engurruñarse ▸conjug 1a◂ VPR to get sad, grow gloomy
enharinar ▸conjug 1a◂ VT to flour
enhebrado SM threading
enhebrar ▸conjug 1a◂ VT to thread
enhestar ▸conjug 1j◂ VT (= *poner vertical*) to set upright
enhiesto ADJ (= *derecho*) erect, upright
enhilar ▸conjug 1a◂ VT [1] [+ *aguja*] to thread
[2] (= *ordenar*) to arrange, put in order
▼ **enhorabuena** SF [1] congratulations *pl;* **¡enhorabuena!** congratulations!; **dar la ~ a algn** to congratulate sb; **estar de ~** to be in luck, be on to a good thing
[2] **~ que ...** thank heavens that ...
enhoramala EXCL good riddance!; **¡vete ~!** go to hell!
enhorquetarse ▸conjug 1a◂ VPR (*Caribe, Cono Sur, Méx*) to sit astride
enhuerar ▸conjug 1a◂ VT to addle
enigma SM enigma
enigmáticamente ADV enigmatically
enigmático ADJ enigmatic
enjabonado Ⓐ ADJ soapy
Ⓑ SM soaping, lathering
enjabonadura SF = **enjabonado B**
enjabonar ▸conjug 1a◂ VT [1] (= *lavar*) [+ *manos, ropa*] to soap, wash; [+ *barba*] to lather
[2] (*) [+ *persona*] (= *adular*) to soft-soap; (= *reprender*) to give sb a dressing-down
enjaezar ▸conjug 1f◂ VT to harness, saddle up
enjalbegado SM, **enjalbegadura** SF whitewashing
enjalbegar ▸conjug 1h◂ VT [+ *pared*] to whitewash; [+ *cara*] to make up
enjambrar ▸conjug 1a◂ Ⓐ VT to hive
Ⓑ VI to swarm
enjambre SM swarm
enjaranarse ▸conjug 1a◂ VPR (*CAm*) to get into debt
enjarciar ▸conjug 1b◂ VT (*Náut*) to rig
enjaretado SM grating, grille
enjaretar ▸conjug 1a◂ Ⓐ VT [1] (*) (= *recitar*) to reel off, spout
[2] (*) (= *endilgar*) **me enjaretó la tarea de ...** he lumbered me with the task of ...
[3] (= *hacer deprisa*) to rush, rush through
[4] (*Cono Sur, Méx*) to slip in
Ⓑ **enjaretarse** VPR **~se la carrera** to shape one's career, mould one's career
enjaular ▸conjug 1a◂ VT [1] (= *guardar*) to cage, put in a cage; **he estado todo el día enjaulado en mi habitación** I've been cooped up in my room all day*
[2] (*) (= *encarcelar*) to jail, lock up, bang up*
enjertar ▸conjug 1a◂ VT = **injertar**
enjetado: ADJ (*Cono Sur, Méx*) cross-looking, scowling
enjetarse: ▸conjug 1a◂ VPR (*Cono Sur, Méx*) (= *enojarse*) to get cross; (= *hacer muecas*) to scowl
enjoyado ADJ [1] [*corona*] bejewelled, set with jewels
[2] [*persona*] **todas las señoras iban enjoyadas al teatro** all the ladies wore jewels to the theatre; **iba demasiado enjoyada** she was dripping with jewellery
enjoyar ▸conjug 1a◂ Ⓐ VT to adorn with jewels, set with precious stones
Ⓑ **enjoyarse** VPR to get all dressed up in jewels
enjuagadientes SM INV mouthwash
enjuagado SM rinsing
enjuagar ▸conjug 1h◂ VT [+ *ropa*] to rinse, rinse out; [+ *boca*] to wash out
enjuague SM [1] (= *líquido*) (*tb* ~ **bucal**) mouthwash
[2] (= *acto*) [*de ropa*] rinsing; [*de boca*] washing, rinsing
[3] (= *intriga*) scheme
enjugamanos SM INV (*LAm*) towel
enjugar ▸conjug 1h◂ Ⓐ VT [1] (= *secar*) [+ *sudor*] to wipe, wipe off; [+ *lágrimas*] to wipe away; [+ *platos*] to wipe, wipe up, dry; [+ *agua*] to wipe up, mop up
[2] [+ *deuda*] to wipe out
Ⓑ **enjugarse** VPR **~se la frente** to wipe one's brow, mop one's brow
enjuiciamiento SM [1] (= *acción*) judgment
[2] (*Jur*) ► **enjuiciamiento civil** lawsuit ► **enjuiciamiento criminal** trial
enjuiciar ▸conjug 1b◂ VT [1] (= *juzgar*) to judge, pass judgment on
[2] (*Jur*) (= *acusar*) to indict; (= *procesar*) to prosecute; (= *sentenciar*) to sentence
enjundia SF [1] (= *sustancia*) substance
[2] (= *fuerza*) strength; **una novela con mucha ~** a very weighty novel
[3] (= *grasa*) animal fat
enjundioso ADJ [1] [*libro, tema*] substantial, meaty
[2] (= *grasiento*) fat
enjuto ADJ [1] (= *flaco*) lean, skinny
[2] [*economía*] lean, lean and fit
[3] (= *seco*) dry, dried
enlabiar* ▸conjug 1b◂ VT to blarney*, bamboozle*, take in
enlabio* SM blarney*, plausible talk
▼ **enlace** SM [1] (= *relación*) connection, relationship
[2] (= *conexión*) (*Elec*) linkage; (*Quím*) bond; (*Ferro*) connection; [*de vías*] crossover; (*en autopista*) motorway junction; (*Mil*) liaison; **los buques no lograron efectuar el ~ en el punto indicado** the ships did not manage to rendezvous at the spot indicated; **estación de ~** junction ► **enlace fijo** fixed link ► **enlace telefónico** telephone link-up
[3] (= *matrimonio*) (*tb* ~ **matrimonial**) marriage; **el ~ de las dos familias** the linking of the two families by marriage
[4] (= *mediador*) link, go-between ► **enlace sindical** shop steward
[5] (*Internet*) link ► **enlace de datos** (*Inform*) data link
enladrillado SM brick paving
enladrillar ▸conjug 1a◂ VT to pave with bricks
enlardar ▸conjug 1a◂ VT (*Culin*) to baste
enlatado Ⓐ ADJ [1] [*alimentos, conservas*] canned, tinned
[2] [*música*] canned
Ⓑ SM canning, tinning
enlatar ▸conjug 1a◂ VT [1] to can, tin
[2] (= *grabar*) to record; (*TV*) to pre-record
enlazar ▸conjug 1f◂ Ⓐ VT [1] (= *unir con lazos*) to bind together; (= *atar*) to tie
[2] [+ *ideas*] to link, connect
[3] (*LAm*) to lasso
Ⓑ VI [*tren, vuelo*] to connect; [*carretera*] to link (up); [*idea, movimiento*] to meet, link (up) (**con** with)
Ⓒ **enlazarse** VPR [*ciudades*] to become linked; [*ideas*] to be connected; [*novios*] to get married; [*dos familias*] to become related by marriage
enlentecer ▸conjug 2d◂ VT to slow down
enlentecimiento SM slowing-down
enlistar ▸conjug 1a◂ VT (*CAm, Caribe, Méx*) = **alistar**
enllavar ▸conjug 1a◂ VT (*CAm*) to lock up
enlodar ▸conjug 1a◂ Ⓐ VT [1] (= *embarrar*) to cover in mud
[2] (*fig*) (= *manchar*) to stain
Ⓑ **enlodarse** VPR [1] (= *embarrarse*) to get muddy
[2] (= *mancharse*) to become stained
enlodazar ▸conjug 1f◂ VT = **enlodar**
enloquecedor ADJ [*ruido, trabajo, experiencia*] maddening; [*dolor de cabeza*] splitting; [*dolor*] excruciating
enloquecedoramente ADV maddeningly; **gritar ~** to shout excruciatingly loudly
enloquecer ▸conjug 2d◂ Ⓐ VT (= *volver loco*) to drive mad; (= *enfurecer*) to madden, drive crazy
Ⓑ VI **le enloquece la música pop** she's mad about pop music
Ⓒ **enloquecerse** VPR to go mad, go out of one's mind
enloquecimiento SM madness
enlosado SM flagstone pavement
enlosar ▸conjug 1a◂ VT to pave (with flagstones)
enlozado ADJ (*LAm*) enamelled, enameled (*EEUU*), glazed
enlozar ▸conjug 1f◂ VT (*LAm*) to enamel, glaze
enlucido SM plaster
enlucidor(a) SM/F plasterer
enlucir ▸conjug 3f◂ VT [+ *pared*] to plaster; [+ *metal*] to polish
enlutado ADJ [*persona*] in mourning, wearing mourning; [*ciudad*] stricken
enlutar ▸conjug 1a◂ Ⓐ VT [1] [+ *persona*] to put into mourning
[2] [+ *ciudad, país*] to plunge into mourning; (= *entristecer*) to sadden, grieve; **el accidente enlutó a la ciudad entera** the accident plunged the whole town into mourning
[3] [+ *vestido*] to put crêpe on
[4] (= *oscurecer*) to darken
Ⓑ **enlutarse** VPR to dress in mourning
enmacetar ▸conjug 1a◂ VT [+ *planta*] to pot (up), put in a pot
enmaderado ADJ [*pared, habitación*] timbered; [*suelo*] boarded
enmaderamiento SM [*de pared, habitación*] timbering; [*de suelo*] boarding
enmaderar ▸conjug 1a◂ VT [+ *pared, habitación*] to timber; [+ *suelo*] to put down floorboards on
enmadrado* ADJ **está ~** he's a mummy's boy, he's tied to his mother's apron strings
enmalezarse ▸conjug 1f◂ VPR (*Andes, Caribe, Cono Sur*) to get overgrown, get covered in scrub
enmaniguarse ▸conjug 1i◂ VPR (*LAm*) to get overgrown with trees
enmantecar ▸conjug 1g◂ VT (*Culin*) to grease, butter

➤ LENGUA Y USO: **enhorabuena** 50.6, 51.1, 51.2, 51.3 **enlace 3** 51.3, 52.1

enmarañar ▸conjug 1a◂ Ⓐ VT [1] [+ *madeja, hilo*] to tangle, tangle up
[2] (= *complicar*) to complicate; **sólo logró ~ más el asunto** he only managed to make matters worse
[3] [+ *persona*] to confuse, perplex
Ⓑ **enmarañarse** VPR [1] (= *enredarse*) to get tangled (up), become entangled
[2] (= *complicarse*) to become involved, become complicated
[3] (= *confundirse*) to get confused
[4] (= *implicarse*) to get involved
[5] [*cielo*] to darken, cloud over

enmarcado SM [1] (= *marco*) frame
[2] (= *acto*) framing

enmarcar ▸conjug 1g◂ Ⓐ VT [+ *cuadro*] to frame; **la catedral enmarcaba perfectamente la ceremonia** the cathedral was the perfect setting for the ceremony
Ⓑ **enmarcarse** VPR **el acuerdo se enmarca dentro del proceso de paz** the agreement is part of the peace process; **su obra se enmarca en las corrientes vanguardistas** his work forms part of the avant garde movements

enmarillecerse ▸conjug 2d◂ VPR (= *amarillear*) to turn yellow; (= *empalidecer*) to turn pale

enmascarado/a SM/F masked man/woman

enmascarar ▸conjug 1a◂ Ⓐ VT [1] [+ *cara*] to mask
[2] [+ *intenciones*] to disguise
Ⓑ **enmascararse** VPR [1] (*lit*) to put on a mask
[2] (*fig*) **~se de** to masquerade as

enmedallado ADJ bemedalled

enmedio ADV = **medio C1**

enmendación SF emendation, correction

enmendar ▸conjug 1j◂ Ⓐ VT [1] (= *corregir*) [+ *texto*] to emend, correct; [+ *ley, conducta*] to amend
[2] [+ *moral*] to reform
[3] [+ *pérdida*] to make good, compensate for
Ⓑ **enmendarse** VPR [*persona*] to mend one's ways

enmicado SM (*Méx*) plastic cover(ing)

enmicar ▸conjug 1g◂ VT (*Méx Téc*) [+ *documento*] to cover in plastic, laminate

enmienda SF [1] (= *corrección*) (*gen*) emendation, correction; (*Jur, Pol*) amendment
► **enmienda a la totalidad** motion for the rejection of a bill
[2] [*de comportamiento*] reform
[3] (= *compensación*) compensation, indemnity

enmohecer ▸conjug 2d◂ Ⓐ VT [1] [+ *metal*] to rust
[2] (*Bot*) to make mouldy, make moldy (*EEUU*)
Ⓑ **enmohecerse** VPR [*metal*] to rust, get rusty; [*planta*] to get mouldy, get moldy (*EEUU*)

enmohecido ADJ [1] [*metal*] rusty, rust-covered
[2] [*planta*] mouldy, moldy (*EEUU*), mildewed

enmonarse* ▸conjug 1a◂ VPR [1] (*con droga*) to go cold turkey‡, suffer withdrawal symptoms
[2] (*LAm*) to get tight*

enmontarse ▸conjug 1a◂ VPR (*CAm, Col, Méx*) to get overgrown

enmoquetado ADJ carpeted

enmoquetador(a) SM/F carpet layer

enmoquetar ▸conjug 1a◂ VT to carpet

enmudecer ▸conjug 2d◂ Ⓐ VT to silence
Ⓑ VI (= *perder el habla*) (*gen*) to go dumb; (*por miedo, sorpresa*) to be dumbstruck
Ⓒ **enmudecerse** VPR (= *callarse*) to remain silent, say nothing; (*por miedo*) to be struck dumb

enmugrar* ▸conjug 1a◂ VT (*LAm*), **enmugrecer*** ▸conjug 2d◂ VT, **enmugrentar*** ▸conjug 1a◂ VT (*Chile*) (= *ensuciar*) to soil, dirty

ennegrecer ▸conjug 2d◂ Ⓐ VT (= *poner negro*) to blacken; (= *oscurecer*) to darken; (= *teñir*) to dye black
Ⓑ VI, **ennegrecerse** VPR (= *ponerse negro*) to turn black; (= *oscurecerse*) to get dark, darken

ennoblecer ▸conjug 2d◂ VT [1] (= *hacer noble*) to ennoble
[2] (= *adornar*) to embellish

ennoblecimiento SM ennoblement

ennoviarse* ▸conjug 1b◂ VPR to start courting

enofilia SF (= *afición*) oenophilia, liking for wines; (= *conocimiento*) expertness in wines

enófilo/a SM/F (= *aficionado*) oenophile, lover of wines; (= *conocedor*) wine expert

enojada SF (*Caribe, Méx*) anger, fit of anger

enojadizo ADJ (*esp LAm*) irritable, short-tempered

enojado ADJ angry, cross, mad (*EEUU*); **dijo, ~** he said angrily

enojar ▸conjug 1a◂ (*esp LAm*) Ⓐ VT (= *encolerizar*) to anger; (= *molestar*) to upset, annoy
Ⓑ **enojarse** VPR (= *enfadarse*) to get angry, lose one's temper; (= *irritarse*) to get annoyed, get cross, get mad (*EEUU*) (**con, contra** with; **por** at, about)

enojo SM [1] (= *enfado*) anger; (= *irritación*) annoyance; **decir con ~** to say angrily
[2] **tener repentinos ~s** to be quick to anger, be easily upset; **de prontos** *o* **repentinos ~s** quick-tempered
[3] **enojos** (= *problemas*) troubles, trials

enojón ADJ (*Chile, Col, Méx*) = **enojadizo**

enojoso ADJ irritating, annoying

enología SF oenology (*frm*), enology (*EEUU frm*), study of wine(-making)

enólogo/a SM/F oenologist, wine expert

enorgullecer ▸conjug 2d◂ Ⓐ VT to fill with pride
Ⓑ **enorgullecerse** VPR to be proud (**de** of), pride o.s. (**de** on)

enorme ADJ [1] (= *muy grande*) enormous, huge
[2] (*) (= *estupendo*) killing*, marvellous; **cuando imita al profe es ~** when he takes off the teacher he's killing*

enormemente ADV enormously; **me gustó ~** I enjoyed it enormously *o* tremendously; **estaba ~ sobrevalorado** it was vastly *o* enormously overrated

enormidad SF [1] (= *inmensidad*) enormousness, hugeness
[2] [*de crimen*] enormity
[3] (= *desatino*) wicked thing, monstrous thing
[4] (*) **me gustó una ~** I liked it enormously *o* tremendously

enoteca SF wine cellar, collection of wines

enqué* SM (*Andes*) **lo traeré si encuentro ~** I'll bring it if I can find something to put it in *o* a bag for it

enquistamiento SM [1] (*Med*) **cuando se produjo el ~ del grano** when the pimple turned into a cyst
[2] (= *atranque*) deadlock; **dado el ~ de la situación** given the current deadlock; **su actitud provocó el ~ de las conversaciones** their attitude caused the negotiations to break down

enquistar ▸conjug 1a◂ Ⓐ VT [+ *conversaciones*] to seal off, shut off, enclose
Ⓑ **enquistarse** VPR [1] (*Med*) to turn into a cyst
[2] [*mal social*] to take hold, fester within

enrabiar ▸conjug 1b◂ Ⓐ VT to enrage
Ⓑ **enrabiarse** VPR to get enraged

enrabietarse ▸conjug 1a◂ VPR to throw a tantrum, get very cross

enrachado ADJ enjoying a run of luck

enraizar ▸conjug 1f◂ VI to take root

enramada SF [1] (= *follaje*) leafy foliage
[2] (*Cono Sur*) (= *cobertizo*) arbour, arbor (*EEUU*), cover made of branches

enramar ▸conjug 1a◂ Ⓐ VT (= *cubrir*) to cover with branches
Ⓑ VI (*Cono Sur*) (= *enverdecer*) to come into leaf

enranciarse ▸conjug 1b◂ VPR to go rancid, get stale

enrarecer ▸conjug 2d◂ Ⓐ VT [1] (= *viciar*) [+ *aire*] to rarefy; [+ *ambiente*] to strain
[2] (= *hacer escasear*) to make scarce
Ⓑ **enrarecerse** VPR [1] [*aire*] to become rarefied, get thin
[2] [*relaciones, ambiente*] to become strained, become tense
[3] (= *escasear*) to become scarce

enrarecido ADJ [*aire*] rarefied; [*relaciones, ambiente*] strained, tense

enrarecimiento SM [1] [*del aire*] rarefaction
[2] [*de relaciones, ambiente*] straining
[3] (= *escasez*) scarceness, rareness

enrastrojarse ▸conjug 1a◂ VPR (*Méx*) to get covered in scrub

enrazado ADJ (*Andes*) [*persona*] half-breed; [*animal*] crossbred

enrazar ▸conjug 1f◂ VT (*Andes*) [+ *personas*] to mix (racially); [+ *animales*] to crossbreed

enredadera SF (*Bot*) climbing plant, creeper
► **enredadera de campo** bindweed

enredador(a) Ⓐ ADJ [1] (= *chismoso*) **es muy ~** he's a stirrer
[2] (= *alborotador*) troublemaking
[3] (= *travieso*) naughty, mischievous
Ⓑ SM/F [1] (= *chismoso*) gossip
[2] (= *alborotador*) troublemaker
[3] (= *travieso*) naughty child

enredar ▸conjug 1a◂ Ⓐ VT [1] [+ *hilos, cuerda*] to tangle up; **este viento te enreda el pelo** your hair gets tangled up in this wind, this wind tangles your hair up
[2] [+ *situación, asunto*] to make complicated, complicate; **con tanta mentira enredó las cosas aún más** with all his lies he made matters even more complicated, with all his lies he complicated matters even more
[3] (*) (= *desordenar*) to get into a mess, mess up; **estos niños lo han enredado todo** these children have got everything into a mess, these children have messed everything up
[4] (*) (= *involucrar*) to get mixed *o* caught up (**en** in); **la han enredado en un asunto turbio** they've got her mixed *o* caught up in some shady deal
[5] (*) (= *entretener*) **no me enredes, que lle-**

go tarde don't hold me back, or I'll be late
6 (*) (= *engañar*) to trick; **le ~on unos timadores** some conmen tricked him
7 (= *enemistar*) to cause trouble among *o* between
8 (*Caza*) [+ *animal*] to net; [+ *trampa*] to set
Ⓑ VI (*) (= *juguetear*) to play around, monkey around*; **¡no enredes!** stop playing around!; **~ con algo** to fiddle with sth; **¡deja ya de ~ con los lápices!** stop fiddling (around) with the pencils, will you?
Ⓒ **enredarse** VPR 1 [*hilos, cuerda*] to get tangled up; **se me ha enredado el pelo** my hair's got all tangled up; **la cinta se enredó en el ventilador** the ribbon got tangled up *o* caught in the fan; **el sedal se enredó en la hélice** the fishing line fouled the propeller
2 [*situación, asunto*] to get complicated
3 (*) (= *involucrarse*) to get mixed up, get involved (**con, en** with); **se enredó en un asunto de drogas** he got mixed up *o* involved in some business to do with drugs
4 (*) (= *liarse*) to get into a tangle*, get into a muddle*; **me enredé haciendo las cuentas** I got into a tangle *o* muddle with the accounts*; **me enredé al pronunciar su nombre** I got tongue-tied when I tried to say his name
5 (*) (*sentimentalmente*) to get involved, get embroiled; **se enredó con una estudiante** he got involved *o* embroiled with a student

enredista* ADJ, SMF (*LAm*) = **enredador**

enredo SM 1 [*de hilos, cuerda*] tangle; **un ~ de pelos** a tangle of hair
2 [*de datos*] (*gen*) maze, tangle; (= *confusión*) mix-up
3 (= *laberinto*) maze
4 (= *asunto turbio*) shady business
5 (= *amorío*) love affair
6 (= *implicación*) embroilment, involvement
7 (*en novela*) complicated situation
8 **enredos** (= *intrigas*) intrigues; (= *mentiras*) mischief *sing*, mischievous lies; **comedia de ~(s)** comedy of intrigue

enredoso/a Ⓐ ADJ 1 (= *complicado*) complicated; (= *tramposo*) tricky
2 (*Méx*) = **enredador A**
Ⓑ SM/F (*Méx*) = **enredador B**

enrejado SM 1 (= *rejas*) grating; [*de ventana*] lattice; (*en jardín*) trellis; (*de jaula*) bars *pl*; **~ de alambre** wire netting, wire netting fence
2 (*Cos*) openwork

enrejar ▸conjug 1a◂ VT 1 (= *poner rejilla*) to put a grating on; (= *cercar*) to fence
2 (*LAm*) (= *poner el ronzal*) to put a halter on
3 (*Méx*) (= *zurcir*) to darn, patch

enrejillado SM small-mesh grille

Enresa SF ABR (*Esp*) = **Empresa Nacional de Residuos Radiactivos**

enrevesado ADJ [*asunto*] difficult, complex; [*mente, carácter*] twisted

enrielar ▸conjug 1a◂ VT 1 (= *poner rieles a*) to lay rails on
2 (*LAm*) [+ *asunto*] to put on the right track

Enrique SM Henry

enriquecer ▸conjug 2d◂ Ⓐ VT to make rich, enrich
Ⓑ **enriquecerse** VPR to get rich; (= *prosperar*) to prosper; **~se a costa ajena** to do well at other people's expense

enriquecido ADJ [*producto*] enriched

enriquecimiento SM enrichment

enriscado ADJ craggy, rocky

enristrar ▸conjug 1a◂ VT 1 [+ *cebollas, ajos*] to (put on a) string
2 [+ *lanza*] to take up
3 [+ *lugar*] to go straight to

enrizar ▸conjug 1f◂ Ⓐ VT to curl
Ⓑ **enrizarse** VPR to curl

enrocar ▸conjug 1g◂ VI (*Ajedrez*) to castle

enrojecer ▸conjug 2d◂ Ⓐ VT (= *poner rojo*) to redden, turn red; (= *ruborizar*) to make blush; [+ *metal*] to make red-hot
Ⓑ VI, **enrojecerse** VPR (= *ruborizarse*) to blush; (*de ira*) to go red (with anger), go red in the face; [*hierro*] to get red-hot

enrojecimiento SM (*gen*) reddening; (= *de rubor*) blushing, blush

enrolar ▸conjug 1a◂ (*esp LAm*) Ⓐ VT (= *reclutar*) to enrol, enroll (*EEUU*), sign on *o* up; (*Mil*) to enlist
Ⓑ **enrolarse** VPR to enrol, enroll (*EEUU*), sign on; (*Mil*) to enlist, join up; (*Dep*) to enter (**en** for)

enrollable ADJ [*colchón, pantalla, persiana*] roll-up *antes de s*; **cinturón ~** inertia-reel seat belt

enrollado ADJ 1 (= *liado*) [*alfombra, pergamino*] rolled (up); [*cuerda, cable*] (*en sí mismo*) coiled (up); (*alrededor de algo*) wound (up); **llevaba el periódico ~ bajo el brazo** he was carrying the newspaper rolled up under his arm; **un hilo ~ en el cable** a wire wound around the cable
2 (*Esp‡*) (= *simpático*) [*persona, música*] cool‡; **es un tío muy ~** he's a really cool guy‡
3 (*Esp‡*) (*en relación amorosa*) **llevan varios meses ~s** they've been going out *o* (*EEUU*) they've been dating for several months; **estar ~ con algn** to be going out with sb, be dating sb (*EEUU*)
4 (*Esp‡*) (*con una actividad*) involved, busy; **parecían muy enrolladas hablando de sus cosas** they seemed very involved *o* busy talking about their own things; **estar ~ con algo** to be busy with sth; **¿todavía estás ~ con los exámenes?** are you still busy with exams?; **siempre te veo ~ con las plantas** you're always busy with your plants; **estar ~ en algo** to be involved in sth; **ahora estoy ~ en política** I'm involved in politics now

enrollamiento SM [*de alfombra, papel*] rolling (up); [*de cuerda, cable*] (*en sí mismo*) coiling (up); (*alrededor de algo*) winding (up)

enrollante ADJ 1 (*) (= *confuso*) confusing
2 (*Esp‡*) (= *atractivo*) smashing*, super*

enrollar ▸conjug 1a◂ Ⓐ VT 1 (= *liar*) [+ *papel, persiana, filete*] to roll (up); [+ *cuerda, cable*] (*en sí mismo*) to coil (up); (*alrededor de algo*) to wind (up)
2 (*Esp‡*) (= *atraer*) **esa tía me enrolla mucho** I'm really into that girl*; **a mí la droga no me enrolla nada** drugs don't do anything for me, I'm not into drugs*
3 (*Esp‡*) (= *enredar*) **no me enrolles más, así no me vas a convencer** don't give me that, you're not going to convince me*; **~ a algn en algo** to get sb involved in sth; **no dejes que te enrolle en sus movidas** don't let him get you involved in his dealings
Ⓑ **enrollarse** VPR 1 (= *liarse*) [*papel*] to roll up; [*cuerda, cable*] (*en sí mismo*) to coil up; (*alrededor de algo*) to wind up; **el cable se le enrolló en la pierna** the cable wound (itself) *o* got wound around his leg
2 (*Esp‡*) (= *extenderse demasiado*) (*al hablar*) to go on*; (*sin decir nada*) to waffle on*; **no veas como se enrolla en las cartas** he certainly goes on a bit in his letters*; **nos enrollamos hablando hasta muy tarde** we were chattering away till very late; **por favor, no te enrolles, que tenemos prisa** please, don't get talking, we've got to hurry; **creo que me he enrollado demasiado en el examen** I think I waffled too much in the exam*; **~se con algo**: **si os enrolláis con el fútbol, será mejor que me vaya** if you get onto football, I'm going to leave; ✦**MODISMO** **~se como una persiana** to go on and on
3 (*Esp‡*) (= *ser simpático*) **venga, enróllate y échanos una mano** come on, be a sport and give us a hand*; **~se bien** to be cool‡; **el camarero se enrolló muy bien y nos puso una copa gratis** the waiter was really nice to us *o* really cool‡ and gave us a free drink; **~se mal** to be uncool‡; **tu madre se enrolla fatal** your mum is so uncool‡
4 (*Esp‡*) [*dos personas*] (= *tener una relación sexual*) to have it off‡, make out (*EEUU**); (= *empezar una relación amorosa*) to get off (together)*, get it on (together) (*EEUU**); **~se con algn** (= *tener una relación sexual*) to have it off with sb‡; (= *empezar una relación amorosa*) to get off with sb*
5 (*Esp‡*) (= *involucrarse*) **~se en algo** to get into sth*, get involved in sth; **se enrolló en el mundo del cine** he got into* *o* got involved in the movie world
6 (*Ven**) (= *confundirse*) to get mixed up; (= *preocuparse*) to get worked up*

enrolle‡ SM bad scene*, pain*

enronquecer ▸conjug 2d◂ Ⓐ VT to make hoarse
Ⓑ VI, **enronquecerse** VPR to grow hoarse

enronquecido ADJ hoarse

enroque SM (*Ajedrez*) castling

enroscado ADJ 1 (= *enrollado*) [*serpiente, cuerda*] coiled
2 (*Andes*) angry

enroscadura SF coil

enroscar ▸conjug 1g◂ Ⓐ VT 1 (= *poner*) [+ *tapón*] to screw on; [+ *tornillo*] to screw in
2 [+ *cable, manguera*] to coil
Ⓑ **enroscarse** VPR [*serpiente*] to coil up; [*gato*] to curl up; **la manguera se le enroscó en la pierna** the hose coiled round his leg; **la serpiente se enroscaba alrededor del árbol** the snake coiled round the tree

enrostrar ▸conjug 1a◂ VT (*LAm*) to reproach

enrulado ADJ (*Cono Sur*) curly

enrular ▸conjug 1a◂ VT (*Andes, Cono Sur*) to curl

enrumbar ▸conjug 1a◂ VI (*Andes, Cono Sur*) to set off

enrutador SM (*Telec*) router

ensacar ▸conjug 1g◂ VT to sack, bag, put into bags

ensalada SF 1 (*Culin*) salad ► **ensalada de col** coleslaw ► **ensalada de frutas** fruit salad ► **ensalada de patatas** potato salad
2 (= *mescolanza*) hotchpotch, hodgepodge (*EEUU*)
3 (= *lío*) mix-up ► **ensalada de tiros*** wild shoot-out

ensaladera SF salad bowl

ensaladilla SF diced vegetable salad ► **ensaladilla rusa** Russian salad

ensalmado ADJ (*LAm*) magic

ensalmador(a) SM/F quack, bonesetter

ensalmar ▸conjug 1a◂ VT [+ *hueso*] to set; [+ *enfermedad*] to treat by quack remedies

ensalme SM (*Andes*) spell, incantation

ensalmo SM (= *encantamiento*) spell, charm; (*Med*) quack remedy, quack treatment; **(como) por ~** as if by magic

ensalzable ADJ praiseworthy, meritorious

ensalzamiento SM [*de persona*] praise; [*de virtudes*] extolling

ensalzar ▸conjug 1f◂ VT [+ *persona*] to praise; [+ *virtudes*] to extol

ensamblado SM (*Aut*) assembly

ensamblador(a) SM/F (= *carpintero*) joiner; (= *ajustador*) fitter; (*Inform*) assembler

ensambladura SF (= *acción*) assembly; (= *juntura*) joint

ensamblaje SM 1 (*Téc*) assembly; [*de astronaves*] docking, link-up; [*de madera*] joint; **planta de ~** assembly plant

2 (*Inform*) assembly language

ensamblar ▸conjug 1a◂ VT (= *montar*) to assemble; [+ *madera*] to joint; [+ *astronaves*] to dock, link up

ensanchador SM (*Téc*) stretcher

ensanchar ▸conjug 1a◂ Ⓐ VT (= *agrandar*) to enlarge, widen; (= *aumentar*) to expand; (*Cos*) to let out

Ⓑ **ensancharse** VPR 1 (= *ampliarse*) [*carretera, río*] to get wider, widen; [*vestido, ropa*] to stretch, get stretched out

2 (= *enorgullecerse*) to be pleased with o.s.; **cada vez que habla de sus hijos se ensancha de orgullo** whenever she talks about her children she fills up with pride

ensanche SM 1 (= *extensión*) [*de ciudad*] enlargement; [*de calle*] widening, expansion; [*de elástico*] stretch, stretching

2 (= *barrio*) suburban development

3 (*Cos*) room to let out

ensangrentado ADJ bloodstained

ensangrentar ▸conjug 1j◂ Ⓐ VT to stain with blood, cover in blood

Ⓑ **ensangrentarse** VPR to become stained with blood; **~se con** *o* **contra** to be cruel to, treat cruelly

ensañado ADJ (= *colérico*) furious; (= *cruel*) cruel, merciless

ensañamiento SM (= *cólera*) rage; (= *crueldad*) cruelty

ensañar ▸conjug 1a◂ Ⓐ VT to enrage

Ⓑ **ensañarse** VPR **~se con** *o* **en** to treat brutally

ensarnarse ▸conjug 1a◂ VPR (*Méx*) to get mangy

ensartada* SF **pegarse una ~** (*Andes*) to be very disappointed, feel let down

ensartador SM (*Cono Sur*) roasting spit

ensartar ▸conjug 1a◂ Ⓐ VT 1 (= *pinchar*) [+ *cuentas*] to string; [+ *aguja*] to thread; [+ *carne*] to spit

2 [+ *ideas*] to string together; [+ *disculpas*] to reel off

3 (*Chile, Méx*) (= *engañar*) to deceive

Ⓑ **ensartarse** VPR 1 (= *implicarse*) to get involved

2 (*Andes, Caribe*) (= *meterse en un aprieto*) to get into a jam*, fall into a trap

3 (*Cono Sur*) (= *salir mal*) to mess things up

ensarte* SM (*Andes*) disappointment, let-down

ensayar ▸conjug 1a◂ Ⓐ VT 1 (= *probar*) to test, try (out)

2 [+ *metal*] to assay

3 (*Mús, Teat*) to rehearse

Ⓑ **ensayarse** VPR 1 (= *practicar*) to practice, practise (*EEUU*)

2 (*Mús, Teat*) to rehearse; **~se a hacer algo** to practise doing sth, practice doing sth (*EEUU*)

ensaye SM assay

ensayista SMF essayist

ensayística SF (= *género literario*) genre of the essay

ensayístico ADJ essay *antes de s*; **obra ensayística** essays *pl*, work in essay form

ensayo SM 1 (= *prueba*) test, trial; (= *experimento*) experiment; (= *intento*) attempt; **de ~** experimental; **pedido de ~** (*Com*) trial order; **viaje de ~** trial run; **vuelo de ~** test flight; **hicimos un ~ de la obra** we rehearsed the play; **hacer algo a modo de ~** to do sth as an experiment ► **ensayo clínico** clinical trial ► **ensayo nuclear** nuclear test

2 [*de metal*] assay

3 (*Literat, Escol etc*) essay

4 (*Mús, Teat*) rehearsal ► **ensayo general** dress rehearsal

5 (*Rugby*) try

ensebado ADJ greased, greasy

enseguida ADV *ver* **seguida 1**

enselvado ADJ wooded

ensenada SF 1 (*Geog*) inlet, cove

2 (*Cono Sur*) small fenced pasture

enseña SF ensign, standard

enseñado ADJ trained, educated; **bien ~** [*perro*] house-trained

enseñante Ⓐ ADJ teaching

Ⓑ SMF teacher

enseñanza SF 1 (= *educación*) education; (= *acción, profesión*) teaching; **primera ~** elementary education; **segunda ~** secondary education ► **enseñanza a distancia** distance learning ► **enseñanza asistida por ordenador** computer-assisted learning ► **enseñanza de niños con dificultades de aprendizaje** remedial teaching, special needs teaching ► **enseñanza general básica** *education course in Spain from 6 to 14* ► **enseñanza primaria** elementary education ► **enseñanza programada** programmed learning, programed learning (*EEUU*) ► **enseñanza secundaria** secondary education ► **enseñanza superior** higher education ► **enseñanza universitaria** university education

2 (= *entrenamiento*) training

3 (= *doctrina*) teaching, doctrine; **la ~ de la Iglesia** the teaching of the Church

enseñar ▸conjug 1a◂ Ⓐ VT 1 (*Educ*) to teach, educate; **~ a algn a hacer algo** to teach sb (how) to do sth; **enseña francés** he teaches French

2 (= *mostrar*) to show; (= *señalar*) to point out; **estás enseñando el sujetador** your bra's showing; **~ algo con el dedo** to point to sth; **nos enseñó el museo** he showed us over *o* around the museum; **te ~é mis pinturas** I'll show you my paintings; **esto nos enseña las dificultades** this reveals the difficulties to us

3 (= *entrenar*) to train

Ⓑ VI to teach, be a teacher

Ⓒ **enseñarse** VPR (*esp LAm*) (= *acostumbrarse*) to become accustomed (**a** to); **no me enseño aquí** I can't settle down here

enseñorearse ▸conjug 1a◂ VPR **~ de** to take possession of, take over

enseres SMPL 1 (= *avíos*) equipment *sing*; **~ domésticos** household goods; **~ eléctricos** electrical appliances

2 (= *efectos personales*) goods and chattels

enseriarse ▸conjug 1b◂ VPR (*Andes, CAm, Caribe*) to look serious

Ensidesa SF ABR (*Esp*) = **Empresa Nacional Siderúrgica, Sociedad Anónima**

ensilado SM ensilage ► **ensilado de patatas** potato clamp

ensiladora SF silo

ensilar ▸conjug 1a◂ VT to store in a silo

ensillar ▸conjug 1a◂ VT to saddle (up)

ensimismamiento SM 1 (*en uno mismo*) absorption

2 (*LAm*) (= *vanidad*) conceit

ensimismarse ▸conjug 1a◂ VPR 1 (*en uno mismo*) to become engrossed, lose o.s.

2 (*LAm*) (= *envanecerse*) to get conceited

ensoberbecer ▸conjug 2d◂ Ⓐ VT to make proud

Ⓑ **ensoberbecerse** VPR 1 [*persona*] to become proud, become arrogant

2 [*mar*] to get rough

ensombrecer ▸conjug 2d◂ Ⓐ VT 1 [+ *cielo*] to darken, cast a shadow over

2 (= *cubrir de sombra*) to overshadow, cast a shadow over

Ⓑ **ensombrecerse** VPR 1 [*cielo*] to darken, grow dark

2 (*fig*) to become gloomy

ensombrerado ADJ with a hat, wearing a hat

ensoñación SF fantasy, fancy, dream; **¡ni por ~!** not a bit of it!, never!

ensoñador(a) Ⓐ ADJ dreamy

Ⓑ SM/F dreamer

ensopar ▸conjug 1a◂ (*LAm*) Ⓐ VT 1 (= *empapar*) to soak, drench

2 [+ *galleta, bizcocho*] to dip, dunk

Ⓑ **ensoparse** VPR [*persona*] to get soaked

ensordecedor ADJ deafening

ensordecer ▸conjug 2d◂ Ⓐ VT [+ *persona*] to deafen; [+ *ruido*] to muffle

Ⓑ VI to go deaf

ensortijar ▸conjug 1a◂ Ⓐ VT 1 [+ *pelo*] to curl

2 [+ *nariz*] to fix a ring in

Ⓑ **ensortijarse** VPR [*pelo*] to curl

ensuciamiento SM soiling, dirtying

ensuciar ▸conjug 1b◂ Ⓐ VT 1 (= *manchar*) to get dirty, dirty; **no me ensuciéis el suelo al entrar** don't get the floor dirty when you come in, don't dirty the floor when you come in

2 (*liter*) [+ *reputación, nombre*] to sully, soil (*liter*)

Ⓑ **ensuciarse** VPR 1 (= *mancharse*) to get dirty; **no te ensucies el vestido** don't get your dress dirty; **me he ensuciado las manos** I've got my hands dirty; **te has ensuciado de barro los pantalones** you've got mud on your trousers

2 [*bebé*] to dirty *o* soil one's nappy

ensueño SM [1] (= *ensoñación*) dream, fantasy
[2] (= *ilusión*) reverie; **de ~** dream-like; **una cocina de ~** a dream kitchen; **mundo de ~** dream world, world of fantasy
[3] **ensueños** (= *fantasías*) visions, fantasies; **¡ni por ~s!** never!

entabicar ▸conjug 1g◂ VT to partition off

entablado SM (= *tablas*) boarding, planking; (= *suelo*) floorboards *pl*

entabladura SF boarding, planking

entablar ▸conjug 1a◂ Ⓐ VT [1] [+ *suelo*] to board (in), board (up)
[2] (= *empezar*) [+ *conversación*] to strike up; [+ *negocio*] to enter into, embark upon; [+ *proceso*] to file; [+ *reclamación*] to put in
[3] (*Ajedrez*) to set up
[4] (*Med*) to splint, put in a splint
Ⓑ VI (*Ajedrez*) to draw
Ⓒ **entablarse** VPR [*viento*] to settle

entable SM [1] (= *tablas*) boarding, planking
[2] (*Ajedrez*) position
[3] (*LAm*) (= *organización*) order, arrangement, disposition
[4] (*Andes*) (= *empresa nueva*) new business
[5] (*Andes*) [*de terrenos vírgenes*] breaking, opening up

entablillar ▸conjug 1a◂ VT (*Med*) to (put in a) splint; **con el brazo entablillado** with his arm in a splint

entalegar ▸conjug 1h◂ VT [1] to bag, put in a bag
[2] (= *acumular*) to hoard, stash away
[3] (‡) (= *enchironar*) to jail

entallado ADJ (*Cos*) waisted, with a waist

entallador(a) SM/F [*de figuras*] sculptor; [*de grabados*] engraver

entalladura SF [1] (= *arte, objeto*) sculpture, carving; (= *grabado*) engraving
[2] (= *corte*) slot, notch, groove

entallar ▸conjug 1a◂ Ⓐ VT [1] (*Cos*) to cut, tailor; (= *ceñir*) to bring in
[2] (*Arte*) (= *esculpir*) to sculpt, carve; (= *grabar*) to engrave; **~ el nombre en un árbol** to carve one's name on a tree
[3] (= *hacer un corte en*) to notch, cut a slot in, cut a groove in
Ⓑ VI to fit (well); **un traje que entalla bien** a well-cut suit

entallecer ▸conjug 2d◂ VI, **entallecerse** VPR to shoot, sprout

entapizado Ⓐ ADJ [1] (= *forrado*) [*mueble*] upholstered (**de** with); [*pared*] lined (**de** with); [*butaca*] covered, upholstered (**de** with)
[2] (*Bot*) overgrown (**de** with)
Ⓑ SM [1] (= *material*) upholstery
[2] (*Méx*) wall-coverings *pl*, tapestries *pl*

entapizar ▸conjug 1f◂ VT [1] (= *forrar*) [+ *mueble*] to upholster (**de** with, in); [+ *pared*] to hang with tapestries; [+ *butaca*] to cover with fabric; (*Cono Sur*) [+ *suelo*] to carpet
[2] (*Bot*) to grow over, cover, spread over

entarascar ▸conjug 1g◂ Ⓐ VT to dress up, doll up
Ⓑ **entarascarse** VPR to dress up, doll up

entarimado SM [1] (= *suelo*) parquet floor
[2] (*de madera*) (= *tablas*) floorboarding, roof boarding; (= *taracea*) inlaid floor
[3] (= *estrado*) dais, stage, platform

entarimar ▸conjug 1a◂ VT to parquet

entarugado SM block flooring

ente SM [1] (= *organización oficial*) body, organization; **el Ente** (*Esp**) *the Spanish state television and radio* ► **ente moral** (*Méx*) non-profit-making organization ► **ente público** public body, public corporation
[2] (*Fil*) entity, being
[3] (*) (= *sujeto*) oddball*

entecarse ▸conjug 1g◂ VPR (*Cono Sur*) to be stubborn

entechar ▸conjug 1a◂ VT (*LAm*) to roof

enteco ADJ weak, sickly, frail

entediarse ▸conjug 1b◂ VPR to get bored

entejar ▸conjug 1a◂ VT (*LAm*) to tile

enteje SM (*LAm*) tiling

Entel SF ABR = **Empresa Nacional de Telecomunicaciones**

entelar ▸conjug 1a◂ VT [+ *pared*] to cover with hangings

entelequia SF [1] (*Fil*) entelechy
[2] (= *plan irrealizable*) pipe dream, pie in the sky

entelerido ADJ [1] (= *temblando*) (*de frío*) shivering with cold; (*de miedo*) shaking with fright, trembling with fear
[2] (*LAm*) (= *débil*) weak
[3] (*LAm*) (= *acongojado*) distressed, upset

entenado/a SM/F stepson/stepdaughter, stepchild

entendederas* SFPL brains; **ser corto de** *o* **tener pocas ~** to be pretty dim; **sus ~ no llegan a más** he has a brain the size of a pea*, he's bird-brained*

entendedor(a) SM/F understanding person; ✦*REFRÁN* **a buen ~, pocas palabras bastan** a word to the wise is sufficient

entender[1] ▸conjug 2g◂ Ⓐ VT [1] (= *comprender*) to understand; **no he entendido la pregunta** I didn't understand the question; **ahora lo entiendo todo** now I understand everything; **entiendo un poco de francés** I (can) understand a little French; **la verdad es que no entiendo el chiste** I don't really get *o* understand the joke; **lo has entendido todo al revés** you've got it all wrong; **no entiendo tu letra** I can't read your writing; **no entiendo cómo has podido hacer eso** I don't understand *o* know how you could do that; **¡a ti no hay quien te entienda!** you're impossible to understand!; **que no te vuelva a ver fumando ¿me has entendido?** don't let me catch you smoking again, do you understand?; **¿entiendes lo que te quiero decir?** do you know what I mean?, do you know what I'm trying to say?; **es un poco raro, tú ya me entiendes** he's a bit odd, if you know what I mean; **dar algo a ~** to imply sth; **dio a ~ que no le gustaba** he implied that he didn't like it; **nos dieron a ~ que querían marcharse** they gave us to understand *o* led us to believe that they wanted to leave; **según él me dio a ~, no está contento en su trabajo** from what he said to me, he is not happy in his job, he gave me to understand that he is not happy in his job; **hacer ~ algo a algn** to make sb understand sth; **hacerse ~** to make o.s. understood; **~ mal** to misunderstand; **si no he entendido mal, esto es lo que queréis decir** unless I've misunderstood what you're saying, this is what you mean; **no quiero que me entiendas mal** don't get me wrong; **no entendió ni una palabra** he didn't understand a word of it; **no entendí una palabra de lo que dijo** I didn't understand a word he said; **no entiendo ni una palabra de ordenadores** I don't understand a thing about computers; ✦*MODISMO* **no ~ ni jota** *o* **ni patata***: **no entendí ni jota** *o* **ni una patata de lo que decían** I didn't have a clue what they were on about; **no entiendo ni jota de alemán*** I don't understand a single word of German
[2] (= *opinar*) to think, believe; **entiendo que sería mejor decírselo** I think *o* believe it would be better to tell him; **yo entiendo que no es correcto hacerlo así** I don't think *o* believe that that's the right way to do it
[3] (= *interpretar*) to understand; **¿tú qué entiendes por libertad?** what do you understand by freedom?; **¿debo ~ que lo niegas?** am I to understand that you deny it?; **me ha parecido ~ que estaban en contra** I understood that they were against it, as I understand it they were against it; **cada uno entiende el amor a su manera** everyone sees love differently, everyone understands something different by love
[4] (*) (= *saber manejar*) to know how to use, know how to work; **¿tú entiendes esta lavadora?** do you know how this washing machine works?, do you know how to use this washing machine?
[5] (= *oír*) to hear; **no se entiende nada** I can't make out *o* hear a thing
Ⓑ VI [1] (= *comprender*) to understand; **¡ya entiendo!** now I understand!, now I get it!; **la vida es así ¿entiendes?** that's life, you know; **~ de algo** to know about sth; **no entiendo de vinos** I don't know much about wine; **Luis sí que entiende de mujeres** Luis certainly knows a thing or two about women; ✦*MODISMO* **no ~ de barcos**: **si le preguntas cualquier cosa, él no entiende de barcos** if you ask him something, he makes out he doesn't know anything about anything
[2] (*Jur*) (= *tener competencia*) **entiende en divorcios** he hears divorce cases; **~ en un asunto** to be in charge of an affair
[3] [*perro, gato*] **entiende por Moncho** he answers to the name of Moncho
[4] (‡) (= *ser homosexual*) to be one of them*
Ⓒ **entenderse** VPR [1] (*uso reflexivo*) to understand o.s.; **si no te entiendes ni tú, ¿quién te va a ~?** if you don't even understand yourself, then how is anyone else going to understand you?; **déjame, que yo me entiendo** leave me alone, I know what I mean; ✦*MODISMOS* **entendérselas**: **que ella se las entienda como pueda** well that's her problem; **allá tú te las entiendas con tus asuntos** you go and sort out your own affairs; **entendérselas con algn**: **van a tener que entendérselas conmigo** they're going to have to deal with me
[2] (*uso recíproco*) **nosotras nos entendemos** we understand each other; **nos entendimos por señas** we communicated using sign language, we used sign language to communicate; **a ver si nos entendemos ¿quién de los dos tiene el dinero?** now let's get this straight, which of the two has got the money?; **ya nos ~emos en el precio** we'll work out a price that we're both happy with; **digamos, para ~nos, que …** let's say, to avoid any misunderstanding, that …; **~se con algn** (= *llevarse bien*) to get on *o* along with sb; (= *tener una relación amorosa*) to have an affair with

sb; **eso no se entiende conmigo** that doesn't concern me, that has nothing to do with me; **~se con algo** to know how to deal with sth
3 (*uso impersonal*) **se entiende que ...** it is understood that ...; **se entiende que no quiera salir con ellos** it's understandable that she doesn't want to go out with them; **¿qué se entiende por estas palabras?** what is meant by these words?; **¿cómo se entiende que no nos llamaras antes?** why didn't you call us first?
4 (= *tratar*) **en caso de duda entiéndase con el cajero** in case of doubt please contact the cashier

entender² SM (= *opinión*) opinion; **a mi ~** in my opinion; *ver tb* **saber D**

entendido/a Ⓐ ADJ 1 (= *comprendido*) understood; **¡entendido!** (= *convenido*) agreed!; **bien ~ que** on the understanding that; **no darse por ~** to pretend not to understand; **tenemos ~ que ...** we understand that ...; **según tenemos ~** as far as we can gather
2 [*persona*] (= *experto*) expert; (= *cualificado*) skilled; (= *sabio*) wise; (= *informado*) well-informed; **ser ~ en** to be well up on
Ⓑ SM/F expert; **según el juicio de los ~s** according to the experts; **el whiskey de los ~s** the connoisseur's whisky

entendimiento SM 1 (= *inteligencia*) understanding, mind; **el ~ humano no tiene límites** human understanding *o* the human mind has no limits; **un hombre de mucho ~** a man of great understanding, a very wise man; **¡este chico no tiene ~!** this boy has no brains!
2 (= *comprensión*) understanding; **medidas para fomentar un mejor ~ de las leyes** measures to foster a better understanding of the laws
3 (= *acuerdo*) understanding; **llegar a un ~** to reach an understanding

entenebrecer ▸conjug 2d◂ Ⓐ VT 1 (= *oscurecer*) to darken, obscure
2 [+ *asunto*] to cloud, obscure; **esto entenebrece más el asunto** this fogs the issue still more
Ⓑ **entenebrecerse** VPR to get dark

entente SF entente

enteradillo/a* SM/F little know-all, smarty*

enterado/a Ⓐ ADJ 1 (= *informado*) (*de una especialidad*) knowledgeable; (*sobre un asunto concreto*) well-informed; **esta muy ~ de política** he's very knowledgeable about politics; **—¿sabes lo que pasó? —sí, estoy ~** "do you know what happened?" — "yes, I know *o* I've heard"; **estar ~ de algo** to know sth; **no estaba ~ de que os fuerais a casar** I didn't know you were getting married; **quedo ~ de que ...** I am now aware that ...; **darse por ~** to get the message
2 (*Chile**) (= *engreído*) snooty*, stuck-up*
Ⓑ SM/F (= *conocedor*) [*de materia*] expert; (*pey*) know-all*, bighead*; **no fue una gran sorpresa para los ~s** it wasn't a great surprise for those in the know*; **ese tío es un ~** that guy is a real know-all *o* bighead*

enteramente ADV entirely, completely

enterar ▸conjug 1a◂ Ⓐ VT 1 (= *informar*) **~ a algn de algo** to inform sb of sth, notify sb of sth, let sb know of sth
2 (*Chile, Méx*) (= *pagar*) [+ *dinero, deuda*] to pay
3 (*Chile*) (= *completar*) [+ *cantidad*] to make up, complete; **hoy entero dos meses sin fumar** it's two months today since I last smoked
Ⓑ **enterarse** VPR 1 (*de noticia, secreto*) 1·1 (*por casualidad*) to hear, find out; **nos enteramos a través de la radio** we heard it on the radio, we found out from the radio; **¿sí? no me había enterado** really? I hadn't heard; **no sabía nada, ahora mismo me entero** I had no idea, this is the first I've heard; **~se de algo** to hear about sth, find out about sth; **no quiero que nadie se entere de esto** I don't want anyone to hear about *o* find out about this; **me enteré de tu accidente por Juan** I heard about *o* found out about your accident from Juan; **me enteré del secuestro a través de la prensa** I read about the kidnapping in the paper; **nos enteramos de que se había ido ayer** we heard *o* found out that he'd gone yesterday
1·2 (*haciendo averiguaciones*) to find out; **entérate y me lo cuentas** find out and let me know; **~se de algo** to find out about sth; **tenemos que ~nos bien de la oferta** we must find out about the details of the offer; **entérate de lo que cuesta** find out what it costs
2 (= *darse cuenta*) to notice; **estaba tan dormido que no se enteró** he was so fast asleep that he didn't notice; **oye, que es a ti, que no te enteras*** hey, you, are you deaf or something?*; **~se de algo** to notice sth; **no se enteró de que le habían quitado la cartera** he didn't notice that his wallet had been stolen; **tú es que no te enteras de nada** you never know what's going on; **todavía no se han enterado de qué tipo de persona es** they still don't know what kind of person he is; ✦*MODISMOS* **te vas a ~ (de quien soy yo** *o* **de lo que vale un peine)** you'll find out what's what*; **para que te enteres** for your information; **he aprobado el examen, para que os enteréis** I've passed the exam, for your information!*
3 (*Esp*) (= *comprender, oír*) to understand; **si hablas tan flojo no me entero** if you talk so quietly I can't understand; **no quiero que vuelvas por aquí ¿te enteras?** I don't want you coming back here, do you understand *o* do you get it?*; **¡a ver si te enteras!** wise up!*; **~se de algo** to understand sth; **no se enteraba de lo que leía** he didn't take in *o* understand what he was reading

entercado* ADJ **~ en hacer algo** (*LAm*) determined to do sth, dead set on doing sth

entereza SF 1 (= *integridad*) integrity
2 (= *firmeza*) firmness ► **entereza de carácter** strength of character

entérico ADJ enteric

enteritis SF INV enteritis

enterito SM (*Arg*) boilersuit

enterizo ADJ in one piece, one-piece *antes de s*

enternecedor ADJ touching

enternecer ▸conjug 2d◂ Ⓐ VT (= *ablandar*) to soften; (= *conmover*) to affect, move (to pity)
Ⓑ **enternecerse** VPR 1 (= *conmoverse*) to be affected, be moved (to pity)
2 (= *ceder*) to relent, give in

entero Ⓐ ADJ 1 (= *completo*) whole, entire; **se comió el paquete ~ de galletas** he ate the whole *o* entire packet of biscuits; **se pasa el día ~ quejándose** he spends the whole *o* entire day complaining; **es famoso en el mundo ~** he's famous the whole world over, he's famous all over the world
2 **por ~** wholly, fully; **me dediqué por ~ a la investigación** I devoted myself wholly *o* fully to research
3 (*Mat*) whole, integral
4 [*persona*] (= *íntegro*) upright; (= *sereno*) composed; **un hombre muy ~** a man of great integrity, a very upright man; **estuvo muy entera durante el funeral** she was very composed *o* she kept her composure during the funeral
5 (*Andes, CAm, Caribe**) (= *idéntico*) identical, similar; **está ~ a su papá** he's just like his dad, he's the spitting image of his dad
6 (= *no castrado*) entire
Ⓑ SM 1 (*Mat*) integer, whole number
2 (*Com, Fin*) point; **las acciones han subido dos ~s** the shares have gone up two points
3 (*LAm*) (= *pago*) payment
4 (*Cono Sur Fin*) balance
5 (*Arg*) boilersuit

enteropostal SM air letter, aerogram

enterradero SM (*Cono Sur*) burial ground

enterrado ADJ [*tesoro, persona*] buried; [*uña*] ingrowing

enterrador(a) SM/F gravedigger

enterramiento SM burial, interment (*frm*)

enterrar ▸conjug 1j◂ VT 1 (= *ocultar en tierra*) to bury
2 (= *olvidarse de*) to bury, forget
3 (*LAm*) [+ *arma*] to thrust (**en** into), bury (**en** in)

enterratorio SM (*Cono Sur*) (= *cementerio*) Indian burial ground; (= *restos*) archaeological remains *pl*, site of archaeological interest

entesar ▸conjug 1j◂ VT to stretch, tauten

entibiar ▸conjug 1b◂ Ⓐ VT 1 [+ *lo caliente*] to cool, cool down
2 [+ *ira*] to cool, cool down
Ⓑ **entibiarse** VPR 1 [*lo caliente*] to become lukewarm
2 [*ira, amistad*] to cool off

entibo SM 1 (*Arquit*) buttress
2 (*Min*) prop

entidad SF 1 (= *esencia*) entity
2 (= *colectividad*) (*Admin, Pol*) body, organization; (*Com, Fin*) firm, company ► **entidad bancaria** bank ► **entidad comercial** company, business ► **entidad crediticia** credit company ► **entidad financiera** financial institution
3 **de ~** of importance

entierrar* ▸conjug 1a◂ VT (*Chile*) [+ *zapatos*] to dirty, make dirty

entierro SM 1 (= *acto*) burial, interment
2 (= *funeral*) funeral; **asistir al ~** to go to the funeral; → CARNAVAL
3 (= *tumba*) grave
4 (*LAm Arqueología*) (buried) treasure

entintar ▸conjug 1a◂ VT 1 (= *llenar de tinta*) [+ *tampón*] to ink; [+ *blanco*] to ink in
2 (= *manchar*) to stain with ink

entizar ▸conjug 1f◂ VT (*LAm Billar*) to chalk

entoldado SM awning

entoldar ▸conjug 1a◂ Ⓐ VT 1 [+ *patio, terraza*] to put an awning over, fit with an awning

2 (= *decorar*) to decorate (*with hangings*)
Ⓑ **entoldarse** VPR 1 (*Meteo*) to become overcast, cloud over
2 [*emoción, alegría*] to be dimmed
3 [*persona*] to give o.s. airs

entomología SF entomology

entomólogo/a SM/F entomologist

entonación SF 1 (*Ling*) intonation
2 (= *arrogancia*) haughtiness

entonado ADJ 1 (*Mús*) in tune
2 (= *arrogante*) haughty, arrogant
3 (*) (= *en forma*) lively, in good form

entonar ▸conjug 1a◂ Ⓐ VT 1 (*Mús*) [+ *canción*] to intone, sing; (*afinando*) to sing in tune; [+ *voz*] to modulate; [+ *nota*] to give, set; [+ *órgano*] to blow
2 [+ *alabanzas*] to sound
3 (*Med*) to tone up
4 (*Arte, Fot*) to tone
5 (= *vigorizar*) to liven up, enliven, invigorate
Ⓑ VI 1 (*Mús*) (= *cantar*) to intone (*frm*), sing; (= *cantar afinadamente*) to be in tune (**con** with)
2 [*colores*] to match
Ⓒ **entonarse** VPR 1 (= *mejorarse*) **toma, un cafecito para ~te** here's a nice cup of coffee to pick *o* perk you up
2 (*) (= *animarse*) to perk up
3 (= *engreírse*) to get arrogant, give o.s. airs

entonces ADV 1 (*uso temporal*) then, at that time; **desde ~** since then; **en aquel ~** at that time; **hasta ~** up till then; **las costumbres de ~** the customs of the time; **el ~ embajador de España** the then Spanish ambassador; **fue ~ que …** it was then that …, that was when …
2 (*uso concesivo*) so, then; **~, ¿qué hacemos?** so, what shall we do?, what shall we do then?; **¿~ cómo que no viniste?** then *o* so why didn't you come?; **pues ~** well then; **¡y ~!** (*Caribe, Cono Sur*) why of course!

entonelar ▸conjug 1a◂ VT to put into barrels, put into casks

entongado* ADJ (*Andes*) cross, riled*

entongar ▸conjug 1h◂ VT 1 (= *apilar*) to pile up, pile in layers
2 (*Andes**) (= *enojar*) to anger

entono SM 1 (*Mús*) intoning, intonation; (*afinando*) being in tune, singing in tune
2 (= *arrogancia*) haughtiness

entontecedor ADJ stupefying

entontecer ▸conjug 2d◂ Ⓐ VT to make silly
Ⓑ **entontecerse** VPR to get silly

entorchado SM 1 (*en uniforme*) gold braid, silver braid
2 (*Mús*) bass string

entorchar ▸conjug 1a◂ VT 1 (= *retorcer*) to twist, twist up
2 [+ *uniforme*] to braid

entornacional ADJ environmental

entornado ADJ [*ojos*] half-closed; [*puerta*] ajar

entornar ▸conjug 1a◂ VT 1 [+ *ojos*] to half-close; (*por el sol*) to screw up; [+ *puerta*] to leave ajar, half-close
2 (= *volcar*) to upset, tip over

entorno SM 1 (= *medioambiente*) environment; (*Literat*) setting, milieu; (= *clima*) climate; (= *escenario*) scene; **las personas de su ~** the people around him; **sacar a algn de su ~** to take sb away from/out of their normal environment; **el ~ cultural** the cultural scene ▸ **entorno natural** natural environment ▸ **entorno social** social setting
2 (*Inform*) environment ▸ **entorno de programación** programming environment ▸ **entorno de red(es)** network environment ▸ **entorno de trabajo** work(ing) environment ▸ **entorno gráfico** graphics environment

entorpecer ▸conjug 2d◂ VT 1 (= *estorbar*) (*gen*) to obstruct, hinder; [+ *proyectos*] to set back; [+ *tráfico*] to slow down, slow up; [+ *trabajo*] to delay, hinder
2 (= *aletargar*) [+ *entendimiento*] to dull, stupefy; [+ *miembro*] to make numb

entorpecimiento SM 1 (= *estorbo*) obstruction; (= *problema*) obstacle; (= *retraso*) delay, slowing-up
2 (= *aletargamiento*) [*del entendimiento*] dullness, stupefaction; [*de un miembro*] numbness

entrabamiento SM (*Chile*) obstruction

entrabar ▸conjug 1a◂ VT (*Chile*) to obstruct

entrada SF 1 (= *lugar de acceso*) entrance; **"entrada"** "way in", "entrance"; **a la ~ del metro** at the entrance to the underground; **le pidieron la identificación a la ~** they asked for some identification at the door; **las ~s a Madrid** roads into Madrid ▸ **entrada de artistas** stage door ▸ **entrada de servicio** tradesman's entrance ▸ **entrada lateral** side entrance ▸ **entrada principal** main entrance
2 (= *vestíbulo*) [*de casa*] hall, entrance hall; [*de hotel*] foyer
3 (= *llegada*) 3·1 (*a un lugar*) **no advirtió la ~ de su padre** she didn't notice her father come in; **sus ~s y salidas de prisión fueron constantes** he was constantly in and out of jail; **hicieron una ~ triunfal en Egipto** they made a triumphal entry into Egypt; **dar ~ a un lugar** to give access to a place; ✦**MODISMO de ~ por salida** (*Méx*): **nunca podemos platicar, tus visitas son siempre de ~ por salida** we never have time to chat, you're always in and out; **una muchacha de ~ por salida** a non-live-in maid, a daily maid
3·2 [*de correspondencia*] arrival; **bandeja de ~s** in-tray
3·3 (*Teat*) (*tb* **~ en escena**) entrance (on stage); **tropezó a la ~** he tripped as he made his entrance
3·4 (*Mús*) [*de instrumento, voz*] entry; **la soprano hizo una ~ muy brusca** the soprano came in very abruptly, the soprano's entry was very abrupt; **el director dio ~ a los vientos** the conductor brought in the wind section
3·5 (*Jur*) (*en un domicilio*) entry; **~ a viva fuerza** forced entry
3·6
▸ **entrada en vigor**: **tras la ~ en vigor de la ley** after the law came into effect *o* force; **la ~ en vigor del nuevo presupuesto tendrá lugar en enero** the new budget will take effect from January, the new budget will come into effect *o* force from January
4 (= *invasión*) [*de militares*] entry; [*de turistas, divisas*] influx; **la ~ de las tropas en 1940** the entry of the troops in 1940; **la ~ masiva de turistas** the huge influx of tourists
5 (= *acceso*) (*a espectáculo*) admission, entry; (*a país*) entry; (*a club, institución, carrera*) admission; **"entrada gratuita"** "admission free"; **la ~ de España en la Comunidad Europea** the entry of Spain into the European Community; **en su discurso de ~ a la Academia** in his introductory *o* opening speech to the Academy; **sus buenas notas le facilitaron la ~ en Medicina** his good marks enabled him to study Medicine; **dar ~ a algn** (*en un lugar*) to allow sb in; (*en club, sociedad*) to admit sb; **no le dimos ~ en nuestra sociedad** he was refused entry to our society, we did not admit him to our society; **prohibir la ~ a algn** to ban sb from entering; **"prohibida la entrada"** "no entry"
6 (= *billete*) ticket; **"no hay entradas"** "sold out"; **media ~** half price; **sacar una ~** to buy a ticket ▸ **entrada de abono** season ticket ▸ **entrada de protocolo** complimentary ticket
7 (= *público*) (*Teat*) audience; (*Dep*) crowd, turnout; **la segunda función contó con una buena ~** there was a good audience for the second performance; **la plaza registró más de media ~** the bullring was over half full; **el sábado hubo una gran ~** there was a big crowd *o* turnout on Saturday
8 (= *recaudación*) (*Teat*) receipts *pl*, takings *pl*; (*Dep*) gate money, receipts *pl*
9 (= *principio*) start; **os deseamos una feliz ~ de año** we wish you all the best for the new year; **de ~** (*desde el principio*) from the start, from the outset; (*al principio*) at first; **de ~ ya nos dijo que no** he said no from the outset, he said no right from the start; **de ~ no se lo quiso creer** at first he refused to believe it; **~ en materia** introduction
10 (*Esp*) (= *primer pago*) (*al comprar una vivienda, coche*) down payment, deposit; **hay que dar un 20% de ~** you have to put down a 20% deposit, you have to make a down payment of 20%; **"compre sin ~"** "no down payment", "no deposit"
11 (*Com*) (*en libro mayor*) entry
12 (= *vía de acceso*) (*Mec*) inlet, intake; (*Elec*) input ▸ **entrada de aire** air intake
13 (*Inform*) input ▸ **entrada de datos** data entry, data input ▸ **entrada de trabajos a distancia** remote job entry ▸ **entrada inmediata** immediate access
14 (*Ftbl*) tackle; **hacer una ~** to tackle sb
15 (*Culin*) starter; **de ~ tomaremos una sopa de verduras** we'll have vegetable soup as a starter
16 [*de diccionario*] entry
17 **entradas** 17·1 (*en el pelo*) receding hairline *sing*; **tener ~s** to have a receding hairline
17·2 (*Fin*) income *sing*; **el total de sus ~s** his total income
▸ **entradas familiares** family income *sing*
▸ **entradas y salidas** income and expenditure *sing*
18 (*Caribe*) (= *ataque*) attack, onslaught; (= *asalto*) assault; (= *paliza*) beating

entradilla SF (*Prensa*) lead-in, opening paragraph

entrado ADJ 1 (= *abundante*) **~ en años** (*euf*) elderly; **~ en carnes** (*euf*) overweight
2 (= *avanzado*) **hasta bien ~ el siglo XIX** until well into the 19th century; **hasta muy entrada la noche** (*antes de medianoche*) until late at night; (*de madrugada*) until the small hours

entrador ADJ 1 (*LAm**) (= *atrevido*) daring, forward
2 (*Cono Sur**) (= *simpático*) charming, likeable

[3] (*Andes, Caribe, Méx*) (= *mujeriego*) amorously inclined
[4] (*CAm*) (= *coqueto*) flirtatious

entramado SM [1] (*Arquit*) (= *estructura*) framework, timber, lumber (*EEUU*); [*de puente*] framework
[2] (= *red*) network

entrambos ADJ PL (*liter*) both

entrampar ▸conjug 1a◂ Ⓐ VT [1] [+ *animal*] to trap, snare
[2] (= *engañar*) to snare, trick
[3] (= *endeudar*) to burden with debts
[4] (= *enredar*) to tangle up
Ⓑ **entramparse** VPR [1] (= *endeudarse*) to get into debt
[2] (= *enredarse*) to get tangled up

entrante Ⓐ ADJ [1] [*mes, semana*] next; **la semana ~** next week
[2] [*ministro, presidente*] new, incoming; [*correo*] incoming; **correo ~ y saliente** incoming and outgoing mail
Ⓑ SM [1] (*Culin*) starter
[2] (*Geog*) inlet
[3] (*Arquit*) recess
[4] ► **entrantes y salientes**† people coming to and leaving a house *etc*

entraña SF [1] **entrañas** (*Anat*) entrails, bowels; **en las ~s de la Tierra** in the bowels of the Earth; ✦*MODISMOS* **arrancar las ~s a algn** to break sb's heart, tear sb's heart out; **dar hasta las ~s** to give one's all; **echar las ~s*** to puke (up)*
[2] (= *lo esencial*) core
[3] **entranas** (= *sentimientos*) heart *sing*, feelings; (= *temperamento*) disposition *sing*; **no tener ~s** to be heartless; **¡hijo de mis ~s!** my precious child!, my beloved son!; **de malas ~s** malicious, evil-minded; **de buenas ~s** well-intentioned, kind-hearted

entrañabilidad SF [1] (= *intimidad*) closeness, intimacy
[2] (= *afabilidad*) loveable nature
[3] (= *encanto*) charm, winning nature

entrañable ADJ [1] (= *querido*) [*amigo*] dear, close; [*amistad*] deep; [*paisaje*] beloved, dearly loved; [*recuerdo*] fond
[2] (= *afectuoso*) affectionate
[3] (= *simpático*) charming, winning

entrañablemente ADV [*amar etc*] dearly, deeply

entrañar ▸conjug 1a◂ Ⓐ VT (= *contener*) to contain; (= *acarrear*) to entail
Ⓑ **entrañarse** VPR to become deeply attached (**con** to)

entrañudo ADJ (*Cono Sur*) [1] (= *valiente*) brave, daring
[2] (= *cruel*) cruel, heartless

entrar ▸conjug 1a◂ Ⓐ VI [1] (*en un lugar*) (*acercándose al hablante*) to come in, enter (*más frm*); (*alejándose del hablante*) to go in, enter (*más frm*); **—¿se puede? —sí, entra** "may I?" — "yes, come in"; **hágalo ~** show him in; **entré en** o (*LAm*) **a la casa** I went into the house; **~on en mi cuarto mientras yo dormía** they came into my room while I was asleep; **la ayudó a ~ en el coche** he helped her (get) into the car; **no me dejaron ~ en la discoteca** I wasn't allowed into the club; **entró en la habitación dando saltos** she bounced into the room; **entró corriendo en la habitación** she ran into the room; **entró tercero en la meta** he crossed the line in third place; **entra frío por la puerta** there's a draught coming in through the door; **el río entra en el lago** the river flows into the lake; **me ha entrado algo en el ojo** I've got something in my eye; **espera un momento, es sólo ~ y salir** wait for me a minute, I won't be long; ✦*MODISMOS* **yo por ahí no entro** that's one thing I won't accept *o* have; **~ en detalles** to go into detail; **no ~ ni salir en un asunto** to play no part in a matter
[2] (= *encajar*) **la maleta no entra en el maletero** the case won't go *o* fit in the boot; **el sofá no entraba por la puerta** the sofa wouldn't go *o* fit through the door; **¿entra uno más?** is there room for one more?, will one more fit?; **estoy lleno, ya no me entra nada más** I'm full, I couldn't eat another thing; **este pantalón no me entra** these trousers don't fit (me); **las historias de este libro entran de lleno en el surrealismo** the stories in this book are genuinely surrealist, the stories in this book come right into the category of surrealism
[3] (= *estar incluido*) **el vino no entra en el precio** the wine is not included (in the price); **eso no entraba en nuestros planes** that wasn't part of our plans; **ese partido entra dentro de la segunda ronda** that is a second-round match; **en un kilo entran cuatro manzanas** you get four apples to the kilo
[4] (= *comenzar*) [4·1] [*persona*] **¿a qué hora entras a clase?** what time do you start school?; **entra a trabajar a las ocho** she starts work at eight o'clock; **~ en una profesión** to take up a profession; **~ en una asociación** to join a society; **al ~ en la madurez** on reaching middle age; **entró de mensajero** he started out as a courier; **entró en la revista como director** he joined the magazine as editor; **entró a formar parte del comité central** he became a member of the central committee
[4·2] **~ en calor** to warm up; **~ en coma** to go into a coma; **~ en contacto con algn** to contact sb
[4·3] [*época, estación*] **en el milenio que entra** in the new millennium; **el mes que entra** the coming month, next month
[5] (*con sensaciones*) **me entró sed** I started to feel thirsty; **me entró sueño** I started to feel sleepy; **me ha entrado hambre al verte comer** watching you eat has made me hungry; **me ~on ganas de reír** I felt like laughing
[6] [*conocimientos, idea*] **no hay forma de que le entre el álgebra** he just can't seem to get the hang of algebra; **no les entra en la cabeza que eso no puede ser así** they can't seem to get it into their heads that this isn't on
[7] (*) (= *soportar*) to bear, stand; **ese tío no me entra** I can't bear *o* stand that fellow
[8] (*Inform*) to access; **~ en el sistema** to access the system
[9] (*Mús*) [*instrumento, voz*] to come in
[10] (*Teat*) to enter
Ⓑ VT [1] (*) [+ *objeto*] (*acercándose al hablante*) to bring in; (*alejándose del hablante*) to take in; **entra las sillas para que no se mojen** bring the chairs in so they don't get wet; **la maestra entró a los niños a clase** the teacher took the children into the classroom; **no podrás ~ el sillón por esa puerta** you won't be able to get the armchair in through that door; **necesitó ayuda para ~ el coche en el garaje** he needed some help getting the car into the garage
[2] (*) (= *abordar a*) to deal with, approach; **sabe ~ a la gente** he knows how to deal with *o* approach people
[3] [+ *futbolista*] to tackle
[4] (*Mil*) to attack

> **ENTRAR**
>
> **Para precisar la manera de entrar**
>
> **Entrar (en)** por regla general se suele traducir por **come in(to)** o por **go in(to)**, según la dirección del movimiento (hacia o en dirección contraria al hablante), pero, **come** y **go** se pueden substituir por otros verbos de movimiento si la frase en español explica la forma en que se entra:
>
> Entró cojeando en Urgencias
> ***He limped into Casualty***
> Acabo de ver a un ratón entrar corriendo en ese agujero
> ***I've just seen a mouse running into that hole***
>
> *Para otros usos y ejemplos ver la entrada.*

entrazado* ADJ (*Cono Sur*) [1] [*persona, vestido*] **mal ~** shabby, ragged; **bien ~** well-dressed, natty*
[2] [*persona, expresión*] **mal ~** nasty-looking; **bien ~** pleasant-looking

entre PREP [1] (= *en medio de*) [1·1] (*dos elementos*) between; **~ las montañas y el mar** between the mountains and the sea; **vendrá ~ las diez y las once** he'll be coming between ten and eleven; **nos veíamos ~ clase y clase** we saw each other between lessons; **~ azul y verde** somewhere between blue and green; **un líquido ~ dulce y amargo** a liquid which is half-sweet, half-sour; **dudo ~ comprar éste o aquél** I'm not sure whether to buy this one or that one; **lo cogió ~ sus manos** she took it in her hands; ✦*MODISMO* **estar ~ la vida y la muerte** to be fighting for one's life; *ver tb* **paréntesis 2, semana**
[1·2] (*más de dos elementos*) among, amongst; **había un baúl ~ las maletas** there was a trunk in among(st) the cases; **¿has buscado ~ las fotografías?** have you looked among(st) the photographs?; **una costumbre muy extendida ~ los romanos** a widespread custom among(st) the Romans; **puedes hablar, estamos ~ amigos** you can speak freely, we're among(st) friends; **paso el día ~ estas cuatro paredes** I spend the whole day within these four walls; **se abrieron paso ~ la multitud** they forced their way through the crowd; **lo vi ~ el público** I saw him in the audience; **~ los que conozco es el mejor** it's the best of those that I know; **empezó a trabajar como mensajero, ~ otras cosas** he started work as a courier, among(st) other things
[2] (*indicando colaboración, participación*) **lo terminamos ~ los dos** between the two of us we finished it; **le compraremos un regalo ~ todos** we'll buy her a present between all of us, we'll all club together to buy her a present; **¿~ cuántos habéis hecho el trabajo?** how many of you did it take to do the work?; **esto lo solucionaremos ~ nosotros** we'll sort that out among(st) *o* between ourselves; **la cuento ~ mis mejores amigas** I count her as one of my best friends; **~ sí: las mujeres ha-**

blaban ~ sí the women were talking among(st) themselves; **los tres hermanos están muy unidos ~ sí** the three brothers are very close to each other
[3] (*uso aditivo*) **~ viaje y alojamiento nos gastamos 80 euros** we spent 80 euros between the travel and the accommodation, the travel and the accommodation came to 80 euros between them; **~ niños y niñas habrá unos veinte en total** there are about twenty in total, if you count boys and girls; **~ que era tarde y hacía frío, decidimos no salir** what with it being late and cold, we decided not to go out; **~ unas cosas y otras no conseguía dormir** what with one thing and another I couldn't sleep; **~ unas cosas y otras se nos hizo de noche** before we knew it, it was night
[4] (*Mat*) **20 ~ 4** 20 divided by 4; **20 ~ 4 es igual a 5** 4 into 20 goes 5 (times)
[5] (*esp LAm**) **~ más estudia más aprende** the more he studies the more he learns
[6] **~ tanto** *ver* **entretanto**

entre... PREF inter...

entreabierto Ⓐ PP *de* **entreabrir**
Ⓑ ADJ (*gen*) half-open; [*puerta*] ajar

entreabrir ▸conjug 3a◂ (*pp* **entreabierto**) VT (*gen*) to half-open, open halfway; [+ *puerta*] to leave ajar

entreacto SM interval, intermission (*EEUU*), entr'acte (*frm*)

entreayudarse ▸conjug 1a◂ VPR to help one another, be of mutual assistance

entrecano ADJ [*pelo*] greyish, grayish (*EEUU*), greying, graying (*EEUU*); [*persona*] going grey *o* (*EEUU*) gray

entrecejo SM space between the eyebrows; **arrugar el ~, fruncir el ~** to frown, wrinkle one's brow

entrecerrar ▸conjug 1j◂ VT (*esp LAm*) (*gen*) to half-close, close halfway; [+ *puerta*] to leave ajar

entrechocar ▸conjug 1g◂ Ⓐ VI [*dientes*] to chatter
Ⓑ **entrechocarse** VPR [1] (= *chocar*) to collide, crash
[2] [*opiniones*] to clash

entrecó SM entrecote, sirloin steak

entrecoger ▸conjug 2c◂ VT [1] to catch, intercept
[2] (= *obligar*) to press, compel

entrecomillado Ⓐ ADJ in inverted commas, in quotes (*EEUU*)
Ⓑ SM inverted commas *pl*, quotes *pl*

entrecomillar ▸conjug 1a◂ VT to place in inverted commas, put inverted commas round

entrecoro SM chancel

entrecortadamente ADV [*respirar*] in a laboured way; [*hablar*] falteringly, hesitatingly

entrecortado ADJ [*respiración*] laboured, labored (*EEUU*), difficult; [*habla*] faltering, hesitant; **con la voz entrecortada** in a faltering voice, in a voice choked with emotion

entrecortar ▸conjug 1a◂ VT [1] [+ *objeto*] to cut halfway through, partially cut
[2] (= *interrumpir*) to cut off, interrupt; [+ *voz*] to cause to falter

entrecot SM entrecote, sirloin steak

entrecruzar ▸conjug 1f◂ Ⓐ VT [1] (= *entrelazar*) to interlace, interweave, intertwine
[2] (*Biol*) to cross, interbreed

> ➤ LENGUA Y USO: **entrega 2** 47.2, 47.3

Ⓑ **entrecruzarse** VPR [1] [*hilos, cintas*] to interweave, intertwine
[2] (*Biol*) to interbreed

entrecubierta SF, **entrecubiertas** SFPL between decks

entredicho SM [1] **estar en ~** (= *ser discutible*) to be questionable, be debatable; **su profesionalidad está** *o* **ha quedado en ~** grave doubts have been cast on his professionalism; **poner algo en ~** (= *cuestionar*) to raise doubts about sth, call sth into question; (= *comprometer*) to jeopardize sth, endanger sth
[2] (= *prohibición*) prohibition, ban; (*Jur*) injunction; **estar en ~** to be under a ban, be banned; **levantar el ~ a** to raise the ban on; **poner algo en ~** (= *prohibir*) to place a ban on sth
[3] (*Cono Sur*) (= *ruptura*) break-up, split
[4] (*Andes*) (= *alarma*) alarm bell

entredós SM [1] (*Cos*) insertion, panel
[2] (= *mueble*) cabinet, dresser

entrefino ADJ [*tela*] medium, medium-quality

entrefuerte ADJ (*LAm*) [*tabaco*] medium strong

▼**entrega** SF [1] (= *acto*) [*de documento, solicitud*] submission; **esta noche es la ~ de premios** tonight is the awards ceremony; **mañana será la ~ de notas** the marks will be given out tomorrow; **tienen que pagar un millón a la ~ de llaves** they have to pay a million on handing over the keys *o* when the keys are handed over; **"entrega de llaves inmediata"** "ready for immediate occupancy"; **hacer ~ de** [+ *regalo, premio, cheque*] to present; **le hizo ~ de la medalla al valor** he presented him with an award for bravery
[2] (*Com*) [*de cartas, mercancías*] delivery; **pagadero a la ~** payable on delivery; **los gastos de ~ no están incluídos** delivery is not included; **si no se efectúa la ~, devuélvase a ...** if undelivered, please return to ...; **la ~ se hará en un plazo de 15 días** it will be delivered within 15 days, delivery within 15 days; **"entrega a domicilio"** "we deliver"; **orden de ~** delivery order ► **entrega contra pago, entrega contra reembolso** cash on delivery
[3] (*al rendirse*) [*de rehenes*] handover; [*de armas*] surrender, handover
[4] (= *sección*) [*de enciclopedia, novela*] instalment, installment (*EEUU*); [*de revista*] issue; [*de serie televisiva*] series; **una novela por ~s** a novel published in instalments, a serialized novel
[5] (= *dedicación*) dedication, devotion; **su ~ a la causa de los indígenas** her dedication to the cause of the native people
[6] (*Dep*) pass

entregado ADJ [1] (= *dedicado*) **estar ~ a** [+ *causa, creencia, actividad, trabajo*] to be dedicated to, be devoted to; **una vida entregada a ayudar a los más necesitados** a life dedicated *o* devoted to helping those most in need; **vive totalmente ~ a la música** his life is totally dedicated *o* devoted to music
[2] (= *sacrificado*) selfless; **es una persona muy entregada** she's a very selfless person

entregar ▸conjug 1h◂ Ⓐ VT [1] (= *dar*) [1·1] [+ *impreso, documento, trabajo*] to hand in, give in, submit (*frm*); **hay que ~ la redacción mañana** the essay has to be handed in *o* given in tomorrow; **el proyecto se ~á a la comisión para que lo estudie** the plan will be put before the commission for them to study; **entregó su alma a Dios** he departed this life; ✦**MODISMO ~las** (*Chile**) to kick the bucket*
[1·2] (*en mano*) (*gen*) to hand over; [+ *regalo*] to give; **me entregó la carta esta mañana** she gave me the letter this morning, she handed over the letter to me this morning
[1·3] [+ *premio, cheque*] to present; **hoy entregan los premios** they are presenting the awards today, the awards ceremony is today
[2] (= *distribuir*) (*gen*) to give out; [+ *correo, pedido*] to deliver; **mañana ~emos las notas del examen** we'll give out the exam marks tomorrow; **"entregamos sus pedidos al día siguiente"** "next day delivery"; **"para entregar a"** (*Com*) (*en envíos*) "for the attention of"
[3] (= *ceder*) [+ *poderes, botín, rehenes*] to hand over; [+ *armas, país*] to hand over, surrender; **~on las joyas a la policía** they handed over the jewels to the police; **el enemigo acabó por ~ las armas** the enemy finally handed over *o* surrendered their weapons; **el juez entregó la custodia del niño a su abuela** the judge gave *o* awarded *o* granted custody of the boy to his grandmother
[4] (*en boda*) [+ *novia*] to give away
Ⓑ **entregarse** VPR [1] (= *rendirse*) to give o.s. up, surrender; **los secuestradores se ~on a la policía** the hijackers gave themselves up *o* surrendered to the police
[2] (= *dejarse dominar*) **~se a** [+ *sueño, tentación*] to succumb to; **se entregó a la desesperación** she gave in to despair; **~se a la bebida** to take to drink
[3] (= *dedicarse*) **~se a algo** to devote o.s. to sth; **se ha entregado por completo al cuidado de su padre** she has devoted herself entirely to looking after her father; **todas las noches me entrego a la lectura de la Biblia** I devote all my evenings to reading the Bible; **~se a algn** (*sexualmente*) to give o.s. to sb; **me entregué a ella sin condiciones** I gave her my unconditional love
[4] (= *adueñarse*) **~se de algo** to take possession of sth

entreguerras: el período de ~ the inter-war period, the period between the wars (*i.e.* 1918-39)

entreguismo SM (*Pol*) (= *apaciguamiento*) appeasement, policy of appeasement; (= *derrotismo*) defeatism; (= *oportunismo*) opportunism; (= *traición*) betrayal, selling-out

entrelazado ADJ intertwined, interlaced, interwoven (**de** with)

entrelazar ▸conjug 1f◂ VT, **entrelazarse** VPR to intertwine, interlace, interweave

entrelistado ADJ striped

entrelucir ▸conjug 3f◂ VI [1] (= *verse*) to show through
[2] (= *relucir*) to gleam, shine dimly

entremás Ⓐ ADV (*Andes, Méx*) (= *además*) moreover; (= *especialmente*) especially
Ⓑ CONJ **~ lo pienso, más convencido estoy** the more I think about it the more convinced I am

entremedias ADV [1] (= *en medio*) in between, halfway; (= *entretanto*) in the meantime
[2] **~ de** between, among

entremedio SM (*LAm*) interval, intermission (*EEUU*)

entremés SM [1] (*Teat, Hist*) interlude, short farce

[2] (*Culin*) side dish; **"entremeses"** "hors d'oeuvres" ► **entremés salado** savoury, savory (*EEUU*)

ENTREMÉS

An **entremés** *is a short farce used as an entertaining interval between the first and second act of a* **comedia**. *It is thought that the* **entremés** *(derived from the Italian* **intermezzo***) was first performed on the Spanish stage in the 16th century and derives from the influential Italian* **Commedia dell'Arte**. *Often using slapstick, stock characters and situations,* **entremeses** *had enormous audience appeal and were written by such distinguished writers as Miguel de Cervantes.*

entremesera SF tray for hors d'oeuvres

entremeter ▸conjug 2a◂ VT (= *insertar*) to insert; (= *poner entre*) to put between

entremeterse *etc ver* **entrometerse** *etc*

entremezclar ▸conjug 1a◂ VT, **entremezclarse** VPR to intermingle; **entremezclado de** interspersed with

entrenador(a) Ⓐ SM/F trainer, coach
Ⓑ SM (*Aer*) trainer, training plane ► **entrenador de pilotaje** flight simulator

entrenamiento SM (= *ejercicios*) training; (= *sesión*) training session; (*por el entrenador*) coaching

entrenar ▸conjug 1a◂ Ⓐ VT (*Dep*) to train, coach; [+ *caballo*] to exercise; **estar entrenado** [+ *futbolista, atleta*] to be in training, be fit
Ⓑ VI to train
Ⓒ **entrenarse** VPR to train

entreno SM = **entrenamiento**

entreoír ▸conjug 3p◂ VT to half-hear, hear indistinctly

entrepágina SF centrefold

entrepaño SM [1] (= *muro*) wall, stretch of wall
[2] (= *panel*) door panel
[3] (= *anaquel*) shelf

entrepierna SF, **entrepiernas** SFPL [1] (*Anat*) crotch, crutch
[2] (= *medida*) inside leg, measurement; ✦*MODISMO* **pasarse algo por la ~**‡ (= *rechazar*) to reject sth totally, throw sth out of the window*; (= *despreciar*) to feel utter contempt for sth

entrepuente SM between-decks

entrerrejado ADJ interwoven, criss-crossed

entrerrenglonar ▸conjug 1a◂ VT to interline, write between the lines of

entresacar ▸conjug 1g◂ VT [1] [+ *información, datos*] (= *seleccionar*) to pick out, select; (= *cribar*) to sift
[2] [+ *pelo, plantas*] to thin out

entresemana SF midweek; (= *días laborables*) working days of the week; **de ~** midweek *antes de s*; (*LAm*) midweek; **cualquier día de ~** any day midweek, any day in the middle of the week

entresijo SM [1] (= *secreto*) secret, mystery; (= *parte oculta*) hidden aspect; (= *dificultad*) difficulty, snag; **este asunto tiene muchos ~s** this business has many ins and outs; **él tiene sus ~s** he's hard to fathom; **se conoce todos los ~s de la justicia** he knows all the ins and outs of the law, he knows the law inside-out
[2] (*Anat*) mesentery

entresuelo SM mezzanine, entresol; (*Teat*) dress circle

entretanto Ⓐ ADV meanwhile, meantime
Ⓑ CONJ **~ esto se produce** until this happens
Ⓒ SM meantime; **en el ~** in the meantime

entretecho SM (*Chile, Col*) attic, garret

entretejer ▸conjug 2a◂ VT [1] [+ *hilos*] to interweave, intertwine
[2] (= *entremezclar*) to interweave

entretejido SM interweaving

entretela SF [1] (*Cos*) interlining
[2] **entretelas** (= *entrañas*) **¡hijo de mis ~s!** my beloved son!, my beloved child!; **confesó sentirse feliz en sus ~s** he admitted feeling really happy deep down; **conozco las ~s del partido** I know the ins and outs of the party, I know the party inside-out

entretelar ▸conjug 1a◂ VT to interline

entretelón SM thick curtain, heavy curtain

entretención SF (*LAm*) (= *entretenimiento*) entertainment

entretener ▸conjug 2k◂ Ⓐ VT [1] (= *divertir*) to entertain, amuse; **nos entretuvo con sus chistes mientras esperábamos** he kept us entertained *o* amused with his jokes while we were waiting; **hacer punto la entretiene** she amuses herself by knitting
[2] (= *retener*) to keep, detain (*más frm*); **pues no le entretengo más** then I won't keep *o* (*más frm*) detain you any longer; **una vecina me entretuvo hablando en las escaleras** a neighbour kept me talking on the stairs
[3] (= *distraer*) **~ a algn** to distract sb's attention; **uno de los ladrones entretuvo a la dependienta** one of the thieves distracted the shop assistant's attention; **~ algo: entretuvieron la espera leyendo** they whiled away the time by reading; **me tomé una tapa para ~ el hambre** I had a snack to take the edge off my hunger
[4] (= *dar largas a*) **me está entreteniendo con mentiras para no pagarme** he's putting me off with lies so as not to pay me
[5] (= *mantener*) [+ *ilusiones*] to nourish; [+ *fuego*] to maintain
Ⓑ VI **la tele entretiene mucho** TV is very entertaining
Ⓒ **entretenerse** VPR [1] (= *divertirse*) to amuse o.s.; **se entretenían contando historias** they amused themselves by telling stories, they kept themselves amused by telling stories
[2] (= *tardar*) to hang about; **¡no te entretengas!** don't hang about!

entretenida SF [1] (= *querida*) mistress; (= *mantenida*) kept woman
[2] **dar (con) la ~ a algn** (*con promesas*) to hold sb off with vague promises, stall sb; (*hablando*) to keep sb talking

entretenido Ⓐ ADJ [*libro, obra de teatro*] entertaining, amusing; [*trabajo*] demanding
Ⓑ SM (*) gigolo, toyboy*

entretenimiento SM [1] (= *diversión*) entertainment, amusement; **hace crucigramas como ~** he does crosswords for entertainment *o* amusement; **es sólo un ~** it's just for amusement; **programa de ~** an entertainment programme
[2] (††) (= *mantenimiento*) upkeep, maintenance; **sólo necesita un ~ mínimo** it only needs minimum maintenance

entretiempo SM (= *primavera*) spring; (= *otoño*) autumn, fall (*EEUU*); **un abrigo de ~** a light coat, a lightweight coat

entrever ▸conjug 2u◂ VT [1] (= *vislumbrar*) to make out; **podía ~ una luz a lo lejos** I could just make out a light in the distance; **dejar ~ algo** to suggest sth, hint at sth; **dejó ~ la posibilidad de que me renovaran el contrato** he suggested that my contract might be renewed, he hinted at the possibility of my contract being renewed; **dejó ~ sus reservas sobre la moneda única** he let it be seen *o* known that he had reservations over the single currency; **estas manifestaciones dejan ~ fisuras en el partido** these demonstrations seem to suggest divisions within the party
[2] (= *adivinar*) to guess; **supo ~ sus verdaderas intenciones** she guessed his true intentions
[3] (= *presentir*) to glimpse; **podemos ~ una solución** we can glimpse a solution

entreverado ADJ [1] [*tocino*] streaky
[2] (= *intercalado*) mixed, interspersed, intermingled (**de** with)
[3] (= *poco uniforme*) patchy

entreverar ▸conjug 1a◂ Ⓐ VT (= *intercalar*) to mix, intermingle
Ⓑ **entreverarse** VPR [1] to be intermingled, be intermixed
[2] (*Cono Sur*) (= *implicarse*) to become mixed up in, get involved in

entrevero SM [1] (*LAm*) mix-up
[2] (*Cono Sur*) (= *desorden*) confusion, disorder; (= *riña*) brawl; (*Mil*) confused cavalry skirmish

entrevía SF (*Ferro*) gauge, gage (*EEUU*); **de ~ angosta** narrow-gauge *antes de s* ► **entrevía angosta** narrow gauge ► **entrevía normal** standard gauge

▼**entrevista** SF [1] (= *conversación*) interview; **hacer una ~ a algn** to interview sb ► **entrevista de trabajo** job interview
[2] (= *reunión*) meeting, conference; **celebrar una ~ con algn** to hold a meeting with sb

entrevistado/a SM/F interviewee, person being interviewed

entrevistador(a) SM/F interviewer

entrevistar ▸conjug 1a◂ Ⓐ VT to interview
Ⓑ **entrevistarse** VPR to meet; **~se con algn** to have a meeting with sb, meet with sb; **el ministro se entrevistó con la reina ayer** the minister had a meeting with *o* met with the queen yesterday; **los vecinos se ~on con el alcalde** the residents were received by the Mayor yesterday

entripado SM (= *secreto*) ghastly secret; (= *resentimiento*) concealed anger, suppressed rage

entripar ▸conjug 1a◂ Ⓐ VT [1] (*Andes**) (= *enfurecer*) to enrage, madden
[2] (*Caribe, Méx*) (= *mojar*) to soak
[3] (*Méx*‡) (= *embarazar*) to put in the family way, put in the club
Ⓑ **entriparse** VPR [1] (*Andes**) (= *enfadarse*) to get cross, get upset
[2] (*Caribe, Méx*) (= *mojarse*) to get soaked

▼**entristecer** ▸conjug 2d◂ Ⓐ VT to sadden, make sad
Ⓑ **entristecerse** VPR to grow sad

➤ LENGUA Y USO: entrevista 1 46.4 entristecer A 51.4

entrometerse ▸conjug 2a◂ VPR (= *interferir*) to meddle, interfere (**en** in, with); (= *molestar*) to intrude

entrometido/a Ⓐ ADJ meddlesome, interfering
Ⓑ SM/F busybody, meddler

entromparse* ▸conjug 1a◂ VPR **1** (= *emborracharse*) to get drunk, get sozzled*
2 (*LAm*) (= *enfadarse*) to get cross, get mad (*EEUU*)

entrón ADJ **1** (*Andes*) (= *entrometido*) meddlesome
2 (*Méx*) (= *animoso*) spirited, daring
3 (*Méx*) (= *coqueto*) flirtatious

entroncar ▸conjug 1g◂ Ⓐ VT to connect, establish a relationship between
Ⓑ VI **1** [*familia*] to be related, be connected (**con** to)
2 (= *estar relacionado*) to be linked, be related (**con** to)
3 (*Ferro*) to join, connect (**con** to)

entronización SF **1** [*de rey*] enthronement
2 (= *ensalzamiento*) exaltation

entronizar ▸conjug 1f◂ VT **1** [+ *rey*] to enthrone **2** (*fig*) (= *ensalzar*) to exalt

entronque SM **1** (= *parentesco*) relationship, link
2 (= *enlace*) connexion, link
3 (*LAm Ferro*) junction

entropía SF entropy

entruchada* SF **1** (= *trampa*) trap, trick
2 (*Cono Sur*) (= *discusión*) slanging match*; (= *conversación*) intimate conversation

entruchar* ▸conjug 1a◂ Ⓐ VT to lure, decoy, lead by the nose
Ⓑ **entrucharse** VPR (*Méx*) (= *entrometerse*) to stick one's nose into other people's affairs

entuerto **1** SM (= *injusticia*) wrong, injustice
2 **entuertos** (*Med*) afterpains

entumecer ▸conjug 2d◂ Ⓐ VT to numb
Ⓑ **entumecerse** VPR **1** [*miembro*] to go numb, go to sleep
2 [*río*] to swell, rise; [*mar*] to surge

entumecido ADJ numb

entumecimiento SM numbness

entumido ADJ **1** (*LAm*) (= *entumecido*) numb
2 (*Andes, Méx*) (= *tímido*) timid

enturbiar ▸conjug 1b◂ Ⓐ VT **1** [+ *líquido*] to muddy, make cloudy
2 (= *complicar*) [+ *asunto*] to confuse, fog; [+ *mente, persona*] to confuse
Ⓑ **enturbiarse** VPR **1** [*líquido*] to get muddy, become cloudy
2 (= *complicarse*) [*asunto*] to become obscured; [*mente, persona*] to get confused
3 [*relaciones*] to be marred

enturcado‡ ADJ (*CAm*) [*persona*] hopping mad*, livid; **un problema ~** a knotty problem

entusiasmante ADJ thrilling, exciting

▼ **entusiasmar** ▸conjug 1a◂ Ⓐ VT (= *apasionar*) to fire with enthusiasm, excite; (= *encantar*) to delight; **me entusiasma el trabajo** I love my work; **no le entusiasma mucho la idea** he's not very keen on the idea
Ⓑ **entusiasmarse** VPR to get enthusiastic, get excited (**con, por** about); **se ha quedado entusiasmada con el vestido** she loves the dress, she is delighted with the dress

entusiasmo SM enthusiasm (**por** for); **con ~** (= *con apasionamiento*) enthusiastically; (= *con interés*) keenly

entusiasta Ⓐ ADJ (= *apasionado*) enthusiastic (**de** about); (= *interesado*) keen (**de** on)
Ⓑ SMF (= *aficionado*) enthusiast, fan*; (= *admirador*) admirer

entusiástico ADJ enthusiastic

enumeración SF (= *listado*) enumeration; (= *cuenta*) count, reckoning

enumerar ▸conjug 1a◂ VT (= *nombrar*) to enumerate; (= *contar*) to count, reckon up

enunciación SF **1** [*de teoría*] enunciation
2 (= *declaración*) declaration

enunciado SM **1** (= *principio*) principle
2 (*Prensa*) heading

enunciar ▸conjug 1b◂ VT [+ *teoría*] to enunciate, state; [+ *idea*] to put forward

enuresis SF INV enuresis

envagonar ▸conjug 1a◂ VT (*LAm*) [+ *mercancías*] to load onto a railway truck

envainar ▸conjug 1a◂ Ⓐ VT **1** [+ *arma*] to sheathe, put in a sheath; **¡envéinala!**‡ shut your trap!‡, shut it!‡
2 (*Andes*) (= *molestar*) to vex, annoy
Ⓑ VI (*Andes*) (= *sucumbir*) to succumb
Ⓒ **envainarse** VPR **1** (*Andes, Caribe**) (*en líos*) to get into trouble; **estar envainado** to be in a jam *o* fix*, be in trouble
2 **envainársela*** to take back what one has said, back down

envalentonamiento SM (= *valor*) boldness; (*pey*) Dutch courage, bravado

envalentonar ▸conjug 1a◂ Ⓐ VT to make bold, embolden
Ⓑ **envalentonarse** VPR (= *cobrar valor*) to pluck up courage; (*pey*) (= *insolentarse*) to become defiant; (= *jactarse*) to brag

envanecer ▸conjug 2d◂ Ⓐ VT to make conceited
Ⓑ **envanecerse** VPR to become conceited, grow vain

envanecido ADJ conceited, stuck-up*

envanecimiento SM conceit, vanity

envaramiento SM (*Méx*) numbness, stiffness

envarar ▸conjug 1a◂ Ⓐ VT to stiffen, make stiff
Ⓑ **envararse** VPR [*pierna, brazo*] to become stiff; [*persona*] to stiffen

envasado SM (*en cajas*) packing; (*en paquetes*) packaging; (*en latas*) canning; (*en botellas, tarros*) bottling

envasador(a) SM/F (*en cajas, paquetes*) packer; (*en latas*) canner; (*en botellas, tarros*) bottler

envasar ▸conjug 1a◂ Ⓐ VT **1** (= *guardar*) (*en cajas*) to pack; (*en paquetes*) to package; (*en botellas, tarros*) to bottle; (*en latas*) to can, tin; (*en tonel*) to barrel; (*en saco*) to sack, bag
2 (*) [+ *vino*] to knock back*
3 (*esp LAm*) **~ un puñal en algn** to plunge a dagger into sb, bury a dagger in sb
Ⓑ VI (*) to tipple, knock it back*

envase SM **1** (= *acto*) (= *empaquetado*) packing, wrapping; (= *embotellado*) bottling; (= *enlatado*) canning
2 (= *recipiente*) container; **precio con ~** price including packing; **~ retornable** returnable container; **géneros sin ~** loose goods, unpackaged *o* unwrapped goods; **~ de vidrio** glass container
3 (= *botella*) (*llena*) bottle; (*vacía*) empty; **~s a devolver** returnable empties
4 (= *lata*) can, tin

envasijar ▸conjug 1a◂ VT (*LAm*) = **envasar A1**

envedijarse ▸conjug 1a◂ VPR **1** (= *enredarse*) [*pelo*] to get tangled; [*ovillo*] to get tangled, become entangled
2 [*personas*] to come to blows

envegarse ▸conjug 1h◂ VPR (*Cono Sur*) to get swampy, turn into a swamp

envejecer ▸conjug 2d◂ Ⓐ VT to age, make look old
Ⓑ VI, **envejecerse** VPR **1** [*persona*] (= *volverse viejo*) to age, get old, grow old; (= *parecer viejo*) to look old; **en dos años se ha envejecido mucho** he's aged a lot these last two years
2 [*ropa, muebles*] to become old-fashioned
3 [*vino*] to mature, age

envejecido ADJ **1** [*persona*] old, aged; (*de aspecto*) old-looking; **está muy ~** he's aged a lot
2 [*piel, madera, tela*] distressed

envejecimiento SM ageing

envelar ▸conjug 1a◂ VI (*Cono Sur Náut*) to hoist the sails; **~las** to run away

envenenador(a) SM/F poisoner

envenenamiento SM poisoning

envenenar ▸conjug 1a◂ Ⓐ VT **1** (*con veneno*) to poison
2 (= *amargar*) to embitter
Ⓑ **envenenarse** VPR **1** (*voluntariamente*) to poison o.s., take poison
2 (*por accidente*) to be poisoned

enverdecer ▸conjug 2r◂ VI to turn green

enveredar ▸conjug 1a◂ VI **~ hacia** to head for, make a beeline for

envergadura SF **1** (= *importancia*) importance; **el edificio sufrió daños de cierta ~** the building suffered considerable *o* substantial damage; **un programa de gran ~** a wide-ranging programme, a programme of considerable scope; **una operación de cierta ~** an operation of some magnitude *o* size; **la obra es de ~** the plan is ambitious
2 (= *tamaño*) scope, magnitude
3 (= *extensión*) (*gen*) expanse, spread; (*Náut*) breadth, beam; (*Aer, Orn*) wingspan; [*de boxeador*] reach

envés SM **1** (= *parte trasera*) [*de tela*] back, wrong side; [*de hoja de planta*] underside; [*de espada*] flat **2** (*Anat**) back

enviado/a SM/F (*Pol*) envoy ► **enviado/a especial** [*de periódico, TV*] special correspondent

▼ **enviar** ▸conjug 1c◂ VT to send; **~ un mensaje a algn** (*por móvil*) to text sb, send sb a text message; **~ a algn a hacer algo** to send sb to do sth; **~ a algn a una misión** to send sb on a mission; **~ por el médico** to send for the doctor, fetch the doctor

enviciador(a) SM/F (*LAm*) drug-pusher

enviciar ▸conjug 1b◂ Ⓐ VT to corrupt
Ⓑ **enviciarse** VPR (= *corromperse*) to get corrupted; **~se con** *o* **en** to become addicted to

envidar ▸conjug 1a◂ VT, VI (*Naipes*) to bid; **~ en falso** to bluff

envidia SF envy, jealousy; **es pura ~** it's sheer *o* pure envy *o* jealousy, he's just jealous; **con este vestido serás la ~ de todas tus amigas** with that dress you'll be the envy of all your friends; **¡qué ~ me da verte tan contenta!** I'm so envious *o* jealous seeing you so happy!; **dar ~ a algn** to make sb envious *o* jealous; **tener ~ a algn** to envy sb, be jealous of sb; ✦***MODISMOS*** **carcomerle** *o* **corroerle a algn la ~** to be eaten up with envy *o* jealousy;

➤ LENGUA Y USO: **entusiasmar A** 34.3 **B** 40.2 **enviar** 47.1, 48.1

estar muerto de ~ to be green with envy; ✦*REFRÁN* **si la ~ fuera tiña (cuántos tiñosos habría)** the world's full of envious people

envidiable ADJ enviable

envidiar ▸conjug 1b◂ VT [1] [+ *persona*] to envy
[2] (= *codiciar*) to desire, covet; **~ algo a algn** to envy sb sth, begrudge sb sth; **su casa no tiene nada que ~ a la tuya** her house is at least as good as yours, her house is quite up to the standard of yours

envidioso ADJ [1] [*de persona*] envious, jealous
[2] (= *codicioso*) covetous

envilecer ▸conjug 2d◂ Ⓐ VT to debase, degrade
Ⓑ **envilecerse** VPR to degrade o.s., lower o.s.; (*implorando*) to grovel, crawl

envilecimiento SM degradation, debasement

envinado ADJ (*Cono Sur*) drunk

▼**envío** SM [1] (= *acción*) (*gen*) sending; (*Com*) dispatch; (*en barco*) shipment; **proponen el ~ de fuerzas de paz** they propose sending peace-keeping forces; **gastos de ~** (cost of) postage and packing, postage and handling (*EEUU*) ► **envío a domicilio** home delivery (service) ► **envío contra reembolso** cash on delivery ► **envío de datos** data transmission ► **envío de segundo curso** second-class mail
[2] (= *mercancías*) (*gen*) consignment, lot; (*Náut*) shipment
[3] (= *dinero*) remittance

envión SM push, shove

envite SM [1] (= *apuesta*) stake
[2] (= *ofrecimiento*) offer, bid; (= *invitación*) invitation
[3] (= *empujón*) push, shove; **al primer ~** from the very start, right away

enviudar ▸conjug 1d◂ VI [*mujer*] to become a widow, be widowed; [*hombre*] to become a widower, be widowed; **~ de la primera mujer** to lose one's first wife; **enviudó tres veces** she lost three husbands

envoltorio SM, **envoltijo** SM bundle, package; *ver tb* **envoltura**

envoltura SF [1] (*gen*) cover; [*de papel*] wrapper, wrapping; (*Bot, Aer*) envelope; (*Mec*) case, casing; (= *vaina*) sheath
[2] **envolturas** [*de bebé*] baby clothes

envolvedero SM, **envolvedor** SM (= *cubierta*) cover; (= *papel*) wrapper, wrapping; (= *sobre*) envelope

envolvente ADJ [1] (= *circundante*) [*ambiente*] surrounding; [*música*] all-enveloping; [*atmósfera*] absorbing; (*Mil*) [*movimiento, maniobra*] encircling, enveloping; **asiento ~** bucket seat; **gafas de sol ~s** wraparound sunglasses *o* shades; **falda ~** wraparound skirt; **parachoques ~** wraparound bumper; **sonido ~** surround sound®
[2] (= *completo*) comprehensive
[3] (*Caribe, Cono Sur*) (= *interesante*) fascinating, intriguing

envolver ▸conjug 2h◂ (*pp* **envuelto**) Ⓐ VT [1] (= *cubrir*) (*con papel*) to wrap (up); (*con ropa*) to wrap (up), cover (up); **¿quiere que se lo envuelva?** shall I wrap it (up) for you?; **dos paquetes envueltos en papel** two parcels wrapped in paper; **llevaba al niño envuelto en una manta** she was carrying the baby wrapped up in a blanket
[2] (= *rodear*) to surround, shroud; **una niebla espesa envolvía el castillo** the castle was surrounded *o* shrouded in thick fog; **su muerte está envuelta en misterio** her death is shrouded in mystery
[3] (= *involucrar*) to involve (**en** in); **lo han envuelto en el tráfico de drogas** they've got him involved in drug trafficking
[4] (*frm*) (= *contener*) to contain; **sus elogios envuelven una censura** there is criticism contained in his praise
Ⓑ **envolverse** VPR [1] (*con ropa*) to wrap o.s. up (**en** in)
[2] (= *involucrarse*) to become involved (**en** in)

envolvimiento SM [1] [*de paquete*] wrapping
[2] (*Mil*) encirclement
[3] (*en asunto, escándalo*) involvement

envuelto PP *de* **envolver**

enyerbar ▸conjug 1a◂ Ⓐ VT (*Andes, Cono Sur, Méx*) (= *hechizar*) to bewitch
Ⓑ **enyerbarse** VPR [1] (*LAm*) [*campo*] to get covered with grass
[2] (*Caribe*) [*trato*] to fail
[3] (*CAm, Méx*) (= *envenenarse*) to poison o.s.
[4] (*Méx*) (= *enamorarse*) to fall madly in love
[5] (*Caribe**) (= *complicarse*) to get complicated

enyesado SM, **enyesadura** SF [1] [*de pared*] plastering
[2] (*Med*) (= *escayola*) plaster cast

enyesar ▸conjug 1a◂ VT [1] [+ *pared*] to plaster
[2] (*Med*) to put in a plaster cast, put in plaster; **le ~on el brazo** his arm was put in a (plaster) cast *o* in plaster; **tener una pierna enyesada** to have one's leg in a (plaster) cast, have a leg in plaster

enyeyado* ADJ (*Caribe*) gloomy, depressed

enyugar ▸conjug 1h◂ VT to yoke

enyuntar ▸conjug 1a◂ VT (*LAm*) to put together, join

enzacatarse ▸conjug 1a◂ VPR (*CAm, Méx*) to get covered with grass

enzarzar ▸conjug 1f◂ Ⓐ VT (*en una disputa*) to involve, entangle, embroil
Ⓑ **enzarzarse** VPR (*en una disputa*) to get involved; (*en problemas*) to get o.s. into trouble; **~se a golpes** to come to blows; **~se en una discusión** to get involved in an argument

enzima SF enzyme

enzocar ▸conjug 1g◂ VT (*Cono Sur*) to insert, put in, fit in

-eo *ver* **Aspects of Word Formation in Spanish 2**

EOI SF ABR (*Esp*) = **Escuela Oficial de Idiomas**;
→ ESCUELA OFICIAL DE IDIOMAS

eólico ADJ wind *antes de s*; **energía eólica** wind power

eón SM aeon, eon (*esp EEUU*)

EP SF ABR (*Esp*) = **Educación Primaria, Enseñanza Primaria**

EP — EDUCACIÓN PRIMARIA

Following the implementation of the 1990 Spanish education reform law, **LOGSE**, *primary education was renamed* **Educación Primaria** *and divided into two* **ciclos** *or stages:* **primer ciclo** *for 6- to 9-year-olds, and* **segundo ciclo** *for 9- to 12-year-olds.*
⇨ *See also* ESO, LOGSE

EPA SF ABR (*Esp*) = **Encuesta de Población Activa**

epa* EXCL, **épale*** EXCL (*LAm*) hey!, wow!, say! (*EEUU*)

epatante* ADJ (= *asombroso*) amazing, astonishing; (= *deslumbrante*) startling, dazzling

epatar* ▸conjug 1a◂ VT (= *asombrar*) to amaze, astonish; (= *deslumbrar*) to startle, dazzle; (= *escandalizar*) to shock; **~ al burgués** to shock the bourgeoisie

epazote SM (*Méx*) herb tea

E.P.D. ABR (= **en paz descanse**) RIP

epi... PREF epi...

épica SF epic poetry

epiceno ADJ (*Ling*) epicene

epicentro SM epicentre, epicenter (*EEUU*)

épico ADJ epic

epicureísmo SM, **epicurismo** SM epicureanism

epicúreo/a ADJ, SM/F epicurean

epidemia SF epidemic

epidémico ADJ epidemic

epidérmico ADJ [1] (= *de la piel*) skin *antes de s*
[2] (= *superficial*) superficial, skin-deep

epidermis SF INV epidermis

Epifanía SF Epiphany, Twelfth Night

epiglotis SF INV epiglottis

epígrafe SM [1] (*en libro, artículo*) epigraph
[2] (*en piedra, metal*) epigraph, inscription

epigrafía SF epigraphy

epigrama SM epigram

epigramático ADJ epigrammatic(al)

epilepsia SF epilepsy

epiléptico/a Ⓐ ADJ epileptic; **ataque ~** epileptic fit, epileptic seizure (*frm*)
Ⓑ SM/F epileptic

epilogar ▸conjug 1h◂ VT (= *resumir*) to sum up; (= *rematar*) to round off, provide a conclusion to

epílogo SM epilogue

episcopado SM [1] (= *cargo*) bishopric
[2] (= *obispos*) bishops *pl*, episcopacy (*frm*)
[3] (= *período*) episcopate (*frm*)

episcopal ADJ [*autoridad, iglesia*] episcopal; [*cargo*] bishopric; **palacio ~** bishop's palace; **sede ~** (= *ciudad*) see; **la Conferencia Episcopal Española** the Synod of Spanish bishops

episcopalista ADJ, SMF Episcopalian

episódico ADJ episodic

episodio SM [*de aventura, suceso*] episode, incident; [*de serie, novela*] episode, part

epistemología SF epistemology

epístola SF epistle, letter

epistolar ADJ epistolary

epistolario SM collected letters *pl*

epitafio SM epitaph

epíteto SM epithet

epitomar ▸conjug 1a◂ VT to summarize

epítome SM summary, epitome (*frm*)

época SF [1] (= *momento histórico*) age, period, epoch (*frm*); **la ~ de Carlos III** the age of Charles III; **durante la ~ isabelina** in Elizabethan times, in the Elizabethan era *o* age; **en aquella ~** at that time, in that period; **muebles de ~** period furniture; **coche de ~** vintage car; **drama de ~** costume drama; **con decoraciones de ~** with period set; **un Picasso de primera ~** an early (period) Picasso; **la ~ azul del artista** the artist's blue

➤ LENGUA Y USO: **envío 1** 47.3

period; **anticiparse a su ~** to be ahead of one's time; **todos tenemos ~s así** we all go through spells like that; **estoy pasando una mala ~** I'm going through a bad patch; **hacer ~** to be epoch-making, be a landmark; **el invento hizo ~** it was an epoch-making invention; **eso hizo ~ en nuestra historia** that was a landmark in our history ► **época de la serpiente de mar** (*hum*) silly season ► **época dorada** golden age ► **época glacial** ice age
2 (*tb* ~ **del año**) (= *temporada*) season, time of year ► **época de celo** (*Zool*) mating season, rutting season ► **época de lluvias** rainy season ► **época de sequía** dry season ► **época monzónica** monsoon season

epopeya SF epic

equi... PREF equi...

equidad SF (= *justicia*) fairness, equity (*frm*); [*de precio*] reasonableness

equidistante ADJ equidistant

equilátero ADJ equilateral

equilibradamente ADV in a balanced way

equilibrado Ⓐ ADJ 1 [*persona*] (= *sensato*) level-headed, sensible; (= *ecuánime*) well-balanced
2 [*dieta*] balanced
3 [*partido*] close
Ⓑ SM ► **equilibrado de ruedas** wheel-balancing

equilibrar ▸conjug 1a◂ Ⓐ VT (*gen*) to balance; [+ *una cosa con otra*] to counterbalance; ~ **gastos e ingresos** to balance outgoings and income; ~ **la balanza de pagos** to restore the balance of payments; ~ **el marcador** to level the score
Ⓑ **equilibrarse** VPR [*persona*] to balance o.s. (**en** on); [*fuerzas*] to counterbalance each other

equilibrio SM 1 (= *estabilidad*) balance; **perturbó el ~ de la balanza** he threw the scales out of balance; **ahora las pesas están en ~** now the weights are evenly balanced; **intentó mantener el ~ sobre la cuerda** he tried to keep his balance on the rope; **mantuvo en ~ el palo sobre su dedo** he balanced the stick on his finger; **perder el ~** to lose one's balance; ✦*MODISMO* **hacer ~s** to do a balancing act ► **equilibrio ecológico** ecological balance ► **equilibrio estable** stable equilibrium ► **equilibrio inestable** unstable equilibrium ► **equilibrio presupuestario** balanced budget
2 (= *armonía*) balance, equilibrium; **existe un ~ estable entre las dos potencias mundiales** there is a stable balance between the two superpowers ► **equilibrio de fuerzas, equilibrio de poderes** balance of power
3 (= *serenidad*) level-headedness

equilibrista SMF 1 (*en circo*) (= *funámbulo*) tightrope walker; (= *acróbata*) acrobat
2 (*LAm*) *politician of shifting allegiance*

equino Ⓐ ADJ equine, horse *antes de s*
Ⓑ SM 1 (= *caballo*) horse; (**carne de**) ~ horsemeat
2 [*de mar*] sea urchin

equinoccial ADJ equinoctial

equinoccio SM equinox ► **equinoccio otoñal** autumnal equinox ► **equinoccio vernal** vernal equinox

equipaje SM 1 (*para viajar*) (= *conjunto de maletas*) luggage, baggage (*EEUU*); (= *avíos*) equipment, kit; **facturar el ~** to register one's luggage; **hacer el ~** to pack, do the packing; **pagar exceso de ~** to pay excess baggage; **compartimento de ~s** luggage compartment, baggage compartment (*esp EEUU*); **zona de recogida de ~s** luggage *o* (*esp EEUU*) baggage collection point ► **equipaje de mano** hand luggage
2 (*Náut*) crew

equipal SM (*Méx*) *wicker chair with seat and back of leather or palm leaves*

equipamiento SM equipment

equipar ▸conjug 1a◂ Ⓐ VT 1 [+ *casa, coche*] to fit, equip (**con, de** with); (*Náut*) to fit out; **~on la cocina con los electrodomésticos más modernos** they fitted *o* equipped the kitchen with the most modern appliances; **el nuevo modelo viene equipado con elevalunas eléctrico** the new model is fitted with electric windows; **un gimnasio muy bien equipado** a very well-equipped gymnasium
2 [+ *persona*] (*con armas, útiles*) to equip (**con, de** with); (*con ropa*) to kit out (**con, de** with); **cuesta mucho dinero ~ a un colegial** it costs a lot of money to get a child kitted out for school; **~on a los obreros con armas** they equipped the workers with weapons; **iban equipados con uniforme de campaña** they were kitted out with battledress
Ⓑ **equiparse** VPR (= *pertrecharse*) to equip o.s. (**con, de** with); **se ~on con cuerdas y linternas** they equipped themselves with ropes and torches

equiparable ADJ comparable (**con** to, with)

equiparación SF comparison

equiparar ▸conjug 1a◂ Ⓐ VT (= *igualar*) to put on the same level, consider equal; (= *comparar*) to compare (**con** with)
Ⓑ **equipararse** VPR **~se con** to be on a level with, rank equally with

equipazo* SM crack team

equipo SM 1 (*Dep*) team ► **equipo de casa** home team ► **equipo de fuera** away team ► **equipo de fútbol** football team ► **equipo de relevos** relay team ► **equipo local** home team ► **equipo titular** A team, first team ► **equipo visitante** visiting team
2 [*de personas*] team; **trabajar en ~** to work as a team ► **equipo cinematográfico móvil** mobile film unit ► **equipo de cámara** camera crew ► **equipo de desactivación de explosivos** bomb-disposal unit ► **equipo de gobierno** government team ► **equipo de rescate, equipo de salvamento, equipo de socorro** (*civil*) rescue team; (*militar*) rescue squad, rescue unit ► **equipo directivo** management team ► **equipo médico** medical team, medical unit
3 (= *utensilios, accesorios*) (*gen*) equipment; (*para deportes*) equipment, kit; **me robaron todo el ~ de esquí** they stole all my skiing equipment *o* gear*; ✦*MODISMO* **caerse con todo el ~*** to make a right mess of things* ► **equipo de alpinismo** climbing gear ► **equipo de alta fidelidad** hi-fi system ► **equipo de caza** hunting gear ► **equipo de fumador** smoker's outfit, smoker's accessories ► **equipo de música** stereo system ► **equipo de novia** trousseau ► **equipo de oficina** office furniture ► **equipo de primeros auxilios** first-aid kit ► **equipo de reparaciones** repair kit ► **equipo físico** (*Inform*) hardware ► **equipo industrial** plant ► **equipo lógico** (*Inform*) software ► **equipo rodante** (*Ferro*) rolling stock

equis SF INV 1 (= *letra*) (name of the letter) X; **rayos ~** X-rays; **cada ~ años** every so many years; **durante ~ años** for X number of years; **pongamos que cuesta ~ dólares** let's suppose it costs X dollars; **averiguar la ~** to find the value of X; **marcar con una ~ la respuesta correcta** put a cross by the correct answer; **tenía que hacer ~ cosas*** I had to do any amount of things
2 (*Andes, CAm**) ✦*MODISMO* **estar en la ~** (= *flaco*) to be all skin and bones; (= *sin dinero*) to be broke*, be skint*

equitación SF 1 (= *acto*) riding; **escuela de ~** riding school
2 (= *arte*) horsemanship

equitativamente ADV (= *con justicia*) equitably, fairly; (= *razonablemente*) reasonably

equitativo ADJ [*distribución, división*] fair; [*precio*] reasonable; [*reparto*] fair, equitable (*frm*); **trato ~** fair deal, square deal

equivalencia SF equivalence

▼**equivalente** Ⓐ ADJ equivalent (**a** to)
Ⓑ SM equivalent

equivaler ▸conjug 2p◂ VI **~ a** to be equivalent to, be equal to; (*en grado, nivel*) to rank as, rank with

equivocación SF (= *error*) mistake, error; (= *descuido*) oversight; (= *malentendido*) misunderstanding; **por ~** by mistake, in error; **ha sido por ~** it was a mistake

equivocado ADJ 1 [*número, dirección*] wrong; [*persona*] mistaken, wrong; **estás ~** you are wrong, you are mistaken (*más frm*)
2 [*afecto, confianza*] misplaced

▼**equivocar** ▸conjug 1g◂ Ⓐ VT 1 (= *confundir*) to get mixed up, mix up; **he equivocado las direcciones de los sobres** I've got the addresses mixed up on the envelopes, I've mixed up the addresses on the envelopes
2 **~ a algn** to make sb make a mistake; **si me hablas mientras escribo me equivocas** if you talk to me while I'm writing, you'll make me make a mistake *o* you'll make me go wrong
3 (= *errar*) **~ el camino** (*lit*) to go the wrong way; (*fig*) to make the wrong choice
Ⓑ **equivocarse** VPR (= *no tener razón*) to be wrong, be mistaken; (= *cometer un error*) to make a mistake; **te equivocas, eso no es así** you're wrong *o* mistaken, it isn't like that; **si crees que voy a dejarte ir, te equivocas** if you think I'm going to let you go, you're wrong *o* mistaken; **me equivoqué muchas veces en el examen** I made a lot of mistakes in the exam; **~se con algn** to be wrong about sb; **la consideraba honesta, pero me equivoqué con ella** I thought she was honest, but I was wrong about her; **~se de algo**: **nos equivocamos de hora y llegamos tarde** we got the time wrong, and we arrived late; **se ~on de tren** they caught the wrong train; **se ~on de casa** they went to the wrong house; **perdone, me he equivocado de número** sorry, (I've got the) wrong number

equívoco Ⓐ ADJ 1 (= *confuso*) equivocal, ambiguous
2 (*LAm*) (= *equivocado*) mistaken
Ⓑ SM 1 (= *malentendido*) misunderstanding
2 (*al hablar*) (= *juego de palabras*) pun, play

➤ LENGUA Y USO: **equivalente A** 32.4 **equivocar B** 39.1

on words; (= *doble sentido*) double meaning; **este tipo de ~s es característico de sus escritos** this kind of wordplay is a characteristic of his writing
[3] (*Méx**) mistake

era[1] *ver* **ser**

era[2] SF (*Hist*) era, age ► **era atómica** atomic age ► **era cristiana, era de Cristo** Christian era ► **era espacial** space age ► **era española, era hispánica** Spanish Era (*from 38 B.C.*) ► **era glacial** ice age

era[3] SF (*Agr*) (*para cereales*) threshing floor; (*para flores*) bed, plot; (*para hortalizas*) patch

erario SM (= *Hacienda*) treasury, exchequer; (= *fondos*) public funds *pl*, public finance; **~ municipal** municipal funds *pl*, council funds *pl*; **con cargo al ~ público** with *o* from public funds

-eras *ver* **Aspects of Word Formation in Spanish 2**

erasmismo SM Erasmism

erasmista ADJ, SMF Erasmist

Erasmo SM Erasmus

erección SF [1] (*Anat*) erection
[2] (*Arquit*) [*de edificio*] erection; [*de monumento*] raising

ereccionarse ▸conjug 1a◂ VPR to become erect

eremita SM (= *ermitaño*) hermit; (= *solitario*) recluse

eremitismo SM living like a hermit, hermit's way of life

ergio SM erg

ergonomía SF ergonomics *sing*

ergonómico ADJ ergonomic

erguido ADJ [1] [*cuerpo*] erect, straight
[2] (= *orgulloso*) proud

erguir ▸conjug 3m◂ Ⓐ VT [1] (= *levantar*) to raise, lift; **~ la cabeza** (*lit*) to hold one's head up; (*fig*) to hold one's head high
[2] (= *enderezar*) to straighten
Ⓑ **erguirse** VPR [1] (= *enderezarse*) (*al ponerse en pie*) to straighten up, stand up straight; (*estando sentado*) to sit up straight
[2] (= *envanecerse*) to swell with pride

-ería *ver* **Aspects of Word Formation in Spanish 2**

erial Ⓐ ADJ uncultivated, untilled
Ⓑ SM (*en campo*) uncultivated land; (*en ciudad*) area of wasteland, piece of waste ground

erigir ▸conjug 3c◂ Ⓐ VT [1] (*Arquit*) [+ *monumento*] to erect; [+ *edificio*] to build
[2] (= *fundar*) to establish, found
[3] **~ a algn en algo** to set sb up as sth
Ⓑ **erigirse** VPR **~ en algo** to set o.s. up as sth

erisipela SF erysipelas *pl*

erizado ADJ [1] (= *de punta*) [*cepillo, cola*] bristly; [*pelo*] spiky; **~ de espinas** covered with thorns
[2] **~ de problemas** bristling with problems

erizar ▸conjug 1f◂ Ⓐ VT [1] **el gato erizó el pelo** the cat bristled, the cat's hair stood on end
[2] [+ *asunto*] to complicate, surround with difficulties
Ⓑ **erizarse** VPR (= *levantar*) [*pelo de animal*] to bristle; [*pelo de persona*] to stand on end; **se me erizó el pelo** my hair stood on end

erizo SM [1] (*Zool*) hedgehog ► **erizo de mar, erizo marino** sea urchin
[2] (*Bot*) burr
[3] (*) (= *persona*) grumpy sort, prickly person*

ermita SF [1] (= *capilla*) chapel, shrine
[2] [*de un ermitaño*] hermitage

ermitaño/a SM/F [1] (= *persona*) hermit
[2] (*Zool*) hermit crab

Ernesto SM Ernest

-ero *ver* **Aspects of Word Formation in Spanish 2**

erogación SF [1] [*de bienes*] distribution
[2] (*LAm*) (= *gasto*) expenditure, outlay
[3] (*Andes, Caribe*) (= *contribución*) contribution, donation

erogar ▸conjug 1h◂ VT [1] [+ *propiedad*] to distribute
[2] (*LAm*) (= *pagar*) to pay; [+ *deuda*] to settle
[3] (*Andes, Cono Sur*) (= *contribuir*) to contribute
[4] (*Méx*) (= *gastar*) to spend, lay out

erógeno ADJ erogenous; **zonas erógenas** erogenous zones

Eros SM Eros

erosión SF (*Geol*) erosion; (*Med*) graze; **causar ~ en** to erode

erosionable ADJ subject to erosion; **un suelo fácilmente ~** a soil which is easily eroded

erosionante ADJ erosive

erosionar ▸conjug 1a◂ Ⓐ VT to erode
Ⓑ **erosionarse** VPR to erode, be eroded

erosivo ADJ erosive

erótico ADJ (*gen*) erotic; [*versos*] love *antes de s*; **el género ~** the genre of love poetry

erotismo SM eroticism

erotizar ▸conjug 1a◂ Ⓐ VT to eroticize
Ⓑ **erotizarse** VPR to be (sexually) stimulated

erotomanía SF eroticism, pathological eroticism

erotómano ADJ erotic, pathologically erotic

errabundear ▸conjug 1a◂ VI to wander, rove

errabundeo SM wanderings *pl*

errabundo ADJ wandering, roving

erradamente ADJ mistakenly

erradicación SF eradication

erradicar ▸conjug 1g◂ VT to eradicate

erradizo ADJ wandering, roving

errado ADJ [1] (= *equivocado*) mistaken, wrong; **estás ~ si piensas que te voy a ayudar** you're mistaken if you think I'm going to help you; **no andas ~ al decir que …** you're not mistaken when you say that …
[2] [*tiro*] wide of the mark

errante ADJ [1] (= *ambulante*) [*trovador*] wandering; [*reportero*] roving; [*vida*] nomadic; [*animal*] stray, lost; **el judío ~** the wandering Jew; **el holandés ~** the flying Dutchman
[2] (= *infiel*) errant; **el marido ~** the errant husband

errar ▸conjug 1k◂ Ⓐ VT [1] (= *equivocar*) [+ *tiro*] to miss with, aim badly; [+ *blanco*] to miss; [+ *vocación*] to miss, mistake; **~ el camino** to lose one's way
[2] (*en obligación*) to fail (*in one's duty to*)
Ⓑ VI [1] (= *vagar*) to wander, rove
[2] (= *equivocarse*) to be mistaken; **~ es cosa humana ◊ de los hombres es ~** to err is human
Ⓒ **errarse** VPR to err, be mistaken

errata SF misprint, printer's error; **fe de ~s** errata; **es ~ por "poder"** it's a misprint for "poder"

errático ADJ erratic

erratismo SM (= *tendencia*) wandering tendencies *pl*, tendency to wander; (= *movimiento*) erratic movement

erre SF (name of the letter) R; ✦**MODISMO ~ que ~** stubbornly, pigheadedly; **y él, ~ que ~, seguía negándolo** he stubbornly went on denying it

erróneamente ADV (= *por equivocación*) mistakenly, erroneously; (= *falsamente*) falsely

erróneo ADJ (= *equivocado*) mistaken, erroneous; (= *falso*) untrue, false

error SM mistake, error (*más frm*); **fue un ~ contárselo a Luisa** it was a mistake to tell Luisa; **salvo ~ u omisión** errors and omissions excepted; **caer en un ~** to make a mistake; **si piensas que lo hizo por tu bien, estás cayendo en un ~** if you think that he did it for your good you're making a mistake; **cometer un ~** to make a mistake; **cometí muchos ~es en el examen** I made a lot of mistakes in the exam; **estar en un ~** to be mistaken, be wrong; **estás en un ~ si piensas que voy a transigir** you're mistaken *o* wrong if you think that I'll give in; **inducir a ~** to be misleading; **estas cifras pueden inducir a ~** these figures could be misleading; **por ~** by mistake ► **error de cálculo** miscalculation ► **error de copia** clerical error ► **error de derecho** legal error ► **error de hecho** factual error, error of fact ► **error de imprenta** misprint ► **error judicial** miscarriage of justice ► **error tipográfico** misprint

ERT ABR [1] (*Esp*) = **Explosivos Río Tinto**
[2] (*Arg*) = **Ente de Radiotelevisión**

ertzaina [er'tʃaina] SMF policeman/policewoman, *member of the autonomous Basque police force*

Ertzaintza [er'tʃaintʃa] SF *autonomous Basque police (force)*

> **ERTZAINTZA**
>
> *The* **Ertzaintza** *is the Basque autonomous police force, recognizable by its distinctive uniform of red sweater, red beret and white truncheon. Madrid has devolved certain policing responsibilities to the Basque government (as well as to Catalonia) but the national police forces,* **Policía Nacional** *and* **Guardia Civil**, *continue to have a role as well.*

eructación SF belch

eructar ▸conjug 1a◂ VI to belch

eructo SM belch

erudición SF learning, scholarship, erudition (*frm*)

eruditamente ADV learnedly

erudito/a Ⓐ ADJ learned, scholarly, erudite (*frm*)
Ⓑ SM/F scholar, learned person; **los ~s en esta materia** those who are expert in this subject, those who really know about this subject; **un ~ a la violeta** (*pey*) a pseudo-intellectual

erupción SF [1] (*Geol*) eruption; **estar en ~** to be erupting; **entrar en ~** to (begin to) erupt ► **erupción solar** solar flare
[2] (*Med*) ► **erupción cutánea** rash, eruption (*frm*)
[3] (= *estallido*) [*de violencia*] outbreak, explosion; [*de ira*] outburst

➤ LENGUA Y USO: **error** 39.1, 45.2

eruptivo ADJ eruptive
E/S ABR (*Inform*) (= **entrada/salida**) I/O
esa ADJ DEM *ver* **ese²**
ésa PRON DEM *ver* **ése**
Esaú SM Esau
esbeltez SF (= *delgadez*) slimness, slenderness; (= *gracilidad*) gracefulness
esbelto ADJ (= *delgado*) slim, slender; (= *grácil*) graceful
esbirro SM [1] (= *ayudante*) henchman, minion; (= *sicario*) killer
[2] (*Caribe*‡) (= *soplón*) grass‡, fink (*EEUU*‡), informer
[3] (*Hist*) (= *alguacil*) bailiff, constable
esbozar ▸conjug 1f◂ VT [1] (*Arte*) to sketch, outline
[2] [+ *plan*] to outline; **~ una sonrisa** to smile a faint smile, force a smile
esbozo SM [1] (*Arte*) sketch
[2] [*de plan*] outline; **con un ~ de sonrisa** with a hint of a smile
escabechado SM pickling, marinating
escabechar ▸conjug 1a◂ VT [1] (*Culin*) to pickle, souse
[2] [+ *canas*] to dye
[3] (*) (= *matar*) to do in*, do away with*
[4] (*Univ**) (= *suspender*) to plough*, to plow (*EEUU**)
escabeche SM [1] (= *salsa*) pickle, brine
[2] (= *pescado*) soused fish
escabechina SF [1] (= *matanza*) slaughter
[2] (*fig*) (= *desastre*) destruction, slaughter; **hacer una ~*** to wreak havoc; (*Univ*) to fail a pile of students
escabel SM footstool, footrest
escabinado SM jury of lay people and judges
escabiosa SF scabious
escabioso ADJ (*Med*) scabious; (*Vet*) scabby, mangy
escabro SM [1] (*Vet*) sheep scab, scabs
[2] (*Bot*) scab
escabrosamente ADV riskily, salaciously
escabrosidad SF [1] [*de terreno*] roughness, ruggedness; [*de superficie*] unevenness
[2] [*de sonido*] harshness
[3] [*de problema*] difficulty, toughness
[4] [*de chiste*] riskiness, salaciousness (*frm*)
escabroso ADJ [1] (= *irregular*) [*terreno*] rough, rugged; [*superficie*] uneven
[2] [*sonido*] harsh
[3] [*problema*] difficult, tough, thorny
[4] [*chiste*] risqué, blue, salacious (*frm*)
escabuche SM weeding hoe
escabullarse ▸conjug 1a◂ VPR (*LAm*), **escabullirse** ▸conjug 3a◂ VPR to slip away *o* off; **~ por** to slip through
escachalandrado* ADJ (*Andes, CAm*) slovenly
escacharrar* ▸conjug 1a◂ Ⓐ VT to bust*
Ⓑ **escacharrarse** VPR to break
escachifollarse* ▸conjug 1a◂ VPR to break, smash
escafandra SF diving suit ► **escafandra autónoma** scuba suit ► **escafandra espacial** spacesuit
escafandrismo SM (= *pesca*) underwater fishing; (= *submarinismo*) deep-sea diving
escafandrista SMF (= *pescador*) underwater fisherman; (= *buzo*) deep-sea diver

escala SF [1] (*en medición, gradación*) scale; **a ~** [*dibujo, mapa, maqueta*] scale *antes de s*; **un mapa hecho a ~** a map drawn to scale, a scale map; **una imitación a ~ reducida de un objeto real** a scaled-down version of a real object; **a ~ real** life-size *antes de s*; **reproducir algo a ~** to reproduce sth to scale ► **escala (abierta de) Richter** Richter scale ► **escala (de) Beaufort** Beaufort scale ► **escala (de) Celsius** Celsius scale ► **escala de colores** colour spectrum, color spectrum (*EEUU*) ► **escala (de) Fahrenheit** Fahrenheit scale ► **escala (de) Kelvin** Kelvin scale ► **escala (de) Mercalli** Mercalli scale ► **escala de salarios** salary scale ► **escala de tiempo** (*Geol*) time scale ► **escala de valores** set of values, scale of values ► **escala graduada** graduated scale ► **escala móvil** (*Téc*) sliding scale; (*Econ*) sliding salary scale ► **escala salarial** salary scale ► **escala social** social ladder, social scale
[2] [*de importancia, extensión*] **la producción a ~ industrial** production on an industrial scale; **un problema a ~ mundial** a global problem, a problem on a worldwide scale; **a** *o* **en gran ~** on a large scale; **a** *o* **en pequeña ~** on a small scale; **un caso de corrupción a pequeña ~** a case of small-scale corruption, a case of corruption on a small scale
[3] (= *parada en ruta*) [3·1] (*Aer*) stopover; **una ~ de dos horas en París** a two-hour stopover in Paris; **un vuelo sin ~s** a non-stop flight; **hacer ~** to stop over; **el vuelo hizo ~ en Brasil** the flight stopped over in Brazil; **hizo dos ~s para repostar** it made two stopovers for refuelling
[3·2] (*Náut*) port of call; **la siguiente ~ es Barcelona** the next port of call is Barcelona; **el buque hizo ~ en Cádiz** the ship put in at Cádiz
► **escala técnica** refuelling *o* (*EEUU*) refueling stop
[4] (= *escalera de mano*) ladder ► **escala de cuerda, escala de viento** rope ladder
[5] (*Mús*) scale ► **escala cromática** chromatic scale ► **escala diatónica** diatonic scale ► **escala musical** musical scale
escalación SF (*Mil, Pol*) escalation
escalada SF [1] [*de montaña*] climb, ascent; **es una ~ fácil** it's an easy climb *o* ascent; **su rápida ~ al poder** his rapid rise to power ► **escalada artificial** artificial climbing ► **escalada en rocas** rock climbing ► **escalada libre** free climbing
[2] (= *aumento*) escalation; **una ~ de la violencia** an escalation of violence; **últimamente ha habido una ~ del/en el conflicto** lately there has been an escalation of/in the conflict, lately the conflict has escalated; **se ha producido una ~ en los precios** prices have escalated
escalador(a) SM/F [1] (*Dep*) (*en alpinismo*) climber, mountaineer; (*en ciclismo*) climber, mountain rider ► **escalador(a) en roca(s)** rock climber
[2] (= *ladrón*) burglar, housebreaker
escalafón SM [1] [*de promoción*] promotion ladder; **ascender en el ~** to go up the ladder, work one's way up
[2] [*de salarios*] salary scale, wage scale
[3] (= *ránking*) table, chart; **en esta industria España ocupa el tercer lugar en el ~ mundial** Spain occupies third place in the world table for this industry
escalamiento SM = **escalada**
escálamo SM thole, tholepin
escalante ADJ escalating; **la crisis ~** the escalating crisis
escalar ▸conjug 1a◂ Ⓐ VT [1] [+ *montaña*] to climb, scale
[2] [+ *casa*] to burgle, burglarize (*EEUU*), break into
[3] (*en la escala social*) to scale, rise to; **~ puestos** to move up
[4] (*Inform*) (= *reducir*) to scale down; (= *aumentar*) to scale up
Ⓑ VI [1] [*alpinista*] to climb
[2] (*en la escala social*) to climb the social ladder, get on, go up in the world*
[3] (*Náut*) to call, put in (**en** at)
[4] (*Mil, Pol*) to escalate
Escalda SM Scheldt
escaldado ADJ [1] (= *escarmentado*) **salir ~: salió ~ del negocio** he got his fingers burned in the deal; **salió escaldada de su matrimonio** she came out of the marriage feeling sadder and wiser; **salió ~ de la experiencia** he was chastened by the experience; *ver tb* **gato A1**
[2] (= *receloso*) wary, cautious
[3] [*mujer*] loose
escaldadura SF [1] (= *quemadura*) scald, scalding
[2] (= *irritación*) chafing
escaldar ▸conjug 1a◂ Ⓐ VT [1] (= *quemar*) to scald; (*Culin*) to blanch
[2] (= *rozar*) to chafe, rub
[3] (= *escarmentar*) to teach a lesson
[4] [+ *metal*] to make red-hot
Ⓑ **escaldarse** VPR [1] (= *quemarse*) to scald o.s., get scalded
[2] (= *rozarse*) to chafe; [*bebé*] to get nappy rash
escalera SF [1] [*de edificio*] stairs *pl*, staircase; **corrió ~s abajo** she ran downstairs *o* down the stairs; **se cayó por las ~s** she fell downstairs *o* down the stairs; **han pintado la ~** they've painted the staircase; **una ~ de mármol** a marble staircase ► **escalera de caracol** spiral staircase ► **escalera de incendios** fire escape ► **escalera de servicio** backstairs *pl* ► **escalera mecánica, escalera móvil** escalator
[2] (*portátil*) ladder ► **escalera de cuerda** rope ladder ► **escalera de mano** ladder ► **escalera de nudos** rope ladder ► **escalera de pintor, escalera de tijera, escalera doble** stepladder, steps *pl* ► **escalera extensible** extension ladder
[3] (*Naipes*) run, sequence; (*en póquer*) straight ► **escalera de color** straight flush
escalerilla SF (*en bricolaje, piscina*) ladder; (*en barco*) gangway, companionway; (*Aer*) steps *pl*
escalfador SM chafing dish
escalfar ▸conjug 1a◂ VT [1] [+ *huevo*] to poach
[2] (*Méx*) (= *desfalcar*) to embezzle
escalilla SF [1] (*Téc*) calibrated scale
[2] [*de ascenso*] promotion ladder
escalinata SF (*interior*) flight of stairs *pl*; (*exterior*) flight of steps, steps *pl*
escalofriado ADJ **estar ~** to feel chilly, feel shivery, feel hot-and-cold

escalofriante ADJ (= *espeluznante*) bloodcurdling, hair-raising; (= *aterrador*) frightening, chilling

escalofriarse ▸conjug 1c◂ VPR [1] (*por fiebre*) to feel chilly, get the shivers, feel hot-and-cold by turns
[2] (*por miedo*) to shiver with fright, get a cold shiver of fright

escalofrío SM [1] (*Med*) chill, feverish chill
[2] (= *temblor*) shiver; **aquello me produjo un ~ de terror** it made me shiver with fear, it sent a shiver down my spine

escalón SM [1] (= *peldaño*) (*gen*) step, stair; [*de escalera de mano*] rung; (= *nivel*) level; [*de cohete*] stage ► **escalón de hielo** ice step
[2] (*al avanzar*) (= *paso*) step; (*al éxito*) stepping stone
[3] (*Mil*) echelon

escalonadamente ADV step by step, in a series of steps

escalonar ▸conjug 1a◂ VT [1] (= *distribuir*) (*gen*) to spread out at intervals; [+ *tierra*] to terrace; [+ *horas de trabajo*] to stagger; [+ *novedad*] to phase in
[2] (*Mil*) to echelon
[3] (*Med*) [+ *dosis*] to regulate

escalopa SF (*Chile*) escalope, cutlet (*EEUU*)

escalope SM escalope, cutlet (*EEUU*) ► **escalope de ternera** escalope of veal, veal cutlet (*EEUU*)

escalopín SM fillet

escalpar ▸conjug 1a◂ VT to scalp

escalpelo SM scalpel

escama SF [1] (*Bot, Zool*) scale
[2] [*de jabón, pintura*] flake; **jabón en ~s** soapflakes
[3] (= *resentimiento*) resentment; (= *sospecha*) suspicion
[4] (*Méx**) cocaine, coke*

escamado ADJ [1] (= *desconfiado*) wary, cautious [2] (*Cono Sur*) (= *harto*) wearied

escamar ▸conjug 1a◂ Ⓐ VT [1] [+ *pez*] to scale, remove the scales from
[2] (= *producir recelo*) to make wary, create distrust in; **eso me escama** that makes me suspicious, that sounds ominous to me
Ⓑ **escamarse** VPR [1] (= *perder escamas*) to scale, scale off, flake off
[2] (= *sospechar*) to get wary, become suspicious; (= *olerse algo*) to smell a rat; **y luego se escamó** and after that he was on his guard

escamocha* SF (*Méx*) leftovers

escamón ADJ (= *que sospecha*) wary, distrustful; (= *nervioso*) apprehensive

escamondar ▸conjug 1a◂ VT [1] [+ *árbol*] to prune
[2] (= *limpiar*) to prune, trim

escamoso ADJ [*pez*] scaly; [*sustancia*] flaky

escamotar ▸conjug 1a◂ VT = **escamotear**

escamoteable ADJ retractable

escamoteador(a) SM/F (= *prestidigitador*) conjurer; (= *estafador*) swindler

escamotear ▸conjug 1a◂ VT [1] (= *hacer desaparecer*) to make vanish, whisk away; [+ *naipe*] to palm; (*Téc*) to retract
[2] (*) (= *robar*) to lift*, pinch*
[3] [+ *hechos, verdad*] to hide, cover up
[4] (= *esquivar*) [+ *responsabilidad*] to shirk

escamoteo SM [1] (= *ilusionismo*) conjuring; (= *truco*) conjuring trick; (= *destreza*) sleight of hand
[2] (*) (= *robo*) lifting*; (= *estafa*) swindling, swindle
[3] (= *ocultación*) concealment
[4] [*de responsabilidad*] shirking

escampar ▸conjug 1a◂ Ⓐ VI [1] (*Meteo*) [*cielo*] to clear; [*lluvia*] to stop; [*tiempo*] to clear up
[2] (*Caribe, Méx*) (*de la lluvia*) to shelter
[3] (*LAm**) (= *largarse*) to clear off*, scarper*
Ⓑ VT [+ *sitio*] to clear out

escampavía SF revenue cutter

escanciador(a) SM/F [1] wine waiter
[2] (*Hist*) cupbearer

escanciar ▸conjug 1b◂ Ⓐ VT [+ *vino*] to pour, pour out, serve; [+ *copa*] to drain
Ⓑ VI to drink (a lot of) wine

escandalera* SF row, uproar

escandalizante ADJ scandalous, shocking

escandalizar ▸conjug 1f◂ Ⓐ VT to scandalize, shock
Ⓑ VI to make a fuss, create a scene
Ⓒ **escandalizarse** VPR to be shocked, be scandalized (**de** at, by); **se escandalizó ante la pintura** he was horrified at the picture, he threw up his hands in horror at the picture

escandallo SM [1] (*Náut*) lead
[2] (*Com*) (= *etiqueta*) price tag; (= *acto*) pricing
[3] (= *prueba*) sampling

escándalo SM [1] (= *tumulto*) scandal, outrage; **¡qué ~!** what a scandal!; **¡es un ~!** it's outrageous *o* shocking!; **precios de ~** (= *caros*) outrageous prices; (= *baratos*) amazing prices; **comportamiento de ~** scandalous behaviour; **un resultado de ~** (= *malo*) a scandalous result; (= *bueno*) a great result, an outstanding result
[2] (= *ruido*) row, uproar; **armar un ~** to make a scene, cause a row *o* an uproar
[3] (= *asombro*) astonishment; **llamar a ~** to cause astonishment, be a shock

escandalosa SF [1] (*Náut*) topsail
[2] (*Andes*) (= *tulipán*) tulip
[3] ✦*MODISMO* **echar la ~** to fly off the handle, curse and swear

escandalosamente ADV [1] (= *sorprendentemente*) [*actuar, hablar*] scandalously, outrageously; [*delinquir*] flagrantly; **~ caro** outrageously expensive
[2] (= *con ruido*) [*romper*] noisily; [*reírse*] loudly, heartily

escandaloso ADJ [1] (= *sorprendente*) [*actuación*] scandalous, shocking; [*delito*] flagrant; [*vida*] scandalous
[2] (= *ruidoso*) [*risa*] hearty, uproarious; [*niño*] noisy
[3] [*color*] loud

Escandinavia SF Scandinavia

escandinavo/a ADJ, SM/F Scandinavian

escandir ▸conjug 3a◂ VT [+ *versos*] to scan

escaneo SM scanning

escáner SM [1] (= *aparato*) scanner
[2] (= *imagen*) scan; **hacerse un ~** to have a scan

escansión SF scansion

escantillón SM pattern, template

escaño SM (= *banco*) bench; (*Pol*) seat

escapada SF [1] (= *huida*) escape, breakout; ✦*MODISMO* **en una ~** in a spare moment; **¿puedes comprarme tabaco en una ~?** have you got a spare moment to buy me some cigarettes?
[2] (= *viaje, salida*) **conseguí hacer una ~ rápida a Bruselas** I managed to get away to Brussels, I managed a quick getaway to Brussels; **las ~s nocturnas del heredero al trono** the heir to the throne's nocturnal jaunts
[3] (*Ciclismo*) breakaway

escapado/a Ⓐ ADJ (= *rápido*) **lo harán ~s** they'll do it like a shot; **irse ~** to rush off; **salió escapada de aquella casa** she rushed out of the house; **tengo que volverme ~ a la tienda** I must get back to the shop double-quick, I have to rush back to the shop
Ⓑ SM/F [1] (= *fugitivo*) fugitive, runaway
[2] (*Ciclismo*) **los ~s** the breakaway group

escapar ▸conjug 1a◂ Ⓐ VI [1] (= *huir*) to escape; **sintió una gran necesidad de ~** he felt a great need to get away *o* escape; **~ a algo**: **no pude ~ a sus encantos** I could not escape her charms; **hay cosas que escapan a nuestro control** some things are beyond our control; **este caso escapa a mi responsabilidad** this case is not my responsibility; **~ de** [+ *cárcel, peligro*] to escape from; [+ *jaula*] to get out of; [+ *situación opresiva*] to escape from, get away from; **logramos ~ de una muerte cierta** we managed to escape certain death; **necesitaba ~ de todo aquello** I needed to escape from *o* get away from all that; **dejar ~** [+ *grito, risa, suspiro*] to let out; [+ *oportunidad*] to let slip; **dejar ~ a algn** to let sb get away; **han dejado ~ al perro** they let the dog get away
[2] (*Dep*) (*en carreras*) to break away; **el ciclista escapó del pelotón** the cyclist broke away from the pack
Ⓑ VT [+ *caballo*] to drive hard
Ⓒ **escaparse** VPR [1] (= *huir*) [*preso*] to escape; [*niño, adolescente*] to run away; **se escapó por la puerta de atrás** he escaped through the back door; **se me ha escapado la paloma** my pigeon has escaped; **me escapé porque no podía aguantar más a mis padres** I ran away because I couldn't stand my parents any longer; **ven aquí, no te me escapes** come here, don't run away; **~se de** [+ *cárcel, peligro*] to escape from; [+ *jaula*] to get out of; [+ *situación opresiva*] to escape from, get away from; **el león se ha escapado del zoológico** the lion has escaped from the zoo; **de ésta no te escapas** you can't get away this time; *ver tb* **pelo 7**
[2] (= *filtrarse*) [*gas, líquido*] to leak, leak out (**por** from)
[3] (= *dejar pasar*) **me voy, que se me escapa el tren** I'm going, or I'll miss my train; **se me había escapado ese detalle** that detail had escaped my notice, I had overlooked *o* missed that detail; **a nadie se le escapa la importancia de esta visita** everybody is aware of *o* realizes the importance of this visit; **no se me escapa que …** I am aware that …, I realize that …; ✦*MODISMO* **~se de las manos**: **la realidad se me escapa de las manos** I'm losing touch with reality, I'm losing my grip on reality; **la situación se les escapó de las manos** they lost control of the situation
[4] (= *dejar salir*) [4-1] [*grito, eructo*] **se me escapó un eructo sin darme cuenta** I accidentally burped *o* let out a burp; **se le escapó un suspiro de alivio** she breathed *o* let out a sigh of relief; **no pude evitar que se me ~a una carcajada** I couldn't help bursting out laughing; **se me escapó una lágrima**

a tear came to my eye
4·2 [*dato, noticia*] **se le escapó la fecha de la reunión** he let slip the date of the meeting
5 (= *soltarse*) 5·1 [*globo, cometa*] to fly away
5·2 [*punto de sutura*] to come undone
5·3 (*Cos*) **se le escapó un punto en la manga** she dropped a stitch in the sleeve
6 (= *hacerse público*) [*información*] to leak, leak out; **se escapó la noticia de que iban a vender la compañía** the news leaked that they were going to sell the firm
7 (= *olvidarse*) to slip one's mind; **ahora mismo se me escapa su nombre** his name escapes me *o* slips my mind right now

escaparate SM 1 (*de tienda*) window, shop window; **ir de** *o* **mirar ~s** to go window-shopping
2 [*de promoción*] showcase
3 (*LAm*) (= *armario*) wardrobe
4 (‡) (= *pecho*) tits‡ *pl*, bosom (*hum*), chest

escaparatismo SM window dressing

escaparatista SMF window dresser

escapatoria SF 1 (= *huida*) [*de lugar*] escape, way out; [*de situación*] way out; **un sitio de donde no había ~ posible** a place from which there was no possible escape *o* way out; **no tienes ~** there is no way out for you; **me temo que eso no te va servir como ~** I'm afraid that excuse isn't going to work
2 (*) *ver* **escapada 1, 2**

escape SM 1 [*de situación opresiva*] escape; **la lectura es mi única forma de ~** reading is my only form of escape; **vía de ~** (*lit*) escape route; (*fig*) (form of) escape; **la televisión es mi única vía de ~** the television is my only (form of) escape; **utilizan el fútbol como una vía de ~ de sus problemas** they use football as an escape from *o* as a way of escaping from their problems; ✦***MODISMO*** **a ~** at full speed; **salir a ~** to rush out
2 (= *fuga*) [*de gas*] leak; [*de líquido, radiación*] leak, leakage; **un ~ de gas** a gas leak
3 (*Mec*) (*tb* **tubo de ~**) exhaust; **gases de ~** exhaust, exhaust fumes; *ver tb* **válvula**, **vía A1**

escapismo SM escapism

escapista ADJ, SMF escapist

escápula SF scapula *pl*, shoulder blade

escapulario SM scapular, scapulary

escaque SM 1 [*de tablero*] square
2 **escaques** (*Hist*) (= *ajedrez*) chess *sing*

escaqueado ADJ checked, chequered, checkered (*EEUU*)

escaquearse‡ ▸conjug 1a◂ VPR (= *irse*) to slope off*; (= *gandulear*) to shirk, skive‡; (= *negar la responsabilidad*) to pass the buck*; (= *rajarse*) to duck out

escara SF (*Med*) crust, slough

escarabajas SFPL firewood *sing*, kindling *sing*

escarabajear ▸conjug 1a◂ Ⓐ VT (*) (= *preocupar*) to bother, worry
Ⓑ VI 1 (*al moverse*) (= *agitarse*) to wriggle, squirm; (= *arrastrarse*) to crawl
2 (= *garabatear*) to scribble, scrawl

escarabajo SM 1 (= *insecto*) beetle ▸ **escarabajo de Colorado, escarabajo de la patata** Colorado beetle
2 (*Téc*) flaw
3 (*) (= *persona*) dwarf, runt
4 (*Aut*) Beetle
5 **escarabajos*** (= *garabatos*) scribble *sing*

escaramujo SM 1 (*Bot*) (= *planta*) wild rose, briar; (= *fruto*) hip, rosehip
2 (*Zool*) goose barnacle
3 (*Caribe*) (= *mal de ojo*) spell, curse

escaramuza SF 1 (*Mil*) skirmish, brush
2 (= *enfrentamiento*) brush

escaramuzar ▸conjug 1f◂ VI to skirmish

escarapela SF 1 (= *insignia*) rosette, cockade
2 (*) (= *riña*) brawl, shindy*

escarapelar ▸conjug 1a◂ Ⓐ VT 1 (*LAm*) (= *descascarar*) to scrape off, scale off, chip off
2 (*Andes*) (= *arrugar*) to crumple, rumple
Ⓑ VI 1 (= *reñir*) to wrangle, quarrel
2 = C
Ⓒ **escarapelarse** VPR 1 (*LAm*) (= *descascararse*) to peel off, flake off
2 (*Andes, Méx*) (= *temblar*) to go weak at the knees, tremble all over

escarbadientes SM INV toothpick

escarbador SM scraper

escarbar ▸conjug 1a◂ Ⓐ VT 1 (= *remover*) [+ *tierra*] to scratch; [+ *fuego*] to poke; [+ *dientes*] to pick
2 (= *investigar*) to investigate, delve into; (= *curiosear*) to pry into
Ⓑ VI 1 to scratch
2 **~ en** = **A2**

escarcear ▸conjug 1a◂ VI (*Cono Sur*) to prance

escarcela SF (*Caza*) pouch, bag

escarceo SM, **escarceos** SMPL 1 [*de caballo*] nervous movement, prance
2 (= *flirteo*) amateur effort; **en mis ~s con la política** in my occasional dealings with politics ▸ **escarceos amorosos** romantic flings, love affairs
3 (= *olas*) small waves *pl*

escarcha SF frost

escarchado ADJ 1 covered in hoarfrost, frosted
2 [*fruta*] crystallized

escarchar ▸conjug 1a◂ Ⓐ VT 1 (*Culin*) [+ *tarta*] to ice; [+ *fruta*] to crystallize
2 (= *helar*) (*gen*) to frost, cover in hoarfrost; [+ *vaso*] to frost
3 (*Cos*) *to embroider with silver or gold*
Ⓑ VI **escarcha** it's frosty, it's freezing

escarchilla SF (*Andes, Caribe*) hail

escarcho SM (red) gurnard

escarda SF 1 (= *acción*) (*lit*) hoeing; (*fig*) weeding out
2 (= *herramienta*) weeding hoe

escardador SM weeding hoe

escardadura SF weeding, hoeing

escardar ▸conjug 1a◂ VT to weed, weed out

escardillo SM weeding hoe

escariador SM reamer

escariar ▸conjug 1b◂ VT to ream

escarificación SF (*Agr, Med*) scarification

escarificador SM scarifier

escarificar ▸conjug 1g◂ VT to scarify

escarlata Ⓐ ADJ INV scarlet
Ⓑ SM (= *color*) scarlet
Ⓒ SF 1 (= *tela*) scarlet cloth
2 (*Med*) scarlet fever

escarlatina SF scarlet fever

escarmenar ▸conjug 1a◂ VT 1 [+ *lana*] to comb
2 (= *castigar*) to punish; **~ algo a algn*** to swindle sb out of sth

escarmentado ADJ wary, cautious; **estoy escarmentada** I've learned my lesson

escarmentar ▸conjug 1j◂ Ⓐ VT to teach a lesson to
Ⓑ VI to learn one's lesson; **¡para que escarmientes!** that'll teach you!; **no escarmientan** they never learn; **escarmenté y no lo volví a hacer** I learned my lesson and never did it again; **~ en cabeza ajena** to learn from someone else's mistakes

escarmiento SM (= *castigo*) punishment; (= *aviso*) lesson, warning; **que esto te sirva de ~** let this be a lesson *o* warning to you; **para ~ de los malhechores** as a lesson *o* warning to wrongdoers

escarnecedor/a Ⓐ ADJ mocking
Ⓑ SM/F scoffer, mocker

escarnecer ▸conjug 2d◂ VT to scoff at, mock, ridicule

escarnio SM (= *insulto*) jibe, taunt; (= *burla*) ridicule; **para mayor ~** to add insult to injury

escarola SF 1 (*Bot*) curly endive, escarole (*EEUU*)
2 (*Méx Cos*) ruff, flounce

escarolar ▸conjug 1a◂ VT (*Méx Cos*) to frill, flounce

escarpa SF 1 (= *cuesta*) slope; (*Geog, Mil*) scarp, escarpment
2 (*Méx*) (= *acera*) pavement, sidewalk (*EEUU*)

escarpado ADJ (= *empinado*) steep, sheer; (= *abrupto*) craggy

escarpadura SF = **escarpa 1**

escarpar ▸conjug 1a◂ VT 1 (*Geog*) to escarp
2 (*Téc*) to rasp

escarpia SF (*gen*) hook; (*para carne*) meat hook; (*Téc*) tenterhook

escarpín SM 1 (= *zapato*) pump; (= *zapatilla*) slipper
2 (= *calcetín*) (*de sobra*) extra sock, outer sock; [*de niña*] ankle sock, anklet (*EEUU*)

escarrancharse* ▸conjug 1a◂ VPR to do the splits

escasamente ADV 1 (= *insuficientemente*) scantily, sparingly
2 (= *apenas*) scarcely, hardly

escasear ▸conjug 1a◂ Ⓐ VI to be scarce
Ⓑ VT (= *escatimar*) to be sparing with, skimp

escasez SF 1 (= *insuficiencia*) shortage, scarcity (*más frm*); **~ de agua** shortage *o* scarcity (*más frm*) of water; **~ de fondos** shortage of funds; **hay ~ de medicamentos** there is a shortage of medicine, medicine is in short supply; **~ de mano de obra/viviendas** labour/housing shortage
2 (= *pobreza*) poverty; **viven en la ~** they live in poverty
3 **escaseces** (= *apuros*) **han pasado muchas escaseces** they suffered great hardships
4 (††) (= *tacañería*) meanness, stinginess

escaso ADJ 1 (= *limitado*) **los alimentos están muy ~s** food is very scarce; **las posibilidades de encontrarlo vivo son muy escasas** the chances of finding him alive are very slim; **habrá escasa visibilidad en las carreteras** visibility on the roads will be poor; **el recital tuvo ~ público** the recital was poorly *o* sparsely attended; **tenemos escasa información del asunto** we have very little information on the subject; **un programa de ~ interés** a programme of limited interest; **un motor de escasa potencia** a not very pow-

erful engine; **iba a escasa distancia del otro coche** he was a short distance behind the other car
[2] **~ de algo** short of sth; **anda ~ de dinero** he's short of money; **estar ~ de víveres** to be short of food; **~ de recursos naturales** poor in natural resources; **una región escasa de población** a thinly populated region; **la fábrica está escasa de personal** the factory is short-staffed
[3] (= *muy justo*) **hay dos toneladas escasas** there are barely *o* scarcely two tons; **duró una hora escasa** it lasted barely *o* scarcely an hour; **tiene 15 años ~s** he's barely *o* hardly 15; **ganar por una cabeza escasa** to win by a short head
[4] (††) (= *tacaño*) mean, stingy

escatimar ▸conjug 1a◂ VT (= *dar poco*) to skimp, be sparing with, stint; (= *reducir*) to curtail, cut down; **no ~ esfuerzos (para)** to spare no effort (to); **no ~ gastos** to spare no expense; **no escatimaba sus alabanzas de …** he was unstinting in his praise of …, he did not stint his praise of …

escatimoso ADJ [1] (= *tacaño*) sparing, scrimpy, mean
[2] (= *taimado*) sly

escatología SF [1] (*de los excrementos*) scatology
[2] (*Fil, Rel*) eschatology

escatológico ADJ [1] (= *de los excrementos*) scatological
[2] (*Fil, Rel*) eschatological

escay SM imitation leather

escayola SF [1] (*Arte*) plaster of Paris
[2] (*Constr*) plaster, plaster of Paris
[3] (*Med*) (= *material*) plaster; (= *férula*) plaster cast, cast

escayolado SM plastering

escayolar ▸conjug 1a◂ VT to put in a plaster cast, put in plaster; **le ~on la pierna** his leg was put in a (plaster) cast *o* in plaster

escena SF [1] (= *escenario*) stage; **¡todo el mundo a ~!** everyone on stage!; **entrar en ~** ◊ **salir a ~** to come on stage, go on stage; **poner en ~** to stage
[2] (= *parte de obra, película*) scene; **la primera ~ del segundo acto** the first scene of the second act ► **escena retrospectiva** flashback
[3] (= *suceso*) scene; **presenciamos ~s terribles** we witnessed terrible scenes; **hacer** *o* **montar una ~** to make a scene
[4] (= *ámbito*) scene; **la ~ internacional** the international scene
[5] **la ~** (= *el teatro*) the stage; **se retiró después de toda una vida dedicada a la ~** she retired after a lifetime in theatre *o* on the stage

escenario SM [1] (*Teat*) stage; **en el ~** on (the) stage
[2] (*Cine*) setting
[3] (*uso figurado*) scene; **el ~ del crimen** the scene of the crime; **el ~ político** the political scene; **la ceremonia tuvo por ~ el auditorio** the ceremony took place in the auditorium

escénico ADJ stage *antes de s*

escenificación SF [*de comedia*] staging; [*de novela*] dramatization; [*de suceso histórico*] re-enactment, reproduction

escenificar ▸conjug 1g◂ VT [+ *comedia*] to stage; [+ *novela*] to dramatize, make a stage version of; [+ *suceso histórico*] to re-enact, reproduce

escenografía SF scenography, stage design

escenógrafo/a SM/F (= *diseñador*) stage designer, theatrical designer; (= *pintor*) scene painter

escenotecnia SF staging, stagecraft

escepticismo SM scepticism, skepticism (*EEUU*)

escéptico/a Ⓐ ADJ sceptical, skeptical (*EEUU*)
Ⓑ SM/F sceptic, skeptic (*EEUU*)

Escila SF Scylla; **~ y Caribdis** Scylla and Charybdis

escindible ADJ fissionable

escindir ▸conjug 3a◂ Ⓐ VT to split, divide; **el partido está escindido** the party is split *o* divided
Ⓑ **escindirse** VPR (= *dividirse*) to split, divide (**en** into); [*facción*] to split off

Escipión SM Scipio

escisión SF [1] (= *división*) split, division; **la ~ del partido** the split in the party
[2] (*Med*) excision (*frm*), surgical removal

escisionismo SM (*Pol*) tendency to split into factions

escisionista ADJ **facción ~** breakaway faction; **tendencia ~** breakaway tendency

esclarecedor ADJ illuminating

esclarecer ▸conjug 2d◂ Ⓐ VT [1] (= *explicar*) [+ *duda, misterio*] to explain, clear up, elucidate; [+ *misterio*] to shed light on; [+ *crimen*] to clear up; [+ *situación*] to clarify
[2] (= *instruir*) to enlighten
[3] (= *ennoblecer*) to ennoble
[4] (= *dar luz*) to light up, illuminate
Ⓑ VI to dawn

esclarecido ADJ illustrious, distinguished

esclarecimiento SM [1] (= *explicación*) explanation, elucidation, clarification
[2] [*de persona*] (= *instrucción*) enlightenment
[3] (= *ennoblecimiento*) ennoblement
[4] (= *iluminación*) illumination

esclava SF bangle, bracelet; *ver tb* **esclavo**

esclavatura SF (*LAm Hist*) [1] (= *esclavos*) slaves *pl*
[2] (= *período*) period of slavery
[3] (= *esclavitud*) slavery

esclavina SF short cloak, cape

esclavismo SM = **esclavitud**

esclavitud SF (*lit, fig*) slavery, servitude, bondage

esclavizar ▸conjug 1f◂ VT to enslave

esclavo/a SM/F slave; **vender a algn como ~** to sell sb into slavery; **ser ~ del tabaco** to be a slave to tobacco ► **esclavo/a blanco/a** white slave ► **esclavo/a sexual** sex slave; *ver tb* **esclava**

esclerosis SF INV [1] (*Med*) sclerosis ► **esclerosis múltiple** multiple sclerosis
[2] (= *fosilización*) fossilization, stagnation

esclerotizado ADJ fossilized, stagnant

esclusa SF [*de canal*] (= *cierre*) lock, sluice; (= *compuerta*) floodgate ► **esclusa de aire** airlock

esclusero/a SM/F lock keeper

-esco *ver* **Aspects of Word Formation in Spanish 2**

escoba Ⓐ SF [1] (*para barrer*) broom, brush; **pasar la ~** to sweep up; ✦*MODISMO* **esto no vende una ~** this is a dead loss ► **escoba mecánica** carpet sweeper
[2] (*Bot*) broom
Ⓑ SM/F (*Dep*) sweeper

escobada SF brush, sweep

escobar ▸conjug 1a◂ VT to sweep, sweep out

escobazo SM [1] (= *golpe*) blow with a broom; **echar a algn a ~s** to kick sb out
[2] (= *barrido*) quick sweep; **dar un ~** to have a quick sweep-up

escobilla SF [1] (= *escoba*) small broom; (*esp LAm*) (= *cepillo*) brush; [*de wáter*] toilet brush ► **escobilla de dientes** (*Andes*) toothbrush
[2] (*Aut*) (= *limpiaparabrisas*) windscreen wiper
[3] (*Aut, Elec*) dynamo brush
[4] (*Bot*) teasel

escobillar ▸conjug 1a◂ Ⓐ VI (*LAm*) to tap one's feet on the floor
Ⓑ VT (*Andes*) (= *cepillar*) to brush; (= *restregar*) to scrub

escobillón SM swab

escobón SM (= *escoba*) large broom, long-handled broom; (= *cepillo*) scrubbing brush; (*de algodón*) swab

escocedor ADJ painful, hurtful

escocedura SF = **escozor**

escocer ▸conjug 2b, 2h◂ Ⓐ VI to sting, smart; **el alcohol te va a ~ un poco** the alcohol will sting *o* smart a little; **me escuece el labio/la herida** my lip/the cut stings *o* is smarting
Ⓑ VT (= *irritar*) to annoy, upset
Ⓒ **escocerse** VPR to chafe, get sore

escocés/esa Ⓐ ADJ [*persona*] Scottish, Scots; [*whisky*] Scotch; **falda escocesa** kilt; **tela escocesa** tartan, plaid
Ⓑ SM/F (= *persona*) Scot, Scotsman/Scotswoman; **los escoceses** the Scots
Ⓒ SM [1] (*Ling*) Scots
[2] (= *whisky*) Scotch ► **escocés de malta** malt whisky

Escocia SF Scotland

escoda SF stonecutter's hammer

escofina SF rasp, file

escofinar ▸conjug 1a◂ VT to rasp, file

escogedor SM (*Agr*) riddle

escogencia SF (*Andes, Caribe*) choice

escoger ▸conjug 2c◂ Ⓐ VT to choose, pick; (*por votación*) to elect; **yo escogí el azul** I chose *o* picked the blue one; **escogió los mejores vinos para la cena** he picked out *o* chose *o* selected the best wines to go with the meal
Ⓑ VI to choose; **no hay mucho donde ~** there isn't much to choose from, there isn't much choice; **hay que ~ entre los dos** you must choose between the two; **puestos a ~, me quedo con éstos** faced with the choice, I'll keep these; **tener donde ~** to have plenty to choose from, have plenty of choice

escogido ADJ [1] (= *seleccionado*) (*gen*) chosen, selected; [*mercancías*] choice, select; [*obras*] selected
[2] [*persona*] **ser muy ~** to be choosy; **ser muy ~ para** *o* **con algo** to be fussy about sth

escogimiento SM choice, selection

escolar Ⓐ ADJ [*edad, vacaciones*] school *antes de s*; **año** *o* **curso ~** school year; *ver tb* **libro 1**
Ⓑ SMF schoolboy/schoolgirl, schoolchild

escolaridad SF schooling, education; **el porcentaje de ~ es elevado** the proportion of those in school is high ► **escolaridad obli-**

gatoria compulsory schooling, compulsory attendance at school

escolarización SF schooling, education; (= *asistencia*) school attendance; (= *alumnos matriculados*) enrolment in school

escolarizar ▸conjug 1f◂ VT (= *educar*) to provide with schooling, educate; (= *matricular*) to enrol in school; (= *mandar*) to send to school; **niños sin ~** children not in school, children receiving no schooling *o* education

escolástica SF, **escolasticismo** SM scholasticism

escolástico Ⓐ ADJ scholastic
Ⓑ SM scholastic, schoolman

escoleta SF (*Méx*) [1] (= *banda*) amateur band
[2] (= *ensayo*) rehearsal, practice (*of an amateur band*)
[3] (= *lección de baile*) dancing lesson

escollar ▸conjug 1a◂ VI [1] (*Andes, Cono Sur Náut*) to hit a reef, strike a rock
[2] (*Cono Sur*) [*empresa*] to fail, come unstuck

escollera SF breakwater, jetty

escollo SM [1] (= *arrecife*) reef, rock
[2] (= *obstáculo oculto*) (*en el camino*) pitfall, stumbling block; (*en actividad*) hidden danger; **los muchos ~s del inglés** the many pitfalls of English

escolopendra SF (*Zool*) centipede

escolta Ⓐ SMF (= *acompañante*) escort; (= *guardaespaldas*) bodyguard; [*de ministro*] minder*
Ⓑ SF escort; **dar ~ a** to escort, accompany

escoltar ▸conjug 1a◂ VT [1] (= *acompañar*) (*gen*) to escort; (*dando protección*) to guard, protect
[2] (*Náut*) to escort, convoy

escombrar ▸conjug 1a◂ VT to clear out, clean out, clear of rubbish

escombrera SF [1] (= *vertedero*) dump, tip
[2] (*Min*) slag heap

escombro[1] SM (= *pez*) mackerel

escombro[2]* SM **armar** *o* **hacer ~** (*Arg*) to kick up a fuss

escombros SMPL (= *basura*) rubbish *sing*, garbage (*EEUU*) *sing*; [*de obra, edificio*] debris *sing*, rubble *sing*; (*Min*) slag *sing*

escondedero SM hiding place

escondeloro SM (*CAm*) hide-and-seek

esconder ▸conjug 2a◂ Ⓐ VT to hide, conceal (**de** from)
Ⓑ **esconderse** VPR (= *ocultarse*) to hide, hide o.s., conceal o.s.; (= *estar escondido*) to be hidden, lurk

escondidas SFPL [1] **a ~** secretly, by stealth; **hacer algo a ~ de algn** to do sth behind sb's back
[2] (*LAm*) hide-and-seek; **jugar a (las) escondida(s)** to play hide-and-seek

escondido SM (*LAm*), **escondidos** SMPL (*LAm*) hide-and-seek

escondite SM [1] (= *escondrijo*) hiding place; (*Caza, Orn*) hide, blind (*EEUU*)
[2] (= *juego*) hide-and-seek; **jugar al ~ con algn** (*lit, fig*) to play hide-and-seek with sb

escondrijo SM (= *escondite*) hiding place, hideout; (= *rincón poco visible*) nook

escoñado/a‡ SM/F has-been*

escoñar‡ ▸conjug 1a◂ Ⓐ VT to smash up, break, shatter
Ⓑ **escoñarse** VPR [1] [*persona*] to hurt o.s.; **estoy escoñado** I'm knackered*
[2] [*máquina*] to break, get broken

escopeta SF [1] (= *arma*) shotgun
► **escopeta de aire comprimido** airgun, air rifle ► **escopeta de cañones recortados** sawn-off shotgun ► **escopeta de dos cañones** double-barrelled gun ► **escopeta de perdigones, escopeta de postas** shotgun ► **escopeta de tiro doble** double-barrelled gun ► **escopeta de viento** airgun, air rifle ► **escopeta paralela** double-barrelled gun ► **escopeta recortada** sawn-off shotgun
[2] (‡) prick‡

escopetado* ADJ, **escopeteado*** ADJ **salir ~** to be off like a shot; **voy ~** I'm in a terrible rush, I must shoot off; **ella hablaba escopetada** her words came in a torrent, her words came pouring out

escopetazo SM [1] (= *disparo*) gunshot
[2] (= *herida*) gunshot wound
[3] (= *noticia*) blow, bombshell
[4] **dar un ~**‡ to have a screw‡

escopetear ▸conjug 1a◂ Ⓐ VT [1] (= *disparar*) to shoot at (with a shotgun)
[2] (*Méx**) to get at, have a dig at*
Ⓑ VI (*Caribe*) (= *contestar*) to answer irritably
Ⓒ **escopetearse** VPR **se ~on en el bosque** they shot at each other in the wood; **se escopetean a injurias** they shower one another with insults, they heap insults upon each other

escopeteo SM [1] (= *disparos*) shooting, volley of shots
[2] [*de injurias, cumplimientos*] shower, lively exchange

escopetero SM gunsmith; (*Mil*) rifleman

escoplear ▸conjug 1a◂ VT to chisel

escoplo SM chisel

escor SM (*LAm*) score

escora SF (*Náut*) [1] (= *línea*) level line, load line
[2] (= *apoyo*) prop, shore
[3] (= *inclinación*) list; **con una ~ de 30 grados** with a thirty-degree list

escoración SF, **escorada** SF [1] (*Náut*) list (**a, hacia** to)
[2] (*fig*) leaning, inclination

escorar ▸conjug 1a◂ (*Náut*) Ⓐ VT to shore up
Ⓑ VI [1] (*Náut*) to list, heel, heel over; **~ a babor** to list to port
[2] (= *inclinarse*) **~ a** *o* **hacia** to lean towards, be inclined towards

escorbútico ADJ scorbutic

escorbuto SM scurvy

escorchar ▸conjug 1a◂ VT [1] to flay, skin
[2] (*Cono Sur*) (= *fastidiar*) to bother, annoy

escoria SF [1] [*de alto horno*] slag, dross
► **escoria básica** basic slag
[2] (= *lo más miserable*) scum, dregs *pl*; **la ~ de la humanidad** the scum *o* dregs of humanity

Escorial SM **el ~** *monastery and palace north of Madrid built by Philip II*

escorial SM [1] (= *vertedero*) dump, slag heap, tip
[2] (*Geol*) bed of lava, deposit of volcanic ash

escorpena SF, **escorpina** SF scorpion fish

Escorpio SM Scorpio; **soy ~** I'm Scorpio

escorpión SM [1] (= *alacrán*) scorpion
[2] (*Astron*) **Escorpión** Scorpio

escorrentía SF [1] (= *torrente*) rush, torrent
[2] (= *derrame*) overflow
[3] (*Agr*) run-off (*of chemicals*) ► **escorrentía superficial** surface run-off

escorzar ▸conjug 1f◂ VT to foreshorten

escorzo SM foreshortening

escota SF sheet

escotado ADJ [*vestido*] low-cut

escotadura SF [1] (*Cos*) low neck, low neckline
[2] (*Teat*) large trap door

escotar ▸conjug 1a◂ Ⓐ VT [1] (*Cos*) [+ *vestido*] to cut low in front; [+ *cuello*] to cut low
[2] [+ *río*] to draw water from
Ⓑ VI (= *pagar su parte*) to pay one's share, chip in

escotch SM (*LAm*) sticky tape

escote SM [1] [*de vestido*] neck, neckline; **un ~ profundo** a plunging neckline; ✦***MODISMO*** **ir** *o* **pagar a ~** (*entre varios*) to share the expenses; (*entre dos*) to go Dutch, go fifty-fifty ► **escote a la caja** round neck ► **escote de bañera** off-the shoulder neckline ► **escote en pico, escote en V** V-neck ► **escote redondo** round neck
[2] [*de mujer*] cleavage

escotilla SF (*Náut*) hatchway, hatch; ✦***MODISMO*** **atrancar las ~s** to batten down the hatches

escotillón SM trap door

escozor SM [1] (= *picor*) stinging, burning
[2] (= *sentimiento*) grief, heartache

escriba SM scribe

escribanía SF [1] (= *mueble*) writing desk
[2] (= *estuche*) writing case
[3] (= *enseres*) (*para escribir*) writing materials *pl*; (*para tintero*) inkstand
[4] (*Jur*) (= *cargo*) clerkship; (= *secretaría judicial*) clerk's office; (*LAm*) (= *notaría*) notary's office

escribano/a Ⓐ SM/F (= *secretario judicial*) court clerk, lawyer's clerk; (*LAm*) (= *notario*) notary, notary public ► **escribano/a municipal** town clerk
Ⓑ SM (*Orn*) bunting ► **escribano cerillo** yellowhammer

escribiente SMF (= *administrador*) clerk; (= *copista*) copyist

▼ **escribir** ▸conjug 3a◂ (*pp* **escrito**) Ⓐ VT, VI [1] [+ *palabra, texto*] to write; **~ a mano** to write in longhand; **~ a máquina** to type; **el que esto escribe** (*gen*) the present writer; (*Prensa*) this correspondent
[2] (*en ortografía*) to spell; **"voy" se escribe con "v"** "voy" is spelled with a "v"; **¿cómo se escribe eso?** how is that spelled?, how do you spell that?
[3] [+ *cheque*] to write out, make out
[4] [+ *música*] to compose, write
Ⓑ **escribirse** VPR [1] [*dos personas*] to write to each other, correspond
[2] **~se con algn** to correspond with sb, write to sb

escrito Ⓐ PP *de* **escribir**
Ⓑ ADJ written, in writing; **examen ~** written exam; **lo ~ arriba** what has been said above
Ⓒ SM [1] (*tb* **texto ~**) writing; (= *documento*) document; (= *original*) manuscript; **por ~** in writing; **acuerdo por ~** written agreement, agreement in writing; **poner por ~** to write down, get down in writing, commit to paper; **tomar algo por ~** to write sth down, take sth down in writing; **no lo creeré hasta que no**

➤ LENGUA Y USO: escribir A1 48.1, 48.2

lo vea por ~ I won't believe it until I see it in black and white *o* in writing
2 (*Jur*) brief
3 **escritos** (*Literat*) writings, works

escritor(a) SM/F writer; **es un ~ consolidado** he's an established writer ► **escritor(a) de material publicitario** copywriter ► **escritor(a) satírico/a** satirist, satirical writer

escritorio SM (= *mueble*) desk, bureau; (= *despacho*) office; **de ~** desktop *antes de s*

escritorzuelo/a SM/F hack, hack writer, scribbler

escritura SF 1 (= *sistema de comunicación*) writing; [*de individuo*] writing, handwriting; **tiene malísima ~** her writing *o* handwriting is terrible; **no acierto a leer su ~** I can't read his writing *o* handwriting; **~ a máquina** typing ► **escritura aérea** skywriting ► **escritura automática** automatic writing ► **escritura corrida** longhand ► **escritura fonética** phonetic script ► **escritura normal** longhand
2 (= *tipo de código*) writing, script ► **escritura china** Chinese writing, Chinese script
3 **Sagrada Escritura** Scripture, Holy Scripture
4 (*Jur*) deed ► **escritura de aprendizaje** indenture ► **escritura de propiedad** title deed ► **escritura de seguro** insurance certificate ► **escritura de traspaso** conveyance, deed of transfer

escriturado ADJ [*capital*] registered

escriturar ▸conjug 1a◂ VT 1 (*Jur*) [+ *documentos*] to formalize legally; [+ *propiedad, casa*] to register (legally)
2 (*Teat*) to book, engage, sign up

escriturario ADJ, **escriturístico** ADJ scriptural

escrófula SF scrofula

escrofuloso ADJ scrofulous

escroto SM scrotum

escrupulizar ▸conjug 1f◂ VT to scruple, hesitate; **no ~ en hacer algo** not to scruple to do sth

escrúpulo SM 1 (= *recelo*) scruple; **falta de ~s** unscrupulousness, lack of scruples; **sin ~** unscrupulous; **no tuvo ~s en hacerlo** he had no qualms about doing it
2 (*con la comida*) fussiness, pernicketiness; **me da ~ beber de ahí** I'm wary about drinking from there
3 (*Farm*) scruple

escrupulosamente ADV scrupulously

escrupulosidad SF scrupulousness

escrupuloso ADJ 1 (= *minucioso*) (*al elegir algo*) particular; (*al hacer algo*) precise
2 (*con la comida*) fussy, pernickety, persnickety (*EEUU*)
3 (= *honesto*) scrupulous

escrushante* SMF (*Arg*) burglar, housebreaker

escrutador(a) Ⓐ ADJ [*mirada*] searching, penetrating
Ⓑ SM/F 1 [*de votos*] returning officer, scrutineer
2 (*Parl*) teller

escrutar ▸conjug 1a◂ VT 1 (= *examinar*) to scrutinize, examine; **parecía que me estaba escrutando con la mirada** he seemed to be scrutinizing *o* examining me with his eyes
2 [+ *votos*] to count

escrutinio SM 1 (= *examen atento*) scrutiny, examination
2 [*de votos*] count, counting

escuadra SF 1 (= *instrumento*) (*para dibujar*) square; (*de carpintero*) carpenter's square; **a ~** square, at right angles; **fuera de ~** out of true ► **escuadra de delineante** set square
2 [*de hombres*] (*Mil*) squad; (*Náut*) squadron ► **escuadra de demolición** demolition squad ► **escuadra de fusilamiento** firing squad
3 (*Aut*) [*de coches*] fleet
4 (*LAm Dep*) team, squad
5 (*Andes*) (= *pistola*) pistol

escuadrar ▸conjug 1a◂ VT (*Téc*) to square

escuadrilla SF (*Aer*) wing, squadron

escuadrón SM (*Mil, Aer*) squadron ► **escuadrón de la muerte** death squad, murder squad ► **escuadrón volante** flying squad

escualidez SF 1 (= *delgadez*) skinniness, scragginess
2 (= *miseria*) squalor, filth

escuálido ADJ 1 (= *delgado*) skinny, scraggy
2 (= *sucio*) squalid, filthy

escualo SM dogfish

escucha Ⓐ SF 1 (= *acción*) listening; (*Radio*) monitoring; **rogamos a nuestros oyentes que permanezcan a la ~** please stay tuned; **estar a la ~** to listen in; **estar de ~** to eavesdrop ► **escucha telefónica** phone tap, wire tap (*EEUU*) ► **escuchas telefónicas** phone tapping, wire tapping (*EEUU*)
2 (*Rel*) chaperon
Ⓑ SMF 1 (*Mil*) scout
2 (*Radio*) monitor

escuchar ▸conjug 1a◂ Ⓐ VT 1 (*con atención*) [+ *música, palabras*] to listen to; [+ *consejo*] to listen to, pay attention to, heed
2 (*esp LAm*) (= *oír*) to hear; **se escucha muy mal** (*Telec*) it's a very bad line *o* (*EEUU*) connection
Ⓑ VI to listen
Ⓒ **escucharse** VPR **le gusta ~se** he likes the sound of his own voice; **se escucha mucho las enfermedades** she's always complaining about her illnesses

escuchimizado* ADJ **estar ~** to be all skin and bones; **es un chico ~** he's a skinny boy

escucho SM (*Andes*) whispered secret

escuchón ADJ (*Andes*) prying, inquisitive

escudar ▸conjug 1a◂ Ⓐ VT to shield
Ⓑ **escudarse** VPR to shield o.s.

escudería SF motor-racing team

escudero SM squire

escudete SM 1 (*Heráldica, Hist*) escutcheon
2 (*Cos*) gusset
3 (*Bot*) white water lily

escudilla SF bowl, basin

escudo SM 1 [*de protección*] shield ► **escudo humano** human shield ► **escudo térmico** heat shield
2 (*Heráldica*) ► **escudo de armas** coat of arms
3 (= *moneda*) escudo

escudriñar ▸conjug 1a◂ VT 1 (= *investigar*) to inquire into, investigate
2 (= *examinar*) to scrutinize

escuela SF 1 (= *colegio*) school; **dejé la ~ a los catorce años** I left school at fourteen; **recuerdo los tiempos de la ~** I remember my schooldays; **ir a la ~** [*alumno, maestro*] to go to school; **fue a la ~ a hablar con el director** he went to the school to speak to the headmaster ► **escuela de párvulos** nursery school, kindergarten ► **escuela de primera enseñanza, escuela elemental** primary school ► **escuela infantil** nursery school ► **escuela primaria** primary school ► **escuela privada** private school, independent school ► **escuela pública** state school, public school (*EEUU*) ► **escuela secundaria** secondary school, high school (*EEUU*)
2 (= *centro de enseñanza*) (*gen*) school; (*Chile*) (= *facultad*) faculty, school ► **escuela de artes y oficios** school of arts and crafts ► **escuela de baile** school of dancing, dance school ► **escuela de ballet** ballet school ► **Escuela de Bellas Artes** art school, art college ► **escuela de chóferes** (*LAm*) driving school ► **escuela de cine** film school ► **escuela de comercio** business school, school of business studies ► **escuela de conducir** (*Col*), **escuela de conductores** (*LAm*) driving school ► **escuela de enfermería** nursing college ► **escuela de equitación** riding school ► **escuela de manejo** (*Méx*) driving school ► **escuela de verano** summer school ► **escuela laboral** technical school, trade school ► **escuela militar** military academy ► **escuela naval** naval academy ► **escuela nocturna** night school ► **escuela normal** teacher training college ► **escuela taller** *vocational training centre* ► **escuela universitaria** *university college offering diploma rather than degree courses*; *ver tb* **buque 1**, **granja**
3 (*) (= *clases*) school; **mañana no hay** *o* **no tenemos ~** there's no school tomorrow; ✦**MODISMO soplarse la ~** (*Esp*) to play truant, skive off*, play hooky (*EEUU**)
4 (= *formación*) experience; **es buen actor pero le falta ~** he's a good actor but he lacks experience; ✦**MODISMO la ~ de la vida** the university of life, the school of life
5 (= *movimiento*) school; **la ~ flamenca** the Flemish school; **la ~ romántica** the Romantic school; **la ~ veneciana** the Venetian school; **un catedrático de la vieja ~** a professor of the old school; **un escritor que ha creado ~** a writer with a great following; → COLEGIO

> **ESCUELA OFICIAL DE IDIOMAS**
>
> *The* **Escuelas Oficiales de Idiomas** *are state-run language schools which offer tuition in a wide range of foreign languages, particularly English and French. Examinations are also open to external candidates and the final qualification, after 5 years' study, the* **Certificado de la Escuela Oficial de Idiomas** *is recognized all over Spain.*

escuelante SMF (*Col, Méx, Ven*) (= *alumno*) pupil

escuelero/a Ⓐ ADJ (*LAm*) school *antes de s*
Ⓑ SM/F 1 (*Andes, Caribe, Cono Sur pey*) (= *maestro*) schoolmaster/schoolmistress
2 (*Andes*) (= *alumno*) schoolboy/schoolgirl; (*) (= *empollón*) swot*, grind (*EEUU**)

escuerzo SM [1] (*Zool*) toad
[2] (= *persona*) runt
escuetamente ADV plainly, baldly
escueto ADJ [*verdad*] plain, naked; [*estilo*] simple; [*explicación, presentación*] concise, succinct
escuincle/a* SM/F (*Méx*), **escuintle/a*** SM/F (*Méx*) [1] (= *niño*) child, kid*
[2] (= *animal*) runt
esculcar ▸conjug 1g◂ VT (*Méx*) to search
esculpir ▸conjug 3a◂ VT [+ *estatua, piedra*] to sculpt; [+ *madera*] to carve; [+ *inscripción*] to cut
esculque SM (*LAm*) body search
escultismo SM = **escutismo**
escultor(a) SM/F sculptor/sculptress
escultórico ADJ sculptural
escultura SF sculpture, carving ► **escultura en madera** wood carving
escultural ADJ [1] (*Arte*) sculptural
[2] [*cuerpo, mujer*] statuesque
escupe* SM (*Prensa*) scoop
escupidera SF [1] (*para escupir*) spittoon, cuspidor (*EEUU*)
[2] (*esp Andes, Cono Sur*) (= *orinal*) chamberpot; ✦*MODISMO* **pedir la ~** to get scared, get the wind up*
escupidor SM [1] (*Andes, Caribe*) (= *recipiente*) spittoon
[2] (*Andes*) (= *estera*) round mat, doormat
escupir ▸conjug 3a◂ Ⓐ VI to spit; **~ a algn** to spit at sb; **~ a la cara de algn** to spit in sb's face; **~ en el suelo** to spit on the ground; ✦*MODISMO* **ser de medio ~*** to be as common as muck*
Ⓑ VT [1] [*persona*] [+ *sangre*] to spit; [+ *comida*] to spit out; [+ *palabra*] to spit, spit out
[2] (= *arrojar*) [+ *llamas*] to belch out, spew
[3] (*) (= *confesar*) to cough*, sing*
escupitajo* SM gob of spit
escurana SF (*LAm*) [1] (= *oscuridad*) darkness
[2] (= *cielo*) overcast sky, threatening sky
escurialense ADJ of/from El Escorial
escurreplatos SM INV plate rack
escurribanda SF [1] (*Med*) [*de vientre*] looseness, diarrhoea, diarrhea (*EEUU*); [*de úlcera*] running
[2] (= *fuga*) escape
[3] (= *paliza*) thrashing
escurrideras SFPL (*Méx, CAm*) = **escurriduras**
escurridero SM draining board, drainboard (*EEUU*)
escurridizo ADJ [1] (= *resbaladizo*) [*superficie, objeto*] slippery; [*nudo*] running
[2] (= *evasivo*) [*carácter*] slippery; [*idea*] elusive
escurrido ADJ [1] (= *delgado*) narrow-hipped, slightly built
[2] (*Andes, Caribe, Méx*) (= *avergonzado*) abashed, ashamed; (= *tímido*) shy
escurridor SM [1] (*Culin*) (= *escurreplatos*) plate rack; (= *colador*) colander
[2] (*Fot*) drying rack
escurriduras SFPL [1] (= *gotas*) drops
[2] (= *heces*) dregs
escurrir ▸conjug 3a◂ Ⓐ VT [+ *ropa*] to wring, wring out; [+ *platos, líquido, botella*] to drain; [+ *verduras*] to strain
Ⓑ VI [*líquido*] to drip
Ⓒ **escurrirse** VPR [1] [*líquido*] to drip
[2] (= *resbalarse*) [*objeto*] to slip, slide; **se me escurrió de entre las manos** it slipped out of my hands
[3] [*comentario*] to slip out
[4] [*persona*] to slip away, sneak off
escúter SM scooter, motor scooter
escutismo SM scouting movement, scouting
esdrújulo ADJ proparoxytone (*frm*), *stressed on the antepenultimate syllable*
ESE ABR (= **estesudeste**) ESE
ese[1] SF name of the letter S; **en forma de ~** S-shaped; ✦*MODISMO* **hacer ~s** [*carretera*] to zigzag, twist and turn; [*coche*] to zigzag; [*borracho*] to reel about
ese[2]**/a** ADJ DEM that; **esa casa** that house; **esos/as** those; **esos dibujos** those drawings; **no conozco al tío ese** I don't know that guy*
ése/a PRON DEM [1] that one; **ése es el mío** that one is mine; **ésos/as** those, those ones; **prefiero ésos** I prefer those ones; **ésos que te compré yo** the ones I bought you
[2] (*en locuciones*) **¡no me vengas con ésas!** don't give me any more of that nonsense!; **y cosas de ésas** and suchlike; **¡no me salgas ahora con ésas!** don't bring all that up again!; **no es una chica de ésas** she's not that kind of girl; **ni por ésas** (= *de ningún modo*) on no account; (= *aun así*) even so
esencia SF [1] (= *base*) [*de teoría*] essence; [*de asunto, problema*] heart; **en ~** essentially, in essence; **quinta ~** quintessence
[2] [*de perfume*] essence
esencial ADJ [1] (= *imprescindible*) essential; **es ~ traer ropa de abrigo** it's essential to bring warm clothing
[2] (= *principal*) essential, main; **lo ~ es que ...** the main *o* essential *o* most important thing is to ...; **he entendido lo ~ de la conversación** I understood the main *o* the most important points of the conversation; **en lo ~: pese a las diferencias, estamos de acuerdo en lo ~** essentially, despite our differences, we are in agreement, despite our differences, we are in agreement on the essentials
[3] [*aceite*] essential
esfagno SM sphagnum
esfera SF [1] (*Geog, Mat*) sphere; **en forma de ~** spherical ► **esfera celeste** celestial sphere ► **esfera terrestre** globe
[2] (*Téc*) [*de reloj*] face ► **esfera impresora** (*Tip*) golfball
[3] (= *campo*) sphere, field; **el proyecto ha sido autorizado por las altas ~s** the project has had the go-ahead from the top authorities *o* the upper echelons ► **esfera de acción** scope, range ► **esfera de actividad** sphere of activity ► **esfera de influencia** sphere of influence
esférico Ⓐ ADJ spherical
Ⓑ SM (*Dep*) football, soccer ball (*EEUU*)
esfero SM (*Col*) ballpoint pen
esferográfico SM (*Col*) ballpoint pen
esferógrafo SM (*Col*) ballpoint pen
esferoide SM spheroid
esfinge SF [1] (= *figura*) sphinx; ✦*MODISMO* **ser como una ~** to be expressionless, have a face like a poker
[2] (*Entomología*) hawk moth
esfínter SM sphincter
esforzadamente ADV vigorously, energetically
esforzado ADJ [1] (= *enérgico*) vigorous, energetic
[2] (= *fuerte*) strong, tough
[3] (= *emprendedor*) enterprising
[4] (= *valiente*) brave
[5] (= *trabajador*) hardworking
esforzar ▸conjug 1f, 1l◂ Ⓐ VT [*voz*] to strain; **no esfuerces la vista** don't strain your eyes
Ⓑ **esforzarse** VPR to exert o.s., make an effort; **hay que ~se más** you must try harder, you must make more effort; **~se en** *o* **por conseguir algo** to struggle *o* strive to achieve sth
esfuerzo SM [1] (*de fuerza física, intelectual*) effort; **sin ~** effortlessly, without strain; **hacer un ~** to make an effort; **no perdonar ~s para conseguir algo** to spare no effort to achieve sth; **no hizo el más mínimo ~ por agradar** he made absolutely no effort at all to be nice, he didn't make the slightest effort to be nice; **bien vale la pena el ~** it's well worth the effort
[2] (= *vigor*) spirit, vigour, vigor (*EEUU*); **con ~** with spirit
[3] (*Mec*) stress
esfumar ▸conjug 1a◂ Ⓐ VT (*Arte*) to tone down, soften
Ⓑ **esfumarse** VPR [1] [*apoyo, esperanzas*] to fade away, melt away
[2] [*persona*] to vanish, make o.s. scarce; **¡esfúmate!*** get lost!*
esfumino SM (*Arte*) stump
esgrima SF [1] (*Dep*) fencing
[2] (= *arte*) swordsmanship
esgrimidor(a) SM/F (*Dep*) fencer
esgrimir ▸conjug 3a◂ Ⓐ VT [1] [+ *espada*] to wield
[2] [+ *argumento*] to use; **~ que** to argue that, maintain that
Ⓑ VI to fence
esgrimista SMF (*LAm*) fencer
esguazar ▸conjug 1f◂ VT to ford
esguince SM [1] (*Med*) sprain
[2] (= *movimiento*) swerve, dodge; **dar un ~** to swerve, dodge
eslabón SM [1] [*de cadena*] link ► **eslabón giratorio** swivel ► **eslabón perdido** (*Biol*) missing link
[2] (*para afilar*) steel
eslabonar ▸conjug 1a◂ VT [1] [+ *eslabones, piezas*] to link, link together
[2] [+ *ideas*] to link, connect
eslálom SM, **eslalon** SM = **slalom**
eslavo/a Ⓐ ADJ Slav, Slavonic
Ⓑ SM/F Slav
Ⓒ SM (*Ling*) Slavonic
eslinga SF (*Náut*) sling
eslingar ▸conjug 1h◂ VT (*Náut*) to sling
eslip SM (*pl* **eslips**) = **slip**
eslogan SM (*pl* **eslogans**) = **slogan**
eslomar ▸conjug 1a◂ VT = **deslomar**
eslora SF (*Náut*) length; **tiene 250m de ~** she is 250m in length
eslovaco/a Ⓐ ADJ Slovak, Slovakian
Ⓑ SM/F Slovak
Eslovaquia SF Slovakia
Eslovenia SF Slovenia
esloveno/a ADJ, SM/F Slovene, Slovenian
esmaltar ▸conjug 1a◂ VT [1] (= *cubrir con esmalte*) [+ *metal*] to enamel; [+ *cerámica,*

porcelana] to glaze; [+ *uñas*] to varnish, paint
[2] (= *adornar*) to adorn (**con, de** with)

esmalte SM [1] (*para metal, diente*) enamel; (*para cerámica, porcelana*) glaze ► **esmalte de uñas** nail varnish, nail polish
[2] (= *objeto*) enamelwork
[3] (= *adorno*) lustre, luster (*EEUU*)

esmeradamente ADV carefully, neatly

esmerado ADJ [1] [*trabajo*] careful, neat
[2] [*persona*] careful, painstaking

esmeralda SF emerald

esmerar ▸conjug 1a◂ Ⓐ VT to polish
Ⓑ **esmerarse** VPR [1] (= *aplicarse*) to take great pains (**en** over); **no se esmera nada en su trabajo** she doesn't take any care over her work; **~se en hacer algo** to take great pains to do sth
[2] (= *hacer lo mejor*) to do one's best

esmerejón SM merlin

esmeril SM emery

esmerilar ▸conjug 1a◂ VT to polish with emery

esmero SM [1] (= *cuidado*) care, carefulness; **con el mayor ~** with the greatest care; **poner ~ en algo** to take great care *o* trouble *o* pains over sth
[2] (= *aseo*) neatness

Esmirna SF Smyrna

esmirriado ADJ puny

esmoladera SF grindstone

esmoquin SM dinner jacket, tuxedo (*EEUU*)

esnifada* SF [*de cola*] sniff; [*de cocaína*] snort*

esnifar* ▸conjug 1a◂ VT [+ *cola*] to sniff; [+ *cocaína*] to snort*

esnife* SM [*de cola*] sniff; [*de cocaína*] snort*

esnob Ⓐ ADJ INV [*persona*] snobbish, stuck-up*; [*coche, restaurante*] posh*, swish*, de luxe
Ⓑ SMF (*pl* **esnobs** [ez'noβ]) snob

esnobear* ▸conjug 1a◂ VT to snub, cold-shoulder

esnobismo SM snobbery, snobbishness

esnobista ADJ snobbish

ESO SF ABR (*Esp*) (= **Enseñanza Secundaria obligatoria**) *compulsory secondary education for 12- to 16-year-olds*

> **ESO**
>
> *As a consequence of the 1990 education reform law,* **LOGSE***, secondary education in Spain is now divided into two stages. The first stage,* **ESO***, or* **Educación Secundaria Obligatoria***, is for 12- to 16-year-olds. It is free and compulsory and includes both vocational and academic subjects. Students are awarded the* **Título de Graduado en Educación Secundaria** *on successful completion at age 16 and can leave school at this point. If they choose to continue their education they go on to the second stage, which consists of either the academically orientated* **Bachillerato** *or the vocational* **Formación Profesional Específica***.*
>
> ⇨ *See also* LOGSE

eso PRON DEM that; **~ no me gusta** I don't like that; **¿qué es ~?** what's that?; **~ de su coche** that business about his car; **¿es verdad ~ que me han contado?** is it true what I've been told?; **¿qué es ~ de que ...?** what's all this about ...?; **¡eso!** that's right!; **~ es** that's it, that's right; **~ sí** yes, of course; **el coche es viejo, ~ sí** the car is certainly old; **~ digo yo** (*indicando acuerdo*) I quite agree; (*respondiendo a pregunta*) that's what I'd like to know; **¡~ no!, ¡~ sí que no!** no way!; **~ creo** I think so; **~ espero** I hope so; **a ~ de las dos** at about two o'clock, round about two; **en ~ llegó el cartero** at that point the postman arrived; **nada de ~** nothing of the kind, far from it; **¡nada de ~!** not a bit of it!; **¿no es ~?** isn't that so?; **por ~** therefore, and so; **por ~ no vine** that's why I didn't come; **no es por ~** that's not the reason, that's not why, it's not because of that; **¿y ~?** why?, how so?*; **y ~ que llovía** in spite of the fact that it was raining

esófago SM oesophagus (*frm*), esophagus (*EEUU frm*), gullet

Esopo SM Aesop

esotérico ADJ esoteric

esoterismo SM [1] (= *culto*) esotericism, cult of the esoteric
[2] (*como género*) esotericism, esoterics *sing*
[3] (= *carácter*) esotericism, esoteric nature

esp. ABR (= **español**) Sp, Span

espabilada* SF (*Andes*) blink; **en una ~** in a jiffy*

espabilado *ver* **despabilado**

espabilar ▸conjug 1a◂ *ver* **despabilar**

espachurrar ▸conjug 1a◂ Ⓐ VT to squash, flatten
Ⓑ **espachurrarse** VPR to get squashed, get flattened

espaciadamente ADV **la revista saldrá más ~** the journal will come out less frequently *o* at longer intervals

espaciado SM (*Inform*) spacing

espaciador SM space bar

espacial ADJ INV [1] (*Aer*) space *antes de s*; **programa ~** space programme; **viajes ~es** space travel
[2] (*Mat*) spatial

espaciar ▸conjug 1b◂ Ⓐ VT [1] [+ *palabras, párrafos*] to space, space out
[2] (*en el tiempo*) [+ *noticia*] to spread; [+ *pagos*] to spread out, stagger; **empezó a ~ más sus visitas** his visits became less frequent, there were longer intervals between his visits
Ⓑ **espaciarse** VPR [1] (*al hablar*) spread o.s., to expatiate (*frm*); **~se en un tema** to enlarge on a subject, expatiate on a subject (*frm*)
[2] (= *relajarse*) to relax, take one's ease

espacio SM [1] (*Astron, Fís, Aer*) space; **exploración del ~** space exploration; **viajar por el ~** to travel in space ► **espacio aéreo** air space ► **espacio exterior, espacio extraterrestre** outer space ► **espacio interestelar** interstellar space ► **espacio sideral** outer space ► **espacio-tiempo** space-time
[2] (= *sitio*) room, space; **no hay ~ para tantas sillas** there isn't room *o* space for so many chairs; **¿me haces un ~ para que me siente?** can you make a bit of room *o* space for me to sit down?; **ocupa mucho ~** it takes up a lot of room; **aquí hay mucho ~ para aparcar** there's lots of room *o* space to park here ► **espacio de maniobra** room for manoeuvre ► **espacio libre** room ► **espacio muerto** clearance
[3] (= *superficie*) space ► **espacio natural** open space ► **espacios verdes** green spaces ► **espacio vital** (*Pol*) living space; [*de persona*] living space
[4] (*en un escrito*) space; **deja más ~ entre las líneas** leave more space between the lines; **un texto mecanografiado a un ~/a doble ~** a single-spaced/double-spaced typescript; **escríbelo a un ~/a doble ~** type it with single spacing/double spacing ► **espacio en blanco** blank space ► **espacio interlineal** interlinear spacing, inter-line spacing
[5] [*de tiempo*] space; **en el ~ de una hora** in the space of an hour; **en el ~ de tres generaciones** in the space of three generations; **por ~ de** for
[6] (*Radio, TV*) (*en la programación*) slot; (= *programa*) programme, program (*EEUU*) ► **espacio electoral** ≈ party political broadcast ► **espacio informativo** news programme ► **espacio publicitario** advertising spot, commercial
[7] (*Mús*) interval
[8] (††) (= *tardanza*) delay, slowness

espacioso ADJ [1] [*cuarto, casa*] spacious, roomy
[2] [*movimiento*] slow, deliberate

espaciotemporal ADJ spatio-temporal

espada Ⓐ SF [1] (= *arma*) sword; **poner a algn a ~** to put sb to the sword; ✦**MODISMOS** **estar hecho una ~** to be as thin as a rake *o* (*EEUU*) rail; **estar entre la ~ y la pared** to be between the devil and the deep blue sea; **la ~ de Damocles** the Sword of Damocles
[2] **espadas** (*Naipes*) *one of the suits in the Spanish card deck, represented by a sword*; → BARAJA ESPAÑOLA
Ⓑ SMF (*Taur*) matador, bullfighter

espadachín SM [1] (*Esgrima*) skilled swordsman
[2] (*pey*) bully, thug

espadaña SF [1] (*Bot*) bulrush
[2] (*Arquit*) steeple, belfry

espadarte SM swordfish

espadazo SM sword thrust, slash with a sword

espadero SM swordsmith

espadín SM [1] (= *espada pequeña*) dress sword, ceremonial sword
[2] [*de espadachín*] picklock
[3] **espadines** (= *pez*) sprats

espadista‡ SMF burglar, lock-picker

espadón SM [1] (= *arma*) broadsword
[2] (*hum*, *) big shot*, top person; (*Mil*) brass hat*

espaguetis SMPL spaghetti *sing*

espalda Ⓐ SF [1] (*Anat*) back; **de ~s a algo** with one's back to sth; **de ~s al sentido de la marcha** facing backwards, with one's back to the engine; **lo mataron por la ~** he was killed from behind; **atar las manos a la ~** to tie sb's hands behind his back; **caer de ~s** to fall on one's back; **estar de ~s** to have one's back turned; **volver la ~** to turn away; (*pey*) to turn tail; **volver la ~ a algn** to cold-shoulder sb, turn one's back on sb; **volverse de ~s** to turn one's back; ✦**MODISMOS** **cubrirse las ~s** to cover o.s., cover one's own back; **dar la ~ a algo/algn** to turn away from sth/sb, face away from sth/sb; **echar algo sobre las ~s** to take sth on, take charge of sth; **hacer algo a ~s de algn** to do sth behind sb's back; **tener las ~s cubiertas** to make sure, be on the safe side; *ver tb* **ancho A1**
[2] (*Dep*) backstroke; **la prueba de 200 me-**

tros ~s the 200 metres backstroke
[3] (*Andes*) (= *destino*) fate, destiny
Ⓑ SMF ► **espalda mojada** (*Méx**) wetback
espaldar SM [1] (*de silla*) back
[2] (*para plantas*) trellis, espalier
[3] **espaldares** (*Dep*) wall bars
espaldarazo SM recognition; **ese concierto supuso su ~ definitivo** that concert finally earned him recognition; **su apoyo ha dado el ~ decisivo al proyecto** his backing has been decisive in setting up the project
espaldera SF [1] (*para plantas*) trellis, espalier
[2] (*para la espalda*) surgical corset
[3] **espalderas** (*Dep*) wall bars
espaldero SM (*Caribe*) bodyguard, henchman
espaldilla SF [1] (*Anat*) shoulder blade
[2] (*Méx Culin*) shoulder of pork
espantá* SF = **espantada**
espantable ADJ = **espantoso**
espantada SF stampede; **dar la ~** to bolt
espantadizo ADJ timid, easily scared
espantado ADJ [1] (= *asustado*) frightened, scared, terrified; **me quedé espantada cuando lo vi con esos pelos** I was horrified when I saw him with that hair
[2] (*LAm*) (= *muy asustado*) sick with fear
espantador ADJ [1] (= *espantoso*) frightening
[2] (*Andes, CAm, Cono Sur*) = **espantadizo**
espantajo SM [1] (= *espantapájaros*) scarecrow
[2] (= *persona*) sight*, fright*
espantamoscas SM INV fly swat
espantapájaros SM INV scarecrow
espantar ▸conjug 1a◂ Ⓐ VT [1] (= *asustar*) (*gen*) to frighten, scare; (*haciendo huir*) to frighten off *o* away, scare off *o* away; **el ruido espantó a las reses** the noise frightened *o* scared the cattle; **espantó a los perros con una escoba** she frightened the dogs off *o* away with a broom; **con ese genio espanta a todas las chicas** with that temper of his he frightens *o* scares all the girls (off *o* away)
[2] (= *horrorizar*) to horrify, appal; **le espantaba la idea de tener que ir solo** he was horrified *o* appalled at the thought of having to go on his own
Ⓑ **espantarse** VPR [1] (= *asustarse*) to get frightened, get scared
[2] (= *horrorizarse*) to be horrified, be appalled (**de** at); **se espantó de verla tan cambiada** he was horrified *o* appalled to see her so changed
[3] (*Caribe*) (= *sospechar*) to get suspicious
espanto SM [1] (= *susto*) fright; *ver tb* **curado A3**
[2] (= *amenaza*) threat, menace
[3] (*LAm*) (= *fantasma*) ghost
[4] (*) (*para exagerar*) **¡qué ~!** how awful!; **hace un frío de ~** it's terribly cold; **es un coche de ~** it's a fabulous *o* tremendous car*
espantosamente ADV [1] (= *con miedo*) frightfully
[2] (*para exagerar*) amazingly
espantosidad SF (*Andes*) terror, fear
espantoso ADJ [1] (= *aterrador*) frightening
[2] (*para exagerar*) **hizo un frío ~** it was absolutely freezing; **llevaba un traje ~** she was wearing an awful *o* a hideous *o* a frightful *o* ghastly* hat; **había un ruido ~** there was a terrible *o* dreadful noise
España SF Spain; **Nueva ~** (*Hist*) New Spain
(*Mexico*); **la ~ de charanga y pandereta** touristy Spain
español(a) Ⓐ ADJ Spanish
Ⓑ SM/F Spaniard; **los ~es** the Spaniards, the Spanish
Ⓒ SM (*Ling*) Spanish ► **español antiguo** Old Spanish ► **español medieval** Medieval Spanish ► **español moderno** Modern Spanish
española SF (*Méx*) spanner
españolada SF (*pey*) *film, show etc giving a clichéd, stereotypical image of Spain*
españolidad SF [1] (= *carácter español*) Spanishness
[2] (= *patriotismo*) Spanish patriotism
españolísimo ADJ SUPERL typically Spanish, unmistakably Spanish, Spanish to the core
españolismo SM [1] (= *amor a lo español*) love of Spain
[2] (= *carácter español*) Spanishness
[3] (*Ling*) Hispanicism
españolista Ⓐ ADJ centralist, unionist (*as opposed to regionalist*)
Ⓑ SMF pro-centralist
españolito* SM ordinary Spaniard, Spanish man in the street; **algún ~** some poor little Spaniard; **cada ~ de a pie** each poor little Spaniard that there is; **no quiero que llegue cualquier ~ y me diga lo que he de hacer** I don't want any old Spaniard to come along and start telling me what to do
españolizar ▸conjug 1f◂ Ⓐ VT to make Spanish, Hispanicize
Ⓑ **españolizarse** VPR to adopt Spanish ways; **se españolizó por completo** he became completely Spanish
esparadrapo SM plaster, sticking plaster, Band-Aid® (*EEUU*)
esparaván SM [1] (*Orn*) sparrowhawk
[2] (*Vet*) spavin
esparavel SM net, casting net
esparceta SF sainfoin
esparcido ADJ [1] (= *desparramado*) scattered
[2] (= *extendido*) widespread
[3] (= *alegre*) cheerful
esparcimiento SM [1] (= *dispersión*) spreading
[2] (= *descanso*) relaxation
[3] (= *diversión*) amusement
esparcir ▸conjug 3b◂ Ⓐ VT [1] (= *desparramar*) to spread, scatter
[2] (= *divulgar*) to disseminate
[3] (= *distraer*) to amuse, divert
Ⓑ **esparcirse** VPR [1] (= *desparramarse*) to spread, spread out, scatter
[2] (= *descansar*) to relax
[3] (= *divertirse*) to amuse o.s.
espárrago SM asparagus; ✦***MODISMOS*** **estar hecho un ~** to be as thin as a rake *o* (*EEUU*) rail; **mandar a algn a freír ~s** to tell sb to get lost, tell sb to go jump in a lake*, tell sb to get stuffed‡, tell sb where to get off*; **¡vete a freír ~s!*** get lost!, go jump in a lake!*, get stuffed!‡
► **espárrago triguero** wild asparagus
esparrancado ADJ [*piernas*] wide apart, spread far apart; [*persona*] with legs wide apart, with legs spread far apart
esparrancarse ▸conjug 1g◂ VPR to spread one's legs, spread one's legs wide apart; **~ sobre algo** to straddle sth
Esparta SF Sparta
espartal SM esparto field
espartano/a Ⓐ ADJ [1] (= *de Esparta*) Spartan
[2] (= *austero*) spartan
Ⓑ SM/F Spartan
esparteña SF = **alpargata**
espartillo SM (*LAm*) esparto, esparto grass
espartizal SM esparto field
esparto SM esparto, esparto grass; ✦***MODISMO*** **estar como el ~** to be all dried up
Espasa SM ✦***MODISMO*** **ser el ~*** to be a walking encyclopedia
espasmo SM spasm
espasmódicamente ADV spasmodically
espasmódico ADJ spasmodic
espasticidad SF spasticity
espástico/a ADJ, SM/F spastic
espatarrarse* ▸conjug 1a◂ VPR [1] (*al sentarse*) to sprawl
[2] = **esparrancarse**
espato SM (*Geol*) spar ► **espato de Islandia** Iceland spar
espátula SF [1] (*Constr*) putty knife; ✦***MODISMO*** **estar hecho una ~** to be as thin as a rake *o* (*EEUU*) rail
[2] (*Arte*) palette knife
[3] (*Culin*) fish slice, spatula
[4] (*Med*) spatula
[5] (*Orn*) spoonbill
especia SF spice
especiado ADJ spiced, spicy
especial Ⓐ ADJ [1] (*para un fin concreto*) [*dieta, permiso*] special; **papel ~ para regalo** gift paper; *ver tb* **educación 1**, **enviado**
[2] (= *extraordinario*) special; **un saludo muy ~ para nuestros compañeros** a special hello to all our colleagues; **de ~ interés es el trabajo de este novelista** the work of this novelist is especially interesting *o* of special interest; **precios ~es para niños** special prices for children
[3] **en ~** especially, particularly; **pedimos disculpas a todos, y en ~ a ...** we apologize to everyone, and especially *o* particularly to ...; **¿desea ver a alguien en ~?** is there anybody in particular you want to see?
[4] (= *quisquilloso*) fussy; **soy muy ~ con la ropa** I'm very fussy about my clothes; **¡qué ~ eres con la comida!** you're such a fussy eater!
[5] (= *extraño*) peculiar; **le encuentro un sabor muy ~ a este café** this coffee has a very peculiar flavour
Ⓑ SM [1] (*TV*) (*tb* **programa ~**) special; **un ~ sobre los Juegos Olímpicos** an Olympic special ► **especial (de) deportes** sports special ► **especial informativo** news special
[2] (*Méx Teat*) show
[3] (*para comer*) (*Cono Sur*) baguette, sub sandwich (*EEUU*); (*Chile*) hot dog
especialidad SF [1] (= *ramo*) speciality, specialty (*EEUU*); **ha elegido la ~ de cirugía** he has chosen to specialize in surgery, he has chosen surgery as his speciality; **hizo dos años de ~** he did a two year specialization; **las matemáticas no son precisamente mi ~** maths is not exactly my speciality *o* strong point
[2] (*Culin*) speciality, specialty (*EEUU*); **"especialidad de la casa"** "speciality of the house"; **las carnes son nuestra ~** the meat dishes are our speciality
[3] (*Farm*) (= *preparado*) medicine

especialista Ⓐ ADJ [*técnico, enfermera*] specialist; **un delantero ~ en tiros libres** a forward who specializes in free kicks; **médico ~** specialist
Ⓑ SMF [1] (*en estudio, profesión*) specialist, expert; **un libro útil tanto para el ~ como para el lector en general** a useful book for both the specialist and the general reader; **es el máximo ~ en biología marina** he is the top authority on marine biology
[2] (*Med, Dep*) specialist; **~ de la piel** skin specialist; **un ~ en 100 metros mariposa** a specialist in the 100 metres butterfly
[3] (*Cine, TV*) stuntman/stuntwoman

especializado ADJ [1] [*personal, público*] specialized; **la creación del periodismo ~** the creation of specialized journalism; **un artículo destinado al lector no ~** an article aimed at the general reader; **una cadena especializada en programas culturales** a channel specializing in cultural programmes
[2] [*obrero*] skilled, trained
[3] [*lenguaje*] technical, specialized

especializarse ▸conjug 1f◂ VPR to specialize (**en** in); **se especializó en Derecho Internacional** he specialized in International Law

especialmente ADV [1] (= *en especial*) especially, particularly; **este problema afecta ~ a los jóvenes** this problem especially *o* particularly affects young people
[2] (= *para un fin concreto*) specially; **un puente ~ construido al efecto** a bridge specially built for the purpose; **un plato ~ recomendado para diabéticos** a dish specially recommended for diabetics

especiar ▸conjug 1b◂ VT to spice

especie SF [1] (*Biol*) species; **la ~ humana** the human race ► **especie amenazada**, **especie en peligro** endangered species ► **especie protegida** protected species
[2] (= *clase*) kind, sort; **una ~ de ...** a kind *o* sort of ...
[3] **en ~** in kind; **pagar en ~** to pay in kind
[4] (= *noticia*) piece of news; **con la ~ de que ...** on the pretext that ...; **corre la ~ de que ha dimitido** there is a rumour that she has resigned, it is rumoured that she has resigned

especificación SF specification

específicamente ADV specifically

especificar ▸conjug 1g◂ VT [+ *cantidad, modelo*] to specify; (*en una lista*) to list, itemize

específico Ⓐ ADJ specific
Ⓑ SM (*Med*) specific

especifidad SF specific nature, specificity

espécimen SM (*pl* **especímenes**) specimen

especioso ADJ specious, plausible

espectacular ADJ spectacular

espectacularidad SF spectacular nature; **de gran ~** very spectacular

espectacularmente ADV spectacularly, in spectacular fashion

espectáculo Ⓐ SM [1] (*Teat*) (= *representación*) show; (= *función*) performance; **sección de ~s** entertainment guide, entertainments section; **el deporte como ~** sport presented as showbusiness; ✦*MODISMO* **dar un ~** to make a scene ► **espectáculo de luz y sonido** sound and light show, son et lumière show ► **espectáculo de variedades** variety show
[2] (= *visión asombrosa*) spectacle; **el ~ de las cataratas** the amazing spectacle *o* sight of the waterfalls, the spectacular waterfalls; **fue un ~ bochornoso** it was an embarrassing spectacle *o* sight
Ⓑ ADJ INV **atletismo ~** athletics on the grand scale; **cine ~** epic films *pl*; **fútbol ~** soccer presented as show-biz; **programa ~** TV variety show; **restaurante ~** restaurant with a floor-show

espectador(a) SM/F [1] (*Cine, Dep, Teat*) spectator; **los ~es** (*Dep*) the spectators; (*Teat*) the audience *sing*
[2] [*de acontecimiento, accidente*] onlooker

espectral ADJ [1] (*Fís*) spectral
[2] (= *fantasmagórico*) ghostly

espectro SM [1] (*Fís*) spectrum; **de amplio ~** wide-ranging, covering a broad spectrum
[2] (= *fantasma*) spectre, specter (*EEUU*), ghost; **el ~ del hambre** the spectre of famine

espectrógrafo SM spectrograph

espectrograma SM spectrogram

espectrometría SF spectrometry

espectrómetro SM spectrometer

espectroscopia SF spectroscopy

espectroscopio SM spectroscope

especulación SF [1] (= *suposición*) speculation
[2] (*Com, Fin*) speculation ► **especulación bursátil** speculation on the stock exchange ► **especulación inmobiliaria** property speculation

especulador(a) SM/F speculator

especular[1] ▸conjug 1a◂ VI [1] (= *hacer cábalas*) to speculate (**sobre** about, on)
[2] (*Com, Fin*) to speculate (**en, con** with)

especular[2] ▸conjug 1a◂ VT (*LAm*) to ruffle the hair of

especular[3] ADJ specular

especulativo ADJ speculative

espéculo SM (*Med*) speculum

espejado ADJ glossy, shining

espejeante ADJ gleaming, glistening

espejear ▸conjug 1a◂ VI to glint

espejeras SFPL (*Caribe*) chafing, chafed patch

espejismo SM [1] (*Ópt*) mirage
[2] (= *ilusión*) mirage, illusion

espejito SM (= *espejo pequeño*) small mirror; [*de bolso*] handbag mirror

espejo SM [1] (= *para mirarse*) mirror; **mirarse al ~** to look at o.s. in the mirror ► **espejo de cuerpo entero** full-length mirror ► **espejo retrovisor** rear-view mirror
[2] (= *reflejo*) mirror, reflection; **un ~ de caballerosidad** a model of chivalry; **la cara es el ~ del alma** the eyes are the windows of the soul
[3] (*Zool*) white patch

espejoso ADJ = **espejado**

espejuelo SM [1] (= *espejo pequeño*) small looking-glass
[2] **espejuelos** lenses, spectacles

espeleoarqueología SF cave archaeology

espeleobuceo SM cave diving

espeleología SF potholing, spelunking (*esp EEUU*), speleology (*frm*)

espeleólogo/a SM/F potholer, spelunker (*esp EEUU*), speleologist (*frm*)

espelta SF (*Bot*) spelt

espelunca SF (*liter*) cave

espeluznante ADJ hair-raising, horrifying

espeluzno SM (*Méx*) = **escalofrío**

▼ **espera** SF [1] (= *acción*) wait; **la ~ fue interminable** it was an endless wait; **tras una ~ de tres horas** after a three-hour wait; **el asunto no tiene ~** the matter is most urgent; **en ~ de su contestación** awaiting your reply; **en ~ de que llegue** waiting for him to arrive; **estar a la ~ de algo** to be expecting sth; **quedo a la ~ de su respuesta** (*en correspondencia*) I look forward to hearing from you
[2] (= *paciencia*) patience; **es que no tienes ~** you have no patience
[3] (*Jur*) stay, respite

esperable ADJ **ser ~** to be hoped for

esperantista SMF Esperantist

esperanto SM Esperanto

esperanza SF hope; **acudimos a ti como última ~** we're turning to you as our last hope; **la nueva ~ del cine español** the bright young hope of Spanish cinema; **hay pocas ~s de que venga** there is little hope that he'll come; **abrigar** *o* **albergar ~s de hacer algo** to cherish hopes of doing sth; **ya no abrigamos ~s de encontrarlo con vida** we no longer hold out any hope of finding him alive; **ser la gran ~ blanca** to be the great white hope; **con la ~ de que ...** in the hope that ...; **dar ~(s) a algn** to give sb hope; **perder la ~** to lose hope; **poner la ~ en algn/algo** to pin one's hopes on sb/sth; **tenemos todas nuestras ~s puestas en él** we have pinned all our hopes on him; **tener ~ en algo** to have hope for sth; **tener ~(s) de hacer algo** to have hope(s) of doing sth; **todavía tengo ~s de que llegue a tiempo** I still hope it will arrive on time; ✦*MODISMOS* **alimentarse** *o* **vivir de ~s** to live on hopes; **¡qué ~!** (*LAm*) some hope!, not on your life!*; **la ~ es lo último que se pierde** there's always hope; **mientras haya vida hay ~** while there's life there's hope ► **esperanza de vida** life expectancy

esperanzado ADJ hopeful; **estar ~ con** *o* **en algo** to be hopeful of sth

esperanzador ADJ [*perspectiva, futuro*] hopeful; [*noticia, resultado, tratamiento*] encouraging, hopeful, promising; **los resultados de la encuesta no pueden ser más ~es** the results of the survey could not be more encouraging *o* hopeful *o* promising

esperanzadoramente ADV encouragingly, promisingly; **los resultados de este año han mejorado ~** there has been an encouraging improvement *o* a promising improvement in this year's results, this year's results have improved encouragingly *o* promisingly

esperanzar ▸conjug 1f◂ VT **~ a algn** to give hope to sb; **las mejoras laborales han esperanzado a los trabajadores** improvements in working conditions have given hope to the workers; **los abogados no quisieron ~lo** the lawyers did not want to raise his hopes *o* get his hopes up

▼ **esperar** ▸conjug 1a◂ Ⓐ VT [1] (= *aguardar*) [+ *tren, persona*] to wait for; **estaba esperando el avión** I was waiting for the plane; **esperaban noticias de los rehenes** they were waiting for *o* awaiting news of the hostages; **fuimos a ~la a la estación** we went to meet her at the station; **nos espera un duro invierno** we've got a hard winter ahead of us; **¡la que te espera cuando llegues a casa!** you're

➤ LENGUA Y USO: **espera 1** 31, 48.2 **esperar A2** 50.1, 35.2, 48.2 **A3** 48.4

(in) for it when you get home!; ✦*MODISMO* **de aquí te espero***: **un lío de aquí te espero*** a tremendous row*; **dijo unas tonterías de aquí te espero** he said some really stupid things

2 (= *desear*) to hope; **espero llegar a tiempo** I hope to arrive on time; **eso espero** I hope so; **han prometido castigar a los culpables y espero que sea así** they've promised to punish those responsible and I hope they will; **—ya nos pagará —espero que sea así** "he'll pay us, you'll see" — "I hope you're right *o* I hope so"; **espero que te haya gustado** I hope you liked it; **espero que vengas** I hope you'll come; **espero que no sea nada grave** I hope it isn't anything serious; **—¿vienen a la fiesta? —espero que sí** "are they coming to the party?" — "I hope so"; **—¿crees que se enfadará? —espero que no** "do you think she will be angry?" — "I hope not"

3 (= *contar con*) to expect; **¿esperas visita?** are you expecting someone?; **espero su llamada en cualquier momento** I expect his call at any moment; **no me esperes antes de las siete** don't expect me before seven; **¿acaso esperas que pague yo?** you're not expecting me to pay, are you?; **llegaron antes de lo que yo esperaba** they arrived sooner than I expected; **esperaban que les pidiera perdón** they were expecting him to apologize; **¿qué esperas, que encima te lo agradezca?** don't expect me to thank you for it as well; **¿qué puedes ~ de él, después de cómo se ha comportado?** what do you expect from him, after the way he has behaved?; **era de ~** it was to be expected; **era de ~ que eso sucediera** it was to be expected that that would happen; **era de ~ que no viniera** it was to be expected that he wouldn't come; **no esperaba menos de ti** I expected nothing *o* no less of you; **llamará cuando menos te lo esperes** he'll call when you least expect it; ✦*MODISMO* **~ algo como agua de mayo** to await sth with eager anticipation

4 [+ *bebé*] **está esperando un hijo** she's expecting (a baby); **está esperando su primer hijo** she's expecting her first child

Ⓑ VI 1 (= *aguardar*) to wait; **~é aquí** I'll wait here; **¡espera un momento, éste no es mi libro!** hold on *o* wait a minute, this isn't my book!; **espera en la puerta, ahora mismo voy** wait at the door, I'm just coming; **~ a *o* hasta que algn haga algo** to wait for sb to do sth; **hacer ~ a algn** keep sb waiting; **su respuesta no se hizo ~** his answer wasn't long in coming; ✦*MODISMOS* **~ desesperando** to hope against hope; **espera y verás** wait and see; **puedes ~ sentado** you've got another think coming; ✦*REFRÁN* **el que espera desespera** a watched pot never boils

2 **~ en algn** to put one's hopes *o* trust in sb; **~ en Dios** to trust in God

Ⓒ **esperarse** VPR 1 (*uso impersonal*) to be expected; **como podía ~se** as was to be expected; **no fue tan bueno como se esperaba** it was not as good as expected; **se espera que asistan más de mil personas** more than a thousand people are expected to attend

2 (*) (= *uso enfático*) **¡espérate un momento!** wait a minute!, hold on a minute!; **espérate a que deje de llover** wait until it stops raining; **¡no es lo que me esperaba!** it's not what I was expecting!; **¡me lo esperaba!** I was expecting this!

> **ESPERAR**
>
> **Esperar** tiene en inglés varias traducciones, entre las que se encuentran **wait (for)**, **await**, **hope** y **expect**.
>
> • Se traduce por **wait** (**for**) cuando **esperar** se refiere al hecho de aguardar la llegada de alguien o de un suceso:
>
> Hice el examen hace dos meses y todavía estoy esperando los resultados
> ***I took the exam two months ago and I'm still waiting for the results***
>
> La esperó media hora y después se fue a casa
> ***He waited half an hour for her and then went home***
>
> • El verbo **await** es un verbo de uso similar a **wait for**, aunque no requiere el uso de la preposición y no es muy corriente en inglés moderno:
>
> Esperaban ansiosamente la llegada del Rey
> ***They eagerly awaited the arrival of the King***
>
> • Se traduce por **hope** cuando deseamos que algo suceda, pero no estamos seguros de si ocurrirá o no:
>
> Espero que no se enfade mucho conmigo
> ***I hope (that) she won't be very annoyed with me***
>
> Después de terminar la carrera espero conseguir un buen trabajo
> ***I hope to get a good job when I finish university***
>
> • Traducimos **esperar** por **expect** cuando estamos muy seguros de que algo va a suceder o cuando hay una razón lógica para que algo suceda:
>
> Espero aprobar porque el examen me salió muy bien
> ***I expect to pass*** *o* ***I expect I'll pass because the exam went very well***
>
> Ha resultado mejor de lo que esperábamos
> ***It was better than we expected***
>
> Está esperando un niño
> ***She's expecting (a baby)***
>
> *Para otros usos y ejemplos ver la entrada.*

esperma SM *o* SF 1 (*Biol*) sperm; **~ de ballena** spermaceti

2 (*Caribe, Col*) (= *vela*) candle

espermatozoide SM, **espermatozoo** SM spermatozoon

espermicida SM spermicide

espermio SM sperm

espernancarse ▸conjug 1g◂ VPR (*LAm*) = **esparrancarse**

esperón SM (*Caribe*) long wait

esperpéntico ADJ 1 (= *absurdo*) absurd, nonsensical

2 (= *grotesco*) grotesque, exaggerated

esperpentización SF presentation in an absurd *o* grotesque *etc* manner, caricaturing

esperpentizar ▸conjug 1f◂ VT to present in an absurd *o* grotesque *etc* way, caricature

esperpento SM 1 (= *persona fea*) fright*, sight*

2 (= *disparate*) nonsense; **lo que dijo no eran más que ~s** what he said was absolute nonsense

3 (*Teat*) *play which focuses on the grotesque*

4 (= *cuento*) macabre story, grotesque tale

> **ESPERPENTO**
>
> ***Esperpento*** *is a type of theatre developed by Ramón del Valle-Inclán (1869-1936) focusing on characters whose physical and psychological characteristics have been deliberately deformed and warped to the point where they become grotesque caricatures. Valle-Inclán used this* ***esperpento*** *as a vehicle for social and political satire.*

espesante SM thickener, thickening agent

espesar ▸conjug 1a◂ Ⓐ VT 1 (= *hacer más espeso*) [+ *líquido, chocolate*] to thicken; [+ *sustancia*] to make dense, make denser

2 (= *hacer más tupido*) [+ *tapiz*] to weave tighter; [+ *jersey, chaqueta*] to knit tighter

Ⓑ **espesarse** VPR [*líquido*] to thicken, get thicker; [*bosque, niebla, humo*] to get denser, get thicker; [*sangre*] to coagulate, solidify

espeso ADJ 1 (*gen*) thick; [*bosque*] dense; [*pasta*] stiff; [*líquido*] thick, heavy

2 (= *sucio*) dirty, untidy

espesor SM (*gen*) thickness; [*de nieve*] depth; **tiene medio metro de ~** it is half a metre thick

espesura SF 1 (= *espesor*) thickness; (= *densidad*) density; **en la ~ de la selva** in the thick *o* heart *o* depths of the jungle

2 (*Bot*) thicket, overgrown place; **se refugiaron en las ~s de la sierra** (*liter*) they took refuge in the mountain fastnesses (*liter*)

3 (= *suciedad*) dirtiness, untidiness

espeta⁑ SM cop*

espetar ▸conjug 1a◂ Ⓐ VT 1 (= *atravesar*) (*gen*) to transfix, pierce, run through; [+ *carne*] to skewer, spit

2 (= *realizar*) [+ *orden*] to rap out; [+ *lección, sermón*] to read; [+ *pregunta*] to fire; **~ algo a algn** to spring sth on sb, broach a subject (unexpectedly) with sb

Ⓑ **espetarse** VPR 1 (= *ponerse cómodo*) to steady o.s., settle o.s.

2 (= *envanecerse*) to get on one's high horse

espetera⁑ SF tits** *pl*

espetón SM 1 (*Culin*) (= *broqueta*) skewer; (= *asador*) spit; (= *clavija*) large pin, iron pin; (= *atizador*) poker

2 (= *pinchazo*) jab, poke

espía Ⓐ SMF spy

Ⓑ ADJ **avión ~** spy plane; **buque ~** spy ship; **satélite ~** spy satellite

espiantar* ▸conjug 1a◂ Ⓐ VT (*Cono Sur*) (= *robar*) to pinch*

Ⓑ VI, **espiantarse** VPR (*Cono Sur*) to scram*, beat it*

espiar ▸conjug 1c◂ Ⓐ VT 1 (= *vigilar*) to spy on, keep (a) watch on

2 (*LAm*) (= *mirar*) to look at, watch

Ⓑ VI to spy

espich* SM (*LAm*) = **espiche**[1]

espicha SF (*Asturias*) cider party

espichar[1] ▸conjug 1a◂ Ⓐ VT 1 ✦*MODISMO* **~la(s)**⁑ to kick the bucket*, peg out⁑

2 (= *pinchar*) to prick

3 (*Cono Sur*) (= *entregar*) to hand over reluctantly, relinquish

4 (*Andes, Cono Sur Téc*) to put a tap on

Ⓑ VI = **A1**

Ⓒ **espicharse** VPR 1 (*LAm*) (= *enflaquecerse*) to get thin

2 (*Andes*) [*neumático*] to go flat
3 (*CAm*) (= *asustarse*) to get scared, get frightened

espichar²* ▸conjug 1a◂ VI (*LAm*) (= *pronunciar un discurso*) to make a speech, speechify*

espiche¹* SM (*LAm*) speech

espiche² SM spike

espidómetro SM (*LAm*) speedometer

espiedo SM (*Cono Sur*) spit

espiga SF 1 (*Bot*) [*de trigo*] ear; [*de flores*] spike
2 (*Téc*) (*gen*) spigot; [*de pestillo*] shaft; [*de cuchillo, herramienta*] tang
3 (= *badajo*) clapper
4 (*Mil*) fuse
5 (*Náut*) masthead

espigadera SF gleaner

espigado ADJ 1 (*Bot*) (= *maduro*) ripe; (= *con grano*) ready to seed
2 [*persona*] tall and slim, willowy

espigador(a) SM/F gleaner

espigar ▸conjug 1h◂ Ⓐ VT 1 [+ *fruta*] to look closely at, scrutinize
2 [+ *libro*] to consult
3 (*Téc*) to pin, peg
Ⓑ VI 1 [*cereales*] to come into ear, form ears; [*flor*] to run to seed
2 = **C**
Ⓒ **espigarse** VPR [*persona joven*] to shoot up, get very tall

espigón SM 1 (*Bot*) ear, spike
2 (*Zool*) sting
3 [*de herramienta*] sharp point, spike
4 (= *malecón*) breakwater

espigueo SM gleaning

espiguero SM (*Méx*) granary

espiguilla SF herring-bone pattern

espín SM porcupine

espina SF 1 (*Bot*) [*de rosal*] thorn; [*de chumbera*] prickle; ✦*MODISMOS* **mala ~** spite, resentment, ill-will; **me da mala ~** it makes me suspicious; **estar en ~s** to be on tenterhooks, be all on edge; **sacarse la ~** to get even, pay off an old score
2 [*de pez*] bone
3 (*Anat*) (*tb* **~ dorsal**) spine; **doblar la ~** to bend over ▸ **espina bífida** spina bifida
4 (= *problema*) worry, suspicion

espinaca SF (*Bot*) spinach; **~s** (*Culin*) spinach *pl*; **no me gustan las ~s** I don't like spinach

espinal ADJ spinal

espinaquer SM spinnaker

espinar ▸conjug 1a◂ Ⓐ VT 1 (= *punzar*) to prick
2 (= *ofender*) to sting, hurt, nettle
Ⓑ **espinarse** VPR to prick o.s.
Ⓒ SM 1 (*Bot*) thicket, thornbrake, thorny place
2 (= *dificultad*) difficulty

espinazo SM spine, backbone; ✦*MODISMO* **doblar el ~*** to knuckle under*

espineta SF (*Mús*) spinet

espingarda SF 1 (*Hist*) (= *cañón*) kind of cannon; (= *mosquete*) Moorish musket
2 (*) (= *chica*) lanky girl

espinglés SM (*hum*) Spanglish

espinilla SF 1 (= *tibia*) shin, shinbone, shank (*EEUU*)
2 (*en la piel*) blackhead

espinillera SF shinpad, shinguard

espinita SF irritation

espino SM ▸ **espino albar, espino blanco** hawthorn ▸ **espino cerval** buckthorn ▸ **espino negro** blackthorn, sloe

espinoso Ⓐ ADJ 1 (= *con espinas*) [*rosal*] thorny; [*chumbera*] prickly; [*pez*] bony
2 [*problema*] knotty, thorny
Ⓑ SM stickleback

espinudo ADJ (*LAm*) = **espinoso A**

espión SM spy

espionaje SM espionage, spying; **novela de ~** spy story ▸ **espionaje industrial** industrial espionage

espíquer SM (*Téc*) speaker

espira SF 1 (*Mat*) spire
2 (*Zool*) whorl, ring
3 (*Elec*) turn

espiráculo SM blow hole, spiracle (*frm*)

espiral Ⓐ ADJ (*gen*) spiral; [*movimiento, línea*] spiral; (*Téc*) helical
Ⓑ SM [*de reloj*] hairspring
Ⓒ SF (= *forma*) (*gen*) spiral; (*anticonceptiva*) coil; (*Téc*) whorl; [*de humo*] spiral; (*Dep*) corkscrew dive; **la ~ inflacionista** the inflationary spiral; **el humo subía en ~** the smoke went spiralling up; **dar vueltas en ~** to spiral

espiralado ADJ spiral

espirar ▸conjug 1a◂ Ⓐ VT [+ *aire, humo*] to breathe out, exhale; [+ *olor*] to give off, give out Ⓑ VI to breathe out, exhale

espirea SF spiraea

espiritado ADJ like a wraith, ghost-like

espiritismo SM spiritualism

espiritista Ⓐ ADJ spiritualist, spiritualistic
Ⓑ SMF spiritualist, spiritualistic

espiritoso ADJ 1 [*bebida*] alcoholic, spirituous (*frm*); **licores espirituosos** spirits
2 [*persona*] spirited, lively

espíritu SM 1 (= *lo inmaterial*) spirit; **pobre de ~** poor in spirit; **levantar el ~ de algn** to raise sb's spirits; **en la letra y en el ~** in the letter and in the spirit ▸ **espíritu de cuerpo** esprit de corps ▸ **espíritu de equipo** team spirit ▸ **espíritu de lucha** fighting spirit ▸ **espíritu guerrero** fighting spirit
2 [*de persona*] (= *mente*) mind; **con ~ amplio** with an open mind; **de ~ crítico** of a critical turn of mind; **edificar el ~ de algn** to improve sb's mind
3 (*Rel*) spirit; ✦*MODISMO* **dar** o **rendir el ~** to give up the ghost ▸ **Espíritu Santo** Holy Ghost, Holy Spirit
4 (= *aparecido*) spirit, ghost ▸ **espíritu maligno** evil spirit
5 (= *alcohol*) spirits *pl*, liquor ▸ **espíritu de vino** spirits of wine *pl*

espiritual Ⓐ ADJ 1 [*vida, patria, poderes*] spiritual
2 (= *fantasmal*) unworldly, ghostly
3 (*Andes, Cono Sur*) (= *gracioso*) funny, witty
Ⓑ SM spiritual, Negro spiritual

espiritualidad SF spirituality

espiritualizar ▸conjug 1f◂ VT to spiritualize

espiritualmente ADV spiritually

espirituoso = **espiritoso**

espita SF 1 (= *grifo*) tap, spigot (*EEUU*) ✦*MODISMO* **abrir la ~ de las lágrimas** to weep buckets* ▸ **espita de entrada del gas** gas tap
2 (*) (= *borracho*) drunkard, boozer*, lush (*EEUU*‡)
3 (‡) [*de hombre*] prick‡

espitar ▸conjug 1a◂ VT to tap, broach

espitoso‡ ADJ (= *eufórico*) hyper*

espléndidamente ADV 1 (= *magníficamente*) splendidly, magnificently
2 (= *generosamente*) lavishly, generously; **se gratificará ~** there will be a generous reward

esplendidez SF 1 (= *magnificencia*) splendour, splendor (*EEUU*), magnificence
2 (= *generosidad*) lavishness, generosity
3 (= *pompa*) pomp

espléndido ADJ 1 (= *magnífico*) splendid, magnificent
2 (= *generoso*) lavish, generous

esplendor SM 1 (= *magnificencia*) splendour, splendor (*EEUU*), magnificence
2 (= *resplandor*) brilliance, radiance

esplendoroso ADJ 1 (= *magnífico*) magnificent
2 (= *resplandeciente*) brilliant, radiant

esplénico ADJ splenetic

espliego SM lavender

esplín SM melancholy, depression, the blues

espolada SF 1 (= *espolazo*) prick with a spur
2 ▸ **espolada de vino*** swig of wine*

espolazo SM prick with a spur

espolear ▸conjug 1a◂ VT 1 [+ *caballo*] to spur, spur on
2 (*para estudiar, ganar*) to spur on

espoleta SF 1 (*Mil*) fuse ▸ **espoleta de tiempo** time-fuse
2 (*Anat*) wishbone

espolón Ⓐ SM 1 (*Zool*) [*de gallo*] spur; [*de caballo*] fetlock
2 (*Geog*) spur (*of a mountain range*)
3 (*Náut*) (= *proa*) stem; (*para atacar*) ram
4 (= *malecón*) sea wall, dike; (= *contrafuerte*) buttress; [*de puente*] cutwater
5 (= *paseo*) promenade
6 (*Med**) chilblain
Ⓑ ADJ (*Andes**) (= *astuto*) sharp, astute

espolvoreador SM dredge

espolvorear ▸conjug 1a◂ VT to dust, sprinkle (**de** with); **espolvoree harina sobre la superficie** dust the surface with flour

espondeo SM spondee

esponja SF 1 (*para el aseo*) sponge; ✦*MODISMOS* **arrojar la ~** to throw in the towel; **beber como una ~** to drink like a fish; **pasemos la ~ por todo aquello** let's forget all about it ▸ **esponja de baño** bath sponge
2 (*) (= *gorrón*) sponger*
3 (*Cono Sur, Méx*‡) (= *bebedor*) drunkard, boozer*, lush (*EEUU*‡)

esponjado ADJ 1 [*material*] spongy; [*toalla, jersey*] fluffy
2 [*persona*] puffed up, pompous

esponjar ▸conjug 1a◂ Ⓐ VT to fluff up, make fluffy
Ⓑ **esponjarse** VPR 1 (= *hacerse esponjoso*) [*lana*] to fluff up, become fluffy; [*masa*] to rise
2 (= *engreírse*) to swell with pride, be puffed up
3 (= *rebosar salud*) to glow with health
4 (= *tener aspecto próspero*) to look prosperous

esponjera SF sponge bag, make-up bag

esponjosidad SF sponginess

esponjoso ADJ [*material*] (= *blando*) spongy; (= *poroso*) porous; [*toalla, jersey*] fluffy, springy

esponsales SMPL betrothal *sing*

esponsor SMF, **espónsor** SMF sponsor

esponsorizar ▸conjug 1f◂ VT to sponsor

espontáneamente ADV spontaneously

espontanearse ▸conjug 1a◂ VPR (= *confesar*) to own up; (= *hablar francamente*) to speak frankly; (= *desahogarse*) to unbosom o.s., open up (**con** to)

espontaneidad SF spontaneity

espontaneísmo SM amateurish enthusiasm, enthusiasm without experience

espontáneo/a Ⓐ ADJ 1 (= *sin reflexión*) spontaneous
2 (= *improvisado*) [*discurso, representación*] impromptu; [*persona*] natural
Ⓑ SM/F 1 (*Taur*) *spectator who rushes into the ring and attempts to take part*
2 (†) (= *bombero*) volunteer fireman/firewoman

espora SF spore

esporádicamente ADV sporadically

esporádico ADJ sporadic

esportillo SM basket, pannier

esportivo ADJ (*LAm*) sporty

esportón SM large basket; ✦*MODISMO* **a esportones** in vast quantities, by the ton

esposar ▸conjug 1a◂ VT to handcuff

esposas SFPL handcuffs; **poner las ~s a algn** to handcuff sb, put sb in handcuffs

esposo/a SM/F husband/wife; **los ~s** husband and wife, the couple

espray SM = **spray**

esprín SM (*CAm*) interior sprung mattress

esprint SM (*pl* **esprints** [es'prin], **esprintes**) sprint

esprínter SMF sprinter

espuela SF 1 (*lit, fig*) spur ► **espuela de caballero** (*Bot*) larkspur
2 (*Andes*) [*de mujer*] feminine charm; (= *coquetería*) coquettishness
3 (*Andes Com*) skill in business, acumen

espueleado ADJ (*Andes, Caribe*) tested, tried

espuelear* ▸conjug 1a◂ VT 1 (*LAm*) (= *espolear*) to spur, spur on
2 (*Andes, Caribe*) (= *probar*) to test, try out

espuelón ADJ (*Andes*) sharp, astute

espuerta SF basket, pannier; ✦*MODISMO* **a ~s** in vast quantities, by the ton

espulgar ▸conjug 1h◂ VT 1 (= *quitar la pulgas a*) to delouse, get the lice *o* fleas out of
2 (†) [+ *obra, novela*] to scrutinize

espuma SF 1 (= *burbujas*) [*de las olas*] surf, foam; [*de jabón, champú*] foam, lather; [*de cerveza*] head; [*de cava, champán*] froth; [*de afeitar*] foam; [*del caldo*] scum; **echar ~** to foam, froth; **el perro echaba ~ por la boca** the dog was foaming *o* frothing at the mouth; **hacer ~** to foam, froth; ✦*MODISMO* **crecer como la ~** to mushroom ► **espuma de afeitar** shaving foam ► **espuma de baño** bubble bath, foam bath ► **espuma de mar** (= *mineral*) meerschaum ► **espuma seca** carpet shampoo
2 (= *gomaespuma*) foam, foam rubber; **un colchón de ~** a foam(-rubber) mattress ► **espuma de caucho**, **espuma de látex** foam rubber
3 (= *tejido*) (*tb* **~ de nylon**) stretch nylon; **medias de ~** stretch tights

espumadera SF, **espumador** SM skimming ladle, skimmer

espumajear ▸conjug 1a◂ VI to foam at the mouth

espumajo SM froth, foam (*at the mouth*)

espumajoso ADJ frothy, foamy

espumar ▸conjug 1a◂ Ⓐ VT (= *quitar espuma a*) to skim off
Ⓑ VI [*cerveza*] to froth, foam; [*vino*] to sparkle

espumarajo SM froth, foam (*at the mouth*); **echar ~s (de rabia)** to splutter with rage

espumear ▸conjug 1a◂ VI to foam

espumilla SF (*LAm*) meringue

espumoso ADJ [*cerveza*] frothy; [*jabón*] foamy; [*baño*] foaming; [*vino*] sparkling

espúreo ADJ, **espurio** ADJ (= *falso*) spurious; [*niño*] illegitimate, bastard

esputar ▸conjug 1a◂ Ⓐ VT to cough up, expectorate (*frm*)
Ⓑ VI to cough up sputum, expectorate (*frm*)

esputo SM (= *escupitajo*) spit, spittle; (*Med*) sputum

esqueje SM cutting

esquela SF 1 (= *anuncio*) notice, announcement ► **esquela de defunción**, **esquela mortuoria** announcement of death, death notice
2 (= *nota*) note
3 (†) (= *carta breve*) short letter ► **esquela amorosa** love letter, billet doux

esquelético ADJ skeletal, skinny*

esqueleto SM 1 (*Anat*) skeleton; ✦*MODISMOS* **menear** *o* **mover el ~*** to strut one's stuff*, dance; **tumbar el ~*** to hit the hay*, hit the sack*, go to bed
2 (= *estructura*) (*gen*) skeleton; (= *de asunto*) bare bones *pl*; [*de edificio*] framework; [*de conferencia, novela*] framework, structure; **en ~** unfinished, incomplete
3 (*Chile Literat*) (= *borrador*) rough draft, outline
4 (*Andes, CAm, Méx*) (= *formulario*) form

esquema SM 1 (*en esbozo*) (= *resumen*) outline; (= *diagrama*) diagram; (= *dibujo*) sketch; **me hice un ~ de la lección** I prepared an outline of the lesson; **un ~ de conexiones eléctricas** a wiring diagram; **le hice un ~ del centro de la ciudad** I did him a sketch map of the centre of town
2 (= *conjunto de ideas*) thinking, way of thinking; **sus ~s mentales están anclados en el pasado** his thinking *o* way of thinking is rooted in the past; **criticó los ~s ideológicos del partido** he criticized the party's ideology; ✦*MODISMOS* **romper ~s** to break the mould; **romperle los ~s a algn***: **no me imaginaba que fueras a hacerte monja, me has roto todos los ~s** I never imagined you'd become a nun, you've really thrown me*
3 (*Rel, Fil*) schema

esquemático ADJ schematic; **un resumen ~** an outline

esquí SM (*pl* **esquís**, **esquíes**) 1 (= *tabla*) ski
2 (*Dep*) skiing; **hacer ~** to go skiing ► **esquí acuático** water skiing ► **esquí alpino** alpine skiing ► **esquí de fondo**, **esquí de travesía** cross-country skiing, ski touring (*EEUU*) ► **esquí náutico** water skiing

esquiable ADJ **pista ~** slope suitable for skiing, slope that can be skied on

esquiador(a) SM/F skier ► **esquiador(a) acuático/a**, **esquiador(a) náutico/a** water skier

esquiar ▸conjug 1c◂ VI to ski

esquife SM skiff

esquijama SM winter pyjamas *pl o* (*EEUU*) pajamas *pl*

esquila[1] SF (= *campanilla*) small bell, handbell; (= *cencerro*) cowbell

esquila[2] SF, **esquilado** SM [*de ovejas*] shearing

esquilador(a) SM/F (= *persona*) (sheep) shearer

esquiladora SF (= *máquina*) shearing machine, clipping machine

esquilar ▸conjug 1a◂ VT [+ *ovejas*] to shear; [+ *pelo*] to clip, crop

esquileo SM shearing

esquilimoso ADJ fastidious, finicky

esquilmar ▸conjug 1a◂ VT 1 [+ *cosecha*] to harvest 2 [+ *tierra*] to impoverish, exhaust
3 (*) [+ *jugador*] to skin*

esquilmo SM harvest, crop, yield

Esquilo SM Aeschylus

esquimal Ⓐ ADJ Eskimo
Ⓑ SMF Eskimo
Ⓒ SM (*Ling*) Eskimo

esquina SF 1 (= *vértice*) corner; **a la vuelta de la ~** (*lit*) around the corner; (*fig*) just around the corner; **las vacaciones están a la vuelta de la ~** the holidays are just around the corner; **sacar de ~** to take a corner kick; **doblar la ~** (*lit*) to turn the corner; (*Cono Sur**) (= *morir*) to die, kick the bucket*; **hacer ~** [*edificio*] to be on the corner; [*calles*] to meet
2 (*Dep*) corner
3 (*LAm*) (= *tienda*) corner shop, village shop
4 **la ~** (*) the game*, prostitution

esquinado ADJ 1 (= *con esquinas*) sharp-cornered, having corners
2 (*Ftbl*) swerving, with a spin on it; **tiro ~** low shot into the corner of the net
3 (*LAm*) [*mueble*] standing in a corner, corner *antes de s*
4 [*persona*] (= *antipático*) unpleasant; (= *difícil*) awkward, prickly; (= *malévolo*) malicious
5 [*noticia*] malicious, ill-intentioned

esquinar ▸conjug 1a◂ Ⓐ VT 1 (*Dep*) to put in a corner
2 (= *hacer esquina con*) to form a corner with
3 (= *estar en la esquina de*) to be on the corner of
4 [+ *madera*] to square, square off
5 [+ *pelota*] to swerve, slice
6 [+ *personas*] to set at odds
Ⓑ VI **~ con** (= *hacer esquina*) to form a corner with; (= *estar en la esquina*) to be on the corner of
Ⓒ **esquinarse** VPR 1 (= *pelearse*) to quarrel, fall out (**con** with)
2 (= *estar resentido*) to get a chip on one's shoulder

esquinazo SM 1 (*) (= *esquina*) corner
2 (*Cono Sur*) (= *serenata*) serenade
3 ✦*MODISMO* **dar ~ a algn** to give sb the slip, shake sb off

esquinera SF 1 (*) (= *prostituta*) tart*, hooker (*EEUU**) 2 (*LAm*) (= *mueble*) corner cupboard

esquinero/a Ⓐ ADJ corner *antes de s*; **farol ~** corner lamppost, lamppost on the corner; **café ~** corner café
Ⓑ SM/F (*) (= *persona*) idler, layabout

esquirla SF splinter

esquirol SMF strikebreaker, blackleg, scab*

esquirolada SF strike-breaking action, work of a scab*

esquirolaje SM, **esquirolismo** SM strike-breaking, blacklegging, scabbing*

esquisto SM schist

esquites SMPL (*CAm, Méx*) popcorn

esquivada SF (*LAm*) evasion, dodge

esquivar ▸conjug 1a◂ Ⓐ VT (= *evitar*) to avoid, shun; (= *evadir*) to dodge, side-step; **~ un golpe** to dodge a blow; **~ el contacto con algn** to avoid meeting sb; **~ hacer algo** to avoid doing sth, be chary of doing sth
Ⓑ **esquivarse** VPR (= *retirarse*) to shy away; (= *evadirse*) to dodge

esquivez SF 1 (= *timidez*) shyness; (= *despego*) unsociability; (= *elusión*) elusiveness; (= *evasiva*) evasiveness
2 (= *desdén*) scorn

esquivo ADJ 1 [*persona*] (= *tímido*) shy; (= *huraño*) unsociable; (= *difícil de encontrar*) elusive; (= *evasivo*) evasive
2 (= *despreciativo*) scornful

esquizo* ADJ, SMF schizo*

esquizofrenia SF schizophrenia

esquizofrénico/a ADJ, SM/F schizophrenic

esquizoide ADJ, SMF schizoid

esta ADJ DEM *ver* **este**

ésta PRON DEM *ver* **éste**

estabilidad SF stability

estabilización SF stabilization

estabilizador Ⓐ ADJ stabilizing
Ⓑ SM (*gen*) stabilizer; (*Aut*) anti-roll bar ► **estabilizador de cola** tailplane, rudder

estabilizante Ⓐ ADJ stabilizing
Ⓑ SM stabilizer

estabilizar ▸conjug 1f◂ Ⓐ VT 1 [+ *objeto*] (= *dar estabilidad a*) to stabilize; (= *fijar*) to make steady
2 [+ *precios*] to stabilize
Ⓑ **estabilizarse** VPR 1 [*objeto, precios*] to become stable, become stabilized
2 [*persona*] to settle down

estable ADJ 1 (= *permanente*) [*pareja, hogar, mercado, bolsa, paz*] stable; [*relación*] stable, steady; [*empleo*] steady; [*inquilino, cliente*] regular
2 (*Fís, Quím*) stable

establecer ▸conjug 2d◂ Ⓐ VT 1 [+ *relación, comunicación*] to establish; **han logrado ~ contacto con el barco** they've managed to make *o* establish contact with the boat; **una reunión para ~ el precio del petróleo** a meeting to set *o* fix oil prices; **han establecido controles policiales** they have set up police checkpoints
2 (= *fundar*) [+ *empresa*] to establish; [+ *colonia*] to settle; **ha establecido su domicilio en Lugo** he's taken up residence in Lugo
3 (= *dictaminar*) to state, lay down; **la ley establece que ...** the law states *o* lays down that ...
4 (= *expresar*) [+ *idea, principio*] to establish; [+ *norma*] to lay down; [+ *criterio*] to set; **para ~ los límites de los poderes del presidente** to establish the extent of the President's powers; **una comisión para ~ la verdad de los hechos** a commission to establish the truth about what happened
5 [+ *récord*] to set
Ⓑ **establecerse** VPR 1 (= *fijar residencia*) to settle; **la familia se estableció en Madrid** the family settled in Madrid
2 (= *abrir un negocio*) to set up (a business), open up (a business); **~se por cuenta propia** to set up on one's own, open up one's own business

establecimiento SM 1 (= *acto*) establishment, setting-up, founding; (= *fundación*) institution; [*de colonias*] establishment
2 (= *local*) (*gen*) establishment; (= *bar*) bar; (= *tienda*) shop; (*Cono Sur*) plant, works *pl* ► **establecimiento central** head office ► **establecimiento comercial** business house, commercial establishment
3 (*Jur*) statute, ordinance

establero SM stableboy, groom

establo SM 1 [*de ganado*] cowshed, stall; (*esp LAm*) (= *granero*) barn; (= *lugar sucio*) pigsty ► **establos de Augías** Augean stables
2 (*Caribe*) (= *garaje*) garage

estaca SF 1 (= *poste*) stake, post; [*de tienda de campaña*] peg; (= *porra*) cudgel, stick; ✦***MODISMO*** **plantar la ~**** to have a crap**
2 (*Agr*) cutting
3 (*LAm Min*) large mining claim, large mining concession
4 (*Andes, Cono Sur*) (= *espuela*) spur
5 ✦***MODISMO*** **arrancar la ~** (*Méx*) to champ at the bit, strain at the leash
6 (*Caribe*) (= *indirecta*) hint; (= *pulla*) taunt

estacada SF 1 (= *cerca*) fence, fencing; (*Mil*) stockade, palisade; (*LAm*) (= *malecón*) dike; ✦***MODISMOS*** **dejar a algn en la ~** to leave sb in the lurch; **estar** *o* **quedar en la ~** (= *estar en apuros*) to be in a jam *o* fix, be left in the lurch; (= *fracasar*) to fail disastrously, be a total disaster*
2 (*LAm*) (= *herida*) wound

estacar ▸conjug 1g◂ Ⓐ VT 1 (*LAm*) (= *herir*) to wound; (= *pinchar*) to prick
2 [+ *tierra, propiedad*] to stake out, stake off
3 [+ *animal*] to tie to a post
4 (*Andes, Caribe*) (= *engañar*) to deceive
Ⓑ **estacarse** VPR 1 (= *quedarse inmóvil*) to stand rooted to the spot, stand stiff as a pole
2 **~se un pie** (*Andes, CAm, Caribe*) to prick o.s. in the foot

estacha SF line, mooring rope

estación SF 1 (*gen*) station ► **estación ballenera** whaling station ► **estación balnearia** (*medicinal*) spa; (*de mar*) seaside resort ► **estación biológica** biological research station ► **estación carbonera** coaling station ► **estación clasificadora** marshalling yard ► **estación cósmica** space station ► **estación de autobuses** bus station ► **estación de bombeo** pumping station ► **estación de cabeza** terminus ► **estación de contenedores** container terminal ► **estación de empalme**, **estación de enlace** junction ► **estación de escucha** listening post ► **estación de esquí** ski resort ► **estación de ferrocarril** railway station ► **estación de fuerza** power station ► **estación de gasolina** petrol station, gas station (*EEUU*) ► **estación de invierno** winter sports resort ► **estación de mercancías** goods station ► **estación de peaje** line of toll booths, toll plaza (*EEUU*) ► **estación depuradora** sewage works, sewage farm ► **estación de rastreo**, **estación de seguimiento** tracking station ► **estación de servicio** service station, petrol station, gas station (*EEUU*) ► **estación de televisión** television station ► **estación de trabajo** (*Inform*) workstation ► **estación de trasbordo** junction ► **estación de vacaciones** holiday resort ► **estación emisora** broadcasting station ► **estación espacial** space station ► **estación invernal** winter sports resort ► **estación marítima** ferry terminal ► **estación meteorológica** weather station ► **estación orbital** orbiting space station ► **estación purificadora de aguas residuales** sewage works, sewage farm ► **estación termal** spa ► **estación terminal** terminus ► **estación transformadora**, **estación transmisora** transmitter ► **estación veraniega** summer resort
2 (*Rel*) **Estaciones del Vía Crucis** Stations of the Cross; ✦***MODISMO*** **correr las estaciones*** to go on a pub crawl*
3 (= *parte del año*) season ► **estación de (las) lluvias** rainy reason ► **estación de plantar** planting season ► **estación muerta** off season, dead season
4 **hacer ~** to make a stop (**en** at, in)

estacional ADJ seasonal

estacionalidad SF seasonal nature, seasonal variation

estacionalmente ADV seasonally, according to the season

estacionamiento SM 1 [*de soldados*] stationing
2 (*Aut*) (= *acción*) parking; (*esp LAm*) (= *sitio*) car park, parking lot (*EEUU*) ► **estacionamiento limitado** restricted parking

estacionar ▸conjug 1a◂ Ⓐ VT 1 [+ *soldados*] to station, place
2 (*Aut*) to park
Ⓑ **estacionarse** VPR (*gen*) to station o.s.; (*Aut*) to park; (= *no moverse*) to remain stationary; **la inflación/la fiebre se ha estacionado** inflation/the fever has stabilized

estacionario ADJ (*gen*) stationary; (*Med*) stable; (*Com, Fin*) slack

estacionómetro SM (*Méx*) parking meter

estacón SM (*LAm*) prick, jab

estada SF (*LAm*) stay

estadía SF 1 (*LAm*) (= *estancia*) stay; (= *duración*) length of stay
2 (*Com*) demurrage
3 (*Náut*) stay in port

estadillo SM (*gen*) survey; (= *inventario*) inventory

estadio SM 1 (= *fase*) stage, phase
2 (*Dep*) stadium
3 (*Mat*) furlong

estadista SMF 1 (*Pol*) statesman/stateswoman
2 (*Mat*) statistician

estadística SF (= *ciencia*) statistics *sing*; **una ~** a figure, a statistic; *ver tb* **estadístico**

estadísticamente ADV statistically

estadístico/a Ⓐ ADJ [*datos, cifras*] statistical
Ⓑ SM/F (= *profesional*) statistician; *ver tb* **estadística**

estadizo ADJ [*comida*] not quite fresh, stale, off

estado SM [1] (= *situación*) [1·1] [*de objeto, proceso*] state; **¿en qué ~ se encuentran las relaciones entre los dos países?** what is the state of relations between the two countries?; **estar en buen ~** [*instalación, alimentos*] to be in good condition; **el ordenador está en perfecto ~** the computer is working perfectly *o* is in perfect working order; **estar en mal ~** [*instalación*] to be in (a) poor condition, be in a bad state; [*alimentos*] to be off; **el techo se encontraba en muy mal ~** the roof was in very poor condition *o* in a very bad state; **tras comer carne en mal ~** after eating meat that was off *o* that had gone off
[1·2] [*de persona*] condition; **el ~ general del paciente** the overall condition of the patient ► **estado civil** marital status ► **estado de alarma, estado de alerta** state of alert ► **estado de ánimo** (*emocional*) mood; (*mental*) state of mind ► **estado de atención** state of alert ► **estado de coma** coma, state of coma ► **estado de cosas** state of affairs; **en este ~ de cosas, lo mejor es convocar nuevas elecciones** given the state of affairs, the best thing to do is call another election; **¿cuál es el ~ de cosas ahora?** what's the state of play now? ► **estado de emergencia, estado de excepción** state of emergency ► **estado de gracia** [*de creyente*] state of grace; [*de político, gobierno*] honeymoon period; [*de deportista*] run of good form ► **estado de guerra** state of war ► **estado de la red** (*Inform*) volume of users ► **estado de salud** condition, state of health ► **estado de sitio** state of siege
[2] (*Fís*) state ► **estado gaseoso** gaseous state ► **estado líquido** solid state ► **estado sólido** solid state
[3] **en ~** (= *embarazada*): **una mujer en ~** an expectant mother; **estar en ~** to be expecting; **quedarse en ~** to become pregnant; **estar en ~ de buena esperanza** to be expecting; **en avanzado ~ de gestación** heavily pregnant, in an advanced state of pregnancy; **estar en ~ interesante** (*hum*) to be expecting, be in the family way*
[4] (= *nación*) state; **los intereses del ~** national *o* state interests; **el Estado español** Spain; **asuntos de ~** affairs of state, state affairs; **hombre de ~** statesman ► **estado asistencial, estado benefactor** welfare state ► **estado colchón** buffer state ► **estado de derecho** democracy ► **estado del bienestar, estado de previsión** welfare state ► **estado policial** police state ► **estado tapón** buffer state; *ver tb* **golpe 10**
[5] (= *región*) (*en EE.UU., México, Brasil*) state
[6] (*Hist*) (= *clase*) estate; **el ~ eclesiástico** the clergy; **~ llano** ◊ **tercer ~** third estate, commoners *pl*
[7] (*Mil*) ► **el Estado Mayor (General)** the (General) Staff
[8] (*Com, Fin*) (= *informe*) report ► **estado de contabilidad** (*Méx*) balance sheet ► **estado de cuenta** bank statement, statement of account (*frm*) ► **estado de cuentas** [*de una empresa*] statement of account ► **estado de pérdidas y ganancias** profit and loss statement ► **estado de reconciliación** reconciliation statement ► **estado financiero** financial statement

estado-ciudad SM (*pl* **estados-ciudad**) city state

estado-nación SM (*pl* **estados-nación**) nation state

Estados Unidos SMPL United States (of America)

estadounidense Ⓐ ADJ American, US *antes de s*, of/from the United States
Ⓑ SMF American; **los ~s** the Americans

estafa SF [1] (= *timo*) swindle, trick
[2] (*Com, Fin*) racket, ramp*

estafador(a) SM/F [1] (= *timador*) swindler, trickster
[2] (*Com, Fin*) racketeer

estafar ▸conjug 1a◂ VT to swindle, defraud, twist*; **~ algo a algn** to swindle sb out of sth, defraud sb of sth; **¡me han estafado!** I've been done!*

estafermo SM [1] (*Hist*) quintain, dummy target
[2] (*) (= *idiota*) twit*, idiot

estafeta Ⓐ SF [1] (= *oficina*) (*tb* **~ de Correos**) sub post office
[2] (= *correo*) post ► **estafeta diplomática** diplomatic post
Ⓑ SMF courier; (*LAm*) [*de drogas*] drug courier, drug runner

estafetero SM postmaster, post-office clerk

estafilococo SM staphylococcus

estagnación SF (*CAm, Caribe*) = **estancamiento**

estaje SM (*CAm*) piecework

estajear ▸conjug 1a◂ VT (*CAm*) (= *trabajar*) to do as piecework; (= *acordar*) to discuss rates and conditions for

estajero/a SM/F (*CAm*) pieceworker

estalactita SF stalactite

estalagmita SF stalagmite

estaliniano ADJ Stalinist

estalinismo SM Stalinism

estalinista ADJ, SMF Stalinist

estallar ▸conjug 1a◂ VI [1] (= *reventar*) [*pólvora, globo*] to explode; [*bomba*] to explode, go off; [*volcán*] to erupt; [*neumático*] to burst; [*vidrio*] to shatter; [*látigo*] to crack; **~ en llanto** to burst into tears; **el parabrisas estalló en pedazos** the windscreen shattered; **hacer ~** to set off; (*fig*) to spark off, start
[2] [*epidemia, guerra, conflicto, sublevación*] to break out; **cuando estalló la guerra** when the war broke out

estallido SM [1] (= *explosión*) explosion; **el gran ~** the big bang
[2] [*de látigo, trueno*] crack
[3] (= *comienzo*) outbreak

estambre SM [1] (*Bot*) stamen
[2] (*de la lana*) worsted, woollen yarn

Estambul SM Istanbul

estamento SM [1] (*Pol*) (*social*) class; (*político*) estate
[2] (= *estrato*) stratum, layer, level

estameña SF serge

estampa SF [1] (*Tip*) (= *imagen*) print; (= *grabado*) engraving; (*en libro*) picture; (*típica, pintoresca, castiza*) vignette ► **estampas de la vida cotidiana** vignettes of everyday life
[2] (= *aspecto*) appearance, aspect; **de magnífica ~** fine-looking, fantastic-looking*; **de ~ poco agradable** unattractive, unpleasant-looking; **ser la propia ~ de algn** to be the very *o* absolute image of sb, be the spitting image of sb*
[3] (†) (= *arte*) printing; (= *máquina*) printing press; **dar un libro a la ~** to publish a book
[4] (†) (= *huella*) imprint

estampación SF (= *acto*) printing; (= *grabado*) engraving; (= *fileteado*) tooling

estampado Ⓐ ADJ printed; **un vestido ~** a print dress
Ⓑ SM [1] (= *impresión*) (*gen*) printing; (*con sello, pie*) stamping
[2] (= *diseño*) pattern
[3] (= *tela*) print

estampar ▸conjug 1a◂ VT [1] (*Tip*) (= *imprimir*) to print; (= *marcar*) to stamp; (= *grabar*) to engrave; (= *filetear*) to tool
[2] (*en la mente, memoria*) to stamp, imprint (**en** on); **quedó estampado en su memoria** it was stamped on her memory
[3] (*) **le estampó un beso en la mejilla** she planted a kiss on his cheek; **le estampó una buena bofetada** he gave him a good slap; **lo estampó contra la pared** she flung him against the wall

estampía: **de ~** ADV suddenly, without warning, unexpectedly

estampida SF [1] (*Agr, Zool*) stampede; **se marchó de ~** he went off like a shot
[2] **de ~** suddenly, without warning, unexpectedly
[3] = **estampido**

estampido SM [*de pistola, fusil*] bang, report; [*de bomba*] blast, bang; [*de trueno*] boom, crash ► **estampido sónico** sonic boom

estampilla SF [1] (= *sello de goma*) seal, stamp, rubber stamp
[2] (*LAm Correos*) stamp

estampillado SM rubber stamping

estampillar ▸conjug 1a◂ VT to rubber-stamp

estampita SF *small religious picture*

estancado ADJ [1] [*agua*] stagnant
[2] [*negociaciones*] at a standstill; **quedarse ~** to get into a rut

estancamiento SM [1] [*de agua*] stagnation
[2] (= *falta de actividad*) [*de asunto, comercio, suministro*] stagnation; [*de negociaciones*] deadlock

estancar ▸conjug 1g◂ Ⓐ VT [1] [+ *aguas*] to hold back, stem
[2] (= *detener*) [+ *progreso*] to hold up, stem; [+ *negociación*] to deadlock; [+ *negocio*] to stop, suspend
[3] (*Com*) to establish a monopoly in, monopolize; (*pey*) to corner
Ⓑ **estancarse** VPR [1] [*agua*] to stagnate, become stagnant
[2] [*economía, industria, persona*] to stagnate

estancia SF [1] (= *permanencia*) stay; **durante su ~ en Londres** during his stay in London
[2] (*liter*) (= *cuarto*) living room
[3] (*LAm*) [*de ganado*] farm, cattle ranch; (= *hacienda*) country estate; (*Caribe*) (= *quinta pequeña*) small farm, smallholding
[4] (*Literat*) stanza

estanciera SF (*Cono Sur*) station wagon

estanciero/a SM/F (*LAm*) farmer, rancher

estanco Ⓐ ADJ (*al agua*) watertight; (*al aire*) airtight
Ⓑ SM [1] (= *expendeduría*) tobacconist's, tobacconist's shop, cigar store (*EEUU*)
[2] (*Andes*) (= *bodega*) liquor store; (=

monopolio) state monopoly, government store where monopoly goods are sold

> **ESTANCO**
>
> *In Spain, an* **estanco** *is a government-licensed tobacconist's, recognizable by the brown and yellow "T" logo of the state tobacco monopoly,* **Tabacalera S.A.**, *which regulates the entire tobacco industry. Tobacco can also be bought at bars and restaurants and* **quioscos**, *but at a higher price. As well as tobacco products the* **estanco** *sells stamps,* **papel timbrado** *(official forms) and coupons for the* **quiniela** *or football pools.*
>
> ⇨ *See also* QUINIELA

estand SM = **stand**

estándar ADJ, SM standard

estandarización SF, **estandardización** SF standardization

estandarizado ADJ, **estandardizado** ADJ standardized

estandarizar ▸conjug 1f◂ VT, **estandardizar** ▸conjug 1f◂ VT to standardize

estandarte SM banner, standard ► **estandarte real** royal standard

estanflación SF stagflation

estánnico ADJ stannic

estanque SM 1 (= *lago*) (*ornamental*) lake; (*pequeño*) pool, pond ► **estanque de juegos, estanque para chapotear** paddling pool
2 (= *depósito*) tank
3 (*Cono Sur*) [*de gasolina*] petrol tank, tank, gas tank (*EEUU*)

estanqueidad SF (*al agua*) watertightness; (*al aire*) air tightness

estanquero/a SM/F tobacconist, tobacco dealer (*EEUU*)

estanquillo SM 1 (*Méx*) booth, kiosk, stall
2 = **estanco B**

estante SM 1 (= *anaquel*) shelf
2 (= *soporte*) rack, stand; (= *estantería*) bookcase
3 (*LAm*) (= *estaca*) prop

estantería SF shelving, shelves *pl*

estantigua SF 1 (= *aparición*) apparition
2 (*) (= *adefesio*) fright*, sight*, scarecrow

estantillo SM (*Andes, Caribe*) prop, support

estañar ▸conjug 1a◂ VT (*Téc*) to tin; (= *soldar*) to solder

estaño SM tin ► **estaño para soldar** solder

estaquear ▸conjug 1a◂ VT (*Cono Sur*) to stretch out between stakes

estaquilla SF [*de madera*] peg; (= *clavo largo*) spike, long nail; (*para tienda*) tent peg

estaquillar ▸conjug 1a◂ VT to pin, peg down *o* out, fasten with pegs

estar

> ▸conjug 1o◂
> A VERBO INTRANSITIVO B VERBO PRONOMINAL
> *Para las expresiones* **estar bien, estar mal,** *ver la otra entrada.*

Ⓐ VERBO INTRANSITIVO

1 ***indicando situación*** to be; **¿dónde estabas?** where were you?; **la última vez que estuve en Roma** the last time I was in Rome; **Madrid está en el centro de España** Madrid is in the centre of Spain; **el monumento está en la plaza** the monument is in the square; **eso no está en sus declaraciones** that's not in any of his statements; **—las tijeras están en el cajón —no, aquí no están** "the scissors are in the drawer" — "no, they're not in here"; **—hola, ¿está Carmen? —no, no está** "hello, is Carmen in?" — "no, I'm afraid she isn't"; **el día que estuve a verlo** the day I went to see him; **está fuera** (*de casa*) she's out; (*de la ciudad/en el extranjero*) she's away; **ya que estamos** while we are at it

2 ***indicando un estado transitorio*** 2·1 (+ *ADJ, ADV*) to be; **está mucho mejor** he's much better; **~ enfermo** *o* **malo** to be ill; **estoy muy cansada** I'm very tired; **¿estás casado o soltero?** are you married or single?; **está vacío** it's empty; **estaba herido** he was injured; **¿cómo estamos?** (*gen*) how are we doing?; (*a otra persona*) how are you?; **con este frío, aquí no se puede ~** it's unbearably cold here; **¡qué bueno está este café!** this coffee's really good!; **mis padres están como siempre** my parents are the same as ever; **¿está libre el baño?** is the bathroom free?; **¿qué tal** *o* **cómo estás?** how are you?; **el récord anterior estaba en 33 segundos** the previous record was *o* stood at 33 seconds

2·2 (+ *PARTICIPIO*) to be; **la radio está rota** the radio is broken; **para las seis ~á terminado** it will be finished by six o'clock; **estaba sentada en la arena** she was sitting on the sand; **está (embarazada) de dos meses** she's two months pregnant; **él no estaba implicado** he wasn't involved; **le está bien empleado por ingenuo** it serves him right for being so naïve

2·3 (+ *GERUNDIO*) to be; **estaba corriendo** he was running; **me está molestando** he's annoying me; **se está muriendo** she's dying; **venga, ya nos estamos yendo, que es tarde** come on, it's time to go, it's late; **está siendo preparado** it's being prepared; **nos estamos engañando** we're deceiving ourselves

3 ***= existir*** to be; **además están los gastos del viaje** then there are the travel expenses; **dejar ~: déjalo ~** just leave him be; **si dejas ~ ese asunto te irán mejor las cosas** you'll do better to let the matter drop

4 ***indicando el aspecto de algo*** to look; **¡qué elegante estás!** you're looking really smart!; **estás más delgado** you've lost weight, you look slimmer; **está más viejo** he looks older; **el sofá ~á mejor al lado de la ventana** the sofa will look better next to the window; **ese tío está muy bueno*** that guy's gorgeous*, that guy's a bit of all right*; **el traje te está grande** that suit is too big for you

5 ***= estar listo*** to be ready; **~á a las cuatro** it'll be ready at four; **en seguida está** it'll be ready in a moment; **dos vueltas más y ya está** two more laps and that'll be it; **¡ya está!** **ya sé lo que podemos hacer** that's it! I know what we can do; **ya estoy** I'm done, that's me*; **¡ya estamos!** (*después de hacer algo*) that's it!; (*dicho con enfado*) that's enough!; **¿estamos?** (*al estar listo*) ready?; (*para pedir conformidad*) are we agreed?, right?, OK?*; **¡ya estuvo!** (*Méx*) that's it!

6 ***indicando fecha, distancia, temperatura*** **estamos en octubre** it's October; **cuando estemos en verano** when it's summer, in the summer

7 ***en estructuras con preposición***

◆ **estar a**: **estamos a 8 de junio** it is the 8th of June, today is the 8th of June; **estábamos a 40°C** it was 40°C; **¿a cuántos estamos?** what's the date?; **¿a cuánto estamos de Madrid?** how far are we from Madrid?; **las uvas están a 1,60 euros** the grapes are one euro 60 cents; **¿a cuánto está el kilo de naranjas?** how much are oranges per kilo?; **estoy a lo que se decida en la reunión** I'm waiting to see what's decided at the meeting; **~ a lo que resulte** to be waiting to see how things turn out

◆ **estar con**: **está con la gripe** he's down with flu, he's got the flu; **estuvo con la enfermedad durante dos años** she had *o* suffered from the disease for two years; **ya está otra vez con el mismo tema** he's harping on about the same old subject again; **ya estoy con ganas de ir** I want to go now; **estoy con ganas de pegarle** I feel like hitting him; **~ con algn**: **yo estoy con él** I'm with him; **los aliados estaban con ellos** the Allies were behind them

◆ **estar de**: **está de buen humor** he's in a good mood; **están de charla** they're having a chat; **está de camarero** he's working as a waiter; **está de jefe temporalmente** he is acting as boss, he is the acting boss; **está de luto** she's in mourning; **¡estoy de nervioso!** I'm so nervous!; **están de paseo** they've gone for a walk; **estaba de uniforme** he was (dressed) in uniform; **están de vacaciones** they are on holiday; **está de viaje en este momento** he's away at the moment

◆ **estar en**: **en eso está el problema** that's (exactly) where the problem is; **el problema está en que ...** the problem lies in the fact that ...; **en ello estamos** we're working on it; **no está en él hacerlo** it is not in his power to do it; **creo que está usted en un error** I think you're mistaken; **no está en sí** she's not in her right mind; **yo estoy en que ...** (= *creer*) I believe that ...

◆ **estar para**: **para eso estamos** (*gen*) that's why we're here, that's what we're here for; (*respondiendo a gracias*) don't mention it; **para eso están los amigos** that's what friends are for; **~ para hacer algo** (= *a punto de*) to be about to do sth, be on the point of doing sth; **está para salir** he's about to leave; **no estoy para bromas** I'm not in the mood for joking; **si alguien llama, no estoy para nadie** if anyone calls, I'm not in

◆ **estar por** (= *en favor de*) [+ *política*] to be in favour *o* (*EEUU*) favor of; [+ *persona*] to support; *ver tb* **hueso 1**

◆ **estar por** + *INFIN*: **la historia de ese hallazgo está por escribir** the story of that discovery is still to be written *o* has yet to be written; **está por ver si es verdad lo que dijeron** it remains to be seen whether what they said is true; **está todavía por hacer** it remains to be done, it is still to be done; **yo estoy por dejarlo** I'm for leaving it, I'm in favour of leaving it; **está por llover** (*LAm*) it's going to rain

◆ **estar sin** + *INFIN*: **las camas estaban sin hacer** the beds were unmade, the beds hadn't been made; **¿todavía estás sin peinar?** haven't you brushed your hair yet?

◆ **estar sobre algn/algo**: **hay que ~ mucho sobre él para que estudie** you have to keep on at him to make sure he studies; **hay que ~ sobre el arroz para que no se pegue** you need to keep a close eye on the rice to make sure it doesn't stick to the pan; **~ sobre sí** to be in control of o.s.

[8] *en oraciones ponderativas* **está que rabia*** he's hopping mad*, he's furious; **estoy que me caigo de sueño** I'm terribly sleepy, I can't keep my eyes open

Ⓑ **estarse** VERBO PRONOMINAL

[1] [= *quedarse*] [1·1] (*en un lugar*) to stay; **puedes ~te con nosotros una semana, si quieres** you can stay with us for a week if you like; **se estuvo dos horas enteras en el cuarto de baño** he was in the bathroom for two whole hours; **yo prefiero ~me en casa** I prefer staying at home

[1·2] (*en un estado*) **usted estése tranquilo, nosotros nos encargaremos de todo** don't you worry, we'll take care of everything; **se estuvo callada un buen rato** she didn't say anything for quite a while, she stayed quiet for quite a while; **¡estáte quieto!** keep *o* stay still!

[2] *uso impersonal* **se está bien aquí** it's nice here; **en la cama se está muy bien** it's nice in bed

---

estarcido SM stencil, stencilled sketch

estarcir ▸conjug 3b◂ VT to stencil

estaribel‡ SM nick‡, can (*EEUU*‡), prison

estárter SM = **stárter**

estatal ADJ [1] (= *del estado*) state *antes de s*
[2] (*Esp*) (= *nacional*) national

estatalismo SM state ownership

estatalista Ⓐ ADJ (*Esp*) national, nationwide
Ⓑ SMF member of a nationwide party

estatalización SF nationalization, taking into public ownership

estatalizar ▸conjug 1f◂ VT to nationalize, take into public ownership

estática SF statics *sing*

estático ADJ [1] (= *fijo*) static
[2] = **extático**

estatificación SF nationalization, taking into public ownership

estatificado ADJ nationalized, publicly-owned

estatificar ▸conjug 1g◂ VT to nationalize, take into public ownership

estatismo SM [1] (= *inmovilidad*) stillness, motionlessness
[2] (*Pol*) state control

estatización SF nationalization, taking into public ownership

estatizar ▸conjug 1f◂ VT to nationalize, take into public ownership

estator SM stator

estatua SF statue

estatuaria SF (*Arte*) statuary

estatuario ADJ statuesque

estatuilla SF statuette, figure

estatuir ▸conjug 3g◂ VT [1] (= *establecer*) to establish; (= *ordenar*) to ordain
[2] (= *probar*) to prove

estatura SF stature, height; **un hombre de 1,80m de ~** a man 1.80m in height; **de ~ normal** of average height

estatus SM INV status

estatutario ADJ statutory

estatuto SM (*Jur*) (*gen*) statute; [*de ciudad*] bylaw; [*de comité*] (standing) rule ► **Estatuto de Autonomía** (*Esp Pol*) statute of autonomy ► **estatutos sociales** (*Com*) articles of association

estay SM stay

este[1] Ⓐ ADJ INV [*zona, área*] east; **el ala ~ del palacio** the east wing of the palace; **la costa ~** the east *o* eastern coast; **íbamos en dirección ~** we were going east *o* eastward(s), we were going in an eastward *o* an easterly direction; **trenes en dirección ~** eastbound trains
Ⓑ SM [1] (*Geog*) East, east; **el sol sale por el Este** the sun rises in the East *o* east; **vientos fuertes del Este** strong east *o* easterly winds; **la casa está orientada hacia el Este** the house is east-facing, the house faces East *o* east
[2] (*Pol*) **el Este** the East; **los países de la Europa del Este** East European countries
[3] (*tb* **zona ~**) east; **al ~ de Toledo** to the east of Toledo; **soy del ~ de Londres** I'm from east London
[4] (*Meteo*) (*tb* **viento del ~**) east wind, easterly wind

este[2]**/a** ADJ DEM [1] (*indicando proximidad*) [1·1] (*sing*) this; **esta silla** this chair; **~ mes** this month; **¿qué habéis hecho ~ fin de semana?** what did you do at the weekend?, what did you do this weekend?; **¿dónde vais a ir ~ fin de semana?** (*dicho un viernes*) where are you going this weekend?; (*dicho un lunes*) where are you going next weekend?
[1·2] **estos/estas** these; **estas tijeras** these scissors, this pair of scissors
[2] (*) (*con valor enfático*) **¡a ver qué quiere ahora el tío ~!** what does that guy want now!*; **¡~ Pedro es un desastre!** that Pedro is a complete disaster!*

éste/a PRON DEM [1] (*sing*) this one; **ésta me gusta más** I prefer this one; **~ no es el que vi ayer** this is not the one I saw yesterday; **¡~ me quiere engañar!** this guy's out to cheat me!; **pero ¿dónde está ~?** where on earth is he?
[2] **éstos/éstas** these; (*en texto*) the latter
[3] (*locuciones*) **en ésta** (*en cartas*) in this town (from where I'm writing); **en éstas**: **en éstas se acerca y dice ...** just then he went up and said ...; **jurar por éstas** to swear by all that is holy
[4] (*esp LAm*) (*como muletilla*) **~ ...** er ..., um ...

estearina SF [1] (*Quím*) stearin
[2] (*LAm*) (= *vela*) candle

esteatita SF soapstone

Esteban SM Stephen

estecolado SM manuring, muck spreading

estela SF [1] (= *rastro*) (*Náut*) wake, wash; (*Aer*) slipstream, trail; **el discurso dejó una larga ~ de comentarios** the speech caused a great deal of comment; **dejaron tras de sí una ~ de muerte** they left a trail of slaughter behind them ► **estela de condensación, estela de humo** vapour trail, vapor trail (*EEUU*)
[2] (= *monumento*) stele, stela

estelar ADJ [1] (*Astron*) stellar
[2] (*Teat*) star *antes de s*; **papel ~** star role; **función ~** all-star show; **combate ~** (*Boxeo*) star bout, star contest

estelarizar ▸conjug 1f◂ VT (*Méx*) **~ en** to star in

estemple SM pit prop

esténcil SM (*LAm*) stencil

estenografía SF shorthand, stenography (*frm*)

estenografiar ▸conjug 1c◂ VT to take down in shorthand

estenográfico ADJ shorthand *antes de s*

estenógrafo/a SM/F shorthand writer

estenotipia SF shorthand typing

estenotipista SMF shorthand typist, steno (*EEUU**)

estentóreamente ADV in a stentorian voice

estentóreo ADJ [*voz*] stentorian (*frm*), booming; [*sonido*] strident

estepa SF [1] (*Geog*) steppe; **la ~ castellana** the Castilian steppe
[2] (*Bot*) rockrose

estepario ADJ steppe *antes de s*

estera SF [1] (= *alfombra*) mat ► **estera de baño** bathmat
[2] (= *tejido*) matting

esteral SM (*Cono Sur*) swamp, marsh

esterar ▸conjug 1a◂ Ⓐ VT to cover with a mat, put a mat on
Ⓑ VI (*) to put on one's winter clothes (*ahead of time*)

estercolamiento SM manuring, muck spreading

estercolar ▸conjug 1a◂ VT to manure

estercolero SM [1] (= *para estiércol*) manure heap, dunghill
[2] (= *lugar sucio*) pigsty, pigpen (*EEUU*), shit hole**

estéreo ADJ, SM stereo; **una televisión en ~** a stereo TV

estéreo... PREF stereo...

estereofonía SF stereo, stereophony

estereofónico ADJ stereo, stereophonic, in stereo

estereoscópico ADJ stereoscopic

estereoscopio SM stereoscope

estereotipación SF stereotyping

estereotipado ADJ stereotyped

estereotipar ▸conjug 1a◂ VT [1] [+ *gesto, frase*] to stereotype
[2] (*Tip*) to stereotype

estereotipo SM [1] (= *modelo*) stereotype
[2] (*Tip*) stereotype

esterero SM ✦*MODISMO* **quedar en el ~** (*Caribe**) to be on one's uppers*

estéril ADJ [1] (= *no fértil*) [*mujer*] barren, sterile, infertile; [*hombre*] sterile; [*terreno*] sterile, barren
[2] [*esfuerzo*] vain, futile

esterilidad SF [1] (= *infertilidad*) [*de mujer*] sterility, infertility; [*de hombre*] sterility; [*de terreno*] sterility, barrenness
[2] [*de esfuerzo*] futility, uselessness

esterilización SF [1] (*contra gérmenes*) sterilization
[2] (*para no ser fértil*) sterilization

esterilizar ▸conjug 1f◂ VT [1] (= *quitar gérmenes*) to sterilize
[2] (= *hacer infértil*) [+ *persona*] to sterilize; [+ *animal*] to sterilize, neuter

esterilla SF [1] (= *alfombrilla*) mat
[2] (= *tejido*) rush matting; **silla de ~** (*Arg*) wicker chair ► **esterilla de alambre** wire mesh

[3] (*Cos*) (*dorado*) gold braid; (*plateado*) silver braid

estérilmente ADV vainly, uselessly, fruitlessly

esterlina ADJ **libra ~** pound sterling

esternón SM breastbone, sternum (*frm*)

estero[1] SM [1] (= *estuario*) estuary
[2] (*LAm*) (= *pantano*) swamp, marsh
[3] (*Cono Sur, Andes*) (= *arroyo*) brook
[4] ✦***MODISMO*** **estar en el ~** (*Caribe**) to be in a fix*

estero[2] SM matting

esteroide SM steroid ► **esteroide anabólico, esteroide anabolizante** anabolic steroid

estertor SM death rattle

estertoroso ADJ stertorous

esteta SMF aesthete, esthete (*EEUU*)

estética SF [1] (*Arte*) aesthetics *sing*, esthetics *sing* (*EEUU*)
[2] (*Med**) **se ha hecho la ~ para quitarse las arrugas** she had cosmetic surgery to remove her wrinkles

esteticién SMF beautician, beauty consultant, beauty specialist

esteticismo SM aestheticism, estheticism (*EEUU*)

esteticista SMF beautician, beauty consultant, beauty specialist

estético ADJ aesthetic, esthetic (*EEUU*); **cirugía estética** cosmetic surgery; **se ha hecho la cirugía estética** he's had cosmetic surgery

estetoscopio SM stethoscope

esteva SF plough handle, plow handle (*EEUU*)

estevado ADJ bow-legged, bandy-legged

estiaje SM [1] [*de río*] low water level
[2] (*indicando duración*) low water

estiba SF [1] (*Mil, Hist*) rammer
[2] (*Náut*) stowage; ✦***MODISMO*** **mudar la ~** to shift the cargo about
[3] (= *acto*) loading
[4] (‡) (= *paliza*) beating up*, bashing*

estibado SM stowage

estibador(a) Ⓐ ADJ **empresa ~a** shipping company
Ⓑ SM/F stevedore, docker

estibar ▸conjug 1a◂ VT [1] (*Náut*) to stow
[2] [+ *lana*] to pack tight, compress

estiércol SM [1] (= *abono*) manure ► **estiércol de caballo** horse manure ► **estiércol líquido** liquid manure
[2] (= *excremento*) dung

Estigio SM Styx

estigio ADJ Stygian

estigma SM [1] (= *marca, deshonra*) stigma
[2] (*Bot*) stigma
[3] **estigmas** (*Rel*) stigmata

estigmatizar ▸conjug 1f◂ VT to stigmatize

estilar ▸conjug 1a◂ VI, **estilarse** VPR [1] (= *estar de moda*) to be in fashion, be in style; **ya no se estila la chistera** top hats aren't in fashion *o* in style anymore
[2] (= *usarse*) to be used; **~ hacer algo** to be customary to do sth

estilete SM [1] (= *arma*) stiletto
[2] [*de tocadiscos*] stylus

estilismo SM fashion design, fashion designing

estilista SMF [1] (*Literat*) stylist
[2] (*Téc*) designer
[3] (*Peluquería*) stylist
[4] (*Natación*) freestyle swimmer

estilística SF stylistics *sing*

estilístico ADJ stylistic

estilización SF (*Téc*) styling

estilizado ADJ stylized; **una joven muy estilizada** a slender young woman

estilizar ▸conjug 1f◂ VT [1] (*Arte*) to stylize
[2] (*Téc*) to design, style

estilo SM [1] (= *manera*) style; **el ~ del escritor** the writer's style; **un comedor ~ Luis XV** a dining-room suite in Louis XV style; **un ~ inconfundible de andar** an unmistakeable way of walking; **al ~ antiguo** in the old style; **un mosaico al ~ de los que se hacían en Roma** a mosaic in the style of those made in Rome; ✦***MODISMO*** **por el ~: algo por el ~** something of the sort *o* kind, something along those lines; **no tenemos nada por el ~** we have nothing in that line; **los banqueros y gentes por el ~** bankers and people like that ► **estilo de vida** way of life; **no me gusta su ~ de vida** I don't like his way of life *o* his lifestyle; **el ~ de vida británico** the British way of life; **un ~ de vida similar al nuestro** a similar lifestyle to ours ► **estilo directo** (*Ling*) direct speech ► **estilo indirecto** (*Ling*) indirect speech, reported speech
[2] (= *elegancia*) style; **una chica con ~** a stylish girl; **tiene mucho ~ vistiendo** he dresses very stylishly
[3] (*Natación*) stroke; **~s** medley; **los 400m ~s** the 400m medley ► **estilo braza** breast stroke ► **estilo libre** freestyle ► **estilo mariposa** butterfly stroke
[4] (= *punzón*) (*para escribir*) stylus; (*de reloj de sol*) gnomon, needle
[5] (*Bot*) style

estilográfica SF fountain pen

estiloso ADJ stylish

estima SF [1] (= *aprecio*) esteem, respect; **se ganó la ~ de todos sus compañeros** he gained the respect *o* esteem of all his friends; **tener a algn en gran ~** to hold sb in high esteem, think very highly of sb
[2] (*Náut*) dead reckoning; **a ~** by dead reckoning

estimable ADJ [1] (= *respetable*) [*persona*] estimable (*frm*), esteemed; **un ~ gesto en favor de la paz** an estimable *o* esteemed gesture for peace; **su ~ carta** (*Com*) your esteemed letter
[2] [*cantidad*] considerable, substantial

estimación SF [1] (= *evaluación*) estimate, valuation
[2] (= *aprecio*) respect; **ha conseguido ganarse la ~ de sus compañeros** he has managed to earn the respect of his colleagues ► **estimación propia** self-esteem

estimado ADJ esteemed, respected; **"Estimado señor Pérez"** "Dear Mr Pérez"

estimador/a SM/F (*Com*) estimator

estimar ▸conjug 1a◂ Ⓐ VT [1] (*Com*) (= *evaluar*) to estimate; (= *valorar*) to value, appraise (*EEUU*) (**en** at); **los daños se ~on en varios millones** the damage was estimated at several million; **~ algo en mil euros** to value sth at a thousand euros; **¡se estima!** thanks very much!, I appreciate it!
[2] (= *respetar*) to respect; **una persona muy estimada por los que lo conocían** a person highly-respected by those who knew him; **~ a algn en mucho** to have a high opinion *o* regard of sb; **~ a algn en poco** to have a low opinion *o* regard of sb
[3] (= *juzgar*) to consider, deem; **lo que usted estime conveniente** whatever you consider *o* deem appropriate
Ⓑ **estimarse** VPR to have a high opinion of o.s.; **si se estima no hará tal cosa** if he has any self-respect he'll do nothing of the sort

estimativamente ADV roughly

estimativo ADJ rough, approximate

estimulante Ⓐ ADJ stimulating
Ⓑ SM stimulant

estimular ▸conjug 1a◂ VT [1] (= *alentar*) [+ *persona*] to encourage; **hay que ~los para que respondan adecuadamente** you must encourage them to answer correctly; **~ a algn a hacer algo** to encourage sb to do sth
[2] (= *favorecer*) [+ *apetito, economía, esfuerzos, ahorro*] to stimulate; [+ *debate*] to promote
[3] [+ *organismo, célula*] to stimulate

estímulo SM [1] (*Psic*) stimulus
[2] (= *incentivo*) incentive

estío SM (*liter*) summer

estipendiar ▸conjug 1b◂ VT to pay a stipend to

estipendiario ADJ, SM stipendiary

estipendio SM [1] (= *sueldo*) [*de empleado*] salary; [*de abogado, notario*] fee
[2] (*Hist*) stipend

estíptico Ⓐ ADJ [1] (*Med*) styptic
[2] (= *estreñido*) constipated
[3] (= *miserable*) mean, miserly
Ⓑ SM styptic

estipulación SF stipulation, condition

estipular ▸conjug 1a◂ VT to stipulate

estirada SF (*Dep*) dive, stretch

estirado Ⓐ ADJ [1] (= *alargado*) stretched
[2] [*persona*] (= *tieso*) stiff, starchy; (= *engreído*) stuck-up*
[3] (= *tacaño*) tight-fisted
Ⓑ SM [*de vidrio*] drawing; [*de pelo*] straightening ► **estirado de piel, estirado facial** face lift

estirador SM (*Téc*) stretcher

estirajar* ▸conjug 1a◂ VT to stretch, stretch out

estiraje SM stretching

estiramiento SM = **estirado B**

estirar ▸conjug 1a◂ Ⓐ VT [1] (= *alargar*) [+ *goma, elástico*] to stretch; [+ *brazos*] to stretch out; [+ *cuello*] to crane; **si lo estiras más se romperá** if you stretch it any more it'll break; **salir a ~ las piernas** to go out and stretch one's legs
[2] (= *aplanar*) [+ *sábana, mantel*] to smooth out; [+ *piel*] to tighten, make taut
[3] (*en el tiempo*) [+ *discurso*] to spin out; **no sé cómo consigue ~ el dinero hasta fin de mes** I don't know how he manages to make his money stretch to the end of the month
[4] (*LAm**) (= *matar*) to bump off*, do away with*; ✦***MODISMO*** **~ la pata** to kick the bucket*
[5] (*Andes*) (= *azotar*) to flog, whip
[6] (*Cono Sur, Méx*) (= *tirar*) to pull, tug at
Ⓑ **estirarse** VPR [1] (= *alargarse*) to stretch
[2] (*Dep*) **el equipo se estiró** the team moved upfield; **el jugador se estiró por la banda** the player ran up the touchline

estirón SM [1] (= *tirón*) pull, tug
[2] **dar** *o* **pegar un ~*** [*niño*] to shoot up*, take a stretch*

estironear ▸conjug 1a◂ VT (*Cono Sur*) to pull hard at, tug sharply at

estirpe SF stock, lineage; **de la ~ regia** of royal stock, of the blood royal

estítico ADJ, SM = **estíptico**

estitiquez SF (*LAm*) constipation

estival ADJ summer *antes de s*

esto PRON DEM this; **~ es difícil** this is difficult; **y ~ ¿qué es?** whatever is this?; **~ es** that is, that is to say; **~ de la boda es un lío*** this wedding business is a hassle*; **por ~** for this reason; **~ …** (*vacilando*) er …, um …; **en ~ entró su madre** at that point his mother came in; **no tiene ni ~ de tonto** he isn't the least *o* slightest bit silly

estocada SF 1 (= *acción*) stab, thrust
2 (= *herida*) stab wound
3 (*Taur*) death blow

Estocolmo SM Stockholm

estofa SF 1 (= *tejido*) quilting, quilted material
2 (= *calidad*) quality; **gente de baja ~** riff-raff*

estofado Ⓐ ADJ 1 (*Culin*) stewed
2 (*Cos*) quilted
Ⓑ SM (*Culin*) stew, hotpot

estofar ▸conjug 1a◂ VT 1 (*Culin*) to stew
2 (*Cos*) to quilt

estoicidad SF stoicism, **estoicismo** SM stoicism

estoico/a Ⓐ ADJ stoic, stoical
Ⓑ SM/F stoic

estola SF stole ► **estola de visón** mink stole

estolidez SF stupidity

estólido ADJ stupid

estomacal ADJ stomach *antes de s*; **trastorno ~** stomach upset

estomagante ADJ 1 [*comida*] indigestible
2 (*) (= *molesto*) upsetting, annoying

estomagar ▸conjug 1h◂ VT 1 (*Med*) to give indigestion to
2 (*) (= *molestar*) to annoy, bother

estómago SM stomach; **dolor de ~** stomach-ache; **"no tomar con el ~ vacío"** "not to be taken on an empty stomach"; **revolver el ~ a algn** to make sb's stomach turn, turn sb's stomach; **tener buen ~** (= *resistir comidas fuertes*) to have a strong stomach; (= *ser insensible*) to be thick-skinned; (= *ser poco escrupuloso*) to have an elastic conscience

estomatólogo/a SM/F stomatologist

Estonia SF Estonia

estonio/a Ⓐ ADJ, SM/F Estonian
Ⓑ SM (*Ling*) Estonian

estopa SF 1 [*del cáñamo*] tow; ✦*MODISMO* **largar ~ a algn*** to bash sb*, hit sb
2 (= *tejido*) burlap ► **estopa de acero** steel wool
3 (*Náut*) oakum
4 (*Caribe*) cotton waste

estopero SM (*Méx Aut*) oil seal

estoperol SM 1 (= *mecha*) tow, wick
2 (*Andes*) (= *tachuela*) brass tack
3 (*Andes*) (= *sartén*) frying pan

estopilla SF cheesecloth

estoque SM 1 (= *arma*) rapier, sword; ✦*MODISMO* **estar hecho un ~** to be as thin as a rake *o* (*EEUU*) rail
2 (*Bot*) gladiolus, gladiola, sword lily

estoquear ▸conjug 1a◂ VT to stab, run through

estorbar ▸conjug 1a◂ Ⓐ VI to be in the way; **estas maletas están estorbando aquí** these cases are in the way here; **siempre estás estorbando** you're always getting in the way
Ⓑ VT 1 (= *obstaculizar*) [+ *paso, avance*] to get in the way of; [+ *trabajo, progreso*] to hinder; [+ *circulación*] to slow down
2 (= *molestar*) to bother

estorbo SM 1 (= *obstáculo*) hindrance, nuisance; **no eres más que un ~** you're just a hindrance *o* nuisance; **no hay ~ para que se haga** there is no obstacle *o* impediment to it being done, there's nothing to get in the way of it being done; **el mayor ~ es el director, que no quiere dar su aprobación** the biggest obstacle is the manager, who won't give his approval
2 (= *molestia*) nuisance

estornino SM starling

estornudar ▸conjug 1a◂ VI to sneeze

estornudo SM sneeze

estoy *ver* **estar**

estrábico ADJ [*persona*] wall-eyed; [*ojo*] squinting, strabismic

estrabismo SM strabismus (*frm*), squint

Estrabón SM Strabo

estrada SF 1 (= *carretera*) road, highway; **batir la ~** (*Mil*) to reconnoitre
2 (*Andes Agr*) section of a rubber plantation (*150 trees*)

estrado SM 1 (= *tarima*) platform; (*Mús*) bandstand ► **estrado del testigo** witness stand
2 **estrados** (*Jur*) law courts; **citar a algn para ~s** to subpoena sb

estrafalario ADJ 1 [*persona, ideas*] odd, eccentric
2 [*ropa*] outlandish

estragado ADJ 1 (= *arruinado*) ruined
2 (= *corrompido*) corrupted, spoiled, perverted
3 (= *depravado*) depraved
4 (= *descuidado*) slovenly, careless, disorderly

estragante ADJ damaging, destructive

estragar ▸conjug 1h◂ VT 1 (= *destrozar*) [+ *estómago*] to ruin; [+ *cuerpo*] to ravage; **un cuerpo estragado por la enfermedad** a body ravaged by disease
2 [+ *gusto*] to corrupt, spoil

estragón SM (*Bot, Culin*) tarragon

estragos SMPL havoc *sing*; **el hambre hizo ~ entre los más necesitados** hunger wreaked havoc with those most in need; **la sequía hizo ~ en el campo** the drought wreaked havoc in the countryside; **el actor que ha causado ~ entre las jovencitas** the actor who has caused a stir with the young girls; **los ~ del tiempo** the ravages of time

estramador SM (*Méx*) comb

estrambólico ADJ (*LAm*) odd, outlandish

estrambote SM (*Literat*) extra lines *pl*, extra verses *pl*, addition

estrambótico ADJ odd, outlandish

estrangis ADV **de ~*** secretly, on the quiet

estrangul SM (*Mús*) mouthpiece

estrangulación SF strangulation

estrangulado ADJ (*Med*) strangulated

estrangulador(a) Ⓐ SM/F (= *persona*) strangler
Ⓑ SM 1 (*Mec*) throttle
2 (*Aut*) choke

estrangulamiento SM 1 (= *acto*) strangulation
2 (*Aut*) narrow stretch of road, bottleneck

estrangular ▸conjug 1a◂ VT 1 [+ *persona*] to strangle, throttle
2 (*Mec*) to throttle
3 (*Aut*) to choke

estranji ADV = **estrangis**

estranqui* SMF = **extranjero B**

estraperlear* ▸conjug 1a◂ VI to deal in black-market goods

estraperlista SMF black marketeer

estraperlo SM black market; **comprar algo de ~** to buy sth on the black market

estrapontín SM (= *asiento extra*) side seat, extra seat; (*Aut*) back seat

Estrasburgo SM Strasbourg

estratagema SF stratagem

estratega SMF strategist; *ver tb* **gabinete 2**

estrategia SF strategy ► **estrategia de la tensión** destabilizing campaign

estratégico ADJ strategic

estratificación SF stratification

estratificado ADJ 1 [*muestreo, sociedad*] stratified
2 [*madera*] laminated

estratificar ▸conjug 1g◂ Ⓐ VT to stratify
Ⓑ **estratificarse** VPR to be stratified

estratigrafía SF stratigraphy

estratigráfico ADJ stratigraphic

estrato SM 1 (= *capa*) stratum
2 (= *nube*) stratus

estratocúmulo SM stratocumulus

estratosfera SF stratosphere

estratosférico ADJ stratospheric

estraza SF rag; **papel de ~** brown paper

estrechamente ADV 1 (= *íntimamente*) closely, intimately
2 (= *austeramente*) austerely

estrechamiento SM 1 [*de valle, calle*] narrowing; **hay un ~ en la calzada** there is a narrowing in the road
2 (= *aumento*) [*de lazos*] tightening; [*de amistades*] strengthening

estrechar ▸conjug 1a◂ Ⓐ VT 1 (= *hacer estrecho*) [+ *calle*] to narrow; [+ *vestido*] to take in; **¿me puedes ~ esta falda?** can you take in this skirt for me?
2 (= *aumentar*) [+ *lazos, relaciones*] to tighten; [+ *amistad*] to strengthen
3 (= *abrazar*) to hug, embrace (*frm*); **me estrechó entre sus brazos** he held me in his arms, he hugged me; **~ la mano a algn** to shake sb's hand, shake hands with sb
4 (= *obligar*) to compel
5 [+ *enemigo*] to press hard
Ⓑ **estrecharse** VPR 1 [*calle*] to narrow, get narrower; **la carretera se estrecha al llegar al puente** the road narrows *o* gets narrower over the bridge
2 (= *abrazarse*) to embrace (*frm*), embrace one another (*frm*), hug; **se ~on la mano** they shook hands
3 (= *aumentar*) [*amistad*] to become stronger, become more intimate; [*lazos, relaciones*] to become closer; **~se con algn** to get very friendly with sb, grow close to sb

4 **~se en los gastos** to economize, cut down on expenditure

estrechez SF 1 (= *angostura*) [*de pasillo, calle*] narrowness; [*de ropa*] tightness
2 (= *dificultad económica*) **está acostumbrado a vivir en la ~** *o* **con ~** he is used to living in straitened circumstances; **hemos pasado muchas estrecheces** we have been through many difficulties *o* hardships ► **estrechez de dinero** shortage of money
3 (= *rigidez*) strictness ► **estrechez de conciencia** small-mindedness ► **estrechez de miras** narrow-mindedness
4 [*de amistad*] closeness

estrecho/a Ⓐ ADJ 1 (= *angosto*) [*calle, pasillo*] narrow; [*zapato, ropa*] tight; **la falda me va muy estrecha** the skirt is very tight on me; **es muy ~ de hombros** he's very narrow-shouldered, he's got very narrow shoulders; **estábamos muy ~s en el asiento trasero** it was a tight squeeze *o* we had to squeeze up tight in the back seat
2 [*amistad, relación*] close; **trabajan en estrecha colaboración con el comité** they work in close collaboration with the committee; **la sometieron a una estrecha vigilancia** they kept her under close supervision *o* a close watch
3 (*sexualmente*) prudish, prim
4 (*de mentalidad*) narrow-minded; **~ de miras** *o* **mente** narrow-minded
Ⓑ SM 1 (*Geog*) strait, straits *pl* ► **Estrecho de Gibraltar** Strait(s) of Gibraltar
2 (†) (= *aprieto*) predicament; **al ~** by force, under compulsion; **poner a algn en el ~ de hacer algo** to put sb in the position of having to do sth
Ⓒ SM/F* prude; **no te hagas la estrecha conmigo** don't act the prude with me

estrechura SF = **estrechez 1, 2**

estregadera SF 1 (= *cepillo*) scrubbing brush
2 (= *fregona*) floor mop
3 [*de puerta*] door scraper, boot scraper

estregar ▸conjug 1h y 1j◂ VT to rub; (*con cepillo*) to scrub, scour

estrella Ⓐ SF 1 (*Astron*) star; ✦***MODISMOS*** **poner a algn sobre las ~s** to praise sb to the skies; **tener buena ~** to be lucky; **tener mala ~** to be unlucky; **ver las ~s** to see stars ► **estrella de Belén** star of Bethlehem ► **estrella de David** Star of David ► **estrella de guía** guiding star ► **estrella del norte** north star ► **estrella de neutrones** neutron star ► **estrella de rabo** comet ► **estrella fija** fixed star ► **estrella fugaz** shooting star ► **estrella neutrónica** neutron star ► **estrella polar** polar star ► **estrella vespertina** evening star; *ver tb* **nacer A1**
2 (*Tip*) asterisk, star; **un hotel de cinco ~s** a five-star hotel
3 (*Cine, Teat*) star; **¿quién es la ~ de la película?** who's the star of the film?, who stars in the film? ► **estrella de cine** film star, movie star (*EEUU*)
4 (*Mil*) star, pip
5 (*Zool*) blaze, white patch ► **estrella de mar** starfish
Ⓑ ADJ INV star *antes de s*; **la atracción ~ de la temporada** the star attraction of the season; **el jugador ~ del equipo** the star player in the team

estrelladera SF slice

estrellado ADJ 1 (= *en forma de estrella*) star-shaped
2 [*cielo*] starry, star-spangled
3 (= *destrozado*) smashed, shattered
4 (*Culin*) [*huevo*] fried

estrellamar SF starfish

estrellar ▸conjug 1a◂ Ⓐ VT 1 (= *hacer chocar*) to smash, shatter; **lo estrelló contra la pared** he smashed it against the wall; **estrelló el balón en el poste** he hammered the ball onto the goalpost; **la corriente amenazaba con ~ el barco contra las rocas** the current threatened to dash the boat on to the rocks
2 (= *decorar con estrellas*) to spangle, cover with stars
3 (*Culin*) [+ *huevo*] to fry
Ⓑ **estrellarse** VPR 1 (= *chocar*) to smash, crash; **el coche se estrelló contra el muro** the car smashed *o* crashed into the wall
2 [*proyecto, plan*] to fail; **~se con** *o* **contra algo** to be thwarted by sth

estrellato SM stardom; **el director que la lanzó al ~** the director who propelled her to stardom

estrellón SM 1 (*esp LAm Aer*) crash; (*Aut*) crash, collision
2 (= *estrella grande*) large star
3 [*de fuegos artificiales*] star firework

estremecedor ADJ alarming, disturbing

estremecer ▸conjug 2d◂ Ⓐ VT to shake
Ⓑ **estremecerse** VPR 1 [*edificio*] to shake
2 [*persona*] (*de miedo*) to tremble (**ante** at; **de** with); (*de horror*) to shudder (**de** with); (*de frío, escalofrío*) to shiver (**de** with)

estremecido ADJ shaking, trembling (**de** with)

estremecimiento SM, **estremezón** (*Col, Ven*) SM 1 (= *sacudida*) shake
2 [*de frío*] shiver, shivering
3 (= *sobresalto*) shock
4 (= *terremoto*) (*Andes, Caribe*) tremor

estrena SF 1 (= *regalo*) good-luck gift, token
2 **estrenas** (*de Navidad*) Christmas presents
3 = **estreno**

estrenar ▸conjug 1a◂ Ⓐ VT 1 (= *usar por primera vez*) [+ *ropa*] to wear for the first time, put on for the first time; [+ *máquina, coche*] to use for the first time; **voy estrenando zapatos** I'm wearing these shoes for the first time; **¿has estrenado ya el coche?** have you tried your new car yet?; **el piso es a ~** it's a brand new flat
2 (*Cine*) to release; (*Teat*) to premiere; **todavía no han estrenado la película** the film hasn't been released yet, the film is not on release yet; **están a punto de ~ el nuevo montaje de "Yerma"** the new production of "Yerma" is about to open
Ⓑ **estrenarse** VPR 1 [*persona*] to make one's debut; **todavía no se ha estrenado como profesora** she still hasn't started working as a teacher; **esta noche todavía no se ha estrenado*** he hasn't pulled so far tonight*
2 (*Cine, Teat*) [*película*] to be released; **la película se estrenó en Junio** the film was released in June
3 (*) to cough up*, pay up

estrenista SMF (*Teat*) first nighter*

estreno SM 1 (= *primer uso*) first use; **hoy voy todo de ~** I'm wearing all new clothes today; **se puso de ~ para la boda** she wore new clothes for the wedding; **fue cuando el ~ del coche nuevo** it was when we went out in the new car for the first time
2 (= *debut*) [*de artista*] debut, first appearance; [*de película*] premiere; [*de obra de teatro*] premiere, first night, first performance; **riguroso ~ mundial** world premiere ► **estreno general** general release
3 (*Caribe*) down payment, deposit

estrenque SM stout esparto rope

estrenuo ADJ vigorous, energetic

estreñido ADJ constipated

estreñimiento SM constipation

estreñir ▸conjug 3h, 3k◂ Ⓐ VT to constipate; **el queso estriñe** cheese causes constipation
Ⓑ **estreñirse** VPR to get constipated

estrepitarse ▸conjug 1a◂ VPR (*Caribe*) to kick up a fuss, make a scene

estrépito SM 1 (= *alboroto*) noise, racket; **reírse con ~** to laugh uproariously
2 (= *bulla*) fuss

estrepitosamente ADV 1 (= *con ruido*) noisily 2 (= *espectacularmente*) spectacularly

estrepitoso ADJ 1 (= *ruidoso*) [*risa, canto*] noisy; [*persona, fiesta*] rowdy; **con aplausos ~s** with loud *o* thunderous applause
2 [*descenso, fracaso*] spectacular

estreptococo SM streptococcus

estreptomicina SF streptomycin

estrés SM stress ► **estrés postraumático** post-traumatic stress

estresado ADJ [*persona*] stressed, stressed out*; [*vida, trabajo*] stressful; **ha estado muy ~ últimamente** he's been very stressed *o* under a lot of stress recently; **lleva una vida muy estresada** he leads a very stressful life

estresante ADJ stressful

estresar ▸conjug 1a◂ VT to cause stress to, put stress on

estría SF 1 (*Anat*) stretch mark
2 (*Arquit*) flute, fluting
3 (*Biol, Geol*) striation

estriado Ⓐ ADJ 1 (*Anat*) stretchmarked
2 (*Arquit*) fluted
3 (*Biol, Geol*) striate, striated
Ⓑ SM 1 (*Arquit*) fluting
2 (*Biol, Geol*) striation

estriar ▸conjug 1c◂ Ⓐ VT to groove, make a groove in
Ⓑ **estriarse** VPR [*piel*] **se estría la piel durante el embarazo** stretch marks appear during pregnancy

estribación SF (*Geog*) spur; **en las estribaciones del Himalaya** in the foothills of the Himalayas

estribar ▸conjug 1a◂ VI **~ en algo: su felicidad estriba en ver contentos a los demás** her happiness comes from seeing other people being happy; **la dificultad estriba en el texto** the difficulty lies in the text; **su prosperidad estriba en esta industria** their prosperity is based on *o* derives from this industry

estribera SF 1 (= *estribo*) stirrup
2 [*de moto*] footrest
3 (*LAm*) saddle strap

estriberón SM stepping stone

estribillo SM 1 (*Literat*) refrain
2 (*Mús*) chorus; **¡siempre con el mismo ~!** it's always the same old story!

estribo SM [1] (= *pieza de apoyo*) [*de jinete*] stirrup; [*de moto*] footrest; ✦*MODISMO* **perder los ~s** (= *enfadarse*) to lose one's temper, blow one's top*; (= *agitarse*) to get hot under the collar
[2] (*en coche*) running board
[3] (*Arquit*) [*de edificio*] buttress; [*de puente*] support
[4] (*Téc*) brace
[5] (*Geog*) spur

estribor SM starboard

estricnina SF strychnine

estricote SM ✦*MODISMO* **andar al ~** (*Caribe**) to live a wild life

estrictamente ADV strictly

estrictez SF (*LAm*) strictness

estricto ADJ strict

estridencia SF stridency, raucousness; **iba vestida sin ~s** she was not loudly dressed

estridente ADJ [1] [*ruido*] strident, raucous
[2] [*color*] loud

estridentemente ADV [1] (= *ruidosamente*) stridently, raucously
[2] (= *vistosamente*) loudly

estridor SM stridency

estrillar ▸conjug 1a◂ VI (*Andes, Cono Sur*) to get cross

estrillo SM (*Andes, Cono Sur*) bad temper, annoyance

estriptís* SM, **estriptise*** SM (*Andes*) striptease

estriptisero/a* SM/F (*Andes*) stripper*, striptease artist

estriptista* SMF stripper*

estro SM [1] (= *inspiración*) inspiration
[2] (*Med, Vet*) oestrus, estrus (*EEUU*)

estrofa SF verse, strophe (*frm*)

estrófico ADJ strophic

estrógeno SM oestrogen, estrogen (*EEUU*)

estroncio SM strontium ► **estroncio 90** strontium 90

estropajo SM [1] (*para fregar*) scourer, scouring pad; ✦*MODISMOS* **poner a algn como un ~** to make sb feel a heel; **servir de ~** to be exploited, be used to do the dirty work ► **estropajo de acero** steel wool
[2] (= *objeto inútil*) worthless object; (= *persona inútil*) dead loss

estropajoso ADJ [1] (= *áspero*) [*lengua*] coated, furry; [*carne*] tough
[2] [*habla*] indistinct; **cuando bebe se le pone la lengua estropajosa** when he drinks he gets tongue-tied
[3] [*pelo*] straggly

estropeado ADJ [1] (= *averiado*) [*lavadora, televisor*] broken; [*ascensor, vehículo*] broken down; **tengo ~ el vídeo** the video is not working *o* has gone wrong *o* is broken
[2] (= *dañado*) [*piel*] damaged; [*carne, fruta*] off; **este jersey está ya muy ~** this jumper is falling apart now; **los muebles están muy ~s** the furniture is in very poor condition
[3] [*persona*] [3·1] (= *afeado*) **la encontré muy estropeada después del parto** she looked the worse for wear after the birth; **lo he visto muy ~ últimamente** he's been looking a real wreck lately*
[3·2] (= *envejecido*) **está muy estropeada para su edad** she looks much older than she is, she looks pretty worn out for her age

estropear ▸conjug 1a◂ Ⓐ VT [1] (= *averiar*) [+ *juguete, lavadora, ascensor*] to break; [+ *vehículo*] to damage
[2] (= *dañar*) [+ *tela, ropa, zapatos*] to ruin; **te vas a ~ la vista** you'll ruin your eyesight; **esa crema le ha estropeado el cutis** that cream has damaged *o* ruined her skin
[3] (= *malograr*) [+ *plan, cosecha, actuación*] to ruin, spoil; **la lluvia nos estropeó la excursión** the rain ruined *o* spoiled our day out; **el final estropeaba la película** the ending ruined *o* spoiled the film; **la luz estropea el vino** light spoils wine, light makes wine go off
[4] (= *afear*) [+ *objeto, habitación*] to ruin the look of, spoil the look of; [+ *vista, panorama*] to ruin, spoil; **estropeó el escritorio pintándolo de blanco** he ruined *o* spoiled the look of the desk by painting it white; **ese sofá estropea el salón** that sofa ruins the look of the living room, that sofa spoils (the look of) the living room; **el centro comercial nos ha estropeado la vista** the shopping centre has ruined *o* spoiled our view
[5] (= *envejecer*) [+ *persona*] **los años la han estropeado** she has aged really badly
Ⓑ **estropearse** VPR [1] (= *averiarse*) [*lavadora, televisor*] to break; [*ascensor, vehículo*] to break down; **se me ha estropeado el vídeo** my video is *o* has broken
[2] (= *dañarse*) [*ropa, zapatos, vista*] to get ruined; [*carne, fruta*] to go off, spoil; **el ante se estropea con la lluvia** suede gets ruined in the rain; **si te lo lavas con este champú no se ~á el pelo** this shampoo won't damage *o* ruin your hair; **se le ha estropeado la cara con el sol** his face has aged from too much sun
[3] (= *malograrse*) [*plan, vacaciones*] to be ruined; **se me ~on todos los planes cuando me quedé sin trabajo** all my plans were ruined when I lost my job; **se nos ~on las vacaciones por culpa del accidente** our holiday was ruined by the accident
[4] [*persona*] (= *afearse*) to lose one's looks; (= *envejecer*) to age; **se ha estropeado mucho desde que está enfermo** he's really lost his looks since he got ill; **no te has estropeado nada con los años** you haven't aged at all

estropicio* SM [1] (= *rotura*) breakage, smashing
[2] (= *trastorno*) harmful effects *pl*; **espero que el retraso no le cause ningún ~** I hope the delay won't cause you any inconvenience
[3] (= *jaleo*) rumpus*

estructura SF [1] [*de poema, célula, organización*] structure ► **estructura atómica** atomic structure ► **estructura del poder** power structure ► **estructura profunda** (*Ling*) deep structure ► **estructura salarial** pay structure ► **estructura superficial** (*Ling*) surface structure
[2] [*de edificio*] frame, framework

estructuración SF [1] (= *acción*) structuring
[2] (= *estructura*) structure

estructural ADJ structural

estructuralismo SM structuralism

estructuralista ADJ, SMF structuralist

estructuralmente ADV structurally

estructurar ▸conjug 1a◂ VT to structure, arrange

estruendo SM [1] (= *ruido*) din
[2] (= *alboroto*) uproar, turmoil
[3] (= *pompa*) pomp

estruendosamente ADV [1] (= *ruidosamente*) noisily, uproariously
[2] (= *aparatosamente*) loudly, obstreperously

estruendoso ADJ [1] (= *ruidoso*) thunderous
[2] (= *escandaloso*) [*derrota, fracaso*] outrageous

estrujado SM [*de uvas*] pressing

estrujadura SF squeeze, press, pressing

estrujar ▸conjug 1a◂ Ⓐ VT [1] (= *exprimir*) to squeeze
[2] (= *apretar*) to press
[3] (= *escurrir*) [+ *bayeta, trapo*] to wring
[4] (= *aprovecharse de*) to drain, bleed white
Ⓑ **estrujarse** VPR ✦*MODISMO* **~se la mollera*** to rack one's brains*

estrujón SM [1] (= *apretón*) squeeze, press
[2] (*) (= *abrazo*) bear hug

Estuardo SM Stuart

estuario SM estuary

estucado Ⓐ ADJ [1] [*papel*] coated
[2] [*pared*] plastered, stuccoed
Ⓑ SM stucco, stucco work

estucar ▸conjug 1g◂ VT to stucco, plaster

estuche SM [1] (= *funda*) [*de gafas, instrumento*] case; [*de lápices*] pencil case; [*de espada*] sheath ► **estuche de afeites** vanity case ► **estuche de aseo** toilet case ► **estuche de cigarros** cigar case ► **estuche de costura** sewing basket ► **estuche de cubiertos** canteen of cutlery ► **estuche de herramientas** toolbox ► **estuche de joyas** jewel box *o* case, jewellery box, jewelry box (*EEUU*)
[2] ✦*MODISMO* **ser un ~*** to be a handyman, be a useful person to have around

estuchero* SM (*Méx*) safebreaker

estuco SM stucco, plaster

estudiado ADJ [*sonrisa, respuesta*] studied; **una persona de gestos muy ~s** a very mannered *o* affected person

estudiantado SM students *pl*, student body

estudiante SMF student; **~ de derecho** law student; **~ de medicina** medical student; **~ de ruso** student of Russian

estudiantil ADJ student *antes de s*; **vida ~** student life; **los problemas ~es** student problems

estudiantina SF student music group; **a la ~** like a student, in the manner of students; → TUNA

estudiantino ADJ student *antes de s*

estudiar ▸conjug 1b◂ Ⓐ VT [1] (= *aprender*) [+ *lección, papel*] to learn; **estoy estudiando francés en una academia** I'm learning French at a language school; **se estudió el papel en media hora** she learned her part in half an hour; **tengo mucho que ~** I've got a lot of work *o* studying to do; **esta tarde tengo que ~ matemáticas** I have to do some maths this evening
[2] (= *cursar*) to study; **estudió arquitectura** he studied architecture; **estoy estudiando piano** I'm studying the piano; **quería que su hijo estudiase una carrera** she wanted her son to go to university *o* to do a degree; **¿qué curso estudias?** what year are you in?
[3] (= *examinar*) [*informe, experimento*] to examine, look into; [*persona*] to study, look into; **el informe estudia los efectos de la sequía** the report examines *o* looks into the effects of the drought; **están estudiando el compor-**

tamiento de los insectos they are studying *o* looking into insect behaviour; **me estudió de pies a cabeza** he looked me up and down

[4] (= *considerar*) to consider, study; **~emos su oferta y ya le contestaremos** we shall consider *o* study your offer and get back to you; **el informe está siendo estudiado** the report is being studied *o* is under consideration; **están estudiando la posibilidad de convocar una huelga** they are looking into the possibility of calling a strike, they are considering calling a strike

Ⓑ VI [1] (= *aprender*) to study; **tienes que ~ más** you have to work *o* study harder; **me tengo que ir a ~ ahora** I must go and do some work *o* studying now

[2] (= *cursar estudios*) to study; **estudió con el Profesor García Montero** she studied under Professor García Montero; **estudia en un colegio de monjas** she goes to a convent school; **dejé de ~ a los trece años** I left school at thirteen; **~ para algo** to study to be sth; **mi hijo estudia para abogado** my son is studying to be a lawyer

estudio SM [1] (= *investigación*) study; **los últimos ~s en lingüística** the latest work *o* studies in linguistics; **en ~s de laboratorio** in laboratory tests *o* studies ► **estudio de campo** field study ► **estudio de casos (prácticos)** case study ► **estudio de desplazamientos y tiempos** (*Com*) time and motion study ► **estudio del trabajo** work study ► **estudio de mercado** market research ► **estudio de viabilidad** feasibility study ► **estudios de motivación** motivational research *sing*; *ver tb* **bolsa 9**, **plan 2**

[2] (= *actividad investigadora*) study; **una vida dedicada al ~** a life devoted to study; **horas de ~** hours of study; **primero el ~ y luego el juego** work first and play later

[3] (= *análisis*) [*de intención de voto, edificio*] survey; **vamos a hacer un ~ del cabello de la víctima** we are going to examine the victim's hair; **ya les hemos entregado el proyecto para su ~** we have already put forward the plan for their consideration; **estar <u>en</u> ~** to be under consideration

[4] **estudios** (= *educación*) education *sing*; **sus padres le pagaron los ~s** her parents paid for her education; **una persona sin ~s** an uneducated person; **<u>cursar</u> ~s de algo** to study sth; **<u>dejar</u> los ~s** (*Escol*) to drop out of school; (*Univ*) to drop out of university; **<u>tener</u> ~s** to have an education, be educated; **tengo algunos ~s de inglés** I've studied some *o* a bit of English ► **estudios primarios** primary education *sing* ► **estudios secundarios** secondary education *sing* ► **estudios superiores** higher education *sing*; **tener ~s superiores de derecho penal** to have studied criminal law to degree level ► **estudios universitarios** university degree *sing*, university studies

[5] (= *erudición*) learning; **un hombre de mucho ~** a man of great learning

[6] (*Arte, Mús*) study; **un ~ de piano** a study *o* étude for piano

[7] (= *lugar de trabajo*) [7·1] (*en una casa*) study

[7·2] (*profesional*) [*de artista, arquitecto*] studio; (*Cono Sur*) [*de abogado*] office

[7·3] (*Cine, Radio, TV*) studio ► **estudio cinematográfico**, **estudio de cine** film studio ► **estudio de diseño** design studio ► **estudio de fotografía** photographer's studio, photographic studio ► **estudio de grabación** recording studio ► **estudio de registro de sonidos** sound-recording studio ► **estudio de televisión** television studio ► **estudio radiofónico** broadcasting studio

[8] (= *apartamento*) studio, studio flat

estudiosamente ADV studiously

estudioso/a Ⓐ ADJ studious

Ⓑ SM/F expert, scholar; **un ~ de la literatura medieval** an expert in *o* a scholar of medieval literature

estufa SF [1] (= *para calentarse*) heater ► **estufa de gas** gas heater ► **estufa de petróleo** oil heater ► **estufa eléctrica** electric fire

[2] (*Agr*) hothouse; ✦*MODISMO* **criar a algn en ~** to pamper sb

[3] (*Méx*) stove

estufilla SF [1] (= *brasero*) small stove, brazier

[2] (*para las manos*) muff

estulticia SF (*liter*) stupidity, foolishness

estultificar ▸conjug 1g◂ (*CAm*) VT **~ a algn** to make sb look stupid, make sb out to be a fool

estulto ADJ (*liter*) stupid, foolish

estupa* Ⓐ SF drug squad

Ⓑ SMF member of the drug squad

estupefacción SF astonishment, amazement

estupefaciente Ⓐ ADJ narcotic

Ⓑ SM narcotic, drug

estupefacto ADJ astonished; **me miró ~** he looked at me in astonishment *o* amazement; **dejar a algn ~** to leave sb speechless

estupendamente ADV marvellously, marvelously (*EEUU*), wonderfully; **estoy ~** I feel great *o* marvellous; **nos lo pasamos ~** we had a fantastic *o* great time*; **le salió ~** he did it very well

▼ **estupendo** ADJ marvellous, marvelous (*EEUU*), great*; **¡estupendo!** that's great!*, splendid!; **—no te preocupes, yo lo hago —¡estupendo!** "don't worry, I'll do it" — "great!"; **tiene un coche ~** he's got a great *o* fantastic car*; **es ~ tocando la trompeta** he's great on the trumpet*

estúpidamente ADV stupidly

estupidez SF [1] (= *cualidad*) stupidity

[2] (= *acto, dicho*) stupid thing; **lo que hizo fue una ~** what he did was stupid, that was a stupid thing to do; **fue una ~ mía** it was a stupid mistake of mine; **deja de decir estupideces** stop talking rubbish* *o* nonsense; **cometer una ~** to do something silly

estupidizador ADJ stupefying

estúpido/a Ⓐ ADJ stupid

Ⓑ SM/F idiot; **ese tío es un ~** that guy's an idiot

estupor SM [1] (= *sorpresa*) amazement, astonishment

[2] (*Med*) stupor

estuprar ▸conjug 1a◂ VT to rape

estupro SM [1] (= *violación*) rape

[2] (*con menor de edad*) sexual intercourse with a minor

estuque SM stucco

estuquería SF stuccoing, stucco work

esturión SM sturgeon

estuve *etc ver* **estar**

esvástica SF swastika

ET ABR (*Esp*) = **Ejército de Tierra**

ETA SF ABR (*Esp Pol*) (= **Euskadi Ta Askatasuna**) ≈ Patria Vasca y Libertad, ETA

-eta *ver* **Aspects of Word Formation in Spanish 2**

etano SM (*Quím*) ethane

etanol SM ethanol

etapa SF [1] [*de viaje*] stage; **en pequeñas ~s** in easy stages; ✦*MODISMO* **quemar ~s** to make rapid progress

[2] (= *fase*) stage, phase; **desarrollo por ~s** phased development, development in stages; **la segunda ~ del plan** the second phase of the plan; **una adquisición proyectada por ~s** a phased takeover; **lo haremos por ~s** we'll do it gradually *o* in stages

[3] (*Dep*) leg, lap

[4] (*Mil*) stopping place

[5] [*de cohete*] stage; **cohete de tres ~s** 3-stage rocket

etario ADJ age *antes de s*; **grupo ~** age group

etarra Ⓐ ADJ of ETA

Ⓑ SMF member of ETA

etc. ABR (= **etcétera**) etc

etcétera Ⓐ ADV and so on

Ⓑ SM long list; **y un largo ~** and a lot more besides, and much much more; **y un largo ~ de autores** and many more authors besides

-ete *ver* **Aspects of Word Formation in Spanish 2**

éter SM ether

etéreo ADJ ethereal

eternamente ADV eternally, everlastingly

eternidad SF eternity; **la espera se me hizo una ~** I waited what felt like an eternity

eternizar ▸conjug 1f◂ Ⓐ VT [1] [+ *vida, personaje*] to perpetuate

[2] [+ *entrevista, viaje*] to drag out

Ⓑ **eternizarse** VPR [1] [*discurso, reunión*] to drag on (forever), go on forever

[2] [*persona*] to take ages*; **se eterniza cada vez que va de compras** she takes ages every time she goes shopping; **~se en hacer algo** to take ages to do sth

eterno ADJ [1] (= *duradero*) eternal, everlasting; **el ~ problema del dinero** the eternal *o* everlasting problem of money

[2] (= *interminable*) never-ending; **el viaje se me hizo ~** I thought the journey would never end, the journey seemed never-ending *o* interminable

ethos ['etos] SM ethos

ética SF ethics ► **ética profesional** professional ethics

ético¹/a Ⓐ ADJ ethical

Ⓑ SM/F ethicist

ético² ADJ (*Med*) consumptive

eticoso* ADJ (*Andes*) fussy, finicky

etileno SM (*Quím*) ethylene

etílico ADJ **alcohol ~** ethyl alcohol; **intoxicación etílica** alcohol poisoning; **en estado ~** intoxicated

etilo SM ethyl

étimo SM etymon

etimología SF etymology

etimológico ADJ etymological

etiología SF aetiology, etiology (*EEUU*)

etíope ADJ, SMF Ethiopian

➤ LENGUA Y USO: **estupendo** 38.1, 38.2, 40.3

Etiopía SF Ethiopia
etiquencia SF (*Caribe, Méx Med*) consumption
etiqueta SF [1] (*pegada*) label; (*atada, grapada*) tag; **despégale la ~ a la camisa** take the label off the shirt; **le han puesto la ~ de cobarde** they've labelled him a coward ► **etiqueta autoadhesiva** sticky label ► **etiqueta del precio** price tag
[2] (= *formalismo*) etiquette; **de ~** formal; **baile de ~** gala ball; **traje de ~** formal dress; **ir de ~** to wear formal dress; **"vestir de ~"** (*en invitación*) "dress: formal"
etiquetación SF, **etiquetado** SM, **etiquetaje** SM labelling
etiquetadora SF labelling machine
etiquetar ▸conjug 1a◂ VT to label; **~ a algn de algo** to label sb (as) sth
etiquetero ADJ formal, ceremonious
etnia SF ethnic group
etnicidad SF ethnicity
étnico ADJ ethnic
etnocéntrico ADJ ethnocentric
etnocentrismo SM ethnocentrism
etnografía SF ethnography
etnográfico ADJ ethnographic
etnología SF ethnology
etnológico ADJ ethnological
etnomusicología SF ethnomusicology
etrusco/a Ⓐ ADJ, SM/F Etruscan
Ⓑ SM (*Ling*) Etruscan
ETS Ⓐ SF ABR (*Med*) (= **enfermedad de transmisión sexual**) STD
Ⓑ SFPL ABR (*Esp*) (= **Escuelas Técnicas Superiores**) *technical colleges offering short degree courses*
ETT SF ABR (*Esp*) = **Empresa de Trabajo Temporal**
EU(A) ABR (*esp LAm*) (= **Estados Unidos (de América)**) US(A)
eucaliptal SM, **eucaliptar** SM eucalyptus plantation
eucalipto SM eucalyptus
eucaristía SF Eucharist
eucarístico ADJ Eucharistic
Euclides SM Euclid
euclidiano ADJ Euclidean
eufemismo SM euphemism
eufemístico ADJ euphemistic
eufonía SF euphony
eufónico ADJ euphonic, euphonious
euforia SF euphoria
eufórico ADJ euphoric
euforizante ADJ **droga ~** drug that produces euphoria
euforizar ▸conjug 1f◂ Ⓐ VT to produce euphoria in, exhilarate
Ⓑ **euforizarse** VPR to become exhilarated
Eufrates SM Euphrates
eugenesia SF eugenics *sing*
eugenésico ADJ eugenic
Eugenio SM Eugene
eugenismo SM eugenics *sing*
eunuco SM eunuch
eurasiático/a ADJ, SM/F Eurasian
eureka EXCL eureka!
euribor SM (*Fin*) Euribor
Eurídice SF Eurydice
Eurípedes SM Euripides
eurítmica SF eurhythmics *sing*
euro SM [1] (= *moneda*) euro
[2] (*liter*) (= *viento*) east wind
euro... PREF Euro...
eurobonos SMPL Eurobonds
eurocalculadora SF euro converter
Eurocámara SF Euro Parliament, European Parliament
eurocheque SM Eurocheque
eurocomisario/a SM/F Euro-commissioner
eurocomunismo SM Eurocommunism
eurocomunista ADJ, SMF Eurocommunist
euroconector SM SCART connector, Euroconnector
Eurocopa SF (*Ftbl*) European Championship
eurócrata SMF Eurocrat
Eurocrédito SM Eurocredit
eurodiputado/a SM/F Euro MP, member of the European Parliament
eurodivisa SF Eurocurrency
eurodólar SM Eurodollar
euroescéptico/a ADJ, SM/F Eurosceptic
eurofanático ADJ fanatically pro-European
eurófilo/a ADJ, SM/F Europhile
eurófobo/a ADJ, SM/F Europhobe
eurofuncionario/a SM/F EU official
euromercado SM Euromarket
euromisil SM short-range nuclear missile
Europa SF Europe
europarlamentario/a SM/F member of the European Parliament
europarlamento SM European Parliament
europeidad SF Europeanness
europeísmo SM Europeanism
europeísta ADJ, SMF pro-European
europeización SF Europeanization
europeizante ADJ, SMF (*LAm*) = **europeísta**
europeizar ▸conjug 1f◂ Ⓐ VT to Europeanize
Ⓑ **europeizarse** VPR to become Europeanized
europeo/a ADJ, SM/F European
Eurotúnel® SM (*estructura*) Channel Tunnel
Eurovisión SF Eurovision
eurozona SF Eurozone
éuscaro ADJ, SM = **euskera**
Euskadi SF the Basque Country ► **Euskadi norte** Pays Basque (*France*)
euskaldún/una Ⓐ ADJ [1] (= *vasco*) Basque
[2] (*Ling*) Basque-speaking
Ⓑ SM/F Basque speaker
euskaldunización SF [1] (*Pol*) conversion to Basque norms [2] (*Ling*) conversion to Basque, *process of making people Basque-speaking*
euskaldunizar ▸conjug 1f◂ VT [1] (*Pol*) to convert to Basque norms [2] (*Ling*) to convert to Basque, make Basque-speaking
euskera SM, **eusquera** SM, **eusquero** SM Basque, the Basque language ► **euskera batua** standard Basque

EUSKERA

Spoken by over half a million people in the Western Pyrenees, Basque, which is a non-Indo-European language, has been one of Spain's **lenguas cooficiales** *(along with* **catalán** *and* **gallego***) since 1982. Originally spoken also in Burgos and the Eastern Pyrenees, it began to lose ground to Castilian from the 13th century onwards. Under Franco its use was prohibited in the media, but it began to experience a revival in the 1950s through semi-clandestine Basque-language schools called* **ikastolas**. *In 1968 the Academy of the Basque Language created a standardized form called* **euskera batua**, *an attempt to homogenize several divergent dialects. Nowadays there is Basque-language radio and television, and under the autonomous government the teaching of the language has become a cornerstone of educational policy.*
⇨ *See also* LENGUAS COOFICIALES

eutanasia SF euthanasia, mercy killing
Eva SF Eve
evacuación SF [1] [*de habitantes, heridos*] evacuation
[2] (*Téc*) waste
[3] (*Med*) evacuation, bowel movement
evacuado/a SM/F evacuee
evacuar ▸conjug 1d◂ VT [1] (= *desocupar*) to evacuate
[2] (*Med*) [+ *llaga*] to drain; **~ el vientre** to have a bowel movement
[3] (*frm*) (= *realizar*) [+ *deber*] to fulfil; [+ *consulta*] to carry out, undertake; [+ *negocio*] to transact; [+ *trato*] to conclude
[4] (*Jur*) [+ *dictamen*] to issue
evacuatorio SM public lavatory
evadido/a SM/F escaped prisoner, escaped convict
evadir ▸conjug 3a◂ Ⓐ VT [1] [+ *problema*] to evade, avoid
[2] (*Fin*) [+ *impuestos*] to evade; [+ *dinero*] to pass, get away with
Ⓑ **evadirse** VPR [1] (= *huir*) (*gen*) to escape; (*de cárcel*) to break out, escape; **~se de la realidad** to escape from reality
[2] (*LAm*‡) to trip‡
evaluación SF [1] (= *valoración*) [*de datos*] evaluation; [*de daños, pérdidas*] assessment ► **evaluación del impacto ambiental** assessment of the impact upon the environment
[2] (*Escol*) (= *acción*) assessment; (= *examen*) test ► **evaluación continua** continuous assessment ► **evaluación escolar** exam (*forming part of end-of-term or end-of-year assessment*)
evaluador(a) SM/F assessor
evaluar ▸conjug 1e◂ VT [1] (= *valorar*) [+ *datos*] to evaluate; [+ *daños, pérdidas*] to assess
[2] (*Escol*) to assess
evaluativo ADJ evaluative
evanescente ADJ evanescent
evangélico ADJ evangelic, evangelical
evangelio SM gospel; **el Evangelio según San Juan** the Gospel according to St John; ✦*MODISMOS* **se aceptan sus ideas como el ~** his ideas are accepted as gospel truth; **lo que habla es el ~** he speaks the gospel truth
evangelismo SM evangelism
Evangelista ADJ **San Juan ~** St John the Evangelist
evangelista SMF evangelist
evangelizador(a) SM/F evangelist
evangelizar ▸conjug 1f◂ VT to evangelize
evaporación SF evaporation
evaporar ▸conjug 1a◂ Ⓐ VT to evaporate
Ⓑ VPR [1] [*líquido*] to evaporate
[2] (*fig*) to vanish o disappear into thin air

evaporizar ▸conjug 1f◂ Ⓐ VT to vaporize
Ⓑ **evaporizarse** VPR to vaporize

evasión SF (= *huida*) [*de lugar*] escape; [*de responsabilidad*] evasion; **literatura de ~** escapist literature ► **evasión de capitales** flight of capital ► **evasión de impuestos**, **evasión fiscal**, **evasión tributaria** tax evasion

evasionario ADJ (*Literat*) escapist

evasionismo SM escapism

evasiva SF 1 (= *pretexto*) excuse; **viene con sus ~s** he avoids a straight answer; **contestar con ~s** to avoid the issue, dodge the issue
2 (= *escapatoria*) loophole, way out

evasivo ADJ [*respuesta*] evasive, noncommittal

evento SM 1 (= *acontecimiento*) event; **con motivo de este ~** to mark this event; **a todo ~** whatever happens
2 (= *incidente*) unforeseen happening
3 (*Dep*) fixture

eventual Ⓐ ADJ 1 (= *posible*) possible
2 (= *temporal*) [*trabajo, obrero*] temporary, casual; [*solución*] stopgap *antes de s*
3 (*LAm*) (= *final*) eventual
Ⓑ SMF temporary worker, casual worker

eventualidad SF 1 (= *posibilidad*) eventuality; **en esa ~** in that eventuality
2 (= *trabajo*) casual employment

eventualmente ADV 1 (= *posiblemente*) possibly; **algún número de la revista se publicará ~** special issues of the journal will be published from time to time
2 (= *por casualidad*) by chance
3 (*LAm*) (= *por fin*) eventually

Everest SM **el (Monte) ~** (Mount) Everest

evidencia SF 1 (= *obviedad*) evidence; **ante la ~ de los hechos, se confesó culpable** faced with the evidence, he pleaded guilty; **negar la ~** to refuse to face (the) facts; **rendirse ante la ~** to face (the) facts
2 (= *ridículo*) **dejar** *o* **poner algo/a algn en ~** to show sth/sb up; **Carlos la puso en ~ delante de todos** Carlos showed her up in front of everyone; **ponerse en ~** to show o.s. up

evidencial ADJ tangible, visible

evidenciar ▸conjug 1b◂ VT 1 (= *probar*) to prove, demonstrate; **~ algo de modo infundible** to give clear proof of sth
2 (= *hacer ver*) to make evident

evidente ADJ obvious, clear, evident; **¡evidente!** naturally!, obviously!

evidentemente ADV obviously, clearly, evidently

evitable ADJ avoidable, preventable; **un accidente fácilmente ~** an accident which could easily be avoided

evitación SF avoidance ► **evitación de accidentes** accident prevention

evitar ▸conjug 1a◂ Ⓐ VT 1 (= *eludir*) to avoid; **quiero ~ ese riesgo** I want to avoid that risk; **intento ~ a Luisa** I'm trying to avoid Luisa; **no pude ~lo** I couldn't help it; **~ hacer algo** to avoid doing sth; **María evita a toda costa encontrarse con él** María avoids bumping into him at all costs
2 (= *ahorrar*) to save; **esto nos ~á muchos problemas** this will save us a lot of problems; **me evita (el) tener que ...** it saves me having to ...
Ⓑ **evitarse** VPR 1 (= *ahorrarse*) to save o.s.; **~se trabajo** to save o.s. trouble; **así me evito tener que ir** that saves me having to go, that way I avoid having to go
2 [*dos personas*] to avoid each other

evocación SF 1 [*de recuerdos*] evocation
2 [*de espíritus*] invocation

evocador ADJ 1 (= *sugestivo*) evocative
2 (*del pasado*) reminiscent (**de** of)

evocar ▸conjug 1g◂ VT 1 (= *recordar*) to evoke, conjure up
2 [+ *espíritu*] to invoke, call up

evocativo ADJ (*LAm*) evocative

evolución SF 1 (*Biol*) evolution
2 (= *desarrollo*) evolution, development
3 (*Med*) progress
4 (*Mil*) manoeuvre, maneuver (*EEUU*)

evolucionar ▸conjug 1a◂ VI 1 (*Biol*) to evolve
2 (= *desarrollarse*) to evolve, develop
3 (*Med*) to progress
4 (*Mil*) to manoeuvre, maneuver (*EEUU*)
5 (*Aer*) to circle

evolucionista ADJ evolutionist

evolutivo ADJ evolutionary

ex Ⓐ PREF ex-, former; **ex secretario** ex-secretary, former secretary; **su ex amante** his former lover, his ex-lover
Ⓑ SMF **mi ex*** my ex*, my ex-husband/ex-wife/ex-boyfriend, *etc*; **un ex del equipo** an ex-member of the team, a former member of the team

exabrupto SM 1 (= *ataque*) broadside
2 (= *observación*) sharp remark, cutting remark

exacción SF 1 (= *acto*) exaction
2 [*de impuestos*] demand

exacerbación SF exacerbation

exacerbante ADJ (*LAm*) 1 (= *irritante*) irritating, provoking
2 (= *agravante*) aggravating

exacerbar ▸conjug 1a◂ VT 1 (= *agravar*) to aggravate, exacerbate
2 (= *irritar*) to irritate

▾**exactamente** ADV exactly; **parecen ~ iguales** they look exactly the same; **sí, eso es, ~** yes, that's right, exactly

exactitud SF 1 (= *precisión*) accuracy; **la ~ del reloj** the accuracy of the watch; **con ~** [*saber, calcular, precisar*] exactly; **no lo sabemos con ~** we don't know exactly; **siguió las instrucciones con ~** he followed the instructions exactly *o* to the letter
2 (= *veracidad*) accuracy; **cuestionó la ~ de su declaración** he questioned the accuracy of her statement
3 (= *fidelidad*) accuracy; **reprodujo el original con increíble ~** he reproduced the original with incredible accuracy

exacto Ⓐ ADJ 1 (= *preciso*) exact; **el precio ~** the exact price; **no recuerdo sus palabras exactas** I can't remember her exact words; **el tren salió a la hora exacta** the train left exactly *o* bang on time; **tus cálculos no son muy ~s** your calculations are not very accurate; **para ser ~** to be exact *o* precise
2 (= *correcto*) correct; **perdone, pero lo que dice no es del todo ~** excuse me, but what you're saying is not entirely correct
3 (= *fiel*) [*copia, versión*] exact
Ⓑ EXCL exactly!, quite right!

exageración SF exaggeration; **dice que lleva diez horas trabajando ¡qué ~!** he says he's been working for ten hours? that's such an exaggeration! *o* what an exaggeration!; — **piden diez millones por esa casa —¡menuda ~!** "they're asking ten million for that house" — "that's way too much! *o* that's a ridiculous amount!"

exageradamente ADV **movía los brazos ~** she was moving her arms in an exaggerated way *o* exaggeratedly; **es ~ prudente** he's excessively cautious, he's over-cautious

exagerado ADJ 1 [*persona*] (*en los gestos*) prone to exaggeration; (*en el vestir*) overdressed, dressy; **¡qué ~ eres!** ◊ **¡no seas ~!** don't exaggerate!, you do exaggerate!; **es un ~ comiendo** he eats an incredible amount; **nos lo contó de forma muy exagerada** he told us in a very exaggerated *o* a completely over-the-top* way
2 [*gesto*] theatrical
3 (= *excesivo*) [*precio*] excessive, steep

exageradura SF (*Caribe*) exaggeration

▾**exagerar** ▸conjug 1a◂ Ⓐ VT to exaggerate; **creo que eso sería ~ las cosas** I think that would be going a bit far *o* overdoing it a bit
Ⓑ VI to exaggerate

exaltación SF 1 (= *ensalzamiento*) exaltation
2 (= *sobreexcitación*) overexcitement, elation
3 (= *fanatismo*) hot-headedness
4 (*Pol*) extremism

exaltado/a Ⓐ ADJ 1 (= *acalorado*) [*humor*] overexcited, elated; [*carácter*] excitable; [*discurso*] impassioned; **los ánimos estaban muy ~s** feelings were running high
2 (= *elevado*) exalted
3 (*Pol*) extreme
Ⓑ SM/F 1 (= *fanático*) hothead
2 (*Pol*) extremist

exaltante ADJ exciting

exaltar ▸conjug 1a◂ Ⓐ VT 1 (= *acalorar*) [+ *persona, manifestante*] to work up, excite; [+ *emoción*] to intensify; [+ *imaginación*] to fire
2 (= *elevar*) to exalt
3 (= *enaltecer*) to raise (**a** to)
Ⓑ **exaltarse** VPR 1 [*persona*] (*gen*) to get excited, get worked up; (*en discusión*) to get heated; **¡no te exaltes!** don't get so worked up *o* hot up!
2 [*emoción*] to run high

exalumno/a SM/F (*esp LAm*) (*Univ*) graduate, former student

examen SM 1 (*Escol*) examination, exam; **hacer un ~** to sit *o* take an examination *o* exam; **presentarse a un ~** to enter for an examination *o* exam, go in for an examination *o* exam ► **examen de admisión** entrance examination *o* exam ► **examen de conciencia**: **hacer ~ de conciencia** to examine one's conscience ► **examen de conducir** driving test ► **examen de ingreso** entrance examination ► **examen de suficiencia** proficiency test ► **examen eliminatorio** qualifying examination ► **examen oral** oral examination ► **examen parcial** (*Univ*) *examination covering part of the course material in a particular subject* ► **examen tipo test** multiple-choice test
2 (= *estudio*) [*de problema*] consideration; [*de zona*] search; **tras el ~ de la situación** after studying the situation; **someter algo a ~** to subject sth to examination *o* scrutiny
3 (*Med*) examination ► **examen ocular** eye test

examinado/a SM/F exam candidate

➤ LENGUA Y USO: **exactamente** 38.1 **exagerar B** 53.1

examinador(a) SM/F examiner

examinando/a SM/F exam candidate

▼**examinar** ▸conjug 1a◂ Ⓐ VT [1] [+ *alumno*] to examine
[2] [+ *producto*] to test
[3] [+ *problema*] to examine, study
[4] [+ *paciente*] to examine
Ⓑ **examinarse** VPR to take an examination *o* exam, be examined (**de** in); **¿cuándo se examinan de inglés?** when are they taking *o* doing their English exam?; **~se para doctor** to take one's doctoral examination

exangüe ADJ [1] (= *sin sangre*) bloodless
[2] (= *débil*) weak

exánime ADJ [1] (= *sin vida*) lifeless
[2] (= *agotado*) exhausted; **caer ~** to fall in a faint

exasperación SF exasperation

exasperador ADJ, **exasperante** ADJ exasperating, infuriating

exasperar ▸conjug 1a◂ Ⓐ VT to exasperate, infuriate
Ⓑ **exasperarse** VPR to get exasperated, lose patience

Exc.ª ABR = **Excelencia**

excarcelación SF release (*from prison*)

excarcelado/a SM/F ex-prisoner, former prisoner

excarcelar ▸conjug 1a◂ VT to release (*from prison*)

excavación SF [1] (= *acto*) excavation
[2] (= *lugar*) excavation, dig

excavador(a) SM/F (= *persona*) excavator, digger

excavadora SF (= *máquina*) digger

excavar ▸conjug 1a◂ VT [1] (*Constr*) to dig, dig out, excavate (*frm*); **excava su madriguera en la tierra** it digs its hole in the earth
[2] (*Arqueología*) to excavate

excedencia SF leave of absence; **pedir la ~** to ask for leave of absence ▸ **excedencia por maternidad** maternity leave ▸ **excedencia primada** voluntary severance ▸ **excedencia voluntaria** unpaid leave

excedentario ADJ surplus *antes de s*; **países ~s** surplus-producing countries

excedente Ⓐ ADJ [*producción*] excess, surplus; [*trabajador*] redundant
Ⓑ SM excess, surplus ▸ **excedente empresarial** profit margin ▸ **excedente laboral** surplus of labour, surplus of labor (*EEUU*), overmanning
Ⓒ SMF person on leave of absence ▸ **excedente forzoso/a** person on compulsory leave of absence

exceder ▸conjug 2a◂ Ⓐ VT [1] (= *superar*) to exceed, surpass; **los beneficios han excedido el millón de euros** profits are in excess of *o* have exceeded a million euros
[2] (= *sobrepasar*) to surpass; **las imágenes excedían cualquier cosa que pudieras imaginar** the pictures surpassed *o* were beyond anything you could imagine
[3] (*en importancia*) to transcend
Ⓑ VI **~ de algo** to exceed sth; **no puede ~ de diez páginas** it cannot exceed ten pages, it cannot be longer than ten pages
Ⓒ **excederse** VPR [1] (= *sobrepasarse*) to excel o.s.
[2] (= *exagerar*) **no te excedas con la bebida** don't overdo it with the drink; **~se en sus funciones** to exceed one's duty

excelencia SF [1] (= *cualidad*) excellence; **por ~** par excellence
[2] (= *fórmula de tratamiento*) **su Excelencia** his Excellency; **sí, Excelencia** yes, your Excellency

excelente ADJ excellent

excelentemente ADV excellently

excelso ADJ lofty, exalted, sublime

excentricidad SF eccentricity

excéntrico/a ADJ, SM/F eccentric

excepción SF exception; **asistieron todos los invitados sin ~** all the guests came without exception; **un libro de ~** an exceptional book; **hacer una ~** to make an exception; **a** *o* **con ~ de** with the exception of, except for; **la ~ confirma la regla** the exception proves the rule

excepcional ADJ [1] (= *anómalo*) [*medidas, circunstancias*] exceptional; **un caso ~** an exceptional case; **aquí las nevadas son ~es** you rarely get any snow here; **de ~ importancia** exceptionally important
[2] (= *muy bueno*) exceptional; **ha obtenido unos resultados ~es** she has achieved exceptional results

excepcionalidad SF exceptional nature

excepcionalmente ADV [1] (= *excelentemente*) exceptionally
[2] (= *como excepción*) as an exception

excepto PREP except, except for; **todos, ~ Juan** everyone, except (for) *o* apart from Juan; **voy cada día, ~ los martes** I go every day, except Tuesdays; **se lo perdono todo, ~ que me mienta** I'll forgive him anything, except lying to me

exceptuar ▸conjug 1e◂ VT [1] (= *excluir*) to except, exclude; **exceptuando a uno de ellos** except for *o* with the exception of (*más frm*) one of them
[2] (*Jur*) to exempt

excesivamente ADV excessively

excesivo ADJ excessive; **con generosidad excesiva** overgenerously

exceso SM [1] (= *demasía*) excess; **en** *o* **por ~** excessively, to excess ▸ **exceso de equipaje** excess luggage, excess baggage (*EEUU*) ▸ **exceso de mano de obra** = **exceso de plantilla** ▸ **exceso de peso** excess weight ▸ **exceso de plantilla** overmanning, overstaffing ▸ **exceso de velocidad** speeding, exceeding the speed limit
[2] (*Com, Fin*) surplus
[3] **excesos** (= *abusos*) (*al beber, comportarse*) excesses; **los ~s de la revolución** the excesses of the revolution; **los ~s cometidos en su juventud** the overindulgences *o* excesses of his youth; **cometer ~s con el alcohol** to drink excessively, drink to excess, overindulge in drink

excipiente SM (*Farm*) excipient

excisión SF (*Med*) excision

excitabilidad SF excitability

excitable ADJ excitable

excitación SF [1] (*Med*) excitation (*frm*); **el café me produce ~** coffee makes me nervy ▸ **excitación sexual** sexual arousal
[2] (*Elec*) excitation
[3] (= *emoción*) excitement

excitante Ⓐ ADJ [1] (*Med*) stimulating
[2] (= *emocionante*) exciting
Ⓑ SM stimulant

excitar ▸conjug 1a◂ Ⓐ VT [1] (= *intranquilizar*) to get worked up, get excited; **no veas el partido porque te excita mucho** don't watch the game, it'll get you worked up *o* excited; **el café me excita** coffee makes me hyper*
[2] (= *entusiasmar*) to make excited; **la buena noticia lo excitó tanto que ya no pudo dormir** the good news made him so excited he couldn't get to sleep
[3] (= *provocar*) [+ *curiosidad*] to arouse, excite; [+ *sentimiento*] to arouse, provoke; [+ *apetito*] to stimulate
[4] (*sexualmente*) to arouse, excite
[5] (*Biol, Elec, Fís*) to excite
[6] (†) (= *incitar*) to rouse, incite; **~ al pueblo a la rebelión** to rouse the populace to rebellion
Ⓑ **excitarse** VPR [1] (= *intranquilizarse*) to get worked up; **no te excites por esa tontería** don't get worked up about such nonsense
[2] (= *entusiasmarse*) to get excited; **se excitó mucho cuando su equipo marcó el gol** she got very excited when her team scored
[3] (*sexualmente*) to get aroused, get excited

exclamación SF [1] (*Ling*) exclamation
[2] (= *grito*) cry

exclamar ▸conjug 1a◂ VT, VI to exclaim, cry out

exclamativo ADJ, **exclamatorio** ADJ exclamatory

exclaustración SF (*Rel*) [*de seglar*] secularization; [*de monje, monja*] expulsion

exclaustrado/a (*Rel*) Ⓐ ADJ [1] (= *secularizado*) secularized
[2] (= *expulsado*) expelled (*from the order*)
Ⓑ SM/F [1] (= *secularizado*) secularized monk/nun
[2] (= *expulsado*) expelled monk/nun

excluido(a) SM/F (*tb* **~ social**) socially-excluded person; **los ~s sociales** the socially-excluded; **me siento un ~** I feel a social outcast

▼**excluir** ▸conjug 3g◂ VT [1] (= *de grupo, herencia*) to exclude (**de** from); **lo han excluido del equipo** he's been dropped from *o* excluded from *o* left out of the team
[2] (= *eliminar*) [+ *solución*] to reject; [+ *posibilidad*] to rule out

exclusión SF exclusion; **con ~ de** excluding

exclusiva SF [1] (*Com*) sole right, sole agency; **tener la ~ de un producto** to be sole agent *o* the sole agents for a product; **no te creas que vas a tener la ~ de coger al niño** don't think you're going to have an exclusive right to *o* exclusive control of the baby; **venta en ~** exclusive sale
[2] (*Periodismo*) exclusive story, exclusive, scoop; **reportaje en ~** exclusive story, exclusive

exclusivamente ADV exclusively

exclusive ADV exclusively; **hasta el uno de enero ~** till the first of January exclusive

exclusividad SF [1] (= *cualidad*) exclusiveness
[2] (*Com*) exclusive rights *pl*, sole rights *pl*

exclusivista ADJ [*club*] exclusive, select; [*grupo*] clannish; [*actitud*] snobbish

exclusivo ADJ [1] (= *único*) sole; **derecho ~** sole right, exclusive right
[2] (= *selecto*) exclusive

➤ LENGUA Y USO: **examinar A3** 53.1, 53.2, 53.4 **excluir 1** 53.4

excluyente ADJ (*LAm*) [*clase, club*] exclusive

excluyentemente ADV exclusively

Excma. ABR = **Excelentísima**

Excmo. ABR = **Excelentísimo**

excombatiente SMF ex-serviceman/servicewoman, veteran

excomulgado/a Ⓐ ADJ [1] (*Rel*) excommunicated
[2] (*) (= *maldito*) blessed*, cursed
Ⓑ SM/F excommunicated person

excomulgar ▸conjug 1h◂ VT to excommunicate

excomunión SF excommunication

excoriación SF [1] (= *desolladura*) graze
[2] (= *rozadura*) chafing

excoriar ▸conjug 1b◂ Ⓐ VT [1] (= *desollar*) to graze
[2] (= *rozar*) to chafe
Ⓑ **excoriarse** VPR to graze o.s.

excrecencia SF excrescence

excreción SF excretion

excremento SM excrement

excretar ▸conjug 1a◂ VT to excrete

exculpación SF [1] [*de obligación*] exoneration
[2] (*Jur*) acquittal

exculpar ▸conjug 1a◂ Ⓐ VT [1] (*de obligación*) to exonerate
[2] (*Jur*) to exonerate (**de** of)
Ⓑ **exculparse** VPR to exonerate o.s.

exculpatorio ADJ **declaración exculpatoria** statement of innocence

excursión SF [1] (*al campo*) excursion, trip, outing; **ir de ~** to go on a trip *o* an excursion *o* an outing ► **excursión a pie** hike ► **excursión campestre** picnic ► **excursión de caza** hunting trip
[2] (= *viaje*) trip, excursion; **una ~ a las Alpujarras** a trip *o* an excursion to the Alpujarras
[3] (*Mil*) raid

excursionar ▸conjug 1a◂ VI to go on a trip, go on an outing

excursionismo SM [1] (*por el campo*) hiking
[2] (= *ir de viaje*) going on trips

excursionista SMF [1] (*por campo, montaña*) hiker
[2] (*en un viaje*) tripper

excurso SM, **excursus** SM INV excursus

▼ **excusa** SF excuse; **buscar una ~** to look for an excuse; **presentar sus ~s** to make one's excuses, excuse o.s.

excusabaraja SF hamper, basket with a lid

excusable ADJ excusable, pardonable

excusado Ⓐ ADJ [1] (= *innecesario*) unnecessary; **~ es decir que …** needless to say …; **pensar en lo ~** to think of something which is quite out of the question
[2] **estar ~ de algo** to be exempt from sth
Ⓑ SM (†) lavatory, comfort station (*EEUU*), toilet

excusar ▸conjug 1a◂ Ⓐ VT [1] (= *disculpar*) to excuse; **excúsame con los otros** apologize to the others for me
[2] (= *evitar*) [+ *disgustos*] to avoid, prevent; **así excusamos disgustos** this way we avoid difficulties; **podemos ~ lo otro** we can forget about the rest of it, we don't have to bother with the rest; **excusamos decirle que …** we don't have to tell you that …; **por eso excuso escribirte más largo** so I can save myself the trouble of writing at greater length
[3] (= *eximir*) to exempt (**de** from)
Ⓑ **excusarse** VPR (= *disculparse*) to apologize (**con** to); **~se de haber hecho algo** to apologize for having done sth

execrable ADJ execrable

execración SF execration

execrar ▸conjug 1a◂ VT to loathe

exégesis SF INV exegesis

exención SF exemption (**de** from); ► **exención contributiva**, **exención de impuestos** tax exemption, tax allowance

exencionar ▸conjug 1a◂ VT = **exentar**

exentar ▸conjug 1a◂ VT [1] (= *eximir*) to exempt (**de** from)
[2] (= *disculpar*) to excuse (**de** from)

exento ADJ [1] (= *libre*) exempt (**de** from), free (**de** from, of); **~ del servicio militar** exempt from military service; **~ de derechos** duty free; **~ de impuestos** tax free; **un libro ~ de interés** a book devoid of interest; **una expedición no exenta de peligros** an expedition not without its dangers
[2] [*lugar*] unobstructed, open
[3] (*Arquit*) free-standing

exequias SFPL (*frm*) funeral rites, exequies (*frm*)

exfoliación SF (*Cos*) exfoliation (*frm*)

exfoliador SM (*Cono Sur*) tear-off pad, loose-leaf notebook

exfoliante SM exfoliant

exfoliar ▸conjug 1b◂ VT to exfoliate

exhalación SF [1] [*de suspiro, gemido*] exhalation
[2] (*Astron*) shooting star; ✦***MODISMO* pasar como una ~** to flash past

exhalar ▸conjug 1a◂ Ⓐ VT [1] (= *arrojar*) [+ *aire*] to exhale; [+ *gas*] to emit, give off
[2] [*persona*] [+ *suspiro*] to breathe; [+ *gemido*] to utter; ✦***MODISMO* ~ el último suspiro** (*euf*) to give up one's last breath, breathe one's last
Ⓑ **exhalarse** VPR to hurry

exhaustivamente ADV exhaustively, thoroughly

exhaustividad SF exhaustiveness, thoroughness

exhaustivo ADJ exhaustive, thorough

exhausto ADJ exhausted

exheredar ▸conjug 1a◂ VT to disinherit

exhibición SF [1] (= *demostración*) show, display; **una impresionante ~ de fuerza** an impressive show of strength; **hay varias esculturas en ~** there are various sculptures on show *o* on display; **no le gusta hacer ~ de sus sentimientos** he doesn't like to show his feelings ► **exhibición aérea** flying display ► **exhibición de escaparate** window display ► **exhibición folklórica** folk festival, display of folk-dancing *etc*
[2] (*Cine*) showing
[3] (*Dep*) exhibition, display; **partido de ~** exhibition match; **una ~ de judo** a judo exhibition *o* display
[4] (*Méx Com*) payment of an instalment *o* (*EEUU*) installment

exhibicionismo SM [1] (= *deseo de exhibirse*) exhibitionism; **no me gusta cómo viste, es puro ~** I don't like the way he dresses, it's pure exhibitionism; **no me gusta la gente que hace tanto ~ de sus conocimientos** I don't like people who are always making a great show of their knowledge *o* who are always showing off how much they know
[2] (*sexual*) exhibitionism (*frm*), indecent exposure

exhibicionista Ⓐ ADJ, SMF exhibitionist
Ⓑ SM (*sexual*) flasher*, exhibitionist (*frm*)

exhibidor SM display case

exhibir ▸conjug 3a◂ Ⓐ VT [1] (= *mostrar*) [+ *cuadros*] to exhibit, put on show; [+ *artículos*] to display; [+ *pasaporte*] to show; [+ *película*] to screen; **los diseños exhibidos en la exposición** the designs on show *o* on display *o* exhibited in the exhibition
[2] (= *mostrar con orgullo*) to show off
[3] (*Méx*) [+ *cantidad*] to pay in cash
Ⓑ **exhibirse** VPR [1] (= *mostrarse en público*) to show o.s. off
[2] (*indecentemente*) to expose o.s.

exhortación SF exhortation

exhortar ▸conjug 1a◂ VT to exhort; **~ a algn a hacer algo** to exhort sb to do sth

exhumación SF exhumation, disinterment

exhumar ▸conjug 1a◂ VT to exhume, disinter

exigencia SF [1] (= *requerimiento*) demand, requirement, exigency (*frm*); **según las ~s de la situación** as the situation requires *o* demands, according to the exigencies of the situation (*frm*); **tener muchas ~s** to be very demanding
[2] (*Caribe*) (= *petición*) request
[3] (*CAm*) (= *escasez*) need, lack

exigente ADJ [*persona, trabajo*] demanding, exacting; **ser ~ con algn** to be demanding *o* exacting of sb, be hard on sb; **es muy ~ con la limpieza** she is very particular about cleanliness

exigir ▸conjug 3c◂ VT [1] [*persona*] (*gen*) to demand; [+ *dimisión*] to demand, call for; **exijo una compensación** I demand compensation; **exigió hablar con el encargado** he demanded to speak to the manager; **exigen al gobierno una bajada de los impuestos** they're demanding that the government lowers taxes; **la maestra nos exige demasiado** our teacher is too demanding, our teacher asks too much of us; **exigen tres años de experiencia** they're asking for *o* they require three years' experience; **exija que le den un recibo** insist on getting a receipt; **~ responsabilidades a algn** to call sb to account
[2] [*situación, trabajo*] to demand, require, call for; **ese puesto exige mucha paciencia** this job demands *o* requires *o* calls for a lot of patience; **el conflicto exige una pronta solución** the conflict requires *o* calls for a quick solution
[3] (*Ven*) (= *demandar*) **~ algo** to ask for sth, request sth; **~ a algn** to beg sb, plead with sb
[4] (†) [+ *impuestos*] to exact, levy (**a** from)

exiguo ADJ [1] [*cantidad*] meagre, meager (*EEUU*)
[2] [*objeto*] (= *pequeño*) tiny

exilado/a ADJ, SM/F = **exiliado**

exilar ▸conjug 1a◂ VT = **exiliar**

exiliado/a Ⓐ ADJ exiled, in exile
Ⓑ SM/F exile

exiliar ▸conjug 1b◂ Ⓐ VT to exile
Ⓑ **exiliarse** VPR to go into exile

exilio SM exile; **estar/vivir en el ~** to be/live in exile; **gobierno en el ~** government in exile

eximente SF grounds for exemption *pl*

eximio ADJ [*persona*] distinguished

➤ LENGUA Y USO: **excusa** 45.2

eximir ▸conjug 3a◂ Ⓐ VT [1] (*de impuestos, servicio militar*) to exempt (**de** from)
[2] (*de obligación*) to free (**de** from); **esto me exime de toda obligación con él** this frees me from any obligation to him
Ⓑ **eximirse** VPR to free o.s.; **~se de hacer algo** to free o.s. from doing sth

existencia SF [1] [*de ser humano, animal*] existence; **desconocía la ~ de ese documento** I was unaware of the existence of that document; **lucha por la ~** struggle for survival; **amargar la ~ a algn** to make sb's life a misery; **quitarse la ~** (*euf*) to do away with o.s., commit suicide
[2] **existencias** (*Com*) stock *sing*; **nuestras ~s de carbón** our coal stocks; **liquidar ~s** to clear stock; **renovar ~s** to restock; **hasta que se acaben las ~s** while stocks last; **sin ~s** out of stock; **tener algo en ~s** to have sth in stock ► **existencias de mercancías** stock-in-trade

existencial ADJ existential

existencialismo SM existentialism

existencialista ADJ, SMF existentialist

existencialmente ADV existentially

existente ADJ [1] (= *que existe*) existing, in existence; **la situación ~ en este momento** the existing *o* present situation, the situation at the moment; **el único documento ~ de la época** the only existing document of *o* from that period
[2] (*Com*) in stock

existir ▸conjug 3a◂ VI [1] (= *ser*) to exist; **esta empresa existe desde hace 90 años** the company has been in existence for 90 years; **no existe tal cosa** there's no such thing
[2] (= *vivir*) to live; **mientras yo exista** as long as I live *o* I'm alive; **dejar de ~** (*euf*) to pass away (*euf*)

exitazo SM [1] (= *gran éxito*) great success
[2] (*Mús, Teat*) smash hit

éxito SM [1] (= *buen resultado*) success; **la operación resultó con ~** the operation was successful *o* was a success; **la tarta que trajiste fue un gran ~** the cake you brought was a great success; **tiene mucho ~ entre los hombres** she's very successful with men, she has a great deal of success with men; **es un hombre de ~** he's a successful man; **tener ~ en algo** to be successful in sth, make a success of sth; **no tener ~** to be unsuccessful, not succeed
[2] (*Mús, Teat*) success, hit; **un ~ rotundo** (*gen*) a resounding success; (*Mús*) a smash hit; **grandes ~s** greatest hits ► **éxito de librería** best seller ► **éxito de taquilla** box-office success ► **éxito de ventas** best seller ► **éxito editorial** best seller
[3] (†) (= *resultado*) result, outcome; **buen ~** happy outcome, success; **con buen ~** successfully; **tener buen ~** to succeed, be successful, have a happy outcome; **tener mal ~** to have an unfortunate outcome, fail, be unsuccessful

exitosamente ADV successfully

exitoso ADJ (*esp LAm*) successful

éxodo SM exodus; **el ~ rural** the drift from the land, the rural exodus; **Éxodo** (*Rel*) Exodus

ex oficio ADJ, ADV ex officio

exoneración SF [1] (= *libramiento*) exoneration
[2] (= *despido*) dismissal

exonerar ▸conjug 1a◂ VT [1] (*de culpa, responsabilidad*) to exonerate (*frm*); (*de un impuesto*) to exempt; **~ a algn de un deber** to free sb from a duty, relieve sb of a duty
[2] [+ *empleado*] to dismiss; **le ~on de sus condecoraciones** they stripped him of his decorations
[3] **~ el vientre** to have a bowel movement

exorbitancia SF exorbitance

exorbitante ADJ exorbitant

exorcismo SM exorcism

exorcista Ⓐ ADJ **prácticas ~s** rites designed to secure exorcism
Ⓑ SMF exorcist

exorcizar ▸conjug 1f◂ VT to exorcise

exordio SM preamble, exordium (*frm*)

exornar ▸conjug 1a◂ VT to adorn, embellish (**de** with)

exosto SM (*LAm Aut*) exhaust

exótica* SF (*Méx*) (= *mujer*) stripper*, striptease artist

exótico ADJ exotic

exotismo SM exoticism

expandible ADJ expansible

expandir ▸conjug 3a◂ Ⓐ VT [1] (= *extender*) (*gen*) to expand; (*Anat*) to expand; (*Com*) to expand, enlarge
[2] [+ *noticia*] to spread; **~ el mercado de un producto** to expand the market for a product; **~ la afición a la lectura** to spread a love of reading
[3] (*Tip, Inform*) **en caracteres expandidos** double width
Ⓑ **expandirse** VPR [1] [*gas, metal*] to expand
[2] (= *extenderse*) [*empresa*] to expand; [*idioma, cultura, noticia*] to spread

expansible ADJ expansible

expansión SF [1] (= *difusión*) [*de empresa, mercado*] expansion; [*de noticia, ideas*] spread; **la ~ económica** economic growth *o* expansion
[2] (= *recreo*) relaxation; (= *placer*) pleasure
[3] (= *efusión*) expansiveness

expansionar ▸conjug 1a◂ Ⓐ VT [+ *mercado*] to expand
Ⓑ **expansionarse** VPR [1] (= *dilatarse*) to expand
[2] (= *relajarse*) to relax
[3] (= *desahogarse*) to unbosom o.s., open one's heart (**con** to)

expansionismo SM expansionism

expansionista ADJ expansionist

expansividad SF expansiveness

expansivo ADJ [1] [*gas*] expansive; **onda expansiva** shock wave
[2] (*Econ*) **una fase/política expansiva** a phase/policy of expansion
[3] [*persona*] expansive

expatriación SF [1] (= *emigración*) expatriation
[2] (= *exilio*) exile

expatriado/a SM/F [1] (= *emigrado*) expatriate
[2] (= *exilado*) exile

expatriarse ▸conjug 1b◂ VPR [1] (= *emigrar*) to emigrate
[2] (= *exiliarse*) to go into exile

expectación SF (= *esperanza*) expectation; (= *ilusión*) excitement; (= *ansia*) eagerness; **crece la ~** excitement is growing, there is mounting excitement

expectante ADJ (= *esperanzador*) expectant; (= *ansioso*) eager; (= *ilusionado*) excited

expectativa SF [1] (= *esperanza*) expectation; **el resultado superó nuestras ~s** the result surpassed our expectations; **no tiene ~s de que le den el empleo** he isn't expecting to get the job ► **expectativa de vida** life expectancy
[2] (= *espera*) **estar a la ~ de algo** to be waiting for sth; **estaban a la ~ de una respuesta** they were waiting for a reply; **estamos a la ~ de conocer los resultados electorales** we are waiting to hear the election results

expectorar ▸conjug 1a◂ VT, VI to expectorate

expedición SF [1] [*de personas*] (*Geog, Mil*) expedition; (*Dep*) away fixture ► **expedición de salvamento** rescue expedition ► **expedición militar** military expedition
[2] (*Com*) shipment, shipping; **gastos de ~** shipping charges
[3] (= *prontitud*) speed, dispatch (*frm*)

expedicionario/a Ⓐ ADJ expeditionary
Ⓑ SM/F member of an expedition

expedidor SM shipping agent, shipper

expedientar ▸conjug 1a◂ VT [1] (= *investigar*) (*gen*) to make a file on, draw up a dossier on; (*Jur*) to start proceedings against
[2] (= *censurar*) to censure, reprimand
[3] (= *expulsar*) to expel
[4] (= *despedir*) (*gen*) to dismiss; [+ *médico*] to strike off the register

expediente SM [1] (= *documento*) (*como historial*) record; (*como dossier*) dossier; (*en forma de ficha*) file; **alumnos con buen/mal ~** pupils with a good/poor track record; ✦*MODISMO* **cubrir el ~** to do the minimum required; **lo haré por cubrir el ~** I'll do it to keep up appearances ► **expediente académico** (*Escol*) student's record, transcript (*EEUU*) ► **expediente policial** police dossier
[2] (*Jur*) (= *acción*) action, proceedings *pl*; (= *papeles*) records of a case *pl*; **abrir** *o* **incoar ~** to start proceedings ► **expediente de regulación de empleo** labour *o* (*EEUU*) labor force adjustment plan ► **expediente disciplinario** disciplinary proceedings *pl* ► **expediente judicial** legal proceedings *pl*
[3] (= *medio*) expedient, means; **recurrir al ~ de hacer algo** to resort to the device of doing sth

expedienteo SM bureaucracy, red tape

expedir ▸conjug 3k◂ VT [+ *mercancías*] to send, ship off; [+ *documento*] to draw up; [+ *orden, billete*] to issue; [+ *negocio*] to deal with, dispatch

expeditar ▸conjug 1a◂ VT (*CAm, Méx*) (= *acelerar*) to expedite (*frm*), hurry along; (= *concluir*) to conclude

expeditivo ADJ expeditious (*frm*), prompt, efficient

expedito ADJ [1] (= *pronto*) expeditious (*frm*), prompt, speedy
[2] [*camino*] clear, free; **dejar ~ el camino para** to clear the way for
[3] (*LAm*) (= *fácil*) easy

expeler ▸conjug 2a◂ VT to expel, eject

expendedor(a) Ⓐ ADJ **máquina ~a** vending machine
Ⓑ SM/F (= *persona*) (*al detalle*) dealer, retailer; (*como intermediario*) agent; (*de tabaco*) tobacconist, tobacco dealer (*EEUU*); (*de lotería*) lottery-ticket seller; (*Teat*) ticket agent

► **expendedor(a) de billetes** ticket clerk, booking clerk ► **expendedor(a) de moneda falsa** distributor of counterfeit money
Ⓒ SM ► **expendedor automático** vending machine ► **expendedor automático de bebidas** drinks (vending) machine

expendeduría SF [*de tabaco*] tobacconist's (shop), cigar store (*EEUU*); [*de lotería*] lottery outlet

expender ▸conjug 2a◂ VT [1] [+ *dinero*] to expend (*frm*), spend
[2] [+ *moneda falsa*] (= *emitir*) to put into circulation; (= *hacer circular*) to pass, circulate
[3] [+ *mercancías*] (= *vender*) to sell, retail; (= *traficar*) to deal in; (= *ser agente de*) to be an agent for, sell on commission

expendio SM [1] (= *gasto*) expense, outlay
[2] (*LAm*) (= *tienda*) small shop ► **expendio de boletos** (*Méx*) ticket office
[3] (*Andes, Cono Sur, Méx*) (= *venta*) retailing, retail selling
[4] ► **expendio de moneda falsa** (*Jur*) issuing false coin, passing false coin

expensar ▸conjug 1a◂ VT (*LAm*) to defray the costs of

expensas SFPL **a ~ de** at the expense of; **a mis ~** at my expense

▼**experiencia** SF [1] (= *acontecimientos*) experience; **una triste ~** a sad experience; **saber por ~** to know by *o* from experience; **aprender por la ~** to learn by experience; **intercambiar ~s** to swap stories ► **experiencia laboral** work experience
[2] (= *experimento*) experiment (**en** on); ► **experiencia clínica** clinical trial ► **experiencia piloto** pilot scheme

experienciar ▸conjug 1b◂ VT = **experimentar**

experimentación SF experimentation

experimentado ADJ experienced

experimental ADJ experimental

experimentalmente ADV experimentally

experimentar ▸conjug 1a◂ Ⓐ VT [1] [+ *método, producto*] to test, try out; **el nuevo fármaco está siendo experimentado** the new drug is being tested
[2] (= *notar*) [+ *cambio*] to experience, go through; [+ *pérdida, deterioro*] to suffer; [+ *aumento*] to show; [+ *sensación*] to feel; **las cifras han experimentado un aumento de un 5 por 100** the figures show an increase of 5%; **no experimenté ninguna sensación nueva** I felt no new sensation; **el enfermo ha experimentado una ligera mejoría** the patient has improved slightly
Ⓑ VI to experiment (**con** with; **en** on)

experimento SM experiment (**con** with; **en** on); **como ~** as an experiment, by way of experiment; **hacer ~s** to experiment (**con** with; **en** on)

experticia SF (*LAm*) expertise

expertización SF expert assessment

expertizar ▸conjug 1f◂ VT to appraise as an expert, give an expert assessment of

experto/a Ⓐ ADJ expert; **es experta en la materia** she's an expert on the subject; **ser ~ en hacer algo** to be an expert at doing sth; **son ~s en restaurar muebles** they are experts at restoring furniture; **eres ~ en meterte en líos** you're an expert at getting into trouble
Ⓑ SM/F expert; **se dejó asesorar por un ~** he sought the advice of an expert, he sought expert advice; **ser un ~ en algo** to be an expert on *o* in sth ► **experto/a contable** auditor, chartered accountant ► **experto/a tributario/a** tax expert

expiación SF expiation (*frm*), atonement

expiar ▸conjug 1c◂ VT to expiate (*frm*), atone for

expiatorio ADJ expiatory

expiración SF expiry, expiration

expirar ▸conjug 1a◂ VI to expire

explanación SF [1] (*Téc*) levelling
[2] (†) (= *explicación*) explanation, elucidation

explanada SF area of level ground ► **explanada de ensillado** saddling enclosure

explanar ▸conjug 1a◂ VT [1] (*Ferro, Téc*) to level, grade
[2] (†) (= *explicar*) to explain, elucidate

explayar ▸conjug 1a◂ Ⓐ VT to extend, expand
Ⓑ **explayarse** VPR [1] (= *esparcirse*) (*gen*) to relax, take it easy; (*en discurso*) to speak at length; **~se a su gusto** to talk one's head off*, talk to one's heart's content; **~se con algn** to confide in sb
[2] (= *extenderse*) to extend, spread

explicable ADJ explicable, explainable; **cosas no fácilmente ~s** things not easily explained, things not easy to explain

explicación SF [1] [*de tema, motivo*] explanation
[2] (= *motivo*) reason (**de** for); **sin dar explicaciones** without giving any reason
[3] (*Univ*) lecture, class

explicaderas SFPL **tener buenas ~** to be good at explaining things (away); (*pey*) to be plausible

explicar ▸conjug 1g◂ Ⓐ VT [1] (= *exponer*) [+ *motivo, tema, cuestión, problema*] to explain; [+ *teoría*] to expound
[2] (*Escol*) [+ *materia*] to lecture in; [+ *curso*] to teach; [+ *clase*] to give, deliver (*frm*)
Ⓑ **explicarse** VPR [1] (*al exponer algo*) to explain, explain o.s.; **¡explíquese usted!** explain yourself!; **explíquese con la mayor brevedad** please be as brief as possible; **se explica con claridad** he states things *o* expresses himself clearly; **esto no se explica fácilmente** this cannot be explained (away) easily, this isn't easy to explain
[2] (*al entender algo*) **no me lo explico** I can't understand it, I can't make it out
[3] (*) (= *pagar*) to cough up*, pay

explicativo ADJ, **explicatorio** ADJ explanatory

explícitamente ADV explicitly

explicitar ▸conjug 1a◂ VT (= *declarar*) to state, assert; (= *aclarar*) to clarify; **~ que ...** to make clear that ...

explícito ADJ explicit

exploración SF [1] [*de terreno, parte del cuerpo*] exploration; (*Mil*) reconnaissance, scouting; (*con radar*) scanning ► **exploración submarina** underwater exploration; (*como deporte*) skin-diving
[2] (*Med*) ► **exploración física** physical examination

explorador(a) Ⓐ SM/F (*Geog*) explorer; (*Mil*) scout
Ⓑ SM [1] (*Med*) probe
[2] (*Radar*) scanner ► **explorador láser** laser scanner
Ⓒ SM/F (boy) scout/(girl) guide *o* (*EEUU*) scout

> **EXPLICAR**
>
> • Cuando **explicar** lleva objeto directo e indirecto, el orden en inglés es normalmente **explain** + **OBJETO DIRECTO** + **to** + **OBJETO INDIRECTO**:
>
> ¿Puedes explicarme eso?
> ***Can you explain that to me?***
> Ya se lo he explicado a mi familia
> ***I've already explained it to my family***
> Os explicaré la situación
> ***I will explain the situation to you***
>
> • Sin embargo, si el objeto directo es una construcción más compleja, en inglés se sigue el mismo orden que en español, sin olvidar el uso de la preposición **to**:
>
> ¿Puedes explicarme por qué no viniste ni llamaste ayer?
> ***Can you explain to me why you didn't come or phone yesterday?***
>
> *Para otros usos y ejemplos ver la entrada.*

explorar ▸conjug 1a◂ Ⓐ VT (*Geog*) to explore; (*Mil*) to reconnoitre; (*Med*) to probe; (*Radar*) to scan
Ⓑ VI to explore; (*Mil*) to reconnoitre, scout

exploratorio ADJ exploratory

explosión SF [1] [*de bomba*] explosion; **15 personas murieron a consecuencia de la ~** 15 people died in the explosion *o* blast; **hacer ~** to explode; **motor de ~** internal combustion engine; **teoría de la gran ~** big bang theory ► **explosión controlada** controlled explosion ► **explosión por simpatía** secondary explosion
[2] [*de cólera*] outburst, explosion
[3] (= *expansión*) explosion ► **explosión demográfica** population explosion

explosionar ▸conjug 1a◂ VT, VI to explode, blow up

explosiva SF (*Ling*) plosive, plosive consonant

explosivo Ⓐ ADJ explosive
Ⓑ SM explosive ► **explosivo de gran potencia, explosivo de ruido** stun grenade ► **explosivo detonante** powerful explosive ► **explosivo plástico** plastic explosive

explotable ADJ exploitable, that can be exploited

explotación SF [1] (= *uso*) [*de recursos, riquezas*] exploitation; [*de planta*] running, operation; [*de mina*] working; **en ~** in operation; **gastos de ~** operating costs, operating expenses ► **explotación a cielo abierto** opencast working, opencast mining, strip mining (*EEUU*) ► **explotación agrícola** farm ► **explotación forestal** forestry ► **explotación ganadera** livestock farm ► **explotación minera** mine ► **explotación petrolífera** oil exploration
[2] (= *uso excesivo*) exploitation

explotador(a) Ⓐ ADJ exploitative
Ⓑ SM/F exploiter

explotar ▸conjug 1a◂ Ⓐ VT [1] (= *usar*) [+ *recursos, riquezas*] to exploit; [+ *planta*] to run, operate; [+ *mina*] to work
[2] (= *usar excesivamente*) [+ *obreros*] to exploit; [+ *situación*] to exploit, make capital out of
[3] [+ *bomba*] to explode
Ⓑ VI [*bomba*] to explode, go off; **~on dos bombas** two bombs exploded *o* went off; **ca-**

➤ LENGUA Y USO: experiencia 1 46.2

yó sin ~ it fell but did not go off, it landed without going off; **juegan con bombas sin ~** they play with unexploded bombs

expoliación SF pillaging, sacking

expoliar ▸conjug 1b◂ VT [1] (= *saquear*) to pillage, sack
[2] (= *desposeer*) to dispossess

expolio SM [1] (= *saqueo*) pillaging, sacking
[2] ✦*MODISMO* **armar un ~** to cause a hullaballoo*

exponencial ADJ exponential

exponente Ⓐ SMF (= *persona*) exponent
Ⓑ SM [1] (*Mat*) index, exponent
[2] (= *ejemplo*) model, prime example; **el tabaco cubano es ~ de calidad** Cuban tobacco is the best of its kind

exponer ▸conjug 2q◂ (*pp* **expuesto**) Ⓐ VT [1] (*al público*) [1·1] (*Arte*) [*museo*] to exhibit, put on show; [*galería, artista*] to show
[1·2] (*Com*) (*en tienda*) to display; (*en feria*) to exhibit
[2] (*a la luz, al agua*) **no debe ~ la cicatriz al sol** he must not expose the scar to the sun
[3] (= *explicar*) [+ *teoría, argumento*] to set out, expound (*frm*); [+ *hechos*] to set out, state; [+ *situación*] to set out
[4] (= *arriesgar*) to risk, put at risk; **expuso su vida por salvarla** he risked his life to save her, he put his life at risk to save her
[5] (*Fot*) to expose
[6] (*Rel*) **~ el Santísimo** to expose the Holy Sacrament
[7] (††) [+ *niño*] to abandon
Ⓑ VI [*pintor, escultor*] to exhibit, show
Ⓒ **exponerse** VPR [1] (= *someterse*) **~se a algo** to expose o.s. to sth; **con ese comentario se expone a las críticas de los periodistas** with that comment she's laying herself open to *o* exposing herself to criticism from the reporters; **le gusta ~se al peligro** she likes exposing herself to danger; **no se exponga al sol durante mucho tiempo** don't go out in the sun for a long time, don't expose yourself to the sun for a long time
[2] (= *arriesgarse*) **~se a hacer algo** to risk doing sth, run the risk of doing sth; **te expones a hacer el ridículo** you're risking making a fool of yourself, you're running the risk of making a fool of yourself; **con eso te expones a que te echen del colegio** that way you're running the risk of being expelled from school

exportable ADJ exportable

exportación SF [1] (= *acto*) export, exportation ► **exportación en pie** live export
[2] (= *artículo*) export, exported article; (= *mercancías*) exports *pl*; **géneros de ~** exports, exported goods; **comercio de ~** export trade

exportador(a) Ⓐ ADJ [*país*] exporting
Ⓑ SM/F exporter

exportar ▸conjug 1a◂ VT to export

exposición SF [1] (= *muestra*) (*Arte*) exhibition; (*Com*) show, fair ► **exposición canina** dog show ► **exposición de modas** fashion show ► **exposición estática** static display ► **exposición itinerante** travelling show, traveling show (*EEUU*) ► **exposición universal** world fair
[2] (= *acto*) (*gen*) exposing, exposure; (*Fot*) exposure; (*Com*) display
[3] (= *enunciado*) [*de hechos*] statement; [*de teoría*] exposition ► **exposición de motivos** (*Jur*) explanatory preamble

exposímetro SM (*Fot*) exposure meter

expósito/a Ⓐ ADJ *ver* **niño B1**
Ⓑ SM/F foundling

expositor(a) Ⓐ SM/F (*Arte*) exhibitor; [*de teoría*] exponent
Ⓑ SM (= *vitrina*) showcase, display case; (= *puesto*) sales stand

exprés Ⓐ ADJ **café ~** espresso; **olla ~** pressure cooker
Ⓑ SM [1] (*LAm*) (= *tren*) express train
[2] (= *café*) espresso coffee

expresado ADJ above-mentioned; **según las cifras expresadas** according to these figures, according to the figures given earlier

expresamente ADV (= *concretamente*) expressly; (= *a propósito*) on purpose, deliberately; (= *claramente*) clearly, plainly; **no lo dijo ~** he didn't say so in so many words

expresar ▸conjug 1a◂ Ⓐ VT [1] (*al hablar*) (= *enunciar*) to express; (= *redactar*) to phrase, put; (= *declarar*) to state, set forth; (= *citar*) to quote; [+ *opiniones, quejas*] to voice; **expresa las opiniones de todos** he is voicing the opinions of us all; **estaba expresado de otro modo** it was worded differently; **el papel no lo expresa** the paper doesn't say so; **usted deberá ~ el número del giro postal** you should quote *o* give *o* state the number of the postal order
[2] [+ *sentimiento*] to show
Ⓑ **expresarse** VPR [1] [*persona*] to express o.s.; **no se expresa bien** he doesn't express himself well
[2] [*cifra, dato*] to be stated; **como abajo se expresa** as is stated below; **el número no se expresa** the number is not given *o* stated

expresión SF [1] (= *acto*) expression; **esta ~ de nuestro agradecimiento** this expression of our gratitude; **han recibido expresiones de solidaridad** they have received messages *o* expressions of solidarity ► **expresión corporal** self-expression through movement
[2] (*Ling*) expression; **la ~ es poco clara** the expression is not very clear ► **expresión familiar** colloquialism, conversational *o* colloquial expression
[3] **expresiones**†† (= *saludos*) greetings, regards

expresionismo SM expressionism

expresionista ADJ, SMF expressionist

expresivamente ADV [1] (= *con expresividad*) expressively
[2] (= *cariñosamente*) tenderly, affectionately

expresividad SF expressiveness

expresivo ADJ (= *que gesticula*) expressive; (= *cariñoso*) tender, affectionate, warm

expreso Ⓐ ADJ [1] (= *explícito*) express; (= *exacto*) specific, clear
[2] [*tren*] express, fast
[3] **café ~** espresso
Ⓑ SM [1] (*Ferro*) express train, fast train
[2] (= *persona*) special messenger
[3] (*Caribe*) (= *autobús*) long-distance coach
Ⓒ ADV express; **mandar algo ~** to send sth express

exprimelimones SM INV lemon squeezer

exprimidera SF squeezer

exprimidor SM (*manual*) lemon squeezer; (*eléctrico*) juice extractor, juicer

exprimir ▸conjug 3a◂ Ⓐ VT [1] [+ *limón, naranja*] to squeeze; [+ *jugo*] to squeeze out, express (*frm*)
[2] [+ *ropa*] to wring out, squeeze dry
[3] (*pey*) [+ *persona*] to exploit
Ⓑ **exprimirse** VPR ✦*MODISMO* **~se el cerebro** *o* **los sesos*** to rack one's brains

ex profeso ADV on purpose, deliberately

expropiación SF [*de casa, terreno*] expropriation; [*de vehículo*] commandeering; **orden de ~** compulsory purchase order ► **expropiación forzosa** compulsory purchase

expropiar ▸conjug 1b◂ VT [+ *casa, terreno*] (*sin indemnización*) to expropriate; (*con indemnización*) to place a compulsory purchase order on; [+ *vehículo*] to commandeer

expuesto Ⓐ PP *de* **exponer**; **según lo arriba ~** according to what has been stated *o* set out above
Ⓑ ADJ [1] [*lugar*] (= *al descubierto*) exposed; (= *peligroso*) dangerous; **partes del cuerpo expuestas al sol** parts of the body exposed to the sun
[2] [*cuadro, mercancías*] on show, on display, on view; **los artículos ~s en el escaparate** the goods displayed in the window
[3] **estar ~ a un riesgo** to be exposed *o* open to a risk

expugnar ▸conjug 1a◂ VT to take by storm

expulsar ▸conjug 1a◂ VT [1] (= *hacer salir*) [+ *alumno, inmigrante*] to expel; [+ *jugador*] to send off, eject (*EEUU*); [+ *intruso, alborotador*] to eject, throw out (**de** from); **la ~on del partido** she was expelled from the party, she was thrown out of the party; **el árbitro lo expulsó del terreno de juego** the referee sent him off the pitch
[2] [+ *gases, humo*] to expel

expulsión SF [1] (= *acto*) [*de gases, humo, persona*] expulsion; [*de país*] deportation; (*Dep*) sending-off, ejection (*EEUU*)
[2] (*Econ*) crowding out effect

expulsor Ⓐ ADJ **asiento ~** (*Aer*) ejector seat
Ⓑ SM (*Téc*) ejector

expurgar ▸conjug 1h◂ VT to expurgate

expurgatorio ADJ expurgatory; **índice ~** (*Rel*) Index

exquisitamente ADV [1] (= *con refinamiento*) exquisitely; (= *deliciosamente*) deliciously, delightfully; (= *excelentemente*) excellently
[2] (*pey*) affectedly

exquisitez SF [1] (= *cualidad*) [*de algo refinado*] exquisiteness; [*de algo excelente*] excellence
[2] [*de comida*] delicacy
[3] (*pey*) affectation

exquisito ADJ [1] (= *excelente*) excellent
[2] (= *refinado*) [*belleza*] exquisite; [*comida*] delicious
[3] (*pey*) (= *afectado*) affected; (= *melindroso*) choosy*, finicky

Ext. ABR [1] (= **Exterior**) ext
[2] (= **Extensión**) ext., extn

extasiar ▸conjug 1c◂ Ⓐ VT to entrance, enrapture, captivate
Ⓑ **extasiarse** VPR to become entranced, go into ecstasies (**ante** over, about)

éxtasis SM INV [1] (= *estado*) (*por arrobamiento*) ecstasy, rapture; (*por trance*) trance; **estar en ~** to be in ecstasy
[2] (= *droga*) ecstasy, E*

extático ADJ ecstatic, rapturous; **lo miró ~** he looked at it ecstatically

extemporal ADJ, **extemporáneo** ADJ [*lluvia*] unseasonable; [*comentario, viaje*] untimely

extender ▸conjug 2g◂ Ⓐ VT [1] (= *desplegar*) [+ *manta, mantel*] to spread out; [+ *alas*] to spread, stretch out; [+ *brazo, pierna, tentáculo*] to stretch out; **extendió el mapa encima de la mesa** he opened out *o* spread out the map on the table; **la Corriente del Golfo extiende su acción beneficiosa hasta el norte de Europa** the beneficial effects of the Gulf Stream reach as far as northern Europe; **~ la mano a algn** to hold out one's hand to sb, extend one's hand to sb (*frm*)
[2] (= *esparcir*) [+ *sellos, arena*] to lay out, spread out; **extendimos el tabaco al sol** we laid *o* spread the tobacco out in the sun
[3] (= *untar*) [+ *crema, mantequilla*] to spread; **la pomada se extiende con cuidado sobre la quemadura** spread the cream carefully on the burn
[4] (= *difundir*) [+ *noticia, rumor*] to spread; [+ *influencia, poder*] to extend
[5] (*frm*) (= *rellenar*) [+ *cheque, receta*] to make out, write out; [+ *certificado*] to issue; **extendí un cheque a su nombre** I made out *o* wrote out a cheque to him
[6] (= *ampliar*) [+ *oferta, contrato*] to extend; **han extendido la oferta hasta mayo** they have extended the offer until May; **han extendido el derecho de cobrar una pensión a las amas de casa** the right to receive a pension has been extended to include housewives
[7] (*Téc*) [+ *alambre*] to draw
Ⓑ **extenderse** VPR [1] (= *propagarse*) [*tumor, rumor, revolución*] to spread (**a** to); **el fuego se extendió por toda la casa** the fire spread throughout the house
[2] (= *ocupar un espacio*) [*terreno, cultivo*] to stretch, extend; [*especie, raza*] to extend; **la mancha de petróleo se extendía hasta la orilla** the oil-slick stretched *o* extended as far as the shore; **la ciudad se extendía a nuestros pies** the city (lay) stretched away beneath us; **ante nosotros se extendía todo un mundo de posibilidades** a whole world of possibilities lay before us
[3] (= *durar*) to last; **su reinado se extendió a lo largo de 50 años** his reign lasted a full 50 years; **el período que se extiende desde principios de siglo hasta los años veinte** the period lasting from the beginning of the century up to the 1920s
[4] (= *explayarse*) **~se en** *o* **sobre** [+ *tema, comentarios, respuestas*] to expand on; **no quisiera ~me demasiado en esta cuestión** I'd rather not expand too much on this subject; **nos extendimos demasiado en el debate** we spent too long on the debate

extendido ADJ [1] (= *desplegado*) [*mantel, mapa*] spread out, outspread; [*alas, brazos*] stretched out, outstretched; **con los brazos ~s** with his arms stretched out, with outstretched arms
[2] (= *propagado*) widespread; **está muy ~ el uso de esa palabra** that word is very widely used, the use of that word is very widespread; **tenía el tumor muy ~** the tumour had spread all over his body

extensamente ADV [1] (= *mucho*) extensively, widely; **ha viajado ~ por Asia** he has travelled extensively *o* widely in Asia
[2] (= *con detalle*) at length, thoroughly; **trató el tema ~** he dealt with the subject at length *o* thoroughly

extensible ADJ [1] [*mesa, escalera*] extending
[2] (= *ampliable*) **un período ~ a tres meses** a period which can be extended to three months; **estas críticas son ~s al resto del equipo** these criticisms can be extended to the rest of the team

extensión SF [1] (= *superficie*) area; **una enorme ~ de agua** an enormous area of water; **grandes extensiones del Reino Unido** large areas of the United Kingdom; **una isla con una ~ similar a la de Europa** an island similar in area to Europe
[2] (= *duración*) length; **la ~ del relato** the length of the story
[3] (= *amplitud*) [*de conocimientos*] extent, range; [*de programa*] scope; [*de significado*] range; **en toda la ~ de la palabra** in every sense of the word; **por ~** by extension; **esto nos afecta a nosotros y, por ~, a todo el país** this affects us and, by extension, the whole country
[4] (= *ampliación*) [*de incendio*] spread; [*de plazo*] extension; **la ~ del regadío a tierras de secano** the extending of irrigation systems to dry lands
[5] [*de cable, cuerda*] extension
[6] (*Telec*) extension; **¿puede ponerme con la ~ 14?** can I have extension 14, please?, can you put me through to extension 14, please?
[7] (*Mús*) [*de instrumento, voz*] range, compass
[8] (*en instituciones*) ► **Extensión Agraria** agricultural advisory service ► **Extensión Universitaria** extramural studies *pl*
[9] (*Internet*) plug-in

extensivo ADJ extensive; **hacer ~ a** to extend to, apply to; **la crítica se hizo extensiva a toda la ciudad** the criticism extended *o* applied to the whole city

extenso ADJ [1] (= *amplio*) [*superficie, objeto*] extensive; [*capítulo, documento*] long, lengthy
[2] (= *completo*) [*estudio, tratado*] extensive; [*conocimientos, vocabulario*] extensive, wide; **un ~ programa de conferencias** an extensive conference programme
[3] (= *detallado*) full, detailed; **estuvo muy ~ en sus explicaciones** his explanations were very detailed, he gave full *o* detailed explanations; **en** *o* **por ~** in full, at length

extensor SM chest expander

extenuación SF exhaustion

extenuado ADJ (= *cansado*) exhausted; (= *débil*) emaciated, wasted

extenuar ▸conjug 1e◂ Ⓐ VT (= *cansar*) to exhaust; (= *debilitar*) to emaciate, weaken
Ⓑ **extenuarse** VPR (= *cansarse*) to get exhausted; (= *debilitarse*) to become emaciated, waste away

exterior Ⓐ ADJ [1] (= *externo*) [*superficie*] outer; [*pared*] external; [*mundo*] exterior, outside; **una habitación ~** a room facing onto the street
[2] (= *extranjero*) [*relaciones, deuda, política*] foreign; [*comercio, ayuda*] foreign, overseas; **asuntos ~es** foreign affairs; **comercio ~** foreign trade, overseas trade; *ver tb* **asunto 3**
Ⓑ SM [1] (= *parte de fuera*) outside, exterior; **el ~ del edificio** the outside *o* exterior of the building; **con el ~ pintado de azul** with the outside painted blue; **salimos al ~ a tomar el aire** we went outside for a breath of fresh air; **el motorista alemán avanzaba por el ~** the German driver was catching up on the outside
[2] **el ~** (= *el extranjero*) abroad; **no hemos recibido noticias del ~** we haven't received any news from abroad; **tanto aquí como en el ~** both here and abroad; **comercio con el ~** foreign trade, overseas trade
[3] **exteriores** (*Cine*) location shots; **rodar en ~es** to film on location
[4] **Exteriores** (*Pol*) the Foreign Ministry, the Foreign Office, the State Department (*EEUU*)

exterioridad SF [1] (= *apariencia*) outward appearance, externals *pl*
[2] **exterioridades** (= *pompa*) pomp *sing*, show *sing*; (= *formas*) formalities

exteriorizar ▸conjug 1f◂ VT (= *expresar*) to express outwardly; (= *mostrar*) to show, reveal

exteriormente ADV outwardly

exterminar ▸conjug 1a◂ VT to exterminate

exterminio SM extermination

externalización SF [*de servicios*] outsourcing

externalizar ▸conjug 1f◂ VT [+ *servicios*] to outsource

externamente ADV externally, outwardly

externo/a Ⓐ ADJ [*influencia*] outside, external; [*superficie*] outer; [*pared*] external; **"medicamento de uso ~"** "medicine for external use only"
Ⓑ SM/F (= *alumno*) day pupil

extinción SF extinction

extinguido ADJ [*animal, volcán*] extinct; [*fuego*] out, extinguished

extinguir ▸conjug 3d◂ Ⓐ VT [1] (= *exterminar*) [+ *fuego*] to extinguish, put out; [+ *sublevación*] to put down
[2] [+ *deuda*] to wipe out
[3] (*Biol*) to exterminate, wipe out
[4] **~ una sentencia** (*Jur*) to serve a sentence
Ⓑ **extinguirse** VPR [1] [*fuego*] to go out
[2] (*Biol*) to die out, become extinct
[3] [*contrato, plazo*] to expire

extinto ADJ [1] [*especie, volcán*] extinct
[2] (*Méx euf*) (= *difunto*) dead, deceased

extintor SM ► **extintor de incendios** fire extinguisher ► **extintor de espuma** foam extinguisher

extirpación SF [1] (= *eliminación*) extirpation (*frm*), eradication
[2] (*Med*) removal

extirpar ▸conjug 1a◂ VT [1] [+ *problema, vicio*] to eradicate, stamp out
[2] (*Med*) to remove (surgically), take out

extorno SM (*Com*) rebate

extorsión SF [1] (*Fin*) (*con intimidación*) extortion, exaction; (*haciendo chantaje*) blackmail
[2] (= *molestia*) inconvenience

extorsionador(a) SM/F (= *intimidador*) extortioner; (= *chantajista*) blackmailer

extorsionar ▸conjug 1a◂ VT [1] (= *usurpar*) to extort money from; **~on a un empresario** they extorted money from a businessman
[2] (= *molestar*) to pester, bother

extorsionista SMF (*Méx*) extortionist, blackmailer

extra Ⓐ ADJ INV [*tiempo*] extra; [*gasolina*] high-octane; **calidad ~** top-quality, best
Ⓑ SMF (*Cine*) extra

Ⓒ SM [1] (*en cuenta*) extra; (*de pago*) bonus
[2] (= *periódico*) special edition, special supplement

extra... PREF extra…

extraacadémico ADJ non-university *adj inv*, (taking place) outside the university

extracción SF [1] (*Med*) [*de diente*] extraction; [*de bala, astilla*] extraction, removal
[2] (*Min*) [*de minerales*] mining, extraction; [*de petróleo*] extraction; [*de pizarra, mármol*] quarrying
[3] (*en sorteo*) **vamos a proceder a la primera ~** we shall now draw the first number
[4] (= *origen*) origins *pl*; **de ~ humilde** of humble origins, from a humble background
[5] (*Mat*) extraction

extracomunitario ADJ **países ~s** countries outside the European Union, non-EU countries

extraconstitucional ADJ unconstitutional

extraconyugal ADJ extramarital, adulterous

extracorto ADJ ultra-short

extractar ▸conjug 1a◂ VT [1] to make extracts from
[2] (= *resumir*) to abridge, summarize

extracto SM [1] (= *resumen*) summary, abstract ▸ **extracto de cuentas** (*Fin*) (bank) statement
[2] (*Farm, Culin*) extract ▸ **extracto de carne** meat extract ▸ **extracto de violeta** violet extract

extractor SM extractor ▸ **extractor de humos** extractor fan

extracurricular ADJ extracurricular, outside the curriculum

extradeportivo ADJ unrelated to sport

extradición SF extradition; **delito sujeto a ~** extraditable offence

extradicionar ▸conjug 1a◂ VT to extradite

extradir ▸conjug 3a◂ VT to extradite

extraditable Ⓐ ADJ subject to extradition
Ⓑ SMF [1] (*Pol*) person subject to extradition
[2] (*esp Col*) prominent drug baron (*wanted by US police*)

extraditar ▸conjug 1a◂ VT to extradite

extraer ▸conjug 2o◂ VT [1] [+ *diente, bala, astilla*] to extract
[2] (*Min*) [+ *minerales*] to mine, extract; [+ *petróleo*] to extract; [+ *pizarra, mármol*] to quarry
[3] [+ *conclusiones*] to draw
[4] (*en sorteo*) to draw
[5] (*Mat*) to extract

extraescolar ADJ **actividad ~** out-of-school activity

extrafino ADJ superfine

extraíble ADJ removable, detachable

extrajudicial ADJ extrajudicial, out of court

extrajurídico ADJ outside the law

extralimitación SF abuse (*of authority*)

extralimitarse ▸conjug 1a◂ VPR to exceed *o* abuse one's authority, overstep the mark

extramarital ADJ extramarital

extramuros ADV outside the city; **~ de** outside

extranjería SF alien status, status of foreigners; **ley de ~** law on aliens

extranjerismo SM foreign word *o* phrase *etc*

extranjerizante ADJ [*ley*] tending to favour foreign ways; [*palabra*] foreign-looking, foreign-sounding

extranjero/a Ⓐ ADJ foreign
Ⓑ SM/F foreigner; (*Jur*) alien
Ⓒ SM **en el ~** abroad; **estar en el ~** to be abroad, be in foreign parts; **ir al ~** to go abroad; **pasó seis años en el ~** he spent six years abroad; **cosas del ~** things from abroad, foreign things

extranjis*: de ~ ADV secretly, on the sly

extrañamente ADV strangely, oddly

extrañamiento SM [1] (= *enajenación*) estrangement (**de** from)
[2] = **extrañeza**
[3] (*Jur*) banishment

extrañar ▸conjug 1a◂ Ⓐ VT [1] (= *sorprender*) to surprise; **eso me extraña** that surprises me, I find that odd; **¡no me ~ía!** I wouldn't be surprised!, it wouldn't surprise me!; **¡ya me extrañaba a mí!** I thought it was a bit strange!; **me extrañaba que no hubieras venido** I was surprised you hadn't come; **me ~ía que …** I'd be surprised if …; **no es de ~ que …** it's hardly surprising that …, it's no wonder that …
[2] (= *echar de menos*) to miss; **esta noche he extrañado mi cama** last night I missed sleeping in my own bed; **extraña mucho a sus padres** he misses his parents a lot
[3] (††) (= *desterrar*) to banish
Ⓑ **extrañarse** VPR [1] (= *sorprenderse*) to be surprised; **~se de algo** to be surprised at sth; **me extrañé de la reacción de tu hermano** I was surprised at your brother's reaction; **se extrañó de vernos juntos** he was surprised to see us together; **~se de que …** to be surprised that …
[2] (††) (= *negarse*) to refuse
[3] (††) [*amigos*] to become estranged, grow apart

extrañeza SF [1] (= *rareza*) strangeness, oddness
[2] (= *asombro*) surprise, amazement; **me miró con ~** he looked at me in surprise
[3] [*de amigos*] estrangement, alienation

extraño/a Ⓐ ADJ [1] (= *raro*) strange; **es muy ~** it's very odd *o* strange; **¡qué ~!** how odd *o* strange!; **parece ~ que …** it seems odd *o* strange that …
[2] (= *ajeno*) **un cuerpo ~** a foreign body; **murió en tierra extraña** he died on foreign soil; **éstas son costumbres extrañas a este país** these are customs which are foreign *o* alien to this country; **este estilo no es ~ a los lectores de su poesía** this style is not unknown to readers of his poetry
Ⓑ SM/F [1] (= *desconocido*) stranger; **no quiero que hables con ~s** I don't want you talking to strangers
[2] (= *extranjero*) foreigner
Ⓒ SM **hacer un ~: el balón hizo un ~** the ball took a bad bounce; **el caballo hizo un ~** the horse shied

extrañoso ADJ (*Andes*) surprised

extraoficial ADJ unofficial, informal

extraoficialmente ADV unofficially, informally

extraordinariamente ADV extraordinarily

extraordinario Ⓐ ADJ [1] (= *especial*) extraordinary; **no tiene nada de ~** there's nothing extraordinary *o* special about it
[2] (= *destacado*) outstanding; [*edición, número, descuento*] special; [*cobro*] supplementary, extra; **por sus servicios ~s** for his outstanding services
[3] (= *insólito*) unusual
Ⓑ SM [1] (*para una ocasión especial*) treat
[2] (*en menú*) special dish, extra dish
[3] (*de publicación*) special issue

extraparlamentario ADJ (taking place) outside parliament

extrapeninsular ADJ outside Iberia, relating to areas outside the Peninsula

extraplano ADJ super-slim

extraplomado ADJ overhanging

extraplomo SM overhang

extrapolable ADJ comparable

extrapolación SF extrapolation

extrapolar ▸conjug 1a◂ VT to extrapolate

extrarradio SM suburbs *pl*, outlying area

extrasensorial ADJ extrasensory

extratasa SF surcharge, extra charge

extraterrenal ADJ, **extraterreno** ADJ (*LAm*) (= *sobrenatural*) supernatural; (= *extraterrestre*) extraterrestrial, from another planet

extraterrestre Ⓐ ADJ from outer space, extraterrestrial
Ⓑ SMF alien, extraterrestrial

extraterritorial ADJ extraterritorial

extravagancia SF [1] (= *cualidad*) [*de aspecto, ropa, persona*] extravagance, outlandishness
[2] (= *capricho*) whim; **tiene sus ~s** he has his oddities *o* peculiarities

extravagante ADJ [*ideas, ropa, persona*] extravagant, outlandish

extravagantemente ADV extravagantly, outlandishly

extravasarse ▸conjug 1a◂ VPR [*líquido*] to leak out, flow out; [*sangre*] to ooze out

extravertido/a ADJ, SM/F = **extrovertido**

extraviado ADJ [*persona, objeto*] lost, missing; [*animal*] lost, stray; **un niño ~** a missing child

extraviar ▸conjug 1c◂ Ⓐ VT [1] [+ *objeto*] to lose, mislay, misplace
[2] (*pey*) [+ *dinero*] to embezzle
[3] (= *desorientar*) [+ *persona*] to mislead, misdirect
Ⓑ **extraviarse** VPR [1] (= *perderse*) [*persona*] to get lost, lose one's way; [*animal*] to stray; [*objeto*] to go missing, go astray; [*carta*] to go astray, get lost in the post
[2] [*persona*] (*moralmente*) to go astray, err, fall into evil ways

extravío SM [1] (= *pérdida*) [*de objeto*] loss, mislaying; [*de animal*] loss
[2] (*moral*) misconduct, erring, evil ways *pl*

extremadamente ADV extremely, exceedingly; **pesticidas ~ peligrosas** extremely *o* exceedingly dangerous pesticides; **una obra ~ original** a highly original work

extremado ADJ extreme; **paisajes de extremada belleza** landscapes of extreme beauty; **un descubrimiento de extremada importancia** an extremely important discovery, a discovery of extreme importance; **lo trató con extremada dureza** he treated him extremely harshly, he treated him with extreme harshness

Extremadura SF Extremadura

extremar ▸conjug 1a◂ Ⓐ VT (= *aumentar al máximo*) **fue necesario ~ las medidas de seguridad** it was necessary to maximize secu-

rity measures; **las personas alérgicas deben ~ las precauciones** allergic people should take extra precautions; **sin ~ el sentimentalismo** without overdoing the sentimentality
Ⓑ **extremarse** VPR to do one's best; **veo que os habéis extremado en la organización** I see that you have done your very best in the organization; **no hace falta que te extremes en la presentación** you don't need to make a special effort in the presentation

extremaunción SF extreme unction

extremeño/a ADJ, SM/F Extremaduran

extremidad SF [1] (= *punta*) tip, extremity; (= *borde*) edge, outermost part
[2] **extremidades** (*Anat*) extremities

extremismo SM extremism

extremista ADJ, SMF extremist

extremo[1] ADJ [1] (= *máximo*) extreme; **una situación de extrema pobreza** a situation of extreme poverty; **en situaciones de calor ~** in extremely hot weather; **el nivel de polen era ~** the pollen count was extremely high; **heridas de extrema gravedad** extremely serious wounds; **en caso ~** as a last resort, if all else fails
[2] (= *alejado*) furthest; **vive en el punto más ~ de la isla** she lives on the furthest *o* most extreme point of the island; *ver tb* **oriente**
[3] (*Pol*) (= *radical*) extreme; **representa lo más ~ de la izquierda** she represents the extreme left wing; **extrema derecha** extreme right, far right; **extrema izquierda** extreme left, far left

extremo[2] Ⓐ SM [1] (= *punta*) end; **vive en el otro ~ de la calle** he lives at the far *o* other end of the street; **agarra la cuerda por este ~** take this end of the rope, take hold of the rope by *o* at this end; **el ~ oriental de la península** the easternmost side *o* point of the peninsula; **de ~ a ~** from one end *o* side to the other; **de un ~ a otro** (*lit*) from one end *o* side to the other; (*fig*) from one extreme to another; ✦*MODISMOS* **ser el ~ opuesto** to be the complete opposite; **ser los dos ~s** to be complete opposites; ✦*REFRÁN* **los ~s se tocan** opposites attract
[2] (= *límite*) extreme; **no me gustan los ~s** I don't like extremes of any kind; **su crueldad alcanzaba ~s insospechados** his cruelty plumbed unheard-of depths; **si la situación se deteriora hasta ese ~ ...** if the situation deteriorates to that extent ...; **en ~** extremely; **la situación era en ~ peligrosa** the situation was extremely dangerous *o* was dangerous in the extreme (*más frm*); **todavía me pesa en ~** I still feel extremely guilty; **hasta el ~** to the full; **estamos explotando los recursos hasta el ~** we are exploiting resources to the full; **es detallista hasta el ~** he pays extremely close attention to detail; **llegar a** *o* **hasta el ~ de**: **hemos llegado al ~ de no decirnos ni hola** it's got to the point now that we don't even say hello to each other; **llegó hasta el ~ de decir que lo mataría** she went as far as to say that she would kill him; **por ahorrar ha llegado al ~ de no comer** he's so desperate to save money he's stopped eating; **en último ~** as a last resort, if all else fails
[3] (= *asunto*) point; **ese ~ no se tocó en la discusión** that point was not touched on during the discussion; **pidieron una rebaja en el rescate, ~ que fue rechazado** they asked for the ransom to be reduced, a condition which was refused
[4] (= *cuidado*) great care
Ⓑ SMF (*Dep*) ► **extremo derecho** right winger; **jugaba de ~ derecho** he played (on the) right wing, he played as a right winger ► **extremo izquierdo** left winger

Extremo Oriente SM Far East

extremoso ADJ [*persona*] (= *efusivo*) gushing, effusive; (= *vehemente*) vehement, extreme in one's attitudes *o* reactions

extrínseco ADJ extrinsic

extrovertido/a Ⓐ ADJ extrovert, outgoing
Ⓑ SM/F extrovert

exuberancia SF [1] [*de persona, conducta*] exuberance
[2] (*Bot*) luxuriance, lushness
[3] (*en el cuerpo*) fullness, buxomness

exuberante ADJ [1] [*persona, conducta*] exuberant
[2] (*Bot*) luxuriant, lush
[3] [*cuerpo, formas*] full, buxom

exudación SF exudation

exudar ▸conjug 1a◂ Ⓐ VT to exude, ooze
Ⓑ VI to exude, ooze out (**de** from)

exultación SF exultation

exultar ▸conjug 1a◂ VI to exult

exvoto SM votive offering

eyaculación SF ejaculation ► **eyaculación precoz** premature ejaculation

eyacular ▸conjug 1a◂ VT, VI to ejaculate

eyectable ADJ **asiento ~** ejector seat

eyectarse ▸conjug 1a◂ VPR (*Aer*) to eject

eyector SM (*Téc*) ejector

-ez *ver* **Aspects of Word Formation in Spanish 2**

Ezequiel SM Ezekiel

EZLN SM ABR (*Méx*) = **Ejército Zapatista de Liberación Nacional**

F f

F[1], **f** ['efe] SF (= *letra*) F, f

F[2] ABR [1] = **fuerza**; **un viento F8** a force eight wind

[2] (= **febrero**) Feb.; **el 23-F** the 23rd February (*date of the Tejero coup attempt, in 1981*)

> **23-F**
>
> ***23-F** refers to the attempted coup d'état carried out in the **Cortes** on 23 February 1981 by a group of **Guardias Civiles** led by Lt. Colonel Antonio Tejero and supported by certain sectors of the army. Members of the Spanish Parliament were held hostage overnight, the national TV station — TVE — was taken over by the military and forced to broadcast nothing but military music and, in some big cities, the army took up positions on the streets. In his role as Supreme Commander of the Armed Forces King Juan Carlos defused the situation by reassuring army commanders that the coup did not have his backing and by pledging his support for democracy. The rebels surrendered the following morning.*

f.ª ABR (*Com*) (= **factura**) inv

fa SM (*Mús*) fa, F ► **fa bemol** F flat ► **fa mayor** F major ► **fa menor** F minor ► **fa sostenido** F sharp

fab. ABR (= **fabricante**) mfr(s)

f.a.b. ABR (= **franco a bordo**) FOB, f.o.b.

fabada SF *rich stew of beans, pork etc*

fabe SF (*Asturias*) bean

fabla SF [1] (*Hist*) pseudo-archaic style

[2] ► **fabla aragonesa** Aragonese dialect

fábrica SF [1] (= *factoría*) factory; **marca de ~** trademark; **precio de ~** price ex-works, price ex-factory ► **fábrica de acero** steel plant, steelworks ► **fábrica de algodón** cotton mill ► **fábrica de cerveza** brewery ► **fábrica de conservas** canning plant, cannery ► **fábrica de gas** gasworks ► **fábrica de moneda** mint ► **fábrica de montaje** assembly plant ► **fábrica de papel** paper mill ► **fábrica de vidrio** glassworks ► **fábrica experimental** pilot plant

[2] (*Arquit*) **de ~** stone, stonework

[3] (= *proceso*) manufacture

[4] (*Andes*) (= *alambique*) still, distillery

fabricación SF manufacture; **de ~ casera** home-made; **de ~ nacional** home-produced; **de ~ propia** our own make; **estar en ~** to be in production ► **fabricación asistida por ordenador** computer-aided manufacturing ► **fabricación de coches** car manufacture ► **fabricación de tejas** tile making ► **fabricación en serie** mass production

fabricante (A) ADJ **la compañía ~** the manufacturer

(B) SMF (*en gran escala*) manufacturer, maker; (*en pequeña escala*) maker; **es ~ de violines** he's a violin-maker

fabricar ►conjug 1g◄ VT [1] (*gen*) to manufacture, make; (= *construir*) to build, construct; **~ en serie** to mass-produce

[2] [+ *mentira*] to fabricate, concoct; [+ *documento*] to fabricate, falsify

fabril ADJ manufacturing, industrial

fabriquero†† SM [1] = **fabricante**

[2] (*Rel*) churchwarden

[3] (*Méx*) (= *destilador*) distillery operator (*in a sugar mill*)

fábula SF [1] (*Literat*) fable; (= *historia*) tale, story

[2] (= *rumor*) rumour, rumor (EEUU); (= *chisme*) (piece of) gossip; (= *mentira*) invention

[3] (*) **es de ~** it's fabulous

[4] (†) (= *argumento*) plot, story

[5] (†) (= *persona*) talk of the town, laughing-stock

fabulario SM collection of fables

fabulista SMF writer of fables

fabulosamente ADV [*barato, bueno*] fabulously; **anoche lo pasaron ~** they had a fabulous time last night

fabuloso ADJ [1] (= *mítico*) mythical, fabulous (*liter*); (= *ficticio*) fabulous (*liter*), imaginary

[2] (*) (= *maravilloso*) fantastic, fabulous; **es francamente ~** it's just fabulous

FACA SM ABR (*Esp*) = **Futuro avión de combate y ataque**

faca SF *large, curved knife with a sharp tip*

facción SF [1] (*Pol*) faction

[2] **facciones** (*Anat*) features; **de facciones irregulares** with o of irregular features

[3] (*Mil*†) duty; **estar de ~** to be on duty

faccioso/a (A) ADJ [*propaganda, jefe*] rebel; [*bando*] breakaway

(B) SM/F (= *rebelde*) rebel; (= *agitador*) agitator

faceta SF [1] (= *aspecto*) facet

[2] [*de cristal, piedra preciosa*] facet

faceto* ADJ (*Méx*) cocksure, arrogant

FACH SF ABR (*Chile*) = **Fuerza Aérea de Chile**

facha[1]* SF [1] (= *aspecto*) look; (= *cara*) face; **la tarta tiene buena ~** the cake looks really good; **esos individuos tienen una mala ~** that bunch look a bit dodgy*; **¿adónde vas con esa ~?** where are you going looking like that?; **tener ~ de** to look like; **tiene ~ de poli** he looks like a copper*; **tiene ~ de buena gente** he looks OK*

[2] (*pey*) **estar hecho una ~** to look a sight*, look terrible; **fachas** (*Méx*) slovenly dress *sing*

[3] **ponerse en ~** (*Náut*) to lie to

facha[2]* (*pey*) [1] ADJ (*Esp*) fascist

[2] SMF (*Esp*) fascist

fachada SF [1] [*de edificio*] façade, front; (= *medida*) frontage; **con ~ al parque** looking towards the park, overlooking the park; **con 15 metros de ~** with a frontage of 15m

[2] (= *apariencia*) façade; **tener mucha ~** to be all show and no substance; **no tiene más que ~** it's all just a façade with him, it's all just show with him; **bajo la ~ de benefactor de las artes** under the guise of a patron of the arts

[3] (*) (= *cara*) mug*

[4] (*Tip*) title page

fachado* ADJ **bien ~** good-looking; **mal ~** ugly, plain

fachenda* (A) SF conceitedness

(B) SMF show-off*

fachendear* ►conjug 1a◄ VI to show off*

fachendista*, **fachendoso/a***, **fachento/a*** (*CAm*) (A) ADJ stuck-up*, snooty*

(B) SM/F show-off*

fachinal* SM (*Cono Sur*) swamp

fachoso* ADJ [1] (= *raro*) ridiculous-looking, odd-looking

[2] (*Andes, Cono Sur*) (= *elegante*) elegant, smart

[3] (*Méx*) (= *engreído*) conceited

facial (A) ADJ [1] (= *del rostro*) facial, face *antes de s*; **crema ~** face cream; **mascarilla ~** pack *o* mask

[2] (*de sello, moneda*) **valor ~** face value

(B) SM face value

fácil (A) ADJ [1] (= *sencillo*) easy; **el examen fue muy ~** the exam was very easy; **no es ~ admitir que se está equivocado** it isn't easy to admit that you're wrong; **no me lo pones nada ~** you aren't making things very easy for me; **los ricos lo tienen todo más ~** rich people have it easy; **~ de hacer** easy to do; **~ de usar** (*gen*) easy to use; (*Inform*) user-friendly

[2] (= *afable*) **nunca tuvo un carácter ~** he was never very easy to get on with; **es de trato ~** he's easy to get on with, he's quite easygoing

[3] (*pey*) [*respuesta*] facile, glib; [*chiste*] obvious

4 (*pey*) [*mujer*] easy
5 (= *probable*) **es ~ que venga** he's quite likely to come, he may well come; **no veo muy ~ que acepten** I don't think they're very likely to accept
Ⓑ ADV (*) easily; **podría costarte 5.000 ~** it could easily cost you 5,000; **te lo arreglo en dos horas ~** I'll fix it for you in two hours, no problem*

facilidad SF 1 (= *sencillez*) easiness; **la aparente ~ de los ejercicios** the apparent easiness of the exercises; **con ~** easily; **se me rompen las uñas con ~** my nails break easily; **con la mayor ~** with the greatest (of) ease
2 (= *habilidad*) **tener ~ para algo** to have a gift for sth; **tiene ~ para las matemáticas** she has a gift for maths, maths comes easy to her; **tener ~ de palabra** to have a way with words
3 **facilidades** (= *condiciones favorables*) **me dieron todas las ~es** they gave me every facility; **"facilidades de pago"** "credit facilities"

facilitar ▸conjug 1a◂ VT 1 (= *hacer fácil*) to make easier, facilitate; **un ordenador facilita mucho el trabajo** a computer makes work much easier; **Internet facilita el acceso a la información** the Internet facilitates access to information; **la nueva autovía ~á la entrada a la capital** the new motorway will give easier access to the capital, the new motorway will facilitate access to the capital
2 (= *proporcionar*) **~ algo a algn** to provide sb with sth, supply sb with sth; **el banco me facilitó la información** the bank provided me with *o* supplied me with the information; **"le agradecería me ~a ..."** "I would be grateful if you would provide *o* supply me with..."
3 (*Cono Sur*) (= *quitar importancia a*) **~ algo** to make sth out to be easier than it really is, play down the difficulty of sth

fácilmente ADV 1 (= *con facilidad*) easily; **hago amigos ~** I make friends easily; **este tipo de cosas no se pueden explicar ~** there's no easy *o* simple explanation for this type of thing, this type of thing cannot be easily explained
2 (= *probablemente*) **andará ~ por los 40** he must be at least 40

facilón* ADJ 1 (= *muy fácil*) [*problema, ejercicio, test*] dead easy*; **este crucigrama es ~** this crossword is dead easy *o* a doddle *o* a cinch*; **tiene un trabajo ~** his job's dead easy *o* a cushy number*
2 (*pey*) (= *manido*) [*comentario, recurso*] trite
3 (*pey*) (= *pegadizo*) [*canción*] trashy*
4 (*hum*) (= *dócil*) [*persona, carácter*] easy*

facilongo* ADJ (*Andes*) **es ~** it's dead easy*, it's a doddle *o* a cinch*

facineroso/a Ⓐ ADJ 1 (= *de delincuente habitual*) criminal
2 (= *malvado*) evil, wicked
Ⓑ SM/F 1 (= *delincuente habitual*) criminal
2 (= *malvado*) evil person, wicked person

facistol Ⓐ ADJ 1 (*Caribe*) (= *descarado*) insolent; (= *vanidoso*) conceited, vain; (= *pedante*) pedantic
2 (*Caribe*) (= *bromista*) **es tan ~** he's full of tricks, he loves playing jokes on people
Ⓑ SM (*Rel*) lectern

facistolería SF (*Andes, Caribe*) (= *descaro*) insolence; (= *jactancia*) conceit, boastfulness

facochero SM warthog

facón SM (*Cono Sur*) long gaucho knife; → GAUCHO

facsímil ADJ, SM, **facsímile** ADJ, SM facsimile

factibilidad SF feasibility; **estudio de ~** feasibility study

factible ADJ feasible

fácticamente (*frm*) ADV actually, in (point of) fact

facticio (*frm*) ADJ factitious (*frm*), artificial

fáctico ADJ real, actual; **los poderes ~s** the powers that be

factor(a) Ⓐ SM/F 1 (*Com*) (= *representante*) agent, factor
2 (*Ferro*) freight clerk
Ⓑ SM 1 (*Mat*) factor
2 (= *elemento*) factor, element; **el ~ suerte** the luck factor, the element of chance; **es un nuevo ~ de la situación** it is a new factor in the situation ► **factor de seguridad** safety factor ► **factor determinante** determining factor ► **factor humano** human factor ► **factor Rh** rhesus factor ► **factor sorpresa** element of surprise ► **factor tiempo** time factor

factoría SF 1 (= *fábrica*) factory ► **factoría de coches** car plant
2 (*Andes*) (= *fundición*) foundry
3 (*Hist*) trading post

factorización SF factoring

factótum SMF 1 (= *manitas*) factotum
2 (= *persona de confianza*) agent, nominee
3 († *pey*) (= *entrometido*) busybody

factual (*frm*) ADJ (= *real*) actual

▼**factura** SF 1 (*Com*) bill, invoice; **pasar** *o* **presentar ~ a algn** to bill *o* invoice sb; **según ~** as per invoice; ✦***MODISMO*** **pasar ~: el escándalo ha pasado ~ a la organización** the scandal has taken its *o* a toll on the organization; **nos pasarán (la) ~ por el apoyo que nos dieron en momentos de crisis** they will call in the favour they did us by supporting us during the crisis ► **factura proforma, factura simulada** pro forma invoice
2 (*frm*) (= *ejecución*) **cuadros de ~ reciente** recently painted pictures, pictures of recent execution; **un thriller psicológico de impecable ~** a perfectly put together *o* constructed psychological thriller
3 (*Cono Sur*) bun, cake

facturación SF 1 (*Com*) (= *acto*) invoicing
2 (*Com*) (= *ventas*) turnover
3 [*de mercancías, equipaje*] (*en aeropuerto*) check-in; (*en puerto, estación*) registration

facturar ▸conjug 1a◂ Ⓐ VT 1 (*Com*) [+ *géneros*] to invoice (for), bill (for); [+ *persona*] to invoice, bill
2 [+ *volumen de ventas*] to turn over, have a turnover of; **la compañía facturó 500 millones en 1997** the company turned over *o* had a turnover of 500 million in 1997
3 [+ *equipaje*] (*en aeropuerto*) to check in; (*en puerto, estación*) to register
Ⓑ VI to check in

facultad SF 1 (= *capacidad*) faculty; **está perdiendo sus ~es** she's losing her faculties; **firmó el testamento en pleno uso de sus ~es** he signed the will in full possession of his faculties ► **facultades mentales** mental faculties, mental powers; **actuó con sus ~es mentales perturbadas** he was mentally disturbed when he did it
2 (= *autoridad*) power, authority; **tener la ~ de hacer algo** to have the power *o* authority to do sth; **tener ~ para hacer algo** to be authorized to do sth
3 (*Univ*) faculty; **está en la ~** he's at the university; **se han quedado a comer en la ~** they stayed to have lunch at the university ► **Facultad de Derecho** Faculty of Law ► **Facultad de Filosofía y Letras** Faculty of Arts

facultar ▸conjug 1a◂ VT **~ a algn para hacer algo** (= *dar autorización*) to authorize sb to do sth, empower sb to do sth; (= *dar derecho*) to entitle sb to do sth

facultativo/a Ⓐ ADJ 1 (= *opcional*) optional, non-compulsory
2 (*Med*) medical; **dictamen ~** medical report; **prescripción facultativa** medical prescription
3 (*Univ*) faculty *antes de s*
Ⓑ SM/F doctor, physician (*frm*)

facundia† SF eloquence; (*pey*) verbosity (*frm*)

facundo† ADJ eloquent; (*pey*) verbose (*frm*)

faena SF 1 (*gen*) task, job, piece of work; (*en el hogar*) chore; (*Mil*) fatigue; **estar de ~** to be at work; **estar en (plena) ~** to be hard at work; **tener mucha ~** to be terribly busy ► **faena doméstica** housework
2 (*) (*tb* **mala ~**) (= *mala pasada*) dirty trick; **hacer una ~ a algn** to play a dirty trick on sb; **¡menuda ~ la que me hizo!** that was a a terrible thing he did to me!
3 (*CAm, Caribe, Méx*) (= *horas extraordinarias*) extra work, overtime
4 (*Taur*) set of passes with the cape; **hizo una ~ maravillosa** he gave a splendid performance (with the cape)
5 (*Cono Sur*) (= *obreros*) gang of workers; (= *local*) work place

faenar ▸conjug 1a◂ Ⓐ VI 1 (= *trabajar*) to work, labour, labor (*EEUU*)
2 [*pescador*] to fish
Ⓑ VT 1 [+ *ganado*] to slaughter
2 (*Cono Sur*) [+ *madera*] to cut

faenero/a SM/F (*Chile*) farm worker, farmhand

fafarechero* (*Col*) ADJ stuck-up*, conceited

fagocitar ▸conjug 1a◂ VT to absorb, gobble up

fagocito SM phagocyte

fagot Ⓐ SM (= *instrumento*) bassoon
Ⓑ SMF (= *músico*) bassoonist

failear ▸conjug 1a◂ VT (*CAm, Cono Sur*) to file

fain ADJ (*CAm*) fine

fainá SF (*Cono Sur*) savoury pastry

fainada SF (*Caribe*), **fainera** SF (*CAm*) silly thing, foolish act

faino ADJ (*Caribe*) rude

faisán SM pheasant

faisanaje SM hanging (of game)

faite (*LAm*) Ⓐ ADJ tough, strong
Ⓑ SM 1 (= *luchador*) tough man, good fighter
2 (*pey*) brawler

faitear* ▸conjug 1a◂ VI (*LAm*) to brawl

faja SF 1 (= *prenda*) girdle, corset ► **faja pantalón** panty girdle
2 (= *cinturón*) belt; [*de tela*] sash
3 (= *tira*) [*de adorno*] strip, band; (*Med*) bandage, support
4 (*Geog*) (= *zona*) strip; **una estrecha ~ de terreno** a narrow strip of land
5 (*Arquit*) band, fascia

➤ LENGUA Y USO: **factura 1** 47.5

6 [*de periódico, impreso*] (*tb* **~ postal**) wrapper, address label
7 (*Andes Aut*) fanbelt
8 (*Méx*) label, title (on spine of book)

fajada SF 1 (*Caribe*) (= *ataque*) attack, rush
2 (*Cono Sur*) (= *paliza*) beating
3 (*Caribe*) (= *decepción*) disappointment

fajar ▸conjug 1a◂ Ⓐ VT 1 (= *envolver*) to wrap; ✦**MODISMO** **¡que lo fajen!** (*Cono Sur, Méx*⁑) tell him to wrap up!*
2 (= *vendar*) to bandage
3 (*LAm*) (= *atacar*) to attack, go for*; (*) (= *golpear*) to beat up
4 (*Cuba*) (= *seducir*) [+ *mujer*] to try to seduce
Ⓑ VI (*LAm*) **~ con algn*** to go for sb, lay into sb*
Ⓒ **fajarse** VPR 1 (= *ponerse una faja*) to put on one's belt
2 (*LAm*) (= *pelearse*) to come to blows, fight; **los boxeadores se ~on duro** the boxers really went for *o* laid into each other*
3 **~se a algn**⁑ to feel sb up⁑

fajilla SF [*de periódicos, revistas, impresos*] wrapper, address label

fajín SM (*Mil*) sash

fajina SF 1 (*Agr*) rick
2 (= *leña*) kindling, brushwood
3 (*Cono Sur*) (= *faena*) task, job (to be done quickly); **tenemos mucha ~** we've a lot to do, we've a tough job on here
4 (*Mil*) (*gen*) bugle call; (*para comer*) call to mess
5 (*Caribe*) (= *horas extraordinarias*) extra work, overtime
6 (*Cono Sur*) hard work; **ropa de ~** working clothes *pl*; **uniforme de ~** fatigues *pl*

fajo SM 1 (= *manojo*) [*de papeles*] bundle, sheaf; [*de billetes*] roll, wad
2 (*Méx*) (= *cinturón*) woman's belt
3 (*Méx*) (= *golpe*) blow
4 (*LAm**) (= *trago*) swig* (of liquor)
5 **fajos**† [*de bebé*] swaddling clothes

falacia SF 1 (= *engaño*) deceit, fraud; (= *error*) fallacy
2 (= *falsedad*) deceitfulness

falange SF 1 (*Anat*) phalange
2 (*Mil*) phalanx
3 **la Falange** (*Esp Pol*) the Falange, *the Spanish Falangist movement*

FALANGE ESPAÑOLA

Founded in 1933 by José Antonio Primo de Rivera, son of the dictator Miguel Primo de Rivera, the **Falange Española** *was a sort of paramilitary fascist party. It grew rapidly in the early months of the Spanish Civil War, particularly after its leader was executed by the Republicans. Franco later merged the* **Falange** *with the* **Carlistas** *to form the* **Falange Española Tradicionalista de las Juntas de Ofensiva Nacional-Sindicalista**. *After the Civil War, the* **FET de las JONS** *was the only legally political party permitted in Franco's Spain. The* **Falange** *is still in existence.*

falangista ADJ, SMF Falangist

falaz ADJ [*individuo*] false, deceitful; [*doctrina*] false, fallacious (*frm*); [*apariencia*] deceptive, misleading

falca SF 1 (*Andes, Caribe, Méx*) (= *transbordador*) river ferryboat
2 (*Andes*) (= *alambique*) small still

falciforme ADJ sickle-shaped

falda SF 1 (= *ropa*) skirt; ✦**MODISMOS** **está cosido** *o* **pegado a las ~s de su madre** he's tied to his mother's apron strings; **estar cosido a las ~s de su mujer** to be dominated by one's wife; **haberse criado bajo las ~s de mamá** to have led a very sheltered life ► **falda de tablas** pleated skirt ► **falda de tubo** straight skirt, pencil skirt ► **falda escocesa** (*gen*) tartan skirt; (= *traje típico escocés*) kilt ► **falda pantalón** culottes *pl*, split skirt ► **falda tableada** pleated skirt
2 (= *regazo*) lap; **sentarse en la ~ de algn** to sit on sb's lap
3 **faldas*** (= *mujeres*) women, ladies; **es muy aficionado a las ~s** he's a great one for the ladies, he's fond of the ladies; **es asunto de ~s** there's a woman behind it somewhere
4 [*de montaña*] (= *ladera*) side; (= *pie*) foot
5 [*de res*] brisket, skirt
6 [*de mesa camilla*] table cover
7 [*de sombrero*] brim

faldear ▸conjug 1a◂ VT [+ *montaña*] to skirt

faldellín SM 1 (†) (= *falda*) short skirt; (= *enagua*) underskirt
2 (*Caribe*) [*de bautizo*] christening robe

faldeo SM (*Cono Sur*) slope, mountainside

faldero ADJ 1 (= *mujeriego*) **hombre ~** ladies' man; **es muy ~** he's a great one for the ladies
2 (= *sumiso*) **perro ~** lapdog

faldicorto ADJ short-skirted

faldilla SF 1 (*Aut*) skirt, apron
2 **faldillas** [*de abrigo*] coat tails; [*de camisa*] shirt tails

faldón SM 1 [*de vestido*] tail, skirt; (= *pliegue*) flap
2 [*de bebé*] long dress
3 (*Arquit*) gable

falena SF moth

falencia SF 1 (*Arg*) (= *bancarrota*) bankruptcy
2 (*Cono Sur*) (= *defecto*) failing, shortcoming
3 (†) (= *error*) error, misstatement

falibilidad SF fallibility

falible ADJ fallible

fálico ADJ phallic

falla SF 1 (*Geol*) fault
2 (= *defecto*) [*de tejido*] flaw; [*de mercancías*] fault, defect; (*LAm*) [*de carácter*] failing; **géneros que tienen ~s** seconds, defective goods
3 (*Esp*) (= *figura*) *huge ornate cardboard figure burnt in Valencia at the Fallas*
4 (*LAm*) (= *error*) error, oversight ► **falla de tiro** (*Mil*) misfire
5 (*LAm Mec*) failure, breakdown ► **falla de encendido** (*Aut*) ignition fault
6 (*LAm*) (= *escasez*) lack, shortage ► **falla en caja** cash shortage
7 (*Andes Naipes*) void

fallada SF (*Naipes*) ruff, trumping

fallar ▸conjug 1a◂ Ⓐ VI 1 [*freno*] to fail; [*plan*] to fail, go wrong; [*cuerda*] to break, give way; [*motor*] to misfire; **le falla la memoria** his memory is failing; **si no me falla la memoria** if my memory serves me correctly *o* right *o* well; **si no me falla la vista** if my eyes don't deceive me; **le falló el corazón** his heart failed; **me ~on las piernas** my legs gave way; **algo falló en sus planes** something went wrong with his plans; **han fallado todas nuestras previsiones** all our predictions have turned out to be wrong; **si le das un caramelo se calla, no falla nunca** if you give him a sweet he'll shut up, it never fails; **no falla, ya has vuelto a llegar tarde*** I knew it, you're late again
2 (= *defraudar*) **~ a algn** to let sb down, fail sb; **me has fallado de nuevo** you've let me down again; **mañana hay reunión, no me falles** there's a meeting tomorrow, don't let me down
3 (*Jur*) to pass judgment; **~ a favor/en contra de algn** to rule in favour of/against sb, find for/against sb
4 (*Naipes*) to trump
Ⓑ VT 1 (= *errar*) **falló las cuatro preguntas** she got all four questions wrong; **fallé el tiro** I missed; **~ el blanco** to miss the target
2 (*Jur*) to deliver judg(e)ment in
3 [+ *premio*] to award
4 (*Naipes*) to trump

Fallas SFPL *Valencian celebration of the feast of St Joseph*

FALLAS

In the week of 19 March (the feast of San José), Valencia honours its patron saint with a spectacular fiesta called **las Fallas**. **Fallas** *is the name given to the huge papier-mâché, cardboard and wooden sculptures depicting politicians and other well-known public figures which, amidst a deafening display of fireworks, are put on bonfires and set alight by members of competing groups, or* **falleros**, *who will have spent the previous year creating and building them. Only the sculpture which is voted best escapes the flames.*

falleba SF door *o* window catch, espagnolette

▼**fallecer** ▸conjug 2d◂ VI to die, pass away (*euf*)

fallecido/a Ⓐ ADJ deceased, late
Ⓑ SM/F deceased

▼**fallecimiento** SM death, demise (*frm*), passing (*euf*)

fallero¹/a Ⓐ ADJ *of/relating to the "Fallas"*
Ⓑ SM/F 1 (= *constructor*) *maker of "Fallas"*
2 (= *participante*) *person who takes part in the "Fallas"* ► **fallera mayor** Fallas queen

fallero² ADJ (*Cono Sur*) work-shy

fallido ADJ 1 [*esfuerzo*] unsuccessful; [*esperanza*] disappointed; [*deuda*] bad, irrecoverable; (*Mec, Mil*) dud; **un tiro ~** a missed shot, a shot wide of the mark *o* target
2 (*Caribe Com*) (= *quebrado*) bankrupt

fallir ▸conjug 3a◂ VI 1 (*Caribe*) (= *quebrar*) to go bankrupt
2 (†) (= *fallar*) to fail
3 (†) (= *caducar*) to run out, expire

▼**fallo** Ⓐ SM 1 (= *mal funcionamiento*) failure; (= *defecto*) fault; **debido a un ~ de los frenos** because of brake failure ► **fallo cardíaco** heart failure ► **fallo de diseño** design fault
2 (= *error*) mistake; **ha sido un ~ decírselo** it was a mistake telling him; **¡qué ~!** what a stupid mistake! ► **fallo humano** human error
3 (*Jur*) [*de un tribunal*] judg(e)ment, ruling; **el ~ fue a su favor** the judg(e)ment *o* ruling was in her favour; **han apelado contra el ~ del jurado** they have appealed against the jury's verdict ► **fallo absolutorio** verdict of not guilty ► **fallo condenatorio** verdict of guilty

➤ LENGUA Y USO: **fallecer** 51.4 **fallecimiento** 51.4 **fallo A2** 45.2

[4] [*de concurso, premio*] decision; **hoy se anunciará el ~ del jurado** the jury's decision will be announced today; **ya se conoce el ~ del concurso de poesía** it is already known who has won the poetry prize
[5] (*Naipes*) void; **tengo ~ a picas** I have a void in spades
(B) ADJ (*Naipes*) **estar ~ a** have a void in

fallón* ADJ (*Ecu*) unreliable

fallutería* SF (*Cono Sur*) [1] (= *hipocresía*) hypocrisy
[2] (= *poca fiabilidad*) untrustworthiness

falluto* ADJ (*Cono Sur*) [1] (= *hipócrita*) hypocritical, two-faced*
[2] (= *poco fiable*) untrustworthy, unreliable
[3] (= *fracasado*) unsuccessful, failed

falo SM phallus

falocracia* SF male domination, male chauvinism

falócrata SM male chauvinist pig*

falocrático ADJ male chauvinist *antes de s*; **actitud falocrática** male chauvinist attitude

falopa‡ SF (*Cono Sur*) hard drugs *pl*

falopearse‡ ▸conjug 1a◂ VPR (*Cono Sur*) to take hard drugs

falopero/a‡ SM/F (*Cono Sur*) druggy‡

falsamente ADV [1] (= *erróneamente*) falsely; **lo han acusado ~** he has been falsely accused
[2] (= *insinceramente*) falsely; **con un aspecto ~ inocente** with a false look of innocence

falsario/a SM/F [1] (= *mentiroso*) liar
[2] (= *falseador*) forger, counterfeiter

falseable ADJ **fácilmente ~** easy to forge, readily forged

falseador(a) SM/F forger, counterfeiter

falsear ▸conjug 1a◂ (A) VT [+ *cifras, datos*] to falsify, doctor; [+ *verdad, hechos*] to distort; [+ *voto*] to rig*, fiddle*; [+ *firma, moneda, documento*] to forge, fake; [+ *cerrojo*] to pick; (*Téc*) to bevel
(B) VI [1] (= *ceder*) to buckle, sag; (*fig*) to flag, slacken
[2] (*Mús*) to be out of tune

falsedad SF [1] [*de acusación, teoría*] falseness, falsity; [*de persona*] falseness, insincerity
[2] (= *mentira*) lie, falsehood (*frm*)

falsete SM [1] (*Mús*) falsetto
[2] [*de cuba*] plug, bung
[3] (*Andes**) hypocrite

falsía SF duplicity (*frm*), falseness

falsificación SF [1] (= *acto*) (= *creación*) forging, faking; (= *alteración*) falsification
[2] (= *objeto*) forgery

falsificador(a) SM/F forger, counterfeiter

falsificar ▸conjug 1g◂ VT [+ *billete, firma, cuadro*] to forge, fake, counterfeit; [+ *resultado, elección*] to rig*, fiddle*; [+ *documento*] (= *crear*) to forge, fake; (= *cambiar*) to falsify

falsilla SF guide (*in copying*)

falso (A) ADJ [1] [*acusación, creencia, rumor*] false; **lo que dices es ~** what you're saying is false *o* untrue; **se inscribió con un nombre ~** she registered under a false name; **ha sido una falsa alarma** it was a false alarm; **~ testimonio** perjury, false testimony
[2] [*firma, pasaporte, joya*] false, fake; [*techo*] false; [*cuadro*] fake; [*moneda*] counterfeit
[3] (= *insincero*) [*persona*] false, insincere; [*sonrisa*] false
[4] [*caballo*] vicious
[5] **en ~**: **coger a algn en ~** to catch sb in a lie; **dar un paso en ~** (*lit*) to trip; (*fig*) to take a false step; **jurar en ~** to commit perjury
(B) SM (*CAm, Méx*) false evidence

▼**falta** SF [1] (= *carencia*) [1·1] [*de recursos, información, control, acuerdo*] lack; **los candidatos demostraron en el examen su absoluta ~ de preparación** in the exam the candidates revealed their total lack of preparation; **es evidente su ~ de voluntad negociadora** it is clear that they have no wish to negotiate; **~ de respeto** disrespect, lack of respect; **la ~ de respeto por las ideas de los demás** disrespect *o* lack of respect for other people's ideas; **¡qué ~ de respeto!** how rude!
[1·2] **a ~ de** in the absence of, for want of; **a ~ de información fiable, nos limitamos a repetir los rumores** in the absence of reliable information, we can merely repeat the rumours, we can merely repeat the rumours, for want of reliable information; **a ~ de champán para celebrarlo, beberemos cerveza** as we don't have any champagne to celebrate with, we'll drink beer; **a ~ de un término/sistema mejor** for want of a better term/system; **a ~ de tres minutos para el final** three minutes from the end; **a ~ de 40kms para la meta el ciclista se retiró** the cyclist withdrew 40kms from the finish; ✦***REFRÁN*** **a ~ de pan, buenas son tortas** half a loaf is better than none
[1·3] **por ~ de** for lack of; **se absolvió al acusado por ~ de pruebas** the defendant was acquitted for lack of evidence; **el rosal se murió por ~ de luz** the rose died due to lack of light
[1·4] **echar algo/a algn en ~** to miss sth/sb; **echo en ~ a mis amigos** I miss my friends; **durante el festival se echaron en ~ a las grandes estrellas** the big names were missing from the festival; *ver tb* **educación 3**
[2] **hacer ~**: **me hace mucha ~ un coche** I really *o* badly* need a car; **a este plato le hace ~ sal** this dish needs more salt; **lo que hace ~ aquí es más disciplina** what's needed here is stricter discipline; **aquí no haces ~** you're not needed here; **no nos hace ~ nada** we've got everything we need, we don't need anything else; **es el hombre que hacía ~** he is the right man for the job; **¡~ hacía!** and about time too!; **si hace ~, voy** if necessary, I'll go, if need be, I'll go; **hacer ~ hacer algo**: **para ser enfermero hace ~ tener vocación** you have to be dedicated to be a nurse; **no hace ~ ser un experto para llegar a esa conclusión** you don't need to be an expert to reach that conclusion; **ahora lo que te hace ~ es recuperar las fuerzas** what you need now is to regain your strength; **¡hace ~ ser tonto para no darse cuenta!** you have to be pretty stupid not to realize!; **hacer ~ que** + SUBJUN: **hace ~ que el agua esté hirviendo** the water must be *o* needs to be boiling; **si hace ~ que os echemos una mano, llamadnos** if you need us to give you a hand, give us a call; **no hace ~ que se lo digas** there's no need for you to tell him; ✦***MODISMO*** **ni ~ que hace** (*iró*): **—¿te han invitado al concierto? —no, ni ~ que me hace** "haven't they invited you to the concert?" — "no, and I couldn't care less"*
[3] (*Escol*) (= *ausencia*) absence; **poner ~ a algn** to mark sb absent, put sb down as absent ► **falta de asistencia** absence; **tiene cinco ~s de asistencia** he has been absent five times
[4] (= *infracción*) [4·1] (*Jur*) offence, offense (*EEUU*); **~ grave** serious offence, serious offense (*EEUU*), serious misconduct; **~ leve** minor offence, minor offense (*EEUU*), misdemeanour, misdemeanor (*EEUU*)
[4·2] (*Ftbl, Balonmano*) foul; (*Tenis*) fault; **ha sido ~** it was a foul *o* fault; **va a sacar la ~** (*Ftbl*) he's going to take the free kick; (*Balonmano*) he's going to take the free throw; **cometer una ~ contra algn** to foul sb; **lanzamiento de ~** (*Ftbl*) free kick
► **falta personal** personal foul
[5] (= *fallo*) [*de persona*] shortcoming, fault; [*de máquina, producto*] flaw, fault; **sacar ~s a algn** to point out sb's shortcomings, find fault with sb; **siempre le está sacando ~s a todo lo que hago** she's always picking holes in everything I do; **sin ~** without fail; **mañana sin ~ recibirá nuestro informe** you will get our report tomorrow without fail ► **falta de ortografía** spelling mistake
[6] (*por estar embarazada*) missed period

faltar ▸conjug 1a◂ VI [1] (= *no haber suficiente*) **faltan profesores** there aren't enough teachers; **a la sopa le falta sal** there isn't enough salt in the soup; **faltan viviendas asequibles** there is a shortage of affordable housing; **faltan dos sillas** we are two chairs short; **~ algo a algn**: **le falta todavía un impreso** you still need another form; **¿te falta dinero?** do you need any money?; **nos falta tiempo para hacerlo** we don't have enough time to do it; **te faltan dos centímetros para poder ser policía** you're two centimetres too short to be a policeman; **no le falta valor** he doesn't lack courage; ✦***MODISMOS*** **¡lo que (me) faltaba!** that's all I needed!; **¡no faltaba** *o* **~ía más!** (= *no hay de qué*) don't mention it!; (= *naturalmente*) of course; (= *¡ni hablar!*) certainly not!, no way!*; **¡no faltaba más que eso!** ◊ **¡lo que faltaba!** (= *¡es el colmo!*) that's the last straw!; (= *¡ni hablar!*) certainly not!, no way!*; **es mejor que sobre que no que falte** better to have too much than too little
[2] (= *no estar*) to be missing; **faltan varios libros del estante** there are several books missing from the shelf; **faltan 20 euros de la caja** there are 20 euros missing from the till; **me falta un bolígrafo** one of my pens is missing; **faltaba de su casa desde hacía un mes** he had been missing for a month; **¿quién falta?** who's missing?, who's not here?; **no podemos irnos, falta Manolo** we can't go, Manolo isn't here yet; **no ~**: **un desayuno en el que no faltan los huevos y el beicon** a breakfast which doesn't fail to include eggs and bacon; **un partido en el que no ~on goles** a match which was not short of goals; **no falta ninguno de los ingredientes de la novela policíaca** all of the ingredients of the detective novel are present; **no falta quien opina que …** there are those who think that …
[3] (= *no ir*) **no he faltado ni una sola vez a las reuniones** I haven't missed a single meeting; **~on tres personas a la reunión** there were three people missing *o* absent from the meeting; **¡no ~é!** I'll be there!; **~ a una cita** (*de negocios*) to miss an appointment, not turn

➤ LENGUA Y USO: falta 1 44.1 2 37.3

up for an appointment; (*con amigo*) not not turn up for a date; **~ a clase** to miss school; **~ al trabajo** to be off work; **nunca falta al trabajo** he's never off work

[4] (= *quedar*) **falta todavía bastante por hacer** there is still quite a lot to be done, quite a lot remains to be done; **falta mucho todavía** there's plenty of time to go yet; **¿falta mucho?** is there long to go?; **¿te falta mucho?** will you be long?; **~ para algo**: **faltan tres semanas para las elecciones** there are three weeks to go to the election, the election is three weeks off; **faltan cinco minutos para que comience la representación** the performance will begin in five minutes; **faltan cinco para las siete** (*LAm*) it's five to seven; **falta poco para las ocho** it's nearly eight o'clock, it's getting on for eight o'clock; **falta poco para que termine el partido** the match is almost over *o* finished

[5] (= *estar a punto de*) **faltó poco para que lo pillara un coche** he was very nearly run down by a car; **le faltaba poco para decírselo** she was about to tell him

[6] (= *insultar*) **¡sin ~!, ¿eh?** keep it polite, right?; **~ a algn** (= *ofender*) to offend sb; (= *ser infiel a*) to be unfaithful to sb; (= *no apoyar*) to fail sb; **~ a algn al respeto** to be rude to sb, be disrespectful to sb

[7] (= *no cumplir*) **~ en algo**: **~ en los pagos** to default on one's payments; **no ~é en comunicárselo** I shall not fail to tell him; *ver tb* **decencia 1**, **palabra 4**, **promesa 1**, **respeto 1**, **verdad 1**

[8] (*euf*) (= *estar muerto*) **desde que falta su madre** since his mother passed away; **cuando falte yo** when I'm gone

falto ADJ [1] (= *carente*) **~ de** [*recursos, información, ideas, inteligencia*] lacking in; **nos pareció un partido ~ de interés** we thought the match was uninteresting *o* lacking in interest; **un hombre ~ de carisma** a man lacking in charisma, a man with no charisma; **un hombre ~ de escrúpulos** an unscrupulous man; **un boxeador ~ de reflejos** a boxer with poor reflexes; **estar ~ de personal** to be short of staff

[2] (†) (*moralmente*) poor, wretched, mean

[3] (*Andes*) (= *fatuo*) fatuous, vain

faltón ADJ [1] (= *negligente*) neglectful, unreliable (*about carrying out duties*) [2] (= *irrespetuoso*) disrespectful [3] (*LAm*) (= *vago*) slack (about work), work-shy

faltoso ADJ [1] (*CAm, Méx*) (= *negligente*) neglectful, unreliable (*about carrying out duties*)

[2] (*CAm, Méx*) (= *irrespetuoso*) disrespectful

[3] (*Andes*) (= *discutidor*) quarrelsome

faltriquera SF [1] (= *bolsillo*) pocket, pouch; [*de reloj*] fob, watch pocket; ✦***MODISMO*** **rascarse la ~** to dig into one's pocket

[2] (= *bolso*) handbag, purse (*EEUU*)

falúa SF (*Náut*) tender

fama SF [1] (= *renombre*) fame; **el libro que le dio ~** the book which made him famous, the book which made his name; **llegar a la ~** to become famous; **tener ~** to be famous; **tus pasteles tienen ~** your cakes are famous; ✦***REFRÁN*** **unos tienen la ~ y otros cardan la lana** some do all the work and others take the credit

[2] (= *reputación*) reputation; **tiene ~ de duro** he has a reputation for being tough; **este restaurante tiene ~ de barato** this restaurant is (well-)known for its cheap food; **tener mala ~** to have a bad reputation; **una casa de mala ~** a house of ill repute

[3] (= *rumor*) report, rumour, rumor (*EEUU*); **corre la ~ de que ...** it is rumoured *o* (*EEUU*) rumored that ...

famélico ADJ starving, famished

familia SF [1] (= *parentela*) family; **¿cómo está la ~?** how is the family?; **es de buena ~** she comes from a good family; **sentirse como en ~** to feel thoroughly at home; **ser como de la ~** to be one of the family; **venir de ~** to run in the family; ✦***MODISMO*** **acordarse de la ~ de algn*** to curse sb, swear at sb ► **familia de acogida** foster family ► **familia monoparental** one-parent family ► **familia nuclear** nuclear family ► **familia numerosa**: **tiene una ~ numerosa** he has a large family; **las ~s numerosas quedan exentas** families with more than four children are exempt ► **familia política** in-laws *pl* ► **familia real** royal family

[2] (= *hijos*) **¿cuándo pensáis tener ~?** when are you thinking of starting a family?; **¿tenéis ya mucha ~?** do you already have lots of children?

[3] (= *pariente*) **Juan no es ~ mía** Juan and I aren't related; **¿sois ~?** are you related?

[4] (= *comunidad*) family; **la gran ~ humana** the great human family; **la ~ socialista** the socialist community

[5] (*Bot, Ling, Zool*) family ► **familia de lenguas** family of languages ► **familia de palabras** word family

[6] (*Tip*) fount

familiar Ⓐ ADJ [1] (= *de la familia*) family *antes de s*; **lazos ~es** family ties; **creció en un ambiente ~ muy alegre** he grew up in a very happy family environment; **"pensión Sol, ambiente familiar"** "pensión Sol, friendly atmosphere"; **coche ~** estate car, station wagon (*EEUU*); **dioses ~es** household gods; **envase ~** family-sized *o* family pack; **en la pensión recibes un trato ~** in the guesthouse they treat you like one of the family

[2] (= *conocido*) familiar; **tu cara me resulta ~** your face looks familiar

[3] [*lenguaje, término*] colloquial

Ⓑ SMF (= *pariente*) relative, relation

familiaridad SF [1] (*en el trato*) familiarity (**con** with); **no le gusta que te tomes esas ~es** he doesn't like you being so familiar with him

[2] [*de estilo*] familiarity, informality

familiarizar ▸conjug 1f◂ Ⓐ VT to familiarize, acquaint; **~ a algn con algo** to familiarize *o* acquaint sb with sth

Ⓑ **familiarizarse** VPR **~se con** to familiarize o.s. with, get to know, make o.s. familiar with

famoseo SM **una revista de ~** a celebrity magazine; **todo lo que hay que saber sobre el ~** everything you need to know about celebrities

famosillo/a* Ⓐ ADJ well-known in limited circles Ⓑ SM/F minor celebrity

famoso/a Ⓐ ADJ [1] (= *célebre*) famous, well-known; **un actor ~** a famous *o* well-known actor; **el pueblo es ~ por su cerámica** the town is famous for its pottery; **es ~ por sus ocurrencias** he's renowned for his witticisms

[2] (*) (= *sonado*) **es otra de sus famosas ocurrencias** it's another of his bright ideas; **aún recuerdo su ~ enfado** I can still remember that time she got angry

Ⓑ SM/F celebrity, famous person; **los ~s** celebrities

fan SMF (*pl* **fans**) fan

fanal SM [1] (*Náut*) (= *farol*) (*en la costa*) harbour beacon, harbor beacon (*EEUU*); (*en barco*) lantern [2] (= *campana*) bell glass [3] (= *pantalla*) [*de lámpara*] chimney [4] (*Méx Aut*) headlight

fanaticada SF (*Caribe*) fans *pl*

fanático/a Ⓐ ADJ fanatical

Ⓑ SM/F (*gen*) fanatic; (*LAm Dep*) fan; **es un ~ del aeromodelismo** he's mad about model aeroplanes; **los ~s de la estrella** the star's fans *o* admirers

fanatismo SM fanaticism

fanatizar ▸conjug 1f◂ VT to arouse fanaticism in

fancine SM = **fanzine**

fandango SM [1] (*Mús*) fandango

[2] (*) (= *jaleo*) row, rumpus*; **se armó un ~** there was a huge row

[3] (*LAm**) (= *fiesta*) rowdy party, booze-up*

fandanguear* ▸conjug 1a◂ VI (*Cono Sur*) to live it up*

fané* ADJ INV [1] (*Cono Sur*) (= *cansado*) worn out, tired out

[2] (*LAm*) (= *arrugado*) messed-up, crumpled

[3] (†) (= *cursi*) vulgar

faneca SF *species of flatfish*

fanega SF [1] *grain measure (in Spain 1.58 bushels, in Mexico 2.57 bushels, in the S. Cone 3.89 bushels)*

[2] *land measure (in Spain 1.59 acres, in the Caribbean 1.73 acres)*

fanfarrear ▸conjug 1a◂ VI = **fanfarronear**

fanfarria SF [1] (*Mús*) fanfare

[2] (*) (= *jactancia*) boasting

fanfarrón/ona Ⓐ ADJ boastful

Ⓑ SM/F boaster, braggart

fanfarronada SF [1] (= *acción*) boasting; **no hace más que ~s** he does nothing but boast

[2] (= *farol*) bluff

fanfarronear ▸conjug 1a◂ VI to boast, talk big*

fanfarronería SF = **fanfarronada**

fangal SM bog, quagmire

fango SM (= *lodo*) mud, mire; (*fig*) mire, dirt

fangoso ADJ muddy, miry

fanguero Ⓐ ADJ (*Cono Sur*) [*animal, jugador*] suited to heavy going

Ⓑ SM (*Caribe, Méx*) [1] (= *fango*) mud, mire

[2] (= *fangal*) bog, quagmire

fantasear ▸conjug 1a◂ VI to dream, fantasize

fantaseo SM dreaming, fantasizing

fantasía SF [1] (= *imaginación*) imagination; **es un producto de su ~** it's a figment of his imagination

[2] (= *cosa imaginada*) fantasy; **son ~s infantiles** they're just children's fantasies; **un mundo de ~** a fantasy world

[3] (*Arte, Literat*) fantasy; (*Mús*) fantasia, fantasy; **tocar por ~** to improvise

[4] **de ~** (= *con adornos, colores*) fancy; **botones de ~** fancy buttons; **joyas de ~** costume jewellery

fantasioso ADJ [1] (= *soñador*) dreamy

[2] (= *presuntuoso*) vain, conceited; **¡fantasiosa!** you're so vain!

fantasma Ⓐ SM [1] (= *aparición*) ghost, phantom (*liter*)

[2] (*TV*) ghost

Ⓑ SMF (*Esp**) (= *fanfarrón*) boaster, braggart

Ⓒ ADJ INV [1] (= *abandonado*) ghost *antes de s*; **buque ~** ghost ship; **ciudad ~** ghost city
[2] (= *inexistente*) phantom *antes de s*; **embarazo ~** phantom pregnancy; **miembro ~** phantom limb; **compañía ~** bogus *o* dummy company

fantasmada* SF bluster, bravado

fantasmagoría SF phantasmagoria

fantasmagórico ADJ phantasmagoric

fantasmal ADJ ghostly, phantom *antes de s*

fantasmear* ▸conjug 1a◂ VI to show off

fantasmón/ona* Ⓐ ADJ boastful
Ⓑ SM/F boaster

fantásticamente ADV fantastically

fantástico Ⓐ ADJ [1] (= *imaginario*) fantastic
[2] (*) (= *estupendo*) fantastic, great*
[3] (= *fanfarrón*) boastful
Ⓑ EXCL (*) great!, fantastic!, terrific!*

fantochada* SF [1] (= *estupidez*) **no digas ~s** don't talk rubbish, don't talk bullshit**; **no hagas ~s** stop messing around
[2] (= *fanfarronada*) **ésa es otra ~ de tu hermana** that's your sister showing off again

fantoche Ⓐ SM [1] (= *títere*) puppet, marionette
[2] (*) (*persona*) (= *mediocre*) mediocrity, nonentity; (= *presumido*) braggart, loudmouth*
Ⓑ ADJ INV puppet *antes de s*; **régimen ~** puppet régime

fantochesco ADJ puppet-like

fantomático ADJ shadowy, mysterious

fanzine SM fanzine

FAO SF ABR [1] (= **Food and Agriculture Organization**) FAO
[2] (= **Fabricación Asistida por Ordenador**) CAM

faquín SM porter

faquir SM fakir

farabute SM (*Cono Sur*) [1] (= *pícaro*) rogue
[2] (= *poco cumplidor*) unreliable person
[3] (= *pobre diablo*) poor wretch

faralá SM (*pl* **faralaes**) [1] (= *volante*) flounce, frill
[2] **faralaes** (*pey*) frills, buttons and bows

farallón SM (*Geog*) headland; (*Geol*) outcrop; (*Cono Sur*) rocky peak

faramalla* SF [1] (= *charla*) humbug, claptrap*; (*Com*) patter, spiel
[2] (= *impostura*) empty show, sham
[3] (*Méx, Chile**) lie
[4] (*Cono Sur*) (= *jactancia*) bragging, boasting

faramallear* ▸conjug 1a◂ VI [1] (*Méx, Chile*) (= *mentir*) to lie
[2] (*Cono Sur*) (= *jactarse*) to brag, boast

faramallero* ADJ (*Cono Sur*) bragging, boastful

farándula SF [1] (*Teat, Hist*) troupe of strolling players; **el mundo de la ~** the theatre *o* (*EEUU*) theater world
[2] (*) (= *charla*) humbug, claptrap*

faranduleo SM trickery

farandulero/a Ⓐ ADJ (*LAm**) = **farolero A**
Ⓑ SM/F [1] (*Teat, Hist*) strolling player
[2] (*) (= *timador*) confidence trickster, con man, swindler

faraón SM Pharaoh

faraónico ADJ (*Hist*) Pharaonic; [*plan, obra*] overambitious

faraute SM [1] (††) herald
[2] (= *entrometido*) busybody

FARC SFPL ABR (*Col*) = **Fuerzas Armadas Revolucionarias de Colombia**

fardada* SF show, display; **pegarse una ~** to show off

fardar* ▸conjug 1a◂ VI [1] [*persona*] (= *lucirse*) to show off, put on a display; (= *jactarse*) to boast; **fardaba de sus amigas** he boasted about his girlfriends
[2] [*objeto*] to be classy; **es un coche que farda mucho** it's a car with a lot of class

farde* SM (= *lucimiento*) showing-off, display; (= *jactancia*) boasting

fardel SM [1] (= *talega*) bag, knapsack
[2] (= *bulto*) bundle

fardo SM [1] (= *bulto*) bundle; (= *bala*) bale, pack
[2] (*fig*) burden; **✦MODISMO pasar el ~** (*Perú**) to pass the buck*

fardón/ona* Ⓐ ADJ [1] [*objeto*] (= *con clase*) classy*, posh; (= *precioso*) nice, great*
[2] (= *elegante*) [*ropa*] natty*; [*persona*] nattily dressed*
[3] (= *vanidoso*) stuck-up*, swanky*
Ⓑ SM/F show-off*

farero/a SM/F lighthouse-keeper

farfulla* Ⓐ SF [1] (= *balbuceo*) spluttering
[2] (= *habla atropellada*) jabbering, gabble
[3] (*LAm*) (= *jactancia*) bragging, boasting
Ⓑ SMF jabberer, gabbler

farfullador ADJ [1] (= *balbuceante*) spluttering; (= *con habla atropellada*) jabbering, gabbling
[2] (*LAm*) (= *jactancioso*) bragging, boastful

farfullar ▸conjug 1a◂ Ⓐ VI [1] (= *balbucear*) to splutter; (= *hablar atropelladamente*) to jabber, gabble
[2] (*LAm*) (= *jactarse*) to brag, boast
Ⓑ VT [1] (*al hablar*) to jabber, gabble
[2] (*al actuar*) to do hastily, botch

farfulleo SM (= *balbuceo*) spluttering; (= *habla atropellada*) jabbering, gabbling

farfullero* ADJ [1] (= *balbuceante*) spluttering; (= *con habla atropellada*) jabbering, gabbling
[2] (*LAm*) = **fanfarrón**

farináceo ADJ starchy, farinaceous (*frm*)

faringe SF pharynx

faringitis SF INV pharyngitis

fariña SF (*Perú, Cono Sur*) coarse manioc flour

fario SM **mal ~** bad luck

farisaico ADJ [1] (*Rel*) Pharisaic(al)
[2] (= *hipócrita*) hypocritical, Pharisaic(al) (*frm*)

fariseo SM [1] (*Rel*) Pharisee
[2] (= *hipócrita*) hypocrite, Pharisee

farlopa* SF (*Esp*) blow*, coke*

farmacéutico/a Ⓐ ADJ [*producto*] pharmaceutical; **la industria farmacéutica** the pharmaceutical *o* drug industry
Ⓑ SM/F (= *persona*) chemist, druggist (*EEUU*), pharmacist (*frm*)

farmacia SF [1] (= *ciencia*) pharmacy
[2] (= *tienda*) chemist's (shop), drugstore (*EEUU*) ► **farmacia de guardia** all-night chemist's

fármaco SM drug, medicine

farmacodependencia SF drug dependency, dependence on drugs

farmacología SF pharmacology

farmacológico ADJ pharmacological

farmacólogo/a SM/F pharmacologist

farmacopea SF pharmacopoeia

faro Ⓐ SM [1] (*Náut*) (= *edificio*) lighthouse; (= *señal*) beacon ► **faro aéreo** air beacon
[2] (*Aut*) headlamp, headlight ► **faro antiniebla** foglamp ► **faro de marcha atrás** reversing light ► **faro halógeno** halogen headlight ► **faro lateral** sidelight ► **faro piloto, faro trasero** rear light, tail light
[3] **faros*** (= *ojos*) peepers*, eyes
Ⓑ ADJ INV (*) **idea ~** bright idea, brilliant idea

farol SM [1] (= *lámpara*) (*en terraza, jardín*) lantern, lamp; (*en la calle*) street lamp; (*Ferro*) headlamp; **✦MODISMOS ¡adelante con los ~es!** press on regardless!; **hacer de ~*** to play gooseberry, be a third wheel (*EEUU*) ► **farol de viento** hurricane lamp
[2] (*) (= *mentira*) (*gen*) lie, fib; (*Naipes*) bluff; **echarse** *o* **marcarse** *o* **tirarse un ~** (*gen*) to shoot a line*, brag; (*Naipes*) to bluff
[3] (*Taur*) flourishing pass
[4] (*Cono Sur*) (= *ventana*) bay window, glassed-in balcony
[5] (= *envase*) *wrapping of tobacco packet*
[6] **faroles** (*LAm**) (= *ojos*) peepers*, eyes

farola SF (= *lámpara*) street lamp; (= *poste*) lamppost

faroladas* SFPL boasting *sing*

farolazo* SM (*CAm, Méx*) swig* (*of liquor*)

farolear* ▸conjug 1a◂ VI (= *presumir*) to boast, brag; (*Naipes*) to bluff

farolero/a Ⓐ ADJ (*) boastful
Ⓑ SM/F [1] (*) (= *fanfarrón*) boaster
[2] (*) (= *mentiroso*) bullshitter**
[3] (= *fabricante*) lamp-maker
[4] (†) (*del alumbrado público*) lamplighter

farolillo SM [1] (*Elec*) fairy-light; (*de papel*) Chinese lantern ► **farolillo rojo** (*Atletismo*) back marker; (*Ftbl*) *team in last place*
[2] (*Bot*) Canterbury bell

farra[1] SF [1] (*esp LAm*) (= *juerga*) party; **ir de ~** to go out partying/drinking
[2] (*Cono Sur*) (= *mofa*) mockery, teasing; **✦MODISMO tomar a algn para la ~** to pull sb's leg

farra[2] SF (= *pez*) salmon trout

fárrago SM hotchpotch, hodgepodge (*EEUU*), jumble

farragoso ADJ (*gen*) cumbersome; [*discurso*] involved, dense

farrear ▸conjug 1a◂ Ⓐ VI (*esp Cono Sur*) to party, be out drinking
Ⓑ **farrearse** VPR [1] (*Cono Sur*) **~se de algn** to tease sb
[2] (*Arg*) [+ *dinero*] to squander

farrero/a Ⓐ ADJ (*Andes, Cono Sur*) merry, fun-loving
Ⓑ SM/F reveller

farrista ADJ [1] (*Cono Sur*) (= *borracho*) hard-drinking, dissipated
[2] (= *juerguista*) boisterous, rowdy

farruco* ADJ stroppy*; **estar** *o* **ponerse ~** to get stroppy*, get aggressive

farruto* ADJ (*Chile pey*) sickly, weak

farsa[1] SF [1] (*Teat*) farce; (*pey*) bad play
[2] (= *engaño*) farce, sham

farsa[2] SF (*Culin*) stuffing

farsante* SMF fraud, phoney*, phony (*EEUU**)

farsear ▸conjug 1a◂ VI (*CAm*) to joke

farsesco ADJ farcical

FAS ABR = **Fuerzas Armadas**

fas: **por ~ o por nefas** ADV rightly or wrongly

FASA SF ABR (*Esp*) = **Fábrica de Automóviles, S.A.**

fascículo SM part, instalment, installment (*EEUU*)

fascinación SF fascination

fascinador ADJ, **fascinante** ADJ fascinating

fascinar ▸conjug 1a◂ VT to fascinate, captivate

fascismo SM fascism

fascista ADJ, SMF fascist

fase SF [1] (= *etapa*) stage, phase; **el proyecto está en ~ de estudio** the project is still under consideration; **estar en ~ ascendente** [*persona*] to be on the way up; [*equipo*] to be on a winning run ► **fase clasificatoria** (*Dep*) qualifying stage ► **fase terminal** terminal phase [2] (*Astron, Biol, Elec*) phase [3] [*de cohete*] stage

fashion ['faʃon] ADJ INV trendy*

faso* SM (*Cono Sur*) cigarette, fag‡

fastidiado* ADJ [1] (= *estropeado*) ruined, bust* [2] **ando ~ del estómago** ◊ **tengo el estómago ~** I've got a dodgy* *o* bad stomach

fastidiar ▸conjug 1b◂ Ⓐ VT [1] (= *molestar*) to annoy; **lo que más me fastidia es tener que decírselo** what annoys me most is having to tell him; **su actitud me fastidia mucho** I find his attitude very annoying; **me fastidia tener que ir** it's a pain having to go*; **¡y encima me insultó ¡no te fastidia!** and on top of that, he was rude to me, can you believe it!

[2] (= *estropear*) [+ *fiesta, plan*] to spoil, ruin; [+ *aparato*] to break; **nos ha fastidiado las vacaciones** it's spoiled *o* ruined our holidays; **¡la hemos fastidiado!** drat!*

Ⓑ VI (= *bromear*) **¡no fastidies!** you're kidding!

Ⓒ **fastidiarse** VPR [1] (= *aguantarse*) **¡a ~se!** ◊ **¡fastídiate!** (that's) tough *o* too bad!*; **¿no le gusta la comida? ¡pues que se fastidie!** he doesn't like the food? well, that's tough!*; **¡para que te fastidies!** so there!*

[2] (= *dañarse*) to hurt; **me he vuelto a ~ la rodilla** I've hurt my knee again, I've done my knee in again

[3] (*) (= *estropearse*) [*fiesta, plan*] to be spoiled, be ruined; [*aparato*] to break down

[4] (*LAm*) (= *aburrirse*) to get bored

fastidio SM [1] (= *molestia*) annoyance, bother; **¡qué ~!** what a nuisance!

[2] (*LAm*) (= *asco*) disgust, repugnance

fastidioso ADJ [1] (= *molesto*) annoying [2] (= *aburrido*) tedious, boring, tiresome [3] (*LAm*) (= *quisquilloso*) fastidious

fasto SM [1] (= *pompa*) pomp, pageantry [2] **fastos** (*Literat*) annals

fastuosamente ADV (= *espléndidamente*) magnificently, splendidly; (= *suntuosamente*) lavishly, sumptuously

fastuoso ADJ [*palacio, carroza*] magnificent, splendid; [*banquete, fiesta*] lavish, sumptuous

fatal Ⓐ ADJ [1] (= *mortal*) [*accidente, desenlace*] fatal

[2] (*) (= *horrible*) awful, terrible; **tiene un inglés ~** his English is awful *o* terrible; **la obra estuvo ~** the play was awful *o* terrible

[3] (= *inevitable*) [*plazo, cita*] unavoidable; **ese comentario ~ firmó su sentencia** that ill-fated *o* disastrous comment sealed his sentence

Ⓑ ADV (*) terribly; **lo pasaron ~** they had an awful *o* a terrible time (of it); **cocina ~** he's an awful *o* a terrible cook; **me encuentro ~** I feel awful *o* terrible

fatalidad SF [1] (= *destino*) fate [2] (= *desdicha*) misfortune, bad luck

fatalismo SM fatalism

fatalista Ⓐ ADJ fatalistic Ⓑ SMF fatalist

fatalizarse ▸conjug 1f◂ VPR [1] (*Andes*) (= *cometer un delito*) to commit a grave crime [2] (*Cono Sur*) (= *sufrir herida*) to seriously hurt o.s.; (*Andes*) (= *sufrir desgracia*) to suffer a series of misfortunes (*as a punishment for a wrong committed*)

fatalmente ADV [1] (= *mortalmente*) fatally [2] (= *inevitablemente*) unavoidably, inevitably [3] (*) (= *muy mal*) disastrously

fatídicamente ADV [1] (= *desgraciadamente*) fatefully, ominously [2] (= *proféticamente*) prophetically

fatídico ADJ [1] (= *desgraciado*) fateful, ominous [2] (= *profético*) prophetic

fatiga SF [1] (= *cansancio*) fatigue (*frm*), tiredness, weariness ► **fatiga cerebral** mental fatigue ► **fatiga muscular** muscle fatigue

[2] (= *ahogo*) breathlessness; **subir las escaleras me causa ~** climbing the stairs makes me breathless, when I climb the stairs I get *o* run out of breath

[3] (= *reparo*) embarrassment; **me da ~ llamar a estas horas de la noche** I'm embarrassed calling at this time of night

[4] **fatigas** (= *penalidades*) hardship *sing*, troubles

[5] (*Téc*) fatigue ► **fatiga del metal** metal fatigue

fatigabilidad SF tendency to tire easily

fatigadamente ADV with difficulty, wearily

fatigar ▸conjug 1h◂ Ⓐ VT [1] (= *cansar*) to tire [2] (= *molestar*) to annoy

Ⓑ **fatigarse** VPR [1] (= *cansarse*) to tire, get tired; **~se al andar** to wear o.s. out walking [2] (= *ahogarse*) to get out of breath, get breathless

fatigosamente ADV painfully, with difficulty

fatigoso ADJ [1] (= *cansado*) tiring, exhausting [2] (*Med*) painful, difficult; **respiración fatigosa** laboured *o* (*EEUU*) labored breathing [3] (= *fastidioso*) trying, tiresome

fato* SM (*Cono Sur*) [1] (= *negocio*) shady deal [2] (= *amorío*) love affair

fatuidad SF [1] (= *necedad*) fatuousness, fatuity [2] (= *vanidad*) conceit

fatuo ADJ [1] (= *necio*) fatuous [2] (= *vanidoso*) conceited; *ver tb* **fuego 1**

fauces SFPL [1] (*Anat*) fauces, gullet *sing*; (*fig*) (= *boca*) jaws [2] (*LAm*) (= *colmillos*) tusks, teeth

faul SM (*pl* **fauls**) (*LAm Dep*) foul

faulear ▸conjug 1a◂ VT (*LAm Dep*) to foul

fauna SF fauna; **toda la ~ del barrio*** all the weirdos in the neighbourhood*

faunístico ADJ faunal; **riqueza faunística** wealth of the fauna

fauno SM faun

Fausto SM Faust

fausto Ⓐ ADJ fortunate, lucky; **~ acontecimiento** happy event; **fausta noticia** happy news; **fausta ocasión** happy occasion

Ⓑ SM splendour, splendor (*EEUU*), magnificence

fautor(a) SM/F (= *cómplice*) accomplice, helper; (= *instigador*) instigator

▼**favor** SM [1] (= *ayuda*) favour, favor (*EEUU*); **~ de venir puntualmente** (*Méx*) please be punctual; **hacer un ~ a algn** to do sb a favour; **¿me puedes hacer un ~?** can you do me a favour?; **¡está para hacerle un ~!‡** she's really something!*; **hacer un flaco ~ a algn** to do no favours to sb; **¿me hace el ~ de bajarme la maleta?** I wonder if you could get my suitcase down for me, please?, could you possibly get my suitcase down for me, please?; **¡haced el ~ de callaros!** will you please be quiet!; **si hace el ~ de pasar** if you'd like *o* care to go in; **si hace ~** (*LAm*) if you don't mind; **pedir un ~ a algn** to ask sb (for) a favour, ask a favour of sb (*más frm*); **por ~** please; **¿me dejan pasar, por ~?** could I get past, please?; **¡por ~! ¡qué calor hace!** goodness me, it's hot today!; ✦**REFRÁN ~ con ~ se paga** one good turn deserves another

[2] (*locuciones*) [2.1] **a favor** in favour; **hay un 50% de gente a ~** 50% of people are in favour; **votos a ~** votes in favour; **¿estás a ~ o en contra?** are you for or against it?; **tener el viento a ~** to have the wind behind one *o* in one's favour

[2.2] **a ~ de** in favour of; **no me convencen sus argumentos a ~ de la huelga** I'm not convinced by his arguments in favour of the strike; **¿está a ~ de poner fin al bloqueo del país?** are you in favour of ending the blockade of the country?; **la balanza está a nuestro ~** the balance is in our favour; **el tiempo corre a nuestro ~** time is on our side; **lo tenía todo a su ~** she had everything going for her; **el partido ya estaba decidido a ~ de la jugadora española** the Spanish player already had the match sewn up; **ir a ~ de la corriente** to go with the flow; **a ~ de la noche** under cover of darkness; **votar a ~ de algo** to vote in favour of sth

[2.3] **en ~ de** [*abdicar, manifestarse*] in favour of; [*intervenir*] on behalf of; [*trabajar, luchar*] for; **el director se manifestó en ~ del cine europeo** the director spoke in favour of *o* expressed his support for the European film industry; **piden a la ONU su intervención en ~ de los detenidos** the UN is being asked to intervene on behalf of those detained; **una recogida de firmas en ~ del indulto de los presos** a petition for the pardon of the prisoners; **siempre abogó en ~ de los más débiles** he always defended the underdog; **se tomarán nuevas medidas en ~ de los ganaderos** new measures are to be taken to help livestock farmers; **el sistema fue perdiendo terreno en ~ de otros métodos más modernos** the system gradually lost ground to more up-to-date methods

[3] (= *apoyo*) [*del rey, dioses*] favour, favor (*EEUU*), protection; [*del público*] support; **gracias al ~ del rey** thanks to the king's protection, thanks to the favour he enjoyed with the king; **la pérdida del ~ popular** the loss of popular support; **la película nunca tuvo el ~ del gran público** the movie never found favour with the general public; **ha sabido ganarse el ~ de la audiencia** she has succeeded in winning the audience's affection; **gozar**

➤ LENGUA Y USO: favor 1 31

del ~ de algn to have sb's support *o* backing, enjoy sb's favour (*frm*); **el partido goza del ~ del 49% de la población** the party has the support *o* backing of 49% of the population; *ver tb* **condición 1**

4 **entrada de ~** complimentary ticket

5 **favores** [*de mujer*] favours, favors (*EEUU*)

favorable ADJ favourable, favorable (*EEUU*); **esperábamos una respuesta ~** we were expecting a favourable reply; **vientos ~s** favourable winds; **~ a algo** in favour of sth; **se mostró ~ al cambio político** he was in favour of political change

favorablemente ADV favourably, favorably (*EEUU*)

favorecedor ADJ [*vestido*] becoming; [*retrato*] flattering

favorecer ▸conjug 2d◂ Ⓐ VT 1 (= *beneficiar*) to be favourable *o* (*EEUU*) favorable to, favour, favor (*EEUU*); **la devaluación ha favorecido a las compañías exportadoras** devaluation has been favourable to *o* has favoured exporting companies; **el sorteo favoreció al equipo canadiense** Canada did well out of the draw; **la suerte no me favoreció** luck was not on my side, fortune did not favour me (*liter*)

2 (= *ayudar a*) [+ *desarrollo, creación, crecimiento*] to contribute to; **las nuevas medidas fiscales ~án la creación de empresas** the new tax measures will contribute to *o* encourage *o* favour the creation of new companies; **puede ~ la aparición de piedras en el riñón** it can contribute to the development of kidney stones

3 (= *tratar con favores*) **~ a algn** to help out sb, do sb favours; **utilizó sus influencias para ~ a sus amigos** she used her influence to help out her friends *o* to do favours for her friends

4 (= *sentar bien*) [*vestido*] to suit, look good on; [*peinado*] to suit; **las faldas largas no te favorecen** long skirts don't suit you *o* look good on you; **la barba no te favorece** the beard doesn't suit you; **el retrato no la favorece** the portrait is not very flattering

Ⓑ VI (= *sentar bien*) to be flattering, look good

favorecido/a Ⓐ ADJ 1 (= *beneficiado*) (*en el trato*) favoured, favored (*EEUU*); (*por la suerte, el dinero*) fortunate; **trato de nación más favorecida** most-favoured nation treatment; **las clases menos favorecidas** the less fortunate classes; **resultó ~ en la lotería con más de un millón de euros** he won over a million euros on the lottery

2 (*físicamente*) **estás muy ~ en esta foto** you look very good in this photo, this is a very good photo of you

Ⓑ SM/F **los ~s con el primer premio** the winners of the first prize, those who won the first prize

favoritismo SM favouritism, favoritism (*EEUU*)

favorito/a ADJ, SM/F favourite, favorite (*EEUU*)

fax SM 1 (= *máquina*) fax (machine); **mandar por ~** to fax, send by fax

2 (= *mensaje*) fax; **mandar un ~** to send a fax

faxear ▸conjug 1a◂ VT to fax, send by fax

faxteléfono SM fax-telephone (machine)

fayuca* SF (*Méx*) smuggling

fayuquear* ▸conjug 1a◂ VT (*Méx*) to smuggle

fayuquero/a* SM/F 1 (*Méx*) smuggler

2 (*Cono Sur*) travelling salesman/saleswoman

fayuto ADJ (*Cono Sur*) = **falluto**

faz SF 1 (= *cara*) face; **en la ~ de la tierra** on the face of the earth; **~ a ~** face to face

2 (= *aspecto*) face, landscape; **estos incendios están cambiando la ~ de nuestro país** these fires are changing the face *o* landscape of our country

3 [*de moneda*] obverse

FC ABR, **f.c.** ABR (= **ferrocarril**) Rly

Fco. ABR = **Francisco**

Fdez. ABR = **Fernández**

Fdo. ABR, **fdo.** ABR (= **firmado**) signed; **Fdo.: D. Josep Pauli i Costa** Signed, Josep Pauli i Costa Esq

FE SF ABR (*Hist*) = **Falange Española** ► **FE de las JONS** = **Falange Española de las Juntas de Ofensiva Nacional Sindicalista**

fe SF 1 (*Rel*) faith (**en** in); **la fe católica** the Catholic faith; ✦*MODISMO* **la fe del carbonero** blind faith; ✦*REFRÁN* **la fe mueve montañas** faith moves mountains

2 (= *confianza*) faith; **tener fe en algn/algo** to have faith in sb/sb; **no tengo fe en los abogados** I have no faith in lawyers; **tiene una fe ciega en ella** he has absolute faith in her; **no tiene fe en la ciencia** he has no faith in science; **dar** *o* **prestar fe a algo** (*frm*) to believe sth, place reliance on sth (*frm*)

3 (= *intención*) faith; **buena fe** good faith; **mala fe** bad faith; **actuar en** *o* **de buena fe** to act in good faith

4 (= *testimonio*) **dar fe de algo** to vouch for sth, testify to sth; **doy fe de ello** I can vouch for *o* testify to that; **en fe de lo cual** (*frm*) in witness whereof (*frm*); **a fe**†† in truth; **a fe mía**†† ◊ **por mi fe**†† by my faith, upon my honour

5 (††) (= *fidelidad*) fidelity

6 (= *certificado*) certificate ► **fe de bautismo** certificate of baptism ► **fe de erratas, fe de errores** (*en libro*) errata; (*en periódico*) correction ► **fe de soltería** proof of single status ► **fe de vida** *certificate testifying that a person is still alive* ► **fe pública** *authority to attest documents*

FEA SF ABR 1 = **Federación Española de Automovilismo**

2 = **Federación Española de Atletismo**

3 (*Hist*) = **Falange Española Auténtica**

fealdad SF ugliness

feamente ADJ hideously, terribly

feb. ABR, **feb.º** ABR (= **febrero**) Feb

feble ADJ feeble, weak

Febo SM Phoebus

febrero SM February; *ver tb* **septiembre**

febril ADJ 1 (*Med*) fevered, feverish

2 [*actividad*] hectic, feverish

febrilmente ADV (*fig*) feverishly, hectically

fecal ADJ faecal, fecal (*EEUU*); **aguas ~es** sewage *sing*

fecha SF 1 (= *día preciso*) date; **¿a qué ~ estamos?** what's the date today?; **han adelantado la ~ de las elecciones** they've brought forward the (date of the) election; **ya tengo ~ para el dentista** I've got an appointment at the dentist's; **la carta tiene ~ del 21 de enero** the letter is dated 21st January; **a partir de esa ~ no volvió a llamar** from then on *o* thereafter he never called again; **a 30 días ~** (*Com*) at 30 days' sight; **con ~ de: una carta con ~ del 15 de agosto** a letter dated 15th August; **hasta la ~** to date, so far; **pasarse de ~** (*Com*) to pass the sell-by date; **este yogur está pasado de ~** this yoghurt is past its sell-by date; **poner la ~** to date; **no se olvide poner la ~ en la solicitud** don't forget to date the form; **en ~ próxima** soon; **sin ~: una carta sin ~** an undated letter, a letter with no date ► **fecha de caducidad** [*de medicamento, tarjeta*] expiry date; [*de alimento*] sell-by date ► **fecha de emisión** date of issue ► **fecha de entrega** delivery date ► **fecha de nacimiento** date of birth ► **fecha de vencimiento** (*Com*) due date ► **fecha de vigencia** (*Com*) effective date ► **fecha futura**: **en alguna ~ futura** at some future date; **un cheque con una ~ futura** a postdated cheque ► **fecha límite** deadline ► **fecha límite de venta** sell-by date ► **fecha tope** [*de finalización*] deadline; [*de entrega*] closing date

2 **fechas** (= *época*) **son ~s de escasa actividad** it's a time of year when there isn't much happening; **siempre viene por estas ~s** he always comes about this time of year; **el año pasado por estas ~s** this time last year; **para esas ~s ya eran diez las víctimas** by then the death toll was already ten; **en breves ~s** (*frm*) shortly

fechable ADJ datable (**en** to)

fechado SM dating

fechador SM date stamp

fechar ▸conjug 1a◂ VT to date

fechoría SF misdeed, misdemeanour, misdemeanor (*EEUU*)

FECOM SM ABR (= **Fondo Europeo de Cooperación Monetaria**) EMCF

fécula SF starch ► **fécula de papa** (*LAm*) potato flour

feculento ADJ starchy

fecundación SF fertilization ► **fecundación artificial** artificial insemination ► **fecundación in vitro** in vitro fertilization

fecundar ▸conjug 1a◂ VT 1 (= *engendrar*) to fertilize; **~ por fertilización cruzada** to cross-fertilize

2 (*liter*) (= *fertilizar*) to make fertile

fecundidad SF 1 [*de hembra*] fertility, fecundity

2 (= *productividad*) fruitfulness, productiveness

fecundizar ▸conjug 1f◂ VT to fertilize

fecundo ADJ 1 [*persona, tierra*] fertile, fecund (*frm*)

2 [*pintor, escritor*] prolific

3 (= *fructífero*) fruitful, productive; **una década fecunda de los grandes economistas** a fruitful *o* productive period for great economists; **~ de palabras** fluent, eloquent; **~ en algo: una época muy fecunda en buenos poetas** a period which produced an abundance *o* a plethora of good poets; **un libro ~ en ideas** a book full of *o* rich in ideas

FED SM ABR (= **Fondo Europeo de Desarrollo**) EDF

FEDER SM ABR (= **Fondo Europeo de Desarrollo Regional**) ERDF

federación SF federation

federal Ⓐ ADJ federal; **Distrito Federal** (*Méx*) Mexico City

➤ LENGUA Y USO: **favorable** 40.2

Ⓑ SMF **los federales** (*Méx*) the federals, the federal police

federalismo SM federalism

federalista ADJ, SMF federalist

federalizar ▸conjug 1f◂ VT to federate, federalize

federar ▸conjug 1a◂ Ⓐ VT to federate

Ⓑ **federarse** VPR [1] (*Pol*) to federate, become federated

[2] (= *hacerse socio*) (*en club, asociación*) to become a member; (*en federación*) to affiliate

federativo ADJ federative

Federico SM Frederick

feérico ADJ fairy *antes de s*

FEF SF ABR = **Federación Española de Fútbol**

féferes SMPL (*LAm*) (*gen*) junk *sing*, lumber *sing*; (= *cosas*) things (in general), thingummyjigs*

fehaciente ADJ [1] (= *fidedigno*) reliable; **de fuentes ~s** from reliable sources

[2] (= *irrefutable*) irrefutable

fehacientemente ADV [1] (= *fidedignamente*) reliably

[2] (= *irrefutablemente*) irrefutably

feíllo* ADJ a bit plain, rather unattractive

FE-JONS [fe'xons] SF ABR (*Hist*) = **Falange Española de las Juntas de Ofensiva Nacional Sindicalista**

felación SF fellatio

feldespato SM felspar

feliciano†‡ SM **echar un ~** to screw**‡

▼**felicidad** SF [1] (= *satisfacción*) happiness; **curva de la ~** pot belly

[2] **¡felicidades!** (= *deseos*) best wishes, congratulations!; (*en cumpleaños*) happy birthday!; **¡mis ~es!** congratulations!

[3] (†) (= *suerte*) good fortune; **viajamos con toda ~** all went well on the journey

▼**felicitación** SF [1] (= *enhorabuena*) **mi ~** *o* **mis felicitaciones al ganador** my congratulations to the winner; **he recibido muchas felicitaciones** lots of people have congratulated me

[2] (= *tarjeta*) greetings card, greeting card (*EEUU*) ► **felicitación de Navidad** Christmas card

▼**felicitar** ▸conjug 1a◂ Ⓐ VT to congratulate; **~ a algn por algo** to congratulate sb on sth; **¡le felicito!** congratulations!, well done!; **~ la Navidad a algn** to wish sb a happy Christmas

Ⓑ **felicitarse** VPR **~se de algo** to be glad about sth

feligrés/esa SM/F parishioner

feligresía SF (= *parroquia*) parish; (= *feligreses*) parishioners *pl*

felino/a Ⓐ ADJ feline, catlike

Ⓑ SM/F feline, cat

Felipe SM Philip

felipismo SM *policies and following of Felipe González, Spanish Prime Minister from 1983 to 1996*

felipista Ⓐ ADJ *relating to Felipe González or his policies*; **la mayoría ~** the pro-Felipe González majority

Ⓑ SMF supporter of Felipe González

▼**feliz** ADJ [1] [*persona, acontecimiento, idea*] happy; **se la ve muy ~** she looks very happy; **el asunto tuvo un final ~** the affair had a happy ending; **¡Feliz Año Nuevo!** Happy New Year!; **hacer ~ a algn** to make sb happy; **"y fueron** *o* **vivieron felices y comieron perdices"** "and they lived happily ever after"

[2] (*frm*) (= *acertado*) [*expresión*] apt

felizmente ADV [1] (*con felicidad*) happily; **vivieron ~ el resto de sus vidas** they lived happily ever after

[2] (= *afortunadamente*) luckily, fortunately; **~ nadie resultó herido** luckily no one was hurt

felón/ona Ⓐ ADJ wicked, treacherous

Ⓑ SM/F wicked person, villain

felonía SF [1] (= *traición*) disloyalty, treachery

[2] (= *crimen*) felony, crime

felpa SF [1] (= *tejido*) [*de toalla, camisa, pañal*] (terry) towelling; [*de sillón, moqueta*] plush; **ositos de ~** furry teddies

[2] (*) (= *paliza*) hiding*; (= *reprimenda*) dressing-down*, ticking-off*; **echarle una ~ a algn** to give sb a dressing-down *o* ticking-off*

felpar ▸conjug 1a◂ VT [1] (= *tapizar*) to cover with plush

[2] (*poét*) (*fig*) to carpet (**de** with)

felpeada* SF (*Cono Sur, Méx*) dressing-down*, ticking-off*

felpear* ▸conjug 1a◂ VT (*Cono Sur, Méx*) to tick off*, scold

felpilla SF chenille

felpudo Ⓐ SM (= *alfombrilla*) doormat

Ⓑ ADJ plush

femenil ADJ [1] (= *femenino*) feminine

[2] (*CAm, Méx Dep*) women's *antes de s*; **equipo ~** women's team

femenino Ⓐ ADJ [1] (*cualidad de mujer*) feminine; **es muy femenina** she's very feminine

[2] [*sexo, representante, población*] female; **el cuerpo ~** the female body

[3] (*Dep*) **deporte ~** women's sport; **equipo ~** women's team

[4] (*Ling*) feminine

Ⓑ SM (*Ling*) feminine

fémina SF (*hum*) woman, female

feminidad SF femininity

feminismo SM feminism

feminista ADJ, SMF feminist

femoral Ⓐ ADJ [*hueso*] femur *antes de s*; [*arteria, vena*] femoral

Ⓑ SF femoral artery

FEMP SF ABR = **Federación Española de Municipios y Provincias**

fémur SM femur

fenecer ▸conjug 2d◂ Ⓐ VI [1] [*persona*] to pass away (*euf*), die

[2] [*actividad*] to come to an end, cease; [*creencia*] to die out

Ⓑ VT (= *terminar*) to finish, conclude

fenecimiento SM [1] [*de persona*] passing (*euf*), death

[2] (= *fin*) end, conclusion

feng shui [ˌfeŋ'ʃuːi] SM feng shui

Fenicia SF Phoenicia

fenicio/a ADJ, SM/F Phoenician

fénico ADJ carbolic; **ácido ~** phenol, carbolic acid

fénix SM phoenix; **el Fénix de los ingenios** the Prince of Wits, the genius of our times (*Lope de Vega, Golden Age dramatist*)

fenol SM phenol, carbolic acid

fenomenal Ⓐ ADJ [1] (= *espectacular*) phenomenal, remarkable

[2] (*) (= *estupendo*) fantastic*, brilliant*

Ⓑ ADV (*) **lo hemos pasado ~** we've had a fantastic *o* brilliant time*; **le va ~** he's getting on fantastically well *o* brilliantly*

fenomenalmente* ADV fantastically well*, brilliantly*

fenómeno Ⓐ SM [1] (*atmosférico, acústico, psíquico*) phenomenon

[2] (= *monstruo*) freak

[3] (= *portento*) genius; **Pedro es un ~** Peter is a genius, Peter is altogether exceptional

Ⓑ ADJ (*) (= *fenomenal*) fantastic*, brilliant*

Ⓒ ADV (*) **lo hemos pasado ~** we had a fantastic *o* brilliant time*; **le va ~** he's getting on fantastically well *o* brilliantly*

feo Ⓐ ADJ [1] (= *sin belleza*) [*persona, casa, ropa*] ugly; **un edificio muy ~** a very ugly building; ✦**MODISMOS más ~ que Picio** *o* **un grajo** as ugly as sin; **bailar con la más fea**: **me tocó bailar con la más fea** I drew the short straw

[2] (= *desagradable*) [*asunto, tiempo*] nasty, unpleasant; [*jugada*] dirty; **tiene la fea costumbre de irse sin despedirse** he has a nasty habit of leaving without saying goodbye; **esto se está poniendo ~** things are getting nasty

[3] (= *de mala educación*) **está muy ~ contestarle así a tu madre** it's very rude *o* it's not nice to answer your mother like that; **está** *o* **queda ~ comerse las uñas en público** it's bad manners to bite your nails in public

[4] (*LAm*) [*olor, comida*] nasty, unpleasant

Ⓑ SM [1] (= *desaire*) **hacer un ~ a algn** to snub sb; **le hizo el ~ de no devolverle la llamada** she snubbed him by not returning his call; **—no puedo ir a tu boda —¿me vas a hacer ese ~?** "I can't come to your wedding" — "but you can't refuse!" *o* "how can you refuse!"

[2] (*) (= *fealdad*) **hoy está con el ~** *o* **de ~ subido** he's looking really ugly today

Ⓒ ADV (*LAm**) bad, badly; **cantar ~** to sing badly; **oler ~** to smell bad, have a nasty smell

FEOGA SM ABR (= **Fondo Europeo de Orientación y de Garantía Agrícola**) EAGGF

feón* ADJ (*LAm*) ugly; **medio ~** rather ugly

feote* ADJ plug-ugly*

feracidad SF fertility, productivity

feralla SF scrap metal

feraz ADJ fertile, productive

féretro SM coffin, casket (*EEUU*)

feri SM (*LAm*) = **ferry**

feria SF [1] (= *muestra comercial*) fair ► **feria comercial** trade fair ► **feria del libro** book fair ► **feria de muestras** trade show, trade exhibition ► **feria de vanidades** empty show, inane spectacle

[2] (= *mercado al aire libre*) market; (*Agr*) show ► **feria agrícola** agricultural show ► **feria de ganado** cattle show

[3] [*de atracciones*] fair, funfair

[4] (= *fiesta*) festival; **durante la ~ habrá corridas de toros todos los días** during the festival there will be bullfights every day; **la Feria de Sevilla** the Seville Fair; ✦**MODISMO irle a algn como en ~** (*Méx**) to go very badly for sb

[5] (= *descanso*) holiday

[6] (*Méx**) (= *cambio*) change, small change

[7] (*CAm*) (= *propina*) tip

feriado Ⓐ ADJ **día ~** holiday

Ⓑ SM (*LAm*) public holiday, bank holiday

ferial Ⓐ ADJ fair *antes de s*, fairground *antes de*

➤ LENGUA Y USO: **felicidad 2** 50.3 **felicitación** 50.6 **felicitar A** 40.4 **feliz 1** 50.1, 50.2

s; **recinto ~** fairground, showground
Ⓑ SM fairground, showground

feriante SMF [1] (= *vendedor*) (*en mercado*) stallholder, trader; (*en feria de muestras*) exhibitor
[2] (= *asistente a feria*) fair-goers

feriar ▸conjug 1b◂ Ⓐ VT [1] (= *comerciar*) to deal in (*in a market, at a fair*)
[2] (= *permutar*) to trade, exchange
[3] (*Méx*) [+ *dinero*] to exchange
[4] (*Andes*) (= *vender barato*) to sell cheap
Ⓑ VI (= *descansar*) to take time off, take a break

ferino ADJ savage, wild; **tos ferina** whooping cough

fermata SF (*Mús*) run

fermentación SF fermentation

fermentado Ⓐ ADJ fermented
Ⓑ SM fermentation

fermentar ▸conjug 1a◂ Ⓐ VI [1] [*vino, queso, compost*] to ferment; **hacer ~** to ferment, cause fermentation in
[2] [*crisis, violencia*] to ferment
Ⓑ VT to ferment

fermento SM [1] [*de queso, cerveza*] ferment
[2] [*de crisis, cambio*] ferment

fermio SM (*Quím*) fermium

Fernando SM, **Fernán**†† SM Ferdinand; ✦***MODISMO*** **te lo han puesto como a ~ VII** they've handed it to you on a plate

ferocidad SF ferocity, ferociousness

ferocísimo ADJ SUPERL *de* **feroz**

Feroe: **las Islas ~** SFPL the Faroe Islands, the Faroes

feromona SF pheromone

feroz ADJ [1] (= *salvaje*) fierce, ferocious; **tengo un hambre ~** I'm starving, I'm famished
[2] (= *cruel*) cruel
[3] (*LAm*) (= *feo*) ugly

ferozmente ADV [1] (= *salvajemente*) fiercely, ferociously
[2] (= *cruelmente*) cruelly

férreo ADJ [1] (= *de hierro*) iron *antes de s*; (*Quím*) ferrous; **metal no ~** non-ferrous metal
[2] (*Ferro*) rail *antes de s*; **vía férrea** railway track *o* line, railroad (*EEUU*)
[3] (= *tenaz*) [*acoso*] fierce, determined; [*cerco, marcaje*] very close, tight; **una voluntad férrea** an iron will
[4] (= *estricto*) [*disciplina, control, embargo*] strict, tight; [*horario*] strict, rigid; [*secreto*] strict; [*silencio*] steely

ferrería SF ironworks, foundry

ferretería SF [1] (= *objetos*) ironmongery, hardware
[2] (= *tienda*) ironmonger's (shop), hardware store (*EEUU*)
[3] = **ferrería**

ferretero/a SM/F ironmonger, hardware dealer (*EEUU*)

férrico ADJ ferric

ferroaleación SF ferro-alloy

ferrobús SM (*Ferro*) diesel car

ferrocarril SM railway, railroad (*EEUU*); **por ~** by rail, by train ► **ferrocarril de cercanías** suburban rail network ► **ferrocarril de cremallera** rack railway ► **ferrocarril de vía estrecha** narrow-gauge railway ► **ferrocarril de vía única** single-track railway ► **ferrocarril elevado** overhead railway, elevated railway, elevated railroad (*EEUU*), el (*EEUU**) ► **ferrocarril funicular** funicular, funicular railway ► **ferrocarril metropolitano** metropolitan railway ► **ferrocarril subterráneo** underground railway

ferrocarrilero/a (*LAm*) ADJ, SM/F = **ferroviario**

ferroprusiato SM (*Arquit, Téc*) blueprint

ferroso ADJ ferrous; **metal no ~** non-ferrous metal

ferrotipo SM (*Fot*) tintype

ferroviario/a Ⓐ ADJ [*red, sistema*] railway *antes de s*, rail *antes de s*, railroad *antes de s* (*EEUU*)
Ⓑ SM/F (= *trabajador*) railwayman/railwaywoman, railway worker, railroad worker (*EEUU*)

ferry ['feri] (*pl* **ferries**) SM ferry

ferry-boat [feri'βot] SM (*LAm*) ferry

fértil ADJ [1] [*tierra, campo*] fertile, rich
[2] [*persona, animal*] fertile
[3] (= *productivo*) [*idioma*] rich, expressive; [*discusión*] fertile, fruitful; [*imaginación*] fertile

fertilidad SF [1] [*del campo*] fertility, richness
[2] [*de persona, animal*] fertility
[3] (= *productividad*) [*de idioma*] richness, expressiveness; [*de periodo*] productivity, richness

fertilización SF fertilization ► **fertilización cruzada** cross-fertilization ► **fertilización in vitro** in vitro fertilization

fertilizante Ⓐ ADJ fertilizing
Ⓑ SM fertilizer

fertilizar ▸conjug 1f◂ VT to fertilize

férula SF [1] (= *vara*) birch, rod
[2] (*Med*) splint
[3] (= *dominio*) rule, domination; **vivir bajo la ~ de un tirano** to live under the iron rule of a tyrant

férvido ADJ fervid, ardent

ferviente ADJ [*devoto, partidario*] fervent; [*deseo, amor, ambición*] burning

fervor SM [1] (*religioso, nacionalista, popular*) fervour, fervor (*EEUU*)
[2] (= *dedicación*) fervour, fervor (*EEUU*), enthusiasm; **estudia con ~** he studies enthusiastically

fervorosamente ADV fervently, passionately

fervoroso ADJ fervent, passionate

festejar ▸conjug 1a◂ VT [1] [+ *persona*] to wine and dine, entertain
[2] (= *celebrar*) to celebrate
[3] (†) (= *cortejar*) to woo, court
[4] (*Méx**) (= *azotar*) to thrash

festejo SM [1] (= *celebración*) celebration; (*Andes*) party; **festejos** (= *fiestas*) festivities
[2] [*de huésped*] wining and dining, entertainment; **hacer ~s a algn** to make a great fuss of sb
[3] (†) (= *cortejo*) wooing, courtship

festín SM feast, banquet

festinar ▸conjug 1a◂ VT [1] (*CAm*) (= *agasajar*) to wine and dine, entertain
[2] (*LAm*) (= *arruinar*) to mess up, ruin (*by being overhasty*)
[3] (*LAm*) (= *acelerar*) to hurry along, speed up

festival SM festival

festivalero/a Ⓐ ADJ festival *antes de s*
Ⓑ SM/F festival-goer

festivamente ADV humorously, jovially

festividad SF [1] (*Rel*) feast, holiday
[2] (*tb* **~es**) (= *celebraciones*) festivities, celebrations
[3] (= *alegría*) gaiety, merrymaking
[4] (= *ingenio*) wit

festivo ADJ [1] (= *no laborable*) **día ~** holiday
[2] (= *alegre*) festive, merry
[3] (= *gracioso*) witty, humorous
[4] (*Literat*) burlesque, comic

festón SM (*Cos*) festoon, scallop; [*de flores*] garland

festonear ▸conjug 1a◂ VT (*Cos*) to festoon, scallop; (*con flores*) to garland

FET SF ABR [1] (*Dep*) = **Federación Española de Tenis**
[2] (*Hist*) (*tb* **~ de las JONS**) = **Falange Española tradicionalista de las Juventudes de Ofensiva Nacional Socialista**

fetal ADJ foetal, fetal (*EEUU*)

fetén†* (*Esp*) Ⓐ ADJ INV [1] (= *estupendo*) smashing*, super*; **una chica ~** a smashing *o* super girl*; **de ~** (= *estupendo*) smashing*, super*
[2] (= *auténtico*) real, authentic
Ⓑ ADV splendidly, marvellously
Ⓒ SF (= *verdad*) truth; **ser la ~** to be gospel truth

fetiche SM fetish

fetichismo SM fetishism

fetichista Ⓐ ADJ fetishistic
Ⓑ SMF fetishist

fetidez SF smelliness, fetidness (*frm*)

fétido ADJ fetid, foul-smelling, stinking

feto SM [1] (*Biol*) foetus, fetus (*EEUU*)
[2] (*) (= *persona fea*) **vaya tío feo, parece un ~** that guy's as ugly as sin*

feúcho* ADJ plain, homely (*EEUU*)

feudal ADJ feudal

feudalismo SM feudalism

feudo SM [1] (*Hist*) fief
[2] (*Dep*) **resultaron ganadores en su ~** they won on their own ground; **el Sevilla no ha perdido ni un punto en su ~** Sevilla haven't lost a single point at home
[3] ► **feudo franco** (*Jur*) freehold

feúra SF (*LAm*) [1] (= *fealdad*) ugliness
[2] **una ~** (= *persona*) an ugly person; (= *cosa*) an ugly thing

FEVE SF ABR = **Ferrocarriles Españoles de Vía Estrecha**

fez SM fez

FF ABR, **f.f.** ABR = **franco (en) fábrica**; **precio FF** price ex-factory

FF.AA. ABR = **Fuerzas Armadas**

FF. CC. ABR, **FFCC** ABR = **Ferrocarriles**

FGD SM ABR (= **Fondo de Garantía de Depósitos**) *supervisory financial body*

fha. ABR (= **fecha**) d

fiabilidad SF reliability, trustworthiness

fiable ADJ reliable, trustworthy

fiaca‡ SF (*Arg*) laziness, apathy

fiado SM [1] **al ~** on credit
[2] (*Jur*) **en ~** on bail

fiador(a) Ⓐ SM/F (*Jur*) (= *persona*) guarantor, bondsman (*EEUU*); **salir ~ por algn** to stand security for sb; (*Jur*) to stand bail for sb
Ⓑ SM [1] (*Mec*) catch; [*de revólver*] safety catch, safety (*EEUU*); [*de cerradura*] tumbler; [*de ventana*] bolt, catch
[2] (†*) (= *trasero*) bottom, backside, butt (*esp EEUU**)
[3] (*Andes, Cono Sur*) [*de perro*] muzzle; [*de casco*] chinstrap

fiambre Ⓐ ADJ [1] (*Culin*) cold, served cold
[2] (*) [*noticia*] old, stale
Ⓑ SM [1] (*Culin*) cold meat, cold cut (*EEUU*); **~s** cold meats, cold cuts (*EEUU*)
[2] (*) (= *cadáver*) corpse, stiff*; **el pobre está ~** the poor guy's stone dead*, the poor guy's cold meat*
[3] (*Cono Sur**) (= *fiesta*) dead party
[4] (*Méx Culin*) *pork, avocado and chili dish*

fiambrera SF [1] (*para almuerzo*) lunch box, dinner pail (*EEUU*)
[2] (*Cono Sur*) (= *nevera*) meat safe, meat store

fiambrería SF (*Andes, Cono Sur*) delicatessen

fianza SF [1] (*Jur*) bail; **bajo ~** on bail ► **fianza carcelera** bail
[2] (*Com*) (= *anticipo*) deposit; (= *garantía*) surety, security, bond ► **fianza de aduana** customs bond ► **fianza de averías** average bond
[3] (= *persona*) surety, guarantor

fiar ▸conjug 1c◂ Ⓐ VT [1] (*Com*) (= *vender*) to sell on credit; (*LAm*) (= *comprar*) to buy on credit; **me fió la comida** he let me have the food on tick* *o* credit
[2] (*frm*) (= *confiar*) **le fié mi secreto** I confided my secret to him
Ⓑ VI [1] (*Com*) to give credit; **"no se fía"** (*en tienda*) "no credit given"; **dejaron de ~le en la tienda** they wouldn't let her have anything on credit anymore
[2] **ser de ~** to be trustworthy, be reliable
Ⓒ **fiarse** VPR [1] (= *confiar*) **~se de algn** to trust sb; **no me fío de él** I don't trust him; **ya no puede uno ~se de nadie** you can't trust anyone any more; **~se de algo** to believe in sth; **no te fíes de lo que digan los periódicos** don't believe what the papers say; **no me fío de su habilidad para resolver el problema** I don't believe in his ability to solve the problem; **no te fíes de las apariencias** don't go *o* judge by appearances; **¡para que te fíes de los amigos!** with friends like that, who needs enemies?; ✦*MODISMO* **¡(cuán *o* tan) largo me lo fiáis!** (*liter, hum*) I'll believe it when I see it!; *ver tb* **pelo 7**
[2] (*frm*) (= *depender*) to rely on; **nos fiamos de usted para conseguirlo** we are relying on you to get it

fiasco SM fiasco

fíat SM (*pl* **fiats**) [1] (= *mandato*) official sanction, fiat
[2] (= *consentimiento*) consent, blessing

fibra SF [1] (*gen*) fibre, fiber (*EEUU*) ► **fibra acrílica** acrylic fibre ► **fibra artificial** man-made fibre ► **fibra de amianto** asbestos fibre ► **fibra de carbono** carbon fibre ► **fibra de coco** coconut fibre ► **fibra de vidrio** fibre glass ► **fibra dietética** dietary fibre ► **fibra ocular** ocular fibre ► **fibra óptica** optical fibre ► **fibra sintética** synthetic fibre
[2] (*en madera*) grain
[3] (*Min*) vein
[4] (= *vigor*) vigour, vigor (*EEUU*); ✦*MODISMO* **despertar la ~ sensible** to strike a chord, evoke ► **fibras del corazón** heartstrings

fibravidrio SM fibreglass

fibrina SF fibrin

fibroóptica SF fibre optics

fibrosis SF INV fibrosis ► **fibrosis cística** cystic fibrosis ► **fibrosis pulmonar** fibrosis of the lungs, pulmonary fibrosis ► **fibrosis quística** cystic fibrosis

fibrositis SF INV fibrositis

fibroso ADJ fibrous

fíbula SF [1] (*Med*) fibula
[2] (*Hist*) fibula, brooch

ficción Ⓐ SF [1] (*Literat*) fiction; **obras de no ~** non-fiction books ► **ficción científica** science fiction
[2] (= *invención*) fiction
[3] (= *mentira*) fabrication
Ⓑ ADJ INV fictitious, make-believe; **historia ~** (piece of) historical fiction, fictionalized history; **reportaje ~** dramatized documentary

ficcioso/a (*Cono Sur*) Ⓐ ADJ (= *simulado*) bluffing; (= *falso*) false, double-dealing
Ⓑ SM/F (= *simulador*) bluffer; (= *falso*) double-dealer

ficha SF [1] (*en juegos*) counter; (*en casino*) chip; (*Telec*) token; ✦*MODISMO* **mover ~** to make a move ► **ficha del dominó** domino ► **ficha de silicio** silicon chip
[2] (= *tarjeta*) card; [*de archivo*] index card, record card; (*en hotel*) registration form ► **ficha antropométrica** anthropometric chart ► **ficha perforada** punched card ► **ficha policial** police dossier, police record ► **ficha técnica** (*TV*) (list of) credits
[3] (*CAm, Caribe*) five-cent piece; (*CAm**) (= *moneda*) coin
[4] (*Méx*) [*de botella*] flat bottle cap
[5] (*Andes*) (*tb* **mala ~**) rogue, villain
[6] (*Dep*) signing-on fee

fichaje SM [1] (*Dep*) (= *acción*) signing, signing-up; (= *dinero*) signing-on fee
[2] (*Dep*) (= *jugador*) signing

fichar ▸conjug 1a◂ Ⓐ VT [1] (= *registrar*) [+ *detenido, trabajador*] to put on file; [+ *dato*] to record, enter (*on a card etc*); **~ a algn** to put sb on file; **está fichado** he's got a record; **lo tenemos fichado** we've got our eye on him
[2] (*Dep*) [+ *jugador*] to sign, sign up
[3] (*Pol*) [+ *nuevos miembros*] to sign up, recruit
[4] (*Caribe*) (= *engañar*) to swindle
Ⓑ VI [1] (*Dep*) [*jugador*] to sign, sign up
[2] [*trabajador*] (*al entrar*) to clock in, clock on; (*al salir*) to clock out, clock off
[3] (*Andes*) (= *morir*) to die

fichero SM [1] (= *archivo*) card index
[2] (= *mueble*) filing cabinet
[3] [*de policía*] records *pl* ► **fichero fotográfico de delincuentes** photographic records of criminals, rogues' gallery (*hum**)
[4] (*Inform*) file ► **fichero activo** active file ► **fichero archivado** archive file ► **fichero de datos** datafile ► **fichero de reserva** back-up file ► **fichero de trabajo** work-file ► **fichero indexado** index file ► **fichero informático** computer file

ficticio ADJ [*nombre, carácter*] fictitious; [*historia, prueba*] fabricated

ficus SM INV rubber plant

FIDA SM ABR (= **Fondo Internacional de Desarrollo Agrícola**) IFAD

fidedigno ADJ reliable, trustworthy; **fuentes fidedignas** reliable sources

fideería SF (*LAm*) pasta factory

fideicomisario/a Ⓐ ADJ trust *antes de s*; **banco ~** trust company Ⓑ SM/F trustee

fideicomiso SM trust

fidelería SF (*LAm*) pasta factory

fidelidad SF [1] (= *lealtad*) (*gen*) faithfulness, loyalty; (*sexual*) faithfulness; **~ a una marca** (*Com*) brand loyalty; **jurar ~ a la República** to swear allegiance to the Republic; **renuncia al cargo por ~ a sus convicciones** he resigned in order to stay true to his principles, he resigned rather than betray his principles
[2] (= *exactitud*) [*de dato*] accuracy
[3] **alta ~** hi-fi

fidelísimo ADJ SUPERL *de* **fiel**

fidelización SF loyalty

fideo SM [1] (*Culin*) noodle; **fideos** noodles
[2] (*) (= *delgado*) beanpole*, string bean (*EEUU**)

fiduciario/a Ⓐ ADJ fiduciary
Ⓑ SM/F fiduciary, trustee

fiebre SF [1] (= *síntoma*) temperature, fever; **tener ~** to have a temperature; **está a *o* tiene 39 de ~** she has a temperature of 39
[2] (= *enfermedad*) fever ► **fiebre aftosa** foot-and-mouth disease ► **fiebre amarilla** yellow fever ► **fiebre del heno** hay fever ► **fiebre de los labios** cold sore ► **fiebre entérica** enteric fever ► **fiebre de Malta** brucellosis ► **fiebre glandular** glandular fever ► **fiebre palúdica** malaria ► **fiebre porcina** swine fever, hog cholera (*EEUU*) ► **fiebre recurrente** relapsing fever ► **fiebre reumática** rheumatic fever ► **fiebre tifoidea** typhoid fever
[3] (= *agitación*) fever; **la ~ del juego** the gambling fever; **la ~ de oro** gold fever
[4] (*Cono Sur*) (= *taimado*) slippery customer*

fiel Ⓐ ADJ [1] (*gen*) faithful, loyal; (*sexualmente*) faithful; **un ~ servidor del partido** a loyal *o* faithful servant of the Party; **seguir siendo ~ a** to remain faithful to, stay true to
[2] [*traducción, relación*] faithful, accurate
Ⓑ SMF (*Rel*) believer; **los ~es** the faithful
Ⓒ SM (*Téc*) [*de balanza*] needle, pointer

fielmente ADV [1] [*servir, apoyar*] faithfully, loyally; **continuó apoyando ~ a su marido** she continued to support her husband faithfully *o* loyally
[2] (= *exactamente*) [*reflejar, describir*] faithfully, accurately

fieltro SM felt; **sombrero de ~** felt hat

fiera Ⓐ SF [1] (*Zool*) wild beast, wild animal; **como una ~ enjaulada** like a caged animal; ✦*MODISMO* **hecho una ~**: **entró hecha una ~** she came in absolutely furious; **ponerse hecho una ~** to be furious, be beside o.s. with rage
[2] (*Taur*) bull
[3] ► **fiera sarda** (*Andes*) expert, top man
Ⓑ SMF fiend; **es una ~ para el deporte** he's a sports fiend; **es un ~ para el trabajo** he's a demon for work

fierecilla SF (*fig*) shrew

fiereza SF [1] (= *ferocidad*) fierceness, ferocity; (*Zool*) wildness
[2] (= *crueldad*) cruelty
[3] (†) (= *fealdad*) deformity, ugliness

fiero Ⓐ ADJ [1] (= *feroz*) fierce, ferocious; (*Zool*) wild; ✦*MODISMO* **no es tan ~ el león como lo pintan** (= *persona*) he's not as bad as he's made out to be; (= *situación*) it's not as bad as it's made out to be
[2] (= *cruel*) cruel
[3] (†) (= *feo*) ugly
Ⓑ **fieros**† SMPL (= *amenazas*) threats; (= *bravatas*) boasts, bragging *sing*; **echar *o* hacer**

~s (= *amenazas*) to utter threats; (= *bravatas*) to boast, brag

fierro SM (*LAm*) 1 (= *hierro*) iron
2 (= *cuchillo*) knife
3 (*Agr*) branding iron, brand
4 (*Aut*) accelerator
5 (*) (= *arma*) gun, weapon
6 **fierros** (*Méx*) (= *dinero*) money *sing*; (*LAm*) (= *resortes*) springs

fiesta SF 1 (= *reunión*) party; **dar** *u* **organizar una ~** to give *o* throw a party; **un ambiente de ~** a party atmosphere; **el país entero está de ~ ante la buena noticia** the whole country is celebrating the good news; ✦*MODISMOS* **no estar para ~s** to be in no mood for jokes; **no sabe de qué va la ~** he hasn't a clue; **para coronar la ~** to round it all off, as a finishing touch; **tener la ~ en paz: no os peleéis, ¡tengamos la ~ en paz!** behave yourselves, don't fight! ► **fiesta de caridad** charity event ► **fiesta de cumpleaños** birthday party ► **fiesta de disfraces** fancy-dress party ► **fiesta familiar** family celebration; *ver tb* **aguar 2**
2 (= *día festivo*) holiday; **mañana es ~** it's a holiday tomorrow; **hacer ~** to take a day off ► **fiesta de la banderita** flag day ► **Fiesta de la Hispanidad** Columbus day ► **Fiesta del Trabajo** Labour day, Labor day (*EEUU*) ► **fiesta fija** immovable feast ► **fiesta nacional** public holiday, bank holiday ► **fiesta movible**, **fiesta móvil** movable feast ► **fiesta patria** (*LAm*) independence day
3 (*Rel*) feast day; **guardar** *o* **santificar las ~s** to observe feast days ► **fiesta de guardar**, **fiesta de precepto** day of obligation
4 (= *festejo*) fiesta, festival; **el pueblo está en ~s** *o* **de ~** the town's having its local fiesta; **la ~ nacional** (*Taur*) bullfighting ► **fiesta de armas** (*Hist*) tournament ► **fiesta mayor** annual festival
5 **fiestas** (= *vacaciones*) holiday, vacation (*EEUU*); **las ~s de Navidad** the Christmas holiday(s); **¡Felices Fiestas!** (*en navidad*) Happy Christmas; **te llamaré después de estas ~s** I'll call you after the holidays
6 **fiestas** (= *carantoñas*) **su perro siempre le hace ~s cuando la ve** the dog is all over her whenever he sees her

FIESTAS

There are a fixed number of public holidays in the Spanish calendar but some dates vary locally. National public holidays include **Navidad** *(25 Dec),* **Reyes** *(6 Jan), the* **Día de los Trabajadores** *(1 May), the* **Día de la Hispanidad/del Pilar** *(12 Oct) and the* **Día de la Constitución** *(6 Dec). Additionally, each autonomous region and town has at its discretion a small number of public holidays that usually coincide with local traditions like a patron saint's day or other celebrations such as* **Carnaval**. *Thus there is a holiday in Madrid for* **San Isidro**, *the city's patron saint, and one in Catalonia for* **Sant Jordi**, *who is the patron saint of the region.*

fiestero ADJ (= *alegre*) happy; (= *juerguista*) fun-loving, party-loving

fiestón* SM, **fiestorro*** SM big party

FIFA SF ABR (= **Fédération Internationale de Football Association**) FIFA

fifar** ►conjug 1a◄ VT (*Arg*) to fuck**, screw**

fifí* SM (*Méx*) playboy

fifiriche* SM 1 (*Costa Rica, Méx*) (= *lechuguino*) dandy, toff*
2 (*CAm, Méx*) (= *enclenque*) weed*

figón SM cheap restaurant

figulino ADJ clay *antes de s*; **arcilla figulina** potter's clay

figura Ⓐ SF 1 (= *estatua*) figure; **una ~ de porcelana** a porcelain figure ► **figura decorativa** (*lit*) decorative motif; (*fig*) figurehead ► **figura de nieve** snowman
2 (= *forma*) shape, form; **una chocolatina con ~ de pez** a fish-shaped chocolate, a chocolate in the shape of a fish
3 (= *silueta*) figure; **tener buena ~** to have a good figure
4 (= *personaje*) figure; **una ~ destacada** an outstanding figure; **es una ~ del toreo** he's a big name in bullfighting, he's a famous bullfighter; **la ~ del partido de hoy** (*Dep*) today's man of the match ► **figura de culto** cult figure ► **figura paterna** father figure
5 (*Geom*) figure ► **figura geométrica** geometric figure
6 (= *ademán*) **hacer ~s** to make faces
7 (*Naipes*) face card; (*Ajedrez*) piece, man
8 (*Ling*) figure ► **figura de dicción**, **figura retórica** figure of speech
9 (*Teat*) character, role; **en la ~ de** in the role of
10 (*Baile, Patinaje*) figure
11 (*Mús*) note
12 (*Astron*) ► **figura celeste** horoscope
13 (††) (= *rostro*) countenance
Ⓑ SM **ser un ~** to be a big name, be somebody

figuración SF 1 (*Cine*) extras *pl*
2 **figuraciones** (= *imaginación*) **eso son figuraciones tuyas** it's just your imagination, you're imagining things

figuradamente ADV figuratively

figurado ADJ figurative

figurante SMF (SF *a veces* **figuranta**) 1 (*Teat*) extra
2 (*fig*) figurehead

figurar ►conjug 1a◄ Ⓐ VI 1 (= *aparecer*) to figure, appear (**como** as; **entre** among); **tu nombre no figura en la lista** your name doesn't figure *o* appear on the list
2 (= *destacar*) **es un don nadie, pero le encanta ~** he's a nobody, but he likes to show off; **una joven que figura mucho en la alta sociedad** a young lady who is prominent in high society
Ⓑ VT (*frm*) 1 (= *representar*) to represent; **cada círculo figura un planeta** each circle represents a planet
2 (= *fingir*) to feign; **figuró una retirada** he feigned a retreat
Ⓒ **figurarse** VPR to imagine; **me figuro que Ana ya habrá llegado** I imagine that Ana will have arrived by now; **¡figúrate lo que sería con un sólo coche!** imagine what it would be like with just one car!; **¿qué te figuras que me preguntó ayer?** what do you think he asked me yesterday?; **no te vayas a ~ que ...** don't go thinking that ...; — **¿te dio vergüenza decírselo? —¡pues, figúrate!** "were you embarrassed to tell him?" — "well, what do you think?"; **ya me lo figuraba** I thought as much

figurativismo SM figurative art

figurativo ADJ figurative

figurilla SF figurine

figurín SM 1 (= *dibujo*) design
2 (= *revista*) fashion magazine
3 (= *persona elegante*) smart dresser

figurinismo SM costume design

figurinista SMF costume designer

figurón SM 1 ► **figurón de proa** (*Náut*) figurehead
2 (*) (= *presuntuoso*) pompous ass*

figuroso ADJ (*Méx*) showy, loud

fija SF 1 (*Andes, Cono Sur Equitación*) favourite, favorite (*EEUU*); **es una ~** it's a cert*; **ésa es la ~** that's for sure
2 (*Téc*†) hinge
3 (†) (*Arquit*) trowel

fijación SF 1 (*Psic*) fixation; **tener (una) ~ con** *o* **por algo/algn** to have a fixation about sth/sb, be fixated on sth/sb; **¡qué ~ tiene con su madre!** he's got a real mother fixation!
2 (= *acto*) (*gen*) fixing; (*con clavos*) securing; **se responsabiliza al grupo de la ~ de carteles** the group is believed to be responsible for putting up posters; **gel de ~ fuerte** extra hold gel ► **fijación de precios** price-fixing
3 **fijaciones** (*Esquí*) (safety) bindings

fijador SM 1 (*Fot*) fixative
2 (= *gomina*) setting lotion

fijamente ADV intently, fixedly; **mirar ~ a algn** to stare at sb, look at sb intently *o* fixedly

fijapelo SM setting lotion

fijar ►conjug 1a◄ Ⓐ VT 1 (= *sujetar*) (*gen, Fot*) to fix; (*con clavos*) to secure; (*con pegamento*) to glue; (*con chinchetas*) to pin up; [+ *pelo*] to set; **un gel para ~ el peinado** a gel to hold your hairstyle in place; **"prohibido fijar carteles"** "stick no bills"
2 (= *centrar*) [+ *atención*] to focus (**en** on); [+ *ojos*] to fix (**en** on); **pero fijemos nuestra atención en otros aspectos del asunto** but let us focus our attention on other aspects of the matter; **le contestó sin vacilar, fijando la mirada en sus ojos** she answered him directly, looking him straight in the eye
3 (= *determinar*) [+ *fecha, hora, precio, plazo*] to fix, set; [+ *límites, servicios mínimos*] to establish; [+ *condiciones*] to lay down; **no hemos fijado aún la fecha de la boda** we haven't fixed *o* set a date for the wedding yet; **~on un plazo de dos meses para llegar a un acuerdo** they set a two-month deadline for an agreement to be reached; **aún no se ha fijado el precio de las acciones** the price of the shares has not yet been fixed; **el Tratado de 1942 fijó los límites entre Perú y Ecuador** the 1942 Treaty established the border between Peru and Ecuador; **la organización ha fijado tres condiciones para volver a la mesa de negociaciones** the organization laid down three conditions for their return to the negotiating table; **el plazo fijado por la ley** the time period established *o* laid down by law
4 [+ *residencia*] to take up; **durante la guerra fijó su residencia en Suiza** during the war he took up residence in Switzerland
Ⓑ **fijarse** VPR 1 (= *prestar atención*) to pay attention; (= *darse cuenta*) to notice; **¿no ves que lo has escrito mal? ¡es que no te fijas!** can't you see you've spelled it wrong?

➤ LENGUA Y USO: **fiesta 1** 52.2 **2** 50.2 **figurar C** 33.2

don't you ever pay any attention to what you're doing?; **voy a hacerlo yo primero, fíjate bien** I'll do it first, watch carefully; **¿han pintado la puerta? no me había fijado** has the door been painted? I hadn't noticed; **~se en algo** (= *prestar atención*) to pay attention to sth; (= *darse cuenta*) to notice sth; **no se fija en lo que hace** he doesn't pay attention to what he is doing; **debería ~se más en lo que dice** he ought to be more careful about *o* think more about what he says; **entre tantos candidatos, es muy difícil que se fijen en mí** out of so many candidates, they're hardly likely to notice me; **¿te has fijado en los colores?** have you noticed the colours?

2 (*uso enfático*) **¡fíjate cómo corre!** (just) look at him run!; **¡fíjate qué precios!** (just) look at these prices!; **¡fíjate lo que me ha dicho!** guess what he just said to me!; **fíjate si será tacaño que ni siquiera les hace un regalo en Navidad** he is so mean he doesn't even give them a present for Christmas; **¿te fijas?** (*esp LAm*) see what I mean?

3 **~se un objetivo** to set (o.s.) a goal; **nos hemos fijado el objetivo de llegar a las próximas Olimpiadas** we've set (ourselves) the goal of getting to the next Olympics; **~se algo como objetivo** to set one's sights on sth

4 (= *establecerse*) **el dolor se me ha fijado en la pierna** the pain has settled in my leg

fijasellos SM INV stamp hinge

fijativo SM fixative

fijeza SF (*gen*) firmness, stability; (= *constancia*) constancy; **mirar con ~ a algn** to stare at sb, look hard at sb

fijo Ⓐ ADJ 1 (= *sujeto*) fixed; **la mesa está fija a la pared** the table is fixed to the wall; *ver tb* **barra 1**, **foto**, **piñón²**

2 (= *inmóvil*) [*mirada*] fixed, steady; [*punto*] fixed; **sentí sus ojos ~s en mí** I felt his eyes fixed on me; **estaba de pie, con la vista fija en el horizonte** he was standing staring at the horizon, he was standing with his gaze fixed on the horizon

3 (= *no variable*) [*fecha, precio*] fixed; **fiestas fijas, como el día de Navidad** fixed holidays, like Christmas Day; **no hay una fecha fija de apertura** there's no definite *o* fixed *o* set date for the opening; **no tengo hora fija para ir al gimnasio** I don't go to the gym at any particular time, I don't have a fixed time for going to the gym; **como soy fotógrafo, no tengo horario ~ de trabajo** being a photographer, I don't have fixed *o* regular work hours; **le ofrecieron una cantidad fija al mes por sus servicios** they offered him a fixed monthly sum for his services; **"sin domicilio ~"** "of no fixed abode"; **imposición a plazo ~** fixed term deposit; **fondos de renta fija** fixed-interest funds

4 (= *regular*) [*sueldo, novio*] steady; [*cliente*] regular; **el padre no tenía trabajo ~** the father didn't have a steady job, the father was not in regular employment (*frm*)

5 (= *permanente*) [*plantilla, contrato, empleado*] permanent; **estoy ~ en la empresa** I have a permanent job in the company; **¿cuándo os van a hacer ~s?** when will you get a permanent contract?

6 [*propósito*] fixed, firm; *ver tb* **idea 3, 5**, **rumbo¹ 1**

7 **de ~*** for sure*; **sé de ~ que no va a estar en casa** I know for sure that he won't be at home*; **de ~ que llueve esta noche** it's definitely going to rain tonight, it's going to rain tonight, that's for sure*

Ⓑ ADV 1 (*) (= *con certeza*) for sure*; **ya sé que no voy a ganar, eso ~** I know I'm not going to win, that's for sure*

2 (= *con fijeza*) fixedly; **miraba muy ~ a su padre** she stared fixedly at her father

fil SM **~ derecho** leapfrog

fila SF 1 (= *hilera*) [*de personas, cosas*] 1·1 (*una tras de otra*) line; **una ~ de coches** a line of cars; **nos colocaron en ~** they lined us up, they put us in a row; **ponerse en ~** to line up, get into line; **salirse de la ~** to step out of line; **una chaqueta de dos ~s de botones** a double-breasted jacket

1·2 (*una al lado de otra*) **había cuatro coches en ~** there were four cars in a row; **aparcar en doble ~** to double-park; **iban andando en ~s de tres** they were walking three abreast

1·3 (*Mil*) **¡en ~!** fall in!; **formar ~s** to form up, fall in; **romper ~s** to fall out, break ranks; **¡rompan ~s!** fall out!, dismiss!

► **fila india**: **en ~ india** in single file

2 [*de asientos*] row; **en primera/segunda ~** in the front/second row ► **fila cero** VIP row

3 **filas** 3·1 (*Mil*) (= *servicio*) **estar en ~s** to be on active service; **incorporarse a ~s** to join up; **llamar a algn a ~s** to call sb up, draft sb (*EEUU*)

3·2 (*Pol*) ranks; **en las ~s del partido** in the ranks of the party; ✦*MODISMO* **cerrar ~s** to close ranks

4 (*) (= *antipatía*) **tener ~ a algn** to have it in for sb*; **el jefe le tiene ~** the boss has it in for him*

5 (*CAm*) (= *cumbre*) peak, summit

filacteria SF phylactery

Filadelfia SF Philadelphia

filamento SM filament

filamentoso ADJ filamentous

filantropía SF philanthropy

filantrópico ADJ philanthropic

filantropismo SM philanthropy

filántropo/a SM/F philanthropist

filar‡ ▸conjug 1a◂ VT 1 (= *calar*) to size up, rumble*

2 (= *observar*) to notice, spot

filarmónica SF philharmonic (orchestra)

filarmónico ADJ philharmonic; **orquesta filarmónica** philharmonic (orchestra)

filatelia SF 1 (= *afición*) philately, stamp collecting

2 (= *tienda*) stamp shop, stamp dealer's

filatélico/a Ⓐ ADJ philatelic

Ⓑ SM/F = **filatelista**

filatelista SMF philatelist, stamp collector

filático ADJ (*Andes*) 1 [*caballo*] vicious

2 [*persona*] (= *travieso*) mischievous; (= *taimado*) crafty; (= *grosero*) rude

filete SM 1 (*Culin*) [*de ternera, cerdo*] steak; [*de pescado*] fillet, filet (*EEUU*); ✦*MODISMO* **darse el ~*** to neck*, pet*; **darse el ~ con algn*** to feel sb*, touch sb up*

2 (*Mec*) [*de tornillo*] worm; (= *rosca*) thread

3 [*de caballo*] snaffle bit

4 (*Cos*) narrow hem

5 (*Tip*) ornamental bar, ornamental line

6 (*Arquit*) fillet

fileteado SM filleting

filetear ▸conjug 1a◂ VT to fillet

filfa* SF 1 (= *fraude*) fraud, hoax

2 (= *falsificación*) fake

3 (= *rumor*) rumour, rumor (*EEUU*)

fili‡ SM pocket; **~ de la buena** breast pocket

filiación SF 1 (*a partido*) affiliation

2 [*de ideas*] connection, relationship

3 (= *señas*) particulars *pl*

4 [*de policía*] records *pl*

filial Ⓐ ADJ 1 (= *de hijo*) filial

2 (*Com*) subsidiary *antes de s*, affiliated

Ⓑ SF (*Com*) subsidiary

filibusterismo SM 1 (*Pol*) filibustering

2 (= *piratería*) buccaneering

filibustero SM pirate, freebooter

filiforme ADJ 1 (*Bot*) thread-like

2 (*hum*) [*persona*] skinny

filigrana SF 1 (*Téc*) filigree (work)

2 (*Tip*) watermark

3 **filigranas** (*fig*) delicate work *sing*; (*Dep*) elegant play *sing*, fancy footwork *sing*

filípica SF harangue, philippic

Filipinas SFPL **las (Islas) ~** the Philippines

filipino/a Ⓐ ADJ Philippine, Filipino

Ⓑ SM/F Filipino

filisteísmo SM Philistinism

filisteo/a ADJ, SM/F Philistine

film SM (*pl* **films**, **filmes**) film, picture, movie (*EEUU*) ► **film transparente** (*Culin*) cling film

filmación SF 1 (= *rodaje*) filming, shooting

2 **filmaciones** footage *sing*

filmador(a) SM/F film maker, moviemaker (*EEUU*)

filmadora SF (= *estudio*) film studio; (= *aparato*) film camera

filmar ▸conjug 1a◂ VT to film, shoot

filme SM = **film**

fílmico ADJ film *antes de s*, movie *antes de s* (*EEUU*); **su carrera fílmica** her film career, her career in films; **obras teatrales y fílmicas** theatrical and screen works, works for stage and screen

filmina SF slide, transparency

filmografía SF filmography; **la ~ de Buñuel** Buñuel's films; **la ~ de la estrella** the star's screen career

filmología SF science of film-making, art of film-making

filmoteca SF film library, film archive

filo¹ SM 1 [*de navaja, espada*] cutting edge, blade; **un arma de doble ~** a double-edged sword; ✦*MODISMOS* **dar ~ a algn** (*Caribe*) to wound sb with a knife; **herir a algn por los mismos ~s††** to pay sb back in his own coin; **pasar al ~ de la espada††** to put to the sword; **vivir en el ~ de la navaja** to live on a knife edge

2 (*con horas*) **al ~ de las doce** just before twelve o'clock; **por ~††** exactly

3 (*Náut*) ► **filo del viento** direction of the wind

4 (*LAm*) (= *de montaña*) ridge

5 (*Andes*) **de ~** resolutely

6 (*Méx**) (= *hambre*) ✦*MODISMO* **tener ~** to be starving

7 (*Cono Sur*) (= *cuento*) tale, tall story

8 (*Cono Sur*) (= *pretendiente*) suitor; (= *novia*) girlfriend; (= *cortejo*) courtship

filo² SM (*Biol*) phylum

filo[3]* SM con-man's accomplice*

...filo SUF ...phile; **francófilo** Francophile

filo... PREF philo..., pro-; **~comunista** pro-communist

filocomunismo SM pro-communist feeling(s)

filocomunista Ⓐ ADJ pro-communist, with communist leanings
Ⓑ SMF pro-communist

filología SF philology ► **Filología Francesa** (= *carrera*) French Studies

filológico ADJ philological

filólogo/a SM/F (= *estudioso*) philologist; (= *estudiante*) language graduate

filomela SF, **filomena** SF (*poét*) nightingale

filón SM (*Min*) vein, lode, seam; (*fig*) gold mine

filongo SM (*Cono Sur*) girlfriend (*of inferior social status*)

filosa* SF [1] (= *navaja*) chiv*, knife
[2] (= *cara*) mug*, face

filoso ADJ [1] (*LAm*) (= *afilado*) sharp
[2] (*Cono Sur**) (= *agudo*) **él es ~** he's sharp, he's really on the ball*; **estar ~ en algo** to be well up on sth
[3] (*CAm*) (= *hambriento*) starving

filosofal ADJ **piedra ~** philosopher's stone

filosofar ▸conjug 1a◂ VI to philosophize

filosofía SF philosophy; **tomarse las cosas con ~** to take things philosophically ► **filosofía de la ciencia** philosophy of science ► **filosofía de la vida** philosophy of life ► **filosofía moral** moral philosophy ► **filosofía natural** natural philosophy; *ver tb* **facultad 3**

filosófico ADJ philosophic, philosophical

filósofo/a SM/F philosopher

filosoviético ADJ pro-Soviet

filote SM (*Andes*) [1] (= *maíz*) ear of green maize, maize silk
[2] **estar en ~** [*niño*] to begin to grow hair

filotear ▸conjug 1a◂ VI (*Andes*) [1] [*maíz*] to come into ear, begin to ripen
[2] [*niño*] to grow hair

filoxera SF phylloxera

filtración SF [1] (*Téc*) (= *proceso*) filtration
[2] (= *fuga*) seepage, leakage, loss
[3] [*de datos*] leak; [*de fondos*] misappropriation

filtrado Ⓐ ADJ [1] [*información*] leaked
[2] **estoy ~** (*Cono Sur**) I'm whacked*
Ⓑ SM filtering

filtrador Ⓐ ADJ filtering
Ⓑ SM filter

filtraje SM filtering

filtrar ▸conjug 1a◂ Ⓐ VT [1] [+ *líquido, luz*] to filter; **hay que ~ el agua** the water needs filtering
[2] [+ *llamadas, visitantes*] to screen
[3] [+ *información, documento, grabación*] to leak
Ⓑ **filtrarse** VPR [1] [*líquido*] to seep, leak; [*luz, sonido*] to filter; **el agua se filtraba por las paredes** water was seeping *o* leaking in through the walls; **el sol se filtraba a través de las cortinas** the sun filtered through the curtains
[2] (= *desaparecer*) [*dinero, bienes*] to disappear

filtro SM [1] (*Téc*) filter; **cigarrillo con ~** filter-tipped cigarette ► **filtro de aire** air filter ► **filtro del aceite** oil filter
[2] (= *selección*) screening ► **filtro de llamadas** call-screening
[3] (*en carretera, de policía*) checkpoint, roadblock
[4] (*Hist*) (= *poción*) love-potion, philtre, philter (*EEUU*)

filudo ADJ (*LAm*) sharp

filván SM (*gen*) feather edge; [*de papel*] deckle edge; [*de cuchillo*] burr

fimbria SF (*Cos*) border, hem

▼ **fin** SM [1] (= *final*) end; **el ~ del mundo** the end of the world; **antes de ~ de mes** before the end of the month; **en la noche de ~ de año** on New Year's Eve; **~ de la cita** end of quote, unquote; **~ de curso** end of the school year; **fiesta de ~ de curso** end-of-year party; **dar ~ a** [+ *ceremonia, actuación*] to bring to a close; [+ *obra, libro*] to finish; [+ *guerra, conflicto*] to bring to an end; **estas palabras dieron ~ a tres años de conflicto** these words brought three years of conflict to an end; **llegar a buen ~** [*aventura*] to have a happy ending; [*plan*] to turn out well; **llevar algo a buen ~** to bring sth to a successful conclusion; **poner ~ a algo** to end sth, put an end to sth; **esta ley pondrá ~ a la discriminación sexual en el trabajo** this law will end *o* will put an end to sexual discrimination in the workplace; **los acuerdos pusieron ~ a doce años de guerra** the agreements ended *o* put an end to twelve years of war; **deseaban poner ~ a sus vidas** they wished to end their lives; **sin ~** endless; **correa sin ~** endless belt; ✦**MODISMO** **llegar a ~ de mes** to make ends meet; **un sueldo que apenas les permite llegar a ~ de mes** a salary that barely enables them to make ends meet ► **fin de fiesta** (*Teat*) grand finale ► **fin de semana** weekend
[2] **a fines de** at the end of; **a ~es de abril** at the end of April; **la crisis de ~es del XIX** the crisis at the end of the 19th century, the late 19th century crisis
[3] (*otras locuciones*) [3·1] **al ~** ◊ **por ~** (*gen*) finally; (*con más énfasis*) at last; **al ~ se ha premiado su esfuerzo** her efforts have finally been rewarded; **tras varios días de marcha, por ~ llegamos a la primera aldea** after several days' walk, we finally came to the first village; **¡al ~ solos!** alone at last!; **¡por ~ te decides a hacer algo!** at last you've decided to do something!; **al ~ y al cabo** after all; **tengo derecho a estar aquí: al ~ y al cabo, soy parte de la familia** I have a right to stay here: after all, I am part of the family; **al ~ y al cabo, lo que importa es que seguimos juntos** at the end of the day, what matters is that we're still together; **a ~ de cuentas** at the end of the day
[3·2] **en ~** (*quitando importancia*) anyway, oh, well; (*para resumir*) in short; **en ~, otro día seguiremos hablando del tema** anyway *o* oh, well, we will carry on discussing this another day; **¡en ~, qué se le va a hacer!** anyway *o* oh, well, there's nothing we can do about it!; **hemos tenido bastantes problemas este año, pero en ~, seguimos adelante** we've had quite a few problems this year, but still *o* anyway, we're still going; **en ~, que no he tenido un momento de descanso** in short, I haven't had a moment's rest
[4] (= *intención*) aim; **se desconocen los ~es de esa organización** the aims of that organization are unknown; **¿con qué ~ se ha organizado esto?** what has been the aim in organizing this?; **a ~ de hacer algo** in order to do sth; **a ~ de que** (+ *SUBJUN*) so that, in order that (*frm*); **se le ha citado como testigo a ~ de que explique sus relaciones con el acusado** he has been called as a witness in order to explain *o* in order that he explain (*frm*) *o* so that he can explain his relationship with the defendant; **con el ~ de hacer algo** in order to do sth; **a tal ~** with this aim in mind, to this end; ✦**REFRÁN** **el ~ justifica los medios** the end justifies the means
[5] (= *propósito*) purpose; **un millón de dólares será destinado a ~es benéficos** a million dollars is to go to charity; **el dinero había sido destinado a otros ~es** the money had been put aside for other purposes; **con ~es experimentales/militares/políticos** for experimental/military/political purposes; **planean intervenir con ~es humanitarios** they are planning to intervene for humanitarian reasons

Fina SF (*forma familiar*) *de* **Josefina**

finado/a Ⓐ ADJ late, deceased; **el ~ presidente** the late president
Ⓑ SM/F deceased
Ⓒ SM (*Téc*) finishing

final Ⓐ ADJ (= *último*) [*momento, capítulo, resultado, decisión*] final; [*objetivo*] ultimate; **los años ~es de la dictadura** the final years of the dictatorship; **estaban deseando ver el producto ~** they were looking forward to seeing the end product; *ver tb* **juicio 4**, **recta**, **punto 2**
Ⓑ SM [1] (= *fin*) [*de ceremonia, vida, aventura, guerra*] end; [*de obra musical*] finale; **hasta el ~ de sus días** till the end of her days; **no vi el ~ de la película** I didn't see the end of the film; **al ~** in the end; **al ~ tuve que darle la razón** in the end I had to admit that he was right; **al ~ de algo** at the end of sth; **el anuncio se realizó ayer al ~ de la reunión** the announcement was made yesterday at the end of the meeting; **al ~ de la calle** at the end of the street; **estamos al ~ de la lista** we are at the bottom of the list
[2] (= *desenlace*) [*de película, libro*] ending; **la novela tiene un ~ inesperado** the novel has an unexpected ending; **un ~ feliz** a happy ending
[3] **a finales de** at the end of; **a ~es del siglo XIX** at the end of the 19th century
Ⓒ SF (*Dep*) final; **consiguieron pasar a la ~** they managed to get through to the final; **cuartos de ~** quarter-finals ► **final de consolación** third-place play-off

finalidad SF [1] (= *propósito*) purpose; **¿qué ~ tendrá todo esto?** what can the purpose of all this be?; **el congreso tuvo como ~ debatir el desarrollo social** the purpose *o* aim of the conference was to discuss social development
[2] (*Fil*) finality

finalista Ⓐ ADJ **los relatos ~s** the short-listed stories; **quedó ~ en dos ocasiones** he was short-listed twice *o* on two occasions
Ⓑ SMF finalist

finalización SF ending, conclusion

finalizar ▸conjug 1f◂ Ⓐ VT to finish; **muchos universitarios no finalizan la carrera** many university students do not finish their degree; **~ la sesión** (*Inform*) to log out, log off; **con el himno se dio por finalizada la ceremonia**

➤ LENGUA Y USO: **fin 4** 35.2

the ceremony came to an end *o* ended with the national anthem
Ⓑ VI to end; **aún no ha finalizado la sesión** the session has not ended yet; **su contrato finaliza el próximo verano** his contract ends *o* comes to an end next summer; **hoy finaliza el plazo para presentar las solicitudes** today is the deadline for submitting applications; **~ con algo** to end with sth; **la jornada finalizó con la prueba de atletismo femenino** the day ended with the women's athletics trials

finalmente ADV [1] (= *al final*) finally, in the end; **~ decidimos ir a Mallorca** finally *o* in the end we decided to go to Majorca; **insistió hasta que, ~, consiguió convencerla** he went on until finally *o* in the end *o* eventually he managed to persuade her
[2] (= *por último*) lastly; **50% están a favor, 30% en contra y, ~, un 20% se muestra indeciso** 50% are in favour, 30% are against and lastly, 20% don't know

finamente ADV [1] (= *elegantemente*) elegantly; (= *educadamente*) politely; (= *delicadamente*) delicately
[2] (= *inteligentemente*) acutely, shrewdly; (= *sutilmente*) subtly

finamiento SM passing*, death

financiación SF financing, funding

financiador(a) SM/F financial backer

financiamiento SM financing, funding

financiar ▸conjug 1b◂ VT to finance, fund

financiera SF finance company, finance house

financiero/a Ⓐ ADJ financial; **el mundo ~** the world of finance, the financial world; **los medios ~s** the financial means
Ⓑ SM/F (= *banquero*) financier

financista Ⓐ ADJ (= *financiero*) financial
Ⓑ SMF (*LAm*) (= *bolsista*) financier; (= *consejero*) financial expert

finanzas SFPL finances

finar ▸conjug 1a◂ Ⓐ VI (= *morir*) to pass away (*euf*), die Ⓑ **finarse** VPR (= *desear*) to long, yearn (**por** for)

finca SF [1] (= *bien inmueble*) property, land, real estate; **cazar en ~ ajena** to poach (*on sb else's property*); **penetrar en ~ ajena** to trespass (*on sb else's property*) ► **finca raíz** (*Andes*) real estate ► **finca urbana** town property
[2] (= *casa de recreo*) country house, country estate; **pasan un mes en su ~** they're spending a month at their country place; **tienen una ~ en Guadalajara** they have a country house *o* country estate in Guadalajara
[3] (= *granja*) farm; (= *minifundio*) small holding; [*de ganado*] ranch ► **finca azucarera** sugar plantation ► **finca cafetera** coffee plantation

fincar ▸conjug 1g◂ Ⓐ VT (*Caribe*) (= *cultivar*) to till, cultivate
Ⓑ VI (*Andes, Méx*) **~ en** (= *consistir*) to consist of, comprise

finchado* ADJ stuck-up*, conceited

fincharse* ▸conjug 1a◂ VPR to become stuck-up*, get conceited

finde* SM ABR (= **fin de semana**) weekend

finés/esa Ⓐ ADJ Finnish
Ⓑ SM/F Finn
Ⓒ SM (*Ling*) Finnish

fineza SF [1] (= *cualidad*) fineness, excellence
[2] [*de modales*] refinement; (= *elegancia*) elegance
[3] (= *acto*) kindness; (= *dádiva*) small gift, token
[4] (= *cumplido*) compliment

fingar‡ ▸conjug 1h◂ VT to nick‡, swipe‡

finger ['finger] SM (*pl* **fingers**) (*Aer*) (telescopic) passenger walkway

fingidamente ADV feignedly

fingido ADJ feigned, false; **con ~ enojo** with feigned annoyance; **nombre ~** assumed name, false name

fingimiento SM pretence, pretense (*EEUU*), feigning

fingir ▸conjug 3c◂ Ⓐ VT to feign; **intenté ~ indiferencia** I tried to feign indifference *o* to appear indifferent; **fingió interés** he pretended to be interested; **~ hacer algo** to pretend to do sth; **finge dormir** *o* **que duerme** he's pretending to be asleep
Ⓑ VI to pretend; **¡no finjas más!** stop pretending!
Ⓒ **fingirse** VPR (*frm*) **~se dormido** to pretend to be asleep; **~se muerto** to play dead, act dead; **~se un sabio** to pretend to be an expert

finiquitar ▸conjug 1a◂ VT [1] (*Fin*) [+ *cuenta*] to settle and close, balance up
[2] (*) [+ *asunto*] to conclude, wind up

finiquito SM (*Com, Fin*) settlement; **dar el ~ a una cuenta** to settle an account; **dar el ~ a algn** to dismiss sb

finisecular ADJ fin-de-siècle *antes de s*, turn-of-the-century *antes de s*

Finisterre SM (*tb* **el Cabo de ~**) Cape Finisterre

finito ADJ finite

finlandés/esa Ⓐ ADJ Finnish
Ⓑ SM/F Finn
Ⓒ SM (*Ling*) Finnish

Finlandia SF Finland

finlandización SF Finlandization, neutralization and subordination (*of one country to another*)

finlandizar ▸conjug 1f◂ VT [+ *país*] to Finlandize, neutralize and subordinate

fino Ⓐ ADJ [1] (= *no grueso*) [*arena, punta, pelo*] fine; [*papel, capa*] thin; [*dedos, cuello*] slender; [*cutis, piel*] smooth; **bolígrafo de punta fina** fine-tipped ballpoint pen
[2] (= *de buena calidad*) [*cristal, porcelana, papel*] fine; [*tabaco*] select; **oro ~** fine gold; *ver tb* **lencería**
[3] (= *cortés*) polite, well-bred; (= *refinado*) refined; **no te hagas la fina** you needn't start putting on airs
[4] (= *agudo*) [*vista*] sharp; [*oído*] acute; **su fina inteligencia analítica** her fine *o* acute analytical intelligence
[5] (= *sutil*) subtle, fine; **me sorprendió su fina ironía** her subtle irony surprised me
[6] [*jerez*] fino, dry
Ⓑ SM (= *jerez*) dry sherry, fino sherry

finolis* ADJ INV affected

finquero SM (*LAm*) farmer

finta SF feint; **hacer ~s** to feint, spar

fintar ▸conjug 1a◂ VI, **fintear** ▸conjug 1a◂ VI (*LAm*) to feint, spar

finura SF [1] (= *buena calidad*) fineness, excellence
[2] (= *cortesía*) politeness, courtesy; (= *refinamiento*) refinement; **¡qué ~!** how refined!, how charming!
[3] (= *sutileza*) subtlety
[4] (= *poco grosor*) fineness

fiñe ADJ (*Caribe*) small, weak, sickly

fiordo SM fiord

fique SM (*Col, Méx, Ven*) [1] (= *fibra*) vegetable fibre *o* (*EEUU*) fiber
[2] (= *cuerda*) rope, cord

firma SF [1] (= *nombre*) signature; (= *acto*) signing; **es de mi ~** I signed that; **seis novelas de su ~** six novels of his, six novels which he has written; **me presentó varios documentos a la ~** he handed me several documents to sign ► **firma de libros** book-signing session
[2] (= *empresa*) firm, company

firmamento SM firmament

firmante Ⓐ ADJ signatory (**de** to)
Ⓑ SMF signatory; **los abajo ~s** the undersigned; **el último ~** the last person signing *o* to sign

firmar ▸conjug 1a◂ Ⓐ VT to sign; **~ un cheque en blanco** to write *o* sign a blank cheque; **~ un contrato** to sign a contract; **firmado y sellado** signed and sealed
Ⓑ VI to sign; **firme aquí** sign here; **no te quejes, si me dieran tu trabajo ~ía ahora mismo** stop complaining, if I was offered your job I'd take it straight away

firme Ⓐ ADJ [1] [*mesa, andamio*] steady; [*terreno*] firm, solid; **mantén la escalera ~** can you hold the ladder steady?
[2] [*paso*] firm, steady; [*voz*] firm; [*mercado, moneda*] steady; [*candidato*] strong; **la libra se ha mantenido ~** the pound has remained steady; **oferta en ~** firm offer; **pedido en ~** firm order
[3] [*amistad, apoyo*] firm, strong; [*decisión, convicción*] firm; **mantenerse ~** to hold one's ground; **se mostró muy ~ con ella** he was very firm with her; **de ~** hard; **trabajar de ~** to work hard; **estar en lo ~**† to be in the right
[4] [*sentencia*] final
[5] (*Mil*) **¡~s!** attention!; **estar en posición de ~s** to stand to attention; **ponerse ~s** to come *o* stand to attention
Ⓑ ADV hard; **trabajar ~** to work hard
Ⓒ SM (*Aut*) road surface; **"firme provisional"** "temporary surface" ► **firme del suelo** (*Arquit*) rubble base (of floor)

firmemente ADV (= *con firmeza*) firmly; (= *bien sujeto*) securely

firmeza SF [1] [*del terreno*] firmness
[2] [*de carácter, convicciones*] strength, firmness; **con ~** firmly; **se negó con ~ a delatarlos** he firmly refused to inform on them

firmita* SF (mere) signature; **echar una ~** to sign on the dotted line (*tb fig*); **¿me echas una ~?** would you sign here please?

firuletes* SMPL (*LAm*) [1] (= *objetos*) knick-knacks
[2] (*al bailar*) gyrations, contortions

fiscal Ⓐ ADJ (= *relativo a impuestos*) fiscal, tax *antes de s*; (= *económico*) fiscal, financial; **año ~** fiscal year, financial year
Ⓑ SMF (SF *a veces* **fiscala**) [1] (*Jur*) public prosecutor, district attorney (*EEUU*) ► **fiscal general del Estado** Director of Public Prosecutions, Attorney-General (*EEUU*)
[2] (*) (= *entrometido*) busybody, meddler

fiscalía SF office of the public prosecutor, District Attorney's office (*EEUU*)

fiscalidad SF (*gen*) taxation; (= *sistema*) tax system; (= *normas*) tax regulations *pl*

fiscalista ADJ **abogado ~** lawyer specializing in tax affairs

fiscalizar ▸conjug 1f◂ VT [1] (= *controlar*) to control; (= *supervisar*) to oversee; (= *registrar*) to inspect (officially)
[2] (= *criticar*) to criticize, find fault with
[3] (*) (= *hurgar*) to pry into

fiscalmente ADV from a tax point of view, taxation-wise

fisco SM treasury, exchequer; **declarar algo al ~** to declare sth to the Inland Revenue *o* (*EEUU*) Internal Revenue Service

fisga SF [1] [*de pesca*] fish spear
[2] (*Guat, Méx Taur*) banderilla
[3] (= *bromas*) banter; **hacer ~ a algn** to tease sb, make fun of sb

fisgar* ▸conjug 1h◂ Ⓐ VT [1] (= *curiosear*) to snoop on*
[2] [+ *pez*] to spear, harpoon
Ⓑ VI [1] (*) (= *curiosear*) to snoop* (**en** on)
[2] (= *mofarse*) to mock

fisgón/ona* Ⓐ ADJ [1] (= *curioso*) nosey*
[2] (= *guasón*) bantering, teasing; (= *mofador*) mocking
Ⓑ SM/F [1] snooper*
[2] (= *guasón*) tease

fisgonear* ▸conjug 1a◂ VI to snoop*

fisgoneo* SM (= *acción*) snooping*; (= *actitud*) nosiness*

física SF physics *sing* ► **física cuántica** quantum physics ► **física de alta(s) energía(s)** high-energy physics ► **física del estado sólido** solid-state physics ► **física de partículas** particle physics ► **física nuclear** nuclear physics ► **física teórica** theoretical physics; *ver tb* **físico**

físicamente ADV physically

físico/a Ⓐ ADJ [1] physical
[2] (*Caribe*) (= *melindroso*) finicky; (= *afectado*) affected
Ⓑ SM/F [1] (= *científico*) physicist ► **físico/a nuclear** nuclear physicist
[2] (†) (= *médico*) physician
Ⓒ SM (*Anat*) physique; (= *aspecto*) appearance, looks *pl*; **de ~ regular** ordinary-looking; *ver tb* **física**

físil ADJ fissile

fisiología SF physiology

fisiológico ADJ physiological

fisiólogo/a SM/F physiologist

fisión SF fission ► **fisión nuclear** nuclear fission

fisionable ADJ fissionable

fisionarse ▸conjug 1a◂ VPR to undergo fission, split

fisionomía SF = **fisonomía**

fisioterapeuta SMF physiotherapist, physical therapist (*EEUU*)

fisioterapia SF physiotherapy, physical therapy (*EEUU*)

fisioterapista SMF (*esp LAm*) physiotherapist, physical therapist (*EEUU*)

fiso‡ SM (*LAm*) mug‡

fisonomía SF [1] (= *cara*) physiognomy, features *pl*
[2] [*de objeto, lugar*] appearance; **la ~ de la ciudad** the appearance of the city

fisonomista SMF **ser buen ~** to have a good memory for faces

fisoterapeuta SMF physiotherapist

fistol SM (*Méx*) tiepin

fístula SF fistula

fisura SF [1] (*en roca*) crack, fissure (*frm*); (*en órgano*) fissure (*frm*); (*en hueso*) crack ► **fisura del paladar, fisura palatina** cleft palate
[2] **sin ~s** [*apoyo, fe, convencimiento*] solid

fitobiología SF phytobiology, plant breeding

fitocultura SF plant breeding

fitófago/a Ⓐ ADJ plant-eating
Ⓑ SM/F plant eater

fitopatología SF phytopathology, plant pathology

fitoplancton SM phytoplankton

fitoquímica SF phytochemistry

fitosanitario Ⓐ ADJ [*productos, industria, problemas, tratamiento*] phytosanitary
Ⓑ SM pesticide

FIV SF ABR (= **fecundación in vitro**) IVF

flaccidez SF flaccidity (*frm*), softness, flabbiness

fláccido ADJ flaccid (*frm*), flabby

flacidez SF = **flaccidez**

flácido ADJ = **fláccido**

flaco Ⓐ ADJ [1] (= *delgado*) thin, skinny*; **años ~s** (*LAm*) lean years; **ponerse ~** (*LAm*) to get thin
[2] (= *débil*) weak, feeble; [*memoria*] bad, short; (*LAm*) [*tierra*] barren; **su punto ~** his weak point, his weakness
Ⓑ SM (= *defecto*) failing; (= *punto débil*) weakness, weak point

flacón ADJ (*Caribe, Cono Sur*) very thin

flacuchento ADJ (*LAm*) very thin

flacura SF [1] (= *delgadez*) thinness, skinniness*
[2] (= *debilidad*) weakness, feebleness

flagelación SF flagellation (*frm*), whipping

flagelar ▸conjug 1a◂ VT [1] (= *azotar*) to flagellate (*frm*), whip
[2] (= *criticar*) to flay, criticize severely

flagelo SM [1] (= *azote*) whip, scourge
[2] (= *calamidad*) scourge, calamity

flagrante ADJ flagrant; **pillar** *o* **sorprender a algn en ~ delito** to catch sb in the act, catch sb redhanded, catch sb in flagrante delicto (*frm*)

flama SF [1] (*Méx*) (= *llama*) flame
[2] (= *destello*) glitter
[3] (= *calor*) stifling heat

flamante ADJ [1] (= *nuevo*) [*automóvil, traje*] brand-new; [*campeón, director*] new
[2] (= *estupendo*) brilliant, fabulous; (= *lujoso*) luxurious, high-class
[3] (= *resplandeciente*) brilliant, flaming

flambeado ADJ flambé

flambear ▸conjug 1a◂ VT to flambé

flamear ▸conjug 1a◂ VI [1] (= *llamear*) to flame, blaze (up)
[2] [*vela*] to flap; [*bandera*] to flutter

flamenco¹ SM (= *ave*) flamingo

flamenco²/a Ⓐ ADJ [1] (*Geog*) Flemish
[2] (*Mús*) flamenco; **cante ~** flamenco
[3] (*pey*) flashy, vulgar, gaudy
[4] **ponerse ~*** (= *engreído*) to get cocky*
[5] (*CAm*) = **flaco**
Ⓑ SM/F (= *persona*) Fleming; **los ~s** the Flemings, the Flemish
Ⓒ SM [1] (*Mús*) flamenco
[2] (*Ling*) Flemish

flamencología SF *study of flamenco music and dance*

flamencólogo/a SM/F *student of flamenco music and dance*

flamenquilla SF marigold

flamígero ADJ **estilo gótico ~** flamboyant Gothic style

flámula SF pennant

flan SM (*dulce*) creme caramel; (*salado*) mould, mold (*EEUU*); ✦***MODISMO*** **estar hecho** *o* **estar como un ~** to shake like a jelly *o* a leaf

flanco SM [1] (= *lado*) [*de animal*] side, flank; [*de persona*] side
[2] (*Mil*) flank; **coger a algn por el ~** to catch sb off guard
[3] (*Geog*) flank

Flandes SM Flanders

flanear* ▸conjug 1a◂ VI to stroll, saunter

flanera SF jelly mould, jelly mold (*EEUU*)

flanquear ▸conjug 1a◂ VT [1] [+ *persona, construcción*] to flank; [+ *calle, costa, río*] to line
[2] (*Mil*) (= *sobrepasar*) to outflank

flaquear ▸conjug 1a◂ VI [1] (= *debilitarse*) (*gen*) to weaken, grow weak; [*esfuerzo*] to slacken, flag; [*salud*] to decline (*frm*), get worse; [*viga*] to give way; **me flaquean las piernas** my legs are like jelly
[2] (= *desanimarse*) to lose heart, become dispirited

flaquencia SF (*LAm*) = **flacura**

flaqueza SF [1] (= *delgadez*) thinness, leanness; (= *debilidad*) feebleness, frailty; **la ~ de su memoria** his poor memory; **la ~ humana** human frailty
[2] **una ~** (= *defecto*) a failing; (= *punto flaco*) a weakness; **las ~s de la carne** the weaknesses of the flesh

flaquísimo ADJ SUPERL *de* **flaco**

flash [flas] SM (*pl* **flashes** ['flases]) [1] (*Fot*) flash, flashlight
[2] (*TV etc*) newsflash
[3] (‡) (= *sorpresa*) shock; **¡qué ~!** what a shock!

flashback ['flasbak] SM (*pl* **flashbacks**) flashback

flato SM [1] (*Med*) **tener ~** to have a stitch
[2] (*LAm*) (= *depresión*) gloom, depression; (*CAm*) (= *temor*) fear, apprehension

flatoso ADJ [1] (*Med*) flatulent
[2] (*CAm, Col, Méx*) (= *deprimido*) depressed; (*CAm*) (= *inquieto*) apprehensive

flatulencia SF flatulence

flatulento ADJ flatulent

flatuoso ADJ flatulent

flauta Ⓐ SF [1] (= *instrumento*) (*tb* **~ travesera**) flute; (*tb* **~ dulce**) recorder; **~ de Pan** panpipes; ✦***MODISMOS*** **estar hecho una ~** to be as thin as a rake; **sonó la ~ (por casualidad)** it was a fluke, it was sheer luck
[2] (= *barra de pan*) French stick, baguette
[3] (*LAm*) ✦***MODISMOS*** **¡~ la ~!** gosh!*; **¡la gran ~!** my God!; **de la gran ~*** terrific*, tremendous*; **¡hijo de la gran ~!**‡ bastard‡, son of a bitch (*EEUU*‡); **¡por la ~!** oh dear!
Ⓑ SMF flautist, flute player, flutist (*EEUU*)

flautín Ⓐ SM (= *instrumento*) piccolo
Ⓑ SMF (= *persona*) piccolo player

flautista SMF flautist, flute player, flutist (*EEUU*); **el ~ de Hamelin** the Pied Piper of Hamelin

flavina SF flavin

flebitis SF INV phlebitis

flecha Ⓐ SF [1] (= *arma*) arrow; (*en juego*) dart; (*Arquit*) spire; [*de billar*] cue rest; **como una ~** like an arrow, like a shot; **con alas en ~** swept-wing, with swept-back wings; **subida en ~** sharp rise; **subir en ~** to rise sharply ► **flecha de dirección** (*Aut*) indicator ► **flecha de mar** squid
[2] (*Andes*) sling; (*Méx Aut*) axle
[3] (*Cono Sur**) (= *coqueta*) flirt
Ⓑ SMF (*Hist**) *member of the Falangist youth movement*

flechado* ADV **el médico vino ~** the doctor came in a flash*; **salir ~** to shoot off*

flechar ▸conjug 1a◂ VT [1] [+ *arco*] to draw
[2] (= *herir*) to wound with an arrow; (= *matar*) to kill with an arrow; (= *disparar*) to shoot (with an arrow)
[3] (*) (= *enamorar*) **~ a algn** to sweep off sb's feet
[4] (*Arg, Méx*) (= *picar*) [*persona*] to prick (*esp with a goad*); [*sol*] to burn, scorch

flechazo SM [1] (= *acción*) bowshot; (= *herida*) arrow wound
[2] (*) (= *amor*) love at first sight; **fue el** o **un ~** it was love at first sight
[3] (*) (= *revelación*) revelation; **aquello fue el ~** then it hit me, that was the moment of revelation

flechero SM (= *soldado*) archer, bowman; (= *artesano*) arrow maker

fleco SM [1] (*Méx*) (= *flequillo*) fringe, bangs *pl* (*EEUU*)
[2] **flecos** [2·1] (= *adorno*) fringe *sing*; **una cazadora de ante con ~s** a fringed suede jacket
[2·2] (= *borde deshilachado*) frayed edge *sing* (*of cloth*)
[2·3] (= *detalles pendientes*) loose ends

flejadora SF strapping machine

flejar ▸conjug 1a◂ VT [1] (*esp LAm*) to strap, secure with metal strips
[2] (*Méx*) [+ *paquete*] to pack

fleje SM (*Téc*) (= *tira*) hoop, metal band; (= *resorte*) spring clip

flema SF [1] (*Med*) phlegm
[2] (= *impasibilidad*) phlegm

flemático ADJ (= *imperturbable*) [*persona*] phlegmatic; [*tono, comportamiento*] matter-of-fact, unruffled

flemón SM gumboil

flemudo ADJ slow, sluggish

flequetería SF (*Andes*) cheating, swindling

flequetero ADJ (*Andes*) tricky, dishonest

flequillo SM fringe, bangs *pl* (*EEUU*)

Flesinga SM Flushing

fleta SF (*Andes, Caribe*) [1] (= *fricción*) rub, rubbing
[2] (= *paliza*) thrashing

fletado* ADJ [1] (*CAm*) sharp, clever
[2] (*Caribe, Méx*) **salir ~*** to be off like a shot

fletador Ⓐ ADJ shipping *antes de s*, freighting *antes de s*
Ⓑ SM [*de avión, barco*] charterer; [*de pasajeros, mercancías*] carrier

fletamiento SM, **fletamento** SM chartering; **contrato de ~** charter

fletán SM **~ negro** Greenland halibut

fletar ▸conjug 1a◂ Ⓐ VT [1] [+ *avión, barco*] to charter; (= *cargar*) to load, freight
[2] (*LAm*) [*autobús*] to hire
[3] (*Cono Sur**) (= *despedir*) to get rid of, fire*; (= *expulsar*) to chuck out*
[4] (*Andes, Cono Sur*) [+ *insultos*] to let fly*; [+ *golpe*] to deal
Ⓑ **fletarse** VPR [1] (*Andes, Caribe, Méx**) (= *largarse*) to get out, beat it*; (*con sigilo*) to slip away, get away unseen; (*Arg*) (= *colarse*) to gatecrash
[2] (*CAm*) (= *enojarse*) to be annoyed, get cross
[3] (*Cono Sur*) **"se fleta"** "for hire"

flete SM [1] (= *alquiler*) [1·1] [*de avión, barco*] charter; **vuelo ~** charter flight
[1·2] (*LAm*) [*de autobús, camión*] hire; (= *precio*) hire charge, hiring fee
[2] (= *carga*) freight; (*Náut, Aer*) cargo; ✦**MODISMO salir sin ~s** (*Andes*) to leave in a hurry, be off like a shot
[3] (= *gastos*) (= *precio del transporte*) freightage, carriage ► **flete debido** freight forward ► **flete pagado** advance freight, prepaid freight ► **flete por cobrar** freight forward ► **flete sobre compras** inward freight
[4] (*LAm*) (= *caballo*) fast horse; [*de carreras*] racehorse; (*Cono Sur*) (= *rocín*) old nag
[5] (*Andes*) (= *amante*) lover, companion
[6] (*) (= *prostitución*) prostitution, the game*
[7] **echarse un ~**** to have a screw**

fletera* SF (*Caribe*) prostitute

fletero/a Ⓐ ADJ (*LAm*) [1] (= *de alquiler*) [*avión*] charter *antes de s*; [*camión*] for hire, for rent (*EEUU*)
[2] (= *de carga*) freight *antes de s*
Ⓑ SM/F [1] (*LAm*) (= *transportista*) haulier; (= *recaudador*) collector of transport charges
[2] (*Andes, Guat*) (= *mozo*) porter

flexibilidad SF (*gen*) flexibility; [*del cuerpo*] suppleness; (*Téc*) pliability; [*de carácter*] flexibility, adaptability ► **flexibilidad laboral, flexibilidad de plantillas** freedom to "restructure", freedom to hire and fire

flexibilización SF [*de control, sanción*] relaxation; [*de horario, programa*] adjusting, adapting ► **flexibilización del mercado laboral, flexibilización del trabajo** *relaxation of laws relating to terms of employment*

flexibilizar ▸conjug 1f◂ VT [+ *control, sanción*] to relax; [+ *horario, programa*] to make (more) flexible, adjust, adapt; [+ *plantilla*] to downsize

flexible Ⓐ ADJ [1] [*material, actitud*] flexible; [*cuerpo*] supple; (*Téc*) pliable; [*sombrero*] soft; **horario ~** flexitime
[2] [*persona*] flexible, open-minded; (*pey*) compliant
Ⓑ SM [1] soft hat
[2] (*Elec*) flex, cord

flexión SF [1] **hacer flexiones (de brazos)** to do press-ups o push-ups; **hacer flexiones de cintura** to touch one's toes; **flexiones de piernas** squats
[2] (*Ling*) inflection ► **flexión nominal** noun inflection ► **flexión verbal** verb inflection
[3] (*Med, Téc*) flexion

flexional ADJ flexional, inflected

flexionar ▸conjug 1a◂ VT (*gen*) to bend; [+ *músculo*] to flex

flexo SM adjustable table-lamp

flipado* ADJ [1] (= *drogado*) stoned*
[2] (= *pasmado*) gobsmacked*; **me quedé ~** I was gobsmacked*

flipante* ADJ [1] (= *estupendo*) great*, smashing*, cool*
[2] (= *pasmoso*) amazing

flipar* ▸conjug 1a◂ Ⓐ VT [1] (= *gustar*) **esto me flipa** I really love this
[2] (= *pasmar*) **me flipó lo que pasó** I was gobsmacked at what happened*
Ⓑ VI [1] (= *pasmarse*) **yo flipaba al ver tanta cosa** I was gobsmacked at all the things I saw*; **¡este tío flipa!** this guy must be kidding!*
[2] (= *pasarlo bien*) to have a great time; **~ con algo** (= *disfrutar*) to really love sth; **yo flipo con esa canción** I really love that song
[3] (= *drogarse*) to get stoned*
Ⓒ **fliparse** VPR [1] **~se por algo** to be mad keen on sth
[2] (= *drogarse*) to get stoned*

flipe* SM [1] (= *experiencia*) amazing experience, startling revelation
[2] (*por drogas*) (= *viaje*) trip*; (= *subida*) high*

flipper* ['fliper] SM pinball machine; **jugar al ~** to play pinball

flirt [flir, fler] SM (*pl* **flirts**) [1] (= *amorío*) fling*
[2] (= *persona*) boyfriend/girlfriend; **la estrella vino con su ~ del momento** the star came with her latest boyfriend

flirteador(a) SM/F flirt

flirtear ▸conjug 1a◂ VI to flirt (**con** with)

flirteo SM [1] (= *coqueteo*) flirting
[2] **un ~** a flirtation

FLN SM ABR (*Pol*) = **Frente de Liberación Nacional**

flojamente ADV weakly, feebly

flojear ▸conjug 1a◂ VI [1] (= *debilitarse*) **me flojean las piernas** my legs are tired
[2] (= *flaquear*) **flojeó en el último examen** she did less well in the last exam; **el ritmo flojea hacia el final** the pace slackens towards the end

flojedad SF = **flojera**

flojel SM [*de tela*] nap; [*de ave*] down

flojera SF [1] (= *debilidad*) weakness, feebleness
[2] (*esp LAm**) (= *pereza*) **me da ~** I can't be bothered

flojo ADJ [1] [*nudo, tuerca*] loose; [*cable, cuerda*] slack; ✦**MODISMO me la trae floja**** I don't give a fuck o bugger**; *ver tb* **cuerda 1**
[2] (= *débil*) [*persona*] weak; [*viento*] light; **está muy ~ después de su enfermedad** he's very weak after his illness; **todavía tengo las piernas muy flojas** my legs are still very weak
[3] (= *mediocre*) [*trabajo, actuación*] poor, feeble; [*estudiante, equipo*] weak, poor; **ha escrito una redacción muy floja** he's written a very poor o feeble essay; **el guión era muy ~** the script was very weak; **está ~ en matemáticas** he's weak in maths
[4] [*té, vino*] weak
[5] [*demanda, mercado*] slack
[6] (= *holgazán*) lazy, idle
[7] (*LAm*) (= *cobarde*) cowardly

floppy ['flopi] SM (*pl* **floppys**) floppy disk

flor Ⓐ SF [1] (*Bot*) flower; **un ramo de ~es** a bunch of flowers; **un vestido de ~es** a floral dress; **~es artificiales** artificial flowers; **~ cortada** (*Com*) cut flowers *pl*; **~es secas**

dried flowers; ✦*MODISMOS* **a ~ de labios** (*LAm*): **siempre anda con una sonrisa a ~ de labios** he always has a slight grin on his face; **de ~** (*Cono Sur*) very good, splendid; **ir de ~ en ~** (*gen*) to flit from flower to flower; (*en cuestiones amorosas*) to flit from one lover to the next; **¡ni ~es!***: **—¿has oído alguna noticia? —¡ni ~es!** "have you heard any news?" — "not a thing"; **de libros sé mucho, pero de cocina ni ~es** I know a lot about books, but I don't know the first thing about cooking*; **de lo prometido, ni ~es** as for what they promised, not a word was mentioned*; **ser ~ de un día**: **su amor fue ~ de un día** their love was short-lived; **su triunfo no fue ~ de un día** his win was no mere flash in the pan; **ser ~ de estufa** to be very delicate ► **flor de lis** fleur-de-lis, fleur-de-lys ► **flor de mano**† artificial flower ► **flor de nieve** snowdrop ► **flor de Pascua** poinsettia ► **flor somnífera** opium poppy

2 **en ~** [*planta, campo*] in flower, in bloom; [*árbol*] in blossom, in flower; [*muchacha*] (*liter*) in the first flower of womanhood (*liter*); **los naranjos en ~** the orange trees in blossom *o* flower

3 **la ~** (= *lo mejor*): **la ~ de la harina** the finest flour; **la ~ del ejército** the elite of the army; **está en la ~ de su carrera deportiva** he is at the peak of his sporting career; **en la ~ de la edad** in the flower of one's youth; **la ~ y nata de la sociedad** the cream of society; **en la ~ de la vida** in the prime of life; ✦*MODISMO* **ser la ~ de la canela** to be the pick of the bunch*

4 **a ~ de agua**: **los peces se veían a ~ de agua** you could see the fish just under the surface of the water; **a ~ de cuño** in mint condition; **a ~ de piel**: **tenía los nervios a ~ de piel** her nerves were all on edge; **tiene la sensibilidad a ~ de piel** she is highly sensitive; **el odio le salía a ~ de piel** his hatred came out into the open, his hatred came to the surface; **a ~ de tierra** at ground level

5 (= *piropo*) compliment, flattering remark; **decir** *o* **echar ~es a algn** to pay compliments to sb, flatter sb

6 [*de ciruela, uva*] bloom

7 [*de cuero*] grain

8 (*Cono Sur**) **~ de**: **~ de caballo** a wonderful horse; **~ de alegre** really happy, very cheerful; **¡~ de discurso se mandó!** what a brilliant talk he gave!; **~ de reloj me regalaste, ya no funciona** (*iró*) what a great watch you bought me, it doesn't work anymore (*iró*); **~ de marido, le pega y no le da plata** (*iró*) her husband is a real gem, he beats her up and gives her no money (*iró*)

9 **ajustado a ~** flush

Ⓑ ADJ (*Cono Sur*) great; **aquí estoy ~** I feel great here; **la fiesta estuvo ~** the party was excellent *o* great

Ⓒ ADV (*Cono Sur**) **hoy me siento ~** I feel great today; **lo pasamos ~** we had a whale of a time*

flora SF flora

floración SF flowering; **en plena ~** in full bloom

floral ADJ floral

florar ▸conjug 1a◂ VI to flower, bloom

florcita SF (*LAm*) little flower

floreado ADJ 1 [*tela*] flowered, floral

2 [*pan*] made with the finest flour, top-quality

3 (*Mús*) elaborate

florear ▸conjug 1a◂ Ⓐ VT 1 [+ *tela*] to decorate *o* pattern with flowers

2 [+ *harina*] to sift

3 [+ *naipes*] to stack

4 (= *adular*) to flatter

Ⓑ VI 1 (*LAm*) (= *florecer*) to flower, bloom

2 (*Mús*) to play a flourish; (*Esgrima*) to flourish

3 (= *piropear*) to flatter

Ⓒ **florearse** VPR (*LAm*) (= *lucirse*) to perform brilliantly; (= *presumir*) to show off

florecer ▸conjug 2d◂ Ⓐ VI 1 (*Bot*) to flower, bloom

2 (= *prosperar*) to flourish, thrive

Ⓑ **florecerse** VPR (= *enmohecer*) to go mouldy, go moldy (*EEUU*)

floreciente ADJ 1 (*Bot*) in flower, flowering, blooming

2 (= *próspero*) flourishing, thriving

florecimiento SM 1 (*Bot*) flowering, blooming

2 (= *prosperidad*) blossoming, flowering

Florencia SF Florence

florentino/a Ⓐ ADJ Florentine

Ⓑ SM/F Florentine

floreo SM 1 (*Esgrima, Mús*) flourish

2 (= *gracia*) witty but insubstantial talk; (= *cumplido*) compliment, nicely-turned phrase; **andarse con ~s** to beat about the bush

florería SF florist's (shop)

florero/a Ⓐ SM/F 1 (= *florista*) (*en tienda, puesto*) florist; (*en la calle*) (street) flower-seller

2 (= *halagador*) flatterer

Ⓑ SM 1 (= *recipiente*) vase; ✦*MODISMO* **estar de ~** to be just for show *o* decoration

2 (*Arte*) (= *cuadro*) flower painting

florescencia SF florescence

floresta SF 1 (= *bosque*) wood, grove; (= *claro*) glade; (*LAm*) (= *selva*) forest, jungle

2 (= *lugar atractivo*) beauty spot; (= *escena rural*) charming rural scene

florete SM (*Esgrima*) foil

floretear ▸conjug 1a◂ VT to decorate with flowers

floretista SMF (*LAm*) fencer

florícola ADJ **el sector ~** the flower-growing sector

floricultor(a) SM/F flower-grower

floricultura SF flower growing

florido ADJ 1 [*campo, jardín*] full of flowers; [*árbol, planta*] in blossom, in flower

2 (= *selecto*) choice, select; **lo más ~ del arte contemporáneo** the pick of contemporary art; **lo más ~ de la sociedad** the cream of society

3 [*estilo*] flowery, florid

florilegio SM anthology

florín SM 1 (*holandés*) guilder

2 (*Hist*) florin

florión/ona SM/F (*Andes*) = **fanfarrón**

floripón SM (*LAm*) = **floripondio 1**

floripondio SM 1 (*pey*) big flower

2 (*Literat*) rhetorical flourish, extravagant figure

3 (*LAm**) (= *hombre*) pansy*, poof**, fag (*EEUU**)

4 (*Andes Bot*) lily of the valley

florista SMF florist

floristería SF florist's (shop)

floristero/a Ⓐ ADJ florist *antes de s*

Ⓑ SM/F florist

florístico ADJ floral

floritura SF flourish

florón SM 1 (*Bot*) big flower

2 (*Arquit*) fleuron, rosette

3 (*Tip*) tailpiece

flota SF 1 [*de buques*] fleet; **la ~ española** the Spanish fleet ► **flota de altura** deep-sea fishing fleet ► **flota de bajura** inshore fishing fleet ► **flota mercante** merchant navy ► **flota pesquera** fishing fleet

2 (*Aer, Aut*) fleet

3 (*Andes*) (= *autobús*) long-distance bus, inter-city bus

4 (*LAm*) (= *muchedumbre*) lot, crowd, heap; **una ~ de** a lot of, a crowd of

5 (*Andes*) (= *jactancia*) boasting, bluster; **echar ~s** (*Andes, CAm, Caribe*) to brag

flotación SF 1 (*Náut*) flotation ► **línea de flotación** waterline

2 (*Fin*) flotation

flotador SM 1 [*de bañista*] (*para la cintura*) rubber ring, life preserver (*EEUU*); (*para los brazos*) (inflatable) armband; (*para las manos*) float

2 [*de hidroavión, para mediciones*] float; [*de cisterna*] ballcock, floater (*EEUU*)

flotante Ⓐ ADJ floating; **de coma ~** (*Inform*) floating-point

Ⓑ SM (*Col*) braggart

flotar ▸conjug 1a◂ VI 1 (*en líquido*) to float

2 [*bandera*] to flutter; **~ al viento** [*cabello*] to stream in the wind

3 (*Fin*) to float

flote SM **a ~** afloat; **mantenerse a ~** [*barco, negocio*] to stay afloat; **poner** *o* **sacar a ~** [+ *barco*] to refloat; [+ *negocio, economía*] to get back on its feet; **salir a ~** [*negocio, economía, persona*] to get back on one's feet; [*secreto*] to come to light

flotilla SF 1 (*Náut*) flotilla, fleet; (*a remolque*) line of vessels being towed, string of barges

2 [*de aviones, taxis etc*] fleet

flou [flo] SM soft focus (effect)

flox [flos] SM phlox

FLS SM ABR (*Nic Pol*) = **Frente de Liberación Sandinista**

fluctuación SF 1 (= *cambio*) fluctuation; **las fluctuaciones de la moda** the ups and downs of fashion

2 (= *indecisión*) uncertainty, hesitation

fluctuante ADJ (*gen*) fluctuating; [*población*] floating

fluctuar ▸conjug 1e◂ VI 1 (= *cambiar*) to fluctuate

2 (= *vacilar*) to waver, hesitate

fluente ADJ fluid, flowing

fluidez SF 1 (*Téc*) fluidity

2 (*fig*) fluency

fluido Ⓐ ADJ (*Téc*) fluid; [*lenguaje*] fluent; [*estilo*] fluid, free-flowing; **la circulación es bastante fluida** traffic is moving quite freely

Ⓑ SM 1 (*Téc*) fluid ► **fluidos corporales** body fluids

2 (*Elec*) current, juice*; **cortar el ~** to cut off the electricity

fluir ▸conjug 3g◂ VI (= *deslizarse*) to flow, run; (= *surgir*) to spring

flujo SM [1] (= *corriente*) flow, stream; **~ de lava** lava flow ► **flujo axial** axial flow ► **flujo de conciencia** stream of consciousness
[2] (*Med*) ► **flujo de vientre** diarrhoea, diarrhea (*EEUU*) ► **flujo menstrual** menstrual flow ► **flujo sanguíneo** flow of blood, blood flow ► **flujo vaginal** vaginal discharge
[3] (= *marea*) incoming tide, rising tide ► **flujo y reflujo** (*lit, fig*) ebb and flow
[4] (*Fís*) ► **flujo eléctrico** electric flux ► **flujo magnético** magnetic flux
[5] (*Com*) ► **flujo de caja, flujo de fondos** cashflow ► **flujo negativo de efectivo** negative cash flow ► **flujo positivo de efectivo** positive cash flow
flujograma SM flow chart
fluminense Ⓐ ADJ of/from Rio de Janeiro
Ⓑ SMF native/inhabitant of Rio de Janeiro; **los ~s** the people of Rio de Janeiro
flúor SM, **fluor** SM [1] (= *gas*) fluorine
[2] (*en agua, pasta de dientes*) fluoride
fluoración SF fluoridation
fluorescencia SF fluorescence
fluorescente Ⓐ ADJ fluorescent
Ⓑ SM (*tb* **tubo ~**) fluorescent tube
fluorización SF fluoridation
fluorizar ▸conjug 1f◂ VT to fluoridate
fluoruro SM fluoride
flus SM (*Col, Ven*) suit of clothes
flute SF champagne glass
fluvial ADJ fluvial, river *antes de s*
flux [flus] SM INV [1] (*Naipes*) flush ► **flux real** royal flush
[2] (*CAm**) (= *suerte*) stroke of luck
[3] (*Méx**) ✦**MODISMOS** **estar** *o* **quedarse a ~** to be completely broke*; **hacer ~** to blow all one's money*
[4] (*Andes, Caribe*) (= *traje*) suit of clothes
FM SF ABR (= **Frecuencia Modulada**) FM
FMI SM ABR (= **Fondo Monetario Internacional**) IMF
FMLN SM ABR (*El Salvador*) = **Frente Farabundo Martí de Liberación Nacional**
FN Ⓐ SM ABR = **Frente Nacional**
Ⓑ SF ABR (*Esp Hist*) = **Fuerza Nueva**
FNMT SF ABR (*Esp*) (= **Fábrica Nacional de Moneda y Timbre**) ≈ Royal Mint, ≈ (US) Mint (*EEUU*)
f.º ABR (= **folio**) fo., fol
fobia SF phobia; **yo a esos aparatos les tengo ~** I hate *o* can't stand these machines ► **fobia a las alturas** fear of heights ► **fobia escolar** fear of going to school
-fobia SUF -phobia; **agorafobia** agoraphobia
fóbico ADJ phobic
-fobo SUF -phobe; **francófobo** francophobe
foca SF [1] (*Zool*) seal; (= *piel*) sealskin ► **foca capuchina** hooded seal ► **foca de fraile** monk seal ► **foca de trompa** elephant seal, sea elephant
[2] (*) (= *persona gorda*) fat lump*
[3] (= *dormilón*) lie-abed
focal ADJ focal
focalizar ▸conjug 1f◂ VT [+ *objeto*] to focus on, get into focus; [+ *atención*] to focus
focha SF coot
foche* ADJ smelly, pongy‡
foco SM [1] (*Mat, Med, Fís*) focus; **estar fuera de ~** (*LAm*) to be out of focus
[2] (= *centro*) focal point, centre, center (*EEUU*); (= *fuente*) source; [*de incendio*] seat; **un ~ de infección** a source of infection
[3] (*Elec*) (*en monumento, estadio*) floodlight; (*en teatro*) spotlight; (*LAm*) (= *bombilla*) lightbulb; (*Aut*) headlamp
fodolí ADJ meddlesome
fodongo* ADJ (*Méx*) (= *vago*) lazy, slovenly; (= *sucio*) filthy
foete SM = **fuete**
fofadal SM (*Agr*) bog, quagmire
fofera* SF, **fofez*** SF flabbiness, podginess
fofo ADJ [1] (= *esponjoso*) soft, spongy
[2] (*) [*persona*] (= *fláccido*) flabby, podgy, pudgy (*EEUU*)
fofoscientos* ADJ umpteen; **fofoscientos mil euros** umpteen thousand euros
fogaje SM [1] (*Méx, Ven*) (= *fiebre*) fever, high temperature; (= *sarpullido*) heat rash; (= *rubor*) flush, blush; (*fig*) fluster
[2] (*Col, Ven*) (= *bochorno*) sultry weather
[3] (*Andes*) (= *fuego*) fire, blaze
fogarada SF, **fogarata** SF (*Cono Sur*) = **fogata**
fogata SF (= *hoguera*) bonfire; (= *llamas*) blaze
fogón SM [1] (*Culin*) range, stove; (*Ferro*) firebox; (*Náut*) galley
[2] [*de cañón, máquina*] vent
[3] (*LAm*) (= *hoguera*) bonfire; (= *hogar*) hearth
fogonazo SM [1] (= *estallido*) flash, explosion
[2] (*Méx*) (= *carajillo*) coffee with brandy
fogonero SM [1] (*Náut*) stoker
[2] (*Ferro*) fireman, stoker
[3] (*Andes*) (*chófer*) chauffeur
fogosidad SF (= *temple*) spirit, mettle; (= *ímpetu*) dash, verve; [*de caballo etc*] friskiness
fogoso ADJ (= *enérgico*) spirited, mettlesome; (= *apasionado*) fiery, ardent; [*caballo etc*] frisky
fogueado ADJ [1] (*LAm*) [*persona*] expert, experienced; (*Méx*) [*animal*] trained
[2] (*Andes*) (= *cansado*) weary
foguear ▸conjug 1a◂ (*LAm*) Ⓐ VT to fire on
Ⓑ **foguearse** VPR (*Mil*) to have one's baptism of fire; (= *acostumbrarse*) to gain experience, become hardened
fogueo SM **bala** *o* **cartucho de ~** blank cartridge; **disparo** *o* **tiro de ~** warning shot; **pistola de ~** starting pistol
foguerear ▸conjug 1a◂ VT (*Caribe, Cono Sur*) [+ *maleza*] to burn off; [+ *fogata*] to set light to
foguista SM (*Cono Sur*) = **fogonero**
foie-gras [fwa'gras] SM INV foie gras
foil SM (*Méx Culin*) foil
foja[1] SF (*Orn*) coot
foja[2] SF (*LAm*) = **hoja 2**
fol. ABR (= **folio**) fo., fol
folclore SM, **folclor** SM = **folklore**
folclórico/a ADJ, SM/F = **folklórico**
folclorista ADJ, SMF = **folklorista**
folclorizar ▸conjug 1f◂ VT = **folklorizar**
folder SM, **fólder** SM (*LAm*) folder
folgo SM foot muff
foliación SF [1] (*Bot*) foliation
[2] (*Tip*) [*de páginas*] numbering
foliar ▸conjug 1b◂ VT to foliate, number the pages of; **páginas sin ~** unnumbered pages
folículo SM follicle ► **folículo piloso** hair follicle
folio SM [1] (*Tip*) (*gen*) folio; (= *encabezamiento*) running title, page heading; **al primer ~** (*fig*) from the very start, at a glance; **en ~** in folio; **libro en ~** folio (book)
[2] (= *hoja*) sheet (of paper); [*de libro, documento*] page; **un documento de diez ~s** a ten-page document
[3] (*tb* **tamaño ~**) A4 size; **doble ~** A3 size; **un ~** an A4 sheet; **~s** A4 paper
[4] (*Andes*) (= *dádiva*) tip; [*de bautismo*] money given as christening present
folk ADJ INV, SM folk
folklore SM [1] folklore
[2] (*) row, shindy*; **se armó un ~** there was a row
folklórico/a Ⓐ ADJ [1] folk *antes de s*; **es muy ~** it's very picturesque, it's full of local colour *o* (*EEUU*) color
[2] (*pey*) frivolous, unserious
Ⓑ SM/F [1] (*Mús*) folk singer
[2] (*pey*) clown, figure of fun
folklorista Ⓐ ADJ [1] folklore *antes de s*
[2] (*pey*) frivolous, unserious
Ⓑ SMF folklorist, specialist in folklore, student of folklore
folklorizar ▸conjug 1f◂ Ⓐ VT to give a popular *o* folksy character to
Ⓑ **folklorizarse** VPR to acquire popular *o* folksy features
follá‡ SF **tener mala ~** to be thoroughly nasty
follada** SF shag**, screw**
follado Ⓐ ADJ **ir ~**** to go like fuck**
Ⓑ SM (*Andes*) petticoat
follador(a)** ADJ shag-happy**
follaje[1] SM [1] (*Bot*) foliage, leaves *pl*; (*Arte*) leaf motif
[2] (= *palabrería*) waffle*, verbiage; (= *adorno*) excessive ornamentation
follaje[2]** SM shagging**, screwing**
follar ▸conjug 1l◂ Ⓐ VT [1] (**) to shag**, screw**
[2] (‡) (= *molestar*) to bother, annoy
[3] (*Téc*) to blow on with the bellows
Ⓑ VI (**) to shag**, screw**
Ⓒ **follarse** VPR [1] (**) to shag**, screw**; **se la folló** he shagged *o* screwed her**; **me lo voy a ~ vivo** I'll have his guts for garters*
[2] (*) (= *ventosear*) to do a silent fart‡
folletería SF leaflets *pl*
folletín SM [1] (*en periódico*) newspaper serial; (*TV*) soap opera, TV serial; (*Radio*) radio serial
[2] (*fig*) drama, saga

> **FOLLETÍN**
> **Folletines** *were originally popular serialized stories that appeared in newspapers and magazines in the 19th and early 20th centuries, often before being published as novels. They usually covered familiar themes such as unrequited love, adultery and family relationships. Nowadays, the word* **folletín** *can refer to radio or TV serials and soaps,* **radionovelas** *or* **telenovelas**, *and people even use* **folletín** *figuratively to talk about any long-running story or intrigue.*

folletinesco ADJ melodramatic
folletinista SMF pulp writer
folletista SMF pamphleteer
folleto SM (*Com*) brochure; (*Pol*) pamphlet; (= *volatín*) leaflet ► **folleto informativo** information leaflet
follín* SM (*Cono Sur*) bad-tempered person

follisca SF (*Andes*) (= *lío*) row; (= *riña*) brawl

follón Ⓐ SM 1 (*) (= *desorden*) mess; **¡qué ~ de papeles!** what a mess of papers!
2 (*) (= *alboroto*) rumpus, row; (= *lío*) trouble; **armar un ~** to make a row, kick up a fuss; **hubo** *o* **se armó un ~ tremendo** there was a hell of a row
3 (*Bot*) sucker
4 (*Andes*) (= *prenda*) petticoat
5 (*Caribe*) (= *juerga de borrachera*) drinking bout
6 (= *cohete*) noiseless rocket
7 (*Méx**) silent fart‡
Ⓑ ADJ (†) 1 (= *perezoso*) lazy, idle
2 (= *arrogante*) arrogant, puffed-up; (= *fanfarrón*) blustering
3 (= *cobarde*) cowardly
4 (*CAm*) [*vestido*] roomy, loose

follonarse* ▸conjug 1a◂ VPR (*Méx*) to do a silent fart‡

follonero/a* Ⓐ ADJ [*persona*] rowdy; [*conducta*] outrageous
Ⓑ SM/F rowdy, troublemaker

fome* ADJ INV (*Chile*) boring, dull

fomentación SF (*Med*) fomentation, poultice

fomentar ▸conjug 1a◂ VT 1 [+ *desarrollo, investigación, ahorro, inversión*] to encourage; [+ *turismo, industria*] to promote, boost; [+ *competitividad, producción*] to boost; [+ *odio, violencia*] to foment; **medidas destinadas a ~ la integración racial** measures aimed at promoting *o* encouraging racial integration
2 (*Med*) to foment, warm
3 (= *incubar*) **la gallina fomenta sus huevos** the hen sits on *o* incubates her eggs

fomento SM 1 (= *ayuda*) promotion, encouragement; [*de ventas*] promotion ► **Ministerio de Fomento** *ministry responsible for public works, buildings etc* 2 (*Med*) poultice

fonador ADJ [*sistema, aparato, órgano*] speech *antes de s*

fonda SF (= *restaurante*) small restaurant; (= *pensión*) boarding house; (*Hist*) inn, tavern; (*Ferro*) buffet; (*Cono Sur*) refreshment stall; (*LAm pey*) cheap restaurant

fondeadero SM (*gen*) anchorage; (*en puerto*) berth

fondeado ADJ 1 (*Náut*) **estar ~** to be anchored, be at anchor
2 (*LAm**) **estar ~** to be in the money, be well heeled*; **quedar ~** to be in the money*

fondear ▸conjug 1a◂ Ⓐ VT 1 [*barco*] (= *anclar*) to anchor; (= *registrar*) to search
2 [+ *profundidad*] to sound
3 (= *examinar*) to examine
4 (*CAm*) (= *financiar*) to provide with money
5 (*Chile*) (= *ocultar*) to hide; (= *ahogar*) to drown
6 (*Caribe*) (= *violar*) to rape
Ⓑ VI [*barco*] to anchor, drop anchor
Ⓒ **fondearse** VPR 1 (*LAm**) (= *enriquecerse*) to get rich; (= *ahorrar*) to save for the future
2 (*LAm**) (= *emborracharse*) to get drunk
3 (*Chile**) (= *ocultarse*) **fondéate, que vienen los pacos** take cover, the police are coming; **anda fondeado de la policía** he's on the run from the police

fondeo SM 1 (*Náut*) anchoring
2 (*Chile*) dumping at sea, drowning at sea

fondero/a SM/F (*LAm*) innkeeper

fondillo SM (*LAm*), **fondillos** SMPL 1 [*de pantalones*] seat
2 (*LAm Anat*) seat, bottom

fondilludo/a* Ⓐ ADJ (*LAm*) big-bottomed
Ⓑ SM/F **es un ~** he's got a big backside

fondista SMF 1 [*de restaurante*] restaurant owner; (*Hist*) innkeeper
2 (*Dep*) long-distance runner

fondo SM 1 (*parte inferior*) [*de caja, botella, lago, mar*] bottom; [*de río*] bed; **descendieron al ~ del cráter** they got down to the bottom of the crater; **los bajos ~s** the underworld; **una maletín con doble ~** a case with a false bottom, a false-bottomed case; **en todo lo que dice hay un doble ~** there's a double meaning in everything he says; **irse al ~** to sink to the bottom; **en el ~ del mar** (*gen*) at the bottom of the sea; (= *en el lecho marino*) on the sea bed; **sin ~** bottomless; ✦*MODISMO* **tocar ~** to reach *o* hit rock bottom; **la economía tocó ~ y el gobierno tuvo que devaluar la moneda** the economy reached *o* hit rock bottom and the government had to devalue the currency; **hemos tocado ~ y todo indica que la recuperación está muy próxima** the market has bottomed out and all the indications are that a recovery is just around the corner
2 (*parte posterior*) [*de pasillo, calle, nave*] end; [*de habitación, armario*] back; **llegaron hasta el ~ de la gruta** they got to the back of the cave; **al ~: su oficina está al ~ a la izquierda** her office is at the end on the left; **al ~ del pasillo** at the end of the corridor; **la barra está al ~ de la cafetería** the bar is at the (far) end of the cafe; **había unas cortinas al ~ del escenario** at the back of the stage there were some curtains
3 (= *profundidad*) [*de cajón, edificio, bañera*] depth; **¿cuánto tiene de ~ el armario?** how deep is the wardrobe?; **tener mucho ~** to be deep; **tener poco ~** [*bañera*] to be shallow; [*cajón, armario*] not to be deep enough
4 (= *lo fundamental*) **en el ~ de esta polémica late el miedo al cambio** at the heart *o* bottom of this controversy lies a fear of change; **la cuestión de ~** the basic *o* fundamental issue; **el problema de ~** the basic *o* fundamental *o* underlying problem; **la forma y el ~** form and content; **llegar al ~ de la cuestión** to get to the bottom of the matter; *ver tb* **artículo 2**
5 (= *segundo plano*) background; **verde sobre ~ rojo** green on a red background; **la historia transcurre sobre un ~ de creciente inquietud social** the story takes place against a background of growing social unrest; **música de ~** background music; **ruido de ~** background noise ► **fondo de escritorio, fondo de pantalla** (*Inform*) (desktop) wallpaper
6 **a fondo** 6·1 (*como adj*) **una investigación a ~** (*policial*) a thorough investigation; [*de estudio*] an in-depth study; **una limpieza a ~** a thorough clean; **una vez al mes hacemos una limpieza a ~** once a month we do a really thorough clean; **una limpieza a ~ de las fuerzas de seguridad** a thorough clean-up of the security forces
6·2 (*como adv*) **no conoce a ~ la situación del país** he does not have a thorough *o* an in-depth knowledge of the country's situation; **la policía investigará a ~ lo ocurrido** the police will conduct a thorough investigation of what happened; **he estudiado a ~ a los escritores del Siglo de Oro** I have studied Golden Age writers in great depth; **aseguró que estudiaría a ~ nuestra propuesta** he promised to look closely at our proposal; **emplearse a ~: tuvo que emplearse a ~ para disuadirlos** he had to use all his skill to dissuade them; **el equipo deberá emplearse a ~ para derrotar a sus adversarios** the team will have to draw on all its resources to beat their opponents; **pisar a ~ el acelerador** to put one's foot down (*on the accelerator*)
7 **en el fondo** 7·1 (= *en nuestro interior*) deep down; **en el ~, es buena persona** deep down he's a good person, he's a good person at heart; **en el ~ de su corazón** in his heart of hearts, deep down
7·2 (= *en realidad*) really; **lo que se debatirá en la reunión, en el ~, es el futuro de la empresa** what is actually *o* really going to be debated in the meeting is the future of the company; **la verdad es que en el ~, no tengo ganas** to be honest, I really don't feel like it; **en el ~ no quiere irse** when it comes down to it, he doesn't want to leave
7·3 (= *en lo fundamental*) fundamentally, essentially; **en el ~ ambos sistemas son muy parecidos** fundamentally *o* essentially, both systems are very similar
8 (*Dep*) **carrera de ~** long-distance race; **esquí de ~** cross-country skiing; **corredor de medio ~** middle-distance runner; **pruebas de medio ~** middle-distance events ► **fondo en carretera** long-distance road-racing
9 (= *dinero*) (*Com, Fin*) fund; (*en póker, entre amigos*) pot, kitty; **tenemos un ~ para imprevistos** we have a contingency fund; **contamos con un ~ de 150.000 euros para becas** we have at our disposal a budget of 150,000 euros for grants; **hemos puesto un ~ para la comida** we have a kitty for the food; **a ~ perdido** [*crédito, inversión*] non-recoverable, non-refundable; **subvención a ~ perdido** capital grant; **su padre le ha prestado bastante dinero a ~ perdido** his father has given him quite a lot of money on permanent loan ► **fondo común** common fund ► **fondo consolidado** consolidated fund ► **fondo de amortización** sinking fund ► **Fondo de Ayuda al Desarrollo** Development Aid Fund ► **Fondo de Cohesión** Cohesion Fund ► **fondo de comercio** goodwill ► **Fondo de Compensación Interterritorial** *system of financial redistribution between the autonomous regions of Spain* ► **fondo de empréstitos** loan fund ► **fondo de inversión** investment fund ► **fondo de pensiones** pension fund ► **fondo de previsión** provident fund ► **fondo ético** (*Fin*) ethical investment fund ► **Fondo Monetario Internacional** International Monetary ► **fondo mutualista** mutual fund
10 **fondos** (= *dinero*) funds; **recaudar ~s** to raise funds; **estar sin ~s** to be out of funds, be broke*; **cheque** *o* **talón sin ~s** bounced cheque, rubber check (*EEUU*); **el cheque no tenía ~s** the cheque bounced ► **fondos bloqueados** frozen assets ► **fondos públicos** public funds ► **fondos reservados** secret funds
11 (= *reserva*) [*de biblioteca, archivo, museo*] collection; **el ~ de arte del museo** the museum's art collection; **hay un ~ de verdad en lo que dice** there is a basis of truth in what

he is saying; **tiene un buen ~ de energías** he has boundless energy ▸ **fondo de armario** basic wardrobe ▸ **fondo editorial** list of titles
12 (= *carácter*) nature, disposition; **de ~ jovial** of cheery *o* cheerful disposition, cheerful-natured; **tiene un ~ de alegría** he is irrepressibly cheerful; **tener buen ~** to be good-natured
13 (*Dep*) (= *resistencia*) stamina; **tener mucho ~** to have a lot of stamina; **tener poco ~** to have no staying power
14 (*Chile, Méx, Ven*) [*de comida, espectáculo*] **como plato de ~ servirán pavo relleno** the main dish will be stuffed turkey; **de ~ actuó el orfeón de carabineros** the main attraction was the police choir
15 (*Méx*) **con** *o* **de ~** serious; **una película de ~** a serious film
16 (*Méx, Ven*) (= *combinación*) petticoat; **medio ~** slip
17 (*Andes*) (= *finca*) country estate
18 (*Chile Culin*) large pot (*to feed a large number of people*)

fondón* ADJ big-bottomed*, broad in the beam*
fondongo SM (*Caribe*) bottom
fonducha SF, **fonducho** SM cheap restaurant
fonema SM phoneme
fonémico ADJ phonemic
fonendoscopio SM phonendoscope
fonética SF phonetics *sing*
fonético ADJ phonetic
fonetista SMF phonetician
foniatra SMF speech therapist
foniatría SF speech therapy
fónico ADJ phonic
fono SM 1 (*Chile Telec*) (= *auricular*) earpiece; (= *número*) telephone number
2 (*Ling*) phone
fonobuzón SM voice mail
fonocaptor SM [*de tocadiscos*] pickup
fonógrafo SM (*esp LAm*) gramophone, phonograph (*EEUU*)
fonología SF phonology
fonológico ADJ phonological
fonoteca SF record library, sound archive
fontanal SM, **fontanar** SM spring
fontanería SF 1 (= *oficio*) plumbing; (= *instalación*) plumbing
2 (= *tienda*) ironmonger's, hardware store
fontanero/a SM/F plumber
footing ['futin] SM jogging; **hacer ~** to jog, go jogging
F.O.P. SFPL ABR = **Fuerzas del Orden Público**
foque SM jib
foquillos SMPL fairy lights
foquismo SM (*LAm Pol*) *a theory of guerrilla warfare advocated by Che Guevara and Fidel Castro*
forajido/a SM/F outlaw, bandit, fugitive from justice
foral ADJ *relative to the fueros, pertaining to the privileges of a town or region*; **parlamento ~** regional parliament; **policía ~** autonomous police; → FUEROS
foramen SM (*Méx*) hole
foráneo/a Ⓐ ADJ foreign
Ⓑ SM/F outsider, stranger
forasta* SMF = **forastero B**
forastero/a Ⓐ ADJ alien, strange
Ⓑ SM/F stranger, outsider
forcejear ▸conjug 1a◂ VI (*gen*) to struggle, wrestle; (= *afanarse*) to strive
forcejeo SM struggle
forcejudo ADV tough, strong, powerful
fórceps SM INV forceps
forcito SM (*LAm*) little Ford (*vehicle*)
forense Ⓐ ADJ forensic; *ver tb* **médico**
Ⓑ SMF (*Med*) forensic scientist; (*Jur*) coroner
forestación SF afforestation
forestal ADJ (*gen*) forest *antes de s*; [*industria*] timber *antes de s*, lumber (*EEUU*) *antes de s*; **cobertura ~** tree cover; *ver tb* **guarda A1**, **repoblación**
forestalista SMF owner of a woodland
forestar ▸conjug 1a◂ VT (*LAm*) to afforest
forfait [for'fe] SM 1 (*Esquí*) ski pass
2 (= *precio*) flat rate, fixed price; **viajes a ~** package tours
3 (*Dep*) (= *ausencia*) absence, non-appearance; (= *retirada*) withdrawal, scratching; **declararse ~** to withdraw; **ganar por ~** to win by default; **hacer ~** to fail to show up
fori‡ SM hankie*, handkerchief
forito SM (*LAm*) = **fotingo**
forja SF 1 (= *fragua*) forge; (= *fundición*) foundry
2 (= *acción*) forging
forjado ADJ **hierro ~** wrought iron
forjar ▸conjug 1a◂ VT 1 [+ *hierro*] to forge, shape
2 (= *crear*) (*gen*) to forge, shape; [+ *sueños, ilusiones*] to build up; **~ un plan** to hammer out a plan; **tratamos de ~ un estado moderno** we are trying to build a modern state
3 [+ *mentiras*] to invent, concoct
forma SF 1 (= *figura*) shape; **tiene ~ de pirámide** it is pyramid-shaped; **hojas de ~ triangular** triangular leaves; **una serie de elementos dispuestos de ~ circular** a series of elements arranged in a circle; **la camisa ha cogido la ~ de la percha** the shirt has been stretched out of shape by the hanger; **nubes de humo con ~ de hongo** mushroom-shaped clouds of smoke; **un pendiente con ~ de animal mitológico** an earring in the shape of a mythological animal; **dar ~ a** [+ *objeto, joya*] to shape; [+ *idea, teoría*] to give shape to; **quiso dar ~ literaria a sus teorías filosóficas** he wanted to put his philosophical theories into literary form; **en ~ de U** U-shaped; **pendientes en ~ de corazón** heart-shaped earrings; **tomar ~** to take shape; **la idea empezó a tomar ~ el año pasado** the idea began to take shape last year
2 (= *modo*) way; **me gusta más de esta ~** I like it better this way; **yo tengo otra ~ de ver las cosas** I see things in a different way; **sólo conozco una ~ llegar hasta allí** I only know one way of getting there *o* one way to get there; **no estoy de acuerdo con su ~ de actuar** I don't agree with his way of doing things; **no hubo ~ de convencerlo** there was no way we could persuade him; **de ~ directa/inmediata/natural** directly/immediately/naturally; **el plan entrará en vigor de ~ inmediata** the plan will take immediate effect, the plan will take effect immediately; **este tema me preocupa de ~ especial** this subject is of particular concern to me; **de esta ~** (*gen*) in this way; (= *por consecuencia*) thus; **queremos controlar los costes y, de esta ~, evitar reducir la plantilla** we want to bring down costs and thus avoid having to downsize; **de todas ~s** anyway, in any case; **pero de todas ~s te agradezco que me lo hayas dicho** but thank you for letting me know anyway, but in any case thank you for letting me know ▸ **forma de pago** method of payment, form of payment ▸ **forma de ser**: **es mi ~ de ser** that's how I am, that's the way I am
3 **de ~ que** (= *en un modo que*) in such a way as, so as; (= *por eso*) so that; **él intentó contestar la pregunta de ~ que no le comprometiese** he tried to answer the question so as *o* in such a way as not to commit himself; **el número de socios fue creciendo cada año, de ~ que en 1989 eran ya varios miles** the number of members grew every year, so that *o* such that by 1989 there were several thousand; **de tal ~ que** (= *en un modo que*) in such a way that; (= *tanto que*) so much that; (= *por eso*) so that; **la noticia se filtró de tal ~ que fueron incapaces de evitarlo** news leaked out in such a way that they were unable to stop it; **la empresa ha crecido de tal ~ que es irreconocible** the company has grown so much *o* to such an extent that it is unrecognizable; **su padre era italiano y su madre polaca, de tal ~ que él siempre se ha sentido europeo** his father was Italian and his mother Polish, so (that) he has always felt himself to be European
4 (*tb* **~ física**) fitness, form; **si no está al cien por cien de ~ no jugará** if he isn't a hundred per cent fit he won't play; **el jugador ha recuperado su ~ física** the player is fit again, the player has regained fitness *o* form; **cuida su ~ física practicando también otros deportes** he keeps fit by playing other sports too; **estar en (buena) ~** (*para hacer deporte*) to be fit, be in good shape; (*para realizar otra actividad*) to be in (good) form; **estar en baja ~** (*lit*) to be not fully fit; (*fig*) to be in bad shape; **estar bajo de ~** to be in poor shape; **mantenerse en ~** to keep fit; **ponerse en ~** to get fit
5 (= *aspecto externo*) form; **la ~ y el fondo** form and content; **es pura ~** it's just for the sake of form, it's a mere formality; **defecto de ~** (*Der*) technicality
6 **formas** (*femeninas*) figure *sing*
7 **formas** (*sociales*) appearances; **guardar** *o* **mantener las ~s** to keep up appearances
8 (*Rel*) **la Sagrada Forma** the Host
9 (= *molde*) (*Téc*) mould, mold (*EEUU*); [*de zapatero*] last; [*de sombrero*] hatter's block; (*Tip*) forme, form (*EEUU*)
10 (*Ling*) [*del verbo*] form
11 (*Tip*) (= *formato*) format
12 (*LAm**) **en ~**: **una fiesta en ~** a proper party, a blowout*; **va a celebrar su cumpleaños en ~** he's going to have a proper *o* a serious* birthday party; **nos aburrimos en ~** we were seriously bored*
13 (*Méx*) form; → MANERA, FORMA, MODO
formación SF 1 (= *creación*) (*gen*) formation; **para prevenir la ~ de hielo** to prevent ice (from) forming, to prevent the formation of ice (*frm*); **se anunció la ~ de un nuevo partido** it was announced that a new party is to be formed; **la ~ de palabras** word formation;

la Europa que está en ~ the Europe that is taking shape *o* that is in formation
[2] (= *aprendizaje*) (*en un campo concreto*) training; (*en conocimientos teóricos*) education; **tenía una ~ musical clásica** she trained as a classical musician, she had a classical musical training; **nuestro objetivo es la ~ de personal técnico** our aim is to train technical staff; **la ~ del profesorado** teacher training; **se nota que tiene ~ universitaria** you can tell he's had a university education *o* background ► **formación laboral**, **formación ocupacional** occupational training ► **formación profesional** vocational training
[3] (= *grupo*) (*político*) party; (*militar*) group; (*musical*) group, band; [*de jugadores*] squad; **las dos principales formaciones de izquierda** the two main left-wing parties; **las grandes formaciones sinfónicas europeas** the great European symphony orchestras; **no ha anunciado todavía la ~ del equipo** he hasn't announced the squad yet ► **formación política** political party
[4] (*Mil*) **en ~** in formation; **en ~ de combate** in battle *o* combat formation
[5] (*Geol, Bot*) formation

formado ADJ formed, shaped; **bien ~** nicely-shaped, well-formed; **hombre (ya) ~** grown man

formal ADJ [1] [*persona*] (= *de fiar*) reliable, dependable; (= *responsable*) responsible; **es un trabajador muy ~** he's a very reliable worker; **un chico muy ~** a very responsible boy; **sé ~ y pórtate bien** be good and behave yourself
[2] [*invitación, protesta*] formal; [*estilo, lenguaje*] formal
[3] (= *oficial*) [*petición, propuesta, compromiso*] official
[4] (*Fil*) formal; **lógica ~** formal logic
[5] (= *estructural*) formal; **el análisis ~ del texto** formal analysis of the text
[6] (*Andes*) (= *afable*) affable, pleasant

formaldehido SM formaldehyde

formaleta SF [1] (*CAm, Col*) (= *construcción*) wooden framework
[2] (*Andes, CAm, Méx*) (= *trampa*) bird trap

formalidad SF [1] (= *requisito*) formality; **son las ~es de costumbre** these are the usual formalities; **es pura ~** it's a pure *o* mere formality, it's just a matter of form
[2] (= *fiabilidad*) reliability; **alabó la ~ de nuestra empresa** he praised our company for its reliability; **se quedó sin clientes por falta de ~** he lost all his customers because of his unreliability; **esta empresa no tiene ~ ninguna** this company is totally unreliable
[3] (= *seriedad*) **¡señores, un poco de ~!** gentlemen, let's be serious!; **¡niños, ~!** kids, behave yourselves!

formalina SF formalin(e)

formalismo SM [1] (*Arte, Literat*) formalism
[2] (*pey*) (= *burocracia*) red tape, useless formalities *pl*; (= *convencionalismo*) conventionalism

formalista Ⓐ ADJ [1] (*Arte, Literat*) formalist
[2] (*pey*) conventional, rigid
Ⓑ SMF [1] (*Arte, Literat*) formalist
[2] (*pey*) stickler for the regulations

formalito* ADJ [*adulto*] respectable; [*niño*] well-behaved

formalizar ▸conjug 1f◂ Ⓐ VT (*Jur*) to formalize; [+ *plan*] to formulate, draw up; [+ *situación*] to put in order, regularize; **~ sus relaciones** to become formally engaged
Ⓑ **formalizarse** VPR [1] (= *ponerse serio*) to grow serious
[2] [*situación*] to be put in order, be regularized; [*relación*] to acquire a proper form, get on to a proper footing
[3] (= *ofenderse*) to take offence

formalote* ADJ stiff, serious

formar ▸conjug 1a◂ Ⓐ VT [1] [+ *figura*] to form, make; **los barracones se disponen formando un cuadrado** the barrack huts are arranged forming *o* making a square; **los curiosos ~on un círculo a su alrededor** the onlookers formed *o* made a circle around him
[2] (= *crear*) [+ *organización, partido, alianza*] to form; **las personas interesadas en ~ un club** people interested in forming a club; **~ gobierno** to form a government; **¿cómo se forma el subjuntivo?** how do you form the subjunctive?; **quieren casarse y ~ una familia** they want to get married and start a family
[3] (= *constituir*) to make up; **los chiitas forman el 60% de la población** the Shiites make up *o* form 60% of the population; **la plantilla la forman 94 bomberos** there are 94 firefighters on the staff; **las dos juntas formaban un dúo de humoristas insuperable** the two of them together made an unbeatable comedy duo; **formamos un buen equipo** we make a good team; **~ equipo con algn** to join forces with sb; **estar formado por** to be made up of; **la asociación está formada por parados y amas de casa** the association is made up of unemployed and housewives; **~ parte de** to be part of; **nuestros soldados ~án parte de las tropas de paz** our soldiers will be part of the peace-keeping force; **el edificio forma parte del recinto de la catedral** the building is *o* forms part of the the cathedral precinct; **sus obras no ~án parte de la colección** his works will not be part of the collection
[4] (= *enseñar*) [+ *personal, monitor, técnico*] to train; [+ *alumno*] to educate
[5] [+ *juicio, opinión*] to form
[6] (*Mil*) to order to fall in; **el sargento formó a los reclutas** the sergeant had the recruits fall in, the sergeant ordered the recruits to fall in
Ⓑ VI [1] (*Mil*) to fall in; **¡a ~!** fall in!
[2] (*Dep*) to line up; **los equipos ~on así: ...** the teams lined up as follows: ...
Ⓒ **formarse** VPR [1] (= *crearse*) to form; **se ~án nubes por la tarde** there will be a build-up of clouds in the afternoon, clouds will form in the afternoon; **remover la salsa para evitar que se formen grumos** stir the sauce to prevent lumps forming; **los vientos que se forman en el Antártico** winds that form *o* develop in the Antarctic; **es inevitable que se formen distintos grupos de opinión** different groups of opinion will inevitably form; **se forman colas diarias en el cine** queues form daily outside the cinema; **en 1955 se formó el segundo gobierno liberal** in 1955 the second liberal government was formed
[2] (= *armarse*) [*jaleo, follón*] **no fue tanto el revuelo que se formó** there wasn't that much of a rumpus; **se formó tal follón que no llegaron a oír el final de su discurso** there was such an uproar that they didn't get to hear the end of his speech
[3] (= *prepararse*) [*profesional, jugador, militar*] to train; [*estudiante*] to study; **se había formado como neurobiólogo** he had trained as a neurobiologist; **París fue la ciudad en la que se formó como pintor** Paris was the city in which he learned the art of painting; **se formó en el mejor colegio de Inglaterra** he studied *o* was educated at the best school in England
[4] (*Mil*) to fall in; **¡fórmense!** fall in!; **se ~on en grupos de a tres** they formed into groups of three
[5] (*Dep*) to line up; **el equipo se formó sin González** the team lined up without Gonzalez
[6] [+ *opinión, impresión*] to form; **¿qué impresión te has formado?** what impression have you formed?; **te formaste una idea equivocada de mí** you got the wrong idea about me

formateado SM formatting

formatear ▸conjug 1a◂ VT to format

formateo SM formatting

formativo ADJ formative

formato SM (*Tip, Inform*) format; (= *tamaño*) [*de papel*] size; **¿de qué ~ lo quiere?** what size do you want?; **papel (de) ~ holandesa** ≈ foolscap; **periódico de ~ reducido** tabloid newspaper ► **formato apaisado** landscape format, landscape ► **formato de registro** record format ► **formato fijo** fixed format ► **formato libre** free format ► **formato vertical** portrait format, portrait

formica® SF Formica®

fórmico ADJ **ácido ~** formic acid

formidable ADJ [1] [*enemigo, problema*] formidable
[2] (= *estupendo*) terrific, tremendous; **¡formidable!** that's great!*, splendid!

formón SM chisel

Formosa SF **la Isla de ~** (*Hist*) Formosa

fórmula SF [1] (*Quím, Mat*) formula ► **fórmula magistral** magistral formula ► **fórmula molecular** molecular formula
[2] (*Med*) ► **fórmula dentaria** dental profile ► **fórmula leucocitaria** leucocyte count
[3] (= *método*) formula; **una ~ para conseguir el éxito** a formula to ensure success ► **fórmula mágica** magic formula
[4] (= *expresión*) ► **fórmula de cortesía** polite set expression
[5] (= *formalidad*) **por pura ~** purely as a matter of form
[6] (*Aut*) **coches de Fórmula 1** Formula 1 cars

formulación SF formulation ► **formulación de datos** data capture

formulaico ADJ formulaic

formular ▸conjug 1a◂ VT [+ *política, teoría*] to formulate; [+ *plan*] to draw up; [+ *pregunta*] pose; [+ *protesta*] to make, lodge; [+ *demanda*] to file, put in; [+ *deseo*] to express

formulario Ⓐ ADJ routine, formulaic
Ⓑ SM [1] (= *impreso*) form; **rellenar un ~** to fill in *o* complete a form ► **formulario de inscripción** registration form ► **formulario de pedido** (*Com*) order form ► **formulario de solicitud** application form
[2] (= *fórmulas*) (*Farm*) formulary, collection of formulae

formulismo SM formulism, red tape

fornicación SF fornication

fornicador(a), **fornicario/a** (A) ADJ fornicating
(B) SM/F fornicator; (= *adúltero*) adulterer/adulteress

fornicar ▸conjug 1g◂ VI to fornicate

fornicio SM fornication

fornido ADJ (= *corpulento*) strapping, hefty; (= *apuesto*) well-built

fornitura SF (*Téc*) movement; (*Cos*) accessories *pl*; (*Mil*) cartridge belt; (*CAm, Caribe*) furniture

foro SM [1] (*Pol, Hist, Internet*) forum; (= *reunión*) forum, (open) meeting
[2] (*Jur*) (= *tribunal*) court of justice; (= *abogados*) bar, legal profession; **el Foro** (*Esp*) Madrid
[3] (*Teat*) upstage area; **desaparecer** *o* **marcharse por el ~** (*lit*) to exit stage left; (*fig*) to do a disappearing act; *ver tb* **mutis**

forofada* SF fans *pl*, supporters *pl*

forofismo SM (volume of) support

forofo/a* SM/F fan, supporter

FORPPA SM ABR (*Esp*) = **Fondo de Ordenación y Regulación de Precios y Productos Agrarios**

FORPRONU SF ABR (= **Fuerza(s) de Protección de las Naciones Unidas**) UNPROFOR, Unprofor

forrado ADJ [1] (= *con forro*) lined; **~ de nilón** lined with nylon; **un libro ~ de pergamino** a book bound in parchment; **un coche ~ de ...** a car upholstered in ...
[2] (*) (= *rico*) **estar ~** to be loaded*, be rolling in it*

forraje SM [1] (*Agr*) (= *alimento*) fodder, forage
[2] (*Agr*) (= *acción*) foraging
[3] (*) (= *mezcla*) hotchpotch, hodgepodge (*EEUU*), mixture

forrajear ▸conjug 1a◂ VI to forage

forrapelotas‡ SMF INV [1] (= *caradura*) rotter*, berk‡
[2] (= *tonto*) idiot

forrar ▸conjug 1a◂ (A) VT [1] (= *poner forro a*) to line (**de** with); (= *acolchar*) to pad; [+ *coche*] to upholster
[2] [+ *libro*] (*como protección*) to cover (**de** with); (= *encuadernar*) to bind (**de** in)
[3] (*Téc*) (*gen*) to line; [+ *tubería, caldera*] to lag
(B) **forrarse** VPR [1] (*) (= *enriquecerse*) to line one's pockets, make a fortune, make a packet*
[2] (*) (*de comida*) to stuff o.s. (**de** with); (*Méx, Guat*) to eat a heavy meal
[3] (*CAm, Méx*) (= *proveerse*) to stock up (**de** with)

forro SM [1] (*gen*) lining; [*de libro*] cover; (*Aut*) upholstery; **con ~ de piel** fur-lined; ✦*MODISMOS* **ni por el ~*** not in the least, not a bit; **no nos parecemos ni por el ~** we are not in the least alike, we are not a bit alike; **limpiar el ~ a algn** (*LAm‡*) to bump sb off‡; **pasarse algo por el ~ de las narices** (‡) not to give a damn about sth*, not to give a toss about sth‡ ► **forro acolchado** padded lining ► **forro polar** fleece, Polartec®
[2] (*Téc*) (*gen*) lining; [*de tubería*] lagging ► **forro de freno** (*Aut*) brake lining
[3] (*Cono Sur**) (= *preservativo*) rubber*, condom
[4] (*Chile*) [*de bicicleta*] tyre, tire (*EEUU*)
[5] (*LAm*) (= *fraude*) swindle, fraud
[6] (*Cono Sur*) (= *talento*) aptitude

forsitia SF forsythia

fortacho SM (*Cono Sur*) strongly-built car, good car; (*pey*) old car, old crock

fortachón* ADJ strong, tough

fortalecer ▸conjug 2d◂ (A) VT [1] (= *reforzar*) [+ *músculos, uña*] to strengthen
[2] [+ *divisa, sistema, posición*] to strengthen
(B) **fortalecerse** VPR [*divisa, poder, opinión*] to become stronger

fortalecimiento SM strengthening

fortaleza SF [1] (*Mil*) fortress, stronghold
[2] (= *fuerza*) strength, toughness; (*moral*) fortitude, strength (of spirit)
[3] (*Cono Sur, Méx‡*) (= *olor*) stench, pong‡

fortificación SF fortification

fortificar ▸conjug 1g◂ VI [1] (*Mil*) to fortify
[2] (= *fortalecer*) to strengthen

fortín SM (= *fuerte*) (small) fort; [*de hormigón*] pillbox

fortísimo ADJ SUPERL *de* **fuerte** (*Mús*) fortissimo

fortuitamente ADV (= *por casualidad*) fortuitously (*frm*), by chance; (= *por accidente*) accidentally

fortuito ADJ (*gen*) fortuitous (*frm*); [*encuentro*] accidental, chance *antes de s*

fortuna SF [1] (= *suerte*) fortune; **la ~ le ha sido adversa** (*liter*) fortune has been unkind to him; **tuvo la buena ~ de heredar la casa** he had the good fortune to inherit the house; **ha tenido la mala ~ de ponerse enferma** she had the misfortune to fall ill; **no tuvo ~ en el concurso** he was unlucky in the competition, he didn't have any luck in the competition; **por ~** luckily, fortunately; **probar ~** to try one's luck
[2] (= *riqueza*) fortune; **heredó una inmensa ~** she inherited a vast fortune; **este piso cuesta una ~** this flat costs a fortune
[3] (*Náut*) (= *tempestad*) storm; **correr ~** to ride out a storm

fortunón* SM huge fortune

fórum SM = **foro**

forúnculo SM boil

forzadamente ADV forcibly, by force; **sonreír ~** to force a smile; **reírse ~** to force a laugh

forzado ADJ [1] (= *obligado*) forced; **verse ~ a hacer algo** to be forced *o* obliged to do sth; **con una sonrisa forzada** with a forced smile
[2] [*puerta, cerradura*] forced
[3] (= *rebuscado*) [*traducción, estilo, metáfora*] forced; *ver tb* **trabajo 1**, **marcha 1**

forzar ▸conjug 1f, 1l◂ VT [1] (= *obligar*) to force; **~ a algn a hacer algo** to force sb to do sth, make sb do sth; **les forzó a dimitir** he forced them to resign, he made them resign
[2] [+ *puerta, cerradura*] to force; (*Mil*) [+ *ciudadela, fuerte*] to storm, take
[3] [+ *ojos, voz*] to strain; [+ *sonrisa*] to force; **estás forzando la vista** you're straining your eyes
[4] (= *violar*) to rape

forzosamente ADV **tiene ~ que ser así** this is the way it has to be; **tuvieron que cerrarlo ~** they had (no alternative but) to close it; **~ lo harás** you'll have no choice but to do it

forzoso ADJ (= *necesario*) necessary; (= *inevitable*) inescapable, unavoidable; (= *obligatorio*) compulsory; **aterrizaje ~** forced landing; **es ~ que** it is inevitable that; **le fue ~ hacerlo** he had no choice but to do it

forzudo/a (A) ADJ (= *fuerte*) tough, brawny
(B) SM/F [*de circo*] strongman/strongwoman; (*pey*) (= *matón*) thug

fosa SF [1] (= *hoyo*) pit; (= *sepultura*) grave ► **fosa atlántica** Atlantic trench ► **fosa común** (*para gente sin familia*) common grave; (*para soldados, prisioneros*) mass grave ► **fosa de reparaciones** (*Aut*) inspection pit ► **fosa fecal** septic tank ► **fosa marina** oceanic trench ► **fosa séptica** septic tank
[2] (*Anat*) cavity ► **fosas nasales** nostrils

fosar ▸conjug 1a◂ VT to dig a ditch *o* trench round

fosco ADJ [1] [*pelo*] wild, disordered
[2] = **hosco**

fosfatina* SF ✦*MODISMO* **estar hecho ~** to be worn out, be shattered*

fosfato SM phosphate

fosforecer ▸conjug 2d◂ VI to phosphoresce (*frm*), glow

fosforera SF [1] (= *fábrica*) match factory
[2] (= *caja*) matchbox

fosforescencia SF phosphorescence

fosforescente ADJ phosphorescent

fosfórico ADJ phosphoric

fosforito* ADJ INV fluorescent; **amarillo ~** fluorescent yellow, luminous yellow

fósforo SM [1] (*Quím*) phosphorus
[2] (*esp LAm*) (= *cerilla*) match
[3] (*Andes*) (= *cápsula fulminante*) percussion cap
[4] (*Méx*) (= *carajillo*) coffee laced with brandy
[5] ✦*MODISMO* **tener ~** (*Cono Sur**) to be shrewd, be sharp
[6] (*CAm*) (= *exaltado*) hothead
[7] (*CAm**) (= *pelirrojo*) redhead

fosforoso ADJ phosphorous

fosgeno SM phosgene

fósil (A) ADJ fossil *antes de s*, fossilized
(B) SM [1] (*Biol*) fossil
[2] (*) (= *viejo*) old crock*, old dodderer*; (= *carroza*) old square*

fosilizado ADJ fossilized

fosilizarse ▸conjug 1f◂ VPR to fossilize, become fossilized

foso SM [1] (= *agujero*) (*redondo*) pit, hole; (*alargado*) ditch, trench; (*en castillo*) moat ► **foso de agua** (*Dep*) water jump ► **foso de reconocimiento** (*Aut*) inspection pit ► **foso generacional** generation gap
[2] (*Teat*) pit; ✦*MODISMO* **irse** *o* **venirse al ~** (*Teat*) to flop* ► **foso de la orquesta** orchestra pit

fotingo* SM (*LAm*) old banger*, jalopy*, clunker (*EEUU**)

foto SF photo, picture; **sacar** *o* **tomar una ~** to take a photo *o* picture (**de** of); ✦*MODISMO* **salir en la ~** to be in the picture, play one's part ► **foto aérea** aerial photo ► **foto de carnet** passport(-size) photo ► **foto de conjunto** group photo ► **foto de familia** [*de familiares*] family photo; [*de colegas*] group photo, team photo ► **foto fija** still, still photo ► **foto robot** quick photo; (= *cabina*) photo booth

foto... PREF photo...

fotoacabado SM photo-finishing

fotocalco SM photoprint

fotocomponedora SF photocomposer

fotocomposición SF filmsetting, photosetting (*EEUU*), photocomposition

fotocompositora SF filmsetting machine, photosetting machine (*EEUU*)

fotoconductor SM photoconductor

fotocontrol SM **resultado comprobado por ~** (*Dep*) photo finish

fotocopia SF [1] (= *copia*) photocopy, print
[2] (= *acción*) photocopying

fotocopiable ADJ photocopiable

fotocopiadora SF (= *máquina*) photocopier, photocopying machine; (= *local*) photocopying shop, photocopier's

fotocopiar ▸conjug 1b◂ VT to photocopy

fotocopista SMF photocopier

fotocopistería SF photocopying shop

fotocromía SF colour photography, color photography (*EEUU*)

fotoeléctrico ADJ photoelectric; **célula fotoeléctrica** photoelectric cell

fotoenvejecimiento SM photo-ageing

foto-finish SF INV, **foto finish** [foto'finis] SF INV photo finish

fotogenia SF photogenic qualities *pl*; **es de una ~ maravillosa** she's wonderfully photogenic

fotogénico ADJ photogenic

fotograbado SM photogravure, photoengraving

fotografía SF [1] (= *arte*) photography ► **fotografía aérea** aerial photography ► **fotografía en color** colour photography, color photography (*EEUU*)
[2] (= *imagen*) photograph; **sacar** *o* **tomar una ~ de algo** to take a photograph of sth ► **fotografía al flash, fotografía al magnesio** flash photograph ► **fotografía de carnet** ≈ passport photograph ► **fotografía en color** colour photograph, color photograph (*EEUU*) ► **fotografía instantánea** snapshot; *ver tb* **foto**

fotografiar ▸conjug 1c◂ Ⓐ VT to photograph
Ⓑ **fotografiarse** VPR to have one's photograph taken

fotográficamente ADV photographically; **le reconocieron ~** they recognized him through photographs

fotográfico ADJ photographic

fotógrafo/a SM/F photographer ► **fotógrafo/a aficionado/a** amateur photographer ► **fotógrafo/a ambulante, fotógrafo/a callejero/a** street photographer ► **fotógrafo/a de estudio** portrait photographer ► **fotógrafo/a de prensa** press photographer

fotograma SM (*Cine*) still

fotogrametría SF photogrammetry

fotomatón SM [1] (= *quiosco*) photo booth; **una foto de ~** a passport photo
[2] (*) (= *foto*) passport photo

fotómetro SM light meter, photometer

fotomodelo SMF photographic model

fotomontaje SM photomontage

fotón SM photon

fotonoticia SF photographic reportage

fotonovela SF *romance or crime story illustrated with photos*

fotoperiodismo SM photojournalism

fotoperiodista SMF photojournalist

fotoprotección SF UV protection

fotoprotector Ⓐ ADJ UV protective
Ⓑ SM UV protectant

fotoquímico ADJ photochemical

foto-robot SF (*pl* **foto-robots**) Photofit picture®

fotorreceptor ADJ photoreceptor

fotorreportaje SM photo story

fotorrobot SF (*pl* **fotorrobots**) = **foto-robot**

fotosensible ADJ photosensitive

fotosensor SM photosensor

fotosíntesis SF INV photosynthesis

fotostatar ▸conjug 1a◂ VT to photostat

fotostato SM photostat

fototeca SF (= *colección*) collection of photographs; (= *archivo*) photographic library

fototopografía SF = **fotogrametría**

fototropismo SM phototropism

fotovoltaico ADJ photovoltaic

fotuto SM [1] (*LAm Mús*) wind instrument (of gourd)
[2] (*Cuba*) (= *bocina*) car horn

foul [faul] (*pl* **fouls**) SM (*LAm*) = **faul**

foulard [fu'lar] SM [*de mujer*] (head)scarf; [*de hombre*] cravat

fox [fos] SM INV foxtrot

FP Ⓐ SF ABR (*Esp Educ*) (= **Formación Profesional**) *vocational courses for 14- to 18-year-olds*
Ⓑ SM ABR (*Pol*) = **Frente Popular**

FPA SF ABR (*Arg, Esp*) = **Formación Profesional Acelerada**

FPLP SM ABR (= **Frente Popular para la Liberación de Palestina**) PFLP

FPMR SM ABR (*Chile*) = **Frente Patriótico Manuel Rodríguez**

Fr. ABR (= **Fray**) Fr

fra. ABR (= **factura**) inv

frac SM (*pl* **fracs** *o* **fraques**) tailcoat, tails *pl*; **ir (vestido) de ~** (*para una ceremonia*) to be in morning dress

fracasado/a Ⓐ ADJ failed, unsuccessful
Ⓑ SM/F failure

fracasar ▸conjug 1a◂ Ⓐ VT (*LAm*) to mess up, make a mess of
Ⓑ VI (*gen*) to fail, be unsuccessful; [*plan*] to fail, fall through

fracaso SM failure; **el ~ de las negociaciones** the failure of the negotiations; **la reforma está condenada al ~** the reform is doomed to failure, the reform is destined to fail; **ir en dirección al ~** to be heading for disaster; **¡es un ~!** he's a disaster!; **es un ~ total** it's a complete disaster ► **fracaso escolar** academic failure ► **fracaso sentimental** disappointment in love

fracción SF [1] (*Mat*) fraction ► **fracción decimal** decimal fraction
[2] (= *parte*) part, fragment
[3] (*Pol etc*) faction, splinter group
[4] (= *repartición*) division, breaking-up (**en** into)

fraccionado ADJ **pago ~** payment by instalments *o* (*EEUU*) installments

fraccionadora SF (*Méx*) estate agent, realtor (*EEUU*)

fraccionalismo SM (*Pol*) factionalism, tendency to form splinter groups

fraccionamiento SM [1] (*gen*) division, breaking-up (**en** into); ► **fraccionamiento de pagos** payment by instalments *o* (*EEUU*) installments ► **fraccionamiento de tierras** land distribution
[2] (*Méx*) housing estate, real estate development (*esp EEUU*)
[3] (*Téc*) [*de petróleo*] cracking

fraccionar ▸conjug 1a◂ VT to divide, break up, split up (**en** into); **~ los pagos** to pay by instalments

fraccionario ADJ fractional; **"se ruega moneda fraccionaria"** "please tender exact fare"

fractura SF [1] (*Med*) fracture ► **fractura complicada** compound fracture ► **fractura múltiple** multiple fracture
[2] (*Jur*) **robo con ~** burglary

fracturar ▸conjug 1a◂ Ⓐ VI to fracture
Ⓑ **fracturarse** VPR to fracture

fragancia SF fragrance, perfume

fragante ADJ [1] (= *perfumado*) fragrant, scented
[2] = **flagrante**

fraganti *ver* **in fraganti**

fragata SF frigate

frágil ADJ [1] [*construcción, material, objeto*] fragile
[2] [*anciano*] frail; [*salud*] delicate; [*acuerdo, sistema*] fragile; **una mujer aparentemente ~** a seemingly fragile woman

fragilidad SF (*gen*) fragility; [*de anciano*] frailty

fragmentación SF fragmentation

fragmentadamente ADV **pagar ~** to pay in instalments *o* (*EEUU*) installments

fragmentado ADJ fragmented; **sólo nos han llegado informaciones fragmentadas** we have only received snippets of information *o* fragmented pieces of information

fragmentar ▸conjug 1a◂ Ⓐ VT to fragment
Ⓑ **fragmentarse** VPR to fragment; **se fragmenta en miles de partículas** it fragments into thousands of particles

fragmentariedad SF (*frm*) fragmentary nature

fragmentario ADJ fragmentary

fragmento SM [1] (= *trozo*) [*de escultura, hueso, bomba, roca*] fragment; [*de vasija*] fragment, shard; **fue alcanzada por ~s de cristales** she was hit by flying glass *o* fragments of glass
[2] (= *extracto*) [*de novela, discurso, obra musical*] passage; (*ya aislado*) excerpt, extract; **a través del tabique se oían ~s de la conversación** you could hear snippets *o* snatches of their conversation through the partition

fragor SM (*gen*) din, clamour, clamor (*EEUU*); [*de trueno*] crash, clash; [*de máquina*] roar

fragoroso ADJ deafening, thunderous

fragosidad SF [1] (= *cualidad*) [*de terreno*] roughness, unevenness; [*de bosque, maleza*] denseness
[2] (= *lugar*) rough spot

fragoso ADJ [*terreno*] rough, uneven; [*bosque*] dense, overgrown

fragua SF forge

fraguado SM [1] [*de metal*] forging
[2] [*de hormigón*] hardening, setting

fraguar ▸conjug 1i◂ Ⓐ VT [1] [+ *metal*] to forge
[2] [+ *plan*] to hatch, concoct
Ⓑ VI [*hormigón*] to harden, set
Ⓒ **fraguarse** VPR [*tormenta*] to blow up; (*fig*) to be brewing

fraile SM [1] (*Rel*) friar, monk ► **fraile de misa y olla**† simple-minded friar ► **fraile descalzo** barefoot monk ► **fraile mendicante** mendicant friar (*gen Franciscan*) ► **fraile predicador** preaching friar, friar preacher
[2] (*Caribe*) (= *bagazo*) bagasse, residue of sugar cane

frailecillo SM (= *ave*) puffin

frailería SF friars *pl*, monks *pl*; (*pey*) priests *pl*

frailesco ADJ, **frailuno** ADJ monkish

frambuesa SF raspberry

frambuesero SM, **frambueso** SM raspberry cane

francachela* SF (= *comida*) spread*; (= *juerga*) spree, binge*

francachón ADJ outspoken, forthright

francamente ADV [1] (= *abiertamente*) frankly; **~, eso está mal** (quite) frankly, I think that's wrong
[2] (= *realmente*) really; **es una obra ~ divertida** it's a really funny play
[3] (= *generosamente*) generously, liberally

francés/esa Ⓐ ADJ French; **a la francesa** in the French manner, French style, the way the French do; ✦*MODISMO* **despedirse a la francesa** to leave without saying goodbye, take French leave; **tortilla francesa** plain omelette, French omelette
Ⓑ SM/F Frenchman/Frenchwoman
Ⓒ SM [1] (*Ling*) French
[2] (**) (= *acto sexual*) blow job**

francesilla SF [1] (*Bot*) buttercup
[2] (*Culin*) French roll

franchute/a* Ⓐ ADJ Frog*, French
Ⓑ SM/F Frog*, Frenchy*
Ⓒ SM (*Ling*) Frog*, French

Francia SF France

fráncico Ⓐ ADJ Frankish
Ⓑ SM (*Ling*) Frankish

francio SM (*Quím*) francium

Francisca SF Frances

franciscano ADJ, SM Franciscan

Francisco SM Francis

francmasón SM freemason

francmasonería SF freemasonry

franco¹ SM (*Fin*) franc

franco² ADJ [1] (= *directo*) frank; **seré ~ contigo** I will be frank with you; **para serte ~** to be frank *o* honest (with you); **si he de ser ~** frankly, to tell you the truth
[2] (= *patente*) clear, evident; **estar en franca decadencia** to be in visible decline; **estar en franca rebeldía** to be in open rebellion
[3] (*Com*) (= *exento*) free; **~ a bordo** free on board; **~ al costado del buque** free alongside ship; **~ de derechos** duty-free; **precio ~ (en) fábrica** price ex-factory, price ex-works; **~ de porte** carriage-free; (*Correos*) post-free; **~ puesto sobre vagón** free on rail
[4] (*Com*) [*puerto*] free; [*camino*] open; **mantener mesa franca** to keep open house
[5] **~ de servicio** (*Mil*) off-duty
[6] (*Cono Sur*) **estar de ~** to be off duty, be on leave
[7] (= *liberal*) generous

franco³ (*Hist*) Ⓐ ADJ Frankish
Ⓑ SM Frank

franco... PREF franco...

francocanadiense ADJ, SMF French-Canadian

francófilo/a ADJ, SM/F Francophile

francófobo/a Ⓐ ADJ francophobe, francophobic *antes de s*
Ⓑ SM/F Francophobe

francófono/a Ⓐ ADJ French-speaking
Ⓑ SM/F French speaker

franco-hispano ADJ Franco-Spanish

francote* ADJ outspoken, blunt

francotirador(a) SM/F [1] (= *tirador*) sniper
[2] (*fig*) freelance, free agent

franela SF [1] (= *tela*) flannel
[2] (*LAm*) (= *camiseta*) T-shirt; (*de ropa interior*) vest, undershirt (*EEUU*)

franelear‡ ▸conjug 1a◂ VI to pet*, make out (*EEUU*‡)

frangollar ▸conjug 1a◂ Ⓐ VT [1] (*Andes, Cono Sur*) (= *chapucear*) to bungle, botch
[2] (*Cono Sur*) [+ *granos*] to grind
Ⓑ VI (*Andes*) to dissemble

frangollero ADJ (*Andes, Cono Sur*) bungling

frangollo SM [1] (*Culin*) (*Andes, Cono Sur*) corn mash; (*Cono Sur*) (= *locro*) meat and maize stew; (*Caribe*) (= *dulce*) *sweet made from mashed bananas*
[2] (*Méx*) dog's dinner*
[3] (*LAm*) (= *alpiste*) birdseed
[4] (*Méx*) (= *lío*) muddle, mess; (= *mezcla*) mixture

frangollón/ona (*LAm*) Ⓐ ADJ bungling
Ⓑ SM/F bungler

franja SF [1] (= *banda*) strip; [*de uniforme*] stripe; **~ de tierra** strip of land; **la ~ de Gaza** the Gaza strip ► **franja de edad** age-group ► **franja horaria** time zone
[2] (= *borde*) fringe, border

franjar ▸conjug 1a◂ VT, **franjear** ▸conjug 1a◂ VT to fringe, trim (**de** with)

franqueadora SF (*Correos*) franking machine

franquear ▸conjug 1a◂ Ⓐ VT [1] [+ *camino*] to clear, open; **~ el paso a algn** to clear the way for sb; **~ la entrada a** to give free entry to
[2] (= *atravesar*) [+ *río*] to cross; [+ *obstáculo*] to negotiate
[3] (*Correos*) to frank, stamp; **una carta franqueada** a post-paid letter; **una carta insuficientemente franqueada** a letter with insufficient postage
[4] [+ *esclavo*] to free, liberate
[5] [+ *derecho*] to grant, concede (**a** to)
Ⓑ **franquearse** VPR (= *sincerarse*) **~se con algn** to have a heart-to-heart talk with sb

franqueo SM (*Correos*) franking; **con ~ insuficiente** with insufficient postage

franqueza SF [1] (= *sinceridad*) frankness; **con ~** frankly; **lo digo con toda ~** I'll be quite frank with you
[2] (= *confianza*) familiarity; **tengo suficiente ~ con él para discrepar** I am on close enough terms with him to disagree
[3] (= *liberalidad*) generosity

franquía SF (*Náut*) room to manoeuvre *o* (*EEUU*) maneuver, searoom

franquicia SF [1] (*Com*) franchise
[2] (= *exención*) exemption (**de** from); ► **franquicia aduanera**, **franquicia arancelaria** exemption from customs duties ► **franquicia de equipaje** (*Aer*) free baggage allowance ► **franquicia postal** Freepost®

franquiciado/a SM/F franchise holder, franchisee

franquiciador(a) SM/F franchisor

franquiciamiento SM franchising

franquiciar ▸conjug 1b◂ VT to franchise

franquismo SM **el ~** (= *período*) the Franco years, the Franco period; (= *política*) the Franco system; **bajo el ~** under Franco; **luchó contra el ~** he fought against Franco

> **FRANQUISMO**
>
> **Franquismo** *is the term used to refer both to the years when General Francisco Franco was the dictator of Spain (from the end of the* **Guerra Civil** *in 1939 to his death in 1975) and to his style of government. He was an authoritarian, right-wing dictator whose political philosophy included imposing traditional Catholic values and making Spain self-sufficient economically. Following a prolonged period of severe isolation from the international community, in the 1960s Spain gradually opened its doors to foreign investment and influence. This coincided with a rise in economic growth and internal political opposition. On his death, Spain became a democratic constitutional monarchy.*

franquista Ⓐ ADJ pro-Franco; **tendencia ~** pro-Franco tendency; **una familia muy ~** a strongly pro-Franco family
Ⓑ SMF supporter of Franco

FRAP SM ABR [1] (*Esp*) = **Frente Revolucionario Antifascista y Patriótico**
[2] (*Chile*) = **Frente de Acción Popular**

fraques SMPL *de* **frac**

frasca SF [1] (= *hojas*) dry leaves *pl*; (= *ramitas*) small twigs *pl*
[2] (*CAm, Méx*) (= *fiesta*) riotous party
[3] ✦*MODISMO* **pegarle a la ~*** to hit the bottle*

frasco SM [1] (= *botella*) bottle; **~ de perfume** perfume bottle; ✦*MODISMOS* **¡chupa del ~!**‡ ◊ **¡toma del ~ (Carrasco)!**‡ stone the crows!* ► **frasco de campaña** (*LAm*) water bottle, canteen
[2] (= *medida*) *liquid measure: Caribe = 2.44 litres, Cono Sur = 21.37 litres*

frase SF (= *oración*) sentence; (= *locución*) phrase, expression; (= *cita*) quotation; **diccionario de ~s** dictionary of quotations ► **frase compleja** complex sentence ► **frase hecha** set phrase; (*pey*) cliché, stock phrase ► **frase lapidaria** axiom

fraseo SM (*Mús*) phrasing

fraseología SF [1] (= *estilo*) phraseology
[2] (*pey*) verbosity, verbiage

Frasquita SF (*forma familiar*) *de* **Francisca**

Frasquito SM (*forma familiar*) *de* **Francisco**

fratás SM (plastering) trowel

fraterna* SF ticking-off*

fraternal ADJ brotherly, fraternal

fraternidad SF brotherhood, fraternity

fraternización SF fraternization

fraternizar ▸conjug 1f◂ VI to fraternize

fraterno ADJ brotherly, fraternal

fratricida Ⓐ ADJ fratricidal
Ⓑ SMF fratricide

fratricidio SM fratricide

fraude SM [1] (= *engaño*) fraud; **por ~** by fraud ► **fraude electoral** electoral fraud ► **fraude fiscal** tax evasion
[2] (= *falta de honradez*) dishonesty, fraudulence

fraudulencia SF fraudulence

fraudulentamente ADV fraudulently, dishonestly

fraudulento ADJ fraudulent, dishonest

fray SM brother, friar; **Fray Juan** Brother John, Friar John

frazada SF (*LAm*) blanket

freático ADJ *ver* **capa 2**

frecuencia SF frequency; **con ~** frequently, often; **alta ~** (*Elec, Radio*) high frequency; **de alta ~** high-frequency ► **frecuencia de onda** wavelength; **estar en la misma ~ de onda** to be on the same wavelength ► **frecuencia de red** mains frequency ► **frecuencia de reloj** clock speed ► **frecuencia modulada** frequency modulation

frecuentador(a) SM/F frequenter

frecuentar ▸conjug 1a◂ VT to frequent

frecuente ADJ [1] (*gen*) frequent; [*costumbre*] common, prevalent; [*vicio*] rife
[2] (*Méx*) (= *familiar*) familiar, over-familiar; **andarse ~ con** to be on close terms with

frecuentemente ADV frequently, often

Fredemo SM ABR (*Perú*) = **Frente Democrático**

freelance [fri'lans] ADJ, SMF INV freelance

freeware [fri'wer] SM freeware

freezer ['friser] SM (*LAm*) freezer

fregada* SF (*CAm, Méx*) (= *embrollo*) mess; (= *problema*) snag; (= *molestia*) nuisance, pain*; ✦**MODISMOS ¡la ~!**‡ you don't say!, never!; **¡me lleva la ~!**‡ well, I'll be damned!*

fregadera* SF (*LAm*) (= *fastidio*) nuisance, pain*

fregadero SM [1] (= *pila*) (kitchen) sink [2] (= *habitación*) scullery [3] (*CAm, Méx**) (= *molestia*) pain in the neck*

fregado/a Ⓐ ADJ [1] (*LAm**) (= *molesto*) annoying
[2] (*LAm**) (= *difícil*) [*trabajo, tarea*] tricky; [*carácter, persona*] fussy
[3] (*LAm**) [*persona*] (= *en mala situación económica*) broke*; (= *deprimido*) down, in a bad way*; (= *dañado, enfermo*) in a bad way*; **le quedó la pierna fregada después del accidente** his leg was in a bad way after the accident*; **ando muy ~ del estómago** my stomach is in a really bad way*
[4] (*LAm**) (= *puñetero*) damn*, lousy*, bloody‡
[5] (*Col, Perú*) (= *astuto*) cunning
[6] (*Chile, Col, Perú, Ven*) (= *estricto*) strict
Ⓑ SM/F (*LAm*) (= *persona difícil*) fussy person
Ⓒ SM [1] (= *acción de fregar*) (*con fregona*) mopping; (*con estropajo, cepillo*) scrubbing; (*con esponja, trapo*) washing; [*de platos*] washing-up
[2] (*) (= *lío*) mess; **está siempre metido en algún ~** he's always involved in shady business
[3] (*) (= *riña*) row

fregador SM [1] (= *fregadero*) sink
[2] (= *trapo*) dishcloth; (= *estropajo*) scourer; (= *fregona*) mop

fregadura SF = **fregado C1**

fregancia SF (*Andes*) = **fregada**

fregandera SF (*Méx*) charwoman, cleaner

fregantina SF (*Andes, Cono Sur*) = **fregada**

fregar ▸conjug 1h, 1j◂ Ⓐ VT [1] (= *limpiar*) (*con fregona*) to mop, wash; (*con estropajo, cepillo*) to scrub; (*con esponja, trapo*) to wash; **~ los cacharros** o **los platos** to wash the dishes, do the washing up, wash up
[2] (*LAm**) (= *fastidiar*) [+ *persona*] annoy; **lo hicieron para ~ a la competencia** they did it to annoy the competition; **¡no me friegues!** (*expresando molestia*) don't be a nuisance!, stop bothering me!; (*expresando asombro*) you're kidding!*; ✦**MODISMO ~ la paciencia** o (*Chile**) **la cachimba a algn** to pester sb*
[3] (*LAm**) (= *malograr*) [+ *planes*] to ruin, mess up; [+ *fiesta*] to ruin; [+ *aparato*] to wreck; **me ~on con el cambio de horario** the timetable change really messed me up; **le ~on el taxi con el choque** his taxi was wrecked in the crash
[4] (*Cono Sur***) to fuck**, screw**
[5] (*Caribe**) (= *pegar*) to beat up; (*Dep*) to beat, thrash
Ⓑ VI [1] (= *fregar los platos*) to wash the dishes, do the washing up, wash up
[2] (= *fregar el suelo*) (*con fregona*) to wash the floor, mop the floor; (*con cepillo*) to scrub the floor
[3] (*LAm**) (= *molestar*) to annoy; **ya viene el vecino a ~ otra vez** here comes the neighbour to annoy us again; **¡no friegues!** (*expresando asombro*) you're kidding!*
Ⓒ **fregarse** VPR (*LAm**) [1] (= *aguantarse*) **unos pocos se llenan los bolsillos y nosotros nos tenemos que ~** a few line their pockets and we have to grin and bear it; **si nos descubren, nos fregamos** if they find us, we've had it o we're done for*
[2] (= *malograrse*) [*planes*] to be ruined, be messed up; [*fiesta*] to be ruined
[3] (= *dañarse*) [+ *pierna, rodilla*] to do in*; **me fregué la espalda levantando sacos** I did my back in lifting sacks*

fregasuelos SM INV mop

fregazón* SM (*Cono Sur*) = **fregada**

fregón* ADJ [1] (*LAm*) (= *molesto*) annoying
[2] (*LAm*) (= *tonto*) silly, stupid
[3] (*Andes, Caribe*) (= *fresco*) brazen, fresh

fregona SF [1] (= *utensilio*) mop
[2] (*) (= *persona*) kitchen maid, dishwasher; (*fig*) · (*pey*) slave, skivvy*; (*Caribe*) (= *sinvergüenza*) shameless hussy

fregota‡ SM waiter

fregoteo* SM = **fregado C1**

freidera SF (*Caribe*) frying pan

freidora SF deep-fat frier

freiduría SF ► **freiduría (de pescado)** fried-fish shop

freír ▸conjug 3l◂ (*pp* **frito**) Ⓐ VT [1] (*Culin*) to fry; ✦**REFRÁN al ~ será el reír** he who laughs last laughs longest
[2] [*sol*] to burn, fry
[3] (*) (= *molestar*) to annoy; (= *acosar*) to harass; (= *atormentar*) to torment; (= *aburrir*) to bore; **~le a algn a preguntas** to bombard sb with questions
[4] (*) (= *matar*) to do in*; **~ a algn a tiros** to riddle sb with bullets
Ⓑ **freírse** VPR [1] (*Culin*) to fry
[2] **~se de calor*** to be roasting
[3] **~sela a algn*** to have sb on*, put sb on (*EEUU**)

frejol SM, **fréjol** SM (*esp Perú*) = **fríjol**

frenada SF, **frenaje** SM (*Aut*) (sudden) braking

frenado SM (*Aut*) braking ► **frenado antibloqueo** anti-lock braking

frenar ▸conjug 1a◂ Ⓐ VT [1] (*Aut, Mec*) to brake
[2] (= *contener*) [+ *inflación, crecimiento, avance, deterioro*] to check, slow down; [+ *pasiones, entusiasmo*] to curb; [+ *enemigo, ataque*] to check, hold back; **su novia tiene que ~le para que no beba tanto** his girlfriend has to restrain him from drinking so much
Ⓑ VI (*Aut*) to brake; **frena, que viene una curva** brake, there's a bend coming up; **~ en seco** to brake sharply o suddenly
Ⓒ **frenarse** VPR (= *contenerse*) to restrain o.s.

frenazo SM (= *acción*) sudden braking; (= *parada*) sudden halt; (= *ruido*) squeal of brakes; **dar un ~** to brake suddenly, brake hard

frenesí SM frenzy

frenéticamente ADV (= *con desenfreno*) frantically, frenziedly; (= *con furia*) furiously, wildly

frenético ADJ (= *desenfrenado*) frantic, frenzied; (= *furioso*) furious, wild; **ponerse ~** to lose one's head

frenillo SM [1] (= *defecto*) **tener ~** to have a speech defect
[2] (*Anat*) [*del pene*] fraenum, frenum (*esp EEUU*)
[3] (= *correa, cuerda*) muzzle

freno SM [1] (*Aut, Mec*) brake; **líquido de ~s** brake fluid; **el pedal del ~** the brake pedal; **echar el ~** o **los ~s** to apply the brake(s); **pisé el ~** I put my foot on the brake, I applied the brake; **soltar el ~** to release the brake; ✦**MODISMO ¡echa el ~, Madaleno!**‡ put a sock in it!* ► **freno de aire** air brake ► **freno de disco** disc brake ► **freno de mano** handbrake, emergency brake (*EEUU*); **poner** o **echar el ~ de mano** to put on the handbrake ► **freno de tambor** drum brake ► **freno de vacío** vacuum brake ► **freno hidráulico** hydraulic brake ► **freno neumático** pneumatic brake ► **freno pedal** foot brake ► **frenos ABS** ABS (brakes), ABS (braking)
[2] [*de caballo*] bit; **morder** o **tascar el ~** (*lit, fig*) to champ at the bit
[3] (= *contención*) brake; **medidas que actúan como ~ al crecimiento económico** measures that act as a brake on economic growth, measures that slow down economic growth; **poner ~ a algo: hay que poner ~ a la especulación** we must curb speculation; **puso ~ a las malas lenguas** he stopped the gossip ► **frenos y contrapesos, frenos y equilibrios** (*Pol*) checks and balances
[4] (*Cono Sur**) (= *hambre*) hunger

frenología SF phrenology

frenólogo/a SM/F phrenologist

frenopático Ⓐ ADJ psychiatric
Ⓑ SM (*Med*) mental home; (* *hum*) loony bin‡

frentazo SM (*Méx*) disappointment, rebuff; **pegarse un ~** to come a cropper*

▼**frente** Ⓐ SF (*Anat*) forehead, brow (*liter*); **arrugar la ~** to frown, knit one's brow; ✦**MODISMOS adornar la ~ a algn*** to cheat on sb*; **con la ~ (muy) alta** with one's head held high; **lo lleva escrito en la ~** it's written all over his face; **~ a ~** face to face; *ver tb* **dedo 2**
Ⓑ SM [1] (= *parte delantera*) front; **al ~** in front; **un ejército con su capitán al ~** an army led by its captain, an army with its captain at the front; **al ~ de**: **entró en Madrid al ~ de las tropas** he led the troops into Madrid, he entered Madrid at the head of his

➤ LENGUA Y USO: frente B5 32.1

troops; **el Madrid sigue al ~ de la clasificación** Madrid still lead the table *o* are still top of the league; **espero seguir al ~ del festival** I hope to continue as director of the festival; **estuvo al ~ del Ministerio de Industria** he was Minister for Industry; **un concierto con Herbert Von Karajan al ~ de la Filarmónica de Berlín** a concert by the Berlin Philharmonic conducted by Herbert Von Karajan; **en ~**: **la casa de en ~** the house opposite; **hacer ~ a** [+ *crisis, problemas*] to tackle; [+ *situación, realidad*] to face up to; **hay que hacer ~ a las dificultades** we have to tackle the problems; **tenemos que hacer ~ a grandes gastos** we are facing considerable expenses; **~ por ~**: **vivimos ~ por ~** we live directly opposite each other; **está ~ por ~ del cine** it's directly opposite the cinema ► **frente de arranque**, **frente de trabajo** (*Min*) coalface
2 **de ~**: **atacar de ~** to make a frontal attack; **chocar de ~** to crash head-on; **ir de ~** to go forward; **mirar de ~** to look (straight) ahead; **seguir de ~** to go straight on, go straight ahead; **viene un coche de ~** there's a car heading straight for us
3 (*Mil, Pol*) front; **formar** *o* **hacer un ~ común con algn** to form a united front with sb; **han formado un ~ contra la corrupción** they have formed an alliance against corruption ► **frente de batalla** battle front ► **frente del oeste** western front ► **Frente Polisario** Polisario Front ► **frente popular** popular front ► **frente unido** united front
4 (*Meteo*) front ► **frente cálido** warm front ► **frente frío** cold front
5 **frente a** 5·1 (= *enfrente de*) opposite; **~ al hotel hay un banco** there's a bank opposite the hotel; **ella está ~ a mí** she is facing *o* opposite me; **el barco encalló ~ a la costa irlandesa** the boat ran aground off the Irish coast
5·2 (= *en presencia de*) **~ a las cámaras** in front of the cameras; **me encontré ~ a una situación difícil** I found myself facing a difficult situation; **ceder ~ a una amenaza** to give way to *o* in the face of a threat
5·3 (= *en oposición a*) **el euro sigue fuerte ~ al dólar** the euro remains strong against the dollar; **logró un 39% de los votos, ~ al 49% de 1990** she got 39% of the vote, as against 49% in 1990; **empataron ~ al Santander** they drew against *o* with Santander; **~ a lo que pensaba, eran franceses** in contrast to what I thought, they were French
6 **~ mío/suyo** (*esp Cono Sur**) in front of me/you, opposite me/you

freo SM channel, strait

fresa Ⓐ SF 1 (*Bot*) (= *fruta*) strawberry; (= *planta*) strawberry plant
2 (*Téc*) milling cutter; [*de dentista*] drill
3 (*Méx* pey*) snob
Ⓑ ADV INV (*Méx**) **la gente ~** the in crowd

fresado SM (*Mec*) milling

fresadora SF (*Mec*) milling machine ► **fresadora de roscar** thread cutter

fresal SM (= *cantero*) strawberry bed; (= *campos*) strawberry fields *pl*

fresar ▸conjug 1a◂ VT (*Mec*) to mill

fresca* SF 1 **la ~**: **saldremos temprano, con la ~** we'll leave early, while it's still cool, we'll leave early, in the cool of the morning; **charlaban en la calle, sentados a la ~** they were sitting in the street chatting in the cool air; **salir a tomar la ~** to go out for a breath of (fresh) air
2 (*) (= *insolencia*) **decir** *o* **soltar cuatro ~s a algn** to give sb a lot of cheek*; *ver tb* **fresco**

frescachón ADJ 1 [*persona*] (= *saludable*) healthy, glowing with health; (= *de buen color*) ruddy
2 (*Náut*) [*viento*] fresh, stiff

frescales* SMF INV rascal, cheeky rascal

fresco/a Ⓐ ADJ 1 (*Culin*) 1·1 (= *no congelado, no cocinado*) fresh; **es mejor comer alimentos ~s** it is best to eat fresh food
1·2 (= *no pasado*) [*carne, fruta*] fresh; [*huevo*] fresh, new-laid; **el pescado está muy ~** the fish is very fresh
1·3 (= *no curado*) [*queso*] unripened; [*salmón*] fresh
2 (= *frío*) 2·1 [*brisa, viento*] cool; **salí a respirar un poco de aire ~** I went outside to get a breath of fresh air
2·2 [*bebida*] cool, cold; [*agua*] (*para beber*) cold; (*en piscina, río*) cool; **una cerveza fresca** a cool *o* cold beer
2·3 [*tiempo*] (*desagradable*) chilly; (*agradable*) cool; **ponte una chaqueta, que la noche está fresca** put a jacket on, it's chilly tonight; **¡qué ~ se estará ahora en la montaña!** it will be so nice and cool just now in the mountains
2·4 [*tela, vestido*] cool
3 (= *reciente*) [*ideas*] fresh; [*pintura*] wet; **la tragedia aún está fresca en mi memoria** the tragic events are still fresh in my memory; **venía contento, con dinero ~ en el bolsillo** he came along looking happy, with fresh money in his pocket; **traigo noticias frescas** I have the latest news; **"pintura fresca"** "wet paint"
4 (= *natural*) [*piel, estilo*] fresh
5 (= *refrescante*) [*colonia, perfume*] refreshing
6 (= *persona*) (= *descansado*) fresh; (= *descarado*) cheeky, sassy (*EEUU*); **prefiero estudiar por las mañanas, cuando aún estoy ~** I prefer studying in the morning while I'm still fresh; **¡qué ~!** what a cheek!*, what a nerve!*; **¡está** *o* **va ~, si cree que le voy a ayudar otra vez!** he couldn't be more wrong if he thinks that I'm going to help him again!, if he thinks I'm going to help him again, he's got another thing coming!; **me lo dijo tan ~** he just said it to me as cool as you like; **me lo dijo y se quedó tan ~** he said it without batting an eyelid; ✦***MODISMO*** **ser más ~ que una lechuga*** to have a lot of nerve*
Ⓑ SM/F (*) (*sinvergüenza*) **¡usted es un ~!** you've got a nerve!*
Ⓒ SM 1 (= *temperatura*) **se sentó a la sombra del árbol buscando el ~** she sat down under the tree, in the cool of its shade; **voy a sentarme fuera, al ~** I'm going to sit outside where it's nice and cool; **el ~ de la mañana** the cool of the morning; **dormir al ~** to sleep in the open air, sleep outdoors; **hace ~** (*desagradable*) it's chilly; (*agradable*) it's cool; **tomar el ~** to get some fresh air; ✦***MODISMO*** **me trae al ~***: **que te lo creas o no, me trae al ~** I couldn't care less whether you believe it or not
2 (*Arte*) fresco; **pintar al ~** to paint in fresco
3 (*Col, Perú, Ven*) (= *bebida*) (*sin gas*) fruit drink; (*con gas*) fizzy fruit drink; *ver tb* **fresca**

frescor SM [*de temperatura, alimentos*] freshness; [*de lugar, bebida*] coolness; **gozar del ~ nocturno** to enjoy the cool night air

frescote ADJ (= *saludable*) healthy, glowing with health, blooming; (= *de buen color*) ruddy; [*mujer*] buxom

frescura SF 1 [*de temperatura, alimentos*] freshness; [*de lugar, bebida*] coolness
2 (= *serenidad*) coolness, calmness; **lo dijo con la mayor ~** she said it without batting an eyelid
3 (*) (= *descaro*) cheek, nerve*; **tiene la mar de ~** he's got the cheek of the devil*; **tuvo la ~ de pedirme dinero** she had the nerve to ask me for money*
4 (= *impertinencia*) cheeky thing (to say), impudent remark; **me dijo unas ~s** he was cheeky to me

fresia SF freesia

fresnada SF ash grove

fresno SM ash (tree)

fresón SM (*Bot*) (= *fruto*) strawberry; (= *planta*) strawberry plant

fresquera SF (= *armario*) meat safe, cooler (*EEUU*); (= *habitación*) cold room

fresquería SF (*LAm*) refreshment stall

fresquito ADJ, SM *ver* **fresco A2, A5, C1**

freudiano/a ADJ, SM/F Freudian

freza SF 1 [*de peces*] (= *huevos*) spawn; (= *acto*) spawning; (= *estación*) spawning
2 (= *excremento*) dung, droppings *pl*

frezadero SM spawning ground

frezar ▸conjug 1f◂ VI to spawn

friable ADJ friable

frialdad SF 1 [*de material, líquido*] coldness
2 (= *indiferencia*) (*en sentimientos, actitudes*) coolness; (*en carácter, mirada*) coldness; **se comportaban con una ~ envidiable** they behaved with enviable coolness; **la novela ha sido acogida con ~ por la crítica** the novel has been given a cool reception by the critics; **reaccionó con ~ ante la noticia** he showed no emotion when he heard the news; **hemos de actuar con ~ y analizar el problema detenidamente** we have to act dispassionately and analyze the problem at length; **ella lo miró con ~** she looked at him coldly

fríamente ADV 1 (= *con indiferencia, sin apasionamiento*) coolly; (= *con hostilidad*) coldly; **luego, cuando pudo pensar ~, se le ocurrió una posible respuesta** later, when she could think about it coolly, she came up with a possible answer; **la propuesta fue acogida ~** the proposal was given a cool reception; **mirado ~, tiene parte de razón en lo que dice** viewed dispassionately, he is partly right in what he says; **el reo miró ~ a los parientes de sus víctimas** the accused looked at with cold detachment at the relatives of his victims
2 (= *a sangre fría*) [*matar*] in cold blood; [*torturar*] coldheartedly

frían *ver* **freír**

frica SF (*Cono Sur*) beating

fricandó SM, **fricasé** SM fricassee

fricativa SF fricative

fricativo ADJ fricative

fricción SF 1 (= *frotamiento*) rub, rubbing; (*Med*) massage
2 (*Mec*) friction
3 (*Pol*) (= *enfrentamiento*) friction, trouble

friccionar ▸conjug 1a◂ VT (= *frotar*) to rub; (*Med*) to rub, massage

friega SF [1] (*gen*) rub, rubbing; (*Med*) massage; (*Dep*) rub-down
[2] (*LAm**) (= *molestia*) nuisance; (= *problema*) bother; (= *lío*) fuss
[3] (*Andes, Cono Sur**) (= *zurra*) thrashing
[4] (*LAm**) (= *idiotez*) silliness, stupidity
[5] (*Andes, Méx**) (= *reprimenda*) ticking-off*

friegaplatos Ⓐ SM INV (= *aparato*) dishwasher
Ⓑ SMF INV (= *persona*) dishwasher, washer-up

friegasuelos SM INV floor mop

frígano SM caddis fly

frigidaire† SM (*LAm*) refrigerator

frigidez SF frigidity

frígido ADJ frigid

frigo* SM (*Esp*) fridge, icebox (*EEUU*)

frigorífico Ⓐ ADJ **camión ~** refrigerator lorry, refrigerator truck (*EEUU*); **instalación frigorífica** cold-storage plant
Ⓑ SM [1] (= *nevera*) refrigerator, fridge, icebox (*EEUU*)
[2] (= *camión*) refrigerator lorry, refrigerator truck (*EEUU*); (*para congelados*) freezer lorry *o* (*EEUU*) truck; (*Náut*) refrigerator ship
[3] (*Cono Sur*) cold-storage plant, meat-packing depot

frigorífico-congelador SM (*pl* **frigoríficos-congeladores**) fridge-freezer

frigorista SMF refrigeration engineer

fríjol SM, **frijol** SM [1] (*esp LAm Bot*) (= *judía*) bean ► **frijol colorado** kidney bean ► **frijol de café** coffee bean ► **frijol de soja** soya bean
[2] **frijoles** (*LAm**) (= *comida*) food *sing*; ✦***MODISMO*** **buscarse los frijoles** (*Cuba**) to earn a crust*, earn a living
[3] ✦***MODISMOS*** **¡frijoles!** (*Caribe*) certainly not!, not on your life!; **echar frijoles** (*Méx*) to blow one's own trumpet; **ser como los frijoles que al primer hervor se arrugan** (*Andes, Méx*) to run at the first sign of trouble
[4] (*Méx*) (= *mofa*) taunt
[5] (*Andes, Méx*) (= *cobarde*) coward

fringolear ▸conjug 1a◂ VT (*Cono Sur*) to thrash, beat

frío Ⓐ ADJ [1] (*en temperatura*) [*agua, aire, invierno, refresco, sopa*] cold; **el agua está muy fría** the water is very cold; **una cervecita bien fría** an ice cold beer; **el café se ha quedado ~** the coffee has got cold; **un sudor ~** a cold sweat; **tienes las manos frías** your hands are cold, you've got cold hands; **me quedé ~** I got cold; ✦***MODISMO*** **~ como el mármol** as cold as ice
[2] (*en sentimientos, actitudes*) [2·1] [*relaciones, acogida, recibimiento*] cool; **sus familia se mostró muy fría con él** his family were very cool towards him
[2·2] (= *desapasionado*) cool; **la mirada fría y penetrante del fotógrafo** the cool, penetrating eye of the photographer; **mantener la cabeza fría** to keep a cool head, keep one's cool
[2·3] (= *insensible, inexpresivo*) cold; **era ~ y calculador** he was cold and calculating; **los ingleses tienen fama de ser muy ~s** the English have a reputation for being cold; **este público es más ~ que el de otras ciudades** this audience is less responsive than those in other cities; **esos asesinos se comportan de forma fría y profesional** they are cold-blooded, professional killers
[2·4] ✦***MODISMOS*** **dejar ~ a algn** (= *indiferente*) to leave sb cold; **todo lo que me digas, me deja ~** everything you say, just leaves me cold; **aquellas revelaciones me dejaron ~** I was stunned by those revelations; **quedarse ~** (= *indiferente*) to be unmoved; (= *pasmado*) to be stunned
[3] [*bala*] spent
Ⓑ SM [1] (= *baja temperatura*) cold; **pese al ~ reinante** despite the cold; **la ola de ~ que azota el país** the cold spell which has gripped the country; **ya han llegado los ~s** the cold weather is here; **una planta resistente al ~** a hardy plant; **laminado en ~** cold-rolled; **hace (mucho) ~** it's (very) cold; **¡qué ~ hace!** it's freezing!, it's so cold! ► **frío industrial** industrial refrigeration ► **frío polar** arctic weather, arctic conditions *pl*
[2] (= *sensación*) cold; **tiritaba de ~** she was shivering with cold; **me entró ~ viendo el partido de fútbol** I got cold at the football match; **coger ~** to catch cold; **pasar ~** to be cold; **tener ~** to be cold, feel cold
[3] **en ~** [3·1] (= *en calma*) **ambas partes tendrán que pactar un acuerdo en ~** the two sides will have to negotiate an agreement with cool heads; **cuando se contemplan las cifras totales en ~** when one calmly *o* coolly considers the total numbers
[3·2] (= *repentinamente*) **me lo dijo en ~ y no supe cómo reaccionar** he sprung it on me out of the blue *o* he told me just like that and I didn't know quite what to say; ✦***MODISMO*** **no dar ni ~ ni calor a algn**: **el hecho de que no me hayan seleccionado no me da ni ~ ni calor** I'm not at all bothered about not being selected; **sus comentarios sobre mí no me dan ni ~ ni calor** his comments about me don't bother me one way or the other, I'm not at all bothered about *o* by his comments
[4] **fríos** (*Andes, CAm, Méx*) (= *fiebre*) intermittent fever *sing*; (= *paludismo*) malaria *sing*

friolento ADJ (*LAm*) sensitive to cold

friolera SF trifle, mere nothing; **gastó la ~ de 1.000 euros** he spent a mere 1,000 euros

friolero ADJ sensitive to cold

friorizado ADJ deep-frozen

frisa SF [1] (= *tela*) frieze
[2] (*Andes, Cono Sur*) (= *pelo*) nap (*on cloth*); (*Cono Sur*) (= *pelusa*) fluff; (*Caribe*) (= *manta*) blanket; ✦***MODISMOS*** **sacar a algn la ~** (*Cono Sur**) to tan sb's hide*; **sacar la ~ a algo** (*Cono Sur**) to make the most of sth

frisar ▸conjug 1a◂ Ⓐ VT [+ *tela*] to frizz, rub
Ⓑ VI **~ en** to border on, be *o* come close to; **frisa en los 50** he's getting on for 50

Frisia SF Friesland

friso SM frieze

fritada SF fry, fry-up*

fritanga SF [1] (= *comida frita*) fry, fry-up*; (*pey*) greasy food
[2] (*Andes, CAm*) (= *guiso*) ≈ hotpot, ≈ stew
[3] (*CAm*) (= *restaurante*) cheap restaurant
[4] (*Cono Sur**) (= *molestia*) pain in the neck*, nuisance

fritanguería SF (*Chile, Perú*) (= *tienda*) fried food shop; (= *puesto*) fried food stall

fritar ▸conjug 1a◂ VT (*LAm*) to fry

frito Ⓐ PP *de* **freír**
Ⓑ ADJ [1] (*gen*) fried; **patatas** *o* (*LAm*) **papas fritas** chips, French fries (*EEUU*)
[2] ✦***MODISMOS*** **dejar ~ a algn*** (= *matar*) to do sb in*, waste sb*; **estar ~*** (= *dormido*) to be kipping*, be out for the count*; (= *muerto*) to have snuffed it‡; (= *excitado*) to be really worked up; (*Caribe, Cono Sur*) (= *acabado*) to be finished, be done for*; **quedarse ~*** (= *dormirse*) to go out like a light; (= *morir*) to snuff it‡; **tener** *o* **traer ~ a algn*** (= *enojar*) to get on sb's nerves; (= *acosar*) to worry sb to death; (= *vencer*) to trounce sb, wipe the floor with sb*; **este trabajo me tiene ~** I'm fed up with this job; **ese hombre me trae ~** I've totally had it with this guy*; **las matemáticas me traen ~** I've totally had it with Maths*, I'm totally fed up with Maths
[3] [*pelo*] frizzy
Ⓒ SM [1] (= *plato*) fry, fried dish ► **fritos variados** mixed grill
[2] ✦***MODISMO*** **gustarle el ~ a algn** (*Cono Sur‡*) **a esa mujer le gusta el ~** she looks like hot stuff*
[3] (*en disco*) hiss, crackling

fritura SF [1] (= *plato*) fried food, fry; **~ de pescado** fried fish; **~ variada** mixed fry
[2] (= *buñuelo*) fritter
[3] (*Telec*) crackling, interference

frívolamente ADV frivolously

frivolidad SF frivolity, frivolousness

frivolité SM (*Cos*) tatting

frivolizar ▸conjug 1f◂ VT (= *trivializar*) to trivialize; (= *quitar importancia a*) to play down

frívolo ADJ frivolous

frivolón ADJ superficial, lightweight

frízer SM (*Cono Sur*) freezer

fronda SF [1] (= *hoja*) frond
[2] **frondas** (= *follaje*) foliage *sing*, leaves

frondís ADJ (*Andes*) dirty

frondosidad SF leafiness, luxuriance

frondoso ADJ leafy, luxuriant

frontal Ⓐ ADJ [1] [*parte, posición*] front; (*Inform*) front-end; **choque ~** head-on collision
[2] [*enfrentamiento*] direct, frontal; [*rechazo*] outright
Ⓑ SM front, front part

frontalmente ADV directly; **chocar ~** to crash *o* collide head-on, have a head-on crash *o* collision; **está situado ~** it is placed on the front; **se oponen ~** they are directly opposed

frontera SF [1] (= *línea divisoria*) frontier, border; (= *zona fronteriza*) frontier zone, borderland
[2] (*Arquit*) façade

fronterizo ADJ frontier *antes de s*, border *antes de s*; **el río ~ con Eslobodia** the river bordering Slobodia *o* forming the border with Slobodia

frontero ADJ opposite, facing

frontis SM INV (*Arquit*) façade

frontispicio SM [1] [*de libro*] frontispiece; (*Arquit*) façade
[2] (*) (= *cara*) face

frontón SM [1] (*Arquit*) pediment
[2] (*Dep*) (= *cancha*) pelota court; (= *pared*) (main) wall (*of a pelota court*)

frotación SF, **frotadura** SF, **frotamiento** SM rub, rubbing; (*Mec*) friction

frotado SM rubbing

frotar ▸conjug 1a◂ Ⓐ VT to rub; [+ *fósforo*] to strike; **quitar algo frotando** to rub sth off

Ⓑ **frotarse** VPR to rub, chafe; **~se las manos** to rub one's hands (together); **frotársela**** to have a wank**, jerk off (EEUU**)

frote SM (= *acción*) rub

frotis SM INV ► **frotis cervical** cervical smear ► **frotis vaginal** vaginal smear

fr(s). ABR (= **franco(s)**) fr

fructífero ADJ fruitful, productive

fructificación SF fruition

fructificar ▸conjug 1g◂ VI [1] (*Bot*) to produce fruit, bear fruit
[2] [*esfuerzos*] to bear fruit; [*plan*] to come to fruition

fructosa SF fructose

fructuosamente ADV fruitfully

fructuoso ADJ fruitful

frufrú SM rustling, rustle

frugal ADJ frugal, thrifty

frugalidad SF frugality

frugalmente ADV frugally (*frm*), thriftily

fruición SF delight; **leer con ~** to read with delight; **beber con ~** to drink with relish; **comer con ~** to eat with relish ► **fruición maliciosa** perverse pleasure *o* delight

frunce SM (*Cos*) gather, shirr

fruncido Ⓐ ADJ [1] (*Cos*) [*tela*] gathered
[2] (*Cono Sur**) (= *remilgado*) prudish, demure; (= *afectado*) affected
Ⓑ SM = **frunce**

fruncimiento SM = **frunce**

fruncir ▸conjug 3b◂ VT [1] (*Cos*) to gather, shirr
[2] [+ *labios*] to purse; **~ el ceño** *o* **entrecejo** to frown, knit one's brow; **~ las cejas** to frown

fruslería SF (= *chuchería*) trinket; (= *nimiedad*) trifle, triviality

frustración SF frustration

frustrado ADJ [*persona*] frustrated; [*intento, plan, atentado*] failed; **delito de homicidio ~** attempted murder; **intento de suicidio ~** failed suicide attempt

frustrante ADJ frustrating

frustrar ▸conjug 1a◂ Ⓐ VT [1] [+ *persona*] to frustrate; [+ *proyecto, aspiración, deseo, sueño*] to thwart; **no quiero ~ sus esperanzas** I don't want to frustrate *o* thwart their hopes; **le frustra no poderse comunicar** he finds it frustrating not being able to communicate
[2] (= *abortar*) [+ *atentado, operación*] to foil; **los guardas ~on el intento de fuga** the guards foiled their escape attempt
Ⓑ **frustrarse** VPR [*persona*] to be frustrated; [*aspiración, deseo*] to be thwarted; [*proyecto*] to be thwarted, fall through; **se frustró enormemente por no poder acabar la carrera** he was terribly frustrated at not being able to finish his studies; **nuestros sueños se ~on** our dreams were dashed *o* shattered

frustre* SM = **frustración**

fruta SF fruit ► **fruta de la pasión** passion fruit ► **fruta del tiempo** seasonal fruit ► **fruta de sartén** fritter ► **fruta escarchada** crystallized fruit ► **fruta prohibida** forbidden fruit ► **frutas confitadas** candied fruits

frutal Ⓐ ADJ fruit-bearing, fruit *antes de s*; **árbol ~** fruit tree
Ⓑ SM fruit tree

frutar ▸conjug 1a◂ VI to fruit, bear fruit

frutera SF fruit dish, fruit bowl

frutería SF fruiterer's (shop), fruit shop, greengrocer's

frutero/a Ⓐ ADJ fruit *antes de s*; **plato ~** fruit dish
Ⓑ SM/F (= *persona*) fruiterer, greengrocer, grocer (*EEUU*)
Ⓒ SM (= *recipiente*) fruit dish, fruit bowl; (= *cesta*) fruit basket

fruticultor(a) SM/F fruit farmer, fruit grower

fruticultura SF fruit growing, fruit farming

frutilla SF (*Andes, Cono Sur*) strawberry

fruto SM [1] (*Bot*) fruit; **dar ~** to fruit, bear fruit ► **fruto del pan** breadfruit ► **frutos del país** (*LAm*) agricultural produce ► **frutos secos** nuts and dried fruit
[2] (= *resultado*) result, product; (= *beneficio*) profit, benefit; [*de esfuerzo*] fruits *pl*; **dar ~** to bear fruit; **sacar ~ de algo** to profit from sth, derive benefit from sth
[3] (= *hijo*) offspring; **el ~ de esta unión** the offspring of this marriage, the fruit *o* product of this union (*liter*) ► **fruto de bendición** legitimate offspring

frutosidad SF fruitiness, fruity flavour *o* (*EEUU*) flavor

FSE SM ABR (= **Fondo Social Europeo**) ESF

FSLN SM ABR (*Nic*) = **Frente Sandinista de Liberación Nacional**

FSM SF ABR (= **Federación Sindical Mundial**) WFTU

fu Ⓐ SM [*de gato*] spit, hiss; ✦*MODISMO* **ni fu ni fa** (= *ni una cosa ni otra*) neither one thing or the other; (= *ni bonito ni feo*) so-so
Ⓑ EXCL ugh!

fuácata* SF (*Cuba, Méx*) ✦*MODISMO* **estar en la ~** to be broke*

fucha EXCL (*Méx*), **fuchi** EXCL (*Méx*) (*asco*) yuk!, ugh!; (*sorpresa*) phew!, wow!

fucilazo SM (flash of) sheet lightning

fuco SM (*Bot*) wrack

fucsia SF fuchsia

fudiño ADJ (*Caribe*) weak, sickly

fudre‡ SM drunk

fue *ver* **ser, ir**

fuego SM [1] (= *llamas*) fire; **buscamos un claro donde hacer ~** we looked for a clearing to make a fire in; **el ~ se declaró en el interior del almacén** the fire broke out inside the warehouse; **¡fuego!** fire!; **apagar el ~** to put out the fire; **atizar el ~** (*lit*) to poke the fire; (*fig*) to stir things up; **encender el ~** to light the fire; **marcar algo a ~** to brand sth; **pegar** *o* **prender ~ a algo** to set fire to sth, set sth on fire; **prendieron ~ a los vehículos** they set fire to the vehicles, they set the vehicles alight *o* on fire; **prender el ~** (*LAm*) to light the fire; **sofocar el ~** to extinguish the fire; ✦*MODISMOS* **echar ~ por los ojos**: **se marchó echando ~ por los ojos** he went off, his eyes blazing; **jugar con ~** to play with fire ► **fuego de artificio** firework; **el procedimiento ha sido sólo un ~ de artificio destinado a calmar a la opinión pública** the proceedings have been mere window dressing aimed at appeasing public opinion; **ha llegado a la cima sin los ~s de artificio típicos de muchas grandes estrellas** she has got to the top without the typical blaze of publicity attached to many big stars ► **fuego fatuo** will-o'-the-wisp ► **fuegos artificiales** fireworks
[2] [*de cocina*] [2·1] (= *quemador*) (*de gas*) burner, ring; (*eléctrico*) ring; **una cocina de gas de cuatro ~s** a four-ring gas cooker
[2·2] (= *calor*) heat, flame; **a ~ lento** on *o* over a low heat, on *o* over a low flame; **se mete en el horno a ~ lento** put in a low oven; **se deja cocer a ~ lento 15 minutos** simmer for 15 minutes, cook on *o* over a low heat for 15 minutes; **a ~ suave** on *o* over a low heat, on *o* over a low flame; **a ~ vivo** on *o* over a high flame, on *o* over a high heat
[3] (*para cigarro*) light; **¿tienes** *o* **me das ~?** have you got a light?; **le pedí ~** I asked him for a light
[4] (*Mil*) fire; **¡fuego!** fire!; **abrir ~ (contra algo/algn)** to open fire (on sth/sb); **¡alto el ~!** cease fire!; **hacer ~ (contra** *o* **sobre algo)** to fire (at sth); **romper el ~** to open fire; ✦*MODISMO* **estar entre dos ~s** to be caught in the crossfire ► **fuego a discreción** (*lit*) fire at will; (*fig*) all-out attack ► **fuego artillero** artillery fire ► **fuego cruzado** crossfire ► **fuego de andanada** (*Náut*) broadside ► **fuego de artillería** artillery fire ► **fuego de mortero** mortar fire ► **fuego graneado**, **fuego nutrido** sustained fire ► **fuego real** live ammunition; *ver tb* **alto**[2] **1**
[5] (= *pasión*) passion, fire; **apagar los ~s de algn** to dampen sb's ardour *o* (*EEUU*) ardor
[6] (*Náut*) beacon, signal fire
[7] (*Med*) (= *erupción*) rash; (*Méx, Chile, Col*) (*en los labios*) cold sore ► **fuego pérsico** shingles *pl*
[8] (= *hogar*) dwelling; **un pueblo de 50 ~s** a village of 50 dwellings

fueguear ▸conjug 1a◂ VT (*CAm*) to set fire to

fueguino /a (*Cono Sur*) Ⓐ ADJ of/from Tierra del Fuego
Ⓑ SM/F native/inhabitant of Tierra del Fuego; **los ~s** the people of Tierra del Fuego

fuel SM fuel oil

fuelle SM [1] (*para el fuego*) bellows *pl*; [*de gaita*] bag; [*de bolso, maleta*] gusset; [*de autobús, tren*] *connecting section*; ✦*MODISMO* **tener el ~ flojo**‡ to fart‡ ► **fuelle de pie** foot pump
[2] (*Aut*) folding top, folding hood (*EEUU*)
[3] (*Fot*) bellows *pl* ► **fuelle quitasol** hood
[4] (= *pulmones*) puff*, breath
[5] (= *aguante*) stamina, staying power; **tener ~** to have the stamina, have the staying power; ✦*MODISMO* **perder ~** to run out of steam
[6] (*) (= *soplón*) grass*

fuel-oil [fuel'oil] SM fuel oil

fuelóleo SM = **fuel**

fuente SF [1] (= *construcción*) fountain; (= *manantial*) spring; ✦*MODISMO* **abrir la ~ de las lágrimas** (*hum*) to open the floodgates* ► **fuente de beber** drinking fountain ► **fuente de río** source of a river ► **fuente de soda** (*LAm*) *café, selling ice-cream and soft drinks*, soda fountain (*EEUU*) ► **fuente termal** hot spring
[2] (*Culin*) serving dish, platter ► **fuente de hornear**, **fuente de horno** ovenproof dish
[3] (= *origen*) source, origin; **de ~ desconocida/fidedigna** from an unknown/a reliable source ► **fuente de alimentación** (*Inform*) power supply ► **fuente de ingresos** source of income ► **fuente de suministro** source of supply

fuer SM **a ~ de** (*liter*) as a; **a ~ de caballero** as a gentleman; **a ~ de hombre honrado** as an honest man

fuera ADV [1] (*de edificio, objeto*) (*indicando posición*) outside; (*indicando dirección*) out; **los niños estaban jugando ~** the children were playing outside; **¡estamos aquí ~!** we're out here!; **el perro tenía la lengua ~** the dog had his tongue hanging out; **llevaba la camisa ~** his shirt was hanging out; **¡fuera!** get out!; **¡segundos ~!** (*Boxeo*) seconds out!; **ir** *o* **salir ~** to go out, go outside; **comer ~** (*al aire libre*) to eat outside; (*en restaurante*) to eat out; **hoy vamos a cenar ~** we're going out for dinner tonight, we're eating out tonight; **de ~** from outside; **trae una silla de ~** bring a chair in from outside; **productos que vienen de ~ de la Unión Europea** products from outside the European Union; **tenemos que traer a alguien de ~** we need to bring somebody from outside in; **desde ~** from outside; **la parte de ~** the outside, the outer part; **por ~** (on the) outside; **lo han pintado sólo por ~** they've only painted it on the outside; **por ~ está duro** it's hard on the outside; **esta camisa se lleva por ~** this shirt is worn outside, this shirt is not tucked in; *ver tb* **lengua 1**

[2] (*de ciudad, trabajo*) **estar ~** to be away, be out of town; **estuvo ~ ocho semanas** he was away for eight weeks; **mis padres llevan varios días ~** my parents have been away for several days

[3] (*tb* **~ del país**) abroad, out of the country; **toda la maquinaria viene de ~** all the machinery comes from abroad; **vienen visitantes de ~ para verlo** people come from abroad to see it; **"¡invasores ~!"** "invaders go home!"; **estar ~** to be abroad; **ir** *o* **salir ~** to go abroad

[4] (*Dep*) [4·1] (*en un partido*) **estar ~** [*pelota*] (*Ftbl*) to be out of play; (*Rugby*) to be in touch; (*Tenis*) to be out; **~ de juego** offside; **~ de tiempo** *after full time*; **estamos ~ de tiempo** time's up; **tirar ~** to shoot wide

[4·2] (*tb* **~ de casa**) away, away from home; **el equipo de ~** the away team; **una victoria ~ de casa** an away win; **jugar ~** to play away (from home)

[5] **~ de** [5·1] (*= en el exterior de*) outside, out of; **estaba ~ de su jaula** it was outside *o* out of its cage; **esperamos ~ de la puerta** we waited outside the door

[5·2] (*= aparte*) apart from, aside from; **pero ~ de eso** but apart *o* aside from that; **~ de que ...** apart from the fact that ...

[5·3] **~ de alcance** out of reach; **~ de combate** (*Mil*) wounded; (*Boxeo*) K.O.ed; **dejar a algn ~ de combate** to knock sb out; **quedar ~ de combate** to be knocked out; **~ de lo común** unusual; **estar ~ de lugar** to be inappropriate, be out of place; **~ de peligro** out of danger; **~ de serie** exceptional; **se ha comprado un coche ~ de serie** he has bought an exceptional car; **es un ~ de serie** he's quite exceptional; **✦MODISMO estar ~ de sí** to be beside o.s.

fueraborda SM INV, **fuera-borda** SM INV, **fuerabordo** SM INV (*= motor*) outboard engine, outboard motor; (*= bote*) dinghy with an outboard engine

fuereño/a SM/F (*Méx*) outsider; (*pey*) rustic, provincial

fuerino/a SM/F (*Cono Sur*) stranger, non-resident

fuero SM [1] (*= carta municipal*) municipal charter; (*= ley local*) local/regional law code; (*= privilegio*) (*tb* **~s**) privilege, exemption; **a ~** according to law; **¿con qué ~?** by what right?; **de ~** de jure, in law

[2] (*= autoridad*) jurisdiction; **el ~ no alcanza a tanto** his authority does not extend that far; **✦MODISMOS en mi ~ interno ...** in my heart of hearts ..., deep down ...; **volver por sus ~s** (*= recuperarse*) to be oneself again; (*= reincidir*) to go back to one's old ways

FUEROS

Fueros *were the charters granted to villages, towns and regions by Spanish monarchs in the Middle Ages and which established their rights and obligations. The* **fueros** *under which the Basques and Navarrese received certain privileges (some fiscal autonomy, their own local administration system and exemption from military service outside their province) became a political football in the 19th Century, being alternately abolished and restored depending on the interests of the monarch or administration in power. Today, Navarre is recognized in the* **Estado de las Autonomías** *as the* **Comunidad Foral de Navarra**.

fuerte Ⓐ ADJ [1] (*persona*) [1·1] (*físicamente*) (*gen*) strong; (*= robusto*) sturdy, powerfully built; (*euf*) (*= obeso*) large; **✦MODISMO ~ como un roble** *o* **un toro** as strong as an ox *o* a horse

[1·2] (*emocionalmente*) strong, tough; **hemos de ser ~s ante la adversidad** we must be strong *o* tough in the face of adversity

[1·3] **estar ~ en filosofía/historia** [*estudiante*] to be strong in philosophy/history

[2] (*= intenso*) [2·1] [*sabor, olor, viento*] strong; [*dolor, calor*] intense; [*lluvia*] heavy; [*ejercicio*] strenuous

[2·2] [*explosión, voz, ruido*] loud; [*golpe*] heavy, hard; [*acento*] strong, thick

[2·3] [*color*] (*= no pálido*) strong; (*= llamativo*) bright; **una blusa de un rosa ~** a bright pink blouse

[2·4] [*impresión*] strong, powerful; [*deseo*] strong, deep; [*fe, objeción*] strong; [*discusión*] heated; **los vecinos tuvieron una discusión muy ~** the neighbours had a heated argument; **en la película se oyen expresiones muy ~s** the film contains strong language; **el taco más ~ que ha pronunciado** the worst swearword he has ever said

[2·5] [*abrazo, beso*] big; **un beso muy ~** (*en cartas*) lots of love; **un ~ abrazo, Carmen** best wishes, Carmen; (*más cariñoso*) love, Carmen

[3] [*bebida, medicamento*] strong; [*comida*] (*= pesada*) heavy; (*= indigesta*) indigestible; **nunca toma cosas ~s, sólo cerveza y vino** he never drinks spirits *o* the hard stuff*, just beer and wine

[4] (*= resistente*) [*cuerda, tela*] strong; [*economía, moneda, país*] strong

[5] (*= importante*) [*aumento, bajada*] sharp; [*crisis*] serious, severe; [*pérdidas*] large, substantial; **la ~ caída de ventas** the sharp drop in sales

[6] (*= impactante*) [*escena*] shocking, disturbing; **me dijo cosas muy ~s que no podría repetir ahora** she said some harsh *o* nasty* things that I couldn't repeat now; **—lo llamó a la oficina y lo despidió en el acto —¡qué ~!*** "he called him at the office and fired him there and then" — "that's outrageous *o* appalling!"

[7] **hacerse ~** (*= protegerse*) to hole up; (*= volverse fuerte*) to gain strength; **un comando se hizo ~ en las montañas** a group of commandos holed up in the mountains; **el fundamentalismo se hace ~ otra vez** fundamentalism is gaining strength again

[8] [*terreno*] rough, difficult

[9] (*Chile*) (*= apestoso*) [*persona*] stinky; **ser** *o* **estar ~ a algo** to stink of sth

Ⓑ ADV [1] (*= con fuerza*) [*golpear*] hard; [*abrazar*] tight, tightly; **pegar ~ al enemigo** to hit the enemy hard; **apostar ~** to bet heavily; **la editorial ha apostado ~ por los nuevos poetas** the publishing house is backing new poets in a big way; **jugar ~** (*lit*) to gamble heavily; (*fig*) to take a gamble

[2] (*= en voz alta*) [*hablar, tocar*] loud, loudly; **toca muy ~** she plays very loud *o* loudly; **¡más ~! ¡que no se le oye aquí atrás!** speak up! we can't hear at the back; **poner la radio más ~** to turn the radio up

[3] (*= gran cantidad*) **desayunar ~** to have a big breakfast; **comer ~** to have a big lunch

Ⓒ SM [1] (*Mil*) fort

[2] (*Mús*) forte

[3] (*= especialidad*) forte, strong point; **el canto no es mi ~** singing is not my forte *o* strong point

[4] (*Chile*) (*= bebida*) hard liquor, hard stuff*

fuertemente ADV [1] (*= con fuerza*) [*golpear*] hard; [*abrazar, apretar*] tightly

[2] (*= mucho*) [*apoyar, favorecer, contrastar*] strongly; [*aumentar, disminuir*] sharply, greatly; **la medida ha sido ~ criticada por los sindicatos** the measure has been strongly criticized by the unions; **hemos conseguido reducir ~ los costes** we have managed to reduce costs greatly

[3] (*+ ADJ*) **un acto ~ emotivo** a highly emotional ceremony; **grupos ~ armados** heavily armed groups; **divisas ~ vinculadas al dólar** currencies closely tied to the dollar

fuerza SF [1] [*de persona*] [1·1] (*física*) strength; **tienes mucha ~** you're very strong; **con ~** [*golpear*] hard; [*abrazar, agarrar, apretar*] tightly, tight; [*aplaudir*] loudly; **le golpeó con toda su ~ en la cabeza** she hit him on the head as hard as she could; **me agarré con ~ a una roca** I held on tight *o* tightly to a rock; **grita con todas tus ~s** shout with all your might; **hacer ~: el médico me ha prohibido que hiciera ~** the doctor has told me not to exert myself; **vamos a intentar levantar la losa: haced ~** let's try and lift up the slab: heave!; **si somos muchos en la manifestación haremos más ~** if there are lots of us at the demonstration we'll be stronger *o* it will lend more force to it; **hacer ~ de vela** to crowd on sail

[1·2] [*de carácter*] strength; **con toda la ~ de su amor** with all the strength of his love; **la ~ creadora de Picasso** Picasso's creative energy; **restar ~s al enemigo** to reduce the enemy's strength; **sentirse con ~s para hacer algo** to have the strength to do sth; **no me siento con ~s para seguir adelante** I don't have the strength to go on; **lo haré**

cuando me sienta con ~s para ello I'll do it when I feel strong enough *o* up to it*; **tener ~s para hacer algo** to be strong enough to do sth, have the strength to do sth; ***✦MODISMOS*** **se le va la ~ por la boca*** he's all talk and no action, he's all mouth*; **sacar ~s de flaqueza** to make a supreme effort, gather all one's strength

► **fuerza de voluntad** willpower; *ver tb* **medir A3**

2 (= *intensidad*) [*de viento*] strength, force; [*de lluvia*] intensity; **el viento empezó a soplar con ~** the wind began to blow strongly; **un viento de ~ seis** a force six wind; **a los pocos minutos rompió a llover con ~** a few minutes later it began to rain heavily; **el agua caía con ~ torrencial** the rain came down in torrents, there was torrential rainfall; **el terremoto ha golpeado con ~ el país** the earthquake has struck the country violently

3 (= *ímpetu*) **en los setenta la mujer entró con ~ en el periodismo** in the seventies women entered journalism in force; **su nombre ha irrumpido con ~ en el mundo artístico** his name has burst onto the art scene; **la ultraderecha renace con ~** the extreme right is making a strong comeback; **la banda terrorista volvió a golpear con ~ ayer** the terrorist group struck another devastating blow yesterday

4 (= *poder*) [*de fe*] strength; [*de argumento*] strength, force, power; [*de la ley*] force; **es un argumento de poca ~** it is not a very strong *o* powerful argument; **les asistía la ~ de la razón** they were helped by the power of reason; **serán castigados con toda la ~ de la ley** they will be punished with the full weight of the law, they will feel the full force of the law; **conquistaron la región por la ~ de las armas** they took the region by force of arms; **cobrar ~** [*rumores*] to grow stronger, gain strength; **la rebelión iba cobrando ~** the rebellion gathered *o* gained strength; **la idea ha cobrado ~ últimamente** the idea has gained in popularity *o* gained momentum recently; **por la ~ de la costumbre** out of habit, from force of habit; **es la ~ de la costumbre** it's force of habit; **con ~ legal** (*Com*) legally binding ► **fuerza mayor** (*Jur*) force majeure; **un caso de ~ mayor** a case of force majeure; **aplazaron el partido por razones de ~ mayor** the match was postponed due to circumstances beyond their control

5 (= *violencia*) force; **recurrir a la ~** to resort to force; **por la ~: quisieron impedirlo por la ~** they tried to prevent it forcibly *o* by force; **tuvieron que separarlos por la ~** they had to separate them by force; **por la ~ no se consigue nada** using force doesn't achieve anything, nothing is achieved by force; **imponer algo por la ~** to impose sth forcibly; **a viva ~: abrió la maleta a viva ~** he forced open the suitcase; **lo arrancaron de allí a viva ~** they wrenched him away forcibly ► **fuerza bruta** brute force

6 (*locuciones*) 6·1 **a ~ de** by; **a ~ de repetirlo acabó creyéndoselo él mismo** by repeating it so much he ended up believing it himself; **a ~ de autodisciplina** by exercising great self control; **bajar kilos a ~ de pedaleo** to lose weight by cycling; **conseguí aprobar a ~ de pasarme horas y horas estudiando** I managed to pass by dint of hours and hours of study; **a ~ de paciencia logró convencerlos** he succeeded in persuading them by dint of great patience

6·2 **a la ~: hacer algo a la ~** to be forced to do sth; **yo no quería, pero tuve que hacerlo a la ~** I didn't want to, but I was forced to do it; **se lo llevaron de su casa a la ~** he was taken from his home by force, he was taken forcibly from his home; **fueron repatriados a la ~** they were forcibly repatriated; **a la ~ tuvo que oírlos: ¡estaba a su lado!** he must have heard them: he was right next to them!; **alimentar a algn a la ~** to force-feed sb; **entrar en un lugar a la ~** [*ladrón*] to break into a place, break in; [*policía, bombero*] to force one's way into a place, enter a place forcibly; ***✦MODISMO*** **a la ~ ahorcan: dejará el ministerio cuando lo haga su jefe, ¡a la ~ ahorcan!** he'll leave the ministry when his boss does — not that he has any choice, anyway *o* life's tough!*

6·3 **en ~ de** by virtue of

6·4 **es ~ hacer algo** it is necessary to do sth; **es ~ reconocer que …** we must recognize that …, it must be admitted that …

6·5 **por ~** inevitably; **una región pobre como la nuestra, por ~ ha de ser más barata** in a poor region like ours prices will inevitably be *o* must be cheaper

7 (*Fís, Mec*) force ► **fuerza ascensional** (*Aer*) buoyancy ► **fuerza centrífuga** centrifugal force ► **fuerza centrípeta** centripetal force ► **fuerza de arrastre** pulling power ► **fuerza de (la) gravedad** force of gravity ► **fuerza de sustentación** (*Aer*) lift ► **fuerza hidráulica** hydraulic power ► **fuerza motriz** (*lit*) motive force; (*fig*) driving force

8 (= *conjunto de personas*) (*Mil, Pol*) force ► **fuerza(s) aérea(s)** air force *sing* ► **fuerza de apoyo** back-up force ► **fuerza de brazos** manpower ► **fuerza de choque** strike force ► **fuerza de disuasión** deterrent ► **fuerza de intervención rápida** rapid intervention force ► **fuerza de pacificación** peace-keeping force ► **fuerza de trabajo** workforce, labour force, labor force (*EEUU*) ► **fuerza de ventas** sales force ► **fuerza disuasoria** deterrent ► **fuerza expedicionaria** expeditionary force ► **fuerza política** political force ► **fuerza pública** police, police force ► **fuerzas aliadas** allied forces ► **fuerzas armadas** armed forces ► **fuerzas del orden (público)** forces of law and order ► **fuerzas de seguridad** security forces ► **fuerzas de tierra** land forces ► **las fuerzas vivas** the powers that be; **las ~s vivas locales** the local power group

9 (*Elec*) power; **han cortado la ~** they've cut off the power

fuese *ver* **ser, ir**

fuetazo SM (*LAm*) lash

fuete (*LAm*) SM whip; **dar ~ a** to whip

fuetear ▸conjug 1a◂ VT (*LAm*) to whip

fuga[1] SF 1 (*gen*) flight, escape; [*de enamorados*] elopement; **darse a la** *o* **ponerse en ~** to flee, take flight; **poner al enemigo en ~** to put the enemy to flight; **le aplicaron la ley de ~(s)** he was shot while trying to escape ► **fuga de capitales** flight of capital (abroad) ► **fuga de cerebros** brain drain ► **fuga de(l) domicilio** running away from home ► **fuga de la cárcel** escape from prison, jailbreak

2 [*de gas*] leak, escape

3 (= *ardor*) ardour, ardor (*EEUU*), impetuosity

fuga[2] SF (*Mús*) fugue

fugacidad SF fleetingness, transitory nature

fugado/a SM/F escapee

fugarse ▸conjug 1h◂ VPR [*preso*] to escape; [*niño, adolescente*] to run away; [*enamorados*] to elope; **se fugó de casa** he ran away from home; **~ de la ley** to abscond from justice

fugaz ADJ 1 [*momento*] fleeting, brief

2 **estrella ~** shooting star

3 (= *esquivo*) elusive

fugazmente ADV fleetingly, briefly

fugitivo/a Ⓐ ADJ 1 fugitive, fleeing

2 = **fugaz 1**

Ⓑ SM/F fugitive

fuguista SMF escaper, jailbreaker

fui, fuimos *etc ver* **ser, ir**

fuina SF marten

ful[1] (*Andes*) Ⓐ ADJ full, full up

Ⓑ SM **marchar a todo ~** to work at full capacity

ful[2]‡ ADJ = **fulastre**

ful[3]‡ SF (= *droga*) hash*

fulana* SF (*pey*) tart‡, slut‡; *ver tb* **fulano**

fulaneo* SM whoring

fulano* SM 1 (= *alguien*) so-and-so; **~ de tal** ◊ **Don Fulano** Mr So-and-so, Joe Bloggs, John Doe (*EEUU*); **Doña Fulana** Mrs So-and-so; **~, zutano y mengano** Tom, Dick and Harry; **me lo dijo ~** somebody or other told me; **no te vas a casar con un ~** you're not going to marry just anybody; **nombramos a ~ y ya está** we nominate some guy and that's that*

2 (= *tío*) guy*; *ver tb* **fulana**

fular SM = **foulard**

fulastre‡ ADJ (= *falso*) false, sham; (= *malo*) bad, rotten*

fulbito SM five-a-side football

fulcro SM fulcrum

fulero/a Ⓐ ADJ 1 [*objeto*] (= *inútil*) useless; (= *malo*) shoddy, cheap, poor-quality; (= *falso*) sham, bogus

2 [*persona*] (= *astuto*) sly; (= *embustero*) lying; (= *torpe*) blundering, incompetent; (= *tramposo*) cheating, deceitful

Ⓑ SM/F (= *astuto*) clever clogs*; (= *embustero*) liar; (= *torpe*) blunderer; (= *tramposo*) cheat

fulgente ADJ, **fúlgido** ADJ dazzling, brilliant

fulgir ▸conjug 3c◂ VI to shine, glow

fulgor SM brilliance, glow; (*fig*) splendour, splendor (*EEUU*)

fulgurante ADJ 1 (= *reluciente*) bright, shining

2 (= *tremendo*) shattering, stunning

fulgurar ▸conjug 1a◂ VI (= *brillar*) to shine, glow; (= *relampaguear*) to flash

fulguroso ADJ (= *brillante*) bright, shining, gleaming; (= *relampagueante*) flashing

fúlica SF coot

full* [ful] Ⓐ ADJ (*LAm*) full; **tenía los dos tanques ~ de gasolina** his two tanks were full of petrol

Ⓑ SM (*Cono Sur*) **a ~: trabajan a ~ para que no quede impune** they are working flat out so he doesn't go unpunished

fullerear* ▸conjug 1a◂ VI (*Andes*) to show off

fullería SF 1 (*Naipes*) (= *acción*) cheating, cardsharping; (= *cualidad*) guile, cunning

2 (= *trampa*) trick
3 (*Andes*) (= *ostentación*) showing-off

fullero/a Ⓐ ADJ 1 (= *tramposo*) cheating, deceitful
2 (= *chapucero*) blundering, incompetent; **hacer algo en plan ~** to botch sth*
Ⓑ SM/F 1 (= *tramposo*) (*gen*) sneak*, tattler (*EEUU*); (*con cartas*) cheat, cardsharp
2 (= *criminal*) crook*
3 (= *chapucero*) blunderer
4 (= *astuto*) clever clogs*
5 (*Andes*) (= *fachendón*) show-off*

fullingue ADJ (*Cono Sur*) 1 [*tabaco*] inferior, poor-quality
2 [*niño*] small, sickly

fulmicotón SM gun cotton

fulminación SF fulmination

fulminador(a) Ⓐ ADJ = **fulminante**
Ⓑ SM/F fulminator (**de** against)

fulminante Ⓐ ADJ 1 [*pólvora*] fulminating; [*mirada*] withering; **cápsula ~** percussion cap
2 (= *súbito*) sudden, fulminant (*frm*); **apoplejía ~** sudden stroke
3 (*) (= *tremendo*) terrific, tremendous; **golpe ~** terrific blow; **tiro ~** (*Ftbl etc*) sizzling shot
Ⓑ SM (*LAm*) percussion cap

fulminantemente ADV without warning; **despedir ~ a algn** to fire sb on the spot*

fulminar ▸conjug 1a◂ Ⓐ VT 1 (= *destruir*) to strike down; **murió fulminado por un rayo** he was struck dead *o* killed by lightning; ✦*MODISMO* **~ a algn con la mirada** to look daggers at sb
2 [+ *amenazas*] to utter (**contra** against)
Ⓑ VI to fulminate, explode

fulo ADJ 1 (*CAm*) (= *rubio*) blond(e), fair
2 (*Cono Sur**) (= *furioso*) furious, hopping mad*

fumada SF [*de cigarro*] puff, drag*

fumadero SM smoke room; **este cuarto es un ~** this room is full of smoke ► **fumadero de opio** opium den

fumado ADJ **estar ~*** to be stoned*

fumador(a) SM/F smoker; **no ~** non-smoker; **en la sección de no ~es** in the no-smoking *o* non-smoking section; **gran ~** heavy smoker ► **fumador(a) de pipa** pipe smoker ► **fumador(a) pasivo/a** passive smoker

fumar ▸conjug 1a◂ Ⓐ VT [+ *cigarro, pipa*] to smoke
Ⓑ VI to smoke; **él fuma en pipa** he smokes a pipe; **¿puedo ~?** can I smoke?; **"prohibido fumar"** "no smoking"; ✦*MODISMO* **~ como un carretero** to smoke like a chimney
Ⓒ **fumarse** VPR 1 (*) [+ *dinero*] to squander, blow*; [+ *clase*] to miss
2 (*Méx**) (= *escaparse*) to vanish, slope off*
3 **fumárselo a algn** (*LAm**) (= *engañar*) to trick sb, swindle sb
4 **~se a algn**** to screw sb**

fumarada SF 1 (= *humo*) puff of smoke
2 (*en pipa*) pipeful

fumata Ⓐ SF 1 (‡) smoking session (*of drugs*)
2 ► **fumata blanca** (*Rel*) (puff of) white smoke; (*fig*) indication of success
Ⓑ SMF (‡) (= *persona*) dope-smoker*
Ⓒ SM (‡) (= *cigarrillo*) fag*

fumeta‡ SMF dope-smoker*

fumeteo* SM smoking

fumigación SF 1 [*de local, ropa*] fumigation
2 (*Agr*) crop-dusting, crop-spraying

fumigar ▸conjug 1h◂ VT 1 [+ *local, ropa*] to fumigate
2 (*Agr*) to dust, spray

fumista SMF 1 (= *de chimeneas*) chimney sweep
2 (= *gandul*) idler, shirker
3 (*Cono Sur*) (= *bromista*) joker, tease

fumo SM (*Caribe*) puff of smoke

fumosidad SF smokiness

fumoso ADJ smoky

funambulesco ADJ grotesque, wildly extravagant

funambulista SMF, **funámbulo/a** SM/F tightrope walker, funambulist (*frm*)

funcia SF (*Andes, CAm hum*) = **función**

función SF 1 (= *actividad*) (*física, de máquina*) function; **el desarrollo de las funciones cerebrales** the development of the brain functions; **el ordenador realiza cinco funciones básicas** the computer performs five basic functions
2 (= *papel*) function; **¿cuál es la ~ del Estado?** what is the function of the State?; **ésa debería ser la ~ de la prensa** that should be the role *o* function of the press; **es una escultura que también cumple** *o* **hace la ~ de puerta** it is a sculpture which also acts as *o* serves as a door; **desempeñar la ~ de director/inspector/secretario** to have *o* hold the position of director/inspector/secretary; **el ministro desempeñará la ~ de mediador** the minister will act as (a) mediator; **la ~ de hacer algo** the task of doing sth; **la ~ de educar corresponde a la escuela** the task of educating falls to the school; **las fuerzas armadas tienen la ~ de proteger el país** the role *o* function of the armed forces is to protect the country
3 **funciones** 3·1 (= *deberes*) duties; **volvió a ejercer sus funciones como alcalde** he returned to carry out his duties as mayor; **en el ejercicio de sus funciones** in the course of her duties; **excederse** *o* **extralimitarse en sus funciones** to exceed one's duties
3·2 **en funciones** [*ministro, alcalde, presidente*] acting *antes de s*; **secretario general en funciones** acting secretary general; **gobierno en funciones** interim government; **entrar en funciones** [*funcionario*] to take up one's duties *o* post; [*ministro, alcalde, presidente*] to take up office, assume office; [*organismo*] to come into being
4 **en ~ de** 4·1 (= *según*) according to; **el dinero se repartirá en ~ de las necesidades de cada país** the money will be distributed according to the needs of each country; **el punto de ebullición del agua varía en ~ de la presión atmosférica** the boiling point of water varies according to atmospheric pressure; **el desarrollo cultural está en ~ de la estructura política de un país** cultural development depends on the political structure of a country
4·2 (= *basándose en*) on the basis of; **los consumidores realizan sus compras en ~ de la calidad y el precio** consumers make their purchases on the basis of quality and price
5 (= *espectáculo*) [*de teatro, ópera*] performance; [*de títeres, variedades, musical*] show; **ir a ver una ~ de circo** to go to the circus
► **función benéfica** charity performance ► **función continua** (*LAm*), **función continuada** (*Cono Sur*) continuous performance ► **función de despedida** farewell performance ► **función de noche** late performance, evening performance ► **función de tarde** matinée
6 **la ~ pública** the civil service
7 (*Mat*) function
8 (*Ling*) function; **~ gramatical** grammatical function

funcional ADJ 1 [*capacidad, actividad*] functional; **analfabetismo ~** functional illiteracy
2 (= *práctico*) [*diseño, casa*] functional

funcionalidad SF functional nature

funcionalismo SM functionalism

funcionamiento SM **lo lubrico cada 2.000 horas de ~** I lubricate it after every 2,000 hours of operation; **es vital para el ~ del sistema nervioso** it's vital for the functioning of the nervous system; **nos explicó el ~ de un carburador** he told us how a carburettor works; **esta máquina no está en ~** this machine is not in operation; **entrar en ~** to come into operation; **poner en ~** to bring into operation

funcionar ▸conjug 1a◂ VI 1 [*aparato, mecanismo*] to work; [*motor*] to work, run; [*sistema*] to work, function; **¿cómo funciona el vídeo?** how does the video work?, how do you work the video?; **funciona con monedas de un euro** it works with one-euro coins; **hacer ~ una máquina** to operate a machine; **"no funciona"** "out of order"
2 [*plan, método*] to work; [*negocio, película*] to be a success; **su primer matrimonio no funcionó** her first marriage did not work out *o* was not a success; **su última novela no ha funcionado tan bien como la anterior** his latest novel hasn't been as successful *o* as much of a success as the previous one

funcionariado SM civil service, bureaucracy

funcionarial ADJ administrative; (*pey*) bureaucratic

funcionario/a SM/F 1 (*tb* **~ público**) civil servant ► **funcionario/a aduanero/a** customs official ► **funcionario/a de policía** police officer ► **funcionario/a de prisiones**, **funcionario/a penitenciario/a** prison officer
2 [*de banco etc*] clerk

funda SF 1 (*gen*) case, cover; [*de disco*] sleeve ► **funda de almohada** pillowcase, pillowslip ► **funda de gafas** spectacles case, glasses case ► **funda de pistola** holster ► **funda protectora del disco** (*Inform*) disk cover ► **funda sobaquera** shoulder holster
2 (= *bolsa*) small bag, holdall
3 [*de diente*] cap
4 (*) (= *condón*) French letter
5 (*Col*) (= *falda*) skirt

fundación SF foundation

fundadamente ADV with good reason, on good grounds

fundado ADJ (= *justificado*) well-founded, justified; **una pretensión mal fundada** an ill-founded claim

fundador(a) SM/F founder

▼**fundamental** ADJ fundamental, basic

fundamentalismo SM fundamentalism

fundamentalista ADJ, SMF fundamentalist

➤ LENGUA Y USO: **fundamental** 53.2, 53.5

fundamentalmente ADV fundamentally, basically; (= *esencialmente*) essentially

fundamentar ▸conjug 1a◂ Ⓐ VT [1] (= *basar*) to base, found (**en** on)
[2] (= *poner las bases de*) to lay the foundations of
Ⓑ **fundamentarse** VPR **~se en** [*persona*] to base o.s. on; [*argumento, teoría*] to be based on

fundamento SM [1] (*Arquit*) foundations *pl*
[2] (= *base*) foundation, basis; (= *razón*) grounds, reason; **eso carece de ~** that is completely without foundation; **creencia sin ~** groundless *o* unfounded belief
[3] (= *formalidad*) reliability, trustworthiness
[4] (*Téc*) weft, woof
[5] **fundamentos** (= *principios*) fundamentals, basic essentials

fundar ▸conjug 1a◂ Ⓐ VT [1] (= *crear*) [+ *institución, asociación, ciudad, revista*] to found; [+ *partido*] to found, set up, establish
[2] (= *basar*) to base (**en** on)
Ⓑ **fundarse** VPR [1] [*institución, asociación, ciudad, revista*] to be founded; [+ *partido*] to be founded, be established, be set up
[2] (= *basarse*) **~se en** [*teoría*] to be based on, be founded on; [*persona*] to base o.s. on; **me fundo en los siguientes hechos** I base my opinion on the following facts

fundente Ⓐ ADJ melting
Ⓑ SM (*Metal*) flux; (*Quím*) dissolvent

fundería SF foundry ► **fundería de hierro** iron foundry

fundición SF [1] (= *acción*) [*de mineral*] smelting; (*en moldes*) casting; [*de lingotes, joyas*] melting down
[2] (= *fábrica*) foundry
[3] (= *hierro fundido*) cast iron
[4] (*Tip*) fount, font (*EEUU*)

fundido/a Ⓐ ADJ [1] [*metal, acero, cera*] molten; **sartén de hierro ~** cast iron frying pan
[2] [*bombilla*] blown
[3] [*queso*] melted
[4] (*) (= *muy cansado*) shattered*, whacked*, pooped (*EEUU**)
[5] (*Perú, Cono Sur**) (= *arruinado*) ruined, bankrupt
[6] (*Chile**) [*niño*] spoilt
Ⓑ SM/F (*Chile**) spoilt brat*
Ⓒ SM [1] (*Cine*) (= *resultado*) fade; (= *acción*) fading ► **fundido a blanco** fade-to-white ► **fundido a negro** fade-to-black ► **fundido de cierre** fade-out ► **fundido en negro** fade-to-black
[2] ► **fundido nuclear** (*Téc*) nuclear meltdown

fundidor(a) SM/F (= *persona*) smelter, founder; (*en fábrica*) foundry worker

fundidora SF (= *fábrica*) foundry

fundillo SM (*LAm*), **fundillos** SMPL (*LAm*) [1] [*del pantalón*] seat
[2] (*) (= *culo*) bum, backside*, ass (*esp EEUU**)

fundir ▸conjug 3a◂ Ⓐ VT [1] (= *derretir*) [1·1] (*para hacer líquido*) [+ *metal, cera, nieve*] to melt; [+ *monedas, lingotes, joyas*] to melt down
[1·2] (*Min*) (*para extraer el metal*) to smelt
[1·3] (*en molde*) [+ *estatuas, cañones*] to cast
[2] [+ *bombilla, fusible*] to blow
[3] (= *fusionar*) [+ *organizaciones, empresas*] to merge, amalgamate; [+ *culturas, movimientos*] to fuse; **intentaba ~ los elementos andaluces con los hindúes** she aimed to fuse Andalusian and Indian elements
[4] (*Cine*) [+ *imágenes*] to fade
[5] (*) [+ *dinero*] to blow*; **nos lo fundimos todo a la ruleta** we blew it all on roulette*
[6] (*Perú, Cono Sur**) (= *arruinar*) ruin; **la nieve nos fundió la cosecha** the snow ruined the crop
[7] (*Chile**) [+ *niño*] to spoil
Ⓑ **fundirse** VPR [1] (= *derretirse*) [*hielo*] to melt
[2] (*Elec*) [*bombilla, fusible*] to blow, go; **se fundieron los plomos** the fuses blew *o* went
[3] (= *fusionarse*) [3·1] [*organizaciones, empresas*] to amalgamate, merge; [*partidos políticos*] to merge; **los ritmos caribeños y el flamenco se ~án durante el festival** Caribbean rhythms and flamenco will fuse together *o* merge in the festival; **~se en algo** [*organizaciones*] to merge to form sth, amalgamate into sth; [*sonidos*] to merge into sth; [*colores, imágenes*] to merge to form sth, blend together to form sth; **ambos museos se fundieron en el Museo Nacional** both museums merged to form *o* (were) amalgamated into the National Museum; **las voces se fundieron en un solo grito** the voices merged into a single cry; **se fundieron en un abrazo** they melted into each other's arms
[3·2] **~se con algo: el cielo se fundía con el mar** the sea and the sky blended *o* merged into one; **la necesidad de ~se con la naturaleza** the need to unite oneself with nature
[4] (*Cine*) [*imagen*] to fade
[5] (*Perú, Cono Sur**) (= *arruinarse*) to be ruined

fundo SM (*Perú, Chile*) landed property, estate; (= *granja*) farm

fundón SM (*Andes, Caribe*) riding-habit

fúnebre ADJ [1] **coche ~** hearse; **pompas ~s** undertaker's, funeral parlor (*EEUU*)
[2] (= *lúgubre*) mournful, funereal (*frm*)

funeral Ⓐ ADJ funeral *antes de s*
Ⓑ **funerales** SMPL (= *exequias*) funeral *sing*; (= *oficio religioso*) funeral service *sing*

funerala* SF ✦*MODISMOS* **marchar a la ~** to march with reversed arms; **ojo a la ~** black eye

funeraria SF undertaker's, funeral parlor (*EEUU*); **director de ~** undertaker, funeral director, mortician (*EEUU*)

funerario ADJ, **funéreo** ADJ funeral *antes de s*

funestamente ADV (= *desastrosamente*) fatally, disastrously; (= *perjudicialmente*) banefully

funestidad SF (*Méx*) calamity

funesto ADJ (= *maldito*) ill-fated; (= *desastroso*) fatal, disastrous; (= *nocivo*) baneful

fungible ADJ (*Jur*) **bienes ~s** perishable goods

fungicida SM fungicide

fungiforme ADJ mushroom-shaped

fungir ▸conjug 3c◂ VI (*CAm, Méx*) (= *actuar*) to act (**de** as); (*Caribe*) to substitute, stand in (**a** for)

fungo SM (*Med*) fungus

fungoideo ADJ fungoid

fungoso ADJ fungous

funguelar‡ ▸conjug 1a◂ VI to pong‡

funicular SM [1] (= *tren*) funicular, funicular railway
[2] (= *teleférico*) cable car

fuñido ADJ [1] (*Caribe*) (= *pendenciero*) quarrelsome; (= *insociable*) unsociable
[2] (*Caribe*) (= *enfermizo*) sickly, feeble

fuñingue ADJ (*Cono Sur*) weak

fuñir‡ (*LAm*) ▸conjug 3h◂ VT **~la** to make a real mess of things, mess things up

furcia** SF tart‡, whore*; **¡furcia!** you slut!‡

furgón SM (*Aut*) truck, van; (*Ferro*) goods van, boxcar (*EEUU*) ► **furgón acorazado** armoured van, armored truck (*EEUU*) ► **furgón blindado** armoured *o* (*EEUU*) armored truck ► **furgón celular** police van, prison van ► **furgón de cola** guard's-van, caboose (*EEUU*) ► **furgón de equipajes** luggage car, baggage car (*EEUU*) ► **furgón de mudanzas** removal van, removal truck (*EEUU*) ► **furgón de reparto** delivery van, delivery truck (*EEUU*) ► **furgón funerario** hearse ► **furgón postal** mail van, post office van

furgonada SF vanload, truckload, wagonload

furgonero SM carter, vanman

furgoneta SF (= *furgón*) (transit) van, pickup (truck) (*EEUU*); (= *coche*) estate (car), station wagon (*EEUU*) ► **furgoneta de reparto** delivery van, delivery truck (*EEUU*)

furia SF (= *rabia*) fury, rage; (= *violencia*) violence; ✦*MODISMOS* **hecho una ~: estar hecho una ~** to be furious; **ponerse hecho una ~** to get mad; **salió hecha una ~** she stormed out; **a la ~** ◊ **a toda ~** (*Cono Sur*) at top speed, real fast (*EEUU**); **trabajar a toda ~** to work like fury

furibundo ADJ (= *furioso*) furious; (= *frenético*) frenzied

furiosamente ADV (= *con rabia*) furiously; (= *con violencia*) violently; (= *frenéticamente*) frantically

furioso ADJ (= *con rabia*) furious; (= *violento*) violent; (= *frenético*) frantic; **estar ~** to be furious; **ponerse ~** to get mad, be furious

furor SM [1] (= *ira*) fury, rage; (= *pasión*) frenzy, passion; **dijo con ~** he said furiously ► **furor uterino** nymphomania
[2] (= *afición*) rage; **hacer ~** to be all the rage*, be a sensation; **tener ~ por** (*LAm*) to have a passion for

furquina SF (*Andes*) short skirt

furriel SM, **furrier** SM quartermaster

furriña SF (*Méx*) anger

furrular* ▸conjug 1a◂ VI to work

furrús* SM switch, swap, change

furrusca* SF (*Andes*) row, brawl

furtivamente ADV furtively

furtivismo SM poaching

furtivo/a Ⓐ ADJ [1] (= *ilegal*) [*persona*] furtive; [*edición*] pirated; **cazador/pescador ~** poacher; **lágrima furtiva** silent tear; **avión ~** stealth bomber
[2] (= *astuto*) sly, stealthy
Ⓑ SM/F (= *persona*) poacher

furular* ▸conjug 1a◂ VI to work

furuminga SF (*Cono Sur*) intrigue, scheme

furúnculo SM (*Med*) boil

fusa SF demisemiquaver, thirty-second note (*EEUU*)

fusca‡ SF, **fusco**‡ SM gun, rod‡

fuselado ADJ streamlined

fuselaje SM fuselage; **de ~ ancho** wide-bodied

fusible SM fuse

fusil SM rifle, gun ► **fusil de asalto** assault rifle

fusilamiento SM [1] (*Jur*) execution (*by firing squad*); (*irregular*) summary execution

2 (*) (= *plagio*) pinching*, plagiarism; [*de producto*] piracy, illegal copying

fusilar ▸conjug 1a◂ VT 1 (= *ejecutar*) to shoot, execute (*by firing squad*)
2 (*Caribe*) (= *matar*) to kill; (*Dep*) [+ *gol*] to shoot
3 (*) (= *plagiar*) (*Literat, Cine*) to pinch*, plagiarize; (*Com*) to pirate, copy illegally

fusilazo SM rifle-shot

fusilería SF gunfire, rifle-fire

fusilero SM rifleman, fusilier

fusión SF 1 (= *unión*) joining, uniting; (*Com*) merger, amalgamation
2 (*Inform*) merge
3 [*de metal*] melting
4 (*Fís*) fusion ► **fusión nuclear** nuclear fusion
5 (*Mús*) crossover

fusionamiento SM (*Com*) merger, amalgamation

fusionar ▸conjug 1a◂ Ⓐ VT (*gen*) to fuse (together); (*Com*) to merge, amalgamate; (*Inform*) to merge
Ⓑ **fusionarse** VPR (*gen*) to fuse; (*Com*) to merge, amalgamate

fusta SF 1 (= *látigo*) riding whip
2 (= *leña*) brushwood, twigs *pl*

fustán SM 1 (= *tela*) fustian
2 (*LAm*) (= *enagua*) petticoat, underskirt; (= *falda*) skirt

fuste SM 1 (= *importancia*) importance; **de ~** important, of some consequence; **de poco ~** unimportant
2 (= *madera*) timber, lumber (*EEUU*); **de ~** wooden
3 [*de lanza*] shaft; [*de chimenea*] shaft
4 (*CAm Anat**) bottom
5 (= *silla*) saddle tree

fustigar ▸conjug 1h◂ VT 1 (= *pegar*) to whip, lash
2 (= *criticar*) to upbraid, give a tongue-lashing to*

futbito SM five-a-side football, five-a-side soccer (*EEUU*)

fútbol SM, **futbol** SM (*LAm*) football, soccer (*esp EEUU*); **~ ofensivo** attacking football ► **fútbol americano** American football ► **fútbol asociación** association football, soccer

futbolero/a Ⓐ ADJ football *antes de s*, soccer *antes de s*
Ⓑ SM/F football supporter, soccer supporter (*EEUU*)

futbolín SM 1 (= *juego*) table football, table soccer (*EEUU*)
2 (*tb* **futbolines**) (= *local*) amusement arcade, amusements *pl*

futbolista SMF footballer, football player, soccer player (*esp EEUU*)

futbolístico ADJ football *antes de s*, soccer *antes de s*

futbolmanía SF football mania, soccer mania (*EEUU*)

fútbol-sala SM, **fútbol sala** SM indoor football, indoor soccer (*EEUU*)

futearse ▸conjug 1a◂ VPR (*Andes*) [*fruta*] to go bad, rot

futesa SF trifle, mere nothing; **futesas** (*en conversación*) small talk *sing*, trivialities

fútil ADJ 1 (= *inútil*) futile
2 (= *sin importancia*) trifling, trivial

futileza SF, **futilidad** SF 1 (= *cualidad*) triviality, trifling nature
2 (*Cono Sur*) trifle, bagatelle; **una ~** a trifle

futing ['futin] SM = **footing**

futón SM futon

futre* SM (*Chile*) toff*, dude (*EEUU**)

futrería SF (*Chile*) 1 (= *conducta*) affected behaviour, affected behavior (*EEUU*)
2 (= *grupo*) group of toffs*, group of dudes (*EEUU**)
3 (= *querencia*) hang-out (*EEUU**)

futura SF (*Jur*) reversion; *ver tb* **futuro**

futurible Ⓐ ADJ (= *venidero*) forthcoming; (= *potencial*) potential; (= *probable*) likely; (= *especulativo*) speculative; (= *digno de ascenso*) promotion-worthy
Ⓑ SMF (*Pol*) (= *dirigente*) potential leader; (= *ministro*) potential minister
Ⓒ SM hot tip, good bet; **es un ~ olímpico** he's a good prospect for the Olympics

futurismo SM futurism

futurista Ⓐ ADJ, **futurístico** ADJ futuristic
Ⓑ SMF futurist

futuro/a Ⓐ ADJ future; **futura madre** mother-to-be; **los equipos más ~s son A y B** the teams with the best prospects are A and B
Ⓑ SM/F (*) fiancé/fiancée
Ⓒ SM 1 future; **en el ~** in (the) future; **en lo ~** ◊ **en un ~** some time in the future; **en un ~ próximo** in the near future; **el ~ se presenta muy oscuro** the future looks bleak; **a ~** (*Chile*) in the future
2 (*Ling*) future (tense)
3 **futuros** (*Com*) futures; *ver tb* **futura**

futurología SF futurology

futurólogo/a SM/F futurologist

G g

G, g[1] [xe] SF (= *letra*) G, g
g[2] ABR (= **gramo(s)**) g, gm(s)
g/ ABR (= **giro**) p.o., m.o. (*EEUU*)
gabacho/a Ⓐ ADJ 1 (* *pey*) (= *francés*) froggy*, Frenchy*
2 (*Geog*) Pyrenean
3 ✦*MODISMO* **le salió gabacha la cosa** (*Andes**) it came to nothing
Ⓑ SM/F 1 (* *pey*) frog*, Frenchy*
2 (*Geog*) Pyrenean villager
3 (*Méx*) (= *extranjero*) foreigner, outsider; (*en Tejas*) white American, Yankee
gabán SM overcoat, topcoat; (*Caribe*) jacket
gabanear ▸conjug 1a◂ Ⓐ VT (*CAm*) to steal
Ⓑ VI (*Méx*) to flee
gabanero SM hall wardrobe
gabarda SF wild rose
gabardina SF 1 (= *abrigo*) raincoat, mackintosh†; **gambas en ~** prawns in batter, battered prawns
2 (= *tela*) gabardine
gabardino/a SM/F (*Méx pey*) white American, Yankee
gabarra SF barge, flatboat
gabarrero/a SM/F bargee, bargeman (*EEUU*)
gabarro SM 1 (*en una tela*) flaw, defect
2 (*Vet*) (= *moquillo*) distemper, pip; [*de caballo*] tumour, tumor (*EEUU*)
3 (*en las cuentas*) error, miscalculation
4 (= *obstáculo*) snag; (= *molestia*) annoyance
gabear ▸conjug 1a◂ VT (*Caribe*) to climb
gabela SF 1 (*Hist*) (= *impuesto*) tax, duty; (= *carga*) burden
2 (*Andes*) (= *ventaja*) advantage, profit
gabinete SM 1 (*profesional*) office ► **gabinete de consulta** consulting-room, doctor's office (*EEUU*) ► **gabinete de diseño** design consultancy ► **gabinete de estrategia** (*Pol*) think-tank ► **gabinete de imagen** public relations office ► **gabinete de prensa** press office ► **gabinete fiscal** tax advisory office ► **gabinete jurídico** (*en empresa*) legal department; (= *bufete*) law firm
2 (*en casa*) (= *despacho*) study, library; (= *salita*) private sitting room; (= *tocador*) boudoir; (*Arte*) studio; **estratega de ~** armchair strategist ► **gabinete de lectura** reading room
3 (*Pol*) cabinet ► **gabinete en la sombra, gabinete fantasma** shadow cabinet
4 (= *laboratorio*) laboratory
5 (= *museo*) museum
6 (= *muebles*) suite of office furniture
7 (*Andes*) (= *balcón*) enclosed balcony
8 ► **gabinete de teléfono** (*Méx*) telephone booth
gablete SM gable
Gabriel SM Gabriel
gacel SM gazelle
gacela SF gazelle
gaceta SF 1 (= *boletín*) gazette, official journal; (*LAm*) (= *diario*) newspaper
2 (*Caribe**) (= *chismoso*) gossip; (= *soplón*) telltale, tattletale (*EEUU*)
gacetero/a SM/F 1 (= *periodista*) newswriter, journalist
2 (= *vendedor*) newspaper seller
gacetilla SF 1 (= *notas sociales*) gossip column; (= *noticias generales*) miscellaneous news section; (= *noticias locales*) local news section; **"Gacetilla"** "News in Brief"
2 (*) (= *chismoso*) gossip; **ella es una ~ con dos patas** she's a dreadful gossip
gacetillero/a SM/F (= *reportero de sociedad*) gossip columnist; (*) (= *periodista*) hack (*pey*)
gacetista SMF gossip
gacha SF 1 thin paste, mush
2 **gachas** (*Culin*) pap; ✦*MODISMO* **se ha hecho unas ~s** she's turned all sentimental ► **gachas de avena** oatmeal porridge
3 (*LAm*) (= *vasija*) earthenware bowl
gachí‡ SF (*pl* **gachís**) bird‡, chick (*EEUU*‡)
gacho ADJ 1 (= *encorvado*) bent down, turned downward; [*cuerno*] down-curved; [*orejas*] drooping, floppy; **sombrero ~** slouch hat; **salió con las orejas gachas** *o* **con la cabeza gacha** he went out all down in the mouth*; ✦*MODISMO* **a cabeza gacha** (*Cono Sur*) obediently
2 **ir a gachas*** to go on all fours
3 (*Méx**) (= *feo*) nasty, ugly; (= *sin suerte*) unlucky
gachó* SM (*pl* **gachós**) guy*, bloke*; **¡gachó!** brother!*; **qué terco eres, ~** man, you're so stubborn
gachón ADJ 1 (*) (= *encantador*) charming, sweet; [*niño*] spoilt
2 (‡) [*mujer*] sexy
gachumbo SM (*LAm*) hollowed-out shell
gachupín/ina SM/F (*Méx*), **gachuzo/a** SM/F (*Méx pey*) Spaniard
gacilla SF (*CAm*) (= *imperdible*) safety pin; (= *broche*) clasp
gaditano/a Ⓐ ADJ of/from Cadiz
Ⓑ SM/F native/inhabitant of Cadiz; **los ~s** the people of Cadiz
GAE SM ABR (*Esp Mil*) = **Grupo Aéreo Embarcado**
gaélico/a Ⓐ ADJ Gaelic
Ⓑ SM/F Gael
Ⓒ SM (*Ling*) Gaelic
gafa SF 1 (= *grapa*) grapple; (= *abrazadera*) clamp
2 **gafas** (*para ver*) glasses, spectacles†, eyeglasses (*EEUU*); (*Dep*) goggles ► **gafas bifocales** bifocals ► **gafas de aro** wire-rimmed glasses ► **gafas de baño, gafas de bucear** diving goggles ► **gafas de cerca** reading glasses ► **gafas de culo de vaso** pebble glasses ► **gafas de esquiar** skiing goggles ► **gafas de leer** reading glasses ► **gafas de media luna** half-moon glasses ► **gafas de motorista** motorcyclist's goggles ► **gafas de protección** safety goggles, protective goggles ► **gafas de sol** sunglasses ► **gafas graduadas** prescription glasses ► **gafas negras, gafas oscuras** dark glasses ► **gafas protectoras** safety goggles, protective goggles ► **gafas sin aros** rimless glasses ► **gafas submarinas** underwater goggles; *ver tb* **gafo**; → PANTALONES, ZAPATOS, GAFAS
gafancia* SF (= *mala suerte*) propensity to attract bad luck; (= *tendencia*) accident-proneness
gafar ▸conjug 1a◂ VT 1 (*) (= *traer mala suerte*) to jinx*, put a jinx on*; (= *estropear*) to mess up; **la máquina parece gafada** the machine is jinxed*, the machine seems to have a jinx on it*
2 (= *arrebatar*) to hook, latch on to
gafe* Ⓐ ADJ **ser ~** to have a jinx*, be jinxed*; **tener un día ~** to have a bad day, have an off day; **un número con ~** an unlucky number
Ⓑ SMF **ser un ~** to have a jinx*, be jinxed*
Ⓒ SM (= *mala suerte*) jinx*
gafete SM clasp, hook and eye
gafo/a Ⓐ ADJ 1 (*LAm*) (= *cansado*) footsore
2 (*Méx*) (= *adormecido*) numb
3 **estar ~** (*CAm**) to be broke*
4 (*Caribe*) (= *no fiable*) unreliable, erratic; (‡) (= *bruto*) thick*
Ⓑ SM/F (*Caribe*) idiot; *ver tb* **gafa**
gafudo ADJ who wears glasses, with glasses
gag SM (*pl* **gags**) gag
gagá* Ⓐ ADJ **estar ~** to be gaga*
Ⓑ SMF old dodderer
gago/a* (*LAm*) Ⓐ ADJ stammering, stuttering
Ⓑ SM/F stammerer, stutterer
gagoso* ADJ (*LAm*) stammering, stuttering

gaguear* ▸conjug 1a◂ VI (*LAm*) to stammer, stutter

gagueo* SM (*LAm*) stammer(ing), stutter(ing)

gaguera* SF (*LAm*) stammer, stutter

gaita Ⓐ SF [1] (*Mús*) bagpipes *pl*; **tocar la ~** to play the bagpipes; ✦**MODISMOS ser como una ~*** to be very demanding; **estar de ~*** to be merry; **estar hecho una ~*** to be a wreck*; **templar ~s*** to pour oil on troubled waters ► **gaita gallega** Galician bagpipes
[2] (*Mús*) (= *flauta*) flute; (= *organillo*) hurdy-gurdy
[3] (*) (= *pescuezo*) neck; ✦**MODISMO sacar la ~** to stick one's neck out
[4] (*) (= *dificultad*) bother, nuisance; **¡qué ~!** what a pain!*; **déjame, que hoy no estoy para ~s** leave me alone, I don't need any hassle today*; **y toda esa ~*** and all that jazz*
[5] (*Méx**) (= *maula*) cheat, trickster
[6] (*Ven*) folk music
Ⓑ SMF (*LAm hum*) (= *gallego*) Galician; (= *español*) Spaniard

gaitero/a Ⓐ SM/F (*Mús*) (bag)piper
Ⓑ ADJ [1] [*color*] gaudy, flashy
[2] [*persona*] buffoonish

gaje SM [1] **en ~ de** (*LAm*) as a token of, as a sign of
[2] **gajes** (= *emolumentos*) pay *sing*, emoluments; (= *beneficios*) perquisites; (= *recompensa*) reward *sing*, bonus *sing*; **~s y emolumentos** (*Com*) perquisites ► **gajes del oficio** (*hum*) occupational hazards, occupational risks

gajo SM [1] [*de naranja*] slice, segment
[2] [*de uvas*] small cluster, bunch
[3] (= *rama*) torn-off branch, torn-off bough
[4] [*de horca*] point, prong
[5] (*Geog*) spur
[6] (*Andes*) curl, ringlet

GAL SMPL ABR (*Esp*) (= **Grupos Antiterroristas de Liberación**) *anti-ETA terrorist group*

gal SMF member of GAL

gala SF [1] (= *fiesta*) show ► **gala benéfica** charity event
[2] **de ~: cena de ~** gala dinner; **función de ~** gala; **uniforme de ~** full-dress uniform; **traje de ~** (*gen*) formal dress; (*Mil*) full dress; **estar de ~** [*ciudad*] to be in festive mood
[3] **galas** (= *ropa*) finery *sing*; (= *joyas*) jewels; **vestir sus mejores ~s** [*persona*] to put on one's Sunday best; [*edificio, ciudad*] to show one's best face ► **galas de novia** bridal attire *sing*
[4] (= *elegancia*) elegance, gracefulness; (= *pompa*) pomp, display; **hacer ~ de algo** (= *jactarse*) to boast of sth; (= *lucirse*) to show sth off; **tener algo a ~** to be proud of sth; **tener a ~ hacer algo** to be proud to do sth
[5] (= *lo más selecto*) pride; **es la ~ de la ciudad** it is the pride of the city; **llevarse las ~s** to win applause
[6] (= *especialidad*) speciality, specialty (*EEUU*)
[7] (*LAm*) (= *regalo*) gift; (= *propina*) tip; *ver tb* **galo**

galáctico ADJ galactic

galafate SM sly thief

galaico ADJ Galician

galán Ⓐ SM [1] (= *hombre apuesto*) handsome fellow; (= *Don Juan*) ladies' man; (*Hist*) young gentleman, courtier
[2] (= *novio*) gallant, beau; (= *pretendiente*) suitor
[3] (*Teat*) male lead; (= *protagonista*) hero; **primer ~** leading man; **joven ~** juvenile lead ► **galán de cine** screen idol
[4] ► **galán de noche** (= *mueble*) clothes-rack and trouser press; (= *planta*) night jasmine
Ⓑ ADV (*LAm**) = **bien**

galanamente† ADV (= *primorosamente*) smartly, sprucely; (= *con elegancia*) elegantly, tastefully

galanas SFPL (*CAm*) **echar ~** to boast, brag; **hacer ~** to do naughty things, be wicked

galancete† SM [1] (= *joven*) handsome young man; (*hum*) dapper little man
[2] (*Teat*) juvenile lead

galancito† SM juvenile lead

galano† ADJ [1] (= *primoroso*) smart, spruce; (= *elegante*) elegant, tasteful; (= *gallardo*) smartly dressed
[2] (*Cuba*) [*vaca*] mottled (*with red and white patches*)

galante ADJ [1] [*hombre*] (= *caballeroso*) gallant; (= *atento*) charming, attentive (*to women*); (= *cortés*) polite, urbane (*frm*)
[2] (††) [*mujer*] flirtatious, flirty; (*pey*) wanton, licentious

galantear ▸conjug 1a◂ VT (= *cortejar*) to court, woo; (= *coquetear*) to flirt with

galantemente ADJ (= *con caballerosidad*) gallantly; (= *con atención*) charmingly, attentively; (= *con cortesía*) politely

galanteo SM (= *corte*) courtship, wooing; (= *coqueteo*) flirting

galantería SF [1] (= *caballerosidad*) gallantry; (= *atención*) charm, attentiveness (*to women*); (= *gentileza*) politeness, urbanity (*frm*)
[2] (= *cumplido*) compliment; (= *piropo*) charming thing to say, gallantry

galanto SM snowdrop

galanura SF (= *gracia*) prettiness; (= *encanto*) charm; (= *gallardía*) elegance, tastefulness

galápago SM [1] (= *tortuga*) freshwater tortoise
[2] (= *molde*) tile mould, tile mold (*EEUU*)
[3] (*Téc*) ingot, pig
[4] (= *montura*) light saddle; (*LAm*) (= *montura de lado*) sidesaddle
[5] [*de bicicleta*] racing saddle

Galápagos SFPL **las (Islas) ~** the Galapagos (Islands)

galapagueño/a Ⓐ ADJ of/from the Galapagos (Islands)
Ⓑ SM/F native/inhabitant of the Galapagos (Islands)

galardón SM (= *premio*) award, prize; (= *recompensa*) reward

galardonado/a SM/F award-winner, prize-winner

galardonar ▸conjug 1a◂ VT [+ *obra, candidato*] to award a prize to, give a prize *o* award to; **ha sido galardonado con el premio Nobel** he was awarded the Nobel prize; **obra galardonada por la Academia** work which won an Academy prize

galaxia SF galaxy

galbana SF laziness, sloth

galbanoso ADJ lazy, slothful

galdosiano ADJ *relating to Benito Pérez Galdós*; **estudios ~s** Galdós studies

galembo SM (*Andes, Caribe*) turkey buzzard

galena SF galena, galenite; *ver tb* **galeno 1**

galeniano ADJ Galenic

Galeno SM Galen

galeno[1]/a SM/F (*Literat hum*) physician; (*LAm*) doctor; *ver tb* **galena**

galeno[2] ADJ [*viento*] moderate, soft

galeón SM galleon

galeote SM galley slave

galera SF [1] (*Náut*) galley; **condenar a algn a ~s** to condemn sb to the galleys
[2] (= *carro*) covered wagon
[3] (*Med*) hospital ward; (*Hist*) women's prison
[4] (*CAm, Méx*) (= *cobertizo*) shed
[5] (*CAm*) (= *matadero*) slaughterhouse
[6] (*LAm*) (= *chistera*) top hat; (= *fieltro*) felt hat, trilby, fedora (*EEUU*); (= *hongo*) bowler hat, derby (*EEUU*)
[7] (*Tip*) galley

galerada SF [1] (*Tip*) galley proof
[2] (= *carga*) wagonload

galería SF [1] (= *espacio*) (*interior, en mina*) gallery; (*exterior*) balcony ► **galería comercial** shopping mall ► **galería de alimentación** food hall ► **galería de arte** art gallery ► **galería de columnas** colonnade ► **galería de la muerte** death row ► **galería de popa** (*Náut*) stern gallery ► **galería de tiro** shooting gallery ► **galería de viento** (*Aer*) wind tunnel ► **galería secreta** secret passage
[2] (*) (= *público*) audience; ✦**MODISMO hacer algo para** *o* **de cara a la ~** to play to the gallery; **ha sido un gesto para la ~** it was just playing to the gallery
[3] (*para cortinas*) pelmet, cornice (*EEUU*)
[4] (*Andes, Caribe*) store

galerista SMF (= *propietario*) gallery owner; (= *director*) art gallery director

galerita SF crested lark

galerna SF, **galerno** SM *violent north-west wind on North coast of Spain*

galerón SM [1] (*CAm*) (= *cobertizo*) shed; (= *tejado*) shed roof
[2] (*Méx*) (= *sala*) hall
[3] (*Caribe*) (= *baile*) folk dance

Gales SM Wales

galés/esa Ⓐ ADJ Welsh
Ⓑ SM/F Welshman/Welshwoman; **los galeses** the Welsh
Ⓒ SM (*Ling*) Welsh

galfaro SM (*Caribe*) little rascal

galga SF [1] (= *instrumento*) gauge, gage (*EEUU*)
[2] (*Geol*) boulder
[3] [*de molino de aceite*] millstone

galgo[1]/a SM/F greyhound; ✦**MODISMOS ¡échale un ~!*** catch him if you can!; **¡vete a espulgar un ~!*** go to blazes! ► **galgo afgano** Afghan (hound) ► **galgo ruso** borzoi, Russian wolfhound

galgo[2]* ADJ, **galgón*** ADJ (*Andes*) sweet-toothed, fond of sweets

galguear* ▸conjug 1a◂ VI (*CAm, Cono Sur*) (= *tener hambre*) to be starving, be ravenous; (= *buscar comida*) to wander about looking for food

Galia SF Gaul

gálibo SM [1] (*Téc*) gauge
[2] (= *luz*) warning light, flashing light

galicano† ADJ [1] (= *galo*) Gallic
[2] (*Rel*) Gallican

galiciano/a ADJ, SM/F Galician

galicismo SM Gallicism

gálico Ⓐ ADJ Gallic
Ⓑ SM syphilis

galicoso/a ADJ, SM/F syphilitic

Galilea SF Galilee

galillo SM uvula

galimatías SM INV (= *asunto*) rigmarole; (= *lenguaje*) gibberish, nonsense

gallada SF [1] (*LAm*) (= *acto atrevido*) bold deed, great achievement; (= *jactancia*) boast
[2] **la ~** (*Cono Sur**) (= *chicos*) the boys*, the lads*; (= *gente*) people

gallardamente ADV (= *con elegancia*) gracefully, elegantly; (= *con magnificencia*) splendidly; (= *con valentía*) bravely; (= *con caballerosidad*) gallantly, dashingly; (= *con nobleza*) nobly

gallardear ▸conjug 1a◂ VI [1] (= *actuar con gracia*) to act with ease and grace; (= *tener buen porte*) to bear o.s. well
[2] (= *pavonearse*) to strut

gallardete SM pennant, streamer

gallardía SF (= *elegancia*) gracefulness; (= *magnificencia*) fineness; (= *valentía*) bravery; (= *caballerosidad*) gallantry, dash; (= *nobleza*) nobleness

gallardo ADJ (= *elegante*) graceful, elegant; (= *magnífico*) fine, splendid; (= *valiente*) brave; (= *caballeroso*) gallant, dashing; (= *noble*) noble

gallareta SF (*LAm*) South American coot

gallear ▸conjug 1a◂ Ⓐ VT [+ *gallina*] to tread
Ⓑ VI [1] (= *destacar*) to excel, stand out
[2] (= *pavonearse*) to strut around; (= *jactarse*) to brag; (= *bravuconear*) to be a bully, chuck one's weight about; (= *gritar*) to bluster, bawl

gallego/a Ⓐ ADJ [1] (= *de Galicia*) Galician
[2] (*LAm pey*) Spanish
Ⓑ SM/F [1] (= *de Galicia*) Galician
[2] (*LAm pey*) Spaniard
Ⓒ SM [1] (*Ling*) Galician
[2] (= *viento*) north-west wind

GALLEGO

Gallego, *a romance language dating back to the 12th century and closely related to Portuguese, is spoken by 80-85% of the inhabitants of* **Galicia**. *During the Franco régime, the use of Galician and other minority national languages was prohibited in the media and in public institutions. It has enjoyed* **lengua cooficial** *status alongside* **castellano** *since 1981. There are several dialects of the language and formal attempts to standardize them in the 1970's were unsuccessful. However, a standard form is now beginning to emerge naturally in the larger urban areas.*
⇨ *See also* LENGUAS COOFICIALES

galleguismo SM [1] (*Ling*) Galleguism, *word or phrase peculiar to Galicia*
[2] (= *sentimiento*) *sense of the differentness of Galicia*; (*Pol*) *doctrine of/belief in Galician autonomy*

galleguista Ⓐ ADJ pro-Galician
Ⓑ SMF pro-Galician

gallera SF [1] (*LAm*) (= *palenque*) cockpit
[2] (*Andes, CAm*) (= *gallinero*) coop (*for gamecocks*); *ver tb* **gallero**

gallería SF (*Caribe*) [1] (= *palenque*) cockpit
[2] (= *egoísmo*) egotism, selfishness

gallero/a Ⓐ ADJ (*LAm, Canarias*) fond of cockfighting
Ⓑ SM/F [1] (*LAm, Canarias*) (= *encargado*) *owner or trainer of fighting cocks*; (= *aficionado*) cockfighting enthusiast
[2] (*Cono Sur*) pilferer; *ver tb* **gallera**

galleta SF [1] (*Culin*) (= *dulce*) biscuit, cookie (*EEUU*); (*Náut*) ship's biscuit, hardtack; (*Cono Sur*) coarse bread; ✦*MODISMO* **ir a toda ~*** to go full-speed ► **galleta para perros** dog biscuit ► **galleta salada** cracker
[2] (*) (= *bofetada*) bash*, slap; **se pegó una ~ con la moto** he had a bad smash on the bike
[3] (*Andes, Cono Sur*) *small bowl for drinking maté*
[4] (*LAm**) confusion, disorder; ✦*MODISMO* **hacerse una ~** (*Cono Sur*) to get muddled ► **galleta del tráfico** (*Ven**) (= *atasco*) traffic jam; (= *burla*) practical joke
[5] (*Cono Sur*) (= *bronca*) ticking-off*; **le dieron una buena ~** they gave him a good ticking-off*
[6] ✦*MODISMOS* **colgar** *o* **dar la ~ a algn** (*Andes, Arg**) (= *despedir*) to sack sb*, fire sb*; (= *plantar*) to jilt sb; (= *rechazar*) to give sb the brush-off*; (= *no hacer caso a*) to give sb the cold shoulder; **tener mucha ~** (*Méx**) to be very strong

galletear ▸conjug 1a◂ VT [1] (*Méx*) (= *golpear*) to belt*, punch
[2] (*Cono Sur*) (= *despedir*) to sack*, fire*

galletero/a Ⓐ SM/F (*Cono Sur*) (= *irritable*) quick-tempered person; (= *pendenciero*) roughneck
Ⓑ SM (= *recipiente*) biscuit tin

gallina Ⓐ SF [1] (= *ave*) hen; ✦*MODISMOS* **acostarse con las ~s** to go to bed early; **cantar la ~** to own up, hold up one's hands; **andar como ~ clueca** (*Méx*) to be as pleased as Punch; **estar como ~ en corral ajeno** (= *estar incómodo*) to be like a fish out of water; (= *no tener libertad*) to have no freedom of movement; **estar como ~ con huevos** to be very distrustful; **¡hasta que meen las ~s!*** pigs might fly!*; **matar la ~ de los huevos de oro** to kill the goose that lays the golden eggs; ✦*REFRÁN* **las ~s de arriba ensucian a las de abajo** (*Chile*) the underdog always suffers ► **gallina ciega** (*CAm, Caribe*) (= *gusano*) white worm; **jugar a la ~ ciega** to play blind man's buff ► **gallina clueca** broody *o* (*EEUU*) brooding hen ► **gallina de agua** coot ► **gallina de bantam** bantam ► **gallina de Guinea** guinea fowl ► **gallina de mar** gurnard ► **gallina ponedora** laying hen
[2] (*Culin*) chicken; **caldo de ~** chicken broth; **~ en pepitoria** *chicken in a sauce made with wine, bread, egg, almonds and pine nuts*
Ⓑ SMF (*) (= *cobarde*) chicken*, coward

gallinacera SF (*Andes pey*) bunch of blacks

gallinaza SF hen droppings *pl*

gallinazo SM (*LAm*) turkey buzzard

gallinería SF [1] (= *gallinas*) flock of hens
[2] (*Com*) (= *tienda*) poultry shop; (= *mercado*) chicken market
[3] (*) (= *cobardía*) cowardice

gallinero/a Ⓐ SM/F [1] (= *criador*) chicken farmer
[2] (= *pollero*) poulterer, poultry dealer
Ⓑ SM [1] (= *criadero*) henhouse, coop; (= *cesta*) poultry basket
[2] (*Teat*) gods *pl*, top gallery
[3] (= *confusión*) hubbub; (= *griterío*) noisy gathering; (= *casa de locos*) madhouse

gallineta SF [1] (*Orn*) (= *chocha*) woodcock; (= *fúlica*) coot; (*LAm*) guinea fowl
[2] ► **gallineta del Atlántico**, **gallineta nórdica** Atlantic redfish

gallinilla SF ► **gallinilla de bantam** bantam

gallipavo SM [1] (= *ave*) turkey
[2] (*Mús*) false note, wrong note

gallito Ⓐ ADJ (*) (= *bravucón*) cocky*, cocksure; **ponerse ~** to get cocky*
Ⓑ SM [1] (= *ave*) cockerel
[2] (= *persona*) tough guy*; **es el ~ del grupo** he's top dog*; **el ~ del mundo** the cock-o'-the-walk
[3] (*Col, Méx Dep*) shuttlecock
[4] (*Andes*) (= *flecha*) small arrow, dart

gallo[1] SM [1] (= *ave*) cock, rooster (*esp EEUU*); (*más pequeño*) cockerel; ✦*MODISMOS* **alzar el ~** (*LAm*) to bawl; **comer ~** (*Andes, CAm**) to suffer a setback; **haber comido ~** (*Méx**) to be in a fighting mood; **como ~ en corral ajeno** like a fish out of water; **entre ~s y medianoche** (*Arg*) on the spur of the moment; **estar como ~ en gallinero** to be highly esteemed, be well thought of; **dormírsele a algn el ~** (*CAm, Méx**) to let an opportunity slip; **no me va nada en el ~** (*Méx**) it doesn't matter to me, it's no skin off my nose*; **levantar el ~** (*LAm*) to bawl; (*Caribe, Méx**) to throw in the towel *o* (*EEUU*) sponge; **matar el ~ a algn** to floor sb, shut sb up*; **en menos que canta un ~** in an instant, in a flash; **otro ~ cantaría** things would be very different; **pelar ~** (*Méx**) (= *salir huyendo*) to make a run for it*; (= *morirse*) to kick the bucket*; **al primer ~** (*Méx*) at midnight; **hay ~ tapado** (*Col*) I smell a rat; **tener mucho ~** to be cocky* ► **gallo de pelea**, **gallo de riña** gamecock, fighting cock ► **gallo lira** black grouse ► **gallo pinto** (*CAm Culin*) beans and rice ► **gallo silvestre** capercaillie; *ver tb* **pata A1.2**, **pelea**, **peso 7.3**
[2] (= *pez*) john dory
[3] (*en la voz*) false note; **soltó un ~** (*al cantar*) he sang a false note; (*al hablar*) his voice cracked; **tengo un ~ en la garganta** I have a frog in my throat
[4] (*) (= *bravucón*) tough guy*; (*LAm*) expert, master; **yo he sido ~ para eso** I was a great one at that
[5] (*Pesca*) cork float
[6] (‡) (= *flema*) spit; (*Méx*) (= *gargajo*) gob of spit‡
[7] (*Méx*) (= *serenata*) street serenade
[8] (*Méx**) (= *ropa usada*) hand-me-down; **anda siempre de ~s** all his clothes are hand-me-downs; **lo visten con los ~s del hermano mayor** they dress him in his brother's hand-me-downs *o* old clothes
[9] (*Andes*) (= *flecha*) dart
[10] (*Col, Méx Dep*) shuttlecock
[11] (*Andes*) [*de bomberos*] hose truck

gallo[2]**/a** SM/F (*Chile*) guy*/girl; **conocí a un ~ estupendo** I met a great guy*; **¡qué galla tan antipática!** she is so unfriendly!

gallofero/a Ⓐ ADJ idle, vagabond
Ⓑ SM/F (= *holgazán*) idler, loafer; (= *vagabundo*) tramp, bum (*EEUU*), hobo (*EEUU*); (= *mendigo*) beggar

gallón* (*Méx*) Ⓐ ADJ cocky*
Ⓑ SM local boss

gallote* Ⓐ ADJ (*CAm, Méx*) cocky*
Ⓑ SM (*CAm*) cop*

gallumbos‡ SMPL underpants

galo/a Ⓐ ADJ (*Hist*) Gallic; (*moderno*) French
Ⓑ SM/F (*Hist*) Gaul; (*moderno*) Frenchman/Frenchwoman; *ver tb* **gala**

galocha SF clog

galón¹ SM (*Cos*) braid; (*Mil*) stripe, chevron; **la acción le valió dos galones** his action gained him a couple of stripes; **quitar los galones a algn** to demote sb

galón² SM (= *medida*) gallon

galonear ▸conjug 1a◂ VT to braid, trim with braid

galopada SF gallop

galopante ADJ (*gen*) galloping; [*inflación*] galloping, runaway; [*déficit*] spiralling; [*paro*] soaring, spiralling; **el número de casos aumentó a un ritmo ~** the number of cases shot up

galopar ▸conjug 1a◂ VI to gallop; **echar a ~** to break into a gallop

galope SM gallop; **a** *o* **al ~** (*lit*) at a gallop; (*fig*) in great haste, in a rush; **a ~ tendido** at full gallop; **alejarse a ~** to gallop off; **desfilar a ~** to gallop past; **llegar a ~** to gallop up; **medio ~** canter

galopín SM [1] (= *pícaro*) ragamuffin, urchin; (= *bribón*) scoundrel; (= *sabelotodo*) smart Aleck*, clever Dick*
[2] (*Náut*) (= *grumete*) cabin boy

galpón SM [1] (*LAm*) (= *cobertizo*) shed, storehouse; (*Aut*) garage
[2] (*Andes*) (= *tejar*) tileworks, pottery

galucha SF (*LAm*) short gallop; (*Caribe*) start of a gallop

galuchar ▸conjug 1a◂ VI (*LAm*) to gallop

galvánico ADJ galvanic

galvanismo SM galvanism

galvanizado ADJ galvanized

galvanizar ▸conjug 1f◂ VT [1] (*Fís*) to electroplate, galvanize
[2] (= *estimular*) to galvanize

galvano SM (*Cono Sur*) commemorative plaque

galvanoplastia SF electroplating

gama¹ SF [1] (= *serie*) range; **una extensa ~ de colores** an extensive range of colours; **alto de ~** ◊ **de ~ alta** top of the range; **bajo de ~** ◊ **de ~ baja** bottom of the range ► **gama de frecuencias** frequency range ► **gama de ondas** wave range ► **gama sonora** sound range
[2] (*Mús*) scale

gama² SF (= *letra*) gamma

gama³ SF (*Zool*) doe (*of fallow deer*); ✦***MODISMO*** **sentársele a algn la ~** (*Cono Sur*) to get discouraged

gamarra SF (*CAm*) halter; ✦***MODISMO*** **llevar a algn de la ~*** to lead sb by the nose

gamba SF [1] (= *marisco*) prawn; **cóctel de ~s** prawn cocktail
[2] (‡) (= *pierna*) leg; ✦***MODISMO*** **meter la ~** to put one's foot in it*
[3] (†‡) 100 pesetas; **media ~** 50 pesetas

gambado ADJ (*Caribe*) knock-kneed

gamberrada SF (= *acto vandálico*) piece of hooliganism; (= *grosería*) loutish thing (to do); (= *broma*) lark*, rag*, piece of horseplay; **hacer ~s** = **gamberrear 1**

gamberrear ▸conjug 1a◂ VI [1] (= *hacer el gamberro*) to go around causing trouble, act like a hooligan; (= *hacer el tonto*) to lark about*, horse around*
[2] (= *gandulear*) to loaf around

gamberrismo SM hooliganism, loutish behaviour

gamberrístico ADJ loutish, ill-bred

gamberro/a Ⓐ ADJ [1] (*pey*) loutish, ill-bred
[2] (= *bromista*) joking, teasing
Ⓑ SM/F [1] (*pey*) hooligan, troublemaker; **hacer el ~** to act like a hooligan
[2] (= *bromista*) joker

gambeta SF [1] [*de caballo*] prance, caper
[2] (*LAm*) (= *esguince*) dodge, avoiding action
[3] (*Dep*) dribble
[4] (*) (= *pretexto*) dodge, pretext

gambito SM gambit

gambuza SF (*Náut*) store, storeroom

gamella SF (= *abrevadero*) trough; (= *artesa*) washtub

gameto SM gamete

gamín/ina* SM/F (*Col*) street urchin

gamma Ⓐ SF (= *letra*) gamma; **radiación ~** gamma radiation
Ⓑ ADJ INV **rayos ~** gamma rays

gamo SM buck (*of fallow deer*)

gamonal SM (*LAm*) = **cacique**

gamonalismo SM (*LAm*) = **caciquismo**

gamulán SM (*Cono Sur*) sheepskin

gamuza SF [1] (*Zool*) chamois
[2] (= *piel*) chamois leather, wash leather; **una cazadora de ~** a suede jacket
[3] (= *paño*) duster, dustcloth (*EEUU*)

▼ **gana** SF [1] **hacer algo con ~s** to do sth willingly *o* enthusiastically; **comer/reírse con ~s** to eat/laugh heartily; **un chico joven y con ~s de trabajar** a young lad willing to work; **jóvenes con ~s de divertirse** young people keen to enjoy themselves; **con ~s de pelea** spoiling for a fight; **dar ~s**: **esto da ~s de comerlo** it makes you want to eat it; **dan ~s de pegarle una patada** you feel like kicking him; **le entran ~s de hacer algo** he gets the urge to do sth; **quedarse con las ~s** to be left disappointed, be left wanting; **nos quedamos con las ~s de saberlo** we never got to find out; **me quedé con las ~s de decirles lo que pensaba** I never got to tell them what I thought; **quitársele a algn las ~s de algo**: **se me han quitado las ~s de ir** I don't feel like going now *o* any more; **hacer algo sin ~s** to do sth reluctantly *o* unwillingly; **tener ~s de hacer algo** to feel like doing sth; **tengo ~s de ir al cine** I feel like going to see a film; **tengo ~s de vomitar** I feel sick, I'm going to be sick; **tengo ~s de ir al servicio** I need (to go to) the loo; **tengo ~s de que llegue el sábado** I'm looking forward to Saturday; **hola, ¿cómo estás? tenía ~s de verte** hi, how are you? I was hoping I'd see you; **tengo unas ~s locas de verte** I can't wait to see you, I'm dying to see you; **tengo pocas ~s de ir** I don't feel like going much, I don't really want to go; **malditas las ~s que tengo de ir*** there's no way I want to go
[2] ✦***MODISMOS*** **de buena ~** gladly; **de buena ~ te ayudaría, pero no puedo** I'd gladly help you, but I can't; **con ~s** (= *de verdad*) really; **ser malo con ~s** to be thoroughly nasty; **hacer lo que le da la ~ a uno** to do as one pleases; **haz lo que te dé la ~** just do as you please; **me visto como me da la ~** I dress the way I want to, I dress as I please; **hazlo como te dé la ~** do it however you like; **¡no me da la ~!** I don't want to!; **porque (no) me da la real ~** because I (don't) damned well want to*; **me da la ~ de** + *INFIN* I feel like + *ger*, I want to + *infin*; **de ~** (*Andes*) (= *sin querer*) unintentionally; (= *en broma*) as a joke, in fun; **hasta las ~s** (*Méx*) right up to the end; **pagar hasta las ~s*** to pay over the odds; **¡las ~s!*** you'll wish you had!; **de mala ~** reluctantly, grudgingly; **no me pega la ~** (*Méx**) I don't feel like it; **siempre hace su regalada ~** (*Méx**) he always goes his own sweet way; **ser ~s de**: **son ~s de molestar** *o* **fastidiar** they're just trying to be awkward; **es ~** (*Andes, Caribe, Méx*) it's a waste of time, there's no point; **tenerle ~s a algn*** to have it in for sb*; **venirle en ~ a algn**: **hacen lo que les viene en ~** they do exactly as they please; **no me viene en ~** I don't feel like it, I can't be bothered; ✦***REFRANES*** **~ tiene de coles quien besa al hortelano** it's just cupboard love; **donde hay ~ hay maña** where there's a will, there's a way

ganadería SF [1] (= *crianza*) cattle raising, stockbreeding; (*en estancia*) ranching
[2] (= *estancia*) stock farm; (= *rancho*) cattle ranch; **toros de ~ de Valdemoro** bulls from the Valdemoro ranch
[3] (= *ganado*) cattle, livestock; (= *raza*) breed, race of cattle

ganadero/a Ⓐ ADJ cattle *antes de s*, stock *antes de s*; (= *de cría*) cattle-raising *antes de s*
Ⓑ SM/F [1] (= *criador*) cattle-raiser, stockbreeder (*EEUU*); (= *hacendado*) rancher
[2] (= *comerciante*) cattle dealer

ganado SM [1] (= *animales*) livestock; (*esp LAm*) (*vacuno*) cattle; (= *rebaño*) herd, flock; **íbamos amontonados como ~** we were packed in like sardines ► **ganado asnal** donkeys *pl* ► **ganado caballar** horses *pl* ► **ganado cabrío** goats *pl* ► **ganado equino** horses *pl* ► **ganado lanar** sheep *pl* ► **ganado mayor** *cattle, horses and mules* ► **ganado menor** *sheep, goats and pigs* ► **ganado mular** mules *pl* ► **ganado ovejuno** sheep *pl* ► **ganado porcino** pigs *pl* ► **ganado vacuno** cattle
[2] (*pey*) (= *gente*) **¡ya verás qué ~ tenemos esta noche!** we've got a right bunch in here tonight!*
[3] (*LAm*) **un ~ de** a crowd *o* mob of

ganador(a) Ⓐ ADJ (= *vencedor*) winning, victorious; **el equipo ~** the winning team; **apostar a ~ y colocado** to back (a horse) each way, back for a win and a place
Ⓑ SM/F winner; (*Fin*) earner; (*que se beneficia*) gainer

ganancia SF [1] (= *beneficio*) gain; (= *aumento*) increase
[2] **ganancias** (*Com, Fin*) (= *ingresos*) earnings; (= *beneficios*) profits; **sacar ~s de algo** to draw profit from sth; **~s y pérdidas** profit and loss; ✦***MODISMO*** **no le arriendo la ~** I don't envy him ► **ganancias brutas** gross profit *sing* ► **ganancias de capital** capital gains ► **ganancias líquidas** net profit *sing*
[3] (*LAm*) (= *propina*) extra, bonus

ganancial Ⓐ ADJ profit *antes de s*; *ver tb* **bien D4**
Ⓑ **gananciales** SMPL joint property *sing*

➤ LENGUA Y USO: **gana 1** 35.4

gananciosola Ⓐ ADJ [1] (= *lucrativo*) gainful
[2] (= *triunfador*) winning; **resultar** *o* **salir ~** to be the gainer
Ⓑ SM/F gainer

ganapán SM [1] (*sin trabajo fijo*) casual labourer *o* (*EEUU*) laborer
[2] (*que hace pequeños arreglos*) odd-job man
[3] (= *palurdo*) lout
[4] (= *recadero*) messenger

ganar ▸conjug 1a◂ Ⓐ VT [1] [+ *sueldo*] to earn; **¿cuánto ganas al mes?** how much do you earn *o* make a month?; **ha ganado mucho dinero** she has made a lot of money
[2] [+ *competición, partido, premio, guerra*] to win; **le ganó cien euros a Rosa** he won a hundred euros from Rosa; **¿quién ganó la carrera?** who won the race?; **si te toca puedes ~ un millón** if you win you could get a million; **~ unas oposiciones para un puesto** to obtain a post by public examination
[3] [+ *contrincante*] to beat; **¡les ganamos!** we beat them!; **ganamos al Olimpic tres a cero** we beat Olimpic three-nil; **no hay quien le gane** there's nobody who can beat him, he's unbeatable; **como orador no hay quien le gane** *o* **no le gana nadie** as a speaker there is no one to touch him, no one outdoes him at speaking
[4] (= *conseguir*) [+ *tiempo, peso, terreno*] to gain; **¿qué gano yo con todo esto?** what do I gain *o* get from all this?; **con eso no ganas nada** that won't get you anywhere; **tierras ganadas al mar** land reclaimed *o* won from the sea; **~ popularidad** to win *o* earn popularity
[5] (= *alcanzar*) [+ *objetivo*] to achieve, attain; **~ la orilla** to reach the shore; **~ la orilla nadando** to swim to the shore
[6] (= *convencer*) to win over; **dejarse ~ por algo** to allow o.s. to be won over by sth
[7] (= *aventajar*) **te gana en inteligencia** he's more intelligent than you; **me gana en pericia** he has more expert knowledge than me; **te gana trabajando** he's a better worker than you
[8] (*Mil*) [+ *plaza, pueblo*] to take, capture
Ⓑ VI [1] (*trabajando*) to earn; **no gano para comprar un piso** I don't earn enough to buy a flat; ✦*MODISMO* **no ganamos para sustos** we have nothing but trouble
[2] (*en competición, guerra*) to win; **~on por cuatro a dos** they won four-two; **~on por 40 votos** they won by 40 votes; **lo importante no es ~** winning isn't the most important thing; **nuestras ideas terminaron ganando** our ideas won out in the end; **dejarse ~** (*con trampas*) to lose on purpose; **se deja ~ por el niño** he lets the kid beat him
[3] (= *mejorar*) to benefit, improve; **la película ~ía mucho si se cortase** the film would greatly benefit from being cut, the film would be greatly improved if it was cut; **hemos ganado con el cambio** we've greatly benefited from the change; **ha ganado mucho en salud** his health has greatly improved; **su juego ha ganado en confianza** her play has become more confident; **salir ganando** to do well; **saldrás ganando** you'll do well out of it; **salí ganando con la venta del coche** I did well out of the sale of the car
Ⓒ **ganarse** VPR [1] [+ *afecto, confianza*] to win; **ha sabido ~se el afecto de todos** she has managed to win everyone's affection; **~se la confianza de algn** to win sb's trust; **~se las antipatías de algn** to make oneself unpopular with sb
[2] [+ *sueldo*] to earn; **~se la vida** to earn a living; **se lo ha ganado** he has earned it *o* deserves it; **se ganó a pulso el título de campeón** he became champion the hard way; **¡te la vas a ~!*** you're for it!*
[3] (*LAm*) (= *acercarse*) to go off; **~se a la cama** to go off to bed; **~se hasta la casa** to get to the house; **el caballo se ganó para el bosque** the horse moved off towards the wood, the horse made for the wood
[4] (= *refugiarse*) to take refuge; **se ganó en la iglesia** he took refuge in the church

gancha‡ SF hash*, pot‡

ganchera SF (*Cono Sur*) matchmaker

ganchero/a SM/F (*Cono Sur*) (= *ayudante*) helper, assistant; (= *factótum*) odd-job man/odd-job woman

ganchete SM ✦*MODISMOS* **mirar al ~** (*Caribe**) to look out of the corner of one's eye (at); **ir de ~** (*LAm*) to go arm-in-arm

ganchillo SM [1] (= *gancho*) crochet hook
[2] (= *labor*) crochet work; **una colcha de ~** a crocheted quilt; **hacer (labores de) ~** to crochet

ganchito® SM *light cheese-flavoured snack,* ≈ Wotsit®

gancho SM [1] (= *garfio*) hook; [*de árbol*] stump; (*Agr*) shepherd's crook; ✦*MODISMOS* **echar el ~ a algn*** to hook sb, capture sb; **estar en ~s** (*LAm‡*) to be hooked on drugs* ► **gancho de carnicero** butcher's hook ► **gancho de remolque** towing hook, trailer hitch
[2] (*LAm*) (= *horquilla*) hairpin; (*para la ropa*) hanger; (*CAm*) (= *imperdible*) safety pin
[3] (*) (= *atractivo sexual*) sex appeal; (= *atractivo popular*) pulling power; **una chica con mucho ~** a girl with lots of sex appeal; **un actor con mucho ~** an actor with great pulling-power; **el nuevo delantero tiene ~** the new forward is a crowd-puller; **esta música tiene ~** this music's really got something; **lo usan de ~ para atraer a la gente** they use it as an attraction to pull the crowds in
[4] [*de timador*] accomplice
[5] (*Boxeo*) (= *golpe*) hook; **un ~ hacia arriba** an uppercut
[6] (*LAm*) (= *ayuda*) help; (= *protección*) protection; ✦*MODISMO* **hacer ~** (*Cono Sur**) to lend a hand
[7] (*Andes*) lady's saddle

ganchoso ADJ, **ganchudo** ADJ hooked, curved

gandalla‡ SMF (*Méx*) [1] (= *vagabundo*) tramp, bum (*EEUU**), hobo (*EEUU*)
[2] (= *arribista*) upstart

gandido ADJ (*Andes*) greedy

gandinga SF (*Caribe*) [1] (*Culin*) thick stew
[2] (*) (= *apatía*) sloth, apathy
[3] (= *vergüenza*) **tener poca ~** to have no sense of shame

gandola SF (*LAm*) articulated truck

gandul(a) Ⓐ ADJ (= *holgazán*) idle, slack; (= *inútil*) good-for-nothing
Ⓑ SM/F (= *holgazán*) idler, slacker; (= *inútil*) good-for-nothing

gandula* SF (*Hist*) law on vagrancy

gandulear ▸conjug 1a◂ VI to idle, loaf around

gandulería SF idleness, loafing

gandulitis SF INV (*hum*) congenital laziness

gane SM (*CAm Dep*) win, victory; **llevarse** *o* **lograr el ~** to win

gang SM (*pl* **gangs**) gang

ganga SF [1] (*Com*) bargain; **¡una verdadera ~!** a genuine bargain!; **precios de ~** bargain prices, giveaway prices
[2] (= *golpe de suerte*) windfall; (= *cosa fácil*) cinch*, gift*; **esto es una ~** this is a gift*
[3] (*Méx**) (= *sarcasmo*) taunt, jeer

Ganges SM **el ~** the Ganges

ganglio SM [1] (*Anat*) [*de células nerviosas*] ganglion; (*linfático*) lymph node
[2] **ganglios‡** [*de mujer*] tits‡

gangosear ▸conjug 1a◂ VI (*Andes, Cono Sur*) [1] (* *pey*) to talk through one's nose, whine
[2] = **ganguear**

gangoseo SM (*Andes, Cono Sur*) = **gangueo**

gangoso ADJ nasal, twanging

gangrena SF gangrene

gangrenar ▸conjug 1a◂ Ⓐ VT [1] (*Med*) to make gangrenous, cause gangrene in
[2] (*Pol*) to infect, destroy
Ⓑ **gangrenarse** VPR to become gangrenous

gangrenoso ADJ gangrenous

gángster ['ganster] SM (*pl* **gángsters** ['ganster]) gangster; (= *pistolero*) gunman

gangsteril ADJ gangster *antes de s*

gangsterismo SM gangsterism

ganguear ▸conjug 1a◂ VI to talk with a nasal accent, speak with a twang

gangueo SM nasal accent, twang

ganoso ADJ [1] (= *afanoso*) anxious, keen; **~ de hacer algo** anxious to do sth, keen to do sth
[2] (*Cono Sur*) [*caballo*] spirited, fiery

gansada* SF (= *acto*) stupid thing (to do), piece of stupidity; (= *broma*) lark, caper*; **decir ~s** to talk nonsense; **hacer ~s** to play the fool, clown around

gansear* ▸conjug 1a◂ VI to play the fool, clown around

ganso/a Ⓐ ADJ (*) [1] (= *grande*) huge, hefty
[2] (= *gandul*) lazy
[3] (= *estúpido*) idiotic; (*pey*) (= *bromista*) play-acting; **¡no seas ~!** don't be an idiot!
[4] (= *atractivo*) hunky*, dishy*; *ver tb* **pasta 5**
Ⓑ SM/F (*) (= *torpe*) idiot, dimwit*; (= *rústico*) country bumpkin, hick (*EEUU**)
Ⓒ SM (= *ave*) (*gen*) goose; (= *macho*) gander; ✦*MODISMO* **hacer el ~** to play the fool, clown around ► **ganso salvaje** wild goose

gánster SM (*pl* **gánsters**) gangster; (= *pistolero*) gunman

Gante SM Ghent

ganzúa Ⓐ SF (= *gancho*) picklock, skeleton key
Ⓑ SMF (= *ladrón*) burglar, thief; (= *sonsacador*) inquisitive person

gañán SM farmhand, labourer, laborer (*EEUU*)

gañido SM [*de perro*] yelp, howl; [*de pájaro*] croak; [*de persona*] wheeze

gañir ▸conjug 3h◂ VI [*perro*] to yelp, howl; [*pájaro*] to croak; [*persona*] to wheeze

gañón* SM, **gañote** SM throat, gullet

gapo‡ SM **echar un ~** to gob‡, spit

GAR SM ABR (*Esp*) (= **Grupo Antiterrorista Rural**) *anti-terrorist branch of the Civil Guard*

garabatear ▸conjug 1a◂ Ⓐ VT to scribble, scrawl
Ⓑ VI 1 (*al escribir*) to scribble, scrawl
2 (= *andar con rodeos*) to beat about the bush
3 (*con gancho*) (= *utilizar*) to use a hook; (= *echar*) to throw out a hook

garabato SM 1 (= *dibujo*) doodle; (= *escritura*) scribble; **una hoja cubierta de ~s ininteligibles** a page full of unintelligible scribbles; **echar un ~** (= *firmar*) to scrawl a signature; **hacer ~s** (= *dibujar*) to doodle; (= *escribir*) to scribble
2 (= *gancho*) hook; (*Náut*) grappling iron; (*Caribe*) long forked pole ➤ **garabato de carnicero** meat hook
3 (*Caribe**) (= *flaco*) beanpole*, string bean (*EEUU**)
4 (*Cono Sur*) (= *palabrota*) swearword; **echar ~s** to swear

garabina SF 1 (*Andes*) (= *bagatela*) trifle, bagatelle; (= *bisutería*) cheap finery
2 (*Caribe*) (= *crisálida*) chrysalis

garabito SM 1 [*de mercado*] market stall
2 (*Cono Sur*) (= *vagabundo*) tramp, bum (*EEUU**), hobo (*EEUU*)

garabullo†‡ SM five pesetas

garaje SM garage; **"duerme en ~"** kept in a garage; **una plaza de ~** a parking space; ✦**MODISMO el ~ La Estrella** (*hum*) the street

garajista SMF (= *dueño*) garage owner; (= *trabajador*) garage attendant

garambaina SF 1 (= *adorno*) cheap finery, tawdry finery
2 (= *carácter chillón*) gaudiness
3 **garambainas** (= *muecas*) affected grimaces; (= *ademanes afectados*) absurd mannerisms; **¡déjate de ~s!** stop your nonsense!
4 **garambainas** (= *escritura*) scribbles

garambetas* SFPL (*Caribe*) 1 = **garambaina 1, 3**
2 **hacer ~** to pull faces

garandumba SF (*Arg*) flatboat, flat river boat

garante Ⓐ ADJ responsible, guaranteeing
Ⓑ SMF (*Fin*) guarantor, surety

▼ **garantía** SF 1 [*de producto*] guarantee, warranty; **bajo** *o* **en ~** under guarantee *o* warranty; **de máxima ~** absolutely guaranteed
2 (= *seguridad*) pledge, security; (= *compromiso*) undertaking, guarantee; **~ de trabajo** job security; **dar ~s a algn** to give sb guarantees; **suspender las ~s (ciudadanas)** to suspend civil rights ➤ **garantías constitucionales** constitutional guarantees
3 (*Jur*) warranty ➤ **garantía escrita** express warranty ➤ **garantía implícita** implied warranty

garantir ▸conjug 3a; defectivo◂ VT 1 (= *garantizar*) to guarantee
2 (*Andes, Caribe, Cono Sur*) (= *asegurar*) to guarantee, assure

garantizadamente ADV genuinely, authentically

garantizado ADJ guaranteed; (= *auténtico*) genuine, authentic

garantizar ▸conjug 1f◂ VT 1 (= *responder de*) [+ *producto, crédito*] to guarantee; **la lavadora está garantizada por dos años** the washing machine is guaranteed for two years, the washing machine has a two-year guarantee; **garantizamos la calidad de nuestros productos** we guarantee the quality of our products
2 (= *avalar*) [+ *persona*] to vouch for
3 (= *asegurar*) to guarantee; **le garantizo que lo recibirá antes del jueves** I guarantee you'll receive it before Thursday; **me van a oír ¡te lo garantizo!** they'll listen to me, I can guarantee it!

garañón SM 1 (*Zool*) (= *asno*) stud jackass; (*LAm*) (= *semental*) stallion
2 (*Cono Sur*) (= *persona*) brothel keeper

garapiña SF 1 (*Culin*) sugar icing, sugar coating
2 (*LAm*) (= *bebida*) iced pineapple drink
3 (*Méx*) (= *robo*) theft

garapiñado ADJ **almendra garapiñada** sugared almond

garapiñar ▸conjug 1a◂ VT 1 [+ *granizado*] to freeze
2 [+ *pastel*] to ice, coat with sugar
3 [+ *fruta*] to candy
4 [+ *nata*] to clot

garapiñera SF ice-cream freezer

garapullo SM (= *rehilete*) dart; (*Taur*) banderilla

garata* SF (*Caribe*) fight, brawl

garatusas SFPL **hacer ~ a algn** to coax sb, wheedle sb

garba SF sheaf

garbanzo SM 1 (= *legumbre*) chickpea; ✦**MODISMOS ganarse los ~s** to earn one's living; **ser el ~ negro de la familia** to be the black sheep of the family
2 ✦**MODISMO de ~** (= *corriente*) ordinary, unpretentious; **gente de ~** humble folk, ordinary people, regular people (*EEUU*)

garbear ▸conjug 1a◂ Ⓐ VT (*) (= *robar*) to pinch*, swipe‡
Ⓑ VI 1 (= *afectar garbo*) to make a show, show off
2 (= *robar*) to steal (*for a living*)
3 (= *buscarse la vida*) to get along, rub along
Ⓒ **garbearse** VPR to get along, rub along

garbeo* SM **darse** *o* **pegarse un ~** (= *dar un paseo*) to go for a stroll; (= *ir por ahí*) to go out, go out and about; (*en coche*) to go for a ride*, go for a spin*

garbera SF stook, shock

garbí SM south-west wind

garbillar ▸conjug 1a◂ VT (*Agr*) to sift, sieve; (*Min*) to sift, screen, riddle

garbillo SM (*para grano*) sieve; (*para mineral*) screen, riddle

garbo SM 1 (= *elegancia*) grace, elegance; (= *porte*) graceful bearing; (= *aire*) jauntiness; [*de mujer*] glamour, glamor (*EEUU*); [*de escrito*] style, stylishness; **hacer algo con ~** to do sth with grace and ease *o* with style; **andar con ~** to walk gracefully; **¡qué ~!** she's so graceful
2 (= *brío*) agility; **empezó a limpiar el cuarto con mucho ~** she went whizzing round the room cleaning up
3 (= *largueza*) magnanimity, generosity

garbosamente ADV 1 (= *con elegancia*) gracefully, elegantly; (*al andar*) jauntily; (= *con estilo*) stylishly
2 (= *con generosidad*) generously

garboso ADJ 1 (= *elegante*) graceful, elegant; [*andar*] jaunty; (= *encantador*) glamorous, alluring; (= *con estilo*) stylish
2 (= *desinteresado*) generous, magnanimous

garceta SF egret

garciamarquiano ADJ *of or relating to Gabriel García Márquez*

garcilla SF little egret ➤ **garcilla bueyera** cattle egret

garçon [gar'son] SM **con pelo a lo ~** with bobbed hair, with hair in a boyish style; *ver tb* **garzón**

gardenia SF gardenia

garduña SF marten

garduño/a SM/F sneak thief

garete SM **irse al ~** [*barco*] to be adrift; (*) [*plan, proyecto etc*] to fall through, bomb (*EEUU**); [*empresa*] to go bust*

garfa SF claw

garfada SF clawing, scratching

garfil* SM (*Méx*) cop*

garfio SM 1 (= *gancho*) hook
2 (*Téc*) (= *arpeo*) grappling iron, claw
3 (*Alpinismo*) (= *pico*) climbing iron

gargajear ▸conjug 1a◂ VI to spit up phlegm, hawk

gargajo SM phlegm, sputum; **echar un ~** to spit up phlegm, hawk

garganta SF 1 (*Anat*) throat, gullet; (= *cuello*) neck; **me duele la ~** I have a sore throat; ✦**MODISMOS le tengo atravesado en la ~** he sticks in my gullet; **mojar la ~** to wet one's whistle*; **tener el agua a la ~** to be in great danger
2 [*del pie*] instep
3 (*Mús*) singing voice; **tener buena ~** to have a good singing voice
4 [*de botella*] neck
5 (*Geog*) (= *barranco*) ravine, gorge; (= *desfiladero*) narrow pass
6 (*Arquit*) [*de columna*] shaft

gargantear ▸conjug 1a◂ VI to warble, quaver, trill

garganteo SM warble, quaver, trill

gargantilla SF choker, necklace

gargantuesco ADJ gargantuan

gárgara SF gargle, gargling; **hacer ~s** to gargle; ✦**MODISMO mandar a algn a hacer ~s*** to tell sb to go to hell; **¡vete a hacer ~s!*** go to blazes!

gargarear ▸conjug 1a◂ VI (*Andes, CAm, Cono Sur*) to gargle

gargarismo SM 1 (= *acto*) gargling
2 (= *líquido*) gargle, gargling solution

gargarizar ▸conjug 1f◂ VI to gargle

gárgol SM groove

gárgola SF gargoyle

garguero SM (= *garganta*) gullet; (= *esófago*) windpipe

garifo ADJ 1 (†) (= *elegante*) spruce, elegant, natty*
2 (*Cono Sur*) (= *astuto*) sharp
3 (*Andes*) (= *engreído*) stuck-up*
4 (*CAm*) (= *hambriento*) hungry
5 **estar ~** (*Andes*) to be broke*

gariga SF (*Méx*) drizzle

garita SF 1 [*de centinela*] sentry box; [*de conserje*] porter's lodge; (*LAm*) [*de policía de tráfico*] stand, box ➤ **garita de control** checkpoint ➤ **garita de señales** (*Ferro*) signal box
2 (= *caseta*) cabin, box
3 [*de camión*] cab

garitea SF (*Andes*) river flatboat

➤ LENGUA Y USO: garantía 2 42.1

garitero/a SM/F (= *dueño*) keeper of a gaming house; (= *jugador*) gambler

garito SM [1] (= *club*) nightclub, nightspot; [*de juego*] gaming house, gambling den
[2] (= *ganancias del juego*) gambling profits *pl*, winnings *pl*

garla SF talk, chatter

garlador(a) Ⓐ ADJ garrulous
Ⓑ SM/F chatterer, great talker

garlito SM [1] (= *red*) fish trap
[2] (= *celada*) snare, trap; **caer en el ~** to fall into the trap; **coger a algn en el ~** to catch sb in the act

garlopa SF jack plane

garnacha SF [1] (= *uva*) garnacha grape; (= *vino*) garnacha (*sweet wine from garnacha grape*)
[2] (*Jur, Hist*) (= *vestidura*) gown, robe; (= *persona*) judge
[3] (*Méx Culin*) *tortilla with meat filling*
[4] ✦*MODISMO* **a la ~** (*CAm**) violently; **¡ni de ~!** (*Caribe**) not on your life!
[5] (*Chile*) (= *ventaja*) advantage, edge

garnachear ▸conjug 1a◂ VT (*Cono Sur*) (= *llevar ventaja a*) to have the edge over

garnucho SM (*Méx*) tap, rap on the nose

Garona SM **el (Río) ~** the Garonne

garpar‡ ▸conjug 1a◂ VT (*Cono Sur*) to pay, fork out*

garra SF [1] (= *pata*) [*de animal*] claw; [*de águila*] talon; (*) [*de persona*] hand, paw*; ✦*MODISMOS* **echar la ~ a algn*** to nab sb*, seize sb; **estar como una ~** (*Andes, Cono Sur*) to be as thin as a rake*
[2] **garras** (= *dominio*) clutches; ✦*MODISMO* **caer en las ~s de algn** to fall into sb's clutches
[3] (*Téc*) claw, hook; (*Mec*) clutch ► **garra de seguridad** safety clutch
[4] (= *fuerza*) bite; (*Dep*) sharpness, edge; **esa canción no tiene ~** that song has no bite to it
[5] (*Méx**) muscular strength
[6] (*Chile**) strip of old leather
[7] **garras** (*Méx**) bits, pieces; ✦*MODISMO* **no hay cuero sin ~s*** nothing is ever perfect
[8] (*Andes*) (= *bolsa*) leather bag

garrafa SF [1] (= *garrafón*) demijohn; (*para agua*) *large glass water container*; **de ~*** (*pey*) [*ginebra, vino*] cheap, dodgy*
[2] (= *licorera*) decanter
[3] (*Arg*) [*de gas*] cylinder

garrafal ADJ (= *enorme*) enormous, terrific; [*error*] monumental, terrible

garrafón SM carboy, demijohn

garrancha* SF [1] (= *espada*) sword
[2] (*Col*) (= *gancho*) hook

garrapata SF [1] (*Zool*) tick
[2] (*Mil**) disabled horse, useless horse

garrapatear ▸conjug 1a◂ VI to scribble, scrawl

garrapatero SM (= *ave*) cowbird, buffalo bird; (*LAm*) tick-eater

garrapaticida Ⓐ ADJ pesticidal
Ⓑ SM insecticide, tick-killing agent

garrapato SM = **garabato 1, 2**

garrapiñada SF sugared almond

garrapiñado ADJ **almendra garrapiñada** sugared almond

garrapiñar ▸conjug 1a◂ VT = **garapiñar**

garrear ▸conjug 1a◂ (*Cono Sur*) Ⓐ VT [1] [+ *animal*] to skin the feet of
[2] (*) (= *robar*) to pinch*
Ⓑ VI (*) to sponge*, live off others

garreo* SM **es de puro ~** (*Cono Sur*) it's a piece of cake*

garrete SM (*Andes, CAm, Cono Sur*) [*de caballo*] hock; [*de persona*] back of the knee

garrido ADJ (*liter*) [1] (= *galano*) neat, smart
[2] (= *atractivo*) [*hombre*] handsome; [*mujer*] pretty

garroba SF carob bean

garrobo SM (*CAm*) (= *lagarto*) iguana; (= *caimán*) small alligator

garrocha SF (*Agr*) goad; (*Taur*) spear; (*Dep*) vaulting pole

garrón SM [1] (*Zool*) [*de ave*] spur; [*de otros animales*] paw; (= *talón*) heel
[2] [*de carne*] shank
[3] (*Arg*) hock; ✦*MODISMO* **vivir de ~** to sponge*, live off others
[4] (*Bot*) snag, spur

garronear* ▸conjug 1a◂ VI (*Arg*) to sponge*, live off others

garrota SF (= *palo*) stick, club; [*de pastor*] crook

garrotazo SM blow with a stick *o* club

garrote SM [1] (= *palo*) stick, club; **la política del ~ y la zanahoria** the carrot-and-stick approach
[2] (*Med*) tourniquet
[3] (*Jur*) (= *ejecución*) garrotte; **dar ~ a algn** to garrotte sb
[4] (*Méx Aut*) brake; ✦*MODISMO* **darse ~*** to check o.s., hold o.s. back

garrotear ▸conjug 1a◂ VT (*LAm*) to club, cudgel

garrotero/a Ⓐ ADJ (*Caribe, Cono Sur**) stingy*
Ⓑ SM/F [1] (*Méx Ferro*) guard, brakeman (*EEUU*)
[2] (*Andes, Cono Sur*) (= *matón*) bully, tough*; (= *pendenciero*) brawler, troublemaker
[3] (*Caribe*) (= *prestamista*) moneylender

garrotillo SM [1] (= *difteria*) croup
[2] (*Cono Sur*) (= *granizada*) summer hail

garrucha SF pulley

garrudo ADJ [1] (*Méx*) (= *forzudo*) tough, muscular
[2] (*Andes*) [*vaca*] terribly thin

garrulería SF chatter

garrulidad SF garrulousness

garrulo/a Ⓐ ADJ loutish
Ⓑ SM/F lout

gárrulo ADJ [1] (= *hablador*) garrulous
[2] [*pájaro*] twittering; [*agua*] babbling, murmuring; [*viento*] noisy

garúa SF [1] (*LAm*) (= *llovizna*) drizzle
[2] (*Caribe*) (= *alboroto*) row, din

garuar ▸conjug 1e◂ VI (*LAm*) to drizzle; ✦*MODISMO* **¡que le garúe fino!** I wish you luck!, I hope it keeps fine for you!

garubar ▸conjug 1a◂ VI (*Cono Sur*) = **garuar**

garufa* SF **ir de ~** (*Cono Sur*) to go on a spree

garuga SF (*Cono Sur*) = **garúa**

garugar ▸conjug 1h◂ VI (*Cono Sur*) = **garuar**

garulla Ⓐ SF [1] (= *uvas*) loose grapes *pl*
[2] (= *gentío*) mob, rabble
Ⓑ SMF (*) urchin, rascal

garullada* SF mob, rabble

garza SF [1] (*tb* **~ real**) heron ► **garza imperial** purple heron
[2] (*Chile*) lager glass, beer glass

garzo ADJ (*liter*) [*ojos*] blue, bluish; [*persona*] blue-eyed

garzón/ona SM/F (*Chile, Uru*) waiter/waitress

gas SM [1] (= *combustible*) gas; **una cocina de ~** a gas cooker; **esta cerveza tiene mucho ~** this beer is very gassy *o* fizzy; **asfixiar con ~ a algn** to gas sb; **agua (mineral) con ~** sparkling (mineral) water; **una bebida con ~** a fizzy drink; **agua (mineral) sin ~** still (mineral) water; **una bebida sin ~** a still drink ► **gas butano** butane, butane gas ► **gas ciudad** town gas ► **gas de (efecto) invernadero** greenhouse gas ► **gas del alumbrado** coal gas ► **gas de los pantanos** marsh gas ► **gas hilarante** laughing gas ► **gases lacrimógenos** tear gas *sing* ► **gas inerte** inert gas ► **gas licuado** liquefied gas; (*Chile*) (*para uso doméstico*) Calor gas® ► **gas mostaza** mustard gas ► **gas natural** natural gas ► **gas nervioso** nerve gas ► **gas noble** noble gas, rare gas ► **gas pobre** producer gas ► **gas propano** propane, propane gas ► **gas tóxico** poison gas
[2] (*CAm, Méx*) (= *gasolina*) petrol, gas (*EEUU*); **darle ~*** to step on the gas*; ✦*MODISMOS* **a medio ~**: **el equipo jugó a medio ~** the team played with the foot off the pedal; **estar ~** (*CAm hum*) to be head over heels in love; **a todo ~** (*Esp Aut*) full out, flat out*; [*trabajar*] flat out*; **el coche iba a todo ~** the car was going full out *o* flat out*; **tenían el aire acondicionado a todo ~** they had the air conditioning full on; **tuvimos que terminarlo a todo ~** we had to work flat out to get it finished*; **la maquinaria electoral funciona ya a todo ~** the electoral machine is now in full swing; **perder ~**: **el equipo comenzó la temporada con fuerza pero ha ido perdiendo ~** the team began the season well but has been losing steam; **los hinchas fueron perdiendo ~ a medida que transcurría el partido** the fans gradually lost enthusiasm as the match progressed
[3] **gases** (= *emanaciones perjudiciales*) fumes; **los ~es tóxicos que se emiten a la atmósfera** the toxic *o* poisonous fumes released into the atmosphere ► **gases de escape** exhaust fumes; **emisiones de ~es de escape** exhaust emissions
[4] **gases** (= *flatulencias*) wind *sing*, flatulence *sing*, gas *sing* (*EEUU*); **tener ~es** to have wind, have gas (*EEUU*)

gasa SF [1] (= *tela*) gauze; [*de luto*] crêpe
[2] (*Med*) gauze, lint; **una ~** a dressing
[3] (= *pañal*) nappy, diaper (*EEUU*)

Gascuña SF Gascony

gaseado ADJ carbonated, aerated

gasear ▸conjug 1a◂ VT to gas, kill with gas

gaseoducto SM gas pipeline

gaseosa SF [1] (= *bebida efervescente*) lemonade
[2] (= *cualquier refresco*) fizzy drink, soda (*EEUU*)

gaseoso ADJ [1] [*estado, densidad, mezcla*] gaseous
[2] [*bebida*] sparkling, fizzy

gásfiter SMF (*pl* **gásfiters**) (*Andes, Cono Sur*) plumber

gasfitería SF (*Andes, Cono Sur*) plumber's (shop)

gasfitero/a SM/F (*Andes, Cono Sur*) plumber

gasificación SF [1] (*Quím*) gasification
[2] [*de ciudad*] supply of piped gas (**de** to)

gasista Ⓐ ADJ gas *antes de s*; **industria ~** gas industry
Ⓑ SMF gas fitter

gasístico ADJ gas *antes de s*

gasoducto SM gas pipeline

gasofa‡ SF juice*, petrol, gas(oline) (*EEUU*)

gas-oil [ga'soil] SM diesel oil

gasóleo SM diesel oil ► **gasóleo B** red diesel ► **gasóleo de calefacción** central heating oil

gasolero SM diesel-powered car

gasolina SF 1 (*Aut*) petrol, gas(oline) (*EEUU*); **echar ~** (*a un vehículo*) to put petrol in; **repostar ~** (*lit*) to fill up with petrol; (‡) (*fig*) to have a drink ► **gasolina con plomo** leaded petrol ► **gasolina de alto octanaje** high octane petrol ► **gasolina de aviación** aviation spirit, aviation fuel ► **gasolina extra** four-star petrol ► **gasolina normal** two-star petrol ► **gasolina sin plomo** unleaded (petrol) ► **gasolina súper** four-star petrol
2 (*Caribe*) (= *gasolinera*) petrol-station, gas station (*EEUU*)

gasolinera SF 1 (*Aut*) petrol station, gas station (*EEUU*)
2 (*Náut*) motorboat

gasolinero/a SM/F (= *dueño*) petrol station owner, gas station owner (*EEUU*); (= *empleado*) petrol pump attendant, gas station attendant (*EEUU*)

gasómetro SM gasometer

gásquet SM (*pl* **gásquets**) (*LAm*) gasket

gastable ADJ expendable

gastado ADJ 1 (= *desgastado*) [*ropa, neumático, superficie*] worn; **tenía el uniforme ~ y sucio** his uniform was worn and dirty; **alfombras de lana muy gastadas** threadbare woollen rugs; **las páginas del libro estaban muy gastadas por el uso** the pages of the book were well-thumbed
2 (= *trillado*) [*metáfora*] stale, hackneyed; [*broma*] old, stale; **un político ~** a washed-up politician*
3 [*pilas*] dead

gastador(a) Ⓐ ADJ extravagant; **es muy ~a** she's very extravagant, she's a big spender
Ⓑ SM/F 1 **es un ~** he's very extravagant, he's a big spender
2 (*Mil*) sapper

gastar ▸conjug 1a◂ Ⓐ VT 1 [+ *dinero*] to spend (**en** on); **han gastado un dineral en el arreglo del coche** they've spent a fortune on fixing the car
2 (= *consumir*) [+ *gasolina, electricidad, agua*] to use; **un radiocasete como éste gasta más pilas** a radio cassette player like this goes through *o* uses more batteries; **he gastado todas las velas que tenía** I've used up all the candles I had
3 (= *desgastar*) [+ *ropa, zapato*] to wear out; [+ *tacones*] to wear down
4 (= *malgastar*) to waste; **~ palabras** to waste one's breath; *ver tb* **saliva**
5 (= *llevar*) [+ *ropa, gafas*] to wear; [+ *barba*] to have; **antes no gastaba gafas** he didn't use to wear glasses; **¿qué número (de zapatos) gasta?** what size (shoes) do you take?; **¿qué talla gasta?** what size are you?
6 [+ *broma*] to play (**a** on); **~ una broma pesada a algn** to play a practical joke *o* a hoax on sb
7 **gastarlas** (*Esp**): **no le repliques, que ya sabes como las gasta** don't answer him back, you know what he's like when he gets angry*
Ⓑ VI 1 (= *gastar dinero*) **a todos nos gusta ~** we all like spending money
2 (= *consumir*) **este coche gasta poco** this car uses very little petrol; **una bombilla normal apenas gasta** a normal light bulb uses hardly any electricity
Ⓒ **gastarse** VPR 1 (= *consumirse*) [*pilas*] to run out; [*vela*] to burn down; **así se gastan antes las pilas** the batteries run out sooner that way
2 (= *desgastarse*) [*suelas, neumáticos*] to wear, wear out; [*tacones*] to wear down
3 (*Esp*) (*enfático*) [+ *dinero*] to spend; **se lo gasta todo en música** he spends all his money on music; **se gastó 400 euros sólo en zapatos** she got through *o* spent 400 euros just on shoes
4 (*enfático*) (= *tener*) **¡vaya genio que te gastas!** what a filthy temper you've got!; **es increíble la intolerancia que se gastan algunas personas** it's amazing how intolerant some people are; **¡vaya humos se gasta la señora!** she's so stuck up!; **hay que tener cuidado con las bromas que se gasta ése** you have to watch out for the jokes he plays on people

Gasteiz SM Vitoria

gasto SM 1 [*de dinero*] **la inversión nos supondría un ~ de varios millones** the investment would involve an expense *o* expenditure of several million; **tenemos que reducir el ~** we must cut costs *o* spending; **no tenías que haberte metido en tanto ~** you needn't have spent so much ► **gasto militar** military spending, military expenditure ► **gasto público** public spending, public expenditure ► **gasto sanitario** health spending, health expenditure ► **gasto social** welfare spending, welfare expenditure
2 **gastos** expenses; **este dinero es para tus ~s** this money is for your expenses; **este mes he tenido muchos ~s** I have had a lot of expenses this month; **un viaje con todos los ~s pagados** an all-expenses-paid trip; **cubrir ~s** to cover (one's) costs ► **gastos administrativos** administrative costs ► **gastos bancarios** bank charges ► **gastos comerciales** business expenses ► **gastos corrientes** (*en empresa*) running costs; (*en la Administración*) revenue expenditure *sing* ► **gastos de administración** administrative costs ► **gastos de comunidad** service charges ► **gastos de conservación** maintenance costs ► **gastos de correo** postal charges ► **gastos de defensa** defence spending *sing*, defense spending *sing* (*EEUU*) ► **gastos de desplazamiento** (*por viaje*) travelling expenses, traveling expenses (*EEUU*); (*por mudanza*) relocation allowance *sing* ► **gastos de distribución** distribution costs ► **gastos de entrega** delivery charge *sing* ► **gastos de envío** postage and packing *sing*, postage and handling *sing* (*EEUU*) ► **gastos de explotación** operating costs ► **gastos de flete** freight charges ► **gastos de mantenimiento** maintenance costs ► **gastos de representación** entertainment allowance *sing* ► **gastos de servicio** service charge *sing* ► **gastos de tramitación** handling charge *sing* ► **gastos de transporte** [*de personal*] travelling expenses, traveling expenses (*EEUU*); [*de mercancías*] freight charges ► **gastos de viaje** travelling expenses, traveling expenses (*EEUU*) ► **gastos fijos** fixed charges ► **gastos generales** overheads, overhead *sing* (*EEUU*) ► **gastos menores (de caja)** petty cash expenses ► **gastos operacionales** operating costs ► **gastos vendidos** accrued charges
3 [*de gas*] flow, rate of flow

gastón¹‡ SM (*CAm*) (= *diarrea*) the runs‡

gastón²* ADJ free-spending

gastoso ADJ extravagant, wasteful

gástrico ADJ gastric

gastritis SF INV gastritis

gastroenteritis SF INV gastroenteritis

gastronomía SF gastronomy

gastronómico ADJ gastronomic

gastrónomo/a SM/F gastronome, gourmet

gastroplastia SF gastroplasty

gastrópodo SM gastropod

gata SF 1 (*Chile, Perú Aut*) jack
2 **a gatas** 2·1 **andar a ~s** to crawl; **subió las escaleras a ~s** he crawled up the stairs; **el niño entró andando a ~s** the baby crawled in; **en este juego tenéis que andar a ~s** in this game you have to crawl on all fours
2·2 (*Cono Sur**) (= *apenas*) barely, by the skin of one's teeth
3 (*Meteo*) hill cloud
4 (= *agujetas*) **tener ~** to ache all over
5 ✦*MODISMOS* **echar la ~** (*CAm**) ◊ **soltar la ~** (*Perú**) to lift*, steal; *ver tb* **gato**

gatada SF 1 (= *movimiento*) *movement o act typical of a cat*
2 (= *arañazos*) scratching, clawing
3 (= *trampa*) artful dodge, sly trick

gatazo* SM ✦*MODISMO* **dar el ~** (*LAm*) to look younger than one is, not to show one's age

gateado Ⓐ ADJ 1 (= *gatuno*) catlike, feline
2 [*mármol*] striped, veined
Ⓑ SM 1 (= *movimiento*) (*al gatear*) crawl, crawling; (*al subir*) climb, climbing
2 (= *arañazos*) scratching, clawing
3 (*Caribe*) hard veined wood (*used in cabinet-making*)

gateamiento SM = **gateado B1, 2**

gatear ▸conjug 1a◂ Ⓐ VI 1 (= *andar a gatas*) to crawl; (= *trepar*) to climb, clamber (**por** up)
2 (*LAm*) to be on the prowl
Ⓑ VT 1 (= *arañar*) to scratch, claw
2 (*) (= *hurtar*) to pinch*, steal
3 (*CAm, Méx**) (= *ligar*) to try to pick up*; (= *seducir*) to seduce

gateo SM crawling

gatera¹ SF 1 (*para gato*) catflap
2 (*Náut*) cat hole; *ver tb* **gatero**

gatera² SF (*Andes*) (= *verdulera*) market woman, stallholder; *ver tb* **gatero**

gatería SF 1 (= *gatos*) cats *pl*, collection of cats
2 (= *pandilla*) gang of louts
3 (= *cualidad*) false modesty

gatero/a Ⓐ ADJ fond of cats
Ⓑ SM/F cat lover; *ver tb* **gatera**

gatillar ▸conjug 1a◂ VT to cock

gatillero SM (*Méx*) hired gun(man), hitman

gatillo SM 1 [*de arma*] trigger; **apretar el ~** to pull *o* press *o* squeeze the trigger

2 (= *herramienta*) [*de dentista*] dental forceps; (*Téc*) clamp
3 (*Zool*) nape of the neck
4 (*) (= *ratero*) young pickpocket, young thief

gatito/a SM/F (*gen*) kitten; (*como término cariñoso*) pussycat

gato¹/a Ⓐ SM/F 1 (*Zool*) (*gen*) cat; (*especificando el sexo*) tomcat/she-cat; **"El ~ con botas"** "Puss in Boots"; ✦*MODISMOS* **dar a algn ~ por liebre** to con sb*; **te han dado ~ por liebre** you've been had *o* conned*, you've been done*; **cuatro ~s**: **no había más que cuatro ~s** there was hardly anyone *o* a soul there; **este programa sólo lo ven cuatro ~s** hardly anyone watches this programme, this programme is only watched by a handful of people; **no son más que cuatro ~s en la oficina** there's only a handful of people in the office; **aquí hay ~ encerrado** there's something fishy (going on) here; **jugar al ~ y al ratón con algn** to play cat and mouse with sb, play a cat-and-mouse game with sb; **lavarse como los ~s** to give o.s. a quick wash; **llevarse el ~ al agua** to win the day, pull it off*; **estar para el ~** (*Chile**) to be in a terrible state*; **esta gripe me tiene para el ~** I'm in a really terrible state with this flu*; **ser ~ viejo** to be an old hand; ✦*REFRANES* **el ~ escaldado del agua fría huye** once bitten twice shy; **de noche todos los ~s son pardos** everything looks the same in the dark ► **gato callejero** stray cat, alley cat (*esp EEUU*) ► **gato de algalia** civet cat ► **gato de Angora** Angora cat ► **gato montés** wild cat ► **gato romano** tabby cat ► **gato siamés** Siamese cat; *ver tb* **defender B2**, **pie 1**
2 (*Esp**) (= *madrileño*) *native of Madrid*
3 (*Méx**) (= *criado*) servant
Ⓑ SM 1 (*Téc*) [*de coche*] jack; (= *torno*) clamp, vice, vise (*EEUU*); (= *grapa*) grab, drag (*EEUU*); (*Méx*) [*de arma*] trigger ► **gato de tornillo** screw jack ► **gato hidráulico** hydraulic jack
2 (*) (= *ladrón*) sneak thief, petty thief
3 (= *baile*) *a popular Argentinian folk dance*
4 (†) (*para el dinero*) money bag
5 (*CAm*) (= *músculo*) muscle
6 (*Méx*) (= *propina*) tip
7 (*Cono Sur*) (= *bolsa de agua*) hot-water bottle; *ver tb* **gata**

gato² SM (*Andes*) open-air market, market place

gatopardo SM ocelot

GATT SM ABR (= **General Agreement on Tariffs and Trade**) GATT

gatuno ADJ catlike, feline

gatuperio SM 1 (= *mezcla*) hotchpotch, hodgepodge (*EEUU*)
2 (= *chanchullo*) shady dealing; (= *fraude*) fraud

gaucano* SM (*Caribe*) *rum-based cocktail*

gaucha† SF (*Cono Sur*) mannish woman

gauchada SF (*Cono Sur*) 1 (= *favor*) kind deed, favour, favor (*EEUU*); **hacer una ~ a algn** to do sb a favour
2 (= *conjunto*) gauchos *pl*
3 (†) (= *acción*) gaucho exploit; (*pey*) gaucho trick

gauchaje SM 1 (*Cono Sur*) (= *personas*) gauchos *pl*; (= *reunión*) gathering of gauchos
2 (*pey*) (= *gentuza*) riffraff, rabble

gauchear ▸conjug 1a◂ VI (*Cono Sur*) to live like a gaucho

gauchesco ADJ (*Cono Sur*) gaucho *antes de s*, of the gauchos; **vida gauchesca** gaucho life

gaucho Ⓐ SM 1 (*LAm*) gaucho; (= *vaquero*) cowboy, herdsman, herder (*EEUU*)
2 (*Cono Sur*) (= *jinete*) good rider, expert horseman
3 (*Andes*) (= *sombrero*) wide-brimmed straw hat
Ⓑ ADJ 1 gaucho *antes de s*, gaucho-like
2 (*Cono Sur**) (= *servicial*) helpful

> **GAUCHO**
>
> ***Gaucho** is the name given to the men who rode the **Pampa**, the plains of Argentina, Uruguay and parts of southern Brazil, earning their living on cattle farms. Important parts of the **gaucho's** traditional costume include the **faja**, a sash worn round the waist, the **facón**, a sheath knife, and **boleadoras**, strips of leather weighted with stones at either end which were used somewhat like lassos to catch cattle. During the 19th century this vast **pampas** area was divided up into large ranches and the free-roaming lifestyle of the **gaucho** gradually disappeared. **Gauchos** were the inspiration for a tradition of **literatura gauchesca**, of which the most famous work is the two-part epic poem "Martín Fierro" written by the Argentine José Hernández between 1872 and 1879 and mourning the loss of the **gaucho** way of life and their persecution as outlaws.*

gaudeamus* SM INV (= *fiesta*) party

gaulista ADJ, SMF Gaullist

gavera SF (*LAm*) crate

gaveta SF (= *cajón*) drawer; (*con llave*) locker; **~ de archivo** filing drawer

gavia SF 1 (*Náut*) (= *vela*) main topsail
2 (*Agr*) (= *zanja*) ditch
3 (= *cuadrilla*) squad of workmen
4 (= *ave*) seagull

gavilán SM 1 (= *ave*) sparrowhawk
2 [*de pluma*] nib
3 [*de espada*] quillon
4 (*LAm*) (= *uñero*) ingrowing toenail

gavilla SF 1 (*Agr*) sheaf
2 (*) (= *pandilla*) gang, band

gavillero SM (*LAm*) gunman

gaviota SF 1 (= *ave*) seagull ► **gaviota argente**, **gaviota argéntea** herring gull
2 (*Méx hum*) flier

gavota SF gavotte

gay Ⓐ ADJ INV gay
Ⓑ SM (*pl* **gays**) gay man, gay

gaya SF 1 (= *ave*) magpie
2 (*en tela*) coloured *o* (*EEUU*) colored stripe

gayo (*liter*) ADJ 1 (= *alegre*) merry, gay; **gaya ciencia** (*Literat, Hist*) art of poetry
2 (= *vistoso*) bright, showy

gayola SF 1 (= *jaula*) cage
2 (*) (= *cárcel*) jail, slammer‡, can (*EEUU**)

gayumbos‡ SMPL underpants

gaza SF (= *lazo*) loop; (*Náut*) bend, bight

gazafatón* SM = **gazapatón**

gazapa* SF fib, lie

gazapatón* SM (= *error*) blunder, slip; (= *disparate*) piece of nonsense

gazapera SF 1 (= *madriguera*) rabbit hole, warren
2 (*) [*de maleantes*] den
3 (= *riña*) brawl, shindy*

gazapo SM 1 (*Zool*) young rabbit
2 (*) (= *disparate*) blunder*, bloomer*; **meter un ~** to make a blunder *o* bloomer*; **cazar un ~** to spot a mistake
3 (= *errata*) printing error, misprint
4 (= *hombre*) (= *taimado*) sly fellow; (*) (= *ladrón*) cat burglar; (*LAm*) (= *mentiroso*) liar
5 (*Caribe*) (= *estafa*) trick

gazmoñería SF, **gazmoñada** SF 1 (= *mojigatería*) prudery, priggishness; (= *beatería*) sanctimoniousness
2 (= *hipocresía*) hypocrisy, cant

gazmoño/a, **gazmoñero/a** Ⓐ ADJ 1 (= *mojigato*) prudish, priggish; (= *puritano*) strait laced; (= *beato*) sanctimonious
2 (= *hipócrita*) hypocritical, canting
Ⓑ SM/F 1 (= *mojigato*) prude, prig; (= *beato*) sanctimonious person
2 (= *hipócrita*) hypocrite

gaznápiro/a SM/F dolt, simpleton

gaznatada‡ SF (*CAm, Caribe, Méx*) smack, slap

gaznate SM 1 (= *pescuezo*) gullet; (= *garganta*) windpipe, throttle; ✦*MODISMO* **refrescar el ~*** to wet one's whistle*
2 (*Méx*) (fruit) fritter

gaznetón/ona Ⓐ ADJ (*Andes, Méx*) loud-mouthed
Ⓑ SM/F loudmouth*

gazpacho SM 1 (*Culin*) *cold vegetable soup*; ✦*REFRÁN* **de ~ no hay empacho** one can never have too much of a good thing
2 (*CAm*) (*bebida*) dregs *pl*; (*comida*) leftovers *pl*

gazuza* SF 1 (= *hambre*) ravenous hunger
2 (*CAm*) (= *alboroto*) din, row
3 (*CAm*) (= *chusma*) common people
4 **es una ~** (*CAm*) she's a wily old bird

GC ABR = **Guardia Civil**

geco SM gecko

géiser SM geyser

geisha ['geiʃa] SF geisha girl

gel SM (*pl* **gels, geles**) gel; **~ de baño** bath gel; **~ de ducha** shower gel

gelatina SF (= *ingrediente*) gelatin(e); (= *postre*) jelly, Jell-O® (*EEUU*) ► **gelatina explosiva** gelignite

gelatinoso ADJ gelatinous

gelidez SF chill, iciness

gélido ADJ chill, icy

gelificarse ▸conjug 1g◂ VPR to gel, coagulate

gelignita SF gelignite

gema SF 1 (= *piedra preciosa*) gem, jewel
2 (*Bot*) (= *botón*) bud

gemelo/a Ⓐ ADJ (= *hermano*) (identical) twin; **torres gemelas** twin towers; **buque ~** sister ship; **es mi alma gemela** we're two of a kind
Ⓑ SM/F (= *hermano*) (identical) twin
Ⓒ SM 1 (= *músculo*) calf muscle
2 [*de camisa*] cufflink
3 (*Náut*) sister ship
4 **gemelos** (= *prismáticos*) binoculars ► **gemelos de campo** field glasses ► **gemelos de teatro** opera glasses
5 **Gemelos** [*del zodíaco*] Gemini, Twins

gemido SM (= *quejido*) groan, moan; (=

lamento) wail, howl; [*de animal*] whine; [*del viento*] howling, wailing

gemidor ADJ (= *que se queja*) groaning, moaning; (= *que se lamenta*) wailing, howling

Géminis Ⓐ SM INV (= *signo*) Gemini
Ⓑ SMF INV (= *persona*) Gemini, Geminian; **soy ~** I'm (a) Gemini
Ⓒ ADJ INV Gemini, Geminian

gemiquear ▸conjug 1a◂ VI (*Cono Sur*) to whine

gemiqueo SM (*Cono Sur*) whining

gemir ▸conjug 3k◂ VI (= *quejarse*) to groan, moan; (= *lamentarse*) to wail, howl; [*animal*] to whine; [*viento*] to howl, wail; **—sí —dijo gimiendo** "yes", he groaned

gen SM gene ► **gen recesivo** recessive gene

Gen. ABR (= **General**) Gen

gen. ABR (*Ling*) 1 (= **género**) gen
2 (= **genitivo**) gen

genciana SF gentian

gendarme SMF (*esp LAm*) policeman/policewoman, gendarme

gendarmería SF (*esp LAm*) police, gendarmerie

gene SM gene

genealogía SF (= *ascendientes*) genealogy; (= *árbol*) family tree; (= *raza*) pedigree

genealógico ADJ genealogical

genealogista SMF genealogist

generación SF 1 (= *acto*) generation; **~ de empleo** employment creation; ✦*MODISMO* **producirse** *o* **surgir por ~ espontánea** to come out of nowhere, come out of the blue
2 (= *grupo*) generation; **la ~ del 27/98** the generation of '27/'98; **las nuevas generaciones** the rising generation; **primera/segunda/tercera/cuarta ~** (*Inform*) first/second/third/fourth generation
3 (= *descendencia*) progeny, offspring; (= *crías*) brood; (= *sucesión*) succession

GENERACIÓN DEL 27/DEL 98

The **Generación del 27** *is the collective name given to a group of writers and poets including Lorca, Alberti, Guillén, Cernuda and Aleixandre, who drew inspiration from earlier Spanish poets as well as from popular folk song and contemporary European art (Dadaism, Surrealism, Cubism). They particularly admired Góngora (1561-1627) and it was their commemoration of the anniversary of his death that earned them the title* **Generación del 27**.

The **Generación del 98** *was the name coined by Azorín for a group of writers (Baroja, Machado, Unamuno, Maeztu, Ganivet, and himself, amongst others) who saw Spain's defeat in the Cuban American war of 1898 as the start of a decline in values. While not all the supposed members of the group accepted their inclusion in it, their work demonstrates shared themes, ideals, and concerns.*

generacional ADJ generation *antes de s*

generacionalmente ADV in terms of generation(s)

generado ADJ **~ por ordenador** (*Inform*) computer-generated

generador Ⓐ ADJ generating; **una demagogia ~a de odio** a demagogy which generates hatred
Ⓑ SM generator ► **generador de programas** (*Inform*) program generator ► **generador eólico** wind turbine

general Ⓐ ADJ 1 (= *común, no detallado*) general; **información de interés ~** information of general interest; **el estado ~ de su salud** his general state of health; **una visión ~ de los problemas del país** an overall *o* general view of the problems of the country; **declaraciones de carácter ~** general comments; **estamos perdiendo de vista el interés ~** we are losing sight of the common interest; **la corrupción es ~ en todo el país** corruption is widespread in the whole country
2 **en ~** 2·1 (*con verbo*) generally, in general; **estoy hablando en ~** I am talking generally *o* in general terms; **en ~, las críticas de la obra han sido favorables** generally (speaking) *o* in general, the play has received favourable criticism
2·2 (*detrás de s*) in general; **literatura, música y arte en ~** literature, music and the arts in general; **el público en ~** the general public
3 **por lo ~** generally; **iban a visitarla, por lo ~, dos o tres veces al año** they generally went to see her two or three times a year; **los resultados son, por lo ~, bastante buenos** in general *o* on the whole, the results are pretty good
Ⓑ SMF (*Mil*) general ► **general de brigada** brigadier general ► **general de división** major general
Ⓒ SM (*Rel*) general
Ⓓ SF 1 (*tb* **carretera ~**) (*Esp*) main road
2 (*tb* **clasificación ~**) (*Ciclismo*) general classification
3 ► **generales de la ley** prescribed personal questions

generala SF 1 (†) (= *persona*) (woman) general; (= *esposa*) general's wife
2 (= *llamamiento*) call to arms, general alert

generalato SM 1 (= *arte, rango*) generalship
2 (= *personas*) generals *pl*
3 (*Méx**) (= *madama*) madame, brothel keeper

generalidad SF 1 generality; (= *mayoría*) mass, majority; **la ~ de los hombres** the majority of men, most men
2 (= *vaguedad*) vague answer, generalization; **¡déjate de ~es!** stop speaking in generalities!
3 **la Generalidad** (*Pol*) = **Generalitat**

generalísimo SM (*Mil*) supreme commander, generalissimo; **el Generalísimo Franco** General Franco

generalista Ⓐ ADJ [*radio, televisión*] general-interest *antes de s*; [*formación*] general; **médico ~** general practitioner
Ⓑ SMF general practitioner, G.P., family practitioner (*EEUU*)

Generalitat SF **la ~ (de Cataluña)** Catalan autonomous government; **la ~ Valenciana** Valencian autonomous government

GENERALITAT

The **Generalitat** *is the autonomous government of Catalonia. The name originally applied to the finance committee of the Catalan parliament, or* **Corts**, *in the early 13th century, but in 1932 was given to the partially devolved government granted to Catalonia under the Second Republic (1931-36). When its leader, Luis Companys, went on to proclaim the "Catalan State of the Spanish Federal Republic" in 1934, Madrid sent in the troops, and imprisoned members of the breakaway* **Generalitat**. *Catalan autonomy was restored under the Popular Front in 1936, but was abolished by Franco after the Civil War. Since his death the* **Generalitat** *has risen again under the 1978 Constitution and Catalonia now enjoys a considerable degree of autonomy from Madrid.*

⇨ *See also* LA CONSTITUCIÓN ESPAÑOLA

generalización SF 1 (= *ampliación*) [*de práctica, tendencia*] spread; [*de conflicto*] widening, spread; **la ~ del uso de herbicidas** the increased use of herbicides
2 (= *afirmación general*) generalization; **hacer generalizaciones** to make generalizations, generalize

generalizado ADJ [*crisis, creencia, guerra*] widespread; **existe la creencia generalizada de que ...** it is commonly *o* widely believed that ..., there is a widely held belief that ...

generalizar ▸conjug 1f◂ Ⓐ VT (= *extender*) [+ *práctica*] to make (more) widespread; [+ *conflicto*] to widen, spread; **el uso ha generalizado una pronunciación distinta** a different pronunciation has become widespread through use; **quieren ~ la situación de Madrid a toda España** they want to apply the situation of Madrid to the whole of Spain
Ⓑ VI (= *hacer generalizaciones*) to generalize; **no se puede ~** you can't generalize
Ⓒ **generalizarse** VPR [*crisis, plaga, costumbre*] to become (more) widespread; [*conflicto*] to widen, spread; **el descontento se está generalizando en todo el país** discontent is spreading *o* becoming more widespread throughout the country; **hoy día se ha generalizado el uso de la palabra "tío"** nowadays the use of the word "tio" has become widespread

generalmente ADV generally

generar ▸conjug 1a◂ VT 1 [+ *electricidad, energía*] to generate
2 [+ *empleo, interés, riqueza*] to generate, create; [+ *problemas, tensiones*] to cause; [+ *beneficios*] to generate; **el turismo ~á muchos puestos de trabajo** tourism will generate *o* create many jobs; **sus comentarios ~on numerosas quejas** his comments generated *o* raised many complaints

generativismo SM generative grammar

generativo ADJ generative

genérico ADJ generic

género SM 1 (= *clase*) kind, type; **personas de ese ~** people of that kind *o* type, people like that; **este festival es el único en su ~** this festival is unique of its kind; **le deseo todo ~ de felicidades** I wish you all the happiness in the world ► **género humano** human race, mankind
2 (*Arte, Literat*) genre, type; **pintor de ~** genre painter; **es todo un ~ de literatura** it is a whole type of literature ► **género chico** (= *sainetes*) (genre of) short farces; (= *zarzuela*) Spanish operetta ► **género literario** literary genre ► **género narrativo** novel genre, fiction
3 (*Ling*) gender; **del ~ masculino** of the masculine gender
4 (*Biol*) (= *especie*) genus
5 **géneros** (*Com*) (= *productos*) goods; (=

mercancías) commodities ► **géneros de lino** linen goods ► **géneros de punto** knitwear *sing*

6 (= *tela*) cloth, material; ✦*MODISMO* **le conozco el ~** I know his sort, I know all about him

generosamente ADV 1 (= *con largueza*) generously

2 (= *con magnanimidad*) nobly, magnanimously

generosidad SF 1 (= *largueza*) generosity

2 (= *magnanimidad*) nobility, magnanimity

3 (*Hist*) nobility

generoso ADJ 1 (= *dadivoso*) generous; **ser ~ con algn** to be generous to sb; **ser ~ con algo** to be generous with sth

2 (= *noble*) noble, magnanimous; **de sangre generosa** of noble blood; **en pecho ~** in a noble heart

3 (*Hist*) highborn, noble

4 [*vino*] rich, full-bodied

genésico ADJ genetic

Génesis SM Genesis

génesis SF INV genesis

genética SF genetics *sing* ► **genética de poblaciones** population genetics; *ver tb* **genético**

genéticamente ADV genetically

geneticista SMF geneticist

genético/a Ⓐ ADJ genetic

Ⓑ SM/F geneticist; *ver tb* **genética**

genetista SMF geneticist

genial ADJ 1 (= *de talento*) brilliant, of genius; **escritor ~** brilliant writer, writer of genius; **fue una idea ~** it was a brilliant idea; **Pablo es ~** Pablo's a genius

2 (= *estupendo*) wonderful, marvellous, marvelous (*EEUU*); **fue una película ~** it was a wonderful *o* marvellous film; **¡eso fue ~!** it was wonderful *o* marvellous!

3 (= *ocurrente*) witty

4 (= *placentero*) pleasant, genial; (= *afable*) cordial, affable

genialidad SF 1 (= *cualidad*) genius

2 (= *acto genial*) stroke of genius, master stroke; **es una ~ suya** (*iró*) it's one of his brilliant ideas

genialmente ADV in an inspired way, brilliantly, with genius

genio SM 1 (= *temperamento*) temper; **¡menudo ~ tiene!** he's got such a temper!; **es una mujer de mucho ~** she's a quick-tempered woman; **tener mal ~** to be bad tempered; **~ vivo** quick temper, hot temper; ✦*MODISMO* **llevar el ~ a algn** (= *seguir la corriente*) to humour sb, humor sb (*EEUU*); (= *no contradecir*) not to dare contradict sb; ✦*REFRÁN* **~ y figura hasta la sepultura** a leopard cannot change his spots

2 (= *carácter*) nature, disposition; **~ alegre** cheerful nature; **tener buen ~** to be good natured, be even tempered; **corto de ~** timid, spiritless; **de ~ franco** of an open nature

3 (= *estado de ánimo*) **estar de buen ~** to be in a good mood; **estar de mal ~** to be in a bad temper, be in a bad mood

4 (= *talento*) genius; **¡eres un ~!** you're a genius!

5 (= *peculiaridad*) genius, peculiarities *pl*; **esto va en contra del ~ de la lengua** this goes against the genius of the language; **el ~ andaluz** the Andalusian spirit, the spirit of Andalucía

6 (= *ser fantástico*) genie

7 (= *divinidad*) spirit ► **genio del mal** evil spirit ► **genio tutelar** guardian spirit

genioso ADJ (*CAm*) bad-tempered

genista SF broom, genista

genital Ⓐ ADJ genital

Ⓑ **genitales** SMPL genitals, genital organs

genitalidad SF sexual activity

genitivo Ⓐ ADJ (= *reproductivo*) generative, reproductive

Ⓑ SM (*Ling*) (= *caso*) genitive ► **genitivo sajón** *possessive genitive with apostrophe*

genocida SMF *person accused or guilty of genocide*

genocidio SM genocide

genoma SM, **genomio** SM genome

Génova SF Genoa

genovés/esa ADJ, SM/F Genoese

gental SM (*Andes*) lot, mass; **un ~ de gente** a mass of people

gente Ⓐ SF 1 (= *personas*) people *pl*; **hay muy poca ~** there are very few people; **no me gusta esa ~** I don't like those people; **España y sus ~s** Spain and its people; **son muy buena ~** they are very nice people; **Juan es buena ~*** Juan is a nice guy*; ✦*MODISMO* **hacer ~** to make a crowd ► **la gente baja** the lower classes *pl* ► **gente (de) bien** (= *los ricos*) well-off people, well-to-do people; (= *los decorosos*) decent people ► **gente bonita** (*Méx*) beautiful people ► **gente de capa parda††** country folk ► **gente de color** coloured people, colored people (*EEUU*) ► **gente de la cuchilla††** butchers *pl* ► **gente de mar** seafaring men *pl* ► **gente de medio pelo** people of limited means, common people ► **gente de paz** peace-loving people; **¡~ de paz!** (*Mil*) friend! ► **gente de pelo††** well-to-do people ► **gente de pluma††** clerks *pl*, penpushers *pl* ► **gente de trato††** tradespeople ► **gente gorda** (*Esp**) well-to-do people, rich people ► **gente guapa**, **gente linda** (*LAm*) beautiful people ► **gente menuda** children *pl* ► **gente natural** (*CAm*) Indians *pl*, natives *pl* ► **gente perdida†** riff-raff ► **gente principal** nobility, gentry; *ver tb* **don[1] 1**

2 (*Méx*) (= *persona*) person; **había dos ~s** there were two people

3 (*) (= *parientes*) family, folks* *pl*; **mi ~** my family, my folks*; ✦*MODISMO* **de ~ en ~** from generation to generation

4 (= *nación*) nation

5 (*Mil*) men *pl*, troops *pl*

6 (= *séquito*) retinue; **el rey y su ~** the king and his retinue

7 (*LAm*) upper-class people *pl*; **ser (buena) ~** to be respectable people

Ⓑ ADJ **es muy ~*** (*Chile*) he's very decent*; (*Méx*) he's very kind

gentecilla SF (= *pobre gente*) unimportant people; (*pey*) (= *gentuza*) rabble, riffraff

genterío SM (*CAm*) = **gentío**

gentil Ⓐ ADJ 1 (= *cortés*) courteous; (*Méx*) (= *amable*) kind, helpful

2 (= *elegante*) graceful, elegant; (= *encantador*) charming

3 (*iró*) pretty, fine; **¡~ cumplido!** a fine compliment!

4 (= *idólatra*) pagan, heathen; (= *no judío*) gentile

Ⓑ SMF (= *idólatra*) pagan, heathen; (= *no judío*) gentile

gentileza SF 1 (= *amabilidad*) kindness; (= *cortesía*) courtesy; **agradezco su ~** I appreciate your kindness; **tuvieron la ~ de invitarme** they were kind enough to invite me; **tenga la ~ de acompañarme** I would appreciate it if you came with me; **"por ~ de ..."** "by courtesy of ..."

2 (= *gracia*) gracefulness; (= *encanto*) charm

3 (= *pompa*) splendour, splendor (*EEUU*)

4 (= *gallardía*) dash, gallantry

gentilhombre SM (*pl* **gentileshombres**) gentleman ► **gentilhombre de cámara** gentleman-in-waiting

gentilicio Ⓐ ADJ (= *de las naciones*) national, tribal; (= *de la familia*) family *antes de s*; **nombre ~** family name

Ⓑ SM *name of the inhabitants of a country or region etc*

gentilidad SF, **gentilismo** SM (= *paganos*) the pagan world; (= *creencias*) heathenism, paganism

gentilmente ADV 1 (= *con amabilidad*) kindly; (= *cortésmente*) courteously, politely; **me cedió ~ el paso** he courteously *o* politely let me past

2 (= *con elegancia*) elegantly, gracefully; (= *con encanto*) charmingly

3 (*iró*) prettily

gentío SM crowd, throng; **había un ~** there were lots of people

gentualla SF = **gentuza**

gentuza SF (*pey*) (= *populacho*) rabble, mob; (= *chusma*) riffraff; **¡qué ~!** what a rabble!*, what a shower!*

genuflexión SF genuflexion

genuflexo ADJ (*Cono Sur*) servile, slavish

genuinamente ADV genuinely

genuino ADJ 1 (= *auténtico*) genuine

2 (*Andes**) smashing*, super*

GEO SMPL ABR (*Esp*) (= **Grupo Especial de Operaciones**) *special police unit*

geo SMF member of GEO

geo... PREF geo...

geoambiental ADJ geoenvironmental

geobiológico ADJ geobiological

geobotánica SF geobotany

geociencia SF geoscience

geoclimático ADJ geoclimatic

geodemografía SF geodemography

geodesía SF geodesy

geodésico ADJ geodesic

geoecología SF geoecology

geoeconómico ADJ geoeconomic

geoestacionario ADJ geostationary

geoestadística SF geostatistics *sing*

geoestrategia SF geostrategy

geoestratégico ADJ geostrategic

geofísica SF geophysics *sing*

geofísico/a Ⓐ ADJ geophysical

Ⓑ SM/F geophysicist

Geofredo SM Geoffrey

geografía SF 1 geography ► **geografía física** physical geography ► **geografía humana** human geography ► **geografía política** political geography

[2] (= *país*) country, territory; **en toda la ~ nacional** all over the country; **recorrer la ~ nacional** to travel all over the country

geográfico ADJ geographical

geógrafo/a SM/F geographer

geohistoria SF, **geo-historia** SF geohistory

geolingüística SF geolinguistics *sing*

geología SF geology

geológico ADJ geological

geólogo/a SM/F geologist

geomagnético ADJ geomagnetic

geometría SF geometry; **de ~ variable** (*Aer*) variable-geometry *antes de s* ► **geometría algebraica** algebraic geometry ► **geometría del espacio** solid geometry

geométrico ADJ geometric(al)

geomorfología SF geomorphology

geopolítica SF geopolitics *sing*

geopolítico ADJ geopolitical

Georgia SF Georgia; **~ del Sur** South Georgia

georgiano/a Ⓐ ADJ, SM/F Georgian
Ⓑ SM (*Ling*) Georgian

geosistema SM geosystem

geostacionario ADJ geostationary

geotermal ADJ geothermal

geranio SM geranium

Gerardo SM Gerard

gerencia SF [1] (= *dirección*) management ► **gerencia de empresas** business management
[2] (= *cargo*) post of manager
[3] (= *oficina*) manager's office
[4] (= *personas*) management, managers *pl*; **alta ~** senior management; **~ intermedia** middle management

gerencial ADJ managerial

gerenciar ▸conjug 1b◂ VT to manage

gerente SMF manager/manageress ► **gerente de fábrica** works manager ► **gerente de ventas** sales manager

geriatra SMF geriatrician

geriatría SF geriatrics *sing*

geriátrico Ⓐ ADJ geriatric; **centro ~** old people's home
Ⓑ SM old people's home

gerifalte SM [1] (= *persona*) important person, bigwig*; **los ~s de la empresa** the company bigwigs*; **estar** *o* **vivir como un ~** to live like a king *o* lord
[2] (= *ave*) gerfalcon

germanesco ADJ **palabra germanesca** underworld slang

germanía SF criminals' slang, underworld slang

germánico ADJ Germanic

germanio SM germanium

germanista SMF Germanist

germanística SF German studies *pl*

germano/a Ⓐ ADJ Germanic, German
Ⓑ SM/F German

germanófilo/a ADJ, SM/F Germanophile

germanófobo/a Ⓐ ADJ anti-German
Ⓑ SM/F Germanophobe

germanófono/a Ⓐ ADJ German-speaking
Ⓑ SM/F German speaker

germanooccidental ADJ, SMF (*Hist*) West German

germanooriental ADJ, SMF (*Hist*) East German

germanoparlante Ⓐ ADJ German-speaking
Ⓑ SMF German speaker

germen SM [1] (= *microorganismo*) germ ► **germen plasma** germ plasma
[2] (= *brote*) germ ► **germen de trigo** wheatgerm
[3] (= *raíz*) germ, seed; (= *origen*) source; **el ~ de una idea** the germ of an idea

germicida Ⓐ ADJ germicidal
Ⓑ SM germicide, germ killer

germinación SF germination

germinar ▸conjug 1a◂ VI to germinate

Gerona SF Gerona

gerontocracia SF gerontocracy

gerontología SF gerontology

gerontólogo/a SM/F gerontologist

Gertrudis SF Gertrude

gerundense Ⓐ ADJ of/from Gerona
Ⓑ SMF native/inhabitant of Gerona; **los ~s** the people of Gerona

gerundiano ADJ bombastic

gerundiar ▸conjug 1b◂ VI (= *hablar*) to speak meaninglessly; (= *escribir*) to write meaninglessly

gerundino SM gerundive

gerundio SM (*Ling*) gerund; ✦***MODISMO*** **andando, que es ~** get a move on — now! ► **gerundio adjetivado** gerundive

gervasio SM (*Andes*) (= *hombre*) guy*; (= *astuto*) smart guy*

gesta SF [1] (= *acción heroica*) heroic deed, epic achievement
[2] (*Literat, Hist*) epic poem, epic; *ver* **cantar C2**

gestación SF [1] (*Biol*) pregnancy, gestation; **los tres primeros meses de ~** the first three months of pregnancy; **en avanzado estado de ~** heavily pregnant; **animales en ~** gestating animals ► **gestación de alquiler** surrogate pregnancy
[2] [*de idea, proyecto*] gestation; **un trabajo de tan larga ~** a project which has been so long in preparation *o* gestation

gestante Ⓐ ADJ expectant
Ⓑ SF expectant mother, pregnant woman

Gestapo SF **la ~** the Gestapo

gestar ▸conjug 1a◂ Ⓐ VT (*Biol*) to gestate
Ⓑ **gestarse** VPR [1] (*Biol*) to gestate
[2] (*fig*) to be conceived

gestear ▸conjug 1a◂ VI = **gesticular**

gesticulación SF gesticulation

gesticular ▸conjug 1a◂ VI (*con ademanes*) to gesticulate; **~ con las manos** to wave one's hands around, gesticulate with one's hands; **~ con los brazos** to wave one's arms around, gesticulate with one's arms; **siempre habla sin ~** (= *sin ademanes*) he never gesticulates when he speaks; (= *sin gestos faciales*) he's always expressionless when he speaks

gestión SF [1] (= *administración*) management; **le despidieron por su mala ~** he was dismissed for bad management ► **gestión de datos** data management ► **gestión de ficheros** file management ► **gestión de personal** personnel management ► **gestión empresarial** business management ► **gestión financiera** financial management ► **gestión forestal** woodland management ► **gestión interna** (*Inform*) housekeeping ► **gestión presupuestaria** budget management

[2] **gestiones** (= *trámites*) **tenía que realizar unas gestiones in Madrid** he had some business to do in Madrid; **hacer las gestiones necesarias para algo** to take the necessary steps for sth; **hacer las gestiones preliminares** to do the groundwork; **el gobierno tendrá que hacer las primeras gestiones** the government will have to make the first move

gestionable ADJ manageable; **difícilmente ~** difficult to manage

gestionar ▸conjug 1a◂ VT [1] (= *administrar*) to manage; **se encargaba de ~ los presupuestos de la empresa** he managed the budgets for his company
[2] (= *tramitar*) [+ *permiso, crédito*] to arrange; **su marido le gestionó el permiso de residencia** her husband arranged her residence permit; **gestionamos la venta de su piso** we will arrange the sale of your flat

gesto SM [1] (= *ademán*) gesture; **con un ~ de cansancio** with a weary gesture; **hacer ~s (a algn)** to make gestures (to sb); **hacer ~s con la(s) mano(s)** to gesture with one's hand(s); **me hizo un ~ para que me sentara** he gestured for me to sit down
[2] (= *expresión*) **hizo** *o* **puso un ~ de alivio** he looked relieved; **hizo** *o* **puso un ~ de asco** he looked disgusted; **hizo** *o* **puso un ~ de extrañeza** he looked surprised; **fruncir el ~** to scowl, look cross; ✦***MODISMO*** **poner mal ~** *o* **torcer el ~** to make a wry face
[3] (= *acción*) gesture; **un ~ de buena voluntad** a goodwill gesture, a gesture of goodwill; **con un ~ generoso remitió la deuda** in a generous gesture he waived the debt

gestología SF study of body-language

gestor(a) Ⓐ ADJ (= *que gestiona*) managing
Ⓑ SM/F manager/manageress; (= *promotor*) promoter; (= *agente*) business agent, representative; (*tb* **~(a) administrativo/a**) *agent undertaking business with government departments, insurance companies etc* ► **gestor(a) de carteras** portfolio manager
Ⓒ SM ► **gestor de bases de datos** database manager ► **gestor de ficheros** file manager

gestora SF (= *comité*) management committee

gestoría SF agency (*for undertaking business with government departments, insurance companies etc*)

> **GESTORÍA**
>
> *In Spain* **gestorías** *are private agencies which specialize in dealing with legal and administrative work. For a fee they carry out the* **trámites** *involved in getting passports, work permits, car documentation, etc and liaise with the Inland Revenue (***Agencia Tributaria***), thereby saving their clients much inconvenience and queueing time.*

gestual ADJ gestural; **lenguaje ~** body-language

gestualidad SF body-language

Getsemaní SM Gethsemane; **el huerto de ~** the garden of Gethsemane

geyser ['ɣeiser] SM geyser

Ghana SF Ghana

ghanés/esa ADJ, SM/F Ghanaian

ghetto SM ghetto

giba SF [1] (= *joroba*) [*de camello*] hump; [*de persona*] hump, hunchback
[2] (‡) (= *molestia*) nuisance, bother

gibado ADJ with a hump, hunchbacked

gibar‡ ▸conjug 1a◂ Ⓐ VT [1] (= *molestar*) to annoy, bother
[2] (= *embaucar*) to put one over on*; (= *tomar la revancha*) to get one's own back on
Ⓑ **gibarse** VPR to put up with it; **se van a ~** they'll have to lump it*

gibón SM gibbon

giboso ADJ with a hump, hunchbacked

Gibraltar SM Gibraltar

gibraltareño/a Ⓐ ADJ of/from Gibraltar, Gibraltarian
Ⓑ SM/F Gibraltarian, native/inhabitant of Gibraltar; **los ~s** the Gibraltarians, the people of Gibraltar

gigabyte [giga'bait] SM gigabyte

giganta SF [1] (= *persona*) giantess, giant
[2] (*Bot*) sunflower

gigante Ⓐ ADJ giant *antes de s*, gigantic; **pantalla ~** giant screen; **tamaño ~** giant size
Ⓑ SM [1] (*Mit*) giant
[2] (= *persona alta*) giant
[3] (= *genio*) giant; **un ~ de la música clásica** one of the giants of classical music
[4] (*en fiestas populares*) giant figure

gigantesco ADJ gigantic, giant *antes de s*

gigantez SF gigantic stature, vast size

gigantismo SM gigantism, giantism

gigantón/ona SM/F (= *muñeco*) giant carnival figure

gigantona SF (*CAm*) (= *baile*) *folk dance with giant masks*

gigoló [dʒigo'lo] SM gigolo

Gijón SM Gijón

gijonés/esa Ⓐ ADJ of/from Gijón
Ⓑ SM/F native/inhabitant of Gijón; **los gijoneses** the people of Gijón

Gil SM Giles

gil* (*esp Cono Sur*) Ⓐ ADJ stupid, silly
Ⓑ SMF fool, twit*

gilar‡ ▸conjug 1a◂ VT to watch, keep tabs on*

gili‡, gilí‡ Ⓐ ADJ [1] (= *tonto*) stupid, silly
[2] (= *vanidoso*) stuck-up*; (= *presumido*) pig-headed*
Ⓑ SMF [1] (= *tonto*) ass‡, prat‡, jerk (*EEUU**); **no seas ~** don't be such an ass *o* prat‡; **hacer el ~** to make an ass *o* prat of o.s.‡
[2] (= *vanidoso*) pompous ass‡

gilipollada‡* SF = **gilipollez**

gilipollas‡* Ⓐ ADJ INV **no seas ~** don't be such a dickhead *o* wanker‡*
Ⓑ SMF INV [1] (= *estúpido*) dickhead‡*, wanker‡*
[2] (= *vanidoso*) pompous ass‡

gilipollear‡* ▸conjug 1a◂ VI to piss about‡*, be a dickhead‡*, be a jerk (*EEUU**)

gilipollesco‡* ADJ bloody stupid‡, bloody idiotic‡

gilipollez‡* SF [1] (= *idiotez*) **es una ~** it's bloody stupid‡; **decir gilipolleces** to talk bullshit‡*
[2] (= *vanidad*) pig-headedness*

gilipuertas‡ ADJ, SMF INV (*euf*) = **gili**

gillete® [xi'lete] SF (= *hoja*) razor blade; (= *maquinilla*) safety razor

gimnasia SF (*Dep*) gymnastics *sing*; (*Escol*) P.E., gym; (= *entrenamiento*) exercises *pl*; **una clase de ~** a P.E. *o* gym lesson; **monitor de ~** (*Escol*) P.E. *o* gym teacher; **mi madre hace ~ todas las mañanas** my mother does exercises every morning; ♦***MODISMO*** **confundir la ~ con la magnesia*** to get things mixed up ► **gimnasia aeróbica** aerobics *sing* ► **gimnasia artística** artistic gymnastics ► **gimnasia correctiva** remedial gymnastics ► **gimnasia de mantenimiento** keep-fit ► **gimnasia deportiva** competitive gymnastics ► **gimnasia mental** mental gymnastics ► **gimnasia respiratoria** breathing exercises *pl* ► **gimnasia rítmica** rhythmic gymnastics ► **gimnasia sobre suelo** floor exercises *pl*

gimnasio SM gymnasium, gym*; **~ múltiple** multigym

gimnasta SMF gymnast

gimnástica SF gymnastics *sing*

gimnástico ADJ [*ejercicio, tabla*] exercise *antes de s*; [*club, asociación*] gymnastic, gymnastics *antes de s*

gimotear ▸conjug 1a◂ VI (= *gemir*) to whine; (= *lamentar*) to wail; (= *lloriquear*) to snivel

gimoteo SM (= *gemido*) whine, whining; (= *lamento*) wailing; (= *lloriqueo*) snivelling, sniveling (*EEUU*)

gincana SF gymkhana

Ginebra[1] SF (*Geog*) Geneva

Ginebra[2] SF (*Hist*) Guinevere

ginebra[1] SF (= *bebida*) gin

ginebra[2]* SF (= *confusión*) bedlam, uproar

ginebrés/esa Ⓐ ADJ of/from Geneva
Ⓑ SM/F native/inhabitant of Geneva; **los ginebreses** the people of Geneva

ginecología SF gynaecology, gynecology (*EEUU*)

ginecológico ADJ gynaecological, gynecological (*EEUU*)

ginecólogo/a SM/F gynaecologist, gynecologist (*EEUU*)

ginesta SF broom

gineta SF genet

gingival ADJ gum *antes de s*, gingival; **campaña de salud ~** campaign for healthy gums

gingivitis SF INV gingivitis

ginkana SF gymkhana

ginseng [jin'sen] SM ginseng

gin-tonic [jin'tonik] SM (*pl* **gin-tonics**) gin and tonic

giña‡ SF (*Caribe*) hatred

Gioconda [dʒo'konda] SF **la ~** (the) Mona Lisa

gira SF [1] (= *viaje*) tour; **estar de ~** to be on tour; **el grupo realiza una ~ por Sudamérica** the group is touring South America, the group is on a tour of South America ► **gira artística** artistic tour ► **gira de conciertos** concert tour ► **gira promocional** promotional tour
[2] (= *excursión*) trip, excursion; (*tb* **~ campestre**) picnic; **ir de ~** to go on a trip *o* an excursion

giradiscos† SM INV record turntable

girado/a SM/F drawee

girador(a) SM/F drawer

giralda SF [1] (= *veleta*) weathercock
[2] **la Giralda** *Seville cathedral tower*

girante ADJ revolving, rotating

girar ▸conjug 1a◂ Ⓐ VT [1] (= *dar vueltas a*) [+ *llave, manivela, volante*] to turn; [+ *peonza, hélice, ruleta*] to spin; **gira la llave de contacto hacia la derecha** turn the ignition key to the right; **~ la cabeza** to turn one's head
[2] (*Com*) [+ *dinero, facturas*] to send; [+ *letra, cheque*] (*gen*) to draw; (*a una persona concreta*) to issue; **le giró 600 euros para que pagara el alquiler** she sent him 600 euros to pay the rent
Ⓑ VI [1] (= *dar vueltas*) [*noria, rueda*] to go (a)round, turn, revolve; [*disco*] to revolve, go (a)round; [*planeta*] to rotate; [*hélice*] to go (a)round, rotate, turn; [*peonza*] to spin; **gira a 1600rpm** it revolves *o* goes (a)round at 1600rpm; **la tierra gira alrededor del sol** the earth revolves around *o* goes (a)round the sun; **el satélite gira alrededor de la tierra** the satellite circles *o* goes (a)round the earth
[2] (= *cambiar de dirección*) to turn (a)round; **al verla giró en redondo** when he saw her he turned right (a)round; **hacer ~** [+ *llave*] to turn; [+ *sillón*] to turn (a)round; **la puerta giró sobre sus bisagras** the door swung on its hinges; **~ sobre sus talones** to turn on one's heel
[3] (= *torcer*) [*vehículo*] to turn; [*camino*] to turn, bend; **el conductor giró bruscamente hacia el otro lado** the driver swerved sharply the other way; **~ a la derecha/izquierda** to turn right/left; **el camino gira a la derecha varios metros más allá** the path turns *o* bends to the right a few metres further on; **el partido ha girado a la izquierda en los últimos años** the party has moved *o* shifted to the left in recent years
[4] **~ alrededor de** *o* **sobre** *o* **en torno a** [+ *tema, ideas*] to revolve around, centre around, center around (*EEUU*); [+ *líder, centro de atención*] to revolve around; **la conversación giraba en torno a las elecciones** the conversation revolved *o* centred around the election; **su última obra gira en torno al tema del amor cortés** his latest work revolves around the subject of courtly love; **el número de asistentes giraba alrededor de 500 personas** there were about 500 people in the audience
[5] **~ en descubierto** (*Com, Fin*) to overdraw
[6] (= *negociar*) to operate, do business; **la compañía gira bajo el nombre de Babel** the company operates under the name of Babel
Ⓒ **girarse** VPR to turn (a)round; **se giró para mirarme** she turned (a)round to look at me

girasol SM sunflower

giratorio ADJ [*movimiento*] circular; [*eje, tambor*] revolving, rotating; [*puerta, escenario*] revolving; [*puente*] swing *antes de s*; [*silla*] swivel *antes de s*

girl* SF [1] (*Teat*) showgirl, chorus girl
[2] (*Dep*) junior player

giro[1] SM [1] (= *vuelta*) (*gen*) turn (**sobre** around); [*de planeta*] (*sobre sí mismo*) rotation; (*alrededor de otro planeta*) revolution; **el avión realizó un ~ de 80 grados** the plane did an 80-degree turn; **con un ~ brusco de cadera** with a sudden twist of the hips; **el coche dio un ~ brusco** the car swerved suddenly; **daba ~s sobre sí misma** she spun round and round ► **giro copernicano** U-turn, complete turnabout ► **giro de 180 grados** (*lit*) U-turn; (*fig*) U-turn, complete turnabout; **la situación ha dado un ~ de 180 grados** the situation has taken a U-turn, there has been a complete

turnabout in the situation
2 (= *cambio*) [*de conversación, acontecimientos*] turn; **el nuevo ~ que dieron ayer los acontecimientos** the new turn events took yesterday; **se produjo un ~ radical en arquitectura** there was a radical change *o* turnabout in architecture; **el electorado ha dado un ~ a la derecha** the electorate has shifted *o* moved to the right
3 (= *envío de dinero*) (*por correo*) money order; (*Com*) draft; **le mandó** *o* **puso un ~ de 400 euros** he sent him a money order for 400 euros ► **giro a la vista** sight draft ► **giro bancario** bank giro, bank draft ► **giro en descubierto** overdraft ► **giro postal** postal order, money order ► **giro postal internacional** international money order ► **giro telegráfico** = **giro postal**
4 (*Ling*) turn of phrase, expression

giro² ADJ (*LAm*) [*gallo*] *with some yellow feathers*

girocompás SM gyrocompass

girola SF ambulatory

Gironda SM Gironde

giroscópico ADJ gyroscopic

giroscopio SM, **giróscopo** SM gyroscope

gis SM 1 (*Méx*) (= *tiza*) chalk
2 (*Andes, Méx*) (= *pizarrín*) slate pencil
3 (*Méx**) (= *bebida*) pulque

gitanada SF (*pey*) 1 (= *acción*) gypsy trick, mean trick
2 (= *halago*) wheedling, cajolery

gitanear ▸conjug 1a◂ VT (*pey*) to wheedle, cajole

gitanería SF 1 (= *grupo*) band of gypsies
2 (= *vida*) gypsy (way of) life
3 (= *dicho*) gypsy saying
4 (*pey*) (= *acción*) wheedling, cajolery

gitanesco ADJ 1 (= *de gitanos*) gypsy *antes de s*
2 (*pey*) (= *taimado*) wily, sly

gitano/a Ⓐ ADJ 1 (*de gitanos*) gypsy *antes de s*; **las costumbres gitanas** gypsy customs
2 (*pey*) (= *camelador*) wheedling, cajoling; (= *taimado*) wily, sly
3 (*) (= *sucio*) dirty
Ⓑ SM/F gypsy; ✦***MODISMOS*** **vivir como ~s*** to live like tramps; **volvió hecho un ~*** he came back in a right mess*

glabro ADJ hairless

glaciación SF glaciation

glacial ADJ 1 [*era*] glacial
2 [*viento*] icy, bitter
3 [*saludo, acogida*] icy, frosty

glaciar SM glacier

gladiador SM gladiator

gladiola SF (*Méx*) gladiolus

gladiolo SM, **gladíolo** SM gladiolus; **un ramo de ~s** a bouquet of gladioli

glamoroso ADJ glamorous

glamour [gla'mur] SM glamour, glamor (*EEUU*)

glamouroso [glamu'roso] ADJ glamorous

glande SM glans

glándula SF (*Anat, Bot*) gland ► **glándula cerrada, glándula de secreción interna** ductless gland ► **glándula endocrina** endocrine gland ► **glándula lagrimal** tear gland ► **glándula mamaria** mammary gland ► **glándula pineal** pineal gland ► **glándula pituitaria** pituitary (gland) ► **glándula prostática** prostate (gland) ► **glándula tiroides** thyroid (gland)

glandular ADJ glandular

glas ADJ INV **azúcar ~** icing sugar

glaseado Ⓐ ADJ (= *brillante*) glazed, glossy; [*tela*] glacé
Ⓑ SM [*de papel, pastel*] glaze

glasear ▸conjug 1a◂ VT 1 [+ *papel*] to glaze
2 (*Culin*) to glacé, glaze

glásnost SF glasnost

glauco ADJ (*liter*) (= *verde claro*) light-green, glaucous; (*esp LAm*) (= *verde*) green

glaucoma SM (*Med*) glaucoma

gleba SF 1 (= *terrón*) clod
2 (*Hist*) glebe

glicerina SF glycerin(e)

glicina SF (*Bot*) wisteria

global ADJ 1 (*en conjunto*) [*cantidad, resultado*] overall, total; [*investigación, análisis*] comprehensive; **estas cifras nos dan una idea ~ del coste** these figures give us an overall picture of the cost
2 (= *mundial*) global; **la aldea ~** the global village

globalidad SF totality; **la ~ del problema** (*en conjunto*) the problem as a whole; (*en sentido amplio*) the problem in its widest sense; **abordar la cuestión en su ~** to tackle the issue in its entirety

globalización SF globalization; **la ~ de la economía** globalization of the economy

globalizador ADJ comprehensive

globalizante ADJ universalizing, world-wide

globalizar ▸conjug 1f◂ VT 1 (= *abarcar*) to encompass, include
2 (= *extender*) to globalize

globalmente ADV 1 [*considerar, examinar*] globally, as a whole
2 (= *en términos generales*) overall

globo SM 1 [*de aire*] balloon ► **globo aerostático** balloon ► **globo cautivo** observation balloon ► **globo de aire caliente** hot-air balloon ► **globo de barrera, globo de protección** barrage-balloon ► **globo dirigible** airship, dirigible ► **globo meteorológico** weather ballon ► **globo sonda** (*Pol*) **lanzar un ~ sonda sobre la posibilidad de convocar un referéndum** to test the political waters regarding the possibility of a referendum
2 (= *esfera*) globe, sphere ► **globo del ojo, globo ocular** eyeball ► **globo de luz** spherical lamp ► **globo terráqueo, globo terrestre** globe
3 (*en un cómic*) balloon
4 [*de chicle*] bubble
5 (‡) (*con drogas*) **cogerse un ~** to get high*; **tener un ~** to be high*
6 (*Ftbl, Tenis*) lob
7 (‡) (= *preservativo*) condom, rubber‡, safe (*EEUU‡*)
8 **globos‡** (= *pechos*) boobs‡
9 **en ~** = **globalmente**

globoso ADJ, **globular** ADJ globular, spherical

glóbulo SM 1 (= *esfera*) globule
2 (*Anat*) blood cell, corpuscle ► **glóbulo blanco** white blood cell, white corpuscle ► **glóbulo rojo** red blood cell, red corpuscle

gloria SF 1 (= *cielo*) glory; **ganarse la ~** to go to heaven; **¡por la ~ de mi madre!** by all that's holy!; **Dios le tenga en su santa ~** God rest his soul
2 (= *delicia*) delight; (= *éxtasis*) bliss; **esta piscina es una ~** this pool is heavenly; ✦***MODISMOS*** **a ~: oler a ~** to smell divine; **saber a ~** to taste heavenly; **dar ~: cocina que da ~** she's a wonderful cook; **está que da ~ verla** she looks wonderful; **estar en la ~** to be in heaven
3 (= *fama*) glory; **cubrirse de ~** (*iró*) to make a fine mess of sth
4 (= *personalidad*) great figure, great*; **una de las grandes ~s del cine** one of the greats* *o* great figures of the cinema; **una vieja ~** a has-been*
5 (*apelativo*) **¡sí, ~!** yes, my love!
6 (‡) (= *droga*) hash*, pot‡

gloriado SM (*Andes*) hot toddy

gloriarse ▸conjug 1b◂ VPR **~ de algo** to boast of sth, be proud of sth; **~ en algo** to glory in sth, rejoice in sth

glorieta SF 1 (= *pérgola*) bower, arbour, arbor (*EEUU*); (= *cenador*) summerhouse
2 (*Aut*) roundabout, traffic circle (*EEUU*); (= *plaza redonda*) circus; (= *cruce*) junction, intersection

glorificación SF glorification

glorificar ▸conjug 1g◂ Ⓐ VT to glorify, praise
Ⓑ **glorificarse** VPR **~se de** *o* **en** to boast of, glory in

Gloriosa SF **la ~** (*Esp Hist*) *the 1868 revolution*; (*Rel*) the Blessed Virgin

gloriosamente ADV gloriously

glorioso ADJ 1 (= *digno de gloria*) glorious; **el ~ alzamiento nacional** (*Esp Hist*) *the Spanish Civil War*
2 (*Rel*) [*santo*] blessed, in glory; [*memoria*] blessed
3 (*pey*) proud, boastful

glosa SF 1 (= *explicación*) gloss; (= *comentario*) comment, note
2 (*Andes*) telling-off

glosar ▸conjug 1a◂ VT (= *explicar*) to gloss; (= *comentar*) to comment on, annotate; (= *criticar*) to criticize

glosario SM glossary

glosopeda SF foot-and-mouth disease

glotal ADJ, **glótico** ADJ glottal

glotis SF INV glottis

glotón/ona Ⓐ ADJ greedy, gluttonous (*frm*)
Ⓑ SM/F glutton
Ⓒ SM (*tb* **~ de América**) wolverine

glotonear ▸conjug 1a◂ VI to be greedy, be gluttonous (*frm*)

glotonería SF greediness, gluttony

glub EXCL gulp!

glucosa SF glucose

gluglú SM 1 [*de agua*] gurgle, gurgling; **hacer ~** to gurgle
2 [*de pavo*] gobble, gobbling; **hacer ~** to gobble

gluglutear ▸conjug 1a◂ VI to gobble

glutamato SM glutamate ► **glutamato monosódico** monosodium glutamate

gluten SM gluten

glúteo Ⓐ ADJ gluteal
Ⓑ SM 1 (= *músculo*) gluteus
2 **glúteos** (= *nalgas*) buttocks, backside *sing*

glutinoso ADJ glutinous

GN ABR (*Nic, Ven*) = **Guardia Nacional**

gneis [neis] SM INV gneiss

gnomo ['nomo] SM gnome

gobelino SM Gobelin tapestry

gobernabilidad SF governability; **llegar a un pacto de ~** to form a government with the support of minority parties

gobernable ADJ [1] (*Pol*) governable; **un pueblo difícilmente ~** an unruly people, a people hard to govern
[2] (*Náut*) navigable, steerable

gobernación SF [1] (= *acto*) governing, government
[2] (= *residencia*) governor's residence; (= *oficina*) governor's office
[3] (*esp LAm Pol*) Ministry of the Interior; **Ministro de la Gobernación** Minister of the Interior, ≈ Home Secretary, ≈ Secretary of the Interior (*EEUU*)

gobernador(a) Ⓐ ADJ [*partido*] governing, ruling
Ⓑ SM/F governor; **el ~ del Banco de España** the governor of the Bank of Spain ► **gobernador(a) civil** civil governor ► **gobernador(a) general** governor general ► **gobernador(a) militar** military governor

gobernalle SM rudder, helm

gobernanta SF [1] [*de hotel*] staff manageress, housekeeper
[2] (*esp LAm*) (= *niñera*) governess

gobernante Ⓐ ADJ ruling, governing; **la clase ~** the ruling *o* governing class
Ⓑ SMF (= *líder*) ruler; **nuestros ~s incumplen sus promesas** our rulers have failed to keep their promises

gobernar ▸conjug 1j◂ Ⓐ VT [1] (*Pol*) to govern, rule
[2] (= *dirigir*) to govern; (= *guiar*) to guide, direct; (= *controlar*) to manage, run; (= *manejar*) to handle
[3] (*Náut*) to steer, sail
Ⓑ VI [1] (*Pol*) to govern, rule; **~ mal** to misgovern
[2] (*Náut*) to handle, steer

gobi‡ SF nick‡, slammer‡, can (*EEUU*‡)

gobierno SM [1] (*Pol*) government; **el ~ español** the Spanish government ► **gobierno autonómico, gobierno autónomo** autonomous government, regional government ► **gobierno central** central government ► **gobierno de coalición** coalition government ► **gobierno de concentración** government of national unity ► **gobierno de gestión** caretaker government ► **el Gobierno de la Nación** central Government ► **gobierno de transición** transition government ► **gobierno directo** direct rule ► **gobierno en funciones** caretaker government ► **gobierno fantasma** shadow cabinet ► **gobierno interino** interim government ► **gobierno militar** military government
[2] (= *dirección*) guidance, direction; (= *gerencia*) management; (= *manejo*) control, handling; **para su ~** for your guidance, for your information; **servir de ~ a algn** to act as a guide to sb, serve as a norm for sb ► **gobierno doméstico, gobierno de la casa** housekeeping, running of the household
[3] (= *puesto*) governorship; (= *edificio*) Government House ► **gobierno civil** (= *puesto*) civil governorship; (= *edificio*) civil governor's residence
[4] (*Náut*) steering; (= *timón*) helm; **buen ~** navigability; **de buen ~** navigable, easily steerable
[5] ✦*MODISMO* **mirar contra el ~** (*Cono Sur*‡) to squint, be boss-eyed*

gobio SM gudgeon

gob.^no^ ABR (= **gobierno**) govt

goce SM (= *disfrute*) enjoyment; (= *posesión*) possession

gocho* SM pig, hog (*EEUU*)

godo/a Ⓐ ADJ (= *gótico*) Gothic
Ⓑ SM/F [1] (*Hist*) Goth
[2] (*LAm Hist*) loyalist; (*pey*) Spaniard; (*Pol*) (= *conservador*) conservative
[3] (*Canarias pey*) (Peninsular) Spaniard

Godofredo SM Godfrey

gofio SM (*Canarias, LAm*) *roasted maize meal often stirred into coffee*

gofre SM waffle

gogó, go-gó Ⓐ SF go-go girl, go-go dancer
Ⓑ ADV (*) **a ~** aplenty, by the bucketful*

gol SM goal; **¡gol!** goal!; **el ~ del empate** the equalizer; **el ~ del honor** the consolation goal; **el ~ de la victoria** the winning goal; **meter** *o* **marcar un ~** to score a goal; ✦*MODISMO* **meter un ~ a algn** to score a point against sb, put one over on sb* ► **gol average** goal average

gola SF [1] (*Anat*) throat, gullet
[2] (*Hist*) [*de armadura*] gorget; [*de adorno*] ruff
[3] (*Arquit*) cyma, ogee

golazo* SM great goal

goleada SF hammering*, thrashing*; **les ganaron por ~** they were hammered *o* thrashed*

goleador(a) Ⓐ ADJ **el equipo más ~** the highest-scoring team, the team which has scored most goals; **aumentó su cuenta ~a** he improved his goal-scoring record
Ⓑ SM/F (goal) scorer; **el máximo ~ de la liga** the top (goal) scorer in the league

golear ▸conjug 1a◂ Ⓐ VT **el Celta fue goleado por el Betis** Celta were hammered *o* thrashed by Betis*; **España goleó a Rumania por seis a cero** Spain hammered *o* thrashed Romania 6-0*; **el portero menos goleado** the keeper who has let in *o* conceded fewest goals; **el equipo más goleado** the team which has conceded most goals
Ⓑ VI to score (a goal)

goleta SF schooner

golf SM [1] (= *juego*) golf; **campo de ~** golf course ► **golf miniatura** miniature golf
[2] (= *pista*) golf course; (= *club*) golf club; (= *chalet*) clubhouse

golfa* SF tart‡, whore*, slut‡

golfada SF loutish behaviour *o* (*EEUU*) behavior, hooliganism

golfán SM water lily

golfante Ⓐ ADJ (= *gamberro*) loutish; (= *delincuente*) delinquent, criminal
Ⓑ SM (= *gamberro*) lout; (= *pillo*) rascal

golfear ▸conjug 1a◂ VI (= *vagabundear*) to idle around, laze around; (= *vivir a la briba*) to live like a street urchin

golferas‡ SM INV = **golfo**²

golfería SF [1] (= *golfos*) louts *pl*; (= *golfillos*) street urchins *pl*
[2] (= *comportamiento*) idling; (= *estilo de vida*) life of idleness; (= *vida callejera*) street life
[3] (= *trampa*) dirty trick

golfillo SM urchin, street urchin

golfismo SM golfing

golfista Ⓐ ADJ golf *antes de s*, golfing *antes de s*
Ⓑ SMF golfer

golfístico ADJ golf *antes de s*, golfing *antes de s*

golfo¹ SM [1] (*Geog*) (= *bahía*) gulf; **la guerra del Golfo** the Gulf War; **la corriente del Golfo** the Gulf Stream ► **Golfo de Méjico** (*Esp*), **Golfo de México** (*LAm*) Gulf of Mexico ► **golfo de Vizcaya** Bay of Biscay ► **Golfo Pérsico** Persian Gulf
[2] (= *mar*) open sea

golfo² SM (= *gamberro*) lout; (= *travieso*) rascal; (= *pilluelo*) street urchin; (= *holgazán*) layabout; **¡menudo ~ estás hecho!** (*hum*) you rascal!

Gólgota SM Golgotha

Goliat SM Goliath

golilla SF [1] (= *adorno*) (*Cos, Hist*) ruff, gorget; [*de magistrado*] magistrate's collar
[2] (*LAm*) (= *bufanda*) neckerchief; ✦*MODISMOS* **alzar ~** (*Méx*) to puff out one's chest; **andar de ~** to be all dressed up; **ajustar la ~** to do one's duty
[3] (*LAm*) [*de ave*] collar, ruff
[4] (*Téc*) flange (*of a pipe*)
[5] (*Caribe*) (= *deuda*) debt
[6] (*Caribe*) (= *trampa*) trick, ruse
[7] **de ~** (*CAm*) (= *gratis*) free, for nothing; (*Caribe**) (= *por casualidad*) by chance, accidentally

gollería SF [1] (= *golosina*) dainty, delicacy
[2] (*) (= *extra*) extra, special treat; **pedir ~s** to ask too much; **es un empleo con muchas ~s** the job has a lot of perks

golleroso ADJ (= *afectado*) affected; (= *puntilloso*) pernickety, persnickety (*EEUU*)

gollete SM (= *garganta*) throat, neck; [*de botella*] neck; **beber a ~** to drink straight from the bottle; ✦*MODISMO* **estar hasta el ~*** (= *harto*) to be up to here*, be fed up*; (= *lleno*) to be full up

golletero/a* SM/F (*LAm*) scrounger*

golondrina SF [1] (= *ave*) swallow; ✦*REFRÁN* **una ~ no hace verano** one swallow does not make a summer ► **golondrina de mar** tern
[2] (= *lancha*) motor launch
[3] (*Cono Sur*) (= *emigrante*) migrant worker
[4] (*Chile Hist*) furniture cart

golondrino SM [1] (= *vagabundo*) tramp, drifter, hobo (*EEUU*); (*Mil*) deserter
[2] (*Med*) *tumour under the armpit*

golondro* SM fancy, yen*, longing; **andar en ~s** to cherish foolish hopes; ✦*MODISMO* **campar de ~** to sponge*, live on other people

golosina SF [1] (= *manjar*) titbit, tidbit (*EEUU*), dainty; (= *dulce*) sweet, piece of candy (*EEUU*)
[2] (= *incentivo*) incentive
[3] (= *bagatela*) trifle; (= *cosa inútil*) useless object
[4] (= *deseo*) desire, longing; (= *antojo*) fancy
[5] (= *gula*) sweet tooth, liking for sweet things; (= *glotonería*) greed

goloso ADJ [1] (*de lo dulce*) sweet-toothed
[2] (*pey*) greedy
[3] (= *apetecible*) attractive, inviting

golpazo SM heavy thump, whack

golpe SM [1] (= *impacto*) hit, knock; (= *choque*) shock, clash; (= *encuentro*) bump; (*con un remo*) stroke; [*del corazón*] beat, throb; **oímos un ~ a la puerta** we heard a knock at the door; **en cuanto compras un coche nuevo tienes un ~** as soon as you buy a new car it gets a knock; **tras el ~ contra el muro tuvo**

que abandonar la carrera after crashing into the wall he had to abandon the race; **dar un ~**: **el coche de atrás nos dio un ~** the car behind ran into us; **dar ~s en la puerta** to hammer at the door; **darse un ~**: **se dio un ~ en la cabeza** he got a bump on his head, he banged his head; **se dio un ~ contra la pared** he hit the wall; **darse ~s de pecho** to beat one's breast; **errar el ~** to fail in an attempt; ✦*MODISMO* **no dar ~*** to be bone idle; ✦*REFRÁN* **a ~ dado no hay quite** (*CAm**) what's done cannot be undone

2 (*dado por una persona a otra*) blow; **le dio un ~ con un palo** he gave him a blow with his stick, he hit him with his stick; **a ~s**: **la emprendieron a ~s contra él** they began to beat him; **le mataron a ~s** they beat him to death; **les molieron a ~s** they beat them up; **los sacaron de la cama a ~s** they were beaten from their beds; **descargar ~s sobre algn** to rain blows on sb ► **golpe aplastante** crushing blow, knockout blow ► **golpe bien dado** hit, well-aimed blow ► **golpe de gracia** coup de grâce ► **golpe mortal** death blow

3 (*Med*) (= *cardenal*) bruise

4 (*en deportes*) (*Ftbl*) kick; (*Boxeo*) (*gen*) blow; (= *puñetazo*) punch; **con un total de 280 ~s** (*Golf*) with a total of 280 strokes; **preparar el ~** (*Golf*) to address the ball ► **golpe bajo** (*Boxeo*) low punch, punch below the belt; **aquello fue un ~ bajo** that was below the belt ► **golpe de acercamiento** (*Golf*) approach shot ► **golpe de castigo** (*Ftbl etc*) penalty kick ► **golpe de martillo** (*Tenis*) smash ► **golpe de penalidad** (*Golf*) penalty stroke ► **golpe de salida** (*Golf*) drive, drive-off ► **golpe franco**, **golpe libre** (*Ftbl*) free kick ► **golpe libre indirecto** indirect free kick

5 (*Téc*) stroke ► **golpe de émbolo** piston stroke

6 (= *desgracia*) blow; **mi ingreso en la cárcel fue un duro ~ para la familia** my imprisonment was a harsh blow to the family; **ha sufrido un duro ~** he has had a hard knock, he has suffered a severe blow; **la policía ha asestado un duro ~ al narcotráfico** the police have dealt a serious blow to drug traffickers; **acusar el ~** to suffer the consequences

7 (= *sorpresa*) surprise; **dar el ~ con algo** to cause a sensation with sth

8 (*) (= *atraco*) job*, heist (*EEUU*); **dieron un ~ en un banco** they did a bank job*; **preparaba su primer ~** he was planning his first job*

9 (= *salida*) witticism, sally; **¡qué ~!** how very clever!, good one!; **el libro tiene unos ~s buenísimos** the book's got some great lines in it

10 (*Pol*) coup ► **golpe blanco** bloodless coup ► **golpe de estado** coup d'état ► **golpe de mano** rising, sudden attack ► **golpe de palacio** palace coup

11 (*otras expresiones*) **a ~ de**: **abrir paso a ~ de machete** to hack out a path with a machete; **lo consiguieron a ~ de talonario** they got it through chequebook power; **al ~** (*Caribe*) instantly; **de ~**: **la puerta se abrió de ~** the door flew open; **cerrar una puerta de ~** to slam a door (shut); **la puerta se cerró de ~** the door slammed shut; **de ~ decidió dejar el trabajo** he suddenly decided to give up work; **de un ~** in one go; ✦*MODISMOS* **ir a ~ de calcetín** o **de alpargata*** to go on shanks's pony; **de ~ y porrazo** suddenly, unexpectedly ► **golpe de agua** heavy fall of rain ► **golpe de calor** heatstroke ► **golpe de efecto** coup de théâtre ► **golpe de fortuna** stroke of luck ► **golpe de gente** crowd of people ► **golpe de mar** heavy sea, surge ► **golpe de sol** sunstroke ► **golpe de suerte** stroke of luck ► **golpe de teatro** coup de théâtre ► **golpe de teléfono** telephone call ► **golpe de timón** change of direction ► **golpe de tos** fit of coughing ► **golpe de viento** gust of wind ► **golpe de vista**: **al primer ~ de vista** at first glance ► **golpe maestro** master stroke, stroke of genius

12 (*Cos*) (= *adorno*) pocket flap; (*Col*) (= *vuelta*) facing

13 (*Méx*) (= *mazo*) sledgehammer

14 (*Caribe**) (= *trago*) swig*, slug* (*of liquor*)

golpeador SM (*LAm*) door knocker

golpeadura SF = **golpeo**

golpear ▸conjug 1a◂ Ⓐ VT 1 (= *dar un golpe a*) to hit; (= *dar golpes a*) [+ *persona, alfombra*] to beat; (*para llamar la atención*) [+ *mesa, puerta, pared*] to bang on; **la ~on en la cabeza con una pistola** (*una vez*) they hit her on the head with a gun; (*varias veces*) they beat her about the head with a gun; **el maestro golpeó el pupitre con la mano** the teacher banged (on) the desk with his hand

2 [*desastre natural*] to hit, strike; **la vida le ha golpeado mucho** life has treated him badly

Ⓑ VI to beat; **la lluvia golpeaba contra los cristales** the rain was beating against the windows

Ⓒ **golpearse** VPR to hit, bang; **me golpeé la cabeza contra el armario** I hit o banged my head on the cupboard

golpecito SM (light) blow, tap; **dar ~s en algo** to tap (on) sth, rap (on) sth

golpeo SM (= *acción*) (*de una vez*) hitting; (*repetidamente*) beating; (*en mesa, puerta, pared*) banging

golpetazo* SM thump; **darse un ~ contra algo** to bang into sth, crash into sth

golpetear ▸conjug 1a◂ VT, VI (= *martillear*) to drum, tap; (= *traquetear*) to rattle

golpeteo SM (= *martilleo*) drumming, tapping; (= *traqueteo*) rattling

golpismo SM (= *tendencia*) *tendency to military coups*; (= *actitud*) *coup d'état mentality*

golpista Ⓐ ADJ **intentona ~** coup attempt; **trama** o **conspiración ~** coup plot o conspiracy

Ⓑ SMF (= *participante*) *participant in a coup*; (= *partidario*) *supporter of a coup*

golpiza SF (*LAm*) (= *paliza*) beating-up, bashing*; **dar una ~ a algn** to beat sb up, bash sb*

goma SF 1 (= *sustancia*) (*Bot*) gum; (= *caucho*) rubber; **unos guantes de ~** a pair of rubber gloves ► **goma 2** plastic explosive ► **goma arábiga** gum arabic ► **goma de mascar** chewing gum ► **goma de pegar** gum, glue ► **goma espuma**, **goma espumosa** foam rubber

2 (= *banda*) (*para el pelo, papeles, paquetes*) rubber band, elastic band; (*en costura*) elastic; (= *tira*) piece of elastic, length of elastic; **jugar** o **saltar a la ~** to skip (*with a long elastic*)

3 (*tb* **~ de borrar**) rubber, eraser

4 (*Cono Sur Aut*) tyre, tire (*EEUU*)

5 (*) (= *preservativo*) condom, sheath

6 (‡) (= *droga*) hash*, pot‡; [*de calidad*] good hash*, good pot‡

7 (*LAm*) [*de zapato*] rubber overshoe

8 (‡) [*de policía*] truncheon

9 (*CAm**) (= *resaca*) hangover; **estar de ~** to have a hangover

goma-espuma SF, **gomaespuma** SF foam rubber

gomal SM (*Andes*) rubber plantation

Gomera SF **la ~** Gomera

gomería SF (*Cono Sur*) tyre o (*EEUU*) tire repair shop

gomero/a Ⓐ ADJ (= *de caucho*) rubber *antes de s*

Ⓑ SM/F 1 (*LAm*) (= *dueño*) rubber planter, rubber producer; (= *trabajador*) rubber-plantation worker

2 (*Cono Sur Aut*) tyre o (*EEUU*) tire mechanic

Ⓒ SM 1 (= *árbol*) rubber tree

2 (= *frasco*) glue container

gomina SF (hair) gel

gominola SF (*azucarada*) Fruit Pastille®; (*no azucarada*) wine gum

gomita SF rubber band, elastic band

Gomorra SF Gomorrah

gomosidad SF gumminess

gomoso Ⓐ ADJ [*líquido*] gummy; [*pan*] rubbery

Ⓑ SM (†*) toff*, dandy

gónada SF gonad

góndola SF 1 (= *vehículo*) (= *barca*) gondola; (*Andes, Chile*) bus ► **góndola de cable** (= *teleférico*) cable car; [*de esquí*] ski-lift ► **góndola del motor** (*Aer*) engine casing

2 (*en supermercado*) gondola

gondolero SM gondolier

gong SM (*pl* **gongs**), **gongo** SM gong

gongorino ADJ *relating to Luis de Góngora*; **estilo ~** Gongoristic style; **estudios ~s** Góngora studies

gongorismo SM Gongorism (*literary style pioneered by Luis de Góngora in the 17th century*); → CULTERANISMO, CONCEPTISMO

gonorrea SF gonorrhoea, gonorrhea (*EEUU*)

gorda SF 1 ✦*MODISMO* **ni ~***: **no tener ni ~** to be skint*, be broke*; **lo hice sin cobrar ni ~** I didn't get a penny for it; **no se oye ni ~** you can hear absolutely nothing; **no entiende ni ~** he doesn't understand a blind thing*

2 **la Gorda** *the 1868 revolution in Spain*; ✦*MODISMOS* **armar la ~*** to kick up a fuss o a stink*; **si no me pagan voy a armar la ~** if they don't pay me I'm going to kick up a fuss o a stink*; **armarse la ~***: **se armó la ~** all hell broke loose; **se armó la ~ cuando volvieron mis padres** there was a hell of a row when my parents came back*

3 (*Méx*) thick tortilla; *ver tb* **gordo**

gordal Ⓐ ADJ fat, big, thick

Ⓑ SM *kind of large olive*

gordinflón/ona* Ⓐ ADJ chubby, podgy, pudgy (*EEUU*); **¡gordinflón!** fatty!*, fatso!*

Ⓑ SM/F fatty*, fatso*

gordito/a* Ⓐ ADJ 1 (= *gordo*) chubby, plump

2 (*Chile*) (= *querido*) darling*

Ⓑ SM/F fatty*, fatso*

gordo/a Ⓐ ADJ 1 [*persona*] (= *obeso*) fat; (= *corpulento*) stout, plump; **está más ~ que nunca** he's fatter than ever; ✦*MODISMO* **caer**

~ a algn*: **ese tipo me cae ~** I can't stand that guy*

2 (*) [*cosa, hecho*] big; **fue el desastre más ~ de su historia** it was the biggest *o* worst disaster in their history; **ha pasado algo muy ~** something major has happened; **una mentira de las gordas** a big fat lie*; **y lo más ~ fue que ...** and then to cap it all ...*

3 [*comida, sustancia*] greasy, oily; **tocino ~** fatty bacon

4 [*agua*] hard

5 [*lienzo, hilo*] coarse

6 (*Chile**) (= *querido*) darling*; *ver tb* **gota A1, perra 2, dedo 1, pez[1] A**

Ⓑ SM/F fat man/woman; **¡gordo!** fatty!*, fatso!*

Ⓒ SM 1 (*Culin*) fat, suet

2 (= *premio*) jackpot, big prize; **ganar el ~** to hit the jackpot, win the big prize; ✦*MODISMO* **sacarse el ~** to bring home the bacon*; *ver tb* **gorda**

EL GORDO

El **Gordo**, *"the big one", refers to a large lottery jackpot, particularly the one offered in the Spanish* **Lotería Nacional** *at Christmas. The* **Sorteo Extraordinario de Navidad** *takes place on 22 December and the jackpot is worth several million pounds. Because of the cost of whole tickets people generally form syndicates so the prize is usually shared out between a number of people.*

⇨ *See also* LOTERÍA

gordolobo SM mullein

gordura SF 1 (= *obesidad*) fat, fatness; (= *corpulencia*) stoutness, plumpness

2 (*Culin*) grease, fat

3 (*Caribe, Cono Sur**) (= *crema*) cream

gorgojear ▸conjug 1a◂ VI = **gorjear**

gorgojeo SM = **gorjeo**

gorgojo SM 1 (= *insecto*) grub, weevil

2 (= *persona*) dwarf, runt

gorgón SM (*Andes*) concrete

gorgoritear ▸conjug 1a◂ VI to trill, warble

gorgorito SM trill, warble; **hacer ~s** to trill, warble

gorgorizar ▸conjug 1f◂ VI to trill, warble

górgoro SM (*Méx*) bubble

gorgotear ▸conjug 1a◂ VI to gurgle

gorgoteo SM gurgle

gorguera SF (= *adorno*) ruff; (*Mil, Hist*) gorget

gori SM ✦*MODISMO* **armar el ~*** to make a row, kick up a fuss

gorigori* SM (= *canto*) gloomy chanting; (*en funeral*) funeral chanting; (= *gemidos*) wailing

gorila Ⓐ SM 1 (*Zool*) gorilla

2 (*) (= *matón*) tough*, thug*; [*de club*] bouncer*; (= *guardaespaldas*) bodyguard, minder*

3 (*Cono Sur Pol**) right-winger; (*Mil*) senior officer

Ⓑ ADJ (*Cono Sur Pol**) reactionary

gorilismo SM thuggery

goriloide SM brute, thug

gorja SF throat, gorge; ✦*MODISMO* **estar de ~*** to be very cheerful

gorjear ▸conjug 1a◂ Ⓐ VI [*ave*] to chirp, trill

Ⓑ **gorjearse** VPR [*niño*] to gurgle, burble

gorjeo SM 1 [*de ave*] chirping, trilling

2 [*de bebé*] gurgling, burbling

gorobeto ADJ (*Andes*) twisted, bent, warped

gorra Ⓐ SF 1 (*para la cabeza*) (*gen*) cap; [*de bebé*] bonnet; (*Mil*) bearskin, busby; ✦*MODISMOS* **pasar la ~** to pass the hat round; **pegar la ~*** to be unfaithful ► **gorra de montar** riding cap ► **gorra de paño** cloth cap ► **gorra de punto** knitted cap ► **gorra de visera** peaked cap ► **gorra de yate** yachting cap

2 ✦*MODISMO* **de ~***: **una comida de ~** a free meal; **andar** *o* **ir** *o* **vivir de ~** to sponge*, scrounge*; **comer de ~** to scrounge a meal*; **entrar de ~** to get in free; **sacar algo de ~** to scrounge sth*; **me vino de ~** (*CAm**) it was a stroke of luck, it came out of the blue

Ⓑ SMF (*) (= *gorrón*) sponger*, cadger*, parasite

gorrazo SM **correr a algn a ~s** to run sb out of town

gorrear ▸conjug 1a◂ Ⓐ VT 1 (*) (= *gorronear*) to scrounge*, cadge*; **siempre me está gorreando cigarrillos** he's always scrounging *o* cadging cigarettes off me*

2 (*Cono Sur‡*) to cuckold

Ⓑ VI (*) to scrounge*, sponge*; **a ver cuándo dejas de ~ y te pagas tú las cosas** when are you going to stop scrounging *o* sponging and pay your own way?*

gorrero/a SM/F 1 cap maker

2 (*) = **gorrón[2]**

gorrinada SF 1 (= *mala pasada*) dirty trick

2 (= *cerdos*) (number of) pigs *pl*

gorrinera SF pigsty, pigpen (*EEUU*)

gorrinería SF 1 (= *porquería*) dirt

2 (= *mala pasada*) dirty trick

gorrino/a SM/F 1 (= *cerdo*) pig, hog (*EEUU*); (= *cochinito*) piglet; **chillaba como un ~** he was squealing like a pig

2 (= *persona*) pig*

gorrión SM 1 (= *ave*) sparrow

2 ✦*MODISMO* **de ~** (*Caribe*) *ver* **gorra A2**

gorrista* SMF = **gorra B**

gorro SM [*de lana*] hat; [*de bebé*] bonnet; ✦*MODISMOS* **estar hasta el ~*** to be fed up*; **hinchar el ~ a algn‡** to get on sb's wick‡; **poner el ~ a algn*** (= *avergonzar*) to embarrass sb; (*Cono Sur, Méx‡*) to be unfaithful to sb, cuckold sb‡ ► **gorro de baño** bathing cap ► **gorro de caña** pith helmet ► **gorro de dormir** nightcap ► **gorro de montaña** Balaclava (helmet) ► **gorro de papel** paper hat ► **gorro de piel** fur hat ► **gorro frigio** Phrygian cap, revolutionary cap

gorrón[1] SM 1 (= *guijarro*) pebble; (= *adoquín*) cobblestone

2 (*Mec*) pivot, journal

gorrón[2]/ona* SM/F (= *aprovechado*) sponger*, cadger*, parasite

gorronear* ▸conjug 1a◂ Ⓐ VT to scrounge*, cadge*; **~ algo a algn** to scrounge *o* cadge sth from sb*; **le gorronean los amigos** his friends scrounge *o* cadge off him*

Ⓑ VI to sponge*, scrounge*

gorroneo* SM sponging*, scrounging*

gorronería* SF 1 (= *abuso*) sponging*, scrounging*

2 (*Andes*) (= *avaricia*) greed, avarice

gospel SM gospel music

gota Ⓐ SF 1 (*de líquido*) drop; (*de sudor*) drop, bead; **unas ~s de coñac** a few drops of brandy; **todo ello mezclado con algunas ~s de humor** all mixed with a few touches of humour; **se añade el aceite ~ a ~** add the oil drop by drop; **van filtrando la información ~ a ~ a la prensa** they let the news leak out to the press in dribs and drabs; **sistema de riego ~ a ~** trickle irrigation; **caer a ~s** to drip; ✦*MODISMOS* **la ~ que colma el vaso** the straw that breaks the camel's back, the last straw; **¡ni ~!** not a bit!; **no bebo ni ~ de alcohol** I don't drink a drop of alcohol; **no corre ni ~ de aire** there isn't a breath of air; **no ver ni ~** to see nothing; **parecerse como dos ~s de agua** to be as like as two peas; **sudar la ~ gorda** to sweat blood ► **gotas amargas** bitters

2 (= *enfermedad*) gout ► **gota caduca, gota coral** epilepsy

3 (*Meteo*) ► **gota fría** *severe weather which brings flooding*

4 ► **gota de leche** (*Chile*) (*fig*) child welfare clinic, welfare food centre

5 **gotas** (= *medicina*) drops ► **gotas nasales** nose drops, nasal drops

Ⓑ SM ► **gota a gota** drip, IV (*EEUU*); **le pusieron el ~ a ~** he was put on a drip

goteado ADJ speckled, spotted

gotear ▸conjug 1a◂ VI 1 [*líquido, grifo, vela*] to drip; [*cañería, recipiente*] to leak; **pintó el techo sin ~** he painted the ceiling without spilling a drop

2 (*Meteo*) to rain lightly

goteo SM 1 [*de líquido, grifo*] dripping; [*de cañería, recipiente*] leak; (= *chorrito*) trickle; **el ~ de cartas de protesta se convirtió en avalancha** the trickle of letters of complaint became a flood; **un constante ~ de dimisiones** a steady flow *o* stream of resignations; **riego por ~** trickle irrigation

2 (*Med*) drip, IV (*EEUU*)

gotera SF 1 (= *filtración*) leak; (= *gotas*) drip; (= *chorrito*) trickle

2 (= *mancha*) damp stain

3 (*Med*) (= *achaque*) chronic ailment; **estar lleno de ~s** to be full of aches and pains, feel a wreck*

4 [*de colgadura*] valance

5 **goteras** (*LAm*) (= *afueras*) outskirts, environs

gotero SM 1 (*Med*) drip, IV (*EEUU*)

2 (*LAm*) [*de laboratorio*] dropper

goterón SM big raindrop

gótico Ⓐ ADJ 1 [*estilo, arte, letra*] Gothic

2 (= *noble*) noble, illustrious

Ⓑ SM (*Ling*) Gothic

gotita SF droplet; **¡una ~ nada más!** [*de bebida*] just a drop!

gotoso ADJ gouty

gouache [gwaʃ] SM gouache

gourmet [gur'me] SMF (*pl* **gourmets** [gur'mes]) gourmet, connoisseur (*of food*)

goyesco ADJ 1 (= *de Goya*) of Goya

2 [*estilo artístico*] Goy(a)esque, *in the style of Goya, after the manner of Goya*

gozada* SF **es una ~** it's brilliant *o* fantastic*; **aquí se está de maravilla, ¡qué ~!** it's wonderful here, sheer heaven!

gozar ▸conjug 1f◂ Ⓐ VT 1 (= *disfrutar*) to enjoy; (= *poseer*) to have, possess

2 (††) [+ *mujer*] to have, seduce

Ⓑ VI 1 (= *disfrutar*) to enjoy o.s., have a good time (**con** with); **~ de algo** (= *disfrutar*) to enjoy sth; (= *tener*) to have sth, possess sth; **~ de buena salud** to enjoy good health
2 (‡) (= *llegar al orgasmo*) to come‡
Ⓒ **gozarse** VPR to enjoy o.s.; **~se en hacer algo** to enjoy doing sth, take pleasure in doing sth

gozne SM hinge

gozo SM 1 (= *placer*) enjoyment, pleasure; (= *complacencia*) delight; (= *júbilo*) joy, rejoicing; **no caber (en sí) de ~** to be overjoyed; **da ~ escucharle** it's a pleasure to listen to him; **es un ~ para los ojos** it's a joy to see, it's a sight for sore eyes; ✦*MODISMO* **¡mi ~ en un pozo!** it's gone down the drain!
2 **gozos** (*Literat, Mús*) *couplets in honour of the Virgin*

gozosamente ADV joyfully; **se lo comunicó ~ a los demás** he joyfully told the others; **aceptaron ~ la ofrenda** they were delighted to accept the gift

gozoso ADJ joyful

gozque SM (= *perro*) small yapping dog; (= *cachorro*) puppy

g.p. ABR, **g/p** ABR (= **giro postal**) p.o., m.o. (*EEUU*)

gr. ABR (= **gramo(s)**) gm(s)

grabación SF recording ► **grabación digital** digital recording ► **grabación en cinta** tape-recording ► **grabación en directo** live recording ► **grabación en vídeo** video recording ► **grabación magnetofónica** tape-recording

grabado Ⓐ ADJ **se me quedó grabada la expresión de la niña** I'll never forget the girl's expression; **tengo grabada en la memoria su cara** her face is engraved *o* etched on my memory
Ⓑ SM (= *impresión*) engraving, print; (*en un libro*) illustration, print ► **grabado al agua fuerte** etching ► **grabado al agua tinta** aquatint ► **grabado en cobre**, **grabado en dulce** copperplate ► **grabado en madera** woodcut ► **grabado rupestre** rock carving

grabador¹ SM tape recorder

grabador²(a) SM/F (= *persona*) engraver

grabadora SF 1 (*tb* **~ de cinta**) tape recorder ► **grabadora de DVDs** (*gen*) DVD recorder; (*en ordenador*) DVD writer, DVD burner ► **grabadora de sonido** voice recorder ► **grabadora de vídeo** video (recorder)
2 (= *empresa*) recording company
3 (*Téc*) graver, cutting tool

grabadura SF engraving

grabar ▸conjug 1a◂ VT 1 (*en madera, metal*) to engrave; **grabó sus iniciales en la medalla** he engraved his initials on the medal; **~ al agua fuerte** to etch
2 [+ *sonidos, imágenes*] (*gen*) to record; (= *hacer una copia en cinta*) to tape; **están grabando su nuevo álbum** they are recording their new album; **un disco grabado en 1960** a record made in 1960; **¿me puedes ~ este CD?** can you tape this CD for me?
3 (= *fijar*) to etch; **lo tengo grabado en la memoria** it's etched on my memory; **lleva el dolor grabado en el rostro** the pain is engraved *o* etched on her face; **~ algo en el ánimo de algn** to impress sth on sb's mind

gracejada* SF (*CAm, Méx*) stupid joke

gracejo SM 1 (= *chispa*) wit, humour, humor (*EEUU*); (*en conversación*) repartee
2 (= *encanto*) charm, grace
3 (*CAm, Méx*) (= *payaso*) clown

▼**gracia** SF 1 (= *diversión*) 1·1 [*de chiste, persona*] **yo no le veo la ~** I don't see what's so funny; **si no lo cuentas bien se le va la ~** if you don't tell it well the joke is lost; **nos lo contó con mucha ~** he told it to us in a very funny *o* amusing way; **ahí está la ~** that's the whole point; **coger** *o* **pescar la ~** to see the point (*of a joke*)
1·2 **hacer ~ a algn**: **a mí no me hace ~ ese humorista** I don't find that comedian funny; **me hace ~ ver a mi padre en la televisión** it's funny seeing my father on television; **me hace ~ que me llamen conservador precisamente ellos** it's funny that they of all people should call me conservative; **no me hacía ~ su aire de superioridad** I didn't like his air of superiority; **al jefe no le va a hacer ninguna ~ que nos vayamos a casa** our boss is not going to be at all happy about us going home; **no me hace mucha ~ la idea de tener que trabajar este domingo** I'm not wild about the idea of having to work this Sunday*
1·3 **tener ~** [*broma, chiste*] to be funny; [*persona*] (= *ser ingenioso*) to be witty; (= *ser divertido*) to be funny, be amusing; **la broma no tuvo ~** the joke wasn't funny; **¡tiene ~ la cosa!** (*iró*) isn't that (just) great! (*iró*); **tendría ~ que se estropeara el despertador justamente hoy** (*iró*) wouldn't it be just great if the alarm didn't go off today of all days? (*iró*); **tiene mucha ~ hablando** he's very witty, he's very funny *o* amusing; **tiene mucha ~ contando chistes** his jokes are really funny
1·4 **¡qué ~!** (*gen*) how funny!; (*iró*) it's great, isn't it?; **¿así que tu hermano y mi hermano se conocen? ¡qué ~!** so your brother and mine know each other — how funny!; **y, ¡qué ~!, me dice el profesor: —señorita, compórtese** and the teacher said to me, it was so funny, "behave yourself, young lady"; **¡qué ~! ¿no? tú de vacaciones y yo aquí estudiando** (*iró*) it's great, isn't it? you are on holiday while I am here studying (*iró*)
1·5 **dar en la ~ de hacer algo** to take to doing sth
2 (= *encanto*) 2·1 (*al moverse*) gracefulness, grace; **se mueve con ~** she moves gracefully; **sin ~** ungraceful, lacking in gracefulness *o* grace; **tener ~** to be graceful
2·2 (*en la personalidad*) charm; **tener ~** [*persona*] to have charm; [*objeto*] to be nice; **no es guapo, pero tiene cierta ~** he's not good-looking but he has a certain charm; **no tiene ninguna ~ vistiendo** she has no dress sense
3 (= *chiste*) joke; **hacer una ~ a algn** to play a prank on sb; **hizo una de sus ~s** he showed himself up once again; **reírle las ~s a algn** to laugh along with sb
4 **gracias** 4·1 (*para expresar agradecimiento*) thanks; **¡~s!** thank you!; **¡muchas ~s!** thank you very much!, thanks a lot!, many thanks! (*más frm*); **dar las ~s a algn** to thank sb (**por** for); **no nos dio ni las ~s** he didn't even say thank you, he didn't even thank us; **llamaba para darte las ~s por todo** I am phoning to thank you for everything; **toma eso, ¡y ~s!** take that and be thankful!; **y ~s que no llegó a más** and we *etc* were lucky to get off so lightly
4·2 **~s a** thanks to; **hemos conseguido esta casa ~s a ellos** it's thanks to them that we got this house; **han sobrevivido ~s a la ayuda internacional** they have survived with the help of *o* thanks to international aid; **la familia se mantiene ~s a que el padre y la madre trabajan** the family manages to support itself thanks to the fact that both parents work; **~s a Dios** thank heaven(s)
5 (*Rel*) grace; **estar en ~ (de Dios)** to be in a state of grace; **por la ~ de Dios** by the grace of God; *ver tb* **obra 1**
6 (*Jur*) mercy, pardon; **medida de ~** pardon; *ver tb* **tiro 1**
7 (= *favor*) favour, favor (*EEUU*); **te concederé la ~ que me pidas** I will grant you whatever favour you request; **caer de la ~ de algn**† fall out of favour with sb; **de ~**† free, gratis; ✦*MODISMOS* **caer en ~ a algn** to warm to sb, take a liking to sb; **me cayó en ~ enseguida** I warmed to him immediately, I took an immediate liking to him; **nunca me cayó en ~ tu suegra** I never really liked your mother-in-law; **hacer a algn ~ de algo** to spare sb sth; **te hago ~ de los detalles** I'll spare you the details
8 (= *benevolencia*) graciousness
9 (*Mit*) **las tres Gracias** the Three Graces
10 **en ~ a**† on account of; **en ~ a la brevedad** for the sake of brevity
11 (†) (= *nombre*) name; **¿cuál es su ~?** what is your name?

graciable ADJ 1 [*persona*] (= *benévolo*) gracious; (= *amable*) kind
2 [*concesión*] easily-granted
3 [*pago*] discretionary

graciablemente ADV 1 [*comportarse*] (= *con benevolencia*) graciously; (= *con amabilidad*) kindly 2 [*pagar*] on a discretionary basis

grácil ADJ [*figura, líneas, movimientos*] graceful; [*talle*] slender

gracilidad SF gracefulness, grace

graciosamente ADV 1 (= *con encanto*) gracefully; (= *con elegancia*) pleasingly, elegantly
2 (= *con humor*) funnily, amusingly; (= *con agudeza*) wittily; (= *payaseando*) comically

graciosidad SF 1 (= *encanto*) grace, gracefulness; (= *elegancia*) elegance; (= *belleza*) beauty
2 (= *humor*) funniness, amusing qualities *pl*; (= *agudeza*) wittiness

gracioso/a Ⓐ ADJ 1 (= *divertido*) funny, amusing; **una situación muy graciosa** a very funny *o* amusing situation; **es de lo más ~** he's really funny *o* amusing; **estás tú muy graciosillo hoy** (*iró*) you're very witty *o* funny today; **lo ~ del caso es que …** the funny *o* amusing thing about it is that …; **lo ~ sería que ganaran ellos, cuando van los últimos** it would be funny if they won, when they're last at the moment; **¡qué ~!** how funny!; **has visto cómo me ha adelantado ese coche ¡qué ~!** (*iró*) did you see how that car overtook me — now that was really clever, wasn't it?
2 (= *mono*) cute; **tiene una nariz muy graciosa** she's got a cute little nose; **un sombrerito muy ~** a lovely *o* cute little hat
3 (*como título*) gracious; **su graciosa Majestad** her gracious Majesty
4 (= *gratuito*) free
Ⓑ SM/F (*iró*) joker*; **habrá sido algún ~** it must have been some joker*; **hacerse el ~** to try to be funny; **¡no se haga el ~!** don't try to

➤ LENGUA Y USO: **gracia 4** 48.1, 49, 52.1, 52.4

be funny!
Ⓒ SM (*Teat, Hist*) comic character, fool

grada SF 1 (= *asiento*) tier, row of seats; **asientos de ~** stands; **la(s) ~(s)** the stands, the terraces, the terracing; **un gol coreado en la(s) ~(s)** a goal which was hailed in the stands *o* on the terraces *o* on the terracing
2 (= *peldaño*) step, stair; (*Rel*) altar step; **gradas** (= *escalinata*) flight *sing* of steps; (*Andes, Cono Sur*) paved terrace *sing* (*in front of a building*)
3 (*Náut*) [*de construcción*] slip; [*de reparaciones*] slipway
4 (= *azada*) harrow ► **grada de disco** disk harrow ► **grada de mano** hoe, cultivator

gradación SF 1 (= *progresión*) gradation; (= *serie*) graded series
2 (*Retórica*) climax; (*Ling*) comparison

gradar ▸conjug 1a◂ VT (*Agr*) (= *allanar*) to harrow; (= *cultivar*) to hoe

gradería SF, **graderío** SM stands *pl*, terraces *pl*, terracing; **ambiente crispado en el graderío** *o* **los graderíos** tense atmosphere in the stands *o* on the terraces *o* on the terracing ► **gradería cubierta** grandstand

grado SM 1 (= *nivel*) degree; **un alto ~ de desarrollo** a high degree of development; **quemaduras de primer/segundo ~** first-/second-degree burns; **parentesco de segundo ~** second-degree kinship; **en alto ~** to a great degree; **la censura dificultó en alto ~ la investigación científica** scientific research was greatly hindered *o* was hindered to a great degree by censorship; **de ~ en ~** step by step, by degrees; **en mayor ~** to a greater degree *o* extent; **en menor ~** to a lesser degree *o* extent; **en mayor o menor ~** to a greater or lesser extent; **en sumo ~** *o* **en ~ sumo**: **era humillante en sumo ~** it was humiliating in the extreme; **me complace en sumo ~** it gives me the greatest pleasure; **en ~ superlativo** in the extreme; **tercer ~ (penitenciario)** (*Esp*) *lowest category within the prison system which allows day release privileges*
2 (*Geog, Mat, Fís*) degree; **la temperatura es de 40 ~s** the temperature is 40 degrees; **estamos a cinco ~s bajo cero** it is five degrees below zero; **un ángulo de 45 ~s** a 45-degree angle; **este vino tiene 12 ~s** this wine is 12 per cent alcohol; **esta cerveza no tiene muchos ~s** this beer is very low in alcohol ► **grado Celsius** degree Celsius ► **grado centígrado** degree centigrade ► **grado Fahrenheit** degree Fahrenheit
3 [*de escalafón*] grade; (*Mil*) rank; **tiene el ~ de teniente** he holds the rank of lieutenant; **un militar de ~ superior** a high-ranking army officer
4 (= *etapa*) stage; **está en el segundo ~ de elaboración** it is now in the second stage of production
5 (*esp LAm Educ*) (= *curso*) year, grade (*EEUU*); (= *título*) degree; **tiene el ~ de licenciado** he is a graduate; **colación de ~s** (*Arg*) conferment of degrees ► **grado universitario** university degree
6 (*Ling*) degree of comparison; **adjetivos en ~ comparativo** comparative adjectives, comparatives; **adjetivos en ~ superlativo** superlative adjectives, superlatives
7 (= *gusto*) **de (buen) ~** willingly; **aceptó las nuevas normas de buen ~** she willingly agreed the new regulations; **de mal ~** unwillingly; ✦MODISMO **de ~ o por (la) fuerza**: **otros muchos países entraron en guerra, de ~ o por la fuerza** many other countries were forced willy-nilly to enter the war; **pues tendrás que ir, de ~ o por la fuerza** well you'll have to go, like it or not
8 [*de escalera*] step
9 **grados** (*Rel*) minor orders

graduable ADJ adjustable, that can be adjusted

graduación SF 1 [*de volumen, temperatura*] adjustment
2 [*de una bebida*] alcoholic strength, proof grading; **bebidas de baja ~** drinks with a low alcohol content ► **graduación octánica** octane rating
3 [*de la vista*] testing
4 (*Univ*) graduation; **baile de ~** graduation ball
5 (*Mil*) (= *rango*) rank; **de alta ~** of high rank, high-ranking

graduado/a Ⓐ ADJ 1 [*escala*] graduated; **gafas graduadas** prescription glasses, glasses with prescription lenses
2 (*Educ*) graduate *antes de s*
3 [*militar*] commissioned
Ⓑ SM/F (= *estudiante*) graduate
Ⓒ SM **graduado escolar** (*Esp*) *formerly, certificate of success in EGB course*

gradual ADJ gradual

gradualidad SF gradualness

gradualismo SM (*esp Pol*) gradualism

gradualista ADJ, SMF gradualist

gradualmente ADV gradually

graduando/a SM/F graduand

graduar ▸conjug 1e◂ Ⓐ VT 1 (= *regular*) [+ *volumen, temperatura*] to adjust; **hay que ~ la salida del agua** the outflow of water has to be regulated
2 (= *medir*) to gauge, measure; (*Téc*) to calibrate; [+ *termómetro*] to graduate; [+ *vista*] to test; **tengo que ~me la vista** I've got to have my eyes tested
3 (*Univ*) to confer a degree on
4 (*Mil*) to confer a rank on; **~ a algn de capitán** to confer the rank of captain on sb
Ⓑ **graduarse** VPR 1 (*Univ*) to graduate, take one's degree; **se graduó en Derecho** he graduated in law
2 (*Mil*) to take a commission (**de** as)

GRAE ABR = **Gramática de la Real Academia Española**

grafía SF spelling; **se inclina por la ~ "gira"** he prefers the spelling "gira"

gráfica SF 1 (= *representación*) (*Mat*) graph; (= *diagrama*) chart ► **gráfica de fiebre**, **gráfica de temperatura** (*Med*) temperature chart
2 (= *empresa*) **"Gráficas Giménez"** "Giménez Graphics"

graficación SF 1 (*Inform*) graphics *sing*
2 (*Mat*) representation on a graph

gráficamente ADV graphically

gráfico Ⓐ ADJ 1 [*diseño, artes*] graphic; **tarjeta gráfica** graphics card; **información gráfica** photographs *pl*, pictures *pl*; **reportero ~** press photographer
2 [*descripción, relato*] graphic
Ⓑ SM 1 (= *diagrama*) chart; (*Mat*) graph ► **gráfico de barras** bar chart ► **gráfico de sectores**, **gráfico de tarta** pie chart
2 **gráficos** (*Inform*) graphics

grafiosis SF INV Dutch elm disease

grafismo SM 1 (*Arte*) graphic art; (*Inform*) computer graphics
2 (= *logotipo*) logo
3 (= *escritura*) graphology

grafista SMF graphic artist, graphic designer

grafiti SMPL graffiti

grafito SM graphite, black lead

grafología SF graphology

grafólogo/a SM/F graphologist

gragea SF 1 (*Med*) sugar-coated pill
2 (= *confite*) small coloured *o* (*EEUU*) colored sweet

graja SF rook

grajea SF (*Andes*) fine shot, birdshot

grajear ▸conjug 1a◂ VI [*ave*] to caw; [*bebé*] to gurgle

grajiento ADJ (*LAm*) smelly

grajilla SF jackdaw

grajo SM 1 (= *cuervo*) rook
2 (*LAm*) (= *olor corporal*) body odour *o* (*EEUU*) odor; [*del sobaco*] underarm smell

Gral. ABR, **gral.** ABR (= **General**) Gen

grama SF (*esp LAm*) (= *hierba*) Bermuda grass; (*Caribe**) (= *césped*) lawn

gramaje SM weight (*of paper etc*)

gramática SF (= *estudio*) grammar; (= *texto*) grammar (book) ► **gramática de casos** case grammar ► **gramática generativa** generative grammar ► **gramática parda** native wit; **saber** *o* **tener mucha ~ parda** to be worldly-wise, know the ways of the world ► **gramática profunda** deep grammar ► **gramática transformacional** transformational grammar; *ver tb* **gramático**

gramatical ADJ grammatical

gramático/a Ⓐ ADJ grammatical
Ⓑ SM/F (= *persona*) grammarian; *ver tb* **gramática**

gramil SM gauge, gage (*EEUU*)

gramilla SF (*LAm*) grass, lawn

gramillar SM (*Cono Sur*) meadow, grassland

gramínea SF grass; (*LAm*) pulse

gramo SM gramme, gram (*EEUU*)

gramófono SM gramophone, phonograph (*EEUU*)

gramola† SF gramophone, phonograph (*EEUU*); (*en bar, cafetería*) jukebox

grampa SF (*esp LAm*) staple

gran *ver* **grande**

grana[1] SF (*Bot*) 1 (= *semilla*) small seed; **dar en ~** to go to seed, run to seed
2 (= *acto*) seeding; (= *estación*) seeding time
3 (*LAm*) (= *pasto*) grass; (*CAm, Méx Dep*) turf

grana[2] SF (*Zool*) cochineal; (= *tinte*) kermes; (= *color*) scarlet; (= *tela*) scarlet cloth; **de ~** scarlet, bright red; ✦MODISMO **ponerse como la ~** to go as red as a beetroot

Granada SF (*Esp*) Granada; (*Caribe*) Grenada

granada SF 1 (*Bot*) pomegranate
2 (= *bomba*) grenade ► **granada anticarro** anti-tank grenade ► **granada de mano** hand grenade ► **granada de metralla** shrapnel shell ► **granada de mortero** mortar shell ► **granada de fragmentación** fragmentation grenade ► **granada de humo** smoke-bomb ► **granada detonadora** stun grenade ► **granada lacrimógena** teargas grenade

granadero SM 1 (*Mil*) grenadier
2 **granaderos** (*Méx*) (= *policía*) riot police

granadilla SF (= *pasionaria*) passionflower; (= *fruto*) passion fruit

granadino/a Ⓐ ADJ of/from Granada
Ⓑ SM/F native/inhabitant of Granada; **los ~s** the people of Granada

granado[1] SM (= *árbol*) pomegranate tree

granado[2] ADJ [1] (= *selecto*) choice, select; (= *notable*) distinguished; **lo más ~ de la sociedad** the cream of society; **lo más ~ de la prosa en lengua española** the pick of Spanish prose writing
[2] (= *maduro*) mature; (= *alto*) full-grown, tall

granangular ADJ **objetivo ~** wide-angle lens

granar ▸conjug 1a◂ VI to seed, run to seed

granate Ⓐ SM [1] (= *mineral*) garnet
[2] (= *color*) deep red, dark crimson
Ⓑ ADJ INV deep red, dark crimson

granazón SF seeding

Gran Bretaña SF Great Britain

Gran Canaria SF Grand Canary

grancanario/a Ⓐ ADJ of/from Grand Canary
Ⓑ SM/F native/inhabitant of Grand Canary; **los ~s** the people of Grand Canary

grande Ⓐ ADJ (*antes de sm sing* **gran**) [1] (*de tamaño*) big, large; (*de estatura*) big, tall; [*número, velocidad*] high, great; **viven en una casa muy ~** they live in a very big *o* large house; **¿cómo es de ~?** how big *o* large is it?, what size is it?; **los zapatos le están muy ~s** the shoes are too big for her; **en cantidades más ~s** in larger *o* greater quantities; **grandísimo** enormous, huge; **un esfuerzo grandísimo** an enormous effort, a huge effort; **un coche grandísimo** a whacking great car*; **¡grandísimo tunante!** you old rogue!; **el gran Buenos Aires** greater Buenos Aires; ✦***MODISMOS*** **a lo ~*** in style; **hacer algo a lo ~** to do sth in style, make a splash doing sth*; **vivir a lo ~** to live in style; **quedarle algo ~ a algn** to be too much for sb, be more than sb can handle; **pasarlo en ~** to have a tremendous time*
[2] (= *importante*) [*artista, hazaña*] great; [*empresa*] big; **un gran pintor** a great painter; **un gran desastre** a great disaster; **es una ventaja muy ~** it's a great advantage; **hay una diferencia no muy ~** there is not a very big *o* great difference; **los ~s bancos internacionales** the big international banks; **las ~s empresas multinacionales** the big multinationals; **la gran mayoría** the great majority
[3] (= *mucho, muy*) great; **con gran placer** with great pleasure; **fueron ~s amigos** they were great friends; **he sentido una gran pena** I felt very sad; **me llevé una alegría muy ~** I felt very happy; **comer con gran apetito** to eat hungrily; **un mes de gran calor** a very hot month; **un programa de gran éxito** a very successful programme; **se estrenó con gran éxito** it was a great success, it went off very well
[4] (*en edad*) (= *mayor*) **ya eres ~, Raúl** you are a big boy now, Raúl; **¿qué piensas hacer cuando seas ~?** what do you want to do when you grow up?
[5] **¡qué ~!** (*Arg**) how funny!
Ⓑ SMF [1] (= *personaje importante*) **los ~s de la industria** the major companies in the industry; **uno de los ~s de la pantalla** one of the screen greats; **los siete ~s** the Big Seven ► **Grande de España** grandee
[2] (*LAm*) (= *adulto*) adult
Ⓒ SF [1] (*Arg*) [*de lotería*] first prize, big prize
[2] (*Andes*‡) (= *cárcel*) clink‡, jail

grandemente ADV greatly, extremely; **~ equivocado** greatly mistaken

grandeza SF [1] (= *nobleza*) nobility; **la ~ de su acción humanitaria** the nobility *o* greatness of his humanitarian action; **~ de alma** *o* **espíritu** magnanimity
[2] [*de artista etc*] greatness
[3] (= *esplendidez*) grandness, impressiveness; (= *ostentación*) grandeur, magnificence
[4] (= *personas*) grandees *pl*; **la Grandeza de España** the Spanish nobility
[5] (= *rango*) status of grandee
[6] (= *tamaño*) size; (= *gran tamaño*) bigness; (= *magnitud*) magnitude

grandilocuencia SF grandiloquence

grandilocuente ADJ, **grandílocuo** ADJ grandiloquent

grandiosidad SF = **grandeza 3**

grandioso ADJ (= *magnífico*) grand, magnificent; (*pey*) grandiose

grandísimo ADJ SUPERL *de* **grande**

grandón ADJ solidly-built

grandor SM size

grandote* ADJ huge

grandullón/ona* Ⓐ ADJ overgrown, oversized
Ⓑ SM/F big kid

grandulón/ona ADJ, SM/F (*Andes*) = **grandullón**

granear ▸conjug 1a◂ VT [1] [+ *semilla*] to sow
[2] (*Téc*) to grain, stipple

granel SM [1] (*Com*) **a ~** (= *en cantidad*) in bulk; (= *sin envasar*) loose; **vender a ~** [+ *líquidos*] to sell by the pint *o* litre; [+ *alimentos*] to sell loose; **vino a ~** wine in bulk *o* in the barrel; **olía a colonia de ~** she smelled of cheap perfume
[2] (= *montón*) heap; **a ~** (= *mucho*) in abundance; (= *a montones*) by the ton; (= *con profusión*) lavishly

granelero SM bulk-carrier

granero SM [1] (= *edificio*) granary, barn
[2] (= *distrito*) granary, corn-producing area; **el ~ de Europa** the breadbasket of Europe

granetario SM precision balance

granete SM punch

granguiñolesco ADJ melodramatic, exaggerated

granilla SF grain (*in cloth*)

granítico ADJ granitic, granite *antes de s*

granito[1] SM (*Geol*) granite

granito[2] SM [1] [*de sal, azúcar etc*] grain; **aportaremos nuestro ~ de arena** we'll do our bit*
[2] (*Med*) pimple

granizada SF [1] (*Meteo*) hailstorm, hail
[2] (*fig*) hail; (= *abundancia*) shower, vast number; **una ~ de balas** a hail of bullets
[3] (*Andes*) (= *bebida*) iced drink

granizado SM (= *bebida*) iced drink; [*de hielo*] slush ► **granizado de café** iced coffee ► **granizado de limón** iced lemon drink

granizal SM (*LAm*) hailstorm

granizar ▸conjug 1f◂ VI (*Meteo*) to hail; (*fig*) to shower, rain

granizo SM hail

granja SF farm; **animales de ~** farm animals; **huevos de ~** free-range eggs; **pollo de ~** free-range chicken ► **granja avícola** chicken farm, poultry farm ► **granja colectiva** collective farm ► **granja de multiplicación** factory farm ► **granja de pollos** chicken farm ► **granja escuela** educational farm ► **granja marina** fish farm

granjear ▸conjug 1a◂ Ⓐ VT [1] (= *adquirir*) [+ *respeto, enemigos*] to earn; **su actitud le granjeó una fama de intolerante** his attitude earned him a reputation as a bigot
[2] (*Andes, Cono Sur*) (= *robar*) to steal
Ⓑ **granjearse** VPR [+ *respeto, enemigos*] to earn

granjería SF [1] (*Com, Fin*) profit, earnings *pl*; (*Agr*) farm earnings *pl*
[2] (= *zootecnia*) farming, husbandry

granjero/a SM/F farmer

grano SM [1] (= *semilla*) [*de cereales*] grain; [*de mostaza*] seed; ✦***MODISMOS*** **ir (directo) al ~** to get to the point; **¡vamos al ~!** let's get to the point!; **no es ~ de anís** it's not just a small thing ► **grano de arroz** grain of rice ► **grano de cacao** cocoa bean ► **grano de café** coffee bean ► **grano de sésamo** sesame seed ► **grano de trigo** grain of wheat ► **granos panificables** bread grains
[2] (= *semillas*) grain; **aquí se almacena el ~** the grain is stored here; ✦***MODISMO*** **apartar el ~ de la paja** to separate the wheat from the chaff
[3] (= *partícula*) grain; (= *punto*) speck; **un ~ de arena** a grain of sand; ✦***MODISMO*** **poner su ~ de arena** to do one's bit*
[4] (*en la piel*) spot, pimple
[5] (*en piedra, madera, fotografía*) grain; **de ~ fino** fine-grained; **de ~ gordo** coarse-grained
[6] (*Farm*) grain
[7] (‡) [*de droga*] fix‡, shot*

granoso ADJ granular, granulated

granuja Ⓐ SMF (= *bribón*) rogue; (*dicho con afecto*) rascal; (= *pilluelo*) urchin, ragamuffin
Ⓑ SF (= *uvas*) loose grapes *pl*; (= *semilla*) grape seed

granujada SF dirty trick; **hacer una ~ a algn** to pull a fast one on sb*; **es una ~** it's a low-down thing to do*

granujería SF (*en conjunto*) rogues *pl*, urchins *pl*

granujiento ADJ, **granujoso** ADJ pimply, spotty

granulación SF granulation

granulado Ⓐ ADJ granulated
Ⓑ SM (*Farm*) **un ~ vitamínico** a vitamin powder

granular[1] ADJ granular

granular[2] ▸conjug 1a◂ Ⓐ VT to granulate
Ⓑ **granularse** VPR [1] (= *superficie*) to granulate, become granulated
[2] (*Med*) to break out in spots, become spotty

gránulo SM granule

granuloso ADJ granular

grapa[1] SF [1] (*para papeles*) staple
[2] (*para cables*) cable clip; (*Mec*) dog clamp; (*Arquit*) cramp

grapa[2] SF (*Cono Sur*) (= *aguardiente*) (cheap) grape liquor, grappa

grapadora SF stapler, stapling gun

grapar ▸conjug 1a◂ VT to staple

GRAPO SMPL ABR (*Esp Pol*) (= **Grupos de Resistencia Antifascista Primero de Octubre**) *terrorist group*

grapo SMF member of GRAPO

grasa Ⓐ SF [1] [*de alimentos*] fat; **alimentos bajos en ~s** low-fat foods; **reducir el consumo de ~s** to cut down on fatty foods; **tener mucha ~** [*carne*] to be fatty; [*guiso, plato*] to be (very) greasy ► **grasa de ballena** blubber ► **grasa de pescado** fish oil ► **grasa no saturada** unsaturated fat ► **grasa saturada** saturated fat ► **grasa vegetal** vegetable fat
[2] (*Anat*) fat; **eliminar ~s** to get rid of fat
[3] (= *suciedad*) grease; **la cocina está llena de ~** the kitchen is really greasy
[4] (*Aut, Mec*) (= *lubrificante*) grease ► **grasa para ejes** axle grease
[5] (*Méx**) (*para el calzado*) shoe polish
[6] (*Arg**) working-class person
[7] **grasas** (= *escorias*) slag *sing*
Ⓑ ADJ (*) [1] (*Arg*) (= *torpe*) stupid, slow
[2] (*Cono Sur pey*) common
Ⓒ SMF **es un ~** (*Cono Sur**) he's common

grasiento ADJ [1] [*guiso, pelo*] greasy
[2] (= *sucio*) greasy

graso ADJ [1] [*alimentos, ácidos*] fatty; [*cutis*] greasy, oily; [*pelo*] greasy
[2] (= *aceitoso*) [*guiso*] greasy, oily

grasoso ADJ greasy

grata SF **su ~ del 8** your letter of the 8th

gratamente ADV pleasantly, pleasingly; **quedé ~ sorprendido** I was pleasantly surprised

gratificación SF [1] (= *recompensa*) reward, recompense; (= *propina*) tip; (= *aguinaldo*) gratuity; [*de sueldo, como prima*] bonus
[2] (= *satisfacción*) gratification

gratificador ADJ gratifying

gratificante ADJ gratifying

gratificar ▸conjug 1g◂ VT [1] (= *recompensar*) to reward, recompense; (*con sueldo extra*) to give a bonus to, pay extra to; (*con propina*) to tip; (*con aguinaldo*) to give a gratuity to; **"se ~á"** "a reward is offered"
[2] (= *satisfacer*) to gratify; (= *complacer*) to give pleasure to, satisfy; [+ *anhelo*] to indulge, gratify

gratinado Ⓐ ADJ au gratin
Ⓑ SM *dish cooked au gratin*; **~ de patatas** potato gratin

gratinador SM grill

gratinar ▸conjug 1a◂ VT to cook au gratin

gratis Ⓐ ADV free, for nothing; **te lo arreglarán ~** they'll fix it (for) free *o* for nothing; **comimos ~** we ate for free *o* nothing; **de ~** (*LAm*) gratis
Ⓑ ADJ free; **la entrada es ~** entry is free

gratitud SF gratitude

grato ADJ [1] (= *placentero*) pleasant, pleasing; (= *satisfactorio*) welcome; **recibir una grata impresión** to get a pleasant impression; **una decisión muy grata para todos** a very welcome decision for everybody; **guarda muy ~s recuerdos de su visita a España** he holds very fond memories of his visit to Spain; **nos es ~ informarle que …** we are pleased to inform you that …
[2] (*Andes*) (= *agradecido*) grateful; **le estoy ~** I am most grateful to you

gratuidad SF [1] (= *cualidad de gratuito*) cost-free status; **debemos garantizar la ~ de la enseñanza** we must ensure that education remains free
[2] (= *arbitrariedad*) gratuitousness; **no comparto la ~ de sus afirmaciones** I can't agree with such gratuitous statements

gratuitamente ADV [1] (= *gratis*) free
[2] [*comentar*] gratuitously; [*acusar*] without foundation

gratuito ADJ [1] (= *gratis*) free, free of charge
[2] [*comentario*] gratuitous, uncalled-for; [*acusación*] unfounded, unjustified

gratulatorio ADJ congratulatory

grava SF (= *guijos*) gravel; (= *piedra molida*) crushed stone; (*en carreteras*) road metal

gravable ADJ taxable, subject to tax

gravamen SM [1] (= *impuesto*) tax; **exento de ~** exempt from tax; **libre de ~** free of tax, tax-free
[2] [*de aduanas*] duty
[3] (= *carga*) burden, obligation; (*Jur*) lien, encumbrance; **libre de ~** free from encumbrances, unencumbered ► **gravamen bancario** banker's lien ► **gravamen del vendedor** vendor's lien ► **gravamen general** general lien

gravar ▸conjug 1a◂ Ⓐ VT [1] (*con impuesto*) to tax; (= *calcular impuestos*) to assess for tax; **~ un producto con un impuesto** to place a tax on a product, tax a product; **los impuestos que gravan esta vivienda** the taxes to which this dwelling is subject
[2] (*con carga, hipoteca*) to burden, encumber (**de** with); (*Jur*) [+ *propiedad*] to place a lien upon; **el préstamo y el interés que se le grava** the loan and the interest charged upon it
Ⓑ **gravarse** VPR (*LAm*) (= *empeorar*) to get worse, become more serious

gravativo ADJ burdensome

grave ADJ [1] (*Med*) [*enfermedad, estado*] serious; **estar ~** to be seriously ill; **hubo 20 heridos ~s** there were 20 people seriously injured
[2] (= *serio*) serious; (= *importante*) important, momentous; **la situación es ~** the situation is serious
[3] [*carácter*] serious, dignified; **y otros hombres ~s** and other worthy men
[4] (*Mús*) [*nota, tono*] low, deep; [*voz*] deep
[5] (*Ling*) [*acento*] grave; [*palabra*] stressed on the penultimate syllable

gravedad SF [1] (*Fís*) gravity ► **gravedad nula** zero gravity
[2] (*Med*) seriousness; **estar enfermo de ~** to be seriously ill; **el herido evoluciona favorablemente, dentro de la ~** the patient is progressing well, but his condition remains serious; **parece que la lesión es de poca ~** it seems that the injury is not serious
[3] (= *seriedad*) seriousness
[4] (= *dignidad*) seriousness, dignity
[5] (*Mús*) depth

gravemente ADV [1] [*afectar, perjudicar*] seriously; **no están ~ afectados** they are not seriously affected; **estar ~ enfermo** to be seriously ill; **resultó ~ herido** he was seriously injured
[2] (= *con solemnidad*) gravely; **habló ~** he spoke gravely

gravera SF gravel bed, gravel pit

gravidez SF pregnancy; **en estado de ~** pregnant; **con pocos miramientos hacia su estado de ~** with little account taken of the fact that she was pregnant

grávido ADJ [1] (= *embarazada*) pregnant; (*Zool*) carrying young, with young
[2] (*liter*) (= *lleno*) full (**de** of), heavy (**de** with); **me sentí ~ de emociones** I was weighed down with emotions, I was full of emotions

gravilla SF gravel

gravitación SF gravitation

gravitacional ADJ gravitational

gravitante ADJ menacing

gravitar ▸conjug 1a◂ VI [1] (*Fís*) to gravitate (**hacia** towards)
[2] (= *girar*) to rotate; **la tierra gravita en torno al sol** the earth rotates round the sun
[3] **~ sobre algn/algo** (= *apoyarse*) to rest on sb/sth; (= *caer sobre*) to bear down on sb/sth; (*fig*) (= *pesar sobre*) to be a burden to sb/sth; (= *amenazar*) to loom over sb/sth

gravitatorio ADJ gravitational

gravoso ADJ [1] (= *caro*) costly, expensive; (= *oneroso*) burdensome; [*precio*] extortionate; **el impuesto es especialmente ~ para las pequeñas empresas** the tax is a particular burden for small businesses
[2] (= *molesto*) burdensome, oppressive; **ser ~ a algn/algo** to be a burden to sb/sth, weigh on sb/sth
[3] (= *insufrible*) tiresome, vexatious

graznar ▸conjug 1a◂ VI [1] [*cuervo*] to croak, caw; [*ganso*] to cackle; [*pato*] to quack
[2] (*pey*) [*cantante*] to croak

graznido SM [*de cuervo*] croak; [*de ganso*] cackle; [*de pato*] quack

grébano/a SM/F (*Cono Sur pey*) Italian, wop**

greca SF border

Grecia SF Greece

greco (*liter*) = **griego**

grecochipriota ADJ, SMF Greek-Cypriot

greda SF (= *arcilla*) clay; (*Téc*) fuller's earth

gredal SM claypit

gredoso ADJ clayey

green [grin] SM (*pl* **greens** [grin]) (*Golf*) green

gregario Ⓐ ADJ [1] [*animal, persona*] gregarious; **tiene un carácter ~** he's a gregarious character; **instinto ~** herd instinct
[2] (= *servil*) servile, slavish
Ⓑ SM (*Dep*) domestic

gregarismo SM gregariousness

gregoriano ADJ Gregorian; **canto ~** Gregorian chant

Gregorio SM Gregory

greguería SF [1] (= *ruido*) hubbub, uproar, hullabaloo
[2] (*Literat*) *brief, humorous and often mildly poetic comment or aphorism about life*

grelos SMPL turnip tops

gremial Ⓐ ADJ [1] (*Hist*) guild *antes de s*
[2] (= *sindical*) trade-union *antes de s*
Ⓑ SM (= *miembro*) guild member

gremialista SMF (*LAm*) trade unionist

gremio SM [1] (= *profesión*) trade, profession; **la jerga del ~** trade jargon; **ser del ~** to be in the trade
[2] (*Hist*) guild, corporation
[3] (= *sindicato*) (trade) union; (= *asociación*) association, organization

greña SF [1] (= *enredo*) tangle, entanglement; **andar a la ~** to bicker, squabble; **estar a la ~ con algn** to be at daggers drawn with sb
[2] **greñas** (= *cabello revuelto*) shock of hair, mat of hair, mop of hair

[3] **en ~** (*Méx*) [*seda*] raw; [*plata*] unpolished; [*azúcar*] unrefined

greñudo ADJ [*cabello*] tangled, matted; [*persona*] dishevelled, disheveled (*EEUU*)

gres SM (= *arcilla*) potter's clay; (= *cerámica*) earthenware, stoneware

gresca SF (= *bulla*) uproar, hubbub; (= *trifulca*) row, shindy*; **andar a la ~** to row, brawl; **armar una ~** to start a fight

grey SF [1] (*Rel*) flock, congregation
[2] [*de ovejas*] flock

Grial SM **Santo ~** Holy Grail

griego/a Ⓐ ADJ Greek, Grecian
Ⓑ SM/F [1] (= *persona*) Greek
[2] (††) (= *tramposo*) cheat
Ⓒ SM [1] (*Ling*) Greek ► **griego antiguo** ancient Greek
[2] (= *lenguaje ininteligible*) gibberish, double Dutch; **hablar en ~** to talk double Dutch; **para mí es ~** it's all Greek to me

grieta SF [1] (= *fisura*) fissure, crack; (= *hendidura*) chink; (= *quiebra*) crevice; (*en la piel*) chap, crack
[2] (*Pol*) rift

grietarse ▸conjug 1a◂ VPR = **agrietar B**

grifa‡ SF (= *droga*) dope*; *ver tb* **grifo**

grifear‡ ▸conjug 1a◂ VI to smoke dope*

grifería[1] SF taps *pl*, faucets *pl* (*EEUU*)

grifería[2] SF (*Caribe*‡) blacks *pl*

grifero/a SM/F (*Andes*) petrol pump attendant, gas pump attendant (*EEUU*)

grifo[1] SM [1] [*de agua*] tap, faucet (*EEUU*); (*a presión*) cock; **agua del ~** tap water; **cerveza (servida) al ~** draught *o* (*EEUU*) draft beer; ✦**MODISMO cerrar el ~** to turn off the tap, cut off the funds
[2] (*LAm*) (= *surtidor de gasolina*) petrol pump, gas pump (*EEUU*); (*Andes*) (= *gasolinera*) petrol station, gas station (*EEUU*); (= *bar*) dive*
[3] (*Cono Sur*) [*de incendios*] fire hydrant

grifo[2]**/a*** Ⓐ ADJ [1] **estar ~** (*Méx*) (= *borracho*) to be plastered*, be soused (*EEUU**); (= *loco*) to be nuts*; (= *drogado*) to be high*, be doped up*
[2] (*Andes*) (= *engreído*) snobbish, stuck-up*
Ⓑ SM/F [1] [*de drogas*] (= *fumador*) dope smoker*; (= *adicto*) dope addict*
[2] (= *borracho*) drunkard; *ver tb* **grifa**

grifo[3]**/a** Ⓐ ADJ [1] [*pelo*] curly, kinky
[2] (*Caribe*†) [*persona*] black
Ⓑ SM/F (*Caribe*†) black man/woman, black person; *ver tb* **grifa**

grifo[4] SM (*Mit*) griffin

grifón SM (= *perro*) griffon; (*mítico*) gryphon

grifota‡ SMF dope smoker*

grigallo SM blackcock

grill [gril] SM [1] (= *aparato*) grill; **asar al ~** to grill
[2] (= *local*) grillroom

grilla SF [1] (= *insecto*) female cricket; ✦**MODISMOS ¡ésa es ~ (y no canta)!*** that's a likely story! (*iró*); **dice la ~ que ...** (*Méx*) there's word going round that ...
[2] (*Andes*) (= *pleito*) row, quarrel

grillado‡ ADJ barmy*

grilladura‡ SF barminess*

grillera SF [1] (= *jaula*) cage for crickets; (= *nido*) cricket hole
[2] (*) (= *casa de locos*) madhouse, bedlam
[3] (‡) (= *furgón*) police wagon

grillete SM fetter, shackle

grillo SM [1] (= *insecto*) cricket ► **grillo cebollero, grillo real** mole cricket
[2] (*Bot*) (= *brote*) shoot, sprout
[3] **grillos** (= *cadenas*) fetters, shackles; (= *esposas*) handcuffs; (= *estorbo*) shackles

grilo‡ SM [1] (= *cárcel*) nick‡, slammer‡, can (*EEUU*‡)
[2] (= *bolsillo*) pocket ► **grilo bueno** right-hand pocket

grima SF [1] **dar ~ a algn** (= *dentera*) to set sb's teeth on edge; (= *irritación*) to get on sb's nerves; **me da ~ sentarme ahí** I can't sit there, it's revolting; **un dato de ~** a bombshell
[2] **una ~ de licor** (*Cono Sur*) a drop of spirits
[3] **en ~** (*Andes*) alone

grimillón SM (*Cono Sur*) lot, heap

grímpola SF pennant

gringada* SF (*LAm*) [1] (= *personas*) (= *extranjeros*) foreigners *pl*; (= *norteamericanos*) Yankees *pl*
[2] (= *canallada*) dirty trick

gringo/a (*LAm*) Ⓐ ADJ [1] (= *extranjero*) foreign; (= *norteamericano*) Yankee, North American
[2] (= *rubio*) blond(e), fair
[3] (††) [*idioma*] foreign, unintelligible
Ⓑ SM/F [1] (= *extranjero*) foreigner; (= *norteamericano*) Yankee, North American
[2] (*Cono Sur*) (= *italiano*) Italian, wop**
[3] (= *rubio*) blond(e), fair-haired person
Ⓒ SM (††) (= *lenguaje ininteligible*) gibberish; **hablar en ~** to talk double Dutch*

> **GRINGO**
>
> *The word* **gringo** *is a derogatory term used in Latin America to refer to white English-speakers, usually Americans, especially in the context of alleged economic, cultural and political interference in Latin America. One rather fanciful theory traces its origin to the Mexican-American War of 1846-48 and the song "Green Grow the Rushes-oh", supposedly sung by the American troops. According to another theory it is a corruption of* **griego** *or "Greek", in the sense of anything foreign and unintelligible, as in the English expression "it's all Greek to me".*

gringolandia* SF (*LAm pey*) USA, Yankeedom*

gringuería SF (*LAm*) foreigners *pl*, gringos *pl*

gripa SF (*LAm*) flu, influenza

gripaje SM seize-up

gripal ADJ flu *antes de s*

gripar* ▸conjug 1a◂ VI to seize up

gripazo SM attack of flu

gripe SF flu, influenza ► **gripe asiática** Asian flu ► **gripe aviar** bird flu, avian flu (*frm*) ► **gripe del cerdo** swine fever

griposo ADJ **estar ~** to have flu

gris Ⓐ ADJ [*color*] grey, gray (*EEUU*); [*día, tiempo, persona*] grey, dull; **~ carbón** charcoal grey; **~ ceniza** ash-grey; **~ marengo** dark grey; **~ perla** pearl-grey; *ver tb* **oso**
Ⓑ SM [1] (= *color*) grey
[2] (*Esp*†*) cop*, *member of the armed police*; **los ~es** the fuzz‡
[3] (*) (= *viento*) **hace un ~** there's a cold wind

grisáceo ADJ greyish, grayish (*EEUU*)

grisalla SF (*Méx*) [1] (= *chatarra*) rusty scrap metal
[2] (= *basura*) rubbish, garbage (*EEUU*)

grisines SMPL (*Arg*) breadsticks

grisma SF (*Cono Sur*) bit, shred

grisoso ADJ (*esp LAm*) greyish, grayish (*EEUU*)

grisú SM firedamp

grisura SF [*de color*] greyness, grayness (*EEUU*); (= *falta de interés*) dullness

grita SF (= *jaleo*) uproar, hubbub; (= *gritos*) shouting; (*Teat*) catcalls *pl*, catcalling, booing; **dar ~ a algn/algo** to boo at sb/sth

gritadera SF (*LAm*) loud shouting, clamour, clamor (*EEUU*)

gritar ▸conjug 1a◂ Ⓐ VI [1] (= *dar voces*) to shout; **¡no grites!** don't shout!; **no sabes hablar sin ~** you can't talk without shouting; **no me grites, que no estoy sorda** don't shout, I'm not deaf; **¡no le grites a tu madre!** don't shout at your mother!; **gritaba de alegría** he shouted for joy
[2] (= *chillar*) to scream; **el enfermo no podía dejar de ~** the patient couldn't stop screaming; **gritaba de dolor** he was screaming with pain
[3] (= *abuchear*) to jeer; **el público gritaba al árbitro** the crowd were jeering the referee
Ⓑ VT [+ *instrucciones, órdenes*] to shout; **le ~on que callara** they shouted at him to be quiet

gritería SF [1] (= *gritos*) shouting, uproar
[2] (*CAm Rel*) festival of the Virgin

griterío SM shouting, uproar

grito SM [1] (= *voz alta*) shout; (= *chillido*) scream; [*de animal*] cry, sound; **a ~s** at the top of one's voice; **¡no des esos ~s!** stop shouting like that!; **llorar a ~s** to weep and wail; **pegar** *o* **lanzar un ~** to cry out; **~s de protesta** shouts of protest; ✦**MODISMOS poner el ~ en el cielo** to scream blue murder*; **pedir algo a ~s**: **esa chica está pidiendo un corte de pelo a ~s** she badly needs a haircut; **a ~ pelado** at the top of one's voice; **es el último ~** it's the very latest, it's the latest thing; **es el último ~ del lujo** it's the last word in luxury; **a voz en ~** at the top of one's voice
[2] (= *abucheo*) jeer
[3] (*LAm*) proclamation; **el ~ de Dolores** *the proclamation of Mexican independence (1810)* ► **grito de independencia** proclamation of independence

gritón ADJ [1] (= *que grita*) shouting
[2] (*pey*) loud-mouthed; **son muy gritones** they're very loud

gro SM grosgrain

groenlandés/esa Ⓐ ADJ Greenland *antes de s*
Ⓑ SM/F Greenlander

Groenlandia SF Greenland

groggy‡ ADJ, **grogui**‡ ADJ (= *atontado*) groggy; (= *impresionado*) shattered, shocked, in a state of shock

groncho/a‡ SM/F (*Cono Sur pey*) worker

grosella SF redcurrant ► **grosella colorada** redcurrant ► **grosella espinosa** gooseberry ► **grosella negra** blackcurrant ► **grosella roja** redcurrant

grosellero SM currant bush ► **grosellero espinoso** gooseberry bush

groseramente ADV (= *descortésmente*) rudely;

(= *con ordinariez*) coarsely; (= *toscamente*) roughly, loutishly

grosería SF [1] (= *mala educación*) rudeness; (= *ordinariez*) coarseness, vulgarity; (= *tosquedad*) roughness
[2] (= *comentario*) rude remark, vulgar remark; (= *palabrota*) swearword

grosero ADJ (= *descortés*) rude; (= *ordinario*) coarse, vulgar; (= *tosco*) rough, loutish; (= *indecente*) indelicate

grosor SM thickness

grosura SF fat, suet

grotesca SF (*Tip*) sans serif

grotescamente ADV (= *de modo ridículo*) grotesquely; (= *de modo absurdo*) bizarrely, absurdly

grotesco ADJ (= *ridículo*) grotesque; (= *absurdo*) bizarre, absurd

grúa SF [1] (*Téc*) crane; (*Náut*) derrick ► **grúa corredera**, **grúa corrediza** travelling crane ► **grúa de pescante** jib crane ► **grúa de puente** overhead crane, gantry crane ► **grúa de torre** tower crane ► **grúa horquilla** (*Chile*) forklift truck ► **grúa móvil** travelling crane
[2] (*Aut*) tow truck, towing vehicle; **avisar** *o* **llamar a la ~** to call for a tow truck; **el coche fue retirado por la ~** the car was towed away

gruesa SF gross, twelve dozen

grueso Ⓐ ADJ [1] (= *obeso*) [*persona*] stout, thickset
[2] [*jersey, pared, libro, tronco*] thick; [*intestino*] large; [*mar*] heavy
[3] (= *basto*) [*tela, humor*] coarse
Ⓑ SM [1] (= *grosor*) thickness
[2] (= *parte principal*) main part, major portion; [*de gente, tropa*] main body, mass; **el ~ del pelotón** (*en carrera*) the pack, the main body of the runners; **va mezclado con el ~ del pasaje** he is mingling with the mass of the passengers
[3] (*Com*) **en ~** in bulk

grujidor SM glass cutter, glazier

grulla SF (*tb* ~ **común**) crane

grullo/a Ⓐ ADJ [1] (*) (= *grosero*) uncouth, rough
[2] (*Méx*) (= *aprovechado*) sponging*, cadging*
[3] (*CAm, Méx*) [*caballo*] grey, gray (*EEUU*)
Ⓑ SM/F bumpkin, yokel, hick (*EEUU**)
Ⓒ SM (*CAm, Méx*) grey horse; (*Cono Sur*) big colt, large stallion

grumete SM (*Náut*) cabin boy, ship's boy

grumo SM [1] (*en salsa*) lump; **una salsa con ~s** a lumpy sauce
[2] [*de sangre*] clot ► **grumo de leche** curd
[3] [*de uvas*] bunch, cluster

grumoso ADJ [1] [*salsa*] lumpy
[2] (= *cuajado*) clotted

gruñido SM [1] [*de animal*] grunt, growl; **dar ~s** to grunt, growl
[2] (= *queja*) grouse*, grumble; **dar ~s** to grouse*, grumble

gruñidor(a) Ⓐ ADJ [1] [*animal*] grunting, growling
[2] [*persona*] grumbling
Ⓑ SM/F grumbler

gruñir ▸conjug 3h◂ VI [1] [*animal*] to grunt, growl
[2] [*persona*] to grouse*, grumble

gruñón/ona Ⓐ ADJ grumpy, grumbling
Ⓑ SM/F grumbler

grupa SF crupper, hindquarters *pl*

grupal ADJ group *antes de s*

grupalmente ADV in groups

grupera SF pillion (seat); **ir en la ~** to sit behind the rider, be carried on the horse's rump

grupi‡ SF groupie*

grupín* SM (*Cono Sur*) crook*; (= *desfalcador*) embezzler; (*en subasta*) false bidder

grupo SM [1] (*gen*) group; (= *equipo*) team; [*de árboles*] cluster, clump; **discusión en ~** group discussion; **reunirse en ~s** to gather in groups ► **grupo de contacto** (*Pol*) contact group ► **grupo de control** control group ► **grupo de encuentro** encounter group ► **grupo de estafas** (*Policía*) fraud squad ► **grupo de estupefacientes** (*Policía*) drug squad ► **grupo de homicidios** (*Policía*) murder squad ► **grupo de investigación** research team, team of researchers ► **grupo del dólar** dollar block ► **grupo de noticias** newsgroup ► **grupo de presión** pressure group, special interest group (*EEUU*) ► **grupo de riesgo** high-risk group ► **grupo de trabajo** working party ► **grupo sanguíneo** blood group ► **grupo testigo** control group
[2] (*Elec, Téc*) unit, plant; (= *montaje*) assembly ► **grupo compresor** compressor unit ► **grupo electrógeno**, **grupo generador** generating set, power plant
[3] (*Cono Sur*) (= *trampa*) trick, con*

grupúsculo SM small group, splinter group

gruta SF cavern, grotto

GT ABR (= **Gran Turismo**) GT

Gta. ABR (*Aut*) = **glorieta**

gua¹ EXCL (*LAm*) (= *preocupación*) oh dear!; (= *sorpresa*) well!; (= *desdén*) get away!*

gua² SM (= *juego*) marbles *pl*; (= *hoyo*) hole for marbles

gua... PREF (*para diversas palabras escritas así en LAm*) *ver tb* **hua...**

guabiroba SF (*Cono Sur*) dugout canoe

guaca SF [1] (*LAm*) (= *sepultura*) (Indian) tomb, funeral mound
[2] (= *tesoro*) buried treasure; [*de armas, droga*] cache
[3] (= *riqueza*) wealth, money; (*Andes, CAm, Caribe, Méx*) (= *hucha*) money box; **hacer ~** (*Andes, Caribe‡*) to make money, make one's pile*; ✦**MODISMO hacer su ~** (*Caribe*) to make hay while the sun shines
[4] (*Caribe*) (= *reprimenda*) ticking-off*
[5] (*Méx*) (= *escopeta*) double-barrelled shotgun
[6] (*Caribe*) large sore

guacal SM (*LAm*) (= *cajón*) wooden crate; (= *calabaza*) gourd, vessel

guacamarón SM (*Caribe*) brave man

guacamaya SF (*LAm*) macaw

guacamayo/a Ⓐ ADJ (*Méx**) absurdly dressed
Ⓑ SM/F (*Caribe pey*) Spaniard
Ⓒ SM (= *ave*) macaw

guacamole SM guacamole

guacamote SM (*Méx*) yucca plant

guacarnaco ADJ [1] (*Andes, Caribe, Cono Sur*) silly, stupid
[2] (*Cono Sur*) long-legged

guachada* SF (*Arg*) dirty trick

guachafita SF (*Ven*) [1] (= *batahola*) hubbub, din; (= *desorden*) disorder
[2] (= *garito*) gambling joint‡
[3] (= *mofa*) mockery, jeering

guachafitero/a (*Ven*) Ⓐ ADJ (= *desorganizado*) chaotic, inefficient
Ⓑ SM/F inefficient person

guachaje SM (*Cono Sur*) (= *animal*) orphaned animal; (= *terneras*) *group of calves separated from their mothers*

guachalomo SM (*Cono Sur*) sirloin steak

guachapear ▸conjug 1a◂ Ⓐ VT [1] (*en agua*) to dabble in, splash about in
[2] (= *estropear*) to botch, mess up
[3] (*Cono Sur**) to pinch*, borrow
[4] (*Andes*) [+ *maleza*] to clear, cut
Ⓑ VI (= *sonar*) to rattle, clatter

guachar ▸conjug 1a◂ VT (*Méx*) to watch

guáchara* SF (*Caribe*) lie

guácharo SM (*CAm*) nightingale

guache¹* SM [1] (*Caribe*) (= *del campo*) rustic, peasant, hick (*EEUU**)
[2] (*Andes, Caribe*) (= *zafio*) uncouth person
[3] (= *vago*) layabout, loafer

guache² SM (*Arte*) gouache

guachicar SM, **guachicarro** SM (*Méx*) parking attendant

guachimán SM (*LAm*) watchman

guachinanga SF (*Caribe*) wooden bar (*on door etc*)

guachinango/a Ⓐ ADJ (*) [1] (*Andes*) (= *zalamero*) smooth; (= *falso*) slimy
[2] (*Caribe*) (= *astuto*) sharp, clever; (= *con labia*) smooth-tongued
Ⓑ SM/F (*) (*Caribe*) [1] (*pey*) Mexican
[2] (= *persona astuta*) clever person
Ⓒ SM (*Caribe, Méx*) (= *pez*) red snapper

guacho/a Ⓐ ADJ [1] (*Andes, Cono Sur*) (= *sin casa*) homeless
[2] (*Andes, Cono Sur*) (= *huérfano*) [*niño*] orphaned; [*animal*] motherless, abandoned
[3] (*Andes, Cono Sur*) [*zapato etc*] odd
[4] (*Méx‡*) (= *capitalino*) of/from Mexico City
Ⓑ SM/F [1] (*Andes, Cono Sur*) (= *expósito*) homeless child, abandoned child; (= *huérfano*) orphan, foundling; (= *animal*) motherless animal; (*) (= *bastardo*) illegitimate child, bastard*
[2] (*Méx‡*) (= *capitalino*) *person from Mexico City*

guadal SM (*Andes, Cono Sur*) sandy bog

Guadalajara SF Guadalajara

guadalajareño/a Ⓐ ADJ of/from Guadalajara
Ⓑ SM/F native/inhabitant of Guadalajara; **los ~s** the people of Guadalajara

guadaloso ADJ (*Cono Sur*) boggy

Guadalquivir SM **el Río ~** the Guadalquivir

guadamecí SM embossed leather

guadaña SF (*Agr*) scythe; **la Guadaña** (*fig*) the Grim Reaper

guadañadora SF mowing machine

guadañar ▸conjug 1a◂ VT to scythe, mow

guadañero SM mower

guadaño SM (*Cuba, Méx*) lighter, small harbour *o* (*EEUU*) harbor boat

Guadiana SM **el ~** the Guadiana; ✦**MODISMO aparece y desaparece como el ~** it keeps coming and going, now you see it now you don't

guadianesco ADJ (= *intermitente*) sporadic, intermittent; (= *quimérico*) will-o'-the-wisp

guágara* SF **echar ~** (*Méx*) to gossip, chew the fat

guagua[1] SF (*Cuba, Canarias*) bus

guagua[2] Ⓐ ADJ (*Andes*) small, little
Ⓑ SF (*Andes, Cono Sur*) [1] (= *bebé*) baby
[2] (= *bagatela*) trifle, small thing; ✦***MODISMO*** **de ~** (*Cuba, Méx*) free, for nothing

guaguarear* ▸conjug 1a◂ VI (*CAm, Méx*) to babble, chatter

guaguatear ▸conjug 1a◂ VT (*CAm, Cono Sur*) to carry in one's arms

guaguatera SF (*Cono Sur*) nurse

guagüero/a Ⓐ ADJ [1] (*Caribe*) (= *gorrón*) sponging*, parasitical
[2] (*Cuba*) bus *antes de s*
Ⓑ SM/F (*Cuba*) (= *chófer*) bus driver

guai* ADJ, ADV = **guay**

guaica SF [1] (*Cono Sur*) (= *cuenta*) rosary bead
[2] (*Andes*) (= *collar*) bead necklace

guaico SM (*Andes*) [1] (= *hondonada*) hollow, dip; (= *barranco*) ravine; (= *hoyo*) hole, pit
[2] (= *estercolero*) dung heap; (= *basurero*) rubbish tip, garbage tip (*EEUU*)
[3] (= *alud*) avalanche

guaina SF [1] (*Arg*) (= *muchacha*) girl, young woman
[2] (*Bol, Chile*) (= *muchacho*) youth, young man

guaino SM (*Cono Sur*) jockey

guaipe SM (*Chile*) (= *estopa*) cotton waste; (= *trapo*) cloth, rag

guáiper SM (*CAm*) windscreen wiper, windshield wiper (*EEUU*)

guaira SF [1] (*CAm*) Indian flute
[2] (*Andes, Cono Sur Min*) earthenware smelting furnace (*for silver ore*)
[3] (*Náut*) triangular sail

guairana SF [1] (*Andes*) [*de cal*] limekiln
[2] = **guaira**

guairo SM (*Cuba, Ven*) small coastal vessel

guairuro SM (*Andes, CAm*) dried seed

guajada* SF (*Méx*) stupid thing

guajalote ADJ, SM (*Caribe, Méx*) = **guajolote**

guaje[1] Ⓐ ADJ (*Méx**) (= *estúpido*) silly, stupid; ✦***MODISMO*** **hacer ~ a algn** to fool sb, take sb in*
Ⓑ SMF (*CAm, Méx**) (= *estúpido*) idiot, fool
Ⓒ SM [1] (*Méx*) (= *calabaza*) gourd, calabash
[2] (*CAm**) (= *trasto*) old thing, piece of junk
[3] (*CAm, Méx*) (= *acacia*) *species of acacia*

guaje[2]**/a** SM/F [1] (*) kid*, child
[2] (*Min*) mining apprentice

guajear* ▸conjug 1a◂ VI (*Méx*) to play the fool, be silly

guajería* SF (*Méx*) [1] (= *estupidez*) idiocy, foolishness
[2] (= *acto*) stupid thing, foolish act

guajiro/a SM/F [1] (*Cuba*) (white) peasant
[2] (*Col, Ven*) *native/inhabitant of the Guajira region*

guajolote (*Méx*) Ⓐ ADJ (*) silly, stupid
Ⓑ SM [1] (= *pavo*) turkey
[2] (*) (= *tonto*) fool, idiot, turkey (*EEUU*)

gualda SF (= *planta*) dyer's greenweed, reseda

gualdo ADJ (= *color*) yellow, golden; *ver tb* **bandera 1**

gualdrapa SF [1] (*Hist*) [*de caballo*] horse blanket
[2] **gualdrapas*** (= *harapos*) tatters, ragged ends
[3] (*CAm**) (= *vagabundo*) down-and-out, bum (*EEUU*), hobo (*EEUU*)

gualdrapear ▸conjug 1a◂ VI [1] (*Náut*) [*velas*] to flap
[2] (*Cuba*) [*caballo*] to walk slowly

gualicho SM [1] (*Andes, Cono Sur*) (= *maleficio*) evil spell; (= *diablo*) devil, evil spirit
[2] (*Arg*) (= *talismán*) good-luck charm, talisman

guallipén SM (*Cono Sur*) fool, idiot

Gualterio SM Walter

guama* SF [1] (*Andes, CAm*) (= *mentira*) lie
[2] (*Andes*) (= *pie*) big foot; (= *mano*) big hand
[3] (*Andes*) (= *desastre*) calamity, disaster

guambito SM (*Andes*) kid*, boy

guambra SMF (*Ecu*) [1] (= *muchacho*) young Indian
[2] (= *niño*) (*gen*) child, baby; (= *indio*) Indian child; (= *mestizo*) mestizo child
[3] (= *amor*) sweetheart

guamiza* SF (*Méx*) beating-up*

guampa SF (*Andes, Cono Sur*) horn

guampara SF (*Caribe*) machete

guámparo SM (*Cono Sur*) (= *cuerno*) horn; (*para beber*) drinking vessel

guampudo ADJ (*Andes, Cono Sur*) horned

guanábana SF [1] (*LAm*) (= *fruta*) soursop, prickly custard apple
[2] (*Andes*) (= *tonto*) fool

guanábano SM soursop (tree)

guanacada* SF (*LAm*) [1] (= *estupidez*) silly thing, foolish act
[2] (= *persona*) simpleton, dimwit*; (= *campesino*) rustic

guanaco/a Ⓐ ADJ (*LAm**) (= *tonto*) simple, silly; (= *torpe*) slow
Ⓑ SM/F (*) [1] (*LAm*) (= *tonto*) simpleton, dimwit*; (= *campesino*) rustic, bumpkin*
[2] (*CAm pey*) (= *salvadoreño*) Salvadorean
Ⓒ SM [1] (*Zool*) guanaco
[2] (*Cono Sur*) (= *antidisturbios*) water cannon

guanajada* SF (*Caribe*) silly thing, foolish act

guanajo/a SM/F (*LAm*) [1] (= *pavo*) turkey
[2] (*) (= *tonto*) fool, idiot

guanay[1] SM (*Chile*) cormorant

guanay[2] SM (*Cono Sur*) (= *remero*) oarsman; (= *estibador*) longshoreman; (= *fortachón*) tough man

guanayerías* SFPL (*Caribe*) silly actions

guanche Ⓐ ADJ Guanche
Ⓑ SMF Guanche (*original inhabitant of Canary Islands*)

guando SM (*Andes, Chile*) stretcher

guanear ▸conjug 1a◂ Ⓐ VT [1] (*Perú Agr*) to fertilize with guano
[2] (*Bol*) (= *ensuciar*) to dirty, soil
Ⓑ VI (*LAm*) [*animales*] to defecate

guanera SF (*LAm*) guano deposit

guanero ADJ (*LAm*) guano *antes de s*

guango* ADJ (*Méx*) (= *holgado*) loose; ✦***MODISMO*** **me viene ~** I couldn't care less*

guanín SM (*Andes, Caribe, Cono Sur Hist*) base gold

guano[1] SM [1] [*de aves marinas*] guano
[2] (*LAm*) (= *estiércol*) dung, manure
[3] (*Cuba**) money, brass*
[4] ✦***MODISMO*** **meter ~** (*Caribe**) to put one's back into it

guano[2] SM (*LAm*) (= *palma*) palm tree; (= *hoja*) palm leaf

guantada SF, **guantazo** SM slap; **dar** *o* **largar una ~ a algn** to give sb a slap, slap sb

guante SM [1] glove; **hacer ~s** (*Dep*) to shadow-box; ✦***MODISMOS*** **ajustarse como un ~** to fit like a glove; **arrojar el ~** to throw down the gauntlet; **de ~ blanco**: **crimen de ~ blanco** white-collar crime; **una campaña electoral de ~ blanco** a clean election campaign; **un partido de ~ blanco** a sporting match; **tratar con ~ blanco** to treat *o* handle with kid gloves; **colgar los ~s** (*Boxeo*) to quit boxing; (= *jubilarse*) to retire; **echar el ~ a algn** to catch hold of sb, seize sb; [*policía*] to catch sb; **echar el ~ a algo** to lay hold of sth; **recoger el ~** to take up the challenge; **ser como un ~** (= *obediente*) to be very meek and mild, be submissive ► **guante con puño** gauntlet ► **guantes de boxeo** boxing gloves ► **guantes de cabritilla** kid gloves ► **guantes de cirujano** surgical gloves ► **guantes de goma** rubber gloves ► **guantes de jardinería** gardening gloves ► **guantes de terciopelo** (*fig*) kid gloves ► **guantes para uso quirúrgico** surgical gloves
[2] (*Chile*) whip, cat-o'nine-tails
[3] **guantes** (= *gratificación*) tip *sing*, commission *sing*

guantear ▸conjug 1a◂ VT (*LAm*) to slap, hit

guantelete SM gauntlet

guantera SF (*Aut*) glove compartment; *ver tb* **guantero**

guantería SF [1] (= *tienda*) glove shop; (= *fábrica*) glove factory
[2] (= *fabricación*) glove making

guantero/a SM/F glover; *ver tb* **guantera**

guantón SM (*LAm*) slap, hit, blow

guañusco* ADJ (*Arg*) [1] (= *marchito*) withered, faded
[2] (= *chamuscado*) burned, burned up

guapear* ▸conjug 1a◂ Ⓐ VI [1] (= *ostentar*) to cut a dash, dress flashily
[2] (= *bravear*) to bluster, swagger
Ⓑ VT (*Andes*) to urge on

guaperas* Ⓐ ADJ INV gorgeous*
Ⓑ SM INV heart-throb*, dream-boy*

guapetón/ona Ⓐ ADJ [1] (= *guapo*) good-looking
[2] (= *elegante*) dashing; (*pey*) flashy
Ⓑ SM/F (= *perdonavidas*) bully

guapeza SF [1] (= *atractivo*) good looks *pl*, attractiveness
[2] (= *elegancia*) smartness, elegance; (*pey*) (= *ostentación*) flashiness
[3] (= *valentía*) boldness, dash; (*pey*) bravado

guapo Ⓐ ADJ [1] (= *atractivo*) [*mujer*] attractive, good-looking; [*hombre*] handsome, good-looking; [*bebé*] beautiful; **va de ~ por la vida** he thinks good looks are all he needs in life
[2] (= *elegante*) smart, elegant; **ir ~** to look smart; **qué ~ estás con ese traje** you look really nice in that suit
[3] (*) (= *bonito*) great*; **qué camiseta más guapa** what a great T-shirt!*; **¿qué tal la película? —¡muy guapa!** "how was the film?" — "great!*"
[4] (*) (*como apelativo*) **¡ven, ~!** (*a un niño*) come here, love!; **¡oye, guapa!** hey!; **¡cállate, ~!** just shut up!
[5] (= *valiente*) bold, dashing; (*Cono Sur, Méx*)

(= *duro*) bold, tough; (= *sin escrúpulos*) unscrupulous

Ⓑ SM [1] (*) (= *valiente*) **¿quién es el ~ que entra primero?** who's got the guts to go in first?*, who's brave enough to go in first?

[2] (*esp LAm*) (= *bravucón*) bully, tough guy; (= *fanfarrón*) braggart

[3] (*CAm Cine*) male lead

guaposo ADJ (*Caribe*) bold, dashing

guapucha* SF (*Andes*) cheating

guapura* SF good looks *pl*

guaquear ▸conjug 1a◂ VI (*Andes, CAm*) to rob tombs *o* graves (*in search of archaeological valuables*)

guaqueo SM (*Andes, CAm*) grave robbing, tomb robbing

guaquero/a SM/F (*Andes, CAm*) grave robber, tomb robber

guara SF [1] (*Andes*) lot, heap

[2] **guaras** (*Cono Sur*) tricks, wiles

guaraca SF (*Andes*) (= *honda*) sling, catapult, slingshot (*EEUU*); (*para trompo*) whip

guaracha SF [1] (*Caribe*) (= *canción*) popular song; (= *baile*) folk dance

[2] (*Caribe**) (= *alboroto*) din, racket; (= *riña*) quarrel; (= *juerga*) party, shindig*

[3] (*Caribe*) (= *banda*) street band

[4] (*Caribe*) (= *chanza*) joke

[5] (*Andes*) litter, rough bed

[6] **guarachas** (*CAm*) old shoes

[7] (*CAm*) = **guarache**

guarache SM (*Méx*) [1] (= *sandalia*) sandal, light shoe

[2] (*Aut*) patch

guarachear* ▸conjug 1a◂ VI (*Caribe*) to revel; (*fig*) to let one's hair down

guaragua SF [1] (*CAm*) (= *mentira*) lie; (= *mentiroso*) liar, tale-teller

[2] (*LAm*) (= *contoneo*) rhythmical movement (*in dancing*)

[3] **guaraguas** (*Andes*) adornments, finery *sing*

guaral SM (*Andes, Caribe*) (= *cuerda*) rope, cord; [*de trompo*] whip

guarangada SF (*LAm*) rude remark

guarango ADJ [1] (*Andes, Cono Sur*) (= *grosero*) [*acto*] rude; [*persona*] uncouth

[2] (*Andes*) (= *sucio*) dirty; (= *harapiento*) ragged

guaranguear ▸conjug 1a◂ VI (*Andes, Cono Sur*) to be rude

guaranguería SF (*Andes, Cono Sur*) rudeness

guaraní Ⓐ ADJ, SMF Guarani

Ⓑ SM (*Ling*) Guarani

> **GUARANÍ**
>
> *Guaraní is an American Indian language of the* **tupí-guaraní** *family and is widely spoken in Paraguay, Brazil, Argentina and Bolivia. In Paraguay it is the majority language and has equal official status with Spanish, which is spoken mainly by non-Indians. In parts of southern Brazil,* **tupí-guaraní** *is the basis for a pidgin known as* **Língua Geral**, *now losing ground to Portuguese. From* **guaraní** *and its sister dialect* **tupí** *come words like "jaguar", "tapir", "toucan" and "tapioca".*

guaranismo SM (*Ling*) *word or expression from the Guarani language*

guarapazo SM (*Andes*) [1] [*de bebida*] shot*, slug*

[2] (= *golpe*) blow, knock; (= *caída*) hard fall

guarapear ▸conjug 1a◂ Ⓐ VI [1] (*Perú*) to drink sugar-cane liquor

[2] (*Caribe*) (= *emborracharse*) to get drunk

Ⓑ **guarapearse** VPR (*Caribe*) to get drunk

guarapo SM (*LAm*) (= *bebida*) sugar-cane liquor; (*Ven*) [*de piña*] fermented pineapple juice; ✦**MODISMOS se le enfrió el ~** (*Caribe**) he lost his nerve; **menear el ~** (*Cuba, Ven*) to get a move on; **volver ~ algo** to tear sth up

guarapón SM (*Andes, Cono Sur*) broad-brimmed hat

guarda Ⓐ SMF [1] (= *vigilante*) [*de parque, cementerio*] keeper; [*de edificio*] security guard ► **guarda de caza, guarda de coto** gamekeeper ► **guarda de dique** lock keeper ► **guarda de pesca** water bailiff, fish (and game) warden (*EEUU*) ► **guarda de seguridad** security guard ► **guarda fluvial** water bailiff ► **guarda forestal** (forest) ranger ► **guarda jurado** (armed) security guard

[2] (*Cono Sur Ferro*) ticket inspector

Ⓑ SF [1] [*de libro*] flyleaf, endpaper

[2] (*Téc*) [*de cerradura*] ward; [*de espada*] guard

[3] (*Cono Sur Cos*) trimming, border

[4] (= *custodia*) [*de lugar, costumbre*] guarding; [*de niño*] guardianship; *ver tb* **ángel 1**

[5] [*de la ley*] observance

guardaagujas SMF INV (*Ferro*) pointsman/pointswoman, switchman/switchwoman (*EEUU*)

guardaalmacén SMF storekeeper

guardabarrera Ⓐ SMF (= *persona*) crossing keeper

Ⓑ SM (*en paso*) level-crossing gate(s), grade-crossing gate(s) (*EEUU*)

guardabarros SM INV mudguard, fender (*EEUU*)

guardabosque SMF, **guardabosques** SMF INV (*en bosque, parque*) ranger, forester; (*en finca*) gamekeeper

guardabrisa SF [1] (= *parabrisas*) windscreen, windshield (*EEUU*)

[2] [*de vela*] shade

[3] (*Méx*) screen

guardacabo SM (*Náut*) thimble

guardacabras SMF INV goatherd

guardacalor SM cosy, cover

guardacamisa SF (*Caribe*) vest, undershirt (*EEUU*)

guardacantón SM (*en las esquinas o caminos*) kerbstone, curbstone (*EEUU*); (= *poste*) roadside post, corner post

guardacoches SMF INV parking attendant

guardacostas Ⓐ SMF INV (= *persona*) coastguard

Ⓑ SM INV (= *barco*) coastguard vessel, revenue cutter

guardador(a) Ⓐ ADJ [1] (= *protector*) protective

[2] (*de orden, ley*) observant, watchful

[3] (*pey*) mean, stingy

Ⓑ SM/F [1] (= *cuidador*) keeper; (= *guarda*) guardian; (= *protector*) protector

[2] [*de la ley*] observer

[3] (*pey*) mean person

guardaespaldas SMF INV bodyguard, minder*

guardaesquinas* SMF INV layabout

guardafango SM mudguard, fender (*EEUU*)

guardafrenos SMF INV guard, conductor (*EEUU*)

guardafuego SM [1] (= *de chimenea*) fireguard

[2] (*Náut*) (= *defensa*) fender

guardagujas SMF INV pointsman/pointswoman, switchman/switchwoman (*EEUU*)

guardajoyas SM INV jewel case

guardajurado SMF (armed) security guard

guardalado SM railing, parapet

guardalmacén SMF storekeeper

guardalodos SM INV mudguard, fender (*EEUU*)

guardamano SM guard (*of a sword*)

guardamechones SM INV locket

guardameta SMF goalkeeper

guardamontes SMPL (*Arg*) rawhide chaps

guardamuebles SM INV furniture repository; **llevar algo a un ~** to put sth in storage

guardapapeles SM INV filing cabinet

guardaparques SMF INV park ranger

guardapelo SM locket

guardapolvo SM [1] (= *cubierta*) dust cover, dust sheet

[2] (= *bata*) dust coat; (= *mono*) overalls *pl*; (= *sobretodo*) outdoor coat

[3] [*de reloj*] inner lid

guardapolvos‡ SM INV [1] (= *condón*) rubber*, safe (*EEUU**)

[2] (*Anat*) pussy**, beaver (*EEUU***)

guardapuerta SF (= *puerta*) outer door, storm door; (= *cortina*) door curtain, draught excluder, draft excluder (*EEUU*)

guardapuntas SM INV top (*of pencil etc*)

guardar ▸conjug 1a◂ Ⓐ VT [1] [+ *objetos*] [1·1] (= *meter*) (*en un lugar*) to put; (*en su sitio*) to put away; **lo guardó en el bolsillo** he put it in his pocket; **no sé dónde he guardado el bolso** I don't know where I've put the bag; **si no vas a jugar más, guarda los juguetes** if you're not going to play any more, put the toys away; **guardó los documentos en el cajón** he put the documents away in the drawer

[1·2] (= *conservar*) to keep; **guardaba el dinero en una caja de seguridad** she kept the money in a safe; **no tira nunca nada, todo lo guarda** he never throws anything away, he hangs on to *o* keeps everything; **guarda tú las entradas del concierto** you hold on to *o* keep the concert tickets; **el grano que se guarda en el almacén** the grain that is stored in the warehouse; **~ algo para sí** to keep sth for o.s.

[1·3] (= *reservar*) to save; **guardo los sellos para mi hermano** I save the stamps for my brother; **te ~é un poco de tarta para cuando vengas** I'll save *o* keep you a bit of cake for when you come; **guárdame un par de entradas** hold *o* save me a couple of tickets, put aside a couple of tickets for me; **guárdame un asiento** keep me a place; **¿puedes ~me el sitio en la cola?** can you keep my place in the queue?; **puedo ~le la habitación sólo hasta mañana** I can only keep *o* hold the room for you till tomorrow

[1·4] (*Inform*) [+ *archivo*] to save

[2] (= *mantener*) [+ *promesa, secreto*] to keep; [+ *recuerdo*] to have; **guardo muy buenos recuerdos de esa época** I have fond memories of that time; **~ el anonimato** to remain anonymous; **~ las apariencias** to keep up appearances; **~ la calma** (*en crisis, desastre*) to keep calm; (*ante una provocación*) to remain

composed; **~ las distancias** to keep one's distance; **~ las formas** to keep up appearances; **~ la línea** (= *mantenerla*) to keep one's figure; (= *cuidarla*) to watch one's figure; **~ en secreto** [+ *objeto, documento*] to keep in secret, keep secretly; [+ *actividad, información*] to keep secret; *ver tb* **cama 1**, **silencio A1**

3 (= *tener*) [+ *relación*] to bear; [+ *semejanza*] to have; **su teoría guarda cierto paralelismo con la de Freud** his theory has a certain parallel with that of Freud

4 (= *sentir*) [+ *rencor*] to bear, have; [+ *respeto*] to have, show; **no le guardo rencor** I have no ill feeling towards him, I bear him no resentment; **los jóvenes de hoy no guardan ningún respeto a sus mayores** young people today have *o* show no respect for their elders

5 (= *cumplir*) [+ *ley*] to observe; **~ los Diez Mandamientos** to follow the Ten Commandments

6 (= *cuidar*) to guard; **un mastín guardaba la entrada** a mastiff guarded the entrance; **los soldados del rey guardan la fortaleza** the king's soldiers are guarding the fortress; **~ a algn de algo** to protect sb from sth; **¡Dios guarde a la Reina!** God save the Queen!; **¡Dios os guarde!**†† may God be with you!

Ⓑ VI **¡guarda!** (*Arg, Chile**) look out!, watch out!

Ⓒ **guardarse** VPR 1 (= *meter*) **me guardé en el bolsillo la foto que me dio** I put the photo he gave me (away) in my pocket; **se guardó rápidamente el paquete de tabaco** he quickly put his cigarettes away

2 (= *conservar*) to keep; **se guardó el dinero del grupo** he kept the group's money for himself, he kept the money that belonged to the group; **¡puedes ~te tus consejos!** you can keep your advice to yourself!

3 **~se de algo** to guard against sth; **debes ~te de las malas compañías** you should guard against bad company; **~se de hacer algo** to be careful not to do sth; **se guardó mucho de reconocer su participación en el asunto** he was careful not to admit his involvement in the affair; **guárdate de no ofenderlo** take care not to upset him; **¡guárdate mucho de hacerlo!** don't you dare!, you'd better not do that!

4 (= *recelar*) to be on one's guard

5 (= *precaverse*) to take care, look out for o.s.*

6 ✦**MODISMO guardársela a algn** to have it in for sb*; **se la guarda desde hace muchos años** she's had it in for him for years; **¡ésta te la guardo!** I won't forget this!, you haven't heard the end *o* last of this!

guardarraya SF 1 (*Cuba, Puerto Rico*) *path between rows of coffee bushes*
2 (*Andes, CAm, Caribe*) boundary

guardarropa Ⓐ SM 1 (*en teatro, discoteca*) cloakroom, checkroom (*EEUU*)
2 (= *armario*) wardrobe
3 (= *ropa*) wardrobe
Ⓑ SMF (= *persona*) cloakroom attendant

guardarropía SF (*Teat*) (= *trajes*) wardrobe; (= *accesorios*) properties *pl*, props* *pl*; ✦**MODISMO de ~** make-believe; (*pey*) sham, fake

guardatiempo SM, **guardatiempos** SM INV timekeeper

guardatrén SMF (*Cono Sur*) guard, conductor (*EEUU*)

guardavalla SMF, **guardavallas** SMF INV (*LAm*) goalkeeper

guardavía SMF (*Ferro*) linesman/lineswoman

guardavidas SMF INV (*Arg*) lifeguard

guardavista SM visor, sunshade

guardería SF (*tb* **~ infantil**) nursery, day nursery, day-care centre *o* (*EEUU*) center; (*en empresa, tienda*) crèche ► **guardería canina** kennels *pl*

guardés/esa SM/F (*gen*) guard; [*de puerta*] doorkeeper; [*de casa de campo*] gatekeeper

guardia Ⓐ SMF (= *policía*) policeman/policewoman; (*Mil*) guardsman ► **guardia civil** civil guard, *police corps with responsibilities outside towns or cities* ► **guardia de tráfico** traffic policeman/policewoman ► **guardia forestal** (forest) ranger, warden ► **guardia jurado** (armed) security guard ► **guardia marina** midshipman ► **guardia municipal**, **guardia urbano/a** police officer (*of the city or town police*) ► **guardias de asalto** riot police; (*Mil*) shock troops

Ⓑ SF 1 (= *vigilancia*) **estar de ~** [*empleado, enfermero, médico*] to be on duty; [*soldado*] to be on sentry duty, be on guard duty; (*Náut*) to be on watch; **médico de ~** doctor on duty, duty doctor; **oficial de ~** officer on duty, duty officer; **puesto de ~** (*Mil*) guard post, sentry box; **hacer ~** [*médico, empleado*] to be on duty; [*soldado*] to do guard duty, do sentry duty; **el soldado que hacía ~** the soldier (who was) on duty; **los fotógrafos hacían ~ junto al juzgado** the photographers were keeping guard outside the court; **montar ~** to stand guard; **los periodistas montaban ~ en la puerta** the journalists were standing guard at the door; **montar la ~** (= *empezarla*) to mount guard; **relevar la ~** to change guard; ✦**MODISMOS bajar la ~** to lower one's guard; **estar en ~** to be on (one's) guard; **poner a algn en ~ (contra algo)** to put sb on one's guard (against sth); **su alusión a mi familia me puso en ~** his reference to my family put me on my guard; **se enciende una luz amarilla para poner en ~ al conductor** a yellow light appears to alert the driver; **ponerse en ~** to be on one's guard; *ver tb* **farmacia 2**, **juzgado**

2 (*tb* **turno de ~**) [*de médico, enfermera*] shift; [*de soldado*] duty session

3 (*Esgrima*) (= *posición*) guard, garde; **estar en ~** to be on guard, be en garde

4 (= *cuerpo*) (*Mil*) guard; ✦**MODISMO la vieja ~** the old guard ► **Guardia Civil** Civil Guard ► **guardia costera** coastguard service ► **guardia de asalto** riot police ► **guardia de honor** guard of honour, guard of honor (*EEUU*) ► **guardia montada** horse guards *pl* ► **guardia municipal** city police, town police ► **Guardia Nacional** (*Nic, Pan*) National Guard, Army ► **guardia pretoriana** (*Hist*) Praetorian Guard; (*pey*) corps of bodyguards ► **Guardia Suiza** Swiss Guard ► **guardia urbana** city police, town police

GUARDIA CIVIL

The **Guardia Civil**, *commonly referred to as* **la Benemérita**, *is the oldest of Spain's various police forces. A paramilitary force like the French* **Gendarmerie**, *it was set up in 1844 to combat banditry in rural areas, but was also used as an instrument of repression in the cities. Under Franco it was resented by many as an oppressive, reactionary force, and was especially hated in the Basque Country. With the return of democracy, Franco's despised* **Policía Armada** *were reformed as the* **Policía Nacional**, *and the present-day role of the* **Guardia Civil** *was redefined. They are mainly stationed in rural areas, and their duties include policing highways and frontiers and taking part in anti-terrorist operations. Their traditional tunics and capes have been replaced by a green uniform, and the famous black patent-leather three-cornered hats are now reserved for ceremonial occasions.*

⇨ *See also* POLICÍA

guardián/ana SM/F 1 (= *defensor*) guardian
2 (= *guarda*) warden, keeper (*EEUU*); (*Zool*) keeper; (= *vigilante*) watchman; *ver tb* **perro A1**

guardiero SM (*Caribe*) watchman (*on an estate*)

guardilla SF (= *desván*) attic, garret; (= *cuarto*) attic room

guardiola* SF piggy bank, money box

guardoso ADJ careful, thrifty; (*pey*) mean

guare SM (*Andes*) punt pole

guarearse* ▸conjug 1a◂ VPR (*CAm*) to get tight*

guarecer ▸conjug 2d◂ Ⓐ VT (= *cobijar*) to protect, give shelter to; (= *preservar*) to preserve
Ⓑ **guarecerse** VPR to shelter, take refuge (**de** from)

guargüero SM (*LAm*) throat, throttle

guari SM (*Cono Sur*) throat, throttle

guaricha SF 1 (*Ven*) (= *joven*) *young unmarried Indian girl*
2 (*Andes, CAm, Caribe*) (= *mujer*) woman; (*vieja*) old bag*
3 (*Andes, CAm, Caribe**) (= *prostituta*) whore

guariche SM (*Andes*) = **guaricha**

guaricho SM (*Caribe*) young farm labourer, young farmhand

guarida SF 1 [*de animales*] den, hideout; [*de persona*] haunt, hideout
2 (*fig*) refuge, shelter; (= *amparo*) cover

guarismo SM figure, numeral; **en ~ y por extenso** in figures and in words

guarnecer ▸conjug 2d◂ VT 1 (= *proveer*) to equip, provide; (= *adornar*) to adorn, garnish; (*Cos*) to trim; (*Téc*) to cover, protect, reinforce; [+ *frenos*] to line; [+ *joya*] to set, mount; [+ *caballo*] to harness
2 (*Culin*) to garnish; **carne guarnecida con cebolla y zanahoria** meat garnished with onion and carrot
3 (*Mil*) to man, garrison
4 (*Arquit*) [+ *pared*] to plaster, stucco

guarnecido SM 1 [*de pared*] plaster, plastering
2 (*Aut*) upholstery

guarnés SM (*Méx*) harness room

guarnición SF 1 (= *acto*) (*de proveer*) equipment, provision; (*de adornar*) adorning; (*Culin*) garnishing
2 (= *adorno*) (*gen*) adornment; (*Cos*) trimming; (*Culin*) garnish; [*de frenos*] lining; [*de joya*] setting, mount; [*de espada*] guard; **ganso con ~ de lombarda y patata** goose with a red cabbage and potato garnish
3 **guarniciones** [*de caballo*] harness *sing*; (=

equipo) gear *sing*; [*de casa*] fittings, fixtures; **guarniciones del alumbrado** light fittings
[4] (*Mil*) garrison
[5] [*de pared*] plastering

guarnicionar ▸conjug 1a◂ VT (*Mil*) to garrison, man

guarnicionero/a SM/F leather worker, leather craftsman/craftswoman; (*para caballos*) harness maker

guaro SM [1] (*CAm*) (= *ron*) liquor, spirits *pl*
[2] (= *ave*) small parrot

guarola* SF (*CAm*) old crock, old banger‡, jalopy (*EEUU*)

guarolo ADJ (*Caribe*) stubborn

guarra SF [1] (*Zool*) sow
[2] (‡ *pey*) (= *mujer*) slut**
[3] (‡) (= *golpe*) punch, bash*; *ver tb* **guarro**

guarrada* SF [1] (= *porquería*) dirty mess, disgusting mess; **hacer una ~** to make a dirty *o* disgusting mess
[2] (= *indecencia*) (= *dicho*) filthy thing (to say), disgusting thing (to say); **ese libro es una ~** that book is a piece of filth*; **decir ~s** to talk filth*; **hacer ~s** to do dirty *o* filthy things
[3] (= *mala pasada*) dirty trick

guarrazo* SM (= *golpe*) **darse** *o* **pegarse un ~** (*gen*) to take a thump*; (*en coche*) to have a smash

guarrear* ▸conjug 1a◂ VT to dirty, mess up

guarrería* SF = **guarrada**

guarrindongo/a* ADJ, SM/F = **guarro**

guarro/a Ⓐ ADJ (*) [1] (= *sucio*) dirty, filthy
[2] (= *indecente*) dirty, filthy; **un chiste ~** a dirty *o* filthy joke
Ⓑ SM/F (*) (= *persona*) (= *sucio*) dirty person; (= *descuidado*) slovenly person; (= *indecente*) filthy person, disgusting person
Ⓒ SM (= *animal*) pig, hog (*EEUU*); *ver tb* **guarra**

guarrusca SF (*Andes*) machete, big knife

guarte†† EXCL look out!, take care!

guarura* SMF (*Méx*) [1] (= *guardaespaldas*) bodyguard, minder*
[2] (= *policía*) cop*

guasa SF [1] (= *chanza*) joking, teasing, kidding*; **con** *o* **de ~** jokingly, in fun; **estar de ~** to be joking *o* kidding; **sonreírse con ~** to smile jokingly; **tomarse algo a ~** to take sth as a joke; **no tengo ganas de ~** I'm not in the mood for jokes
[2] (= *sosería*) dullness, insipidness
[3] (*CAm*) (= *suerte*) luck; *ver tb* **guaso**

guasábara SF (*Andes, Caribe*) [1] (*Hist*) [*de esclavos*] uprising
[2] (††) (= *clamor*) clamour, clamor (*EEUU*), uproar

guasada‡ SF (*Cono Sur*) obscenity

guasamaco ADJ (*Cono Sur*) rough, coarse

guasanga SF [1] (*CAm, Cuba, Méx*) (= *bulla*) din, uproar
[2] (*CAm*) (= *chiste*) joke

guasca[1] SF [1] (*LAm*) (= *correa*) leather strap, rawhide thong; (*Andes*) (= *látigo*) riding whip, crop; **dar ~** (= *azotar*) to whip, flog; ✦*MODISMOS* **dar ~ a algo** (*Cono Sur*) to insist stubbornly on sth; **¡déle ~ no más!** (*Cono Sur*) keep at it!; **dar ~ a algn** (*Andes*) to wind sb up*; **pisarse la ~** (*Andes, Cono Sur*‡) to fall into the trap; **volverse ~** (*Andes*) to be full of longing
[2] (*Cono Sur*‡*) prick**

guasca[2] SF (*Andes*) mountain peak

guascaro ADJ (*Andes*) impulsive

guascazo SM (*LAm*) (= *latigazo*) lash; (= *golpe*) blow, punch

guasch [gwaʃ] SM gouache

guasearse ▸conjug 1a◂ VPR to joke, tease, kid*; **~ de algo/algn** to poke fun at sth/sb

guasería* SF (*Andes, Cono Sur*) rudeness

guaserío SM (*Cono Sur*) rabble

guaso/a* (*Andes, Caribe, Cono Sur*) Ⓐ ADJ [1] (= *grosero*) coarse, rough
[2] (*Cono Sur*) (= *tímido*) shy
[3] (= *sencillo*) simple, unsophisticated
Ⓑ SM/F [1] (*Chile*) (= *campesino*) peasant, countryman/woman, hick (*EEUU**); (= *vaquero*) cowboy/cowgirl
[2] (*Cono Sur*) (= *grosero*) uncouth person
Ⓒ SM (*Cuba*) (= *bulla*) merry din; (= *parranda*) merrymaking, revelry; *ver tb* **guasa**

guasón/ona Ⓐ ADJ [1] (= *bromista*) joking, teasing; **se pusieron en plan ~** they started joking around *o* teasing
[2] (= *burlón*) mocking; **en tono ~** in a mocking tone
Ⓑ SM/F (= *bromista*) joker, tease; (= *ocurrente*) wag, wit

guasqueada* SF (*LAm*) (= *latigazo*) lash; (= *azotaina*) whipping, flogging

guasquear ▸conjug 1a◂ Ⓐ VT (*LAm**) (= *azotar*) to whip, flog
Ⓑ VI (*Chile*) to crack

guata[1] SF [1] (= *algodón*) raw cotton; (= *relleno*) padding
[2] (*Andes*) (= *cuerda*) twine, cord
[3] (*Cuba*) (= *mentira*) lie, fib
[4] (*Andes**) (= *amigo*) inseparable friend, bosom pal

guata[2] SF [1] (*Andes, Cono Sur*) (= *panza*) paunch, belly; **echar ~** (*Chile**) to get fat
[2] **guatas** (*Cono Sur Culin*) tripe *sing*
[3] (*Cono Sur*) warping, bulging

guata[3] SMF (*Andes*) *inhabitant of the interior*

guataca Ⓐ SF (*Caribe*) [1] (= *azada*) small hoe; (= *pala de madera*) wooden shovel
[2] (*Anat*) big ear
Ⓑ SMF (= *lameculos*) crawler*, creep‡, brown-nose (*EEUU*‡)

guataco ADJ [1] (*Andes pey*) (= *indio*) Indian, native
[2] (*CAm, Méx**) (= *gordito*) chubby, plump

guatal SM (*CAm*) hillock

guate SM [1] (*CAm*) [*de maíz*] maize plantation
[2] (*) (*Ven*) (= *serrano*) highlander; (*Caribe*) (= *colombiano*) Colombian
[3] (*Andes**) (= *amigo*) bosom pal

guateado ADJ quilted

guatearse ▸conjug 1a◂ VPR (*Chile*) to warp, bulge

Guatemala SF Guatemala; ✦*MODISMO* **salir de ~ y entrar en Guatepeor** to jump out of the frying pan into the fire

guatemalteco/a Ⓐ ADJ Guatemalan, of/from Guatemala
Ⓑ SM/F Guatemalan; **los ~s** the people of Guatemala

guatemaltequismo SM *word or phrase peculiar to Guatemala*

guateque SM party, binge*

guatero SM (*Chile*) hot water bottle

guatitas SFPL (*Chile*) tripe *sing*

guato‡ SM (*LAm*) joint‡, reefer‡

guatón* ADJ (*Chile*) (= *barrigón*) fat, pot-bellied; (= *regordete*) plump; **sí, ~** yes, darling

guatuso ADJ (*CAm*) blond(e), fair

guau Ⓐ EXCL [1] (*de perro*) woof!, bow-wow!
[2] (*de sorpresa*) wow!*
Ⓑ SM (= *ladrido*) bark

guay* Ⓐ ADJ super*, smashing*
Ⓑ ADV **pasarlo ~** to have a super *o* smashing time*

guaya SF (*Ven*) steel cable

guayaba SF [1] (*LAm Bot*) guava; (= *jalea*) guava jelly
[2] (*LAm**) (= *mentira*) fib, lie
[3] (*LAm*) (= *tobillo*) ankle
[4] (*CAm*) (= *beso*) kiss; (‡) (= *boca*) gob‡
[5] **la ~** (*CAm*) power

guayabal SM grove of guava trees

guayabear* ▸conjug 1a◂ Ⓐ VT (*CAm*) (= *besar*) to kiss
Ⓑ VI (*LAm*) (= *mentir*) to lie, tell fibs

guayabera SF (*LAm*) (= *camisa*) *loose shirt with large pockets*; (= *chaqueta*) lightweight jacket

guayabero* ADJ (*LAm*) lying, deceitful

guayabo SM [1] (*Bot*) guava tree
[2] (*Andes*) (= *pena*) grief, sorrow
[3] (*Ven*) (= *murria*) nostalgia
[4] (*Andes, Cono Sur**) (= *resaca*) hangover
[5] (*) (= *guapa*) pretty girl, smasher*; **está hecha un ~** (= *atractiva*) she looks marvellous; (= *joven*) she looks very young
[6] (*Méx***) pussy**, beaver (*EEUU***)

guayaca Ⓐ ADJ (*Cono Sur*) (= *torpe*) slow, dull; (= *corto*) simple-minded
Ⓑ SF (*LAm*) (= *bolso*) bag, purse (*EEUU*)

guayacán SM lignum vitae

Guayana SF Guyana, Guiana ► **Guayana Británica** British Guiana ► **Guayana Francesa** French Guiana ► **Guayana Holandesa** Dutch Guiana

guayanés/esa ADJ, SM/F Guyanese

guayar ▸conjug 1a◂ VT (*Caribe*) to grate

guayo SM (*Caribe*) [1] (*Culin*) grater
[2] (*Mús**) bad street band

guayuco SM (*Col, Ven*) loincloth

guayunga SF (*Andes*) lot, heap

gubernamental Ⓐ ADJ (*gen*) governmental, government *antes de s*; [*facción*] loyalist; **organización no ~** non-governmental organization
Ⓑ SMF (*leal*) loyalist, government supporter; (*Mil*) government soldier

gubernamentalización SF (increase in) government intervention *o* control

gubernativo ADJ government *antes de s*, governmental; **los delegados ~s** the government delegates; **la decisión gubernativa** the government's decision; **por orden gubernativa** by order of the government

gubia SF gouge

güe... (*para diversas palabras escritas así esp en LAm*) *ver tb* **hue...** *p. ej.* **güevón**; *ver* **huevón**

guedeja SF [1] (= *mechón*) lock
[2] (= *cabellera*) long hair
[3] [*de león*] mane

güegüecho Ⓐ ADJ [1] (*Andes, CAm**) (= *tonto*) silly, stupid
[2] (*CAm, Méx Med*) suffering from goitre *o* (*EEUU*) goiter
Ⓑ SM [1] (*CAm, Méx Med*) goitre, goiter (*EEUU*)

2 (CAm) (= ave) turkey
3 (CAm*) (= bohío) hovel

güeñi SM (Cono Sur) (= chico) boy; (= criado) servant

guepardo SM cheetah

güerequeque SM (Andes) plover

Guernesey SM Guernsey

güero ADJ (CAm, Méx) (= rubio) blond(e), fair; (de tez) fair, light-skinned

guerra SF 1 (Mil, Pol) war; (= arte) warfare; **Primera Guerra Mundial** First World War; **Segunda Guerra Mundial** Second World War; **de ~** military, war antes de s; **Ministerio de Guerra** Ministry of War, War Office, War Department (EEUU); **declarar la ~** to declare war (**a** on); **estar en ~** to be at war (**con** with); **hacer la ~** to wage war (**a** on); ► **guerra a muerte** war to the bitter end ► **guerra atómica** atomic war(fare) ► **guerra bacteriana**, **guerra bacteriológica** germ warfare ► **guerra biológica** biological warfare ► **guerra caliente** hot war, shooting war ► **guerra civil** civil war ► **guerra comercial** trade war ► **guerra convencional** conventional warfare ► **guerra de agotamiento**, **guerra de desgaste** war of attrition ► **guerra de bandas** gang warfare ► **guerra de guerrillas** guerrilla warfare ► **Guerra de la Independencia** (LAm) War of Independence; (Esp) Peninsular War ► **guerra de las galaxias** Star Wars ► **Guerra de los Cien Años** Hundred Years' War ► **Guerra de los Treinta Años** Thirty Years' War ► **Guerra del Transvaal** Boer War ► **guerra de nervios** war of nerves ► **guerra de precios** price war ► **Guerra de Sucesión** War of Spanish Succession ► **guerra de trincheras** trench warfare ► **guerra económica** economic warfare ► **guerra nuclear** nuclear war(fare) ► **guerra psicológica** psychological warfare ► **guerra química** chemical warfare ► **guerra relámpago** blitzkrieg, lightning war (EEUU) ► **guerra santa** holy war, crusade ► **guerra sin cuartel** all-out war ► **guerra sucia** dirty war; ver tb **declarar A1**
2 (= problemas) **dar ~** (gen) to be a nuisance (**a** to), make trouble (**a** for); [niño] to carry on; **pedir** o **querer ~** (gen) to look for trouble; (*) (sexualmente) to feel randy o horny*
3 (= juego) billiards

GUERRA CIVIL ESPAÑOLA

Spain's political climate was extremely volatile in the 1930s, under the Second Republic, with various sectors of society all vying for power. The elections of February 1936 were won by a coalition of socialist and anarchist groups known as the **Frente Popular** *or* **FP**, *and were followed by a period of strikes, uprisings and social disorder. On 18 July of that year, General Francisco Franco led a military coup. In the ensuing war Franco's side was known as the* **Nacionales** *and the government forces as the* **Republicanos**. *Neither army was well-equipped, so foreign support was a decisive factor: the USSR sent aid to the Republicans and volunteers from all over Europe formed* **Brigadas Internacionales** *(International Brigades) to fight with them. Fascist Italy and Germany sent troops and weapons to Franco. The fighting was bitter and protracted, and the Nationalists' superior firepower finally triumphed. The war ended officially on 1 April 1939, when Franco proclaimed himself* **Jefe del Estado**, *a position he held for the next 36 years.*
⇨ See also FRANQUISMO

guerrear ▸conjug 1a◂ VI (= pelear) to wage war, fight; (fig) to put up a fight, resist

guerrera SF (= chaqueta) combat jacket; (Mil) military jacket; (= abrigo) trench coat

guerrero/a Ⓐ ADJ 1 (= belicoso) war antes de s; **espíritu ~** fighting spirit; **hazañas guerreras** fighting exploits
2 (de carácter) warlike; **un pueblo ~** a warlike people; **virtudes guerreras** warlike virtues
3 (= en guerra) warring; **tribus guerreras** warring tribes
Ⓑ SM/F (= soldado) warrior, soldier
Ⓒ SM (Caribe*) rum and vodka-based cocktail

guerrilla SF 1 (= grupo) guerrillas pl; (= fuerzas) guerrilla forces pl
2 (= guerra) guerrilla warfare

guerrillear ▸conjug 1a◂ VI to wage guerrilla warfare

guerrillero/a Ⓐ ADJ guerrilla antes de s; **líder ~** guerrilla leader
Ⓑ SM/F guerrilla (fighter); (= maqui) partisan ► **guerrillero/a urbano/a** urban guerrilla

guerrista Ⓐ ADJ (= luchador) combative, fighting
Ⓑ SMF (Esp Pol) supporter of Alfonso Guerra

güesear‡ ▸conjug 1a◂ VT (CAm) to wash

gueto SM ghetto

güevo SM ✦**MODISMO a** o **de ~** (Méx) by hook or by crook

güevón/ona* (LAm) ADJ, SM/F = **huevón**

güi... (para diversas palabras escritas así en LAm) ver tb **hui...**

guía Ⓐ SF 1 (= libro) guidebook (**de** to); (= manual) handbook; [de teléfono] directory ► **guía de campo** (Biol) field guide ► **guía de carga** (Ferro) waybill ► **guía de datos** data directory ► **guía del ocio** "what's on" guide ► **guía del turista** tourist guide ► **guía de teléfonos** telephone directory ► **guía del viajero** traveller's o (EEUU) traveler's guide ► **guía gastronómica** food guide ► **guía oficial de ferrocarriles** (Ferro) official timetable ► **guía telefónica** telephone directory ► **guía turística** tourist guide
2 (= orientación) guidance; (= acto) guiding; **para que le sirva de ~** for your guidance ► **guía vocacional** vocational guidance
3 (Inform) prompt
4 (Mec) guide; [de bicicleta] handlebars pl; (= caballo) leader, front horse; **guías** (= riendas) reins ► **guía sonora** (Cine) soundtrack
Ⓑ SMF (= persona) guide; (= dirigente) leader; (= consejero) adviser ► **guía de turismo** tourist guide
Ⓒ ADJ INV guide antes de s, guiding; **manual ~** guidebook; **cable ~** guiding wire, guide rope

guiado SM guiding, guidance; [de misil] guiding

guiar ▸conjug 1c◂ Ⓐ VT 1 (gen) to guide; (= dirigir) to lead, direct; (= controlar) to manage; (= orientar) to advise; **no te dejes ~ por la propaganda** don't be influenced o led by propaganda
2 (Aut) to drive; (Náut) to steer; (Aer) to pilot
3 (Bot) to train
Ⓑ **guiarse** VPR **~se por algo** to be guided by sth, be ruled by sth, go by sth; **no hay que ~se por lo que dice la televisión** you don't have to be guided o ruled o go by what's on television; **~se por el sentido común** to follow common sense

güicoy SM (CAm Bot) courgette, zucchini (EEUU)

Guido SM Guy

guija[1] SF (= piedra) pebble; (en camino) cobble, cobblestone

guija[2] SF (Bot) vetch

guijarral SM (= terreno) stony place; (= playa) shingle, pebbles pl

guijarro SM (= piedra) pebble; (en camino) cobblestone, cobble

guijarroso ADJ [terreno] stony; [camino] cobbled; [playa] pebbly, shingly

guijo SM 1 (= grava) gravel; (para caminos) granite chips pl; (en la playa) shingle
2 (Mec) (= gorrón) shaft of wheel

güila[1] SF 1 (Méx) (= prostituta) whore, tart‡, slut‡
2 (Chile*) (= andrajos) rags pl, tatters pl
3 (CAm) (= trompito) small spinning top

güila[2]* SMF (CAm) kid*

güiliento ADJ (Cono Sur) ragged, tattered

guillado* ADJ cracked*, crazy; **estar ~** to be off one's trolley*

guillame SM (Téc) rabbet plane

guillarse* ▸conjug 1a◂ VPR 1 to go crazy, go round the twist*
2 **guillárselas** (= irse) to beat it*; (= morir) to kick the bucket‡

Guillermo SM William

guillotina SF guillotine; (para papel) paper cutter; **ventana de ~** sash window

guillotinado SM guillotining

guillotinar ▸conjug 1a◂ VT to guillotine

güilo ADJ (Méx) (= tullido) maimed, crippled; (fig) weak, sickly

güincha SF (Andes, Cono Sur) 1 (= ribete) narrow strip of cloth; (= cinta) ribbon; (= para pelo) hair ribbon
2 (Dep) (= meta) tape, finishing line; (= salida) starting line
3 (= cinta métrica) measuring tape, tape measure
4 **¡las ~s!** rubbish!, forget it!

güinche SM (Arg) (= torno) winch, hoist; (= grúa) crane

güinchero SM (LAm) winch operator; [de grúa] crane operator

guinda SF 1 (= fruta) morello cherry, mazzard cherry, sour cherry (EEUU); ✦**MODISMOS ponerse como una ~** to turn scarlet; **échale ~s al pavo** would you believe it!
2 (= remate) **la ~ (del pastel)** the icing on the cake; **como ~** to cap o top it all; **y como ~ la actuación de Madonna** and to cap o top it all we had Madonna's performance; **poner la ~** (= rematar bien) to put the icing on the cake; (= terminar) to add the finishing touches; **puso la ~ con un gol en el último minuto** his goal in the last minute was the icing on the cake; **poner la ~ a la oferta** to top off the offer, add a final attraction to the offer; **aquello puso la ~ final** (iró) that was the last straw
3 (Náut) height of masts
4 (Caribe) guttering, spout

[5] **eso es una ~** (*Cono Sur*⁑) that's simple, it's a cinch⁑
[6] **guindas** (*Cono Sur*⁑) balls⁑, bollocks⁑

guindalejo SM (*Andes, Caribe*) (= *ropa vieja*) old clothes *pl*; (= *trastos*) junk, lumber

guindaleza SF (*Náut*) hawser

guindar ▸conjug 1a◂ Ⓐ VT [1] (⁑) (= *robar*) to pinch*, swipe*
[2] (⁑) [+ *contrato, trabajo*] to win (*against competition*), land
[3] (*Caribe*) (= *colgar*) to hang up
Ⓑ **guindarse** VPR [1] (= *descolgarse*) to hang (down)
[2] (*) (= *ahorcarse*) to hang o.s.; (= *morirse*) to kick the bucket*

guindaste SM (*Náut*) jib crane

guinde⁑ SM nicking⁑, thieving; **un ~** a job*

guindilla Ⓐ SF (= *pimiento*) chili, hot pepper; **~ roja** red chilli; **~ verde** green chilli
Ⓑ SMF (*Esp**) (= *policía*) cop*

guindo[1] SM mazzard cherry tree, morello cherry tree; ✦*MODISMO* **caer del ~*** to twig*, to cotton on*

guindo[2] SM (*CAm*) ravine

guindola SF (*Náut*) lifebuoy

guindón⁑ SM thief

Guinea SF Guinea ▸ **Guinea Ecuatorial** Equatorial Guinea ▸ **Guinea Española** Spanish Guinea

guinea SF (= *moneda*) guinea; *ver tb* **guineo**

Guinea-Bissau SF Guinea-Bissau

guineo[1]**/a** Ⓐ ADJ Guinea(n), of/from Guinea
Ⓑ SM/F Guinea(n); *ver tb* **guinea**

guineo[2] SM (*LAm*) banana

guiña SF [1] (*Andes, Caribe*) bad luck
[2] (*Andes*) witchcraft

guiñada SF [1] (= *guiño*) wink
[2] (*Aer, Náut*) yaw

guiñapo SM [1] (= *andrajo*) rag, tatter; ✦*MODISMO* **poner a algn como un ~** to shower sb with insults
[2] (= *dejado*) slovenly person; (= *granuja*) ragamuffin; (= *réprobo*) rogue, reprobate

guiñar ▸conjug 1a◂ Ⓐ VT to wink; **~ el ojo a algn** to wink at sb
Ⓑ VI [1] (*con un ojo*) to wink
[2] (*Aer, Náut*) to yaw

guiño SM [1] (*con un ojo*) wink; **hacer ~s a algn** to wink at sb; (*amantes*) to make eyes at sb; **~ cómplice** (*lit*) knowing wink; (= *apoyo*) tacit support
[2] (*Aer, Náut*) yaw

guiñol SM (*Teat*) puppet theatre *o* (*EEUU*) theater, Punch and Judy show

guiñolista SMF puppeteer

guión SM [1] (*Radio, TV*) script; (*Cine*) (*como transcripción*) script; (*como obra*) screenplay; **salirse del ~** to depart from the script, improvise; **el premio al mejor ~** the prize for the best screenplay
[2] (*Literat*) (= *resumen*) summary, outline; (= *aclaración*) explanatory text
[3] (*Tip*) hyphen, dash
[4] (= *pendón*) royal standard; (*Rel*) processional cross, processional banner
[5] (*Orn*) ▸ **guión de codornices** corncrake

guionista SMF scriptwriter

guionizar ▸conjug 1f◂ VT to script, write the script for

guipar⁑ ▸conjug 1a◂ VT [1] (= *ver*) to see
[2] (= *entender*) to cotton on to*, catch on to
[3] (= *percibir*) to spot, catch sight of

güipil SM (*CAm, Méx*) *Indian regional dress or blouse*

Guipúzcoa SF Guipúzcoa

guipuzcoano/a Ⓐ ADJ of/from Guipúzcoa
Ⓑ SM/F native/inhabitant of Guipúzcoa; **los ~s** the people of Guipúzcoa

guiri Ⓐ SMF (*) (= *extranjero*) foreigner; (= *turista*) tourist
Ⓑ SM [1] (*) (= *policía*) policeman; (= *guardia civil*) civil guard
[2] (*Hist*) Carlist soldier
[3] **en el ~**⁑ abroad, in foreign parts

guirigay SM [1] (= *griterío*) hubbub, uproar; (= *confusión*) chaos, confusion; **¡esto es un ~!** the place is like a bear garden!
[2] (= *lenguaje confuso*) gibberish, jargon

guirizapa SF (*Caribe*) quarrel, squabble

guirlache SM *type of nougat*

guirnalda SF (= *tira, collar*) garland; (*en entierro*) wreath; (*Arte*) garland, floral motif

güiro* SM [1] (*Caribe*) (= *calabaza*) gourd
[2] (*Mús*) musical instrument
[3] (*Caribe*) (= *cabeza*) head, nut⁑, noggin (*EEUU*⁑)
[4] (*CAm*) (= *bebé*) small baby
[5] (*Caribe*) (= *mujerzuela*) loose woman
[6] (*Andes*) (= *brote de maíz*) maize shoot

güirro Ⓐ ADJ (*LAm*) weak, sickly
Ⓑ SM (*CAm*) small baby

guisa SF [1] **a ~ de: se puso una cinta a ~ de pulsera** she wore a strap like a bracelet; **usando el bastón a ~ de batuta** using his walking stick like *o* as a baton
[2] **de tal ~** in such a way (**que** that)

guisado Ⓐ ADJ **carne guisada** beef stew, beef casserole
Ⓑ SM stew; **~ de alubias** bean casserole

guisador(a) SM/F, **guisandero/a** SM/F cook

guisante SM pea ▸ **guisante de olor** sweet pea

guisar ▸conjug 1a◂ Ⓐ VT [1] (*Culin*) (= *cocinar*) to cook; (= *en salsa*) to stew; ✦*REFRÁN* **él se lo guisa, él se lo come** he's made his bed, so he can lie in it
[2] (*) (= *tramar*) to cook up*; **¿qué estarán guisando?** what can they be cooking up?*
Ⓑ VI to cook; **me paso el día guisando** I spend the day cooking
Ⓒ **guisarse** VPR (*) (= *tramarse*) **¿qué se estará guisando en la asamblea?** what are they cooking up in the meeting, I wonder?*

güisingue SM (*Andes*) whip

güisinguear ▸conjug 1a◂ VT (*Andes*) to whip

guiso SM [1] (= *guisado*) stew
[2] (= *aliño*) seasoning

guisote SM (*pey*) (= *guiso*) hash, poor-quality stew; (= *mezcla*) concoction; (= *comida*) grub*, nosh⁑, chow (*EEUU*⁑)

güisquería SF night club

güisqui SM whisky

guita SF [1] (= *cuerda*) twine; (= *bramante*) packthread
[2] (⁑) (= *dinero*) dough*, cash; **¿cuánta ~?** how much dough* *o* cash?; **aflojar** *o* **soltar la ~** to cough up*, stump up*, fork out*

güita⁑ SF (*Méx*) dough*

guitarra Ⓐ SF (= *instrumento*) guitar; ✦*MODISMOS* **chafar la ~ a algn** to queer sb's pitch; **ser como ~ en un entierro** to be quite out of place, strike the wrong note; **estar con la ~ bien/mal templada** to be in a good/bad mood ▸ **guitarra baja** bass guitar ▸ **guitarra clásica** classical guitar ▸ **guitarra eléctrica** electrical guitar
Ⓑ SMF guitarist ▸ **guitarra solista** (*en concierto*) solo guitarist; (*en grupo*) lead guitar

guitarrear ▸conjug 1a◂ VI to play the guitar, strum a guitar

guitarreo SM strum(ming)

guitarrero/a SM/F (electric) guitarist

guitarrista SMF guitarist

guitarrón SM [1] (*Méx Mús*) large guitar
[2] (*CAm*) (= *abeja*) bee

güito SM [1] (= *hueso*) stone
[2] **güitos**⁑ balls⁑

güizcal SM (*CAm Bot*) chayote

gula SF gluttony, greed

gulag SM (*pl* **gulags**) gulag

gulash [gu'laʃ] SM INV goulash

guloso ADJ gluttonous (*frm*), greedy

gulusmear ▸conjug 1a◂ VI [1] (= *comer*) to nibble titbits
[2] (= *oler*) to sniff the cooking
[3] (= *curiosear*) to snoop

guma⁑ SF hen

gumarra* SM (*Méx*) cop*

gurguciar ▸conjug 1b◂ Ⓐ VT (*CAm*) to sniff at, sniff out
Ⓑ VI (*Méx**) (= *gruñir*) to grunt, snort

guri⁑ SM (= *policía*) cop*; (*Mil*) soldier

gurí* SM (*Cono Sur*) (*pl* **gurís, guríes** *o* **gurises**)
[1] (†) (= *mestizo*) mestizo, Indian child, child of mixed race
[2] (= *muchacho*) boy, kid*

guripa* SM [1] (*Mil*) soldier; (= *policía*) cop*
[2] (= *pillo*) rascal, rogue; (= *tonto*) berk⁑
[3] (= *sujeto*) bloke*, guy*

gurisa* SF (*Cono Sur*) [1] (†) (= *mestiza*) Indian child, child of mixed race
[2] (= *chica*) girl, bird*, chick (*EEUU**); (= *esposa*) young wife

gurrí SM (*Col, Ecu*) wild duck

gurrumina* SF [1] (*Andes*) (= *molestia*) bother, nuisance; (= *tristeza*) sadness
[2] (*Méx*) (= *fruslería*) trifle, mere nothing

gurrumino/a* Ⓐ ADJ [1] (= *débil*) weak, sickly; (= *insignificante*) small, puny
[2] [*marido*] complaisant, indulgent
[3] (*Andes*) (= *cobarde*) cowardly
[4] (*CAm*) (= *listo*) clever, sharp
Ⓑ SM/F [1] (*Méx*) (= *chiquillo*) child
[2] (*LAm*) (= *persona astuta*) sharp customer*
Ⓒ SM (= *cornudo*) cuckold; (= *marido complaciente*) complaisant husband, indulgent husband

gurrupié SM [1] (*Méx*) (*en los garitos*) croupier
[2] (*Caribe, Andes*) (= *falso postor*) false bidder
[3] (*Caribe**) (= *amigo*) pal*, buddy (*esp EEUU*)

gurú SMF (*pl* **gurús**) guru

gurupié SM = **gurrupié**

gus SM (*Andes*) turkey buzzard

gusa* SF hunger; **tener ~** to be hungry

gusanera SF [1] (= *nido*) nest of maggots; (= *lugar*) breeding ground for maggots
[2] (*Cuba*⁑ *pey*) **la ~** Miami (*home of refugee Cubans since 1959*)

3 (= *montón*) bunch, lot; **una ~ de chiquillos** a bunch of kids

gusaniento ADJ worm-eaten

gusanillo SM 1 (*) (= *hambre*) **me anda el ~** I feel peckish; **cómete una manzana para matar el ~** have an apple to keep you going
2 (*) (= *interés*) bug*; **le entró el ~ de la gimnasia** he caught the keep-fit bug*, he got hooked on keep-fit*
3 (= *espiral*) spiral binding; **encuadernado en ~** spiral bound
4 **el ~ de la conciencia*** the prickings of conscience

gusano Ⓐ SM 1 (*gen*) worm; [*de tierra*] earthworm; [*de mosca*] maggot; [*de mariposa, polilla*] caterpillar; ✦*MODISMO* **criar ~s** to be dead and buried, be pushing up the daisies* ► **gusano de la carne** maggot ► **gusano de la conciencia** remorse ► **gusano de luz** glow worm ► **gusano de seda** silkworm
2 (= *persona*) worm; (= *ser despreciable*) contemptible person; (= *persona dócil*) meek creature
3 (*Inform*) worm
4 (*Cuba*‡ *pey*) *nickname for Cuban refugees post-1959*
Ⓑ ADJ (*Cuba*‡ *pey*) Cuban-refugee *antes de s*

gusanoso ADJ worm-eaten

gusarapo SM 1 (= *renacuajo*) tadpole
2 (*) (= *bicho*) bug, creature
3 (*) (= *persona*) worm*

gusgo ADJ (*Méx*) sweet-toothed

gustación SF tasting, trying

gustado ADJ (*LAm*) popular; **un plato muy ~** a very popular dish

▼**gustar** ▸conjug 1a◂ Ⓐ VI 1 (*con complemento personal*) 1·1 (*con sustantivo*) **me gusta el té** I like tea; **¿te gustó México?** did you like Mexico?; **no me gusta mucho** I don't like it very much; **le gustan mucho los niños** she loves children, she's very fond of children, she likes children a lot; **¿te ha gustado la película?** did you enjoy the film?; **el rojo es el que más me gusta** I like the red one best; **eso es, así me gusta** that's right, that's the way I like it; **me gusta como canta** I like the way she sings
1·2 (+ *INFIN*) **¿te gusta jugar a las cartas?** do you like playing cards?; **no me gusta nada levantarme temprano** I hate getting up early, I don't like getting up early at all; **no me ~ía nada estar en su lugar** I'd hate to be *o* I really wouldn't like to be in his place *o* shoes; **le gusta mucho jugar al fútbol** he's a keen footballer, he likes playing *o* to play football; **le gusta llegar con tiempo de sobra a una cita** she likes to get to her appointments with time to spare
1·3 **~ que** (+ *SUBJUN*): **no le gusta que lo llamen Pepe** he doesn't like being *o* to be called Pepe; **le gusta que la cena esté en la mesa cuando llega a casa** he likes his supper to be on the table when he gets home; **no me gustó que no invitaran a mi hija a la boda** I didn't like the fact that *o* I was annoyed that my daughter wasn't invited to the wedding; **me gusta mucho que me den masajes** I love having massages; **¿te ~ía que te llevara al cine?** would you like me to take you to the cinema?, would you like it if I took you to the cinema?
1·4 (= *sentir atracción por*) **a mi amiga le gusta Carlos** my friend fancies* *o* likes *o* is keen on Carlos
2 (*sin complemento explícito*) **es una película que siempre gusta** it's a film that never fails to please; **la obra no gustó** the play was not a success; **mi número ya no gusta** my act isn't popular any more
3 (*en frases de cortesía*) **¿gusta usted?** would you like some?, may I offer you some?; **si usted gusta** if you please, if you don't mind; **como usted guste** as you wish, as you please†; **cuando gusten** (*invitando a pasar*) when you're ready; **puede venir por aquí cuando guste** you can come here whenever you like *o* wish
4 **~ de algo** to like sth; **vivía recluido y no gustaba de compañía** he was a recluse and did not like company; **la novela ideal para quienes no gusten de obras largas** the ideal novel for people who don't like *o* enjoy long books; **~ de hacer algo** to like to do sth; **Josechu, como gustan de llamarlo en su familia** Josechu, as his family like to call him; **una expresión que gustan de repetir los escritores del XVIII** an expression that 18th century writers like to use *o* are fond of using frequently
Ⓑ VT 1 (= *probar*) to taste, sample; **después de ~ la buena vida** after tasting the good life
2 (*LAm*) **gusto un café** I'd like a coffee; **¿~ía un poco de vino?** would you like some wine?; **si gustan pasar a la sala de espera** would you like to go through to the waiting room?

gustazo* SM great pleasure; **me di el ~ de levantarme a las doce** I treated myself to a lie-in till twelve

gustillo SM **coger el ~ a algo** to get *o* grow to like sth

gustirrinín* SM = **gusto 4**

▼**gusto** SM 1 (= *sentido*) taste; **agregue azúcar a ~** add sugar to taste
2 [*de comida*] taste, flavour, flavor (*EEUU*); **tiene un ~ amargo** it has a bitter taste *o* flavour, it tastes bitter; **le noto un ~ a almendras** it tastes of almonds; **helado de tres ~s** Neapolitan ice cream
3 (= *sentido estético*) taste; **tenemos los mismos ~s** we have the same tastes; **es demasiado grande para mi ~** it's too big for my taste; **he decorado la habitación a mi ~** I've decorated the room to my taste; **al ~ de hoy** *o* **según el ~ de hoy** in the taste of today; **ser persona de ~** to be a person of taste; **tiene ~ para vestir** she dresses with taste, she has taste in clothes; **una habitación decorada con ~** a tastefully decorated room; **buen ~** good taste; **no es de buen ~ decir eso** it's not in good taste to say that; **tiene buen ~ para combinar colores** she has good taste in combining colours; **un decorado de buen ~** tasteful décor; **mal ~** bad taste; **es de un mal ~ extraordinario** it is in extraordinarily bad taste; **una broma de muy mal ~** a joke in very poor taste; **un comentario de mal ~** a tasteless remark; ✦*REFRANES* **sobre ~s no hay disputa** ◊ **de ~s no hay nada escrito** there's no accounting for tastes
4 (= *placer*) pleasure; **a ~: aquí me encuentro** *o* **siento a ~** I feel at home *o* ease here; **tengo los pies a ~ y calientes** my feet are nice and warm; **acomodarse a su ~** to make o.s. at home, make o.s. comfortable; **con mucho ~** with pleasure; **lo haré con mucho ~** I'll be glad to do it, I'll be only too happy to do it; **con sumo ~** with great pleasure; **comer con ~** to eat heartily; **dar ~ a algn** to please sb, give pleasure to sb; **lo compré para dar ~ a los chiquillos** I bought it to please the kids; **da ~ hacerlo** it's nice to do it; **da ~ trabajar contigo** it's a pleasure to work with you; **da ~ verlos tan contentos** it's lovely to see them so happy; **tienen un entusiasmo que da ~** they show a wonderful enthusiasm; **leo por ~** I read for pleasure; **no lo hago por ~** I don't do it out of choice; **es por ~ que siga allí** (*LAm*) you'll wait there in vain; **tener el ~ de hacer algo** to have the pleasure of doing sth
5 (= *agrado*) liking; **al ~ de** to the liking of; **ser del ~ de algn** to be to sb's liking; **coger el ~ a algo** ◊ **tomar ~ a algo** to take a liking to sth; **tener ~ por algo** to have a liking for sth
6 (*en presentaciones*) **¡mucho ~!** ◊ **¡tanto ~!** ◊ **¡~ verlo!** (*LAm**) how do you do?, pleased to meet you; **el ~ es mío** how do you do?, the pleasure is (all) mine; **(tengo) mucho ~ en conocerle** I'm very pleased to meet you; **tengo mucho ~ en presentar al Sr Peláez** allow me to introduce Mr Peláez
7 (= *antojo*) whim, fancy; **a ~** at will, according to one's fancy
8 (*Cono Sur*) (= *estilo*) style, design, colour; (= *gama*) range, assortment

gustosamente ADV gladly, willingly; **accedí ~ a su petición** I gladly *o* willingly agreed to their request; **se sometió ~ a las preguntas de los periodistas** she gladly *o* willingly answered the journalists' questions; **aprovecho ~ esta oportunidad para desearle lo mejor** I am delighted to have this opportunity to wish you the best

gustoso ADJ 1 (= *complacido*) gladly; **lo hizo ~** he did it gladly; **acepto ~ su ofrecimiento** I gladly accept your offer
2 (= *sabroso*) tasty
3 (= *agradable*) [*lectura*] enjoyable; [*sensación*] pleasant, pleasing

gutapercha SF gutta-percha

gutifarra SF (*LAm*) = **butifarra**

gutural ADJ (*Ling*) guttural; (= *de la garganta*) throaty

Guyana SF Guyana

guyanés/esa ADJ, SM/F Guyanese, Guyanan

➤ LENGUA Y USO: **gustar A1** 28.1, 34.1, 34.2, 34.3, 35.4, 52.3 **gusto 4** 38.3, 52.1, 52.4

H h

H^{1}, **h**^{1} ['atʃe] SF (= *letra*) H, h

H^{2} ABR [1] = **hectárea(s)**
[2] (*Quím*) (= **hidrógeno**) H

h^{2} ABR (= **hora**) h., hr.

H. ABR [1] (*Fin*) (= **haber**) Cr
[2] (*Rel*) (= **Hermano**) Br., Bro.

h. ABR [1] (= **hacia**) c
[2] (= **habitantes**) pop

Ha ABR = **hectárea(s)**

ha^{1} EXCL oh!

ha^{2} *ver* **haber**

haba SF [1] (= *legumbre*) broad bean; [*de café*] coffee bean; ✦*MODISMOS* **en todas partes cuecen ~s** it's the same the whole world over; **son ~s contadas** (*para expresar escasez*) they are few and far between; (= *es seguro*) it's a sure thing, it's a dead cert* ► **haba de las Indias** sweet pea ► **haba de soja** soya bean ► **haba verde** young broad bean
[2] (*Vet*) tumour, tumor (*EEUU*)
[3] (**) (= *pene*) prick**

Habana SF **La ~** Havana

habanera SF (*Mús*) habanera

habanero/a Ⓐ ADJ of/from Havana
Ⓑ SM/F native/inhabitant of Havana; **los ~s** the people of Havana

habano/a Ⓐ ADJ, SM/F = **habanero**
Ⓑ SM (= *puro*) Havana cigar

hábeas corpus SM habeas corpus

▼**haber** ►conjug 2j◄ Ⓐ V AUX [1] (*en tiempos compuestos*) to have; **he comido** I have *o* I've eaten; **había ido al cine** he had gone *o* he'd gone to the cinema; **lo hubiéramos hecho** we would have done it; **¡~lo dicho!** you should have said!; **¡hubieran visto la casa!** (*esp LAm**) you should have seen the house!; **pero, ¿habráse visto (cosa igual)?** well, have you ever seen anything like it?; **de ~lo sabido** if I had known, if I'd known
[2] **~ de** [2·1] (*indicando obligación*) **he de hacerlo** I have to do it, I must do it; **hemos de tener paciencia** we must be patient; **has de saber que …** you should know that …; **¿qué he de hacer?** what am I to do?; **los has de ver** (*LAm*) you'll see them
[2·2] (*indicando suposición*) **han de ser las nueve** it must be about nine o'clock; **ha de llegar hoy** (*esp LAm*) he should get here today; **has de estar equivocado** (*esp LAm*) you must be mistaken
Ⓑ V IMPERS [1] **hay** (*con sustantivo en singular*) there is; (*con sustantivo en plural*) there are; **hay un hombre en la calle** there is a man in the street; **hay mucho que hacer** there is so much to be done; **hubo una guerra** there was a war; **no hubo discusión** there was no discussion; **¿habrá tiempo?** will there be time?; **tomará lo que haya** he'll take whatever there is; **lo que hay es que …** it's like this …, the thing is …; **algo debe de ~ para que se comporte así** there must be some reason for him acting like that; **hay sol** the sun is shining, it's sunny; **hay dos hombres en la calle** there are two men in the street; **no hay plátanos** there are no bananas; **ha habido problemas** there have been problems; **habían muchas personas** (*LAm*) there were many people there; **¿cuánto hay de aquí a Cuzco?** how far is it from here to Cuzco?; **los hay excelentes** some are excellent; **los hay buenos y malos** some are good and some are bad; **los hay que están confusos y asustados** some (people) are confused and afraid; **las hay en negro y blanco** they are available in black and white; **oportunistas los hay en todas partes** you'll find opportunists everywhere, there are always opportunists, wherever you go; **no hay**: **no hay nada mejor que …** there's nothing better than …; **no hay como esta playa para disfrutar del surf** there's nothing like this beach for surfing; **no hay más que hablar** there's no more to be said, there's nothing more to say; **no hay quien te entienda** there's no understanding you; **¡aquí no hay quien duerma!** it's impossible to get any sleep round here!; **¡no hay de qué!** don't mention it!, not at all!; **¿qué hay?** (= *¿qué pasa?*) what's up?; (= *¿qué tal?*) how's it going?, how are things?; **¡qué hubo!** (*Chile, Méx, Ven**) how's it going?, how are things?; ✦*MODISMOS* **como hay pocos** ◊ **donde los haya**: **un amigo como hay pocos** *o* **donde los haya** a friend in a million; **de lo que no hay**: **¡eres de lo que no hay!** you're unbelievable!; **si los hay**: **buen chico si los hay** a good lad if ever there was one
[2] (*Com*) **"¡mejores no hay!"** "there's none better!"; **¡hay helado!** (*dicho a voces*) ice cream!; (*en cartel*) ice cream sold; **¿hay puros?** do you have any cigars?; **"no hay entradas** *o* **localidades"** "sold out"
[3] **hay que**: **hay que trabajar** one has to work, everyone must work; **hay que hacer algo** something has to be done; **hay que hacerlo** it has to be done; **no hay que hacer nada** you don't have to do anything; **hay que ser fuertes** we must be strong; **hay que trabajar más** (*como mandato*) you must work harder; **no hay que olvidar que …** we mustn't forget that …; **no hay que tomarlo a mal** there's no reason to take it badly, you mustn't get upset about it; **¡había que decírselo!** we'll have to tell him!; **¡había que verlo!** you should have seen it!; **no hay más que**: **no hay más que leer las normas** all you have to do is read the rules; **no hay más que haber viajado un poco para saberlo** anyone who has done a bit of travelling would know; ✦*MODISMO* **¡hay que ver!** (*sorpresa*) well I never!
[4] (*indicando tiempo*) **tres años ha** (*frm*) three years ago; **años ha que no les veo** (*frm, hum*) I haven't seen them for years
Ⓒ VT [1] (= *ocurrir*) **en el encuentro habido ayer** in yesterday's game; **el descenso de temperatura habida ayer** the fall in temperature recorded yesterday; **la lista de las víctimas habidas** the list of casualties; ✦*MODISMO* **habidos y por ~**: **se trataron todos los temas habidos y por ~** they discussed every subject under the sun
[2] (= *tener*) **un hijo habido fuera del matrimonio** a child born out of wedlock; **los dos hijos habidos en su primer matrimonio** the two children from her first marriage; **Pepe, que Dios haya en su gloria** Pepe, God rest his soul; **bien haya …** (*Rel*) blessed be …
[3] (*liter*) (= *obtener*) **lee cuantos libros puede ~** he reads all the books he can lay his hands on
Ⓓ **haberse** VPR [1] **habérselas con algn** (= *tener delante*) to be up against sb; (= *enfrentarse*) to have it out with sb; **tenemos que habérnoslas con un enemigo despiadado** we are up against a ruthless enemy
[2] (††) (= *comportarse*) to comport o.s. (*frm*); **se ha habido con honradez** he has comported himself honourably
Ⓔ SM [1] (*en balance*) credit side; **¿cuánto tengo en el ~?** how much do I have in my account?; **la autora tiene seis libros en su ~** the author has six books to her credit; **asentar** *o* **pasar algo al ~ de algn** to credit sth to sb
[2] **haberes** (= *ingresos*) salary *sing*; (= *bienes*) assets; **no percibieron sus ~es** they weren't paid

habichuela SF kidney bean; ✦*MODISMO* **ganarse las ~s** to earn one's living

hábil ADJ [1] (= *diestro*) skilful, skillful (*EEUU*); **un político ~** a skilful politician; **fue una ~ estrategia diplomática** it was a skilful piece of diplomacy; **es muy ~ con la aguja** he's very handy *o* good with a needle; **¡muy ~! ya me has vuelto a endilgar el trabajo** (*hum*)

➤ LENGUA Y USO: **haber B2** 37.1 **B3** 37.1, 37.2

very clever! you've landed me with the job again; **ser ~ para algo** to be good at sth; **es muy ~ para la carpintería** he's very good at carpentry; **Juan es muy ~ aparcando el coche** Juan is very good at parking the car; **es muy ~ para solucionar conflictos** he has a real knack for resolving conflicts
[2] (*Jur*) competent; *ver tb* **día 1**

habilidad SF [1] (= *capacidad*) ability; (= *destreza*) skill; **tiene mucha ~ para la pintura** she's a very able painter; **un hombre de gran ~ política** a man of great political skill; **su ~ con el balón era de leyenda** his ball skills were legendary; **tiene una gran ~ para evitar enfrentamientos** he's very skilful *o* clever at avoiding confrontation; **tiene ~ manual** he's good *o* clever with his hands; **con ~: le sacó el secreto con ~** he cleverly *o* skilfully got the secret out of him; **defendió su argumento con ~** he defended his argument skilfully *o* cleverly ► **habilidades sociales** social skills
[2] (*Jur*) competence

habilidoso ADJ handy, good with one's hands

habilitación SF [1] (= *título*) qualification, entitlement
[2] [*de casa*] fitting out
[3] (*Fin*) (*con dinero*) financing; (*Cono Sur*) (= *crédito*) credit in kind; (*CAm, Méx*) (= *anticipo*) advance, sub*
[4] (= *oficina*) paymaster's, payroll office (*EEUU*)
[5] (*Cono Sur*) (= *sociedad*) *offer of a partnership to an employee*

habilitado/a SM/F paymaster

habilitar ►conjug 1a◄ VT [1] [+ *persona*] (= *dar derecho a*) to qualify, entitle; (= *permitir*) to enable; (= *autorizar*) to empower, authorize
[2] (= *preparar*) to equip, fit out; **las aulas están habilitadas con televisores** the rooms are equipped with TVs
[3] (*Fin*) (*con dinero*) to finance; **~ a algn** (*Cono Sur Agr*) to make sb a loan in kind (*with the next crop as security*), give sb credit facilities; (*CAm, Méx**) (= *dar un anticipo*) to give sb an advance, sub sb*
[4] (*Cono Sur Com*) to take into partnership
[5] (*CAm Agr*) to cover, serve
[6] (*Caribe*) (= *fastidiar*) to annoy, bother

hábilmente ADV [1] (= *diestramente*) skilfully, skillfully (*EEUU*)
[2] (= *capazmente*) ably, expertly
[3] (= *inteligentemente*) cleverly, smartly
[4] (*pey*) (= *con argucias*) cunningly

habiloso* ADJ (*Cono Sur*) clever, skilful, skillful (*EEUU*)

habitabilidad SF (*gen*) habitability

habitable ADJ inhabitable

habitación SF [1] (= *cuarto*) room ► **habitación de matrimonio, habitación doble** double room ► **habitación individual** single room ► **habitación para invitados** guest room
[2] (*Biol*) habitat, habitation

habitacional ADJ (*Cono Sur*) housing *antes de s*

habitáculo SM (*para vivir*) living space; (*en vehículo*) inside, interior

habitado ADJ [*isla, pueblo*] inhabited; [*casa, habitación*] lived-in; [*satélite, cohete*] manned

habitante Ⓐ SMF [1] (*gen*) inhabitant; **una ciudad de 10.000 ~s** a town of 10,000 inhabitants *o* people, a town with a population of 10,000
[2] (= *vecino*) resident
[3] (= *inquilino*) occupant, tenant
Ⓑ SM (*hum*) (= *piojo*) louse; **tener ~s** to have lice, have nits*

habitar ►conjug 1a◄ Ⓐ VT [+ *zona, territorio*] to inhabit, live in; [+ *casa*] to live in, occupy, be the occupant of
Ⓑ VI (= *vivir*) to live

hábitat SM (*pl* **hábitats** ['aβitas]) habitat

hábito SM [1] (= *costumbre*) habit; **una droga que crea ~** a habit-forming drug; **tener el ~ de hacer algo** to be in the habit of doing sth ► **hábitos de consumo** buying habits
[2] (*Rel*) habit; ✦**MODISMOS colgar los ~s** to leave the priesthood; **tomar el ~** [*hombre*] to take holy orders, become a monk; [*mujer*] to take the veil, become a nun ► **hábito monástico** monastic habit

habituado/a SM/F habitué

habitual Ⓐ ADJ (= *acostumbrado*) habitual, customary, usual; [*cliente, lector*] regular; [*criminal*] hardened; **mi restaurante ~** my usual restaurant; **como lector ~ de su revista** as a regular reader of your magazine
Ⓑ SMF [*de bar, tienda*] regular

habituar ►conjug 1e◄ Ⓐ VT to accustom (**a** to)
Ⓑ **habituarse** VPR **~se a** to become accustomed to, get used to

habla SF [1] (= *facultad*) speech; **dejar a algn sin ~** to leave sb speechless; **perder el ~** to lose the power of speech
[2] (*Ling*) (= *idioma*) language; (= *dialecto*) dialect, speech; **de ~ francesa** French-speaking
[3] (= *acción*) **¡Benjamín al ~!** (*Telec*) Benjamín speaking!; **estar al ~** (*Telec*) to be on the line, be speaking; (*Náut*) to be within hailing distance; **ponerse al ~ con algn** to get in touch with sb; ✦**MODISMO negar** *o* **quitar el ~ a algn** to stop speaking to sb, not be on speaking terms with sb

hablachento ADJ (*Caribe*) talkative

hablada SF [1] (*Cono Sur*) (= *charla*) speech
[2] (*Méx*) **habladas** (= *fanfarronada*) boast
[3] (*Andes**) (= *bronca*) scolding, telling-off*
[4] (*CAm, Cono Sur, Méx*) (= *indirecta*) hint, innuendo; (= *chisme*) rumour, piece of gossip; ✦**MODISMO echar ~s** to drop hints, make innuendoes

habladera SF [1] (*LAm*) talking, noise of talking
[2] (*Cono Sur, Méx*) = **habladuría**

habladero SM (*Caribe**) piece of gossip

hablado ADJ [1] (= *dicho*) spoken; **la palabra hablada** the spoken word
[2] **bien ~** well-spoken; **mal ~** coarse, foul-mouthed

hablador(a) Ⓐ ADJ [1] (= *parlanchín*) talkative, chatty*
[2] (= *chismoso*) gossipy, given to gossip
[3] (*Méx*) (= *jactancioso*) boastful; (= *amenazador*) bullying
[4] (*Caribe, Méx**) (= *mentiroso*) lying; (= *gritón*) loud-mouthed
Ⓑ SM/F [1] (= *locuaz*) great talker, chatterbox*
[2] (= *chismoso*) gossip

habladuría SF [1] (= *rumor*) rumour, rumor (*EEUU*)
[2] (= *injuria*) nasty remark
[3] (= *chisme*) piece of gossip
[4] **habladurías** gossip *sing*, scandal *sing*, tittle-tattle* *sing*

hablanchín ADJ talkative, garrulous

hablante Ⓐ ADJ speaking
Ⓑ SMF speaker

-hablante SUF *en palabras compuestas* **castellanohablante** (*adj*) Castilian-speaking; (*nmf*) Castilian speaker

hablantín ADJ = **hablanchín**

hablantina SF [1] (*Andes*) (*sin sentido*) gibberish, meaningless torrent
[2] (*Andes, Caribe*) (= *cháchara*) empty talk, idle chatter
[3] (*Caribe*) (= *algarabía*) hubbub, din

hablantino ADJ (*Andes, Caribe*), **hablantinoso** ADJ (*Andes, Caribe*) = **hablador A1, 2**

hablar ►conjug 1a◄ Ⓐ VI to speak, talk (**a, con** to; **de** about, of); **necesito ~ contigo** I need to talk *o* speak to you; **acabamos de ~ del premio** we were just talking *o* speaking about the prize; **¡mira quién fue a ~!** look who's talking!; **los datos hablan por sí solos** the facts speak for themselves; **que hable él** let him speak, let him have his say; **¡hable!** ◊ **¡puede ~!** (*Telec*) you're through!, go ahead! (*EEUU*); **¿quién habla?** (*Telec*) who's calling?, who is it?; **~ alto** to speak *o* talk loudly; **~ bajo** to speak *o* talk quietly, speak *o* talk in a low voice; **~ claro** (*fig*) to speak plainly *o* bluntly; **dar que ~ a la gente** to make people talk, cause tongues to wag; **hablaba en broma** she was joking; **vamos a ~ en confianza** this is between you and me; **¿hablas en serio?** are you serious?; **hacer ~ a algn** to make sb talk; **el vino hace ~** wine loosens people's tongues; **~ por ~** to talk for talking's sake, talk for the sake of it; **~ por teléfono** to speak on the phone; **hablamos por teléfono todos los días** we speak on the phone every day, we phone each other every day; **acabo de ~ por teléfono con ella** I was just on the phone to her; **~ solo** to talk *o* speak to o.s.; ✦**MODISMOS ¡ni ~!: —¿vas a ayudarle en la mudanza? —¡ni ~!** "are you going to help him with the move?" — "no way!" *o* "you must be joking!"; **de eso ni ~** that's out of the question; **hablando del rey de Roma ...** talk of the devil ...; *ver tb* **cristiano C2, plata 3**
Ⓑ VT [1] [+ *idioma*] to speak; **habla bien el portugués** he speaks good Portuguese, he speaks Portuguese well; **"se habla inglés"** "English spoken"; **en el Brasil se habla portugués** they speak Portuguese in Brazil
[2] (= *tratar de*) **hay que ~lo todo** we need to discuss everything; **eso habrá que ~lo con tu padre** you'll have to discuss that with your father; **no hay más que ~** there's nothing more to be said about it; **exijo que se haga lo que yo digo y no hay más que ~** you will do what I say and that's that; **me gustan las películas de vaqueros y no hay más que ~** I happen to like westerns and I don't see why I should have to justify it
[3] (*Méx Telec*) to (tele)phone
Ⓒ **hablarse** VPR [1] (*uso impersonal*) **se habla de que van a comprarlo** there is talk of their buying it; **pagaremos los cinco millones y**

no se hable más we'll pay the five million and that'll be an end to it; **si es su deber que lo hagan y no se hable más** if it's their duty then they should do it and there's nothing more to be said

2 (*uso recíproco*) **no se hablan** they are not on speaking terms, they are not speaking (to each other); **no me hablo con él** I'm not speaking to him, I'm not on speaking terms with him

HABLAR

¿"Speak" o "talk"?

- Se traduce por **speak** cuando **hablar** tiene un sentido general, es decir, hace referencia a la emisión de sonidos articulados:

  Estaba tan conmocionado que no podía hablar

  He was so shocked that he was unable to speak

  Su padre antes tartamudeaba al hablar

  Her father used to stutter when he spoke

- También se emplea **speak** cuando nos referimos a la capacidad de **hablar** un idioma:

  Habla francés y alemán

  She speaks French and German

- Cuando **hablar** implica la participación de más de una persona, es decir, se trata de una conversación, una charla, o un comentario, entonces se traduce por **talk**.

  Es una de esas personas que no para de hablar

  He's one of those people who won't stop talking

- Para traducir la construcción **hablar con alguien** podemos utilizar **talk to** (**talk with** en el inglés de EE.UU.) o, si el uso es más formal, se puede emplear **speak to** (**speak with** en el inglés de EE.UU.):

  Vi a Manolo hablando animadamente con un grupo de turistas

  I saw Manolo talking** o **speaking animatedly to** o **with a group of tourists

- Si queremos especificar el idioma en que se desarrolla la conversación, se puede emplear tanto **talk** como **speak**, aunque éste último se usa en un lenguaje más formal:

  Me sorprendió bastante verla hablar en francés con tanta soltura

  I was surprised to see her talking** o **speaking (in) French so fluently

Para otros usos y ejemplos ver la entrada.

hablilla SF (= *rumor*) rumour, rumor (*EEUU*), story; (= *habladuría*) piece of gossip

hablista SMF good speaker, elegant user of language

habloteo SM incomprehensible talk

habré *etc ver* **haber**

Habsburgo SM Hapsburg

hacedero† ADJ practicable, feasible

hacedor(a) SM/F (*gen*) maker; (*Literat*) poet; **el (Supremo) Hacedor** the Creator, the Maker

hacendado/a Ⓐ ADJ landed, property-owning Ⓑ SM/F (= *propietario*) (*de tierras*) landowner; (*LAm*) (*de ganado*) rancher; (*Caribe*) (*de ingenio*) sugar-plantation owner

hacendario ADJ (*Méx*) treasury *antes de s*, budgetary

hacendista SMF economist, financial expert

hacendoso ADJ 1 (= *trabajador*) industrious, hard-working

2 (= *ocupado*) busy, bustling

hacer

▸conjug 2r◂

A VERBO TRANSITIVO | C VERBO IMPERSONAL

B VERBO INTRANSITIVO | D VERBO PRONOMINAL

*Para las expresiones **hacer añicos, hacer gracia, hacerse ilusiones, hacer pedazos, hacerse de rogar, hacer el tonto, hacer las veces de** ver la otra entrada.*

Ⓐ VERBO TRANSITIVO

1 ***indicando actividad en general*** to do; **¿qué haces?** what are you doing?; **¿qué haces ahí?** what are you doing there?; **no sé qué ~** I don't know what to do; **hace y deshace las cosas a su antojo** she does as she pleases; **¡eso no se hace!** that's not done!; **no hizo nada por ayudarnos** she didn't do anything to help us; **haz todo lo posible por llegar a tiempo** do everything possible to arrive on time; **~ el amor** to make love; **~ la guerra** to wage war; ✦***MODISMOS*** **¡qué le vamos a ~!** what can you do?, there's nothing you can do; **~ algo por hacer**: **no tiene sentido ~ las cosas por ~las** there's no point doing things just for the sake of it; **¡la hemos hecho buena!** (*iró*) we've really gone and done it now!*; **ya ha hecho otra de las suyas** he's been up to his old tricks again

2 ***en lugar de otro verbo*** to do; **él protestó y yo hice lo mismo** he protested and I did the same; **no viene tanto como lo solía ~** he doesn't come as much as he used to

3 ***= crear*** [+ *coche, escultura, juguete, ropa, pastel*] to make; [+ *casa*] to build; [+ *dibujo*] to do; [+ *novela, sinfonía*] to write; **~ dinero** to make money; **le cuesta trabajo ~ amigos** he finds it hard to make friends

4 ***= realizar*** [+ *apuesta, discurso, objeción*] to make; [+ *deporte, deberes*] to do; [+ *caca, pipí*] to do; [+ *nudo*] to tie; [+ *pregunta*] to ask; [+ *visita*] to pay; [+ *milagros*] to do, work; **el gato hizo miau** the cat went miaow, the cat miaowed; **el árbol no hace mucha sombra** the tree isn't very shady, the tree doesn't provide a lot of shade; **¿me puedes ~ el nudo de la corbata?** could you knot my tie for me?; **~ un favor a algn** to do sb a favour; **~ un gesto** (*con la cara*) to make *o* pull a face; (*con la mano*) to make a sign; **~ un recado** to do *o* run an errand; **~ ruido** to make a noise; **~ sitio** to make room; **~ tiempo** to kill time

5 ***= preparar*** [+ *cama, comida*] to make; **~ el pelo/las uñas a algn** to do sb's hair/nails; **~ la barba a algn** to trim sb's beard; **~ las maletas** to pack one's bags

6 ***= dedicarse a*** **¿qué hace tu padre?** what does your father do?; **está haciendo turismo en África** he's gone touring in Africa; **~ cine** to make films; **~ teatro** to act

7 ***= actuar*** **~ un papel** to play a role *o* part; **~ el papel de malo** to play the (part of the) villain

8 ***= sumar*** to make; **6 y 3 hacen 9** 6 and 3 make 9; **éste hace 100** this one makes 100; **y cincuenta céntimos, hacen diez euros** and fifty cents change, which makes ten euros; **éste hace el corredor número 100 en atravesar la meta** he's the 100th runner to cross the finishing line

9 ***= cumplir*** **voy a ~ 30 años la próxima semana** I'm going to be 30 next week, it's my 30th birthday next week

10 ***= obligar*** (+ *INFIN*) to make; **les hice venir** I made them come; **siempre consigue ~me reír** she always manages to make me laugh; **le gustaba ~me rabiar** he enjoyed making me mad; **hágale entrar** show him in, have him come in; **me lo hizo saber** he told me about it, he informed me of it; **~ que** (+ *SUBJUN*): **yo haré que vengan** I'll make sure they come

11 ***= mandar*** (+ *INFIN*) **hizo construirse un palacio** she had a palace built; **hicieron pintar la fachada del colegio** they had the front of the school painted

12 ***= transformar*** (+ *ADJ*) to make; **esto lo hará más difícil** this will make it more difficult; **~ feliz a algn** to make sb happy; **te hace más delgado** it makes you look slimmer; **has hecho de mí un hombre muy feliz** you've made me a very happy man

13 ***= pensar*** to think; **yo le hacía más viejo** I thought he was older, I had him down as being older; **te hacíamos en el Perú** we thought you were in Peru

14 ***= acostumbrar*** **~ el cuerpo al frío** to get one's body used to the cold

15 ***= ejercitar*** **~ dedos** to do finger exercises; **~ piernas** to stretch one's legs

16 **~ a algn con** (= *proveer*): **me hizo con dinero** he provided me with money

Ⓑ VERBO INTRANSITIVO

1 ***= comportarse*** **haces bien en esperar** you're right to wait; **haces mal no contestando a sus llamadas** it's wrong of you not to answer his calls; **~ como que** *o* **como si** to make as if; **hizo como que no se daba cuenta** *o* **como si no se diera cuenta** he made as if he hadn't noticed, he pretended not to have noticed; **hizo como si me fuera a pegar** he made as if to strike me

2 **dar que ~** to cause trouble; **dieron que ~ a la policía** they caused *o* gave the police quite a bit of trouble

3 ***= importar*** **no le hace** (*LAm*) it doesn't matter, never mind; ✦***MODISMO*** **¡no le hagas!** (*Méx**) don't give me that!*

4 ***= ser apropiado*** **¿hace?** will it do?, is it all right?; (= *¿de acuerdo?*) is it a deal?; **la llave hace a todas las puertas** the key fits all the doors; **hace a todo** he's good for anything

5 ***= apetecer*** **¿te hace que vayamos a tomar unas copas?** how about going for a drink?, what do you say we go for a drink?; **¿te hace un cigarrillo?** how about a cigarette?, do you fancy a cigarette?

6 ***seguido de preposición***

◆ **hacer de** (*Teat*) to play the part of; **~ de malo** to play the villain

◆ **hacer por** (= *intentar*) **haz por verlo si puedes** try to get round to seeing him if you can; **~ por hacer algo** to try to do sth, make an effort to do sth

Ⓒ VERBO IMPERSONAL

1 ***con expresiones de tiempo atmosférico*** to be; **hace calor/frío** it's hot/cold; **hizo dos grados bajo cero** it was two degrees below zero; **¿qué tiempo hace?** what's the weather like?; **ojalá haga buen tiempo** I hope the weather's nice

2 ***con expresiones temporales*** **hace tres años que se fue** he left three years ago, it's

three years since he left; **hace tres años que no lo veo** I haven't seen him for three years, it's three years since I (last) saw him; **ha estado aquí hasta hace poco** he was here only a short while ago; **no hace mucho** not long ago; **hace un mes que voy** I've been going for a month; **¿hace mucho que esperas?** have you been waiting long?; **hace de esto varios años** it is some years since this happened; **desde hace cuatro años** for four years; **está perdido desde hace 15 días** it's been missing for a fortnight
3 *LAm = haber, tener* **hace sed** I'm thirsty; **hace sueño** I'm sleepy
Ⓓ **hacerse** VERBO PRONOMINAL
1 *= realizar, crear* **~se algo** [*uno mismo*] to make o.s. sth; [*otra persona*] to have sth made; **se hizo un jersey** he made himself a jumper; **¿os hicisteis muchas fotos?** did you take a lot of photos?; **todos los días me hago 3km andando** I walk 3km every day; **~se un retrato** to have one's portrait painted; **se hizo la cirugía estética** she had plastic surgery; **~se caca** to soil one's pants; **~se pipí** to wet o.s.; ver tb **idea 1**, **nudo**[2] **1**
2 *= cocinarse* **todavía se está haciendo la comida** the meal's still cooking; **deja que se haga bien la carne** make sure the meat is well done
3 (+ *INFIN*) 3·1 (= *conseguir*) **deberías ~te oír** you should make your voice heard; **la respuesta no se hizo esperar** the answer was not long in coming
3·2 (= *mandar*) **se hizo traer caviar directamente de Rusia** she had caviar sent over from Russia; **se hizo cortar el pelo** she had her hair cut; **~se afeitar la barba** to have one's beard trimmed; **me estoy haciendo confeccionar un traje** I'm having a suit made
4 *= reflexivo* **se hizo a sí mismo** he's a self-made man
5 *recíproco* **se hacían caricias** they were caressing each other; **~se cortesías mutuamente** to exchange courtesies
6 *= llegar a ser* 6·1 (+ *SUSTANTIVO*) to become; **se hicieron amigos** they became friends; **~se enfermera** to become a nurse; **el sofá se hace cama** the sofa can be turned into a bed
6·2 (+ *ADJ*) **~se cristiano** to become a Christian; **quiere ~se famoso** he wants to be famous; **esto se está haciendo pesado** this is getting *o* becoming tedious; **se está haciendo viejo** he's getting old; **se hace tarde** it's getting late; **~se grande** to grow tall; **con tanto ruido se me hace imposible trabajar** I can't work with all this noise
7 *= parecer* **se me hizo largo/pesado el viaje** the journey felt long/boring; **se me hace que ...** (*esp LAm*) it seems to me that ..., I get the impression that ...; **se me hace que nos están engañando** it seems to me that *o* I get the impression that we're being deceived
8 ** = fingirse* **~se el interesante** to act all high and mighty; **~se de nuevas** to act all innocent; **~se el sordo** to pretend not to hear
9 *= moverse* **~se atrás** to move back; **~se a un lado** (*de pie*) to move to one side; (*sentado*) to move over; **hazte para allá, que me siente** move up that way a bit so I can sit down
10 *seguido de preposición*
◆ **hacerse a** (= *acostumbrarse*) to get used to; **~se a una idea** to get used to an idea; **~se a hacer algo** to get used to doing sth; **¿te has hecho ya a levantarte temprano?** have you got used to getting up early yet?
◆ **hacerse con** [+ *información*] to get hold of; [+ *ciudad, fortaleza*] to take; **logró ~se con una copia** he managed to get hold of a copy; **se hizo con una importante fortuna** he amassed a large fortune; **~se con el control de algo** to gain control of sth; **finalmente se hicieron con la victoria** they eventually managed to win

hacha[1] SF 1 (= *herramienta*) axe, ax (*EEUU*); (*pequeña*) hatchet; ✦*MODISMOS* **desenterrar el ~ de guerra** to renew hostilities; **enterrar el ~ de guerra** to bury the hatchet ► **hacha de armas** battle-axe
2 ✦*MODISMOS* **dar con el ~ a algn** (*Cono Sur**) to tear sb off a strip*; **de ~** (*Chile*) unexpectedly, without warning; **estar con el ~** (*Cono Sur**) to have a hangover*; **de ~ y tiza** (*Cono Sur**) tough, virile; (*pey*) brawling; **serun ~*: María es un ~** María is a real star; **es un ~ para el fútbol** he's brilliant at football, he's a brilliant footballer
hacha[2] SF 1 (= *vela*) large candle
2 (= *haz de paja*) bundle of straw
hacha[3] ADJ (*Méx*) ✦*MODISMOS* **estar ~** to be ready; **ser ~ para la ropa** to be hard on one's clothes
hachador(a) SM/F (*CAm*) lumberjack
hachar ▸conjug 1a◂ VT (*LAm*) = **hachear**
hachazo SM 1 (= *golpe*) blow with an axe, blow with an ax (*EEUU*)
2 (*LAm*) (= *herida*) gash, axe wound, ax wound (*EEUU*)
3 (*Andes*) [*de caballo*] bolt, dash
hache SF (name of the letter) H; ✦*MODISMOS* **llámalo ~** call it what you will; **por ~ o por be** for one reason or another; **volverse ~s y erres** (*Andes*) ◊ **volverse ~s y cúes** (*Cono Sur*) to come to nothing, fall through
hachear ▸conjug 1a◂ Ⓐ VT (= *partir*) to hew, cut, cut down
Ⓑ VI (= *empuñar*) to wield an axe
hachemita ADJ Hashemite, Jordanian
hachero[1]**/a** SM/F 1 (= *leñador*) lumberjack
2 (*Mil*) sapper
hachero[2] SM torch stand, sconce
hacheta SF (*gen*) adze; (*pequeña*) small axe, hatchet
hachís SM, **hachich** SM hashish, hash
hacho SM (= *fuego*) beacon; (= *colina*) beacon hill
hachón SM large torch, firebrand
hachuela SF = **hacheta**
hacia PREP 1 (*indicando dirección*) towards, in the direction of; **ir ~ las montañas** to go towards the mountains; **eso está más ~ el este** that's further (over) to the east, that's more in an easterly direction; **vamos ~ allá** let's go in that direction, let's go over that way; **¿~ dónde vamos?** where are we going?; **~ abajo** down, downwards; **~ adelante** forwards; **~ arriba** up, upwards; **~ atrás** backwards
2 (*con expresiones temporales*) about, near; **~ las cinco** about five, around five; **~ mediodía** about noon, around noon
3 (= *ante*) towards; **su hostilidad ~ la empresa** his hostility towards the firm
hacienda SF 1 (= *finca*) country estate; (*LAm*) ranch; (*Caribe*) sugar plantation
2 (= *bienes*) property
3 (*Cono Sur*) (= *ganado*) cattle, livestock
4 (*Fin*) 4·1 (*tb* **Ministerio de Hacienda**) ≈ Treasury, ≈ Exchequer, ≈ Treasury Department (*EEUU*); **Hacienda me debe mucho dinero** the Inland Revenue owes me a lot of money
4·2 (*tb* **delegación de Hacienda**) tax office
4·3 (*tb* **~ pública**) **supondría un desembolso enorme para la ~ pública** it would involve a massive outlay of public funds *o* money; **ha defraudado a la ~ pública** he has defrauded the public purse
5 **haciendas**† (*domésticas*) household chores
hacina SF (= *montón*) pile, heap; (*Agr*) stack, rick
hacinado ADJ 1 (= *amontonado*) [*cosas*] heaped(-up), piled(-up); (*Agr*) stacked(-up); [*gente, animales*] crowded together, packed together; **vivían ~s** they lived on top of each other; **la gente estaba hacinada** people were crowded *o* packed together
2 (= *acumulado*) accumulated
hacinamiento SM 1 (= *amontonamiento*) [*de cosas*] heaping (up), piling (up); (*Agr*) stacking; [*de gente, animales*] crowding, overcrowding
2 (= *acumulación*) accumulation
hacinar ▸conjug 1a◂ Ⓐ VT 1 (= *amontonar*) [+ *cosas, objetos*] to heap (up), pile (up); (*Agr*) to stack, put into a stack, put into a rick; [+ *gente, animales*] to cram
2 (= *acumular*) to accumulate, amass
3 (†) (= *ahorrar*) to hoard
Ⓑ **hacinarse** VPR **~se en** [*gente, animales*] to pack into, cram into
hada SF fairy; **cuento de ~s** fairy tale ► **hada buena** good fairy ► **hada madrina** fairy godmother
hado SM (*frm*) fate, destiny
haga *ver* **hacer**
hágalo usted mismo SM do-it-yourself
hagiografía SF hagiography
hagiógrafo/a SM/F hagiographer
hago *ver* **hacer**
haiga†* SM (*Esp*) big car, posh car*
haiku ['haiku] SM haiku
Haití SM Haiti
haitiano/a Ⓐ ADJ of/from Haiti
Ⓑ SM/F native/inhabitant of Haiti; **los ~s** the people of Haiti
hala EXCL 1 (*mostrando sorpresa*) (*gen*) wow!; (= *qué exageración*) come off it!*
2 (= *vamos*) come on!, let's go!
3 (= *deprisa*) get on with it!*, hurry up!
4 **no quiero, ¡hala!** I don't want to, so there!
5 (*Náut*) heave!
halaco SM (*CAm*) piece of junk, useless object
halagador(a) Ⓐ ADJ 1 (= *adulador*) [*retrato, opinión*] flattering
2 (= *agradable*) [*propuesta*] pleasing, gratifying
Ⓑ SM/F [*persona*] flatterer
halagar ▸conjug 1h◂ VT 1 (= *adular*) to flatter
2 (= *agradar*) to please, gratify; **es una perspectiva que me halaga** it's a pleasant prospect
3 (†) (= *mostrar afecto*) to show affection to
halago SM 1 (= *adulación*) flattery
2 (= *gusto*) pleasure, delight; (= *satisfacción*) gratification
3 (†) (= *atracción*) attraction; **los ~s de la**

vida en el campo the attractions of country life

halagüeño ADJ 1 (= *prometedor*) [*perspectiva*] promising, rosy
2 (= *adulador*) [*opinión, observación*] flattering
3 (= *agradable*) pleasing; (= *atractivo*) attractive, alluring

halar ▸conjug 1a◂ VT, VI (*LAm*) = **jalar**

halcón SM 1 (*Zool*) falcon ▸ **halcón abejero** honey buzzard ▸ **halcón común, halcón peregrino** peregrine falcon
2 (*Pol*) hawk, hardliner; **los halcones y las palomas** the hawks and the doves
3 (*Méx*) (= *matón a sueldo*) *young government-sponsored thug*

halconería SF falconry

halconero/a SM/F falconer

halda SF 1 (= *falda*) skirt; ✦**MODISMO de ~s o de mangas** at all costs, by hook or by crook
2 (= *arpillera*) sackcloth, coarse wrapping material

hale EXCL = **hala 2,3**

haleche SM anchovy

halibut [ali'βu] SM (*pl* **halibuts** [ali'βu]) halibut

hálito SM (*frm*) 1 (= *aliento*) breath
2 (= *vapor*) vapour, vapor (*EEUU*), exhalation
3 (*poét*) gentle breeze

halitosis SF INV halitosis (*frm*), bad breath

hall [xol] SM (*pl* **halls, halles** [xol]) [*de casa*] hall; [*de teatro, cine*] foyer; [*de hotel*] lounge, foyer

hallaca SF (*Ven*) tamale

hallador(a) SM/F finder

hallar ▸conjug 1a◂ Ⓐ VT 1 (= *encontrar*) 1·1 [+ *objeto, persona, respuesta, solución*] to find; **~án a los otros invitados en el salón** you will find the other guests in the living room; **el cadáver fue hallado ayer** the body was found yesterday; **tenemos que ~ una salida a la crisis** we have to find a way out of the crisis; **hallé a tu hermano muy cambiado** I thought your brother had changed a lot
1·2 [+ *apoyo, oposición*] to meet with; **halló la oposición de todos los vecinos** he met with opposition from all the neighbours; **no halló la aprobación que esperaba para su proyecto** his plan did not meet with the approval he had hoped for; **halló la muerte en la montaña** he met his death on the mountain
2 (= *descubrir*) [+ *método*] to find, discover; **halló el modo de producirlo sintéticamente** he found *o* discovered a way to produce it synthetically; **~on que el estado del enfermo era peor de lo que creían** they found *o* discovered that the patient's condition was worse than they had thought
3 (= *averiguar*) [+ *motivo, razón*] to find out; [+ *información*] to obtain; **halló el motivo por el que no vinieron** he found out the reason why they hadn't come
4 (*Jur*) **ser hallado culpable de algo** to be found guilty of sth
Ⓑ **hallarse** VPR 1 (= *estar*) 1·1 (*indicando posición*) to be; **nos hallamos en Sevilla** we are in Seville; **la plaza en la que se halla la catedral** the square which the cathedral is in, the square in which the cathedral stands; **se hallan entre las cien personas más ricas del mundo** they are among the hundred richest people in the world
1·2 (*indicando estado*) to be; **sólo ocho de las islas se hallan habitadas** only eight of the islands are inhabited; **en la reunión se hallaban presentes todos los directivos** all the directors were present at the meeting
2 (= *encontrarse*) to find o.s.; **de repente me hallé en medio de un grupo de desconocidos** I suddenly found myself in the middle of a group of strangers; **nos hallamos ante un ensayo excepcional** we're talking about *o* this is an exceptional essay; **~se con: se halló con numerosos obstáculos** she found herself up against numerous obstacles; **me hallé con que tenía más dinero del que pensaba** I realized that I had more money than I had thought
3 (= *sentirse*) to feel; **sentado aquí me hallo a gusto** it's so nice sitting here, I feel very relaxed *o* good sitting here; **es muy tímido, no se halla en las fiestas** he's very shy, he feels uncomfortable *o* awkward at parties; **no me hallo en una casa tan grande** I don't feel comfortable *o* right in such a big house

hallazgo SM 1 (= *acto*) discovery; **fue detenido tras el ~ de unos documentos que le incriminaban** he was arrested following the discovery of incriminating documents
2 (= *descubrimiento*) [*de la ciencia*] discovery; (*por investigador, institución*) finding; **los últimos ~s científicos** the latest scientific discoveries; **la revista en la que el investigador ha difundido sus ~s** the journal in which the researcher published his findings
3 (= *cosa hallada*) find; **el nuevo guitarra del grupo ha sido un ~** the band's new guitarist was a real find
4 (= *recompensa*) reward; **"500 pesos de hallazgo"** "500 pesos reward"

halo SM 1 [*de luna, sol*] halo
2 [*de santo*] halo
3 (= *fama*) aura

halogenado ADJ halogenated

halógeno Ⓐ ADJ halogenous, halogen *antes de s*; **lámpara halógena** halogen lamp
Ⓑ SM halogen

halón SM (*LAm*) = **jalón 3**

haltera Ⓐ SF (*Dep*) 1 (= *barra*) dumb-bell, bar-bell
2 **halteras** (= *pesos*) weights
Ⓑ SMF [*persona*] weight-lifter

halterofilia SF weight-lifting

halterófilo/a SM/F weight-lifter

hamaca SF 1 (= *cama*) hammock
2 (*Cono Sur*) (= *mecedora*) rocking chair; (= *columpio*) swing ▸ **hamaca plegable** deckchair

hamacar ▸conjug 1g◂ (*LAm*), **hamaquear** ▸conjug 1a◂ (*LAm*) Ⓐ VT 1 (= *mecer*) to rock
2 (= *columpiar*) to swing
3 (*Méx**) **~ a algn** to keep sb on tenterhooks
4 (*Caribe*) (= *golpear*) to beat
Ⓑ **hamacarse** VPR (*esp LAm*) **hamaquearse** VPR (*LAm*) 1 (= *mecerse*) to rock
2 (= *columpiarse*) to swing

hambre SF 1 (= *necesidad de comer*) hunger; **una huelga de ~** a hunger strike; **estar con ~** to be hungry; **vengo con mucha ~** I'm terribly hungry, I'm starving*; **dar ~ a algn** to make sb hungry; **entrar ~: me está entrando ~** I'm starting to feel hungry, I'm getting hungry; **matar de ~ a algn** to starve sb to death; **en el colegio nos mataban de ~** they starved us at school; **morir de ~** to die of hunger, starve to death; **padecer** *o* **pasar ~** to go hungry; **quedarse con ~: se han quedado con ~** they are still hungry; **tener ~** to be hungry; ✦**MODISMOS engañar** *o* **entretener el ~** to stave off hunger; **tengo un ~ que no veo*** I'm absolutely starving*; **tener un ~ canina** *o* **de lobo** to be ravenous, be ravenously hungry; **se ha juntado el ~ con las ganas de comer** what an explosive combination they are!, they're a right pair!; **ser más listo que el ~*** to be razor sharp*, be as sharp as a needle; **matar el ~** to keep one going, take the edge off one's appetite; ✦**REFRÁN a buen ~ no hay pan duro** beggars can't be choosers; *ver tb* **muerto C2, salario**
2 (= *escasez general*) famine; **la guerra ha traído muerte y ~ al país** the war has brought death and famine to the country
3 (= *deseo*) **~ de algo** hunger for sth; **políticos con ~ de poder** politicians with a hunger for power; **el ~ de gloria del protagonista** the hero's hunger for glory; **tener ~ de justicia/triunfos** to be hungry for justice/victory

hambreado ADJ (*LAm*) = **hambriento**

hambreador(a) SM/F (*Chile, Perú*) [*de personas*] exploiter

hambrear ▸conjug 1a◂ Ⓐ VT (*Chile*) 1 (= *explotar*) [+ *personas*] to exploit
2 (= *hacer pasar hambre*) to starve
Ⓑ VI to starve, be hungry

hambriento/a Ⓐ ADJ 1 (= *con hambre*) hungry; (= *famélico*) starving; **venimos ~s** we're starving*, we're very hungry; **unas tristes imágenes de niños ~s** very sad pictures of hungry *o* starving children
2 **~ de** hungry for; **políticos ~s de poder** politicians hungry for power; **están ~s de afecto** they are starved of affection
Ⓑ SM/F (*con hambre*) hungry person; (*en situación desesperada*) starving person; **los ~s** the hungry; **dar de comer al ~** to feed the hungry

hambrón* ADJ (*Esp*) greedy

hambruna SF 1 famine
2 (*Andes, Cono Sur*) = **hambrusia**

hambrusia SF (*Col, Méx*) ravenous hunger; **tener ~** to be famished

Hamburgo SM Hamburg

hamburgués/esa Ⓐ ADJ of/from Hamburg
Ⓑ SM/F native/inhabitant of Hamburg; **los hamburgueses** the people of Hamburg

hamburguesa SF hamburger, burger

hamburguesera SF hamburger-maker

hamburguesería SF burger bar, burger joint*

hamo SM fish-hook

hampa SF (*gen*) criminal underworld; **gente del ~** criminals, riffraff; (*Hist*) rogue's life, vagrancy

hampesco ADJ underworld *antes de s*, criminal

hampón/ona SM/F thug

hámster SM (*pl* **hámsters**) hamster

han *ver* **haber**

hand [xan] SM (*CAm Dep*) handball

hándbol ['xandbol] SM handball

handbolista SMF handball player

handicap SM, **hándicap** SM (*pl* **handicaps, hándicaps**) handicap

handling ['xanlin] SM (*Aer*) baggage handling

hangar SM (*Aer*) hangar

Hannover SM, **Hannóver** SM Hanover

Hanovre SM Hanover

hápax SM INV hapax, nonce-word

happening ['xapenin] SM (*pl* **happenings**) (*Arte*) happening

haragán/ana Ⓐ ADJ (= *vago*) idle, lazy
Ⓑ SM/F (= *holgazán*) layabout, idler
Ⓒ SM (*Caribe*) (= *fregona*) mop

haragana* SF (*CAm*) (= *silla reclinable*) reclining chair

haraganear ▸conjug 1a◂ VI to idle, loaf about, laze around

haraganería SF idleness, laziness

harakiri SM hara-kiri; **hacerse el ~** to commit hara-kiri

harapiento ADJ tattered, in rags

harapo SM [1] (= *andrajo*) rag; ✦*MODISMO* **estar hecho un ~** to go about dressed in rags
[2] **harapos** (*Méx*‡) clothes, clobber‡, threads (*EEUU**)

haraposo ADJ = **harapiento**

haraquiri SM = **harakiri**

hard [xar] SM hardware

hardware ['xarwer] SM hardware, computer hardware

haré *ver* **hacer**

harén SM harem

harina SF [1] flour; ✦*MODISMOS* **eso es ~ de otro costal** that's a different kettle of fish, that's another story; **estar en ~s** (*Andes**) to be broke*; **meterse en ~** to get down to it ► **harina con levadura** self-raising flour ► **harina de arroz** ground rice ► **harina de avena** oatmeal ► **harina de flor** extra fine flour ► **harina de huesos** bonemeal ► **harina de maíz** cornflour, corn starch (*EEUU*) ► **harina de patata** potato flour ► **harina de pescado** fish-meal ► **harina de soja** soya flour ► **harina de trigo** wheat flour ► **harina integral** wholemeal flour ► **harina lacteada** malted milk ► **harina leudante** (*Cono Sur*) *ver* **harina con levadura**
[2] (*Andes*) (= *pedacito*) small piece; **una ~ de pan** a bit of bread
[3] (*Caribe*‡) (= *dinero*) money, dough‡

harinear ▸conjug 1a◂ VI (*Caribe*) to drizzle

harineo SM (*Caribe*) drizzle

harinero/a Ⓐ ADJ flour *antes de s*
Ⓑ SM/F (= *comerciante*) flour merchant
Ⓒ SM (= *recipiente*) flour bin

harinoso ADJ floury

harnear ▸conjug 1a◂ VT (*LAm*) to sieve, sift

harnero SM sieve

harpagón‡ ADJ (*Andes*) very thin, skinny

harpillera SF sacking, sackcloth

hartar ▸conjug 1a◂ Ⓐ VT [1] (= *cansar*) **me harta tanta televisión** I get tired of *o* fed up with* *o* sick of* watching so much television; **los estás hartando con tantas bobadas** they're getting tired of *o* fed up with* *o* sick of* your fooling around; **ya me está hartando que siempre me hable de lo mismo** I'm getting tired of *o* fed up with* *o* sick of* him always talking about the same thing
[2] (= *atiborrar*) **~ a algn a** *o* **de** [+ *comida, alcohol*] to fill sb full of; **nos hartan a chistes malos** we get fed up with* *o* sick of* *o* tired of their bad jokes; **el maestro los harta a deberes** their teacher overloads them with homework; **lo ~on a palos** they gave him a real beating
[3] (*CAm*) (= *maldecir de*) to malign, slander
Ⓑ VI (= *cansar*) **todos estos tópicos manidos ya hartan** all these worn-out clichés get so boring, you get tired of *o* get fed up with* *o* sick of* all these worn-out clichés
Ⓒ **hartarse** VPR [1] (= *cansarse*) to get fed up*; **un día se ~á y se marchará** one of these days she'll get tired *o* get fed up* of it all and leave; **~se de algo/algn** to get tired of sth/sb, get fed up with sth/sb*, get sick of sth/sb*; **me estoy hartando de todo esto** I'm getting tired of *o* fed up with* *o* sick of* all this; **ya me he hartado de esperar** I've had enough of waiting, I'm tired of *o* fed up with* *o* sick of* waiting; **se hartó de que siempre lo hicieran blanco de sus burlas** he got fed up with* *o* sick of* *o* tired of always being the butt of their jokes
[2] (= *atiborrarse*) **~se de** [+ *comida*] to gorge o.s. on, stuff o.s. with*; **se ~on de uvas** they gorged themselves on grapes, they stuffed themselves with grapes*; **le gustaría poder ~se de marisco** he'd like to be able to have a real blowout on seafood; **me harté de agua** I drank gallons *o* loads of water*
[3] (= *saciarse*) **~se a** *o* **de algo**: **en esa exposición puedes ~te de cultura griega** in that exhibition you can get your fill of Greek culture; **fui al museo para ~me de buena pintura** I went to the museum to see plenty of good paintings; **~se a** *o* **de hacer algo**: **en vacaciones me harté a** *o* **de tomar el sol** I sunbathed all day on holiday; **nos hartamos de reír** we laughed till we were fit to burst; **comieron hasta ~se** they gorged *o* stuffed* themselves; **bebieron champán hasta ~se** they drank their fill of champagne; **dormimos hasta ~nos** we slept as long as we wanted

hartazgo SM [*de comida*] surfeit, glut; **darse un ~** [*de comida*] to eat too much, overeat; [*de noticias, televisión*] to have too much

▼**harto** Ⓐ ADJ [1] (= *cansado*) fed up*; **¡ya estamos ~s!** we've had enough!, we're fed up!*; **¡me tienes ~!** I'm fed up with you!*; **estar ~ de algo/algn** to be tired of sth/sb, be fed up with sth/sb*, be sick of sth/sb*; **estaban un poco ~s de tanta publicidad** they were a bit tired of all the publicity, they were a bit fed up with *o* sick of all the publicity*; **está ~ de su jefe** he's fed up with *o* sick of his boss*; **estar ~ de hacer algo** to be tired of doing sth, be fed up of doing sth*, be sick of doing sth*; **está ~ de no tener dinero** he's tired *o* fed up* *o* sick of* not having any money; **estar ~ de que** (+ *SUBJUN*) to be fed up with* + *ger*, be sick of* + *ger*; **estamos ~s de que lleguen siempre tarde** we're tired of *o* fed up with* *o* sick of* them arriving late
[2] (= *lleno*) **~ de algo** stuffed with sth*
[3] (= *mucho*) [3·1] (*frm*) **ocurre con harta frecuencia** it happens very often *o* very frequently; **tienen hartas razones para sentirse ofendidos** they have plenty of reasons to feel offended
[3·2] (*LAm*) plenty of, a lot of; **usaste harta harina** you used plenty of *o* a lot of flour; **~s chilenos** plenty of *o* a lot of Chileans; **ha habido ~s accidentes** there have been a lot of *o* plenty of accidents
Ⓑ ADV [1] (*con adjetivo*) [1·1] (*frm*) very, extremely; **una tarea ~ difícil** a very difficult task, an extremely difficult task
[1·2] (*LAm*) very; **llegaron ~ cansados** they were very tired when they arrived
[2] (*LAm*) (*con adverbio*) very; **lo sé ~ bien** I know that very well *o* all too well
[3] (*LAm*) (*con verbo*) a lot; **te quiero ~** I love you a lot; **dormí ~ anoche** I slept a lot last night
Ⓒ PRON (*LAm*) **hace ~ que no lo veo** it's been a long time since I saw him; **—¿queda leche? —sí, harta** "is there any milk left?" — "yes, lots"; **falta ~ para llegar** there's still a long way to go

hartón* Ⓐ SM [1] **darse un ~ de algo** to stuff oneself with sth*; **me di un ~ de pasteles** I stuffed myself with cakes; **se dio un ~ de leer novelas policíacas** he had a binge of reading crime novels; **nos dimos un ~ de reír** we killed ourselves laughing; **me di un ~ de llorar en el cine** I cried my eyes out in the cinema
[2] (*LAm*) (= *banana*) large banana
Ⓑ ADJ (*CAm, Méx, Ven*) gluttonous

hartura SF [1] (= *cansancio*) **otra vez fútbol, ¡qué ~!** football again, I'm fed up with it! *o* I'm sick of it!*; **muchos votaron a la oposición por ~ hacia el gobierno** many people voted for the opposition because they had had enough of *o* they were tired of the government
[2] (= *hartazgo*) **la comida picante da sensación de ~** spicy food leaves you feeling full
[3] (*frm*) (= *abundancia*) abundance, plenty; **con ~** in abundance, in plenty

has *ver* **haber**

has ABR = **hectáreas**

hasídico ADJ Hassidic

hasidita SMF Hassid

hasta Ⓐ PREP [1] (*en el espacio*) (*gen*) to, as far as; (= *hacia arriba*) up to; (= *hacia abajo*) down to; **fuimos juntos ~ el primer pueblo, luego nos separamos** we went to *o* as far as the first village together, then we split up; **sus tierras llegan ~ las montañas** their lands stretch to *o* as far as the mountains; **te acompaño, pero sólo ~ el final de la calle** I'll go with you, but only to *o* up to *o* down to the end of the street; **con las lluvias el agua subió ~ aquí** with all the rain the water came up to here; **el vestido me llega ~ las rodillas** the dress comes down to my knees; **¿~ dónde ... ?** how far ... ?; **¿~ dónde vais?** how far are you going?; **~ tan lejos** that far, as far as that; **—fuimos andando ~ la ermita —¿~ tan lejos?** "we walked to *o* as far as the chapel" — "that far?" *o* "as far as that?"; **no creía que íbamos a llegar ~ tan lejos** I didn't think we'd get this far
[2] (*en el tiempo*) until, till; **se va a quedar ~ el martes** she's staying until *o* till Tuesday; **no me levanto ~ las nueve** I don't get up until *o* till nine o'clock; **no iré ~ después de la reunión** I won't go until *o* till after the meeting; **falta una semana ~ los exámenes** there's a week to go to *o* until *o* till the exams; **¿siempre escuchas música ~ tan tarde?** do you always listen to music so late (at night)?; **el ~ ayer presidente de nuestro club** the hitherto president of our club (*frm*); **~ ahora** so far, up to now; **~ ahora nadie se ha quejado** so far no one has complained, no one has complained up to now; **~ ahora no se había quejado nadie** no one had complained before *o* until now *o* till now; **tuve problemas al principio, pero luego las co-**

sas se tranquilizaron y ~ ahora I had problems at the beginning but then things calmed down and since then it's been OK; **¿~ cuándo ... ?** how long ... for?; **¿~ cuándo podemos seguir así?** how long can we carry on like this for?; **¿~ cuándo os quedáis?** how long are you staying (for)?; **~ entonces** until then, (up) till then; **~ la fecha** to date; **~ el momento** so far, up to now, thus far (*frm*); **~ nueva orden** until further notice
[3] (*con cantidades*) (*gen*) up to; (*con valor enfático*) as much as/as many as; **puedes gastar ~ 200 euros** you can spend up to 200 euros; **duerme ~ diez horas diarias** he sleeps up to ten hours a day; **podemos llegar a producir ~ 50 toneladas** we can produce as much as 50 tons; **llegó a haber ~ 500 invitados** there were as many as 500 guests
[4] (*en expresiones de despedida*) **~ ahora** see you in a minute; **~ la vista** see you, so long; **~ luego** see you, bye*; **~ más ver** see you again; **~ nunca** I hope I never see you again; **~ otra** see you again; **~ pronto** see you soon; **~ siempre*** goodbye, farewell (*frm*)
[5] (*CAm, Col, Méx*) not ... until, not ... till; **~ mañana viene** he's not coming until *o* till tomorrow; **lo hizo ~ el martes** he didn't do it until *o* till Tuesday; **~ hoy lo conocí** I only met him today, I hadn't met him until *o* till today
Ⓑ CONJ [1] **~ que** until, till; **vivió aquí ~ que murió su mujer** he lived here until *o* till his wife died; **no me iré ~ que (no) me lo des** I won't go until *o* till you give it to me
[2] (+ *INFIN*) until, till; **no se fueron ~ acabar** they didn't leave until *o* till they were finished
Ⓒ ADV (= *incluso*) even; **~ en Valencia hiela a veces** even in Valencia it freezes sometimes; **la música estaba tan alta que se oía ~ desde la calle** the music was so loud that you could even hear it from the street

hastiador ADJ = **hastiante**

hastial SM (*Arquit*) gable end

hastiante ADJ [1] (= *que cansa*) wearisome
[2] (= *que aburre*) boring
[3] (= *asqueante*) sickening

hastiar ▸conjug 1c◂ Ⓐ VT [1] (= *cansar*) to weary
[2] (= *aburrir*) to bore
[3] (= *asquear*) to sicken, disgust
Ⓑ **hastiarse** VPR **~se de** to tire of, get fed up with*

hastío SM [1] (= *cansancio*) weariness
[2] (= *aburrimiento*) boredom
[3] (= *asco*) disgust

hatajo SM lot, collection; **un ~ de sinvergüenzas** a bunch of crooks

hatillo SM = **hato**

hato SM [1] [*de ropa*] bundle; ✦**MODISMOS echarse el ~ a cuestas** ◊ **liar el ~** to pack up; **~ y garabato** (*Andes, Caribe**) all that one has; **menear el ~ a algn** to beat sb up*; **revolver el ~** to stir up trouble
[2] (*Agr*) [*de ganado*] herd; [*de ovejas*] flock
[3] [*de gente*] group, crowd; (*pey*) bunch, gang
[4] [*de objetos, observaciones*] lot, heap
[5] (*LAm*) (= *rancho*) cattle ranch
[6] (= *víveres*) provisions *pl*
[7] (= *choza*) shepherd's hut
[8] (= *parada*) stopping place (*of migratory flocks*)

Hawai SM (*tb* **Islas ~**) Hawaii

HASTA

La preposición **hasta** tiene varias traducciones posibles, dependiendo de si se emplea en expresiones de tiempo o de lugar.

En expresiones de tiempo

• Generalmente se traduce por **till** o **until**. **Till** tiene un uso más informal que **until** y no suele ir al principio de la frase.

El paquete no me llegó hasta dos semanas después
The parcel did not arrive until** o **till two weeks later

Hasta entonces las cosas nos iban bien
Until then things were going well for us

• Además, **hasta** también se puede traducir por **to** en la construcción **desde ... hasta ...**:

Estoy aquí todos los días desde las ocho hasta las tres
I'm here every day from eight until** o **till** o **to three

Te estuve esperando desde las once de la mañana hasta la una de la tarde
I was waiting for you from eleven in the morning until** o **till** o **to one in the afternoon

En expresiones de lugar

• Cuando usamos **hasta** en expresiones de lugar, podemos traducirlo por **(up/down) to** o por **as far as**:

Caminó hasta el borde del acantilado
He walked (up) to** o **as far as the edge of the cliff

¿Vamos hasta la orilla?
Shall we go down to the shore?

Ya anda solo hasta el sofá
He can already walk on his own as far as** o **(up) to the sofa

Para otros usos y ejemplos ver la entrada.

hawaianas SFPL (*esp LAm*) (= *chanclas*) flip flops, thongs

hawaiano/a Ⓐ ADJ of/from Hawaii
Ⓑ SM/F native/inhabitant of Hawaii; **los ~s** the people of Hawaii

hay *ver* **haber**

haya[1] *ver* **haber**

haya[2] SF beech, beech tree

Haya SF **La ~** The Hague

hayaca SF (*Andes*) tamale; (*Caribe*) *stuffed cornmeal pasty*

hayal SM, **hayedo** SM beechwood

hayo SM (*Bot*) coca, coca leaves

hayuco SM beechnut; **hayucos** beechnuts, beechmast *sing*

haz[1] SM [1] (= *manojo*) bundle, bunch; [*de trigo*] sheaf; [*de paja*] truss
[2] (= *rayo*) beam ► **haz de electrones** electron beam ► **haz de luz** beam of light ► **haz de partículas** particle beam ► **haz láser** laser beam
[3] **haces** (*Hist, Pol*) fasces

haz[2] SF [1] (= *lado derecho*) right side
[2] (= *superficie*) face, surface; **de dos haces** two-faced ► **haz de la tierra** face of the earth

haz[3] *ver* **hacer**

haza SF small field, plot of arable land

hazaña SF feat, exploit, deed; **las ~s del héroe** the hero's exploits, the hero's great deeds; **sería una ~** it would be a great achievement, it would be a great thing to do

hazañería SF fuss, exaggerated show, histrionics *pl*

hazañero ADJ [*persona*] dramatic, histrionic, given to making a great fuss; [*acción*] histrionic, exaggerated

hazañoso ADJ [*persona*] heroic, gallant, dauntless; [*acción*] heroic, doughty

hazmerreír SMF INV laughing stock

HB SM ABR (*Esp Pol*) = **Herri Batasuna**

he[1] *ver* **haber**

he[2] ADV (*frm*) **he aquí** here is, here are; **¡heme aquí!** here I am!; **¡helo aquí!** here it is!; **¡helos allí!** there they are!; **he aquí la razón de que ...** ◊ **he aquí por qué ...** that is why ...; **he aquí los resultados** these are the results, here you have the results

heavy ['xeβi] (*pl* **heavies, heavys**) Ⓐ ADJ [1] [*música, grupo*] heavy metal
[2] (*) (= *duro*) heavy*
Ⓑ SMF heavy metal fan
Ⓒ SM (= *música*) heavy metal

hebdomadario (*frm*) Ⓐ ADJ weekly
Ⓑ SM weekly

hebilla SF buckle, clasp

hebra SF [1] [*de hilo*] thread
[2] (*Bot*) (= *fibra*) fibre, fiber (*EEUU*); [*de madera*] grain; [*de gusano de seda*] thread; **tabaco de ~** loose tobacco
[3] [*de metal*] vein, streak
[4] **hebras** (*poét*) hair
[5] ✦**MODISMOS de una ~** (*Cono Sur, Méx**) all at once; **pegar la ~** (= *entablar conversación*) to start *o* strike up a conversation; (= *hablar mucho*) to chatter, talk nineteen to the dozen; **no quedar ni ~** (*Andes**): **no quedó ni ~ de comida** there wasn't a scrap of food left; **romperse la ~** (*Méx**): **se rompió la ~ entre los dos amigos** the two friends fell out

hebraico ADJ Hebraic

hebraísta SMF Hebraist

hebreo/a Ⓐ ADJ Hebrew
Ⓑ SM/F Hebrew; **los ~s** the Hebrews
Ⓒ SM (*Ling*) Hebrew; ✦**MODISMO jurar en ~**† to blow one's top*

Hébridas SFPL Hebrides

hebroso ADJ (= *fibroso*) fibrous; [*carne*] stringy

hecatombe SF [1] (= *catástrofe*) disaster; **¡aquello fue la ~!** what a disaster that was!
[2] (= *carnicería*) slaughter, butchery
[3] (*Hist*) hecatomb

heces SFPL *ver* **hez**

hechicería SF [1] (= *brujería*) sorcery, witchcraft
[2] (= *maleficio*) spell
[3] (= *encantamiento*) spell, charm

hechicero/a Ⓐ ADJ [1] [*rito, poder*] magic, magical
[2] [*labios, ojos*] enchanting, bewitching
Ⓑ SM/F (= *brujo*) sorcerer/sorceress, wizard/witch; [*de tribu*] witch doctor

hechizante ADJ enchanting, bewitching

hechizar ▸conjug 1f◂ VT [1] (= *embrujar*) to bewitch, cast a spell on
[2] (= *cautivar*) to fascinate, charm, enchant

hechizo Ⓐ ADJ (*Andes, Cono Sur, Méx*) home-made, locally produced, craft *antes de s*
Ⓑ SM [1] (= *brujería*) sorcery, witchcraft
[2] (= *encantamiento*) enchantment; (= *maleficio*) spell; **un ~** a magic spell, a charm
[3] (= *atracción*) fascination
[4] **~s** (= *encantos*) charms

▼**hecho** Ⓐ PP *de* **hacer**
Ⓑ ADJ [1] (= *realizado*) done; **bien ~** well done; **mal ~** badly done; **si le dijiste que no fuera, mal ~** if you told him not to go, then you were wrong *o* you shouldn't have; **¡hecho!** (= *de acuerdo*) agreed!, it's a deal!; ✦***MODISMO*** **lo ~, ~ está** what's done cannot be undone; ✦***REFRÁN*** **a lo ~ pecho** it's no use crying over spilt milk
[2] (= *manufacturado*) made; **¿de qué está ~?** what's it made of?; **bien ~** well made; **mal ~** poorly made; **~ a mano** handmade; **~ a máquina** machine-made; **~ a la medida** made-to-measure; **se compra la ropa hecha** he buys his clothes off-the-peg
[3] (= *acabado*) done, finished; (= *listo*) ready; **el trabajo ya está ~** the work is done *o* finished; **¿está hecha la comida?** is dinner ready?
[4] (*Culin*) [4·1] (= *maduro*) [*queso, vino*] mature; [*fruta*] ripe
[4·2] (= *cocinado*) **muy ~** (= *bien*) well-cooked; (= *demasiado*) overdone; **no muy ~** ◊ **poco ~** underdone, undercooked; **un filete poco** *o* **no muy ~** a rare steak
[5] (= *convertido en*) **el baño está ~ un asco** the bathroom is disgusting; **usted está ~ un chaval** you look so young!; **ella, hecha una furia, se lanzó** she hurled herself furiously; **estará hecha una mujercita** she must be quite grown up now
[6] [*persona*] **bien ~** well-proportioned; **mal ~** ill-proportioned; ✦***MODISMO*** **~ y derecho**: **un hombre ~ y derecho** a (fully) grown man; **soldados ~s y derechos** proper soldiers
[7] (= *acostumbrado*) **estar ~ a** to be used to
Ⓒ SM [1] (= *acto*) **los vecinos quieren ~s** the residents want action; **~s, y** *o* **que no palabras** actions speak louder than words ► **hecho consumado** fait accompli ► **hecho de armas** feat of arms ► **Hechos de los Apóstoles** Acts of the Apostles
[2] (= *realidad*) fact; (= *suceso*) event; **es un ~** it's a fact; **es un ~ conocido** it's a well-known fact; **el ~ es que ...** the fact is that ...; **volvamos a los ~s** let's get back to the facts; **hay que clarificar los ~s** the facts must be clarified; **un ~ histórico** (= *acontecimiento*) an historic event; (= *dato*) a historical fact; **los ~s acaecidos ayer** yesterday's events; **el lugar de los ~s** the scene of the incident; ► **hecho imponible** (*Fin*) taxable source of income
[3] **de ~** in fact, as a matter of fact; **de ~, yo no sé nada de eso** in fact *o* as a matter of fact, I don't know anything about that
[4] (*Jur*) **de ~ y de derecho** de facto and de jure

hechor[1](a) SM/F [1] (*Jur*) perpetrator
[2] (*Cono Sur*) = **malhechor**

hechor[2] SM (*LAm*) (= *semental*) stud donkey

hechura SF [1] (*Cos*) (= *confección*) making-up, confection (*frm*); (= *corte*) cut; **de ~ sastre** tailor-made; **las ~s** the cost of making up
[2] (= *forma*) form, shape; **a ~ de** like, after the manner of; ✦***MODISMOS*** **no tener una ~** (*LAm*) to be a dead loss; **tener ~s de algo** to show an aptitude for sth
[3] [*cuadro, escultura*] craftsmanship, workmanship; **de exquisita ~** of exquisite workmanship
[4] (= *creación*) (*gen*) making, creation, product; [*persona*] creature, puppet; **él es una ~ del ministro** he is a creature *o* puppet of the minister; **no tiene ~** it can't be done; **somos ~ de Dios** we are God's handiwork

hectárea SF hectare (= *2.471 acres*)

héctico ADJ (*frm*) consumptive

hectogramo SM hectogramme, hectogram (*EEUU*)

hectolitro SM hectolitre, hectoliter (*EEUU*)

Héctor SM Hector

heder ▸conjug 2g◂ VI [1] (= *apestar*) to stink (**a** of), reek (**a** of)
[2] (= *molestar*) to be annoying

hediondez SF [1] (= *olor*) stink, stench
[2] (= *cosa*) stinking thing

hediondo ADJ [1] (= *maloliente*) stinking, foul-smelling
[2] (= *asqueroso*) repulsive
[3] (= *sucio*) filthy
[4] (= *obsceno*) obscene
[5] (= *inaguantable*) annoying, unbearable

hedonismo SM hedonism

hedonista Ⓐ ADJ hedonistic
Ⓑ SMF hedonist

hedor SM stink (**a** of), stench (**a** of)

hegemonía SF hegemony

hégira SF Hegira

helada SF frost ► **helada blanca** hoarfrost ► **helada de madrugada** early-morning frost

heladamente ADV icily

heladera SF (*Cono Sur*) refrigerator, fridge*, icebox (*EEUU*); *ver tb* **heladero**

heladería SF ice-cream parlour, ice-cream parlor (*EEUU*)

heladero/a Ⓐ ADJ ice-cream *antes de s*
Ⓑ SM/F ice-cream seller; *ver tb* **heladera**

helado Ⓐ ADJ [1] (= *congelado*) [*lago, río*] frozen; [*carretera*] icy
[2] (= *muy frío*) [*bebida, comida*] ice-cold; [*mirada*] frosty, icy; **¡estoy ~!** I'm frozen!, I'm freezing!; **¡tengo las manos heladas!** my hands are frozen *o* freezing *o* like ice!; **me quedé ~ de frío** I was frozen
[3] (= *pasmado*) **dejar ~ a algn** to dumbfound sb; **¡me deja usted ~!** you amaze me!; **¡me quedé ~!** (*de sorpresa*) I couldn't believe it!; (*de miedo*) I was scared stiff!
[4] (*Caribe Culin*) iced, frosted
Ⓑ SM ice cream

helador ADJ [*viento*] icy, freezing; **hace un frío ~** it's icy cold, it's perishing cold, it's freezing cold

heladora SF [1] (= *máquina*) ice-cream maker
[2] [*de nevera*] freezer unit, freezing compartment, freezer; (*esp Cono Sur*) refrigerator, fridge*, icebox (*EEUU*)

helaje SM (*Andes*) (= *frío intenso*) intense cold; (= *sensación*) chill

helar ▸conjug 1j◂ Ⓐ VT [1] (*Meteo*) to freeze, ice up
[2] (= *congelar*) [+ *líquido*] to freeze; [+ *bebidas*] to ice, chill
[3] (= *pasmar*) to dumbfound, amaze
[4] (= *aterrar*) to scare to death
Ⓑ VI (= *hacer frío*) (*Meteo*) to freeze
Ⓒ **helarse** VPR [1] (*Aer, Ferro*) to ice up, freeze up
[2] (= *congelarse*) [*líquido*] to freeze; [*plantas*] to be killed by frost; [*lago, río*] to freeze over
[3] [*persona*] **¡me estoy helando!** I'm freezing!; ✦***MODISMO*** **se me heló la sangre (en las venas)** my blood ran cold

helecho SM bracken, fern

Helena SF Helen

helénico ADJ Hellenic, Ancient Greek

heleno/a SM/F Hellene, Ancient Greek

Helesponto SM Hellespont

hélice SF [1] (= *espiral*) (*figura*) spiral; (*Anat, Elec, Mat*) helix ► **hélice doble** double helix
[2] (*Aer*) propeller, airscrew
[3] (*Náut*) propeller, screw

helicoidal ADJ spiral, helicoidal, helical

helicóptero SM helicopter ► **helicóptero artillado, helicóptero de ataque, helicóptero de combate** helicopter gunship ► **helicóptero de salvamento** rescue helicopter ► **helicóptero fumigador** crop-spraying helicopter

heliesquí SM heli-skiing

helio SM helium

helio... PREF helio...

helioesquí SM heli-skiing

heliógrafo SM heliograph

heliosfera SF heliosphere

heliosismología SF helioseismology

helioterapia SF heliotherapy (*frm*), sunray treatment

heliotipia SF heliotype

heliotropo SM heliotrope

helipuerto SM heliport

helitransportar ▸conjug 1a◂ VT (*gen*) to transport by helicopter; (*Mil*) to helicopter (in)

helmántico/a Ⓐ ADJ of/from Salamanca
Ⓑ SM/F native/inhabitant of Salamanca; **los ~s** the people of Salamanca

helvético/a Ⓐ ADJ of/from Switzerland
Ⓑ SM/F native/inhabitant of Switzerland; **los ~s** the people of Switzerland

hematíe SM red (blood) corpuscle

hematología SF haematology, hematology (*EEUU*)

hematoma SM bruise

hembra SF [1] (*Bot, Zool*) female; **el pájaro ~** the hen, the female bird; **el armiño ~** the female stoat, the she-stoat
[2] (= *mujer*) woman, female; **"hembra"** "female"; **cinco hijos: dos varones y tres ~s** five children: two boys and three girls
[3] (*Mec*) nut ► **hembra de terraja** die
[4] (*Cos*) eye; **macho y ~** hook and eye

hembraje SM (*LAm*) female flock, female herd; (*hum*) womenfolk

hembrería* SF (*Caribe, Méx*), **hembrerío*** SM gaggle of women, crowd of women

hembrilla SF (*Mec*) nut, eyebolt

hembrista SMF (*hum*) feminist

hemerográfico ADJ newspaper *antes de s*

hemeroteca SF newspaper library

hemiciclo SM [1] (= *anfiteatro*) semicircular theatre, semicircular theater (*EEUU*)
[2] (*Pol*) (= *sala*) chamber; (= *zona central*) floor

➤ LENGUA Y USO: **hecho** C3 53.3

hemiplejía SF hemiplegia (*frm*), stroke
hemisferio SM hemisphere
hemistiquio SM hemistich
hemo... PREF haemo..., hemo... (*EEUU*)
hemodiálisis SF INV haemodialysis, hemodialysis (*EEUU*)
hemodinámica SF haemodynamics *sing*
hemodinámico ADJ haemodynamic
hemodonación SF donation of blood
hemofilia SF haemophilia, hemophilia (*EEUU*)
hemofílico/a ADJ, SM/F haemophiliac, hemophiliac (*EEUU*)
hemoglobina SF haemoglobin, hemoglobin (*EEUU*)
hemograma SM haemogram, hemogram (*EEUU*)
hemorragia SF 1 (*Med*) haemorrhage, hemorrhage (*EEUU*), bleeding; **cortar una ~** to stop the bleeding; **morir por ~** to bleed to death ► **hemorragia cerebral** cerebral haemorrhage, brain haemorrhage ► **hemorragia nasal** nosebleed
2 [*de científicos, técnicos*] drain
hemorroides SFPL haemorrhoids, hemorrhoids (*EEUU*), piles
hemos *ver* **haber**
henal SM hayloft
henar SM meadow, hayfield
henchir ▸conjug 3h◂ Ⓐ VT to fill (up) (**de** with), stuff* (**de** with)
Ⓑ **henchirse** VPR 1 (*gen*) to swell; **~se de comida** to stuff o.s. with food*
2 (*de orgullo*) to swell with pride
Hendaya SF Hendaye
hendedura SF = **hendidura**
hender ▸conjug 2g◂ VT 1 (= *resquebrajar*) to crack
2 (= *cortar*) to cleave, split
3 (= *surcar*) [+ *olas*] to cleave, breast
hendidura SF 1 (= *grieta*) (*en pared, superficie*) crack
2 (= *corte*) cleft, split
3 (*Geol*) rift, fissure
hendija SF (*LAm*) crack, crevice
hendir ▸conjug 3i◂ VT = **hender**
henequén SM (*LAm*) 1 (= *planta*) agave, henequen
2 (= *fibra*) agave fibre, agave fiber (*EEUU*), henequen
henificación SF haymaking, tedding
henificar ▸conjug 1g◂ VT to ted
henil SM hayloft
heniquén SM (*Caribe, Méx*) = **henequén**
heno SM hay
heñir ▸conjug 3h y 3k◂ VT to knead
hepático ADJ hepatic (*frm*), liver *antes de s*; **trasplante ~** liver transplant
hepatitis SF INV hepatitis
hepato... PREF hepato..., hepat...
heptagonal ADJ heptagonal
heptágono SM heptagon
heptámetro SM heptameter
heptatlón SM heptathlon
heráldica SF heraldry
heráldico ADJ heraldic
heraldo SM herald
herales† SMPL trousers, pants (*EEUU*)
herbáceo ADJ herbaceous
herbajar ▸conjug 1a◂, **herbajear** ▸conjug 1a◂ Ⓐ VT to graze, put out to pasture
Ⓑ VI to graze
herbaje SM 1 (*gen*) herbage; (= *pasto*) grass, pasture
2 (*Náut*) coarse woollen cloth
herbario[1] Ⓐ ADJ herbal
Ⓑ SM (= *colección*) herbarium (*frm*), plant collection
herbario[2]**/a** SM/F (*gen*) herbalist; (= *botánico*) botanist
herbazal SM grassland, pasture
herbicida SM weed-killer ► **herbicida selectivo** selective weed-killer
herbívoro/a Ⓐ ADJ herbivorous
Ⓑ SM/F herbivore
herbodietética SF 1 **productos de ~** health food products
2 (= *tienda*) health food shop
herbodietético ADJ health food *antes de s*
herbolario[1] SM 1 (= *tienda*) herbalist's (shop), health food shop
2 (= *colección*) herbarium (*frm*), plant collection
herbolario[2]**/a** Ⓐ ADJ (†) (= *alocado*) crazy, cracked*
Ⓑ SM/F (= *persona*) herbalist
herboristería SF herbalist's, herbalist's shop
herborizar ▸conjug 1f◂ VI (= *recoger hierbas*) to gather herbs, pick herbs; (*como coleccionista*) to botanize, collect plants
herboso ADJ grassy
hercio SM hertz
hercúleo ADJ Herculean
Hércules SM 1 (*Mit*) Hercules
2 [*de circo*] strong man; **es un ~** he's awfully strong
heredabilidad SF inheritability
heredable ADJ inheritable, that can be inherited
heredad SF 1 (= *hacienda*) country estate, farm
2 (= *terreno cultivado*) landed property
heredar ▸conjug 1a◂ 1 VT [+ *dinero, tradición, problema*] to inherit; **heredó un título nobiliario** he inherited a title; **ha heredado las deudas de su padre** he has inherited his father's debts; **el rey heredó el trono en 1865** the king succeeded to the throne in 1865
2 [+ *rasgo*] to inherit; **ha heredado el pelo rubio de su madre** he's inherited his mother's blond hair, he gets his blond hair from his mother
3 [+ *ropa, libros*] to inherit; **los libros de texto que he heredado de mi hermano** the textbooks I inherited from my brother; **siempre hereda la ropa de su hermana mayor** her clothes are always handed down from her elder sister
4 [+ *persona*] (†) to name as one's heir
5 (*LAm*) (= *legar*) to leave, bequeath
heredero/a SM/F heir/heiress (**de** to), inheritor (**de** of); **príncipe ~** crown prince ► **heredero/a de la corona** heir to the crown ► **heredero/a del trono** heir to the throne ► **heredero/a forzoso/a** heir apparent ► **heredero/a presunto/a** heir presumptive
hereditario ADJ hereditary
hereje Ⓐ ADJ 1 (*Cono Sur**) (= *irrespetuoso*) disrespectful
2 (*Andes, Caribe*) (= *excesivo*) excessive; **un trabajo ~*** a heavy task
Ⓑ SMF heretic
herejía SF 1 (*Rel*) heresy
2 (= *trampa*) dirty trick
3 (= *injuria*) insult
4 (*Andes, Méx*) silly remark, gaffe
herencia SF 1 [*de propiedad, valores*] inheritance, legacy; **malgastó la ~ del padre** he squandered his father's legacy, he squandered the inheritance he had from his father; **me dejó las joyas en ~** she left *o* bequeathed me her jewels; **recibieron la finca en ~** they inherited the estate; **es parte de la ~ cultural de los españoles** it's part of the cultural heritage of the Spanish, it's part of Spanish heritage; **la ~ cultural que recibimos de los romanos** the cultural legacy of the Romans ► **herencia yacente** unsettled estate
2 (*Biol*) heredity ► **herencia genética** genetic inheritance
hereque (*Caribe*) SM 1 (*Med*) skin disease
2 (*Bot*) *disease of coffee*
heresiarca SMF heresiarch, arch-heretic
herético ADJ heretical
herida SF 1 (*física*) (*por arma*) wound; (*por accidente*) injury; **una ~ de bala** a bullet wound; **me sangraba la ~ del brazo** (*de arma*) the wound in my arm was bleeding; (*por caída, golpe*) the cut on my arm was bleeding; **me he hecho una ~ en la frente** I've got a cut on my forehead; **murió a causa de las ~s del accidente** he died from injuries received in the accident; **sufrió ~s graves** he was seriously injured; **las ~s internas en el seno del partido** the rifts *o* splits within the party ► **herida abierta** open wound; **una ~ abierta en la conciencia española** an open wound *o* running sore on the Spanish conscience ► **herida contusa** bruise ► **herida de bala** bullet wound
2 (= *ofensa*) insult; ✦**MODISMOS** **hurgar en la ~**: **evitó mencionar el divorcio para no hurgar en la ~** he avoided mentioning the divorce so as to let sleeping dogs lie; **lamerse las ~s** to lick one's wounds
herido/a Ⓐ ADJ 1 (*físicamente*) (*gen*) injured; (*en tiroteo, atentado, guerra*) wounded; **había un hombre ~ en el suelo** there was an injured man lying on the ground; **un soldado ~** a wounded soldier; **un policía resultó ~ en el tiroteo** a policeman was injured *o* wounded in the shooting; **estaba ~ de muerte** ◊ **estaba mortalmente ~** he was fatally injured
2 (*emocionalmente*) hurt; **Susana se sintió herida por lo que le dijiste** Susana was hurt by what you said to her; **me sentí herida en mi amor propio** it was a blow to my self-esteem; **tiene el orgullo ~** his pride has been hurt *o* wounded
Ⓑ SM/F (= *lesionado*) (*gen*) injured person; (*en tiroteo, atentado, guerra*) wounded person; **había un ~ en el parque** there was an injured man in the park; **hubo dos ~s en el accidente** two people were injured *o* hurt in the accident; **hubo cinco ~s leves** five people were slightly injured *o* hurt; **se llevaron a los ~s al hospital** they took the casualties *o* injured (people) to hospital; **el número de los ~s en el accidente** the number of casualties *o* people injured in the accident; **asistieron a**

los ~s en las trincheras they helped the wounded in the trenches; **los ~s de guerra** the war wounded
Ⓒ SM (*Cono Sur*) ditch, channel

herir ▸conjug 3i◂ VT 1 (= *lesionar*) (*gen*) to injure, hurt; (*con arma*) to wound; **~ a algn en el brazo** to wound sb in the arm
2 (= *ofender*) to hurt; **me hirió en lo más hondo** it really hurt me deep down
3 (= *irritar*) [*sol, luz*] to beat down on; **un color que hiere la vista** a colour which offends the eye
4 (*liter*) (= *golpear*) to beat, strike, hit
5 (*Mús*) to pluck, play

hermafrodita ADJ, SMF hermaphrodite

hermanable ADJ 1 (*de hermano*) fraternal
2 (= *compatible*) compatible
3 (= *a tono*) matching, that can be matched

hermanamiento SM **~ de ciudades** town-twinning

hermanar ▸conjug 1a◂ VT 1 (= *hacer juego*) to match
2 (= *unir*) [+ *ciudades*] to twin, make sister cities (*EEUU*)
3 (= *armonizar*) to harmonize, bring into harmony
4 (*Cono Sur*) (= *hacer pares*) to pair

hermanastro/a SM/F (*con padre o madre común*) half brother/sister; (*sin vínculo sanguíneo*) stepbrother/stepsister

hermandad SF 1 (= *grupo*) [*de hombres*] brotherhood, fraternity; [*de mujeres*] sisterhood; **Santa Hermandad** (*Hist*) rural police (*15th to 19th centuries*)
2 (= *sindicato*) association

hermanita SF little sister ► **hermanitas de la caridad** Little Sisters of Charity, Sisters of Mercy

hermano/a Ⓐ ADJ [*barco*] sister *antes de s*; **ciudades hermanas** twin towns
Ⓑ SM/F 1 brother/sister; **por favor, indique el número de ~s/as** please state number of siblings; **somos ~s de madre** we have the same mother; **medio ~** half-brother/-sister; **primo ~** first cousin; **mis ~s** (= *sólo chicos*) my brothers; (= *chicos y chicas*) my brothers and sisters; **Gonzalo y Luís son como ~s** Gonzalo and Luís are like brothers; **Rosa y Fernando son como ~s** Rosa and Fernando are like brother and sister ► **hermano/a carnal** full brother/sister ► **hermano de armas** brother-in-arms ► **hermano/a de leche** foster brother/sister ► **hermano/a de sangre** blood brother/sister ► **hermano/a gemelo/a** twin brother/sister ► **hermano/a mayor** elder brother/sister, big brother/sister* ► **hermano/a político/a** brother-in-law/sister-in-law ► **hermanos/as siameses/as** Siamese twins
2 (*Rel*) brother/sister; **hermanos** brethren ► **hermano/a lego/a** lay brother/sister
3 [*de un par*] pair; **no encuentro el ~ de este calcetín** I can't find the pair for this sock
4 (*LAm*) (= *espectro*) ghost

hermenéutica SF hermeneutics *sing*

hermética SF hermetic philosophy, hermetics *sing*

herméticamente ADV hermetically

hermeticidad SF hermetic nature, hermeticism

hermético ADJ 1 (= *cerrado*) (*gen*) hermetic; (*al aire*) airtight; (*al agua*) watertight
2 (= *inescrutable*) [*teoría*] watertight; [*misterio*] impenetrable; [*persona*] reserved, secretive

hermetismo SM (= *inescrutabilidad*) [*de teoría, misterio*] tight secrecy, close secrecy; [*de persona*] silence, reserve; **acordaron la paz con gran ~** they agreed the peace in the utmost secrecy

hermetizar ▸conjug 1f◂ VT to seal off, close off

hermosamente ADV beautifully, handsomely

hermosear ▸conjug 1a◂ VT (*frm*) to beautify, embellish

hermoso ADJ 1 (= *bello*) beautiful, lovely; **la casa tiene un ~ jardín** the house has a beautiful *o* lovely garden; **un día ~** a beautiful *o* lovely day
2 (= *robusto, saludable*) **¡qué niño tan ~!** what a fine-looking boy!; **seis ~s toros** six magnificent bulls
3 (= *grande*) nice and big; **el coche tiene un maletero muy ~** the car has a nice big boot, the car's boot is nice and big; **me sirvió una hermosa porción de queso** she gave me a nice big chunk of cheese
4 (= *noble*) **un ~ gesto** a noble gesture

hermosura SF 1 (= *cualidad*) beauty
2 (= *persona, cosa hermosa*) **esta modelo es una ~** this model is a beauty, this model is beautiful; **¡qué ~ de niño!** what a lovely *o* beautiful child!

hernia SF rupture, hernia ► **hernia de disco, hernia discal** slipped disc ► **hernia estrangulada** strangulated hernia ► **hernia hiatal** hiatus hernia

herniarse ▸conjug 1b◂ VPR (*Med*) to rupture o.s.; **no trabajes tanto que te vas a herniar** (*iró*) don't work so hard, you're going to give yourself a hernia (*iró*)

Herodes SM Herod; ✦***MODISMOS*** **hacer lo de ~*** to put up with it; **ir de ~ a Pilatos** to be driven from pillar to post

héroe SM hero

heroicamente ADV heroically

heroicidad SF 1 (= *cualidad*) heroism
2 (= *proeza*) heroic deed

heroico ADJ heroic

heroicocómico ADJ mock-heroic

heroína[1] SF (= *mujer*) heroine

heroína[2] SF (= *droga*) heroin

heroinomanía SF heroin addiction

heroinómano/a SM/F heroin addict

heroísmo SM heroism

herpes SM INV (*Med*) (*en los labios, genitales*) herpes; (= *culebrilla*) shingles ► **herpes genital** genital herpes ► **herpes labial** cold sore, labial herpes (*frm*)

herrada SF 1 (*Col*) [*de caballo*] shoeing
2 (= *cubo*) bucket
3 (*Andes Agr*) branding

herrador SM farrier, blacksmith

herradura SF horseshoe; **camino de ~** bridle path; **curva en ~** (*Aut*) hairpin bend; ✦***MODISMO*** **mostrar las ~s** to bolt, show a clean pair of heels

herraje SM 1 (*en puerta, mueble*) ironwork, iron fittings *pl*
2 (*Méx*) silver harness fittings *pl*
3 (*Cono Sur*) (= *herradura*) horseshoe

herramental SM toolkit, toolbag

herramienta SF 1 (*gen*) tool; **herramientas** set of tools ► **herramienta de filo** edge tool ► **herramienta de mano** hand tool ► **herramienta mecánica** power tool
2 (*hum*) [*de toro*] horns *pl*; (= *dientes*) teeth *pl*

herranza SF (*Andes*) branding

herrar ▸conjug 1j◂ VT 1 (*Agr*) [+ *caballo*] to shoe; [+ *ganado*] to brand
2 (*Téc*) to bind with iron, trim with ironwork

herrería SF 1 (= *taller*) smithy, blacksmith's, blacksmith's workshop (*EEUU*)
2 (= *oficio*) blacksmith's trade
3 (†) (= *fábrica*) ironworks
4 (††) (= *alboroto*) uproar, tumult

herrerillo SM (*Orn*) tit

herrero/a SM/F blacksmith, smith; ✦***REFRÁN*** **en casa del ~ (cuchillo de palo)** there's none worse shod than the shoemaker's wife ► **herrero/a de grueso** foundry worker

herrete SM (= *cabo*) metal tip, ferrule; (*LAm*) branding-iron, brand

Herri Batasuna SM *Basque pro-independence political party*

herribatasuno/a Ⓐ ADJ of Herri Batasuna
Ⓑ SM/F (= *miembro*) member of Herri Batasuna; (= *simpatizante*) supporter of Herri Batasuna

herrumbre SF 1 (= *óxido*) rust
2 (*Bot*) rust
3 (= *gusto*) iron taste

herrumbroso ADJ rusty

hertzio SM hertz

hervederas* SFPL (*Caribe*) heartburn, indigestion

hervidero SM 1 [*de gente*] swarm, throng, crowd; **un ~ de gente** a swarm of people
2 (*Pol*) hotbed; **un ~ de disturbios** a hotbed of unrest
3 (= *manantial*) hot spring

hervido Ⓐ ADJ (*gen*) boiled
Ⓑ SM (*LAm*) (= *guiso*) stew

hervidor SM kettle

hervidora SF ► **hervidora de agua** water heater

hervir ▸conjug 3i◂ Ⓐ VT to boil
Ⓑ VI 1 [*agua, leche*] to boil; **~ a fuego lento** to simmer; **dejar de ~** to go off the boil, stop boiling; **empezar** *o* **romper a ~** to come to the boil, begin to boil; ✦***MODISMO*** **¡me hierve la sangre!** it makes my blood boil!
2 (= *burbujear*) [*líquido*] to bubble, seethe; [*mar*] to seethe, surge
3 (= *persona*) **hiervo en deseos de ...** I'm just itching to ...; **el público hervía de emoción** the audience was carried away with *o* bubbling with excitement
4 **~ de** *o* **en** (= *estar lleno de*) to swarm with; **la cama hervía de pulgas** the bed was swarming *o* alive with fleas

hervor SM 1 [*de agua, leche*] boiling; **dar un ~ a algo** to boil sth once; **alzar el ~** *o* **levantar el ~** to come to the boil
2 (*popular, emocional*) ardour, ardor (*EEUU*)

hervoroso ADJ 1 [*líquido*] boiling, seething; [*sol*] burning
2 = **fervoroso**

heteo/a (*Hist*) Ⓐ ADJ of/from Anatolia
Ⓑ SM/F native/inhabitant of Anatolia; **los ~s** the people of Anatolia

hetero* ADJ, SMF = **heterosexual**

heterodoxia SF heterodoxy

heterodoxo ADJ heterodox, unorthodox

heterogeneidad SF heterogeneous nature, heterogeneity (*frm*)

heterogéneo ADJ heterogeneous

heteronimia SF heteronomy

heterónimo SM heteronym

heterónomo ADJ heteronomous

heterosexual ADJ, SMF heterosexual

heterosexualidad SF heterosexuality

heticarse ▸conjug 1g◂ VPR (*Caribe*) to contract tuberculosis

hético ADJ consumptive

hetiquencia SF (*Caribe*) tuberculosis

heurístico ADJ heuristic

hexadecimal ADJ hexadecimal

hexagonal ADJ hexagonal

hexágono SM hexagon

hexámetro SM hexameter

hez SF 1 **heces** (*Med*) faeces, feces (*EEUU*); [*de vino*] lees
2 (*frm*) (= *escoria*) dregs, scum; **la ~ de la sociedad** the dregs o scum of society

hg ABR (= **hectogramo(s)**) hg

hiatal ADJ [+ *hernia*] hiatus *antes de s*, hiatal

hiato SM (*Ling*) hiatus

hibernación SF hibernation; **estar en ~** to be in hibernation

hibernal ADJ (*frm*) wintry, winter *antes de s*

hibernar ▸conjug 1a◂ VI to hibernate

hibisco SM hibiscus

hibridación SF, **hibridaje** SM hybridization

hibridar ▸conjug 1a◂ VT, VI to hybridize

hibridismo SM hybridism

hibridizar ▸conjug 1f◂ VT 1 (*Biol*) to hybridize
2 [+ *paisaje*] to lend a mixed appearance to, produce a hybrid appearance in

híbrido Ⓐ ADJ hybrid
Ⓑ SM hybrid

hice *etc ver* **hacer**

hidalgo/a Ⓐ ADJ 1 (= *caballeroso*) noble
2 (= *honrado*) honourable, honorable (*EEUU*)
3 (= *generoso*) generous
Ⓑ SM/F nobleman/noblewoman
Ⓒ SM (*Méx Hist*) *10-peso gold coin*

hidalguía SF 1 (= *nobleza*) nobility
2 (= *honradez*) nobility, honourableness, honorableness (*EEUU*)
3 (= *generosidad*) generosity

hideputa** SM = **hijodeputa**

Hidra SF (*Mit*) Hydra

hidra SF hydra

hidratación SF [*de la piel*] moisturizing

hidratante Ⓐ ADJ moisturizing; **crema ~** moisturizing cream
Ⓑ SF moisturizing cream, moisturizer

hidratar ▸conjug 1a◂ Ⓐ VT 1 [+ *piel*] to moisturize
2 (*Quím*) to hydrate
Ⓑ **hidratarse** VPR to put on moisturizing cream

hidrato SM hydrate ► **hidrato de carbono** carbohydrate

hidráulica SF hydraulics *sing*

hidráulico ADJ hydraulic (*frm*), water *antes de s*; **fuerza hidráulica** water power, hydraulic power

hídrico ADJ water *antes de s*

hidro... PREF hydro..., water-

hidroala SM hydrofoil

hidroavión SM seaplane, flying boat

hidrocarburo SM hydrocarbon

hidrocefalia SF (*Med*) hydrocephalus, water on the brain

hidrodeslizador SM hovercraft

hidrodinámica SF hydrodynamics *sing*

hidroeléctrica SF hydroelectric power station

hidroeléctrico ADJ hydroelectric; **central hidroeléctrica** hydro(electricity) station

hidroesfera SF hydrosphere

hidrófilo ADJ absorbent; **algodón ~** cotton wool, absorbent cotton (*EEUU*)

hidrofobia SF hydrophobia (*frm*), rabies

hidrofóbico ADJ, **hidrófobo** ADJ hydrophobic

hidrofoil SM hydrofoil

hidrofuerza SF hydropower

hidrófugo Ⓐ ADJ water-repellent, damp-proof
Ⓑ SM water repellent

hidrógeno SM hydrogen

hidrografía SF hydrography

hidrólisis SF INV hydrolysis

hidrolizar ▸conjug 1f◂ Ⓐ VT to hydrolyze
Ⓑ **hidrolizarse** VPR to hydrolyze

hidrológico ADJ water *antes de s*; **recursos ~s** water resources

hidromasaje SM hydromassage

hidropesía SF dropsy

hidrópico ADJ dropsical

hidroplano SM hydroplane

hidroponia SF hydroponics *sing*, aquiculture

hidropónico ADJ hydroponic

hidrosfera SF hydrosphere

hidrosoluble ADJ soluble in water, water-soluble

hidroterapia SF hydrotherapy ► **hidroterapia del colon** colonic irrigation

hidrovía SF waterway

hidróxido SM hydroxide ► **hidróxido amónico** ammonium hydroxide

hiedra SF ivy

hiel SF 1 (*Anat*) gall, bile; ✦**MODISMO echar la ~*** to sweat blood*, slog away*
2 (= *amargura*) bitterness; **no tener ~** to be very sweet-tempered
3 **hieles** (= *adversidades*) troubles, upsets

hiela *ver* **helar**

hielera SF (*Chile, Méx*) (= *nevera*) refrigerator, fridge*; (= *bandeja*) ice tray

hielo SM 1 (= *agua helada*) ice; **con ~** (*bebida*) with ice, on the rocks*; ✦**MODISMOS ser más frío que el ~** to be as cold as ice; **romper el ~** to break the ice ► **hielo a la deriva, hielo flotante, hielo movedizo** drift ice ► **hielo picado** crushed ice ► **hielo seco** dry ice
2 (= *helada*) frost

hiena SF 1 (= *animal*) hyena
2 (= *persona cruel*) vulture; ✦**MODISMOS hecho una ~** furious; **ponerse como una ~** to get furious, hit the roof*

hierático ADJ (*frm*) [*figura, postura*] hieratic, hieratical; [*aspecto*] stern, severe

hieratismo SM (*frm*) 1 [*de figura, postura*] hieratic attitude
2 (= *solemnidad*) solemnity, stateliness

hierba SF 1 (= *pasto*) grass; **mala ~** weed; ✦**MODISMOS oír** o **sentir** o **ver crecer la ~** to be pretty smart; **pisar mala ~** to have bad luck; **y otras ~s** and so forth, and suchlike; ✦**REFRÁN mala ~ nunca muere** it's a case of the proverbial bad penny ► **hierba artificial** artificial playing surface, Astroturf® ► **hierba cana** groundsel ► **hierba de San Juan** St John's-wort ► **hierba gatera** catmint ► **hierba lombriguera** ragwort ► **hierba mate** (*esp Cono Sur*) maté ► **hierba mora** nightshade ► **hierba rastrera** cotton grass
2 (*Med*) herb, medicinal plant; **cura de ~s** herbal cure; **infusión de ~s** herbal tea
3 (*Culin*) herb; **a las finas ~s** cooked with herbs
4 (*) (= *droga*) grass*, pot*

hierbabuena SF mint

hierbajo SM weed

hierbajoso ADJ weedy, weed-infested

hierbaluisa SF lemon verbena, aloysia (*frm*)

hierra SF (*LAm*) branding

hierro SM 1 (= *metal*) iron; **de ~** iron *antes de s*; ✦**MODISMOS fuerte como el ~** like iron, tough; **llevar ~ a Vizcaya** to carry coals to Newcastle; **machacar en ~ frío** to flog a dead horse, beat one's head against a brick wall; **quitar ~** to minimize sth, cut things down to their proper size ► **hierro acanalado** corrugated iron ► **hierro batido** wrought iron ► **hierro bruto** crude iron, pig iron ► **hierro colado** cast iron ► **hierro de fundición** cast iron ► **hierro en lingotes** pig iron ► **hierro forjado** wrought iron ► **hierro fundido** cast iron ► **hierro ondulado** corrugated iron ► **hierro viejo** scrap iron, old iron; *ver tb* **fierro**
2 (= *objeto*) iron object; (= *herramienta*) tool; [*de flecha, lanza*] head; ✦**REFRÁN quien a ~ mata, a ~ muere** those that live by the sword die by the sword
3 (*Agr*) branding-iron
4 (*Golf*) iron; **hierros** irons

hi-fi [i'fi] SM (*pl* **hi-fis**) hi-fi

higa SF 1 (= *gesto*) rude sign, obscene gesture
2 (= *burla*) **dar ~ a** to jeer at, mock; ✦**MODISMO no le importa una ~*** he doesn't give a damn*, he doesn't give a toss*

hígado SM 1 (*Anat*) liver; ✦**MODISMOS castigar el ~*** to knock it back*; **ser un ~** (*CAm, Méx**) to be a pain in the neck*; **tener ~ de indio** (*CAm, Méx*) to be a disagreeable sort
2 **hígados** (*fig*) guts, pluck *sing*; ✦**MODISMO echar los ~s** to sweat one's guts out*

higadoso ADJ **ser ~** (*CAm, Méx**) to be a pain in the neck*

highball SM (*LAm*) (= *cóctel*) cocktail, highball (*EEUU*)

higiene SF hygiene ► **higiene íntima** personal hygiene

higiénico ADJ hygienic; **papel ~** toilet paper

higienización SF cleaning, cleansing

higienizado ADJ sterilized

higienizar ▸conjug 1f◂ Ⓐ VT 1 (= *limpiar*) to clean, cleanse
2 (= *desinfectar*) to sterilize
Ⓑ **higienizarse** VPR (*Cono Sur*) (= *lavarse*) to wash oneself

higo SM 1 (*Bot*) fig, green fig; ✦**MODISMOS de ~s a brevas** once in a blue moon; **estar hecho un ~** to be all crumpled up; **(no) me importa un ~** I couldn't care less; **ser un ~ mustio** to be weakly ► **higo chumbo, higo**

de tuna prickly pear ► **higo paso, higo seco** dried fig
2 (*Vet*) thrush
3 (✱✱) (= *coño*) cunt✱✱

higuera SF fig tree; ✦*MODISMOS* **caer de una ~** to come down to earth with a bump; **estar en la ~** to be daydreaming, be up in the clouds ► **higuera chumba, higuera de tuna** prickly pear cactus, Indian fig tree ► **higuera del infierno, higuera infernal** castor-oil plant

higuerilla SF (*Méx*) castor-oil plant

hijadeputa✱✱ SF, **hijaputa**✱✱ SF bitch✱, cow✱

hijastro/a SM/F stepson/stepdaughter

hijo/a SM/F 1 son/daughter; **una pareja sin ~s** a childless couple; **¿cuántos ~s tiene Amelia?** how many children does Amelia have?; **¿cuántos ~s tiene a su cargo?** how many dependent children do you have?; **Pedro Gutiérrez, ~** Pedro Gutiérrez Junior; **su novio le hizo un ~*** her boyfriend got her pregnant; **nombrar a algn ~ predilecto de la ciudad** to name sb a favourite son of the city; **ser ~ único** to be an only child; **el Hijo de Dios** the Son of God; ✦*MODISMOS* **cada** *o* **todo ~ de vecino** any Tom, Dick or Harry*; **como todo ~ de vecino** like everyone else, like the next man; **hacer a algn un ~ macho** (*LAm*) to do sb harm; **soy ~ de mis obras** I'm a self-made man ► **hijo/a adoptivo/a** adopted child ► **hijo/a biológico/a** natural child, biological child ► **hijo de la chingada** (*Méx*✱✱) bastard✱✱, son of a bitch✱✱ ► **hijo/a de leche** foster child ► **hijo/a de papá** rich kid* ► **hijo/a de puta**✱✱ (= *hombre*) bastard✱✱, son of a bitch✱✱ (= *mujer*) bitch✱, cow✱ ► **hijo/a natural** illegitimate child ► **hijo/a político/a** son-in-law/daugher-in-law ► **hijo pródigo** prodigal son
2 [*de un pueblo, un país*] son; **es ~ de Madrid** he hails from Madrid, he is from Madrid
3 **hijos** (= *descendientes*) **todos somos ~s de Dios** we are all God's children
4 (*uso vocativo*) **¡~ de mi alma!** my precious child!; **¡ay ~, qué pesado eres!** you're such a pain!; **¡hijo(s)!** ◊ **¡híjole!** (*Méx**) Christ!✱, good God!*

hijodeputa✱✱ SM, **hijoputa**✱✱ SM bastard✱✱, son of a bitch (*EEUU*✱✱)

hijoputada✱✱ SF dirty trick

hijoputesco✱✱ ADJ rotten*, dirty

hijoputez✱✱ SF dirty trick

hijuela SF 1 (= *filial*) offshoot, branch
2 (*Jur*) (= *propiedades*) *estate of a deceased person*; (= *parte*) share, portion, inheritance; (= *legado*) list of bequests
3 (*Andes, Cono Sur*) plot of land
4 (*Cos*) piece of material (*for widening a garment*)
5 (*Agr*) small irrigation channel
6 (*Méx Min*) seam of ore
7 (*Andes, Cono Sur*) rural property

hijuelo SM 1 (*Zool*) young
2 (*Bot*) shoot
3 (*Andes*) (= *camino*) side road, minor road

hijuemadre✱✱ EXCL (*CAm*) bloody hell!✱✱, goddammit (*EEUU*✱), Jesus Christ!✱✱

hijueputa✱✱ SM (*LAm*) bastard✱✱, son of a bitch (*EEUU*✱✱)

hijuna✱✱ EXCL (*LAm*) you bastard!✱✱, you son of a bitch! (*EEUU*✱✱)

hila† SF 1 (= *fila*) row, line; **a la ~** in a row, in single file
2 (= *cuerda*) thin gut
3 **hilas** (*Med*) lint

hilacha SF 1 (= *hilo*) ravelled thread, loose thread ► **hilacha de vidrio** spun glass
2 **hilachas** (*Méx*) (= *andrajos*) rags
3 ✦*MODISMO* **mostrar la ~** (*Cono Sur*) to show o.s. in one's true colours *o* (*EEUU*) colors

hilachento ADJ (*LAm*) 1 (= *persona*) ragged
2 [*ropa*] (= *deshilachado*) frayed; (= *raído*) shabby

hilacho SM 1 (= *hilo*) = **hilacha 1**
2 **hilachos** = **hilacha 2**
3 ✦*MODISMO* **dar vuelo al ~** (*Méx**) to have a wild time

hilachudo ADJ (*Méx*) = **hilachento**

hilada SF 1 (= *fila*) row, line
2 (*Arquit*) course

hilado Ⓐ ADJ spun; **seda hilada** spun silk
Ⓑ SM 1 (= *acto*) spinning
2 (= *hilo*) thread, yarn

hilador(a) Ⓐ SM/F (= *persona*) spinner
Ⓑ SF (*Téc*) spinning jenny

hilandería SF 1 (= *oficio*) spinning
2 (= *fábrica*) spinning mill ► **hilandería de algodón** cotton mill

hilandero/a SM/F spinner

hilangos SMPL (*Andes*) rags, tatters

hilar ▸conjug 1a◂ VT 1 (*Cos*) to spin
2 (= *relacionar*) to reason, infer; ✦*MODISMOS* **~ (muy) delgado** ◊ **~ fino** to split hairs; **~ delgado** (*Cono Sur*) to be dying, be on one's last legs*

hilaracha SF = **hilacha**

hilarante ADJ hilarious; **gas ~** laughing gas

hilaridad SF hilarity

hilatura SF spinning

hilaza SF yarn, coarse thread; ✦*MODISMO* **descubrir la ~** to show o.s. in one's true colours *o* (*EEUU*) colors

hilazón SF connection

hilera SF 1 (= *fila*) (*gen*) row, line; (*Mil*) rank, file; (*Arquit*) course; (*Agr*) row, drill
2 (*Cos*) fine thread

hilo SM 1 (*Cos*) thread, yarn; **tela de ~** (*Méx*) linen cloth; **coser al ~** to sew on the straight, sew with the weave; ✦*MODISMOS* **a ~** continuously, uninterruptedly; **al ~** in a row, on the trot, running; **contar algo del ~ al ovillo** to tell sth without omitting a single detail; **dar mucho ~ que torcer** to cause a lot of trouble; **escapar con el ~ en una pata** (*Caribe, Cono Sur**) to get out of a tight corner, wriggle out of a jam*; **estar al ~** to be watchful, be on the look-out; **estar hecho un ~** to be as thin as a rake; **mover los ~s** to pull strings; **pender de un ~** to hang by a thread ► **hilo dental** dental floss ► **hilo de perlas** string of pearls ► **hilo de zurcir** darning wool
2 (= *cable*) [*de metal*] thin wire; [*de electricidad*] wire, flex; [*de teléfono*] line ► **hilo de tierra** earth wire, ground wire (*EEUU*) ► **hilo directo** direct line, hot line ► **hilo musical** piped music
3 (= *chorro*) [*de líquido*] thin stream, trickle; [*de gente*] thin line; ✦*MODISMOS* **decir algo con un ~ de voz** to say sth in a thin *o* barely audible voice; **irse tras el ~ de la gente** to follow the crowd ► **hilo de humo** thin line of smoke, plume of smoke
4 (*Bot*) fibre, fiber (*EEUU*), filament
5 (= *lino*) linen; **traje de ~** linen dress *o* suit ► **hilo de bramante** twine ► **hilo de Escocia** lisle, strong cotton
6 (= *curso*) [*de conversación*] thread; [*de vida*] course; [*de pensamientos*] train; **el ~ conductor** the theme *o* leitmotiv; **coger el ~** to pick up the thread; **perder el ~** to lose the thread; **seguir el ~** [*de razonamiento*] to follow, understand ► **hilo argumental** story line, plot

hilván SM 1 (*Cos*) (= *hilo suelto*) tacking, basting (*EEUU*)
2 (*Cono Sur*) (= *hilo*) tacking thread, basting thread (*EEUU*)
3 (*Caribe*) (= *dobladillo*) hem

hilvanar ▸conjug 1a◂ VT 1 (*Cos*) to tack, baste (*EEUU*)
2 (= *preparar*) [+ *trabajo, discurso*] to cobble together; **bien hilvanado** well put together, well constructed
3 (= *relacionar*) to string together

Himalaya SM **el ~** the Himalayas

himalayo ADJ Himalayan

himen SM hymen, maidenhead (*liter*)

himeneo SM 1 (*liter*) nuptials *pl*, wedding
2 (*poét*) epithalamium

himnario SM hymnal, hymnbook

himno SM hymn ► **himno nacional** national anthem

hincada SF 1 (*Chile, Ecu*) (*de rodillas*) genuflection (*frm*)
2 (*Caribe*) (= *hincadura*) thrust
3 (*Caribe*) (= *dolor*) sharp pain, stabbing pain

hincadura SF thrust, thrusting, driving

hincapié SM **hacer ~ en** (= *recalcar*) to emphasize, stress; (= *insistir en*) to insist on, demand; **hizo ~ en la necesidad de revisar el reglamento** she emphasized *o* stressed the need to revise the regulations

hincapilotes SM INV (*Cono Sur*) pile-driver

hincar ▸conjug 1g◂ Ⓐ VT (= *meter*) [+ *objeto punzante*] to thrust, drive (**en** into); [+ *pie*] to set (firmly) (**en** on); **hincó el bastón en el suelo** he stuck his stick in the ground, he thrust his stick into the ground; **hincó la mirada en ella** he fixed his gaze on her, he stared at her fixedly; ✦*MODISMO* **~la*** (= *trabajar mucho*) to slog*, work hard; *ver tb* **diente 2**, **rodilla 1**
Ⓑ **hincarse** VPR **~se de rodillas** (*esp LAm*) to kneel, kneel down

hincha[1] SF 1 (= *antipatía*) **tener ~ a algn** to have a grudge against sb; **tomar ~ a algn** to take a dislike to sb
2 (*Cono Sur**) (= *aburrimiento*) **¡qué ~!** what a bore!

hincha[2] SMF 1 (*Dep*) fan, supporter; **los ~s del Madrid** the Madrid supporters
2 (*Perú**) (= *amigo*) pal*, mate*, buddy (*esp EEUU**)

hinchable ADJ inflatable

hinchabolas✱✱ SMF INV (*Cono Sur*) = **hinchapelotas**

hinchada SF supporters *pl*, fans *pl*

hinchado ADJ 1 (= *inflamado*) swollen
2 (= *vanidoso*) [*persona*] swollen-headed, conceited; [*estilo*] pompous, high-flown

hinchador SM 1 ► **hinchador de ruedas** tyre inflator
2 (*Cono Sur*✱) pest, bloody nuisance✱

hinchante* ADJ [1] (= *molesto*) annoying, tiresome
[2] (= *gracioso*) funny
hinchapelotas** SM INV (*Cono Sur*) **es un ~** he's a pain in the arse**, he's a pain in the ass (*EEUU***)
hinchar ▸conjug 1a◂ Ⓐ VT [1] [+ *vientre*] to distend, enlarge; [+ *globo*] to blow up, inflate, pump up
[2] (= *exagerar*) to exaggerate
[3] (*Cono Sur**) (= *molestar*) to annoy, upset; **me hincha todo el tiempo** he keeps on at me all the time
Ⓑ **hincharse** VPR [1] (= *inflamarse*) [*herida, tobillo*] to swell, swell up; [*vientre*] to get distended (*frm*), get bloated
[2] (= *hartarse*) **~se de** [+ *comida*] to stuff o.s. with*; **se ~on de gambas** they stuffed themselves with prawns*; **me hinché de agua** I drank gallons *o* loads of water*; **~se a** *o* **de hacer algo: ~se a** *o* **de correr** to run like mad; **~se de reír** to have a good laugh, split one's sides laughing
[3] (= *engreírse*) to get conceited, become vain, get swollen-headed
[4] (*) (= *enriquecerse*) to make a pile*, make a mint*
hinchazón SF [1] (*Med*) [*de herida, tobillo*] swelling; (= *bulto*) bump, lump
[2] (*frm*) (= *arrogancia*) conceit
[3] (*frm*) [*de estilo*] pomposity
hinco SM (*Cono Sur*) post, stake
hindi SM Hindi
hindú ADJ, SMF [1] (*Rel*) Hindu
[2] (= *de la India*) Indian
hinduismo SM Hinduism
hiniesta SF (*Bot*) broom
hinojo[1] SM (*Bot, Culin*) fennel
hinojo[2] SM (††) **de ~s** on bended knee; **postrarse de ~s** to kneel (down), go down on one's knees
hip EXCL hic
hipar ▸conjug 1a◂ VI [1] (= *tener hipo*) to hiccup, hiccough
[2] [*perro*] to pant
[3] **~ por algo** to long for sth, yearn for sth; **~ por hacer algo** to long to do sth, yearn to do sth
[4] (= *gimotear*) to whine
[5] (= *estar exhausto*) to be worn out, be exhausted
hipato* ADJ [1] (*Andes*) (= *repleto*) full, swollen
[2] (*Andes, Caribe*) (= *pálido*) pale, anaemic, anemic (*EEUU*); (= *soso*) tasteless
hipear ▸conjug 1a◂ VI (*Méx*) = **hipar**
hiper* Ⓐ SM INV hypermarket
Ⓑ ADJ (= *fantástico*) mega*, wicked*
hiper... PREF hyper...
hiperacidez SF hyperacidity
hiperactividad SF hyperactivity
hiperactivo ADJ hyperactive
hiperagudo ADJ abnormally acute
hipérbaton SM (*pl* **hipérbatos**) hyperbaton
hipérbola SF hyperbola
hipérbole SF hyperbole
hiperbólico ADJ hyperbolic (*frm*), hyperbolical (*frm*), exaggerated
hipercorrección SF hypercorrection
hipercrítico ADJ hypercritical
hiperenlace SM (*Internet*) hyperlink
hiperexcitación SF hyperexcitement
hiperexcitado ADJ over-excited
hiperglucemia SF hyperglycaemia, hyperglycemia (*EEUU*)
hiperinflación SF runaway inflation, hyperinflation
hipermedia SM INV hypermedia
hipermercado SM hypermarket
hipermetropía SF, **hiperopía** SF long-sightedness, far-sightedness (*EEUU*), long-sight; **tener ~** to be long-sighted
hipermillonario ADJ [*acuerdo, ganancias*] multi-million pound/dollar *etc antes de s*
hipernervioso ADJ excessively nervous, highly strung
hiperrealismo SM hyper-realism
hipersensibilidad SF hypersensitivity (*frm*), over-sensitiveness, touchiness
hipersensible ADJ hypersensitive, oversensitive, touchy
hipersensitivo ADJ hypersensitive
hipersónico ADJ supersonic
hipertensión SF hypertension, high blood pressure
hipertenso ADJ having high blood pressure, with high blood pressure; **ser ~** to have high blood pressure
hipertexto SM hypertext
hipertrofia SF hypertrophy
hipervínculo SM hyperlink
hipervitaminosis SF INV hypervitaminosis
hipiar ▸conjug 1b◂ VI (*Méx*) = **hipar**
hípico ADJ horse *antes de s*, equine (*frm*); **club ~** riding club
hipido SM whine, whimper
hipismo SM horse-racing
hipnosis SF INV hypnosis
hipnoterapia SF hypnotherapy
hipnótico ADJ, SM hypnotic
hipnotismo SM hypnotism
hipnotista SMF hypnotist
hipnotizable ADJ susceptible to hypnosis
hipnotizador(a) Ⓐ ADJ hypnotizing
Ⓑ SM/F hypnotist
hipnotizante SMF hypnotist
hipnotizar ▸conjug 1f◂ VT [1] (*Psic*) to hypnotize [2] (= *hechizar*) to mesmerize
hipo SM [1] (*gen*) hiccups *pl*, hiccoughs *pl*; **quitar el ~ a algn** to cure sb's hiccups; **tener ~** to have hiccups; ✦***MODISMO*** **que quita el ~** breathtaking
[2] (††) (= *deseo*) longing, yearning; **tener ~ por** to long for, crave
[3] (††) (= *asco*) disgust
hipo... PREF hypo...
hipoalergénico ADJ hypoallergenic
hipocalórico ADJ low-calorie *antes de s*
hipocampo SM sea horse
hipocondria SF, **hipocondría** SF hypochondria
hipocondriaco, hipocondríaco/a Ⓐ ADJ hypochondriac, hypochondriacal
Ⓑ SM/F hypochondriac
hipocorístico ADJ **nombre ~** pet name, *affectionate form of a name p.ej. Merche = Mercedes, Jim = James*
Hipócrates SM Hippocrates
hipocrático ADJ **juramento ~** Hippocratic oath
hipocresía SF hypocrisy
hipócrita Ⓐ ADJ hypocritical
Ⓑ SMF hypocrite
hipócritamente ADV hypocritically
hipodérmico ADJ hypodermic; **aguja hipodérmica** hypodermic needle
hipódromo SM [*de caballos*] racecourse, racetrack (*EEUU*); (*Hist*) hippodrome
hipoglucemia SF hypoglycaemia, hypoglycemia (*EEUU*)
hipónimo SM hyponym
hipopótamo SM hippopotamus, hippo
hiposulfito SM ► **hiposulfito sódico** (*Fot*) hypo, sodium thiosulphate
hipoteca SF mortgage; **segunda ~** second mortgage, remortgage; **levantar una ~** to raise a mortgage; **redimir una ~** to pay off a mortgage ► **hipoteca dotal** endowment mortgage
hipotecar ▸conjug 1g◂ Ⓐ VT [+ *propiedades*] to mortgage; [+ *futuro*] to jeopardize
Ⓑ **hipotecarse** VPR (= *comprometerse*) to commit o.s.
hipotecario ADJ mortgage *antes de s*
hipotensión SF low blood pressure
hipotenso/a Ⓐ ADJ **ser ~** to have low blood pressure
Ⓑ SM/F person with low blood pressure
hipotensor ADJ hypotensive
hipotenusa SF hypotenuse
hipotermia SF hypothermia
hipótesis SF INV [1] (= *suposición*) hypothesis, supposition
[2] (= *teoría*) theory, idea; **es sólo una ~** it's just an idea *o* a theory
hipotéticamente ADV hypothetically
hipotético ADJ hypothetic, hypothetical
hipotetizar ▸conjug 1f◂ VI to hypothesize
hippie ['xipi] ADJ, SMF, **hippy** ['xipi] ADJ, SMF (*pl* **hippies**) hippy
hippioso/a* [xi'pjoso] Ⓐ ADJ hippyish
Ⓑ SM/F hippy type
hippismo [xi'pismo] SM hippy movement; **los años del ~** the hippy years
hiriente ADJ [1] [*observación, tono*] wounding, cutting
[2] [*contraste*] striking
hirsutez SF hairiness
hirsuto ADJ [1] [*persona*] hairy, hirsute (*frm*); [*barba*] bristly
[2] (= *brusco*) brusque, gruff
hirvición* SF (*Andes*) abundance, multitude
hirviendo *ver* **hervir**
hirviente ADJ boiling, seething
hisca SF birdlime
hisopear ▸conjug 1a◂ VT (*Rel*) to sprinkle with holy water, asperse (*frm*)
hisopo SM [1] (*Rel*) sprinkler, aspergillum (*frm*)
[2] (*Bot*) hyssop
[3] (*LAm*) (= *brocha*) paintbrush
[4] (*Cono Sur*) [*de algodón*] cotton bud, Q-tip® (*EEUU*)
[5] (*Cono Sur*) (= *trapo*) dishcloth
hispalense (*liter*) Ⓐ ADJ of/from Sevilla
Ⓑ SMF native/inhabitant of Sevilla; **los ~s** the people of Sevilla
Híspalis SF (*liter*) Seville

Hispania SF (*Hist*) Hispania, Roman Spain
hispánico ADJ Hispanic (*frm*), Spanish
hispanidad SF [1] (*gen*) Spanishness, Spanish characteristics *pl*
[2] (*Pol*) Spanish world, Hispanic world (*frm*); **Día de la Hispanidad** Columbus Day (*12 October*)

DÍA DE LA HISPANIDAD

***El Día de la Hispanidad**, on 12 October, is a national holiday in Spain in honour of Columbus's arrival in the Americas. It is also a holiday in other Spanish-speaking countries where it is called the **Día de la Raza**.*

hispanismo SM [1] *word etc borrowed from Spanish*, hispanicism (*frm*)
[2] (*Univ*) Hispanism, Hispanic studies *pl*; **el ~ holandés** Hispanic studies in Holland
hispanista SMF (*Univ*) hispanist, hispanicist
hispanística SF Hispanic studies *pl*
hispanizar ▸conjug 1f◂ VT to Hispanicize
hispano/a Ⓐ ADJ [1] (= *español*) Spanish, Hispanic (*frm*)
[2] (= *latinoamericano*) Hispanic
Ⓑ SM/F [1] (= *español*) Spaniard
[2] (= *latinoamericano*) Spanish-speaking American (*EEUU*), Hispanic
hispano-... PREF Hispano-..., Spanish-...; **pacto ~italiano** Hispano-Italian pact
Hispanoamérica SF Spanish America, Latin America
hispanoamericano/a ADJ, SM/F Spanish American, Latin American
hispanoárabe ADJ Hispano-Arabic
hispanófilo/a SM/F Hispanophile
hispanófobo/a SM/F hispanophobe
hispanohablante Ⓐ ADJ Spanish-speaking
Ⓑ SMF Spanish speaker
hispanomarroquí ADJ Spanish-Moroccan
hispanoparlante ADJ, SMF = **hispanohablante**
hispinglés SM (*hum*) Spanglish
histamínico ADJ histamine *antes de s*
histerectomía SF hysterectomy
histeria SF hysteria ► **histeria colectiva** mass hysteria
histéricamente ADV hysterically
histérico /a Ⓐ ADJ [1] (*Med*) hysterical; **paroxismo ~** hysterics *pl*
[2] (= *nervioso*) **no seas tan ~** don't get so worked up; **¡me pone ~!*** it drives me mad!, it drives me up the wall*
Ⓑ SM/F [1] (*Med*) hysteric
[2] (= *nervioso*) **no hagas caso, son unos ~s** pay no attention, they're always having hysterics
histerismo SM [1] (*Med*) hysteria
[2] (= *nerviosismo*) hysterics *pl*
histerizarse ▸conjug 1f◂ VPR to get hysterical
histograma SM histogram
histología SF histology
historia SF [1] [*de país, institución*] history; **la ~ del cine** the history of film *o* cinema; **es licenciado en ~** he has a degree in history, he has a history degree; **es un récord absoluto en la ~ del torneo** it is a tournament record; **nuestros problemas ya son ~** the problems we had are history now; ✦***MODISMOS*** **hacer ~** to make history; **un acuerdo que hará ~** an agreement that will make history; **un atleta que ha hecho ~ en el mundo del deporte** an athlete who has made sporting history; **pasar a la ~: pasará a la ~ como la primera mujer en el espacio** she will go down in history as the first woman in space; **ese modelo de coche ya ha pasado a la ~** that model of car is a thing of the past; **nuestro problema ya pasó a la ~** our problem is a thing of the past *o* has long since disappeared; **picar en ~†** to be a serious matter; **ser de ~†** to be famous; (*pey*) to be notorious; **tener ~** [*objeto*] to have an interesting history; [*suceso*] to be interesting; **tiene ~ cómo conseguimos este libro** how we got hold of this book is an interesting story, there's an interesting story behind how we got hold of this book
► **historia antigua** ancient history
► **historia clínica** medical history
► **historia del arte** history of art, art history
► **historia moderna** modern history
► **historia natural** natural history
► **Historia Sagrada** Biblical history; (*en la escuela*) (†) Scripture ► **historia universal** world history
[2] (= *relato*) story; **esta ~ es larga de contar** it's a long story; **cuéntame con detalles toda la ~** tell me the whole story in detail; **ésta es la ~ de una princesita** this is the story of a little princess; **la ~ de siempre** *o* **la misma ~** *o* **la ~ de todos los días** the same old story; **una ~ de amor** a love story
[3] (= *enredo*) story; **¡ahora no me cuentes la ~ de tu vida!** don't tell me your whole life story now!; **tu vecina siempre viene con ~s** your neighbour is always gossiping
[4] (= *excusa*) (*sobre algo pasado*) excuse, story; (*sobre algo presente o futuro*) excuse; **seguro que te viene con alguna ~** she's sure to give you some excuse *o* tell you some story; **¿así que has estado trabajando hasta ahora? ¡no me vengas con ~s** *o* **déjate de ~s!** so you've been working right up to now, have you? don't give me any of your stories!; **dijo que llegaba tarde por no se qué ~** he said he was going to be late for some reason or other
[5] (*) (= *lío*) business*; **andan metidos en una ~ un poco rara** they're mixed up in a rather funny business*
[6] (*) (= *romance*) fling*; **tener una ~ con algn** to have a fling with sb*
historiado ADJ [1] (*Arte*) historiated (*frm*), storiated (*frm*)
[2] (= *con exceso de adorno*) over-elaborate, fussy
historiador(a) SM/F [1] (= *estudioso*) historian ► **historiador(a) de arte** art historian
[2] (= *cronista*) chronicler, recorder
historia-ficción SF historical novels *pl*
historial Ⓐ ADJ historical
Ⓑ SM [1] (*en archivo*) [*de acontecimiento*] record; [*de persona*] curriculum vitae, c.v., résumé (*EEUU*)
[2] (*Med*) case history
[3] (*tb* **~ de ventas**) sales history
historiar ▸conjug 1b◂ VT [1] [*escritor*] to write the history of; [*libro*] to tell the history of, recount the history of; **este desarrollo cultural es historiado en una nueva obra** the history of this cultural development is recorded in a new book
[2] (*Arte*) to depict
historicismo SM historicism
historicista ADJ historicist
histórico/a Ⓐ ADJ [1] (= *de la historia*) [*perspectiva, contexto, investigación*] historical; **una película basada en hechos ~s** a film based on historical facts; **las novelas históricas son mis preferidas** I'm particularly keen on historical novels; **el patrimonio ~ del país** the country's heritage
[2] (= *importante*) [*acontecimiento, encuentro*] historic; [*récord*] all-time; **este es un momento ~** this is a historic moment; **el centro** *o* **casco ~ de la ciudad** the historic city centre; **el dólar marcó un nuevo mínimo ~ frente al yen** the dollar hit an all-time low against the yen
[3] [*miembro, socio*] (= *de hace tiempo*) long-serving; (= *desde el principio*) founder; **los ~s fundadores del partido** the founding fathers of the party; **miembro ~** (*de hace tiempo*) long-serving member; (*desde el principio*) founder member
Ⓑ SM/F **el Atlético, uno de los ~s del fútbol español** Atlético, one of the oldest teams in Spanish football
historiero ADJ (*Cono Sur*) gossipy
historieta SF [1] (*con viñetas*) strip cartoon, comic strip
[2] (= *anécdota*) tale
historietista SMF strip cartoonist
historificar ▸conjug 1g◂ VT to consign to the history books
historiografía SF historiography (*frm*), writing of history
historiógrafo/a SM/F historiographer
histrión SM (*liter*) [1] (= *actor*) actor, player; (= *farsante*) playactor
[2] (= *bufón*) buffoon
histriónico ADJ histrionic
histrionismo SM [1] (*Teat*) acting, art of acting
[2] (= *oratoria*) histrionics *pl*
[3] (= *actores*) actors *pl*, theatre people *pl*
hita SF [1] (*Téc*) brad, headless nail
[2] = **hito**
hitita Ⓐ ADJ (*Hist*) Hittite, of/from Anatolia Ⓑ SMF (*Hist*) Hittite, native/inhabitant of Anatolia; **los ~s** the Hittites, the people of Anatolia
Ⓒ SM (*Ling*) Hittite
hitleriano ADJ Hitlerian
hito SM [1] (= *acontecimiento*) landmark, milestone; **es un ~ en nuestra historia** it is a landmark in our history; **esto marca un ~ histórico** this marks a historical milestone
[2] (= *señal*) (*para límites*) boundary post; (*para distancias*) milestone; (*Aut*) (= *cono*) cone, traffic cone; ✦***MODISMO*** **mirar a algn de ~ en ~** to stare at sb ► **hito kilométrico** kilometre stone
[3] (*Dep*) quoits
[4] (*Mil lit*) target; (*fig*) aim, goal; ✦***MODISMOS*** **a ~** fixedly; **dar en el ~** to hit the nail on the head; **mudar de ~** to change one's tactics
hizo *ver* **hacer**
hl ABR (= **hectolitro(s)**) hl
hm ABR (= **hectómetro(s)**) hm
Hna(s). ABR (= **Hermana(s)**) Sr(s)
Hno(s). ABR (= **Hermano(s)**) Bro(s)
hobby ['xobi] SM (*pl* **hobbys** ['xobis]) hobby

hocicada* SF **darse una ~ con la puerta** to bash one's face against the door*; **darse una ~ en el suelo** to fall flat on one's face

hocicar ▸conjug 1g◂ Ⓐ VT [*cerdo*] to root among; [*persona*] to nuzzle
Ⓑ VI 1 [*cerdo*] to root; [*persona*] to nuzzle
2 (*Náut*) to pitch
3 (= *caer*) to fall on one's face
4 (= *enfrentarse*) to run into trouble, come up against it
5 (†) [*amantes*] to pet; **~ con** o **en** to put one's nose against, put one's nose into

hocico SM 1 [*de animal*] snout, nose
2 [*de persona*] (= *cara*) mug*; (= *nariz*) snout*; **caer de ~s** to fall (flat) on one's face; **cerrar el ~‡** to shut one's trap‡, belt up‡; **dar de ~s contra algo** to bump o walk into sth; ✦*MODISMOS* **estar de ~s** to be in a bad mood; **meter el ~** to meddle, poke one's nose in; **poner ~** to scowl; **torcer el ~** to make a (wry) face, look cross

hocicón* ADJ (*Andes*) angry, cross

hocicudo* ADJ (*Andes, Caribe*) (= *con mala cara*) scowling; (= *de mal humor*) grumpy*

hociquear ▸conjug 1a◂ VT, VI = **hocicar**

hociquera SF (*Andes, Caribe*) muzzle

hockey ['oki, 'xoki] SM hockey, field hockey (*EEUU*) ► **hockey sobre hielo** ice hockey, hockey (*EEUU*) ► **hockey sobre hierba** hockey ► **hockey sobre patines** roller hockey

hodierno†† ADJ (= *diariamente*) daily; (= *frecuente*) frequent

hogaño†† ADV (= *este año*) this year; (= *actualmente*) these days, nowadays

hogar SM 1 (= *casa*) home; **dejó el ~ familiar a los veinte años** he left home at the age of twenty; **artículos del** o **para el ~** household goods; **labores del ~** housework; **se han quedado sin ~** they have become homeless; **~, dulce ~** home, sweet home ► **hogar conyugal** conjugal home ► **hogar de acogida** (*para huérfanos, refugiados*) home ► **hogar de ancianos** old folk's home, old people's home ► **hogar del pensionista** senior citizens' social club
2 (= *chimenea*) hearth (*liter*); **se sentaron al calor del ~** they sat around the fire; **se recuperó al calor del ~** he recuperated in the comfort of his own home
3 (*Téc*) furnace; (*Ferro*) firebox
4 (*Esp Educ*) home economics

hogareño ADJ [*cocina*] home *antes de s*; [*ambiente*] homely; [*persona*] home-loving

hogaza SF large loaf

hoguera SF 1 (= *fogata*) bonfire; **la casa estaba hecha una ~** the house was ablaze, the house was an inferno; → SAN JUAN
2 (*Hist*) stake; **murió en la ~** he was burned at the stake

hoja SF 1 (*Bot*) [*de árbol, planta*] leaf; [*de hierba*] blade; **de ~ ancha** broad-leaved; **de ~ caduca** deciduous; **de ~ perenne** evergreen; **la ~** (*LAm*‡) pot*, hash* ► **hoja de parra** fig leaf
2 [*de papel*] leaf, sheet; (= *página*) page; (= *formulario*) form, document; **~s sueltas** loose sheets, loose-leaf paper *sing*; **volver la ~** (*lit*) to turn the page; (= *cambiar de tema*) to change the subject; (= *cambiar de actividad*) to turn over a new leaf; ✦*MODISMO* **doblar la ~** to change the subject ► **hoja de cálculo** spreadsheet ► **hoja de cumplido** compliments slip ► **hoja de embalaje** packing-slip ► **hoja de guarda** flyleaf ► **hoja de inscripción** registration form ► **hoja de pedido** order form ► **hoja de reclamación** complaint form ► **hoja de ruta** waybill ► **hoja de servicio(s)** record (of service) ► **hoja de trabajo** (*Inform*) worksheet ► **hoja de vida** (*Andes*) curriculum vitae, résumé (*EEUU*), CV ► **hoja electrónica** spreadsheet ► **hoja informativa** leaflet, handout ► **hoja parroquial** parish magazine ► **hoja volante, hoja volandera** leaflet, handbill
3 (*Téc*) [*de metal*] sheet; [*de espada, patín*] blade ► **hoja de afeitar** razor blade ► **hoja de estaño** tinfoil ► **hoja de lata** tin, tinplate ► **hoja plegadiza** flap (*of table etc*)
4 [*de puerta, de madera*] leaf; [*de cristal*] sheet, pane
5 ► **hoja de tocino** side of bacon, flitch

hojalata SF tin, tinplate; (*LAm*) corrugated iron

hojalatada SF (*Méx Aut*) panel beating

hojalatería SF 1 (= *obra*) tinwork
2 (= *establecimiento*) tinsmith's, tinsmith's shop
3 (*LAm*) (= *objetos*) tinware

hojalaterío SM (*Andes, CAm, Méx*) tinware

hojalatero/a SM/F tinsmith

hojaldre SM, **hojalda** SF (*LAm*), **hojaldra** SF (*LAm*) puff pastry

hojarasca SF 1 (= *hojas*) dead leaves *pl*, fallen leaves *pl*
2 (*frm*) (*al hablar*) empty verbiage, waffle*

hojear ▸conjug 1a◂ Ⓐ VT 1 (= *pasar las hojas de*) to turn the pages of, leaf through
2 (= *leer rápidamente*) to skim through, glance through
Ⓑ VI 1 (*Méx Bot*) to put out leaves
2 (*CAm, Méx Agr*) to eat leaves
3 [*superficie*] to scale off, flake off

hojerío SM (*CAm*) leaves, foliage

hojoso ADJ leafy

hojuela SF 1 (*Bot*) leaflet, little leaf
2 (= *lámina*) [*de cereal, pintura*] flake; [*de metal*] foil, thin sheet ► **hojuela de estaño** tinfoil
3 (*Culin*) pancake; (*Caribe, Méx*) puff pastry

hola EXCL hello!, hullo!, hi!*

holán SM 1 (= *tejido*) cambric, fine linen
2 (*Méx*) (= *volante*) flounce, frill

Holanda SF Holland

holandés/esa Ⓐ ADJ Dutch, of/from Holland
Ⓑ SM/F native/inhabitant of Holland; **los holandeses** the people of Holland, the Dutch; **el ~ errante** the Flying Dutchman
Ⓒ SM (*Ling*) Dutch

holandesa SF (*Tip*) quarto sheet

holding ['xoldin] SM (*pl* **holdings** ['xoldin]) holding company

holgadamente ADV 1 (= *ampliamente*) loosely, comfortably; **caben ~** they fit in easily, they go in with room to spare; **ganaron las elecciones ~** they won the elections easily o comfortably
2 (= *cómodamente*) **vivir ~** to live comfortably, be comfortably off

holgado ADJ 1 [*ropa*] (= *suelto*) loose, comfortable, baggy; **demasiado ~** too big
2 (= *amplio*) roomy; **así quedará el cuarto más ~** this will make more space in the room; **consiguieron una victoria holgada** they won easily o comfortably
3 (= *cómodo*) comfortably off, well-to-do; **vida holgada** comfortable life, life of ease

holganza SF (*frm*) 1 (= *inactividad*) idleness; (= *descanso*) rest; (= *ocio*) leisure, ease
2 (= *diversión*) amusement, enjoyment

holgar ▸conjug 1h, 1l◂ Ⓐ VI 1 (= *descansar*) to rest, take one's ease
2 (= *no trabajar*) to be idle, be out of work
3 (*frm*) [*objeto*] to lie unused
4 (*frm*) (= *sobrar*) to be unnecessary, be superfluous; **huelga decir que …** it goes without saying that …; **huelga toda protesta** no protest is necessary, it is not necessary to protest
5 (= *estar contento*) **huelgo de saberlo** I'm delighted to hear it
Ⓑ **holgarse** VPR (*frm*) to amuse o.s., enjoy o.s.; **~se con algo** to take pleasure in sth; **~se con una noticia** to be pleased about a piece of news; **~se de que …** to be pleased that …, be glad that …

holgazán/ana Ⓐ ADJ idle, lazy
Ⓑ SM/F idler, loafer, layabout*

holgazanear ▸conjug 1a◂ VI to laze around, loaf about

holgazanería SF laziness, loafing

holgazanitis SF INV (*hum*) congenital laziness, work-shyness

holgorio SM = **jolgorio**

holgura SF 1 (= *anchura*) (*Cos*) looseness, fullness; (*Mec*) play, free movement
2 (= *bienestar*) comfortable living; **vivir con ~** to live comfortably
3 (†) (= *goce*) enjoyment; (= *alegría*) merriment, merrymaking

hollar ▸conjug 1l◂ VT (*frm*) 1 (= *pisar*) to tread, tread on
2 (= *pisotear*) to trample down
3 (= *humillar*) to humiliate

hollejo SM (*Bot*) skin, peel

hollín SM soot

holliniento ADJ, **hollinoso** ADJ sooty, covered in soot

holocausto SM 1 (*Hist*) **el Holocausto** the Holocaust
2 (= *desastre*) ► **holocausto nuclear** nuclear holocaust
3 (*Rel*) (= *sacrificio*) burnt offering, sacrifice

holografía SF holograph

holograma SM hologram

hombracho SM, **hombrachón** SM hulking great brute, big tough fellow

hombrada SF manly deed, brave act; **¡vaya ~** (*iró*) how brave!

hombradía SF manliness, courage, guts*

hombre Ⓐ SM 1 (= *varón adulto*) man; (= *especie humana*) mankind; **¡ven aquí si eres ~!** come over here if you're a real man!; **ayúdale, que el ~ ya no puede más** help him, the poor man's exhausted; **es otro ~ desde que se casó** he's been a different man since he got married; **es ~ de pocas palabras** he is a man of few words; **¡~ al agua!** man overboard!; **el abominable ~ de las nieves** the abominable snowman; **creerse muy ~**: **se cree muy ~** he thinks he's a real hard man; **pobre ~**: **el pobre ~ se quedó sin nadie** the poor man o poor devil ended up all alone; **no le hagas caso, es un pobre ~** don't take any notice, he's just a sad little man*; ✦*MODISMOS* **como un solo ~**: **contestaron**

como un solo ~ they answered with one voice; **desde que el ~ es ~** always, since the year dot; **hablar de ~ a ~** to talk man to man; **ser un ~ de pelo en pecho** to be a real man, be a he-man; **ser un ~ hecho y derecho** to be a grown man; **si lo compras, me haces un ~*** if you buy it, you'll be doing me a big favour; ✦*REFRÁN* **el ~ propone y Dios dispone** man proposes, God disposes ► **hombre blanco** white man ► **hombre bueno** honest man, good man ► **hombre de armas** man-at-arms ► **hombre de bien** honest man, good man ► **hombre de confianza** right-hand man ► **hombre de estado** statesman ► **hombre de la calle**: **el ~ de la calle no entiende el problema** the average person can't understand the problem ► **hombre de las cavernas** caveman ► **hombre del día** man of the moment ► **hombre de letras** man of letters ► **hombre de leyes** lawyer, attorney (-at-law) (*EEUU*) ► **hombre del saco** bogeyman ► **hombre del tiempo** weatherman ► **hombre de mar** seafaring man, seaman ► **hombre de mundo** man of the world ► **hombre de negocios** businessman ► **hombre de paja** stooge* ► **hombre de pro**, **hombre de provecho** worthy *o* good man ► **hombre fuerte**: **el ~ fuerte del partido** the strong man of the party ► **hombre lobo** werewolf ► **hombre medio**: **el ~ medio** the man in the street, the average person ► **hombre mosca** trapeze artist ► **hombre muerto**: **¡si no te rindes eres ~ muerto!** surrender or you're a dead man! ► **hombre mundano** man-about-town ► **hombre orquesta** one-man band

2 (= *miembro de ejército, equipo*) man

Ⓑ EXCL **—¿me haces un favor? —sí, ~** "would you do me a favour?" — "(yes) of course"; **—¿vendrás? —¡~ claro!** "are you coming?" — "you bet!"; **¡venga, ~, haz un esfuerzo!** come on, make an effort!; **¡~, no me vengas con eso!** oh please *o* oh come on, don't give me that!; **~, yo creo que ...** well, I think that ...; **¡~, Pedro! ¿qué tal?** hey, Pedro! how's things?; **¡vaya, ~, qué mala suerte has tenido!** dear oh dear, what terrible luck!

hombre-anuncio SM (*pl* **hombres-anuncio**) sandwich-board man

hombrear[1] ▸conjug 1a◂ VI [*joven*] to act grown-up, play the man; [*hombre*] to act tough

hombrear[2] ▸conjug 1a◂ Ⓐ VT 1 (= *empujar*) to shoulder, push with one's shoulder

2 (*Andes, Cono Sur, Méx*) (= *ayudar*) to help, lend a hand to

Ⓑ VI **~ con algn** to try to keep up with sb, strive to equal sb

Ⓒ **hombrearse** VPR = **B**

hombrecillo SM 1 (= *persona*) little man, little fellow

2 (*Bot*) hop

hombre-gol SM (*pl* **hombres-gol**) striker who can score goals

hombre-lobo SM (*pl* **hombres-lobo**) werewolf

hombre-masa SM (*pl* **hombres-masa**) ordinary man, man in the street

hombre-mito SM (*pl* **hombres-mito**) man who is a myth in his own lifetime

hombre-mono SM (*pl* **hombres-mono**) ape-man

hombrera SF 1 (*Cos*) (= *almohadilla*) shoulder pad; (= *tirante*) shoulder strap

2 (*Mil*) epaulette

hombre-rana SM (*pl* **hombres-rana**) frogman

hombretón SM big strong fellow

hombría SF manliness ► **hombría de bien** honesty, uprightness

hombrillo SM (*Caribe Aut*) hard shoulder, berm (*EEUU*)

hombro SM shoulder; **a ~s** on one's shoulders; **¡armas al ~!** ◊ **¡sobre el ~ armas!** shoulder arms!; **cargar algo sobre los ~s** to shoulder sth; **echarse algo al ~** to shoulder sth, take sth upon o.s.; **en ~s**: **sacar a algn en ~s** to carry sb out on their shoulders; **el vencedor salió en ~s** the victor was carried out shoulder-high; **encogerse de ~s** to shrug one's shoulders, shrug; **enderezar los ~s** to square one's shoulders, straighten up; ✦*MODISMOS* **arrimar el ~** to put one's shoulder to the wheel, lend a hand; **~ con ~** shoulder to shoulder; **mirar a algn por encima del ~** to look down on sb, look down one's nose at sb; **poner el ~** to put one's shoulder to the wheel, lend a hand

hombruno ADJ mannish, butch*

homenaje Ⓐ SM 1 (= *tributo*) tribute; **en ~ a algn** in honour of sb; **rendir** *o* **tributar ~ a** to pay a tribute to, pay homage to; **rendir el último ~** to pay one's last respects

2 (= *celebración*) celebration, gathering (*in honour of sb*)

3 (*LAm*) (= *regalo*) gift, favour, favor (*EEUU*)

Ⓑ ADJ INV **una cena-~ para don Manuel** a dinner in honour *o* (*EEUU*) honor of don Manuel; **un concierto-~ para el compositor** a concert in honour *o* (*EEUU*) honor of the composer; **libro-~** homage volume; **partido-~** benefit match, testimonial game

homenajeado/a SM/F **el ~** the person being honoured *o* (*EEUU*) honored, the guest of honour *o* (*EEUU*) honor

homenajear ▸conjug 1a◂ VT to honour, honor (*EEUU*), pay tribute to

homeópata SMF homeopath

homeopatía SF homeopathy

homeopático ADJ homeopathic

homérico ADJ Homeric

Homero SM Homer

homicida Ⓐ ADJ homicidal; **el arma ~** the murder weapon

Ⓑ SMF murderer/murderess

homicidio SM (= *intencionado*) murder, homicide (*frm*); (= *involuntario*) manslaughter ► **homicidio frustrado** attempted murder

homilía SF homily

homínido SM hominid

homoerótico ADJ homo-erotic

homofobia SF homophobia

homofóbico ADJ homophobic

homófobo/a Ⓐ ADJ homophobic

Ⓑ SM/F homophobe

homogeneidad SF homogeneity

homogeneización SF levelling down, leveling down (*EEUU*), equalization

homogeneizante, **homogeneizador** Ⓐ ADJ homogenizing; **una tendencia ~** a tendency for homogenization

Ⓑ SM homogenizer

homogeneizar ▸conjug 1f◂ VT, **homogenizar** ▸conjug 1f◂ VT to homogenize, level down, equalize

homogéneo ADJ homogeneous

homógrafo SM homograph

homologable ADJ equivalent (**a, con** to), comparable (**a, con** to)

homologación SF 1 (= *aprobación*) official approval; **el nuevo medicamento ha recibido la ~ de la UE** the new drug has received EU approval, the new drug has been licensed by the EU

2 (= *equiparación*) **le han denegado la ~ del título** they refused to recognize her qualification as equivalent; **favorecía la ~ de lo popular y lo culto** he was in favour of equal status for popular and high culture

3 (*Dep*) ratification, recognition

homologado ADJ officially approved

homologar ▸conjug 1h◂ VT 1 (= *aprobar*) to approve officially, sanction

2 (= *equiparar*) to bring into line, standardize

3 (*Dep*) [+ *récord*] to ratify, recognize

homólogo/a Ⓐ ADJ equivalent (**de** to)

Ⓑ SM/F counterpart, opposite number

homónimo Ⓐ ADJ homonymous

Ⓑ SM 1 (*Ling*) homonym

2 (= *tocayo*) namesake

homosexual ADJ, SMF homosexual

homosexualidad SF, **homosexualismo** SM homosexuality

honda SF (*de cuero*) sling; (*elástica*) catapult, slingshot (*EEUU*)

hondear[1] ▸conjug 1a◂ VT (*Náut*) (= *sondear*) to sound; (= *descargar*) to unload

hondear[2] ▸conjug 1a◂ VT (*LAm*) to hit with a catapult *o* (*EEUU*) slingshot

hondo Ⓐ ADJ 1 (= *profundo*) deep; **plato ~** soup plate; **en lo más ~ de la piscina** at the deep end (of the pool); **la hirió en lo más ~ de su ser** he wounded her to the depths of her being, she was cut to the quick

2 (= *intenso*) deep, profound; **con ~ pesar** with deep *o* profound sorrow

Ⓑ ADV **respirar ~** to breathe deeply

Ⓒ SM **el ~** the depth(s) *pl*

hondón SM 1 [*de taza, valle*] bottom

2 [*de espuela*] footrest

3 [*de aguja*] eye

hondonada SF 1 (= *valle*) hollow, dip

2 (= *barranco*) gully, ravine

hondura SF 1 (= *profundidad*) depth, profundity (*frm*)

2 (= *lugar*) depth, deep place; ✦*MODISMO* **meterse en ~s** to get out of one's depth, get into deep water

Honduras SF Honduras ► **Honduras Británica** (*Hist*) British Honduras

hondureñismo SM *word or phrase peculiar to Honduras*

hondureño/a Ⓐ ADJ of/from Honduras

Ⓑ SM/F native/inhabitant of Honduras; **los ~s** the people of Honduras

honestamente ADV 1 (= *sinceramente*) honestly; **dime ~ lo que piensas** tell me honestly what you think

2 (= *honradamente*) honourably, honorably (*EEUU*); **cumple ~ con su deber** she carries out her duty honourably; **se comportó ~ y nos devolvió lo nuestro** he did the decent

thing and gave us back what was rightly ours
3 (= *decentemente*) decently

honestidad SF 1 (= *sinceridad*) honesty; **te diré con ~ lo que pienso** I'll tell you honestly what I think
2 (= *honradez*) honour, honor (*EEUU*); **puso en duda la ~ del presidente** he called into question the president's honour
3 (= *decencia*) decency

honesto ADJ 1 (= *sincero*) honest; **sé ~ y dime lo que piensas** be honest and tell me what you think
2 (= *honrado*) honourable, honorable (*EEUU*); **hay pocos políticos ~s** there are very few honourable politicians; **es muy ~ y sabe reconocer sus errores** he's very honest and is able to recognize his mistakes
3 (= *decente*) decent

hongkonés/esa, **hongkongués/esa** Ⓐ ADJ of/from Hong Kong
Ⓑ SM/F native/inhabitant of Hong Kong; **los hongkoneses** the people of Hong Kong

hongo SM 1 (*Bot*) fungus
2 (*Med*) fungal growth; **tengo ~s en los pies** I have athlete's foot, I have a fungal growth on my feet
3 (= *seta*) (*comestible*) mushroom; (*venenoso*) toadstool; **un enorme ~ de humo** an enormous mushroom cloud of smoke; ✦*MODISMO* **crecen** *o* **proliferan como ~s** they sprout up like mushrooms
4 (= *sombrero*) bowler hat, derby (*EEUU*)

honkonés/esa ADJ, SM/F = **hongkonés**

Honolulú SM Honolulu

honor SM 1 (= *cualidad*) honour, honor (*EEUU*); **en ~ a la verdad** to be fair; **en ~ de algn** in sb's honour; **hacer ~ a** to honour; **hacer ~ a su fama** to live up to it's *etc* reputation; **hacer ~ a un compromiso** to honour a pledge; **hacer ~ a su firma** to honour one's signature; **tener el ~ de hacer algo** to have the honour of doing sth, be proud to do sth
► **honor profesional** professional etiquette
2 **honores** honours, honors (*EEUU*); **sepultar a algn con todos los ~es militares** to bury sb with full military honours; **hacer los ~es de la casa** to do the honours of the house; **hacer los debidos ~es a una comida** to do full justice to a meal
3 (= *gloria*) glory; **Antonio Machado, ~ de esta ciudad** Antonio Machado, who is this city's claim to fame
4 [*de mujer*] honour, honor (*EEUU*), virtue

honorabilidad SF 1 (= *cualidad*) honourableness (*frm*), honour, honor (*EEUU*), worthiness
2 (= *persona*) distinguished person

honorable ADJ honourable, honorable (*EEUU*), worthy

honorario ADJ honorary, honorific

honorarios SMPL fees, professional fees, charges

honorífico ADJ honourable, honorable (*EEUU*); **cargo ~** honorary post; **mención honorífica** honourable mention

honra SF 1 (= *orgullo*) honour, honor (*EEUU*), pride; **tener algo a mucha ~** to be proud of sth, consider sth an honour; **tener a mucha ~ hacer algo** to be proud to do sth, consider it an honour to do sth; **¡y a mucha ~!** and proud of it! ► **honra personal** personal honour
2 (†) (= *virginidad*) honour, honor (*EEUU*), virtue
3 ► **honras fúnebres** funeral rites, last honours; *ver tb* **atentado B**

honradamente ADV 1 (= *honestamente*) honestly
2 (= *honorablemente*) honourably, honorably (*EEUU*), uprightly

honradez SF 1 (= *honestidad*) honesty
2 (= *integridad*) uprightness, integrity, honourableness (*frm*)

honrado ADJ 1 (= *honesto*) honest; **hombre ~** honest man, decent man
2 (= *honorable*) honourable, honorable (*EEUU*), upright

honrar ▸conjug 1a◂ Ⓐ VT 1 (= *enorgullecer*) to honour, honor (*EEUU*); **un gesto que le honra** a gesture to be proud of
2 (= *respetar*) to honour, honor (*EEUU*), revere (*frm*)
3 (*Com*) to honour, honor (*EEUU*)
Ⓑ **honrarse** VPR **~se con algo** to be honoured *o* (*EEUU*) honored by sth; **me honro con su amistad** I am honoured by his friendship, I am privileged to be his friend; **~se de hacer algo** to be honoured to do sth, consider it an honour to do sth

honrilla SF ✦*MODISMO* **por la negra ~** out of concern for what people will say, for the sake of appearances

honrosamente ADV honourably, honorably (*EEUU*)

honroso ADJ 1 (= *honorable*) honourable, honorable (*EEUU*)
2 (= *respetable*) respectable; **es una profesión honrosa** it is a respectable profession

hontanar SM spring, group of springs

hopa[1] SF cassock

hopa[2] EXCL 1 (*Cono Sur*) (= *¡deja!*) stop it!, that hurts!
2 (*Andes, CAm, Méx*) (= *saludo*) hullo!
3 (*Arg*) (*a animales*) whoa!

hopo[1] ['xopo] SM (fox's) brush, tail

hopo[2] EXCL out!, get out!

hora SF 1 (= *periodo de tiempo*) hour; **el viaje dura una ~** the journey lasts an hour; **durante dos ~s** for two hours; **dos ~s de reloj** two hours exactly; **esperamos ~s** we waited for hours; **ocho euros la ~** eight euros an hour; **echar ~s** to put the hours in; **media ~** half an hour; **la media ~ del bocadillo** half-hour break at work, ≈ tea break; **por ~s** by the hour; **trabajar por ~s** to work on an hourly basis *o* by the hour; **sueldo por ~** hourly wage; **asistenta por ~s** daily (help)
► **horas de comercio** business hours
► **horas de consulta** opening hours (*of surgery*) ► **horas de mayor audiencia** (*TV*) prime time *sing* ► **horas de oficina** business hours, office hours ► **horas de trabajo** working hours ► **horas de visita** visiting hours ► **horas de vuelo** (*Aer*) flying time *sing*; (*fig*) (= *experiencia*) experience *sing*; (*fig*) (= *antigüedad*) seniority *sing* ► **horas extra**, **horas extraordinarias** overtime *sing*; **hacer ~s (extra)** to work overtime ► **horas libres** free time *sing*, spare time *sing* ► **horas muertas** dead period *sing*; **se pasa las ~s muertas viendo la tele** he spends hour after hour watching telly
2 (= *momento*) 2·1 (*concreto*) time; **¿qué ~ es?** what time is it?, what's the time?; **¿tienes ~?** have you got the time?; **¿a qué ~?** (at) what time?; **¿a qué ~ llega?** what time is he arriving?; **¡la ~!** ◊ **¡es la ~!** time's up!; **llegar a la ~** to arrive on time; **a la ~ en punto** on the dot; **a la ~ justa** in the nick of time; **a la ~ de pagar ...** when it comes to paying ...; **a altas ~s (de la madrugada)** in the small hours; **a una ~ avanzada** at a late hour; **dar la ~** [*reloj*] to strike (the hour); **poner el reloj en ~** to set one's watch; **no comer entre ~s** not to eat between meals; **a estas ~s**: **a estas ~s ya deben de estar en París** they must be in Paris by now; **ayer a estas ~s** at this time yesterday
2·2 (*oportuno*) **buena ~**: **es buena ~ para empezar** it's a good time to start; **llegas a buena ~** you've arrived just in time; **en buena ~** at just the right time; **es ~ de hacer algo** it is time to do sth; **es ~ de irnos** it's time we went, it's time for us to go; **éstas no son ~s de llegar a casa** this is no time to get home, what sort of a time is this to get home?; **le ha llegado la ~** her time has come; **mala ~**: **es mala ~** it's a bad time; **en mala ~ se lo dije** I shouldn't have told her; **en la ~ de su muerte** at the moment of his death; **a primera ~** first thing in the morning; **a última ~** at the last moment, at the last minute; **dejar las cosas hasta última ~** to leave things until the last moment *o* minute; **cambios de última ~** last-minute changes; **noticias de última ~** last-minute news; **"última hora"** (*noticias*) "stop press"; **la ~ de la verdad** the moment of truth; **¡ya era ~!** and about time too!; **ya es** *o* **va siendo ~ de que te vayas** it is high time (that) you went, it is about time (that) you went; ✦*MODISMOS* **¡a buena(s) ~(s) (mangas verdes)!** it's too late now!; **¡a buenas ~s llegas!** this is a fine time for you to arrive!; **a buena ~(s) te vuelvo a prestar nada** that's the last time I lend you anything; **no ver la ~ de algo** to be hardly able to wait for sth, look forward impatiently to sth
► **hora bruja** witching hour ► **hora cero** zero hour; **desde las cero ~s** from midnight
► **hora de apertura** opening time ► **hora de cenar** dinnertime ► **hora de comer** (*gen*) mealtime; (*a mediodía*) lunchtime ► **hora de entrada**: **la ~ de entrada a la oficina** the time when we start work at the office ► **hora de las brujas** witching hour ► **hora de recreo** playtime, recess (*EEUU*) ► **hora de salida** [*de tren, avión, bus*] time of departure; [*de carrera*] starting time; [*de escuela, trabajo*] finishing time ► **hora estimada de llegada** estimated time of arrival ► **hora insular canaria** *local time in the Canary Islands* ► **hora judicial** *time when the courts start hearing cases* ► **hora local** local time ► **hora media de Greenwich** Greenwich mean time ► **hora oficial** official time, standard time ► **hora peninsular** *local time in mainland Spain* ► **hora pico** (*Méx*) rush hour ► **hora punta** [*del tráfico*] rush hour ► **horas punta** [*de electricidad, teléfono*] peak hours ► **hora suprema** one's last hour, hour of death ► **horas valle** off-peak times ► **hora universal** universal time
3 (*Educ*) period; **después de inglés tenemos una ~ libre** after English we have a free period ► **horas de clase** (= *horas lectivas*) teaching hours; (= *horas de colegio*) school hours; **van a reducir las ~s de clase** teach-

ing hours are going to be cut; **doy ocho ~s de clase** [*profesor*] I teach for eight hours; **en ~s de clase** during school hours
[4] (= *cita*) appointment; **dar ~ a algn** to give sb an appointment; **pedir ~** to ask for an appointment; **tener ~** to have an appointment; **tengo ~ para el dentista** I've got an appointment at the dentist's
[5] (*Rel*) **libro de ~s** book of hours ► **horas canónicas** canonical hours

horaciano ADJ Horatian

Horacio SM Horace

horadar ▸conjug 1a◂ VT (= *perforar*) to drill, perforate (*frm*); [+ *túnel*] to make

hora-hombre SF (*pl* **horas-hombre**) man-hour

horario (A) SM [1] [*de trabajo, trenes*] timetable; **el ~ de verano empieza hoy** summer time starts today, the clocks go forward today; **"horario de invierno: abierto solo mañanas"** "winter hours: open mornings only"; **llegar a ~** (*LAm*) to arrive on time, be on schedule ► **horario comercial** business hours *pl* ► **horario de atención al público** public opening hours *pl* ► **horario de máxima audiencia** (*TV*) peak viewing time, prime time ► **horario de oficina** office hours *pl* ► **horario de visitas** [*de hospital*] visiting hours *pl*; [*de médico*] surgery hours *pl* ► **horario flexible** flexitime ► **horario intensivo** continuous working day ► **horario partido** split shift(s)
[2] [*de reloj*] hour hand
(B) ADJ (= *cada hora*) hourly; *ver tb* **huso, señal 7**

horca SF [1] [*de ejecución*] gallows, gibbet; **condenar a algn a la ~** to condemn sb *o* send sb to the gallows
[2] (*Agr*) pitchfork
[3] [*de ajos*] string
[4] (*Caribe*) (= *regalo*) birthday present, *present given on one's saint's day*

horcadura SF fork (*of a tree*)

horcajadas SFPL **a ~** astride

horcajadura SF (*Anat*) crotch

horcajo SM [1] (*Agr*) yoke
[2] [*de árbol, río*] fork

horcar ▸conjug 1g◂ VT (*LAm*) = **ahorcar**

horchata SF [*de chufas*] tiger nut milk; [*de almendras*] almond milk

horchatería SF refreshment stall

horcón SM [1] (= *horca*) pitchfork
[2] (*para frutales*) forked prop
[3] (*LAm*) (*para techo*) prop, support

horda SF horde

hordiate SM barley water

horero SM (*Andes, Méx*) hour hand

horita* ADV (*esp Méx*) = **ahorita**

horizontal (A) ADJ horizontal
(B) SF horizontal position; **se desplaza en ~** it moves horizontally; **lleva una raya en ~ sobre el logotipo** it has a horizontal line on the logo; ✦**MODISMO coger** *o* **tomar la ~*** to crash out*

horizontalmente ADV horizontally

horizonte SM [1] (= *línea*) horizon; **la línea del ~** the horizon; **en el ~ del año 2000** around the year 2000
[2] **horizontes** (= *perspectivas*) **este descubrimiento abrirá nuevos ~s** this discovery will open up new horizons; **el partido tiene unos ~s muy estrechos** the party has limited horizons *o* ambitions

horma SF [1] (*Téc*) form, mould, mold (*EEUU*); [*de calzado*] last, shoetree; ✦**MODISMO encontrar(se) con la ~ de su zapato** to meet one's match ► **horma de sombrero** hat block
[2] (= *muro*) dry-stone wall

hormadoras SFPL (*Andes*) petticoat *sing*

hormiga SF [1] (*Entomología*) ant; ✦**MODISMO ser una ~*** (= *trabajador*) to be hard-working; (= *ahorrativo*) to be thrifty ► **hormiga blanca** white ant ► **hormiga león** antlion, antlion fly ► **hormiga obrera** worker ant ► **hormiga roja** red ant
[2] **hormigas** (*Med*) (= *picor*) itch *sing*; (= *hormigueo*) pins and needles

hormigón SM concrete ► **hormigón armado** reinforced concrete ► **hormigón pretensado** pre-stressed concrete

hormigonera SF concrete mixer

hormigonero ADJ concrete *antes de s*

hormiguear ▸conjug 1a◂ VI [1] [*parte del cuerpo*] (*al quedarse insensible*) to tingle; (= *hacer cosquillas*) to tickle; (= *picar*) to itch; **me hormiguea el pie** I've got pins and needles in my foot
[2] [*gente, animales*] to swarm, teem

hormigueo SM [1] (*en el cuerpo*) (*al quedarse insensible*) tingling; (= *cosquilleo*) ticklish feeling, pins and needles; (*al picar*) itch, itching
[2] (= *inquietud*) anxiety, uneasiness
[3] [*de gente, animales*] swarming

hormiguero (A) ADJ ant-eating; **oso ~** anteater
(B) SM [1] (*Entomología*) ants' nest, ant hill
[2] [*de gente*] **aquello era un ~** it was swarming with people

hormiguillo SM = **hormigueo 1,2**

hormiguita* SF **ser una ~** (= *muy trabajador*) to be hard-working, be always beavering away; (= *ahorrativo*) to be thrifty

hormona SF hormone ► **hormona de(l) crecimiento** growth hormone

hormonal ADJ hormonal

hormonarse ▸conjug 1a◂ VPR to have hormone treatment

hornacina SF niche, vaulted niche

hornada SF [1] [*de pan*] batch
[2] [*de estudiantes, políticos*] collection, crop

hornalla SF (*Cono Sur*) (= *horno*) oven; [*de estufa*] hotplate, burner (*EEUU*), ring

hornazo SM [1] (= *pastel*) Easter pie (*decorated with eggs*)
[2] [*de pasteles, pan*] batch

horneado SM cooking (time), baking (time)

hornear ▸conjug 1a◂ (A) VT to cook, bake
(B) VI to bake

hornero/a SM/F baker

hornillo SM [1] (*Culin*) (*gen*) cooker, stove; (*portátil*) portable stove ► **hornillo de gas** gas ring ► **hornillo eléctrico** hotplate, burner (*EEUU*)
[2] (*Téc*) small furnace
[3] [*de pipa*] bowl
[4] (*Mil, Hist*) mine

horno SM [1] (*Culin*) oven, stove; **¡esta casa es un ~!** it's like an oven in here!; **al ~** baked; **asar al ~** to bake; **meter un plato al ~ fuerte** to put a dish into a high oven; **resistente al ~** ovenproof; ✦**MODISMO no está el ~ para bollos** this is the wrong moment ► **horno de leña** wood-fired oven ► **horno microondas** microwave oven
[2] (*Téc*) furnace; (*para cerámica*) kiln; **alto(s) ~(s)** blast furnace *sing* ► **horno crematorio** crematorium ► **horno de cal** lime kiln ► **horno de fundición** smelting furnace ► **horno de ladrillos** brick kiln
[3] [*de pipa*] bowl

horóscopo SM horoscope; **leer el ~** to read one's stars *o* horoscope

horqueta SF [1] (*Agr*) pitchfork
[2] (*Bot*) fork of a tree
[3] (*LAm*) [*de camino*] fork

horquetear ▸conjug 1a◂ (A) VT (*Cono Sur*) [+ *oído*] to prick up; [+ *persona*] to listen suspiciously to
(B) VI [1] (*Méx*) (= *ahorcajarse*) to sit astride, straddle
[2] (*LAm*) (= *enramar*) to grow branches, put out branches

horquilla SF [1] (*para pelo*) hairpin, hairclip
[2] (*Agr*) (*para heno*) pitchfork; (*para cavar*) garden fork
[3] (*Mec*) (*en bicicleta*) fork; (*para carga*) yoke
[4] (*Telec*) rest, cradle
[5] [*de zanco*] footrest
[6] (*Com*) [*de salarios*] wage levels *pl*; [*de inflación*] bracket

horrarse ▸conjug 1a◂ VPR (*LAm Agr*) to abort

horrendo ADJ [1] (= *aterrador*) [*crimen*] horrific, ghastly*
[2] (= *horrible*) [*ropa, zapatos*] hideous, ghastly*; [*película, libro*] dreadful; [*frío, calor*] terrible, dreadful, awful; **tengo un hambre ~** I'm terribly hungry

hórreo SM raised granary

horrible ADJ [1] (= *espantoso*) [*accidente, crimen, matanza*] horrific; **una pesadilla ~** a horrible nightmare
[2] (= *feo*) [*persona, objeto, ropa, cuadro*] hideous; **ella es guapa pero su novio es ~** she's pretty but her boyfriend's hideous; **hizo un tiempo ~** the weather was horrible; **tienes una letra ~** your handwriting is terrible
[3] (= *malo, perverso*) horrible; **¡qué hombre tan ~!** what a horrible man!
[4] (= *insoportable*) terrible; **tengo un dolor de cabeza ~** I've got a terrible headache; **hizo un calor ~** it was terribly hot, the heat was terrible; **la conferencia fue un rollo ~*** the lecture was a real drag*

horriblemente ADV horribly, dreadfully

horripilante ADJ (= *espeluznante*) [*escena*] hair-raising, horrifying; [*persona*] creepy*, terrifying

horripilar ▸conjug 1a◂ (A) VT **~ a algn** to make sb's hair stand on end, horrify sb, give sb the creeps*
(B) **horripilarse** VPR to be horrified, be terrified; **era para ~se** it was enough to make your hair stand on end

horro ADJ (*frm*) [1] (= *exento*) free, exempt, enfranchised; **~ de** bereft of, devoid of
[2] (*Biol*) sterile

horror SM [1] (= *miedo*) horror (**a** of), dread (**a** of); **¡qué ~!** how awful *o* dreadful!, how ghastly!*; **tener ~ a algo** to have a horror of sth; **la fiesta fue un ~*** the party was ghastly*, the party was dreadful; **se dicen ~es de la cocina inglesa*** awful things are said about English cooking; **tener algo en ~** (*frm*) to detest sth, loathe sth

2 (= *acto*) atrocity, terrible thing; **los ~es de la guerra** the horrors of war
3 (*) (= *mucho*) **me gusta ~es** *o* **un ~** I love it; **hoy he trabajado un ~** today I worked awfully hard; **me duele ~es** it's really painful, it hurts like mad *o* like hell*; **se divirtieron ~es** they had a tremendous *o* fantastic time*; **ella sabe ~es** she knows a hell of a lot*

horrorizar ▸conjug 1f◂ Ⓐ VT to horrify, terrify
Ⓑ **horrorizarse** VPR to be horrified, be terrified

horrorosamente ADV 1 (= *aterradoramente*) horrifyingly
2 [*sufrir, doler*] horribly, frightfully
3 [*vestir, peinarse*] dreadfully, awfully

horroroso ADJ 1 (= *aterrador*) dreadful, ghastly*
2 (= *horrible*) [*ropa, peinado*] hideous, horrific; [*dolor*] terrible; [*película, libro*] dreadful; **tengo un sueño ~** I feel really sleepy

horrura SF 1 (= *suciedad*) filth, dirt
2 (= *basura*) rubbish, garbage (*EEUU*)

hortaliza SF 1 (= *verdura*) vegetable; **hortalizas** vegetables, garden produce
2 (*Méx*) (= *huerto*) vegetable garden

hortelano/a SM/F 1 (= *jardinero*) gardener
2 (*Com*) market gardener, truck farmer (*EEUU*)

hortensia SF hydrangea

hortera[1]* (*Esp*) Ⓐ ADJ INV 1 (= *de mal gusto*) [*decoración*] tacky*, tasteless, vulgar; [*persona*] lacking in taste; [*gustos*] terrible, crude
2 (†) (= *fingido*) fraud, sham
Ⓑ SMF **es un ~** his taste stinks*, he has lousy taste*

hortera[2]† SF wooden bowl

hortera[3]† SM shop-assistant, grocer's boy

horterada* SF (*Esp*) vulgarity; **ese vestido es una ~** that dress is a sight*

horterez* SF (*Esp*), **horterismo*** SM (*Esp*) coarseness, vulgarity

horterizar* ▸conjug 1f◂ (*Esp*) VT to coarsen, cheapen, make vulgar

hortícola Ⓐ ADJ horticultural, garden *antes de s*
Ⓑ SMF = **horticultor 1**

horticultor(a) SM/F 1 horticulturist, gardener
2 (*en vivero*) nurseryman

horticultura SF horticulture, gardening

horticulturista SMF horticulturalist, horticulturist

hortofrutícola ADJ fruit and vegetable *antes de s*

hortofruticultura SF fruit and vegetable growing

hosco ADJ 1 [*persona*] sullen, grim (*liter*)
2 [*tiempo, lugar, ambiente*] gloomy

hospedador SM (*Biol*) host

hospedaje SM (cost of) board and lodging

hospedar ▸conjug 1a◂ Ⓐ VT 1 (= *alojar*) to lodge, give a room to
2 (= *recibir*) to receive as a guest, entertain
Ⓑ **hospedarse** VPR to stay, lodge (**en** at)

hospedería SF 1 (= *posada*) hostelry, inn
2 (*en convento*) guest quarters *pl*

hospedero/a SM/F 1 (= *posadero*) landlord/landlady, innkeeper
2 (= *anfitrión*) host/hostess

hospiciano/a SM/F, **hospiciante** SMF (*LAm*) orphan (*living in an orphanage*)

hospicio SM 1 (*para niños*) orphanage
2 (*para pobres*) (*Hist*) poorhouse; (*Rel*) hospice
3 (*Cono Sur*) (*para ancianos*) old people's home

hospital SM hospital, infirmary ▸ **hospital de aislamiento** isolation hospital ▸ **hospital de campaña** field hospital ▸ **hospital de contagiosos** isolation hospital ▸ **hospital de día** day hospital ▸ **hospital de sangre** field dressing station

HOSPITAL

Uso del artículo

En inglés el uso del artículo delante de **hospital** depende del motivo por el que alguien haya acudido al centro hospitalario:

- Se traduce **al hospital** por **to hospital**, **en el hospital** por **in hospital** y **desde el hospital** por **from hospital** cuando alguien está o va a ser ingresado allí:

  La llevaron con urgencia al hospital como consecuencia de un infarto
  She was rushed to hospital following a heart attack
  Después del accidente estuvo tres meses en el hospital
  Following the accident, she was in hospital for three months

- Se traduce **al hospital** por **to the hospital**, **en el hospital** por **at the hospital** y **desde el hospital** por **from the hospital** cuando alguien va o está allí por otros motivos. También se emplea el artículo cuando se trata de consultas externas:

  Este lunes tengo que ir al hospital a una revisión
  I've got to go to the hospital on Monday for a check-up
  Mi hermana trabaja en el hospital
  My sister works at the hospital

Para otros usos y ejemplos ver la entrada.

hospitalariamente ADV hospitably

hospitalario ADJ 1 (= *acogedor*) hospitable
2 (*Med*) hospital *antes de s*; **estancia hospitalaria** stay in hospital; **atención hospitalaria** hospital treatment

hospitalidad SF hospitality

hospitalización SF hospitalization

hospitalizar ▸conjug 1f◂ Ⓐ VT to send to hospital, take to hospital, hospitalize (*frm*); **estuvo hospitalizado tres meses** he spent three months in hospital
Ⓑ **hospitalizarse** VPR (*LAm*) to go into hospital

hosquedad SF 1 [*de persona*] sullenness, grimness (*liter*)
2 [*del tiempo, lugar*] gloominess

hostal SM cheap hotel, boarding house

hostelería SF 1 (= *industria*) hotel trade, hotel business; **empresa de ~** catering company
2 (= *gerencia*) hotel management

hostelero/a Ⓐ ADJ catering *antes de s*; **sector ~** hotel and catering industry
Ⓑ SM/F innkeeper, landlord/landlady

hostería SF 1 (= *posada*) inn, hostelry
2 (*Cono Sur*) (= *hotel*) hotel

hostia SF 1 (*Rel*) host, consecrated wafer
2 (**) (= *golpe*) punch, bash*; (= *choque*) bang, bash*, smash; **dar de ~s a algn** to kick the shit out of sb**; **liarse a ~s** to get into a scrap*; **le pegué dos ~s** I walloped him a couple of times*
3 (**) (*como exclamación*) **¡hostia!** (*indicando sorpresa*) Christ almighty!‡, bloody hell!‡; (*indicando fastidio*) damn it all!
4 (**) (*como intensificador*) **de la ~**: **ese inspector de la ~** that bloody inspector‡; **había un tráfico de la ~** the traffic was bloody awful‡; **una tormenta de la ~** a storm and a half*; **ni ~**: **no entiendo ni ~** I don't understand a damn *o* bloody word of it*; **¡qué ~(s)!** (*para negar*) get away!, never!, no way!*; (*indicando rechazo*) bollocks!**; **¿qué ~s quieres?** what the hell do you want?*; **¡qué libros ni qué ~s!** books, my foot!* *o* my arse!**
5 (**) **mala ~**: **estar de mala ~** to be in a filthy* *o* shitty** mood; **tener mala ~** (= *mal carácter*) to have a nasty streak; (= *mala suerte*) to have rotten luck
6 (**) ✦**MODISMOS** **déjate de ~s** stop pissing around**, stop faffing around*; **echar ~s** to shout blue murder*, go up the wall*; **hacer un par como unas ~s** to muck it all up*; **ir a toda ~** to go like the clappers*; **no tiene media ~** he's no use at all, he's a dead loss*; **salió cagando** *o* **echando ~s** he shot out like a bat out of hell; **ser la ~**: **¡ese tío es la ~!** (*con admiración*) he's a hell of a guy!*; (*con enfado*) what a shit he is!**; **y toda la ~** and all the rest

hostiar** ▸conjug 1b◂ VT to wallop*, sock*, bash*

hostiazo** SM bash*, sock*

hostigamiento SM 1 (= *acoso*) harassment
2 (*con vara, látigo*) lashing, whipping

hostigar ▸conjug 1h◂ VT 1 (= *molestar*) to harass, plague, pester
2 (= *dar latigazos*) to lash, whip
3 (*LAm*) [+ *comida*] to surfeit, cloy

hostigoso ADJ (*Andes, Cono Sur*) [*comida*] sickly, cloying; [*persona*] annoying, tedious

hostil ADJ hostile

hostilidad SF 1 (= *cualidad*) hostility
2 (= *acto*) hostile act; **iniciar las ~es** to start hostilities

hostilizar ▸conjug 1f◂ VT (*Mil*) to harry, harass, worry

hostión** SM (= *golpe, choque*) bash*; **su padre le dio** *o* **pegó un buen ~** her father gave her a good walloping; **se dio** *o* **pegó un ~ contra el árbol** he smashed into a tree

hotel SM 1 (*Com*) hotel ▸ **hotel alojamiento** (*Cono Sur*), **hotel garaje** (*Méx*) *hotel where one pays by the hour*
2 (‡) (= *cárcel*) (*tb* **~ del Estado, ~ rejas**) nick‡, prison
3 (*Mil*) glasshouse‡

hotelería SF = **hostelería**

hotelero/a Ⓐ ADJ hotel *antes de s*; **la industria hotelera** the hotel trade
Ⓑ SM/F hotelkeeper, hotel manager/manageress, hotelier

hotelito SM (*gen*) small house; (*de vacaciones*) cottage, vacation retreat, second home

hoy ADV 1 (= *en este día*) today; **¿a qué día estamos ~?** what day is it today?; **~ hace un mes de su boda** their wedding was a month ago today; **de ~**: **en el correo de ~** in

today's post; **el día de ~** (*Esp*) this very day; **de ~ en adelante** from now on; **de ~ no pasa que le escriba** I'll write to him this very day; **está para llegar de ~ a mañana** he could arrive any day now; **desde ~** from now on; **de ~ en ocho días** a week today; **de ~ en quince días** today fortnight, a fortnight today; **hasta ~: eso me prometió, ¡y hasta ~!** that's what he promised me, and I've heard no more about it!; **~ mismo: —¿cuándo quieres empezar? —~ mismo** "when do you want to start?" — "today"; **por ~: por ~ hemos terminado** that's all for today; ✦***MODISMO*** **~ por ti, mañana por mí** you can do the same for me some time
2 (= *en la actualidad*) today, nowadays; **~ todo es mejor que antes** things are better today *o* nowadays than before; **la juventud de ~** the youth of today; **~ (en) día** nowadays; **~ por ~** at the present time, right now

hoya SF 1 (= *agujero*) pit, hole ► **hoya de arena** (*Golf*) bunker, sand trap (*EEUU*)
2 (= *tumba*) grave
3 (*Geog*) vale, valley; (*LAm*) [*de río*] riverbed, river basin
4 (*Agr*) seedbed

hoyada SF hollow, depression

hoyador SM (*LAm*) dibber, seed drill

hoyanco SM (*Méx Aut*) pothole, hole in the road

hoyar ▸conjug 1a◂ VT (*CAm, Caribe, Méx*) to make holes (*for sowing seeds*)

hoyito SM (*en la cara*) dimple

hoyo SM 1 (= *agujero*) hole; **en el ~ 18** (*Golf*) at the 18th hole
2 (= *hondura*) pit
3 (= *tumba*) grave
4 (*Med*) pockmark
5 (= *hueco*) hollow, cavity
6 ✦***MODISMO*** **irse al ~** (*Cono Sur**) to get into an awful jam*, face ruin; *ver tb* **muerto C2**

hoyuelo SM dimple

hoz SF 1 (*Agr*) sickle; **la ~ y el martillo** the hammer and sickle
2 (*Geog*) gorge, narrow pass, defile (*frm*)
3 ✦***MODISMO*** **de ~ y coz** wildly, recklessly

hozar ▸conjug 1f◂ VT [*cerdo*] to root in, root among

hros. ABR = **herederos**

hs ABR (= **horas**) h., hrs

hua... PREF *ver* **gua...**

huaca SF = **guaca**

huacalón ADJ (*Méx*) 1 (= *gordo*) fat
2 (= *de voz áspera*) gravel-voiced

huacarear‡ ▸conjug 1a◂ VI (*LAm*) to throw up*

huacha SF (*Andes*) washer

huachafería SF (*Andes*) 1 (= *gente*) middle-class snobs *pl*, social climbers *pl*
2 (= *actitud*) snobbery, airs and graces

huachafo/a (*Andes*) (A) ADJ = **cursi**
(B) SM/F middle-class snob, social climber
(C) SM (*Caribe*) funny man, comic

huacho (A) SM 1 (*Andes*) *section of a lottery ticket*
2 (*Méx**) *common soldier*
(B) ADJ (*Méx*) = **guacho A**

huaco (A) SM (*Andes Hist*) *ancient Peruvian pottery artefact*
(B) ADJ (*LAm*) (= *sin dientes*) toothless

huahua SF (*LAm*) = **guagua**

huaica SF (*Andes*) bargain sale

huaico SM (*Andes*) alluvium

huaipe SM (*Chile*) cotton waste

huáncar SM (*Andes*), **huáncara** SF (*Andes*) Indian drum

huaquero/a SM/F (*Andes*) = **guaquero**

huaraca SF (*Andes*) = **guaraca**

huarache SM (*Méx*) (= *sandalia*) sandal

huáscar* SM (*Chile*) water cannon truck (*used by police*)

huasicama SMF (*Andes*) Indian servant

huasipungo SM (*Andes Agr*) (Indian's) tied plot of land

huaso/a SM/F (*Chile*) = **guaso B**

huasteca SF **la Huasteca** *the region round the Gulf of Mexico*

huatal SM (*LAm*) = **guatal**

huave SMF (*Méx*) Huave Indian

huayco SM 1 (*Andes, Chile*) (= *alud*) landslide of mud and rock; *ver tb* **guaico**
2 (*Andes*) (= *matón a sueldo*) paid thug

huayno SM (*Andes, Chile*) *folk song and dance*; → CHICHA

hube *etc ver* **haber**

hucha SF 1 (*para ahorrar*) money box; (*para caridad*) collecting tin
2 (= *ahorros*) savings *pl*; **tener una buena ~** to have a nice little nest egg, have money laid by
3 (†) (= *arca*) chest

hueca‡ SF pansy‡, queer‡, fag (*EEUU*‡)

hueco (A) ADJ 1 [*árbol, tubo*] hollow; **una nuez hueca** an empty walnut shell; ✦***MODISMO*** **tener la cabeza hueca** to be empty-headed
2 [*lana, tierra*] soft
3 [*blusa, chaqueta*] loose
4 [*sonido*] hollow; [*voz*] booming, resonant
5 (= *insustancial*) [*palabras, promesas, retórica*] empty; **un discurso retórico y ~** a speech full of empty rhetoric
6 (= *pedante*) [*estilo, lenguaje*] pompous
7 [*persona*] (= *orgulloso*) proud; (= *engreído*) conceited, smug; **el niño se puso muy ~ cuando lo nombraron ganador** the boy was very proud when he was declared the winner; **la típica rubia hueca** (*pey*) the usual blonde bimbo*
(B) SM 1 (= *agujero*) (*en valla, muro*) hole; **se ha caído un pájaro por el ~ de la chimenea** a bird has fallen down the chimney; **el ~ del ascensor** the lift *o* (*EEUU*) elevator shaft; **el ~ de la escalera** the stairwell; **el ~ de la puerta** the doorway
2 (= *espacio libre*) space; (*entre árboles*) gap, opening; **en este ~ voy a poner la lavadora** I'm going to put the washing machine in this (empty) space; **no hay ni un ~ para aparcar** there isn't a single parking space; **el ~ que quedaba entre las dos mesas** the gap *o* space between the two tables; **sólo hay ~s en la primera fila** the only places *o* spaces are in the front row; **en su corazón no hay ~ para el rencor** there is no room in his heart for rancour; **hacer (un) ~ a algn** to make space for sb; **¿me haces un ~?** can you make some room for me?
3 (*en texto*) gap, blank
4 (*en mercado, organización*) gap; **en el mercado hay un ~ para una revista de este tipo** there is a gap in the market for this type of magazine; **abrirse** *o* **hacerse un ~** to carve *o* create a niche for oneself; **aspiran a abrirse un ~ en el mundo de la música pop** they are hoping to carve *o* create a niche for themselves in the pop world; **llenar** *u* **ocupar un ~** to fill a gap; **deja un ~ que será difícil llenar** he leaves a gap which will be hard to fill
5 (= *cavidad*) hollow; **el ~ de la mano** the hollow of the *o* one's hand; **suena a ~** it sounds hollow
6 (= *nicho*) recess, alcove
7 (= *en una empresa*) vacancy
8 [*de tiempo*] **en cuanto tenga un ~ hablará contigo** he will talk to you as soon as he has a gap in his schedule *o* as soon as he can fit you in; **hizo un ~ en su programa para recibirlos** he made space in his schedule to see them, he managed to fit them into his schedule
9 (*Méx*‡) (= *homosexual*) queer‡, faggot (*EEUU*‡)
10 (*Tip*) = **huecograbado**

huecograbado SM (*Tip*) photogravure

huela *etc ver* **oler**

huelán (*Cono Sur*) ADJ 1 (= *inmaduro*) (*gen*) immature, not fully developed; [*madera*] unseasoned; [*hierba*] withered; [*trigo*] unripe
2 **una persona huelana** a person who has come down in the world

huelebraguetas‡ SMF INV private eye*

hueleguisos* SMF INV (*Andes*) sponger*, scrounger*

huelehuele* SMF (*Caribe*) idiot

huelga SF 1 [*de trabajo*] strike, stoppage, walkout; **los obreros en ~** the workers on strike, the striking workers; **estar en ~** to be on strike; **declarar la ~** ◊ **declararse en ~** ◊ **hacer ~** ◊ **ir a la ~** ◊ **ponerse en ~** to go on strike, come out on strike ► **huelga (a la) japonesa** *industrial action characterized by overproduction by the workforce* ► **huelga de brazos caídos** sit-down strike ► **huelga de celo** work-to-rule, go-slow, slowdown (strike) (*EEUU*) ► **huelga de hambre** hunger strike ► **huelga de hostigamiento** guerrilla strike ► **huelga de pago de alquiler** rent strike ► **huelga de reglamento** work-to-rule, go-slow, slowdown (strike) (*EEUU*) ► **huelga general** general strike ► **huelga oficial** official strike ► **huelga patronal** lock-out ► **huelga por solidaridad** sympathy strike ► **huelga rotatoria** rotating strike ► **huelga salvaje** wildcat strike
2 (= *descanso*) rest, repose (*frm*)
3 (*Mec*) play, free movement

huelgo SM (*frm*) 1 (= *aliento*) breath; **tomar ~** to take breath, pause
2 (= *espacio*) room, space; **entra con ~** it goes in easily, it goes in with room to spare
3 (*Mec*) play, free movement

huelguear ▸conjug 1a◂ VI (*Andes*) to strike, be on strike

huelguismo SM strike mentality, readiness to strike

huelguista SMF striker

huelguístico ADJ strike *antes de s*; **movimiento ~** wave of strikes; **el panorama ~** the strike scene

huella SF 1 (*en el suelo*) (= *pisada*) footprint, footstep; [*de coche, animal*] track; **seguir las ~s de algn** to follow in sb's footsteps

► **huella dactilar**, **huella digital** fingerprint ► **huella genética** genetic fingerprint
2 (= *rastro*) trace; **sin dejar ~** without leaving a trace, leaving no sign; **se le notaban las ~s del sufrimiento** you could see the signs of her suffering
3 (= *impronta*) **el presidente dejó ~ inconfundible en el partido** the president left his unmistakable mark *o* stamp on the party; **aquello dejó una ~ imborrable** it left an indelible memory
4 (= *acto*) tread, treading
5 [*de escalera*] tread

huellear ▸conjug 1a◂ VT (*Andes*) to track, follow the trail of

huellero ADJ **perro ~** (*Andes*) tracker dog

huello†† SM *condition of the ground etc (for walking)*; **camino de buen ~** good road for walking; **camino de mal ~** bad road for walking, badly-surfaced road

Huelva SF Huelva

huemul SM (*Cono Sur*) southern Andean deer

huérfano/a Ⓐ ADJ 1 [*niño*] orphaned; **una niña huérfana de madre** a motherless child, a child that has lost her mother
2 (= *desprovisto*) **~ de** [+ *seguridad, protección*] devoid of; [+ *cariño, amor*] bereft of (*frm*), starved of
Ⓑ SM/F orphan

huero ADJ 1 [*palabras, acciones*] empty, sterile; **un discurso ~** an empty speech
2 [*huevo*] rotten
3 (*CAm, Méx*) = **güero**

huerta SF 1 (= *huerto*) vegetable garden, kitchen garden (*EEUU*)
2 (*Esp*) **la huerta murciana/valenciana** the fertile, irrigated region of Murcia/Valencia
3 (*Andes*) [*de cacao*] cocoa plantation

huertano/a Ⓐ ADJ (*Esp*) of/from the "huerta"
Ⓑ SM/F 1 (= *hortelano*) market gardener, truck farmer (*EEUU*)
2 (*Esp*) (= *habitante*) inhabitant of the "huerta"; (= *hortelano*) farmer (of the "huerta")

huertero/a SM/F (*LAm*) gardener

huerto SM [*de verduras*] kitchen garden; (*comercial*) (small) market garden, truck garden (*EEUU*); [*de árboles frutales*] orchard; (*en casa pequeña*) back garden; **el Huerto de los Olivos** the Mount of Olives; ✦*MODISMO* **llevarse a algn al ~*** (= *engañar*) to put one over on sb*, lead sb up the garden path*; (*a la cama*) to go to bed with sb, sleep with sb, go for a roll in the hay with sb*

huesa SF grave

huesear‡ ▸conjug 1a◂ VI (*LAm*) to beg

huesecillo SM small bone

huesería SM (*Andes*) unsaleable merchandise

huesillo SM (*Andes, Cono Sur*) sun-dried peach

huesista* SMF (*Méx*) *person with a soft job*

hueso SM 1 (*Anat*) bone; **sin ~** boneless; **una blusa de color ~** an off-white blouse; ✦*MODISMOS* **dar con los ~s en**: **dio con sus ~s en la cárcel** he landed *o* ended up in jail; **estar calado** *o* **empapado hasta los ~s** to be soaked to the skin; **estar en los ~s** to be nothing but skin and bone; **estar por los ~s de algn*** to be crazy about sb*; **no dejar ~ sano a algn** to pull sb to pieces; **pinchar en ~*** to come up against a brick wall; **ser un saco de ~s*** to be a bag of bones*; **la sin ~*** the tongue; **darle a la sin ~*** to talk a lot; **irse de la sin ~** ◊ **soltar la sin ~*** to shoot one's mouth off*; **tener los ~s molidos** to be dog-tired ► **hueso de santo** *filled roll of marzipan*
2 (*Bot*) stone, pit (*EEUU*); **aceitunas sin ~** pitted olives; ✦*MODISMOS* **ser un ~***: **las matemáticas son un ~** maths is a nightmare; **su profesor es un ~** her teacher is terribly strict; **ser un ~ duro de roer*** to be a hard nut to crack
3 (*CAm, Méx*) (= *sinecura*) government job, sinecure; (= *puesto cómodo*) soft job
4 (*Andes*) mule; ✦*MODISMO* **ser ~** to be stingy
5 ► **hueso colorado** (*Méx*) strong northerly wind

huesoso ADJ (*esp LAm*) bony, bone *antes de s*

huésped(a) Ⓐ SM/F 1 (= *invitado*) (*en casa, hotel*) guest; (*en pensión*) lodger, roomer (*EEUU*), boarder; ✦*MODISMO* **hacerse los dedos ~es**: **se le hacen los dedos ~es cada vez que oye hablar de dinero** he rubs his hands at the first mention of money
2 (= *anfitrión*) host/hostess
3 (††) (= *posadero*) innkeeper, landlord/landlady; ✦*MODISMO* **no contar con la ~a** to reckon without one's host
Ⓑ ADJ **ordenador ~** host computer; **hembra ~** host female

hueste SF (*liter*) 1 (= *ejército*) host (*liter*), army
2 (= *muchedumbre*) crowd, mass
3 (= *partidarios*) followers *pl*

huesudo ADJ bony, big-boned

hueva SF 1 (*tb* **~s**) (*Culin*) roe; (*Zool*) eggs, spawn *sing* ► **hueva de lisa** (*Méx*) cod roe ► **huevas de lumpo** German caviar *sing*
2 **huevas** (*Chile***) (= *testículos*) balls**

huevada SF 1 (*Andes, Cono Sur*‡) (= *comentario*) stupid remark; (= *acto*) stupid thing (to do); (= *idea*) crazy idea; **huevadas** (= *tonterías*) nonsense, rubbish*, crap**
2 (*LAm*) [*de huevos*] nest of eggs, clutch of eggs
3 **una ~**‡ (*como adv*) a hell of a lot*; **se divirtió una ~** he had a tremendous *o* fantastic time*

huevear* ▸conjug 1a◂ VI (*Chile*) to mess about*

huevera SF 1 (*para guardar huevos*) egg box
2 (‡) (= *suspensorio*) jockstrap

huevería SF *shop that specializes in selling eggs*

huevero ADJ egg *antes de s*; **industria huevera** egg industry

huevo SM 1 (*Biol, Culin*) egg; ✦*MODISMOS* **andar sobre ~s** to go very gingerly; **hacerle ~ a algo** (*CAm*‡) to face up to sth; **parecerse como un ~ a una castaña*** to be like chalk and cheese; **pensar en los ~s del gallo** (*Andes, CAm*) to be in a daydream; **poner algo a ~**: **nos lo han puesto a ~*** they've made it easy for us; **¡que te frían un ~!**‡ get knotted!‡; **ser como el ~ de Colón** to be simple, be easy ► **huevo a la copa** (*Andes, Chile*) boiled egg ► **huevo amelcochado** (*CAm*) (soft-)boiled egg ► **huevo cocido** hard-boiled egg ► **huevo crudo** raw egg ► **huevo de color** (*LAm*) brown egg ► **huevo de corral** free-range egg ► **huevo de Pascua** Easter egg ► **huevo de Paslama** (*CAm*) turtle's egg ► **huevo duro** hard-boiled egg ► **huevo en cáscara** (soft-)boiled egg ► **huevo escalfado** poached egg ► **huevo estrellado** fried egg ► **huevo fresco** freshly-laid egg, new-laid egg ► **huevo frito** fried egg ► **huevo moreno** brown egg ► **huevo pasado por agua** soft-boiled egg ► **huevos al plato** *fried egg in tomato sauce served with ham and peas* ► **huevos pericos**, **huevos revueltos** scrambled eggs ► **huevo tibio** (*Andes, CAm, Méx*) soft-boiled egg
2 (**) (= *testículo*) ball**; **—me debes diez euros —¡un ~!** "you owe me ten euros" — "bollocks!"**; ✦*MODISMOS* **estar hasta los ~s de algo** *o* **algn**: **estoy hasta los ~s de este niño** I've had a fucking bellyful of this kid**; **estar hasta los ~s de hacer algo**: **estoy hasta los ~s de estudiar** I'm fucking fed up with studying**; **se necesitan ~s para hacer eso** you need balls to do that**; **se me pusieron los ~s de corbata** it put the fear of God into me*; **no tuve ~s de contestarle** I didn't have the balls to answer back**; **tuve que hacerlo por ~s** I had to do it, I had no fucking choice**
3 **un ~**** (*como adv*) (= *mucho*) a hell of a lot‡; **le queremos un ~** we like him a hell of a lot‡; **sufrí un ~** I suffered like hell‡; **nos costó un ~ terminarlo** it was one hell of a job to finish it‡; **el ordenador me costó un ~** the computer cost me an arm and a leg*, the computer cost me a bomb*
4 (*Cos*) darning egg
5 (*LAm*) (= *vago*) idler, loafer; (= *imbécil*) idiot; (= *cobarde*) coward

huevón/ona‡ Ⓐ ADJ 1 (= *flojo*) lazy, idle
2 (*LAm*) (= *estúpido*) stupid, thick*
3 (= *lento*) slow
4 (*Chile*) (= *cobarde*) cowardly, chicken*, yellow*
Ⓑ SM/F (= *holgazán*) lazy sod**, skiver*, layabout*; (= *imbécil*) stupid idiot*, bloody fool‡

Hugo SM Hugh, Hugo

hugonote/a ADJ, SM/F Huguenot

hui... (*para palabras que en LAm se escriben así*) *ver tb* **gui..., güi...** *p.ej.* **huinche**; *ver* **güinche**

huida SF 1 (= *fuga*) escape, flight (*liter*); **tras la ~ del general** following the general's escape; **la ~ de Egipto** (*Biblia*) the flight from Egypt; **los refugiados abandonaron muchas de sus posesiones en la ~** the refugees abandoned many of their possessions when they fled; **no consiguieron evitar la ~ de los prisioneros** they were unable to prevent the prisoners from getting away *o* escaping, they were unable to prevent the prisoners' escape; **el plan es una ~ hacia adelante** the plan is a bit of a leap in the dark; **emprender la ~** to take flight
2 [*de capital, inversores*] flight
3 [*de un caballo*] bolt; *ver tb* **huido**

huidizo ADJ 1 (= *esquivo*) [*persona*] elusive; [*mirada*] evasive
2 (= *tímido*) shy, timid
3 (= *fugaz*) [*impresión, luz*] fleeting
4 (*Anat*) [*barbilla*] wispy; [*frente*] receding

huido/a Ⓐ ADJ 1 (= *escapado*) [*criminal*] fugitive; [*esclavo*] runaway; **los tres terroristas ~s** the three terrorists on the run, the three fugitive terrorists; **lleva más de un año ~ de la justicia** he has been a fugitive from justice *o* he has been on the run for over a year; **los rusos ~s del Palacio de Invierno** the Russians that had fled from the Winter Palace
2 (= *receloso*) elusive; **anda ~ desde que cerró el negocio** he's been rather elusive since he closed down the business; **ha estado muy ~ de la gente desde que se divorció**

he's been very wary of people since he got divorced
Ⓑ SM/F fugitive; *ver tb* **huida**

huilas* SFPL (*Chile*) (= *andrajos*) rags

huile SM (*Méx*) roasting grill

huilón ADJ (*Andes*) elusive

huincha SF (*Andes, Cono Sur*) = **güincha**

huipil SM (*CAm, Méx*) Indian regional dress *o* blouse

huir ▸conjug 3g◂ Ⓐ VI 1 (= *escapar*) to run away, flee (*liter*); **huyó despavorido cuando comenzaron los disparos** he ran away *o* (*liter*) fled in terror when the shooting started; **los ladrones huyeron en un vehículo robado** the robbers made their getaway *o* (*liter*) fled in a stolen vehicle; **huyeron a Chipre** they escaped *o* (*liter*) fled to Cyprus; **~ de** [+ *enemigo, catástrofe, pobreza*] to flee from; [+ *cárcel, peligro*] to escape from; [+ *familia*] to run away from; **los refugiados que huyeron de la guerra civil** the refugees who fled the civil war; **~ de su casa** [*refugiados, civiles*] to flee (from) one's home; [*adolescente*] to run away from home; **~ de la justicia** to fly from justice, fly from the law; **huyó del país** he fled the country
2 (= *evitar*) **~ de** [+ *protagonismo, publicidad, tópicos*] to avoid; [+ *calor, frío*] to escape, escape from; **huye de los periodistas como de la peste** she avoids journalists like the plague; **se metió en una iglesia huyendo del calor** he went into a church to escape (from) the heat; **se drogan para ~ de la realidad** they take drugs to escape (from) reality
3 (*frm*) [*tiempo*] to fly, fly by; **los años huyen sin darse uno cuenta** the years fly by without you realizing
Ⓑ VT (= *esquivar*) to avoid; **parece como si tu hijo te huyera** your son seems to be avoiding you
Ⓒ **huirse** VPR (*Méx*) to escape; **decidieron ~se** they decided to escape; **~se con algn** to escape with sb

huira SF (*Andes, Cono Sur*) 1 (= *cuerda*) rope; ✦**MODISMOS dar ~ a algn*** to thrash sb; **sacar las ~s a algn*** to beat sb up*
2 (= *cabestro*) halter, tether

huiro SM (*Andes, Cono Sur*) seaweed

huisache (*LAm*) Ⓐ SM (= *árbol*) species of acacia
Ⓑ SMF (= *leguleyo*) unqualified lawyer

huisachear ▸conjug 1a◂ VI (*CAm, Méx*) 1 (= *litigar*) to go to law, engage in litigation
2 (*) (= *ejercer sin título*) to practise law without a qualification

huisachería SF (*CAm, Méx*) 1 (= *tretas*) lawyer's tricks *pl*, legal intricacies *pl*
2 (= *ejercicio fraudulento*) *practice of law without a qualification*

huisachero SM (*CAm, Méx*) 1 (= *leguleyo*) shyster lawyer, unqualified lawyer
2 (= *plumífero*) scribbler, pen-pusher

huitlacoche SM (*CAm, Méx*) black mushroom

huizache SM (*CAm, Méx*) = **huisache**

hulado SM (*CAm*) 1 (= *tela*) oilskin, rubberized cloth
2 (= *capa*) oilskin

hula-hop [xula'xop] SM Hula-Hoop®

hular SM (*Méx*) rubber plantation

hule[1] SM 1 (= *goma*) rubber
2 (= *tela*) oilskin, oilcloth
3 (*CAm, Méx*) (= *árbol*) rubber tree
4 (*Méx**) (= *preservativo*) condom, rubber*

hule[2] SM (*Taur*) goring, row; ✦**MODISMO habrá ~** someone's going to get it*

hulear ▸conjug 1a◂ VI (*CAm*) to extract rubber

hulero/a Ⓐ ADJ (*CAm*) rubber *antes de s*
Ⓑ SM/F rubber tapper

hulla SF soft coal

hullera SF colliery, coalmine

hullero ADJ coal *antes de s*

huloso ADJ (*CAm*) rubbery, elastic

humanamente ADV 1 [*posible, comprensible*] humanly
2 (= *con humanidad*) humanely

humanar ▸conjug 1a◂ Ⓐ VT to humanize
Ⓑ **humanarse** VPR 1 (= *humanizarse*) to become more human
2 **~se a** + INFIN (*LAm*) to condescend to + *infin*
3 (*Rel*) [*Cristo*] to become man

humanidad SF 1 (= *género humano*) humanity, mankind
2 (= *benevolencia*) humanity, humaneness (*frm*)
3 (*) (= *gordura*) corpulence
4 **humanidades** (*Educ*) humanities

humanismo SM humanism

humanista SMF humanist

humanístico ADJ humanistic

humanitario/a Ⓐ ADJ 1 [*ayuda, labor, misión*] humanitarian
2 (= *benévolo*) humane
Ⓑ SM/F humanitarian

humanitarismo SM humanitarianism

humanización SF humanization

humanizador ADJ humanizing

humanizar ▸conjug 1f◂ Ⓐ VT to humanize, make more human
Ⓑ **humanizarse** VPR to become more human

humano Ⓐ ADJ 1 [*vida, existencia, derechos*] human; **ser ~** human being; ✦**REFRÁN equivocarse es ~** to err is human
2 (= *benévolo*) humane
3 (*Educ*) **ciencias humanas** humanities
Ⓑ SM human, human being

humanoide ADJ, SMF humanoid

humarasca SF (*CAm*), **humareda** SF cloud of smoke

humazo SM dense smoke, cloud of smoke; ✦**MODISMO dar ~ a algn** to get rid of sb

humeante ADJ 1 [*pipa, madera*] smoking; [*mecha, restos*] smouldering, smoldering (*EEUU*); [*cañón, escopeta*] smoking
2 [*caldo, sopa*] steaming

humear ▸conjug 1a◂ Ⓐ VI 1 (= *soltar humo*) [*fuego, chimenea*] to smoke, give out smoke
2 (= *soltar vapor*) to steam
3 [*memoria, rencor*] to be still alive, linger on
4 (= *presumir*) to give o.s. airs, be conceited
Ⓑ VT 1 (*Andes, Caribe, Méx*) (= *fumigar*) to fumigate
2 (*Méx**) (= *golpear*) to beat, thrash

humectador SM 1 [*de ambiente*] humidifier
2 [*de cigarrillos, tabaco*] humidor

humectante ADJ moisturizing

humectar ▸conjug 1a◂ VT = **humedecer**

húmeda* SF **la ~** the tongue

humedad SF 1 (*en atmósfera*) humidity; **en Barcelona siempre hay mucha ~** in Barcelona it's always very humid ▸ **humedad absoluta** absolute humidity ▸ **humedad relativa** relative humidity
2 (*en pared, techo*) damp, dampness; **hay manchas de ~ en el techo** there are stains of damp on the ceiling; **aquí huele a ~** this place smells of damp; ✦**MODISMO sentir la ~** (*Andes, Caribe**) to have to answer for one's actions

humedal SM wetland

humedecedor SM humidifier

humedecer ▸conjug 2d◂ Ⓐ VT 1 (= *mojar*) [+ *camisa, ropa*] to moisten, dampen; [+ *suelo, sello*] to wet; [+ *piel, labios*] to moisten, wet
2 [+ *ambiente*] to humidify
Ⓑ **humedecerse** VPR to get damp, get wet; **se le humedecieron los ojos** his eyes filled with tears, tears came into his eyes

húmedo ADJ [*clima*] damp; [*calor*] humid; [*ropa, pared*] damp; [*pelo*] damp, wet; [*labios, tierra, bizcocho*] moist

HÚMEDO

Para traducir el adjetivo **húmedo** en inglés hay que tener en cuenta la diferencia entre: **damp**, **moist**, **humid** y **wet**.

- Se traduce por **damp** cuando **húmedo** se utiliza para describir cosas que han estado mojadas y que todavía no se han secado del todo:

No salgas con el pelo húmedo
Don't go out with your hair damp
...el olor de la tierra húmeda...
...the smell of damp earth...
Pásele un trapo húmedo
Wipe it with a damp cloth

- Se traduce por **moist** cuando queremos sugerir que el hecho de que esté o sea **húmedo** le da un carácter agradable o atractivo.

El pastel estaba húmedo y esponjoso
The cake was moist and smooth
Hay que mantener las raíces húmedas
The roots must be kept moist

- En contextos científicos se traduce por **humid** cuando se refiere a condiciones atmosféricas:

...el clima caluroso y húmedo de Chipre...
...the hot and humid climate of Cyprus...

- También referido al tiempo atmosférico, pero en un lenguaje menos científico, lo traducimos por **wet** cuando se refiere a un tiempo lluvioso:

Hemos tenido un verano muy húmedo
We've had a very wet summer

humera SF (*Caribe*) cloud of smoke

humero SM 1 (= *tubo*) [*de chimenea*] chimney, smokestack; [*de calentador, cocina*] flue
2 (*Andes*) (= *humareda*) cloud of smoke

húmero SM humerus

humidificar ▸conjug 1g◂ VT to humidify

humildad SF 1 [*de carácter*] humbleness, humility
2 (= *docilidad*) meekness
3 [*de origen*] humbleness, lowliness

humilde ADJ 1 (= *no orgulloso*) [*carácter, opinión, comida*] humble; [*voz*] small
2 (= *pobre*) [*clase, vivienda*] low, modest; [*origen*] lowly, humble; **son gente ~** they are humble *o* poor people

humildemente ADV humbly

humillación SF 1 (= *sumisión*) humiliation; **¡qué ~!** I'm so humiliated!, how humiliating!
2 (= *acto*) humbling

humillante ADJ humiliating

humillar ▸conjug 1a◂ Ⓐ VT [1] (= *rebajar*) [+ *persona*] to humiliate, humble
[2] (*Mil*) [+ *enemigos, rebeldes*] to crush
[3] (*frm*) [+ *cabeza*] to bow, lower
Ⓑ **humillarse** VPR (= *doblegarse*) to humble o.s.; **~se a** *o* **ante** to bow to, bow down before

humita SF (*Andes, Cono Sur*) [1] (*Culin*) (= *tamal*) tamale; (= *maíz molido*) ground maize, ground corn (*EEUU*)
[2] (*Chile*) bow tie

humo SM [1] (= *de fuego, cigarro*) smoke; (= *gases*) fumes *pl*; (= *vapor*) vapour, vapor (*EEUU*), steam; **echar ~** (*lit*) to smoke; (*fig*) to be fuming; ✦*MODISMOS* **convertirse en ~** to vanish without a trace; **hacerse ~** ◊ **irse todo en ~** (*Andes, Cono Sur**) to disappear, clear off*, scarper*; **írsele al ~ a algn** (*LAm*) to jump sb*; **a ~ de pajas** thoughtlessly, heedlessly; **ni hablaba a ~ de pajas** nor was he talking idly; **quedó en ~ de pajas** it all came to nothing; **tomar la del ~**‡ to beat it*; ✦*REFRANES* **lo que hace ~ es porque está ardiendo** ◊ **donde se hace ~ es porque hay fuego** there's no smoke without fire
[2] **humos** (= *vanidad*) conceit *sing*, airs; **tener muchos ~s** to think a lot of o.s., have a big head; ✦*MODISMOS* **bajar los ~s a algn** to take sb down a peg (or two); **darse ~s** to brag, boast; **vender ~s** to brag, talk big*
[3] **humos**† (= *hogares*) homes, hearths

humor[1] SM [1] (= *estado de ánimo*) mood, humour, humor (*EEUU*), temper; **buen ~** good humour, good mood; **en un tono de mal ~** in an ill-tempered tone; **estar de buen/mal ~** to be in a good/bad mood, be in a good/bad temper; **me pone de mal ~** it puts me in a bad mood; **no tengo ~ para fiestas** I'm not in a party mood; **seguir el ~ a algn** to humour sb, go along with sb's mood; ✦*MODISMO* **un ~ de perros** a filthy mood *o* temper
[2] (= *gracia*) humour, humor (*EEUU*), humorousness (*frm*) ► **humor negro** black humour

humor[2] SM (*Med, Biol*) humour, humor (*EEUU*)

humorada SF [1] (= *broma*) witticism, joke
[2] (= *capricho*) caprice, whim

humorado ADJ **bien ~** good-humoured, good-tempered; **mal ~** bad-tempered, cross, peevish

humorismo SM [1] [*de carácter, momento*] humour, humor (*EEUU*), humorousness (*frm*)
[2] (*Teat*) stand-up comedy

humorista SMF [1] (= *cómico*) stand-up comedian/comedienne; (= *dibujante*) cartoonist; (= *escritor*) humorist
[2] (= *persona graciosa*) joker

humorísticamente ADV humorously

humorístico ADJ humorous, funny, facetious (*pey*)

humoso ADJ smoky

humus SM humus

hundible ADJ sinkable

hundido ADJ [1] [*barco, huellas*] sunken
[2] [*ojos*] deep-set, hollow
[3] (= *desmoralizado*) downcast, demoralized

hundimiento SM [1] [*de barco*] sinking
[2] (= *colapso*) [*de edificio, familia, empresa*] collapse, ruin, fall; [*de terreno*] cave-in, subsidence

hundir ▸conjug 3a◂ Ⓐ VT [1] (*en agua*) to sink
[2] (= *destruir*) [+ *edificio*] to ruin, destroy, cause the collapse of; [+ *plan*] to sink, ruin
[3] (= *desmoralizar*) to demoralize; **me hundes en la miseria** you are driving me to ruin
Ⓑ **hundirse** VPR [1] (*en agua*) [*barco*] to sink; [*nadador*] to plunge, go down; **se hundió en el estudio de la historia** he immersed himself in the study of history, he became absorbed in the study of history; **se hundió en la meditación** he became lost in thought
[2] (= *derrumbarse*) [*edificio*] to collapse, fall down, tumble down; [*terreno*] to cave in, subside
[3] (= *económicamente*) **el negocio se hundió** the business failed *o* went under *o* went to the wall; **se hundieron los precios** prices slumped; **la economía se hundió** the economy collapsed
[4] (= *moralmente*) to collapse, break down; **~se en la miseria** to get really low *o* depressed

húngaro/a Ⓐ ADJ of/from Hungary
Ⓑ SM/F native/inhabitant of Hungary
Ⓒ SM (*Ling*) Hungarian

Hungría SF Hungary

huno SM Hun

huracán SM hurricane

huracanado ADJ **viento ~** hurricane-force wind, gale-force wind

huraco SM (*LAm*) hole

hurañía SF (*frm*) [1] (= *timidez*) shyness
[2] (= *insociabilidad*) unsociableness
[3] (= *esquivez*) elusiveness

huraño ADJ [1] (= *tímido*) shy
[2] (= *poco sociable*) unsociable
[3] (= *esquivo*) shy, elusive

hure SM (*Andes*) large pot

hureque SM (*Andes*) = **huraco**

hurgar ▸conjug 1h◂ Ⓐ VT [1] [+ *herida*] to poke, poke at, jab; [+ *fuego*] to poke, rake
[2] (*LAm*) = **hurguetear**
[3] (†) (= *incitar*) to stir up, provoke
Ⓑ VI (= *curiosear*) **~ en** to rummage in; **~ en el bolsillo** to feel in one's pocket, rummage in one's pocket
Ⓒ **hurgarse** VPR **~se la nariz** to pick one's nose

hurgón SM [1] [*de fuego*] poker, fire rake
[2] (= *estocada*) thrust, stab

hurgonada SF, **hurgonazo** SM poke, jab

hurgonear ▸conjug 1a◂ VT [+ *fuego*] to poke, rake, rake out; [+ *adversario*] to thrust at, jab, jab at

hurgonero SM poker, fire rake

hurguete* SM (*Cono Sur*) nosy parker*, busybody

hurguetear ▸conjug 1a◂ VT (*LAm*) [1] (= *rebuscar*) to finger, turn over, rummage inquisitively among
[2] (= *fisgonear*) to poke one's nose into*, pry into

hurí SF houri

hurón Ⓐ ADJ [1] (= *huraño*) unsociable
[2] (*Cono Sur**) (= *glotón*) greedy
Ⓑ SM [1] (*Zool*) ferret
[2] (= *huraño*) unsociable person
[3] (= *fisgón*) (*pey*) busybody, nosy parker*, snooper*

huronear ▸conjug 1a◂ VI (= *fisgar*) to pry, snoop around*

huronera SF [1] (*Zool*) [*de hurón*] ferret hole; [*de oso, león*] den, lair
[2] (= *escondrijo*) hiding place

hurra EXCL hurray!, hurrah!

hurtadillas SFPL **a ~** stealthily, on the sly*

hurtar ▸conjug 1a◂ Ⓐ VT [1] (= *robar*) to steal; **pretenden ~ al país las elecciones** they are trying to deprive the country of (the chance of holding) elections
[2] **~ el cuerpo** to dodge, move out of the way
[3] [*mar, río*] to eat away, erode
[4] (= *plagiar*) to plagiarize, pinch*, lift*
Ⓑ **hurtarse** VPR (*frm*) [1] (= *retirarse*) to withdraw
[2] (= *irse*) to make off
[3] (= *no tomar parte*) to keep out of the way

hurto SM [1] (= *robo*) robbery; (*Jur*) larceny; **cometió un ~** he committed a robbery; ✦*MODISMO* **a ~** (*frm*) stealthily, by stealth, on the sly*
[2] (= *botín*) (piece of) stolen property, loot, thing stolen

húsar SM hussar

husillo SM [1] (*Mec*) spindle, shaft
[2] [*de prensa*] screw, worm
[3] (= *conducto*) drain

husma SF (*frm*) snooping*, prying; **andar a la ~** to go snooping around*, go prying; **andar a la ~ de algo** to go prying for *o* after sth

husmear ▸conjug 1a◂ Ⓐ VT [1] (= *olisquear*) to scent, get wind of
[2] (= *fisgonear*) to pry into, sniff out*
Ⓑ VI (= *oler mal*) to smell bad

husmeo SM [1] (= *olisqueo*) scenting
[2] (= *fisgoneo*) prying, snooping*

husmo SM (*frm*) high smell, strong smell, gaminess; ✦*MODISMO* **estar al ~** to watch one's chance

huso SM [1] (*Téc*) (*para tejer*) spindle; [*de torno*] drum
[2] ► **huso horario** (*Geog*) time zone
[3] (*Col**) kneecap

hutu ADJ, SMF Hutu

huy EXCL (*de dolor*) ow!, ouch!; (*de asombro*) wow!; (*de sorpresa*) well!, oh!, jeez! (*EEUU*); (*de alivio*) phew!; **¡~, perdona!** oops, sorry!

huyente ADJ (*frm*) [*frente*] receding

huyón/ona (*LAm*) Ⓐ ADJ [1] (= *cobarde*) cowardly
[2] (= *huraño*) unsociable
Ⓑ SM/F [1] (= *cobarde*) coward
[2] (= *huraño*) unsociable person

Hz ABR (= **hertzio, hercio**) Hz

I i

I, i [i] SF (= *letra*) I, i ► **I griega** Y, y

IA SF ABR (= **inteligencia artificial**) AI

IAC SF ABR (*LAm*) (= **ingeniería asistida por computador**) CAE

IAE SM ABR (*Esp*) (= **Impuesto de** *o* **sobre Actividades Económicas**) *tax on commercial and professional activities*

-iano *ver* **Aspects of Word Formation in Spanish 2**

IAO SF ABR 1 (= **instrucción asistida por ordenador**) CAI
2 (= **ingeniería asistida por ordenador**) CAE

IB ABR = **Iberia, Líneas Aéreas de España, Sociedad Anónima**

ib. ABR (= **ibídem**) ib, ibid

iba *etc ver* **ir**

Iberia SF Iberia

ibérico ADJ Iberian; **la Península Ibérica** the Iberian Peninsula

ibero/a ADJ, SM/F, **íbero/a** ADJ, SM/F Iberian

Iberoamérica SF Latin America

iberoamericano/a ADJ, SM/F Latin American

ibex SM INV ibex

IBI SM ABR (*Esp*) (= **Impuesto de** *o* **sobre Bienes Inmuebles**) rates, real estate tax (*EEUU*)

íbice SM ibex

ibicenco/a Ⓐ ADJ of/from Ibiza
Ⓑ SM/F native/inhabitant of Ibiza; **los ~s** the people of Ibiza

ibíd. ABR (= **ibídem**) ib, ibid

-ibilidad *ver* **Aspects of Word Formation in Spanish 2**

ibis SF INV ibis

Ibiza SF Ibiza

-ible *ver* **Aspects of Word Formation in Spanish 2**

ibón SM Pyrenean lake, tarn

ícaro SM (*LAm Dep*) hang-glider

ICE SM ABR (*Esp*) 1 (*Educ*) = **Instituto de Ciencias de la Educación**
2 (*Com*) = **Instituto de Ciencias Económicas**

iceberg SM ['iθeβer] (*pl* **icebergs** ['iθeβer]) iceberg; **la punta** *o* **cabeza del ~** the tip of the iceberg

ICEX SM ABR (*Esp*) = **Instituto de Comercio Exterior**

ICH SM ABR (*Esp*) = **Instituto de Cultura Hispánica**

ICI SM ABR (*Esp*) = **Instituto de Cooperación Iberoamericana**

ICO SM ABR (*Esp*) = **Instituto de Crédito Oficial**

-ico, -ica *ver* **Aspects of Word Formation in Spanish 2**

ICONA SM ABR, **Icona** SM ABR (*Esp*) (= **Instituto para la Conservación de la Naturaleza**) ≈ NCC

icono SM (*Arte, Inform*) icon

iconoclasia SF, **iconoclastia** SF iconoclasm

iconoclasta Ⓐ ADJ iconoclastic
Ⓑ SMF iconoclast

iconografía SF iconography

iconográfico ADJ iconographic

ictericia SF jaundice

ictio- PREF ichthyo-

ictiofauna SF fish *pl*, fishes *pl*

ICYT SM ABR = **Instituto de Información y Documentación sobre Ciencia y Tecnología**

id[1] SM id

id[2] *ver* **ir**

I+D ABR (= **Investigación y Desarrollo**) R&D

íd. ABR (= **ídem**) do

ida SF 1 (= *movimiento*) departure; **viaje de ~** outward journey; **partido de ~** away leg; **~ y vuelta** round trip; **billete de ~ y vuelta** return (ticket), round trip ticket (*EEUU*); **~s y venidas** comings and goings; **✦MODISMOS en dos ~s y venidas** in an instant; **dejar las ~s por las venidas** to miss the boat
2 (*Caza*) track, trail
3 (= *acto precipitado*) rash act

IDCA SM ABR = **Instituto de Desarrollo Cooperativo en América**

iddish ['idiʃ] SM Yiddish

IDE SF ABR (= **Iniciativa de Defensa Estratégica**) SDI

idea SF 1 (= *concepto*) idea; **tenía una ~ muy distinta de Rusia** I had a very different idea of what Russia was like; **tenía una ~ falsa de mí** he had a false impression of me, he had the wrong idea about me; **formarse una ~ de algo** to form an impression of sth; **hacerse una ~ de algo** to get an idea of sth; **no es fácil hacerse una ~ del proyecto** it's not easy to get an idea of the project; **hacerse una ~ equivocada de algn** to get a false impression of sb, get the wrong idea about sb; **hazte a la ~ de que no va a volver nunca** you'd better get used to the idea that she's never coming back; *ver tb* **preconcebido**
2 (= *sugerencia*) idea; **tengo una gran ~** I've had a great idea; **¡qué ~! ¿por qué no vamos a Marruecos?** I've got an idea! why don't we go to Morocco?; **necesitamos a gente con ~s** we need people with (fresh) ideas; **~s para cuidar su cabello** hair care tips; **~ brillante** ◊ **~ genial** brilliant idea, brainwave; **✦MODISMO ~s de bombero** (*Esp*) bright ideas (*iró*), hairbrained schemes*
3 (= *intención*) idea, intention; **mi ~ era salir temprano** I had intended to leave early, my idea *o* intention was to leave early; **cambiar de ~** to change one's mind; **no hemos conseguido que cambiara de ~** we haven't been able to change her mind; **~ fija** fixed idea; **salió del país con una ~ fija: no volver nunca** he left the country with one fixed idea: never to return; **su ~ fija era marcharse a Francia** she had this fixed idea about going to France; **ir con la ~ de hacer algo** to mean to do sth; **no iba nunca con la ~ de perjudicar a nadie** it was never his intention to harm anybody, he never meant to harm anybody; **tiene muy mala ~** his intentions are not good, he's a nasty piece of work*; **tuvo muy mala ~ al hacer las preguntas** his questions were really malicious *o* nasty; **nos preparó una trampa a mala ~** he played a nasty trick on us; **lo hizo sin mala ~** he didn't mean any harm; **metérsele una ~ en la cabeza a algn**: **cuando se le mete una ~ en la cabeza no hay quien se la saque** once he gets an idea into his head no one can talk him out of it; **tener ~ de hacer algo** (*en el pasado*) to mean to do sth; (*en el futuro*) to be thinking of doing sth; **tenía ~ de traerme varias botellas de vodka** I meant *o* I was meaning to bring some bottles of vodka; **✦MODISMO tener ~ a algn** (*Cono Sur*) to have it in for sb
4 (= *conocimiento*) idea; **no tengo mucha ~ de cocina** I haven't got much (of an) idea about cooking; **—¿a qué hora llega Sara? —no tengo ni ~** "what time is Sara arriving?" — "I've got no idea"; **¡ni ~!** no idea!; **tener ~ de algo** to have an idea of sth; **¿tienes ~ de la hora que es?** do you have any idea of the time?; **¡no tienes ~ de las ganas que tenía de verte!** you have no idea how much I wanted to see you!; **no tenía ni ~ de que te fueras a casar** I had no idea that you were getting married; **no tener la menor ~** not to have the faintest *o* the foggiest idea; **cuando me fui a Alemania no tenía la menor ~ de alemán** when I went to Germany I couldn't speak a word of German; *ver tb* **pajolero 1, remoto 3**
5 **ideas** (= *opiniones*) ideas; **lo expulsaron por sus ~s políticas** they expelled him be-

cause of his political beliefs *o* ideas; **tengo las ~s muy claras con respecto al aborto** my position on abortion is very clear; **yo soy de ~s fijas** I have very fixed ideas about things; **una persona de ~s conservadoras/liberales/radicales** a conservative/liberal/radical-minded person

ideación SF conception, thinking-out

ideal Ⓐ ADJ ideal; **es el marido ~** he is the ideal husband; **un mundo ~** an ideal world; **nuestra casa ~** our dream house *o* home; **lo ~ es poder hacerlo tú mismo** ideally you would be able to do it yourself, the ideal thing is to be able to do it yourself; **lo ~ sería que el aparcamiento fuera gratis** ideally the parking would be free, the ideal thing would be for the parking to be free; **lo ~ para ella sería un piso en el centro** the ideal thing for her would be a flat in the centre of town
Ⓑ SM [1] (= *modelo*) ideal; **el ~ de belleza masculina** the ideal of masculine beauty
[2] (= *deseo*) ideal; **mi ~ es vivir junto al mar** my ideal is to live by the sea
[3] **ideales** (= *valores*) ideals; **jóvenes sin ~es** young people with no ideals

idealismo SM idealism

idealista Ⓐ ADJ idealistic
Ⓑ SMF idealist

idealización SF idealization

idealizar ▸conjug 1f◂ VT to idealize

idealmente ADV ideally

idear ▸conjug 1a◂ VT [1] [+ *proyecto, teoría*] to devise, think up; **siempre está ideando excusas para no ayudarme** he's always thinking up excuses to avoid helping me
[2] (= *diseñar*) [+ *edificio*] to design; [+ *invento, máquina*] to design, devise; **la máquina ideada por Turing** the machine that Turing designed *o* devised; **una bombilla ideada para ...** a lightbulb designed to ...

ideario SM ideology; **el ~ de la organización** the thinking of the organization

ideático ADJ [1] (*LAm*) (= *excéntrico*) eccentric, odd [2] (*CAm*) (= *inventivo*) ingenious

IDEM SM ABR (*Esp*) = **Instituto de los Derechos de la Mujer**

ídem ADV (*en lengua escrita*) idem; (*en lengua hablada*) ditto; ✦**MODISMO** ~ **de ~***: **yo dije que no, y ella ~ de ~** I said no and she said (exactly) the same

idénticamente ADV identically

idéntico ADJ identical; **estas sillas son idénticas** these chairs are identical *o* exactly the same; **este cuadro es ~ a este otro** this picture is identical to *o* exactly the same as this other one; **llevaba una falda idéntica a la mía** she was wearing an identical skirt to mine; **ser ~ a algn** to be the spitting image of sb*

identidad SF [1] (= *rasgos distintivos*) identity; **carnet de ~** identity card ► **identidad corporativa** corporate identity
[2] (= *igualdad*) identity; **la ~ de intereses** the identity of interests

identificable ADJ identifiable

identificación SF identification ► **identificación errónea** mistaken identity

identificador(a) Ⓐ ADJ identifying
Ⓑ SM/F identifier
Ⓒ SM ► **identificador de llamadas** caller ID

identificar ▸conjug 1g◂ Ⓐ VT [1] (= *reconocer*) to identify; **han identificado al ladrón** they have identified the thief; **aún no han identificado las causas de la tragedia** the causes of the tragedy have still not been identified; **una víctima sin ~** an unidentified victim
[2] (= *equiparar*) **no identifiques violencia con juventud** don't think that young people and violence automatically go together; **siempre la identificaban con causas humanitarias** she was always identified *o* associated with humanitarian causes
Ⓑ **identificarse** VPR [1] (= *demostrar la identidad*) to identify o.s.; **se identificó como el padre del niño** he identified himself as the child's father; **la policía les pidió que se ~an** the police asked them to show their identity cards
[2] **~se con** to identify with; **muchos jóvenes se identifican con este personaje** many young people identify with this character; **se identificaba con las víctimas del racismo** he identified with victims of racism

identificatorio ADJ identifying

ideograma SM ideogram

ideología SF ideology

ideológicamente ADV ideologically

ideológico ADJ ideological

ideólogo/a SM/F ideologist

ideoso ADJ (*Méx*) (= *maniático*) obsessive; (= *caprichoso*) wilful

idílico ADJ idyllic

idilio SM [1] (= *romance*) romance, love affair
[2] (*Literat*) idyll

idiolecto SM idiolect

idioma SM language; **los ~s de trabajo de la UE** the working languages of the EU

idiomaticidad SF idiomatic nature

idiomático ADJ idiomatic; **giro ~** idiom, idiomatic expression

idiosincrasia SF idiosyncrasy

idiosincrásico ADJ idiosyncratic

idiota Ⓐ ADJ idiotic, stupid
Ⓑ SMF idiot; **¡idiota!** you idiot!

idiotez SF idiocy; **¡eso es una ~!** that's nonsense!; **decir idioteces** to talk rubbish; **hacer idioteces** to do silly things

idiotismo SM [1] (*Ling*) idiom, idiomatic expression
[2] (= *ignorancia*) ignorance

idiotizado ADJ stupefied; **al verla se quedaron como ~s** when they saw her they were stupefied; **~s por el consumo de droga** stupefied *o* zombified by drugs

idiotizar ▸conjug 1f◂ VT [1] (= *volver idiota a*) to stupefy
[2] (*LAm*) (= *volver loco a*) **~ a algn** to drive sb crazy

IDO SM ABR (*Esp*) = **Instituto de Denominaciones de Origen**

ido Ⓐ ADJ (*) [1] (= *despistado*) absent-minded; **estar ~** to be miles away
[2] (= *chiflado*) crazy, nuts*; **estar ~ (de la cabeza)** to be crazy
[3] (*CAm, Méx*) **estar ~** to be drunk
Ⓑ SMPL **los ~s** the dead, the departed

idólatra Ⓐ ADJ idolatrous
Ⓑ SMF idolator/idolatress

idolatrar ▸conjug 1a◂ VT [1] [+ *dios*] to worship
[2] [+ *amado, cantante*] to idolize

idolatría SF idolatry

idolátrico ADJ idolatrous

ídolo SM idol

idoneidad SF [1] (= *conveniencia*) suitability, fitness
[2] (= *capacidad*) aptitude

idoneizar ▸conjug 1f◂ VT to make suitable

idóneo ADJ [1] (= *apropiado*) suitable, fit
[2] (*Méx*) (*genuino*) genuine

idus SMPL ides

i.e. ABR = **id est** (= *lo mismo*) i.e.

IEE SM ABR [1] (*Admin*) = **Instituto Español de Emigración**
[2] (*Esp Com*) = **Instituto de Estudios Económicos**

IEI SM ABR (*Esp*) = **Instituto de Educación e Investigación**

IEM SM ABR (*Esp*) = **Instituto de Enseñanza Media**

iglesia SF church; **casarse por la ~** to get married in church, have a church wedding; ✦**MODISMOS casarse por detrás de la ~** to move in together; **¡con la ~ hemos topado!** now we're really up against it!; **llevar a algn a la ~** to lead sb to the altar ► **Iglesia Anglicana** Church of England, Anglican Church ► **iglesia catedral** cathedral ► **Iglesia Católica** Catholic Church ► **iglesia colegial** collegiate church ► **iglesia parroquial** parish church

IGLESIA

Uso del artículo

En inglés el uso del artículo delante de **church** depende del motivo por el que alguien se encuentre en el edificio.

- Se traduce **a la iglesia** por **to church**, **en la iglesia** por **in church**, **desde la iglesia** por **from church**, *etc*, cuando alguien va o está allí para asistir al servicio religioso:

  Vamos a la iglesia todos los domingos
  We go to church every Sunday

- Se traduce **a la iglesia** por **to the church**, **en la iglesia** por **at the church** y **desde la iglesia** por **from the church**, *etc* cuando alguien va o está allí por otros motivos:

  Mi padre ha ido a la iglesia a arreglar las ventanas
  My father has gone to the church to fix the windows

Para otros usos y ejemplos ver la entrada.

iglesiero* ADJ (*LAm*) churchy*, church-going

iglú SM igloo

IGN SM ABR (*Esp, Hond*) = **Instituto Geográfico Nacional**

Ignacio SM Ignatius

ignaro ADJ (*frm*) ignorant

ígneo ADJ igneous

ignición SF ignition

ignifugación SF fireproofing

ignífugo ADJ fireproof, fire-resistant

igníscible ADJ flammable, easy to ignite

ignominia SF [1] (= *deshonor*) disgrace, ignominy; **es una ~ que ...** it's a disgrace that ...
[2] (= *acto*) disgraceful act

ignominiosamente ADV ignominiously

ignominioso ADJ ignominious, disgraceful

➤ LENGUA Y USO: **idioma** 46.3

ignorado ADJ (= *desconocido*) unknown; (= *poco conocido*) obscure, little-known

ignorancia SF ignorance; **por ~** through ignorance

ignorante Ⓐ ADJ ignorant
Ⓑ SMF ignoramus

ignorar ▸conjug 1a◂ VT [1] (= *desconocer*) to not know, be ignorant of; **ignoramos su paradero** we don't know his whereabouts; **lo ignoro por completo** I've absolutely no idea; **no ignoro que ...** I am fully aware that ..., I am not unaware that ...
[2] (= *no tener en cuenta*) to ignore

ignoto ADJ (*liter*) (= *desconocido*) unknown; (= *no descubierto*) undiscovered

igual Ⓐ ADJ [1] (= *idéntico*) **todas las casas son ~es** all the houses are the same; **son todos ~es** they're all the same; **llevaban la corbata ~** they were wearing the same tie; **son únicamente ~es en apariencia** they are alike in appearance only; **~ a: éste es ~ al otro** this one is like the other one, this one is the same as the other one; **había vendido ya dos vestidos ~es a ése** I had already sold two dresses like that one; **no he visto nunca cosa ~** I never saw the like *o* anything like it; **partes ~es** equal shares; **se dividieron el dinero en partes ~es** they divided the money into equal shares; **~ que: tengo una falda ~ que la tuya** I've got a skirt just like yours, I've got a skirt the same as yours; **es ~ que su madre** (*físicamente*) she looks just like her mother; (*en la personalidad*) she's just like her mother
[2] **~ de: es ~ de útil pero más barato** it's just as useful but cheaper; **estoy ~ de sorprendido que tú** I am just as surprised as you are; **las dos habitaciones son ~ de grandes** the two rooms are the same size
[3] (*en rango, jerarquía*) equal; **todos somos ~es ante la ley** we are all equal in the eyes of the law; **somos ~es en derechos y en deberes** we have the same rights and obligations
[4] (*Mat*) equal; **un kilómetro es ~ a 1.000 metros** a kilometre is equal to 1,000 metres, a kilometre equals 1,000 metres; **X es ~ a Y** X is equal to Y
[5] (= *constante*) [*ritmo*] steady; [*presión, temperatura*] steady, constant; [*clima*] constant; [*terreno*] even
[6] (*Dep*) **ir ~es** to be level; **quince ~es** fifteen all; **cuarenta ~es** deuce
Ⓑ ADV [1] (= *de la misma forma*) **se visten ~** they dress the same
[2] (*locuciones*) [2·1] **da ~** ◊ **es ~** it makes no difference, it's all the same; **da** *o* **es ~ hoy que mañana** today or tomorrow, it doesn't matter *o* it makes no difference; **me da ~** ◊ **me es ~** it's all the same to me, I don't mind
[2·2] **por ~** equally; **esta norma se aplica a todos por ~** this rule applies equally to everyone
[2·3] **~ que** (= *como*): **~ que cualquier otro** just like anybody else; **le gusta Brahms, ~ que a mí** like me, he is fond of Brahms; **al ~ que: los chilenos, al ~ que los argentinos, estiman que ...** the Chileans, (just) like the Argentinians, think that ...
[3] (*Esp**) (= *quizás*) maybe; **~ no lo saben** maybe they don't know, they may not know; **~ voy al cine** I may go to the cinema
[4] (*esp Cono Sur**) (= *a pesar de todo*) just the same, still; **era inocente pero me expulsaron ~** I was innocent but they threw me out just the same, I was innocent but they still threw me out
Ⓒ SMF (*en la misma escala social*) equal; (*en la misma clase, trabajo*) peer; **estaba mucho más contento entre sus ~es** he felt much happier being amongst his equals; **se sentía como una extraña entre sus ~es** she felt like a stranger among her peers; **sus ~es en edad y clase social** people of his age and social class; **tratar a algn de ~ a ~** to treat sb as an equal
Ⓓ SM [1] (*Mat*) equals sign, equal sign (*EEUU*)
[2] (= *comparación*) **no tener ~** to be unrivalled, have no equal; **su crueldad hacía ellos no tenía ~** their cruelty towards them was unparalleled; **sin ~** unrivalled; **el paisaje es de una belleza sin ~** the countryside is unrivalled in its beauty
[3] **iguales** (= *lotería*) lottery tickets

iguala SF [1] (*Com*) (= *acuerdo*) agreement; (= *cuota*) agreed fee
[2] (= *igualación*) equalization, tying (*EEUU*)

igualación SF [1] (= *nivelación*) [*de suelo, césped*] levelling, leveling (*EEUU*); **la tendencia a la ~ de los precios** the tendency to balance prices, the tendency towards balancing prices; **han ofrecido la ~ de los sueldos para todos** they have offered to give everybody the same salary; **buscan la ~ de todos los ciudadanos ante la ley** they are seeking to make all citizens equal before the law
[2] (*Mat*) equating

igualada SF (*Dep*) [1] (= *tanto*) equalizer
[2] (= *igualdad de puntos*) level score; **rompió la ~** he broke the deadlock; **todavía tenemos la ~ en el marcador** the scores are still level

igualado ADJ [1] (= *a la misma altura*) neck and neck; **los dos atletas iban muy ~s** the two athletes were running neck and neck; **los dos partidos van ~s en las encuestas** the two parties are running neck and neck in the opinion polls; **el partido quedó ~ a dos** the match finished two all
[2] (*indicando posición*) [*competidores, equipos*] evenly-matched; [*competición, partido*] even, evenly-matched; **el marcador** *o* **el partido estaba ~ a 84 puntos** the scores were level at 84-84; **los dos equipos están ~s a puntos** both teams are level on points
[3] [*suelo, césped*] levelled off, leveled off (*EEUU*)
[4] (*CAm, Méx**) (= *irrespetuoso*) disrespectful (*to people of a higher class*)

igualar ▸conjug 1a◂ Ⓐ VT [1] (= *hacer igual*) [1·1] [+ *cantidades, sueldos*] to make equal, make the same; [+ *resultado*] to equal; **a final de año nos ~án el sueldo a todos** at the end of the year they are going to make all our salaries equal *o* the same; **ha conseguido ~ el número de partidos ganados** she has managed to win the same number of matches; **conseguimos ~ el número de votos** we managed to equal the number of votes; **~ algo a** *o* **con algo** to make sth the same as sth; **han igualado mi sueldo al vuestro** they've put us on the same salary, they've made my salary the same as yours; **si igualamos la x a 2** if x is equal to 2
[1·2] (*Dep*) [+ *marca, récord*] to equal; **a los tres minutos el equipo visitante igualó el marcador** three minutes later, the away team scored the equalizer *o* equalized; **~ el partido** to draw the match, equalize; **~ a puntos a** *o* **con algn** to be level on points with sb
[2] [+ *suelo, superficie*] to level, level off; **quiero que me iguales el flequillo** can you just even up the fringe?; **~ algo con algo** to make sth level with sth
[3] (= *poner al mismo nivel*) [+ *precios*] to match, equal; [+ *derechos, fuerzas*] to place on an equal footing; **el museo ha igualado el precio ofrecido por el coleccionista** the museum has matched *o* equalled the price offered by the collector; **la constitución iguala los derechos de todos los ciudadanos** the constitution grants equal rights to all citizens; **~ a algn en belleza** to match sb's beauty; **nadie le igualaba en sabiduría** there was none as wise as he; **a final de curso consiguió ~ a su hermano en las notas** at the end of the year she managed to get the same marks as her brother
[4] (*Com*) [+ *venta*] to agree upon
Ⓑ VI [1] (= *ser igual*) **~ con algo** to match sth; **el bolso iguala con los zapatos** the handbag matches the shoes; **~ en belleza** to be equally beautiful; **igualan en número de representantes** they have the same number *o* an equal number of representatives
[2] (*Dep*) (= *empatar*) to score the equalizer, equalize
[3] (*Com*) to come to an agreement
[4] (*CAm, Méx**) to be too familiar, be cheeky*
Ⓒ **igualarse** VPR (= *compararse*) **~se a** *o* **con algn** to be on the same level as sb; **su único deseo era ~se con los más ricos que él** his only desire was to be on the same level as those richer than him; **su familia no puede ~se con la nuestra** his family doesn't compare with *o* to ours

igualatorio SM (*Med*) insurance group

igualdad SF [1] (= *equivalencia*) equality; **~ de derechos** equal rights; **~ de oportunidades** equal opportunities; **~ de salario** equal pay; **en ~ de condiciones** on an equal basis, on an equal footing
[2] (= *uniformidad*) [*de superficie*] evenness; [*de rasgos, formas*] similarity

igualitario ADJ egalitarian

igualitarismo SM egalitarianism

igualito ADJ (*diminutivo de* **igual**) exactly the same, identical; **los dos son ~s** they're the spitting image of each other

igualización SF equalization, tying (*EEUU*)

igualmente ADV [1] (= *del mismo modo*) equally; **todos mis estudiantes son ~ vagos** all my students are equally lazy, my students are all as lazy as each other; **aunque se lo prohíbas, lo hará ~** even if you tell him not to, he'll do it anyway *o* just the same
[2] (= *también*) likewise; **~, los pensionistas quedan exentos** likewise, pensioners are exempt
[3] (*en saludo*) likewise, the same to you; **—¡Feliz Navidad! —gracias, ~** "Happy Christmas!" — "thanks, likewise *o* the same to you"; **—muchos recuerdos a tus padres —gracias, ~** "give my regards to your parents" — "I will, and to yours too"
[4] (= *uniformemente*) evenly

iguana SF iguana

IHS ABR (= **Jesús**) IHS

Ill SM ABR (*Méx*) = **Instituto Indigenista Interamericano**

ijada SF, **ijar** SM [1] (= *costado*) [*de animal*] flank; [*de persona*] side
[2] (= *dolor*) stitch, pain in the side; ✦*MODISMO* **esto tiene su ~** this has its weak side

ijadear ▸conjug 1a◂ VI (*Zool*) to pant

ikastola SF *school in which Basque is the language of instruction*; → EUSKERA

ikurriña SF *Basque national flag*

-il *ver* **Aspects of Word Formation in Spanish 2**

ilación SF (= *inferencia*) inference; (= *nexo*) connection, relationship

ILARI [i'lari] SM ABR = **Instituto Latinoamericano de Relaciones Internacionales**

ilativo ADJ inferential; (*Ling*) illative

ilegal ADJ illegal, unlawful

ilegalidad SF illegality, unlawfulness; **trabajar en la ~** to work illegally

ilegalización SF outlawing, banning

ilegalizar ▸conjug 1f◂ VT to outlaw, make illegal, ban

ilegalmente ADV illegally, unlawfully

ilegible ADJ illegible, unreadable

ilegítimamente ADV illegitimately

ilegitimar ▸conjug 1a◂ VT to make illegal

ilegitimidad SF illegitimacy

ilegitimizar ▸conjug 1f◂ VT = **ilegitimar**

ilegítimo ADJ [1] (= *no legítimo*) illegitimate
[2] (= *ilegal*) unlawful
[3] (= *falso*) false, spurious

ilerdense Ⓐ ADJ of/from Lérida
Ⓑ SMF native/inhabitant of Lérida; **los ~s** the people of Lérida

ileso ADJ [1] (= *sin lesiones*) unhurt, unharmed; **los pasajeros resultaron ~s** the passengers were unhurt *o* unharmed; **salió ~** he escaped unscathed
[2] (= *sin tocar*) untouched

iletrado ADJ (= *analfabeto*) illiterate; (= *inculto*) uneducated

Ilíada SF Iliad

iliberal ADJ illiberal

ilícitamente ADV illicitly, illegally, unlawfully

ilicitano/a Ⓐ ADJ of/from Elche
Ⓑ SM/F native/inhabitant of Elche; **los ~s** the people of Elche

ilícito ADJ illicit, unlawful

ilimitado ADJ unlimited, limitless

iliterato ADJ illiterate

illanco SM (*Andes*) slow stream, quiet-flowing stream

-illo, -illa *ver* **Aspects of Word Formation in Spanish 2**

Ilma. ABR = **Ilustrísima**

Ilmo. ABR = **Ilustrísimo**

ilocalizable ADJ **ayer seguía ~** he could still not be found yesterday, he was still nowhere to be found yesterday

ilógicamente ADV illogically

ilógico ADJ illogical

ILPES SM ABR = **Instituto Latinoamericano de Planificación Económica y Social**

ilu* SF = **ilusión 3**

iluminación SF [1] (= *alumbrado*) (*en casa, calle*) lighting; (*en estadio*) floodlighting; **~ indirecta** indirect lighting
[2] (= *conocimiento*) enlightenment

iluminado/a Ⓐ ADJ [1] (= *alumbrado*) illuminated, lit
[2] (= *con conocimiento*) enlightened
[3] **estar ~**‡ (= *borracho*) to be lit up*; (= *drogado*) to be high*
Ⓑ SM/F visionary; **los Iluminados** the Illuminati

iluminador(a) Ⓐ ADJ illuminating
Ⓑ SM/F illuminator

iluminar ▸conjug 1a◂ Ⓐ VT [1] [+ *cuarto, calle, ciudad*] to light; [+ *estadio, edificio, monumento*] to light up; **una sola bombilla iluminaba el cuarto** the room was lit by a single bulb; **la felicidad iluminó su rostro** his face lit up with happiness
[2] [+ *grabado, ilustración*] to illuminate
[3] [+ *teoría, tesis*] to illustrate
[4] (*Rel*) to enlighten
Ⓑ **iluminarse** VPR (= *alegrarse*) [*cara, expresión*] to light up; **se le iluminó el rostro al verla** his face lit up when he saw her; **el cielo se iluminó con los fuegos artificiales** the sky was lit up with fireworks, fireworks lit up the sky

iluminista SMF (*Cine, TV*) electrician, lighting engineer

ilusión SF [1] (= *imagen no real*) illusion; **todo es ~** it's all an illusion ► **ilusión óptica** optical illusion
[2] (= *esperanza*) **su ~ era comprarlo** her dream was to buy it; **tendió la mano con ~** she put her hand out hopefully; **hacerse ilusiones** to get one's hopes up; **no te hagas ilusiones** don't get your hopes up; **se hace la ~ de que …** she fondly imagines that …; **no me hago muchas ilusiones de que …** I am not very hopeful that …; **poner su ~ en algo** to pin one's hopes on sth
[3] (= *entusiasmo*) excitement; **¡qué ~!** how exciting!; **¡qué ~ verte aquí!** it's really great to see you here!; **trabajar con ~** to work with a will; **el viaje me hace mucha ~** I am so looking forward to the trip; **tu carta me hizo mucha ~** I was thrilled to get your letter; **me hace una gran ~ que …** it gives me a thrill that …

ilusionadamente ADV (= *con esperanza*) with high hopes; (= *con emoción*) excitedly

ilusionado ADJ (= *esperanzado*) hopeful; (= *entusiasmado*) excited; **estaba ~ con el viaje a Francia** he was looking forward to going to France; **joven ~** young hopeful

ilusionante ADJ exciting

ilusionar ▸conjug 1a◂ Ⓐ VT [1] (= *entusiasmar*) to excite, thrill; **me ilusiona mucho el viaje** I'm really excited about the journey
[2] (= *alentar falsamente*) **~ a algn** to get sb's hopes up
Ⓑ **ilusionarse** VPR [1] (= *entusiasmarse*) to get excited
[2] (*falsamente*) to get one's hopes up; **no te ilusiones** don't get your hopes up

ilusionismo SM conjuring

ilusionista SMF conjurer, illusionist

iluso/a Ⓐ ADJ (= *crédulo*) gullible; **¡pobre ~!** poor deluded creature!; **¡~ de mí!** silly me!
Ⓑ SM/F (= *soñador*) dreamer; **¡iluso!** you're hopeful!

ilusorio ADJ (= *irreal*) illusory; (= *sin valor*) empty; (= *sin efecto*) ineffective

ilustración SF [1] (= *ejemplo*) illustration
[2] [*de libro*] picture, illustration
[3] (= *instrucción*) learning, erudition; **la Ilustración** the Enlightenment, the Age of Enlightenment

ilustrado ADJ [1] [*libro*] illustrated
[2] [*persona*] (= *culto*) learned, erudite; (= *progresista*) enlightened

ilustrador(a) Ⓐ ADJ [1] (= *que aclara*) illustrative
[2] (= *instructivo*) enlightening
Ⓑ SM/F illustrator

▼ **ilustrar** ▸conjug 1a◂ Ⓐ VT [1] [+ *libro*] to illustrate
[2] [+ *tema*] to explain, illustrate
[3] (= *instruir*) to instruct, enlighten
[4] (†) (= *hacer ilustre*) to make illustrious, make famous
Ⓑ **ilustrarse** VPR [1] (= *instruirse*) to acquire knowledge
[2] (†) (= *hacerse ilustre*) to become illustrious, become famous

ilustrativo ADJ illustrative

ilustre ADJ illustrious, famous

ilustrísimo ADJ most illustrious; **Su Ilustrísima**† (*al referirse a un obispo*) His Grace; **Vuestra Ilustrísima**† (*al dirigirse a un obispo*) Your Grace, Your Lordship

IM SM ABR = **Instituto de la Mujer**

IMAC SM ABR (= **Instituto de Mediación, Arbitraje y Conciliación**) ≈ ACAS

imagen SF [1] (*Fot, Ópt*) image; (= *en foto, dibujo, TV*) picture; **las imágenes del accidente** the pictures *o* images of the accident; **es una ~ muy hermosa de tu madre** it's a beautiful picture of your mother; **~ en movimiento** moving image; ✦*REFRÁN* **una ~ vale más que mil palabras** a picture is worth a thousand words ► **imágenes de archivo** library pictures ► **imagen especular** mirror image ► **imagen fija** still ► **imagen virtual** virtual image
[2] (= *reflejo*) reflection; **vio su ~ reflejada en el lago** she saw her reflection in the lake; **le gustaba contemplar su ~ en el espejo** he liked looking at himself *o* at his reflection in the mirror; ✦*MODISMOS* **a (la) ~ y semejanza de uno** in one's own image; **Dios creó al hombre a su ~ y semejanza** God created man in his own image; **los ha educado a su ~ y semejanza** she has brought them up to be just like her; **un campeonato a ~ y semejanza de los que se celebran en Francia** a championship of exactly the same kind as those held in France; **ser la misma** *o* **la viva ~ de algn** to be the living *o* spitting* image of sb; **ser la viva ~ de algo** to be the picture of sth; **era la viva ~ de la desesperación** he was the picture of despair; **es la viva ~ de la felicidad** she is happiness personified, she is the picture of happiness
[3] (= *representación mental*) image, picture; **tenía otra ~ de ti** I had a different image *o* picture of you; **guardo una ~ borrosa del accidente** I only have a vague picture of the accident in my mind
[4] (= *aspecto*) image; **Luis cuida mucho su ~** Luis takes great care over his appearance *o* image; **eso contrasta con su ~ de tipo duro** that contradicts with his tough guy image; **la ~ del partido** the party's image; **un cambio de ~** a change of image ► **imagen**

➤ LENGUA Y USO: **ilustrar A2** 53.5

de marca brand image ► **imagen pública** public image
[5] (*Rel*) [*de madera, pintura*] image; [*de piedra*] statue; ✦*MODISMO* **quedar para vestir imágenes** to be an old maid
[6] (*Literat*) (= *metáfora*) image; **un texto con gran abundancia de imágenes** a text full of images *o* imagery ► **imágenes poéticas** poetic imagery *sing*

imaginable ADJ imaginable, conceivable; **una hermosura más allá de lo ~** a beauty beyond all belief (*liter*); **su descaro va más allá de lo ~** he has an unbelievable cheek; **no es ~ que …** it is difficult to imagine *o* conceive that …

imaginación SF [1] imagination; **tiene mucha ~** he's got a great imagination; **eso es todo obra de tu ~** it's all a figment of your imagination; **no te dejes llevar por la ~** don't let your imagination run away with you; **no se me pasó por la ~ que …** it never even occurred to me that …; **ni por ~** on no account ► **imaginación creativa** creative imagination; ► **imaginación poética** poetic imagination
[2] **imaginaciones** (= *lo imaginado*) **eso son imaginaciones tuyas** you're imagining things

imaginar ▸conjug 1a◂ Ⓐ VT [1] (= *suponer*) to imagine; **no puedes ~ cuánto he deseado que llegara este momento** you can't imagine how much I've been looking forward to this moment; **imagino que necesitaréis unas vacaciones** I imagine *o* suppose *o* guess* that you'll need a holiday; **imagina que tuvieras mucho dinero, ¿qué harías?** suppose *o* imagine that you had a lot of money — what would you do?; **ya estás imaginando cosas** you're just imagining things
[2] (= *visualizar*) to imagine; **imaginad un mundo sin guerras** imagine a world without war
[3] (= *inventar*) [+ *plan, método*] to think up
Ⓑ **imaginarse** VPR [1] (= *suponer*) to imagine; **no te puedes ~ lo mal que iba todo** you can't imagine how bad things were; **—no sabes lo cansados que estamos —sí, ya me imagino** "you've no idea how tired we are" — "yes, I can imagine"; **¡pues, imagínate, se nos averió el coche en plena montaña!** just imagine, the car broke down right up in the mountains!; **—¿lo habéis pasado bien? —imagínate** "did you have a good time?" — "what do you think? *o* we sure did"; **~se que** (*en suposiciones*) to imagine that, suppose that, guess that*; (*en oraciones condicionales*) to imagine that, suppose that; **me imagino que tendrás ganas de descansar** I imagine *o* suppose *o* guess* you'll need a rest; **no me imaginaba que tuvieras un hermano** I never imagined *o* guessed* you had a brother; **imagínate que os pasa algo** suppose something happens to you; **me imagino que sí** I should think so, I (would) imagine so
[2] (= *visualizar*) to imagine, picture; **imagínatela cubierta de nieve** imagine *o* picture it covered in snow; **me la imaginaba más joven** I had imagined *o* pictured her as being younger

imaginaria SF (*Mil*) reserve, nightguard

imaginario Ⓐ ADJ imaginary; **el mundo de lo ~** the imaginary world
Ⓑ SM [1] (*Literat*) imagery
[2] (= *imaginación*) imagination; **el ~ de un niño** a child's imagination

imaginativa SF [1] (= *imaginación*) imagination, imaginativeness
[2] (= *sentido común*) common sense

imaginativo ADJ imaginative; **una sátira nada imaginativa** a very unimaginative satire; **el mundo de lo ~** the imaginary world

imaginería SF [1] (*Rel*) images *pl*, statues *pl*
[2] (*Literat*) imagery

imaginero/a SM/F maker/painter of religious images

imam SM, **imán**[1] SM (*Rel*) imam

imán[2] SM magnet ► **imán de herradura** horseshoe magnet

imantación SF, **imanación** SF magnetization

imantar ▸conjug 1a◂ VT, **imanar** ▸conjug 1a◂ VT to magnetize

imbatibilidad SF unbeatable character; (*Dep*) unbeaten record

imbatible ADJ unbeatable

imbatido ADJ unbeaten

imbebible ADJ undrinkable

imbécil Ⓐ ADJ [1] (= *idiota*) silly, stupid
[2] (*Med*) imbecile
Ⓑ SMF [1] (= *idiota*) imbecile, idiot; **¡imbécil!** you idiot!
[2] (*Med*) imbecile

imbecilidad SF [1] (= *idiotez*) stupidity, idiocy; **decir ~es** to say silly things
[2] (*Med*) imbecility

imbecilizar ▸conjug 1f◂ VT (= *idiotizar*) to reduce to a state of idiocy; (*por alcohol, drogas*) to stupefy

imberbe ADJ beardless

imbíbito ADJ (*CAm, Méx*) included (*in the bill*)

imbombera SF (*Ven Med*) pernicious anaemia, pernicious anemia (*EEUU*)

imbombo ADJ (*Ven*) anaemic, anemic (*EEUU*)

imbornal SM [1] (*Náut*) scupper
[2] (*Arquit*) gutter
[3] ✦*MODISMO* **irse por los ~es** (*LAm**) to go off at a tangent

imborrable ADJ [*tinta*] indelible; [*recuerdo*] indelible, unforgettable

imbricación SF [1] [*de placas*] overlapping
[2] [*de aspectos, asuntos*] interweaving, interdependence

imbricado ADJ [1] [*placa*] overlapping
[2] [*asunto*] interwoven

imbricar ▸conjug 1g◂ Ⓐ VT [1] (= *superponer*) to overlap
[2] (= *entrelazar*) to interweave
Ⓑ **imbricarse** VPR [1] [*placas*] to overlap
[2] [*asuntos, problemas*] to be interwoven

imbuir ▸conjug 3g◂ VT to imbue, infuse (**de, en** with); **imbuido de la cultura de** imbued with the culture of; **una tradición imbuida de cierto romanticismo** a tradition imbued with a certain romanticism

imbunchar ▸conjug 1a◂ VT (*Chile*) [1] (= *encantar*) to bewitch
[2] (= *estafar*) to swindle, cheat

imbunche SM (*Cono Sur*) [1] (= *hechizo*) spell, piece of witchcraft
[2] (= *brujo*) sorcerer, wizard
[3] (= *confusión*) mess

IMCE SM ABR = **Instituto Mejicano de Comercio Exterior**

IMEC SF ABR (*Esp*) = **Instrucción Militar de la Escala de Complemento**

imitable ADJ [1] (= *copiable*) imitable
[2] (= *digno de imitación*) worthy of imitation

imitación SF [1] (= *copia*) imitation; **a ~ de** in imitation of; **desconfíe de las imitaciones** beware of imitations; **de ~** imitation *antes de s*; **joyas de ~** imitation jewellery *o* (*EEUU*) jewelry; **un bolso de ~ piel** an imitation leather bag; **una pistola de ~** a fake gun
[2] (*Teat*) impression, impersonation

imitador(a) Ⓐ ADJ imitative
Ⓑ SM/F [1] (= *plagiario*) imitator
[2] (= *seguidor*) follower
[3] (*Teat*) impressionist, impersonator

imitar ▸conjug 1a◂ VT [1] (= *emular*) to imitate; **Susana imita a sus padres en todo** Susana copies everything her parents do; **se limita a ~ a los mejores autores** he confines himself to aping the best authors
[2] (= *por diversión*) to imitate, mimic; **¡deja ya de ~me!** stop imitating *o* mimicking me!; **sabe ~ muy bien mi firma** he can imitate *o* copy my signature really well; **sabe ~ todos los acentos** he can imitate any accent; **el humorista imitó al rey** the comedian did an impression of the king
[3] (= *parecerse a*) **imita el tacto de la seda** it simulates the feel of silk; **estos pendientes imitan el oro** these earrings are meant to look like gold

imitativo ADJ imitative

impaciencia SF impatience

impacientar ▸conjug 1a◂ Ⓐ VT [1] [*lentitud, retraso*] to make impatient
[2] (= *exasperar*) to exasperate
Ⓑ **impacientarse** VPR [1] (*por falta de tiempo*) to get impatient (**ante, por** about, at; **con** with)
[2] (= *exasperarse*) to lose patience, get worked up

impaciente ADJ [1] (= *sin paciencia*) impatient (**por** to); **~ por empezar** impatient to start; **¡estoy ~!** I can't wait!
[2] (= *irritable*) impatient

impacientemente ADV [1] (= *sin paciencia*) impatiently
[2] (= *con exasperación*) impatiently

impactante ADJ (= *impresionante*) striking, impressive; (= *contundente*) shattering; (= *abrumador*) crushing, overwhelming

impactar ▸conjug 1a◂ Ⓐ VT to impress, have an impact on
Ⓑ VI [1] (= *chocar*) to crash (**contra** against; **en** into)
[2] (= *afectar*) **~ en** to affect
Ⓒ **impactarse** VPR **~se ante** *o* **por algo** to be overawed by sth

impacto SM [1] (= *golpe*) [*de vehículo, disparo*] impact; (*LAm*) punch, blow ► **impacto de bala** bullethole
[2] (= *efecto*) [*de noticia, cambios, leyes*] impact; **~ ambiental** environmental impact; **~ político** political impact

impagable ADJ (*lit*) unpayable; (*fig*) priceless

impagado ADJ unpaid

impagador(a) SM/F defaulter, non-payer

impago Ⓐ ADJ (*Cono Sur*) unpaid
Ⓑ SM non-payment, failure to pay

impajaritable* ADJ (*Cono Sur*) necessary, imperative

impalpable ADJ impalpable

impar Ⓐ ADJ [1] (*Mat*) odd; **los números ~es** the odd numbers
[2] (= *único*) unique
Ⓑ SM odd number

imparable ADJ unstoppable

imparablemente ADV unstoppably

imparcial ADJ impartial, fair

imparcialidad SF impartiality

imparcialmente ADV impartially

impartible ADJ indivisible

impartición SF teaching

impartir ▸conjug 3a◂ VT [+ *instrucción*] to impart (*frm*), give; [+ *orden*] to give

impasibilidad SF impassiveness, impassivity; **le golpeó en el rostro ante la ~ de todos los que pasaban por allí** he hit her in the face and no-one passing by took any notice; **los precios siguen bajando ante la ~ del gobierno** the government remains unmoved *o* impassive despite the continual fall in prices

impasible ADJ impassive

impasse [im'pas] SM *o* SF [1] (= *estancamiento*) impasse
[2] (*Bridge*) finesse; **hacer el ~ a algn** to finesse against sb

impávidamente ADV [1] (= *intrépidamente*) intrepidly; (= *impasiblemente*) dauntlessly
[2] (*LAm*) (= *con insolencia*) cheekily

impavidez SF [1] (= *valor*) intrepidity; (= *impasibilidad*) dauntlessness
[2] (*LAm*) (= *insolencia*) cheek, cheekiness, sass (*EEUU**)

impávido ADJ [1] (= *valiente*) intrepid; (= *impasible*) dauntless, undaunted
[2] (*LAm*) (= *insolente*) cheeky, sassy (*EEUU**)

IMPE SM ABR (*Esp*) = **Instituto de la Mediana y Pequeña Empresa**

impecable ADJ impeccable, faultless

impecablemente ADV impeccably, faultlessly

impedido/a Ⓐ ADJ disabled; **estar ~ para algo** to be unfit for sth; **me veo ~ para ayudar** I am not in a position to help
Ⓑ SM/F disabled person

impedimenta SF (*Mil*) impedimenta *pl*

impedimento SM [1] (= *dificultad*) impediment, hindrance; **pidieron a los republicanos que no pusieran ~s al nombramiento** they asked the republicans not to block the appointment; **nos ponen ~s para evitar que lo hagamos** they are putting obstacles in our way to prevent us doing it
[2] (*Med*) disability, handicap; **~ del habla** speech impediment

impedir ▸conjug 3k◂ VT [1] (= *parar*) to prevent, stop; **trataron de ~ la huida de los presos** they tried to prevent the prisoners escaping *o* the prisoners' escape; **~ a algn el acceso al edificio** to prevent sb from entering the building; **lo que no se puede ~** what cannot be prevented; **a mí nadie me lo va a ~** nobody's going to stop me; **~ a algn hacer algo** ◊ **~ que algn haga algo** to prevent sb (from) doing sth, stop sb doing sth; **esto no impide que ...** this does not alter the fact that ...; **~ el paso** to block the way; **un camión nos impedía el paso** a lorry was blocking our way
[2] (= *dificultar*) (*con obstáculos*) to impede, obstruct; (*con problemas*) to hinder, hamper

impeditivo ADJ preventive

➤ LENGUA Y USO: **impensable** 43.3

impeler ▸conjug 2a◂ VT [1] (= *empujar*) to drive, propel
[2] (= *incitar*) to drive, urge, impel; **~ a algn a hacer algo** to drive *o* impel sb to do sth; **impelido por la necesidad** driven by need

impenetrabilidad SF impenetrability

impenetrable ADJ [1] (= *no atravesable*) [*bosque*] impenetrable
[2] (= *impermeable*) impervious
[3] (= *incomprensible*) obscure, impenetrable

impenitencia SF impenitence

impenitente ADJ unrepentant, impenitent

impensable ADJ unthinkable

impensadamente ADV [1] (= *inesperadamente*) unexpectedly
[2] (= *por casualidad*) at random, by chance

impensado ADJ [1] (= *inesperado*) unexpected, unforeseen
[2] (= *casual*) random, chance *antes de s*

impepinable* ADJ certain

impepinablemente* ADV inevitably; **~ se le olvida** he's sure to forget, he always forgets

imperante ADJ ruling, prevailing

imperar ▸conjug 1a◂ VI [1] (= *prevalecer*) [*condiciones*] to prevail; [*precio*] to be in force, be current
[2] (= *mandar*) [*rey*] to rule, reign; [*jefe, capitán*] to be in command

imperativamente ADV [1] (= *obligatoriamente*) imperatively
[2] [*decir*] imperiously, in a commanding tone

imperatividad SF imperative nature, imperativeness

imperativo Ⓐ ADJ (*gen*) imperative; [*tono*] commanding, imperative
Ⓑ SM [1] (= *necesidad*) imperative
► **imperativo categórico** moral imperative
[2] (*Ling*) imperative, imperative mood

imperceptibilidad SF imperceptibility

imperceptible ADJ imperceptible

imperceptiblemente ADV imperceptibly

imperdible SM safety pin

imperdonable ADJ unforgivable, unpardonable, inexcusable

imperdonablemente ADV unforgivably, unpardonably, inexcusably

imperecedero ADJ [*recuerdo*] immortal, undying; [*legado*] eternal; [*fama*] eternal, everlasting

imperfección SF [1] (= *cualidad*) imperfection
[2] (= *fallo*) flaw, fault

imperfeccionar ▸conjug 1a◂ VT (*Cono Sur*) to spoil

imperfectamente ADV imperfectly

imperfecto Ⓐ ADJ [1] [*producto, método*] imperfect, flawed
[2] (*Ling*) imperfect
Ⓑ SM (*Ling*) imperfect, imperfect tense

imperial Ⓐ ADJ imperial
Ⓑ SF (*en carruaje*) imperial

imperialismo SM imperialism

imperialista Ⓐ ADJ imperialist, imperialistic
Ⓑ SMF imperialist

imperialmente ADV imperially

impericia SF [1] (= *torpeza*) unskilfulness, unskillfulness (*EEUU*)
[2] (= *inexperiencia*) inexperience; **a prueba de ~** foolproof

imperio SM [1] (*Pol*) empire; **Imperio Español** Spanish Empire; ✦**MODISMOS vale un ~** ◊ **vale siete ~s** it's worth a fortune
[2] (= *autoridad*) rule; **el ~ de la ley** the rule of law
[3] (= *orgullo*) haughtiness, pride

imperiosamente ADV [1] (= *con autoritarismo*) imperiously
[2] (= *urgentemente*) urgently

imperiosidad SF [1] (= *autoritarismo*) imperiousness
[2] (= *urgencia*) pressing necessity, overriding need

imperioso ADJ [1] (= *autoritario*) imperious
[2] (= *urgente*) pressing, urgent; **necesidad imperiosa** pressing need, absolute necessity

imperito ADJ (= *inhábil*) inexpert, unskilled; (= *inexperto*) inexperienced; (= *torpe*) clumsy

impermanente ADJ impermanent

impermeabilidad SF impermeability, imperviousness

impermeabilización SF [1] (*Téc*) waterproofing
[2] (*Aut*) undersealing
[3] [*de frontera*] sealing

impermeabilizar ▸conjug 1f◂ VT [1] (*Téc*) to waterproof, make watertight
[2] (*Aut*) to underseal
[3] [+ *frontera*] to seal off

impermeable Ⓐ ADJ [1] (*al agua*) waterproof
[2] (= *impenetrable*) impermeable (**a** to), impervious
Ⓑ SM [1] (*prenda*) raincoat, mac*
[2] (‡) (= *preservativo*) French letter*

impersonal ADJ impersonal

impersonalidad SF impersonality, impersonal nature

impersonalismo SM [1] (= *cualidad*) impersonality, impersonal nature
[2] (*LAm*) disinterestedness

impersonalmente ADV impersonally

impertérrito ADJ [1] (= *sin miedo*) unafraid
[2] (= *impávido*) unshaken, unmoved

impertinencia SF [1] (= *insolencia*) impertinence
[2] (= *comentario*) impertinent remark
[3] (*frm*) (= *irrelevancia*) irrelevance

impertinente Ⓐ ADJ [1] (= *insolente*) impertinent
[2] (*frm*) (= *irrelevante*) irrelevant, not pertinent
Ⓑ **impertinentes** SMPL lorgnette *sing*

impertinentemente ADV [1] (= *insolentemente*) impertinently
[2] (*frm*) (= *irrelevantemente*) irrelevantly

imperturbable ADJ (= *no cambiable*) imperturbable; (= *sereno*) unruffled; (= *impasible*) impassive

imperturbablemente ADV (= *sin cambios*) imperturbably; (= *impasiblemente*) impassively

imperturbado ADJ unperturbed

impétigo SM impetigo

impetrar ▸conjug 1a◂ VT [1] (= *rogar*) to beg for, beseech
[2] (= *obtener*) to obtain, win

ímpetu SM [1] (= *impulso*) impetus; (*Mec*) momentum
[2] (= *acometida*) rush, onrush
[3] (*al hacer algo*) (= *impulsividad*) impetuousness, impetuosity; (= *violencia*) violence

impetuosamente ADV (= *con impulsividad*) impetuously, impulsively; (= *con violencia*) violently

impetuosidad SF impetuosity, impetuousness

impetuoso ADJ [1] [*persona*] impetuous, impulsive
[2] [*acto*] hasty, impetuous
[3] [*corriente*] rushing, violent

impiadoso ADJ (*LAm*) impious

impiedad SF [1] (*Rel*) impiety, ungodliness
[2] (= *crueldad*) cruelty, pitilessness

impío ADJ [1] (*Rel*) impious, ungodly
[2] (= *cruel*) cruel, pitiless

implacable ADJ implacable, relentless

implacablemente ADV implacably, relentlessly

implantable ADJ that can be implanted

implantación SF [1] [*de modelo, ley*] implementation; **la ~ del nuevo sistema educativo** the implementation of the new education system; **la ~ de la dictadura** the installing of the dictatorship
[2] [*de costumbre, ideología*] **una costumbre de reciente ~** a custom that has only recently become established *o* taken root; **tras la ~ del capitalismo** since capitalism became established *o* took root; **esta moda no tuvo ~ en España** this fashion never caught on in Spain
[3] [*de empresa*] establishment, setting up
[4] (= *popularidad*) **un partido con escasa ~ en las ciudades** a party with little support in the cities; **un idioma de fuerte ~ en Nueva York** a language which is firmly established in New York
[5] (*Med*) [*de miembro*] implantation

implantar ▸conjug 1a◂ Ⓐ VT [1] [+ *reforma, sistema, modelo*] to implement; [+ *castigo, medidas*] to bring in; [+ *toque de queda*] to impose; **hemos implantado el uso obligatorio del gallego** we have brought in *o* implemented compulsory Galician; **cuando ~on la dictadura** when the dictatorship was installed; **han vuelto a ~ la pena de muerte** they have brought back the death penalty
[2] [+ *costumbre, ideas*] to introduce; **los americanos han implantado sus costumbres en Europa** the Americans have introduced their customs to Europe
[3] [+ *empresa*] to establish, set up
[4] (*Med*) to implant
Ⓑ **implantarse** VPR to become established; **se ha implantado el uso del catalán en la vida diaria** Catalan has become established in everyday life; **la nueva moda se ha implantado entre los jóvenes** the new fashion has caught on among young people

implante SM implant

implementar ▸conjug 1a◂ Ⓐ VT to implement
Ⓑ VI to help, give aid

implemento SM [1] (= *herramienta*) implement, tool
[2] (*LAm*) means

implicación SF [1] (= *complicidad*) involvement
[2] (= *significado*) implication
[3] (= *contradicción*) contradiction (in terms)

implicancia SF (*LAm*) implication

implicar ▸conjug 1g◂ VT [1] (= *involucrar*) to involve; **las partes implicadas** the interested parties, the parties concerned
[2] (= *significar*) to imply; **esto no implica que ...** this does not mean that ...

implícitamente ADV implicitly

implícito ADJ implicit

imploración SF supplication, entreaty

implorante ADJ [*mirada, mano*] imploring

implorar ▸conjug 1a◂ VT to implore, beg, beseech (*liter*); **~ a algn que haga algo** to implore *o* beg sb to do sth, beseech sb to do sth (*liter*)

implosionar ▸conjug 1a◂ VI, **implotar** ▸conjug 1a◂ VI to implode

implume ADJ [1] (= *sin plumas*) featherless, unfledged
[2] (= *sin vello*) unfledged

impolítico ADJ [1] (= *imprudente*) impolitic, imprudent
[2] (= *no diplomático*) tactless, undiplomatic
[3] (= *descortés*) impolite

impoluto ADJ unpolluted, pure

imponderable Ⓐ ADJ imponderable
Ⓑ **imponderables** SMPL imponderables

imponencia SF [1] (*LAm*) (= *lo impresionante*) impressiveness
[2] (= *majestuosidad*) stateliness, grandness

imponente Ⓐ ADJ [1] (= *que asusta*) [*persona, castillo, montaña*] imposing
[2] (= *magnífico*) [*aspecto*] stunning; [*edificio, fachada*] impressive; [*paisaje, representación*] stunning, impressive; **ibas ~ con ese vestido** you looked stunning in that dress; **vivía en una ~ mansión** she lived in an imposing *o* impressive mansion
Ⓑ SMF [1] (*Fin*) depositor
[2] (*Chile*) Social Security contributor

imponer ▸conjug 2q◂ (*pp* **impuesto**) Ⓐ VT [1] (= *poner*) [+ *castigo, obligación*] to impose; [+ *tarea*] to set; **~ sanciones comerciales a un país** to impose trade sanctions against *o* on a country; **no quiero ~te nada, sólo darte un buen consejo** I don't want to force you to do anything *o* I don't want to impose anything on you, just to give you some good advice; **el juez le impuso una pena de tres años de prisión** the judge gave him a three-year prison sentence; **no le impusieron ningún castigo al portero** the goalkeeper was not penalized
[2] (*frm*) (= *conceder*) [+ *medalla*] to award; **a la princesa le impusieron el nombre de Mercedes** the princess was given the name Mercedes, the princess was named Mercedes
[3] (= *hacer prevalecer*) [+ *voluntad, costumbre*] to impose; [+ *norma*] to enforce; [+ *miedo*] to instil; [+ *condición*] to lay down, impose; [+ *enseñanza, uso*] to make compulsory; **trató de ~ su punto de vista** he tried to impose his viewpoint; **su trabajo le impone un ritmo de vida muy acelerado** her work forces her to lead a very fast lifestyle; **quieren ~ la enseñanza del catalán** they want to make the teaching of Catalan compulsory; **han impuesto por la fuerza el velo a las mujeres** women have been forced to wear the veil; **han impuesto a la fuerza la enseñanza religiosa** they have enforced religious education; **~ la moda** to set the trend; **este año han impuesto la moda del acid jazz** this year acid jazz is the trend; **algunos creadores japoneses imponen su moda en Occidente** some Japanese designers have successfully brought their fashions over to the West; **~ respeto** to command respect; **la autoridad siempre impone respeto** authority always commands respect; **tu padre me impone mucho respeto** I find your father very intimidating; **~ el ritmo** to set the pace
[4] (*Com, Fin*) [+ *dinero*] to deposit; [+ *impuesto*] to put (**a, sobre** on), levy (**a, sobre** on); **hemos impuesto tres millones a plazo fijo** we have deposited three million for a fixed term; **han impuesto nuevas tasas sobre los servicios básicos** they have put *o* levied new taxes on essential services
[5] (= *instruir*) **~ a algn en algo** to instruct sb in sth
[6] (*Rel*) **~ las manos sobre algn** to lay hands on sb
[7] (*Chile*) to pay (in contributions), pay (in Social Security)
Ⓑ VI [1] (= *intimidar*) [*persona*] to command respect; [*edificio*] to be imposing; [*arma*] to be intimidating; **su forma de hablar en público impone** his style of public speaking commands respect; **el castillo imponía un poco al entrar** the castle was rather imposing as you went in; **¿no te impone dormir solo?** don't you find it rather scary sleeping on your own?
[2] (*Chile*) to pay contributions, pay one's Social Security
Ⓒ **imponerse** VPR [1] (= *obligarse*) [+ *horario, tarea*] to set o.s.; **nos hemos impuesto un horario de trabajo muy duro** we've set ourselves a very heavy work schedule
[2] (= *hacerse respetar*) to assert one's authority, assert o.s.; **sabe ~se cuando hace falta** he knows how to assert his authority *o* himself when necessary; **~se a** *o* **sobre algn** to assert one's authority over sb; **el clero consiguió ~se al Gobierno** the clergy managed to assert its authority over the government; **siempre acaba imponiéndose sobre sus hermanas** he always ends up getting his own way with his sisters
[3] (= *prevalecer*) [*criterio*] to prevail; [*moda*] to become fashionable; **al final se impuso un criterio de sabiduría** wisdom prevailed in the end; **se está imponiendo otra vez la ropa deportiva** sportswear is coming into fashion again; **la minifalda no ha llegado a ~se esta temporada** the mini-skirt hasn't caught on this season
[4] (*frm*) (= *ser necesario*) [*cambio*] to be needed; [*conclusión*] to be inescapable; **se impone la necesidad de una gran reforma** there is an urgent need for extensive reform; **la conclusión se impone** the conclusion is inescapable
[5] (*Dep*) (= *vencer*) to win; **el Barcelona se impuso en el último minuto** Barcelona won (the match) in the last minute; **el Valencia se impuso por tres a cero al Oviedo** Valencia defeated *o* beat Oviedo three nil; *ver tb* **sprint**
[6] (= *instruirse*) **~se en algo** to acquaint o.s. with sth
[7] (*Méx**) (= *acostumbrarse*) **~se a algo** to become accustomed to sth; **~se a hacer algo** to become accustomed to doing sth

imponible ADJ [1] (*Fin*) [*riqueza, hecho*] taxable, subject to tax; [*importación*] dutiable, subject to duty; **no ~** tax-free, tax-exempt (*EEUU*); *ver tb* **base A4**
[2] (*) [*ropa*] unwearable

impopular ADJ unpopular

impopularidad SF unpopularity

importación SF [1] (= *acto*) importation; **la ~ de coches** the importation of cars; **de ~** [*producto, artículo*] imported; [*comercio, permiso*] import *antes de s*; **whisky de ~** imported whisky

[2] **importaciones** (= *mercancías*) imports

importador(a) Ⓐ ADJ importing

Ⓑ SM/F importer

▼ **importancia** SF importance; **tu ayuda ha sido de gran ~** your help has been very important *o* of great importance; **un autor de ~ universal** an author of worldwide renown; **¿y eso qué ~ tiene?** and how is that important *o* significant?, and what significance does that have?; **no te preocupes, no tiene ~** don't worry, it's not important; **carecer de ~** to be unimportant; **de cierta ~** [*empresa, asunto*] of some importance, important; [*herida*] serious; **conceder** *o* **dar mucha ~ a algo** to attach great importance to sth; **no quiero darle más ~ de la que tiene, pero ...** I don't want to make an issue of this but ...; **darse ~** to give o.s. airs; **quitar** *o* **restar ~ a algo** to make light of sth, play down the importance of sth; **sin ~** [*herida, comentario*] minor; **son detalles sin ~** these are minor details

▼ **importante** ADJ [1] (= *trascendental*) [*información, persona*] important; [*acontecimiento*] significant, important; [*papel, factor, parte*] important, major; [*cambio*] significant, major; **se trata de algo ~** it's important; **tu padre es un hombre ~** your father's an important man; **uno de los momentos más ~s de mi vida** one of the most significant *o* important moments in my life; **un paso ~ para la democracia** an important *o* a big *o* a major step for democracy; **dárselas de ~** to give o.s. airs; **lo ~ es ...** the main thing is ...; **lo ~ es participar** the main thing is taking part; **lo más ~ en la vida** the most important thing in life; **poco ~** unimportant; **es ~ que** it is important that; **es ~ que expreses tu opinión** it's important for you to express your opinion

[2] (*como intensificador*) [*cantidad, pérdida*] considerable; [*herida*] serious; [*retraso*] considerable, serious; **una ~ suma de dinero** a considerable amount of money

importantizarse* ▸conjug 1f◂ VPR (*Caribe*) to give o.s. airs

importar¹ ▸conjug 1a◂ VT (*Com*) to import (**de** from)

▼ **importar²** ▸conjug 1a◂ Ⓐ VI [1] (= *ser importante*) to matter; **¿qué importa que no seamos ricos?** what does it matter if *o* that we're not rich?; **—llegaremos allí un poco tarde —no importa** "we'll be there a bit late" — "never mind *o* it doesn't matter"; **lo que importa es la calidad** the important thing is the quality, what matters is the quality; **¿y eso qué importa?** what does that matter?; **el color importa mucho en su pintura** colour is important in her painting, colour plays an important part in her painting; **lo comprará a no importa qué precio** he'll buy it at any price; **no importa el tiempo que haga, allí estaremos** we'll be there whatever the weather

[2] (*con complemento de persona*) [2·1] (= *interesar*) **sí que me importa tu opinión** your opinion does matter to me, I do care about your opinion; **¿a quién le importa lo que yo diga?** who cares (about) what I say?; **no le importa nada de lo que pase** he doesn't care about anything that happens, he's not bothered about anything; **tú me importas más que nada** I care about you more than anything, you mean more to me than anything; **¿y a ti qué te importa?** what business is it of yours?; **¡a ti eso no te importa!** it's nothing to do with you!, it's none of your business!; **meterse en lo que a uno no le importa** to poke one's nose into other people's business; **deja ya de meterte en lo que no te importa** stop poking your nose into other people's business; **no quisiera meterme en lo que no me importa, pero ...** I know it's none of my business, but ...; ✦*MODISMOS* **(no) me importa un bledo** *o* **un comino** *o* **un pito** *o* **un rábano*** I couldn't care less*, I don't give a damn‡; **(no) me importa un carajo** *o* **un huevo**** I don't give a shit** *o* a toss‡; **tú no le importas un carajo** he doesn't give a shit** *o* a toss‡ about you

[2·2] (= *molestar*) **¿te ~ía prestarme este libro?** would you mind lending me this book?, could you lend me this book?; **si no le importa, me gustaría que me enviaran la factura** if it's not too much trouble, I'd like you to send me the bill; **—¿quieres venir al concierto? —pues no me ~ía** "do you want to come to the concert?" — "I wouldn't mind"; **¿te importa si fumo?** do you mind if I smoke?; **no ~ a algn hacer algo**: **no me importa esperar** I don't mind waiting; **si os hace falta alguien, a mí no me ~ía ayudaros** if you need somebody, I'd be happy to help *o* I don't mind helping; **no me importa que llegues un poco tarde** I don't mind if you're a bit late, I don't mind you being a bit late

Ⓑ VT (*frm*) [*artículo, producto*] to cost; [*gastos, beneficios*] to amount to; **¿cuánto importa esta lámpara?** how much does this lamp cost?; **los gastos de transporte ~on 2.000 euros** transport costs amounted to 2,000 euros

▼ **importe** SM [1] (= *valor*) [*de compra, gastos, cheque*] amount; **el ~ de esta factura** the amount of this bill; **¿a cuánto asciende el ~ de los gastos?** how much do the expenses amount to *o* come to?; **el ~ de la recaudación** (*Cine, Teat*) box office takings *pl*; (*Dep*) gate receipts *pl*; **por ~ de** to the value of; **un préstamo por ~ de 10.000 euros** a loan to the value of 10,000 euros; **cheques por un ~ total de 20 millones** cheques to the total value of 20 million ► **importe global** grand total

[2] (= *coste*) cost; **el ~ de la mano de obra** the cost of labour

importunación SF pestering ► **importunación sexual** sexual harassment

importunar ▸conjug 1a◂ VT to bother, pester

importunidad SF (= *acción*) pestering; (= *efecto*) annoyance, nuisance

importuno ADJ [1] (= *fastidioso*) annoying

[2] (= *inoportuno*) inopportune, inappropriate

imposibilidad SF [1] [*de suceso, acción*] impossibility

[2] (= *incapacidad*) **mi ~ para hacerlo** my inability to do it

imposibilitado ADJ [1] (*Med*) disabled; **estar** *o* **verse ~ para hacer algo** to be unable to do sth, be prevented from doing sth

[2] (*Fin*) without means

imposibilitar ▸conjug 1a◂ VT [1] (*Med*) to disable

[2] (= *impedir*) to make impossible, prevent; **esto me imposibilita hacerlo** this makes it impossible for me to do it, this prevents me from doing it

▼ **imposible** Ⓐ ADJ [1] (= *no posible*) impossible; **es ~** it's impossible, it's out of the question; **es ~ de predecir** it's impossible to predict; **hacer lo ~ por hacer algo** to do one's utmost to do sth; **¡parece ~!** you'd never believe it!

[2] (= *inaguantable*) impossible

[3] (= *difícil*) impossible

[4] (*LAm*) (= *descuidado*) slovenly, dirty; (= *repugnante*) repulsive

Ⓑ SM **un ~** (*tarea*) an impossible task; (*objetivo*) an impossible goal; **lo que voy a pedir es un ~** what I'm about to ask is impossible, I'm about to ask for the impossible; **perseguía un ~** he was pursuing an impossible dream *o* aim

imposición SF [1] (= *introducción*) [*de obligación, multa*] imposition; [*de ley, moda*] introduction; **la ~ de la moneda única** the introduction of the single currency; **ante todo tenía que conseguir la ~ de su voluntad** above all he had to impose his will; **no me gustan las imposiciones** I don't like people making demands on me

[2] [*de medallas*] **la ceremonia de ~ de medallas** the medal ceremony

[3] (= *impuesto*) taxation; **doble ~** double taxation ► **imposición directa** direct taxation ► **imposición indirecta** indirect taxation

[4] (= *ingreso*) deposit; **efectuar una ~** to make a deposit ► **imposición a plazo (fijo)** fixed-term deposit

[5] (*Tip*) imposition

[6] (*Rel*) ► **imposición de manos** laying on of hands

[7] (*Chile*) Social Security contribution

impositiva SF (*LAm*) tax office

impositivamente ADV for tax purposes, with regard to taxation

impositivo ADJ [1] (*Fin*) tax *antes de s*; **sistema ~** tax system

[2] (*Andes, Cono Sur*) (= *autoritario*) domineering; (= *imperativo*) imperative

impositor(a) SM/F (*Fin*) depositor

impostar ▸conjug 1a◂ VT **~ la voz** to project one's voice

impostergable ADJ **una cita ~** an appointment that cannot be put off

impostor(a) SM/F [1] (= *charlatán*) impostor

[2] (= *calumniador*) slanderer

impostura SF [1] (= *fraude*) imposture

[2] (= *calumnia*) slur, slander

impotable ADJ undrinkable

impotencia SF [1] (*para hacer algo*) impotence, helplessness

[2] (*Med*) impotence

impotente ADJ [1] (*para hacer algo*) impotent, helpless

[2] (*Med*) impotent

impracticabilidad SF impracticability

impracticable ADJ [1] (= *irrealizable*) impracti-

➤ LENGUA Y USO: **importancia** 53.6 **importante 1** 53 **importar² A1** 34.5 **A2** 31, 36.1 **importe 1** 47.5

cable, unworkable
2 [*carretera*] impassable
imprecación SF imprecation, curse
imprecar ▸conjug 1g◂ VT to curse
imprecisable ADJ indeterminable
imprecisión SF lack of precision, vagueness
impreciso ADJ imprecise, vague
impredecibilidad SF unpredictability
impredecible ADJ, **impredictible** ADJ (*LAm*) unpredictable
impregnación SF impregnation
impregnar ▸conjug 1a◂ VT 1 (= *humedecer*) to impregnate
2 (= *saturar*) to soak
3 [*olor, sentimiento*] to pervade
impremeditado ADJ unpremeditated
imprenta SF 1 (= *acto*) printing; **dar** *o* **entregar a la ~** to send for printing
2 (= *máquina*) press
3 (= *taller*) printer's
4 (= *impresos*) printed matter; *ver tb* **letra 1**
imprentar ▸conjug 1a◂ VT 1 (*Cono Sur*) to put a permanent crease into
2 (*LAm*) to mark
impreparado ADJ unprepared
imprescindible ADJ essential, indispensable; **cosas ~s** essentials; **es ~ que …** it is essential that …; **lo más ~** the bare essentials
impresentable ADJ (= *no presentable*) unpresentable; [*acto*] disgraceful; **estás ~** you look a state; **Juan es ~** you can't take Juan anywhere
▼**impresión** SF 1 (= *sensación*) impression; **¿qué ~ te produjo?** what was your impression of it?; **cambiar impresiones** to exchange views; **causar (una) buena ~ a algn** [*persona*] to make a good impression on sb; [*actividad, ciudad*] to impress sb; **dar la ~ de**: **da la ~ de ser un autor maduro** he appears to be a mature author; **daba la ~ de no caber en la caja** it looked as if it wouldn't fit in the box; **me da la ~ de que …** I get the impression that …; **de ~** (*Esp**) fabulous*; **¡estabas de ~ con ese vestido!** you looked fabulous in that dress!*; **hacer buena ~ a algn** = **causar (una) buena impresión a algn**; **intercambiar impresiones** to exchange views; **primera ~** first impression; **se deja llevar por las primeras impresiones** he's easily swayed by first impressions; **la primera ~ es la que vale** it's the first impression that counts; **tener la ~ de que …** to have the impression that …
2 (= *susto*) shock; **el agua fría da ~ al principio** the cold water is a bit of a shock at first; **su muerte me causó una gran ~** her death was a great shock to me; **me llevé una fuerte ~ cuando me enteré** I got a terrible shock when I found out
3 (= *huella*) imprint ► **impresión dactilar, impresión digital** fingerprint
4 (*Tip*) (= *acción*) printing; (= *resultado*) print; (= *tirada*) print-run; **un error de ~** a printing error; **la ~ es tan mala que resulta difícil de leer** the print is so bad that it's difficult to read; **una ~ de 5.000 ejemplares** a print-run of 5,000 copies ► **impresión en color(es)** colour printing, color printing (*EEUU*)
5 (*Inform*) (= *acción*) printing; (= *resultado*) printout
6 (*Fot*) print
7 (*Biol, Psic*) imprinting
impresionable ADJ impressionable
impresionado ADJ 1 (= *sorprendido, asustado*) affected
2 (*Fot*) exposed; **excesivamente ~** overexposed
impresionante ADJ 1 (= *maravilloso*) [*edificio, acto*] impressive; [*espectáculo*] striking
2 (= *conmovedor*) moving, affecting
3 (= *espantoso*) shocking
impresionar ▸conjug 1a◂ Ⓐ VT 1 (*Téc*) [+ *disco*] to cut; [+ *foto*] to expose; **película sin ~** unexposed film
2 [+ *persona*] (= *causar impresión a*) to impress, strike; (= *conmover*) to move, affect; (= *horrorizar*) to shock; **no se deja ~ fácilmente** he is not easily impressed; **la noticia de su muerte me impresionó mucho** the news of his death had a profound effect on me
Ⓑ VI (= *causar impresión*) to make an impression; **lo hace sólo para ~** he does it just to impress
Ⓒ **impresionarse** VPR 1 (= *sorprenderse, asustarse*) to be affected
2 (= *conmoverse*) to be moved, be affected
impresionismo SM impressionism
impresionista Ⓐ ADJ impressionist, impressionistic
Ⓑ SMF impressionist
impreso Ⓐ PP *de* **imprimir**
Ⓑ ADJ [*papel, libro, material*] printed
Ⓒ SM 1 (= *formulario*) form; **un ~ de beca** a grant application form; **cumplimentar** (*frm*) *o* **rellenar un ~** to fill in a form, fill out a form ► **impreso de solicitud** application form
2 **"impresos"** (*en sobre*) printed matter *sing*
impresor(a) SM/F printer
impresora SF (*Inform*) printer ► **impresora (de) calidad carta** letter-quality printer ► **impresora de chorro de tinta** ink-jet printer ► **impresora de impacto** impact printer ► **impresora de inyección de burbujas** bubble-jet printer ► **impresora (de) láser** laser printer ► **impresora de línea** line-printer ► **impresora de margarita** daisy-wheel printer ► **impresora de matriz de puntos** dot-matrix printer ► **impresora de no impacto** non-impact printer ► **impresora en paralelo** parallel printer ► **impresora matricial** dot-matrix printer
imprevisibilidad SF [*de suceso, problema*] unforeseeable nature; [*de persona*] unpredictability
imprevisible ADJ [*suceso, problema*] unforeseeable; [*persona*] unpredictable
imprevisión SF lack of foresight
imprevisor ADJ lacking foresight, improvident (*frm*)
imprevisto Ⓐ ADJ unforeseen, unexpected
Ⓑ SM (= *suceso*) contingency; **~s** (= *gastos*) incidentals, unforeseen expenses; (= *emergencias*) contingencies; **si no surgen ~s** if noth- ing unexpected occurs
imprimar ▸conjug 1a◂ VT (*Arte*) to prime
imprimátur SM imprimatur
imprimible ADJ printable
imprimir ▸conjug 3a◂ (*pp* **imprimido** *en tiempos compuestos; pp* **impreso** *como adj*) VT 1 (*Tip*) [+ *libro, folleto, billetes*] to print; **"impreso en Montevideo"** "printed in Montevideo"
2 (*Inform*) [+ *documento, página*] to print out
3 (= *marcar*) [+ *nombre, número*] to print; **dejó sus huellas impresas en el jarrón** he left his fingerprints on the vase; **estar impreso en algo** to be engraved on sth; **el accidente quedó impreso en su memoria** the accident was imprinted on his memory; **el dolor estaba impreso en su rostro** pain was written all over his face
4 (= *transmitir*) [+ *estilo*] to stamp; [+ *ritmo*] to set; [+ *velocidad*] to introduce; **el director imprimió su sello a la orquesta** the conductor put his own stamp on the orchestra; **imprime a sus escritos un particular encanto** she brings a special charm to her writing; **el equipo no ha encontrado la forma de ~ velocidad a su juego** the team have not found a way to speed up their game; **~ carácter** to be character-building; **haber vivido en Madrid le ha imprimido carácter** living in Madrid has been a character-building experience (for him) *o* has been character-building for him; **sus lecturas infantiles han imprimido carácter en su obra** his childhood reading has given character to his work
5 (*Biol*) to imprint (**a** on)
improbabilidad SF improbability, unlikelihood
improbable ADJ improbable, unlikely
improbar ▸conjug 1l◂ VT (*Caribe*) to fail to approve, not approve
improbidad SF dishonesty
ímprobo ADJ 1 (= *persona*) dishonest, corrupt
2 (= *enorme*) [*tarea, esfuerzo*] enormous
improcedencia SF 1 (= *no idoneidad*) unsuitability, inappropriateness
2 (*Jur*) inadmissibility
improcedente ADJ 1 (= *inadecuado*) unsuitable, inappropriate
2 (*Jur*) inadmissible; **despido ~** unfair dismissal
improductividad SF unproductiveness
improductivo ADJ unproductive
impronta SF 1 (*Arte*) (= *marca*) stamp, impression; [*de relieve*] rubbing; [*de hueco*] cast, mould, mold (*EEUU*)
2 (= *rastro*) stamp, mark
impronunciable ADJ unpronounceable
improperio SM insult; **soltar ~s** to curse
impropiamente ADV 1 (= *inadecuadamente*) inappropriately, unsuitably
2 (= *incorrectamente*) improperly
impropicio ADJ inauspicious, unpropitious
impropiedad SF 1 (= *inadecuación*) inappropriateness, unsuitability
2 (= *incorrección*) [*de estilo, palabras*] impropriety, infelicity (*frm*)
impropio ADJ 1 (= *inadecuado*) inappropriate, unsuitable; **~ de** *o* **para** inappropriate for
2 (= *incorrecto*) [*estilo, palabras*] improper, incorrect
improrrogable ADJ [*fecha, plazo*] that cannot be extended
impróvidamente ADV improvidently
impróvido ADJ improvident
improvisación SF [*de acción*] improvisation; (*Mús*) extemporization; (*Teat*) ad-lib
improvisadamente ADV 1 (= *de repente*) unexpectedly, suddenly
2 (= *sin preparación*) at the drop of a hat

➤ LENGUA Y USO: imposible A1 39, 43, 52.5 impresión 1 33.2

improvisado ADJ [*discurso*] improvised; [*reparación*] makeshift; [*música*] impromptu

improvisamente ADV unexpectedly, suddenly

improvisar ▸conjug 1a◂ VT [+ *discurso*] to improvise; [+ *comida*] to rustle up*; [+ *música*] to extemporize; [+ *representación*] to ad-lib

improviso Ⓐ ADJ [1] (= *imprevisto*) unexpected, unforeseen

[2] **de ~** unexpectedly, suddenly; [*dicho*] off the cuff; [*hecho*] on the spur of the moment; **coger** *o* **pillar de ~** to catch unawares; **hablar de ~** to speak off the cuff; **tocar de ~** to play impromptu

Ⓑ SM **en un ~** (*Andes**) suddenly, without warning

improvisto ADJ unexpected, unforeseen; **de ~** unexpectedly, suddenly

imprudencia SF [1] (= *cualidad*) (*al hacer algo*) imprudence, rashness; (*al averiguar algo*) indiscretion

[2] (= *acción*) **fue una ~ del conductor** it was the driver's carelessness ► **imprudencia temeraria** criminal negligence; **ser acusado de conducir con ~ temeraria** to be charged with dangerous driving

imprudente ADJ [1] (= *irreflexivo*) imprudent, rash

[2] (= *indiscreto*) indiscreet

[3] [*conductor*] careless

imprudentemente ADV [1] (= *sin reflexionar*) unwisely, imprudently

[2] (= *indiscretamente*) indiscreetly

[3] [*conducir*] carelessly

Impte. ABR (= **Importe**) amt

impúber ADJ prepubescent, immature

impublicable ADJ unprintable

impudencia SF shamelessness, brazenness

impudente ADJ shameless, brazen

impúdicamente ADV (= *sin vergüenza*) immodestly, shamelessly; (= *obscenamente*) lewdly; (= *con lascivia*) lecherously

impudicia SF (= *desvergüenza*) immodesty, shamelessness; (= *obscenidad*) lewdness; (= *lascivia*) lechery

impúdico ADJ (= *desvergonzado*) immodest, shameless; (= *obsceno*) lewd; (= *lascivo*) lecherous

impudor SM = **impudicia**

impuesto Ⓐ PP *de* **imponer**

Ⓑ ADJ **estar ~ en** to be well versed in; **estar** *o* **quedar ~ de** to be informed about

Ⓒ SM (*al estado*) tax (**sobre** on); (*en operaciones de compraventa*) duty (**sobre** on), levy (**sobre** on); **~s** taxes, taxation *sing*; **antes de ~s** pre-tax; **beneficios antes de ~s** pre-tax profits; **¿cuánto ganas antes de ~s?** how much do you earn before tax?; **libre de ~s** [*inversión, mercancías*] tax-free; [*bebida, perfume, tabaco*] duty-free; **sujeto a ~** taxable ► **impuesto al valor agregado** value added tax ► **impuesto comunitario** community tax ► **impuesto de actividades económicas** business tax ► **impuesto de bienes inmuebles** property tax ► **impuesto de circulación** road tax ► **impuesto del timbre** stamp duty ► **impuesto de lujo** luxury tax ► **impuesto de plusvalía** capital gains tax ► **impuesto de radicación** property tax ► **impuesto de sociedades** corporation tax ► **impuesto de transferencia de capital** capital transfer tax ► **impuesto de venta** sales tax ► **impuesto directo** direct tax ► **impuesto ecológico** eco-tax, green tax ► **impuesto revolucionario** *protection money paid to terrorists* ► **impuesto sobre apuestas** betting tax ► **impuesto sobre bienes inmuebles** property tax ► **impuesto sobre el capital** capital levy ► **Impuesto sobre (el) Valor Añadido, Impuesto sobre (el) Valor Agregado** (*LAm*) Value Added Tax ► **impuesto sobre espectáculos** entertainment tax ► **impuesto sobre la propiedad** property tax, rate (*EEUU*) ► **impuesto sobre la renta de las personas físicas** income tax ► **impuesto sobre la riqueza** wealth tax ► **impuesto sobre los bienes heredados** inheritance tax, estate duty ► **impuesto verde** green tax

impugnación SF challenge, contestation

impugnar ▸conjug 1a◂ VT [+ *decisión, fallo*] to contest, challenge; [+ *teoría*] to refute; [+ *motivos, testimonio*] to impeach

impulsador SM (*Aer*) booster

impulsar ▸conjug 1a◂ VT [1] (*Mec*) to drive, propel

[2] [+ *persona*] to drive, impel; **impulsado por el miedo** driven (on) by fear

[3] [+ *deporte, inversión*] to promote

impulsión SF impulsion

impulsividad SF impulsiveness

impulsivo ADJ impulsive; **compra impulsiva** impulse buying

impulso SM [1] (= *empuje*) **le dio tanto ~ que la tiró del columpio** he gave her such a push that she fell off the swing; **llevaba tanto ~ que no pudo parar a tiempo** she was going so fast she couldn't stop in time; **coger** *o* **tomar ~** to gather momentum

[2] (= *estímulo*) boost; **un ~ a la economía** a boost to the economy; **esto dará un ~ a las negociaciones** this will give the negotiations a boost; **este director ha dado un ~ a la empresa** this director has given the company fresh impetus *o* a boost

[3] (= *deseo instintivo*) impulse; **un ~ repentino** a sudden impulse; **mi primer ~ fue salir corriendo** my first instinct was to run away; **no pude resistir el ~ de abrazarla** I couldn't resist the impulse *o* urge to embrace her; **a ~s del miedo** driven (on) by fear ► **impulso sexual** sexual urge, sex drive

[4] (*Fís, Fisiol*) impulse ► **impulso eléctrico** electrical impulse ► **impulso nervioso** nerve impulse

impulsor(a) Ⓐ ADJ drive *antes de s*, driving

Ⓑ SM/F (= *persona*) promoter, instigator

Ⓒ SM (*Mec*) drive; (*Aer*) booster

impune ADJ unpunished

impunemente ADV with impunity

impunidad SF impunity

impuntual ADJ unpunctual

impuntualidad SF unpunctuality

impureza SF [1] [*de sustancia, agua*] impurity

[2] [*de persona, pensamiento*] impurity

impurificar ▸conjug 1g◂ VT [1] (= *adulterar*) to adulterate, make impure

[2] (= *corromper*) to corrupt, defile

impuro ADJ [1] [*sustancia, agua*] impure

[2] [*persona, pensamiento*] impure

imputable ADJ **fracasos que son ~s a** failures which can be attributed to, failures which are attributable to

imputación SF accusation, imputation

imputar ▸conjug 1a◂ VT **~ a** to impute to, attribute to; **los hechos que se les imputan** the acts with which they are charged

imputrescible ADJ (*frm*) (*gen*) rot-proof; (*pey*) non-biodegradable

in* ADJ INV in*; **es el estilo más in** this is the really in style*; **lo in es hablar de ...** the in thing is to talk about ...; **lo que llevan los más in** what people who are really with it are wearing*

-ín, -ina *ver* **Aspects of Word Formation in Spanish 2**

inabarcable ADJ vast, extensive

inabordable ADJ unapproachable

inacabable ADJ endless, interminable

inacabablemente ADV endlessly, interminably

inacabado ADJ [*trabajo, libro*] unfinished; [*problema*] unresolved

inaccesibilidad SF inaccessibility

inaccesible ADJ [*torre, montaña*] inaccessible; [*precio*] prohibitive; [*persona*] aloof

inacción SF (= *falta de actividad*) inactivity; (= *ociosidad*) inactivity, idleness

inacentuado ADJ unaccented, unstressed

inaceptabilidad SF unacceptability

▼**inaceptable** ADJ unacceptable

inactividad SF [1] [*de persona*] (= *falta de actividad*) inactivity; (= *pereza*) idleness

[2] (*Com, Fin*) [*de mercado*] sluggishness

inactivo/a Ⓐ ADJ [1] [*persona*] (= *sin actividad*) inactive; (= *perezoso*) idle

[2] [*volcán*] dormant, inactive

[3] (*Com, Fin*) [*mercado*] sluggish; [*población*] non-working

Ⓑ SM/F **los ~s** the non-working population

inactual ADJ (= *no válido*) lacking present validity, no longer applicable; (= *caduco*) old-fashioned, out-of-date

inadaptable ADJ unadaptable

inadaptación SF [1] (= *falta de adaptación*) inability to adapt; **~ social** maladjustment

[2] (*Med*) rejection

inadaptado/a Ⓐ ADJ maladjusted (**a** to)

Ⓑ SM/F misfit, maladjusted person ► **inadaptado/a social** social misfit

inadecuación SF [*de recursos, medidas*] inadequacy; [*de película, momento*] unsuitability, inappropriateness

inadecuado ADJ [*recurso, medida*] inadequate; [*película, momento*] unsuitable, inappropriate

inadmisibilidad SF unacceptable nature

inadmisible ADJ unacceptable

inadvertencia SF [1] (= *cualidad*) inadvertence; **por ~** inadvertently

[2] **una ~** an oversight, a slip

inadvertidamente ADV inadvertently

inadvertido ADJ [1] (= *no notado*) unnoticed, unobserved; **pasar ~** to go unnoticed, escape notice

[2] (= *despistado*) inattentive

inafectado ADJ unaffected

inagotabilidad SF [*de recursos*] inexhaustibility; (= *resistencia*) tireless nature

inagotable ADJ [*recursos*] inexhaustible; [*persona, paciencia*] tireless

inaguantable ADJ intolerable, unbearable

➤ LENGUA Y USO: inaceptable 41

inaguantablemente ADV intolerably, unbearably

inajenable ADJ [1] *[billete]* non-transferable
[2] *(Jur)* inalienable

inalámbrico Ⓐ ADJ wireless; *(Telec)* cordless
Ⓑ SM (= *micrófono*) wireless mike; (= *teléfono*) cordless telephone

in albis ADV **quedarse ~** (= *no saber*) to be left in the dark; (= *fracasar*) to get nothing for one's trouble

inalcanzable ADJ unattainable

inalienable ADJ inalienable

inalterabilidad SF *[de materia]* inalterability, unchanging nature; *[de persona, cualidad]* immutability

inalterable ADJ *[materia]* inalterable, unchanging; *[persona, cualidad]* immutable; *[cara]* impassive; *[color]* permanent, fast; *[lustre]* permanent

inalterado ADJ unchanged, unaltered

inamistoso ADJ unfriendly

inamovible ADJ [1] (= *fijo*) fixed, immovable
[2] *(Téc)* undetachable

inanición SF [1] (= *hambre*) starvation; **morir de ~** to die of starvation
[2] *(Med)* inanition

inanidad SF inanity

inanimado ADJ inanimate

inánime ADJ lifeless

INAP SM ABR *(Esp)* = **Instituto Nacional de la Administración Pública**

inapagable ADJ *[sed]* unquenchable; *[fuego, incendio]* inextinguishable

inapeable ADJ [1] (= *oscuro*) incomprehensible
[2] (= *terco*) obstinate, stubborn

inapelabilidad SF finality, unappealable nature

inapelable ADJ [1] *(Jur)* unappealable, not open to appeal; **las decisiones de los jueces serán ~s** the judges' decisions will be final
[2] (= *irremediable*) irremediable, inevitable

inapercibido ADJ unperceived

inapetencia SF lack of appetite, loss of appetite

inapetente ADJ **estar ~** to have no appetite, not to be hungry

inaplazable ADJ which cannot be put off *o* postponed, pressing

inaplicable ADJ not applicable

inaplicado ADJ slack, lazy

inapreciable ADJ [1] *[diferencia]* imperceptible
[2] *(de valor)* invaluable, inestimable

inaprehensible ADJ, **inaprensible** ADJ [1] (= *complicado*) indefinite, hard to pin down
[2] (= *escurridizo*) hard to grasp

inaptitud SF unsuitability

inapto ADJ unsuited (**para** to)

inarmónico ADJ *(lit)* unharmonious; *(fig)* cacophonous

inarrugable ADJ crease-resistant

inarticulado ADJ inarticulate

inasequible ADJ (= *inalcanzable*) unattainable, out of reach; (= *indisponible*) unobtainable

inasistencia SF absence

inastillable ADJ shatterproof

inasumible ADJ unacceptable

inatacable ADJ unassailable

inatención SF inattention (**a** to), lack of attention (**a** to)

inatento ADJ inattentive

inaudible ADJ inaudible

inaudito ADJ *(gen)* unheard-of; (= *sin precedente*) unprecedented; (= *increíble*) outrageous

inauguración SF *[de teatro, exposición]* opening, inauguration *(frm)*; *[de monumento]* unveiling; *[de casa]* house-warming party; *[de curso]* start; *(Com)* setting up; **ceremonia de ~** inauguration ceremony, opening ceremony
► **inauguración privada** *(Arte)* private viewing

inaugural ADJ *[ceremonia, competición, discurso]* opening, inaugural; *[concierto]* opening; *[viaje]* maiden *antes de s*

inaugurar ▸conjug 1a◂ VT [+ *edificio*] to inaugurate; [+ *exposición*] to open (formally); [+ *estatua*] to unveil

inautenticidad SF lack of authenticity

inauténtico ADJ inauthentic, not genuine, false

INB SM ABR *(Esp Escol)* = **Instituto Nacional de Bachillerato**

INBA SM ABR *(Méx)* = **Instituto Nacional de Bellas Artes**

INBAD SM ABR *(Esp)* = **Instituto Nacional de Bachillerato a Distancia**

INC SM ABR *(Esp)* [1] = **Instituto Nacional de Colonización**
[2] *(Com)* = **Instituto Nacional de Consumo**

inc. ABR (= **inclusive**) inc.

inca SMF Inca

incachable* ADJ *(LAm)* useless

INCAE SM ABR = **Instituto Centroamericano de Administración de Empresas**

incaico ADJ Inca *antes de s*

incalculable ADJ incalculable

incalificable ADJ indescribable, unspeakable

incalificablemente ADV indescribably, unspeakably

incanato SM *(Perú)* (= *época*) Inca period; (= *reinado*) reign *(of an Inca)*

incandescencia SF incandescence *(frm)*, white heat

incandescente ADJ [1] *[hierro, bombilla]* incandescent *(frm)*, white hot
[2] *[mirada]* burning, passionate

incansable ADJ tireless, untiring

incansablemente ADV tirelessly, untiringly

incapacidad SF [1] (= *falta de capacidad*) (*para una actividad*) inability; (*para una profesión*) incompetence; **~ de concentración** inability to concentrate; **su ~ de respuesta** his failure to reply; **~ de** *o* **para hacer algo** inability to do sth ► **incapacidad laboral permanente** invalidity ► **incapacidad laboral transitoria, incapacidad temporal** temporary disability
[2] (= *discapacidad*) *(física)* physical handicap, disability; *(mental)* mental handicap
[3] *(Jur)* *(tb* **~ legal***)* legal incapacity

incapacitación SF **proceso de ~ presidencial** impeachment of a president

incapacitado ADJ [1] (= *inadecuado*) unfit (**para** for)
[2] (= *descalificado*) disqualified
[3] (= *minusválido*) handicapped, disabled

incapacitante ADJ incapacitating

incapacitar ▸conjug 1a◂ VT [1] (= *invalidar*) to incapacitate, handicap
[2] *(Jur)* to disqualify (**para** for)

▼ **incapaz** Ⓐ ADJ [1] **ser ~: no es que sea ~, es que no tengo fuerzas** it's not that I can't do it, I just haven't got the strength; **no sé cómo puedes engañarlo, yo sería ~** I don't know how you can deceive him, I could never do a thing like that; **ser ~ de hacer algo** (= *no atreverse, no querer*) to never do sth, be incapable of doing sth *(frm)*; (= *no poder*) to be unable to do sth; **¿es que eres ~ de hablar en serio?** can't you ever talk seriously?, aren't you capable of talking seriously? *(frm)*; **la policía se mostró ~ de prevenir la tragedia** the police proved unable to prevent the tragedy; **ser ~ para algo** to be useless at sth; **soy ~ para la física** I'm useless at physics
[2] (= *incompetente*) incompetent
[3] *(Jur)* unfit; **fue declarado ~ de administrar sus bienes** he was declared unfit to manage his property
[4] *(CAm)* *[niño]* trying, difficult
Ⓑ SMF incompetent, incompetent fool

incapturable ADJ unattainable

incardinar ▸conjug 1a◂ VT *(frm)* to include *(as an integral part)*

incario SM *(Perú)* Inca period

incasable ADJ unmarriageable

incásico ADJ *(LAm)* Inca *antes de s*

incatalogable ADJ (= *indefinible*) indefinable; (= *poco convencional*) off-beat; **persona ~** person who refuses to be pigeon-holed

incautación SF seizure, confiscation

incautamente ADV unwarily, incautiously

incautar ▸conjug 1a◂ Ⓐ VT to seize, confiscate
Ⓑ **incautarse** VPR **~se de** *(Jur)* to seize, confiscate; (= *intervenir*) to take possession of

incauto ADJ [1] (= *crédulo*) gullible
[2] (= *imprevisor*) unwary, incautious

incendiar ▸conjug 1b◂ Ⓐ VT to set fire to, set alight
Ⓑ **incendiarse** VPR (= *empezar a arder*) to catch fire; (= *quemarse*) to burn down

incendiario/a Ⓐ ADJ [1] *[bomba, mecanismo]* incendiary
[2] *[discurso, escrito]* inflammatory
Ⓑ SM/F fire-raiser, arsonist ► **incendiario/a de la guerra** warmonger

incendiarismo SM arson

incendio SM fire; ✦*MODISMO* **echar** *o* **hablar ~s de algn** *(Andes, Cono Sur)* to sling mud at sb ► **incendio forestal** forest fire ► **incendio intencionado, incendio provocado** arson attack

incensar ▸conjug 1j◂ VT [1] *(Rel)* to cense, incense
[2] (= *halagar*) to flatter

incensario SM censer

incentivación SF [1] (= *motivación*) motivation
[2] *(Fin)* (= *sistema*) incentive scheme; (= *prima*) productivity bonus

incentivar ▸conjug la◂ VT to encourage; **baja incentivada** voluntary redundancy

incentivo SM incentive; **baja por ~** voluntary redundancy ► **incentivo fiscal** tax incentive

incertidumbre SF uncertainty

incesante ADJ incessant, unceasing

incesantemente ADV incessantly, unceasingly

➤ LENGUA Y USO: **incapaz A1** 43.4

incesto SM incest

incestuoso ADJ incestuous

incidencia SF [1] (*Mat*) incidence
[2] (= *suceso*) incident
[3] (= *impacto*) impact, effect; **la huelga tuvo escasa ~** the strike had little impact

incidentado ADJ [1] (= *con percances*) eventful
[2] (= *descontrolado*) unruly, riotous, turbulent

incidental ADJ incidental

incidente (A) SM [1] (= *contratiempo*) hitch; **la manifestación transcurrió sin ~s** the demonstration passed off without incident; **un viaje sin ~s** a trouble-free journey
[2] (= *disputa*) incident; **un desagradable ~ entre los dos jugadores** an unpleasant incident between the two players; **~ diplomático** diplomatic incident
(B) ADJ incidental

incidentemente ADV incidentally

incidir ▸conjug 3a◂ (A) VI [1] **~ en** (= *afectar*) to influence, affect; (= *recaer sobre*) to have a bearing on; **~ en un error** to make a mistake; **el impuesto incide más en ellos** the tax affects them most, the tax hits them hardest; **la familia ha incidido fuertemente en la historia** the family has influenced history a lot
[2] (= *hacer hincapié*) **~ en un tema** to stress a subject
(B) VT (*Med*) to incise

incienso SM [1] (*Rel*) incense
[2] (= *halagos*) flattery

inciertamente ADV uncertainly

incierto ADJ (= *dudoso*) uncertain; (= *inconstante*) inconstant; (= *inseguro*) insecure

incineración SF [*de basuras*] incineration; [*de cadáveres*] cremation

incinerador SM, **incineradora** SF incinerator
► **incinerador de residuos sólidos** solid-waste incinerator

incinerar ▸conjug 1a◂ VT [+ *basuras*] to incinerate, burn; [+ *cadáver*] to cremate

incipiente ADJ incipient

incircunciso ADJ uncircumcised

incisión SF incision

incisividad SF incisiveness

incisivo (A) ADJ [1] (= *cortante*) sharp, cutting
[2] (= *mordaz*) incisive
(B) SM incisor

inciso SM [1] (= *observación*) digression, aside; **hacer un ~** to make an aside
[2] (= *interrupción*) interjection, interruption
[3] (*Ling*) (= *oración*) interpolated clause; (= *coma*) comma
[4] (*Jur*) subsection

incitación SF incitement (**a** to)

incitante ADJ provocative

incitar ▸conjug 1a◂ VT to incite; **~ a algn a hacer algo** to urge sb to do sth; **~ a algn contra otro** to incite sb against another person

incívico/a (A) ADJ antisocial
(B) SM/F antisocial person

incivil ADJ uncivil, rude

incivilidad SF [1] (= *cualidad*) incivility, rudeness
[2] **una ~** an incivility, a piece of rudeness

incivilizado ADJ uncivilized

incivismo SM *antisocial behaviour or outlook etc*

inclasificable ADJ unclassifiable

inclemencia SF (*Meteo*) harshness, inclemency; **la ~ del tiempo** the inclemency of the weather; **dejar algo a la ~** to leave sth exposed to the weather *o* the elements

inclemente ADJ (*Meteo*) harsh, inclement

inclinación SF [1] [*de terreno*] slope, gradient; [*de objeto*] lean, list; **la ~ del terreno** the slope of the ground, the gradient (of the ground); **la ~ de la Torre de Pisa** the lean of the Tower of Pisa; **un poste con una ~ de siete grados** a post with a seven-degree lean *o* list ► **inclinación lateral** (*Aer*) bank ► **inclinación magnética** magnetic dip, magnetic inclination
[2] (= *reverencia*) bow; **hizo una profunda ~ ante el rey** he made a deep bow before the king; **María me saludó con una ~ de cabeza** María greeted me with a nod; **el presidente dio su aprobación con una ~ de cabeza** the president nodded (his) approval
[3] (= *tendencia*) inclination; **su ~ natural es conservadora** his natural inclination is conservative, he's conservative by inclination; **no tengo ~ política concreta** I have no particular political inclinations *o* leanings; **tiene inclinaciones artísticas** she has artistic inclinations, she's artistically inclined; **tiene ~ a tomárselo todo a risa** he's inclined to treat everything as a joke; **tener ~ hacia la poesía** to have a penchant for poetry, have poetic leanings ► **inclinación sexual** sexual preferences *pl*

inclinado ADJ [1] (*en ángulo*) [*terreno, línea*] sloping; [*plano*] inclined; **la torre inclinada de Pisa** the leaning tower of Pisa
[2] **estar ~ a hacer algo** to be inclined to do sth; **sentirse ~ a hacer algo** to feel inclined to do sth

inclinar ▸conjug 1a◂ (A) VT [1] (= *ladear*) [+ *objeto vertical*] to tilt, lean; **el peso de los abrigos inclinó el perchero** the hatstand was tilting *o* leaning under the weight of the coats; **inclinó el plato para acabarse la sopa** he tilted his plate to finish off his soup; **inclinó el respaldo del asiento** he reclined his seat; **inclina el cuadro hacia la derecha** slope *o* tilt the picture to the right
[2] [+ *cabeza*] to lean; **inclinó la cabeza para olerle el cabello** she leant her head forward to smell his hair; **para afirmar inclinó la cabeza** he nodded (his) agreement; **~on la cabeza ante el altar** they bowed their heads before the altar
[3] (= *resolver*) [+ *balanza*] to tip; **los indecisos ~on la balanza hacia la izquierda** the floating voters tipped the balance in favour of the left; **este gol inclinó el marcador a su favor** this goal tipped the balance in their favour
[4] (= *predisponer*) to incline; **la crisis inclina a los consumidores hacia el ahorro** the recession inclines consumers to save their money
[5] (= *decidir*) **eso la inclinó a pensar que yo era el culpable** that led her to think that I was guilty; **el informe lo inclinó a cambiar de estrategia** the report swayed him in favour of changing his strategy
(B) **inclinarse** VPR [1] [*objeto vertical*] to lean, tilt
[2] (= *encorvarse*) to stoop, bend; **Balbino se inclinó sobre el muro** Balbino leant over the wall; **Amelia se inclinó hacia delante para coger el bolso** Amelia leant forward to pick up the bag; **me incliné hacia atrás para ponerme cómodo** I leant back to make myself comfortable; **nos inclinamos ante el rey** we bowed to the king
[3] (= *tender*) **me inclino a favor de la moneda única** I'm inclined to be in favour of the single currency; **me inclino a pensar que no es verdad** I am inclined to *o* I tend to think that it's not true; **entre los dos, me inclino por el segundo** of the two, I'm inclined to go for the second *o* I tend to prefer the second

ínclito ADJ (*frm, liter*) illustrious, renowned

incluir ▸conjug 3g◂ VT [1] (= *comprender*) to include, contain; **todo incluido** (*Com*) inclusive, all-in
[2] (= *agregar*) to include; (*en carta*) to enclose

inclusa SF foundling hospital

inclusero/a SM/F foundling

inclusión SF inclusion; **con ~ de** including

inclusivamente ADV inclusive, inclusively

inclusive ADV inclusive; **del 1 al 10, ambos ~** from the 1st to the 10th inclusive; **hasta el próximo domingo ~** up to and including next Sunday

inclusivo ADJ inclusive

incluso (A) ADV [1] (= *aun*) even; **~ le pegó** he even hit her; **no resulta sencillo ni ~ para nosotros** it isn't simple, (not) even for us; **estaba sonriente e ~ alegre** she was smiling and happy even
[2] (= *incluyendo*) including; **nos gustó a todos, ~ a los más testarudos** we all liked it, even *o* including the most stubborn of us
(B) ADJ enclosed

incoación SF inception

incoar ▸conjug 1a◂ VT to start, initiate

incobrable (A) ADJ irrecoverable
(B) **incobrables** SMPL irrecoverable debts, bad debts

incógnita SF [1] (*Mat*) unknown quantity; **despejar la ~** to find the unknown quantity
[2] (*por averiguar*) (= *misterio*) mystery; (= *razón oculta*) hidden motive; **queda en pie la ~ sobre su influencia** there is still a question mark over his influence

incógnito (A) ADJ unknown
(B) SM incognito; **viajar de ~** to travel incognito

incognoscible ADJ unknowable

incoherencia SF [1] (= *falta de sentido*) (*en pensamiento, ideas*) incoherence; (*en comportamiento, respuestas*) inconsistency
[2] (= *falta de conexión*) disconnectedness
[3] **incoherencias** nonsense *sing*

incoherente ADJ [1] (= *sin sentido*) [*pensamiento, ideas*] incoherent; [*comportamiento, respuestas*] inconsistent; **es ~ con sus ideas** he's inconsistent in his thinking
[2] (= *inconexo*) disconnected

incoloro ADJ [*líquido, luz*] colourless, colorless (*EEUU*); [*barniz*] clear

incólume ADJ (= *ileso*) unhurt, unharmed; **salió ~ del accidente** he emerged unharmed *o* unscathed from the accident

incombustible ADJ [*mueble, ropa*] fire-resistant; [*tela*] fireproof

incomible ADJ inedible, uneatable

incómodamente ADV (= *sin comodidad*) uncomfortably; (= *con molestias*) inconveniently

incomodar ▸conjug 1a◂ (A) VT [1] (= *causar molestia*) to inconvenience, trouble

2 (= *causar vergüenza*) to make feel uncomfortable, embarrass

3 (= *enfadar*) to annoy

Ⓑ **incomodarse** VPR 1 (= *tomarse molestia*) to put o.s. out; **¡no se incomode!** don't bother!, don't trouble yourself!

2 (= *avergonzarse*) to feel uncomfortable, feel embarrassed

3 (= *enfadarse*) to get annoyed (**con** with)

incomodidad SF 1 (= *falta de comodidad*) discomfort

2 (= *inoportunidad*) inconvenience

3 (= *fastidio*) annoyance, irritation

incomodo SM = **incomodidad 3**

incómodo Ⓐ ADJ 1 [*sofá, situación*] uncomfortable; **un paquete ~ de llevar** an awkward *o* cumbersome package to carry; **sentirse ~** to feel ill at ease, feel uncomfortable; **me resultaba ~ estar con los dos a la vez** I felt ill at ease *o* uncomfortable being with both of them together

2 [*persona*] tiresome, annoying

3 **estar ~ con algn** (*Cono Sur*) to be angry with sb, be fed up with sb*

Ⓑ SM (*LAm*) = **incomodidad 3**

incomparable ADJ incomparable

incomparablemente ADV incomparably

incomparecencia SF failure to appear (*in court etc*), non-appearance

incomparecimiento SM **pleito perdido por ~** suit lost by default *o* failure to appear; **pleito ganado por ~** undefended suit

incompasivo ADJ (= *indiferente*) unsympathetic; (= *despiadado*) pitiless

incompatibilidad SF incompatibility; **~ de caracteres** mutual incompatibility; **~ de intereses** conflict of interests; **ley de ~es** *law regulating the holding of multiple posts*

incompatibilizar ▸conjug 1f◂ VT to make incompatible, render incompatible

incompatible ADJ incompatible

incompetencia SF incompetence

incompetente ADJ incompetent

incompletamente ADV incompletely

incompleto ADJ incomplete

incomprendido/a Ⓐ ADJ [*persona*] misunderstood; [*genio*] not appreciated

Ⓑ SM/F (= *persona*) misunderstood person

incomprensibilidad SF incomprehensibility

incomprensible ADJ incomprehensible

incomprensión SF 1 [*de padres, mayores*] incomprehension, lack of understanding

2 (= *subestimación*) lack of appreciation

incomprobable ADJ unprovable

incomunicación SF 1 (= *aislamiento*) (*gen*) isolation; (*para presos*) solitary confinement; **ello permite la ~ de los detenidos** it allows those detained to be held incommunicado

2 (= *falta de comunicación*) lack of communication

incomunicado ADJ 1 (= *aislado*) isolated, cut off

2 [*preso*] in solitary confinement

incomunicar ▸conjug 1g◂ Ⓐ VT 1 (= *aislar*) to cut off, isolate

2 [+ *preso*] to put in solitary confinement; **~ a un detenido** to refuse a prisoner access to a lawyer

Ⓑ **incomunicarse** VPR to isolate o.s., cut o.s. off

inconcebible ADJ inconceivable

inconcebiblemente ADV inconceivably

inconciliable ADJ irreconcilable

inconcluso ADJ unfinished, incomplete

inconcluyente ADJ inconclusive

inconcreción SF vagueness

inconcreto ADJ vague

inconcuso ADJ indisputable, incontrovertible

▼ **incondicional** Ⓐ ADJ 1 (= *sin condiciones*) [*retirada, fianza, amor, garantía*] unconditional; [*fe*] complete, unquestioning; [*apoyo*] wholehearted, unconditional; [*afirmación*] unqualified; [*partidario*] staunch, stalwart

2 (*LAm pey*) servile, fawning

Ⓑ SMF 1 (= *partidario*) stalwart, staunch supporter

2 (*pey*) (= *intransigente*) diehard, hardliner

3 (*LAm*) yes man*

incondicionalidad SF 1 (= *apoyo*) unconditional support

2 (= *lealtad*) unquestioning loyalty

incondicionalismo SM (*LAm*) toadyism, servility

incondicionalmente ADV (= *sin condiciones*) unconditionally, unreservedly; (= *sin reservas*) implicitly, unquestioningly; (= *totalmente*) wholeheartedly; (= *con devoción*) staunchly

inconexión SF [*de datos*] unconnectedness; [*de ideas*] disconnectedness; [*de lenguaje, palabras*] incoherence

inconexo ADJ [*datos*] unrelated, unconnected; [*ideas*] disconnected, disjointed; [*texto*] disjointed; [*lenguaje, palabras*] incoherent

inconfesable ADJ shameful, disgraceful

inconfeso ADJ [*reo*] who refuses to confess; **homosexual ~** closet homosexual

inconforme ADJ nonconformist; **estar** *o* **mostrarse ~ con algo** (*CAm*) to disagree with sth

inconformismo SM non-conformism

inconformista ADJ, SMF non-conformist

inconfundible ADJ unmistakable

inconfundiblemente ADV unmistakably

incongruencia SF 1 (= *falta de coherencia*) inconsistency, contradiction; **notó la ~ de su razonamiento** he spotted the inconsistency *o* contradiction in his argument

2 (= *cosa incoherente*) **el paciente decía ~s** the patient was talking incoherently; **¡deja de decir ~s!** stop talking nonsense!

incongruente ADJ, **incongruo** ADJ incongruous

inconmensurable ADJ 1 (= *enorme*) immeasurable, vast

2 (= *fantástico*) fantastic

3 (*Mat*) incommensurate

inconmovible ADJ [*persona*] unmoved; [*creencia, fe*] unshakeable

inconmutable ADJ immutable

inconocible ADJ 1 (= *que no se puede conocer*) unknowable; **lo ~** the unknowable

2 (*LAm**) (= *irreconocible*) unrecognizable

inconquistable ADJ [*reino*] unconquerable; [*espíritu, fuerza*] unconquerable, unyielding

inconsciencia SF 1 (*Med*) unconsciousness

2 (= *ignorancia*) unawareness

3 (= *irreflexión*) thoughtlessness

inconsciente Ⓐ ADJ 1 (*Med*) unconscious; **lo ~** the unconscious; **lo encontraron ~** they found him unconscious

2 (= *ignorante*) unaware (**de** of), oblivious (**de** to)

3 (= *involuntario*) unwitting

4 (= *irresponsable*) thoughtless; **es más ~ que malo** he's thoughtless rather than wicked; **son gente ~** they're thoughtless people

Ⓑ SM unconscious; **el ~ colectivo** the collective unconscious

inconscientemente ADV 1 (= *sin saber*) unconsciously

2 (= *sin querer*) unwittingly

3 (= *sin pensar*) thoughtlessly

inconsecuencia SF inconsistency

inconsecuente ADJ inconsistent

inconsideración SF 1 (= *desconsideración*) inconsiderateness, thoughtlessness

2 (= *precipitación*) rashness, haste

inconsideradamente ADV 1 (= *sin consideración*) inconsiderately, thoughtlessly

2 (= *precipitadamente*) rashly, hastily

inconsiderado ADJ 1 (= *desconsiderado*) inconsiderate, thoughtless

2 (= *precipitado*) rash, hasty

inconsistencia SF [*de superficie*] unevenness; [*de argumento*] weakness; [*de tierra*] looseness; [*de tela*] flimsiness; [*de masa*] lumpiness

inconsistente ADJ [*superficie*] uneven; [*argumento*] weak; [*tierra*] loose; [*tela*] flimsy; [*masa*] lumpy

inconsolable ADJ inconsolable

inconstancia SF 1 [*de equipo, sistema*] inconstancy

2 [*de tiempo*] changeability

3 (= *veleidad*) fickleness

inconstante ADJ 1 [*equipo, sistema*] inconstant

2 [*tiempo*] changeable

3 [*persona*] (= *veleidoso*) fickle; (= *poco firme*) unsteady; **un amigo ~** a fairweather friend

inconstantemente ADV (= *sin regularidad*) inconstantly; (= *caprichosamente*) in a fickle way

inconstitucional ADJ unconstitutional

inconstitucionalidad SF unconstitutional nature

inconstitucionalmente ADV unconstitutionally

inconsumible ADJ unfit for consumption

incontable ADJ countless, innumerable

incontaminante ADJ non-polluting

incontenible ADJ uncontrollable, unstoppable

incontestable ADJ 1 (= *innegable*) [*argumento*] undeniable, indisputable; [*evidencia, prueba*] irrefutable

2 [*pregunta*] unanswerable

incontestablemente ADV undeniably, indisputably

incontestado ADJ (= *sin respuesta*) unanswered; (= *sin objeciones*) unchallenged, unquestioned; (= *indiscutible*) undisputed

incontinencia SF (*tb Med*) incontinence ► **incontinencia verbal** verbal diarrhoea

incontinente Ⓐ ADJ (*tb Med*) incontinent

Ⓑ ADV = **incontinenti**

incontinenti ADV at once, instantly, forthwith (*frm o liter*)

incontrastable ADJ [*dificultad*] insuperable;

➤ LENGUA Y USO: **incondicional A1** 38.1

[*argumento*] unanswerable; [*persona*] unshakeable, unyielding

incontrolable ADJ uncontrollable

incontrolablemente ADV uncontrollably

incontrolado/a Ⓐ ADJ (= *sin control*) uncontrolled; (= *sin permiso*) unauthorized; (= *violento*) violent, wild
Ⓑ SM/F 1 (= *persona violenta*) violent person (*esp policeman, etc who acts outside the law*)
2 (*Pol*) strong-arm man, bully-boy

incontrovertible ADJ incontrovertible, indisputable

incontrovertido ADJ undisputed

inconveniencia SF 1 (= *inoportunidad*) inappropriateness
2 (= *comentario*) tactless remark
3 (= *acto*) improper thing to do, wrong thing to do

▼ **inconveniente** Ⓐ ADJ inappropriate; **protestar ahora sería del todo ~** it would be inappropriate to complain now; **es ~ hacer públicos esos temas** it is not appropriate to make these matters public
Ⓑ SM 1 (= *problema*) problem; **surgieron muchos ~s y finalmente desistí** a lot of problems arose and in the end I gave up; **el ~ es que es muy caro** the problem *o* trouble is that it's very expensive
2 (= *desventaja*) disadvantage; **tiene el ~ de que consume mucha gasolina** it has the disadvantage of using a lot of petrol; **ventajas e ~s** advantages and disadvantages
3 (= *objeción*) objection; **no hay ~ en pagar a plazos** there is no objection to you paying in instalments; **¿hay ~ en pagar con tarjeta?** is it all right to pay by card?; **¿tienes algún ~ en venir?** do you mind coming?; **preferiría que se fuera, si no tiene ~** I'd rather you went, if you don't mind; **no tengo ningún ~** I don't mind; **no veo ~ en que llames desde aquí** there's no reason why you shouldn't phone from here; **poner (un) ~** to object; **mi madre pone ~s a todo lo que hago** my mother objects to everything I do

inconvertibilidad SF inconvertibility

inconvertible ADJ inconvertible

incordiante* Ⓐ ADJ annoying
Ⓑ SMF troublemaker

incordiar* ▸conjug 1b◂ Ⓐ VT to annoy, pester, bug*; **siempre me está incordiando con preguntas tontas** he's always pestering *o* annoying me with silly questions
Ⓑ VI **¡no incordies!** stop it!, behave yourself!; **tus hijos nunca incordian** your children are never a nuisance

incordio* SM pain*, nuisance

incorporación SF (*gen*) incorporation; (*a filas*) enlisting, enlistment; **la ~ del ejército al gabinete** the inclusion of the Army in the Cabinet; **"sueldo a convenir, ~ inmediata"** "salary negotiable, start immediately"

incorporado ADJ (*Téc*) built-in; **con antena incorporada** with built-in aerial

incorporal ADJ = **incorpóreo**

incorporar ▸conjug 1a◂ Ⓐ VT 1 (= *añadir*) (*gen*) to incorporate (**a, en** into, in); (*Culin*) to mix in, add; **~ a filas** (*Mil*) to call up, enlist
2 (= *involucrar*) to involve (**a** in, with)
3 (= *abarcar*) to embody
4 (= *levantar*) **~ a algn** to sit sb up (*in bed*)
5 (*Teat*) **Rosana incorpora al personaje de Julieta** Rosana plays the part of Julieta
Ⓑ **incorporarse** VPR 1 [*persona acostada*] to sit up; **~se en la cama** to sit up in bed
2 **~se a** [+ *regimiento, asociación*] to join; **~se a una empresa** to join a company; **~se a filas** to join up, enlist; **~se al trabajo** to start work, report for work

incorpóreo ADJ 1 (= *sin cuerpo*) incorporeal
2 (= *inmaterial*) intangible

incorrección SF 1 [*de datos*] incorrectness, inaccuracy
2 (= *descortesía*) discourtesy; **fue una incorrección no informarles** it was bad manners *o* impolite not to inform them; **cometer una ~** to commit a faux pas
3 (*Ling*) mistake

incorrectamente ADV 1 (= *equivocadamente*) incorrectly
2 (= *con descortesía*) discourteously

incorrecto ADJ 1 [*dato*] incorrect, wrong
2 [*conducta*] (= *descortés*) discourteous, bad-mannered; (= *irregular*) improper; **ser ~ con algn** to take liberties with sb
3 [*facciones*] irregular, odd

incorregible ADJ incorrigible

incorrosible ADJ rustproof

incorruptible ADJ incorruptible

incorrupto ADJ 1 (= *no descompuesto*) incorrupt
2 (= *no pervertido*) uncorrupted

incredibilidad SF incredibility

incredulidad SF (= *desconfianza*) incredulity; (= *escepticismo*) scepticism, skepticism (*EEUU*)

incrédulo/a Ⓐ ADJ (= *desconfiado*) incredulous; (= *escéptico*) sceptical, skeptical (*EEUU*)
Ⓑ SM/F sceptic, skeptic (*EEUU*)

increíble ADJ incredible, unbelievable; **es ~ que ...** it is incredible *o* unbelievable that ...

increíblemente ADV incredibly, unbelievably

incremental ADJ incremental

incrementar ▸conjug 1a◂ Ⓐ VT to increase
Ⓑ **incrementarse** VPR to increase

incremento SM [*de conocimiento*] increase, gain; [*de precio, sueldo, productividad*] increase, rise; **tomar ~** to increase ► **incremento de temperatura** rise in temperature ► **incremento salarial** pay rise

increpación SF reprimand, rebuke

increpar ▸conjug 1a◂ VT to reprimand, rebuke

in crescendo ADV **ir ~** to increase, spiral upwards

incriminación SF incrimination

incriminar ▸conjug 1a◂ VT 1 (*Jur*) (= *sugerir culpa de*) to incriminate; (= *acusar*) to accuse; **las pruebas los incriminan** the evidence incriminates them; **varios testigos la incriminan** several witnesses accuse her
2 (= *criminalizar*) to make a crime of, consider criminal
3 (= *exagerar*) to magnify

incruento ADJ bloodless

incrúspido* ADJ (*LAm*) (= *torpe*) clumsy; (= *desmañado*) ham-fisted

incrustación SF 1 (= *acto*) (*lit*) incrustation; (*fig*) grafting
2 (*Arte*) inlay, inlaid work
3 (*Téc*) scale

incrustar ▸conjug 1a◂ Ⓐ VT 1 (= *introducir*) (*lit*) to incrust; (*fig*) to graft
2 [+ *joyas*] to inlay; **una espada incrustada de pedrería** a sword encrusted with precious stones
3 (*Téc*) to set (**en** into)
Ⓑ **incrustarse** VPR **~se en** [*bala*] to lodge in, embed itself in; **se le ha incrustado esta idea en la mente** he's got this idea firmly fixed in his head

incuantificable ADJ unquantifiable

incubación SF incubation

incubadora SF incubator

incubar ▸conjug 1a◂ Ⓐ VT to incubate
Ⓑ **incubarse** VPR to incubate

íncubo SM (*frm*) 1 (= *diablo*) incubus
2 (= *pesadilla*) nightmare

incuestionable ADJ unquestionable, unchallengeable

incuestionablemente ADV unquestionably

inculcar ▸conjug 1g◂ Ⓐ VT to instil, instill (*EEUU*), inculcate (**en** in, into)
Ⓑ **inculcarse** VPR (= *obstinarse*) to be obstinate

inculpable ADJ blameless, guiltless

inculpación SF (*gen*) accusation; (*Jur*) charge

inculpado/a SM/F accused person; **el ~** the accused, the defendant

inculpar ▸conjug 1a◂ VT (*gen*) to accuse (**de** of); (*Jur*) to charge (**de** with); **los crímenes que se le inculpan** the crimes with which he is charged

incultamente ADV (= *iletradamente*) in an uncultured way; (= *groseramente*) uncouthly

incultivable ADJ uncultivable

inculto ADJ 1 [*persona*] (= *iletrado*) uncultured, uneducated; (= *incivilizado*) uncivilized; (= *grosero*) uncouth
2 (*Agr*) uncultivated; **dejar un terreno ~** to leave land uncultivated

incultura SF (= *ignorancia*) lack of culture; (= *grosería*) uncouthness

incumbencia SF (= *obligación*) obligation, duty; (= *competencia*) concern; **no es de mi ~** it is no concern of mine, it is not my job

incumbir ▸conjug 3a◂ VI **esto sólo incumbe a los implicados** this only concerns those involved; **no me incumbe a mí** it is no concern of mine, it is not my job; **le incumbe hacerlo** that is his job, it is his duty to do it

incumplible ADJ unattainable

incumplido ADJ unfulfilled

incumplimiento SM **~ de las promesas electorales** failure to keep electoral promises; **~ de una orden** failure to comply with an order; **~ de contrato** breach of contract; **lo expulsaron por ~ del deber** he was expelled for failing to carry out his duties

incumplir ▸conjug 3a◂ VT [+ *regla*] to break, fail to observe; [+ *promesa*] to break, fail to keep; [+ *contrato*] to breach

incunable SM incunable, incunabulum; **~s** incunabula

incurable Ⓐ ADJ 1 (*Med*) incurable
2 (= *incorregible*) hopeless, irremediable
Ⓑ SMF incurable

incuria SF 1 (= *negligencia*) negligence; **por ~** through negligence
2 (= *dejadez*) carelessness, shiftlessness

incurrir ▸conjug 3a◂ VI **~ en** [+ *error*] to make; [+ *crimen*] to commit; [+ *deuda, odio*] to incur; [+ *desastre*] to fall victim to

➤ LENGUA Y USO: **inconveniente B2** 53.4 **B3** 28.1, 36.1, 36.2, 38.1

incursión SF raid, incursion ► **incursión aérea** air raid

incursionar ▸conjug 1a◂ VI **~ en** to make a raid into, penetrate into; **~ en un tema** to tackle a subject, broach a subject

indagación SF investigation, inquiry

indagador(a) SM/F investigator (**de** into, of), inquirer (**de** into)

indagar ▸conjug 1h◂ VT (= *investigar*) to investigate, inquire into; (= *averiguar*) to find out, ascertain

indagatoria SF (*Méx*) investigation, inquiry

indagatorio ADJ investigatory

indebidamente ADV (= *injustificadamente*) unduly; (= *incorrectamente*) improperly; (= *injustamente*) illegally, wrongfully

indebido ADJ (= *injustificado*) undue; (= *incorrecto*) improper; (= *injusto*) illegal, wrongful

INDEC SM ABR (*Arg*) = **Instituto Nacional de Estadísticas y Censos**

indecencia SF [1] (= *cualidad*) (= *falta de decencia*) indecency; (= *obscenidad*) obscenity
[2] (= *acto*) indecent act; (= *palabra*) indecent thing
[3] (= *porquería*) filth

indecente ADJ [1] [*persona*] (= *falto de decencia*) indecent; (= *obsceno*) obscene; **algún empleadillo ~** some wretched clerk; **es una persona ~** he's shameless; **¡indecente!** you brute!
[2] (= *asqueroso*) filthy; **la calle está ~ de lodo** the street is terribly muddy; **un cuchitril ~** a filthy pigsty of a place

indecentemente ADV [1] (= *sin decencia*) indecently
[2] (= *obscenamente*) obscenely

indecible ADJ unspeakable, indescribable; **sufrir lo ~** to suffer terribly

indeciblemente ADV unspeakably, indescribably

indecisión SF indecision

indeciso/a Ⓐ ADJ [1] [*persona*] indecisive; **estoy ~** I'm undecided; **¡soy tan ~!** I can never make up my mind!
[2] [*tema*] (= *por decidir*) undecided; (= *indefinido*) vague
[3] [*resultado*] indecisive
Ⓑ SM/F (*Pol*) (*en votación*) undecided voter; (*en encuesta*) don't know

indeclarable ADJ undeclarable

indeclinable ADJ [1] (*Ling*) indeclinable
[2] (= *inevitable*) unavoidable

indecoro SM indecorum, unseemliness

indecorosamente ADV indecorously

indecoroso ADJ unseemly, indecorous

indefectible ADJ unfailing

indefectiblemente ADV unfailingly

indefendible ADJ indefensible

indefensión SF defencelessness, defenselessness (*EEUU*)

indefenso ADJ defenceless, defenseless (*EEUU*)

indefinible ADJ indefinable

indefinición SF [1] (= *falta de definición*) lack of definition
[2] (= *vaguedad*) absence of clarity, vagueness

indefinidamente ADV indefinitely

indefinido ADJ [1] (= *ilimitado*) indefinite; **por tiempo ~** indefinitely
[2] (= *vago*) undefined, vague
[3] (*Ling*) indefinite

indeformabilidad SF ability to keep its shape

indeformable ADJ that keeps its shape

indeleble ADJ indelible

indelicadeza SF indelicacy; **cometió** *o* **tuvo la ~ de preguntarle la edad** he was tactless enough to ask her age

indelicado ADJ indelicate

indemne ADJ [*persona*] unharmed, unhurt; [*objeto*] undamaged

indemnidad SF indemnity

indemnizable ADJ that can be indemnified, recoverable

indemnización SF [1] (= *acto*) indemnification
[2] (= *suma*) compensation, indemnity; **pagó mil dólares de ~** he paid one thousand dollars in damages *o* in compensation ► **indemnización compensatoria** financial compensation ► **indemnización por daños y perjuicios** damages *pl* ► **indemnización por despido** redundancy pay ► **indemnización por enfermedad** statutory sick pay
[3] **indemnizaciones** (*Mil, Pol*) reparations

indemnizar ▸conjug 1f◂ VT to compensate, indemnify

indemnizatorio ADJ compensatory

indemostrable ADJ indemonstrable

independencia SF independence; **con ~ de (que)** irrespective of (whether)

independentismo SM independence movement

independentista Ⓐ ADJ pro-independence *antes de s*
Ⓑ SMF pro-independence campaigner

independiente Ⓐ ADJ [1] (*gen*) independent; **hacerse ~** to become independent
[2] [*piso etc*] self-contained
[3] (*Inform*) stand-alone
Ⓑ SMF independent

independientemente ADV independently; **~ de que** irrespective *o* regardless of whether

independista Ⓐ ADJ pro-independence *antes de s*
Ⓑ SMF pro-independent

independizar ▸conjug 1f◂ Ⓐ VT to make independent
Ⓑ **independizarse** VPR to become independent (**de** of), gain independence (**de** from); **el país se independizó en 1962** the country became independent in 1962, the country gained independence in 1962; **~se económicamente** to become economically independent; **~se de los padres** to become independent from one's parents

indesarraigable ADJ ineradicable

indescifrable ADJ [*código*] indecipherable, undecipherable; [*misterio*] impenetrable

indescriptible ADJ indescribable

indescriptiblemente ADV indescribably

indeseable Ⓐ ADJ undesirable
Ⓑ SMF undesirable

indeseado ADJ unwanted

indesligable ADJ inseparable (**de** from)

indesmallable ADJ [*medias*] ladder-proof, run-resist

indesmayable ADJ unfaltering

indesmentible ADJ undeniable

indespegable ADJ that will not come unstuck

indestructible ADJ indestructible

indetectable ADJ undetectable

indeterminación SF (*al hablar*) indeterminacy, vagueness; (= *sobre el futuro*) indeterminacy, uncertainty; **principio de ~** uncertainty principle, indeterminacy principle

indeterminado ADJ [1] (= *impreciso*) indeterminate; [*resultado*] inconclusive; **un número ~ de personas** an indeterminate number of people
[2] (= *indefinido*) indefinite; **por (un) tiempo ~** indefinitely
[3] [*persona*] irresolute
[4] (*Ling*) indefinite

indexación SF (*Fin*) indexation, index-linking; (*Inform*) indexing

indexado ADJ (*Fin*) index-linked

indexar ▸conjug 1a◂ VT (*Fin*) to index-link

India SF **la ~** India; **las ~s** the Indies ► **Indias Occidentales** West Indies ► **Indias Orientales** East Indies

indiada SF [1] (*LAm*) (= *grupo*) group of Indians; (*Cono Sur pey*) mob
[2] (*LAm*) (= *acto*) *typically Indian thing to do or say*

indiana SF printed calico

indiano/a Ⓐ ADJ American, Spanish-American
Ⓑ SM/F *Spaniard who has made good in America*; ✦*MODISMO* **~ de hilo negro** miser

indicación SF [1] (= *señal*) sign; **me hizo una ~ con la mano** he gestured *o* signalled to me with his hand, he made a sign to me with his hand; **~ al margen** note in the margin, margin note
[2] (= *consejo*) hint, suggestion; **aprovechó la ~** he took the hint; **por ~ de algn** at the suggestion of sb; **me pongo en contacto con usted por ~ del Sr. Gómez** I'm writing to you at the suggestion of Sr Gómez; **he dejado de fumar por ~ del médico** I've stopped smoking on medical advice *o* on the doctor's advice
[3] [*de termómetro*] reading
[4] (*Med*) sign, symptom
[5] **indicaciones** (= *instrucciones*) instructions, directions; **me dio algunas indicaciones sobre el manejo del aparato** he gave me instructions *o* directions about how to use the machine; **seguiré sus indicaciones** I will follow your instructions *o* directions; **"indicaciones de uso"** "instructions for use"

indicado ADJ [1] (= *adecuado*) suitable; **un comentario muy poco ~** a highly inappropriate remark; **eres la persona indicada para este puesto** you are the right person for this job; **no es el momento más ~ para hablar de eso** it isn't the best *o* right moment to talk about this; **tú eres la menos indicada para protestar** you're the last person who should complain; **ser lo más/menos ~** to be the best/worst thing (**para** for); **eso es lo más ~ en este caso** that's the best thing to do in this case
[2] (= *señalado*) [*fecha, hora*] specified

indicador Ⓐ ADJ **luces ~as** indicator lights; **sigue los carteles ~es** follow the road signs; *ver tb* **papel 1**
Ⓑ SM [1] (= *señal*) sign; **es ~ de su mala salud** it is a sign of his ill health; **el que la novela tenga un premio no es un ~ de su ca-**

lidad the fact that it has won a prize doesn't mean it's a quality novel ► **indicador de carretera** road sign
[2] (*Téc*) (= *aparato*) gauge, gage (*EEUU*); (= *aguja*) pointer ► **indicador de dirección** (*Aut*) indicator ► **indicador de encendido** power-on indicator ► **indicador del nivel de gasolina** (*Aut*) fuel gauge ► **indicador del nivel del aceite** (*Aut*) oil gauge ► **indicador de velocidad** (*Aut*) speedometer
[3] (*Econ*) indicator; (*Bolsa*) index ► **indicador económico** economic indicator
[4] (*Inform*) flag

indicar ▸conjug 1g◂ VT [1] (= *señalar*) to show; **me indicó el camino** he showed me the way; **¿me puede usted ~ dónde está el museo?** can you tell me *o* show me where the museum is?; **indica con un rotulador rojo dónde están los errores** use a red felt-tip pen to indicate *o* show where the mistakes are; **me indicó un punto en el mapa** he showed me *o* pointed out a point on the map
[2] (= *decir*) [*señal, policía*] to indicate; [*portavoz, fuentes*] to state, point out, indicate; **esta señal indica que tenemos que detenernos** this sign indicates that we have to stop; **el policía nos indicó que parásemos** the policeman gestured *o* indicated to us to stop; **según me indicaba en su carta** as you indicated in your letter; **hice lo que usted me indicó** I did as you instructed; **me indicó con el dedo que me callase** he gestured to me to be quiet; **según ~on fuentes policiales** as police sources have stated *o* pointed out *o* indicated
[3] (= *mostrar*) [+ *cantidad, temperatura*] to show; [+ *subida, victoria*] to point to; **el precio viene indicado en la etiqueta** the price is shown on the label; **su actitud indicaba una enorme falta de interés** her attitude showed an enormous lack of interest; **las previsiones del tiempo indican una subida de las temperaturas** the weather forecast points to a rise in temperatures; **no hay nada que indique lo contrario** there's nothing to suggest otherwise, there is no indication to the contrary; **como indica el informe** as shown in the report; **todo parece ~ que van a ganar las elecciones** there is every indication *o* sign that they will win the election, everything points to them winning the election; **como su (propio) nombre indica**: **la otitis, como su propio nombre indica, es una inflamación del oído** otitis, as its name suggests, is an inflammation of the ear
[4] (*frm*) (= *recomendar*) [*abogado, médico*] to tell, say; **haz lo que te indique el médico** do as the doctor tells you, do as the doctor says

indicativo Ⓐ ADJ [1] (= *sintomático*) **ser ~ de algo** to be indicative of sth; **esto es ~ del nuevo rumbo de la empresa** this is indicative of the company's new direction; **es un síntoma ~ de que la situación está mejorando** this is indicative of the fact that the situation is improving
[2] (= *recomendado*) [*horario, precio*] recommended; **el precio ~ de la leche** the recommended price of milk
Ⓑ SM [1] (*Ling*) indicative; **presente de ~** present indicative
[2] (*Radio*) call sign, call letters *pl* (*EEUU*)
[3] (*Aut*) ► **indicativo de nacionalidad** national identification plate

índice SM [1] [*de libro, publicación*] index ► **índice alfabético** alphabetical index ► **índice de materias**, **índice temático** table of contents ► **índice toponímico** place index
[2] (= *catálogo*) (library) catalogue, (library) catalog (*EEUU*)
[3] (*Estadística*) rate; **por debajo del ~ de pobreza** below the poverty line ► **índice de audiencia** (*TV*) audience ratings *pl* ► **índice de mortalidad** death rate, mortality rate ► **índice de natalidad** birth rate ► **índice de ocupación** occupancy rate ► **índice de participación electoral** electoral turnout ► **índice de vida** life expectancy
[4] (*Econ*) index ► **índice al por menor** retail price index ► **índice de deuda** debt ratio ► **índice del coste de (la) vida** cost-of-living index ► **índice de precios al consumo** retail price index ► **índice Dow Jones** Dow Jones Average
[5] (*Mec*) ► **índice de compresión** compression ratio
[6] (= *prueba*) sign, indication; **es un ~ claro de que el plan ha fracasado** it's a clear sign *o* indication that the plan has failed
[7] (*Téc*) (= *aguja*) pointer, needle; (= *manecilla*) hand
[8] (*Anat*) (*tb* **dedo ~**) index finger, forefinger
[9] (*Rel*) **el Índice** the Index ► **Índice expurgatorio** Index

indiciación SF indexing; (*Fin*) index-linking

indiciario ADJ **prueba indiciaria** circumstantial proof

indicio SM [1] (= *señal*) (*gen*) indication, sign; [*de gratitud*] token; [*de droga*] trace; (*Inform*) marker, mark; **es ~ de** it is an indication of, it is a sign of; **no hay el menor ~ de él** there isn't the faintest sign of him, there isn't the least trace of him; **dar ~s de sorpresa** to show some surprise
[2] **indicios** (*Jur*) evidence *sing*, circumstantial evidence *sing* (**de** to); ► **indicios de culpabilidad** evidence of guilt ► **indicios de delito** evidence of a crime

indiferencia SF lack of interest (**hacia** in, towards), indifference (*frm*) (**hacia** towards); **sentía una terrible ~ ante todo** she felt a terrible lack of interest in everything; **ella aparentaba ~** she pretended to be indifferent, she feigned indifference; **nos trató con ~** he treated us with indifference; **ante la ~ de los políticos** faced by the indifference of politicians

indiferente ADJ [1] (= *impasible*) [*actitud, mirada*] indifferent; **un grupo de transeúntes ~s** a group of unconcerned passers-by; **dejar ~ a algn**: **esas imágenes no pueden dejarnos ~s** those images cannot fail to move us; **todo lo deja ~** he's so indifferent to everything; **permanecer** *o* **quedarse ~** to remain indifferent (**a, ante** to); **no podemos permanecer ~s ante esta terrible situación** we cannot remain indifferent to this terrible situation; **se mostró ~ a sus encantos** he remained indifferent to her charms; **se mostró ~ a la hora de decidir** when it came to making a decision he showed no interest; **ser ~ a algo** to be indifferent to sth
[2] (= *que da igual*) **a mí la política me es ~** politics doesn't interest me; **—¿desea salir por la mañana o por la tarde? —me es ~** "do you want to leave in the morning or the afternoon?" — "it makes no difference to me *o* I don't mind"; **es ~ que vengáis hoy o mañana** it makes no difference *o* it doesn't matter whether you come today or tomorrow; **hablar de cosas ~s** to talk about trivialities

indiferentemente ADV [1] (= *sin diferencia*) indistinctly; **sinónimos usados ~ en el texto** synonyms used indistinctly in the text; **~ de algo** regardless of sth
[2] (= *sin interés*) indifferently; **la miró ~** he looked at her with indifference, he looked at her indifferently

indiferentismo SM (*Rel*) scepticism, indifferentism

indígena Ⓐ ADJ [1] (= *nativo*) indigenous (**de** to), native (**de** to)
[2] (*LAm*) Indian
Ⓑ SMF [1] (= *nativo*) native
[2] (*LAm*) Indian

indigencia SF poverty, destitution

indigenismo SM [1] (= *movimiento*) indigenism, pro-Indian political movement; (= *estudio*) study of Indian societies and cultures
[2] (*Ling*) *word/phrase borrowed from a native language*

indigenista Ⓐ ADJ pro-Indian; **propaganda ~** pro-Indian propaganda
Ⓑ SMF (= *estudiante*) student of Indian cultures; (*Pol*) supporter *o* promoter of Indian cultures

indigente Ⓐ ADJ destitute
Ⓑ SMF destitute person

indigerible ADJ indigestible, undigestible

indigestar ▸conjug 1a◂ Ⓐ VT to give indigestion
Ⓑ **indigestarse** VPR [1] [*persona*] to get indigestion
[2] [*comida*] to cause indigestion; **esa carne se me indigestó** that meat gave me indigestion
[3] (= *ser insoportable*) **ese tío se me indigesta** I can't stand that guy*
[4] (*LAm*) (= *inquietarse*) to get worried, get alarmed

indigestible ADJ indigestible

indigestión SF indigestion

indigesto ADJ [1] [*alimento*] indigestible, hard to digest; [*artículo, libro*] indigestible, difficult to get through
[2] (= *confuso*) muddled, badly thought-out

indignación SF indignation, anger; **descargar la ~ sobre algn** to vent one's spleen on sb, take out one's anger on sb

indignado ADJ indignant, angry (**con, contra** with; **por** at, about)

indignamente ADV [1] (= *sin mérito*) unworthily
[2] (= *despreciablemente*) contemptibly, meanly

indignante ADJ outrageous, infuriating

indignar ▸conjug 1a◂ Ⓐ VT (= *enfadar*) to anger, make indignant; (= *provocar*) to provoke, stir up
Ⓑ **indignarse** VPR to get angry; **¡es para ~se!** it's infuriating!; **~se con algn** to get angry with sb; **~se por algo** to get indignant about sth, get angry about sth

indignidad SF [1] (= *falta de mérito*) unworthiness

[2] (= *vileza*) unworthy act; **sufrir la ~ de hacer algo** to suffer the indignity of doing sth
[3] (= *insulto*) indignity, insult

indigno ADJ [1] (= *impropio*) unworthy; **tales comentarios son ~s de un ministro** such comments are unworthy of a minister
[2] (= *desmerecedor*) unworthy; **ser ~ de algo** to be unworthy of sth; **eres indigna de nuestra confianza** you are unworthy *o* not worthy of our trust
[3] (= *despreciable*) despicable; **el más ~ de los delitos** the most despicable of crimes

índigo SM indigo

indino* ADJ [1] (= *insolente*) cheeky*, sassy (*EEUU**)
[2] (*Andes, Caribe*) (= *tacaño*) mean, stingy

indio/a Ⓐ ADJ [1] [*persona*] Indian
[2] (= *azul*) blue
Ⓑ SM/F [1] Indian
[2] ✦*MODISMOS* **hacer el ~*** to play the fool; **salirle el ~ a algn** (*CAm, Cono Sur**): **le salió el ~** he behaved like a boor; **ser el ~ gorrón*** to live by scrounging*; **subírsele el ~ a algn** (*Cono Sur*): **se le subió el ~*** he got over-excited
Ⓒ SM ► **indio viejo** (*CAm, Méx Culin*) *stewed meat with maize and herbs*

indirecta SF hint; **lanzar** *o* **soltar una ~** to drop a hint; **(re)coger la ~** to take the hint; ✦*MODISMO* **~ del padre Cobos**† broad hint

indirectamente ADV indirectly

indirecto ADJ [1] [*apoyo, control, causa, respuesta*] indirect; [*referencia*] oblique; [*amenaza, crítica*] veiled; **estaba ayudando a los opresores de modo ~** he was indirectly helping the oppressors, in a roundabout way he was helping the oppressors; **de modo ~ me dijo que me fuera** he hinted that I should go; **fue una manera indirecta de pedir dinero** it was a indirect *o* roundabout way of asking for money
[2] [*impuesto, coste*] indirect
[3] [*iluminación, luz*] indirect
[4] (*Gram*) [*complemento, estilo*] indirect

indiscernible ADJ indiscernible

indisciplina SF [1] (= *falta de disciplina*) indiscipline, lack of discipline
[2] (*Mil*) insubordination

indisciplinado ADJ [1] [*niño, alumno*] undisciplined
[2] [*soldado*] insubordinate

indisciplinarse ▸conjug 1a◂ VPR [1] [*niño, alumno*] to get out of control
[2] [*soldado*] to be insubordinate

indiscreción SF [1] (= *falta de discreción*) indiscretion
[2] (= *acto, dicho*) gaffe, faux pas; **si no es ~** if I may say so; **cometió la ~ de decírmelo** he was tactless enough to tell me

indiscretamente ADV (= *sin discreción*) indiscreetly; (= *sin tacto*) tactlessly

indiscreto ADJ (= *falto de discreción*) indiscreet; (= *falto de tacto*) tactless

indiscriminadamente ADV indiscriminately

indiscriminado ADJ indiscriminate

indisculpable ADJ inexcusable, unforgivable

▼ **indiscutible** ADJ indisputable, unquestionable

▼ **indiscutiblemente** ADV indisputably, unquestionably

indisimulable ADJ that cannot be disguised

indisimulado ADJ undisguised

indisociable ADJ inseparable (**de** from)

indisolubilidad SF indissolubility

indisoluble ADJ [1] [*matrimonio*] indissoluble
[2] [*sustancia*] insoluble

indisolublemente ADV indissolubly

▼ **indispensable** ADJ indispensable, essential

indisponer ▸conjug 2q◂ Ⓐ VT [1] (*Med*) to upset, make ill
[2] (= *ofender*) to upset
[3] (= *enemistar*) **~ a algn con otro** to set sb against another person
[4] [+ *plan*] to spoil, upset
Ⓑ **indisponerse** VPR [1] (*Med*) to become ill, fall ill
[2] **~se con algn** to fall out with sb

indisponible ADJ not available, unavailable

indisposición SF [1] (*Med*) indisposition
[2] (= *desgana*) disinclination, unwillingness

indispuesto ADJ [1] (*Med*) indisposed, unwell; **sentirse ~** to feel unwell
[2] (= *sin ganas*) disinclined, unwilling

indisputable ADJ (= *indiscutible*) indisputable, unquestioned; (= *incontestado*) unchallenged

indistinción SF [1] (= *falta de distinción*) (*en colores*) indistinctness; (*en conceptos*) vagueness
[2] (= *falta de discriminación*) lack of discrimination

indistinguible ADJ indistinguishable (**de** from)

indistintamente ADV [1] (= *sin distinción*) without distinction; (= *sin discriminación*) indiscriminately; **pueden firmar ~** either may sign (*joint holder of the account etc*)
[2] (= *no claramente*) vaguely, indistinctly

indistinto ADJ [1] (= *poco claro*) indistinct, vague; (= *borroso*) faint, dim
[2] (= *indiscriminado*) indiscriminate; **permiten el uso ~ del inglés y el español** they allow indiscriminate use of Spanish and English
[3] (= *indiferente*) **es ~** it makes no difference, it doesn't matter

individua SF (*pey*) woman

individual Ⓐ ADJ [1] [*trabajo, necesidades, características*] individual
[2] [*cama, cuarto*] single
[3] (*Andes, Cono Sur**) (= *idéntico*) identical; **es ~ a su padre** he is the spitting image of his father
Ⓑ SM (*Dep*) singles *pl*, singles match; **~ femenino/masculino** women's/men's singles *pl*

individualidad SF individuality

individualismo SM individualism

individualista Ⓐ ADJ individualistic
Ⓑ SMF individualist

individualizar ▸conjug 1f◂ Ⓐ VT [1] (= *diferenciar*) **le resultaba difícil ~ con precisión a unos de otros** it was difficult for him to pick out one individual from another; **este método está basado en la capacidad de ~ genes diferentes** this method is based on the ability to pick out individual genes
[2] [+ *tratamiento, situación*] to individualize; **estos importantes hallazgos permitirán ~ el tratamiento** these important discoveries will allow us to individualize the treatment *o* tailor the treatment to the individual; **~ la enseñanza** to tailor *o* target teaching to each individual's needs
Ⓑ VI **prefiero no ~** I prefer not to pick out any individuals *o* single anyone out

individualmente ADV individually

individuar ▸conjug 1e◂ VT, VI = **individualizar**

individuo Ⓐ ADJ individual
Ⓑ SM [1] (= *persona*) (*gen*) individual; (*pey*) individual, character; **el ~ en cuestión** the person in question
[2] (= *socio*) member, fellow

indivisibilidad SF indivisibility

indivisible ADJ indivisible

indiviso ADJ undivided

indización SF (*Fin*) index-linking; (*Inform*) indexing

indizado Ⓐ ADJ (*Fin*) index-linked; (*Inform*) indexed
Ⓑ SM indexing

indizar ▸conjug 1f◂ VT (*Fin*) to index-link; (*Inform*) to index

INDO SM ABR (*Com*) = **Instituto Nacional de Denominaciones de Origen**

Indo SM (*Geog*) Indus

indo/a ADJ, SM/F Indian, Hindu

indo... PREF Indo...

Indochina SF Indochina

indócil ADJ (= *difícil*) unmanageable; (= *testarudo*) headstrong; (= *rebelde*) disobedient

indocilidad SF (= *carácter difícil*) unmanageability; (= *testarudez*) headstrong character; (= *rebeldía*) disobedience

indocto ADJ ignorant, unlearned

indoctrinar ▸conjug 1a◂ VT (= *enseñar*) to indoctrinate; (*pey*) to brainwash

indocumentado/a Ⓐ ADJ not carrying identity papers
Ⓑ SM/F person who carries no identity papers; (*Méx*) illegal immigrant

indoeuropeo/a Ⓐ ADJ, SM/F Indo-European
Ⓑ SM (*Ling*) Indo-European

índole SF [1] (= *naturaleza*) nature
[2] (= *tipo*) kind, sort; **cosas de esta ~** things of this kind

indolencia SF (= *pereza*) indolence, laziness; (= *abulia*) apathy; (= *languidez*) listlessness

indolente ADJ (= *perezoso*) indolent, lazy; (= *abúlico*) apathetic; (= *lánguido*) listless

indoloro ADJ painless

indomable ADJ [*espíritu*] indomitable; [*animal*] untameable; [*pelo*] unmanageable; [*energía*] boundless

indomado ADJ wild, untamed

indomesticable ADJ untameable

indomiciliado ADJ homeless

indómito ADJ = **indomable**

Indonesia SF Indonesia

indonesio/a ADJ, SM/F Indonesian

indormia* SF (*Andes, Caribe*) trick, wangle*, wheeze*

Indostán SM Hindustan

indostanés/esa ADJ, SM/F Hindustani

indostaní SM (*Ling*) Hindustani

indostánico Ⓐ ADJ Hindustani
Ⓑ SM (*Ling*) Hindustani

indotado ADJ without a dowry

indte. ABR = **indistintamente**

Indubán SM ABR (*Esp Fin*) = **Banco de Financiación Industrial**

indubitable ADJ indubitable, undoubted

➤ LENGUA Y USO: **indiscutible** 42.1 **indiscutiblemente** 53.6 **indispensable** 37.1

indubitablemente ADV indubitably, undoubtedly

inducción SF 1 (*Fil, Elec*) induction; **por ~** by induction, inductively
2 (= *persuasión*) inducement

inducido SM (*Elec*) armature

inducir ▸conjug 3n◂ VT 1 (*Fil*) to infer
2 (*Elec*) to induce
3 (= *empujar, llevar*) to induce; **~ a algn a hacer algo** to induce sb to do sth; **~ a algn a error** to lead sb into error

inductivo ADJ inductive; **pregunta inductiva** leading question

inductor(a) Ⓐ SM/F instigator
Ⓑ SM (*Elec, Biol*) inductor

▼ **indudable** ADJ [*talento, encanto, lealtad*] undoubted, unquestionable; **de ~ importancia** of undoubted *o* unquestionable importance; **su inteligencia es ~** his intelligence is not in doubt, his intelligence is undeniable; **es ~ que es de Picasso** there is no doubt that it is by Picasso; **es el mejor, eso es ~** he's the best, there's no doubt about that

indudablemente ADV undoubtedly, unquestionably

indulgencia SF 1 (= *tolerancia*) (*tb Rel*) indulgence; **proceder sin ~ contra algn** to proceed ruthlessly against sb ► **indulgencia plenaria** plenary indulgence
2 (*para perdonar*) leniency

indulgente ADJ (= *tolerante*) indulgent; (*para perdonar*) lenient (**con** towards)

indulgentemente ADV (= *con tolerancia*) indulgently; (*para perdonar*) leniently

indultar ▸conjug 1a◂ Ⓐ VT 1 (= *perdonar*) to pardon, reprieve
2 (= *eximir*) to exempt (**de** from), excuse (**de** from)
Ⓑ **indultarse** VPR 1 (*Andes*) (= *entrometerse*) to meddle, pry
2 (*Caribe**) to get o.s. out of a jam*

indulto SM 1 (= *perdón*) pardon, reprieve
2 (= *exención*) exemption

indumentaria SF 1 (= *ropa*) clothing, dress
2 (= *estudio*) costume, history of costume

indumentario ADJ clothing *antes de s*; **elegancia indumentaria** elegance of dress, sartorial elegance

indumento SM clothing, apparel, dress

industria SF 1 (*Com*) industry; **la zona con más ~ del país** the most industrialized area of the country ► **industria agropecuaria** farming and fishing ► **industria artesanal** cottage industry ► **industria automovilística** car industry, automobile industry (*EEUU*) ► **industria básica** basic industry ► **industria casera** cottage industry ► **industria del automóvil** car industry, automobile industry (*EEUU*) ► **industria del ocio** leisure industry ► **industria ligera** light industry ► **industria militar** weapons industry, defence industry ► **industria pesada** heavy industry ► **industria petrolífera** oil industry ► **industria siderúrgica** iron and steel industry
2 (= *fábrica*) factory
3 (= *dedicación*) industry, industriousness
4 (†) (= *maña*) ingenuity, skill, expertise; **de ~** on purpose

industrial Ⓐ ADJ 1 (= *de la industria*) industrial
2 (= *no casero*) factory-made, industrially produced
3 (*) (= *enorme*) huge, massive; **en cantidades ~es** in huge amounts; **hay basura acumulada en cantidades ~es** there's a huge amount of rubbish piled up
Ⓑ SMF industrialist

industrialismo SM industrialism

industrialista SMF (*LAm*) industrialist

industrialización SF industrialization

industrializar ▸conjug 1f◂ Ⓐ VT to industrialize
Ⓑ **industrializarse** VPR to become industrialized

industriarse ▸conjug 1b◂ VPR to manage, find a way; **industriárselas para hacer algo** to manage to do sth

industriosamente ADV 1 (= *con diligencia*) industriously
2 (= *con maña*) skilfully, skillfully (*EEUU*), resourcefully

industrioso ADJ 1 (= *diligente*) industrious
2 (= *mañoso*) resourceful

INE SM ABR (*Esp*) = **Instituto Nacional de Estadística**

inédito ADJ 1 [*texto*] unpublished; **un texto rigurosamente ~** a text never published previously in any form
2 (= *nuevo*) new; **una experiencia inédita** a completely new experience
3 (= *nunca visto*) hitherto unheard-of

ineducable ADJ ineducable

ineducado ADJ 1 (= *sin instrucción*) uneducated
2 (= *maleducado*) ill-bred, bad-mannered

INEF SM ABR = **Instituto Nacional de Educación Física**

inefable ADJ indescribable, ineffable

inefectivo ADJ (*LAm*) ineffective

ineficacia SF 1 [*de medida*] ineffectiveness
2 [*de proceso*] inefficiency; [*de gobierno, persona*] inefficiency, incompetence

ineficaz ADJ 1 [*medida*] ineffective
2 (= *inútil*) [*proceso*] inefficient; [*gobierno, persona*] inefficient, incompetent

ineficazmente ADV 1 (= *sin resultado*) ineffectively, ineffectually
2 (= *sin eficiencia*) inefficiently

ineficiencia SF inefficiency

ineficiente ADJ inefficient

inelástico ADJ inelastic, rigid

inelegancia SF inelegance, lack of elegance

inelegante ADJ inelegant

inelegantemente ADV inelegantly

inelegibilidad SF ineligibility

inelegible ADJ ineligible

ineluctable ADJ (*liter*) ineluctable (*liter*)

ineludible ADJ unavoidable, inescapable

INEM SM ABR (*Esp*) 1 (= **Instituto Nacional de Empleo**) *employment organization*
2 = **Instituto Nacional de Enseñanza Media**

INEN SM ABR (*Méx*) = **Instituto Nacional de Energía Nuclear**

inenarrable ADJ inexpressible

inencogible ADJ shrink-resistant

inepcia SF 1 (= *ineptitud*) ineptitude, incompetence
2 (= *necedad*) stupidity
3 (= *impropiedad*) unsuitability
4 (= *dicho*) silly thing to say; (= *acto*) silly thing to do; **decir ~s** to talk rubbish

ineptitud SF ineptitude, incompetence

inepto ADJ inept, incompetent; **~ de toda ineptitud** utterly incompetent

inequívoco ADJ (= *sin ambigüedad*) unequivocal, unambiguous; (= *inconfundible*) unmistakable

inercia SF 1 (*Fís*) inertia
2 (= *indolencia*) inertia; **por ~** through force of habit, out of habit

inerme ADJ (= *sin armas*) unarmed; (= *indefenso*) defenceless, defenseless (*EEUU*)

inerte ADJ 1 (*Fís*) inert
2 (= *sin vida*) lifeless; (= *inmóvil*) inert, motionless

Inés SF Agnes

inescrupuloso ADJ unscrupulous

inescrutabilidad SF inscrutability

inescrutable ADJ inscrutable

inespecífico ADJ unspecific, non-specific

inesperadamente ADV (= *por sorpresa*) unexpectedly; (= *de repente*) without warning, suddenly

inesperado ADJ (= *imprevisto*) unexpected; (= *repentino*) sudden

inesquivable ADJ unavoidable

inestabilidad SF instability, unsteadiness ► **inestabilidad laboral** lack of job security

inestabilizar ▸conjug 1f◂ Ⓐ VT to destabilize
Ⓑ **inestabilizarse** VPR to become unstable

inestable ADJ unstable, unsteady

inestimable ADJ inestimable, invaluable

inevitabilidad SF inevitability

▼ **inevitable** ADJ inevitable

inevitablemente ADV inevitably, unavoidably

inexactitud SF (= *imprecisión*) inaccuracy; (= *falsedad*) incorrectness, wrongness

inexacto ADJ (= *no preciso*) inaccurate; (= *no cierto*) incorrect, untrue

inexcusable ADJ 1 [*conducta*] inexcusable, unforgivable
2 [*conclusión*] inevitable, unavoidable; **una visita ~** a trip not to be missed

inexcusablemente ADV 1 (= *imperdonablemente*) inexcusably, unforgivably
2 (= *ineludiblemente*) inevitably, unavoidably; **el depósito será devuelto ~ si ...** the deposit will be returned as a matter of obligation if ...

inexhausto ADJ inexhaustible, unending

inexistencia SF non-existence

inexistente ADJ non-existent

inexorabilidad SF inexorability

inexorable ADJ inexorable

inexorablemente ADV inexorably

inexperiencia SF (= *falta de experiencia*) inexperience, lack of experience; (= *torpeza*) lack of skill

inexperimentado ADJ inexperienced

inexperto ADJ (= *novato*) inexperienced; (= *torpe*) unskilled, inexpert

inexplicable ADJ inexplicable

inexplicablemente ADV inexplicably

inexplicado ADJ unexplained

inexplorado ADJ [*terreno, campo, tema*] unexplored; [*ruta*] uncharted

➤ LENGUA Y USO: **indudable** 53.6 **inevitable** 42.1

inexplotado ADJ unexploited, unused
inexportable ADJ that cannot be exported
inexpresable ADJ inexpressible
inexpresividad SF inexpressiveness, expressionlessness
inexpresivo ADJ expressionless, inexpressive
inexpuesto ADJ (*Fot*) unexposed
inexpugnabilidad SF impregnability
inexpugnable ADJ impregnable
inextinguible ADJ eternal, inextinguishable
inextirpable ADJ ineradicable
in extremis ADV [1] (= *en el último momento*) at the very last moment
[2] (= *como último recurso*) as a last resort
[3] (= *moribundo*) **estar ~** to be at death's door
inextricable ADJ [*relación, lío*] inextricable; [*bosque*] impenetrable
infalibilidad SF infallibility; **~ pontificia** papal infallibility
infalible ADJ [1] [*persona*] infallible
[2] [*aparato, plan*] foolproof
[3] [*puntería*] unerring
[4] (= *inevitable*) certain, sure
infaliblemente ADV [1] (= *sin equivocarse*) infallibly
[2] (= *siempre*) unfailingly
[3] (= *de modo certero*) unerringly, unfailingly, without fail
infaltable ADJ (*LAm*) not to be missed
infamación SF defamation
infamador(a) Ⓐ ADJ defamatory, slanderous
Ⓑ SM/F slanderer
infamante ADJ shameful, degrading
infamar ▸conjug 1a◂ VT (= *difamar*) to defame, slander; (= *deshonrar*) to dishonour, dishonor (*EEUU*)
infamatorio ADJ defamatory, slanderous
infame Ⓐ ADJ (= *odioso*) [*persona*] odious; [*tarea*] thankless; **esto es ~** this is monstrous
Ⓑ SMF vile person, villain
infamia SF [1] (= *calumnia*) calumny, slur
[2] (= *deshonra*) disgrace, ignominy; **sufrió la ~ de ser declarado culpable** he suffered the disgrace *o* ignominy of being found guilty
[3] (= *canallada*) despicable act; **engañar a un amigo es una ~** it's despicable to deceive a friend; **recalentar el café es una ~** (*hum*) reheating coffee is a crime
[4] (= *carácter infame*) infamy; **la ~ de sus actos** the infamy of his acts
infancia SF [1] [*de una persona*] childhood; [*de proyecto, teoría*] infancy; **es un amigo de la ~** he's a childhood friend; **en mi ~ nunca tuve juguetes** as a child I never had toys; **en su más tierna ~** in his tenderest youth (*liter o hum*); **la investigación genética se halla todavía en su ~** genetic research is still in its infancy; **durante la ~ de la humanidad** in mankind's infancy; *ver tb* **jardín**
[2] (= *niños*) children; **Día Internacional de la Infancia** International Children's Day
infante/a SM/F Ⓐ (*Hist*) infante/infanta, prince/princess
Ⓑ SM [1] (*Mil, Hist*) infantryman ► **infante de marina** marine
[2] (= *niño*) infant; **tierno ~** young child
infantería SF infantry ► **infantería de marina** marines *pl*
infanticida SMF infanticide, child killer
infanticidio SM infanticide

infantil ADJ [1] [*educación, población, prostitución, psicología*] child *antes de s*; [*sonrisa, mirada*] childish, childlike; [*enfermedad*] children's, childhood *antes de s*; [*hospital, libro, programa*] children's; [*mortalidad*] infant, child *antes de s*
[2] (*pey*) childish, infantile
[3] (*Dep*) ≈ youth
infantilada* SF **es una ~** it's such a childish thing to do
infantilismo SM infantilism
infantiloide ADJ childish, puerile
infanzón/a SM/F (*Hist*) *member of the lowest rank of the nobility*
infartante* ADJ heart-stopping
infarto SM [1] (*tb* **~ de miocardio**) heart attack
[2] **de ~*** heart-stopping
infatigable ADJ tireless, untiring
infatigablemente ADV tirelessly, untiringly
infatuación SF vanity, conceit
infatuar ▸conjug 1d◂ Ⓐ VT to make conceited
Ⓑ **infatuarse** VPR to get conceited (**con** about)
infausto ADJ (= *infortunado*) unlucky; (= *funesto*) ill-starred, ill-fated
INFE SM ABR = **Instituto de Fomento de las Exportaciones**
infección SF infection
infecciosidad SF infectiousness
infeccioso ADJ infectious
infectar ▸conjug 1a◂ Ⓐ VT [1] (*Med*) to infect
[2] (= *pervertir*) to pervert, corrupt
Ⓑ **infectarse** VPR [1] (*Med*) to become infected (**de** with)
[2] (= *pervertirse*) to become perverted, become corrupted
infecto ADJ [1] (*Med*) infected (**de** with)
[2] (= *repugnante*) disgusting
infectocontagioso ADJ infectious, transmittable
infecundidad SF [1] [*de mujer*] infertility, sterility
[2] [*de tierra*] infertility, barrenness
infecundo ADJ [1] [*mujer*] infertile, sterile; **la época infecunda de la mujer** woman's infertile period
[2] [*tierra*] infertile, barren
[3] [*esfuerzo*] fruitless
infelicidad SF unhappiness
infeliz Ⓐ ADJ [1] (= *desgraciado*) [*persona*] unhappy; [*vida*] unhappy, wretched; [*tentativa*] unsuccessful
[2] (= *bonachón*) kindhearted, good-natured; (*pey*) gullible
Ⓑ SMF [1] (= *desgraciado*) poor unfortunate, poor wretch; **vi cómo golpeaban a un ~** I saw them hitting some poor unfortunate *o* wretch
[2] (= *bonachón*) kindhearted person, good-natured person; (*pey*) gullible fool
infelizmente ADV unhappily, unfortunately
infelizón* SM, **infelizote*** SM = **infeliz B1**
inferencia SF inference; **por ~** by inference
inferible ADJ inferable
▼**inferior** Ⓐ ADJ [1] (*en el espacio*) lower; **la parte ~** the lower part; **las extremidades ~es** the lower limbs; **labio ~** bottom *o* lower lip; **el piso ~ del edificio** the ground floor of the building; **el apartamento ~ al mío** the flat below mine
[2] (*en categoría, jerarquía*) inferior; **de calidad ~** of inferior quality, inferior; **los organismos ~es de la creación** the lower forms of life; **están en un puesto ~ al nuestro en la liga** they're just below us in the league; **en una posición ~ en la lista** further down the list; **le es ~ en talento** he is inferior to him in talent; **tú no eres ~ a nadie** you're as good as anyone else
[3] (*con cantidades, números*) lower; **sacó una nota ~ a la esperada** he got a lower mark than expected; **temperaturas ~es a los 20°** temperatures lower than 20°, temperatures below 20°; **renta per cápita ~ a la media** per capita income lower than *o* below the average; **cualquier número ~ a nueve** any number under *o* below *o* less than nine; **ingresos ~es a los dos millones** income below two million; **la cantidad de personas fue ~ a la del año pasado** there were fewer people than last year
Ⓑ SMF subordinate; **habla con mucho respeto a sus ~es** he's very respectful to his subordinates
inferioridad SF inferiority; **complejo de ~** inferiority complex; **estar** *o* **encontrarse en ~ de condiciones** to be at a disadvantage
inferir ▸conjug 3i◂ VT [1] (= *deducir*) to infer, deduce; **~ una cosa de otra** to infer one thing from another
[2] (= *causar*) [+ *herida*] to inflict (**a, en** on); [+ *insulto*] to offer (**a** to)
infernáculo SM hopscotch
infernal ADJ infernal, hellish; **un ruido ~** a dreadful racket*
infernillo SM = **infiernillo**
infértil ADJ infertile
infestación SF infestation
infestado ADJ **~ de** [+ *parásitos, gérmenes*] infested with; **~ de cucarachas** cockroach-infested; **~ de turistas/mendigos** crawling with tourists/beggars
infestante ADJ invasive, pervasive
infestar ▸conjug 1a◂ VT [1] (= *infectar*) to infect
[2] (= *invadir*) to overrun, invade
[3] [*insectos*] to infest
infibulación SF infibulation
infibulado ADJ infibulated
inficionar ▸conjug 1a◂ VT = **infectar**
infidelidad SF [1] (*en pareja*) infidelity, unfaithfulness ► **infidelidad conyugal** marital infidelity
[2] (*Rel*) unbelief, lack of faith
[3] (†) (= *conjunto de infieles*) unbelievers *pl*, infidels *pl*
infidencia SF [1] (= *deslealtad*) disloyalty, faithlessness; (= *traición*) treason
[2] (= *acto*) disloyal act
[3] (*Jur*) breach of trust
infiel Ⓐ ADJ [1] (= *desleal*) unfaithful (**a, para, con** to); **fue ~ a su mujer** he was unfaithful to his wife
[2] (*Rel*) unbelieving, infidel
[3] (= *erróneo*) unfaithful, inaccurate; **la memoria le fue ~** his memory failed him
Ⓑ SMF (*Rel*) unbeliever, infidel
infielmente ADV [1] (= *con deslealtad*) unfaithfully, disloyally
[2] (= *con error*) inaccurately

➤ LENGUA Y USO: **inferior A2** 32.3

infiernillo SM (*tb* ~ **de alcohol**) spirit lamp, spirit stove ► **infiernillo campestre** camp stove ► **infiernillo de gasolina** petrol stove

infierno SM 1 (*Rel*) hell; **la ciudad era un ~ (de llamas)** the city was a blazing inferno; **vivieron un ~** they went through hell; ✦*MODISMOS* **está en el quinto ~*** it's at the back of beyond; **mandar a algn al quinto ~*** to tell sb to go to hell*; **¡vete al ~!*** go to hell!*
2 (= *lugar*) (*horrible*) hellhole*; (*ruidoso*) madhouse*

infijo SM infix

infiltración SF infiltration

infiltrado/a SM/F infiltrator

infiltrar ▸conjug 1a◂ Ⓐ VT 1 [+ *espía, policía*] to infiltrate; **han infiltrado un agente en la organización** they have infiltrated an agent into the organization
2 (*Med*) to infiltrate
Ⓑ **infiltrarse** VPR 1 [*espía, agente*] to infiltrate; **el detective se infiltró en la banda de mafiosos** the detective infiltrated the mafia ring; **consiguieron ~se en territorio rumano** they succeeded in infiltrating into Romanian territory; **se infiltró en la red informática de la NASA** he hacked into NASA's computer network
2 [*ideas, costumbres*] to permeate; **el liberalismo se fue infiltrando entre los intelectuales** liberalism gradually permeated the intelligentsia
3 [*líquido*] to seep; [*luz*] to filter; **la humedad se había ido infiltrando en el techo** the damp had seeped through the ceiling

ínfimo ADJ [*calidad, grado*] very poor; [*cantidad, participación, porcentaje, nivel*] very small, tiny; **de ínfima calidad** very poor quality *antes de s*; **la ayuda que le dieron fue ínfima** the help they afforded him was next to nothing; **viven en ínfimas condiciones** they live in dreadful *o* appalling conditions; **precios ~s** knockdown prices

infinidad SF 1 (*Mat*) infinity
2 (= *gran cantidad*) **~ de veces** countless times, innumerable times; **hay ~ de personas que creen ...** any number of people believe ..., there's no end of people who believe ...; **hablan una ~ de lenguas** they speak a huge number of languages; **durante una ~ de días** for days on end

infinitamente ADJ infinitely; **te lo agradeceré ~** I'd be deeply *o* immensely grateful to you; **lo sintió ~** he was deeply sorry

infinitesimal ADJ infinitesimal

infinitivo Ⓐ ADJ infinitive Ⓑ SM infinitive

infinito Ⓐ ADJ [*universo, variedad*] infinite; [*entusiasmo, posibilidades*] boundless; **con paciencia infinita** with infinite patience; **sonrió con infinita tristeza** she smiled with immense sadness; **tuve que copiarlo infinitas veces** I had to copy it out countless times *o* over and over again; **hasta lo ~** ad infinitum
Ⓑ ADV infinitely, immensely; **se lo agradezco ~** I'm deeply *o* immensely grateful to you
Ⓒ SM (*Mat*) infinity; **el ~** (*Fil*) the infinite; **así podríamos seguir hasta el ~** we could go on like this for ever *o* indefinitely

infinitud SF = **infinidad**

inflable ADJ inflatable

inflación SF 1 (*gen, Econ*) inflation ► **inflación subyacente** underlying inflation
2 (= *hinchazón*) swelling
3 (= *vanidad*) pride, conceit

inflacionario ADJ inflationary; **una política económica inflacionaria** an inflationary economic policy

inflacionismo SM inflation

inflacionista ADJ inflationary

inflado SM inflating, pumping up

inflador SM (*LAm*) bicycle pump

inflagaitas* SMF INV twit*

inflamabilidad SF inflammability

inflamable ADJ inflammable

inflamación SF 1 (*Med*) inflammation
2 (*Fís*) ignition, combustion

inflamar ▸conjug 1a◂ Ⓐ VT 1 (*Med*) to inflame
2 (= *enardecer*) to inflame, arouse
3 (= *prender fuego a*) to set on fire, ignite
Ⓑ **inflamarse** VPR 1 (*Med*) to become inflamed
2 (= *enardecerse*) to become inflamed (**de** with), become aroused
3 (= *encenderse*) to catch fire, ignite; **se inflama fácilmente** it is highly inflammable

inflamatorio ADJ inflammatory

inflapollas‡ SM INV berk‡, wimp‡

inflar ▸conjug 1a◂ Ⓐ VT 1 [+ *neumático, globo*] to inflate, blow up
2 (= *exagerar*) (*gen*) to exaggerate; [+ *precios*] to inflate
3 (= *engreír*) to make conceited
4 (*Econ*) to reinflate
5 (*Cono Sur*) to heed, pay attention to
Ⓑ VI (*Méx**) to booze*, drink
Ⓒ **inflarse** VPR 1 (= *hincharse*) to swell
2 (= *engreírse*) to get conceited; **~se de orgullo** to swell with pride

inflatorio ADJ inflationary

inflexibilidad SF inflexibility

inflexible ADJ (= *rígido*) inflexible; (= *inconmovible*) unbending, unyielding; **~ a los ruegos** unmoved by appeals, unresponsive to appeals; **regla ~** strict rule, hard-and-fast rule

inflexión SF inflection

infligir ▸conjug 3c◂ VT to inflict (**a** on)

influencia SF 1 (= *influjo*) influence; **Cervantes ejerció gran ~ en su poesía** Cervantes had a great influence on his poetry; **sus pinturas tienen ~ modernista** his pictures show a modernist influence; **la tele tiene ~ negativa sobre mis hijos** telly has *o* is a bad influence on my children; **ya no tiene ~ dentro del gobierno** he now has no influence in the government; **tiene ~ con el jefe** she has influence with the boss; **actuó bajo la ~ de las drogas** he acted under the influence of drugs
2 **influencias** (= *contactos*) contacts; **siempre se vale de sus ~s** he always uses his contacts; *ver tb* **tráfico 3**

influenciable ADJ impressionable, easily influenced

influenciar ▸conjug 1b◂ VT to influence

influenza SF (*esp LAm*) influenza, flu

influir ▸conjug 3g◂ Ⓐ VT to influence; **A, influido por B ...** A, influenced by B ...
Ⓑ VI 1 to have influence, carry weight; **es hombre que influye** he's a man of influence, he carries a lot of weight
2 **~ en** *o* **sobre** (*gen*) to influence; (= *contribuir a*) to have a hand in

influjo SM influence (**sobre** on)

influyente ADJ influential

infografía SF computer graphics

infopista SF information superhighway

▼**información** SF 1 (= *datos*) information; (= *oficina*) information desk; (*Telec*) Directory Enquiries, Directory Assistance (*EEUU*); **¿dónde podría obtener más ~?** where could I get more information?; **si desean más** *o* **mayor ~** if you require further information; **pasaron toda la ~ a la policía** they passed on all the information *o* the details to the police; **pregunte en ~** ask at information *o* at the information desk; **~ internacional ¿dígame?** international enquiries, can I help you?; **le han dado una ~ falsa** you've been given false information; **"Información"** "Information", "Enquiries" ► **información genética** genetic information
2 (= *noticias*) news; **según las últimas informaciones** according to the latest reports *o* news; **les daremos más ~ dentro de unos minutos** we will give you some more information in a few minutes ► **información caliente** hot tip ► **información deportiva** (*en prensa, radio*) sports section; (*en TV*) sports news ► **información financiera** (*en prensa, radio*) financial section; (*en TV*) financial news ► **información internacional** foreign news
3 (*Jur*) judicial inquiry, investigation; **abrir una ~** to begin proceedings
4 (*Inform*) (= *datos*) data *pl*; *ver tb* **tratamiento 3**
5 (*Mil*) intelligence

informado ADJ 1 (= *enterado*) **estar ~** to be informed (**de, sobre** about); **estaba ~ de todo** he was informed about everything; **tenemos derecho a estar ~s** we have a right to know, we have a right to information; **bien ~** well-informed; **según fuentes bien informadas** according to well-informed sources; **mal ~** misinformed, badly informed; **si eso es lo que crees, estás muy mal informada** if that's what you think you're misinformed *o* you've been badly informed; **mantener ~ a algn** to keep sb informed
2 [*trabajador*] **bien ~** with good references

informador(a) Ⓐ ADJ **la comisión ~a** the inquiry commission, the commission of inquiry; **una charla ~a** an informative talk; **el equipo ~ de esta cadena** this channel's team of reporters
Ⓑ SM/F 1 [*de una noticia*] informant; [*de la policía*] informer ► **informador(a) turístico/a** tourist guide
2 (= *periodista*) journalist; **los ~es de la prensa** the media, the representatives of the media ► **informador(a) gráfico/a** press photographer

informal ADJ 1 [*persona*] unreliable
2 [*charla, lenguaje, cena*] informal; [*ropa*] casual, informal; **reunión ~** informal meeting
3 (*LAm*) (= *no oficial*) **el sector ~ de la economía** the unofficial sector of the economy, the black economy

informalidad SF 1 [*de persona*] unreliability
2 [*de lenguaje, reunión*] informality; (*en el vestir*) casualness

informalmente ADV informally; **vestir ~** to dress informally, dress casually

informante SMF [*de una noticia*] informant; [*de la policía*] informer

➤ LENGUA Y USO: **información 1** 48.3

▼ **informar** ▸conjug 1a◂ Ⓐ VT [1] (= *dar información a*) **¿dónde te han informado?** where did you get your information?; **le han informado mal** you've been misinformed, you've been badly informed; **~ a algn de algo** to inform sb of sth, tell sb about sth; **nadie me informó del cambio de planes** no one informed me of *o* told me about the change of plan; **le informé de lo que pasaba** I informed him of what was happening, I told him what was happening; **el portavoz informó a la prensa de los cambios en el gobierno** the spokesman briefed the press on the changes in the government, the spokesman informed the press about the changes in the government; **~ a algn sobre algo** to inform sb about sth, give sb information on sth; **¿me puede usted ~ sobre las becas al extranjero?** can you tell me about overseas grants here?, can you give me information on overseas grants here?

[2] (= *comunicar*) **~ que** to report that; **la policía informó que las causas del accidente no estaban claras** the police reported that the cause of the accident was not clear; **~ a algn que** to tell sb that, inform sb that; **nadie me informó que se hubiera pasado la reunión a otro día** no one told *o* informed me that the meeting had been changed to another day; **nos complace ~le que ha resultado ganadora** we are pleased to inform you that you are the winner

[3] (*frm*) (= *caracterizar*) **la seriedad informa su carácter** she's extremely serious by nature; **la preocupación por el bien general debe ~ sus actuaciones** their actions should be guided *o* governed by concern for the common good

Ⓑ VI [1] (= *dar noticias*) [*portavoz, fuentes*] to state, point out, indicate; **se ha producido un nuevo atentado terrorista, ~on fuentes policiales** police sources have reported a new terrorist attack; **el criminal había sido detenido, según ~on fuentes oficiales** according to official sources, the criminal had been arrested; **nuestros representantes ~án de los motivos de la huelga** our representatives will announce the reasons for the strike; **~ de que** to report that; **acaban de ~ de que se ha cometido un atentado** a terrorist attack has just been reported, we have just received reports of a terrorist attack; **~ sobre algo** to report on sth; **una rueda de prensa para ~ sobre el incendio** a press conference to report on the fire; **no informó sobre el traspaso del jugador** he gave no information on the player's transfer

[2] (*Jur*) [*delator*] to inform (**contra** against); [*abogado*] to sum up

Ⓒ **informarse** VPR (= *obtener información*) to find out, get information; **te puedes ~ en la oficina de turismo** you can find out in the tourist office, you can get some information from the tourist office; **¿te has informado bien?** are you sure your information is correct?; **~se de** *o* **sobre algo** to find out about sth; **antes de comprar nada, infórmate de las condiciones de pago** before you buy anything find out about the terms of payment; **he estado informándome sobre los cursos de verano** I've been enquiring about *o* finding out about summer courses

informática SF computing ► **informática gráfica** computer graphics; *ver tb* **informático**

informáticamente ADV computationally; **controlado ~** controlled by computer, computer-controlled

informático/a Ⓐ ADJ computer *antes de s*; **centro ~** computer centre; **servicios ~s** computer services

Ⓑ SM/F (= *técnico*) computer expert; (= *programador*) computer programmer

Ⓒ SM computer equipment; *ver tb* **informática**

informatividad SF informative nature

informativo Ⓐ ADJ [1] (= *que informa*) informative; **un libro muy ~** a very informative book; **un folleto ~** an information leaflet; **boletín ~** news bulletin

[2] [*comité*] consultative, advisory

Ⓑ SM (*Radio, TV*) news programme, news program (*EEUU*)

informatización SF computerization

informatizar ▸conjug 1f◂ VT to computerize

informe[1] ADJ [*bulto, figura*] shapeless

informe[2] SM [1] (= *escrito*) report (**sobre** on); **el ~ de la comisión** the committee's report; **han redactado un ~ sobre la corrupción** they have drafted a report on corruption; **~ médico/policial/técnico** medical/police/technical report ► **informe de prensa** press release

[2] **informes** (= *datos*) information *sing*; [*de trabajador*] references; **según mis ~s** according to my information; **dar ~s sobre algn/algo** to give information about sb/sth; **pedir ~s de** *o* **sobre algo** to ask for information about sth; **pedir ~s de** *o* **sobre algn** (*para trabajo*) to follow up sb's references; **tomar ~s** to gather information

[3] (*Jur*) report; **según el ~ del forense** according to the forensic report ► **informe del juez** summing-up, summation (*EEUU*) ► **informe jurídico** pleadings *pl*

[4] (*Com*) report ► **informe anual** annual report ► **informe de gestión** chairman's report

[5] (*Pol*) White Paper

infortunado ADJ unfortunate, unlucky

infortunio SM (= *mala suerte*) misfortune, ill luck; (= *accidente*) mishap

infra... PREF infra..., under...

infraalimentación SF, **infralimentación** SF undernourishment

infraalimentado ADJ, **infralimentado** ADJ underfed, undernourished

infracción SF [*de ley*] infringement (**de** of); [*de acuerdo*] breach (**de** of); [*de norma*] offence (**de** against), violation (*EEUU*) (**de** of); ► **infracción de contrato** breach of contract ► **infracción de tráfico** traffic offence, driving offence, traffic violation (*EEUU*)

infractor(a) SM/F offender (**de** against)

infradesarrollado ADJ under-developed

infradesarrollo SM under-development

infradotado/a Ⓐ ADJ [1] (= *falto de recursos*) undersupplied, short of resources; (= *falto de personal*) understaffed

[2] (*pey*) [*persona*] subnormal

Ⓑ SM/F (*pey*) moron*

infraestimación SF underestimate

infraestimar ▸conjug 1a◂ VT to underestimate

infraestructura SF infrastructure

in fraganti ADV **coger** *o* **pillar** *o* **sorprender ~ a algn** to catch sb redhanded

infrahumano ADJ subhuman

infraliteratura SF pulp fiction

inframundo SM underworld

infrangible ADJ unbreakable

infranqueable ADJ [*obstáculo físico*] impassable; [*abismo, distancia*] unbridgeable; [*dificultad*] insurmountable, insuperable

infrarrojo ADJ infrared

infrascrito/a, **infraescrito/a** Ⓐ ADJ (= *que firma*) undersigned; (= *mencionado*) undermentioned

Ⓑ SM/F **el ~** the undersigned; (*LAm hum*) the present speaker, I myself

infrautilización SF under-use

infrautilizado ADJ [*servicios, músculos*] under-used; [*recursos*] untapped

infrautilizar ▸conjug 1f◂ VT to under-use

infravaloración SF [1] (= *subvaloración*) undervaluing

[2] (= *subestimación*) underestimate

infravalorar ▸conjug 1a◂ VT [1] (= *subvalorar*) to undervalue

[2] (= *subestimar*) to underestimate

infravaluar ▸conjug 1e◂ VT [1] (= *subestimar*) to underestimate

[2] (= *quitar importancia a*) to play down

infravivienda SF sub-standard housing

infrecuencia SF infrequency

infrecuente ADJ infrequent

infringir ▸conjug 3c◂ VT to infringe, contravene

infructuosamente ADV (= *sin resultado*) fruitlessly; (= *sin éxito*) unsuccessfully; (= *sin beneficio*) unprofitably

infructuoso ADJ [*búsqueda, esfuerzo, negociación*] fruitless; [*intento*] unsuccessful; [*empresa, operación*] unprofitable

ínfulas SFPL (= *vanidad*) conceit *sing*; (= *disparates*) pretentious nonsense *sing*; **darse ~** to get all high and mighty; **tener (muchas) ~ de algo** to fancy o.s. as sth; **un joven con ~ de escritor** a young man who fancies himself as a writer

infumable ADJ [1] [*cigarro, tabaco*] unsmokable

[2] (*) (= *insoportable*) [*persona*] unbearable, intolerable; [*espectáculo, película*] unwatchable; [*libro*] unreadable

infundado ADJ unfounded, groundless

infundia* SF (*LAm*) fat

infundio SM (= *mentira*) fib; (= *cuento malicioso*) malicious story

infundir ▸conjug 3a◂ VT to instil, instill (*EEUU*) (**a, en** into); **~ ánimo a algn** to encourage sb; **~ confianza/respeto** to inspire confidence/respect; **~ miedo a algn** to fill sb with fear, scare sb; **~ sospechas** to arouse suspicion; **~ un espíritu nuevo a un club** to inject new life into a club

infusión SF infusion ► **infusión de hierbas** herbal tea ► **infusión de manzanilla** camomile tea

infuso ADJ *ver* **ciencia 1**

Ing. ABR = **ingeniero/ingeniera**

ingeniar ▸conjug 1a◂ Ⓐ VT to devise, think up

Ⓑ **ingeniarse** VPR **~se con algo** to manage with sth, make do with sth; **ingeniárselas para hacer algo** to manage to do sth

➤ LENGUA Y USO: **informar A1** 48.3

ingeniería SF engineering ► **ingeniería civil** civil engineering ► **ingeniería de control** control engineering ► **ingeniería de sistemas** (*Inform*) systems engineering ► **ingeniería eléctrica** electrical engineering ► **ingeniería financiera** financial engineering ► **ingeniería genética** genetic engineering ► **ingeniería química** chemical engineering ► **ingeniería social** social engineering

Ingeniero SM (*esp Méx*) graduate; (*título*) sir; **Ing. Quintanilla** ≈ Dr. Quintanilla

ingeniero/a SM/F (SF *a veces* **ingeniero**) engineer; **mi hermana es ingeniera** *o* ~ my sister's an engineer ► **ingeniero/a aeronáutico/a** aeronautical engineer ► **ingeniero/a agrónomo/a** agronomist, agricultural expert ► **ingeniero/a de caminos, canales y puertos** civil engineer ► **ingeniero/a de mantenimiento** maintenance engineer ► **ingeniero/a de minas** mining engineer ► **ingeniero/a de montes** forestry expert ► **ingeniero/a de sonido** sound engineer ► **ingeniero/a de telecomunicaciones** telecommunications engineer ► **ingeniero/a de vuelo** flight engineer ► **ingeniero/a forestal** forestry expert ► **ingeniero/a industrial** industrial engineer ► **ingeniero/a naval** naval architect ► **ingeniero/a químico/a** chemical engineer

ingenio SM 1 (= *inventiva*) ingenuity, inventiveness; (= *talento*) talent; (= *gracia*) wit; **aguzar el ~** to sharpen one's wits
2 (= *persona*) wit
3 (*Mec*) apparatus, device; (*Mil*) device ► **ingenio nuclear** nuclear device
4 (= *fábrica*) mill, plant ► **ingenio azucarero, ingenio de azúcar** sugar mill, sugar refinery
5 (*Andes*) [*de acero*] steel works; (= *fundición*) foundry

ingeniosamente ADV 1 (= *inteligentemente*) ingeniously, cleverly
2 (= *con gracia*) wittily

ingeniosidad SF 1 (= *maña*) ingenuity, ingeniousness
2 (= *idea*) clever idea
3 (= *agudeza*) wittiness

ingenioso ADJ 1 (= *mañoso*) clever, resourceful; [*invento, sistema*] ingenious
2 (= *agudo*) witty

ingénito ADJ innate, inborn

ingente ADJ huge, enormous

ingenuamente ADV naïvely, ingenuously

ingenuidad SF naïveté, ingenuousness

➤ **ingenuo** ADJ naïve, ingenuous

ingerido* ADJ (*Méx*) (= *enfermo*) ill, under the weather; (= *abatido*) downcast

ingerir ▸conjug 3i◂ VT (= *tragar*) to swallow; (= *tomar*) to consume, ingest (*frm*); **el automovilista había ingerido tres litros de alcohol** the motorist had drunk *o* consumed three litres of alcohol

ingesta SF consumption, ingestion (*frm*), intake; **la ~ de alcohol** alcohol consumption; **la ~ diaria de hierro** the daily intake of iron ► **ingesta compulsiva** compulsive eating

ingestión SF consumption, ingestion (*frm*); **~ de fruta** fruit consumption; **~ máxima al día** maximum daily intake; **la ~ de vitamina C parece ser beneficiosa** taking vitamin C seems to be beneficial

➤ LENGUA Y USO: **ingenuo** 53.1

Inglaterra SF England; **la batalla de ~** the Battle of Britain (1940)

ingle SF groin

inglés/esa Ⓐ ADJ English; **montar a la inglesa** to ride sidesaddle
Ⓑ SM/F Englishman/Englishwoman; **los ingleses** the English, English people
Ⓒ SM (*Ling*) English

inglesismo SM anglicism

inglete SM (= *ángulo*) angle of 45°; (= *ensambladura*) mitre joint

ingobernabilidad SF [*de aparato*] uncontrollable nature; [*de país, ciudad*] ungovernable nature; [*de embarcación*] unsteerability

ingobernable ADJ [*aparato*] uncontrollable; [*país, ciudad*] ungovernable; [*embarcación*] unsteerable, impossible to steer

ingratitud SF ingratitude

ingrato/a Ⓐ ADJ [*persona*] ungrateful; [*tarea*] thankless, unrewarding; [*sabor*] unpleasant, disagreeable; **¡ingrato!** you're so ungrateful!
Ⓑ SM/F ungrateful person; **¡eres un ~!** you're so ungrateful!

ingravidez SF weightlessness

ingrávido ADJ (= *sin peso*) weightless; (*liter*) (= *ligero*) very light

ingrediente SM 1 [*de comida, compuesto*] ingredient
2 **ingredientes** (*Arg*) (= *tapas*) appetizers

ingresado/a SM/F 1 (= *enfermo*) patient
2 (= *preso*) prisoner
3 (*Univ*) entrant, new student

ingresar ▸conjug 1a◂ Ⓐ VT 1 (*Esp Fin*) [+ *dinero, cheque*] to pay in, deposit; [+ *ganancias*] to take; **quería ~ este cheque** I'd like to pay in this cheque *o* to deposit this cheque; **he ingresado 500 euros en mi cuenta/en el banco** I've paid 500 euros into my account/the bank, I've deposited 500 euros in my account/the bank; **se han ingresado 200 dólares en su cuenta** 200 dollars have been credited to your account; **ingresamos unas tres mil libras en las rebajas** we took about three thousand pounds in the sales; **ingresa 2.500 euros al mes** he earns 2,500 euros a month
2 (= *internar*) 2·1 (*en institución*) **la ~on en la cárcel hace dos días** she was put in prison *o* sent to prison two days ago; **la cárcel donde están ingresados los terroristas** the prison where the terrorists are being held; **~ a algn en un colegio** to enrol sb in a school, send sb to a school
2·2 (*en hospital*) to admit (**en** to); **lo ~on en la unidad de cuidados intensivos** he was admitted to the intensive care unit; **un paciente ingresado a consecuencia de una intoxicación** a patient admitted to hospital *o* (*EEUU*) to the hospital as a result of food poisoning; **María continúa ingresada** María is still in hospital
Ⓑ VI 1 (= *entrar*) 1·1 (*en institución*) to join; **han ingresado 500 nuevos socios en el club** 500 new members have joined the club; **fue la primera mujer que ingresó en** *o* (*LAm*) **a la Academia** she was the first woman to be elected to the Academy *o* to become a member of the Academy; **~ en** *o* (*LAm*) **a la cárcel** to go to prison, be sent to prison; **~ en** *o* (*LAm*) **a un colegio** to enter a school; **~ en el** *o* (*LAm*) **al ejército** to join the army, join up; **ingresó en el ejército británico a los 20 años** he joined the British army at the age of 20; **~ en** *o* (*LAm*) **a una sociedad** to become a member of a club, join a club; **~ en** *o* (*LAm*) **a la universidad** to start university, begin one's university studies
1·2 (*Med*) **~ cadáver** to be dead on arrival; **~ en el hospital** to be admitted to hospital, be admitted to the hospital (*EEUU*), go into hospital, go into the hospital (*EEUU*); **falleció poco después de ~ en el hospital** she died shortly after being admitted to hospital, she died shortly after she went into hospital; **el agente se encuentra ingresado en el hospital universitario** the police officer is a patient in the university hospital
2 (*Fin*) [*dinero*] to come in; **el dinero que ingresa en Hacienda** the money which comes into the Treasury; **hoy no ha ingresado mucho en caja** we haven't taken much today
Ⓒ **ingresarse** VPR (*Méx*) (*en club, institución*) to join, become a member; (*en el ejército*) to join up

ingreso SM 1 (= *entrada*) 1·1 (*en institución*) admission (**en** into); **el ~ de España en la OTAN** Spain's admission into NATO; **tras su ~ en la Academia** after he joined the Academy, after his admission to the Academy; **después de su ~ en la marina** after he joined the navy; **examen de ~** (*Univ*) entrance examination; **~ en prisión** imprisonment; **el juez ordenó su ~ en prisión** the judge ordered him to be sent to prison, the judge ordered his imprisonment
1·2 (*en hospital*) admission (**en** to); **ha habido un aumento en el número de ~s** there has been an increase in the number of admissions; **tras su ~ en el hospital** after being admitted to hospital, after his admission to hospital; **¿a qué hora se produjo el ~?** what time was he admitted?
2 (*Fin*) 2·1 (*Esp*) (= *depósito*) deposit; **¿de cuánto es el ~?** how much are you paying in?, how much are you depositing?; **hacer un ~** to pay in some money, make a deposit
2·2 **ingresos** [*de persona, empresa*] income *sing*; [*de país, multinacional*] revenue *sing*; **el trabajo es mi única fuente de ~s** work is my only source of income; **las personas con ~s inferiores a 1.000 euros** people with incomes below 1,000 euros; **los ~s del Estado han disminuido este año** State revenue has gone down this year; **~s y gastos** [*de persona, empresa*] income and outgoings, income and expenditure; [*de país, multinacional*] income and expenditure; **~s por algo** revenue from sth; **los ~s por publicidad** advertising revenue, revenue from advertising; **~s por impuestos** tax revenue; **vivir con arreglo a los ~s** to live within one's income ► **ingresos anuales** [*de persona, empresa*] annual income *sing*; [*de país, multinacional*] annual revenue *sing* ► **ingresos brutos** gross income *sing* ► **ingresos de taquilla** (*Cine, Teat*) box-office takings; (*Dep*) ticket sales ► **ingresos devengados** earned income *sing* ► **ingresos exentos de impuestos** non-taxable income *sing* ► **ingresos gravables** taxable income *sing* ► **ingresos netos** net income *sing* ► **ingresos personales disponibles** disposable personal income *sing*
3 (= *lugar de acceso*) entrance

íngrimo* ADJ **~ y solo** (*esp LAm*) all alone, completely alone

inguandia SF (*Andes*) fib, tale

inguinal ADJ inguinal (*frm*), groin *antes de s*

INH SM ABR = **Instituto Nacional de Hidrocarburos**

inhábil ADJ [1] [*persona*] (= *torpe*) unskilful, unskillful (*EEUU*), clumsy; (= *incompetente*) incompetent; (= *no apto*) unfit (**para** for; **para hacer algo** to do sth)
[2] **día ~** non-working day; **ese día ha sido declarado ~** that day has been declared a holiday; **en horas ~es** outside office hours; **un mes parlamentariamente ~** a month when parliament is not in session
[3] [*testigo*] ineligible

inhabilidad SF (= *torpeza*) unskilfulness, unskillfulness (*EEUU*), clumsiness; (= *incompetencia*) incompetence; (= *incapacidad*) unfitness (**para** for); (*para un cargo*) ineligibility; [*de testigo*] ineligibility

inhabilitación SF [1] (*Pol, Jur*) disqualification
[2] (*Med*) disablement; *ver tb* **nota A1**

inhabilitar ▸conjug 1a◂ VT [1] (*Pol, Jur*) to disqualify; **el alcalde fue inhabilitado por seis años** the mayor was disqualified *o* barred from holding office for six years; **los funcionarios responsables han sido inhabilitados** the civil servants responsible have been suspended; **~ a algn para algo/hacer algo** to disqualify sb from sth/doing sth
[2] (*Med*) to disable, render unfit

inhabitable ADJ uninhabitable

inhabitado ADJ uninhabited

inhabituado ADJ unaccustomed (**a** to)

inhabitual ADJ unusual, out of the ordinary, exceptional

inhalación SF [1] [*de gases*] inhalation; **~ de colas/pegamento** glue-sniffing ► **inhalación de humo** smoke inhalation
[2] **inhalaciones** (*Med*) inhalations

inhalador SM inhaler

inhalante SM inhalant

inhalar ▸conjug 1a◂ VT [+ *gases*] to inhale; [+ *cola, pegamento*] to sniff

inherente ADJ inherent (**a** in); **la función ~ a un oficio** the duties attached to an office

inhibición SF inhibition

inhibidor Ⓐ ADJ inhibiting
Ⓑ SM inhibitor ► **inhibidor del apetito** appetite depressant ► **inhibidor del crecimiento** growth inhibitor

inhibir ▸conjug 3a◂ Ⓐ VT [1] (= *reprimir*) to inhibit
[2] (*Jur*) to restrain, stay
Ⓑ **inhibirse** VPR [1] (= *no actuar*) to keep out (**de** of), stay away (**de** from)
[2] (= *abstenerse*) to refrain (**de** from)
[3] (*Biol, Quim*) to be inhibited

inhibitorio ADJ inhibitory

inhospitalario ADJ inhospitable

inhospitalidad SF inhospitality

inhóspito ADJ inhospitable

inhumación SF burial, interment (*frm*)

inhumanamente ADV (= *de forma no humana*) inhumanly; (= *sin compasión*) uncompassionately

inhumanidad SF inhumanity

inhumano ADJ [1] (= *no humano*) inhuman
[2] (= *falto de compasión*) inhumane
[3] (*Cono Sur*) dirty, disgusting

inhumar ▸conjug 1a◂ VT to bury, inter (*frm*)

INI SM ABR [1] (*Esp*) (= **Instituto Nacional de Industria**) ≈ National Enterprise Board
[2] (*Chile*) = **Instituto Nacional de Investigaciones**

INIA SM ABR [1] (*Esp Agr*) = **Instituto Nacional de Investigación Agraria**
[2] (*Méx*) = **Instituto Nacional de Investigaciones Agrícolas**

iniciación SF [1] (= *comienzo*) beginning
[2] (= *introducción*) introduction; **curso de ~** introductory course
[3] (*Rel*) initiation; **ceremonia de ~** initiation ceremony; **rito de ~** initiation rite

iniciado/a Ⓐ ADJ initiated
Ⓑ SM/F initiate (*frm*); **para los ~s/no ~s** for the initiated/the uninitiated

iniciador(a) Ⓐ SM/F [*de plan*] initiator; [*de técnica, práctica*] pioneer
Ⓑ SM [*de bomba*] primer, priming device

inicial Ⓐ ADJ [*posición, velocidad, respuesta*] initial; [*sueldo, alineación*] starting; **capital ~** initial capital, starting capital; **salió a la venta con un precio ~ de tres millones** it went on sale at a starting price of three million
Ⓑ SF [1] (= *letra*) initial
[2] (*Caribe*) deposit, down payment

inicialar ▸conjug 1a◂ VT to initial

inicializar ▸conjug 1f◂ VT [1] (= *poner iniciales a*) to initial
[2] (*Inform*) to initialize

iniciar ▸conjug 1b◂ Ⓐ VT [1] [+ *actividad*] (= *comenzar*) to begin, start, initiate (*frm*); (= *dar origen a*) to originate; (= *fundar*) to pioneer; **~ la sesión** (*Inform*) to log in, log on
[2] (*en conocimientos, secta*) to initiate (**en** into); **~ a algn en un secreto** to let sb into a secret
Ⓑ **iniciarse** VPR [1] (= *comenzar*) to begin, start
[2] **~se como actor/escritor** to start out as an actor/writer, take one's first steps as an actor/writer; **~se como fumador** to start smoking, take up smoking; **~se en política** to start out in politics; **~se en un deporte** to start a new sport

iniciático ADJ **ritos ~s** initiation rites

iniciativa SF [1] (= *capacidad emprendedora*) initiative; **~ de paz** peace initiative; **bajo su ~** on his initiative; **por ~ propia** on one's own initiative; **carecer de ~** to lack initiative; **tomar la ~** to take the initiative ► **iniciativa privada** private enterprise
[2] (= *liderazgo*) leadership

inicio SM start, beginning

inicuamente (*frm*) ADV wickedly, iniquitously (*frm*)

inicuo (*frm*) ADJ wicked, iniquitous (*frm*)

inidentificable ADJ unidentifiable

inidentificado ADJ unidentified

inigualable ADJ [*calidad*] unsurpassable; [*belleza, reputación*] matchless; [*oferta, precio*] unbeatable

inigualado ADJ [*fama, récord, duración*] unequalled, unequaled (*EEUU*); [*belleza, encanto*] unparalleled, unrivalled, unrivaled (*EEUU*)

inimaginable ADJ unimaginable, inconceivable

inimitable ADJ inimitable

ininflamable ADJ non-flammable, fire-resistant

ininteligente ADJ unintelligent

ininteligibilidad SF unintelligibility

ininteligible ADJ unintelligible

ininterrumpidamente ADV (= *continuamente*) continuously, without a break; (= *a un ritmo constante*) steadily; (= *sin interrupción*) uninterruptedly; **la canción suena ~ en la radio** the song is played continuously *o* nonstop on the radio; **dos coleccionistas pujaron ~** two collectors bid continuously; **los salarios han crecido ~** salaries have risen steadily; **continúan ~ las tareas de búsqueda** the search continues uninterrupted

ininterrumpido ADJ (= *sin interrupción*) (*gen*) uninterrupted; [*proceso*] continuous; [*progreso*] steady, sustained; **20 horas de música ininterrumpida** 20 hours of non-stop *o* uninterrupted music; **llovió de forma ininterrumpida** it rained continuously *o* non-stop; **la película se proyecta de manera ininterrumpida** the film is shown uninterrupted *o* without a break

iniquidad SF (= *maldad*) wickedness, iniquity (*frm*); (= *injusticia*) injustice

in itinere ADV (*frm*) **siniestros ~** accidents which happen on one's way to or from work

injerencia SF interference (**en** in), meddling (**en** in)

injerir ▸conjug 3i◂ Ⓐ VT [1] (= *introducir*) to insert (**en** into), introduce (**en** into)
[2] (*Agr*) to graft (**en** on, on to)
Ⓑ **injerirse** VPR to interfere (**en** in), meddle (**en** in)

injertar ▸conjug 1a◂ VT [1] (*Agr, Med*) to graft (**en** on, on to)
[2] [+ *vida*] to inject (**en** into)

injerto SM [1] (= *acción*) grafting
[2] (*Agr, Med*) graft; **~ de piel** skin graft; **~ de médula ósea** bone marrow transplant; **~ de genes** gene implant

injuria SF [1] (= *insulto*) insult; (*Jur*) slander; **~s** abuse *sing*, insults; **cubrir/llenar a algn de ~s** to heap abuse on sb; **demandar a algn por ~s** ◊ **presentar una querella por ~s contra algn** to sue sb for slander
[2] (†† *liter*) (= *daño*) **las ~s del tiempo** the ravages of time

injuriar ▸conjug 1b◂ VT [1] (= *insultar*) (*gen*) to insult, abuse; (*Jur*) to slander
[2] (†† *liter*) (= *dañar*) to damage, harm

injuriosamente ADV [1] (= *insultantemente*) insultingly, offensively; (*Jur*) slanderously
[2] (†† *liter*) (= *de modo dañino*) harmfully

injurioso ADJ [1] (= *insultante*) insulting, offensive; (*Jur*) slanderous
[2] (†† *liter*) (= *dañino*) harmful, damaging

injustamente ADV (= *con injusticia*) unjustly, unfairly; (= *indebidamente*) wrongfully

injusticia SF (= *falta de justicia*) injustice; (= *falta de equidad*) unfairness; **es una ~** (= *inmerecido*) it's unjust, it's an injustice; (= *no equitativo*) it's unfair; **una solemne ~** a terrible injustice; **con ~** unjustly

injustificable ADJ unjustifiable

injustificadamente ADV unjustifiably

injustificado ADJ unjustified

injusto ADJ [*castigo, crítica*] unjust, unfair; [*detención*] wrongful; [*despido, norma, persona, reparto*] unfair; **ser ~ con algn** to be unfair to sb

INLE SM ABR = **Instituto Nacional del Libro Español**

inllevable ADJ unbearable, intolerable

inmaculado ADJ [1] (= *limpio*) [*baño, cocina*] immaculate, spotless; [*persona, ropa*] immaculate; [*honradez, reputación*] impeccable
[2] (*Rel*) **la Inmaculada (Concepción)** the Immaculate Conception; **María Inmaculada** Immaculate Mary

inmadurez SF immaturity

inmaduro ADJ [*persona*] immature; [*fruta*] unripe

inmancable ADJ (*Andes, Caribe*) unfailing, infallible

inmanejable ADJ unmanageable

inmanencia SF immanence

inmanente ADJ immanent

inmarchitable ADJ, **inmarcesible** ADJ undying, unfading

inmaterial ADJ immaterial

INME SM ABR = **Instituto Nacional de Moneda Extranjera**

inmediaciones SFPL surrounding area *sing*, vicinity *sing*; **en las ~ del bosque** in the area around the forest, in the vicinity of the forest

inmediata* SF **la ~** the natural thing, the first thing

inmediatamente ADV [1] (= *al momento*) immediately, at once
[2] **~ de su llegada** immediately after they arrive; **desmoldar ~ de sacarlo del horno** turn out immediately after removing from the oven; **~ de recibido** immediately on receipt

inmediatez SF immediacy

inmediato ADJ [1] (= *sin mediar intervalo*) immediate
[2] (= *rápido*) prompt; **de ~** immediately; **en lo ~** ◊ **en el futuro ~** in the immediate future
[3] [*lugar*] (= *contiguo*) adjoining; (= *próximo*) neighbouring, neighboring (*EEUU*); **~ a** close to, next to

inmejorable ADJ (= *excelente*) (*gen*) excellent, superb; [*precio, récord*] unbeatable; **~s recomendaciones** excellent references; **de calidad ~** top-quality

inmejorablemente ADV excellently, superbly; **portarse ~** to behave perfectly

inmemorial ADJ, **inmemorable** ADJ immemorial; **desde tiempo ~** from time immemorial

inmensamente ADV immensely, vastly; **~ rico** immensely rich, enormously wealthy

inmensidad SF immensity, vastness

inmenso ADJ [*llanura, océano, fortuna*] vast, immense; [*objeto, ciudad, número*] enormous; [*alegría, tristeza, esfuerzo*] tremendous, immense; [*talento*] enormous, immense; **la inmensa mayoría** the vast majority; **sentí un ~ vacío tras su muerte** I felt a vast emptiness after his death; **Leonor tiene un corazón ~** Leonor is enormously big-hearted

inmensurable ADJ immeasurable

inmerecidamente ADV undeservedly

inmerecido ADJ, **inmérito** ADJ undeserved

inmergir ▸conjug 3c◂ VT to immerse

inmersión SF [1] (= *sumergimiento*) (*gen*) immersion; [*de buzo*] dive; (*en pesca submarina*) skin-diving, underwater fishing
[2] (*Téc, Fot*) **tanque de ~** immersion tank
[3] (*en tema, idioma*) immersion; **periodos de ~ en el extranjero** periods of intensive exposure abroad

inmerso ADJ [1] (= *sumergido*) immersed
[2] (*en actividades, ideas*) immersed (**en** in); **~ en sus meditaciones** deep in thought

inmigración SF immigration

inmigrado/a SM/F immigrant

inmigrante ADJ, SMF immigrant

inmigrar ▸conjug 1a◂ VI to immigrate

inminencia SF imminence

inminente ADJ imminent

inmiscuirse ▸conjug 3g◂ VPR to interfere, meddle (**en** in)

inmisericorde ADJ merciless, pitiless

inmisericordemente ADV mercilessly, pitilessly

inmisericordioso ADJ merciless, pitiless

inmobiliaria SF [1] (= *agencia de venta*) estate agent, real estate agency (*EEUU*)
[2] (= *constructora*) property developer

inmobiliario ADJ real estate *antes de s*, property *antes de s*; **agente ~** estate agent, real estate agent (*EEUU*), realtor (*EEUU*); **venta inmobiliaria** sale of property

inmoderación SF lack of moderation

inmoderadamente ADV immoderately

inmoderado ADJ immoderate

inmodestamente ADV immodestly

inmodestia SF immodesty

inmodesto ADJ immodest

inmodificable ADJ that cannot be modified

inmolación SF sacrifice, immolation (*frm*)

inmolar ▸conjug 1a◂ VT sacrifice, to immolate (*frm*)

inmoral ADJ immoral

inmoralidad SF [1] (= *cualidad*) immorality
[2] (= *acto*) immoral act; **es una ~** it's immoral

inmortal ADJ, SMF immortal

inmortalidad SF immortality

inmortalizar ▸conjug 1f◂ VT to immortalize

inmotivación SF lack of motivation

inmotivado ADJ [*acción, asesinato*] motiveless; [*sospecha*] groundless

inmoto ADJ (*frm*) unmoved

inmovible ADJ immovable

inmóvil ADJ (= *quieto*) still, motionless; (= *inamovible*) immovable; **quedar ~** (*gen*) to stand still *o* motionless; (*Aut*) to remain stationary

inmovilidad SF [1] [*de persona*] (= *inamovilidad*) immovability; (= *inactividad*) immobility
[2] [*del mar*] stillness

inmovilismo SM (= *estancamiento*) stagnation; (= *oposición al cambio*) resistance to change; (*Pol*) (= *ideología*) ultraconservatism; (= *política*) do-nothing policy

inmovilista ADJ (= *estancado*) stagnant; (= *opuesto al cambio*) resistant to change; (*Pol*) ultraconservative; → APERTURISMO

inmovilización SF [1] [*de persona, vehículo*] immobilization; **~ de vehículos con cepo** vehicle clamping; **~ de coches** *o* **carros** (*Méx*) traffic jam
[2] (= *paralización*) paralysing

inmovilizado SM capital assets *pl*, fixed assets *pl*

inmovilizar ▸conjug 1f◂ VT [1] [+ *persona, vehículo*] to immobilize
[2] (= *paralizar*) to paralyse, bring to a standstill
[3] (*Fin*) [+ *capital*] to tie up

inmueble Ⓐ ADJ **bienes ~s** real estate *sing*, real property *sing* (*EEUU*)
Ⓑ SM [1] (= *edificio*) property, building
[2] **inmuebles** (= *bienes*) real estate *sing*, real property *sing* (*EEUU*); (= *edificios*) buildings, properties

inmundicia SF [1] (= *inmoralidad*) filth, dirt; **esto es una ~** this is absolutely disgusting
[2] **inmundicias** (= *basura*) rubbish *sing*, garbage *sing* (*EEUU*)

inmundo ADJ filthy, dirty

inmune ADJ [1] (*Med*) immune (**a** against, to)
[2] (= *no afectado*) immune (**a** to); **~ a las críticas** immune to criticism
[3] (= *exento*) exempt (**de** from)

inmunidad SF [1] (*Pol, Med*) immunity
► **inmunidad diplomática** diplomatic immunity ► **inmunidad parlamentaria** parliamentary immunity
[2] (= *exención*) exemption

inmunitario ADJ immune; **respuesta inmunitaria** immune response; **sistema ~** immune system

inmunización SF immunization

inmunizar ▸conjug 1f◂ VT to immunize

inmunodefensivo ADJ **sistema ~** immune defence system

inmunodeficiencia SF immunodeficiency

inmunodeprimido ADJ immunodeficient

inmunología SF immunology

inmunológico ADJ immune; **sistema ~** immune system; **tolerancia inmunológica** immunological tolerance; **instituto ~** immunology institute

inmunólogo/a SM/F immunologist

inmunorreacción SF immune reaction

inmunorrespuesta SF immune response

inmunosupresivo ADJ, SM immunosuppressive

inmunosupresor Ⓐ ADJ immunosuppressive
Ⓑ SM immunosuppressant

inmunoterapia SF immunotherapy

inmutabilidad SF immutability

inmutable ADJ [*principio, sociedad*] unchanging; [*persona*] impassive; **aguantó ~ los insultos** she took the insults impassively

inmutarse ▸conjug 1a◂ VPR to get perturbed, get worked up; **ni se inmutó** he didn't bat an eyelid, he didn't turn a hair; **siguió sin ~** he carried on unperturbed; **las cosas van mal, pero ¿quién se inmuta?** things are going badly, but who's worrying *o* bothered?

innato ADJ innate, inborn

innatural ADJ unnatural

innavegable ADJ [*río, canal*] unnavigable; [*barco*] unseaworthy

innecesariamente ADV unnecessarily

innecesario ADJ unnecessary

▼ **innegable** ADJ undeniable

innegociable ADJ non-negotiable

innoble ADJ ignoble

innocuo ADJ = **inocuo**

innombrable ADJ unmentionable

innominado ADJ nameless, unnamed

➤ LENGUA Y USO: **innegable** 53.1

innovación SF innovation
innovador(a) Ⓐ ADJ innovative
Ⓑ SM/F innovator
innovar ▸conjug 1a◂ Ⓐ VT to introduce
Ⓑ VI to innovate
innovativo ADJ innovative, innovatory
innumerable ADJ, **innúmero** ADJ countless, innumerable
inobediencia SF disobedience
inobediente ADJ disobedient
inobjetable ADJ [*declaración, victoria*] indisputable; [*método, trabajo*] unobjectionable; [*origen*] undisputed; [*liderazgo*] unassailable; [*fuente, honradez*] unimpeachable; [*comportamiento*] impeccable
inobservado ADJ unobserved
inobservancia SF [*de norma*] non-observance; [*de obligaciones*] neglect; [*de ley*] violation, breaking
inocencia SF [*de acusado*] innocence; (= *ingenuidad*) innocence, naïveté
Inocencio SM Innocent
inocentada SF 1 practical joke, April Fool joke; → DÍA DE LOS (SANTOS) INOCENTES
2 (= *simpleza*) (= *dicho*) naïve remark; (= *error*) blunder
inocente[1] Ⓐ ADJ 1 (= *sin culpa*) innocent (**de** of); (*Jur*) not guilty, innocent; **fueron declarados ~s** they were found not guilty; **siempre se ha declarado ~** he has always pleaded his innocence
2 (= *ingenuo*) naïve
3 (= *inofensivo*) harmless
Ⓑ SMF 1 (= *ingenuo*) innocent person
2 (= *bobo*) simpleton; **el día de los (Santos) Inocentes** ≈ April Fools' Day, ≈ All Fools' Day

> **DÍA DE LOS (SANTOS) INOCENTES**
>
> *28 December,* **el día de los (Santos) Inocentes**, *is when the Catholic Church in Spain commemorates the New Testament story of King Herod's slaughter of the innocent children of Judaea. Like our April Fools' Day, Spaniards play practical jokes or* **inocentadas** *on each other. A typical example is sticking a* **monigote**, *a cut-out paper figure, on someone's back. Whenever someone falls for a trick, the practical joker cries out "***Inocente!***"*

inocente[2] SM 1 (*Andes, Cono Sur*) avocado pear
2 (*Andes*) masquerade
inocentemente ADV innocently
inocentón/ona* Ⓐ ADJ gullible, naïve
Ⓑ SM/F simpleton
inocuidad SF harmlessness, innocuousness (*frm*)
inoculación SF inoculation
inocular ▸conjug 1a◂ VT 1 (*Med*) to inoculate (**contra** against; **de** with)
2 [+ *idea, característica*] to inject; **inocula a sus personajes una gran profundidad** he injects a great deal of depth into his characters; **inoculó a los franceses la doctrina de la soberanía del pueblo** he infused the French with the doctrine of the sovereignty of the people
3 (= *pervertir*) to corrupt (**de** with), contaminate (**de** with)
inocuo ADJ innocuous, harmless
inodoro Ⓐ ADJ odourless, odorless (*EEUU*)
Ⓑ SM toilet, lavatory ► **inodoro químico** chemical toilet
inofensivo ADJ inoffensive, harmless
inoficioso* ADJ (*LAm*) useless
inolvidable ADJ unforgettable
inolvidablemente ADV unforgettably
inope† ADJ impecunious, indigent
inoperable ADJ 1 (*Med*) inoperable
2 [*aparato, vehículo*] inoperative
3 [*plan, sistema*] unworkable
inoperancia SF 1 [*de plan*] inoperative character
2 [*de autoridades, policía*] ineffectiveness
3 (*LAm*) (= *inutilidad*) uselessness, fruitlessness
inoperante ADJ 1 (= *inviable*) [*plan*] inoperative; [*decisión*] ineffective
2 (*LAm*) (= *inútil*) useless, fruitless; (= *inactivo*) inactive, out of use
inopia SF indigence, poverty; ✦*MODISMO* **estar en la ~** (= *no saber*) to be in the dark, have no idea; (= *estar despistado*) to be dreaming, be far away
inopinadamente ADV unexpectedly
inopinado ADJ unexpected
inoportunamente ADV 1 (= *a destiempo*) inopportunely, at a bad time
2 (= *causando molestia*) inconveniently
3 (= *de modo impropio*) inappropriately
inoportunidad SF 1 [*de momento*] inopportuneness, untimeliness
2 (= *molestia*) inconvenience
3 [*de comportamiento, comentario*] inappropriateness
inoportuno ADJ 1 [*momento*] inopportune, untimely
2 (= *molesto*) inconvenient
3 [*comportamiento, comentario*] inappropriate
inorgánico ADJ inorganic
inoxidable ADJ (*gen*) rustproof; [*acero*] stainless
inquebrantable ADJ [*fe*] unshakeable, unyielding; [*fidelidad, lealtad*] unswerving; [*entusiasmo*] undying; [*unidad, voluntad*] unbreakable; [*salud*] robust, stout
inquietador ADJ = **inquietante**
inquietamente ADV 1 (= *con preocupación*) anxiously, worriedly
2 (= *agitadamente*) restlessly
inquietante ADJ worrying, disturbing
inquietar ▸conjug 1a◂ Ⓐ VT to worry
Ⓑ **inquietarse** VPR to worry; **¡no te inquietes!** don't worry!
inquieto ADJ 1 (= *preocupado*) anxious, worried; **estar ~ por algo** to be anxious about sth, be worried about sth
2 (= *agitado*) restless, unsettled
inquietud SF 1 (= *preocupación*) concern; **expresaron su ~ por el futuro de sus hijos** they expressed their concern for their children's future; **los rumores han provocado ~ entre los inversores** the rumours have aroused concern among investors; **aumenta la ~ por la proliferación de armas nucleares** concern is growing over the proliferation of nuclear weapons; **esperaban su llamada con ~** they anxiously awaited her call
2 (= *interés*) interest; **mi hijo no tiene ninguna ~** my son isn't interested in anything, my son has no interest in anything; **es persona de ~es culturales** she has an interest in culture, she has cultural interests
inquilinaje SM 1 (*Cono Sur*) = **inquilinato**
2 (*Méx*) tenants *pl*
inquilinato SM 1 (= *arrendamiento*) tenancy; (*Jur*) lease, leasehold; **contrato de ~** tenancy agreement
2 (= *alquiler*) rent; **impuesto de ~** rates *pl*
3 (*Arg, Col, Uru*) (= *edificio*) tenement house; (*pey*) slum
inquilino/a SM/F (= *arrendatario*) tenant; (*Com*) lessee; (*Chile Agr*) tenant farmer; **~ de renta antigua** long-standing tenant, protected tenant
inquina SF (= *aversión*) dislike, aversion; (= *rencor*) ill will; **tener ~ a algn** to have a grudge against sb, have it in for sb*
inquiridor(a) Ⓐ ADJ inquiring
Ⓑ SM/F (= *que pregunta*) inquirer; (= *investigador*) investigator
inquiriente SMF inquirer
inquirir ▸conjug 3i◂ Ⓐ VT to investigate, look into
Ⓑ VI to inquire; **~ sobre algo** to make inquiries about sth, inquire into sth
inquisición SF 1 (= *indagación*) inquiry, investigation
2 (*Hist*) ► **la (Santa) Inquisición** the (Spanish) Inquisition
inquisidor SM inquisitor
inquisitivo ADJ inquisitive, curious
inquisitorial ADJ inquisitorial
inrayable ADJ scratch-proof
INRI ABR INRI
inri SM **para más ~*** to make matters worse
insaciable ADJ insatiable
insaciablemente ADV insatiably
insalubre ADJ (= *insano*) (*gen*) unhealthy, insalubrious (*frm*); [*condiciones*] insanitary
insalubridad SF unhealthiness
INSALUD SM ABR (*Esp*), **Insalud** SM ABR (*Esp*) = **Instituto Nacional de la Salud**
insalvable ADJ insuperable
insanable ADJ incurable
insania SF insanity
insano ADJ 1 (= *loco*) insane, mad
2 (= *malsano*) unhealthy
insatisfacción SF dissatisfaction
insatisfactorio ADJ unsatisfactory
insatisfecho ADJ [*condición, deseo*] unsatisfied; [*persona*] dissatisfied
insaturado ADJ unsaturated
inscribir ▸conjug 3a◂ (*pp* **inscrito**) Ⓐ VT 1 (= *grabar*) [+ *nombre, iniciales*] to inscribe (**en** on); **el anillo tenía inscrita la fecha de su boda** the ring had the date of the wedding inscribed on it
2 (= *apuntar*) 2·1 [+ *persona*] (*en lista*) to put down; (*en colegio, curso*) to enrol, enroll (*EEUU*); **he inscrito mi nombre en la lista** I've put my name down on the list
2·2 (*Jur*) [+ *contrato, nacimiento*] to register; **~ en el registro** to enter in the register, register; **todos los nacimientos están inscritos en el registro** all births are entered in the register, all births are registered; **hemos inscrito la casa en el registro de la propiedad** we've had the house registered

2·3 **~ algo en el orden del día** to put sth on the agenda
3 (*Mat*) [+ *figura, polígono*] to inscribe
Ⓑ **inscribirse** VPR 1 (= *apuntarse*) (*en colegio, curso*) to enrol, enroll (*EEUU*), register; (*en partido político*) to join; (*en concurso, competición*) to enter; (*en lista*) to put one's name down, register; **todos los participantes deben ~se antes del 1 de mayo** all participants should enrol *o* register before the 1st of May; **me he inscrito en el concurso de cuentos** I've entered the story-writing competition; **de los 25 equipos inscritos, sólo se presentaron 14** of the 25 teams on the list, only 14 turned up; **~se en el censo electoral** to register o.s. on the electoral roll *o* to vote; **me he inscrito en el censo de residentes extranjeros** I've registered (myself) as a foreign resident; **~se en el registro** [*pareja*] to sign the marriage register
2 (= *incluirse*) **~se dentro de** *o* **en** [+ *movimiento, tradición*] to fall within; [+ *clasificación*] to be classed among; **la novela se inscribe dentro de la tradición del realismo mágico** the novel falls within the tradition of magic realism; **esta pieza se inscribe en la línea de los grandes oratorios de la época** this piece can be classed among the great oratorios of the period; **esta reunión se inscribe en el marco de un ciclo de conferencias** this meeting forms part of a series of lectures; **la política del gobierno se inscribe dentro de un marco europeo** the government's policy follows the European framework

inscripción SF 1 (= *texto grabado*) (*gen*) inscription; (*Tip*) lettering
2 (= *acto*) (*en concurso*) entry; (*en curso*) enrolment, enrollment (*EEUU*); (*en congreso*) registration; **las inscripciones deberán realizarse entre el 1 y el 5 de marzo** those interested should enrol *o* (*EEUU*) enroll between the 1st and the 5th of March, enrolment will take place from the 1st to the 5th of March; **el plazo de ~ en el curso finaliza el día 3 de mayo** course applications will be accepted until the 3rd of May, the closing date *o* deadline for enrolment on the course is May 3rd; **~ en el censo electoral** registration on the electoral roll; **~ en el registro** registration; *ver tb* **boletín**

inscripto PP (*Arg*) *de* **inscribir**

inscrito/a Ⓐ PP *de* **inscribir**
Ⓑ ADJ (*Mat*) inscribed; **el triángulo queda ~ dentro de la circunferencia** the triangle is inscribed within the circumference
Ⓒ SM/F (= *persona registrada*) **el 25% de los ~s en el censo** 25% of those registered on the census; **hemos alcanzado la cifra de doscientos ~s para el concurso** more than two hundred entries have been received for the competition

insecticida SM insecticide

insectívoro ADJ insectivorous

insecto SM insect

inseguridad SF 1 (= *peligro*) lack of safety ► **inseguridad ciudadana** lack of safety in the streets, decline in law and order
2 (= *falta de confianza*) insecurity
3 (= *falta de estabilidad*) unsteadiness
4 (= *incertidumbre*) uncertainty ► **inseguridad laboral** lack of job security

inseguro ADJ 1 (= *peligroso*) [*zona, negocio, conducción*] unsafe
2 (= *sin confianza*) insecure; **se sienten ~s** they feel insecure
3 (= *sin estabilidad*) [*paso, estructura*] unsteady
4 (= *incierto*) [*clima*] unpredictable; [*persona*] uncertain, unsure (**de** about, of); [*futuro*] insecure

inseminación SF insemination ► **inseminación artificial** artificial insemination

inseminar ▸conjug 1a◂ VT to inseminate

insensatez SF foolishness, stupidity; **cometieron la ~ de no negociar** they were foolish *o* stupid enough not to negotiate; **lo que propones es una ~** what you are proposing is foolish *o* stupid; **dice unas insensateces increíbles** he says such foolish *o* stupid things

insensato ADJ foolish, stupid

insensibilidad SF 1 (= *indiferencia*) insensitivity, unfeeling nature
2 (*Med*) (= *falta de conocimiento*) insensibility, unconsciousness; (= *entumecimiento*) numbness

insensibilizar ▸conjug 1f◂ VT 1 [+ *persona*] (*ante emociones, problemas*) to render insensitive; (*ante sufrimiento*) to render unfeeling
2 (*Med*) (= *anestesiar*) to anaesthetize, anesthetize (*EEUU*); (*a alérgenos*) to desensitize

insensible ADJ 1 [*persona*] (= *indiferente*) insensitive (**a** to); (= *no afectado*) unaffected (**a** by)
2 [*cambio*] imperceptible
3 (*Med*) (= *inconsciente*) insensible, unconscious; (= *entumecido*) numb

insensiblemente ADV imperceptibly

inseparable ADJ inseparable

inseparablemente ADV inseparably

insepulto ADJ unburied; **funeral** *o* **misa (de) corpore ~** funeral mass

inserción SF insertion

INSERSO SM ABR (*Esp*), **Inserso** SM ABR (*Esp*) = **Instituto Nacional de Servicios Sociales**

insertable ADJ plug-in

insertar ▸conjug 1a◂ VT to insert

inserto Ⓐ ADJ **problemas en los que está ~ el gobierno** problems with which the government finds itself involved
Ⓑ SM insert

inservible ADJ (= *inútil*) useless; (= *averiado*) out of order

insidia SF 1 (= *trampa*) snare, trap
2 (= *acto*) malicious act
3 (= *mala intención*) maliciousness

insidiosamente ADV (= *engañando*) insidiously; (= *a traición*) treacherously

insidioso ADJ (= *engañoso*) insidious, deceptive; (= *traicionero*) treacherous

insigne ADJ (= *distinguido*) distinguished; (= *famoso*) famous

insignia SF 1 (= *distintivo*) badge, button (*EEUU*), emblem; **luce la ~ del club** he is sporting the club's badge *o* emblem
2 (= *estandarte*) flag, banner; (*Náut*) pennant
3 **insignias** [*de dignidad, poder*] insignia

insignificancia SF 1 (*cualidad*) insignificance
2 (= *cosa insignificante*) trifle

insignificante ADJ [*asunto, cantidad, detalle, accidente*] insignificant, trivial; [*persona*] insignificant

insinceridad SF insincerity

insincero ADJ insincere

insinuación SF insinuation; **hacer insinuaciones sobre algo** to make insinuations about sth, drop hints about sth; **insinuaciones eróticas/amorosas** sexual/amorous advances

insinuador ADJ insinuating

insinuante ADJ 1 (= *sugerente*) [*tono, movimiento*] insinuating; [*mirada, insinuación, ropa*] suggestive
2 (= *zalamero*) ingratiating
3 (= *taimado*) cunning, crafty

insinuar ▸conjug 1e◂ Ⓐ VT 1 (= *sugerir*) to insinuate, hint at; **~ que ...** to insinuate *o* imply that ...
2 **~ una observación** to slip in a comment
3 **~ una sonrisa** to give the hint of a smile
Ⓑ **insinuarse** VPR 1 (= *entreverse*) to begin to appear
2 **~se a algn** to make advances to sb
3 **~se con algn** to ingratiate o.s. with sb
4 **~se en algo** (= *introducirse*) to worm one's way into sth; **~se en el ánimo de algn** to work one's way gradually into sb's mind

insipidez SF [*de comida*] insipidness, tastelessness; [*de espectáculo, persona*] dullness, tediousness

insípido ADJ [*comida*] insipid, tasteless; [*espectáculo, persona*] dull, tedious

insistencia SF [*de persona*] insistence (**en** on); [*de quejas*] persistence; **a ~ de** at the insistence of; **se repite con ~ machacona** it is repeated with wearisome insistence

insistente ADJ [*persona*] insistent; [*quejas*] persistent

insistentemente ADV (*gen*) insistently; [*pedir, quejarse*] persistently

▼**insistir** ▸conjug 3a◂ VI 1 (= *perseverar*) **bueno, si insistes** all right, if you insist; **insistió en que se trataba de un error** she insisted that it was a mistake, she was adamant that it was a mistake; **insistió en que nos quedásemos a cenar** she insisted that we should stay to supper; **insisto en que todos abandonen la sala** I insist that everyone leave *o* leaves the room; **no insistas, que no pienso ir** don't keep on about it because I'm not going; **yo le decía que no, pero él insistía** I said no, but he kept on and on about it; **insiste y al final lo conseguirás** keep at it and you'll get there in the end; **si no te contestan, insiste** if they don't answer, keep trying; **insistieron en casarse en junio** they were adamant that they should get married in June
2 (= *enfatizar*) **~ en** *o* **sobre algo** to stress *o* emphasize sth

in situ ADV on the spot, in situ (*frm*)

insobornable ADJ incorruptible

insociabilidad SF unsociability

insociable ADJ unsociable

insolación SF 1 (*Med*) sunstroke; **coger una ~** to get sunstroke
2 (*Meteo*) sunshine; **horas de ~** hours of sunshine; **la ~ media diaria es de ...** the average hours of daily sunshine is ...

insolar ▸conjug 1a◂ Ⓐ VT to expose to the sun, put in the sun
Ⓑ **insolarse** VPR to get sunstroke

insolencia SF insolence; **lo que han hecho me parece una ~** I think what they did was really rude

➤ LENGUA Y USO: insistir 1 35.4

insolentarse ▸conjug 1a◂ VPR to become insolent, become rude; **~ con algn** to be insolent to sb, be rude to sb

insolente ADJ [1] (= *descarado*) insolent, rude
[2] (= *altivo*) haughty, contemptuous

insolentemente ADV [1] (= *con descaro*) insolently, rudely
[2] (= *con altivez*) haughtily, contemptuously

insolidaridad SF lack of solidarity

insolidario ADJ unsupportive; **hacerse ~ de algo** to dissociate o.s. from sth

insolidarizarse ▸conjug 1f◂ VPR **~ con algo** to dissociate oneself from sth

insólitamente ADV unusually, unwontedly (*frm*)

insólito ADJ unusual, unwonted (*frm*)

insolubilidad SF insolubility

insoluble ADJ insoluble

insolvencia SF insolvency, bankruptcy

insolvente ADJ insolvent, bankrupt

insomne Ⓐ ADJ sleepless, insomniac
Ⓑ SMF insomniac

insomnio SM sleeplessness, insomnia

insondable ADJ [*abismo, mar*] bottomless; [*misterio*] unfathomable (*liter*), impenetrable

insonorización SF soundproofing

insonorizado ADJ soundproof; **estar ~** to be soundproofed

insonorizar ▸conjug 1f◂ VT to soundproof

insonoro ADJ noiseless, soundless

insoportable ADJ unbearable, intolerable

insoportablemente ADV unbearably, intolerably

insoria SF (*Caribe*) insignificant thing; **una ~** a minimal amount

insoslayable ADJ unavoidable

insoslayablemente ADV unavoidably

insospechable ADJ beyond suspicion

insospechado ADJ unsuspected

▼ **insostenible** ADJ untenable

inspección SF (= *revisión*) inspection, examination; (= *control*) check ► **la Inspección de Hacienda** ≈ Inland Revenue, ≈ Internal Revenue Service (*EEUU*); **nos amenazan con una ~ de Hacienda** we have been threatened with a tax inspection, they have threatened us with an Inland Revenue inspection ► **Inspección de Trabajo** ≈ Industrial Relations Commission ► **inspección médica** medical examination ► **inspección ocular** visual inspection *o* examination ► **inspección técnica de vehículos** roadworthiness test, ≈ MOT test

inspeccionar ▸conjug 1a◂ VT (= *examinar*) to inspect; (= *controlar*) to check; (= *supervisar*) to supervise; (*Inform*) to peek

inspector(a) SM/F [1] (*gen*) inspector; (= *supervisor*) supervisor ► **inspector(a) de aduanas** customs officer ► **inspector(a) de enseñanza** school inspector ► **inspector(a) de Hacienda** tax inspector ► **inspector(a) de policía** police inspector
[2] (*Cono Sur*) [*de autobús*] conductor

inspectorado SM inspectorate

inspiración SF [1] [*de artista*] inspiration; **le vino la ~ para componer la canción** she got the inspiration to compose the song; **ballets de ~ española** Spanish-inspired ballets; **chaqueta de ~ náutica** a sailor-style jacket
[2] (*Med*) inhalation

inspirado ADJ inspired; **el poeta estaba poco ~** the poet was not very inspired, the poet was uninspired

inspirador/a Ⓐ ADJ inspiring, inspirational
Ⓑ SM/F (= *que da idea*) inspirer; (= *creador*) creator, originator

inspirar ▸conjug 1a◂ Ⓐ VT [1] [+ *artista*] to inspire; **eso no inspira confianza al consumidor** that does not inspire confidence in the consumer; **prefiero ~ respeto a ~ miedo** I prefer to inspire respect rather than instill fear
[2] (*Med*) to inhale, breathe in
Ⓑ **inspirarse** VPR **~se en algo** to be inspired by sth, find inspiration in sth

inspirativo ADJ [*discurso*] inspirational

INSS SM ABR (*Esp*) = **Instituto Nacional de Seguridad Social**

Inst. ABR, **Instº** ABR = **Instituto**

instable ADJ = **inestable**

instalación SF [1] (= *conexión*) [*de equipo, luz*] installation; **el técnico se encargará de hacer la ~ eléctrica** the technician will put in the electrics *o* (*frm*) take care of the electrical installation
[2] (= *montaje*) [*de oficina, fábrica*] setting up; [*de tienda de campaña*] pitching
[3] (= *equipo*) [*de luz, gas*] system; **han venido a arreglar la ~ de la luz** they've come to mend the electrical system *o* the wiring ► **instalación de fuerza** power plant ► **instalación eléctrica** electricity system, wiring ► **instalación sanitaria** sanitation facilities *pl*
[4] **instalaciones** [4·1] (= *recinto*) installations; **durante su recorrido por las instalaciones del museo** during her visit round the museum
[4·2] (= *servicios*) facilities; **el centro deportivo cuenta con excelentes instalaciones** the sports centre has excellent facilities
► **instalaciones deportivas** (= *recinto*) sports grounds; (= *servicios*) sports facilities ► **instalaciones portuarias** harbour installations ► **instalaciones recreativas** (= *recinto*) recreational areas; (= *servicios*) recreational facilities
[5] (*Arte*) installation

instalador(a) Ⓐ ADJ [*empresa, persona*] installation *antes de s*; **el técnico ~** the installation engineer
Ⓑ SM/F fitter ► **instalador(a) electricista, instalador(a) eléctrico/a** electrician ► **instalador(a) sanitario/a** plumber

instalar ▸conjug 1a◂ Ⓐ VT [1] (= *conectar*) [+ *calefacción, teléfono*] to install, instal (*EEUU*); [+ *luz, gas*] to connect, connect up, put in; [+ *antena*] to put up, erect (*frm*); [+ *lavadora, lavaplatos*] to install, instal (*EEUU*), plumb in; [+ *ordenador, vídeo*] to set up; [+ *sistema de control*] to install, instal (*EEUU*), put into operation; [+ *sistema operativo*] to install, instal (*EEUU*); **¿te han instalado ya el teléfono?** have you had the phone put in yet?, are you on the phone yet?; **hemos instalado un nuevo sistema de vigilancia** we've installed a new security system, we've put a new security system into operation; **ya tenemos instalado el lavaplatos** the dishwasher is in now; **he tenido que ~ una batería nueva en el coche** I've had to put a new battery in the car
[2] (= *montar*) [+ *consulta, oficina*] to set up, open; [+ *campamento, fábrica, espectáculo, exposición*] to set up; [+ *tienda de campaña*] to pitch; **la primera galería de arte que se instala en la ciudad** the first art gallery to be opened in town; **la escultura fue instalada en el centro del escenario** the sculpture was erected in the middle of the stage
[3] [+ *persona*] to put, install; **lo instaló en el cuarto de invitados** she put *o* installed him in the guest room; **el ejército lo instaló en el poder** the army put him into power
Ⓑ **instalarse** VPR **~se en** [+ *casa, oficina*] to settle into; [+ *ciudad*] to set up home in, settle in; [+ *país*] to settle in; **cuando estemos ya instalados os invitaremos a cenar** when we're settled in, we'll invite you round for dinner; **¿cuándo os ~éis en las nuevas oficinas?** when are you moving to the new offices?; **en 1940 me instalé definitivamente en España** in 1940 I settled in Spain for good; **me instalé en el sofá y de allí no me moví** I sat *o* settled myself down on the sofa and didn't move from there; **~se en el poder** to take power, get into power; **el partido ha conseguido ~se en el poder** the party has managed to take power *o* get into power; **el general se instaló en el poder tras el golpe de estado** the general took power after the coup d'état

instancia SF [1] (= *solicitud*) application, request; (*Jur*) petition; **a ~(s) de algn** at the request of sb, at sb's request; **pedir algo con ~** to demand sth insistently, demand sth urgently
[2] (= *formulario*) application form
[3] (= *momento*) **de primera ~** first of all; **en última ~** (= *como último recurso*) as a last resort; (= *en definitiva*) in the last analysis
[4] (*Pol*) (= *autoridad*) authority; (= *organismo*) agency; **altas ~s** high authorities ► **instancias del poder** corridors of power ► **instancias internacionales** international authorities

instantánea SF [1] (*Fot*) snap, snapshot
[2] (*) tart*, whore

instantáneamente ADV instantaneously, instantly

instantáneo ADJ [*respuesta, comunicación*] instantaneous; [*acceso, éxito, fracaso*] instant *antes de s*; **café ~** instant coffee; **la bala le produjo la muerte instantánea** the bullet killed him instantly

instante SM moment, instant; **se detuvo un ~** he stopped for a moment; **al ~** right now, at once; **(a) cada ~** all the time, every single moment; **en un ~** in a flash; **en ese** *o* **aquel mismo ~** at that precise moment; **hace un ~** a moment ago; **por ~s** incessantly

instantemente ADV insistently, urgently

instar ▸conjug 1a◂ Ⓐ VT to urge, press; **~ a algn a hacer algo** ◊ **~ a algn para que haga algo** to urge sb to do sth; **me instó a que hablase** he urged me to speak
Ⓑ VI to be urgent, be pressing

instauración SF [1] (= *establecimiento*) establishment, setting-up
[2] (= *renovación*) restoration, renewal

instaurar ▸conjug 1a◂ VT [1] (= *establecer*) to establish, set up
[2] (= *renovar*) to restore, renew

➤ LENGUA Y USO: **insostenible** 53.3

instigación SF instigation; **a ~ de algn** at the instigation of sb, at sb's instigation

instigador(a) SM/F instigator ► **instigador(a) de un delito** instigator of a crime; (*Jur*) accessory before the fact

instigar ▸conjug 1h◂ VT to incite; **~ a algn a hacer algo** to incite *o* induce sb to do sth; **~ a la sublevación** to incite to riot

instilar ▸conjug 1a◂ VT to instil, instill (*EEUU*) (**en** into)

instintivamente ADV instinctively

instintivo ADJ instinctive

instinto SM 1 (*de conducta*) (*gen*) instinct; **por ~** instinctively ► **instinto asesino, instinto de matar** killer instinct ► **instinto de supervivencia** survival instinct ► **instinto maternal** maternal instinct ► **instinto sexual** sexual urge
2 (= *impulso*) impulse, urge

institución SF 1 (= *organismo*) institution; **instituciones hospitalarias** hospitals; **un inspector de instituciones penitenciarias** an inspector of prisons; **esa tienda es toda una ~ en la ciudad** that shop is something of an institution in the city ► **institución benéfica, institución de beneficencia** charitable foundation, charitable organization ► **institución pública** public institution, public body
2 (= *acción*) establishment
3 **instituciones** (*en nación, sociedad*) institutions

institucional ADJ institutional

institucionalizado ADJ institutionalized

institucionalizar ▸conjug 1f◂ Ⓐ VT to institutionalize
Ⓑ **institucionalizarse** VPR to become institutionalized

instituir ▸conjug 3g◂ VT 1 (= *establecer*) [+ *ley, reforma*] to institute, establish; [+ *costumbre, norma, premio*] to establish
2 (= *fundar*) to found, set up

instituto SM 1 (= *organismo*) institute, institution; **~ financiero** financial institution; **los ~s armados** the army, the military; **el benemérito ~** the Civil Guard ► **instituto de belleza** (*Esp*) beauty parlour, beauty parlor (*EEUU*) ► **Instituto de la Mujer** Institute of Women's Affairs ► **Instituto Nacional de Empleo (INEM)** ≈ Department of Employment ► **Instituto Nacional de Industria (INI)** (*Esp Hist*) ≈ Board of Trade
2 (*Esp Educ*) ≈ secondary school, ≈ high school (*EEUU*); **nos conocemos desde que íbamos al ~** we've known each other since we were at secondary school together ► **Instituto Nacional de Bachillerato** ≈ state secondary school, ≈ high school (*EEUU*)
3 (= *regla*) (*gen*) principle, rule; (*Rel*) rule

institutriz SF governess

instrucción SF 1 (*Educ*) education; **recibió su ~ musical en Viena** he received his musical education in Vienna; **una persona de vasta ~** a highly educated person; **tener poca ~ en algo** to have a limited knowledge of sth ► **instrucción primaria** primary education ► **instrucción programada** programmed teaching ► **instrucción pública** state education
2 (*Mil*) (= *período*) training; (= *ejercicio*) drill; **hizo la ~ en Almería** he did his military training in Almería; **los soldados estaban haciendo la ~ en el patio** the soldiers were being drilled in the courtyard; **un vuelo de ~** a training flight ► **instrucción militar** military training
3 (*Dep*) coaching, training
4 (*Jur*) (*tb* **~ del sumario**) preliminary investigation; *ver tb* **juez 1, juzgado**
5 (*Inform*) statement
6 **instrucciones** (= *indicaciones*) instructions; **de acuerdo con tus instrucciones** in accordance with your instructions; **seguí sus instrucciones al pie de la letra** I followed her instructions to the letter; **recibir instrucciones** to receive instructions *o* orders; (*Mil*) to be briefed; **hemos recibido instrucciones de no decir nada** we've received instructions *o* orders to say nothing ► **instrucciones de funcionamiento** operating instructions ► **instrucciones de uso, instrucciones para el uso** directions for use

instructivo ADJ 1 (= *educativo*) educational
2 (= *revelador*) [*conclusión, reunión*] enlightening; [*ejemplo*] instructive

instructor(a) Ⓐ ADJ [*cabo, sargento*] training; [*fiscal, juez*] examining
Ⓑ SM/F 1 (*Dep*) coach, trainer ► **instructor(a) de vuelo** flight instructor
2 (*Mil*) instructor
3 (*Jur*) examining magistrate ► **instructor(a) de diligencias** *judge appointed to look into a case*

instruido ADJ 1 (= *educado*) well-educated; **estar ~ en algo** to be educated in sth
2 (= *informado*) well-informed

instruir ▸conjug 3g◂ Ⓐ VT 1 (= *formar*) 1·1 (*Educ*) [+ *estudiante*] to instruct; [+ *profesional*] to train; **he sido instruido para ejercer como abogado** I have been trained as a lawyer; **~ a algn en algo** to instruct sb in sth, train sb in sth; **me instruyeron en el manejo del fusil** I was taught how to use a gun; **fuimos instruidos en el arte del engaño** we were taught the art of deception, we were instructed *o* trained in the art of deception
1·2 (*Dep*) to coach, train
1·3 (*Mil*) to train
2 (*Jur*) (= *tramitar*) [+ *caso, causa*] to try, hear; **el juez que instruye la causa** the judge who is trying *o* hearing the case; **~ las diligencias** *o* **el sumario** to institute proceedings
Ⓑ VI (= *enseñar*) **la experiencia instruye mucho** experience is a great teacher; **juegos que instruyen** educational games; **el viajar instruye mucho** travel broadens the mind; **ya lo he instruido de nuestros proyectos** I've already explained our plans to him; **este libro los ~á con detalle sobre el modo de hacerlo** this book will give you detailed information *o* instructions (on *o* about) how to do it
Ⓒ **instruirse** VPR to learn, teach o.s. (**de** about)

instrumentación SF orchestration, scoring

instrumental Ⓐ ADJ 1 (*Mús*) instrumental
2 (*Der*) **prueba ~** documentary evidence
Ⓑ SM 1 (= *conjunto de instrumentos*) instruments *pl*, set of instruments; **el ~ de laboratorio** the laboratory instruments; **el ~ quirúrgico** the surgical instruments
2 (*Ling*) instrumental, instrumental case

instrumentalista SMF instrumentalist

instrumentalización SF exploitation

instrumentalizar ▸conjug 1f◂ VT 1 (= *llevar a cabo*) to carry out
2 **~ a algn** (= *utilizar*) to use sb as a tool, make cynical use of sb; (= *explotar*) to exploit sb, manipulate sb

instrumentar ▸conjug 1a◂ VT 1 (*Mús*) to score, orchestrate; **está instrumentado para …** it is scored for …
2 [+ *medidas, plan*] to implement, bring in
3 [+ *campaña*] to orchestrate
4 (= *manipular*) to manipulate

instrumentista SMF 1 (*Mús*) (= *músico*) instrumentalist; (= *fabricante*) instrument maker; **~ de cuerda** string player
2 (*Med*) theatre nurse
3 (*Mec*) machinist

instrumento SM 1 (*Mús*) instrument ► **instrumento de cuerda** string instrument ► **instrumento de época** period instrument ► **instrumento de percusión** percussion instrument ► **instrumento de tecla** keyboard instrument ► **instrumento de viento** wind instrument ► **instrumento musical, instrumento músico** musical instrument
2 (*Téc*) (= *aparato*) instrument; (= *herramienta*) tool, implement; **volar por ~s** to fly on instruments ► **instrumento auditivo** listening device ► **instrumento de precisión** precision instrument ► **instrumentos científicos** scientific instruments ► **instrumentos de mando** (*Aer*) controls ► **instrumentos quirúrgicos** surgical instruments ► **instrumentos topográficos** surveying instruments
3 (= *medio*) instrument, tool; **fue solamente el ~ del dictador** he was just a tool in the dictator's hands
4 (*Jur*) deed, legal document ► **instrumento de venta** bill of sale
5 (**) (= *pene*) tool**

insubordinación SF (= *desobediencia*) insubordination; (= *falta de disciplina*) unruliness, rebelliousness

insubordinado ADJ (= *desobediente*) insubordinate; (= *indisciplinado*) unruly, rebellious

insubordinar ▸conjug 1a◂ Ⓐ VT to stir up, rouse to rebellion
Ⓑ **insubordinarse** VPR to rebel; **~se contra el gobierno** to rise up *o* rebel against the government

insubsanable ADJ [*error*] irreparable; [*problema*] insoluble

insubstituible ADJ = **insustituible**

insudar ▸conjug 1a◂ VI (*liter*) to toil away

insuficiencia SF 1 (= *escasez*) insufficiency; **~ de franqueo** underpaid postage
2 (= *carencia*) lack, shortage; **~ de recursos** lack of resources; **debido a la ~ de personal** due to shortage of staff
3 (= *incompetencia*) incompetence
4 (*Med*) ► **insuficiencia cardíaca** heart failure ► **insuficiencia renal** kidney failure ► **insuficiencia respiratoria** shortage of breath
5 **insuficiencias** (= *fallos*) inadequacies; (= *carencias*) deficiencies; **existen muchas ~s en el sistema judicial** there are many inadequacies in the judicial system; **~s en la dieta alimenticia** deficiencies in the diet

insuficiente Ⓐ ADJ inadequate; **la explicación dada es ~** the explanation given is inadequate; **estos cambios son claramente ~s**

these changes are clearly inadequate *o* insufficient; **el dinero recolectado es ~ para hacer la obra** the money collected is insufficient *o* not sufficient to do the work; **tu nota es ~ para hacer derecho** this mark is not good enough for you to do law
Ⓑ SM fail; **me han puesto tres ~s** I've had three fails

insuficientemente ADV insufficiently, inadequately

insuflar ▸conjug 1a◂ VT [1] (*Med*) **~ aire a algo** to blow air into something
[2] (*liter*) **sus palabras ~on vida al proyecto** his words breathed life into the project; **insufló aires de esperanza a la vida política** he breathed new hope into politics

insufrible ADJ unbearable, insufferable

insufriblemente ADV unbearably, insufferably

insular ADJ island *antes de s*

insularidad SF insularity

insulina SF insulin

insulinodependiente ADJ insulin-dependent

insulsez SF [1] [*de comida*] tastelessness
[2] [*de charla, persona*] dullness

insulso ADJ [1] [*comida*] tasteless, insipid
[2] [*charla, persona*] dull

insultante ADJ insulting

insultar ▸conjug 1a◂ VT to insult

insulto SM [1] (= *ofensa*) insult (**para** to)
[2] (*Méx**) (= *indigestión*) bellyache*, stomachache

insumergible ADJ unsinkable

insumisión SF [1] (= *rebeldía*) rebelliousness
[2] (*Esp Mil*) *refusal to do military service or community service*

insumiso Ⓐ ADJ rebellious
Ⓑ SM [1] (*Esp Mil*) *man who refuses to do military service or community service*
[2] **insumisos** (*Méx Econ*) (= *entradas*) input *sing*, input materials

> **INSUMISO**
>
> *In Spain most men are required to do national service. If they object on conscientious grounds, they are legally entitled to opt to do the longer community-based alternative,* **Prestación Social Sustitutoria (PSS)**. *Those who refuse to do either form of service are called* **insumisos**. *Many* **insumisos** *argue that the discrimination against men inherent in the system is unconstitutional and the exploitation, as they see it, of unpaid labour is unlawful. Penalties for* **insumisión** *(refusal to do either form of service) can be severe, and may include prison sentences.*
> ⇨ *See also* MILI, PRESTACIÓN SOCIAL SUSTITUTORIA

insumo SM [1] (*Cono Sur*) (= *componente*) component, ingredient
[2] (*esp LAm*) **insumos** (*Econ*) supplies, input, materials

insuperable ADJ [*problema*] insurmountable; [*precio*] unbeatable; [*calidad*] unsurpassable

insuperado ADJ unsurpassed

insurgencia SF [1] (= *acto*) rebellion, uprising
[2] (= *fuerzas*) insurgent forces *pl*

insurgente ADJ, SMF insurgent

insurrección SF revolt, insurrection

insurreccional ADJ insurrectionary

insurreccionar ▸conjug 1a◂ Ⓐ VT to incite to rebel
Ⓑ **insurreccionarse** VPR to rebel, revolt

insurrecto/a ADJ, SM/F rebel, insurgent

insustancial ADJ insubstantial

insustituible ADJ irreplaceable

INTA SM ABR [1] (*Esp Aer*) = **Instituto Nacional de Técnica Aerospacial**
[2] (*Arg Agr*) = **Instituto Nacional de Tecnología Agropecuaria**
[3] (*Guat*) = **Instituto Nacional de Transformación Agraria**

intachable ADJ [1] (= *perfecto*) faultless, perfect
[2] [*conducta*] irreproachable

intacto ADJ [1] (= *sin tocar*) untouched; **dejó el desayuno casi ~** she left her breakfast almost untouched
[2] (= *no dañado*) intact, undamaged; **el vehículo estaba ~** the vehicle was intact *o* undamaged; **conserva ~ su sentido del humor** his sense of humor is intact *o* unaffected; **su prestigio sigue ~** his reputation remains intact

intangible Ⓐ ADJ intangible
Ⓑ SM intangible, intangible asset

integérrimo ADJ SUPERL *de* **íntegro**

integración SF [1] (= *incorporación*) integration; **la ~ de España en la UE** Spain's integration into the EU; **~ racial** racial integration
[2] (*Elec*) integration; **~ a muy gran escala** very large-scale integration; **~ a pequeña escala** small-scale integration

integrado ADJ [1] (*Elec*) [*circuito*] integrated
[2] (*Inform*) [*software*] integrated

integrador ADJ **política ~a** policy of integration, integrationist policy; **proceso ~** process of integration

integral Ⓐ ADJ [1] (= *entero*) [*cereal*] wholegrain; [*arroz*] brown; [*pan, harina*] wholemeal
[2] (= *total*) [*plan, reforma, servicio*] comprehensive, all-round; **para el cuidado ~ de la salud** for comprehensive *o* all-round health care; **educación ~** all-round education; **un desnudo ~** a full frontal
[3] (= *integrante*) integral, built-in; **una parte ~ de** an integral part of
[4] (= *redomado*) total, complete; **un idiota ~** a total *o* complete fool
[5] (*Mat*) integral
Ⓑ SF (*Mat*) integral

íntegramente ADV [1] (= *completamente*) entirely; **un concierto ~ dedicado a Mozart** a concert entirely devoted to Mozart; **el periódico reprodujo ~ la carta** the newspaper published the letter in full
[2] (= *con integridad*) uprightly, with integrity

integrante Ⓐ ADJ [*parte, elemento*] integral; [*país*] member *antes de s*; **es parte ~ de nuestra existencia** it is an integral part of our existence; **los estados ~s de la Unión Europea** the member states of the European Union
Ⓑ SMF member

integrar ▸conjug 1a◂ Ⓐ VT [1] (= *componer*) to make up; **la exposición la integran 150 fotografías** the exhibition is made up of 150 photographs; **una enciclopedia integrada por 12 volúmenes** an encyclopaedia consisting of 12 volumes
[2] (= *incorporar*) [+ *funciones, servicios*] to incorporate, include; **este programa integra diversas funciones** this program incorporates *o* includes various functions; **han integrado bien los muebles en el resto de la decoración** they have integrated *o* incorporated the furniture very well into the rest of the decor; **~ a algn en algo** to integrate sb into sth; **un programa para ~ a los presos en el mercado laboral** a programme to integrate prisoners into the labour market; **quieren ~ a su club en la federación deportiva** they want their club to become a member of *o* join the sports federation
[3] (*Mat*) to integrate
[4] (*Fin*) (= *reembolsar*) to repay, reimburse; (*Cono Sur*) (= *pagar*) to pay up
Ⓑ **integrarse** VPR [1] (= *adaptarse*) **~se en** [+ *grupo*] to fit into, integrate into; [+ *conjunto, entorno*] to blend with; **no le costó nada ~se en la clase** he had no difficulty fitting *o* integrating into the class; **la casa se integra perfectamente en el paisaje** the house blends perfectly with *o* into the landscape
[2] (= *unirse*) **~se en** [+ *asociación, conjunto*] to join; **el año en que España se integró plenamente en la Alianza Atlántica** the year Spain became a full member of the Atlantic Alliance; **el significante y el significado se integran en un solo elemento lingüístico** the signifier and the meaning join to form a single linguistic element

integridad SF [1] (= *totalidad*) wholeness, completeness; **en su ~** completely, as a whole; **publicaron el texto en su ~** they published the text in full *o* in its entirety; **~ física** personal safety, physical well being; **peligró su ~ física** she put her personal safety at risk; **delito contra la ~ de la persona** crime against the person
[2] (= *honradez*) integrity
[3] (*Inform*) integrity
[4] (†) (= *virginidad*) virginity

integrismo SM [1] (= *conservadurismo*) entrenched traditionalism
[2] (*Rel*) fundamentalism; **el ~ islámico** Islamic fundamentalism

integrista Ⓐ ADJ [1] (= *conservador*) traditionalist
[2] (*Rel*) fundamentalist
Ⓑ SMF [1] (= *conservador*) traditionalist
[2] (*Rel*) fundamentalist ▸ **integrista islámico** Islamic fundamentalist

íntegro ADJ [1] (= *completo*) [*cantidad, pago*] whole; [*condena*] full; [*grabación, texto*] unabridged; **dedica su sueldo ~ a la hipoteca** his whole salary goes towards the mortgage; **cumplió la pena íntegra** he served his sentence in full, he served his full sentence; **han publicado la versión íntegra del texto** they've published an unabridged version of the text; **el libro jamás se publicó ~** the book was never published in full; **en versión íntegra** [*película*] uncut; [*novela*] unabridged
[2] (= *honrado*) upright

integumento SM integument

intelecto SM, **intelectiva** SF intellect

intelectual ADJ, SMF intellectual

intelectuala* SF (*hum*) bluestocking

intelectualidad SF [1] (= *personas*) intelligentsia, intellectuals *pl*
[2] (*cualidad*) intellectuality, intellectual character

intelectualmente ADV intellectually

intelectualoide ADJ, SMF pseudo-intellectual

inteligencia SF [1] (= *capacidad*) intelligence ► **inteligencia artificial** artificial intelligence ► **inteligencia máquina** machine intelligence ► **inteligencia verbal** verbal skills *pl*, verbal ability
[2] (= *persona inteligente*) mind, intellect; **es una de las grandes ~s del partido** he is one of the great minds *o* intellects of the party
[3] (*Mil*) intelligence; **servicio de ~** intelligence service
[4] **la ~** (= *intelectuales*) the intelligentsia
[5] (= *comprensión*) understanding
[6] (= *acuerdo*) agreement

inteligente ADJ [1] [*persona, animal, pregunta, comentario*] intelligent; **¿hay vida ~ en Marte?** is there intelligent life on Mars?
[2] (*Inform*) intelligent; [*misil, edificio, tarjeta*] smart

inteligentemente ADV intelligently

inteligibilidad SF intelligibility

inteligible ADJ intelligible

inteligiblemente ADV intelligibly

intemperancia SF intemperance

intemperante ADJ intemperate

intemperie SF **la ~** the elements *pl*; **estar a la ~** to be out in the open, be at the mercy of the elements; **crema para proteger la piel de la ~** cream to protect the skin against the elements; **aguantar la ~** to put up with the elements, put up with wind and weather; **una cara curtida a la ~** a weatherbeaten face, a face tanned by wind and weather; **dejar a algn a la ~** to leave sb unprotected

intempestivamente ADV in an untimely way, at a bad time

intempestivo ADJ untimely; **regresar a casa a horas intempestivas** to return home at an ungodly hour

intemporal ADJ timeless

▼**intención** SF [1] (= *propósito*) intention; **causar daño no era la ~ de mi cliente** it was not my client's intention to cause any damage (*frm*); **perdona, no ha sido mi ~ despertarte** sorry, I didn't mean to wake you; **lo hizo con la mejor ~ del mundo** he did it with the best (of) intentions; **la ~ desestabilizadora de sus palabras** the disruptive intent of his words; **su ~ era que yo le pagara la entrada** he meant me to pay for his ticket; **su ~ era muy otra** he had something very different in mind; **no, gracias, pero se agradece la ~** no, but thanks for thinking of me, no thanks, but it was a kind thought; **la ~ es lo que cuenta** it's the thought that counts; **con ~** (= *a propósito*) deliberately, intentionally; **esto está hecho con ~** this was deliberate, this was no accident; **mencionó lo del divorcio con mala** *o* **mucha ~** he spitefully mentioned the divorce; **la ~ de hacer algo: ha dejado clara su ~ de venir** he has made it clear that he intends to come; **no lo dijo con la ~ de ofenderla** he didn't say it with the intention of offending her, he didn't say it to offend her; **sonrió con la ~ de animarme** he smiled to try to cheer me up; **sin la menor ~ de generalizar** without wishing to generalize; **tenemos la ~ de salir temprano** we intend *o* plan to start out early; **no tengo la menor** *o* **más mínima ~ de pedir perdón** I haven't got the slightest intention of apologizing, I have no intention of apologizing; **sin ~** without meaning to; **aunque lo haya hecho sin ~** even if he did it without meaning to, even if he didn't mean to do it ► **intención de voto** voting intention
[2] **intenciones** (= *planes*) intentions, plans; **no te fíes, no sabes sus intenciones** don't trust him, you don't know what he has in mind; **¿cuáles son tus intenciones para el año próximo?** what are your plans for next year?; **tener buenas intenciones** to mean well, have good intentions; **tener malas intenciones** to be up to no good; ✦**REFRÁN de buenas intenciones está el infierno lleno** the road to hell is paved with good intentions
[3] **doble** *o* **segunda ~** double meaning; **lo dijo con segunda** *o* **doble ~** there was a double meaning to what he said

intencionadamente ADV [1] (= *a propósito*) deliberately, on purpose
[2] (= *con mala intención*) nastily

intencionado ADJ [1] (= *deliberado*) deliberate, intentional
[2] **bien ~** [*persona*] well-meaning, well-intentioned; [*acto*] well-meant, well-intentioned
[3] **mal ~** [*persona*] ill-meaning, hostile; [*acto*] ill-meant, ill-intentioned

intencional ADJ intentional

intencionalidad SF [1] (= *propósito*) purpose, intention; **la ~ del incendio** the fact that the fire was deliberately started
[2] **una pregunta cargada de ~** a loaded question

intencionalmente ADV intentionally

intendencia SF [1] (= *dirección*) management, administration
[2] (= *oficina*) manager's office
[3] (*Mil*) (*tb* **cuerpo de ~**) ≈ service corps, ≈ quartermaster corps (*EEUU*)
[4] (*Arg*) (= *alcaldía*) mayoralty; (= *cargo de gobernador*) governorship

intendente SMF [1] (= *director*) manager
[2] (*Mil*) ► **intendente de ejército** quartermaster general
[3] (*LAm Hist*) governor
[4] (*Arg*) (= *alcalde*) mayor; (*Arg, Chile*) (= *gobernador*) provincial governor
[5] (*Méx, Ecu*) (= *policía*) police inspector

intensamente ADV [1] (= *con intensidad*) intensely
[2] (= *con fuerza, vehemencia*) powerfully, strongly
[3] (= *vivamente*) vividly, profoundly

intensar ▸conjug 1a◂ Ⓐ VT to intensify
Ⓑ **intensarse** VPR to intensify

intensidad SF [1] (*Elec, Téc*) strength; [*de terremoto, sonido*] intensity ► **intensidad luminosa** luminous intensity
[2] [*de color, olor, dolor*] intensity; [*de recuerdo*] vividness; [*de emoción, sentimiento*] strength; **la ~ de su mirada la atemorizó** the intensity of his gaze frightened her; **Manuel vivió con ~** Manuel lived life to the full; **ha aumentado la ~ del tráfico** the volume of traffic has increased; **nevaba con gran ~** it was snowing heavily *o* hard

intensificación SF intensification

intensificar ▸conjug 1g◂ Ⓐ VT to intensify
Ⓑ **intensificarse** VPR to intensify

intensión SF intensity, intenseness

intensivamente ADV intensively

intensivo ADJ [*búsqueda, tratamiento*] intensive; [*curso*] intensive, crash *antes de s*

intenso ADJ [*frío, dolor, actividad*] intense; [*emoción*] powerful, strong; [*recuerdo*] vivid; [*color*] deep, intense; [*bronceado*] deep; [*corriente eléctrica*] strong

intentar ▸conjug 1a◂ VT to try, attempt (*frm*); **hemos intentado un acuerdo** we've tried *o* attempted (*frm*) to reach an agreement; **¿por qué no lo intentas otra vez?** why don't you try again?; **¡venga, inténtalo!** come on, have a go *o* have a try!; **lo he intentado con regalos, pero no consigo animarla** I've tried (giving her) presents, but I just can't cheer her up; **lo ha intentado con todo** he has tried everything; **con ~lo nada se pierde** ◊ **por ~lo que no quede** there's no harm in trying; **~ hacer algo** to try to do sth, attempt to do sth (*frm*); **~emos llegar a la cima** we shall try *o* attempt (*frm*) to reach the summit; **llevo todo el día intentando hablar contigo** I've been trying to talk to you all day; **intente no fumar** try not to smoke; **~ que** + *SUBJUN*: **llevan años intentando que se celebre el juicio** they've spent years trying to bring the case to trial; **intenta que te lo dejen más barato** try and get *o* try to get them to reduce the price; **intenta que no se enteren tus padres** try not to let your parents find out

intento SM [1] (= *tentativa*) attempt; **al primer ~** at the first attempt; **fracasó en su ~ de batir el récord mundial** he failed in his attempt to beat the world record; **~ fallido** *o* **fracasado** failed attempt ► **intento de asesinato** (= *acción*) murder attempt; (= *cargo*) attempted murder ► **intento de soborno** attempted bribe ► **intento de suicidio** suicide attempt ► **intento de violación** attempted rape
[2] (= *propósito*) (*Méx*) intention; **de ~**† (*Méx, Col*) by design

intentona SF [1] (= *tentativa*) foolhardy attempt, wild attempt
[2] (*Pol*) putsch, rising ► **intentona golpista** failed coup (d'état), attempted coup (d'état)

ínter SM (*Andes, Cono Sur Rel*) curate

inter... PREF inter...

interacción SF interaction; **"interacciones"** (*Farm*) "not to be taken with..."

interaccionar ▸conjug 1a◂ VI to interact (**con** with)

interactivo ADJ interactive; **computación interactiva** (*Inform*) interactive computing

interactuación SF interaction

interactuar ▸conjug 1e◂ VI to interact (**con** with)

interamericano ADJ inter-American

interandino ADJ inter-Andean, concerning areas on both sides of the Andes

interanual ADJ **promedio ~** year-on-year average; **variación ~** variation from year to year

interbancario ADJ inter-bank *antes de s*

interbibliotecario ADJ inter-library *antes de s*; **préstamo ~** inter-library loan

intercalación SF [1] (= *inserción*) [*de comentarios, imágenes*] insertion, interspersing; [*de cultivos*] insertion, alternating
[2] (*Inform*) merging

intercalar ▸conjug 1a◂ VT [1] (= *insertar*) [+ *pausa, ejemplo*] to put in, include; [+ *comentarios, cultivos*] to intersperse, alternate; [+ *actividad*] to fit in, combine; **deberías ~ al-**

➤ LENGUA Y USO: **intención 1** 35.1, 35.2, 35.3, 45.4

gún ejemplo you should put in *o* include the odd example; **hemos intercalado unas imágenes con otras** we have interspersed *o* alternated some images with others; **una gira mundial que ~á con el rodaje** a world tour which he will fit in with the filming; **intercala en su obra ideas innovadoras con recuerdos de su pasado** in her work she alternates innovative ideas with memories of her past; **~ algo en algo** to insert sth into sth; **en el texto se han intercalado bastantes fotografías** a number of photographs have been inserted into the text; **intercaló unas palabras de agradecimiento en su discurso** he incorporated a few words of thanks into his speech; **~ algo entre** [+ *imágenes, objetos*] to insert sth between; [+ *cultivos*] to intersperse sth between, alternate sth with; **intercalaba pétalos entre las páginas de los libros** he inserted *o* put petals between the pages of the books; **daban unos aperitivos intercalados entre los platos** they served aperitifs between courses

2 (*Inform*) [+ *archivos, texto*] to merge

intercambiable ADJ interchangeable

intercambiar ▸conjug 1b◂ VT [+ *impresiones, presos, ideas, dinero*] to exchange; [+ *sellos, fotos*] to swap, exchange

intercambio SM [*de impresiones, de presos, ideas, dinero*] exchange; [*de sellos, fotos*] swap, exchange; **hice ~ con una chica inglesa** I went *o* did an exchange with an English girl; **me junto con un estudiante de español y hacemos ~ de conversación** I get together with a Spanish student to exchange conversation

interceder ▸conjug 2a◂ VI to intercede; **~ con el juez por el acusado** to intercede with the judge on the defendant's behalf, plead with the judge for the defendant

intercentros ADJ INV **comité ~** joint committee (*with representatives from all the different workplaces*)

interceptación SF 1 [*de correspondencia, misil*] interception

2 (*Aut*) stoppage, holdup

interceptar ▸conjug 1a◂ VT 1 [+ *correspondencia, misil, balón*] to intercept

2 (*Aut*) [+ *tráfico*] to stop, hold up; [+ *carretera*] to block, cut off

interceptor SM 1 (= *persona*) interceptor

2 (*Mec*) trap, separator

intercesión SF 1 (= *mediación*) mediation; **la ~ del alcalde no sirvió de nada** the mayor's mediation served no purpose

2 (*Rel*) intercession; **un milagro atribuido a la ~ del santo** a miracle attributed to the intercession of the saint

intercesor(a) SM/F 1 (= *mediador*) mediator

2 (*Rel*) intercessor

interclasista ADJ 1 (= *entre clases*) inter-class, which crosses class barriers

2 (= *sin clases*) classless

inter-club ADJ inter-club, between two clubs

intercomunicación SF intercommunication

intercomunicador SM intercom

intercomunicar ▸conjug 1g◂ VT to link

intercomunión SF intercommunion

interconectar ▸conjug 1a◂ VT to interconnect

interconectividad SF interconnectivity

interconexión SF interconnection

interconfesional ADJ interdenominational

interconsonántico ADJ interconsonantal

intercontinental ADJ intercontinental

intercultural ADJ intercultural

interdecir ▸conjug 3o◂ VT (*frm*) to forbid, prohibit

interdepartamental ADJ interdepartmental

interdependencia SF interdependence

interdependiente ADJ interdependent

interdicción SF prohibition, interdiction

interdicto SM prohibition, ban; (*Jur, Rel*) interdict

interdisciplinar ADJ, **interdisciplinario** ADJ interdisciplinary

interdisciplinariedad SF interdisciplinary nature

interés SM 1 (= *valor*) interest; **una cuestión de ~ general** a question of general interest; **un edificio de ~ histórico** a building of historic interest; **ese asunto no tiene ~ para nosotros** this matter is of no interest to us

2 (= *curiosidad*) interest; **el tema despertó** *o* **suscitó el ~ del público** the topic aroused public interest; **ha seguido con gran ~ la campaña electoral** he has followed the electoral campaign with great interest; **esperar algo con ~** to await sth with interest; **mostrar ~ en** *o* **por algo** to show (an) interest in sth; **poner ~ en algo** to take an interest in sth; **puse verdadero ~ en aprender inglés** I took a real interest in learning English; **sentir** *o* **tener ~ por algo** to be interested in sth; **si tienes ~ por el piso, todavía está a la venta** if you're interested in the flat, it's still for sale; **siento auténtico ~ por los idiomas** I have a real interest *o* I am really interested in languages; **sentir** *o* **tener ~ por hacer algo** to be interested in doing sth

3 (= *beneficio*) 3·1 [*de persona, país*] interest; **no deberías dejarte llevar por el ~** you shouldn't let yourself be swayed by personal interest; **¿qué ~ tienes tú en que pierdan el partido?** what's your interest in their losing the match?; **te lo digo por tu propio ~** I'm telling you for your own benefit *o* in your own interest; **en ~ del país ha renunciado a la reelección** in the interest(s) of the country he is not standing for re-election

3·2 (*Fin*) interest; **un préstamo a** *o* **con un ~ del 9 por ciento** a loan at 9 per cent interest; **los intereses de mi cuenta** the interest on my account; **dar ~** [*capital, inversión*] to yield interest; [*banco, cuenta*] to pay interest; **mi capital me da un ~ del 5,3 por ciento** my capital yields an interest of 5.3 per cent; **devengar ~** to accrue interest, earn interest; **tasa** (*LAm*) *o* **tipo de ~** interest rate

► **intereses acumulados** accrued interest *sing* ► **interés compuesto** compound interest ► **interés controlador** controlling interest ► **interés devengado** accrued interest, earned interest ► **intereses por cobrar** interest receivable *sing* ► **intereses por pagar** interest payable *sing* ► **interés simple** simple interest

4 **intereses** 4·1 (*Com*) interests; **hay intereses económicos por medio** there are financial interests involved; **tengo que defender mis intereses** I have to look after my own interests; **los intereses españoles en África** Spanish interests in Africa; **un conflicto de intereses** a conflict of interests; **tener intereses en algo** to have interests *o* a stake in sth; **tiene intereses en varias compañías extranjeras** he has interests *o* a stake in several foreign companies

4·2 (= *aficiones*) interests; **¿qué intereses tienes?** what are your interests?; **fomentar los intereses de algn** to foster sb's interest in sth

► **intereses creados** vested interests

interesadamente ADV **mintieron ~** they lied to protect their own interests *o* in their own interests; **actuaron ~** they had ulterior motives in acting as they did, they acted to protect their own interests; **he dejado de actuar ~** I've stopped acting purely in my own interest

interesado/a Ⓐ ADJ 1 (= *con interés*) interested; **las partes interesadas tendrán que firmar el contrato mañana** the interested parties will have to sign the contract tomorrow; **las personas interesadas pueden llamar al 900 100 100** anyone interested can phone 900 100 100; **estar ~ en** *o* **por algo** to be interested in sth; **nadie estaba ~ por la casa** nobody was interested in the house; **estoy ~ en recibir más información** I'm interested in receiving some more information; **estamos muy ~s en el proyecto** we have a great interest in the project, we are very interested in the project

2 (= *egoísta*) self-interested, selfish; **lo veo muy ~** he seems really self-interested *o* selfish to me; **su ayuda era muy interesada** she had her own interests at heart in helping us; **actuar de forma interesada** to act selfishly

Ⓑ SM/F 1 (= *persona interesada*) **los ~s pueden escribir una postal con sus datos** anyone interested *o* those interested should send a postcard with their personal details; **hace falta el consentimiento de los ~s** we need the consent of those concerned; **~ en algo**: **una cita indispensable para todos los ~s en el jazz** a must for all those interested in jazz *o* for all jazz fans; **soy el primer ~ en ganar** I have the greatest interest in winning

2 (= *persona egoísta*) **eres un ~** you always act out of self-interest, you're always on the lookout for yourself

interesante ADJ [*persona, película*] interesting; [*precio, sueldo*] attractive; **hacerse el/la ~** to try to attract attention

interesar ▸conjug 1a◂ Ⓐ VI 1 (= *despertar interés*) 1·1 [*tema, propuesta*] to be of interest, interest; **un tema que interesa a los jóvenes** a subject of interest to young people, a subject which interests young people; **esa propuesta no nos interesa** we're not interested in that proposal, that proposal is of no interest to us

1·2 [*actividad, persona*] **no me interesan los toros** I'm not interested in bullfighting; **sólo le interesa el dinero** his only interest is money, all he's interested in is money; **no me interesa en absoluto como persona** I'm not the slightest bit interested in him as a person

2 (= *concernir*) **~ a algn** to concern sb; **el asunto interesa a todos** the matter concerns everybody; **a ti no te interesa lo que yo esté haciendo** what I'm doing is no concern of yours; **a quien pueda ~** (*frm*) to whom it may concern (*frm*)

3 (= *convenir*) **ese tipo de negocios no in-**

➤ LENGUA Y USO: interés 1 35.4 interesante 53.6

teresa that sort of business is not worth our while; **no dice nada porque no le interesa desde el punto de vista judicial** he doesn't say anything because, from a legal point of view, it's not in his interest; **este coche podría ~te** this car could be of interest (to you), this car might interest you; **cuando algo no le interesa, cambia de tema** whenever he feels uncomfortable about something, he changes the subject; **~ía conocer más datos antes de decidirnos** it would be useful to have more details before making a decision; **te podría ~ invertir en bolsa** it could be interesting for you to invest on the stock market; **me interesa más este hotel** this hotel suits me better

Ⓑ VT [1] **~ a algn en algo** to interest sb in sth; **no logré ~lo en mi trabajo** I failed to get him interested in my work

[2] (*Med*) [+ *órgano, nervio*] to affect; **la herida interesa la región lumbar** the injury affects the lumbar region

[3] (*Com*) **el portador interesa cinco euros en …** the bearer has a stake of five euros in …

Ⓒ **interesarse** VPR [1] **~se por algo** to show an interest in sth, take an interest in sth, be interested in sth; **no se interesa por nada** he shows *o* takes no interest in anything, he's not interested in anything; **se interesó por el trabajo de los campesinos** he showed *o* took an interest in the work of the country people

[2] **~se por algn** (= *preocuparse*) to show concern for sb; (= *preguntar*) to inquire about sb, ask after sb; **si tú no haces un esfuerzo nadie se va a ~ por ti** if you don't make an effort no one will show any concern for *o* interest in you; **en la fiesta nadie se interesaba por ella** nobody paid any attention to her at the party; **llamó para ~se por su salud** she called to inquire about *o* ask after his health

[3] (*Com*) **~se en una empresa** to have an interest *o* a stake in a company

interestatal ADJ inter-state

interestelar ADJ interstellar

interétnico ADJ interracial

interface SM *o* SF, **interfaz** SM *o* SF (*Inform*) interface ► **interface de serie** serial interface ► **interface de usuario** user interface ► **interface gráfica** graphical interface

interfase SF (*Inform*) = **interface**

interfecto/a Ⓐ ADJ killed, murdered

Ⓑ SM/F [1] (= *víctima*) murder victim

[2] (*) (= *individuo*) your man/woman*

interferencia SF [1] (*Radio, Telec*) interference; (*deliberada*) jamming; (= *escucha telefónica*) tapping

[2] (*Inform*) glitch

[3] (*Ling*) interference

[4] (= *injerencia*) interference (**en** in); **no ~** non-interference

interferir ▸conjug 3i◂ Ⓐ VT [1] (= *obstaculizar*) to interfere with, get in the way of

[2] (*Radio, Telec*) to interfere with; (*con intención*) to jam; [+ *teléfono*] to tap

[3] (= *injerirse en*) to interfere in, meddle in; **interfieren la vida privada de los ciudadanos** they interfere *o* meddle in people's private lives

Ⓑ VI to interfere (**en** in, with)

Ⓒ **interferirse** VPR to interfere (**en** in, with); **no está en posición de ~se en el conflicto** he is in no position to interfere in the conflict

interferón SM interferon

interfijo SM infix

interfono SM intercom, entryphone

intergeneracional ADJ intergenerational, between generations

intergubernamental ADJ intergovernmental

interín, ínterin Ⓐ SM [1] (= *intervalo*) interim; **en el ~** in the meantime, in the interim (*frm*); **en el ~ se ha producido otro caso similar** in the meantime another similar case has appeared

[2] (= *período vacante*) short period; **el ~ en que el secretario sustituyó a la ministra** the (short) period during which the secretary stood in for the minister; **desempeña las funciones del director durante el ~** he deputizes for his manager in his absence

Ⓑ CONJ while, until

interinamente ADV [1] (= *temporalmente*) temporarily; **el Presidente ha sido sustituido ~ por el ministro del Interior** the President has temporarily been replaced by the Interior Minister

[2] (= *entretanto*) in the interim, meanwhile

interinar ▸conjug 1a◂ VT [+ *puesto*] to occupy temporarily, occupy in an acting capacity

interinato SM [1] (*Cono Sur*) (= *temporalidad*) temporary nature

[2] (*Cono Sur*) (= *período*) period in a temporary post *o* position

[3] (*CAm Med*) residence, internship (*EEUU*)

interinidad SF (= *estado*) temporary nature; (= *estatus*) provisional status; (= *empleo*) temporary work; **situación de ~** temporary state (of affairs); (*en puesto*) temporary status

interino/a Ⓐ ADJ [*empleo, empleado*] temporary; [*alcalde, director*] acting *antes de s*; [*medida*] stopgap, interim; **acuerdo ~** interim accord, interim agreement; **gobierno ~** interim government; **informe ~** interim report, progress report; **profesor(a) ~/a** supply teacher, substitute teacher (*EEUU*)

Ⓑ SM/F temporary holder of a post, acting official; (*Teat*) stand-in; (*Med*) locum, on-call doctor (*EEUU*)

Ⓒ SF (= *asistenta*) non-resident maid

interior Ⓐ ADJ [1] [*espacio*] interior; [*patio*] inner, interior; [*escalera*] internal, interior; [*bolsillo*] inside; [*paz, fuerza*] inner; **la parte ~ de la casa** the inside *o* interior of the house; **en la parte ~** inside, on the inside; **habitación/piso ~** room/flat without a view onto the street; **pista ~** (*Dep*) inside lane; **un joven con mucha vida ~** a reflective young man; *ver tb* **ropa**

[2] (= *nacional*) [*comercio, política, mercado*] domestic

[3] (*Geog*) inland

Ⓑ SM [1] (= *parte interna*) inside, interior; **el ~ quedó destrozado por el fuego** the inside *o* interior was destroyed by the fire; **el ~ de la cueva** the inside *o* interior of the cave; **se dirigieron al ~ del edificio** they went inside the building; **el cuerpo fue hallado en el ~ de un vehículo** the body was found inside a vehicle; **busque su regalo en el ~ del paquete** look for your free gift inside the packet; **plantas de ~** house plants; **diseño de ~es** interior design; **decoración de ~es** interior decoration

[2] (= *alma*) soul; **esto refleja un ~ atormentado** that reflects a soul in torment; **en mi ~ seguía amándola** in my heart I loved her still; **dije para mi ~** I said to myself

[3] (*Geog*) interior; **una tribu del ~ del Brasil** a tribe from the Brazilian interior; **no soy de la costa, soy del ~** I'm not from the coast, I'm from inland; **mañana lloverá en las zonas del ~** tomorrow there will be rain in inland areas

[4] ► **(Ministerio del) Interior** (*Pol*) ≈ Home Office, ≈ Justice Department (*EEUU*)

[5] (*Dep*) inside-forward ► **interior derecho** inside-right ► **interior izquierdo** inside-left

[6] **interiores** (*Cine*) interiors; **el estudio donde ruedan los ~es** the studio where they shoot the interiors

[7] **interiores** (*Col, Ven*) (= *calzoncillos*) (under)pants, shorts (*EEUU*)

interioridad SF [1] [*de persona*] inner being; **en su ~, sabe que …** (*CAm*) in his heart he knows that …, deep down he knows that …

[2] **interioridades** (= *intimidades*) private *o* personal matters; (= *detalles*) ins and outs; **desconocen las ~es del mercado** they don't know all the ins and outs of the market; **vivió de cerca las ~es de la reforma** he was intimately acquainted with the ins and outs of the reform

interiorismo SM interior decoration, interior design

interiorista SMF interior decorator, interior designer

interiorizar ▸conjug 1f◂ Ⓐ VT [1] (*Psic*) to internalize

[2] (*Chile*) to inform (**de, sobre** about)

Ⓑ **interiorizarse** VPR **~se de/sobre algo** to familiarize o.s. with sth

interiormente ADV (= *internamente*) internally; (*de persona*) inwardly; **han remodelado el edificio ~** the building has been redesigned internally; **~ me siento estremecido** inwardly I'm shaking

interjección SF interjection

interlínea SF (*Inform*) line feed

interlineado SM space/writing between the lines

interlineal ADJ interlinear

interlinear ▸conjug 1a◂ VT [1] (*al escribir*) to interline, write between the lines

[2] (*Tip*) to space, lead

interlocutor(a) SM/F (*gen*) speaker, interlocutor (*frm*); (*al teléfono*) person at the other end of the line; **mi ~** the person I was speaking to, the person who spoke to me ► **interlocutor(a) válido/a** (*Pol*) official negotiator, official spokesman ► **interlocutores sociales** social partners

intérlope Ⓐ ADJ (*Méx*) (= *fraudulento*) fraudulent

Ⓑ SM (*Com*) interloper, unauthorized trader

interludio SM interlude, intermission (*EEUU*)

intermediación SF (*gen*) mediation; (*Fin*) brokerage

intermediario/a Ⓐ ADJ intermediary

Ⓑ SM/F [1] (= *mediador*) (*gen*) intermediary, go-between; (*Com*) middle-man

[2] (*en disputa*) mediator

intermedio Ⓐ ADJ [1] [*etapa, grupo, nivel*] intermediate; [*periodo*] intervening; **omitió un**

paso ~ del razonamiento he missed out an intermediate stage in the reasoning; **los estratos sociales ~s** the middle classes; **un punto ~ entre colonialismo e independencia** a halfway house between colonialism and independence; **en un punto ~ entre Córdoba y Montoro** halfway between Córdoba and Montoro; **un tono ~ entre gris y negro** a shade halfway between grey and black
[2] [*tamaño, talla*] medium; **de tamaño ~** medium-sized
Ⓑ SM [1] (*Teat*) interval; (*TV*) break; (*Cine*) intermission
[2] **por ~ de** by means of, through the intermediary of

intermezzo [inter'metso] SM intermezzo

interminable ADJ endless, interminable

interminablemente ADV endlessly, interminably

interministerial ADJ interdepartmental, interministerial; **comité/comisión ~** interdepartmental committee/commission, interministerial committee/commission

intermisión SF intermission, interval

intermitencia SF intermittence

intermitente Ⓐ ADJ (*gen*) intermittent; [*guerra*] sporadic; [*huelga, negociaciones*] on-off; [*luz*] flashing; [*lluvia, nieve*] sporadic, intermittent; **se escuchan disparos de forma ~** shots can be heard now and again *o* intermittently
Ⓑ SM [1] (*Aut*) indicator, turn signal (*EEUU*)
[2] (*Inform*) indicator light

internación SF internment

internacional Ⓐ ADJ international
Ⓑ SMF international; **la Internacional** (= *himno*) the Internationale; **la Internacional Socialista** the Socialist International

internacionalidad SF international nature

internacionalismo SM internationalism

internacionalista Ⓐ ADJ internationalist
Ⓑ SMF [1] (= *partidario*) internationalist
[2] (*Jur*) internationalist

internacionalizar ▸conjug 1f◂ Ⓐ VT to internationalize
Ⓑ **internacionalizarse** VPR to become international

internacionalmente ADV internationally

internada SF (*Dep*) run

internado/a Ⓐ ADJ **estar ~ en** to be (a patient) in
Ⓑ SM/F (*Mil*) internee; (*Escol*) boarder; (*Med*) patient
Ⓒ SM [1] (= *colegio*) boarding school; (= *acto*) boarding
[2] (= *alumnos*) boarders *pl*

internalización SF internalization

internalizar ▸conjug 1f◂ VT to internalize

internamente ADV (*gen*) internally; (*de persona*) inside, deep down; **parece frío, pero ~ es muy emotivo** he seems cold, but inside *o* deep down he's very emotional

internamiento SM (*Pol*) internment; (*Med*) admission (*to hospital*)

internar ▸conjug 1a◂ Ⓐ VT [1] (= *ingresar*) (*Mil*) to intern; (*Med*) to admit (**en** to); **~ a algn en un manicomio** to commit sb to a psychiatric hospital
[2] (= *enviar tierra adentro*) to send inland
Ⓑ **internarse** VPR [1] (= *avanzar*) to advance deep, penetrate; **el jugador se internó por la derecha** the player cut inside from the right; **~se en algo** to go into *o* right inside sth; **se internó en el edificio** he disappeared into the building; **~se en un país** to go into the interior of a country; **se ~on por los pasillos** they went deep into the corridors
[2] **~se en un tema** to study a subject in depth, go deeply into a subject

internauta SMF Net user, Internet user

Internet SM *o* SF, **internet** SM *o* SF Internet

interno/a Ⓐ ADJ internal; **la política interna** internal politics, domestic politics; **por vía interna** (*Med*) internally; **paredes internas** interior walls; **criada interna** live-in servant
Ⓑ SM/F [1] (*Escol*) boarder
[2] (*Med*) houseman, intern (*EEUU*)
[3] (= *preso*) inmate, prisoner
Ⓒ SM (*Cono Sur Telec*) extension, telephone extension

interparlamentario ADJ interparliamentary

interpelación SF (*frm*) appeal, plea

interpelante SMF (*frm*) questioner

interpelar ▸conjug 1a◂ VT (*frm*) [1] (= *dirigirse a*) to address, speak to; (*Pol*) to ask for explanations, question
[2] (†) (= *implorar*) to implore, beseech

interpenetrarse ▸conjug 1a◂ VPR to overlap

interpersonal ADJ interpersonal; **relaciones ~es** interpersonal relationships

interplanetario ADJ interplanetary

Interpol SF ABR (= **International Criminal Police Organisation**) Interpol

interpolación SF interpolation

interpolar ▸conjug 1a◂ VT (= *intercalar*) to interpolate; (= *interrumpir*) to interrupt briefly

interponer ▸conjug 2q◂ Ⓐ VT [1] (= *insertar*) to interpose (*frm*), insert
[2] (*Jur*) [+ *apelación*] to lodge
[3] (*en discurso*) to interpose, interject
Ⓑ **interponerse** VPR [*persona*] to intervene; [*obstáculo*] to stand in the way; **no pensamos ~nos** we do not intend to intervene; **se interpuso en su camino** he blocked his path, he stood in his way; **se interpuso entre los dos para que no riñeran** he came between the two of them to stop them fighting; **grandes obstáculos se interponen en la solución del conflicto** there are great obstacles standing in the way of a solution to the conflict

interposición SF [1] (= *inserción*) insertion
[2] (*Jur*) lodging, formulation
[3] (*en discurso*) interjection

interpretable ADJ interpretable

interpretación SF [1] [*de texto, mensaje*] interpretation; **mala ~** misinterpretation, misunderstanding; **admite diversas interpretaciones** it can be interpreted in several different ways
[2] (= *traducción hablada*) interpreting; **~ simultánea** simultaneous interpreting
[3] (*Mús, Teat*) performance; **~ en directo** live performance

interpretar ▸conjug 1a◂ VT [1] [+ *texto, mensaje*] to interpret; **~ mal** to misinterpret, misunderstand
[2] (*Ling*) to interpret; **~ del chino al ruso** to interpret from Chinese into Russian
[3] (*Mús* [+ *pieza*] to play, perform; [+ *canción*] to sing; (*Teat*) [+ *papel*] to play

interpretativo ADJ interpretative

intérprete Ⓐ SMF [1] (*Ling*) interpreter
► **intérprete de conferencias** conference interpreter ► **intérprete de enlace** liaison interpreter
[2] (*Mús*) (= *músico*) performer; (= *cantante*) singer
Ⓑ SM (*Inform*) interpreter

interprofesional ADJ **acuerdo ~** inter-trade agreement; **salario mínimo ~** minimum wage

interprovincial SM (*Andes*) long-distance bus, coach

interracial ADJ interracial

interregno SM (*Hist, Pol*) interregnum; (*LAm*) interval, intervening period; **en el ~** in the meantime

interrelación SF interrelation

interrelacionado ADJ interrelated

interrelacionar ▸conjug 1a◂ VT to interrelate

interrogación SF [1] (= *interrogatorio*) questioning, interrogation
[2] (= *pregunta*) question; (*Inform*) inquiry
[3] (*Tip*) (= *signo de interrogación*) question mark

interrogador(a) SM/F interrogator, questioner

➤ **interrogante** Ⓐ ADJ questioning
Ⓑ SMF (= *persona*) interrogator, questioner
Ⓒ SM *o* SF (= *signo*) question mark; (= *incógnita*) question mark, query; (= *pregunta*) question, query

interrogar ▸conjug 1h◂ VT to interrogate, question; (*Jur*) [+ *testigo, detenido*] to question, examine

interrogativo Ⓐ ADJ interrogative
Ⓑ SM interrogative

interrogatorio SM [1] (= *preguntas*) interrogation, questioning; (*tras una misión*) debriefing
[2] (*Jur*) questioning, examination
[3] (= *cuestionario*) questionnaire

interrumpir ▸conjug 3a◂ Ⓐ VT [1] (= *cesar*) (*gen*) to interrupt; [+ *vacaciones*] to cut short; [+ *tráfico*] to block, hold up; [+ *embarazo*] to terminate
[2] (*Elec*) [+ *luz*] to switch off; [+ *suministro*] to cut off
[3] (*Inform*) to abort
Ⓑ VI to interrupt

interrupción SF (*gen*) interruption; [*de trabajo*] holdup ► **interrupción de emisión** break in transmission ► **interrupción (voluntaria) del embarazo** termination ► **interrupción del fluido eléctrico** power cut, power failure

interruptor SM (*Elec*) switch ► **interruptor con regulador de intensidad** dimmer switch ► **interruptor de dos direcciones** two-way switch ► **interruptor de seguridad** safety switch

intersecarse ▸conjug 1g◂ VPR to intersect

intersección SF intersection; (*Aut*) junction

intersexual ADJ [*animal, persona*] sexually ambiguous; [*acercamiento, enfrentamiento*] between the sexes

intersexualidad SF sexual ambiguity

intersticio SM (= *espacio*) interstice (*frm*); (= *grieta*) crack; (= *intervalo*) interval, gap

intertanto (*LAm*) Ⓐ ADV meanwhile
Ⓑ CONJ **~ que él llegue** until he comes, while we wait for him to come
Ⓒ SM **en el ~** in the meantime

intertextualidad SF intertextuality

intertítulo SM caption, subtitle

➤ LENGUA Y USO: **interrogante** C 53.6

interurbano Ⓐ ADJ [*autobús, transporte, llamada*] long-distance; [*tren*] inter-city
Ⓑ SM (*CAm*) inter-city taxi

intervalo SM [1] [*de tiempo*] (*tb Mús*) interval; (= *descanso*) break; **a ~s** (*gen*) at intervals; (= *de vez en cuando*) every now and then; **a ~s de dos horas** at two hour intervals
[2] (= *espacio libre*) gap; **situados a ~s de dos metros** placed at two metre intervals; **~s de nubes** cloudy spells *o* intervals; **mantener el ~ de seguridad** (*Aut*) to keep one's distance

intervención SF [1] (= *actuación*) intervention (**en** in); **fue necesaria la ~ de la policía** police intervention was necessary; **su ~ en la discusión** his contribution to the discussion; **política de no ~** policy of non-intervention
[2] (= *discurso*) speech
[3] (*Mús, Teat*) performance
[4] (*Med*) (*tb* **~ quirúrgica**) operation
[5] (= *control*) (*en producción*) supervision, control; (*en empresa*) intervention; (*LAm*) [*de sindicatos*] government takeover
[6] [*de contrabando, droga*] seizure, confiscation
[7] (= *auditoría*) audit, auditing
[8] (*Telec*) tapping

intervencionismo SM interventionism

intervencionista Ⓐ ADJ interventionist; **no ~** (*Com*) non-interventionist, laissez-faire
Ⓑ SMF interventionist

intervenir ▸conjug 3r◂ Ⓐ VI [1] (= *tomar parte*) to take part; **no intervino en el debate** he did not take part in the debate; **la reyerta en la que intervino el acusado** the brawl in which the defendant took part *o* was involved
[2] (= *injerirse*) to intervene; **España rehusó ~ militarmente** Spain refused to intervene militarily; **la policía intervino para separar a las dos pandillas** the police intervened to separate the two gangs
[3] (= *mediar*) **el presidente intervino para que se pudiera llegar a un acuerdo** the president mediated *o* interceded so that an agreement could be reached; **intervino para que los sacaran de la cárcel** he used his influence to get them out of prison; **las circunstancias que intervinieron en mi dimisión** the circumstances that influenced my resignation; **él no intervino en la decisión** he did not have a hand in the decision
Ⓑ VT [1] (= *controlar*) to take over, take control of; **la junta militar intervino todas las cadenas estatales** the junta took over *o* took control of all the state-run channels; **el gobierno intervino a los ferroviarios** the government took over *o* took control of the railworkers' union
[2] (*Com*) [+ *cuenta*] to audit; [+ *banco, empresa*] to take into administration; [+ *cuenta, bienes*] to freeze
[3] (*Med*) to operate on; **lo intervinieron quirúrgicamente** he was operated on
[4] [+ *droga, armas, patrimonio, bienes*] to confiscate, seize
[5] [+ *teléfono*] to tap

interventor(a) SM/F [1] (= *inspector*) inspector, supervisor; (*en elecciones*) scrutineer, canvasser (*EEUU*) ► **interventor(a) de cuentas** auditor [2] ► **interventor(a) judicial** receiver, official receiver; (*LAm*) government-appointed manager

interviniente SMF participant

➤ LENGUA Y USO: **intolerable** 34.3

interviú SF (a veces SM), **interview** SF (a veces SM) interview; **hacer una ~ a algn** to interview sb

interviuvar ▸conjug 1a◂ VT to interview, have an interview with

intestado/a ADJ, SM/F intestate

intestinal ADJ intestinal

intestino Ⓐ ADJ (*frm*) (= *interno*) internal; [*lucha*] internecine
Ⓑ SM intestine, gut; **cáncer de ~** intestinal cancer; **síndrome de ~ irritable** irritable bowel syndrome ► **intestino ciego** caecum ► **intestino delgado** small intestine ► **intestino grueso** large intestine

inti SM (*Perú*) *former Peruvian monetary unit*

Intifada SF, **intifada** SF Intifada

intimación SF announcement, notification

íntimamente ADV intimately; **estar ~ ligado/relacionado a algn/algo** to be closely linked/related to sb/sth

intimar ▸conjug 1a◂ Ⓐ VT [1] (= *notificar*) to announce, notify
[2] (= *mandar*) to order, require
Ⓑ VI **ahora intiman mucho** they're very friendly now; **~ con algn** to be friends with sb
Ⓒ **intimarse** VPR [1] = **B**
[2] (= *hacer amistad*) to become friendly (**con** with)

intimidación SF intimidation; *ver tb* **disparo 1**

intimidad SF [1] (= *amistad*) intimacy, familiarity; **disfrutar de la ~ de algn** to be on close terms with sb; **entrar en ~ con algn** to become friendly with sb
[2] (= *ámbito privado*) privacy; **celebró su cumpleaños en la ~ familiar** he celebrated his birthday in the privacy of his family; **conocido en la ~ como Josemari** known in private life as Josemari; **la ceremonia se celebró en la ~** the wedding was a private affair
[3] **intimidades** (= *cosas personales*) personal matters, private matters; (*euf*) (= *genitales*) private parts (*euf*), privates (*euf hum*)

intimidador ADJ intimidating

intimidar ▸conjug 1a◂ Ⓐ VT to intimidate, scare
Ⓑ **intimidarse** VPR (= *temer*) to be intimidated; (= *asustarse*) to get scared

intimidatorio ADJ intimidating

intimista ADJ intimate, private

íntimo/a Ⓐ ADJ [*secreto, confesión*] intimate; [*amigo, relación*] close, intimate; [*pensamientos, sentimientos*] innermost; [*vida*] personal, private; **una boda íntima** a quiet wedding, a private wedding; **una cena íntima** a romantic meal; **una fiesta íntima** a private party; **es ~ amigo mío** he is a very close friend of mine; **en lo más ~ de mi corazón** in my heart of hearts
Ⓑ SM/F close friend; **sólo lo saben sus ~s** only her close friends know

intitular ▸conjug 1a◂ VT to entitle

intocable Ⓐ ADJ [1] (= *sagrado*) sacred, sacrosanct; **la Constitución es ~** the Constitution is sacred *o* sacrosanct; **sigue líder ~ en los Campeonatos del Mundo** he is still the runaway leader in the World Championships
[2] [*tema*] taboo
Ⓑ SMF (*en la India*) untouchable

▼ **intolerable** ADJ intolerable, unbearable

intolerancia SF [1] (*cualidad*) intolerance
[2] (*Med*) intolerance; **~ a la lactosa** intolerance to lactose; **tiene ~ al sol** he's allergic to direct sunlight

intolerante Ⓐ ADJ intolerant (**con** of)
Ⓑ SMF intolerant person

intonso ADJ [1] (= *con pelo largo*) [*persona*] with long hair; [*barba*] unshorn, shaggy
[2] [*libro*] untrimmed, with edges untrimmed
[3] (= *grosero*) boorish

intoxicación SF [1] (*Med*) poisoning ► **intoxicación alimenticia** food poisoning ► **intoxicación etílica** alcohol poisoning; (*euf*) drunkenness
[2] (*Pol*) indoctrination; **campaña de ~ informativa** campaign of media indoctrination

intoxicador(a) Ⓐ ADJ [1] intoxicating
[2] (*Pol*) misleading, deceptive
Ⓑ SM/F indoctrinator

intoxicar ▸conjug 1g◂ Ⓐ VT [1] (*Med*) to poison
[2] (*Pol*) to indoctrinate
Ⓑ **intoxicarse** VPR [1] (*Med*) (*con sustancia tóxica*) to be poisoned; (*con alimentos*) to get food poisoning
[2] (*con drogas*) to drug o.s.; (*con alcohol*) to get intoxicated

intra... PREF intra...

intracomunitario ADJ within the EC

intraducible ADJ untranslatable

intragable ADJ (= *desagradable*) unpalatable; (= *insoportable*) intolerable; (= *no aceptable*) unacceptable

intramatrimonial ADJ **agresión ~** violence within a marriage, violence between husband and wife

intramuros ADV within the city, within the walls

intranet [intra'net] SF intranet

intranquilidad SF (= *preocupación*) worry, anxiety; (= *desasosiego*) restlessness

intranquilizar ▸conjug 1f◂ Ⓐ VT to worry, make uneasy
Ⓑ **intranquilizarse** VPR to get worried, feel uneasy

intranquilo ADJ (= *preocupado*) worried, anxious; (= *desasosegado*) restless; **estaban ~s por nuestra tardanza** they were worried *o* anxious because we were late

intranscendencia SF = **intrascendencia**

intranscendente ADJ = **intrascendente**

intranscribible ADJ unprintable

intransferible ADJ not transferable

intransigencia SF intransigence

intransigente Ⓐ ADJ (*gen*) intransigent; (= *que no cede*) unyielding; (= *fanático*) diehard
Ⓑ SMF diehard

intransitable ADJ impassable

intransitivo ADJ, SM intransitive

intrascendencia SF unimportance, insignificance

intrascendente ADJ unimportant, insignificant

intratable ADJ [1] [*persona*] difficult; **¡son ~s!** they're impossible!
[2] (*Med*) untreatable

intrauterino ADJ intrauterine

intravenoso ADJ intravenous

intrépidamente ADV intrepidly

intrepidez SF intrepidness, intrepidity

intrépido ADJ intrepid

intricado ADJ = **intrincado**

intriga SF (= *maquinación*) intrigue; (= *ardid*) plot, scheme; (*Teat*) plot; **novela de ~** thriller; **película de ~** thriller ► **intriga secundaria** subplot

intrigante Ⓐ ADJ [1] (= *enredador*) scheming [2] (= *interesante*) intriguing Ⓑ SMF schemer

intrigar ▸conjug 1h◂ Ⓐ VT [1] (= *interesar*) to intrigue; **lo que más me intriga del caso es ...** the most intriguing aspect of the case is ...; **me tienes intrigada** you've got me intrigued [2] (*LAm*) [+ *asunto*] to conduct in a surprising way Ⓑ VI to scheme, plot Ⓒ **intrigarse** VPR (*LAm*) to be intrigued

intrincadamente ADV [1] (= *complejamente*) intricately; **los dos asuntos están ~ vinculados** the two matters are intricately linked [2] (= *formando una trama*) densely, impenetrably

intrincado ADJ [1] (= *complejo*) complicated; (= *enmarañado*) intricate; **un laberinto ~** an intricate maze; **explorábamos los ~s recovecos** we explored the hidden corners; **un hombre de carácter ~** a man with a complex character [2] [*bosque*] dense

intrincar ▸conjug 1g◂ VT (= *complicar*) to confuse, complicate; (= *enredar*) to entangle

intríngulis* SM INV (= *pega*) hidden snag, catch*; (= *misterio*) puzzle, mystery; (= *secreto*) (hidden) secret; (= *motivo*) ulterior motive; **ahí está el ~** that's the secret; **tiene su ~** it's quite tricky*, it's not as easy as it looks

intrínsecamente ADV intrinsically, inherently

intrínseco ADJ intrinsic, inherent

intro... PREF intro...

▼**introducción** SF [1] [*de texto*] introduction; **"Introducción a la gramática española"** "Introduction to Spanish Grammar"; **un curso de ~ al psicoanálisis** an introductory course in psychoanalysis [2] (= *inserción*) insertion; **la ~ del tubo puede causar heridas** inserting the tube *o* the insertion of the tube can cause injury, the tube's insertion could cause injury [3] (= *llegada*) [*de mercancías, cambios*] introduction; **la ~ de la moneda única** the introduction of a single currency; **la revolución que supuso la ~ del vídeo en los hogares** the revolution caused by the arrival of the video in the home; **se dedicaba a la ~ de heroína en España** he was involved in smuggling heroin into Spain; **~ de contrabando** smuggling [4] (*Inform*) [*de datos*] input

introducir ▸conjug 3n◂ Ⓐ VT [1] (= *meter*) [1·1] [+ *mano, pie*] to put, place (**en** in(to)); [+ *moneda, llave*] to put, insert (**en** in(to)); **introdujo los pies en el agua** he put *o* placed his feet in(to) the water; **no podía ~ la llave en la cerradura** he couldn't get the key in(to) the lock; **introduzca la moneda/el disquete en la ranura** insert the coin/the diskette in(to) the slot; **introdujo la carta por debajo de la puerta** he slipped the letter under the door [1·2] [+ *enfermedad, mercancías*] to bring (**en** into), introduce (**en** into); [+ *contrabando, droga*] to bring (**en** in(to)); **cualquier animal puede ~ la rabia en el país** any animal could bring *o* introduce rabies into the country; **el tabaco introducido ilegalmente en Europa** the tobacco brought into Europe illegally; **esa bebida hace ya años que se introdujo en España** that drink was introduced in Spain *o* was brought onto the Spanish market years ago; **~ algo de contrabando** to smuggle sth (**en** into); **~ algo en el mercado** to bring sth onto the market, introduce sth into the market [1·3] **~ a algn en** [+ *habitación*] to show sb into; [+ *situación real*] to introduce sb to; [+ *situación irreal*] to transport sb to; **el mayordomo nos introdujo hasta el salón** the butler showed us into the drawing room; **quería ~la en la alta sociedad** he wanted to introduce her to high society; **su poesía nos introduce en un mundo de felicidad** his poetry transports us to a world of happiness; **la novela nos introduce en el Egipto de Cleopatra** the novel takes us back to the Egypt of Cleopatra [2] (= *empezar*) [+ *cultivo, ley, método*] to introduce; **poco a poco se fueron introduciendo las tradiciones árabes** Arab traditions were gradually introduced; **para ~ el tema, empezaré hablando de política exterior** to introduce the subject, I'll begin by discussing foreign policy; **~ la ley del divorcio causó muchos problemas** the introduction of the divorce law caused many problems, introducing the divorce law was very problematic [3] (= *realizar*) [+ *medidas, reformas*] to bring in, introduce; **quieren ~ cambios en la legislación** they want to make changes to the current legislation, they want to introduce changes into the current legislation; **las reformas se ~án gradualmente a lo largo de los próximos tres años** the reforms will be phased in over the next three years, the reforms will be brought in *o* introduced gradually over the next three years; **se deben ~ mejoras en el diseño del folleto** improvements need to be made to the pamphlet design [4] (*Inform*) [+ *datos*] to input, enter Ⓑ **introducirse** VPR [1] (= *meterse*) [*astilla, cristal*] to lodge; **la espina se me introdujo por debajo de la uña** the thorn lodged under my nail; **el balón se introdujo a través de los palos** the ball went in through the goalposts; **~se en algo** to get into sth, enter sth; **cuando el virus se introduce en el organismo** when the virus gets into *o* enters the organism; **se introdujo en el sótano a través de un agujero** he got into the basement through a hole; **el coche se introdujo despacio en el garaje** the car entered the garage slowly; **hemos logrado ~nos en el mercado europeo** we've managed to break *o* get into the European market; **muchas palabras se introducen en nuestro idioma procedentes del inglés** many words pass into our language from English [2] (= *entrometerse*) to interfere, meddle

introductor(a) Ⓐ ADJ introductory Ⓑ SM/F **el ~ de la música atonal en España** the man who introduced atonal music in Spain; **fue la ~a de esa técnica en Latinoamérica** she was the one who introduced that technique in Latin America ► **introductor(a) de datos** data inputter ► **introductor(a) de embajadores** *head of Protocol in the Foreign Affairs Department*

introductorio ADJ [1] (*Literat*) [*curso, discurso*] introductory; [*poema, relato*] opening [2] (*Mús*) [*movimiento*] opening

introito SM [1] (*Teat*) prologue, prolog (EEUU) [2] (*Rel*) introit

intromisión SF [1] (= *injerencia*) interference [2] (= *inserción*) introduction, insertion

introspección SF introspection

introspectivo ADJ introspective

introversión SF introversion

introvertido/a Ⓐ ADJ introverted Ⓑ SM/F introvert

intrusión SF (= *intromisión*) intrusion; (*Jur*) trespass ► **intrusión informática** hacking

intrusismo SM infiltration

intruso/a Ⓐ ADJ intrusive Ⓑ SM/F (*gen*) intruder; (= *extraño*) outsider; (*en fiesta*) gatecrasher; (*Jur*) trespasser; (*Mil, Pol*) infiltrator ► **intruso/a informático/a** hacker

intuible ADJ that can be intuited

intuición SF intuition; **por ~** intuitively

intuir ▸conjug 3g◂ Ⓐ VT (= *saber*) to know intuitively; (= *sentir*) to sense, feel; **intuyo que alguien me sigue** I have a feeling I'm being followed Ⓑ **intuirse** VPR **eso se intuye** that can be guessed; **se intuye que ...** one can tell intuitively that ..., one can guess that ...; **el hombre se intuye observado** the man has a feeling he is under observation

intuitivamente ADV intuitively

intuitivo ADJ intuitive

intumescencia SF intumescence (*frm*), swelling

intumescente ADJ intumescent (*frm*), swollen

inuit ADJ, SMF Inuit

inundación SF (*acción*) flooding; (*efecto*) flood

inundadizo ADJ (*LAm*) liable to flooding

inundar ▸conjug 1a◂ VT [1] (*con agua*) to flood; **la lluvia inundó la campiña** the rain flooded the countryside, the rain left the countryside under water [2] (*con productos*) to flood (**de, en** with), swamp (**de, en** with); **~ el mercado de un producto** to flood the market with a product; **quedamos inundados de ofertas** offers rained in on us, we were flooded *o* swamped with offers [3] [*gente*] to flood, swamp [4] [*pena, sensación*] to overwhelm, sweep over

inusitado ADJ unusual, rare

inusual ADJ unusual

inusualmente ADV unusually

inútil Ⓐ ADJ [1] (= *vano*) [*intento, esfuerzo*] unsuccessful, fruitless; **lo intenté todo, pero fue ~** I tried everything, but it was no use *o* useless; **es ~ que usted proteste** it's no good *o* use you protesting, there's no point in protesting; **es ~ seguir intentándolo** there's no point in keeping on trying [2] (= *inepto*) useless*, hopeless* [3] (= *inválido*) disabled; **ha quedado ~ a causa de la artritis** she is completely disabled by arthritis [4] (= *inservible*) useless; **tira todos los trastos ~es** throw away all that useless junk [5] (*Mil*) unfit; **lo han declarado ~ para el**

➤ LENGUA Y USO: **introducción 1** 53.1

servicio militar he has been declared unfit for military service

Ⓑ SMF **¡tu hermana es una ~!** your sister is useless *o* hopeless!*

inutilidad SF uselessness; **constituir ~** to render inelegible, bar

inutilizable ADJ unusable, unfit for use

inutilización SF [*de mecanismo*] disablement; [*de sello*] cancellation

inutilizar ▸conjug 1f◂ Ⓐ VT (= *hacer inútil*) (*gen*) to make useless, render useless; [+ *mecanismo*] to disable, put out of action; [+ *sello*] to cancel; **el cañón quedó inutilizado** the cannon was put out of action; **las carreteras han quedado inutilizadas** the roads have become unuseable; **la mano derecha le quedó inutilizada** he lost the use of his right hand

Ⓑ **inutilizarse** VPR to become useless; [*mecanismo*] to be disabled

inútilmente ADV (= *sin utilidad*) uselessly; (= *en vano*) vainly, fruitlessly

INV SM ABR (*Esp*) = **Instituto Nacional de la Vivienda**

invadeable ADJ [*carretera, puente*] impassable; [*situación, problema*] unsurmountable

invadir ▸conjug 3a◂ VT [1] (= *atacar*) [+ *célula, país*] to invade; [+ *espacio aéreo, aguas jurisdiccionales*] to violate, enter; **los turistas invaden nuestras costas** tourists descend upon *o* invade our coasts; **las malas hierbas/los insectos invadieron el trigal** the wheatfield was overrun with weeds/insects; **los pájaros invadieron la plantación** birds swooped down onto the field; **~ la intimidad de algn** to invade sb's privacy

[2] (= *ocupar*) [2·1] [*multitud*] (*gen*) to pour into/onto; (*protestando*) to storm into/onto; **los fans invadieron el estadio/el escenario** the fans poured into the stadium/onto the stage; **los manifestantes invadieron la ciudad/las calles** the protesters stormed into the city/onto the streets

[2·2] [*vehículo*] to go into/onto; **el camión invadió el carril contrario/la pista de despegue** the lorry went into the wrong lane/onto the runway

[3] **~ a algn** [*sentimiento*] to overcome sb; **la invadió una gran tristeza** she was filled with great sadness, a great sadness overcame her; **el miedo había invadido su cuerpo** she was overcome by fear, she was filled with fear, fear overcame her

[4] (*Com*) [*producto*] to encroach on; **los vinos franceses invaden los mercados europeos** French wines are encroaching on European markets; **la televisión invadió nuestros hogares** television invaded our homes

[5] (*Jur*) to encroach upon; **el abogado intentó ~ las funciones del juez** the solicitor attempted to encroach upon the judge's prerogatives; **el delegado invadió atribuciones que no le correspondían** the delegate went beyond the powers vested in him

invalidación SF [*de certificado, resultado*] invalidation, nullification; [*de una decisión*] reversal

invalidante ADJ disabling, incapacitating

invalidar ▸conjug 1a◂ VT [+ *certificado, resultado*] to invalidate, nullify; [+ *decisión*] to reverse; [+ *leyes*] to repeal

invalidez SF [1] (*Med*) disability, disablement; **solicitar la ~ (laboral)** to apply for disability benefit ► **invalidez permanente** permanent disability

[2] (*Jur*) invalidity

inválido/a Ⓐ ADJ [1] (*Med*) disabled

[2] (*Jur*) invalid, null and void; **declarar inválida una elección** to declare an election void

Ⓑ SM/F (*Med*) disabled person; **~ de guerra** disabled ex-serviceman

invaluable ADJ (*LAm*) invaluable

invariable ADJ invariable

invariablemente ADV invariably

invariancia SF invariability, lack of variation

invasión SF [1] [*de país, cultivos*] invasion; **la ~ aliada de Italia** the allied invasion of Italy; **una ~ de películas norteamericanas** an invasion of American films

[2] [*de pista, calzada*] presence; **la ~ de la pista por un avión de carga causó el accidente** the accident was caused by the presence of a cargo plane on the runway

[3] (*Jur*) [*de derechos*] encroachment; [*de funciones, poderes*] usurpation

[4] (*Col*) (= *chabolas*) shantytown

invasor(a) Ⓐ ADJ [*ejército, pueblo*] invading; [*tumor*] invasive

Ⓑ SM/F invader; **la resistencia contra el ~ extranjero** resistance against the foreign invader

invectiva SF (*frm*) invective; **una ~** a tirade

invectivar ▸conjug 1a◂ VT (*frm*) (= *arremeter*) to inveigh against (*frm*); (= *insultar*) to heap abuse upon

invencibilidad SF invincibility

invencible ADJ [*enemigo, rival*] invincible, unbeatable; [*obstáculo*] insurmountable, insuperable; **La (Armada) Invencible** the (Spanish Armada) (*1588*)

invenciblemente ADV invincibly, unbeatably

invención SF [1] (= *invento*) invention; **la ~ de la imprenta** the invention of printing

[2] (= *mentira*) invention, fabrication; (*Literat*) invention, fiction

invendible ADJ unsaleable, unsellable

invendido Ⓐ ADJ unsold

Ⓑ SM unsold item

inventar ▸conjug 1a◂ Ⓐ VT (*gen*) to invent; [+ *plan*] to devise; [+ *historia, excusa*] to invent, concoct

Ⓑ **inventarse** VPR [+ *historia, excusa*] to invent, concoct

inventariado SM detailed account

inventariar ▸conjug 1b◂ VT to inventory, make an inventory of

inventario SM inventory; **~ continuo** continuous inventory; **hacer el ~** (*Com*) to do the stocktaking, take inventory (*EEUU*); **"cerrado por ~"** "closed for stocktaking", "closed for inventory" (*EEUU*)

inventiva SF (= *imaginación*) inventiveness; (= *ingenio*) ingenuity, resourcefulness

inventivo ADJ (= *imaginativo*) inventive; (= *ingenioso*) ingenious, resourceful

invento SM invention; ✦**MODISMO** **~ del tebeo*** silly idea

inventor(a) SM/F inventor

inverificable ADJ unverifiable

invernáculo SM greenhouse

invernada SF [1] (= *estación*) winter season

[2] (= *hibernación*) hibernation

[3] (*Andes, Cono Sur*) (= *pasto*) winter pasture

[4] (*Caribe*) (= *tempestad*) heavy rainstorm

invernadero Ⓐ SM [1] (*para plantas*) greenhouse; (*con temperatura elevada*) hothouse

[2] (*LAm*) (= *pasto*) winter pasture

[3] (= *lugar de recreo*) winter resort

Ⓑ ADJ INV **efecto ~** greenhouse effect; **gases ~** greenhouse gases

invernal ADJ winter *antes de s*; [*clima, frío*] wintry

invernante Ⓐ ADJ over-wintering

Ⓑ SM (*Orn*) over-wintering species, winter visitor

invernar ▸conjug 1j◂ Ⓐ VI [1] (= *pasar el invierno*) to winter, spend the winter; (*Zool*) to hibernate

[2] (*Cono Sur*) [*ganado*] to pasture (and fatten) in winter

Ⓑ VT (*Cono Sur*) [+ *ganado*] to pasture (and fatten) in winter

invernazo* SM (*Caribe*) rainy season (*July to September*)

inverne SM (*LAm*) (= *pasto*) winter pasturing; (= *engorde*) winter fattening

invernizo ADJ wintry

inverosímil ADJ (= *improbable*) unlikely, improbable; (= *increíble*) implausible

inverosimilitud SF (= *improbabilidad*) unlikeliness, improbability; (= *incredibilidad*) implausibility

inversamente ADV inversely; **e ~** and vice versa

inversión SF [1] (*Com, Fin*) investment (**en** in) ► **inversión de capital(es)** capital investment ► **inversiones extranjeras** foreign investment *sing*

[2] [*de esfuerzo, tiempo*] investment

[3] [*de orden, dirección*] inversion; (*Elec*) reversal; (*Aut, Mec*) reversing ► **inversión de marcha** reversing, backing ► **inversión sexual** homosexuality ► **inversión térmica** temperature inversion

inversionista SMF (*Com, Fin*) investor

inverso ADJ [1] (= *contrario*) opposite; **en sentido ~** in the opposite direction; **en orden ~** in reverse order; **por orden ~ de antigüedad** in reverse order of seniority; **a la inversa** the other way round; (*al contrario*) on the contrary

[2] [*cara*] reverse

[3] (*Mat*) inverse

inversor(a) Ⓐ ADJ investment *antes de s*

Ⓑ SM/F (*Com, Fin*) investor ► **inversor(a) financiero/a** investments manager ► **inversor(a) inmobiliario/a** property investor ► **inversor(a) institucional** institutional investor

invertebrado ADJ, SM invertebrate

invertido/a Ⓐ ADJ [1] (= *al revés*) [*imagen, objeto*] inverted, upside-down; [*orden*] reversed; **escritura invertida** mirror writing; **la pirámide invertida** the inverted pyramid

[2] (†) (= *homosexual*) homosexual

Ⓑ SM/F (†) invert†, homosexual

invertir ▸conjug 3i◂ Ⓐ VT [1] (*Com, Fin*) to invest (**en** in)

[2] [+ *esfuerzo, tiempo*] to invest (**en** on), put in (**en** on); **invirtieron una hora en recorrer diez kilómetros** they spent an hour covering ten kilometres

[3] [+ *figura, objeto*] (= *volcar*) to invert, turn upside down; (= *poner al revés*) to put the oth-

er way round, reverse
[4] (= *cambiar*) [+ *orden*] to change, invert; [+ *dirección*] to reverse
[5] (*Mat*) to invert
Ⓑ VI ~ **en algo** to invest in sth
Ⓒ VPR [*papeles, relación de fuerzas, tendencia*] to be reversed

investidura SF investiture; **discurso de ~** investiture speech; **votación de ~** (*Pol*) vote of confidence (*in the new prime minister*)

investigación SF [1] [*de accidente, delito*] (*por la policía*) investigation; (*por un comité*) inquiry; **la ~ policial del robo** the police investigation of the robbery; **la ~ de los dos casos de corrupción** the inquiry into the two cases of corruption; **ha ordenado la ~ de las cuentas bancarias** he has ordered their bank accounts to be investigated; **una comisión de ~** a committee of inquiry
[2] (*científica, académica*) research; **están realizando una ~ sobre el ADN** they're doing research into *o* on DNA; **hace trabajo de ~** he's doing research work; **un trabajo de ~ sobre el barroco** a research project on the baroque, a piece of research on the baroque ► **investigación de mercado** market research ► **investigación operativa** operational research, operations research ► **investigación y desarrollo** research and development

investigador(a) Ⓐ ADJ (*gen*) investigative; (*en ciencia*) research *antes de s*; **equipo ~** (*en periodismo, policía*) team of investigators; (*en ciencia*) research team; **labor ~a** (*de periodista, policía*) investigative work; (*en ciencia*) research; **capacidad ~a** research ability; **han nombrado una comisión ~a sobre el caso** a commission of enquiry has been appointed to the case
Ⓑ SM/F [1] (= *periodista, policía*) investigator ► **investigador(a) privado/a** private investigator *o* detective
[2] (= *científico*) research worker, researcher; [*de doctorado*] research student

investigar ▸conjug 1h◂ Ⓐ VT [1] [+ *accidente, crimen, queja, hechos*] to investigate; [+ *cuentas, patrimonio*] to audit; **el juez ordenó ~ sus actividades financieras** the judge ordered an investigation of their financial activities
[2] (*Univ*) to research, do research into
[3] (= *tantear*) to check out; **quédate aquí y yo ~é el terreno** stay here and I'll check out the lie of the land*
Ⓑ VI [1] [*policía, comité*] to investigate
[2] (*Univ*) to do research; **una beca para ~ sobre el SIDA** a grant to do research into AIDS

investigativo ADJ investigative

investir ▸conjug 3k◂ VT **fue investido doctor honoris causa** he was granted an honorary doctorate; **será investido presidente** he will be sworn in as president; **fue investido como Príncipe de Gales** the title of Prince of Wales was conferred on him; ~ **a algn con o de algo** to confer sth on sb

inveterado ADJ [*fumador, pecador*] inveterate; [*criminal*] hardened; [*hábito*] deep-seated, well-established

inviabilidad SF (= *imposibilidad*) unfeasibility, unviability; [*de reclamación*] invalidity

inviable ADJ (= *imposible*) unfeasible, unviable, non-viable; [*reclamación*] invalid

invicto ADJ [*pueblo*] unconquered; [*equipo*] unbeaten

invidencia SF blindness

invidente Ⓐ ADJ blind
Ⓑ SMF blind person

invierno SM [1] (= *estación*) winter; **deportes de ~** winter sports ► **invierno nuclear** nuclear winter
[2] (*Andes, CAm, Caribe*) (= *meses de lluvia*) rainy season
[3] (*Caribe*) (= *aguacero*) heavy shower

inviolabilidad SF inviolability ► **inviolabilidad parlamentaria** parliamentary immunity

inviolable ADJ inviolable

inviolado ADJ inviolate

invisibilidad SF invisibility

invisible Ⓐ ADJ invisible; **importaciones ~s** invisible imports; **exportaciones ~s** invisible exports
Ⓑ SM (*Arg*) hairpin

▼**invitación** SF invitation (**a** to); **a ~ de algn** at sb's invitation

invitado/a Ⓐ ADJ invited; **estrella invitada** guest star
Ⓑ SM/F guest ► **invitado/a de honor** guest of honour ► **invitado/a de piedra** unwanted guest ► **invitado/a estelar** star guest

▼**invitar** ▸conjug 1a◂ VT [1] (*gen*) to invite; **me invitó al cine** she invited me to the cinema; **me invitó a Marbella** she invited me to go to Marbella; **invito yo** it's on me; **os invito a una cerveza** I'll buy *o* stand you all a beer; **nos invitó a cenar (fuera)** she took us out for a meal; **dio las gracias a los que lo habían invitado** he thanked his hosts
[2] (= *incitar*) to invite; ~ **a algn a hacer algo** to invite sb to do sth; (*exhortando*) to call on sb to do sth; ~ **a algn a la violencia** to incite sb to violence
[3] (= *atraer*) to entice; **una frase que invita a comprar** a slogan which entices you to buy

in vitro ADJ, ADV in vitro; **fecundación** *o* **fertilización ~** in vitro fertilization

invocación SF invocation; **una ~ a la Virgen** an invocation of *o* to the Virgin; **una ~ de auxilio** a plea for help

invocar ▸conjug 1g◂ VT [1] (= *citar*) to cite, invoke
[2] [+ *derecho, principio*] to cite, invoke; ~ **la ley** to invoke the law
[3] (= *rogar*) (*gen*) to invoke, appeal for; [+ *divinidad, santo*] to invoke, call on; ~ **la ayuda de algn** to appeal for *o* invoke sb's help
[4] (*Inform*) to call

involución SF (*Pol*) regression ► **involución demográfica** demographic regression

involucionismo SM (*Pol*) reaction; (*en sentido amplio*) reactionary forces *pl*

involucionista (*Pol*) Ⓐ ADJ regressive, reactionary
Ⓑ SMF reactionary

involucración SF, **involucramiento** SM involvement

involucrar ▸conjug 1a◂ Ⓐ VT [1] (= *implicar*) to involve; ~ **a algn en algo** to involve sb in sth, mix sb up in sth; **andar involucrado en** to be mixed up in; **las personas involucradas en el caso** the people involved in the affair
[2] (= *mezclar*) to jumble up, mix up; **lo tiene todo involucrado** he's got it all mixed up; ~ **algo en un discurso** to bring sth irrelevant into a speech
Ⓑ **involucrarse** VPR [1] (= *participar*) to get involved (**en** in)
[2] (= *entrometerse*) to meddle, interfere (**en** in)

involuntariamente ADV (= *sin voluntad*) involuntarily; (= *sin intención*) unintentionally

involuntario ADJ [*gesto, movimiento*] involuntary; [*ofensa*] unintentional; [*agente, causante*] unwitting; **homicidio ~** involuntary manslaughter

involutivo ADJ (*Pol*) reactionary

invulnerabilidad SF invulnerability

invulnerable ADJ invulnerable

inyección SF [1] (*Med*) (= *acción, sustancia*) injection; **una ~ de morfina** an injection of morphine, a morphine injection; **ha venido a ponerme una ~** he's come to give me an injection; **se pone una ~ diaria** she gives herself an injection every day ► **inyección intramuscular** intramuscular injection ► **inyección intravenosa** intravenous injection ► **inyección letal** lethal injection ► **inyección subcutánea** subcutaneous injection
[2] [*de dinero, fondos*] injection; **una ~ financiera de 300 millones de euros** a cash injection of 300 million euros
[3] [*de optimismo, energía*] injection; **una ~ de moral para el equipo** a shot in the arm for the team
[4] (*Mec*) injection; **motor de ~** fuel injection engine; **impresión por ~ de burbujas** bubble-jet printing ► **inyección electrónica** electronic fuel injection

inyectable Ⓐ ADJ injectable; **"administración por vía oral o ~"** "to be taken orally or by injection"
Ⓑ SM (= *inyección*) injection; (= *vacuna*) vaccine

inyectado ADJ **ojos ~s en sangre** bloodshot eyes

inyectar ▸conjug 1a◂ Ⓐ VT [1] (*Med*) to inject (**en** into); ~ **algo en algn** to inject sb with sth; **le ~on un antibiótico** he had an antibiotic injection
[2] [+ *optimismo, dinero*] to inject; **~on optimismo al mercado** they injected optimism into the market
[3] (*Mec*) to inject
Ⓑ **inyectarse** VPR to give o.s. an injection, inject o.s.

inyector SM (*en motor*) injector; (*en horno, fragua*) nozzle

ion SM ion

iónico ADJ ionic

ionizador SM ionizer, negative ionizer

ionizar ▸conjug 1f◂ VT to ionize

ionosfera SF ionosphere

IORTV ABR = **Instituto Oficial de Radiodifusión y Televisión**

iota SF iota

IPC SM ABR (= **índice de precios al consumo**) RPI, CPI (*esp EEUU*)

ipecacuana SF ipecacuanha, ipecac (*EEUU*)

➤ LENGUA Y USO: **invitación** 52.1, 52.4 **invitar** 52.1, 52.4

IPM SM ABR (= **índice de precios al por menor**) RPI

iPod® SM iPod®

ipomea SF (*Bot*) morning glory

IPPV SM ABR = **Instituto para la Promoción Pública de la Vivienda**

ir

▸conjug 3s◂
A VERBO INTRANSITIVO
B VERBO AUXILIAR
C VERBO PRONOMINAL

Para las expresiones ***ir de vacaciones, ir de veras, ir dado, irse de la lengua****, ver la otra entrada.*

Ⓐ VERBO INTRANSITIVO

1 *= marchar* 1·1 (*indicando movimiento, acción*) to go; **anoche fuimos al cine** we went to the cinema last night; **¿has ido alguna vez a Quito?** have you ever been to Quito?; **¿a qué colegio vas?** what school do you go to?; **esta carretera va a Huesca** this road goes to Huesca, this is the road to Huesca; **íbamos hacia Sevilla** we were going towards Seville; **ir hasta León** to go as far as León; **ir despacio** to go slow(ly); **ir con tiento** to go carefully *o* cautiously; **¡ya voy!** ◊ **¡ahora voy!** coming!, I'll be right there!; **vamos a casa** let's go home; **¿quién va?** (*Mil*) who goes there?

1·2 (*indicando la forma de transporte*) **ir andando** to walk, go on foot; **tuvimos que ir andando** we had to walk *o* go on foot; **¿vas a ir andando o en autobús?** are you walking or going by bus?; **ir en avión** to fly; **ir en bicicleta** to ride; **ir a caballo** to ride; **fui en coche** I went by car, I drove; **ir a pie** = **ir andando**; **fui en tren** I went by train *o* rail

1·3 (*con complemento*) **iba muy bien vestido** he was very well dressed; **este reloj va atrasado** this clock is slow; **iban muertos de risa por la calle** they were killing themselves laughing as they went down the street

1·4 **ir (a) por** to go and get; **voy (a) por el paraguas** I'll go and get the umbrella; **voy por el médico** I'll go and fetch *o* get the doctor; **voy a por él** (*a buscarle*) I'll go and get him; (*a atacarle*) I'm going to get him; **sólo van a por las pelas*** they're only in it for the money

2 *indicando proceso* 2·1 [*persona*] **¿cómo va el paciente?** how's the patient doing?; **el enfermo va mejor** the patient is improving *o* doing better; **el enfermo va peor** the patient has got worse

2·2 [*acción, obra*] to go; **¿cómo va el ensayo?** how's the essay going?, how are you getting on with the essay?; **¿cómo va el partido?** what's the score?; **¿cómo va eso?** how are things (going)?; **todo va bien** everything's fine, everything's going well; **los resultados van a mejor** the results are improving *o* getting better

2·3 **ir por**: **¿te has leído ya el libro? ¿por dónde vas?** have you read the book yet? whereabouts are you? *o* how far have you got?; **ir por la mitad de algo** to be halfway through sth; **la película ya va por la mitad** it's already half way through the film; **íbamos por la mitad de nuestro viaje** we were half way there

3 *indicando manera, posición* **ese cuadro debería ir encima del sofá** that picture should go over the sofa; **lo que te dijo iba en serio** he meant what he said (to you)

4 *= extenderse* to go, stretch; **la pradera va desde la montaña hasta el mar** the grasslands go *o* stretch from the mountains to the sea; **en lo que va de año** so far this year; **en lo que va de semana hemos recibido cientos de llamadas** we've had hundreds of calls so far this week; **en lo que va desde 1950 hasta nuestros días** from 1950 up until now

5 *indicando distancia, diferencia* **va mucho de uno a otro** there's a lot of difference between them; **¡lo que va del padre al hijo!** what a difference there is between father and son!, father and son are nothing like each other!; **de 7 a 9 van 2** the difference between 7 and 9 is 2; (*en resta*) 7 from 9 leaves 2

6 *indicando acumulación* **con éste van 30** that makes 30 (with this one); **van ya tres llamadas y no contesta** we've called him three times and he doesn't answer

7 *en apuestas* **van cinco pesos a que no lo haces** I bet you five pesos you won't do it; **¿cuánto va?** how much do you bet?

8 *= vestir* **ir con pantalones** to be wearing trousers; **¿con qué ropa** *o* **cómo fuiste a la boda?** what did you wear to the wedding?; **iba de rojo** she was dressed in red, she was wearing red; **la que va de negro** the girl in black; *ver tb* **etiqueta 2**

9 **irle a algn** 9·1 (*indicando importancia*) **nos va mucho en esto** we have a lot riding on this; **le va la vida en ello** his life depends on it; ✦*MODISMO* **ni me va ni me viene** it's nothing to do with me

9·2 (*indicando situación*) **¿cómo te va?** how are things?, how are you doing?; **¿cómo te va en los estudios?** how are you getting on with your studies?; **¡que te vaya bien!** take care!

9·3 (= *sentar*) to suit; **¿me va bien esto?** does this suit me?; **no le va bien el sombrero** the hat doesn't suit her

9·4 (*) (= *gustar*) **no me va nada ese rollo** I'm not into that sort of thing*; **ese tipo de gente no me va** I don't get on with that type of people; **le va al Cruz Azul** (*Méx Dep*) he supports Cruz Azul

10 *seguido de preposición*

- **ir con** (= *acompañar, combinar*) to go with; **no quería ir con ella a ninguna parte** I didn't want to go anywhere with her; **iba con su madre** he was with his mother; **esta fotocopia debe ir con la carta** this photocopy has to go (in) with the letter; **yo voy con el Real Madrid** I support Real Madrid; **el marrón no va bien con el azul** brown and blue don't go together; **eso de ser famosa no va con ella** being famous doesn't agree with her
- **ir de**: **¿de qué va la película?** what's the film about?; **la película va nada más que de sexo** the film is all sex; **no sabe de qué va el rollo*** he doesn't know what it's all about; **va de intelectual por la vida*** he acts the intellectual all the time; **¿de qué vas?*** what are you on about?*
- **ir para**: **va para los 40** he's getting on for 40, he's knocking on 40; **va para viejo** he's getting old; **va para arquitecto** he's going to be an architect; **va para cinco años que entré en la Universidad** it's getting on for five years since I started University
- **ir por** (*indicando intención*) **eso no va por usted** I wasn't referring to you, that wasn't meant for you; **¡va por los novios!** (here's) to the bride and groom!
- **ir tras** to go after; **se dio cuenta de que iban tras él** he realized they were after him; **ir tras una chica** to chase (after) a girl

11 *otras locuciones* **a lo que iba** as I was saying; **ir a algn con algo**: **siempre le iba con sus problemas** he always went to her with his problems; **¿dónde vas?**: **—¿le regalamos un equipo de música? —¿dónde vas? con un libro tiene bastante** "shall we give him a stereo?" — "what do you mean? a book is fine"; **—¿le pido disculpas? —¿dónde vas? deja que sea él quien se disculpe** "shall I apologize?" — "what are you talking about? let him be the one to apologize"; **si vamos a eso** for that matter; **a eso voy** I'm coming to that; **pues, a eso voy** that's what I mean, that's what I'm getting at; **es el no va más*** it's the ultimate; **ir de mal en peor** to go from bad to worse; **ir a lo suyo** to do one's own thing; (*pey*) to look after Number One; **aquí cada uno va a lo suyo** everyone does their own thing here; **ir y venir**: **era un constante ir y venir de ambulancias** ambulances were constantly coming and going; **llevo todo el día yendo y viniendo de un lado al otro de la ciudad** I've spent all day going from one end of town to the other; **cuando tú vas, yo ya he venido** I've been there before, I've seen it all before; **ir y**: **ahora va y me dice que no viene** now he goes and tells me he's not coming; **fue y se marchó** (*Méx**) he just upped and left*; *ver tb* **lejos A1**

12 *exclamaciones*

- **¡vaya!** (*indicando sorpresa*) well!; (*indicando enfado*) damn!; **¡vaya! ¿qué haces tú por aquí?** well, what a surprise! what are you doing here?; **¡vaya, vaya!** well I'm blowed!*; **¡vaya coche!** what a car!, that's some car!; **¡vaya susto que me pegué!** I got such a fright!, what a fright I got!; **¡vaya con el niño!** that damn kid!*
- **¡vamos!** (*dando ánimos*) come on!; (*para ponerse en marcha*) let's go!; **¡vamos! ¡di algo!** come on! say something!; **vamos, no es difícil** come on, it's not difficult; **una chica, vamos, una mujer** a girl, well, a woman; **es molesto, pero ¡vamos!** it's a nuisance, but there it is
- **¡qué va!**: **—¿no me vas a echar la bronca ? —no, qué va** "you're not going to tell me off, are you?" — "of course I'm not"; **¿perder la liga? ¡qué va, hombre!** lose the league? you must be joking!

Ⓑ VERBO AUXILIAR

- **ir a** + *INFIN* to go; **fui a verle** I went to see him; **vamos a hacerlo** (*afirmando*) we are going to do it; (*exhortando*) let's do it; **tras muchas vueltas fuimos a dar con la calle Serrano** after driving round for ages we eventually found Serrano Street; **¿cómo lo iba a tener?** how could he have had it?; **¡no lo va a saber!** of course he knows!; **¿no irás a decirme que no lo sabías?** you're not going to tell me you didn't know?; **¿no irá a soplar?‡** I hope he's not going to split on us*; **no vaya a ser que ...**: **no salgas no vaya a ser que venga** don't go out in case she comes
- **ir** + *GERUND*: **iba anocheciendo** it was getting dark; **iban fumando** they were smoking; **¿quién va ganando?** who's winning?; **fueron hablando todo el camino** they talked the whole way there; **como iba diciendo** as I was saying; **¡voy corriendo!** I'll be right

there!; **id pensando en el tema que queréis tratar** be *o* start thinking about the subject you want to deal with; **hemos ido consiguiendo lo que queríamos** we found what we wanted eventually; **voy comprendiendo que …** I am beginning to see that …

◆ **ir** + *PARTICIPIO*: **van escritas tres cartas** that's three letters I've written; **va vendido todo** everything has been sold

Ⓒ **irse** VERBO PRONOMINAL

1 ***uso impersonal*** **por aquí se va a Toledo** this is the way to Toledo; **¿por dónde se va al aeropuerto?** which is the way *o* which way is it to the airport?

2 ***= marcharse*** to go, leave; **se fueron** they went, they left; **se fue de la reunión sin decir nada** she left the meeting without saying anything; **es hora de irnos** it's time we were going; **me voy, ¡hasta luego!** I'm off, see you!; **vete a hacer los deberes** go and do your homework; **se le fue un hijo a Alemania** one of her sons went to Germany; **¡vete!** go away!, get out!; **¡no te vayas!** don't go!; **¡vámonos!** let's go!; (*antes de subirse al tren, barco*) all aboard!; **¡nos fuimos!** (*LAm**) let's go!, off we go!*; **me voy de con usted** (*CAm*) I'm leaving you

3 ***= actuar*** **vete con cuidado cuando habléis de este tema** you should tread carefully when you mention that subject

4 ***= salirse*** (*por agujero*) to leak out; (*por el borde*) to overflow; **se fue el vino** the wine leaked out; **el líquido se fue por una ranura** the liquid ran out along a groove; **se me fue la leche** the milk boiled over; **a la cerveza se le ha ido el gas** the beer has gone flat

5 ***= vaciarse*** (*por agujero*) to leak; (*por el borde*) to overflow; **el neumático se va** the tyre is losing air

6 ***= desaparecer*** [*luz*] to go out; **se fue la luz** the lights went out; **la mancha se va sólo con agua** you can only get the stain out with water

7 ***= terminarse*** **írsele a algn: se me va el sueldo en autobuses** all my wages go on bus fares; **rápido, que se nos va el tiempo** be quick, we're running out of time; **no se me va este dolor de espalda** I can't seem to get rid of this backache; **hoy no se me va la mala leche** I can't seem to get out of my bad mood today; **no se le va el enfado** he's still angry

8 ***= perder el equilibrio*** **parecía que me iba para atrás cuando andaba** I felt as if I were falling over backwards when I walked; **se le fue la pierna y tropezó** her leg went (from under her) and she tripped; *ver tb* **mano A4, pie 2**

9 ***euf = morirse*** (*en presente*) to be dying; (*en pasado*) to pass away; **se nos va el amo** the master is dying; **se nos fue hace tres años** he passed away three years ago

10 ***euf = ventosear*** to break wind; (= *orinar*) to wet o.s.; (= *defecar*) to soil o.s.

11 ***‡ = eyacular*** to come‡

ira SF [*de persona*] anger, rage; [*de elementos*] fury, violence; **ha provocado la ~ de los críticos** he has incurred the wrath of the critics; **las uvas de la ~** the grapes of wrath

iracundia SF (= *propensión*) irascibility (*frm*); (= *cólera*) rage, ire (*liter*)

iracundo ADJ (= *propenso a la ira*) irascible (*frm*); (= *colérico*) irate

Irak SM Iraq

iraki ADJ, SMF = **iraquí**

Irán SM Iran

iranés/esa ADJ, SM/F = **iraní**

iraní Ⓐ ADJ, SMF Iranian
Ⓑ SM (*Ling*) Iranian

iranio ADJ (*Hist*) = **iraní**

Iraq SM Iraq

iraquí ADJ, SMF Iraqi

irascibilidad SF irascibility (*frm*)

irascible ADJ irascible (*frm*)

irguiendo *etc ver* **erguir**

iribú SM (*Arg Orn*) turkey buzzard

iridiscente ADJ iridescent

iridología SF iridology

iris SM INV 1 (*Anat*) iris; ✦***MODISMO*** **hacer un ~** (*LAm**) to wink
2 (*Meteo*) rainbow

irisación SF iridescence

irisado ADJ iridescent

irisar ▸conjug 1a◂ VI to be iridescent

Irlanda SF Ireland; **la República de ~** the Republic of Ireland ► **Irlanda del Norte** Northern Ireland

irlandés/esa Ⓐ ADJ Irish; **café ~** Irish coffee
Ⓑ SM/F Irishman/Irishwoman; **los irlandeses** the Irish
Ⓒ SM (*Ling*) Irish

ironía SF 1 (*gen*) irony; **con ~** ironically; (= *con burla*) sarcastically
2 (= *comentario*) sarcastic remark

irónicamente ADV ironically

irónico ADJ (*gen*) ironic, ironical; (= *mordaz*) sarcastic

ironizar ▸conjug 1f◂ Ⓐ VT to ridicule
Ⓑ VI to speak ironically; **~ sobre algo** to be sarcastic about sth; **ironizó ella** she said ironically

IRPF SM ABR (*Esp*) (= **impuesto sobre la renta de las personas físicas**) ≈ personal income tax

irracional Ⓐ ADJ irrational; **un ser ~** an irrational being
Ⓑ SMF irrational person

irracionalidad SF irrationality

irracionalmente ADV irrationally

irradiación SF irradiation

irradiar ▸conjug 1b◂ VT 1 (= *emanar*) to irradiate, radiate
2 (*Med*) to irradiate

irrayable ADJ scratch-proof

irrazonable ADJ unreasonable

irreal ADJ unreal

irrealidad SF unreality

irrealista ADJ unrealistic

irrealizable ADJ (*gen*) unrealizable; [*meta*] unrealistic, impossible; [*plan*] unworkable

irrebatible ADJ irrefutable, unanswerable

irrechazable ADJ irresistible

irrecomendable ADJ inadvisable

irreconciliable ADJ irreconcilable

irreconocible ADJ unrecognizable

irrecuperable ADJ irrecoverable, irretrievable

irrecurrible ADJ **la decisión es ~** there is no appeal against this decision

irrecusable ADJ unimpeachable

irredentismo SM irredentism

irredentista ADJ, SMF irredentist

irredento ADJ unrepentant, inveterate; **un machista ~** a dyed-in-the-wool chauvinist; **el sur ~** the godforsaken south

irredimible ADJ irredeemable

irreducible ADJ 1 (= *mínimo*) irreducible
2 [*diferencias*] irreconcilable

irreductible ADJ 1 (= *invencible*) [*enemigo, oposición, voluntad*] implacable, unyielding; [*obstáculo*] insurmountable; **el sector ~ de los terroristas** the hardline faction of the terrorists
2 [*espíritu, optimismo*] irrepressible

irreembolsable ADJ non-returnable

irreemplazable ADJ irreplaceable

irreflexión SF (= *falta de reflexión*) thoughtlessness; (= *ímpetu*) rashness, impetuosity

irreflexivamente ADV (= *sin reflexionar*) thoughtlessly, unthinkingly; (= *impetuosamente*) rashly

irreflexivo ADJ 1 [*persona*] (= *inconsciente*) thoughtless, unthinking; (= *impetuoso*) rash, impetuous
2 [*acto*] rash, ill-considered

irreformable ADJ unreformable

irrefrenable ADJ [*violencia*] unrestrained, uncontrollable; [*persona*] irrepressible; [*deseo*] unstoppable

irrefutable ADJ irrefutable, unanswerable

irregular ADJ 1 (= *desigual*) 1·1 [*superficie, terreno*] uneven; [*contorno, línea*] crooked; [*rasgos*] irregular; [*filo*] jagged
1·2 [*latido, ritmo*] irregular; [*rendimiento*] irregular, erratic; [*jugador, equipo*] inconsistent; [*año, vida*] chaotic; **tiene el sueño ~** he has an irregular sleep pattern; **el corazón le latía de forma ~** his heart was beating irregularly; **el índice de asistencia ha sido bastante ~ este año** attendance has been quite irregular *o* erratic this year; **el comportamiento ~ de la Bolsa** the erratic behaviour of the stock market; **he tenido un año muy ~** I've had quite a chaotic year; **a intervalos ~es** at irregular intervals
2 (= *no legal*) **la situación de la pareja es algo ~** the couple's situation is somewhat irregular; **han cometido ciertas acciones ~es** they have been involved in certain irregularities; **extranjeros en situación ~** foreigners registered illegally; **Hans admitió su comportamiento ~** Hans admitted his unlawful behaviour
3 (*Ling*) [*verbo*] irregular
4 (*Mat*) [*polígono, figura*] irregular

irregularidad SF 1 (= *desigualdad*) 1·1 [*de superficie, terreno*] irregularity, unevenness; **las ~es del terreno** the unevenness of the terrain
1·2 [*de latido, ritmo, lluvias*] irregularity; [*de jugador, equipo*] inconsistency, erratic performance; **noté la ~ de su pulso** I noticed that his pulse was erratic; **la ~ del equipo se demostró una vez más en el último partido** the team's inconsistency *o* erratic performance was noticeable again in their last match
2 (= *ilegalidad*) irregularity; **~es administrativas** administrative irregularities; **~es contables** irregularities in the accounts; **~es fiscales** tax irregularities; **~es urbanísticas** irregu-

larities in town planning procedures
[3] (*Ling*) irregularity
irregularmente ADV [1] (= *desigualmente*) irregularly
[2] (= *ilegalmente*) illegally
irrelevante ADJ irrelevant
irreligioso ADJ irreligious (*frm*), ungodly (*pey*)
irrellenable ADJ [*botella, encendedor*] disposable
irremediable ADJ [*daño, decadencia*] irremediable; [*pérdida*] irreparable, irretrievable; [*vicio*] incurable
irremediablemente ADV [1] (= *inevitablemente*) inevitably; **~ habrá una inclinación hacia la izquierda** inevitably there will be a swing to the left
[2] (= *irreparablemente*) irremediably; **una oportunidad ~ perdida** an opportunity irremediably lost, an opportunity lost forever; **el matrimonio estaba ~ roto** the marriage had broken down hopelessly *o* irretrievably
irremisible ADJ irremissible
irremisiblemente ADV irremissibly; **~ perdido** irretrievably lost, lost beyond hope of recovery
irremontable ADJ insurmountable
irremunerado ADJ unremunerated
irrentable ADJ unprofitable
irrenunciable ADJ [*derecho*] inalienable; [*condición*] absolute; [*deber*] unavoidable, inescapable; **una aspiración ~** an aspiration which can never be given up
irreparable ADJ irreparable
irreparablemente ADV irreparably
irrepetible ADJ unrepeatable
irreprensible ADJ irreproachable
irreprimible ADJ irrepressible
irreprochable ADJ irreproachable
irreproducible ADJ unrepeatable
irresistible ADJ irresistible; (*pey*) unbearable, insufferable
irresistiblemente ADV irresistibly
irresoluble ADJ (= *insoluble*) unsolvable; (= *sin resolver*) unresolved
irresolución SF hesitation, indecision
irresoluto ADJ [1] (= *perplejo*) indecisive
[2] (= *sin resolver*) unresolved
irrespetar ▸conjug 1a◂ VT (*LAm*) to show disrespect to *o* for
irrespeto SM disrespect
irrespetuosamente ADV disrespectfully
irrespetuoso ADJ disrespectful
irrespirable ADJ unbreathable
irresponsabilidad SF irresponsibility
irresponsable ADJ irresponsible
irrestricto ADJ (*LAm*) **apoyo ~** unconditional support
irresuelto ADJ = **irresoluto 1**
irreverencia SF irreverence
irreverente ADJ irreverent; **un chiste ~** an irreverent joke
irreversible ADJ irreversible
irrevocable ADJ irrevocable
irrevocablemente ADV irrevocably
irrigación SF irrigation; **~ por aspersión** irrigation using sprinkler (system); **~ por goteo** trickle irrigation
irrigador SM sprinkler
irrigar ▸conjug 1h◂ VT [1] (= *regar*) to irrigate
[2] [+ *cerebro, músculo*] to feed, supply with blood
irrisible ADJ laughable, absurd
irrisión SF [1] (= *mofa*) derision, ridicule
[2] (= *hazmerreír*) laughing stock
irrisorio ADJ (= *ridículo*) derisory, ridiculous; [*precio*] absurdly low
irritabilidad SF irritability
irritable ADJ irritable
irritación SF irritation
irritador ADJ irritating
irritante Ⓐ ADJ irritating
Ⓑ SM irritant
irritar ▸conjug 1a◂ Ⓐ VT [1] (= *enfadar*) to irritate
[2] (*Med*) to irritate; **tengo la garganta irritada** I've got a sore throat
[3] [+ *celos, pasiones*] to stir up, inflame
Ⓑ **irritarse** VPR to get irritated; **~se por algo** to get irritated about *o* at sth, get annoyed about *o* at sth; **~se con algn** to get irritated with sb, get annoyed with sb
irrogar ▸conjug 1h◂ VT (*Jur*) to occasion
irrompible ADJ unbreakable
irrumpir ▸conjug 3a◂ VI **~ en** to burst into; **los agentes irrumpieron en el bar** the policemen burst into the bar; **los tanques irrumpieron en la plaza** the tanks burst onto the square
irrupción SF **la mujer está haciendo su ~ en el mundo laboral** women are breaking into the world of employment; **acaba de hacer su ~ en el mundo de la música country** she has just burst onto the country music scene
IRTP SM ABR (*Esp*) (= **impuesto sobre el rendimiento del trabajo personal**) ≈ PAYE
IRYDA SM ABR = **Instituto para la Reforma y el Desarrollo Agrario**
Isaac SM Isaac
Isabel SF Isabel, Elizabeth; **la reina ~ II** Queen Elizabeth II
isabelino ADJ **la España isabelina** Isabelline Spain, the Spain of Isabel II; **la Inglaterra isabelina** Elizabethan England, the England of Elizabeth I
Isabelita SF (*forma familiar*) *de* **Isabel**
Isaías SM Isaiah
iscocoro‡ SM (*CAm pey*) Indian
ISDE SM ABR (*Esp*) = **Instituto Superior de Dirección de Empresas**
Iseo SF Iseult, Isolde
isidrada SF, **isidros** SMPL celebration of St Isidore (*patron saint of Madrid*)
-ísimo *ver* **Aspects of Word Formation in Spanish 2**
isla SF [1] (*Geog*) island; **una ~ desierta** a desert island ► **Islas Baleares** Balearic Islands ► **Islas Británicas** British Isles ► **Islas Canarias** Canary Islands ► **Islas Filipinas** Philippine Islands, Philippines ► **Islas Malvinas** Falkland Islands; *ver el segundo elemento para otros nombres*
[2] (*Arquit*) block
[3] (*Aut*) traffic island
Islam SM Islam
islámico ADJ Islamic
islamismo SM (*Rel*) Islam; (= *integrismo*) Islamic fundamentalism
islamista ADJ, SMF (*Rel*) Islamist; (= *integrista*) Islamic fundamentalist
islamización SF Islamization
islamizante ADJ Islamicizing
islamizar ▸conjug 1f◂ VT to Islamize, convert to Islam
islamofobia SF Islamophobia
islandés/esa Ⓐ ADJ Icelandic
Ⓑ SM/F Icelander
Ⓒ SM (*Ling*) Icelandic
Islandia SF Iceland
islándico ADJ Icelandic
isleño/a Ⓐ ADJ island *antes de s*
Ⓑ SM/F islander
isleta SF islet
islote SM small island
ismo SM ism
-ismo *ver* **Aspects of Word Formation in Spanish 2**
iso... PREF iso...
isobara SF, **isóbara** SF isobar
isoca SF (*Cono Sur*) caterpillar, grub
isohispa SF contour line
Isolde SF Iseult, Isolde
isométrica SF isometrics *sing*, isometric exercises *pl*
isométrico ADJ isometric
isósceles ADJ **triángulo ~** isosceles triangle
isoterma SF isotherm
isotérmico ADJ [1] (= *con aislamiento*) [*ropa*] thermal; [*recipiente*] insulated; [*vehículo*] refrigerated
[2] (*Geog*) isothermal
isotónico ADJ isotonic
isótopo SM isotope
Israel SM Israel
israelí ADJ, SMF Israeli
israelita ADJ, SMF Israelite
-ista *ver* **Aspects of Word Formation in Spanish 2**
istmeño/a Ⓐ ADJ of/from the Isthmus (*often Panamanian*)
Ⓑ SM/F native/inhabitant of the Isthmus (*often Panamanian*)
istmo SM isthmus; **el Istmo** (*Méx*) the isthmus of Tehuantepec ► **istmo de Panamá** Isthmus of Panama
itacate SM (*Méx*) provisions *pl* (*for journey*), food
Italia SF Italy
italianismo SM italianism, *word/phrase etc borrowed from Italian*
italiano/a Ⓐ ADJ, SM/F Italian
Ⓑ SM (*Ling*) Italian
itálica SF italic; **en ~** in italics
ítem Ⓐ SM item Ⓑ ADV also, likewise
itemizar ▸conjug 1f◂ VT (*Chile*) (= *enumerar*) to itemize, list; (= *dividir*) to divide into sections
iterar ▸conjug 1a◂ VT to repeat
iterativo ADJ iterative
itinerante ADJ [*biblioteca, exposición*] travelling, traveling (EEUU); [*compañía de teatro*] touring; **comando ~** mobile terrorist unit; **embajador ~** roving ambassador, ambassador at large
itinerario SM [1] (= *ruta*) itinerary, route
[2] (*Méx Ferro*) timetable
-itis *ver* **Aspects of Word Formation in Spanish 2**

-ito, **-ita** *ver* **Aspects of Word Formation in Spanish 2**

ITV SF ABR (*Esp*) (= **Inspección Técnica de Vehículos**) ≈ MOT

IU SF ABR (*Esp Pol*) (= **Izquierda Unida**) *Spanish coalition of left-wing parties*

i/v ABR = **ida y vuelta**

IVA SM ABR (= **impuesto sobre el valor añadido** o (*LAm*) **agregado**) VAT

Ivan SM Ivan; **~ el Terrible** Ivan the Terrible

IVP SM ABR = **Instituto Venezolano de Petroquímica**

ixtle SM (*Méx*) fibre, fiber (*EEUU*)

iza* SF whore

izada SF (*LAm*) lifting, raising

izado SM **~ de la bandera** raising o hoisting the flag

izamiento SM raising, hoisting

-izante *ver* **Aspects of Word Formation in Spanish 2**

izar ▸conjug 1f◂ VT [+ *bandera*] to hoist, raise; [+ *velas*] to hoist, run up; **la bandera está izada** the flag is flying

izcuinche SM (*Méx*), **izcuintle** SM (*Méx*) [1] (= *perro*) mangy dog, mongrel
[2] (*) (= *chiquillo*) kid*; (= *pilluelo*) urchin

izda. ABR L, l

izdo. ABR (= **izquierdo**) L, l

-izo *ver* **Aspects of Word Formation in Spanish 2**

izq. ABR, **izq.°** ABR, **izqdo.** ABR (= **izquierdo**) L, l

izq.ª ABR, **izqda.** ABR (= **izquierda**) L, l

izquierda SF [1] (= *mano*) left hand; (= *lado*) left, left-hand side; **sólo sabe escribir con la ~** he can only write with his left hand; **mi casa está a la ~** my house is on the left o on the left-hand side; **está a la ~ de tu hermano** he's to the left of your brother; **el árbol de la ~** the tree on the left o on the left-hand side; **tuerza por la tercera a la ~** take the third turn on the left o on the left-hand side; **conducen por la ~** they drive on the left o on the left-hand side; *ver tb* **cero 1**
[2] (*Pol*) **la ~** the left (wing); **la extrema ~** the extreme left (wing); **ser de ~s** to be on the left ► **Izquierda Unida** *Spanish coalition of left-wing parties*

izquierdismo SM leftism, *left-wing outlook or tendencies etc*

izquierdista Ⓐ ADJ left-wing
Ⓑ SMF left-winger

izquierdo ADJ [1] (*gen*) left; **metió el balón por el lado ~ del portero** he placed the ball to the goalkeeper's left, he placed the ball left of the goalkeeper; **el lateral ~ del Barcelona** the Barcelona left-winger; **las dos ruedas del lado ~** the two wheels on the left-hand side
[2] (= *zurdo*) left-handed

izquierdoso/a* (*pey*) Ⓐ ADJ leftish
Ⓑ SM/F lefty*

J j

J, j ['xota] SF (= *letra*) J, j

ja[1] EXCL ha!

ja[2]‡ SF (= *mujer*) wife; (= *novia*) bird‡, chick (*EEUU*‡)

jaba SF [1] (*Cuba*) (= *cesto*) straw basket
[2] (*CAm, Méx*) (= *caja*) crate
[3] (*Caribe*) (= *bolsa*) beggar's bag, poverty; ✦*MODISMOS* **llevar** *o* **tener algo en ~*** to have sth up one's sleeve; **no poder ver a otro con ~ grande*** to envy sb; **soltar la ~** to go up in the world; **tomar la ~** to be reduced to begging
[4] (*LAm Bot*) = **haba 1**

jabado ADJ [1] (*Caribe, Méx*) white with brown patches
[2] (= *indeciso*) hesitant, undecided

jabalí SM wild boar ► **jabalí verrugoso** wart-hog

jabalina SF [1] (*Dep*) javelin
[2] (*Zool*) wild sow

jabato Ⓐ ADJ [1] (= *valiente*) brave, bold
[2] (*Caribe, Méx*) (= *grosero*) rude, gruff; (= *malhumorado*) ill-tempered
Ⓑ SM [1] (*Zool*) young wild boar; **portarse como un ~** to be very brave
[2] (*) (= *persona*) tough guy*

jábega SF [1] (= *red*) sweep net, dragnet
[2] (= *barca*) fishing smack

jabón SM [1] (*para lavar*) soap; **una pastilla de ~** a bar of soap; ✦*MODISMO* **no es lo mismo ~ que hilo negro** (*Andes, Caribe*) they're as different as chalk and cheese ► **jabón de afeitar** shaving soap ► **jabón de olor** toilet soap ► **jabón de sastre** tailor's chalk, French chalk ► **jabón de tocador** toilet soap ► **jabón en escamas** soapflakes ► **jabón en polvo** soap powder, washing powder, (powdered) laundry detergent (*EEUU*) ► **jabón líquido** liquid soap
[2] (*) (= *adulación*) flattery; **dar ~ a algn** to soft-soap sb
[3] (†) (= *reprimenda*) **dar un ~ a algn** to tell sb off
[4] (*Caribe, Cono Sur, Méx*) (= *susto*) fright, scare; **agarrarse un ~** to get a fright

jabonada SF [1] = **jabonadura 1**
[2] (*LAm*) (= *bronca*) telling-off

jabonado SM [1] (= *acción*) soaping
[2] (= *ropa*) wash, laundry
[3] (= *bronca*) telling-off

jabonadura SF [1] (= *acción*) soaping
[2] **jabonaduras** (= *espuma*) lather *sing*, soap-suds
[3] (*) (= *al regañar*) telling-off; **dar una ~ a algn** to tell sb off

jabonar ▸conjug 1a◂ VT [1] (*con jabón*) (*gen*) to soap; [+ *barba*] to lather
[2] (*) (= *reprender*) to tell off

jaboncillo SM [1] (*para lavar*) small bar of soap
[2] (*tb* **~ de sastre**) tailor's chalk, French chalk

jabonera SF soapdish

jabonería SF soap factory

jabonete SM small bar of soap

jabonoso ADJ soapy

jabuco SM (*Caribe*) (= *caja*) large basket, big crate; (= *bolsa*) bag; ✦*MODISMO* **dar ~ a algn** to snub sb, give sb the cold shoulder

jaca SF (= *caballo pequeño*) pony, small horse; (= *yegua*) mare; (*en lenguaje infantil*) horse; (*Caribe*) gelding

jacal SM (*CAm, Caribe, Méx*) shack, hut; ✦*MODISMO* **no tiene ~ donde meterse** he's without a roof over his head; ✦*REFRÁN* **al ~ viejo no le faltan goteras** old age is bound to have its problems

jacalear* ▸conjug 1a◂ VI (*Méx*) to go around gossiping

jacalón SM (*Méx*) (= *cobertizo*) shed; (= *casucha*) shack, hovel; (*Teat**) fleapit*

jácara†† SF [1] (*Literat*) *comic ballad of low life*
[2] (*Mús*) *a merry dance*
[3] (= *personas*) *band of night revellers*; **estar de ~** to be very merry
[4] (= *molestia*) pain*, nuisance
[5] (= *cuento*) fib, story

jacarandá SM *o* SF (*pl* **jacarandaes, jacarandás**) jacaranda, jacaranda tree

jacarandoso ADJ (= *alegre*) merry, jolly; (= *airoso*) spirited, lively

jacaré SM (*LAm*) alligator

jacarear†† ▸conjug 1a◂ VI [1] (*Mús*) (= *cantar*) to sing in the streets at nights; (= *dar serenatas*) to go serenading
[2] (= *armar un escándalo*) to cause a commotion
[3] (= *insultar*) to be rude, make offensive remarks

jacarero/a†† Ⓐ ADJ merry, fun-loving
Ⓑ SM/F amusing person, wag

jácena SF girder, main beam

jachís SM = **hachís**

jachudo ADJ (*Andes*) (= *fuerte*) strong, tough; (= *terco*) obstinate

jacinto SM [1] (*Bot*) hyacinth
[2] (*Min*) jacinth

jaco SM [1] (= *caballo*) small horse, young horse; (*pey*) nag, hack
[2] (‡) (= *heroína*) horse‡, heroin

jacobeo ADJ (*Rel*) of St James; **la devoción jacobea** the devotion to St James, the cult of St James; **la ruta jacobea** the pilgrims' road to Santiago de Compostela

jacobino/a ADJ, SM/F Jacobin

Jacobo SM Jacob

jactancia SF (= *autoalabanzas*) boasting; (= *orgullo*) boastfulness

jactanciosamente ADV boastfully

jactancioso ADJ boastful

jactarse ▸conjug 1a◂ VPR to boast, brag; **~ de algo** to boast about *o* of sth; **~ de hacer algo** to boast of doing sth

jacuzzi® [ja'kuzi] SM (*pl* **jacuzzis**) Jacuzzi®

jade SM jade

jadeante ADJ panting, gasping

jadear ▸conjug 1a◂ VI to pant, gasp for breath

jadeo SM panting, gasping

Jaén SM Jaen

jaez SM [1] (*para el caballo*) harness; **jaeces** trappings
[2] (= *ralea*) kind, sort; **y gente de ese ~** and people of that sort

jaguar SM jaguar

jagüel SM (*LAm*), **jagüey** SM (*LAm*) pool

jai‡ SF bird‡, chick (*EEUU*‡), dame*

jai alai SM pelota

jaiba Ⓐ SF [1] (*LAm*) (= *cangrejo*) crab
[2] (*Andes*) (= *boca*) mouth; ✦*MODISMO* **abrir la ~** to show o.s. greedy for money
Ⓑ SMF (*Caribe, Méx**) sharp customer*

jaibol SM (*LAm*) highball (*EEUU*)

jaibón* ADJ (*CAm*) stuck-up*, pretentious, snobbish

jáilaif* (*LAm*) Ⓐ ADJ high-life *antes de s*
Ⓑ SF high life

jailoso ADJ (*Andes*) (*gen*) well-bred; (*pey*) stuck-up*, pretentious, snobbish

Jaime SM James; ✦*MODISMO* **hacer el Jaimito*** to horse around*

jalada SF (*Méx*) [1] (= *tirón*) pull, tug, heave
[2] (= *reprimenda*) ticking-off*
[3] (*Andes**) (*Univ*) failure

jaladera SF (*Méx*) handle

jalador SM (*LAm*) door-handle

jalamecate* SM (*LAm*) toady, creep‡

jalapeño SM (*Méx*) jalapeno pepper

jalar ▸conjug 1a◂ Ⓐ VT [1] (*LAm*) (= *tirar de*) to pull; (= *arrastrar*) (*tb Náut*) to haul; **no le jales el pelo** don't pull his hair
[2] (*Méx**) (= *llevar*) to pick up, give a lift to
[3] (*LAm Pol*) to draw, attract, win
[4] (*LAm*) (= *trabajar*) to work hard at
[5] (*Andes, Caribe**) (= *hacer*) to make, do, perform
[6] (*Esp**) (= *comer*) to eat
Ⓑ VI [1] (*LAm*) (= *tirar*) to pull; **~ de** to pull at, tug at
[2] (*Méx**) **eso le jala** she's big on that*, she's a fan of that
[3] (*LAm*) (= *irse*) to go off; **~ para su casa** to go off home
[4] (*CAm, Méx*) [*novios*] to be courting
[5] (*LAm*) (= *trabajar*) to work hard
[6] (*Andes*⁑) [*estudiante*] to flunk*, fail
[7] (*Méx*) (= *exagerar*) to exaggerate
[8] (⁑) (= *correr*) to run
[9] (*Méx*) (= *tener influencia*) to have pull*
[10] (*Andes*⁑) (= *fumar*) to smoke dope*
Ⓒ **jalarse** VPR [1] (*LAm*) (= *irse*) to go off
[2] (*LAm*) (= *emborracharse*) to get drunk
[3] (*CAm**) [*novios*] to be courting
[4] (**⁑) (= *masturbarse*) to wank**⁑

jalbegar ▸conjug 1h◂ VT to whitewash

jalbegue SM (= *pintura*) whitewash; (= *acción*) whitewashing

jalde ADJ, **jaldo** ADJ bright yellow

jalea SF jelly; ✦**MODISMO hacerse una ~**† (= *enamorado*) to be madly in love; (= *amable*) to be a creep⁑ ► **jalea de guayaba** guava jelly ► **jalea real** royal jelly

jalear ▸conjug 1a◂ Ⓐ VT [1] (*haciendo ruido*) [+ *bailaor*] to cheer on; [+ *perros*] to urge on
[2] (*Méx*) (= *burlarse*) to jeer at
Ⓑ VI (*Méx*) to amuse o.s. noisily

jaleo SM [1] (*) (= *ruido*) row, racket; **armar un ~** to kick up a row
[2] (*) (= *confusión*) mess, muddle; (= *problema*) hassle; **es un ~ acordarse de tantos nombres** it's such a hassle having to remember all those names; **con tanto botón me armo unos ~s** I get into such a mess *o* muddle with all these buttons; **se armó un ~ tremendo** all hell broke loose*
[3] (*) (= *juerga*) binge*; **estar de ~** to be having a good time
[4] (*Mús*) shouting and clapping (*to encourage dancers*)
[5] (*Caza*) hallooing

jaleoso ADJ noisy, rowdy, boisterous

jalisciense ADJ of/from Jalisco

jalisco[1]⁑ ADJ (*CAm, Méx*) plastered⁑, stoned (*EEUU*⁑)

jalisco[2] SM (*CAm, Méx*) straw hat

jallo ADJ (*Méx*) (= *ostentoso*) showy, flashy; (= *quisquilloso*) touchy

jalón SM [1] (= *poste*) (*gen*) stake, pole; [*de agrimensor*] surveying rod
[2] (= *hito*) milestone, watershed; **esto marca un ~ en ...** this is a milestone in ...
[3] (*LAm*) (= *tirón*) pull, tug; (= *robo*) snatch*; **hacer algo de un ~** (*Col, Méx*) to do sth in one go
[4] (*LAm*) (= *distancia*) distance, stretch; **hay un buen ~** it's a good *o* fair way
[5] (*CAm, Méx**) (= *trago*) swig*, drink
[6] (*CAm*) (= *amante*) lover, sweetheart; (= *pretendiente*) suitor

jalona SF (*CAm*) flirt, flighty girl

jalonamiento SM staking out, marking out

jalonar ▸conjug 1a◂ VT to stake out, mark out; **el camino está jalonado por plazas fuertes** the route is marked out by a series of strongholds, a line of strongholds marks the route

jalonazo SM (*CAm, Méx*) pull, tug

jalonear ▸conjug 1a◂ Ⓐ VT (*Méx*) to pull, tug
Ⓑ VI [1] (*CAm, Méx*) (= *tirar*) to pull, tug
[2] (*Méx*) (= *regatear*) to haggle

jalonero⁑ SM bag-snatcher

jalufa⁑ SF hunger; **pasar** *o* **tener ~** to be hungry

Jamaica SF Jamaica

jamaica[1] SF (*CAm, Méx*) jumble sale, charity sale (*EEUU*)

jamaica[2] SF (*Caribe, Méx Bot*) hibiscus

jamaicano/a ADJ, SM/F, **jamaiquino/a** (*LAm*) ADJ, SM/F Jamaican

jamancia⁑ SF [1] (= *comida*) grub⁑, chow (*EEUU*⁑)
[2] (= *hambre*) hunger; **pasar** *o* **tener ~** to be hungry

jamar* ▸conjug 1a◂ Ⓐ VT to stuff o.s. with*
Ⓑ VI to eat, stuff o.s.*
Ⓒ **jamarse** VPR **se lo jamó todo** he scoffed the lot*

jamás ADV never; (*con negación, en interrogación*) ever; **¡jamás!** never!; **¿se vio ~ tal cosa?** did you ever see such a thing?; **el mejor amigo que ~ ha existido** the best friend ever; **¡~ de los jamases!** never in your life!

jamba SF jamb ► **jamba de puerta** doorjamb, doorpost (*EEUU*); *ver tb* **jambo**

jambado* ADJ (*Méx*) greedy, gluttonous; **estar ~** to be feeling over-full

jambarse ▸conjug 1a◂ VPR (*CAm, Méx*) to overeat

jambo/a⁑ SM/F (= *hombre*) bloke⁑, geezer⁑; (= *mujer*) bird⁑, dame*; *ver tb* **jamba**

jamelgo SM nag, old hack

jamón Ⓐ SM [1] [*de cerdo*] ham; ✦**MODISMO ¡y un ~ (con chorreras)!*** get away!*, my foot!* ► **jamón cocido** boiled ham ► **jamón de pata negra** *type of top-quality Parma ham made from a special breed of pig that has black legs* ► **jamón dulce** boiled ham ► **jamón serrano** ≈ Parma ham ► **jamón (de) York** boiled ham
[2] (*) [*de persona*] thigh, ham*
[3] (*Caribe*) (= *ganga*) bargain
[4] (*Caribe*) (= *conflicto*) difficulty
Ⓑ ADJ (*) [*persona*] dishy*; **un plato que está ~** a delicious meal

jamona* SF buxom woman

jampa SF (*Andes, Méx*) (= *umbral*) threshold; (= *puerta*) doorway

jámparo SM (*Andes*) canoe, small boat

jamurar* ▸conjug 1a◂ VT (*Andes*) to rinse

jan SM (*Caribe Agr*) seed drill; ✦**MODISMO ensartarse en los ~es** to get involved in an unprofitable piece of business

jandinga⁑ SF (*Caribe*) grub⁑, chow (*EEUU*⁑)

janearse ▸conjug 1a◂ VPR (*Caribe*) [1] (= *saltar*) to leap into the saddle
[2] (*) (= *pararse*) to come to a complete stop

jangada[1] SF (*Náut*) raft

jangada[2] SF (= *disparate*) stupid remark; (= *trampa*) dirty trick

Jano SM Janus

janpa SF = **jampa**

Japón SM Japan

japonés/esa Ⓐ ADJ, SM/F Japanese
Ⓑ SM (*Ling*) Japanese

japuta SF pomfret

jaque SM [1] (*Ajedrez*) check; **dar ~ a algn** to put sb in check; **¡~ (al rey)!** check!; **~ continuo** continuous check; ✦**MODISMO tener en ~ a algn** to hold a sword over sb's head ► **jaque mate** checkmate; **dar ~ mate a algn** to checkmate sb, mate sb
[2] (*) (= *matón*) bully

jaquear ▸conjug 1a◂ VT [1] (*Ajedrez*) to check
[2] (*Mil*) (*fig*) to harass; **quedar jaqueado** to be rendered powerless

jaqueca SF [1] (= *dolor*) (severe) headache, migraine; ✦**MODISMO dar ~ a algn** (= *aburrir*) to bore sb; (= *acosar*) to bother sb, pester sb
[2] (*Cono Sur*) (= *resaca*) hangover

jaquetón* SM bully, braggart

jáquima SF [1] (*LAm*) [*de caballo*] headstall
[2] (*CAm, Méx**) (= *borrachera*) drunkenness, drunken state

jaquimón SM (*LAm*) headstall, halter

jara[1] SF [1] (*Bot*) rockrose, cistus
[2] (= *mata*) clump, thicket
[3] (= *dardo*) dart
[4] **la ~** (*Méx**) the cops* *pl*

jara[2] SF (*Andes*) halt, rest

jarabe SM [1] (= *líquido*) syrup; **~ contra** *o* **para la tos** cough syrup *o* mixture; ✦**MODISMO dar ~ a algn*** to butter sb up* ► **jarabe de arce** maple syrup ► **jarabe de glucosa** glucose syrup ► **jarabe de palo*** beating ► **jarabe de pico** mere words, blarney
[2] ► **jarabe tapatío** Mexican hat dance

jaral SM [1] (= *terreno*) thicket
[2] (= *asunto espinoso*) thorny question

jaramago SM hedge mustard

jarana SF [1] (*) (= *juerga*) binge*; **andar/ir de ~** to be/go out on the town
[2] (*Méx Mús*) small guitar
[3] (*Perú*) (= *baile*) dance
[4] (*Caribe*) (= *banda*) dance band
[5] (*CAm*) (= *deuda*) debt
[6] (*Andes*) (= *embuste*) fib
[7] (*LAm*) (= *broma*) practical joke, hoax; **la ~ sale a la cara** (*CAm*) a joke can come back on you

jaranear ▸conjug 1a◂ Ⓐ VI [1] (*) (= *divertirse*) to be out on the town
[2] (*CAm*) (= *endeudarse*) to get into debt
Ⓑ VT (*Andes, CAm*) to cheat, swindle

jaranero ADJ [1] (*) (= *juerguista*) merry, roistering
[2] (*CAm*) (= *tramposo*) deceitful, tricky
[3] (*Méx Mús*) jarana player

jaranista* ADJ (*LAm*) = **jaranero 1**

jarano SM (*Méx*) broad hat, sombrero

jarcha SF kharja

jarcia SF [1] (*Náut*) (*tb* **~s**) rigging
[2] [*de pesca*] fishing tackle
[3] (*Cuba, Méx*) (= *cuerda*) rope (*made from agave fibre*)
[4] (*CAm*) agave
[5] (= *montón*) heap, mess

jardín SM garden, flower garden; ✦**MODISMO ser un ~ de rosas** to be a bed of roses ► **jardín alpestre** rock garden ► **jardín botánico** botanical garden ► **jardín de infancia**, **jardín de infantes** (*LAm*) kindergarten, nursery school ► **jardín rocoso** rock garden ► **jardín zoológico** zoo

jardinaje SM (*LAm*) gardening

jardinera SF 1 (*para plantas*) (*en ventana, balcón*) window box; (*en la calle*) flower bed
2 **a la ~** (*Culin*) jardiniere
3 (*Cono Sur*) (= *carrito*) barrow, cart
4 (*Chile*) (= *pantalón*) overalls *pl*, dungarees *pl*
5 (*Andes*) (= *abrigo*) jacket; *ver tb* **jardinero**

jardinería SF gardening

jardinero/a Ⓐ SM/F gardener
Ⓑ SM (*Cono Sur*) (= *pantalón*) overalls *pl*, dungarees *pl*; [*de niño*] romper suit; *ver tb* **jardinera**

jarea* SF (*Méx*) hunger

jarear ▸conjug 1a◂ VI (*Andes*) to halt, stop for a rest

jarearse* ▸conjug 1a◂ VPR (*Méx*) 1 (*de hambre*) to be starving*
2 (= *huir*) to flee

jareta SF 1 (*Cos*) (= *dobladillo*) casing; (= *adorno*) tuck
2 (*Náut*) (= *cabo*) cable, rope; (= *red*) netting
3 (*CAm, Cono Sur*) (= *bragueta*) fly, flies *pl*
4 (*Caribe*) (= *contratiempo*) snag, setback

jarete SM (*Caribe*) paddle

jari* SM row, racket

jarifo ADJ (*liter*) elegant, showy, spruce

jaripeo* SM (*Méx*) horse show

jaro SM arum lily

jarocho/a Ⓐ ADJ of/from Veracruz
Ⓑ SM/F native/inhabitant of Veracruz; **los ~s** the people of Veracruz

jarope SM 1 (= *jarabe*) syrup
2 (*) brew, concoction, nasty drink; **resultó un ~ poco agradable** it was a bitter pill to swallow

jarra SF [*de leche*] jug, pitcher (*EEUU*); [*de cerveza*] mug, tankard; **de** *o* **en ~s** with arms akimbo

jarrada SF (*LAm*) jugful, pitcherful (*EEUU*)

jarrete SM 1 (*Anat*) back of the knee; (*Zool*) hock
2 (*Andes*) (= *talón*) heel

jarro SM jug, pitcher (*EEUU*); ✦**MODISMOS caer como un ~ de agua fría** to come as a complete shock; **echar un ~ de agua fría a una idea** to pour cold water on an idea

jarrón SM 1 (*para flores*) vase
2 (*Arqueología*) urn

jartón* ADJ (*CAm, Méx*) greedy, gluttonous

Jartum SM, **Jartún** SM Khartoum

jaspe SM jasper

jaspeado ADJ speckled, mottled

jaspear ▸conjug 1a◂ Ⓐ VT to speckle, marble to streak
Ⓑ **jaspearse** VPR (*Caribe**) to get cross

jato SM 1 (= *ternero*) calf
2 (*Caribe*) (= *perro*) stray dog, mongrel
3 (*Méx*) (= *carga*) load
4 (*Andes*) (= *silla de montar*) saddle
5 (*LAm*) = **hato**

Jauja SF, **jauja** SF 1 **¡esto es ~!** this is the life!; **vivir en ~** to live in luxury; **¿estamos aquí o en ~?** where do you think you are?
2 (*Cono Sur**) (= *chisme*) rumour, tale

jaula SF 1 (*para animales*) (*tb Min*) cage
2 [*de embalaje*] crate
3 [*de demente*] cell
4 (*Aut*) lock-up garage
5 (*Caribe**) Black Maria*, paddy wagon (*EEUU**)
6 (*Méx Ferro**) open truck
7 ✦**MODISMO hacer ~** (*Méx*) to dig one's heels in

jauría SF pack of hounds

Java SF Java

java* SF (*Caribe*) trick

jay‡ SF = **jai**

jayán SM 1 (= *forzudo*) big strong man; (*pey*) hulking great brute, tough guy*
2 (*CAm*‡) (= *grosero*) foul-mouthed person

jayares‡ SMPL bread‡, money

jáyaro* ADJ (*Andes*) rough, uncouth

jazmín SM jasmine ► **jazmín de la India, jazmín del Cabo** gardenia

jazz [jaθ, jas] SM jazz

jazzista Ⓐ ADJ jazz *antes de s*, jazzy
Ⓑ SMF jazz player

jazzístico ADJ jazz *antes de s*

J.C. ABR (= **Jesucristo**) JC

jeans [jins, dʒins] SMPL jeans

jebe SM 1 (*LAm*) (= *planta*) rubber plant; (= *goma*) rubber
2 (*Cono Sur*) (= *elástico*) elastic
3 (= *porra*) club, cudgel; ✦**MODISMO llevar ~** to suffer a lot
4 (**) (= *trasero*) arse**, ass (*EEUU***)
5 (*Andes*‡) (= *preservativo*) French letter, rubber*

jebero SM (*LAm*) rubber-plantation worker

jeep [jip] SM jeep

jefatura SF 1 (= *liderato*) leadership; **bajo la ~ de** under the leadership of; **ha dimitido de la ~ del partido** she has resigned the party leadership
2 (= *sede*) headquarters *pl* ► **Jefatura de la aviación civil** ≈ Civil Aviation Authority, ≈ Federal Aviation Administration (*EEUU*) ► **jefatura de policía** police headquarters *pl*
3 (*Caribe*) (= *registro*) registry office

jefazo* SM big shot*, big noise*

jefe/a SM/F 1 (= *superior*) boss; (= *director*) head; (*Pol*) leader; (*Com*) manager; (*Mil*) officer in command; [*de tribu*] chief; **comandante en ~** commander-in-chief; **¿quién es el ~ aquí?** who's in charge around here? ► **jefe/a civil** (*Caribe*) registrar ► **jefe/a de almacén** warehouse manager/manageress ► **jefe/a de bomberos** fire chief, chief fire officer ► **jefe/a de cabina** (*Aer*) chief steward/stewardess ► **jefe/a de camareros** head waiter/waitress ► **jefe/a de cocina** head chef ► **jefe/a de equipo** team leader ► **jefe/a de estación** station master, station manager ► **jefe/a de estado** head of state ► **jefe/a de estado mayor** chief of staff ► **jefe/a de estudios** (*Escol*) director of studies ► **jefe/a de filas** (*Pol*) party leader ► **jefe/a de máquinas** (*Náut*) chief engineer ► **jefe/a de márketing** marketing manager ► **jefe/a de obras** site manager ► **jefe/a de oficina** office manager/manageress ► **jefe/a de personal** personnel manager ► **jefe/a de pista** ringmaster ► **jefe/a de plató** (*Cine, TV*) floor manager ► **jefe/a de producción** production manager ► **jefe/a de protocolo** chief of protocol ► **jefe/a de realización** (*Cine, TV*) production manager ► **jefe/a de redacción** editor-in-chief ► **jefe/a de sala** head waiter/waitress ► **jefe/a de taller** foreman ► **jefe/a de tren** guard, conductor (*EEUU*) ► **jefe/a de ventas** sales manager ► **jefe/a ejecutivo/a** chief executive ► **jefe/a supremo/a** commander-in-chief
2 (*como apelativo*) **¡oiga ~!** hey!, mate!*; **sí, mi ~** (*esp LAm*) yes, sir *o* boss

Jehová SM Jehovah

jején SM 1 (*LAm Zool*) gnat; ✦**MODISMO sabe donde el ~ puso el huevo** (*Caribe*) he's pretty smart
2 (*Andes, Méx**) (= *montón*) loads*, masses; **un ~ de** loads of*
3 (*Méx**) (= *multitud*) mob

jelenque* SM (*Méx*) din, racket

jemeres SMPL **los ~ rojos** the Khmer Rouge

jemiquear ▸conjug 1a◂ VI (*Cono Sur*) = **jeremiquear**

JEN [xen] SF ABR (*Esp*) (= **Junta de Energía Nuclear**) ≈ AEA, ≈ AEC (*EEUU*)

jengibre SM ginger

jenízaro Ⓐ ADJ mixed, hybrid
Ⓑ SM (*Hist*) janissary

Jenofonte SM Xenophon

jeque SM sheik(h)

jerarca SM leader, chief, heirarch (*frm*)

jerarquía SF hierarchy; **una persona de ~** a high-ranking person

jerárquico ADJ hierarchic, hierarchical

jerarquización SF [*de organismo*] hierarchical structuring; [*de elementos*] arranging in order (of importance)

jerarquizado ADJ hierarchical

jerarquizar ▸conjug 1f◂ VT [+ *organismo*] to give a hierarchical structure to; [+ *elementos*] to arrange in order (of importance)

jeremiada SF jeremiad

Jeremías SM Jeremy; (*Biblia*) Jeremiah

jeremías* SMF INV moaner*, whinger*

jeremiquear ▸conjug 1a◂ VI (*LAm*) (= *lloriquear*) to snivel, whimper; (= *regañar*) to nag

Jerez SF ► **Jerez de la Frontera** Jerez

jerez SM sherry

> **JEREZ**
>
> ***Jerez*** *is a specific term for the fortified white wine from the* ***denominación de origen*** *area around Jerez de la Frontera in Andalusia. There are many varieties, which are not always equivalent to the sherries sold in Britain. The name given to each variety depends on the exact conditions of manufacture, such as the amount of yeast mould which is allowed to grow on the surface of the wine, and the blending process. The main types are:* ***fino*** *(very dry and pale),* ***amontillado*** *(dry, with a nutty flavour) and* ***oloroso*** *(darker colour, full flavour). A special type of* ***fino*** *called* ***manzanilla*** *(literally, "camomile tea") is produced only in the town of Sanlúcar de Barrameda, where the sea air is supposed to give it a salty tang.*
>
> ⇨ *See also* DENOMINACIÓN DE ORIGEN, SOLERA

jerezano/a Ⓐ ADJ of/from Jerez
Ⓑ SM/F native/inhabitant of Jerez; **los ~s** the people of Jerez

jerga[1] SF 1 (= *lenguaje*) jargon ► **jerga de germanía** criminal slang ► **jerga informática** computer jargon ► **jerga publicitaria**

sales jargon
2 (= *galimatías*) gibberish

jerga[2] SF 1 (= *tela*) coarse cloth, sackcloth
2 (*Méx*) floor cloth
3 (*LAm*) (= *manta*) horse blanket
4 (*Andes*) coarse cloak

jergal ADJ jargon *antes de s*

jergón SM 1 (= *colchón*) palliasse, straw mattress
2 (= *vestido*) sack* (*ill-fitting garment*)
3 (*) (= *persona*) awkward-looking person, oaf

jeribeque SM **hacer ~s** to make faces, grimace

Jericó SM Jericho

jerigonza SF 1 (= *galimatías*) gibberish
2 (= *lenguaje*) jargon
3 (= *estupidez*) silly thing

jeringa SF 1 (*Med*) syringe ► **jeringa de engrase** grease gun ► **jeringa de un solo uso** disposable syringe
2 (*) (= *molestia*) nuisance

jeringador* ADJ annoying

jeringar ▸conjug 1h◂ Ⓐ VT 1 (*) (= *fastidiar*) to annoy, plague; **¡nos ha jeringado!** he's pulled a sly one on us!*; (*con menosprecio*) wouldn't we all!
2 (= *inyectar*) to syringe
Ⓑ **jeringarse** VPR (*) to put up with it; **¡que se jeringue!** he can lump it!*

jeringazo SM (= *acción*) syringing; (= *chorro*) squirt

jeringón/ona* (*LAm*) Ⓐ ADJ annoying
Ⓑ SM/F pest, pain*

jeringuear* ▸conjug 1a◂ VT (*LAm*) = **jeringar A1**

jeringuilla[1] SF syringe ► **jeringuilla desechable** disposable syringe

jeringuilla[2] SF (*Bot*) mock orange, syringa

Jerjes SM Xerxes

jeró⁑ SM clock⁑, mug⁑

jeroglífico Ⓐ ADJ hieroglyphic
Ⓑ SM 1 (= *escritura*) hieroglyph, hieroglyphic
2 (= *situación, juego*) puzzle

jerónimo[1] ADJ, SM (*Rel*) Hieronymite

jerónimo[2] SM ✦*MODISMO* **sin ~ de duda** (*LAm hum*) without a shadow of doubt

Jerónimo SM Jerome

jersei SM (*pl* **jerseis** *o* **jerséis**), **jersey** SM (*pl* **jerseys**) sweater, pullover, jumper, jersey ► **jersey amarillo** (*Ciclismo*) yellow jersey

Jerusalén SF Jerusalem

jeruza⁑ SF (*CAm*) clink⁑, jail, can (*EEUU**)

Jesucristo SM Jesus Christ

jesuita Ⓐ ADJ 1 (*Rel*) Jesuit
2 (= *hipócrita*) Jesuitic, Jesuitical
Ⓑ SM 1 (*Rel*) Jesuit
2 (= *hipócrita*) hypocrite

jesuítico ADJ Jesuitic, Jesuitical

Jesús SM Jesus; **¡Jesús!** (*indicando sorpresa*) good heavens!; (*al estornudar*) bless you!; ✦*MODISMO* **en un decir ~** before you could say Jack Robinson

jet [jet] (*pl* **jets**) Ⓐ SM (*Aer*) jet, jet plane
Ⓑ SF **la ~** the jet-set

jeta Ⓐ SF 1 (*) (= *cara*) face, mug*, dial*; **te romperé la ~** I'll smash your face in⁑; ✦*MODISMO* **estirar la ~** (*Cono Sur*⁑) to kick the bucket*
2 (= *hocico*) [*de animal*] snout; (*) [*de persona*] gob*
3 (*) (= *ceño*) frown, scowl; **poner ~** to frown, scowl
4 (*) (= *descaro*) cheek*, nerve*; **¡qué ~ tienes!** you've got a nerve!*; **se quedó con mi libro por la ~** the cheeky thing kept my book
Ⓑ SMF **ser un(a) ~*** to have a nerve*, have a cheek*

jetazo* SM bash*, punch

jetear ▸conjug 1a◂ VI (*Cono Sur*) to eat at someone else's expense

jet lag SM INV jet lag; **tener ~** to be jet-lagged

jetón ADJ, **jetudo** ADJ 1 (= *de labios gruesos*) thick-lipped
2 (*Cono Sur*) stupid

jet ski ['jeteski] SM jet ski

Jezabel SF Jezebel

ji EXCL **¡ji, ji, ji!** (*imitando la risa*) hee, hee, hee!; (*iró*) tee hee!

jibarear ▸conjug 1a◂ VI (*Caribe*) to flirt

jíbaro/a Ⓐ ADJ 1 [*pueblo*] Jivaro
2 (*Caribe, Méx*) (= *rústico*) country *antes de s*, rustic; (= *huraño*) sullen
Ⓑ SM/F 1 (= *indígena*) Jivaro
2 (*Caribe, Méx*) peasant
3 (*CAm*⁑) (= *traficante*) dealer, drug dealer
Ⓒ SM (*Caribe*) (= *animal*) wild animal

jibia Ⓐ SF (*Zool*) cuttlefish
Ⓑ SM (⁑) (= *homosexual*) queer⁑, poof (*pey*⁑), fag (*EEUU pey*⁑)

jícama SF (*CAm, Méx*) edible tuber

jícara SF 1 (= *taza*) chocolate cup
2 (*CAm, Méx*) (= *vasija*) gourd; ✦*MODISMOS* **bailar la ~ a algn*** to soft-soap sb*; **sacar la ~ a algn** to dance attendance on sb
3 (*CAm**) (= *cabeza*) head

jicarazo SM 1 (= *veneno*) (cup of) poison, poisonous drink
2 (*CAm, Méx*) (= *taza*) cupful

jícaro SM (*CAm, Méx*) 1 (*Bot*) calabash tree
2 (= *plato*) bowl

jicarón ADJ (*CAm*) big-headed

jicarudo ADJ (*Méx**) broad-faced, broad-browed

jiche SM (*CAm, Méx*) tendon, sinew

jicote SM (*CAm, Méx*) wasp

jicotera SF (*CAm, Méx*) (= *nido*) wasps' nest; (= *zumbido*) buzzing of wasps; ✦*MODISMO* **armar una ~** to kick up a row

jienense, jiennense Ⓐ ADJ of/from Jaén
Ⓑ SMF native/inhabitant of Jaén; **los ~s** the people of Jaén

jifero Ⓐ ADJ (*) filthy
Ⓑ SM 1 (= *matarife*) slaughterer, butcher
2 (= *cuchillo*) butcher's knife

jifia SF swordfish

jijona SM soft nougat (*made in Jijona*); → TURRÓN

jilguero SM goldfinch; **¡mi ~!*** my angel!

jilibioso* ADJ (*Cono Sur*) (= *lloroso*) weepy, tearful; (= *delicado*) finicky, hard to please; [*caballo*] nervous

jilipollas⁎⁎ SMF INV asshole⁎⁎

jilote SM (*CAm, Méx*) (= *elote*) green ear of maize *o* (*EEUU*) corn; (= *maíz verde*) young maize, young corn (*EEUU*)

jilotear ▸conjug 1a◂ VI (*CAm, Méx*) to come into ear

jimagua (*Caribe*) Ⓐ ADJ identical
Ⓑ SMF twin

jimba SF 1 (*Andes*) (= *trenza*) pigtail, plait, braid (*EEUU*)
2 (*Méx*) (= *bambú*) bamboo
3 (*Méx**) (= *borrachera*) drunkenness

jimbal SM (*Méx*) bamboo thicket

jimbito SM (*CAm*) (= *avispa*) small wasp; (= *nido*) wasps' nest

jimbo ADJ (*Méx*) drunk

jimeno⁑ SM (*Méx*) cop*

jimio SM = **simio**

jinaiste* SM (*Méx*) bunch of kids

jincar* ▸conjug 1g◂ VT (*CAm*) to spike

jindama* SF fear, funk*

jindarse* ▸conjug 1a◂ VPR **se lo jindó todo** he scoffed the lot*

jineta[1] SF (*esp LAm*) horsewoman, rider; **a la ~** with short stirrups

jineta[2] SF (*Zool*) genet

jinete SM horseman, rider; (*Mil*) cavalryman

jinetear ▸conjug 1a◂ Ⓐ VT 1 (*LAm*) (= *montar*) to ride; (= *domar*) to break in; ✦*MODISMO* **~ la burra** (*CAm*) to go the whole hog, stake everything
2 (*Méx**) [+ *fondos*] to misappropriate
Ⓑ VI to ride around
Ⓒ **jinetearse** VPR 1 (*Andes, Méx*) (= *no caerse*) to stay in the saddle; (*fig*) (*) to hang on, keep going
2 (*Andes*) (= *ser presumido*) to be vain

jinetera* (*Cuba*) SF prostitute

jingoísmo SM jingoism

jingoísta Ⓐ ADJ jingoistic
Ⓑ SMF jingoist, jingo

jiote SM (*Méx*) rash, impetigo

jipa SF (*Andes*) Panama hat, straw hat

jipar* ▸conjug 1a◂ VT **le tengo jipado** I've got him taped*, I've got him all sized up

jipatera SF (*Andes, Caribe, Méx*), **jipatez** SF (*Caribe, Méx*) paleness, wanness

jipato ADJ (*LAm*) (= *pálido*) pale, wan; (= *enclenque*) sickly, frail; (= *soso*) tasteless

jipe SM (*Andes, Méx*), **jipi**[1] SM Panama hat, straw hat

jipi[2] SMF hippy

jipijapa (*LAm*) Ⓐ SF (= *paja*) fine woven straw
Ⓑ SM (*esp LAm*) (= *sombrero*) Panama hat, straw hat

jipioso/a* Ⓐ ADJ hippyish
Ⓑ SM/F hippy type

jipismo SM hippy movement

jira[1] SF [*de tela*] strip

jira[2] SF (= *excursión*) excursion, outing; (*tb* **~ campestre**) picnic

jirafa SF 1 (*Zool*) giraffe
2 (*TV, Cine*) boom

jiribilla SF (*Méx*) spin, turn; ✦*MODISMO* **tener ~** (*Caribe*) (*gen*) to have its awkward points; [*persona*] to be anxious

jirimiquear ▸conjug 1a◂ VI (*LAm*) = **jeremiquear**

jirón SM 1 (= *andrajo*) rag, shred; **hacer algo jirones** to tear sth to shreds; **hecho jirones** in shreds *o* tatters
2 (= *parte*) bit, shred
3 (*Perú*) (= *calle*) street

jit* [xit] SM (*pl* **jits** [xit]) (*LAm*) hit

jitazo SM (*Méx*) hit, blow; (*Dep*) hit, stroke

jitomate SM (*Méx*) tomato

jiu-jitsu SM jiu-jitsu

JJ.OO. ABR = **Juegos Olímpicos**

jo* EXCL (*para expresar disgusto*) oh!, aw!; (*para expresar sorpresa*) wow!, blimey!*, jeez! (*EEUU**); **¡jo, otra vez!** oh no, not again!, aw no, not again!; **¡jo, jo!** (*al reír*) ho ho!, ha ha!

Job SM Job

jobar* EXCL (*para expresar disgusto*) oh!, aw!; (*para expresar sorpresa*) wow!, blimey!*, jeez! (*EEUU**)

jobo SM [1] (*CAm, Méx Bot*) cedar, cedar tree
[2] (*CAm**) (= *aguardiente*) spirits

jockey ['joki] SM (*pl* **jockeys** ['jokis]) jockey

joco ADJ [1] (*CAm, Méx*) (= *amargo*) sharp, bitter
[2] (*Andes*) (= *hueco*) hollow

jocolote* SM (*CAm*) hut, shack

jocoque SM (*Méx*), **jocoqui** SM (*Méx*) sour milk, sour cream

jocosamente ADV humorously, comically

jocoserio ADJ seriocomic

jocosidad SF [1] (= *cualidad*) humour, humor (*EEUU*), jocularity (*frm*)
[2] (= *chiste*) joke

jocoso ADJ humorous, jocular

joda✱ SF (*esp LAm*) [1] (= *molestia*) bloody nuisance‡
[2] (= *broma*) joke; **lo dijo en ~** he said it as a joke

jodedera✱ SF screwing✱

joder✱ ▸conjug 2a◂ Ⓐ VT [1] (= *copular*) to fuck✱, screw✱
[2] (= *fastidiar*) to piss off✱; **me jode que crea que he sido yo** it pisses me off that he thinks it was me✱; **me jodió mucho que perdiera Colombia** I was really pissed off when Colombia lost✱; **me jode tener que pagarlo yo todo** it's a bugger having to pay for it all myself✱, it pisses me off having to pay for it all myself✱; **¡deja ya de ~me de una vez!** stop bugging me!*, stop being such a pain in the arse!‡; **si te deniegan la prórroga esta vez, te han jodido** if they refuse you an extension this time, you've had it* *o* you're fucked✱; ✦***MODISMO*** **no te jode** (*Esp*): **¡no te jode! ¡ahora dice que es amigo nuestro!** can you believe it! — now he's calling himself a friend of ours; **si yo tuviera un coche así también podría ir a esa velocidad,¡no te jode!** if I had a car like that I could go that fast as well, no problem *o* (*EEUU**) no sweat; **a mí también me gustaría ser rico, ¡no te jode!** I'd like to be rich too, wouldn't we all!
[3] (= *estropear*) [+ *aparato*] to bust*, bugger up✱; [+ *planes*] to screw up‡, bugger up✱; **¡me has jodido el reloj!** you've bust* *o* buggered up✱ my watch!, you've busted my watch (*EEUU**); **lo que hacen es ~nos la vida al resto** what they do is fuck✱ *o* screw* *o* bugger✱ things up for the rest of us; ✦***MODISMO*** **~la** to mess things up*, screw things up*; **en cuanto abres la boca la jodes** as soon as you open your mouth you mess *o* screw* things up; **¡la jodimos!** now we've blown it!*
Ⓑ VI [1] (= *copular*) to fuck✱, screw✱
[2] (= *fastidiar*) **ya sé que jode tener que levantarse tan temprano** I know it's a drag* *o* a pain in the arse✱ *o* ass (*EEUU*✱) having to get up so early; **son ganas de ~** they're just trying to be awkward; ✦***MODISMO*** **¡no jodas!** (*indicando sorpresa*) bloody hell!‡, you're kidding!*; (*indicando rechazo*) you must be joking!*
Ⓒ **joderse** VPR [1] (= *fastidiarse*) **ellos a hacerse ricos y los demás a ~se** they get rich and the rest of us can go to hell‡ *o* can go screw ourselves✱; **¡(es que) hay que ~se!** for fuck's sake!✱; **¡que se joda!** screw him!✱; **si no les gusta ¡que se jodan!** if they don't like it, tough shit!✱; **¡te jodes!** tough shit!✱
[2] (= *estropearse*) **se me ha jodido el coche** the car's had it*, the car's buggered‡; **cuando llegó él se jodió todo** when he arrived it messed* *o* screwed✱ everything up
[3] **~se la espalda/una pierna** to do one's back/leg in*; **se jodió el pie jugando al fútbol** he did his foot in playing football*
Ⓓ EXCL (*Esp*) shit!‡, bloody hell!‡; **¡joder! no me esperaba este regalo** shit!‡ *o* bloody hell!‡, I didn't expect a present like this; **cállate ya ¡joder!** for Christ's sake, shut up!*, shut the fuck up!✱, shut up for fuck's sake!✱; **esto hay que celebrarlo, ¡joder!** come on, this calls for a celebration!, hell, this we have to celebrate!‡; **pero ¿cómo no iba a asustarme, ~?** well, of course I was frightened, for Christ's sake, who wouldn't be?*; **~ con: ¡~ con el pesado ese! ¡no se va a callar nunca!** God* *o* Christ*, isn't that pain in the arse ever going to shut up!; **¡~ con tu hermanito! ¡matrícula de honor!** shit✱ *o* God* *o* Christ‡, I can't believe your brother got a distinction!

jodido✱ ADJ [1] (*con ser*) [*situación*] bloody awkward‡; **va a ser ~ tener que enfrentarse a él** it'll be bloody‡ *o* damn‡ awkward having to confront him; **la cárcel es muy jodida** it's bloody‡ *o* damn‡ hard being in jail; **es un libro ~** it's a bloody difficult book‡, it's a helluva difficult book*
[2] (*con estar*) [2·1] [*persona*] (= *en mal estado*) in a bad way, fucked✱, buggered✱; (= *desanimado*) pissed off✱
[2·2] (= *estropeado*) (= *aparato, vehículo*) bust*, busted (*EEUU**)
[3] (= *maldito*) damn‡, bloody‡; **¡qué guapo es el muy ~!** he's damn‡ *o* bloody‡ good-looking!; **ni un jodido euro** not one bloody euro‡; **¡el ~ coche no arranca otra vez!** the damn‡ *o* bloody‡ *o* fucking✱ car won't start again!
[4] (*LAm**) (= *molesto*) damned annoying‡, bloody annoying‡; **esa clienta es muy jodida** she's a bloody annoying customer‡
[5] (*LAm*) [*persona*] (= *egoísta*) selfish; (= *malo*) evil, wicked; (= *exigente*) awkward; (= *zalamero*) smarmy, greasy

jodienda✱ SF [1] (= *acto sexual*) fucking✱
[2] (= *fastidio*) fucking nuisance✱

jodón✱ ADJ (*LAm*) [1] (= *molesto*) bloody annoying‡; **es tan ~** he loves arsing about✱
[2] (= *tramposo*) slippery

jodontón✱ ADJ randy*, oversexed

jofaina SF washbasin, bathroom sink (*EEUU*)

jogging ['joɣin] SM [1] (*Dep*) jogging; **hacer ~** to jog
[2] (*Arg*) (= *ropa*) jogging suit

jojoba SF jojoba

jojoto Ⓐ ADJ (*Caribe*) [*fruta*] (= *manchado*) bruised; (= *inmaduro*) green, underripe; [*maíz*] tender
Ⓑ SM (*Ven*) (ear of) corn *o* maize

jol SM hall, lobby

jolgórico ADJ riotous, hilarious

jolgorio SM fun, revelry; **ir de ~** to go on a binge

jolín* EXCL, **jolines*** EXCL flip!*

jolinche ADJ, **jolino** ADJ (*Méx*) short-tailed, bob-tailed

jolón SM (*Méx*) (= *avispa*) wasp; (= *avispero*) wasps' nest

jolongo SM [1] (*Caribe*) (= *bolsa*) shoulder-bag
[2] (*) (= *problema*) problem

jolote SM (*CAm, Méx*) turkey

joma SF (*Méx*) hump

jombado ADJ (*Méx*), **jombeado** ADJ (*Méx*) hunchbacked

Jonás SM Jonah

Jonatás SM Jonathan

jónico ADJ Ionic

jonja SF (*Cono Sur*) mimicry

jonjear ▸conjug 1a◂ VT (*Cono Sur*) to tease, make fun of

jonjolear* ▸conjug 1a◂ VT (*Andes*) to spoil

jonrón SM (*esp LAm*) (= *béisbol*) home run

jonronear ▸conjug 1a◂ VI (*LAm Dep*) to make a home run

JONS [xons] SFPL ABR (*Esp Hist*) = **Juntas de Ofensiva Nacional Sindicalista**

jopé‡ EXCL (*para expresar disgusto*) oh!, aw!; (*para expresar sorpresa*) wow!, blimey!*, jeez! (*EEUU**)

jopo[1] SM brush, tail

jopo[2] EXCL out!, get out!

jora SF (*LAm*) *maize specially prepared for making high-grade chicha*

Jordán SM Jordan, Jordan river; ✦***MODISMO*** **ir al ~** to be rejuvenated

Jordania SF Jordan

jordano/a ADJ, SM/F Jordanian

jorga* SF (*Andes*) gang

Jorge SM George

jorgón SM (*Andes*) lot, abundance

jorguín/ina SM/F sorcerer/sorceress

jorguinería SF sorcery, witchcraft

jornada SF [1] (= *tiempo de trabajo*) **media ~** half day ► **jornada anual** working days in the year ► **jornada completa** full (working) day ► **jornada continua** = **jornada intensiva** ► **jornada de ocho horas** eight-hour day ► **jornada inglesa** five-day week ► **jornada intensiva** *full day's work with no lunch break* ► **jornada laboral** (*al día*) working day; (*a la semana*) working week; (*al año*) working year ► **jornada legal** maximum legal working hours ► **jornada partida** split shift ► **jornada semanal** working week
[2] (= *día*) day ► **jornada de huelga** day of industrial action ► **jornada de lucha** day of action ► **jornada de movilización** day of action, day of protest ► **jornada de reflexión** (*Pol*) day before the election (*on which campaigning is banned*) ► **jornada informativa** open day, open house (*EEUU*)
[3] [*de viaje*] day's journey; (= *etapa*) stage (of a journey); **a largas ~s** (*Mil*) by forced marches
[4] (*Mil*) expedition; **la ~ de Orán** the expedition against Oran
[5] **jornadas** (*Univ*) congress, conference; **"Jornadas Cervantinas"** "Conference on Cervantes"
[6] (= *vida*) lifetime, life span

[7] (*Teat, Hist*) act
[8] (*Cono Sur*) (= *sueldo*) day's wage

jornadista SMF (*Univ*) conference member, delegate

jornal SM (= *sueldo*) (day's) wage; (= *trabajo*) day's work; **política de ~es y precios** prices and incomes policy; **trabajar a ~** to be paid by the day ► **jornal mínimo** minimum wage

jornalero/a SM/F (day) labourer, (day) laborer (*EEUU*)

joro SM (*Caribe*) small basket

joroba SF [1] [*de persona, camello*] hump
[2] (*) (= *fastidio*) pain*, drag*

jorobado/a Ⓐ ADJ [1] (= *con chepa*) hunch-backed
[2] (*) (= *fastidiado*) **ando algo ~ con la espalda** my back's giving me a bit of trouble, my back's playing up a bit*; **la artritis lo tiene ~** arthritis makes his life a misery
[3] (*) [*tema, asunto, decisión*] tricky
Ⓑ SM/F (= *con chepa*) hunchback

jorobar* ►conjug 1a◄ Ⓐ VT [1] (= *fastidiar*) to annoy; **lo que más me joroba es que no reconozcan mi trabajo** what annoys me most is that they don't acknowledge the work I do; **esa música me está empezando a ~** that music is beginning to get on my nerves; **¡no me jorobes!** get off my back!
[2] (= *estropear*) [+ *aparato*] to mess up, wreck; [+ *planes, fiesta*] to bust*, ruin, screw up‡
Ⓑ VI **sólo lo hace por ~** he only does it to be annoying
Ⓒ **jorobarse** VPR [1] (= *aguantarse*) **no puedo hacer nada, así que tendré que ~me** there's nothing I can do, so I'll just have to grin and bear it; **pues ¡que se jorobe!** well, he can lump it!*; **¡hay que ~se!** for God's sake!*, bloody hell!‡
[2] (= *estropearse*) [*aparato*] to be wrecked, be bust*; [*planes*] to be ruined; [*fiesta*] to be ruined
[3] **~se una pierna/una rodilla** to do one's leg/a knee in*

jorobeta SF (*Cono Sur*) nuisance

jorobón ADJ (*LAm*) annoying

joronche* SM (*Méx*) hunchback

jorongo SM (*Méx*) poncho, sleeveless poncho

joropo SM (*Ven Mús*) *(national) Venezuelan dance*

jorro SM (*Caribe*) poor-quality cigarette

jorungo* ADJ (*Caribe*) (= *molesto*) annoying, irritating

José SM Joseph

Josefina SF Josephine

Josué SM Joshua

jota[1] SF [1] (name of the letter) J; ✦**MODISMO sin faltar una ~** to a T
[2] ✦**MODISMO ni ~**: **no entendió ni ~** he didn't understand a word of it; **no saber ni ~** to have no idea
[3] (*Mús*) *Spanish dance and tune, esp Aragonese*
[4] (*Naipes*) knave, jack

jota[2] SF (*Andes, Cono Sur Orn*) vulture

jote SM (*Cono Sur*) [1] (= *buitre*) buzzard
[2] (= *cometa*) large kite
[3] (= *desagradecido*) ungrateful person
[4] (= *cura*) priest

joto* Ⓐ ADJ (*Méx*) effeminate
Ⓑ SM [1] (*Méx*) effeminate person, queer‡, fag (*EEUU*‡)
[2] (*Andes*) bundle

jovato/a* SM/F (*Cono Sur*) old man/old woman

joven Ⓐ ADJ [*persona, animal*] young; [*aspecto*] youthful
Ⓑ SMF young man/young woman; (*como apelativo*) young man/young lady; **los jóvenes** young people, youth, the young; **¡joven!** (*Méx*) (*al cliente*) (yes), sir?; (*al empleado*) excuse me!

jovencito/a SM/F youngster

jovial ADJ jolly, cheerful

jovialidad SF jolliness, cheerfulness

jovialmente ADV in a jolly way, cheerfully

joya SF [1] (= *adorno*) jewel, gem; **~s** jewels, jewellery, jewelry (*EEUU*) ► **joyas de fantasía** costume jewellery, imitation jewellery
[2] (= *objeto preciado*) gem, treasure
[3] [*de novia*] trousseau

joyería SF [1] (= *tienda*) jeweller's o (*EEUU*) jeweler's (shop)
[2] (= *joyas*) jewellery, jewelry (*EEUU*), jewels

joyero/a Ⓐ SM/F jeweller, jeweler (*EEUU*)
Ⓑ SM (= *estuche*) jewel case

joystick ['joiestik] (*pl* **joysticks**) SM joystick

Jruschov SM Khrushchev

juagar ►conjug 1h◄ VT (*Andes*) = **enjuagar**

Juan SM John; **San ~ Bautista** St John the Baptist; **San ~ Evangelista** St John the Evangelist; **San ~ de la Cruz** St John of the Cross; **un buen ~** a good-natured fool; **ser un Don ~** to be a Romeo ► **Juan Lanas** (*CAm pey*) simpleton; (= *marido*) henpecked husband ► **Juan Palomo** (= *solitario*) lone wolf, loner; (= *egoísta*) *person who looks after Number One* ► **Juan Vainas** = **Juan Lanas** ► **Juan Zoquete** country bumpkin

juan* SM (*Méx*) common soldier

Juana SF Joan, Jean, Jane; **~ de Arco** Joan of Arc

juana SF [1] (*Andes*) (= *prostituta*) whore
[2] (*Méx**) marijuana
[3] (*CAm**) cop*

juancarlismo SM *support for King Juan Carlos I*

juancarlista Ⓐ ADJ *of or relating to King Juan Carlos I*; **ser ~** to be a supporter of King Juan Carlos I
Ⓑ SMF supporter of King Juan Carlos I

juancho SM (*Andes*) boyfriend, lover

juanete SM [1] (*en el pie*) bunion
[2] (*Náut*) topgallant sail
[3] (*Andes, CAm*) (= *cadera*) hip

juanillo* SM (*Andes, Cono Sur*) bribe

juapao SM (*Caribe*) beating, thrashing

jubilación SF [1] (= *acción*) retirement ► **jubilación anticipada** early retirement ► **jubilación forzosa** compulsory retirement ► **jubilación voluntaria** voluntary retirement
[2] (= *pensión*) retirement pension

jubilado/a Ⓐ ADJ [1] [*trabajador*] retired; **vivir ~** to live in retirement
[2] (*Andes, Caribe**) (= *sagaz*) wise
[3] (*Andes**) (= *lerdo*) thick*, slow-witted
Ⓑ SM/F retired person, pensioner

jubilar ►conjug 1a◄ Ⓐ VT [1] [+ *trabajador*] to pension off, retire
[2] (*hum*, *) (= *desechar*) [+ *objeto*] to discard; [+ *persona*] to put out to grass
Ⓑ **jubilarse** VPR [1] [*trabajador*] to retire; **~se anticipadamente** to take early retirement, retire early
[2] (*CAm*) (= *hacer novillos*) to play truant
[3] (*Caribe**) (= *instruirse*) to gain experience
[4] (*Andes**) (= *deteriorarse*) to deteriorate, go downhill; (= *enloquecer*) to lose one's head

jubileo SM (*Rel*) jubilee

júbilo SM joy, rejoicing, jubilation; **con ~** joyfully

jubiloso ADJ jubilant

jubón SM [*de hombre*] doublet, jerkin; [*de mujer*] bodice

jud SM (*CAm Aut*) bonnet, hood (*EEUU*)

Judá SM Judah

judaico ADJ Jewish, Judaic

judaísmo SM Judaism

judaizante Ⓐ ADJ Judaizing
Ⓑ SMF Judaizer

Judas SM [1] (= *nombre*) Judas
[2] (= *muñeco*) Easter effigy

judas SM INV [1] (= *traidor*) traitor, betrayer
[2] (= *muñeco*) Easter effigy
[3] (= *mirilla*) peephole
[4] (*Cono Sur**) snooper*

Judea SF Judea

judeoespañol ADJ, SM Judeo-Spanish

judería SF [1] (= *barrio*) Jewish quarter
[2] (= *judíos*) Jewry
[3] (*CAm, Méx**) (= *travesura*) prank

judía SF bean ► **judía blanca** haricot bean ► **judía colorada** runner bean ► **judía de la peladilla**, **judía de Lima** Lima bean ► **judía escarlata** runner bean ► **judía pinta** pinto bean ► **judía verde** green bean; *ver tb* **judío**

judiada SF [1] (= *acto cruel*) cruel thing
[2] (*Fin*) extortion

judicatura SF [1] (= *jueces*) judiciary
[2] (= *cargo*) office of judge

judicial ADJ judicial; **recurrir a la vía ~** to go to law, have recourse to law

judío/a Ⓐ ADJ [1] [*pueblo, religión*] Jewish
[2] (*pey*) (= *tacaño*) mean, miserly
Ⓑ SM/F Jew/Jewess, Jewish man/woman; *ver tb* **judía**

Judit SF Judith

judo SM judo

judoca SMF, **judoka** SMF judoist, judoka

juego[1] *ver* **jugar**

juego[2] SM [1] (= *acto*) play; **se acabó el tiempo de ~** it's time to stop playing; **el balón está en ~** the ball is in play; **estar fuera de ~** [*jugador*] to be offside; [*balón*] to be out of play; **por ~** for fun ► **juego duro** rough play ► **juego limpio** fair play ► **juego sucio** (*Ftbl*) foul play, dirty play; (*fig*) dirty tricks *pl*
[2] (*como entretenimiento*) game; **es solamente un ~** it's only a game; **el ~ del ajedrez** the game of chess; **"~ terminado"** "game over"; ✦**MODISMO ser un ~ de niños** to be child's play ► **juego de azar** game of chance ► **juego de cartas** card game ► **juego de destreza** game of skill ► **juego de la cuna** cat's cradle ► **el juego de la oca** ≈ snakes and ladders ► **juego de manos** conjuring trick ► **juego de mesa** board game ► **juego de ordenador** computer game ► **juego de palabras** pun, play on words ► **juego de rol** role-playing game ► **juego de salón**, **juego de sociedad** parlour game ► **juego educativo** educational game ► **juego infantil** childrens' game, game for children ► **juegos malabares** juggling; **hacer ~s malabares con algo** to juggle sth

3 **juegos** (*Dep*) (= *competición*) ► **juegos atléticos** (*LAm*) athletics championships ► **Juegos Olímpicos** Olympic Games ► **Juegos Olímpicos de Invierno** Winter Olympics

4 (= *jugada*) (*en tenis*) game; (*de cartas*) hand; (*en bridge*) rubber; **~, set y partido** game, set and match

5 (*con apuestas*) gambling; **el ~ es un vicio** gambling is a vice; **lo perdió todo en el ~** he gambled everything away, he lost everything through gambling; **¡hagan ~!** place your bets!; ✦*MODISMOS* **estar en ~** to be at stake; **lo que está en ~** what is at stake; **hay diversos intereses en ~** there are various interests at stake; **los factores que entran en ~** the factors that come into play; **poner algo en ~** (= *arriesgar*) to place sth at risk; (= *recurrir a*) to bring sth to bear

6 (= *estrategia*) game; **le conozco** *o* **veo el ~** I know his little game, I know what he's up to; ✦*MODISMOS* **seguir el ~ a algn** to play along with sb; **hacer un ~ doble** to be playing a double game

7 (= *conjunto*) [*de vajilla*] set, service; [*de muebles*] suite; [*de herramientas*] kit; **con falda a ~** with skirt to match, with matching skirt; **las cortinas hacen ~ con el sofá** the curtains match the sofa, the curtains go with the sofa ► **juego de bolas** (*Mec*) ball bearing, set of ball bearings ► **juego de café** coffee set, coffee service ► **juego de cama** set of matching bedlinen ► **juego de campanas** peal of bells ► **juego de caracteres** character set ► **juego de comedor** dining-room suite ► **juego de luces** (*de árbol de Navidad*) fairy lights *pl*; (*en fiesta, espectáculo*) decorative lights *pl* ► **juego de mesa** dinner service ► **juego de programas** (*Inform*) suite, suite of programmes ► **juego de té** tea set, tea service

8 [*de mecanismo*] play, movement; **el ~ de la rodilla** the movement of the knee; **estar en ~** to be in gear

9 (= *efecto*) play; **el ~ de las luces sobre el agua** the play of light on the water; **el ~ de los colores** the interplay of the colours

10 (*Pelota*) (= *pista*) court; **en el ~ de pelota** on the pelota court

juepucha‡ EXCL (*Cono Sur*) well I'm damned!

juerga* SF binge*; **ir de ~** to go out for a good time; **correr grandes ~s** to live it up*; **¡vaya ~ que nos vamos a correr!** we'll have a great time!

juergata‡ SF = juerga

juerguearse* ▸conjug 1a◂ VPR to live it up*

juerguista SMF reveller

juev. ABR (= **jueves**) Thur, Thurs

jueves SM INV Thursday; ✦*MODISMO* **no es nada del otro ~** it's nothing to write home about ► **Jueves Santo** Maundy Thursday; *ver tb* **sábado**

juez SMF (SF *a veces* **jueza**) 1 (*Jur*) judge; ✦*MODISMO* **ser ~ y parte** to be an interested party ► **juez árbitro** arbitrator, referee ► **juez de diligencias, juez de instrucción** examining magistrate ► **juez de paz** justice of the peace, magistrate ► **juez de primera instancia, juez instructor** examining magistrate ► **juez municipal** magistrate

2 (*Dep*) judge ► **juez de banda, juez de línea** (*Ftbl*) linesman; (*Rugby*) touch judge; (*Tenis*) umpire ► **juez de salida** starter ► **juez de silla** umpire

jugable ADJ playable

jugada SF 1 (*Dep*) piece of play; (*Ftbl, Ajedrez*) move; **una bonita ~** a lovely piece of play, a lovely move; **hacer una ~** to make a move ► **jugada a balón parado** (*Ftbl*) set piece ► **jugada de pizarra** textbook move

2 (*Golf*) stroke, shot

3 **(mala) ~** dirty trick; **hacer** *o* **gastar una mala ~ a algn** to play a dirty trick on sb

4 (*Méx*) dodge

jugado ADJ (*Andes*) expert, skilled

jugador(a) SM/F 1 [*de deporte, juegos de mesa*] player ► **jugador(a) de ajedrez** chess player ► **jugador(a) de baloncesto** basketball player ► **jugador(a) de fútbol** footballer, football player ► **jugador(a) de manos**† conjurer

2 [*de apuestas*] gambler ► **jugador(a) de bolsa** stock market speculator

jugar ▸conjug 1h, 1n◂ Ⓐ VI 1 [*niño, deportista*] to play; **¡si seguís así yo no juego!** if you carry on like that I'm not playing!; **~ a algo** to play sth; **~ al ajedrez** to play chess; **~ al tenis** to play tennis; **~ a la lotería** to play the lottery; **~ a la ruleta** to play roulette; **~ a los dados** to play dice; **~ al escondite** to play hide-and-seek; **~ con algo** to play with sth; **no le gusta ~ con muñecas** he doesn't like playing with dolls; **está jugando con el ordenador** she's playing on the computer; **~ contra algn** to play (against) sb; **hoy juegan contra el Celtic** today they're playing (against) Celtic; ✦*MODISMOS* **~ con fuego** to play with fire; **~ con ventaja** to be at an advantage, have the advantage; **~ limpio** to play fair; **~ sucio** to play dirty; **de jugando** (*Caribe**) in fun, for fun

2 (= *hacer una jugada*) 2·1 (*en ajedrez, parchís*) to move; **¿quién juega?** whose move *o* turn *o* go is it?

2·2 (*con cartas*) to play; **¿quién juega?** whose turn *o* go is it?

3 (= *pretender ser*) **~ a algo** to play at being sth; **sólo está jugando a detective** he's only playing at being a detective; **yo no juego a ser estrella de Hollywood** I'm not playing at being a Hollywood star; **vamos a ~ a que yo soy la madre y tú el hijo** let's pretend that I'm the mother and you the son

4 **~ con** 4·1 (= *manosear*) (*gen*) to play around with, mess around with; (*distraídamente*) to toy with, fiddle with; **no juegues con el enchufe, que es peligroso** don't play *o* mess around with the plug — it's dangerous; **estaba jugando con un bolígrafo mientras hablaba** he was toying *o* fiddling with a pen while he spoke

4·2 (= *no tomar en serio*) [*sentimientos*] to play with; **solamente está jugando contigo** he's just leading you on; **es importante permanecer en el poder, pero no a costa de ~ con la opinión pública** it is important to stay in power, but not if it means gambling with public opinion; **con la salud no se juega** you can't put your health at risk

4·3 (= *utilizar*) to play with; **esta obra juega con el tema del teatro dentro del teatro** this work plays with the idea of a play within a play

5 (= *influir*) **~ en contra de algo/algn** to work against sth/sb; **su inexperiencia jugaba en contra suya** his inexperience worked against him; **la posición del sol jugaba en contra de nuestro equipo** the position of the sun put our team at a disadvantage; **~ a favor de algo/algn** [*situación*] to work in sth/sb's favour *o* (*EEUU*) favor; [*tiempo, destino*] to be on sb's side; **las ventajas de una moneda débil siguen jugando a su favor** the advantages of a weak currency continue to work in their favour; **existe otro elemento que juega a favor del acusado** there is another factor that should go *o* work in favour of the defendant; **has estudiado mucho y eso juega a tu favor** you have studied a lot and that should work in your favour

6 (= *apostar*) to gamble

7 (*Bolsa*) to speculate; **~ al alza** to bet on a bull market; **~ a la baja** to bet on a bear market; **~ a la bolsa** to play the stock market

8 (*LAm Mec*) to move about

Ⓑ VT 1 [+ *partida, partido*] to play; **el partido se juega hoy** the match will be played today; ✦*MODISMOS* **~ la baza de algo**: **la oposición ~á la baza de la moción de censura** the opposition will play its trump card and move a motion of censure; **jugársela a algn*** to do the dirty on sb*; **su hermano se la jugó** his brother did the dirty on him*; **¡me la han jugado!** I've been had!*; **su mujer se la jugaba con otro** (*LAm*) his wife was two-timing him*; *ver tb* **baza 2**

2 [+ *papel*] to play; **juegan un papel fundamental en el desarrollo del país** they play a fundamental role in the country's development

3 (= *apostar*) to bet; **~ cinco dólares a una carta** to bet *o* put five dollars on a card

4 (*LAm*) [+ *fútbol, tenis, ajedrez, póker*] to play

5 (††) [+ *espada, florete*] to handle, wield

Ⓒ **jugarse** VPR 1 [+ *dinero*] (= *apostar*) to bet, stake; (= *perder*) to gamble away; **se jugó 500 dólares** he bet *o* staked 500 dollars; **se jugó la fortuna a la ruleta** he gambled away his fortune at roulette; **jugárselo todo a una carta** (*lit*) to bet everything on one card; (*fig*) to put all one's eggs in one basket

2 (*como reto*) to bet; **me juego lo que quieras a que no te atreves** I bet you anything you won't dare; **¿qué te juegas a que tengo razón?** what do you bet I'm right?, what's the betting I'm right?

3 (= *exponerse a perder*) 3·1 (*en una apuesta consciente*) to stake; **nos jugamos mucho en esta operación** we're staking a lot on this operation; **jugárselo todo en algo** to stake everything on sth; **ambos equipos se lo juegan todo hoy** both teams are staking everything on today's match; ✦*MODISMOS* **jugársela**: **conducir más deprisa hubiera sido jugársela** to drive any faster would have been too risky; **España se la juega ante Italia esta noche** Spain is staking everything on their match with Italy tonight; **~se el todo por el todo** to take the plunge

3·2 (= *sin darse cuenta*) **nos estamos jugando el futuro de la democracia** the future of democracy is at stake here; **¿qué nos jugamos en las próximas elecciones?** what is at stake for us in the next election?; **esto es ~se la vida** this means risking one's life

jugarreta SF dirty trick; **hacer una ~ a algn** to play a dirty trick on sb

juglar SM minstrel, jongleur

juglaresco ADJ **arte ~** art of the minstrel(s); **estilo ~** minstrel style, popular style

juglaría SF minstrelsy, art of the minstrel(s)

jugo SM 1 (= *líquido*) (*gen*) juice; [*de carne*] gravy; [*de árbol*] sap ► **jugo de naranja** orange juice ► **jugos digestivos** digestive juices ► **jugos gástricos** gastric juices
2 (= *sustancia*) essence, substance; **sacar el ~ a algo** to get the most out of sth

jugosidad SF juiciness, succulence

jugoso ADJ 1 [*alimento*] juicy, succulent
2 (= *rentable*) [*aumento, reducción*] substantial, considerable; [*negocio*] profitable; **un discurso ~** a speech that gives/gave plenty of food for thought

jugué, juguemos *etc ver* **jugar**

juguera SF (*Cono Sur*) blender, liquidizer

juguete SM 1 (= *objeto*) toy; **un cañón de ~** a toy gun ► **juguete educativo** educational toy
2 (*uso figurado*) toy, plaything; **fue el ~ de las olas** the waves tossed it about as if it were their plaything
3 (= *chiste*) joke
4 (*Teat*) skit, sketch

juguetear ▸conjug 1a◂ VI to play, sport; **~ con** to play with, sport with

jugueteo SM playing, romping

juguetería SF 1 (= *tienda*) toyshop
2 (= *industria*) toy business

juguetero/a Ⓐ ADJ toy *antes de s*
Ⓑ SM/F toyshop owner
Ⓒ SM (= *mueble*) whatnot

juguetón ADJ playful

juicio SM 1 (= *inteligencia*) judgment, reason
2 (= *sensatez*) good sense; **asentar el ~** to come to one's senses; **lo dejo a su ~** I leave it to your discretion; **estar en su sano ~** to be in one's right mind; **estar fuera de ~** to be out of one's mind; **perder el ~** to go mad; **no tener ~** ◊ **tener poco ~** to lack common sense; **tener mucho ~** to be sensible
3 (= *opinión*) opinion; **a mi ~** in my opinion ► **juicio de valor** value judgment
4 (*Jur*) (= *proceso*) trial; (= *veredicto*) verdict, judgment; **llevar a algn a ~** to take sb to court ► **juicio civil** criminal trial ► **juicio con jurado** trial by jury ► **juicio criminal** criminal trial ► **juicio de Dios** trial by ordeal ► **juicio en rebeldía** judgment by default ► **Juicio Final** Last Judgment ► **juicio sumario** summary trial

juicioso ADJ sensible, judicious

juilipío SM (*Andes*) sparrow

juilón⁑ ADJ (*Méx*) yellow

JUJEM [xu'xem] SF ABR (*Esp Mil*) = **Junta de Jefes del Estado Mayor**

jul. ABR (= **julio**) Jul, July

julai⁑ SM, **jula**⁑ SM 1 (= *idiota*) twit*, berk⁑
2 (= *homosexual*) poofter⁑

julandra⁑ SM, **julandrón**⁑ SM = **julai**

julepe SM 1 (*Naipes*) *card game*
2 (*) (= *reprimenda*) telling-off*, dressing-down*
3 (*LAm**) (= *susto*) scare, fright; **irse** *o* **salir de ~** (*Andes*) to run away in terror
4 (*Caribe, Méx**) (= *trabajo*) bind*
5 **meter un ~** (*Andes*) to hurry on, speed up
6 (= *bebida*) julep

julepear* ▸conjug 1a◂ Ⓐ VT 1 (*Cono Sur*) (= *asustar*) to scare, frighten
2 (*Méx*) (= *cansar*) to wear out, tire out
3 (*Andes*) (= *apresurar*) to hurry along, speed up
Ⓑ **julepearse** VPR (*Cono Sur*) (= *asustarse*) to get scared; (= *estar atento*) to smell danger

julia* SF (*Méx*) Black Maria*, paddy wagon (*EEUU**)

Julián SM, **Juliano** SM Julian

juliana SF (*Culin*) julienne; **cortar en ~** to cut into thin shreds, cut into julienne strips

Julieta SF Juliet

Julio SM Julius; **~ César** Julius Caesar

julio SM July; *ver tb* **septiembre**

juma* SF drunkenness, drunken state

jumadera* SF (*Méx*) 1 drunkenness, drunken state
2 (= *humareda*) cloud of smoke

jumado* ADJ drunk, plastered*

jumar* ▸conjug 1a◂ Ⓐ VI to pong⁑, stink
Ⓑ **jumarse** VPR to get drunk

jumatán* SM (*Caribe*) drunkard

jumazo⁑ SM (*Caribe*) fag⁑

jumbo SM jumbo, jumbo jet

jumeado* ADJ (*Andes*) drunk, tight*

jumelar⁑ ▸conjug 1a◂ VI to pong⁑, stink

jumento SM (= *animal*) donkey; (= *insulto*) dolt

jumo* ADJ (*LAm*) drunk, plastered*

jumper ['dʒumper] SM (*pl* **jumpers**) (*Cono Sur*) sleeveless sweater

jun. ABR (= **junio**) Jun

junar⁑ ▸conjug 1a◂ Ⓐ VT (= *ver*) to see; (= *mirar*) to watch
Ⓑ VI (*Cono Sur*) to keep a look-out

juncal Ⓐ ADJ 1 (*Bot*) rushy, reedy
2 (= *esbelto*) willowy, lissom
Ⓑ SM reed bed

juncar SM reed bed

juncia SF sedge

junco[1] SM (= *planta*) rush, reed

junco[2] SM (= *barco*) junk

juncoso ADJ 1 (*Bot*) rushy, reedy, reed-like
2 [*lugar*] covered in rushes

jungla SF jungle ► **jungla de asfalto** concrete jungle

junguiano/a ADJ, SM/F Jungian

junio SM June; *ver* **septiembre**

junior ['dʒunjor], **júnior**[1] ['dʒunjor] Ⓐ ADJ INV junior
Ⓑ SMF (*pl* **juniors** *o* **júniors**) junior
Ⓒ SM (*Cono Sur*) office boy

júnior[2] SM (*pl* **juniores**) (*Rel*) novice monk, junior novice

Juno SF Juno

junquera SF rush, bulrush

junquillo SM 1 (*Bot*) jonquil
2 (= *bastón*) rattan; (= *madera*) strip of light wood
3 (*Caribe, Méx*) gold necklace

junta SF 1 (= *reunión*) meeting; **celebrar** *o* **convocar una ~** to hold a meeting ► **junta de acreedores** meeting of creditors ► **junta general de accionistas** general meeting of shareholders ► **junta general extraordinaria** extraordinary general meeting, special meeting (*EEUU*)
2 (= *comité*) (*gen*) council, committee; (*Com, Fin*) board; **la ~ de la asociación** the committee of the association ► **junta de gobierno** governing body ► **junta de portavoces** (*Parl*) House business committee ► **junta directiva** board of directors ► **junta electoral** electoral board ► **junta municipal** council ► **junta rectora** governing body
3 (*Mil*) junta ► **junta militar** military junta
4 (*Esp Pol*) *name given to the governments of some autonomous areas in Spain*
5 (*Téc*) (= *acoplamiento*) joint; (= *arandela*) washer, gasket ► **junta cardán**, **junta universal** universal joint
6 (*LAm*) (= *amistad*) **las malas ~s** the wrong kind of people; **le prohibieron las ~s con esa gente** they forbade him to go out with those people

juntadero SM (*Cono Sur*) meeting place

juntamente ADV 1 **~ con** together with; **entregó su currículum ~ con los documentos justificativos** he handed in his CV together with the supporting documents
2 (= *conjuntamente*) together; **ella y yo ~** she and I together
3 (= *al mismo tiempo*) **eran todos, ~, verdugos y víctimas** all of them were both executioners and victims, all of them were executioners as well as victims

juntar ▸conjug 1a◂ Ⓐ VT 1 (= *colocar juntos*) to put together; **juntó las manos en actitud de plegaria** she put her hands together as if praying; **~on varias mesas** they put several tables together; **junta el armario a la pared** put the cupboard against the wall; **~ dinero** (= *ahorrar*) to save, save up; (= *reunir fondos*) to raise funds, fundraise; **estoy juntando dinero para comprarme una bicicleta** I'm saving up to buy a bicycle
2 (= *reunir*) [+ *amigos, conocidos*] to get together; [+ *participantes, concursantes*] to bring together; **juntó a sus amigos para darles la noticia** he got his friends together to tell them the news; **¿cómo consiguió el director ~ tantas estrellas en una misma película?** how did the director manage to bring together so many stars *o* get so many stars together in one film?; **la final ha juntado a los dos mejores equipos del mundo** the final has brought together the two best teams in the world
3 (= *coleccionar*) [+ *sellos, objetos*] to collect
4 (= *entornar*) [+ *puerta, ventana*] to push to
Ⓑ **juntarse** VPR 1 (= *reunirse*) 1·1 (*para una cita*) to get together, meet up; **por la tarde nos juntamos todos para jugar a las cartas** in the afternoons we all get together *o* meet up to play cards; **~se con algn** to get together with sb, meet up with sb; **a veces se juntan con otros matrimonios y salen por ahí** they sometimes get together *o* meet up with other couples and go out somewhere
1·2 (*en asamblea, trabajo*) to meet; **solían ~se en ese local** they used to meet on those premises
1·3 (*sin citarse*) to come together; **en el estadio se ~án hoy bastantes figuras del fútbol** many famous figures in football will come together in the stadium today; **en la sala apenas se ~on dos docenas de personas** less than two dozen people assembled in the hall; **se ~on más de cinco mil personas para oírlo** more than five thousand people assembled *o* came together to listen to him
2 (= *unirse*) **se fue juntando mucha más gente por el camino** many more people joined them along the way; **se juntan un es-**

permatozoide y un óvulo a sperm and an egg join together; **~se a** *o* **con algn** to join up with sb; **salimos de París por la mañana y en Calais se nos juntó Pedro** we left Paris in the morning and Pedro joined up with us *o* met up with us in Calais; **se juntó a otros dos músicos para crear un nuevo grupo** he joined up with two other musicians to create a new band

[3] (= *arrimarse*) [*varias personas*] to move closer together; **si te juntas un poco más cabremos todos en el banco** if you move up a bit we can all get on the bench

[4] (= *relacionarse*) [*pareja*] to get together; **~se con algn** (*gen*) to mix with sb; (*en pareja*) to get together with sb; **allí se puede uno ~ con la crema de la sociedad** there you can mix with the cream of society; **no me gusta que te juntes con esa gente** I don't like you going round *o* mixing with those people

[5] (= *ocurrir a la vez*) to come together; **en su poesía se juntan elementos tradicionales y renovadores** traditional and new elements come together in his poetry; **la semana pasada se me juntó todo** it was just one thing after another last week; **se ~on dos bodas el mismo día** there were two marriages on the same day; **se te va a ~ el desayuno con la comida** you'll be having breakfast at the same time as your lunch

[6] [*empresas, asociaciones*] to merge; **ambas coordinadoras se ~on en una organización central** both coordinating committees merged to form a centralized organization

[7] [*líneas, caminos*] to meet, join

[8] (*Zool*) to mate, copulate

juntillas *ver* **pie 1**

junto Ⓐ ADJ [1] (= *unido, acompañado*) together; **mételo todo ~ en la maleta** put it all together in the suitcase; **se pone todo ~ en un plato y se sirve** arrange it all in a dish and serve; **sinfín, como sustantivo, se escribe ~** when it is a noun, "sinfín" is written as one word; **nunca había visto tantos libros ~s** I had never seen so many books together in one place; **llevamos quince años ~s** we've been together for fifteen years; **fuimos ~s** we went together; **todos ~s** all together; **trabajar ~s** to work together; **vivir ~s** to live together; ✦***MODISMO*** **~s pero no revueltos** (*hum*) close to each other *o* together, but not in each other's pockets

[2] (= *cercano*) close together; **tenía los ojos muy ~s** his eyes were very close together; **poneos más ~s, que no cabéis en la foto** move a bit closer together, I can't get you all in (the photo)

[3] (= *al mismo tiempo*) together; **las vi entrar juntas** I saw them go in together; **ocurrió todo ~** it happened all at once

Ⓑ ADV [1] **~ a** [1·1] (= *cerca de*) close to, near; **20.000 personas seguían acampadas ~ a la frontera** 20,000 people were still camped close to *o* near the border; **tienen un chalet ~ al mar** they have a house close to *o* near the sea

[1·2] (= *al lado de*) next to, beside; **fue enterrado ~ a su padre** he was buried next to *o* beside his father; **José permanecía de pie, ~ a la puerta** José remained standing by the door

[1·3] (= *en compañía de*) with, together with; **celebró su aniversario ~ a su familia** he celebrated his anniversary (together) with his family; **expresó su deseo de volver ~ a su marido** she expressed a wish to go back to her husband

[1·4] (= *conjuntamente*) together with, along with; **nuestro equipo es, ~ al italiano, el mejor de la liga** together with the Italian team, ours is the best in the league

[2] **~ con** [2·1] (= *en compañía de*) with, together with; **fue detenido ~ con otros cuatro terroristas** he was arrested (together) with four other terrorists; **machacar los ajos en el mortero ~ con el perejil** crush the garlic in the mortar (together) with the parsley

[2·2] (= *conjuntamente*) together with; **el paro es, ~ con el terrorismo, nuestro mayor problema** together with terrorism, unemployment is our biggest problem

[3] **en ~**† in all, all together

[4] **(de) por ~**† (*Com*) wholesale

juntura SF (*Anat, Téc*) joint

jupa SF (*CAm, Méx*) [1] (= *calabaza*) gourd

[2] (‡) (= *cabeza*) head, nut‡, noggin (*EEUU**)

jupata‡ SF jacket

jupiarse ▸conjug 1b◂ VPR (*CAm*) to get drunk

Júpiter SM Jupiter

jura[1] SF (= *juramento*) oath, pledge ► **jura de (la) bandera** (taking the) oath of loyalty *o* allegiance

jura[2]‡ Ⓐ SM (*CAm, Caribe*) cop*

Ⓑ SF **la ~** the cops* *pl*, the fuzz‡

juraco* SM (*CAm*) hole

jurado Ⓐ SM (= *tribunal*) (*Jur*) jury; (*en concurso, TV*) panel (*of judges*)

Ⓑ SMF (= *miembro*) (*Jur*) juror; (*en concurso, TV*) judge

Ⓒ ADJ [*declaración*] sworn; *ver tb* **guarda A1, guardia A, traductor**

juramentar ▸conjug 1a◂ Ⓐ VT to swear in, administer the oath to

Ⓑ **juramentarse** VPR to be sworn in, take the oath

juramento SM [1] (= *promesa*) oath; **bajo ~** on oath; **prestar ~** to take the oath (**sobre** on); **tomar ~ a algn** to swear sb in ► **juramento de fidelidad** oath of loyalty ► **juramento hipocrático** Hippocratic oath

[2] (= *blasfemia*) oath, curse; **decir ~s** to swear

jurar ▸conjug 1a◂ Ⓐ VT [1] (*solemnemente*) to swear; **juró haberlo visto entrar** she swore she had seen him come in; **juró vengarse de ellos** he swore to avenge himself on them; **~ decir la verdad** to swear to tell the truth; **~ (la) bandera** to pledge allegiance (to the flag); **~ el cargo** to be sworn in; **~ la Constitución** to pledge allegiance to the Constitution; **lo juro por mi honor** I swear on my honour; **lo juro por mi madre** I swear to God; ✦***MODISMO*** **tenérsela jurada a algn** (*como venganza personal*) to have it in for sb; (*a nivel político, profesional*) to be after sb's blood

[2] (*uso enfático*) to swear; **no he oído nada, se lo juro** I didn't hear a thing, I swear; **te juro que fue el peor momento de mi vida** I swear it was the worst moment of my life; **~ía que estaba allí hace un momento** I could have sworn he was there a moment ago; **—yo no entiendo mucho de esto —no hace falta que lo jures, guapo** (*iró*) "I don't know much about this sort of thing" — "sure you don't, pal"*

Ⓑ VI (= *blasfemar*) to swear; **¡no jures!** don't swear!; **~ en falso** to commit perjury; ✦***MODISMO*** **~ como un carretero** to swear like a trooper

jurdós‡ SM bread‡, money

jurel SM [1] (= *pez*) horse mackerel

[2] **coger ~*** to get a fright

jurero/a SM/F (*Andes, Cono Sur*) perjurer, false witness

jurgo SM (*Andes*), **jurgonera** SF (*Andes*) = **jorga**

jurídico ADJ legal, juridical; **departamento ~** (*Com*) legal department

jurisdicción SF [1] (= *autoridad*) jurisdiction

[2] (= *distrito*) district, administrative area

jurisdiccional ADJ **aguas ~es** territorial waters

jurispericia SF jurisprudence

jurisperito/a SM/F jurist, legal expert

jurisprudencia SF jurisprudence

jurista SMF jurist

juro SM (= *derecho*) right of perpetual ownership; (= *pago*) annuity, pension; **a ~** (*Andes, Caribe*) ◊ **de ~** certainly

justa SF [1] (*Hist*) joust, tournament

[2] (= *competición*) contest

justamente ADV [1] (= *exactamente*) [1·1] (= *coincidiendo con algo*) just; **la fábrica se instaló en los setenta, ~ cuando estalló la crisis energética** the factory was set up in the seventies, just when the energy crisis broke out; **lo sorprendente es que lo eligieran a él, ~ ahora que …** what is surprising is that he was chosen, just when …; **ocurrió hace ~ un año** it happened exactly a year ago; **~ lo contrario** exactly the opposite

[1·2] (= *referido a cosa, lugar*) exactly, precisely; **es aquí ~ donde está la originalidad del autor** it is precisely in this where the author's originality lies; **ésas son ~ las que no están en venta** those are precisely the ones which are not for sale

[2] (= *con justicia*) justly; **los monumentos por los que la ciudad es ~ famosa** the monuments for which the city is justly famous

[3] (= *escasamente*) frugally; **viven muy ~ con la pensión** they live very frugally on their pension

justar ▸conjug 1a◂ VI to joust, tilt

justicia Ⓐ SF (*gen*) justice; (= *equidad*) fairness, equity; (= *derecho*) right; **de ~** justly, deservedly; **lo estimo de ~** I think it fair; **es de ~ añadir que** it is only fair to add that; **en ~** by rights; **hacer ~ a** to do justice to; **tomarse la ~ por su mano** to take the law into one's own hands ► **justicia gratuita** legal aid ► **justicia poética** poetic justice ► **justicia social** social justice

Ⓑ SM (††) *representative of authority*; **~s y ladrones** cops and robbers*

justiciable ADJ [1] (= *procesable*) actionable

[2] [*decisión*] subject to review by a court

justicialismo SM (*Arg Hist, Pol*) *political movement founded by Perón*; → PERONISMO

justicieramente ADV justly

justiciero ADJ (strictly) just, righteous

justificable ADJ justifiable

▼**justificación** SF justification ► **justificación automática** (*Inform*) automatic justification

justificado ADJ justified; **no ~** unjustified

➤ LENGUA Y USO: **justificación** 53.3

justificante SM [*de dinero*] receipt; [*de enfermedad*] sick note

justificar ▸conjug 1g◂ Ⓐ VT [1] (= *explicar*) to account for, explain; **tendrá que ~ su ausencia del trabajo** she will have to account for *o* explain her absence from work; **el gobierno no pudo ~ el aumento del gasto** the government was unable to account for *o* explain the increase in expenditure; **justificó las compras con facturas** he accounted for his purchases with receipts

[2] (= *excusar*) [+ *decisión, comportamiento*] to justify, excuse; **nada justifica tal violencia** nothing can justify *o* excuse such violence; **siempre justifica a sus hijos ante sus amigas** she always defends her sons to her friends; **es un criminal y no pretendo ~lo** he's a criminal and I'm not trying to make excuses for him

[3] (*Inform, Tip*) to justify

Ⓑ **justificarse** VPR to justify o.s., make excuses for o.s.; **no intentes ~te porque no tienes razón** don't try and justify yourself *o* make excuses for yourself because you're in the wrong; **se justificó diciendo que el tren llegó tarde** he justified himself *o* made his excuses saying the train was late

justificativo ADJ **documento ~** voucher, certificate

justillo SM jerkin

justipreciar ▸conjug 1b◂ VT to evaluate, appraise

justiprecio SM evaluation, appraisal

▼**justo** Ⓐ ADJ [1] (= *con justicia*) [*castigo, sentencia, solución, decisión, sociedad*] fair, just; [*juicio, premio, árbitro, juez*] fair; [*causa*] just; **el pacto me pareció muy ~** the agreement seemed very fair to me; **no es ~ que ganen más los hombres que las mujeres** it's not fair that men should earn more than women; **pero seamos ~s ...** but let's be fair ...; **el premio ha sido ~** the prize was fairly won; **un reparto más ~ de la riqueza** a more equitable *o* just distribution of wealth

[2] (= *exacto*) [*precio, medidas*] exact; **cuesta 10 euros justos** it costs exactly 10 euros; **nació a los tres años ~s de que terminara la guerra** he was born exactly three years after the war ended; **valorar algo en su justa medida** to appreciate sth for its true worth; **tengo el tiempo ~ para tomarme un café** I've got just enough time to have a coffee; **estamos los ~s para jugar al bridge** there's just the right number of us to play bridge

[3] (= *preciso*) **encontró la palabra justa** she found exactly *o* just the right word; **vino en el momento ~** he came just at the right moment

[4] (= *escaso*) **vivimos muy ~s** we have only just enough to live on; **~ de: vamos un poco ~s de tiempo** we're a bit pushed for time; **llegaste muy ~ de tiempo** you only just made it; **el equipo ha llegado a estas alturas de la competición muy ~ de fuerzas** the team have struggled to get this far in the competition; **ando ~ de dinero** money's a bit tight at the moment; **vive con lo ~** he just manages to make ends meet

[5] (= *apretado*) [*ropa*] tight; **el traje me queda** *o* **me viene** *o* **me está muy ~** the suit is very tight for *o* on me; **entramos todos en el coche, pero muy ~s** we all got into the car, but it was a real squeeze

Ⓑ ADV [1] (= *exactamente*) (*gen*) just; (*con cantidades*) exactly; **eso es ~ lo que iba a decir** that's just *o* exactly what I was going to say; **llegó ~ cuando yo salía** she arrived just *o* exactly as I was leaving; **vino ~ a tiempo** he came just in time; **su casa está ~ enfrente del cine** his house is just *o* right opposite the cinema; **¡justo!** that's it!, right!, exactly!; **me costó ~ el doble que a ti** it cost me exactly double what it cost you; **~ lo contrario** exactly the opposite

[2] (= *escasamente*) **vivir muy ~** to just manage to make ends meet, have only just enough to live on

Ⓒ SMPL **los ~s** (*Rel*) the just; ✦*MODISMO* **pagan ~s por pecadores** the innocent pay for the sins of the guilty

jute SM (*CAm*) edible snail

juvenil Ⓐ ADJ [1] [*persona*] youthful; **de aspecto ~** youthful in appearance; **en los años ~es** in one's early years, in one's youth; **obra ~** early work

[2] [*equipo, torneo*] junior

Ⓑ SMF (*Dep*) junior, junior player

juventud SF [1] (= *época*) youth; **en mi ~ no había ordenadores** in my youth *o* when I was young there were no computers; **pecados de ~** youthful indiscretions; ✦*MODISMO* **¡~, divino tesoro!** what it is to be young!

[2] (= *los jóvenes*) young people; **la ~ de hoy** ◊ **la ~ actual** young people today, the youth of today; **la ~ española** Spanish young people; ✦*MODISMO* **~ no conoce virtud** boys will be boys ► **Juventudes Comunistas** Young Communists

[3] (= *cualidad*) youth; **su cutis aún conserva su ~** her complexion is still young

juyungo/a SM/F (*Ecu*) black, mulatto

juzgado SM court ► **juzgado de guardia** police court; **esto es de ~ de guardia** (*fig*) this is an absolute outrage ► **juzgado de instrucción** examining magistrate's court ► **juzgado de lo penal** criminal court ► **juzgado de lo social** social court ► **juzgado de menores** juvenile court ► **juzgado de primera instancia** court of first instance

juzgar ▸conjug 1h◂ VT [1] (= *emitir un juicio*) to judge; **júzguelo usted misma** judge for yourself; **juzgue usted mi sorpresa** imagine my surprise; **~ mal** to misjudge; **a ~ por** to judge by, judging by; **a ~ por lo que hemos visto** to judge by *o* from what we have seen

[2] (= *considerar*) to think, consider; **lo juzgo mi deber** I consider *o* (*frm*) deem it my duty

juzgón ADJ (*CAm, Méx*) hypercritical, carping

➤ LENGUA Y USO: justo B1 40.2

K k

K, k [ka] SF (= *letra*) K, k

K SM ABR (= **kilobyte**) K

ka SF (name of the letter) K

kabuki SM kabuki

Kadsastán SM Kazakhstan

kafkiano ADJ Kafkaesque

káiser SM Kaiser

kaki SM = **caqui**

kamikaze SM kamikaze

Kampuchea SF Kampuchea

kampucheano/a ADJ, SM/F Kampuchean

kaperuj SM (*Andes*) embroidered shawl

kaput* [ka'pu] ADJ kaput*; **hacer ~** to go kaput*, go phut*

karaoke SM karaoke

kárate SM, **karate** SM karate

karateka SMF, **karateca** SMF karate expert

karma SM karma

karting ['kartin] SM, **kárting** ['kartin] SM go-kart racing

KAS SF ABR (= **Koordinadora Abertzale Sozialista**) *Basque nationalist umbrella group*

Katar SM Qatar

katiuska Ⓐ ADJ (*Esp*) **botas ~s** wellington boots Ⓑ SF wellington, wellington boot

kayac SM, **kayak** SM kayak

kazajo/a Ⓐ ADJ, SM/F Kazak, Kazakh
Ⓑ SM (*Ling*) Kazak, Kazakh

Kazajistán SM Kazakhstan

k/c ABR (= **kilociclo(s)**) kc

kebab SM (*pl* **kebabs**) kebab

kedada* SF (*Internet*) gathering *o* meeting (*arranged over the Internet*)

kéfir SM (*Andes*) *type of yoghurt*

Kenia SF Kenya

keniano/a ADJ, SM/F Kenyan

keniata ADJ, SMF Kenyan

kepis SM INV, **kepí** SM *military style round cap or hat*

kermes SM, **kermesse** SM charity fair, bazaar

kerosén SM (*LAm*), **kerosene** SM (*LAm*), **keroseno** SM, **kerosina** SF (*CAm*) kerosene, paraffin

ketchup ['ketʃap, 'ketʃup] SM ketchup, catsup (*EEUU*)

keynesiano/a ADJ, SM/F Keynesian

kg ABR (= **kilogramo(s)**) kg

KHz ABR (= **kilohertzio(s), kilohercio(s)**) KHz

kibutz [ki'βuts] SM (*pl* **kibutzim, kibutz**) kibbutz

kiki⁑ SM joint⁑, reefer⁑

kiko SM *snack of salted, toasted maize*

kikongo SM Kikongo

kilate SM = **quilate**

kilo SM 1 (= *unidad de peso*) kilo; **los ~s de más** those extra kilos; **cuarto de ~** a quarter of a kilo, 250 grams
2 (*) (= *un millón de pesetas*) one million pesetas; **un cuarto de ~** a quarter of a million pesetas, 250,000 pesetas
3 (*) (*como adv*) (= *mucho*) a lot, load*

> **KILOS, METROS, AÑOS**
>
> En inglés cuando la unidad de medida precede al nombre como adjetivo compuesto, debe escribirse en singular y unida por un guión al número correspondiente. En el resto de los casos se emplea en plural, como en español:
>
> Una caja de bombones de dos kilos/La caja de bombones pesa dos kilos
> ***A two-kilo box of chocolates/The box of chocolates weighs two kilos***
> Una regla de 20cms/La regla mide 20cms
> ***A 20-centimetre ruler/The ruler is 20 centimetres long***
> Un muchacho de quince años/El muchacho tiene quince años
> ***A fifteen-year-old boy/The boy is fifteen years old***

kilobyte ['kilobait] SM kilobyte

kilocaloría SF kilocalorie, Calorie

kilociclo SM kilocycle

kilogramo SM kilogramme, kilogram (*EEUU*)

kilohercio SM, **kilohertzio** SM kilohertz

kilolitro SM kilolitre, kiloliter (*EEUU*)

kilometraje SM ≈ mileage

kilometrar ▸conjug 1a◂ VT to measure, measure in kilometres

kilométrico ADJ 1 (*de kilómetro*) kilometric; **(billete) ~** (*Ferro*) ≈ mileage ticket
2 (*) (= *muy largo*) very long; **palabra kilométrica** very long word

kilómetro SM kilometre, kilometer (*EEUU*); **~ cero** (= *punto de partida*) starting point; (*central*) central point; → KILOS, METROS, AÑOS

kilooctecto SM kilobyte

kilopondio SM kilogramme-force

kilotón SM kiloton

kilovatio SM kilowatt

kilovatio-hora SM kilowatt-hour; **kilovatios-hora** kilowatt-hours

kimona SF (*Cuba, Méx*), **kimono** SM kimono

kínder SM (*LAm*), **kindergarten** SM (*LAm*) kindergarten, nursery school

kinesiología SF kinesiology

kión SM (*Andes*) ginger

kiosco SM = **quiosco**

kiosquero/a SM/F = **quiosquero**

Kirguizistán SM Kyrgyzstan

kit SM (*pl* **kits**) kit ► **kit de montaje** self-assembly kit

kitsch [kitʃ] ADJ INV, SM kitsch

kiwi SM 1 (= *ave*) kiwi
2 (= *fruta*) kiwi fruit

klaxon SM horn; **tocar el ~** to blow the horn, toot (the horn)

klínex SM INV tissue, Kleenex®

km ABR (= **kilómetro(s)**) km

km/h ABR (= **kilómetros por hora**) km/h, kmh

knock-out ['nokau] SM, **K.O.** [kaw] SM (= *acto*) knockout; (= *golpe*) knockout blow; **dejar a algn ~** to knock sb out; *ver tb* **noqueo** *etc*

kodak [ko'ðak] SF (*pl* **kodaks** [ko'ðak]) small camera

kohl SM (*para ojos*) kohl

koljós SM (*pl* **koljoses**), **koljoz** [kol'xos] SM (*pl* **koljozi**) kolkhoz

kosovar Ⓐ ADJ Kosovan, Kosovo *antes de s*
Ⓑ SMF Kosovar

Kosovo SM Kosovo

k.p.h. ABR (= **kilómetros por hora**) km/h, kmh

k.p.l. ABR = **kilómetros por litro**

krausismo SM *philosophy and doctrine of K.C.F. Krause*

krausista Ⓐ ADJ Krausist, of Krause
Ⓑ SMF follower of Krause

kuchen SM (*Chile*) fancy cake, fancy German-style cake

Kurdistán SM Kurdistan

kurdo/a Ⓐ ADJ Kurdish
Ⓑ SM/F Kurd
Ⓒ SM (*Ling*) Kurdish

Kuwait SM Kuwait

kuwaití ADJ, SMF Kuwaiti

kv ABR (= **kilovoltio(s)**) kV, kv

kv/h ABR (= **kilovoltios-hora**) kV/h, kv/h

kw ABR (= **kilovatio(s)**) kW, kw

kw/h ABR (= **kilovatios-hora**) kW/h, kw/h

L l

L, l ['ele] SF (= *letra*) L, l

l ABR 1 (= **litro(s)**) l
2 (= **libro**) bk
3 (*Jur*) = **ley**

L/ ABR (= **Letra de Cambio**) B/E, BE

la[1] ART DEF 1 (*con sustantivos*) the; **la mujer** the woman; **La India** India
2 **la de**: **mi casa y la de usted** my house and yours; **esta chica y la del sombrero verde** this girl and the one in the green hat; **la de Pedro es mejor** Peter's is better; **y la de todos los demás** and everybody else's, and that of everybody else; **ir a la de Pepe** to go to Pepe's place; **la de Rodríguez** Mrs Rodríguez; **¡la de goles que marcó!** what a lot of goals he scored!; **¡la de veces que se equivoca!** how often he's wrong!; *ver tb* **el**

la[2] PRON PERS (*refiriéndose a ella*) her; (*refiriéndose a usted*) you; (*refiriéndose a una cosa, un animal*) it; *ver tb* **lo, laísmo**

la[3] SM (*Mús*) la, A; **la menor** A minor

laberintero ADJ (*Méx*) = **laberintoso**

laberíntico ADJ (*gen*) labyrinthine; [*edificio*] rambling

laberinto SM 1 (= *enredo*) [*de corredores, calles*] labyrinth, maze; (*en parque*) maze; [*de situaciones, ideas, reglas*] labyrinth, maze
2 (*esp LAm**) (= *griterío*) row, racket

laberintoso ADJ (*Méx*) 1 (= *ruidoso*) rowdy, brawling
2 (= *chismoso*) gossipy

labia SF fluency; (*pey*) glibness, glib tongue; **tener mucha ~** to have the gift of the gab*

labial ADJ, SF labial

labihendido ADJ harelipped

labio SM (*Anat*) lip; [*de vasija*] edge, rim, lip; **labios** lips, mouth *sing*; **lamerse los ~s** to lick one's lips; **leer los ~s** to lip-read; ✦***MODISMOS*** **de ~s para afuera**: **es muy valiente de ~s para afuera** he comes over brave enough, he seems brave on the face of it; **no descoser los ~s** to keep one's mouth shut; **no morderse los ~s** to be very outspoken, pull no punches; **sin despegar los ~s** without uttering a word ► **labio inferior** lower lip ► **labios mayores** labia majora ► **labio leporino** harelip, cleft lip ► **labios menores** labia minora ► **labio superior** upper lip

labiodental ADJ, SF labiodental

labiolectura SF, **labiología** SF lip-reading

labiosear* ▸conjug 1a◂ VT (*CAm*) to flatter

labiosidad* SF (*Andes, CAm*) flattery

labioso ADJ (*LAm*) 1 (= *hablador*) talkative
2 (= *lisonjero*) flattering
3 (= *persuasivo*) persuasive, glib
4 (= *taimado*) sly

labor SF 1 (= *trabajo*) labour, labor (*EEUU*), work; **"profesión: sus labores"** (*en censo, formulario*) "occupation: housewife"; **una ~** job, task, piece of work ► **labor de chinos** tedious job ► **labor de equipo** teamwork ► **labores domésticas** household chores ► **labor social** work for a good cause, work in a good cause
2 (= *costura*) sewing, needlework; (= *bordado*) embroidery; (= *punto*) knitting; **una ~** a piece of sewing ► **labor de aguja** needlework ► **labor de ganchillo** crochet, crocheting ► **labores de punto** knitting
3 (*Agr*) (= *arada*) ploughing, plowing (*EEUU*); (= *cultivo*) farm work, cultivation
4 **labores** (*Min*) workings
5 (*CAm, Caribe*) (= *parcela*) small farm, smallholding

laborable ADJ 1 [*jornada, semana*] working; **día ~** working day
2 [*tierra, terreno*] arable

laboral ADJ (*gen*) labour *antes de s*, labor (*EEUU*) *antes de s*, work *antes de s*; [*jornada, horario*] working

laboralista ADJ labour *antes de s*, labor *antes de s* (*EEUU*); **abogado ~** labour lawyer

laboralmente ADV **~ productivo** productive in terms of work

laborar ▸conjug 1a◂ Ⓐ VT 1 (*frm*) (= *trabajar*) to work
2 (*Agr*) to work, till (*liter*)
Ⓑ VI 1 (*frm*) (= *trabajar*) to work
2 (= *intrigar*) to scheme, plot

laboratorio SM laboratory ► **laboratorio de idiomas** language laboratory ► **laboratorio espacial** space laboratory

laborear ▸conjug 1a◂ VT (= *trabajar*) to work; (*Agr*) to work, till (*liter*)

laboreo SM (= *trabajo*) working; (*Agr*) working, cultivation, tilling (*liter*)

laborero SM (*Andes, Cono Sur*) foreman

laboriosamente ADV 1 (= *con dedicación*) industriously
2 (= *con minuciosidad*) painstakingly
3 (= *con dificultad*) with great difficulty

laboriosidad SF 1 (= *dedicación*) industry
2 (= *minuciosidad*) painstaking skill
3 (= *dificultad*) laboriousness

laborioso ADJ 1 (= *dedicado, constante*) hard-working, industrious
2 (= *minucioso*) painstaking
3 (= *dificultoso*) [*trabajo, negociaciones*] laborious, difficult

laborismo SM Labour Movement

laborista Ⓐ ADJ Labour *antes de s*; **Partido Laborista** Labour Party
Ⓑ SMF 1 (*en Gran Bretaña*) (*Pol*) Labour Party member, Labour supporter
2 (*CAm*) (= *trabajador*) small farmer, smallholder

laborterapia SF work-therapy

labra SF carving, working, cutting

labradío ADJ arable

labrado Ⓐ ADJ (= *trabajado*) worked; [*metal*] wrought; [*madera*] carved; [*tela*] patterned, embroidered
Ⓑ SM cultivated field; **labrados** cultivated land *sing*

Labrador SM (*Geog*) Labrador

labrador(a) SM/F 1 (= *propietario*) (peasant) farmer
2 (= *labriego*) farm labourer, farmhand, farmworker; (= *campesino*) peasant
3 (= *perro*) Labrador

labrantín/ina SM/F small farmer

labrantío ADJ arable

labranza SF cultivation, farming, tilling (*liter*); **tierras de ~** farmland

labrar ▸conjug 1a◂ Ⓐ VT 1 (= *trabajar*) to work; [+ *metal*] to work; [+ *madera*] to carve; [+ *tierra*] to work, farm, till (*liter*); [+ *tela*] to embroider
2 [+ *imagen*] to create; [+ *fortuna*] to amass
Ⓑ **labrarse** VPR **~se un porvenir** to carve out a future for o.s.

labriego/a SM/F farmhand, labourer, peasant

laburante* SM (*Cono Sur*) worker

laburar* ▸conjug 1a◂ VI (*Cono Sur*) to work

laburno SM laburnum

laburo* SM (*Cono Sur*) (= *trabajo*) work; (= *puesto*) job; **¡qué ~!** what a job!

laca SF 1 (= *gomorresina*) shellac; (= *barniz*) lacquer; [*de pelo*] hairspray ► **laca de uñas, laca para uñas** nail polish, nail varnish
2 (= *color*) lake
3 (*Cono Sur*) = **lacra**

lacado SM lacquer

lacar ▸conjug 1g◂ VT to lacquer

lacayo SM 1 (= *criado*) footman
2 (*pey*) (= *adulador*) lackey

laceada SF (*Cono Sur*) whipping

lacear ▸conjug 1a◂ VT 1 (*Caza*) (= *atrapar*) to snare, trap
2 (*Andes Caza*) [+ *ganado*] to lasso
3 (*Arg*) (= *zurrar*) to whip
4 (= *adornar*) to beribbon, adorn with bows; (= *atar*) to tie with a bow; (*CAm, Méx*) [+ *carga*] to tie on firmly, strap securely

laceración SF 1 [*de cuerpo*] laceration
2 [*de reputación, nombre*] damage

lacerante ADJ 1 [*dolor*] excruciating
2 [*palabras, comentarios*] wounding, cutting

lacerar ▸conjug 1a◂ VT 1 (= *herir*) to lacerate
2 (= *perjudicar*) to damage

laceria SF (*frm*) 1 (= *pobreza*) poverty, want
2 (= *sufrimiento*) distress, wretchedness

lacero/a SM/F dog-catcher

lacha SF (= *honor*) sense of honour; (= *vergüenza*) sense of shame

lachear* ▸conjug 1a◂ VT (*Cono Sur*) to chat up*

lacho* SM (*Chile, Perú*) lover

laciar ▸conjug 1b◂ VT (*LAm*) [+ *pelo rizado*] to straighten

Lacio SM Latium

lacio ADJ 1 [*pelo*] lank, straight
2 [*movimiento*] limp, languid
3 (*Bot*) withered, faded

lacón SM shoulder of pork

lacónicamente ADV laconically, tersely

lacónico ADJ laconic, terse

laconismo SM laconic style, laconic manner, terseness

lacra SF 1 (*Med*) scar, trace; (*LAm*) (= *llaga*) sore, ulcer; (= *costra*) scab
2 (*social, moral*) blot, blemish; **la prostitución es una ~ social** prostitution is a blot on society

lacrado ADJ (wax-)sealed

lacrar[1] ▸conjug 1a◂ Ⓐ VT 1 (*Med*) (= *dañar*) to damage the health of, harm; (= *contagiar*) to infect
2 [+ *intereses*] to be prejudicial to, be against
Ⓑ **lacrarse** VPR **~se con algo** to suffer harm *o* damage *o* loss from sth; **~se con el trabajo excesivo** to harm o.s. through overwork

lacrar[2] ▸conjug 1a◂ VT to seal (*with sealing wax*)

lacre Ⓐ ADJ (*LAm*) bright red
Ⓑ SM 1 (= *cera*) sealing wax
2 (*Chile*) (= *color*) red colour, red color (*EEUU*)

lacrimógeno ADJ 1 [*humo, vapor*] tear-producing; **gas ~** tear gas
2 [*canción, historia*] highly sentimental, weepy*; **novela lacrimógena** tear-jerker

lacrimoso ADJ tearful, lachrymose (*frm*)

lacrosse [la'kros] SF lacrosse

lactación SF, **lactancia** SF lactation; [*de niño*] breast-feeding ► **lactancia artificial** bottle-feeding

lactante Ⓐ ADJ **mujer ~** nursing mother
Ⓑ SMF breast-fed baby

lactar ▸conjug 1a◂ Ⓐ VT to breast-feed, nurse; (*Zool*) feed on milk
Ⓑ VI to suckle, breast-feed

lácteo ADJ milk *antes de s*, lacteal (*frm*); **productos ~s** dairy products

láctico ADJ lactic

lacto-ovo-vegetariano/a ADJ, SM/F lacto-ovo-vegetarian

lactosa SF lactose

lactosuero SM whey, buttermilk

lacustre ADJ (*frm*) (*gen*) lake *antes de s*, lacustrine (*frm*); (*LAm*) marshy

ladeado ADJ 1 (= *inclinado*) tilted, leaning, inclined
2 (*Arg*) (= *descuidado*) slovenly
3 (*Cono Sur**) (= *taimado*) crooked*
4 (*Cono Sur**) (= *enfadado*) **andar ~** to be in a bad temper; **andar ~ con algn** to be in a huff with sb

ladear ▸conjug 1a◂ Ⓐ VT 1 (= *inclinar*) to tilt, tip; (*Aer*) to bank, turn; [+ *cabeza*] to tilt, put on one side
2 [+ *montaña*] to skirt, go round the side of
Ⓑ VI 1 (= *inclinarse*) to tilt, tip, lean
2 (= *apartarse*) to turn aside, turn off
Ⓒ **ladearse** VPR 1 (= *inclinarse*) to lean (**a** towards); (= *torcerse*) to bend; (*Dep*) to swerve; (*Aer*) to bank, turn
2 (*Chile**) (= *enamorarse*) to fall in love (**con** with)
3 **~se con** to be equal to, be even with

ladeo SM (= *inclinación*) tilt, leaning; (*Aer*) banking, turning

ladera SF hillside

ladero/a Ⓐ ADJ side *antes de s*, lateral
Ⓑ SM/F (*Arg**) helper, backer

ladilla SF crab louse; ✦**MODISMO** **¡qué ~!** (*Caribe**) what a pain!*

ladillento ADJ (*CAm, Méx*) lousy

ladillo SM (*Prensa*) subhead, subtitle

ladinazo ADJ (*Cono Sur*) cunning, shrewd

ladino/a Ⓐ ADJ 1 (= *astuto*) smart, shrewd; (= *taimado*) cunning, wily
2 (*LAm*) [*indio*] Spanish-speaking
3 (*CAm, Méx*) (= *mestizo*) half-breed, mestizo; (= *blanco*) non-Indian, white, of Spanish descent
4 (*LAm*) (= *adulador*) smooth-tongued, smarmy*
5 (*Méx**) [*voz*] high-pitched, fluty
Ⓑ SM/F 1 (*LAm*) (= *indio*) Spanish-speaking Indian
2 (*CAm, Méx*) (= *mestizo*) half-breed, mestizo; (= *blanco*) non-Indian, white
Ⓒ SM (*Ling*) Ladin (*Rhaeto-Romance dialect*); [*de sefardíes*] Ladino, Sephardic, Judeo-Spanish

lado SM 1 (= *lateral*) side; **~ derecho** right side, right-hand side; **~ izquierdo** left side, left-hand side; **a los dos ~s de la carretera** on both sides of the road; **al otro ~ de la calle** on the other side of the street, across the street; **llevar algo al otro ~ del río** to take sth across *o* over the river; **a un ~ y a otro** on all sides, all around; **es primo mío por el ~ de mi padre** he's a cousin on my father's side; **~ a ~** side by side; **<u>de</u> ~** sideways; **poner algo de ~** to put sth sideways; **lleva el sombrero de ~** she wears her hat at an angle; **duermo de ~** I sleep on my side; **<u>echarse</u>** *o* **<u>hacerse</u> a un ~** [*persona*] to move to one side, step aside; [*vehículo*] to swerve out of the way; **<u>por</u> su ~**: **se fue cada uno por su ~** they went their separate ways; **salieron corriendo cada uno por su ~** they all ran off in different directions; ✦**MODISMOS** **dar a algn de ~** to give sb the cold shoulder; **a mí eso me da de ~** I couldn't care less about that; **dejar a un ~** to leave aside, forget; **echar a un ~** to cast aside; **mirar a algn de (medio) ~** to look down on sb; **poner a un ~** to put aside
2 (= *aspecto*) side; **todo tiene su ~ bueno** everything has its good side; **vamos a ver un ~ distinto de la cuestión** we're going to look at a different aspect of the issue; **ése es su ~ débil** that's her weak point; **<u>por</u> un ~ ..., por otro ~ ...** on the one hand ..., on the other hand ...; **por ese ~, creo que está bien** in that respect, I think it's all right
3 (= *lugar*) **ponlo en <u>cualquier</u> ~** put it anywhere; **<u>otro</u> ~**: **tiene que estar en otro ~** it must be somewhere else; **ir de un ~ a otro** to go to and fro, walk up and down; **estuvo de un ~ para otro toda la mañana** she was up and down all morning, she was running around all morning; **por <u>todos</u> ~s**: **me lo encuentro por todos ~s** I bump into him everywhere I go; **rodeado de agua por todos ~s** surrounded by water on all sides, completely surrounded by water; **ir a todos ~s** to go all over
4 (*indicando proximidad*) **no se movió del ~ de su madre** she never left her mother's side; **estar <u>al</u> ~** to be near; **el cine está aquí al ~** the cinema is just round the corner, the cinema is very near; **la mesa de al ~** the next table; **la casa de al ~** the house next door; **al ~ <u>de</u>**: **la silla que está al ~ del armario** the chair beside the wardrobe; **viven al ~ de nosotros** they live next door to us; **al ~ de aquello, esto no es nada** compared to that, this is nothing; **al ~ de ella, tú pareces una belleza** compared to her, you seem really beautiful; **a <u>mi/tu</u> ~**: **Felipe se sentó a mi ~** Felipe sat beside me; **estuvo a mi ~ todo el tiempo** she was at my side the whole time; **los buenos ratos que he pasado a su ~** the good times I've had with her
5 (= *bando*) (*Mil*) flank; (*Pol*) faction; **yo estoy de su ~** I'm on his side, I'm with him; **ponerse al ~ de algn** to side with sb
6 (*Mat*) side; **un triángulo tiene tres ~s** triangles have three sides; **un polígono de cinco ~s** a five-sided polygon
7 (*Dep*) end; **cambiar de ~** to change ends
8 (†) (= *favor*) favour, protection; **tener buenos ~s** to have good connections

ladrar ▸conjug 1a◂ VI [*perro*] to bark; [*persona*] to yell; [*tripas*] to rumble; ✦**MODISMOS** **está que ladra*** he's hopping mad*; **esta semana estoy ladrando** (*Caribe**) I'm flat broke this week*; **ladran, luego andamos** you can tell it's having some effect

ladrería SF (*Andes, Caribe*), **ladrerío** SM (*Méx*) barking

ladrido SM 1 [*de perro*] bark, barking
2 (= *grito*) yell; **se enfadó y nos dio unos ~s** he got angry and yelled at us
3 (†) (= *calumnia*) slander

ladrillado SM [*de ladrillos*] brick floor; [*de azulejos*] tile floor

ladrillar ▸conjug 1a◂ Ⓐ VT to brick, pave with bricks
Ⓑ SM brickworks

ladrillazo SM **dar un ~ a algn** to throw a brick at sb

ladrillera SF, **ladrillería** SF brickworks

ladrillo SM 1 (*Constr*) brick; ✦**MODISMO** **ser un ~***: **este libro es un ~** this book is really hard going* ► **ladrillo de fuego, ladrillo refractario** firebrick ► **ladrillo ventilador** air-brick
2 (= *azulejo*) tile
3 [*de chocolate*] block

ladrón/ona Ⓐ ADJ thieving
Ⓑ SM/F thief; **¡al ~!** stop thief! ► **ladrón de corazones** ladykiller ► **ladrón/ona de guante blanco** white-collar criminal
Ⓒ SM (*Elec*) adaptor

ladronera SF [1] (= *guarida*) den of thieves
[2] (†) (*acto*) robbery, theft

lagaña SF = **legaña**

lagar SM [*de vino*] winepress; (= *edificio*) winery; [*de aceite*] oil press

lagarta SF [1] alligator; (‡) (= *zorra*) bitch‡; **¡lagarta!** you bitch!‡
[2] (*Entomología*) gipsy moth ► **lagarta falsa** lackey moth; *ver tb* **lagarto**

lagartear* ▸conjug 1a◂ VT [1] (*Cono Sur*) (= *inmovilizar*) to pinion, pin down
[2] (*Andes*) (= *falsear*) to fiddle*, wangle*

lagartera SF lizard hole

lagartija SF [1] (*Zool*) (small) lizard, wall lizard
[2] (*Méx**) (= *salvavidas*) lifeguard
[3] (= *ejercicio*) press-up

lagarto SM [1] (*Zool*) lizard; (*LAm*) (= *caimán*) alligator; ✦MODISMO **¡lagarto, lagarto!** (= *cuidado*) look out!; (= *toca madera*) touch wood!; (*Andes, Méx*) (= *Dios nos libre*) God forbid! ► **lagarto de Indias** alligator ► **lagarto verde** green lizard
[2] (= *taimado*) devious person, sly person, fox
[3] (*CAm, Méx**) (= *codicioso*) get-rich-quick type*; (*Andes**) (= *sableador*) scrounger*, sponger*; (*Andes**) (= *especulador*) profiteer
[4] (*Méx**) (= *astuto*) sharp customer, smart operator; *ver tb* **lagarta**

lagartón ADJ [1] (= *listo*) sharp, shrewd; (= *taimado*) sly
[2] (*CAm, Méx*) (= *codicioso*) greedy

lagartona‡ SF (= *zorra*) bitch‡

lago SM lake; (*escocés*) loch; **los Grandes Lagos** the Great Lakes

Lagos SM Lagos

lágrima SF (*gen*) tear; (= *gota*) drop; **beberse las ~s** to hold back one's tears; **derramar una lagrimita** (*iró*) to shed a tear; **deshacerse en ~s** to dissolve into tears; **echar una ~** to shed a tear; **llorar a ~ viva** to cry one's heart out; **nadie soltará una ~ por eso** nobody is going to shed a tear over that; **se me saltaron las ~s** tears came to my eyes ► **lágrimas de cocodrilo** crocodile tears ► **lágrimas de don Pedro** (*Cono Sur*) June rains

lagrimal SM corner of the eye

lagrimar ▸conjug 1a◂ VI to cry

lagrimea SF **tener ~** to have streaming eyes

lagrimear ▸conjug 1a◂ VI [1] [*persona*] (= *ser llorica*) to shed tears easily; (= *estar lloroso*) to be tearful
[2] [*ojos*] to water, fill with tears

lagrimilla SF (*Cono Sur*) unfermented grape juice

lagrimoso ADJ [*persona*] tearful, lachrymose (*frm*); [*ojos*] watery

laguna SF [1] (*Geog*) (*en el interior*) pool; (*en la costa*) lagoon
[2] (*en conocimientos*) gap; **sabe bien el inglés, pero tiene muchas ~s** he knows English well but has many gaps
[3] (*en libro, manuscrito*) gap, lacuna (*frm*)
[4] (*en proceso*) hiatus, gap, break

lagunajo SM (*Caribe*), **lagunato** SM (*Caribe*) (= *estanque*) pool, pond; (= *charco*) puddle

lagunoso ADJ marshy, swampy

laicado SM laity

laical ADJ lay

laicidad SF (*LAm*), **laicismo** SM laicism (*doctrine of the independence of the state from church interference*)

laicizar ▸conjug 1f◂ VT to laicize

laico/a Ⓐ ADJ [1] (= *seglar*) [*misionero, predicador*] lay
[2] [*estado, educación, colegio*] secular; **educación laica** secular education
Ⓑ SM/F layman/laywoman

laísmo SM *use of "la" and "las" as indirect objects*; → LEÍSMO, LOÍSMO, LAÍSMO

laísta Ⓐ ADJ *that uses "la" and "las" as indirect objects*
Ⓑ SMF *user of "la" and "las" as indirect objects*

laja¹ SF [1] (*LAm*) (= *piedra*) sandstone; (= *roca*) rock
[2] (*Andes*) (= *lugar*) steep ground

laja² SF (*Andes*) fine rope

laja³‡ SF (= *chica*) bird‡, chick (*EEUU*‡), dame*

Lalo SM (*LAm*) (*forma familiar*) *de* **Eduardo**

lama¹ SF [1] (= *cieno*) mud, slime, ooze
[2] (*LAm*) (= *moho*) mould, mold (*EEUU*), verdigris; (*Min*) crushed ore
[3] (*Méx*) (= *musgo*) moss

lama² SM (*Rel*) lama

lama³ SF [*de persiana*] slat

lama⁴ SF (= *tejido*) lamé

lambada SF lambada

lambarear* ▸conjug 1a◂ VI (*Caribe*) to wander aimlessly about

lambeculo‡ SMF (*LAm*) creep‡, bootlicker*

lambeladrillos* SM INV (*Andes*) hypocrite

lambeplatos* SMF INV (*LAm*) [1] (= *lameculos*) bootlicker*
[2] (= *persona desgraciada*) poor wretch

lamber ▸conjug 2a◂ VT (*LAm*) [1] = **lamer**
[2] (= *adular*) to fawn on, suck up to*

lambeta‡ SMF (*Cono Sur*) creep‡, bootlicker*

lambetazo SM (*LAm*) (= *lametón*) lick

lambetear ▸conjug 1a◂ VT (*LAm*) [1] (= *lamer*) to lick
[2] (*) (= *adular*) to suck up to*

lambiche ADJ (*Méx*) = **lambiscón**

lambida SF (*LAm*) lick

lambido* ADJ [1] (*LAm*) (= *vano*) affected, vain
[2] (*Méx, CAm*) (= *cínico*) shameless, cynical
[3] (= *desvergonzado*) cheeky*, sassy (*EEUU**)

lambioche* ADJ (*Méx*) fawning, servile

lambiscón* (*LAm*) ADJ [1] (= *adulón*) fawning
[2] (= *glotón*) greedy

lambisconear ▸conjug 1a◂ (*LAm*) Ⓐ VT [1] (*) (= *adular*) to suck up to*
[2] (= *lamer*) to lick
Ⓑ VI (*) (= *adular*) to creep*, crawl*

lambisconería* SF (*LAm*) [1] (= *coba*) crawling*, brown-nosing (*EEUU*‡), fawning
[2] (= *gula*) greediness, gluttony

lambisquear ▸conjug 1a◂ VI (*Méx*) to look for sweets o (*EEUU*) candies

lambón ADJ (*LAm*) = **lambioche**

lambraña SMF (*Andes*) wretch

lambrijo* ADJ (*Méx*) skinny

lambrusquear ▸conjug 1a◂ VT (*Cono Sur*) to lick

lambuzo ADJ (*Andes, Caribe, Méx*) [1] (= *glotón*) greedy, gluttonous (*frm*)
[2] (= *desvergonzado*) shameless, brazen

lamé SM lamé

lameculismo‡ SM arselicking**, crawling‡, brown-nosing (*EEUU*‡)

lameculos‡ SMF INV arselicker**, crawler‡, brown-nose (*EEUU*‡)

lamedura SF lick, licking

lamentable ADJ [*conducta*] deplorable; [*injusticia*] shameful; [*error*] regrettable; [*escena, aspecto, estado*] sorry, pitiful; [*pérdida*] sad; **es ~ que ...** it is regrettable that ...

lamentablemente ADV regrettably, unfortunately

lamentación SF sorrow, lamentation (*frm*); **ahora no sirven lamentaciones** it's no good crying over spilt milk

▼ **lamentar** ▸conjug 1a◂ Ⓐ VT (= *sentir*) to be sorry about, regret; [+ *pérdida*] to lament, bewail, bemoan (*frm*); **lamentamos la muerte de su marido** we're sorry to hear of your husband's death; **no hay que ~ víctimas** fortunately there were no casualties; **lamento lo que pasó** I'm sorry about what happened; **~ que** to be sorry that, regret that; **lamentamos mucho que ...** we very much regret that ...
Ⓑ **lamentarse** VPR [1] (= *quejarse*) to complain; **ahora de nada sirve ~se** there's no point complaining now; **~se de algo: se lamenta del tiempo malgastado** he regrets the time he wasted; **se lamenta de su mala suerte** he's cursing his bad luck
[2] (*frm*) (= *llorar*) to lament; **el país entero se lamenta por la pérdida del presidente** the whole country is mourning o (*frm*) lamenting the loss of the president

lamento SM lament, lamentation (*frm*), moan, wail

lamentoso ADJ (*LAm*) [1] (= *penoso*) = **lamentable**
[2] (= *quejoso*) plaintive

lameplatos SMF INV [1] (= *pobre*) pauper, scavenger
[2] (*Méx**) (= *adulón*) toady
[3] (*Méx**) (= *parásito*) scrounger*
[4] (*Méx**) (= *inútil*) disaster

lamer ▸conjug 2a◂ Ⓐ VT [1] (*con la lengua*) to lick
[2] [*olas*] to lap (against)
[3] (= *pasar rozando*) to graze
Ⓑ **lamerse** VPR ✦MODISMO **que no se lame‡: un problema que no se lame** a bloody great problem‡

lametada SF lick; [*de ola*] lap

lametazo SM lick; [*del sol*] touch, caress

lamido Ⓐ ADJ [1] (= *flaco*) very thin, emaciated (*frm*); (= *pálido*) pale
[2] (= *afectado*) prim, affected
Ⓑ SM (*Téc*) lapping

lámina¹ SF (*gen*) sheet; (*Fot, Tip*) plate; (= *grabado*) engraving; (*en libro*) plate, illustration; (*Inform*) chip ► **lámina de queso** slice of cheese ► **lámina de silicio** silicon wafer ► **láminas de acero** sheet steel *sing*

lámina² SMF (*Andes*) rogue, rascal

laminado Ⓐ ADJ [1] (*gen*) laminate(d)
[2] (*Téc*) sheet *antes de s*, rolled; **cobre ~** sheet copper, rolled copper
Ⓑ SM laminate

laminador SM, **laminadora** SF rolling mill

laminar ▸conjug 1a◂ VT (*gen*) to laminate; (*Téc*) to roll

➤ LENGUA Y USO: lamentar A 36.3, 39.2, 45.3, 46.6, 47.2, 47.3, 48.4

lamiscar ▸conjug 1g◂ VT to lick greedily, lick noisily

lampa SF (*Chile, Perú*) (= *azada*) hoe; (= *pico*) pick, pickax (*EEUU*)

lampacear ▸conjug 1a◂ VT (*CAm*) [+ *piso*] to mop

lampalagua SF (*Chile*) mythical snake

lampalague SF (*Cono Sur*) 1 (= *serpiente*) boa constrictor
2 (= *glotón*) glutton

lampancia* SF ravenous hunger

lampante* SMF beggar

lampar* ▸conjug 1a◂ VI to beg

lámpara Ⓐ SF 1 (*Elec*) lamp, light; (*Radio*) valve, tube (*EEUU*); **lámparas** (*LAm*) (= *ojos*) eyes; ✦***MODISMOS*** **atizar la ~*** to fill up the glasses; **quebrar la ~** (*Caribe**) to ruin everything, blow it‡ ► **lámpara bronceador** sun lamp ► **lámpara de Aladino** Aladdin's lamp ► **lámpara de alcohol** spirit lamp, alcohol lamp (*EEUU*) ► **lámpara de arco** arc-lamp ► **lámpara de bolsillo** torch, flashlight ► **lámpara de cuarzo** quartz lamp ► **lámpara de escritorio** desk-lamp ► **lámpara de gas** gas lamp ► **lámpara de lectura** reading lamp ► **lámpara de mesa** table lamp ► **lámpara de pared** wall light ► **lámpara de pie** standard lamp ► **lámpara de señales** signalling lamp ► **lámpara de sol artificial** sun lamp ► **lámpara de soldar** blowlamp, blowtorch ► **lámpara de techo** overhead lamp ► **lámpara flexo** adjustable table lamp ► **lámpara plegable** angle-poise lamp ► **lámpara solar ultravioleta** sun lamp
2 (= *mancha*) stain, dirty mark
Ⓑ SMF (*Caribe*) (= *ladrón*) thief; (= *estafador*) con man*

lamparazo SM (*Méx*) gulp

lamparilla SF 1 (= *lámpara*) small lamp
2 (*Bot*) aspen

lamparín SM (*Chile, Perú*) (= *quinqué*) paraffin lamp; (*Cono Sur*) (= *vela*) candle

lámparo ADJ (*Andes*) penniless, broke*

lamparón SM 1 (*Med*) scrofula
2 (= *mancha*) large grease spot

lampazo¹ SM (*Bot*) burdock

lampazo² SM 1 (*LAm*) (= *escobilla*) floor mop
2 (*Andes, Caribe*) (= *azotamiento*) whipping
3 (*Náut*) swab

lampear ▸conjug 1a◂ VT (*Andes*) (*con pala*) to shovel; (*con azada*) to hoe

lampiño ADJ (= *sin pelo*) hairless; (= *sin barba*) beardless

lampión SM lantern

lampista SMF plumber

lampistería SF electrical shop

lampón¹ ADJ (*Andes*) starving, hungry

lampón² SM (*Andes*) (= *pala*) spade; (= *azada*) hoe

lamprea SF 1 (= *pez*) lamprey
2 (*Med*) sore, ulcer

lamprear ▸conjug 1a◂ VT (*CAm*) to whip

lana¹ SF 1 (*gen*) wool; (= *vellón*) fleece; (= *tela*) woollen cloth, woolen cloth (*EEUU*); (*para labores*) knitting wool; **de ~** ◊ **hecho de ~** wool *antes de s*, woollen, woolen (*EEUU*); ✦***REFRÁN*** **ir por ~ y volver trasquilado** to get more than one bargained for ► **lana de acero** steel wool ► **lana para labores** knitting wool ► **lana virgen** pure new wool
2 **lanas*** (*hum*) long hair *sing*, locks
3 (*Andes, Méx**) (= *dinero*) money, dough*
4 (*Andes, Méx*) (= *mentira*) lie
5 (*CAm*) (= *estafador*) swindler

lana² SF (*CAm*) = **lama¹ 2**

lanar ADJ wool-bearing, wool *antes de s*; **ganado ~** sheep

lance SM 1 (= *episodio*) incident, event ► **lance de fortuna** stroke of luck
2 (= *momento difícil*) critical moment, difficult moment
3 (= *riña*) row, quarrel ► **lance de honor** affair of honour, affair of honor (*EEUU*), duel
4 [*de red*] throw, cast
5 (*Pesca*) catch
6 (*Dep*) move, piece of play
7 (= *accidente*) chance, accident
8 **tirarse (a) un ~** (*Cono Sur*) to take a chance
9 (*Com*) **de ~** secondhand, cheap; **libros de ~** secondhand books; **comprar algo de ~** to buy sth secondhand, buy sth cheap
10 (*Cono Sur*) (= *agachada*) duck, dodge; **sacar ~** to dodge, duck away
11 (*Cono Sur*) (= *parte*) section, range; **casa de tres ~s** house in three sections

lancear ▸conjug 1a◂ VT to spear

lancero Ⓐ SM 1 (*Mil*) lancer
2 **lanceros** (*Mús*) lancers
Ⓑ SMF (*Cono Sur*) (= *soñador*) dreamer, blind optimist

lanceta SF 1 (*Med*) lancet; **abrir con ~** to lance
2 (*LAm*) (= *aguijada*) goad; [*de insecto*] sting

lancha¹ SF 1 (= *barca*) (small) boat; [*de motor*] launch ► **lancha cañonera** gunboat ► **lancha de carga** lighter, barge ► **lancha de carreras** speedboat ► **lancha de desembarco, lancha de desembarque** landing craft ► **lancha de pesca** fishing boat ► **lancha de salvamento, lancha de socorro** lifeboat ► **lancha fuera borda** outboard dinghy ► **lancha hinchable, lancha inflable** inflatable dinghy ► **lancha motora** motorboat, speedboat ► **lancha neumática** rubber dinghy, raft (*EEUU*) ► **lancha patrullera** patrol boat ► **lancha rápida** speedboat ► **lancha salvavidas** lifeboat ► **lancha torpedera** torpedo boat
2 (*Cono Sur**) police car

lancha² SF (*Andes*) 1 (= *niebla*) mist, fog
2 (= *helada*) (hoar)frost

lanchaje SM (*Méx*) freight charge

lanchar ▸conjug 1a◂ VI (*Andes*) 1 (= *encapotarse*) to become overcast
2 (= *helar*) to freeze

lanchero/a SM/F 1 (= *barquero*) boatman/boatwoman; [*de lancha de carga*] lighterman/lighterwoman, bargee, bargeman/bargewoman (*EEUU*)
2 (*Caribe*) *Cuban refugee*

lanchón SM lighter, barge ► **lanchón de desembarco** landing craft

lancinante ADJ (*frm*) [*dolor*] piercing

lancinar ▸conjug 1a◂ VT (*frm*) to lance, pierce

Landas SFPL **las ~** the Landes

landó SM 1 (= *carruaje*) landau
2 (*Andes Mús*) Peruvian folk music

landre SF ✦***MODISMO*** **¡mala ~ te coma!** curse you!

lanería SF 1 (= *géneros*) woollen goods, woolen goods (*EEUU*)
2 (= *tienda*) wool shop

lanero/a Ⓐ ADJ wool *antes de s*, woollen, woolen (*EEUU*); **la industria lanera** the wool industry
Ⓑ SM/F (= *persona*) wool dealer
Ⓒ SM (= *almacén*) wool warehouse

lángara‡ SMF (*Méx*) slippery individual*

lángaro ADJ 1 (*CAm*) (= *vago*) vagrant, wandering, idle
2 (*Andes, Méx*) (= *hambriento*) starving, poverty-stricken
3 (*Méx*) (= *malo*) wicked; (= *taimado*) sly, untrustworthy
4 (*CAm*) (= *larguirucho*) lanky

langarucho ADJ (*CAm, Méx*), **langarote** ADJ (*Andes*) lanky

langosta SF 1 [*de mar*] lobster; [*de río*] crayfish
2 (= *insecto*) locust

langostera SF lobster pot

langostino SM, **langostín** SM prawn; (*grande*) king prawn

langostinero ADJ **barco ~** prawn-fishing boat

languceta ADJ (*Cono Sur*), **languciento** ADJ (*Cono Sur, Méx*), **langucio** ADJ (*Cono Sur*) 1 (= *hambriento*) starving
2 (= *enclenque*) sickly

lánguidamente ADV (= *sin espíritu*) languidly; (= *débilmente*) weakly, listlessly

languidecer ▸conjug 2d◂ VI to languish

languidez SF (= *falta de espíritu*) languor (*liter*), lassitude (*frm*); (= *debilidad*) listlessness

lánguido ADJ (*gen*) languid (*liter*); (= *débil*) weak, listless

languso ADJ (*Méx*) 1 (= *taimado*) sly, shrewd
2 (= *larguirucho*) lanky

lanilla SF 1 (= *flojel*) nap
2 (= *tela*) thin flannel cloth

lanolina SF lanolin(e)

lanoso ADJ woolly, wooly (*EEUU*), fleecy

lanudo ADJ 1 (= *lanoso*) woolly, wooly (*EEUU*), fleecy
2 (*Méx**) (= *rico*) well off
3 (*Andes, Caribe*) (= *maleducado*) rustic, uncouth

lanza Ⓐ SF 1 (*Mil*) lance, spear; ✦***MODISMOS*** **estar ~ en ristre** to be ready for action; **medir ~s** to cross swords; **romper una ~ por algn** to back sb to the hilt; **ser una ~** (= *ser hábil*) to be pretty sharp; (*Méx*) to be sly, be a rogue
2 (*en carruajes*) shaft
3 [*de manguera*] nozzle
Ⓑ SMF 1 (*LAm**) (= *estafador*) cheat, shark*
2 (*Chile**) (= *ratero*) pickpocket, thief; (*Cono Sur*) (= *tironista*) bag-snatcher

lanzabengalas SM INV flare

lanzabombas SM INV (*Aer*) bomb release; (*Mil*) mortar

lanzacohetes SM INV rocket launcher ► **lanzacohetes múltiple** multiple rocket launcher

lanzada SF (= *golpe*) spear thrust; (= *herida*) spear wound

lanzadera SF shuttle ► **lanzadera de misiles** missile launcher ► **lanzadera espacial** space shuttle

lanzadestellos SM INV (*Aut*) flashing light

lanzado/a Ⓐ ADJ 1 **ser ~*** 1·1 (*al hacer algo*) **es un tío muy ~** he's very full of confidence, he's really single-minded
1·2 (*en las relaciones*) to be forward; **¡qué ~ es!** he's so forward!; **es muy lanzada con los hombres** she's very forward with men
2 (*) (*al moverse*) **salió ~ de la casa** he rushed out of the house; **ir ~*** [*coche, moto*] to tear along; **el coche iba ~** the car was tearing along; **¿dónde va tan ~?** where's he going in such a rush?; **no deberías ir tan ~ en los negocios** you shouldn't rush into things in business matters
3 (*sexualmente*) **estar ~**‡ to be horny‡
Ⓑ SM/F (*) **ese tío es un ~** that guy is full of confidence*
Ⓒ SM (*Pesca*) spinning

lanzador(a) Ⓐ ADJ [*avión, cohete*] launch *antes de s*
Ⓑ SM/F 1 (= *persona*) (*Cricket*) bowler; (*Béisbol*) pitcher; **es un experto ~ de faltas** (*Ftbl*) he's an expert at free kicks
► **lanzador(a) de bala** (*LAm*) shot-putter
► **lanzador(a) de cuchillos** knife thrower
► **lanzador(a) de jabalina** javelin thrower
► **lanzador(a) de martillo** hammer thrower
► **lanzador(a) de peso** shot-putter
2 [*de cohetes, misiles*] launcher
3 [*de producto, moda*] promoter

lanzaespumas SM INV foam extinguisher

lanzagranadas SM INV grenade launcher, mortar

lanzallamas SM INV flamethrower

lanzamiento SM 1 [*de objeto*] (*gen*) throwing; (*con violencia*) hurling; (*desde el aire*) dropping; **la manifestación acabó con ~ de objetos contra la policía** the demonstration ended with people hurling things at the police; **~ en paracaídas** parachuting, parachute jumping
2 (*Dep*) (*con la pierna*) kick; (*hacia portería, canasta*) shot; **falló el ~ del penalti** he missed the penalty (kick); **un ~ de tres puntos** a three-point field goal ► **lanzamiento a canasta** shot at basket ► **lanzamiento de bala** (*LAm*) the shot put ► **lanzamiento de disco** the discus ► **lanzamiento de falta** (*Ftbl*) free kick ► **lanzamiento de jabalina** the javelin ► **lanzamiento de martillo** the hammer ► **lanzamiento de penaltis** penalty shoot-out ► **lanzamiento de peso** the shot put
3 [*de nave espacial, misil*] launch
4 (*Com, Fin*) [*de acciones, producto*] launch; [*de disco*] release; **oferta de ~** promotional offer; **~ publicitario** advertising campaign
5 (*Jur*) repossession

lanzaminas SM INV minelayer

lanzamisiles SM INV missile launcher

lanzar ▸conjug 1f◂ Ⓐ VT 1 [+ *objeto, piedra*] (*gen*) to throw; (*con violencia*) to hurl, fling; **lánzame la pelota** throw me the ball; **~on botes de humo contra los manifestantes** they threw *o* hurled smoke bombs at the demonstrators; **la explosión lanzó algunas piedras al cielo** the explosion threw *o* flung stones into the sky; **~ algo/a algn al suelo** (*gen*) to throw sth/sb to the ground; (*con violencia*) to hurl sth/sb to the ground
2 (= *disparar*) [+ *flecha, proyectil*] to fire; [+ *cohete, misil*] (*hacia el aire*) to launch; (*hacia tierra*) to drop; **una bomba lanzada desde un avión enemigo** a bomb dropped from an enemy aircraft
3 (*Dep*) [+ *disco, jabalina, balón*] to throw; [+ *peso*] to put; [+ *pelota*] (*Béisbol*) to pitch; (*Cricket*) to bowl; **~ una falta** (*Ftbl*) to take a free kick; **~ un penalti** to take a penalty
4 (= *emitir*) [+ *mensaje*] to deliver; [+ *insulto, ataque*] to hurl; [+ *indirecta*] to drop; [+ *desafío*] to issue, throw down; [+ *grito, suspiro*] to let out; **lanzó un mensaje tranquilizador a la población** he delivered a reassuring message to the people; **las autoridades han lanzado un nuevo mensaje a los inversores** the authorities have issued a new message to investors; **la emisora lanzó duros ataques contra el presidente** the radio station launched harsh attacks against the president; **~on al aire la idea de reducir los impuestos** they floated the idea of reducing taxes; **~ críticas contra algn** to criticize sb, level criticism against sb (*frm*); **se ~on algunos gritos apoyando al ejército** a few shouts went out in support of the army; **~ una mirada** to shoot a glance *o* look; *ver tb* **llamamiento**
5 (*Com*) [+ *producto, moda*] to launch, bring out; [+ *disco*] to release, bring out; **han lanzado al mercado un nuevo modelo** they have brought out a new model, they have released a new model onto the market; **fue el primer banco que lanzó al mercado bonos hipotecarios** it was the first bank to issue mortgage bonds
6 (*Mil*) [+ *campaña, ataque*] to launch
7 (= *vomitar*) to bring up
8 (*Bot*) [+ *hojas, flores*] to come out in, put out
9 (*Jur*) to dispossess; **lo ~on de sus tierras** he was dispossessed of his land
Ⓑ **lanzarse** VPR 1 (= *arrojarse*) (*al suelo, al vacío*) to throw o.s.; (*al agua*) to throw o.s., jump; **se lanzó por el precipicio** he threw himself off the precipice; **se ~on al suelo** they threw *o* flung themselves to the ground; **de un salto se lanzó al río** he jumped into the river; **los perros se ~on sobre los restos de comida** the dogs pounced on the leftovers; **~se sobre algn** to pounce on sb, leap on sb; **el vigilante se lanzó sobre el ladrón** the guard pounced *o* leapt on the robber; **la muchedumbre se lanzó sobre él** the crowd rushed towards *o* crowded round him; **~se en paracaídas** to parachute; **~se en picado** to dive, swoop down; **el águila se lanzó en picado a por su presa** the eagle swooped towards its prey
2 (= *ir rápidamente*) to hurtle; **se ~on hacia la salida** they hurtled towards the exit; **~se a hacer algo: se ~on a comprar acciones** they rushed to buy shares; **la policía se lanzó a buscar al asesino** the police launched a murder hunt
3 (*) (= *decidirse*) to take the plunge*; **llevábamos años pensando montar un negocio hasta que nos lanzamos** after years wanting to set up a business, we finally took the plunge*
4 **~se a** (= *dedicarse*): **no tienen dinero para ~se a la construcción de nuevas viviendas** they don't have the funds to embark upon *o* undertake new housing projects; **se lanzó a la política en 1963** she went into *o* took up politics in 1963; **decidió ~se a la carrera presidencial** he decided to enter the presidential race

Lanzarote SM 1 (= *isla*) Lanzarote
2 (= *personaje*) Lancelot

lanzaroteño/a Ⓐ ADJ of/from Lanzarote
Ⓑ SM/F native/inhabitant of Lanzarote; **los ~s** the people of Lanzarote

lanzatorpedos SM INV torpedo tube

laña SF clamp, rivet

lañar ▸conjug 1a◂ VT 1 (*Téc*) to clamp (together), rivet
2 (‡) (= *robar*) to nick‡, steal

Laos SM Laos

laosiano/a ADJ, SM/F Laotian

lapa SF 1 (*Zool*) limpet; ✦**MODISMO pegarse a algn como una ~** to stick to sb like a limpet
2 (*Andes, Cono Sur Bot*) half gourd (*used as bowl*)
3 (*Andes*) (= *sombrero*) large flat-topped hat

lapalada SF (*Méx*) drizzle

La Palma SF (*en Canarias*) La Palma

laparoscopia SF laparoscopy

laparoscópico ADJ laparoscopic

lape ADJ (*Cono Sur*) 1 (= *enredado*) matted
2 [*baile*] merry, lively

lapicera SF (*Cono Sur*) (= *pluma*) fountain pen; (= *bolígrafo*) ballpoint pen

lapicero SM 1 (= *portaminas*) propelling pencil, mechanical pencil (*EEUU*) ► **lapicero hemostático** styptic pencil
2 (*Esp*) (= *lápiz*) pencil; (*LAm*) (= *pluma*) fountain pen
3 (**) (= *pene*) prick**

lápida SF gravestone, tombstone ► **lápida conmemorativa** commemorative stone plaque ► **lápida mortuoria** tombstone, gravestone ► **lápida mural** stone plaque let into a wall ► **lápida sepulcral** tombstone

lapidar ▸conjug 1a◂ VT 1 [+ *persona*] to stone
2 (*LAm*) [+ *joyas*] to cut

lapidario/a Ⓐ ADJ lapidary; **frase lapidaria** immortal phrase
Ⓑ SM/F lapidary

lapislázuli SM lapis lazuli

lápiz SM 1 (*gen*) pencil; [*de color*] crayon; **escribir algo a** *o* **con ~** to write sth in pencil; **está añadido a ~** it is added in pencil, it is pencilled in; ✦**MODISMO meter ~ a** to sign ► **lápiz a pasta** (*Cono Sur*) ball-point pen ► **lápiz de carbón** charcoal pencil ► **lápiz de carmín** lipstick ► **lápiz de cejas** eyebrow pencil ► **lápiz de labios** lipstick ► **lápiz de luz, lápiz electrónico** light pen ► **lápiz de ojos** eyebrow pencil ► **lápiz (de) plomo** lead pencil ► **lápiz labial** lipstick ► **lápiz lector** data pen ► **lápiz negro** (*en la censura*) blue pencil ► **lápiz óptico** light pen
2 (*Min*) black lead, graphite

lapo* SM 1 (*Esp*) (= *escupitajo*) spit
2 (= *golpe*) punch, bash*, swipe; ✦**MODISMO de un ~** (*LAm*) at one go
3 (*Andes, Caribe*) swig*
4 (*Caribe*) (= *inocente*) simple soul

lapón/ona Ⓐ ADJ of/from Lapland
Ⓑ SM/F native/inhabitant of Lapland; **los lapones** the people of Lapland
Ⓒ SM (*Ling*) Lapp

Laponia SF Lapland

lapso SM 1 (= *tiempo*) lapse; **en un ~ de cinco días** in (the space of) five days ► **lapso**

de tiempo interval of time, space of time
2 (= *error*) mistake, error

lapsus SM INV (*frm*) lapse, mistake ► **lapsus calami** slip of the pen ► **lapsus de memoria** lapse of memory ► **lapsus freudiano** Freudian slip ► **lapsus linguae** slip of the tongue

laqueado ADJ lacquered, varnished

laquear ▸conjug 1a◂ VT (*gen*) to lacquer; [+ *uñas*] to varnish, paint

LAR SF ABR (*Esp Jur*) = **Ley de Arrendamientos Rústicos**

lardar ▸conjug 1a◂ VT, **lardear** ▸conjug 1a◂ VT to lard, baste

lardo SM lard, animal fat

lardoso ADJ (*gen*) lardy, fatty; (= *grasiento*) greasy

larga SF 1 ✦*MODISMOS* **a la ~** in the long run; **dar ~s a algo/algn** to put sth/sb off; **estamos cansados de que nos den ~s** we're tired of being put off all the time; **si te pregunta por el dinero, tú dale ~s** if he asks you about the money, just fob him off*; **saberla ~** to know what's what*
2 (*Aut*) (*tb* **luz ~**) full beam; **pon las ~s** put the headlights on full beam
3 (*Taur*) pass with the cape
4 (*Dep*) length; *ver tb* **largo**

largada SF (*Dep*) start

largamente ADV 1 (= *por mucho tiempo*) a long time; **el conflicto podría extenderse ~** the conflict could drag on (a long time)
2 (= *con detalle*) at length; **su libro trata ~ de este tema** his book deals with this subject at length; **habló ~ de la crisis** he spoke at length about the crisis
3 (= *abundantemente*) [*compensar*] **esto compensa ~ el esfuerzo** this fully compensates the effort; **han rentabilizado ~ su inversión** they have received a handsome return on their investment
4 (= *cómodamente*) **vivir ~** to live comfortably *o* at ease

largar ▸conjug 1h◂ Ⓐ VT 1 (‡) (= *dar*) 1·1 [+ *discurso, regañina*] to give; [+ *exclamación, suspiro*] to let out; **le largó una bronca tremenda** she gave him a good ticking-off*; **nos largó un rollo interminable sobre los viejos tiempos** he gave us a never-ending spiel about the old days*, he rabbited on forever about the old days*; **no sabe hablar sin ~ insultos** he can't open his mouth without letting fly *o* without insulting someone
1·2 [+ *dinero*] to give; **le largó una buena propina** he gave him a good tip; **lárgame la pasta** hand over the cash*
1·3 [+ *golpe, mordisco*] to give; **me largó un puñetazo en la boca** he punched me in the mouth, he gave me a punch in the mouth; **le ~on una buena paliza** he was badly beaten up
2 (‡) (= *expulsar*) [+ *empleado*] to kick out‡, give the boot‡; [+ *alumno, huésped*] to kick out‡, chuck out‡
3 (‡) (= *endilgar*) **~ a algn** [+ *tarea, trabajo*] to dump on sb*, foist (off) on sb; [+ *animal, niño*] to dump on sb*; **siempre nos larga lo que ella no quiere hacer** she always dumps* *o* foists (off) what she doesn't want to do herself on us; **me ~on a los niños** they dumped their kids on me*
4 (‡) (= *deshacerse de*) [+ *novio, marido*] to ditch*, dump*
5 (*Náut*) [+ *bandera, vela*] to unfurl; [+ *barca*] to put out; [+ *cuerda*] (= *soltar*) to let out, pay out; (= *aflojar*) to loosen, slacken; **~ amarras** to cast off; **~ lastre** to drop ballast
6 (*Cono Sur, Méx**) (= *lanzar*) to throw, hurl
7 (*Cono Sur, Méx Dep*) to start
Ⓑ VI (‡) 1 (*Esp*) (= *hablar*) to go on*, rabbit on*; **hay que ver lo que largas** you don't half go on *o* rabbit on*; **~ contra algn** to bad-mouth sb‡; **siempre estás largando contra todo el mundo** you're always bad-mouthing everybody‡
2 (= *revelar un secreto*) to spill the beans*; **venga, larga** come on, spill the beans*; **no hay forma de que largue** there's no way he'll spit it out‡
Ⓒ **largarse** VPR 1 (*) (= *irse*) to be off*, leave; **yo me largo** I'm off now*, I'm leaving now; **es hora de que nos larguemos** it's time for us to leave *o* be off*; **¡larguémonos de aquí!** let's get out of here!*; **¡lárgate!** get lost!*, clear off!*; **~se de casa** to leave home; **~se del trabajo** to quit one's job
2 (*Náut*) to set sail, start out
3 (*Cono Sur*) (= *empezar*) to start, begin; **~se a hacer algo** to start *o* begin doing *o* to do sth
4 (*Cono Sur*) (= *tirarse*) **se largó de cabeza al agua** he dived into the water; **~se un eructo** to let out a burp; **~se un pedo*** to let off a fart‡

largavistas SM INV (*Cono Sur Téc*) (= *gemelos*) binoculars *pl*

largo Ⓐ ADJ 1 (*indicando longitud*) [*pasillo, pelo, uñas*] long; **el sofá es muy ~ para esa pared** the sofa is too long for that wall; **esa chaqueta te está** *o* **te queda larga** that jacket is too long for you; **me gusta llevar el pelo ~** I like to wear my hair long; **una camiseta interior de manga larga** a long-sleeved vest; **ser ~ de piernas** to have long legs; **ponerse de ~** (= *vestirse*) to wear a long dress/skirt; (= *debutar*) to make one's début; **¿hay que ponerse de ~ para la cena?** do we have to wear evening dress to the dinner?; ✦*MODISMO* **ser ~ de lengua*** to be a blabbermouth*; *ver tb* **diente 2**, **luz 2**, **mano A2**, **puesta 1**, **vestir C1**
2 (*indicando distancia*) [*distancia, camino*] long; **nos queda todavía un ~ camino** we still have a long way to go; **un misil de ~ alcance** a long-range missile; **pasar de ~** [*persona, autobús*] to go past; [*momento, oportunidad*] to go by; **pasamos de ~ por Valencia** we went straight past Valencia; **no podemos dejar pasar de ~ esta oportunidad** we can't let this opportunity go by; **de ~ recorrido** [*vuelo*] long-haul *antes de s*; [*tren, autobús*] long-distance *antes de s*; **seguir de ~*** (= *no parar*) to keep on going; (= *pasar de lado*) to pass by
3 (*indicando duración*) [*espera, viaje, sílaba, película*] long; **es muy ~ de contar** it's a long story; **murió tras una larga enfermedad** he died after a lengthy *o* long illness; **pasaron tres ~s años** three long years went by; **el resultado de ~s años de investigación** the result of many years of research; **hacerse ~**: **no se me hizo nada larga la clase** the class didn't seem at all long to me; **esta película se está haciendo larguísima** this film is really dragging on*; **para ~**: **la reunión va para ~** the meeting looks like being a long one, the meeting looks like going on for some time yet; **cada vez que coge el teléfono tiene para ~** every time he picks up the phone he stays on it for ages; **tengo para ~ hasta que termine** I've got a long way to go before I finish; **a ~ plazo** in the long term; **venir de ~**: **este problema viene de ~** this problem goes back a long way, this problem started way back*; ✦*MODISMOS* **hablar ~ y tendido sobre algo** to talk at great length about sth; **tú y yo tenemos que hablar ~ y tendido** you and I have to have a long talk; **ser más ~ que un día sin pan** to take forever
4 (= *indicando exceso*) good; **tardó media hora larga** he took a good half-hour; **un kilo ~ de uvas** just over a kilo of grapes
5 (*) [*persona*] tall; **tú que eres tan ~, alcánzame ese tarro** you're tall, can you reach that jar for me?; **se cayó al suelo cuan ~ era**† *o* **todo lo ~ que era** he fell flat on his face, he measured his length on the floor†
6 (*locuciones*) **a lo ~** (= *longitudinalmente*) lengthways; (= *a lo lejos*) (far and away) in the distance; **corté la tabla a lo ~** I sawed the board lengthways; **échate a lo ~** stretch yourself full out; **se ve un pico a lo ~** (far and away) in the distance you can see a mountain peak; **a lo ~ de** [+ *río, pared*] along; [+ *día, mes, año*] all through, throughout; **viajó a lo ~ y a lo ancho de Europa** he travelled the length and breadth of Europe; **había palmeras a lo ~ de todo el paseo marítimo** there were palm tress all along the promenade; **a lo ~ de los últimos años hemos viajado mucho** we have travelled a lot over the last few years; **trabajó mucho a lo ~ de su vida** she worked hard all through *o* throughout her life; **el tiempo mejorará a lo ~ de la semana** the weather will improve in the course of the week; **a lo más ~** at the most
7 (*Esp**) (= *astuto*) sharp; **es un tío muy ~** he's a very sharp guy
8 (*Esp*) (= *generoso*) generous; **tirar de ~** to be extravagant
9 (*Esp*) [*cuerda*] loose, slack
10 (*Esp Agr*) [*cosecha*] abundant, plentiful
Ⓑ SM 1 (= *longitud*) length; **¿cuánto tiene de ~?** how long is it?, what's its length?; **tiene nueve metros de ~** it is nine metres long
2 (= *unidad de medida*) [*de falda, piscina*] length; [*de cortina*] drop; **~ de pernera** leg length; **hice diez ~s seguidos** I swam ten lengths without stopping
3 (*Cine*) (*tb* **~metraje**) feature film
4 (*Mús*) largo
Ⓒ ADV (*) **¡~ (de aquí)!** clear off!, get lost!

largometraje SM full-length film, feature film

largón/ona‡ SM/F spy, informer

largona SF 1 (*Andes, Cono Sur*) (= *demora*) delay
2 **largonas** (*Andes*) **dar ~s a algo*** to keep putting sth off
3 (*Cono Sur*) (= *descanso*) **darse una ~*** to take a rest

largor SM length

largucho ADJ (*LAm*) lanky

larguero Ⓐ ADJ (*Cono Sur*) 1 (*) (= *largo*) long, lengthy; [*discurso*] wordy, long-drawn-out
2 (*Dep*) trained for long-distance running
3 (= *lento*) slow-working, slow
4 (*) (= *generoso*) generous, lavish; (= *copioso*) abundant, copious

Ⓑ SM (*Arquit*) crossbeam; [*de puerta*] jamb; (*Dep*) crossbar; (*en cama*) bolster

largueza SF generosity, largesse (*frm*)

larguirucho ADJ lanky, gangling

larguísimo ADJ (*superl*) *de* **largo**

largura SF length

largurucho ADJ (*LAm*) lanky, gangling

lárice SM larch

laringe SF larynx

laringitis SF INV laryngitis

larva SF larva, grub, maggot

larvado ADJ hidden, latent; **permanecer ~** to be latent, remain dormant

las[1] ART DEF FPL *ver* **los**[1]

las[2] PRON PERS *ver* **los**[2]

lasaña SF lasagne, lasagna

lasca SF [*de piedra*] chip; [*de comida*] slice

lascadura SF (*Méx*) [1] (= *rozadura*) graze, abrasion (*frm*)
[2] (= *herida*) injury

lascar ▸conjug 1g◂ Ⓐ VT [1] (*Méx*) [+ *piel*] to graze, bruise; [+ *piedra*] to chip, chip off
[2] (*Náut*) to slacken
Ⓑ VI (*Méx*) to chip off, flake off

lascivamente ADV lewdly, lasciviously

lascivia SF lust, lewdness, lasciviousness

lascivo ADJ [*gesto, mirada, comentario*] lewd, lascivious; [*persona*] lecherous, lascivious

láser SM laser; **rayo ~** laser beam

láser disc SM INV, **láserdisc** SM INV laser disc

lasérico ADJ laser *antes de s*

laserterapia SF laser therapy

lasitud (*liter*) SF lassitude (*liter*), weariness

laso (*liter*) ADJ [1] (= *cansado*) weary
[2] (= *lánguido*) languid (*liter*), limp
[3] (= *débil*) weak

Las Palmas SFPL (*en Canarias*) La Palma, Las Palmas

▼**lástima** SF [1] (= *pena*) pity, shame; **es una ~** it's a pity *o* shame; **es ~ que …** it's a pity *o* shame that …, it's too bad that …; **dar ~**: **toda esta pobreza me da mucha ~** such poverty makes me really sad; **es tan desgraciado que da ~** he's so unhappy I feel really sorry for him *o* I really pity him; **es una película tan mala que da ~** it's a pathetic film, it's an awful film, it's such a pathetically bad film; **¡qué ~!**: **—hemos perdido —¡qué ~!** "we've lost" — "what a shame! *o* what a pity! *o* that's too bad!"; **¡qué ~ de hombre!** isn't he pitiful?; **sentir** *o* **tener ~ de algn** to feel sorry for sb
[2] (= *escena lastimosa*) pitiful sight; **estar hecho una ~** to be in a sorry *o* dreadful state
[3] (*frm*) (= *queja*) complaint, tale of woe

lastimada SF (*CAm, Méx*) = **lastimadura**

lastimador ADJ harmful

lastimadura SF (*LAm*) [1] (= *herida*) graze
[2] (= *moretón*) bruise

lastimar ▸conjug 1a◂ Ⓐ VT [1] (= *hacer daño*) to hurt; **me lastimó** he hurt me
[2] (= *ofender*) to hurt
Ⓑ **lastimarse** VPR [1] (= *herirse*) to hurt o.s.; **se lastimó el brazo** he hurt his arm
[2] **~se de** (= *quejarse*) to complain about; (= *apiadarse*) to feel sorry for, pity

lastimero ADJ [1] (= *dañoso*) harmful
[2] = **lastimoso**

lastimón SM (*LAm*) = **lastimadura**

lastimosamente ADV pitifully, pathetically

lastimoso ADJ pitiful, pathetic

lastrante ADJ burdensome

lastrar ▸conjug 1a◂ VT [1] [+ *embarcación, globo*] to ballast
[2] (= *obstaculizar*) to burden, weigh down

lastre SM [1] (*Náut, Téc*) ballast; **en ~** (*Náut*) in ballast
[2] (= *inconveniente*) burden
[3] (= *sentido común*) good sense, good judgment
[4] (*Cono Sur*‡) (= *comida*) grub*, chow (*EEUU*‡)

lata SF [1] (= *envase*) [*de comida*] tin, can; [*de bebida*] can; **sardinas en ~** tinned sardines, canned sardines; **un cuatro ~s*** (= *coche viejo*) an old banger*; (= *Renault 4L*) Renault 4L
[2] (= *metal*) tinplate; **suena a ~** it sounds tinny
[3] (*Andes*) (= *comida*) food, daily ration ► **lata petitoria** collecting tin (*for charity*)
[4] (*) (= *molestia*) nuisance, pain*, drag*; **es una ~ tener que …** it's a nuisance *o* pain* *o* drag* having to …; **¡qué ~!** ◊ **¡vaya (una) ~!** what a nuisance! *o* drag!* *o* pain!*; **dar la ~** to be a nuisance, be a pain*; **dar la ~ a algn** to pester sb, go on at sb*; **dar ~** (*Andes, CAm**) (= *parlotear*) to babble on; (*Andes**) (= *insistir*) to nag, go on
[5] (= *censura*) **dar ~ a algn** (*Caribe*) to condemn sb, censure sb
[6] (= *madera*) lath
[7] (‡) (= *dinero*) dough‡; ✦***MODISMOS* estar en la(s) ~(s)** ◊ **estar sin ~s** (*Andes, CAm*) to be penniless, be broke*

latazo* SM nuisance, pain*

latear* ▸conjug 1a◂ VI (*LAm*) [1] (= *dar la lata*) to be a nuisance, be annoying
[2] (= *hablar*) to babble on

latente ADJ [1] (*gen*) latent
[2] (*LAm*) (= *vivo*) alive, intense, vigorous

lateral Ⓐ ADJ [1] [*calle, puerta, salida*] side *antes de s*
[2] (*en genealogía*) [*línea, parentesco*] indirect
[3] (*Fonética, Téc*) lateral
Ⓑ SM [1] [*de avenida*] side street
[2] **laterales** (*Teat*) wings
Ⓒ SMF (*Dep*) winger ► **lateral derecho** right winger ► **lateral izquierdo** left winger

lateralmente ADV sideways, laterally (*frm*)

latería SF [1] (*CAm*) (= *hojalata*) tin, tinplate
[2] (*Caribe, Cono Sur*) (= *hojalatería*) tinsmith's, tinsmith's workshop, tinworks

laterío SM (*Méx*) tinned goods *pl*, canned goods *pl*

latero SM (*LAm*) [1] (= *oficio*) tinsmith
[2] (*) (= *latoso*) bore, drag*

látex SM latex

latido SM [1] (= *palpitación*) [*de corazón*] beat, beating; [*de herida, dolor*] throb, throbbing
[2] [*de perro*] bark

latifundio SM large estate

latifundista SMF *owner of a large estate*

latigazo SM [1] (*con látigo*) (= *golpe*) lash; (= *chasquido*) crack (*of the whip*)
[2] [*de electricidad*] shock
[3] (= *insultos*) tongue lashing
[4] [*de bebida*] swig*

látigo SM [1] (= *instrumento*) whip
[2] (*Andes*) (= *sonido*) crack (*of the whip*)
[3] (*Cono Sur Dep*) finishing post, finishing line; ✦***MODISMO* salir al ~** to complete a task
[4] (*Andes, Cono Sur*) (= *jinete*) horseman, rider

latigudo ADJ (*LAm*) leathery

latigueada SF (*Andes, CAm, Cono Sur*) whipping, thrashing

latiguear ▸conjug 1a◂ VT (*LAm*) to whip, thrash

latiguera SF (*Andes*) whipping, thrashing

latiguillo SM [1] (= *muletilla*) cliché, overworked phrase
[2] (*Teat*) hamming

latín SM [1] (*Ling*) Latin; **bajo ~** Low Latin; ✦***MODISMO* saber (mucho) ~*** to be pretty sharp ► **latín clásico** Classical Latin ► **latín tardío** Late Latin ► **latín vulgar** Vulgar Latin
[2] **latines** Latin tags

latinajo SM (= *latín macarrónico*) dog Latin, bad Latin; **~s** Latin tags; **echar ~s** to come out with learned quotations and references

latinidad SF latinity

latinismo SM Latinism

latinista SMF Latinist

latinización SF latinization

latinizar ▸conjug 1f◂ VT, VI to latinize

latino/a Ⓐ ADJ [1] (= *latinoamericano*) Latin American
[2] (*Hist*) Latin
Ⓑ SM/F [1] (= *latinoamericano*) Latin American; **los ~s** Latin Americans; ✦***MODISMO* te cantan los cinco ~s**†* your feet smell
[2] (*Hist*) native/inhabitant of Latium; **los ~s** the people of Latium

Latinoamérica SF Latin America

latinoamericano/a ADJ, SM/F Latin American

latir ▸conjug 3a◂ VI [1] [*corazón*] to beat; [*herida*] to throb
[2] (= *estar latente*) to lie, lie hidden, lurk
[3] [*perro*] to bark
[4] (*Andes, Méx**) **me late que todo saldrá bien** something tells me that everything will turn out all right

latitud SF [1] (*Geog*) latitude; **a 45 grados de ~ sur** 45 degrees south
[2] (= *área*) area; **por estas ~es** in these parts
[3] (= *extensión*) breadth

latitudinal ADJ latitudinal

LATN SF ABR (*Par Aer*) = **Líneas Aéreas de Transporte Nacional**

lato ADJ (*frm*) [*territorio*] broad, wide; [*sentido*] broad

latón SM [1] (= *metal*) brass
[2] (*Cono Sur*) (= *recipiente*) large tin container; (*Andes*) (= *cubo*) tin bucket

latoso/a* Ⓐ ADJ (= *molesto*) annoying, tiresome; (= *pesado*) boring, tedious
Ⓑ SM/F bore, pain*, drag*

latrocinio SM larceny

Latvia SF Latvia

latvio/a Ⓐ ADJ Latvian
Ⓑ SM/F Latvian; **los ~s** the Latvians
Ⓒ SM (*Ling*) Latvian, Lettish

LAU SF ABR (*Esp Jur*) = **Ley de Arrendamientos Urbanos**

lauca SF (*Cono Sur*) baldness, loss of hair

laucadura SF (*Cono Sur*) baldness

laucar ▸conjug 1g◂ VT (*Cono Sur*) to fleece, shear, remove the hair *o* wool from

laucha SF [1] (*Cono Sur Zool*) *small mouse*; ✦***MODISMOS* aguaitar la ~** ◊ **catear la ~** to

➤ LENGUA Y USO: lástima 1 45.3

bide one's time; **ser una ~** ◊ **ser una lauchita** to be very sharp *o* quick
2 (*Arg*) (= *viejo verde*) dirty old man
3 (*) (= *flacón*) weed*
4 (*Andes*) expert

lauco ADJ (*Cono Sur*) bald, hairless

laúd SM (*Mús*) lute

laudable ADJ laudable, praiseworthy

laudablemente ADV laudably

láudano SM laudanum

laudatorio ADJ (*frm*) laudatory (*frm*)

laudo SM (*Jur*) decision, finding ► **laudo de obligado cumplimiento** binding decision

laureado/a (*frm*) Ⓐ ADJ [*persona*] honoured, honored (*EEUU*), distinguished; [*obra*] prize-winning; **poeta ~** poet laureate
Ⓑ SM/F (= *premiado*) prizewinner

laurear ▸conjug 1a◂ VT (*frm*) 1 (= *galardonar*) to honour, honor (*EEUU*)
2 (*Hist*) (= *coronar*) to crown with laurel

laurel SM 1 (*Bot*) laurel; **hojas de ~** (*Culin*) bay leaves ► **laurel cerezo** cherry laurel
2 **laureles** (= *gloria*) laurels; (= *premio*) honour *sing*, honor (*EEUU*); ✦*MODISMO* **descansar** *o* **dormirse en los ~es** to rest on one's laurels

laurencio SM (*Quím*) lawrencium

lauréola SF 1 (= *corona*) laurel wreath, crown of laurel; (= *auréola*) halo
2 (*Bot*) daphne

lauro SM 1 (= *árbol*) laurel
2 **lauros** laurels

Lausana SF Lausanne

lava[1] SF (*Geol*) lava

lava[2] SF (*Min*) washing

lavable ADJ washable

lavabo SM 1 (= *pila*) washbasin, washstand†
2 (= *cuarto de baño*) bathroom, washroom (*EEUU*), toilet; (*en lugar público*) toilet, rest room (*EEUU*); **¿dónde está el ~ de señoras, por favor?** where is the ladies, please?

lavacara SF (*Andes*) washbasin

lavacaras* SMF INV toady, creep*

lavacoches SM INV car wash

lavada SF wash

lavadero SM 1 (= *lavandería*) laundry, wash house; (*en río*) washing place; [*de casa*] utility room
2 (*LAm Min*) gold-bearing sands (*in river*)

lavado SM 1 [*de ropa, vehículo*] wash, washing; **le di dos ~s al jersey** I gave the jumper two washes, I washed the jumper twice; **yo me encargaré del ~ de la ropa** I'll take care of the washing; **la furgoneta quedará como nueva después de un buen ~** the van will look like new after a good wash; **prelavado y ~** pre-wash and wash ► **lavado a mano** hand-wash ► **lavado de automóviles** carwash ► **lavado de cabeza** shampoo ► **lavado en seco** dry cleaning
2 (*Med*) ► **lavado de estómago, lavado gástrico**: **le hicieron un ~ de estómago** he had his stomach pumped ► **lavado intestinal** enema ► **lavado vaginal** douche
3 (*fig*) **campaña de ~ de imagen** image campaign ► **lavado de bonos** bond-washing ► **lavado de cara** face lift ► **lavado de cerebro** brainwashing; **le han hecho un ~ de cerebro** he's been brainwashed ► **lavado de dinero** money-laundering

lavador SM 1 (*Cono Sur*) (= *fregadero*) sink
2 (*Cono Sur*) (= *aseo*) lavatory, toilet, washroom (*EEUU*)

lavadora SF 1 [*de ropa*] washing machine ► **lavadora de carga frontal** front-loading washing machine, front-loader ► **lavadora de carga superior** top-loading washing machine, top-loader ► **lavadora de coches** car wash ► **lavadora de platos** dishwasher ► **lavadora secadora** washer-drier
2 (*Andes*) (= *persona*) laundress, washerwoman

lavadura SF 1 (= *lavado*) washing
2 (= *agua sucia*) dirty water

lavafaros SM INV headlamp washer

lavafrutas SM INV finger bowl

lavagallos SM (*Andes, Caribe*) firewater

lavaje SM (*Cono Sur*) 1 = **lavadura**
2 (*Med*) enema

lavaluneta SM rear window washer

lavamanos SM INV washbasin

lavanda SF (*Bot*) lavender; **agua de ~** lavender water

lavandera SF 1 (= *mujer*) laundress, washerwoman
2 (*Orn*) wagtail

lavandería SF laundry ► **lavandería automática** launderette, laundromat (*EEUU*) ► **lavandería industrial** industrial laundry

lavandina SF (*Cono Sur*) bleach

lavándula SF = **lavanda**

lavaojos SM INV eye bath

lavaparabrisas SM INV windscreen washer, windshield washer (*EEUU*)

lavapiés SM INV footbath (*at the beach*)

lavaplatos Ⓐ SM INV 1 (= *aparato*) dishwasher
2 (*Chile, Col, Méx*) (= *fregadero*) sink
Ⓑ SMF INV (= *empleado*) washer-up, dishwasher

lavar ▸conjug 1a◂ Ⓐ VT 1 (= *limpiar*) to wash; **lávale la cabeza a la niña** wash the child's hair; **~ los platos** to wash the dishes, do the washing up; **~ en seco** to dry-clean; **~ y marcar** to shampoo and set; **tejanos lavados a la piedra** stonewashed jeans; **camisa de lava y pon** drip-dry shirt
2 [+ *dinero*] to launder
3 [+ *honor, ofensa, pecado*] to wash away
4 (*Min*) to wash
Ⓑ **lavarse** VPR to wash, have a wash; **tengo que ~me antes de salir** I need to wash *o* have a wash before going out; **~se los dientes** to clean one's teeth; **me lavé las manos antes de comer** I washed my hands before eating; **el gobierno se lavó las manos ante este asunto** the government washed their hands of the whole affair

lavasecadora SF washer-dryer

lavaseco SM (*Chile*) (= *tintorería*) drycleaner's

lavativa SF 1 (*Med*) enema
2 (†) (= *molestia*) nuisance, bother, bore

lavatorio SM 1 (†) (= *pila*) washstand†
2 (*LAm*) (= *cuarto de baño*) bathroom, washroom (*EEUU*)
3 (*Med*) lotion

lavavajillas SM INV (= *aparato*) dishwasher; (= *detergente*) washing-up liquid, (liquid) dish soap (*EEUU*)

lavazas SFPL dishwater *sing*, dirty water *sing*, slops

lavoteo* SM quick wash, cat-lick*

laxante ADJ, SM laxative

laxar ▸conjug 1a◂ VT [+ *vientre*] to loosen

laxativo ADJ laxative

laxitud SF (*frm*) laxity, laxness, slackness

laxo ADJ (*frm*) lax, slack

laya SF 1 (= *pala*) spade ► **laya de puntas** (garden) fork
2 (*liter*) (= *tipo*) kind, sort; **de esta ~** of this kind *o* sort

lazada SF (*decorativa*) bow; [*de zapatos*] knot

lazar ▸conjug 1f◂ Ⓐ VT 1 (= *atrapar con lazo*) to lasso, rope
2 (*Méx*) = **enlazar A**
Ⓑ VI (*CAm*) [*tren*] to connect

lazareto SM (*Hist*) leper hospital, isolation hospital

lazariento ADJ (*CAm, Cono Sur, Méx*) leprous

lazarillo SM blind person's guide

lazarino/a Ⓐ ADJ leprous
Ⓑ SM/F leper

Lázaro SM Lazarus

lazo SM 1 (= *nudo*) (*para asegurar*) knot; (*decorativo*) bow ► **lazo corredizo** slipknot ► **lazo de zapato** shoelace
2 (*Agr*) lasso, lariat
3 (*Caza*) snare, trap; ✦*MODISMOS* **caer en el ~** to fall into the trap; **tender un ~ a algn** to set *o* lay a trap for sb
4 (*Aut*) hairpin bend
5 **lazos** (= *vínculos*) ties; **~s familiares** family ties; **los ~s culturales entre los dos países** cultural ties between the two countries; **~s de parentesco** ties of blood

L/C SF ABR (= **Letra de Cambio**) B/E, BE

Lda. ABR = **Licenciada**

Ldo. ABR = **Licenciado**

le PRON PERS 1 (*directo*) (= *a él*) him; (= *a usted*) you; **no le veo** I don't see him; **¿le ayudo?** shall I help you?
2 (*indirecto*) (= *a él, ella*) (to) him, (to) her, (to) it; (= *a usted*) (to) you; **le hablé** I spoke to him, I spoke to her; **quiero darle esto** I want to give you this; **le he comprado esto** I bought this for you; **una de las mejores actuaciones que le hemos visto** one of the best performances we have seen from him; **no se le conoce otra obra** no other work of his is known; *ver tb* **leísmo**

lea‡ SF tart‡, slut‡, whore

leal ADJ [*persona*] loyal, faithful; [*competencia*] fair

lealmente ADV loyally, faithfully

lealtad SF loyalty, fidelity ► **lealtad de marca** brand loyalty, loyalty to a brand

leandra†‡ SF one peseta

Leandro SM Leander

leasing ['lizin] SM (= *operación*) leasing ► **leasing financiero** finance lease ► **leasing operativo** operational lease

lebrato SM leveret

lebrel SM greyhound

lebrillo SM earthenware bowl

lebrón* ADJ (*Méx*) 1 (= *astuto*) sharp, wide-awake
2 (= *arrogante*) boastful
3 (= *taimado*) sly

LEC SF ABR (*Esp Jur*) = **Ley de Enjuiciamiento Civil**

lección SF (= *tema*) lesson; (= *clase*) lesson, class; **dar lecciones** to teach, give lessons; ✦*MODISMOS* **aprenderse la ~** to learn one's lesson; **dar una ~ a algn** to teach sb a lesson; **saberse la ~*** to know what the score is*; **servir de ~**: **¡qué te sirva de ~!** let that be a lesson to you! ► **lección magistral** master class ► **lección particular** private lesson ► **lección práctica** object lesson (**de** in)

lecha SF milt, roe, soft roe

lechada SF [1] (*Constr*) (= *lavado*) whitewash; (*para fijar baldosas*) [*de masilla*] grout; [*de papel*] pulp
[2] (*Méx*) [*de leche*] milking
[3] (‡‡) (= *semen*) spunk‡‡

lechal Ⓐ ADJ sucking, suckling; **cordero ~** baby lamb, young lamb
Ⓑ SM milk, milky juice

lechar ▸conjug 1a◂ VT [1] (*LAm*) (= *ordeñar*) to milk
[2] (*Andes, CAm*) (= *amamantar*) to suckle
[3] (*CAm, Méx**) (= *blanquear*) to whitewash

lechazo[1] SM young lamb

lechazo[2]‡ SM [1] (= *golpe*) bash, swipe
[2] (= *choque*) bash, bang

leche SF [1] [*de mamífero*] milk; **se ha cortado la ~** the milk has gone off; **café con ~** white coffee, coffee with milk; **chocolate con ~** milk chocolate; ✦*MODISMO* **estar con** *o* **tener la ~ en los labios** to be young and inexperienced, be wet behind the ears ► **leche completa** full-cream milk, whole milk ► **leche condensada** condensed milk ► **leche de larga duración, leche de larga vida** long-life milk ► **leche del día** fresh milk ► **leche descremada, leche desnatada** skimmed milk ► **leche en polvo** powdered milk ► **leche entera** full-cream milk, whole milk ► **leche evaporada** evaporated milk ► **leche frita** *dessert made of milk thickened with flour, coated with egg and fried* ► **leche homogeneizada** homogenized milk ► **leche materna** mother's milk ► **leche merengada** milkshake flavoured with cinnamon ► **leche pasteurizada** pasteurised milk ► **leche semidesnatada** semi-skimmed milk ► **leche sin desnatar** (*Esp*) whole milk ► **leche UHT** long-life milk, UHT milk
[2] (*Bot*) milk, milky juice; (*Bol*) rubber; (*Caribe*) rubber tree ► **leche de coco** coconut milk
[3] (= *loción*) ► **leche corporal** body lotion ► **leche hidratante** moisturizer, moisturizing lotion ► **leche limpiadora** cleanser, cleansing milk
[4] (‡‡) (= *semen*) cum‡‡, spunk‡‡
[5] (‡) (= *golpe*) **darse una ~** to come a cropper*; **se ha dado una ~ con la moto** he came a cropper on his motorbike*; **¡te voy a dar una ~!** I'll thump you!*; **se liaron a ~s** they laid into each other*, they started swinging at each other*
[6] ✦*MODISMO* **ser la ~**‡ (= *el colmo*) **cantando es la ~** (= *bueno*) when he sings he's a bloody marvel‡; (= *malo*) when he sings he's bloody awful‡; **nunca se acuerdan de llamar, ¡son la ~!** they never think to call, they're unbelievable!
[7] (‡) (*como interjección*) **¡leche!** hell!, shit‡‡; **¡leches!** (= *ni hablar*) no way!*, get away!
[8] (‡) (*con valor enfático*) **de la ~**‡ bloody‡; **hace un calor de la ~** it's bloody hot; **¡este tráfico de la ~ me tiene frita!** I'm fed up with this bloody traffic!; **ni ~** *o* **~s**: **no entiende ni ~** he doesn't understand a bloody thing‡; **qué ~**: **¿qué ~ quieres?** what the hell do you want?‡; **¡qué coche ni qué ~!** car my foot!*
[9] (*indicando velocidad*) ✦*MODISMOS* **ir a toda ~**‡ to go like the clappers*; **salió echando** *o* **cagando ~s**‡‡ he went like a bat out of hell*
[10] **mala ~**‡ bad blood, ill-feeling; **aquí hay mucha mala ~** there's a lot of bad blood *o* ill-feeling here; **un tío con muy** *o* **mucha mala ~** a nasty piece of work*; **estar de mala ~** to be in a shitty mood‡; **poner a algn de mala ~** to piss sb off‡‡; **tener mala ~** to be a nasty piece of work*
[11] (‡) (= *lío*) **tuvimos que rellenar informes, impresos y toda esa ~** we had to fill in reports, forms and all that jazz*
[12] (*esp LAm*) (= *suerte*) good luck; **¡qué ~ tienes!** you lucky *o* jammy* devil!

lecheada SF (*Cono Sur*) = **lechada**

lechear ▸conjug 1a◂ VT (*LAm*) to milk

lechecillas SFPL sweetbreads

lechera SF [1] (= *recipiente*) milk can, milk churn
[2] (*LAm*) (= *vaca*) cow
[3] (*) [*de policía*] police car; *ver tb* **lechero**

lechería SF [1] (= *establecimiento*) dairy, creamery; (*Andes, Cono Sur*) (= *sala de ordeño*) milking parlour
[2] (*Cono Sur*) (= *vacas*) cows *pl*, herd
[3] (*LAm*) (= *tacañería*) meanness

lecherita SF milk jug

lechero/a Ⓐ ADJ [1] [*producción, cuota*] milk *antes de s*; [*productos, vaca*] dairy *antes de s*; **ganado ~** dairy cattle
[2] (*LAm**) (= *suertudo*) lucky
[3] (*Méx**) (= *tacaño*) mean, stingy*
[4] (*Caribe*) (= *codicioso*) greedy, grasping
Ⓑ SM/F (= *granjero*) dairy farmer; (= *distribuidor*) milkman/milkwoman; *ver tb* **lechera**

lechigada SF [*de animales*] litter, brood; [*de maleantes*] gang

lecho SM [1] (= *cama*) bed ► **lecho de enfermo** sickbed ► **lecho de muerte** deathbed ► **lecho de rosas** bed of roses ► **lecho mortuorio** deathbed
[2] (*Agr*) bedding ► **lecho de siembra** seedbed
[3] (= *fondo*) [*de río*] bed; [*de mar, lago*] bottom; [*de océano*] bottom, floor; (*Geol*) layer ► **lecho del mar** seabed ► **lecho de roca** bedrock ► **lecho marino** seabed

lechón/ona SM/F [1] (= *cochinillo*) piglet; (*Culin*) sucking pig, suckling pig (*EEUU*)
[2] (= *desaseado*) pig*, slob*

lechoncillo SM piglet; (*Culin*) sucking pig, suckling pig (*EEUU*)

lechosa SF (*Ven*) papaya (*fruit*)

lechosidad SF milkiness

lechoso ADJ [1] [*líquido*] milky
[2] (*LAm**) (= *suertudo*) lucky, jammy*

lechucear ▸conjug 1a◂ VI (*Andes*) to be on night duty

lechucero/a (*Andes*) Ⓐ SM/F (= *obrero*) nightshift worker; (= *taxista*) taxi driver (*who works at night*)
Ⓑ SM (= *taxi*) night taxi

lechudo ADJ (*LAm*) lucky, jammy*

lechuga SF [1] (*Bot*) lettuce ► **lechuga Cos, lechuga francesa, lechuga orejona** (*Méx*) cos lettuce; *ver tb* **fresco A6**
[2] (*Cos*) frill, flounce
[3] (= *billete*) (*Esp*†‡) 1000 peseta note; (*Caribe*) banknote
[4] (*euf*) = **leche 7**

lechuguilla SF (*Cos*) frill, flounce, ruff

lechuguino SM [1] (*Bot*) young lettuce
[2] (†) (= *persona*) dandy†

lechuza SF [1] (*Orn*) owl ► **lechuza común** barn owl
[2] (*Cono Sur, Méx*) (= *albino*) albino
[3] (*Caribe, Méx*‡) (= *puta*) whore

lechuzo/a* SM/F [1] (= *feo*) ugly devil*
[2] (= *lerdo*) dimwit*

leco‡ ADJ (*Méx*) nuts*, round the bend*

lectivo ADJ school *antes de s*; **año ~** school year

lectoescritura SF reading and writing

lector(a) Ⓐ ADJ **el público ~** the reading public
Ⓑ SM/F [1] (= *persona*) reader ► **lector(a) de cartas** fortune-teller
[2] (*Escol, Univ*) (conversation) assistant
Ⓒ SM (= *aparato*) reader ► **lector de código de barras** bar code scanner ► **lector de discos compactos** CD player, compact disc player ► **lector de disco óptico** optical disc scanner ► **lector de fichas** card reader ► **lector de tarjeta magnética** magnetic card reader ► **lector óptico de caracteres** optical character reader, optical character scanner

lectorado SM [1] [*de periódico*] readership
[2] (*Univ*) assistantship

lectura SF [1] (= *acción*) reading; **dar ~ a** to read (publicly); **sala de ~** reading room; **segunda ~** (*Esp Pol*) second reading ► **lectura del pensamiento** mind-reading ► **lectura dramatizada** dramatization, dramatized reading ► **lectura labial** lip-reading
[2] (= *obra*) reading matter; **lista de ~s recomendadas** reading list
[3] (= *interpretación*) reading; **hay varias ~s posibles de los resultados electorales** the election results can be read in various ways, there are various possible readings of the election results

leer ▸conjug 2e◂ Ⓐ VT to read; **~ el pensamiento a algn** to read sb's mind *o* thoughts; **~ la mano a algn** to read sb's palm; **~ los labios** to lip-read; **~ para sí** to read to oneself; ✦*MODISMO* **~ la cartilla a algn** to tell sb off
Ⓑ VI to read; **"al que leyere"** "to the reader"; **~ entre líneas** to read between the lines; **~ en voz alta** to read aloud; **~ en voz baja** to read quietly

lefa‡‡ SF spunk‡‡

lega SF lay sister

legación SF legation

legado SM [1] (= *enviado*) legate
[2] (*Jur*) legacy, bequest

legajar ▸conjug 1a◂ VT (*Andes, Cono Sur, Méx*) to file

legajo SM file, bundle (of papers)

legal ADJ [1] (= *de ley*) legal
[2] [*persona*] (= *de confianza*) trustworthy,

truthful, reliable; **es un tío ~*** he's a good bloke*
3 (= *sin antecedentes*) [*archivo*] clean*; [*persona*] clean*, with no police record
4 (*Andes*) (= *excelente*) great*

legalidad SF legality, lawfulness

legalista ADJ legalistic

legalización SF [*de partido, droga, situación*] legalization; [*de documentos*] authentication

legalizar ▸conjug 1f◂ VT [+ *partido, situación*] to legalize; [+ *documentos*] to authenticate

legalmente ADV legally, lawfully

légamo SM (= *cieno*) slime, mud; (= *arcilla*) clay

legamoso ADJ (= *viscoso*) slimy; (= *arcilloso*) clayey

legaña SF sleep, rheum

legañoso ADJ bleary

legar ▸conjug 1h◂ VT to bequeath, leave (**a** to)

legatario/a SM/F legatee

legendario ADJ legendary

leggings ['leγins] SMPL leggings

legía* SM legionnaire, *member of the Spanish Foreign Legion*

legibilidad SF legibility

legible ADJ legible; **~ por máquina** (*Inform*) machine-readable

legiblemente ADV legibly

legión SF legion; **la Legión** (*Esp*) the Spanish Legion; **son ~** they are legion ► **Legión de Honor** Legion of Honour, Legion of Honor (*EEUU*) ► **Legión Extranjera** Foreign Legion

legionario Ⓐ ADJ legionary
Ⓑ SM (*Hist*) legionary; (*Mil*) legionnaire

legionella SF legionnaire's disease

legislación SF legislation, laws *pl*; **~ antimonopolio** (*Com*) anti-trust laws, anti-trust legislation

legislador(a) SM/F legislator

legislar ▸conjug 1a◂ VI to legislate

legislativas SFPL parliamentary elections

legislativo ADJ legislative

legislatura SF (*Pol*) 1 (= *mandato*) term of office, period of office; (= *año parlamentario*) session; **agotar la ~** to serve out one's term (of office)
2 (*LAm*) (= *cuerpo*) legislature, legislative body

legista Ⓐ SMF (= *jurista*) jurist, legist; (= *estudiante*) law student
Ⓑ ADJ (*LAm*) **médico ~** forensic expert, criminal pathologist

legítima* SF **la ~** my better half

legitimación SF legitimation

legítimamente ADV 1 (= *legalmente*) legitimately, rightfully
2 (= *auténticamente*) genuinely

legitimar ▸conjug 1a◂ Ⓐ VT [+ *comportamiento*] to legitimize; [+ *documento, firma*] to authenticate; [+ *divorcio, elecciones, situación ilegal*] to legalize
Ⓑ **legitimarse** VPR to establish one's title, establish one's claim; **considerarse legitimado para hacer algo** to consider o.s. entitled to do sth

legitimidad SF 1 [*de petición*] legitimacy
2 [*de documento, firma*] authenticity

legitimista ADJ, SMF royalist, legitimist

legitimización SF legitimization

legitimizar ▸conjug 1f◂ VT = **legitimar**

legítimo ADJ 1 [*dueño*] legitimate, rightful; [*derecho*] legitimate; [*esposo*] lawful; **en legítima defensa** in self-defence
2 (= *auténtico*) [*firma, cuadro*] authentic, genuine; (*Aut*) [*repuestos*] genuine

lego/a Ⓐ ADJ 1 (*Rel*) [*hermano, predicador*] lay
2 (= *ignorante*) ignorant, uninformed
Ⓑ SM/F 1 (*Rel*) lay brother/lay sister; **los ~s** the laity
2 (= *desconocedor*) layman/laywoman, layperson

legón SM hoe

legración SF, **legrado** SM (*Med*) D & C, scrape*

legua SF league; ✦**MODISMO eso se ve** *o* **se nota a la ~** you can tell it a mile away

leguaje SM 1 (*CAm*) (= *distancia*) distance in leagues
2 (*Andes*) (= *gastos de viaje*) travelling expenses

leguleyo/a SM/F pettifogging lawyer, shyster (*EEUU*)

legumbre SF (= *seca*) pulse; (= *fresca*) vegetable

leguminosa SF (*Bot*) (= *planta*) leguminous plant; (= *grano*) pulse

leguminoso ADJ leguminous

lehendakari SMF *head of the Basque autonomous government*

leíble ADJ legible

leída SF (*LAm*) reading; **dar una ~ a*** to read; **de una ~** in one go

Leiden SM Leyden

leído ADJ [*persona*] well-read; [*libro*] widely read; **ser muy ~** to be well-read

leísmo SM *use of "le" instead of "lo" and "la" as direct objects*

> **LEÍSMO, LOÍSMO, LAÍSMO**
>
> *These terms refer to the reversal of the standard distinction between direct and indirect object pronouns for people in Spanish. Normally* **lo(s)** *and* **la(s)** *are the direct object pronouns (eg:* **Lo/La vi ayer** *I saw him/her yesterday) and* **le(s)** *the indirect equivalents (eg:* **Le di tu recado** *I gave him/her your message).* **Leísmo** *involves replacing* **lo(s)** *and* **la(s)** *with* **le(s)** *(eg:* **Le vi ayer**), *while* **loísmo** *and* **laísmo** *mean using* **lo(s)** *and* **la(s)** *instead of* **le(s)** *(eg:* **Lo/La di tu recado**). *Whereas* **leísmo** *is relatively socially acceptable,* **loísmo** *and* **laísmo** *tend to be frowned upon.*

leísta Ⓐ ADJ *that uses "le" instead of "lo" and "la" as direct objects*
Ⓑ SMF *user of "le" instead of "lo" and "la"*

lejanía SF (= *distancia*) remoteness; **en la ~** in the distance

lejano ADJ 1 (*en el espacio, en el tiempo*) distant; **en un futuro no muy ~** in the not too distant future; **en aquellas épocas lejanas** in those distant *o* far-off times; **un país ~** a far-off country; **Lejano Oeste** Far West; **Lejano Oriente** Far East
2 [*pariente*] distant

lejas ADJ PL **de ~ tierras** of/from some distant land

lejía[1] SF 1 (= *líquido*) bleach
2 (†*) (= *reprensión*) dressing-down*

lejía[2] SM = **legía**

lejísimos ADV (*superl*) *de* **lejos**

lejos Ⓐ ADV 1 (*en el espacio*) far, far away; **¿está ~?** is it far (away)?; **está muy ~** it's a long way (away), it's really far (away); **el cine queda demasiado ~ para ir andando** the cinema is too far to walk; **a lo ~** in the distance; **de** *o* **desde ~** at *o* from a distance, from afar (*liter*); **los curiosos observaban la escena desde ~** bystanders observed the scene at *o* from a distance; **prefiero ver los relámpagos de bien ~** I prefer watching lightning from a good distance *o* from a long way off; **veo mal de ~** I am short-sighted; **el equipo español iba seguido de ~ por Alemania** the Spanish team was followed at a distance by Germany, the Spanish team was followed, a long way behind, by Germany; **más ~** further away; **siéntate un poco más ~** sit a bit further away; ✦**MODISMOS ir demasiado ~** to go too far, overstep the mark; **llevar algo demasiado ~** to take sth too far; **llegar ~** to go far; **ese chico llegará ~** that boy will go far; **sin ir más ~**: **Javier, sin ir más ~, tuvo el mismo problema** Javier, as it happens, had the same problem; **hoy, sin ir más ~, la he visto dos veces** in fact *o* as it happens, I've seen her twice today; *ver tb* **mundanal**
2 **~ de algo** a long way from sth, far from sth; **está ~ de la oficina** it is a long way *o* far from the office; **vivo lejísimos de aquí** I live miles away from here; **~ de asustarse, los niños estaban encantados con la tormenta** far from being scared, the children really loved the storm; **estaba ~ de saber lo que iba a pasar** little did I know what would happen; **en eso no andaba él muy ~** he wasn't far off the mark on that point; **nada más ~ de mi intención que hacerte daño** harming you was the last thing on my mind; **nada más ~ de la realidad** nothing could be further from the truth
3 (*en el tiempo*) far off; **junio ya no está tan ~** June is not so far off now; **está ~ el día en que podamos comprarnos una casa** the day we can afford a house is still a long way off; **¡qué ~ me parecen las vacaciones!** the holidays seem so far off!; **venir de ~**: **su amistad viene de ~** their friendship goes back a long way
4 (*Cono Sur*) (= *con mucho*) easily; **es ~ la más inteligente** she's the most intelligent by far, she's easily the most intelligent; **ganaron ~** they won easily
Ⓑ SM 1 (= *aspecto*) **tiene buen ~** it looks good from a distance
2 (*Arte*) [*de cuadro*] background
3 (*Esp*) (*en la vista*) **tengo mal el ~** I am short-sighted

lejura SF 1 (*Andes*) distance
2 **lejuras** (*Cono Sur*) remote place, remote area

lele* ADJ, SMF (*LAm*) = **lelo**

lelo/a Ⓐ ADJ (= *tonto*) slow; **quedarse ~** to be stunned
Ⓑ SM/F (= *tonto*) halfwit; **parece que te ven cara de ~** they seem to think you're totally stupid, they seem to think you were born yesterday

lema SM 1 (*Pol*) slogan
2 (= *máxima*) motto
3 (*en diccionario*) headword

lem(m)ing ['lemin] SM lemming

lempira SM (*Hond*) *monetary unit of Honduras*

lempo (*Andes*) Ⓐ ADJ (= *grande*) big, large
Ⓑ SM (= *pedazo*) bit, piece; **un ~ de caballo** a big horse

lémur SM lemur

lencería SF [1] (= *ropa interior*) lingerie; **~ fina** fine lingerie
[2] (= *ropa blanca*) linen; **~ fina** fine linen
[3] (†) (= *armario*) linen cupboard
[4] (†) (= *tienda*) draper's, draper's shop

lencero/a SM/F draper

lendakari SM = **lehendakari**

lendroso ADJ lousy, infested with lice

lengón ADJ (*Andes*) = **lenguón**

lengua SF [1] (*Anat*) tongue; **me he mordido la ~** I've bitten my tongue; **beber con la ~** to lap up; **mala ~** gossip; **según las malas ~s ...** according to gossip ...; **sacar la ~: abra la boca y saque la ~** open your mouth and put *o* stick your tongue out; **no le saques la ~ a tu hermana** don't stick your tongue out at your sister; ✦*MODISMOS* **andar en ~s** to be the talk of the town; **atar la ~ a algn** to silence sb; **buscar la ~ a algn** to pick a quarrel with sb; **¿te ha comido la ~ el gato?** has the cat got your tongue?; **darle a la ~** to chatter, talk too much; **darse la ~*** to french-kiss; **hacerse ~s de algn/algo** to praise sb/sth to the skies, rave about sb/sth; **irse de la ~** to let the cat out of the bag; **llegar con la ~ fuera** to arrive out of breath; **morderse la ~** to hold one's tongue, bite one's lip *o* tongue; **nacer con la ~ fuera** to be born idle; **no morderse la ~** not to mince one's words, not to pull one's punches; **no tener pelos en la ~** not to mince one's words, not to pull one's punches; **tener algo en la punta de la ~** to have sth on the tip of one's tongue; **soltar la ~*** to spill the beans*; **tener mucha ~*** to be lippy*, be cheeky*; **tirar de la ~ a algn** to draw sb out, make sb talk ► **lengua de trapo** baby talk ► **lengua larga** (*LAm*), **lengua viperina** sharp tongue, vicious tongue; *ver tb* **largo A1**, **trabar C1**
[2] [*de campana*] tongue, clapper
[3] (*Geog*) ► **lengua de tierra** spit of land, tongue of land
[4] (*Ling*) language, tongue; (*Esp Escol*) Spanish language (*as a school subject*); **hablar en ~** (*Andes*) to speak Quichua ► **lengua de destino** target language ► **lengua de origen** source language ► **lengua de trabajo** working language ► **lengua franca** lingua franca ► **lengua madre** parent language ► **lengua materna** mother tongue ► **lengua minoritaria** minority language ► **lengua moderna** modern language ► **lengua muerta** dead language ► **lengua oficial** official language ► **lengua viva** living language

> **LENGUAS COOFICIALES**
>
> *Under the Spanish constitution* **catalán, euskera and gallego** *are* **lenguas oficiales** *and enjoy the same status as* **castellano** *in the autonomous regions in which they are spoken. These languages are also known as* **lenguas cooficiales** *to show they enjoy equal status with Spanish. The regional governments actively promote their use through the media and the education system.*
>
> ⇨ *See also* CATALÁN, EUSKERA, GALLEGO

lenguado SM sole

lenguaje SM [1] (*gen*) language; **en ~ llano** in plain English ► **lenguaje comercial** business language ► **lenguaje corporal** body language ► **lenguaje de gestos** sign language ► **lenguaje de las manos** sign language ► **lenguaje del cuerpo** body language ► **lenguaje de los signos** sign language ► **lenguaje formal** formal language ► **lenguaje fuente** source language ► **lenguaje gestual** sign language ► **lenguaje objeto** target language ► **lenguaje periodístico** journalese ► **lenguaje vulgar** common speech
[2] (*Literat*) style
[3] (*Inform*) language ► **lenguaje de alto nivel** high-level language ► **lenguaje de bajo nivel** low-level language ► **lenguaje de programación** program(m)ing language ► **lenguaje ensamblador** assembly language ► **lenguaje informático**, **lenguaje máquina** machine language

lenguaraz ADJ (= *charlatán*) garrulous, talkative; (= *mal hablado*) foul-mouthed

lenguaz ADJ garrulous

lengüeta Ⓐ SF [1] (*gen*) tab; [*de zapatos*] tongue; [*de balanza*] needle, pointer; [*de flecha*] barb
[2] (*Mús*) reed
[3] (*Anat*) epiglottis
[4] (*LAm*) (= *cortapapeles*) paper knife
[5] (*LAm Cos*) edging (*of a petticoat*)
Ⓑ SMF (*LAm*) (= *hablador*) chatterbox*; (= *chismoso*) gossip

lengüetada SF, **lengüetazo** SM lick

lengüetear ▸conjug 1a◂ (*LAm*) Ⓐ VT (= *lamer*) to lick Ⓑ VI [1] (= *sacar la lengua*) to stick one's tongue out [2] (*Caribe*) (= *parlotear*) to jabber away, chatter away

lengüeterías SFPL (*LAm*) gossip *sing*, tittle-tattle *sing*

lengüetero ADJ (*Caribe*) (= *hablador*) garrulous; (= *chismoso*) gossipy

lengüicorto* ADJ shy, timid

lengüilargo ADJ (*Caribe*), **lengüisucio** ADJ (*Caribe*) foul-mouthed

lenguón/ona (*LAm*) Ⓐ ADJ [1] (= *chismoso*) gossipy; (= *hablador*) garrulous
[2] (= *franco*) outspoken
Ⓑ SM/F gossip

lenidad SF lenience

Lenin SM Lenin

Leningrado SM Leningrad

leninismo SM Leninism

leninista ADJ, SMF Leninist

lenitivo Ⓐ ADJ lenitive
Ⓑ SM lenitive, palliative

lenocinio SM pimping, procuring; **casa de ~** brothel

lentamente ADV slowly; **bébelo ~** drink it slowly; **el tráfico circulaba muy ~** the traffic was very slow-moving *o* was going very slowly; **la libra ha subido ~ en el último año** the pound has edged upwards in the last year, the pound has risen slowly in the last year

lente SF (*a veces* SM) [1] (*gen*) lens ► **lente de aumento** magnifying glass ► **lente de gran ángulo**, **lente granangular** wide-angle lens ► **lentes de contacto** contact lenses ► **lentes progresivas** varifocal lenses ► **lente zoom** zoom lens
[2] **lentes** (*esp LAm*) (= *gafas*) glasses, spectacles ► **lentes bifocales** bifocals

lenteja SF [1] (= *grano*) lentil
[2] **lentejas** (= *guiso*) lentil soup *sing*; ✦*MODISMO* **ganarse las ~s** to earn one's crust

lentejuela SF sequin, spangle

lentificar ▸conjug 1g◂ Ⓐ VT to slow down
Ⓑ **lentificarse** VPR to slow down

lentilla SF contact lens; **lentillas** contact lenses ► **lentillas blandas** soft (contact) lenses ► **lentillas duras** hard (contact) lenses ► **lentillas semirígidas** gas permeable (contact) lenses

lentitud SF slowness; **con ~** slowly

lento Ⓐ ADJ [*ritmo, movimiento, caída*] slow; [*tráfico, película*] slow, slow-moving; **una muerte lenta** a lingering *o* slow death; **la circulación iba muy lenta esta mañana** traffic was very slow *o* slow-moving this morning; **¡qué ~s pasan los días!** the days go so slowly!; **es muy ~ en el trabajo** he's a very slow worker; **la economía está creciendo a un ritmo ~** the economy is growing sluggishly *o* slowly; **~ pero seguro** slowly but surely; *ver tb* **cámara A1**, **fuego 2.2**, **paso² A4**
Ⓑ ADV slowly; **trabaja muy ~** he works very slowly; **habla tan ~ que casi no la entiendo** she speaks so slowly that I can hardly understand her

lentorro* ADJ sluggish, slow

leña SF [1] (*para el fuego*) firewood; **hacer ~** to gather firewood; ✦*MODISMOS* **echar ~ al fuego** to add fuel to the fire *o* flames; **llevar ~ al monte** to carry coals to Newcastle ► **leña de oveja** (*Cono Sur*) sheep droppings
[2] (*) (= *golpes*) thrashing, hiding; **dar ~ a algn** ◊ **cargar** *o* **hartar de ~ a algn** to thrash sb, give sb a good hiding; **repartir ~** to lash out; **sacudirle ~ a algn** to give sb (some) stick*, lay into sb*; **trincar ~** to sweat blood

leñador(a) SM/F woodcutter, logger

leñar ▸conjug 1a◂ VT (*Cono Sur, Méx*), **leñatear** ▸conjug 1a◂ VT (*Andes*) (= *hacer leña*) to make into firewood; (= *cortar leña*) to cut up for firewood

leñateo SM (*Andes, CAm*) woodpile

leñatero/a SM/F (*Cono Sur*) woodcutter, logger

leñazo* SM [1] (= *golpe*) knock
[2] (= *choque*) bash*

leñe* EXCL heck*; **¿dónde ~ ...?** where the heck ...?

leñera SF woodshed

leñero/a SM/F (= *comerciante*) timber merchant

leño SM [1] (= *tronco*) log, lumber (*EEUU*); ✦*MODISMOS* **dormir como un ~** to sleep like a log; **hacer ~ del árbol caído** to kick sb when he's down
[2] (*) (= *zoquete*) dolt*, blockhead*

leñoso ADJ woody

Leo SM (*Zodíaco*) Leo

León SM [1] (= *nombre*) Leon, Leo
[2] (*Geog*) (*en España*) León

león SM [1] (*Zool*) lion; (*LAm*) puma; ✦*MODISMOS* **estar hecho un ~** to be furious; **ponerse como un ~** to be furious, get mad ► **león marino** sea lion; *ver tb* **fiero A1**
[2] **leones**‡ (= *dados*) loaded dice

leona SF [1] (*Zool*) (*fig*) lioness
[2] (*) (= *portera*) porter, concierge
[3] (‡) (= *puta*) tart‡, slut‡
[4] (*Chile*) (= *confusión*) confusion, mix-up*

leonado ADJ tawny, fawn-colored (*EEUU*)

leonera SF [1] (= *jaula*) lion's cage; (= *cueva*) lion's den; **parece una ~** the place is a tip*
[2] (*Cono Sur*) (= *celda*) communal prison cell
[3] (*Andes*) (= *reunión*) noisy gathering

leonés/esa Ⓐ ADJ of/from León
Ⓑ SM/F native/inhabitant of León; **los leoneses** the people of León
Ⓒ SM (*Ling*) Leonese

leonino ADJ [1] (*Literat*) leonine
[2] [*contrato*] unfair, one-sided

Leonor SF Eleanor

leontina SF watch chain

leopardo SM leopard ► **leopardo cazador** cheetah

leopoldina SF fob, short watch chain

leotardo SM [1] [*de bailarina*] leotard
[2] **leotardos** woollen tights, woolen pantyhose (*EEUU*)

Lepe SM ✦**MODISMOS ir donde las ~** (*Cono Sur*) to make a bloomer* (*in calculating*); **saber más que ~*** to be pretty smart; **ser más tonto que ~*** to be a complete twit*

leperada* SF (*CAm, Méx*) (*en el habla*) coarse remark; (= *acto*) dirty trick, rotten thing (to do)*

lépero/a* Ⓐ ADJ [1] (*CAm, Méx*) (= *grosero*) rude, uncouth
[2] (*Andes*) **estar ~** to be broke*
Ⓑ SM/F [1] (*CAm, Méx*) (= *grosero*) rude person, uncouth person
[2] (*Méx*) (= *plebeyo*) low-class person, guttersnipe (*pey*)

leperusco* ADJ (*Méx*) low-class, plebeian; (*pey*) rotten*, villainous

lepidopterólogo/a SM/F lepidopterist

lepidópteros SMPL lepidoptera, butterflies and moths

lepisma SF silverfish

leporino ADJ leporine, hare-like; **labio ~** harelip, cleft lip

lepra SF leprosy ► **lepra de montaña** (*LAm*) mountain leprosy, leishmaniasis (*frm*)

leprosario SM (*Méx*), **leprosería** SF leper colony

leproso/a Ⓐ ADJ leprous
Ⓑ SM/F leper

lerdear ▸conjug 1a◂ Ⓐ VI (*CAm, Arg*) (*sin prisa*) to do things very slowly; (*sin ganas*) to drag one's feet*
Ⓑ **lerdearse** VPR to be slow (*about doing things*), drag one's feet*

lerdera SF (*CAm*) = **lerdez**

lerdez SF, **lerdeza** SF (*CAm*) [1] (= *lentitud*) slowness
[2] (= *estupidez*) slow-wittedness
[3] (= *patosería*) clumsiness
[4] (= *pesadez*) heaviness, sluggishness

lerdo ADJ [1] (= *lento*) slow
[2] (= *de pocas luces*) slow-witted
[3] (= *patoso*) clumsy
[4] (= *pesado*) heavy, sluggish

lerdura SF (*Cono Sur*) = **lerdez**

lerén* SM (*Andes*) [1] (= *tipo*) bloke*, guy*
[2] (= *de baja estatura*) midget

Lérida SF Lerida

leridano/a Ⓐ ADJ of/from Lérida
Ⓑ SM/F native/inhabitant of Lérida; **los ~s** the people of Lérida

les PRON PERS [1] (*directo*) (= *a ellos, ellas*) them; (= *a ustedes*) you
[2] (*indirecto*) (= *a ellos, ellas*) (to) them; (= *a ustedes*) (to) you; *ver tb* **le**

lesbiana SF lesbian

lesbianismo SM lesbianism

lésbico ADJ, **lesbio** ADJ lesbian

lesera* SF (*Andes, Cono Sur*) (= *estupidez*) stupidity; (= *tontería*) nonsense

leseras* SFPL (*Cono Sur*) (= *tonterías*) nonsense *sing*

lesión SF [1] (= *herida*) wound, lesion; (*Dep*) injury ► **lesión cerebral** brain damage ► **lesión de ligamentos** injured ligament
[2] (*Jur*) **agresión con lesiones** assault and battery
[3] (= *agravio*) damage

lesionado ADJ (= *herido*) hurt; (*Dep*) injured

lesionar ▸conjug 1a◂ Ⓐ VT (= *dañar*) to hurt; (= *herir*) injure
Ⓑ **lesionarse** VPR to injure oneself; **~se la pierna** to injure one's leg

lesividad SF harmfulness

lesivo ADJ [1] (= *dañino*) harmful, damaging
[2] (= *perjudicial*) detrimental

lesna SF awl

leso ADJ (*frm*) [1] (= *ofendido*) hurt; **crimen de lesa patria** high treason; **crimen de lesa humanidad** crime against humanity; **lesa majestad** lese-majesty; **crimen de lesa majestad** lese-majesty, treason
[2] (*LAm**) (= *necio*) simple, stupid; **hacer ~ a algn** (*Cono Sur*) to play a trick on sb; ✦**MODISMOS no está para ~** (*Cono Sur*) he's not easily taken in; **hacerse el ~** to pretend not to know, pretend not to notice

Lesoto SM Lesotho

lesura* SF (*Chile*) stupidity

letal ADJ deadly, lethal

letalidad SF (*frm*) deadliness, lethal nature; **la enfermedad tiene una elevada ~** there is a high death rate from this disease

letanía SF [1] (*Rel*) litany
[2] (= *retahíla*) long list, litany

letárgico ADJ lethargic

letargo SM lethargy

Lete(o) SM Lethe

letón/ona Ⓐ ADJ Latvian
Ⓑ SM/F Latvian; **los letones** the Latvians
Ⓒ SM (*Ling*) Latvian, Lettish

Letonia SF Latvia

letra SF [1] (*Tip*) letter; ✦**MODISMOS decir a una mujer las cuatro ~s**†* to call a woman a slut; **poner unas** *o* **dos** *o* **cuatro ~s a algn** to drop sb a line; ✦**REFRÁN la ~ con sangre entra** spare the rod and spoil the child ► **letra bastardilla**, **letra cursiva** italics *pl*, italic type (*EEUU*) ► **letra de imprenta**, **letra de molde** print; **escriba su nombre en ~s de imprenta** *o* **de molde** please print your name in block letters ► **letra gótica** Gothic script ► **letra inicial** initial letter ► **letra mayúscula** capital letter ► **letra menuda** small print ► **letra minúscula** small letter ► **letra muerta** dead letter ► **letra negrilla**, **letra negrita** bold type, heavy type ► **letra pequeña** small print ► **letra redonda** roman, roman type (*EEUU*) ► **letras sagradas** Scripture ► **letra versal** capital letter ► **letra versalita** small capital ► **letra voladita** superscript (type)
[2] (= *escritura*) handwriting, writing; **no le entiendo la ~** I can't read his handwriting *o* writing; ✦**MODISMO despacito y buena ~** easy does it
[3] (= *sentido literal*) letter, literal meaning; **a la ~** to the letter; **atarse a la ~** (*frm*) to stick to the literal meaning; *ver tb* **pie 4**
[4] (*Com*) (= *pago*) instalment, installment (*EEUU*); **le faltan cinco ~s para acabar de pagar el coche** she still has five instalments to make on the car; **pagar a ~ vista** to pay on sight ► **letra abierta** letter of credit ► **letra aceptada** accepted letter ► **letra a la vista** sight draft ► **letra bancaria** banker's draft, bank draft ► **letra de cambio** bill (of exchange), draft ► **letra de crédito** letter of credit ► **letra del Tesoro** Treasury bill ► **letra de patente** letters patent *pl*
[5] [*de canción*] words *pl*, lyrics *pl*
[6] **letras** (= *cultura*) letters, learning *sing*; **un hombre de ~s** a man of letters; **primeras ~s** elementary education, the three Rs
[7] **letras** (*Escol, Univ*) (= *humanidades*) arts; **voy a hacer dos asignaturas de ~s** I'm going to study two arts subjects; **Filosofía y Letras** humanities

letrado/a Ⓐ ADJ [1] (= *culto*) learned; (*pey*) pedantic
[2] (*Jur*) legal; **derecho a la asistencia letrada** right to have a lawyer present
Ⓑ SM/F lawyer, counsel, attorney (*EEUU*) ► **letrado/a de oficio** court-appointed counsel

letrero SM [1] (*en tienda*) sign, notice; (*en carretera*) sign ► **letrero luminoso** neon sign
[2] (*en moneda*) inscription

letrina SF latrine, privy; **el río es una ~** the river is an open sewer

letrista SMF (*Mús*) songwriter, lyricist

leucemia SF leukaemia, leukemia (*EEUU*)

leucémico/a SM/F leukaemia *o* (*EEUU*) leukemia sufferer

leucocito SM (*Med*) leucocyte, leukocyte (*EEUU*)

leucoma SF leucoma

leudante ADJ *ver* **harina**

leudar ▸conjug 1a◂ Ⓐ VT to leaven
Ⓑ **leudarse** VPR [*pan*] to rise

leva SF [1] (*Náut*) weighing anchor
[2] (*Mil*) levy
[3] (*Mec*) cam
[4] (*Andes, CAm*) (= *estafa*) trick, swindle, ruse
[5] ✦**MODISMOS bajar la ~ a algn** (*Andes, Cono Sur*) to do sb a mischief; **caer de ~** (*CAm*) to play the fool; **echar ~s** (*Andes, Méx**) (= *jactarse*) to boast; (*Andes**) (= *amenazar*) to bluster, utter threats; **encender la ~ a algn** (*Caribe**) to give sb a good hiding*; **ponerse la ~** (*Andes*) (= *largarse*) to beat it*; (= *hacer novillos*) (*) to play truant; (= *faltar al trabajo*) to skive off work*

levadizo ADJ that can be raised; **puente ~** drawbridge

levado SM raising; **sistema de ~** raising mechanism

levadura SF [1] yeast ► **levadura de cerveza** brewer's yeast ► **levadura de panadero** baker's yeast ► **levadura en polvo** baking powder

2 ✦*MODISMO* **mala ~** (*euf*) = **mala leche**; *ver* **leche 10**

levantada SF (*Perú*) (= *alzamiento*) raising

levantado ADJ (= *despierto*) up; **no me esperes ~** don't wait up for me

levantador(a) SM/F ► **levantador(a) de pesos** weight lifter

levantamiento SM 1 (= *alzado*) [*de objeto*] raising, lifting; (*con una grúa*) hoisting ► **levantamiento de pesas** weight-lifting
2 [*de prohibición, embargo*] lifting; **el ~ de las sanciones económicas** the lifting of economic sanctions; **el ~ de la veda de caza** the opening of the hunting season
3 (*Arquit*) [*de edificio, monumento*] construction; [*de plano*] drawing up
4 (*Jur*) **se procedió al ~ del acta de denuncia** they proceeded to issue a formal report; **~ del cadáver** removal of the body
5 (*Pol*) uprising, revolt
6 (*Geog*) survey; **~ cartográfico** topographical survey, mapping

levantamuertos* SM INV (*Andes Culin*) vegetable broth

levantar ▸conjug 1a◂ Ⓐ VT 1 (= *alzar*) 1·1 [+ *peso, objeto*] to lift; (*con una grúa*) to hoist; **¿puedes ~ un poco la silla?** can you lift the chair up a bit?; **era imposible ~lo del suelo** it was impossible to lift it off the floor; **levantemos las copas por los novios** let's raise our glasses to the bride and groom; **la grúa levantó el coche hasta la plataforma** the crane hoisted the car onto the platform
1·2 [+ *pierna, cabeza, cejas*] to raise; **levanta la pierna derecha** raise your right leg; **levantemos los corazones** let us lift up our hearts; **~ la mano** to put one's hand up, raise one's hand; **levantó la mano para pedir la vez** she put her hand up *o* raised her hand to ask for a turn; **a mí no me levanta la mano nadie** nobody raises their hand to me; **~ la mirada** *o* **los ojos** *o* **la vista** to look up; **no levantó la mirada del libro cuando entramos** she didn't raise her eyes from her book *o* she didn't look up from the book when we came in; ✦*MODISMO* **si tu padre ~a la cabeza ...** your father must be turning in his grave; **si su mujer ~a la cabeza y lo viera casado otra vez se volvería a morir** his wife would turn in her grave to see him married again; *ver tb* **cabeza A2**, **tapa 1**
1·3 [+ *cortina, falda*] to lift, lift up; [+ *persiana, telón*] to raise; **el viento le levantó la falda** the wind lifted her skirt (up); **~ polvo** to raise dust
2 (= *poner de pie*) 2·1 **~ a algn** (*del suelo*) to lift sb, lift sb up; (*de la cama*) to get sb up; **pesaba tanto que no pude ~la del suelo** she was so heavy that I couldn't lift her off the ground; **cuando se sienta en ese sofá no hay quien lo levante** once he sits on that sofa no one can get him off it; **su actuación levantó al público de sus asientos** her performance brought the audience to their feet
2·2 [+ *objeto caído*] to pick up
3 (= *erigir*) [+ *edificio, pared*] to put up; [+ *monumento*] to erect, put up
4 (= *fundar*) [+ *empresa, imperio*] to found, establish; **levantó un gran imperio comercial** he founded *o* established a great commercial empire
5 (= *dar un empuje*) to build up; **todos los trabajadores ayudaron a ~ la empresa** all the workers helped to build up the company; **tenemos que ~ de nuevo la economía** we've got to get the economy back on its feet
6 [+ *ánimo, moral*] to lift, raise; **necesito algo que me levante la moral** I need something to lift *o* raise my spirits
7 [+ *tono, volumen*] to raise; **levanta la voz, que no te oigo** speak up — I can't hear you; **¡no levantes la voz!** keep your voice down!; **a mí nadie me levanta la voz** nobody raises their voice to me
8 (= *desmontar*) [+ *tienda de campaña*] to take down; **~ el campamento** to strike camp; **~ la casa** to move out; **~ la mesa** (*LAm*) to clear the table
9 (= *producir*) [+ *sospechas*] to arouse; [+ *dolor*] to give; [+ *rumor*] to spark off; **tantos gritos me levantan dolor de cabeza** all this shouting is giving me a headache; **el reportaje ha levantado rumores de un posible divorcio** the report has sparked off rumours of a possible divorce; **~ falso testimonio** (*Jur*) to give false testimony; (*Rel*) to bear false witness; *ver tb* **ampolla**
10 (= *terminar*) [+ *prohibición, embargo*] to lift; [+ *veda*] to end; **esta semana se levanta la veda** the close season ends this week; **se ha levantado la prohibición de la caza de la ballena** the ban on whaling has been lifted; **~ el castigo a algn** to let sb off; **se ~á el castigo a los que pidan perdón** those who apologize will be let off (their punishment)
11 (*Jur*) 11·1 [+ *censo*] to take; [+ *atestado*] to make; [+ *sesión*] to adjourn; **se levanta la sesión** court is adjourned; *ver tb* **acta 1**
11·2 [+ *cadáver*] to remove
12 (*Arquit*) [+ *plano*] to make, draw up
13 (*Caza*) to flush out; *ver tb* **liebre 1**, **vuelo² 1**
14 (*Mil*) [+ *ejército*] to raise
15 (= *sublevar*) (*Pol*) **la corrupción política levantó al pueblo contra el gobierno** political corruption turned people against the government
16 (*Naipes*) (= *coger*) to pick; (= *superar*) to beat
17 (*) (= *ganar*) [+ *dinero*] to make, earn
18 (*) (= *robar*) to pinch*, swipe*
19 (*Ven‡*) (= *arrestar*) to nick‡, arrest
20 (*Col, Perú, Ven**) [+ *mujer*] to pick up*
Ⓑ VI 1 (*hum*) [*persona*] **no levanta del suelo más de metro y medio** she's no more than five foot from head to toe
2 (*Naipes*) to cut the pack; **levanta, es tu turno** cut the pack, it's your turn
Ⓒ **levantarse** VPR 1 (= *alzarse*) 1·1 (*de la cama, del suelo*) to get up; **me levanto todos los días a las ocho** I get up at eight every day; **¡venga, levántate!** come on, get out of bed *o* get up!; **se cayó y no podía ~se** she fell down and couldn't get up; **ya se levanta y anda un poco** he's getting up and about now; ✦*MODISMO* **~se con** *o* (*Andes*) **en el pie izquierdo** to get out of bed on the wrong side
1·2 (*de un asiento*) to get up, stand up; **se ~on todos cuando entró el obispo** everyone got up *o* stood up *o* rose to their feet (*frm*) when the bishop entered; **levántense** please stand; **nadie se levanta de la mesa hasta que no lo diga yo** no one gets up from the table until I say so
2 (= *erguirse*) [*edificio, monumento*] to stand; **en la plaza se levanta el monumento a Salazar** in the square stands the monument to Salazar; **la torre se levanta por encima de los demás edificios** the tower rises *o* stands above the other buildings
3 (= *despegarse*) 3·1 (*Constr*) [*pintura*] to come off, peel off; [*baldosa, suelo*] to come up; **el suelo estaba todo levantado** the floor had all come up
3·2 [*piel*] to peel
4 (*Meteo*) 4·1 (= *disiparse*) [*niebla, nubes*] to lift
4·2 (= *producirse*) [*viento*] to get up; **se está levantando un viento terrible** there's a terrible wind getting up; **se ~on olas de tres metros** ten foot waves rose up
5 (= *sublevarse*) to rise, rise up
6 (*Rel*) (= *resucitar*) to rise
7 (*) (= *apoderarse*) **~se con algo** to make off with sth
8 (*Col, Perú, Ven**) [+ *mujer*] (= *ligarse a*) to pick up*; (= *acostarse con*) to get off with*

levantaválvulas SM INV valve tappet

levante¹ SM (*Geog*) 1 (= *este*) east
2 (*tb* **viento de ~**) east wind

levante² SM 1 (*Caribe Pol*) uprising
2 (*Caribe*) (= *arreo*) driving of cattle
3 (*Andes*) (= *arrogancia*) arrogance, haughtiness
4 **dar** *o* **pegar un ~ a algn** (*Cono Sur**) to give sb a dressing-down*
5 (*Cono Sur**) (= *encuentro*) pick-up*; **hacer un ~ a algn** to pick sb up*
6 **hacer un ~** (*Caribe**) to fall in love

Levante SM 1 (= *este de España*) east coast
2 (= *oriente*) Levant; **el ~** the Levant, the (Near) East

levantino/a Ⓐ ADJ 1 (= *del Levante español*) of/from the eastern coast *o* provinces of Spain
2 (= *oriental*) Levantine
Ⓑ SM/F 1 (= *del Levante español*) native/inhabitant of the eastern provinces of Spain; **los ~s** the people of the east of Spain
2 (= *oriental*) Levantine

levantisco ADJ [*persona*] rebellious; [*país*] turbulent, troubled

levar ▸conjug 1a◂ Ⓐ VT 1 (*Mil*) to levy, recruit (by force)
2 (*Náut*) **~ anclas** to weigh anchor
Ⓑ **levarse** VPR to weigh anchor, set sail

leve ADJ 1 (= *sin importancia*) minor; **cometió una falta ~** he committed a minor offence; **sólo tiene heridas ~s** he only has minor injuries
2 (= *suave*) [*brisa*] light; [*sonrisa*] slight; **asintió con un ~ movimiento de cabeza** she gave a slight nod of agreement
3 (= *ligero*) [*carga, peso*] light
4 (*frm*) (= *muy fino*) light, fine; **un ~ velo** a light veil

levedad SF 1 (= *poca importancia*) **debido a la ~ de las heridas** because the injuries were not serious
2 (*frm*) (*en peso*) lightness
3 (*frm*) (*en grosor*) fineness

levemente ADV 1 (= *superficialmente*) slightly; **ocho personas resultaron ayer ~ heridas** eight people were slightly hurt yesterday
2 (= *ligeramente*) lightly; **se le notaba ~ aturdido** he appeared to be slightly stunned
3 (= *suavemente*) **el aire empezó a soplar ~** a light breeze stirred the air

leviatán SM leviathan

levita¹ SF frock coat

levita² SM Levite

levitación SF levitation

levitar ▸conjug 1a◂ VI to levitate

Levítico SM Leviticus

lexema SM lexeme

lexicalizador Ⓐ ADJ lexicalizing
Ⓑ SM lexicalizer

lexicalizar ▸conjug 1f◂ Ⓐ VT to lexicalize
Ⓑ **lexicalizarse** VPR to be lexicalized

léxico Ⓐ ADJ lexical
Ⓑ SM (= *lexicón*) lexicon; (= *diccionario*) dictionary; (= *vocabulario*) vocabulary; (= *lista de palabras*) word list

lexicografía SF lexicography

lexicográfico ADJ lexicographical

lexicógrafo/a SM/F lexicographer

lexicología SF lexicology

lexicólogo/a SM/F lexicologist

lexicón SM lexicon

lexicosemántico ADJ lexico-semantic

ley SF [1] (= *precepto*) law; **aprobar** *o* **votar una ~** to pass a law; **todos somos iguales ante la ~** we are all equal before the law; **está por encima de la ~** he's above the law; **está fuera de la ~** he's outside the law; **un fuera de la ~** an outlaw; **de acuerdo con la ~** ◊ **según la ~** in accordance with the law, by law, in law; ✦*MODISMOS* **con todas las de la ~**: **quieren crear una fundación con todas las de la ~** they want to set up a fully-fledged charitable trust; **va a protestar, y con todas las de la ~** he's going to complain and rightly so; **quiere celebrar su aniversario con todas las de la ~** she wants to celebrate her anniversary in style; **hecha la ~ hecha la trampa** ◊ **el que hace la ~ hace la trampa** every law has a loophole ► **ley cambiaria** currency exchange regulations ► **ley de extranjería** immigration laws ► **ley de fugas**: **se le aplicó la ~ de fugas** he was shot while trying to escape ► **ley fundamental** constitutional law ► **ley marcial** martial law ► **ley orgánica** constitutional law ► **ley seca** prohibition law
[2] (= *regla no escrita*) law ► **ley de la calle** mob law, lynch law ► **ley de la selva** law of the jungle ► **ley del embudo** unfair law ► **ley del más fuerte** (principle of) might is right ► **ley del Talión** (*Hist*) lex talionis; (*fig*) (principle of) an eye for an eye and a tooth for a tooth
[3] (= *principio científico*) law ► **ley de la gravedad** law of gravity ► **ley de la oferta y la demanda** law of supply and demand ► **ley natural** (*Fís*) law of nature; (*Ética*) natural law
[4] (*Dep*) rule, law ► **ley de la ventaja** advantage rule
[5] (*Rel*) **la ~ de Dios** the rule of God, God's law ► **ley de Moisés** the law of Moses
[6] (*Metal*) **oro de ~** pure gold, standard gold; **bajo de ~** base; **ser de (buena) ~** to be genuine; **ser de mala ~** to be a bad character
[7] (†) (= *lealtad*) loyalty, devotion; **tener/tomar ~ a algn** to be/become devoted to sb

leyenda SF [1] (= *historia*) legend ► **leyenda negra** (= *mala fama*) bad reputation; (*Hist*) *view of the Conquest of Latin America which emphasised the negative side of Spanish involvement*
[2] (= *inscripción*) [*de moneda, medalla, lápida*] legend, inscription
[3] [*de cuadro, grabado, mapa*] (= *encabezamiento*) heading; (= *pie*) caption
[4] (= *eslogan*) slogan

leyendo *etc ver* **leer**

leyente SMF reader

leyista SM (*Caribe*) pettifogging lawyer, shyster

leyoso ADJ (*Andes*) cunning, sly

lezna SF awl

lía SF (*LAm*) plaited esparto grass

liado* ADJ (= *ocupado*) **Pedro está muy ~, así que he venido yo en su lugar** Pedro is tied up so I've come instead

liana SF liana

liante/a* SM/F [1] (= *enredador*) mischief-maker
[2] (= *persona difícil*) awkward customer*
[3] (= *timador*) con man*, swindler
[4] (= *chismoso*) gossip

liar ▸conjug 1c◂ Ⓐ VT [1] [+ *fardos, paquetes*] (= *atar*) to tie up; (= *envolver*) to wrap (up); **lía este paquete con una cuerda** tie up this parcel with some string; *ver tb* **bártulos, petate 2**
[2] [+ *cigarrillo*] to roll
[3] (= *confundir*) to confuse; **me ~on con tantas explicaciones** they confused me with all their explanations; **¡no me líes!** (= *no me confundas*) don't confuse me!; (= *no me metas en problemas*) don't get me into trouble!
[4] **~la*** (= *provocar una discusión*) to stir up trouble; (= *hacer algo mal*) to make a mess of things; **¡la liamos!** we've done it now!*
[5] **~las†‡** (= *irse*) to beat it*; (= *morir*) to peg out‡
Ⓑ **liarse** VPR [1] (= *confundirse*) to get muddled up; **explícalo mejor, que ya te has vuelto a ~** explain it a bit better, you've got all muddled up again
[2] (*) (*sentimentalmente*) **~se con algn** to have an affair with sb, get involved with sb; **se ha liado con su jefe** she's having an affair with her boss
[3] **~se a*** (+ *INFIN*): **nos liamos a hablar y se nos pasó la hora** we got talking and we forgot the time; **nos liamos a ver fotos y estuve allí toda la tarde** we got to looking through photos and I stayed there all evening
[4] **~se a golpes** *o* **a palos*** to lay into one another*; *ver tb* **manta¹ 1**

lib. ABR (= **libro**) bk

libación SF libation; **libaciones** libations, potations

libanés/esa Ⓐ ADJ Lebanese
Ⓑ SM/F Lebanese, Lebanese man/woman; **los libaneses** the Lebanese, the people of the Lebanon

Líbano SM **el ~** the Lebanon

libar ▸conjug 1a◂ Ⓐ VT [1] (= *succionar*) to suck
[2] (= *sorber*) to sip
[3] (= *degustar*) to taste
Ⓑ VI (*LAm**) (= *beber*) to booze*

libelista SMF lampoonist, writer of lampoons

libelo SM [1] (= *sátira*) lampoon (**contra** of), satire (**contra** on)
[2] (*Jur*) libel

libélula SF dragonfly

liberación SF (*gen*) liberation; [*de preso*] release; [*de precios*] deregulation ► **liberación de la mujer** women's liberation

liberacionista* SF women's libber*

liberado/a Ⓐ ADJ [1] (*gen*) liberated
[2] [*de partido, sindicato*] full-time, professional; [*de organización*] full-time
[3] (*Com, Fin*) paid-up, paid-in (*EEUU*)
Ⓑ SM/F (*Pol*) [*de sindicato, partido, organización*] full-time official

liberal Ⓐ ADJ [1] (*Pol*) liberal
[2] (= *tolerante*) liberal, open-minded
[3] (= *generoso*) liberal, generous
[4] [*profesión*] liberal
Ⓑ SMF liberal

liberalidad SF [1] (= *generosidad*) liberality (*frm*), generosity
[2] [*de ideas, costumbres*] liberalism

liberalismo SM liberalism

liberalización SF liberalization

liberalizador ADJ liberalizing

liberalizar ▸conjug 1f◂ VT to liberalize; [+ *mercado*] to deregulate

liberalmente ADV (= *libremente*) freely; (= *generosamente*) liberally, generously

liberar ▸conjug 1a◂ Ⓐ VT [1] [+ *rehén*] to free, release; [+ *país, pueblo*] to liberate
[2] **~ a algn de** [+ *carga, obligación*] to free sb of *o* from; [+ *peligro*] to save sb from; **la han liberado de una gran responsabilidad** they have freed her of a great responsibility; **~ a algn de un pago** to exempt sb from a payment
[3] (*Fin*) [+ *precios*] to deregulate; [+ *acción*] to pay in full; [+ *deuda*] to release; [+ *tipo de cambio*] to float
[4] [+ *energía, oxígeno*] to release
Ⓑ **liberarse** VPR [1] **~se de algo** to free o.s. from sth; **el preso se liberó de las esposas** the prisoner freed himself from *o* got free of the handcuffs; **se ha liberado de su complejo de inferioridad** he has rid himself of his inferiority complex
[2] (*socialmente*) to liberate o.s.; **las mujeres empiezan a ~se** women are beginning to liberate themselves

Liberia SF Liberia

liberiano/a Ⓐ ADJ Liberian
Ⓑ SM/F Liberian; **los ~s** the Liberians, the people of Liberia

líbero SMF (*Dep*) sweeper

libérrimo ADJ entirely free, absolutely free

libertad SF [1] (*gen*) freedom; **disfrutamos de la ~ de la vida en el campo** we enjoy the freedom of life in the country; **no tengo ~ para hacer lo que quiera** I'm not free to do what I want, I don't have the freedom to do what I want; **estar en ~** to be free; **poner a algn en ~** to set sb free ► **libertad bajo fianza** release on bail ► **libertad bajo palabra** parole ► **libertad condicional** probation; **estar en ~ condicional** to be on probation ► **libertad de asociación** freedom of association ► **libertad de cátedra** academic freedom, freedom to teach ► **libertad de comercio** free trade ► **libertad de conciencia** freedom of conscience ► **libertad de cultos** freedom of worship ► **libertad de empresa** free enterprise ► **libertad de expresión** freedom of speech ► **libertad de imprenta, libertad de prensa** freedom of the press ► **libertad de voto** free vote ► **libertades civiles** civil liberties ► **libertad vigilada** probation; **estar en ~ vigilada** to be on probation
[2] (= *confianza*) **hablar con entera** *o* **total ~** to speak freely; **tomarse la ~ de hacer algo** to take the liberty of doing sth; **tomarse mu-**

chas o **demasiadas ~es con algn** to take too many liberties with sb

libertador(a) Ⓐ ADJ liberating
Ⓑ SM/F liberator; **El Libertador** (*LAm Hist*) the Liberator (*Simón Bolívar*)

libertar ▸conjug 1a◂ VT [1] (= *poner en libertad*) to set free, release
[2] (= *eximir*) [*de deber, obligación*] to release; [*de impuestos, ley*] to exempt
[3] (= *salvar*) to save (**de** from); **~ a algn de la muerte** to save sb from death

libertario/a ADJ, SM/F libertarian

libertinaje SM licentiousness (*frm*), profligacy (*frm*)

libertino/a Ⓐ ADJ [1] (= *inmoral*) loose-living, profligate (*frm*)
[2] (*Rel, Hist*) freethinking
Ⓑ SM/F [1] (= *juerguista*) libertine
[2] (*Rel, Hist*) freethinker

liberto/a Ⓐ ADJ [*esclavo*] freed, liberated
Ⓑ SM/F freedman/freedwoman

Libia SF Libya

libídine SF (*frm*) (= *lujuria*) lewdness, lasciviousness; (= *líbido*) libido

libidinoso ADJ lustful, libidinous (*frm*)

libido SF libido

libio/a Ⓐ ADJ Libyan
Ⓑ SM/F Libyan; **los ~s** the Libyans, the people of Libia

liborio* ADJ Cuban

Libra SF (*Zodíaco*) Libra

libra SF [1] (= *moneda*) pound ▸ **libra esterlina** pound sterling
[2] (= *unidad de peso*) pound
[3] (*Perú Hist*) 10 soles note;
→ KILOS, METROS, AÑOS

libraco* SM (= *aburrido*) boring book, trashy book*; (= *grande*) old tome

librado/a Ⓐ ADJ **salir bien/mal ~ de algo** to come out of sth well/badly
Ⓑ SM/F (*Com*) drawee

librador(a) SM/F (*Com*) drawer

libramiento SM [1] (*gen*) deliverance
[2] (*Com*) order of payment

librante SMF (*Com*) drawer

libranza SF [1] (*Com*) order of payment ▸ **libranza de correos, libranza postal** (*LAm*) postal order, money order
[2] [*de trabajador*] time off

librar ▸conjug 1a◂ Ⓐ VT [1] (= *liberar*) **~ a algn de** [+ *preocupación, responsabilidad*] to free sb from o of; [+ *peligro*] to save sb from; **¡Dios me libre!** Heaven forbid!; **¡líbreme Dios de maldecir a nadie!** heaven forbid that I should curse anyone!
[2] [+ *batalla*] to fight
[3] (*Com*) to draw; [+ *cheque*] to make out; **~ a cargo de** to draw on
[4] [+ *sentencia*] to pass; [+ *decreto*] to issue
[5] (*frm*) [+ *secreto*] to reveal
[6] (†) [+ *esperanza, confianza*] to place (**en** en)
Ⓑ VI [1] (*en el trabajo*) **libro los sábados** I have Saturdays off; **trabaja seis horas y libra dos** he works six hours and has two hours off; **libro a las tres** I'm free at three, I finish work at three
[2] (†) (= *parir*) to give birth
[3] (†) **~ bien** to succeed; **~ mal** to fail
Ⓒ **librarse** VPR [1] (= *eximirse*) **~se de algo/algn** to escape from sth/sb; **se ha librado del servicio militar** he has escaped military service; **se han librado del castigo** they have escaped punishment; **logró ~se de sus captores** he managed to escape from his captors
[2] (= *deshacerse*) **~se de algn/algo** to get rid of sb/sth; **por fin nos hemos librado de él** we've finally got rid of him

libre Ⓐ ADJ [1] (*gen*) free (**de** from, of); **cada cual es ~ de hacer lo que quiera** everyone is free to do as they wish; **¿estás ~?** are you free?; **el martes estoy ~, así que podemos quedar** I'm free on Tuesday so we can meet up
[2] (= *exento*) **~ de derechos** duty-free; **~ de franqueo** post-free; **~ de impuestos** free of tax; **estar ~ de servicio** to be off duty
[3] (= *sin ocupar*) [*plaza*] vacant, unoccupied; **¿está ~ este asiento?** is this seat free?; **"libre"** [*parking*] "spaces"; [*taxi*] "for hire"
[4] [*tiempo*] spare, free
[5] **al aire ~** in the open air
[6] **por ~** (= *por cuenta propia*): **examinarse por ~** to take one's exams as an independent candidate; **trabajar por ~** to freelance; **ir** o **funcionar por ~** to go it alone
[7] (*Dep, Natación*) **los 200 metros ~s** the 200 metres freestyle; **estilo ~** freestyle; *ver tb* **saque A1, tiro 3**
[8] [*traducción, adaptación, verso*] free
[9] **~ a bordo** (*Com*) free on board
[10] (†) (= *inmoral*) loose, immoral; **de vida ~** loose-living, immoral
Ⓑ SM [1] (*Dep*) (= *tiro*) free kick ▸ **libre directo** direct free kick ▸ **libre indirecto** indirect free kick
[2] (*Méx*) taxi
Ⓒ SMF (*Dep*) (= *jugador*) sweeper

librea Ⓐ SF livery, uniform
Ⓑ SM (*Cono Sur*) footman

librecambio SM free trade

librecambismo SM free trade

librecambista Ⓐ ADJ free-trade *antes de s*
Ⓑ SMF free trader

librepensador(a) SM/F freethinker

librepensamiento SM freethinking

librera SF (*LAm*) bookcase

librería SF [1] (= *tienda*) bookshop, bookstore (*EEUU*) ▸ **librería anticuaria, librería de antiguo** antiquarian bookshop ▸ **librería de ocasión, librería de viejo** secondhand bookshop
[2] (= *estante*) bookcase; (= *biblioteca*) library
[3] (= *comercio*) book trade

librero[1]/a SM/F (= *persona*) bookseller ▸ **librero/a de viejo** secondhand bookseller

librero[2] SM (*LAm*) (= *estante*) bookcase

libresco ADJ bookish

libreta SF [1] (= *cuaderno*) notebook ▸ **libreta de anillas** spiral-bound notebook ▸ **libreta de direcciones** address book
[2] (*Com*) (= *cartilla*) account book; (= *cuenta*) savings account ▸ **libreta de ahorros** savings book ▸ **libreta de depósitos** bank book, pass book
[3] (*Cono Sur Aut*) driving licence, driver's license (*EEUU*)
[4] (*LAm*) ▸ **libreta militar** certificate of military service
[5] [*de pan*] one-pound loaf

librete SM booklet

libretista SMF librettist

libreto SM [1] [*de ópera*] libretto
[2] (*LAm*) (= *guión*) script, film script

libro SM [1] (= *obra impresa*) book; ✦***MODISMOS*** **ser como un ~ abierto** to be an open book; **ahorcar** o **arrimar** o **colgar los ~s** to give up studying; **hablar como un ~** (= *con precisión*) to know what one is talking about; (= *con pedantería*) to sound like a text book ▸ **libro de bolsillo** paperback ▸ **libro de cabecera** bedside book ▸ **libro de cocina** cookery book, cookbook (*EEUU*) ▸ **libro de consulta** reference book ▸ **libro de cuentos** storybook ▸ **libro de estilo** style book ▸ **libro de imágenes** picture-book ▸ **libro de lectura** reader ▸ **libro desplegable** pop-up book ▸ **libro de texto** textbook ▸ **libro electrónico** e-book ▸ **libro encuadernado, libro en pasta** hardback (book) ▸ **libro en rústica** paperback (book) ▸ **libro escolar** (= *informe*) school report; [*de texto*] schoolbook ▸ **libro mágico, libro móvil** pop-up book ▸ **libro usado** second-hand book
[2] (= *registro*) book; **llevar los ~s** (*Com*) to keep the books o accounts ▸ **libro de actas** minute book ▸ **libro de apuntes** notebook ▸ **libro de caja** cash book, petty cash book ▸ **libro de caja auxiliar** petty cash book ▸ **libro de contabilidad** account book ▸ **libro de cría** register of pedigrees ▸ **libro de cuentas** account book ▸ **libro de familia** *booklet containing family details (marriage, births) used for official purposes* ▸ **libro de honor** visitors' book ▸ **libro de orígenes** register of pedigrees ▸ **libro de pedidos** order book ▸ **libro de reclamaciones** complaints book ▸ **libro de ruta** itinerary ▸ **libro de visitas** visitors' book ▸ **libro de vuelos** (*Aer*) logbook ▸ **libro diario** journal ▸ **libro genealógico** (*Agr*) herd-book ▸ **libro mayor** ledger ▸ **libro parroquial** parish register ▸ **libro talonario** receipt book
[3] (*Pol*) ▸ **libro blanco** white paper ▸ **libro rojo** red paper ▸ **libro verde** green paper

librote SM big book, tome

Lic. ABR (*esp Méx*) = **Licenciado/Licenciada**

licencia SF [1] (= *documento*) licence, license (*EEUU*) ▸ **licencia de armas** gun licence, gun permit (*EEUU*) ▸ **licencia de caza** game licence, hunting permit ▸ **licencia de conducir, licencia de conductor** driving licence, driver's license (*EEUU*) ▸ **licencia de construcción** ≈ planning permission ▸ **licencia de exportación** (*Com*) export licence ▸ **licencia de manejar** (*LAm*) driving licence, driver's license (*EEUU*) ▸ **licencia de matrimonio** marriage licence ▸ **licencia de obras** building permit, planning permission ▸ **licencia de piloto, licencia de vuelo** pilot's licence ▸ **licencia fiscal** *registration with the Spanish Inland Revenue necessary for any commercial activity*
[2] (*Mil*) leave, furlough (*EEUU*)
[3] [*de trabajo*] leave; **estar de ~** to be on leave; **ir de ~** to go on leave ▸ **licencia absoluta** discharge ▸ **licencia de maternidad** maternity leave ▸ **licencia honrosa** honourable discharge ▸ **licencia por enfermedad** sick leave ▸ **licencia sin sueldo** unpaid leave
[4] (*frm*) (= *permiso*) permission; **sin mi ~** without my permission; **dar su ~** to give one's permission, grant permission
[5] (= *libertinaje*) licence

[6] (*Literat*) ► **licencia poética** poetic licence

[7] (*Univ*†) degree

licenciado/a SM/F [1] (*Univ*) graduate; **Licenciado en Filosofía y Letras** Bachelor of Arts

[2] (*Méx, CAm*) (= *abogado*) lawyer, attorney(-at-law) (*EEUU*); **el ~ Gutiérrez nos lleva el caso** Mr. Gutiérrez is conducting the case

[3] (*esp Méx*) (= *título*) ≈ Dr; **el Licenciado Papacostas nos dice que ...** Dr Papacostas tells us that ...

[4] (*Mil*) *soldier having completed national service*

licenciar ▸conjug 1b◂ Ⓐ VT [1] (*Univ*) to confer a degree on

[2] (*Mil*) to discharge

[3] (*Com*) [+ *patente*] to license

[4] (*frm*) (= *permitir*) to permit, allow

Ⓑ **licenciarse** VPR [1] (*Univ*) to graduate, take one's degree; **~se en Derecho** to graduate in law, get a degree in law

[2] (*Mil*) to be discharged

licenciatario/a SM/F licensee

licenciatura SF [1] (= *título*) degree

[2] (= *estudios*) degree course, course of study (*EEUU*)

[3] (= *ceremonia*) graduation

> **LICENCIATURA**
>
> *Until recently most Spanish degree courses lasted five years. Students would be awarded a* **diplomatura** *(general degree) if they completed three years of study, and they would get their* **licenciatura** *(honours degree) after another two years. Now, under new* **planes de estudio**, *or curricula,* **licenciaturas** *take four years. The first two years are referred to as the* **primer ciclo** *and the final two years as the* **segundo ciclo**.

licencioso ADJ licentious

liceo SM [1] (= *centro cultural*) lyceum

[2] (*LAm*) (= *instituto*) secondary school, junior high school (*EEUU*)

licha‡ SF, **liche**‡ SF street

lichi SM lychee

líchigo SM (*Andes*) provisions, food

licitación SF [1] (*en contratación pública*) *bidding for a public contract*

[2] (*en subasta*) bidding (*at auction*)

licitador(a) SM/F [1] (*en contratación pública*) bidder

[2] (*LAm*) (= *subastador*) auctioneer

licitar ▸conjug 1a◂ Ⓐ VT [1] (*en contratación pública*) to tender for

[2] (*en subasta*) (= *pujar*) to bid for

[3] (*LAm*) (= *vender*) to sell by auction

Ⓑ VI to bid

lícito ADJ [1] (*Jur*) [*permiso*] legal; [*comercio*] legitimate, legal; [*conducta*] legal, lawful, licit (*frm*)

[2] (*frm*) (= *justo*) right, reasonable; **no es lícita tanta desigualdad social** such levels of social inequality are not right *o* are unreasonable

[3] (*frm*) (= *permisible*) permissible; **si es ~ preguntarlo** if one may ask

licitud SF [1] (= *legalidad*) legality, lawfulness; **la controversia sobre la ~ del aborto** the controversy about whether abortion should be permitted

[2] (= *justicia*) rightness, fairness

licor SM [1] (= *bebida dulce*) liqueur ► **licor de frutas** fruit liqueur

[2] **licores** (= *alcohol*) spirits *pl*, liquor *sing* (*EEUU*)

[3] (= *líquido*) liquid

licorera SF [1] (= *botella*) decanter

[2] (= *empresa*) distillery

licorería SF (*LAm*) distillery

licorero/a Ⓐ ADJ **empresa ~** distillery; **industria ~** alcohol *o* drinks industry

Ⓑ SM/F (*LAm*) distiller

licorista SMF (= *fabricante*) distiller; (= *comerciante*) liquor dealer, liquor seller

licoroso ADJ [*vino*] strong, of high alcoholic content

licra® SF Lycra®

licuación SF liquefaction (*frm*), melting

licuado SM (*tb* **~ de frutas**) (*LAm*) milk shake

licuadora SF (*Culin*) blender, liquidizer

licuar ▸conjug 1d◂ VT [1] (*Culin*) to blend, liquidize

[2] (*Fís, Quím*) to liquefy, turn into liquid; [+ *nieve*] to melt

licuefacción SF liquefaction

lid SF (*frm*) [1] (= *combate*) fight, combat

[2] (= *disputa*) dispute; **en buena ~** (*lit*) in (a) fair fight; (*fig*) fair and square

líder Ⓐ ADJ INV top, leading, foremost; **marca ~** leading brand, brand leader

Ⓑ SMF (*Pol*) leader; (*Dep*) leader, league leader, top club ► **líder del mercado** market leader

liderar ▸conjug 1a◂ VT to lead, head

liderato SM, **liderazgo** SM (*gen*) leadership; (*Dep*) lead, leadership

lidia SF [1] (*Taur*) (= *espectáculo, arte*) bullfighting; (= *corrida*) bullfight; **toro de ~** fighting bull

[2] (*frm*) (= *lucha*) struggle, fight

[3] (*LAm*) (= *molestia*) trouble, nuisance; **dar ~** to be trying, be a nuisance

lidiador(a) SM/F (*gen*) fighter; (*Taur*) bullfighter

lidiar ▸conjug 1b◂ Ⓐ VT (*Taur*) to fight

Ⓑ VI to fight (**con, contra** against; **por** for)

liebre SF [1] (*Zool*) hare; ✦***MODISMOS*** **coger una ~*** to come a cropper*, take a flat beating (*EEUU*); **levantar la ~** to blow the gaff*, let the cat out of the bag; **ser ~ corrida** (*Méx**) to be an old hand; *ver tb* **gato¹ 1**

[2] (= *cobarde*) coward

[3] (*Chile*) (= *microbús*) minibus

Lieja SF Liège

liencillo SM (*LAm*) thick cotton material

liendre SF nit

lienzo SM [1] (= *tela*) linen; **un ~** a piece of linen

[2] (*Arte*) canvas

[3] (= *pañuelo*) handkerchief

[4] (*Arquit*) (= *muro*) wall; (= *fachada*) face, front

[5] (*LAm*) [*de valla*] section of fence

[6] (*Méx*) (= *corral*) corral, pen

liftar ▸conjug 1a◂ VT (*Dep*) [+ *pelota*] to loft

lifting SM face-lift; **hacerse un ~** to get a face-lift, have a face-lift

liga SF [1] (*Pol, Dep*) league

[2] (= *faja*) suspender, garter (*EEUU*)

[3] (*para sujetar*) elastic band

[4] (= *muérdago*) mistletoe

[5] (= *sustancia viscosa*) birdlime

[6] (*CAm, Méx*) (= *unión*) binding

[7] (*Metal*) alloy

[8] (*Andes**) (= *amigo*) bosom friend

[9] (*) (= *persona*) pick-up‡

ligado SM [1] (*Mús*) (*entre dos notas*) slur, tie; (= *pasaje*) legato passage

[2] (*Tip*) ligature

ligadura SF [1] (*Med*) ligature ► **ligadura de trompas** tubal ligation

[2] **ligaduras** [*de cuerda, correa*] bonds, ties; (*entre personas*) ties; **eres demasiado joven para ~s** you're too young to tie yourself down to one person; **todavía tienes las marcas de las ~s** you still have the marks from the ropes when you were tied up

[3] (*Mús*) ligature, tie

[4] (*Náut*) lashing

ligamento SM ligament; **romperse un ~** to tear a ligament

ligamiento SM [1] (= *atadura*) tying

[2] [*familiar, comercial*] tie

ligar ▸conjug 1h◂ Ⓐ VT [1] (= *atar*) (*gen*) to tie, bind; (*Med*) to bind up, put a ligature on

[2] (= *mezclar*) [+ *metales*] to alloy, mix; [+ *bebidas*] to mix; [+ *salsa*] to thicken

[3] (= *unir*) to join, bind together; **estar ligado por contrato a** to be bound by contract to

[4] (*) (= *conquistar*) to pick up*, get off with*, pull*

[5] (*) (= *birlar*) to pinch*

[6] (*) (= *conseguir*) to get hold of, lay one's hands on

[7] (*) (= *comprar*) to buy

[8] (*) (= *detener*) to nick*

[9] (*Caribe*) (= *contratar*) to contract in advance for

Ⓑ VI [1] (= *ir juntos*) to mix well, blend well, go well together

[2] (*) (= *conquistar*) to pull*; **salieron dispuestas a ~** they went out to try to pick up a man *o* to pull*; **Pepe y Ana han ligado** Pepe and Ana have paired up

[3] (*Caribe, Méx**) (= *tener suerte*) to have a bit of luck, be lucky; **la cosa le ligó** (*Andes, CAm*) the affair went well for him

[4] (*Caribe, Méx*) (= *mirar*) to look, stare

[5] **le ligó su deseo** (*Andes, Caribe**) her wish came true

Ⓒ **ligarse** VPR [1] (= *unirse*) to unite, join together

[2] (*) (= *conquistar*) to get off with*; **~se a** *o* **con algn** to get off with sb*

[3] (= *comprometerse*) to bind o.s., commit o.s.

ligazón SF [1] (*Náut*) rib

[2] (= *unión*) connection, bond, link

ligeramente ADV [1] (*con adjetivos*) slightly; **la foto estaba ~ desenfocada** the photo was slightly out of focus; **me siento ~ cansada** I feel rather tired

[2] (= *con verbos*) [2·1] (= *levemente*) [*oler, saber*] slightly; [*asar, cocer*] lightly; [*desplazarse, moverse, cambiar*] slightly; **las acciones han bajado ~ esta semana** the shares have dropped slightly *o* a little this week; **se ha recuperado ~** he's made a slight recovery

[2·2] (= *rápidamente*) [*correr, andar*] quickly; [*tocar*] lightly, gently

[2·3] (= *sin sensatez*) [*actuar*] flippantly; **no deberías actuar tan ~** you shouldn't act so flippantly; **hay decisiones que no se pueden tomar ~** there are some decisions which can't be taken lightly

ligerear ▸conjug 1a◂ VI (*Cono Sur*) to walk fast, move quickly

ligereza SF 1 [*de objeto, material, tejido*] lightness
2 (= *rapidez*) speed, swiftness
3 (= *agilidad*) agility, nimbleness; **~ mental** mental agility
4 (= *falta de sensatez*) flippancy; **actuar con ~** to act flippantly; **hablar con ~** to speak without thinking; **juzgar algo con ~** to jump to conclusions about sth, judge sth hastily ► **ligereza de espíritu** light-heartedness
5 (= *dicho imprudente*) flippant remark; (= *hecho imprudente*) indiscretion; **lo que dijo era sólo una ~** what she said was just a flippant remark; **cometí la ~ de contárselo todo** I was foolish enough to tell him everything

ligero Ⓐ ADJ 1 (= *poco pesado*) [*paquete, gas, metal, comida*] light; [*tela*] light, lightweight, thin; [*material*] lightweight; **una blusa ligera** a light *o* lightweight *o* thin blouse; **construido con materiales ~s** built from lightweight materials; **hemos cenado algo ~** we had something light for dinner; **viajar ~ de equipaje** to travel light; **~ de ropa** lightly dressed; **vas muy ~ de ropa para esta época del año** you're very lightly *o* flimsily dressed for this time of the year; **fotos de chicas ligeras de ropa** photos of scantily clad girls; **tener el sueño ~** to be a light sleeper; **~ como una pluma** as light as a feather
2 (= *leve*) [*viento, caricia*] light; [*ruido*] slight; [*perfume, fragancia*] delicate; **sopla un ~ viento** a light wind is blowing; **el más ~ ruido lo despierta** he wakes at the slightest noise
3 (= *poco importante*) [*enfermedad*] minor; [*castigo*] light
4 (= *rápido*) swift; **~ de dedos** quick-fingered; **~ de pies** light-footed, quick; ✦***MODISMO*** **~ como una bala** *o* **el viento** as quick as a flash, like the wind; *ver tb* **paso² 4**
5 (= *ágil*) agile; **después del régimen me siento mucho más ligera** after the diet I feel a lot lighter on my feet *o* a lot more agile
6 (= *superficial*) [*conocimiento*] slight; [*sospecha*] sneaking; **un ~ conocimiento de alemán** a slight knowledge *o* a smattering of German; **tengo la ligera sospecha de que nos hemos equivocado** I have a sneaking suspicion that we've made a mistake
7 (= *frívolo*) [*carácter, persona*] flippant, frivolous; [*comentario, tema*] flippant; [*mujer*] (*pey*, †) loose†; **no deberías ser tan ligera con estos asuntos** you shouldn't be so flippant *o* frivolous about these things; *ver tb* **casco 5**
8 (= *sin complicaciones*) [*novela, película*] lightweight; [*conversación, contexto*] light-hearted
9 **a la ligera** (= *irreflexivamente*) rashly; (= *rápidamente*) quickly; **no se pueden hacer las cosas a la ligera** you shouldn't act so rashly; **es obvio que lo has hecho muy a la ligera** it's obvious that you rushed it *o* did it too quickly; **no podemos juzgar su conducta a la ligera** we shouldn't jump to conclusions about his behaviour, we shouldn't judge his behaviour so hastily; **tomarse algo a la ligera** not to take sth seriously
Ⓑ ADV (= *rápido*) [*andar, correr*] quickly; **ella corrió ~ por el puente** she ran quickly over the bridge; **venga, ~, que nos vamos** get a move on, we're going; **de ~** rashly, thoughtlessly

light [laɪt] ADJ INV [*tabaco*] low-tar *antes de s*; [*comida*] low-calorie; [*plan, política*] watered-down, toned-down

lignito SM lignite

ligón¹ SM hoe

ligón²/ona* Ⓐ ADJ 1 [*persona*] flirtatious; **es muy ~** he's a great one for the girls
2 [*prenda*] (= *bonita*) attractive; (= *sexy*) provocative, sexy
Ⓑ SM/F **es una ligona** she's successful with the men, she has no problem pulling the men*

ligoteo* SM **es un sitio de ~** it's a pick-up joint*; **ese amigo tuyo siempre está de ~** that friend of yours is always on the pull*, that friend of yours is always after the women *o* eyeing up the talent*; **el ~ electrónico** computer dating

ligue* Ⓐ SM 1 (= *conquista*) **ir de ~** to look for sb to get off with*, go eyeing up the talent*
2 (= *amorío*) affair
Ⓑ SMF (= *persona*) pick-up*, date, boyfriend/girlfriend ► **ligue de una noche** one-night stand

liguero¹ SM suspender belt, garter belt (*EEUU*)

liguero² ADJ (*Dep*) league *antes de s*; **líder ~** league leader

liguilla SF (*Dep*) (= *torneo*) small tournament; (*para ascender*) mini-league, *group of teams which play off to determine promotion*

ligur (*Hist*) Ⓐ ADJ Ligurian
Ⓑ SMF Ligurian; **los ~os** the Ligurians, the people of Liguria

ligustro SM privet

lija SF 1 (*Zool*) dogfish
2 (*Téc*) (= *papel de lija*) sandpaper ► **lija esmeril** emery paper
3 **darse ~** (*Caribe**) to give o.s. airs

lijadora SF sander, sanding machine

lijar ▸conjug 1a◂ VT to sandpaper, sand down

lijoso* ADJ (*Caribe*) vain, stuck-up*

Lila SF Lille

lila¹ SF (*Bot*) lilac

lila² SM 1 (= *color*) lilac
2 (= *idiota*) twit*, wimp*; (= *crédulo*) sucker*

lila³‡ SM (*Esp*) 5000 pesetas

lilailas* SFPL tricks

lile* ADJ (*Cono Sur*) weak, sickly

liliche* SM (*CAm*) piece of junk

liliputiense ADJ, SMF Lilliputian

liliquear* ▸conjug 1a◂ VI (*Chile*) to tremble nervously, shake

Lima SF Lima

lima¹ SF (*Bot*) lime, sweet-lime tree

lima² SF (*Téc*) 1 (= *herramienta*) file; ✦***MODISMO*** **comer como una ~** to eat like a horse ► **lima de uñas, lima para las uñas** nail file, fingernail file (*EEUU*)
2 (= *pulido*) [*de superficie*] polishing; **dar la última ~ a una obra** to put the finishing touches to a work

lima³†‡ SF (= *camisa*) shirt

limadura SF 1 (*gen*) filing
2 **limaduras** (= *virutas*) filings

limar ▸conjug 1a◂ VT 1 (*Téc*) (*con lima*) to file down, file off
2 [+ *uñas*] to file
3 (= *pulir*) [+ *artículo, obra*] to polish up; [+ *diferencias*] to iron out

limatón SM (*LAm*) crossbeam, roofbeam

limaza SF slug

limazo SM slime, sliminess

limbo SM 1 (*Bot, Mat*) limb
2 (*Rel*) limbo; **estar en el ~** (*Rel*) to be in limbo; (= *estar distraído*) to be miles away

limeño/a Ⓐ ADJ of/from Lima
Ⓑ SM/F native/inhabitant of Lima; **los ~s** the people of Lima

limero SM lime (tree)

limeta SF 1 (*Cono Sur*) (= *frente*) broad brow; (= *calva*) bald head
2 (*LAm*) (= *botella*) flagon, bottle

liminar ADJ preliminary, introductory

limitación SF 1 (= *restricción*) limitation; **exigen la ~ de los poderes del gobierno** they demand a limitation of the government's powers; **intervinieron todos los diputados sin ~ de tiempo** all the MPs took part without being subject to a time limit ► **limitación de armamentos** arms limitation ► **limitación de velocidad** speed limit
2 **limitaciones** (= *deficiencias*) limitations; **no lo haré porque conozco mis limitaciones** I won't do it because I know my limitations

limitado ADJ 1 (*gen*) limited; **sociedad limitada** (*Com*) limited company, corporation (*EEUU*)
2 (= *lerdo*) slow-witted, dim*

limitador SM (*Aut*) limiter ► **limitador de ruido** limiter ► **limitador de velocidad** speed limiter

▼**limitar** ▸conjug 1a◂ Ⓐ VT (= *restringir*) to limit, restrict; **nos han limitado el número de visitas** they have limited *o* restricted the number of visits we can have; **~on el tiempo del examen a dos horas** the exam time was limited to two hours; **hay que ~ el consumo de alcohol entre los adolescentes** alcohol consumption among young people should be restricted
Ⓑ VI **~ con** to border on; **España limita al norte con Francia** Spain borders on France to the north
Ⓒ **limitarse** VPR **~se a hacer algo** to limit *o* confine o.s. to doing sth; **no nos limitemos a tratar los aspectos económicos** let's not limit *o* confine ourselves to the economic aspects; **me he limitado a corregir unos cuantos errores** all I've done is correct a few mistakes, I've just corrected a few mistakes, that's all; **tú limítate a escuchar** just be quiet and listen

limitativo ADJ, **limitatorio** ADJ limiting, restrictive

límite Ⓐ SM 1 (*gen*) limit; **podrá presentarse cualquiera, sin ~ de edad** anyone can apply, regardless *o* irrespective of age, anyone can apply, there's no age limit; **eran exámenes larguísimos, sin ~ de tiempo** the exams were very long, there was no time limit; **como** *o* **de ~**: **tenemos como** *o* **de ~ el sábado para presentar el trabajo** the deadline for submitting our work is Saturday; **no tener ~s** to know no bounds; **poner (un) ~ a**: **han puesto un ~ de participantes** they have put a limit *o* restriction on the number of participants; **nos pusieron un ~ de dinero para gastar** they put a restriction on *o* limited the

➤ LENGUA Y USO: limitar C 53.2

amount of money we had to spend; **quieren poner ~ a sus ambiciones políticas** they want to limit his political ambitions; **pretenden poner ~ a la investigación sobre embriones** they aim to put tighter controls on research into embryos, they aim to restrict *o* curb research into embryos; **sin ~s** limitless ► **límite de crédito** (*Com*) credit limit ► **límite de gastos** spending limit ► **límite de velocidad** speed limit
[2] (*Geog, Pol*) boundary, border ► **límite forestal** tree line, timber line
[3] (*Inform*) ► **límite de página** page break
[4] (= *final*) end
Ⓑ ADJ INV extreme, maximum; **caso ~** extreme case; **competición ~** out-and-out contest; **concentración ~** maximum concentration; **jornada ~ semanal** maximum possible working week; **sentencia ~** definitive ruling; **situaciones ~** extreme situations; **someter una máquina a pruebas ~** to test a machine to the limit

limítrofe ADJ bordering, neighbouring, neighboring (*EEUU*)

limo SM [1] (= *barro*) slime, mud
[2] (‡) (= *bolso*) handbag, purse (*EEUU*)

limón SM [1] (*Bot*) lemon; (*Caribe*) lime
[2] **limones‡** tits‡

limonada SF (*natural*) lemonade; (*artificial*) lemon squash ► **limonada natural** fresh lemonade, lemonade (*EEUU*); *ver tb* **chicha[1] A1**

limonado ADJ lemon, lemon-coloured, lemon-colored (*EEUU*)

limonar SM lemon grove

limonero SM lemon tree

limosina SF limousine

limosna SF charity, alms†; **¡una ~, señor!** can you spare something, sir?; **pedir ~** to beg; **vivir de ~** to live by begging, live on charity

limosnear ▸conjug 1a◂ VI to beg

limosnera SF collecting tin (*for charity*)

limosnero/a Ⓐ ADJ (= *caritativo*) charitable
Ⓑ SM/F [1] (*Hist*) almoner
[2] (*LAm*) (= *mendigo*) beggar

limoso ADJ slimy, muddy

limpia Ⓐ SF [1] (= *acto de limpiar*) cleaning
[2] (*CAm, Méx Agr*) weeding, clearing
[3] (*Pol*) (= *purga*) clean-up, purge
[4] (*Andes, Cono Sur, Méx*) (= *azotes*) beating
Ⓑ SM [1] (*) (= *persona*) bootblack; (= *niño*) shoeshine boy
[2] (*Aut*) windscreen wiper, windshield wiper (*EEUU*)

limpiabarros SM INV (= *utensilio*) scraper, boot scraper; (= *felpudo*) doormat

limpiabotas SMF INV bootblack

limpiacabezales SM INV head-cleaner

limpiachimeneas SMF INV chimney sweep

limpiacoches SMF INV (= *persona*) street car-washer

limpiacristales Ⓐ SM INV [1] (= *líquido*) window-cleaning fluid; (= *trapo*) cleaning cloth
[2] (*Aut*) windscreen wiper
Ⓑ SMF INV (= *persona*) window cleaner

limpiada SF [1] (*LAm*) (= *acto de limpiar*) clean, clean-up
[2] (*Cono Sur*) (*en bosque*) clearing

limpiadientes SM INV toothpick

limpiador(a) Ⓐ ADJ [*líquido, crema*] cleansing
Ⓑ SM/F (= *persona*) cleaner

limpiadura SF [1] (= *acto de limpiar*) cleaning, cleaning-up
[2] **limpiaduras** dirt *sing*, dust *sing*, scourings

limpiafaros SM INV headlamp wiper

limpiahogares SM INV household cleaning fluid

limpiahornos SM INV oven cleaner

limpialuneta SM ► **limpialuneta trasero**, **limpialuneta posterior** rear windscreen wiper, rear wiper

limpiamanos SM INV (*CAm, Méx*) hand towel

limpiamente ADV [1] (= *con pulcritud*) cleanly
[2] (= *honestamente*) honestly; **nos ganaron ~** they beat us fair and square
[3] (= *hábilmente*) skilfully, skillfully (*EEUU*); **hace las jugadas muy ~** he makes the moves with great skill, he makes the moves very neatly

limpiametales SM INV metal polish

limpiamuebles SM INV furniture polish

limpiaparabrisas SM INV windscreen wiper, windshield wiper (*EEUU*)

limpiapiés SM INV (= *utensilio*) scraper, boot scraper; (*Méx*) (= *estera*) doormat

limpiapipas SM INV pipe cleaner

limpiaplicador SM (*Méx*) cotton bud, Q-tip® (*EEUU*)

limpiaplumas SM INV penwiper

limpiar ▸conjug 1b◂ Ⓐ VT [1] [+ *casa*] to tidy, tidy up, clean; [+ *cara, piel*] to cleanse; [+ *marca*] to wipe off, clean off; [+ *maquillaje*] to remove; [+ *zapatos*] to polish, shine; **~ en seco** to dry-clean
[2] (*Culin*) [+ *conejo*] to clean; [+ *pescado*] to gut
[3] (= *enjugar*) to wipe, wipe off; **~ las narices a un niño** to wipe a child's nose
[4] (*Mil*) to mop up; (*Policía*) to clean up
[5] (*Bot*) to prune, cut back
[6] (*) (*en el juego*) to clean out*
[7] (‡) (= *robar*) to swipe*, nick*
[8] (*Méx**) (= *pegar*) to hit, bash*, beat up
[9] (‡) (= *matar*) to do in‡
Ⓑ **limpiarse** VPR to clean o.s., wipe o.s.; **~se las narices** to blow one's nose

limpiaventanas SMF INV [1] (= *persona*) window cleaner
[2] (= *líquido*) window-cleaning fluid

limpiavía SM (*LAm*) cowcatcher

límpido ADJ (*frm*) limpid

limpieza SF [1] (= *acción*) cleaning; **la mujer** *o* **señora de la ~** the cleaning lady; **hacer la ~** to do the cleaning ► **limpieza en seco** dry cleaning ► **limpieza general** spring cleaning
[2] (*Pol*) purge; (*Mil*) mopping-up; (*Policía*) clean-up ► **limpieza étnica** ethnic cleansing
[3] (= *estado*) cleanness ► **limpieza de sangre** racial purity
[4] **con ~** (= *con integridad*) fair and square; **nos ha ganado con ~** he beat us fair and square
[5] (= *destreza*) skill; **hace las jugadas con mucha ~** he makes the moves with great skill, he makes the moves very neatly

limpio Ⓐ ADJ [1] [*casa, cuarto*] clean; **~ de algo** free from sth, clear of sth; ✦**MODISMO más ~ que los chorros del oro** as clean as can be
[2] (= *despejado*) clear; **el cielo estaba ~ de nubes** there was a cloudless sky, there was not a cloud in the sky
[3] [*líquidos*] pure, clean
[4] (*en lo moral*) pure; (= *honesto*) honest
[5] (*Dep*) [*jugada*] fair
[6] (*Fin*) clear, net; **50 dólares de ganancia limpia** 50 dollars of clear profit
[7] (*) (= *sin dinero*) **estar ~** to be broke; **quedar(se) ~** to be cleaned out*
[8] (*) (*enfático*) **a pedrada limpia**: **se defendieron a pedrada limpia** they defended themselves with nothing but stones; **a puñetazo ~** with bare fists
Ⓑ SM [1] **en ~** (*Fin*) clear, net; **copia en ~** fair copy; **pasar** *o* **poner algo en ~** to make a fair *o* neat *o* clean copy of sth; **poner un texto en ~** to tidy a text up, produce a final version of a text; ✦**MODISMOS sacar algo en ~** to make sense of sth; **no pude sacar nada en ~** I couldn't make anything of it
[2] (*Méx*) (= *claro de bosque*) clearing (*in a wood*), treeless area, bare ground
Ⓒ ADV **jugar ~** to play fair

limpión SM [1] (= *acto*) wipe, (quick) clean; **dar un ~ a algo** to give sth a wipe
[2] (†) (= *trapo*) cleaning rag, cleaning cloth; (*Andes, CAm, Caribe*) dishcloth
[3] (†) (= *persona*) cleaner
[4] (*Andes**) (= *regañina*) ticking-off*

limpito ADJ nice and clean

limusina SF limousine

lina SF (*Cono Sur*) [1] [*de lana*] skein of coarse wool
[2] (= *trenza*) pigtail, long hair

linaje SM [1] (= *familia*) lineage, descent; **de ~ de reyes** descended from royalty, of royal descent; **de ~ honrado** of good parentage
[2] (= *clase*) class, kind; **de otro ~** of another kind ► **linaje humano** mankind
[3] **linajes** (= *familias*) (local) nobility *sing*, noble families

linajudo ADJ highborn, noble, blue-blooded

linar SM flax field

linaza SF linseed

lince Ⓐ SM [1] (*Zool*) lynx; (*CAm, Méx*) wild cat; ✦**MODISMOS ser un ~** (= *observador*) to be very sharp-eyed; (= *astuto*) to be very shrewd *o* sharp; **tener ojos de ~** to be very sharp-eyed ► **lince ibérico** pardal lynx, Spanish lynx
[2] (*LAm*) (= *agudeza*) sharpness
Ⓑ ADJ ✦**MODISMOS ojos ~s** eagle eyes; **es muy ~** (= *observador*) he's very sharp-eyed; (= *astuto*) he's very shrewd *o* sharp

linchamiento SM lynching

linchar ▸conjug 1a◂ VT to lynch

linche SM (*Andes*) (= *mochila*) knapsack; **linches** (*Méx*†) (= *alforjas*) saddlebags

lindamente ADV [1] (= *con belleza*) prettily; (= *con delicadeza*) daintily; (= *con elegancia*) elegantly
[2] (*iró*) well
[3] (*esp LAm*) (= *excelentemente*) excellently, marvellously

lindante ADJ bordering (**con** on), adjacent (**con** to), adjoining

lindar ▸conjug 1a◂ VI **~ con: mis tierras lindan con las suyas** my land borders on theirs; **el banco linda con el ayuntamiento** the bank is adjacent to the town hall; **eso linda con el racismo** that is bordering on racism

linde SM *o* SF boundary

lindero Ⓐ ADJ (= *limítrofe*) adjoining, bordering
Ⓑ SM (= *borde*) edge, border; (= *linde*) boundary

lindeza SF [1] (= *belleza*) prettiness
[2] (*esp LAm*) (= *amabilidad*) niceness
[3] **lindezas** (= *cosas bonitas*) pretty things; (*iró*) (= *insultos*) insults, improprieties
[4] (= *ocurrencia*) witticism

lindo Ⓐ ADJ (*esp LAm*) [1] (= *bonito*) nice, lovely, pretty; **un ~ coche** a nice car, a fine car
[2] (*iró*) fine, pretty
[3] (= *excelente*) fine, excellent, first-rate; **un ~ partido** a first-rate game; **un ~ concierto** a good concert; ✦***MODISMO*** **de lo ~** a lot, a great deal; **jugaron de lo ~** they played fantastically, they played a first-rate game
Ⓑ ADV (*LAm*) nicely, well; **baila ~** she dances beautifully
Ⓒ SM (*Hist*) fop

lindura SF [1] (*esp Cono Sur*) (= *belleza*) prettiness, loveliness; **está hecha una ~*** she looks really pretty *o* lovely
[2] (*Caribe, Cono Sur*) [*persona*] (= *campeón*) ace, champion; (= *experto*) expert; **ella es una ~ en el vestir** she dresses beautifully
[3] (*LAm*) (= *objeto*) lovely thing

línea Ⓐ SF [1] (= *raya*) line; **dibujó una ~ recta** he drew a straight line; **primera ~ de playa** sea-front; **en ~** (= *alineado*) in (a) line, in a row; **en ~ recta** in a straight line; **tirar una ~** (*Arte*) to draw a line; **en toda la ~** [*ganar, vencer*] outright; [*derrotar*] totally; ✦***MODISMO*** **ser de una** *o* **una sola ~** (*Caribe, Cono Sur**) to be as straight as a die, be absolutely straight ► **línea a trazos** broken line ► **línea de base** (*Agrimensura*) base-line ► **línea de cambio de fecha** International Date Line ► **línea de carga** load-line ► **línea de flotación** (*Náut*) water line ► **línea de la vida** life line ► **línea del biquini** bikini line ► **línea de montaje** assembly line, production line ► **línea de puntos** dotted line ► **línea discontinua** (*Aut*) broken line ► **línea divisoria** dividing line
[2] (*en un escrito*) line; **leer entre ~s** to read between the lines; ✦***MODISMO*** **poner unas ~s a algn** to drop a line to sb
[3] (*Com*) (= *género, gama*) line; **es único en su ~** it is unique in its line, it is the only one of its kind; **en esa ~ no tenemos nada** we have nothing in that line; **de primera ~** first-rate, top-ranking ► **línea blanca** white goods *pl* ► **línea marrón** brown goods *pl*
[4] (*Elec*) line, cable ► **línea aérea** overhead cable ► **línea de alta tensión** high-tension cable ► **línea de conducción eléctrica** power line
[5] (*Telec*) line; **me he quedado sin ~** I've been cut off; **han cortado la ~** I've *o* we've been cut off ► **línea caliente** hot line ► **línea compartida** shared line ► **línea derivada** extension ► **línea de socorro** helpline, telephone helpline ► **línea directa** direct line ► **línea erótica** sex-line ► **línea exterior** outside line ► **línea gratuita** freephone ► **línea roja** hot line ► **línea telefónica** telephone line ► **línea (telefónica) de ayuda** helpline, telephone helpline
[6] (*Mil*) line; **cerrar ~s** to close ranks; **de ~** regular, front-line; **primera ~** front line ► **línea de alto el fuego** ceasefire line ► **línea de batalla** line of battle, battle line ► **línea de fuego** firing line
[7] (*Aer, Ferro*) **autobús de ~** service bus, regular bus ► **línea aérea** airline ► **línea de abastecimiento** supply line ► **línea férrea** railway, railroad (*EEUU*) ► **línea regular** scheduled service
[8] (*Dep*) line ► **línea de balón muerto** dead-ball line ► **línea de banda** sideline, touchline ► **línea de centro** halfway line ► **línea de fondo** by-line ► **línea de gol** goal-line ► **línea delantera** forward line ► **línea de llegada** finishing-line ► **línea de medio campo** halfway line ► **línea de meta** (*en fútbol*) goal-line; (*en carrera*) finishing-line ► **línea de puerta** goal-line ► **línea de saque** baseline, service line ► **línea de toque** touchline ► **línea lateral** sideline, touchline
[9] (*Inform*) **en ~** on-line; **fuera de ~** off-line ► **línea de estado, línea de situación** status line
[10] (= *talle*) figure; **guardar** *o* **conservar la ~** to keep one's figure (trim)
[11] (= *moda*) **la ~ de 2000** the 2000 look
[12] [*de pensamiento, acción*] line; **explicar algo a grandes ~s** *o* **en sus ~s generales** to set sth out in broad outline, give the broad outline of sth ► **línea de conducta** course of action ► **línea de partido** party line ► **línea dura** (*Pol*) hard line
[13] (*genealógica*) line; **en ~ directa** in an unbroken line ► **línea de sangre** blood line ► **línea sucesoria** line of succession, order of succession
Ⓑ SMF (*Dep*) linesman, assistant referee

lineal ADJ (*gen*) linear; (*Inform*) on-line; **aumento ~ de sueldos** across-the-board pay increase; **dibujo ~** line drawing; **impuesto ~** flat-rate tax

linealidad SF linearity

lineamento SM lineament

linear ▸conjug 1a◂ VT [1] (*gen*) to line, draw lines on
[2] (*Arte*) to sketch, outline

linense Ⓐ ADJ of/from La Línea
Ⓑ SMF native/inhabitant of La Línea; **los ~s** the people of La Línea

linfa SF lymph

linfático ADJ lymphatic

linfocito SM (*Med*) lymphocyte

lingotazo* SM swig*, shot*

lingote SM ingot

lingüista SMF linguist

lingüística SF linguistics *sing* ► **lingüística aplicada** applied linguistics ► **lingüística computacional** computational linguistics ► **lingüística de contrastes** contrastive linguistics

lingüístico ADJ linguistic

linier SMF (*pl* **liniers**) (*Dep*) linesman, assistant referee

linimento SM liniment

lino SM [1] (*Bot*) flax
[2] (*Cono Sur*) (= *linaza*) linseed
[3] (= *ropa fina*) linen; (= *lona*) canvas; **géneros de ~** linen goods

linóleo SM lino, linoleum

linón SM lawn (*fabric*)

linotipia SF, **linotipo** SM linotype

linotipista SMF linotype operator

linterna SF [1] (*eléctrica*) torch, flashlight (*EEUU*); (= *farolillo*) lantern ► **linterna mágica** magic lantern ► **linterna roja** back marker
[2] (*Arquit*) lantern
[3] **linternas** (*Méx hum*) (= *ojos*) eyes

linyera SM (*Cono Sur*) (= *vagabundo*) tramp, bum (*EEUU**)

lío SM [1] (= *fardo*) bundle; (*Cono Sur*) truss
[2] (*) (= *jaleo*) fuss; (= *confusión*) muddle, mix-up; **ese ~ de los pasaportes** that fuss about the passports; **en mi mesa hay un ~ enorme de papeles** my desk is in a real muddle with all these bits of paper; **armar un ~** to make a fuss, kick up a fuss; **armarse un ~**: **se armó un ~ tremendo** there was a terrific fuss; **hacerse un ~** to get into a muddle, get mixed up; **se hizo un ~ con tantos nombres** he got into a muddle with all the names
[3] (= *aprieto*) **meterse en un ~** to get into trouble
[4] (*) (= *amorío*) affair; **tener un ~ con algn** to be having an affair with sb ► **lío de faldas** affair
[5] (= *cotilleo*) tale, piece of gossip; **¡no me vengas con ~s!** less of your tales!

liofilizado ADJ freeze-dried

Liorna† SF Leghorn

lioso ADJ gossipy

lipa SF (*Caribe*) belly

lipes SF INV (*LAm*) (*tb* **piedra ~**) blue vitriol

lipidia Ⓐ SF [1] (*CAm*) (= *pobreza*) poverty
[2] (*Chile, Perú*) (= *diarrea*) the runs*
Ⓑ SMF (*Caribe, Méx*) nuisance, pest

lipidiar ▸conjug 1b◂ VT (*Caribe, Méx*) to annoy, bother, pester

lipidioso ADJ (*Caribe, Méx*) (= *impertinente*) cheeky; (= *molesto*) annoying

lipoaspiración SF liposuction

lipocito SM fat particle

lipoescultura SF liposculpture

lipólisis SF INV lipolysis

lipón ADJ (*Caribe*) fat, pot-bellied

lipoplastia SF liposculpture

liposoma SM liposome

liposucción SF liposuction

lipotimia SF faint, blackout

lique‡† SM kick; **dar el ~ a algn** to kick sb out; **darse el ~** to clear out*

liquen SM lichen

líquida SF (*Ling*) liquid

➤ **liquidación** SF [1] (*Com, Fin*) [*de compañía, negocio*] liquidation, winding-up; [*de cuenta, deuda*] settlement; **entrar en ~** to go into liquidation; **vender en ~** to sell up ► **liquidación forzosa, liquidación obligatoria** compulsory liquidation
[2] (= *rebajas*) sale; **venta de ~** (clearance) sale ► **liquidación por cierre del negocio** closing-down sale ► **liquidación por fin de temporada** end-of-season sale
[3] (*por despido*) redundancy pay; **oficina** *o* **sección de ~** accounts section, payments office
[4] (*Quím*) liquefaction
[5] (*Pol*) liquidation

liquidador(a) SM/F liquidator

liquidar ▸conjug 1a◂ Ⓐ VT [1] [+ *cuenta*] to settle; [+ *empresa, negocio*] to wind up, liquidate; [+ *deuda*] to settle, pay off, clear; [+ *existencias*] to sell off, sell up
[2] [+ *asunto, problema*] to deal with; **ya he-**

➤ LENGUA Y USO: **liquidación 1** 47.5

mos liquidado la cuestión we've dealt with that issue now; **le pides perdón y asunto liquidado** just say you are sorry and that'll be the end of it

[3] (*) (= *gastar*) to go through*, blow*; **ha liquidado en un mes todos sus ahorros** she went through *o* blew all her savings in one month

[4] (*) (= *matar*) to bump off*

[5] (*Pol*) (= *eliminar*) to liquidate

[6] (*LAm*) (= *destrozar*) to destroy, ruin

[7] (*Méx*) [+ *obreros*] to pay off

[8] (*Quím*) to liquefy

Ⓑ **liquidarse** VPR [1] (*) (= *gastarse*) to blow*; **se han liquidado todos sus ahorros** they have blown all their savings

[2] (*Quím*) to liquefy

liquidez SF [1] [*de líquido, sustancia*] liquidity, fluidity

[2] (*Fin*) liquidity

líquido Ⓐ ADJ [1] [*sustancia*] liquid, fluid; **el ~ elemento** water

[2] (*Fin*) net; **ganancia líquida** net profit

[3] (*CAm, Méx*) (= *exacto*) exact; **cuatro varas líquidas** exactly four yards

[4] (*Ling*) liquid

Ⓑ SM [1] (*gen*) liquid, fluid ► **líquido anticongelante** antifreeze ► **líquido de frenos** brake fluid ► **líquido seminal** seminal fluid ► **líquidos corporales** body fluids ► **líquido sinovial** synovial fluid

[2] (*Fin*) (= *efectivo*) ready cash, ready money ► **líquido imponible** net taxable income

liquiliqui SM (*Caribe*) Venezuelan national dress

lira SF [1] (*Mús*) lyre

[2] (*Literat*) *5-line stanza popular in the 16th century*

[3] (= *moneda*) lira

lírica SF lyrical poetry

lírico/a Ⓐ ADJ [1] (*Literat*) lyric(al); (*Teat*) musical

[2] (*LAm*) [*persona*] full of idealistic plans; [*plan, idea*] Utopian, fantastic

Ⓑ SM/F (*LAm*) (= *soñador*) dreamer, Utopian

lirio SM iris ► **lirio de los valles** lily of the valley

lirismo SM [1] (*gen*) lyricism

[2] (*LAm*) (= *sueños*) dreams *pl*, Utopia; (= *manera de ser*) fantasy, Utopianism

lirón SM [1] (*Zool*) dormouse

[2] (= *dormilón*) sleepyhead; ✦*MODISMO* **dormir como un ~** to sleep like a log

lirondo ADJ *ver* **mondo**

lis SF lily

lisa SF [1] (*Caribe**) (= *cerveza*) beer

[2] (*Andes*) (= *pez*) mullet; *ver tb* **liso**

lisamente ADV evenly, smoothly

Lisboa SF Lisbon

lisboeta, lisbonense Ⓐ ADJ of/from Lisbon

Ⓑ SMF native/inhabitant of Lisbon; **los ~s** the people of Lisbon

lisérgico ADJ **ácido ~** lysergic acid

lisiado/a Ⓐ ADJ crippled, lame

Ⓑ SM/F cripple; **un ~ de guerra** a wounded ex-serviceman

lisiar ▸conjug 1b◂ VT (*gen*) to injure (permanently), hurt (seriously); (= *tullir*) to cripple, maim

liso Ⓐ ADJ [1] [*terreno, superficie*] smooth, even; [*neumático*] bald; ✦*MODISMO* **~ como la palma de la mano** as smooth as glass

[2] [*pelo*] straight

[3] [*mar*] calm

[4] (*Dep*) **los 400 metros ~s** the 400-metre flat race

[5] (= *sin adornos*) plain, unadorned; (= *de un solo color*) plain; ✦*MODISMOS* **irse ~** (*Caribe**) to leave without a word; **la tiene lisa*** he's got it made*; **lisa y llanamente** (= *en términos sencillos*) plainly, in plain language; (= *evidentemente*) quite simply; **~ y llano** plain, simple, straightforward

[6] (*Andes, Cono Sur*) (= *grosero*) rude

[7] (*LAm**) (= *descarado*) fresh*, cheeky, sassy (*EEUU*)

[8] (*) (= *de poco pecho*) flat-chested

Ⓑ SM (*Cono Sur*) tall beer glass; *ver tb* **lisa**

lisol SM lysol

lisonja SF flattery

lisonjear ▸conjug 1a◂ VT [1] (= *alabar*) to flatter

[2] (= *agradar*) to please, delight

lisonjeramente ADV [1] (= *aduladoramente*) flatteringly

[2] (= *agradablemente*) pleasingly, agreeably

lisonjero/a Ⓐ ADJ [1] (= *adulador*) flattering

[2] (= *agradable*) pleasing, agreeable

Ⓑ SM/F flatterer

lista SF [1] [*de nombres, elementos*] list; (*Mil*) roll, roll call; (*en escuela*) register, school list (*EEUU*); **pasar ~** (*Mil*) to call the roll; (*Escol*) to call the register; ✦*MODISMO* **pasar ~ a algn** to call sb to account ► **lista cerrada** (*Pol*) closed list ► **lista de boda** wedding list ► **lista de comidas** menu ► **lista de correos** poste restante, general delivery (*EEUU*) ► **lista de direcciones** mailing list ► **lista de encuentros** (*Dep*) fixture list ► **lista de espera** waiting list ► **lista de éxitos** (*Mús*) charts *pl* ► **lista de pagos** payroll ► **lista de platos** menu ► **lista de precios** price list ► **lista de premios** honours list ► **lista de raya** (*Méx*) payroll ► **lista de tandas** duty roster, rota ► **lista de vinos** wine list ► **lista electoral** electoral roll, register of voters ► **lista negra** blacklist ► **listas de audiencia** ratings, audience rating *sing*

[2] (= *tira*) [*de tela*] strip; [*de papel*] slip

[3] (= *raya*) stripe; **tela a ~s** striped material

listadillo SM (*Andes, Caribe, Méx*) striped, (white and blue) cotton cloth

listado[1] Ⓐ ADJ striped

Ⓑ SM (*Andes, Caribe*) = **listadillo**

listado[2] SM (= *lista*) list, listing; (*Com, Inform*) listing, printout ► **listado de comprobación** checklist ► **listado paginado** paged listing

listar ▸conjug 1a◂ VT to list, enter on a list; (*Inform*) to list

listeria SF listeria

listero/a SM/F timekeeper, wages clerk

listillo/a SM/F know-all, smart Aleck*

listín SM [1] (*Telec*) ► **listín telefónico, listín de teléfonos** telephone directory

[2] (*Caribe*) (= *periódico*) newspaper

listo Ⓐ ADJ [1] (= *dispuesto*) ready; **¿estás ~?** are you ready?; **me pongo las lentillas y ~** I'll just put my lenses in and I'll be ready; **¡preparados, ~s, ya!** ready, steady, go!; **la cena está ya lista** dinner's ready; **~ para algo** ready for sth; **todo está ~ para el concierto** everything is ready for the concert; **¿~s para el ataque?** ready to attack?; **"listo para usar"** "ready to use", "ready for use"; **ya estoy lista para salir** I'm ready to go out

[2] (= *terminado*) finished; **una última lectura y ~** one last read through and that's it *o* it's finished; **la traducción tendrá que estar lista para mañana** the translation will have to be finished for tomorrow; ✦*MODISMO* **estar** *o* **ir ~***: **pues está lista si espera que yo la llame** well, if she expects me to call her she's got another think coming; **¿que quieres ir al cine? ¡estás ~!** so you want to go to the cinema? no way!*; **—el tren va con retraso —¡pues estamos ~s!** "the train is running late" — "well, we've had it now* *o* we've really had it now!"*

[3] (= *inteligente*) clever, bright, smart*; **el más ~ de la clase** the cleverest *o* brightest *o* smartest* in the class; **¿te crees muy lista, verdad?** you think you're really smart, don't you?; **tú, ~, ¿a qué no sabes una cosa?** (*iró*) OK, cleverclogs *o* wise guy, I bet you don't know this*; **se las da de ~** he thinks he's so clever; **va de lista por la vida** she goes round thinking she knows it all; **pasarse de ~** to be too clever by half; ✦*MODISMO* **ser más ~ que el hambre** to be as sharp as a needle

[4] (*Chile, Col, Perú*) (= *de acuerdo*) OK; **¡listo!** OK!

Ⓑ SMF [1] (= *inteligente*) clever one, smart one*

[2] (*pey*) cleverclogs*, smart arse**, smart ass (*EEUU**); **siempre hay algún ~ que te hace una pregunta** there's always some cleverclogs* *o* smart arse** who asks you a question

listón SM [1] [*de madera*] strip, lath; (*Dep*) bar; [*de goma, metal*] strip; (*Arquit*) fillet

[2] (= *nivel*) level; **bajar el ~** to make things too easy ► **listón de la pobreza** poverty line ► **listón de los precios** price level

[3] (*Cos*) ribbon

lisura SF [1] [*de terreno, superficie*] evenness, smoothness; [*de pelo*] straightness; [*del mar*] calmness

[2] (= *sinceridad*) sincerity; (= *ingenuidad*) naïvety

[3] (*Andes, Cono Sur*) (= *grosería*) rude remark, cheeky remark

[4] (*LAm*) (= *descaro*) impudence, brazenness

lisurero ADJ (*Perú*), **lisuriento** ADJ (*Perú*) rude, cheeky, sassy (*EEUU*)

litera SF [1] (*en alcoba*) bunk, bunk bed; (*Náut, Ferro*) bunk, berth; (*Ferro*) couchette

[2] (*Hist*) (= *carruaje*) litter

literal ADJ literal

literalmente ADV literally (*tb fig*)

literario ADJ literary

literato/a SM/F man/woman of letters

literatura SF literature ► **literatura comparada** (study of) comparative literature ► **literatura de evasión** escapist literature ► **literatura de kiosco** cheap literature

litigación SF litigation

litigante SMF litigant

litigar ▸conjug 1h◂ Ⓐ VT to dispute at law

Ⓑ VI [1] (*Jur*) to go to law

[2] (*frm*) (= *discutir*) to argue, dispute

litigio SM [1] (*Jur*) litigation; (= *pleito*) lawsuit

[2] (*frm*) (= *disputa*) dispute; **en ~** in dispute; **el asunto en ~** the matter under debate

litigioso ADJ litigious, contentious

litio SM lithium

litisexpensas SFPL (*Jur*) costs

litografía SF [1] (= *proceso*) lithography
[2] (= *cuadro*) lithograph

litografiar ▸conjug 1c◂ VT to lithograph

litoral Ⓐ ADJ coastal, littoral (*frm*)
Ⓑ SM seaboard, coast, littoral (*frm*)

litre SM (*Cono Sur*) rash

litri* ADJ affected, dandified

litro¹ SM litre, liter (*EEUU*);
→ KILOS, METROS, AÑOS

litro² SM (*Cono Sur*) coarse woollen *o* (*EEUU*) woolen cloth

litrona* SF litre *o* (*EEUU*) liter bottle

Lituania SF Lithuania

lituano/a Ⓐ ADJ Lithuanian
Ⓑ SM/F Lithuanian; **los ~s** the Lithuanians, the people of Lithuania
Ⓒ SM (*Ling*) Lithuanian

liturgia SF liturgy

litúrgico ADJ liturgical

livianamente ADV [1] (= *de forma inconstante*) in a fickle way
[2] (= *frívolamente*) frivolously, in a trivial way
[3] (= *lascivamente*) lewdly

liviandad SF [1] (= *de poco peso*) lightness
[2] (= *inconstancia*) fickleness
[3] (= *frivolidad*) frivolity, triviality
[4] (= *lascivia*) lewdness

liviano Ⓐ ADJ [1] (= *ligero*) light
[2] (= *inconstante*) fickle
[3] (= *frívolo*) frivolous, trivial
[4] (= *lascivo*) lewd
Ⓑ **livianos** SMPL lights, lungs

lividez SF [1] (= *palidez*) pallor, paleness
[2] (= *amoratamiento*) lividness

lívido ADJ [1] (= *pálido*) pallid, pale, livid
[2] (= *amoratado*) black and blue, livid

living ['liβin] SM (*pl* **livings** ['liβin]) (*LAm*) living room, lounge

lixiviar ▸conjug 1b◂ Ⓐ VT to leach
Ⓑ **lixiviarse** VPR to leach

liza SF (*Hist*) lists *pl*; (*fig*) contest

Ll, ll ['eʎe] SF *former letter in the Spanish alphabet*

llacsa SF (*Cono Sur*) molten metal

llaga SF [1] (= *úlcera*) ulcer, sore; ✦*MODISMO* **¡por las ~s (de Cristo)!** damnation!
[2] (= *sufrimiento*) affliction, torment; **las ~s de la guerra** the havoc of war, the afflictions of war; ✦*MODISMO* **renovar la ~** to open up an old wound; *ver tb* **dedo 1**

llagar ▸conjug 1h◂ VT to cause a sore on, wound

llalla SF (*Cono Sur*) = **yaya**

llama¹ SF (*Zool*) llama

llama² SF [1] [*de fuego*] flame; **arder sin ~** to smoulder, smolder (*EEUU*); **en ~s** burning, ablaze, in flames; **entregar algo a las ~s** to commit sth to the flames; **estallar en ~s** to burst into flames; ✦*MODISMO* **salir de las ~s y caer en las brasas** to jump out of the frying pan into the fire ► **llama piloto** pilot light (*on stove*) ► **llama solar** solar flare
[2] [*de amor, pasión*] flame, fire; [*de esperanza, libertad*] spark

▼**llamada** SF [1] (*Telec*) call; **gracias por su ~** thank you for your call; **ahora le paso la ~** I'll put you through now; **devolver una ~** to phone back; **hacer una ~** to make a call; **desde este teléfono no se pueden hacer ~s al extranjero** you can't make international calls from this telephone; **¿puedo hacer una ~?** can I use your phone?, can I make a call? ► **llamada a cobro revertido** reverse charge call, collect call (*EEUU*) ► **llamada a larga distancia, llamada de larga distancia** (*LAm*) long-distance call, trunk call ► **llamada internacional** international call ► **llamada interprovincial** *call made between towns in different provinces* ► **llamada interurbana** *call made between different towns within the same province* ► **llamada local, llamada metropolitana** local call ► **llamada por cobrar** (*Chile, Méx*) = **llamada a cobro revertido** ► **llamada provincial** = **llamada interurbana** ► **llamada telefónica** telephone call ► **llamada urbana** local call
[2] (*a la puerta*) (*con el puño*) knock; (*con el timbre*) ring
[3] (= *aviso*) call; **última ~ para los pasajeros con destino Bruselas** last call for passengers flying to Brussels; **la ~ del deber** the call of duty; **la ~ de la selva** the call of the wild; **acudir a la ~ de algn** to answer sb's call; **la enfermera acudió rápidamente a mi ~** the nurse came quickly when I called her, the nurse answered my call quickly ► **llamada al orden** call to order ► **llamada de alerta** (*lit*) alert; (*fig*) warning, alarm call ► **llamada de socorro** call for help
[4] (= *gesto*) signal, gesture
[5] (*Tip*) mark; **haz una ~ al margen** make a mark in the margin
[6] (*Inform*) ► **llamada a procedimiento** procedure call
[7] (*Mil*) (*tb* **~ a las armas**) call to arms

llamado Ⓐ ADJ [1] (= *con el nombre de*) [*persona*] named, called; [*lugar*] called; **un chico ~ Manuel** a boy named *o* called Manuel; **un hotel ~ Miramar** a hotel called Miramar
[2] (= *conocido*) so-called; **la llamada generación beat** the so-called beat generation; **ordenadores paralelos, así ~s por que funcionan simultáneamente** parallel computers, so called because they work simultaneously; **el cubo de Rubik, así ~ en honor a su inventor** Rubik's cube, named after its inventor
[3] (= *destinado*) **me sentía ~ a hacerlo** I felt destined to do it; **esta ley está llamada a desaparecer** this law is bound *o* destined to disappear; **estar ~ al fracaso** to be doomed to failure
[4] (= *convocado*) **jóvenes ~s a prestar el servicio militar** young men called up (for military service)
Ⓑ SM [1] (*Arg*) call, phone call
[2] (*LAm*) (= *llamamiento*) appeal

llamador¹ SM (*en la puerta*) (= *aldaba*) doorknocker; (= *timbre*) bell

llamador²(a) SM/F (= *visitante*) caller

llamamiento SM call; **un ~ al diálogo** a call for dialogue; **hacer *o* lanzar un ~ (a algo)** to make *o* issue an appeal *o* call (for sth); **el presidente hizo un ~ a la unidad nacional** the president called for national unity, the president made *o* issued an appeal *o* a call for national unity; **han hecho un ~ a la población pidiendo donaciones de sangre** they have appealed for blood donations, they have appealed to people to give blood ► **llamamiento a filas** (*Mil*) call-up, draft (*EEUU*) ► **llamamiento de socorro** call for help

▼**llamar** ▸conjug 1a◂ Ⓐ VT [1] (= *nombrar*) to call; **mis amigos me llaman Mari** my friends call me Mari; **¿cómo van a ~ al niño?** what are they going to name *o* call the baby?; **me llamó imbécil** he called me an idiot; **la llamó de todo** he called her every name under the sun; *ver tb* **hache**
[2] (= *considerar*) to call; **eso yo lo llamo un auténtico robo** that's what I call daylight robbery*; **lo que se dio en ~ la nueva generación** what became known as the new generation, what came to be called the new generation; **el mal llamado problema** what people wrongly consider a problem
[3] (= *avisar*) [+ *médico, fontanero*] to call; [+ *taxi*] (*por teléfono*) to call; (*con la mano*) to hail; **te estuve llamando a voces** I was shouting for you; **me llamó con la mano para que me acercara** he beckoned me over; **no te metas donde no te llaman*** don't poke your nose in where it's not wanted*; **~ a algn a escena** to call sb to the stage; **~ a algn al orden** to call sb to order; *ver tb* **mandar A1**
[4] (*Telec*) (*tb* **~ por teléfono**) to call, ring, phone; **que me llamen a las siete** ask them to call *o* ring *o* phone me at seven; **te llaman desde París** they're calling you *o* they're on the phone from Paris; **¿quién me llama?** who's on the phone?
[5] (= *atraer*) **el ejército llama a muchos jóvenes** the army appeals to a lot of young people; **el chocolate no me llama demasiado** I'm not all that keen on chocolate; *ver tb* **atención 1**
[6] (= *convocar*) to call, summon (*frm*); **lo ~on a palacio** he was called *o* summoned (*frm*) to the palace; **Dios lo ha llamado a su lado** (*euf*) he has been called to God; **~ a algn a filas** to call sb up; **pronto seremos llamados a las urnas** an election/a referendum will soon be called; *ver tb* **llamado A3**
Ⓑ VI [1] (*Telec*) [*persona*] to call, ring, phone; [*teléfono*] to ring; **¿quién llama?** who's calling?; **ha llamado Maribel** Maribel called *o* rang *o* phoned
[2] (*a la puerta*) (*con el puño*) to knock; (*al timbre*) to ring; **"entren sin llamar"** "enter without knocking"; **llamé pero el timbre no sonaba** I rang the bell but it didn't work; **¿quién llama?** who's there?, who is it?; **están llamando** there's someone at the door
Ⓒ **llamarse** VPR [1] [*persona, lugar*] to be called; **mi primo se llama Benjamín** my cousin's name is Benjamín, mi cousin is called Benjamín; **¿cómo te llamas?** what's your name?; **se llama Mari Paz** her name is Mari Paz; **¿sabes cómo se llama la película?** do you know the name of the film?, do you know what the film is called?; **¡como me llamo Manuel que lo haré!** I'll do it, as sure as my name's Manuel!
[2] (*Esp**) (= *costar*) **¿cómo se llama esto?** how much is this?, what's the damage?‡

llamarada SF [1] [*de fuego*] flare-up, sudden blaze
[2] (*en rostro*) flush
[3] [*de indignación, ira*] blaze, outburst

llamarón SM (*Andes, CAm, Cono Sur*) = **llamarada**

llamativo ADJ (= *vistoso*) [*color*] loud, bright; **se**

➤ LENGUA Y USO: **llamada 1** 27 **llamar A4** 27 **B1** 27

viste de modo ~ she wears very striking clothes

llame SM (*Cono Sur*) bird trap

llameante ADJ blazing

llamear ▸conjug 1a◂ VI to blaze, flame

llamón* ADJ (*Méx*) whining, whingeing*

llampo SM (*Andes, Cono Sur*) ore, pulverized ore

llana SF 1 (*Geog*) plain
2 (*Arquit*) trowel

llanada SF plain

llanamente ADV 1 (= *lisamente*) smoothly, evenly
2 (= *sin ostentaciones*) plainly, simply
3 (= *sinceramente*) openly, frankly
4 (= *claramente*) clearly, straightforwardly; *ver tb* **liso A5**

llanca SF (*LAm*) copper ore

llanear ▸conjug 1a◂ VI (*Aut*) to cruise, coast along

llanero/a SM/F 1 (*esp Ven*) plainsman/plainswoman ▸ **llanero solitario** lone ranger
2 (*Caribe*) (= *vaquero*) cowboy

llaneza SF 1 (= *franqueza*) openness, frankness
2 (= *sencillez*) plainness, simplicity; (= *claridad*) clearness, straightforwardness

llanito/a* SM/F Gibraltarian

llano Ⓐ ADJ 1 [*superficie, terreno*] (= *sin desniveles*) flat; (= *no inclinado*) level
2 (= *sencillo*) [*persona, trato*] straightforward; [*estilo, lenguaje*] simple; **en lenguaje ~** in plain language *o* terms
3 **palabra llana** *word with the stress on the penultimate syllable*
Ⓑ SM plain; **Los Llanos** (*Ven Geog*) Venezuelan Plains

llanque SM (*Andes*) rustic sandal

llanta SF 1 [*de rueda*] rim ▸ **llanta de oruga** caterpillar track ▸ **llantas de aleación** alloy wheels
2 (*esp LAm*) (= *neumático*) tyre, tire (*EEUU*)
3 (*Caribe*) (= *anillo*) large finger-ring

llantén SM plantain

llantera* SF (= *lloros*) sobbing; (= *berridos*) bawling

llantería* SF (*Cono Sur*) weeping and wailing

llantina* SF sobbing; **¡no empieces con la ~!** cut out the sob stuff!*

llanto SM 1 (= *lloro*) crying, tears *pl*; **se oía el ~ de un niño en la otra habitación** you could hear a child crying in the next room; **¡deja ya el ~!** stop crying!; **todo acaba en ~** everything ends in tears; **estaba al borde del ~** he was close to tears; **romper en ~** to burst into tears
2 (= *lamento*) moaning, lamentation
3 (*Literat*) dirge, lament, funeral lament

llanura SF 1 (*Geog*) plain; (= *pradera*) prairie
2 (= *lisura*) flatness, smoothness, evenness

llapa SF (*LAm*) *ver* **yapa**

llapango* ADJ (*Andes*) barefoot

llapingacho SM (*Andes*) ≈ cheese omelette

llaretá SF (*Andes*) dried llama dung

llauto SM (*Andes*) headband

llave SF 1 [*de puerta*] key; **bajo ~** under lock and key; **cerrar con ~** to lock; **cerrar una puerta con ~** to lock a door; **echar (la) ~ (a)** to lock up; **"llave en mano"** "with vacant possession"; **✦MODISMOS guardar algo bajo siete ~s** to keep sth under lock and key; **¡por las ~s de San Pedro!** by heaven!; **tener las ~s de la caja** to hold the purse strings ▸ **llave de cambio** shift key ▸ **llave de contacto** (*Aut*) ignition key ▸ **llave espacial** spacing bar ▸ **llave maestra** skeleton key, master key
2 [*de gas, agua*] tap, faucet (*EEUU*); (*Elec*) switch ▸ **llave de bola** ballcock, floater (*EEUU*) ▸ **llave de cierre** stopcock ▸ **llave de flotador** ballcock, floater (*EEUU*) ▸ **llave de paso** [*del agua*] stopcock; [*del gas*] mains tap; **cerrar la ~ de paso del agua/gas** to turn the water/gas off at the mains ▸ **llave de riego** hydrant
3 (*Mec*) spanner ▸ **llave ajustable** adjustable spanner ▸ **llave de carraca** ratchet spanner, ratchet wrench (*EEUU*) ▸ **llave de ruedas (en cruz)** wheel brace ▸ **llave inglesa** monkey wrench
4 (*Mús*) stop, key
5 (*Tip*) curly bracket, brace bracket
6 (*Dep*) [*de lucha libre*] lock; [*de judo*] hold
7 [*de escopeta*] lock
8 (*Cono Sur Arquit*) beam, joist
9 **llaves** (*Méx Taur*) horns

llavero SM 1 (= *objeto*) key ring
2 (†) (*persona, tb* **~ de cárcel**) turnkey

llavín SM latch key

llegada SF 1 [*de un viaje*] arrival
2 (*Dep*) (= *meta*) finishing line

llegar

▸conjug 1h◂
Ⓐ VERBO INTRANSITIVO
Ⓑ VERBO TRANSITIVO
Ⓒ VERBO PRONOMINAL

Para las expresiones ***llegar al alma, llegar lejos, llegar a las manos,*** *ver la otra entrada.*

Ⓐ VERBO INTRANSITIVO

1 **movimiento, destino, procedencia** to arrive; **Carmen no ha llegado todavía** Carmen hasn't arrived yet; **~on cubiertos de barro** they arrived covered in mud; **avíseme cuando llegue** tell me when he arrives *o* comes; **está recién llegado de Roma** he recently arrived from Rome; **por fin hemos llegado** we're here at last; **el vuelo ~á a las 14:15** the flight gets in at 14:15; **~á en tren/autobús** he will come by train/bus; **no llegues tarde** don't be late; **~ a: cuando llegamos a Bilbao estaba lloviendo** when we got to *o* arrived in Bilbao it was raining; **¿a qué hora llegaste a casa?** what time did you get home?; **los vehículos están llegando a la línea de salida** the cars are approaching the starting line; **~le a alguien: ¿te ha llegado ya el paquete?** have you got the parcel yet?; **estar al ~: Carlos debe de estar al ~** Carlos should be arriving any minute now; **el verano está al ~** summer is just around the corner; **hacer ~ algo a algn: hacer ~ una carta a algn** to send sb a letter; **¿le puedes hacer ~ este recado?** could you give her this message?; **¿le has hecho ~ el dinero?** did you get the money to her?; **✦MODISMOS ~le** (*LAm*): **le llegó el año pasado** he died last year; **me llega** (*Andes**) I don't give a damn; **✦REFRÁN el que primero llegue, ése la calza** first come first served; *ver tb* **santo B2**

2 **= alcanzar** 2·1 (*con las manos*) to reach; **¿me puedes quitar la cortina? yo no llego** could you take the curtain down for me? I can't reach; **no llego al estante de arriba** I can't reach the top shelf
2·2 (*indicando distancia, nivel*) **esta cuerda no llega** this rope isn't long enough, this rope won't reach; **me llegó muy hondo lo que me dijo** what she said made a very deep impression on me; **el tema de la película no me llega** the subject of the film does nothing for me *o* leaves me cold; **~ a** *o* **hasta** to come up to; **el agua me llegaba hasta las rodillas** the water came up to my knees; **soy bajita y justo le llego al hombro** I'm short and I only just come up to his shoulder; **el vestido le llega hasta los pies** the dress comes *o* goes down to her feet; **los pies no le llegaban al suelo** her feet weren't touching the floor; **la cola llegaba hasta la puerta** the queue went *o* reached back as far as the door; **el tren sólo llega hasta Burgos** the train only goes as far as Burgos; **me llega al corazón ver tanto sufrimiento** seeing so much suffering touches me to the heart; **✦MODISMOS ¡hasta allí podíamos ~!** that's the limit!, what a nerve!; **a tanto no llego**: **soy bastante inteligente pero a tanto no llego** I'm reasonably clever, but not enough to do that; **podría dejarle un millón, pero dos no, a tanto no llego** I might let her have a million, but not two, I'm not prepared to go as far as that; *ver tb* **camisa 1**, **suela 1**
2·3 (*indicando duración*) to last; **el pobrecito no ~á a las Navidades** the poor thing won't make it to *o* last till Christmas; **este abrigo no te llega al próximo invierno** this coat won't last till next winter; **le falta un año para ~ a la jubilación** he has a year to go till *o* before he retires

3

◆ **llegar a + SUSTANTIVO** 3·1 (= *conseguir*) [+ *acuerdo, conclusión*] to reach, come to; **llegó a la felicidad completa** she attained total happiness; **¿cómo has conseguido ~ a la fama?** how did you manage to achieve fame *o* become famous?; **le costó pero llegó a arquitecto** it wasn't easy, but he eventually managed to become an architect; **por fin ha llegado a catedrático** he's finally made it to professor
3·2 (*con cantidades*) to come to; **los gastos totales ~on a 1.000 euros** the total expenditure came to 1,000 euros; **el importe llega a 50 pesos** the total is 50 pesos; **el público no llegaba a 200 espectadores** there were fewer than 200 spectators there; **la audiencia de este programa ha llegado a cinco millones** (*Radio*) as many as five million people have listened to this programme; (*TV*) the viewing figures for this programme have been as high as five million

4

◆ **llegar a + INFIN** 4·1 (= *conseguir*) **llegó a conocer a varios directores de cine** she met *o* got to know several film directors; **no llego a comprenderlo** I just can't understand it; **el producto puede ~ a tener éxito** the product could be a success; **si lo llego a saber** if I had known; **~ a ser famoso/el jefe** to become famous/the boss; **Julia llegó a ser presidenta** Julia became president; **~ a ver: no llegó a ver la película terminada** he never saw the film finished; **el proyecto no llegó a ver la luz** the project never saw the light of day; **temí no ~ a ver el año nuevo** I feared I wouldn't live to see the new year, I feared I wouldn't make it to the new year

[4·2] (*como algo extremo*) **llegué a estar tan mal, que casi no podía moverme** I got so bad, I could hardly move; **llegamos a sospechar de él** we came to suspect him; **puede ~ a alcanzar los 300km/h** it can reach speeds of up to 300km/h; **este pez puede ~ a alcanzar los dos metros de largo** this fish can grow as long as two metres; **la popularidad que un actor puede ~ a alcanzar a través de la televisión** the popularity an actor can come to attain from being on television; **¿llegó a creer que sería campeón del mundo?** did you ever believe you'd be world champion?; **yo había llegado a creer que estábamos en el camino de superar ese problema** I had really started to believe that we were on the way to overcoming that problem; **llegué a creérmelo** I came to believe it; **llegó al punto de robarle** he even went so far as to rob her

[5] [= *bastar*] to be enough; **con dos euros no me llega** two euros isn't enough; **con ese dinero no le va a ~** you won't have enough money; **no me llega para ropa nueva** I can't afford to buy new clothes; **hacer ~ el sueldo a fin de mes** to make ends meet; **hacer ~ el dinero** to make one's money last

[6] [*momento, acontecimiento*] to come; **~á un día en que sea rico** the day will come when I'm rich; **cuando llegó la paz** when peace came; **se fueron cuando llegó la noche** they left at nightfall

Ⓑ VERBO TRANSITIVO

[= *acercar*] to bring up, bring over

Ⓒ **llegarse** VERBO PRONOMINAL **voy a ~me por el banco** I'm going down *o* over to the bank; **llégate a su casa y dile que ...** go over to his house and tell him…; **llégate a mi casa mañana** come round tomorrow; **llégate más a mí** come closer to me

LLEGAR

Llegar a

A la hora de traducir **llegar a** al inglés, tenemos que diferenciar entre **arrive in** y **arrive at**.

- Empleamos **arrive in** con países, ciudades, pueblos, *etc*:

  Esperamos llegar a Italia el día 11 de junio

  We expect to arrive in Italy on 11th June

  Llegaremos a Córdoba dentro de dos horas

  We'll be arriving in Cordoba in two hours' time

- En cambio, se traduce por **arrive at** cuando nos referimos a lugares más pequeños, como aeropuertos, estaciones, *etc*. La expresión **llegar a casa** es una excepción, ya que se traduce por **arrive/get home**, es decir, sin preposición:

  Llegamos al aeropuerto con cuatro horas de retraso

  We arrived at the airport four hours late

  Llegué a casa completamente agotada

  I arrived home completely exhausted

Para otros usos y ejemplos ver la entrada.

lleísmo SM *pronunciation of Spanish "y" as "ll"*

llenador ADJ (*Cono Sur*) [*comida*] filling, satisfying

llenar ▸conjug 1a◂ Ⓐ VT [1] (= *rellenar*) [+ *cubo, vaso*] to fill; [+ *bañera*] to run; [+ *cajón, maleta*] to fill; **llenó tanto la maleta que no podía cerrarla** he packed *o* filled the suitcase so full that he couldn't shut it; **no sabía cómo ~ las tardes** she didn't know how to fill her evenings; **no me llenes el vaso** don't fill my glass (up to the top); **no me llenes mucho el plato** don't give me too much food; **¿puede ~ aquí?** (*en un bar*) the same again, please; **siempre llena los auditorios** he always gets full houses; **~ con *o* de algo** [+ *contenedor*] to fill with sth; [+ *superficie*] to cover with sth; **llenó las estanterías de libros** she filled the shelves with books; **llenó la pizarra de nombres** he covered the blackboard with names; ✦***MODISMO*** **le llenó la cabeza de pájaros** he filled her head with nonsense

[2] (= *ocupar*) to fill; **los coches ~on el centro de la ciudad** the town centre was filled with cars; **las cajas llenan todo el maletero** the boxes take up *o* fill the whole boot; **~ un hueco** to fill a gap; **llena un hueco que había en el mercado** it fills a gap in the market; **no podía ~ el hueco dejado por su antecesor** he couldn't fill his predecessor's shoes

[3] (= *satisfacer*) [+ *deseo*] to fulfil, fulfill (*EEUU*), satisfy; **este trabajo no me llena** I don't find this job satisfying *o* fulfilling; **mi vida no me llena** I'm not getting enough out of life; **no me termina de ~ este libro** this book doesn't really convince me; **sus nietos han llenado su vejez** his grandchildren have gladdened his old age (*liter*)

[4] (= *colmar*) **~ a algn de** [+ *inquietud, dudas*] to fill sb with; **sus hijos lo ~on de orgullo** his children filled him with pride; **su tono de voz la llenó de inquietud** his tone of voice made her feel uneasy, his tone of voice filled her with unease (*liter*); **lo ~on de insultos** they heaped insults upon him, they hurled abuse at him; **verte nos llenó de alegría** we were delighted to see you; **lo ~on de atenciones** they showered him with attention, they made a great fuss of him; **nos ~on de elogios** they showered praise on us

[5] (= *cumplimentar*) [+ *documento, impreso*] to fill in, fill out (*EEUU*)

Ⓑ VI [*comida*] to be filling; **esta sopa no llena nada** this soup isn't really very filling, this soup doesn't really fill you up

Ⓒ **llenarse** VPR [1] (= *ocuparse completamente*) to fill, fill up; **la sala se fue llenando rápidamente** the hall was filling up fast; **los viernes siempre se llena el restaurante** the restaurant always gets full *o* fills up on Fridays; **~se de algo** to fill (up) with sth; **la habitación se llenó de humo** the room filled with smoke; **los ojos se les ~on de lágrimas** tears welled up in their eyes, their eyes filled with tears; ✦***MODISMO*** **~se hasta la bandera *o* hasta los topes** to be full to bursting, be packed out, be packed to the rafters

[2] (= *colmarse*) **con esa tarta me he llenado** I'm full after that cake; **lo único que quiere es ~se los bolsillos** all he wants is to line his pockets*; **aquí se llena uno bien la barriga*** you can really stuff yourself here*; **se llenó los bolsillos de caramelos** she filled her pockets with sweets, she stuffed her pockets full of sweets; **~se de** [+ *orgullo, alegría*] to be filled with; [+ *comida*] to stuff o.s. with*; **con eso se ~án de gloria** that will cover them in glory; **en un año se llenó de deudas** after a year he was up to his neck in debt; **se me llenó la espalda de ronchas** my back came out in a rash all over

[3] (= *cubrirse*) to get covered; **los libros se han llenado de polvo** the books have got covered in dust; **me he llenado los dedos de tinta** I've got ink all over my fingers, my fingers are covered in ink; **el techo se llenó de humedad** damp appeared all over the ceiling

[4] (*frm*) (= *enfadarse*) to get cross, get annoyed

llenazo* SM (= *entradas agotadas*) sellout; (*Teat, Dep*) (= *asientos ocupados*) full house; **ayer hubo ~ en el concierto** there was a full house for the concert yesterday, yesterday's concert was a sellout; **hubo un ~ total en el estadio** the stadium was totally packed out

llenazón SM (*Méx*) blown-out feeling, indigestion

lleno Ⓐ ADJ [1] (= *completo*) [*plato, vaso*] full; [*teatro, tren*] full; **el depósito está ~** the tank is full; **no me pongas el plato muy ~** don't give me too much food; **¡~, por favor!** (*en una gasolinera*) fill her up, please!; **no hables con la boca llena** don't talk with your mouth full; **el autobús iba ~** the bus was full (up); **~ hasta el borde** full to the brim; ✦***MODISMO*** **~ a reventar *o* hasta la bandera *o* hasta los topes** full to bursting, packed out, packed to the rafters

[2] **~ de** [2·1] [*espacio*] full of; [*superficie*] covered in; **le gusta tener la casa llena de gente** she likes to have the house full of people; **los muebles están ~s de polvo** the furniture is covered in dust; **llevaba el traje ~ de manchas** his suit was covered in stains

[2·2] [*complejos, problemas*] full of; [*odio, esperanza*] filled with; **un viaje ~ de aventuras** a journey full of adventures; **estaba ~ de dudas** I was filled with doubt; **una mirada llena de odio** a hateful look, a look full of hate; **llegué ~ de alegría** I arrived in high spirits

[3] **de ~** directly; **los cambios nos afectarán de ~** the changes will affect us directly; **nos daba el sol de ~** the sun was (shining) directly on us; **la bala le alcanzó de ~ en el corazón** the bullet hit him straight in the heart; **está dedicado de ~ a su familia** he is entirely dedicated to his family; **el impacto le dio de ~ en la cara** he took the impact full in the face; **acertaste de ~ con ese comentario** you've hit the nail on the head (with that remark), that remark was spot on

[4] (= *saciado*) full, full up*

[5] (= *regordete*) plump, chubby

[6] (*Astron*) [*luna*] full; **hoy es luna llena** there is a full moon today

Ⓑ SM [1] (= *aforo completo*) (*gen*) sellout; (*Cine, Teat*) full house; **ayer hubo ~ en el concierto** there was a full house for the concert yesterday, yesterday's concert was a sellout ► **lleno absoluto, lleno hasta la bandera, lleno total** (*Cine, Teat*) packed house; (*Dep*) capacity crowd; **el espectáculo sigue representándose con ~s absolutos** the show continues to play to

packed houses
2 (*Astron*) full moon

llevadero ADJ bearable, tolerable

llevar

▸conjug 1a◂
A VERBO TRANSITIVO C VERBO PRONOMINAL
B VERBO INTRANSITIVO
*Para las expresiones **llevar adelante, llevar la contraria, llevar las de perder, llevar a la práctica, llevar a término, llevar ventaja,** ver la otra entrada.*

Ⓐ VERBO TRANSITIVO

1 *= transportar* (*con los brazos*) to carry; (*indicando el punto de destino*) to take; (*en vehículo*) to transport; **yo llevaba la maleta** I was carrying the case; **es muy pesado para ~lo entre los dos** it's too heavy for the two of us to carry; **no te olvides de ~ un paraguas** make sure you take an umbrella with you; **lleva los vasos a la cocina** can you take the glasses to the kitchen?; **"comida para ~"** "food to take away", "take-away food"; **¿es para ~?** is it to take away?

2 (*tb* **~ puesto**) to wear; **¿hay que ~ corbata a la reunión?** do we have to wear a tie to the meeting?; **llevaba puesto un sombrero muy raro** she had a very odd hat on, she was wearing a very odd hat

3 (*tb* **~ encima**) **sólo llevo diez euros** I've only got ten euros on me; **no llevo dinero (encima)** I haven't got any money on me; **¡la que llevaba encima aquella noche!*** he was really smashed that night!*

4 *= tener* 4·1 [+ *barba, pelo*] to have; **lleva barba** he has a beard; **lleva el pelo corto** he has short hair

4·2 [+ *adorno, ingrediente*] to have; **esta raqueta no lleva el precio** this racket doesn't have the price on it; **este pastel no lleva harina** this cake doesn't have any flour in it; **lleva un rótulo que dice ...** it has a label (on it) which says ...; **el tren no lleva coche-comedor** the train doesn't have a dining car; **lleva mucha sal** it's very salty; **¿qué lleva el pollo que está tan bueno?** what's in this chicken that makes it taste so good?

4·3 [+ *armas, nombre, título*] to have, bear (*frm*); **~á el nombre de la madre** she will be named after her mother; **el libro lleva el título de ...** the book has the title of ..., the book is entitled ...

5 *+ persona* 5·1 (= *acompañar, conducir*) to take; **voy a ~ a los niños al colegio** I'm going to take the children to school; **lo llevamos al teatro** we took him to the theatre; **¿adónde me llevan?** where are you taking me?; **a ver ¿cuándo me llevas a cenar?** when are you going to take me out for a meal?

5·2 (*en coche*) to drive; **Sofía nos llevó a casa** Sofía gave us a lift home, Sofía drove us home; **yo voy en esa dirección, ¿quieres que te lleve?** I'm going that way, do you want a lift?

6 *= conducir* 6·1 [+ *vehículo*] to drive; **lleva muy bien el coche** she drives the car very well; **yo llevé el coche hasta Santander** I drove the car to Santander

6·2 [+ *persona, entidad*] **este camino nos lleva a Bogotá** this road takes us to Bogotá; **ha llevado al país a una guerra** he has led the country into a war; **llevó a su empresa a la bancarrota** he caused his company to go bankrupt, he bankrupted his company; **dejarse ~** to get carried away; **se dejaba ~ por las olas** he allowed the waves to carry him away; **no te dejes ~ por las apariencias** don't be taken in *o* deceived by appearances; **si te dejas ~ por él, acabarás mal** if you fall in with him, you'll be in trouble

7 *= dirigir* [+ *negocio, tienda*] to run; **~ una finca** to run an estate; **lleva todos sus negocios en secreto** he conducts all his business in secret; **~ la casa** to run the household; **lleva muy bien la casa** she's a very good housewife; **¿quién lleva la cuenta?** who is keeping count?; **~ las cuentas** *o* **los libros** (*Com*) to keep the books; **~ una materia** (*Méx*) to study a subject; *ver tb* **compás 1**

8 *= aportar* to bring; **la madre es quien lleva el dinero a la casa** it is the mother who brings home the money; **llevó la tranquilidad a todos** he brought peace to everyone; **seguro que llevas alegría a tu familia** I'm sure you're making your family happy

9 *= adelantar en* **mi hermana mayor me lleva ocho años** my elder sister is eight years older than me; **él me lleva una cabeza** he's a head taller than me

10 *= inducir* **~ a algn a creer que ...** to lead sb to think that ..., make sb think that ...; **esto me lleva a pensar que ...** this leads me to think that ...

11 *= tolerar* **~ las desgracias con paciencia** to bear misfortunes patiently; **¿cómo lleva lo de su hijo?** how's she coping with what happened to her son?; **lleva muy bien sus sesenta años** he's doing very well for sixty; **tiene mucho genio y hay que saber ~lo** he's very bad-tempered and you have to know how to deal with him

12 *indicando tiempo* 12·1 (= *haber estado*) to be; **¿cuánto tiempo llevas aquí?** how long have you been here?; **llevo horas esperando aquí** I've been waiting here for hours; **el tren lleva una hora de retraso** the train is an hour late; **llevo tres meses buscándolo** I have been looking for it for three months

12·2 (= *tardar*) to take; **el trabajo me ~á tres días** the work will take me three days; **~á varias horas reparar la avería** it will take several hours to carry out the repairs

13 *= cobrar* to charge; **me llevó 80 euros por arreglar el televisor** he charged me 80 euros for fixing the television; **no quería ~me nada** he didn't want to charge me, he didn't want to take any money

14 *= ir por* **¿qué dirección llevaba?** what direction was he going in?, which way was he going?; **lleva camino de ser como su padre** it looks like he's going to turn out just like his father

15 *+ vida* to lead; **~ una vida tranquila** to live *o* lead a quiet life

16 (+ PARTICIPIO) **llevo estudiados tres capítulos** I have covered three chapters; **llevaba hecha la mitad** he had done half of it; **lleva conseguidas muchas victorias** he has won many victories

17 *= producir* (*Com, Fin*) to bear; (*Agr*) to bear, produce; **los bonos llevan un 8% de interés** the bonds pay *o* bear interest at 8%; **no lleva fruto este año** it has no fruit this year, it hasn't produced any fruit this year

Ⓑ VERBO INTRANSITIVO

carretera to go, lead; **esta carretera lleva a La Paz** this road goes *o* leads to La Paz

Ⓒ **llevarse** VERBO PRONOMINAL

1 *= tomar consigo* to take; **se llevó todo mi dinero** he took all my money; **puedes ~te el disco que quieras** take whichever record you want; **¿puedo ~me este libro?** can I borrow this book?; **llévatelo** take it (with you); **—¿le gusta? —sí, me lo llevo** (*al comprar*) "do you like it?" — "yes, I'll take it"; **los ladrones se ~on la caja** the thieves took the safe (away); **se ~on más de diez mil euros en joyas** they got away with more than ten thousand euros' worth of jewels

2 *+ persona* (= *acompañar*) **se lo ~on al cine** they took him off to the cinema; **el padre se llevó a su hijo** the father took his son away; **~se a algn por delante** (= *atropellar*) to run sb over; (*LAm*) (= *ofender*) to offend sb; (= *maltratar*) to ride roughshod over sb; **el camión se llevó una farola por delante** the truck went off the road and took a lamppost with it; **la riada se llevó el pueblo por delante** the village was swept away by *o* in the flood, the flood took the village with it; **el viento se llevó por delante los tejados de las casas** the wind blew the roofs off the houses; **una infección en el riñón se lo llevó por delante** he died from a kidney infection; **esa ley se llevó por delante los derechos de los trabajadores** this law swept away *o* rode roughshod over the rights of the workers; **✦MODISMO ¡que se lo lleve el diablo!** to hell with it!

3 *= conseguir* [+ *premio*] to win; **se llevó el primer premio** she won first prize; **siempre me llevo la peor parte** I always come off worst; **✦MODISMOS llevársela***: **¡no lo toques o te la llevas!** don't touch it or you'll live to regret it!; **¡tú te la llevas!** (*en juegos*) you're it!

4 *= sufrir* **me llevé una gran decepción** I was very disappointed; **me llevé una alegría** I was so happy; **se llevó un buen susto** he got a real fright

5 *= arrastrar* **el mar se lleva la arena** the sea washes the sand away; **el viento se llevó las nubes** the wind blew the clouds away; **el viento se llevó una rama** the wind tore off a branch; **la espada se le llevó dos dedos** the sword took off two of his fingers; **✦MODISMO las palabras se las lleva el viento** words are not binding

6 *en el trato* **~se bien** to get on well (together); **no se lleva bien con el jefe** he doesn't get on *o* along with the boss; **me llevo bien con mi hermano** I get on well with my brother; **nos llevamos muy mal** we get on very badly; *ver tb* **matar B, perro 2**

7 *= estar de moda* to be in fashion, be all the rage; **se llevan los lunares** polka dots are in fashion *o* all the rage; **se vuelven a ~ las gafas negras** dark glasses are coming back into fashion

8 *con cantidades* **mi hermano y yo nos llevamos tres años** there are three years between my brother and me; **de doce me llevo una** (*Mat*) that makes twelve so carry one

llicla SF (*Andes*) woollen *o* (*EEUU*) woolen shawl

llicta SF (*Andes*) quinine paste

llimo ADJ (*Cono Sur*) (= *de orejas pequeñas*) small-eared; (= *sin orejas*) earless

llocalla SM (*Andes*) boy

lloquena SF (*Andes*) fish spear, harpoon

llora SF (*Caribe*) wake

llorado ADJ (*frm*) [*difunto*] late lamented (*frm*); [*muerte*] lamented (*frm*); **nuestro ~ poeta** our late lamented poet; **no ~** unlamented, unmourned

llorar ▸conjug 1a◂ Ⓐ VT 1 [+ *lágrimas*] to weep, cry; ✦*MODISMO* **~ lágrimas de cocodrilo** to weep crocodile tears
2 (*liter*) (= *lamentar*) [+ *a difunto*] to mourn; [+ *muerte*] to mourn, lament; [+ *desgracia*] to bemoan; [+ *actitud*] to lament, regret; **nadie lo ha llorado** nobody mourned *o* lamented his death, nobody mourned him; **algún día ~ás tu ligereza** some day you will regret your flippant behaviour; **lloran la pérdida de su libertad** they long for their lost freedom
Ⓑ VI 1 to cry, weep (*liter*); **¡no llores!** don't cry!; **me dieron** *o* **me entraron ganas de ~** I felt like crying; **se puso a ~ desconsoladamente** she began to cry *o* weep (*liter*) inconsolably; **Rosa lloraba en silencio** Rosa cried *o* wept (*liter*) silently; **~ de algo** to cry with sth; **estuve llorando de alegría** I was crying with happiness; **lloramos de risa** we laughed until we cried, we cried with laughter; **echarse a ~** to start to cry; **hacer ~ a algn** to make sb cry; **no hay nada que me pueda hacer ~** nothing can make me cry; **~ por algo/algn: no llores más por ella, es una idiota** don't cry over her anymore, she's an idiot; **lloraba por cualquier cosa** she would cry at *o* over the slightest thing; **no lloréis por mí cuando me vaya** don't cry for me when I'm gone; **romper a ~** to burst into tears; ✦*MODISMOS* **~ a cuajo** to sob one's heart out†; **~ a mares** *o* **a moco tendido** *o* **a rienda suelta** to cry one's eyes out; **~ a moco y baba**† to sob one's heart out†; **~ como una criatura** to cry like a baby; **ser de** *o* **para ~** (*iró*) to be enough to make you cry *o* weep; **el concierto fue como para ~** the concert was enough to make you cry *o* weep; ✦*REFRÁN* **el que no llora no mama** if you don't ask you don't get
2 [*ojos*] to water; **me lloran los ojos** my eyes are watering
3 (= *rogar*) **~ a algn** to moan to sb; **llórale un poco a tu madre y ya verás ...** if you moan a bit to your mother, you'll see ...
4 (*Chile**) (= *favorecer*) **a este rincón le llora un sofá** a sofa would look good in that corner; **a ti te llora el rojo** you look good in red, red looks good on you
5 (*Andes, Caribe*) (= *favorecer poco*) to be very unbecoming

llorera* SF fit of crying; **una buena ~** a good cry

lloretas* SMF INV (*Andes, CAm*) crybaby

llorica* Ⓐ ADJ **no seas ~** don't be such a crybaby*
Ⓑ SMF crybaby*

lloricón* ADJ [*persona*] weepy*, tearful; [*película, literatura*] tear-jerking*

lloriquear ▸conjug 1a◂ VI to snivel, whimper

lloriqueo SM snivelling, sniveling (*EEUU*), whimpering

llorisquear ▸conjug 1a◂ VI (*Caribe, Cono Sur*) = **lloriquear**

llorisqueo SM (*Caribe, Cono Sur*) = **lloriqueo**

lloro SM 1 (= *llanto*) crying, weeping, tears *pl*; (= *berrido*) wailing
2 (*en grabación*) wow

llorón/ona Ⓐ ADJ 1 (= *que llora*) **era muy ~ de pequeño** he was a real crybaby when he was little*; **es una mujer muy llorona** she cries very easily; *ver tb* **sauce**
2 (= *quejica*) **no seas tan ~** don't be such a moaner *o* whinger*
Ⓑ SM/F 1 (= *que llora*) crybaby*
2 (= *quejica*) moaner*, whinger*

llorona SF 1 (= *plañidera*) hired mourner
2 (*Méx*) *spectre of a wailing woman who wanders the streets*
3 (*Cono Sur*) (= *llanto*) **le dio la ~** she got all weepy
4 (*Andes, Cono Sur*) **lloronas** large spurs

lloroso ADJ [*tono, voz*] tearful; [*ojos*] watery; **—¿me has echado de menos? —le dijo con voz llorosa** "have you missed me?," she said tearfully *o* in a tearful voice; **tenía los ojos ~s por la alergia** her eyes were watering from hayfever, her eyes were all watery from hayfever; **se le pusieron los ojos ~s cuando le regañaron** she was close to tears when they told her off

llovedera SF (*Andes, CAm, Caribe*), **llovedero** SM (*Cono Sur*) (period of) continuous rain; (= *época*) rainy season; (= *tormenta*) rainstorm

llovedizo ADJ 1 [*techo*] leaky
2 **agua llovediza** rainwater

llover ▸conjug 2h◂ VI 1 (*Meteo*) to rain; **está lloviendo** it is raining; ✦*MODISMOS* **~ a cántaros** to rain cats and dogs, pour (down); **como llovido del cielo**: **llegar** *o* **venir (como) llovido del cielo** (*inesperado*) to come (totally) out of the blue; (*muy oportuno*) to be a godsend, come just at the right time; **~ a mares** to rain cats and dogs, pour (down); **está llovido en la milpita** (*Méx**) we're having a run of bad luck, we're going through a bad patch; **~ sobre mojado**: **luego llovió sobre mojado** then on top of all that something else happened; **ya ha llovido desde entonces** ◊ **ha llovido mucho desde entonces** a lot of water has flowed under the bridge since then; **nunca llueve a gusto de todos** you can't please everybody; **¡cómo ahora llueve pepinos** *o* **uvas!** (*Andes*) rubbish!; **siempre que llueve escampa** (*Caribe*) every cloud has a silver lining; **llueva o truene** rain or shine, come what may
2 **~le a algn**: **le llovieron regalos encima** he was showered with gifts

llovida SF (*LAm*) rain, shower

llovido SM stowaway

llovizna SF drizzle

lloviznar ▸conjug 1a◂ VI to drizzle

lloviznoso ADJ drizzly

llueca SF broody hen

lluqui ADJ (*Andes*) left-handed

lluvia SF 1 (*Meteo*) rain; (= *cantidad*) rainfall; **día de ~** rainy day; **intensa ~** heavy rain; **la ~ caída en el mes de enero** the rainfall in January, the January rainfall; ✦*REFRÁN* **la ~ cae sobre los buenos como sobre los malos** it rains on the just as well as on the unjust ► **lluvia ácida** acid rain ► **lluvia artificial** cloud seeding ► **lluvia de estrellas fugaces**, **lluvia de meteoros** meteor shower ► **lluvia de oro** (*Bot*) laburnum ► **lluvia menuda** drizzle, fine rain ► **lluvia radiactiva** (radioactive) fallout ► **lluvias monzónicas** monsoon rains ► **lluvia torrencial** torrential rain
2 (= *abundancia*) [*de balas, misiles*] hail; [*de insultos*] stream, barrage; [*de regalos*] shower; [*de infortunios*] string
3 [*de insecticida, laca*] spray; [*de regadera*] rose
4 (*Cono Sur*) (= *ducha*) shower, shower bath

lluvioso ADJ rainy, wet

lo[1] ART DEF 1 (*con adjetivos*) 1·1 **el gusto por lo bello** a taste for beautiful things; **no me gusta lo picante** I don't like spicy things; **subimos a lo más alto del edificio** we went right to the top of the building; **lo difícil fue convencerla** the difficult part was convincing her; **lo difícil es que ...** the difficult thing is that ...; **yo defiendo lo mío** I defend what is mine; **la física no es lo mío** physics isn't my thing; **en vista de lo ocurrido** in view of what has happened; **sufre lo indecible** she suffers terribly; **lo insospechado del caso** what was unsuspected about the matter; **lo totalmente inesperado del descubrimiento** the completely unexpected nature of the discovery; **ven lo más pronto posible** come as soon as you possibly can; **es de lo más divertido** it's so *o* really funny; **es de lo mejor que hay en el mercado** it's among the best you can get; **lo mejor/peor de la película** the best/worst thing about the film; **lo peor fue que no pudimos entrar** the worst thing was we couldn't get in
1·2 (*referido a un estilo*) **construido a lo campesino** built in the peasant style; **viste a lo americano** he dresses in the American style, he dresses like an American; **un peinado a lo afro** an afro hairstyle; **un peinado a lo mohicano** a mohican
1·3 (*con valor enfático*) **no saben lo aburrido que es** they don't know how boring it is; **me doy cuenta de lo amables que son** I realize how kind they are; **sabes lo mucho que me gusta** you know (just) how much I like it
2 **lo de**: **lo de ayer** what happened yesterday; **olvida lo de ayer** forget what happened yesterday, forget about yesterday; **lo de siempre** the usual; **lo de la boda** the business about the wedding; **lo de Rumasa** the Rumasa affair; **lo de no traer dinero ya no es una excusa** saying you don't have any money on you is no excuse; **fui (a) lo de Pablo** (*Cono Sur*) (= *a casa de*) I went to Pablo's place
3 **lo que** 3·1 (*relativo*) what; **lo que más me gusta es nadar** what I like most is swimming; **lo que digo es ...** what I say is ...; **repito lo que he dicho antes** I repeat what I said earlier; **¡sí hombre, lo que (yo) he dicho!** yes, just like I said!; **toma lo que quieras** take what *o* whatever you want; **todo lo que puedas** as much as *o* whatever you can; **empezó a tocar, lo que le fastidió** she began to play, which annoyed him, to his annoyance, she began to play; **lo que es eso ...** as for that ...; **en lo que a mi concierne** as far as I'm concerned; **cuesta más de lo que crees** it costs more than you think; **lo que pasa es que ...** the thing is ...; **lo que sea** whatever
3·2 (*con valor intensificador*) **¡lo que has tardado!** how long you've taken!, you've taken so long!; **¡lo que sufre un hombre honrado!** what *o* the things an honourable man has to suffer!; **¡lo que cuesta vivir!** the cost of living is so high!; **es lo que se dice feo** he's undeniably ugly; **es lo que se dice un hombre** he's a real man

[3·3] **a lo que** (*LAm*) (*en cuanto*) as soon as; **a lo que me vio me saludó** as soon as he saw me he said hello
[3·4] **en lo que ...** whilst ...

lo² PRON PERS [1] (*refiriéndose a él*) him; **¿lo habéis invitado?** have you invited him?; **no lo conozco** I don't know him; **lo han despedido** he's been sacked
[2] (*refiriéndose a usted*) you; **yo a usted lo conozco** I know you
[3] (*refiriéndose a una cosa, un animal*) it; **no lo veo** I can't see it; **lo tengo aquí** I have it here; **voy a pensarlo** I'll think about it; **¿el té lo tomas con leche?** do you take milk in your tea?; **no lo sabía** I didn't know; **lo sé** I know; **ya lo creo** I should think so; **no lo hay** there isn't any; **¿te acuerdas de lo bien que lo pasamos?** do you remember what a good time we had?; **¡con lo mal que lo pasamos!** we had such an awful time!
[4] (*referido a un estado, cualidad*) **no parece lista pero lo es** she doesn't seem clever but she is; **guapa sí que lo es** she's certainly pretty; **—¿estás cansado? —sí, lo estoy** "are you tired?" — "yes, I am"

loa SF [1] (= *elogio*) praise
[2] (*Teat, Hist*) prologue, playlet
[3] (*CAm, Méx**) (= *regañada*) reproof

loable ADV praiseworthy, laudable, commendable

loablemente ADV commendably

LOAPA SF ABR (*Esp Jur*) = **Ley Orgánica de Armonización del Proceso Autonómico**

loar ▸conjug 1a◂ VT to praise

lob SM lob

loba SF [1] (*Zool*) she-wolf
[2] (*Agr*) ridge (between furrows)

lobanillo SM wen, cyst

lobato/a SM/F wolf cub

lobby ['loβi] SM (*pl* **lobbys** ['loβi]) lobby, pressure group; **hacer ~** to lobby (**a favor de** for)

lobelia SF lobelia

lobero ADJ **perro ~** wolfhound

lobezno/a SM/F wolf cub

lobito SM (*Cono Sur*) (*tb* **~ de río**) otter

lobo Ⓐ SM [1] (*Zool*) wolf; ✦*MODISMOS* **arrojar a algn a los ~s** to throw sb to the wolves; **gritar ¡al ~!** to cry wolf; **¡menos ~s (Caperucita)!** tell me another one!; **pillar un ~**‡ to get plastered‡; **son ~s de una camada** they're birds of a feather ► **lobo de mar** old salt, sea dog; (*Chile*) seal ► **lobo gris** grey wolf, timber wolf ► **lobo marino** seal ► **lobo rojo** red wolf
[2] (*Méx**) (= *guardia*) traffic cop*
Ⓑ ADJ (*Chile**) (= *huraño*) shy

lobotomía SF lobotomy

lóbrego ADJ dark, gloomy

lobreguez SF darkness, gloom(iness)

lóbulo SM lobe

lobuno ADJ wolfish, wolflike

LOC SM ABR (*Inform*) (= **lector óptico de caracteres**) OCR

loca SF [1] (‡) (= *homosexual*) queen‡; **es una ~** he's a real queen‡
[2] (*Cono Sur*‡) (= *prostituta*) whore
[3] ✦*MODISMO* **darle la ~ a algn** (*Cono Sur*) to get cross, get into a temper; *ver tb* **loco**

local Ⓐ ADJ [*cultura, producción*] local; **equipo ~** home team
Ⓑ SM [1] [*de negocio*] premises *pl*; **en el ~** on the premises ► **local comercial** (*gen*) business premises *pl*; (*sin ocupar*) shop unit
[2] (= *lugar*) place

localidad SF [1] (= *pueblo*) town, place, locality (*frm*)
[2] (*Teat*) (= *asiento*) seat; (= *entrada*) ticket; **"no hay localidades"** "house full", "sold out"; **sacar ~es** to get tickets
[3] (= *lugar*) location

localismo SM localism

localizable ADJ **el director no estaba ~** we couldn't get hold of the director; **difícilmente/fácilmente ~** [*objeto, lugar*] hard/easy to find; [*persona*] hard/easy to get hold of

localización SF [1] [*de supervivientes*] finding; **el temporal dificultó la ~ del naufragio** the storm made it difficult to find *o* locate the wreck
[2] [*de llamada*] tracing; **la ~ de la llamada fue cuestión de segundos** it took a matter of seconds to trace the call
[3] [*de enfermedad, dolor*] localization
[4] (*frm*) (= *ubicación*) siting, location, placing

localizado ADJ localized

localizador SM pager, beeper

localizar ▸conjug 1f◂ Ⓐ VT [1] (= *encontrar*) to find, locate; **¿dónde se puede ~ al Sr Gómez?** where can I find *o* get hold of Mr Gómez?
[2] [+ *llamada telefónica*] to trace
[3] (*Med*) to localize
[4] (*frm*) (= *colocar*) to site, locate, place; **el lugar donde van a ~ la nueva industria** the place where the new industry is to be sited
Ⓑ VPR [1] (*Méx*) (= *situarse*) to be located
[2] [*dolor*] to be localized

localmente ADV locally

locamente ADV madly, wildly; **~ enamorado** madly in love

locatario/a SM/F (*LAm*) tenant, lessee

locatis* SMF INV crackpot

locería SF [1] (*LAm*) (= *loza*) pottery; (= *loza fina*) china, chinaware
[2] (*Méx*) (= *vajilla*) crockery

locero/a SM/F (*LAm*) potter

locha SF loach

loche SM (*Andes*) (= *bermejo*) ginger colour

locho ADJ (*Andes*) (= *bermejo*) ginger, reddish

loción SF lotion ► **loción capilar** hair restorer ► **loción facial** (*para limpiar*) cleanser; (*para tonificar*) toner ► **loción para después del afeitado** aftershave lotion ► **loción para el cabello** hair restorer

lock-out ['lokaut] SM (*pl* **lock-outs** ['lokaut]) lockout

loco/a Ⓐ ADJ [1] (= *no cuerdo*) mad, crazy; **¿estás ~?** are you mad *o* crazy?; **no seas ~, eso es muy arriesgado** don't be stupid, that's very risky; **una brújula loca** *a compass whose needle no longer points north*; **estaba ~ de alegría** he was mad *o* wild with joy; **andar** *o* **estar ~ con algo** (= *preocupado*) to be worried to death about sth; (= *contento*) to be crazy about sth; **ando ~ con el examen** the exam is driving me crazy; **está loca con su moto nueva** she's crazy about her new motorbike; **está ~ por algn/algo**: **está ~ por esa chica** he's mad *o* crazy about that girl; **anda** *o* **está loca por irse a Inglaterra** she's mad keen to go to England; **tener** *o* **traer ~ a algn**: **este asunto me tiene** *o* **trae ~** this business is driving me crazy; **volver ~ a algn** to drive sb mad, drive sb round the bend; **el marisco me vuelve ~** I'm crazy about seafood; **volverse ~** to go insane, go mad; **estoy para volverme ~** I'm at my wits' end; **este caos es para volverse ~** this is absolute chaos; ✦*MODISMOS* **estar ~ de atar** *o* **de remate** to be stark raving mad; **estar más ~ que una cabra** to be as mad as a hatter; **no lo hago ni ~*** no way will I do that*; **hacer algo a lo ~** to do sth any old how; **~ de verano** (*Cono Sur*) cracked, crazy
[2] (= *frenético*) hectic; **hoy he tenido un día ~** I've had a really hectic day today
[3] (*) (= *enorme*) **llevo una prisa loca** I'm in a tremendous *o* real rush*; **he tenido una suerte loca** I've been fantastically lucky*
Ⓑ SM/F lunatic, madman/madwoman; **el ~ de César se ha comprado otro coche** that lunatic *o* madman César has bought another car; **ésta es una casa de ~s** this place is a madhouse; **correr como un ~** to run like mad; **gritar como un ~** to shout like a madman, shout one's head off; **hacerse el ~** to act the fool; **es un ~ perdido** he's stark raving mad; **ponerse como un ~** to start acting like a madman/madwoman; ✦*MODISMO* **cada ~ con su tema** everyone has their own axe to grind
Ⓒ SM (*Chile*) abalone, false abalone

locomoción SF [1] (= *desplazamiento*) locomotion
[2] (*LAm*) (= *transporte*) transport ► **locomoción colectiva** public transport

locomotividad SF power of locomotion

locomotor(a)/triz ADJ [1] [*vehículo, aparato*] locomotive
[2] (*Anat*) [*sistema, aparato, conducta*] locomotor

locomotora SF [1] (*Ferro*) engine, locomotive ► **locomotora de maniobras** shunting engine, switch engine (*EEUU*) ► **locomotora de vapor** steam locomotive
[2] [*de la economía, del desarrollo*] driving force

locomotriz ADJ *ver* **locomotor**

locomóvil SF traction engine

locrear ▸conjug 1a◂ VI (*LAm*) to eat, have a meal

locro SM (*LAm*) *meat and vegetable stew*

locuacidad SF (*frm*) loquacity (*frm*), talkativeness

locuaz ADJ (*frm*) loquacious (*frm*), talkative

locución SF [1] (= *giro idiomático*) expression, phrase
[2] (*TV*) **"locución"** "voice", "reader"

locuelo/a* Ⓐ ADJ daft, loony*
Ⓑ SM/F loony*, crackpot*

locumba¹* (*Perú*), **locumbeta*** (*Perú*) Ⓐ ADJ INV (= *loco*) crazy*, nuts*
Ⓑ SMF INV nutter*

locumba²* (*Perú*) SF grape liquor

▼ **locura** SF [1] (= *demencia*) madness, insanity; **un ataque de ~** a fit of madness
[2] (= *exceso*) **¡qué ~!** it's madness!; **me gusta con ~*** I'm crazy about it; **es una casa de ~*** it's a smashing house*; **precios de ~*** fantastic prices; **tener** *o* **sentir ~ por algn** to be crazy about sb; **tiene ~ por su sobrino** she's crazy about her nephew
[3] (= *acto*) **es capaz de hacer cualquier ~**

➤ LENGUA Y USO: locura 3 29.3

he is capable of any madness; **no hagas ~s** don't do anything crazy; **ser una ~** to be madness; **es una ~ ir sola** it's madness to go on your own

locutor(a) SM/F (*Radio, TV*) (*entre programas, en anuncios*) announcer; (*TV*) [*de noticias*] newscaster, newsreader; (= *comentarista*) commentator ► **locutor(a) de continuidad** (*TV, Radio*) linkman/linkwoman ► **locutor(a) deportivo/a** sports commentator

locutorio SM [1] (*Telec*) telephone box, telephone booth
[2] (*para visitas*) [*de cárcel*] visiting room; (*Rel*) parlour, parlor (*EEUU*)
[3] ► **locutorio radiofónico** studio

lodacero SM (*Andes*), **lodazal** SM quagmire, mudhole

LODE SF ABR (*Esp*) = **Ley Orgánica Reguladora del Derecho a la Educación**

lodo SM (= *barro*) mud, mire (*liter*); **lodos** (*Med*) mudbath *sing*; (*Min*) sludge *sing* ► **lodo de depuradora** sewage sludge

lodoso ADJ muddy

loft SM loft

log ABR (= **logaritmo**) log

loga SF [1] (*CAm*) (= *eulogía*) eulogy; ✦*MODISMO* **echar una ~ a algn*** (*iró*) to tell sb off*
[2] (*Cono Sur*) (= *balada*) ballad, short poem

logaritmo SM logarithm

logia SF [1] (*Mil*) [*de masones*] lodge
[2] (*Arquit*) loggia

lógica SF logic; ✦*MODISMO* **ser de una ~ aplastante** to be blindingly obvious ► **lógica booleana** Boolean logic ► **lógica borrosa**, **lógica difusa** fuzzy logic ► **lógica simbólica** symbolic logic; *ver tb* **lógico**

logical SM software

▼**lógicamente** ADV logically

logicial SM software

lógico/a Ⓐ ADJ [1] (*relativo a la lógica*) [*conclusión, razonamiento, planteamiento*] logical
[2] (= *normal*) natural; **como es ~** naturally; **es ~** it's only natural; **es ~ que ...** it stands to reason that ..., it's understandable that ...; **—ayudaría a su hijo antes que al tuyo —¡lógico!** "I would help my son before yours" — "well, naturally!"; **lo más ~ sería ...** (+ *INFIN*) the most sensible thing would be to ... + *infin*
[3] (*Inform*) logic *antes de s*
Ⓑ SM/F logician; *ver tb* **lógica**

login SM login

logística SF logistics *pl*

logístico ADJ logistic

logo SM logo

logopeda SMF speech therapist

logopedia SF speech therapy

logoprocesadora SF word processor

logoterapeuta SMF speech therapist

logoterapia SF speech therapy

logotipo SM logo

logradamente ADV successfully

logrado ADJ successful

lograr ▸conjug 1a◂ VT [+ *trabajo*] to get, obtain (*frm*); [+ *vacaciones*] to get; [+ *éxito, victoria*] to achieve; [+ *perfección*] to attain; **logra cuanto quiere** he gets whatever he wants; **por fin lo logró** eventually he managed it; **~ hacer algo** to manage to do sth, succeed in doing sth; **~ que algn haga algo** to (manage to) get sb to do sth

logrear ▸conjug 1a◂ VI to lend money at interest, be a moneylender

logrero/a SM/F [1] (= *prestamista*) moneylender, profiteer (*pey*)
[2] (*LAm*) (= *gorrón*) sponger*, parasite

logro SM [1] (= *éxito*) achievement, attainment (*frm*); **uno de sus mayores ~s** one of his greatest achievements
[2] (*Com, Fin*) profit; **a ~** at (a high rate of) interest

logroñés/esa Ⓐ ADJ of/from Logroño
Ⓑ SM/F native/inhabitant of Logroño; **los logroñeses** the people of Logroño

LOGSE SF ABR = **Ley de Ordenación General del Sistema Educativo**

> **LOGSE**
>
> *Spain's* **Ley de Ordenación General del Sistema Educativo** *(1990) provided for a new educational system which began to be implemented in the 1991-92 academic year. Amongst other things, it raised the school-leaving age from 14 to 16 and introduced compulsory vocational training for all students. Religious education became optional and special-needs provision was incorporated into mainstream education. Following the implementation of the* **LOGSE**, *compulsory education is divided into* **Educación Primaria** *(EP) and* **Educación Secundaria Obligatoria** *(ESO).*
>
> ⇨ *See also* EP, ESO

Loira SM Loire

loísmo SM *use of "lo" instead of "le" as indirect object*; → LEÍSMO, LOÍSMO, LAÍSMO

loísta Ⓐ ADJ *that uses "lo" instead of "le" as indirect object*
Ⓑ SMF *user of "lo" instead of "le"*

Lola SF, **Lolita** SF (*formas familiares*) *de* **María de los Dolores**

lolailo/a* SM/F (*pey*) gypsy

lolo/a* SM/F (*Chile*) boy/girl, teenager, teen (*EEUU**)

loma SF [1] (= *colina*) hillock, low ridge
[2] (*Cono Sur**) ✦*MODISMO* **en la ~ del diablo** *o* **del quinoto** at the back of beyond*
[3] (*) (= *mano*) mitt*

lomada SF (*Cono Sur*) = **loma**

lomaje SM (*Cono Sur*) low ridge

lombarda SF (*Agr*) red cabbage; *ver tb* **lombardo**

Lombardía SF Lombardy

lombardo/a Ⓐ ADJ of/from Lombardy
Ⓑ SM/F native/inhabitant of Lombardy; **los ~s** the people of Lombardy; *ver tb* **lombarda**

lombriciento ADJ (*LAm*) suffering from worms

lombriz SF worm, earthworm ► **lombriz de mar** lugworm ► **lombriz intestinal**, **lombriz solitaria** tapeworm

lomería SF, **lomerío** SM (*LAm*) low hills *pl*, series of ridges

lometón SM (*Caribe, Méx*) isolated hillock

lomillería SF (*Cono Sur*) [1] (= *taller*) harness maker's; (= *tienda*) harness shop
[2] (= *equipo*) harness, harness accessories *pl*

lomillero/a SM/F (*Cono Sur*) (= *fabricante*) harness maker; (= *vendedor*) harness seller

lomillo SM [1] (*Cos*) cross-stitch
[2] **lomillos** (*LAm*) (= *almohadillas*) pads (of a pack saddle)

lomo SM [1] (*Anat*) back; [*de cerdo*] loin ► **lomo embuchado** (*Esp*) cured loin of pork
[2] **lomos** (= *costillas*) ribs; **iba a ~s de una mula** he was riding a mule
[3] [*de libro*] spine
[4] [*de cuchillo*] back, blunt edge
[5] (*Agr*) (= *tierra*) ridge
[6] (*Arg*) ► **lomo de burro*** speed hump, speed ramp

lona[1] SF (= *tejido*) canvas; (*Náut*) sailcloth; (= *arpillera*) sackcloth; **la ~** (*Dep*) the canvas, the ring; ✦*MODISMO* **estar en la ~** (*Andes, Caribe**) to be broke*

lona[2]* ADJ INV (*Cono Sur*) **estar ~** to be knackered*, be worn out

loncha SF = **lonja**[1]

lonchar ▸conjug 1a◂ (*LAm*) Ⓐ VT to have for lunch
Ⓑ VI to have lunch, lunch

lonche SM (*LAm*) (= *comida*) lunch; (= *merienda*) tea, afternoon snack

lonchera SF (*Andes*) lunch box

lonchería SF (*LAm*) lunch counter, snack bar, diner (*EEUU*)

loncho SM (*Andes*) bit, piece, slice

londinense Ⓐ ADJ London *antes de s*
Ⓑ SMF Londoner; **los ~s** Londoners

Londres SM London

londri SM (*LAm*) laundry

loneta SF (*Cono Sur*) thin canvas

longa SF (*Andes*) Indian girl

longanimidad SF (*liter*) forbearance (*frm*), magnanimity

longánimo ADJ (*liter*) forbearing (*frm*), magnanimous

longaniza SF [1] (= *salchicha*) *long pork sausage*; *ver tb* **perro A2**
[2] (*Cono Sur*) (= *serie*) string, series
[3] (**) (= *pene*) prick**

longevidad SF longevity

longevo ADJ long-lived; **las mujeres son más longevas que los hombres** women live longer than men

longitud SF [1] (= *largo*) length; **salto de ~** (*Dep*) long jump ► **longitud de onda** wavelength [2] (*Geog*) longitude

longitudinal ADJ longitudinal

longitudinalmente ADV longitudinally (*frm*), lengthways

longo/a SM/F (*Ecu*) young Indian

longui* SM ✦*MODISMO* **hacerse el ~** (= *desentenderse*) to pretend not to know; (= *fingir desinterés*) to pretend not to be interested; (= *guardar secreto*) not to let on, keep mum*

lonja[1] SF [1] (= *loncha*) slice; [*de tocino*] rasher
[2] (*Cono Sur*) (= *cuero*) strip of leather; ✦*MODISMO* **sacar ~s a algn** to give sb a good thrashing

lonja[2] SF [1] (*Com*) market, exchange; ✦*MODISMO* **manipular la ~** to rig the market ► **lonja de granos** corn exchange ► **lonja de pescado** fish market
[2] (= *tienda*) grocer's (shop)

lonjear ▸conjug 1a◂ VT (*Cono Sur*) [1] [+ *cuero*] to cut into strips [2] (= *zurrar*) to thrash

➤ LENGUA Y USO: **lógicamente** 53.6

lonjista SMF grocer

lontananza SF [*de cuadro*] background; **en ~** far away, in the distance

loor SM (*liter*) praise

LOPJ SF ABR (*Esp Jur*) = **Ley Orgánica del Poder Judicial**

loquear* ▸conjug 1a◂ VI [1] (= *hacer locuras*) to play the fool
[2] (= *divertirse*) to lark about*, have a high old time*

loqueo* SM (*Cono Sur*) uproar, hullaballoo

loquera* SF [1] (= *manicomio*) madhouse, loony bin*
[2] (*LAm*) (= *locura*) madness; *ver tb* **loquero[1]**

loquería* SF (*LAm*) madhouse, lunatic asylum

loquero[1]/a* SM/F (= *enfermero*) psychiatric nurse; *ver tb* **loquera**

loquero[2]* SM [1] (*Arg*) (= *bullicio*) row, racket; *ver tb* **loquera**
[2] (*Cono Sur*) (*fig*) (= *manicomio*) **esta oficina es un ~** this office is a madhouse

loquina SF (*Andes*) foolish thing, idiocy

loquincho* ADJ (*Cono Sur*) crazy

lor SM lord

lora SF [1] (*LAm Orn*) (female) parrot
[2] (*Cono Sur**) (= *fea*) old boot*
[3] (= *habladora*) chatterbox*
[4] (*Andes, Caribe*) (= *herida*) severe wound, open wound; *ver* **loro**

lord [lor] SM (*pl* **lores**) lord

Lorena SF Lorraine

Lorenzo SM Laurence, Lawrence

lorna⁑ ADJ INV (*Cono Sur*) daft*, crackpot*

loro Ⓐ SM [1] (= *ave*) parrot
[2] (⁑) (= *radio*) radio; (= *radiocasete*) radio-cassette; ✦**MODISMO** **estar al ~**⁑ (= *alerta*) to be on the alert; (= *informado*) to know the score*; **hay que estar al ~** you need to be on the alert; **está al ~ de lo que pasa** he's in touch with what's going on; **¡al ~!** watch out!
[3] (= *charlatán*) chatterbox*; **mi hermana es un ~, no para de hablar** my sister's a chatterbox, she never stops talking
[4] (*) (= *mujer fea*) old bag*, old bat*
[5] (*Cono Sur*) (= *en robo*) thieves' lookout man
[6] (*Cono Sur Med*) bedpan
[7] (*Cono Sur*) (= *moco*) **sacar los ~s*** to pick one's nose
[8] (*Caribe*) (= *cuchillo*) pointed and curved knife; *ver tb* **lora**
Ⓑ ADJ dark brown

lorquiano ADJ relating to Federico García Lorca; **estudios ~s** Lorca studies; **las influencias lorquianas** Lorca's influences

los[1]/las[1] ART DEF M/FPL the; **los chicos juegan en el parque** the kids are playing in the park; **las sillas que compramos** the chairs we bought; **mis libros y ~ de usted** my books and yours; **las de Juan son verdes** John's are green; **una inocentada de las de niño pequeño** a practical joke typical of a small child; *ver tb* **el**

los[2]/las[2] PRON PERS (*refiriéndose a ellos, ellas*) them; (*refiriéndose a ustedes*) you; **les dije a los niños que ~ subiría al parque** I told the children that I would take them to the park; **no te ~ lleves, que aún no ~ he leído** don't take them away, I haven't read them yet; **señoras, yo las guiaré hasta la salida** ladies, I'll show you the way out; **¿~ hay?** are there any?; **~ hay y muy buenos** there are some and very good they are too

losa SF (stone) slab, flagstone ► **losa radiante** (*Arg*) underfloor heating ► **losa sepulcral** gravestone, tombstone

losange SM [1] (= *forma*) diamond (shape)
[2] (*Mat*) rhombus, rhomb
[3] (*Dep*) diamond
[4] (*Heráldica*) lozenge

loseta SF [*de moqueta*] carpet tile; [*de cerámica*] floor tile

lota SF burbot

lote[1] SM [1] [*de herencia, reparto*] portion, share
[2] (*en subasta*) lot; **el ~ 37 es una estantería de caoba** lot 37 is a mahogany bookcase
[3] (*Inform*) batch
[4] (*LAm*) (= *solar*) lot, piece of land, building site
[5] (*LAm**) [*de drogas*] cache (*of drugs*)
[6] (⁑) ✦**MODISMO** **darse** *o* **pegarse el ~ con algn** to make it with sb⁑
[7] (= *medida*) (*Méx*) *about 100 hectares*; (*Cono Sur*) *about 400 hectares*
[8] ✦**MODISMO** **al ~** (*Cono Sur*) any old how*

lote[2]* SM (*Cono Sur*) (= *imbécil*) idiot, clot*

lotear ▸conjug 1a◂ VT (*esp Cono Sur*) to divide into lots

loteo SM (*esp Cono Sur*) division into lots

lotería SF lottery; **jugar a la ~** to play the lottery; **le cayó** *o* **le tocó la ~** ◊ **se sacó la ~** (*LAm*) (= *ganar*) he won the big prize in the lottery; (*fig*) he struck lucky ► **Lotería Nacional** National Lottery ► **lotería primitiva** *weekly state-run lottery*

> **LOTERÍA**
>
> *There are two state-run lotteries in Spain: the* **Lotería Primitiva** *and the* **Lotería Nacional**, *with money raised going directly to the government. The* **Primitiva**, *which is weekly, is similar to the British National Lottery in that players choose six numbers, including a bonus number* (**complementario**), *out of a total of 49. There are also several other similar draws each week, for which players can buy a multiple-draw ticket called a* **bono-loto**. *The* **Lotería Nacional** *works differently: people buy numbered tickets, which, if their number comes up, will entitle them to a share in the prize money with others who have the same numbered ticket. Whole numbers are quite costly, so people tend to buy either* **décimos** *or smaller* **participaciones**. *Several dozen prizes are won in each of the ordinary weekly draws,* **sorteos ordinarios**. *Every year there are also a number of* **sorteos extraordinarios**, *the most famous being the Christmas draw, or* **sorteo de Navidad**, *and the* **sorteo del Niño** *at the Epiphany.*
>
> ⇨*See also* EL GORDO, ONCE

lotero/a SM/F seller of lottery tickets

lotificación SF (*CAm, Méx*) division into lots

lotificar ▸conjug 1g◂ VT (*CAm, Méx*) to divide into lots

lotización SF (*Andes*) division into lots

lotizar ▸conjug 1f◂ VT (*Andes*) to divide into lots

loto[1] SM lotus

loto[2]* SF lottery

Lovaina SF Louvain

loza SF [1] (= *vajilla*) crockery; **hacer la ~** to wash up
[2] (= *cerámica*) pottery ► **loza fina** china, chinaware

lozanamente ADV [1] (*Bot*) (= *frondosamente*) luxuriantly, profusely
[2] (= *vigorosamente*) vigorously

lozanear ▸conjug 1a◂ VI (*Bot*) to flourish, do well, flourish; [*persona*] to bloom

lozanía SF [1] (*Bot*) (= *frondosidad*) lushness, luxuriance; (= *frescura*) freshness
[2] [*de persona*] (= *vigor*) vigour, vigor (*EEUU*), healthiness
[3] [*del rostro, mejillas*] freshness

lozano ADJ [1] (*Bot*) (= *frondoso*) lush, luxuriant; (= *fresco*) fresh; [*persona, animal*] (= *vigoroso*) vigorous, full of life; (= *saludable*) healthy-looking
[2] (= *seguro de sí*) self-assured; (= *arrogante*) arrogant

LRU SF ABR (*Esp Jur*) = **Ley de Reforma Universitaria**

LSD SM ABR (= **lysergic acid diethylamide**) LSD

lúa†⁑ SF one peseta

lubina SF sea bass

lubricación SF lubrication

lubricador Ⓐ ADJ lubricating
Ⓑ SM lubricator

lubricante Ⓐ ADJ [1] [*aceite, sustancia*] lubricant, lubricating
[2] (*) [*persona*] greasy*
Ⓑ SM lubricant

lubricar ▸conjug 1g◂ VT to lubricate

lubricidad SF [1] (= *deslizamiento*) slipperiness
[2] (= *lujuria*) lewdness, lubricity (*frm*)

lúbrico ADJ [1] (= *resbaladizo*) slippery
[2] (= *lujurioso*) lewd, lubricious (*frm*)

lubrificación SF lubrication

lubrificante Ⓐ ADJ lubricant, lubricating
Ⓑ SM lubricant

lubrificar ▸conjug 1f◂ VT = **lubricar**

luca* SF (*Cono Sur*) 1000 pesos

Lucano SM Lucan

Lucas SM Luke, Lucas; (*Rel*) Luke

lucas* ADJ INV (*Méx*) crazy, cracked*

lucecitas SFPL fairy-lights

lucense Ⓐ ADJ of/from Lugo
Ⓑ SMF native/inhabitant of Lugo; **los ~s** the people of Lugo

lucera SF skylight

Lucerna SF Lucerne

lucerna SF chandelier

lucernario SM skylight

lucero SM [1] (*Astron*) bright star; (= *Venus*) Venus ► **lucero del alba, lucero de la mañana** morning star ► **lucero de la tarde, lucero vespertino** evening star
[2] (*frm*) (= *brillo*) (= *esplendor*) brilliance, radiance

Lucha SF (*forma familiar*) *de* **Luz, Lucía**

lucha SF [1] (= *combate*) fight; (= *esfuerzo*) struggle (**por** for); **~ a muerte** fight to the bitter end, fight to the death; **la ~ contra la droga** the fight against drugs; **la ~ por la supervivencia** the fight *o* struggle for survival; **esta vida es una ~** life is a struggle; **abandonar la ~** to give up the struggle ► **lucha armada**

armed struggle ► **lucha contraincendios** fire-fighting ► **lucha de clases** class struggle

[2] (*Dep*) ► **lucha grecorromana**, **lucha libre** wrestling

luchador(a) Ⓐ ADJ combative

Ⓑ SM/F (= *combatiente*) fighter; (*Dep*) wrestler; **~ por la libertad** freedom fighter

luchar ►conjug 1a◄ VI [1] (= *combatir*) to fight; (= *esforzarse*) to struggle (**por algo** for sth); **luchó en el bando republicano** he fought on the Republican side; **tuvo que ~ mucho en la vida** life was a constant struggle for her; **~ con** *o* **contra algo/algn** to fight (against) sth/sb; **~on contra la corrupción** they fought against corruption; **el enfermo luchaba con la muerte** the sick man was fighting for his life; **luchaba con los mandos** he was struggling *o* wrestling with the controls

[2] (*Dep*) to wrestle (**con** with)

luche SM (*Cono Sur*) [1] (= *juego*) hopscotch

[2] (*Bot*) *an edible seaweed*

Lucía SF Lucy

lucidez SF [1] (= *perspicacia*) lucidity, clarity; **demuestra gran ~ al resolver los problemas** she's very lucid *o* clear when solving problems

[2] (*tb* **~ mental**) lucidity; **es demente, pero tiene momentos de ~ (mental)** she's insane but has moments of lucidity, she's insane but has her lucid moments

[3] (*CAm, Cono Sur*) (= *brillantez*) brilliance

lucido ADJ [1] (= *espléndido*) splendid, magnificent; **fue una boda muy lucida** it was a splendid *o* magnificent wedding; **la actriz tuvo una actuación muy lucida** the actress gave a splendid *o* magnificent *o* stunning performance

[2] **estar ~** ◊ **quedar(se) ~** (*iró*) to make a mess of things; **¡estamos ~s!** a fine mess we're in!; **~s estaríamos si ...** it would be awful if ...

lúcido ADJ [1] [*persona*] **ser/estar ~** to be lucid

[2] [*observación, comentario, análisis*] lucid

luciente ADJ bright, shining, brilliant

luciérnaga SF glow-worm

Lucifer SM Lucifer

lucimiento SM [1] (= *brillo*) brilliance, sparkle; **hacer algo con ~** to do sth outstandingly well *o* very successfully

[2] (= *ostentación*) show, ostentation

lucio[1] SM (= *pez*) pike

lucio[2] ADJ (*frm*) = **lúcido**

lución SM slow-worm

lucir ►conjug 3f◄ Ⓐ VI [1] (= *brillar*) to shine; **lucían las estrellas** the stars were shining

[2] (= *destacar*) to excel; **no lucía en los estudios** he did not excel as a student

[3] (= *aprovechar*) **trabaja mucho, pero no le luce el esfuerzo** he works hard but it doesn't do him much good; ✦***MODISMO* así le/te/me luce el pelo**: **nunca estudia y así le luce el pelo** he never studies and it shows

[4] (*LAm*) (= *parecer*) to look, seem; **(te) luce lindo** it looks nice (on you)

Ⓑ VT (= *ostentar*) to show off; [+ *ropa*] to sport; **~ las habilidades** to show off one's talents; **lucía un traje nuevo** he was sporting a new suit; **siempre va luciendo escote** she always wears low-cut dresses

Ⓒ **lucirse** VPR [1] (= *destacar*) to excel; **Carlos se lució en el examen** Carlos excelled in the exam; **se lució con un gol** he distinguished himself with a goal

[2] (= *hacer el ridículo*) (*iró*) to excel o.s.; **¡te has lucido!** you've excelled yourself!

lucrarse ►conjug 1a◄ VPR to do well out of a deal; (*pey*) feather one's (own) nest

lucrativo ADJ lucrative, profitable; **organización no lucrativa** non-profitmaking organization, not-for-profit organization

Lucrecia SF Lucretia

Lucrecio SM Lucretius

lucro SM profit; **~s y daños** (*Fin*) profit and loss; *ver tb* **afán 1**

luctuoso ADJ (*frm*) mournful, sad

lucubración SF (*frm*) lucubration (*frm*); **déjate de lucubraciones y vamos al grano** come down off the clouds and let's talk sense

lúcuma* SF [1] (*Chile, Perú, Bol*) (= *fruta*) *variety of eggfruit*; (= *berenjena*) aubergine, eggplant (*EEUU*)

[2] ✦***MODISMOS* coger la ~** (*Caribe**) (= *enojarse*) to get mad*; (= *afanarse*) to keep at it; **dar la ~** (*Méx**) (= *empeñarse*) to keep trying

ludibrio SM (*frm*) mockery, derision

lúdico ADJ ludic (*liter*), playful

ludir ►conjug 3a◄ VT to rub (**con, contra** against)

ludoparque SM sports centre, sports complex

ludópata Ⓐ ADJ addicted to gambling

Ⓑ SMF compulsive gambler, gambling addict

ludopatía SF compulsive gambling, addiction to gambling

ludoteca SF children's play-centre

▼ **luego** Ⓐ ADV [1] (*en el tiempo*) [1·1] (*referido al pasado*) then; **—quedamos en un bar —¿y ~ qué pasó?** "we met in a bar" — "and then what happened?"; **vimos una película y ~ fuimos a cenar** we saw a film and later (on) *o* afterwards *o* then went out for dinner

[1·2] (*referido al futuro*) later (on), afterwards; **te lo dejo pero ~ me lo devuelves** you can borrow it but you have to give me it back later (on) *o* afterwards; **~ vuelvo** I'll be back later (on); **te veo ~** I'll see you later (on) *o* then; **~ de** after; **~ de eso** after that; **~ de cenar se fue** he left after dinner; **¡hasta ~!** bye!, see you!, see you later!; **~ que ...** (*LAm*) (*tan pronto como*) as soon as ...; (*después que*) after ...

[1·3] (*LAm*) (= *pronto*) soon; **lo vamos a saber muy ~** we'll find out really soon; **espéralo que lueguito viene** wait for him, he's coming in a minute; **empieza siempre con entusiasmo pero lueguito se aburre** he's very enthusiastic at the beginning but he gets bored quickly; **luego luego** (*esp Méx**) straight away

[1·4] (*Andes, Caribe, Méx*) (= *de vez en cuando*) sometimes, from time to time

[2] (*en el espacio*) then; **primero está la cocina y ~ el comedor** the kitchen is first, then the dining room; **primero va usted y ~ yo** you're first and I'm next, you're first and then it's me

[3] (= *además*) then; **~ tenemos estos otros colores** then we have these other colours

[4] (*Méx*) (= *muy cerca*) right here, right there

[5] **desde ~** of course; *ver tb* **desde 4**

Ⓑ CONJ (= *así que*) therefore; **pienso, ~ existo** I think, therefore I am; **~ x es igual a 7** therefore x equals 7

lueguito ADV [1] (*LAm*) (= *inmediatamente*) at once, right now, immediately

[2] (*Chile, CAm, Méx**) (= *cerca*) near, nearby; **aquí ~** close by here, very near here

luengo†† ADJ long

lúes SF syphilis

▼ **lugar** SM [1] (= *sitio*) place; **dejó las joyas en ~ seguro** she left the jewels in a safe place; **es un ~ muy bonito** it is a lovely spot *o* place; **devolver un libro a su ~** to put a book back in its place; **el concierto será en un ~ cerrado** the concert will take place indoors *o* at an indoor venue; **el ~ del crimen** the scene of the crime; **algún ~** somewhere; **una emisión desde algún ~ de Europa** a broadcast from somewhere in Europe; **lo escondió en algún ~ de la casa** she hid it somewhere around the house; **los Santos Lugares** the Holy Places; ✦***MODISMO* poner las cosas en su ~** to put things straight ► **lugar común** cliché, commonplace ► **lugar de encuentro** meeting-place ► **lugar geométrico** locus; *ver tb* **composición 3**

[2] (= *posición*) [2·1] (*en lista, carrera, trabajo*) **ocupa un buen ~ en la empresa** she has a good position *o* post at the company; **ocupar el ~ de algn** to take sb's place; **llegó en último ~** he came last; **en primer ~: se han clasificado en primer ~** they have qualified in first place; **en primer ~, me gustaría agradecer la invitación** first of all *o* firstly, I would like to thank you for inviting me

[2·2] (= *situación*) **yo, en tu ~, no iría** I wouldn't go if I were you; **usted póngase en mi ~** put yourself in my place *o* shoes; **en su ~, ¡descanso!** (*Mil*) stand easy!; **dejar a algn en buen/mal ~** [*comportamiento*] to reflect well/badly on sb; [*persona*] to make sb look good/bad; **estar fuera de ~** to be out of place, **sentirse fuera de ~** to feel out of place; ✦***MODISMO* encontrar un ~ bajo el sol** to find a place in the sun

[2·3] **en ~ de** instead of; **vino el portavoz en ~ del ministro** the spokesman came instead of the minister, the spokesman came in the minister's place; **¿puedo asistir yo en su ~?** can I go instead?; **en ~ de escribir, me llamó por teléfono** instead of writing, he called me; **en ~ de ir a la piscina, ¿por qué no vamos a la playa?** why don't we go to the beach instead of the swimming pool?

[3] (= *ocasión*) opportunity, chance; **si se me da el ~** if I have the opportunity *o* chance; **no hubo ~ para decir lo que pensaba** there was no opportunity to say what I thought; **no hay ~ para preocupaciones** there is no cause for concern; **dar ~ a algo** to give rise to sth, lead to sth; **dejar ~ a algo** to leave room for sth; **los datos no dejan ~ a dudas** the figures leave no room for doubt; **la situación no dejaba ~ al optimismo** the situation left little room for *o* gave few grounds for optimism; **sin ~ a dudas** without doubt, undoubtedly; **no ha ~: una reacción tan fuerte, francamente no ha ~** there is no need for such a violent response; **—¡protesto! —no ha ~** (*Jur*) "objection!" — "overruled"; **tener ~** to take place, happen, occur; ✦***MODISMO* a como dé** *o* **diera ~** (*Méx*) (= *de cualquier manera*) somehow or other, one way or another; (= *a toda costa*) at any cost

➤ LENGUA Y USO: **luego A5** 39.1 **lugar 2·3** 53.1, 53.2, 53.5

[4] (= *espacio*) room, space; **no hay ~ para escribir nada más** there's no room *o* space to write any more; **¿hay ~?** is there any room?; **hacer ~ para algo** to make room for sth
[5] (= *localidad*) place; **En un ~ de la Mancha ...** Somewhere in La Mancha ...; **del ~** local; **un vino del ~** a local wine; **las gentes del ~** the local people, the locals ► **lugar de nacimiento** (*gen*) birthplace; (*en impreso*) place of birth ► **lugar de trabajo** workplace

lugareño/a Ⓐ ADJ [1] (= *local*) local
[2] (*Méx*) (= *regional*) regional; (= *nativo*) native
Ⓑ SM/F local

lugarteniente SM deputy, substitute (*EEUU*)

Lugo SM Lugo

lugo SM (*Andes Zool*) ram

lugre SM lugger

lúgubre ADJ (= *triste*) mournful, lugubrious (*frm*), dismal; [*voz, tono*] sombre, somber (*EEUU*), mournful

luir ▸conjug 3g◂ VT (*Cono Sur*) [1] (= *arrugar*) to rumple, mess up
[2] [+ *cerámica*] to polish

Luis SM Louis

Luisa SF Louise

Luisiana SF Louisiana

lujo SM [1] (= *fasto*) luxury; **vivir con ~** to live in luxury; **hoy en día comer carne es un ~** eating meat is a luxury these days; **de ~** luxury *antes de s*; **un coche de ~** a luxury car; **permitirse el ~ de hacer algo** to allow o.s. the luxury of doing sth ► **lujo asiático***: **¿te vas al Caribe? ¡vaya ~ asiático!** so you're off to the Caribbean? what a life of luxury!
[2] (= *abundancia*) profusion, wealth, abundance; **con todo ~ de detalles** with a wealth of detail

lujosamente ADV [1] (= *con fasto*) luxuriously
[2] (= *profusamente*) profusely

lujoso ADJ [1] (= *fastuoso*) luxurious
[2] (= *profuso*) profuse

lujuria SF [1] [*sexual*] lust, lechery, lewdness
[2] [*de vegetación*] lushness, abundance
[3] [*de poder*] excess

lujuriante ADJ (*frm*) [1] [*vegetación*] luxuriant, lush; [*aroma*] delicious, inviting
[2] (= *lujurioso*) lustful, lecherous, lewd

lujuriar ▸conjug 1b◂ VI (*frm*) to lust

lujurioso ADJ lustful, lecherous, lewd

lullir‡ ▸conjug 3h◂ VT (*Andes, CAm, Méx*) to rub (**con, contra** against, on)

lulo¹/a (*Cono Sur*) Ⓐ ADJ (*) [1] (= *desgarbado*) lanky
[2] (= *torpe*) dull, slow
Ⓑ SM/F (= *persona desgarbada*) lanky person

lulo² SM [1] (*Chile**) (= *bulto*) bundle; (= *rizo*) kiss curl
[2] ✦**MODISMO al ~** (*Caribe**) one after another
[3] ► **lulo del ojo** (*Andes*) eyeball

lulú SMF (*tb* **~ de Pomerania**) Pomeranian, pom

luma* SF (*Cono Sur*) [1] (= *bastón*) police truncheon
[2] (= *reprimenda*) ticking-off*

lumbago SM lumbago

lumbalgia SF lumbago

lumbar ADJ lumbar

lumbre SF [1] (= *fuego*) fire; **a la ~** ◊ **cerca de la ~** near the fire, by the fireside; ✦**MODISMO echar ~ por los ojos** to be furious
[2] (†) (*para cigarro*) light; **¿me das ~?** ◊ **¿tienes ~?** have you got a light?
[3] (= *luz*) light; (= *brillo*) brightness, brilliance ► **lumbre del agua** surface of the water
[4] (†) (*Arquit*) (= *claraboya*) skylight; (= *abertura*) light, opening (*in a wall*)

lumbrera SF [1] (= *genio*) leading light, luminary; **estaba rodeado de ~s literarias** he was surrounded by leading literary figures
[2] (= *claraboya*) skylight
[3] (= *cuerpo luminoso*) luminary (*liter*)
[4] (*Mec*) vent, port ► **lumbrera de admisión** inlet ► **lumbrera de escape** exhaust vent
[5] (*Méx Taur, Teat*) box

lumi‡ SF whore

luminar SM = **lumbrera 1**

luminaria SF (*Rel*) altar lamp; **luminarias** illuminations, lights

luminescencia SF luminescence

luminescente ADJ luminescent

lumínico ADJ light *antes de s*

luminosidad SF [1] (= *resplandor*) brightness, luminosity (*frm*)
[2] [*de una ocurrencia, explicación*] brilliance

luminoso Ⓐ ADJ [1] (*gen*) bright, shining; [*letrero*] illuminated; [*esfera, reloj*] luminous
[2] [*idea*] bright, brilliant; [*exposición*] brilliant
Ⓑ SM (*Com*) neon sign; (*Dep*) electronic scoreboard

luminotecnia SF lighting

luminotécnico ADJ lighting *antes de s*; **efectos ~s** lighting effects

lumpen Ⓐ ADJ INV lumpen; **el Madrid ~** the Madrid underclass
Ⓑ SM INV underclass, lumpen

lumpo SM lumpfish; **caviar de ~** lumpfish caviar; **huevas de ~** lumpfish roe

luna SF [1] (= *astro*) moon; **claro de ~** moonlight; **media ~** half moon; ✦**MODISMOS estar de buena/mala ~** to be in a good/bad mood; **estar en la ~** to have one's head in the clouds; **estar en la ~ de Valencia** to be in a dream world; **hablar de la ~: eso es hablar de la ~** that's nonsense; **quedarse a la ~ de Valencia** to be disappointed, be left in the lurch; **quedarse en la ~ de Paita** (*Andes**) to be struck dumb ► **luna creciente** crescent moon, waxing moon ► **luna de miel** [*de novios*] honeymoon; (*fig, Pol*) honeymoon (period) ► **luna llena** full moon ► **luna menguante** waning moon ► **luna nueva** new moon
[2] (= *vidrio*) (= *escaparate*) plate glass; (= *espejo*) mirror; [*de gafas*] lens; (*Aut*) window; [*de ventana*] pane; [*de puerta*] panel ► **luna térmica** (*Aut*) heated rear window

lunar Ⓐ ADJ lunar
Ⓑ SM [1] (*Anat*) mole ► **lunar postizo** beauty spot
[2] (*en tejido*) polka-dot, spot; **de ~es** polka-dot; **un vestido de ~es** a polka-dot dress
[3] (= *defecto*) flaw, blemish; (*moral*) stain, blot

lunarejo ADJ (*LAm*) spotty, spotty-faced

lunático/a ADJ, SM/F lunatic

lunch [lunʃ] SM (*pl* **lunchs** [lunʃ]) lunch; (= *refrigerio*) midday snack; (*en celebración, fiesta*) midday reception, cold buffet

lunchería SF (*LAm*) = **lonchería**

lunes SM INV Monday; ✦**MODISMOS hacer San Lunes** (*LAm**) to stay away from work on Monday; **no ocurre cada ~ y cada martes** it doesn't happen every day of the week; *ver tb* **sábado**

luneta SF [1] [*de gafas*] lens; (*Aut*) window ► **luneta trasera** rear window ► **luneta trasera térmica** heated rear window
[2] (= *media luna*) halfmoon shape, crescent
[3] (*Méx Teat*†) stall

lunfa* SM (*Cono Sur*) thief

lunfardismo SM (*Cono Sur*) (= *palabra*) slang word

lunfardo SM [1] (*Arg*) *local slang of Buenos Aires*
[2] (*Cono Sur*) criminal slang, language of the underworld

lupa SF magnifying glass; **ha examinado el discurso con ~** she has gone over the speech with a fine tooth comb

lupanar†† SM brothel

Lupe SF (*forma familiar*) *de* **Guadalupe**

lupia¹ SF [1] (= *lobanillo*) wen, cyst
[2] **lupias** (*Andes*) (= *cantidad pequeña*) small amount of money *sing*; (= *cambio*) small change *sing*

lupia²* SMF (*CAm*) quack*

lúpulo SM (*Bot*) hop, hops *pl*

luquete SM (*Cono Sur*) [1] (*Agr*) unploughed patch of land
[2] (= *calva*) bald patch
[3] (= *mancha*) grease spot

lurio* (*Méx*) ADJ (= *enamorado*) in love; (= *loco*) crazy, cracked*

lusitano/a Ⓐ ADJ Portuguese; (*Hist*) Lusitanian
Ⓑ SM/F Portuguese man/woman, native/inhabitant of Portugal; (*Hist*) Lusitanian; **los ~s** the Portuguese

luso/a ADJ, SM/F = **lusitano**

lustrabotas SMF INV (*LAm*) bootblack, shoeshine boy/girl

lustrada* SM (*LAm*) (= *acto*) shine, shoeshine

lustrador¹(a) SM/F (*LAm*) (= *limpiabotas*) bootblack, shoeshine boy/girl

lustrador² SM (*Téc*) polisher

lustradora SF polishing machine

lustrar ▸conjug 1a◂ VT (*esp LAm*) to shine, polish

lustre SM [1] (= *brillo*) shine, lustre, luster (*EEUU*), gloss; **dar ~ a** to polish, put a shine on
[2] (= *sustancia*) polish ► **lustre para calzado** shoe polish ► **lustre para metales** metal polish
[3] (= *prestigio*) lustre, luster (*EEUU*), glory

lustrín SM (*Chile*) shoeshine box, shoeshine stand

lustrina SF [1] (*Cono Sur*) *shiny material of alpaca*
[2] (*Andes*) (= *tela*) silk cloth
[3] (*Cono Sur*) (= *betún*) shoe polish

lustro SM period of five years, five year period, lustrum (*frm*)

lustroso ADJ [1] (= *brillante*) [*zapatos*] shiny; [*pelo*] glossy, shiny
[2] (= *saludable*) healthy-looking

lutencio SM (*Quím*) lutetium

luteranismo SM Lutheranism

luterano/a ADJ, SM/F Lutheran

Lutero SM Luther

luto SM mourning; **medio ~** half-mourning; **dejar el ~** to come out of mourning; **estar de ~** ◊ **llevar ~** ◊ **vestir(se) de ~** to be in mourning (**por** for); ► **luto riguroso** deep mourning

luxación SF (*Med*) dislocation

Luxemburgo SM Luxembourg

luxemburgués/esa Ⓐ ADJ of/from Luxembourg
Ⓑ SM/F native/inhabitant of Luxembourg; **los luxemburgueses** the people of Luxembourg

luz SF [1] (= *claridad*) light; **una casa con mucha ~** a very bright house, a house that gets a lot of light; **necesito más ~ para leer** I can't read in this light; **a media ~**: **la habitación estaba a media ~** the room was in half-darkness; **estábamos allí tumbados a media ~** we were lying there in the half-darkness; **poner una lámpara a media ~** to dim a light; **a primera ~** at first light; **quitar** *o* **tapar la ~ a algn** to be in sb's light; **aparta de ahí, que me quitas** *o* **tapas la ~** get out of the way, you're in my light; ✦*MODISMOS* **entre dos luces** (= *al atardecer*) at twilight; (= *al amanecer*) at dawn, at daybreak; **estar entre dos luces*** (= *borracho*) to be mellow, be tipsy; **hacer ~ de gas a algn** to confuse sb; **negar la ~ del día a algn** to concede absolutely nothing to sb; **ver la ~ al final del túnel** to see light at the end of the tunnel ► **luz cenital** light from above ► **luz del día**: **se despierta con la ~ del día** she wakes up when it gets light *o* (*liter*) at first light; **con la ~ del día lo veremos de otra manera** we'll see things differently in the cold light of day; ✦*MODISMO* **tan claro como la ~ del día** as clear as daylight ► **luz de (la) luna**: **a la ~ de la luna** by the light of the moon, by moonlight ► **luz de las velas**: **a la ~ de las velas** by candlelight ► **luz del sol** sunlight; **me molesta la ~ del sol** the sunlight hurts my eyes ► **luz eléctrica** electric light ► **luz natural** natural light ► **luz solar** sunlight ► **luz ultravioleta** ultraviolet light ► **luz y sombra** light and shade ► **luz y sonido**: **un espectáculo de ~ y sonido** a son et lumière show; *ver tb* **brillar**

[2] (= *lámpara, foco*) light; **me dejé la ~ encendida** I left the light on; **se ha fundido la ~ de la cocina** the light has gone in the kitchen; **las luces de la ciudad** the city lights; **apagar la ~** to switch *o* turn *o* put the light off; **encender** *o* (*LAm*) **prender** *o* **poner la ~** to switch *o* turn *o* put the light on; ✦*MODISMO* **hacer algo con ~ y taquígrafos** to do sth openly; **reunirse sin ~ ni taquígrafos** to meet behind closed doors ► **luces cortas** dipped headlights, low beams (*EEUU*); **poner las luces cortas** to dip one's headlights, dim one's headlights (*EEUU*) ► **luces de aterrizaje** (*Aer*) landing lights ► **luces de balización** (*Aer*) runway lights ► **luces de carretera** full-beam headlights; **poner las luces de carretera** to put one's headlights on full beam *o* (*EEUU*) high beam ► **luces de cruce** dipped headlights; **poner las luces de cruce** to dip one's headlights, dim one's headlights (*EEUU*) ► **luces de detención** brake lights ► **luces de estacionamiento** parking lights ► **luces de frenado, luces de freno** brake lights ► **luces de gálibo** clearance lights ► **luces de navegación** navigation lights ► **luces de posición** sidelights ► **luces de tráfico** traffic lights ► **luces largas** = **luces de carretera** ► **luces traseras** rear lights, tail lamps ► **luz de Bengala** (*Mil*) flare, star-shell; (*LAm*) (= *fuego de artificio*) sparkler ► **luz de cortesía** courtesy light; (*CAm*) sidelight ► **luz de costado** sidelight ► **luz de giro** direction indicator ► **luz de situación** sidelight, parking light ► **luz intermitente** flashing light ► **luz piloto** sidelight, parking light ► **luz relámpago** (*Fot*) flashlight ► **luz roja** red light ► **luz verde** green light; **dar ~ verde a un proyecto** to give a project the go-ahead *o* the green light; **recibir ~ verde** to get the go-ahead *o* the green light ► **luz vuelta** (*Méx*) direction indicator; *ver tb* **traje**[2]

[3] (= *suministro de electricidad*) electricity; **no hay ~ en todo el edificio** there's no electricity in the whole building; **les cortaron la ~** their electricity (supply) was cut off; **se ha ido la ~** the lights have gone out; **¿cuánto has pagado de ~ este mes?** how much was your electricity bill this month?

[4] (*tb* **~ pública**) ✦*MODISMOS* **sacar a la ~** [+ *secreto*] to bring to light; [+ *libro, disco*] to bring out; **salir a la ~** [*secreto*] to come to light; [*libro, disco*] to come out; **el año en que el periódico salió a la ~** the year in which the newspaper first came out; **la última vez que el periódico salió a la ~** the last time the newspaper was published; **ver la ~** [*libro, disco*] to appear, come out

[5] (*Med*) **dar a ~** [+ *niño*] to give birth; **acaba de dar a ~ (a) una niña** she has just given birth to a baby girl

[6] (*Cono Sur*) (= *ventaja*) **dar ~ a algn** to give sb a start; **te doy diez metros de ~** I'll give you ten metres' start

[7] (= *aclaración*) light; **a la ~ de lo que hemos visto** in the light of what we've seen; **a la ~ de un nuevo descubrimiento** in the light of a new discovery; **arrojar ~ sobre algo** to cast *o* shed *o* throw light on sth; **estudiar algo a nueva ~** to study sth in a new light; ✦*MODISMO* **a todas luces** by any reckoning

[8] (*Arquit*) [*de puerta, hueco*] span; [*de edificio*] window, opening; [*de puente*] span

[9] **luces** (= *inteligencia*) intelligence *sing*; **corto de luces** ◊ **de pocas luces** dim, stupid

[10] (*Hist, Literat*) **el Siglo de las Luces** the Age of Enlightenment

[11] (*Cono Sur*) (= *distancia*) *distance between two objects* ► **luz al suelo** clearance (*under a vehicle*)

[12] (*Andes**) dough*, money

lycra® ['laikra] SF Lycra®

Lyón SM Lyons

➤ LENGUA Y USO: luz 7 44.1

M m

M[1], **m**[1] ['eme] SF (= *letra*) M, m

M[2] ABR 1 (= **mediano**) M
2 (= *marzo*) Mar; **11-M** March 11, *date of the Madrid train bombing in 2004*

m[2] ABR 1 (= **metro(s)**) m; m^2 (= **metros cuadrados**) sq. m., m^2; m^3 (= **metros cúbicos**) cu. m., m^3
2 (= **masculino**) masc., m

M. ABR 1 = **Madrid**
2 (*Ferro*) = **Metropolitano**
3 (*Geog*) = **Meridiano**

m. ABR 1 (= **murió**) d
2 (= **mes**) m
3 (= **monte**) Mt

M-19 SM ABR (*Col Pol*) = **Movimiento 19 de Abril**

M.ª ABR = **María**

maca[1] SF 1 (= *defecto*) flaw, defect
2 (= *mancha*) (*gen*) spot; (*en fruta*) bruise, blemish

maca[2] SF (*Caribe*) (= *loro*) parrot

maca[3]‡ SM = **macarra**

macabeo/a Ⓐ ADJ Maccabean; *ver tb* **rollo A5**
Ⓑ SM/F Maccabee

macabí SM 1 (*Andes*) shrewd person
2 (*Caribe*) bandit

macabro ADJ macabre

macaco Ⓐ ADJ (*) 1 (*LAm*) (= *deforme*) deformed, misshapen; (= *feo*) ugly
2 (*CAm, Caribe*) (= *tonto*) silly
Ⓑ SM 1 (*Zool*) macaque
2 (*Cono Sur pey*) Brazilian
3 (*Caribe*) big shot*, bigwig
4 (*Méx*) bogey

macadamizar ▸conjug 1f◂ VT to macadamize, tarmac

macadán SM macadam

macagua SF 1 (*LAm*) (= *ave*) laughing falcon
2 (*Ven*) (= *serpiente*) *poisonous snake*

macana SF 1 (*LAm*) (= *porra*) (*gen*) club, cudgel; [*de policía*] truncheon, billy (club) (*EEUU*); (*Hist*) Indian club *o* cudgel
2 (*Andes, Cono Sur**) (= *mentira*) lie; **¡macana!** it's all lies!; **macanas** (= *tonterías*) rubbish *sing*, nonsense *sing*
3 (*Cono Sur**) (= *contrariedad*) pain*, nuisance; **¡qué ~! el ascensor no funciona** what a pain* *o* nuisance! the lift's not working
4 (*Cono Sur**) (= *chapuza*) bad job
5 (*Cono Sur**) (= *charla*) long boring conversation
6 (*Caribe*) **de ~** undoubtedly; **es de ~ que ...** of course ...

macanazo SM 1 (*Caribe*) blow (*with a club, cudgel*)
2 (*Cono Sur*) = **macana 2, 4**

macaneador(a)* (*Cono Sur*) Ⓐ ADJ (= *mentiroso*) deceitful; (= *poco fiable*) unreliable
Ⓑ SM/F charlatan

macanear* ▸conjug 1a◂ Ⓐ VI 1 (*esp Andes, Cono Sur*) (= *mentir*) to lie; (= *exagerar*) to exaggerate wildly, tell tall stories; (= *decir tonterías*) to talk nonsense, talk rubbish; (= *hacer tonterías*) to mess about
2 (*LAm**) (= *trabajar*) to work hard, keep one's nose to the grindstone
Ⓑ VT 1 (*Caribe*) (= *aporrear*) to beat, hit
2 (*Caribe*) (*en jardín, huerta*) to weed, clear of weeds
3 (*Caribe*) [+ *asunto*] to handle

macanero* ADJ (*Andes, Cono Sur*) (= *que dice tonterías*) given to talking nonsense, silly; (= *fantasioso*) given to telling tall stories

macanudo* ADJ 1 (*LAm*) (= *estupendo*) great*, fantastic* 2 (*Andes*) (= *duro*) [*trabajo*] tough, difficult; [*persona*] strong, tough 3 (*Cono Sur, Méx*) (= *abultado*) swollen, overlarge 4 (*Cono Sur*) (= *exagerado*) disproportionate

Macao SM Macao

macaquear ▸conjug 1a◂ Ⓐ VT (*CAm*) (= *robar*) to steal
Ⓑ VI (*Cono Sur*) (= *hacer gestos*) to make faces

macarra‡ SM (*Esp*) 1 (= *bruto*) lout, thug; (= *mal vestido*) vulgar, flashy type; **tiene aspecto de ~** he looks really vulgar and flashy
2 (= *chulo*) pimp

macarrada‡ SF **lo que hiciste fue una ~** that was a really loutish thing of you to do

macarrón[1] SM (*tb* **~ de almendras**) macaroon

macarrón[2] SM (*Náut*) bulwark, stanchion

macarrones SMPL (= *pasta*) macaroni

macarrónico ADJ macaronic

macarse ▸conjug 1g◂ VPR to go bad, rot

macear ▸conjug 1a◂ Ⓐ VT to hammer, pound
Ⓑ VI 1 (= *insistir*) = **machacar B1**
2 (*CAm**) to bet

Macedonia SF Macedonia

macedonia SF ▸ **macedonia de frutas** fruit salad

macedonio/a Ⓐ ADJ, SM/F Macedonian
Ⓑ SM (*Ling*) Macedonian

maceración SF 1 (*Culin*) [*de fruta*] soaking, maceration; [*de carne*] marinading; **dejar en ~** [+ *fruta*] to leave to soak; [+ *carne*] to marinate
2 (= *vergüenza*) mortification

macerado SM maceration

macerar ▸conjug 1a◂ Ⓐ VT 1 (*Culin*) [+ *fruta*] to soak, macerate; [+ *carne*] to marinate
2 (= *avergonzar*) to mortify
Ⓑ **macerarse** VPR 1 (*Culin*) [*fruta*] to soak, macerate; [*carne*] to marinate
2 (= *mortificarse*) to mortify o.s.

macero SM macebearer

maceta Ⓐ SF 1 [*de flores*] (= *tiesto*) flowerpot, plant pot; (*Cono Sur*) (= *ramo*) bouquet, bunch of flowers
2 (= *martillo*) (*gen*) mallet, small hammer; [*de cantero*] stonecutter's hammer
3 (*Méx**) (= *cabeza*) nut*, noggin (*EEUU**); **ser duro de ~** (*Andes, Cono Sur*) to be thick in the head*
Ⓑ ADJ (*) 1 (*Andes, Cono Sur*) thick*, slow; **ponerse ~** to get old
2 (*Caribe*) stingy*, tight*

macetero SM 1 (= *soporte*) flowerpot stand, flowerpot holder
2 (*LAm*) (= *maceta*) flowerpot

macetón SM tub

macha SF (*Andes, Caribe*) mannish woman, butch woman (*pey)

machaca Ⓐ SF (= *aparato*) crusher, pounder
Ⓑ SMF (*) (= *persona*) nag, pest

machacadora SF crusher, pounder

machacante ADJ [*publicidad*] constant; [*estribillo*] monotonous, insistent

machacar ▸conjug 1g◂ Ⓐ VT 1 (= *triturar*) to crush; **machacó los ajos en el mortero** he crushed the garlic in the mortar
2 (*) (= *aniquilar*) [+ *contrincante*] to thrash; (*en discusión*) to crush, flatten; **el equipo visitante los machacó** they were thrashed by the visiting team
3 [+ *precio*] to slash
4 (*) [+ *lección, asignatura*] to swot (up)*
5 (*Esp**) (= *insistir sobre*) to go on about; **deja ya de ~ siempre lo mismo** stop going on and on about the same thing
6 (*Baloncesto**) to dunk, slam dunk
Ⓑ VI (*) 1 (*Esp*) (= *insistir*) to go on; **¡no machaques!** don't go on so!, stop harping on about it!; **~ con** *o* **sobre algo** to go on about sth; *ver tb* **hierro 1**
2 (= *empollar*) to swot*
Ⓒ **machacarse** VPR 1 (*) [+ *dinero, herencia, sueldo*] to blow*
2 **machacársela** (*Esp***) to wank**; **¡a mí me la machaca!** I couldn't give a fuck!**

machacón/ona Ⓐ ADJ (= *insistente*) insistent; (= *monótono*) monotonous, repetitive; (=

pesado) tiresome, wearisome; **con insistencia machacona** with tiresome *o* wearisome insistence
Ⓑ SM/F pest, bore
machaconamente ADV (= *con insistencia*) insistently; (= *con monotonía*) monotonously, repetitively; (= *con pesadez*) tiresomely
machaconeo SM, **machaconería** SF (= *insistencia*) insistence; (= *monotonía*) monotony, repetitiveness
machada* SF [1] courageous act, heroic deed; (*pey*) piece of macho bravado; **fue una ~** it was a piece of macho bravado
[2] (= *dicho*) macho remark
machado SM hatchet
machamartillo SM ✦*MODISMO* **a ~: eran cristianos a ~** they were staunch Christians; **creer a ~** (= *firmemente*) to believe firmly; (= *ciegamente*) to believe blindly; **cumplir algo a ~** to carry out sth to the letter
machango ADJ (*Cono Sur*) tedious
machaque* SM dunk, slam dunk
machaquear ▸conjug 1a◂ VT, VI (*Méx*) = **machacar**
machaqueo SM crushing, pounding
machaquería SF (= *insistencia*) insistence; (= *monotonía*) monotony; (= *fastidio*) tiresomeness
macharse⁑ ▸conjug 1a◂ VPR (*Cono Sur*) to get drunk
machetazo SM (*esp LAm*) [1] (= *golpe*) blow with a machete
[2] (= *instrumento*) large machete
machete¹ SM machete
machete² ADJ mean, stingy
machetear ▸conjug 1a◂ Ⓐ VT (*LAm*) [1] [+ *caña*] to cut (*with a machete*)
[2] [+ *persona*] to slash (*with a machete*)
[3] (*Andes*) (= *vender barato*) to sell cheap
Ⓑ VI (*Méx*) [1] (= *obstinarse*) to keep on, persevere
[2] (= *trabajar*) to slog away, hammer away
machetero SM [1] (*esp LAm Agr*) cane cutter
[2] (*Méx*) (= *cargador*) porter, stevedore
[3] (*Méx**) (= *estudiante*) plodder*
[4] (*Caribe**) revolutionary; **~ de salón** armchair revolutionary
[5] (*Caribe*) (= *soldado*) soldier
machi SM (*Cono Sur*), **machí** SM (*Cono Sur*) medicine man
machiega SF (*tb* **abeja ~**) queen bee
machihembrado SM dovetail, dovetail joint
machihembrar ▸conjug 1a◂ VT to dovetail
machina SF [1] (*Mec*) (= *grúa*) crane, derrick; (= *mazo*) pile driver
[2] (*Caribe*) (= *tiovivo*) merry-go-round, carousel (*EEUU*)
machirulo* (*Esp*) Ⓐ ADJ [*niña*] tomboyish; [*mujer*] mannish, butch (* *pey*)
Ⓑ SM (= *niña*) tomboy; (= *mujer*) mannish woman, butch woman (* *pey*)
machismo SM [1] (*pey*) male chauvinism, machismo
[2] [*de hombre*] (= *orgullo*) male pride, maleness; (= *virilidad*) virility, masculinity
machista Ⓐ ADJ male chauvinist(ic), macho *antes de s*
Ⓑ SMF male chauvinist
machito¹ SM (*Méx*) fried offal
machito² SM ✦*MODISMO* **estar montado** *o* **subido en el ~** to be well placed, be riding high
macho Ⓐ ADJ [1] (*Biol*) male; **la flor ~** the male flower; **una rata ~** a male rat
[2] (*) (= *viril*) manly, brave; **mi niño es muy ~ y no llora** my kid is very manly *o* brave and doesn't cry; **se cree muy ~** he thinks he's very macho*
[3] (*Mec*) male
[4] (*Andes*) (= *fantástico*) splendid, terrific*
Ⓑ SM [1] (*Biol*) male ▸ **macho cabrío** he-goat, billy-goat
[2] (*) (= *hombretón*) macho man*, he-man*
[3] (*) (*uso apelativo*) mate*, buddy (*EEUU**); **vale, ~, no te enfades*** all right, mate, no need to get mad*
[4] (= *mulo*) mule ▸ **macho de varas** leading mule
[5] (*Mec*) male screw; ✦*MODISMO* **atarse** *o* **apretarse los ~s** to pluck up one's courage
[6] (*Elec*) male plug
[7] (*Cos*) hook
[8] (= *mazo*) sledgehammer
[9] (*Arquit*) buttress
[10] ✦*MODISMO* **parar el ~ a algn** (*LAm*) to take the wind out of sb's sails
[11] (*CAm Mil*) US marine
[12] (*Esp*†⁑) five peseta coin
machón SM buttress
machona* SF (*Andes, Caribe, Cono Sur*) (= *niña*) tomboy; (= *mujer*) mannish woman, butch woman (* *pey*)
machorra⁑ SF dyke⁑*, lesbian
machota SF [1] (*) (= *mujer*) mannish woman, butch woman (* *pey*)
[2] (= *mazo*) (*gen*) hammer, mallet; (*de apisonar*) tamper
[3] ✦*MODISMO* **a la ~** (*Andes, Caribe**) carelessly; (*CAm*) rudely, roughly
machote SM [1] (*) tough guy*, he-man*
[2] (*Méx*) (= *borrador*) rough draft, sketch; (= *modelo*) model
[3] (*Méx*) (= *impreso*) blank form
machucadura SF bruise
machucar ▸conjug 1g◂ VT [1] (= *aplastar*) to pound, crush; (= *golpear*) to beat; (= *abollar*) to dent; (= *dañar*) to knock about, damage
[2] (*Med*) to bruise
[3] (*Andes, Caribe, Méx*) [+ *caballo*] to tire out (*before a race*)
[4] (*Caribe*) [+ *ropa*] to rinse through
machucho ADJ [1] (= *mayor*) elderly, getting on in years
[2] (= *prudente*) prudent; (= *tranquilo*) sedate; (= *juicioso*) sensible
[3] (*Andes, Méx**) (= *taimado*) cunning, sly
machucón SM (*Méx*) bruise
macia SF mace
macicez SF (= *solidez*) massiveness, solidity; (= *gordura*) stoutness
macilento ADJ (= *pálido*) wan, pale; (= *demacrado*) haggard, gaunt
macillo SM (*Mús*) hammer
macis SF INV mace
maciza SF (*LAm*) chipboard, Masonite® (*EEUU*)
macizar ▸conjug 1f◂ VT to fill up, fill in, pack solid
macizo Ⓐ ADJ [1] (= *no hueco*) solid; **una mesa de roble ~** a solid oak table; **~ de gente** solid with people
[2] (= *fuerte*) [*objeto*] solidly made; [*persona*] stout, well-built
[3] (= *grande*) massive
[4] (*) (= *atractivo*) gorgeous*; **está maciza** she's gorgeous*
Ⓑ SM [1] (*Geog*) massif
[2] [*de plantas*] clump
[3] (*Arquit*) [*de pared*] stretch, section (*of a wall*); [*de edificios*] group
[4] (= *masa*) mass
[5] (*Aut*) solid tyre, solid tire (*EEUU*)
Ⓒ ADV (*CAm, Méx*) quickly, fast
macizorro⁑ ADJ [*hombre*] hunky*; [*mujer*] well-stacked*
maco⁑ SM [1] (= *cárcel*) nick*, prison
[2] (*Mil*) glasshouse
macollo SM bunch, cluster
macramé SM macramé
macro SF (*Inform*) macro
macró* SM (*Cono Sur*) pimp
macro... PREF macro...
macrobiótico ADJ macrobiotic
macrocefalia SF [1] (*Anat*) macrocephaly
[2] [*de administración, entidad*] top-heaviness
macrocefálico ADJ [1] (*Anat*) macrocephalic
[2] [*administración, entidad*] top-heavy
macrocomando SM (*Inform*) macro (command)
macroconcierto SM mega-gig*
macrocosmos SM INV, **macrocosmo** SM macrocosm
macroeconomía SF macroeconomics *sing*
macroeconómico ADJ macroeconomic
macroestructura SF macrostructure
macrófago SM macrophage
macrofotografía SF macrophotography
macrojuicio SM mega-trial
macromolecular ADJ macromolecular
macronivel SM macro level
macroproceso SM mega-trial
macroproyecto SM large-scale project
macuache* ADJ (*Méx*) rough, coarse
macuco* Ⓐ ADJ [1] (*Andes, Cono Sur*) (= *taimado*) crafty, cunning
[2] (*Andes*) (= *inútil*) old and useless
[3] (*Andes, Cono Sur*) (= *grande*) big; (= *demasiado grande*) overgrown
Ⓑ SM (*Andes, Cono Sur**) (= *grandullón*) overgrown boy, big lad
macuenco ADJ [1] (*Caribe**) (= *flaco*) thin, skinny; (= *débil*) weak, feeble
[2] (*Caribe*) (= *inútil*) useless
[3] (*Andes*) (= *demasiado grande*) big; (= *muy crecido*) overgrown, extra large; (*) (= *estupendo*) great*, fantastic*
mácula SF [1] (*liter*) (= *mancha*) blemish, stain; **sin ~** [*objeto*] immaculate; [*interpretación, actuación*] faultless; [*historial, pasado*] unblemished
[2] (*Anat*) blind spot
[3] (*Astron*) (*tb* **~ solar**) sunspot
[4] (= *trampa*) trick, fraud
macular ▸conjug 1a◂ VT to stain, spot
macundales SMPL (*Andes, Caribe*), **macundos** SMPL (*Caribe*) (= *trastos*) things, gear* *sing*, junk* *sing*; (= *negocios*) affairs, business *sing*
macutazo⁑ SM (= *rumor*) rumour, rumor (*EEUU*); (= *bulo*) hoax

macuto SM [1] (= *mochila*) [*de soldado*] backpack; [*de colegial*] satchel
[2] (*Caribe*) begging basket
Madagascar SM Madagascar
madalena SF (*Culin*) fairy cake
madaleno‡ SM secret policeman
madama SF (*LAm*), **madame** SF madam, brothel keeper
madeja (A) SF [*de lana*] skein, hank; [*de pelo*] tangle, mop; **una ~ de nervios** a bundle of nerves; ✦*MODISMOS* **desenredar la ~ de algo** to get to the bottom of sth; **se está enredando la ~** the plot thickens, things are getting complicated; **tirar de la ~** to put two and two together
(B) SMF (= *persona*) layabout, idler
madera¹ SF [1] (= *material*) (*gen*) wood; (*para la construcción, carpintería*) timber; **dame esa ~** give me that piece of wood; **una silla de ~** a wooden chair; **está hecho de ~** it's made of wood; **una escultura en ~** a wooden sculpture; ✦*MODISMO* **¡toca ~!** touch wood!, knock on wood! (*EEUU*) ► **madera contrachapada** plywood ► **madera de balsa** balsa wood ► **madera dura** hardwood ► **madera fósil** lignite ► **madera maciza** solid wood ► **madera (multi)laminada**, **madera terciada** plywood
[2] **tener ~ de algo** to have the makings of sth; **tiene ~ de futbolista** he's got the makings of a footballer
[3] (*Mús*) woodwind section (*of the orchestra*)
[4] (*Ftbl**) **la ~** the woodwork
[5] (*Zool*) *horny part of hoof*
madera² SM (= *vino*) Madeira
Madera SF Madeira
maderable ADJ timber-yielding
maderaje SM, **maderamen** SM (= *madera*) timber, lumber (*EEUU*), wood; (= *trabajo*) woodwork
maderero/a (A) SM/F timber merchant
(B) ADJ wood *antes de s*, timber *antes de s*; **industria maderera** timber industry; **productos ~s** wood products
maderismo SM (*Méx Pol*) *reform movement led by Madero*
maderista SMF (*Méx Pol*) supporter of Madero
madero SM [1] [*de construcción*] (= *tabla*) (piece of) timber; (= *viga*) beam; (= *tronco*) log
[2] (*Náut*) ship, vessel
[3] (*) (= *idiota*) blockhead*
[4] (*Esp*‡) (= *policía*) cop*, pig‡
Madona SF Madonna
madrastra SF stepmother
madraza SF doting mother, devoted mother
madrazo* SM (*Méx*) hard blow
madre (A) SF [1] (= *pariente*) mother; **ser ~** to be a mother; **futura ~** mother-to-be; **su señora ~** (*esp Méx*) your mother; **sin ~** motherless; **¡~ mía!** good heavens! ► **madre adoptiva** adoptive mother ► **madre biológica** biological mother ► **madre de alquiler** surrogate mother ► **madre de Dios** Mother of God; **¡~ de Dios!** good heavens! ► **madre de familia** mother ► **madre genética** biological mother ► **madre nodriza** surrogate mother ► **la Madre Patria** the Mother Country, the Old Country ► **madre política** mother-in-law ► **madre soltera** single mother, unmarried mother ► **madre trabajadora** working mother
[2] (*Rel*) (*en convento*) mother; (*en asilo*) matron ► **madre superiora** Mother Superior
[3] ✦*MODISMOS* **como su ~ lo echó al mundo** *o* **lo parió*** in his birthday suit*, starkers*; **ni ~*** not a dicky bird*, not a sausage*; **ciento y la ~*** hundreds of people; **ahí está la ~ del cordero*** that's just the trouble, that's the crux of the matter; **darle a algn en la ~** (*Méx**) to wallop sb*, thump sb; **mentarle la ~ a algn** to insult sb (*violently*); **¡(me cago en) la ~ que te parió!**‡‡ fuck off!‡‡; **no tener ~: él no tiene ~*** he's a real swine*; **esto no tiene ~*** this is the limit; **a toda ~** ◊ **de la ~** (*LAm*‡) great*, fantastic*; **¡tu ~!**‡‡ up yours!‡‡, get stuffed!‡‡; *ver tb* **puto A**
[4] (= *origen*) origin, cradle
[5] [*de río*] bed; **salirse de ~** [*río*] to burst its banks; [*persona*] to lose all self-control; [*proceso*] to go beyond its normal limits; ✦*MODISMO* **sacar de ~ a algn** to upset sb
[6] [*de vino*] dregs *pl*, sediment
[7] (*Agr*) (= *acequia*) main channel, main irrigation ditch; (= *alcantarilla*) main sewer
[8] (*en juegos*) home
[9] (*Anat*) womb
[10] (*Andes*) dead skin, scab
[11] (‡) queer‡, fag (*EEUU*‡)
(B) ADJ [1] (= *de origen*) **acequia ~** main channel; **alcantarilla ~** main sewer; **buque ~** mother ship; **lengua ~** (*Ling*) parent language
[2] **color ~** dominant colour; **la cuestión ~** the chief problem, the central problem
[3] (*LAm**) **una regañada ~** a real telling-off*, one hell of a telling-off‡
madrejón SM (*Cono Sur*) watercourse
madreperla SF (= *nácar*) mother-of-pearl; (= *ostra*) pearl oyster ► **madreperla de río** freshwater mussel
madreselva SF honeysuckle ► **madreselva siempreverde** Cape honeysuckle
Madrid SM Madrid
madridista (A) ADJ *of or relating to Real Madrid football club*
(B) SMF (= *jugador*) Real Madrid player; (= *hincha*) Real Madrid supporter; **los ~s** Real Madrid
madrigal SM madrigal
madriguera SF [1] (= *refugio*) [*de animales*] den, burrow; [*de conejos*] warren; [*de tejones*] set
[2] [*de ladrones*] den
madrileño/a (A) ADJ of/from Madrid; **la madrileña calle de Alcalá** (= *de Madrid*) Alcalá Street in Madrid; (= *representativa de Madrid*) Alcalá Street, the archetypical Madrid street; **la madrileñísima Cibeles** Cibeles Square which is so typical of Madrid
(B) SM/F native/inhabitant of Madrid; **los ~s** the people of Madrid
Madriles* SMPL **los ~** Madrid
madrina SF [1] [*de bautizo*] godmother; [*de boda*] ≈ matron of honour; [*de asociación, inauguración*] patron, patroness; *ver tb* **hada**
[2] (*Arquit*) prop, shore
[3] (*Téc*) brace
[4] (*Agr*) lead mare
[5] (*LAm*) (= *animal*) tame animal (*used in breaking in or catching others*)
[6] (*Méx**) police informer
madriza‡ SF (*Méx*) bashing*, beating-up*
madroño SM [1] (*Bot*) strawberry tree, arbutus
[2] (= *borla*) tassel
madrugada SF (= *noche*) early morning, small hours *pl*; (= *alba*) dawn, daybreak; **de ~** in the small hours; **levantarse de ~** to get up early *o* at the crack of dawn; **a las cuatro de la ~** at four o'clock in the morning, at four a.m.
madrugador(a) (A) ADJ **ser ~** to be an early riser
(B) SM/F early riser
madrugar ▸conjug 1h◂ (A) VI [1] (= *levantarse temprano*) (*una vez*) to get up early, get up at the crack of dawn; (*por costumbre*) to be an early riser; ✦*REFRANES* **a quien madruga, Dios le ayuda** the early bird catches the worm; **no por mucho ~ amanece más temprano** time will take its course
[2] (= *anticiparse*) to be quick off the mark
[3] (= *precipitarse*) to jump the gun
(B) VT **~ a algn** (= *adelantarse*) to get in ahead of sb; (*CAm*) (= *matar*) to bump sb off*
madrugón SM **darse** *o* **pegarse un ~** to get up really early *o* at the crack of dawn
maduración SF [*de fruta*] ripening; [*de persona, idea*] maturing
madurar ▸conjug 1a◂ (A) VI [1] [*fruta*] to ripen
[2] [*persona*] to mature
[3] [*idea, plan*] to mature
(B) VT [1] [+ *fruta*] to ripen
[2] [+ *persona*] (= *hacer mayor*) to mature; (= *hacer fuerte*) to toughen, toughen up
[3] [+ *idea, plan*] to think out
(C) **madurarse** VPR to ripen
madurez SF [1] [*de fruta*] ripeness
[2] [*de carácter, edad*] maturity; **revela una ~ nada frecuente en una primera novela** she shows a rare maturity for a first novel
maduro (A) ADJ [1] [*fruta*] ripe; **poco ~** underripe
[2] [*persona, carácter*] mature; **de edad madura** middle-aged; **el clima no está ~ para esas negociaciones** the climate is not ripe for such negotiations; ✦*MODISMO* **el divieso está ~** the boil is about to burst
(B) SM (*Col*) plantain
MAE SM ABR (*Esp Pol*) = **Ministerio de Asuntos Exteriores**
maesa SF queen bee
maestra SF [1] (= *abeja*) queen bee
[2] (*Arquit*) guide line; *ver tb* **maestro**
maestranza SF [1] (*Mil*) arsenal, armoury, armory (*EEUU*)
[2] (*Náut*) naval dockyard
[3] (= *personal*) *staff of an arsenal/a dockyard*
[4] (*LAm*) machine shop
maestrazgo SM (*Hist*) office of grand master
maestre SM (*Hist*) grand master (*of a military order*)
maestrear ▸conjug 1a◂ VT [1] (= *dirigir*) to direct, manage
[2] (*Agr*) to prune
maestría SF [1] [*de persona*] (= *dominio*) mastery; (= *habilidad*) skill, expertise
[2] (*LAm Univ*) master's degree
[3] (*Esp Educ*) *vocational qualification*
maestro/a (A) SM/F [1] (= *profesor*) teacher; **mi tía es maestra** my aunt's a teacher ► **maestro/a de escuela** schoolteacher
[2] (*en un arte, un oficio*) master ► **maestro/a albañil** master mason ► **maestro/a de armas** fencing master ► **maestro/a de ceremonias** master of ceremonies ► **maestro/a**

de cocina head chef ► **maestro/a de esgrima** fencing master ► **maestro/a de obras** foreman ► **maestro sastre** master tailor
Ⓑ SM [1] (= *autoridad*) authority; **el ~ de todos los medievalistas españoles** the greatest authority among the Spanish medievalists, the doyen of Spanish medievalists; **beber en los grandes ~s** to absorb wisdom from the great teachers
[2] (*esp LAm*) (= *oficial*) skilled workman, craftsman ► **maestro de caminos** skilled road-construction man
[3] (*Mús*) maestro; **el ~ Falla** the great musician *o* composer Falla; **¡música, ~!** music, maestro!; **"Los ~s cantores"** "The Mastersingers" ► **maestro de coros** choirmaster
[4] (*Ajedrez*) master; **Kasparov, uno de los grandes ~s** Kasparov, one of the grand masters
Ⓒ ADJ [1] (*Téc*) (= *principal*) main; **cloaca maestra** main sewer; **llave maestra** master key, pass key; **plan ~** master plan; **viga maestra** main beam; *ver tb* **obra 2.2**
[2] (*Zool*) [*animal*] trained; **halcón ~** trained hawk; *ver tb* **abeja, maestra**

mafafa SF (*LAm*) marijuana

mafia SF mafia; **la Mafia** the Mafia; **ese departamento es una ~*** that department is very cliquey* *o* is a bit of a mafia

mafioso/a Ⓐ ADJ Mafia *antes de s*
Ⓑ SM/F (= *de la Mafia*) mafioso, member of the Mafia; (= *criminal*) gangster, mobster (*EEUU*)

Magallanes SM **Estrecho de ~** Magellan Strait

magancear ▸conjug 1a◂ VI (*Andes, Cono Sur*) to idle, laze around

maganto ADJ [1] (= *macilento*) wan, wasted
[2] (= *preocupado*) worried
[3] (= *soso*) lifeless, dull

maganza* SF (*Andes*) idleness, laziness

maganzón/ona* SM/F (*LAm*) lazy person, idler

maganzonería* SF (*LAm*) = **maganza**

magazine SM (*TV*) magazine

Magdalena SF Magdalen, Madeleine; **La ~** Mary Magdalene; ✦**MODISMO llorar como una ~** to cry one's eyes out

magdalena SF (*Culin*) fairy cake

magenta SF magenta

magia SF magic; **la ~ de su música** the magic of his music; **por arte de ~** (as if) by magic ► **magia blanca** white magic ► **magia negra** black magic

magiar ADJ, SMF Magyar

mágico Ⓐ ADJ [1] (= *con poderes*) [*alfombra, varita, fórmula, palabras*] magic; [*poderes, propiedades*] magical
[2] (= *especial*) [*momentos, cualidad*] magical; **fue una noche mágica** it was a magical evening
Ⓑ SM magician

magín* SM (= *fantasía*) imagination; (= *mente*) mind; **darle al ~** to have a think; **me vienen al ~ un par de frases** a couple of phrases come to mind; **todo eso salió de su ~** it all came out of his own head

magisterio SM [1] (= *enseñanza*) teaching; (= *profesión*) teaching, teaching profession; (= *formación*) teacher training, teacher education (*EEUU*); (= *maestros*) teachers *pl*; **dedicarse al ~** to go in for teaching; **ejerció el ~ durante 40 años** she taught *o* was a teacher for 40 years
[2] **Magisterio** (*CAm Univ*) Department of Education
[3] (= *maestría*) mastery
[4] (= *pedantería*) pompousness, pedantry

magistrado/a SM/F [1] (*Jur*) magistrate, judge
[2] (*LAm Pol*) **Primer Magistrado** head of state, President

magistral Ⓐ ADJ [1] (= *genial*) [*actuación, obra*] masterly; **cantó el aria de forma ~** she gave a masterly rendition of the aria
[2] [*actitud, tono*] (*gen*) magisterial; (*pey*) pompous, pedantic
Ⓑ SM (*tb* **reloj ~**) master clock

magistratura SF (= *cargo*) magistracy, judgeship; (= *jueces*) judges *pl*, magistracy; **alta ~** highest authority ► **Magistratura de trabajo** industrial tribunal

magma SM magma

magnánimamente ADV magnanimously

magnanimidad SF magnanimity

magnánimo ADJ magnanimous

magnate SMF tycoon, magnate; **un ~ de la prensa** a press baron; **los ~s de la industria** industrial magnates

magnavoz SM (*Méx*) loudspeaker, loudhailer

magnesia SF magnesia; ✦**MODISMO confundir la gimnasia con la ~** to confuse two totally different things

magnesio SM [1] (*Quím*) magnesium
[2] (*Fot*) flash, flashlight

magnéticamente ADV magnetically

magnético ADJ (*lit, fig*) magnetic

magnetismo SM (*lit, fig*) magnetism ► **magnetismo animal** animal magnetism

magnetizable ADJ magnetizable

magnetizar ▸conjug 1f◂ VT to magnetize

magneto SF magneto

magnetofón SM, **magnetófono** SM tape recorder ► **magnetófono de bolsillo** personal stereo ► **magnetófono de cinta abierta** reel-to-reel tape recorder

magnetofónico ADJ **cinta magnetofónica** recording tape; **grabado en cinta magnetofónica** tape-recorded

magnetómetro SM magnetometer

magnetoscopio SM video recorder

magnetosfera SF magnetosphere

magnetoterapia SF magnetic therapy

magnicida SMF assassin (*of an important person*)

magnicidio SM assassination (*of an important person*)

magníficamente ADV magnificently, splendidly

magnificar ▸conjug 1g◂ VT [1] (= *exagerar*) to exaggerate, blow up out of all proportion
[2] (= *alabar*) to praise, extol

magnificencia SF [1] (= *grandeza*) magnificence, splendour, splendor (*EEUU*)
[2] (= *generosidad*) generosity

magnífico ADJ magnificent, wonderful; **es un jugador ~** he's a magnificent *o* wonderful player; **tenemos un ~ profesor** we have a magnificent *o* wonderful teacher; **Ortega estuvo ~** Ortega was magnificent; **¡magnífico!** excellent!, splendid!; **rector ~** (*Esp Univ*) honourable Chancellor, honorable Chancellor (*EEUU*)

magnitud SF magnitude; **de primera ~** (*Astron*) first-magnitude; (*fig*) first-rate *antes de s*, of the first order; **un problema de gran ~** a major problem

magno ADJ (*liter*) great; *ver tb* **Alejandro, aula, carta 3**

magnolia SF magnolia

mago/a SM/F [1] (= *prestidigitador*) magician
[2] (*en cuentos*) magician, wizard/sorceress; **el Mago de Oz** the Wizard of Oz; **los Reyes Magos** the Three Wise Men, the Magi (*frm*); **es un ~ de las finanzas** he's a financial wizard

magra SF [1] [*de carne*] lean part
[2] (= *loncha*) (*gen*) slice; [*de beicon*] rasher
[3] **¡magra!‡** rubbish!*, not on your nelly!*
[4] (*Esp*) (= *casa*) house

magrear‡ ▸conjug 1a◂ VT (*Esp*) to touch up*, grope*

Magreb SM Maghreb

magrebí ADJ, SMF Maghrebi

magreo‡ SM (*Esp*) touching up*, groping*

magrez SF leanness

magro Ⓐ ADJ [1] (= *sin grasa*) [*carne*] lean; [*porción*] meagre, meager (*EEUU*)
[2] [*persona*] lean
[3] [*resultado*] poor; [*sueldo*] meagre, meager (*EEUU*)
[4] [*tierra*] poor
Ⓑ SM loin

magrura SF leanness

magua SF (*Caribe*) disappointment; (= *fracaso*) failure; (= *revés*) setback

maguarse* ▸conjug 1i◂ VPR (*Caribe*) [1] [*fiesta*] to be a failure, be spoiled
[2] [*persona*] (= *decepcionarse*) to be disappointed; (= *deprimirse*) to get depressed

maguer (*liter*) Ⓐ PREP in spite of, despite
Ⓑ CONJ although

maguey SM maguey

maguillo SM wild apple tree

magulladura SF bruise

magullamiento SM bruising

magullar ▸conjug 1a◂ Ⓐ VT (= *amoratar*) to bruise; (= *dañar*) to hurt, damage; (= *golpear*) to batter, bash*; (*Andes, Caribe*) to crumple, rumple Ⓑ **magullarse** VPR (= *hacerse un moratón*) to get bruised; (= *hacerse daño*) to get hurt

magullón SM (*LAm*) bruise

Maguncia SF Mainz

maharajá SM maharajah; ✦**MODISMO vivir como un ~** to live like a prince

mahdi SM Mahdi

Mahoma SM Mohammed, Mahomet

mahometano/a ADJ, SM/F Muslim

mahometismo SM Islam

mahonesa SF mayonnaise

mai‡ SM joint‡

maicena® SF cornflour, cornstarch (*EEUU*)

maicero ADJ maize *antes de s*, corn *antes de s* (*EEUU*)

maicillo SM (*Chile*) gravel, road gravel

mail* SM e-mail

mailing ['mailin] SM (*pl* **mailings** ['mailin]) mailshot; **hacer un ~** to do a mailshot ► **mailing electoral** postal canvassing

maillot [ma'jot] SM (*Dep*) jersey; **el ~ amarillo** the yellow jersey

maitines SMPL matins

maître ['metre] SM head waiter

maíz SM maize, corn (*EEUU*), sweetcorn; **~ en la mazorca** corn on the cob; ✦*MODISMOS* **coger a algn asando ~** (*Caribe*) to catch sb red-handed; **dar a algn ~ tostado** (*Andes*) to give sb their comeuppance

maizal SM maize field, cornfield (*EEUU*)

maizena® SF cornflour, cornstarch (*EEUU*)

maizudo ADJ (*CAm*) rich, wealthy

maja SF pestle; *ver tb* **majo**

majada SF [1] (= *corral*) sheep pen
[2] (= *estiércol*) dung
[3] (*Cono Sur*) [*de ovejas*] flock; [*de cabras*] herd

majaderear ▸conjug 1a◂ VT (*LAm*) to annoy

majadería SF [1] (= *cualidad*) (= *tontería*) silliness; (= *sinsentido*) absurdity
[2] **una ~** a silly thing, an absurdity; **majaderías** nonsense *sing*; **decir ~s** to talk nonsense; **hacer ~s** to be silly

majadero/a Ⓐ ADJ (= *tonto*) silly, stupid
Ⓑ SM/F (= *tonto*) idiot, fool; **¡majadero!** you idiot!
Ⓒ SM [1] (*Téc*) pestle
[2] (*Cos*) bobbin

majador SM pestle

majagranzas†* SMF INV = **majadero**

majagua SF (*Caribe*) [1] (*Dep*) baseball bat
[2] (*) (= *traje*) suit

majar ▸conjug 1a◂ VT [1] (= *aplastar*) to pound, crush; (*Med*) to bruise
[2] (*) (= *molestar*) to bother, pester

majara‡, majareta‡ Ⓐ ADJ nuts*, crackers*; **estás ~** you're nuts *o* crackers*
Ⓑ SMF nutter*

maje Ⓐ ADJ (*Méx‡*) gullible; **hacer ~ al marido** to cheat on one's husband
Ⓑ SMF (*Méx‡*) sucker‡
Ⓒ SM (*CAm**) bloke*, guy*

majestad SF majesty; **Su Majestad** His/Her Majesty; **(Vuestra) Majestad** Your Majesty

majestuosamente ADV majestically

majestuosidad SF majesty

majestuoso ADJ majestic

majete* Ⓐ ADJ nice
Ⓑ SM guy*, bloke*; **tranquilo, ~** relax, man*

majeza SF [1] (= *atractivo*) good looks *pl*, attractiveness
[2] (= *belleza*) loveliness
[3] (= *elegancia*) smartness; (*pey*) flashiness

majo/a Ⓐ ADJ (*Esp*) [1] [*persona*] (= *agradable*) nice; (= *guapo*) attractive, good-looking
[2] [*cosa*] nice; **¡qué blusa tan maja!** what a nice blouse!
[3] (*uso apelativo*) **¡hola maja! ¿qué tal te va?** hello, love! how's things?; **oye, majo, haz el favor de callarte** do me a favour, will you just shut up?
Ⓑ SM/F (*Hist*) *inhabitant of the working-class neighbourhoods of Madrid in the 18th and 19th centuries*; *ver tb* **maja**

majong [ma'xon] SM mahjong

majuela SF haw, hawthorn berry

majuelo SM [1] (= *vid*) young vine
[2] (= *espino*) hawthorn

mal Ⓐ ADV [1] (= *imperfectamente*) badly; **el negocio les va ~** their business is doing badly; **está muy ~ escrito** it's very badly written; **han escrito ~ mi apellido** they've spelt my surname wrong; **me entendió ~** he misunderstood me; **creo que me expliqué ~** I don't think I explained what I meant properly; **oigo/veo ~** I can't hear/see well; **lo hice lo menos ~ que pude** I did it as well as I could; **si ~ no recuerdo** if my memory serves me right, if I remember correctly; **~ puedo hablar yo de este asunto** I'm hardly the right person to talk to about this
[2] (= *reprobablemente*) **se portó muy ~ con su mejor amiga** she behaved very badly towards her best friend; **hacer ~**: **hace ~ en mentir** he is wrong to lie
[3] (= *insuficientemente*) poorly; **la habitación estaba ~ iluminada** the room was poorly lit; **este disco se vendió muy ~** this record sold very poorly, this record had very poor sales; **sus hijos estaban ~ alimentados** her children were underfed; **un trabajo ~ pagado** a badly paid job; **comer ~**: **en este restaurante se come ~** the food isn't very good in this restaurant; **la niña come ~** the girl isn't eating properly, the girl is off her food; **por falta de dinero comemos ~** we aren't able to eat properly because we don't have enough money
[4] (= *sin salud*) ill; **su padre está bastante ~** her father's pretty ill; **encontrarse** *o* **sentirse ~** to feel ill
[5] (= *desagradablemente*) **lo pasé muy ~ en la fiesta** I had a very bad time at the party; **les fue muy ~ en Inglaterra** things went very badly for them in England; **¡no está ~ este vino!** this wine isn't bad!; **no estaría ~ ir mañana de excursión** I wouldn't mind going on a trip tomorrow; **caer ~ algn**: **me cae ~ su amigo** I don't like his friend; **decir** *o* **hablar ~ de algn** to speak ill of sb; **llevarse ~**: **me llevo ~ con él** I don't get on with him; **los dos hermanos se llevan muy ~** the two brothers don't get on at all; **oler ~**: **esta habitación huele ~** this room smells (bad); **pensar ~ de algn** to think badly of sb; **saber ~**: **sabe ~** it doesn't taste nice
[6] (*otras locuciones*) **estar a ~ con algn** to be on bad terms with sb; **¡menos ~!** thank goodness!; **menos ~ que …** it's just as well (that) …, it's a good job (that) …; **ir de ~ en peor** to go from bad to worse; **~ que bien** more or less, just about; **~ que bien lo hemos solucionado** we've more or less *o* just about managed to solve it; **~ que bien vamos tirando** we're just about managing to get by; **tomarse algo (a) ~** to take sth the wrong way
Ⓑ CONJ **~ que le pese** whether he likes it or not
Ⓒ ADJ *ver* **malo A**
Ⓓ SM [1] (= *maldad*) **el ~** evil; **el bien y el ~** good and evil; **caer en el ~** to fall into evil ways; **combatir el ~** (*frm*) to fight against evil; **echar algo a ~** to despise sth
[2] (= *perjuicio*) harm; **no le deseo ningún ~** I don't wish him any harm *o* ill; **hacer ~ a algn** to do sb harm; **el ~ ya está hecho** the harm *o* damage is done now; **no hay ningún ~** there's no harm done; **¡~ haya quien …!** (*frm*) a curse on whoever …!; **dar ~ a algn** to make sb suffer; **darse ~** to torment o.s.; **un ~ menor** the lesser of two evils; **rebajamos los precios, como ~ menor** we cut the prices, as the lesser of two evils; **esa solución no me satisface, pero es un ~ menor** I'm not happy with that solution, but it could have been worse; **parar en ~** to come to a bad end; ✦*REFRANES* **no hay ~ que por bien no venga** it's an ill wind that blows nobody any good; **~ de muchos consuelo de tontos** that's no consolation
[3] (= *problema*) ill; **los ~es de la economía** the ills afflicting the economy
[4] (*Med*) disease, illness ► **mal caduco** epilepsy ► **mal de altura** altitude sickness ► **mal de amores** lovesickness; **sufre ~ de amores** she's lovesick ► **mal de Chagas** Chagas' disease ► **mal de la tierra** homesickness ► **mal de mar** seasickness ► **mal francés** (*Hist*) syphilis
[5] ► **mal de ojo** evil eye; **le echaron el ~ de ojo** they gave him the evil eye
[6] (*LAm Med*) epileptic fit

mala¹ SF bad luck

mala² SF (= *saco*) mailbag; (= *correo*) mail, post

malabar ADJ **juegos ~es** juggling *sing*

malabarismo SM [1] (= *juegos malabares*) juggling
[2] **malabarismos** (= *complicaciones*) juggling *sing*, balancing act *sing*; **hacer ~s** (*lit*) to juggle; (*fig*) to do a balancing act

malabarista SMF juggler

malacate SM [1] (= *torno*) winch, capstan
[2] (*CAm*) (= *huso*) spindle

malaconsejado ADJ ill-advised

malaconsejar ▸conjug 1a◂ VT to give bad advice to

malacostumbrado ADJ [1] (= *de malos hábitos*) given to bad habits
[2] (= *consentido*) spoiled, pampered

malacostumbrar ▸conjug 1a◂ VT **~ a algn** (*gen*) to get sb into bad habits; (= *consentir*) to spoil sb

malacrianza SF (*LAm*) rudeness

Málaga SF Malaga

malage SM = **malaje**

malagradecido ADJ ungrateful

malagueño/a Ⓐ ADJ of/from Málaga
Ⓑ SM/F native/inhabitant of Málaga; **los ~s** the people of Málaga

Malaisia SF Malaysia

malaisio/a ADJ, SM/F Malaysian

malaje* SM [1] (= *mala sombra*) malign influence; (= *mala suerte*) bad luck; **soy un ~** I'm bad luck
[2] (= *sosería*) dullness, lifelessness; (= *falta de encanto*) lack of charm
[3] (= *malévolo*) nasty piece of work*; (= *soso*) bore, pain*

malaleche* Ⓐ ADJ nasty, horrible
Ⓑ SMF nasty person

malamente ADV [1] (*) (= *mal*) badly; **el asunto acabó ~** the affair ended badly; **estar ~ de dinero** to be badly off for money
[2] (= *difícilmente*) **~ podrán vencer** they have little chance of winning; **en el sofá ~ caben dos personas** the sofa is only just big enough for two people; **tenemos gasolina ~ para …** we barely *o* hardly have enough petrol to …

malandante ADJ unfortunate

malandanza SF misfortune

malandrín/ina SM/F (*hum*) scoundrel, rogue

malandro‡ SM (*Caribe*) scrounger*

malanga Ⓐ ADJ (*Caribe**) thick*
Ⓑ SF (*Caribe, Méx*) *tuber resembling a sweet potato*

malapata* SMF (= *patoso*) clumsy thing; (= *aburrido*) bore; (= *pesado*) pest, nuisance

malapropismo SM malapropism

malaria SF malaria

Malasia SF Malaysia

malasio/a ADJ, SM/F Malaysian

malasombra* SMF = **malapata**

Malaui SM, **Malawi** SM Malawi

malauiano/a ADJ, SM/F Malawian

malaúva* Ⓐ ADJ mean, miserable
Ⓑ SMF miserable creature, miserable sod**

malavenido ADJ **estar ~s** to be in disagreement *o* in conflict; **una pareja malavenida** an unsuited *o* incompatible couple

malaventura SF misfortune

malaventurado ADJ unfortunate

Malaya SF Malaya

malaya SF (*Chile*) steak

malayo/a Ⓐ ADJ Malay, Malayan
Ⓑ SM/F Malay
Ⓒ SM (*Ling*) Malay

Malaysia SF Malaysia

malbaratar ▸conjug 1a◂ VT (= *malvender*) to sell off cheap, sell at a loss; (= *malgastar*) to squander

malcarado ADJ (= *feo*) ugly; (= *enfadado*) grim-faced

malcasado ADJ (= *infeliz*) unhappily married; (= *infiel*) errant, unfaithful

malcasarse ▸conjug 1a◂ VPR to make an unhappy marriage

malcomer ▸conjug 2a◂ VI to eat badly

malcontento/a Ⓐ ADJ discontented
Ⓑ SM/F malcontent

malcriadez SF (*LAm*) bad manners *pl*, rudeness

malcriado ADJ (= *grosero*) bad-mannered, rude; (= *consentido*) spoiled, pampered

malcriar ▸conjug 1c◂ VT to spoil, pamper

maldad SF 1 (= *cualidad*) evil, wickedness
2 **una ~** a wicked thing

maldecir ▸conjug 3o◂ Ⓐ VT 1 (*con maldición*) to curse; **maldecía mi mala suerte** I cursed my bad luck
2 (= *odiar*) to loathe, detest
Ⓑ VI to curse; **~ de algn/algo** (= *hablar mal*) to speak ill of sb/sth; (= *quejarse*) to complain bitterly about sb/sth

maldiciendo *etc ver* **maldecir**

maldiciente Ⓐ ADJ (= *quejoso*) grumbling; (= *grosero*) foul-mouthed
Ⓑ SMF (= *quejoso*) grumbler; (= *descontento*) malcontent; (= *difamador*) slanderer

maldición SF curse; **la ~ de la bruja** the witch's curse; **¡maldición!** damn!, curse it!; **parece que ha caído una ~ sobre este programa** this programme seems to be cursed

maldiga *etc ver* **maldecir**

maldispuesto ADJ 1 (= *enfermo*) ill, indisposed
2 (*contra alguien*) ill-disposed

maldita SF 1 (= *lengua*) tongue; ✦**MODISMO soltar la ~** (= *hablar mucho*) to talk too much; (= *enojarse*) to explode, blow up
2 (*Caribe*) (= *llaga*) sore, swelling; (= *picadura*) insect bite

malditismo SM aura of doom

maldito Ⓐ ADJ 1 (= *condenado*) damned; **poeta ~** accursed poet
2 (*Rel*) accursed
3 (*) (*uso enfático*) damn*; **¡maldita sea!** damn it!*; **ese ~ libro** that damn book*; **ese ~ niño** that wretched child; **¡~ el día en que lo conocí!** curse the day I met him!; **¡malditas las ganas que tengo de verle!** I really don't feel like seeing him!; **no le encuentro maldita la gracia** I don't see what's so damn funny*; **no entiende maldita la cosa** he doesn't understand a damn thing*; **no le hace ~ (el) caso** he doesn't take a blind bit of notice; **~ lo que me importa** I don't give a damn*
4 (= *maligno*) wicked
5 (*Méx**) (= *taimado*) crafty
Ⓑ SM **el ~** (*Rel*) the Evil One, the devil

maldormir ▸conjug 3j◂ VI to sleep badly, sleep in fits and starts

maleabilidad SF malleability

maleable ADJ malleable

maleado ADJ (*LAm*) corrupt

maleante Ⓐ SMF (= *malhechor*) crook, villain; (= *vago*) vagrant
Ⓑ ADJ (= *malo*) wicked; (= *pícaro*) villainous; (= *indeseable*) unsavoury, unsavory (*EEUU*)

malear ▸conjug 1a◂ Ⓐ VT 1 (= *corromper*) to corrupt, pervert
2 (= *dañar*) to damage, harm
3 [+ *tierra*] to sour
Ⓑ **malearse** VPR 1 (= *corromperse*) to be corrupted
2 (= *dañarse*) to spoil, be harmed

malecón SM pier, jetty

maledicencia SF slander, scandal

maledicente ADJ slanderous, scandalous

maleducado ADJ bad-mannered, rude

maleducar ▸conjug 1g◂ VT to spoil

maleficiar ▸conjug 1b◂ VT 1 (= *hechizar*) to bewitch, cast an evil spell on
2 (= *dañar*) to harm, damage

maleficio SM 1 (= *hechizo*) curse, spell
2 (= *brujería*) witchcraft

maléfico ADJ evil

malejo* ADJ rather bad, pretty bad

malencarado ADJ sour-faced

malentendido SM misunderstanding

malestar SM 1 (= *incomodidad*) discomfort; **uno de los síntomas es un ~ generalizado** one of the symptoms is a general feeling of discomfort; **sentía un ligero ~** he felt slightly unwell; **el medicamento le produjo ~ en el estómago** the medicine upset his stomach
2 (= *inquietud*) unease; **enseguida adivinó su ~** he immediately sensed her unease; **su conducta le causó un profundo ~** his behaviour disturbed her deeply
3 (= *descontento*) discontent; **las nuevas medidas han causado ~ entre la población** the new measures have aroused discontent among the population

maleta[1] Ⓐ SF 1 (*para equipaje*) case, suitcase; **fuimos a retirar nuestras ~s de la consigna** we went to get our luggage from the left-luggage office; **hacer la(s) ~(s)** (*lit*) to pack; (*fig*) to pack one's bags; **ya puede ir preparando las ~s** he's on his way out, he can start packing his bags
2 (*Aut*) boot, trunk (*EEUU*)
3 (*Cono Sur*) [*de caballo*] saddlebag
4 (*CAm*) (= *fajo de ropa*) bundle of clothes
5 (*Andes, Caribe*) (= *joroba*) hump
Ⓑ SMF 1 (*) (= *persona inepta*) (*gen*) dead loss*; (*Taur*) clumsy beginner; (*Dep*) useless player
2 (*LAm*) (= *vago*) lazy person, idler

maleta[2] ADJ 1 (*LAm*) (= *travieso*) naughty, mischievous; (= *malo*) wicked
2 (*Andes, Cono Sur*) (= *tonto*) stupid; (= *inútil*) useless
3 (*Cono Sur*) (= *astuto*) sly
4 (*LAm*) (= *vago*) lazy
5 (*CAm, Méx*) (= *torpe*) ham-fisted

maletazo SM bump (*with a suitcase*)

maletera SF 1 (*LAm Aut*) boot, trunk (*EEUU*)
2 (*Andes, Méx*) [*de caballo*] saddlebag
3 (*Cono Sur*) (= *cortabolsas*) pickpocket

maletero SM 1 (*Aut*) boot, trunk (*EEUU*)
2 (= *mozo*) porter
3 (*Cono Sur*) (= *ladrón*) pickpocket

maletilla SMF (*Taur*) *aspiring bullfighter*

maletín SM (= *maleta*) small case; (= *portafolios*) briefcase, attaché case; [*de colegial*] satchel; [*de médico*] bag ► **maletín de excursiones** picnic case ► **maletín de grupa** saddlebag ► **maletín de viaje** travel bag

maletón ADJ (*Andes*) hunchbacked

maletudo/a (*Andes, Caribe*) Ⓐ ADJ hunchbacked
Ⓑ SM/F hunchback

malevo/a SM/F (*Cono Sur*) malefactor

malevolencia SF malevolence, spite; **por ~** out of spite; **sin ~ para nadie** without meaning to offend anyone

malévolo ADJ, **malevolente** ADJ malevolent, malicious

maleza SF 1 (= *malas hierbas*) weeds *pl*
2 (= *espesura*) [*de matas*] undergrowth; [*de zarza*] thicket; [*de broza*] brushwood; **fueron abriéndose camino entre la ~** they gradually beat a path through the undergrowth
3 (*Cono Sur*) (= *pus*) pus
4 (*CAm*) (= *enfermedad*) sickness, illness

malezal SM 1 (*Caribe, Cono Sur*) (= *hierbas*) mass of weeds
2 (*Cono Sur Med*) pus

malfamado ADJ notorious

malformación SF malformation

malformado ADJ malformed

Malgache SM Malagasy

malgache ADJ, SMF Madagascan

malgastador(a) Ⓐ ADJ spendthrift *antes de s*, wasteful
Ⓑ SM/F spendthrift

malgastar ▸conjug 1a◂ VT [+ *tiempo, esfuerzo*] to waste; [+ *recursos, dinero*] to squander, waste; [+ *salud*] to ruin

malgeniado ADJ (*LAm*), **malgenioso** ADJ (*LAm*) bad-tempered

malhabido ADJ [*ganancia*] ill-gotten

malhablado/a Ⓐ ADJ foul-mouthed
Ⓑ SM/F **es un ~** he has a foul mouth (on him), he's so foul-mouthed

malhadado ADJ ill-fated, ill-starred

malhaya EXCL (*LAm*) damn!; **¡~ sea!** damn him!*

malhecho Ⓐ ADJ (*) ugly, misshapen
Ⓑ SM misdeed

malhechor(a) SM/F delinquent, criminal; **banda de ~es** bunch of delinquents

malherido ADJ badly injured, seriously injured

malhumorado ADJ bad-tempered

mali** SM joint**

malicia SF [1] (= *mala intención*) malice, spite; **lo dije sin ~** I said it without malice
[2] (= *picardía*) [*de persona*] mischief; [*de mirada*] mischievousness; [*de chiste*] naughtiness; **sonrió con ~** she smiled mischievously; **contó un chiste con mucha ~** he told a very naughty joke
[3] (= *astucia*) slyness, guile; **el niño tiene demasiada ~ para su edad** that child is too knowing for his age
[4] **malicias** (= *sospechas*) suspicions; **tengo mis ~s** I have my suspicions
[5] [*de animal*] viciousness

maliciarse ▸conjug 1b◂ VPR to suspect, have one's suspicions; **ya me lo maliciaba** I thought as much, it's just what I suspected

maliciosamente ADV [1] (= *con mala intención*) maliciously, spitefully
[2] (= *con picardía*) mischievously
[3] (= *con astucia*) slyly

malicioso ADJ [1] (= *malintencionado*) malicious, spiteful
[2] (= *pícaro*) mischievous; **una mirada maliciosa** a mischievous look
[3] (= *astuto*) sly, crafty
[4] (= *malo*) wicked, evil

malignidad SF [1] (*Med*) malignancy
[2] [*de persona*] (= *maldad*) evil nature; (= *daño*) harmfulness; (= *rencor*) malice

malignizarse ▸conjug 1f◂ VPR [*célula, tumor*] to become malignant

maligno Ⓐ ADJ [1] (*Med*) malignant
[2] (= *perverso*) [*persona*] evil; [*influencia*] pernicious, harmful; [*actitud, observación*] malicious
Ⓑ SM **el ~** the Devil, the Evil One

Malinche SF (*Méx*) *mistress of Cortés*

malinchismo SM (*Méx*) *tendency to favour things foreign*

malinformar ▸conjug 1a◂ VT to misinform

malintencionadamente ADV maliciously

malintencionado ADJ [*persona, comentario*] malicious

malinterpretación SF misinterpretation

malinterpretar ▸conjug 1a◂ VT to misinterpret

malísimamente ADV very badly, dreadfully

malísimo ADJ very bad, dreadful

malito ADJ **estar ~** to be in poor shape, be rather poorly

malla SF [1] [*de red*] mesh; (= *red*) network; **hacer ~** to knit; **medias de ~** fishnet stockings
▸ **malla de alambre** wire mesh, wire netting
[2] (*para ballet, gimnasia*) leotard; **mallas** (= *leotardos*) tights *pl*, pantyhose (*EEUU*); (*sin pie*) leggings
[3] (*LAm*) (*tb* **~ de baño**) swimming costume, swimsuit
[4] (*Dep*) **las ~s** the net *sing*; **dio con el balón en el fondo de las ~s** he placed the ball into the back of the net
[5] (*Hist*) chain mail; *ver tb* **cota**[1]

mallo SM mallet

Mallorca SF Majorca

mallorquín/ina Ⓐ ADJ, SM/F Majorcan
Ⓑ SM (*Ling*) Majorcan

malmandado ADJ (= *desobediente*) disobedient; (= *terco*) obstinate, bloody-minded*

malmirado ADJ [1] (= *mal considerado*) **estar ~** to be disliked
[2] (= *desconsiderado*) thoughtless, inconsiderate

malmodado‡ ADJ (*Caribe, Méx*) (= *hosco*) heavy-handed, rough; (= *insolente*) rude, insolent

malnacido/a* SM/F swine*

malnutrición SF malnutrition

malnutrido ADJ malnourished

malo/a Ⓐ ADJ (*antes de sm sing* **mal**) [1] (= *perjudicial*) bad; **es ~ para la salud** it's bad for your health; ✦*REFRÁN* **más vale lo ~ conocido (que lo bueno por conocer)** better the devil you know (than the devil you don't)
[2] (= *imperfecto*) bad; **esta película es bastante mala** this is a pretty bad film; **un chiste malísimo** a really bad joke, a terrible joke; **este papel es ~ para escribir** this paper is bad for writing; **mala calidad** poor quality; **es una tela muy mala** it's a very poor-quality material; **joyas malas** fake jewels; **ni un(a) mal(a) ...** ◊ **no hay ni un mal bar para tomar algo** there isn't a single little bar where we can get a drink
[3] (= *adverso*) bad; **he tenido mala suerte** I've had bad luck, I've been unlucky; **eso es una mala señal** that's a bad sign; **—es tarde y no ha llamado —¡malo!** "it's late and she hasn't called" — "oh dear!"; **~ sería que no ganáramos** it would be a disaster if we didn't win; **lo ~ es que ...** the trouble is (that) ...; *ver tb* **pata A6**
[4] (= *desagradable*) bad; **un mal día** a bad day; **el tiempo estuvo muy ~ todo el verano** we had really bad weather all summer; **un olor muy ~** a bad *o* nasty smell
[5] (= *podrido*) **esta carne está mala** this meat's off
[6] (= *reprobable*) wrong; **¿qué tiene de ~?** what's wrong with that?; **¿qué tiene de ~ comer helados en invierno?** what's wrong with eating ice cream in winter?; **van por mal camino** they'll come to no good if they carry on like this; **es una mala persona** he's a bad person; **una bruja mala** a wicked witch; *ver tb* **arte 2, idea 3, leche 10, lengua 1, manera 2, pasada 5, trato 4, uva 1**
[7] (= *travieso*) naughty; **¡no seas ~!** don't be naughty!
[8] (= *enfermo*) ill; **mi hija está mala** my daughter's ill; **tienes muy mala cara** you look awful *o* really ill; **se puso ~ después de comer** he started to feel ill after lunch; **me puse ~ de reírme** I nearly died laughing; **tengo mala la garganta** I've got a sore throat
[9] (= *inepto*) bad; **ser ~ para algo** to be bad at sth; **soy muy mala para la física** I'm very bad at physics
[10] (= *difícil*) hard, difficult; **es un animal ~ de domesticar** it's a hard *o* difficult animal to tame; **es muy ~ de vencer** he's very hard *o* difficult to beat
[11] ✦*MODISMOS* **a la mala** (*LAm*) (= *a la fuerza*) by force, forcibly; (= *de forma traicionera*) treacherously; **andar a malas con algn** to be on bad terms with sb; **ponerse a malas con algn** to fall out with sb; **estar de malas** (= *de mal humor*) to be in a bad mood; (= *sin suerte*) to be out of luck; **venir de malas** to have evil intentions; **por las malas** by force, willy-nilly
Ⓑ SM/F (= *personaje*) (*Teat*) villain; (*Cine*) baddie*
Ⓒ SM **el ~** (*Rel*) the Evil One, the Devil

maloca SF [1] (*Cono Sur Hist*) Indian raid
[2] (*Andes*) Indian village

malogrado ADJ [1] (= *difunto*) **el ~ ministro** the late-lamented minister
[2] (= *fracasado*) [*proyecto*] abortive, ill-fated; [*esfuerzo*] wasted

malograr ▸conjug 1a◂ Ⓐ VT (= *arruinar*) to spoil, ruin; (= *desperdiciar*) to waste
Ⓑ **malograrse** VPR [1] (= *fracasar*) to fail; (= *decepcionar*) to fail to come up to expectations, not fulfil its promise
[2] (*esp Perú*) [*máquina*] to go wrong, break down
[3] [*persona*] to die before one's time

malogro SM [1] (= *fracaso*) failure; (= *desperdicio*) waste
[2] (= *muerte*) early death, untimely end

maloliente ADJ stinking, smelly

malón SM (*LAm*) [1] (*Hist*) Indian raid
[2] (= *persona*) tough, thug

malpagar ▸conjug 1h◂ VT to pay badly, underpay

malparado ADJ **salir ~** to come off badly; **salir ~ de algo** to get the worst of sth

malparar ▸conjug 1a◂ VT (= *dañar*) to damage; (= *estropear*) to harm, impair; (= *maltratar*) to ill-treat

malparido/a‡ SM/F son of a bitch‡, bastard‡

malparir ▸conjug 3a◂ VI to have a miscarriage, miscarry

malparto SM miscarriage

malpensado ADJ evil-minded; **¡no seas ~!** why do you always have to think the worst of people!

malpensar ▸conjug 1j◂ VI **~ de algn** to think ill of sb

malqueda* SMF shifty sort, unreliable type

malquerencia SF dislike

malquerer ▸conjug 2t◂ VT to dislike

malquerido ADJ unloved

malquistar ▸conjug 1a◂ Ⓐ VT **~ a dos personas** to cause a rift between two people
Ⓑ **malquistarse** VPR [*dos personas*] to fall out, become estranged; **~se con algn** to fall out with sb, become estranged from sb

malquisto ADJ **estar ~** to be disliked, be unpopular; **los dos están ~s** they have fallen out with each other, they have become estranged

malrotar ▸conjug 1a◂ VT to squander

malsano ADJ [1] [*clima*] unhealthy
[2] (= *perverso*) [*curiosidad, fascinación*] morbid; [*mente*] sick, morbid

malsín SM (= *difamador*) slanderer; (= *soplón*) informer, taleteller

malsonante ADJ rude, nasty; **usar palabras ~s** to use rude words *o* bad language

malsufrido ADJ impatient

Malta SF Malta

malta SF [1] (= *cereal*) malt; **whisky de ~** malt whisky
[2] (*Chile*) dark beer

malteada SF (*LAm*) malted milk shake

malteado Ⓐ ADJ malted
Ⓑ SM malting

maltear ▸conjug 1a◂ VT to malt

maltés/esa Ⓐ ADJ, SM/F Maltese
Ⓑ SM (*Ling*) Maltese

maltirar ▸conjug 1a◂ VI to scrape by, scrape a living

maltón SM (*LAm*), **maltoncillo** SM (*LAm*) (= *animal*) young animal; (= *niño*) child

maltraer ▸conjug 2o◂ VI 1 (= *maltratar*) to ill-treat; ✦*MODISMO* **llevar** *o* **traer a ~ a algn** [*persona*] to give sb nothing but trouble; [*problema*] to be the bane of sb's life
2 (= *injuriar*) to insult, abuse

maltraído ADJ (*LAm*) shabby, untidy

maltratado ADJ [*bebé, mujer*] battered

maltratamiento SM = **maltrato**

maltratar ▸conjug 1a◂ VT 1 [+ *persona*] (= *tratar mal*) to ill-treat, maltreat; (= *pegar*) to batter
2 [+ *cosas*] to handle roughly
3 (*tb* ~ **de palabra**) to abuse, insult

maltrato SM 1 (= *conducta*) (*al tratar mal*) mistreatment, ill-treatment; (*al pegar*) battering ▸ **maltrato conyugal** wife-battering ▸ **maltrato infantil** child-battering ▸ **maltrato psicológico** psychological abuse
2 [*de cosas*] rough handling
3 (= *insultos*) abuse, insults *pl*

maltrecho ADJ 1 [*objeto*] battered, knocked-about; **las maltrechas arcas de la organización** the organization's depleted coffers
2 [*persona*] (= *herida*) injured; (= *agotada*) worn out; **dejar ~ a algn** to leave sb in a bad way; **los ~s líderes del partido** the beleaguered party leaders

malucho* ADJ (*Med*) poorly, under the weather*

malura* SF (*Cono Sur*) (= *dolor*) pain, discomfort; (= *malestar*) sickness, indisposition ▸ **malura de estómago** stomach ache

malva Ⓐ ADJ INV [*color*] mauve
Ⓑ SF (*Bot*) mallow; **(de) color de ~** mauve; ✦*MODISMOS* **criar ~s** ◊ **estar criando ~s** (*Esp**) to be pushing up the daisies*; **estar como una ~** to be very meek and mild ▸ **malva loca**, **malva real**, **malva rósea** hollyhock

malvado/a Ⓐ ADJ evil, wicked
Ⓑ SM/F villain

malvaloca SF hollyhock

malvarrosa SF hollyhock

malvasía SF malmsey

malvavisco SM marshmallow

malvender ▸conjug 2a◂ VT to sell off cheap, sell at a loss

malversación SF embezzlement, misappropriation ▸ **malversación de fondos** embezzlement, misappropriation of funds

malversador(a) SM/F embezzler

malversar ▸conjug 1a◂ VT 1 (*Fin*) to embezzle, misappropriate; **~ fondos** to embezzle *o* misappropriate funds
2 (= *distorsionar*) to distort

Malvinas SFPL (*tb* **Islas ~**) Falkland Islands, Falklands

malvinés/esa Ⓐ ADJ of/from the Falkland Islands
Ⓑ SM/F Falkland islander

malviviente SMF, ADJ (*Méx*) = **maleante**

malvivir ▸conjug 3a◂ VI to live badly, live poorly; **malviven de lo que pueden** they scrape by as best they can

malvón SM (*LAm*) geranium

mama SF 1 (*Med*) (= *glándula*) mammary gland; (= *pecho*) breast; **cáncer de ~** breast cancer
2 = **mamá 1**

mamá* SF 1 (= *madre*) mum*, mummy*, mom(my) (*EEUU**); **futura ~** mother-to-be
2 (*esp CAm, Caribe, Méx*) [*de cortesía*] mother ▸ **mamá grande** (*Col*) grandmother

mamacallos* SMF INV (*Esp*) useless person

mamacita* SF (*LAm*) 1 (= *madre*) mummy*, mommy (*EEUU**), mum*, mom (*EEUU**)
2 **¡eh, ~!** hey, gorgeous!*

mamacona‡ SF (*Andes*) old lady

mamada SF 1 (= *chupada*) suck
2 (**‡) blow job**‡
3 (‡) (= *borrachera*) binge*
4 (*LAm**) (= *cosa fácil*) cinch*; (= *ganga*) snip*, bargain; (= *trabajo*) cushy number

mamadera SF 1 (*LAm*) (= *tetilla*) rubber teat; (= *biberón*) feeding bottle
2 **mamaderas**‡ boobs‡

mamado ADJ 1 (‡) (= *borracho*) smashed*, sloshed*
2 (*) (= *fácil*) dead easy*
3 (*Caribe**) (= *tonto*) silly, stupid

mamagrande SF (*LAm*) grandmother; *ver tb* **mamá 2**

mamaíta* SF = **mamá 1**

mamalón ADJ (*Caribe*) (= *vago*) idle; (= *gorrón*) sponging

mamamama* SF (*Andes*) grandma*

mamandurria* SF (= *empleo*) cushy job*; (= *sueldo*) fat salary; (= *gajes*) rich pickings *pl*

mamantear ▸conjug 1a◂ VT (*LAm*) 1 (= *mamar*) to nurse, feed
2 (= *mimar*) to spoil, pamper

mamaón SM (*Méx*) tipsy cake

mamar ▸conjug 1a◂ Ⓐ VT 1 [+ *leche, pecho*] to suck
2 (= *asimilar*) **lo mamó desde pequeño** he grew up with it from childhood; **nació mamando el oficio** he was born to the trade; **todavía no han mamado suficiente democracia** democracy hasn't become a way of life yet
3 (*) (= *devorar*) [+ *comida*] to wolf down, bolt; [+ *recursos*] to milk, suck dry; [+ *fondos*] to pocket (illegally); **¡cómo la mamamos!** this is the life!, we never had it so good!
4 (**‡) (= *sexualmente*) to suck off**‡, give a blow job**‡
Ⓑ VI 1 [*bebé*] to suck; **dar de ~ a un bebé** to feed a baby; **dar de ~ a una cría** to suckle a baby; ✦*MODISMO* **¡no mames!** (*Méx*‡) come off it!*, don't give me that!*
2 (‡) (= *beber*) to booze*, drink
Ⓒ **mamarse** VPR 1 (‡) (= *emborracharse*) to get smashed‡, get sloshed*
2 (*) [+ *puesto, ventaja*] to wangle*
3 **~se a algn*** (*LAm*) (= *engañar*) to take sb for a ride*; (*CAm*) (= *matar*) to do sb in‡
4 **~se un susto*** to give o.s. a fright
5 (*Andes**) (= *rajarse*) to go back on one's word

mamario ADJ mammary

mamarrachada* SF (= *acción*) stupid thing; (= *objeto*) monstrosity*, sight*

mamarracho/a* Ⓐ SM/F (= *persona*) sight*; **estaba hecho un ~** he looked a sight *o* a complete mess*
Ⓑ SM (= *objeto*) monstrosity*, sight*; (= *obra, trabajo*) mess, botch; (= *cuadro*) daub

mamá-señora SF (*LAm*) grandmother

mambo SM (*Mús*) mambo

mameluca‡ SF (*Cono Sur*) whore

mameluco SM 1 (*Hist*) Mameluke
2 (*LAm*) (= *mono*) overalls *pl*; (*tb* **~s de niño**) rompers *pl*, romper suit
3 (*LAm Hist*) Brazilian mestizo, half-breed
4 (*) (= *idiota*) chump*, idiot

mameo‡ SM **cogerse un ~** to get plastered*, get smashed*

mamerto/a SM/F twit*, idiot

mamey SM (*LAm*) mammee apple, mamey; ✦*MODISMO* **ser ~ colorado** (*Caribe**) to be out of this world

mameyal SM (*LAm*) mamey plantation

mamífero Ⓐ ADJ mammalian, mammal *antes de s*
Ⓑ SM mammal

Mammón SM Mammon

mamografía SF mammography

mamola SF **dar** *o* **hacer la ~ a algn** (*lit*) to tickle *o* chuck sb under the chin; (*fig*) to take sb for a ride*

mamón Ⓐ SM 1 (= *bebé*) small baby, baby at the breast
2 (**‡) (= *idiota*) prick**‡, wanker**‡
3 (‡) (= *gorrón*) scrounger*; (= *indeseable*) rotter*, swine*; **¡qué suerte tienes, ~!** you lucky sod!‡
4 (*Bot*) sucker, shoot
5 (*Andes, Cono Sur*) (= *árbol*) papaya tree; (= *fruta*) papaya
6 (*Cono Sur, Méx*) suck
7 (*CAm*) (= *palo*) club, stick
8 (*Méx*) (= *bizcocho*) soft sponge cake
Ⓑ ADJ 1 [*niño*] small, suckling
2 (*Méx**) (= *bruto*) thick*; (= *engreído*) cocky*

mamonada‡ SF **eso es una ~** that's bloody stupid‡

mamoncete‡ SM (little) bastard**‡

mamonear ▸conjug 1a◂ VT 1 (*CAm*) (= *golpear*) to beat
2 (*Caribe*) (= *aplazar*) (*gen*) to postpone; [+ *tiempo*] to waste

mamotrético* ADJ (= *enorme*) gigantic; (= *inmanejable*) unwieldy

mamotreto* SM 1 (= *libro*) hefty volume; (= *objeto*) monstrosity*, useless great object
2 (*esp LAm*) (= *aparato*) contraption; (= *bulto*) lump; (= *coche viejo*) old banger*, jalopy (*EEUU*)
3 (*Méx*) (= *inútil*) dead loss*

mampara SF screen, partition

mamparo SM (*Náut, Aer*) bulkhead

mamplora‡ SM (*CAm*) queer‡, fag (*EEUU*‡)

mamporrera* SF madame, brothel-keeper

mamporro* SM (= *golpe*) (*con la mano*) clout*, bash*; (*al caer*) bump; **atizar** *o* **sacudir un ~ a algn** to give sb a clout *o* bash*; **liarse a ~s con algn** to come to blows with sb

mampostería SF masonry

mampuesto SM 1 (= *piedra*) rough stone
2 (= *muro*) wall
3 (*LAm*) [*de fusil*] rest
4 **de ~** spare, emergency *antes de s*

mamúa‡ SF (*Cono Sur*) **agarrarse una ~** to get plastered*

mamuchi* SF mumsy*

mamut SM (*pl* **mamuts**) mammoth

mana SF (*LAm*) 1 (= *manantial*) spring
2 (= *alimento*) manna

maná SM manna

manada SF [1] (*Zool*) [*de ganado*] herd; [*de lobos*] pack; [*de leones*] pride
[2] (*) [*de gente*] crowd, mob; **los periodistas llegaron en ~** a swarm *o* pack of journalists arrived

manadero SM herdsman, drover

manager, **mánager** ['manaʒer] SMF (*pl* **managers** *o* **mánagers**) manager

Managua SF Managua

managua, **managüense** Ⓐ ADJ INV of/from Managua
Ⓑ SMF native/inhabitant of Managua; **los ~s** the people of Managua

manantial Ⓐ SM [1] (= *fuente*) spring; **agua de ~** spring water ▸ **manantial termal** hot spring
[2] [*de riqueza, conflicto*] (= *origen*) source, origin; (= *causa*) cause
Ⓑ ADJ **agua ~** running water, flowing water

manantío ADJ running, flowing

manar ▸conjug 1a◂ Ⓐ VT to run with, flow with; **la herida manaba sangre** blood gushed from the wound
Ⓑ VI [1] [*líquido*] (*gen*) to run, flow; (*a chorros*) to pour out, stream; (= *surgir*) to well up
[2] (= *abundar*) to abound, be plentiful; **~ en algo** to abound in sth

manatí SM manatee, sea cow

manazas* Ⓐ SMF INV **ser (un) ~** to be clumsy
Ⓑ SFPL (= *manos*) big mitts*

manazo SM (*LAm*) slap

mancar ▸conjug 1g◂ Ⓐ VT [1] (= *mutilar*) to maim, cripple
[2] (*Cono Sur*) **~ el tiro** to miss
Ⓑ VI (*Andes**) (= *fracasar*) to blow it*; (*Escol*) to fail

mancarrón* SM [1] (*Cono Sur*) (= *caballo*) nag
[2] (*Andes, Cono Sur*) (= *obrero*) disabled workman
[3] (*Andes, Cono Sur*) (= *presa*) small dam

manceba†† SF (= *amante*) lover, mistress; (= *concubina*) concubine

mancebía†† SF brothel

mancebo†† SM [1] (= *joven*) youth, young man
[2] (= *soltero*) bachelor
[3] (*Com*) clerk
[4] (*Farm*) assistant, dispenser

mancera SF plough handle

Mancha SF **La ~** La Mancha

mancha SF [1] (= *marca*) [*de aceite, comida, pintura, sangre*] stain; [*de óxido, bolígrafo*] mark; [*de pintura de labios*] smudge; **había ~s de sangre por el suelo** there were bloodstains on the floor; **procura que no te caigan ~s en la camisa** try not to get stains on your shirt; **me cayó una ~ de tinta en la carta** a drop of ink fell on the letter; **las ~s de grasa salen mejor con agua caliente** oil stains come out better with hot water; **han salido ~s de humedad en la pared** damp patches have appeared on the wall; **quitar una ~** to get a mark *o* stain out, get a mark *o* stain off; ✦*MODISMO* **extenderse como una ~ de aceite** [*enfermedad, noticia*] to spread like wildfire; [*movimiento, tendencia*] to spread far and wide
[2] (= *área*) [*de hielo, vegetación*] patch; (*en el Sol, en un planeta*) spot; **~s de bosque bajo** patches of scrubland ▸ **mancha de petróleo** oil slick ▸ **mancha solar** sunspot
[3] (*Zool*) (*grande*) patch; (*redonda*) spot; **un cachorro blanco con ~s marrones** a white puppy with brown patches; **los leopardos tienen la piel a ~s** leopards have spotted coats *o* spots
[4] (= *deshonra*) stain; **una ~ en su honor** a stain on his honour; **la expulsión del colegio fue una ~ en su expediente** his expulsion from school was a black mark *o* a blot on his record; **esa derrota fue la única ~ en una excelente temporada** that defeat was the only blot on an otherwise excellent season; **la ~ del pecado** the taint of sin; **sin ~** [*conducta*] impeccable; [*expediente*] unblemished; [*alma*] pure
[5] (*Med*) [*de sarampión, rubeola*] spot; (*en el pulmón*) shadow; **le han salido unas ~s rojizas en la cara** his face has come out in reddish spots ▸ **mancha amarilla** [*de retina*] yellow spot ▸ **mancha de nacimiento** birthmark ▸ **manchas del sarampión** measles spots
[6] (*Arte*) shading, shaded area ▸ **mancha de color** (*en pintura*) splash of colour *o* (*EEUU*) color; (*en fotografía*) patch of colour *o* (*EEUU*) color
[7] (*CAm, Méx*) [*de langostas*] cloud, swarm; [*de peces*] school, shoal; [*de gente*] swarm
[8] (*Arg, Uru*) (= *juego*) **la ~** tag
[9] (*Perú**) [*de amigos*] gang

manchado ADJ [1] (= *sucio*) stained, dirty; **esta camisa está manchada** this shirt is stained *o* dirty; **su traje estaba completamente ~** his suit was completely covered in stains; **~ de algo**: **la acera estaba manchada de sangre** the pavement was stained with blood; **tenía la chaqueta manchada de café** his jacket had coffee stains on it *o* was stained with coffee; **un par de botas manchadas de barro** a pair of mud-stained boots; **tenía los dedos ~s de tinta** she had ink stains on her fingers, she had ink-stained fingers; **el folio estaba ~ de tinta** the sheet of paper was smudged with ink
[2] (*Zool*) [*caballo, perro*] (*con manchas pequeñas*) spotted; (*con manchas más grandes*) dappled; [*ave*] speckled; **el caballo tiene el lomo ~** the horse has dappled markings on its back
[3] (= *sin honra*) [*reputación*] tarnished; **estaba ~ por el pecado original** he bore the taint of original sin
[4] (*Arte*) shaded

manchar ▸conjug 1a◂ Ⓐ VT [1] (= *ensuciar*) to get dirty, stain; **te has manchado el vestido** you've got your dress dirty, you've stained your dress, there's dirt on your dress; **ten cuidado de no ~me** be careful you don't get me dirty *o* stain my clothes; **~ algo de algo** (*gen*) to stain sth with sth; (*más sucio*) to get sth covered in sth; **me has manchado de pintura** you've got paint on me
[2] (= *desprestigiar*) [+ *honor, imagen*] to tarnish
Ⓑ VI to stain; **este vino no mancha** this wine doesn't stain
Ⓒ **mancharse** VPR [1] (= *ensuciarse*) to get dirty; **no lo toques que te puedes ~** don't touch it or you'll get dirty!; **¿cómo se te ha manchado la chaqueta?** how did you get your jacket dirty?; **~se de algo**: **se me ~on los dedos de sangre** I got blood *o* bloodstains on my fingers; **te has manchado la boca de chocolate** you've got chocolate *o* chocolate stains round your mouth; **me he manchado el traje de barro/de tinta** I got my suit covered in mud/ink, I got mud/ink all over my suit; ✦*MODISMO* **~se las manos** to get one's hands dirty, dirty one's hands
[2] (= *deshonrarse*) to tarnish one's reputation

manchego/a Ⓐ ADJ of/from La Mancha
Ⓑ SM/F native/inhabitant of La Mancha; **los ~s** the people of La Mancha

mancheta SF [*de libro*] blurb; [*de periódico*] masthead

manchón[1] SM [1] (= *mancha*) large stain, big spot
[2] (*Bot*) patch of dense vegetation

manchón[2] SM (*Cono Sur*) muff

Manchuria SF Manchuria

manchuriano/a ADJ, SM/F Manchurian

mancilla SF stain, blemish; **sin ~** unblemished; (*Rel*) immaculate, pure

mancillar ▸conjug 1a◂ VT to stain, sully (*liter*)

manco/a Ⓐ ADJ [1] (*de una mano*) one-handed; (*de un brazo*) one-armed; (= *sin brazos*) armless; **quedó ~ de la izquierda** he lost his left hand
[2] (= *incompleto*) half-finished
[3] (= *defectuoso*) defective, faulty
[4] ✦*MODISMO* **no ser ~** (= *astuto*) to be nobody's fool; (= *útil*) to be useful *o* handy; (= *sin escrúpulos*) to be pretty sharp; **Alarcos, jugador que tampoco es ~** Alarcos, who is a pretty useful player himself; **no ser ~ en algo** to be pretty good at sth
Ⓑ SM/F (*de una mano*) one-handed person; (*de un brazo*) one-armed person; (= *sin brazos*) armless person, person with no arms
Ⓒ SM (*Cono Sur*) (= *caballo*) nag

mancomún: **de ~** ADV = **mancomunadamente**

mancomunadamente ADV (= *en conjunto*) jointly, together; (= *por voluntad común*) by common consent; **obrar ~ con algn** to act jointly with sb

mancomunado ADJ joint, jointly held

mancomunar ▸conjug 1a◂ Ⓐ VT [1] (= *unir*) [+ *personas*] to unite, associate; [+ *intereses*] to combine; [+ *recursos*] to pool
[2] (*Jur*) to make jointly responsible
Ⓑ **mancomunarse** VPR to unite

mancomunidad SF [1] (= *unión*) union, association
[2] (= *comunidad*) (*gen*) community; [*de recursos*] pool
[3] (*Jur*) joint responsibility
[4] (*Pol*) commonwealth; **la Mancomunidad Británica** the British Commonwealth

mancornar ▸conjug 1l◂ VT [1] [+ *toro*] (= *agarrar*) to seize by the horns; (*con una cuerda*) to hobble
[2] (= *unir*) to join, couple

mancornas SFPL (*LAm*), **mancuernas** SFPL (*Méx*), **mancuernillas** SFPL (*CAm, Méx*) cufflinks

manda SF [1] (= *legado*) bequest
[2] (*LAm*) (= *voto*) religious vow

mandadero/a SM/F (= *recadero*) errand boy/girl; (= *mensajero*) messenger

mandado/a Ⓐ SM/F [1] (*pey*) (= *subordinado*) dogsbody*; **yo aquí no soy más que un ~** here I just obey instructions, I'm just a dogsbody* *o* a minion here
[2] (*Méx**) (= *aprovechado*) opportunist; **no seas ~** don't take advantage of the situation

Ⓑ SM [1] (= *recado*) errand; **hacer un ~** to do *o* run an errand; **ir a (hacer) los ~s** to do the shopping
[2] (= *orden*) order
[3] (*Méx*) **el ~** the shopping; **ir al ~** to do the shopping

mandamás SMF INV boss*, bigwig*

mandamiento SM [1] (*Rel*) commandment; **los Diez Mandamientos** the Ten Commandments
[2] (*Jur*) (*tb* **~ judicial**) writ, warrant; **notificar a algn un ~ judicial** to serve a writ on sb ► **mandamiento de ejecución** warrant of execution ► **mandamiento de entrada y registro** (*Esp*) search warrant ► **mandamiento de prisión** warrant of commitment
[3] (*Esp Fin*) ► **mandamiento de pago** banker's order
[4] (= *orden*) order, command

mandanga SF [1] (*) (= *cachaza*) slowness; **¡qué ~ tienes!** you take your time, don't you!
[2] (*) (= *cuento*) tale, story; (= *excusa*) excuse; (= *paparrucha*) rubbish*; **¡no me vengas con ~s!*** don't give me that rubbish!*, who are you trying to kid?*; **hay que dejarse de ~s y decirlo bien claro** you have to stop beating about the bush and say it straight out; **deberían obligarle a dimitir sin más ~s** he should be forced to resign, no two ways about it*; **¡tiene ~!** this is too much!
[3] (‡) (= *golpe*) bash*
[4] (‡) (= *droga*) pot*, grass*

mandanguero/a‡ SM/F (= *fumador*) potsmoker*; (= *vendedor*) dealer in pot *o* grass*

mandar ►conjug 1a◄ Ⓐ VT [1] (= *ordenar, encargar*) to tell; **haz lo que te manden** do as you are told; **no me gusta que me manden** I don't like being told what to do; **¿hoy no te han mandado deberes?** haven't they given you any homework today?; **¿qué manda usted?** (*esp LAm*) can I help you?; **¿manda usted algo más?** (*esp LAm*) would you like anything else?; **~ (a algn) (a) hacer algo**: **lo mandé a comprar pan** I sent him (out) for bread *o* to buy some bread; **me he mandado hacer un traje** I'm having a suit made; **tuvimos que ~ arreglar el coche** we had to put the car in for repairs, we had to have the car repaired; **¿quién diablos me ~ía a mí meterme en esto?*** why on earth did I get mixed up in this?*; **¿quién te manda ser tan tonto?** how could you be so stupid?; **~ callar a algn** (*gen*) to tell sb to be quiet; (*con autoridad*) to order sb to be quiet; **~ llamar a algn** to send for sb; **he mandado llamar al electricista** I've sent for the electrician; **mandó llamar a todas las monjas al patio** she summoned all the nuns to the courtyard; **~ salir a algn** to order sb out; **~ venir a algn** = **mandar llamar a algn**; **~ a algn (a) por algo** to send sb (out) for sth *o* to do sth; **lo mandé a por el periódico** I sent him (out) for the paper *o* to buy the paper; **~ a algn que haga algo** (*gen*) to tell sb to do sth; (*con autoridad*) to order sb to do sth; **me han mandado que deje de fumar** I've been advised *o* told to stop smoking; ✦*MODISMO* **como está mandado** (*Esp**) **se casará por la iglesia como está mandado** she'll have a church wedding as one would expect; **lo hizo como estaba mandado** he did the right thing*
[2] (= *enviar*) to send; **me han mandado un paquete de Madrid** I've got *o* I've been sent a parcel from Madrid; **lo ~on como representante de la empresa** he was sent to represent the company, he was sent as the company's representative; **he mandado a los niños a la cama** I've sent the children to bed; **~ algo por correo** to post sth, mail sth (*EEUU*); **te ~é mi dirección por correo electrónico** I'll send you my address by e-mail, I'll e-mail you my address; **~ recuerdos a algn** to send one's love to sb, send one's regards to sb (*frm*); *ver tb* **carajo A3**, **mierda A1**, **mona 1**, **paseo 1**, **porra 6**
[3] (= *estar al mando de*) [+ *batallón*] to lead, command; [+ *trabajadores, policías*] to be in charge of; **mandaba la brigada de bomberos** he was in charge of the fire brigade
[4] (*Dep*) to send, hit; **mandó la pelota fuera del campo de golf** he sent *o* hit the ball off the golf course; **mandó el balón al poste** she hit the post with the ball
[5] (*Med*) to prescribe; **le han mandado antibióticos** she has been prescribed antibiotics
[6] (= *legar*) to leave, bequeath (*frm*)
[7] (*LAm*) (= *lanzar*) to throw, hurl
[8] (*LAm**) **~ un golpe a algn** to hit sb; **~ una patada a algn** to give sb a a kick, kick sb; **le mandó una bofetada** she slapped him
[9] (*LAm*) (= *tirar*) to throw away
[10] (*LAm*) [+ *caballo*] to break in
[11] (*Cono Sur Dep*) to start
Ⓑ VI [1] (= *estar al mando*) (*gen*) to be in charge; (*Mil*) to be in command; **¿quién manda aquí?** who's in charge here?; **aquí mando yo** I'm the boss here, I'm in charge here; **~ en algo** to be in charge of sth; (*Mil*) to be in command of sth; **los que mandan en este país** the people that run this country; **mandaba en todo un ejército** he was in command of an entire army
[2] (= *ordenar*) **¡mande usted!** at your service!, what can I do for you?; **de nada, a ~** don't mention it, (I'm) at your service!; **¿mande?** (*esp Méx*) (= *¿cómo dice?*) pardon?, what did you say?; (*invitando a hablar*) yes?; **le gusta ~** (*pey*) he likes bossing people around; **según manda la ley** (*Jur*) in accordance with the law; *ver tb* **canon 2**, **Dios 3**
Ⓒ **mandarse** VPR [1] [*enfermo*] to get about by o.s., manage unaided
[2] [*habitaciones*] to communicate (**con** with)
[3] (*LAm**) **mándese entrar** *o* **pasar** please come in; **~se cambiar** (*Andes, Cono Sur*) ◊ **~se mudar** (*Arg, Uru*) to up and leave*; **¡mándate cambiar!** beat it!*, clear off!*; ✦*MODISMO* **~se (guarda) abajo** (*Chile**) to come down, come crashing down
[4] (*LAm*) **~se con algn** to be rude to sb, be bossy with sb
[5] (*Caribe, Cono Sur*) (= *irse*) to go away, slip away; (= *desaparecer*) to disappear secretly
[6] (*LAm**) [+ *comida*] to scoff*, polish off*; [+ *bebida, trago*] to knock back*
[7] (*Andes**) [+ *gol*] to score; [+ *mentira*] to come out with; **se manda cada discurso** he's such an amazing speaker; **se manda unas metidas de pata ...** he's always putting his foot in his mouth*
[8] (*Méx**) (= *aprovecharse*) to take advantage (of the situation)

mandarín SM [1] (*Hist, Ling*) Mandarin
[2] (*pey*) petty bureaucrat

mandarina SF [1] (*Bot*) mandarin, tangerine; ✦*MODISMO* **¡chúpate esa ~!** (*Esp‡*) get that!*, hark at him!
[2] (*Ling*) Mandarin

mandarino SM mandarin (orange) tree

mandatario/a SM/F [1] (*Jur*) agent, attorney
[2] (= *dirigente*) leader; (*esp LAm Pol*) (*tb* **primer ~**) Head of State; **los altos ~s de la Iglesia** Church leaders

mandato SM [1] (= *orden*) mandate; **bajo ~ de la ONU** under UN mandate; **según un ~ constitucional** according to the constitution ► **mandato judicial** court order
[2] (= *período de mando*) term of office, mandate (*frm*); **se acerca el final de su ~** his term of office *o* his mandate (*frm*) is coming to an end; **la duración de su ~ fue de cuatro años** he was in office for four years; **bajo** *o* **durante el ~ de algn** during sb's term of office *o* mandate (*frm*); **territorio bajo ~** mandated territory
[3] (*Jur*) (= *estatutos*) terms of reference *pl*; (= *poder*) power of attorney; **eso no forma parte de mi ~** that is not in my brief
[4] (*Inform*) command
[5] (*Com*) ► **mandato internacional** international money order
[6] (*Rel*) maundy

mandíbula SF (*Anat, Téc*) jaw; (*Zool*) mandible; ✦*MODISMO* **reírse a ~ batiente** to laugh one's head off

mandil SM [1] (= *delantal*) apron; [*de albañil*] (leather) apron; (= *bata*) pinafore dress
[2] (*LAm*) horse blanket

mandilón SM [1] (= *babi*) smock, pinafore dress
[2] (= *overol*) overalls *pl*
[3] (*) (= *cobarde*) coward

mandinga* Ⓐ SM [1] (*LAm*) (= *diablo*) devil; (= *duende*) goblin; (*malévolo*) evil spirit
[2] (*Andes, Caribe*) (= *negro*) black
Ⓑ ADJ [1] (*CAm, Cono Sur*) (= *afeminado*) effeminate
[2] (*Caribe, Cono Sur*) (= *pícaro*) impish, mischievous

mandioca SF cassava, manioc

mandiocal SM (*LAm*) cassava plot

mando SM [1] (= *poder*) command; **ha entregado el ~ al teniente** he's handed over command to the lieutenant; **están bajo el ~ del ejercito alemán** they are under the command of the German army; **el Mando de las Fuerzas Aéreas** the Air Force Command; **al ~ de** [+ *pelotón, flota*] in command of; [+ *asociación, expedición, país*] in charge of; [+ *capitán, jefe*] under the command *o* orders of, led by; **con ella al ~, mejorarán las cosas** with her in charge, things will get better; **lo pusieron al ~ de la campaña electoral** they put him in charge of the electoral campaign; **un grupo al ~ de las labores de rescate** a group leading the rescue operations; **estuvo al ~ del país durante muchos años** he was in power for many years, he led the country for many years; **las tropas estaban al ~ de un general extranjero** the troops were under the command *o* orders of a foreign general *o* were led by a foreign general; **alto ~** high command; **tomar el ~** (*Mil*) to take command; (*Dep*) to take the lead ► **mando supremo** commander-in-chief; *ver tb* **dote 2**, **voz 3**

2 [*de máquina, vehículo*] control; **no podía controlar los ~s** she couldn't operate the controls; **a los ~s de algo** at the controls of sth; **cuadro de ~s** control panel; **~ a la izquierda** left-hand drive; **palanca de ~** [*de máquina*] control lever; [*de avión*] joystick; **tablero de ~s** control panel ► **mando a distancia** remote control ► **mando de teclado** push-button control ► **mando selector** control knob

3 (= *período de mando*) term of office

4 **mandos** (= *autoridades*) (*Mil*) high-ranking officers, senior officers; (*Pol*) high-ranking members, senior members ► **mandos intermedios, mandos medios** (*LAm Com*) middle management ► **mandos militares** high-ranking officers, senior officers

mandoble SM 1 (= *golpe*) two-handed blow

2 (= *espada*) broadsword, large sword

3 (*) (= *rapapolvo*) ticking-off*

mandolina SF mandolin

mandón/ona Ⓐ ADJ (*) bossy

Ⓑ SM/F (*) bossy-boots*

Ⓒ SM 1 (*Cono Sur Min*) mine foreman

2 (*Chile*) (*en carreras*) starter

mandonear* ▸conjug 1a◂ VT **~ a algn** to boss sb around

mandrágora SF mandrake

mandria Ⓐ ADJ worthless

Ⓑ SM useless individual, weakling

mandril[1] SM (*Zool*) mandrill

mandril[2] SM (*Téc*) mandrel

manduca* SF grub*, chow (*EEUU*‡), nosh*

manducar* ▸conjug 1g◂ VT to scoff*, stuff o.s. with

manducatoria‡ SF grub*, eats* *pl*, chow (*EEUU*‡)

manea SF hobble

maneador SM (*LAm*) hobble; (*Cono Sur*) whip; (*Méx*) halter

manear ▸conjug 1a◂ Ⓐ VT to hobble

Ⓑ **manearse** VPR (*Andes, Méx*) to trip over one's own feet

manecilla SF 1 (*Téc*) (*gen*) pointer; [*de reloj*] hand ► **manecilla grande** minute hand ► **manecilla pequeña** hour hand

2 [*de libro*] clasp

maneco ADJ (*Méx*) 1 (= *tullido*) (*gen*) maimed, deformed; (*de manos*) with deformed hands; (*de pies*) with deformed feet

2 (= *patizambo*) knock-kneed

manejabilidad SF [*de asunto*] manageability; [*de herramienta*] handiness, ease of use; [*de vehículo*] handling

manejable ADJ [*asunto, pelo*] manageable; [*aparato, libro*] user-friendly, easy to use; [*vehículo*] manoeuvrable, maneuvrable (*EEUU*)

manejador(a) Ⓐ ADJ manipulative

Ⓑ SM/F (*LAm Aut*) driver, motorist

manejar ▸conjug 1a◂ Ⓐ VT 1 (= *usar*) [+ *herramienta, arma*] to handle, use; [+ *máquina*] to operate; [+ *idioma*] to use

2 (= *dirigir*) [+ *negocio, empresa*] to run; [+ *asuntos*] to look after

3 [+ *dinero*] to handle; **manejan cifras elevadísimas** they handle huge sums (of money)

4 **~ a algn: mi tía maneja a su marido** my aunt keeps her husband under her thumb

5 (*LAm Aut*) to drive

Ⓑ VI 1 **"manejar con cuidado"** "handle with care"

2 (*LAm Aut*) to drive; **el examen de ~** the driving test

Ⓒ **manejarse** VPR 1 (*Esp*) (= *desenvolverse*) to manage; **no te preocupes, puedo ~me** *o* **manejármelas yo sola** don't worry, I can manage on my own; **se maneja bien en inglés** he gets along fine in English; **se maneja bien con los chiquillos** she's good with the kids; **¿cómo te (las) manejas para estudiar y trabajar?** how do you manage to study and work at the same time?; **ya empieza a ~se con ayuda de las muletas** she's beginning to get about with the aid of crutches

2 (= *comportarse*) to act, behave

manejo SM 1 (= *uso*) [*de herramienta, arma*] use; [*de máquina*] operation; [*de idioma*] use; **una herramienta de fácil ~** a tool that is easy-to-use

2 (*Com*) [*de negocio, empresa*] running; [*de dinero, fondos*] handling; **se encarga del ~ de los asuntos de la empresa** he takes charge of looking after their business affairs; **llevar todo el ~ de algo** to be in sole charge of sth

3 **tener buen ~ de** [+ *idioma, tema*] to have a good command of; **tiene un buen ~ del alemán** she has a good command of German; **demostró tener un gran ~ de la situación** he demonstrated a thorough command of the situation

4 **manejos** (= *intrigas*) dealings; **turbios ~s** shady dealings

5 (*LAm Aut*) driving

▼ **manera** SF 1 (= *modo*) way; **hay varias ~s de hacerlo** there are various ways of doing it; **eso no es ~ de tratar a un animal** that's not the way to treat an animal, that's no way to treat an animal; **hazlo de la ~ que sea** do it however *o* the way you like; **de una ~ u otra** (in) one way or another; **¡llovía de una ~!** it was really pouring down!; **¡nunca he visto nevar de esta ~!** I've never seen it snow like this!; **no hubo ~ de convencerla** there was no convincing her, there was no way we could convince her; **a mi/tu/*etc* ~** my/your/*etc* way; **lo hice a mi ~** I did it my way; **a mi ~ de ver, tenemos dos opciones** the way I see it, we have two options; **a la ~ de algn/algo**: **siguen arando a la ~ de sus abuelos** they still plough as *o* in the way their grandfathers did; **una novela escrita a la ~ de Kafka** a novel written in a Kafkaesque manner *o* in the style of Kafka; **de ~ perfecta** perfectly, in a perfect way; **nos recibió de ~ cortés** he received us courteously *o* in a courteous way; **de esta ~** (in) this way, (in) this fashion; **de la misma ~** (in) the same way, (in) the same fashion ► **manera de ser**: **es su ~ de ser** that's the way she is; **cada uno tiene una ~ de ser** everyone has their own character

2 (*locuciones*) **de alguna ~** (= *en cierto modo*) to some extent; (= *de cualquier modo*) somehow; (*al principio de frase*) in a way, in some ways; **en cierta ~** in a way, to a certain extent; **de cualquier ~** (= *sin cuidado*) any old how; (= *de todos modos*) anyway; **en gran ~** to a large extent; **de mala ~**: **le pegó de mala ~** he hit her really hard; **lo estafaron de mala ~*** they really ripped him off*; **me contestó de muy mala ~** he answered me very rudely; **ese tío se enrolla de mala ~*** that guy just can't stop jabbering*; **de ninguna ~**: **eso no lo vamos a aceptar de ninguna ~** there's no way we are going to accept that; **de ninguna ~ deben paralizarse las obras** on no account must the work stop; **no quiero de ninguna ~ implicarla en esto** I don't want to involve her in this in any way; **no se parece de ninguna ~ a lo que habíamos imaginado** it's nothing like we had imagined; **¡de ninguna ~!** certainly not!, no way!; **de otra ~** (= *de otro modo*) in a different way; (= *por otra parte*) otherwise; **los jóvenes entienden el mundo de otra ~** young people see the world in a different way; **las cosas podrían haber sido de otra ~** things could have been different; **no podía ser de otra ~** it couldn't be any other way; **de otra ~, no es posible entender su actitud** otherwise, it's impossible to understand his attitude; **dicho de otra ~** in other words, to put it another way; **sobre ~** exceedingly; **de tal ~ que …** in such a way that …; **de todas ~s** anyway, in any case

3 **de ~ que** (*antes de verbo*) so; (*después de verbo*) so that; **¿de ~ que esto no te gusta?** so you don't like this?; **lo hizo de ~ que nadie se dio cuenta** he did it so that nobody noticed

4 **maneras** (= *modales*) manners; **buenas ~s** good manners; **se lo dije con buenas ~s** I told him politely; **malas ~s** bad manners, rudeness; **con muy malas ~s** very rudely; **tener ~s** (*LAm*) to have good manners, be well-mannered

5 (*liter*) (= *tipo*) kind; **otra ~ de valentía** another kind of courage

6 (*Arte, Literat*) (= *estilo*) style; **las diferentes ~s de Picasso** Picasso's different styles

MANERA, FORMA, MODO

De manera + ADJETIVO

• Cuando **de manera + ADJETIVO** añade información sobre una acción, la traducción más frecuente al inglés es un adverbio terminado en **-ly**. En inglés este tipo de adverbio es mucho más común que el equivalente **-mente** español:

Todos estos cambios ocurren de manera natural

All these changes happen naturally

La Constitución prohíbe de manera expresa la especulación inmobiliaria

The Constitution expressly forbids speculation in real estate

• **De manera + ADJETIVO** también se puede traducir por **in a + ADJETIVO + way** si no existe un adverbio terminado en **-ly** que equivalga al adjetivo:

Se lo dijo de manera amistosa

He said it to her in a friendly way

• En los casos en que se quiere hacer hincapié en la manera de hacer algo, se puede utilizar tanto un adverbio en **-ly** como la construcción **in a + ADJETIVO + way**, aunque ésta última posibilidad es más frecuente:

Tienes que intentar comportarte de manera responsable

You must try to behave responsibly *o* ***in a responsible way***

Ellos podrán ayudarte a manejar tu negocio de manera profesional

They'll be able to help you run your business professionally *o* ***in a professional way***

Para otros usos y ejemplos ver las entradas manera, forma y modo.

maneta SF lever

maneto ADJ (*Andes, CAm, Caribe*) = **maneco**

manflor‡ SM, **manflorita**‡ SM (*LAm*) pansy‡ (*pey*), queer‡ (*pey*), fag (*EEUU*‡)

➤ LENGUA Y USO: **manera 1** 53.5

manga SF [1] (*en ropa*) sleeve; **estar en ~s de camisa** to be in shirtsleeves; **~ japonesa** batwing sleeve; **~ ra(n)glan** raglan sleeve; **de ~ corta/larga** short-/long-sleeved; **sin ~s** sleeveless; ✦*MODISMOS* **andar ~ por hombro** to be a mess, be all over the place; **con el nuevo jefe todo anda ~ por hombro** with this new boss everything's in a mess *o* all over the place; **la casa está ~ por hombro** the house is a mess; **bajo ~*** under the counter; **estar de ~** to be in league; **hacer ~s y capirotes de algn** to ignore sb completely; **pegar las ~s*** to kick the bucket*; **ser de** *o* **tener ~ ancha** (= *tolerante*) to be easy-going; (= *poco severo*) to be too lenient; (*pey*) (= *sin escrúpulos*) to be unscrupulous; **sacarse algo de la ~** to come up with sth; **traer algo en la ~** to have sth up one's sleeve; *ver tb* **corte[1] 7**
[2] (= *manguera*) (*tb* **~ de riego**) hose, hosepipe ► **manga de incendios** fire hose
[3] (*Culin*) (= *colador*) strainer; [*de pastelería*] piping bag ► **manga pastelera** piping bag
[4] (*Aer*) windsock ► **manga de mariposas** butterfly net
[5] (*Geog*) [*de agua*] stretch; [*de nubes*] cloudburst; **tormentas con espesas ~s de agua** storms with heavy squally showers ► **manga de viento** whirlwind ► **manga marina** waterspout
[6] (*Náut*) beam, breadth
[7] (*Dep*) [*de competición*] round, stage; (*Tenis*) set; (*Bridge*) game; **ir a ~** to go to game ► **manga clasificatoria** qualifying round ► **manga de consolación** runners-up play-off
[8] (*LAm*) (= *multitud*) crowd, mob
[9] (*LAm Agr*) funnel, narrow entrance
[10] (*CAm*) poncho, coarse blanket ► **manga de agua** rain cape
[11] (= *bolso*) travelling bag, traveling bag (*EEUU*)

mangal SM (*LAm*) [1] = **manglar**
[2] (*Méx**) (= *trampa*) dirty trick
[3] (*Andes*) (= *plantío*) mango plantation

mangana SF lasso, lariat

mangancia* SF [1] (= *timo*) swindle, racket
[2] (= *robo*) (*gen*) thieving, pilfering; (*en tienda*) shoplifting
[3] (= *gorronería*) scrounging*
[4] (= *cuento*) story, fib

manganear ▶conjug 1a◀ Ⓐ VT [1] (*Perú*) (= *molestar*) to bother, annoy
[2] (= *coger con lazo*) to lasso
[3] (*CAm, Cono Sur*) (= *saquear*) to pillage, plunder; (*) (= *robar*) to pinch*, nick*
Ⓑ VI (*Caribe*) to loaf, hang about

manganeso SM manganese

manganeta SF (*LAm*), **manganilla** SF [1] (= *juego de manos*) sleight of hand
[2] (= *engaño*) trick, deceit
[3] (= *timo*) swindle, racket

mangante* Ⓐ SMF [1] (= *ladrón*) (*gen*) thief; (*en tienda*) shoplifter
[2] (= *mendigo*) beggar
[3] (= *gorrón*) scrounger*, freeloader*
[4] (= *caradura*) rotter*, villain
Ⓑ ADJ (= *caradura*) brazen

manganzón ADJ (= *perezoso*) lazy

mangar* ▶conjug 1h◀ Ⓐ VT [1] (= *robar*) to pinch*, nick*
[2] (= *mendigar*) to scrounge*
Ⓑ VI (= *robar*) (*gen*) to pilfer*; (*en tienda*) to shoplift; (*Cono Sur*) to scrounge*

mangazón* ADJ (*LAm*) lazy

manglar SM mangrove swamp

mangle SM (*Bot*) mangrove

mango[1] SM [1] (*Bot*) mango
[2] (*Cono Sur‡*) dough‡, dosh‡
[3] (*Méx**) good-looking lad

mango[2] SM [1] (= *asa*) handle ► **mango de escoba** (*para barrer*) broomstick; (*Aer*) joystick ► **mango de pluma** penholder
[2] (*Arg**) (= *dinero*) dough‡, dosh‡

mangón SM (*Andes*) (= *prado*) pasture; (= *estancia*) cattle ranch

mangoneador(a)* SM/F [1] (= *entrometido*) meddler; (= *mandón*) bossyboots*
[2] (*Méx*) (= *oficial corrupto*) grafter, corrupt official

mangonear* ▶conjug 1a◀ Ⓐ VT [1] [+ *persona*] to boss about*
[2] (= *birlar*) to pinch*, nick*
[3] (*LAm*) (= *saquear*) to pillage, plunder
Ⓑ VI [1] (= *entrometerse*) to meddle, interfere (**en** in); (= *interesarse*) to dabble (**en** in)
[2] (= *ser mandón*) (*con personas*) to boss people about; (*con asuntos*) to run everything
[3] (*LAm*) (= *estafar*) (*gen*) to graft, be on the fiddle*; (*Pol*) to fix things, fiddle the results*

mangoneo* SM [1] (= *entrometimiento*) meddling, interference
[2] (*con personas*) (= *control*) bossing people about; (= *descaro*) brazenness
[3] (*LAm*) (= *estafa*) (*gen*) graft*, fiddling*; (*Pol*) fixing (of results)

mangoneón/a*, **mangonero/a*** Ⓐ ADJ (= *entrometido*) meddlesome, interfering; (= *mandón*) bossy; (= *descarado*) brazen
Ⓑ SM/F (= *entrometido*) busybody; (= *mandón*) bossy individual; (= *descarado*) brazen sort

mangosta SF mongoose

manguear ▶conjug 1a◀ (*LAm*) Ⓐ VT [+ *ganado*] to drive; [+ *caza*] to beat, put up
Ⓑ VI (*) [1] (*Andes, Caribe*) (= *gandulear*) to skive*
[2] (*Cono Sur*) (= *sablear*) to scrounge*

mangueo* SM (= *robo*) thieving, pilfering; (= *gorroneo*) scrounging*

manguera SF [1] [*de riego*] hose, hosepipe ► **manguera antidisturbios** water-cannon ► **manguera de aspiración** suction pump ► **manguera de incendios** fire hose
[2] (*Andes*) [*de bicicleta*] bicycle tyre, inner tube
[3] (*Meteo*) waterspout
[4] (*Cono Sur*) corral, yard

mangui‡ SMF (= *ladrón*) thief; (= *ratero*) small-time crook*; (= *canalla*) villain, rotter*

manguillo SM (*Méx*) penholder

manguito SM [1] (*para manos*) muff
[2] (*Téc*) sleeve, coupling ► **manguito incandescente** gas mantle

mangurrina* SF bash*, wallop*

mangurrino* ADJ rotten*, worthless

manguta‡ SMF (= *ladrón*) small-time thief; (= *indeseable*) good-for-nothing

mani* SF demo*

maní SM (*pl* **maníes** *o* **manises**) [1] (*esp LAm*) (= *cacahuete*) peanut; (= *planta*) groundnut plant
[2] (*Caribe**) (= *dinero*) dough‡, dosh‡
[3] **¡maní!** (*Cono Sur*) never!

manía SF [1] (*Med*) mania ► **manía de grandezas** megalomania ► **manía persecutoria** persecution mania
[2] [*de persona*] (= *costumbre*) odd habit; (= *rareza*) peculiarity, oddity; (= *capricho*) fad, whim; **tiene sus ~s** he has his little ways; **tiene la ~ de comerse las uñas** he has the annoying habit of biting his nails; **le ha dado la ~ de salir sin abrigo** he's taken to going out without a coat
[3] [*de grupo*] (= *afición*) mania; (= *moda*) rage, craze; **la ~ del fútbol** football fever, the football craze; **la ~ de la minifalda** the craze for miniskirts; **tiene la ~ de las motos** he's obsessed with motorbikes, he's motorbike-crazy*
[4] (= *antipatía*) dislike; **coger ~ a algn** to take a dislike to sb; **tener ~ a algn** to dislike sb; **tengo ~ a los bichos** I can't stand insects; **el maestro me tiene ~** the teacher's got it in for me

maniabierto ADJ (*Caribe*) lavish, generous

maníaco/a, **maniaco/a** Ⓐ ADJ maniac, maniacal
Ⓑ SM/F maniac ► **maníaco/a sexual** sex maniac

maniaco-depresivo/a ADJ, SM/F manic depressive

maniatar ▶conjug 1a◀ VT [1] **~ a algn** (*con cuerdas*) to tie sb's hands; (*con esposas*) to handcuff sb
[2] [+ *animal*] to hobble

maniático/a Ⓐ ADJ [1] (= *con manías*) maniac, maniacal; (= *fanático*) fanatical; (= *obsesionado*) obsessive
[2] (= *loco*) crazy; (= *excéntrico*) eccentric, cranky*; (= *delicado*) fussy
[3] (= *terco*) stubborn
Ⓑ SM/F (= *obsesionado*) maniac; (= *fanático*) fanatic; (= *excéntrico*) crank*; **sólo piensa en no pisar las rayas de las aceras, es un ~** his only concern is not to step on the lines on the pavement, he's obsessed; **~ de la ecología** ecology fanatic, ecology freak*; **es un ~ de la puntuación** he is obsessive about punctuation; **es un ~ del fútbol** he's football-crazy

manicero/a SM/F (*LAm*) peanut seller

manicomio SM lunatic asylum, insane asylum (*EEUU*), mental hospital; **no quiero ir a parar a un ~** I don't want to end up in the loony bin*; **ese día la ciudad es un ~** on that day the city goes mad *o* is like a madhouse

manicura SF manicure; **hacerse la ~** (*uno mismo*) to do one's nails; (*por profesional*) to have a manicure; **se me puede estropear la ~** I could ruin my nails

manicuro/a SM/F manicurist

manida SF lair, den

manido ADJ [1] (= *trillado*) [*tema*] trite, stale; [*frase*] hackneyed
[2] (= *pasado*) [*carne*] high, gamy; [*frutos secos*] stale

manierismo SM mannerism

manierista ADJ, SMF mannerist

manifa* SF demo*

manifestación SF [1] (*Pol*) (= *desfile*) demonstration; (= *concentración*) mass meeting, rally
[2] (= *muestra*) [*de emoción*] display, show; (= *señal*) sign; **manifestaciones de alegría/júbilo** jubilation; **han recibido muchas manifestaciones de apoyo** they have received a lot of support; **manifestaciones de duelo** expressions of grief; **una gran ~ de entusiasmo** a great show of enthusiasm
[3] (= *declaración*) statement, declaration
[4] (*Chile*) (*tb* ~ **social**) social occasion
[5] ► **manifestación de impuesto** (*Méx*) tax return

manifestante SMF demonstrator

manifestar ▸conjug 1j◂ Ⓐ VT [1] (= *declarar*) to declare; **el presidente manifestó que no firmaría el acuerdo** the president declared that he would not sign the agreement; **~on su solidaridad con los damnificados** they declared their sympathy with the victims
[2] [+ *emociones*] to show; **manifiesta un sincero arrepentimiento** he shows genuine regret; **nos manifestaba un gran cariño** he showed us great affection
Ⓑ **manifestarse** VPR [1] (= *declararse*) **el presidente se ha manifestado a favor del pacto** the president came out in favour of the agreement
[2] (*Pol*) to demonstrate; **los estudiantes se ~on en contra de la nueva ley** the students demonstrated against the new law
[3] (= *mostrarse*) to be apparent, be evident; **su pesimismo se manifiesta en todas sus obras** his pessimism is apparent *o* evident in all his works

manifiesto Ⓐ ADJ (= *claro*) (*gen*) clear, manifest; [*error*] glaring, obvious; [*verdad*] manifest; **poner algo de ~** (= *aclarar*) to make sth clear; (= *revelar*) to reveal sth; **quiero poner de ~ que ...** I wish to state that ...; **quedar ~** to be plain, be clear
Ⓑ SM [1] (*Pol, Arte*) (= *programa*) manifesto ► **el Manifiesto Comunista** the Communist Manifesto
[2] (*Náut*) manifest

manigua (*LAm*) SF [1] [*de terreno*] (= *ciénaga*) swamp; (= *maleza*) scrubland; (= *selva*) jungle; (= *campo*) countryside; **irse a la ~**†† to take to the hills (*in revolt*)
[2] **agarrar ~** (*Caribe**) to get flustered

manigual SM (*Caribe*) = **manigua**

manigueta SF [1] (= *mango*) handle; (= *manivela*) crank; (*Cono Sur Aut*) starting handle
[2] (= *maniota*) hobble

manija SF [1] (= *mango*) (*gen*) handle; (*Arg*) [*de puerta*] door knob
[2] (*Mec*) clamp, collar
[3] (*Ferro*) coupling
[4] (*Agr*) hobble
[5] (*Cono Sur*) (= *vaso*) mug, tankard
[6] (*Cono Sur Aut*) starting handle; **dar ~ a algn** to egg sb on

Manila SF Manila

manilargo ADJ [1] (= *generoso*) open-handed, generous
[2] (*esp LAm**) (= *ladrón*) light-fingered

manilense Ⓐ ADJ of/from Manila
Ⓑ SMF native/inhabitant of Manila; **los ~s** the people of Manila

manileño/a ADJ, SM/F = **manilense**

➤ LENGUA Y USO: **manifestar A1** 53.5

manilla SF [1] [*de puerta*] handle, door handle
[2] (= *mango*) handle
[3] [*de reloj*] hand
[4] [*de tabaco*] bundle
[5] (= *pulsera*) bracelet ► **manillas (de hierro)** (= *grilletes*) manacles, handcuffs

manillar SM handlebars *pl*

maniobra SF [1] (= *giro*) (*Aut*) manoeuvre, maneuver (*EEUU*); (*Ferro*) shunting, switching (*EEUU*); **hacer ~s** (*Aut*) to manoeuvre, maneuver (*EEUU*); (*Ferro*) to shunt, switch (*EEUU*)
[2] (*Náut*) (= *operación*) manoeuvre, maneuver (*EEUU*); (= *aparejo*) gear, rigging
[3] **maniobras** (*Mil*) manoeuvres, maneuvers (*EEUU*); **estar de ~s** to be on manoeuvres
[4] (= *estratagema*) manoeuvre, maneuver (*EEUU*), move; **una ~ política** a political manoeuvre; **fue una hábil ~ para expulsar al jefe** it was a clever manoeuvre *o* move to get rid of the boss ► **maniobra dilatoria** delaying tactic

maniobrabilidad SF [*de vehículo*] manoeuvrability, maneuverability (*EEUU*); [*de aparato*] handling qualities, ease of use

maniobrable ADJ [*vehículo*] manoeuvrable; [*aparato*] easy to handle *o* use

maniobrar ▸conjug 1a◂ Ⓐ VT [1] [+ *aparato, vehículo*] (= *manejar*) to handle, operate; (= *mover*) to manoeuvre, maneuver (*EEUU*)
[2] (*Ferro*) to shunt
Ⓑ VI to manoeuvre, maneuver (*EEUU*)

maniota SF hobble

manipulable ADJ [1] (*Téc*) operable, that can be operated; **aparatos ~s por el visitante** devices that can be operated by the visitor
[2] (*Biol*) controllable
[3] [*persona*] easily manipulated

manipulación SF [1] (= *manejo*) [*de alimentos*] handling; [*de pieza, máquina*] manipulation
[2] [*de información, resultados*] manipulation ► **manipulación genética** genetic manipulation
[3] (*Med*) manipulation

manipulado SM handling

manipulador(a) Ⓐ ADJ manipulative
Ⓑ SM/F [1] [*de mercancías*] handler ► **manipulador(a) de alimentos** person who handles food ► **manipulador(a) de marionetas** puppeteer
[2] (= *mangoneador*) manipulator
Ⓒ SM (*Elec, Telec*) key, tapper

manipular ▸conjug 1a◂ Ⓐ VT [1] (= *manejar*) [+ *alimentos, géneros*] to handle; [+ *aparato*] to operate, use
[2] (= *mangonear*) to manipulate
Ⓑ VI **~ con** *o* **en algo** to manipulate sth

manipulativo ADJ manipulative

manipuleo SM (= *mangoneo*) manipulation; (= *trampas*) fiddling

maniqueísmo SM [1] (*Hist*) Manicheism, Manichaeism
[2] (= *tendencia a simplificar*) *tendency to see things in black and white*; **discutir sin ~s** to discuss without taking up extreme positions

maniqueísta ADJ Manichean, Manichaean

maniqueo/a Ⓐ ADJ [1] (*Hist*) Manichean, Manichaean
[2] (= *simplista*) black and white
[3] (= *extremista*) extremist
Ⓑ SM/F [1] (*Hist*) Manichean, Manichaean
[2] (= *simplista*) *person who tends to see things in black and white terms*

maniquí Ⓐ SMF (*) poser*
Ⓑ SM [1] (= *muñeco*) [*de sastre, escaparate*] dummy, mannequin; (*Esgrima*) dummy figure
[2] (= *títere*) puppet
Ⓒ SF (= *modelo*) model

manir ▸conjug 3a◂ Ⓐ VT [+ *carne*] to hang
Ⓑ **manirse** VPR (*CAm*) to go off

manirroto/a Ⓐ ADJ extravagant, lavish
Ⓑ SM/F spendthrift

manisero (*LAm*) = **manicero**

manisuelto/a Ⓐ ADJ extravagant
Ⓑ SM/F spendthrift

manita SF little hand; **echar una ~ a algn** to lend sb a hand; ✦MODISMOS **hacer ~s** to canoodle, make out (*EEUU**) (**con** with); **tener ~s de plata** *o* **de oro** to be very skilful ► **manitas de cerdo** pig's trotters

manitas* SMF INV handyman/handywoman; **ser (un(a)) ~** to be handy, be good with one's hands

manito[1] SM (*Méx*) pal*, buddy (*EEUU**); (*en conversación*) mate*, pal*

manito[2]* SM (*LAm*) = **manita**

manivacío ADJ empty-handed

manivela SF crank, handle ► **manivela de arranque** starting handle

manjar SM [1] (= *delicia*) delicacy; **~ exquisito** tasty morsel; **~ espiritual** food for the mind, spiritual sustenance
[2] (*Cono Sur*) (= *leche condensada*) heated condensed milk ► **manjar blanco** blancmange ► **manjar dulce** (*Andes*) fudge
[3] (*CAm, Méx*) suit

mano[1]

[A] SUSTANTIVO FEMENINO	[B] SUSTANTIVO MASCULINO

Ⓐ SUSTANTIVO FEMENINO

Para las expresiones ***manos arriba, al alcance de la mano, frotarse las manos****, ver la otra entrada.*

[1] [*Anat*] hand; **lo hice con mis propias ~s** I made it with my own hands, I made it myself; **el asesino salió con las ~s en alto** the murderer came out with his hands up *o* with his hands in the air; **votar a ~ alzada** to vote by a show of hands; **dar la ~ a algn** (*para saludar*) to shake hands with sb; (*para andar, apoyarse*) to take sb by the hand; **darse la ~** *o* **las ~s** to shake hands; **recibir algo de ~s de algn** to receive sth from sb; **los dos iban de la ~** the two were walking hand-in-hand, the two were walking along holding hands; **llevar a algn de la ~** to lead sb by the hand; **¡~s a la obra!** (*como orden*) to work!; (*para darse ánimo*) let's get on with it!, (let's) get down to work; **¡las ~s quietas!** hands off!, keep your hands to yourself!; **¡venga esa ~!** shake!, put it there!

◆ **a mano** (= *sin máquina*) by hand; (= *cerca*) handy, at hand; (= *asequible*) handy, to hand; **cosió los pantalones a ~** she sewed the trousers by hand, she hand-sewed the trousers; **escribir a ~** to write in longhand, write out (by hand); **escrito a ~** handwritten; **bordado a ~** hand-embroidered; **hecho a ~** handmade; **¿tienes un bolígrafo a ~?** have you got a pen handy *o* to hand?; **la tienda**

me queda *o* **me pilla* muy a ~** the shop is very handy for me, the shop is very close *o* nearby

◆ **en mano**: **a entregar en ~** to deliver by hand; **se presentó en el ayuntamiento pistola en ~** he turned up at the town hall with a gun in his hand; **carta en ~** letter delivered by hand; **"piso disponible, llave en mano"** (*para alquilar*) "flat available for immediate occupancy"; (*para comprar*) "flat available for immediate possession"; *ver tb* **estrechar A3**, **levantar A1.2**, **robo 1**

[2] ✦*MODISMOS* **abrir la ~** to open up, loosen up; (= *dejarse*) to let one's standards slip; **a ~ airada** violently; **bajo ~** (= *secretamente*) in secret, on the quiet; **cargar la ~** (= *exagerar*) to overdo it; (= *cobrar demasiado*) to overcharge; (= *exigir*) to press too hard, be too exacting; **en ese colegio le cargan la ~** they ask too much of her *o* put too much pressure on her at that school; **no cargues la ~ con las especias** don't put too much spice in; **coger a algn con las ~s en la masa** to catch sb red-handed; **dar de ~** to knock off*, stop working; **le das la ~ y se toma el codo** give him an inch and he'll take a mile; **dar una ~ a algn** (*LAm*) to lend *o* give sb a hand; **de ~s a boca** unexpectedly, suddenly; **estar con una ~ adelante y otra atrás** to be broke*; **estar ~ sobre ~** to be idle, be out of work; **echar ~ a** to lay hands on; **echar ~ de** to make use of, resort to; **echar una ~ a algn** to lend *o* give sb a hand; **ganar a algn por la ~** to beat sb to it; **llegar a las ~s** to come to blows; **a ~s llenas** lavishly, generously; **~ a ~**: **se bebieron la botella ~ a ~** they drank the bottle between (the two of) them; **meter ~ a algn*** to touch sb up*; **meter ~ a algo**: **hay que meterle ~ a la corrupción** we have to deal with *o* tackle corruption; **tengo que meterle ~ a las matemáticas** I need to get stuck into my maths*; **pasar la ~ a algn** (= *ser permisivo*) to be lenient with sb; (*LAm*) (= *adular*) to flatter sb, suck up to sb*; **ponerle a algn la ~ encima**: **¡como me pongas la ~ encima ...!** if you lay one finger on me ...!; **poner la ~ en el fuego**: **yo no pondría la ~ en el fuego por Juan** I wouldn't risk my neck for Juan, I wouldn't put myself on the line for Juan; **yo pondría la ~ en el fuego por su inocencia** I'd stake my life on his being innocent; **¡qué ~!** (*Ven*) not likely!; **sentar la ~ a algn** (= *pegar*) to beat sb; **tener las ~s largas** (= *ser propenso a robar*) to be light-fingered; (= *ser propenso a pegar*) to be apt to hit out; **tener las ~s libres** to have full *o* free rein, be given full *o* free rein, be free (to do sth); **traerse algo entre ~s**: **¿qué os traéis entre ~s?** what are you up to?; **se trae entre ~s varios asuntos a la vez** he's dealing with several matters at once; **untar la ~ a algn** to grease sb's palm; **con las ~s vacías** empty-handed; **se fue de las negociaciones con las ~s vacías** he left the negotiations empty-handed; **vivir de la ~ a la boca** to live from hand to mouth ► **mano derecha** right-hand man; **Pedro es mi ~ derecha** Pedro is my right-hand man ► **mano de santo** sure remedy; **fue ~ de santo** it came just right, it was just what the doctor ordered ► **mano dura** harsh treatment; (*Pol*) firm hand ► **manos de mantequilla** butterfingers

[3] [= *posesión*] hand; **cambiar de ~s** to change hands; **la casa ha cambiado varias veces de ~** the house has changed hands several times, the house has had several owners; **de primera ~** (at) first-hand; **conocemos la noticia de primera ~** we got the news first-hand; **se ha comprado un coche de primera ~** he has bought a (brand) new car; **de segunda ~** second-hand; **ropa de segunda ~** second-hand *o* used clothes

[4] [= *control*] **está en tus ~s** it's up to you; **ha hecho cuanto ha estado en su ~** he has done all *o* everything in his power; **de buena ~** on good authority; **en buenas ~s** in good hands

◆ **a manos de** at the hands of; **murió a ~s de los mafiosos** he died at the hands of the mafia; **la carta nunca llegó a ~s del jefe** the letter never reached the boss, the letter never came into the hands of the boss

◆ **en manos de** in the hands of; **hemos puesto el asunto en ~s del abogado** we have placed the matter in the hands of our lawyer; **me pongo en tus ~s** I place myself entirely in your hands; **el armamento cayó en ~s de los traficantes** the weapons fell into the hands of arms dealers; ✦*MODISMOS* **írsele a algn la ~ con algo**: **se te ha ido la ~ con la sal** you overdid it with the salt; **írsele algo de las ~s a algn**: **el asunto se le fue de las ~s** he lost all control of the affair; **dejado de la ~ de Dios** godforsaken; **tomarse la justicia por su ~** to take the law into one's own hands

[5] [= *habilidad*] **¡qué ~s tiene!** he's so clever with his hands!; **tener buena ~**: **tiene buena ~ para aparcar** she's good at parking; **tener buena ~ para la cocina** to be a good cook; **tiene buena ~ con los niños** she's good with children; **tener (buena) ~ para las plantas** to have green fingers; **tener mala ~** to be clumsy, be awkward ► **mano izquierda**: **tiene ~ izquierda con los animales** he's got a way with animals

[6] [= *lado*] side; **a ~ derecha** on the right-hand side; **a ~ izquierda** on the left-hand side

[7] [= *trabajadores*] **manos** hands, workers; **contratar ~s** to sign up *o* take on workers ► **mano de obra** labour, labor (*EEUU*), manpower ► **mano de obra directa** direct labour ► **mano de obra especializada** skilled labour

[8] [*Dep*] handling, handball; **¡mano!** handball!

[9] [*Zool*] [*de mono*] hand; [*de perro, gato, oso, león*] front paw; [*de caballo*] forefoot, front hoof; [*de ave*] foot; (= *trompa*) trunk ► **manos de cerdo** (*Culin*) pig's trotters

[10] [= *instrumento*] [*de reloj*] hand ► **mano de almirez, mano de mortero** pestle

[11] [= *capa*] [*de pintura*] coat; [*de jabón*] wash, soaping; **dar una ~ de jabón a la ropa** to give the clothes a wash *o* soaping

[12] [*Juegos, Naipes*] (= *partida*) round, game; (= *conjunto de cartas*) hand; **echar una ~ de mus** to have a game *o* round of mus; **ser** *o* **tener la ~** to lead; **soy ~** it's my lead

[13] [= *lote*] lot, series; (*Andes, CAm, Cono Sur, Méx*) *group of things of the same kind*; (*LAm*) [*de plátanos*] bunch, hand; **le dio una ~ de bofetadas** he punched him several times; **una ~ de papel** a quire of paper (*24 or 25 sheets*)

[14] [*Mús*] scale

[15] [*LAm* = *desgracia*] misfortune, mishap; (= *suceso imprevisto*) unexpected event

[16] [*LAm* = *suerte*] **¡qué ~!** what a stroke of luck!

[17] [*LAm Aut*] direction ► **mano única** one-way street

Ⓑ SUSTANTIVO MASCULINO

► **mano a mano**: **hubo un ~ a ~ entre los dos políticos en el parlamento** the two politicians slogged it out between them in parliament; **la corrida será un ~ a ~ entre los dos toreros** the bullfight will be a two-way contest with the two bullfighters

---

mano² SM (*Méx*) (*en conversación*) mate*, pal*

manoizquierdoso ADJ (= *astuto*) knowing, cunning; (= *sofisticado*) sophisticated

manojo SM [1] (= *conjunto*) handful, bunch; **un ~ de llaves** a bunch of keys; **un ~ de hierba** a tuft of grass; **un ~ de pillos** a bunch of rogues; ✦*MODISMO* **estar hecho** *o* **ser un ~ de nervios** to be a bundle *o* bag of nerves
[2] (*Caribe*) bundle of raw tobacco (*about 2lbs*)

manola‡ SF [1] (= *jeringuilla*) needle, syringe
[2] (†) *Madrid woman of the people, characterized by flamboyant zarzuela-type costume*

manoletina SF (*Taur*) *a kind of pass with the cape*

Manolo SM (*forma familiar*) *de* **Manuel**

manolo SM toff*; (*esp Madrid*) *Madrid man of the people, characterized by flamboyant zarzuela-type costume*

manómetro SM pressure gauge, manometer (*frm*)

manopla SF [1] (= *guante*) (*gen*) mitten; [*de cocina*] oven glove; [*de baño*] bath mitt
[2] (*Hist, Téc*) gauntlet
[3] (*LAm*) (= *puño de hierro*) knuckle-duster
[4] (*Cono Sur*) (= *llave inglesa*) spanner

manoseado ADJ [*libro*] well-thumbed; [*tema*] hackneyed, well-worn

manosear ▸conjug 1a◂ VT [1] [+ *objeto*] (= *tocar*) to handle, paw*; (= *desordenar*) to rumple; (= *jugar con*) to fiddle with, mess about with [2] (*LAm*) [+ *persona*] to touch up*, grope* [3] [+ *tema*] to overwork, repeat

manoseo SM [1] [*de objetos*] (*gen*) handling, pawing*; (*desordenando*) rumpling
[2] (*LAm*) [*de persona*] touching up*, groping*
[3] [*de tema*] overworking, repetition

manos libres Ⓐ SM INV [*teléfono, dispositivo*] hands-free
Ⓑ SM INV hands-free kit, hands-free set

manotada SF [1] (= *golpe*) slap, smack
[2] (*LAm*) (= *puñado*) handful, fistful

manotazo SM slap, smack; **dar un ~ a algn** to give sb a slap, slap sb; **le partió el labio de un ~** she split his lip with a smack in the mouth; **se lo quité de un ~** I swiped it off him

manoteador SM (*Cono Sur, Méx*) [1] (= *ladrón*) (*gen*) thief; [*de bolsos*] bag-snatcher [2] (= *estafador*) fiddler* [3] (= *aspaventero*) gesticulator

manotear ▸conjug 1a◂ Ⓐ VT (= *dar palmadas*) to slap, smack Ⓑ VI [1] (= *gesticular*) to gesticulate [2] (*Cono Sur, Méx**) (= *arrancar*) to bag-snatch; (= *robar*) to steal

manoteo SM [1] (= *gestos*) gesticulation
[2] (*Cono Sur, Méx**) (= *robo*) theft, robbery; (= *estafa*) fiddling*

manque* CONJ (*esp LAm*) = **aunque**

manquear ▸conjug 1a◂ VI [1] (= *estar lisiado*) to

be maimed, be crippled
[2] (= *fingir*) to pretend to be crippled
[3] (*Cono Sur, Méx*) (= *cojear*) to limp

manquedad SF, **manquera** SF [1] (= *incapacidad*) disablement
[2] (= *defecto*) defect

mansalino ADJ (*Cono Sur*) (= *enorme*) huge; (= *extraordinario*) extraordinary; (= *excelente*) excellent

mansalva SF **a ~** (= *mucho*) in abundance; (= *a gran escala*) on a large scale; (= *sin riesgo*) without risk; **gastan dinero a ~** they spend money as if there were no tomorrow; **ese profesor suspende a ~** that teacher fails pupils left, right and centre; **le dispararon a ~** they shot him before he could defend himself; **estar a ~ de algo** to be safe from sth

mansamente ADV gently, meekly

mansarda SF (*esp LAm*) attic

mansedumbre SF [1] [*de persona*] gentleness, meekness
[2] [*de animal*] tameness

mansión SF mansion

manso Ⓐ ADJ [1] [*persona*] meek, gentle
[2] [*animal*] tame
[3] (*Chile**) (= *tremendo*) huge, tremendous
Ⓑ SM (*Esp‡*) mattress

manta[1] SF [1] (*para taparse*) blanket; ✦*MODISMOS* **a ~**: **repartieron vino y comida a ~** they handed out food and wine in abundance; **llovía a ~** it was raining buckets; **la policía dio palos a ~** the police didn't hold back with their truncheons; **liarse la ~ a la cabeza** to take the plunge; **tirar de la ~** to let the cat out of the bag, give the game away ► **manta de viaje** travelling rug, traveling rug (*EEUU*) ► **manta eléctrica** electric blanket ► **manta ignífuga** fire blanket
[2] (*LAm*) (= *calicó*) *coarse cotton cloth*; (= *poncho*) poncho
[3] (*) (= *paliza*) hiding; **les dieron una buena ~ de palos** they gave them a good hiding *o* beating with a stick
[4] (*Zool*) manta ray

manta[2]* Ⓐ ADJ bone-idle
Ⓑ SMF idler, slacker
Ⓒ SF idleness

mantadril SM (*CAm*) denim

mantarraya SF (*LAm*) manta ray

mantear ▸conjug 1a◂ VT [1] (= *lanzar*) to toss in a blanket
[2] (*Caribe*) (= *maltratar*) to ill-treat, abuse
[3] (*Caribe*) (= *golpear*) to beat up

manteca SF [1] (= *grasa*) fat, animal fat ► **manteca de cerdo** lard
[2] (*esp Cono Sur*) (= *mantequilla*) butter ► **manteca de cacahuete** peanut butter ► **manteca de cacao** cocoa butter ► **manteca de vaca** butter ► **manteca vegetal** vegetable fat
[3] (‡) (= *dinero*) dough‡, dosh‡; (= *géneros*) goods *pl*
[4] (*LAm‡*) (= *marihuana*) pot*, grass*
[5] (*Andes*) (= *criada*) servant girl

mantecada SF small cake, iced bun

mantecado SM *Christmas sweet made from flour, almonds and lard*

mantecón* SM milksop, mollycoddle

mantecoso ADJ (= *grasiento*) greasy; (= *cremoso*) creamy, buttery; **queso ~** soft cheese

➤ LENGUA Y USO: **mantener A6** 53.5

mantel SM (*para comer*) tablecloth; (*Rel*) altar cloth; **una cena de ~ largo** (*Cono Sur**) a formal dinner; **levantar los ~es** to clear the table; **poner los ~es** to lay the table ► **mantel individual** place mat

mantelería SF table linen; **una ~ blanca** a set of white table linen

mantelillo SM table runner

mantelito SM doily

mantención SF (*LAm*) = **manutención**

mantenedor(a) SM/F (*Esp*) [*de certamen*] chairman/chairwoman, chairperson, president ► **mantenedor(a) de la familia** breadwinner

mantener ▸conjug 2k◂ Ⓐ VT [1] (= *sostener*) (*gen*) to hold; [+ *puente, techo*] to support; **mantén la caja un momento** hold the box a minute; **los pilares que mantienen el puente** the pillars which support the bridge
[2] (= *preservar*) [2·1] (*en un lugar*) to store, keep; **"una vez abierto manténgase refrigerado"** "once opened keep in a refrigerator"; **"manténgase en un lugar fresco y seco"** "store in a cool dry place"
[2·2] (*en un estado o situación*) to keep; **la ilusión es lo único que lo mantiene vivo** hope is the only thing that keeps him alive *o* going; **hay que ~ actualizada la base de datos** we have to keep the database up to date; **para ~ el motor en buen estado** to keep the engine in good condition; **"mantenga limpia su ciudad"** keep your city clean; **"manténgase fuera del alcance de los niños"** "keep out of the reach of children"; **~ algo caliente** to keep sth hot; **~ algo en equilibrio** to balance sth, keep sth balanced; **~ algo en secreto** to keep sth a secret; **mantuvo en secreto que tenía dos hijos** she kept her two children a secret; *ver tb* **raya**[1] **1**
[3] (= *conservar*) [+ *opinión*] to maintain, hold; [+ *costumbre, ideales*] to keep up, maintain; [+ *disciplina*] to maintain, keep; [+ *promesa*] to keep; **un alto porcentaje mantenía su opinión sobre la crisis** a high percentage maintained *o* held their opinion about the crisis; **me marcho manteniendo mi opinión** I'm leaving, but I stand by my opinion; **una civilización que lucha por ~ sus tradiciones** a civilization struggling to uphold *o* maintain its traditions; **eran partidarios de ~ el antiguo orden social** they were in favour of preserving the old social order; **~ el orden público** to keep the peace; **al conducir hay que ~ la distancia de seguridad** you have to keep (at) a safe distance when driving; **~ el equilibrio** to keep one's balance; **le cuesta ~ el equilibrio** he finds it difficult to keep his balance; **hemos conseguido ~ el equilibrio entre ingresos y gastos** we have managed to maintain a balance between income and expenditure; **~ el fuego** to keep the fire going; **~ la línea** to keep one's figure, keep in shape; **~ la paz** to keep the peace, maintain peace; ✦*MODISMO* **mantenella y no enmendalla** (*Esp*) to stand one's ground; *ver tb* **calma 1**, **distancia 1**
[4] (*económicamente*) to support, maintain; **ahora tiene una familia que ~** now he has a family to support *o* maintain; **ya no pienso ~la más** I refuse to keep *o* support *o* maintain her any longer
[5] [+ *conversación, contacto*] to maintain, hold; **es incapaz de ~ una conversación coherente** he is incapable of maintaining *o* holding a coherent conversation; **en las conversaciones que hemos mantenido con el presidente** in the talks we have held with the president; **¿han mantenido ustedes relaciones sexuales?** have you had sexual relations?; *ver tb* **correspondencia 2**
[6] (= *afirmar*) to maintain; **siempre he mantenido lo contrario** I've always maintained the opposite
Ⓑ **mantenerse** VPR [1] (= *sostenerse*) to be supported; **el techo se mantiene con cuatro columnas** the roof is supported by four columns; **~se en pie** [*persona*] to stand up, stay on one's feet; [*edificio*] to be still standing; **la iglesia es lo único que se mantiene en pie** only the church is still standing
[2] (*en un estado o situación*) to stay, remain; **se mantenía despierto a base de pastillas** he stayed *o* remained awake by taking pills; **el precio del petróleo se mantendrá estable** the price of oil will remain stable; **el motor se mantiene en perfectas condiciones** the engine is still in perfect condition; **"manténgase a su derecha"** (*Aut*) "keep right", "keep to the right"; **~se en contacto** to keep in touch (**con** with); **¿os seguís manteniendo en contacto?** do you still keep in touch?; **se mantenía en contacto telefónico permanente con su familia** he maintained permanent telephone contact with his family; **~se al día en algo** to keep up to date with sth; **~se en forma** to keep fit, keep in shape; **~se en su puesto** keep *o* retain one's post; **~se en vigor** [*costumbre*] to remain in existence; [*ley*] to remain in force; ✦*MODISMO* **~se en su sitio** *o* **en sus trece*** to stand one's ground, stick to one's guns; *ver tb* **firme A3**, **flote**
[3] (*económicamente*) to support o.s.
[4] (= *alimentarse*) **~se a base de algo** to live on sth; **se mantiene a base de verduras** he lives on vegetables

mantenibilidad SF ease of maintenance

mantenido/a Ⓐ ADJ [1] [*esfuerzo, tensión*] constant
[2] [*persona*] kept
Ⓑ SM/F (= *amante*) kept man/kept woman
Ⓒ SM (*CAm, Méx**) (= *proxeneta*) pimp; (= *aprovechado*) sponger*, parasite

mantenimiento SM [1] (= *continuación*) maintenance; **el ~ de la paz** the maintenance of peace; **el ~ de las tradiciones** the upholding of traditions; **tras el ~ de las conversaciones de paz** after maintaining *o* holding peace talks
[2] (= *conservación*) (*Mec, Téc*) maintenance; **el ~ de las carreteras** upkeep of the roads, road maintenance; **el coste del ~ de una familia** the upkeep of a family, the cost of running a family; **costes** *o* **gastos de ~** maintenance costs, upkeep; **servicio de ~** maintenance service
[3] (*Dep*) keep-fit; **clase de ~** keep-fit class; **ejercicios** *o* **gimnasia de ~** keep-fit exercises

manteo SM [*de hombre*] long cloak; [*de mujer*] full skirt

mantequera SF [1] (*para batir*) churn
[2] (*para servir*) butter dish

mantequería SF (*LAm*) (= *lechería*) dairy, creamery; (= *ultramarinos*) grocer's, grocer's shop

mantequilla SF butter; **pan con ~** bread and butter; **tostadas con ~** buttered toast; **manos de ~** butter fingers ► **mantequilla de cacahuete** peanut butter

mantequillera SF butter dish

mantilla SF [1] [*de mujer*] mantilla ► **mantilla de blonda**, **mantilla de encajes** lace mantilla
[2] [*de bebé*] **mantillas** baby clothes; ✦*MODISMOS* **estar en ~s** [*persona*] to be very naive; [*proyecto, técnica*] to be in its infancy; **dejar a algn en ~s** to leave sb in the dark

mantillo SM humus, mould, mold (*EEUU*)

mantillón SM [1] (*CAm, Méx*) (= *manta*) horse-blanket
[2] (*Méx**) (= *amante*) kept man/woman (*pey*); (= *parásito*) sponger

mantis SF INV ► **mantis religiosa** praying mantis

manto SM [1] (= *capa*) (*para abrigarse*) cloak; (*Rel, Jur*) robe, gown
[2] (*Zool*) mantle
[3] (*liter*) (= *velo*) **cuando la noche tiende su ~** when the world is cloaked in darkness; **un ~ de nieve cubría la colina** a blanket of snow covered the hill
[4] (*Min*) layer, stratum
[5] (*tb* **~ de chimenea**) mantel

mantón SM shawl ► **mantón de manila** embroidered shawl

mantra SM mantra

mantudo ADJ [1] [*ave*] with drooping wings
[2] (*CAm*) (= *disfrazado*) masked, in disguise

manuable ADJ handy, easy to handle

manual Ⓐ ADJ [1] (= *de manos*) manual; **habilidad ~** manual dexterity; **tener habilidad ~** to be clever with one's hands; **trabajo ~** manual labour, manual labor (*EEUU*)
[2] = **manuable**
Ⓑ SM manual, guide ► **manual de consulta** reference book, reference manual ► **manual de estilo** style book, style guide ► **manual de funcionamiento** operating manual ► **manual de instrucciones** instruction manual ► **manual del usuario** user's manual ► **manual de mantenimiento** service manual, maintenance manual ► **manual de operación** instructions manual ► **manual de reparaciones** repair manual ► **manual sexual** sex manual

manualidades SFPL handicrafts, craftwork *sing*; **hacer ~** to do craftwork; **talleres de ~** craft workshops

manualmente ADV manually, by hand

manubrio SM [1] (*Mec*) (= *manivela*) handle, crank; (= *torno*) winch
[2] (*Mús*) barrel organ
[3] (*LAm*) [*de bicicleta*] handlebar, handlebars *pl*
[4] (*Par Aut*) steering wheel

manudo ADJ (*LAm*) with big hands

Manuel SM Emmanuel

manuelita SF (*Caribe*) rolled pancake

manufactura SF [1] (= *fabricación*) manufacture
[2] (= *producto*) product
[3] (= *fábrica*) factory

manufacturado ADJ manufactured

manufacturar ▸conjug 1a◂ VT to manufacture

manufacturero/a Ⓐ ADJ manufacturing
Ⓑ SM/F (*esp LAm*) manufacturer, manufacturing company

manumitir ▸conjug 3a◂ VT to manumit

manú(s)⁑ SM (*Esp*) bloke*

manuscrito Ⓐ ADJ handwritten
Ⓑ SM manuscript ► **manuscritos del Mar Muerto** Dead Sea scrolls

manutención SF [1] [*de una familia*] maintenance, upkeep; **le pasa la ~ para sus hijos** he pays for their children's maintenance *o* upkeep; **gastos de ~** maintenance costs, upkeep
[2] (*Mec, Téc*) maintenance

manyar⁑ ▸conjug 1a◂ VT, VI (*Caribe, Cono Sur*) to eat

manzana SF [1] (= *fruta*) apple; **~ ácida** cooking apple; **~ de mesa** eating apple; **~ de sidra** cider apple; **~ silvestre** wild apple, crabapple; **tarta de ~** apple tart; ✦*MODISMO* **~ de la discordia** bone of contention
[2] ► **manzana de Adán** (*esp LAm Anat*) Adam's apple
[3] [*de casas*] block (of houses)
[4] (= *medida*) (*CAm*) *land measure (= 1.75 acres)*; (*Cono Sur*) *land measure (= 2.5 acres)*

manzanal SM [1] (= *huerto*) apple orchard
[2] (= *manzano*) apple tree

manzanar SM apple orchard

manzanilla SF [1] (*Bot*) (= *flor*) camomile; (= *infusión*) camomile tea
[2] (= *jerez*) manzanilla sherry
[3] (= *aceituna*) *a variety of small olive*

manzano SM apple tree

maña SF [1] (= *habilidad*) skill; **tiene mucha ~ para hacer arreglos caseros** he's a dab hand at mending things around the house
[2] (= *ardid*) trick; **con ~** craftily, slyly; **malas ~s** (*gen*) bad habits; [*de niño*] naughty ways

mañana Ⓐ ADV tomorrow; **~ por la ~** tomorrow morning; **~ por la noche** tomorrow night; **¡hasta ~!** see you tomorrow!; **pasado ~** the day after tomorrow; **~ temprano** early tomorrow; **~ será otro día** tomorrow's another day
Ⓑ SM future; **el ~ es incierto** the future is uncertain, tomorrow is uncertain; **el día de ~** in the future
Ⓒ SF morning; **la ~ siguiente** the following morning; **a las siete de la ~** at seven o'clock in the morning, at seven a.m.; **de** *o* **por la ~** in the morning; **muy de ~** very early in the morning; **en la ~ de ayer** yesterday morning; **en la ~ de hoy** this morning; **de la noche a la ~** overnight

mañanero/a Ⓐ ADJ [1] (= *madrugador*) **ser ~** to be an early riser
[2] (= *matutino*) morning *antes de s*
Ⓑ SM/F early riser

mañanita SF [1] (= *mañana*) early morning; **de ~** very early in the morning, at the crack of dawn
[2] (= *chal*) bed jacket
[3] **mañanitas** (*Méx*) (= *canción*) serenade *sing*

mañear ▸conjug 1a◂ Ⓐ VT to manage cleverly, contrive skilfully
Ⓑ VI [1] (*con ingenio*) to act shrewdly, go about things cunningly
[2] (*con picardía*) to get up to one's tricks

mañero ADJ [1] = **mañoso 1**
[2] (*Cono Sur*) [*animal*] (= *fiero*) vicious; (= *obstinado*) obstinate; (= *asustadizo*) nervous, skittish

maño/a ADJ, SM/F Aragonese

mañosamente ADV [1] (= *ingeniosamente*) cleverly, ingeniously, skilfully, skillfully (*EEUU*)
[2] (= *con picardía*) craftily, cunningly

mañosear ▸conjug 1a◂ VI (*Andes, Cono Sur*) [*niño*] to be difficult (*esp about food*)

mañoso/a Ⓐ ADJ [1] [*persona*] (= *hábil*) clever, ingenious; (= *astuto*) crafty, cunning
[2] (*Andes*) (= *perezoso*) lazy
[3] (*LAm*) [*animal*] (= *violento*) vicious; (= *terco*) obstinate; (= *tímido*) shy, nervous; (*Andes, Cono Sur, Méx*) difficult (*esp about food*)
Ⓑ SM/F (*CAm*) (= *ladrón*) thief

maoísmo SM Maoism

maoísta ADJ, SMF Maoist

Mao Zedong SM Mao Tse-tung

MAPA SM ABR (= **Ministerio de Agricultura, Pesca y Alimentación**) ≈ MAFF, ≈ USDA (*EEUU*)

mapa SM map; **el ~ político** (= *escena*) the political scene; (= *abanico*) the political spectrum ✦*MODISMO* **desaparecer del ~** to vanish off the face of the earth ► **mapa de carreteras** road map ► **mapa del tiempo** weather map ► **mapa en relieve** relief map ► **mapa geológico** geological map ► **mapa hipsométrico** contour map ► **mapa meteorológico** weather map ► **mapa mural** wall map

mapache SM racoon, raccoon

mapamundi SM [1] (= *mapa*) world map
[2] (*) (= *trasero*) bottom

mapeado SM mapping

mapeango ADJ (*Caribe, Méx*), **mapiango** ADJ (*Caribe, Méx*) useless, incompetent

mapear ▸conjug 1a◂ VT to map

mapuche (*a veces en fem* **mapucha**) (*esp Chile*)
Ⓐ ADJ Mapuche, Araucanian
Ⓑ SMF Mapuche (Indian), Araucanian (Indian); → ARAUCANO
Ⓒ SM (*Ling*) Mapuche, Araucanian

mapurito SM (*CAm*) skunk

maque SM lacquer

maquear ▸conjug 1a◂ Ⓐ VT to lacquer
Ⓑ **maquearse** VPR (⁑) to get ready (to go out), get dressed up; **ir (bien) maqueado** to be all dressed up

maqueta SF [1] (= *modelo*) model, scale model, mock-up
[2] (= *libro*) dummy, fake (*EEUU*)
[3] (*Mús*) demo, demo tape

maquetación SF layout, design

maquetar ▸conjug 1a◂ VT, **maquetear** ▸conjug 1a◂ VT to lay out, design

maquetista SMF (*Arquit*) model maker; (*Tip*) typesetter

maqueto SM (*pey*) immigrant worker (*in the Basque Country*)

maquiavélico ADJ Machiavellian

Maquiavelo SM Machiavelli

maquiladora SF (*Méx Com*) bonded assembly plant

maquilar ▸conjug 1a◂ VT (*Méx*) to assemble

maquillador(a) SM/F (*Teat*) make-up artist

maquillaje SM [1] (= *pintura*) make-up; (= *acto*) making up ► **maquillaje base**, **maquillaje de fondo** foundation
[2] (*) [*de cuentas*] massaging*

maquillar ▸conjug 1a◂ Ⓐ VT [1] (= *persona*) to make up
[2] (*) [+ *cifras, cuentas*] to massage*
Ⓑ **maquillarse** VPR to make o.s. up

máquina SF 1 (= *aparato*) (*gen*) machine; **a toda ~** at full speed; **coser algo a ~** to machine-sew sth; **entrar en ~** to go to press; **escribir a ~** to type; **escrito a ~** typed, typewritten; **hecho a ~** machine-made; **pasar algo a ~** to type sth (up); ✦*MODISMO* **forzar la ~** (= *ir deprisa*) to go full steam ahead; (= *abusar de las posibilidades*) to pull out all the stops ► **máquina copiadora** copier, copying machine ► **máquina cosechadora** combine harvester, combine ► **máquina de afeitar** razor, safety razor ► **máquina de afeitar eléctrica** electric razor, shaver ► **máquina de azar** fruit machine ► **máquina de bolas*** pinball machine ► **máquina de calcular** calculator ► **máquina de contabilidad** adding machine ► **máquina de coser** sewing machine ► **máquina de discos** jukebox ► **máquina de escribir** typewriter ► **máquina de franquear** franking machine ► **máquina de hacer punto** knitting machine ► **máquina de lavar** washing machine ► **máquina de sumar** adding machine ► **máquina de tabaco*** cigarette machine ► **máquina de tejer, máquina de tricotar** knitting machine ► **máquina de vapor** steam engine ► **máquina excavadora** mechanical digger, steam shovel (*EEUU*) ► **máquina expendedora** vending machine ► **máquina fotográfica** camera ► **máquina franqueadora** franking machine ► **máquina herramienta** machine tool ► **máquina ordeñadora** milking machine ► **máquina picadora** mincer ► **máquina quitanieves** snowplough, snowplow (*EEUU*) ► **máquina registradora** (*LAm*) cash register ► **máquina tejedora** knitting machine ► **máquina tragaperras** fruit machine, one-armed bandit; (*Com*) vending machine
2 (*Transportes*) [*de tren*] engine, locomotive; (*) (= *moto*) motorbike; (*CAm, Cuba*) (= *coche*) car; (= *taxi*) taxi
3 (*Fot*) camera
4 (*Pol*) machine ► **máquina electoral** electoral machine
5 (= *maquinaria*) machinery, workings *pl*; (= *plan*) scheme of things

maquinación SF machination, plot

maquinador(a) SM/F schemer, plotter

maquinal ADJ mechanical

maquinalmente ADV mechanically

maquinar ▸conjug 1a◂ VT, VI to plot

maquinaria SF 1 (= *conjunto de máquinas*) machinery ► **maquinaria agrícola** agricultural machinery, farm implements *pl* ► **maquinaria pesada** heavy plant
2 (= *mecanismo*) mechanism; **la ~ de un reloj** the mechanism of a watch
3 (*Pol*) machine; **la ~ electoral** the campaign machine; **la ~ propagandística** the propaganda machine

maquinilla SF (= *máquina*) small machine; (= *torno*) winch; (*para el pelo*) clippers *pl*; **~ para liar cigarrillos** cigarette(-rolling) machine ► **maquinilla de afeitar** razor, safety razor ► **maquinilla eléctrica** electric razor, shaver

maquinista SMF 1 (*Ferro*) engine driver, engineer (*EEUU*); (*Náut*) engineer
2 (*Téc*) operator, machinist
3 (*Teat*) scene-shifter; (*Cine*) cameraman's assistant

maquis SM INV (= *movimiento*) resistance movement, maquis; (= *persona*) member of the resistance, maquis

mar[1] SM (*a veces* SF) 1 (*Geog*) sea; **el fondo del ~** the bottom of the sea, the seabed; **una casa al lado del ~** a house by the sea *o* on the coast; **el avión cayó en el ~** the plane came down in the sea; **el** *o* **la ~ estaba en calma** the sea was calm; **iban navegando en ~ abierto** they were sailing on the open sea; **~ adentro** [*ir, llevar*] out to sea; [*estar*] out at sea; **en alta ~** on the high seas; **un buque de alta ~** an ocean-going vessel; **pesca de alta ~** deep-sea fishing; **~ arbolada** heavy sea; **caer(se) al ~** (*desde tierra*) to fall into the sea; (*desde un barco*) to fall overboard; **echarse a la ~** to set sail; **~ de fondo** (*lit*) groundswell; (*fig*) underlying tension; **~ gruesa** heavy sea; **hacerse a la ~** (*liter*) [*barco*] to set sail, put to sea (*frm*); [*marinero*] to set sail; **~ picada** choppy sea; **por ~** by sea, by boat; **toda la mercancía llegará por ~** all the goods will arrive by sea *o* by boat; **~ rizada** rough sea; **los siete ~es** the seven seas; ✦*MODISMOS* **arar en el ~** to labour in vain; **eso es hablar de la ~** that's just wishful thinking, that's just pie in the sky*; **me cago en la ~ (salada)** (*Esp*‡) shit!‡; **mecachis en la ~** (*Esp euf*) sugar!; ✦*REFRÁN* **quien no se arriesga no pasa la ~** nothing ventured, nothing gained ► **mar Adriático** Adriatic Sea ► **mar Báltico** Baltic Sea ► **mar Cantábrico** Cantabrian Sea (*Bay of Biscay*) ► **mar Caribe** Caribbean Sea ► **mar Caspio** Caspian Sea ► **mar de arena** (*poét*) sand dunes *pl*, desert wastes *pl* (*poét*) ► **mar de las Antillas** Caribbean Sea ► **mar del Norte** North Sea ► **mar Egeo** Aegean Sea ► **mar interior** inland sea ► **mar Jónico** Ionian Sea ► **mar Mediterráneo** Mediterranean Sea ► **mar Muerto** Dead Sea ► **mar Negro** Black Sea ► **mar Rojo** Red Sea ► **mar Tirreno** Tyrrhenian Sea; *ver tb* **brazo 4, golpe 11**
2 (= *marea*) tide; **hay demasiada ~ para salir de pesca** the tide is too high to go fishing ► **mar llena** high tide
3 (= *abundancia*) 3·1 **un ~ de diferencia** a world of difference; **hay un ~ de diferencia entre las dos expresiones** there is a world of difference between the two expressions; **existe un ~ de diferencia entre nosotros** we're poles apart; **estar hecho un ~ de dudas** to be full of doubt, be beset with doubts (*frm*); **estar hecho un ~ de lágrimas** to be in floods of tears; **se fue hecha un ~ de lágrimas** she left in floods of tears
3·2 **a ~es**: **estaba llorando a ~es** she was crying her eyes out; **estaba sudando a ~es** he was sweating buckets*; **estuvo lloviendo a ~es todo el camino** it was raining cats and dogs *o* it was pouring (down) the whole way; **el vino corría a ~es en la fiesta** wine flowed like water at the party
3·3 ✦*MODISMO* **la ~ de***: **tengo la ~ de cosas que hacer** I've got no end of things to do; **hace la ~ de tiempo que no la veo** I haven't seen her for ages; **es la ~ de guapa** she's ever so pretty; **estoy la ~ de contento** I'm ever so happy, I'm over the moon*; **lo hemos pasado la ~ de bien** we had a whale of a time* *o* a great time; **en Lisboa vivimos la ~ de bien** we live ever so well in Lisbon, we love living in Lisbon; **ese traje te queda la ~ de bien** that suit looks wonderful on you

mar[2] SF (*euf*) *de* **madre** *in obscene expressions*

mar[3] EXCL (*Mil*) march!

mar. ABR (= **marzo**) Mar

mara* SF crowd, gang*

marabunta SF 1 [*de hormigas*] plague
2 (= *multitud*) crowd
3 (= *daños*) havoc, ravages *pl*

maraca SF 1 (*Mús*) maraca
2 (*Cono Sur*) (= *prostituta*) whore
3 (*Andes, Caribe*) (= *inútil*) dead loss*

maraco* SM (*Caribe*) youngest child, baby of the family

maracucho/a Ⓐ ADJ of/from Maracaibo
Ⓑ SM/F native/inhabitant of Maracaibo; **los ~s** the people of Maracaibo

maracuyá SM passion fruit

marajá SM = **maharajá**

maraña SF 1 (= *maleza*) thicket, tangle of plants
2 [*de hilos*] tangle
3 (= *enredo*) mess, tangle; **una ~ de pasillos** a maze *o* labyrinth of passages; **una ~ de burocracia** a bureaucratic maze *o* labyrinth; **una ~ de mentiras** a web of lies
4 (*) (= *truco*) trick, ruse
5 (*Andes*) small tip

marañero/a Ⓐ ADJ scheming
Ⓑ SM/F schemer

marañón SM (*Bot*) cashew

maraquear ▸conjug 1a◂ VT (*LAm*) to shake, rattle

maraquero SM (*Andes, Caribe*) maraca player

marar‡ ▸conjug 1a◂ VT 1 (= *matar*) to do in*
2 (= *pegar*) to bash*, beat up*

marasmo SM 1 (*Med*) wasting, atrophy
2 (= *estancamiento*) paralysis, stagnation; **hay que sacar al país del ~ económico en que está sumido** we have to pull the country out of its economic stagnation

maratón SM (*a veces* SF) marathon ► **maratón radiofónico** radiothon

maratoniano/a Ⓐ ADJ marathon *antes de s*
Ⓑ SM/F marathon runner

maratonista ADJ, SMF = **maratoniano**

maravedí SM (*pl* **maravedís** *o* **maravedises**) *old Spanish coin*

maravilla SF 1 (= *prodigio*) wonder; **las ~s de la tecnología** the wonders of technology; **¡qué ~ de tiempo tenemos!** what wonderful weather we're having!; **el concierto fue una ~** the concert was wonderful, it was a wonderful concert; **pinta que es una ~** she paints in the most wonderful way; **contar** *o* **hablar ~s de algn/algo** to rave about sb/sth; **hacer ~s** to work wonders; **una dieta que hace ~s con tu silueta** a diet that works wonders for your figure; **hace ~s con la flauta** she plays the flute like a dream; **las siete ~s del mundo** the seven wonders of the world; ✦*MODISMOS* **a ~** (*Esp*) ◊ **a las mil ~s** ◊ **de ~** wonderfully, wonderfully well, marvellously; **el horno funciona a las mil ~s** the oven works wonderfully (well) *o* beautifully *o* marvellously; **representa a ~ ese tipo de poesía** he is a wonderful *o* marvellous exponent of that type of poetry; **siempre nos hemos llevado de ~** we've always got on like a house on fire* *o* wonderfully (well) *o* marvellously; **—¿cómo te va con el coche nuevo?**

—¡de ~! "how are you getting on with the new car?" — "really well!" *o* "great!*"; **este dinero me viene de ~** this money couldn't have come at a better time
2 (= *asombro*) amazement; **para ~ de todos se puso a cantar** to the amazement of us all she burst into song
3 (*Bot*) (= *caléndula*) marigold; (= *enredadera*) morning glory; (*Chile*) (= *girasol*) sunflower

maravillar ▸conjug 1a◂ Ⓐ VT to astonish, amaze; **su actuación maravilló a todo el mundo** his performance astonished *o* amazed everybody, everybody was astonished *o* amazed at his performance
Ⓑ **maravillarse** VPR **~se con** *o* **de algo** to be astonished *o* amazed at *o* by sth; **nos maravillamos con su increíble paciencia** we were astonished *o* amazed at *o* by his incredible patience, we marvelled at his incredible patience

maravillosamente ADV wonderfully, marvellously, marvelously (*EEUU*); **una figura ~ tallada** a wonderfully *o* marvellously carved figure; **ese vestido te sienta ~** you look wonderful *o* marvellous in that dress

maravilloso ADJ 1 (= *magnífico*) wonderful, marvellous, marvelous (*EEUU*); **tengo dos hijos ~s** I have two wonderful *o* marvellous children; **he tenido una maravillosa idea** I've had a wonderful *o* marvellous idea
2 (= *mágico*) magic; **la lámpara maravillosa de Aladino** Aladdin's magic lamp

marbellí Ⓐ ADJ of/from Marbella
Ⓑ SMF native/inhabitant of Marbella; **los ~es** the people of Marbella

marbete SM 1 (= *etiqueta*) label, tag ► **marbete engomado** sticker
2 (*Cos*) edge, border

marca SF 1 (= *señal*) mark; **dejó una ~ al principio del libro** he left a mark at the beginning of the book; **se te nota la ~ del bañador** I can see your tan line*, I can see the mark where your swimming costume was; **haz una ~ en la casilla correcta** tick the appropriate box; **la película lleva la ~ inconfundible de su director** the film bears all the hallmarks of its director; **sello de ~** hallmark ► **marca de agua** watermark ► **marca de la casa**: **un vino ~ de la casa** a house wine; **la mala educación parece ser la ~ de la casa** bad manners seem to be the norm here ► **marca de ley** hallmark ► **marca de nacimiento** birthmark ► **marca transparente** watermark
2 (= *huella*) [*de pie*] footprint, footmark; [*de dedos*] fingerprint; **seguí las ~s que habían dejado sobre la arena** I followed the tracks they had left in the sand, I followed their footprints *o* footmarks in the sand
3 (*Com*) [*de comida, jabón, tabaco*] brand; [*de electrodoméstico, coche*] make; [*de ropa*] label; **¿qué ~ de tabaco fumas?** what brand do you smoke?; **¿de qué ~ es tu televisor?** what make is your television?; **venden productos de su propia ~** they sell own-brand goods; **siempre va vestido de ~** he always wears fashion labels; **ropa de ~** designer-label clothes, designer-label clothing; ✦*MODISMO* **de ~ mayor*** [*susto, borrachera*] incredible; **es un imbécil de ~ mayor** he's a total idiot* ► **marca de calidad** quality mark ► **marca de fábrica** trademark ► **marca registrada** registered trademark; *ver tb* **imagen 4**
4 (*Dep*) [*de especialidad*] record; [*de deportista*] best time; **su mejor ~ personal** his personal best (time); **batir una ~** to break a record; **establecer una ~** to set a record; **acaba de establecer la mejor ~ de la temporada** he's just set the best time of the season; **mejorar** *o* **superar una ~** to break a record
5 (*Náut*) (*en tierra*) seamark; (*en el mar*) marker, buoy
6 (*Naipes*) bid
7 (*en el ganado*) (= *señal*) brand; (= *acción*) branding
8 (= *herramienta*) brand, iron
9 (*Hist*) march, frontier area; **la Marca Hispánica** the Spanish March (*Catalonia*)

marcable ADJ (*Naipes*) biddable

marcación SF 1 (*Náut*) bearing
2 (*Telec*) dialling, dialing (*EEUU*) ► **marcación automática** autodial, automatic dial

marcadamente ADV markedly

marcado Ⓐ ADJ marked; **con ~ acento argentino** with a marked Argentinian accent; **ese vestido le hacía las caderas muy marcadas** that dress accentuated her hips *o* made her hips stand out; **su visita tiene un ~ significado político** his visit has a strong political significance
Ⓑ SM 1 [*de pelo*] set
2 [*de ganado*] branding

marcador(a) Ⓐ SM 1 (*Dep*) scoreboard; **el ~ va dos a uno** the score is 2-1; **dieron la vuelta al ~** they turned the match round; **abrir** *o* **inaugurar el ~** to open the scoring ► **marcador electrónico** electronic scoreboard; *ver tb* **igualar A1.2**
2 (= *indicador*) (*gen*) marker; [*de libro*] bookmark ► **marcador de caminos** road sign
3 (*LAm*) (= *rotulador*) marker
4 (*Billar*) marker
5 (*Telec*) dial
Ⓑ SM/F (*Esp*) scorer

marcaje SM 1 (*Dep*) marking; (= *entrada*) tackle, tackling ► **marcaje al hombre**, **marcaje personal** man-marking, one-to-one marking ► **marcaje por zonas**, **marcaje zonal** zonal *o* defence marking
2 [*de criminal*] shadowing, following; **hacer ~ a algn** to shadow sb, tail sb

marcapasos SM INV pacemaker

▼marcar ▸conjug 1g◂ Ⓐ VT 1 (= *señalar*) 1·1 [+ *objeto, ropa*] to mark; [+ *ganado*] to brand; **ha marcado las toallas con mis iniciales** she has put my initials on the towels, she has marked the towels with my initials; **el accidente lo dejó marcado para siempre** the accident marked him for life; **seguimos el procedimiento marcado por la ley** we followed the procedures required *o* laid down by law; **¿qué precio marca la etiqueta?** (*Com*) what's the price (marked) on the label?; **están marcando las camisas** (*Com*) they are putting prices on the shirts, they are pricing the shirts
1·2 [+ *límites*] to mark; **el Mediterráneo marca los límites por el este** the Mediterranean marks the eastern limit
1·3 (*Inform*) [+ *bloque, texto*] to flag
1·4 (*Mús*) [+ *partitura*] to mark up
2 [*experiencia, suceso*] to mark; **ese encuentro la ~ía para siempre** that meeting would mark her for life; **una vida marcada por el sufrimiento** a life marked by suffering
3 [*termómetro*] to read; **mi reloj marca las dos** it's two o'clock by my watch, my watch says two o'clock; **este reloj marca la hora exacta** this watch keeps the right time
4 (= *designar*) [+ *tarea*] to assign; [+ *política, estrategia*] to lay down; [+ *directrices, pautas*] to lay down, give; [+ *comienzo, periodo*] to mark; **la empresa nos ha marcado algunas pautas a seguir** the company has given us *o* has issued some guidelines to follow; **la paz marcó el comienzo de una nueva era** peace marked the beginning of a new era; **esta obra marca el paso de la música medieval a la renacentista** this work marks the transition from medieval to renaissance music; **como marca la ley** as specified by law; *ver tb* **hito 1**, **pauta 1**
5 (= *hacer resaltar*) to accentuate; **ese vestido te marca mucho las caderas** that dress really accentuates your hips *o* makes your hips stand out; *ver tb* **paquete A7**
6 (= *seguir*) [+ *sospechoso*] to shadow, tail
7 (*Dep*) 7·1 [+ *gol*] to score
7·2 [+ *tiempo*] to record, clock; **ha marcado un tiempo de 9,46** he recorded *o* clocked a time of 9.46
7·3 [+ *jugador, contrario*] to mark, shadow; (*Méx*) to tackle
8 (*Mús*) **~ el compás** to keep time, beat time; *ver tb* **paso² A4**
9 (*Telec*) to dial
10 (*Naipes*) to bid
11 (*Peluquería*) to set; **he ido a que me marquen el pelo** I went to get my hair set
Ⓑ VI 1 (*Dep*) to score
2 (*Telec*) to dial
3 (*Peluquería*) to set; **"lavar y marcar"** "shampoo and set"
Ⓒ **marcarse** VPR 1 [*figura, formas*] to stand out; **se le marcan mucho las venas de las manos** the veins on his hands really stand out; **~se con relieve** to stand out in relief
2 (*Esp**) **¿nos marcamos un baile?** do you fancy a dance?; **se marcó un detalle bien majo conmigo** that was a really nice touch of hers; *ver tb* **farol 2**
3 (*Peluquería*) **~se el pelo** to have one's hair set, have one's hair styled
4 (*Náut*) to take one's bearings

marcha SF 1 [*de soldados, manifestantes*] march; **una ~ de protesta** a protest march; **el batallón salió de ~ hacia el campamento** the battalion marched towards the camp; **¡en ~!** let's go!, let's get going; (*Mil*) forward march!; **abrir la ~** to head the march; **cerrar la ~** to bring up the rear; **encabezar la ~** to head the march; **ponerse en ~** [*persona*] (*lit*) to set off; (*fig*) to set about; [*máquina, motor*] to start; **antes de ponerse en ~, se recomienda que revisen sus vehículos** before setting off, we recommend that you check your vehicles; **ya se han puesto en ~ para preparar la querella** they have already set a lawsuit in motion, they have already set about bringing a lawsuit ► **marcha a pie** [*de caminantes*] (= *excursión*) hike; (= *actividad*) hiking; [*de manifestantes*] march ► **marcha forzada** forced march; **hemos trabajado a ~s forzadas** we've been working against the clock; **intenta recuperar a ~s forzadas su imagen pública** he is trying to rebuild his public image as quickly as possible ► **marcha**

➤ LENGUA Y USO: marcar A9 27

triunfal [*de ejército*] triumphal march; (*hacia la meta*) winning run
2 (= *partida*) departure; **su ~ fue muy precipitada** her departure was very sudden; **tras tu ~** after you left; **¿a qué hora tenéis la ~?** (*Esp**) what time do you set off?
3 (= *velocidad*) speed; **¡vaya ~ que llevas!** (*Esp*) what a speed you go at!; **he tardado en coger la ~ pero ya estoy al día** it took me a while to get into it *o* to get the hang of it but I'm on top of it now*; **"marcha moderada"** (*Aut*) "slow"; **acelerar la ~** to speed up, go faster; **deberíamos acelerar un poco la ~** we should speed up a little *o* go a little faster; **moderar la ~** to slow down; **a toda ~** at top speed; **un coche venía a toda ~ cuesta abajo** a car was coming down the hill at full *o* top speed; **han elaborado el informe a toda ~** the report has been prepared at top speed
4 (*Mús*) march ► **marcha fúnebre** funeral march ► **marcha militar** military march ► **marcha nupcial** wedding march ► **la Marcha Real** *Spanish national anthem*
5 (*Aut*) gear; **meter la cuarta ~** to change into fourth gear; **cambiar de ~** to change gear; **~ corta/directa** low/top gear; **~ larga** high gear; **primera ~** first gear ► **marcha atrás** (*en vehículo*) reverse, reverse gear; (*en negociaciones*) withdrawal; (*) (*en el acto sexual*) withdrawal; **fue ~ atrás unos cuantos metros** he reversed a few metres; **dar ~ atrás** (*con un vehículo*) to reverse, put the car/van/*etc* into reverse; (*en negociaciones, en el acto sexual*) to withdraw; **a última hora han dado ~ atrás** they pulled out *o* withdrew at the last minute; **si pudiese dar ~ atrás en el tiempo ...** if I could go back in time ...
6 **en ~** (= *en funcionamiento*) [*máquina, sistema*] in operation; [*motor*] running; [*electrodoméstico, ordenador*] on; [*proyecto*] under way, in progress, on the go; **un país en ~** a country on the move *o* that is going places; **la televisión ha estado en ~ todo el día** the television has been on all day; **nos apeamos del autobús en ~** we got off the bus while it was moving; **tiene varios proyectos en ~** he has various projects under way *o* in progress *o* on the go; **poner en ~** [+ *máquina, motor*] to start; [+ *electrodoméstico, ordenador*] to turn on; [+ *proyecto, actividad*] to set in motion; [+ *ley, resolución*] to implement
7 (*Dep*) (= *carrera*) walk; (= *excursión*) walk, hike; **ganó los 20kms ~** he won the 20km walk ► **marcha atlética, marcha de competición** walk
8 (= *desarrollo*) [*de enfermedad*] course; [*de huracán*] progress; **la ~ de los acontecimientos** the course of events; **la larga ~ de las conversaciones** the long drawn-out process *o* course of the talks; ✦***MODISMO* sobre la ~** (= *en el momento*) there and then; (= *durante una actividad*) as I/you/*etc* go along; **le hicieron los análisis sobre la ~** he had his tests done there and then; **los cambios los haremos sobre la ~** we'll make the changes as we go along
9 (*Esp*⁑) (= *animación*) **no tengo ganas de ~** I don't feel like going out; **un sitio con mucha ~** a very lively place, a place with a lot of action⁑; **yo necesito un novio que me dé ~** I need a boyfriend with a bit of life; **en Granada hay mucha ~ por la noche** Granada has a great nightlife; **¿dónde está la ~ de Vigo?** where's the nightlife in Vigo?, where are the good bars in Vigo?; **me va la ~ tecno** I'm really into techno⁑; **les pegan y no se quejan, parece que les va la ~** they get hit but never complain, it seems they like a bit of suffering; **estar/ir** *o* **salir de ~** (*a bares*) to be out/go out (on the town)*; (*a discotecas*) to be out/go (out) clubbing*; **estuvimos de ~ hasta las cinco** we were out (on the town) *o* out clubbing until five in the morning*; **¿estuviste de ~ hasta muy tarde?** were you out very late last night?; **hace siglos que no vamos de ~** we haven't had a night out *o* been out for ages, we haven't been out on the town *o* (out) clubbing for ages*; **tener ~*** [*persona, música*] to be lively; [*ciudad*] to be full of action, be buzzing*; **mi abuela tiene mucha ~** my grandma is really lively; **hoy no tengo ninguna ~** I'm not in a very lively mood tonight
10 (*Méx Aut*) self-starter, self-starter motor
11 (*Caribe*) [*de caballo*] slow trot

marchador(a) SM/F walker

marchamo SM (= *etiqueta*) label, tag; [*de aduana*] customs mark; (*fig*) stamp

marchand SMF art dealer

marchantaje SM (*LAm*) clients *pl*, clientele

marchante/a SM/F 1 (= *comerciante*) dealer, merchant ► **marchante de arte** art dealer
2 (*LAm**) (= *cliente*) client, customer; (= *vendedor*) (*ambulante*) pedlar, peddler (*EEUU*); (*en mercado*) stall holder
3 (*Caribe*) (= *embaucador*) trickster

marchantía* SF (*CAm, Caribe*) clients *pl*, clientele

marchar ▸conjug 1a◂ Ⓐ VI 1 (= *ir*) to go; (= *andar*) to walk; **~on a pie** they went on foot; **~on hacia el pueblo** they walked towards the village
2 (*Mil*) to march
3 **¡marchando, que llegamos tarde!** get a move on, we'll be late!; **—¡un café! —¡marchando!** "a coffee, please" — "right away, sir!"
4 [*mecanismo*] to work; **mi reloj no marcha** my watch isn't working; **el motor no marcha** the engine isn't working, the engine won't work; **el motor marcha mal** the engine isn't running properly; **~ en vacío** to idle
5 (= *desarrollarse*) to go; **todo marcha bien** everything is going well; **el proyecto marcha** the plan is working (out); **el negocio no marcha** the business is getting nowhere; **¿cómo marcha eso** *o* **marchan las cosas?** (*esp LAm*) how's it going?, how are things?
6 (*Caribe, Cono Sur*) [*caballo*] to trot
7 (*Méx**) to do military service
Ⓑ **marcharse** VPR to go (away), leave; **¿os marcháis?** are you leaving?; **con permiso, me marcho** if you don't mind I must go; **es tarde, me marcho a casa** it's late, I'm going home; **me marché de casa a los veinte años** I left home when I was twenty; **¿cuándo te marchas de vacaciones?** when are you going on holiday?; **se marchó de la capital** he left the capital; **~se a otro sitio** to go somewhere else

marchista SMF 1 (= *manifestante*) marcher, protest marcher
2 (*LAm Dep*) walker

marchitar ▸conjug 1a◂ Ⓐ VT to wither, dry up
Ⓑ **marchitarse** VPR 1 [*flores*] to wither, fade
2 [*belleza, juventud*] to fade
3 [*esperanzas*] to fade; [*ideales*] to fade away
4 [*persona*] to languish, fade away

marchitez SF withered state, faded condition

marchito ADJ [*flores*] withered; [*belleza, juventud, esperanzas*] faded

marchoso/a* Ⓐ ADJ (= *animado*) lively; **he conocido a gente muy marchosa** I've met some really lively people; **es un tío muy ~** he's really into going out, he's really lively
Ⓑ SM/F **es un ~ profesional** (*hum*) he's really into the action⁑; **un sitio para los más ~s** a place for those who can really take the pace*

Marcial SM Martial

marcial ADJ [*ley*] martial; [*porte, disciplina*] military

marcianitos SMPL (= *juego*) space-invaders

marciano/a ADJ, SM/F Martian

marco Ⓐ SM 1 (*Arquit, Arte*) frame; **~ para cuadro** picture frame; **poner ~ a un cuadro** to frame a picture ► **marco de la chimenea** mantelpiece ► **marco de la puerta** doorframe ► **marco de ventana** window frame
2 (*Dep*) goal posts *pl*, goal
3 (= *escenario*) setting; **un ~ incomparable** a perfect setting; **el paisaje ofreció un bello ~ para la fiesta** the countryside made a splendid setting for the festivity
4 (= *contexto*) framework ► **marco de referencia** frame of reference ► **marco institucional** institutional framework ► **marco jurídico** judicial framework ► **marco legal** legal framework
5 (*Fin*) mark
6 [*de pesos*] standard
Ⓑ ADJ INV **acuerdo ~** framework agreement; **ley ~** framework law; **plan ~** draft *o* framework plan; **programa ~** framework programme

márcola SF pruning hook

Marcos SM Mark

marduga* SMF (*CAm*) tramp

marea SF 1 (*Geog*) tide ► **marea alta** high tide, high water ► **marea baja** low tide, low water ► **marea creciente** rising tide ► **marea menguante** ebb tide ► **marea muerta** neap tide ► **marea negra** oil slick ► **marea viva** spring tide
2 (= *flujo*) tide; **la ~ de la rebelión** the tide of revolt; **una auténtica ~ humana** a real flood of people
3 (= *brisa*) light sea breeze
4 (= *llovizna*) drizzle; (*Cono Sur*) sea mist

mareado ADJ 1 **estar ~** (= *con náuseas*) to be *o* feel sick; (*en coche*) to be *o* feel carsick; (*en barco*) to be *o* feel seasick; (*en avión*) to be *o* feel airsick; (= *aturdido*) to feel dizzy
2 (= *achispado*) tipsy

mareaje SM 1 (= *marinería*) navigation, seamanship
2 (= *rumbo*) ship's course

marear ▸conjug 1a◂ Ⓐ VT 1 (*Med*) **~ a algn** to make sb feel sick; **el olor a alquitrán me marea** the smell of tar makes me feel sick; **el fuerte oleaje me marea** the swell is making me feel seasick
2 (= *aturdir*) **~ a algn** to make sb (feel) dizzy; **las alturas me marean** heights make me (feel) dizzy
3 (= *emborrachar*) **~ a algn** to make sb feel drunk *o* light-headed

4 (= *confundir*) **no grites tanto, que me mareas** don't shout so much, I can't hear myself think; **¡decídete y no me marees más!** make up your mind and stop going on at me!
5 (*Caribe, Méx*) (= *engañar*) to cheat
Ⓑ VI (††) (*Náut*) to sail, navigate
Ⓒ **marearse** VPR 1 (*Med*) to feel sick; (*en coche*) to get carsick, get travel-sick; (*en barco*) to get seasick; **se mareó con el calor** he felt sick because of the heat, the heat made him feel sick; **¿te mareas cuando vas en barco?** do you get seasick when you travel by boat?; **siempre me mareo en el coche** I always get carsick
2 (= *aturdirse*) to feel dizzy; **te ~ás si das tantas vueltas** you'll get dizzy going round like that
3 (= *emborracharse*) to get drunk *o* light-headed
4 (= *confundirse*) to get confused
5 (= *preocuparse*) **no te marees con esto** don't bother your head about this
6 (*Caribe, Cono Sur*) [*paño*] to fade

marejada SF 1 (*Náut*) swell, heavy sea
2 (= *oleada*) [*de descontento, protesta*] wave, upsurge

marejadilla SF slight swell

maremagno SM, **maremágnum** SM 1 (= *cantidad*) ocean, sea
2 (= *confusión*) confusion

maremoto SM (= *movimiento sísmico*) seaquake; (= *ola*) tidal wave

marengo ADJ INV **gris ~** dark grey

mareo SM 1 (*Med*) sickness; (*en coche*) carsickness, travel sickness; (*en mar*) seasickness; (*en avión*) airsickness
2 (= *aturdimiento*) dizziness, giddiness; **le dio un ~ a causa del calor** the heat made her feel dizzy
3 (= *confusión*) **¡qué ~ de cifras!** all these numbers are making me dizzy
4 (= *pesadez*) pain*, nuisance; **es un ~ tener que ...** it is a pain *o* nuisance having to ...; **¡qué ~ de hombre!** what a pest that man is!

mareomotriz ADJ [*energía*] wave *antes de s*, tidal *antes de s*; **central ~** tidal power station

marfil SM 1 (= *material*) ivory; **(de) color ~** ivory, ivory-coloured *o* (*EEUU*) ivory-colored
2 (*LAm*) (= *peine*) fine-toothed comb

marfileño ADJ ivory

marga SF marl, loam

margal SM (= *terreno*) marly patch; (= *hoyo*) marl pit

margarina SF margarine

Margarita SF Margaret

margarita SF 1 (*Bot*) daisy; **deshojar la ~** (= *juego*) to play "she loves me, she loves me not"; (= *dudar*) to waver; ✦**MODISMOS criar ~s*** to be pushing up the daisies*; **ir a coger ~s*** to (go and) spend a penny*
2 (= *perla*) pearl; ✦**MODISMO echar ~s a los cerdos** to cast pearls before swine
3 (*Zool*) winkle
4 (*Tip*) daisywheel
5 (= *cóctel*) margarita (*cocktail of tequila and lime or lemon juice*)

margen Ⓐ SM 1 [*de página*] margin; **una nota al ~** a marginal note, a note in the margin; **un comentario al ~** an aside
2 (= *espacio*) **ganaron las elecciones por un escaso ~** they won the election by a narrow margin; **existe un amplio ~ para el fraude** there is plenty of scope for fraud; **la victoria no daba ~ para pensar que ...** the victory did not give any reason to think that ...; **en un escaso ~ de tiempo** in a short space of time; **dejen un ~ de una semana para la entrega** allow a week for delivery ► **margen de acción, margen de actuación** scope for action, room for manoeuvre, room for maneuver (*EEUU*) ► **margen de confianza, margen de credibilidad** credibility gap ► **margen de error** margin of error ► **margen de maniobra** = **margen de acción** ► **margen de seguridad** safety margin
3 **al ~ de** [+ *opinión, resultado*] regardless of, despite; **al ~ de lo que tú digas** regardless of *o* despite what you say; **una vida al ~ del sistema** a life on the fringes of society; **al ~ de la ley** outside the law; **al ~ de que las acusaciones sean o no fundadas** whether the accusations are true or not; **dejar algo al ~** to leave sth aside, set sth aside; **dejando al ~ nuestras creencias, la idea es muy buena** leaving *o* setting aside our beliefs, it's a very good idea; **lo dejaron** *o* **mantuvieron al ~ de las negociaciones** they excluded him from the negotiations, they left him out of the negotiations; **mantenerse** *o* **quedarse al ~ de** [+ *negociaciones, situación, escándalo*] to keep out of, stay out of; [+ *sociedad, vida pública*] to remain on the sidelines of, remain on the fringes of
4 (*Econ*) (= *beneficio*) margin; **la competencia ha reducido nuestros márgenes** our margins have been squeezed by the competition ► **margen bruto** gross margin ► **margen comercial** mark-up ► **margen de beneficio** profit margin ► **margen de explotación** trading profit ► **margen de fluctuación** rate of fluctuation ► **margen de ganancia(s)** profit margin ► **margen neto** net margin
Ⓑ SF [*de río*] bank; **la ~ derecha del Tajo** the right bank of the Tagus

marginación SF 1 (= *aislamiento*) [*de persona*] alienation; [*de grupo*] alienation, marginalization; **tiene miedo a la ~** she's scared of being alienated; **la ~ que sienten los inmigrantes** the alienation *o* marginalization felt by immigrants ► **marginación social** (= *discriminación*) social alienation; (= *pobreza*) social deprivation
2 (= *discriminación*) discrimination; **la ~ laboral de la mujer** discrimination against women in the workplace
3 (= *población marginada*) marginalization; **países con un alto índice de ~** countries with a high rate of marginalization

marginado/a Ⓐ ADJ 1 (= *aislado*) marginalized; **un poeta ~ a lo largo de su vida** a poet marginalized during his lifetime; **estar** *o* **quedar ~ de algo** (= *aislado*) to be alienated from sth; (= *excluido*) to be excluded from sth; **siguen estando ~s de la sociedad** they remain alienated from society; **estos países han quedado ~s del comercio internacional** these countries have been excluded from international trading; **sentirse ~** to feel discriminated against; **los agricultores se sienten ~s por la nueva ley** farmers feel discriminated against as a result of the new law
2 (= *pobre*) deprived; **una de las zonas más marginadas de Madrid** one of the most deprived areas in *o* of Madrid
Ⓑ SM/F (*por elección*) outsider, drop-out*; (*por discriminación*) underprivileged person, deprived person; **los ~s de nuestra sociedad** the underprivileged in our society

marginal ADJ 1 (= *al margen*) [*corrección, nota*] marginal, in the margin; **una nota ~** a marginal note, a note in the margin; **una observación ~** an aside
2 (= *pobre*) deprived; **un barrio ~** a deprived neighbourhood
3 (= *alternativo*) [*teatro*] fringe *antes de s*; [*publicación*] underground *antes de s*; [*artista*] alternative
4 (= *poco importante*) [*asunto*] marginal; [*papel, personaje*] minor; **la literatura ocupa una situación ~ en nuestra sociedad** literature holds a marginal position in our society
5 (*Econ*) [*coste, tipo*] marginal

marginalidad SF 1 [*de persona*] state of alienation
2 [*de grupo*] marginalization; **zonas de ~** marginalized areas

marginalización SF marginalization, exclusion

marginalizar ▸conjug 1f◂ VT to marginalize, exclude

marginar ▸conjug 1a◂ Ⓐ VT 1 (= *aislar*) [+ *persona*] to alienate; [+ *grupo*] to marginalize; **la marginaban en la escuela** she was alienated at school; **la sociedad margina a los toxicómanos** society marginalizes drug addicts; **la televisión margina los programas culturales** cultural programmes are marginalized on television
2 (= *discriminar*) **no se ~á a nadie por su ideología** nobody will be discriminated against because of their ideology
3 (= *excluir*) to push out (**de** of), exclude (**de** from); **acabaron marginándola del grupo** they ended up pushing her out of the group *o* excluding her from the group
4 (*Tip*) [+ *texto*] to write notes in the margin of; [+ *página*] to leave margins on
Ⓑ **marginarse** VPR to alienate oneself (**de** from)

margoso ADJ marly, loamy

margullo SM (*Caribe Bot*) shoot, runner

Mari SF (*forma familiar*) de **María**

María SF Mary; **Santa ~, madre de Dios** Holy Mary, mother of God ► **María Antonieta** Marie Antoinette ► **María Estuardo** Mary Stuart ► **María Magdalena** Mary Magdalene ► **María Santísima** the Virgin Mary

maría[1]* SF (*Esp*) (= *marihuana*) grass*, pot*

maría[2]* SF (*hum, pey*) (= *ama de casa*) housewife

maría[3]* SF (*Escol*) unimportant subject; ✦**MODISMO las tres ~s** (*Hist*) *religious instruction, civics and PE*

maría[4]* SF (*Méx*) *female Indian immigrant from the country to Mexico City*

maría[5]* SF (= *caja de caudales*) peter*, safe

mariachi Ⓐ ADJ (*Méx*) mariachi
Ⓑ SM (= *música*) mariachi music; (= *conjunto*) mariachi band
Ⓒ SMF (= *persona*) mariachi musician

CONJUNTO MARIACHI

The **conjuntos mariachis**, *bands of itinerant Mexican musicians, are mostly to be seen in the Plaza Garibaldi in Mexico City, wearing their* *traditional **charro** costumes: sequin-studded cowboy-style suits and wide-brimmed Mexican hats. Besides being a major tourist attraction, they provide music in the form of love songs for weddings, birthdays and **quinceañeras** (coming-out balls for Mexican girls who have reached their 15th birthday). The term **mariachi** is said to derive from the French word for wedding.*

marial ADJ, **mariano** ADJ Marian
marianismo SM Marianism
maribén‡ SF (*Esp*) death
marica Ⓐ SF (= *urraca*) magpie
Ⓑ SM 1 (*) (= *cobarde*) sissy
2 (‡) = **maricón**
Maricastaña SF **en los días** *o* **en tiempos de ~** way back, in the good old days; **son ideas trasnochadas del año de maricastaña** those ideas are out of the Ark; **va vestida como en tiempos de ~** her clothes are so old-fashioned
maricón‡ SM 1 (= *homosexual*) queer‡, fag (*EEUU*‡), poof‡; **¡~ el último!** the last one's a sissy!*
2 (= *sinvergüenza*) bastard**‡; **¡~ de mierda!** you bastard!**‡
mariconada‡ SF 1 (= *mala pasada*) dirty trick
2 (= *tontería*) **¡déjate ya de ~s!** stop pissing about!‡, stop behaving like a prat *o* (*EEUU*) jerk!*
mariconear* ▸conjug 1a◂ VI to camp it up (*pey*)
mariconeo* SM homosexual activities *pl*
mariconera* SF (man's) handbag
maridaje SM 1 (= *unión*) marriage, combination; **un ~ de tradiciones orientales y españolas** a marriage *o* combination of oriental and Spanish traditions; **un perfecto ~ gastronómico** a perfect gastronomic combination
2 (= *conexión*) close association; (*Pol pey*) unholy alliance
3 (= *matrimonio*) (= *vida*) conjugal life; (= *unión*) marriage ties *pl*
maridar ▸conjug 1a◂ VT 1 (= *combinar*) to combine, marry
2 (= *casar*) to marry
marido SM husband
marielito* SM (*Caribe*) Cuban exile
marihuana SF, **mariguana** SF, **marijuana** SF marijuana
marihuanero/a, **mariguanero/a**, **marijuanero/a** Ⓐ ADJ marijuana *antes de s*
Ⓑ SM/F (= *cultivador*) marijuana grower; (= *fumador*) marijuana smoker
marimacha* SF (*Andes*) = **marimacho**
marimacho* Ⓐ ADJ butch*, mannish
Ⓑ SM mannish woman, butch woman (* *pey*)
marimandón/ona* Ⓐ ADJ overbearing, bossy
Ⓑ SM/F bossyboots*
marimba Ⓐ SF 1 (*Mús*) (= *xilófono*) marimba; (= *tambor*) *kind of drum*; (*Caribe, Cono Sur*) *out-of-tune instrument*
2 (*Cono Sur*) (= *paliza*) beating
3 (*Andes Med*) large goitre
Ⓑ ADJ (*CAm, Caribe*) cowardly
marimoña SF buttercup
marimorena SF fuss, row; **armar la ~** to kick up a fuss *o* a row
marina SF 1 (= *organización*) navy; (= *barcos*) fleet; **la ~ española** the Spanish navy, the Spanish fleet; **servir en la ~** to serve in the navy ► **marina de guerra** navy ► **marina mercante** merchant navy, merchant marine (*EEUU*)
2 (= *marinería*) seamanship; (= *navegación*) navigation; **término de ~** nautical term
3 (*Geog*) coast, coastal area
4 (*Arte*) seascape
marinar ▸conjug 1a◂ VT to marinate, marinade
marinera SF 1 (= *blusa*) matelot top
2 (*Perú*) (= *baile*) *Peruvian folk dance*; *ver tb* **marinero**
marinería SF 1 (= *arte*) seamanship
2 (= *tripulación*) ship's crew; (= *marineros*) seamen *pl*, sailors *pl*
marinero Ⓐ ADJ 1 = **marino A**
2 [*gente*] seafaring
3 [*barco*] seaworthy
4 **a la marinera** sailor-fashion; **mejillones a la marinera** (*Culin*) moules marinières
Ⓑ SM (*gen*) sailor, mariner (*liter*); (= *hombre de mar*) seafarer, seaman; **gorra de ~** sailor's cap; **traje de ~** sailor suit; **niños vestidos de ~** children in sailor suits ► **marinero de agua dulce** fair-weather sailor, landlubber ► **marinero de cubierta** deckhand ► **marinero de primera** able seaman; *ver tb* **marinera**
marinesco ADJ seamanly; **a la marinesca** in a seamanlike way, sailor-fashion
marino Ⓐ ADJ sea *antes de s*, marine; **pez ~** sea fish; **fauna marina** marine life, sea creatures *pl*
Ⓑ SM (= *marinero*) sailor, seaman; (= *oficial*) naval officer ► **marino mercante** merchant seaman
mariolatría SF Mariolatry
marioneta SF puppet, marionette; **es una ~ en manos del ejército** he is the army's puppet; **régimen ~** puppet régime
marionetista SMF puppeteer
mariposa SF 1 (*Entomología*) butterfly ► **mariposa cabeza de muerte**, **mariposa de calavera** death's head moth ► **mariposa de la col** cabbage white butterfly ► **mariposa nocturna** moth
2 (*Natación*) butterfly; **100 metros ~** 100 metres butterfly; **nadaba en el estilo ~** she was swimming butterfly
3 (= *tuerca*) wing nut, butterfly nut
4 ► **mariposa cervical** orthopaedic pillow, butterfly pillow
5 (*Andes, CAm*) (= *juguete*) toy windmill
6 (*Andes*) (= *juego*) blind-man's buff
7 (*) (= *homosexual*) poof‡, fag (*EEUU*‡), fairy*
mariposear ▸conjug 1a◂ VI 1 (= *revolotear*) to flutter about, flit to and fro
2 (= *ser inconstante*) to be fickle; (= *coquetear*) to flit from one girl/man to the next; **~ alrededor de algn** to dance attendance on sb, be constantly fluttering round sb
mariposilla SF small moth; [*de ropa*] clothes-moth
mariposo* SM poof‡, fag (*EEUU*‡), fairy*
mariposón* SM 1 (= *flirteador*) flirt, Romeo*
2 (= *homosexual*) poof‡, fag (*EEUU*‡), fairy*
Mariquita SF (*forma familiar*) de **María**
mariquita Ⓐ SF 1 (= *insecto*) ladybird, ladybug (*EEUU*)
2 (*Orn*) parakeet
3 (*Méx*‡) pot*, grass*
Ⓑ SM (*) (= *homosexual*) poof‡, fag (*EEUU*‡), fairy*
marisabidilla SF know-all
mariscada SF seafood platter
mariscador(a) SM/F gatherer of shellfish
mariscal SM 1 (*Mil*) marshal ► **mariscal de campo** field marshal
2 (*Hist*) blacksmith, farrier
3 (*Chile*) (= *guiso*) seafood stew
mariscala SF (= *esposa*) marshal's wife
mariscar ▸conjug 1g◂ Ⓐ VI (= *pescar*) to gather shellfish
Ⓑ VT (‡) (= *robar*) to nick*, swipe*
marisco SM shellfish, seafood; **no me gusta el ~** ◊ **no me gustan los ~s** I don't like shellfish *o* seafood
marisma SF (= *pantano*) salt marsh; (= *tierras de arena*) mud flats *pl*; **las ~s del Guadalquivir** the Guadalquivir marshes
marisqueo SM shellfishing
marisquería SF (= *restaurante*) shellfish bar, seafood restaurant; (= *tienda*) seafood shop
marisquero ADJ shellfish *antes de s*, seafood *antes de s*; **barco ~** shellfishing boat
marital ADJ marital; **convivencia ~** living together as husband and wife; **hacer vida ~** to live together as husband and wife; **obligaciones ~es** marital duties; **problemas ~es** marital problems
maritatas SFPL (*esp LAm*), **maritates** SMPL (*CAm, Méx*) gear *sing*, tackle *sing*, tools; (*pey*) things, junk* *sing*
marítimo ADJ (*de barcos, costeño*) maritime; (*de navegación*) shipping *antes de s*; (*del mar*) marine, sea *antes de s*; **ciudad marítima** coastal town; **ruta marítima** sea route, seaway; **seguro ~** marine insurance; *ver tb* **estación 1**, **paseo 2**
maritornes* SF INV 1 (= *criada*) slovenly maidservant
2 (= *putilla*) tart‡, slut‡
marjal SM marsh, fen
márketing ['marketin] SM marketing ► **márketing directo** direct marketing
marmaja‡ SF (*Méx*) dough*, money
marmellas‡ SFPL (*Esp*) tits‡, breasts
marmita SF 1 (*Culin*) pot; (*Mil*) mess tin
2 (*Geol*) (*tb* **~ de gigante**) pothole
marmitón SM kitchen boy, scullion
mármol SM marble; [*de cocina*] (= *encimera*) worktop; (*para picar*) chopping-block
marmolejo SM small marble column
marmolería SF marble mason's (workshop) ► **marmolería funeraria** monumental masonry
marmolista SMF monumental mason
marmóreo ADJ marble *antes de s*, marmoreal (*frm*)
marmosete SM (*Tip*) vignette
marmota SF 1 (*Zool*) marmot; **✦MODISMO dormir como una ~** to sleep like a log ► **marmota de Alemania** hamster ► **marmota de América** woodchuck, whistler (*EEUU*)
2 (= *dormilón*) sleepyhead*
3 (*) (= *criada*) maid, servant
maroma SF 1 (= *cuerda*) rope
2 (*LAm*) (= *cuerda floja*) tightrope

[3] **maromas** (*LAm*) acrobatics *pl*, acrobatic stunts; **hacer ~s** = **maromear**

maromear ▸conjug 1a◂ VI (*LAm*) [1] (*en cuerda floja*) to walk the tightrope; (= *hacer volatines*) to do acrobatics, do acrobatic stunts
[2] (*Pol*) (= *ser diplomático*) to do a balancing act; (= *ser chaquetero*) to change one's political allegiance

maromero/a SM/F (*LAm*) [1] (= *funámbulo*) tightrope walker; (= *acróbata*) acrobat
[2] (= *político*) opportunist (politician)

maromo* SM (*esp Esp*) bloke*, guy*

marona* SF **tiene 60 años y ~** (*Caribe*) he's well over sixty

marqués/esa SM/F marquis/marchioness

marquesina SF (= *cobertizo*) glass canopy, porch; (= *techo*) glass roof, cantilever roof; [*de parada*] bus shelter; [*de tienda de campaña*] fly sheet; (*Ferro*) roof, cab (*of locomotive*)

marquetería SF marquetry

márquetin SM marketing

marquezote SM (*CAm*) sweet bread

marquito SM slide mounting

marrajo Ⓐ ADJ [*toro*] vicious, dangerous; [*persona*] sly
Ⓑ SM [1] (= *tiburón*) shark
[2] (*Méx*) (= *tacaño*) skinflint
[3] (= *candado*) padlock

marramizar ▸conjug 1f◂ VI [*gato*] to howl, caterwaul

marrana SF [1] (*Zool*) sow
[2] (*) (= *mujer*) slut; *ver tb* **marrano**

marranada* SF, **marranería*** SF [1] (= *inmundicia*) filthiness
[2] (= *acto*) filthy act; **decir ~s** to talk filth
[3] (= *mala pasada*) dirty trick

marrano/a Ⓐ ADJ (*) filthy, dirty
Ⓑ SM (*Zool*) pig, hog (*EEUU*)
Ⓒ SM/F [1] (*) (= *persona*) (*despreciable*) swine*; (*sucio*) dirty pig*
[2] (*Hist*) converted Jew; *ver tb* **marrana**

Marraquech SM, **Marraqués** SM Marrakech, Marrakesh

marrar ▸conjug 1a◂ Ⓐ VT **~ el tiro/golpe** to miss
Ⓑ VI [1] [*disparo*] to miss
[2] [*comentario*] to miss the mark; [*plan*] to fail, go wrong; **no me marra una** everything's going well for me

marras ADV [1] **de ~: es el problema de ~** it's the same old problem; **el individuo de ~** you-know-who; **volver a lo de ~** to go back over the same old stuff
[2] (*Andes**) **hace ~ que no lo veo** it's ages since I saw him

marrazo SM (*Méx*) (= *bayoneta*) bayonet; (= *pico*) mattock; (= *cuchillo*) short machete

marrocata⁑ SF Moroccan hashish

marrón Ⓐ ADJ brown
Ⓑ SM [1] (= *color*) brown
[2] (*Culin*) ► **marrón glacé** marron glacé
[3] (⁑) (= *acusación*) charge; (= *condena*) sentence; (= *situación comprometida*) mess; **le dieron cinco años de ~** they gave him five years' bird*; **le pillaron de** o **en un ~** they caught him red-handed; ✦**MODISMO comerse un ~** to own up
[4] (⁑) (= *policía*) pig⁑, cop*
[5] (*LAm Hist*) maroon
[6] (*Andes*) (= *papillote*) curlpaper
[7] (*Caribe*) (= *café con leche*) coffee with milk

marroncito SM (*Caribe*) coffee with milk

marroquí Ⓐ ADJ, SMF Moroccan
Ⓑ SM (= *piel*) morocco, morocco leather

marroquinería SF [1] (= *artículos*) (fine) leather goods *pl*; (= *tienda*) leather goods shop
[2] (= *arte*) (fine) leatherwork

marrubio SM (*Bot*) horehound

marrueco/a ADJ, SM/F = **marroquí A**

Marruecos SM Morocco; **el ~ Español** (*Hist*) Spanish Morocco

marrullería SF [1] (= *cualidad*) smoothness, glibness
[2] (= *excusa*) plausible excuse
[3] **marrullerías** (= *engatusamiento*) cajolery *sing*, wheedling *sing*; (*Dep*) dirty play *sing*

marrullero/a Ⓐ ADJ (= *lenguaraz*) smooth, glib; (= *engatusador*) cajoling, wheedling; [*equipo, jugador*] dirty
Ⓑ SM/F smooth type, smoothie*

Marsella SF Marseilles

Marsellesa SF Marseillaise

marsopa SF porpoise

marsupial ADJ, SM marsupial

mart. ABR (= **martes**) Tue, Tues

marta SF (= *animal*) (pine) marten; (= *piel*) sable
► **marta cebellina, marta cibelina** sable

martajar ▸conjug 1a◂ VT (*CAm, Méx*) [1] [+ *maíz*] to pound, grind
[2] **~ el español** to speak broken Spanish

Marte SM Mars

martellina SF sledgehammer

martes SM INV Tuesday; **~ y trece** ≈ Friday 13th ► **martes de carnaval, martes de carnestolendas** Shrove Tuesday; *ver tb* **sábado**; → CARNAVAL

> **MARTES Y TRECE**
> *According to Spanish superstition Tuesday is an unlucky day, even more so if it falls on the 13th of the month. As the proverb goes, "***En martes, ni te cases ni te embarques***".*

martiano/a (*Cuba Pol*) Ⓐ ADJ supporting the ideas of José Martí
Ⓑ SM/F supporter of José Martí

martillada SF hammer blow, blow with a hammer

martillar ▸conjug 1a◂ VT, VI = **martillear**

martillazo SM (heavy) blow with a hammer; **recibió un ~ en la cabeza** he was hit on the head with a hammer, he received a hammer blow to the head; **me di un ~ en el dedo** I hit my finger with the hammer; **a ~s: destrozar algo a ~s** to smash sth to pieces with a hammer; **dar forma a algo a ~s** to hammer sth out, hammer sth into shape

martilleante ADJ insistent, repetitious

martillear ▸conjug 1a◂ Ⓐ VT [1] (= *golpear*) [+ *puerta*] to hammer on, pound on; [+ *piano*] to pound away at; (= *machacar*) to pound
[2] (= *atormentar*) to worry, torment
Ⓑ VI [*motor*] to knock

martilleo SM hammering; (= *machaqueo*) pounding

martillero/a SM/F (*Andes, Caribe*) auctioneer

martillo SM [1] (*tb Dep*) hammer; [*de presidente de asamblea*] gavel ► **martillo de hielo** ice-pick ► **martillo de madera** mallet ► **martillo de orejas** claw-hammer ► **martillo mecánico** power hammer ► **martillo neumático, martillo picador** pneumatic drill, jackhammer (*EEUU*) ► **martillo pilón** steam hammer ► **martillo sacaclavos** claw hammer
[2] (*Com*) auction room
[3] (*Arquit*) house that sticks out from the row; (*LAm*) wing (*of a building*)
[4] (= *persona*) hammer, scourge

Martín SM Martin; **San ~** (= *santo*) St Martin; (= *fiesta*) Martinmas; (*Agr*) *season for slaughtering pigs*; ✦**REFRÁN a cada cerdo** o **puerco le llega su San ~** everyone comes to his day of reckoning; *ver tb* **veranillo**

martín SM ► **martín pescador** kingfisher

martinete SM [1] [*de construcción*] drop hammer, pile driver
[2] (*Mús*) hammer
[3] (*Zool*) heron

martingala SF (= *truco*) trick, ruse; (*LAm pey*) trick, fiddle*

Martinica SF Martinique

mártir SMF martyr

martirio SM [1] (*Rel*) martyrdom
[2] (= *tormento*) torment, torture; (= *persona*) pain* ► **martirio chino** Chinese torture

martirizador ADJ agonizing, excruciating

martirizante ADJ = **martirizador**

martirizar ▸conjug 1f◂ VT [1] (*Rel*) to martyr
[2] (= *atormentar*) to torture, torment

martirologio SM martyrology

Marucha SF, **Maruja** SF (*formas familiares*) *de* **María**

marucha SF (*Andes*) rump steak

maruja* SF traditional housewife; **soy una ~** I'm only a housewife

marujeo* SM chitchat, gossip

marula SF (*Méx*) teat, nipple (*EEUU*)

marullero ADJ = **marrullero**

marusa SF (*Caribe*) shoulder bag

maruto SM (*Caribe*) [1] (*Anat*) navel
[2] (*Med*) (= *verruga*) wart; (= *moradura*) bruise, welt

marxismo SM Marxism

marxista ADJ, SMF Marxist

marzal ADJ March *antes de s*, of March

marzo SM March; *ver tb* **septiembre**

mas CONJ but

más

> [A] ADVERBIO [C] SUSTANTIVO
> [B] ADJETIVO MASCULINO
> *Para expresiones como* ***más aún, más de la cuenta, a más tardar, las más de las veces****, ver la otra entrada.*

Ⓐ ADVERBIO

[1] comparativo [1.1] (*con adjetivo, adverbio*) more; **~ cómodo** more comfortable; **~ inteligente** more intelligent

La mayoría de los adjetivos y adverbios de una sílaba o de dos sílabas teminados en "-y" forman el comparativo añadiendo la terminación "-er". A veces se produce un cambio ortográfico.

~ barato cheaper; **~ grande** bigger; **~ joven** younger; **~ largo** longer; **~ feliz** happier; **~ lejos** further; **~ deprisa** faster, more quickly; **vete ~ lejos de la cámara** move further away from the camera; **échate ~ hacia la derecha** move more o further to the right

1·2 (*con verbo*) **¿quieres ~?** would you like some more?; **ahora salgo ~** I go out more these days; **últimamente nos vemos ~** we've been seeing more of each other lately; **correr ~** to run faster; **durar ~** to last longer; **me gusta ~ sin chocolate** I like it better *o* I prefer it without chocolate; **trabajar ~** to work harder

1·3 (*con numerales, sustantivos*) **quisiera dos libros ~** I'd like another two books, I'd like two more books; **un kilómetro ~ y llegaremos** one more kilometre and we'll be there; **ahora pesa veinte kilos ~** he's twenty kilos heavier now, he weighs twenty kilos more now; **sólo se lo repetiré una vez ~** I will only repeat it once more *o* one more time; **¡no aguanto aquí ni un minuto ~!** I can't stand it here a minute longer!

1·4 **~ de** more than; **no tiene ~ de dieciséis años** he isn't more than sixteen; **se estima en ~ de mil** it is reckoned at more than a thousand; **en la clase somos ~ de diez** there are over ten *o* more than ten of us in the class; **son ~ de las diez** it's past *o* gone *o* after ten o'clock; **~ de lo que yo creía** more than I thought; **lo hizo con ~ destreza de la que esperaba** he did it more skilfully than he had expected

1·5 **~ que** more than; **el alemán es ~ difícil que el inglés** German is more difficult *o* harder than English; **tiene ~ dinero que yo** he has more money than I do *o* than me; **él ha viajado ~ que yo** he has travelled more (widely) than I have *o* than me; **se trata de voluntad ~ que de fuerza** it's a question of willpower rather than of strength, it's more a question of willpower than of strength; *ver tb* **cada 3**

2 *superlativo* 2·1 (*con adjetivos, sustantivos*) most; **su película ~ innovadora** his most innovative film; **él es el ~ inteligente** he is the most intelligent (one)

La mayoría de los adjetivos y adverbios de una sílaba o de dos sílabas teminados en "-y" forman el superlativo añadiendo la terminación "-est". A veces se produce un cambio ortográfico.

el bolígrafo ~ barato the cheapest pen; **el niño ~ joven** the youngest child; **el coche ~ grande** the biggest car; **el punto ~ lejano** the furthest point; **la persona ~ feliz** the happiest person; **siempre está donde haya ~ diversión** he's always to be found where the most fun is going on

2·2 (*con verbos*) **salió cuando ~ llovía** he left when it was raining the heaviest *o* the hardest, he left when the rain was at its heaviest; **el/la que ~**: **él es el que sabe ~** he's the one who knows (the) most; **es el que ~ viene a verme** he's the one who comes to see me (the) most (often); **el que ~ me gusta es el de flores** the one I like (the) best *o* most is the flowery one; **fue el que ~ trabajó** he was the one who worked (the) hardest; **trabaja tanto como el que ~** he works as hard as anyone

2·3 **~... de**: **el ~ alto de la clase** the tallest in the class; **ella es la ~ guapa de todas** she is the prettiest of them all; **el tren ~ rápido del mundo** the fastest train in the world

2·4 **lo ~ posible** as much as possible; **lo ~ temprano** the earliest; **lo ~ que puede** as much as he can; **a lo ~** at (the) most; **un libro de lo ~ divertido** a most *o* highly amusing book; **es un hombre de lo ~ honrado** he's entirely honest; **todo lo ~** at (the) most; *ver tb* **quien 2.3**

3 **algo ~**: **quisiera decirle algo ~** there's something else I wanted to say to you; **¿desea algo ~?** would you like anything else?; **no dijo nada ~** he didn't say anything else, he said nothing else; **no lo sabe nadie ~** no one else knows, nobody else knows; **¿qué ~?** what else?; **¿quién ~?** anybody else?; *ver tb* **nada A2.2**, **nadie 1**

4 *al sumar* and, plus; **14 ~ 20 menos 12 es igual a 22** 14 plus 20 minus 12 equals 22; **dos ~ tres (son) cinco** two and *o* plus three is five; **seremos nosotros ~ los niños** it will be us plus the kids; **éstos, ~ los que ya teníamos, hacen 200** these together with *o* plus the ones we had before, make 200; **España ~ Portugal** Spain together with Portugal

5 *en frases negativas* 5·1 (*con sentido restrictivo*) **no veo ~ solución que ...** I see no other solution than *o* but to ...; **no hay ~ que mirar alrededor para darse cuenta** you only have to look around you to see; **al final no fue ~ que un susto** it gave us a fright, but that's all; **no hace ~ de tres semanas** only *o* just three weeks ago, no more than three weeks ago

5·2 (= *otra vez*) **no vengas ~ por aquí** don't come round here any more; **nunca ~ le ofreceré mi ayuda** I'll never offer to help her again

6 *con valor intensivo* **qué ... ~**: **¡qué perro ~ feo!** what an ugly dog!; **¡es ~ bueno!** he's (ever) so kind!

7

◆ **de más**: **tenemos uno de ~** we have one too many; **trae una manta de ~** bring an extra blanket; **estar de ~** to be unnecessary, be superfluous; **aquí yo estoy de ~** I'm not needed here, I'm in the way here; **unas copas no estarían de ~** a few drinks wouldn't do any harm; **no estará (por) de ~ preguntar** there's no harm in asking

8

◆ **no más** (*LAm*) just, only; **así no ~** just like that; **ayer no ~** just *o* only yesterday; **dos días no ~** just *o* only two days; **¡espera no ~!** just you wait!; **pruébelo no ~** just try it; **siga no ~** just carry on; **habían llegado no ~** they had just arrived; **no ~ llegué me echaron** no sooner had I arrived than they threw me out; **vengo no ~ a verlo** I've come just to see it; **¡pase no ~!** (= *entre*) please *o* do go in; (= *venga*) please *o* do come in; **siéntese no ~** please *o* do sit down; **sírvase no ~** please *o* do help yourself; **hasta no ~** to the utmost, to the limit

9 *otras locuciones* **es ~** what's more, furthermore, moreover; **creo que eso es así, es ~, podría asegurártelo** I believe that it is the case, and what's more *o* furthermore *o* moreover I could prove it to you; **dos ~, dos menos** give or take two; **ni ~ ni menos**: **él es uno ~ de entre nosotros, ni ~ ni menos** he's just one of the group, that's all; **desciende de ni ~ ni menos que de Carlomagno** he is descended from none other than Charlemagne, he is descended from Charlemagne no less; **~ o menos**: **me dijo ~ o menos lo mismo de ayer** he said more or less the same thing to me yesterday; **me levanté a las siete ~ o menos** I got up at around *o* about seven o'clock; **por ~ que**: **por ~ que se esfuerce** however much *o* hard he tries, no matter how (hard) he tries; **por ~ veces que se lo he dicho** no matter how many times I've told him; **por ~ que quisiera ayudar** much as I should like to help; **sin ~ (ni ~)** without further ado; ✦*MODISMOS* **a ~ no poder**: **está lloviendo a ~ no poder** it really is pouring down; **esa noche bebimos a ~ no poder** that night we drank until we could drink no more, we really had a lot to drink that night; **corrimos a ~ no poder** we ran as fast as we could; **a ~ y mejor**: **está nevando a ~ y mejor** it really is snowing, it's snowing and then some; **ir a ~**: **discutieron, pero la cosa no fue a ~** they argued, but things didn't get out of hand; **el problema de la droga va a ~** the drugs problem is getting out of hand *o* out of control; *ver tb* **allá 1**, **bien A9**, **dar B3**, **nunca**, **valer B5**

Ⓑ ADJETIVO

(*) **esta es ~ casa que la otra** this is a better house than the last one; **es ~ hombre** he's more of a man

Ⓒ SUSTANTIVO MASCULINO

1 *Mat* plus, plus sign

2 ✦*MODISMO* **tiene sus ~ y sus menos** it has its good and its bad points, there are things to be said on both sides

masa¹ SF 1 [*de pan*] dough
2 (*Cono Sur*) (= *pastelillo*) small bun, teacake; (*Andes, Cono Sur*) (= *hojaldre*) puff pastry ► **masa quebrada** short pastry, shortcrust pastry
3 (= *argamasa*) mortar

masa² SF 1 (= *conjunto*) mass; **una ~ de gente** a mass of people; **una ~ de aire** a mass of air; **una ~ de nubes** a bank of clouds ► **masa coral** choir
2 (= *volumen*) mass; ✦*MODISMO* **llevar algo en la ~ de la sangre** to have sth in one's blood, have a natural inclination towards sth ► **masa atómica** atomic mass ► **masa crítica** (*Fís*) critical mass; (*fig*) (= *mínimo*) requisite number ► **masa encefálica** brain matter ► **masa molecular** molecular mass ► **masa polar** polar icecap
3 (*Sociol*) **las ~s** the masses; **los medios de comunicación de ~s** the mass media
4 **en ~** (= *en multitud*) en masse; **fueron en ~ a recibir al equipo** they went en masse to greet the team; **protestaron en ~** they held a mass protest; **producir algo en ~** to mass-produce sth; **despidos en ~** mass redundancies
5 (*Econ, Fin*) ► **masa de acreedores** body of creditors ► **masa monetaria** money supply ► **masa salarial** total wage bill
6 (*Elec*) earth, ground (*EEUU*); **conectar un aparato con ~** to earth *o* (*EEUU*) ground an appliance

masacrar ▸conjug 1a◂ VT to massacre

masacre SF massacre

masacrear* ▸conjug 1a◂ VT (*Caribe*) to touch up*

masada SF farm

masadero/a SM/F farmer

masaje SM massage; **dar (un) ~ a algn** to give sb a massage; **salón de ~** massage parlour ► **masaje cardíaco** cardiac massage

masajear ▸conjug 1a◂ VT to massage

masajista SMF masseur/masseuse; (*Dep*) physio* ► **masajista terapéutico/a** physio-therapist

masar* ▸conjug 1a◂ VT to massage

masato SM (*Andes, CAm*) (= *bebida*) *drink made from fermented maize, bananas, yucca etc*; (*Andes*) (= *dulce de coco*) *coconut sweet*; (*Andes*) [*de plátanos*] *banana custard*

mascada SF [1] (*LAm*) (= *tabaco*) plug of chewing tobacco
[2] (*CAm*) (= *ahorros*) nest egg; (*Cono Sur*) (= *ganancias*) illicit gains *pl*; (= *tajada*) rake-off*, cut
[3] (*Andes, CAm*) (= *tesoro*) buried treasure
[4] (*CAm**) (= *reprimenda*) rebuke
[5] (*Méx*) (= *pañuelo*) silk handkerchief *o* scarf

mascado* ADJ (*CAm*) creased, rumpled

mascadura SF chewing

mascar ▸conjug 1g◂ Ⓐ VT [1] (= *masticar*) to chew
[2] (*) [+ *palabras*] to mumble, mutter; ✦***MODISMOS*** **~ un asunto** ◊ **dar mascado un asunto** to explain sth in very simple terms
Ⓑ VI (= *masticar*) to chew; (*esp LAm*) (= *mascar tabaco*) to chew tobacco; (*Andes*) (= *mascar coca*) to chew coca
Ⓒ **mascarse** VPR to sense; **en la plaza de toros se mascaba la tragedia** you could sense tragedy in the bullring

máscara Ⓐ SF [1] (= *careta*) mask; **baile de ~s** masked ball; **~ para esgrima** fencing mask ► **máscara antigás** gas mask ► **máscara de oxígeno** oxygen mask ► **máscara facial** face mask *o* pack
[2] **máscaras** (= *mascarada*) masque *sing*, masquerade *sing*
[3] (= *apariencia*) mask; (= *disfraz*) disguise; **bajo su ~ de cinismo** beneath his mask of cynicism; **quitar la ~ a algn** to unmask sb; **quitarse la ~** to reveal o.s.
[4] (= *rímel*) (*tb* **~ de pestañas**) mascara
Ⓑ SMF masked person

mascarada SF [1] (= *fiesta*) masque, masquerade
[2] (= *farsa*) charade, masquerade

mascarilla SF (= *máscara*) (*tb Med*) mask; (*en cosmética*) face mask *o* pack ► **mascarilla capilar** (= *sustancia*) hair oil; (= *tratamiento*) hair-conditioning treatment ► **mascarilla de arcilla** mudpack ► **mascarilla facial** face mask, face pack ► **mascarilla de oxígeno** oxygen mask ► **mascarilla mortuoria** death mask

mascarón SM large mask ► **mascarón de proa** figurehead

mascota SF [1] [*de club, acontecimiento*] mascot
[2] (= *animal doméstico*) pet

masculinidad SF masculinity, manliness

masculinizador ADJ, **masculinizante** ADJ masculinizing

masculinizar ▸conjug 1f◂ VT to make more masculine; (*Biol*) to masculinize

masculino Ⓐ ADJ [1] (*Biol*) male; [*apariencia*] masculine, manly; **ropa masculina** men's clothing, menswear
[2] (*Ling*) masculine
Ⓑ SM (*Ling*) masculine

mascullar ▸conjug 1a◂ VT to mumble, mutter

masectomía SF mastectomy

masera SF kneading trough

masía SF (*Aragón, Cataluña*) farm

MASCULINO

Masculino se traduce al inglés por **male** y **masculine**.

• **Masculino** se traduce por **male** cuando nos referimos a la condición masculina de los seres vivos (en oposición al sexo femenino):

Un veinticinco por ciento de la población masculina sobrepasa ya el metro ochenta de estatura
Twenty five per cent of the male population is now six foot or over

• Se traduce por **masculine** para referirse a las cualidades y características que tradicionalmente se han relacionado con los hombres:

Una mujer tosca de rasgos más bien masculinos
A rough woman with rather masculine features

• También se utiliza en el ámbito gramatical:

Escribe cinco palabras españolas del género masculino que terminen en -e
Write five masculine words in Spanish ending in -e

Para otros usos y ejemplos ver la entrada.

---

masificación SF (= *abarrotamiento*) overcrowding; (= *propagación*) growth, spread; **la ~ de la universidad** overcrowding in universities; **la ~ de la producción de alimentos** mass production of food; **la ~ de la cultura** the bringing of culture to the masses

masificado ADJ (= *abarrotado*) overcrowded; (= *de masas*) mass *antes de s*; **una sociedad masificada** a mass society; **el esquí es ahora un deporte ~** skiing is a sport practised by everyone these days

masificarse ▸conjug 1g◂ VPR (= *abarrotarse*) to get overcrowded; (= *crecer demasiado*) to get too big

masilla SF (*para ventanas*) putty; (*para agujeros*) filler

masillo SM (*Caribe*) plaster

masita SF (*LAm*) small cake, pastry

masitero SM (*Andes, Caribe, Cono Sur*) pastry cook, confectioner

masivamente ADV en masse; **votaron ~ al partido socialista** they voted en masse for the socialist party; **la huelga fue apoyada ~** there was overwhelming support for the strike

masivo ADJ [*ataque, dosis etc*] massive; [*evacuación, ejecución*] mass *antes de s*; **se espera una asistencia masiva** a huge turnout is expected; **reunión masiva** mass meeting

masmediático ADJ mass-media *antes de s*; **mucha atención masmediática** a lot of attention from the mass media

masoca* Ⓐ ADJ masochistic
Ⓑ SMF masochist

masocotudo ADJ (*Andes, Cono Sur*) = **amazacotado**

masón SM (free)mason

masonería SF (free)masonry

masónico ADJ masonic

masoquismo SM masochism

masoquista Ⓐ ADJ masochistic
Ⓑ SMF masochist

masoterapia SF massage (therapy)

mastate SM (*CAm, Méx Hist*) loincloth

mastectomía SF mastectomy

mastelero SM topmast

master, máster Ⓐ ADJ [*copia*] master
Ⓑ SM (*pl* **masters**) [1] (*Univ*) master's degree (**en** in); ► **Master de Administración de Empresas** Master of Business Administration, MBA
[2] (*Cine, Mús*) master copy
[3] (*Dep*) masters' (competition); **el Master de Augusta** the Augusta Masters

masticación SF chewing, mastication (*frm*)

masticar ▸conjug 1g◂ VT to chew, masticate (*frm*)

mástil SM [1] (= *palo*) pole; (= *sostén*) support; (*para bandera*) flagpole; (*Náut*) mast; (*Arquit*) upright ► **mástil de tienda** tent pole
[2] [*de guitarra*] neck
[3] [*de pluma*] shaft

mastín SM mastiff ► **mastín danés** Great Dane ► **mastín del Pirineo** Pyrenean mountain dog, Great Pyrenees (*EEUU*)

mastique SM (= *escayola*) plaster; (= *cemento*) cement; (= *masilla*) putty

mastitis SF INV mastitis

masto SM (*Agr, Hort*) stock (*for grafting*)

mastodonte SM [1] (= *animal*) mastodon
[2] (*) (= *persona*) (great) hulk*; (= *organización*) behemoth; (= *máquina*) huge great thing*

mastodóntico ADJ colossal, huge

mastoides ADJ, SF INV mastoid

mastuerzo SM [1] (*Bot*) cress; (*tb* **~ de agua**) watercress
[2] (*) (= *persona*) clodhopper*

masturbación SF masturbation

masturbar ▸conjug 1a◂ Ⓐ VT to masturbate
Ⓑ **masturbarse** VPR to masturbate

masturbatorio ADJ masturbatory

Mat. ABR = **Matemáticas**

mata SF [1] (= *arbusto*) bush, shrub; (*esp LAm*) (= *planta*) plant; (*en tiesto*) potted plant ► **mata de coco** (*Caribe*) coconut palm ► **mata de plátano** (*Caribe*) banana tree ► **mata rubia** kermes oak
[2] (= *ramita*) sprig; (= *manojo*) tuft; (= *raíz*) clump; (= *ramo*) bunch
[3] **matas** (= *matorral*) thicket *sing*, scrub *sing*, bushes
[4] (*Agr*) (= *terreno*) field, plot; (*Andes*) (= *huerto*) orchard
[5] (*LAm*) (= *arboleda*) clump, grove; (*LAm*) (= *bosque*) forest ► **mata de bananos** banana plantation
[6] ► **mata de pelo** mop of hair

mataburros SM INV (*Caribe, Cono Sur hum*) dictionary

matacaballo ADV ✦***MODISMO*** **a ~** at breakneck speed

matacán SM [1] (*Andes, Caribe*) (= *cervato*) fawn, young deer
[2] (*CAm*) (= *ternero*) calf

matachín SM bully

matadero SM [1] [*de ganado*] slaughterhouse, abattoir (*frm*); **son como las ovejas que van al ~** they go like lambs to the slaughter
[2] (*) (= *trabajo*) killer*, exhausting task
[3] (*Méx, Cono Sur**) (= *prostíbulo*) brothel

matador(a) Ⓐ ADJ [1] (= *que mata*) killing
[2] (*) (= *horrible*) horrible; (= *ridículo*) ridicu-

lous; (= *absurdo*) absurd; **el vestido te está ~** that dress looks terrible on you
Ⓑ SM/F [1] (= *asesino*) killer
[2] (*Taur*) matador, bullfighter

matadura SF sore

matafuego SM fire extinguisher

matagigantes SM INV giant-killer

matalahúga SF, **matalahúva** SF aniseed

matalobos SM INV aconite, wolf's-bane

matalón Ⓐ ADJ [*caballo*] old, worn-out
Ⓑ SM nag

matalotaje SM [1] (*Náut*) ship's stores
[2] (*) (= *revoltijo*) jumble, mess

matambre SM (*Cono Sur*) stuffed rolled beef

matamoros SM INV swashbuckler, braggart

matamoscas SM INV (= *paleta*) fly swat; (= *papel*) flypaper; (= *aerosol*) fly spray

matanza SF [1] (*en batalla*) slaughter, killing; (*Agr*) slaughtering; (= *temporada*) slaughtering season; (*fig*) slaughter, massacre
[2] (*Caribe*) (= *matadero*) slaughterhouse; (*Andes*) (= *tienda*) butcher's, butcher's shop; (*CAm*) (= *mercado*) meat market

mataperrada* SF (*Andes, Cono Sur*) (= *broma*) prank; (= *granujada*) dirty trick

mataperrear* ▸conjug 1a◂ VI (*Andes, Cono Sur*) to wander the streets

mataperros* SM INV (= *niño*) urchin; (= *adolescente*) hooligan

matapolillas SM INV mothballs *pl*

matar ▸conjug 1a◂ Ⓐ VT [1] [+ *persona*] to kill; [+ *reses, ganado*] to kill, slaughter; **la mató en un ataque de celos** he killed her in a fit of jealousy; **el jefe me va a ~** the boss will kill me; **~ a algn a golpes** to beat sb to death; **~ a algn a disgustos** to make sb's life a misery; **así me maten** for the life of me; **que me maten si ...** I'll be damned if ...; ✦*MODISMOS* **~las callando** to go about things slyly; **entre todos la ~on (y ella sola se murió)** they are all to blame
[2] [+ *tiempo, pelota*] to kill; [+ *sed*] to quench; [+ *sello*] to postmark, cancel; [+ *pieza*] (*en ajedrez*) to take; [+ *cal*] to slake; [+ *ángulo, borde*] to file down; [+ *color*] to dull; **cómete una manzana para ~ el hambre** have an apple to keep you going
[3] (*) (= *molestar*) **los zapatos me están matando** these shoes are killing me*; **me mata tener que trabajar en sábado** it's a pain having to work on a Saturday*
[4] (*) (= *sorprender*) **¿se van a casar? ¡me has matado!** they're getting married? you're kidding!*
Ⓑ VI to kill; **no ~ás** (*Rel*) thou shalt not kill; **entrar a ~** (*Taur*) to go in for the kill; ✦*MODISMO* **estar** *o* **llevarse a ~ con algn** to be at daggers drawn with sb
Ⓒ **matarse** VPR [1] (= *suicidarse*) to kill o.s.; **se mató de un tiro** he shot himself
[2] (= *morir*) to be killed, get killed; **se ~on en un accidente de aviación** they were killed in a plane crash
[3] (= *esforzarse*) to kill o.s.; **convendría revisar estas facturas, pero no te mates** these invoices need checking but don't kill yourself; **~se trabajando** *o* **a trabajar** to kill o.s. with work; **se mata para mantener a su familia** he has to work like crazy to keep his family; **se mata por sacar buenas notas** he goes all out to get good marks

matarife SM [1] [*de animales*] slaughterman, butcher ► **matarife de caballos** knacker
[2] (= *matón*) thug

matarratas SM INV [1] (= *veneno*) rat poison
[2] (*) (= *alcohol*) rotgut, bad liquor

matasanos* SM INV quack (doctor)

matasellado SM postmark, franking

matasellar ▸conjug 1a◂ VT to postmark, frank

matasellos SM INV (= *marca*) postmark; (= *instrumento*) franking machine; **la carta tenía ~ de Madrid** the letter was postmarked Madrid ► **matasellos de puño** hand stamp

matasiete SM braggart, bully

matasuegras SM INV party blower

matasuelo SM ✦*MODISMO* **darse un ~** (*Andes**) to come a cropper*, take a flat beating (*EEUU*)

matate SM (*CAm*) canvas bag

matazón SF (*Andes, CAm, Caribe*) = **matanza**

match [matʃ] SM (*pl* **matchs** [matʃ]) match, game (*EEUU*)

mate[1] ADJ (= *sin brillo*) matt; [*sonido*] dull

mate[2] SM (*Ajedrez*) mate; **dar ~ a** to mate, checkmate

mate[3] SM (*LAm*) [1] (= *bebida*) maté ► **mate cocido** maté infusion ► **mate de coca** coca leaf tea ► **mate de menta** mint tea
[2] (= *vasija*) gourd, maté pot; ✦*MODISMOS* **pegar ~** (*CAm*) to go crazy; **tener mucho ~** (*CAm*) to be sharp
[3] (*Cono Sur**) (= *cabeza*) head, nut*, noggin (*EEUU**)

mate[4] SM (*Tenis*) smash

matear[1] ▸conjug 1a◂ Ⓐ VT (*Agr*) to plant at regular intervals, sow in groups
Ⓑ VI [1] (*Bot*) to sprout (thickly)
[2] [*perro*] to hunt among the bushes

matear[2] ▸conjug 1a◂ VI (*LAm*) to drink maté

matear[3] ▸conjug 1a◂ VT (*Cono Sur*) [1] (*Ajedrez*) to checkmate
[2] (= *mezclar*) to mix

matemáticamente ADV [1] (*Mat*) mathematically
[2] (= *exactamente*) exactly; **siempre llegan ~ a la misma hora** they always arrive at exactly the the same time; **las dos versiones coinciden casi ~** the two versions tally in almost every detail
[3] (*Dep*) **nuestro equipo se sitúa ~ en Primera División** mathematically, our team is guaranteed a place in the First Division

matemáticas SFPL, **matemática** SF mathematics *sing* ► **matemáticas aplicadas** applied mathematics ► **matemáticas puras** pure mathematics

matemático/a Ⓐ ADJ [1] (*Mat*) mathematical; [*cálculo*] precise
[2] (= *exacto*) exact; **con puntualidad matemática** dead on time
[3] (*Dep*) **con esa victoria aseguró el ascenso ~** with that win they made sure of promotion
[4] **es ~** (= *no falla*): **¡es ~!, ¡cada vez que me siento, suena el teléfono!** it's like clockwork!, every time I sit down the phone rings!
Ⓑ SM/F mathematician, math specialist (*EEUU*)

Mateo SM Matthew; **el evangelio según San ~** the Gospel according to St Matthew; **la Pasión según San ~** the St Matthew Passion

materia SF [1] (*Fís*) matter; (= *material*) material, substance; **~ inorgánica** inorganic matter; **~ vegetal** vegetable matter; **una ~ esponjosa y blanda** a soft spongy material *o* substance; **hay ~ para escribir varios libros** there is enough material to write several books; **hay mucha ~ para investigar** there is a lot of material to research; **ya tenéis ~ para pensar** that should give you something to think about *o* food for thought ► **materia colorante** dyestuff ► **materia fecal** faeces *pl*, feces *pl* (*EEUU*) ► **materia grasa** fat ► **materia gris** grey *o* (*EEUU*) gray matter ► **materia prima** raw material
[2] (= *tema*) subject matter; (*Escol*) subject; **índice de ~s** table of contents; **en ~ de** as regards; **entrar en ~** to get down to business, get to the point; **son expertos en la ~** they are experts on the subject; **será ~ de muchas discusiones** it will be the subject of a lot of debate ► **materia optativa** (*Escol*) option, optional subject

material Ⓐ ADJ [1] [*ayuda, valor etc*] material; **bienestar ~** material well-being
[2] (= *físico*) physical; **la presencia ~ de algn** sb's physical *o* bodily presence; **dolor ~** physical pain; **daños ~es** physical damage, damage to property
[3] (= *real*) **la imposibilidad ~ de ...** the physical impossibility of ...; **el autor ~ del hecho** the actual perpetrator of the deed; **no tengo tiempo ~ para ir** I literally don't have time to go
Ⓑ SM [1] (= *materia*) material; **hecho de mal ~** made of poor-quality material(s); **tengo ya ~ para una novela** I've got enough material now for a novel ► **material de construcción** building materials *pl* ► **material de desecho** waste material ► **materiales de derribo** rubble *sing* ► **materiales plásticos** plastics ► **material impreso** printed matter ► **material reciclado** recycled material
[2] (= *equipo*) equipment ► **material bélico, material de guerra** war material, military equipment ► **material de envasado** packaging materials *pl* ► **material de limpieza** cleaning materials *pl* ► **material de oficina** office supplies *pl*, stationery ► **material deportivo** sports equipment ► **material escolar** school equipment ► **materiales didácticos** teaching materials ► **material fotográfico** photographic equipment ► **material informático** hardware ► **material móvil, material rodante** rolling stock
[3] (*Tip*) copy
[4] (*) (= *cuero*) leather
[5] **de ~** (*LAm*) made of bricks, brick-built

materialidad SF (= *naturaleza*) (material) nature; (= *apariencia*) outward appearance; **percibe solamente la ~ del asunto** he sees only the superficial aspects of the question; **es menos la ~ del insulto que ...** it's not so much the insult itself as ...

materialismo SM materialism ► **materialismo dialéctico** dialectical materialism

materialista Ⓐ ADJ materialist(ic)
Ⓑ SMF materialist
Ⓒ SM [1] (*Méx*) (= *camionero*) lorry driver, truckdriver (*EEUU*)
[2] (*Méx*) (= *contratista*) building contractor

materializable ADJ realizable, attainable

materialización SF materialization

materializar ▸conjug 1f◂ Ⓐ VT to materialize
Ⓑ **materializarse** VPR to materialize

materialmente ADV [1] (= *de manera material*) materially; **no ha beneficiado ~ a este pueblo** it has brought no material benefit to this town
[2] (= *físicamente*) physically; **~ posible** physically possible; **se vio ~ asaltada por los fans** she was physically assaulted by the fans
[3] (= *absolutamente*) absolutely; **nos es ~ imposible** it is quite *o* absolutely impossible for us; **estaba ~ mojado** he was absolutely soaked

maternal Ⓐ ADJ [*instinto*] maternal; [*amor*] motherly, maternal; [*leche*] mother's; [*faja, sujetador*] maternity *antes de s*; **baja ~** maternity leave
Ⓑ SM (*Caribe*) (= *guardería*) nursery

maternidad SF [1] (= *estado*) motherhood, maternity
[2] (= *hospital*) (*tb* **casa de ~**) maternity hospital

materno ADJ [*lengua*] mother *antes de s*; [*amor, tono*] motherly, maternal; [*casa*] mother's; **el hogar ~** one's childhood home; **el útero ~** the mother's womb; **abuelo ~** maternal grandfather, grandfather on one's mother's side; **leche materna** mother's milk; **hospital ~-infantil** maternity hospital

matero ADJ (*Cono Sur*) [1] (= *de mate*) of maté, relating to maté
[2] [*persona*] fond of drinking maté

mates* SFPL maths* *sing*, math *sing* (*EEUU*)

matete* SM (*Cono Sur*) [1] (= *revoltijo*) mess, hash*
[2] (= *riña*) quarrel, brawl
[3] (= *confusión*) confusion

Matilde SF Mat(h)ilda

matinal Ⓐ ADJ morning *antes de s*
Ⓑ SF matinée

matinée SM [1] (*Teat*) matinée
[2] (*Andes*) (= *fiesta infantil*) children's party

matiz SM [1] [*de color*] shade
[2] [*de sentido*] shade, nuance; (= *ironía*) touch

matización SF [1] (*Arte*) blending
[2] (= *teñido*) tinging, tinting
[3] (= *aclaración*) qualification; **conviene hacer algunas matizaciones al respecto** some clarifications are required; **esta opinión, con ciertas matizaciones, es compartida por todos** this opinion, with certain qualifications, is shared by everyone; **quiero hacer una ~** I'd like to qualify *o* clarify that

matizado ADJ **~ de** *o* **en** tinged with, touched with (*tb fig*); **una explicación más matizada** a more thorough *o* exhaustive explanation

matizar ▸conjug 1f◂ VT [1] (*Arte*) to blend; [+ *tono*] to vary, introduce some variety into; [+ *contraste, intensidad de colores*] to tone down
[2] (= *teñir*) to tinge, tint (**de** with)
[3] (= *aclarar*) to qualify; **creo que deberías ~ lo que acabas de decir** I think what you just said needs qualifying; **~ que ...** to explain that ..., point out that ...; **el ministro defendió su postura, aunque matizó que ...** the minister defended his position, although he explained *o* pointed out that ...

matojal SM (*Caribe*), **matojo** SM (*Andes, Caribe, Méx*) = **matorral**

matón SM (= *bravucón*) thug; (*en el colegio*) bully, thug ▸ **matón de barrio** local thug, local bully-boy*

matonismo SM (= *bravuconería*) thuggery; (*en el colegio*) bullying

matorral SM (= *conjunto de matas*) thicket, bushes *pl*; (= *terreno*) scrubland

matorro SM (*Andes*) = **matorral**

matra SF (*Cono Sur*) horse blanket

matraca Ⓐ SF [1] (= *carraca*) rattle
[2] (*) (= *lata*) nuisance, pain*; (= *burla*) teasing, banter; **dar la ~ a algn** (= *molestar*) to pester sb; (= *burlarse de*) to tease sb
[3] (*Andes‡*) (= *marihuana*) hash*, pot*
[4] **matracas** (*Escol‡*) maths* *sing*, math *sing* (*EEUU*)
[5] (*Méx**) (= *metralleta*) machine gun
Ⓑ SMF (*) (= *persona*) nuisance, pain*

matraquear ▸conjug 1a◂ VT [1] (= *hacer sonar*) to rattle
[2] (*) = **dar la matraca**; *ver* **matraca A2**

matraz SM flask

matreraje SM (*Cono Sur*) banditry

matrero (*LAm*) Ⓐ ADJ [1] (= *astuto*) cunning, sly
[2] (= *desconfiado*) suspicious, distrustful
Ⓑ SM (= *bandido*) bandit, brigand; (= *fugitivo*) fugitive from justice; (= *tramposo*) trickster

matriarca SF matriarch

matriarcado SM matriarchy

matriarcal ADJ matriarchal

matricería SF die-stamping

matricida SMF matricide

matricidio SM matricide

matrícula SF [1] (= *inscripción*) registration, enrolment, enrollment (*EEUU*); **el plazo de ~ finaliza el día 15** the last day for registration *o* enrolment is the 15th; **fui a la universidad a hacer la ~** I went to University to matriculate; **tasas de ~** registration fees
[2] (= *nota*) ▸ **matrícula de honor** *top marks in a subject at university with the right to free registration the following year*
[3] (= *alumnado*) roll
[4] (*Aut*) (= *número*) registration number, license number (*EEUU*); (= *placa*) number plate, license plate (*EEUU*); **un coche con ~ de Toledo** a car with a Toledo number plate ▸ **matrícula de encargo** personalized number plate
[5] (*Náut*) registration; **un buque de ~ extranjera** a ship with foreign registration, a foreign-registered ship; **un barco con ~ de Bilbao** a Bilbao-registered boat
[6] (= *registro*) register

matriculación SF [1] (= *inscripción*) registration, enrolment, enrollment (*EEUU*)
[2] [*de barco, vehículo*] registration

matricular ▸conjug 1a◂ Ⓐ VT [1] (= *inscribir*) to register, enrol, enroll (*EEUU*)
[2] [+ *barco, vehículo*] to register
Ⓑ **matricularse** VPR to register, enrol; **~se en el curso de ...** to sign on *o* enrol *o* (*EEUU*) enroll for the course in ...

matrilineal ADJ matrilineal

matrilinealidad SF matrilineal descent

matrimonial ADJ matrimonial; **agencia ~** marriage bureau; **enlace ~** wedding; **vida ~** married life, conjugal life (*frm*); **capitulaciones ~es** marriage settlement *sing*

matrimonialista ADJ **abogado ~** lawyer specializing in matrimonial cases

matrimoniar ▸conjug 1b◂ VI to marry, get married

matrimonio SM [1] (= *institución*) marriage, matrimony (*frm*); **contraer ~ (con algn)** to marry (sb); **tras 26 años de ~** after 26 years of marriage; **hacer vida de ~** to live together as man and wife; **hacer uso del ~** (*hum*) to make love ▸ **matrimonio abierto** open marriage ▸ **matrimonio canónico** canonical marriage ▸ **matrimonio civil** civil marriage ▸ **matrimonio clandestino** secret marriage ▸ **matrimonio consensual** common-law marriage ▸ **matrimonio de conveniencia, matrimonio de interés** marriage of convenience ▸ **matrimonio religioso** church wedding
[2] (= *pareja*) (married) couple; **el ~ García** the Garcías, Mr and Mrs García; **cama de ~** double bed

matritense ADJ, SMF = **madrileño**

matriz Ⓐ SF [1] (*Anat*) womb, uterus
[2] (*Téc*) mould, mold (*EEUU*), die; (*Tip*) matrix
[3] [*de talonario*] stub, counterfoil
[4] (*Jur*) original, master copy
[5] (*Mat*) matrix; (*Inform*) array
Ⓑ ADJ **casa ~** (*Com*) (= *sede*) head office; (= *compañía*) parent company; (= *convento*) parent house

matrona SF [1] (= *mujer*) matron
[2] (= *comadrona*) midwife

matronal ADJ matronly

matungo‡ (*Caribe, Cono Sur*) Ⓐ ADJ old, worn-out
Ⓑ SM (= *caballo*) old horse, nag; (= *persona*) beanpole*, string bean (*EEUU**)

maturrango Ⓐ ADJ (*Cono Sur*) (= *torpe*) clumsy, awkward; (*Andes, Cono Sur*) [*jinete*] poor, incompetent
Ⓑ SM (*Andes, Cono Sur*) poor rider, incompetent horseman

Matusalén SM Methuselah

matute SM [1] (= *acto*) smuggling, contraband; **de ~** (= *de contrabando*) smuggled, contraband *antes de s*; (= *en secreto*) secretly, on the sly; **se colaron de ~** they sneakily jumped the queue; **introducir una idea de ~** to surreptitiously slip an idea in
[2] (= *géneros*) smuggled goods *pl*, contraband
[3] (= *casa de juego*) gambling den

matuteo SM smuggling, contraband

matutero SM smuggler

matutino Ⓐ ADJ morning *antes de s*
Ⓑ SM morning newspaper

maula Ⓐ ADJ [*animal*] useless, lazy; [*persona*] good-for-nothing, unreliable
Ⓑ SMF [1] (= *vago*) idler, slacker
[2] (= *tramposo*) cheat, trickster; (= *moroso*) bad payer
Ⓒ SF [1] (= *retal*) remnant; (= *trasto*) piece of junk, useless object; (= *persona*) dead loss*
[2] (= *truco*) dirty trick

maulería SF cunning, trickiness

maulero SM [1] (= *tramposo*) cheat, trickster; (= *engañador*) swindler
[2] (= *ilusionista*) conjurer

maullar ▸conjug 1a◂ VI to mew, miaow

maullido SM mew, miaow

Mauricio[1] SM Maurice

Mauricio[2] SM (*Geog*) Mauritius ▸ **Isla Mauricio** Mauritius

Mauritania SF Mauritania

mauritano/a ADJ, SM/F Mauritanian

maurofilia SF (*Hist*) *admiration for the Moors and Moorish culture*

maurofobia SF (*Hist*) *hatred of the Moors and Moorish culture*

mausoleo SM mausoleum

máx. ABR (= **máximo**) max

maxi PREF maxi…

maxiabrigo SM maxi-coat

maxifalda SF maxiskirt

maxilar Ⓐ ADJ maxillary
Ⓑ SM jaw, jawbone; **recibió un puñetazo en el ~** he received a punch in the jaw

maxilofacial ADJ maxillofacial

máxima[1] SF (= *frase*) maxim

máxima[2] SF (*Meteo*) maximum (temperature), high; **~s de 44 grados en Sevilla y Córdoba** top temperatures *o* highs of 44 degrees in Seville and Córdoba

maximalismo SM maximalism

maximalista ADJ, SMF maximalist

máxime ADV (= *sobre todo*) especially; (= *principalmente*) principally; **y ~ cuando …** and all the more so when …

maximización SF maximization

maximizar ▸conjug 1f◂ VT to maximize

máximo Ⓐ ADJ [*altura, temperatura, velocidad, carga*] maximum; **el ~ dirigente** the leader; **~ jefe** *o* **líder** (*esp LAm*) President, leader; **llegar al punto ~** to reach the highest point; **lo ~ en ordenadores** the last word in computers; **acortaron el viaje lo ~ posible** they shortened their journey as much as they could
Ⓑ SM maximum; **un ~ de 100 euros** a maximum of 100 euros; **el ~ de tiempo que se te permite** the maximum time you're allowed; **al ~** to the maximum; **debemos aprovechar al ~ nuestros recursos** we must exploit our resources to the maximum, we must make the best of the resources we have; **sube la calefacción al ~** put the heating up as high as it'll go; **como ~** (= *como mucho*) at the most, at the outside; (= *como muy tarde*) at the latest; **te costará 5.000 como ~** it'll cost you 5,000 at the most; **llegaré a las nueve como ~** I'll be there by nine o'clock at the latest ► **máximo histórico** all-time high

máximum SM maximum

maxisencillo SM, **maxisingle** SM twelve-inch (record)

maxtate SM (*Méx*) straw basket

may. ABR (= **mayúscula(s)**) cap, caps

maya[1] SF [1] (*Bot*) daisy
[2] (= *muchacha*) May Queen

maya[2] (*Hist*) Ⓐ ADJ Mayan
Ⓑ SMF Maya, Mayan; **los ~** the Maya(s)

mayal SM flail

mayestático ADJ majestic, royal; **el plural ~** the royal "we"

mayo SM [1] (= *mes*) May; **el primero de ~** May Day; **el ~ francés** May 68; *ver tb* **septiembre**
[2] (= *palo*) maypole

mayólica SF (*Andes*) wall tile

mayonesa SF mayonnaise

mayor Ⓐ ADJ [1] (*comparativo*) [1·1] (= *más grande*) **necesitamos una habitación ~** we need a bigger *o* larger room; **un ~ número de visitantes** a larger *o* greater number of visitors, more visitors; **son temas de ~ importancia** they are more important issues, they are issues of greater importance; **sin ~es complicaciones** without further ado; **la ~ parte de los ciudadanos** most citizens; **ser ~ que algo**: **mi casa es ~ que la suya** my house is bigger *o* larger than his; **el índice de paro es ~ que hace un año** unemployment is higher than (it was) a year ago; ✦**MODISMO llegar a ~es** [*situación*] to get out of hand, get out of control
[1·2] (= *de más edad*) older; **es mi hermana ~** she's my older *o* elder sister; **Emilio es el ~ de los dos** Emilio is the older of the two; **~ que algn** older than sb; **Paco es ~ que Nacho** Paco is older than Nacho; **es tres años ~ que yo** he is three years older than me; **vivió con un hombre muchos años ~ que ella** she lived with a man many years her senior, she lived with a man who was several years older than her
[2] (*superlativo*) [2·1] (= *más grande*) **esta es la ~ iglesia del mundo** this is the biggest *o* largest church in the world; **su ~ problema** his biggest *o* greatest problem; **su ~ enemigo** his biggest *o* greatest enemy; **viven en la ~ miseria** they live in the greatest *o* utmost poverty; **hacer algo con el ~ cuidado** to do sth with the greatest *o* utmost care
[2·2] (= *de más edad*) oldest; **Juan es el ~** Juan is the oldest; **mi hijo (el) ~** my oldest *o* eldest son
[3] (= *principal*) [*plaza, mástil*] main; [*altar, misa*] high; **calle ~** high street, main street (*EEUU*); *ver tb* **colegio 1**, **libro 2**
[4] (= *adulto*) grown-up, adult; **nuestros hijos ya son ~es** our children are grown-up now; **las personas ~es** grown-ups, adults; **ya eres muy ~ para hacer esas tonterías** you're too old now to do silly things like that; **ser ~ de edad** to be of age; **hacerse ~** to grow up
[5] (= *de edad avanzada*) old, elderly; **mis padres son muy ~es** my parents are very old
[6] (= *jefe*) head *antes de s*; **el cocinero ~** the head chef; **montero ~** head huntsman
[7] (*Mús*) major
Ⓑ SMF [1] (= *adulto*) grown-up, adult; **los ~es se fueron a una fiesta** the grown-ups *o* adults went to a party; **los ~es no hacen cosas así** grown-ups don't do things like that ► **mayor de edad** adult, *person who is legally of age*
[2] (= *anciano*) **los ~es** elderly people; **¡más respeto con los ~es!** be more respectful to your elders (and betters)!
[3] (*LAm Mil*) major
Ⓒ SM **al por ~** wholesale; **vender al por ~** to sell wholesale; **repartir golpes al por ~** to throw punches left, right and centre

mayoral SM [1] (= *capataz*) foreman, overseer
[2] [*de finca*] farm manager, steward; [*de ovejas*] head shepherd
[3] (*Hist*) (= *cochero*) coachman

mayorazgo SM [1] (= *institución*) primogeniture
[2] (= *tierras*) entailed estate
[3] (= *hijo*) eldest son, first-born

mayorcito ADJ **eres ~ ya** you're a big boy now; **ya es ~ para saber lo que hace** he's old enough to know what he's doing; **ya eres un poco ~ para hacer eso** you're too old now to be doing that

mayordomo SM [*de casa*] butler; [*de hacienda*] steward; (*Cono Sur*) (= *capataz*) foreman; (*Andes*) (= *criado*) servant; (*LAm Rel*) patron (saint)

mayorear* ▸conjug 1a◂ VI (*CAm*) to be in charge, be the boss

mayoreo SM (*LAm*) wholesale (trade)

mayorete SF majorette

mayoría SF [1] (= *mayor parte*) majority; **la ~ de los españoles** the majority of Spaniards, most Spaniards; **la ~ de las veces** usually, on most occasions; **en la ~ de los casos** in most cases; **en su ~** mostly; **islas inhabitadas en su ~** islands, most of which are *o* which are mostly uninhabited; **una ~ del 20 por ciento** a 20 per cent majority; **una ~ de las cuatro quintas partes** a four-fifths majority; **la abrumadora ~** the overwhelming majority; **por una ~ arrolladora** by an overwhelming majority; **gobierno de la ~** majority rule; **la inmensa ~** the vast majority ► **mayoría absoluta** absolute majority ► **mayoría minoritaria** simple majority, relative majority ► **mayoría relativa** simple majority, relative majority ► **mayoría silenciosa** silent majority ► **mayoría simple** simple majority
[2] ► **mayoría de edad** adulthood, majority ► **mayoría de edad penal** age of majority; **cumplir** *o* **llegar a la ~ de edad** to come of age

mayorista Ⓐ ADJ wholesale
Ⓑ SMF wholesaler

mayoritariamente ADV [1] (= *principalmente*) mainly, mostly; **gente ~ joven** mainly *o* mostly young people, young people for the most part
[2] (*al votar*) by a majority; **el Parlamento votó ~ en contra de la reforma** a majority of the Parliament voted against the reform

mayoritario ADJ majority *antes de s*; **gobierno/accionista ~** majority government/shareholder

mayormente ADV (= *principalmente*) chiefly, mainly; (= *especialmente*) especially; (= *tanto más*) all the more so; **no me interesa ~** I'm not especially *o* particularly interested, I'm not all that interested

mayúscula SF capital (letter); (*Tip*) upper case letter; **se escribe con ~** it's written with a capital (letter); **con el título en ~s** with the title in capitals *o* capital letters; **la Literatura, con ~s** literature with a capital L, heavyweight literature; **un intelectual con ~s** an intellectual with a capital I, a heavyweight intellectual

mayúsculo ADJ [1] [*letra*] capital
[2] (= *enorme*) tremendous; **un susto ~** a tremendous fright *o* scare; **un error ~** a tremendous mistake

maza SF [1] (= *arma*) mace; (*Dep*) bat; (*Polo*) stick, mallet; (*Mús*) drumstick; [*de taco de billar*] handle; (*Téc*) flail; [*de cáñamo, lino*] brake; **la declaración del Gobierno cayó como una ~ sobre la oposición** the government statement was a bombshell for the opposition ► **maza de fraga** drop hammer ► **maza de gimnasia** Indian club
[2] (*) (= *persona*) bore
[3] (*LAm*) [*de rueda*] hub
[4] (*Andes, Caribe*) [*de ingenio*] drum (of a sugar mill)

mazacote SM [1] (*Culin*) **el arroz se ha hecho un ~** the rice is just one sticky mass
[2] (= *hormigón*) concrete
[3] (*Arte*) (= *mezcla*) mess, hotchpotch, hodge-

➤ LENGUA Y USO: **mayoría 1** 53.1

podge (*EEUU*); (= *monstruosidad*) eyesore, monstrosity
[4] (*CAm, Méx*) (= *dulce*) sweet mixture
[5] (*) (= *lata*) bore
[6] (*Caribe*‡) (= *culo*) arse‡, ass (*EEUU*‡)

mazacotudo ADJ = **amazacotado**

mazada SF [1] (= *golpe*) bash*, blow (with a club)
[2] (*fig*) blow; **fue una ~ para él** it came as a blow to him; **dar ~ a algn** to hurt sb, injure sb

mazamorra (*LAm*) SF [1] [*de maíz*] maize mush, maize porridge; (*pey*) mush
[2] (= *ampolla*) blister

mazamorrero/a* (*Andes*) Ⓐ ADJ of/from Lima
Ⓑ SM/F native/inhabitant of Lima; **los ~s** the people of Lima

mazapán SM marzipan

mazazo SM heavy blow; **fue un ~ para él** it came as a real blow to him; **la noticia cayó como un ~** the news was a bombshell; **el Gobierno asestó ayer un auténtico ~ a la oposición** the government dealt a real blow to the opposition yesterday

mazmorra SF dungeon

mazo SM [1] (= *martillo*) mallet; [*de mortero*] pestle; (= *porra*) club; [*de croquet*] mallet; [*de campana*] clapper; (*Agr*) flail; ❖*REFRÁN* **a Dios rogando y con el ~ dando** God helps those who help themselves
[2] (= *manojo*) bunch, handful; (= *fardo*) bundle, packet, package (*EEUU*); [*de papeles*] sheaf, bundle; [*de naipes*] pack; [*de billetes*] wad, roll
[3] (*) (= *persona*) bore

mazorca SF [1] [*de maíz*] cob, ear ► **mazorca de maíz** corncob
[2] (*Téc*) spindle
[3] (*Cono Sur*) (= *gobierno*) despotic government; (= *banda*) political gang

mazota SF (*Andes, Méx*) = **mazorca 1**

mazote SM (*Andes, Méx*) handful; **de a ~** free

Mb ABR (= **megabyte**) Mb

mb ABR (= **milibar(es)**) mb

Mbytes ABR (= **megabytes**) Mbytes

MCCA SM ABR (= **Mercado Común Centroamericano**) CACM

MCD SM ABR (= **Máximo Común Divisor**) HCF

MCM SM ABR (= **Mínimo Común Múltiplo**) LCM

MDP SM ABR (*Chile*) = **Movimiento Democrático Popular**

me PRON PERS [1] (*como complemento directo*) me; **me llamó por teléfono** he telephoned *o* rang me; **ya no me quiere** he doesn't love me any more
[2] (*como complemento indirecto*) (to) me; **¡dámelo!** give it to me!; **me lo compró** (*de mí*) he bought it from me; (*para mí*) he bought it for me; **me lo presentó mi primo** my cousin introduced him to me; **¿por qué me lo preguntas?** why do you ask?; **me lo dijeron ayer** they told me yesterday
[3] (*con partes del cuerpo, ropa*) **me rompí el brazo** I broke my arm; **me lavé la cara** I washed my face; **me quité el abrigo** I took my coat off; **se me está cayendo el pelo** my hair is falling out
[4] (*uso enfático*) **me lo comí todo** I ate it all up; **se me ha caído el bolígrafo** I've dropped my pen; **me preparé un café** I made myself a coffee
[5] (*uso reflexivo o pronominal*) **me lavé** I washed (myself); **me miré al espejo** I looked at myself in the mirror; **me voy a enfadar** I'm going to get cross; **me marcho** I am going

meada‡ SF [1] (= *orina*) piss‡; **echar una ~** to have a piss *o* a slash‡
[2] (= *mancha*) urine mark, urine stain

meadero‡ SM bog‡, loo*, john (*EEUU*‡)

meado‡ ADJ [1] **esto está ~** it's a cinch*, it's dead easy*
[2] (*Cono Sur*) **estar ~** to be pissed‡

meados‡ SMPL piss‡ *sing*

meaja SF crumb

meandro SM meander

meapilas‡ Ⓐ ADJ sanctimonious, holier-than-thou
Ⓑ SMF INV (= *santito*) goody-goody*

mear‡ ▸conjug 1a◂ Ⓐ VT [1] (= *orinar*) to piss on‡
[2] (= *humillar, ganar*) to piss on‡
Ⓑ VI to piss‡, have *o* (*EEUU*) take a piss‡; ❖*MODISMO* **~ fuera del tiesto** to miss the point completely
Ⓒ **mearse** VPR to wet o.s.; **~se de risa** to piss o.s. laughing‡

MEC SM ABR (*Esp*) = **Ministerio de Educación y Ciencia**

meca[1] SF **la ~ del cine** the Mecca of the film world

meca[2]‡ EXCL (*Chile*) shit!‡

meca[3]* SF (*Andes*) prostitute

Meca SF **La ~** Mecca

mecachis* EXCL (*Esp*) (*euf de* **¡me cago!**) sugar!*, shoot!*; **~ en la mar** sugar!*, shoot!*

mecánica SF [1] (= *técnica*) mechanics *sing* ► **mecánica de precisión** precision engineering
[2] (= *mecanismo*) mechanism, works
[3] (= *funcionamiento*) mechanics *pl*; **la ~ del concurso es sencilla** the mechanics of the competition are simple; **la ~ parlamentaria** parliamentary procedure; **la ~ electoral** electoral procedure

mecánicamente ADV mechanically

mecanicista ADJ mechanistic

mecánico/a Ⓐ ADJ [1] (*gen*) mechanical; (*con motor*) power *antes de s*; (= *de máquinas*) machine *antes de s*
[2] [*gesto, trabajo*] mechanical
Ⓑ SM/F [*de coches*] mechanic, grease monkey (*EEUU**); (= *operario*) machinist; (= *ajustador*) fitter, repair man/woman; (*Aer*) rigger, fitter; (= *conductor*) driver, chauffeur ► **mecánico/a de vuelo** flight engineer

mecanismo SM [1] [*de reloj, cerradura, fusil*] mechanism ► **mecanismo de dirección** steering gear ► **mecanismo de seguridad** safety mechanism
[2] (= *procedimiento*) mechanism; **el ~ electoral** the electoral procedure ► **mecanismo de defensa** defence mechanism

mecanización SF mechanization

mecanizado ADJ mechanized

mecanizar ▸conjug 1f◂ VT to mechanize

mecano® SM Meccano®

mecanografía SF typing ► **mecanografía al tacto** touch-typing

mecanografiado Ⓐ ADJ typewritten
Ⓑ SM (= *texto*) typescript; (= *acción*) typing

mecanografiar ▸conjug 1c◂ VT to type

mecanógrafo/a SM/F typist

mecapal SM (*CAm, Méx*) leather strap (*for carrying*)

mecapalero SM (*CAm, Méx*) porter

mecatazo SM (*CAm*) [1] (= *golpe*) lash
[2] (*) (= *trago*) swig*

mecate SM [1] (*CAm, Méx*) (= *cuerda*) rope, twine; (= *fibra*) strip of pita fibre; **¡es todo ~!** (*Méx**) it's terrific!; ❖*MODISMO* **jalear el ~ a algn*** to suck up to sb*
[2] (*Méx**) (= *persona*) boor, oaf

mecateada SF (*CAm, Méx*) lashing, beating

mecatear[1] ▸conjug 1a◂ Ⓐ VT [1] (*CAm, Méx*) (= *atar*) to tie up; (= *azotar*) to lash, whip
[2] (*LAm**) (= *dar coba a*) to suck up to*
Ⓑ **mecatearse** VPR (*Méx*‡) **~se** ◊ **mecateárselas** to beat it*, leg it*

mecatear[2] ▸conjug 1a◂ VI (*Andes*) to eat cakes

mecatero‡ SM (*LAm*) creep*, toady

mecato SM (*Andes*) cakes *pl*, pastries *pl*

mecedor Ⓐ ADJ rocking
Ⓑ SM [1] (= *columpio*) swing
[2] (*CAm, Caribe, Méx*) (= *silla*) rocking chair
[3] (*Caribe*) (= *cuchara*) stirrer

mecedora SF rocking chair

Mecenas SM Maecenas

mecenas SMF INV patron; **~ de las artes** patron of the arts

mecenazgo SM patronage

mecer ▸conjug 2b◂ Ⓐ VT [1] [+ *cuna, niño*] to rock; (*en columpio*) to swing; [+ *rama*] to cause to sway, move to and fro; [*olas*] [+ *barco*] to rock
[2] [+ *líquido*] to stir; [+ *recipiente*] to shake
Ⓑ **mecerse** VPR (*en mecedora*) to rock (to and fro); (*en columpio*) to swing; [*rama*] to sway, move to and fro

mecha SF [1] [*de vela, lámpara*] wick; [*de explosivo*] fuse; **encender la ~** (*lit, fig*) to light the fuse; ❖*MODISMOS* **aguantar ~** to grin and bear it; **tener mucha ~ para algo** to be very good at sth, have a knack for sth; **a toda ~*** at full speed ► **mecha lenta** slow fuse ► **mecha tardía** time fuse
[2] [*de pelo*] = **mechón[1]**
[3] **mechas** (*en el pelo*) highlights
[4] [*de tocino*] rasher
[5] (*Andes, Cono Sur Téc*) bit (*of brace*)
[6] (*Andes, Caribe**) (= *broma*) joke
[7] (*LAm*) (= *miedo*) fear
[8] (*) (= *ratería*) shoplifting
[9] (*Andes*) (= *baratija*) trinket

mechado ADJ **carne mechada** larded meat; **~ de anglicismos** full of Anglicisms

mechar ▸conjug 1a◂ VT (*Culin*) (= *poner tocino*) to lard; (= *rellenar*) to stuff

mechero[1] SM [1] (= *encendedor*) cigarette lighter; (= *estufa*) burner; (*Andes, Cono Sur*) (= *candil*) oil lamp ► **mechero Bunsen** Bunsen burner ► **mechero de gas** gas burner ► **mechero encendedor**, **mechero piloto** pilot light
[2] (*CAm, Méx*) [*de pelo*] mop of hair
[3] (‡) (= *pene*) prick‡

mechero[2]/a* SM/F [1] (= *ladrón*) shoplifter
[2] (*Caribe*) (= *bromista*) joker

mechificar* ▸conjug 1g◂ VT (*Andes, Caribe*) (= *engañar*) to trick, deceive; (= *mofarse de*) to mock

mecho SM (*Andes, CAm*) (= *vela*) candle; (= *cabo*) candle end; (= *candelero*) candlestick

mechón[1] SM [*de pelo*] lock; (= *hilos*) bundle

mechón²/ona* SM/F (*Chile*) fresher, freshman

mechudo ADJ (*LAm*) tousled, unkempt

meción SM (*CAm, Caribe*) jerk, jolt

meco* ADJ (*CAm, Méx*) (= *ordinario*) coarse, vulgar; (= *bruto*) thick*; (= *salvaje*) uncivilized, wild; (*Hist*) wild (Indian)

medalla SF (*Dep, Mil*) medal; (= *joya*) medallion; **una ~ de la Virgen** a medallion with the Virgin Mary on it; **ser ~ de bronce/plata/oro** to be a bronze/silver/gold medallist *o* (*EEUU*) medalist, get a bronze/silver/gold (medal) ► **medalla al valor** medal for bravery

medallero SM medal table

medallista SMF [1] (*Dep*) medallist, medalist (*EEUU*) ► **medallista de bronce** bronze medallist ► **medallista de oro** gold medallist ► **medallista de plata** silver medallist
[2] (= *diseñador*) medal designer

medallón SM [1] (= *medalla*) medallion
[2] (= *relicario*) locket
[3] (*Culin*) medallion, médaillon ► **medallón de pescado** fish cake

médano SM, **medaño** SM (*en tierra*) sand dune; (*en el mar*) sandbank

media SF [1] **medias** (= *hasta la cintura*) tights, pantyhose *sing* (*EEUU*); (*hasta el muslo*) stockings ► **medias de compresión** support tights ► **medias de malla** (*hasta el muslo*) fishnet stockings; (*hasta la cintura*) fishnet tights ► **medias de red**, **medias de rejilla** = **medias de malla** ► **medias pantalón** (*Col*) tights *pl*; → PANTALONES, ZAPATOS, GAFAS
[2] (*LAm*) (= *calcetín*) sock
[3] **de ~** [*aguja*] knitting *antes de s*; [*punto*] plain; **hacer ~** to knit
[4] (*Dep*) midfield
[5] (= *promedio*) average; **100 de ~ al día** an average of 100 a day; **dan una ~ de cinco conciertos al mes** they give an average of five concerts a month ► **media aritmética** arithmetic mean ► **media ponderada** weighted average
[6] ► **media de cerveza** 1/4 litre bottle of beer

mediación SF mediation, intercession; **por ~ de** through

mediado ADJ [1] [*local*] half-full, half-empty; [*trabajo*] half-completed; **el local estaba ~** the place was half-full *o* half-empty; **mediada la tarde** halfway through the afternoon; **llevo ~ el trabajo** I am halfway through the job, I have completed half the work
[2] **a ~s de marzo** in the middle of March, halfway through March; **a ~s del siglo pasado** around the middle of the last century

mediador(a) SM/F mediator

mediagua SF (*Cono Sur*) hut, shack

medial ADJ medial

medialuna SF (*LAm*) croissant

mediana SF [1] (*Aut*) central reservation, median (*EEUU*)
[2] (*Mat*) median

medianamente ADV [1] (= *bastante*) fairly; **una calle ~ concurrida** a fairly busy street; **me gusta comer ~ bien** I like to eat at least fairly well; **cualquier persona ~ sensata** any half-sensible person
[2] (= *regular*) moderately; **un trabajo ~ bueno** a moderately good piece of work; **quedó ~ en los exámenes** he did moderately well in the exams

medianera SF (*Andes, Cono Sur*) party wall, dividing wall

medianería SF [1] (= *pared*) party wall
[2] (*Caribe, Méx Com*) partnership; (*Agr*) sharecropping

medianero Ⓐ ADJ [1] [*pared*] party *antes de s*, dividing *antes de s*; [*valla*] boundary *antes de s*
[2] [*vecino*] adjacent, next
Ⓑ SM [1] [*de casa*] owner of the adjoining house (or property *etc*)
[2] (*Caribe, Méx*) (= *socio*) partner; (*Agr*) share-cropper

medianía SF [1] (= *promedio*) average; (= *punto medio*) halfway point; (*Econ*) moderate means *pl*, modest circumstances *pl*; (*en sociedad*) undistinguished social position
[2] (= *mediocridad*) mediocrity; **no pasa de ser una ~** he's no better than average, he's little more than mediocre
[3] (*Com*) middleman

mediano ADJ [1] (= *regular*) average; (*en tamaño*) medium-sized; [*empresa*] medium-sized; **una bomba de mediana potencia** a medium-sized bomb; **una cebolla mediana** a medium onion; **camisetas de talla mediana** medium T-shirts; **es ~ de estatura** he is of average *o* medium height; **de mediana edad** middle-aged
[2] (= *del medio*) middle; **es el hermano ~** he is the middle brother
[3] (= *indiferente*) mediocre, average

medianoche SF midnight; **a ~** at midnight

▼ **mediante** PREP [1] (= *por medio de*) by means of; **izan las cajas ~ una polea** the crates are lifted by means of a pulley; **se comunicaban ~ mensajes en clave** they communicated by means of coded messages; **se comunican ~ gestos** they communicate through signs; **lograron abrir la puerta ~ una palanca** they managed to open the door with a metal bar; **vigilaban el edificio ~ cámaras ocultas** hidden cameras were used to keep a watch on the building; **un diseño ~ ordenador** a computer-generated design
[2] **Dios ~** God willing; **volveré, Dios ~, el lunes** I'll be back on Monday, God willing

mediar ▸conjug 1b◂ VI [1] (= *estar en medio*) to be halfway through; (= *llegar a la mitad*) to get to the middle, get halfway; [*tiempo*] to elapse, pass; **entre A y B median 30kms** it is 30kms from A to B; **media un abismo entre los dos gobiernos** the two governments are poles apart; **entre los dos sucesos ~on varios años** the two events were separated by several years, several years elapsed between the two events; **mediaba el otoño** autumn was half over, it was halfway through autumn; **mediaba el mes de julio** it was halfway through July
[2] (= *ocurrir*) to come up, happen; (= *intervenir*) to intervene; (= *existir*) to exist; **pero medió la muerte de su madre** but his mother's death intervened; **media el hecho de que ...** we must take into account the fact that ...; **median relaciones cordiales entre los dos** cordial relations exist between the two; **sin ~ palabra se abalanzó sobre ellos** he fell upon them without a word
[3] (= *interceder*) to mediate (**en** in; **entre** between), intervene; **~ en favor de algn** ◊ **~ por algn** to intercede *o* intervene on sb's behalf; **~ con algn** to intercede with sb

mediático ADJ media *antes de s*

mediatizar ▸conjug 1f◂ VT [1] (= *estorbar*) to interfere with, obstruct; (= *influir*) to influence
[2] (*Pol*) to annexe, take control of

medible ADJ (= *mensurable*) measurable; (= *observable*) detectable, appreciable

medicación SF (= *medicinas*) medication; (= *tratamiento*) medication, treatment

médicamente ADV medically

medicamento SM medicine ► **medicamento de patente** patent medicine

medicamentoso ADJ **incompatibilidad medicamentosa** incompatibility between drugs; **el tratamiento ~ será diferente** the drugs prescribed will vary

medicar ▸conjug 1g◂ Ⓐ VT to give medicine to; **estar medicado** to be on medication; **jabón medicado** medicated soap
Ⓑ **medicarse** VPR to take medicine

medicastro SM (*pey*) quack (doctor)

medicina SF [1] (= *ciencia*) medicine; **estudia ~ en la universidad** he's studying medicine at university; **un estudiante de ~** a medical student ► **medicina de empresa** industrial medicine ► **medicina forense** forensic medicine ► **medicina general** general medicine, general practice ► **medicina homeopática** homeopathic medicine ► **medicina interna** internal medicine ► **medicina legal** forensic medicine, legal medicine ► **medicina natural** natural medicine ► **medicina preventiva** preventive medicine
[2] (= *medicamento*) medicine; **¿te has tomado ya la ~?** have you taken your medicine yet?

medicinal ADJ medicinal

medicinar ▸conjug 1a◂ Ⓐ VT to give medicine to
Ⓑ **medicinarse** VPR to take medicine; **~se con algo** to dose o.s. with sth

medición SF [1] [*de presión, distancia*] (= *acción*) measuring; (= *resultado*) measurement; **pronto comenzarán los trabajos de ~** measuring *o* measurement works will begin soon; **un nuevo método de ~** a new measuring system; **¿cómo se realiza la ~ de la temperatura?** how is the temperature measured?; **un método de ~ de audiencias** an audience tracking system; **aparatos de ~** measuring instruments; **hacer mediciones** to take measurements; **instrumentos de ~** measuring instruments
[2] (*Literat*) [*de versos*] measuring, scansion

médico/a Ⓐ ADJ medical; **asistencia médica** medical attention; **receta médica** prescription
Ⓑ SM/F doctor ► **médico/a de cabecera** family doctor, GP ► **médico/a (de medicina) general** general practitioner ► **médico/a dentista** dental surgeon ► **médico/a deportivo/a** sports doctor ► **médico/a forense** forensic surgeon, expert in forensic medicine; (*Jur*) coroner ► **médico/a interno/a** houseman, intern (*EEUU*) ► **médico/a naturista** naturopath ► **médico/a partero/a** obstetrician ► **médico/a pediatra**, **médico/a puericultor(a)** paediatrician ► **médico/a residente** houseman, intern (*EEUU*) ► **médico/a rural** country doctor

➤ LENGUA Y USO: mediante 1 44.1

medida SF [1] (= *unidad de medida*) measure; **una ~ de harina y dos de azúcar** one measure of flour and two of sugar; **puedes usar un vaso como ~** you can use a glass as a measure; **la libra es una ~ de peso** the pound is a measure of weight; ✦**MODISMO esto colma la ~** this is the last straw ▸ **medida agraria** land measure ▸ **medida de capacidad** cubic measure ▸ **medida de superficie** square measure ▸ **medida de volumen** cubic measure ▸ **medida para áridos** dry measure ▸ **medida para líquidos** liquid measure

[2] (= *medición*) measuring, measurement; **la ~ del tiempo se realizará con unos cronómetros especiales** time will be measured using some special chronometers

[3] **medidas** (= *dimensiones*) measurements; **¿qué ~s tiene la mesa?** what are the measurements of the table?; **¿cuáles son tus ~s?** what are your measurements?; **tomar las ~s a algn/algo** (*lit*) to measure sb/sth, take sb's/sth's measurements; (*fig*) to size sb/sth up*; **tómale bien las ~s antes de proponerle nada** make sure you've got him well sized up before you propose anything

[4] (= *proporción*) **no sé en qué ~ nos afectará la nueva ley** I don't know to what extent the new law will affect us; **en cierta ~** to a certain extent; **en gran ~** to a great extent; **en menor ~** to a lesser extent; **en la ~ de lo posible** as far as possible, insofar as it is possible; **a ~ que** as; **a ~ que vaya bajando el nivel** as the level goes down; **a ~ que van pasando los días** as the days go by; **en la ~ en que** (+ *indic*) in that; (+ *subjun*) if; **el relato era bueno en la ~ en que reflejaba el ambiente de la época** the story was good in that it reflected the atmosphere of the time; **sólo cambiarán el tratamiento en la ~ en que los resultados sean negativos** the treatment will only be altered if the results are negative

[5] (*Cos*) **a (la) ~** [*ropa, zapatos*] made to measure; [*trabajo, vacaciones*] tailor-made; **un traje (hecho) a la ~** a made-to-measure suit; **no tenemos un sombrero a su ~** we don't have a hat in your size *o* to fit you; **un papel hecho a su ~** a tailor-made role; **le respondió a la ~ de las circunstancias** she replied as the circumstances required; **lo hice a la ~ de tus deseos** I did it according to your wishes; **un hotel a la ~ de tus necesidades** a hotel that suits all your needs; **de** *o* **sobre ~** (*Chile*) [*ropa, zapatos*] made-to-measure; **venir a (la) ~** (*lit*) to be the right size; (*fig*) to be tailor-made; **este pantalón me viene a ~** these trousers are just the right size; **este trabajo me viene a la ~** this job is tailor-made for me

[6] (*LAm*) (= *talla*) size; **¿cuál es su ~?** what size do you take?; **¿qué ~ de cuello tiene usted?** what collar size are you?, what is your collar measurement?; **ropa a sobre ~** (*Méx*) outsize clothing

[7] (= *disposición*) measure; **~s destinadas a reducir el desempleo** measures aimed at reducing unemployment; **adoptar** *o* **tomar ~s** to take measures, take steps; **una de las ~s urgentes adoptadas** one of the emergency measures *o* steps taken ▸ **medida cautelar**, **medida de precaución** precautionary measure ▸ **medida de presión** form of pressure ▸ **medida preventiva** preventive measure ▸ **medida represiva** form of repression ▸ **medidas de seguridad** (*contra ataques, robos*) security measures; (*contra incendios*) safety measures ▸ **medidas represivas** repressive measures; *ver tb* **paquete 3**

[8] (= *moderación*) **con ~** in moderation; **sin ~** to excess; **bebía sin ~** he drank to excess; **gastos sin ~** excessive spending

[9] [*de versos*] (= *medición*) measuring, scansion; (= *longitud*) measure

medidor(a) Ⓐ ADJ measuring
Ⓑ SM/F (= *persona*) measurer
Ⓒ SM (*esp LAm*) (= *aparato*) meter ▸ **medidor de agua** water meter ▸ **medidor de lluvia** rain gauge ▸ **medidor de presión** pressure gauge ▸ **medidor Geiger** Geiger counter

mediero/a SM/F (*LAm*) share-cropper

medieval ADJ medieval

medievalismo SM medievalism

medievalista SMF medievalist

medievo SM Middle Ages *pl*

medio Ⓐ ADJ [1] (= *la mitad de*) half; **nos queda media botella** we've half a bottle left; **~ limón** half a lemon; **~ litro** half a litre; **acudió media ciudad** half the town turned up; **~ luto** half-mourning; **media pensión** (*en hotel*) half-board; **media hora** half an hour; **estuve esperando media hora** I was waiting for half an hour; **el enfermo ha empeorado en la última media hora** the patient has got worse in the last half hour; **una hora y media** an hour and a half; **tardamos tres horas y media en llegar** we took three and a half hours to get there; **son las ocho y media** it's half past eight; **media luna** (*Astron*) half-moon; **en forma de media luna** crescent-shaped; **la Media Luna** (*en el Islam*) the Crescent; *ver tb* **asta**, **luz 1**, **mundo 2**, **naranja A3**, **palabra 1**, **voz 1**, **vuelta 1**

[2] (= *intermedio*) **la clase media** the middle class; **café de media mañana** mid-morning coffee; **a media tarde** halfway through the afternoon; **a ~ camino**: **estamos a ~ camino** we're halfway there; **a ~ camino entre Madrid y Barcelona** halfway between Madrid and Barcelona; *ver tb* **plazo**

[3] (= *promedio*) average; **la temperatura media** the average temperature; *ver tb* **término 2**

[4] (= *normal*) average; **el francés ~** the average Frenchman; **el hombre ~** the man in the street

[5] **a medias**: **lo dejó hecho a medias** he left it half-done; **está escrito a medias** it's half-written; **estoy satisfecho sólo a medias** I am only partly satisfied; **una verdad a medias** a half truth; **ir a medias** to go fifty-fifty; **lo pagamos a medias** we share *o* split the cost

Ⓑ ADV [1] (*con adjetivo*) half; **está ~ borracha** she's half drunk; **~ dormido** half asleep; **es ~ tonto** he's not very bright, he's a bit on the slow side

[2] (*con verbo, adverbio*) **está a ~ escribir/terminar** it is half-written/finished; **~ se sonrió** she gave a half-smile; **lo dijo ~ en broma** he was only half-joking; **Ana ~ se enamoró de Gonzalo** Ana kind of fell in love with Gonzalo; **eso no está ni ~ bien** that isn't even close to being right

[3] (*LAm*) (= *bastante*) rather, quite, pretty*; **fue ~ difícil** it was pretty hard

Ⓒ SM [1] (= *centro*) middle, centre, center (*EEUU*); **justo en el ~ de la plaza hay una fuente** there's a fountain right in the middle *o* centre of the square; **coger algo por el ~** to take sth round the middle; **el justo ~** a happy medium; **de en ~**: **la casa de en ~** the middle house; **quitar algo de en ~** to get sth out of the way; **quitarse de en ~** to get out of the way; **de por ~**: **hay droga de por ~** drugs are involved; **hay dificultades de por ~** there are difficulties in the way; **meterse de por ~** to intervene; **día (de) por ~** (*LAm*) every other day; **en ~**: **iba a besarla, pero él se puso en ~** I was going to kiss her, but he got between us; **no dejes las cosas por en ~** don't leave your things in the middle of the floor; **en ~ de la plaza** in the middle of the square; **en ~ de tanta confusión** in the midst of such confusion; **en ~ de todos ellos** among all of them; **por ~ de**: **pasar por ~ de** to go through (the middle of); ✦**MODISMO de ~ a ~**: **equivocarse de ~ a ~** to be completely wrong

[2] (*Dep*) midfielder ▸ **medio apertura** (*Rugby*) fly-half ▸ **medio centro** centre-half ▸ **medio (de) melé** (*Rugby*) scrum-half

[3] (= *método*) means *pl*, way; **lo intentaré por todos los ~s (posibles)** I'll try everything possible; **no hay ~ de conseguirlo** there is no way of getting it, it's impossible to get; **poner todos los ~s para hacer algo** ◊ **no regatear ~s para hacer algo** to spare no effort to do sth; **por ~ de**: **se mueve por ~ de poleas** it moves by means of *o* using a pulley system; **me avisó por ~ de mi vecino** she let me know through my neighbour; **respira por ~ de las agallas** it breathes through *o* using *o* by means of its gills; **lo consiguió por ~ de chantajes** he obtained it by *o* through blackmail ▸ **medio de transporte** means of transport

[4] **los medios** (*tb* **los ~s de comunicación** *o* **difusión**) the media; **los ~s de comunicación de masas** the mass media; **los ~s informativos** the news media

[5] **medios** (= *recursos*) means, resources; **es un hombre de (muchos) ~s** he's a man of means; **no tienen ~s económicos suficientes** they do not have sufficient financial resources

[6] (*Biol*) (*tb* **~ ambiente**) environment

[7] (= *círculo*) circle; **en los ~s financieros** in financial circles; **encontrarse en su ~** to be in one's element *o* milieu

medioambiental ADJ environmental

medioambientalista SMF environmentalist

medioambiente SM environment

mediocampista SMF midfield player

mediocampo SM midfield

mediocre ADJ average; (*pey*) mediocre

mediocridad SF (*pey*) mediocrity; **es una ~** he's a nonentity

mediodía SM [1] (= *las doce*) midday, noon; (= *hora de comer*) ≈ lunchtime; **a ~** (= *a las doce*) at midday *o* noon; (= *a la hora de comer*) ≈ at lunchtime

[2] (*Geog*) south; **el ~ de Francia** the French Midi

medioevo SM Middle Ages *pl*

mediofondista SMF middle-distance runner

mediofondo SM (*Caribe*) petticoat

mediogrande ADJ medium large

mediometraje SM medium-length film

mediooeste SM Midwest

mediooriental ADJ Middle Eastern

Medio Oriente SM Middle East

mediopensionista SMF day pupil, day student

mediopequeño ADJ medium small

mediquillo SM (*pey*) quack (doctor)

medir ▸conjug 3k◂ Ⓐ VT [1] (= *tomar la medida de*) [+ *habitación, ángulo*] to measure; [+ *distancia, temperatura*] to measure, gauge, gage (*EEUU*); [+ *tierra*] to survey, plot; **~ algo por millas** to measure sth in miles; ✦**MODISMOS ~ a algn (con la vista)** to size sb up*; **~ las calles** (*Méx**) to hang around on the streets*
[2] (= *calcular*) to weigh up; **deberías ~ las consecuencias de lo que dices** you should consider *o* weigh up the consequences of what you say; **deberíamos ~ los pros y los contras de esta decisión** we should weigh up the pros and cons of this decision
[3] (= *enfrentar*) **los dos púgiles ~án sus fuerzas** the two boxers will be pitted against each other *o* will take each other on; *ver tb* **rasero**
[4] (= *moderar*) [+ *comentarios*] to choose carefully; **mide tus palabras** (*aconsejando*) choose your words carefully; (*regañando*) mind your language
[5] (*Literat*) to scan; **¿cómo se mide este verso?** how does this line scan?
Ⓑ VI to measure, be; **el tablero mide 80 por 20** the board measures *o* is 80 by 20; **¿cuánto mides?** how tall are you?; **mido 1,80m** I am 1.80m; **la caja mide 20cm de ancho** the box is 20cm wide; **mide 88cm de pecho** her bust measurement is 88cms
Ⓒ **medirse** VPR [1] (= *tomarse la medida*) (*uno mismo*) to measure o.s.; [+ *cintura, pecho*] to measure
[2] (= *enfrentarse*) **~se con algn** to take on sb; **una final en la que se ~án los dos equipos** a final in which the two teams will be pitted against each other *o* will take each other on
[3] (= *moderarse*) to restrain o.s.; **deberías ~te un poco en tus actos** you should act with a bit more restraint *o* restrain yourself a bit
[4] (*Méx**) (= *no perder la calma*) to keep one's head
[5] (*Col, Méx*) [+ *sombrero, zapatos*] to try on

meditabundo ADJ pensive, thoughtful

meditación SF meditation; **meditaciones** meditations (**sobre** on); ► **meditación trascendental** transcendental meditation

meditar ▸conjug 1a◂ Ⓐ VT (= *pensar*) to ponder, meditate (on); [+ *plan*] to think out
Ⓑ VI to meditate, ponder

mediterraneidad SF Mediterranean feel *o* spirit; **un concepto de ~ muy interesante** a very interesting notion of what being Mediterranean is

Mediterráneo SM **el ~** the Mediterranean; ✦**MODISMO descubrir el ~*** to reinvent the wheel

mediterráneo ADJ [1] (*Geog*) Mediterranean
[2] (= *sin salida al mar*) land-locked

médium SMF (*pl* **médiums**) (= *persona*) medium

mediúmnico ADJ **sesión mediúmnica** session with a medium; **revelaciones mediúmnicas** revelations from a medium

medo SM **los ~s y los persas** the Medes and the Persians

➤ LENGUA Y USO: **mejor A1** 28.1, 29.2

medra SF (= *aumento*) increase, growth; (= *mejora*) improvement; (*Econ*) prosperity

medrar ▸conjug 1a◂ VI (= *aumentar*) to increase, grow; (= *mejorar*) to improve, do well; (= *prosperar*) to prosper, thrive; [*animal, planta etc*] to grow, thrive; **¡medrados estamos!** (*iró*) we're in a real pickle now!

medro SM = **medra**

medroso ADJ fearful, timid

médula SF, **medula** SF [1] (*Anat*) marrow, medulla (*frm*) ► **médula espinal** spinal cord ► **médula ósea** bone marrow; **hasta la ~** (*fig*) to the core; **es irlandés hasta la ~** he is Irish through and through; **estoy convencido hasta la ~** I am totally *o* absolutely convinced; **estoy mojado hasta la ~** I am soaked to the skin [2] (*Bot*) pith [3] (= *esencia*) essence

medular ADJ [1] (*Anat*) bone-marrow *antes de s*; **trasplante ~** bone-marrow transplant
[2] (= *fundamental*) central, fundamental, essential

medusa SF jellyfish

Mefistófeles SM Mephistopheles

mefítico ADJ mephitic(al)

mefitismo SM mephitis

mega... PREF mega...

megabyte ['megabait] SM megabyte

megaciclo SM megacycle

megafonía SF (= *sistema*) public address system; (*en la calle*) loudspeakers *pl*

megáfono SM megaphone

megahercio SM, **megaherzio** SM megahertz

megalítico ADJ megalithic

megalito SM megalith

megalomanía SF megalomania

megalómano/a SM/F megalomaniac

megalópolis SF INV megalopolis, super-city

megaocteto SM megabyte

megapíxel SM (*pl* **megapixels** *o* **megapíxeles**) megapixel

megatón SM megaton

megavatio SM megawatt

megavoltio SM megavolt

meiga SF (*Galicia*) wise woman, witch

mejicanismo SM Mexicanism, *word o phrase etc peculiar to Mexico*

mejicano/a ADJ, SM/F Mexican

Méjico SM Mexico

mejido ADJ [*huevo*] beaten

mejilla SF cheek

mejillón SM mussel

mejillonera SF mussel-bed

mejillonero ADJ mussel *antes de s*; **industria mejillonera** mussel industry

▼**mejor** Ⓐ ADJ [1] (*comparativo*) [1·1] (= *más bueno*) [*resultado, producto*] better; [*calidad, oferta*] better, higher; **a falta de otra cosa ~ que hacer** for lack of anything better to do; **nunca he visto nada ~** I've never seen anything better; **es ~ de lo que creía** it's better than I thought; **y lo que es ~** and even better, and better still; **~ que algo** better than sth; **éste es ~ que aquél** this one is better than that one; **no hay nada ~ que una buena comida** there's nothing better than a good meal
[1·2] (= *preferible*) **ser ~** to be better; **sería ~ callarse** it'd be better to keep quiet; **hubiera sido ~ no decir nada** it would have been better to say nothing; **será ~ que te vayas** you'd better go
[2] (*superlativo*) [2·1] (*de dos*) better; **de estos dos refrescos, ¿cuál es el ~?** which is the better (out) of these two drinks?
[2·2] (*de varios*) [*persona, producto*] best; [*calidad*] top, highest; [*oferta*] highest, best; **¿quién es tu ~ amigo?** who is your best friend?; **está entre las diez ~es** she is among the ten best; **ser el ~ de la clase** to be the best in the class, be top of the class; **es el ~ de todos** he's the best of all; **vive el ~ momento de su carrera deportiva** he is at the peak of his sporting career; **un jamón de la ~ calidad** a top quality ham, a ham of the highest quality; ✦**MODISMO llevarse la ~ parte** to take the lion's share
[2·3] **lo ~** the best; **os deseo (todo) lo ~** I wish you all the best, my best wishes (to you); **lo ~ de España es el clima** the best thing about Spain is the climate; **lo ~ del caso es que ...** the good thing is that ..., the best part of it is that ...; **os deseo lo ~ del mundo** I wish you all the best; **tengo unos abuelos que son lo ~ del mundo** my grandparents are the best in the world; **tenéis que hacerlo lo ~ posible** you have to do the best you can, you have to do your best; **lo hice lo ~ que pude** I did it the best I could, I did it as well as I could; **lo ~ que podemos hacer es callarnos** the best thing we can do is keep quiet; **estar en lo ~ de la vida** to be in the prime of life; *ver tb* **partir A3**
Ⓑ ADV [1] (*comparativo de bien*) better; **ahora lo entiendo todo un poco ~** I understand everything a bit better now; **yo canto ~ que tú** I can sing better than you; **lo hace cada vez ~** he's getting better and better; **¿te sientes algo ~?** do you feel any better?; **ahora estoy un poco ~ de dinero** I'm a bit better off now; **así está mucho ~** it's much better like that; **¡pues si no quieres venir con nosotros, ~!** well, if you don't want to come with us, so much the better!; **~ dicho** or rather, or I should say; **lleva tres años en Inglaterra, o ~ dicho, en el Reino Unido** she's been in England, or rather *o* or I should say the United Kingdom, for three years; **mucho ~** much better, a lot better*; **~ o peor**: **~ o peor, ya saldremos adelante** for better or (for) worse, we'll come through this; **~ que ~** *o* **tanto ~** so much the better, all the better; *ver tb* **nunca**
[2] (*superlativo de bien*) best; **¿quién es el que lo hace ~?** who does it best?; **éste es el texto ~ redactado de todos** this text is the best written of all
[3] (= *preferiblemente*) **~ quedamos otro día** why don't we meet another day?, it'd be better if we met another day; **~ vámonos** we'd better go; **tú, ~ te callas*** you'd better keep quiet*; **~ me voy*** I'd better go; *ver tb* **cuanto B2**
[4] **a lo ~** maybe; **a lo ~ viene mañana** he might come tomorrow, maybe he'll come tomorrow; **a lo ~ hasta nos toca la lotería** we might even win the lottery; **—¿crees que lloverá hoy? —a lo ~** "do you think it will rain today?" — "maybe" *o* "it might"

mejora SF [1] (= *progreso*) improvement
[2] (= *aumento*) increase; **~s de productividad** increases in productivity
[3] **mejoras** (= *obras*) improvements, altera-

tions
[4] (*en subasta*) higher bid
[5] (*Méx Agr*) weeding

mejorable ADJ improvable

mejoramiento SM improvement

mejorana SF marjoram

mejorar ▸conjug 1a◂ Ⓐ VT [1] [+ *servicio, resultados*] to improve; [+ *enfermo*] to make better; (= *realzar*) to enhance; [+ *oferta*] to raise, improve; [+ *récord*] to break; (*Inform*) to upgrade; ✦*MODISMO* **mejorando lo presente** present company excepted
[2] **~ a algn** (= *ser mejor que*) to be better than sb
Ⓑ VI [1] [*situación*] to improve, get better; (*Meteo*) to improve, clear up; (*Fin*) to improve, pick up; [*enfermo*] to get better; **han mejorado de actitud/imagen** their attitude/image has improved; **los negocios mejoran** business is picking up; **está mejorado de sus dolores** the pain has gone away
[2] (*en subasta*) to raise one's bid
Ⓒ **mejorarse** VPR to get better, improve; **¡que se mejore!** get well soon!

mejorcito ADJ **lo ~ del programa** the best thing in the programme; **lo ~ de la clientela** the top customers; **este queso es de lo ~ que hay*** this cheese is the best you can get

mejoría SF improvement; **¡que siga la ~!** I hope the improvement continues

mejunje SM [1] (= *mezcla*) (*gen*) concoction; (= *bebida*) brew
[2] (*) (= *fraude*) fraud
[3] (*LAm**) (= *lío*) mess, mix-up

melado Ⓐ ADJ [*color*] honey-coloured *o* (*EEUU*) -colored
Ⓑ SM treacle, syrup; (*LAm*) [*de caña*] cane syrup

meladura SF (*Caribe, Méx*) cane syrup

melancolía SF melancholy, sadness; (*Med*) melancholia

melancólicamente ADV (= *con tristeza*) sadly, in a melancholy way; (= *soñando*) wistfully

melancólico ADJ (= *triste*) melancholy, sad; (= *soñador*) wistful

melanésico ADJ Melanesian

melanesio/a ADJ, SM/F Melanesian

melanina SF melanin

melanismo SM melanism

melanoma SM melanoma ► **melanoma maligno** malignant melanoma

melarchía SF (*CAm*) = **melancolía**

melaza SF treacle, molasses *pl* (*EEUU*)

melcocha SF (= *melaza*) treacle, molasses *pl* (*EEUU*); (= *azúcar de cande*) candy, molasses toffee

melcochado ADJ [*fruta*] candied; (*de color*) golden, honey-coloured *o* (*EEUU*) -colored

melcocharse ▸conjug 1a◂ VPR to thicken (*in boiling*)

mele* SM bash*, punch

melé SF, **mêlée** [me'le] SF (*Rugby*) scrum; (= *follón*) melee, confusion

melena SF [1] [*de persona*] long hair; **lleva una ~ rubia** she has long blond hair; ✦*MODISMOS* **andar a la ~** to be at daggers drawn; **soltarse la ~** to let one's hair down
[2] [*de león*] mane
[3] **melenas** (*pey*) (= *greñas*) mop of hair *sing*

melenas* SM INV = **melenudo B**

melenudo/a* Ⓐ ADJ long-haired
Ⓑ SM long-haired guy

melga SF (*Cono Sur, Méx*) *plot of land prepared for sowing*

melifluo ADJ sickly sweet

melillense Ⓐ ADJ of/from Melilla
Ⓑ SMF native/inhabitant of Melilla; **los ~s** the people of Melilla

melindre SM [1] (= *bollo*) sweet cake, iced bun; (= *buñuelo*) honey fritter
[2] **melindres** (= *afectación*) affected ways; (= *aprensión*) squeamishness *sing*; (= *mojigatería*) prudery *sing*, prudishness *sing*; **déjate de ~s y cómelo** don't be so finicky, just eat it; **no me vengas con ~s y elige el que más te guste** stop humming and hawing and choose the one you like best; **gastar ~s** = **melindrear**

melindrear ▸conjug 1a◂ VI (= *ser afectado*) to be affected; (= *ser aprensivo*) to be squeamish; (= *ser mojigato*) to be prudish; (= *ser quisquilloso*) to be finicky, be terribly fussy

melindroso ADJ (= *afectado*) affected; (= *aprensivo*) squeamish; (= *mojigato*) prudish; (= *quisquilloso*) finicky, fussy

meliorativo ADJ ameliorative

melisca SF (*Cono Sur*) gleaning

mella SF [1] (= *rotura*) nick, notch; (*en dientes*) gap
[2] ✦*MODISMO* **hacer ~ en algo/algn** (= *impresión*) to make an impression on sth/sb
[3] **la crisis ha hecho ~ en los bolsillos de los europeos** Europeans are feeling the pinch because of the crisis; **la compra de unos terrenos parece haber hecho ~ en su imagen** the purchase of some land seems to have damaged his image; **la fatiga habrá hecho ~ en los reflejos de muchos corredores** fatigue will have affected the reflexes of many runners

mellado ADJ [1] [*filo*] jagged, nicked
[2] [*persona*] gap-toothed; (*Cono Sur*) (= *con labio leporino*) hare-lipped

mellar ▸conjug 1a◂ VT [1] [+ *cuchillo, filo*] to nick, notch; [+ *diente*] to chip; [+ *madera*] to take a chip out of
[2] (= *dañar*) to damage, harm; [+ *afán*] to hold back; [+ *entusiasmo*] to dampen

mellizo/a ADJ, SM/F twin

melo* SM = **melodrama**

melocotón SM (= *fruto*) peach; (= *árbol*) peach tree

melocotonero SM peach tree

melodía SF [1] (= *música*) melody, tune; **una ~ conocida** a familiar tune
[2] (= *cualidad*) melodiousness

melódico ADJ melodic

melodiosamente ADV melodiously, tunefully

melodiosidad SF melodiousness

melodioso ADJ melodious, tuneful

melodrama SM melodrama

melodramáticamente ADV melodramatically

melodramático ADJ melodramatic

melómano/a SM/F music lover

melón¹ SM [1] (*Bot*) melon; ✦*REFRÁN* **los melones, a cata** the proof of the pudding is in the eating
[2] (*) (= *cabeza*) head, nut*, noggin (*EEUU**); **estrujarse el ~** to rack one's brains
[3] (*) (= *tonto*) twit*, lemon*
[4] **melones**** (= *pechos*) melons**, tits**

melón² SM (*Zool*) = **meloncillo**

melonada* SF silly thing, stupid remark

melonar SM bed of melons, melon plot

meloncillo SM (*Zool*) ichneumon, *kind of mongoose*

melopea* SF **coger** *o* **agarrar** *o* **pillar una ~** to get sloshed *o* plastered*

melosidad SF [1] (= *dulzura*) sweetness
[2] (= *empalago*) [*de persona, voz*] sickly-sweetness; [*de canción, música*] schmaltziness, sickly-sweetness

meloso ADJ [1] (= *dulce*) sweet
[2] (= *empalagoso*) [*persona, voz*] sickly-sweet; [*canción, música*] schmaltzy, sickly-sweet

membrana SF [1] (= *capa*) membrane; (*Orn*) membrane, web ► **membrana mucosa** mucous membrane ► **membrana virginal** hymen
[2] (*Cono Sur Med*) diphtheria

membranoso ADJ membranous

membresía SF (*Méx*) membership

membretado ADJ **papel ~** headed notepaper

membrete SM letterhead, heading; **papel con ~** headed notepaper

membrillero SM quince tree

membrillo SM [1] (= *fruta*) quince; **(carne de) ~** quince jelly
[2] (*) (= *tonto*) fool, idiot
[3] (*) (= *cobarde*) softie*, coward
[4] (*) (= *chivato*) nark*, grass*

membrudo ADJ burly, brawny, tough

memela SF (*CAm, Méx*) (= *tortilla*) maize tortilla; (*rellena*) *fried tortilla filled with beans*

memez* SF stupid thing; **eso es una ~** that's stupid; **decir memeces** to talk rubbish

memo¹/a* Ⓐ ADJ silly, stupid
Ⓑ SM/F idiot

memo²* SM memo*, memorandum

memorabilia SF memorabilia

memorable ADJ memorable

memorablemente ADV memorably

memorando SM, **memorándum** SM (*pl* **memorándums**) [1] (= *nota*) memorandum
[2] (= *libreta*) notebook

memoria SF [1] (= *facultad*) memory; **lo había olvidado ¡qué ~ la mía!** I'd forgotten, what a terrible memory I have!; **el accidente se le había borrado** *o* **ido de la ~** he had forgotten about the accident, he had erased the accident from his memory; **de ~** [*aprender, saber*] by heart; [*hablar, recitar, tocar*] from memory; **si no me falla la ~** if my memory serves me right, if I remember right(ly) *o* correctly; **falta de ~** (*permanente*) poor memory, forgetfulness; (*repentina*) lapse of memory; **hacer ~** to try to remember; **hacer ~ de algo** to recall sth; **perder la ~** to lose one's memory; **pérdida de ~** loss of memory; **refrescar la ~ a algn** to refresh sb's memory, jog sb's memory; **tener buena/mala/poca ~** to have a good/bad/poor memory; **traer algo a la ~** to bring sth back; **una canción que trae momentos pasados a la ~** a song that brings back the past *o* reminds you of the past; **venir a la ~**: **¡en este sitio me vienen tantos recuerdos a la ~!** this place brings back so many memories!; **no me viene su número a la ~** her number's slipped my mind, I can't remember her number; ✦*MODISMO* **tener (una) ~ de elefante** to have the memory of an el-

➤ LENGUA Y USO: mejorar B1 50.4

ephant ► **memoria asociativa** associative memory ► **memoria fotográfica** photographic memory
[2] (= *recuerdo*) memory; **ha sido fiel a la ~ de su esposa** he has been faithful to his wife's memory; **fue un discurso digno de ~** it was a speech worth remembering *o* a highly memorable speech; **a la** *o* **en ~ de algn** [*acto, monumento*] in memory of sb; **un homenaje a la ~ de las víctimas de la guerra** a tribute to the memory of *o* in memory of war victims; **hemos guardado un minuto de silencio en su ~** we observed a minute's silence in his memory; **haber** *o* **quedar ~ de algo**: **la peor tormenta de la que hay ~** the worst storm in living memory; **el único suceso del que me queda ~** the only event I remember *o* of which I have any memory ► **memoria colectiva** collective memory ► **memoria histórica** historical memory
[3] (= *informe*) (*gen*) report; (*Educ*) paper; **tenemos que presentar una ~ de todas nuestras actividades** we have to present a report on all our activities ► **memoria anual** annual report ► **memoria de licenciatura** dissertation
[4] (= *relación*) record; **una ~ de todos los libros adquiridos** a record of all the books acquired
[5] (*Inform*) memory ► **memoria auxiliar** backing storage ► **memoria burbuja** bubble memory ► **memoria central** main memory ► **memoria de acceso aleatorio** random access memory, RAM ► **memoria del teclado** keyboard memory ► **memoria de núcleos** core memory ► **memoria de sólo lectura** read-only memory, ROM ► **memoria externa** external storage ► **memoria intermedia** buffer ► **memoria interna** internal storage, main memory ► **memoria muerta** read-only memory, ROM ► **memoria principal** main memory ► **memoria programable** programmable read-only memory ► **memoria RAM** RAM ► **memoria ROM** ROM ► **memoria virtual** virtual memory
[6] **memorias** [6·1] (*Literat*) (= *autobiografía*) memoirs, records
[6·2] (†) **dar ~s a algn** to send *o* give one's regards to sb

memorial SM (= *escrito*) memorial; (*Jur*) brief

memorialista SMF amanuensis

memorión* (A) ADJ **es muy ~** he has an amazing memory
(B) SM amazing memory

memorioso ADJ **es muy ~** he has a very good memory

memorista ADJ (*esp LAm*) **es ~** he just memorizes things

memorístico ADJ [*concurso*] memory *antes de s*; [*aprendizaje, educación*] rote *antes de s*; **una prueba memorística** a memory test; **enseñanza memorística** rote learning, learning by rote

memorización SF memorizing

memorizar ▸conjug 1f◂ VT to memorize

mena SF ore

menaje SM [1] (= *muebles*) furniture, furnishings *pl*
[2] (= *utensilios*) (*tb* **artículos de ~**) household items *pl*; **sección de ~** (*en tienda*) hardware and kitchen department
[3] (= *tareas*) housework; (= *economía doméstica*) housekeeping
[4] (= *familia*) family, household; **vida de ~** (*LAm*) family life, domestic life ► **menaje de tres** ménage à trois

menarquía SF menarche

menchevique ADJ, SMF Menshevik

Menchu SF (*forma familiar*) *de* **Carmen**

mención SF mention ► **mención honorífica** honourable *o* (*EEUU*) honorable mention; **hacer ~ de algo** to mention sth

mencionado ADJ aforementioned

mencionar ▸conjug 1a◂ VT to mention; **sin ~ ...** not to mention ..., let alone ...; **dejar de ~** to fail to mention

menda* (A) PRON (*tb* **~s**) (= *yo*) yours truly; **lo tuvo que hacer este ~ (lerenda)** yours truly had to do it*, muggins here had to do it*; **el ~ no está de acuerdo** I, for one, don't agree
(B) SMF (= *persona*) **un ~** a bloke*, a guy*

mendacidad SF [1] (= *cualidad*) untruthfulness, mendacity (*frm*)
[2] (= *mentira*) untruth

mendaz ADJ untruthful, mendacious (*frm*)

mendeliano ADJ Mendelian

mendelismo SM Mendelism, Mendelianism

mendicante (A) ADJ [1] (*Rel*) mendicant; **las órdenes ~s** the mendicant orders
[2] [*actitud*] begging
(B) SMF [1] (*Rel*) mendicant
[2] (= *mendigo*) beggar

mendicidad SF begging, mendicity (*frm*)

mendigar ▸conjug 1h◂ (A) VT to beg for
(B) VI to beg

mendigo/a (A) SM/F beggar
(B) ADJ (*Méx**) (= *cobarde*) yellow*, yellow-bellied*

mendrugo SM [1] (= *trozo*) (*tb* **~ de pan**) crust of bread
[2] (*) (= *tonto*) dimwit*

meneado ADJ (*Caribe*) drunk

meneallo: **más vale no ~*** let sleeping dogs lie, the less said the better

menear ▸conjug 1a◂ (A) VT [1] [+ *cola*] to wag; [+ *cabeza*] to shake; [+ *líquido*] to stir; [+ *pelo*] to toss; [+ *caderas*] to swing; **sin ~ un dedo** without lifting a finger; **peor es ~lo** it's best not to stir things up; ✦**MODISMO** **¡me la menean!**** I don't give a shit!**
[2] [+ *asunto*] to get on with, get moving on; [+ *negocio*] to handle, conduct
[3] **~ cálamo** to wield a pen
(B) **menearse** VPR [1] (*gen*) to shake; [*cola*] to wag; (= *contonearse*) to swing, sway; **yo de aquí no me meneo** I'm staying right here, I'm staying put; ✦**MODISMOS** **de no te menees***: **un vapuleo de no te menees** a good hiding; **una multa de las que no te menees** a hefty fine; **~se** *o* **meneársela**** to wank**
[2] (= *apresurarse*) to get a move on; **¡~se!** get going!, jump to it!

Menelao SM Menelaus

meneo SM [1] [*de cola*] wag; [*de cabeza*] shake, toss; [*de líquido*] stir, stirring; [*de caderas*] swing(ing), sway(ing); (= *sacudida*) jerk, jolt; **dar un ~ a algo** to jerk sth
[2] (*) (= *paliza*) hiding*; (= *bronca*) dressing-down*
[3] (= *actividad*) = **movida 1**

menequear ▸conjug 1a◂ VT (*Cono Sur, Méx*),

menequetear ▸conjug 1a◂ VT (*Cono Sur, Méx*) to shake, wag

menequeo SM (*Cono Sur, Méx*), **menequeteo** SM (*Cono Sur, Méx*) shaking, wagging

menester SM [1] **ser ~** (*frm*) (= *ser necesario*) **es ~ hacer algo** we must do something, it is necessary to do something; **cuando sea ~** when necessary; **todo es ~** everything is welcome
[2] (= *trabajo*) job; (= *recado*) errand; **salir para un ~** to go out on an errand
[3] **menesteres** (= *deberes*) duties, business *sing*; (= *ocupación*) occupation *sing*; (= *función*) function *sing*; **no estamos capacitados para esos ~es** we are not trained to do that; **venden un aparatito para esos ~es** you can buy a little machine to do those jobs; ✦**MODISMO** **hacer sus ~es** (*euf*) to do one's business
[4] **menesteres** (*Téc*) gear *sing*, tools

menesteroso/a (A) ADJ needy
(B) SM/F **los ~s** the needy

menestra SF (*tb* **~ de verduras**) vegetable stew

menestral SMF (*a veces* SF **menestrala**) skilled worker, artisan

menestrón SM (*Andes*) ≈ minestrone soup

mengano/a SM/F Mr/Mrs/Miss so-and-so; *ver tb* **fulano**

mengua SF [1] (= *disminución*) decrease, reduction; (= *decadencia*) decay, decline; **ir en ~ de algo** to be to the detriment of sth; **en ~ de la unidad del partido** to the detriment of party unity; **sin ~** (= *íntegro*) complete, whole; (= *intacto*) intact, untouched; **sin ~ de la relación de compañerismo** without affecting one's relationship as colleagues
[2] (= *falta*) lack; (= *pérdida*) loss
[3] (= *pobreza*) poverty
[4] [*de persona*] (= *debilidad*) spinelessness, weakness of character
[5] (= *descrédito*) discredit; **ir en ~ de algn** to be to sb's discredit

menguadamente ADV [1] (= *desgraciadamente*) wretchedly; (= *cobardemente*) cravenly (*liter*); (= *sin fuerza*) weakly, spinelessly
[2] (= *con tacañería*) meanly
[3] (= *estúpidamente*) foolishly

menguado (A) ADJ [1] (= *disminuido*) [*ejército, tropas*] depleted; [*esfuerzos*] diminished; [*fuerzas, presupuesto*] reduced; **un hombre de menguada estatura** a diminutive man
[2] (= *desgraciado*) wretched, miserable; (= *cobarde*) cowardly, craven (*liter*); (= *débil*) weak, spineless
[3] (= *tacaño*) mean
[4] (= *tonto*) foolish
[5] (= *aciago*) unlucky; **en hora menguada** at an unlucky moment
[6] **medias menguadas** fully-fashioned stockings
(B) SM (*en labor de punto*) decrease

menguante (A) ADJ (= *que disminuye*) decreasing, diminishing; (= *decadente*) decaying; [*luna*] waning; [*marea*] ebb *antes de s*
(B) SF [1] (*Náut*) ebb tide
[2] [*de luna*] waning; *ver tb* **cuarto B2**
[3] (= *decadencia*) decay, decline; **estar en ~** to be in decline

menguar ▸conjug 1i◂ (A) VT [1] (= *disminuir*) to lessen, reduce; [+ *labor de punto*] to decrease
[2] (= *desacreditar*) to discredit
(B) VI [1] (= *disminuir*) to decrease, dwindle;

➤ LENGUA Y USO: **mencionar** 53.2

[*número, nivel del agua*] to go down; [*marea*] to go out, ebb; [*luna*] to wane
2 (= *decaer*) to wane, decay, decline

mengue* SM the devil; **¡malos ~s te lleven!** go to hell!*

meninges* SFPL ✦*MODISMO* **estrujarse las ~** to rack one's brains

meningitis SF INV meningitis

menisco SM meniscus

menjunje SM, **menjurje** SM = **mejunje**

menopausia SF menopause

menopáusico ADJ menopausal

menor Ⓐ ADJ 1 (*comparativo*) 1·1 (*de tamaño*) smaller; **una caja de ~ tamaño** a smaller box; **los libros están ordenados de ~ a mayor** the books are arranged by size, from small to large
1·2 (*de cantidad*) fewer, less; **necesito una cantidad ~ de botellas** I need fewer bottles; **echa sal en ~ cantidad** add less salt; **~ que algo** less than sth; **su aportación es diez veces ~ que la nuestra** his contribution is ten times less than ours; **tres es ~ que siete** three is less than seven
1·3 (*de importancia, tiempo*) **heridas de ~ importancia** minor injuries; **existe un ~ control en las aduanas** customs controls are not as strict *o* tight as they were; **el crecimiento de la economía es cada vez ~** the economy is growing at an ever slower rate; **viene con ~ frecuencia que antes** she doesn't come as often now; **en ~ grado** to a lesser extent
1·4 (*de edad*) younger; **mis dos hermanos ~es** my two younger brothers; **si eres ~ de 18 años no puedes entrar** if you are under 18 you can't go in; **~ que algn** younger than sb; **soy tres años ~ que mi marido** I am three years younger than my husband; **ser ~ de edad** to be under age; (*Jur*) to be a minor; **dos jóvenes ~es de edad se han escapado de su casa** two under-age youngsters have run away from home
1·5 (*Mús*) minor; **concierto en Mi ~** concerto in E minor
1·6 (*Rel*) [*orden*] minor
2 (*superlativo*) 2·1 [*de tamaño*] smallest; **es el país de ~ tamaño de Europa** it is the smallest country in Europe; **éste es el ~ de todos** this is the smallest of all
2·2 [*de cantidad*] lowest, smallest; **el partido de ~ asistencia de la liga** the match with the lowest *o* smallest attendance in the league; **realizó la vuelta en el ~ número de golpes** he finished the round in the lowest number of shots; **hagan el ~ ruido posible** make as little noise as possible; **se despierta con el ~ ruido** he wakes up at the slightest noise
2·3 [*de importancia, tiempo*] least; **no le doy la ~ importancia** I don't attach the slightest *o* least importance to it; **no tiene la ~ importancia** it is not in the least important; **en el ~ tiempo posible** in the shortest possible time; *ver tb* **idea 4**
2·4 [*de edad*] youngest; **éste es Miguel, mi hijo ~** this is Miguel, my youngest son
Ⓑ SMF (= *niño*) child, minor (*frm*); **un programa educativo para ~es** an educational programme for children; **los ~es deben ir acompañados** children who are under age *o* minors (*frm*) must be accompanied; **lo detuvieron por vender drogas a ~es** he was arrested for selling drugs to minors; **un ~ de 15 años** a boy of 15; **un campeonato para ~es de 16 años** a championship for under-16s; **apto/no apto para ~es** suitable/not suitable for (young) children; **"apto para menores acompañados"** (*Cine*) ≈ "certificate PG"
► **menor de edad** (*Jur*) minor; **los ~es de edad** those who are under age, minors; **delitos cometidos por ~es de edad** crimes committed by minors; *ver tb* **tribunal 1**
Ⓒ SM 1 (*Com*) **(al) por ~** retail *antes de s*; **venta (al) por ~** retail sales; **un establecimiento de venta al por ~** a retail establishment
2 (*Esp*) **contar algo al por ~** to recount sth in detail

Menorca SF Minorca

menoría SF 1 (*Jur*) minority
2 (= *inferioridad*) inferiority; (= *subordinación*) subordination

menorista (*LAm*) Ⓐ ADJ retail *antes de s*
Ⓑ SMF retailer

menorquín/ina ADJ, SM/F Minorcan

menos Ⓐ ADV 1 (*comparativo*) less; **ahora salgo ~** I go out less these days; **últimamente nos vemos ~** we've been seeing less of each other recently; **me gusta cada vez ~** I like it less and less; **una película ~ conocida** a less well-known film; **Juan está ~ deprimido** Juan is less depressed; **es ~ difícil de lo que parece** it's less difficult than it seems; **~ aún** even less; **este me gusta ~ aún** I like this one even less; **~ de** (*con sustantivos incontables, medidas, dinero, tiempo*) less than; (*con sustantivos contables*) fewer than; **está a ~ de tres horas en tren** it's less than three hours away by train; **llegamos en ~ de diez minutos** we got there in less than *o* in under ten minutes; **~ de lo que piensas** less than you think; **tiene ~ de dieciocho años** he's under eighteen; **~ de 50 cajas** fewer than 50 boxes; **en ~ de nada** in no time at all; **por ~ de nada** for no reason at all; **~ que** less than; **me gusta ~ que el otro** I like it less than the other one; **trabaja ~ que yo** he doesn't work as hard as I do; **éste es ~ caro que aquél** this one is less expensive than that one; **lo hizo ~ cuidadosamente que ayer** he did it less carefully than yesterday
2 (*superlativo*) least; **su película ~ innovadora** his least innovative film; **es el ~ inteligente de los cuatro** he is the least intelligent of the four; **el chico ~ desobediente de la clase** the least disobedient boy in the class; **es el que habla ~** he's the one who talks (the) least; **fue el que trabajó ~** he was the one who did the least work
3 **al ~** at least; **hay al ~ cien personas** there are at least a hundred people; **si al ~ lloviera** if only it would rain; **de ~**: **hay siete de ~** we're seven short, there are seven missing; **me dieron un paquete con medio kilo de ~** they gave me a packet which was half a kilo short *o* under weight; **me han pagado dos libras de ~** they have underpaid me by two pounds; **darse de ~** to underestimate o.s.; **hacer a algn de ~** to put sb down; **echar de ~ a algn** to miss sb; **ir a ~** to come down in the world; **lo ~ diez** at least ten; **lo ~ posible** as little as possible; **es lo ~ que se puede esperar** it's the least one can expect; **eso es lo de ~** that's the least of it; **¡~ mal!** thank goodness!; **¡~ mal que habéis venido!** thank goodness you've come!; **era nada ~ que un rey** he was a king, no less; **no es para ~** quite right too; **por lo ~** at least; **¡qué ~!**: **—le di un euro de propina —¡qué ~!** "I tipped her a euro" — "that was the least you could do!"; **¿qué ~ que darle las gracias?** the least we can do is say thanks!; **quedarse en ~**: **no se quedó en ~** he was not to be outdone; **tener a ~ hacer algo** to consider it beneath o.s. to do sth; **venir a ~** to come down in the world; **y ~**: **no quiero verle y ~ visitarle** I don't want to see him, let alone visit him; **¡ya será ~!** come off it!; *ver tb* **cuando B2, poder**
Ⓑ ADJ 1 (*comparativo*) (*con sustantivos incontables, medidas, dinero, tiempo*) less; (*con sustantivos contables*) fewer; **~ harina** less flour; **~ gatos** fewer cats; **aquí hay ~ gente** there are fewer people here; **~ ... que**: **A tiene ~ ventajas que B** A has fewer advantages than B; **Ana tiene ~ años que Carlos** Ana is younger than Carlos; **no soy ~ hombre que él*** I'm as much of a man as he is; **éste es ~ coche que el anterior*** this is not as good a car as the last one; **ser ~ que**: **ganaremos porque son ~ que nosotros** we'll win because there are fewer of them than there are of us; **para no ser ~ que los vecinos** to keep up with the neighbours
2 (*superlativo*) (*con sustantivos incontables, medidas, dinero, tiempo*) least; (*con sustantivos contables*) fewest; **el método que lleva ~ tiempo** the method which takes (the) least time; **es el que ~ culpa tiene** he is the least to blame; **el examen con ~ errores** the exam paper with the fewest mistakes
Ⓒ PREP 1 (= *excepto*) except; **todos ~ él** everybody except him; **¡todo ~ eso!** anything but that!
2 (*Mat*) (*para restar*) minus, less; **cinco ~ dos** five minus *o* less two; **siete ~ dos (son) cinco** seven minus two is five; **son las siete ~ veinte** it's twenty to seven
Ⓓ CONJ **a ~ que** unless; **no iré a ~ que me acompañes** I won't go unless you come with me
Ⓔ SM 1 (*Mat*) minus sign
2 **los ~** the minority
3 *ver tb* **más 2**

menoscabar ▸conjug 1a◂ VT 1 (= *disminuir*) to lessen, reduce; (= *dañar*) to damage
2 (= *desacreditar*) to discredit

menoscabo SM (= *disminución*) lessening, reduction; (= *daño*) damage; **con** *o* **en ~ de** to the detriment of; **reducción de jornada sin ~ salarial** reduction in the working day with no loss of salary; **debe haber cierta reserva, sin ~ de la amistad** certain things must remain in confidence, without being detrimental to one's friendship; **sufrir ~** to be damaged

menospreciable ADJ contemptible

menospreciador ADJ scornful, contemptuous

menospreciar ▸conjug 1b◂ VT 1 (= *despreciar*) to scorn, despise
2 (= *ofender*) to slight
3 (= *subestimar*) to underrate, underestimate

menospreciativo ADJ (= *despreciativo*) scornful, contemptuous; (= *ofensivo*) slighting

menosprecio SM 1 (= *desdén*) scorn, contempt
2 (= *subestimación*) underrating, underestimation
3 (= *falta de respeto*) disrespect; **con ~ del**

sexo de la víctima without regard for the sex of the victim

mensáfono SM bleeper, pager

mensaje SM (*gen*) message; (*) (*por móvil*) text (message); **un ~ de apoyo** a message of support ► **mensaje de buenos augurios** goodwill message ► **mensaje de error** (*Inform*) error message ► **mensaje de la corona** (*Parl*) Queen's/King's speech ► **mensaje de texto** text message; **envío de ~s de texto** text messaging; **enviar ~s de texto/un ~ de texto a algn** to text sb ► **mensaje subliminal** subliminal message

mensajería SF [1] [*de paquetes*] (= *servicio*) courier service; (= *empresa*) courier firm
[2] [*de avisos*] (= *servicio*) messaging service; (= *empresa*) courier firm ► **mensajería electrónica** electronic messaging, electronic message handling

mensajero/a SM/F [1] (*para empresa de mensajería*) courier [2] (= *recadero*) messenger

menso* ADJ (*Chile, Méx*) silly, stupid

menstruación SF menstruation

menstrual ADJ menstrual; **dolores ~es** period pains

menstruar ▸conjug 1e◂ VI to menstruate

menstruo SM [1] (= *menstruación*) menstruation [2] (= *sangre*) menses *pl*

mensual ADJ monthly; **50 dólares ~es** 50 dollars a month

mensualidad SF (= *salario*) monthly salary; (= *plazo*) monthly instalment *o* (*EEUU*) installment, monthly payment; **se puede pagar en diez ~es** payment can be made in ten monthly instalments

mensualmente ADV monthly

mensuario SM (*LAm*) monthly (magazine)

ménsula SF (= *repisa*) bracket; (*Arquit*) corbel

mensura SF measurement

mensurable ADJ measurable

mensuración SF mensuration

menta[1] SF mint; **un caramelo de ~** a mint sweet ► **menta romana**, **menta verde** spearmint

menta[2] SF [1] (*Arg**) (= *fama*) reputation
[2] **mentas** (*Chile**) (= *chismes*) rumours, rumors (*EEUU*), gossip *sing*

mentada SF (*Méx*) serious insult; **hacerle a algn una ~** to seriously insult sb

mentado ADJ [1] (= *mencionado*) aforementioned [2] (= *famoso*) well-known, famous

mental ADJ [*esfuerzo, salud*] mental; [*capacidad, trabajo*] intellectual

mentalidad SF mentality; **tiene ~ de criminal** he has a criminal mentality; **tienes (una) ~ de un niño de tres años** you've got the mentality of a three-year old; **tiene una ~ muy abierta** he is very open-minded, he's got a very open outlook

mentalización SF [1] (= *preparación*) mental preparation; **la importancia de la ~ de los jugadores en la victoria** the importance of players' mental preparation to achieving victory
[2] (= *concienciación*) **la ~ de la opinión pública respecto al problema del paro** the raising of public awareness about the problem of unemployment; **campañas de ~ contra la bebida** campaigns to raise awareness of the risks of drinking
[3] (= *persuasión*) persuasion; (*pey*) brainwashing

mentalizado ADJ **están ~s para imponerse a cualquier dificultad** they are mentally prepared to overcome any problem; **el equipo salió ~ para el triunfo** the team went out with their minds set on victory

mentalizar ▸conjug 1f◂ Ⓐ VT [1] (= *preparar*) to prepare mentally
[2] (= *concienciar*) to make aware
[3] (= *persuadir*) to persuade, convince; (*pey*) to brainwash
Ⓑ **mentalizarse** VPR [1] (= *prepararse*) to prepare o.s. mentally; **me había mentalizado para lo peor** I had prepared myself for the worst
[2] (= *concienciarse*) to become aware (**de** of)

mentalmente ADV mentally

mentar ▸conjug 1j◂ VT to mention; **~ la madre a algn** (*esp Méx*) to insult sb seriously

mentas* SFPL (*Andes, Cono Sur*) [1] (= *reputación*) good name *sing*, reputation *sing*; **una persona de buenas ~** a highly-regarded *o* well-respected person
[2] (= *chismes*) rumours, rumors (*EEUU*), gossip *sing*

mente SF [1] (= *pensamiento*) mind; **tiene una ~ analítica** he's got an analytical mind; **irse algo de la ~**: **se le fue completamente de la ~** it completely slipped his mind; **quitarse algo de la ~**: **no me lo puedo quitar de la ~** I can't get it out of my mind; **tener en ~ hacer algo** to be thinking of doing sth; **tiene en ~ cambiar de empleo** he's thinking of changing jobs; **traer a la ~** to call to mind; **venir a la ~** to come to mind ► **mente consciente** conscious mind ► **mente subconsciente** subconscious mind
[2] (= *mentalidad*) **tiene una ~ muy abierta** she's very open-minded, she's got a very open outlook
[3] (= *intelectual*) mind; **una de las grandes ~s de nuestro tiempo** one of the great minds of our time

mentecatería SF, **mentecatez** SF stupidity, foolishness

mentecato/a Ⓐ ADJ silly, stupid
Ⓑ SM/F idiot, fool

mentidero SM gossip shop*

mentir ▸conjug 3i◂ VI to lie; **nos mintió** he lied to us; **miente quien diga que hubo un acuerdo** whoever says there was an agreement is lying; **~ no está bien** it's wrong to tell lies; **no he mentido en mi vida** I've never told a lie in all my life; **¡miento!** sorry!, I'm wrong!, my mistake!; **¡esta carta no me dejará ~!** this letter will bear me out *o* confirm what I say

mentira SF [1] (= *embuste*) lie; **¡mentira!** it's a lie!; **no digas ~s** don't tell lies; **sus ~s le causaron problemas** his lying got him into trouble; **coger a algn en una ~** to catch sb in a lie; **de ~**: **una pistola de ~** a toy pistol; **parecer ~**: **aunque parezca ~** however incredible it seems, strange though it may seem; **¡parece ~!** it's unbelievable!, I can't *o* don't believe it!; **parece ~ que no te acuerdes** I can't believe that you don't remember; ✦***MODISMOS*** **una ~ como una casa** *o* **como una catedral** *o* **un templo** a whopping great lie*; **la ~ tiene las patas cortas** ◊ **no hay ~ que no salga** truth will out ► **mentira caritativa**, **mentira oficiosa** (*Cono Sur*), **mentira piadosa**, **mentira reverenda** (*Cono Sur*) white lie
[2] (*en uñas*) white mark (*on fingernail*)
[3] (= *errata*) erratum

mentirijillas* SFPL **es** *o* **va de ~** it's only a joke; (*a niño*) it's only pretend *o* make-believe; **lloraba de ~** she was pretending to cry; **jugar de ~** to play for fun (*ie not for money*)

mentirilla SF fib*, white lie

mentirosillo/a SM/F fibber*

mentiroso/a Ⓐ ADJ [1] (= *que miente*) lying; **¡es tan ~!** he's such a liar!; **¡mentiroso!** you liar!
[2] [*texto*] full of errors, full of misprints
Ⓑ SM/F (= *que miente*) liar; **~ profesional** compulsive liar

mentís SM INV denial; **dar el ~ a algo** to refute sth, deny sth

mentol SM menthol

mentolado ADJ mentholated

mentolatum* SM **ser un ~** (*Cono Sur*) to be a jack of all trades

mentón SM chin ► **doble mentón** double chin

mentor SM mentor

menú SM [1] [*de comida*] menu ► **menú de la casa** main menu, standard menu ► **menú del día** (*Esp*) set meal
[2] (*Inform*) menu; **guiado por ~** (*Inform*) menu-driven ► **menú desplegable** pull-down menu, drop-down menu

menudear ▸conjug 1a◂ Ⓐ VI [1] (= *ser frecuente*) to be frequent, happen frequently; [*misiles, insultos*] to come thick and fast; **en la campaña menudean las acusaciones** accusations are flying thick and fast in the campaign; **un texto en el que menudean las erratas** a text full of mistakes
[2] (*al explicarse*) to go into great detail
[3] (*Cono Sur, Méx*) (= *abundar*) to abound; (= *proliferar*) to increase, grow in number
Ⓑ VT [1] (= *repetir*) to repeat frequently, do repeatedly; **menudea sus visitas** he often comes to visit
[2] (*LAm*) (= *vender*) to sell retail

menudencia SF [1] (= *bagatela*) trifle, small thing; **~s** odds and ends
[2] (= *minuciosidad*) minuteness; (= *exactitud*) exactness; (= *meticulosidad*) meticulousness
[3] **menudencias** (*Culin*) [*de cerdo*] offal *sing*; (= *menudillos*) [*de ave*] giblets

menudeo SM (*Com*) retail trade; **vender al ~** to sell retail

menudez SF smallness, minuteness

menudillos SMPL giblets

menudo Ⓐ ADJ [1] (= *pequeño*) small, minute; [*persona*] diminutive, slight; (*fig*) slight, insignificant; **moneda menuda** small change; **la gente menuda** the little ones, kids*; ✦***MODISMOS*** **a la menuda** ◊ **por la menuda** (*Com*) retail; **contar algo por ~** to tell sth in detail
[2] (*uso admirativo*) **¡~ lío!** what a mess!; **¡menuda plancha!** what a boob!*; **¡menuda vidorra nos vamos a dar!** we won't half live it up!*; **¡menuda me la han hecho!** they've really gone and pulled a fast one on me!*; **¡~ viento hizo anoche!** it wasn't half windy last night!*
[3] (= *minucioso*) exact, meticulous

Ⓑ ADV **a ~** often
Ⓒ SM [1] (= *dinero*) small change
[2] **menudos** (*Culin*) offal *sing*; [*de ave*] giblets; (*Méx*) (= *guisado*) tripe stew *sing*

meñique SM (*tb* **dedo ~**) little finger

meódromo‡ SM bog‡, loo*, john (*EEUU*‡)

meollo SM [1] (*Anat*) marrow
[2] [*de asunto*] heart, crux; **el ~ de la cuestión** the heart *o* crux of the matter
[3] [*de persona*] brains *pl*; **estrujarse el ~** to rack one's brains
[4] [*de pan*] crumb, soft part

meón/ona* Ⓐ ADJ **es muy ~** [*niño*] he's always wetting himself; [*adulto*] he's got a weak bladder
Ⓑ SM/F [1] **este niño es un ~** this boy's always wetting himself
[2] (= *bebé*) baby, baby boy/baby girl

meos‡ SMPL piss** *sing*

meque* SM (*Caribe*) rap

mequetrefe SMF (= *inútil*) good-for-nothing; (= *curiosón*) busybody

meramente ADV merely, only

merca SF (*Méx*) (= *compra*) shopping, purchases *pl*; (*Cono Sur*) (= *contrabando*) contraband goods *pl*

mercachifle SM [1] (*pey*) (= *comerciante*) small-time trader; (= *vendedor ambulante*) hawker, huckster
[2] (= *avaricioso*) money grabber

mercadear ▸conjug 1a◂ Ⓐ VT (= *vender*) to market; (= *regatear*) to haggle over
Ⓑ VI to deal, trade

mercadeo SM marketing

mercader SM (*esp Hist*) merchant

mercadería SF merchandise; **~s** goods, merchandise *sing*

mercadillo SM street market; (*benéfico*) (charity) bazaar

mercado SM market; **inundar el ~ de algo** to flood the market with sth; **salir al ~** to come on to the market ► **mercado bursátil** stock market ► **mercado cambiario** foreign exchange market ► **mercado cautivo** captive market ► **Mercado Común** Common Market ► **mercado de demanda** seller's market ► **mercado de dinero** money market ► **mercado de divisas** currency market, foreign exchange market ► **mercado de futuros** futures market ► **mercado de la vivienda** housing market ► **mercado de oferta** buyer's market ► **mercado de productos básicos** commodity market ► **mercado de signo favorable al comprador, mercado de compradores** buyer's market ► **mercado de signo favorable al vendedor, mercado de vendedores** seller's market ► **mercado de trabajo** labour *o* (*EEUU*) labor market ► **mercado de valores** stock market ► **mercado de viejo** flea market ► **mercado en alza** bull market ► **mercado en baja** bear market ► **mercado exterior** foreign market, overseas market ► **mercado inmobiliario** property market ► **mercado interior** domestic market ► **mercado laboral** labour *o* (*EEUU*) labor market ► **mercado libre** free market (**de** in); ► **mercado mundial** world market ► **mercado nacional** domestic market ► **mercado negro** black market ► **mercado objetivo** target market ► **mercado persa** (*Cono Sur*) cut-price store ► **mercado único** single market

mercadológico ADJ market *antes de s*, marketing *antes de s*

mercadotecnia SF marketing; **estudios de ~** market research

mercadotécnico ADJ marketing *antes de s*

mercancía Ⓐ SF merchandise; **~s** goods, merchandise *sing* ► **mercancías en depósito** bonded goods ► **mercancías de general** (*Náut*) general cargo *sing* ► **mercancías perecederas** perishable goods
Ⓑ SM INV **mercancías** goods train *sing*, freight train *sing* (*EEUU*)

mercante Ⓐ ADJ merchant *antes de s*; *ver tb* **buque 1, marina 1**
Ⓑ SM merchantman, merchant ship

mercantil ADJ (*gen*) mercantile, commercial; [*derecho*] commercial; *ver tb* **registro 2, sociedad 3**

mercantilismo SM mercantilism

mercantilización SF commercialization; **la ~ de la cultura** the commercialization of culture

mercantilizar ▸conjug 1f◂ VT to commercialize

mercar†† ▸conjug 1g◂ Ⓐ VT to buy
Ⓑ **mercarse** VPR **~se algo** to get sth

merced SF [1] (†) (= *favor*) favour, favor (*EEUU*); **hacer a algn la ~ de hacer algo** to do sb the favour of doing sth; **tenga la ~ de hacerlo** please be so good as to do it
[2] **merced a** thanks to
[3] **estar a la ~ de algo/algn** to be at the mercy of sth/sb; **el barco quedó a la ~ de los vientos** the boat was left to the mercy of the winds
[4] (*antaño*) **vuestra ~** your worship, sir

mercedario/a ADJ, SM/F Mercedarian

mercenario Ⓐ ADJ mercenary
Ⓑ SM (*Mil*) mercenary; (*Agr*) day labourer; (*pey*) (= *asalariado*) hireling

mercería SF [1] (= *artículos*) haberdashery, notions *pl* (*EEUU*)
[2] (= *tienda*) haberdasher's (shop), notions store (*EEUU*); (*Caribe, Méx*) (= *lencería*) draper's (shop), dry-goods store (*EEUU*); (*Cono Sur*) (= *ferretería*) ironmonger's, hardware store

mercero/a SM/F haberdasher, notions dealer (*EEUU*); (*Andes, Caribe, Méx*) draper

Merche SF (*forma familiar*) *de* **Mercedes**

merchero/a* SM/F petty criminal, delinquent

Mercosur SM ABR (= **Mercado Común del Cono Sur**) *Argentina, Brazil, Paraguay and Uruguay*

mercromina® SF Mercurochrome®

mercurial ADJ mercurial

Mercurio SM Mercury

mercurio SM mercury

mercurocromo SM Mercurochrome®

merdoso‡ ADJ filthy

merecedor ADJ deserving, worthy (**de** of); **es ~ de aplauso** it is to be applauded; **~ de confianza** trustworthy; **~ de crédito** solvent; **hacerse ~ de algo** to earn sth; **ser ~ de algo** to deserve sth, be deserving of sth

merecer ▸conjug 2d◂ Ⓐ VT [1] [+ *recompensa, castigo*] to deserve; **~ hacer algo** to deserve to do sth; **merece (que se le dé) el premio** he deserves (to receive) the prize; **no merece sino elogios** she deserves nothing but praise; **el trato que él nos merece** the treatment he deserves from us; **merece la pena** it's worth it; **no merece la pena discutir** it's not worth arguing
[2] (*Andes*) (= *atrapar*) to catch; (= *robar*) to snatch, pinch*; (= *encontrar*) to find
Ⓑ VI to be deserving, be worthy; **~ mucho** to be very deserving
Ⓒ **merecerse** VPR **~se algo** to deserve sth; **te mereces el premio** you deserve the prize; **tienes unos hijos que no te los mereces** you don't deserve your children; **te mereces eso y más** you deserve that and more; **se lo mereció** he deserved it, he got what he deserved; **se lo merece por tonto** (it) serves him right for being so stupid

merecidamente ADV deservedly

merecido Ⓐ ADJ [*premio, descanso*] well-deserved; **bien ~ lo tiene** it serves him right
Ⓑ SM just deserts *pl*; **llevarse su ~** to get one's just deserts

merecimiento SM [1] (= *lo merecido*) just deserts *pl*
[2] (= *mérito*) merit, worthiness; **perdimos con todo ~** we deserved to lose; **lo logró sin ningún ~** she didn't deserve to achieve it; **otra persona de mayor ~** another more deserving person

merendar* ▸conjug 1j◂ Ⓐ VI to have an afternoon snack, have tea; (*en el campo*) to have a picnic
Ⓑ VT [1] (= *comer*) to have as an afternoon snack, have for tea
[2] (= *mirar*) **~ lo que escribe otro** to look at what somebody else is writing; **~ las cartas de otro** to peep at sb else's cards
Ⓒ **merendarse** VPR [1] **~se a algn** [+ *adversario*] to thrash sb*, walk all over sb*; (*LAm*) (= *matar*) to bump sb off*; (*Andes*) (= *pegar*) to beat sb up*; (*Cono Sur*) (= *estafar*) to fleece sb*
[2] (= *acabar con*) [+ *libro*] to devour; [+ *país, territorio*] to take over
[3] **~se una fortuna** to squander a fortune

merendero SM (= *café*) open-air café, snack bar; (*en el campo*) picnic area; (*Méx*) (= *restaurán*) café, lunch counter

merendola* SF (= *fiesta*) tea party; (*campestre*) picnic

merengar‡ ▸conjug 1h◂ VT to upset, annoy

merengue Ⓐ ADJ (*) of/relating to Real Madrid F.C.
Ⓑ SM [1] (*Culin*) meringue
[2] (= *persona*) (= *blandengue*) wimp*, weed*; (*LAm*) (= *enfermizo*) sickly person
[3] (*Andes, Caribe*) (= *baile*) merengue
[4] (*Cono Sur**) (= *alboroto*) row, fuss
Ⓒ SMPL **los ~s*** Real Madrid F.C.

meretriz SF prostitute

mergo SM cormorant

meridiana SF [1] (= *diván*) divan, couch; (†) chaise longue; (= *cama*) day bed
[2] **a la ~** at noon

meridianamente ADV clearly, with complete clarity; **eso queda ~ claro** that is crystal clear

meridiano Ⓐ ADJ [1] [*calor*] midday *antes de s*; **la hora meridiana** noon
[2] [*luz*] very bright
[3] [*hecho*] clear as day, crystal-clear; **lo veo con claridad meridiana** I can see it perfectly clearly; **sus razones eran claras y meridia-**

nas her reasons were crystal-clear
Ⓑ SM (*Astron, Geog*) meridian

meridional Ⓐ ADJ southern
Ⓑ SMF southerner

merienda SF tea, afternoon snack; [*de viaje*] packed meal; (*en el campo*) picnic; (*Andes*) supper; **ir de ~** to go for a picnic; ✦*MODISMO* **juntar ~s** to join forces, pool one's resources ► **merienda-cena** high tea, early evening meal ► **merienda de negros*** (= *confusión*) bedlam, free-for-all; (= *chanchullo*) crooked deal

merino Ⓐ ADJ merino
Ⓑ SMF (= *oveja*) merino (sheep)
Ⓒ SM (= *lana*) merino wool

mérito SM [1] (= *valor*) merit, worth; **de ~** of merit, worthy; **una obra de gran ~ artístico** a work of great artistic merit; **restar ~ de algo** to detract from sth; **tener ~: eso tiene mucho ~** that's very commendable; **el chico tiene mucho ~** he's a worthy lad; **hizo ~s suficientes para merecer el honor** he had done enough to deserve the honour; **la han ascendido por ~s** she was promoted on merit; **alega los siguientes ~s** he quotes the following facts in support; **"serán ~s los idiomas"** (*en anuncio*) "languages an advantage"; ✦*MODISMO* **hacer ~s** to strive for recognition ► **méritos de guerra** mention in dispatches *sing*
[2] (= *mención*) **hacer ~ de algo** to mention sth

meritocracia SF meritocracy

meritócrata SMF meritocrat

meritoriaje SM actor's apprenticeship

meritorio/a Ⓐ ADJ (= *de mérito*) meritorious (*frm*), worthy; (= *merecedor*) deserving; **~ de alabanza** praiseworthy; **hizo una meritoria labor en beneficio de la infancia** her work in aid of children was commendable; **su meritoria actuación del domingo** his commendable performance on Sunday; **consiguió una meritoria sexta posición** he came a well-deserved sixth
Ⓑ SM/F unpaid trainee

merla SF = **mirlo**

merlan SM whiting

merlango SM haddock

Merlín SM Merlin; ✦*MODISMO* **saber más que ~** to know all there is to know

merlo¹ SM (= *pez*) black wrasse

merlo²* SM (*LAm*) (= *persona*) idiot

merlucera SF *type of fishing boat, used especially for fishing hake*

merluza SF [1] (= *pez*) hake
[2] (*) (= *borrachera*) **coger una ~** to get sozzled*; **estar con la ~*** to be sozzled*

merluzo/a* Ⓐ ADJ silly, stupid
Ⓑ SM/F idiot

merma SF (= *disminución*) [*de interés, ganancia*] decrease; (*al secarse*) shrinkage; (= *pérdida*) loss; **sin ~ de calidad** without loss of quality, without compromising on quality; **para que su honor no sufra ~** so that his honour is not diminished

mermar ▸conjug 1a◂ Ⓐ VT (= *disminuir*) [+ *crecimiento, capacidad*] to reduce; [+ *autoridad, prestigio*] to undermine; [+ *reservas*] to deplete; [+ *pago, raciones*] to cut
Ⓑ VI, **mermarse** VPR (= *disminuir*) to decrease, dwindle; [*reservas*] to become depleted; [*líquido*] to go down; [*carne*] to shrink

mermelada SF jam ► **mermelada de albaricoques** apricot jam ► **mermelada de naranja** marmalade

mero¹ Ⓐ ADJ [1] (= *simple*) mere, simple; **el ~ hecho de ...** the mere *o* simple fact of ...; **les detuvieron por el ~ hecho de protestar** they were arrested merely *o* simply for protesting; **soy un ~ espectador** I'm only *o* just a spectator; **es algo más que un ~ producto de consumo** it is more than just a consumer product, it is more than a mere consumer product; **fue una mera casualidad** it was pure coincidence
[2] (*Méx*) (= *exacto*) precise, exact; **a la mera hora** (*lit*) right on time; (*) (*fig*) when it comes down to it*
[3] (*Méx*) (= *justo*) right; **en el momento ~** at the right moment
[4] (*Méx*) (= *mismo*) **el ~ centro** the very centre; **la mera verdad** the plain truth; **el ~ Pedro** Pedro himself; **en la mera calle** right there on the street; **en la mera esquina** right on the corner; **tu ~ papá** your own father
Ⓑ ADV [1] (*CAm, Méx*) (= *justo*) right, just; **aquí ~** (= *exacto*) right here, just here; (= *cerca*) near here; **¡eso ~!** right!, you've got it!
[2] (*CAm, Méx*) **ahora ~** (= *ahora mismo*) right now; (= *pronto*) in a minute; **¡ya ~!*** just coming!; **ya ~ llega** he'll be here any minute now; **él va ~ adelante** he's just ahead
[3] (*CAm*) (= *de verdad*) really, truly
[4] (*Méx*) (= *muy*) very
[5] (*Méx*) (= *hace poco*) just; **ahora ~ llegó** he's just got here
[6] (*Andes*) (= *sólo*) only
Ⓒ SM **el ~ ~** (*Méx**) the boss*

mero² SM (*Pesca*) grouper

merodeador(a) Ⓐ ADJ prowling; [*pandilla, tropas*] marauding
Ⓑ SM/F prowler

merodear ▸conjug 1a◂ VI [1] (= *rondar*) to prowl (about); [*pandillas, tropas*] to maraud; **vio a un hombre merodeando entre los coches** she saw a man prowling around among the cars
[2] (*Méx*) to make money by illicit means

merodeo SM (= *acecho*) prowling; [*de pandillas, tropas*] marauding

merolico* SM (*Méx*) (= *curandero*) quack*; (= *vendedor*) street salesman

merovingio/a ADJ, SM/F Merovingian

mersa* (*Arg*), **merza*** (*Arg*) Ⓐ ADJ INV (= *de mal gusto*) common, naff*; (= *ostentoso*) flashy
Ⓑ SMF INV common person
Ⓒ SF (= *hampa*) mob, gang

mes SM [1] month; **al ~ llegó él** he came a month later; **50 dólares al ~** 50 dollars a month; **el ~ corriente** this month; **el ~ que viene** ◊ **el ~ próximo** next month ► **mes lunar** lunar month
[2] (= *sueldo*) month's pay; (= *renta*) month's rent; (= *pago*) monthly payment; **facilidades de pago 36 ~es** 36 months credit available
[3] (*Med**) **estar con** *o* **tener el ~** to have one's period

mesa SF [1] table; [*de despacho*] desk; **¡a la ~!** dinner's ready!; **bendecir la ~** to say grace; **de ~: vino de ~** table wine; **poner la ~** to lay the table; **recoger la ~** ◊ **quitar la ~** to clear the table; **sentarse a la ~** to sit down to table; **servir la ~** to wait at table; ✦*MODISMO* **estar sobre la ~** [*asunto*] to be on the table, be under consideration *o* discussion ► **mesa auxiliar** side table, occasional table ► **mesa de alas abatibles** gate-leg(ged) table ► **mesa de billar** billiard table ► **mesa de café**, **mesa de centro** coffee table ► **mesa de comedor** dining table ► **mesa de despacho** office desk ► **mesa de juntas** conference table ► **mesa de mezclas** mixer, mixing desk ► **mesa de negociación** negotiating table ► **mesa de noche** bedside table, night stand *o* table (EEUU) ► **mesa de operaciones** operating table ► **mesa de tijera** folding table ► **mesa de trabajo** desk ► **mesa(s) nido** nest of tables ► **mesa operatoria** operating table ► **mesa ratona** (*Cono Sur*) coffee table ► **mesa redonda** (*Pol*) (= *discusión*) round table; (= *conferencia*) round-table conference; (*Hist*) Round Table
[2] (= *personas*) (= *comité*) committee; [*de empresa*] board; (*en mitin*) platform ► **Mesa de la Cámara**, **Mesa del Parlamento** parliamentary assembly ► **mesa electoral** *officials in charge of a polling station* ► **Mesa Nacional** National Committee
[3] (= *pensión*) board; **~ y cama** bed and board; **tener a algn a ~ y mantel** to give sb free board
[4] (*Geog*) (= *meseta*) tableland, plateau
[5] (*Arquit*) landing
[6] [*de herramienta*] side, flat

mesada SF [1] (= *dinero*) monthly payment
[2] (*Arg*) worktop

mesana SF mizzen

mesarse ▸conjug 1a◂ VPR **~ el pelo** *o* **los cabellos** to tear one's hair (out); **~ la barba** to pull one's beard

mescalina SF mescaline

mescolanza SF = **mezcolanza**

mesenterio SM mesentery

mesero/a SM/F (*Méx*) waiter/waitress

meseta SF [1] (*Geog*) tableland, plateau
[2] (*Arquit*) landing

mesetario ADJ (*Esp*) (= *de la meseta*) of/from the Castilian meseta; (= *castellano*) Castilian

mesiánico ADJ messianic

Mesías SM INV Messiah

mesilla SF [1] (*pequeña*) small table; (*auxiliar*) side table, occasional table ► **mesilla de noche** bedside table, night stand *o* (EEUU) table ► **mesilla de ruedas** trolley, cart (EEUU) ► **mesilla plegable** folding table
[2] (*Caribe*) market stall

mesmeriano ADJ mesmeric

mesmerismo SM mesmerism

mesmerizante ADJ mesmerizing

mesmerizar ▸conjug 1f◂ VT to mesmerize

mesnada SF [1] (*Hist*) armed retinue
[2] **mesnadas** (= *partidarios*) followers, supporters; **las ~s del orden** the forces of order

Mesoamérica SF Middle America (*Mexico, Central America and the West Indies*)

mesoamericano/a ADJ, SM/F Middle American

mesolítico Ⓐ ADJ Mesolithic
Ⓑ SM **el ~** the Mesolithic

mesolito SM mesolith

mesomorfo SM mesomorph

mesón[1] SM [1] (*Hist*) inn; (*moderno*) *restaurant and bar with period décor*, olde worlde inn
[2] (*CAm*) (= *pensión*) lodging house, rooming house (*EEUU*)
[3] (*Chile, Ven*) (= *mostrador*) counter
[4] (*Cono Sur*) (= *mesa grande*) large table

mesón[2] SM (*Fís*) meson

mesonero/a SM/F [1] (††) innkeeper
[2] (*en bar*) landlord/landlady
[3] (*Caribe*) waiter/waitress

mesteño (*Méx*) Ⓐ ADJ [*caballo*] wild, untamed
Ⓑ SM mustang

mestizaje SM [1] (= *cruce*) crossbreeding, miscegenation (*frm*)
[2] (= *grupo de mestizos*) mestizos *pl*, half-castes (*pey*) *pl*

mestizar ▸conjug 1f◂ VT [+ *raza*] to crossbreed; [+ *razas*] to mix (*by crossbreeding*)

mestizo/a Ⓐ ADJ [*persona*] mixed-race; [*sociedad*] racially mixed; [*raza*] mixed; [*animal*] crossbred, mongrel (*pey*); [*planta*] hybrid
Ⓑ SM/F (= *persona*) mestizo, half-caste (*pey*); (= *animal*) crossbreed, mongrel (*pey*); (= *planta*) hybrid

mesura SF [1] (= *moderación*) moderation, restraint; **con ~** in moderation; **gastan dinero sin ~** they spend money like water
[2] (= *calma*) calm

mesurado ADJ [1] (= *moderado*) moderate, restrained; **estilo ~** restrained style; **precios ~s** reasonable prices
[2] (= *tranquilo*) calm

mesurar ▸conjug 1a◂ Ⓐ VT [1] (= *contener*) to restrain
[2] (*Ecu*) (= *medir*) to measure
Ⓑ **mesurarse** VPR to restrain o.s., act with restraint

meta Ⓐ SF [1] (*Ftbl*) goal; (*en hípica*) winning post; (*Atletismo*) finishing line; **chutar a ~** to shoot at goal; **entrar en** *o* **pasar por ~** to cross the finishing line ► **meta volante** (*en ciclismo*) bonus sprint
[2] (= *objetivo*) goal, aim; **¿cuál es tu ~ en la vida?** what is your goal *o* aim in life?; **fijarse una ~** to set o.s. a goal
Ⓑ SMF (= *portero*) (goal)keeper

meta... PREF meta...

metabólico ADJ metabolic

metabolismo SM metabolism

metabolizador ADJ metabolizing

metabolizar ▸conjug 1f◂ VT to metabolize

metacarpiano SM metacarpal

metacrilato SM methacrylate

metadona SF methadone

metafísica SF metaphysics *sing*

metafísico /a Ⓐ ADJ metaphysical
Ⓑ SM/F metaphysician

metáfora SF metaphor

metafórico ADJ metaphoric(al)

metal SM [1] (= *material*) metal; (*Mús*) brass; **el vil ~** filthy lucre ► **metal en láminas, metal laminado** sheet metal ► **metal noble** precious metal ► **metal pesado** heavy metal
[2] [*de voz*] timbre

metalenguaje SM metalanguage

metalero ADJ (*Andes, Cono Sur*) metal *antes de s*

metálico Ⓐ ADJ [*objeto*] metal *antes de s*; [*color, sonido, brillo*] metallic; **un Cadillac azul ~** a metallic blue Cadillac
Ⓑ SM (= *dinero*) cash; (= *moneda*) coin; (*en barras*) specie, bullion; **pagar en ~** to pay (in) cash; **premio en ~** cash prize

metalista SMF metalworker

metalistería SF metalwork

metaliteratura SF metaliterature

metalizado ADJ [1] [*pintura*] metallic
[2] (= *materialista*) mercenary, only interested in making money; **el mundo actual está ~** the modern world revolves around money

metalizar ▸conjug 1f◂ Ⓐ VT [+ *material*] to metallize
Ⓑ **metalizarse** VPR [1] [*persona*] to become mercenary
[2] [*material*] to become metallized

metalmecánico ADJ **industria metalmecánica** (*Cono Sur*) metallurgical industry

metalurgia SF metallurgy

metalúrgico/a Ⓐ ADJ metallurgic(al); **industria metalúrgica** engineering industry
Ⓑ SM/F (= *trabajador*) metalworker; (= *científico*) metallurgist

metamórfico ADJ metamorphic

metamorfosear ▸conjug 1a◂ Ⓐ VT to metamorphose (*frm*), transform (**en** into)
Ⓑ **metamorfosearse** VPR to be metamorphosed (*frm*), be transformed

metamorfosis SF INV metamorphosis (*frm*), transformation

metano SM methane

metástasis SF INV metastasis

metastatizar ▸conjug 1f◂ VI, **metastizar** ▸conjug 1f◂ VI to metastasize

metatarsiano SM metatarsal

metate SM (*CAm, Méx*) flat stone for grinding

metátesis SF INV metathesis

metedor[1] SM [*de bebé*] nappy liner

metedor[2](a)†† SM/F (= *contrabandista*) smuggler

metedura SF ► **metedura de pata*** blunder, clanger*

meteduría SF smuggling

metejón* SM [1] (*Cono Sur*) violent love
[2] (*Andes*) (= *enredo*) mess

metelón ADJ (*Méx*) meddling

metempsicosis SF INV metempsychosis

meteórico ADJ meteoric

meteorito SM meteorite

meteoro SM meteor

meteoroide SM meteoroid

meteorología SF meteorology

meteorológico ADJ meteorological, weather *antes de s*; **boletín** *o* **parte ~** weather report

meteorologista SMF meteorologist

meteorólogo/a SM/F meteorologist

metepatas* SMF INV **eres un ~** you're always putting your foot in it

meter ▸conjug 2a◂ Ⓐ VT [1] (= *poner, introducir*) to put; **¿dónde has metido las llaves?** where have you put the keys?; **metió el palo por el aro** she stuck *o* put the stick through the ring; **mete las hamacas que está lloviendo** bring the hammocks in, it's raining; **~ algo __en__ algo** to put sth in(to) sth; **metió la mano en el bolsillo** she put her hand in(to) her pocket; **metió el dedo en la sopa** he dipped *o* put his finger in the soup; **tienes que ~ la pieza en su sitio** you have to fit *o* put the part in the correct place; **consiguió ~ toda la ropa en la maleta** she managed to get *o* fit all the clothes in(to) the suitcase; **~ dinero en el banco** to put money in the bank; **¿quién le metió esas ideas en la cabeza?** who gave him those ideas?; ✦**MODISMO a todo ~*** (= *rápido*) as fast as possible; **está lloviendo a todo ~** it's pelting with rain, it's pelting down; **le están dando antibióticos a todo ~** he's being stuffed with antibiotics*
[2] (*Dep*) to score; **~ un gol** to score a goal
[3] (*Cos*) (*para estrechar*) to take in; (*para acortar*) to take up; **métele la falda que le queda larga** take her skirt up a bit, it's too long
[4] (*Aut*) [+ *marcha*] to go into; **mete primera** go into first gear; **¡mete el acelerador!** put your foot down!
[5] (= *internar*) **~ a algn en la cárcel** to put sb in prison; **lo metieron en un colegio privado** they put him in *o* sent him to a private school
[6] (*en una profesión*) **lo metieron a trabajar en el banco** they got him a job in a bank; **metieron a su hija (a) monja** they sent their daughter to a convent; **lo metieron a** *o* **de fontanero** they apprenticed him to a plumber
[7] (= *implicar*) **~ a algn en algo** to get sb involved in sth; **él me metió en el negocio** he got me involved in the business; **tú me metiste en este lío** you got me into this mess; **no metas a mi madre en esto** don't drag *o* bring my mother into this; **Luis metió a Fernando en muchos disgustos** Luis let Fernando in for a lot of trouble
[8] (= *ocasionar*) **~ __miedo__ a algn** to scare *o* frighten sb; **~ __prisa__ a algn** to hurry sb, make sb get a move on; **tenemos que ~le prisa a Adela** we need to hurry Adela, we need to make Adela get a move on; **¡no me metas prisa!** don't rush me!; **~ __ruido__** to make a noise; **~ un __susto__ a algn** to give sb a fright
[9] (*) (= *dar*) **le metieron un golpe en la cabeza** they hit him on the head; **le metió una torta delante de todos** she hit him in front of everyone
[10] (*) (= *endosar*) **me han metido dos billetes falsos** they gave me two false banknotes; **me metieron una multa por no llevar puesto el cinturón** I was fined for not wearing a seat belt; **nos metió un rollo inacabable** he went on and on for ages; **le metieron cinco años de cárcel** they gave him five years in prison; **nos van a ~ más trabajo** they're going to lumber us with more work
[11] (*) (= *aplicar*) **me metió la maquinilla y me peló al cero** he took the clippers to me and shaved all my hair off; **le quedaba largo el traje y le metió las tijeras** her dress was too long, so she took the scissors to it
[12] (*) (= *hacer entender*) **no hay quien le meta que aquello era mentira** nobody seems able to make him understand that it was a lie, nobody is able to get it into his head that it was a lie
[13] **~las** (*Andes*‡) to beat it*
Ⓑ **meterse** VPR [1] (= *introducirse*) **métete por la primera calle a la derecha** take the first street on the right; **¿dónde se habrá metido el lápiz?** where can the pencil have got to?; **no sabía dónde ~se de pura vergüenza** she was so ashamed, she didn't know where to hide; **~se __en__ algo**: **después de comer siempre se mete en el despacho** after lunch she always goes into her study *o*

shuts herself away in her study; **se metió en la tienda** she went into the shop; **se metió en la cama** she got into bed; **se metió en un agujero** he got into a hole; **se metieron en el agua nada más llegar** they got straight into the water as soon as they arrived; **se me metió una avispa en el coche** a wasp got into my car; **el río se mete en el mar** the river flows into the sea; **un trozo de tierra que se mete en el mar** a finger of land that sticks out into the sea

[2] (= *introducir*) **métete la camisa** tuck your shirt in; **~se una buena cena*** to have a good dinner; **~se un pico**‡ to give o.s. a fix‡; ✦*MODISMO* **¡métetelo donde te quepa!**‡ you can stuff it!‡

[3] (= *involucrarse*) **~se en algo**: **se metió en un negocio turbio** he got involved in a shady affair; **~se en política** to go into politics; **~se en líos** to get into trouble; **se metió en peligro** he got into danger; **no te metas en explicaciones** don't bother giving any explanations; **me metí mucho en la película** I really got into *o* got involved in the film

[4] (= *entrometerse*) **~se en algo** to interfere in sth, meddle in sth; **¿por qué te metes (en esto)?** why are you interfering (in this matter)?; **¡no te metas en lo que no te importa!** ◊ **¡no te metas donde no te llaman!** mind your own business!

[5] (*de profesión*) **~se a algo**: **~se a monja** to become a nun; **~se a escritor** to become a writer; **~se de algo**: **~se de aprendiz en un oficio** to go into trade as an apprentice

[6] **~se a hacer algo** (= *emprender*) to start doing sth, start to do sth; **se metió a pintar todas las paredes de la casa** he started painting *o* to paint the whole house

[7] **~se con algn*** (= *provocar*) to pick on sb*; (= *burlarse de*) to tease sb

meterete/a* (*Arg*), **metete/a*** (*Chile, Méx*) Ⓐ ADJ interfering
Ⓑ SM/F busybody, meddler

metiche* ADJ (*CAm, Chile, Méx*) interfering, meddling

meticón/ona* Ⓐ ADJ interfering, meddling
Ⓑ SM/F busybody, meddler

meticulosamente ADV meticulously, scrupulously

meticulosidad SF meticulousness, scrupulousness

meticuloso ADJ meticulous

metida* SF = **metedura**

metido* Ⓐ ADJ [1] **estar muy ~ en algo** to be deeply involved in sth; **anda ~ en un lío** he's in a bit of trouble

[2] **~ en años** elderly, advanced in years; **está algo metidita en años** she's getting on a bit now; **~ en carnes** plump

[3] **~ en sí mismo** introspective

[4] **estar muy ~ con algn** to be well in with sb

[5] (*LAm*) (= *entrometido*) interfering, meddling

[6] (*Caribe, Cono Sur**) (= *bebido*) half cut*

Ⓑ SM [1] (= *reprimenda*) ticking-off; **dar** *o* **pegar un ~ a algn** to give sb a ticking-off

[2] (‡) (= *sablazo*) **pegar un ~ a algn** to touch sb for money*

[3] (*) (= *golpe*) bash*; (= *empujón*) shove; **le pegó un buen ~ a la tarta** she took a good chunk out of the cake

metijón/ona* SM/F busybody, meddler

metílico ADJ, **metilado** ADJ **alcohol ~** methylated spirit

metilo SM methyl

metimiento SM [1] (= *inserción*) insertion
[2] (*) (= *influencia*) influence, pull*

metódicamente ADV methodically

metódico ADJ methodical

metodismo SM Methodism

metodista ADJ, SMF Methodist

método SM [1] (= *procedimiento*) method; **sus ~s de enseñanza son un poco anticuados** his teaching methods are a bit old-fashioned; **el mejor ~ para acabar con los gérmenes** the best way of killing off germs ► **método anticonceptivo** method of contraception ► **método audiovisual** audiovisual method ► **método del ritmo** rhythm method

[2] (= *organización*) **no obtienen resultados porque les falta ~** they don't get any results because they are not methodical (enough); **trabajar con ~** to work methodically

[3] (= *manual*) manual

metodología SF methodology

metodológico ADJ methodological

metomentodo* Ⓐ ADJ INV interfering, meddling Ⓑ SMF busybody, meddler

metonimia SF metonymy

metraje SM [1] (*Cine*) length; **cinta de largo ~** feature(-length) film; *ver tb* **cortometraje**, **mediometraje**, **largometraje**
[2] (= *distancia*) distance

metralla SF [1] (*Mil*) shrapnel
[2] (*) (= *calderilla*) coppers *pl*, small change

metralleta SF submachine gun, tommy gun

métrica SF metrics *sing*

métrico ADJ metric(al); **cinta métrica** tape measure

metro¹ SM [1] (= *medida*) metre, meter (*EEUU*); **~s por segundo** metres per second; **mide tres ~s de largo** it's three metres long; **vender algo por ~s** to sell sth by the metre ► **metro cuadrado** square metre ► **metro cúbico** cubic metre; → KILOS, METROS, AÑOS

[2] (= *regla*) rule, ruler; (= *cinta métrica*) tape measure

[3] (*Literat*) metre, meter (*EEUU*)

metro² SM underground, tube, subway (*EEUU*)

metrobús SM combined bus and underground railway ticket

metrónomo SM metronome

metrópoli SF (= *ciudad*) metropolis; [*de imperio*] mother country

metropolitano Ⓐ ADJ metropolitan; **área metropolitana de Madrid** Greater Madrid
Ⓑ SM [1] (*Rel*) metropolitan
[2] (= *tren*) = **metro²**

metrosexual ADJ, SM metrosexual

mexicano/a ADJ, SM/F Mexican

México SM Mexico

mezanine SM mezzanine

mezcal SM (*Méx*) mescal

mezcla SF [1] (= *acción*) [*de ingredientes, colores*] mixing; [*de razas, culturas*] mixing; [*de sonidos*] mixing; [*de cafés, tabacos, whiskies*] blending; **la ~ de lo dulce y lo amargo** mixing sweet and sour flavours; *ver tb* **mesa 1**

[2] (= *resultado*) [*de ingredientes, colores*] mixture; [*de razas, culturas*] mix; [*de cafés, tabacos, whiskies*] blend; **añade más agua a la ~** add some more water to the mixture; **sin ~** [*sustancia*] pure; [*gasolina*] unadulterated; **costumbres transmitidas sin ~ de influencias externas** customs passed on without any external influence ► **mezcla explosiva** (*lit*) explosive mixture; (*fig*) lethal combination; **los dos hermanos formaban una ~ explosiva** the two brothers formed a lethal combination

[3] (*Mús*) mix

[4] (*Constr*) mortar

[5] (*Cos*) blend, mix

mezclado SM mixing; **el proceso de ~** the mixing process

mezclador(a) Ⓐ ADJ [*vaso, mesa*] mixing
Ⓑ SM/F (*Radio, TV*) (= *persona*) mixer ► **mezclador(a) de imágenes** vision mixer ► **mezclador(a) de sonido** sound mixer, dubbing mixer
Ⓒ SM [1] (*Radio, TV*) (= *aparato*) (*tb* **~ de sonido**) mixer, mixing desk ► **mezclador de vídeo**, **mezclador de video** (*LAm*) video mixer
[2] (*Culin*) (*tb* **vaso ~**) mixing bowl

mezcladora SF mixer; (*tb* **~ de sonido**) mixer, mixing desk ► **mezcladora de hormigón** concrete mixer

mezclar ▸conjug 1a◂ Ⓐ VT [1] (= *combinar*) [+ *ingredientes, colores*] to mix, mix together; [+ *estilos*] to mix, combine; [+ *personas*] to mix; **los materiales deben ~se muy despacio** the materials should be mixed (together) very slowly; **no mezcles los colores en la paleta** don't mix the colours on the palette; **un artista que mezcla estilos diferentes en su obra** an artist who mixes *o* combines different styles in his work; **han mezclado a niños de distintos niveles en la misma clase** they have mixed children of different abilities in the same class; **~ algo con algo** to mix sth with sth; **he mezclado el agua caliente con la fría** I've mixed the hot and cold water together, I've mixed the hot water with the cold; **no se debe ~ la religión con la política** one shouldn't mix religion with politics; **la banda sonora mezcla la música tradicional con el rock** the soundtrack is a mixture of traditional and rock music; **la harina y el azúcar se mezclan por partes iguales** equal quantities of flour and sugar are mixed (together); **la comida china mezcla sabores salados y dulces** Chinese food combines *o* mixes savoury and sweet flavours

[2] (= *confundir, desordenar*) [+ *fotos, papeles*] to mix up, mess up; [+ *idiomas*] to mix up, muddle up; [+ *naipes*] to shuffle; **¿quién me ha mezclado todos los papeles?** who's mixed *o* messed up all my papers?; **cuando habla mezcla los dos idiomas** when he talks he mixes *o* muddles up the two languages

[3] [+ *café, tabaco, whisky*] to blend

[4] (*Mús*) [+ *sonido*] to mix

[5] (= *implicar*) **~ a algn en algo** to involve sb in sth, get sb involved in sth; **no quiero que me mezcles en ese asunto** I don't want you to involve me *o* get me involved in that business

Ⓑ VI (*) (*con bebidas alcohólicas*) to mix (one's) drinks; **no me gusta ~** I don't like mixing (my) drinks

Ⓒ **mezclarse** VPR [1] (= *combinarse*) [*ingredientes, colores*] to mix; [*culturas, elementos*] to mix, combine; **el aceite y el agua no se mezclan** oil and water don't mix; **en la película se mezclan la realidad y la ficción** the

film mixes *o* combines reality and fiction; **lo que sentía era amor mezclado con odio** what she felt was a mixture of love and hate
[2] (= *confundirse*) [*papeles, intereses*] to get mixed up; **se me han mezclado todos los documentos** all my documents have got mixed up; **los problemas políticos se mezclan con los amorosos** political issues get mixed up with romantic ones; **la vi ~se entre la multitud** I saw her merge into the crowd; **los muertos se mezclaban con los supervivientes** the dead lay amongst the survivors
[3] (= *involucrarse*) **~se en algo** to get involved in sth; **procura no ~te en eso** try not to get involved *o* get mixed up in that
[4] (= *relacionarse*) **~se con algn** to mix with sb, get involved with sb; **no quiero que te mezcles con esa gente** I don't want you mixing with *o* getting involved with those people

mezclillo SM (*Cono Sur*) denim

mezcolanza SF hotchpotch, hodgepodge (*EEUU*), jumble

mezquinamente ADV meanly

mezquinar ▸conjug 1a◂ (*LAm*) (A) VT [1] **~ algo** to be stingy with sth, skimp on sth
[2] (*Cono Sur*) **~ el cuerpo** to dodge, swerve
[3] (*Andes*) **~ a algn** to defend sb; **~ a un niño** to let a child off a punishment
(B) VI to be mean, be stingy

mezquindad SF [1] (= *tacañería*) meanness, stinginess
[2] (= *insignificancia*) paltriness, wretchedness; **esa cantidad es una ~** that amount's a pittance
[3] (= *acto vil*) mean thing (to do)

mezquino/a (A) ADJ [1] (= *tacaño*) mean, stingy [2] (= *insignificante*) [*pago*] miserable, paltry
(B) SM/F [1] (= *tacaño*) mean person, miser
[2] (*LAm*) (= *verruga*) wart

mezquita SF mosque

mezquite SM (*Méx*) mesquite (tree *o* shrub)

mezzanine [metsa'nine] SM mezzanine; (*Andes Teat*) circle

mezzosoprano [metsoso'prano] SF mezzo-soprano

M.F. ABR (= **modulación de frecuencia**) FM

mg ABR (= **miligramo(s)**) mg

MHz ABR (= **megahertzio(s), megahercio(s)**) MHz

mi[1] ADJ POSES my

mi[2] SM (*Mús*) E ► **mi mayor** E major

mí PRON (*después de prep*) me, myself; **unos para ti y otros para mí** some for you and some for me; **tengo confianza en mí mismo** I have confidence in myself; **¡a mí con ésas!** come off it!*, tell me another!; **¿y a mí qué?** so what?, what has that got to do with me?; **¡a mí!** (= *socorro*) help!; **para mí no hay duda** as far as I'm concerned there's no doubt; **por mí puede ir** as far as I'm concerned she can go; **por mí mismo** by myself

miaja SF [1] (= *migaja*) crumb
[2] (= *poquito*) tiny bit; **ni (una) ~** not the least little bit
[3] (*como adv*) a bit; **me quiere una ~** she likes me a bit

mialgia SF myalgia

miasma SM miasma

miasmático ADJ miasmic

miau SM mew, miaow; ✦***MODISMO*** **hizo ~ como el gato** you couldn't see him for dust

Mibor SM ABR = **Madrid inter-bank offered rate**

mica[1] SF [1] (*Min*) mica
[2] (*Caribe Aut*) sidelight

mica[2] SF (*Andes*) (= *orinal*) chamber pot

mica[3]* SF (*CAm*) (= *borrachera*) **ponerse una ~** to get drunk

micada SF (*CAm, Méx*) flourish

micción SF (*Med frm*) urination

miccionar ▸conjug 1a◂ VI (*Med frm*) to urinate

miche SM [1] (*Méx*) (= *gato*) cat
[2] (*Caribe*) (= *licor*) liquor, spirits *pl*
[3] (*Cono Sur*) (= *juego*) game of marbles
[4] (*CAm*) (= *pelea*) fight, brawl

michelín* SM spare tyre*, spare tire (*EEUU**), roll of fat; **yo no tengo michelines como otras** I haven't got a spare tyre like some people*

michi SM (*Andes*) noughts and crosses, tick-tack-toe (*EEUU*)

michino/a SM/F, **micho/a*** SM/F puss, pussy cat

micifuz* SM puss, pussycat

mico SM [1] (*Zool*) long-tailed monkey; (*como término genérico*) monkey; **¡cállate, ~!*** (*a niño*) shut up, you little monkey!; ✦***MODISMO*** **volverse ~: se volvió ~ buscándolo** he was getting into a real state looking for it
[2] (*) **ser un ~** (= *feo*) to be an ugly devil
[3] (*CAm***) (= *vagina*) fanny**, twat**

micoleón SM (*CAm*) kinkajou

micología SF mycology

micra SF micron

micrero/a SM/F (*Andes, Cono Sur*) minibus driver; (*Cono Sur*) bus driver

micro[1] SM (*Radio*) mike*

micro[2] SM (= *microbús*) (*Andes, Cono Sur*) (*de corta distancia*) minibus; (*Cono Sur*) (*de larga distancia*) bus

micro[3] SM (*Inform*) micro, microcomputer

micro... PREF micro...

microalgas SFPL micro-algae

microbiano ADJ microbial

microbio SM microbe (*frm*), germ

microbiología SF microbiology

microbiológico ADJ microbiological

microbiólogo/a SM/F microbiologist

microbús SM minibus

microcasete SM *o* SF, **micro-cassette** SM *o* SF micro-cassette player, mini-cassette player

microchip SM (*pl* **microchips**) microchip

microcircuitería SF microcircuitry

microcircuito SM microcircuit

microcirugía SF microsurgery

microclima SM microclimate

microcomputador SM, **microcomputadora** SF micro, microcomputer

microcosmos SM INV microcosm

microcrédito SM microcredit

microeconomía SF microeconomics *sing*

microeconómico ADJ microeconomic

microelectrónica SF microelectronics *sing*

microelectrónico ADJ microelectronic

microemisor ADJ microtransmitter *antes de s*

microespaciado SM microspacing

microfalda SF micro-skirt

microficha SF microfiche

microfilm SM (*pl* **microfilms** *o* **microfilmes**) microfilm

microfilmar ▸conjug 1a◂ VT to microfilm

micrófono SM [1] (*Radio, TV*) microphone; **hablar por el ~** to speak over the microphone ► **micrófono espía** hidden microphone, bug ► **micrófono inalámbrico**, **micrófono sin hilos** cordless microphone
[2] [*de ordenador*] mouthpiece

microforma SF microform

microfotografiar ▸conjug 1c◂ VT to microphotograph

microfundio SM smallholding, small farm

micrograbador SM micro-cassette recorder, mini-cassette recorder

microinformática SF microcomputing

microinyectar ▸conjug 1a◂ VT to microinject

microlentillas SFPL contact lenses

micrómetro SM micrometer

microonda SF microwave

microondas SM INV (*tb* **horno ~**) microwave (oven); **apto para ~** microwavable, suitable for microwaving

microordenador SM microcomputer

microorganismo SM microorganism

micropastilla SF (*Inform*) chip, wafer

microplaqueta SF, **microplaquita** SF ► **microplaqueta de silicio** silicon chip

microprocesador SM microprocessor

microprograma SM (*Inform*) microprogram

micropunto SM microdot

microscopía SF microscopy

microscópico ADJ microscopic; **se controló por observación microscópica** it was monitored through *o* with a microscope; **vistos a través del examen ~** seen through a microscope

microscopio SM microscope ► **microscopio electrónico** electron microscope

microsegundo SM microsecond

microsurco SM microgroove

microtaxi SM minicab

microtecnia SF, **microtecnología** SF microtechnology

microtécnica SF, **microtecnología** SF microtechnology

microtenis SM INV (*LAm*) table-tennis

microtransmisor SM micro-transmitter

Midas SM Midas; **ser un rey ~** to have the Midas touch

midi SM, **midifalda** SF midiskirt

MIE SM ABR (*Esp*) = **Ministerio de Industria y Energía**

miéchica EXCL (*LAm euf*) sugar!*, shoot!*

miedica* SMF chicken*, coward

mieditis* SF INV (= *nervios*) jitters*; **me da ~** it gives me the jitters; **tengo ~** I'm scared *o* petrified

miedo SM [1] fear; **~ a las represalias** fear of reprisals; **¡qué ~!** how scary!; **coger ~ a algo** to become afraid of sth; **dar ~** to scare; **me da ~ subir al tejado** I'm scared to go up on the roof; **le daba ~ hacerlo** he was afraid *o* scared to do it; **me da ~ dejar solo al niño** I'm frightened to leave the child alone; **de ~**: **una película de ~** a horror film; **entrar ~ a algn**: **me entró un ~ terrible** I suddenly felt terribly scared; **meter ~ a algn** to scare *o* frighten sb; **pasar ~**: **pasé mucho ~ viendo la película** I was very scared watching the

film; **perder el ~ a algo** to lose one's fear of sth; **por ~ a** o **de algo** for fear of sth; **por ~ a** o **de quedar en ridículo** for fear of looking ridiculous; **por ~ de que ...** for fear that ...; **tener ~** to be scared o frightened; **no tengas ~** don't be scared o frightened; **tener ~ a** o **de algn/algo** to be afraid of sb/sth; **tengo ~ a morir** I'm afraid of dying; **tenemos ~ a** o **de que nos ataquen** we're afraid that they may attack us; **tengo ~ de que le ocurra algo** I'm scared something will happen to him; **tener ~ de** o **a hacer algo** to be afraid to do sth, be afraid of doing sth; ✦*MODISMO* **meterle el ~ en el cuerpo a algn** to scare the wits out of sb, scare the pants off sb* ► **miedo al público** (*Teat*) stage fright ► **miedo cerval** great fear ► **miedo escénico** stage fright
2 (*) **de ~** (= *increíble*): **es un coche de ~** it's a fantastic car; **lo pasamos de ~** we had a fantastic time; **hace un frío de ~** it's freezing; **mi madre cocina de ~** my mum's a fantastic cook

miedoso/a Ⓐ ADJ (= *cobarde*) scared; **¿por qué eres tan ~?** why are you always so scared of everything; **no seas ~, que no te hace nada** don't be scared, it's not going to hurt you
Ⓑ SM/F coward

miel SF [*de abejas*] honey; (= *melaza*) (*tb* **~ de caña, ~ negra**) molasses; **las ~es del triunfo** the sweet taste of success; ✦*MODISMOS* **~ sobre hojuelas**: **me gusta el trabajo, y si está bien pagado, pues es ~ sobre hojuelas** I enjoy the work, and if it's also well-paid, so much the better; **dejar a algn con la ~ en los labios** to leave sb feeling cheated; **quedarse con la ~ en los labios** to be left feeling cheated; ✦*REFRANES* **hazte de ~ y te comerán las moscas** if you are too nice people will take advantage of you; **no hay ~ sin hiel** there's no rose without a thorn

mielero SM honeypot

mielga SF alfalfa

miembro Ⓐ SM 1 (*Anat*) limb, member ► **miembro viril** male member, penis
2 (*Ling, Mat*) member
Ⓑ SMF [*de club*] member; [*de institución, academia*] fellow, associate; **no ~** non-member; **hacerse ~ de** to become a member of, join
Ⓒ ADJ member *antes de s*; **los países ~s** the member states

mientes SFPL **¡ni por ~!** never!, not on your life!; **parar ~ en algo** to reflect on sth; **traer a las ~** to recall; **se le vino a las ~** it occurred to him

▼**mientras** Ⓐ CONJ 1 (= *durante*) while; **sonreía ~ hablaba** he smiled as he spoke; **~ él estaba fuera** while he was out; **fue bonito ~ duró** it was nice while it lasted; **~ duró la guerra** while o when the war was on
2 (*expresando condición*) as long as; **seguiré ~ pueda caminar** I'll carry on (for) as long as I can still walk; **no podemos comenzar ~ no venga** we can't start until he comes
3 (= *en tanto que*) while, whereas; **tú trabajas ~ que yo estoy en el paro** you're working while o whereas I'm unemployed
4 (*esp LAm*) (= *cuanto*) **~ más lo repetía, menos lo creía** the more he repeated it the less I believed him; **~ más tienen más quieren** the more they have the more they want
Ⓑ ADV (*tb* **~ tanto**) (= *entre tanto*) meanwhile, in the meantime; **llegaré en seguida, ~ (tanto), prepáralo todo** I'll be right there, meanwhile o in the meantime, you get it all ready

➤ LENGUA Y USO: mientras A3 32.1

mierc. ABR (= **miércoles**) Wed, Weds

miércoles SM INV Wednesday ► **miércoles de ceniza** Ash Wednesday; *ver* **sábado**

mierda** Ⓐ SF 1 (= *excremento*) shit**, crap**; **una ~ de perro** some dog shit**; **estar hecho una ~** (= *sucio*) to be filthy; (= *cansado*) to be knackered*; **irse a la ~**: **nuestros planes se han ido a la ~** our plans have gone down the pan*; **¡vete a la ~!** go to hell!‡, piss off!**; **mandar a algn a la ~** to tell sb to piss off**
2 (= *suciedad*) crap**; **había mucha ~ debajo de la alfombra** there was a lot of crap under the carpet**; **tienes la casa llena de ~** your house is filthy, your house is a pigsty
3 (= *cosa sin valor*) crap**; **el libro es una ~** the book is crap**; **es una ~ de coche** it's a crappy car**; **—¿cuánto te han pagado? —una ~** "how much did they pay you?" — "a pittance"; **de ~** crappy**; **una película de ~** a crappy film**; **esos políticos de ~** those crappy politicians**
4 (= *borrachera*) **coger** o **pillar una ~** to get pissed‡, get sloshed‡
5 (= *suerte*) **marcó un gol de pura ~** he scored a goal by an almighty fluke
6 (*uso enfático*) **¿qué ~ quieres?** what the hell do you want?‡
7 (= *hachís*) shit**
Ⓑ SMF (= *persona*) **tu hermana es una ~** your sister is a shit**; **es un (don) ~** he's a little shit**, he's a nobody
Ⓒ EXCL shit!**; **¡mierda! ya me he equivocado** shit, I've made a mistake**; **—¡ven aquí! —¡una ~!** "come here!" — "piss off!"**

mierdoso‡ ADJ filthy

mies SF 1 (= *cereal*) (ripe) corn, (ripe) grain
2 (= *temporada*) harvest time
3 **mieses** cornfields

miga SF 1 [*de pan*] **la ~** the inside part of the bread, the crumb; **se separa la corteza de la ~** remove the crust from the bread
2 **migas** (*Culin*) fried breadcrumbs; ✦*MODISMO* **hacer buenas ~s con algn** to get on well with sb
3 (= *sustancia*) substance; **esto tiene su ~** there's more to this than meets the eye
4 (= *pedazo*) bit; **hacer algo ~s** to break o smash sth to pieces; **hacer ~s a algn** to shatter sb; **tener los pies hechos ~s** to be footsore

migajas SFPL 1 [*de pan*] crumbs
2 (= *trocitos*) bits; (= *sobras*) scraps; **tuvieron que contentarse con las ~ del reparto** they had to be content with the scraps when it was shared out

migar ▸conjug 1h◂ VT to crumble

migra* SF (*LAm*) immigration police o authorities

migración SF migration

migraña SF migraine

migrañoso/a SM/F migraine sufferer

migrar ▸conjug 1a◂ VI to migrate

migratorio ADJ migratory

Miguel SM Michael; **~ Ángel** (= *artista*) Michelangelo

mijo SM millet

mil ADJ INV, PRON, SM a o one thousand; **tres ~ coches** three thousand cars; **~ doscientos dólares** one thousand two hundred dollars; **~ veces** a thousand times, thousands of times; **~es y ~es** thousands and thousands; ✦*MODISMO* **a las ~*** at some ungodly hour*; *ver tb* **seis**

miladi SF milady

milagrero/a* Ⓐ ADJ 1 (= *que cree en milagros*) **personas milagreras** people who believe in miracles
2 [*curación*] miracle *antes de s*, miraculous; [*poder*] miraculous; [*persona*] with miraculous powers
Ⓑ SM/F 1 (= *que cree en milagros*) believer in miracles
2 (= *que hace milagros*) miracle-worker

milagro Ⓐ SM (*Rel*) miracle; (*fig*) miracle, wonder; **es un ~ que ...** it is a miracle o wonder that ...; **~ (sería) que ...** it would be a miracle if ...; **de ~**: **se salvaron de ~** they had a miraculous escape, it was a miracle they escaped; **vivir de ~** to somehow manage to keep body and soul together; **ese CD aquí no se consigue ni de ~** you can't get that CD here for love nor money; **hacer ~s**: **un buen maquillaje puede hacer ~s** decent make-up can work wonders; **no podemos hacer ~s** we can't work miracles ► **milagro económico** economic miracle
Ⓑ ADJ INV miracle *antes de s*, miraculous; **cura ~** miracle cure; **entrenador ~** super-coach, wonder-coach

milagrosa* SF (*Rel*) *image of the Virgin Mary believed to perform miracles*; *ver tb* **milagroso**

milagrosamente ADV miraculously

milagroso ADJ miraculous; *ver tb* **milagrosa**

Milán SM Milan

milanesa SF (*esp LAm Culin*) escalope, schnitzel

milano SM (*Orn*) kite ► **milano real** red kite

mildeu SM, **mildiu** SM, **mildiú** SM mildew

mildo ADJ (*Cono Sur*) timid, shy

milenariamente ADV **un pueblo ~ libre** a people which has been free since time immemorial

milenario Ⓐ ADJ (= *de mil años*) thousand-year-old *antes de s*; (= *antiquísimo*) ancient, age-old
Ⓑ SM millennium

milenio SM millennium

milenrama SF yarrow

milésima SF thousandth; **ganó con 91 ~s de ventaja** she won by 91 thousandths of a second; **una ~ de segundo** a thousandth of a second; (*fig*) a split second

milésimo/a Ⓐ ADJ thousandth
Ⓑ SM thousandth; **hasta el ~** to three decimal places; *ver tb* **sexto**

milhojas SM o SF INV (= *pastel*) millefeuille, *cake made with puff pastry, filled with meringue*

mili* SF military service; **un amigo que está en la ~** a friend who is doing his military service; **hacer la ~** to do one's military service

MILI

La **mili** *is the colloquial term used in Spain to refer to the compulsory military service* (**servicio militar**) *which men are drafted into at 18. Exemption is possible on medical grounds and in certain family situations, while students and those living abroad can obtain a deferment*

*(**prórroga**) which allows them to put off doing their military service until a more convenient time. Conscientious objectors (**objetores de conciencia**) can choose to do a longer period of community service, known as **Prestación Social Sustitutoria** (**PSS**) instead of military service. Over recent years, the length of **la mili** has been reduced to the current nine months, but there is still plenty of opposition to it and the number of those who refuse to do either military or community service, called **insumisos**, has increased. Plans are in place to phase out military service and establish a professional army.*

⇨ See also INSUMISO, PRESTACIÓN SOCIAL SUSTITUTORIA

miliar ADJ **piedra ~** milestone

milibar SM millibar

milicia SF 1 (= *arte*) art of war; (= *profesión*) military profession
2 (= *tropa*) militia; **~s armadas** armed militias
3 (= *militares*) military
4 (= *servicio militar*) military service

miliciano/a SM/F militiaman/militiawoman; (*Andes, Cono Sur*) (= *conscripto*) conscript, draftee (*EEUU*)

milico* SM 1 (*Andes, Cono Sur pey*) (= *soldado*) soldier; (= *soldado raso*) squaddie*; **los ~s** the military
2 (*Andes*) = **miliciano**

miligramo SM milligramme, milligram (*EEUU*)

mililitro SM millilitre, milliliter (*EEUU*)

milimetrado ADJ (*fig*) minutely calculated; **papel ~** graph paper

milimétricamente ADV precisely, minutely, down to the last detail; **analizan las cuentas ~** they go through the accounts down to the last detail; **todo está ~ preparado** every last detail is prepared; **las previsiones se han cumplido ~** things have turned out exactly as foreseen

milimétrico ADJ (= *preciso*) precise, minute; **con precisión milimétrica** with pinpoint accuracy

milímetro SM millimetre, millimeter (*EEUU*); **no hemos avanzado ni un ~** we have got absolutely nowhere; **no ceder ni un ~** not to give an inch; **sin salirse un ~ del programa** keeping strictly to the programme; **lo calculó al** *o* **hasta el ~** he calculated it very precisely; **coinciden casi al ~** they tally in almost every detail; **cumplen las instrucciones al ~** they carry out their orders to the letter

milisegundo SM millisecond

militancia SF 1 (*en partido*) membership; **está prohibida su ~ en los partidos políticos** they are not permitted to be a member of *o* join a political party; **dejó el partido tras casi 20 años de ~** she left the party after almost 20 years as a member ► **militancia de base** rank-and-file members *pl*
2 (= *afiliación*) **¿cuál es su ~ política?** what is his political affiliation?

militante Ⓐ ADJ (= *radical*) militant; **una feminista ~** a militant feminist
Ⓑ SMF [*de partido*] member ► **militante de base** rank and file member

militantismo SM militancy

militar Ⓐ ADJ military; **ciencia ~** art of war
Ⓑ SM (= *soldado*) soldier, military man; (*en la mili*) serviceman; **los ~es** the military
Ⓒ ▸conjug 1a◂ VI 1 (*Mil*) to serve (*in the army*)
2 (*Pol*) **~ en un partido** to be a member of a party

militarada SF military rising, putsch

militarismo SM militarism

militarista Ⓐ ADJ militaristic
Ⓑ SMF militarist

militarización SF militarization

militarizar ▸conjug 1f◂ VT to militarize

militarote SM (*LAm pey*) rough soldier

milla SF mile ► **milla marina** nautical mile; → KILOS, METROS, AÑOS

millar SM thousand; **a ~es** by the thousand; **los había a ~es** there were thousands of them

millarada SF (about a) thousand

millardo SM thousand million, billion

millas-pasajero SFPL passenger miles

millo SM, **millón**[1] SM (*esp LAm*) (variety of) millet

millón[2] SM million; **un ~** a *o* one million; **un ~ y medio de visitantes** a million and a half visitors, one-and-a-half million visitors; **un ~ de sellos** a *o* one million stamps; **tres ~es de niños** three million children; **millones de años** millions of years; **¡un ~ de gracias!** thanks a million!, thanks ever so much!

millonada* SF **costó una ~** it cost a fortune; **lo vendió por una ~** he sold it for a fortune

millonario/a SM/F millionaire/millionairess

millonésima SF millionth

millonésimo/a ADJ, SM/F millionth

milonga (*Cono Sur*) SF 1 (*) (= *mentirilla*) fib*, tale
2 (= *baile*) *type of dance and music from the River Plate Region*
3 (= *fiesta*) party
4 (= *cotilleo*) gossip

milonguero/a SM/F 1 (*Mús*) singer of milongas
2 (*Cono Sur*) (= *fiestero*) partylover

milor SM, **milord** [mi'lor] SM milord; **vive como un ~** he lives like a lord

milpa SF (*CAm, Méx*) (= *plantación*) maize field, cornfield (*EEUU*); (= *planta*) maize, corn (*EEUU*)

milpear ▸conjug 1a◂ (*CAm, Méx*) Ⓐ VT to prepare for the sowing of maize, prepare for the sowing of corn (*EEUU*)
Ⓑ VI 1 (= *plantar*) to sow a field with maize, sow a field with corn (*EEUU*)
2 [*maíz*] (= *brotar*) to sprout

milpero/a SM/F (*CAm, Méx*) maize grower, corn grower (*EEUU*)

milpiés SM INV millipede

milrayas ADJ INV **pantalón ~** fine pin-stripe trousers

miltomate SM (*CAm, Méx*) *small green or white tomato*

mimado ADJ spoiled, pampered

mimar ▸conjug 1a◂ VT to spoil, pamper

mimbre SM *o* SF 1 (*Bot*) osier, willow
2 (= *material*) wicker; **de ~** wicker *antes de s*, wickerwork *antes de s*; ✦**MODISMO con este ~ hay que hacer el cesto** one has to make the best of what one has

mimbrearse ▸conjug 1a◂ VPR to sway

mimbrera SF osier

mimbreral SM osier bed

mimeografiar ▸conjug 1c◂ VT to mimeograph

mimeógrafo SM mimeograph

miméticamente ADV mimetically, by way of imitation

mimético ADJ mimetic, imitation *antes de s*

mimetismo SM mimicry

mimetizar ▸conjug 1f◂ (*esp LAm*) Ⓐ VT (= *imitar*) to imitate
Ⓑ **mimetizarse** VPR 1 (*Zool*) to change colour, change color (*EEUU*)
2 (*Mil*) to camouflage o.s.

mímica SF 1 (= *arte*) mime; (= *lenguaje*) sign language; (= *gestos*) gesticulation
2 (= *imitación*) imitation, mimicry

mímico ADJ mimic; **intérprete ~** sign language interpreter; **lenguaje ~** sign language

mimo/a Ⓐ SM/F (*Teat*) mime
Ⓑ SM 1 (*Teat*) mime
2 (= *copia*) **hacer ~ de algo** to mime sth
3 (= *caricia*) cuddle; **una casa diseñada con ~** a house designed with loving care; **manejó el balón con ~** he caressed the ball; **escribe con ~** she's very careful in the way she writes; **dar ~s a algn** (= *consentir*) to spoil *o* pamper sb

mimosa SF mimosa

mimoso ADJ 1 (= *cariñoso*) affectionate; **es muy mimosa con su novio** she's very affectionate towards her boyfriend; **¡no te pongas tan ~!** don't be so clingy!
2 (= *mimado*) spoilt, pampered

Min. ABR (= **Ministerio**) Min; **~ de AA.EE.** FO, ≈ FCO; **~ de D.** MOD

min. ABR 1 (= **minuto(s)**) m, min
2 (= **minúscula(s)**) lc, l.c.

mín. ABR (= **mínimo**) min

mina[1] SF 1 (*Min*) mine ► **mina a cielo abierto** opencast mine, open cut mine (*EEUU*) ► **mina de carbón, mina hullera** coal mine
2 (= *galería*) gallery; (= *pozo*) shaft
3 (*Mil, Náut*) mine ► **mina antipersonal** anti-personnel mine ► **mina terrestre** land mine
4 [*de lápiz*] lead
5 (= *ganga*) (*tb* **~ de oro**) gold mine; **este negocio es una ~ (de oro)** this business is a gold mine ► **mina de información** mine of information

mina[2]‡ SF (*Cono Sur*) (= *mujer*) bird*, chick (*EEUU*‡)

minada SF (*Mil*) mining

minador(a) Ⓐ SM 1 (*Mil*) sapper
2 (*Náut*) (*tb* **buque ~**) minelayer
Ⓑ SM/F (*Min*) mining engineer

minar ▸conjug 1a◂ VT 1 (*Min, Mil, Náut*) to mine
2 (= *debilitar*) to undermine

minarete SM minaret

mineral Ⓐ ADJ mineral
Ⓑ SM 1 (*Geol*) mineral
2 (*Min*) ore ► **mineral de hierro** iron ore
3 (*Chile*) (= *mina*) mine

mineralero SM ore-carrier

mineralizar ▸conjug 1f◂ VT to mineralize

mineralogía SF mineralogy

mineralogista SMF mineralogist

minería SF mining

minero/a Ⓐ ADJ mining Ⓑ SM/F miner ► **minero/a de carbón** coalminer ► **minero/a de interior** face worker

Minerva SF Minerva

minestrone SF minestrone

minga1** SF prick**

minga2 SF (*LAm*) 1 (= *trabajo*) voluntary communal labour *o* (*EEUU*) labor, cooperative work
2 (= *equipo*) crew *o* gang of cooperative workers

mingaco SM (*Andes, Cono Sur*) = **minga**2 **1**

mingar ▸conjug 1h◂ Ⓐ VI (*LAm*) (= *trabajar*) to work communally, work cooperatively
Ⓑ VT 1 (*Andes, Cono Sur*) [+ *trabajadores*] to call together for a communal task
2 (*Andes*) (= *atacar*) to set (up)on, attack

mingitorio SM, **mingitorios** SMPL (*hum*) urinal

Mingo SM (*forma familiar*) *de* **Domingo**

mini Ⓐ SM 1 (*Aut*) Mini
2 (*Inform*) minicomputer
Ⓑ SF (= *falda*) mini, miniskirt

mini... PREF mini...; **~coche** minicar

miniacería SF small steelworks

miniar ▸conjug 1b◂ VT [+ *manuscrito*] to illuminate

miniatura Ⓐ ADJ miniature; **golf ~** crazy golf
Ⓑ SF miniature; **en ~** in miniature; **una réplica exacta de la casa en ~** an exact replica of the house in miniature; **relojes en ~** miniature clocks; **un barco en ~** a model ship

miniaturista SMF miniaturist

miniaturización SF miniaturization

miniaturizar ▸conjug 1f◂ VT to miniaturize

minibar SM minibar

minicadena SF mini hi-fi, mini stereo system

minicalculadora SF pocket calculator

minicasino SM small gambling club

minicines SMPL *cinema with several small screens*

minicomputador SM minicomputer

MiniDisc®, **minidisc** SM (= *disco*) MiniDisc®, minidisc; (= *aparato*) MiniDisc® (player), minidisc (player)

minidisco SM diskette

miniestadio SM small sports arena

minifalda SF miniskirt

minifaldero/a Ⓐ ADJ miniskirted; **una chica minifaldera** a girl in a miniskirt
Ⓑ SF **una atrevida minifaldera** a daring girl in a miniskirt; **las minifalderas** girls in miniskirts

minifundio SM smallholding, small farm

minifundismo SM 1 (*Agr*) *small-scale farming*
2 (*fig*) (= *fragmentación*) tendency to fragment, fragmentation; **~ sindical** parochial trade unionism (*pey*)

minifundista SMF smallholder

minigira SF short tour

minigolf SM crazy golf

minihorno SM small oven

mínima SF (*Meteo*) low, lowest temperature; *ver tb* **mínimo**

minimal ADJ minimalist

minimalismo SM minimalism

minimalista ADJ, SMF minimalist

minimalizar ▸conjug 1f◂ VT to minimize

mínimamente ADV **la población se verá afectada ~** the population will be minimally affected; **si fueras ~ inteligente** if you had a modicum of intelligence; **la situación no es ni ~ aceptable** the situation is not acceptable in the slightest

minimizar ▸conjug 1f◂ VT 1 (= *reducir al mínimo*) [+ *gastos, efectos*] to minimize; **han minimizado el empleo de insecticidas** they have minimized the use of insecticides
2 (= *quitar importancia a*) [+ *problema, suceso*] to make light of, minimize, play down; **el ministro minimizó las pérdidas económicas** the minister made light of *o* played down *o* minimized the economic losses

mínimo Ⓐ ADJ 1 (= *inferior*) [*nivel, cantidad*] minimum; **no llegaron a alcanzar el nivel ~ exigido** they did not manage to reach the minimum level required; **la temperatura mínima fue de 15 grados** the minimum temperature was 15 degrees; **quería conseguirlo todo con el ~ esfuerzo** he wanted to achieve everything with a *o* the minimum of effort; **"tarifa mínima: 2 euros"** "minimum fare: 2 euros"; **el tamaño ~ del dibujo deberá ser de 20 x 30 centímetros** the drawing should not be less than 20 x 30 centimetres; **lo ~: es lo ~ que podemos hacer** it's the least we can do; **intente hablar lo ~ posible** try and talk as little as possible; **lo más ~** the least *o* the slightest; **el dinero no me interesa lo más ~** I'm not the least *o* the slightest bit interested in money; **los sueldos no se verán afectados en lo más ~** salaries will not be affected in the least *o* in the slightest; **precio ~** minimum price; **en un tiempo ~** in no time at all; **el microondas calienta la comida en un tiempo ~** the microwave heats up food in next to no time *o* in no time at all; **~ común denominador** lowest common denominator
2 (= *muy pequeño*) [*habitación, letra*] tiny, minute; [*detalle*] minute; [*gasto, beneficio*] minimal; **escribía con una letra mínima** his writing was tiny *o* minute; **una habitación de tamaño ~** a tiny room; **esto es sólo una mínima parte de lo que hemos gastado** this is just a tiny fraction of what we have spent; **este teléfono ocupa un espacio ~** this telephone takes up hardly any space; **me contó hasta el más ~ detalle** he told me everything in minute detail; **un vehículo de consumo ~** a vehicle with minimal fuel consumption
3 [*plazo*] **no existe un plazo ~ para entregar el trabajo** there's no set date for the work to be handed in
Ⓑ SM 1 (= *cantidad mínima*) minimum; **¿cuál es el ~?** what is the minimum?; **bajo ~s** (*Esp*) [*credibilidad, moral*] at rock bottom; [*consumo, presupuesto*] very low; **el equipo salió al campo con la moral bajo ~s** the team took to the field with their morale at rock bottom; **su credibilidad se halla bajo ~s** his credibility is at an all-time low; **con el presupuesto bajo ~s** with the budget cut back to a minimum, with a very low budget; **como ~** at least; **eso costará, como ~, 40 euros** that will cost at least 40 euros; **como ~ te he llamado cinco veces** I've phoned you at least five times; **un ~ de algo** a minimum of sth; **necesitas hacer un ~ de esfuerzo** you need to make a minimum of effort; **necesitamos un ~ de dos millones** we need a minimum of two million; **si tuviera un ~ de vergüenza no vendría más por aquí** if he had any shame at all he wouldn't come back here; **necesito un ~ de intimidad** I need a modicum of privacy; **reducir algo al ~** to keep *o* reduce sth to a minimum; **han intentado reducir los gastos al ~** they have tried to keep *o* reduce expenditure to a minimum
2 (*Fin*) record low, lowest point; **hoy se ha llegado en la bolsa al ~ anual** today the stock exchange reached this year's record low *o* lowest point ► **mínimo histórico** all-time low
3 (*Mat*) [*de una función*] minimum
4 (*Meteo*) ► **mínimo de presión** low-pressure area, trough; *ver tb* **mínima**
5 (*Caribe Aut*) choke

mínimum SM minimum

minina* SF (*Esp*) (= *pene*) willy*, peter (*EEUU***)

minino/a SM/F (= *gato*) puss, pussycat

minio SM red lead, minium

miniordenador SM minicomputer

minipíldora SF minipill

Minipimer® SM electric mixer

miniserie SF miniseries

ministerial ADJ (*de ministro, ministerio*) ministerial; **reunión ~** cabinet meeting

ministerio SM 1 (*Pol*) ministry, department (*esp EEUU*) ► **Ministerio de Asuntos Exteriores** Foreign Office, State Department (*EEUU*) ► **Ministerio de Comercio e Industria** Department of Trade and Industry ► **Ministerio de (la) Gobernación** *o* **del Interior** ≈ Home Office, Department of the Interior (*EEUU*) ► **Ministerio de Hacienda** Treasury, Treasury Department (*EEUU*) ► **Ministerio Fiscal** Attorney General's office
2 (*Jur*) **el ~ público** the Prosecution, the State Prosecutor (*EEUU*)

ministrable SMF (= *candidato*) candidate for minister

ministro/a SM/F (*en gobierno*) minister, secretary (*esp EEUU*); **primer ~** prime minister; **consejo de ~s** (= *grupo*) cabinet; (= *reunión*) cabinet meeting ► **ministro/a de Asuntos Exteriores** Foreign Secretary, Secretary of State (*EEUU*) ► **ministro/a de Hacienda** Chancellor of the Exchequer, Secretary of the Treasury (*EEUU*) ► **ministro/a de (la) Gobernación, ministro/a del Interior** Home Secretary, Secretary of the Interior (*EEUU*) ► **ministro/a en la sombra** shadow minister ► **ministro/a en visita** (*Chile*) examining magistrate ► **ministro/a portavoz** government spokesperson ► **ministro/a sin cartera** minister without portfolio

minivacaciones SFPL minibreak *sing*

minoración SF reduction, diminution

minorar ▸conjug 1a◂ VT to reduce, diminish

minoría SF minority; **estar en ~** to be in a *o* the minority; **gobernar en ~** to govern without an overall majority ► **minoría de edad** minority ► **minoría étnica** ethnic minority

minoridad SF minority (*of age*)

minorista Ⓐ ADJ retail *antes de s*
Ⓑ SMF retailer

minoritario ADJ minority *antes de s*; **gobierno ~** minority government

Minotauro SM Minotaur

minucia SF 1 (= *detalle insignificante*) trifle, insignificant detail; **describir algo con ~** to describe sth in detail; **minucias** petty details, minutiae

[2] (= *bagatela*) mere nothing

minuciosamente ADV [*limpiar*] thoroughly, meticulously; [*examinar, inspeccionar*] minutely; **analizó ~ las diferencias** he analysed the differences in minute detail; **marfiles tallados ~** delicately carved pieces of ivory

minuciosidad SF **lo limpió con ~** she cleaned it thoroughly *o* meticulously; **debes inspeccionarlo con ~** you should inspect it thoroughly; **describió la situación con ~** she described the situation in minute detail

minucioso ADJ [1] (= *meticuloso*) thorough, meticulous

[2] (= *detallado*) very detailed

minué SM minuet

minuetto SM minuet

minúscula SF small letter; (*Tip*) lower case letter; **se escribe con ~** [*la primera letra*] it is written with a small letter; [*toda una frase*] it is written in small letters *o* lower case letters; **la verdad con ~** truth with a small T

minúsculo ADJ [1] (= *muy pequeño*) tiny, minuscule

[2] (*Tip*) **letra minúscula** lower-case letter; **en letra minúscula** in lower-case letters

minusvalía SF [1] (*Med*) disability, handicap; **personas con ~** disabled people ► **minusvalía física** physical disability *o* handicap ► **minusvalía psíquica** mental disability *o* handicap

[2] (*Com*) depreciation, capital loss

minusvalidez SF disablement, disability

minusválido/a Ⓐ ADJ (*físico*) physically handicapped, physically disabled; (*psíquico*) mentally handicapped, mentally disabled

Ⓑ SM/F disabled person, handicapped person; **los ~s** the disabled ► **minusválido/a físico/a** physically handicapped person, physically disabled person ► **minusválido/a psíquico/a** mentally handicapped person, mentally disabled person

minusvalorar ▸conjug 1a◂ Ⓐ VT to undervalue, underestimate

Ⓑ **minusvalorarse** VPR to hold o.s. in low esteem, have a low opinion of o.s.

minusvalorizar ▸conjug 1f◂ VT to undervalue

minuta SF [1] [*de abogado*] lawyer's bill

[2] (= *menú*) menu

[3] (= *borrador*) rough draft, first draft

[4] (= *lista*) list, roll

[5] (*Arg*) quick meal

[6] (*Caribe, Cono Sur*) **a la ~** rolled in breadcrumbs

[7] (*Cono Sur*) (= *basura*) junk, trash; (= *tienda*) junk shop

[8] (*CAm*) (= *bebida*) flavoured ice drink

minutado SM, **minutaje** SM timing, running time

minutar ▸conjug 1a◂ VT [1] [+ *contrato*] to draft

[2] [+ *cliente*] to bill

minutario SM minute book

minutero SM (= *manecilla*) minute hand; (= *reloj*) timer

minutisa SF sweet william

minuto SM minute; **llegó al ~** she arrived one minute later; **volverá dentro de un ~** she'll be back in a minute; **a medida que pasaban los ~s** as the minutes ticked by; **guardar un ~ de silencio** to observe a minute's silence; ✦***MODISMO*** **tengo los ~s contados** I have no time to spare

miñango* SM (*Andes, Cono Sur*) bit, small piece; **hecho ~s** smashed to pieces, in smithereens

Miño SM **el (río) ~** the Miño

miñoco SM (*Andes*) grimace

miñón ADJ (*LAm*) sweet, cute

mío Ⓐ ADJ POSES mine; **es ~** it's mine; **no es amigo ~** he's no friend of mine; **¡Dios ~!** my God!, good heavens!; **¡hijo ~!** my dear boy!

Ⓑ PRON POSES [1] **el ~/la mía** mine; **éste es el ~** this one's mine; **la mía está en el armario** mine's in the cupboard; **lo ~**: **lo ~ es tuyo** what is mine is yours, what belongs to me belongs to you; **he puesto lo ~ en esta caja** I've put my stuff *o* things in this box; **lo ~ con Ana acabó hace tiempo** Ana and I finished a while ago; **lo ~ son los deportes** I'm a sports person myself; **el tenis no es lo ~** tennis is not for me, tennis is not my cup of tea *o* my thing

[2] **los ~s** (= *mis familiares*) my folks, my family; **echo de menos a los ~s** I miss my folks

[3] **la mía** (= *mi oportunidad*): **¡ésta es la mía, entraré ahora que no me ven!** now's my chance, I'll slip in now while they aren't watching!

miocardio SM myocardium (*frm*); *ver tb* **infarto**

Mioceno SM **el ~** the Miocene

miope Ⓐ ADJ short-sighted, near-sighted (*EEUU*), myopic (*frm*)

Ⓑ SMF short-sighted person, near-sighted person (*EEUU*), myopic person (*frm*)

miopía SF short-sightedness, near-sightedness (*EEUU*), myopia (*frm*)

miosis SF INV miosis, myosis

miosotis SF INV myosotis, myosote, forget-me-not

MIPS SMPL ABR (= **millones de instrucciones por segundo**) MIPS

MIR SM ABR [1] (*Esp Med*) = **Médico interno residente**

[2] (*Bol*) = **Movimiento de Izquierda Revolucionaria**

mira SF [1] (*Mil, Téc*) sight; ✦***MODISMO*** **estar con** *o* **tener la ~ puesta en algo** to have one's sights set on sth ► **mira de bombardeo** bombsight ► **mira telescópica** telescopic sight

[2] (= *intención*) aim, intention; **con la ~ de hacer algo** with the aim of doing sth; **con ~s a** with a view to; **llevar una ~ interesada** to have (only) one's own interests at heart; **tener ~s sobre algo/algn** to have designs on sth/sb

[3] **miras** (= *actitud*): **corto de ~s** narrow-minded; **amplio** *o* **ancho de ~s** (= *tolerante*) broad-minded; **de ~s estrechas** narrow-minded

[4] **estar a la ~** to be on the lookout (**de** for)

[5] (= *torre*) watchtower; (= *puesto*) lookout post

mirada SF [1] (= *forma de mirar*) look; **tiene una ~ melancólica** he has a sad look about him; **con una ~ triste** with a sad look in his eyes; **tenía la ~ penetrante** she had a penetrating gaze; **no podía resistir su ~** I couldn't resist those eyes; **con la ~ fija en el infinito** staring into space; ✦***MODISMO*** **hay ~s que matan** if looks could kill

[2] (= *acto*) (*rápida*) glance; (*detenida*) gaze; **le dirigió una ~ de sospecha** he gave her a suspicious look *o* glance, he looked *o* glanced at her suspiciously; **le echó una ~ por encima del hombro** she gave him a condescending look, she looked at him condescendingly; **era capaz de aguantarle** *o* **resistirle la ~ a cualquiera** he could outstare anybody, he could stare anybody out; **nos dirigimos una ~ de complicidad** we glanced at each other knowingly; **tuvo que aguantar las ~s compasivas de toda la familia** he had to suffer the pitying looks of the whole family; **echar una ~ de <u>reojo</u>** *o* **de <u>soslayo</u> a algo/algn** to look out of the corner of one's eye at sth/sb, cast a sidelong glance at sth/sb ► **mirada perdida**: **tenía la ~ perdida en el horizonte** she was gazing into the distance; **tenían la ~ perdida de quienes están próximos a la locura** they had the empty look of people on the verge of madness

[3] (= *vista*) **recorrió la habitación con la ~** he looked around the room; **<u>apartar</u> la ~ (de algn/algo)** to look away (from sb/sth); **sin apartar la ~ de ella** without looking away from her; **<u>bajar</u> la ~** to look down; **<u>clavar</u> la ~ en algo/algn** to fix one's eyes on sth/sb; **<u>desviar</u> la ~ (de algn/algo)** (*lit*) to look away (from sb/sth), avert one's eyes (from sb/sth); (*fig*) to turn one's back (on sb/sth); **es sólo una excusa para desviar su ~ de los verdaderos problemas** it's just an excuse to turn their backs on the real problems; **<u>dirigir</u> la ~ a** *o* **hacia algn/algo** (*lit*) to look at sb/sth; (*fig*) to turn one's attention to sb/sth; **dirigió la ~ a Rosa** he looked at Rosa; **ahora están dirigiendo su ~ hacia los más necesitados** they are now turning their attention to those most in need; **<u>echar</u> una ~ a algn/algo** (*varias veces*) to keep an eye on sb/sth, check on sb/sth; (*una sola vez*) to have a look at sb/sth; **échale una miradita al arroz de vez en cuando** keep an eye *o* check on the rice every now and then; **echa una ~ a ver si te has dejado la luz encendida** have a look to see if you've left the light on; **antes de irse a dormir les echó una ~ a los niños** before going to bed he had a look in on the children *o* he had a quick look at the children; **le echó una última ~ a la casa antes de irse** she had a *o* one last look at the house before leaving; **le deberíais echar una última ~ al examen** you should give your exam paper a final read through; **<u>levantar</u> la ~** to look up, raise one's eyes; **al vernos entrar levantó la ~** on seeing us enter, he looked up *o* raised his eyes; **no levantó la ~ del libro** he didn't take his eyes off the book; **tener la ~ <u>puesta</u> en algo** (*lit*) to have one's gaze fixed on sth; (*fig*) to be looking towards sth, have one's sights set on sth; **<u>seguir</u> algo/a algn con la ~** to follow sth/sb with one's eyes; **<u>volver</u> la ~** to look back; **salió de la casa sin volver la ~** she left the house without looking back; **si volvemos la ~ hacia atrás, nos daremos cuenta de nuestros errores** if we look back we will realize our mistakes; **volvió su ~ a Amelia** she looked round at Amelia *o* turned her eyes towards Amelia; **volvió la ~ a su izquierda** he looked round to his left, he turned his eyes to the left; *ver tb* **devorar 1**

[4] **miradas** (= *atención*): **todas las ~s estarán puestas en el jugador brasileño** all

eyes will be on the Brazilian player; **me fui, huyendo de las ~s de todo el pueblo** I left, fleeing from the prying eyes of the whole village

miradero SM [1] (= *lugar*) vantage point, lookout

[2] (= *atracción*) centre of attention, center of attention (*EEUU*)

mirado ADJ [1] (= *estimado*) **bien ~** well *o* highly thought of, highly regarded; **no estaba bien ~ que llevaran falda corta** wearing short skirts was frowned upon; **mal ~** *ver* **malmirado**

[2] (= *sensato*) sensible; (= *cauto*) cautious, careful; (= *considerado*) considerate, thoughtful; (= *educado*) well-behaved; **ser ~ en los gastos** to watch what one spends, be a careful spender

[3] (*pey*) finicky*, fussy

[4] **bien ~ ...** all things considered ..., when you think about it ...

mirador SM [1] (= *lugar de observación*) viewpoint, vantage point

[2] (= *ventana*) bay window; (= *balcón*) (enclosed) balcony

[3] (*Náut*) ► **mirador de popa** stern gallery

miraguano SM (*LAm*) (type of) kapok tree, kapok

miramiento SM [1] (= *consideración*) considerateness; (= *cortesía*) courtesy; **sin ~** without consideration

[2] (= *circunspección*) care, caution; (*pey*) (= *timidez*) timidity, excessive caution

[3] **miramientos** (= *respeto*) respect *sing*; (= *cortesías*) courtesies, attentions; **andar con ~s** to tread carefully; **sin ~s** unceremoniously

miranda†* SF **estar de ~** (= *gandulear*) to be loafing *o* lazing around; (= *no participar*) to be an onlooker

mirar ►conjug 1a◄ Ⓐ VT [1] (= *ver*) to look at; **estaba mirando la foto** she was looking at the photo; **me miró con tristeza** she looked at me sadly; **miraban boquiabiertos el nuevo aparato** they stared open-mouthed at the new machine; **~ a algn de arriba abajo** to look sb up and down; **~ algo/a algn de reojo** *o* **de través** to look at sth/sb out of the corner of one's eye; **~ fijamente algo/a algn** to gaze *o* stare at sth/sb; **~ algo por encima** to glance over sth; ✦**MODISMOS** **~ bien** *o* **con buenos ojos a algn** to approve of sb; **~ mal** *o* **con malos ojos a algn** to disapprove of sb; **de mírame y no me toques** delicate, fragile; *ver tb* **hombro**

[2] (= *observar*) to watch; **se quedó mirando cómo jugaban los niños** she stood watching the children play; **miraba los barcos** she was watching the boats; **estuvo mirando la tele todo el día** he spent all day watching TV

[3] (= *comprobar*) **le ~on la maleta en la aduana** they searched his suitcase at customs; **mira que no hierva el agua** make sure the water doesn't boil; **mira a ver lo que hace el niño** go and see *o* check what the boy's up to; **mira a ver si ha venido el taxi** (look and) see if the taxi has come; **míralo en el diccionario** look it up in the dictionary

[4] (= *pensar en*) **no mira las dificultades** he doesn't think of the difficulties; **lo hago mirando el porvenir** I'm doing it with the future in mind; **¡no gastes más, mira que no tenemos dinero!** don't spend any more, remember we've no money!; **mirándolo bien**: **bien mirado** *o* **si bien se mira** *o* **mirándolo bien, la situación no es tan grave** all in all, the situation isn't that bad, if you really think about it, the situation isn't all that bad; **bien mirado** *o* **mirándolo bien, creo que lo haré más tarde** on second thoughts, I think I'll do it later

[5] (= *ser cuidadoso con*) **mira mucho el dinero** he's very careful with money; **deberías ~ lo que gastas** you should watch what you spend; **mira mucho todos los detalles** she pays great attention to detail

[6] (*uso exclamativo*) [6·1] (*en imperativo*) **¡mira qué cuadro tan bonito!** look, what a pretty painting!; **¡mira cómo me has puesto de agua!** look, you've covered me in water!; **¡mira lo que has hecho!** (just) look what you've done!; **¡mira quién fue a hablar!** look who's talking!; **¡mira (bien) lo que haces!** watch what you do!; **¡mira con quién hablas!** just remember who you're talking to!

[6·2] (*indicando sorpresa, disgusto*) **mira que**: **¡mira que es tonto!** he's so stupid!; **¡mira que te avisé!** didn't I warn you?; **¡mira que ponerse a llover ahora!** it would have to start raining right now!

[6·3] (*indicando esperanza, temor*) **mira que si**: **¡mira que si ganas!** imagine if you win!; **¡mira que si no viene!** just suppose he doesn't come!; **¡mira que si es mentira!** just suppose it isn't true!, what if it isn't true?

[7] (*LAm*) (= *ver*) to see; **¿lo miras?** can you see it?

Ⓑ VI [1] (*con la vista*) to look; **me vio pero miró hacia otro lado** she saw me, but she looked the other way; **estaba mirando por la ventana** he was looking out of the window; **miré por el agujero** I looked through the hole; **miró alrededor para ver si veía a alguien** she looked around to see if she could see anyone; **~ de reojo** *o* **de través** to look out of the corner of one's eye

[2] (= *comprobar*) to look; **¿has mirado en el cajón?** have you looked in the drawer?

[3] (= *estar orientado hacia*) to face; **la casa mira al sur** the house faces south; **el balcón mira al jardín** the balcony looks out onto the garden

[4] (= *cuidar*) **~ por algn** to look after sb, take care of sb; **debes de ~ por tus hermanos** you should look after *o* take care of your brothers; **mira mucho por su ropa** she takes great care of her clothes; **sólo mira por sus intereses** he only looks after his own interests; **tienes que ~ por ti mismo** you have to look out for yourself

[5] (*uso exclamativo*) [5·1] (*en imperativo*) **¡mira! un ratón** look, a mouse!; **mira, yo creo que ...** look, I think that ...; **mira, déjame en paz ahora** look, just leave me alone now; **mire usted, yo no tengo por qué aguantar esto** look here, I don't have to put up with this

[5·2] (*indicando sorpresa, admiración*) **mira si**: **¡mira si estaría buena la sopa que todos repitieron!** the soup was so good that everyone had seconds!; **¡mira si es listo el niño!** what a clever boy he is!; ✦**MODISMO** **¡(pues) mira por dónde ...!** you'll never believe it!

[6] **~ a** (= *proponerse*) to aim at; **este proyecto mira a mejorar la calidad del agua** this project is aimed at improving water quality

[7] (*frm*) **por lo que mira a** as for, as regards

Ⓒ **mirarse** VPR [1] (*reflexivo*) to look at o.s.; **~se al** *o* **en el espejo** to look at o.s. in the mirror

[2] (*recíproco*) to look at each other *o* one another; **Juan y María se ~on asombrados** Juan and María looked at each other *o* one another in amazement; **los amantes se ~on a los ojos** the lovers looked into each other's eyes

[3] **se mire por donde se mire** whichever way you look at it

[4] **~se mucho** *o* **muy bien de hacer algo** to think carefully before doing sth

mirasol SM sunflower

miríada SF myriad; **~(s) de moscas** myriads of flies, a myriad of flies

mirilla SF (*en puerta*) peephole, spyhole; (*Fot*) viewfinder

miriñaque SM [1] (*Hist*) crinoline, hoop skirt

[2] (*Cono Sur Ferro*) cowcatcher

[3] (*Caribe, Méx*) (= *tela*) thin cotton cloth

miriópodo SM myriapod

miristiquívoro ADJ myristicivorous

mirlarse ►conjug 1a◄ VPR to put on airs, act important

mirlo SM [1] (*Orn*) blackbird ► **mirlo blanco** (*fig*) rare bird

[2] (= *presuntuosidad*) self-importance, pompousness

[3] (⁑) (= *lengua*) tongue; ✦**MODISMO** **achantar el ~** to shut one's trap*

mirobrigense Ⓐ ADJ of/from Ciudad Rodrigo

Ⓑ SMF native/inhabitant of Ciudad Rodrigo; **los ~s** the people of Ciudad Rodrigo

mirón/ona* Ⓐ ADJ nosey*, curious

Ⓑ SM/F (= *espectador*) onlooker; (= *mirón*) nosey-parker*; (= *voyer*) voyeur, peeping Tom; **estar de ~** to stand around watching, stand around doing nothing; **ir de ~** to go along just to watch; ✦**MODISMO** **los mirones son de piedra** those watching the game are not allowed to speak

mironismo* SM voyeurism

mirra SF [1] (= *resina*) myrrh

[2] (*Caribe*) (*trocito*) small piece

mirtilo SM bilberry, whortleberry

mirto SM myrtle

mis SF = **miss**

misa SF mass; **vamos a ~ todos los domingos** we go to mass every Sunday; **dijeron/celebraron ~ en la catedral** they said/celebrated mass in the cathedral; ✦**MODISMOS** **como en ~**: **los niños estaban como en ~** the children were really quiet; **decir ~**: **¡por mí, que digan ~!** let them say what they like!; **estar en ~ y repicando** to have one's cake and eat it; **ir a ~**: **lo que yo diga va a ~** what I say goes; **no saber de la ~ la media** *o* **la mitad** not to know anything about it, not to have a clue; **ser como ~ de pobre** to last all too short a time ► **misa cantada** sung mass ► **misa de campaña** open-air mass ► **misa de corpore insepulto**, **misa de cuerpo presente** funeral mass ► **misa de difuntos** requiem mass ► **misa del alba** early morning mass ► **misa del domingo** Sunday mass ► **misa del gallo** midnight mass (*on Christmas Eve*) ► **misa mayor** high mass ► **misa negra** black mass ► **misa rezada** low mass ► **misa solemne** high mass

misacantano SM (= *sacerdote*) ordained priest; (*en primera misa*) *priest saying his first mass*

misal SM missal
misantropía SF misanthropy
misantrópico ADJ misanthropic
misántropo/a SM/F misanthrope, misanthropist
misario SM acolyte (*frm*), altar boy
miscelánea SF [1] (*frm*) (= *mezcla*) miscellany
[2] (*Méx*) (= *tienda*) corner shop
misceláneo ADJ miscellaneous
misera SF lobster
miserable Ⓐ ADJ [1] (= *tacaño*) mean, stingy; (= *avaro*) miserly
[2] [*sueldo*] miserable, paltry
[3] (= *vil*) vile, despicable
[4] [*lugar, habitación*] squalid, wretched
[5] (= *desdichado*) wretched
Ⓑ SMF [1] (= *desgraciado*) wretch
[2] (= *canalla*) swine, wretch; **¡miserable!** you miserable wretch!
miserando ADJ (*esp LAm*) pitiful
miseria SF [1] (= *pobreza*) poverty, destitution; **caer en la ~** to fall into poverty; **vivir en la ~** to live in poverty
[2] (= *insignificancia*) **una ~** a pittance
[3] (= *tacañería*) meanness, stinginess
[4] (†) (= *parásitos*) fleas *pl*, lice *pl*; **estar lleno de ~** to be covered with vermin
misericordia SF compassion, mercy; **Señor, ten ~ de nosotros** (*Rel*) Lord, have mercy upon us
misericordioso ADJ merciful; **Alá es ~** Allah is merciful; **mentira misericordiosa** white lie; **obras misericordiosas** charitable works
misero* ADJ churchy, fond of going to church
mísero ADJ [1] (= *tacaño*) mean, stingy; (= *avaro*) miserly
[2] [*sueldo*] miserable, paltry
[3] (= *vil*) vile, despicable
[4] [*lugar, habitación*] squalid, wretched
[5] (= *desdichado*) wretched
misérrimo ADJ SUPERL *ver* **mísero**
Misiá* SF (*Cono Sur*), **Misia*** SF (*Cono Sur*) (*tratamiento*) Missis*, Missus*; **~ Eugenia** Miss Eugenia
misil SM missile ► **misil antiaéreo** anti-aircraft missile ► **misil antimisil** anti-missile missile ► **misil autodirigido** guided missile ► **misil balístico** ballistic missile ► **misil buscador del calor** heat-seeking missile ► **misil de alcance medio** medium-range missile ► **misil (de) crucero** cruise missile ► **misil tierra-aire** ground-to-air missile
misilístico ADJ missile *antes de s*
misión SF [1] (= *cometido*) mission; (= *tarea*) task; (*Pol*) assignment ► **misión de buena voluntad** goodwill mission ► **misión humanitaria** humanitarian mission ► **misión investigadora** fact-finding mission
[2] (= *delegación*) mission ► **misión comercial** trade mission ► **misión diplomática** diplomatic mission
[3] **misiones** (*Rel*) overseas missions, missionary work *sing*
misional ADJ missionary
misionero/a SM/F missionary; **postura** *o* **posición del ~** missionary position
Misisipí SM Mississippi
misiva SF missive
miskito SM Miskito

mismamente* ADV (= *sólo*) only, just; (= *textualmente*) literally; (= *incluso*) even; (= *en realidad*) really, actually; **~ anoche estuve allí** I was there only *o* just last night; **~ cerca de mi casa hay uno** there's actually one right near my house
mismísimo Ⓐ ADJ SUPERL very (same); **con mis ~s ojos** with my own eyes; **es usted el ~ diablo** you're the devil incarnate; **este niño es el ~ demonio** this child is a real little devil; **estuvo el ~ obispo** the bishop himself was there; **es el ~ que yo perdí** it's the very (same) one I lost
Ⓑ SMPL **los ~s: estoy hasta los ~s*** I'm up to here with it*

▼ **mismo** Ⓐ ADJ [1] (= *igual*) same; **el ~ coche** the same car; **estos dos vestidos son de la misma talla** these two dresses are the same size; **respondieron al ~ tiempo** they answered together, they answered at the same time; **el ~ ... que** the same ... as; **lleva la misma falda que ayer** she's wearing the same skirt as yesterday; **tengo el ~ dinero que tú** I've got the same amount of money as you; **tiene el ~ pelo que su padre** his hair's the same as his father's
[2] (*reflexivo*) **hablaba consigo ~** he was talking to himself; **lo hizo por sí ~** he did it by himself; **perjudicarse a sí ~** to harm oneself; *ver tb* **valer C2**
[3] (*enfático*) [3·1] (*relativo a personas*) **yo ~ lo vi** I saw it myself, I saw it with my own eyes; **estuvo el ~ ministro** the minister himself was there; **ni ella misma lo sabe** she doesn't even know herself; **ella misma se hace los vestidos** she makes her own dresses; **—¿quién responde? —a ver, tú ~** "who's going to answer?" — "well, why don't you answer yourself!"
[3·2] (*relativo a cosas*) **—¿cuál quieres? —ese ~** "which one do you want?" — "that one there"; **—¡es un canalla! —eso ~ pienso yo** "he's a swine!" — "my thoughts exactly"; **viven en el ~ centro de Córdoba** they live right in the centre of Córdoba; **en todos los países europeos, España misma incluida** in all European countries, including Spain itself; **Ana es la generosidad misma** Ana is generosity itself, Ana is the epitome of generosity; **en ese ~ momento** at that very moment; **por eso ~: era pobre y por eso ~ su ascenso tiene más mérito** he was poor and for that very reason his promotion is all the more commendable
[4] (*como pronombre*) **es el ~ que nos alquilaron el año pasado** it's the same one they rented us last year; **—¿y qué edad tienes tú? —la misma que él** "and how old are you?" — "I'm the same age as him"; **no es la misma desde su divorcio** she hasn't been the same since her divorce; **—¿es usted la señorita Sánchez? —¡la misma!** "are you Miss Sánchez?" — "I am indeed!"; **leyó el texto pero no reveló el origen del ~** he read the text without revealing its source; ✦***MODISMO*** **estamos en las mismas** we're no better off than before, we're no further forward
[5] **lo mismo** [5·1] (= *la misma cosa*) the same (thing); **los políticos siempre dicen lo ~** politicians always say the same (thing); **hizo lo ~ que ayer** he did the same as yesterday; **¡hombre, no es lo ~!** it's not the same (thing) at all!; **—son unos canallas —lo ~ digo yo** "they're swine" — "that's (exactly) what I say"; **—¡enhorabuena! —lo ~ digo** "congratulations!" — "likewise" *o* "the same to you"; **—eres un sinvergüenza —lo ~ te digo** "you're completely shameless" — "you too" *o* "so are you"; **nos contó lo ~ de siempre** she told us the usual story; **—¿qué desea de beber? —lo ~ (de antes), por favor** "what would you like to drink?" — "(the) same again, please"; **cuando le interese a él, o lo que es lo ~, nunca** when it suits him, in other words never; **por lo ~: no es inteligente y por lo ~ tiene que estudiar el doble** he's not clever, which is exactly why he has to study twice as hard; **lo ~ que: le dijo lo ~ que yo** she told him the same thing *o* the same as she told me; **le multaron por lo ~ que a mi** she got fined for the same thing as me; **no es lo ~ hablar en público que en privado** it's not the same thing to talk in public as to talk in private
[5·2] **dar lo ~: da lo ~** it's all the same, it makes no difference; **me da lo ~** ◊ **lo ~ me da** I don't mind, it's all the same to me; **da lo ~ que vengas hoy o mañana** it doesn't matter whether you come today or tomorrow
[5·3] (*) (= *a lo mejor*) **lo ~ no vienen** maybe they won't come; **no lo sé todavía, pero lo ~ voy** I don't know yet, but I may well come; **pídeselo, lo ~ te lo presta** ask him for it; you never know, he may lend it to you
[5·4] **lo ~ que** (= *al igual que*): **en Europa, lo ~ que en América** in Europe, (just) as in America; **lo ~ que usted es médico yo soy ingeniero** just as you are a doctor, so I am an engineer; **suspendí el examen, lo ~ que Íñigo** I failed the exam, just like Íñigo; **yo, lo ~ que mi padre, odio el baloncesto** I hate basketball, just like my father; **nos divertimos lo ~ que si hubiéramos ido al baile** we had just as good a time as if we had gone to the dance
[5·5] **lo ~ ... que** (= *tanto ... como*): **lo ~ te puede criticar que alabar** she's just as likely to criticize you as to praise you; **lo ~ puede durar una hora que dos** it could last anywhere between one and two hours; **aquí lo ~ te venden una vajilla que una bicicleta** they'll sell you anything here, from a dinner service to a bicycle; **lo ~ si viene que si no viene** whether he comes or not
Ⓑ ADV (*enfático*) **delante ~ de la casa** right in front of the house; **en la capital ~ hay barrios de chabolas** even in the capital there are shanty towns; **ahora ~** (= *inmediatamente*) right away *o* now; (= *hace un momento*) just now; **hazlo ahora ~** do it right away *o* now; **ahora ~ acabo de hablar con él** I've just been talking to him, I was talking to him only a moment ago; **aquí ~: —¿dónde lo pongo? —aquí ~** "where shall I put it?" — "right here"; **aquí ~ acampamos el año pasado** this is the exact spot where we camped last year; **así ~: —¿cómo quieres el filete? —así ~ está bien** "how would you like your steak?" — "it's fine as it is"; **ayer ~** only yesterday; **hoy ~: he llegado hoy ~** I just arrived today; **me dijo que me contestarían hoy ~** he told me they'd give me an answer today; **mañana ~: llegará mañana ~** he's arriving tomorrow, no less; **me contestarán mañana ~** they'll give me an answer tomorrow

➤ LENGUA Y USO: **mismo** A1 32.3, 32.4 A5 32.4, 34.5

misogamia SF misogamy
misógamo/a SM/F misogamist
misoginia SF misogyny
misógino SM misogynist
miss [mis] SF beauty queen; **concurso de ~es** beauty contest ► **Miss España 1997** Miss Spain 1997
míster SM 1 (*Dep*) trainer, coach
2 († *hum*) (= *británico*) (any) Briton
misterio SM 1 (= *incógnita*) mystery; **no hay ~** there's no mystery about it; **ahora conozco mejor los ~s del país** now I know more of the country's secrets; **una novela de ~** a mystery (story)
2 (= *secreto*) secrecy; **¿a qué viene tanto ~?** why all this secrecy?, why are you being so mysterious?; **obrar con ~** to act in secret
3 (*Teat*) mystery play
misteriosamente ADV mysteriously
misterioso ADJ mysterious
mística SF, **misticismo** SM mysticism
místico/a Ⓐ ADJ mystic(al)
Ⓑ SM/F mystic
mistificación SF mystification
mistificar ▸conjug 1g◂ VT to mystify
mistongo* ADJ (*Cono Sur*) wretched, miserable
Misuri SM Missouri
mita (*Andes, Cono Sur Hist*) SF (= *dinero*) *tax paid by Indians*; (= *trabajo*) *common service to landlord*
mitad SF 1 half; **basta tomar la ~ de un comprimido** half a tablet is enough; **me queda la ~** I have half left; **a ~ de precio** half-price; **reducir en una ~** to cut by half, halve; (*Culin*) to reduce by half; **~ (y) ~** half-and-half; **paguemos ~ y ~** let's go halves; **es ~ blanco y ~ rojo** it's half white and half red; ✦*MODISMO* **mi otra ~** my other half, my better half
2 (*Dep*) half; **la primera ~** the first half
3 (= *centro*) middle; **a ~ de la comida** in the middle of the meal, halfway through the meal; **está a ~ de camino entre Madrid y Barcelona** it's halfway between Madrid and Barcelona; **en ~ de la calle** in the middle of the street; **el depósito está a la ~** the tank is half empty; **ya estamos a la ~** we're halfway there; **hacia la ~ de la película** about halfway through the film; **atravesar de ~ a ~** to pierce right through; **cortar por la ~** to cut in half; **corta las uvas por la ~** cut the grapes in half; **doblado por la ~** folded in half; ✦*MODISMO* **me parte por la ~** it upsets my plans
mítico ADJ mythical
mitificar ▸conjug 1g◂ VT to mythologize, convert into a myth
mitigación SF mitigation (*frm*); (= *de dolor*) relief; [*de sed*] quenching
mitigar ▸conjug 1h◂ VT (*gen*) to mitigate (*frm*); [+ *dolor*] to relieve, ease; [+ *sed*] to quench; [+ *ira*] to calm, appease; [+ *temores*] to allay; [+ *calor*] to reduce; [+ *soledad*] to alleviate, relieve
mitin SM 1 (*Pol*) rally
2 (= *discurso*) political speech; **dar un ~** to make a speech
mitinear ▸conjug 1a◂ VI to make a (political) speech; (*pey*) to make a rabble-rousing speech
mitinero /a Ⓐ ADJ demagogic, rabble-rousing
Ⓑ SM/F demagogue, rabble-rouser
mitinesco ADJ rabble-rousing
mito SM myth; **este hombre es un ~ del cine** this man is a film legend
mitología SF mythology
mitológico ADJ mythological
mitómano/a SM/F 1 (= *idólatra*) mythomaniac
2 (*Psic*) person who exaggerates
mitón SM mitten
mitote SM (*Méx*) 1 (*Hist*) Aztec ritual/dance
2 (= *pelea*) brawl
3 (*) (= *jaleo*) uproar
4 (*) (= *charla*) chat; **estar en el ~** to have a chat
Mitra SM Mithras
mitra SF 1 (= *gorro*) mitre, miter (*EEUU*)
2 (= *obispado*) bishopric; (= *arzobispado*) archbishopric
mitrado SM bishop, prelate
mitraico ADJ Mithraic
mitraísmo SM Mithraism
mítulo SM mussel
mixomatosis SF INV myxomatosis
Mixteca SF (*Méx*) southern Mexico
mixteco SM **el ~** (*Méx Hist*) (= *pueblo*) the Mixtecs; (= *civilización*) Mixtec civilization
mixtificar ▸conjug 1g◂ VT = **mistificar**
mixtión SF (*frm*) mixture
mixto Ⓐ ADJ (= *mezclado*) mixed; [*comité*] joint; [*empresa*] joint
Ⓑ SM 1 (= *sandwich*) *(toasted) cheese and ham sandwich*
2 (= *fósforo*) match
3 (*Mil*) explosive compound
4 (*Ferro*) passenger and goods train
mixtolobo SM Alsatian (dog)
mixtura SF (*frm*) mixture
mixturar ▸conjug 1a◂ VT (*frm*) to mix
Mk ABR (= **Marco**) Mk
ml ABR (= **mililitro(s)**) ml
MLN SM ABR (*LAm*) = **Movimiento de Liberación Nacional**
mm ABR (= **milímetro(s)**) mm
M.N. ABR, **m/n** ABR (*LAm*) = **moneda nacional**
mnemotécnica SF, **mnemónica** SF mnemonics *sing*
mnemotécnico ADJ mnemonic
Mnez. ABR = **Martínez**
MNR SM ABR (*Bol*) = **Movimiento Nacionalista Revolucionario**
M.º ABR 1 (*Pol*) (= **Ministerio**) Min
2 (*Escol*) = **Maestro**
m/o ABR (*Com*) = **mi orden**
moai SM (*pl* **moais**) (*Chile*) Easter Island statue
moaré SM moiré
mobiliario SM (= *muebles*) furniture ► **mobiliario auxiliar** small pieces of furniture *pl* ► **mobiliario de cocina** (= *armarios*) kitchen units *pl* ► **mobiliario de cuarto de baño** bathroom fittings *pl* ► **mobiliario de oficina** office furniture ► **mobiliario sanitario** sanitary ware, bathroom fittings *pl* ► **mobiliario urbano** street furniture
moblaje SM = **mobiliario**
MOC SM ABR (*Esp*) = **Movimiento de Objeción de Conciencia**
moca[1] SM (*Culin*) mocha
moca[2] SF (*Méx*) coffee-flavoured cake/biscuit
moca[3] SF (= *barrizal*) quagmire, muddy place
mocarro* SM snot*
mocasín SM moccasin
mocear† ▸conjug 1a◂ VI to play around, live a bit wildly, sow one's wild oats
mocedad† SF 1 (= *juventud*) youth; **en mis ~es** in my youth, in my young days
2 **mocedades** (= *travesuras*) youthful pranks; (= *vida licenciosa*) wild living *sing*; **pasar las ~es** to sow one's wild oats
moceril† ADJ youthful
mocerío† SM young people *pl*, lads and lasses *pl*
mocero† ADJ (= *libertino*) rakish, loose-living; (= *mujeriego*) fond of the girls
mocetón/ona† SM/F strapping youth/girl
mocha‡ SF (*Esp*) nut*, noggin (*EEUU**)
mochales* ADJ (*Esp*) **estar ~** to be nuts *o* crazy*; **estar ~ por algn** to be nuts *o* crazy about sb*
mochar ▸conjug 1a◂ VT 1 (*LAm*) (= *cortar*) to chop off (clumsily), hack off
2 (*Andes**) (= *despedir*) to fire*, sack*
3 (*Cono Sur*) (= *robar*) to pinch*, nick*
4 = **desmochar**
moche SM = **troche**
mochila SF 1 rucksack, knapsack, backpack; (*Mil*) pack; **turistas de ~** backpackers; **viajar en plan de ~** to backpack; ✦*MODISMO* **tener algo casi en la ~*** to have sth almost in the bag* ► **mochila portabebés** baby-carrier, baby-sling
2 [*de bicicleta*] pannier
3 (*Cono Sur*) (= *cartera*) satchel
mochilear ▸conjug 1a◂ VI to backpack, go backpacking
mochilero/a SM/F backpacker
mocho/a Ⓐ ADJ 1 (= *desafilado*) blunt, short
2 [*árbol*] lopped, pollarded; [*vaca*] hornless, polled; [*torre*] flat-topped; [*muñón*] stubby
3 (= *mutilado*) mutilated; (*Caribe*) (= *manco*) one-armed
4 (*Andes*) (= *grande*) big, huge
5 (*Méx*) (= *reaccionario*) reactionary; (= *beato*) sanctimonious
Ⓑ SM/F 1 (*CAm**) (= *huérfano*) orphan
2 (*Méx*) (= *reaccionario*) reactionary; (= *beato*) sanctimonious person
Ⓒ SM 1 [*de utensilio*] blunt end, thick end; [*de cigarrillo*] butt
2 (*) (= *carga*) = **mochuelo 2**
3 (*Andes, Caribe**) (= *caballo*) nag
mochuelo SM 1 (*Orn*) (*tb* **~ común**) little owl; ✦*MODISMO* **cada ~ a su olivo** let's all go back to our own homes
2 ✦*MODISMOS* **cargar con el ~** to get landed with it; **colgar** *o* **echar el ~ a algn** to lumber sb with the job*; (= *culpa*) to make sb carry the can*; (= *crimen*) to frame sb
moción SF 1 (*Parl*) motion; **hacer** *o* **presentar una ~** to propose *o* table a motion ► **moción compuesta** composite motion ► **moción de censura** motion of censure, censure motion ► **moción de confianza** vote of confidence
2 (= *movimiento*) motion
mocionante SMF (*CAm, Méx*) proposer (of a motion)
mocionar ▸conjug 1a◂ VT (*CAm, Méx*) to move, propose
mocito/a† Ⓐ ADJ very young
Ⓑ SM/F youngster; **mocitas casaderas** girls

of marriageable age; **está hecha una mocita** she's a very grown-up young lady

moco SM [1] mucus, snot*; **limpiarse los ~s** to blow one's nose; **sorberse los ~s** to sniff; **tener ~s** to have a runny nose; ✦*MODISMOS* **llorar a ~ tendido** to cry one's eyes out; **soltar el ~** to burst into tears; **tirarse el ~*** (= *mentir*) to lie; (= *exagerar*) to exaggerate, shoot a line*; (= *jactarse*) to brag
[2] (*Orn*) crest; ✦*MODISMO* **no es ~ de pavo** (= *es importante*) it's no trifle, it's not to be sneezed at; (= *es grave*) you can't laugh this one off
[3] (= *mecha*) snuff, burnt wick; (= *cera derretida*) candle drippings *pl*; **a ~ de candil** by candlelight
[4] (*Téc*) slag

mocoso/a* SM/F brat; **ese ~ no tiene derecho a opinar** that little brat has no right to give his opinion; **no puedes salir solo porque eres un ~** you can't go out on your own because you're just a kid; **un ~ de 19 años** a snotty-nosed youth of 19*

moda SF fashion; **la ~ de primavera** spring fashion; **el rap es la última ~** rap is the latest craze *o* fashion; **en los noventa llegó la ~ del acid-jazz** in the nineties acid-jazz became fashionable *o* trendy*; **la ~ esa de salir tarde por la noche** that habit of going out late at night; **ha vuelto la ~ de la minifalda** mini-skirts are back in (fashion) again; **es sólo una ~ pasajera** it's just a passing fad; **a la ~** fashionable; **un sombrero a la ~** a fashionable hat; **un vestido a la ~ de París** a dress in the Paris fashion *o* style; **tienes que ponerte** *o* **vestirte un poco más a la ~** you should try and dress a bit more fashionably; **siempre va vestida a la última ~** she always dresses in the latest fashion; **estar de ~** to be in fashion, be fashionable, be in*, be all the rage*, be trendy*; **los vaqueros ajustados están muy de ~** tight jeans are really fashionable *o* in fashion, tight jeans are all the rage *o* really trendy *o* really in*; **esa teoría está muy de ~ ahora** that theory is very trendy* *o* fashionable at the moment; **pasado de ~** out of fashion, old-fashioned, outdated, out*; **pasarse de ~** to go out of fashion; **ponerse de ~** to become fashionable, get trendy*; **esta zona se está poniendo muy de ~** this area is becoming very fashionable, this area is getting very trendy*; *ver tb* **imponer A3**

modal ADJ modal

modales SMPL manners; **te lo daré si lo pides con buenos ~** I'll give it to you if you ask nicely *o* politely

modalidad SF [1] (= *tipo*) form, type; **una nueva ~ de contrato** a new form *o* type of contract ► **modalidad de pago** (*Com*) method of payment
[2] (*Dep*) category; **es campeón de Europa en la ~ de cross-country** he's the European champion in the cross-country category; **ha ganado una medalla en la ~ de salto de altura** he won a medal in the high-jump
[3] (*Ling, Fil*) modality
[4] (*Inform*) mode ► **modalidad de texto** text mode

modelado SM modelling

modelador(a) SM/F modeller

modelaje SM modelling

modelar ▸conjug 1a◂ Ⓐ VT (= *dar forma a*) to shape, form; [*escultor*] to sculpt; [*alfarero*] to model; **la vida nos modela** life moulds *o* (*EEUU*) molds us; **~ el futuro** to shape the future
Ⓑ **modelarse** VPR **~se sobre algn** to model o.s. on sb

modélicamente ADV in a model *o* an exemplary fashion

modélico ADJ model, exemplary

modelismo SM modelling, model-making

modelista SMF model-maker, modeller

modelización SF modelling, creation of models ► **modelización cognoscitiva** cognitive modelling ► **modelización informática** computer modelling ► **modelización matemática** mathematical modelling

modelizar ▸conjug 1f◂ VT to model, make a model of

modelo Ⓐ SM [1] (= *tipo*) model; **se fabrica en varios ~s** it comes in several models; **un coche último ~** the latest-model car
[2] (= *ejemplo*) **presentar algo como ~** to hold sth up as a model; **servir de ~** to serve as a model; **tomar por ~** to take as a model; **~ de maridos** model husband; **~ de vida** lifestyle, way of life ► **modelo a escala** scale model ► **modelo estándar** standard model
[3] (= *patrón*) pattern; (*para hacer punto*) pattern
[4] (= *prenda*) model, design; **un ~ de Valentino** a Valentino model *o* design
Ⓑ SMF (*Arte, Fot, Moda*) model; **desfile de ~s** fashion show; **servir de ~ a un pintor** to sit *o* pose for a painter ► **modelo de alta costura** fashion model, haute couture model ► **modelo de portada** cover girl
Ⓒ ADJ INV (= *ejemplar*) model, exemplary; **cárcel ~** model prison; **niño ~** model child

módem SM (*pl* **módems**) modem

moderación SF [1] (= *mesura*) moderation; **le recomiendo ~ en la comida** I recommend you (to) eat in moderation; **con ~** [*actuar*] with restraint; [*beber, comer*] in moderation; [*crecer*] moderately; **fume con ~** smoke in moderation; **deberías hablar con ~** you should speak in a moderate tone
[2] (*Econ*) **ha sido necesaria una ~ del gasto** we have had to cut *o* reduce expenses ► **moderación salarial** wage restraint
[3] [*de debate, coloquio*] **la ~ del debate correrá a cargo de ...** the debate will be chaired by ...

moderadamente ADV moderately

moderado ADJ moderate; **un candidato de izquierda moderada** a moderate left-wing candidate; **es muy ~ en la expresión** he is very moderate in tone; **vientos de ~s a fuertes** moderate to strong winds

moderador(a) Ⓐ ADJ [*papel, poder*] moderating
Ⓑ SM/F [1] (*en un debate, coloquio*) moderator, chairperson; (*TV*) presenter
[2] (*Pol*) moderator; **el ministro actuó de ~ en las conversaciones** the minister acted as a moderator in the talks
Ⓒ SM (*Fís*) moderator

moderar ▸conjug 1a◂ Ⓐ VT [1] (= *controlar*) [1.1] [+ *impulsos, emociones*] to restrain, control; [+ *violencia, deseo*] to curb, control; [+ *ambición, opiniones, actitud*] to moderate; **lo convencieron para que ~a su postura** they persuaded him to moderate his position; **he tenido que ~ mis aspiraciones** I've had to lower my sights
[1.2] [+ *palabras, lenguaje, tono*] to tone down, mind; **ambos líderes han ido moderando su lenguaje** both leaders have gradually toned down their language; **por favor, caballero, modere sus palabras** please, sir, mind your language; **moderen su lenguaje en este tribunal** I will not have such language in court
[2] (= *reducir*) [+ *gastos, consumo*] to cut, reduce; [+ *velocidad*] to reduce; [+ *tensión*] to ease; **medidas para ~ la inflación** measures to curb *o* cut *o* reduce inflation; **modere su velocidad** reduce your speed, slow down; *ver tb* **marcha 3**
[3] [+ *debate, coloquio*] to chair, moderate; **la mesa redonda fue moderada por Jesús Sánchez** the round table was chaired by Jesús Sánchez
Ⓑ **moderarse** VPR [1] [*persona*] to restrain o.s., control o.s.; **prometo ~me más la próxima vez** I promise to restrain *o* control myself a bit more next time; **iba a decir una grosería, pero me ~é** I was going to say a rude word but I won't; **tuvo que ~se en sus palabras** he had to tone down his language; **hemos tenido que ~nos un poco en los gastos** we've had to cut down our spending a little
[2] [*inflación, precio*] **se están moderando los precios** prices are being kept in check *o* being held back; **la inflación se moderó relativamente** inflation slowed slightly

modernamente ADV (= *actualmente*) nowadays, in modern times; (= *recientemente*) recently

modernez* SF modernity

modernidad SF modernity

modernismo SM modernism

modernista Ⓐ ADJ modernist(ic)
Ⓑ SMF modernist

modernización SF modernization

modernizador/a Ⓐ ADJ modernizing
Ⓑ SM/F modernizer

modernizar ▸conjug 1f◂ Ⓐ VT to modernize
Ⓑ **modernizarse** VPR to modernize, move with the times

moderno/a Ⓐ ADJ [1] (= *actual*) modern; **una revista dirigida a la mujer moderna** a magazine aimed at the modern woman, a magazine for the woman of today; **siempre va vestida muy moderna** she always wears very trendy clothes*, she always dresses very trendily*; **tiene un equipo de música muy ~** he's got a very up-to-date hi-fi; **le gusta todo lo ~** he likes all things modern; **tienes unos abuelos muy ~s** your grandparents are very with it*; **a la moderna**† in the modern way
[2] (*Hist*) modern; **la edad moderna** the modern period
Ⓑ SM/F trendy*

modestamente ADV [1] (= *humildemente*) modestly; **—no estoy de acuerdo —dijo ~** "I don't agree," he said modestly; **yo creo, ~, que están equivocados** in my humble opinion, they are wrong; **contribuyeron ~ a la causa** they contributed to the cause in a modest way
[2] (= *sin lujo*) modestly; **~ vestido** modestly dressed; **vivía ~** he lived modestly

modestia SF [1] (= *humildad*) modesty; **~ aparte, no soy mal cocinero** though I say so myself *o* (*frm*) modesty aside, I'm not a bad cook; **con ~** modestly; **vive con ~** he lives modestly; **le respondió con ~** she answered modestly; **falsa ~** false modesty
[2] (= *escasez*) **con ~ de medios** with quite limited resources; **pese a la ~ de sus recursos económicos** despite her limited means
[3] (= *falta de lujo*) modesty; **me sorprendió la ~ de su casa** I was surprised by how humble *o* modest his house was
[4] (†) (= *recato*) modesty

modesto ADJ [1] (= *humilde*) modest; **no seas tan ~** don't be so modest; **era hijo de un ~ contable** he was the son of a modest accountant; **en mi modesta opinión** in my humble opinion
[2] (= *de poca importancia*) modest; **vivía de un sueldo ~** he lived on a modest salary; **nuestra modesta aportación a la causa** our modest *o* humble contribution to the cause; **un ~ paso hacia la paz** a modest step towards peace
[3] (= *sin lujo*) modest; **se alojaron en una modesta pensión** they stayed in a modest guesthouse; **visten de forma muy modesta** they dress very modestly
[4] (†) (= *recatado*) [*mujer*] modest

modex SM (*Caribe*) press-on sanitary towel

modicidad SF (*frm*) reasonableness, moderateness

módico ADJ [*precio*] reasonable, modest; [*suma*] modest

modificable ADJ modifiable, that can be modified; **los precios son ~s** prices are subject to change

modificación SF (*en producto, vehículo*) modification; (*en texto*) change, alteration; (*en precio*) change ► **modificación de (la) conducta** behaviour modification; **técnicas de ~ de conducta** behaviour modification techniques

modificar ▸conjug 1g◂ VT [+ *producto, vehículo*] to modify; [+ *texto*] to change, alter; [+ *vida*] to change

modismo SM idiom

modistilla SF seamstress

modisto/a SM/F (= *sastre*) dressmaker; [*de alta costura*] fashion designer, couturier ► **modisto/a de sombreros** milliner

modo SM [1] (= *manera*) way, manner (*frm*); **los han distribuido del siguiente ~** they have been distributed in the following way *o* (*frm*) manner; **¿no hay otro ~ de hacerlo?** isn't there another way of doing it?; **no me gusta su ~ de actuar** I don't like the way he does things; **de un ~ u otro** one way or another; **a mi ~ de pensar** *o* **ver** in my view, the way I see it ► **modo de empleo** instructions for use ► **modo de gobierno** form of government ► **modo de producción** mode of production ► **modo de vida** way of life; → MANERA, FORMA, MODO
[2] (*locuciones*) **a mi/tu ~** (in) my/your (own) way; **cada uno lo interpreta a su ~** everyone interprets it in his or her own way; **a ~ de** as; **utilizó una bolsa a ~ de maleta** she used a bag as a suitcase; **a ~ de ejemplo/respuesta** by way of example/reply; **en ~ alguno** = **de ningún modo**; **en cierto ~** in a way, to a certain extent; **de cualquier ~** (*antes de verbo*) anyway, in any case; (= *después de verbo*) anyhow; **de cualquier ~, ahora tenemos que irnos** we have to go now anyway *o* in any case; **hazlo de cualquier ~** do it anyway you like, do it anyhow, do it any old how*; **de ~** (+ *ADJ*): **tenemos que actuar de ~ coherente** we must act consistently; **eso nos afectará de ~ directo** this will have a direct effect on us, this will affect us directly; **el accidente influyó de ~ negativo en el niño** the accident had a negative effect on the child; **de ese ~** (*antes de verbo*) (in) this way; (*después de verbo*) like that; **de ese ~ no habrá problemas** this way there won't be any problems; **no hables de ese ~** don't talk like that; **grosso ~** broadly speaking; **ésa fue, grosso ~, la contestación que nos dio** broadly speaking, that was the answer he gave us; **de igual ~** = **del mismo modo**; **de mal ~** rudely; **me lo pidió de muy mal ~** he asked me for it very rudely; **del mismo ~** in the same way; **todos van vestidos del mismo ~** they are all dressed the same *o* in the same way; **del mismo ~ sucedió con los agricultores** the same thing happened with the farmers; **del mismo ~ que** in the same way as *o* that, just as; **de ningún ~**: **no quiero de ningún ~ implicarla en esto** I don't want to involve her in this in any way; **no puedo permitir eso de ningún ~** there's no way I can allow that; **no se parece de ningún ~ a lo que habíamos imaginado** it's nothing like we had imagined; **¡de ningún ~!** certainly not!, no way!*; **de todos ~s** anyway, all the same, in any case; **aunque no me dejes, me iré de todos ~s** even if you don't let me, I'll go anyway *o* all the same *o* in any case; **aunque lo esperaba, de todos ~s me sorprendió** even though I was expecting it, I was still surprised
[3] **de ~ que** (*antes de verbo*) so; (*después de verbo*) so that; **¡de ~ que eras tú el que llamaba!** so it was you that was calling!; **apílalos de ~ que no se caigan** stack them up so (that) they won't fall over
[4] (*Esp frm*) (= *moderación*) moderation; **bebe con ~** drink in moderation
[5] (*LAm*) **¡ni ~!** (= *de ninguna manera*) no way*, not a chance*; (= *no hay otra alternativa*) what else can I/you *etc* do?; **ni ~ que lo va a hacer** no way she's going to do it; **si no me quieres, ni ~** if you don't love me, what else can I do?
[6] **modos** (= *modales*) manners; **buenos ~s** good manners; **con buenos ~s** politely; **malos ~s** bad manners; **me contestó con muy malos ~s** he answered me very rudely
[7] (*Ling*) [*del verbo*] mood; **de ~** manner *antes de s*; **adverbio de ~** manner adverb ► **modo adverbial** adverbial phrase ► **modo conjuntivo** conjunctional phrase ► **modo imperativo** imperative mood ► **modo indicativo** indicative mood ► **modo subjuntivo** subjunctive mood
[8] (*Inform*) mode
[9] (*Mús*) mode; **~ mayor/menor** major/minor mode

modorra SF [1] (= *sueño*) drowsiness; **me entró la ~** I began to feel drowsy; **sacudirse la ~** to rouse o.s.
[2] (*Vet*) staggers

modorro ADJ [1] (= *soñoliento*) drowsy
[2] (*) (= *tonto*) dull, stupid
[3] [*fruta*] soft, squashy

modosito ADJ, **modoso** ADJ (= *educado*) well-mannered; (= *recatado*) demure

modulación SF modulation ► **modulación de frecuencia** (*Radio*) frequency modulation

modulado ADJ modulated

modulador SM modulator

modulador-demodulador SM (*Inform*) modem

modular ▸conjug 1a◂ Ⓐ ADJ modular
Ⓑ VT to modulate
Ⓒ SM (*Cono Sur*) shelf unit

modularidad SF modularity

módulo SM [1] (*Educ*) module
[2] [*de mobiliario*] unit; **estantería por ~s** modular *o* combination shelving units *pl*
[3] (*Andes*) platform
[4] (*Espacio*) ► **módulo de mando** command module ► **módulo lunar** lunar module

moer SM moiré

mofa SF (= *burla*) mockery, ridicule; **hacer ~ de algo/algn** to scoff at sth/sb, make fun of sth/sb; **exponer a algn a la ~ pública** to hold sb up to public ridicule; **es una ~ de nuestras creencias** it makes a mockery of our beliefs

mofador(a) Ⓐ ADJ mocking, scoffing, sneering
Ⓑ SM/F mocker, derider

mofar ▸conjug 1a◂ Ⓐ VI to mock, scoff, sneer
Ⓑ **mofarse** VPR **~se de algo/algn** to mock sth/sb, scoff at sth/sb, sneer at sth/sb

mofeta SF [1] (*Zool*) skunk
[2] (*Min*) firedamp
[3] (‡) (= *pedo*) fart‡

mofinco‡ SM (*Caribe*) firewater*, gut-rot*

mofle SM (*LAm Aut*) silencer, muffler (*EEUU*)

moflete SM (= *mejilla*) chubby cheek

mofletudo ADJ chubby-cheeked

mogol SM [1] = **mongol**
[2] (*Hist*) **el Gran Mogol** the Great Mogul

Mogolia SF = **Mongolia**

mogólico/a ADJ, SM/F = **mongólico**

mogolla SF (*Andes, Cono Sur*) bargain

mogollón* Ⓐ SM [1] (= *gran cantidad*) loads *pl*, masses *pl*; **(un) ~ de gente** ◊ **gente a ~** loads *o* masses of people; **tengo (un) ~ de discos** I've got loads *o* masses of records
[2] (= *confusión*) commotion, upheaval; (= *lío*) fuss, row; **hay mucho ~ aquí** it's a bit wild here
[3] **de ~** (= *gratis*): **colarse de ~ en un sitio** to get into a place without paying; **comer de ~** to scrounge a meal*; **lograr un puesto de ~** to wangle a job*
Ⓑ ADV (= *mucho*) **me gusta ~** I think it's great *o* fantastic*

mogollónico* ADJ huge, massive

mogote SM (= *otero*) flat-topped hillock; (= *montón*) heap, pile; [*de gavillas*] stack

mohair [mo'xair, mo'air] SM mohair

mohín SM (= *pucheros*) pout; **hacer un ~** to make a face; **con un leve ~ de extrañeza** with a faintly surprised expression

mohína SF [1] (= *enfado*) annoyance, displeasure
[2] (= *mal humor*) the sulks
[3] (= *tristeza*) depression; **ser fácil a las ~s** to be easily depressed

mohíno ADJ [1] (= *enfadado*) annoyed
[2] (= *malhumorado*) sulky, sullen
[3] (= *triste*) sad, depressed; **se fue ~ y cabizbajo** he went off, sad and downcast

➤ LENGUA Y USO: **modo 2** 53.5

moho SM 1 (*en metal*) rust
2 (*en alimentos*) mould, mold (*EEUU*), mildew; **cubierto de ~** mouldy, moldy (*EEUU*); **olor a ~** musty smell; ✦*MODISMOS* **no cría ~** he's always on the go, he doesn't let the grass grow under his feet; **no dejar criar ~ a algn** to keep sb on the go

mohoso ADJ 1 [*metal*] rusty
2 [*alimento*] mouldy, moldy (*EEUU*); [*olor, sabor*] musty
3 [*chiste*] stale

Moisés SM Moses

moisés SM INV (= *cuna*) Moses basket, cradle; (*portátil*) carrycot

moja⁑ SF (= *puñalada*) stab, thrust; (= *herida*) stab wound

mojada SF 1 (*con agua*) wetting, soaking
2 (= *herida*) stab (wound)

mojado Ⓐ ADJ (= *húmedo*) damp, wet; (= *empapado*) soaked, drenched; **le pasé por la frente un trapo ~** I mopped her brow with a damp cloth; **por la mañana la hierba estaba mojada** the grass was wet in the morning; **llegamos a casa completamente ~s** we were completely soaked *o* drenched when we got home; *ver tb* **llover**
Ⓑ SM (*Méx*) wetback (*EEUU*), illegal immigrant

mojama SF salted tuna; ✦*MODISMOS* **está más seco que una ~** he's as wrinkled as a prune; **estar más tieso que la ~** to be practically in the grave; **~ tiesa**: **todo escritor que no sea una ~ tiesa** any writer worth his salt

mojar ▸conjug 1a◂ Ⓐ VT 1 (*involuntariamente*) to get wet; (*voluntariamente*) to wet; (= *humedecer*) to damp(en), moisten; (= *empapar*) to drench, soak; **¡no mojes la alfombra!** don't get the carpet wet!; **~ la cabeza al niño** to wet the baby's head; **el niño ha mojado la cama** the baby's wet the bed; **moja un poco el trapo** dampen the cloth; **la lluvia nos mojó a todos** we all got soaked in the rain; **moje ligeramente el sello** moisten the stamp a little; **~ la ropa en agua** to soak *o* steep the washing in water
2 (= *meter*) to dip; **~ el pan en el café** to dip *o* dunk one's bread in one's coffee; **~ la pluma en la tinta** to dip one's pen into the ink
3 (*) [+ *triunfo*] to celebrate with a drink
4 ✦*MODISMOS* **~la** ◊ **~ el churro**⁑ to dip one's wick⁑
5 (*Ling*) to palatalize
6 (= *apuñalar*) to stab
7 (*Caribe*) [+ *camarero*] to tip; (*) (= *sobornar*) to bribe
Ⓑ VI **~ en** (= *hacer pinitos*) to dabble in; (= *entrometerse*) to meddle *o* get involved in
Ⓒ **mojarse** VPR 1 (= *humedecerse*) 1·1 (*reflexivo*) to get wet; **~se hasta los huesos** to get soaked to the skin
1·2 **~se el pelo** (*involuntariamente*) to get one's hair wet; (*voluntariamente*) to wet one's hair; **me he mojado las mangas** I got my sleeves wet
2 (*) (= *comprometerse*) to get one's feet wet; **no se mojó** he kept out of it, he didn't get involved
3 ✦*MODISMO* **~se las orejas** (*Cono Sur*) to give way, back down

mojarra SF 1 (⁑) (= *lengua*) tongue
2 (*LAm*) (= *cuchillo*) short broad knife
3 (= *pez*) *type of bream*

mojera SF whitebeam

mojicón SM 1 (= *bizcocho*) sponge cake; (= *bollo*) bun
2 (*) (= *bofetada*) punch in the face, slap

mojiganga SF 1 (= *farsa*) farce, piece of clowning
2 (*Hist*) masquerade, mummery

mojigatería SF (= *beatería*) sanctimoniousness; (= *puritanismo*) prudery, prudishness

mojigato/a Ⓐ ADJ (= *santurrón*) sanctimonious; (= *puritano*) prudish, strait-laced
Ⓑ SM/F (= *santurrón*) sanctimonious person; (= *puritano*) prude

mojinete SM [*de techo*] ridge; [*de muro*] tiling, coping; (*Cono Sur*) (= *aguilón*) gable

mojito SM (*Cuba*) *long drink with a base of rum*

mojo SM (*esp Méx*) garlic sauce

mojón¹ SM 1 (= *piedra*) boundary stone; (*tb* **~ kilométrico**) milestone
2 (= *montón*) heap, pile
3 (*Andes*⁑) (= *mierda*) shit⁑, crap⁑

mojón²/ona SM/F (*Caribe*⁑) (= *bruto*) idiot, thickhead*; (= *chaparro*) shortie*

mol. ABR (*Fís*) (= **molécula**) mol

mola SF rounded mountain

molar¹ SM molar

molar²⁑ ▸conjug 1a◂ VI (*Esp*) 1 (= *gustar*) **lo que más me mola es …** what I'm really into is …*; **tía, me molas mucho** I'm crazy about you baby*; **¡cómo mola esa moto!** that bike is really cool!⁑; **¿te mola un pitillo?** do you fancy a smoke?*; **no me mola** I don't go for that*, I don't fancy that
2 (= *estar de moda*) to be in*; **eso mola mucho ahora** that's very in right now*, that's all the rage now
3 (= *dar tono*) to be classy*, be real posh*
4 (= *valer*) to be OK*; **por partes iguales, ¿mola?** equal shares then, OK?*
5 (= *marchar*) **la cosa no mola** it's not going well at all

molcajete SM (*esp Méx*) mortar

Moldavia SF Moldavia

moldavo/a ADJ, SM/F Moldavian, Moldovan

molde SM 1 (*Culin, Téc*) mould, mold (*EEUU*); (= *vaciado*) cast; (*Tip*) form; ✦*MODISMO* **romper ~s** to break the mould ► **molde de corona** ring mould *o* (*EEUU*) mold
2 (*Cos*) (= *patrón*) pattern; (= *aguja*) knitting needle
3 (= *modelo*) model
4 ✦*MODISMO* **de ~** (= *perfecto*) perfect, just right; **el vestido le está de ~** the dress is just right for her; **esto me viene de ~** this is just what I want *o* need, this is just the job*; *ver tb* **letra 1**, **pan 1**

moldeable ADJ [*material*] malleable; [*carácter, persona*] easily influenced, impressionable

moldeado SM 1 (= *modelado*) moulding, molding (*EEUU*); (*en yeso*) casting
2 [*del pelo*] soft perm

moldear ▸conjug 1a◂ VT 1 (= *modelar*) to mould, mold (*EEUU*); (*en yeso*) to cast
2 [+ *pelo*] to give a soft perm
3 [+ *persona*] to mould, mold (*EEUU*), shape

moldeo SM moulding, molding (*EEUU*)

moldura SF 1 (= *marco*) frame ► **moldura lateral** (*Aut*) side stripe
2 (*Arquit*) moulding, molding (*EEUU*)

mole¹ SF (= *masa*) mass, bulk; (= *edificio*) pile; **la enorme ~ del buque** the vast bulk of the ship; **ese edificio/hombre es una ~** that building/man is massive; **se sentó con toda su ~** he sat down with his full bulk *o* weight

mole² (*Méx*) SM (= *salsa*) thick chilli sauce; (= *plato*) meat in chilli sauce; ✦*MODISMO* **ser el ~ de algn*** to be sb's favourite thing ► **mole de olla** meat stew ► **mole poblano** *meat dish from Puebla*

molécula SF molecule

molecular ADJ molecular

moledor Ⓐ ADJ grinding, crushing
Ⓑ SM grinder, crusher

moledora SF (*Téc*) grinder, crusher

moledura SF 1 (= *acción*) [*de café*] grinding; [*de trigo*] milling
2 (*) (= *agotamiento*) **¡qué ~ traigo!** I'm shattered*

moler ▸conjug 2h◂ VT 1 [+ *café*] to grind; [+ *trigo*] to mill; (= *machacar*) to crush; (= *pulverizar*) to pound; ✦*MODISMO* **~ a algn a palos** to give sb a beating
2 (= *fastidiar*) to annoy; (= *aburrir*) to bore

▼ **molestar** ▸conjug 1a◂ Ⓐ VT 1 (= *importunar*) to bother, annoy; **¿no la estarán molestando, verdad?** they're not bothering *o* annoying you, are they?; **no la molestes más con tus tonterías** stop pestering *o* bothering *o* annoying her with your silly games
2 (= *interrumpir*) to disturb; **que no me moleste nadie** I don't want to be disturbed by anyone; **siento ~te, pero necesito que me ayudes** I'm sorry to disturb *o* trouble *o* bother you, but I need your help
3 (= *ofender*) to upset; **espero no haberte molestado** I hope I didn't upset you
Ⓑ VI 1 (= *importunar*) to be a nuisance; **quita de en medio, que siempre estás molestando** get out of the way, you're always being a nuisance; **no quisiera ~, pero necesito hablar contigo** I don't want to bother you *o* be a nuisance, but I need to talk to you; **"no molestar"** "(please) do not disturb"; **me molesta mucho que me hablen así** it really annoys *o* irritates me when they talk to me like that; **ese ruido me molesta** that noise is bothering *o* annoying *o* irritating me; **me molesta el jarrón, ¿puedes apartarlo?** the vase is in the way, can you move it?; **me molesta tener que repetirlo** it annoys me to have to repeat it
2 (= *incomodar*) to feel uncomfortable, bother; **¿te molesta el humo?** does the smoke bother you?; **me está empezando a ~ la herida** the injury is starting to play up* *o* bother me; **me molesta al tragar** it hurts when I swallow; **la radio no me molesta para estudiar** the radio doesn't bother me when I'm studying; **si le sigue molestando, acuda a su médico** if it goes on giving you trouble, see your doctor
3 (= *ofender*) to upset; **me molestó mucho lo que dijiste** what you said really upset me; **le molestó que no lo invitárais a la fiesta** he was hurt that you didn't invite him to the party
4 (= *importar*) (*en preguntas*) **¿le molesta la radio?** does the radio bother you?, do you mind the radio being on?; **¿te ~ía prestarme un paraguas?** would you mind lending me an umbrella?; **¿le molesta que abra la ventana**

➤ LENGUA Y USO: molestar A1 36.1

o **si abro la ventana?** do you mind if I open the window?

Ⓒ **molestarse** VPR [1] (= *tomarse la molestia*) to bother o.s.; **no se moleste, prefiero estar de pie** don't trouble *o* bother yourself, I prefer to stand; **—¿quiere que abra la ventana? —por mí no se moleste** "shall I open the window?" — "don't mind me"; **no te molestes por él, sabe arreglárselas solo** don't put yourself out for him, he can manage on his own; **~se en hacer algo** to take the trouble to do sth; **se molestó en llevarnos al aeropuerto** she took the trouble to drive us to the airport, she went to the trouble of driving us to the airport; **no te molestes en venir a por mí** don't bother to come and pick me up, you needn't take the trouble to come and pick me up; **ni siquiera te has molestado en responder a mis cartas** you didn't even bother to answer my letters

[2] (= *disgustarse*) (*con enfado*) to get annoyed, get upset; (*con ofensa*) to take offence, take offense (*EEUU*); **no deberías ~te, lo hizo sin mala intención** you shouldn't get annoyed *o* upset/take offence, he didn't mean any harm; **~se con algn** to get annoyed *o* cross with sb; **~se por algo** to get annoyed at sth, get upset about sth; **se molesta por nada** he gets annoyed at *o* upset about the slightest thing; **¿te has molestado por ese comentario?** did that comment upset *o* offend you?

molestia SF [1] (= *trastorno*) bother, trouble; **el retraso nos causó muchas ~s** the delay caused us a lot of bother *o* trouble; **¿me podrías llevar a casa, si no es mucha ~?** could you take me home, if it's not too much bother *o* trouble?; **andar con muletas es una gran ~** walking with crutches is a real nuisance *o* bother; **perdone la ~, pero …** sorry to bother you, but …; **¡no es ninguna ~, estaré encantado de ayudarte!** it's no trouble at all, I'll be happy to help!; **"perdonen las ~s"** "we apologize for any inconvenience"; **ahorrarse la ~ de hacer algo** to save o.s. the bother *o* trouble of doing sth; **tomarse la ~ de hacer algo** to take the trouble to do sth; **se tomaron la ~ de visitarlos en persona** they took the trouble to visit them in person; **no tenías que haberte tomado la ~** you shouldn't have bothered *o* taken the trouble, you shouldn't have put yourself out

[2] (*Med*) discomfort; **al andar noto una pequeña ~** I feel a slight discomfort when I walk; **si persisten las ~s, consulte a un especialista** if the discomfort *o* trouble persists, consult a specialist; **tengo una pequeña ~ en la garganta** I have a bit of a sore throat; **tengo ~s en el estómago** I have an upset stomach

molesto ADJ [1] (= *que causa molestia*) [*tos, picor, ruido, persona*] irritating, annoying; [*olor, síntoma*] unpleasant; **es una persona muy molesta** he's a very irritating *o* annoying person; **es sumamente ~ que …** it's extremely irritating *o* annoying that …; **una sensación bastante molesta** quite an uncomfortable *o* unpleasant feeling; **lo único ~ es el viaje** the only nuisance is the journey, the only annoying thing is the journey; **si no es ~ para usted** if it's no trouble to you *o* no bother for you

[2] (= *que incomoda*) [*asiento, ropa*] uncomfortable; [*tarea*] annoying; [*situación*] awkward, embarrassing; **las faldas ajustadas son muy molestas** tight skirts are very uncomfortable

[3] (= *incómodo*) [*persona*] uncomfortable; **me sentía ~ en la fiesta** I felt uneasy *o* uncomfortable at the party; **me siento ~ cada vez que me hace un regalo** I feel awkward *o* embarrassed whenever she gives me a present; **estaba ~ por la inyección** he was in some discomfort o pain after the injection

[4] (= *enfadado*) [*persona*] annoyed; **estaba muy molesta con su actitud** she was very annoyed at their attitude; **¿estás ~ conmigo por lo que dije?** are you annoyed at me for what I said?

[5] (= *disgustado*) [*persona*] upset; **¿estás molesta por algo que haya pasado?** are you upset about something that's happened?

molestoso ADJ (*LAm*) annoying

molibdeno SM molybdenum

molicie SF [1] (= *blandura*) softness

[2] (= *comodidad*) **reblandecido por la ~ de la vida moderna** made complacent by the comforts *o* ease of modern life; **una vida sin concesiones de ~** a life with no concessions to luxury *o* comfort

[3] (= *afeminamiento*) effeminacy

molido ADJ [1] [*café, especias*] ground

[2] **estar ~*** (= *cansado*) to be shattered*; **estoy ~ de tanto viajar** I'm shattered with all this travelling*; **tengo todo el cuerpo ~** I'm aching all over; **tengo los riñones ~s** my back is killing me*

molienda SF [1] (= *acto*) [*de café*] grinding; [*de trigo*] milling

[2] (= *cantidad*) *quantity of grain to be ground*

[3] (*) (= *cansancio*) weariness

[4] (*) (= *molestia*) nuisance

moliente ADJ *ver* **corriente A3**

molinero/a SM/F miller

molinete SM (toy) windmill

molinillo SM [1] (*para moler*) hand mill ► **molinillo de aceite** olive press ► **molinillo de café** coffee mill *o* grinder ► **molinillo de carne** mincer

[2] (= *juguete*) (toy) windmill, pinwheel (*EEUU*)

molino SM [1] (*gen*) mill; (= *trituradora*) grinder ► **molino de agua** water mill ► **molino de cubo** waterwheel ► **molino de viento** windmill

[2] (*) (= *persona*) fidget

molla SF [*de persona*] fleshy part; [*de carne*] lean part; [*de fruta*] flesh; [*de pan*] doughy part

mollar ADJ [1] [*fruta*] (= *blanda*) soft; (= *fácil de pelar*) easy to peel; [*almendra*] easily shelled

[2] [*carne*] boned, boneless

[3] (*) [*trabajo*] cushy*, easy

[4] (*) (= *crédulo*) gullible

mollate SM plonk*

molledo SM [1] [*del brazo*] fleshy part

[2] [*de pan*] doughy part

molleja SF [1] [*de ave*] gizzard

[2] **mollejas** [*de res, cordero*] sweetbreads

mollejón* SM softie*; (*pey*) fat slob*

mollera SF [1] (*) (= *seso*) brains *pl*, sense; **tener buena ~** to have brains, be brainy; **✦MODISMOS cerrado** *o* **duro de ~** (= *estúpido*) dense*, dim*; (= *terco*) pig-headed; **no les cabe en la ~** they just can't get their heads round it*; **secar la ~ a algn** to drive sb crazy

[2] (= *coronilla*) crown of the head

mollete SM [1] (*Culin*) muffin

[2] [*del brazo*] fleshy part

[3] (= *mejilla*) fat cheek

molo SM (*Cono Sur*) breakwater, mole

molón‡ ADJ [1] (*Esp*) (= *bueno*) fantastic*, brilliant*

[2] (*Esp*) (= *elegante*) posh*, classy*

[3] (*CAm, Méx*) (= *pesado*) tiresome

molondra‡ SF bonce*

molote SM [1] (*Méx*) (= *ovillo*) ball of wool

[2] (*Méx Culin*) fried maize pancake

[3] (*Andes, Méx*) (= *jugarreta*) dirty trick

[4] (*CAm, Caribe, Méx*) (= *alboroto*) riot, commotion

molotov ADJ INV **cóctel ~** Molotov cocktail, petrol bomb

molturar ▸conjug 1a◂ VT to grind, mill

Molucas SFPL **las (Islas) ~** the Moluccas, the Molucca Islands

molusco SM mollusc, mollusk (*EEUU*)

momentáneamente ADV momentarily

momentáneo ADJ momentary

momento SM [1] (= *instante*) moment; **la miró un ~** he looked at her for a moment; **espera un ~** hold on a minute *o* moment; **—¡Juan, ven aquí! —¡un ~!** "come here, Juan" — "just a minute *o* moment!"; **llegará dentro de un ~** she'll be here in a minute *o* moment; **está protestando desde el ~ en que llegó** he's been complaining from the moment he arrived; **hace un ~** just a moment ago; **en ese preciso ~ se paró el coche** at that very moment *o* right then, the car stopped; **éste es un ~ histórico** this is a historic moment; **no paró de hablar ni un solo ~** he never stopped talking for a single second; **no creí ni por un ~ que llegaría a divorciarse** I never thought for a moment that she'd get divorced; **llegará en breves ~s** she'll be here shortly; **en este ~** at the moment, right now; **en este ~ el doctor no puede atenderle** the doctor can't see you at the moment *o* right now; **no dejó de apoyarme en ningún ~** she never stopped supporting me for a moment; **en un primer ~** at first; **en un primer ~ creí que era un resfriado** at first I thought it was a cold; **estuvo a mi lado en todo ~** he was at my side the whole time; **en un ~** in next to no time; **limpió el cuarto en un ~** he cleaned the room in next to no time

[2] (= *rato*) **los mejores ~s del partido** the highlights of the match; **pasamos ~s inolvidables en Madrid** we had an unforgettable time in Madrid

[3] (= *época*) time; **en el ~ actual** at the present time; **deben usarse las técnicas disponibles en el ~** the currently available techniques should be used; **del ~**: **la música más representativa del ~** the music which is most representative of current trends; **el grupo favorito del ~** the most popular group at the moment

[4] (= *coyuntura*) **nuestra empresa pasa por un ~ magnífico** our company is doing splendidly at the moment; **atravesamos un ~ difícil** we are going through a difficult time *o* patch; **el actor estaba en su mejor ~** the actor was in his prime; **llegué en buen ~** I arrived at a good time; **ha llegado el ~ de hacer algo** the time has come to do sth; **en el ~ oportuno** at the right time; **ser buen/mal ~ para hacer algo** to be a good/bad time to do

sth; **es el mejor ~ para invertir en bolsa** it's the ideal time to invest in the stock market; **todo se hará en su ~** we'll do everything in good time o when the time comes; **ya te avisarán en su ~** they'll let you know in due course

5 (*otras locuciones*) **al ~** at once; **a cada ~ se despertaba y pedía agua** she kept waking up and asking for water, she was constantly waking up and asking for water; **en cualquier ~** any time now; **puede llegar en cualquier ~** she could arrive at any moment; **en un ~ dado**: **en un ~ dado, conseguí sujetarlo del brazo** at one stage I managed to grab hold of his arm; **en un ~ dado, yo mismo puedo echarte una mano** I could give you a hand some time, if necessary; **de ~** for the moment; **de ~ continúa en el trabajo** he's staying in the job for the time being o for the moment; **de ~ déjalo y piénsatelo mejor** leave it for the moment and think it over; **de ~ no lo reconocí, pero luego recordé su cara** at first I didn't recognize him, but then I remembered his face; **desde el ~ en que**: **los impuestos, desde el ~ en que son obligatorios, son una extorsión** since taxes are compulsory, they amount to extortion; **en el ~** straight away; **la llamé y acudió en el ~** I called her and she came over straight away; **de un ~ a otro** any minute now; **en el ~ menos pensado** when least expected; **esas cosas pasan en el ~ menos pensado** those things happen when you least expect them; **por ~s** by the minute; **está cambiando por ~s** it is changing by the minute; **por el ~** for the time being, for now

6 (*Mec*) momentum, moment

momería SF mummery, clowning

momia SF mummy; **parece una ~** she looks like a zombie; **no te quedes ahí como una ~** don't stand there like a dummy

momificación SF mummification

momificar ▸conjug 1g◂ Ⓐ VT to mummify

Ⓑ **momificarse** VPR to mummify, become mummified

momio[1] Ⓐ SM (= *ganga*) bargain; (= *extra*) extra; (= *sinecura*) cushy job*; (= *trato*) profitable deal; **de ~** free

Ⓑ ADJ [*carne*] lean

momio[2]**/a*** (*Chile*) Ⓐ ADJ reactionary, right-wing *antes de s*

Ⓑ SM/F 1 (= *carroza*) square*, fuddy-duddy*

2 (*Pol*) reactionary, right winger

momo SM 1 (= *cara*) funny face

2 (= *payasadas*) clowning, buffoonery

mona SF 1 (*Zool*) (= *hembra*) female monkey; (= *especie*) Barbary ape; ✦*MODISMO* **mandar a algn a freír ~s*** to tell sb where to go*, tell sb to get lost*; ✦*REFRÁN* **aunque la ~ se vista de seda (~ se queda)** you can't make a silk purse out of a sow's ear

2 (*) (= *copión*) copycat*

3 (*) (= *borrachera*) **coger** o **pillar una ~** to get sloshed o plastered*; **dormir la ~** to sleep it off

4 ► **mona de Pascua** Easter cake

5 (*LAm**) (= *droga*) *Colombian golden marijuana*

6 ✦*MODISMO* **andar** o **estar como la ~** (*Cono Sur*) (= *sin dinero*) to be broke*; (= *desgraciado*) to feel terrible; *ver tb* **mono**[3] **B**

monacal ADJ monastic

monacato SM monasticism, monastic life ► **monacato femenino** convent life, life as a nun

monacillo SM acolyte, altar boy

Mónaco SM Monaco

monada SF 1 (= *cosa*) **la casa es una ~** the house is gorgeous o lovely; **¡qué ~!** isn't it gorgeous o lovely?; **¡qué ~ de perrito!** what a cute o lovely little dog!

2 (= *chica*) pretty girl; **¡hola, ~!** hello gorgeous o beautiful!*

3 (= *tontería*) **deja de hacer ~s** stop clowning around

4 [*de niño*] charming habit, sweet little way

5 (*) **monadas** (= *zalamería*) flattery *sing*

6 (= *cualidad*) silliness, childishness

mónada SF monad

monaguillo SM, **monago** SM altar boy, acolyte

monarca SMF monarch

monarquía SF monarchy

monárquico/a Ⓐ ADJ monarchic(al); (*Pol*) royalist, monarchist

Ⓑ SM/F royalist, monarchist

monarquismo SM monarchism

monarquista SM monarchist

monasterio SM [*de hombres*] monastery; [*de mujeres*] convent

monástico ADJ monastic

Moncho SM (*forma familiar*) *de* **Ramón**

Moncloa SF **la ~** *official residence of the Spanish prime minister (Madrid)*

monclovita ADJ of the Moncloa palace, of the prime minister, prime ministerial

monda[1] SF 1 (= *peladura*) [*de naranja*] peel; [*de patata*] peelings *pl*; [*de plátano*] skin

2 (= *acción*) peeling

3 (= *poda*) pruning; (= *temporada*) pruning season

4 (*LAm**) (= *paliza*) beating

monda[2]* SF **¡es la ~!** (= *fantástico*) it's great!*, it's fantastic!*; (= *el colmo*) (*refiriéndose a algo*) it's the limit!; (*refiriéndose a algn*) he's the limit o end!*; [*algo divertido*] it's a scream*; [*persona divertida*] he's a scream*; **este nuevo baile es la ~** (= *fantástico*) this new dance is great o fantastic*; (*pey*) this new dance is the pits*

mondadientes SM INV toothpick

mondador SM (*Méx*) shredder

mondadura SF = **monda**[1] **1**

mondante* ADJ **es un chaval ~** he's a scream*; **nos pasó una cosa ~** something hilarious o really funny happened to us

mondar ▸conjug 1a◂ Ⓐ VT 1 [+ *fruta, patata*] to peel; [+ *nueces, guisantes*] to shell; [+ *palo*] to pare, remove the bark from

2 (*) [+ *persona*] (= *cortar el pelo*) to scalp*; (= *desplumar*) to fleece*, clean out*

3 (= *podar*) to prune

4 (= *limpiar*) (*gen*) to clean, cleanse; [+ *canal*] to clean out

5 (*LAm**) (= *pegar*) to beat (up), thrash; (*Caribe*) **~ a algn** to wipe the floor with sb*

Ⓑ **mondarse** VPR 1 (*tb* **~se de risa**) (*) to die laughing*

2 **~se los dientes** to pick one's teeth

mondo ADJ 1 [*cabeza*] completely shorn

2 (= *sin añadidura*) plain; **el asunto ~ es esto** the plain fact of the matter is this; **tiene su sueldo ~ y nada más** he has just what he earns, nothing more; ✦*MODISMO* **~ y lirondo*** pure and simple

3 (*) (= *sin dinero*) **me he quedado ~** I'm cleaned out*, I haven't a cent

mondongo SM (= *entrañas*) guts *pl*, insides *pl*; (= *callos*) tripe

mondongudo ADJ (*esp Cono Sur*) paunchy, pot-bellied

monear ▸conjug 1a◂ VI 1 (= *comportarse*) to monkey around, clown around; (= *hacer muecas*) to make faces

2 (*Cono Sur, Méx**) (= *jactarse*) to boast, swank*

moneda SF 1 (= *pieza*) coin; **una ~ falsa** a counterfeit coin; **una ~ de cinco dólares** a five-dollar piece; **la máquina funciona con ~s** the machine is coin-operated; **tirar una ~ al aire** to toss a coin ► **moneda menuda**, **moneda suelta** small change

2 [*de un país*] currency; **en ~ española** in Spanish money; **la casa de la ~** the mint; ✦*MODISMO* **pagar a algn con** o **en la misma ~** to pay sb back in his own coin o in kind ► **moneda blanda** soft currency ► **moneda convertible** convertible currency ► **moneda corriente** currency; ✦*MODISMO* **es ~ corriente** it's a common occurrence ► **moneda débil** soft currency ► **moneda decimal** decimal currency ► **moneda de curso legal** legal tender ► **moneda dura** hard currency ► **moneda fraccionaria** money in small denominations ► **moneda fuerte** hard currency ► **moneda nacional** national currency; **el precio es 1.000 pesos, ~ nacional** (*LAm*) the price is 1,000 pesos ► **moneda única** single currency

monedar ▸conjug 1a◂ VT, **monedear** ▸conjug 1a◂ VT to mint, coin

monedero SM 1 (*para monedas*) purse, coin purse (*EEUU*)

2 ► **monedero falso** counterfeiter

monegasco/a Ⓐ ADJ of/from Monaco, Monegasque; **el principado ~** the Principality of Monaco

Ⓑ SM/F native/inhabitant of Monaco, Monegasque; **los ~s** the people of Monaco

monería SF 1 (= *mueca*) funny face, monkey face; (= *imitación*) mimicry

2 (= *payasada*) antic, prank; **hacer ~s** to monkey around, clown around

3 (= *banalidad*) trifle, triviality

monetario ADJ monetary

monetarismo SM monetarism

monetarista ADJ, SMF monetarist

mongol(a) Ⓐ ADJ, SM/F Mongol, Mongolian

Ⓑ SM (*Ling*) Mongolian

Mongolia SF Mongolia

mongólico/a Ⓐ ADJ 1 (*Med*†) mongoloid†; **niños ~s** children with Down's syndrome

2 (*pey*) (= *estúpido*) moronic; **ideas mongólicas** moronic ideas

3 (= *mongol*) Mongolian

Ⓑ SM/F 1 (*Med*†) Down's syndrome sufferer

2 (*pey*) (= *estúpido*) moron*

3 (= *mongol*) Mongolian

mongolismo† SM Down's syndrome, mongolism†

moni* SF (*LAm*) money

monicaco/a* SM/F twit*

monicongo SM (*LAm*) cartoon film

monigote SM [1] (= *muñeco*) rag doll; [*de papel*] paper doll; ✦*MODISMO* **hacer el ~** to fool around, clown around ► **monigote de nieve** snowman ► **monigote de paja** straw man ► **monigote de tebeo** cartoon character; → DÍA DE LOS (SANTOS) INOCENTES
[2] (= *niño*) little monkey
[3] (*sin personalidad*) weak character
[4] (= *garabato*) doodle

monises‡ SMPL brass* *sing*, dough* *sing*

monitor(a) Ⓐ SM/F (= *persona*) (*Dep*) instructor, coach; [*de gira*] group leader ► **monitor(a) de campamento** camp leader ► **monitor(a) de esquí** ski instructor ► **monitor(a) de natación** swimming instructor ► **monitor(a) deportivo/a** (*gen*) sports coach; (*en escuela*) games coach
Ⓑ SM (*tb Inform, Téc*) monitor

monitoreado SM monitoring

monitorear ▸conjug 1a◂ VT to monitor

monitorio ADJ admonitory

monitorización SF monitoring

monitorizar ▸conjug 1f◂ VT to monitor

monja SF nun ► **monja de clausura** cloistered nun, nun in a closed order

monje SM [1] (*Rel*) monk
[2] (*Caribe*) (= *dinero*) five-peso note

monjil Ⓐ ADJ (*lit*) nun's; (*fig*) (*pey*) excessively demure
Ⓑ SM (*hábito*) nun's habit

mono[1] SM [1] (*Zool*) monkey; **¡mono!** (*a niño*) you little monkey! ► **mono araña** spider monkey ► **mono aullador** howler monkey
[2] (‡) [*de drogadicto*] withdrawal symptoms *pl*, cold turkey*; **estar con el ~** to be suffering withdrawal symptoms, have gone cold turkey*; **tener ~ de fama** to crave fame
[3] (= *traje de faena*) overalls *pl*, boiler suit; [*de calle*] jumpsuit; (*con peto*) dungarees *pl* ► **mono de aviador** flying suit ► **mono de esquí** ski suit ► **mono de vuelo** flying suit
[4] (*) (= *hombre feo*) ugly devil
[5] (= *figura*) *cartoon or caricature figure*; **monos** (*Cono Sur*) doodles ► **monos animados** (*Cono Sur*) cartoons
[6] (*Naipes*) joker
[7] (‡) (*policía*) cop*
[8] (*) (= *seña*) sign (*between lovers*); **hacerse ~s** to make eyes at each other
[9] (*Caribe**) (= *deuda*) debt
[10] ✦*MODISMOS* **tener ~s en la cara: no me mirarían más ni que tuviera ~s en la cara** they couldn't have stared at me more if I had come from the moon; **estar de ~s** to be at daggers drawn; **meter los ~s a algn** (*LAm*) to put the wind up sb*; **ser un ~ de repetición** to repeat things like a parrot; **ser el último ~** to be a nobody ► **mono de imitación** copycat*

mono[2] ADJ [1] (= *bonito*) pretty, lovely; (= *simpático*) nice, cute; **una chica muy mona** a lovely *o* very pretty girl; **¡qué sombrero más ~!** what a nice *o* cute little hat!
[2] (*Mús*) mono

mono[3]**/a** Ⓐ ADJ (*LAm*) (= *amarillo*) yellow; (= *rubio*) blond; (= *rojizo*) reddish blond
Ⓑ SM/F (*Col*) (= *rubio*) blond(e) (person); *ver tb* **mona**

mono... PREF mono...

monocarril SM monorail

monocasco SM monohull

monocigótico ADJ, **monocigoto** ADJ monozygotic

monocolor ADJ one-colour, of a single colour; **gobierno ~** one-party government

monocorde ADJ [1] (*Mús*) single-stringed
[2] (= *monótono*) monotonous, unvaried

monocromo Ⓐ ADJ monochrome; (*TV*) black-and-white
Ⓑ SM monochrome

monóculo SM monocle

monocultivo SM single crop farming, monoculture; **el ~ es un peligro para muchos países** in many countries dependence upon a single crop is risky

monofónico ADJ monophonic

monogamia SF monogamy

monógamo ADJ monogamous

monografía SF monograph

monográfico Ⓐ ADJ monographic; **estudio ~** monograph; **número ~** [*de revista*] issue devoted to a single subject; **programa ~** programme devoted to a single subject
Ⓑ SM monograph, special edition

monograma SM monogram

monokini SM topless swimsuit

monolingüe Ⓐ ADJ monolingual
Ⓑ SMF monoglot

monolingüismo SM monolingualism

monolítico ADJ monolithic

monolitismo SM (= *naturaleza*) monolithic nature; (= *sistema*) monolithic system

monolito SM monolith

monologar ▸conjug 1h◂ VI to soliloquize; (*Teat*) to give a monologue

monólogo SM monologue, monolog (*EEUU*) ► **monólogo interior** stream of consciousness

monomando SM mixer tap, mixing faucet (*EEUU*)

monomanía SF (*gen*) mania, obsession; (*Psic*) monomania

monomaniaco/a ADJ, SM/F, **monomaníaco/a** ADJ, SM/F monomaniac

monomio SM monomial

monomotor ADJ single-engined

monono* ADJ (*Cono Sur*) (= *atractivo*) lovely, pretty; (= *acicalado*) dressed up

mononucleado ADJ mononuclear

mononucleosis SF INV ► **mononucleosis infecciosa** glandular fever

monoparental ADJ **familia ~** single-parent family, one-parent family

monoparentalidad SF single parenthood

monopartidismo SM single-party system

monopatín SM skateboard

monopatinaje SM skateboarding

monoplano SM monoplane

monoplaza SM single-seater

monopolio SM monopoly ► **monopolio total** absolute monopoly

monopolista ADJ, SMF monopolist

monopolístico ADJ monopolistic

monopolización SF monopolization

monopolizador ADJ [1] (*Econ*) monopolistic; **una empresa ~a del mercado** a company with a monopoly in the market
[2] [*persona*] **un niño ~ del cariño materno** a child who monopolizes his mother's attention

monopolizar ▸conjug 1f◂ VT to monopolize

monopsonio SM monopsony

monoquini SM = **monokini**

monorrail SM monorail

monorrimo ADJ [*estrofa*] having the same rhyme throughout

monosabio SM [1] (*Zool*) trained monkey
[2] (*Taur*) picador's assistant (*employee who leads the horse team dragging the dead bull*)

monosilábico ADJ monosyllabic

monosílabo Ⓐ ADJ monosyllabic
Ⓑ SM monosyllable; **responder con ~s** to answer in monosyllables

monoteísmo SM monotheism

monoteísta Ⓐ ADJ monotheistic
Ⓑ SMF monotheist

monotema SM **ése fue el ~ de la entrevista** that was the only issue discussed in the interview; **su ~ de siempre** his old hobbyhorse

monotemático ADJ on a single subject

monoterapia SF monotherapy, single-drug therapy

monotipia SF Monotype®

monotonía SF [1] (= *uniformidad*) (*gen*) monotony; [*de voz, sonido*] monotone
[2] (= *aburrimiento*) monotony; **la ~ (de la existencia) cotidiana** the daily grind

monótono ADJ [1] (= *uniforme*) [*voz, sonido*] monotonous
[2] (= *aburrido*) [*trabajo, discurso*] tedious, monotonous; [*vida*] dreary, humdrum

monousuario ADJ (*Inform*) single-user

monovalente ADJ monovalent, univalent

monovía ADJ INV monorail *antes de s*

monovolumen Ⓐ ADJ **vehículo ~** people carrier, minivan (*EEUU*)
Ⓑ SM people carrier, minivan (*EEUU*)

monóxido SM monoxide ► **monóxido de carbono** carbon monoxide ► **monóxido de cloro** chlorine monoxide

Mons. ABR (= **Monseñor**) Mgr, Mons, Msgr

monseñor SM monsignor

monserga SF (= *pesadez*) boring spiel*; (= *tontería*) drivel*; **dar la ~** (= *fastidiar*) to be irritating; (= *aburrir*) be a bore; **¡no me vengas con ~s!** (= *no molestes*) give it a rest!; (= *no te enrolles*) don't talk drivel!*

monstruo Ⓐ SM [1] (*Mit*) monster; **el ~ del lago Ness** the Loch Ness monster
[2] (= *engendro*) freak*, monster; **~ de circo** circus freak
[3] (= *persona malvada*) monster; **su jefe es un ~** her boss is a monster; **ese niño es un monstruito** that child is a little monster
[4] (= *prodigio*) giant; **es un ~ del ajedrez** he's a fantastic chess player; **es un ~ jugando al fútbol** he's a sensational footballer; **Borges, ~ sagrado de la literatura sudamericana** Borges, the revered figure of South American literature
[5] (= *cosa enorme*) monster; **¡mira, vaya ~ de camión!** look at that lorry, what a monster!
Ⓑ ADJ INV (*) (= *maravilloso*) [1] fantastic, brilliant; **idea ~** fantastic *o* brilliant idea
[2] (= *grande*) huge; **mitin ~** huge meeting; **dos proyectos ~** two huge projects

monstruosidad SF [1] (= *cosa fea*) monstrosity; **¡qué ~ de casa!** what a monstrosity of a

house!
[2] (= *crueldad*) atrocity
[3] (= *deformidad*) **la ~ de sus facciones** his monstrous features

monstruoso ADJ [1] (= *terrible*) monstrous; **es ~ que ...** it is monstrous that ...
[2] (= *horrible*) monstrous, hideous; (= *deforme*) freak *antes de s*
[3] (= *enorme*) monstrous, huge

monta SF [1] (= *suma*) total, sum
[2] (*en equitación*) (= *caballo*) mount; (= *acción*) mounting
[3] (= *apareamiento*) mating; (= *temporada de apareamiento*) mating season
[4] ♦*MODISMO* **de poca ~** third-rate *antes de s*; **un cantante/hotel de poca ~** a third-rate singer/hotel; **un ladrón de poca ~** a small-time thief

montacargas SM INV service lift, freight elevator (*EEUU*)

montada SF **la ~** (*CAm*) the mounted rural police

montadito SM (*Esp*) small sandwich

montado Ⓐ ADJ [1] [*persona*] **iba ~ a caballo** he was riding a horse, he was on horseback; **estaba montada en la bicicleta** she was riding her bicycle; **artillería montada** horse artillery; **guardia montada** horse guards *pl*; **policía montada** mounted police
[2] [*caballo*] saddled
[3] (*Esp Culin*) [*nata*] whipped; [*clara*] whisked
[4] (*Esp**) ♦*MODISMO* **estar ~ (en el dólar)** to be rolling in it*, be loaded*
Ⓑ SM (*Esp*) small sandwich ► **montado de lomo** *hot sandwich made with pork loin*

montador(a) Ⓐ SM/F [1] (*Téc*) [*de máquinas, aparatos*] fitter; [*de joyas*] setter
[2] (*Cine, TV*) film editor ► **montador(a) de escena** set designer
Ⓑ SM (= *poyo*) (*para montar*) mounting block

montadura SF [1] (= *acto*) mounting
[2] = **montura 3**

montaje SM [1] (*Téc*) [*de estantería, aparato*] assembly; [*de ordenador*] set up; [*de joyas*] setting; **instrucciones para el ~** assembly instructions; **el telescopio se encuentra en fase de ~** the telescope is being assembled; **para el ~ de la estantería basta con un destornillador** to put up *o* assemble the shelves all you need is a screwdriver; *ver tb* **cadena 6**
[2] [*de exposición*] mounting, setting up; [*de obra de teatro*] staging; **el ~ de la exposición durará tres semanas** mounting *o* setting up the exhibition will take three weeks; **un nuevo ~ de una obra de Jean Genet** a new staging of one of Jean Genet's plays
[3] (*) (= *engaño*) set-up*; **el accidente fue sólo un ~** the accident was just a set-up*; **todo era un ~ policial** the whole thing was set up by the police *o* was a police set-up* ► **montaje publicitario** advertising stunt, publicity stunt
[4] (*Cine, Fot*) montage ► **montaje fotográfico** photomontage
[5] (*Radio*) hookup

montante SM [1] (= *suma*) total ► **montante compensatorio monetario** amount of financial compensation
[2] (= *poste*) upright, post; (= *soporte*) stanchion; (*Arquit*) [*de puerta*] transom; [*de ventana*] mullion
[3] (= *ventana*) fanlight, transom (*EEUU*)

montaña Ⓐ SF [1] (= *monte*) mountain; **una ~ de papeles** a mountain of papers; **~ de mantequilla** butter mountain; ♦*MODISMO* **hacer una ~ de un granito de arena** to make a mountain out of a molehill ► **montaña rusa** roller coaster, big dipper ► **Montañas Rocosas** Rocky Mountains
[2] (= *zona*) (= *sierra*) mountains *pl*; **pasamos un mes en la ~** we spent a month in the mountains
[3] (*LAm*) (= *bosque*) forest
Ⓑ SMF ► **montaña del Pirineo** Pyrenean mountain dog, Great Pyrenees (*EEUU*)

montañero/a Ⓐ SM/F mountaineer, climber
Ⓑ ADJ mountain *antes de s*

montañés/esa Ⓐ ADJ [1] (= *de montaña*) mountain *antes de s*; (= *de tierras altas*) highland *antes de s*
[2] (= *de Santander*) of/from the Santander region
Ⓑ SM/F [1] (*gen*) highlander
[2] [*de Santander*] native/inhabitant of the Santander region

montañismo SM mountaineering, mountain climbing

montañoso ADJ mountainous

montaplatos SM INV dumb waiter

montar ▸conjug 1a◂ Ⓐ VT [1] (= *cabalgar*) to ride; **montaba una yegua blanca** she was riding a white mare
[2] (= *subir*) **~ a algn en** *o* **sobre algo** to lift sb onto sth, sit sb on sth; **se lo montó sobre las rodillas** she lifted him onto her knees, she sat him on her knees
[3] (*Téc*) [+ *estantería, ventana*] to assemble, put together; [+ *coche*] to assemble; [+ *tienda de campaña*] to put up, pitch
[4] (= *instalar*) [+ *consulta, oficina*] to set up, open; [+ *galería de arte, tienda*] to open; [+ *campamento, espectáculo*] to set up; [+ *exposición*] to set up, mount; **han montado una tienda de animales** they've opened a pet shop; **~ una casa** to set up house *o* home; **~ un negocio** to set up *o* start up a business
[5] (= *engarzar*) [+ *joya*] to set; [+ *pistola*] to cock; [+ *reloj, resorte*] to wind, wind up; **una perla montada sobre un anillo de oro** a pearl set in a gold ring
[6] (*Fot*) [+ *foto, diapositiva*] to mount
[7] (= *organizar*) [+ *operación*] to mount; [+ *sistema de control*] to put into operation; **toda la operación se montó en una semana** the whole operation was mounted in a week; **la policía montó un fuerte dispositivo de seguridad** the police put strict security measures into operation; **~ guardia** to stand guard
[8] (*Esp**) (= *crear*) **~ una bronca** *o* **un escándalo** to kick up a fuss/scandal*; **¡menudo escándalo se montó con lo de la boda!** what a fuss they kicked up about that wedding!*; **~ un número** *o* **un show** to make a scene; **nos montó un show sin motivo ninguno** he made a big scene for no reason at all
[9] (= *solapar*) **~ algo sobre algo** to overlap sth with sth; **han montado unos colores sobre otros** they have overlapped some colours with others
[10] (*Cine*) [+ *película*] to edit
[11] (*Teat*) [+ *decorado*] to put up; [+ *obra*] to stage, put on; **~on la obra con muy bajo presupuesto** they staged *o* put on the play on a small budget
[12] (*Esp Culin*) [+ *nata*] to whip; [+ *clara*] to whisk, beat; **~ la clara a punto de nieve** to whisk *o* beat the egg white until stiff
[13] (= *aparear*) (*Zool*) [+ *yegua, vaca*] to mount; (**) [+ *persona*] to mount**
[14] (*Cos*) [+ *puntos*] to cast on
Ⓑ VI [1] (= *ir a caballo*) to ride; **antes montaba a diario** I used to go riding every day; **monta para una cuadra de carreras** he rides for a racing stable; **¿tú montas bien a caballo?** do you ride well?
[2] (= *subirse*) [2·1] (*a un caballo*) to get on, mount; **ayúdame a ~** help me up, help me to get on *o* to mount
[2·2] (*en un vehículo*) **~ en avión** to fly, travel by air *o* by plane; **~ en barco** to travel by boat; **~ en bicicleta** to ride a bicycle, cycle; **aprendí a ~ en bici a los seis años** I learned to ride a bike *o* to cycle when I was six; *ver tb* **cólera A1**
[3] (*Fin*) (= *sumar*) [*factura, gastos*] to amount to, come to; **el total monta (a) 2.500 euros** the total amounts *o* comes to 2,500 euros; ♦*REFRÁN* **tanto monta (monta tanto, Isabel como Fernando)** (*Esp*) it makes no difference, it's all the same; **tanto monta que vengas o no** it makes no difference *o* it's all the same whether you come or not
[4] (= *solapar*) **~ sobre algo** to overlap sth, cover part of sth; **el mapa monta sobre el texto** the map overlaps the text, the map covers part of the text; **el texto está montado sobre la foto** the text covers part of the photo
Ⓒ **montarse** VPR [1] (= *subirse*) **~se en** [+ *coche*] to get in(to); [+ *autobús, tren*] to get on(to); [+ *caballo, bicicleta*] to get on(to), mount; [+ *atracción de feria*] to go on; **¿te has montado alguna vez en avión?** have you ever been on a plane?, have you ever flown?; **~se en barco** to get on a boat, travel by boat
[2] ♦*MODISMOS* **montárselo** (*Esp**) (= *organizarse*) **montátelo como puedas** you'll have to manage the best you can; **¡tú sí que te lo has montado bien!** ◊ **¡tú sí que lo tienes bien montado!** you're on to a good thing there!*, you've got it made!*; **se lo montó fatal con lo del regalo** he messed things up with the present*; **se lo ha montado muy mal contigo** he's behaved very badly towards you; **~se en el dólar** to make big money*

montaraz ADJ (= *salvaje*) wild, untamed; (= *tosco*) rough, coarse; (= *huraño*) unsociable

montarrón SM (*Andes*) forest

monte SM [1] (= *montaña*) mountain; (= *cerro*) hill; **el Monte de los Olivos** the Mount of Olives; **el Monte Sinaí** Mount Sinai; **los ~s Pirineos** the Pyrenees; **los Montes Urales** the Urals; **los ~s Apalaches** the Appalachian Mountains; **los ~s Cárpatos** the Carpathian Mountains; ♦*MODISMO* **echarse al ~** to take to the hills
[2] (= *campo*) countryside, country; (= *bosque*) woodland; **los domingos salimos al ~ a pasear** on Sundays we go walking in the countryside; **un conejo de ~** a wild rabbit; **batir el ~** to beat for game, go hunting; ♦*MODISMOS* **hacérsele un ~ a algn**: **todo se le hace un ~** he makes mountains out of molehills; **no todo el ~ es orégano** it's not all plain sailing ► **monte alto** forest

► **monte bajo** scrub
3 ► **monte de piedad** pawnshop
4 (*Naipes*) (= *baraja*) pile; (= *banca*) bank
5 ► **monte de Venus** mons veneris
6 (*CAm, Caribe*) (= *alrededores*) outskirts *pl*, surrounding country; (*Méx*) (= *hierba*) grass, pasture
7 (*LAm**) (= *hachís*) hash*, pot*

montear ▸conjug 1a◂ VT to hunt

montecillo SM mound, hump

montepío SM 1 (= *sociedad*) friendly society; (= *fondo*) charitable fund for dependents
2 (*Andes, Cono Sur*) (= *viudedad*) widow's pension
3 (= *monte de piedad*) pawnshop

montera SF 1 (= *sombrero*) cloth cap; [*de torero*] bullfighter's hat; ✦*MODISMO* **ponerse algo por ~** to laugh at sth; *ver tb* **mundo 5**
2 (*Téc*) rise
3 (*Arquit*) skylight; *ver tb* **montero**

montería SF 1 (= *arte*) hunting; (= *caza*) hunt, chase
2 (= *animales*) game
3 (= *personas*) hunting party
4 (= *lugar*) hunting ground
5 (*Arte*) hunting scene
6 (*Andes*) (= *canoa*) canoe
7 (*CAm*) (= *concesión*) concession
8 (*CAm, Méx*) (= *madería*) logging camp

montero/a SM/F (= *cazador*) hunter; (= *ojeador*) beater; *ver tb* **montera**

montés ADJ wild

montevideano/a ADJ, SM/F Montevidean

montículo SM mound, hump

monto SM amount; **un cheque por un ~ aproximado de nueve millones** a cheque for approximately nine million

montón SM 1 (*gen*) heap, pile; [*de nieve*] pile; ✦*MODISMOS* **del ~** ordinary, average; **un hombre del ~** just an ordinary *o* average chap; **salirse del ~** to stand out from the crowd; **en ~** all jumbled together
2 (*) (= *mucho*) **sabe un ~** he knows loads*; **tenemos montones** we've got loads *o* masses*; **un ~ de** loads of*, masses of*; **un ~ de gente** loads of people*, masses of people*; **tardaron un ~ de tiempo** they took ages; **tengo un ~ de cosas que decirte** I've got loads to tell you*; **a montones**: **ejemplos hay a montones** there is no shortage of examples; **tenía baches a montones** it was full of potholes

montonera SF (*LAm*) 1 (= *montón*) pile, heap; (*Andes*) (= *almiar*) haystack
2 (= *guerrilla*) band of guerrilla fighters
3 (*Cono Sur Hist*) troop of mounted rebels

montonero/a Ⓐ ADJ 1 (*Cono Sur*) urban guerrilla *antes de s*
2 (*LAm*) (= *autoritario*) overbearing
Ⓑ SM/F urban guerrilla; **los Montoneros** *armed wing of the Peronist movement in Argentina*

montuno ADJ 1 (= *de montaña*) mountain *antes de s*; (= *de bosque*) forest *antes de s*
2 (*LAm*) (= *salvaje*) wild, untamed; (= *rústico*) rustic

montuosidad SF hilliness, mountainous nature

montuoso ADJ hilly, mountainous

montura SF 1 [*de gafas*] frame; [*de joya*] mount, setting
2 (= *animal*) mount
3 (= *silla*) saddle; (= *arreos*) harness, trappings *pl*; **cabalgar sin ~** to ride bareback

monumental ADJ 1 (= *de monumentos*) **conjunto ~** collection of historical monuments; **la riqueza ~ del país** the country's wealth of monuments; **un catálogo ~ de España** a catalogue of the (historical) monuments of Spain
2 (= *enorme*) [*esfuerzo, error, éxito*] monumental; [*atasco*] enormous; [*bronca, paliza*] tremendous
3 (*) (= *excelente*) tremendous*, terrific*

monumentalidad SF monumental character

monumentalismo SM *tendency to construct vast buildings or monuments*

monumento SM 1 (= *construcción*) monument; **el ~ a la paz** the monument to peace, the peace monument; **visitar los ~s de una ciudad** to visit a city's historical buildings ► **monumento a los caídos** war memorial ► **monumento al soldado desconocido** tomb of the unknown soldier ► **monumento histórico-artístico** (= *edificio*) listed building; (= *zona*) ≈ conservation area ► **monumentos prehistóricos** prehistoric remains
2 (*) (= *mujer*) beauty
3 **monumentos** (= *documentos*) documents, source material *sing*

monzón SM monsoon

monzónico ADJ monsoon *antes de s*; **lluvias monzónicas** monsoon rains

moña SF 1 (= *lazo*) bow; (= *cinta*) ribbon
2 (*) (= *muñeca*) doll
3 (*) (= *borrachera*) **cogerse una ~** to get sloshed*; **estar con la ~** to be sloshed*

moño SM 1 [*de pelo*] bun, chignon; (*en lo alto de la cabeza*) topknot; [*de caballo*] forelock; **se peina con un ~ alto** she piles her hair on top of her head; **hacerse (un) ~** to put one's hair up (in a bun); **agarrarse del ~** to pull each other's hair out; ✦*MODISMOS* **estar hasta el ~*** to be fed up to the back teeth*; **estar con el ~ torcido** (*Caribe, Méx*) to have got out of the wrong side of the bed; **ponerse ~s*** to give o.s. airs
2 (*Orn*) crest
3 (= *lazo*) bow
4 **moños** (= *adornos*) fripperies, buttons and bows
5 (*LAm*) (= *altivez*) pride, haughtiness; ✦*MODISMOS* **bajar el ~ a algn** to take sb down a peg; **agachar el ~** (*Cono Sur**) to give in
6 (*Cono Sur*) bar

mopa SF mop

moquear ▸conjug 1a◂ VI to have a runny nose

moquera SF, **moqueo** SM **tener ~** to have a runny nose

moquero* SM hankie*

moqueta SF fitted carpet

moquete SM punch on the nose

moquillo SM [*de perro, gato*] distemper; [*de ave*] pip

mor: **por ~ de** PREP because of, on account of; **por ~ de la amistad** for friendship's sake

mora[1] SF 1 (*Bot*) (= *zarzamora*) blackberry; [*del moral*] mulberry
2 (*Andes*) (= *bala*) bullet
3 (*Méx**) (= *droga*) pot*, grass*

mora[2] SF (*Fin, Jur*) delay; **ponerse en ~** to default

mora[3] SF (*Cono Sur*) (= *morcilla*) black pudding, blood sausage (*EEUU*)

morada SF 1 (= *casa*) dwelling (*liter*), abode (*liter*), dwelling place; **bienvenido a mi humilde ~** welcome to my humble abode; **no tener ~ fija** to be of no fixed abode ► **última morada** final resting place; *ver tb* **allanamiento 4**
2 (= *estadía*) stay, period of residence

morado Ⓐ ADJ purple; **terciopelo ~** purple velvet; **ojo ~** black eye; ✦*MODISMOS* **pasarlas moradas** to have a tough time of it; **ponerse ~ (de algo)*** to stuff one's face (with sth)*
Ⓑ SM 1 (= *color*) purple
2 (= *cardenal*) bruise

morador(a) SM/F inhabitant

moradura SF bruise

moral[1] SM (*Bot*) mulberry tree

moral[2] Ⓐ ADJ 1 (= *ético*) moral; **toda persona necesita una formación ~** everyone needs a moral education; **tenemos la obligación ~ de ayudarle** we are morally obliged to help him, we have a moral obligation to help him
2 (= *espiritual*) moral; **demostró una gran fortaleza ~** he showed great moral strength; **le daremos todo el apoyo ~ que necesite** we will give her all the moral support she needs; **ideas que quedan dentro del plano ~** ideas which fall within the sphere of morality
Ⓑ SF 1 (= *ética, moralidad*) morality, morals *pl*; **la ~ cristiana** Christian morality, Christian morals; **una película de dudosa ~** a film of dubious morality *o* morals; **no existe una ~ absoluta** there isn't an absolute morality; **doble ~** double standards *pl*; **faltar a la ~** to behave immorally
2 (= *estado de ánimo*) morale; **intentó subirle la ~ al equipo** he tried to boost the team's morale; **la victoria nos dio mucha ~** the victory boosted our morale; **tener baja la ~** ◊ **estar bajo de ~** to feel a bit low; **ando muy bajo de ~ últimamente** I've been feeling a bit low lately; **levantar la ~ a algn** to raise sb's spirits *o* morale; **la ~ de las tropas estaba por los suelos** the morale of the troops was at rock bottom; **la ~ se me cayó por los suelos cuando la vi con otro hombre** my heart sank when I saw her with another man; ✦*MODISMO* **tener más ~ que el alcoyano** (*Esp**) to keep going against all the odds, have real fighting spirit
3 (= *valor*) moral courage; **yo no habría tenido ~ para hablarles así** I wouldn't have had the moral courage to speak to them like that

moraleja SF moral

moralidad SF 1 (= *moral*) [*de persona, acto*] morality, morals *pl*; **una obra de ~ dudosa** a play of dubious morality *o* morals; **su falta de ~** his immorality; **faltar a la ~** to behave immorally
2 (= *moraleja*) moral

moralina SF moral

moralista Ⓐ ADJ moralistic
Ⓑ SMF moralist

moralizador(a) Ⓐ ADJ moralizing, moralistic; **la literatura ~a de la época** the moralizing *o* moralistic literature of the period; **su actitud**

era ~a his attitude was moralistic, he had a moralistic attitude
Ⓑ SM/F moralizer

moralizante ADJ moralizing, moralistic; **sus novelas tienen un tono ~** his novels have a moralizing *o* moralistic tone; **el relato era bastante ~** the story was quite moralistic

moralizar ▸conjug 1f◂ Ⓐ VT to raise the moral standards of; **quiso ~ el país** he wanted to raise the country's moral standards
Ⓑ VI to moralize; **en su afán de ~** in their eagerness to moralize

moralmente ADV morally; **me sentía ~ obligado** I felt morally obliged; **~ no está bien** morally speaking, it's no good

morapio* SM cheap red wine*

morar ▸conjug 1a◂ VI (= *vivir*) dwell (*liter*), to live; (= *alojarse*) to stay

moratón SM bruise

moratoria SF moratorium

morbidez SF softness, delicacy

morbididad SF = **morbilidad**

mórbido ADJ [1] (= *enfermo*) morbid
[2] (= *suave*) soft, delicate

morbilidad SF morbidity, sickness rate

morbo SM [1] (*) (= *curiosidad*) morbid curiosity; **la prensa amarilla alimenta el ~ de la gente** the gutter press feeds people's morbid curiosity
[2] (*) (= *atractivo sexual*) **no es guapa pero tiene ~** she's not pretty but she's sexy
[3] (*Med*) (= *enfermedad*) disease, illness

morbosidad SF [1] (= *curiosidad*) morbid curiosity, morbid interest
[2] (= *enfermedad*) morbidity, sickness
[3] (= *estadística*) morbidity, sick rate

morboso ADJ [1] (= *malsano*) [*persona, mente*] morbid; [*espectáculo*] gruesome; **curiosidad morbosa** morbid curiosity
[2] (= *atractivo*) sexually attractive
[3] (= *enfermo*) morbid, sickly; [*clima, zona*] unhealthy

morcilla SF [1] (*Culin*) blood sausage, black pudding; (*Méx*) (= *callos*) tripe; ✦*MODISMO* **¡que te den ~!‡** get stuffed!‡
[2] (*Teat*) ad lib
[3] (‡‡) (= *pene*) prick‡‡
[4] (*Caribe*) (= *mentira*) lie

morcillo Ⓐ ADJ [*caballo*] black with reddish hairs
Ⓑ SM (= *carne*) shank (*of beef*)

morcón SM [1] (*Culin*) large blood sausage
[2] (*) (= *rechoncho*) stocky person
[3] (*) (= *descuidado*) sloppy individual, slob*

mordacidad SF sharpness, bite; **no posee ni la gracia ni la ~ de Wilder** he has neither the humour nor the acid wit of Wilder; **con ~** sharply

mordaga‡ SF, **mordaguera‡** SF **coger** *o* **pillar una ~** to get plastered*

mordaz ADJ [*crítica, persona*] sharp, scathing; [*estilo*] incisive; [*humor*] caustic

mordaza SF [1] (*en la boca*) gag
[2] (*Téc*) clamp

mordazmente ADV bitingly, scathingly

mordedura SF bite; **una ~ de serpiente** a snake bite

mordelón Ⓐ ADJ [1] (*LAm*) [*perro*] prone to bite
[2] (*CAm, Méx**) (= *sobornable*) given to taking bribes
Ⓑ SM (*Méx‡*) traffic cop*

morder ▸conjug 2h◂ Ⓐ VT [1] (*con los dientes*) to bite
[2] (= *corroer*) (*Quím*) to corrode, eat away; [+ *recursos*] to eat into
[3] (*Mec*) [+ *embrague*] to catch
[4] (*CAm, Méx*) (= *exigir soborno*) to take a bribe from
[5] (*Méx*) (= *estafar*) to cheat
[6] (*) (= *denigrar*) to gossip about, run down
[7] (‡) (= *reconocer*) to recognize
Ⓑ VI to bite; ✦*MODISMO* **está que muerde** he's hopping mad
Ⓒ **morderse** VPR to bite; **~se las uñas** to bite one's nails; ✦*MODISMO* **~se la lengua** to bite one's tongue

mordicar ▸conjug 1g◂ VI to smart, sting

mordida SF [1] (= *mordisco*) bite
[2] (*CAm, Méx*) (= *soborno*) bribe; (= *tajada*) rake-off*, cut*; (= *acción*) bribery

mordiscar ▸conjug 1g◂ = **mordisquear**

mordisco SM [1] (= *bocado*) bite; **el perro me dio un ~** the dog bit me; **le arrancó la oreja de un ~** he took his ear off in one bite; **deshacer algo a ~s** to bite sth to pieces
[2] (= *trozo*) bite
[3] (‡) (= *beso*) love bite, hickey (EEUU)

mordisquear ▸conjug 1a◂ Ⓐ VT (*gen*) to nibble (at); [*caballo*] to champ
Ⓑ VI (*gen*) to nibble; [*caballo*] to champ

morena[1] SF (*Geol*) moraine

morena[2] SF (= *pez*) moray

morenal SM (*CAm*) shanty town

morenear ▸conjug 1a◂ Ⓐ VT to tan
Ⓑ **morenearse** VPR to tan

morenez SF suntan, brownness

moreno/a Ⓐ ADJ [1] [*persona*] (= *de pelo moreno*) dark-haired; (= *de tez morena*) dark(-skinned), swarthy; (= *bronceado*) brown, tanned; (*euf*) coloured, colored (EEUU); (*Andes, Caribe*) mulatto; **ponerse ~** to tan, go brown
[2] [*pelo*] (dark) brown; [*azúcar, pan*] brown
Ⓑ SM/F [*de pelo*] dark-haired man/woman; [*de tez*] dark(-skinned) man/woman; **una morena** a brunette
Ⓒ SM tan

morera SF mulberry tree

morería SF (*Hist*) (= *territorio*) Moorish lands *pl*, Moorish territory; (= *barrio*) Moorish quarter

moretón SM bruise

morfa‡ SF = **morfina**

morfar‡ ▸conjug 1a◂ (*Cono Sur*) Ⓐ VT to eat, scoff*
Ⓑ VI to eat, nosh*, chow down (EEUU*); **ni siquiera les alcanza para ~** they don't even have enough money to pay for grub‡

morfema SM morpheme

morfémico ADJ morphemic

morfi‡ SM (*Cono Sur*) grub*, nosh*, chow (EEUU*)

morfina SF morphine

morfinomanía SF morphine addiction

morfinómano/a Ⓐ ADJ addicted to morphine
Ⓑ SM/F morphine addict

morfofonología SF morphophonology

morfología SF morphology

morfológico ADJ morphological

morfón‡ ADJ (*Cono Sur*) piggish, greedy

morfosintaxis SF INV morphosyntax

morganático ADJ morganatic

morgue SF (*esp LAm*) morgue

moribundo/a Ⓐ ADJ [1] [*persona*] dying; **estaba ~** he was dying, he was at death's door
[2] [*proceso, negocio*] moribund; **el régimen está ~** the regime is moribund *o* on the way out
Ⓑ SM/F dying person; **los ~s** the dying

moricho SM (*Caribe*) hammock

morigeración SF restraint, moderation

morigerado ADJ well-behaved, law-abiding

morigerar ▸conjug 1a◂ VT to restrain, moderate

morillo SM firedog

▼ **morir** ▸conjug 3j◂ (*pp* **muerto**) Ⓐ VI [1] [*persona, animal, planta*] to die; **ha muerto de repente** she died suddenly; **murió a consecuencia de un infarto** he died as a result of a heart attack; **lo asfixió hasta ~** she suffocated him to death; **¡muera el tirano!** down with the tyrant!, death to the tyrant!; **~ ahogado** to drown; **~ ahorcado** (*por un verdugo*) to be hanged; (*suicidándose*) to be found hanged; **murió ahorcado en su celda** he was found hanged in his cell; **~ asesinado** [*persona*] to be murdered; [*personaje público*] to be assassinated; **~ de algo** to die of sth; **murió de cáncer/del corazón** he died of cancer/of a heart attack; **~ de frío** to die of cold, freeze to death; **~ de hambre** to die of hunger, starve to death; **~ de muerte natural** to die a natural death, die of natural causes; **~ de vejez** *o* **de viejo** to die of old age; **~ por algo** to die for sth; **no merece la pena ~ por amor** it is not worth dying for love; ✦*MODISMO* **~ al pie del cañón** to die with one's boots on; *ver tb* **bota 1**
[2] (= *extinguirse*) [*civilización*] to die, die out, come to an end; [*amor*] to die; [*fuego*] to die down; [*luz*] to fade; **con él moría toda una generación** with him died an entire generation; **moría el día** (*liter*) the day was drawing to a close (*liter*); **las olas iban a ~ a la playa** (*liter*) the waves ran out on the beach; **ese camino muere en la ermita** that path comes to an end at the chapel; ✦*MODISMO* **y allí muere** (*LAm*) and that's all there is to it
Ⓑ **morirse** VPR [1] [*persona, animal, planta*] to die; **se murió tras una larga enfermedad** he died after a long illness; **se acaba de ~ su abuelo** her grandfather has just died; **se le ha muerto el gato** her cat has died; **¡ojalá** *o* **así se muera!** I hope he drops dead!; **~se de algo** to die of sth; **se murió de una pulmonía** she died of pneumonia
[2] (*) (*para exagerar*) to die; **por poco me muero cuando me lo contaron** I nearly died when they told me*; **si me descubren me muero** I'll die if they find me out*; **¡muérete! primero se casa con una millonaria y luego se divorcia** you'll never guess what! first he marries a millionairess, then he gets divorced*; **¡no se va a ~ por llamar por teléfono alguna vez!** it wouldn't kill him to ring me some time!*; **¡que me muera si miento!** cross my heart and hope to die!*, may God strike me dead if I'm lying!*; **~se de algo**: **en esta casa me muero de frío** I'm freezing in this house; **¡me muero de hambre!** I'm starving!; **¡me muero de sed!** I'm dying of thirst!*; **me moría de pena de verla llorar** it broke my heart to see her cry; **se moría de envidia** he was green with envy; **por poco**

➤ LENGUA Y USO: **morir A1** 51.4

me muero de vergüenza I nearly died of embarrassment*; **me moría de miedo** I was scared stiff*; **se van a ~ de risa** they'll kill themselves laughing*; **la película era para ~se de risa** the film was hilarious *o* incredibly funny; **~se de ganas de hacer algo** to be dying to do sth*; **me moría de ganas de verte** I was dying to see you*; **~se por algo** (*de deseo*) to be dying for sth*; (*de afición*) to be crazy *o* mad about sth*; **¡me muero por una cerveza fresquita!** I'm dying for *o* I could murder a nice cold beer!*; **se muere por el fútbol** he's crazy *o* mad about football*; **~se por algn** to be crazy *o* mad about sb*; **~se por hacer algo** to be dying to do sth*; **me muero por tener una moto** I'm dying to have a motorbike*; **✦MODISMO de** *o* **para ~se**: **ese jamón estaba de** *o* **para ~se** that ham was just amazing!*; **el Caribe es como para ~se** the Caribbean is just amazing!*; **las fotos del terremoto eran para ~se** the pictures of the earthquake were just horrific*

3 (= *entumecerse*) [*brazo, pierna*] to go to sleep, go numb

morisco/a Ⓐ ADJ Moorish; (*Arquit*) Moorish

Ⓑ SM/F 1 (*Hist*) Moslem convert to Christianity, subject Moslem (*of 15th and 16th centuries*)

2 (*Méx*) (= *cuarterón*) quadroon

morisma SF Moors *pl*

morisqueta SF fraud, dirty trick

mormón/ona SM/F Mormon

mormónico ADJ Mormon

mormonismo SM Mormonism

moro/a Ⓐ ADJ 1 (*Hist*) Moorish

2 (*Esp* pey*) (= *del norte de Africa*) North African

3 (*Esp**) (= *machista*) macho*

4 [*caballo*] dappled, piebald

Ⓑ SM/F 1 (*Hist*) Moor; **✦MODISMOS ¡hay ~s en la costa!** watch out!; **no hay ~s en la costa** the coast is clear; **dar a ~ muerto gran lanzada** to kick a man when he's down

2 (*Esp* pey*) (= *del norte de Africa*) North African

3 (*LAm*) (= *caballo*) piebald (horse)

Ⓒ SM 1 (*) (= *marido*) domineering husband

2 **~s y cristianos** (*Caribe**) (*Culin*) rice with black beans

3 (*Esp**) (= *Marruecos*) Morocco; **bajar al ~** to go to Morocco

4 (*Mús**) wrong note

morocha SF (*Caribe*) double-barrelled gun

morocho (*LAm*) Ⓐ ADJ 1 [*pelo*] dark; [*persona*] dark, swarthy; [*chica*] brunette; **de piel morocha** dark-skinned

2 (= *fuerte*) strong, tough; (= *apuesto*) well-built; (= *bien conservado*) well-preserved

3 (*Caribe*) (= *gemelo*) twin

Ⓑ SM 1 (= *maíz*) hard maize, corn (*EEUU*)

2 (= *persona*) tough guy*

3 **morochos** (*Ven*) (= *gemelos*) twins

morón SM hillock

morondanga SF hotchpotch, hodgepodge (*EEUU*)

morondo ADJ 1 (= *calvo*) bald; (= *sin hojas*) leafless, bare

2 (= *mondo*) bare, plain

moronga SF (*CAm, Méx*) black pudding, blood sausage (*EEUU*)

morosidad SF 1 (*Fin*) slowness in paying; (= *atrasos*) arrears *pl*

2 (= *lentitud*) slowness; (= *apatía*) apathy

moroso/a Ⓐ ADJ 1 (*Fin*) slow to pay; **deudor ~** slow payer, defaulter

2 (= *lento*) slow; **una película de acción morosa** a slow-moving film; **delectación morosa** lingering enjoyment

Ⓑ SM/F (*Fin*) bad debtor, defaulter; **cartera de ~s** bad debts *pl*

morra SF top of the head; **✦MODISMO andar a la ~** to exchange blows

morrada* SF 1 (= *cabezazo*) (*contra objeto*) bang on the head; (*contra otra persona, animal*) butt; **darse una ~** to fall flat on one's face

2 (= *bofetada*) bash*, punch

morral SM 1 (= *mochila*) haversack, knapsack; [*de caza*] pouch, game bag; [*de caballo*] nose-bag

2 (*) (= *matón*) lout, rough type

morralla SF 1 (= *peces*) small fry, little fish

2 (= *cosas*) junk*; (= *basura*) rubbish, garbage (*EEUU*)

3 (= *personas*) rabble, riff-raff

4 (*Méx*) (= *calderilla*) small change

morrazo* SM (= *golpe*) thump

morrear* ▸conjug 1a◂ VT, VI to snog*, neck

morrena SF moraine

morreo* SM snogging*, necking

morrera‡ SF (= *labios*) lips *pl*; (= *boca*) kisser*

morrillo SM (*Zool*) fleshy part of the neck; (*) (= *cuello*) neck, back of the neck

morriña SF (*Esp*) homesickness; **tener ~** to be homesick

morriñoso ADJ homesick

morrión SM helmet, morion

morrito* SM **hacer ~s** to pout

morro SM 1 (*Zool*) snout, nose

2 (*Esp**) (= *labio*) (thick) lip; **beber a ~** to drink from the bottle; **¡cierra los ~s!** shut your trap!‡; **dar a algn en los ~s** (*lit*) to bash sb*; (*fig*) to get one's own back on sb; **partir los ~s a algn** to bash sb's face in*; **✦MODISMOS estar de ~(s)** to be in a bad mood; **estar de ~(s) con algn** to be cross with sb; **poner ~** ◊ **torcer el ~** (= *ofenderse*) to look cross; (= *hacer una mueca*) to turn up one's nose; **poner morritos** to look sullen

3 (‡) (= *descaro*) cheek*, nerve*; **tener ~** to have a cheek*, have a nerve*; **¡qué ~ tienes!** you've got a nerve!*; **echarle mucho ~** to have a real nerve*; **✦MODISMOS tiene un ~ que se lo pisa*** he's got a real brass neck*; **por el ~**: **me lo quedé por el ~** I just held on to it and to hell with them!*

4 (*Aer, Aut etc*) nose; **caer de ~** to nose-dive

5 (*Geog*) (= *promontorio*) headland, promontory; (= *cerro*) small rounded hill

6 (= *guijarro*) pebble

morrocotudo* ADJ 1 (= *fantástico*) smashing*, terrific*

2 (= *grande*) [*riña, golpe*] tremendous; [*susto*] terrible

3 (*Andes*) (= *rico*) rich

4 (*Cono Sur*) (= *torpe*) clumsy, awkward

morrocoy SM (*CAm*) turtle

morrocoyo SM (*Caribe*) 1 (*Zool*) turtle

2 (‡) (= *gordo*) fat person, fatty‡

3 (= *tullido*) cripple

morrón Ⓐ ADJ **pimiento ~** sweet red pepper

Ⓑ SM 1 (= *pimiento*) sweet red pepper

2 (*Esp**) (= *golpe*) blow; **se dio un ~ con la puerta** he banged into the door and hurt his face

morrongo/a SM/F cat

morronguero* ADJ (*Caribe*) 1 (= *tacaño*) stingy

2 (= *cobarde*) yellow*

morroñoso ADJ 1 (*CAm*) (= *áspero*) rough

2 (*Andes*) (= *pequeño*) small; (= *endeble*) feeble; (= *miserable*) wretched, poverty-stricken

morrudo ADJ 1 (= *de labios gruesos*) thick-lipped

2 (*Cono Sur*) (= *musculoso*) tough, brawny

morsa SF walrus

morse SM Morse code

mortadela SF mortadella

mortaja SF 1 [*de muerto*] shroud

2 (*Téc*) mortise

3 (*LAm**) (= *papel*) cigarette paper

mortal Ⓐ ADJ 1 [*ser*] mortal

2 [*herida, golpe*] fatal, deadly; [*disparo, accidente*] fatal; [*veneno, virus, sustancia, dosis*] deadly, lethal; [*peligro*] mortal; **la película es un aburrimiento ~** the film is a real bore; **salto ~** somersault

3 [*pecado*] mortal; [*odio*] deadly

4 **quedarse ~†** to be thunderstruck

5 **✦MODISMO las señas son ~es†** there's no escaping the evidence

Ⓑ SMF (= *ser*) mortal; **como cualquier ~** just like anybody else

Ⓒ SM (= *salto*) somersault; **doble ~** double somersault

mortalidad SF 1 (= *condición de mortal*) mortality

2 (*en demografía*) mortality; (*en accidente*) death toll ▸ **mortalidad infantil** infant mortality

mortalmente ADV fatally; **le disparó ~ en el abdomen** he shot him fatally in the stomach; **resultó ~ herido** he was mortally wounded; **pecar ~** to commit a mortal sin

mortandad SF 1 (= *víctimas*) (*humanas*) loss of life; (*animales*) death

2 (= *matanza*) slaughter, carnage

mortecino ADJ 1 [*luz*] dim, faint; [*color*] dull; [*fuego, llamas*] dying

2 (= *débil*) weak, failing; **hacer la mortecina** to pretend to be dead

morterada* SF **gana una ~** he earns a small fortune, he earns a tidy bit*

mortero SM mortar

mortífero ADJ deadly, lethal

mortificación SF 1 (= *sufrimiento*) torture; **era una ~ para él** it was torture *o* hell for him

2 (= *humillación*) humiliation

3 (*Rel*) mortification

mortificar ▸conjug 1g◂ Ⓐ VT 1 (= *atormentar*) to torment, plague; **sus compañeros les mortifican con crueldad** their workmates treat them cruelly; **me han mortificado toda la noche los mosquitos** I was tormented all night by the mosquitos; **estos zapatos me mortifican** these shoes are killing me

2 (= *humillar*) to humiliate

3 (*Rel*) **~ la carne** to mortify the flesh

4 (*Med*) to damage seriously

Ⓑ **mortificarse** VPR 1 (= *atormentarse*) to torment o.s., distress o.s.

2 (*Rel*) to mortify the flesh

[3] (*CAm, Méx*) (= *avergonzarse*) to feel ashamed, be mortified

mortuorio ADJ mortuary; **casa mortuoria** home of the deceased; **coche ~** hearse; **esquela mortuoria** death notice

morueco SM ram

moruno ADJ (*pey*) Moorish; *ver tb* **pincho 4**

morza SF (*Cono Sur*) carpenter's vice

Mosa SM **el (río) ~** the Meuse

mosaico¹ ADJ Mosaic, of Moses

mosaico² SM [1] (*Arte*) (*gen*) mosaic; (= *pavimento*) tessellated pavement; **un ~ romano** a Roman mosaic; **un suelo de ~** a mosaic floor ► **mosaico de madera** marquetry

[2] (= *conjunto*) **un ~ de grupos étnicos** a whole spectrum of ethnic groups

mosca Ⓐ SF [1] (= *insecto*) fly; **pescar a la ~** to fish with a fly, fly-fish; ✦*MODISMOS* **asarse las ~s: se asaban las ~s** it was baking hot; **caer como ~s** to drop like flies; **cazar ~s** to daydream; **mandar a algn a capar ~s*** to tell sb to go to blazes*; **papar ~s** to daydream; **por si las ~s*** just in case; **me llevaré el impermeable por si las ~s** I'll take my raincoat just in case; **¿qué ~ te/le ha picado?*** what's got into you/him?; **tener la ~ en** *o* **detrás de la oreja*** to smell a rat* ► **mosca artificial** (*en pesca*) fly ► **mosca azul**, **mosca blanca** whitefly ► **mosca de burro** horsefly ► **mosca de España** Spanish fly, cantharides ► **mosca de la carne** meat fly ► **mosca de la fruta** fruit fly ► **mosca doméstica** house fly ► **mosca drosofila** drosophila, fruit fly ► **mosca muerta** = **mosquita** ► **mosca tsetsé** tsetse fly

[2] (*) (= *pesado*) pest

[3] (†) (= *dinero*) dough*; ✦*MODISMO* **aflojar** *o* **soltar la ~** to fork out*, stump up

[4] (†) (= *barba*) small goatee beard

[5] **moscas** (= *centellas*) sparks ► **moscas volantes** spots before the eyes, floaters

[6] (*Méx**) (= *parásito*) sponger*

Ⓑ ADJ INV (*Esp**) ✦*MODISMOS* **estar ~** (= *suspicaz*) to be suspicious, smell a rat*; (= *preocupado*) to be worried; **estar ~ con algn** (= *enfadado*) to be cross *o* annoyed with sb

moscada ADJ **nuez ~** nutmeg

moscarda SF bluebottle, blowfly

moscardón SM [1] (= *moscarda*) bluebottle, blowfly; (= *abejón*) hornet

[2] (*) (= *persona molesta*) pest, nuisance

moscatel¹ ADJ, SM muscatel

moscatel² SM [1] (= *pesado*) bore, pest

[2] (= *mocetón*) big lad, overgrown lad

moscón SM [1] (= *insecto*) bluebottle, blowfly

[2] (*Bot*) maple

[3] (*) (= *pesado*) pest, nuisance

moscoso* SM day off (*for personal matters, not deducted from annual leave*)

moscovita ADJ, SMF Muscovite

Moscú SM Moscow

Mosela SM Moselle

mosqueado ADJ [1] (*) (= *enfadado*) cross, angry

[2] (*) (= *desconfiado*) suspicious; **ya andaba yo ~** I already had my suspicions

[3] (= *moteado*) spotted

mosqueador SM (*para moscas*) (= *instrumento*) fly-whisk; (= *cola*) tail

mosqueante* ADJ [1] (= *molesto*) annoying, irritating

[2] (= *sospechoso*) suspicious, fishy*

mosquearse* ▸conjug 1a◂ VPR [1] (= *enfadarse*) to get cross, get annoyed; (= *ofenderse*) to get offended

[2] (= *desconfiar*) to smell a rat*

[3] (= *preocuparse*) to worry; **me mosqueé porque a las once no había llamado** I got worried because he hadn't called by eleven

mosqueo* SM **coger** *o* **pillar** *o* **llevarse un ~** (= *enfadarse*) to get cross, get annoyed; (= *ofenderse*) to get offended; (= *desconfiar*) to smell a rat*; (= *preocuparse*) to worry

mosquete SM musket

mosquetero SM (*Hist, Mil*) musketeer; (*Teat*) groundling

mosquita SF **~ muerta** hypocrite; **hacerse la ~ muerta** to look as if butter wouldn't melt in one's mouth

mosquitero SM mosquito net

mosquito SM (*gen*) mosquito; (*pequeño*) gnat

mosso SM **Mossos d'esquadra** *Catalan autonomous police*

mostacera SF, **mostacero** SM mustard pot

mostacho SM moustache, mustache (*EEUU*)

mostachón SM macaroon

mostacilla SF (*Andes*) bead necklace

mostaza SF [1] (*Culin*) mustard; **~ de Dijon** (French) Dijon mustard; **~ inglesa** English mustard; **un vestido ~** a mustard-yellow dress

[2] (*Andes, Méx‡*) pot*, hash*

mostela SF sheaf

mosto SM [*de uva*] grape juice; (*en la elaboración de vino*) must

mostrador SM [1] [*de tienda*] counter; [*de café, bar*] bar; [*de oficina, biblioteca*] desk ► **mostrador de caja** cash desk ► **mostrador de facturación** check-in desk ► **mostrador de tránsito** transit desk

[2] [*de reloj*] face, dial

[3] (‡) (= *pecho*) tits** *pl*

mostrar ▸conjug 1l◂ Ⓐ VT (= *señalar, explicar*) to show; (= *exponer*) to display, exhibit; **nos mostró el camino** he showed us the way; **~ en pantalla** (*Inform*) to display

Ⓑ **mostrarse** VPR (+ *ADJ*) **se mostró interesado en la oferta** he was interested *o* showed interest in the offer; **se mostró partidario de aceptar la propuesta** he was in favour of accepting the proposal

mostrenco/a Ⓐ ADJ [1] (*) [*persona*] (= *bruto*) oafish; (= *poco inteligente*) dense, slow; (= *gordo*) fat

[2] (*) [*objeto*] crude, roughly made

[3] (††) (= *sin dueño*) ownerless, unclaimed; (= *sin hogar*) homeless, rootless

Ⓑ SM/F (*) oaf

mostro* ADJ (*Andes*) great*, superb

mota SF [1] (= *partícula*) speck, tiny bit; **~ de polvo** speck of dust; **~ de carbonilla** smut, speck of coal dust; ✦*REFRÁN* **ver la ~ en el ojo ajeno** to see the mote in sb else's eye

[2] (= *dibujo*) dot; **una mariposa blanca con ~s azules** a white butterfly speckled with blue; **a ~s** [*dibujo*] dotted

[3] (*en tela*) (= *nudillo*) burl; (= *jaspeado*) fleck

[4] (= *defecto*) fault, blemish

[5] **no hace (ni) ~ de aire** there isn't a breath of air

[6] (*Geog*) hillock

[7] (= *mojón*) boundary mark; (= *césped*) turf, clod (*used to block off irrigation channel*)

[8] (*LAm*) (= *pelo*) lock of wavy hair

[9] (*Andes, Caribe, Méx*) (= *borla*) powder puff

[10] (*LAm*) (= *lana*) tuft (*of wool*)

[11] (*LAm*) (= *planta*) marijuana plant; (= *droga*) grass*, pot‡; *ver tb* **moto²**

mote¹ SM [1] (= *apodo*) nickname; **le pusieron el ~ de "el abuelo"** they nicknamed him *o* they gave him the nickname "Grandad"

[2] (*Hist*) motto, device

mote² SM [1] (*Andes, Cono Sur*) (= *trigo*) boiled wheat; (= *maíz*) boiled maize, boiled corn (*EEUU*) ► **mote con huesillos** (*Chile*) maize and peach drink

[2] (*Cono Sur*) ✦*MODISMOS* **pelar ~** to gossip; **como ~** in large numbers

moteado ADJ [1] [*piel*] (= *con manchas pequeñas*) speckled; (= *con manchas grandes*) dappled, mottled; **un caballo gris ~** a dapple-grey horse

[2] [*tela*] (*de forma irregular*) flecked; (= *con lunares*) dotted

motear ▸conjug 1a◂ VT to speck (**de** with)

motejar ▸conjug 1a◂ VT to nickname; **~ a algn de algo** to brand sb sth, accuse sb of being sth

motel SM motel

motero/a* SM/F biker*

motete SM motet

motín SM [*de presos*] riot; (*en barco, de tropas*) mutiny ► **motín carcelario** prison riot

motivación SF [1] (= *estimulación*) motivation

[2] (= *motivo*) motive

motivacional ADJ motivational

motivar ▸conjug 1a◂ VT [1] (= *estimular*) to motivate; **los estudios ya no la motivan** she is no longer motivated by her studies

[2] (= *causar*) to cause; **un retraso motivado por circunstancias ajenas a su voluntad** a delay caused by circumstances beyond his control

[3] (= *explicar*) to justify, explain; **motivó su decisión con razonamientos muy válidos** she had some very sound reasons to justify her decision

▼ **motivo** Ⓐ SM [1] (= *causa*) reason; **dejó el trabajo por ~s personales** he left the job for personal reasons; **por cuyo ~** for which reason; **fue ~ de descalificación del atleta** it was the reason for the athlete's disqualification; **con este** *o* **tal ~** for this reason; **con ~ de** (= *debido a*) because of, owing to; (= *en ocasión de*) on the occasion of; **se informatizará el sistema con ~ de las elecciones** the system will be computerized because of *o* owing to the elections; **con ~ de nuestra boda le invitamos a ...** on the occasion of our wedding we invite you to ...; **~ de**: **me dio ~ de preocupación** it gave me cause for concern; **la decisión fue ~ de críticas** the decision became the object of criticism; **sin ~** for no reason, without good reason; **dejó de hablarme sin ~** he stopped talking to me for no reason; **ser ~ sobrado** *o* **suficiente**: **es ~ suficiente** *o* **sobrado para seguir votándolo** that's reason enough to continue voting for him, that's all the more reason to continue voting for him; **hay suficientes** *o* **sobrados ~s para odiarlo** there are more than enough reasons for hating him ► **motivos de divorcio** grounds for divorce ► **motivos ocultos**

➤ LENGUA Y USO: motivo A1 44.1

ulterior motives

[2] (= *móvil*) motive; **¿cuál fue el ~ del crimen?** what was the motive for the crime?

[3] (*Arte, Mús*) motif; **decorado con ~s orientales** decorated with oriental motifs ► **motivo conductor** leitmotif ► **motivo decorativo** decorative motif ► **motivo ornamental** ornamental motif

Ⓑ ADJ motive

moto[1] SF (motor)bike; **voy al trabajo en ~** I travel to work by (motor)bike; ✦***MODISMOS*** **ir como una ~**‡ to be in a rush; **ponerse como una ~**‡ (*sexualmente*) to get really turned on‡, get horny‡; (*con droga*) to get high*; (= *cabrearse*) to go off one's head* ► **moto acuática, moto de agua** jet ski

moto[2]**/a** Ⓐ ADJ [1] (*CAm*) orphaned, abandoned

[2] (*Andes*) tailless

Ⓑ SM/F (*CAm*) orphan; *ver tb* **mota**

motobomba SF motor pump, fire engine

motocarro SM *light delivery van with three wheels*

motocicleta SF motorcycle, motorbike; **~ con sidecar** motorbike *o* motorcycle with a sidecar

motociclismo SM motorcycling

motociclista SMF motorcyclist ► **motociclista de escolta** outrider

moto-cross SM INV motocross

motocultor SM cultivator

motón SM pulley

motonauta SMF jet skier

motonáutica SF motorboat racing, speedboat racing

motonave SF motor ship, motor vessel

motoneta SF (*LAm*) (motor) scooter

motoneurona SF motor neurone

motonieve SF snowmobile

motoniveladora SF bulldozer

motor Ⓐ ADJ [1] (*Téc*) motive, motor (*EEUU*); **potencia ~a** motive power

[2] (*Anat*) motor

Ⓑ SM motor, engine; **~ eléctrico** electric motor *o* engine; **un ~ de seis cilindros** a six-cylinder engine; **con seis ~es** six-engined; **con ~** power-driven; **aviación con ~** powered flight ► **motor a chorro, motor a reacción** jet engine ► **motor de arranque** starter, starter motor ► **motor de aviación** aircraft engine ► **motor de búsqueda** (*Internet*) search engine ► **motor de combustión interna, motor de explosión** internal combustion engine ► **motor de inyección** fuel-injected engine ► **motor delantero** front-mounted engine ► **motor de puesta en marcha** starter, starter motor ► **motor diesel** diesel engine ► **motor fuera (de) borda** outboard motor ► **motor refrigerado por aire** air-cooled engine ► **motor trasero** rear-mounted engine

motora SF, **motorbote** SM motorboat, speedboat

motorismo SM motorcycling

motorista SMF [1] (= *motociclista*) motorcyclist

[2] (*esp LAm*) (= *automovilista*) motorist, driver

motorístico ADJ motor-racing *antes de s*

motorización SF [1] (= *acto*) motorization; (= *mecanización*) mechanization

[2] (= *capacidad*) engine size

motorizado ADJ motorized; [*tropas*] mechanized, motorized; **trineo ~** motor sleigh; **un largo convoy ~** a long convoy of vehicles; **en autobús u otro medio ~** by bus or some other means of transport; **patrulla motorizada** motorized patrol, mobile unit; **personas no motorizadas** people who do not own a car, people who do not have their own transport; **estar ~*** to have wheels*, have a car

motorizar ▸conjug 1f◂ Ⓐ VT (*Mil, Téc*) to motorize

Ⓑ **motorizarse** VPR (*hum*, *) to get o.s. some wheels*

motosegadora SF motor mower, motorized lawn mower

motosierra SF power saw

motoso ADJ (*LAm*) [*pelo*] kinky

motricidad SF [1] (= *capacidad*) mobility

[2] (*Fisiol*) motor functions *pl*

motriz ADJ [1] (*Téc*) motive, motor (*EEUU*); **potencia ~** motive power; **fuerza ~** driving force

[2] (*Anat*) motor; **la actividad ~** motor functions

motu: **de ~ propio** ADV of one's own accord

motudo ADJ (*Cono Sur*) [*pelo*] kinky

mousse [muːs] SF (*a veces* SM) [1] (*Culin*) mousse ► **mousse de chocolate** chocolate mousse

[2] [*de pelo*] (styling) mousse; [*de afeitar*] shaving foam

movedizo ADJ [1] (= *no fijo*) [*terreno, suelo*] moving, shifting; [*objeto*] movable; [*persona, animal*] restless; *ver tb* **arena 1**

[2] (= *cambiante*) [*persona*] fickle; [*situación*] unsettled, changeable

mover ▸conjug 2h◂ Ⓐ VT [1] (= *cambiar de posición*) [1·1] [+ *objeto, mano, pierna*] to move; **no muevas la mesa** don't move the table; **~ a algn de algún sitio** to move sb from somewhere; **de aquí no nos mueve nadie** we're staying right here, we're not moving from here; **"no nos ~án"** "we shall not be moved"

[1·2] (*en juegos*) [+ *ficha, pieza*] to move

[2] (= *agitar*) to stir; **muévelo para que no se pegue** stir it *o* give it a stir so that it doesn't stick; **el perro se acercó moviendo la cola** the dog came up to us wagging its tail; **el viento movía sus cabellos** the wind blew her hair; **~ la cabeza** (*para negar*) to shake one's head; (*para asentir*) to nod, nod one's head; **movió la cabeza negando la pregunta** she shook her head in answer to the question; **movió la cabeza afirmativamente** she nodded (her head)

[3] (*Mec*) (= *accionar*) [+ *máquina*] to work, power; **el agua movía el molino** the water turned *o* drove the wheel; **el vapor mueve el émbolo** the steam drives *o* works the piston

[4] (= *incitar*) **el interés propio nos mueve a todos** self-interest motivates all of us; **lo hice movida por la curiosidad** it was curiosity that prompted *o* moved me to do it; **actuaba movido por sus instintos** he acted on his instincts; **su mensaje movía a las masas** his message roused the masses; **~ a algn a algo** to move sb to sth; **su pobreza te mueve a la compasión** their poverty moves you to pity; **~ a algn a las lágrimas** to move sb to tears; **~ a algn a la risa** to make sb laugh; **~ a algn a hacer algo** to prompt sb to do sth, move sb to do sth; **¿qué fue lo que te movió a actuar de ese modo?** what prompted *o* moved you to act in that way?

[5] (= *agilizar*) [+ *asunto, tema*] to push; [+ *trámite*] to handle; **ella le movió todo el papeleo** she handled all the paperwork for him; **~ una guerra contra algn** to wage war on sb; **~ un pleito contra algn** to start proceedings against sb

[6] [+ *dinero*] to move, handle; **esta empresa mueve miles de millones anualmente** this company moves *o* handles thousands of millions each year; **el tráfico de armas mueve mucho dinero** arms trading involves *o* moves a lot of money

[7] (*) [+ *droga*] to push

Ⓑ VI [1] (*en juegos*) to move; **¿con qué ficha has movido?** what piece have you moved?; **¿a quién le toca ~?** whose move is it?

[2] (= *incitar*) **~ a algo**: **esta situación mueve a la risa** this situation makes you (want to) laugh

[3] (*Bot*) to bud, sprout

Ⓒ **moverse** VPR [1] (= *cambiar de posición o lugar*) to move; **se mueve con dificultad** he has difficulty moving, he finds it difficult to move; **no te muevas, que te voy a hacer una foto** keep still *o* don't move, I'm going to take your photo; **se mueve mucho en la cama** she fidgets *o* moves around a lot in bed; **muévete un poco para allá** move up a bit; **no te muevas de ahí hasta que yo vuelva** stay right there *o* don't move until I come back; **lleva horas sin ~se de ese sofá** he hasn't moved *o* stirred from that sofa in hours; **no hay quien la haga ~se** no one can get her to move; **la máquina se movía sola** the machine moved on its own

[2] (= *agitarse*) [*mar*] to be rough; [*barco*] to roll; [*cortina, hojas*] to move; **las cortinas se movían con el viento** the curtains stirred *o* moved in the wind; **¿se ha movido mucho el barco?** was the sea rough?

[3] (= *ponerse en marcha*) to move o.s., get a move on*; **¡venga, muévete, que tenemos prisa!** come on, move yourself *o* get a move on, we're in a hurry!*

[4] (= *ser activo*) [*persona*] to be on the move*, be on the go*; [*ciudad*] to be lively; **esta moviéndose continuamente** she's always on the move *o* go*; **tuvo que ~se mucho para conseguir ese trabajo** he had to pull out all the stops to get that job; **Londres es una ciudad que se mueve** London is a really lively city

[5] (= *relacionarse*) (*en un ambiente*) to move; (*entre cierta gente*) to mix; **siempre me he movido en ambientes financieros** I have always moved in financial circles; **se mueve mucho entre aristócratas** he mixes a lot with the aristocracy

movible ADJ [1] (= *no fijo*) [*objeto*] movable, *ver tb* **fiesta 2**

[2] (= *voluble*) [*carácter, persona*] fickle

movida SF [1] (*) (= *animación*) scene*; **un bar en el centro de la ~** a bar at the heart of the club scene*; **la ~ cultural** the cultural scene*; **la ~ madrileña** the Madrid scene*; **la ~ está en la costa** the coast is where it's at‡

[2] (‡) (= *asunto*) thing, stuff‡; **a mí no me va esa ~** I'm not into that scene* *o* stuff‡; **la ~ es que ...** the thing is that ...; **¡qué ~! ¡ahora tengo que ponerme a trabajar!** what a pain! I've got to get down to work now!*; **ese**

tío anda en ~s raras that guy is into really weird stuff‡
[3] (*Esp**) (= *pelea*) trouble; **cuando vuelva a casa me espera una buena ~** there's going to be real trouble when I get home*
[4] (*Ajedrez*) move ► **movida clave** key-move
[5] (*Pol*) movement
[6] (*Chile*‡) bash*, do*

MOVIDA MADRILEÑA

The **Movida Madrileña** *was a cultural movement which sprang up in Madrid towards the end of the* **Transición a la Democracia** *(Transition to Democracy — 1975-82). In post-Franco Spain many were glad to shake off Catholic social and sexual mores and to experiment. This was the period that saw the emergence of exciting and innovative film directors like Pedro Almodóvar and bands like Radio Futura and Alaska y los Pegamoides. At the same time the media, music and fashion industries sought to distance themselves from the mass-produced popular culture of the US and UK and establish their own Spanish identity.*

movido ADJ [1] (*Fot*) blurred; **la foto ha salido un poco movida** the photo has come out a bit blurred
[2] [*persona*] (= *activo*) on the move*, on the go*; (= *inquieto*) restless; **es una persona muy movida** he's always on the move *o* go*
[3] (= *agitado*) [3·1] [*mar*] rough, choppy; [*viaje*] (*en barco*) rough; (*en avión*) bumpy
[3·2] [*día, semana*] hectic, busy; [*reunión, sesión*] stormy; **he tenido una mañana muy movida** I had a very hectic *o* busy morning; **sabíamos que la reunión sería bastante movidita** we knew that the meeting would be quite stormy
[4] (*Andes, CAm*) [*huevo*] soft-shelled
[5] (*CAm*) (= *débil*) weak, feeble; (= *lento*) slow, sluggish; (= *indeciso*) irresolute

movidón* SM rave-up*, wild party, hot party (*EEUU*)

móvil Ⓐ SM [1] (= *motivo*) motive; **un crimen sin ~ aparente** a crime with no apparent motive; **el ~ del asesinato** the motive for the murder; **éste es el verdadero ~ de su política** this is the real reason behind his policies
[2] (= *teléfono*) mobile (phone)
[3] (*Arte*) mobile
Ⓑ ADJ [*teléfono, unidad*] mobile

movilidad SF mobility ► **movilidad ascendente** upward mobility ► **movilidad social** social mobility

movilización SF [1] (*Mil*) mobilization
[2] (*Pol*) (= *manifestación*) **habrá varias jornadas de ~** there will be several days of industrial action; **una llamada a la ~ de los trabajadores** a call for the mobilization of the workforce
[3] (*Fin*) ► **movilización de capital** raising of capital ► **movilización de recursos** mobilization of resources

movilizar ▸conjug 1f◂ VT [1] (= *organizar*) to mobilize
[2] (*Cono Sur*) to unblock, free
[3] (*Chile*) to transport

movimiento SM [1] (*Mec, Fís*) movement; **el ~ ascendente del aire** the upward movement of the air; **~ hacia abajo/arriba** downward/upward movement; ✦*REFRÁN* **el ~ se demuestra andando** actions speak louder than words ► **movimiento acelerado** acceleration ► **movimiento continuo** continuous movement, continuous motion ► **movimiento de pinza** pincer movement ► **movimiento de rotación** rotatory movement ► **movimiento de traslación** orbital movement *o* motion ► **movimiento ondulatorio** wave movement, wave motion ► **movimiento perpetuo** perpetual motion ► **movimiento retardado** deceleration ► **movimiento sísmico** seismic tremor
[2] (= *desplazamiento*) [*de persona, animal*] movement; **todos nuestros ~s fueron filmados** all our movements were filmed; **esta máquina puede detectar el menor ~** this machine can detect the slightest movement; **he hecho un mal ~ con el hombro** I moved my shoulder awkwardly; **no hagas ningún ~** don't move a muscle, don't make a move; **~ de cabeza** (*para negar*) shake; (*para asentir*) nod ► **movimiento en falso** false move; **¡un ~ en falso y disparo!** one false move and I'll shoot!; **hizo un ~ en falso y tropezó** he missed his step and tripped over ► **movimiento migratorio** migratory movement
[3] **en ~** [*figura, persona*] moving; [*vehículo*] in motion; **una célula en ~** a moving cell *o* a cell in motion; **a lo lejos vi una figura en ~** I saw a moving figure in the distance; **está siempre en ~** (*fig*) she's always on the move *o* go*; **mantener algo en ~** to keep sth moving *o* in motion; **poner en ~** [+ *máquina, motor*] to set in motion; [+ *vehículo*] to get going; [+ *actividad, negocio*] to start, start up; **nos pusimos en ~ demasiado tarde** we got going too late
[4] (*Fin, Com*) [*de cuenta*] transaction; [*de dinero*] movement; **¿puedo consultar los ~s de mi cuenta?** can I have a statement of my account?; **"últimos ~s"** "latest transactions"; **hubo mucho ~ de dinero en el mercado** there was a lot of movement in the money market; **el ~ de los precios** changes in prices; **el ~ ascensional de los precios de las acciones** the upward movement of share prices ► **movimiento de caja** cash flow ► **movimiento de efectivo** cash flow ► **movimiento de mercancías** turnover, volume of business ► **movimientos de existencias** stock movements
[5] (= *actividad*) (*en oficina, tribunal*) activity; (*en aeropuerto, carretera*) traffic; **hoy ha habido mucho ~ en la Bolsa** there was a lot of activity on the Stock Market today; **un día de poco ~ en la Bolsa** a light trading day on the Stock Market; **el ~ de pasajeros ha sido intenso estos días** passenger traffic has been very heavy in recent days; **un día de poco ~ en las carreteras** a day with little traffic on the roads ► **movimiento máximo** (*Aut*) peak traffic
[6] (= *tendencia*) movement; **el ~ de liberación de la mujer** the women's liberation movement; **el Movimiento (Nacional)** (*Esp Hist*) *the Falangist Movement* ► **movimiento obrero** workers' movement ► **movimiento pacifista** pacifist movement ► **movimiento sindical** trade union movement
[7] (*Mús*) [*de compás*] tempo; [*de sinfonía*] movement
[8] (*Inform*) ► **movimiento de bloques** block move
[9] (= *jugada*) move

moviola® SF [1] (*Cine*) Moviola®
[2] (= *repetición*) action replay

mozalbete SM lad

Mozambique SM Mozambique

mozambiqueño/a ADJ, SM/F Mozambican

mozárabe Ⓐ ADJ Mozarabic
Ⓑ SMF Mozarab; → RECONQUISTA
Ⓒ SM (*Ling*) Mozarabic

mozarrón SM big lad, strapping young fellow

mozo/a Ⓐ ADJ [1] (= *joven*) young; **en sus años ~s** in his youth, in his young days
[2] (= *soltero*) single, unmarried
Ⓑ SM/F [1] (= *joven*) lad/girl; **buena moza** good-looking girl
[2] (= *criado*) servant ► **moza de taberna** (*Esp*†) barmaid
Ⓒ SM (= *camarero*) waiter; (*Ferro etc*) porter ► **mozo de almacén** warehouse assistant ► **mozo de caballos** groom ► **mozo de café** waiter ► **mozo de cámara** cabin boy ► **mozo de cuadra** stable boy ► **mozo de cuerda, mozo de equipajes, mozo de estación** porter ► **mozo de hotel** bellboy, bellhop (*EEUU*) ► **mozo de laboratorio** laboratory assistant ► **mozo de panadería** baker's boy

mozuelo/a SM/F lad/girl

MP3 SM MP3; **reproductor de** ~ MP3 player

MPAIAC SM ABR (*Esp*) = **Movimiento para la Autodeterminación y la Independencia del Archipiélago Canario**

MRTA SM ABR (*Perú*) = **Movimiento Revolucionario Túpac Amaru**

ms. ABR, **mss.** ABR (= **manuscrito**) MS., ms.

Mtro. ABR = **Maestro**

mu‡ Ⓐ SM ✦*MODISMO* **no decir ni mu** not to say a word
Ⓑ SF **¡achanta la mu!** (*Méx*) shut your face!‡

muaré SM moiré

mucamo/a SM/F (*Andes, Cono Sur*) houseboy/maid, servant

muceta SF cape

muchá SMF (*LAm*) = **muchacho A**

muchachada SF [1] (= *travesura*) childish prank
[2] (*LAm*) (= *grupo de jóvenes*) group of young people, bunch of kids*

muchacha-guía SF (*pl* **muchachas-guías**) girl guide, girl scout (*EEUU*)

muchachería SF [1] (= *travesura*) childish prank [2] (= *muchachos*) boys and girls *pl*, kids* *pl*; (= *pandilla*) group of young people, bunch of kids*

muchachil ADJ boyish/girlish

muchacho/a Ⓐ SM/F [1] (= *joven*) boy /girl
[2] (*tb* **~ de servicio**) (= *hombre*) servant; (= *mujer*) maid, servant
Ⓑ SM (*Chile*) (= *cuña*) wedge; (*LAm*) (= *abrazadera*) clamp; (*Cono Sur*) [*de zapato*] shoehorn; (*Andes*) (= *lámpara*) miner's lamp; (= *sostén*) prop

muchedumbre SF [1] [*de personas*] crowd, throng; (*pey*) mob, herd; **una ~ de admiradores** a crowd of admirers
[2] [*de pájaros*] flock

muchísimo Ⓐ ADJ a lot of, lots of; **había muchísima gente** there were a lot of people, there were lots of people; **había muchísima comida** there was a lot of food, there was lots of food; **hace ~ tiempo** a very long time ago, ages ago

Ⓑ ADV very much, a lot; **me quiere ~** he loves me very much *o* a lot, he really loves me; **llovía ~** it was raining really *o* very hard, it was pouring down

mucho Ⓐ ADJ [1] *(en singular) (en oraciones afirmativas)* a lot of, lots of; *(en oraciones interrogativas y negativas)* a lot of, much; **tengo ~ dinero** I have a lot of *o* lots of money; **había mucha gente** there were a lot of *o* lots of people there; **¿tienes ~ trabajo?** do you have a lot of *o* much work?; **no tengo ~ dinero** I don't have a lot of *o* much money; **hace ~ calor** it's very hot; **tengo ~ frío** I'm very cold; **tengo mucha hambre** I'm very hungry; **tengo mucha sed** I'm very thirsty; **tuve mucha suerte** I was very lucky; **no hace ~ tiempo** not long ago; **llevo aquí ~ tiempo** I've been here a long time

[2] *(en plural) (en oraciones afirmativas)* a lot of, lots of; *(en oraciones interrogativas y negativas)* a lot of, many; **tiene muchas plantas** he has got a lot of *o* lots of plants; **muchas personas creen que no** a lot of *o* lots of people don't think so; **se lo he dicho muchas veces** I've told him many *o* lots of times; **¿había ~s niños en el parque?** were there a lot of *o* many children in the park?; **no había ~s patos en el lago** there weren't a lot of *o* many ducks on the lake

[3] (*) *(con singular colectivo)* **había ~ borracho** there were a lot of *o* lots of drunks there; **hay ~ tonto suelto** there are a lot of *o* lots of idiots around; **~ beso, pero luego me critica por la espalda** she's all kisses, but then she criticizes me behind my back

[4] *(= demasiado)* **es ~ dinero para un niño** it's too much money for a child; **es mucha mujer para ti*** that woman is too much for you; **ésta es mucha casa para nosotros*** this house is too big for us

Ⓑ PRON [1] *(en singular)* [1·1] *(en frases afirmativas)* a lot, lots; *(en frases interrogativas y negativas)* a lot, much; **tengo ~ que hacer** I have a lot *o* lots to do; **tiene la culpa de ~ de lo que pasa** he's to blame for a lot of *o* much of what has happened; **el plan tiene ~ de positivo** there's a lot about the plan that is positive; **su discurso tiene ~ de fascista** his rhetoric contains a lot of fascist elements; **¿has aprendido ~ en este trabajo?** have you learnt a lot *o* much from this job?; **no tengo ~ que hacer** I haven't got a lot *o* much to do; **—¿cuánto vino queda? —mucho** "how much wine is left?" — "a lot" *o* "lots"

[1·2] *(referido a tiempo)* long; **¿te vas a quedar ~?** are you staying long?; **no tardes ~** don't be long; **¿falta ~ para llegar?** will it be long till we arrive?; **—¿cuánto nos queda para acabar? —mucho** "how long till we finish?" — "ages"; **hace ~ que no salgo a bailar** it's a long time *o* ages since I went out dancing

[2] *(en plural) (en frases afirmativas)* a lot, lots; *(en frases interrogativas y negativas)* a lot, many; **somos ~s** there are a lot of *o* lots of us; **son ~s los que no quieren** there are a lot *o* lots who don't want to; **~s dicen que ...** a lot of *o* lots of *o* many people say that ...; **~s de los ausentes** many of *o* a lot of those absent; **—¿hay manzanas? —sí, pero no muchas** "are there any apples?" — "yes, but not many *o* not a lot"; **¿vinieron ~s?** did many *o* a lot of people come?; **—¿cuántos había? —muchos** "how many were there?" — "a lot" *o* "lots"

Ⓒ ADV [1] *(= en gran cantidad)* a lot; **come ~** she eats a lot; **te quiero ~** I love you very much *o* a lot; **viene ~** he comes often *o* a lot; **me gusta ~ el jazz** I really like jazz, I like jazz a lot; **sí señor, me gusta y ~** I do indeed like it and I like it a lot; **—son 75 euros —es mucho** "that will be 75 euros" — "that's a lot"; **alegrarse ~** to be very glad; **correr ~** to run fast; **lo siento ~** I'm very *o* really sorry; **¡~ lo sientes tú!*** a fat lot you care!*; **trabajar ~** to work hard; **~ antes** long before; **~ más** much *o* a lot more; **~ menos** much *o* a lot less; **muy ~: se guardará muy ~ de hacerlo*** he'll jolly well be careful not to do it*; **si no es ~ pedir** if that's not asking too much; **eso es ~ pedir** it's a lot to ask; **pensárselo ~: se lo pensó ~ antes de contestar** he thought long and hard about it before replying; **~ peor** much *o* a lot worse

[2] *(en respuestas)* **—¿estás cansado? —¡mucho!** "are you tired?" — "I certainly am!"; **—¿te gusta? —no mucho** "do you like it?" — "not really"

[3] *(otras locuciones)* **como ~** at (the) most; **como ~ leo un libro al mes** at (the) most I read one book a month; **con ~** by far, far and away; **fue, con ~, el mejor** he was by far the best, he was far and away the best; **no se puede comparar, ni con ~, a ninguna de nuestras ideas** it bears no comparison at all *o* you can't begin to compare it with any of our ideas; **cuando ~** *(frm)* at (the) most; **tener a algn en ~** to think highly of sb; **ni ~ menos: Juan no es ni ~ menos el que era** Juan is nothing like the man he was; **mi intención no era insultarte, ni ~ menos** I in no way intended to insult you, I didn't intend to insult you, far from it; **por ~ que: por ~ que estudies** however hard you study; **por ~ que lo quieras no debes mimarlo** no matter how much you love him, you shouldn't spoil him

mucilaginoso ADJ mucilaginous

mucílago SM mucilage

mucosa SF *(= membrana)* mucous membrane; *(= secreción)* mucus

mucosidad SF mucus

mucoso ADJ mucous

múcura SF *(Andes, Caribe)* earthenware jug

muda SF [1] *[de ropa]* change of underwear

[2] *(Zool) [de piel]* slough; *[de pelo, plumaje]* moult, molt *(EEUU)*

[3] *[de la voz]* breaking

mudable ADJ, **mudadizo** ADJ [1] *(= variable)* changeable, variable

[2] *[persona]* fickle

mudanza SF [1] *(= cambio)* change; **sufrir ~** to undergo a change

[2] *[de casa]* move; **estar de ~** to be moving; **mudanzas** removals; **camión de ~s** removal van, moving van *(EEUU)*; **empresa de ~s** removals company, moving company *(EEUU)*

[3] *(Baile)* figure

[4] **mudanzas** *(= inconstancia)* fickleness *sing*, moodiness *sing*

mudar ▸conjug 1a◂ Ⓐ VT [1] *(= cambiar)* to change; *(= transformar)* to change, turn **(en** into); **esto mudó la tristeza en alegría** this changed *o* turned the sadness into joy; **le mudan las sábanas todos los días** they change his sheets every day; **le han mudado a otra oficina** they've moved him to another office

[2] *(Zool) [+ piel]* to shed; *[+ pelo, plumaje]* to moult, molt *(EEUU)*

Ⓑ VI [1] *(= cambiar)* **~ de** to change; **he mudado de parecer** I've changed my mind; **~ de color** to change colour; **su cara mudó de color** his face changed colour; *ver tb* **mandar C3**

[2] *(Zool)* **~ de** *[+ piel]* to shed; *[+ pelo, plumaje]* to moult, molt *(EEUU)*

Ⓒ **mudarse** VPR [1] *(tb* **~se de ropa***)* to change one's clothes

[2] *(tb* **~se de casa***)* to move, move house

[3] *[voz]* to break

mudéjar Ⓐ ADJ Mudejar

Ⓑ SMF *(Hist)* Mudejar *(Moslem permitted to live under Christian rule)*; → RECONQUISTA

mudejarismo SM *Mudejar character or style*

mudenco ADJ *(CAm) (= tartamudo)* stuttering; *(= tonto)* stupid

mudengo ADJ *(Andes)* silly

mudez SF dumbness

mudo ADJ [1] *(Med)* dumb, mute *(frm)*; **es ~ de nacimiento** he was born dumb *o (frm)* mute

[2] *(= callado)* silent, mute; **sufrió con resignación muda** he suffered with silent *o* mute resignation; **no podemos permanecer ~s ante lo que está ocurriendo** we cannot remain silent in the face of what is happening; **ser testigo ~ de algo** to stand in mute witness *o* testimony to sth; **quedarse ~ (de)** to be struck dumb (with); **quedarse ~ de asombro** to be left speechless, be dumbfounded; **se quedó ~ durante tres horas** he did not speak for three hours; **quedarse ~ de envidia** *(Esp)* to be green with envy

[3] *(Ling) [letra]* mute, silent; *[consonante]* voiceless

[4] *[película]* silent

[5] **papel ~** *(Teat)* walk-on part

[6] *(Andes, CAm) (= tonto)* foolish, silly

mueblaje SM = **mobiliario**

MUEBLE

- Para traducir la palabra **mueble** al inglés, hay que recordar que el sustantivo **furniture** es incontable y lleva el verbo en singular:

  Los muebles del comedor son muy antiguos

  The dining-room furniture is very old

- Si queremos traducir expresiones en las que se habla de un solo mueble, o en las que se precisa el número de muebles, utilizamos la construcción **piece/pieces of furniture**:

  Éste es un mueble muy valioso

  This is a very valuable piece of furniture

  He comprado un par de muebles antiguos

  I bought one or two pieces of antique furniture

Para otros usos y ejemplos ver la entrada.

mueble Ⓐ ADJ movable; **bienes ~s** movable *o* personal property *sing*

Ⓑ SM [1] *(= objeto)* piece of furniture; **~s** furniture *sing*; **con ~s** furnished; **sin ~s** unfurnished; **~s y enseres** furniture and fittings; ✦***MODISMO*** **salvar los ~s** to save face ► **mueble de elementos adicionables** unit, piece of unit furniture ► **mueble librería** bookcase ► **muebles de cocina** kitchen units ► **muebles de época** period furniture

sing ► **muebles de oficina** office furniture *sing*
[2] (*Méx**) (= *coche*) car

mueblé* SM brothel

mueble-bar SM cocktail cabinet, drinks cabinet

mueblería SF (= *fábrica*) furniture factory; (= *tienda*) furniture shop

mueca SF (wry) face, grimace; **hacer ~s** to make faces, pull faces (**a** at); **una ~ de asco/estupor/desesperación** a disgusted/astonished/despairing expression

muela SF [1] (*Anat*) (*gen*) tooth; (*para especificar*) back tooth, molar; **dolor de ~s** toothache; ✦*MODISMOS* **está que echa las ~s** he's hopping mad; **hacer la ~** (*Caribe*‡) to skive‡ ► **muela del juicio** wisdom tooth
[2] (*Téc*) [*de molino*] millstone; [*de afilar*] grindstone
[3] (*Geog*) (= *cerro*) mound, hillock
[4] (*Andes*) gluttony
[5] (*Caribe*) trickery

muellaje SM wharfage

muelle¹ Ⓐ SM (= *resorte*) spring; **colchón de ~s** interior sprung mattress ► **muelle helicoidal** coil spring ► **muelle real** mainspring
Ⓑ ADJ [1] (= *blando*) soft; (= *delicado*) delicate; (= *elástico*) springy, bouncy
[2] [*vida*] soft, easy

muelle² SM [1] (*Náut*) (= *puerto*) wharf, quay; (= *malecón*) pier; **cargador de ~s** docker ► **muelle de atraque** (*Náut*) mooring quay; (*Aer*) docking bay
[2] (*Ferro*) (*tb* ~ **de carga**) loading bay

muenda SF (*Andes*) thrashing

muera *etc ver* **morir**

muérdago SM mistletoe

muerdo* SM bite

muérgano/a Ⓐ SM/F (*Andes*) (= *desharrapado*) shabby person; (*Andes*) (= *maleducado*) ill-bred person, lout
Ⓑ SM [1] (*Andes, Caribe*) (= *cacharro*) useless object, piece of junk
[2] (*Andes*) (= *caballo*) vicious horse

muermo/a* (*Esp*) Ⓐ ADJ (= *pesado*) boring; (= *aburrido*) wet*
Ⓑ SM/F (= *pesado*) crashing bore*; (= *aburrido*) drip*, wet fish*
Ⓒ SM [1] (= *aburrimiento*) boredom; (= *depresión*) the blues* *pl*
[2] (= *asunto*) bore
[3] [*de droga*] bad trip*

muerte SF [1] (= *por enfermedad, accidente*) death; **tuvo una buena ~** he had a good death, he died a good death; **hasta que la ~ nos separe** till death us do part; **murió de ~ natural** he died a natural death *o* of natural causes; **se debatía entre la vida y la ~** he was fighting for his life; **una lucha a ~** a fight to the death; **defenderé mis derechos a ~** I will defend my rights to the death; **mantuvo una guerra a ~ con la enfermedad** he fought his illness to the bitter end; **luchar a ~** to fight to the death; **odiar algo/a algn a ~** to detest sth/sb, loathe sth/sb; **causar la ~ a algn** to kill sb, cause the death of sb; **las heridas que le causaron la ~** the injuries that killed him *o* caused his death; **encontrar la ~** to die, meet one's death; **herido de ~** fatally injured; **el ciervo escapó herido de ~** the deer escaped fatally injured; **la democracia estaba herida de ~** democracy was on its last legs; **pena de ~** death sentence; **estar a las puertas de la ~** to be at death's door; **un susto de ~** a terrible fright; **me diste un susto de ~** you scared me to death, you gave me a terrible fright; ✦*MODISMOS* **estar de ~** (*Esp**) to be out-of-this-world*; (*Chile**) to be extremely upset; **la comida estaba de ~** the meal was out of this world*; **de mala ~*** [*trabajo, película*] crappy**, crap** *antes de s*; [*casa, pueblo*] grotty‡; **nos detuvimos en un pueblucho de mala ~** we stopped in a grotty little town‡; **era un hotel de mala ~** the hotel was a real dump‡, the hotel was really grotty‡; **cada ~ de obispo** (*LAm**) once in a blue moon; **ser la ~*** (= *ser horrible*) to be hell*; (= *ser estupendo*) to be amazing*; **este trabajo es la ~** this job is really hell*; **este calor es la ~** this heat is killing me*; **esa noria es la ~** that big wheel is amazing* ► **muerte cerebral** brain death ► **muerte civil** loss of civil rights ► **muerte clínica**: **en situación de ~ clínica** clinically dead ► **muerte súbita** (*Med*) sudden death; (*Tenis*) tie-break; (*Golf*) sudden death play-off; (*Ftbl*) sudden death ► **muerte prematura** premature death ► **muerte repentina** sudden death ► **muerte violenta** violent death; *ver tb* **vida 1**
[2] (= *asesinato*) murder; **fue declarado culpable de varias ~s** he was found guilty of various murders; **dar ~ a algn** to kill sb ► **muerte a mano airada** violent death
[3] (= *desaparición*) [*de imperio, civilización*] death, demise (*frm*); **la ~ de las civilizaciones indígenas** the death *o* demise of native civilizations

muerto/a Ⓐ PP *de* **morir**
Ⓑ ADJ [1] [*persona, animal*] dead; **mis abuelos están ~s** my grandparents are dead; **el golpe lo dejó medio ~** the blow left him half-dead; **resultó ~ en el acto** he died instantly; **~ en acción** *o* **campaña** killed in action; **dar por ~ a algn** to give sb up for dead; **ser ~ a tiros** to be shot, be shot dead; **vivo o ~** dead or alive; ✦*MODISMOS* **estar más ~ que vivo** to be more dead than alive; **estar ~ y enterrado*** ◊ **estar más ~ que una piedra*** ◊ **estar más que ~*** to be as dead as a doornail*, be as dead as a dodo*, be stone dead*; **no tener donde caerse ~** not to have a penny to one's name; *ver tb* **ángulo, cal, lengua 4, marea 1, naturaleza 6, punto 7, tiempo 6, vía A2**
[2] (*) (*para exagerar*) [2·1] (= *cansado*) dead tired*, ready to drop*; **después del viaje estábamos ~s** we were dead tired *o* ready to drop after the journey*; **caí muerta en la cama** I dropped flat out on the bed
[2·2] (= *sin animación*) dead; **en invierno este pueblo está ~** this town is dead in winter
[2·3] **estar ~ de algo**: **estaba ~ de la envidia** I was green with envy; **me voy a la cama, que estoy muerta de sueño** I'm going to bed, I'm dead tired*; **estaba ~ de miedo** I was scared to death; **estaba ~ del aburrimiento** he was dead bored; **estoy muerta de cansancio** I'm dead tired *o* dog tired*, I'm ready to drop*; **comes como si estuvieras ~ de hambre** you're eating as if you were starving hungry; **estar ~ de risa** [*persona*] to laugh one's head off, kill o.s. laughing; [*casa*] to let go to rack and ruin; (*Esp*) [*ropa*] to be gathering dust; **estaba ~ de risa con sus chistes** I laughed my head off at his jokes, I killed myself laughing at his jokes; **compró una casa para tenerla muerta de risa** he bought a house and let it go to rack and ruin*; **el piano sigue ahí ~ de risa** the piano is still there gathering dust; **el solar sigue todavía ~ de risa** nothing has been done yet with that plot of land
[3] (= *relajado*) [*brazo, mano*] limp; **se me quedó la mano muerta** my hand went limp; **deja el brazo ~** let your arm go limp
[4] (= *apagado*) [*color*] dull
Ⓒ SM/F [1] (= *persona muerta*) (*en accidente, guerra*) **¿ha habido ~s en el accidente?** was anyone killed in the accident?; **el conflicto ha causado 45.000 ~s** the conflict has caused 45,000 deaths *o* the deaths of 45,000 people; **el número de ~s va en aumento** the death toll *o* the number of deaths is rising; **doblar a ~** to toll the death knell; **los ~s** the dead; **resucitó de entre los ~s** he rose from the dead; **los ~s vivientes** the living dead; **tocar a ~** to toll the death knell; ✦*MODISMOS* **¡me cago en los ~s!** (*Esp***) fucking hell!**; **¡te lo juro por mis ~s!*** I swear on my mother's grave!*; **un ~ de hambre** a nobody; **ni ~***: **no me pondría ese traje ni ~** I wouldn't be seen dead in that suit*; **resucitar a un ~**: **esta sopa resucita a un ~** (*hum*) this soup really hits the spot*
[2] (*) (= *cadáver*) body; **han encontrado un ~ en el río** they have found a (dead) body in the river; **el ~ fue trasladado en avión** the body was taken by plane; **hacer el ~** to float; **¿sabes hacer el ~ boca arriba?** can you float on your back?; **hacerse el ~** to pretend to be dead; ✦*MODISMO* **callarse como un ~** to keep dead quiet; ✦*REFRANES* **los ~s no hablan** dead men tell no tales; **el ~ al hoyo y el vivo al bollo** dead men have no friends
Ⓓ SM [1] (*) (= *tarea pesada*) drag*; **¡vaya ~ que nos ha caído encima!** (*Esp*) what a drag!*; **lo siento, pero te ha tocado a ti el ~ de decírselo al jefe** I'm sorry, but you've drawn the short straw — you've got to tell the boss; ✦*MODISMOS* **cargar con el ~** to carry the can*, take the rap*; **ese ~ yo no me lo cargo, yo soy inocente** I'm not taking the blame *o* rap*, I'm innocent; **cargar con el ~ de hacer algo** to be lumbered with doing sth*; **siempre me cargan con el ~ de cuidar a los niños** I always get lumbered with looking after the children; **cargar** *o* **echar el ~ a algn** to pin the blame on sb; **a mí no me cargas tú ese ~, yo no tengo nada que ver en este asunto** don't try and pin the blame on me, I've got nothing to do with this
[2] (*Naipes*) dummy

DÍA DE LOS MUERTOS

November 2, All Souls' Day, called the **Día de los Muertos** *elsewhere in the Spanish-speaking world and* **Día de los Difuntos** *in Spain, is the day when Christians throughout the Spanish-speaking world traditionally honour their dead. In Mexico the festivities are particularly spectacular with a week-long festival, starting on November 1, in which Christian and ancient pagan customs are married. November 1 itself is for children who have died, while November 2 is set aside for adults. Families meet to take food, flowers and sweets in the shape of skeletons, coffins and crosses to the graves of* *their loved ones. In Spain people celebrate the* **Día de los Difuntos** *by taking flowers to the cemetery.*

muesca SF 1 (= *hendidura*) notch, nick; (*para encajar*) groove, slot
2 (= *marca*) mark

muesli SM muesli

muestra SF 1 (= *señal*) sign, indication; **no ir es ~ de desprecio** not going is a sign of contempt; **es (una) ~ de cariño** it is a token of affection; **dar ~s de algo** to show signs of sth; ✦*MODISMO* **para ~ (basta) un botón** by way of example; **¿que si es listo? para ~ un botón, ha sacado un diez en el examen** is he clever? by way of example he got full marks in the exam
2 (= *prueba*) proof; **eso es (la) ~ de que estaba mintiendo** this is proof that he was lying
3 (*Com*) sample ► **muestra gratuita** free sample
4 (*Med*) sample, specimen
5 (= *exposición*) trade fair
6 (= *en estadística*) sample ► **muestra aleatoria, muestra al azar** random sample ► **muestra representativa** representative sample
7 (*Cos*) pattern
8 (= *esfera de reloj*) face
9 (†) [*de tienda*] sign, signboard

muestral ADJ sample *antes de s*

muestrario SM 1 (= *muestras*) collection of samples; (= *libro*) pattern book
2 [*de personajes, objetos*] collection

muestrear ▸conjug 1a◂ VT to sample

muestreo SM (= *acto*) sampling; (= *muestra*) sample; **hacer un ~ de la población** to select a sample of the population

mueva *etc ver* **mover**

mufa* SF (*Cono Sur*) (= *mala suerte*) bad luck, misfortune; (= *mal humor*) bad mood; (= *aburrimiento*) boredom, tedium

mufado* ADJ (*Cono Sur*) **estar ~** to be in a bad mood

mugido SM 1 [*de vaca*] moo; [*de toro*] bellow
2 [*de dolor*] roar, howl

mugir ▸conjug 3c◂ VI 1 [*vaca*] to moo; [*toro*] to bellow
2 (*con dolor*) to roar, howl

mugre SF (= *suciedad*) dirt; (= *inmundicia*) filth; (= *grasa*) grime, grease; ✦*MODISMO* **sacarse la ~** (*Cono Sur**) (= *trabajar*) to work like a dog*; (= *sufrir un percance*) to have a nasty accident

mugriento ADJ (= *sucio*) dirty, filthy; (= *grasiento*) grimy, greasy

mugrón SM (= *vástago*) shoot, sprout; [*de vid*] sucker, layer

mugroso ADJ (*LAm*) dirty, mucky*

muguete SM lily of the valley

mui‡ SF = **muy B**

muina* SF (*Méx*) **me da la ~** it gets on my nerves

mujahedín SM, **mujahidín** SM, **mujaidín** SM mujaheddin

mujer SF 1 woman; **ser muy ~** ◊ **ser toda una ~** to be a real woman; **ser muy ~ de su casa** to be very house-proud; **nombre de ~** woman's name; **ropa de ~** women's clothes *o* clothing; **hacerse ~** to become a woman ► **mujer bandera**† striking woman ► **mujer de la limpieza** cleaning lady, cleaning woman, cleaner ► **mujer de la vida** (*euf*), **mujer de mala vida** prostitute ► **mujer de negocios** businesswoman ► **mujer de vida alegre** loose woman ► **mujer empresaria** businesswoman ► **mujer fatal** femme fatale ► **mujer objeto** sex object ► **mujer piloto** (woman) pilot ► **mujer policía** policewoman ► **mujer pública** (*euf*) prostitute ► **mujer sacerdote** woman priest
2 (= *esposa*) wife; **mi ~** my wife; **mi futura ~** my wife-to-be; **tomar ~** to take a wife ► **mujer maltratada** battered wife
3 (*uso apelativo*) (*en oración directa no se traduce*) **¡déjalo, mujer, no te preocupes!** forget about it, don't worry!; **¡mujer, no digas esas cosas!** please! don't say such things!

mujeraza* SF shrew

mujercita SF little woman, little lady

mujerengo ADJ (*CAm, Cono Sur*) 1 (= *afeminado*) effeminate
2 (= *mujeriego*) **es muy ~** he's a real womanizer

mujerero ADJ (*LAm*) **es muy ~** he's a real womanizer

mujeriego Ⓐ ADJ 1 [*hombre*] **es muy ~** he's a real womanizer
2 **cabalgar a mujeriegas** to ride sidesaddle
Ⓑ SM womanizer

mujeril ADJ womanly

mujerío* SM (*Esp*) **ir de ~** (= *de putas*) to go whoring; (= *de ligue*) to go looking for a woman

mujer-objeto SF (*pl* **mujeres-objeto**) (female) sex object

mujerona SF big woman

mujer-rana SF diver

mujerzuela‡ SF tart‡, slut‡

mújol SM grey mullet

mula SF 1 (= *animal*) mule; ✦*MODISMO* **más terco que una ~** as stubborn as a mule
2 (*Méx*) (= *bravucón*) tough guy
3 (*Méx*) (= *trastos*) junk, trash (*EEUU*)
4 (*CAm*) (= *vergüenza*) shame
5 (*Andes*) (= *pipa*) pipe
6 (*Andes*) (= *idiota*) idiot
7 (*Cono Sur**) (= *mentira*) lie; (= *engaño*) trick; ✦*MODISMOS* **meter la ~** to tell lies; **meter la ~ a algn** to trick sb

mulada SF drove of mules

muladar SM 1 (= *estercolero*) dungheap
2 (= *casa*) pigsty, pigpen (*EEUU*)

mulato/a ADJ, SM/F mulatto

mulé‡ SM **dar ~ a algn** to bump sb off*

mulero/a SM/F 1 (= *mozo*) muleteer
2 (*Cono Sur**) (= *mentiroso*) liar

muleta SF 1 (*para andar*) crutch
2 (*Taur*) *matador's stick with red cloth attached*
3 (= *apoyo*) prop, support

muletazo SM *movement of the "muleta" in bullfighting*

muletilla SF 1 (= *frase*) pet word, tag
2 (= *bastón*) cross-handled cane; (*Téc*) (= *botón*) wooden toggle, wooden button
3 (*Taur*) = **muleta 2**

muletón SM flannelette

mulillas SFPL *team of mules which drag the dead bull from the bullring*

mullido Ⓐ ADJ 1 [*cama, sofá, alfombra, hierba*] soft, springy; [*almohada, terreno*] soft; [*pelo, tela*] fluffy
2 **dejar a algn ~*** to wear sb out
Ⓑ SM (= *relleno*) stuffing, filling

mullir ▸conjug 3a◂ VT 1 (= *ablandar*) to soften; [+ *almohada*] to fluff up; [+ *cama*] to shake up; [+ *tierra*] to hoe, fork over
2 [+ *plantas*] to hoe round, loosen the earth round

mullo SM (red) mullet

mulo SM mule; ✦*MODISMO* **trabaja como un ~** he works like a dog

mulón ADJ (*Andes, Cono Sur*) (= *tartamudo*) stammering; [*niño*] slow in learning to talk, backward

multa SF fine; **echar** *o* **poner una ~ a algn** to fine sb ► **multa de tráfico** traffic fine ► **multa por aparcamiento indebido** parking ticket

multar ▸conjug 1a◂ VT to fine; **~ a algn con 100 dólares** to fine sb 100 dollars

multi... PREF multi...

multiacceso ADJ (*Inform*) multi-access

multicampeón/ona SM/F several times champion

multicanal ADJ (*TV*) multichannel

multicapa ADJ INV multilayer(ed)

multicine SM multiscreen cinema, multiplex

multicolor ADJ [*camisa, bandera, pájaro*] multicoloured, multicolored (*EEUU*); [*espectáculo*] colourful, colorful (*EEUU*); [*planta, diseño*] variegated

multiconferencia SF three-way call

multiconfesional ADJ multidenominational

multicopiar ▸conjug 1b◂ VT to duplicate

multicopista SF duplicator; **a ~** duplicated, mimeographed

multicultural ADJ multicultural

multiculturalidad SF multiculturalism

multidimensional ADJ multidimensional

multidireccional ADJ multidirectional

multidisciplinar ADJ, **multidisciplinario** ADJ multidisciplinary; **estudio ~** multidisciplinary study, cross-disciplinary study

multifacético ADJ many-sided, multifaceted; **un hombre ~** a man of many talents

multifamiliar ADJ **edificio ~** block of flats, apartment block (*EEUU*)

multifásico ADJ polyphase

multiforme ADJ multiform, multifarious

multifuncional ADJ multifunctional

multigrado ADJ multigrade

multilaminar ADJ **madera ~** plywood

multilateral ADJ, **multilátero** ADJ multilateral

multilingüe ADJ multilingual

multimedia ADJ INV multimedia *antes de s*

multimillonario/a Ⓐ SM/F multimillionaire/multimillionairess
Ⓑ ADJ 1 (= *persona*) **ser ~** to be a multimillionaire/multimillionairess
2 **un contrato ~** (*de euros*) a multi-million euro contract; (*de dólares*) a multi-million dollar contract

multimotor Ⓐ ADJ multi-engined
Ⓑ SM multi-engined aircraft

multinacional Ⓐ ADJ multinational
Ⓑ SF multinational, multinational company

multiorgánico ADJ **donante ~** multiple organ donor

multipartidismo SM multi-party system

multipartidista ADJ multi-party *antes de s*

múltiple ADJ [1] [*colisión, embarazo, fractura*] multiple; **enchufe ~** multiple socket; **misiles de cabeza ~** multiple-warhead missiles; **preguntas de elección ~** multiple choice questions; **orgasmo ~** multiple orgasm
[2] **múltiples** (= *muchos*) [*aplicaciones, problemas, ocasiones*] many, numerous; **esta mesa tiene ~s usos** this table has many *o* numerous uses, this is a multipurpose table
[3] (*Inform*) **de tarea ~** multi-task; **de usuario ~** multi-user

multiplexor SM multiplexor

multiplicación SF [1] (*Mat, Biol*) multiplication
[2] (= *aumento*) increase; **gracias a la ~ de los satélites de comunicación** thanks to the rapid increase in the number of communications satellites; **la ~ de los panes y los peces** (*Rel*) the feeding of the five thousand, the miracle of the loaves and the fishes

multiplicado SM multiplicand

multiplicador Ⓐ ADJ **efecto ~** multiplier effect
Ⓑ SM multiplier

multiplicar ▸conjug 1g◂ Ⓐ VT (*Mat*) to multiply (**por** by); (= *aumentar*) to increase, multiply
Ⓑ **multiplicarse** VPR [1] (*Mat, Biol*) to multiply; (= *aumentar*) to increase, multiply
[2] [*persona*] to be everywhere at once; **no puedo ~me** I can't be in half a dozen places at once, I've only got one pair of hands

multiplicidad SF multiplicity, great variety

múltiplo Ⓐ ADJ multiple
Ⓑ SM multiple ► **mínimo común múltiplo** lowest common multiple

multiprocesador SM multiprocessor

multiprocesamiento SM, **multiproceso** SM multiprocessing

multipropiedad SF time-share; **el sistema de ~** time-sharing

multirracial ADJ multiracial

multirregional ADJ multi-regional

multirregulable ADJ adjustable (to a variety of positions)

multirreincidencia SF persistent offending

multirreincidente SMF persistent offender

multirriesgo ADJ INV **póliza ~** fully comprehensive policy, all-risks policy

multisecular ADJ age-old, centuries-old

multitarea Ⓐ ADJ INV multitasking
Ⓑ SF multitask

multitud SF [1] (= *gentío*) crowd; **una ~ de curiosos y periodistas** a crowd of curious onlookers and journalists; **la ~** the crowd, the masses *pl*
[2] **~ de: tengo ~ de cosas que hacer** I've got a mountain of things to do; **existen ~ de posibilidades** there are any number of possibilities

multitudinario ADJ [*manifestación*] mass *antes de s*; [*reunión*] large; [*recepción*] tumultuous; **asamblea multitudinaria** mass meeting

multiuso ADJ INV multipurpose

multiusuario ADJ INV multiuser

multiviaje ADJ INV **billete ~** multiple-journey ticket

mun. ABR = **municipio**

mundanal ADJ worldly; **lejos del ~ ruido** far from the madding crowd (*liter*); **alejarse del ~ ruido** to get away from it all

mundanalidad SF (*liter*) worldliness

mundanería SF worldliness

mundano/a Ⓐ ADJ [1] (= *del mundo*) worldly
[2] (= *de alta sociedad*) society *antes de s*; (= *de moda*) fashionable; **son gente muy mundana** they're great society people; **una reunión mundana** a fashionable gathering, a gathering of society people
Ⓑ SM/F society person, socialite

mundial Ⓐ ADJ [*acontecimiento, esfuerzo, organismo*] worldwide; [*economía, figura, población*] world *antes de s*; **una crisis a escala ~** a crisis on a worldwide scale, a global crisis; **las comunicaciones ~es** worldwide communications; **la primera guerra ~** the First World War, World War I; **la segunda guerra ~** the Second World War, World War II
Ⓑ SM world championship; **el Mundial** *o* **los Mundiales (de Fútbol)** the World Cup; **el Mundial** *o* **los Mundiales de Atletismo** the Athletics World Cup *o* Championship

mundialización SF globalization

mundialmente ADV worldwide, universally; **~ famoso** world-famous; **hacer algo ~ popular** to make sth universally popular; **una palabra ~ utilizada** a word used throughout *o* all over the world; **un especialista ~ conocido** a world-famous specialist, a specialist of world renown

mundillo SM world, circle; **en el ~ teatral** in the theatre world, in theatrical circles

mundo SM [1] (= *lo creado*) world; **la Copa del Mundo** the World Cup; **no hay nada mejor en el ~** there's nothing better in the whole (wide) world; **artistas de todo el ~ exponen sus obras** artists from all over the world are exhibiting their work; **la prensa de todo el ~ dio la noticia** the world press reported the news; **es conocido en todo el ~** he is known throughout the world *o* the world over; **es lo que más desea en el ~** it's what she wants most in (all) the world; **el ~ antiguo** ancient world; **el Nuevo Mundo** the New World; **el otro ~** the next world, the hereafter; **irse al otro ~** to pass away; **el Tercer Mundo** the Third World; **el Viejo Mundo** the Old World; *ver tb* **hombre A1**
[2] (= *humanidad*) **medio ~** almost everybody; **conoce a medio ~** he knows almost everybody; **estaba medio ~** there were loads of people there; **todo el ~** everyone, everybody
[3] (= *ámbito*) world; **el ~ de la moda** the fashion world; **el ~ hispánico** the Hispanic world; **en el ~ de las ideas** in the world *o* realm of ideas; **en el ~ científico** in scientific circles; **el ~ del espectáculo** show business; **incorporarse al ~ del trabajo** to get a job; **no piensa volver al ~ de la política** she doesn't intend to return to politics
[4] (= *vida mundana*) world; **decidió volver la espalda al ~** he decided to abandon worldly things; **los placeres del ~** worldly pleasures; **las tentaciones del ~** the temptations of the flesh
[5] ✦***MODISMOS*** **así va el ~** no wonder things are as they are; **correr ~** to see the world; **ha corrido mucho ~** he's been around a bit; **echar a algn al ~** to bring sb into the world; **echarse al ~** (*euf*) to go on the streets; **desde que el ~ es ~** since time began; **se le cayó el ~ encima** his world fell apart; **por esos ~s (de Dios)** all over, here there and everywhere; **no es el fin del ~** it's not the end of the world; **aunque se hunda el ~** come what may; **no por eso se hundirá el ~** it won't be the end of the world; **por nada del** *o* **en el ~** not for all the world; **no lo cambiaría por nada del ~** I wouldn't change it for anything in the world *o* for all the world; **no es nada del otro ~** it's nothing special *o* to write home about; **hacer algo del otro ~** to do sth quite extraordinary; **ponerse el ~ por montera**: **se cansó de trabajar en una oficina, se puso el ~ por montera y se hizo artista** he grew tired of working in an office, so he threw caution to the wind and became an artist; **se puso el ~ por montera y se fue a vivir al campo** he decided to go and live in the country and damn the consequences; **el ~ es un pañuelo** it's a small world; **tener mucho ~** to be very experienced, know one's way around; **tener poco ~** to be wet behind the ears, be inexperienced; **traer a algn al ~** to bring sb into the world; **como Dios lo trajo al ~** stark naked, as naked as the day he was born; **venir al ~** to come into the world, be born; **tal como vino al ~** stark naked; **ver ~** to see the world; **ha visto mucho ~** he's been around a bit; *ver tb* **comer C1**
[6] **un ~** (= *mucho*): **había todo un ~ de posibilidades** there was a whole world of possibilities; **hay un ~ de distancia entre las dos ideologías** the two ideologies are worlds apart; **no debemos hacer un ~ de sus comentarios** there's no need to blow her comments out of proportion, we shouldn't read too much into her comments

mundología SF worldly wisdom, experience of the world, savoir-faire

mundonuevo SM peep show

Munich SM Munich

munición SF [1] (*tb* **municiones**) (= *balas*) ammunition, munitions *pl*; (= *pertrechos*) stores *pl*, supplies *pl*; **fábrica de municiones** munitions factory ► **municiones de boca** provisions, rations
[2] (*Mil*) **de ~** army *antes de s*, service *antes de s*; **botas de ~** army boots
[3] (*CAm*) uniform

municionera SF (*Caribe*) ammunition pouch

municipal Ⓐ ADJ [*elección*] municipal; [*concejo*] town *antes de s*, local; [*empleado, oficina*] council *antes de s*; [*impuesto*] local, council *antes de s*; [*piscina*] public; **la empresa ~ de transportes** the municipal transport company
Ⓑ SMF (= *guardia*) local policeman/policewoman

municipalidad SF [1] (= *distrito*) municipality
[2] (= *ayuntamiento*) town council, local council
[3] (= *edificio*) town hall

municipio SM [1] (= *distrito*) municipality; (= *población*) town
[2] (= *ayuntamiento*) town council, local council
[3] (= *edificio*) town hall

munificencia SF munificence
munífico ADJ munificent
muniqués/esa Ⓐ ADJ of/from Munich
Ⓑ SM/F native/inhabitant of Munich; **los muniqueses** the people of Munich
muñeca SF [1] (*Anat*) wrist
[2] (= *juguete*) doll ► **muñeca de trapo** rag doll ► **muñeca rusa** Russian doll
[3] (‡) (= *chica*) doll‡, chick (*EEUU*‡)
[4] (= *trapo*) polishing rag
[5] (*Andes, Cono Sur*) (= *mutualidad*) friendly society, benefit society (*EEUU*)
[6] (*Cono Sur**) (= *influencia*) pull, influence
muñeco SM [1] (= *juguete*) (*con forma humana*) doll; (= *con forma animal*) toy ► **muñeco de peluche** soft toy
[2] [*de ventrílocuo*] dummy; [*de marionetas*] puppet; (= *efigie*) [*de político, famoso*] effigy; (= *dibujo*) figure; (= *espantapájaros*) scarecrow ► **muñeco de guante** glove puppet ► **muñeco de nieve** snowman
[3] (= *pelele*) puppet, pawn
[4] (*) (= *niño*) sweetie*, little angel
[5] (*) (*lío*) row, shindy*
[6] **muñecos** (*Andes*) **me entraron los ~s** I had butterflies in my stomach
muñeira SF *a popular Galician dance*
muñequado* ADJ (*Andes*) jumpy, nervous
muñequera SF wristband
muñequero/a SM/F puppeteer
muñir ▸conjug 3h◂ VT [1] (= *convocar*) to summon, call, convoke
[2] (*pey*) (= *amañar*) to rig, fix
muñón SM [1] (*Anat*) stump
[2] (*Mec*) pivot, journal; [*de cañón*] trunnion
mural Ⓐ ADJ mural, wall *antes de s*; **mapa ~** wall map; **periódico ~** wall newspaper
Ⓑ SM mural
muralismo SM muralism
muralista ADJ, SMF muralist
muralla SF [1] [*de ciudad*] (= *muro*) (city) wall, walls *pl*; (= *terraplén*) rampart ► **la Gran Muralla china** the Great Wall of China
[2] (*LAm*) (= *pared*) wall
murar ▸conjug 1a◂ VT to wall
Murcia SF Murcia
murciano/a Ⓐ ADJ of/from Murcia, Murcian
Ⓑ SM/F native/inhabitant of Murcia, Murcian
murciélago SM bat
murga SF [1] (*) (= *lata*) nuisance, bind*; **dar la ~** to be a pain*, be a pest
[2] (= *banda*) band of street musicians
murguista SM [1] (= *músico*) street musician; (*hum*, *) bad musician
[2] (*) (= *pesado*) bore
múrido SM rodent
murmullo SM [1] (= *susurro*) murmur(ing), whisper(ing); (= *queja*) muttering
[2] [*de hojas, viento*] rustle, rustling; [*de agua*] murmur; (= *ruido confuso*) hum(ming)
murmuración SF gossip
murmurador(a) Ⓐ ADJ (= *chismoso*) gossiping; (= *criticón*) backbiting
Ⓑ SM/F (= *chismoso*) gossip; (= *criticón*) backbiter
murmurar ▸conjug 1a◂ Ⓐ VT (= *susurrar*) to murmur, whisper; (= *quejarse*) to mutter; **murmuró unas palabras de agradecimiento** she murmured a few words of thanks; **la tranquilizaba murmurando palabras en su oído** he calmed her by whispering in her ear
Ⓑ VI [1] (= *cotillear*) to gossip (**de** about); (= *quejarse*) to grumble, mutter (**de** about); **siempre están murmurando del jefe** they're always grumbling o muttering about the boss
[2] [*hojas*] to rustle; [*viento*] to whisper; [*agua*] to murmur
muro SM wall; **enfrentarse con un ~ de silencio** to come up against a wall of silence ► **muro de Berlín** Berlin Wall ► **muro de contención** retaining wall ► **Muro de las Lamentaciones** Wailing Wall
murria SF depression, the blues *pl*; **tener ~** to be down in the dumps*, feel blue
murrio ADJ depressed
murruco* ADJ (*CAm*) curly-haired
mus[1] SM *a card game*
mus[2]* SM ✦**MODISMO sin decir ni ~** without saying a word; *ver tb* **tus**[2]
musa SF Muse; **las ~s** the Muses
musaraña SF [1] (*Zool*) shrew
[2] (= *mota*) speck floating in the eye; ✦**MODISMOS mirar a las ~s** to stare vacantly o into space; **pensar en las ~s** to daydream
musculación SF muscle-building
muscular ADJ muscular
musculatura SF muscles *pl*, musculature (*frm*); **la ~ abdominal** the abdominal muscles; **combinar ~ con inteligencia** to have brains as well as brawn
músculo SM muscle
musculoso ADJ (= *de muchos músculos*) muscular; (= *fortachón*) muscly*
museística SF museum studies
museístico ADJ museum *antes de s*
muselina SF muslin
museo SM (*gen*) museum; [*de pintura, escultura*] museum, gallery ► **museo de arte moderno** modern art gallery ► **museo de cera** wax museum, waxworks ► **museo de historia natural** natural history museum ► **museo de pintura** art gallery
museografía SF museography
musgaño SM shrew
musgo SM moss ► **musgo irlandés** carrageen moss
musgoso ADJ mossy, moss-covered
música SF [1] music; **poner ~ a algo** to set sth to music; ✦**MODISMOS irse con la ~ a otra parte** to clear off*; **¡vete con la ~ a otra parte!** clear off!*; **me suena a ~ de caballitos** it sounds all too familiar ► **música ambiental, música ambiente** background music ► **música antigua** early music ► **música celestial** heavenly music; **sus ideas me suenan a ~ celestial** (*iró*) his ideas sound like hot air to me ► **música clásica** classical music ► **música concreta** concrete music ► **música coreada** choral music ► **música culta** classical music ► **música de cámara** chamber music ► **música de fondo** background music ► **música de las esferas, música de los planetas** music of the spheres ► **música disco** disco music ► **música enlatada** canned music, piped music ► **música étnica** world music ► **música folk** folk music ► **música ligera** light music ► **música militar** military music ► **música pop** pop music ► **música rock** rock music ► **música sacra, música sagrada** sacred music
[2] (= *banda*) band
[3] **músicas*** (= *tonterías*) drivel *sing*; **no estoy para ~s** I'm not in the mood to listen to such drivel
[4] (*Esp*†) (= *cartera*) wallet, billfold (*EEUU*); (= *dinero*) bread‡, money; *ver tb* **músico**
musical ADJ, SM musical
musicalidad SF musicality, musical quality
musicalizar ▸conjug 1f◂ VT to set to music
musicar ▸conjug 1g◂ VT to set to music
músico/a Ⓐ ADJ musical
Ⓑ SM/F [1] (= *instrumentista*) musician; **~s de jazz** jazz musicians ► **músico callejero** street musician, busker ► **músico mayor** bandmaster
[2] (= *compositor*) musician; *ver tb* **música**
musicología SF musicology
musicólogo/a SM/F musicologist
musiqueo SM monotonous sound
musiquilla SF (= *melodía*) tune ► **musiquilla de fondo** background music
musitar ▸conjug 1a◂ VT, VI to mumble, mutter
muslada‡ SF, **muslamen‡** SM thighs *pl*
muslera SF Tubigrip®, thigh strap
muslime ADJ, SMF Moslem
muslímico ADJ Moslem
muslo SM thigh
mustango SM mustang
mustela SF weasel
mustiarse ▸conjug 1b◂ VPR to wither, wilt
mustio ADJ [1] [*planta*] withered; [*lechuga*] limp
[2] [*tela, bandera*] faded
[3] [*persona*] depressed, gloomy
[4] (*Méx**) (= *hipócrita*) hypocritical
musulmán/ana ADJ, SM/F Moslem
mutabilidad SF mutability (*frm*), changeableness
mutable ADJ (= *que puede mutar*) mutable; (= *variable*) mutable (*frm*), changeable
mutación SF [1] (= *cambio*) change
[2] (*Biol*) mutation
[3] (*Ling*) mutation
[4] (*Teat*) scene change
mutagene SM mutagen
mutágeno Ⓐ ADJ mutagenic
Ⓑ SM mutagen
mutante ADJ, SMF mutant
mutar ▸conjug 1a◂ Ⓐ VI to mutate
Ⓑ VT [1] (*Biol*) to mutate
[2] (= *cambiar*) to transform, alter
Ⓒ **mutarse** VPR to mutate (**en** into)
mutil SM (*Hist*) Carlist soldier
mutilación SF mutilation
mutilado/a Ⓐ ADJ [1] [*persona*] crippled, disabled; [*cadáver*] mutilated
[2] [*escultura, monumento*] vandalized, defaced
Ⓑ SM/F cripple, disabled person ► **mutilado/a de guerra** disabled veteran
mutilar ▸conjug 1a◂ VT [1] (*gen*) to mutilate; (= *lisiar*) to cripple, disable
[2] [+ *escultura, monumento*] to vandalize, deface; [+ *texto*] to butcher, hack about
mutis SM INV (*Teat*) exit; **¡mutis!** sh!; **tú ~** you keep quiet; **hacer ~** (*Teat*) (= *retirarse*) to exit; (*fig*) to say nothing, keep quiet; ✦**MODISMO hacer ~ por el foro** to make o.s. scarce*
mutismo SM (= *silencio*) silence; **guardar un ~ absoluto** to remain tight-lipped
mutua SF friendly society, benefit society (*EEUU*)

mutual SF (*Andes, Cono Sur*) friendly society, benefit society (*EEUU*)

mutualidad SF [1] (= *asociación*) friendly society, benefit society (*EEUU*)

[2] (= *reciprocidad*) reciprocity, reciprocal nature

[3] (= *ayuda*) mutual aid, reciprocal aid

mutualista Ⓐ ADJ mutualist

Ⓑ SMF *member or associate of a friendly society or benefit society*

Ⓒ SF (*Cono Sur*) friendly society, benefit society (*EEUU*)

mutuamente ADV mutually, reciprocally

mutuo ADJ (= *recíproco*) mutual; (= *conjunto*) joint

muy Ⓐ ADJ [1] (= *mucho*) very; **~ bueno** very good; **eso es ~ español** that's very Spanish; **fue una reacción ~ suya** it was a very typical reaction of his; **somos ~ amigos** we're great friends; **es ~ hombre** he's very manly; **es ~ mujer** she's a real woman; **~ bien/tarde/mucho** very well/late/much; **~ bien, que venga** all right, he can come (along); **Muy Señor mío** Dear Sir; **~ pero que ~ guapo** really, really handsome; **~ de**: **~ de noche** very late at night; **~ de mañana** very early in the morning; **eso es ~ de él** that's just like him; **yo soy ~ de la siesta** I'm very fond of a siesta; **su apoyo es ~ de agradecer** his support is very much appreciated; **es ~ de sentir** (*frm*) it is much to be regretted; **el/la ~**: **el ~ tonto de Pedro** that great idiot Pedro; **las ~ presumidas se gastaron todo en ropa** they're so self-obsessed they spent all their money on clothes; **¡el ~ bandido!** the rascal!; **por ~**: **por ~ cansado que estés** however tired you are, no matter how tired you are

[2] (= *demasiado*) too; **ya es ~ tarde para cenar** it's too late to have dinner now; **es ~ joven para salir contigo** she's too young to be going out with you

[3] (*con participio*) greatly, highly; **~ buscado** highly sought-after; **fue un tema ~ comentado** the topic was very much discussed

Ⓑ SF (†) (= *lengua*) tongue; (= *boca*) trap‡, mouth; ✦***MODISMOS*** **achantar la ~** to shut one's trap‡; **irse de la ~** to spill the beans*; **largar por la ~** to natter*

N n

N¹, n ['ene] SF (= *letra*) N, n

N² (A) SF ABR (*Aut*) = **nacional**
(B) ABR 1 (= **Norte**) N
2 (= **noviembre**) Nov; **20-N** *20th November, day of Franco's death*
3 (*LAm*) = **Moneda Nacional**; **le entregaron sólo N$2.000** they only gave him 2,000 new pesos

> **20-N**
>
> ***20-N** is commonly used as shorthand to refer to the anniversary of General Franco's death on 20 November 1975. Every year supporters of the far right hold a commemorative rally in Madrid's Plaza de Oriente, the scene of many of Franco's speeches to the people.*

n. ABR 1 = **nuestro/nuestra**
2 (= **nacido**) b
3 (= **número**) no., No.

na* PRON, **ná*** PRON = **nada**

naba SF (*Bot*) swede, rutabaga (*EEUU*)

nabab SM nabob

nabina SF rapeseed

nabiza SF (*Esp*) turnip greens *pl*

nabo SM 1 (*Bot*) turnip; (= *raíz gruesa*) root vegetable ► **nabo gallego** rape ► **nabo sueco** swede, rutabaga (*EEUU*)
2 (*Anat*) root of the tail
3 (*Arquit*) newel, stair post
4 (*Náut*) mast
5 (**) (= *pene*) prick**

Nabucodonosor SM Nebuchadnezzar

nácar SM mother-of-pearl, nacre (*frm*)

nacarado ADJ, **nacarino** ADJ mother-of-pearl *antes de s*, pearly

nacatamal SM (*CAm, Méx*) *maize, meat and rice wrapped in banana leaf*

nacatete SM (*Méx*), **nacatón/ona** SM/F (*CAm, Méx*) unfledged chick

nacedera SF (*CAm*) (*tb* **cerca ~**) hedge

nacencia SF (*LAm*) = **nacimiento**

nacer ►conjug 2d◄ (A) VI 1 [*persona, animal*] to be born; [*ave, insecto, reptil*] to hatch; **nací en Cuba** I was born in Cuba; **cuando nazca el niño** when the baby is born; **nació para poeta** he was born to be a poet; **no nació para sufrir** she was not born to suffer; **al ~** at birth; **~ en el seno de una familia adinerada** to be born into a wealthy family; **~ muerto** to be stillborn; **~ antes de tiempo** to be born prematurely; ✦***MODISMOS*** **¡oye, que no nací ayer!** I wasn't born yesterday, you know!; **~ con estrella** to be born under a lucky star; **~ de pie** to be born lucky; **nadie nace enseñado** we all have to learn; **~ parado** (*Andes**) to be born with a silver spoon in one's mouth; **volver a ~** to have a lucky escape; ✦***REFRÁN*** **unos nacen con estrella y otros estrellados** fortune smiles on some but not on others
2 [*planta*] (*gen*) to sprout, bud; (= *aparecer*) to come up; [*pelo, plumas*] to grow, sprout; **le nacieron alas** it sprouted wings
3 [*estrella, sol*] to rise; [*día*] to dawn
4 [*agua*] to spring up, appear, begin to flow; [*camino*] to begin, start (**de** from; **en** in)
5 [*revolución, miedo*] to spring (**de** from); [*idea*] to come (**de** from), originate, have its origin (**de, en** in); **el error nace del hecho de que …** the error springs o stems from the fact that …; **entre ellos ha nacido una fuerte simpatía** a strong friendship has sprung up between them; **nació una sospecha en su mente** a suspicion formed in her mind; **¿de dónde nace la idea?** where does the idea come from?
6 **~ a: con esa exposición nació a la vida artística** that exhibition saw the beginning of his artistic career; **~ al amor** to awaken to love
(B) **nacerse** VPR 1 (*Bot*) to bud, sprout
2 (*Cos*) to split

Nacho SM (*forma familiar*) *de* **Ignacio**

nacido (A) ADJ born; **~ de padres ricos** born of wealthy parents; **~ a la libertad** born free; **~ para el amor** born to love; **recién ~** newborn; **ser bien ~** (= *de noble linaje*) to be of noble birth; (= *educado*) to be well-bred; **ser mal ~** (= *mala persona*) to be mean, be wicked; (= *maleducado*) to be ill-mannered, be ill-bred; *ver tb* **malnacido**
(B) SM **los ~s a finales de siglo** those born o people born at the end of the century; ✦***MODISMOS*** **ningún ~** nobody; **todos los ~s** everybody, all mankind

naciente (A) ADJ (= *que nace*) nascent (*frm*); (= *nuevo*) new, recent; (= *creciente*) growing; [*sol*] rising; **el ~ interés por …** the new-found o growing interest in …
(B) SM 1 (= *este*) east
2 **nacientes** (*Cono Sur*) (= *manantial*) spring *sing*, source *sing*

▼**nacimiento** SM 1 (*gen*) birth; (*Orn etc*) hatching; **de ~: ciego de ~** blind from birth, born blind; **un tonto de ~** a born fool; **este defecto lo tiene de ~** he has had this defect since birth, he was born with this defect ► **nacimiento sin violencia** painless childbirth
2 (= *estirpe*) birth, family; **de ~ noble** of noble birth, of noble family
3 (= *manantial*) spring, source
4 [*del pelo*] roots *pl*
5 (= *origen*) [*de nación*] birth; [*de amistad*] beginning, start; **el partido tuvo su ~ en …** the party had its origins in …; **dar ~ a** to give rise to
6 (*Arte, Rel*) nativity (scene)

nación (A) SF (= *país*) nation; (= *pueblo*) people; **de ~ española** of Spanish nationality; **trato de ~ más favorecida** most favoured nation treatment ► **Naciones Unidas** United Nations
(B) SMF (*Cono Sur*) (= *extranjero*) foreigner

nacional (A) ADJ (= *de la nación*) national; (*Econ, Com*) domestic, home *antes de s*; **la deuda ~** national debt; **los periódicos ~es** national newspapers; **la economía ~** the domestic economy; **sólo consumen productos ~es** they buy only home-produced goods o British, Spanish goods etc; **lloverá en todo el territorio ~** there will be rain throughout the country; **páginas de ~** (*Prensa*) home news pages; **"vuelos nacionales"** "domestic flights"; *ver tb* **carretera, fiesta 2, moneda 2**
(B) SMF 1 (*LAm*) (= *ciudadano*) national
2 **los ~es** (*en la guerra civil española*) the Franco forces

nacionalcatolicismo SM *Spanish Catholicism considered as an ally of Franco*

nacionalidad SF 1 (*gen*) nationality; **ser de ~ argentina** to be of Argentinian nationality, have Argentinian citizenship; **tener doble ~** to have dual nationality
2 (*Esp Pol*) (= *región autonómica*) autonomous region

nacionalismo SM nationalism

nacionalista (A) ADJ nationalist, nationalistic
(B) SMF nationalist

nacionalización SF 1 [*de persona*] naturalization
2 [*de industria*] nationalization

nacionalizado ADJ [*persona*] naturalized; [*industria*] nationalized; **un chileno ~ español** a Chilean who has become a naturalized Spaniard

nacionalizar ►conjug 1f◄ (A) VT [+ *persona*] to naturalize; [+ *industria*] to nationalize
(B) **nacionalizarse** VPR [*persona*] to become naturalized; [*industria*] to be nationalized; **~se**

➤ LENGUA Y USO: nacimiento 1 51.1

español to become a Spanish citizen, become a naturalized Spaniard

nacionalsocialismo SM national socialism

naco* Ⓐ ADJ (*Méx*) (= *bobo*) stupid; (= *cobarde*) yellow*
Ⓑ SM [1] (*CAm*) (= *cobarde*) coward; (= *endeble*) weakling, milksop
[2] (*Andes, Cono Sur*) (= *tabaco*) plug of tobacco
[3] (*Andes*) (= *maíz*) *maize kernels cooked with salt*; (= *puré de patatas*) mashed potatoes
[4] (*Cono Sur*) (= *susto*) fright, scare

nada Ⓐ PRON [1] (= *ninguna cosa*) (*con el verbo inglés en forma afirmativa*) nothing; (*con el verbo inglés en forma negativa*) anything; **no dijo ~ en toda la tarde** he said nothing all afternoon, he didn't say anything all afternoon; **no encontrarás ~ que te guste** you won't find anything you like; **no hay ~ como un café después de comer** there's nothing like a coffee after your meal, nothing beats a coffee after your meal; **—¿qué has comprado? —nada** "what have you bought?" — "nothing"; **no entiende ~** he doesn't understand a thing *o* anything; **~ de**: **no sabe ~ de español** he knows no Spanish at all, he doesn't know any Spanish at all; **no tiene ~ de particular** there's nothing special about it; **—¿qué te cuentas? —~ de particular** "what's new?" — "nothing much" *o* "not a lot"; **no creo que ~ de eso te convenga** I don't think that's what you want at all; **¡~ de eso!** not a bit of it!; **¡~ de marcharse!** forget about leaving!; **~ de ~** absolutely nothing, nothing at all; **✦MODISMOS ¡de eso ~, monada!*** no way, José!*; **esto y ~, es lo mismo** it all boils down to nothing; *ver tb* **ahí 2**
[2] (*en locuciones*) [2·1] (*con verbo*) **estuvo en ~ que lo perdiesen** they very nearly lost it; **no me falta de ~** I've got everything I need; **a la cocina no le falta de ~** the kitchen has everything; **hace ~** just a moment ago; **no se parecen en ~** they're not at all alike; **quedar(se) en ~** to come to nothing; **no reparar en ~** to stop at nothing; **no servir para ~** to be utterly useless; **no sirves para ~** you're utterly useless; **no sirve de ~ que os quejéis** there's no point in you complaining; **no ha sido ~** it's nothing, it doesn't matter
[2·2] (*con preposición, adverbio*) **antes de ~**: **antes de ~ tengo que telefonear** before I do anything else I must make a phone call; **se fue antes de ~** she left almost at once; **a cada ~** (*LAm**) constantly; **casi ~**: **no costó casi ~** it cost next to nothing; **¡había unas cien mil personas! ¡casi ~!** there were no fewer than a hundred thousand people there!; **como si ~**: **se lo advertí, pero como si ~** I warned him but it was as if I hadn't spoken; **le dijo que estaba despedido y se quedó como si ~** she told him he was fired and he didn't even bat an eyelid; **de ~**: **—¡gracias! —de ~** "thanks!" — "don't mention it" *o* "you're welcome"; **fue una mentira de ~** it was only a little lie; **¡tanto revuelo por un premio de ~!** all that fuss over such a silly little prize!; **dentro de ~** very soon; **~ más**: **—¿desea algo más? —~ más, gracias** "can I get you anything else?" — "no, that's all thank you"; **no dijo ~ más** he didn't say anything else, he said nothing else; **son las siete ~ más** it's only seven o'clock; **quiero uno ~ más** I only want one; **encendió la tele ~ más llegar** he turned on the TV as soon as he got in; **ocurrió ~ más iniciado el partido** it happened just after the beginning of the game; **estas flores aparecen ~ más terminado el invierno** these flowers come out just after the winter is over *o* as soon as the winter is over; **~ más que estoy muy cansado** (*Andes, Méx*) it's just that I'm very tired; **(~ más y) ~ menos que ...** (no more and) no less than ...; **han ganado ~ menos que un coche** they've won a car, no less; **entró ~ menos que el rey** who should come in but the king!; **ni ~** or anything; **es raro que no haya llamado ni ~** it's odd that she hasn't called or anything; **no quiere comer ni ~** he won't even eat; **pues no es feo ni ~** (*iró*) he's not ugly ... much!; **para ~** at all; **no los mencionó para ~** he never mentioned them at all; **—¿te gusta? —para ~** "do you like it?" — "not at all"; **por ~**: **por ~ se echa a llorar** she's always crying over nothing *o* for no reason at all; **no me subiría a un avión por ~ del mundo** I wouldn't get on a plane for anything in the world; **no por ~ le llaman "apestoso"** he's not called "smelly" for nothing; **no por ~ decidimos comprar** we had good reason to buy; **por ~ y menos puedes hacerte un vestido** you can make your own dress for next to nothing; **¡por ~!** (*Cono Sur*) not at all!, don't mention it!; **por menos de ~** for two pins
[3] (*como coletilla*) **pues ~, me voy** well, I'm off then; **—¿qué pasó? —pues ~, que estuve esperando y no llegó** "what happened?" — "well, I was there waiting and he didn't arrive"; **y ~, al final nos fuimos** anyway, in the end we left
[4] (*Tenis*) love; **treinta-~** thirty-love
Ⓑ ADV not at all, by no means; **no es ~ fácil** it's not at all easy, it's by no means easy; **esto no me gusta ~** I don't like this at all; **no está ~ triste** he isn't sad at all; **pues no eres tú ~ ambicioso** (*iró*) well you're not very ambitious, are you? ... much!
Ⓒ SF **la ~** the void; **el avión pareció salir de la ~** the aircraft seemed to come from nowhere

nadaderas SFPL water wings

nadador(a) SM/F swimmer

nadar ▸conjug 1a◂ VI [1] (*gen*) to swim; (= *flotar*) to float; (*Andes*) (= *bañarse*) to take a bath; **¿no sabes ~?** can't you swim?; **~ a braza** to do (the) breaststroke, swim breaststroke; **~ a crol** to do the crawl, swim crawl; **~ a espalda** to do backstroke, swim backstroke; **~ a mariposa** to do (the) butterfly, swim butterfly; **✦MODISMOS ~ contra corriente** to go against the tide; **~ en la abundancia** to be rolling in it*, be rolling in money*; **querer ~ y guardar la ropa** to want to have it both ways, want to have one's cake and eat it; *ver tb* **agua 4**
[2] (*en prenda, zapatos*) **en estos pantalones va nadando** these trousers are much too big for him, he's lost inside these trousers

nadería SF **discutir por ~s** to argue over nothing *o* over stupid things; **me regaló una ~** she gave me a little nothing, she gave me a small trifle

nadie PRON [1] (= *ninguna persona*) (*verbo inglés en afirmativo*) nobody, no one; (*verbo inglés en negativo*) anybody, anyone; **~ lo tiene** ◊ **no lo tiene ~** nobody has it; **no he visto a ~** I haven't seen anybody; **casi ~** hardly anybody; **lo hace como ~** she does it really well; **~ más** nobody else, no one else; **vino mi familia y ~ más** just my family came and nobody *o* no one else; **no vi a ~ más que a Juan** I didn't see anybody apart from *o* except Juan; **no lo sabe ~ más que tú** nobody else knows, apart from you, nobody but you knows
[2] (= *persona insignificante*) **no es ~** he's nobody (that matters); **✦MODISMO es un don ~** he's a nobody, he's a nonentity

nadir SM nadir

nadita* (*esp LAm*) = **nada**

nado SM **cruzar** *o* **pasar a ~** to swim across

nafta SF (= *hidrocarburo*) naphtha; (*Arg*) (= *gasolina*) petrol, gasoline (*EEUU*)

naftaleno SM naphthalene, naphthaline

naftalina SF [1] (*Quím*) naphthalene, naphthaline
[2] (*para la ropa*) mothballs *pl*

nagual SM [1] (*CAm, Méx*) (= *brujo*) sorcerer, wizard
[2] (*Méx**) (= *mentira*) lie
[3] (*CAm*) (= *mascota*) inseparable companion

nagualear‡ ▸conjug 1a◂ VI (*Méx*) [1] (= *mentir*) to lie
[2] (= *robar*) to nick things*
[3] (= *jaranear*) to paint the town red

naguas SFPL (*LAm*) petticoat *sing*

nagüeta SF (*CAm*) overskirt

nahual SM (*CAm, Méx Mit*) spirit, phantom; (= *doble*) double; (*) (= *ladrón*) cat burglar

náhuatl Ⓐ ADJ INV Nahuatl
Ⓑ SMF INV Nahuatl Indian
Ⓒ SM (*Ling*) Nahuatl language

NÁHUATL

***Náhuatl** is the indigenous Mexican language that was once spoken by the Aztecs and which has given us such words as "tomato", "avocado" "chocolate" and "chilli". The first book to be printed on the American continent was a catechism in **náhuatl**, edited by a Franciscan monk in 1539. Today **náhuatl** is spoken in the central plateau of Mexico by a million bilingual and monolingual speakers.*

naide* PRON (*hum*) = **nadie**

naif Ⓐ ADJ (*pl* **naifs** *o* **naif**) (*Arte*) naive, primitivist
Ⓑ SM naive art

nailon SM nylon

naipe SM (= *carta*) playing card; **naipes** cards; **una baraja de ~s** a pack *o* deck of cards
► **naipe de figura** court card, picture card

naipeador ADJ (*Cono Sur*) fond of cards

naipear ▸conjug 1a◂ VI (*Cono Sur*) to play cards

naja‡ SF **✦MODISMOS de ~(s)** at full speed, like the clappers*; **darse** *o* **salir de ~s** to get out, beat it*

najarse‡ ▸conjug 1a◂ VPR to beat it*

najencia‡ EXCL scram!*

nal. ABR (= **nacional**) nat

nalga SF buttock; **nalgas** buttocks, backside *sing*; **darse de ~s** to fall on one's backside

nalgada SF [1] (*Culin*) ham
[2] (= *azote*) smack on the bottom; **nalgadas** spanking *sing*

nalgudo ADJ, **nalgón** ADJ (*Andes*), **nalguiento** ADJ (*Andes*) big-bottomed *antes de s*, broad in the beam*

Namibia SF Namibia

namibio/a Ⓐ ADJ Namibian
Ⓑ SM/F Namibian; **los ~s** the Namibians, the people of Namibia

nana[1] SF [1] (*Mús*) lullaby, cradlesong
[2] (*CAm, Méx*) (= *nodriza*) wet nurse; (= *niñera*) nursemaid
[3] (= *pelele*) Babygro®, rompers *pl*; *ver tb* **nano**

nana[2] SF [1] (= *abuela*) grandma*, granny*; *ver tb* **año**
[2] (*CAm*) (= *mamá*) mum*, mom (*EEUU**), mummy*, mommy (*EEUU**); *ver tb* **nano**

nana[3]* SF (*Cono Sur*) (= *dolor*) pain; *ver tb* **nano**

nanai* EXCL, **nanay*** EXCL (*tb* **~ de la China**) no way!*; **me hizo ver que ~ (de la China)** he made me see there was nothing doing, he showed me it just wasn't on*

nano/a‡ SM/F kid*; *ver tb* **nana**

nanopartícula SF nanoparticle

nanotechnología SF nanotechnology

nao SF (*Hist*) ship

napa SF imitation leather

napalm SM napalm

napia* SF, **napias*** SFPL snout*, hooter*

napo‡ SM 1000-peseta note

Napoleón SM Napoleon

napoleón SM (*Chile*) (= *alicates*) pliers *pl*, pair of pliers

napoleónico ADJ Napoleonic

Nápoles SM Naples

napolitano/a Ⓐ ADJ of/from Naples, Neapolitan Ⓑ SM/F Neapolitan; **los ~s** the Neapolitans, the people of Naples

narajái‡ SM (*Esp*) priest

naranja Ⓐ SF [1] (= *fruta*) orange ► **naranja amarga**, **naranja cajel** Seville orange ► **naranja navel** navel orange ► **naranja sanguina** blood orange ► **naranja zajarí** Seville orange
[2] (*) ✦*MODISMOS* **¡naranjas!** ◊ **¡~s de la China!** no way!*, nothing doing!*; **encontrar su media ~** to meet one's match; **esperar la media ~** to wait for Mr Right/one's ideal woman; **mi media ~** my better half
[3] (*Caribe*) bitter orange
Ⓑ ADJ INV [*color*] orange
Ⓒ SM (= *color*) orange

naranjada SF orangeade, orange squash

naranjado ADJ orange, orange-coloured

naranjal SM orange grove

naranjero/a Ⓐ ADJ [*país, comarca, región*] orange-growing Ⓑ SM/F (= *agricultor*) orange grower; (= *vendedor*) orange seller Ⓒ SM (= *árbol*) orange tree

naranjo SM orange tree

Narbona SF Narbonne

narcisismo SM narcissism

narcisista Ⓐ ADJ narcissistic
Ⓑ SMF narcissist

Narciso SM Narcissus

narciso SM [1] (*Bot*) narcissus ► **narciso atrompetado**, **narciso trompón** daffodil
[2] (= *presumido*) narcissist

narco* Ⓐ SMF = **narcotraficante**
Ⓑ SM = **narcotráfico**

narco... PREF narco..., drug(s) *antes de s*

narcocorrupción SF drugs-related corruption

narcodependencia SF drug dependency, drug dependence

narcodólar SM drug dollar; **~es** drug money *sing*

narcoguerrilla SF drug terrorists *pl*

narcosis SF INV narcosis

narcoterrorismo SM drug-related terrorism, narco-terrorism

narcótico Ⓐ ADJ narcotic
Ⓑ SM [1] (*gen*) narcotic; (= *somnífero*) sleeping pill, sleeping tablet
[2] **narcóticos** (= *estupefacientes*) narcotics

narcotismo SM narcosis, narcotism

narcotizante ADJ, SM narcotic

narcotizar ▸conjug 1f◂ VT to drug, narcotize (*frm*)

narcotraficante SMF drug(s) trafficker, drug dealer

narcotráfico SM drug trafficking *o* dealing

nardo SM nard, spikenard

narguile SM hookah

naricear* ▸conjug 1a◂ VT (*Andes*) [1] (= *olfatear*) to smell (out)
[2] (= *curiosear*) to poke one's nose into

narigada SF (*LAm*) snuff

narigón Ⓐ ADJ big-nosed
Ⓑ SM (*Méx*) nose ring

narigudo ADJ big-nosed

narigueta ADJ (*Cono Sur*) big-nosed

nariz SF [1] (*Anat*) nose; **tengo un grano en la ~** I have a spot on my nose; **tengo la ~ tapada** I have a blocked nose, my nose is blocked; **no te metas el dedo en la ~** don't pick your nose; **tiene las narices muy grandes** he has a very big nose; **hablar con** *o* **por la ~** to talk through one's nose ► **nariz aguileña** aquiline nose ► **nariz chata** snub nose ► **nariz de boxeador** boxer's nose ► **nariz griega** Greek profile ► **nariz respingona** turned-up nose; *ver tb* **sangre A1**, **sonarse B2, C**
[2] ✦*MODISMOS* **darle en la ~ a algn***: **me da en la ~ que no está diciendo la verdad** I get the feeling *o* something tells me that she is not telling the truth; **darse de narices con algo/algn*** to bump into sth/sb*; **darse de narices con la puerta** to bump into the door*; **darse de narices contra el suelo** to fall flat on one's face; **de las narices** (*Esp**) damn*, bloody‡; **ya estamos otra vez con el ruidito ese de las narices** there's that damn* *o* bloody‡ noise again; **de narices** (*Esp**): **me echó una bronca de narices** he gave me a hell of a telling off*; **hace un frío de narices** it's absolutely freezing*; **era guapa de narices** she was a real stunner*; **he dormido de narices** I slept really well; **me encuentro de narices** I feel fantastic *o* great; **delante de** *o* **en las narices de algn***: **le roboron el coche en sus propias narices** they stole his car right under his nose*; **estar hasta las narices (de algo/algn)*** to be fed up to the back teeth (with sth/sb)*; **hinchar las narices a algn** (*Esp**) to get up sb's nose*; **ese tío me hincha las narices** that guy really gets up my nose*; **hinchársele las narices a algn** (*Esp**) **se le hincharon las narices** he blew his top*, he hit the roof; **meter las narices en algo*** to poke one's nose into sth; **pasarse algo por las narices***: **eso me lo paso por las narices*** I couldn't care less* *o* I don't give two hoots* about that; **por narices** (*Esp**) **dijo que su hija no iba y por narices tuvo que ser así** she said that her daughter was not going and that was that; **con una alineación así tienen que ganar por narices** with a lineup like this they'd better win; **esto tiene que estar listo para el lunes por narices** this has to be ready by Monday no matter what; **pasar** *o* **restregar por las narices***: **le gustaba pasar a su novia por las narices de su ex** he liked to show off his girlfriend under the eyes of his ex; **siempre nos están restregando por las narices que tienen mucho dinero** they're always showing off in front of our eyes that they have money; **romper las narices a algn*** to smash sb's face in*; **hazlo o te rompo las narices** do it or I'll smash your face in*; **tener narices** (*Esp**) **¡tiene narices la cosa!** it's outrageous!; **tocar las narices a algn** (*Esp**) **ya me está tocando las narices con sus comentarios** his comments really get up my nose; **me toca las narices lo que diga ella** I don't give a damn what she says*; **tocarse las narices*** to sit around twiddling one's thumbs; **en esa oficina se están todo el día tocando las narices** they sit around all day twiddling their thumbs in that office; **no ven más allá de sus narices*** they can't see beyond the end of their nose; *ver tb* **palmo 1**
[3] (*Esp**) (*frases de sentido exclamativo*) **¡narices!** rubbish!, nonsense!; **¿dónde narices están mis calcetines?** where on earth are my socks?*; **¿qué días de fiesta ni que narices? ¡aquí todo el mundo trabaja!** holidays! what are you talking about? here everybody has to work!
[4] (= *olfato*) nose, sense of smell; **perros de presa con muy buena ~** gun dogs with a good nose *o* keen sense of smell
[5] [*del vino*] nose

narizota* SF big nose

narizotas* SMF INV (*Esp*) **ser un ~** to have a really big nose

narizudo ADJ (*CAm, Méx*) big-nosed

narpias* SFPL = **napia**

narración SF (= *relato, versión*) account; (*Literat*) narration

narrador(a) SM/F narrator

narrar ▸conjug 1a◂ VT [+ *historia*] to tell; [+ *suceso, aventuras, experiencia*] to recount

narrativa SF [1] (= *narración*) narrative, story
[2] (= *arte*) narrative skill, skill in storytelling
[3] (= *género*) fiction

narrativo ADJ narrative

narval SM narwhal

NASA SF ABR (= **National Aeronautics and Space Administration**) NASA

nasa SF [1] [*de pan*] bread bin
[2] (*Pesca*) basket, creel; (= *trampa*) fish trap

nasal ADJ, SF nasal

nasalidad SF nasality

nasalización SF nasalization

nasalizar ▸conjug 1f◂ VT to nasalize

nasalmente ADV nasally

naso* SM (*Cono Sur*) nose, conk*, schnozzle (*esp EEUU‡*), hooter*

N.ª S.ra ABR = **Nuestra Señora**

nasti‡ EXCL (*tb* **~ de plasti**) no way!*; **¡de eso ~, (monasti)!** no way!*

nata SF [1] (*Esp*) (*gen*) cream; (*en leche cocida*) skin ► **nata batida** whipped cream ► **nata líquida** cream ► **nata montada** whipped cream ► **nata para montar** whipping cream
[2] (*fig*) cream; **la flor y ~ de la sociedad** the cream of society

natación SF [1] (*gen*) swimming
[2] (= *estilo*) style (of swimming), stroke ► **natación a braza** breast-stroke ► **natación de costado** sidestroke ► **natación de espalda** backstroke ► **natación de pecho** breast-stroke ► **natación en cuchillo** side-stroke ► **natación sincronizada** synchronized swimming ► **natación submarina** (*gen*) underwater swimming; (*con aparato respiratorio*) skin diving

natal ADJ [*país*] native; [*pueblo*] home *antes de s*

natalicio Ⓐ ADJ birthday *antes de s*
Ⓑ SM birthday

natalidad SF birth rate

natalista ADJ **una política ~** a policy aimed at raising the birth rate

natatorio Ⓐ ADJ **técnica natatoria** swimming technique; **vejiga natatoria** air bladder
Ⓑ SM (*Arg*) swimming pool

natillas SFPL (*Esp*) custard *sing* ► **natillas de huevo** egg custard *sing*

natividad SF nativity

nativo/a Ⓐ ADJ [1] [*persona, país*] native; **lengua nativa** mother tongue
[2] (= *innato*) natural, innate
[3] (*Min*) native
Ⓑ SM/F native

nato ADJ [1] (*gen*) born; **un actor ~** a born actor; **un criminal ~** a natural-born criminal; **es un pintor ~** he's a natural painter
[2] (*por derecho*) ex officio; **el secretario es miembro ~ de …** the secretary is ex officio a member of …

natura†† SF [1] (= *naturaleza*) nature; **contra ~: un pecado contra ~** a sin against nature; **inclinaciones contra ~** unnatural leanings
[2] (= *genitales*) genitals *pl*

naturaca* EXCL naturally!, natch!*

natural Ⓐ ADJ [1] (= *no artificial*) [*calor*] natural; [*luz, frontera*] natural; [*seda*] pure; [*flor*] real; **los fenómenos ~es** natural phenomena; **es rubia ~** she's a natural blonde
[2] (= *fresco*) fresh; **fruta ~** fresh fruit
[3] (= *sin aditivos*) natural; **yogur ~** natural yoghurt; **con ingredientes ~es** with natural ingredients
[4] (= *a temperatura ambiente*) **este vino se sirve ~** this wine should be served at room temperature
[5] (= *innato*) natural; **tiene un talento ~ para la música** she has a natural talent for music; **la bondad es ~ en él** kindness is in his nature, it's in his nature to be kind
[6] (= *normal*) natural; **es ~ que estés cansado** it's natural that you should be tired; **es lo más ~ del mundo** it's perfectly natural, it's the most natural thing in the world
[7] (= *no afectado*) natural; **has salido muy ~ en la foto** you look very natural in the photo
[8] (= *ilegítimo*) illegitimate; **hijo ~** illegitimate child
[9] (= *nativo*) **es ~ de Córdoba** he is a native of Cordoba; **¿de dónde es usted ~?** where are you from?, where were you born?
[10] **de tamaño ~** life-size(d)
[11] (*Mús*) natural
Ⓑ SMF native; **un ~ de Badajoz** a native of Badajoz
Ⓒ SM [1] (= *carácter*) nature; **un ~ optimista** an optimistic nature; **es de ~ reservado** he's reserved by nature
[2] **al ~: fruta al ~** (= *sin aditamentos*) fruit in its own juice; **está muy guapa al ~** she is very pretty just as she is (without make-up); **se sirve al ~** (= *a temperatura ambiente*) it is served at room temperature
[3] (*Arte*) **del ~: pintar del ~** to paint from life; **clase de dibujo del ~** life class
[4] (*Taur*) *type of pass*

naturaleza SF [1] (= *universo físico*) nature; **las leyes de la ~** the laws of nature; **las ciencias de la ~** the natural science(s)
[2] (= *campo*) nature; **viven en plena ~** they live surrounded by nature
[3] (= *carácter*) nature; **son de ~ tímida** they're shy by nature; **es despistado por ~** he's naturally absent-minded; **la ~ humana** human nature
[4] (= *constitución*) constitution; **es de ~ fuerte** he has a strong constitution
[5] (= *especie*) nature; **situaciones de ~ poco común** situations of an unusual nature
[6] (*Arte*) ► **naturaleza muerta** still life
[7] (†) (*Pol*) nationality; **el joven es suizo de ~** the young man is Swiss by nationality
[8] **romper la ~**† to start to menstruate

naturalidad SF naturalness; **con la mayor ~ (del mundo)** as if it were the most natural thing in the world; **se levantó y siguió caminando con la mayor ~ del mundo** she picked herself up and carried on walking as if nothing had happened; **lo dijo con la mayor ~** he said it in a perfectly ordinary voice; **hacer algo con ~** to do sth in a natural way

naturalismo SM [1] (*Arte*) naturalism; (= *realismo*) realism
[2] (= *nudismo*) naturism

naturalista Ⓐ ADJ (*Arte*) naturalistic; (= *realista*) realistic
Ⓑ SMF [1] (*Arte*) naturalist
[2] (= *nudista*) naturist

naturalización SF naturalization

naturalizar ▸conjug 1f◂ Ⓐ VT to naturalize
Ⓑ **naturalizarse** VPR to become naturalized

naturalmente ADV [1] (= *de modo natural*) in a natural way
[2] (= *por supuesto*) **¡naturalmente!** naturally!, of course!

naturismo SM [1] (= *nudismo*) naturism
[2] (= *naturopatía*) naturopathy

naturista SMF [1] (= *nudista*) naturist
[2] (= *naturópata*) naturopath

naturópata SMF naturopath

naturopatía SF naturopathy

naufragar ▸conjug 1h◂ VI [1] [*barco*] to be wrecked, sink; [*gente*] to be shipwrecked
[2] [*película, obra, asunto*] to fail; [*negocio*] to go under, fail

naufragio SM [1] (*Náut*) shipwreck
[2] (*fig*) failure, ruin

náufrago/a Ⓐ ADJ shipwrecked
Ⓑ SM/F shipwrecked person, castaway

náusea SF (= *malestar físico*) nausea, sick feeling; (= *repulsión*) disgust, repulsion; **dar ~s a** to nauseate, sicken, disgust; **tener ~s** (*lit*) to feel nauseated, feel sick; (*fig*) to be nauseated, be sickened

nauseabundo ADJ nauseating, sickening

náutica SF navigation, seamanship

náutico ADJ nautical; **club ~** yacht club

nautilo SM nautilus

navaja SF [1] (= *cuchillo*) clasp knife, penknife ► **navaja automática** flick knife ► **navaja barbera** cutthroat razor ► **navaja de afeitar** razor ► **navaja de muelle, navaja de resorte** flick knife ► **navaja multiuso(s)** Swiss army knife
[2] (= *molusco*) razor shell
[3] (*Zool*) (= *colmillo*) tusk
[4] (*Entomología*) sting
[5] (*pey*) (= *lengua*) sharp tongue, evil tongue

navajada SF, **navajazo** SM knife wound, slash, gash

navajeo SM (*con navaja*) knifing, stabbing; (*fig*) infighting; (*por la espalda*) back-stabbing, stabbing in the back

navajero/a SM/F *criminal who carries a knife*

naval ADJ [*base*] naval; [*oficial*] navy *antes de s*, naval; [*compañía, industria*] shipping *antes de s*; [*constructor*] ship *antes de s*; [*capitán*] sea *antes de s*; [*bloqueo*] naval

Navarra SF Navarre

navarrica ADJ, SMF = **navarro**

navarro/a Ⓐ ADJ of/from Navarre
Ⓑ SM/F native/inhabitant of Navarre; **los ~s** the people of Navarre

nave SF [1] (*Náut*) ship, vessel; ✦***MODISMOS*** **la Nave de San Pedro** (*Rel*) the Roman Catholic Church; **quemar las ~s** to burn one's boats ► **nave insignia** flagship
[2] (*Aer*) ► **nave espacial** spaceship, spacecraft
[3] (*Arquit*) [*de iglesia*] nave; [*de fábrica etc*] bay ► **nave central** nave ► **nave lateral** aisle
[4] (= *almacén*) warehouse ► **nave de laminación** rolling mill ► **nave industrial** factory premises *pl*
[5] (*Méx**) (= *coche*) car

navegabilidad SF [*de río, canal*] navigability; [*de barco*] seaworthiness

navegable ADJ [*río, canal*] navigable; [*barco*] seaworthy

navegación SF (= *arte*) navigation; (= *buques*) ships *pl*, shipping; (= *viaje*) sea voyage; **cerrado a la ~** closed to shipping ► **navegación aérea** (= *acción*) aerial navigation; (= *tráfico*) air traffic ► **navegación a vela** sailing ► **navegación costera** coastal traffic ► **navegación fluvial** river navigation

navegador(a) Ⓐ SM/F navigator
Ⓑ SM (*Internet*) browser

navegante SMF [1] (= *marinero*) seafarer; **un pueblo de ~s** a seafaring nation ► **navegante a vela** yachtsman/yachtswoman
[2] (= *que lleva el rumbo*) navigator

navegar ▸conjug 1h◂ Ⓐ VT [1] (*Náut*) to sail; **~ a 15 nudos** to sail at 15 knots, go at 15 knots; **~ a (la) vela** to sail, go sailing
[2] (*Inform*) **~ por Internet** to surf the Net
Ⓑ VT [1] [*barco*] to sail; **~ los mares** to sail the seas
[2] [*avión*] to fly
[3] (= *llevar el rumbo*) to navigate

Navidad SF Christmas; **(día de) ~** Christmas Day; **¡feliz ~!** happy Christmas!; **Navidades** Christmas (time); **por ~es** at Christmas (time)

➤ LENGUA Y USO: **Navidad** 50.2

navideño ADJ Christmas *antes de s*
naviera SF shipping company
naviero/a Ⓐ ADJ shipping *antes de s*
Ⓑ SM/F shipowner
navío SM ship ► **navío de alto bordo, navío de línea** (*Hist*) ship of the line
náyade SF naiad
naylón SM nylon
nazarenas SFPL (*Andes, Cono Sur*) large gaucho spurs
nazareno/a Ⓐ ADJ (*Hist*) Nazarene
Ⓑ SM/F [1] (*Hist*) Nazarene
[2] (*Rel*) penitent in a Holy Week procession; → [SEMANA SANTA]
Ⓒ SM (*) [1] (= *fraude*) con trick*
[2] (= *persona*) con man*
Nazaret SM Nazareth
nazi ADJ, SMF Nazi
nazismo SM Nazism
nazista ADJ Nazi
NB ABR (= **nota bene**) NB
N. de la R. ABR = **nota de la redacción**
N. de la T ABR = **Nota de la Traductora**
N. del T ABR = **Nota del Traductor**
NE ABR (= **nordeste**) NE
neblina SF [1] (*Meteo*) mist, mistiness
[2] (*fig*) fog
neblinoso ADJ misty
nebulizador SM nebulizer
nebulosa SF nebula
nebulosidad SF [1] (*Astron*) nebulosity; [*del cielo*] cloudiness; [*del aire*] mistiness; (= *penumbra*) gloominess
[2] (= *imprecisión*) vagueness; (= *oscuridad*) obscurity
nebuloso ADJ [1] (*Astron*) nebular, nebulous; [*cielo*] cloudy; [*aire*] misty; (= *tétrico*) dark, gloomy
[2] (= *impreciso*) nebulous, vague; (= *oscuro*) obscure
necedad SF [1] (= *cualidad*) crassness, foolishness, silliness
[2] (= *cosa tonta*) **una ~** a silly thing; **~es** nonsense *sing*
necesariamente ADV necessarily; **el escalador más rápido no es ~ el mejor** the quickest climber is not necessarily the best; **no tenemos que estar allí ~** we don't necessarily need to be there
▼ **necesario** ADJ [1] (*tras sustantivo*) necessary; **los empleados carecen de la formación necesaria** the employees lack the necessary training; **no quiero estar aquí más del tiempo ~** I don't want to be here any longer than necessary; **no disponen del dinero ~ para acabar las obras** they do not have the money they need *o* the money necessary to finish the work; **haremos todo lo ~ para avanzar en las conversaciones de paz** we will do everything (that is) necessary to advance the peace talks; **ésta es una condición necesaria para que una democracia funcione** this is a necessary condition for a democracy to work; **no gastes más de lo estrictamente ~** don't spend more than is strictly necessary
[2] **hacer ~**: **estos graves incidentes hicieron necesaria la intervención de la policía** these serious incidents made it necessary for the police to intervene, these serious incidents made police intervention necessary; **hacerse ~**: **se hace necesaria una completa renovación antes de la próxima temporada** a complete overhaul is now necessary *o* required before next season; **se hizo necesaria la intervención del estado en la economía** state intervention in the economy became necessary *o* was required
[3] **ser ~** to be needed, be necessary; **no será necesaria la intervención del ejército** no military intervention will be needed *o* necessary; **para hacerse monja son ~s dos años en el noviciado** it takes two years as a novice to become a nun; **fueron necesarias varias reuniones para llegar a un acuerdo** a number of meetings were needed to reach an agreement; **haremos huelga si es ~** if necessary we will go on strike, we will go on strike if need be; **si fuera ~** if necessary, if need be, if it should be necessary; **de ser ~** if necessary, if need be
[4] **es ~ hacer algo**: **es muy ~ tener una infraestructura sólida** it is essential *o* vital to have a solid infrastructure; **para ir a Francia no es ~ tener pasaporte** you don't need a passport *o* it is not necessary to have a passport to go to France; **es ~ que** + *SUBJUN*: **era ~ que continuara con el tratamiento** he needed to continue *o* it was necessary for him to continue with the treatment; **no es ~ que le pidas disculpas** there is no need for you to apologize to him
neceser SM toilet bag ► **neceser de belleza** vanity case ► **neceser de costura** workbox ► **neceser de fin de semana** overnight bag, weekend bag
necesidad SF [1] (= *urgencia*) [1·1] **la ~ de algo** the need for sth; **la ~ de que la OTAN cumpla su promesa** the need for NATO to carry out its promise; **hay ~ de discreción en este momento** there is a need for discretion at this moment; **la ~ de hacer algo** the need to do sth; **se habló de la ~ de encontrar una nueva vía de diálogo** the need to find a new approach to the talks was discussed; **no hay ~ de hacerlo** there is no need to do it; **tener ~ de algo** to need sth; **tienen ~ urgente de ayuda alimenticia** they urgently need food aid, they are in urgent need of food aid; **con la nueva tarjeta bancaria no tendrá ~ de llevar dinero** with the new bank card you won't need to carry money with you; **y ¿qué ~ tienes de irte a un hotel habiendo camas en casa?** why would you need to go to a hotel when there are spare beds at home?; ✦*MODISMO* **hacer de la ~ virtud** to make a virtue of necessity; ✦*REFRÁN* **la ~ aguza el ingenio** necessity is the mother of invention
[1·2] **de ~**: **en caso de ~** in an emergency; **una situación de ~** an emergency; **una herida mortal de ~** a fatal wound; **artículos** *o* **productos de primera ~** basic essentials, staple items
[1·3] **por ~**: **tuve que aprenderlo por ~** I had to learn it out of necessity; **el que se llame John no significa que tenga que ser inglés por ~** the fact that he is called John does not necessarily mean that he is English
[1·4] **sin ~**: **no corra riesgos sin ~** don't take unnecessary risks; **sin ~ de algo** without the need for sth; **podemos llegar a un acuerdo sin ~ de que intervenga el director** we can come to an agreement without any need for the director to intervene; **ahora podemos ir de compras sin ~ de movernos de casa** now we can go shopping without needing to leave the house
[1·5] (= *cosa necesaria*) (*personal*) need; (*objetiva*) necessity; **satisfacer las ~es de algn** to satisfy sb's needs; **para un representante un coche no es un lujo, es una ~** for a sales rep, a car is not a luxury, it's a necessity
[2] (= *pobreza*) need; **están en la mayor ~** they are in great need
[3] (= *apuro*) tight spot; **encontrarse en una ~** to be in a tight spot
[4] **necesidades** [4·1] (= *privaciones*) hardships; **pasar ~es** to suffer hardship *o* hardships
[4·2] ✦*MODISMO* **hacer sus ~es** (*euf*) to relieve o.s.
necesitado Ⓐ ADJ [1] (= *falto*) **andar** *o* **estar** *o* **verse ~ de algo** to need sth; **estamos ~s de mano de obra** we need workers, we are in need of labour; **anda ~ de afecto** he's in need of affection, he needs affection
[2] (= *pobre*) in need; **ayuda a familias necesitadas** help for needy families, help for families in need; **las naciones más necesitadas** the nations in greatest need
Ⓑ SMPL **los ~s** the needy
▼ **necesitar** ▸conjug 1a◂ Ⓐ VT to need; **necesitamos dos más** we need two more; **para comprarse un barco así se necesita mucho dinero** you need a lot of money to buy a boat like that; **póngase en contacto con nosotros si necesita más información** get in touch with us if you need *o* (*frm*) require more information; **"se necesita coche"** "car wanted"; **~ hacer algo** to need to do sth; **no necesitas hacerlo** you don't need to do it, you needn't do it; **necesito verte ahora mismo** I need to see you right now; **se necesita ser caradura para presentarse sin avisar** you'd have to be cheeky to turn up without warning; **~ que** + *SUBJUN*: **necesito que me lo mandes urgentemente** I need you to send it to me urgently; **no necesito que nadie me lo recuerde** I don't need to be reminded, I don't need anyone to remind me
Ⓑ VI **~ de algo** to need sth; **el ser humano necesita del oxígeno para vivir** human beings need oxygen to survive
neciamente ADV foolishly, stupidly
necio/a Ⓐ ADJ [1] (= *tonto*) foolish, stupid
[2] (*Méx*) (= *terco*) stubborn, pig-headed
[3] (*Andes*) (= *displicente*) peevish
[4] (*Andes, Caribe, Cono Sur*) (= *quisquilloso*) touchy, hypersensitive
[5] (*CAm*) [*enfermedad*] hard to shake off
Ⓑ SM/F fool
nécora SF small crab
necrófago SM ghoul
necrofilia SF necrophilia
necrófilo/a ADJ, SM/F necrophiliac
necrología SF, **necrológica** SF (= *lista*) obituary column; (= *noticia*) obituary
necrológico ADJ obituary *antes de s*
necromancia SF, **necromancía** SF necromancy
necrópolis SF INV necropolis
necropsia SF autopsy

➤ LENGUA Y USO: **necesario 3** 37.2 **necesitar A** 37.1

necrosar ▸conjug 1a◂ Ⓐ VT, VI to necrotize
Ⓑ **necrosarse** VPR to necrotize

necrosis SF INV necrosis

necrotizar ▸conjug 1f◂ Ⓐ VT, VI to necrotize
Ⓑ **necrotizarse** VPR to necrotize

néctar SM (*lit, fig*) nectar; **~ de melocotón** peach nectar

nectarina SF nectarine

neerlandés/esa Ⓐ ADJ Dutch
Ⓑ SM/F Dutchman/Dutchwoman; **los neerlandeses** the Dutch
Ⓒ SM (*Ling*) Dutch

nefando ADJ (*liter*) unspeakable, abominable

nefario ADJ (*liter*) nefarious

nefasto ADJ 1 (= *funesto*) [*viaje*] ill-fated; [*año*] unlucky; [*resultado*] unfortunate; [*influencia*] pernicious; [*corrupción*] harmful, damaging; [*alcohol, ácido*] harmful
2 (*LAm*) (= *atroz*) dreadful, terrible

nefato* ADJ (*Caribe*) stupid, dim*

nefrítico ADJ nephritic

nefritis SF INV nephritis

negación SF 1 (*gen*) negation; (= *negativa*) denial
2 (*Ling*) negative

negado/a Ⓐ ADJ hopeless, useless; **ser ~ para algo** to be hopeless *o* useless at sth
Ⓑ SM/F **es un ~** he's hopeless *o* useless, he's a dead loss*

▼ **negar** ▸conjug 1h, 1j◂ Ⓐ VT 1 (= *desmentir*) to deny; **niega haber robado los documentos** he denies having stolen the documents; **el ministro ha negado todas las acusaciones** the minister has denied all the accusations; **no me ~ás que ha valido la pena** you can't deny it's been worth it; **negó que lo hubieran despedido** he denied that they had sacked him, he denied having been sacked
2 (= *rehusar*) to refuse, deny (**a** to); **le ~on el paso por la frontera** they refused to let him cross the border; **nos ~on la entrada al edificio** we were refused *o* denied entry to the building; **~ el saludo a algn** to blank sb*, snub sb*; **~ la mano a algn** to refuse to shake hands with sb
3 (*frm*) [+ *persona*] to disown; **negó a su hija** he disowned his daughter
Ⓑ VI **~ con la cabeza** to shake one's head
Ⓒ **negarse** VPR 1 **~se a hacer algo** to refuse to do sth; **se negó a pagar la multa** he refused to pay the fine
2 **~se a la evidencia** to deny the obvious

negativa SF refusal; **me sorprendió su ~ a cooperar** I was surprised at his refusal to cooperate ► **negativa rotunda** flat refusal

negativamente ADV negatively; **contestar ~** to answer in the negative; **valorar algo ~** to take a negative view of sth

negatividad SF, **negativismo** SM negative attitude

negativizar ▸conjug 1f◂ VT to neutralize

negativo Ⓐ ADJ 1 (*gen*) negative; **voto ~** vote against, no vote
2 (*Mat*) minus
3 (*Fot*) negative
Ⓑ SM (*Fot*) negative

negligencia SF negligence

negligente Ⓐ ADJ negligent
Ⓑ SMF careless person

negligentemente ADV negligently

negociabilidad SF negotiability

negociable ADJ negotiable

negociación SF (*gen*) negotiation; (= *transacción*) deal, transaction; [*de cheque*] clearance; **entrar en negociaciones con** to enter into negotiations with ► **negociación colectiva de salarios** collective bargaining

negociadamente ADV **resolver un problema ~** to settle a problem by negotiation

negociado SM 1 (= *sección*) department, section
2 (*Andes, Cono Sur*) (= *negocio turbio*) shady deal
3 (*Cono Sur*) (= *establecimiento*) shop, store (*EEUU*)

negociador(a) Ⓐ ADJ negotiating; **comisión ~a** negotiating committee
Ⓑ SM/F negotiator

negociante SMF businessman/businesswoman

negociar ▸conjug 1b◂ Ⓐ VT to negotiate
Ⓑ VI 1 (*Pol etc*) to negotiate
2 (*Com*) **~ en** *o* **con** to deal in, trade in

negocio SM 1 (*Com, Fin*) (= *empresa*) business; (= *tienda*) shop, store (*EEUU*); **el ~ del espectáculo** show business; **el ~ del libro** the book trade; **montar un ~** to set up *o* start a business; **traspasar un ~** to transfer a business, sell a business
2 (= *transacción*) deal, transaction; **el ~ es el ~** business is business; **hacer un buen ~** to pull off a good deal; **¡hiciste un buen ~!** (*iró*) that was a fine deal you did!; **un ~ redondo** a real bargain, a really good deal; ✦*MODISMO* **cuidar de su propio ~** to look after one's own interests, look after number one ► **negocio sucio, negocio turbio** shady deal
3 **negocios** (*Com, Fin*) business *sing*, trade *sing*; **el mundo de los ~s** the business world; **estar en viaje de ~s** to be (away) on business; **hablar de ~s** to talk business; **hombre/mujer de ~s** businessman/businesswoman; **retirarse de los ~s** to retire from business; ✦*REFRÁN* **a malos ~s sombrero de copa** one must make the best of a bad job
4 (= *asunto*) affair; **eso es ~ tuyo** that's your affair; **mal ~** bad business; **¡mal ~!** it looks bad!
5 (*Andes, Cono Sur*) (= *firma*) firm, company; (= *casa*) place of business
6 (*Andes, Caribe**) **el ~** the fact, the truth; **pero el ~ es que …** but the fact is that …
7 (*Andes*) (= *cuento*) tale, piece of gossip

negocioso ADJ (= *diligente*) industrious; (*en las maneras*) businesslike

negra SF 1 (*Mús*) crotchet, quarter note (*EEUU*)
2 (= *mala suerte*) bad luck; **ése me trae la ~** he brings me bad luck; **le tocó la ~** he had bad luck; **tener la ~** to be out of luck, be having a run of bad luck
3 (*Ajedrez*) black piece
4 (*CAm*) black mark; *ver tb* **negro**

negrada SF (*LAm*) 1 (*Hist*) (= *grupo*) group of Negroes, Negroes *pl*
2 (= *fraude*) cheat, fraud

negrear ▸conjug 1a◂ VI 1 (= *ponerse negro*) to go black, turn black; (= *parecer negro*) to appear black
2 (= *tirar a negro*) to be blackish

negrería SF (*LAm*), **negrerío** SM (*LAm*) = **negrada 1**

negrero SM (*Hist*) slave trader; (= *explotador*) exploiter of labour *o* (*EEUU*) labor, slave driver*

negriazul ADJ black and blue; **la nueva estrella ~** (*Dep*) the new star to wear the black and blue strip

negrilla SF 1 (*Tip*) = **negrita**
2 (*Bot*) elm

negrita SF 1 (*Tip*) boldface; **en ~** in bold (type), in boldface
2 (*CAm*) black mark

negrito[1] SM golliwog

negrito[2] SM (*Caribe*) black coffee

negritud SF negritude

negro/a Ⓐ ADJ 1 [*color, pelo*] black; [*ojos, tabaco*] dark; [*raza*] black, Negro†; ✦*MODISMOS* **más ~ que el azabache** jet-black; **~ como boca de lobo** ◊ **~ como un pozo** pitch-black, pitch-dark
2 (= *moreno*) [*piel*] dark, swarthy; (*por el sol*) tanned, brown; **ponerse ~** to go brown, tan
3 (= *sucio*) filthy, black
4 [*estado de ánimo, humor*] black, gloomy; [*suerte*] terrible, atrocious; **la cosa se pone negra** it's not going well, it looks bad; **lo ve todo ~** he always sees the negative side of things, he's terribly pessimistic about everything; ✦*MODISMOS* **ve muy ~ el porvenir** he's very gloomy about the future; **pasarlas negras** to have a tough time of it; **verse ~** to be in a jam*; **verse ~ para hacer algo** to have one's work cut out to do sth; **nos vimos ~s para salir del apuro** we had a tough time getting out of it; **vérselas negras** to find o.s. in trouble
5 (*) (= *enfadado*) cross, peeved*; **estoy ~ con esto** I'm getting desperate about it; **poner ~ a algn** to make sb cross, upset sb; **ponerse ~** to get cross, cut up rough
6 (= *ilegal*) black; **dinero ~** hot money; **economía negra** black economy; **mercado ~** black market
7 (*Pol*) fascist; **terrorismo ~** fascist terrorism
Ⓑ SM 1 (= *color*) black; **en ~** (*Fot*) in black and white ► **negro de humo** lampblack
2 (*Caribe*) (= *café*) black coffee
Ⓒ SM/F 1 (= *persona*) black, coloured person†, Negro†; **¡no somos ~s!** we won't stand for it!, you can't do that to us!; ✦*MODISMO* **trabajar como un ~** to work like a dog, slave away*
2 (*) (= *escritor*) ghostwriter
3 **mi ~** (*Andes, Cono Sur**) (= *cariño*) darling, honey; *ver tb* **negra**

negroide ADJ negroid

negrura SF blackness

negruzco ADJ blackish

nel: EXCL (*Méx*) yep*

neli: ADV = **nada**

nema SF (*Méx Admin*) seal

neme SM (*Andes*) asphalt

nemotécnica SF = **mnemotécnica**

nene/a SM/F 1 (= *niño pequeño*) baby, small child
2 (*uso apelativo*) **¡sí, nena!** (*a mujer*) yes dear!, yes darling!; **¿vamos al cine, ~?** (*a hombre*) shall we go to the cinema, darling?

nenúfar SM water lily

neo SM neon

neo... PREF neo…

neoaristotelismo SM neo-Aristotelianism

➤ LENGUA Y USO: **negar A1** 53.6 **C1** 35.5, 39.3

neocapitalista ADJ, SMF neo-capitalist
neocelandés/esa Ⓐ ADJ of/from New Zealand
Ⓑ SM/F New Zealander; **los neocelandeses** the New Zealanders
neoclasicismo SM neoclassicism
neoclásico ADJ neoclassical
neocolonialismo SM neocolonialism
neofascismo SM neofascism
neofascista ADJ, SMF neofascist
neófito/a SM/F neophyte
neogótico ADJ neogothic
neoimpresionismo SM neo-impressionism
neolatino ADJ **lenguas neolatinas** Romance languages
neolengua SF newspeak
neolítico ADJ neolithic
neologismo SM neologism
neón SM (= *gas, luz*) neon
neonatal ADJ [*asistencia*] neonatal
neonato/a SM/F newborn baby
neonatólogo/a SM/F neonatologist
neonazi ADJ, SMF neonazi
neonazista ADJ neonazi
neoplatónico ADJ neoplatonic
neoplatonismo SM neoplatonism
neoplatonista SMF neoplatonist
neoyorquino/a Ⓐ ADJ of/from New York
Ⓑ SM/F New Yorker; **los ~s** the New Yorkers
neozelandés/esa Ⓐ ADJ of/from New Zealand Ⓑ SM/F New Zealander; **los neozelandeses** the New Zealanders
Nepal SM Nepal
nepalés/esa, nepalí Ⓐ ADJ Nepalese
Ⓑ SM/F Nepalese; **los nepaleses** the Nepalese
nepotismo SM nepotism
Neptuno SM Neptune
nereida SF nereid
Nerón SM Nero
nervadura SF (*Arquit*) ribs *pl*; (*Bot, Entomología*) nervure (*frm*), vein
nervio SM [1] (*Anat*) nerve; (*en carne*) sinew; **este filete tiene mucho ~** this steak is very sinewy *o* gristly ► **nervio ciático** sciatic nerve ► **nervio dental** nerve of the tooth ► **nervio óptico** optic nerve
[2] **nervios** (= *ansiedad*) nerves; ✦**MODISMOS crispar los ~s a algn** to get *o* grate on sb's nerves; **de los ~s***: **estoy de los ~s** my nerves are on edge; **poner de los ~s a algn** to get on sb's nerves, put sb's nerves on edge; **ponerse de los ~s** to get wound up*; **tener ~s de acero** to have nerves of steel; **tener los ~s como las cuerdas de un violín** to be as jumpy as a cat; **tener los ~s destrozados** ◊ **estar destrozado de los ~s** to be a nervous wreck; **tener los ~s a flor de piel** to be ready to explode; **poner los ~s de punta a algn** to get *o* grate on sb's nerves
[3] (*Arquit, Tip, Bot*) rib; [*de insectos*] vein; (*Mús*) string; [*de libro*] rib
[4] (= *vigor*) vigour, vigor (*EEUU*), strength; **tener ~** to have character; **un hombre sin ~** a spineless man, a weak man; ✦**MODISMO ser puro ~** to live on one's nerves
[5] [*de persona, sociedad*] (= *eje*) leading light, guiding spirit; **él es el ~ de la sociedad** he is the guiding spirit of the club
[6] [*de cuestión, problema*] (= *fondo*) crux, heart
nerviosamente ADV nervously
nerviosera SF attack of nerves
nerviosismo SF, **nerviosidad** SM nervousness, nerves *pl*; (= *agitación*) agitation, restlessness
nervioso ADJ [1] (*Anat*) nerve *antes de s*, nervous; **centro ~** nerve centre; **crisis nerviosa** nervous breakdown; **depresión nerviosa** nervous depression; **sistema ~** nervous system; **ataque ~** (attack of) hysterics
[2] (= *excitable*) **ser ~** to be highly strung, be nervous; **es un niño muy ~** he's a very highly strung *o* nervous child; **los foxterriers son muy ~s** fox terriers are very highly strung
[3] (= *intranquilo*) **estar ~** to be nervous; **está nerviosa porque tiene un examen** she's nervous because she has an exam; **está muy ~ porque aún no han llegado** he's very anxious because they haven't arrived yet; **esperaban ~s los resultados** they waited nervously to hear the results; **los caballos estaban ~s antes de la tormenta** the horses were restless before the storm; **poner ~ a algn** to make sb nervous; **ponerse ~** to get nervous; **me pongo muy nerviosa en las entrevistas** I get very nervous in interviews; **¡no te pongas ~!** keep cool!*
nervoso ADJ [1] [*persona*] = **nervioso 2,3**
[2] [*carne*] sinewy, tough
nervudo ADJ [1] (= *robusto*) tough
[2] [*mano, brazo*] sinewy
nesga SF (*Cos*) flare, gore
nesgado ADJ (*Cos*) flared
nesgar ▸conjug 1h◂ VT (*Cos*) to flare, gore
netamente ADV (= *claramente*) clearly; (= *puramente*) purely; (= *genuinamente*) genuinely; **una construcción ~ española** a purely Spanish construction, a genuinely Spanish construction
neto ADJ [1] (*Com, Fin*) net; **peso ~** net weight; **sueldo ~** net salary, salary after deductions
[2] (= *claro*) clear; **un perfil ~** a clear outline
neumático Ⓐ ADJ [*martillo, bomba*] pneumatic; [*freno*] air *antes de s*, pneumatic
Ⓑ SM [*de rueda*] tyre, tire (*EEUU*) ► **neumático balón** balloon tyre ► **neumático de recambio, neumático de repuesto** spare tyre ► **neumático radial** radial tyre ► **neumático sin cámara** tubeless tyre
neumoconiosis SF INV pneumoconiosis
neumonía SF pneumonia ► **neumonía asiática** SARS
neura* SF [1] (= *manía*) obsession; **¡menuda ~ te ha cogido con lo de adelgazar!** you've got a real obsession with losing weight!; **tiene la ~ de lavarse continuamente las manos** he's obsessed with washing his hands all the time
[2] (= *depresión*) **estar con la ~**: **está con la ~ desde que la despidieron** she's been very down since she lost her job
neural ADJ neural
neuralgia SF neuralgia
neurálgico ADJ [1] (*Med*) neuralgic, nerve *antes de s*
[2] (*fig*) [*centro*] nerve *antes de s*; [*punto*] crucial, key *antes de s*
neuras* SMF INV **es un ~** he's neurotic
neurastenia SF [1] (*Med*) neurasthenia (*frm*), nervous exhaustion
[2] (*fig*) nerviness, excitability
neurasténico ADJ [1] (*Med*) neurasthenic
[2] (*fig*) neurotic, nervy, excitable
neuritis SF INV neuritis
neuro... PREF neuro...
neuroanatomía SF neuroanatomy
neurobiología SF neurobiology
neurociencia SF neuroscience
neurocirugía SF neurosurgery
neurocirujano/a SM/F neurosurgeon
neuroléptico SM (*Farm*) neuroleptic
neurología SF neurology
neurólogo/a SM/F neurologist
neurona SF neuron, nerve cell
neurópata SMF neuropath
neuropatía SF neuropathy
neuropático ADJ neuropathic
neuropatológico ADJ neuropathological
neuropsicología SF neuropsychology
neuropsicólogo/a SM/F neuropsychologist
neuropsiquiatra SMF neuropsychiatrist
neuropsiquiatría SF neuropsychiatry
neurosiquiatra SMF neuropsychiatrist
neurosiquiatría SF neuropsychiatry
neurosis SF INV neurosis ► **neurosis de guerra** shell shock
neurótico/a ADJ, SM/F neurotic
neurotizar ▸conjug 1f◂ Ⓐ VT to make neurotic
Ⓑ **neurotizarse** VPR to become neurotic
neurotransmisor SM neurotransmitter
neutral ADJ, SMF neutral
neutralidad SF neutrality
neutralismo SM neutralism
neutralista ADJ, SMF neutralist
neutralización SF neutralization
neutralizar ▸conjug 1f◂ Ⓐ VT (*gen*) to neutralize; [+ *tendencia, influencia*] to counteract
Ⓑ **neutralizarse** VPR (*gen*) to neutralize each other; [*influencias*] to cancel (each other) out
neutro Ⓐ ADJ [1] (*gen*) neutral
[2] (*Biol*) neuter, sexless; **abeja neutra** worker bee
[3] (*Ling*) neuter; **género ~** neuter; **verbo ~** intransitive verb
Ⓑ SM (*Ling*) neuter
neutrón SM neutron
nevada SF snowfall
nevado Ⓐ ADJ [1] (= *cubierto de nieve*) snow-covered; [*montaña*] snow-capped
[2] (*fig*) snowy, snow-white
Ⓑ SM (*LAm*) snow-capped mountain
nevar ▸conjug 1j◂ Ⓐ VI to snow
Ⓑ VT to whiten
nevasca SF snowstorm
nevazón SF (*Andes, Cono Sur*) snowstorm
nevera SF [1] (= *frigorífico*) refrigerator, fridge*, icebox (*EEUU*)
[2] (= *casa, habitación*) icebox
nevera-congelador SF fridge-freezer
nevero SM snowfield, ice field, place of perpetual snow
nevisca SF light snowfall, flurry of snow
neviscar ▸conjug 1g◂ VI to snow lightly
nevoso ADJ snowy
newtoniano ADJ Newtonian
newtonio SM newton

nexo SM link, connection, nexus (*frm*)

n/f. ABR = **nuestro favor**

n/g. ABR = **nuestro giro**

ni CONJ [1] (= *y no*) (*con verbo negativo en inglés*) or; (*con verbo afirmativo en inglés*) nor; **no le gustan las plantas ni los animales** he doesn't like plants or animals; **no bebe ni fuma** he doesn't smoke or drink; **un edificio sin puertas ni ventanas** a building without doors or windows; **—a mí no me gusta —ni a mí** "I don't like it" — "nor do I" *o* "neither do I"; **ni... ni ...**: **no tenía ni amigos ni familiares** he had no friends and no family (either), he had no friends or family, he had neither friends nor family; **no es ni blanco ni negro** it's not black and it's not white (either), it's neither black nor white; **no vinieron ni Juan ni Pedro** Juan didn't come and neither did Pedro, neither Juan nor Pedro came; **ni vino ni llamó por teléfono** he didn't come and he didn't phone (either), he neither came nor phoned; **ni lo sé ni me importa** I don't know and I don't care; **ni que lo hagas bien ni que lo hagas mal te dirán nada** whether you do it well or badly, they won't say anything
[2] (*para dar más énfasis*) even; **no sabe ni dónde está Moscú** he doesn't even know where Moscow is; **ni a ti te lo dirá** he won't tell even *you*; **no lo compraría ni aunque tuviera dinero** I wouldn't buy it even if I had the money; **no tengo ni idea** I have no idea; **no ha llamado ni nada** he hasn't phoned or anything; **ni se sabe** God knows, who knows?; **ni siquiera** not even; **ni siquiera nos ha visto** he didn't even see us; **ni siquiera me llamó** he didn't even phone me; **ni uno**: **—¿cuántos tienes? —ni uno** "how many have you got?" — "not a single one" *o* "none"; **no hemos comprado ni un regalo** we haven't bought a single present; **no me ha dicho ni una palabra desde que llegó** she hasn't said a single word to me since she got here; **ni uno de sus parientes lo ha felicitado** not (a single) one of his relatives has congratulated him; **no tengo ni un duro** I haven't got a penny
[3] (*exclamaciones*) **¡ni hablar!** no way!, not on your life!; **¿yo? ¿votar a ésos? ¡ni hablar!** me vote for them? no way! *o* not on your life!; **¡ni por ésas!**: **he intentado convencerla prometiéndole un regalo, pero ni por ésas** I tried to persuade her with a present but even that didn't work; **ni que**: **siempre cuidando de él, ¡ni que fueras su madre!** you're always taking care of him, anyone would think you were his mother!; **vaya unos humos que tiene, ¡ni que fuese un dios!** he's so arrogant, he must think he's God!; **¡pero tú qué te has creído!, ¡ni que yo fuese tonto!** you must think I'm stupid or something!; **¡qué curso ni qué curso! ¡yo he aprendido por mi cuenta!** what are you talking about, taking a course? I've studied by myself!
[4] **ni bien** (*Arg, Uru*) as soon as; **ni bien me fui, sonó el teléfono** as soon as I left, the phone rang

Niágara SM Niagara

niara SF (*Agr*) stack, rick

nica ADJ, SMF (*CAm pey*) Nicaraguan

nicabar* ▸conjug 1a◂ VT to rip off*, nick*

Nicaragua SF Nicaragua

nicaragüense Ⓐ ADJ Nicaraguan
Ⓑ SMF Nicaraguan; **los ~s** the Nicaraguans

nicaragüismo SM *word/phrase peculiar to Nicaragua*

nicho SM (*gen*) niche; (= *receso*) recess ► **nicho ecológico** ecological niche

nick SM (*Internet*) nickname, user name, nick

Nico SM (*forma familiar*) *de* **Nicolás**

Nicolás SM Nicholas

nicotiana SF nicotiana, tobacco plant

nicotina SF nicotine

nicotínico ADJ nicotinic, nicotine *antes de s*

nidada SF [*de huevos*] clutch; [*de pajarillos*] brood

nidal SM [1] (*Orn*) nest; (= *nido artificial*) nesting box [2] [*de dinero*] nest egg [3] (*) (= *guarida*) haunt, hang-out*; (= *escondite*) hiding place

nidificación SF nesting, nest-building

nidificante ADJ **ave ~** nesting bird

nidificar ▸conjug 1g◂ VI to nest

nido SM [1] (*gen*) nest; ✦**MODISMOS caer del ~** to come down to earth with a bump; **parece que se ha caído de un ~** he's a bit wet behind the ears*; **manchar el propio ~** to foul one's own nest ► **nido de abeja** (*en tela*) honeycomb pattern ► **nido de amor** lovenest ► **nido de víboras** nest of vipers
[2] (= *escondrijo*) hiding place; **un ~ de ladrones** a den of thieves
[3] [*de conflictos*] hotbed; [*de discusiones*] focus; **el reparto de premios fue un ~ de polémicas** the prize giving gave rise to heated arguments
[4] (*en hospital*) baby unit
[5] [*de bebé*] (= *camita*) cot; (= *corralito*) playpen
[6] (= *emplazamiento*) ► **nido de ametralladoras** machine-gun nest

niebla SF [1] (= *bruma*) fog; **un día de ~** a foggy day; **hay ~** it is foggy ► **niebla artificial** smoke screen ► **niebla de humo** smog
[2] (*en asunto, negocio*) confusion
[3] (*Bot*) mildew

niego, niegue *etc ver* **negar**

nietísimo/a SM/F (*hum*) extra-special grandchild

nieto/a SM/F [1] (*lit*) grandson/granddaughter; **~s** grandchildren
[2] (*fig*) descendant

nieva *etc ver* **nevar**

nieve SF [1] (*Meteo*) snow; **~ abundante** *o* **copiosa** heavy snow; **copo de ~** snowflake; **las primeras ~s** the first snows, the first snowfall ► **nieve artificial** artificial snow ► **nieve en polvo** powdery snow ► **nieves perpetuas** perpetual snow
[2] (*Culin*) **a punto de ~** stiff, beaten stiff; **batir a punto de ~** to beat until stiff
[3] (*LAm*) (= *polo*) ice lolly; (= *sorbete*) sorbet, water-ice
[4] (‡) (= *cocaína*) snow*, coke*
[5] (*TV*) (= *interferencia*) snow

NIF SM ABR (= **número de identificación fiscal**) *ID number used for tax purposes*

Nigeria SF Nigeria

nigeriano/a Ⓐ ADJ Nigerian
Ⓑ SM/F Nigerian; **los ~s** the Nigerians

night* [naɪt] SM nightclub

nigromancia SF necromancy

nigromante SM necromancer

nigua SF (*Ant, CAm*) (= *pulga*) chigoe, chigger

nihilismo SM nihilism

nihilista Ⓐ ADJ nihilistic
Ⓑ SMF nihilist

niki SM (*Esp*) T-shirt

Nilo SM Nile

nilón [ni'lon] SM nylon

nimbo SM [1] (*Arte, Astron, Rel*) halo
[2] (*Meteo*) nimbus

nimbostrato SM nimbostratus

nimiamente ADV trivially

nimiedad SF [1] (= *cualidad*) insignificance, triviality
[2] **una ~** a trifle, a tiny detail; **riñeron por una ~** they quarrelled over nothing
[3] (= *minuciosidad*) meticulousness; (*pey*) fussiness; (= *prolijidad*) long-windedness
[4] (= *exceso*) excess

nimiez SF trifle, bagatelle

nimio ADJ [1] (= *insignificante*) insignificant, trivial; **un sinfín de detalles ~s** endless trivial details
[2] [*persona*] (= *minucioso*) meticulous; (*pey*) fussy (about details); (= *prolijo*) long-winded
[3] (= *excesivo*) excessive (**en** in)

ninchi‡ SM [1] (= *imbécil*) berk*, twit*
[2] (= *niño*) kid*, child
[3] (= *amigo*) pal*, buddy (*EEUU**)

ninfa SF [1] (*Mit*) nymph
[2] (*Esp‡*) (= *chica*) bird*, chick (*EEUU‡*)

ninfeta SF, **ninfilla** SF, **ninfita** SF nymphet

ninfómana SF nymphomaniac

ninfomanía SF nymphomania

ninfómano ADJ nymphomaniac

nínfula SF nymphet

ningún ADJ *ver* **ninguno**

ningunear* ▸conjug 1a◂ VT (*esp CAm, Méx*) **~ a algn** (= *hacer el vacío a*) to pretend that sb doesn't exist, ignore sb; (= *despreciar*) to look down one's nose at sb; (= *empequeñecer*) to make sb feel small; (= *tratar mal*) to treat sb like dirt*

ninguneo* SM (*esp CAm, Méx*) **le condenaron al ~** they completely ostracized him

ninguno Ⓐ ADJ (*con verbo negativo en inglés*) any; (*con verbo afirmativo en inglés*) no; **no practica ningún deporte** he doesn't do any sport, he does no sport; **no hay ningún riesgo de contagio** there is no risk of infection; **no voy a ninguna parte** I'm not going anywhere; **no es ningún tonto** he's no fool; **no es molestia ninguna** it's no trouble at all
Ⓑ PRON [1] (*entre más de dos*) (*con verbo negativo en inglés*) any; (*con verbo afirmativo en inglés*) none; **hizo cuatro exámenes pero no aprobó ~** he took four exams but didn't pass any (of them); **—¿cuál te gusta? —ninguno** "which one do you like?" — "none of them"; **~ de: no me creo ninguna de sus historias** I don't believe any of his stories; **no me interesa ~ de ellos** I'm not interested in any of them; **no lo sabe ~ de sus amigos** none of his friends know
[2] (*entre dos*) (*con verbo negativo en inglés*) either; (*con verbo afirmativo en inglés*) neither; **no me gusta ~ (de los dos)** I don't like either (of them); **no os quiero ver a ~ de los dos por aquí** I don't want to see either of

you round here; **no nos ha escrito ~ de los dos** neither of them has written to us; **~ de los dos equipos pasará a la final** neither of the teams *o* neither team will get through to the final
[3] (= *nadie*) nobody, no-one; **lo hace como ~** he does it like nobody *o* no-one else; **los invité a los dos pero no vino ~** I invited both but neither of them came

NINGUNO

Adjetivo

• Se traduce por **any** si el verbo va en forma negativa y por **no** si el verbo va en forma afirmativa. En general es más frecuente usar **not** + **any** (salvo como sujeto, posición en la que se debe emplear **no**), ya que **no** se utiliza normalmente con carácter más enfático:

No tengo ninguna pregunta
I haven't got any questions
No se ha cometido ningún delito
No crime has been committed
No fui a ningún sitio
I didn't go anywhere
No hay ningún peligro
There is no danger, There isn't any danger

NOTA: Hay que tener en cuenta que el sustantivo que sigue a **any** va en plural si es contable, como en el primer ejemplo.

• Con palabras que poseen un sentido negativo tales como **hardly**, **without** y **never** hay que utilizar **any**:

Conseguí hacerlo sin ninguna ayuda
I managed to do it without any help

Pronombre

• El uso de los pronombres **any** y **none** sigue las mismas pautas que los adjetivos **any** y **no**, ya que se emplea preferiblemente la forma **any** con verbos en forma negativa y **none** si la forma es afirmativa, e igualmente se prefiere la forma **none** para la posición de sujeto:

No quiero ninguno de éstos
I don't want any of these
No me gusta ninguno de ellos
I don't like any of them
No queda ninguno
There are none left
No va a venir ninguno de sus amigos
None of her friends is *o* ***are coming***

NOTA: Si el verbo va detrás de **none** puede ir tanto en singular como en plural.

• En lugar de **none** y **any**, si **ninguno** se refiere a dos personas o cosas se emplea **neither** y **either**, siguiendo las mismas reglas anotadas anteriormente:

Ninguno de los dos equipos está jugando bien
Neither of the teams *o* ***Neither team is playing well***
No conozco a ninguno de los dos
I don't know either of them

NOTA: El verbo va en singular si sigue a **neither**.

⇨ *Ver tb* ALGUNO, ALGO
Para otros usos y ejemplos ver la entrada.

niña SF [1] ► **niña bonita*** (*en lotería*) (= *15*) number fifteen; **ser la ~ bonita de algn** to be the apple of sb's eye
[2] [*de los ojos*] pupil; **ser la ~ de los ojos de algn** to be the apple of sb's eye; *ver tb* **niño B1**

niñada SF = **niñería 2**

niñato* Ⓐ ADJ **no seas tan ~** don't be so childish, don't be such a baby
Ⓑ SM (*pey*) (= *niño*) kid*

niñear ▸conjug 1a◂ VI to act childishly

niñera SF nanny, child's nurse (*EEUU*), nursemaid†

niñería SF [1] (= *cualidad*) childishness
[2] (= *acto*) childish thing; (= *trivialidad*) silly thing, triviality; **llora por cualquier ~** she cries at the slightest thing

niñero ADJ fond of children

niñez SF [*de persona*] childhood; [*de proyecto, teoría*] infancy

niño/a Ⓐ ADJ [1] (= *joven*) young; (*pey*) childish; **es muy ~ todavía** he's still very young; **¡no seas ~!** don't be so childish!
[2] (*Andes*) [*fruta*] green, unripe
Ⓑ SM/F [1] (= *crío*) child, (little) boy/(little) girl; **los ~s** the children; **de ~** as a child; **desde ~** since childhood, since I *etc* was a child; ✦***MODISMOS*** **ser el ~ mimado de algn** to be sb's pet; **¡qué coche ni qué ~ muerto!*** all this nonsense about a car!, car my foot!*; **como ~ con zapatos nuevos** (*por regalo, compra*) like a child with a new toy, as pleased as punch; (*por noticia, sorpresa*) as pleased as punch ► **niño/a bien, niño/a bonito/a** Hooray Henry*; **el ~ bonito del toreo** the golden boy of bullfighting ► **niño/a de la calle** street kid ► **niño/a expósito/a** foundling ► **niño/a pera, niño/a pijo/a*** pampered child, daddy's boy/girl ► **niño/a prodigio/a** child prodigy ► **niño/a terrible** enfant terrible
[2] (= *bebé*) baby; **va a tener un ~** she's going to have a baby; **hacer un ~ a una** to get a girl in the family way; **cuando nazca el ~** when the baby is born, when the child is born ► **niño/a azul** blue baby ► **el Niño de la bola** (*lit*) the infant Jesus; (*fig*) fortune's favourite ► **niño/a de pecho** babe-in-arms ► **el Niño Jesús** the Christ-child; (*con menos formalidad*) the Baby Jesus ► **niño/a probeta** test-tube baby
[3] (*) (*uso apelativo*) **¡~, que te vas a caer!** watch out, lad, you're going to fall!; **¡niña, no seas tan tonta!** don't be such a silly girl!
[4] (*LAm esp Hist*) (= *título*) master/mistress, sir/miss; **el ~ Francisco** (young) master Francisco
[5] (*Cono Sur*) undesirable; *ver tb* **niña**

nipón/ona Ⓐ ADJ Japanese
Ⓑ SM/F Japanese; **los nipones** the Japanese

nipos‡ SMPL dough* *sing*, cash* *sing*

níquel SM [1] (*gen*) nickel; (*Téc*) nickel-plating
[2] (*LAm*) (= *moneda*) small coin, nickel (*EEUU*); **~es** (*Cono Sur, Méx*) dough* *sing*

niquelado Ⓐ ADJ nickel-plated
Ⓑ SM nickel plating

niquelar ▸conjug 1a◂ Ⓐ VT to nickel-plate
Ⓑ VI (*Esp‡*) to shoot a line*

niquelera SF (*Andes*) purse, coin purse (*EEUU*)

niqui SM T-shirt

nirvana SM Nirvana

níspero SM, **níspola** SF medlar

nítidamente ADV clearly, sharply

nitidez SF [1] [*de imagen, fotografía*] sharpness, clarity; [*de aire, agua*] clarity
[2] [*de explicación, orden*] clarity; [*de conducta*] irreproachability

nítido ADJ [1] [*imagen, fotografía*] sharp, clear; [*aire, agua*] clear
[2] [*explicación, orden*] clear; [*conducta*] irreproachable

nitral SM nitrate deposit, saltpetre bed, saltpeter bed (*EEUU*)

nitrato SM nitrate ► **nitrato de cloro** chlorine nitrate ► **nitrato potásico** potassium nitrate

nitrera SF (*Cono Sur*) nitrate deposit

nítrico ADJ nitric

nitro SM nitre, niter (*EEUU*), saltpetre, saltpeter (*EEUU*)

nitrobenceno SM nitrobenzene

nitrogenado ADJ nitrogenous

nitrógeno SM nitrogen

nitroglicerina SF nitroglycerin(e)

nitroso ADJ nitrous

nivel SM [1] (= *altura*) level, height; **a 900m sobre el ~ del mar** at 900m above sea level; **la nieve alcanzó un ~ de 1,5m** the snow reached a depth of 1.5m; **a ~** (*gen*) level, flush; (= *horizontal*) horizontal; **al ~ de** on a level with, at the same height as, on the same level as; **paso a ~** level crossing, grade crossing (*EEUU*) ► **nivel de(l) aceite** (*Aut etc*) oil level ► **nivel de crucero** cruising altitude ► **nivel del agua** water level ► **nivel del mar** sea level ► **nivel freático** water table
[2] (*escolar, cultural*) level, standard; **el ~ cultural del país** the cultural standard of the country; **alto ~ de empleo** high level of employment; **conferencia al más alto ~** ◊ **conferencia de alto ~** high-level conference, top-level conference; **de primer ~** top-level; **a ~ internacional** at an international level; **estar al ~ de** to be equal to, be on a level with; **estar al ~ de las circunstancias** to rise to the occasion; **no está al ~ de los demás** he is not up to the standard of the others; ✦***MODISMO*** **dar el ~** to come up to scratch ► **nivel de vida** standard of living ► **niveles de audiencia** ratings, audience rating *sing*; (*TV*) viewing figures
[3] (= *instrumento*) (*tb* **~ de aire, ~ de burbuja**) spirit level
[4] **a ~ de** (= *en cuanto a*) as for, as regards; (= *como*) as; (= *a tono con*) in keeping with; **a ~ de ministro es un desastre** as a minister he's a disaster; **a ~ de viajes** so far as travel is concerned, regarding travel

nivelación SF [1] [*de superficie*] levelling (out), leveling (out) (*EEUU*)
[2] [*de presupuesto*] balancing

nivelado Ⓐ ADJ [1] [*superficie*] level, flat; (*Téc*) flush
[2] [*presupuesto*] balanced
Ⓑ SM levelling, leveling (*EEUU*)

niveladora SF bulldozer

nivelar ▸conjug 1a◂ VT [1] [+ *superficie*] to level (out); (*Ferro*) to grade
[2] [+ *diferencias, deficiencias*] to even (out), even (up)
[3] [+ *presupuesto*] to balance (**con** against), adjust (**con** to); [+ *déficit*] to cover

níveo ADJ (*liter*) snowy, snow-white

nivosidad SF snowfall, (depth of) snow

nixtamal SM (*CAm, Méx*) (= *maíz cocido*) boiled maize, boiled corn (*EEUU*)

Niza SF Nice

n/l. ABR = **nuestra letra**

NN ABR (= **ningún nombre**) no name (*mark on grave of unknown person*)

NNE ABR (= **nornordeste**) NNE

NNO ABR (= **nornoroeste**) NNW

NN.UU. SFPL ABR (= **Naciones Unidas**) UN

N.° ABR, **n.°** ABR (= **número**) No., no.

NO ABR (= **noroeste**) NW

no Ⓐ ADV [1] (= *para negar*) [1·1] (*en respuestas independientes*) no; (*con adverbios*) not; **—¿quieres un café? —no, gracias** "would you like a coffee?" — "no, thanks"; **—¿quieres venir? —no** "do you want to come?" — "no" *o* "no, I don't"; **—¿te gusta? —no mucho** "do you like it?" — "not really"; **todavía no** not yet; **¡no a la bajada de sueldos!** no to wage cuts!; **¡yo no!** not me!, not I!†

[1·2] (*para formar la negación de los verbos*) **no sé** I don't know; **María no habla inglés** María doesn't speak English; **no puedo ir esta noche** I can't come tonight; **no tengo tiempo** I haven't got time; **no debes preocuparte** you mustn't worry; **no hace frío** it isn't cold

[1·3] **que no**: **decir que no** to say no; **creo que no** I don't think so; **me rogó que no lo hiciera** he asked me not to do it; **—¿eras tú el que llamaba? —¡que no, que no era yo!** "was it you who was calling?" — "no, I've already told you it wasn't!"; **¡a que no eres capaz!** I bet you can't!; **¡a que no lo sabes!** I bet you don't know!

[1·4] (*con doble negación*) **no conozco a nadie** I don't know anyone; **no quiero nada** I don't want anything, I want nothing; *ver tb* **de 23, bien B2, más A5.1, A8, sí[1] 1**

[2] (*para confirmar*) **esto es tuyo, ¿no?** this is yours, isn't it?; **fueron al cine, ¿no?** they went to the cinema, didn't they?; **puedo salir esta noche, ¿no?** I can go out tonight, can't I?

[3] (*para enfatizar*) **es mejor que lo diga que no que se calle** it's better that he should speak up rather than saying nothing; **hasta que no pagues no te lo darán** they won't give it to you until you pay; **¿pues no va y le da el dinero a ella?** so what does he do? he goes and gives the money to her!

[4] (*modificando a adjetivos y sustantivos*) non-; **pacto de no agresión** non-aggression pact; **los países no alineados** the non-aligned nations; **no beligerancia** non-belligerence; **el no conformismo** non-conformism; **los no fumadores** non-smokers; **la política de no intervención** the policy of non-intervention, the non-intervention policy; **no renovable** non-renewable; **la no necesidad del latín en partes de la misa** the fact that Latin is not obligatory in parts of the mass; ✦***MODISMO*** **el no va más** the ultimate; **lo que en los sesenta era el no va más** what was the ultimate in the sixties; **ese barco es el no va más del lujo** that boat is the ultimate in luxury

Ⓑ SM **un no contundente** a resounding no; **le dieron un no por respuesta** they answered him no; **no hubo ni un solo no en la votación** not a single person voted no

n/o. ABR = **nuestra orden**

Nobel SM [1] (*tb* **Premio ~**) Nobel Prize

[2] (= *persona*) Nobel prizewinner

nobiliario ADJ [1] **título ~** title

[2] [*libro*] genealogical

nobilizar ▸conjug 1f◂ VT to enhance, dignify, ennoble

noble Ⓐ ADJ [1] (= *aristocrático*) noble

[2] (= *honrado*) noble

[3] [*madera*] fine

Ⓑ SMF nobleman/noblewoman; **los ~s** the nobility *sing*, the nobles

noblemente ADV nobly

nobleza SF [1] (= *cualidad*) nobility; **~ obliga** noblesse oblige

[2] (= *aristocracia*) nobility

nobuk SM nubuck

nocaut SM (*LAm*), **nocáut** SM (*LAm*) knockout

nocautear ▸conjug 1a◂ VT (*LAm*) to knock out, K.O.*

nocdáun SM (*LAm*) knockdown

noche SF [1] (= *parte del día*) night; **a las once de la ~** at eleven o'clock at night; **la alarma no dejó de sonar en toda la ~** the alarm didn't stop ringing all night; **"Las mil y una ~s"** "The Arabian Nights"; **a la ~** (*Arg, Uru*) = **por la noche**; **ayer ~** last night; **¡buenas ~s!** (= *al atardecer*) good evening!; (= *al despedirse o al acostarse*) good night!; **de ~** (*como adv*) at night; (*como adj*) night *antes de s*; **tiene miedo a salir de ~ a la calle** she is afraid to go out after dark *o* at night; **viajaban de ~ y dormían durante el día** they travelled by night and slept during the day; **crema de ~** night cream; **turno de ~** night shift; **traje de ~** evening dress; **en la ~** (*LAm*) = **por la noche**; **en la ~ de ayer** last night; **en la ~ de hoy** tonight; **en la ~ del martes** on Tuesday night; **hasta muy entrada la ~** till late into the night, into the small hours; **esta ~** (= *hoy por la noche*) tonight; (= *anoche*) last night; **¿qué hay en la tele esta ~?** what's on TV tonight?; **no he podido dormir esta ~** I couldn't sleep last night; **hacer ~ en un sitio** to spend the night somewhere; **media ~** midnight; **por la ~** at night; **cuando se echa una siesta luego por la ~ no duerme** when he has a siesta, he doesn't sleep at night; **mañana por la ~** tomorrow night; **el lunes por la ~** on Monday night; ✦***MODISMOS*** **de la ~ a la mañana** overnight; **pasar la ~ en blanco** *o* **(de claro) en claro** *o* **en vela** to have a sleepless night; **perderse en la ~ de los tiempos** to be lost in the mists of time ▸ **noche de amor** night of passion ▸ **noche de bodas** wedding-night ▸ **noche de estreno** (*Teat*) first night, opening night ▸ **noche de los cuchillos largos** night of the long knives ▸ **noche toledana** sleepless night ▸ **Noche Vieja** New Year's Eve; *ver tb* **función 5, gato A1**

[2] (= *oscuridad*) **al caer la ~** at nightfall; **ya es ~ cerrada** it's completely dark now; **es de ~** it is dark; **ahora es de ~ y no se ve nada** it's dark now and you can't see a thing; **cuando sea de ~, volveremos al refugio** when night falls *o* when it's dark, we'll return to the shelter; **hacerse de ~** to get dark

[3] **la ~** (= *vida nocturna*) nightlife; **aquí se vive intensamente la ~** the nightlife is very lively here; **es el local de moda de la ~ neoyorquina** it is the trendiest nightspot on the New York scene

Nochebuena SF Christmas Eve

> **NOCHEBUENA**
>
> *Traditional Christmas celebrations in Spanish-speaking countries mainly take place on the night of* **Nochebuena**, *Christmas Eve. These include a large Christmas meal, going to Midnight Mass,* **Misa del Gallo**, *and, in Spain, watching the seasonal message from the King on TV. Presents are traditionally given at the Epiphany by* **los Reyes Magos**, *the Three Kings, but due to ever increasing Anglo-Saxon influence some people also give presents on Christmas Day.*
>
> ⇨ *See also* DÍA DE REYES

nochecita SF (*LAm*) dusk, nightfall

nocherniego Ⓐ ADJ nocturnal, given to wandering about at night

Ⓑ SM night owl

nochero/a Ⓐ ADJ (*LAm*) nocturnal

Ⓑ SM/F (*Guat*) night worker

Ⓒ SM [1] (*Chile, Col*) (= *vigilante*) night watchman

[2] (*Col*) (= *mesilla*) bedside table, night stand (*EEUU*)

Nochevieja SF, **nochevieja** SF New Year's Eve

> **NOCHEVIEJA**
>
> **Nochevieja**, *or New Year's Eve, is one of the most important seasonal celebrations in Spanish-speaking countries. Whereas* **Nochebuena** *is traditionally spent at home with the family,* **Nochevieja** *is an occasion for going out. In Spain, the highlight of the evening is* **las campanadas**, *the chimes of the* **Puerta del Sol** *clock in Madrid, which are broadcast live to usher in the New Year, like Big Ben in the UK. As the bells strike it is traditional to eat twelve grapes, one for each chime, a custom known as* **las uvas de la suerte** *or* **las doce uvas**.

nochote SM (*Méx*) cactus beer

noción SF [1] (= *idea*) notion, idea; **no tener la menor ~ de algo** not to have the faintest idea about sth

[2] **nociones** (= *conocimientos*) [*de electrónica, música*] basics, rudiments; [*de lenguas*] smattering *sing*; **tiene algunas nociones de árabe** he has a smattering of Arabic

nocional ADJ notional

nocividad SF harmfulness

nocivo ADJ harmful, injurious (*frm*) (**para** to)

noctambulear ▸conjug 1a◂ VI to wander about at night

noctambulismo SM sleepwalking, somnambulism (*frm*)

noctámbulo/a Ⓐ ADJ active at night

Ⓑ SM/F (= *sonámbulo*) sleepwalker; (= *jaranero*) night owl

noctiluca SF (*Entomología*) glow-worm

noctívago/a ADJ, SM/F = **noctámbulo**

nocturnidad SF evening hours *pl*, night hours *pl*; **con la agravante de la ~** made more serious by the fact that it was done at night; **obrar con ~** to operate under cover of darkness

nocturno Ⓐ ADJ [1] [*servicio, tarifa, ceguera*] night *antes de s*; **un vuelo ~** a night flight; **locales ~s** nightspots; **vigilante ~** night watch-

man; **el barrio no tiene mucho ambiente ~** there's not much nightlife in the area; **clases nocturnas** evening classes, night school (*EEUU*); **su primera salida nocturna de las vacaciones** her first night out during the holidays
2 (*Zool, Bot*) nocturnal
Ⓑ SM 1 (*Mús*) nocturne
2 (*Escol*) evening classes *pl*, night school (*EEUU*)

nodo[1] SM node

nodo[2] SM, **No-do** SM (*Cine, Hist*) newsreel

nodriza SF wet nurse; **barco ~** supply ship

nodular ADJ nodular

nódulo SM nodule

Noé SM Noah

nogal SM (= *madera*) walnut; (= *árbol*) walnut tree

noguera SF walnut tree

noluntad SF unwillingness, reluctance

nómada Ⓐ ADJ nomadic
Ⓑ SMF nomad

nomadear ▸conjug 1a◂ VI to wander

nomadeo SM wanderings *pl*

nomadismo SM nomadism

nomás ADV (*LAm*) (*gen*) just; (= *tan sólo*) only; *ver tb* **más A5.1, A8**

nombradía SF fame, renown

nombrado ADJ 1 (= *susodicho*) aforementioned
2 (= *famoso*) famous, renowned

nombramiento SM 1 (*gen*) naming; (= *designación*) designation
2 (*para un puesto etc*) nomination, appointment; (*Mil*) commission
3 (= *mención*) mention

nombrar ▸conjug 1a◂ VT 1 (*gen*) to name; (= *designar*) to designate
2 (*para puesto, cargo*) to nominate, appoint; (*Mil*) to commission; **~ a algn embajador** to appoint sb ambassador
3 (= *mencionar*) to mention

nombre SM 1 [*de persona, cosa*] name; **~ y apellidos** name in full, full name; **de rey no tenía más que el ~** he was king in name only; **a ~ de**: **un sobre a ~ de ...** an envelope addressed to ...; **no hay nadie a ~ de María** there's no one by the name of María; **bajo el ~ de** under the name of; **de ~** by name; **de ~ García** García by name; **conocer a algn de ~** to know sb by name; **no existe sino de ~** it exists in name only; **era rey tan sólo de ~** he was king in name only; **en ~ de** in the name of, on behalf of; **en ~ de la libertad** in the name of liberty; **¡abran en ~ de la ley!** open up in the name of the law!; **poner ~ a** to call, name; **¿qué ~ le van a poner?** what are they going to call him?; **por ~** by the name of, called; **sin ~** nameless; ✦*MODISMOS* **llamar a las cosas por su ~** to call a spade a spade; **no tener ~**: **su conducta no tiene ~** his conduct is utterly despicable ► **nombre artístico** [*de escritor*] pen-name, nom de plume; [*de actor*] stage name ► **nombre comercial** trade name ► **nombre de bautismo** Christian name, given name (*EEUU*) ► **nombre de familia** family name ► **nombre de fichero** (*Inform*) file name ► **nombre de lugar** place name ► **nombre de pila** first name, Christian name, given name (*EEUU*) ► **nombre de religión** name in religion ► **nombre de soltera** maiden name ► **nombre gentilicio** family name ► **nombre social** corporate name
2 (*Ling*) noun ► **nombre abstracto** abstract noun ► **nombre colectivo** collective noun ► **nombre común** common noun ► **nombre concreto** concrete noun ► **nombre propio** proper name
3 (= *reputación*) name, reputation; **se ha hecho un ~ en el mundo editorial** she's made a name for herself in the world of publishing; **tiene ~ en el mundo entero** it has a worldwide reputation; **un médico de ~** a famous *o* renowned doctor

nomenclátor SM, **nomenclador** SM catalogue of names

nomenclatura SF nomenclature

nomeolvides SF INV 1 (*Bot*) forget-me-not
2 [*pulsera*] bracelet (*with lover's name etc*)

nómina SF 1 (= *lista de empleados*) payroll; **tiene una ~ de 500 personas** he has 500 on his payroll; **entrar en ~** to be put on the payroll; **estar en ~** to be on the staff
2 (= *sueldo*) salary; (= *hoja de pago*) payslip; **cobrar la ~** to get paid, get one's pay-packet

nominación SF (*esp LAm*) nomination

nominal ADJ 1 [*cargo*] nominal; [*jefe, rey*] in name only
2 [*valor*] face *antes de s*, nominal; [*sueldo etc*] nominal
3 (*Ling*) noun *antes de s*

nominalismo SM nominalism

nominalización SF nominalization

nominalizar ▸conjug 1f◂ VT to nominalize

nominalmente ADV nominally, in name; **al menos ~** at least in name

nominar ▸conjug 1a◂ VT to nominate

nominativo Ⓐ ADJ 1 (*Ling*) nominative
2 (*Com, Fin*) **el cheque será ~ a favor de García** the cheque should be made out *o* made payable to García
Ⓑ SM (*Ling*) nominative

non Ⓐ ADJ [*número*] odd
Ⓑ SM (= *impar*) odd number; **los ~es** the odd ones; **pares y ~es** odds and evens; **estar de ~** (= *persona*) to be odd man out; (*fig*) to be useless; **queda uno de ~** there's an odd one, there's one left over; **un zapato de ~** an odd shoe; ✦*MODISMO* **andar de ~es** to have nothing to do, be at a loose end

nonada SF trifle, mere nothing

nonagenario/a Ⓐ ADJ nonagenarian, ninety-year-old
Ⓑ SM/F nonagenarian

nonagésimo ADJ ninetieth; *ver* **sexto A**

nonato ADJ (= *no nacido*) unborn; (*mediante cesárea*) not born naturally, born by Caesarean section

noneco ADJ (*CAm*), **nonejo** ADJ (*CAm*) thick*

nones* ADV no; **decir que ~** to say no, flatly refuse; **¡nones!** no way!*

noningentésimo ADJ nine-hundredth

nono[1] ADJ ninth

nono[2]**/a*** SM/F (*Cono Sur*) granddad*/grandma*

nopal SM prickly pear

nopalera SF patch of prickly pears

noqueada SF (*esp LAm*) (= *acto*) knockout; (= *golpe*) knockout blow

noqueado* ADJ (*LAm*) shattered*, knackered*, pooped (*EEUU**)

noquear ▸conjug 1a◂ VT (*esp LAm*) to knock out, K.O*

noqueo SM (*esp LAm*) knockout

noratlántico ADJ north-Atlantic

noray SM bollard

norcoreano/a Ⓐ ADJ North Korean
Ⓑ SM/F North Korean; **los ~s** the North Koreans

nordeste Ⓐ ADJ [*región, parte*] north-east, north-eastern; [*dirección*] north-easterly; [*viento*] north-east, north-easterly
Ⓑ SM 1 (= *región*) northeast
2 (= *viento*) north-east wind

nordestino ADJ north-eastern

nórdico/a Ⓐ ADJ 1 (*gen*) northern, northerly; **es la ciudad más nórdica de Europa** it is the most northerly city in Europe
2 (*Hist*) Nordic, Norse
Ⓑ SM/F 1 (*gen*) northerner
2 (*Hist*) Norseman
Ⓒ SM (*Ling*) Norse

noreste ADJ, SM = **nordeste**

noria SF 1 (*Agr*) waterwheel
2 [*de feria*] big wheel, Ferris wheel (*EEUU*)

norirlandés/esa Ⓐ ADJ Northern Irish
Ⓑ SM/F native/inhabitant of Northern Ireland; **los norirlandeses** the people of Northern Ireland

norma SF 1 (= *regla*) (*gen, tb Educ*) rule; (*oficial*) regulation; **los centros educativos tienen autonomía para elaborar sus propias ~s** schools and colleges have the power to make their own rules; **la primera ~ de autodefensa** the first rule of self-defence; **el comercio internacional está sujeto a ciertas ~s** international trade is subject to certain regulations; **una nueva ~ europea sobre emisiones acústicas** a new European regulation on sound emissions; **como** *o* **por ~ general** as a general rule, as a rule of thumb; **tener por ~ hacer algo** to make it a rule to do sth; **tengo por ~ no hablar nunca de estos temas** I make it a rule never to talk about such matters ► **norma de comprobación** (*Fís*) control ► **normas de conducta** (*sociales*) rules of behaviour; [*de periódico, empresa*] policy *sing* ► **norma de vida** principle ► **normas de seguridad** safety regulations
2 (= *situación, costumbre*) norm; **un país donde la pobreza es la ~** a country where poverty is the norm; **es ~ ofrecer una copa de bienvenida** it is standard practice *o* it is the norm to offer a complimentary drink; **como es ~ en estos casos** as is standard practice *o* as is the norm in these cases
3 **la ~** (*Ling*) the standard form; **la ~ andaluza** standard Andalusian Spanish
4 (*Arquit, Téc*) square

normal Ⓐ ADJ (= *usual*) normal; **una persona ~** a normal person; **es perfectamente ~** it's perfectly normal; **es ~ que quiera divertirse** it's only normal that he wants to enjoy himself; **no es ~ que no quiera venir** it's unusual for him not to want to come; **lleva una vida muy ~** he leads a very ordinary life; **~ y corriente** ordinary; **—¿es guapo? —no, ~ y corriente** "is he handsome?" — "no, just ordinary"; **como alumno es ~ y corriente** he's an average pupil
Ⓑ SF (= *gasolina*) three-star petrol, regular gas (*EEUU*)

3 (*Téc*) standard; (*Mat, Quím*) normal
4 **Escuela Normal** (*esp LAm*) teacher training college

normalidad SF normality, normalcy (*EEUU*); **la situación ha vuelto a la ~** the situation has returned to normality *o* normal; **se comportaba con total ~** he was behaving perfectly normally; **el acto discurrió con toda ~** the ceremony passed off without incident

normalillo ADJ, **normalito** ADJ quite ordinary, run-of-the-mill

normalista (*LAm*) Ⓐ ADJ INV [*de estudiante*] student teacher *antes de s*; [*de maestro*] schoolteacher *antes de s*
Ⓑ SMF (= *estudiante*) student teacher; (= *maestro*) schoolteacher

normalización SF 1 [*de relaciones, servicio, situación*] normalization; **la ~ del uso del catalán en las escuelas** the standardization of Catalan in the schools ► **normalización lingüística** *policy of making the local language official within an autonomous region*
2 (*Com, Téc*) standardization

normalizado ADJ (*Com, Téc*) standard, standardized

normalizar ▸conjug 1f◂ Ⓐ VT 1 [+ *relaciones, servicio, situación*] to restore to normal, normalize
2 (*Com, Téc*) to standardize
Ⓑ **normalizarse** VPR to return to normal, normalize; **el servicio se normalizó a mediodía** the service returned to normal at midday

▼**normalmente** ADV (*gen*) normally; (= *usualmente*) usually

Normandía SF Normandy

normando/a Ⓐ ADJ 1 (*gen*) of/from Normandy; (*Hist*) Norman; **las Islas Normandas** the Channel Islands
2 (= *vikingo*) Norse
Ⓑ SM/F 1 (*gen*) native/inhabitant of Normandy; (*Hist*) Norman; **los ~s** the people of Normandy; (*Hist*) the Normans
2 (= *vikingo*) Norseman

normar ▸conjug 1a◂ VT (*LAm*) to lay down rules for, establish norms for

normativa SF rules *pl*, regulations *pl*, guidelines *pl*; **según la ~ vigente** according to current rules *o* regulations *o* guidelines

normativo ADJ 1 (= *preceptivo*) [*aspecto, carácter*] normative; [*gramática*] prescriptive; **es ~ en todos los coches nuevos** it is mandatory in all new cars
2 (= *legal*) **el marco ~ vigente** the existing regulatory framework; **el actual vacío ~** the present lack of regulation

noroccidental ADJ north-western

noroeste Ⓐ ADJ [*región*] north-west, north-western; [*dirección*] north-westerly; [*viento*] north-west, north-westerly
Ⓑ SM 1 (= *región*) north-west
2 (= *viento*) north-west wind

nororiental ADJ north-eastern

norsa SF (*LAm*) (= *enfermera*) nurse; (= *institutriz*) governess; (= *niñera*) nursemaid

nortada SF (steady) northerly wind

norte Ⓐ ADJ [*región*] northern; [*dirección*] northerly; [*viento*] north; **el hemisferio ~** the northern hemisphere; **la zona ~ de la ciudad** the northern part of the city, the north of the city; **en la costa ~** on the north coast
Ⓑ SM 1 (= *punto cardinal*) north ► **norte magnético** magnetic north
2 [*de región, país*] north; **el ~ del país** the north of the country; **al ~ de Huelva** to the north of Huelva; **eso cae más hacia el ~** that lies further (to the) north; **viajábamos hacia el ~** we were travelling north; **en la parte del ~** in the northern part; **vientos del ~** northerly winds
3 (= *viento*) north wind
4 (= *meta*) aim, objective; **aún no ha encontrado su ~ en la vida** she still hasn't found her aim in life; **pregunta sin ~** aimless question; **perder el ~** to lose one's way, go astray
5 (*Caribe*) (= *Estados Unidos*) ≈ United States
6 (*Caribe*) (= *llovizna*) drizzle

norteafricano/a Ⓐ ADJ North African
Ⓑ SM/F North African man/woman; **los ~s** the people of North Africa

Norteamérica SF North America

norteamericano/a Ⓐ ADJ North American; (*de Estados Unidos*) American
Ⓑ SM/F North American; (*de Estados Unidos*) American; **los ~s** the North Americans, the people of North America; (*de Estados Unidos*) the Americans

nortear ▸conjug 1a◂ VI (*Andes, CAm, Caribe*) **nortea** the north wind is blowing

norteño/a Ⓐ ADJ northern
Ⓑ SM/F northerner

nortino/a (*Andes, Cono Sur*) Ⓐ ADJ northern
Ⓑ SM/F northerner

Noruega SF Norway

noruego/a Ⓐ ADJ Norwegian
Ⓑ SM/F Norwegian; **los ~s** the Norwegians
Ⓒ SM (*Ling*) Norwegian

norvietnamés/esa (*LAm*) Ⓐ ADJ North Vietnamese
Ⓑ SM/F North Vietnamese man/North Vietnamese woman; **los norvietnameses** the North Vietnamese, the people of North Vietnam

norvietnamita Ⓐ ADJ North Vietnamese
Ⓑ SMF North Vietnamese man/North Vietnamese woman; **los ~s** the North Vietnamese, the people of North Vietnam

nos PRON PERS PL 1 (*directo*) us; **~ quiere mucho** she loves us dearly; **~ vinieron a ver** they came to see us
2 (*indirecto*) us; **~ dio un consejo** he gave us some advice; **~ lo compró** (*de nosotros*) he bought it from us; (*para nosotros*) he bought it for us; **~ tienen que arreglar el ordenador** they have to fix the computer for us; **~ dolían los pies** our feet were hurting
3 (*reflexivo*) ourselves; **tenemos que defendernos** we must defend ourselves; **~ lavamos** we washed; **~ levantamos a las siete** we get up at seven; **~ pusimos los abrigos** we put our coats on
4 (*mutuo*) each other; **~ dimos un beso** we gave each other a kiss; **no ~ hablamos** we don't speak to each other; **~ hemos enamorado** we fell in love

nosocomio SM (*esp LAm*) hospital

nosotros/as PRON PERS PL 1 (*sujeto*) we; **~ no somos italianos** we are not Italian; **se lo podemos llevar ~ mismos** we can deliver it to you ourselves
2 (*tras prep y conj*) us; **tu hermano vino con ~** your brother came with us; **no irán sin ~** they won't go without us; **no pedimos nada para ~** we ask nothing for ourselves; **han jugado peor que nosotras** they played worse than us

nostalgia SF [*del pasado*] nostalgia; [*de casa, patria, amigos*] homesickness

nostálgico ADJ [*del pasado*] nostalgic; (*de casa, patria, amigos*) homesick

nostalgioso ADJ (*Cono Sur*) = **nostálgico**

nota Ⓐ SF 1 (= *mensaje corto*) note; (*Admin*) memo; **te he dejado una ~ encima de la mesa** I've left you a note on the table ► **nota de aviso** advice note ► **nota de entrega** delivery note ► **nota de inhabilitación** (*Aut*) endorsement (*on licence*) ► **nota de quita y pon** Post-it®
2 (= *apunte*) note; **tomar ~s** to take notes; **tomar (buena) ~ (de algo)** (*fijarse*) to take (good) note (of sth)
3 (= *comentario*) note; **texto con ~s de ...** text edited with notes by ..., text annotated by ... ► **nota a pie de página** footnote ► **notas al margen** marginal notes
4 (*Escol*) mark, grade (*EEUU*); **sacar buenas ~s** to get good marks; **ir para** *o* **a por ~*** to go *o* aim for a high mark; **¿ya te han dado las ~s?** have you had your report yet?
5 (*Mús*) note; **entonar la ~** to pitch a note; **dar la ~** (*lit*) to give the keynote; (*fig*) to get oneself noticed, act up ► **nota discordante** (*lit*) discordant note, discord; **sus críticas fueron la única ~ discordante** his criticisms struck the only discordant note; **Juan siempre tiene que dar la ~ discordante** Juan always has to disagree ► **nota dominante** (*lit*) dominant note; (*fig*) dominant feature *o* element
6 (= *adorno, detalle*) **una ~ de color** a colourful note; **una ~ de buen gusto** a tasteful note
7 (*Prensa*) note ► **nota de la redacción** editor's note ► **nota de prensa** press release ► **nota de sociedad** gossip column ► **nota informativa** press release
8 **digno de ~** (= *notable*) notable, worthy of note
9 (*Com*) (= *recibo*) receipt; (= *vale*) IOU; (*Méx*) (= *cuenta*) bill ► **nota de cargo**, **nota de débito** debit note ► **nota de crédito** credit note ► **nota de gastos** expense account
10 (†) (= *reputación*) reputation; **de ~** of note, famous; **de mala ~** notorious; **tiene ~ de tacaño** he has a reputation for meanness
11 (*LAm*‡) effects *pl* of drugs
Ⓑ SM **notas**‡ (= *tío*) bloke‡, dude (*EEUU*‡)

notabilidad SF 1 (= *cualidad*) noteworthiness, notability
2 (= *persona notable*) notable person

▼**notable** Ⓐ ADJ 1 (= *destacado*) notable; **una actuación verdaderamente ~** an outstanding performance, a truly notable performance; **un poema ~ por su belleza lírica** a poem notable for its lyrical beauty; **la exposición reúne a pintores tan ~s como ...** the exhibition brings together such notable *o* distinguished painters as ...
2 (= *considerable*) [*aumento, mejoría, diferencia*] significant, considerable; **el enfermo ha experimentado una ~ mejoría** the patient has experienced a significant *o* considerable improvement; **la disminución de la contaminación ha sido ~** there has been a significant *o* considerable reduction in pollution; **la obra fue un fracaso ~** the play was a

➤ LENGUA Y USO: **normalmente** 53.1 **notable A1** 53.1

signal failure

Ⓑ SM (*Esp*) (= *calificación*) *mark or grade between 7 and 8 out of 10*; **he sacado un ~** ≈ I got a B

Ⓒ SMPL **los ~s** the notables

notablemente ADV [*mejorar, disminuir, aumentar*] significantly, considerably; **nuestro déficit es ~ superior a la media** our deficit is significantly *o* considerably above average; **apareció ~ cansado** he appeared visibly tired

notación SF notation ► **notación binaria** binary notation ► **notación hexadecimal** hexadecimal notation ► **notación musical** musical notation

notar ▸conjug 1a◂ Ⓐ VT [1] (= *darse cuenta de*) to notice; **no lo había notado** I hadn't noticed; **los usuarios apenas han notado los efectos de la huelga** customers have hardly noticed the effects of the strike; **noté que la gente la miraba** I noticed people looking at her, I noticed that people were looking at her; **un niño nota cuando hay tensión en casa** a child can tell when there is tension at home; **dejarse ~**: **la subida de los precios se dejará ~ sobre todo en los alimentos** the rise in prices will be most noticeable in the case of food; **su ausencia en el equipo se dejó ~ ayer** his absence from the team was noticeable yesterday; **hacer ~ algo** to point sth out; **le hice ~ que había sido él, no yo, quien dio la orden** I pointed out to him that it had been him and not me who had given the order; **hacerse ~**: **los resultados se hicieron ~ sin tardanza** the consequences soon became apparent; **sólo se comportan así para hacerse ~** they only behave like that to get noticed *o* get attention; **la esposa del presidente apenas se ha hecho ~ en todo este tiempo** the president's wife has been almost invisible all this time

[2] (= *sentir*) [+ *dolor, pinchazo, frío*] to feel; **no noto frío alguno** I don't feel at all cold; **empiezo a ~ el cansancio** I'm beginning to feel tired

[3] (+ *ADJ*) **te noto muy cambiado** you seem very different; **lo noté preocupado** he seemed worried (to me); **he notado la casa más silenciosa últimamente** the house has seemed quieter recently; **te noto raro** you're acting strangely

[4] (= *anotar*) to note down

[5] (= *marcar*) to mark, indicate

[6] [+ *persona*] (= *criticar*) to criticize; (= *desacreditar*) to discredit; **~ a algn de algo** to brand sb as sth, criticize sb for being sth

Ⓑ **notarse** VPR [1] (*uso impersonal*) [1·1] (= *ser obvio*) to be noticeable; **en la reunión se notó mucho la ausencia de la antigua directora** the absence of the former director was very noticeable at the meeting; **notársele algo a algn: —estás disgustada, ¿verdad? —sí, ¿se me nota mucho?** "you're upset, aren't you?" — "yes, is it (that) obvious?"; **no se le nota que es extranjero** you can't tell he's a foreigner, you wouldn't know he's a foreigner; **se le notaba muy agitado** he was obviously very agitated; **~se que**: **se notaba que no se sentía muy seguro de sí mismo** you could tell he didn't feel very confident, he obviously didn't feel very confident; **¡se nota que acabas de cobrar!** you can tell you've just been paid!, you've obviously just been paid!; **no se notaba que acabaran de limpiar la escalera** you wouldn't know they had just cleaned the stairs

[1·2] (= *sentirse*) to be felt; **el impacto de la subida de los precios se ~á en febrero** the impact of the price increases will be felt in February; **la inflación se ha notado en el bolsillo de los españoles** the Spanish have felt the effect of inflation on their pocket; **fue un terremoto tan pequeño que no se notó** it was such a small earthquake that it went unnoticed *o* that no-one felt it

[1·3] (= *verse*) [*mancha, defecto*] to show; **no se nota nada la mancha** the stain doesn't show at all; **notársele algo a algn: —tienes una carrera en la media —¿se me nota mucho?** "you've got a ladder in your tights" — "does it show much?"; **sólo se le nota la edad en la cara** his age only shows in his face

[2] (*uso reflexivo*) to feel; **me noto más relajado** I feel more relaxed; **me noto con menos energía estos días** I've been feeling less energetic recently

notaría SF [1] (= *profesión*) profession of notary; **gastos de ~** legal fees, lawyer's fees

[2] (= *despacho*) notary's office

notariado SM [1] (= *profesión*) profession of notary

[2] (= *notarios*) notaries *pl*

notarial ADJ (*gen*) notarial; [*estilo*] legal, lawyer's

notarialmente ADV by legal process; **recurrir ~ a algn** to bring a legal action against sb; **tiene que certificarse ~** it must be legally certified, it must be certified before a commissioner for oaths

notario/a SM/F notary, notary public, attorney-at-law (*EEUU*)

notebook ['notbuk] SM notebook, notebook computer

NOTICIA

- Para traducir la palabra **noticia** al inglés, hay que tener en cuenta que el sustantivo **news** es incontable y lleva el verbo en singular:

  Las noticias de hoy no son nada buenas
  Today's news isn't very good
  Cuando recibió la noticia se puso a llorar
  When she received the news she burst into tears

- Cuando queremos precisar que se trata de una noticia en particular o de un número determinado de noticias utilizamos la expresión **piece/pieces of news**:

  Había dos noticias que nos parecieron preocupantes
  There were two pieces of news that we found worrying

Para otros usos y ejemplos ver la entrada.

▼ **noticia** SF [1] (= *información*) news; **¿hay alguna ~?** any news?; **eso no es ~** that's not news; **tengo una buena ~ que darte** I've got some good news for you; **fue una ~ excelente para la economía** it was an excellent piece of news for the economy; **la última ~ fue sobre las inundaciones** the last news item was about the flooding; **vi las ~s de las nueve** I watched the nine o'clock news; **según nuestras ~s** according to our information; **estar atrasado de ~s** to be behind the times, lack up-to-date information; **¡~s frescas!** (*iró*) tell me a new one! ► **noticia bomba*** bombshell* ► **noticia de portada** front-page news, headline news

[2] (= *conocimiento*) **tener ~s de algn** to have news of sb; **hace tiempo que no tenemos ~s suyas** we haven't heard from her for a long time; **no tener ~ de algo** to know nothing about a matter; **no tenemos ~ de su paradero** we have no idea of his whereabouts

noticiable ADJ newsworthy

noticiar ▸conjug 1b◂ VT to notify

noticiario SM (*TV, Radio*) news bulletin; (*Cine*) newsreel

noticiero Ⓐ ADJ [1] (*TV, Radio*) news *antes de s*

[2] (= *portador de noticias*) news-bearing, news-giving

Ⓑ SM [1] (= *periódico*) newspaper, gazette

[2] (*LAm TV*) news bulletin; (*Caribe Cine*) newsreel

notición* SM bombshell

noticioso Ⓐ ADJ [1] (*esp LAm*) [*reportaje*] news *antes de s*; [*fuente etc*] well-informed; [*suceso*] newsworthy; **agencia noticiosa** news agency; **texto ~** news report

[2] (†) **~ de que usted quería verme ...** hearing that you wished to see me ...

Ⓑ SM (*LAm TV, Radio*) news bulletin

notificación SF notification

notificar ▸conjug 1g◂ VT to notify, inform

notoriamente ADV (= *obviamente*) obviously; (= *evidentemente*) glaringly, blatantly, flagrantly; **una sentencia ~ injusta** a glaringly unjust sentence

notoriedad SF (= *fama*) fame, renown; (= *dominio público*) wide knowledge; **hechos de amplia ~** widely-known facts

notorio ADJ [1] (= *conocido*) well-known, publicly known; (= *famoso*) famous; **es ~ que ...** it is well-known that ...; **un hecho ~** a well-known fact

[2] (= *obvio*) obvious; [*error*] glaring, blatant, flagrant

nov. ABR (= **noviembre**) Nov

novador(a) Ⓐ ADJ innovating, revolutionary

Ⓑ SM/F innovator

noval ADJ [*tierra*] newly-broken

novamás* SM INV **es el ~** (= *lo mejor*) it's the ultimate; (= *lo último*) it's the latest thing

novatada SF [1] (= *burla*) rag, ragging, hazing (*EEUU*)

[2] (= *error*) beginner's mistake, elementary blunder; ✦**MODISMO** **pagar la ~** to learn the hard way

novato/a Ⓐ ADJ raw, green

Ⓑ SM/F beginner, tyro

novecientos/as Ⓐ ADJ, PRON (*gen*) nine hundred; (*ordinal*) nine hundredth; **línea** *o* **número ~** freefone number

Ⓑ SM nine hundred; **en el ~** in the twentieth century; *ver tb* **seiscientos**

novedad SF [1] (= *cualidad*) novelty, newness; **la ~ del método sorprendió a todos** the novelty *o* newness of the method surprised everyone

[2] (= *cosa nueva*) novelty; **hace tiempo que la reflexología ha dejado de ser (una) ~** reflexology ceased to be a novelty a long time ago; **las ~es discográficas** new releases; **las últimas ~es en moda infantil** the latest in children's fashions; **¿llegó tarde? ¡vaya ~!**

➤ LENGUA Y USO: noticia 1 48.1, 48.2

(*iró*) so he was late? surprise, surprise!

3 (= *cambio*) **llegar sin ~** to arrive safely; **la jornada ha transcurrido sin ~** it has been a quiet day, it has been a normal day; **el enfermo sigue sin ~** the patient's condition is unchanged; **sin ~ en el frente** (*Mil hum*) all quiet on the Western front

4 **novedades** (= *noticias*) news; **cuéntame todas las ~es** tell me all the news

novedoso ADJ 1 [*idea, método*] novel, new, original

2 (*Cono Sur, Méx*) = **novelesco**

novel Ⓐ ADJ (= *nuevo*) new; (= *inexperto*) inexperienced; **una escritora ~** a new writer

Ⓑ SMF (= *principiante*) beginner, novice

novela SF novel; **la ~ española en el siglo XX** the 20th century Spanish novel ► **novela de amor** love story, romance ► **novela de aprendizaje** Bildungsroman, *novel concerned with a person's formative years* ► **novela de ciencia ficción** science fiction novel ► **novela de misterio** mystery (story) ► **novela epistolar** epistolary novel ► **novela gótica** Gothic novel ► **novela histórica** historical novel ► **novela iniciática** Bildungsroman, *novel concerned with a person's formative years* ► **novela negra** thriller ► **novela policíaca** detective story, whodunit* ► **novela por entregas** serial ► **novela radiofónica** radio serial ► **novela río** saga ► **novela rosa** romantic novel

novelación SF fictionalization

novelado ADJ fictionalized

novelar ▸conjug 1a◂ Ⓐ VT to make a novel out of, fictionalize

Ⓑ VI to write novels

novelero/a Ⓐ ADJ 1 (= *imaginativo*) highly imaginative

2 (= *romántico*) dreamy, romantic

3 (= *aficionado*) (*a novedades*) fond of novelty; (*a novelas*) fond of novels; (*a habladurías*) gossipy, fond of gossiping

4 [*cuento, historia*] romantic, novelettish

Ⓑ SM/F novel reader

novelesco ADJ 1 (*Literat*) fictional; **el género ~** fiction, the novel

2 (= *romántico*) romantic, fantastic, novelettish; [*aventura etc*] storybook *antes de s*

novelista SMF novelist

novelística SF **la ~** fiction, the novel

novelón* SM big novel, epic (novel); (*pey*) pulp novel

novelucha SF (*pey*) cheap novel, pulp novel

novena SF (*Rel*) novena

noveno ADJ ninth; *ver tb* **sexto**

noventa ADJ INV, PRON, SM (*gen*) ninety; (*ordinal*) ninetieth; **los (años) ~** the nineties; **los escritores del ~ y ocho** the writers of the 1898 Generation; *ver tb* **seis**

noventayochista ADJ **un escritor ~** a writer of the 1898 Generation

noventón/ona Ⓐ ADJ ninety-year-old, ninetyish

Ⓑ SM/F person of about ninety

novia‡ SF (*Mil*) rifle, gun, rod (*EEUU*); *ver tb* **novio**

noviar ▸conjug 1b◂ VI **~ con** (*Cono Sur*) to go out with, date, court (*frm*)

noviazgo SM engagement

noviciado SM (*gen*) apprenticeship, training; (*Rel*) novitiate

novicio/a SM/F (*gen*) beginner, novice; (= *aprendiz*) apprentice; (*Rel*) novice

noviembre SM November; *ver tb* **septiembre**

noviero* ADJ **es muy ~** (*gen*) he has had lots of girlfriends; (= *enamoradizo*) he's always falling in love

novilla SF heifer

novillada SF (*Taur*) training fight (*bullfight with young bulls and novice bullfighters*)

novillero/a SM/F 1 (*Taur*) apprentice bullfighter, novice

2 (*Escol**) truant

novillo SM 1 (*Zool*) young bull, bullock, steer (*EEUU*)

2 **novillos** (*Taur*) = **novillada**

3 ✦***MODISMO*** **hacer ~s** (*gen*) to stay away, not turn up, skive off*; (*Escol*) to play truant, play hooky (*EEUU**), skive off*

novilunio SM (*Astron*) new moon

novio/a SM/F (= *amigo*) boyfriend/girlfriend, sweetheart†; (= *prometido*) fiancé/fiancée; (*en boda*) (bride)groom/bride; (= *recién casado*) newly-married man/woman; **los ~s** (= *prometidos*) the engaged couple; (*en boda*) the bride and groom; (= *recién casados*) the newly-weds; **ser ~s formales** to be formally engaged; **viaje de ~s** honeymoon

novísimo ADJ (*gen*) newest, latest, most recent; (*Com*) brand-new

ns ABR (= **no sabe(n)**) *don't know(s)*

N.S. ABR = **Nuestro Señor**

ns/nc ABR (= **no sabe(n)/no contesta(n)**) *don't knows*

N.T. ABR 1 (*Rel*) (= **Nuevo Testamento**) NT

2 (*Téc*) = **nuevas tecnologías**

ntra. ABR = **nuestra**

ntro. ABR = **nuestro**

NU SFPL ABR (= **Naciones Unidas**) UN

nubada SF, **nubarrada** SF 1 (= *chaparrón*) downpour, sudden heavy shower

2 (*fig*) abundance

nubarrón SM storm cloud

nube SF 1 (*gen*) cloud ► **nube de lluvia** rain-cloud ► **nube de tormenta** storm cloud ► **nube de verano** (*lit*) summer shower; (*fig*) brief burst of annoyance

2 [*de humo, insectos, polvo*] cloud; [*de gente*] crowd, multitude; **una ~ de periodistas** a crowd *o* pack of journalists; **una ~ de críticas** a storm of criticism; **una ~ de pordioseros** a swarm of beggars

3 (*Med*) (*en el ojo*) cloud, film

4 ✦***MODISMOS*** **andar por las ~s** ◊ **estar en las ~s** to have one's head in the clouds; **estar en una ~** to be on cloud nine; **los precios están por las ~s** prices are sky high; **poner a algn en** *o* **por** *o* **sobre las ~s** to praise sb to the skies; **ponerse por las ~s** [*persona*] to go up the wall*; [*precio*] to rocket, soar

5 (= *golosina*) candyfloss, cotton candy (*EEUU*)

núbil ADJ nubile

nublado Ⓐ ADJ [*cielo*] cloudy, overcast

Ⓑ SM 1 (= *nube*) storm cloud, black cloud

2 (= *amenaza*) threat; (= *peligro*) impending danger

3 (= *enfado*) anger, black mood; ✦***MODISMO*** **pasó el ~** the trouble's over

4 (= *multitud*) swarm, crowd, multitude

nublar ▸conjug 1a◂ Ⓐ VT 1 (*gen*) to darken, obscure

2 [+ *vista, mente*] to cloud; [+ *razón*] to affect, cloud; [+ *felicidad*] to cloud, mar

Ⓑ **nublarse** VPR to become cloudy, cloud over

nublazón SM (*LAm*) = **nublado B**

nublo ADJ (*LAm*) cloudy

nubloso ADJ 1 [*cielo*] cloudy

2 (= *desafortunado*) unlucky, unfortunate; (= *triste*) gloomy

nubosidad SF cloudiness, clouds *pl*; **habrá ~ de desarrollo** *o* **evolución** it will become increasingly cloudy

nuboso ADJ cloudy

nubuck SM nubuck

nuca SF nape (of the neck), back of the neck

nuclear Ⓐ ADJ (*gen*) nuclear; **central ~** nuclear power station

Ⓑ SF (= *central nuclear*) nuclear power station

Ⓒ ▸conjug 1a◂ VT 1 (= *reunir*) to bring together; (= *combinar*) to combine; (= *concentrar*) to concentrate; [+ *miembros etc*] to provide a focus for, act as a forum for

2 (= *liderar*) to lead

nuclearización SF (= *proceso*) introduction of nuclear energy (**de** to); [*de un país*] conversion to nuclear energy

nuclearizado ADJ **países ~s** countries possessing nuclear weapons

nuclearizarse ▸conjug 1f◂ VPR 1 (*Elec*) to build nuclear power stations, go nuclear

2 (*Mil*) to make *o* acquire nuclear weapons

nucleizar ▸conjug 1f◂ VT = **nuclear B**

núcleo SM (*Biol, Fís, Quím*) nucleus; (*Elec*) core; (*Bot*) kernel, stone; (*fig*) core, essence ► **núcleo de población** population centre, population center (*EEUU*) ► **núcleo duro** hard core ► **núcleo rural** (new) village, village settlement ► **núcleo tormentoso** thunderstorm ► **núcleo urbano** city centre, city center (*EEUU*)

nudillo SM knuckle

nudismo SM nudism

nudista SMF nudist

nudo[1] ADJ **nuda propiedad** bare ownership, bare title to property

nudo[2] SM 1 (*en hilo, cuerda*) knot; **el ~ de la corbata** the tie knot; **no sabe hacerse el ~ de la corbata** he doesn't know how to do up his tie; **atar con un ~** to tie in a knot; ✦***MODISMO*** **un ~ en la garganta** a lump in one's throat; **se me hizo un ~ en la garganta** I got a lump in my throat ► **nudo corredizo** slipknot ► **nudo de rizos** reef knot ► **nudo gordiano** Gordian knot ► **nudo llano, nudo marinero** reef knot

2 [*de carreteras, ferrocarriles*] junction

3 (= *vínculo*) bond, tie

4 [*de problema, cuestión*] core, crux; [*de obra, narración*] crisis, point of greatest complexity

5 (*en tallo*) node; (*en madera*) knot

nudoso ADJ [*madera*] knotty, full of knots; [*tronco*] gnarled; [*bastón*] knobbly, knobby (*EEUU*)

nueces SFPL *de* **nuez**

nuégado SM nougat

nuera SF daughter-in-law

nuestro/a Ⓐ ADJ POSES our; (*tras sustantivo*) of ours; **~ perro** our dog; **~s hijos** our children; **un barco ~** a boat of ours, one of our boats; **un amigo ~** a friend of ours

Ⓑ PRON POSES ours; **—¿de quién es esto? —es ~** "whose is this?" — "it's ours"; **esta casa es la nuestra** this house is ours; **es el ~** it is ours; **el tenis no nos gusta, lo ~ es el fútbol** we don't like tennis, we're more into football; **no servimos para pintar, lo ~ es la fotografía** we're no use at painting, we're better at photography; **los ~s** (= *nuestra familia*) our people, our family; (*Dep*) (= *nuestro equipo*) our men, our side; **es de los ~s** he's one of ours, he's one of us

nueva SF (= *noticia*) piece of news; **~s** news; ✦*MODISMOS* **coger a algn de ~s** to take sb by surprise; **me cogió de ~s** it took me by surprise, it was news to me; **hacerse de ~s** to pretend to be surprised

Nueva Caledonia SF New Caledonia

Nueva Delhi SF New Delhi

Nueva Escocia SF Nova Scotia

Nueva Gales SF (*tb* **~ del Sur**) New South Wales

Nueva Guinea SF New Guinea

Nueva Inglaterra SF New England

nuevamente ADV again

nuevaolero ADJ new-wave *antes de s*

Nueva Orleáns SF New Orleans

Nueva York SF New York

Nueva Zelanda SF, **Nueva Zelandia** SF (*LAm*) New Zealand

nueve Ⓐ ADJ INV, PRON (*gen*) nine; (*ordinal, en la fecha*) ninth; **las ~** nine o'clock; **le escribí el día ~** I wrote to him on the ninth

Ⓑ SM (= *número*) nine; (= *fecha*) ninth; *ver tb* **seis**

nuevecito ADJ brand-new

nuevo ADJ [1] (= *no usado*) new; **ha presentado su nueva película** he launched his new film; **la casa es nueva** the house is new; **la casa está nueva** the house is as good as new; **como ~: estos pantalones están como ~s** these trousers are just like new; **con una mano de pintura quedará como ~** it'll look like new after a coat of paint; **después de una buena siesta quedarás como ~** you'll feel like new after a good nap; ✦*MODISMO* **no hay nada ~ bajo el sol** there's nothing new under the sun

[2] (= *recién llegado*) new; **es ~ en el oficio** he's new to the trade; **es ~ en la ciudad** he's new to the town; **soy ~ en el colegio** I'm new at the school

[3] **de ~** (= *otra vez*) again; **tuve que leer el libro de ~** I had to read the book again

nuevomejicano/a Ⓐ ADJ New Mexican

Ⓑ SM/F New Mexican; **los ~s** the New Mexicans, the people of New Mexico

Nuevo Méjico SM New Mexico

nuez SF [1] (= *fruto*) (*gen*) nut; [*del nogal*] walnut; (*Méx*) pecan nut ► **nuez de Brasil** Brazil nut ► **nuez de Castilla** (*Méx*) walnut ► **nuez de Pará** Brazil nut ► **nuez moscada** nutmeg ► **nuez nogal** (*Méx*) walnut

[2] (*Anat*) (*tb* **~ de Adán**) Adam's apple

nulidad SF [1] (*Jur*) nullity

[2] (= *incapacidad*) incompetence, incapacity

[3] (= *persona*) nonentity; **es una ~** he's a dead loss*, he's useless

nulo Ⓐ ADJ [1] (*Jur*) void, null, null and void; **~ y sin efecto** null and void; **el matrimonio fue declarado ~** the marriage was annulled

[2] [*persona*] useless*, hopeless*; **es ~ para la música** he's useless at music*

[3] (*en boxeo*) **combate ~** draw

Ⓑ **nulos** SMPL (*Naipes*) misère *sing*; **bridge con ~s** bridge with the misère variation

núm. ABR (= **número**) No., no.

Numancia SF [1] (*Hist*) Numantia

[2] (*fig*) *symbol of heroic or last-ditch resistance*

numantino/a Ⓐ ADJ [1] (*Hist*) of/from Numantia

[2] [*resistencia*] heroic, last-ditch; (*pey*) diehard, stubborn

Ⓑ SM/F native/inhabitant of Numantia; **los ~s** the people of Numantia

numen SM [1] (*Literat*) (= *inspiración*) inspiration ► **numen poético** poetic inspiration

[2] (= *deidad*) numen

numeración SF [1] (= *acto*) numeration, numbering

[2] (= *números*) numbers *pl*, numerals *pl* ► **numeración arábiga** Arabic numerals *pl* ► **numeración de línea** (*Inform*) line numbering ► **numeración romana** Roman numerals *pl*

numerador SM numerator

numeral Ⓐ ADJ numeral, number *antes de s*

Ⓑ SM numeral

numerar ▸conjug 1a◂ Ⓐ VT (*gen*) to number; **páginas sin ~** unnumbered pages

Ⓑ **numerarse** VPR (*Mil etc*) to number off

numerario Ⓐ ADJ [1] (*del número*) numerary

[2] [*socio, miembro*] full; [*catedrático*] tenured; **profesor ~** permanent member of teaching staff; **no ~** non-established

Ⓑ SM (*Fin*) cash, hard cash

numerero* ADJ over-the-top, outrageous

numéricamente ADV numerically

numérico ADJ (*gen*) numerical; (*Inform*) numeric

numerito SM (*Teat*) short act; [*de relleno*] fill-in act; ✦*MODISMO* **montar el** o **un ~*** to make a scene, kick up a fuss

número SM [1] (*Mat*) number; **en ~s redondos** in round numbers; **estar en ~s rojos** to be in the red; **volver a ~s negros** to get back into the black, return to profitability; **de ~: miembro de ~** full member; **profesor de ~** tenured teacher, teacher with a permanent post; **echar** o **hacer ~s*** to do one's sums, number-crunch; **sin ~: calle Aribau, sin ~** Aribau street, no number; **problemas sin ~** countless problems ► **número arábigo** Arabic numeral ► **número binario** (*Inform*) binary number ► **número cardinal** cardinal number ► **número de identificación fiscal** *ID number used for tax purposes* ► **número de lote** batch number, batch code ► **número de matrícula** (*Aut*) registration number ► **número de referencia** reference number ► **número de serie** serial number ► **número de teléfono** telephone number, phone number ► **número dos** (*lit*) number two; **el ~ dos del partido** the second in command of the party, the number two of the party ► **número entero** whole number ► **número fraccionario** fraction ► **número impar** odd number ► **número negativo** negative number ► **número ordinal** ordinal number ► **número par** even number ► **número perfecto** perfect number ► **número personal de identificación** (= *clave*) personal identification number ► **número primo** prime number ► **número quebrado** fraction ► **número romano** Roman numeral ► **número uno** number one; **para mí, Sinatra será siempre el ~ uno** for me Sinatra will always be number one; **el jugador ~ uno de su país** the number one player in his country, the top player in his country

[2] [*de zapatos*] size

[3] [*de periódico, revista*] number, issue ► **número atrasado** back number ► **número cero** dummy number, dummy run ► **número extraordinario** special edition, special issue ► **número suelto** single issue

[4] (= *billete de lotería*) ticket

[5] (*Teat*) act, number; ✦*MODISMO* **montar el** o **un ~*** to make a scene, kick up a fuss

[6] (*Gram*) number

[7] (*Mil*) man; (= *soldado raso*) private; (= *policía*) policeman; **un sargento y cuatro ~s** a sergeant and four men

numerología SF numerology

numeroso ADJ numerous; **familia numerosa** large family

numerus clausus SM *system of restricted entry (to university etc)*, quota system

numísmata SMF numismatist

numismática SF numismatics *sing*

numismático/a Ⓐ ADJ numismatic

Ⓑ SM/F numismatist

núms. ABR (= **números**) Nos, nos

nunca ADV never; **no viene ~** he never comes; **~ volveré a confiar en ella** I'll never trust her again; **ninguno de nosotros había esquiado ~** neither of us had ever skied before; **¿has visto ~ cosa igual?** have you ever seen anything like this?; **casi ~ me escribe** he hardly ever writes to me; **¡hasta ~!** I don't care if I never see you again!; **~ jamás** never ever; **no lo he visto ~ jamás** I've never ever seen it; **no lo haré ~ jamás** I'll never ever do it again; **~ más: no lo hizo ~ más** he never did it again; **no lo veré ~ más** I'll never see him again; **más que ~** more than ever; **~ mejor dicho: el primer paso hacia el coche popular lo dio — ~ mejor dicho — el Volkswagen (coche del pueblo, en alemán)** the first step towards a popular car was the appropriately-named Volkswagen (people's car in German); ✦*REFRÁN* **~ es tarde si la dicha es buena** better late than never

nunciatura SF nunciature

nuncio SM [1] (*Rel*) nuncio; ✦*MODISMOS* **¡cuéntaselo al ~!** tell that to the marines!; **¡que lo haga el ~!** get somebody else to do it! ► **nuncio apostólico**, **nuncio pontificio** papal nuncio

[2] (= *mensajero*) messenger; (*liter*) herald, harbinger ► **nuncio de la primavera** harbinger of spring

nunquita ADV (*LAm*) = **nunca**

nupcial ADJ wedding *antes de s*, nuptial (*frm*)

nupcialidad SF rate of marriage, marriage statistics

nupcias SFPL wedding *sing*, nuptials (*frm*); **casarse en segundas ~** to marry again, get married for the second time, remarry; **Jesús, que se casó en segundas ~ con Rosa** Jesús, who got married for the second time to Rosa

nurse ['nurse] SF [1] (*LAm*) (= *enfermera*) nurse

[2] (= *institutriz*) governess; (= *niñera*) nursemaid

nutria SF otter
nutrición SF nutrition
nutricional ADJ nutritional
nutricionista SMF nutritionist
nutrido ADJ [1] (= *alimentado*) **bien ~** well-nourished; **mal ~** undernourished, malnourished
[2] (= *grande*) large, considerable; (= *numeroso*) numerous; (= *abundante*) abundant; **una nutrida concurrencia** a large crowd, a large attendance; **~ de** full of, abounding in (*frm*); **fuego ~** (*Mil*) heavy fire; **~s aplausos** enthusiastic applause
nutriente SM nutrient
nutrimento SM nutriment, nourishment
nutrir ▸conjug 3a◂ Ⓐ VT [1] (= *alimentar*) to feed, nourish
[2] (= *fortalecer*) [+ *confianza, relaciones*] strengthen
[3] (= *proveer*) (*de agua, ayuda*) to provide
[4] (= *llenar*) to fill
Ⓑ **nutrirse** VPR [1] (= *alimentarse*) to receive nourishment
[2] (= *fortalecerse*) to feed (**de** on)
[3] (= *abastecerse*) **el acuífero del que se venía nutriendo el río** the aquifer which fed the river; **las multinacionales que se nutren de las ayudas públicas** the multinationals which have been benefitting from State aid
nutritivo ADJ nutritious, nourishing; **valor ~** nutritional value, food value
nylon ['nailon] SM nylon

Ñ ñ

Ñ, ñ ['eɲe] SF (= *letra*) Ñ, ñ
ña* SF (*LAm*) = **doña**
ñaca* EXCL (*para dar envidia*) so there!
ñaca-ñaca: SM rumpy-pumpy:
ñácara SF (*CAm*) ulcer, sore
ñaco SM (*Méx*) popcorn
ñafiar ▸conjug 1b◂ VT (*Caribe*) to pilfer
ñam* EXCL **¡ñam ñam!** yum yum!*
ñame SM yam
ñandú SM (*Cono Sur*) South American ostrich, rhea
ñandutí SM (*Cono Sur*) Paraguayan lace
ñanga SF [1] (*CAm*) (= *pantano*) marsh, swampy ground
[2] (*Andes*) (= *trozo*) bit, small portion
ñangada SF (*CAm*) [1] (= *mordedura*) nip, bite
[2] (*) (= *tontería*) **¡qué ~ hiciste!** that was a stupid thing to do!
ñangado ADJ (*Caribe*) (= *patizambo*) knock-kneed; (= *estevado*) bow-legged
ñangara SMF (*Caribe Pol*) guerrilla
ñango* ADJ (*LAm*) awkward, clumsy
ñangotarse* ▸conjug 1a◂ VPR (*Andes, Caribe*)
[1] (= *agacharse*) to squat, crouch down
[2] (= *desanimarse*) to lose heart
ñangué SM **en los tiempos de ~** (*Andes**) way back, in the dim and distant past
ñaña* SF (*LAm*) (= *nodriza*) nursemaid, wet nurse
ñaño/a* (*LAm*) Ⓐ ADJ [*amigo*] close; (= *consentido*) spoiled
Ⓑ SM/F (= *amigo*) friend; (= *hermano mayor*) elder brother/sister
ñapa SF (*LAm*) (= *prima*) extra, bonus; (= *propina*) tip; **de ~** as an extra
ñapango SM (*Col*) mulatto, mestizo
ñaque SM junk
ñata[1] SF (*Andes*) (= *muerte*) death
ñata[2]* SF (*LAm*), **ñatas*** SFPL (*LAm*) nose, conk*
ñato ADJ (*LAm*) flat-nosed, snub-nosed
ñau EXCL (*LAm*) mew, miaow; **hacer ~ ~** (*lit*) to miaow, mew; (= *arañar*) to scratch
ñauar ▸conjug 1a◂ VI (*LAm*) to miaow, mew
ñeque* SM (*Andes, Cono Sur*) (= *fuerza*) strength
ñique* SM (*CAm, Cono Sur*) (= *cabezazo*) butt with the head; (*CAm*) (= *puñetazo*) punch
ñiquiñaque SM [1] (= *trastos*) trash, junk
[2] (= *persona*) worthless individual
ñisca SF [1] (*Andes, CAm, Cono Sur*) (= *pedazo*) bit, small piece
[2] (*Andes, CAm:*) (= *excremento*) crap**
ño* SM (*LAm*) = **don**[2]
ñoca SF (*Andes*) crack, fissure
ñoco ADJ (*LAm*) (= *sin un dedo*) lacking a finger; (= *manco*) one-handed
ñola SF [1] (*Andes, CAm:*) (= *excremento*) crap**
[2] (*CAm**) (= *úlcera*) ulcer, sore
ñongarse ▸conjug 1h◂ VPR (*Andes*) [1] (= *agacharse*) to squat, crouch down
[2] **~ el pie** to twist one's foot
ñongo ADJ [1] (*Caribe, Cono Sur, Méx**) (= *estúpido*) stupid; (*Cono Sur*) (= *lento*) slow, lazy; (= *perdido*) good-for-nothing; (= *humilde*) creepy
[2] (*Andes, Caribe*) (= *lisiado*) crippled
[3] (*Caribe*) (= *tramposo*) tricky, deceitful; (= *feo*) unsightly; (= *infausto*) of ill omen; (= *quisquilloso*) touchy
ñoña** SF (*Chile, Ecu*) shit**; *ver tb* **ñoño**
ñoñería SF, **ñoñez** SF [1] (= *sosería*) insipidness
[2] (= *falta de carácter*) spinelessness; (= *melindres*) fussiness
ñoño/a Ⓐ ADJ [1] (= *soso*) characterless, insipid
[2] [*persona*] (= *débil*) spineless; (= *melindroso*) fussy, finicky
Ⓑ SM/F spineless person, drip*; *ver tb* **ñoña**
ñoqui SM [1] **ñoquis** (*Culin*) gnocchi
[2] (*Cono Sur**) (= *golpe*) thump
ñorba SF (*Andes*), **ñorbo** SM (*Andes*) passion-flower
ñorda** SF turd**, shit**; **¡una ~!** get away!*; **ser una ~** to be a shit**
ñu SM gnu
ñuco ADJ (*Andes*) [*animal*] dehorned; [*persona*] limbless
ñudo: **al ~** ADV (*LAm*) in vain
ñudoso ADJ = **nudoso**
ñufla* Ⓐ ADJ worthless
Ⓑ SF (*Cono Sur*) piece of junk
ñuño* SF (*Andes*) wet-nurse
ñusca: SF (*Andes*) crap**
ñusta SF (*Andes Hist*) princess of royal blood
ñutir ▸conjug 3a◂ VI (*Andes*) to grunt
ñuto* ADJ (*Andes*) crushed, ground

O o

O[1], **o** [o] SF (= *letra*) O, o

O[2] ABR 1 (*Geog*) (= **oeste**) W
2 (= **octubre**) Oct.

o[1] CONJ or; **o ... o** either ... or; *ver tb* **ser A3**

o[2] ABR (*Com*) (= **orden**) o

ó CONJ or; **5 ó 6** 5 or 6

OACI SF ABR (= **Organización de la Aviación Civil Internacional**) ICAO

oasis SM INV oasis

ob. ABR, **obpo.** ABR (= **obispo**) Bp

obcecación SF (= *ofuscación*) blindness; (= *terquedad*) blind obstinacy; **en un momento de ~** in a moment of blind rage

obcecadamente ADV (= *con ofuscación*) blindly; (= *con terquedad*) obstinately, stubbornly, obdurately (*frm*)

obcecado ADJ (= *ofuscado*) blind, mentally blinded; (= *terco*) obstinate, stubborn, obdurate (*frm*); (= *trastornado*) disturbed

obcecar ▸conjug 1g◂ Ⓐ VT (= *ofuscar*) to blind (mentally); (= *trastornar*) to disturb the mind of; **el amor lo ha obcecado** love has blinded him (to all else)
Ⓑ **obcecarse** VPR to become obsessed; **~se con una idea** to become obsessed with an idea

ob. cit. ABR (= **obra citada**) op. cit.

obducción SF obduction

obedecer ▸conjug 2d◂ VT, VI 1 [+ *persona, norma*] to obey; **~ a algn** to obey sb, do as sb says
2 (= *deberse*) **~ a algo** to be due to sth; **los síntomas obedecen a una reacción alérgica** the symptoms are due to an allergic reaction; **su viaje obedece a dos motivos** there are two reasons for his journey, his journey is due to two reasons; **~ al hecho de que ...** to be due to ..., arise from ...
3 [*mecanismo*] to respond; **el volante no me obedecía** the steering wheel did not respond

obediencia SF obedience

obediente ADJ obedient

obelisco SM 1 (= *monumento*) obelisk
2 (*Tip*) dagger

obenques SMPL (*Náut*) shrouds

obertura SF overture

obesidad SF obesity

obeso ADJ obese

óbice SM obstacle, impediment; **eso no es ~ para que lo haga** that should not prevent him (from) *o* stop him doing it

obispado SM bishopric

➤ LENGUA Y USO: **objetivo B1** 35.2

obispo SM bishop

óbito SM (*liter*) death

obituario SM 1 (= *esquela*) obituary; (= *sección de periódico*) obituary section
2 (*Rel*) (= *registro*) register of deaths and burials

objeción SF objection; **poner objeciones** to object, make *o* raise objections; **no ponen ninguna ~** they don't object, they make *o* raise no objection ► **objeción de conciencia** conscientious objection

objetable ADJ (= *criticable*) open to objection; (= *inaceptable*) objectionable

objetante SMF (*gen*) objector; (*en mitin*) heckler

objetar ▸conjug 1a◂ Ⓐ VT (*gen*) to object to; [+ *argumento, plan*] to put forward, present; **¿algo que ~?** any objections?; **le objeté que no había dinero suficiente** I pointed out to him that there was not enough money
Ⓑ VI (*Mil*) to be a conscientious objector

objetivamente ADV objectively

objetivar ▸conjug 1a◂ VT to objectify, put in objective terms

objetividad SF objectivity

▼ **objetivo** Ⓐ ADJ objective
Ⓑ SM 1 (= *propósito*) objective, aim
2 (*Mil*) objective, target
3 (*Fot*) lens ► **objetivo zoom** zoom lens

objeto SM 1 (= *cosa*) object; **"objetos perdidos"** "lost property" ► **objeto contundente** blunt instrument ► **objeto de arte** objet d'art ► **objetos de escritorio** writing materials ► **objetos de regalo** giftware *sing*, gifts ► **objetos de tocador** toilet articles ► **objetos de valor** valuables ► **objeto sexual** sex object ► **objeto volante no identificado** unidentified flying object
2 (= *propósito*) object, aim; **desconocían el ~ de su visita** they did not know the object *o* aim of his visit; **al** *o* **con ~ de hacer algo** with the object *o* aim of doing sth; **estas medidas tienen por ~ reducir la inflación** the aim of these measures is to reduce inflation; **no tiene ~ que sigas preguntándome** there's no point in you continuing to ask me, it's no use you continuing to ask me
3 (= *blanco*) object; **me hizo ~ de sus obsesiones** I became the object of his obsessions; **fue ~ de sus burlas** she was the butt of their jokes; **fue ~ de un asalto** he was the target of an attack, he suffered an attack
4 (*Ling*) object ► **objeto directo** direct object ► **objeto indirecto** indirect object

objetor(a) SM/F objector ► **objetor(a) de conciencia** conscientious objector

> **OBJETOR DE CONCIENCIA**
> *The number of conscientious objectors to military service in Spain initially started to rise in the 1960s even though under the Francoist government of the time they could expect to be tried in a military court and to receive a long prison sentence. In the 1970s objectors tended to be assigned to non-fighting units like the medical corps and a law was finally passed in 1984 giving them legal status. In 1988 an alternative non-military programme* (**Prestación Social Sustitutoria** *or* **PSS**) *was developed allowing objectors to do social and community work. Events like Spain's membership of NATO in 1986 and the Gulf War in 1990 triggered a dramatic increase in the numbers of conscientious objectors.*
> ⇨ *See also* INSUMISO, PRESTACIÓN SOCIAL SUSTITUTORIA

oblación SF oblation, offering

oblar ▸conjug 1a◂ VT (*Cono Sur*) [+ *deuda*] to pay in cash

oblata SF oblation, offering

oblea SF 1 (= *galleta*) (*Culin*) wafer-thin slice; (*Rel*) wafer; ✦**MODISMO quedar como una ~** to be as thin as a rake
2 (*Inform*) chip, wafer
3 (*Cono Sur Correos*) stamp

oblicua SF (*Mat*) oblique line

oblicuamente ADV obliquely

oblicuar ▸conjug 1d◂ Ⓐ VT to slant, place obliquely, cant, tilt
Ⓑ VI to deviate from the perpendicular

oblicuidad SF obliquity, oblique angle, oblique position

oblicuo ADJ [*línea*] oblique; [*ojos*] slanting; [*mirada*] sidelong

obligación SF 1 (= *responsabilidad*) obligation, duty; **cumplir con una ~** to fulfil an obligation; **faltar a sus obligaciones** to fail in one's obligations *o* duty, neglect one's obligations *o* duty; **tener ~ de hacer algo** to have a duty to do sth, be under an obligation to do sth; ✦**REFRÁN primero es la ~ que la devoción** business before pleasure
2 (*Com, Fin*) bond, security ► **obligación convertible** convertible bond, convertible debenture ► **obligación de banco** bank bill ► **obligaciones del Estado** government

bonds, government securities ► **obligación tributaria** (*Méx*) tax liability

obligacional ADJ compulsory, binding

obligacionista SMF bondholder

obligado Ⓐ ADJ [1] (= *forzado*) forced; **no estás ~ a dar dinero** you're not being forced to give money; **se vieron ~s a vender su casa** they were forced to sell their house; **no te sientas obligada a venir** don't feel obliged to come

[2] (= *obligatorio*) **normas de ~ cumplimiento** regulations that must be complied with

[3] (= *inexcusable*) **es ~ hacerle una visita** you're expected to pay her a visit; **este museo es visita obligada para el amante del arte** this museum is a must for the art lover

[4] (*frm*) (= *agradecido*) **estar** *o* **quedar ~ a algn** to be obliged to sb, be in sb's debt

Ⓑ SM (*Mús*) obbligato

▼**obligar** ▸conjug 1h◂ Ⓐ VT [1] (= *forzar*) to force; **~ a algn a hacer algo** to force sb to do sth; **me han obligado a venir** they forced me to come; **la obligan a estudiar francés** they make her study French

[2] [*ley, norma*] **la disposición obliga a todos los contribuyentes** all taxpayers are bound to observe this requirement, this requirement is binding on all taxpayers

[3] (= *empujar*) to force; **sólo se puede cerrar el cajón obligándolo** you can't get the drawer shut except by forcing it

Ⓑ **obligarse** VPR **tengo que ~me a ir al gimnasio cada día** I have to force myself to go to the gym every day; **me obligo a cumplir los términos del contrato** (*frm*) I undertake to fulfil the terms of the contract

obligatoriamente ADV [1] (= *preceptivamente*) compulsorily

[2] (= *forzosamente*) of necessity

obligatoriedad SF obligatory nature; **de ~ jurídica** legally binding

▼**obligatorio** ADJ (= *preceptivo*) (*gen*) obligatory, compulsory; [*promesa, acuerdo*] binding; **es ~ hacerlo** it is obligatory to do it; **escolaridad obligatoria** compulsory schooling

obliteración SF (*Med*) obliteration

obliterar ▸conjug 1a◂ VT [1] (*Med*) (*gen*) to obliterate; [+ *herida*] to staunch

[2] (= *inutilizar*) to obliterate, destroy

oblongo ADJ oblong

obnubilación SF = **ofuscación**

obnubilar ▸conjug 1a◂ VT = **ofuscar 2**

oboe Ⓐ SM (= *instrumento*) oboe

Ⓑ SMF (= *músico*) oboist, oboe player

oboísta SMF oboist

óbolo SM mite, small contribution; **~ de San Pedro** Peter's pence

obra SF [1] (= *acción*) deed; **hoy he hecho una buena ~** I did a good deed today; **pecar de ~** to sin by deed; **buenas ~s** good works, good deeds; **ser ~ de algn** to be sb's doing; **esto no puede ser ~ de mi hijo** this can't be my son's doing; **la policía cree que podría ser ~ de la Mafia** the police think this could be the work of the Mafia; **poner por ~ un plan** to set a plan in motion; **por ~ (y gracia) de** thanks to; **un país destrozado por ~ del turismo** a country totally spoilt by tourism; **una gimnasta convertida en ídolo mundial por ~ y gracia de su entrenador** a gymnast who became a world famous idol thanks to her coach; **por ~ y gracia del Espíritu Santo** (*Rel*) through the working of the Holy Spirit, by the power of the Holy Spirit; **cree que el trabajo va a estar terminado mañana por ~ y gracia del Espíritu Santo** (*iró*) he thinks that the work will miraculously get done tomorrow; ✦***MODISMO*** **ser ~ de romanos** to be a huge task, be a herculean task; ✦***REFRÁN*** **~s son amores y no buenas razones** actions speak louder than words ► **obra benéfica** (= *acción*) charitable deed; (= *organización*) charitable organization, charity; **el dinero se destinará a ~s benéficas** the money will go to charity ► **obra de caridad** charitable deed, act of charity ► **obra de misericordia** (*Rel*) work of mercy ► **obra pía** religious foundation ► **obra piadosa** charitable deed ► **obra social** (= *organización*) *benevolent fund for arts, sports etc*; (= *labor*) charitable work

[2] [*de creación artística*] [2·1] (= *producción total*) (*Arte, Literat, Teat, Mús*) work; **la vida y la ~ de San Juan de la Cruz** the life and work of Saint John of the Cross; **el tema de la muerte en la ~ de Lorca** the subject of death in Lorca *o* in Lorca's work

[2·2] (= *pieza*) (*Arte, Mús*) work; (*Teat*) play; (*Literat*) book, work; **una ~ de Goya** a work *o* painting by Goya; **una ~ de Lope de Vega** a play by Lope de Vega; **las ~s de Cervantes** the works of Cervantes; **~s completas** complete works, collected works

► **obra de arte** work of art ► **obra de consulta** reference book ► **obra de divulgación** *non-fiction book aimed at a popular audience* ► **obra de teatro, obra dramática** play ► **obra maestra** masterpiece ► **obra teatral** play

[3] (*Constr*) [3·1] (= *edificio en construcción*) building site, construction site; **hemos estado visitando la ~** we've been visiting the building *o* construction site; **¿cuándo acaban la ~?** when do they finish the building work?; ✦***MODISMO*** **ser** *o* **parecer la ~ del Escorial** to be a never-ending job

[3·2] **de ~** [*chimenea*] brick *antes de s*; [*estantería, armario*] built-in

[3·3] **obras** (*en edificio*) building work *sing*, construction work *sing*; (*en carretera*) roadworks; **las ~s de construcción del hospital** building *o* construction work on the hospital; **las ~s de remodelación del estadio** redevelopment work at the stadium; **las ~s de ampliación del aeropuerto** work on expanding the airport; **los vecinos están de ~s** they're having building work done next door, they have the builders in next door*; **"obras"** (*en edificio*) "building under construction"; (*en carretera*) "roadworks"; **"cerrado por obras"** "closed for refurbishment"; **"página en obras"** (*Internet*) "site under construction"; **la autopista está en ~s** there are roadworks on the motorway; **estamos haciendo ~s en la cocina** we're having some building work done in the kitchen

► **obras públicas** public works; **Ministerio de Obras Públicas** Ministry of Public Works ► **obras viales, obras viarias** roadworks

[4] (= *ejecución*) workmanship; **la ~ es buena pero los materiales son de mala calidad** the workmanship is good but the materials are of a poor quality; ✦***MODISMO*** **poner manos a la ~** to get down to work; *ver tb* **mano A7**

[5] (*Chile*) brickwork

[6] **~ de** about; **en ~ de ocho semanas** in about eight weeks

[7] **la Obra** (*Esp Rel*) Opus Dei; → OPUS DEI

obradera* SF (*Andes, CAm euf*) diarrhoea, diarrhea (*EEUU*)

obrador SM [*de artesano*] workshop, workroom; [*de pastelería*] bakery

obraje SM [1] (*Cono Sur*) (= *aserradero*) sawmill, timberyard

[2] (*Méx*) (= *carnicería*) pork butcher's, pork butcher's shop

[3] (*Andes*) (= *fábrica textil*) textile plant

obrajero SM [1] (*Cono Sur*) (= *maderero*) timber merchant

[2] (*Bol*) (= *artesano*) craftsman, skilled worker

[3] (*Méx*) (= *carnicero*) pork butcher

obrar ▸conjug 1a◂ Ⓐ VI [1] (= *actuar*) to act; **~on correctamente en todo momento** they acted correctly at all times; **debemos ~ de acuerdo con nuestra conciencia** we must act in accordance with our consciences; **~ con precaución** to act cautiously

[2] (= *tener efecto*) [*medicinas*] to work, have an effect

[3] (*frm*) (= *estar*) **~ en manos** *o* **en poder de algn** to be in sb's possession; **los dos documentos obran ya en poder del abogado** both documents are now in the possession of the lawyer

[4] (= *hacer obras*) to have building work done, do building work

[5] (*euf*) (= *defecar*) to go*, go to the toilet *o* (*EEUU*) bathroom, pass a stool (*euf*)

Ⓑ VT [1] (*frm*) [+ *mejoría*] to make; [+ *milagro*] to work; **el medicamento no obró ningún efecto en el enfermo** the medicine had no effect on *o* did not work on the patient

[2] (= *trabajar*) [+ *madera*] to work

[3] (*Cono Sur*) (= *construir*) to build

obrerado SM work force

obrerismo SM labour movement, labor movement (*EEUU*)

obrero/a Ⓐ ADJ [*clase*] working; [*movimiento*] labour *antes de s*, labor *antes de s* (*EEUU*); **condiciones obreras** working conditions

Ⓑ SM/F (= *empleado*) worker; (= *peón*) labourer, laborer (*EEUU*) ► **obrero/a autónomo/a** self-employed worker ► **obrero/a cualificado/a** skilled worker ► **obrero/a escenógrafo/a** stagehand ► **obrero/a especializado/a** skilled worker ► **obrero/a portuario/a** dock worker

obscenamente ADV obscenely

obscenidad SF obscenity

obsceno ADJ obscene

obscu... *ver* **oscu...**

obsecuente ADJ humble, obsequious

obseder ▸conjug 2a◂ VT (*LAm*) to obsess

obsequiar ▸conjug 1b◂ VT [1] (= *regalar*) **le ~on un reloj** they presented him with a watch, they gave him a watch

[2] (*Esp*) (= *agasajar*) **lo van a ~ con un banquete** they are going to hold a dinner in his honour *o* (*EEUU*) honor

obsequio SM [1] (= *regalo*) (*gen*) gift, present; (*para jubilado*) presentation; (*Com*) free gift; **ejemplar de ~** complimentary copy

[2] (*frm*) (= *agasajo*) courtesy, kindness; **en ~ de** in honour *o* (*EEUU*) honor of; **hágame el ~ de** + *INFIN* do me the kindness of + *ger*

➤ LENGUA Y USO: **obligar A1** 37.1, 37.3 **obligatorio** 37.1, 37.3

obsequiosamente ADV [1] (= *servicialmente*) deferentially, obligingly
[2] (= *aduladoramente*) obsequiously
obsequiosidad SF [1] (= *amabilidad*) deference, complaisance
[2] (= *adulación*) obsequiousness
obsequioso ADJ [1] (= *servicial*) deferential, obliging
[2] (= *adulador*) obsequious
[3] (*Méx*) (= *dadivoso*) fond of giving presents
observable ADJ observable
observación SF [1] (= *acto*) (*gen*) observation; (*Jur*) observance; **estar en ~** to be under observation ► **observación de aves** birdwatching ► **observación postal** interception of mail
[2] (= *comentario*) remark, comment, observation; **hacer una ~** to make a remark *o* comment *o* observation, comment
[3] (= *objeción*) objection; **hacer una ~ a** to raise an objection to
observador(a) Ⓐ ADJ observant
Ⓑ SM/F observer ► **observador(a) extranjero/a** foreign observer
observancia SF observance
observar ▸conjug 1a◂ VT [1] (= *mirar*) to observe, watch; (*Astron*) to observe
[2] (= *notar*) to see, notice; **se observa una mejoría** you can see *o* detect an improvement; **~ que** to observe that, notice that
[3] (*LAm*) **~ algo a algn** to point sth out to sb, draw sb's attention to sth
[4] [+ *leyes*] to observe; [+ *reglas*] to abide by, adhere to; **~ buena conducta** (*Perú*) to behave o.s.
[5] (= *mostrar*) to show, give signs of
observatorio SM observatory ► **observatorio del tiempo, observatorio meteorológico** weather station
obsesión SF obsession
obsesionante ADJ [*recuerdo*] haunting; [*manía, afición*] obsessive
obsesionar ▸conjug 1a◂ VT [*recuerdo*] to haunt; [*manía, afición*] to obsess; **estar obsesionado con** *o* **por algo** to be obsessed by sth
obsesivo ADJ obsessive
obseso ADJ obsessed
obsidiana SF obsidian
obsolescencia SF obsolescence ► **obsolescencia incorporada** (*Com*) built-in obsolescence
obsoleto ADJ obsolete
obstaculización SF hindering, hampering
obstaculizar ▸conjug 1f◂ VT [+ *negociaciones, progreso*] to hinder, hamper; [+ *tráfico*] to hold up
obstáculo SM [1] (*físico*) obstacle; *ver tb* **carrera 2**
[2] (= *dificultad*) obstacle, hindrance; **no es ~ para que yo lo haga** that does not prevent me (from) *o* stop me doing it; **poner ~s a algo/algn** to hinder sth/sb
obstante: **no ~** Ⓐ ADV [1] (= *sin embargo*) nevertheless, however
[2] (= *de todos modos*) all the same
Ⓑ PREP (= *a pesar de*) in spite of
obstar ▸conjug 1a◂ VI **~ a** *o* **para** to hinder, prevent; **eso no obsta para que lo haga** that does not prevent him (from) *o* stop him doing it
obstetra SMF obstetrician
obstetricia SF obstetrics *sing*
obstétrico/a Ⓐ ADJ obstetric(al)
Ⓑ SM/F obstetrician
obstinación SF obstinacy, stubbornness
obstinadamente ADV obstinately, stubbornly
obstinado ADJ obstinate, stubborn
obstinarse ▸conjug 1a◂ VPR to be obstinate; **~ en hacer algo** to persist in doing sth, insist on doing sth
obstrucción SF obstruction
obstruccionar ▸conjug 1a◂ VT (*esp LAm*) to obstruct
obstruccionismo SM (*gen*) obstructionism; (*Pol*) filibustering
obstruccionista Ⓐ ADJ (*gen*) obstructionist, obstructive; (*Pol*) filibustering
Ⓑ SMF (*gen*) obstructionist; (*Pol*) filibusterer
obstructivismo SM obstructiveness
obstructivo ADJ, **obstructor** ADJ obstructive
obstruir ▸conjug 3g◂ VT [1] (= *bloquear*) [+ *carretera, vena*] to obstruct; [+ *desagüe, tubería*] to block, clog; (*Dep*) to block
[2] [+ *desarrollo, proceso*] to hinder, hamper, hold up
obtención SF **el único requisito que se exige para la ~ del permiso** the only requirement for obtaining the permit; **esta medida facilitará la ~ de préstamos** this measure will make it easier to obtain a loan; **las ventas de acciones orientadas a la ~ rápida de beneficios** the sale of shares with a view to receiving a quick return
obtener ▸conjug 2k◂ VT [+ *resultado, información, permiso*] to get, obtain; [+ *mayoría, votos*] to win, obtain; [+ *premio, medalla, victoria*] to win; [+ *apoyo*] to gain, get, obtain; [+ *beneficios*] to make; **esperamos ~ mejores resultados este año** we are hoping to get *o* obtain *o* achieve better results this year; **los socialistas obtuvieron la mayoría absoluta** the socialists won *o* obtained an absolute majority; **ambos obtuvieron el premio Nobel en 1993** they both won the Nobel prize in 1993; **el equipo español confía en ~ la victoria** the Spanish team is confident of victory; **la empresa está obteniendo grandes beneficios** the company is making large profits; **con la venta de los derechos la editorial obtuvo varios millones de dólares** the publishers got several million dollars from the sale of the copyright; **nunca obtuvo respuesta** he never got *o* received a reply; **el acusado obtuvo la libertad provisional** the accused was granted bail
obtenible ADV [*información, resultado*] obtainable; [*meta*] achievable
obturación SF (*gen*) plugging, sealing, stopping; [*de diente*] filling; **velocidad de ~** (*Fot*) shutter speed
obturador SM (*gen*) plug, seal; (*Aut*) choke; (*Fot*) shutter
obturar ▸conjug 1a◂ VT (*gen*) to plug, seal, stop (up); [+ *diente*] to fill
obtuso ADJ [1] (= *sin punta*) blunt
[2] (*Mat*) obtuse
[3] (*de mente, entendimiento*) obtuse
obús SM [1] (*Mil*) (= *cañón*) howitzer; (= *proyectil*) shell
[2] (*Aut*) tyre valve, tire valve (*EEUU*)
obvención SF bonus, perquisite
obvencional ADJ [1] (= *adicional*) bonus, extra
[2] (= *incidental*) incidental
obviamente ADV obviously
obviar ▸conjug 1c◂ Ⓐ VT [1] (= *evitar*) (*gen*) to obviate, get round, avoid; **~ un problema** to get round a problem
[2] (= *no mencionar*) to leave out; **obvió los detalles más peliagudos** he left out the more awkward details
Ⓑ VI (= *estorbar*) to stand in the way
obviedad SF [1] (= *cualidad*) obvious nature, obviousness
[2] **una ~** an obvious remark; **la respuesta parece ser una ~** the answer seems to be obvious
obvio ADJ obvious
OC ABR (= **onda corta**) SW
oca SF [1] (= *ganso*) goose; ✦***MODISMO*** **¡es la ~!*** it's the tops!*
[2] **la Oca** (= *juego*) *board game similar to snakes and ladders*
[3] (*Andes*) (= *planta*) oca (*root vegetable*)
ocasión SF [1] (= *vez*) occasion; **en aquella ~** on that occasion; **en algunas ocasiones** sometimes; **venir en una mala ~** to come at a bad time; **con ~ de** on the occasion of
[2] (= *oportunidad*) chance, opportunity; **el delantero perdió una magnífica ~ de gol** the forward missed a great goal scoring opportunity *o* a great chance of scoring; **aprovechar la ~** to take one's chance, seize one's opportunity; **dar a algn la ~ de hacer algo** to give sb the chance *o* opportunity of doing sth; ✦***MODISMO*** **la ~ la pintan calva** it's an offer one can't refuse
[3] (= *motivo*) cause; **no hay ~ para quejarse** there is no cause for complaint
[4] **de ~** (*Com*) secondhand, used; **librería de ~** secondhand bookshop
[5] (*LAm*) (= *ganga*) bargain; **precio de ~** bargain price, reduced price
ocasional ADJ [1] (= *accidental*) chance, accidental
[2] (= *eventual*) [*trabajo*] casual, temporary; [*lluvia, visita, fumador*] occasional; **sólo consigue trabajo ~** he can only find casual *o* temporary work
ocasionalmente ADV [1] (= *accidentalmente*) by chance, accidentally
[2] (= *de vez en cuando*) occasionally
ocasionar ▸conjug 1a◂ VT to cause; **lamento ~le tantas molestias** I'm sorry to cause you *o* to be so much trouble; **la espesa niebla ocasionó el accidente** the accident was caused by thick fog
ocaso SM [1] (*Astron*) [*del sol*] sunset, sundown (*EEUU*); [*de astro*] setting
[2] [*de civilización*] decline; **en el ~ de su vida** in his declining years, in the twilight of his life (*liter*)
[3] (*Geog*) west
occidental Ⓐ ADJ western
Ⓑ SMF westerner
occidentalidad SF (*Pol*) allegiance to the western bloc, pro-Western stance
occidentalista ADJ (*Pol*) pro-Western
occidentalizado ADJ westernized
occidentalizar ▸conjug 1f◂ VT to westernize
Occidente SM (*Pol*) the West, the Western world
occidente SM west

occipucio SM occiput

occiso/a SM/F (*Jur*) **el ~** (*gen*) the deceased; [*de asesinato*] the victim

Occitania SF Occitania

OCDE SF ABR (= **Organización para la Cooperación y el Desarrollo Económico**) OECD

oceanario SM oceanarium

Oceanía SF Oceania

oceánico ADJ oceanic

océano SM ocean ► **Océano Atlántico** Atlantic Ocean ► **Océano Glacial Ártico** Arctic Ocean ► **Océano Índico** Indian Ocean ► **Océano Pacífico** Pacific Ocean

oceanografía SF oceanography

oceanográfico ADJ oceanographic

oceanógrafo/a SM/F oceanographer

ocelote SM ocelot

ochar* ▸conjug 1a◂ (*Cono Sur*) Ⓐ VT [1] [+ *perro*] to urge on, provoke to attack
[2] (= *espiar*) to spy on
Ⓑ VI (= *ladrar*) to bark

ochavado ADJ octagonal

ochavo SM ochavo; ✦*MODISMO* **no tener ni un ~*** to be broke*

ochenta ADJ INV, PRON, SM eighty; (*ordinal*) eightieth; **los (años) ~** the eighties; *ver tb* **seis**

ochentón/ona Ⓐ ADJ eighty-year-old *antes de s*, eightyish
Ⓑ SM/F person of about eighty

ocho Ⓐ ADJ INV, PRON (*gen*) eight; (*ordinal, en la fecha*) eighth; **las ~** eight o'clock; **le escribí el día ~** I wrote to him on the eighth; **dentro de ~ días** within a week
Ⓑ SM [1] (= *número*) eight; (= *fecha*) eighth
[2] **ochos** (*Cos*) cable stitch *sing*; *ver tb* **seis**

ochocentista ADJ nineteenth-century *antes de s*

ochocientos/as ADJ, PRON, SM (*gen*) eight hundred; (*ordinal*) eight hundredth; *ver tb* **seiscientos**

ochote SM choir of eight voices

OCI SF ABR (*Ven, Perú Pol*) = **Oficina Central de Información**

ocio SM [1] (= *tiempo libre*) leisure; **ratos de ~** leisure time, spare time, free time; **cultura del ~** leisure culture; **guía del ~** what's on
[2] (= *inactividad*) idleness
[3] **ocios** (= *actividades*) leisure pursuits

ociosamente ADV idly

ociosear* ▸conjug 1a◂ VI (*Cono Sur*) (*gen*) to be at leisure; (*pey*) to laze around, loaf about

ociosidad SF idleness; ✦*REFRÁN* **la ~ es la madre de todos los vicios** the devil finds work for idle hands

ocioso ADJ [1] [*persona*] idle
[2] (= *inútil*) [*acto*] useless, pointless; [*promesa*] idle, empty; **dinero ~** money lying idle; **es ~ especular** there is no point in speculating

oclusión SF [1] (*Ling*) occlusion ► **oclusión glotal** glottal stop
[2] (*Meteo*) occluded front

oclusiva SF (*Ling*) occlusive, plosive

oclusivo ADJ (*Ling*) occlusive, plosive

ocote SM (*CAm, Méx*) [1] (*Bot*) ocote pine
[2] (= *tea*) torch; ✦*MODISMO* **echar ~** to make trouble

ocozoal SM (*Méx*) rattlesnake, rattler (*EEUU**)

-ocracia *ver* **Aspects of Word Formation in Spanish 2**

ocre SM ochre ► **ocre amarillo** yellow ochre ► **ocre rojo** red ochre

OCSHA SF ABR (*Rel*) = **Obra de la Cooperación Sacerdotal Hispanoamericana**

oct. ABR (= **octubre**) Oct

octaedro SM octahedron

octagonal ADJ octagonal

octágono SM octagon

octanaje SM (*Téc*) octane number; **de alto ~** high-octane *antes de s*

octano SM octane

octava SF (*Mús, Literat*) octave

octavilla SF pamphlet, leaflet

octavín SM piccolo

Octavio SM Octavian

octavo Ⓐ ADJ eighth
Ⓑ SM [1] (= *número*) eighth; *ver tb* **sexto**
[2] (*Tip*) **libro en ~** octavo book
[3] (*Dep*) ► **octavos de final** quarterfinals
[4] [*de droga*] small dose, small shot*

octeto SM (*Mús*) octet; (*Inform*) byte

octogenario/a ADJ, SM/F octogenarian, eighty-year-old

octogésimo ADJ eightieth; *ver tb* **sexto A**

octosílabo Ⓐ ADJ octosyllabic
Ⓑ SM octosyllable

octubre SM October; *ver tb* **septiembre**

OCU SF ABR (*Esp*) = **Organización de Consumidores y Usuarios**

ocular Ⓐ ADJ ocular (*frm*), eye *antes de s*; **mediante examen ~** by visual inspection, with the eye; **testigo ~** eyewitness
Ⓑ SM eyepiece

oculista SMF oculist, eye doctor (*EEUU*)

ocultación SF, **ocultamiento** SM hiding, concealment

ocultamente ADV (= *secretamente*) secretly; (= *misteriosamente*) mysteriously; (= *furtivamente*) stealthily

ocultar ▸conjug 1a◂ Ⓐ VT [1] [+ *objeto, mancha*] to hide (**a, de** from), conceal (**a, de** from)
[2] [+ *sentimientos, intenciones*] to hide, conceal
Ⓑ **ocultarse** VPR to hide (o.s.); **~se con** *o* **tras algo** to hide behind sth; **~se a la vista** to keep out of sight; **no se me oculta que ...** I am fully aware that...; **se me oculta la razón** I cannot see the reason, the reason is a mystery to me

ocultismo SM occultism

ocultista SMF occultist

oculto ADJ [1] (= *escondido*) hidden, concealed; **permanecer ~** to stay hidden
[2] (= *misterioso*) (*gen*) mysterious; [*pensamiento*] inner, secret; [*motivo*] ulterior
[3] [*poderes*] occult; *ver tb* **ciencia 2**

ocupa‡ SMF squatter

ocupable ADJ [*persona*] employable; [*puesto, posición*] available; **plaza ~** job available, position available

ocupación SF [1] (= *empleo*) (*en general*) employment; (*en concreto*) occupation; **ha bajado el nivel de ~ entre los jóvenes** the level of employment among young people has dropped; **desea volver a su ~ habitual, la enseñanza** he wishes to return to his usual occupation, teaching
[2] (= *actividad*) activity; **lee mucho cuando sus ocupaciones políticas se lo permiten** he reads a lot when his political activities allow it; **abandonaron sus ocupaciones para unirse a la manifestación** they stopped what they were doing to join the march
[3] [*de viviendas*] (= *acción*) occupation; (= *nivel de ocupación*) occupancy; **para fomentar la ~ de viviendas rurales** to encourage the occupation of rural dwellings; **la ~ hotelera ha aumentado este año** hotel occupancy has increased this year; **"se alquila piso, ~ inmediata"** "apartment available for immediate rent"
[4] (*Mil, Pol*) occupation; **durante la ~ de la embajada por los guerrilleros** during the occupation of the embassy by the guerrillas; **las fuerzas de ~** the occupying forces

ocupacional ADJ [*actividad, taller, terapia, salud*] occupational; **formación ~** job training

ocupado/a Ⓐ ADJ [1] [*sitio, asiento, plaza*] taken; [*habitación*] taken, occupied; [*retrete*] engaged; **¿está ocupada esta silla?** is this seat taken?; **todas las habitaciones del hotel están ocupadas** all the rooms in the hotel are taken *o* occupied; **el vuelo está todo ~** the flight is completely full; **¿está ~ el baño?** is the toilet occupied *o* engaged?; **"ocupado"** "engaged"
[2] (*Telec*) engaged, busy (*EEUU*); **la línea está ocupada** the line is engaged *o* busy; **señal de ~** engaged tone, busy signal (*EEUU*); **da señal de ~** the line is engaged *o* busy
[3] (*Pol, Mil*) [*territorio, país*] occupied
[4] [*persona*] [4·1] (= *atareado*) busy (**con** with); **estoy muy ~** I'm very busy; **estaba ocupada lavando el coche** she was busy washing the car; **no podía abrir la puerta porque tenía las dos manos ocupadas** I couldn't open the door because my hands were full *o* I had my hands full
[4·2] (= *empleado*) in work, working; **la población ocupada** the working population
[5] (*Esp††*) (= *embarazada*) pregnant
Ⓑ SM/F **el porcentaje de ~s** the percentage of people in work

ocupante Ⓐ ADJ (*Pol, Mil*) [*tropas, país*] occupying
Ⓑ SMF [1] [*de vehículo*] occupant; [*de vivienda*] occupant, occupier; **ningún ~ del vehículo resultó herido** none of the occupants of the vehicle were injured; **~s ilegales de viviendas** squatters
[2] (*Pol, Mil*) [*de país*] occupier; **el ~ ruso** the occupying Russians, the Russian occupiers

▼ **ocupar** ▸conjug 1a◂ Ⓐ VT [1] [+ *espacio*] to take up; **la noticia ocupaba dos páginas del periódico** the story took up two pages in the newspaper; **el armario ocupa toda la pared** the wardrobe takes up *o* covers the length of the wall; **el nuevo museo se construirá en el espacio que ocupaba el antiguo** the new museum is to be built on the site of the old one
[2] [+ *posición*] **el equipo español ocupa el puesto número diez en la clasificación** the Spanish team are tenth *o* are in tenth place in the league table; **la posición que ocupa nuestra empresa en el mercado europeo** our company's position in the European market, the position that our company occupies *o* has *o* holds in the European market; **vuelvan a ~ sus asientos** go back to your seats
[3] (*Com*) [+ *puesto, cargo*] to hold; [+ *vacante*] to fill; **la persona que ocupaba el cargo antes que ella** her predecessor in the post, the

➤ LENGUA Y USO: **ocupar B1** 53.2

person who held the post before her; **desde 1990 ocupa un escaño en el parlamento** he has held a seat in parliament since 1990; **~á su escaño el próximo mes** he will take his seat next month; **él ocupó el puesto que quedó vacante cuando me jubilé** he filled the position left vacant when I retired
4 (*Mil, Pol*) [+ *ciudad, país*] to occupy; **los obreros ~on la fábrica** the workers occupied the factory
5 (= *habitar*) [+ *vivienda*] to live in, occupy; [+ *local*] to occupy; **la vivienda que ocupan desde hace dos años** the house they have been living in *o* have occupied for the last two years; **los jóvenes que ~on la vivienda abandonada** the youths that squatted *o* occupied the empty building; **la agencia ocupa el último piso del edificio** the agency has *o* occupies the top floor of the building; **la fundación ocupa un piso en el centro de Barcelona** the foundation is based in *o* occupies a flat in the centre of Barcelona; **la celda que ocupa ahora** the cell he currently occupies
6 [+ *tiempo*] [*labor, acción*] take up; [*persona*] to spend; **los niños y las labores de la casa me ocupan mucho tiempo** the children and the housework take up a lot of my time; **escribir el artículo me ocupó toda la mañana** my whole morning was taken up with writing the article; **ocupa sus ratos libres pintando** he spends his spare time painting; **no sabe en qué ~ su tiempo libre** he doesn't know how to fill *o* spend his spare time
7 (= *dar trabajo a*) to employ; **la agricultura ocupa a un 10% de la población activa** 10% of the working population is employed in agriculture, agriculture employs 10% of the working population
8 (= *concernir*) **pero, volviendo al tema que nos ocupa …** however, returning to the subject under discussion …, however, returning to the subject we are concerned with *o* that concerns us …; **en el caso que nos ocupa** in this particular case, in the case under discussion
9 (= *confiscar*) to confiscate; **les ~on todo el contrabando** all their smuggled goods were seized *o* confiscated; **la policía le ocupó la navaja** the police confiscated his knife
10 (*Méx*) (= *usar*) to use; **¿está ocupando la pluma?** are you using the pen?
Ⓑ **ocuparse** VPR 1 **~se de** 1·1 (*como profesión, obligación*) to deal with; **este organismo se ocupa de conceder las licencias** this organization deals with the issuing of licences; **me ~é de ello mañana a primera hora** I will deal with it first thing tomorrow; **los servicios de seguridad no se ocupan de cuestiones económicas** the security services do not deal with economic matters; **no tiene tiempo para ~se de esos asuntos** she doesn't have time to deal with those matters; **no es ésta la primera vez que nos hemos ocupado de su obra** this is not the first time that we have discussed *o* looked at his work; **ella es quien se ocupó de los detalles de la boda** it was her that took care of *o* saw to the details of the wedding
1·2 (*por interés*) to take an interest in; **los críticos no se ~on del libro** the book was ignored by the critics, the critics took no interest in the book; **me ocupo muy poco de las tareas domésticas** I don't bother much with *o* about the housework, I take very little interest in the housework; **¡tú ocúpate de lo tuyo!** mind your own business!
1·3 (= *cuidar de*) [+ *enfermo, niños*] to take care of, look after; [+ *enemigo*] to take care of
1·4 [*libro, conferencia, programa*] **el libro se ocupa de los aspectos económicos del problema** the book deals with the economic aspects of the problem; **el programa de esta noche se ~á de las elecciones en Francia** tonight's programme will take a look at the French elections; **nos ocupamos ahora de la información deportiva** (*Radio, TV*) and now a look at today's sports
2 **~se en: varias empresas se ocupan en proyectos de este tipo** a number of companies are involved in projects of this kind; **tras jubilarse sólo se ocupaba en cuidar el jardín** after retiring she only spent her time doing the garden

ocurrencia SF 1 (= *idea*) idea; **tuvo una ~ genial** he had a brilliant idea; **¡vaya ~!** (*iró*) what a bright idea!; **tuvo la ~ de lavarse los zapatos en la lavadora** (*iró*) he had the bright idea of washing his shoes in the washing machine
2 (= *dicho gracioso*) funny remark; **este niño tiene unas ~s divertidísimas** this child comes out with the funniest remarks
3 (*frm*) (= *acontecimiento*) occurrence

ocurrente ADJ 1 (= *chistoso*) witty
2 (= *listo*) bright, clever
3 (= *gracioso*) entertaining, amusing

ocurrido ADJ 1 (= *sucedido*) **lo ~** what has/had happened
2 (*Andes*) (= *gracioso*) witty, funny

ocurrir ▸conjug 3a◂ Ⓐ VI to happen; **ha ocurrido algo horrible** something terrible has happened; **lo que ocurrió podría haberse evitado** what happened could have been avoided; **por lo que pudiera ~** because of what might happen; **ocurre que …** it (so) happens that …; **¿qué ocurre?** what's going on?; **¿qué te ocurre?** what's the matter?; **lo que ocurre es que …** the thing is …
Ⓑ **ocurrirse** VPR **se nos ocurrió una idea buenísima** we had a brilliant idea; **¿se te ocurre algo?** can you think of anything?; **se le ocurrió hacerlo** he thought of doing it; **¡ni se te ocurra (hacerlo)!** don't even think about (doing) it!; **¡se te ocurren unas cosas!** you've got some right ideas!; **si se le ocurre huir** if he takes it into his head to escape; **¿cómo no se te ocurrió pensar que …?** didn't it cross your mind that ...?; **se me ocurre que …** it occurs to me that …; **nunca se me había ocurrido** it had never crossed my mind; **¿a quién se le ocurre presentarse a medianoche?** who in their right mind would turn up in the middle of the night?

oda SF ode

odalisca SF odalisque

ODECA SF ABR (= **Organización de los Estados Centroamericanos**) OCAS

ODEPA SF ABR = **Organización Deportiva Panamericana**

odiar ▸conjug 1b◂ VT 1 (= *sentir odio por*) to hate
2 (*Chile*) (= *molestar*) to pester, annoy; (= *aburrir*) to bore

odio SM 1 (*gen*) hatred; **almacenar ~** to store up hatred; **tener ~ a algn** to hate sb ► **odio de clase** class hatred ► **odio de sangre** feud, vendetta ► **odio mortal** mortal hatred
2 (*Chile*) (= *molestia*) nuisance, bother

odiosear* ▸conjug 1a◂ VT (*Chile*) to pester, annoy

odiosidad SF 1 (*gen*) odiousness, hatefulness; (= *repelencia*) nastiness
2 (*Arg, Chile, Perú*) (= *molestia*) nuisance, annoyance

odioso ADJ 1 (= *detestable*) odious, hateful, detestable
2 (= *repelente*) nasty, unpleasant; **hacerse ~ a algn** to become a nuisance to sb
3 (*Arg, Chile, Perú*) (= *molesto*) annoying

Odisea SF Odyssey

odisea SF odyssey, epic journey; **fue toda una ~** it was a real odyssey

Odiseo SM Odysseus

odómetro SM milometer, odometer (*EEUU*)

odonto- PREF odonto-

odontología SF dentistry, odontology

odontólogo/a SM/F dentist, dental surgeon, odontologist

odorífero ADJ, **odorífico** ADJ sweet-smelling, odoriferous (*frm*)

odre SM 1 (= *recipiente*) wineskin
2 (*) (= *borracho*) drunk, drunkard, old soak*

OEA SF ABR (= **Organización de Estados Americanos**) OAS

OECE SF ABR (= **Organización Europea de Cooperación Económica**) OEEC

OELA SF ABR = **Organización de Estados Latinoamericanos**

oeste Ⓐ ADJ [*región*] western; [*dirección*] westerly; [*viento*] west, westerly; **la zona ~ de la ciudad** the western part of the city, the west of the city; **en la costa ~** on the west coast
Ⓑ SM 1 (= *punto cardinal*) west
2 [*de región, país*] west; **el ~ del país** the west of the country; **al ~ de Girona** to the west of Girona; **eso cae más hacia el ~** that lies further (to the) west; **viajábamos hacia el ~** we were travelling west; **en la parte del ~** in the western part; **vientos del ~** westerly winds; **una película del Oeste** a Western
3 (= *viento*) west wind

Ofelia SF Ophelia

ofender ▸conjug 2a◂ Ⓐ VT 1 (= *agraviar*) to offend; **por temor a ~lo** for fear of offending him; **perdona si te he ofendido** I'm sorry if I've offended you; **(dicho) sin ánimo de ~, no es que tu marido sea un santo** no offence meant, but your husband's no saint; **no ofendas la memoria de tu madre** don't insult your mother's memory
2 [+ *sentido*] to offend, be offensive to; **~ a la vista** to offend the eye
3 (*Méx‡*) [+ *mujer*] to touch up‡, feel‡
Ⓑ **ofenderse** VPR to take offence *o* (*EEUU*) offense; **se ofendió porque no lo invitaron** he took offence at not being invited; **no te ofendas por lo que te voy a decir** don't be offended by what I'm going to tell you

ofendido ADJ offended; **darse por ~** to take offence *o* (*EEUU*) offense

ofensa SF 1 (= *insulto*) offence, offense (*EEUU*)
2 (= *desprecio*) slight

ofensiva SF offensive; **pasar a la ~** to go on the offensive; **tomar la ~** to take the offensive ► **ofensiva de paz** peace offensive

ofensivamente ADV (*Dep*) in attack

➤ LENGUA Y USO: **ocurrir B** 28.1, 28.2

ofensivo ADJ [1] (= *de ataque*) (*tb Mil*) offensive
[2] [*conducta, palabra*] offensive, rude, insulting

ofensor(a) Ⓐ ADJ offending
Ⓑ SM/F offender

oferta SF [1] (= *ofrecimiento*) offer
[2] (*Com*) (*gen*) offer; (*para contrato, concurso*) tender; (*en subasta*) bid; (*Econ*) supply; (= *ganga*) special offer; **estar de** *o* **en ~** to be on offer; **la ley de la ~ y la demanda** the law of supply and demand; **la ~ es superior a la demanda** supply exceeds demand ▸ **oferta cerrada** sealed bid ▸ **oferta condicional** conditional offer ▸ **oferta excedentaria** excess supply ▸ **oferta monetaria** money supply ▸ **oferta promocional** promotional offer ▸ **oferta pública de adquisición (de acciones)** takeover bid ▸ **oferta pública de venta (de acciones)** share offer ▸ **ofertas de trabajo** (*en periódico*) situations vacant (column), job openings (*EEUU*)
[3] (= *regalo*) gift, present

ofertante SMF (*Com*) bidder

ofertar ▸conjug 1a◂ VT [1] (*esp LAm*) (= *ofrecer*) [+ *suma de dinero, producto*] to offer
[2] (*Com*) (*en concurso*) to tender; (*en subasta*) to bid
[3] (= *ofrecer barato*) to sell on special offer

ofertorio SM offertory

off [of] SM **en ~** (*Cine*) off-screen; (*Teat*) offstage; **pasa algo en ~** (*Cine*) something happens off-screen; **hay una discusión en ~** there is an argument offstage; **poner un aparato en ~** to switch a machine off; **ruido en ~** background noise; *ver tb* **voz 1**

office ['ofis] SM [1] (*Esp Arquit*) (= *comedor pequeño*) breakfast room; (= *trascocina*) scullery; (= *despensa*) pantry; (= *lavadero*) utility room
[2] (*Aer*) galley

offset ['ofset] SM (*Tip*) offset

offside [of'sai] SM (*Dep*) offside; **¡offside!** offside!; **estar en ~** (*Dep*) to be offside

oficial Ⓐ ADJ [*viaje, documento, comunicado*] official
Ⓑ SMF (*a veces* SF **oficiala**) [1] (*Mil*) officer; **primer ~** (*Náut*) first mate ▸ **oficial de enlace** liaison officer ▸ **oficial de guardia** (*Náut*) officer of the watch ▸ **oficial del día** orderly officer ▸ **oficial de marina** naval officer ▸ **oficial ejecutivo** executive officer ▸ **oficial médico** medical officer ▸ **oficial pagador** paymaster
[2] (= *obrero*) (*en fábrica*) skilled worker; (*en taller artesano*) craftsman/craftswoman; (*por cuenta ajena*) journeyman; (*en oficina*) clerk ▸ **oficial mayor** chief clerk

oficialada SF (*Cono Sur, Méx*) = **oficialidad**

oficialidad SF (*Mil*) officers *pl*

oficialismo SM [1] (= *tendencia*) [*de un partido*] party-liners *pl*; [*del gobierno*] pro-government political forces *pl*
[2] (*LAm*) (= *autoridades*) **el ~** government authorities, the ruling *o* governing party

oficialista Ⓐ ADJ (*LAm*) (= *del gobierno*) (pro-) government *antes de s*, of the party in power; **el candidato ~** the ruling *o* governing party's candidate
Ⓑ SMF [1] [*del partido*] party-liner
[2] (*LAm*) [*del gobierno*] government supporter

oficializar ▸conjug 1f◂ VT to make official, give official status to

oficialmente ADV officially

oficiante SM (*Rel*) celebrant, officiant

oficiar ▸conjug 1b◂ Ⓐ VT [1] (*Rel*) [+ *misa*] to celebrate; [+ *funeral, boda*] to conduct, officiate at
[2] (= *informar*) to inform officially
Ⓑ VI [1] (*Rel*) to officiate
[2] **~ de** to officiate as, act as

oficina SF [1] (= *despacho*) (*gen*) office; (*Mil*) orderly room; (*Farm*) laboratory; (*Téc*) workshop; **horas de ~** office hours ▸ **oficina de colocación, oficina de empleo** job centre ▸ **oficina de información** information bureau ▸ **oficina de objetos perdidos** lost property office, lost-and-found department (*EEUU*) ▸ **oficina de prensa** press office ▸ **oficina meteorológica** weather bureau ▸ **oficina paisaje** open-plan office
[2] (*Chile Min*) nitrate works

oficinesco ADJ [1] [*ambiente, mobiliario*] office *antes de s*; [*versión*] clerical
[2] (*pey*) bureaucratic

oficinista SMF office worker, clerk; **los ~s** office workers

oficio SM [1] (= *profesión*) trade; **aprender un ~** to learn a trade; **sabe su ~** he knows his job; **los deberes del ~** the duties of the post; **mi ~ es enseñar** my job is to teach; **un profesional con mucho ~** a seasoned professional; **tiene mucho ~** he is very experienced; ✦*MODISMOS* **sin ~ ni beneficio**: **un pobre temporero sin ~ ni beneficio** just a poor seasonal worker without a penny to his name; **se encontró sin ~ ni beneficio al salir del colegio** he found himself with no means of earning a living when he left school; **es un vago sin ~ ni beneficio** he's a good-for-nothing layabout; **ser del ~** (= *ser experto*) to be an old hand; (= *prostituirse*) to be on the game*
[2] (= *función*) function; **el ~ de esta pieza es de …** what this part does is …
[3] **de ~: miembro de ~** ex officio member; **matones de ~** professional thugs; **fue enterrado de ~** he was buried at the State's expense; **le informaremos de ~** we will inform you officially; *ver tb* **abogado 1**
[4] (= *comunicado*) official letter
[5] (*Rel*) service, mass ▸ **oficio de difuntos** funeral service, mass for the dead, office for the dead ▸ **oficio divino** divine office
[6] **Santo Oficio** (*Hist*) Holy Office, Inquisition
[7] **buenos ~s** good offices; **ofrecer sus buenos ~s** to offer one's good offices
[8] (= *trascocina*) scullery

oficiosamente ADV [1] (= *extraoficialmente*) unofficially
[2] (= *con entrometimiento*) officiously
[3] (= *solícitamente*) helpfully, obligingly

oficiosidad SF [1] (= *entrometimiento*) officiousness
[2] (= *solicitud*) helpfulness, obligingness

oficioso ADJ [1] (= *extraoficial*) unofficial, informal; **de fuente oficiosa** from an unofficial source
[2] (= *entrometido*) officious
[3] (= *solícito*) helpful, obliging; **mentira oficiosa** white lie

-ófilo SUF *p.ej* **anglófilo**

ofimática SF office automation, office computerization

ofimático ADJ **sistema ~** office computer system; **gestión ofimática integrada** integrated computer system for office management

Ofines SF ABR = **Oficina Internacional de Información y Observación del Español**

-ófobo SUF *p.ej.* **anglófobo**

-ófono SUF *p.ej.* **anglófono**

▼**ofrecer** ▸conjug 2d◂ Ⓐ VT [1] (= *presentar voluntariamente*) [1·1] [+ *servicios, ayuda, trabajo, dinero*] to offer; **nos ofreció un té** he offered us tea; **me ofrecieron la posibilidad de trabajar para ellos** they offered me the chance to work for them; **¿cuánto te ofrecieron por el coche?** how much did they offer you for the car?; **~ hacer algo** to offer to do sth; **el club le ha ofrecido prorrogar su contrato** the club has offered to extend his contract; **me ofrecieron participar en la coproducción** they asked me if I would like to take part in the co-production
[1·2] [+ *espectáculo, programa*] (*en TV*) to show; **varias cadenas ofrecen el partido en directo** several channels are showing the match live; **los principales espectáculos que ofrece el festival** the main events featured in the festival; **la Filarmónica ~á un concierto el día de Navidad** the Philharmonic are giving a concert on Christmas Day
[1·3] (*frm*) [+ *respetos*] to pay (*frm*); **~ la bienvenida a algn** to welcome sb
[2] (= *tener*) [2·1] [+ *ventaja*] to offer; [+ *oportunidad, garantías*] to offer, give; [+ *solución*] to offer, provide; **el formato electrónico ofrece algunas ventajas** the electronic format offers some advantages; **la sanidad pública ofrece más posibilidades de investigación** public health care offers *o* provides more scope for research; **no ofrece las suficientes garantías** it's not sufficiently reliable; **no ~ duda**: **la gravedad del caso no ofrece duda** there is no doubt about the seriousness of the case; **el resultado no ofrecía dudas** the result left no room for doubt
[2·2] [+ *dificultad*] to present; **el caso no ofrece dificultad alguna** the case presents no difficulty; **el ladrón no ofreció resistencia** the burglar did not put up a struggle, the burglar offered no resistance (*frm*)
[2·3] [+ *imagen*] to present; **el partido necesita ~ una imagen de estabilidad** the party needs to present an image of stability; **el palacio abandonado ofrecía un aspecto desolador** the deserted palace looked depressingly bleak; **la zona ofrece un deprimente espectáculo a sus visitantes** the area is a depressing sight for visitors
[3] (= *celebrar*) [+ *acto, fiesta, cena*] to hold, give; **un portavoz del Ministerio ofreció una rueda de prensa** a Ministry spokesman gave *o* held a press conference; **los compañeros le ofrecieron una comida de despedida** her colleagues held a farewell lunch for her
[4] [+ *sacrificio, víctima*] to offer up; **ofrecieron un cordero en sacrificio a los dioses** they offered up a lamb to the gods; **ofrecieron su vida por la causa** they gave their lives for the cause
[5] (*Rel*) to make a vow; **ha ofrecido que va a dejar de fumar** he made a vow to stop smoking

➤ LENGUA Y USO: ofrecer A1 30

Ⓑ **ofrecerse** VPR [1] [*persona*] **un joven se ofreció como guía** a young man offered to act as a guide; **la vecina se ha ofrecido para cualquier cosa que necesitemos** the woman next door offered to help us in any way she could; **~se a** *o* **para hacer algo** to offer to do sth; **me ofrecí a acompañarla hasta la puerta** I offered to see her to the door; **"profesor de inglés se ofrece para dar clases particulares"** "English teacher offers private tuition"; **~se (como) voluntario** to volunteer (**a** for)
[2] **ofrecérsele a algn** [*oportunidad*] to offer itself (to sb), present itself (to sb); [*obstáculo, dificultad*] to present itself (to sb); **se le ofreció una maravillosa oportunidad** a wonderful opportunity offered *o* presented itself (to him); **se le ofrece ahora la oportunidad de demostrar su valía** he has now been given *o* he now has the opportunity to prove himself; **los obstáculos que se le ofrecieron** the obstacles that she was now faced with, the obstacles that had presented themselves; **un hermoso espectáculo se ofrecía ante sus ojos** (*liter*) a beautiful sight presented itself to her eyes (*liter*)
[3] (*frm*) (= *desear*) **buenos días, ¿qué se le ofrece?** good morning, what can I do for you? *o* what would you like?; **¿se le ofrece algo?** is there anything I can do for you?
[4] (= *ocurrir*) to occur; **se me ofrece una duda** I have a doubt, a problem has occurred to me; **¿qué se ofrece?** what's going on?, what's happening?

ofrecimiento SM offer

ofrenda SF [1] (= *tributo*) tribute; (*Rel*) offering ► **ofrenda floral** floral tribute
[2] (= *regalo*) gift

ofrendar ▸conjug 1a◂ VT [1] (= *ofrecer*) to give, contribute
[2] (*Rel*) to offer up

oftalmía SF ophthalmia

oftálmico ADJ ophthalmic

oftalmología SF ophthalmology

oftalmólogo/a SM/F ophthalmologist

ofuscación SF, **ofuscamiento** SM [1] [*de la vista*] blurring
[2] (*al pensar*) bewilderment, confusion; (*al actuar*) blindness

ofuscar ▸conjug 1g◂ Ⓐ VT [1] [*luz*] to dazzle
[2] [+ *persona*] (= *confundir*) to bewilder, confuse; (= *cegar*) to blind; **estar ofuscado por la cólera** to be blinded by rage
Ⓑ **ofuscarse** VPR **~se por algo** to be blinded by sth

Ogino SM, **ogino** SM **método ~** rhythm method (*of birth-control*)

ogro SM ogre

oh EXCL oh!

ohmio SM ohm

oíble ADJ audible

OIC SF ABR [1] (= **Organización Internacional del Comercio**) ITO
[2] = **Organización Interamericana del Café**

OICE SF ABR = **Organización Interamericana de Cooperación Económica**

OICI SF ABR (= **Organización Interamericana de Cooperación Intermunicipal**) IAMO

OID SF ABR = **Oficina de Información Diplomática**

oída SF hearing; **de** *o* **por ~s** by *o* from hearsay

➤ LENGUA Y USO: **ojalá B1** 45.2, 52.5

-oide *ver* **Aspects of Word Formation in Spanish 2**

oído SM [1] (*Anat*) ear; **le estarán zumbando los ~s** his ears must be burning; **decir algo al ~ de algn** to whisper sth to sb, whisper sth in sb's ear; ✦**MODISMOS aguzar los ~s** to prick up one's ears; **aplicar el ~** to listen carefully; **¡~ a la caja!** pay attention!; **dar ~s a algo** (= *escuchar*) to listen to sth; (= *creer*) to believe sth; **entra por un ~ y sale por otro** it goes in one ear and out (of) the other; **hacer ~s a algo** to pay attention to sth, take heed of sth; **hacer ~s sordos a algo** to turn a deaf ear to sth; **llegar a ~s de algn** to come to sb's attention; **¡~ al parche!** pay attention!; **prestar ~(s) a algo** to give ear to sth; **regalarle a algn el ~** *o* **los ~s** to flatter sb, sweet-talk sb; **ser todo ~s** to be all ears; *ver tb* **crédito 1** ► **oído externo** external ear ► **oído interno** inner ear ► **oído medio** middle ear
[2] (= *sentido*) (sense of) hearing; **duro de ~** hard of hearing; **es una canción que se pega al ~** it's a catchy song; **tiene un ~ muy fino** he has a very keen sense of hearing
[3] (*Mús*) ear; **de ~** by ear; **siempre toca de ~** she always plays by ear; **tener (buen) ~** to have a good ear

oidor SM (*Hist*) judge

OIEA SM *o* SF ABR (= **Organismo** *u* **Organización Internacional de la Energía Atómica**) IAEA

oigo *etc ver* **oír**

OIN SF ABR (= **Organización Internacional de Normalización**) ISO

OIP SF ABR (*Aer*) = **Organización Iberoamericana de Pilotos**

OIR SF ABR (= **Organización Internacional para los Refugiados**) IRO

oír ▸conjug 3p◂ Ⓐ VT [1] (= *percibir sonidos*) to hear; **he oído un ruido** I heard a noise; **¿me oyes bien desde tu habitación?** can you hear me all right from your room?; **le oí abrir la puerta** I heard him open the door, I heard him opening the door; **—la han despedido —¡no me digas! —como lo oyes** "she's been sacked" — "no, really!" — "she has, I'm telling you"; **~ hablar de algn** to hear about *o* of sb; **he oído decir que …** I've heard it said that …, rumour *o* (*EEUU*) rumor has it that …; ✦**MODISMOS lo oyó como quien oye llover** she paid no attention, she turned a deaf ear to it; **¡me van a ~!** they'll be having a few words from me!
[2] (= *escuchar*) to listen to; **~ la radio** to listen to the radio; **óyeme bien, no vuelvas a hacerlo** now listen to what I'm telling you, don't do it again; **no han querido ~ nuestras quejas** they didn't want to listen to our complaints; **fui a ~ un concierto** I went to see a concert, I attended a concert
[3] [+ *misa*] to attend, hear
[4] [+ *confesión*] to hear
[5] [+ *ruego*] to heed, answer; **¡Dios te oiga!** I just hope you're right!
Ⓑ VI [1] (= *percibir sonidos*) to hear; **~ mal** (= *ser medio sordo*) to be hard of hearing; (*al teléfono*) to be unable to hear (properly)
[2] **~ de algn** (*LAm*) to hear from sb
[3] (*en exclamaciones*) **¡oye, que te dejas el cambio!** hey, you've forgotten your change!; **oiga, ¿es usted el encargado?** excuse me, are you in charge?; **¡oye, que yo no he dicho eso!** hold on *o* just a minute, that's not what I said!; **¡oiga!** (*Telec*) hello?

OIT SF ABR (= **Oficina** *u* **Organización Internacional del Trabajo**) ILO

ojada SF (*Andes*) skylight

ojal SM buttonhole, boutonniere (*EEUU*)

▼ **ojalá** Ⓐ EXCL **—mañana puede que haga sol —¡ojalá!** "it might be sunny tomorrow" — "I hope so!" *o* "I hope it will be!"; **—¿te darán el trabajo? —¡ojalá!** "will you get the job?" — "let's hope so!"
Ⓑ CONJ [1] **¡~ venga pronto!** I wish he'd come!, I hope he comes soon!; **¡~ que gane la carrera!** let's hope she wins the race!; **—¿vendrás con nosotros? —¡~ pudiera!** "will you come with us?" — "I wish I could!"; **¡~ pudiera andar de nuevo!** if only he could walk again!
[2] (*LAm*) (= *aunque*) even though; **no lo haré, ~ me maten** I won't do it even if they kill me

ojazos SMPL (= *ojos grandes*) big eyes, wide eyes; (= *ojos bonitos*) lovely big eyes; **echar los ~ a algn** to make eyes at sb

OJD SF ABR (= **Oficina de Justificación de la Difusión**) *office which keeps statistics of newspaper circulations*

OJE SF ABR = **Organización Juvenil Española**

ojeada SF glance; **echar una ~ a algo** to glance at sth, take a quick look at sth

ojeador(a) SM/F (*Caza*) beater; (*Dep*) talent scout, talent spotter

ojear[1] ▸conjug 1a◂ VT (*gen*) to eye; (*fijamente*) to stare at; **voy a ~ cómo va el trabajo** I'm going to see how the work is getting on

ojear[2] ▸conjug 1a◂ VT [1] (= *ahuyentar*) to drive away, shoo away
[2] (*Caza*) to beat, put up
[3] (*Cono Sur*) (= *hechizar*) to put the evil eye on

ojén SM anisette

ojeo SM (*Caza*) beating

ojeras SFPL bags under the eyes; **tener ~** to have bags under the eyes

ojeriza SF spite, ill will; **tener ~ a algn** to have a grudge against sb, have it in for sb*

ojeroso ADJ haggard; **estar ~** to have bags under the eyes

ojete SM [1] (*Cos*) eyelet
[2] (**) (= *ano*) arsehole**, asshole (*EEUU***)

ojiabierto ADJ wide-eyed

ojillos SMPL (*brillantes*) bright eyes; (*bonitos*) lovely eyes; (*pícaros*) roguish eyes; **¡tiene unos ~!** you should see the eyes she's got!

ojímetro SM **a ~*** roughly, at a rough guess

ojinegro ADJ black-eyed

ojito SM [1] ✦**MODISMOS hacer ~s a algn*** to make eyes at sb, give sb the eye; **poner ~s a algn** to look longingly at sb; **ser el ~ derecho de algn** to be the apple of sb's eye
[2] (= *cuidado*) **¡ojito!** careful!, look out!

ojituerto ADJ cross-eyed

ojiva SF [1] (*Arquit*) pointed arch, ogive
[2] (*Mil*) warhead

ojival ADJ ogival, pointed

ojo SM [1] (*Anat*) eye; ✦**MODISMOS a ~ (de buen cubero)**: **calculé a ~ (de buen cubero) cuántas personas había** I roughly calculated *o* made a rough guess at how many people were there; **no hace falta medir la harina, échala a ~** there's no need to weigh out the flour, just add roughly the right amount; **abrir los ~s (a algo)** to open one's eyes (to sth); **abrirle los ~s a algn** to open sb's eyes; **en un abrir y cerrar de ~s** in the twinkling of an eye; **avivar el ~** to be on the alert; **mirar** *o* **ver algo con buenos ~s** to look kindly on sth, approve of sth; **con los ~s cerrados** ◊ **a ~s cerrados** without a second thought; **lo aceptaría con los ~s cerrados** I'd accept it without a second thought; **cerrar los ~s a** *o* **ante algo** to shut one's eyes to sth; **tener ~ clínico** to have good intuition; **costar un ~ de la cara*** to cost an arm and a leg*; **dar en los ~s** to be conspicuous; **ser el ~ derecho de algn** to be the apple of sb's eye; **echar un ~ a algo/algn** to keep an eye on sth/sb; **tener el ~ echado a algn/algo** to have one's eye on sb/sth; **le tiene echado el ~ a Elisa desde que llegó** he's had his eye on Elisa ever since he arrived; **le tengo echado el ~ a ese vestido** I've got my eye on that dress; **tener a algn entre ~s** to have it in for sb; **hacer del ~**† to wink; **mirar** *o* **ver algo con malos ~s** to disapprove of sth; **veían con malos ~s que se hubiese nacionalizado español** they disapproved of him adopting Spanish nationality; **¡no es nada lo del ~!** (*iró*) it's no big deal!; **no pegué ~ en toda la noche** I didn't get a wink of sleep all night; **se le salieron los ~s de las órbitas** his eyes popped out of his head; **se le pusieron los ~s como platos** she was wide-eyed with amazement; **poner ~s a algn** to look longingly at sb; **en mis propios ~s** before my very eyes; **no quitar ~ a algo/algn** not to take one's eyes off sth/sb; **salir de ~** to be obvious; **tener (buen) ~ para algo** to have a good eye for sth, be a good judge of sth; **ser todo ~s** to be all eyes; **a ~s vistas** visibly; ✦*REFRANES* **~ por ~, (diente por diente)** an eye for an eye, (a tooth for a tooth); **~s que no ven, corazón que no siente** out of sight, out of mind ► **ojo a la funerala***, **ojo a la virulé***, **ojo a la pava*** shiner* ► **ojo amoratado** black eye ► **ojo de cristal** glass eye ► **ojo de pez** (*Fot*) fish-eye lens ► **ojo mágico** magic eye ► **ojos almendrados** almond eyes; *ver tb* **avizor A, dichoso 2, niña 3**

2 **ojos** (= *vista*): **pasar los ~s por algo** to look sth over; **paseó los ~s por la sala** he looked round the hall; **torcer los ~s** to squint; ✦*MODISMOS* **a los ~s de algn** in sb's eyes; **clavar los ~s en algo/algn** to fix one's gaze on sth/sb, stare at sth/sb; **comerse** *o* **devorar a algn con los ~s** (*con deseo*) to devour sb with one's eyes; (*con ira*) to look daggers at sb; **entrar por los ~s**: **esa comida no me termina de entrar por los ~s** that meal is not exactly mouth-watering; **los anuncios bien hechos nos entran por los ~s** well-made adverts captivate us; **irse los ~s tras algo/algn**: **se le fueron los ~s tras la chica** he couldn't keep his eyes off the girl; **tener los ~s puestos en algo** (= *prestar atención a*) to centre one's attention on sth; (= *desear*) to have one's heart set on sth; **España tiene los ~s puestos en los novios reales** all eyes in Spain are on the royal couple; **recrear los ~s en algo/algn** to feast one's eyes on sth/sb; **saltar a los ~s** to be blindingly obvious

3 (= *cuidado*) **¡ojo!** careful!, look out!; **¡ojo! es muy mentiroso** be careful! he's an awful liar; **~ con el escalón** mind the step; **hay que tener mucho ~ con los carteristas** one must be very careful of *o* beware pickpockets; **ir con ~** to keep one's eyes open for trouble

4 (= *orificio*) [*de aguja*] eye; [*de queso*] hole; [*de puente*] span; **el ~ de la cerradura** *o* (*LAm*) **llave** the keyhole; **un puente de cuatro ~s** a bridge with four arches *o* spans ► **ojo de buey** (*Náut*) porthole ► **ojo del culo**⁑ hole⁑, arsehole⁑⁑, asshole (*EEUU*⁑⁑) ► **ojo del huracán** eye of the hurricane; **el presidente vuelve a estar en el ~ del huracán** the president is once again at the centre of a controversy

5 (*LAm*) (= *depósito natural*) ► **ojo de agua** pool, natural pool

ojón ADJ (*LAm*) big-eyed, with big eyes

ojota SF 1 (*LAm*) (= *sandalia*) rough sandal 2 (*Andes, Cono Sur*) (= *piel de llama*) *tanned llama leather*

ojotes* SMPL (*Andes, CAm pey*) bulging eyes, goggle eyes; (*bonitos*) lovely big eyes

ojuelos SMPL = **ojillos**

okapi SM okapi

okupa⁑ SMF squatter

OL ABR (= **onda larga**) LW

ola SF 1 [*de mar*] wave; **la ~** (*en un estadio*) the Mexican wave; **la nueva ~** [*de moda*] the new wave; [*de personas*] the new generation; (*Mús, Cine*) the new wave; ✦*MODISMOS* **batir las ~s** to ply the seas; **estar en la cresta de la ~** to be on the crest of a wave; **hacer ~s** to make waves, rock the boat ► **ola de marea** tidal wave ► **ola sísmica** tidal wave

2 (= *abundancia*) [*de indignación, prosperidad*] wave; [*de atentados, huelgas*] spate; [*de gripe*] (sudden) outbreak ► **ola de calor** heat wave ► **ola de frío** cold spell, cold snap ► **ola delictiva** crime wave

OLADE SF ABR = **Organización Latinoamericana de Energía**

OLAVU SF ABR = **Organización Latinoamericana del Vino y de la Uva**

olé EXCL bravo!

oleada SF 1 (*Náut*) big wave 2 (= *gran cantidad*) [*de jóvenes, artistas*] wave; [*de atentados, huelgas*] spate; [*de inflación*] surge; **una gran ~ de gente** a great surge of people; **la primera ~ del ataque** the first wave of the attack

oleaginosa SF oil product

oleaginoso ADJ oily, oleaginous (*frm*)

oleaje SM swell, surge

olear[1] ▸conjug 1a◂ VI to wave, flutter

olear[2] ▸conjug 1a◂ VT to shout "olé" to, cheer, encourage

oleícola ADJ oil *antes de s*, olive-oil *antes de s*

oleicultor(a) SM/F olive-grower

oleicultura SF olive-growing

óleo SM 1 (*gen*) oil; **santo(s) ~(s)** (*Rel*) holy oil(s)

2 (*Arte*) oil painting; **pintar al ~** to paint in oils

3 (*LAm*) (= *bautismo*) baptism

oleo... PREF oleo...

oleoducto SM pipeline, oil pipeline

oleoso ADJ oily

oler ▸conjug 2i◂ Ⓐ VT 1 (= *percibir por la nariz*) to smell; **me gusta ~ las flores** I like smelling the flowers

2 (*) (= *sospechar*) to suspect; **ha olido lo que estás tramando** he suspects what you're up to, he's smelt a rat*

3 (*) (= *curiosear*) to poke one's nose into*; **siempre anda oliendo lo que hacen los demás** he's always poking his nose into other people's affairs

Ⓑ VI 1 (= *despedir olor*) to smell (**a** of, like); **huele muy bien** [*comida*] it smells very good; [*flor, perfume*] it smells very nice; **huele fatal** it smells foul; **huele que apesta** it stinks; **¡qué mal huelen estos zapatos!** these shoes smell awful!; **huele a humedad** it smells of damp; **huele a tabaco** it smells of cigarette smoke; **aquí huele a quemado** there's a smell of burning in here; **le huele el aliento** his breath smells; **te huelen los pies** your feet smell; **huele que alimenta*** (= *muy bien*) it smells heavenly; (= *muy mal*) it smells foul, it stinks to high heaven*

2 (*indicando desconfianza*) **sus excusas me huelen a camelo*** his excuses sound a bit fishy to me*; ✦*MODISMO* **~ a chamusquina**: **todo esto me huele a chamusquina** the whole thing sounds fishy to me

Ⓒ **olerse** VPR (*) (= *sospechar*) to suspect; **nadie se había olido nada** nobody had suspected anything; **se olía que no iban a venir** he had the feeling *o* suspicion that they weren't going to come

oletear ▸conjug 1a◂ VT (*Andes*) to pry into

oletón ADJ (*Andes*) prying

olfa* SMF (*Cono Sur*) (= *lameculos*) creep*, bootlicker*, brown-nose (*EEUU*⁑); (= *admirador*) admirer, follower

olfacción SF smelling, act of smelling, olfaction (*frm*)

olfatear ▸conjug 1a◂ VT 1 [+ *comida*] to smell, sniff; [+ *presa*] to scent, smell out 2 (= *curiosear*) to pry into, poke one's nose into

olfativo ADJ olfactory

olfato SM 1 (= *sentido*) smell, sense of smell 2 (= *instinto*) instinct, intuition

olfatorio ADJ olfactory

oliente ADJ **bien ~** sweet-smelling; **mal ~** foul-smelling

oligarca SMF oligarch

oligarquía SF oligarchy

oligárquico ADJ oligarchic, oligarchical

oligo... PREF oligo...

oligoelemento SM trace element

oligofrénico/a Ⓐ ADJ mentally handicapped Ⓑ SM/F mentally handicapped person

oligopolio SM oligopoly

oligopolístico ADJ oligopolistic

oligopsonio SM oligopsony

olimpiada SF, **olimpíada** SF Olympiad; **las Olimpiadas** the Olympics; **Olimpiada de Invierno** Winter Olympics

olímpicamente* ADV **pasó de nosotros ~*** he completely snubbed us

olímpico/a Ⓐ ADJ 1 [*deporte, título*] Olympic; (*Hist*) Olympian

2 (*) (= *enorme*) **nos despreció de forma olímpica** he was utterly contemptuous of us; **fue una sesión de trabajo olímpica** it was a marathon work session

3 (= *despectivo*) dismissive

Ⓑ SM/F Olympic athlete

olimpismo SM (= *movimiento*) Olympic movement; (= *juegos*) Olympic Games *pl*

Olimpo SM Olympus

oliscar ▸conjug 1g◂ Ⓐ VT [1] (= *olfatear*) to smell, sniff (gently)
[2] (= *curiosear*) to investigate, look into
Ⓑ VI (= *apestar*) to start to smell (bad)

olisco ADJ (*Cono Sur*), **oliscón** ADJ (*Andes*), **oliscoso** ADJ (*LAm*) [*carne*] high*

olisquear ▸conjug 1a◂ VT, VI = **oliscar**

oliva Ⓐ SF [1] (= *aceituna*) olive; **(color) verde ~** olive green
[2] (= *árbol*) olive tree
[3] (*Orn*) = **lechuza**
Ⓑ ADJ INV olive

oliváceo ADJ olive, olive-green

olivar SM olive grove

olivarero/a Ⓐ ADJ olive *antes de s*
Ⓑ SM/F olive-producer, olive-oil producer

Oliverio SM Oliver

olivero ADJ olive *antes de s*, olive-growing *antes de s*; **región olivera** olive-growing region

olivicultor(a) SM/F olive grower

olivicultura SF olive growing

olivo SM olive tree; ✦*MODISMO* **tomar el ~**‡ to beat it*

olla SF [1] (= *cacharro*) pot, pan; ✦*MODISMO* **se me va la ~*** (*por volverse loco*) I'm losing my head; (*hablando sin parar*) I'm going over the top; (*por borrachera*) I'm out of my head*; (*al perder el hilo*) I'm losing the thread, I'm getting lost ▸ **olla a presión, olla de presión** pressure cooker ▸ **olla exprés** pressure cooker
[2] (*Culin*) stew ▸ **olla podrida** hotpot
[3] (*en río*) eddy, whirlpool
[4] (*Alpinismo*) chimney
[5] ▸ **olla común, olla popular** (*Cono Sur*) soup kitchen

ollar SM [*de caballo*] nostril

ollero/a SM/F (= *artesano*) *maker of pots and pans*; (= *vendedor*) *dealer in pots and pans*

olmeca Ⓐ ADJ Olmec
Ⓑ SMF Olmec; **los ~s** the Olmecs

olmeda SF, **olmedo** SM elm grove

olmo SM elm, elm tree ▸ **olmo campestre** common elm ▸ **olmo de montaña** wych elm

ológrafo ADJ, SM holograph

olor SM [1] (*gen*) smell (**a** of); **buen ~** nice smell; **mal ~** bad smell, nasty smell; **tiene mal ~** it smells horrible ▸ **olor a quemado** smell of burning ▸ **olor corporal** body odour *o* (*EEUU*) odor
[2] (= *atracción*) smell; **acudir al ~ del dinero** to be attracted by the smell of money
[3] (= *fama*) ▸ **olor de santidad** odour of sanctity
[4] **olores** (*Cono Sur, Méx Culin*) spices

olorcillo SM (*ligero*) faint smell; (*delicado*) delicate aroma; (*pey*) whiff (**a** of)

oloroso Ⓐ ADJ sweet-smelling, fragrant, scented
Ⓑ SM (= *jerez*) oloroso, oloroso sherry

olote SM (*CAm, Méx*) [1] (*Agr*) (= *mazorca*) corncob; (= *tallo*) maize stalk
[2] **un ~** a nobody, a nonentity

olotear ▸conjug 1a◂ VI (*CAm, Méx*) to gather maize *o* (*EEUU*) corn, harvest maize *o* (*EEUU*) corn

olotera SF (*CAm, Méx*) [1] (= *montón*) heap of corncobs
[2] (= *máquina*) maize thresher

OLP SF ABR (= **Organización para la Liberación de Palestina**) PLO

olvidadizo ADJ [1] (= *desmemoriado*) forgetful
[2] (= *ingrato*) ungrateful

olvidado ADJ [1] (= *abandonado*) forgotten; **~ de Dios** godforsaken
[2] = **olvidadizo**

olvidar ▸conjug 1a◂ Ⓐ VT [1] (= *no acordarse de*) to forget; **he olvidado su nombre** I've forgotten his name; **~ hacer algo** to forget to do sth; **no olvides comprar el pan** don't forget to buy the bread; **¡olvídame!*** get lost!*
[2] (= *dejar olvidado*) to forget, leave behind, leave; **no olvides los guantes** don't forget your gloves, don't leave your gloves behind; **olvidé las llaves encima de la mesa** I left the keys on top of the table; **olvidé el paraguas en la tienda** I left my umbrella in the shop
[3] (= *omitir*) to leave out, omit
Ⓑ **olvidarse** VPR [1] (= *no acordarse*) to forget; **se me olvidó por completo** I forgot all about it; **se me olvida la fecha** I forget the date, I can't think of the date; **~se de hacer algo** to forget to do sth; **me olvidé de decírtelo** I forgot to tell you
[2] (= *dejarse olvidado*) to forget, leave behind, leave; **se me olvidó el paraguas** I forgot my umbrella, I left my umbrella behind; **me he olvidado el maletín en casa** I have left my briefcase at home
[3] (*fig*) (*pey*) to forget o.s.

> **OLVIDAR**
>
> Si se **nos olvida un objeto** en algún lugar, **olvidar** se puede traducir por **forget**, **leave** o **leave behind**:
>
> • Por regla general, si no mencionamos el lugar donde se nos ha olvidado, **olvidar** se traduce por **forget** o **leave behind**:
>
> He olvidado la cartera
> ***I have forgotten my wallet, I have left my wallet behind***
> No olvides el pasaporte
> ***Don't forget your passport, Don't leave your passport behind***
>
> • Si mencionamos el lugar donde se nos ha olvidado, **olvidar** se suele traducir por **leave**:
>
> He olvidado la cartera en el restaurante
> ***I have left my wallet in the restaurant***
>
> *Para otros usos y ejemplos ver la entrada.*

olvido SM [1] (*absoluto*) oblivion; **caer en el ~** to fall into oblivion; **echar al ~** to forget; **enterrar** *o* **hundir en el ~** to cast into oblivion (*liter*); **rescatar del ~** to rescue from oblivion
[2] (= *estado*) forgetfulness
[3] (= *descuido*) slip, oversight; **ha sido por ~** it was an oversight

olvidón ADJ (*Andes*) forgetful

OM ABR [1] (*Pol*) = **Orden Ministerial**
[2] (*Radio*) (= **onda media**) MW

Omán SM Oman

ombligo SM navel, belly button*; ✦*MODISMOS* **se le arrugó** *o* **encogió el ~** he got cold feet*; **meter a algn el ~ para dentro*** to put the wind up sb*; **mirarse el ~** to contemplate one's navel

ombliguera SF (*Andes*) striptease artiste

ombú SM (*Arg*) ombú, ombú tree

ombudsman SM ombudsman

OMC SF ABR (= **Organización Mundial del Comercio**) WTO

omega SF omega

OMG SM ABR (= **Organismo Modificado Genéticamente**) GMO

OMI SF ABR (= **Organización Marítima Internacional**) IMO

OMIC SF ABR (*Esp*) = **Oficina Municipal de Información al Consumidor**

ominoso ADJ [1] (= *de mal agüero*) ominous
[2] (= *pasmoso*) awful, dreadful

omisión SF [1] (*gen*) omission, oversight; **su ~ de hacer algo** his failure to do sth ▸ **omisión de auxilio** (*Jur*) failure to give assistance, failure to go to somebody's aid
[2] (= *descuido*) slip, oversight

omiso ADJ **hacer caso ~ de algo** to ignore sth

omitir ▸conjug 3a◂ VT [1] (= *no decir*) to leave out, miss out, omit
[2] **~ hacer algo** to omit to do sth, fail to do sth

OMM SF ABR (= **Organización Meteorológica Mundial**) WMO

omni... PREF omni...

ómnibus Ⓐ ADJ **tren ~** slow train
Ⓑ SM [1] (*Aut, Hist*) omnibus
[2] (*LAm*) bus

omnibús SM (*Cono Sur*) bus

omnicomprensivo ADJ all-inclusive

omnidireccional ADJ omnidirectional

omnímodo ADJ (*gen*) all-embracing; [*poder*] absolute

omnipotencia SF omnipotence

omnipotente ADJ omnipotent, all-powerful

omnipresencia SF omnipresence

omnipresente ADJ omnipresent

omnisapiente ADJ omniscient, all-knowing

omnisciencia SF omniscience

omnisciente ADJ, **omniscio** ADJ omniscient, all-knowing

omnívoro ADJ omnivorous

omoplato SM, **omóplato** SM shoulder blade

OMS SF ABR (= **Organización Mundial de la Salud**) WHO

OMT SF ABR (*Esp*) = **Oficina Municipal de Transportes**

-ón, -ona *ver* **Aspects of Word Formation in Spanish 2**

onanismo SM onanism

onanista Ⓐ ADJ onanistic
Ⓑ SMF onanist

ONCE SF ABR (*Esp*) = **Organización Nacional de Ciegos Españoles**

> **ONCE**
>
> *The* **Organización Nacional de Ciegos Españoles** *began life as a charity for the blind and is now one of the wealthiest and most successful organizations in Spain, with a wide-ranging sphere of activity, including assisting other disabled groups. The popular lottery which it set up to provide employment for its members is now its main source of income, generating plentiful capital for investment. One of* **ONCE***'s main roles is to provide educational, occupational and rehabilitation centres for its members and to help them to achieve financial independence and social integration.*

once Ⓐ ADJ INV, PRON (*gen*) eleven; (*ordinal, en la fecha*) eleventh; **las ~** eleven o'clock; **le escribí el día ~** I wrote to him on the eleventh; ✦*MODISMOS* **tomar las ~*** to have elevenses*; **tomar ~** *o* **la(s) ~** *o a veces* **~s** (*Chile*) to have afternoon tea, have an afternoon snack
Ⓑ SM (*gen*) eleven; (= *fecha*) eleventh; (*Ftbl*) team; **el ~ titular** the first team; *ver tb* **seis**

oncear ▸conjug 1a◂ VI (*Andes*) to have an afternoon snack

onceavo/a ADJ, SM/F, **onceno/a** ADJ, SM/F eleventh; *ver tb* **sexto A**

11-S SM 9-11

oncogén SM oncogene

oncología SF oncology ► **oncología clínica** clinical oncology

oncólogo/a SM/F oncologist

onda SF [1] (*gen*) wave; **tratamiento de ~ ultravioleta** ultra-violet treatment ► **onda corta** short wave; **de ~ corta** shortwave *antes de s* ► **onda de choque** shock wave ► **onda de radio** radio wave ► **onda expansiva** shock wave ► **onda explosiva** blast, shock wave ► **onda extracorta** ultra-short wave ► **onda larga** long wave ► **onda luminosa** light wave ► **onda media** medium wave ► **ondas cerebrales** brain waves ► **onda sísmica** shock wave ► **onda sonora** sound wave
[2] (*) (= *ambiente*) wavelength; **estamos en la misma ~** we're on the same wavelength; **¡qué buena ~!*** that's great!*; ✦*MODISMOS* **agarrar** *o* **coger la ~** (= *entender*) to get it*, get the point*; (= *coger el tino*) to get the hang of it; **estar en la ~*** (= *de moda*) to be in*; (= *al tanto*) to be on the ball*, be up to date; [*persona*] (= *a la moda*) to be hip*; **estar en ~‡** (= *drogado*) to be high‡ (*on drugs*); **estar en ~ gay** to be into the gay thing*; **se merece un regalo en su ~*** he deserves a present he'll really like; **estar fuera de ~** to be out of touch; **perder la ~*** to lose one's touch; **¿qué ~?** (*LAm**) what's up?*
[3] (*Cos*) scallop

ondeante ADJ = **ondulante**

ondear ▸conjug 1a◂ Ⓐ VT [1] [+ *bandera*] to wave
[2] (*Cos*) to pink, scallop
Ⓑ VI [1] (= *moverse*) [*agua*] to ripple; [*bandera*] to fly, flutter; [*pelo*] to flow; **la bandera ondea en lo alto del edificio** the flag flies from the top of the building; **la bandera ondea a media asta** the flag is flying at half mast
[2] (= *flotar al viento*) to stream
Ⓒ **ondearse** VPR to swing, sway

ondia* EXCL (*euf*) = **hostia**

ondímetro SM wave meter

ondina SF undine, water nymph

ondulación SF [1] [*de movimiento*] undulation, wavy motion; (*en agua*) wave, ripple; (*en pelo*) wave ► **ondulación permanente†** permanent wave
[2] **ondulaciones** (*en paisaje*) undulations, ups and downs; (*en terreno*) unevenness *sing*

ondulado Ⓐ ADJ [*carretera*] uneven, rough; [*paisaje, terreno*] undulating, rolling; [*superficie*] undulating, uneven; [*cartón, hierro*] corrugated; [*pelo*] wavy
Ⓑ SM (*en pelo*) wave

ondulante ADJ [1] [*movimiento*] (*gen*) undulating; (= *de lado a lado*) from side to side, (gently) swaying
[2] [*sonido*] rising and falling
[3] = **ondulado A**

ondular ▸conjug 1a◂ Ⓐ VT [+ *pelo*] to wave; [+ *cuerpo*] to wiggle; **hacerse ~ el pelo** to have one's hair waved
Ⓑ VI, **ondularse** VPR (*gen*) to undulate; (= *balancearse*) to sway

ondulatorio ADJ undulatory, wavy

oneroso ADJ [1] (= *pesado*) onerous, burdensome
[2] (*Jur*) onerous

ONG SF ABR (= **Organización No Gubernamental**) NGO

ónice SM onyx

onírico ADJ oneiric, dream *antes de s*

ónix SM onyx

ONL SF ABR (= **Organización No Lucrativa**) non-profit-making organization

on line [ˈonˈlain] ADJ, ADV on-line

ONO ABR (= **oesnoroeste**) WNW

onomástica SF [1] [*del nombre*] saint's day; → SANTO
[2] (= *ciencia*) onomastics *sing*, study of personal names

onomástico Ⓐ ADJ onomastic, name *antes de s*, of names; **fiesta onomástica** saint's day; **índice ~** index of names; **lista onomástica** list of names
Ⓑ SM saint's day, name day

onomatopeya SF onomatopoeia

onomatopéyico ADJ onomatopoeic

ontología SF ontology

ontológico ADJ ontological

ONU SF ABR (= **Organización de las Naciones Unidas**) UNO; **la ~** the UN

onubense Ⓐ ADJ of/from Huelva
Ⓑ SMF native/inhabitant of Huelva; **los ~s** the people of Huelva

ONUDI SF ABR (= **Organización de las Naciones Unidas para el Desarrollo Industrial**) UNIDO

onusiano ADJ United Nations *antes de s*

onza[1] SF ounce

onza[2] SF (*LAm Zool*) snow leopard, ounce

onzavo/a ADJ, SM/F eleventh; *ver tb* **sexto A**

oolítico ADJ oolitic

oolito SM oolite

O.P. ABR [1] = **Obras Públicas**
[2] (*Rel*) (= **Orden de Predicadores**) O.S.D.

op. ABR (= **opus**) op

OPA SF ABR (= **oferta pública de adquisición**) *takeover bid* ► **OPA hostil** hostile takeover bid

opa[1] Ⓐ ADJ (*Andes, Arg*) [1] (= *sordomudo*) deaf and dumb
[2] (*) (= *tonto*) stupid; (= *retrasado*) mentally retarded
Ⓑ SMF (*) (= *tonto*) idiot

opa[2] EXCL (*Arg*) stop it!

opacar ▸conjug 1g◂ (*LAm*) Ⓐ VT [1] (= *hacer opaco*) to make opaque; (= *oscurecer*) to darken; (= *empañar*) to mist up; (= *deslustrar*) to dull, tarnish
[2] [+ *persona*] to outshine, overshadow
Ⓑ **opacarse** VPR [1] (*LAm*) (= *hacerse opaco*) to become opaque; (= *oscurecerse*) to darken, get dark; (= *empañarse*) to mist up; (= *deslustrarse*) to lose its shine, become tarnished
[2] (*Andes, CAm*) [*cielo*] to cloud over

opacidad SF [1] (= *falta de transparencia*) opacity, opaqueness
[2] (= *falta de brillo*) dullness, lifelessness
[3] (= *tristeza*) gloominess, sadness

opaco ADJ [1] (= *no transparente*) opaque; **una pantalla opaca a los rayos X** a screen which does not let X-rays through, a screen opaque to X-rays
[2] (= *sin brillo*) dull, lifeless
[3] (= *triste*) gloomy, sad

opado ADJ (*Andes, Caribe*) pale

OPAEP SF ABR (= **Organización de Países Árabes Exportadores de Petróleo**) OAPEC

opalescencia SF opalescence

opalescente ADJ opalescent

ópalo SM opal

opaparado ADJ (*Andes*) bewildered

opar ▸conjug 1a◂ VT, VI to put in a takeover bid (for); *ver tb* **OPA**

opción SF [1] (= *elección*) option; **opciones por defecto** default options; **no hay ~** there is no other option, there is no alternative *o* choice
[2] (= *derecho*) right, option; **tiene ~ a viajar gratis** he has the right *o* option to travel free
[3] (*Com*) option (**a** on); **con ~ a** *o* **para ocho más** with an option on eight more; **este dispositivo es de ~** this gadget is optional; **suscribir una ~ para la compra de algo** to take out an option on sth ► **opción a compra, opción de adquisición, opción de compra** (*gen*) option to buy, option to purchase; (*en Bolsa*) call option ► **opción de venta** (*en Bolsa*) put option

opcional ADJ optional

opcionalmente ADV optionally

op. cit. ABR (= **opere citato**) op. cit.

Op.D. ABR (*Rel*) = **Opus Dei**

opear* ▸conjug 1a◂ VI (*Andes, Cono Sur*) to act the fool, fool about

open [ˈopen] SM INV (*Golf*) open

OPEP SF ABR (= **Organización de Países Exportadores del Petróleo**) OPEC

ópera SF (*Teat*) (= *género*) opera; (= *edificio*) opera, opera house; **gran ~** grand opera ► **ópera bufa** comic opera ► **ópera prima** debut, first work

operable ADJ [*cataratas, tumor*] operable; [*regulaciones*] workable; [*medidas*] workable, feasible

operación SF [1] (= *acción*) operation ► **operaciones de rescate, operaciones de salvamento** rescue operations ► **operación retorno** (*Esp*) *effort to control traffic returning to a big city after a major holiday*
[2] (*Med*) operation; **una ~ de estómago** a stomach operation, an operation on the stomach ► **operación a corazón abierto** open-heart surgery ► **operación cesárea** Caesarean, Caesarean operation ► **operación quirúrgica** surgical operation
[3] (*Mil*) operation ► **operaciones conjuntas** joint operations ► **operación de ablandamiento** softening-up operation ► **operación de limpia, operación de limpieza** mopping up operation
[4] (*Com*) transaction, deal ► **operación a plazo** forward transaction ► **operaciones bursátiles, operaciones de bolsa** stock-exchange transactions ► **operación "llave en mano"** turnkey operation ► **operación**

mercantil business deal
5 (*Mat*) operation
6 (*LAm Min*) operation, working, exploitation; (*Com*) management
7 ► **operaciones accesorias** (*Inform*) housekeeping *sing*

operacional ADJ operational

operador(a) SM/F (*gen*) operator; (*Med*) surgeon; (*Cine*) [*de rodaje*] cameraman/camerawoman; [*de proyección*] projectionist ► **operador(a) de cabina** projectionist, operator ► **operador(a) de grúa** winchman ► **operador(a) del telégrafo** (*LAm*) telegraph operator ► **operador(a) de sistemas** systems operator ► **operador(a) de télex** telex operator ► **operador(a) turístico/a** tour operator

operante ADJ 1 (= *en funcionamiento*) operating
2 (= *influente*) powerful, influential; **los medios más ~s del país** the most influential circles in the country

operar ▸conjug 1a◂ Ⓐ VT 1 (= *producir*) [+ *cambio*] to produce, bring about; [+ *cura*] to effect; [+ *milagro*] to work
2 (*Med*) [+ *paciente*] to operate on; **~ a algn de apendicitis** to operate on sb for appendicitis
3 [+ *máquina*] to operate, use
4 (= *dirigir*) [+ *negocio*] to manage, run; [+ *mina*] to work, exploit
Ⓑ VI 1 (*gen, Mat*) to operate
2 (*Com*) to deal, do business; **hoy no se ha operado en la bolsa** there has been no dealing *o* trading on the stock exchange today
Ⓒ **operarse** VPR 1 (= *producirse*) to occur, come about; **se han operado grandes cambios** great changes have been made *o* have come about, there have been great changes
2 (*Med*) to have an operation (**de** for)

operario/a SM/F (*gen*) operative; (*esp LAm*) (= *obrero*) worker ► **operario/a de máquina** machinist

ópera-rock SF (*pl* **óperas-rock**) rock opera

operatividad SF 1 [*de proyecto*] operating capacity
2 (= *eficacia*) effectiveness, efficiency

operativizar ▸conjug 1f◂ VT to put into operation, make operative

operativo Ⓐ ADJ operative
Ⓑ SM (*Cono Sur*) (*esp militar, policial*) operation

opereta SF operetta, light opera

opería SF (*Andes, Cono Sur*) stupidity

operista SMF opera singer

operístico ADJ operatic, opera *antes de s*

operófilo/a SM/F opera-lover

operoso* ADJ (*Caribe*) irritable

opiáceo SM opiate

opiarse* ▸conjug 1b◂ VPR (*Cono Sur*) to get bored, get fed up*

opiata SF opiate

opimo ADJ plentiful, abundant, rich

opinable ADJ debatable, open to a variety of opinions

▼**opinar** ▸conjug 1a◂ Ⓐ VT to think; **~ que ...** to think that ..., be of the opinion that ...
Ⓑ VI 1 (= *pensar*) to think
2 **~ bien de algo/algn** to think well of sth/sb, have a good *o* high opinion of sth/sb
3 (= *dar su opinión*) to give one's opinion; **fueron opinando uno tras otro** they gave their opinions in turn; **hubo un 7% que no quiso ~** (*en sondeo*) there were 7% "don't knows"

▼**opinión** SF opinion, view; **en mi ~** in my opinion *o* view; **ser de la ~ (de) que ...** to be of the opinion that ..., take the view that ...; **cambiar de ~** to change one's mind; **compartir la ~ de algn** to share sb's opinion *o* view; **formarse una ~** to form an opinion; **mudar de ~** to have a change of mind *o* opinion ► **opinión pública** public opinion

opio SM 1 (= *sustancia*) opium; ✦**MODISMO dar el ~ a algn*** to enchant sb, captivate sb; **ella le dio el ~** she swept him off his feet
2 (*Cono Sur**) (= *tostón*) drag*; **la película es un ~** the film is a drag*

opiómano/a SM/F opium addict

opíparo ADJ [*banquete*] sumptuous

oponente Ⓐ ADJ opposing, contrary
Ⓑ SMF opponent

▼**oponer** ▸conjug 2q◂ (*pp* **opuesto**) Ⓐ VT 1 [+ *resistencia*] to put up
2 [+ *argumentos*] to set out; **estaba en desacuerdo y opuso sus razones** he set out the reasons for his disagreement
3 (= *poner contra*) **opusieron un dique contra el mar** they built a dike as a defence against the sea
Ⓑ **oponerse** VPR to be opposed; (*mutuamente*) to oppose each other; **yo no me opongo** I don't object; **~se a algo** to oppose sth; **se opone rotundamente a ello** he is flatly opposed to it

Oporto SM Oporto

oporto SM port

oportunamente ADV 1 (*en el tiempo*) opportunely
2 (= *pertinentemente*) appropriately

oportunidad SF 1 (= *ocasión*) chance, opportunity; **darle una/otra ~ a algn** to give sb a/another chance; **tener la ~ de hacer algo** to have a chance to do sth, have the chance of doing sth; **no tuvo la ~ de ir** he didn't have a chance to go; **a** *o* **en la primera ~** at the first opportunity
2 (= *vez*) occasion, time; **en dos ~es** on two occasions
3 (*Jur*) **igualdad de ~es** equality of opportunity
4 **"oportunidades"** (= *rebajas*) "bargains"
5 (= *cualidad*) opportuneness, timeliness

oportunismo SM opportunism

oportunista Ⓐ ADJ opportunist, opportunistic
Ⓑ SMF opportunist

oportuno ADJ 1 [*ocasión*] opportune; **en el momento ~** at an opportune moment, at the right moment; **su llamada no pudo ser más oportuna** his call could not have come at a better moment, his call could not have been better timed
2 (= *pertinente*) appropriate; **no me ha parecido ~ decírselo** I didn't think it appropriate to tell him; **una respuesta oportuna** an apt reply; **sería ~ hacerlo en seguida** it would be best to do it at once
3 [*persona*] **¡ella siempre tan oportuna!** (*iró*) you can always rely on her!

oposición SF 1 (*gen*) opposition ► **oposición frontal** direct opposition, total opposition
2 (*Esp*) (*tb* **oposiciones**) *Civil Service examination*; **hay varias plazas de libre ~** *o* **de ~ libre** there are several places that will be filled on the basis of a competitive examination; **sacar unas oposiciones** to be successful in a public competition; **hacer oposiciones a ...** ◊ **presentarse a unas oposiciones a ...** to sit an examination for ...; **hacer oposiciones para una cátedra** to compete for a chair

OPOSICIONES

***Oposiciones** are exams that applicants for lifetime public-sector jobs must pass. The exams are held every year, every other year or every five years, depending on the speciality. The candidates (**opositores**) must sit a series of written exams and/or attend interviews. Some applicants can spend years studying for and re-sitting exams, so preparing candidates for **oposiciones** is a major source of students for many **academias**. All public-sector appointments that are open to competition are published in the **BOE**, an official government publication.*

⇨ *See also* ACADEMIA, BOE

oposicional ADJ opposition *antes de s*

oposicionista Ⓐ ADJ opposition *antes de s*
Ⓑ SMF member of the opposition

opositar ▸conjug 1a◂ VI (*Esp*) to go in for a public competition (*for a post*), sit for a public entrance/promotion examination

opositor(a) Ⓐ ADJ (= *contrario*) opposing; (*Pol*) opposition *antes de s*, of the opposition; **el líder ~** the leader of the opposition
Ⓑ SM/F 1 (*Univ*) competitor, candidate (**a** for)
2 (*Pol*) opponent

opresión SF 1 (= *sensación*) oppression; [*de situación, lugar*] oppressiveness
2 (*Med*) difficulty in breathing, tightness of the chest; **sentir ~** to find it difficult to breathe

opresivo ADJ oppressive

opresor(a) Ⓐ ADJ oppressive
Ⓑ SM/F oppressor

oprimente ADJ oppressive

oprimir ▸conjug 3a◂ VT 1 (= *apretar*) [+ *objeto*] to squeeze, press, exert pressure on; [+ *gas*] to compress; **la blusa me estaba oprimiendo el cuello** the blouse was too tight on my neck
2 [+ *botón, tecla*] to press
3 [+ *pueblo, nación*] (= *tiranizar*) to oppress; (= *cargar*) to burden, weigh down; (= *aplastar*) to crush

oprobio SM (*frm*) opprobrium (*frm*), ignominy

oprobioso ADJ (*frm*) opprobrious (*frm*), ignominious

optar ▸conjug 1a◂ VI 1 (*gen*) to choose, decide; **~ entre** to choose *o* decide between; **~ por** to choose, decide on, opt for; **~ por hacer algo** to choose to do sth, opt to do sth
2 **~ a** to compete for; **~ a un premio** to compete for a prize; **(poder) ~ a** to (have the right to) apply for *or* go in for; **ellos no pueden ~ a las becas** they are not entitled to apply for the scholarships

optativa SF (*Educ*) option, elective (*EEUU*)

optativamente ADV optionally

optativo Ⓐ ADJ 1 (= *opcional*) optional

➤ LENGUA Y USO: **opinar B1** 33.1 **opinión** 29.2, 33.1, 33.2, 34.5, 38.1, 53.3, 53.5 **oponer B** 41

2 (*Ling*) optative
Ⓑ SM (*Ling*) optative

óptica SF 1 (= *ciencia*) optics *sing*
2 (= *tienda*) optician's
3 (= *punto de vista*) viewpoint, point of view; **desde esta ~** from this point of view

óptico/a Ⓐ ADJ [*instrumentos, fibra*] optical; [*nervio*] optic; **fue sólo una ilusión óptica** it was just an optical illusion
Ⓑ SM/F optician

óptico-cinético SM light show

optimación SF optimization

óptimamente ADV ideally

optimar ▸conjug 1a◂ VT to optimize

optimismo SM optimism ► **optimismo cauto, optimismo matizado** cautious optimism

optimista Ⓐ ADJ optimistic, hopeful
Ⓑ SMF optimist

optimización SF optimization

optimizar ▸conjug 1f◂ VT to optimize

óptimo Ⓐ ADJ ideal, optimum *antes de s*; **condiciones óptimas para la navegación a vela** ideal *o* optimum conditions for sailing; **hemos obtenido ~s resultados con este producto** we've had top *o* the best results with this product
Ⓑ SM ► **óptimo de población** (*Econ*) optimum population

optometrista SMF optometrist

opuesto Ⓐ PP *de* **oponer**
Ⓑ ADJ 1 [*ángulo, lado*] opposite; **están en el extremo ~ de la ciudad** they are on the opposite side of town; **chocó con un coche que venía en dirección opuesta** he crashed into a car coming in the opposite direction
2 (*Dep*) [*equipo*] opposing
3 [*intereses, versiones*] conflicting; **tenemos gustos ~s** we have very different tastes
4 **ser ~ a algo** to be opposed to sth

opugnar ▸conjug 1a◂ VT to attack

opulencia SF 1 (= *lujo*) luxury; (= *riqueza*) opulence, affluence; **vivir en la ~** to live in luxury; **sociedad de la ~** affluent society
2 (= *abundancia*) **la ~ de sus cabellos** the luxuriance of her hair; **la ~ de sus carnes** her abundant *o* ample flesh (*liter o hum*)

opulento ADJ 1 (= *lujoso*) luxurious; (= *rico*) opulent, affluent
2 (= *abundante*) abundant

opuncia SF (*Méx*) prickly pear

opus SM (*Mús*) opus

opúsculo SM tract, brief treatise

OPUS DEI

The **Opus Dei**, *also referred to as* **la Obra**, *is an influential Catholic association formed in 1928 by the Spaniard José María Escrivá de Balaguer with the aim of spreading Christian principles in society. It has a a direct link to the Vatican by virtue of a special "Personal Prelature" granted by John Paul II in 1982, which in practice means that it enjoys complete independence from local diocesan authorities. During the Franco era members of the* **Opus** *formed the intellectual backbone of the régime, and the technocrats who engineered the "economic miracle" of the 1950s and 60s were drawn largely from its number. Members of the* **Opus** *are particularly well-represented in educational circles: the universities of Pamplona in Spain and Piura in Peru are run by it.*

opusdeísta SMF member of Opus Dei

OPV SF ABR (= **Oferta Pública de Venta (de acciones)**) *share offer*

oquedad SF 1 (= *cavidad*) hollow, cavity
2 [*de escrito, habla*] emptiness, hollowness
3 (= *vacío*) void

oquedal SM wood of grown timber, plantation

ORA SF ABR = **Operación de Regulación de Aparcamientos**

ora ADV (*frm*) **~ A, ~ B** (*uso temporal*) now A, now B; (= *a veces*) sometimes A, sometimes B

oración SF 1 (*Rel*) prayer; **oraciones por la paz** prayers for peace; **estar en ~** to be at prayer
2 (*Ling*) sentence; **partes de la ~** parts of speech ► **oración compuesta** complex sentence ► **oración directa** direct speech ► **oración indirecta** indirect speech, reported speech ► **oración subordinada** subordinate clause
3 (= *discurso*) oration (*frm*), speech; **pronunciar una ~** to make a speech ► **oración fúnebre** funeral oration
4 (*LAm*) (= *invocación*) pagan invocation, magic charm

oracional ADJ sentence *antes de s*

oráculo SM oracle

orador(a) SM/F speaker, orator (*frm*)

oral ADJ oral; **por vía ~** (*Med*) orally

órale* EXCL (*Méx*) (= *¡venga!*) come on!; (= *¡oiga!*) hey!

orangután SM orangutan

orante Ⓐ ADJ **actitud ~** kneeling position, attitude of prayer
Ⓑ SMF (= *persona*) worshipper, person at prayer

orar ▸conjug 1a◂ VI 1 (*Rel*) to pray (**a** to; **por** for)
2 (= *disertar*) to speak, make a speech

orate SMF lunatic

orático ADJ (*CAm*) crazy, lunatic

oratoria SF oratory; **concurso de ~** public speaking competition

oratorio Ⓐ ADJ oratorical
Ⓑ SM (*Mús*) oratorio; (*Rel*) oratory, chapel

orbe SM 1 (= *globo*) orb, sphere
2 (= *mundo*) world; **en todo el ~** all over the world *o* globe

órbita SF 1 (*gen*) orbit; **entrar en ~ alrededor de la luna** to go into orbit round the moon; **estar en ~** to be in orbit; **poner en ~** to put in orbit; **está fuera de su ~ de acción** it's outside his field
2 (*Anat*) (*ocular*) socket, eye-socket

orbital ADJ orbital

orbitar ▸conjug 1a◂ VT to orbit

orca SF killer whale

Órcadas SFPL Orkneys, Orkney Islands

órdago: **de ~*** ADJ (*gen*) fantastic; (*pey*) awful, tremendous*; **tienen un yate de ~** they've got a fantastic yacht; **se cogieron una borrachera de ~** they got well and truly drunk

ordalías SFPL (*Hist*) ordeal *sing*, trial *sing* by ordeal

orden Ⓐ SM 1 (*en colocación, sucesión*) 1·1 (*con objetos, personas*) order; **fueron archivados por ~ alfabético** they were filed alphabetically *o* in alphabetical order; **se fueron sentando por ~ de llegada** they sat down in order of arrival; **por ~ de antigüedad** in order of seniority; **por ~ cronológico** in chronological order; **por ~ de importancia** in order of importance; **poner ~ en algo** to sort sth out; **el ministro supo poner ~ en el departamento** the minister managed to sort out *o* put some order into the department; **los policías trataban de poner ~ en aquel caos de tráfico** the police attempted to sort out the traffic chaos; **voy a poner ~ en mi mesa** I'm going to tidy up my desk
1·2 **en ~** in order; **todo en ~, mi capitán** everything is in order, captain; **en ~ de combate** in battle order; **poner en ~** [+ *papeles, documentos*] to sort out; **en unas cuantas horas consiguieron poner todas sus cosas en ~** in a few hours they managed to sort everything out; **poner en ~ las ideas** to sort out one's ideas; ✦*MODISMOS* **poner la casa en ~** to put one's house in order; **sin ~ ni concierto** without rhyme or reason
► **orden del día** agenda ► **orden natural** natural order ► **orden sucesorio** order of succession
2 (*tb* **~ social**) order; **el ~ establecido** the established order; **las fuerzas del ~** the forces of law and order; **llamar al ~** to call to order; **mantener el ~** to keep order; **restablecer el ~** to restore *o* reestablish order ► **orden público** public order, law and order; **fueron detenidos por alterar el ~ público** they were arrested for breach of the peace *o* for disturbing the peace
3 (= *tipo*) nature; **motivos de ~ moral** moral reasons; **en otro ~ de cosas …** at the same time …, meanwhile …; **de primer ~** [*figura*] leading; [*factor*] of prime importance, prime; **una figura política de primer ~** a leading political figure; **un pensador de primer ~** a first-rate thinker; **un problema de primer ~** a major problem; **en todos los órdenes** on all fronts
4 **del ~ de** in the order of, in the region of; **el coste sería del ~ de diez millones de dólares** the cost would be in the order *o* region of ten million dollars; **necesitamos del ~ de 1.500 euros para comprarlo** we need approximately 1,500 euros to buy it
5 **en ~ a** (= *con miras a*) with a view to; (= *en cuanto a*) with regard to; **en ~ a hacer algo** in order to do sth
6 (*Arquit*) order ► **orden corintio** Corinthian order ► **orden dórico** Doric order ► **orden jónico** Ionic order
7 (*Biol*) order
8 (*Rel*) (*tb* **~ sacerdotal**) ordination
Ⓑ SF 1 (= *mandato*) order; **¡es una ~!** (and) that's an order!; **tenemos órdenes de no dejar pasar a nadie** we are under orders not to let anybody through; **dar una ~ a algn** to give sb an order, order sb; **dar (la) ~ de hacer algo** to give the order to do sth; **hasta nueva ~** until further notice; **por ~ de** by order of; **fue encarcelado por ~ del juez** he was imprisoned by order of the judge; ✦*MODISMO* **estar a la ~ del día**: **los robos están a la ~ del día en esta zona** robberies have become the norm in this area; **en los setenta llevar coleta estaba a la ~ del día** in the seventies ponytails were the latest thing ► **orden de allanamiento** (*LAm*) search war-

rant ► **orden de arresto, orden de búsqueda y captura** arrest warrant ► **orden de citación** (*Méx*), **orden de comparación** (*Méx*) summons, subpoena (*EEUU*) ► **orden de desalojo** eviction order ► **orden de detención** arrest warrant ► **orden del día** (*Mil*) order of the day ► **orden de registro** search warrant ► **orden judicial** court order ► **orden ministerial** ministerial order, ministerial decree

[2] **a la ~** [2·1] (*Mil*) yes, sir!

[2·2] (*LAm*) (*en tienda*) what can I get you?; (= *no hay de qué*) you're welcome, don't mention it!; **estoy a la ~ para lo que necesites** if there is anything you need, just ask

[2·3] **a las órdenes de algn** (*Mil*) at sb's command; (*en la policía*) under sb's instructions *o* orders; (*en otros trabajos*) under sb; **el personal que estará a las órdenes del nuevo director** the staff who will be working under the new director; **¡a sus órdenes!** (*Mil*) yes sir; (*esp LAm*) at your service

[3] (*Mil, Hist, Rel*) (= *institución*) order; **la Orden de Calatrava** the Order of Calatrava; **la Orden de San Benito** the Benedictine Order ► **orden de caballería** order of knighthood ► **orden militar** military order ► **orden monástica** monastic order ► **orden religiosa** religious order

[4] **órdenes** (*Rel*) orders ► **órdenes mayores** major orders ► **órdenes menores** minor orders ► **órdenes sagradas** holy orders

[5] (*Com, Fin*) order; (*Méx*) (= *pedido*) order; **cheques a la ~ de Suárez** cheques (to be made) payable to Suárez ► **orden bancaria** banker's order ► **orden de compra** purchase order ► **orden de pago** money order

[6] (*Méx*) (= *ración*) dish

ordenación SF [1] (= *colocación*) (*estado*) order, arrangement; (*acción*) ordering, arranging ► **ordenación del territorio, ordenación territorial** town and country planning ► **ordenación del tráfico** traffic planning ► **ordenación urbana** town planning

[2] (*Rel*) ordination

ordenada SF ordinate

ordenadamente ADV [*entrar, salir*] in an orderly fashion; [*trabajar*] in an organized *o* ordered manner; **evacuaron ~ a los heridos** they evacuated the wounded in an orderly fashion; **~ colocados** neatly arranged

ordenado ADJ [1] (= *en orden*) [*habitación, escritorio*] tidy; [*oficina*] well-organized, ordered; **tiene toda la casa muy limpia y ordenada** she keeps the house very clean and tidy; **llevan una vida normal y ordenada** they lead a normal, ordered *o* orderly life; **los niños entraron de forma ordenada en el museo** the children entered the museum in an orderly fashion

[2] [*persona*] (*al colocar algo*) tidy; (*en el trabajo*) organized

[3] (*Rel*) ordained, in holy orders

ordenador SM computer; **pasar a ~** to type up on computer ► **ordenador analógico** analogue computer, analog computer (*EEUU*) ► **ordenador central** mainframe computer ► **ordenador de gestión** business computer ► **ordenador de (sobre)mesa** desktop computer ► **ordenador doméstico** home computer ► **ordenador personal** personal computer ► **ordenador portátil** (*gen*) portable computer; (*pequeño*) laptop computer ► **ordenador torre** tower unit ► **ordenador transportable** portable computer

ordenamiento SM [1] (*Jur*) (= *leyes*) legislation; **el nuevo ~ eléctrico** the new legislation on electricity ► **ordenamiento constitucional** constitution ► **ordenamiento jurídico** legal system

[2] (*al colocar algo*) ordering, arranging

ordenancista SMF disciplinarian, martinet

ordenando SM (*Rel*) ordinand

ordenanza Ⓐ SF (= *decreto*) ordinance, decree; **honores de ~** official honours; **ser de ~** to be the rule ► **ordenanzas municipales** bylaws

Ⓑ SMF [1] (*en oficina*) messenger

[2] (= *bedel*) porter

[3] (*Mil*) orderly

ordenar ▸conjug 1a◂ Ⓐ VT [1] (= *poner en orden*) (*siguiendo un sistema*) to arrange; (*colocando en su sitio*) to tidy; (*Inform*) to sort; **hay que ~ los recibos por fechas** we have to put the receipts in order of date, we have to arrange the receipts by date; **voy a ~ mis libros** I'm going to sort out *o* organize my books; **ordenó los relatos cronológicamente** he arranged the stories chronologically *o* in chronological order; **nunca ordena sus papeles** he never tidies his paperwork; **~ sus asuntos** to put one's affairs in order; **~ su vida** to put *o* get one's life in order

[2] (= *mandar*) to order; **la juez ordenó su detención** the judge ordered his arrest; **les habían ordenado que siguieran al vehículo** they had been ordered to follow the vehicle; **un tono de ordeno y mando** a dictatorial tone

[3] (*Rel*) to ordain; **fue ordenado sacerdote en octubre** he was ordained as a priest in October

Ⓑ **ordenarse** VPR (*Rel*) to be ordained

ordeña SF (*LAm*) milking

ordeñadero SM milking pail

ordeñadora SF milking machine

ordeñar ▸conjug 1a◂ VT [+ *vaca, oveja*] to milk; [+ *aceitunas*] to harvest

ordeño SM, **ordeñe** SM (*Caribe*) [*de leche*] milking; [*de aceitunas*] harvest

órdiga‡ SF **¡la ~!** (*Esp*) bloody hell!‡

ordinal ADJ, SM ordinal

ordinariamente ADV ordinarily, usually

ordinariez SF [1] (= *cualidad*) coarseness, vulgarity, commonness

[2] **una ~** a coarse remark

ordinario Ⓐ ADJ [1] (= *normal*) ordinary; **de ~** usually; **de ~ coge el autobús para ir a trabajar** he usually takes the bus to work

[2] (= *vulgar*) [*persona*] common; [*comportamiento, modales*] coarse; **son gente muy ordinaria** they're very common people; **sólo cuenta chistes ~s** he only tells crude jokes

Ⓑ SM [1] (*Rel*) ordinary ► **ordinario de la misa** Ordinary of the mass

[2] (†) (= *gastos*) daily household expenses *pl*

[3] (†) (= *recadero*) carrier, delivery man

ordinograma SM (*gen*) organization chart; [*de flujo*] flowchart

orear ▸conjug 1a◂ Ⓐ VT [+ *casa, habitación*] to air

Ⓑ **orearse** VPR [1] [*ropa*] to air

[2] [*persona*] to get some fresh air, take a breather

orégano SM [1] (= *hierba*) oregano

[2] (*Méx*‡) (= *marihuana*) grass‡

oreja Ⓐ SF [1] (*Anat*) ear; ✦*MODISMOS* **aguzar las ~s** to prick up one's ears; **calentar las ~s a algn** (= *pegar*) to box sb's ears; (= *irritar*) to get on sb's nerves; (= *despachar*) to send sb away with a flea in his ear*; **chafar la ~** to have a kip*; **descubrir** *o* **enseñar la ~** (= *traicionarse*) to give o.s. away, show one's true colours; (= *aparecer*) to show up; **con las ~s gachas** with one's tail between one's legs, crestfallen; **estar hasta las ~s de algo** to be up to one's ears *o* eyes in sth*; **hacer ~s** to listen to sense, see sense; **hacer ~s de mercader** to turn a deaf ear; **pegar la ~ (en algo)** to eavesdrop (on sth), listen in (on *o* to sth); **planchar ~**‡ = **chafar la oreja**; **ponerle a algn las ~s coloradas** to embarrass sb; **sonreír de ~ a ~** (*con alegría*) to beam; (*con autosatisfacción*) to grin from ear to ear; **verle las ~s al lobo** to get a sudden fright; **vérsele la ~ a algn***: **se le ve la ~** you can see his little game*; *ver tb* **tirón**[1] **1**

[2] (= *pieza*) [*de sillón*] wing; [*de zapato*] tab; [*de jarra*] handle; [*de envase de zumo, leche*] flap; [*de martillo*] claw; [*de libro*] flap; [*de tambor*] lug

[3] (*LAm*) (= *curiosidad*) curiosity; (= *escucha*) eavesdropping; (= *prudencia*) caution

Ⓑ SMF (‡) (= *soplón*) grass*, fink (*EEUU**), informer

orejano/a Ⓐ ADJ [1] (*Andes, Cono Sur*) [*ganado*] unbranded, ownerless

[2] (*LAm*) (= *tímido*) shy, easily scared; (= *huraño*) unsociable

[3] (*Caribe*) (= *cauteloso*) cautious

Ⓑ SM/F (*CAm, Caribe*) peasant, countryman/countrywoman

orejear ▸conjug 1a◂ VI [1] (*LAm*) (= *escuchar*) to eavesdrop

[2] (*Cono Sur**) (*Naipes*) to show one's cards one by one

[3] (*Andes, Caribe, Cono Sur*) (= *sospechar*) to be suspicious, be distrustful

orejera SF [1] (*para el frío*) earflap

[2] (*Agr*) mouldboard, moldboard (*EEUU*)

orejero Ⓐ ADJ (*) [1] (*LAm*) (= *receloso*) suspicious; (= *prudente*) cautious

[2] (*Cono Sur*) (= *chismoso*) telltale, tattletale (*EEUU*)

[3] (*Andes*) (= *rencoroso*) malicious

Ⓑ SM [1] [*de sillón*] wing chair

[2] (*Cono Sur**) (= *hombre de confianza*) boss's right-hand man

orejeta SF (*Téc*) lug

orejón Ⓐ ADJ [1] (*esp LAm*) = **orejudo**

[2] (*CAm, Méx*) (= *tosco*) rough, coarse

[3] (*Andes*) (= *distraído*) absent-minded

Ⓑ SM [1] (= *tirón*) pull on the ear

[2] [*de fruta*] *strip of dried peach/apricot*

[3] (*Andes Hist*) *Inca officer*

[4] (*Andes Med*) goitre, goiter (*EEUU*)

[5] (*Andes*) (= *vaquero*) herdsman; (= *llanero*) plainsman

[6] (*Méx*‡) (= *marido*) cuckold

orejonas SFPL (*Andes, Caribe*) big spurs

orejudo ADJ big-eared, with big ears

orensano/a Ⓐ ADJ of/from Orense

Ⓑ SM/F native/inhabitant of Orense; **los ~s** the people of Orense

Orense SM Orense

orfanato SM, **orfanatorio** SM (*LAm*) orphanage

orfandad SF [1] (= *estado*) orphanage (*frm*)
[2] (= *desamparo*) helplessness, destitution

orfebre SMF silversmith, goldsmith

orfebrería SF [1] (= *oficio*) silversmithing, goldsmithing, craftsmanship in precious metals
[2] (= *objetos*) [*de oro*] gold articles *pl*; [*de plata*] silverware

orfelinato SM orphanage

Orfeo SM Orpheus

orfeón SM choral society

organdí SM organdie

orgánicamente ADV organically

orgánico ADJ organic; *ver tb* **ley 1**

organigrama SM [*de entidad, empresa*] organization chart; (*Inform*) flow chart

organillero SM organ grinder

organillo SM barrel organ, hurdy-gurdy

organismo SM [1] (*Biol*) organism
[2] (*Pol*) (*gen*) organization; (= *institución*) body, institution; (= *agencia*) agency ▸ **organismo de sondaje** polling organization ▸ **Organismo Internacional de Energía Atómica** International Atomic Energy Agency ▸ **organismo rector** governing body, Board of Trustees (*EEUU*) ▸ **organismos de gobierno** organs of government, government bodies

organista SMF organist

organito SM (*Cono Sur*) = **organillo**

organización SF organization ▸ **Organización de Estados Americanos** Organization of American States ▸ **Organización de las Naciones Unidas** United Nations Organization ▸ **organización no gubernamental** non-governmental organization; *ver tb* **OPEP**

organizadamente ADV in an organized way

organizador(a) Ⓐ ADJ organizing; **el comité ~** the organizing committee
Ⓑ SM/F organizer

organizar ▸conjug 1f◂ Ⓐ VT [1] [+ *fiesta, espectáculo*] to organize
[2] (*) [+ *jaleo, pelea*] **los marineros ~on un auténtico alboroto** the sailors created *o* made a real commotion; **¡menuda has organizado!** you've really stirred things up, haven't you!
Ⓑ **organizarse** VPR [1] [*persona*] to organize o.s., get o.s. organized; **te tienes que ~ mejor** you need to organize yourself better, you need to get yourself better organized
[2] (*) [*jaleo, pelea*] **se organizó una pelea tremenda** there was a terrific punch-up*

organizativo ADJ organizational

órgano SM [1] (*Anat, Mec*) organ ▸ **órgano del habla** speech organ ▸ **órgano sexual** sexual organ, sex organ
[2] (*Mús*) organ ▸ **órgano eléctrico** electric organ
[3] (= *medio*) means, medium ▸ **órgano de enlace** means of communication

organofosfato SM organophosphate

orgásmico ADJ orgasmic

orgasmo SM orgasm

orgía SF orgy

orgiástico ADJ orgiastic

orgullo SM [1] (= *satisfacción*) pride; **eres el ~ de la familia** you're the pride of the family; **me llena de ~ ver crecer a mis hijos** it makes me really proud to see my children growing up
[2] (= *altanería*) pride; **su ~ le costará caro** his pride will cost him dear; **su ~ le impedía disculparse** he was too proud to say sorry

orgullosamente ADV proudly

orgulloso ADJ [1] (= *satisfecho*) proud; **estar ~ de algo/algn** to be proud of sth/sb; **estar ~ de hacer algo** to be proud to do sth
[2] (= *altanero*) proud; **es muy orgullosa y nunca saluda** she's very proud, she never says hello

oricio SM sea-urchin

orientable ADJ adjustable

orientación SF [1] [*de casa*] aspect; [*de habitación*] position, orientation; (= *dirección*) direction; **una casa con ~ sur** a house facing south; **la ~ actual del partido** the party's present course *o* position ▸ **orientación sexual** sexual orientation
[2] (= *guía*) guidance, orientation; **me ayudó en la ~ bibliográfica** he helped me with bibliographical information; **lo hizo para mi ~** he did it for my guidance ▸ **orientación profesional** careers guidance ▸ **orientación vocacional** vocational guidance
[3] (*Dep*) orienteering

orientador(a) SM/F careers adviser, (school) counselor (*EEUU*)

oriental Ⓐ ADJ [1] [*persona*] oriental; [*región, zona*] eastern
[2] (*Cono Sur*) (= *uruguayo*) Uruguayan; **la Banda Oriental** Uruguay
[3] (*Cuba*) of/from Oriente province
Ⓑ SMF [1] (= *persona de Oriente*) oriental
[2] (*Cono Sur*) (= *uruguayo*) Uruguayan
[3] (*Cuba*) native/inhabitant of Oriente province; **los ~es** the people of Oriente province

orientalismo SM orientalism

orientalista ADJ, SMF orientalist

orientar ▸conjug 1a◂ Ⓐ VT [1] (= *situar*) **~ algo hacia** *o* **a algo** to position sth to face sth; **~on la parabólica hacia el norte** they positioned the satellite dish to face north, they put the satellite dish facing north; **la casa está orientada hacia el suroeste** the house faces south-west, the house looks south-west
[2] (= *enfocar*) to direct; **tenemos que ~ nuestros esfuerzos hacia un aumento de la productividad** we must direct our efforts towards improving productivity; **hay que ~ las investigaciones en otro sentido** we shall have to follow a different path of enquiry; **cómics orientados a un público adulto** comics oriented *o* targeted at adult readers
[3] (= *guiar*) to guide; **me ha orientado en la materia** he has guided me through the subject, he has given me guidance about the subject
[4] (*Náut*) [+ *vela*] to trim
Ⓑ **orientarse** VPR [1] (= *encontrar el camino*) to get one's bearings; **es difícil ~se en esta ciudad** it's hard to get one's bearings in this city, it's hard to find one's way around in this city
[2] (= *tender*) **su estilo se orienta hacia lo abstracto** his style tends towards the abstract

orientativamente ADV by way of guidance

orientativo ADJ guiding, illustrative; **los pesos reseñados son puramente ~s** the weights shown are for guidance only

oriente SM [1] (= *este*) east
[2] **el Oriente** the Orient, the East; **el Cercano** *o* **Próximo Oriente** the Near East; **el Extremo** *o* **Lejano Oriente** the Far East; **el Oriente Medio** the Middle East
[3] (= *viento*) east wind
[4] [*de masones*] masonic lodge

orificación SF gold filling

orificar ▸conjug 1g◂ VT [+ *muela*] to fill with gold

orificio SM (= *agujero*) orifice (*frm*), hole; (*para aire, gas*) vent ▸ **orificio de bala** bullet hole ▸ **orificio de entrada** (*en herida*) point of entry ▸ **orificio de salida** (*en herida*) point of exit

origen SM [1] (= *causa, principio*) origin; **el ~ del hombre** the origin of man; **un trabajo de investigación sobre los orígenes del flamenco** a piece of research on the origins of flamenco; **la policía está investigando el ~ de las llamadas telefónicas** the police are investigating the source of the phone calls; **dar ~ a** [+ *rumores, movimiento, organización*] to give rise to; **esta situación ha dado ~ a múltiples procesos judiciales** this situation has given rise to numerous lawsuits; **el Big Bang, la gran explosión que dio ~ al Universo** the Big Bang, the great explosion that created the Universe; **de ~: proteínas de ~ animal/vegetal** animal/vegetable proteins; **problemas de ~ psicológico** psychological problems, problems of psychological origin; **un deporte de ~ inglés** a sport of English origin, a sport originally from England; **desde sus orígenes** [*de movimiento, corriente*] from its origins; [*de ciudad, país*] from the very beginning, right from the start; **una historia de la medicina desde sus orígenes hasta nuestros días** a history of medicine from its origins up to the present day; **en su ~** originally; **la obra fue escrita en su ~ para cuatro voces** the work was originally written for four voices; **en su ~ la organización no tenía más de veinte miembros** at the outset *o* at the start *o* originally the organization had no more than twenty members; **tener su ~ en** [+ *lugar*] to originate in; [+ *inicio*] to originate from; [+ *fecha*] to date back to; **la paella tuvo su ~ en Valencia** paella had its origin *o* originated in Valencia; **el vals tiene su ~ en las danzas austriacas "Ländler"** the waltz originates *o* comes from Austrian Ländler dances; **el fuego tuvo su ~ en un cortocircuito** the fire was caused by a short circuit; **tiene su ~ en el siglo XV** it dates back to the 15th century
[2] [*de persona*] background, origins *pl*; **son gente de ~ humilde** they are from a humble background, they are of humble origins; **sabemos poco de sus orígenes** we know little about his background; **de ~ argentino/árabe** of Argentinian/Arab origin *o* (*más frm*) extraction; **país de ~** country of origin, native country
[3] **en ~** (*Com, Fin*) at source; **el reciclado de residuos en ~** the recycling of waste at source; **este impuesto se retiene en ~** this tax is deducted at source

original Ⓐ ADJ [1] (= *inicial*) [*idea, documento, idioma*] original; [*edición*] first; **van a intentar devolver la zona a su estado ~** they are going to try to return the area to its original state; *ver tb* **pecado 1**

2 (= *novedoso*) original; **el guión tiene poco de ~** the script is not very original

3 (= *raro*) unusual, original; (= *extravagante*) eccentric; **él siempre tiene que ser tan ~** (*iró*) he always has to be so different

4 (= *creativo*) original; **es un escritor muy ~** he's a very original writer

5 (= *procedente*) **ser ~ de** [*planta, animal*] to be native to

Ⓑ SM 1 (= *modelo*) original; **no se parece en nada al ~** it doesn't look anything like the original

2 (*Tip*) (*tb* **~ de imprenta**) manuscript, original, copy

originalidad SF 1 (= *novedad*) originality

2 (= *excentricidad*) eccentricity

originalmente ADV originally

originar ▸conjug 1a◂ Ⓐ VT to cause; **el terremoto originó la estampida de los elefantes** the earthquake caused the elephants to stampede; **la lucha de clases originó el conflicto** the class struggle led to *o* gave rise to the conflict; **están buscando las causas que ~on el fuego** they're looking for the cause of the fire

Ⓑ **originarse** VPR [*enfermedad, crisis, conflicto, incendio*] to start, originate; [*universo*] to begin; **la saeta se origina en la antigua música religiosa cristiana** "saeta" originates in ancient Christian religious music; **casi un 30% de la deuda externa del Tercer Mundo se origina por la compra de armas** nearly 30% of foreign debt in the Third World results from arms purchases

originariamente ADV originally

originario ADJ 1 (= *inicial*) original; **el sentido ~ del término** the original sense of the term; **en su forma originaria** in its original form; **país ~** country of origin, native country

2 **~ de** [*animal, planta*] native to; [*persona*] from; **el lichi es ~ de China** lychees originated in China, the lychee is native to China; **un joven ~ de Cabo Verde** a young man from Cape Verde; **los escoceses son ~s de Irlanda** the Scottish originally came from Ireland

orilla SF 1 (= *borde*) [*de río*] bank; [*de lago*] shore, edge; [*de mesa*] edge; [*de taza*] rim, lip; **la ~ del mar** the seashore; **a ~s de** on the banks of; **vive ~ de mi casa*** he lives next door to me

2 (*Cos*) (= *orillo*) selvage; (= *dobladillo*) hem

3 (*LAm*) (= *acera*) pavement, sidewalk (*EEUU*)

4 ✦**MODISMO de ~** (*Caribe*) (= *sin importancia*) trivial, of no account; (= *sin valor*) worthless

5 **orillas** (*LAm*) (= *arrabales*) outlying districts; (*pey*) poor quarter *sing*; (*Méx*) shanty town *sing*

orillar ▸conjug 1a◂ VT 1 [+ *lago, bosque*] to skirt, go round

2 (= *esquivar*) [+ *dificultad*] to avoid, get round; [+ *tema*] to touch briefly on

3 (= *arreglar*) [+ *negocio*] to put in order, tidy up; [+ *obstáculo*] to overcome

4 (= *concluir*) to wind up

5 (*Cos*) to edge (**de** with), trim (**de** with)

6 **~ a algn a hacer algo** (*Méx*) to lead sb to do sth

orillero/a (*LAm*) Ⓐ ADJ (*gen*) lower-class, working-class; (= *arrabalero*) common, vulgar

Ⓑ SM/F (*gen*) lower-class person, working-class person; (= *arrabalero*) common person, vulgar person

orillo SM selvage

orín¹ SM rust; **tomarse de ~** to get rusty

orín² SM, **orina** SF urine

orinacamas SM INV dandelion

orinal SM 1 (= *bacín*) chamber pot; [*de niños*] potty ► **orinal de cama** bedpan

2 (*Mil**) tin hat*, helmet

orinar ▸conjug 1a◂ Ⓐ VI (*gen*) to urinate

Ⓑ VT **~ sangre** to pass blood (*in the urine*)

Ⓒ **orinarse** VPR to wet o.s.; **~se en la cama** to wet one's bed; **~se encima** to wet o.s.

orines SMPL urine *sing*

Orinoco SM **el río ~** the Orinoco River

orita* (*LAm*) = **ahorita**

oriundo/a Ⓐ ADJ **~ de** [*planta, animal*] indigenous to, native to; **el melocotón, aunque ~ de China, se propagó rápidamente por el Oriente Medio** the peach, although indigenous *o* native to China, rapidly spread through the Middle East; **Pepa es oriunda de Granada** Pepa comes from *o* (*hum*) hails from Granada

Ⓑ SM/F (= *nativo*) native, inhabitant

orla SF, **orladura** SF 1 (= *borde*) [*de vestido, cuadro*] border; [*de flecos*] fringe ► **orla litoral** coastal strip

2 (= *ribete*) trimming

3 (*Educ*) (= *fotografía*) class graduation photograph

orlar ▸conjug 1a◂ VT to edge (**con, de** with), trim (**con, de** with)

ornamentación SF ornamentation, adornment

ornamental ADJ ornamental

ornamentar ▸conjug 1a◂ VT to adorn (**de** with)

ornamento SM 1 (= *adorno*) ornament, adornment

2 **ornamentos** (*Rel*) vestments; (= *cualidades*) good qualities

ornar ▸conjug 1a◂ VT to adorn (**de** with)

ornato SM adornment, decoration

ornitofauna SF birds *pl*, bird population

ornitología SF ornithology

ornitológico ADJ ornithological

ornitólogo/a SM/F ornithologist

ornitorrinco SM platypus

oro SM 1 (= *metal*) gold; **de ~** gold *antes de s*, golden (*frec liter*); **regla de ~** golden rule; **tiene una voz de ~** she has a wonderful voice; ✦**MODISMOS apalear ~** to be rolling in money; **de ~ y azul** very smart and elegant, all dressed up; **como un ~** like new; **es de ~** he's a treasure; **guardar algo como ~ en paño** to treasure sth; **hacerse de ~** to make a fortune; **prometer el ~ y el moro** to promise the moon; ✦**REFRÁN no es ~ todo lo que reluce** all that glitters is not gold ► **oro amarillo** yellow gold ► **oro batido** gold leaf ► **oro en barras** gold bars *pl*, bullion ► **oro en polvo** gold dust ► **oro laminado** rolled gold ► **oro molido** ormolu ► **oro negro** black gold, oil ► **oro viejo** old gold

2 **oros** (*Esp*) (*Naipes*) *one of the suits in the Spanish card deck, represented by gold coins*; → BARAJA ESPAÑOLA

orografía SF orography

orográfico ADJ orographical

orondo ADJ 1 (= *grueso*) [*persona*] potbellied, big-bellied; [*vasija*] rounded, potbellied

2 (= *satisfecho*) smug, self-satisfied; (= *pomposo*) pompous

3 (*LAm*) (= *sereno*) calm, serene

oropel SM tinsel; **de ~** flashy, gaudy; ✦**MODISMO gastar mucho ~** to make a pretence of being wealthy

oropéndola SF golden oriole

oroya SF (*Andes*) 1 (= *cesta*) *basket of a rope bridge*

2 (*Ferro*) funicular railway

orozuz SM liquorice

orquesta SF orchestra ► **orquesta de baile** dance band ► **orquesta de cámara** chamber orchestra ► **orquesta de cuerda** string orchestra ► **orquesta de jazz** jazz band ► **orquesta sinfónica** symphony orchestra

orquestación SF orchestration (*tb fig*)

orquestal ADJ orchestral

orquestar ▸conjug 1a◂ VT to orchestrate (*tb fig*)

orquestina SF band

orquídea SF orchid

orsay SM = **offside**

ortiga SF nettle, stinging nettle

orto¹ SM sunrise

orto²** SM (*Cono Sur*) (= *culo*) arse**, ass (*EEUU***); (= *ano*) arsehole**, asshole**

orto... PREF ortho...

ortodoncia SF orthodontics *sing*, dental orthopedics *sing* (*EEUU*)

ortodoncista SMF orthodontist

ortodoxia SF orthodoxy

ortodoxo ADJ orthodox

ortofonista SMF speech therapist

ortografía SF spelling, orthography (*frm*)

ortográfico ADJ spelling *antes de s*, orthographic(al) (*frm*); **reforma ortográfica** spelling reform

ortopeda SMF orthopaedist, orthopedist (*EEUU*)

ortopedia SF orthopaedics *sing*, orthopedics *sing* (*EEUU*)

ortopédico ADJ orthopaedic, orthopedic (*EEUU*)

ortopedista SMF orthopaedist, orthopedist (*EEUU*)

oruga SF 1 (= *gusano*) caterpillar

2 (*Bot*) rocket

3 (= *vehículo*) (*Téc*) caterpillar, caterpillar track; (*Mil*) tracked personnel carrier; **tractor de ~** caterpillar tractor

orujo SM 1 (= *bebida*) *liquor distilled from grape remains*

2 (= *restos*) marc

orza¹ SF (= *jarra*) glazed earthenware jar

orza² SF (*Náut*) luff, luffing; ✦**MODISMO ir de ~** to be on the wrong track

orzar ▸conjug 1f◂ VI (*Náut*) to luff

orzuelo SM (*Med*) stye

os¹ PRON PERS PL 1 (*directo*) you; **os quiero mucho** I love you very much; **no os oigo** I can't hear you

2 (*indirecto*) you; **os lo di** I gave it to you; **os lo compré** (= *de vosotros*) I bought it from you; (= *para vosotros*) I bought it for you; **¿os han arreglado ya el ordenador?** have they fixed the computer for you yet?

3 (*reflexivo*) yourselves; **¿os habéis hecho daño?** did you hurt yourselves?; **lavaos las**

manos wash your hands; **cuando os marchéis** when you leave; **no hace falta que os quitéis el abrigo** you don't need to take your coats off

[4] (*mutuo*) each other; **quiero que os pidáis perdón** I want you to say sorry to each other; **¿os conocéis?** have you met?, do you know each other?

os² EXCL shoo!

osa SF [1] (= *animal*) she-bear; ✦**MODISMOS** **¡anda la ~!*** what a carry-on!*; **¡la ~!*** gosh!*

[2] (*Astron*) ► **Osa Mayor** Ursa Major, Great Bear ► **Osa Menor** Ursa Minor, Little Bear

osadamente ADV daringly, boldly

osadía SF [1] (= *audacia*) daring, boldness

[2] (= *descaro*) impudence, audacity, temerity

osado ADJ [1] (= *audaz*) daring, bold

[2] (= *descarado*) impudent, audacious

osamenta SF [1] (= *esqueleto*) skeleton

[2] (= *huesos*) bones *pl*

osar ▸conjug 1a◂ VI to dare; **~ hacer algo** to dare to do sth

osario SM ossuary, charnel house

Oscar SM, **óscar** SM Oscar

oscarizado/a Ⓐ ADJ Oscar-winning

Ⓑ SM/F Oscar winner

OSCE SF ABR (= **Organización para la Seguridad y Cooperación en Europa**) OSCE

oscense Ⓐ ADJ of/from Huesca

Ⓑ SMF native/inhabitant of Huesca; **los ~s** the people of Huesca

oscilación SF [1] [*de péndulo*] swinging, swaying, oscillation

[2] [*de luz*] winking, blinking; [*de llama*] flickering

[3] [*de precios, peso, temperatura*] fluctuation

[4] [*de parecer, pensar*] hesitation, wavering

oscilador Ⓐ ADJ oscillating

Ⓑ SM oscillator

oscilante ADJ oscillating (*frm*)

oscilar ▸conjug 1a◂ VI [1] [*péndulo*] to swing, oscillate

[2] [*luz*] to wink, blink; [*llama*] to flicker

[3] [*precio, peso, temperatura*] to fluctuate (**entre** between); [*calidad, diseño*] to vary (**entre** between); [*distancia, intensidad*] to range (**entre** between); **la distancia oscila entre los 100 y 500m** the distance ranges between 100 and 500m *o* from 100 to 500m; **los precios oscilan mucho** prices are fluctuating a lot

[4] (= *dudar*) to hesitate (**entre** between), waver (**entre** between); **oscila entre la alegría y el pesimismo** his mood swings from cheerfulness to pessimism

oscilatorio ADJ oscillatory

osciloscopio SM oscilloscope

oscular ▸conjug 1a◂ VT (*liter*) to osculate (*frm, hum*), kiss

ósculo SM (*liter*) osculation (*frm, hum*), kiss

oscuramente ADV obscurely

oscurana SF [1] (*CAm*) [*de polvo*] cloud of volcanic dust

[2] (*Andes**) (= *oscuridad*) darkness

oscurantismo SM obscurantism

oscurantista ADJ, SMF obscurantist

oscurear ▸conjug 1a◂ VT, VI (*Méx*) = **oscurecer**

oscurecer ▸conjug 2d◂ Ⓐ VT [1] [+ *color, espacio*] to darken

[2] (= *quitar importancia a*) [+ *cuestión*] to confuse, cloud; [+ *rival*] to overshadow, put in the shade; [+ *fama*] to tarnish

[3] (*Arte*) to shade

Ⓑ VI, **oscurecerse** VPR to grow dark, get dark

oscurecimiento SM [1] [*de color, piel*] darkening

[2] [*de memoria*] failing

oscuridad SF [1] (= *ausencia de luz*) **tiene pánico a la ~** he's terrified of the dark; **la ~ envolvía el pueblo** the village was wrapped in darkness; **pasaba horas sentado en la ~** he would sit for hours in the dark *o* in darkness

[2] [*de texto, explicación*] obscurity; **la ~ de su prosa** the obscurity of his prose

[3] (= *anonimato*) obscurity; **salir de la ~** to emerge from obscurity

oscuro ADJ [1] (= *sin luz*) dark; **¡qué casa tan oscura!** what a dark house!

[2] [*color, cielo, día*] dark; **un hermoso azul ~** a beautiful dark blue; **tiene el pelo castaño ~** she has dark brown hair

[3] [*texto, explicación*] obscure

[4] (= *sospechoso*) **oscuras intenciones** dubious intentions, sinister intentions; **un asunto ~** a shady business

[5] (= *incierto*) [*porvenir, futuro*] uncertain; **de origen ~** of obscure origin(s)

[6] (= *poco conocido*) obscure; **un ~ escritor** an obscure writer

[7] **a oscuras** in the dark, in darkness

óseo ADJ [1] (*gen*) bony

[2] (*Med*) osseous, bone *antes de s*

osezno SM bear cub

osificación SF ossification

osificar ▸conjug 1g◂ Ⓐ VT to ossify

Ⓑ **osificarse** VPR to ossify, become ossified

-osis *ver* **Aspects of Word Formation in Spanish 2**

osito SM [1] (= *juguete*) teddy, teddy bear ► **osito de felpa**, **osito de peluche** teddy, teddy bear ► **osito panda** panda

[2] (*Cono Sur*) [*de bebé*] Babygro®

osmosis SF INV, **ósmosis** SF INV osmosis

osmótico ADJ osmotic

OSO ABR (= **oessudoeste**) WSW

oso SM bear; ✦**MODISMOS** **hacer el ~** to play the fool; **ser un ~** to be a prickly sort ► **oso blanco** polar bear ► **oso colmenero** (*LAm*) anteater ► **oso de las cavernas** cave bear ► **oso de peluche** teddy bear ► **oso gris** grizzly, grizzly bear ► **oso hormiguero** anteater ► **oso marsupial** koala bear ► **oso panda** panda ► **oso pardo** brown bear ► **oso perezoso** sloth

Ostende SM Ostend

ostensible ADJ obvious, evident; **hacer algo ~** to make sth quite clear; (*LAm*) to express sth, register sth; **procurar no hacerse ~** to keep out of the way, lie low

ostensiblemente ADV [1] (= *evidentemente*) obviously, evidently

[2] (= *visiblemente*) visibly, openly; **se mostró ~ conmovido** he was visibly moved

ostensorio SM monstrance

ostenta SF (*Andes, Cono Sur*) = **ostentación**

ostentación SF [1] (= *exhibición*) ostentation

[2] (= *acto*) show, display; **hacer ~ de** to flaunt, parade, show off

ostentar ▸conjug 1a◂ VT [1] (= *exhibir*) to show; (= *hacer gala de*) to flaunt, parade, show off

[2] (= *tener*) [+ *poderes legales*] to have, possess; [+ *cargo, título*] to have, hold; **~ el título mundial en patinaje sobre hielo** to hold the world title in ice-skating; **ostenta todavía las cicatrices** he still has *o* carries the scars

ostentativo ADJ ostentatious

ostentosamente ADV ostentatiously

ostentoso ADJ ostentatious

osteo... PREF osteo...

osteoartritis SF INV osteoarthritis

osteópata SMF osteopath

osteopatía SF osteopathy

osteoporosis SF INV osteoporosis

osti: EXCL = **hostia**

ostión SM (*esp LAm*) large oyster

ostionería SF (*LAm*) (= *tienda*) sea food shop; (= *restaurante*) sea food restaurant; (= *bar*) oyster bar

ostra Ⓐ SF [1] (*Zool*) oyster ► **ostra perlera** pearl oyster; *ver tb* **aburrir B**

[2] (= *persona*) (*pesado*) bore; (*huraño*) shrinking violet; (= *cliente fijo*) regular; **es una ~** he's a fixture here

Ⓑ **ostras*** EXCL (*euf*) (*denota sorpresa*) crikey!*; (*denota enfado o desagrado*) sugar!*, shoot! (*EEUU**)

ostracismo SM ostracism

ostracista ADJ discriminatory

ostral SM oyster bed

ostrería SF oyster bar

ostrero SM [1] (= *lugar*) oyster bed

[2] (*Orn*) oystercatcher

osuno ADJ bear-like

OTAN SF ABR (= **Organización del Tratado del Atlántico Norte**) NATO

otánico ADJ NATO *antes de s*

otanista SMF supporter of NATO

otario/a* (*Cono Sur*) Ⓐ ADJ gullible

Ⓑ SM/F sucker*

OTASE SF ABR (= **Organización del Tratado del Sudeste Asiático**) SEATO

otate SM (*Méx*) (= *caña*) cane, stick; (= *junco*) reed, rush

-ote, -ota *ver* **Aspects of Word Formation in Spanish 2**

oteadero SM look-out post

otear ▸conjug 1a◂ VT [1] [+ *horizonte*] to scan

[2] [+ *objeto lejano*] (*desde arriba*) to look down on, look down over; (*de forma poco clara*) to make out, glimpse

[3] (= *espiar*) to watch (from above), spy on

[4] (= *examinar*) to examine, look into

Otelo SM Othello

otero SM low hill, hillock, knoll

OTI SF ABR (*TV*) = **Organización de la Televisión Iberoamericana**

otitis SF INV inflammation of the ear, otitis (*frm*) ► **otitis media** inflammation of the middle ear, otitis media (*frm*)

otomano/a (*Hist*) Ⓐ ADJ Ottoman

Ⓑ SM/F Ottoman; **los ~s** the Ottomans

otomía SF (*Méx*) atrocity; **hacer ~s*** to get up to no good, misbehave

Otón SM Otto

otoñada SF autumn, autumn time, fall (*EEUU*)

otoñal ADJ autumnal, autumn *antes de s*, fall *antes de s* (*EEUU*)

otoño SM (= *estación*) autumn, fall (*EEUU*); **en el ~ de la vida** in the autumn of one's life

otorgamiento SM 1 (= *concesión*) [*de privilegio, ayuda, permiso, independencia*] granting; [*de premio*] awarding
2 (*Jur*) (= *acción*) execution; (= *documento*) legal document, deed; **~ de una escritura** execution of a deed

otorgar ▸conjug 1h◂ VT 1 (= *conceder*) [+ *privilegio, ayuda, independencia, permiso*] to grant (**a** to); [+ *premio*] to award (**a** to); [+ *poderes, título*] to confer (**a** on); [+ *esfuerzo, tiempo*] to devote (**a** to)
2 (*Jur*) (= *ejecutar*) to execute; [+ *testamento*] to make
3 (= *consentir en*) to consent to, agree to

otoronco SM (*Andes Zool*) mountain bear

otorrino SMF ear, nose and throat specialist, ENT specialist

otorrinolaringología SF otolaryngology (*frm*), otorhinolaryngology (*frm*)

otorrinolaringólogo SMF ear, nose and throat specialist, otolaryngologist (*frm*)

otramente†† ADV in a different way, differently

otredad SF (*liter*) otherness

otro Ⓐ ADJ 1 (= *diferente*) (*en singular*) another; (*en plural*) other; **dame otra revista** give me another magazine; **necesito ~ destornillador más grande** I need a bigger screwdriver; **tengo ~s planes** I have other plans; **no puedo venir ningún ~ día** I can't come any other day; **¿tiene algún ~ modelo?** do you have any other models?; **¿hay alguna otra manera de hacerlo?** is there any other way of doing it?; **son ~s tiempos** times have changed; **de ~ modo** otherwise; **le pago, de ~ modo no lo haría** I'm paying her, otherwise she wouldn't do it; **está en otra parte** it's somewhere else; **por otra parte** on the other hand; **por otra parte, he de admitir que me gusta** on the other hand, I have to admit I like it; **~ tanto**: **Juan me insultó y Antonio hizo ~ tanto** Juan insulted me and so did Antonio; **ayer subió tres puntos y hoy aumentará ~ tanto** it went up by three points yesterday and will rise by the same amount today; *ver tb* **mundo 1, 5**
2 (= *uno más*) (*en singular, con cifras*) another; (*en plural*) other; **¿quieres otra taza de café?** would you like another cup of coffee?; **tropezamos con otra nueva dificultad** we came up against yet another difficulty; **va a ser ~ Hitler** he's going to be a second *o* another Hitler; **luego me enseñó ~s trajes** then he showed me some other dresses; **después volvió con ~s ocho libros** then he came back with another eight books *o* with eight more books; **otra cosa**: **me gustaría preguntarle otra cosa** I'd like to ask you something else; **¿desea alguna otra cosa?** would you like anything else?; **otra vez** again
3 (*en una secuencia temporal*) 3·1 (*en el futuro*) next; **yo me bajé aquí y él en la otra parada** I got off here and he got off at the next stop; **se fue y a la otra semana me escribió*** he left and wrote to me the next week
3·2 (*en el pasado*) other; **me encontré con él el ~ día** I met him the other day
Ⓑ PRON 1 (= *diferente*) (*en singular*) another, another one; (*en plural*) others; **—he perdido mi lápiz —no importa, tengo ~** "I have lost my pencil" — "it doesn't matter, I've got another (one)"; **tengo ~s en el almacén** I've got some others in the warehouse; **todos los países europeos y alguno que ~ de África** all the countries in Europe and some from Africa; **es más eficaz que ningún ~** it's more efficient than any other one; **el ~** the other one; **lo ~ no importa** the rest doesn't matter
2 (= *uno más*) (*en singular*) another, another one; (*en plural*) others; **¿quieres ~?** do you want another (one)?; **¿me puede enseñar ~s?** could you show me some others *o* more?; **se me perdieron y me dieron ~s** I lost them, but they gave me some more; **¡otra!** (*en concierto*) encore!; (*en bar*) (the) same again, please
3 (*en una secuencia temporal*) **un día sí y ~ no** every other day; **el jueves que viene no, el ~** a week on Thursday
4 (*referido a personas*) (*en singular*) somebody else; (*en plural*) others; **que lo haga ~** let somebody else do it; **tomé el sombrero de ~** I took somebody else's hat; **parece otra desde que se casó** she's a different person since she got married; **como dijo el ~** as somebody *o* someone said; **no fue ~ que el obispo** it was none other than the bishop; **unos creen que ganará, ~s que perderá** some think he'll win, others that he'll lose; **no sabe adaptarse a las costumbres de los ~s** he doesn't know how to fit in with other people; **uno y ~** both, both of them; **unos y ~s coinciden en que …** both sides *o* groups agree that …, they all agree that …; **están enamorados el uno del ~** they're in love with each other; ✦*MODISMO* **¡~ que tal (baila)!** here we go again!

otrora (*liter*) Ⓐ ADV (= *antiguamente*) formerly, in olden times
Ⓑ ADJ INV one-time, former; **el ~ señor del país** the one-time ruler of the country

otrosí ADV (†† *frm*) furthermore

OUA SF ABR (= **Organización de la Unidad Africana**) OAU

OUAA SF ABR (= **Organización de la Unidad Afro-americana**) OAAU

ouija SF, **oui-ja®** SF Ouija® board

ourensano/a ADJ, SM/F = **orensano**

output ['autpu] SM (*pl* **outputs** ['autpu]) (*Inform*) printout

ovación SF ovation

ovacionar ▸conjug 1a◂ VT to cheer, applaud, give an ovation to

oval ADJ, **ovalado** ADJ oval

óvalo SM 1 (= *figura*) oval
2 (*Méx Med*) pessary

ovárico ADJ [*tejido, hormonas, quiste*] ovarian

ovario SM ovary

ovas SFPL fish eggs, roe *sing*

oveja SF 1 (= *animal*) (*sin distinción de sexo*) sheep; (= *hembra*) ewe; ✦*MODISMOS* **apartar las ~s de los cabritos** to separate the sheep from the goats; **cargar con la ~ muerta** to be left holding the baby; **ser la ~ negra de la familia** to be the black sheep of the family; ✦*REFRÁN* **cada ~ con su pareja** birds of a feather flock together
2 (*Cono Sur*) (= *prostituta*) whore

ovejera SF (*Méx*) sheepfold

ovejería SF (*Chile*) (= *ovejas*) sheep *pl*; (= *actividad*) sheep farming; (= *hacienda*) sheep farm

ovejero SM sheepdog ▸ **ovejero alemán** German shepherd, German shepherd dog, Alsatian

ovejita* SF (*Arg*) whore

ovejo SM (*LAm*), **ovejón** SM (*LAm*) ram

ovejuno ADJ 1 (*Agr*) sheep *antes de s*; **ganado ~** sheep
2 (= *parecido a la oveja*) sheeplike

overbooking [oβer'βukin] SM overbooking

overear ▸conjug 1a◂ VT (*Andes, Cono Sur Culin*) to cook to a golden colour, brown

overol SM (*LAm*) overalls *pl*

ovetense Ⓐ ADJ of/from Oviedo
Ⓑ SMF native/inhabitant of Oviedo; **los ~s** the people of Oviedo

Ovidio SM Ovid

oviducto SM oviduct

Oviedo SM Oviedo

oviforme ADJ egg-shaped, oviform (*frm*)

ovillar ▸conjug 1a◂ Ⓐ VT to wind, wind into a ball
Ⓑ **ovillarse** VPR to curl up into a ball

ovillo SM 1 [*de lana, cuerda*] ball; **hacerse un ~** (*gen*) to curl up into a ball; [*de miedo*] to cower; (*en el habla*) to get tied up in knots
2 (= *enredo*) tangle

ovino Ⓐ ADJ ovine (*frm*), sheep *antes de s*; **ganado ~** sheep
Ⓑ SM (= *animales*) sheep *pl*; **carne de ~** [*de oveja añeja*] mutton; [*de cordero*] lamb

ovíparo ADJ oviparous

OVNI SM ABR (= **objeto volante** o **volador no identificado**) UFO

ovoide Ⓐ ADJ ovoid (*frm*), egg-shaped
Ⓑ SM 1 (= *figura*) ovoid
2 (*LAm Dep*) rugby ball

ovolactovegetariano/a ADJ, SM/F lacto-ovo-vegetarian

ovovegetariano/a ADJ, SM/F ovo-vegetarian

ovulación SF ovulation

ovular ▸conjug 1a◂ VI to ovulate

óvulo SM ovule, ovum

ox [os] EXCL shoo!

oxálico ADJ oxalic

oxear ▸conjug 1a◂ VT to shoo away

oxiacanta SF hawthorn

oxiacetilénico ADJ oxyacetylene *antes de s*; **soplete ~** oxyacetylene torch

oxidación SF 1 [*de metal*] rusting
2 (*Quím*) oxidation

oxidado ADJ 1 [*metal*] rusty
2 (*Quím*) oxidized

oxidar ▸conjug 1a◂ Ⓐ VT 1 [+ *metal*] to rust
2 (*Quím*) to oxidize
Ⓑ **oxidarse** VPR 1 [*metal*] to rust, go rusty
2 (*Quím*) to oxidize

óxido SM 1 (*en metal*) rust
2 (*Quím*) oxide ▸ **óxido de hierro** iron oxide ▸ **óxido nítrico** nitric oxide ▸ **óxido nitroso** nitrous oxide

oxigenación SF oxygenation

oxigenado Ⓐ ADJ 1 (*Quím*) oxygenated
2 [*pelo*] bleached; **una rubia oxigenada** a peroxide blonde
Ⓑ SM peroxide (*for hair*)

oxigenar ▸conjug 1a◂ Ⓐ VT to oxygenate
Ⓑ **oxigenarse** VPR 1 (*gen*) to become oxygenated
2 [*persona*] to get some fresh air

oxígeno SM oxygen

oxímoron SM oxymoron

oxte EXCL (†) (*a animal*) shoo!; (*a persona*) get out!, hop it!*; ✦*MODISMO* **sin decir ~ ni moxte** without a word

oye, **oyendo** *etc ver* **oír**

oyente SMF [1] (*Radio*) listener; **queridos ~s** dear listeners
[2] (*Univ*) unregistered student, occasional student, auditor (*EEUU*); **voy de ~ a las clases de Derecho Romano** I attend the classes on Roman Law as an unregistered student

ozono SM ozone

ozonosfera SF ozonosphere

P p

P, p [pe] SF (= *letra*) P, p
P. ABR 1 (*Rel*) (= **Padre**) F., Fr.
2 = **Papa**
3 (= **presidente**) P
4 (= **Príncipe**) P
p. ABR 1 (*Tip*) (= **página**) p
2 (*Cos*) = **punto**
p.ª ABR = **para**
pa* PREP *informal or humorous pronunciation of "para"*
p.a. ABR 1 = **por autorización**
2 = **por ausencia**
PAAU SFPL ABR = **Pruebas para el Acceso a la Universidad**
pabellón SM 1 (*Arquit*) [*de muestras, exposiciones*] pavilion; [*de jardín*] summerhouse; [*de hospital*] (= *ala*) wing; (= *anexo*) block, section ► **pabellón de aduanas** customs house ► **pabellón de caza** shooting box ► **pabellón de conciertos** bandstand ► **pabellón de hidroterapia** pumproom ► **pabellón de música** bandstand ► **pabellón deportivo, pabellón polideportivo** sports hall
2 (= *carpa*) bell tent
3 (*Med*) ► **pabellón de la oreja** outer ear
4 [*de cama*] canopy
5 (*Mús*) [*de trompeta*] mouth
6 (*Mil*) stack
7 (*Náut etc*) (= *bandera*) flag; **un buque de ~ panameño** a ship flying the Panamanian flag ► **pabellón de conveniencia** flag of convenience ► **pabellón nacional** national flag
pabilo SM, **pábilo** SM wick
Pablo SM Paul
pábulo SM 1 (= *motivo*) food, fuel; (= *estímulo*) encouragement; **dar ~ a** to feed, encourage; **dar ~ a las llamas** to add fuel to the flames; **dar ~ a los rumores** to fuel rumours
2 (*liter*) (= *alimento*) food
PAC SF ABR (= **Política Agraria Común**) CAP
Paca SF (*forma familiar*) *de* **Francisca**
paca¹ SF (*Agr*) bale
paca² SF (*LAm Zool*) paca, spotted cavy
pacapaca SF (*Andes*) owl; ✦*MODISMO* **le vino la ~*** it all went wrong for him
pacatería SF (*pey*) 1 (= *timidez*) timidity
2 (= *modestia*) excessive modesty, prudishness
pacato ADJ (*pey*) 1 (= *tímido*) timid
2 (= *modesto*) excessively modest, prudish
pacense Ⓐ ADJ of/from Badajoz
Ⓑ SMF native/inhabitant of Badajoz; **los ~s** the people of Badajoz
paceño/a Ⓐ ADJ of/from La Paz
Ⓑ SM/F native/inhabitant of La Paz; **los ~s** the people of La Paz
pacer ▸conjug 2d◂ Ⓐ VT 1 [+ *hierba*] to eat, graze 2 [+ *ganado*] to graze, pasture
Ⓑ VI to graze
pacha SF (*CAm*) baby's bottle
pachá SM pasha; ✦*MODISMO* **vivir como un ~** to live like a king
pachacho* ADJ (*Cono Sur*) (= *rechoncho*) chubby; (= *achaparrado*) squat
pachaco* ADJ (*CAm*) weak, feeble
pachamama SF (*Andes, Cono Sur*) Mother Earth, the earth mother
pachamanca SF (*Perú*) barbecue
pachanga* SF 1 (= *fiesta*) lively party; (= *juerga*) binge*, booze-up‡
2 (*Caribe*) (= *lío*) mix-up
3 (*Mús*) Cuban dance
pachanguear* ▸conjug 1a◂ VI to go on a spree
pachanguero* ADJ 1 (= *bullicioso*) noisy, rowdy 2 [*música*] catchy
pacharán SM sloe brandy
pacho* ADJ 1 (*CAm, Cono Sur**) [*persona*] (= *rechoncho*) chubby; (= *achaparrado*) squat
2 (*CAm*) [*objeto*] flat, flattened; [*sombrero*] flat-brimmed
3 (*Caribe*) (= *calmoso*) phlegmatic
pachocha* SF (*LAm*) = **pachorra**
pachol SM (*Méx*) mat of hair
pachón Ⓐ ADJ 1 (*) [*persona*] lackadaisical
2 (*CAm, Cono Sur**) (= *peludo*) shaggy, hairy; (*CAm, Méx**) (= *lanudo*) woolly, wooly (*EEUU*)
3 (*Andes**) (= *gordito*) plump
4 (*Andes**) (= *lerdo*) dim*, dense*
Ⓑ SM 1 (= *perro*) basset hound
2 (*) (= *persona*) dull person, slow sort
pachorra* SF (= *indolencia*) slowness, sluggishness; (= *tranquilidad*) calmness; **Juan, con su santa ~ ...** Juan, as slow as ever ...
pachorrada* SF (*Caribe, Cono Sur*) blunder, gaffe
pachorrear* ▸conjug 1a◂ VI (*CAm*) to be slow, be sluggish
pachorriento* ADJ (*Andes, Cono Sur*), **pachorro*** ADJ (*Andes, Caribe*), **pachorrudo*** ADJ
1 (= *indolente*) slow, sluggish
2 (= *tranquilo*) calm
pachotada* SF (*Andes, Méx*) = **patochada**
pachucho* ADJ [*fruta*] overripe; [*persona*] off-colour, off-color (*EEUU*), poorly
pachuco/a* (*Méx*) Ⓐ ADJ (= *llamativo*) flashy, flashily dressed
Ⓑ SM/F 1 (*pey*) (= *chicano*) Chicano, Mexican-American
2 (= *bien vestido*) sharp dresser, snappy dresser
pachulí SM 1 (= *planta, perfume*) patchouli
2 (*Esp*‡) (= *tío*) bloke‡, guy*
paciencia SF patience; **¡paciencia!** (*gen*) be patient!; (*Cono Sur*) that's just too bad!; **acabársele** *o* **agotársele la ~ a algn: se me acaba** *o* **agota la ~** my patience is running out *o* wearing thin; **armarse** *o* **cargarse** *o* **revestirse de ~** to resolve to be patient; **perder la ~** to lose patience; **tener ~** to be patient; **no tengo más ~** my patience is at an end; ✦*MODISMO* **¡~ y barajar!** keep trying!, don't give up!
paciencioso ADJ (*Andes, Cono Sur*) long-suffering
paciente ADJ, SMF patient
pacientemente ADV patiently
pacienzudo* ADJ very patient, long-suffering
pacificación SF pacification
pacificador(a) Ⓐ ADJ pacifying, peace-making; **operación ~a** peace-keeping operation
Ⓑ SM/F peacemaker
pacíficamente ADV pacifically, peaceably
pacificar ▸conjug 1g◂ Ⓐ VT 1 (*Mil*) to pacify
2 (= *calmar*) to calm; (= *apaciguar*) to appease
3 (= *reconciliar*) to bring together, reconcile
Ⓑ **pacificarse** VPR to calm down
Pacífico SM (*tb* **Océano ~**) Pacific (Ocean)
pacífico ADJ [*lugar, proceso, arreglo*] peaceful; [*carácter*] peaceable; [*ciudadano*] peace-loving
pacifismo SM pacifism
pacifista ADJ, SMF pacifist
pack SM [*de yogures, latas*] pack; [*de vacaciones*] package
Paco SM (*forma familiar*) *de* **Francisco**; ✦*MODISMO* **ya vendrá el tío ~ con la rebaja** they *etc* will soon come down to earth (with a bump)
paco¹ SM (*Mil Hist*) sniper, sharpshooter
paco²‡ SM (*LAm*) cop‡, policeman
paco³ Ⓐ ADJ (*Andes, Cono Sur*) (= *rojizo*) reddish
Ⓑ SM (*Andes, Cono Sur*) (= *mamífero*) alpaca
pacota* SF (*Méx*) 1 (= *género*) = **pacotilla 1**
2 (= *persona*) layabout*
pacotada* SF (*Andes*) blunder, gaffe

pacotilla SF [1] (= *género*) trash, junk, inferior stuff; **de ~** trashy, shoddy; **hacer su ~** to be doing nicely, make a nice profit
[2] (*Andes, CAm, Cono Sur*) rabble, crowd, mob

pacotillero Ⓐ ADJ (*Andes*) (= *rústico*) rude, uncouth
Ⓑ SM (*Andes, Caribe, Cono Sur*) (= *vendedor ambulante*) pedlar, peddler (*EEUU*), hawker

pactable ADJ negotiable

pactar ▸conjug 1a◂ Ⓐ VT [1] (= *acordar*) to agree to; **~ una tregua** to agree to a truce
[2] (= *estipular*) to stipulate
Ⓑ VI [1] (= *llegar a un acuerdo*) to come to an agreement, make a pact
[2] (= *transigir*) to compromise

pacto SM agreement, pact; **hacer un ~** to make an agreement, make a pact; **romper un ~** to break an agreement; ✦***MODISMO*** **hacer un ~ con el diablo** to make a pact with the devil ► **Pacto Andino** Andean Pact ► **pacto de caballeros** gentlemen's agreement ► **pacto de no agresión** non-aggression pact ► **pacto de recompra** repurchase agreement ► **Pacto de Varsovia** Warsaw Pact ► **pacto entre caballeros** gentlemen's agreement ► **pacto social** (*gen*) social contract; [*de salarios*] wages settlement

> **PACTOS DE LA MONCLOA**
> *In the unstable political environment that followed Franco's death and the narrow victory of Adolfo Suárez's* **UCD** *party in the 1977 general election, it became obvious that a great deal of cross-party cooperation would be needed if progress in Spain were to be made. The result was the* **Pactos de la Moncloa**, *named after the prime minister's official residence, where the pacts were signed in October 1977. They were designed to bring together all political groups in a spirit of consensus in order to push through vital legislation, specifically the Constitution, but also budgets and regional policies.*
> ⇨ *See also* LA CONSTITUCIÓN ESPAÑOLA

padecer ▸conjug 2d◂ Ⓐ VI to suffer; **ha padecido mucho** she has suffered a lot; **~ de** to suffer from; **padece del corazón** he has heart trouble; **ella padece por todos** she suffers on everybody's account; **padece en su amor propio** his self-respect suffers; **se embala bien para que no padezca en el viaje** it is well packed so that it will not get damaged on the journey
Ⓑ VT [1] (= *sufrir*) to suffer; **eso hace ~ el metal de los goznes** that puts a strain on the metal of the hinges
[2] (= *aguantar*) [+ *malos tratos, adversidades*] to endure, put up with; **~ un error** to labour under a misapprehension

padecimiento SM (*gen*) suffering; (*Med*) ailment

pádel SM paddle tennis

padrastro SM [1] (= *pariente*) stepfather
[2] (*en dedo*) hangnail
[3] (†) (= *mal padre*) harsh father, cruel parent
[4] (†) (= *dificultad*) obstacle, difficulty

padrazo SM indulgent father

padre Ⓐ SM [1] (= *progenitor*) father; (*Zool*) father, sire; **lo quiero como a un ~** I love him as you would a father; **su señor ~** your father; **Gutiérrez ~** Gutiérrez senior, the elder Gutiérrez; ✦***MODISMOS*** **de ~ y muy señor mío**: **una paliza de ~ y muy señor mío** an almighty thrashing, the father and mother of a thrashing; **no tiene ~ ni madre, ni perrito que le ladre** he is (all) alone in the world ► **padre de familia** family man; (*Jur*) head of a household ► **padre político** father-in-law ► **padre soltero** single father
[2] **padres** (= *padre y madre*) parents
[3] (*Rel*) father; **el Padre Las Casas** Father Las Casas ► **padre espiritual** confessor ► **Padre Nuestro** Lord's Prayer, Our Father ► **Padre Santo** Holy Father ► **padres de la Iglesia** Church Fathers
[4] [*de disciplina*] father; **es el ~ de la lingüística moderna** he is the father of modern linguistics
[5] (*) **¡mi ~!** you don't say!*; **¡tu ~!** up yours!‡; **¡eres mi ~!** you're a marvel!
Ⓑ ADJ (*) (= *enorme*) huge; **un éxito ~** a huge success; **se armó un lío ~** there was an almighty row; **darse una vida ~** to live the life of Riley*

padrejón SM (*Arg*) stallion

padrenuestro SM Lord's Prayer; ✦***MODISMO*** **en menos que se reza un ~** in no time at all

padrillo SM (*Andes, Cono Sur*) stallion

padrinazgo SM [1] (*Rel*) godfathership
[2] (= *patrocinio*) sponsorship, patronage; (= *protección*) protection

padrino SM [1] (*en bautizo*) godfather; **padrinos** godparents
[2] (*en boda*) ≈ best man
[3] (*en duelo*) second
[4] [*de mafia*] godfather
[5] (= *patrocinador*) sponsor, patron
[6] (†‡) (= *víctima*) sucker‡, victim

padrísimo* ADJ (*Méx*) = **padre B**

padrón SM [1] (= *censo*) census; (*Pol*) electoral register, electoral roll; [*de miembros*] register
[2] (*Téc*) pattern
[3] (= *columna*) commemorative column, inscribed column
[4] (= *infamia*) stain, blot; **será un ~ (de ignominia) para todos nosotros** it will be a disgrace for all of us
[5] (*LAm Agr*) stud; (= *caballo*) stallion; (*Andes*) (= *toro padre*) breeding bull
[6] (*Chile Aut*) car registration documents *pl*
[7] (*) (= *padrazo*) indulgent father

padrote SM [1] (*CAm, Méx**) (= *chulo*) pimp
[2] (*LAm*) (= *caballo*) stallion; (= *toro*) breeding bull

paella SF [1] (*Culin*) paella
[2] (= *recipiente*) paella dish

paellada SF paella party

paellera SF [1] (*Culin*) (= *recipiente*) paella dish
[2] (*hum*) dish aerial, dish antenna (*EEUU*), TV satellite dish

paellero/a Ⓐ ADJ [*arroz, ingredientes*] paella *antes de s* Ⓑ SM/F (= *cocinero*) paella cook

paf EXCL wham!, zap!

pág. ABR (= **página**) p

paga SF [1] (= *sueldo*) (*semanal*) wages *pl*; (*mensual*) salary; [*de jubilado, viuda*] pension; [*de niño*] pocket money; **14 ~s al año** 14 yearly payments; **día de ~** payday ► **paga de Navidad** Christmas bonus (*equivalent to a month's salary*) ► **paga extra, paga extraordinaria** salary bonus (*usually paid in July and December*)
[2] (*Com*) (= *pago*) payment; **entrega contra ~** cash on delivery

> **PAGA EXTRAORDINARIA**
> *Most long-term and permanent employment contracts in Spain stipulate that annual salary will be paid in 14 instalments. This means that most Spanish workers receive twice the normal monthly wage in June and December. These extra payments are generally known as* **paga extraordinaria** *or* **paga extra**.

pagadero ADJ payable; **una hipoteca pagadera en diez años** a mortgage payable over ten years; **~ a plazos** payable in instalments; **~ al portador** payable to bearer; **~ a la entrega** payable on delivery

pagado ADJ [1] (= *ya abonado*) [*impuesto, factura, vacaciones*] paid; **con todos los gastos ~s** with all expenses paid; **"no pagado"** "unpaid"; **~ por adelantado** paid in advance, prepaid; *ver tb* **porte 1**
[2] (= *con sueldo*) [*asesino, mercenario*] hired; **el futbolista mejor ~ de la historia** the most highly paid *o* the best paid footballer in history
[3] (= *satisfecho*) [*persona*] **~ de uno mismo** self-satisfied, smug

pagador(a) Ⓐ ADJ **la entidad ~a** the payer
Ⓑ SM/F [1] (= *persona*) payer; **ser buen/mal ~** to be a good/bad payer
[2] (*Mil*) (*tb* **oficial ~**) paymaster

pagaduría SF (*gen*) pay office, cashier's office; (*Mil*) paymaster's office

paganini* SMF **ser el ~** to be the one who pays

paganismo SM paganism, heathenism

pagano/a Ⓐ ADJ (*Rel*) pagan, heathen
Ⓑ SM/F [1] (*Rel*) pagan, heathen
[2] (*) = **paganini**
[3] (= *chivo expiatorio*) scapegoat, dupe, victim

pagar ▸conjug 1h◂ Ⓐ VT [1] (= *abonar*) [+ *factura, rescate, sueldo*] to pay; [+ *compra*] to pay for; [+ *intereses, hipoteca*] to pay off, repay; **paga 200 dólares de alquiler** he pays 200 dollars in rent; **los menores de tres años no pagan entrada** children under three get in free; **ya han pagado las bebidas** the drinks have been paid for; **su tío le paga los estudios** his uncle is paying for his education; **estamos pagando la hipoteca del piso** we're paying off *o* repaying the mortgage on the flat; **cantidad a ~** amount payable; **"a pagar en destino"** (*Correos*) "postage due"; **~ algo con tarjeta de crédito** to pay for sth by credit card; **¿lo puede ~ con dólares?** can I pay in dollars?; **~ algo al contado** *o* **en efectivo** *o* **en metálico** to pay cash for sth, pay for sth in cash; **~ algo a plazos** to pay for sth in instalments *o* (*EEUU*) installments; **~ algo por** to pay sth for; **¿cuánto pagasteis por el coche?** how much did you pay for the car?; **hemos pagado un precio muy alto por haberlo traicionado** betraying him cost us dear, we paid a high price for betraying him; ✦***MODISMOS*** **ni aunque me paguen** not if you paid me; **~ a algn con la misma moneda** to give sb a taste of their own medicine; *ver tb* **pato 2, plato 1, vidrio 1**
[2] (= *costar*) to cost; **el pavo se está pagando a 23 euros el kilo** turkey costs 23 euros a kilo at the moment; **sus cuadros se pagan a**

peso de oro his paintings fetch a very high price

3 (= *corresponder*) [+ *ayuda, favor*] to repay; [+ *visita*] to return; **¿cómo puedo ~te lo que has hecho por mis hijos?** how can I repay you for what you've done for my children?

4 (= *sufrir las consecuencias de*) **lo pagó con su vida** he paid for it with his life; **pagó su error con diez años de cárcel** his mistake cost him ten years in jail; ✦*MODISMOS* **~ algo caro** to pay dearly for sth; **¡lo ~ás caro!** you'll pay dearly for this!; **~las: ¡las vas a ~!** you've got it coming to you!*, you'll pay for this!; **¡me las ~ás todas juntas!** I'll get you for this!; **¡que Dios se lo pague!** God bless you!; ✦*REFRÁN* **el que la hace la paga** you have to face the consequences for what you do

Ⓑ VI 1 (= *satisfacer un pago*) to pay; **hoy pago yo** I'm paying today, it's my turn to pay today; **en este trabajo pagan bien** this job pays well

2 (*Col, Méx*) (= *compensar*) to pay; **el negocio no paga** the business doesn't pay

Ⓒ **pagarse** VPR 1 [+ *estudios, gastos*] to pay for; **yo me lo pago todo** I support myself, I pay for everything myself; **él mismo está pagándose sus estudios** he's paying for his own education

2 (= *vanagloriarse*) **~se de algo** to be pleased with sth; **se paga mucho de su pelo** she's terribly vain about her hair; **~se de uno mismo** to be conceited, be full of o.s.*

pagaré SM promissory note, IOU ► **pagaré del Tesoro** Treasury bill, Treasury bond

página SF page; **anuncio a toda ~** ◊ **anuncio a ~ entera** full-page advertisement; **primera ~** front page; ✦*MODISMO* **currarse la ~**‡ to try it on* ► **página de inicio** (*Internet*) home page ► **páginas amarillas, páginas doradas** (*Arg*) Yellow Pages® ► **página web** Web page

paginación SF pagination

paginar ▸conjug 1a◂ VT to paginate, number the pages of; **con seis hojas sin ~** with six unnumbered pages

▼**pago**[1] Ⓐ SM 1 (*Fin*) payment; **el primer ~ fue de 150 euros** the first payment was 150 euros; **tras el ~ de la primera letra** after paying the first instalment; **atrasarse en los ~s** to be in arrears; **huésped de ~** paying guest; **día de ~** payday; **suspender ~s** to stop payments ► **pago a cuenta** payment on account ► **pago adelantado** advance payment ► **pago a la entrega** cash on delivery ► **pago a la orden** direct debit ► **pago a la presentación de factura** payment on invoice ► **pago al contado** cash payment ► **pago anticipado** advance payment ► **pago a plazos** payment by instalments *o* (*EEUU*) installments ► **pago a título gracioso** ex gratia payment ► **pago contra reembolso** cash on delivery ► **pago domiciliado** direct debit ► **pago en especie** payment in kind ► **pago fraccionado** payment in instalments *o* (*EEUU*) installments, part-payment ► **pago inicial** down payment, deposit ► **pago íntegro** gross payment ► **pago por resultados** payment by results ► **pago por visión** pay per view ► **pago simbólico** token payment; *ver tb* **balanza 2, colegio 1, condición 1, suspensión 3**

2 (= *recompensa*) return, reward; **este es el ~ que me dais por mis esfuerzos** this is what you give me in return for *o* as a reward for my efforts; **en ~ de** *o* **por algo** in return for sth, as a reward for sth

Ⓑ ADJ paid; **estar ~** (*lit*) to be paid; (*fig*) to be even, be quits

pago[2] SM (= *zona*) district; (= *finca*) estate (*esp planted with vines or olives*); (*Cono Sur*) region, area; (= *tierra natal*) home turf; **por estos ~s** round here, in this neck of the woods*

pago[3] (*Arg*) PP *de* **pagar**

pagoda SF pagoda

pagote* SM scapegoat

págs. ABR (= **páginas**) pp

pagua SF 1 (*Cono Sur*) (= *hernia*) hernia; (= *hinchazón*) large swelling

2 (*Méx*) large avocado pear

paguacha SF (*Cono Sur*) 1 = **pagua 1**

2 (= *melón*) large melon

3 (‡) (= *cabeza*) nut*, noggin (*EEUU**), bonce*

paguala SF (*Caribe*) swordfish

pai SM (*LAm*) pie

paiche SM (*Andes*) dried salted fish

paila SF 1 (*esp Chile*) (= *sartén*) frying pan; (= *cacerola*) large pan

2 (*Cono Sur*) (= *comida*) meal of fried food

pailero/a SM/F 1 (*Andes, Méx**) (= *italiano*) immigrant Italian, Wop**

2 (*CAm, Caribe, Méx*) (= *cobrero*) coppersmith; (= *calderero*) tinker

pailón SM 1 (*Andes, Caribe*) (= *cazo*) pot, pan

2 (*Andes, CAm Geog*) (= *cuenca*) bowl

3 (*Caribe*) (= *remolino*) whirlpool

paíño SM petrel

pairo SM **estar al ~** (*Náut*) to lie to; ✦*MODISMO* **quedarse al ~** to sit back and do nothing

país SM 1 (= *nación*) country; **los ~es miembros** *o* **participantes** the member countries ► **país de las maravillas** wonderland ► **país de nunca jamás** never-never land ► **país deudor** debtor nation ► **país en desarrollo, país en vías de desarrollo** developing nation ► **país natal** native land ► **país satélite** satellite country *o* state

2 (= *tierra*) land, region; **vino del ~** local wine

3 (*Arte*) (= *paisaje*) landscape

paisa* SMF (*LAm*) = **paisano B3**

paisaje SM 1 (= *terreno*) landscape; **el ~ montañoso del Tirol** the mountainous landscape of Tyrol ► **paisaje interior** state of mind

2 (= *vista panorámica*) **estaba contemplando el ~** I was looking at the scenery; **desde aquí se divisa un ~ magnífico** you get a magnificent view from here

3 (*Arte*) landscape

paisajismo SM (*Arte*) landscape painting; [*de jardines*] landscaping, landscape gardening

paisajista SMF (= *pintor*) landscape painter; (= *jardinero*) landscape gardener

paisajístico ADJ landscape *antes de s*, scenic

paisanada SF (*Cono Sur*) (*gen*) group of peasants; (*colectivamente*) peasants *pl*

paisanaje SM 1 (= *población civil*) civil population

2 (*Arg*) (*gen*) group of peasants; (*colectivamente*) peasants *pl*

paisano/a Ⓐ ADJ (= *del mismo país*) from the same country; (= *de la misma región*) from the same region; (= *del mismo pueblo*) from the same town

Ⓑ SM/F 1 (= *civil*) civilian; **traje de ~** plain clothes *pl*; **vestir de ~** [*soldado*] to be wearing civilian clothes, be in civvies*; [*policía*] to be in plain clothes

2 (= *del mismo país*) compatriot, fellow countryman/countrywoman; **es ~ mío** he's a fellow countryman (of mine); (= *del mismo pueblo*) person from the same town; (= *de la misma región*) person from the same region

3 (*esp Arg*) (= *campesino*) peasant

4 (*Cono Sur*) (= *extranjero*) foreigner; (*Cono Sur*) (= *árabe*) Arab; (*Méx*) (= *español*) Spaniard; (*Andes, Cono Sur*) (= *chino*) Chinaman/Chinese woman

Países Bajos SMPL **los ~** (= *Holanda*) the Netherlands; (*Hist*) the Low countries

paisito* SM (*Uru*) homeland

País Vasco SM **el ~** the Basque Country

paja SF 1 (*Agr*) straw; (*de beber*) straw; (*LAm*) (= *leña*) dried brushwood; **sombrero de ~** straw hat; **techo de ~** thatched roof; **hombre de ~*** front man*; ✦*MODISMOS* **lo hizo en un quitarme las ~s*** she did it in a jiffy*; **riñeron por un quítame allá esas ~s** they quarrelled *o* (*EEUU*) quarreled over nothing; ✦*REFRÁN* **ver la ~ en el ojo ajeno y no la viga en el propio** to see the mote in sb else's eye and not the beam in one's own

2 (*fig*) trash, rubbish, garbage (*EEUU*); (*en libro, ensayo*) padding, waffle*; **hinchar un libro con mucha ~** to pad a book out; **meter ~** to waffle

3 (**‡) (= *masturbación*) **hacerse una ~** ◊ **volarse la ~** (*CAm*) to wank**‡, jerk off‡

4 (*Andes, Chile*) ► **paja brava** tall altiplano grass

5 (*Andes, CAm*) (*tb* **~ de agua**) (= *grifo*) tap, faucet (*EEUU*); (= *canal*) canal

6 (*Cono Sur*‡) (= *droga*) dope‡

7 (*CAm*‡) (= *mentira*) lie, fib*

pajar SM straw loft

pájara SF 1 (*Orn*) hen, hen bird; (= *perdiz hembra*) hen partridge

2 (*) (= *mujer taimada*) sneaky bitch*; (= *ladrona*) thieving woman

3 (*Dep*) (= *desfallecimiento*) collapse

4 (= *pájaro de papel*) paper bird; (= *cometa*) kite

5 ► **pájara pinta** (game of) forfeits

6 ✦*MODISMO* **dar ~ a algn** (*Andes, CAm*) to swindle sb

pajarada SF (*Andes*) flock of birds

pajarear ▸conjug 1a◂ Ⓐ VT 1 (*LAm*) [+ *pájaros*] to scare, keep off

2 (*Andes*) (= *observar*) to watch intently

3 (*Andes*) (= *matar*) to murder

Ⓑ VI 1 (*) (= *holgazanear*) to loaf; (= *vagar*) to loiter

2 (*LAm*) [*caballo*] to shy

3 (*Cono Sur**) (= *estar distraído*) to have one's head in the clouds

4 (*Méx**) (= *escuchar*) to keep an ear open

pajarera SF aviar; *ver tb* **pajarero**

pajarería SF 1 (= *tienda*) pet shop

2 (= *bandada de pájaros*) large flock of birds

3 (*Caribe**) (= *vanidad*) vanity

pajarero/a Ⓐ ADJ 1 (*Orn*) bird *antes de s*

2 [*persona*] (= *alegre*) merry, fun-loving; (= *chistoso*) facetious, waggish

3 [*ropa*] flashy, loud

➤ LENGUA Y USO: **pago**[1] **A1** 47.5

4 (*LAm*) [*caballo*] nervous
5 (*Caribe**) (= *entrometido*) meddlesome
Ⓑ SM/F (*Com*) bird dealer; (= *cazador*) bird catcher; (= *criador*) bird breeder, bird fancier; (*Andes, CAm*) (= *ahuyentador*) bird-scarer; *ver tb* **pajarera**

pajarilla SF paper kite; ✦*MODISMO* **se le alegraron las ~s*** he laughed himself silly*

pajarita SF 1 (= *corbata*) bow tie
2 (= *pájaro de papel*) paper bird; (= *cometa*) paper kite
3 (*Orn*) ► **pajarita de las nieves** white wagtail

pajarito SM 1 (*Orn*) (= *cría*) baby bird, fledgling; (*hum*) birdie
2 (= *persona*) very small person; ✦*MODISMOS* **me lo dijo un ~** a little bird told me; **quedarse como un ~** to die peacefully
3 (*Caribe*) (= *bichito*) bug, insect

pájaro Ⓐ SM 1 (*Orn*) bird; ✦*MODISMOS* **matar dos ~s de un tiro** to kill two birds with one stone; **quedarse como un ~** to die peacefully; **tener la cabeza a ~s** ◊ **tener la cabeza llena de ~s** ◊ **tener ~s en la cabeza** to be featherbrained; ✦*REFRÁN* **más vale ~ en mano que ciento volando** a bird in the hand is worth two in the bush ► **pájaro azul** bluebird ► **pájaro bobo** penguin ► **pájaro cantarín, pájaro cantor** songbird ► **pájaro carpintero** woodpecker ► **pájaro de mal agüero** bird of ill omen ► **pájaro mosca** (*Esp*) hummingbird
2 (*) (= *astuto*) clever fellow, sharp sort ► **pájaro bravo** (*Ven**) smart Alec* ► **pájaro de cuenta** (= *importante*) big shot*, big noise*; (= *de cuidado*) nasty piece of work; (= *taimado*) wily bird
3 (**) (= *pene*) prick**
4 (*Caribe*‡) (= *homosexual*) queer‡, poof‡, fag (*EEUU*‡)
Ⓑ ADJ 1 (*Cono Sur*) (= *atolondrado*) scatty, featherbrained
2 (*Cono Sur*) (= *sospechoso*) shady, dubious
3 (*Cono Sur*) (= *chillón*) loud, flashy
4 (*Caribe*‡) (= *afeminado*) poofy‡, queer‡
5 (*Cono Sur*) (= *distraído*) vague, distracted

pajarón/ona* (*Cono Sur*) Ⓐ ADJ vague, ineffectual, stupid
Ⓑ SM/F 1 (= *poco fiable*) untrustworthy sort; (= *ineficaz*) unbusinesslike person
2 (= *charro*) flashily dressed person

pajarota* SF (*Esp*) false rumour, canard

pajarraca* SF to-do*, fuss

pajarraco SM 1 (*Orn*) big ugly bird
2 (*) (= *pillo*) slyboots*

paje SM (*gen*) page; (*Náut*) cabin boy

pajel SM sea-bream

pajera SF straw loft

pajero/a Ⓐ SM/F 1 (**) (*en sentido sexual*) tosser**, wanker**
2 (*CAm**) (= *mentiroso*) liar
3 (*CAm*) (= *fontanero*) plumber
Ⓑ ADJ (*CAm**) (= *mentiroso*) fibbing*

pajilla SF 1 (*CAm, Caribe, Méx*) (= *sombrero*) straw hat
2 (*LAm*) (= *cigarrillo*) *type of cigarette made from rolled maize*

pajita SF (drinking) straw; ✦*MODISMO* **quedarse mascando ~** (*Caribe**) to be left feeling foolish

pajizo ADJ 1 (= *de paja*) straw, made of straw; [*techo*] thatched
2 [*color*] straw-coloured, straw-colored (*EEUU*)

pajolero‡ ADJ (*Esp*) 1 (= *condenado*) bloody‡, damn(ed)*; **no tener ni pajolera idea** not to have a clue*
2 (= *tonto*) stupid
3 (= *travieso*) naughty, mischievous
4 (= *molesto*) irritating

pajón* ADJ (*Méx*) [*pelo*] (= *lacio*) lank; (= *crespo*) curly

pajonal SM (*LAm*) scrubland

pajoso ADJ 1 [*grano*] full of chaff
2 [*color*] straw-coloured; (= *como paja*) like straw

pajuela SF (= *tira*) spill; (*Andes*) (= *fósforo*) match; (*Andes, Cono Sur, Méx*) (= *de dientes*) toothpick; (*Caribe Mús*) plectrum; ✦*MODISMO* **el tiempo de la ~** olden days, bygone times

pajúo* ADJ (*Caribe*) daft, stupid

Pakistán SM Pakistan

pakistaní Ⓐ ADJ Pakistani
Ⓑ SMF Pakistani; **los ~es** the Pakistanis

pala SF 1 (*para cavar*) spade; (*para nieve, carbón, tierra*) shovel ► **pala cargadora** mechanical loader ► **pala de patatas** potato fork ► **pala excavadora** digger ► **pala mecánica** power shovel ► **pala quitanieves** snowplough, snowplow (*EEUU*) ► **pala topadora** (*Arg*) bulldozer
2 (*Culin*) slice ► **pala para el pescado** fish slice
3 (*Dep, Béisbol*) bat; (*en ping-pong*) bat, paddle (*EEUU*); (*en tenis*) racket; **jugar a ~** to play beach-tennis
4 [*de hélice, remo*] blade
5 ► **pala matamoscas** fly swat
6 [*de zapato*] vamp
7 (‡) (= *mano*) mitt‡; **¡choca la ~!** shake on it!*
8 (†) (= *astucia*) cunning, wiliness

palabra SF 1 (= *vocablo*) word; **un título de dos ~s** a two-word title; **lo tradujo ~ por ~** he translated it word for word; **me lo resumió en dos ~s** he summarized it for me in a couple of words; **¿me permiten decir unas ~s?** could I say a few words?; **eso no son más que ~s** those are just (empty) words; **no tengo ~s** *o* **me faltan ~s para expresar lo que siento** I haven't got the *o* there aren't words to express how I feel, words fail to express how I feel; **tuvo ~s de elogio para el ministro** he had words of praise for the minister; **sin decir** *o* **chistar* ~** without a word; **no dijo ni media ~** he didn't give us the slightest hint; **no entiendo ~** I can't understand a word; **es ~ de Dios** it is the word of God; **con buenas ~s: me lo dijo con muy buenas ~s** he told me as cool as you like*; **nos entretenía con buenas ~s, pero nunca nos daba el dinero** he palmed us off with smooth talk, but he never gave us the money; **medias ~s** hints; **lo dijo todo con medias ~s** he said everything indirectly; **en una ~** in a word; **¡ni una ~ más!** not another word!; ✦*MODISMOS* **coger a algn la ~** (= *creer*) to take sb at his word; (= *obligar*) to keep sb to his word; **comerse las ~s** to mumble; **no cruzar (una) ~ con algn** not to say a word to sb; **decir la última ~** to have the last word; **dejar a algn con la ~ en la boca** to cut sb off in mid-sentence; **me dejó con la ~ en la boca y se fue de la habitación** he walked out of the room while I was in mid-sentence; **gastar ~s** to waste one's breath; **medir las ~s** to choose one's words carefully; **negar la ~ de Dios a algn** to concede absolutely nothing to sb; **quitar la ~ de la boca a algn** to take the words right out of sb's mouth; **tener unas ~s con algn** to have words with sb; **trabarse de ~s** to wrangle, squabble; **tener la última ~** to have the final say; ✦*REFRANES* **a ~s necias, oídos sordos** it's best not to listen to the silly things people say; **las ~s se las lleva el viento** words count for nothing ► **palabra clave** keyword ► **palabras cruzadas** (*LAm*) (= *crucigrama*) crossword *sing*; **un juego de ~s cruzadas** a word puzzle ► **palabras gruesas** crude language *sing* ► **palabras mayores†** offensive language *sing*; ✦*MODISMO* **ser ~s mayores** (= *ser importante*): **¿te han hecho directora? ¡eso ya son ~s mayores!** so you've been appointed director, that's really something!; *ver tb* **juego² 2**
2 (= *facultad de hablar*) **la ~** speech; **perdió el uso de la ~** he lost the power of speech; **tiene el don de la ~** ◊ **es de ~ fácil** he has a way with words, he has the gift of the gab*; **de ~: he pecado sólo de ~** I've sinned in word only; **nos acusó de ~** he accused us verbally; **dirigir la ~ a algn: hace tiempo que no me dirige la ~** he hasn't spoken to me for a long time
3 (*frm*) (= *turno para hablar*) floor; **ceder la ~ a algn** ◊ **conceder la ~ a algn** to give sb the floor, invite sb to speak; **pedir la ~** to ask for the floor, ask to be allowed to speak; **tener la ~** to have the floor; **tiene la ~ el señor presidente** the president has the floor; **yo no tengo la ~** it's not for me to say; **tomar la ~** to take the floor, speak; **hacer uso de la ~** to take the floor, speak
4 (= *promesa*) word; **es hombre de ~** he is a man of his word; **cumplió su ~** he kept his word, he was true to his word; **~ que yo no tengo nada que ver*** I've got nothing to do with it, (I) promise!; **—¿de verdad que no sabías nada? —¡palabra!** *o* (*hum*) **¡palabrita del Niño Jesús!** "you really didn't know anything?" — "cross my heart and hope to die!"; **bajo ~** (*Mil*) on parole; **dar** *o* **empeñar su ~** to give one's word; **faltar a su ~** to go back on *o* break one's word ► **palabra de casamiento: dar ~ de casamiento** to promise to marry ► **palabra de honor** word of honour, word of honor (*EEUU*); **¿me das tu ~ de honor de que no dirás nada?** do you give me your word of honour you won't say anything?; **¡~ de honor!** word of honour!

palabrear ▸conjug 1a◂ VT 1 (*Andes, Cono Sur*) (= *acordar*) to agree verbally to; **~ a algn** to promise to marry sb
2 (*Cono Sur*) (= *insultar*) to abuse

palabreja SF (*gen*) strange word; (= *palabrota*) swearword

palabrería SF, **palabrerío** SM verbiage, hot air

palabrero/a Ⓐ ADJ wordy, long-winded
Ⓑ SM/F windbag‡

palabro* SM (= *palabrota*) swearword; (= *palabra rara*) odd word; (= *palabra petulante*) pretentious term; (= *barbarismo*) barbarism

palabrota SF swearword

palabrudo* ADJ (*Cono Sur*) foulmouthed

palacete SM small palace

palacial ADJ (*LAm*) palatial

palaciego Ⓐ ADJ palace *antes de s*, court *antes de s*
Ⓑ SM (= *persona*) courtier

palacio SM (*gen*) palace; (= *mansión*) mansion; **el ~ del marqués de Mudéjar** the house of the Marquis of Mudéjar; **ir a ~** to go to court; **tener un puesto en ~** to have a post at court ► **palacio de congresos** conference centre, conference hall ► **palacio de deportes** sports centre ► **palacio de justicia** courthouse ► **Palacio de las Comunicaciones** (*en Madrid*) General Post Office ► **palacio de los deportes** sports centre ► **palacio episcopal** bishop's palace ► **palacio municipal** city hall ► **Palacio Nacional** (*p.ej. en Guatemala*) Parliament Building ► **palacio real** royal palace

palada SF 1 (*con pala*) shovelful, spadeful
2 (*con remo*) stroke

paladar SM 1 (*Anat*) (hard) palate, roof of the mouth
2 (= *gusto*) palate; **tener un ~ delicado** to have a delicate palate

paladear ▸conjug 1a◂ VT (*gen*) to taste; (= *degustar*) to savour, savor (*EEUU*); **beber algo paladeándolo** to have a sip of sth (to see what it tastes like)

paladeo SM (*gen*) tasting; (= *degustación*) [*de comida*] savouring, savoring (*EEUU*); [*de bebida*] sipping

paladín SM 1 (*Hist*) paladin
2 [*de la libertad, justicia*] champion

paladinamente (*liter*) ADV (= *públicamente*) openly, publicly; (= *claramente*) clearly

paladino (*liter*) ADJ (= *público*) open, public; (= *claro*) clear; **más ~ no puede ser** it couldn't be clearer

palafrén SM palfrey

palafrenero SM groom

palana SF (*Andes*) 1 (= *pala*) shovel, spade
2 (= *azadón*) hoe

palanca SF 1 (= *barra*) lever ► **palanca de arranque** kick-starter ► **palanca de cambio** gear lever, gearshift (*EEUU*) ► **palanca de freno** brake lever ► **palanca de mando** joystick
2 (*) (= *influencia*) pull, influence; **mover ~s** to pull strings; **tener ~** to have pull, know people in the right places ► **palancas del poder** levers of power
3 (*Andes, Méx*) [*de barca*] punting pole

palangana Ⓐ SF 1 (= *jofaina*) washbasin, washbowl (*EEUU*)
2 (*Andes, CAm*) (= *fuente*) platter, serving dish
Ⓑ SMF 1 (*Cono Sur**) (= *intruso*) intruder
2 (*LAm*) (= *frívolo*) shallow person
3 (*LAm*) (= *charlatán*) charlatan
4 (*LAm*) (= *jactancioso*) braggart

palanganear* ▸conjug 1a◂ VI (*LAm*) to brag, show off*

palanganero SM washstand

palangre SM fishing line (*with multiple hooks*)

palanquear ▸conjug 1a◂ Ⓐ VT 1 (*Andes, CAm*) (= *apalancar*) to lever (along), move with a lever
2 (*Andes, Caribe, Méx*) [+ *barca*] to punt, pole along
3 (*Cono Sur**) (= *ayudar*) **¿quién te palanqueó?** who got you fixed up?
Ⓑ VI (*Andes, Caribe, Cono Sur**) to pull strings

palanquera SF stockade

palanquero SM 1 (*Andes, Cono Sur Ferro*) brakeman
2 (*Andes*) (= *leñador*) lumberman
3 (*Cono Sur**) (= *ladrón*) burglar, housebreaker

palanqueta SF 1 (*gen*) small lever; [*de forzar puertas*] jemmy, crowbar
2 (*Cono Sur, Méx*) (= *peso*) weight

palanquetazo* SM break-in, burglary

palanquista* SM burglar

p'alante‡ ADV = **para adelante**; *ver* **adelante 1**

palapa SF (*Méx*) 1 (= *palmera*) palm tree
2 (*como tejado*) palm roof

palatal ADJ, SF palatal

palatalizar ▸conjug 1f◂ Ⓐ VT to palatalize
Ⓑ **palatalizarse** VPR to palatalize

palatinado SM palatinate

palatino ADJ 1 (*Pol*) palace *antes de s*, court *antes de s*; (*del palatinado*) palatine
2 (*Anat*) palatal

palatosquisis SF INV cleft palate

palca SF (*Andes*) crossroads *sing*

palco SM (*Teat*) box; (*Ftbl*) director's box ► **palco de autoridades**, **palco de honor** royal box, box for distinguished persons ► **palco de la presidencia** (*Taur*) president's box ► **palco de proscenio** stage box ► **palco presidencial** (*Taur*) president's box

palde SM (*Cono Sur*) (= *herramienta*) *pointed digging tool*; (= *puñal*) dagger

palé SM *board game similar to Monopoly*

palear ▸conjug 1a◂ Ⓐ VT 1 (*LAm*) [+ *barca*] to punt, pole
2 (*LAm*) [+ *tierra*] to shovel; [+ *zanja*] to dig
3 (*Cono Sur*) [+ *granos*] to thresh
Ⓑ VI [*piragüista*] to paddle

palenque SM 1 (= *estacada*) stockade, palisade
2 (= *recinto*) arena, ring; [*de gallos*] pit
3 (*Cono Sur*) [*de caballos*] tethering post
4 (*Cono Sur**) (= *alboroto*) din, racket

palenquear ▸conjug 1a◂ VT (*Cono Sur*) to tether

palentino/a Ⓐ ADJ of/from Palencia
Ⓑ SM/F native/inhabitant of Palencia; **los ~s** the people of Palencia

paleo... PREF paleo...

paleografía SF paleography

paleógrafo/a SM/F paleographer

paleolítico ADJ paleolithic

paleontología SF paleontology

paleontólogo/a SM/F paleontologist

palero* Ⓐ ADJ (*Andes*) big-headed*
Ⓑ SM (*Méx*) front man*

Palestina SF Palestine

palestino/a Ⓐ ADJ Palestinian
Ⓑ SM/F Palestinian; **los ~s** the Palestinians

palestra SF (*Hist*) arena; (= *liza*) lists *pl*; **salir** *o* **saltar a la ~** (= *participar*) to take the floor; (= *darse a conocer*) to come to the fore

paleta Ⓐ SF 1 (*para cavar*) small shovel, small spade; [*de albañil*] trowel; (*Culin*) (*con ranuras*) fish slice; (= *plana*) spatula; (*para el fuego*) fire shovel
2 (*Arte*) palette
3 (*Téc*) [*de turbina*] blade; [*de noria*] paddle, bucket; (= *plataforma*) pallet
4 (*Anat*) shoulder blade
5 (*LAm*) (= *polo*) ice lolly, popsicle (*EEUU*)
6 (*LAm*) (= *pala*) wooden paddle for beating clothes
7 (*LAm Culin*) topside of beef
Ⓑ SM (*) (= *albañil*) building worker, brickie*; *ver tb* **paleto**

paletada SF shovelful, spadeful

paletear ▸conjug 1a◂ Ⓐ VT (*Cono Sur*) [+ *caballo*] to pat; (*fig*) to flatter
Ⓑ VI (*Cono Sur*) to be out of work

paletería¹ SF (*Culin*) palate, sense of taste

paletería²* SF collection of yokels, shower‡

paletero SM (*Andes*) tuberculosis

paletilla SF shoulder blade

paletización SF (*Com*) palletization

paleto/a Ⓐ ADJ (*) boorish, stupid
Ⓑ SM/F (*) yokel, country bumpkin, hick (*EEUU*); *ver tb* **paleta**
Ⓒ SM (*Zool*) fallow deer

palia SF altar cloth, pall

paliacate SM (*Méx*) kerchief, scarf

paliar ▸conjug 1b◂ VT 1 (= *mitigar*) [+ *dolor*] to relieve, alleviate, palliate (*frm*); [+ *efectos*] to lessen, mitigate, palliate (*frm*); [+ *importancia*] to diminish
2 (= *disimular*) [+ *defecto*] to conceal, gloss over; [+ *ofensa*] to mitigate, excuse

paliativo Ⓐ ADJ palliative, mitigating
Ⓑ SM palliative; **sin ~s** [*desastre, fracaso*] unmitigated; [*rechazo*] unreserved; [*vulgaridad*] utter; **un edificio feo sin ~s** an ugly building with no redeeming features; **condenar sin ~s** to condemn unreservedly

palidecer ▸conjug 2d◂ VI turn pale

palidez SF paleness, pallor

pálido ADJ (*gen*) pale, pallid; (= *enfermizo*) sickly

palidoso ADJ (*Andes*) = **pálido**

palier SM 1 (*Mec*) bearing
2 (= *plataforma*) pallet
3 (*Arg*) (= *descanso*) landing

palillo SM 1 (= *mondadientes*) (*tb* **~ de dientes**) toothpick; **unas piernas como ~s de dientes** legs like matchsticks
2 (*Mús*) [*de tambor, batería*] drumstick; **palillos** (= *instrumento*) castanets
3 (*para comida oriental*) chopstick
4 (* *hum*) very thin person; ✦**MODISMO estar hecho un ~** to be as thin as a rake
5 (*Taur**) banderilla
6 (*Cono Sur*) (= *aguja de tejer*) knitting needle
7 (*CAm, Méx*) (= *portalápices*) penholder

palimpsesto SM palimpsest

palíndromo SM palindrome

palinodia† SF recantation; **cantar la ~** to recant

palio SM 1 (= *dosel*) canopy
2 (*Rel*) pallium; ✦**MODISMO recibir bajo ~ a algn** to roll out the red carpet for sb
3 (††) (= *manto*) cloak

palique* SM chat, chitchat; **darle al ~** ◊ **estar de ~** to chat, natter

palista SMF (*Dep*) canoeist

palito SM (*Arg*) ice lolly, Popsicle (*EEUU*)

palitroque SM 1 (*) (= *palo*) stick
2 (*Taur**) banderilla

3 (*Cono Sur*) (= *juego*) skittles *pl*, bowling (*EEUU*); (= *local*) skittle alley, bowling alley (*EEUU*)

paliza Ⓐ SF 1 (= *tunda*) beating, thrashing; **dar** *o* **propinar una ~ a algn** to give sb a beating, beat sb up*; **los críticos le dieron una ~ a la novela** the critics panned *o* slated the novel*
2 (*) (= *pesadez*) bore; **el viaje fue una ~** the journey was a real bore *o* drag*; **dar la ~** to be a pain; **darse la ~** (*al estudiar, trabajar*) to slog away; (*al tocarse, besarse*) to be all over each other
3 (*) (*Dep etc*) drubbing, thrashing; **el Betis le dio una ~ al Barcelona** Betis gave Barcelona a real thrashing, Betis thrashed Barcelona
Ⓑ SMF INV (*) (= *pesado*) bore, pain*

palizada SF 1 (= *valla*) fence, palisade
2 (= *cercado*) fenced enclosure

palizas* SMF INV bore, pain*

palla SF (*Andes Hist*) Inca princess

pallador SM (*LAm*) = **payador**

pallar¹ ▸conjug 1a◂ VT (*Min*) to extract; (*Agr*) to glean

pallar² SM (*Andes, Cono Sur*) Lima bean

pallasa SF mattress

pallasca SF (*Andes, Cono Sur*), **pallaso** SM (*Andes, Cono Sur*) mattress

Palma SF ► **Palma de Mallorca** Palma

palma SF 1 (*Anat*) palm; **leerle la ~ de la mano a algn** to read sb's palm; ✦***MODISMOS*** **conocer algo como la ~ de la mano** to know sth like the back of one's hand; **ser liso** *o* **llano como la ~ de la mano** to be as flat as a pancake; **llevar a algn en ~s** *o* **palmitas** to wait on sb hand and foot
2 **palmas** (= *aplausos*) clapping *sing*, applause *sing*; **batir** *o* **dar** *o* **hacer ~s** to clap (one's hands), applaud; **tocar las ~s** to clap in time ► **palmas de tango** slow hand-clap
3 (*Bot*) palm (tree); (= *hoja*) palm leaf; ✦***MODISMO*** **llevarse la ~**: **las tres son muy antipáticas, pero Ana se lleva la ~** the three of them are very unfriendly, but Ana wins hands down

palmada SF 1 [*de amistad*] slap, pat; **darse una ~ en la frente** to clap one's hand to one's brow
2 **palmadas** (= *aplausos*) clapping *sing*, applause *sing*; ✦***MODISMO*** **dar ~s** to clap (one's hands), applaud

palmadita SF pat, light tap

palmado⁑ ADJ (*CAm*) skint⁑, flat broke*

palmar¹ SM (*Bot*) palm grove, cluster of palms

palmar²⁑ ▸conjug 1a◂ Ⓐ VI 1 (= *morir*) to kick the bucket*, peg out⁑
2 (*en juego*) to lose
Ⓑ VT ✦***MODISMO*** **~la** to kick the bucket*, to peg out⁑

palmar³ ADJ, **palmario** ADJ obvious, self-evident

palmarés SM 1 (*Dep*) [*de ganadores*] list of winners
2 (= *historial*) record

palmarote⁑ SM (*Caribe*) yokel, hick (*EEUU**)

palmatoria SF 1 [*de vela*] candlestick
2 [*de castigo*] cane

palmazón* SM ✦***MODISMO*** **estar en el ~** (*CAm*) to be broke*

palmeado ADJ [*pata*] webbed

palmear ▸conjug 1a◂ Ⓐ VT (*LAm*) [+ *perro etc*] to pat
Ⓑ VI to clap

palmense Ⓐ ADJ of/from Las Palmas
Ⓑ SMF native/inhabitant of Las Palmas; **los ~s** the people of Las Palmas

palmera SF, **palmero¹** SM (*Andes, Cono Sur, Méx*) palm (tree); ✦***MODISMO*** **estar en la ~*** to be broke* ► **palmera datilera** date palm

palmero²/a Ⓐ ADJ of/from La Palma
Ⓑ SM/F native/inhabitant of La Palma; **los ~s** the people of La Palma

palmeta SF (= *vara*) cane; (= *acto*) caning, swish with a cane

palmetazo SM 1 (= *acto*) caning, swish with a cane
2 (= *desaire*) slap in the face

palmillas SFPL = **palmitas**

palmípedo ADJ web-footed

palmista SMF (*LAm*) palmist

palmiste SM (= *grano*) palm kernel; (= *aceite*) palm oil

palmitas SFPL ✦***MODISMO*** **tener** *o* **llevar** *o* **traer a algn en ~** (= *mimar*) to spoil sb; (= *tratar con cuidado*) to handle sb with kid gloves

palmito SM (*LAm*) palm heart

palmo SM 1 (= *medida*) span; (*fig*) few inches *pl*, small amount; ✦***MODISMOS*** **~ a ~** inch by inch; **avanzar ~ a ~** to inch forward; **conocer el terreno ~ a ~** *o* **a ~s** to know every inch of the ground; **tener medido el terreno a ~s** to know every inch of the ground; **con un ~ de lengua fuera** with his tongue hanging out; **crecer a ~s** to shoot up; **dejar a algn con un ~ de narices** to disappoint sb, let sb down; **no hay un ~ de A a B** there's hardly any distance *o* difference between A and B; **no levantaba un ~ del suelo cuando ...** he was knee-high to a grasshopper when ...
2 (*CAm***) (= *coño*) cunt**

palmotear ▸conjug 1a◂ VI to clap, applaud

palmoteo SM clapping, applause

palo SM 1 (= *vara*) (*de poco grosor*) stick; (*fijo en el suelo*) post; [*de telégrafos, tienda de campaña*] pole; [*de herramienta*] handle, shaft; **le pegó con un ~** he hit him with a stick; **las gallinas estaban subidas en el ~** the hens were sitting on the perch; **el ~ de la fregona** the mop handle; **política de ~ y zanahoria** carrot and stick policy; ✦***MODISMOS*** **estar hecho un ~** to be as thin *o* skinny as a rake; **meter ~s en las ruedas** to throw a spanner in the works; **más tieso que un ~**: **andaba más tieso que un ~** he walked bolt upright; **te voy a poner más tieso que un ~** I'm going to give you a good hiding; ✦***REFRÁN*** **de tal ~ tal astilla** like father like son ► **palo de escoba** broomstick ► **palo ensebado** greasy pole
2 (= *madera*) **cuchara de ~** wooden spoon; **pata de ~** wooden leg, peg leg
3 (= *golpe*) blow; **un par de ~s es lo que tú necesitas** what you need is a good hiding; **dar** *o* **pegar un ~ a algn** (= *golpear*) to hit sb with a stick; (*) (= *timar*) to rip sb off*; **los críticos le dieron un ~ a la obra** the critics slated the play*; **vaya ~ me pegaron en ese restaurante** they really ripped me off in that restaurant*; **dar de ~s a algn** to give sb a beating; ✦***MODISMOS*** **andar a ~s*** to be always squabbling *o* fighting; **dar ~s de ciego** (*peleando*) to lash out wildly; (*buscando una solución*) to take a stab in the dark; **no dar** *o* **pegar (ni) ~ al agua*** to not lift a finger; **moler a algn a ~s** to give sb a beating; **ni a ~s***: **ni a ~s va a aprender la lección** there's no way he's going to learn the lesson*; **ni a ~s me voy yo de aquí dejándote sola** wild horses wouldn't make me go off and leave you on your own, there's no way I would go off and leave you on your own*
4 (*) (= *disgusto*) bummer⁑, nightmare*; **es un ~ que te bajen el sueldo** it's a real bummer⁑ *o* nightmare* that they're cutting your salary; **¡qué ~ si suspendo!** it'll be a real bummer⁑ *o* nightmare* if I fail!; **dar ~**: **me daría ~ que se enterase** I would hate it if he found out; **llevarse un ~**: **nos llevamos un ~ muy gordo cuando descubrimos la verdad** it was a real blow when we found out the truth; **Manuel se ha llevado un gran ~ con Luisa** Manuel has been badly let down by Luisa
5 (*Náut*) mast; ✦***MODISMO*** **a ~ seco** [*navegar*] under bare poles; [*comer, beber*] **nos tomamos el vino a ~ seco** we had the wine on its own; **nos comimos el jamón a ~ seco** we had the ham on its own, we had the ham with nothing to wash it down; **no pasa un día a ~ seco** (*Ven*) he never goes a single day without a drink; **vermut a ~ seco** straight vermouth; ✦***REFRÁN*** **que cada ~ aguante su vela** everyone should face up to their responsibilities ► **palo de mesana** mizzenmast ► **palo de trinquete** foremast ► **palo mayor** mainmast
6 (*Dep*) 6·1 [*de portería*] post; **el balón se coló entre los ~s** the ball went between the posts
6·2 (*para golpear*) (*en hockey*) stick; (*en golf*) club
► **palo de golf** golf club
7 (= *de uva*) stalk
8 (*Tip*) (*de b, d*) upstroke; (*de p, q*) downstroke; **hace los ~s muy largos** he makes long strokes
9 (*Naipes*) suit; **cambiar de ~** to change suit; **seguir el ~** to follow suit ► **palo del triunfo** trump suit, trumps *pl*
10 (*Mús*) (*en flamenco*) style
11 (*esp LAm Bot*) tree ► **palo de hule** (*CAm*) rubber tree ► **palo de mango** mango tree ► **palo dulce** liquorice root ► **palo (de) rosa** rosewood ► **palo santo** lignum vitae
12 (*Ven**) [*de licor*] swig*, slug*; **pegarse unos ~s** to have a few drinks; ✦***MODISMOS*** **darse al ~** to take to drink; **a medio ~** half-drunk
13 (*Chile**) ✦***MODISMO*** **tirar el ~*** to brag ► **palo blanco** man of straw ► **palo grueso** big shot*
14 (*Méx***) (= *acto sexual*) screw**; **echar un ~** to have a screw**
15 (*Col, Ven*) **un ~ de**: **un ~ de casa** a marvellous house; **es un ~ de hombre** he's a great guy; **cayó un ~ de agua** the rain came pouring down, there was a huge downpour*

paloma SF 1 (*Orn*) dove, pigeon; **¡palomita!** darling! ► **paloma buscadora de blancos** homing pigeon ► **paloma de la paz** dove of peace ► **paloma mensajera** carrier pigeon, homing pigeon ► **paloma torcaz** wood pigeon, ringdove
2 (= *persona*) meek and mild person; (*Pol*)

dove ► **paloma sin hiel** pet, lamb
[3] (= *ejercicio*) handstand
[4] (*CAm, Caribe, Méx*) (= *cometa*) kite
[5] **palomas** (*Náut*) white horses, whitecaps (*EEUU*)

palomar SM dovecot(e)

palomear ▸conjug 1a◂ VT [1] (*Caribe*) (= *engañar*) to swindle
[2] (*Andes*) [+ *enemigos*] to hunt down one by one; (= *tirar a matar*) to shoot to kill, shoot dead; (= *matar a traición*) to shoot down in cold blood

palomilla SF [1] (*Entomología*) moth; (*esp*) grain moth; (= *crisálida*) nymph, chrysalis
[2] (*Téc*) (= *tuerca*) wing nut
[3] (= *soporte*) wall bracket, angle iron
[4] [*de caballo*] back, backbone
[5] (*Andes, Cono Sur**) (= *niño vagabundo*) urchin, ragamuffin; (*CAm, Cono Sur, Méx**) [*de niños*] mob of kids*; (= *pandilla*) crowd of layabouts, band of hooligans

palomino Ⓐ ADJ (*Andes, Cono Sur, Méx*) [*caballo*] palomino *antes de s*; (= *blanco*) white
Ⓑ SM [1] (*Orn*) young pigeon
[2] (*Andes, Cono Sur, Méx*) (= *caballo palomino*) palomino (horse); (= *caballo blanco*) white horse
[3] (*) (*en ropa interior*) skidmark*

palomita SF [1] (*Méx*) (= *aprobación*) tick
[2] (*Dep*) full-length dive
[3] **palomitas** (*tb* **~s de maíz**) popcorn *sing*

palomo Ⓐ ADJ (*Andes, Cono Sur, Méx*) = **palomino A**
Ⓑ SM (cock) pigeon ► **palomo de arcilla** clay pigeon

palotada† SF ✦*MODISMO* **no dar ~** (= *no trabajar*) not to do a stroke of work; (= *no hacer nada*) to do nothing; (= *hacerlo mal*) to get nothing right

palote SM [1] (*en escritura*) (*gen*) downstroke; (*en forma de "S"*) pothook
[2] (*Mús*) drumstick
[3] (*Caribe, Cono Sur Culin*) [*de amasar*] rolling pin
[4] (*Cono Sur**) (= *persona*) beanpole*, stringbean (*EEUU**)

palotear ▸conjug 1a◂ VI to bicker, wrangle

paloteo SM bickering, wrangling

palpable ADJ [1] (*con las manos*) palpable, tangible
[2] (= *claro, evidente*) palpable, obvious, palpable

palpamiento SM (*LAm*) frisking, body-search

palpar ▸conjug 1a◂ Ⓐ VT [1] (= *tocar*) to touch, feel; (= *tantear*) to feel one's way along; (*amorosamente*) to caress, fondle; (*esp LAm*) [+ *sospechoso*] to frisk
[2] (= *notar*) to appreciate, understand; **ahora palpa las consecuencias** now he's really feeling the consequences; **ya ~ás lo que es esto** one day you'll really understand all this
Ⓑ **palparse** VPR [*miedo, ansiedad*] to be felt; **se palpaba el descontento** you could feel the restlessness; **hay una enemistad que se palpa** you can feel the hostility, the hostility is tangible

palpitación SF (*gen*) palpitation; (*nerviosa*) quiver, quivering; (*con fuerza*) flutter, fluttering

palpitante ADJ [1] (*gen*) palpitating; [*corazón*] throbbing
[2] [*interés, cuestión*] burning

palpitar ▸conjug 1a◂ VI [1] (*gen*) to palpitate; [*corazón*] to throb, beat; (*nerviosamente*) to quiver; (*con fuerza*) to flutter
[2] (*fig*) to throb; **en la poesía palpita la emoción** the poem throbs with emotion
[3] (*Cono Sur*) ✦*MODISMOS* **me palpita** I have a hunch; **ya me palpitaba el fracaso** I had a hunch it would be a failure

pálpito SM, **palpite** SM hunch; **tener un ~** to have a hunch

palquista‡ SM cat burglar

palta SF (*Andes, Cono Sur*) avocado (pear)

palto SM (*Andes, Cono Sur*) avocado (pear) tree

paltó SM (*esp LAm*) topcoat, overcoat

palúdico ADJ [1] [*pantano, terreno*] marshy
[2] (*Med*) malarial

paludismo SM malaria

palurdo/a* Ⓐ ADJ coarse, uncouth
Ⓑ SM/F (= *paleto*) yokel, hick (*EEUU**); (*pey*) lout

palustre[1] SM (*Téc*) trowel

palustre[2] ADJ marsh *antes de s*

pamela SF sun hat, picture hat

pamema SF [1] (= *bagatela*) trivial thing, trifle
[2] **pamemas** (= *aspavientos*) fuss *sing*; **¡déjate de ~s!** stop your fussing!; **deja de decir ~s** stop talking nonsense
[3] **pamemas** (= *halagos*) flattery *sing*; (= *persuasión*) coaxing *sing*, wheedling *sing*

pampa[1] SF [1] (*LAm Geog*) pampa(s), prairie; **la Pampa** the Pampas; → GAUCHO
[2] (*Cono Sur Min*) *region of nitrate deposits*; (= *descampado*) *open area on the outskirts of a town*
[3] (*Andes*) (*en la sierra*) *high grassy plateau*
[4] ✦*MODISMOS* **a** o **en la ~** (*LAm**) in the open; **en ~** (*LAm**) in the nude; **estar en ~ y la vía** (*Cono Sur**) to be flat broke*; **quedarse en ~** (*Cono Sur**) to come to nothing, fall through

pampa[2] Ⓐ ADJ [1] (*Andes, Cono Sur**) [*negocio*] shady, dishonest
[2] (*Andes*) (= *endeble*) weak, feeble
Ⓑ SMF (*Arg*) (pampean) Indian
Ⓒ SM (*Ling*) *language of the pampean Indians*

pámpana SF vine leaf; ✦*MODISMO* **zurrar la ~ a algn** (*Esp*†*) to give sb a hiding*

pámpano SM vine shoot, vine tendril

pampeano/a (*LAm*) Ⓐ ADJ of/from the pampas
Ⓑ SM/F native/inhabitant of the pampas; **los ~s** the people of the pampas

pampear[1] ▸conjug 1a◂ VI (*Cono Sur*) to travel over the pampas

pampear[2] ▸conjug 1a◂ VT (*Andes*) [1] (= *tocar*) to tap, pat (on the shoulder)
[2] [+ *masa*] to roll out

pampero/a (*LAm*) Ⓐ ADJ of/from the pampas
Ⓑ SM/F native/inhabitant of the pampas; **los ~s** the people of the pampas
Ⓒ SM (*Meteo*) strong westerly wind (*blowing over the pampas from the Andes*)

pampinflar‡ ▸conjug 1a◂ VT **¡me la pampinflas!** you stupid git!‡

pampino/a Ⓐ ADJ (*LAm*) of/from the Chilean pampas
Ⓑ SM/F (*Cono Sur*) native/inhabitant of the Chilean pampas; **los ~s** the people of the Chilean pampas

pamplina SF [1] (*) (= *tontería*) silly remark; **¡pamplinas!** rubbish!, nonsense!; **eso son ~s** that's a load of rubbish; **sin más ~s** without any more beating about the bush
[2] (*) (= *aspaviento*) fuss
[3] (*) (= *zalamería*) soft soap*; **no me vengas con ~s** don't come to me with that soft soap*
[4] (*Bot*) chickweed

pamplinero* ADJ [1] (= *tonto*) silly, nonsensical
[2] (= *aspaventero*) given to making a great fuss
[3] (= *zalamero*) sweet-talking

pamplonada SF (*LAm*) (= *trivialidad*) triviality; (= *tontería*) silly thing, piece of nonsense

pamplonés/esa ADJ, SM/F = **pamplonica**

pamplonica Ⓐ ADJ of/from Pamplona
Ⓑ SMF native/inhabitant of Pamplona; **los ~s** the people of Pamplona

pampon SM (*Andes*) open space, open ground

pamporcino SM cyclamen

pan SM [1] (*Culin*) bread; (= *hogaza*) loaf; **les gusta mucho el ~ con mantequilla** they love bread and butter; **compré dos ~es** I bought two loaves; **estar a ~ y agua** to be on bread and water ► **pan blanco**, **pan candeal** white bread ► **pan casero** home-made bread ► **pan cenceño** unleavened bread ► **pan de centeno** rye bread ► **pan de flor** white bread ► **pan de molde** tin loaf ► **pan duro** stale bread ► **pan francés** (*Arg*) baguette ► **pan integral** wholemeal bread ► **pan lactal** (*Arg*) sandwich loaf ► **pan moreno** brown bread ► **pan rallado** breadcrumbs *pl*
[2] (= *bloque*) ► **pan de azúcar** sugar loaf ► **pan de hierba** turf, sod ► **pan de higos** block of dried figs ► **pan de jabón** bar o cake of soap
[3] (*Agr*) wheat; **un año de mucho ~** a year of a heavy wheat crop
[4] (*Téc*) gold o silver leaf
[5] ✦*MODISMOS* **con su ~ se lo coma** that's his look-out; **contigo ~ y cebolla** (with you I'd gladly have) love in a cottage; **echar ~es** (*Andes, Cono Sur*) to boast, brag; **ganarse el ~** to earn one's living; **hacer un ~ como unas hostias** to make a real mistake o gaffe; **llamar al ~ ~ y al vino vino** to call a spade a spade; **más bueno que el ~***: **estar más bueno que el ~** [*persona*] to be gorgeous, be dishy*; **ser más bueno que el ~** to be as good as gold; **ser ~ comido**: **eso es ~ comido** it's a piece of cake, it's a cinch; **ser el ~ nuestro de cada día**: **aquí los atracos son el ~ nuestro de cada día** muggings happen all the time around here; **venderse como ~ bendito** to sell like hot cakes

pan... PREF pan...; *p.ej.* **panasiático** pan-Asiatic

pana[1] SF (= *paño*) corduroy

pana[2] SF (*Chile Aut*) breakdown; **quedar en ~** to break down

pana[3] SF (*Chile*) [1] (= *hígado*) liver
[2] (*) (= *valor*) guts* *pl*, courage; ✦*MODISMO* **se le heló la ~** (*Cono Sur*) he lost his nerve
[3] ✦*MODISMO* **tirar ~s** (*Andes**) to put on airs

pana[4] SMF (*Caribe*) (= *compañero*) pal*, buddy (*EEUU*)

panacea SF panacea

panaché SM mixed salad

panadería SF [1] (= *tienda*) baker's (shop), bakery
[2] (= *oficio*) breadmaking

panadero/a SM/F baker

panadizo SM (*Med*) whitlow

panal SM honeycomb

Panamá SM Panama

panamá SM panama hat

panameñismo SM *word/phrase peculiar to Panama*

panameño/a Ⓐ ADJ Panamanian
Ⓑ SM/F Panamanian; **los ~s** the Panamanians

panamericanismo SM Pan-Americanism

panamericano Ⓐ ADJ Pan-American
Ⓑ SF **la Panamericana** the Pan-American highway

panamitos SMPL (*Andes*), **panamos** SMPL (*Andes*) 1 (= *judías*) beans
2 (*fig*) food *sing*, daily bread *sing*

panca SF (*Andes*) dry leaf of maize

pancarta SF placard, banner

panceta SF (*Arg*) streaky bacon

pancha* SF = **panza**

panchanguero* ADJ 1 (= *ruidoso*) noisy, rowdy
2 (*Méx*) (= *alegre*) merry; (= *chistoso*) witty
3 (*Méx*) (= *campechano*) expansive

pancho[1] ADJ (= *tranquilo*) calm, unruffled; **estar tan ~** (*Cono Sur, Esp*) to remain perfectly calm, not turn a hair

pancho[2] Ⓐ ADJ 1 (*Cono Sur*) (= *marrón*) brown, tan
2 (*Andes, Caribe*) (= *aplastado*) broad and flat; (= *achaparrado*) squat; ✦*MODISMO* **ni tan ~ ni tan ancho** (*Caribe*⁑) neither one thing nor the other
Ⓑ SM (*Arg Culin*) hot dog

pancho[3] SM (= *pez*) young sea-bream

Pancho SM (*forma familiar*) *de* **Francisco**

pancista ADJ, SMF opportunist

pancita SF (*Méx Culin*) tripe

pancito SM (*LAm*) (bread) roll

páncreas SM INV pancreas

pancreático ADJ pancreatic

pancromático ADJ panchromatic

panda[1] SMF (*Zool*) panda

panda[2] SF = **pandilla**

panda[3] SF (*Caribe*) = **pandeo**

pandear ▸conjug 1a◂ VI, **pandearse** VPR [*madera*] to bend, warp; [*pared*] to sag, bulge

pandemonio SM, **pandemónium** SM pandemonium; **fue el ~*** all hell broke loose, there was pandemonium

pandeo SM [*de madera*] bend; [*de pared, tejado*] sag(ging), bulge, bulging

pandereta SF tambourine; ✦*MODISMOS* **la España de ~*** tourist Spain; **zumbar la ~ a algn** (*Esp**) to tan sb's hide*

panderetear ▸conjug 1a◂ VI to play the tambourine

pandero SM 1 (*Mús*) tambourine
2 (*) (= *culo*) backside, butt (*EEUU*⁑)
3 (†) (= *cometa*) kite
4 (†*) (= *tonto*) idiot

pandibó⁑ SM slammer⁑, can (*EEUU**), prison

pandilla SF 1 [*de amigos*] group of friends; **ayer salí con la ~ de mi hermano** I went out with my brother's friends yesterday
2 [*de criminales*] gang; [*de gamberros*] bunch, load

pandillero/a SM/F (*esp LAm*) member of a gang

pando ADJ 1 [*pared*] bulging; [*madera*] warped; [*viga*] sagging
2 [*río, persona*] slow
3 [*plato*] shallow; [*terreno*] flat
4 (*CAm*) (= *oprimido*) oppressed
5 (*CAm**) (= *saciado*) full (up)
6 (*CAm, Méx*) (*de hombros*) round-shouldered

Pandora SF ✦*MODISMO* **la caja de ~** Pandora's box

pandorga SF 1 (*) (= *jamona*) fat woman
2 (= *cometa*) kite
3 (*Andes**) (= *molestia*) bother, nuisance
4 (*Andes*) (= *mentira*) lie
5 (*Méx**) (= *broma*) (*gen*) practical joke; (*estudiantil*) student prank

pandorgo ADJ 1 (*Méx*) (= *lerdo*) dim, stupid
2 (*Caribe*) (= *gordinflón*) fat and slow-moving

pane SM (*Andes Aut*) breakdown

panear ▸conjug 1a◂ VI (*Andes, Cono Sur*) to boast, show off

panecillo SM (bread) roll

panegírico SM panegyric

panel SM 1 [*de pared, puerta*] panel; **~es** (*Arquit*) panelling *sing*, paneling (*EEUU*) ► **panel de información de vuelos** flight information board ► **panel de instrumentos** (*Aut*) dashboard ► **panel de mandos** (*Aer etc*) control panel, controls *pl* ► **panel explicativo** display panel ► **panel solar** solar panel
2 (= *jurado*) panel ► **panel de audiencia** TV viewers' panel

panela SF 1 (*LAm Culin*) brown sugar loaf
2 (*Méx*) (= *sombrero*) straw hat
3 (*Andes, Méx**) (= *pesado*) bore, drag; (= *zalamero*) creep⁑

panelería SF panelling, paneling (*EEUU*)

panera SF bread basket

pánfilo ADJ 1 (= *crédulo*) simple, gullible; (= *tonto*) stupid; (= *lento*) sluggish, lethargic
2 (*Andes*) (= *pálido*) pale, discoloured, discolored (*EEUU*)

panfletario ADJ [*estilo*] highly-coloured, highly-colored (*EEUU*); [*propaganda*] cheap, demagogic

panfletista SMF (*gen*) pamphleteer; (*esp LAm*) satirist, lampoonist

panfleto SM (*gen*) pamphlet; (*esp LAm*) lampoon

panga SF (*CAm, Méx*) (= *lancha*) barge, lighter; (= *transbordador*) ferry(boat)

pangolín SM scaly anteater

paniaguado SM 1 (= *criado*) servant
2 (= *protegido*) protégé

paniaguarse ▸conjug 1i◂ VPR (*Méx*) to become friends, pal up*

pánico Ⓐ ADJ panic *antes de s*
Ⓑ SM 1 (= *miedo*) panic; **el ~ comprador** panic buying; **yo le tengo un ~ tremendo** I'm scared stiff of him
2 ✦*MODISMO* **de ~*** excellent, brilliant

paniego ADJ (*Agr*) **tierra paniega** wheatland

panificable ADJ **granos ~s** bread grains

panificación SF breadmaking

panificadora SF bakery

panil SM (*Cono Sur*) celery

panizo SM 1 (*Bot*) (= *mijo*) millet; (= *maíz*) maize
2 (*Chile*) [*de mineral*] mineral deposit
3 (*Chile*) (= *tesoro*) treasure; (= *negocio*) gold mine

panocha SF, **panoja** SF 1 (*Bot*) [*de maíz*] corncob; [*de trigo*] ear of wheat
2 (*Méx*) (= *azúcar*) unrefined brown sugar; (= *dulce*) brown sugar candy
3 (*Andes, CAm, Cono Sur*) (= *torta*) *large pancake of maize and cheese*
4 (*) (= *dinero*) brass*, dough*
5 (*Méx*⁑) (= *vulva*) cunt⁑

panocho/a Ⓐ ADJ of/from Murcia
Ⓑ SM/F native/inhabitant of Murcia; **los ~s** the Murcians, the people of Murcia
Ⓒ SM (*Ling*) Murcian dialect

panoli* SMF, **panolis*** SMF INV chump*, idiot

panoplia SF 1 (= *armadura*) panoply
2 (= *colección de armas*) collection of arms

panorama SM 1 (*gen*) panorama (*tb fig*); (= *vista*) view; (= *perspectiva*) outlook; **el ~ actual político** the present political scene
2 (*Arte, Fot*) view

panorámica SF general view, survey

panorámico ADJ panoramic; **punto ~** viewpoint, vantage point

panoramizar ▸conjug 1f◂ VTI (*Cine*) to pan

panqué SM (*CAm, Caribe*), **panqueque** SM (*LAm*) pancake

panquequera SF (*LAm*) pancake iron

panquequería SF (*LAm*) pancake house

pantaleta SF (*LAm*), **pantaletas** SFPL (*LAm*) (= *bombachos*) bloomers, drawers; (= *bragas*) panties

pantalla SF 1 [*de lámpara*] shade, lampshade
2 (*Cine*) screen; **los personajes de la ~** screen personalities; **la pequeña ~** the small screen, the TV; **llevar una historia a la ~** to film a story ► **pantalla acústica** baffle ► **pantalla de televisión** television screen ► **pantalla de vídeo** video screen ► **pantalla grande** big screen ► **pantalla plana** flat screen
3 (*Inform*) screen, display ► **pantalla de ayuda** help screen ► **pantalla de cristal líquido** liquid crystal display ► **pantalla de plasma** plasma screen ► **pantalla de radar** radar screen ► **pantalla de rayos** (*en aeropuerto*) X-ray security apparatus ► **pantalla táctil** touch screen
4 (*CAm*) (= *abanico*) fan
5 (*fig*) front; (= *señuelo*) decoy; **servir de ~ a algo** to be a front for sth; ✦*MODISMO* **hacer la ~** (*Dep*) to protect the goalkeeper
6 [*de chimenea*] fireguard
7 (= *biombo*) screen
8 (*LAm*) (= *esbirro*) henchman
9 (*CAm*) (= *espejo*) large mirror

pantalón SM, **pantalones** SMPL 1 trousers, pants (*EEUU*); **un ~ ◊ unos pantalones ◊ un par de pantalones** a pair of trousers *o* (*EEUU*) pants; **bajarse los pantalones** (*lit*) to take *o* pull one's trousers down; (*Esp**) (*fig*) to swallow one's pride; ✦*MODISMOS* **es ella la que lleva los pantalones*** she's the one who wears the trousers; **llevar los pantalones bien puestos** (*Caribe**) to have guts ► **pantalones cortos** shorts ► **pantalones de corsario** pirate trousers ► **pantalones de esquí** ski pants ► **pantalón de montar** riding breeches *pl* ► **pantalón pitillo** drainpipe trousers *pl* ► **pantalones tejanos, pantalones vaqueros** jeans
2 (*Andes*) (= *hombre*) man, male
3 (*Caribe*) (= *coraje*) guts, courage

PANTALONES, ZAPATOS, GAFAS

Uso de "pair"

- Para especificar el número de objetos que constan de dos piezas que forman parte de un juego de dos, se debe usar en inglés el partitivo **pair of** + SUSTANTIVO:

Tengo dos pares de zapatos
I've got two pairs of shoes

- La misma regla se aplica cuando se trata de objetos compuestos por dos piezas simétricas:

¿Cuántos pantalones meto en la maleta?
How many pairs of trousers shall I pack?

! Si no queremos especificar el número de objetos, no es necesario utilizar **pair**:

¿Puede arreglarme las gafas?
I wondered if you could mend my glasses?

*Para otros usos y ejemplos ver las entradas **gafa, pantalón** y **zapato**.*

pantanal SM marshland
pantano SM [1] (= *embalse*) reservoir
[2] (= *ciénaga*) bog, marsh
[3] (†) (= *atolladero*) fix*, mess*; **salir de un ~** to get out of a jam*
pantanoso ADJ [1] [*terreno, región*] boggy, marshy
[2] [*situación*] difficult, tricky*
panteísmo SM pantheism
panteísta Ⓐ ADJ pantheistic
Ⓑ SMF pantheist
panteón SM [1] (= *monumento*) pantheon; **el ~ de los reyes** the burial place of the royal family ► **panteón familiar** family vault
[2] (*LAm*) (= *cementerio*) cemetery
[3] (*Cono Sur*) (= *mineral*) ore, mineral
panteonero SM (*LAm*) gravedigger
pantera SF [1] (*Zool*) (*gen*) panther; (*Caribe*) (= *jaguar*) jaguar
[2] (*Méx*) (= *matón*) heavy*; (= *atrevido*) risk-taker
pantimedias SFPL (*Méx*) tights, pantyhose (*EEUU*)
pantis SMPL tights, pantyhose (*EEUU*)
pantógrafo SM pantograph
pantomima SF mime
pantoque SM (*Náut*) bilge; **agua de ~** bilge water
pantorra* SF (fat) calf
pantorrilla SF [1] (*Anat*) calf
[2] (*Andes*) (= *vanidad*) vanity
pantorrilludo ADJ [1] (= *de piernas gordas*) thick-calved
[2] (*Andes**) (= *vanidoso*) vain
pants SMPL (*LAm*) tracksuit *sing*, sweat suit *sing* (*EEUU*)
pantufla SF, **pantuflo** SM (carpet) slipper
panty SM, **pantys** SMPL tights, pantyhose (*EEUU*)
panucho SM (*Méx*) stuffed tortilla
panudo/a* (*Andes*) Ⓐ ADJ boastful, bragging
Ⓑ SM/F loudmouth*
panul SM (*Cono Sur*) celery
panza* SF belly, paunch; **estrellarse de ~** to do a belly flop, make a pancake landing ► **panza de burro** (*Alpinismo*) overhang ► **panza mojada** (*Méx**) wetback (*EEUU*)
panzada* SF [1] (= *hartazgo*) **darse una ~ de algo: nos dimos una ~ de cordero** we stuffed ourselves with lamb; **me he dado una buena ~ de dormir** I had a really good sleep
[2] (= *golpe*) (*en el agua*) belly flop; **aterrizaje de ~** belly landing
panzazo SM [1] (*Andes, Cono Sur*) (= *golpe*) belly flop
[2] (*Méx*) = **panzada 1**
[3] ✦*MODISMO* **pasar de ~** (*LAm‡*) to get through by the skin of one's teeth
panzón ADJ, **panzudo** ADJ paunchy, potbellied
pañal SM [1] [*de bebé*] nappy, diaper (*EEUU*); ✦*MODISMOS* **estar todavía en ~es** [*persona*] to be still wet behind the ears; [*ciencia, técnica*] to be still in its infancy; **yo de informática estoy todavía en ~es** when it comes to computing, I'm still a little wet behind the ears; **esto ha dejado en ~es a los rivales** this has left the competition way behind ► **pañal desechable** disposable nappy
[2] [*de camisa*] shirt-tail
[3] **pañales** (= *canastilla*) baby clothes; ✦*MODISMOS* **criarse en buenos ~es** to be born with a silver spoon in one's mouth; **de humildes ~es** of humble origins
pañería SF (= *géneros*) drapery; (= *tienda*) draper's (shop), dry-goods store (*EEUU*)
pañero/a SM/F draper, dry-goods dealer (*EEUU*), clothier
pañete SM [1] (= *tela*) light cloth
[2] **pañetes** (= *calzones*) shorts, trunks
[3] (*Andes*) (= *enlucido*) coat of fine plaster
[4] (*Cono Sur*) [*del caballo*] horse blanket
pañí¹ SM (*Cono Sur*) sun trap
pañí²‡ SF ✦*MODISMO* **dar la ~** to give a tip-off, tip the wink*
pañito SM (*Esp*) [*de mesa*] table-runner; [*de bandeja*] traycloth
paño SM [1] (= *tela*) cloth; ✦*MODISMOS* **conocerse el ~** to know the score*; **le conozco el ~** I know his sort; ✦*REFRÁN* **el buen ~ en el arca se vende** good wine needs no bush
[2] (= *pieza*) cloth; (= *trapo*) duster; ✦*MODISMO* **jugar a dos ~s** to play a double game ► **paño de altar** altar cloth ► **paño de cocina** dishcloth ► **paño de lágrimas**: **soy su ~ de lágrimas** I'm a shoulder for him to cry on ► **paño de los platos** tea towel ► **paño de manos** hand towel ► **paño de secar** tea towel ► **paño higiénico** (*Esp*†) sanitary towel, sanitary napkin (*EEUU*) ► **paño mortuorio** pall ► **paños calientes** half measures; **no andarse con ~s calientes** (*para solucionar algo*) not to go in for half-measures; (*al criticar algo*) to pull no punches; **poner ~s calientes** to make a half-hearted attempt ► **paños tibios** (*fig*) half-measures
[3] (*Cos*) (= *ancho*) piece of cloth, width
[4] **paños** (= *ropa*) clothes; (*Arte*) drapes ► **paños menores** underwear *sing*
[5] **al ~** (*Teat*) offstage
[6] (*Arquit*) wall section
[7] (*en cristal*) cloud of mist; [*de diamante*] flaw
[8] (*Caribe*) (= *red*) fishing net
[9] (*Andes*) (= *tierra*) plot of land
pañol SM (*Náut*) store, storeroom ► **pañol del agua** water store ► **pañol del carbón** coal bunker
pañolada SF (*Taur, Ftbl*) *form of protest at bullfights and football matches where the crowd all wave their handkerchiefs in the air*
pañoleta SF [1] [*de mujer*] (*sobre los hombros*) shawl; (*sobre la cabeza*) headscarf
[2] [*de torero*] tie
pañolón SM shawl
pañuelo SM (*para limpiarse*) handkerchief; (*para la cabeza*) scarf, headscarf; (*para el cuello*) scarf; [*de hombre*] cravat ► **pañuelo de papel** paper handkerchief
papa¹ SM (*Rel*) pope ► **papa negro** black pope (*General of the Jesuits*)
papa² SF [1] (*esp LAm*) (= *patata*) potato; ✦*MODISMOS* **cuando las ~s queman** (*Cono Sur*) when things hot up; **echar las ~s** (*Esp**) to throw up*; **ni ~***: **no entiendo ni ~** I don't understand a word; **no oyó ni ~** he didn't hear a thing; **no sabe ni ~** he hasn't got a clue ► **papa dulce** sweet potato ► **papas colchas** (*CAm*) crisps, potato chips (*EEUU*) ► **papas fritas** chips, French fries (*EEUU*)
[2] (*Méx**) (= *mentira*) fib*
[3] (*Cono Sur**) (= *golpe*) bash*
[4] (*Caribe**) (= *trabajo fácil*) soft job*
[5] (*Méx*) (= *sopa*) porridge, gruel; (*Cono Sur*) (= *de bebé*) baby food
papa³ ADJ INV (*Cono Sur**) jolly good*, first-rate
papá* SM dad*, daddy*, pop (*EEUU**); **mis ~s** my mum and dad*, my mom and pop (*EEUU*) ► **papá grande** (*Méx*) grandfather, grandpa* ► **Papá Noel** Father Christmas; *ver tb* **hijo**
papachar* ▸conjug 1a◂ (*Méx*) VT [1] (= *acariciar*) to caress, stroke
[2] (= *mimar*) to pamper, spoil
papachos* SMPL (*Méx*) (= *caricias*) caresses; (= *abrazos*) cuddles
papacote (*CAm*) Ⓐ SM (= *cometa*) kite
Ⓑ SMF (= *persona influyente*) bigwig, big shot*
papada SF [*de persona*] double chin; [*de animal*] dewlap
papadeno/a‡ SM/F (*Caribe*) Jehovah's Witness
papadilla SF dewlap
papado SM papacy
papagayo SM [1] (= *pájaro*) parrot
[2] (= *charlatán*) chatterbox; **como un ~** parrot-fashion; **deja de repetir todo lo que digo como un ~** don't just repeat what I say parrot-fashion
[3] (*Caribe, Méx*) (= *cometa*) large kite
[4] (*Andes*) (= *bacinilla*) bedpan
papaíto* SM dad*, daddy*, pop (*EEUU**)
papal¹ ADJ (*Rel*) papal
papal² SM (*LAm*) potato field
papalina SF [1] (= *gorro*) (*con orejeras*) cap with earflaps; (*de esquiar*) ski-cap; (*para atar al cuello*) bonnet; (= *toca*) mobcap
[2] (*) (= *juerga*) binge*; **coger una ~** to get plastered*
[3] **papalinas** (*CAm*) (= *patatas fritas*) (*Culin*) crisps, potato chips (*EEUU*)
papalón* SM (*Méx*) rat*, swine*
papalote SM (*CAm, Méx*) [1] (= *cometa*) kite
[2] (= *molino*) [*de niño*] windmill
papalotear* ▸conjug 1a◂ VI [1] (*CAm, Méx*) (= *vagabundear*) to wander about
[2] (*Méx*) (= *agonizar*) to give one's last gasp
papamoscas SM INV [1] (*Orn*) flycatcher
[2] = **papanatas**
papamóvil SM popemobile
papanatas* SM INV sucker*, simpleton
papanatería SF, **papanatismo** SM gullibility, simple-mindedness
papandujo* ADJ (*Esp*) soft, overripe

papapa SF (*CAm*) stupidity

papar* ▸conjug 1a◂ Ⓐ VT (= *tragar*) to swallow, gulp (down)
Ⓑ **paparse** VPR 1 (= *comer*) to scoff*; **se lo papó todo** he scoffed the lot*; ✦*MODISMO* **¡pápate ésa!** (*Esp*) put that in your pipe and smoke it!*
2 (= *recibir un golpe*) to get a sudden knock, be hit real hard*

paparazzo [papa'ratso] SM (*pl* **paparazzi**) paparazzo; **los paparazzi** the paparazzi

paparrucha* SF, **paparruchada*** SF 1 (= *disparate*) silly thing; **~s** rubbish *sing*, nonsense *sing*
2 (†) (= *chapuza*) worthless object
3 (†) (= *infundio*) hoax

paparruta SMF (*Cono Sur*) humbug

paparulo* SM (*Cono Sur*) sucker⁑

papas* SFPL (= *gachas*) pap *sing*, mushy food *sing*; (= *comida*) grub⁑ *sing*, chow *sing* (*EEUU*⁑)

papaya SF 1 (= *fruta*) papaya, pawpaw
2 (*Caribe*⁂) (= *vulva*) fanny⁂, beaver (*esp EEUU*⁂)

papayo SM papaya tree, pawpaw tree

papear⁑ ▸conjug 1a◂ VI to eat, scoff*

papel SM 1 (= *material*) paper; **una bolsa de ~** a paper bag; **un ~** (*pequeño*) a piece of paper; (= *hoja, folio*) a sheet of paper; **lo escribí en un ~** I wrote it on a piece of paper; **sobre el ~** on paper ► **papel absorbente** kitchen roll ► **papel atrapamoscas** flypaper ► **papel biblia** India paper ► **papel carbón** carbon paper ► **papel cel(l)o** adhesive tape ► **papel continuo** continuous feed paper ► **papel craft** (*CAm, Méx*) waxed paper ► **papel charol** shiny wrapping paper ► **papel cuadriculado** squared paper, graph paper ► **papel de aluminio** tinfoil, aluminium o (*EEUU*) aluminum foil ► **papel de arroz** rice paper ► **papel de calcar, papel de calco** tracing paper ► **papel de cartas** notepaper ► **papel de celofán** Cellophane® ► **papel de China** India paper ► **papel de desecho** waste paper ► **papel de embalaje, papel de embalar** wrapping paper ► **papel de empapelar** wallpaper ► **papel de envolver** wrapping paper ► **papel de estaño** tinfoil, aluminium o (*EEUU*) aluminum foil ► **papel de estraza** (grey) wrapping paper ► **papel de excusado**† toilet paper ► **papel de filtro** filter paper ► **papel de fumar** cigarette paper; **entre ellos no cabía un ~ de fumar** (*Esp*) you couldn't have got a razor's edge between them ► **papel de grasa** greaseproof paper ► **papel de lija** sandpaper ► **papel de mano** handmade paper ► **papel de oficio** (*LAm*) official foolscap paper ► **papel de paja de arroz** rice paper ► **papel de paredes** wallpaper ► **papel de plata** silver paper ► **papel de regalo** gift wrap, wrapping paper ► **papel (de) seda** tissue paper ► **papel de tina** handmade paper ► **papel de tornasol** litmus paper ► **papel encerado** wax(ed) paper ► **papel engomado** gummed paper ► **papel estucado** art paper ► **papel fiduciario** fiduciary issue, fiat currency ► **papel higiénico** toilet paper ► **papel indicador** litmus paper ► **papel madera** (*Cono Sur*) brown wrapping paper ► **papel mojado** scrap of paper, worthless bit of paper; **el documento no es más que ~ mojado** the document isn't worth the paper it's written on ► **papel ondulado** corrugated paper ► **papel para máquina de escribir** typing paper ► **papel pautado** ruled paper ► **papel pergamino** parchment paper ► **papel pintado** wallpaper ► **papel prensa** newsprint ► **papel reciclado** recycled paper ► **papel sanitario** (*Méx*) toilet paper ► **papel secante** blotting paper ► **papel sellado** stamped paper ► **papel timbrado** stamp, stamp paper ► **papel transparente** tracing paper ► **papel usado, papeles usados** wastepaper *sing* ► **papel vegetal** film ► **papel vitela** vellum paper
2 **papeles** (= *documentos*) papers, documents; (= *carnet*) identification papers; **los ~es, por favor** your papers, please; **tiene los ~es en regla** his papers are in order; **los sin ~es** illegal immigrants; ✦*MODISMO* **perder los ~es** to lose it
3 (= *actuación*) (*Cine, Teat*) part, role; (*fig*) role; **hizo el ~ de Cleopatra** she played the part of Cleopatra; **el ~ del gobierno en este asunto** the government's role in this matter; **tuvo que desempeñar un ~ secundario** he had to play second fiddle, he had to take a minor role; **jugó un ~ muy importante en las negociaciones** he played a very important part in the negotiations; **hacer buen/mal ~** to make a good/bad impression; **el equipo hizo un buen ~ en el torneo** the team did well in the tournament ► **papel estelar** star part
4 (= *billetes*) **mil dólares en ~** a thousand dollars in notes ► **papel moneda** paper money, banknotes *pl*
5 (*Fin*) (= *bonos*) stocks and shares *pl* ► **papel del Estado** government bonds *pl*
6 (*Esp*⁑) 1,000-peseta note; (*Andes*) one-peso note
7 (*LAm*) (= *bolsa*) bag

> **PAPEL**
>
> El sustantivo **papel** se puede traducir en inglés por **paper** o por **piece of paper**.
>
> • Lo traducimos por **paper** cuando nos referimos al **papel** como material:
>
> ¿Todo el mundo tiene lápiz y papel?
> ***Has everybody got a pencil and paper?***
>
> • Si **papel** se refiere a una hoja de papel no lo traducimos por **paper**, sino por **a piece of paper** si nos referimos a un trozo de papel pequeño y por **a sheet of paper** si nos referimos a una hoja de papel o a un folio:
>
> ¿Has visto el papel en el que estaba apuntando mis notas?
> ***Have you seen that sheet of paper I was making notes on?***
> Apúntalo en este papel
> ***Write it down on this piece of paper***
>
> • Si nos referimos a varias hojas o trozos de papel en blanco utilizamos **sheets** o **pieces**:
>
> Necesitamos varios papeles
> ***We need several pieces of paper***
>
> • Si nos referimos a **papeles** que ya están escritos, se pueden traducir por **papers**:
>
> Tengo que ordenar todos estos papeles
> ***I must sort out all these papers***
>
> *Para otros usos y ejemplos ver la entrada.*

papela⁑ SF (*Esp*) 1 (= *documento*) (*gen*) paper, document; (= *carné*) identity card, ID
2 (= *droga*) = **papelina**

papelada SF (*Col*) pretence

papelear ▸conjug 1a◂ VI 1 (= *revolver papeles*) to rummage through papers
2 (= *atraer la atención*) to make a splash, draw attention to o.s.

papeleo SM (= *trámites*) paperwork; (*pey*) red tape

papelera SF 1 (= *recipiente*) (*en la oficina, en casa*) wastepaper bin, wastepaper basket; (*en la calle*) litter bin, trash can (*EEUU*); (*Inform*) (*tb* **~ de reciclaje**) wastebasket
2 (= *fábrica*) paper mill
3 (= *escritorio*) writing desk

papelería SF 1 (= *tienda*) stationer's (shop)
2 (= *artículos de escribir*) stationery
3 (= *montón*) mass of papers, heap of papers; (= *lío*) sheaf of papers

papelerío SM (*LAm*) = **papelería 3**

papelero/a Ⓐ ADJ 1 (*Com*) paper *antes de s*
2 (= *farolero*) pretentious
Ⓑ SM/F 1 (= *fabricante*) paper manufacturer
2 (= *vendedor*) [*de artículos de escribir*] stationer; (*Méx*) [*de periódicos*] newspaper seller
3 (*Cono Sur*) (= *hazmerreír*) ridiculous person

papeleta SF 1 (*gen*) slip of paper; (= *ficha*) index card, file card; [*de rifa*] ticket; (*Univ*) (*tb* **~ de examen**) *exam results slip*; (*CAm*) [*de visita*] visiting card, calling card (*EEUU*); ✦*MODISMO* **¡vaya ~!** this is a tough one! ► **papeleta de empeño** pawn ticket ► **papeleta de examen** (*Univ*) *exam results slip*
2 (*Pol*) ballot paper, voting paper ► **papeleta en blanco** blank ballot paper ► **papeleta nula** spoiled ballot paper
3 (*LAm*) (= *bolsa*) bag
4 (*Andes**) (= *multa*) fine

papelillo SM 1 (= *papel*) cigarette paper
2 (= *cigarro*) cigarette
3 (*Med*) sachet

papelina* SF paper, sheet (*containing drug*)

papelista SMF (*Caribe, Cono Sur*) = **picapleitos**

papelito SM 1 (= *trozo de papel*) slip of paper, bit of paper
2 (*Teat, Cine*) minor role, bit part

papelón/ona Ⓐ SM/F (= *impostor*) impostor; (= *engreído*) show-off*
Ⓑ SM 1 (*Teat, Cine*) leading role, big part; ✦*MODISMO* **hacer un ~** to show o.s. up, make o.s. a laughing stock
2 (= *papel usado*) (piece of) wastepaper; (= *cartulina*) pasteboard
3 (*Andes, Caribe*) (= *pan de azúcar*) sugar loaf

papelonero ADJ (*Cono Sur*) ridiculous

papelote SM (*pey*), **papelucho** SM (*pey*) (*gen*) useless bit of paper; (*sin valor*) worthless document; (*Literat*) trashy piece of writing

papeo⁑ SM 1 (= *comida*) grub⁑, chow (*EEUU*⁑), food 2 (= *el comer*) eating

papera SF 1 (= *bocio*) goitre, goiter (*EEUU*)
2 **paperas** (= *enfermedad*) mumps *sing*

papero/a Ⓐ ADJ 1 (*LAm*) [*exportación, producción*] potato *antes de s*
2 (*Méx*) (= *embustero*) lying, deceitful
Ⓑ SM/F (*Agr*) potato grower; (*Com*) potato dealer

papi* SM dad*, daddy*, pop (*EEUU**)

papiamento SM (*Ling*) Papiamento

papila SF papilla ► **papila gustativa** taste bud

papilla SF 1 [*de bebé*] baby food; ✦*MODISMO* **estar hecho ~*** (= *cansado*) to be shattered*;

(= *roto*) to be smashed to pieces
[2] (†) (= *astucia*) guile, deceit

papillote SM buttered paper, greased paper; **en ~** (*Culin*) en papillote

papiloma SM wart, papilloma (*frm*)
► **papiloma genital** genital wart

papilomavirus SM INV papillomavirus

papira⁑ SF letter

papiro SM papyrus

pápiro⁑ SM (*Esp*) (= *billete*) 1,000 peseta note; **~s** (= *dinero*) brass* *sing*, cash *sing*; **tener afán de ~s** to be greedy for money

papiroflexia SF origami

papirotazo SM, **papirote** SM flick

papismo SM (*pey*) papism

papista Ⓐ ADJ (*pey*) papist; ✦*MODISMO* **es más ~ que el papa** he's more Catholic than the Pope
Ⓑ SMF papist

papo SM [1] (= *papada*) double chin, jowl; [*de ave*] crop; [*de animal*] dewlap; ✦*MODISMOS* **estar de ~ de mona** (*Esp**) to be first-rate; **pasarlo de ~ de mona** (*Esp**) to have a super time*
[2] (= *bocio*) goitre, goiter (*EEUU*)
[3] (⁑) (= *vulva*) pussy⁑

paprika SF paprika

papudo ADJ [*persona*] double-chinned, with a heavy jowl; (*Zool*) dewlapped

papujado ADJ swollen, puffed up

papujo ADJ [1] (*Méx*) (= *hinchado*) swollen, puffed up; (*Andes*) (*de mejillas*) chubby-cheeked
[2] (*Méx*) (= *anémico*) anaemic, anemic (*EEUU*); (= *macilento*) wan; (= *enfermizo*) sickly

paquebote SM packet boat

paquero SM (*Méx*) swindler, crook

paquete Ⓐ SM [1] [*de correos*] (*grande*) parcel; (*pequeño*) package; **me mandaron un ~ por correo** I got a parcel in the post; ✦*MODISMO* **ir** *o* **viajar de ~*** (*en moto*) to ride pillion
► **paquete bomba** parcel bomb ► **paquetes postales** (*como servicio*) parcel post *sing*
[2] [*de cigarrillos, galletas*] packet, pack (*EEUU*); [*de harina, azúcar*] bag
[3] (*Fin, Inform*) (= *conjunto*) package
► **paquete accionarial, paquete de acciones** parcel of shares ► **paquete de aplicaciones** software package ► **paquete de beneficios** benefits package ► **paquete de medidas** package of measures ► **paquete estadístico** statistical package ► **paquete integrado** integrated package
[4] (*) (= *persona torpe*) **ser un ~** to be useless, be a dead loss*; **es un auténtico ~ para las matemáticas** he's completely useless at maths
[5] (*) (= *castigo*) **el sargento le metió un ~ por abandonar su puesto** the sergeant threw the book at him for leaving his post; **nos van a pegar un ~ si nos saltamos las clases** we'll get a rocket if we skip classes*
[6] (*) (= *bebé*) **dejar a una con el ~** to put a woman in the family way; **soltar el ~** to give birth
[7] (⁑) (= *genitales masculinos*) bulge, lunchbox⁑; ✦*MODISMO* **marcar ~** to wear very tight trousers
[8] (*) (= *pañal*) (*limpio*) nappy; (*sucio*) dirty nappy; **aún lleva ~ por las noches** she still wears a nappy at night
[9] (*Náut*) packet (boat)
[10] (†*) (= *majo*) dandy; **estar hecho un ~** to be all dressed up, be dressed in style
[11] (*Med*⁑) dose (of VD)⁑
[12] (*LAm*) (= *cosa pesada*) nuisance, bore; **¡menudo ~! ◊ ¡vaya ~!** what a bore!
[13] ✦*MODISMO* **darse ~** (*esp CAm, Méx*) to give o.s. airs
[14] (*Méx*) (= *asunto*) tough job, hard one
[15] (*Cono Sur*⁑) queer⁑, poof⁑, fag (*EEUU*⁑)
[16] (*LAm*) (= *vacaciones*) package holiday
Ⓑ ADJ INV (*Andes, Arg**) elegant, chic

paquetear ▸conjug 1a◂ VI (*LAm*) to be very smart

paquete-bomba SM (*pl* **paquetes-bomba**) parcel bomb

paquetería SF [1] (= *paquetes*) parcels *pl*; **servicio de ~** parcel service
[2] (*Cono Sur**) **¡qué ~!** how elegant!; **se puso toda su ~** she put on her Sunday best; **¡vaya ~ que lleva!** she's wearing everything but the kitchen sink!*

paquetero/a* SM/F card sharper

paquetudo* ADJ (*LAm*) [1] = **paquete B**
[2] (= *orgulloso*) stuck-up*

paquidermo SM pachyderm

paquistaní = **pakistaní**

Paquita SF (*forma familiar*) *de* **Francisca**

Paquito SM (*forma familiar*) *de* **Francisco**

PAR SM ABR (*Esp*) = **Partido Aragonés Regionalista**

par Ⓐ ADJ [1] [*número*] even
[2] (= *igual*) equal; **son ~es en altura** they're of equal height
Ⓑ SM [1] (= *pareja*) pair; (= *número indeterminado*) couple; **un ~ de guantes** a pair of gloves; **a ~es** in pairs, in twos; **por un ~ de dólares** for a couple of dollars; **un ~ de veces** a couple of times; **le dio un ~ de bofetadas** he slapped him a couple of times; ✦*MODISMO* **de tres ~es de narices***: **se cogió un cabreo de tres ~es de narices** he went totally off his head*; **te piden un currículum de tres ~es de narices** they are asking for an amazing CV ► **par de fuerzas** (*Mec*) couple ► **par de torsión** (*Mec*) torque
[2] (= *igual*) equal; **está al ~ de los mejores** it is on a par with the best; **caminar al ~ de algn** to walk abreast of sb; **sin ~** unparalleled, peerless (*frm*); **no tener ~** to be unparalleled *o* peerless (*frm*)
[3] (*Mat*) even number; **~es o nones** odds or evens
[4] (*Golf*) par; **dos bajo ~** two under par; **lo hizo con cuatro por debajo del ~** he did it in four under par; **bajar del ~** to finish under par
[5] ✦*MODISMO* **de ~ en ~** wide open
[6] (*Pol*) peer; **los doce ~es** the twelve peers
Ⓒ SF [1] (*esp Com, Fin*) par; **estar por encima de la ~** to be above *o* over par; **estar por debajo de la ~** to be under *o* below par; **a la ~** (= *al mismo nivel*) on a par; (= *a la vez*) at the same time; **las acciones de las hidroeléctricas están a la ~** shares in the hydroelectric companies are at par; **caminaban a la ~** they were walking alongside each other, they were walking side by side
[2] **a la ~ que: es útil a la ~ que divertido** it is both useful and amusing, it is useful as well as being amusing

> **PAR**
>
> A la hora de traducir **par (de)** seguido de un sustantivo, hay que tener en cuenta la diferencia entre **pair (of)** y **couple (of)**.
>
> • Se traduce por **pair (of)** cuando nos referimos a objetos que normalmente se usan por **pares**:
>
> ...tres pares de guantes...
> ***...three pairs of gloves...***
> Voy a necesitar dos pares más de calcetines
> ***I'll need two more pairs of socks***
>
> • Lo traducimos por **couple (of)** en los demás casos, en los que **un par de** se puede emplear además en el sentido más vago de "dos o más de dos":
>
> Me he comprado un par de camisas
> ***I've bought a couple of shirts***
> Regresaré en un par de minutos
> ***I'll be back in a couple of minutes***
>
> ⇨ *Ver tb* PANTALONES, ZAPATOS, GAFAS
> *Para otros usos y ejemplos ver la entrada.*

para[1] PREP [1] (*indicando finalidad, uso*) for; **un regalo ~ ti** a present for you; **psicológicamente no estoy preparado ~ eso** I'm not psychologically ready for that; **es demasiado cara ~ nosotros** it's too dear for us, it's beyond our means; **no tengo ~ el viaje** I haven't got enough money for the trip; **léelo ~ ti** read it to yourself; **nació ~ poeta** he was born to be a poet; **ya no estoy ~ estos trotes** I'm not up to this sort of thing anymore; **yo no valgo ~ esto** I'm no good at this; **una taza ~ café** a coffee cup; **laca ~ el pelo** hairspray; **~ esto, podíamos habernos quedado en casa** if this is it, we might as well have stayed at home
[2] **~ que** [2·1] (+ *SUBJUN*) **lo traje ~ que lo vieras** I brought it so (that) you could see it; **es ~ que lo leas** it's for you to read; **un regalo ~ que te acuerdes de mí** a present for you to remember me by; **~ que eso fuera posible tendrías que trabajar mucho** you would have to work hard for that to be possible
[2·2] (*en preguntas*) **¿~ qué lo quieres?** why do you want it?, what do you want it for?; **¿~ qué sirve?** what's it for?; **—¿por qué no se lo dices? —¿~ qué?** "why don't you tell her?" — "what's the point *o* use?"; **tú ya has pasado por eso, ¿~ qué te voy a contar?** you've already been through that, so there's no point *o* use me telling you; ✦*MODISMO* **que ~ qué***: **tengo un hambre que ~ qué** (*uso enfático*) I'm absolutely starving*; **hay un embotellamiento que ~ qué** there's a huge traffic jam
[3] (+ *INFIN*) [3·1] (*indicando finalidad*) to; **lo hizo ~ salvarse** he did it (in order) to save himself; **~ comprarlo necesitas cinco dólares más** to buy it you need another five dollars; **estoy ahorrando ~ comprarme una moto** I'm saving up to buy a motorbike, I'm saving up for a motorbike; **entré despacito ~ no despertarla** I went in slowly so as not to wake her; **no es ~ comer** it's not for eating, it's not to be eaten; **tengo bastante ~ vivir** I have enough to live on; **es muy tarde ~ salir** it's too late to go out
[3·2] (*indicando secuencia temporal*) **se casaron ~ separarse en seguida** they married only to separate soon after; **el rey visitará Argentina ~ volar después a Chile** the king will visit

Argentina and then fly on to Chile

4 (*con expresiones de tiempo*) **con esto tengo ~ rato** this will take me a while; **lo dejamos ~ mañana** let's leave it till tomorrow; **tengo muchos deberes ~ mañana** I have a lot of homework to do for tomorrow; **lo recordaré ~ siempre** I'll remember it forever; **ahora ~ las vacaciones de agosto hará un año** it'll be a year ago this *o* come the August holiday; **va ~ un año desde la última vez** it's getting on for a year since the last time; **lo tendré listo ~ fin de mes** I'll have it ready by *o* for the end of the month; **~ entonces ya era tarde** it was already too late by then; **~ las dos estaba lloviendo** by two o'clock it was raining; **un cuarto ~ las diez** (*LAm*) a quarter to ten; **son cinco ~ las ocho** (*LAm*) it's five to eight

5 (*indicando dirección*) **~ atrás** back, backwards; **~ la derecha** to the right; **el autobús ~ Marbella** the bus for Marbella, the Marbella bus; **iba ~ el metro** I was going towards the underground; **ir ~ casa** to go home, head for home; **salir ~ Panamá** to leave for Panama

6 (*indicando opiniones*) **~ mí que miente** in my opinion *o* if you ask me he's lying; **no hay niño feo ~ una madre** all mothers think their baby is beautiful

7 (*en comparaciones*) **es mucho ~ lo que suele dar** this is a lot in comparison with what he usually gives; **¿quién es usted ~ gritarme así?** who are you to shout at me like that?; **~ profesor habla muy mal** he doesn't speak very clearly for a teacher; **~ ser un niño lo hace muy bien** he does it very well for a child; **~ patatas, las de mi pueblo** if it's potatoes you want, look no further than my home town; **~ ruidosos, los españoles** there's nobody like the Spaniards for being noisy

8 (*indicando trato*) **~ con** to, towards; **tan amable ~ con todos** so kind to *o* towards everybody; *ver tb* **estar A7**, **ir A10**

para²* SM paratrooper, para*

para... PREF para...

parabellum® SM INV (automatic) pistol; **balas del calibre 9mm Parabellum** 9mm Parabellum bullets

parabién SM congratulations *pl*; **dar el ~ a algn** to congratulate sb (**por** on)

parábola SF 1 (*Mat*) parabola

2 (*Literat*) parable

parabólica SF satellite dish

parabólico ADJ parabolic

parabrisas SM INV windscreen, windshield (*EEUU*)

paraca¹* SM paratrooper, para*

paraca² SF (*Andes*) *strong wind from the sea*

paracaídas SM INV parachute; **lanzar algo en ~** to send sth down by parachute; **aterrizar en ~ en un lugar** to parachute into a place; **lanzarse** *o* **saltar** *o* **tirarse en ~** (*gen*) to parachute; (*en emergencia*) to parachute, bale out; (*una sola vez*) to do a parachute jump

paracaidismo SM 1 (*Dep, Mil*) parachuting ► **paracaidismo acrobático** skydiving

2 (*Méx**) (= *ocupación*) squatting

paracaidista SMF 1 (*gen*) parachutist; (*Mil*) paratrooper; (*acrobático*) skydiver; **los ~s** (*Mil*) the paratroops

2 (*Méx**) (= *ocupante*) squatter

3 (*Méx**) (= *colado*) gatecrasher

paracetamol SM paracetamol

parachispas SM INV fireguard, fire screen

parachoques SM INV (*Aut*) bumper, fender (*EEUU*); (*Ferro*) buffer; (*Mec*) shock absorber

parada SF 1 (= *acción*) stop; **hicimos varias ~s en el camino** we made several stops on the way; **un tren sin ~s** a direct train; **el autobús hace ~ en Valencia** the bus stops at Valencia; **correr en ~** to run on the spot, run in place (*EEUU*); **hacer una ~ a algn** (*Chile**) to stop sb ► **parada cardíaca** cardiac arrest ► **parada de manos** (*Chile*) handstand ► **parada en firme** (*Equitación*) dead stop, dead halt ► **parada en seco** sudden stop

2 (= *lugar*) stop; **la próxima ~ es la nuestra** the next stop is ours ► **parada de autobús** bus stop ► **parada de taxis** taxi rank ► **parada discrecional** request stop ► **parada y fonda** food and shelter; **hicimos ~ y fonda en un monasterio** they gave us food and shelter in a monastery

3 [*de caballos*] relay, team

4 (= *desfile*) (*Mil*) parade; **formar en ~** to parade; ✦*MODISMO* **ir a todas las ~s** (*Chile*) to be up for anything* ► **parada nupcial** (*Orn*) courtship display

5 (*Dep*) save, stop

6 (*Mús*) pause

7 (*Esgrima*) parry

8 (*en el juego*) bet, stake

9 (= *presa*) dam

10 (*Agr*) stud farm

11 (*Cono Sur*) (= *vanidad*) snobbery, pretension; (= *jactancia*) boastfulness; ✦*MODISMO* **hacer la ~***: **hizo la ~ como que estudiaba** he put on a show of studying*; **no me dio asiento, sólo hizo la ~** he made as if to give me his seat, but didn't

12 (*Chile**) (= *traje*) outfit

13 (*Perú*) open market, farmer's market (*EEUU*)

paradear* ▸conjug 1a◂ VI (*Cono Sur*) to brag, show off; **~ con algo** to brag about sth, show sth off

paradero SM 1 (*gen*) whereabouts *pl*; **averiguar el ~ de algn** to ascertain sb's whereabouts; **García se halla en ~ desconocido** García's whereabouts are unknown; **no sabemos su ~** we do not know his whereabouts

2 (= *fin*) end; **seguramente tendrá mal ~** he'll surely come to a bad end

3 (*Andes, Cono Sur*) [*de autobús*] bus stop

4 (*LAm*) (= *apeadero*) wayside halt

paradigma SM paradigm

paradigmático ADJ paradigmatic

paradisiaco ADJ, **paradisíaco** ADJ heavenly

parado/a Ⓐ ADJ 1 (= *detenido*) **me quedé ~ para que no me oyese** I stood still so that he couldn't hear me; **estuve un momento ~ delante de su puerta** I stopped for a moment in front of his door; **¿por qué no nos echas una mano en vez de estar ahí ~?** can't you give us a hand instead of just standing there *o* around?; **no le gusta estar ~, siempre encuentra algo que hacer** he doesn't like to be idle *o* doing nothing, he always finds himself something to do; **¿qué hace ese coche ahí ~?** what's that car doing standing there?; **la producción estuvo parada durante unos meses** production was at a standstill *o* stopped for a few months; **salida parada** (*Dep*) standing start

2 (*Esp*) (= *sin trabajo*) unemployed; **llevo dos años parada** I've been out of work *o* unemployed for two years; **se ha quedado ~ hace poco tiempo** he was made redundant a short time ago

3 (= *desconcertado*) **me quedé ~ sin saber qué hacer después** I was taken aback and did not know what to do next; **me dejó ~ con lo que me dijo** what he said really took me aback, I was really taken aback by what he said

4 (*LAm*) (= *de pie*) standing (up); **estuve ~ durante dos horas** I was standing for two hours; ✦*MODISMO* **caer ~ (como los gatos)** to land on one's feet

5 (*Esp**) **ser ~** (= *ser tímido*) to be tongue-tied; (= *tener poca iniciativa*) to be a wimp*

6 (*Caribe, Cono Sur*) (= *engreído*) vain

7 **bien/mal ~**: **en este libro la mujer queda muy bien parada** women are shown in a good light in this book, women come out well in this book; **la crítica ha dejado mal parada a la película** the film got a battering from the critics; **salir bien/mal ~**: **salió mejor ~ de lo que cabía esperar** he came out of it better than could be expected; **salió muy mal ~ del accidente** he was in a bad way after the accident; **la imagen del partido ha salido muy mal parada de todo este escándalo** the party's image has suffered because of this scandal

8 (*Andes, Caribe*) (= *afortunado*) **estar bien ~** to be lucky; **estar mal ~** to be unlucky

9 (*Méx, Col*) **estar bien ~ con algn** to be well in with sb*

10 (*LAm*) (= *hacia arriba*) [*pelo*] stiff; [*poste*] upright; [*orejas*] pricked-up; **con la cola parada** with its tail held high

11 (*Méx, Ven*) (= *levantado*) up, out of bed

12 (*Chile*) (= *en huelga*) (out) on strike

Ⓑ SM/F (*Esp*) unemployed person; **Miguel López, un ~ de 27 años ...** Miguel López, an unemployed, 27 year old man ...; **el número de ~s** the number of people out of work *o* the number of unemployed; **los ~s de larga duración** the long-term unemployed

Ⓒ SM 1 (*Ven*) **dar un ~ a algn** = **hacer una parada a algn**

2 (*Méx*) (= *parecido*) air, look, resemblance; **tener ~ de algn** to look like sb

paradoja SF paradox

paradójicamente ADV paradoxically

▼ **paradójico** ADJ paradoxical

paradón* SM (*Dep*) great save, fantastic stop*

parador SM (*Esp*) (*tb* **~ nacional de turismo**) (state-run) tourist hotel; (*Hist*) inn

PARADOR NACIONAL

In the early days of the Spanish tourist industry in the 1950s, the government set up a network of high-class tourist hotels known as ***paradores****. They are sited in rural beauty spots and places of historical interest, often in converted castles and monasteries. There are currently 57 paradors, all rated at 3 stars or above and aiming to provide a high standard of accommodation with the emphasis on local character and cuisine.*

paraestatal ADJ [*organismo*] public; [*actividad*] semi-official

➤ LENGUA Y USO: **paradójico** 53.3

parafernalia SF paraphernalia

parafina SF (*sólida*) paraffin wax; (*Cono Sur*) (= *combustible*) paraffin ► **parafina líquida** liquid paraffin

parafinado ADJ waxed, waterproofed

parafrasear ▸conjug 1a◂ VT to paraphrase

paráfrasis SF INV paraphrase

paragolpes SM INV (*Cono Sur Aut*) bumper, fender (*EEUU*)

parágrafo SM (*Caribe*) paragraph

paraguas SM INV [1] (*para la lluvia*) umbrella ► **paraguas nuclear** nuclear umbrella ► **paraguas protector** protective umbrella
[2] (*) (= *condón*) rubber*, French letter‡
[3] (*Andes, Caribe, Méx*) (= *seta comestible*) mushroom; (= *hongo venenoso*) toadstool; (= *moho*) fungus

Paraguay SM Paraguay

paraguayismo SM *word or phrase peculiar to Paraguay*

paraguayo/a Ⓐ ADJ of/from Paraguay
Ⓑ SM/F native/inhabitant of Paraguay; **los ~s** the people of Paraguay
Ⓒ SM [1] (*Andes*) (= *látigo*) whip
[2] (*Caribe*) (= *machete*) long straight knife

paragüero/a Ⓐ ADJ (*hum*) of/from Orense
Ⓑ SM/F (*hum*) native/inhabitant of Orense; **los ~s** the people of Orense
Ⓒ SM umbrella stand

paraíso SM [1] (*Rel*) paradise, heaven ► **paraíso fiscal** tax haven ► **paraíso terrenal** Garden of Eden
[2] (*Teat*) upper gallery, gods *pl*

paraje SM place, spot

paral SM (*Méx*) (= *madero*) post; (= *puntal*) shore, prop

paralela SF [1] (= *línea*) parallel (line)
[2] **paralelas** (*Dep*) parallel bars ► **paralelas asimétricas** asymmetric bars

paralelamente ADV [1] (= *en la misma dirección*) **la carretera avanza ~ a la vía del tren** the road runs parallel to the rail track
[2] (= *al mismo tiempo*) **los ministros de finanzas se reunieron ~ en Washington** the Finance Ministers held a parallel meeting in Washington; **~ a esta expansión económica tuvieron lugar importantes cambios sociales** significant social changes occurred in parallel with the economic expansion; **~, los rebeldes prosiguen su campaña de terror** similarly, the rebels are continuing with their campaign of terror

paralelismo SM parallelism, parallel

paralelo Ⓐ ADJ [1] [*líneas*] parallel (**a** to); [*vidas, caracteres*] parallel
[2] (= *no oficial*) unofficial, irregular; (*pey*) illegal; **importaciones paralelas** unauthorized imports, illegal imports; **medicina paralela** alternative medicine
Ⓑ SM parallel; **en ~** (*Elec*) in parallel; **en ~ con** in parallel with; **rodar en ~** [*ciclistas*] to cycle two abreast; **un éxito sin ~** an unparalleled success

paralelogramo SM parallelogram

paralimpiada SF = **paraolimpiada**

paralímpico/a ADJ, SM/F = **paraolímpico**

parálisis SF INV paralysis ► **parálisis cerebral** cerebral palsy ► **parálisis infantil** infantile paralysis ► **parálisis progresiva** creeping paralysis

paralítico/a ADJ, SM/F paralytic

paralización SF (*gen*) stoppage; (*Med*) paralysation, paralyzation; (*fig*) blocking; (*Com*) stagnation; **la ~ fue total** everything came to a complete standstill

paralizador ADJ, **paralizante** ADJ [*miedo, gas*] paralysing, paralyzing

paralizar ▸conjug 1f◂ Ⓐ VT (*gen*) to stop; (*Med*) to paralyse, paralyze; [+ *tráfico*] to bring to a standstill; **estar paralizado de un brazo** to be paralysed in one arm; **estar paralizado de miedo** to be paralysed with fright
Ⓑ **paralizarse** VPR [1] [*pierna, brazo*] to become paralysed
[2] [*demanda, inversiones, obra*] to grind to a halt

paramar[1] SM (*Andes, Caribe*) *season of wind and snow*

paramar[2] ▸conjug 1a◂ VI (*Andes, Caribe*), **paramear** ▸conjug 1a◂ VI (*Andes, Caribe*) to drizzle

paramédico ADJ paramedic, paramedical

paramento SM [1] (= *adorno*) ornamental cover; [*de caballo*] trappings *pl*; (= *colgadura*) hangings *pl* ► **paramentos sacerdotales** liturgical vestments
[2] [*de pared, piedra*] face

paramera SF [1] (*Geog*) high moorland
[2] (*Caribe*) (= *malestar*) mountain sickness

paramero/a Ⓐ ADJ (*Andes, Caribe Geog*) upland, highland
Ⓑ SM/F (= *persona*) highlander

parámetro SM parameter

paramilitar ADJ, SMF paramilitary

páramo SM [1] (= *brezal*) bleak plateau, high moor
[2] (= *descampado*) waste land
[3] (*Andes*) (= *llovizna*) drizzle; (= *tormenta*) blizzard
[4] (*Caribe*) (= *cumbres*) mountain heights *pl*

paramoso ADJ (*Andes*) drizzly

paramotor SM paramotor

paramuno ADJ (*Andes*) upland, highland

paranera SF (*LAm*) grassland

parangón SM comparison; **no tiene ~ en otro país** there is nothing comparable in any other country; **sin ~** incomparable, matchless

parangonable ADJ comparable (**con** to)

parangonar ▸conjug 1a◂ VT to compare (**con** to)

paraninfo SM (*Univ*) (= *salón de actos*) assembly hall; (= *auditorio*) auditorium

paranoia SF paranoia

paranoico/a ADJ, SM/F paranoid

paranoide ADJ paranoid

paranormal ADJ paranormal

paranza SF (*Caza*) hide, blind (*EEUU*)

paraolimpiada SF, **paraolimpiadas** SFPL Paralympics, Paralympic Games

paraolímpico/a Ⓐ ADJ Paralympic; **Juegos Paraolímpicos** Paralympics, Paralympic Games
Ⓑ SM/F Paralympic athlete

parapente SM (= *deporte*) paragliding; (= *aparato*) paraglider

parapetarse ▸conjug 1a◂ VPR [1] (= *protegerse*) to protect o.s., shelter (**tras** behind)
[2] (*fig*) **~ tras media docena de excusas** to take refuge in half a dozen excuses

parapeto SM [1] (*como defensa*) (*gen*) defence, defense (*EEUU*), barricade; (*Mil*) parapet
[2] [*de puente, escalera*] parapet

paraplejia SF, **paraplejía** SF paraplegia

parapléjico/a ADJ, SM/F paraplegic

parapsicología SF parapsychology

parar ▸conjug 1a◂ Ⓐ VT [1] [+ *persona, coche, respiración*] to stop; **me paró a punta de pistola** he stopped me at gunpoint; **nos paró la policía** we were stopped by the police; **~on el tráfico en el centro** they stopped the traffic in the centre; **no hay quien pare el avance tecnológico** there is no stopping technological progress
[2] [+ *tiro, penalti, gol*] to save, stop; [+ *pase*] to intercept, cut off; [+ *golpe*] to ward off; (*Esgrima*) to parry
[3] [+ *atención*] to fix (**en** on); *ver tb* **mientes**
[4] (*Naipes*) to bet, stake
[5] (†) (= *conducir*) to lead; **ahí le paró esa manera de vida** that's where that way of life led him
[6] (†) (= *arreglar*) to prepare, arrange
[7] (*LAm*) (= *levantar*) to raise; (= *poner de pie*) to stand upright
[8] **~la con algn** (*Andes**) to take it out on sb
Ⓑ VI [1] (= *detenerse, terminar*) to stop; **¡pare!** stop!; **el autobús para enfrente** the bus stops opposite; **paramos a echar gasolina** we stopped to get some petrol; **¡no para! siempre está haciendo algo** he never stops! he's always doing something; **¡y no para!** [*hablante*] he just goes on and on!; **no ~á hasta conseguirlo** he won't stop *o* give up until he gets it; **~ en seco** to stop dead; **sin ~**: **los teléfonos sonaban sin ~** the phones never stopped ringing; **lloraba sin ~** he didn't stop crying; **fumaba sin ~** she smoked non-stop, she chain-smoked; **hablar sin ~** to talk non-stop; **estuvo una semana lloviendo sin ~** it rained uninterruptedly *o* without a break for a week; ✦***MODISMO*** **¡dónde va a ~!***: **es mucho mejor éste ¡dónde va a ~!** this one's much better, there's no comparison!
[2] **~ de hacer algo** to stop doing sth; **ha parado de llover** it has stopped raining; **no para de quejarse** he never stops complaining, he complains all the time; ✦***MODISMO*** **y para de contar*** and that's that
[3] **ir a ~** to end up; **la empresa podría ir a ~ a manos extranjeras** the firm could end up in foreign hands; **nos equivocamos de tren y fuimos a ~ a Manchester** we got on the wrong train and ended up in Manchester; **fueron a ~ a la comisaría** they ended up at the police station; **la herencia fue a ~ a manos de su primo** the inheritance went to his cousin; **no sabemos en qué va a ir a ~ todo esto** we don't know where all this is going to end; **¿dónde habrá ido a ~ todo aquel dinero?** what can have become of *o* happened to all that money?; **¿dónde vamos a ir a ~?** where's it all going to end?, what is the world coming to?
[4] (= *hospedarse*) to stay (**en** at); **siempre paro en este hotel** I always stay at this hotel
[5] (= *hacer huelga*) to go on strike
[6] **~ con algn** (*Andes**) to hang about with sb
[7] [*perro*] to point
Ⓒ **pararse** VPR [1] [*persona*] to stop; [*coche*] to stop, pull up; [*proceso*] to stop, come to a halt; [*trabajo*] to stop, come to a standstill; **se paró en la puerta** he stopped at the door; **no se**

paran ante nada they will let nothing stop them; **el reloj se ha parado** the clock has stopped; **~se a hacer algo** to stop to do sth, pause to do sth
2 **~se en algo** (= *prestar atención*) to pay attention to sth
3 (*LAm*) (= *ponerse de pie*) to stand (up); (*de la cama*) to get up; [*pelo*] to stand on end
4 (*Tip*) to set
5 (*LAm**) (= *enriquecerse*) to make one's pile*, get rich

pararrayos SM INV lightning conductor, lightning rod (*EEUU*)

parasitar ▸conjug 1a◂ Ⓐ VT to parasitize
Ⓑ VI **~ en** to parasitize

parasitario ADJ, **parasítico** ADJ parasitic(al)

parasitismo SM parasitism

parásito Ⓐ ADJ parasitic (**de** on)
Ⓑ SM 1 (*Biol*) parasite (*tb fig*)
2 **parásitos** (*Radio*) atmospherics *pl*, statics *sing*
3 (*CAm*) squatter

parasitología SF parasitology

parasitólogo/a SM/F parasitologist

parasitosis SF INV parasitism

parasol SM parasol, sunshade

parateatral ADJ theatre-related, quasi-dramatic

paratifoidea SF paratyphoid

paratopes SM INV (*Ferro*) buffer

parcamente ADV (= *frugalmente*) frugally, sparingly; (= *moderadamente*) moderately

Parcas SFPL **las ~** the Parcae, the Fates

parcela SF 1 (= *solar*) plot, piece of ground; (*Agr*) smallholding
2 [*de conocimientos, autonomía*] (= *parte*) part, portion; (= *área*) area ► **parcela de poder** (*político*) power base; (*de influencia*) sphere of influence

parcelar ▸conjug 1a◂ VT (*gen*) to divide into plots; [+ *finca*] to break up, parcel out

parcelario ADJ **tierra parcelaria** land divided into plots

parcelero/a SM/F, **parcelista** SMF owner of a plot, smallholder

parchar ▸conjug 1a◂ VT (*esp LAm*) to patch, put a patch on

parche SM 1 (= *pieza*) patch; (*para un ojo*) eye patch; ✦***MODISMO*** **pegar un ~ a algn*** to put one over on sb* ► **parche de nicotina** nicotine patch
2 (*provisional*) temporary remedy, stopgap solution; **poner ~s** to paper over the cracks
3 (*Med*) (= *cataplasma*) poultice; (*Chile*) (= *tirita*) sticking plaster, Band-Aid® (*EEUU*)
4 (*Mús*) (= *piel de tambor*) drumhead; (= *tambor*) drum; ✦***MODISMO*** **dar el ~** to busk

parchear[1] ▸conjug 1a◂ VT to patch (up)

parchear[2]‡ ▸conjug 1a◂ VT to feel‡, touch up‡

parcheo SM temporary remedies *pl*, stopgap solutions *pl*

parchís SM *board game similar to ludo*, Parcheesi® (*EEUU*)

parchita SF (*Caribe*) passion fruit

parcho SM (*Caribe*) = **parche**

parcial Ⓐ ADJ 1 (= *incompleto*) partial; **eclipse ~** partial eclipse; **examen ~** mid-term exam; **a tiempo ~** part-time
2 (= *no ecuánime*) biased, partial; (*Pol*) partisan
Ⓑ SM (= *examen*) mid-term exam

parcialidad SF 1 (= *falta de ecuanimidad*) partiality, bias; (*Pol*) partisanship
2 (= *grupo*) (*gen*) faction, group; (*de rebeldes*) rebel group

parcidad SF = **parquedad**

parco ADJ (*gen*) frugal, sparing; (= *moderado*) moderate, temperate; (*en el gasto*) parsimonious; **muy ~ en comer** very frugal in one's eating habits; **~ en elogios** sparing in one's praises

parcómetro SM parking meter

pardal SM 1 (*Orn*) (= *gorrión*) sparrow; (= *pardillo*) linnet
2 (*Bot*) aconite
3 (†*) (= *pillo*) sly fellow, rogue; **¡pardal!** (*a niño*) you rascal!

pardear ▸conjug 1a◂ VI to look brown(ish)

pardiez†† EXCL good heavens!, by gad!††

pardillo/a Ⓐ SM/F 1 (*) (= *ingenuo*) simpleton
2 (*) (= *rústico*) yokel, hick (*EEUU**)
Ⓑ SM 1 (*tb* **~ común**) linnet
2 (= *paño*) brown cloth

pardo/a Ⓐ ADJ 1 [*color*] grey-brown, brownish-grey
2 [*cielo*] overcast
3 [*voz*] flat, dull
Ⓑ SM/F (*Caribe, Cono Sur pey*) (= *mulato*) mulatto, half-breed; (*Méx*‡) (= *persona humilde*) poor devil

pardusco ADJ = **pardo**

pareado Ⓐ ADJ 1 [*verso*] rhyming
2 [*chalet*] semi-detached
Ⓑ SM couplet

parear ▸conjug 1a◂ Ⓐ VT 1 (= *emparejar*) to pair up
2 (*Biol*) to mate, pair
Ⓑ VI (*Caribe*‡) to skive‡
Ⓒ **parearse** VPR to pair off

▼ **parecer** Ⓐ SM 1 (= *opinión*) opinion, view; **a mi ~** in my opinion *o* view; **somos del mismo ~** we are of the same opinion *o* view; **cambiar** *o* **mudar de ~** to change one's mind
2 (†) (= *aspecto*) **de buen ~** good-looking, handsome; **de mal ~** unattractive
Ⓑ ▸conjug 2d◂ VI 1 (*uso copulativo*) 1·1 (*por el aspecto*) (+ *ADJ*) to look; (+ *SUSTANTIVO*) to look like; **esos zapatos no parecen muy cómodos** those shoes don't look very comfortable; **pareces más joven** you look younger; **parece una modelo** she looks like a model; **¡pareces una reina!** you look like a queen!; **una casa que parece un palacio** a house that looks like a palace; **parece una foca*** she's huge *o* enormous*; **estos guantes parecen de seda** these gloves feel like silk
1·2 (= *por el carácter, el comportamiento*) to seem; **parece muy afectado por la noticia** he seems very upset by the news; **parecía una persona muy amable** she seemed very nice; **desde que se divorció no parece la misma** since she got divorced she seems a different person
2 (*uso impersonal*) (= *dar la impresión de*) to seem; **todo parecía indicar que estaba interesado** everything seemed to point towards him being interested; **aunque no lo parezca** surprising though it may seem *o* (*más frm*) appear; **así parece** so it seems *o* (*más frm*) appears; **al ~** ◊ **a lo que parece** apparently, seemingly; **parece como si** + *SUBJUN*: **parece como si quisiera ocultar algo** it's as if he were trying to hide something; **en mi sueño parecía como si volara** in my dream it was as if I was flying; **parece que** + *INDIC*: **parece que va a llover** it looks as though *o* as if it's going to rain, it looks like rain; **parece que fue ayer** it seems only yesterday; **parece que huele a gas** I think I can smell gas; **según parece** apparently, seemingly; **parece ser que** + *INDIC*: **parece ser que van a aumentar las temperaturas** it seems *o* (*más frm*) appears (that) it's going to get warmer; **parece ser que ha habido algún problema** it seems *o* (*más frm*) appears (that) there has been a problem
3 (*indicando opinión*) **~le a algn: ¿qué os pareció la película?** what did you think of the film?; **¿no te parece extraño que no haya llamado?** don't you think it's strange that she hasn't called?; **me parece bien que vayas** I think it's a good idea for you to go; **te llamaré luego, si te parece bien** I'll phone you later, if that's all right with *o* by you; **¡me parece muy mal!** I think it's shocking!; **si a usted no le parece mal** if you don't mind; **me parece mentira que haya pasado tanto tiempo** I can't believe it has been so long; **podríamos ir al cine si te parece** we could go to the cinema if you like; **vamos a la piscina, ¿te parece?** what do you say we go to the swimming pool?, what about going to the swimming pool?; **como te parezca** as you wish; **~ que: me parece que se está haciendo tarde** it's getting rather late, I think; **me parece que sí** I think so; **me parece que no** I don't think so; **¿te parece que está bien no acudir a una cita?** do you think it's acceptable not to turn up for an appointment?
4 (†) (= *aparecer*) to appear; [*objeto perdido*] to turn up; **pareció el sol entre las nubes** the sun appeared through the clouds; **ya parecieron los guantes** the gloves have turned up; **¡ya pareció aquello!** so that was it!
Ⓒ **parecerse** VPR 1 (= *asemejarse*) **~se a algn** (*en el aspecto*) to look like sb, be like sb; (*en el carácter*) to be like sb; **en esta foto se parece mucho a su abuelo** in this photo he looks *o* is a lot like his grandfather; **el retrato no se le parece** the portrait isn't a bit like him; **es muy sensible, se parece a su madre** she's very sensitive, she's like her mother; **~se a algo** to look like sth, be like sth; **su jersey se parece al mío** his jumper looks *o* is like mine; **ni cosa que se parezca** nor anything of the sort
2 (*uso recíproco*) (*en el aspecto*) to look alike, be alike; (*en el carácter*) to be alike; **son hermanas pero no se parecen mucho** they're sisters but they don't look *o* they aren't very much alike; **¿en qué se parecen estos dos objetos?** what's the similarity between these two objects?, in what way are these two objects alike?

parecidamente ADV similarly, equally

▼ **parecido** Ⓐ ADJ 1 (= *similar*) similar; **tienen apellidos ~s** they have similar surnames; **las casas son todas parecidas** the houses are all similar *o* alike; **nunca he visto cosa parecida** I've never seen anything like it; **ser ~ a algo** to be similar to sth, be like sth; **mi reloj es muy ~ al tuyo** my watch is very similar to yours, my watch is very like yours; **ser ~ a**

➤ LENGUA Y USO: parecer A1 33.2, 53.5 B3 28.1, 34.1, 36.1 C 32.5 parecido B 32.4

algn (*de aspecto*) to look like sb; (*de carácter*) to be like sb
[2] **bien ~** good-looking, nice-looking, handsome; **no es mal parecida** she's not bad-looking
Ⓑ SM resemblance, likeness; **yo no te veo el ~ con tu hermano** I can't see the resemblance *o* likeness between you and your brother; **hay un gran ~ entre las dos historias** there is a great resemblance *o* likeness between the two stories, the two stories are very alike; **tiene un cierto ~ con Marlon Brando** he bears a slight resemblance to Marlon Brando

parecimiento SM [1] (*Cono Sur, Méx*) = **parecido B**
[2] (*Cono Sur*) (= *comparecencia*) appearance; (= *aparición*) apparition

pared SF [1] [*de edificio, habitación*] wall; **estar ~ con ~ con algo** to be right next door to sth; **estar cara a la ~** (*Escol*) to be stood in the corner; ✦***MODISMOS*** **entre cuatro ~es**: **se pasa la vida entre cuatro ~es** he spends his life cooped up at home; **hablar a la ~**: **es como hablarle a la ~** it's like talking to a brick wall; **las ~es oyen** the walls have ears; **ponerse (blanco) como la ~** to go as white as a sheet; **subirse por las ~es*** to go up the wall* ► **pared de carga** load-bearing wall ► **pared divisoria** dividing wall ► **pared maestra** main wall ► **pared medianera** party wall
[2] (*Anat*) wall ► **pared arterial** arterial wall ► **pared abdominal** abdominal wall ► **pared celular** cell wall
[3] (*Alpinismo*) face wall
[4] (*Ftbl*) **hacer la ~** to make *o* do a one-two*

paredeño ADJ adjoining, next-door (**con** to)

paredón SM [1] (*Arquit*) (= *muro*) thick wall; [*de ruinas*] standing wall
[2] [*de roca*] wall of rock, rock face
[3] (*Mil*) **¡al ~!** put him up against the wall and shoot him!; **llevar a algn al ~** to put sb up against the wall, shoot sb

pareja SF [1] (= *par*) pair; **en este juego hay que formar ~s** for this game you have to get into pairs
[2] [*de esposos, compañeros sentimentales*] couple; **había varias ~s bailando** there were several couples dancing; **vivir en ~** to live as a couple; **nuestra vida como ~** our life together; **llevamos una relación de ~** we are an item ► **pareja abierta** open marriage ► **pareja de hecho** unmarried couple ► **pareja reproductora** (*Orn*) breeding pair
[3] (= *compañero*) partner; (= *cónyuge*) spouse; **vino con su ~** he came with his partner ► **pareja de baile** dancing partner ► **pareja estable** regular partner
[4] [*de calcetín, guante, zapato*] **no encuentro la ~ de este zapato** I can't find the shoe that goes with this one *o* my other shoe
[5] [*de hijos*] **ya tenemos la parejita** now we've got one of each
[6] [*de guardias civiles*] *pair of Civil Guard officers on patrol*
[7] (*LAm*) (= *caballos*) pair (*of horses*); [*de tiro*] team (*of draught animals*); [*de bueyes*] yoke (*of oxen*)

parejamente ADV equally

parejería* SF (*Caribe*) vanity, conceit

parejero Ⓐ ADJ (*Caribe**) (= *demasiado confiado*) cheeky, sassy (*EEUU**); (= *presumido*) cocky, over-confident
Ⓑ SM [1] (*LAm*) (= *caballo*) racehorse
[2] (*Caribe**) (= *persona*) hanger-on

PAREJA

Para traducir el sustantivo **pareja** referido a dos personas, hay que tener en cuenta la diferencia entre los sustantivos **pair** y **couple**:

- Se traduce por **couple** cuando se trata de un matrimonio o de dos personas que parecen tener una relación íntima, o cuando se refiere a una pareja de baile:

En Salford conocí a una pareja de Ecuador
In Salford I met a couple from Ecuador
Algunas parejas prefieren no tener hijos
Some couples prefer not to have children
Había muchas parejas mayores bailando
There were a lot of older couples dancing

- En un contexto de trabajo o de competiciones deportivas o cuando a la **pareja** no se le asocia ningún vínculo afectivo, se traduce por **pair**:

Ahora vamos a trabajar por parejas
Now we're going to work in pairs
Detuvieron a la pareja al cruzar la frontera
The pair were arrested when they were crossing the border

- La expresión **pareja de** se puede traducir tanto por **couple of** como por **pair of** cuando tiene el sentido de **par de**:

Una pareja de pillos me robaron el reloj
A couple** o **A pair of thugs stole my watch
⇨ *Ver tb* PAR
Para otros usos y ejemplos ver la entrada.

parejo Ⓐ ADJ [1] (= *igual*) similar, alike; **seis todos ~s** six all the same; **ir ~s** to be neck and neck; **ir ~ con** to be on a par with; **por ~** on a par
[2] (*LAm*) (= *nivelado*) (*Téc*) even, flush; [*terreno*] flat, level
Ⓑ ADV (*LAm*) (= *al mismo tiempo*) at the same time, together
Ⓒ SM (*CAm, Caribe*) [*de baile*] dancing partner

paremiología SF study of proverbs

parentela SF relations *pl*, family

parenteral ADJ parenteral; **inyección ~** intravenous injection

parentesco SM relationship, kinship

paréntesis SM INV [1] (*Tip*) parenthesis, bracket ► **paréntesis cuadrados** square brackets
[2] (*Ling*) (= *pausa*) parenthesis; (= *digresión*) digression; (= *aparte*) aside; **hacer un ~** (*en discurso, escrito*) to digress; **entre ~** (*como adj*) parenthetical, incidental; (*como adv*) parenthetically, incidentally; **y, entre ~ …** and, by the way …, and I may add in passing …
[3] (= *intervalo*) interval, break; (= *hueco*) gap; (= *descanso*) lull; **el ~ vacacional** the break for the holidays; **hacer un ~** to take a break

pareo[1] SM (*tradicional*) pareo; [*de playa*] beach wrap; (= *chal*) rectangular shawl

pareo[2] SM (*gen*) matching; (= *unión*) pairing off; (*Zool*) mating

paria SMF pariah

parián SM (*Méx*) market

parida SF [1] (*) (= *dicho*) silly thing, stupid remark; **salir con una ~** to come out with a silly remark; **~s** nonsense *sing* ► **parida mental** dumb idea*
[2] (= *mujer*) *woman who has recently given birth*

paridad SF [1] (= *igualdad*) parity, equality; (= *semejanza*) similarity
[2] (= *comparación*) comparison

parido* ADJ **bien ~** good-looking

paridora ADJ FEM fertile, productive

parienta SF **la ~*** the wife*, the missus*

pariente/a Ⓐ SM/F (= *familiar*) relative, relation; **un medio ~** a distant relative *o* relation; **un ~ pobre** a poor relation; **es un ~ político** he's related to me by marriage; **los ~s políticos** the in-laws
Ⓑ SM **el ~*** the old man*, my hubby*

parietal Ⓐ ADJ parietal
Ⓑ SM parietal bone

parihuela SF, **parihuelas** SFPL stretcher

paripé* SM **hacer** *o* **montar el ~** to put on a show

parir ▸conjug 3a◂ Ⓐ VI [*mujer*] to give birth, have a baby; [*yegua*] to foal; [*vaca*] to calve; [*cerda*] to farrow; [*perra*] to pup; ✦***MODISMOS*** **éramos pocos y parió la abuela*** that's the limit*; **poner a ~ a algn*** to slag sb off*
Ⓑ VT [1] (= *dar a luz*) [*mujer*] to give birth to, have, bear (*frm*); [*animal*] to have; **¡la madre que te parió!**** you bastard!**
[2] (= *producir*) to produce; **ha parido una magnífica novela** he has produced a brilliant novel
[3] **~la*** to drop a clanger*

París SM Paris

parisién ADJ Parisian

parisiense ADJ, SMF, **parisino/a** ADJ, SM/F Parisian

paritario ADJ peer *antes de s*; **grupo ~** peer group

paritorio SM delivery room

parka SF parka

parking ['parkin] SM (*pl* **parkings**), **párking** ['parkin] SM (*pl* **párkings**) car park, parking lot (*EEUU*)

párkinson SM, **Parkinson** SM Parkinson's (disease)

parla SF chatter, gossip

parlador ADJ talkative

parlamentar ▸conjug 1a◂ VI (*gen*) to converse, talk; (*Mil*) to parley

parlamentario/a Ⓐ ADJ parliamentary
Ⓑ SM/F (= *diputado*) M.P., member of parliament; (*más veterano*) parliamentarian ► **parlamentario/a autónomo/a** member of a regional parliament

parlamento SM [1] (*Pol*) parliament ► **parlamento autónomo** regional parliament ► **Parlamento Europeo** European Parliament
[2] (= *discurso*) speech
[3] (*Mil*) parley

parlana SF (*CAm*) turtle

parlanchín/ina* Ⓐ ADJ talkative
Ⓑ SM/F chatterbox*

parlante Ⓐ ADJ talking
Ⓑ SM (*LAm*) loudspeaker

-parlante SUF (*en palabras compuestas*) **castellanoparlante** (*como adjetivo*) Castilian-speaking; (*como sustantivo*) Castilian speaker

parlar ▸conjug 1a◂ VI [1] (*) [*persona*] to chatter (away), talk (a lot)
[2] [*pájaro*] to chatter

parlero ADJ [1] (= *hablador*) talkative, garrulous; (= *chismoso*) gossipy

[2] [*pájaro*] talking; (= *cantor*) singing, song *antes de s*
[3] [*arroyo*] musical; [*ojos*] expressive

parleta* SF chat, small talk

parlotear* ▸conjug 1a◂ VI to chatter, prattle

parloteo* SM chatter, prattle

PARM SM ABR (*Méx*) = **Partido Auténtico de la Revolución Mexicana**

parmesano Ⓐ ADJ Parmesan; **queso ~** Parmesan cheese
Ⓑ SM Parmesan

Parnaso SM Parnassus

parné‡ SM dough‡, cash*

paro[1] SM (*Orn*) tit

paro[2] SM [1] (= *desempleo*) unemployment; **índice de ~** level of unemployment; **estar en ~** to be unemployed; **lo han enviado al ~** they have put him out of a job, they have made him unemployed ► **paro cíclico** cyclical unemployment ► **paro encubierto** underemployment ► **paro estacional** seasonal unemployment ► **paro obrero** unemployment
[2] (= *subsidio*) unemployment benefit, unemployment insurance (*EEUU*); **cobrar el ~** to be on the dole*, receive unemployment benefit (*frm*)
[3] (= *interrupción*) stoppage; **se produjo un ~ en la cadena de montaje** there was a stoppage on the assembly line ► **paro biológico** (*Pesca*) temporary fishing ban ► **paro cardíaco** cardiac arrest ► **paro del sistema** (*Inform*) system shutdown ► **paro forzoso** enforced stoppage ► **paro técnico** technical breakdown
[4] (= *huelga*) strike; **un ~ de tres días** a three-day strike; **hay ~ en la industria** work in the industry is at a standstill
[5] (*Andes, Caribe Dados*) throw
[6] **en ~** (*Andes*) (= *de una vez*) all at once, in one go

parodia SF [1] (= *imitación*) parody, takeoff*
[2] [*de la justicia, investigación*] travesty

parodiar ▸conjug 1b◂ VT to parody, take off*

paródico ADJ parodic

parodista SMF parodist, writer of parodies

parola SF [1] (*cualidad*) (= *soltura*) fluency; (= *verborrea*) verbosity; (= *labia*) gift of the gab*
[2] (= *charla*) (*gen*) chitchat; (*cansina*) tiresome talk; **son ~s** (*Cono Sur**) it's all hot air*

parolimpiada SF = **paraolimpiada**

parolímpico/a ADJ, SM/F = **paraolímpico**

parón SM **la obras sufrieron un ~ ayer** building work came to a halt yesterday; **tras un ~ por la lluvia, continuó el partido** after rain had halted play, the matched restarted; **parones en una de las líneas del metro** stoppages on one of the underground lines

paroxismo SM paroxysm ► **paroxismo de risa** convulsions *pl* of laughter ► **paroxismo histérico** hysterics *pl*

parpadear ▸conjug 1a◂ VI [*ojos*] to blink; [*luz*] to flicker; [*estrella*] to twinkle

parpadeo SM [*de ojos*] blinking; [*de luz*] flickering; [*de estrella*] twinkling

párpado SM eyelid; **restregarse los ~s** to rub one's eyes

parpichuela‡ SF **hacerse una ~** to wank‡

parque SM [1] (= *terreno, recinto*) park ► **parque acuático** water park ► **parque central** (*Méx*) town square ► **parque de atracciones** amusement park ► **parque de chatarra** scrap yard ► **parque de estacionamiento** car park, parking lot (*EEUU*) ► **parque eólico** wind farm ► **parque infantil** children's playground ► **parque nacional** national park ► **parque natural** nature reserve ► **parque tecnológico** technology park ► **parque temático** theme park ► **parque zoológico** zoo
[2] [*de material*] depot ► **parque de artillería** artillery depot, artillery stores *pl* ► **parque de bomberos** fire station, fire *o* station house (*EEUU*)
[3] [*de vehículos*] fleet; **el ~ nacional de automóviles** the total number of cars in the country; **el ~ provincial de tractores** the number of tractors in use in the province ► **parque automovilístico** car fleet; (*en carreras*) ► **parque cerrado** parc fermé ► **parque móvil** fleet of official cars
[4] (*para niños*) playpen
[5] (*Méx*) (= *munición*) ammunition, ammo*; (= *depósito*) ammunition dump
[6] (*LAm*) (= *equipo*) equipment

parqué SM, **parquet** [par'ke] SM (*pl* **parquets** [par'kes]) [1] (= *entarimado*) parquet
[2] (*Fin*) **el ~** the Floor (*of the stock exchange*); (*fig*) the stock market

parqueadero SM (*LAm*) car park, parking lot (*EEUU*)

parquear ▸conjug 1a◂ VT, VI (*LAm*) to park

parquedad SF (= *frugalidad*) frugality, sparingness; (= *moderación*) moderation

parqueo SM (*LAm*) [1] (= *acto*) parking
[2] (= *aparcamiento*) car-park, parking lot (*EEUU*)

parquímetro SM parking meter

párr. ABR (= **párrafo**) par, para

parra SF (*Bot*) grapevine; (= *trepadora*) climbing vine; ✦**MODISMO subirse a la ~*** (= *engreírse*) to get all high and mighty; (= *enfadarse*) to blow one's top*

parrafada* SF [1] (= *charla*) chat, talk; **echar la ~** to have a chat
[2] (= *discurso*) spiel*, talk; **soltar** *o* **tirarse una ~** to give a lengthy spiel*

párrafo SM paragraph; **hacer ~ aparte** (*lit*) to start a new paragraph; (*fig*) to change the subject; ✦**MODISMO echar un ~ (con algn)*** to have a chat (with sb)

parral SM vine arbour, vine arbor (*EEUU*)

parrampán* SM (*Pan*) pretentious person

parranda SF [1] (*) (= *juerga*) spree; **andar** *o* **ir de ~** to go out on the town*
[2] (*Andes, Cono Sur, Méx*) [*de cosas*] lot, heap; [*de personas*] group; **una ~ de** a lot of

parrandear* ▸conjug 1a◂ VI to go on a binge*

parricida SMF parricide

parricidio SM parricide

parrilla SF [1] (*Culin*) grill; **carne a la ~** grilled meat
[2] (*Dep*) (*tb* **~ de salida**) [*de coches*] starting grid; [*de caballos*] starting stalls
[3] (*Aut*) [*de radiador*] radiator grille; (*LAm*) (= *baca*) roof rack
[4] [*de bicicleta*] carrier
[5] (= *restaurante*) grillroom, steak restaurant

parrillada SF [1] (= *plato*) (mixed) grill; (*en barbacoa*) barbecue
[2] (*Cono Sur*) (= *restaurante*) grillroom, steak restaurant

párroco SM parish priest

parroquia SF [1] (*Rel*) (= *zona*) parish; (= *iglesia*) parish church; (= *feligreses*) parishioners *pl*
[2] (= *clientes*) customers *pl*, clientele; **hoy hay poca ~** there aren't many customers today; **una tienda con mucha ~** a shop with a large clientele, a well-patronized shop

parroquial ADJ parochial, parish *antes de s*

parroquiano/a SM/F [1] (*Rel*) parishioner
[2] (*Com*) patron, customer; **ser ~ de** to shop regularly at, patronize

parsi SMF Parsee

parsimonia SF [1] (= *calma*) calmness; (= *flema*) phlegmatic nature; **con ~** calmly, unhurriedly
[2] (= *frugalidad*) sparingness; (*con el dinero*) carefulness

parsimonioso ADJ [1] (= *tranquilo*) calm, unhurried; (= *flemático*) phlegmatic
[2] (= *frugal*) sparing; (*con el dinero*) careful

parte[1] SM [1] (= *informe*) report; **dar ~ a algn** to report to sb; **han dado ~ del robo a la policía** they have reported the break-in to the police ► **parte de alta** certificate of starting employment ► **parte de baja (laboral)** (*por enfermedad*) doctor's note; (*por cese*) certificate of leaving employment, ≈ P45 ► **parte de defunción** death certificate ► **parte facultativo, parte médico** medical report, medical bulletin ► **parte meteorológico** weather forecast, weather report
[2] (*Mil*) dispatch, communiqué ► **parte de guerra** military communiqué, war report
[3] (*Radio*†) news bulletin; **el ~ de las tres** the three o'clock news (bulletin)
[4] (*Cono Sur*) [*de boda*] wedding invitation; (*Aut*) speeding ticket

▼**parte**[2] SF [1] (= *sección*) part; **el examen consta de dos ~s** the exam consists of two parts; **¿en qué ~ del libro te has quedado?** where are you in the book?, which bit of the book are you on at the moment?; **~ de lo que pasa es culpa mía** I'm partly to blame for the situation; **la ~ de abajo** the bottom; **la ~ de arriba** the top; **la ~ de atrás** the back; **la cuarta ~** a quarter; **han perdido la cuarta ~ de las ganancias** they've lost a quarter of the profits; **la ~ delantera** the front; **ser ~ esencial de algo** to be an essential part of sth; **la mayor ~ de algo**: **pasé la mayor ~ del tiempo leyendo** I spent most of the time reading; **la mayor ~ de los españoles** most Spanish people; **—¿os queda dinero? —sí, aunque ya hemos gastado la mayor ~** "do you have any money left?" — "yes, though we've spent most of it"; **la tercera ~** a third; **reducir algo en una tercera ~** to reduce sth by a third ► **parte de la oración** part of speech
[2] (*en locuciones*) **de ~ de**: **llamo de ~ de Juan** I'm calling on behalf of Juan; **de ~ de todos nosotros** on behalf of us all; **salúdalo de mi ~** give him my regards; **dale esto de mi ~** give her this from me; **¿de ~ de quién?** (*al teléfono*) who's calling?; **en ~** partly, in part; **se debe en ~ a su falta de experiencia** it's partly due to his lack of experience, it's due in part to his lack of experience; **tienes razón sólo en ~** you're only partly right; **formar ~ de algo**: **¿cuándo entró a formar ~ de la organización?** when did she join the

➤ LENGUA Y USO: parte[2] 2 48.2, 49, 50.6, 53.5

organization?; **no formaba ~ del equipo** he was not in the team; **forma ~ de sus obligaciones** it is part of his duties; **en gran ~** to a large extent; **por otra ~** on the other hand; **por una ~ ... por otra (parte)** on the one hand, ... on the other; **por ~ de** on the part of; **exige un gran esfuerzo por ~ de los alumnos** it requires a great effort on the part of *o* from the pupils; **yo por mi ~, no estoy de acuerdo** I, for my part, disagree; **¡vayamos por ~s!** let's take it one step at a time!

3 (= *participación*) share; **mi ~ de la herencia** my share of the inheritance; **como ~ del pago** in part exchange; **a ~s iguales** in equal shares; **ir a la ~** to go shares; **tener ~ en algo** to share in sth; **tomar ~ (en algo)** to take part (in sth); **¿cuántos corredores tomarán ~ en la prueba?** how many runners will take part in the race?; **yo no tomé ~ en ese asunto** I had no part in it; ✦*MODISMOS* **llevarse la mejor ~** to come off best, get the best of it; **poner de su ~** to do one's bit *o* share; **tienes que poner de tu ~** you have to do your bit *o* share; **quedarse con la ~ del león** to take the lion's share; *ver tb* **partir 3**

4 (= *lugar*) part; **¿de qué ~ de Inglaterra eres?** what part of England are you from?; **¿en qué ~ de la ciudad vives?** where *o* whereabouts in the city do you live?; **en alguna ~** somewhere; **en alguna ~ de Europa** somewhere in Europe; **en cualquier ~** anywhere; **en ninguna ~** nowhere; **en ninguna ~ del país** nowhere in the country; **por ahí no se va a ninguna ~** (*lit*) that way doesn't lead anywhere; (*fig*) that will get us nowhere; **ir a otra ~** to go somewhere else; **debe de estar en otra ~** it must be somewhere else; **en** *o* **por todas ~s** everywhere; **en todas ~s de España** all over Spain; ✦*MODISMOS* **en las cinco ~s del mundo** (*Esp*) in the four corners of the earth; **de una ~ a otra** back and forth, to and fro; **tomar algo en buena ~**† to take sth in good part; **echar algo a mala ~**† to look on sth with disapproval; **de algún** *o* **un tiempo a esta ~** for some time now; **en salva sea la ~** (*Esp euf*) (= *trasero*) **le dio una patada en salva sea la ~** she gave him a kick up the behind; *ver tb* **haba**

5 (= *bando*) side; **estar de ~ de algn** to be on sb's side; **estoy de tu ~** I'm on your side; **¿de ~ de quién estás tú?** whose side are you on?; **todo está de su ~** everything is in his favour; **ponerse de ~ de algn** to side with sb, take sb's side

6 (*indicando parentesco*) side; **es primo por ~ de madre** he's a cousin on my mother's side

7 (*Dep*) (*en partido*) half; **primera ~** first half; **segunda ~** second half

8 (*Teat*) part

9 (*Jur*) (*en contrato*) party; **las ~s contratantes** the parties to the contract; **el documento debe ser firmado por ambas ~s** the document should be signed by both parties; **sin la intervención de terceras ~s** without the involvement of third parties; ✦*MODISMO* **ser juez y ~** to be judge and jury (*in one's own case*) ► **parte actora** plaintiff ► **parte acusadora** prosecution ► **parte contraria** opposing party

10 **partes** (*euf*) (= *genitales*) private parts (*euf*), privates (*euf*); **recibió un golpe en sus ~s** he was hit in the privates (*euf*) ► **partes íntimas**, **partes pudendas** private parts

11 **partes**† (= *cualidades*) parts, qualities, talents; **buenas ~s** good parts

12 (*Méx*) spare part

parteaguas SM INV (*LAm*) (*gen*) divide, ridge; (= *línea divisoria*) watershed ► **parteaguas continental** continental divide

partear ▸conjug 1a◂ VT to deliver

parteluz SM mullion

partenaire [parte'ner] SMF partner

partenogénesis SF INV parthenogenesis

Partenón SM Parthenon

partenueces SM INV nutcracker

partero/a SM/F 1 (= *comadrona*) midwife/male midwife

2 (*Méx*) (= *obstetra*) obstetrician; (= *ginecólogo*) gynaecologist, gynecologist (*EEUU*)

parterre SM 1 [*de flores*] flower bed

2 (*Teat*) stalls *pl*

partición SF (= *reparto*) division, sharing-out; (*Pol*) partition; (*Mat*) division

participación SF 1 (= *acto*) **negó su ~ en el atentado** he denied taking part *o* any involvement in the attack; **queremos fomentar la ~ de los ciudadanos en la política** we want to encourage public participation *o* involvement in politics; **habló de ello durante su ~ en el programa** he spoke about it when he was on the programme ► **participación electoral** turnout

2 (*Fin*) (= *parte*) share; (= *inversión*) holding, interest; **la ~ de la empresa Ceresa en Rodex** Ceresa's holding in Rodex ► **participación accionarial** holding, shareholding ► **participación en el mercado** market share ► **participación en los beneficios** profit-sharing ► **participación minoritaria** minority interest

3 (= *número de participantes*) entry; **hubo una nutrida ~** there was a big entry, there were a lot of entries

4 (= *parte*) share; [*de lotería*] (share in a) lottery ticket; → LOTERÍA

5 (= *aviso*) notice, notification; **dar ~ de algo** to give notice of sth ► **participación de boda** notice of a forthcoming wedding

participante Ⓐ ADJ participating; **los países ~s** the participating countries

Ⓑ SMF (*gen*) participant; (*Dep*) entrant

participar ▸conjug 1a◂ Ⓐ VI 1 (= *tomar parte*) to take part, participate (*frm*); **~ en un concurso** to take part *o* participate in a competition; **20 países ~án en la cumbre** 20 countries will take part in the summit; **~ en una carrera** to take part in a race

2 (*Fin*) **~ en una empresa** to own shares in a company; **~ de los beneficios** to share in the profits; **~ de** *o* **en una herencia** to share in an estate

3 (= *compartir*) **~ de una cualidad/opinión** to share a quality/an opinion

Ⓑ VT (*frm*) (= *informar*) to inform; **~ algo a algn** to inform sb of sth

participativo ADJ [*sociedad, público*] participative; [*deporte, juego*] participative, participatory; [*democracia*] participatory

partícipe SMF (*gen*) participant; (*Com*) interested party; **hacer ~ a algn de algo** (= *informar*) to inform sb of sth; (= *compartir*) to share sth with sb; (= *implicar*) to make sb party to sth

participial ADJ participial

participio SM (*Ling*) participle ► **participio activo** present participle ► **participio de pasado** past participle ► **participio (de) presente** present participle ► **participio de pretérito**, **participio pasivo** past participle

partícula SF particle ► **partícula alfa** alpha particle ► **partícula atómica** atomic particle ► **partícula elemental** elementary particle

particular Ⓐ ADJ 1 (= *especial*) special; **nada de ~** nothing special; **el vestido no tiene nada de ~** the dress is nothing special; **lo que tiene de ~ es que ...** what's remarkable about it is that ...

2 (= *específico*) **en este caso ~** in this particular case; **tiene un sabor ~** it has a flavour of its own; **en ~** in particular; **me gustan todas, pero ésta en ~** I like all of them, but this one in particular

3 (= *privado*) [*secretario, coche*] private; **clase ~** private lesson; **casa ~** private home

Ⓑ SM (= *asunto*) matter; **no dijo mucho sobre este ~** he didn't say much about this matter; **sin otro ~, se despide atentamente ...** (*en correspondencia*) yours faithfully, sincerely yours (*EEUU*)

Ⓒ SMF (= *persona*) (private) individual; **no comerciamos con ~es** we don't do business with individuals

particularidad SF 1 (= *propiedad*) particularity, peculiarity; (= *rasgo distintivo*) special feature, characteristic; **tiene la ~ de que ...** one of its special features is (that) ..., it has the characteristic that ...

2 (= *amistad*) friendship, intimacy

particularizar ▸conjug 1f◂ Ⓐ VT 1 (= *distinguir*) to distinguish, characterize

2 (= *especificar*) to specify

3 (= *singularizar*) to single out

4 (= *preferir*) to prefer

5 (= *pormenorizar*) to particularize, give details about

Ⓑ **particularizarse** VPR 1 (= *distinguirse*) [*cosa*] to distinguish itself, stand out; [*persona*] to make one's mark

2 **~se con algn** to single sb out (*for special treatment etc*)

particularmente ADV 1 (= *especialmente*) particularly, specially

2 (= *personalmente*) privately, personally

partida SF 1 (= *documento*) certificate ► **partida bautismal**, **partida de bautismo** baptismal certificate ► **partida de defunción** death certificate ► **partida de matrimonio** marriage certificate ► **partida de nacimiento** birth certificate

2 (*Fin*) [*de cuenta*] entry, item; [*de presupuesto*] item, heading ► **partida doble** double entry; **por ~ doble** on two accounts ► **partida simple** single entry

3 (*Com*) (= *envío*) consignment; **han enviado una ~ de 10.000 euros** they have sent a consignment worth 10,000 euros

4 (*Naipes, Ajedrez*) game; **echar una ~** to have a game; ✦*MODISMO* **jugarle una mala ~ a algn** to play a dirty trick on sb

5 (= *salida*) departure

6 (= *grupo*) party; (*Mil*) band, group ► **partida de campo** picnic (party) ► **partida de caza** hunting party

partidario/a Ⓐ ADJ **ser ~ de algo** to be in favour *o* (*EEUU*) favor of sth; **ser ~ de hacer algo** to be in favour of doing sth
Ⓑ SM/F [1] (= *defensor*) [*de persona*] supporter, follower; [*de idea, movimiento*] supporter; **el candidato a la presidencia tiene muchos ~s** the presidential candidate has many supporters *o* followers; **los ~s del aborto** supporters *o* those in favour of abortion, those who support abortion
[2] (*Andes, Caribe*) (= *aparcero*) sharecropper

partidillo SM (*Dep*) practice game

partidismo SM partisanship

partidista Ⓐ ADJ partisan, party *antes de s*
Ⓑ SMF partisan

partido SM [1] (*Pol*) party; **sistema de ~ único** one-party system; **tomar ~** to take sides; **tomar ~ por algo/algn** to side with sth/sb ► **partido de la oposición** opposition party ► **partido político** political party ► **Partido Verde** Green Party
[2] (*Dep*) game, match ► **partido amistoso** friendly (game *o* match) ► **partido de casa** home game *o* match ► **partido de desempate** replay ► **partido de dobles** (*Tenis*) doubles match, game of doubles ► **partido de exhibición** exhibition game *o* match ► **partido de fútbol** football game *o* match ► **partido (de) homenaje** benefit game *o* match ► **partido de ida** away game *o* match, first leg ► **partido de vuelta** return game *o* match, second leg ► **partido internacional** international (match)
[3] (= *provecho*) **sacar ~ de algo** to make the most of sth
[4] **ser un buen ~** [*persona*] to be a good match
[5] (= *distrito*) district, administrative area ► **partido judicial** *district under the jurisdiction of a local court*
[6] (*frm*) (= *apoyo*) support; **tiene ~ entre todas las clases sociales** he has support among all social classes
[7] (*frm*) **darse a ~** ◊ **venir(se) a ~** to give way
[8] (*Cono Sur Naipes*) hand
[9] (*Andes, Caribe*) (= *aparcería*) crop share

partija SF [1] (= *partición*) partition, division
[2] (*pey*) = **parte²**

partiota SF (*Caribe*) dollar bill

partir ▸conjug 3a◂ Ⓐ VT [1] (= *dividir*) [+ *tarta, sandía, baraja*] to cut; [+ *tableta de chocolate*] to break; [+ *tronco*] to split; **parte la barra de pan por la mitad** (*con cuchillo*) cut the baguette in half; (*con las manos*) break the baguette in half; **¿te parto un trozo de queso?** shall I cut you (off) a piece of cheese?
[2] (= *romper*) [+ *hueso, diente*] to break; [+ *rama*] to break off; [+ *nuez, almendra*] to crack; **se sentó en la mesa y la partió** he sat on the table and broke it in two; **partió el plato en varios trozos** he broke the plate into several pieces; **la piedra no llegó a ~ el cristal** the stone didn't break the window; **le partió el labio de un puñetazo** he gave him a punch and split his lip; **¡te voy a ~ la cara!*** I'm going to smash your face in!*; **~ la cabeza a algn** to split sb's head open; ✦*MODISMO* **~ el corazón a algn** to break sb's heart
[3] (= *distribuir*) to share out; (= *compartir*) to share; **~ algo con otros** to share sth with others; ✦*REFRÁN* **quien parte y reparte se queda con la mejor parte** the person in charge of sharing out always keeps the biggest bit for himself
[4] (*) (= *fastidiar*) to mess up*; **no soporto estas reuniones a las 11, me parten toda la mañana** I hate these 11 o'clock meetings, they mess up the whole morning*; **salir a comprar ya me ha partido la tarde** going shopping has wasted my whole afternoon
Ⓑ VI [1] (= *ponerse en camino*) [*persona, expedición*] to set off; [*tren, avión*] to depart (**de** from; **para** for; **hacia** in the direction of); **~emos a primera hora de la mañana** we'll set off first thing in the morning; **la expedición ~á mañana de París** the expedition will set out *o* depart from Paris tomorrow; **partieron del puerto de Palos con destino a América** they set sail for America from the port of Palos
[2] **~ de algo** to start from sth; **hemos partido de un supuesto falso** we have started from a false assumption; **partiendo de la base de que …** working on the principle that …, assuming that …; **¿de quién partió la idea?** whose idea was it?
[3] **a ~ de** from; **a ~ de hoy** from today; **a ~ de mañana** from tomorrow; **a ~ del lunes** from Monday, starting on Monday; **a ~ de ahora** from now on; **la tercera casa a ~ de la esquina** the third house from the corner; **a ~ del puente la carretera se estrecha** the road gets narrower after the bridge; **¿qué podemos deducir a ~ de estos datos?** what can we deduce from these data?
Ⓒ **partirse** VPR [1] (= *romperse*) to break; **el remo se partió en dos** the oar broke in two; **me he partido un brazo** I've broken my arm; **se le partió el labio del golpe** the blow split his lip; ✦*MODISMO* **~se de risa** to split one's sides laughing
[2] (†) (= *irse*) to leave; (= *ponerse en camino*) to set off

partisano/a ADJ, SM/F partisan

partitivo ADJ partitive

partitura SF (*Mús*) score

parto SM [1] (*Med*) (*gen*) birth, delivery; (= *contracciones*) labour, labor (*EEUU*); (*Zool*) parturition; **asistir en un ~** to deliver a baby; **estar de ~** to be in labour; **tuvo un ~ difícil** it was a difficult birth; **mal ~** miscarriage; **murió de ~** she died in childbirth; ✦*MODISMO* **costar un ~** to be a real effort ► **parto múltiple** multiple birth ► **parto natural** natural childbirth ► **parto prematuro** premature birth ► **parto provocado** induced labour ► **parto sin dolor** painless childbirth
[2] (= *creación*) product, creation; **el ensayo ha sido un ~ difícil** I sweated blood over the essay ► **parto del ingenio** brainchild ► **parto de los montes** anticlimax, bathos

parturición SF parturition

parturienta SF (*antes del parto*) woman in labour, woman in labor (*EEUU*); (*después del parto*) woman who has just given birth

party (*pl* **partys**) SM (*gen*) party; (= *cóctel*) cocktail party, reception

parva SF [1] [*de trigo, cebada, centeno*] unthreshed grain
[2] (= *montón*) heap, pile

parvada SF (*LAm*) flock

parvedad SF (*con nombres incontables*) small amount; (*con nombres contables*) small number; **una ~** a tiny bit; **~ de recursos** limited resources *pl*, scant resources *pl*

parvulario SM nursery school, kindergarten

parvulista SMF nursery teacher

párvulo/a SM/F (*gen*) infant, child; (*Escol*) infant; **colegio de ~s** nursery school

pasa SF raisin; ✦*MODISMO* **está hecho una ~*** he's as shrivelled as a prune ► **pasa de Corinto** currant ► **pasa de Esmirna** sultana

pasable ADJ [1] (= *tolerable*) passable, tolerable
[2] (*LAm*) [*arroyo etc*] fordable
[3] (*Cono Sur*) (= *vendible*) saleable

pasablemente ADV passably, tolerably (well)

pasabocas SMPL (*Col*) tasty snacks

pasacalle SM passacaglia

pasacintas SM INV suspender-belt, garter belt (*EEUU*)

pasada SF [1] [*de pintura, barniz*] coat; (*con un trapo*) wipe; **dale dos ~s de jabón a la ropa** soap the clothes twice; **le di una ~ con la plancha a la camisa** I ran the iron over the shirt
[2] (*Cos*) (= *puntada*) **dale una ~ al pantalón** give it a quick sew
[3] **de ~** in passing; **me comentó de ~ que no vendría mañana** she mentioned in passing that she wouldn't be coming tomorrow; **ya que vas al estanco de ~ cómprame unos sellos** (*LAm*) if you are going to the tobacconist's could you buy me some stamps while you're there *o* while you're at it; **sólo estoy aquí de ~** (*LAm*) I'm only just passing by *o* through
[4] (*) (= *barbaridad*) **¡este coche es una ~!** this car is amazing!; **¿has visto cómo ha saltado? ¡qué ~!** did you see him jump? amazing!; **¡qué ~! me han cobrado 75 euros** what a rip-off! they charged me 75 euros*; **una ~ de …*** (= *un montón de*) lots of …, tons of …*; **había una ~ de gente** there were lots *o* tons* of people
[5] (= *jugarreta*) **hacerle** *o* **jugarle una mala ~ a algn** to play a dirty trick on sb
[6] (*CAm, Cono Sur**) (= *reprimenda*) telling-off*
[7] (*Col*) (= *vergüenza*) shame, embarrassment

pasadera SF stepping stone

pasadero Ⓐ ADJ (= *tolerable*) passable, tolerable; (*Aut etc*) passable, open
Ⓑ SM (= *piedra*) stepping stone

pasadizo SM (*interior*) passage; (*entre calles*) passageway, alley

pasado Ⓐ ADJ [1] [*tiempo*] **el jueves ~** last Thursday; **el mes ~** last month; **~ mañana** the day after tomorrow; **~s dos días** after two days; **ya eran pasadas las seis** it was already after six; **lo ~** the past; ✦*MODISMO* **lo ~, ~ (está)** let bygones be bygones
[2] (*Culin*) (= *en mal estado*) [*pan*] stale; [*fruta*] overripe; **esta leche está pasada** this milk is off
[3] (*Culin*) (= *muy hecho*) [*carne*] overdone; [*arroz, pasta*] overcooked; **me gustan los filetes muy ~s** I like my steaks very well done; **la carne estaba demasiado pasada** the meat was overdone; **huevo ~ por agua** soft-boiled egg
[4] (= *no actual*) [*ropa, zapatos*] old-fashioned; [*noticia*] stale; [*idea, costumbre*] antiquated, out-of-date
[5] (= *muy usado*) worn; **esta tela está muy pasada y se rompe con facilidad** this material is very worn and it tears easily; **estar ~ de vueltas** *o* **de rosca** [*grifo, tuerca*] to be worn; [*persona*] to have seen it all before
[6] [*belleza*] faded

➤ LENGUA Y USO: **partidario A** 38.1, 40.3

7 (*) (= *borracho, drogado*) **estar ~** to be out of one's box*
Ⓑ SM 1 **el ~** the past; ✦*MODISMO* **el ~, ~ (está)** let bygones be bygones
2 [*de persona*] past; **tiene un ~ muy turbio** he has a very murky past
3 (*Ling*) past (tense)

pasador(a) Ⓐ SM/F (= *contrabandista*) smuggler; (*LAm*) (= *correo*) drug courier
Ⓑ SM 1 (*Culin*) (*gen*) colander; [*de té*] strainer
2 (*Téc*) (= *filtro*) filter; (= *pestillo*) bolt, fastener; [*de bisagra*] pin
3 [*de corbata*] tie pin; [*de camisa*] collar stud
4 [*de pelo*] hairpin
5 **pasadores** (= *gemelos*) cufflinks; (*LAm*) (= *cordones*) shoelaces

pasaje SM 1 (= *acción*) passage, passing; (*Náut*) voyage, crossing
2 (*esp LAm*) (= *boleto*) ticket ► **pasaje electrónico** e-ticket
3 (= *tarifa*) fare; **cobrar el ~** to collect fares
4 (= *viajeros*) passengers *pl*
5 (= *callejón*) passageway, alleyway; (*con tiendas*) arcade; (*Caribe, Cono Sur, Méx*) cul-de-sac
6 (*Literat, Mús*) passage
7 (*Andes, Caribe*) (= *cuento*) story, anecdote
8 (*Andes*) (= *pisos*) tenement building

pasajeramente ADV fleetingly

pasajero/a Ⓐ ADJ 1 [*momento*] fleeting, passing; **ave ~** bird of passage, migratory bird
2 [*sitio*] busy Ⓑ SM/F passenger Ⓒ SM (*Méx*) ferryman

pasamanos SM INV, **pasamano** SM 1 (*Arquit*) (*gen*) handrail, rail; [*de escalera*] banister
2 (*Cono Sur Ferro etc*) strap (*for standing passenger*)
3 (*Cos*) braid
4 (*Cono Sur*) (= *propina*) tip

pasamontañas SM Balaclava (helmet), ski mask

pasandito* ADV (*CAm, Méx*) on tiptoe

pasante SMF 1 (*gen*) assistant; (*Jur*) articled clerk
2 (*Escol*†) assistant teacher; (= *tutor*) tutor

pasapalos SMPL (*Méx, Ven*) tasty snacks

pasapasa SM sleight of hand

pasaportar* ▸conjug 1a◂ VT to bump off*

pasaporte SM passport; ✦*MODISMO* **dar el ~ a algn*** (= *despedir*) to boot sb out*; (= *matar*) to bump sb off*

pasapurés SM INV, **pasapuré** SM manual food mill

pasar

▸conjug 1a◂
A VERBO INTRANSITIVO
B VERBO TRANSITIVO
C VERBO PRONOMINAL
D SUSTANTIVO MASCULINO

Para las expresiones ***pasar lista, pasar de moda, pasar desapercibido, pasarse de rosca****, ver la otra entrada*

Ⓐ VERBO INTRANSITIVO
1 = *ocurrir* 1·1 [*suceso*] to happen; **¿qué pasó?** what happened?; **¿pasa algo?** is anything up?, is anything wrong?, is anything the matter?; **como si no hubiese pasado nada** as if nothing had happened; **aquí pasa algo misterioso** there's something odd going on here; **siempre pasa igual** *o* **lo mismo** it's always the same; **¿qué pasa?** what's happening?, what's going on?, what's up?; (*como saludo*) how's things?*; **¿qué pasa que no entra?** why doesn't she come in?; **¿qué pasa contigo?** what's up with you?; (*) (*como saludo*) how's it going?*; **¿qué ha pasado con ella?** what's become of her?; **lo que pasa es que ...** well, you see..., the thing is that ...; **pase lo que pase** whatever happens, come what may
1·2 **~le a algn: nunca me pasa nada** nothing ever happens to me; **no me ha pasado otra (igual) en la vida** nothing like this has ever happened to me before; **siempre me pasa lo mismo, lo pierdo todo** it's always the same, I keep losing things; **tuvo un accidente, pero por suerte no le pasó nada** he had an accident, but fortunately he wasn't hurt; **esto te pasa por no hacerme caso** this is what comes of not listening to me, this wouldn't have happened (to you) if you'd listened to me; **¿qué te pasa?** what's the matter?; **¿qué le pasa a ése?** what's the matter with him?
2 = *cambiar de lugar* 2·1 [*objeto*] **la cuerda pasa de un lado a otro de la calle** the rope goes from one side of the street to the other; **cuando muera la empresa ~á al hijo** when he dies the company will go to his son; **la foto fue pasando de mano en mano** the photo was passed around; **pasó de mis manos a las suyas** it passed from my hands into his
2·2 [*persona*] to go; **~ a un cuarto contiguo** to go into an adjoining room; **~ de Inglaterra al Canadá** to go from England to Canada
3 = *entrar* **¡pase!** come in!; (*cediendo el paso*) after you!; **no se puede ~** you can't go through, you can't go in; **pasamos directamente a ver al jefe** we went straight in to see the boss; **los moros ~on a España** the Moors crossed over into Spain; **hacer ~ a algn** to show sb in
4 = *transitar* **pasó una bicicleta** a bicycle went past; **¿a qué hora pasa el cartero?** what time does the postman come?; **ya ha pasado el tren de las cinco** (= *sin hacer parada*) the five o'clock train has already gone by; (= *haciendo parada*) the five o'clock train has already been and gone; **¿ha pasado ya el camión de la basura?** have the dustmen been?; **~ de largo** to go *o* pass by; **~ por: el autobús pasa por delante de nuestra casa** the bus goes past our house; **ese autobús no pasa por aquí** that bus doesn't come this way
5 = *acercarse a* **tengo que ~ por el banco** I've got to go to the bank; **~é por la tienda mañana** I'll go *o* pop into the shop tomorrow; **tendrá que ~ por mi despacho** he'll have to come to my office; **pase por caja** please pay at the cash desk; **~é por tu casa** I'll drop in
◆ **pasar a** + *INFIN*: **te ~é a buscar a las ocho** I'll pick you up at eight; **pasa a verme cuando quieras** come round whenever you like
6 = *cambiar de situación* to go; **el equipo ha pasado a primera división** the team has gone up to the first division; **y luego ~on a otra cosa** and then they went on to something else; **ha pasado de ser tímida a no tenerle miedo a nada** she has gone from being shy to fearing nothing; **~ de teniente a general** to go from lieutenant to general; **~ a ser** to become; **en muy poco tiempo ha pasado a ser un gran profesional** he has become a real professional in a very short space of time
7 = *transcurrir* [*tiempo*] to pass, go by; **han pasado cuatro años** four years have passed *o* gone by; **el tiempo pasa deprisa** time passes *o* goes so quickly; **¡cómo pasa el tiempo!** how time flies!; **ya ha pasado una hora** it's been an hour already
8 = *acabar* [*problema, situación*] to be over; [*efectos*] to wear off; **ha pasado la crisis** the crisis is over; **ya pasó aquello** that's all over (and done with) now
9 = *aceptarse* **puede ~** it's passable, it's OK; **por esta vez pase** I'll let it go this time; **que me llames carroza, pase, pero fascista, no** you can call me an old fuddy-duddy if you like, but not a fascist
10
◆ **pasar por** 10·1 (= *atravesar, caber*) to go through; **el hilo pasa por el agujero** the thread goes through the hole; **pasamos por un túnel muy largo** we went through a very long tunnel; **no pasamos por el pueblo** we didn't go through the village; **el río pasa por la ciudad** the river flows *o* goes through the city; **~ por la aduana** to go through customs; **está pasando por un mal momento** he's going through a bad patch; **no creo que el sofá pase por esa puerta** I don't think the settee will go through the door
10·2 (= *depender de*) to depend on; **el futuro de la empresa pasa por este acuerdo** the company's future depends on *o* hangs on this agreement
10·3 (= *ser considerado*) to pass as; **podrían perfectamente ~ por gemelos** they could easily pass as twins; **Juan pasa por francés** most people think Juan is French; **hacerse ~ por** to pass o.s. off as; **se hace ~ por médico** he passes himself off as a doctor
11 *otras formas preposicionales*
◆ **pasar a** + *INFIN* (= *empezar*) **paso ahora a explicar mi postura** I will now go on to explain my position; **~ a decir algo** to go on to say sth; **ya va siendo hora de ~ a la acción** it is time for action
◆ **pasar de** (= *exceder*) **pasa ya de los 70** he's over 70; **esto pasa de ser una broma** this is beyond a joke; **no pasa de ser un jugador mediocre** he's no more than an average player; **no pasan de 60 los que lo tienen** those who have it do not number more than 60, fewer than 60 people have it; **yo de ahí no paso** that's as far as I'm prepared to go; **de ésta no pasa** this is the very last time; **de hoy no pasa que le escriba** I'll write to him this very day
◆ **pasar sin**: **tendrá que ~ sin coche** he'll have to get by *o* manage without a car; **no puede ~ sin ella** he can't manage without her
12 *Naipes* to pass; **yo paso** pass
13 *esp Esp* = mostrarse indiferente* **yo paso** count me out; **~ de algo/algn: yo paso de política** I'm not into politics; **paso de todo** I couldn't care less; **pasa olímpicamente de todo lo que le dicen** he doesn't take the blindest bit of notice of anything they say to him; **paso de ti, chaval** I couldn't care less about you, pal

Ⓑ VERBO TRANSITIVO
1 = *dar, entregar* (*gen*) to pass; (*en una serie*) to pass on; **¿me pasas la sal, por favor?**

➤ LENGUA Y USO: pasar A1 44.1 A11 53.2

could you pass (me) the salt, please?; **le pasó el sobre** he handed *o* passed her the envelope; **pásale una nota con disimulo** slip him a note; **cuando termines pásasela a Isabel** when you've finished pass it on to Isabel

2 *= traspasar* [+ *río, frontera*] to cross; [+ *límite*] to go beyond; **el túnel pasa la montaña** the tunnel goes right through the mountain; **esto pasa los límites de lo razonable** this goes beyond the realm of what is reasonable

3 *= llevar* **nos ~on a ver al director** they took us to see the manager; **nos ~on a otra habitación** they moved us into another room; **he pasado mi despacho al dormitorio** I've moved my office into the bedroom

4 *= hacer atravesar* **pasa el alambre por este agujero** put the wire through this hole; **pasó el hilo por el ojo de la aguja** she threaded the thread through the eye of the needle

5 *= colar* to strain; **~ el café por el colador** to strain the coffee

6 *= introducir* [+ *moneda falsa*] to pass (off); [+ *contrabando*] to smuggle; **han pasado billetes falsos** they've passed (off) forged notes; **han pasado un alijo de cocaína por la frontera** a consignment of cocaine has been smuggled across the border

7 *= hacer deslizar* **voy a ~le un trapo** I'm going to wipe it down; **~ la mano por algo** to run one's hand over sth; **~ el cepillo por el pelo** to run a brush through one's hair; **~ la aspiradora por la alfombra** to vacuum the carpet, run the vacuum cleaner over the carpet; **~ la aspiradora** to do the vacuuming

8 *= deslizar* to slip; **le pasó el brazo por los hombros/la cintura** she slipped *o* put her arm around his shoulders/waist

9 *= contagiar* to give; **me has pasado tu catarro** you've given me your cold

10 *= volver* [+ *página*] to turn; ♦*MODISMO* **~ página** to make a fresh start

11 *= escribir* **~ algo a limpio** to make a neat *o* fair *o* clean copy of sth; **~ algo a máquina** to type sth up

12 *= tragar* (*lit*) to swallow; (*fig*) to bear, stand; **no puedo ~ esta pastilla** I can't swallow this pill, I can't get this pill down; **no puedo ~ a ese hombre** I can't bear *o* stand that man

13 *= tolerar* **se lo pasan todo** they let him get away with anything; **no te voy a ~ más** I'm not going to indulge you any more

14 *= aprobar* [+ *examen*] to pass

15 *= proyectar* [+ *película, programa*] to show, screen

16 *= poner en contacto* **te paso con Pedro** (*al mismo teléfono*) I'll put you on to Pedro; (*a distinto teléfono*) I'll put you through to Pedro

17 *= realizar* **pasa consulta** *o* **visita a unas 700 personas diarias** he sees 700 patients a day; *ver tb* revista 3

18 *= superar* **los pasa a todos en inteligencia** she's more intelligent than any of them; **para ganar debes ~ a muchos contrincantes** to win you have to beat a lot of opponents; **me pasa ya 3cm** he's already 3cm taller than I am

19 *Aut* to pass, overtake

20 *= omitir* **~ algo por alto** to overlook sth; **~ por alto un detalle** to overlook a detail

21 *+ tiempo* to spend; **~ las vacaciones** to spend one's holidays; **voy a ~ el fin de semana con ella** I'm going to spend the weekend with her; **fuimos a ~ el día en la playa** we went to the seaside for the day; **lo ~emos tan ricamente** we'll have such a good time

♦ **pasarlo** + *ADV*: **~lo bien** to have a good time; **¡que lo pases bien!** have a good time!, enjoy yourself!; **~lo mal** to have a bad time; **lo pasamos muy mal** we had an awful time

22 *= dejar atrás* **hemos pasado el aniversario** the anniversary has passed, the anniversary is behind us; **ya hemos pasado lo peor** we're over the worst now, the worst is behind us now

23 *= sufrir* **ha pasado una mala racha** she's been through a bad patch; **ha pasado muchas enfermedades** he's had a lot of illnesses; **~ frío** to be cold; **~ hambre** to be hungry

24 *Cono Sur* = engañar* to cheat, swindle

Ⓒ **pasarse** VERBO PRONOMINAL

1 *= cesar* **¿se te ha pasado el mareo?** have you stopped feeling dizzy?; **ya se te ~á** [*enfado, disgusto*] you'll get over it; [*dolor*] it'll stop

2 *= perder* to miss; **se me pasó el turno** I missed my turn; **que no se te pase la oportunidad** don't miss this chance

3 *= trasladarse* to go over; **~se al enemigo** to go over to the enemy

4 *= estropearse* [*flor etc*] to fade; [*carne, pescado*] to go bad *o* off; [*fruta*] to go bad *o* soft; [*ropa*] to show signs of wear, get threadbare; **no se ~á si se tapa la botella** it will keep if you put the cap back on the bottle

5 *= recocerse* **se ha pasado el arroz** the rice is overcooked

6 *tornillo, tuerca* to get overscrewed

7 ** = excederse* **está bien hacer ejercicio pero no hay que ~se** it's good to exercise but there's no point in overdoing it; **¡no te pases, o nos echarán del bar!** steady on *o* cool it or they'll throw us out of the bar!*; **¡no te pases, que te voy a dar una torta!** just watch it or I'll smack you in the face!; **¡te has pasado, tío!** (*censurando*) you've really gone and done it now!; (*felicitando*) well done, man!*, nice one!*; **se pasa en mostrar agradecimiento** he overdoes the gratitude; **te has pasado mucho con ella, gritándole así** you went much too far shouting at her like that; **~se de**: **se pasa de bueno/generoso** he's too good/generous; **~se de listo** to be too clever by half; **~se de la raya** to go too far, overstep the mark

8 *+ tiempo* to spend; **se ha pasado todo el día leyendo** he has spent the whole day reading

9 *= olvidarse de* **se le pasó la fecha del examen** he forgot the date of the exam; **se me pasó llamarle** I forgot to ring him

10 **no se le pasa nada** nothing escapes him, he doesn't miss a thing

11 *seguido de preposición*

♦ **pasarse por** [+ *lugar*] **pásate por casa si tienes tiempo** come round if you've got time; **ya que tienes que ~te por el banco ingrésame este talón** seeing as you have to go to the bank anyway, you can pay this cheque in for me; **se me pasó por la cabeza** *o* **imaginación** it crossed my mind

♦ **pasarse sin algo** to do without sth

Ⓓ SUSTANTIVO MASCULINO

(†) **un modesto ~** a modest competence; **tener un buen ~** to be well off

---

PASAR

En expresiones temporales

- Se traduce por **spend** cuando **pasar** tiene un uso transitivo y queremos indicar un período de tiempo concreto, seguido de la actividad que en ese tiempo se desarrolla, o del lugar:

  Me pasé la tarde escribiendo cartas
  I spent the evening writing letters
  Ha pasado toda su vida en el campo
  He has spent his whole life in the country

- En cambio, cuando se describe la forma en que se pasa el tiempo mediante un adjetivo, se debe emplear en inglés la construcción **have** + **(a)** + **ADJETIVO** + **SUSTANTIVO**:

  Pasamos una tarde entretenida
  We had a lovely afternoon
  Pasamos un rato estupendo jugando al squash
  We had a fantastic time playing squash

NOTA: la expresión **pasar el rato** se traduce por **pass the time**:

  No sé qué hacer para pasar el rato
  I don't know what to do to pass the time

- Cuando el uso es intransitivo, **pasar** se traduce por **pass** *o* **go by**.

  A medida que pasaba el tiempo se deprimía cada vez más
  As time passed *o* ***went by, he became more and more depressed***

Para otros usos y ejemplos ver la entrada.

---

pasarela SF (= *puente*) footbridge; (*Teat*) catwalk, walkway; [*de modelos*] catwalk; (*Náut*) gangway, gangplank ► **pasarela telescópica** airport walkway, jetty walkway

pasarrato SM (*Caribe, Méx*) = **pasatiempo**

pasatiempo SM 1 (= *entretenimiento*) pastime; (= *afición*) hobby
2 **pasatiempos** (*en periódicos, revistas*) puzzles

pascana SF 1 (*Andes, Cono Sur*) (= *fonda*) wayside inn
2 (*Andes, Cono Sur*) (= *etapa*) stage, part (of a journey)
3 (*Andes*) *part of a journey done without stopping*

pascícola ADJ grazing *antes de s*, pasture *antes de s*

Pascua SF 1 (= *Navidad*) Christmas time, Christmas period; (= *Epifanía*) Epiphany; **¡felices ~s!** merry Christmas! ► **Pascua(s) de Navidad** Christmas
2 (*en Semana Santa*) Easter ► **Pascua de Pentecostés** Pentecost, Whitsun, Whitsuntide ► **Pascua de Resurrección**, **Pascua florida** Easter
3 ► **Pascua de los hebreos**, **Pascua de los judíos** Passover
4 ♦*MODISMOS* **de ~s a Ramos** once in a blue moon; **estar como unas ~s** to be as happy as a lark; **hacer la ~ a algn*** (= *molestar*) to annoy sb, bug sb*; (= *perjudicar*) to do the dirty on sb; **¡que se hagan la ~!** (*Esp**) they can lump it!; **y santas ~s** and that's that, and that's the lot

pascual ADJ Paschal; **cordero ~** (older) lamb

pascualina SF (*Arg, Uru*) *spinach and cheese quiche*

pase SM [1] (= *documento*) pass ► **pase de embarque** (*Aer*) boarding pass ► **pase de favor** (*Pol*) safe conduct; (= *invitación*) complimentary ticket ► **pase de prensa** press pass ► **pase de temporada** (*Teat, Mús*) season ticket ► **pase pernocta** (*Mil*) overnight pass
[2] (*Cine*) showing ► **pase de modas, pase de modelos** fashion show
[3] (*Com*) permit
[4] (*Jur*) licence, license (EEUU)
[5] (*Dep*) pass ► **pase adelante** forward pass ► **pase (hacia) atrás** back pass
[6] ► **pase de lista** (*Mil*) roll call
[7] (*Taur*) ► **pase de pecho** chest-level pass
[8] (‡) (= *contrabando*) drug smuggling; (*LAm*‡) (= *dosis*) fix‡

paseandero ADJ (*Cono Sur*) fond of strolling

paseante SMF [1] (*gen*) walker, stroller; (= *transeúnte*) passer-by; (*tb* **~ en corte**) (*pey*) loafer, idler
[2] (†) (= *pretendiente*) suitor

pasear ▸conjug 1a◂ Ⓐ VT [1] [+ *perro, niño*] to take for a walk, walk
[2] (= *exhibir*) [+ *ropa, coche*] to parade, show off
[3] **~ la calle a una muchacha** (*Esp*†) to walk up and down the street where a girl lives
[4] (*CAm*) [+ *dinero*] to squander
[5] (*Esp Hist**) = **dar el paseo a**
Ⓑ VI, **pasearse** VPR [1] (*gen*) to go for a walk, go for a stroll; (= *de un lado a otro*) to walk about, walk up and down; **~ en bicicleta** to go for a ride, go cycling; **~ en coche** to go for a drive, go for a run in the car; **~ a caballo** to ride, go riding; **~ en bote** to go sailing
[2] (*Esp*) (= *estar ocioso*) to idle, loaf about
[3] **~se por un tema** (*Esp*) to deal superficially with a subject
[4] **~se** (*Méx*) to take a day off

paseíllo SM (*Taur*) *ceremonial entry of bullfighters*

paseíto SM little walk, gentle stroll

paseo SM [1] (*gen*) walk, stroll; (= *excursión*) outing; **dar un ~** (*andando*) to go for a walk *o* stroll, take a walk *o* stroll; (*en coche*) to go for a ride; **estar de ~** to be out for a walk; **llevar** *o* **sacar a un niño de ~** to take a child out for a walk; **✦MODISMOS dar el ~ a algn*** to take sb for a ride*; **enviar** *o* **mandar a ~*** [+ *estudios, trabajo*] to jack in*; **enviar** *o* **mandar a algn a ~*** to tell sb to go to blazes*, send sb packing, chuck sb out; **no va a ser un ~** (*Esp*) it's not going to be easy; **¡vete a ~!‡** get lost!‡ ► **paseo a caballo** ride (on horseback) ► **paseo de vigilancia** round, tour of inspection ► **paseo en barco** boat trip ► **paseo en bicicleta** (bike) ride ► **paseo en coche** drive, ride ► **paseo espacial** space walk ► **paseo por la naturaleza** nature trail
[2] (= *avenida*) parade, avenue ► **paseo marítimo** promenade, esplanade
[3] (= *distancia*) short walk; **entre las dos casas no hay más que un ~** it's only a short walk between the two houses
[4] ► **paseo cívico** (*Méx*) procession, fiesta procession
[5] (*Esp**) (*Hist*) *(journey leading to the) summary execution of a political opponent*; **dar el ~ a algn** (*Hist*) to execute sb summarily; (*moderno*) to bump sb off‡

pasero SM (*Andes*) ferryman

pashá SM = **pachá**

pasible ADJ (*liter*) able to endure, long-suffering

pasillear ▸conjug 1a◂ VI (*Parl*) to engage in lobby discussions, lobby

pasilleo SM lobby discussions *pl*, lobbying

pasillo SM [1] (= *corredor*) (*en casa, oficina*) corridor; (*en avión, teatro*) aisle ► **pasillo aéreo** air corridor, air lane ► **pasillo móvil, pasillo rodante** travelator
[2] (*Pol*) lobby; **hacer ~s** to engage in lobby discussions, lobby
[3] (*Teat*) (= *pieza corta*) short piece, sketch

pasión SF [1] (= *amor intenso*) passion; **noches de ~** nights of passion; **la quería con ~** he loved her passionately; **tener ~ por algn** to love sb passionately
[2] (= *gran afición*) passion; **le gusta el cine con ~** he's passionate about films, he's mad about films; **tener ~ por algo** to have a passion for sth; **tiene ~ por los animales** he has a passion for animals, he loves animals
[3] (= *exaltación*) passion; **lo mató cegada por la ~** she killed him in a blind fit of passion; **defendía su postura con ~** she argued her case with passion *o* passionately
[4] (*Rel*) **la Pasión** the Passion

pasional ADJ passionate; **crimen ~** crime of passion

pasionaria SF passionflower

pasito ADV (*Col*) gently, softly

pasiva SF (*Ling*) passive (voice)

pasivamente ADV passively

pasividad SF passiveness, passivity

pasivo Ⓐ ADJ [1] [+ *persona, comportamiento*] passive; **es un niño muy ~ y nunca toma la iniciativa** he is a very passive child, he never takes the initiative
[2] (*Ling*) passive; **la voz pasiva** the passive voice
Ⓑ SM (*Com, Fin*) liabilities *pl*; [*de cuenta*] debit side ► **pasivo circulante, pasivo corriente** current liabilities *pl* ► **pasivo diferido** deferred liabilities *pl*

pasma‡ (*Esp*) Ⓐ SMF cop*
Ⓑ SF **la ~** the fuzz‡, the cops* *pl*

pasmado ADJ [1] (= *asombrado*) astonished, amazed; **dejar ~ a algn** to astonish *o* amaze sb; **estar** *o* **quedar ~ de** to be amazed at, be astonished at; **mirar con cara de ~** to look in astonishment at
[2] (= *atontado*) stunned, dumbfounded; **se quedó ahí ~** he just stood there gaping; **¡oye, ~!*** hey, you dope!
[3] (= *frío*) frozen stiff; (*Bot*) frostbitten
[4] (*LAm*) [*herida*] infected; [*persona*] unhealthy-looking, ill-looking
[5] (*CAm, Méx*) (= *estúpido*) stupid; (= *torpe*) clumsy
[6] (*LAm*) [*fruta*] overripe

pasmar ▸conjug 1a◂ Ⓐ VT [1] (= *asombrar*) to amaze, astonish
[2] (= *atontar*) to stun, dumbfound
[3] (= *enfriar*) to chill to the bone; (*Bot*) to nip, cut
Ⓑ **pasmarse** VPR [1] (= *asombrarse*) to be amazed, be astonished (**de** at); (= *maravillarse*) to marvel, wonder (**de** at)
[2] (= *estar helado*) to be chilled to the bone; (= *resfriarse*) to catch a chill
[3] (*LAm Med*) (= *infectarse*) to become infected; (= *enfermar*) to fall ill; (*con trismo*) to get lockjaw; (*con fiebre*) to catch a fever
[4] [*colores*] to fade
[5] (*Caribe, Méx*) [*fruta*] to wither

pasmarota SF, **pasmarotada** SF display of shocked surprise, exaggerated reaction

pasmarote* SMF idiot, halfwit; **¡no te quedes ahí como un ~!** don't just stand there like an idiot!

pasmazón SM (*CAm, Caribe, Méx*) = **pasmo**

pasmo SM [1] (= *asombro*) amazement, astonishment; (= *admiración*) wonder; **es el ~ de cuantos lo ven** it is a marvel *o* a source of wonder to all who see it
[2] (= *enfriamiento*) chill; **le dio un ~*** he was frozen stiff
[3] (*Med*) (= *trismo*) lockjaw, tetanus
[4] (*LAm*) (= *fiebre*) fever

pasmosamente ADV (= *asombrosamente*) amazingly, astonishingly; (= *admirablemente*) wonderfully

pasmoso ADJ (= *asombroso*) amazing, astonishing; (= *admirable*) wonderful

paso[1] ADJ dried; **higo ~** dried fig; **ciruela pasa** prune; **uva pasa** raisin

paso[2] Ⓐ SM [1] (= *acción de pasar*) **contemplaban el ~ de la procesión desde un balcón** they watched the procession go by from a balcony; **para evitar el ~ del aire** to prevent the air getting through; **por estas fechas tiene lugar el ~ de las cigüeñas por nuestra región** this is the time of year when the storks fly over our region; **los detuvieron en el ~ del estrecho** they were arrested while crossing the channel; **el presidente, a su ~ por nuestra ciudad ...** the president, during his visit to our city ...; **el huracán arrasó con todo lo que encontró a su ~** the hurricane flattened everything in its path; **con el ~ del tiempo** with (the passing of) time; **"prohibido el paso"** "no entry"; **ceder el ~** to give way, yield (EEUU); **"ceda el ~"** "give way", "yield" (EEUU); **dar ~ a algo**: **el invierno dio ~ a la primavera** winter gave way to spring; **ahora vamos a dar ~ a nuestro corresponsal en Lisboa** we now go over to our correspondent in Lisbon; **las protestas dieron ~ a una huelga** the protests led to *o* were followed by a strike; **de ~**: **mencionaron el tema sólo de ~** they only mentioned the matter in passing; **¿puedes ir al supermercado, de ~ que vas a la farmacia?** could you go to the supermarket on your way to the chemist's?; **de ~ recuérdale que tiene un libro nuestro** remind him that he's got a book of ours while you're at it; **el banco me pilla de ~** the bank is on my way; **dicho sea de ~** incidentally; **entrar de ~** to drop in; **estar de ~** to be passing through; **están sólo de ~ por Barcelona** they're just passing through Barcelona ► **paso del Ecuador** *party or trip organized by university students to celebrate the halfway stage in their degree course* ► **paso franco, paso libre** free passage; *ver tb* **ave**
[2] (= *camino*) way; (*Arquit*) passage; (*Geog*) pass; (*Náut*) strait; **estás en mitad del ~** you're blocking the way; **¡paso!** make way!; **la policía le abría ~** the police cleared a path for him; **abrirse ~** to make one's way; **se abrió ~ entre la multitud** he made his way through the crowd; **se abrió ~ a tiros** he shot his way through; **se abrieron ~ luchando** they fought their way through; **cerrar el ~**

to block the way; **dejar el ~ libre** to leave the way open; **dejar ~ a algn** to let sb past; **impedir el ~** to block the way; ✦***MODISMOS*** **salir al ~ a algn** to collar sb; **salir al ~ de algo** to be quick to deny sth; **han salido al ~ de la acusación** they've been quick to deny the accusation; **salir del ~** to get out of trouble ► **paso a desnivel, paso a distinto nivel** (*Aut*) flyover, overpass (*EEUU*) ► **paso a nivel** level crossing, grade crossing (*EEUU*) ► **paso a nivel sin barrera** unguarded level crossing ► **paso (de) cebra** (*Esp*) zebra crossing, crosswalk (*EEUU*) ► **paso de peatones** pedestrian crossing, crosswalk (*EEUU*) ► **paso elevado** (*Aut*) flyover, overpass (*EEUU*) ► **paso fronterizo** border crossing ► **paso inferior** underpass, subway ► **paso salmonero** salmon ladder ► **paso subterráneo** underpass, subway ► **paso superior** (*Aut*) flyover, overpass (*EEUU*)

3 (*al andar*) (= *acción*) step; (= *ruido*) footstep; (= *huella*) footprint; **he oído ~s** I heard footsteps; **coger el ~** to fall into step; **dar un ~** to take a step; **¿ha dado ya sus primeros ~s?** has she taken her first steps yet?; **no da ni un ~ sin ella** he never goes anywhere without her; **dirigir sus ~s hacia** to head towards; **dar un ~ en falso** (= *tropezar*) to miss one's footing; (= *equivocarse*) to make a false move; **hacer ~s** (*Baloncesto*) to travel (with the ball); **volvió sobre sus ~s** she retraced her steps; ✦***MODISMOS*** **a cada ~** at every step, at every turn; **a ~s agigantados** by leaps and bounds; **el proyecto avanza a ~s agigantados** the project is advancing by leaps and bounds; **la demanda aumenta a ~s agigantados** demand is increasing at a rate of knots *o* extremely quickly; **andar en malos ~s** to be mixed up in shady affairs; **dar un mal ~** make a false move; **~ a ~** step by step; **por sus ~s contados** step by step, systematically; **seguir los ~s a algn** to tail sb; **seguir los ~s de algn** to follow in sb's footsteps ► **paso adelante** (*lit, fig*) step forward ► **paso a dos** pas de deux ► **paso atrás** (*lit, fig*) step backwards; **dio un ~ atrás** he took a step backwards

4 (= *modo de andar*) [*de persona*] walk, gait; [*de caballo*] gait; **caminaba con ~ decidido** he was walking purposefully; **acelerar el ~** to go faster, speed up; **aflojar el ~** to slow down; **apretar** *o* **avivar el ~** to go faster, speed up; **a buen ~** at a good pace; **iba andando a buen ~** I was walking at a good pace; **las conversaciones marchan a buen ~** the talks are proceeding at a good pace *o* rate; **establecer el ~** to make the pace, set the pace; **a ~ lento** at a slow pace, slowly; **a ~ ligero** (*gen*) at a swift pace; (*Mil*) at the double; **llevar el ~** to keep in step, keep time; **marcar el ~** (*gen*) to keep time; (*Mil*) to mark time; **a ~ redoblado** (*LAm Mil*) at the double; **romper el ~** to break step; ✦***MODISMO*** **a ~ de tortuga** at a snail's pace ► **paso de ambladura, paso de andadura** (*Equitación*) amble ► **paso de ganso** (*LAm*), **paso de (la) oca** goose step ► **paso de vals** waltz step

5 (= *ritmo*) rate, pace; **a este ~** at this rate; **a este ~ no terminarán nunca** at this rate they'll never finish; **al ~ que vamos no acabaremos nunca** at the rate we're going we'll never finish

6 (= *distancia*) **vive a un ~ de aquí** he lives round the corner from here; **estaba a unos diez ~s** it was about ten paces away; **de eso al terrorismo no hay más que un ~** it's a small step from there to terrorism

7 (= *avance*) step; **es un ~ hacia nuestro objetivo** it's a step towards our objective; **el matrimonio es un ~ muy importante en la vida** marriage is an important step in life; ✦***MODISMOS*** **dar el primer ~** ◊ **dar los primeros ~s** to make the first move

8 (*Téc*) [*de tornillo*] pitch; [*de contador, teléfono*] unit

9 (*Teat, Hist*) sketch, interlude

10 (*Rel*) (*en procesión*) *float in Holy Week procession, with statues representing part of Easter story*; → SEMANA SANTA

11 ► **paso de armas** (*Mil, Hist*) passage of arms

12 (*LAm*) (= *vado*) ford

Ⓑ ADV softly, gently; **¡paso!** not so fast!, easy there!

pasodoble SM paso doble

pasón⁑ SM = **pasada 4**

pasoso ADJ 1 (*LAm*) (= *poroso*) porous, permeable; (= *absorbente*) absorbent

2 (*Cono Sur*) (= *sudoroso*) perspiring, sweaty

3 (*Andes Med*) contagious

pasota* Ⓐ ADJ INV 1 (*Esp*) [*persona*] **Jesús va de ~ por la vida** Jesús doesn't care much about anything; **filosofía ~** couldn't-care-less attitude

2 (*Méx*) (= *pasado de moda*) passé, out of fashion

Ⓑ SMF **eres un ~** you just don't care, do you?

pasote* SM (*Esp*) (= *ultraje*) outrage; (= *exceso*) exaggeration

pasotismo SM (*Esp*) couldn't-care-less attitude

paspa SF (*Andes*), **paspadura** SF (*Andes, Cono Sur*) chapped skin, cracked skin

pasparse ▸conjug 1a◂ VPR (*Andes, Cono Sur*) [*piel*] to chap, crack

paspartú SM passe-partout

pasquín SM 1 (*Pol*) wall poster

2 (*Literat*) skit, lampoon

pássim ADV passim

pasta SF 1 (= *masa*) paste ► **pasta de celulosa** wood pulp ► **pasta de coca** cocaine paste ► **pasta de dientes** toothpaste ► **pasta de madera** wood pulp ► **pasta dentífrica** toothpaste ► **pasta de papel** paper pulp

2 [*de pan*] dough; (*en repostería*) pastry; (= *pastelillo*) biscuit, cookie (*EEUU*) ► **pasta quebrada** shortcrust pastry ► **pastas de té** biscuits, cookies (*EEUU*)

3 (= *macarrones, fideos*) pasta ► **pasta al huevo** egg pasta ► **pasta de sopa** pasta for soup

4 (*para untar*) paste ► **pasta de anchoas** anchovy paste ► **pasta de carne** meat paste

5 (*) (= *dinero*) money, cash, dough*; **¡suelta la ~!** hand over the dough!*; **me ha costado una ~ gansa** it cost me an arm and a leg*

6 (*Tip*) boards *pl*; **media ~** half-binding; **libro en ~** hardback ► **pasta española** marbled leather binding

7 (= *talante*) **tiene ~ de futbolista** he has the makings of a footballer; **ser de buena ~** to be a good sort

pastaje SM (*Andes, CAm, Cono Sur*), **pastal** SM (*LAm*) (= *pastizal*) pasture, grazing land; (= *pasto*) grass, pasture

pastar ▸conjug 1a◂ VT, VI to graze

pastear ▸conjug 1a◂ VT to graze

pastejón SM solid mass, lump

pastel Ⓐ SM 1 (*Culin*) (= *dulce*) cake; [*de carne*] pie; **"pasteles"** "pastry" *sing*, "confectionery" *sing*; ✦***MODISMO*** **repartirse el ~** to divide up the cake *o* (*EEUU*) pie ► **pastel de boda** wedding cake ► **pastel de cumpleaños** birthday cake

2 (*Arte*) pastel; **pintura al ~** pastel drawing

3 (*) (= *chanchullo*) scam*; **se descubrió el ~** the scam came to light*

4 (†) (= *chapuza*) botch, mess

Ⓑ ADJ pastel; **tono ~** pastel shade

pastelado SM (*Caribe*) choc-ice, ice-cream bar (*EEUU*)

pastelear ▸conjug 1a◂ VI 1 (= *trampear*) to go in for sharp practice; (= *maquinar*) to plot; (= *chanchullear*) to make cynical compromises

2 (= *temporizar*) to stall, spin it out to gain time

3 (*) (= *adular*) to creep*, be a bootlicker*

pastelería SF 1 (= *arte*) pastry-making, (art of) confectionery

2 (= *pasteles*) cakes *pl*, pastries *pl*

3 (= *tienda*) baker's, cake shop

pastelero/a Ⓐ ADJ 1 (*Culin*) **masa pastelera** pastry; **rodillo ~** rolling-pin

2 ✦***MODISMO*** **no tengo ni pastelera idea*** (*euf*) I haven't a clue*

3 (*Cono Sur*) (= *intrigante*) meddlesome, intriguing

Ⓑ SM/F 1 (*Culin*) pastry cook

2 (*Com*) baker

3 (*LAm Pol*) turncoat

4 (*Andes*⁑) (= *traficante*) drug trafficker

pastelillo SM (*Culin*) tart ► **pastelillo de hígado de ganso** (*Esp*) pâté de foie gras ► **pastelillo de mantequilla** (*Esp*) pat of butter

pastelón SM (*Cono Sur*) large paving stone

pasterizar ▸conjug 1f◂ VT = **pasteurizar**

pasteurización SF pasteurization

pasteurizado ADJ pasteurized

pasteurizar ▸conjug 1f◂ VT to pasteurize

pastiche SM pastiche

pastilla Ⓐ SF 1 (*Med*) tablet, pill; (= *anticonceptivo*) Pill ► **pastilla para la tos** cough drop

2 (*de jabón*) bar; (*de chocolate*) piece, square; ✦***MODISMO*** **ir a toda ~** (*Esp**) to go full-belt* ► **pastilla de caldo** stock cube ► **pastilla de freno(s)** (*Aut*) brake pad *o* shoe ► **pastilla de fuego** firelighter

3 (*Inform*) chip ► **pastilla de silicio** silicon chip

Ⓑ ADJ INV (*Esp*⁑) (= *aburrido*) deadly boring

pastillero¹/a⁑ SM/F pill popper⁑

pastillero² SM pillbox

pastinaca SF parsnip

pastizal SM pasture

pastizara⁑ SF **una ~** a whole heap of money*

pasto SM 1 (*Agr*) (= *acción*) grazing; (= *sitio*) pasture; (= *hierba*) grass, pasture; (= *pienso*) feed, fodder; (*LAm*) (= *césped*) lawn; **derecho de ~** grazing rights; **un sitio abundante en ~s** a place with rich grazing; **echar el ganado al ~** to put the animals out to pasture ► **pasto seco** fodder

2 (*fig*) (= *alimento*) food, nourishment; [*del fuego*] fuel; **es ~ de la murmuración** it is a

subject for gossip; **fue ~ del fuego** *o* **de las llamas** the flames devoured it; **ser ~ de la actualidad** to be newsworthy; **sirvió de ~ a los mirones** the onlookers lapped it up* ► **pasto espiritual** spiritual nourishment

3 ✦*MODISMO* **a todo ~*** abundantly; **beber a todo ~** to drink for all one is worth, drink to excess; **cita refranes a todo ~** he quotes vast quantities of proverbs; **correr a todo ~** to run like hell*; **había fruta a todo ~** there was fruit in unlimited quantities

4 **vino de ~** ordinary wine

5 (*Méx*‡) (= *hierba*) grass‡, pot‡

pastón‡ SM **un ~** a whole heap of money*

pastor(a) Ⓐ SM/F 1 (*Agr*) [*de ovejas*] shepherd/shepherdess; [*de cabras*] goatherd; [*de vacas*] cowherd; **el Buen Pastor** the Good Shepherd

2 (*Rel*) minister, clergyman/clergywoman

Ⓑ SM (*Zool*) sheepdog; **viejo ~ inglés** old English sheepdog ► **pastor alemán** Alsatian, German shepherd ► **pastor escocés** rough collie

pastorada SF Nativity procession, moving tableau of the Nativity

pastoral Ⓐ ADJ pastoral

Ⓑ SF 1 (*Literat*) pastoral

2 (*Rel*) pastoral letter

pastorear ▸conjug 1a◂ VT 1 (*Agr*) to shepherd; [+ *rebaño*] to pasture, graze; (= *cuidar*) to look after

2 (*Rel*) to guide, shepherd

3 (*LAm**) (= *acechar*) to lie in wait for

4 (*CAm*) (= *mimar*) to spoil, pamper

pastorela SF (*Literat*) pastourelle

pastoreo SM grazing

pastoril ADJ (*Literat*) pastoral

pastoso ADJ 1 [*masa*] doughy; [*pasta*] pasty

2 [*lengua*] furry; [*voz, vino*] rich, mellow

3 (*Cono Sur*) (= *con hierba*) grassy

4 (*Andes**) (= *vago*) lazy

pastura SF 1 (= *campo*) pasture

2 (= *comida*) food, fodder, feed

pasturaje SM common pasture

pasudo ADJ (*Méx*) [*pelo*] kinky

pat SM (*pl* **pats** [pat]) putt

pat. ABR (= **patente**) pat.

pata Ⓐ SF 1 (*Zool*) 1·1 (= *pierna*) leg; **~ delantera** front leg; **~ trasera** back *o* hind leg; **pantalones de ~ de elefante** flared trousers, flares; **de ~ negra** (*Esp*) [*cerdo, jamón*] prime; **un fútbol de ~ negra** top-notch football*

1·2 (= *pie*) [*de mamífero*] (*tb Peletería*) paw; [*de ave*] foot

► **pata de cabra** (*Téc*) crowbar ► **pata de cangrejo** crab stick ► **pata de gallo** (*en tela*) houndstooth check; (†) (= *disparate*) silly remark, piece of nonsense; **una chaqueta de ~ de gallo** a houndstooth jacket ► **pata hendida** cloven hoof ► **patas de gallo** (*en el ojo*) crow's feet

2 (*) [*de persona*] leg; **quita la ~, que no veo** get your leg out of the way, I can't see*; **es un diccionario con dos ~s** (*hum*) he's a walking dictionary, he's a dictionary on legs (*hum*); **a ~*** on foot, on Shanks' pony*, on Shanks' mare (*EEUU**); **a la ~ coja** hopping; **entró saltando a la ~ coja** he came hopping in; **a cuatro ~s** on all fours ► **pata de palo** wooden leg, peg leg

3 [*de mueble*] leg; **~s arriba** (= *invertido*) upside down; (= *revuelto*) in a complete mess, topsy-turvy*; **después de la mudanza estaba toda la casa ~s arriba** after the move the whole house was in a complete mess *o* was topsy-turvy*

4 (*Chile*) (= *etapa*) stage, leg

5 **patas** (*Chile**) (= *caradura*) cheek* *sing*; **tener ~s** to be brash, be cheeky*

6 ✦*MODISMOS* **a la ~** (*Chile**) to the letter; **enseñar la ~** to give oneself away; **estirar la ~*** to kick the bucket*; **hacer la ~ a algn** (*Chile**) to soft-soap sb*, suck up to sb*; **hacer algo con las ~s** (*Col, Méx**) to make a pig's ear of sth*; **a la ~ la llana** (*Esp**) **estaba escrito a la ~ la llana** it was written in plain language; **aunque se ha hecho famosa, se sigue comportando a la ~ la llana** although she has become famous, she is as down to earth as ever; **mala ~** bad luck; **trae mala ~ casarse en martes** it's bad luck to get married on a Tuesday; **¡qué mala ~ tuviste!** you were really unlucky!; **meter ~** (*Cono Sur Aut*) to step on the gas*; **meter la ~** to put one's foot in it; **a ~ pelada** (*Chile, Perú**) in bare feet*; **sacar la ~** to give oneself away; **saltar en una ~** (*Cono Sur*) to jump with joy; **ser ~** (*Arg*) to be game*, be up for it*; **es ~ para todo** he's game for anything*, he's up for anything*; **ser ~ de perro** (*Chile, Méx**) to have itchy feet; *ver tb* **metedura, pato**

Ⓑ SM (*Andes**) 1 (= *amigo*) pal*, mate*, buddy (*EEUU*)

2 (= *tipo*) bloke‡

pataca SF Jerusalem artichoke

patache SM 1 (= *barca*) flat-bottomed boat

2 (*Andes*) (= *sopa*) soup; (‡) (= *comida*) food, grub‡, chow (*EEUU*‡)

patacho SM 1 (*Cono Sur*) (= *lancha*) flat-bottomed boat

2 (*CAm, Méx*) (= *recua*) train of mules

patacón SM 1 (*Andes Culin*) slice of fried banana

2 (*Cono Sur*) (= *moretón*) bruise, welt

patada SF 1 (= *puntapié*) kick; **una ~ en la espinilla** a kick in the shin; **abrieron la puerta de una ~** they kicked the door open; **a ~s: echar a algn a ~s** to kick *o* boot sb out; **tratar a algn a ~s** to treat sb very badly *o* like dirt*; **dar ~s** to kick; **ya noto como da pataditas** I can feel it kicking now; **dar** *o* **meter** *o* **pegar una ~ a algn/algo** to kick sb/sth, give sb/sth a kick; **le dio una fuerte ~ al balón** he kicked the ball hard, he gave the ball a hard kick; **¡como te meta una ~ en el culo, verás!*** if you don't watch it, I'll give you a kick up the arse!*; **cada vez que habla le mete una ~ al diccionario** (*hum*) every time he opens his mouth his words come out all wrong; **dar ~s en el suelo** to stamp (the floor)

2 ✦*MODISMOS* **a ~s*** (= *en gran cantidad*) **ejemplos de eso los hay a ~s** there are loads of examples of that*; **había comida a ~s** there was loads *o* heaps of food*; **a las ~s** (*LAm**) really badly; **hace todo a las ~s** he makes a real mess of everything, he does everything really badly; **dar la ~ a*** [+ *empleado*] to kick out*, give the boot to*; [+ *novio, marido*] to ditch*, dump*; **darse ~s por algo: la gente se daba ~s por conseguir una entrada** people would do anything to get a ticket; **dar cien ~s a algn*** to bug sb*; **me da cien ~s no poder hablar con libertad** it bugs me that I can't speak freely*; **de la ~** (*CAm, Méx**) **me fue de la ~** it was a disaster, it all went pear-shaped on me*; **me cae de la ~** I can't stand the sight of him*; **en dos ~s*** (= *sin esfuerzo*) with no trouble at all; (= *en seguida*) in a jiffy*; **caer** *o* **sentar como una ~ en el estómago*** [*bebida, comida*] to upset one's stomach; [*acción*] to be like a kick in the teeth; **me cayó** *o* **sentó como una ~ en los cojones**‡‡ it really pissed me off‡‡

patadón* SM (= *puntapié*) big kick; (*Dep*) long kick, long ball, long clearance

patagón/ona Ⓐ ADJ Patagonian

Ⓑ SM/F native/inhabitant of Patagonia; **los patagones** the people of Patagonia

Patagonia SF Patagonia; **voy a la ~** I'm going to Patagonia

patagónico ADJ Patagonian

patalear ▸conjug 1a◂ VI 1 (*en el suelo*) to stamp (angrily)

2 [*bebé, niño*] to kick out

3 (= *protestar*) to protest; (= *montar follón*) to make a fuss; **por mí, que patalee** as far as I'm concerned he can make all the fuss he likes

pataleo SM 1 (*en el suelo*) stamping

2 (*en el aire*) kicking

3 (= *protesta*) protest; (= *follón*) scene, fuss; **derecho al ~** right to protest; **tener derecho al ~** to have the right to complain

pataleta* SF 1 (= *rabieta*) tantrum

2 (*Med*) (= *soponcio*) fit, convulsion

3 **dar ~s** (*LAm*) [*niño*] to stamp one's feet

patán SM rustic, yokel, hick (*EEUU**); (*pey*) lout

pataplaf EXCL, **pataplás** EXCL, **pataplún** EXCL (*LAm*) bang!, crash!

patarata† SF 1 (= *afectación*) gush, affectation; (= *aspaviento*) emotional fuss, excessive show of feeling

2 (= *disparate*) silly thing; (= *bagatela*) triviality; **~s** nonsense *sing*, tomfoolery *sing*

pataratero† ADJ 1 (= *afectado*) gushing, affected

2 (= *tonto*) silly

pataruco ADJ (*Caribe*) 1 (= *tosco*) coarse, rough

2 (= *cobarde*) cowardly

patasca SF (*Andes Culin*) *pork stew with corn*; ✦*MODISMO* **armar una ~*** to kick up a racket

patata SF (*Esp*) 1 (= *tubérculo*) potato; **puré de ~s** mashed potatoes *pl* ► **patata caliente** (*fig*) hot potato ► **patata de siembra** seed potato ► **patatas bravas** *fried potatoes with spicy tomato sauce* ► **patatas con su piel** jacket potatoes ► **patatas deshechas** mashed potatoes ► **patatas enteras** jacket potatoes ► **patatas fritas** (*en tiras*) chips, French fries (*EEUU*); (*de bolsa*) crisps, potato chips (*EEUU*) ► **patatas nuevas** new potatoes ► **patata temprana** early potato

2 ✦*MODISMOS* **ni ~*** nothing at all; **no entendió ni ~** he didn't understand a single word; **(no) me importa una ~** ◊ **no se me da una ~** I don't care two hoots; **pasar la ~ caliente*** to pass the buck*; **ser una ~*** to be rubbish*

3 (‡‡) (= *vulva*) fanny‡‡, beaver (*esp EEUU*‡‡)

patatal SM, **patatar** SM potato field, potato patch

patatera SF potato plant

patatero* ADJ **oficial ~** ranker; *ver tb* **rollo 5**

patatín*: ✦*MODISMOS* **en el año ~** in such-and-such a year; **que (si) ~, que (si) patatán** this, that and the other; **y ~ patatán** and so on

patato* ADJ (*Caribe*), **patatuco*** ADJ (*Caribe*) short

patatús* SM (= *ataque*) fit*; (= *desmayo*) dizzy spell; **le daría un ~ si lo supiera** he'd have a fit if he knew*

paté SM pâté

pateada SF 1 (*Cono Sur*) (= *paseo largo*) long tiring walk
2 = **pateadura**

pateador SM (*Dep*) kicker

pateadura SF, **pateamiento** SM 1 (*con los pies*) stamping, kicking
2 (*en discusión*) vehement denial; (*más agresiva*) violent interjection; (*Teat*) noisy protest, catcalls *pl*

patear[1] ▸conjug 1a◂ Ⓐ VT 1 (*en el suelo*) to stamp on; (= *dar patadas a*) to kick, boot; (*Dep*) [+ *pelota*] to kick
2 (*Esp**) (= *andar por*) to tramp round; **tuve que ~ toda la ciudad** I had to tramp round the whole town
3 (= *maltratar*) to treat roughly, treat inconsiderately; (*Teat*) (= *abuchear*) to boo, jeer
4 (*Caribe*) (= *insultar*) to abuse
5 **la comida me ha pateado** (*Cono Sur**) the meal has upset my stomach
Ⓑ VI 1 (= *patalear*) to stamp one's foot; (*Teat*) to stamp
2 (*LAm*) [*arma, animal*] to kick
3 (*) (= *ir a pata*) to walk (it); (*Cono Sur*) to go long distances on foot
4 (*) (= *ir y venir*) to be always on the go, bustle about
Ⓒ **patearse** VPR (*) 1 (= *recorrer a pie*) **nos hemos pateado Madrid** we explored *o* did Madrid on foot
2 (= *malgastar*) **~se el dinero** to blow one's money*

patear[2] ▸conjug 1a◂ VI to putt

patena SF paten

patentado ADJ patent(ed), proprietary (*frm*); **marca patentada** registered trade mark

patentar ▸conjug 1a◂ VT to patent

patente Ⓐ ADJ 1 [*mentira, muestra*] clear; **es prueba ~ de su ineficacia** it's clear proof of his inefficiency; **me decepcionó su ~ desinterés** I was disappointed by his patent *o* clear lack of interest; **su enojo era ~** his annoyance was plain to see, he was plainly *o* patently *o* clearly annoyed; **la culpabilidad era ~ en su rostro** he had guilt written all over his face; **hacer algo ~** to reveal sth, show sth clearly; **aquella reacción hizo ~ su rencor** that reaction clearly showed *o* revealed his resentment; **quedar ~** to become patently clear *o* obvious; **con ese comentario su ignorancia quedó ~** with that comment his ignorance became patently clear *o* obvious
2 (*Com*) patent
3 (*Cono Sur**) (= *excelente*) superb, great
Ⓑ SF 1 [*de invento, producto*] patent; **derechos de ~** patent rights; **de ~** (*Cono Sur*) first-rate ► **patente de invención** patent
2 (*Jur*) (= *permiso*) licence, license (*EEUU*), authorization ► **patente de corso** (*Hist*) letter(s) of marque; **se cree que tiene ~ de corso** he thinks he's got a licence to do whatever he pleases ► **patente de navegación** ship's registration certificate ► **patente de privilegio** letters patent ► **patente de sanidad** bill of health
3 (*Cono Sur Aut*) licence plate, license plate (*EEUU*); (= *carnet*) driving licence, driver's license (*EEUU*)
Ⓒ SM (*Caribe*) patent medicine

patentizar ▸conjug 1f◂ Ⓐ VT to show, make evident
Ⓑ **patentizarse** VPR to show plainly, become obvious

pateo SM stamping

páter* SM (*Mil*) padre*

patera SF (*Esp*) boat, small boat (*often used for illegal immigration*)

paterfamilias SM INV paterfamilias

paternal ADJ fatherly, paternal

paternalismo SM paternalism; (*pey*) patronizing attitude

paternalista Ⓐ ADJ paternalistic; (*pey*) patronizing
Ⓑ SMF paternalist; (*pey*) patronizing person

paternalmente ADV paternally, in a fatherly fashion

paternidad SF 1 (= *estado, situación*) fatherhood, parenthood
2 (*Jur*) paternity; **prueba de ~** paternity test ► **paternidad literaria** authorship

paterno ADJ paternal; **abuelo ~** paternal grandfather

patero* ADJ 1 (*Cono Sur*) (= *adulador*) fawning
2 (*Andes*) (= *embustero*) slippery, wily

patéticamente ADV pathetically, movingly, poignantly

patético ADJ 1 (= *digno de lástima*) pathetic, moving
2 (*Cono Sur*) (= *evidente*) clear, evident
3 (*Andes**) (= *andador*) **es muy ~** he loves walking

patetismo SM pathos, poignancy

patiabierto ADJ bow-legged

patibulario ADJ 1 (= *horroroso*) horrifying, harrowing
2 [*persona*] sinister

patíbulo SM scaffold, gallows

paticorto ADJ short-legged

patidifuso* ADJ (= *estupefacto*) astounded, taken aback; (= *perplejo*) nonplussed; **dejar a algn ~** (= *estupefacto*) to take sb aback; (= *perplejo*) to nonplus sb

patiestevado ADJ bandy-legged

patihendido ADJ cloven-hoofed

patilargo ADJ long-legged

patilla SF 1 [*de gafas*] sidepiece, temple (*EEUU*); [*de vestido*] pocket flap
2 [*de hombre*] sideburn; (= *rizo*) kiss curl; ✦*MODISMO* **tener ~s*** to have a brass neck*
3 (*Arg*) (= *banco*) bench
4 (*Caribe, Col*) (= *sandía*) watermelon
5 (*Inform*) pin
6 (*Cono Sur Bot*) layer

patimocho ADJ (*LAm*) lame

patín SM 1 (*gen*) skate; [*de trineo*] runner; (*Aer*) skid; **patines** (*Cono Sur*) soft overslippers ► **patín de cola** (*Aer*) tailskid ► **patín de cuchilla, patín de hielo** ice skate ► **patín de ruedas** roller skate ► **patines en línea** rollerblades
2 (= *patinete*) scooter
3 (*Náut*) ► **patín de pedal, patín playero** pedalo, pedal-boat
4 (*Aut**) old banger‡

pátina SF patina

patinadero SM skating rink

patinado ADJ shiny, glossy

patinador(a) SM/F skater

patinadura SF (*Caribe*) skid, skidding

patinaje SM 1 (*Dep*) skating ► **patinaje artístico, patinaje de figuras** figure skating ► **patinaje sobre hielo** ice-skating ► **patinaje sobre ruedas** roller-skating
2 (*Aut*) skidding

patinar ▸conjug 1a◂ VI 1 (*con patines*) (*sobre ruedas*) to roller-skate; (*sobre hielo*) to skate, ice-skate
2 (= *resbalar*) [*coche*] to skid; [*persona*] to slide; **el suelo estaba húmedo y patiné** the ground was wet and I slid
3 (*) (= *equivocarse*) to make a blunder, boob*
4 (*Arg**) to fail

patinazo SM 1 (*Aut*) skid
2 (*) (= *error*) boob*, blunder; **dar** *o* **pegar un ~** to blunder, make a boob*

patinete SM, **patineta** SF scooter

patio SM 1 [*de casa*] courtyard; [*de escuela*] playground; ✦*MODISMOS* **¡cómo está el ~!***: **¡cómo está el ~! hoy todos están de mal humor** what an atmosphere! everybody is in a bad mood today!; **¡cómo está el ~! varios diputados se han liado a puñetazos** several MPs got involved in a punch-up — what's the world coming to?; **llevar el ~** to rule the roost ► **patio de armas** parade ground ► **patio de luces** well (*of a building*) ► **patio de operaciones** floor (*of the stock exchange*) ► **patio de recreo** playground
2 (*Teat*) pit ► **patio de butacas** stalls *pl*, orchestra (*EEUU*)
3 (*Méx Ferro*) shunting yard

patiquín SM (*Caribe*) fop, dandy

patita SF *ver* **calle 2.1**

patitieso* ADJ 1 (= *paralizado*) **me quedé patitiesa** (*de frío*) I was frozen stiff; (*de miedo*) I was scared stiff
2 (*fig*) = **patidifuso**
3 (= *presumido*) stuck-up*, conceited

patito SM duckling; ✦*MODISMO* **los dos ~s*** all the twos*, twenty-two ► **patito feo** ugly duckling

patituerto ADJ bandy-legged

patizambo ADJ knock-kneed

pato SM 1 (*Orn*) duck ✦*MODISMOS* **pagar el ~*** to carry the can*; **ser el ~ de la boda** *o* **fiesta** (*LAm*) to be a laughing stock; **salga ~ o gallareta** (*LAm*) whatever the results ► **pato a la naranja** duck à l'orange ► **pato colorado** red-crested pochard ► **pato de reclamo** decoy duck ► **pato (macho)** drake ► **pato malvasía** white-headed duck ► **pato real, pato silvestre** mallard, wild duck
2 (*) (= *persona aburrida*) bore; **estar hecho un ~** to be terribly dull
3 (= *torpe*) **ser un ~** to be clumsy
4 (*) (= *aburrimiento*) boredom; (= *período aburrido*) boring time; (= *fiesta*) bore, drag
5 (*Andes**) (= *gorrón*) sponger*; **viajar de ~** to stow away
6 (*Andes**) (= *inocentón*) sucker‡
7 (*Méx*) ✦*MODISMO* **hacer el ~** *o* **hacerse ~**

to act the fool
[8] (*Cono Sur**) **ser un ~ o estar ~** to be broke*; ✦*MODISMO* **pasarse de ~ a ganso** to go too far
[9] (*LAm*) (= *bacineta*) bedpan

patochada SF blunder, bloomer*

patógeno SM pathogen

patojo/a* Ⓐ ADJ (*LAm*) lame
Ⓑ SM/F (*Andes, CAm*) (= *niño*) child; (= *novio*) sweetheart, boyfriend/girlfriend; (*pey*) urchin, ragamuffin

patología SF pathology

patológico ADJ pathological

patólogo/a SM/F pathologist

patomachera* SF (*Caribe*) slanging match*

patoso/a* Ⓐ ADJ [1] (= *torpe*) clumsy
[2] (= *molesto*) troublesome; **ponerse ~** to make trouble
Ⓑ SM/F [1] (= *torpe*) clumsy oaf
[2] (= *sabihondo*) clever Dick*, smart Aleck*
[3] (= *agitador*) troublemaker

patota* SF [1] (*Cono Sur*) (= *pandilla*) street gang, mob of young thugs; (= *grupo*) large group
[2] (*Caribe, Cono Sur*) (= *amigos*) mob, crowd (of friends)

patotear* ▸conjug 1a◂ VT (*Cono Sur*) to beat up*

patotero* SM (*Cono Sur*) rowdy, young thug

patraña SF [1] (= *embuste*) tall story
[2] (= *narración confusa*) rigmarole, long involved story

patraquear ▸conjug 1a◂ VT (*Cono Sur*) [+ *objeto*] to steal; [+ *persona*] to hold up, mug*

patraquero/a SM/F (*Cono Sur*) (= *ladrón*) thief; (= *atracador*) holdup man/woman, mugger*

patria SF native land, fatherland; **madre ~** mother country; **luchar por la ~** to fight for one's country; ✦*MODISMO* **hacer ~** to fly the flag* ► **patria adoptiva** adopted country ► **patria chica** home town, home area

patriada SF (*Cono Sur Hist*) rising, revolt

patriarca SM patriarch

patriarcado SM patriarchy

patriarcal ADJ patriarchal

Patricia SF Patricia

Patricio SM Patrick

patricio/a ADJ, SM/F patrician

patrilineal ADJ patrilineal

patrimonial ADJ hereditary

patrimonio SM [1] (= *bienes*) (*adquiridos*) assets *pl*, wealth; (*heredados*) inheritance, patrimony (*frm*); (*dejados en herencia*) estate; **su ~ personal es de 300 millones** his personal assets are 300 million, his personal wealth is some 300 million; **el ~ heredado por mis padres** my parents' inheritance *o* (*frm*) patrimony; **dejó un ~ valorado en miles de millones** his estate was valued at thousands of millions; **gestión de ~s** asset management
[2] [*artístico, cultural*] heritage ► **patrimonio de la humanidad** world heritage ► **patrimonio nacional** national heritage
[3] (*Com*) net worth, capital resources *pl*

patrio ADJ [1] (*Pol*) native, home *antes de s*; **el suelo ~** one's native land, one's native soil; **amor ~** love of one's country, patriotism
[2] (*Jur*) [*poder*] paternal

patriota Ⓐ ADJ patriotic
Ⓑ SMF patriot
Ⓒ SM (*CAm*) banana

patriotería SF, **patrioterismo** SM (= *chauvinismo*) chauvinism; (= *jingoísmo*) jingoism

patriotero/a Ⓐ ADJ (= *chauvinista*) chauvinistic; (= *jingoísta*) jingoistic
Ⓑ SM/F (= *chauvinista*) chauvinist; (= *jingoísta*) jingoist

patrióticamente ADV patriotically

patriótico ADJ patriotic

patriotismo SM patriotism

patrocinado/a SM/F (*Jur*) client

patrocinador(a) Ⓐ ADJ sponsoring; **empresa ~a** sponsor, sponsoring company
Ⓑ SM/F (*Com*) sponsor; [*de artes, causas benéficas*] patron/patroness; (= *promotor*) promoter

patrocinar ▸conjug 1a◂ VT (*Com*) to sponsor; [+ *artes, causas benéficas*] to act as patron to; (= *respaldar*) to back, support; **un movimiento patrocinado por …** a movement under the auspices of *o* under the patronage of …

patrocinazgo SM (*Com*) sponsorship; [*de artes, causas benéficas*] patronage

patrocinio SM (*Com*) sponsorship; [*de artes, causas benéficas*] patronage; (= *respaldo*) backing, support ► **patrocinio empresarial** commercial sponsorship

patrón/ona Ⓐ SM/F [1] (= *jefe*) boss*; (= *dueño*) employer, owner; (*Hist*) [*de esclavo*] master/mistress
[2] [*de pensión*] landlord/landlady
[3] (*Náut*) (*gen*) skipper; [*de barco mercante*] master/mistress
[4] (*Rel*) (*tb* **santo ~**) (= *santo*) patron saint; (= *virgen*) patron
[5] (= *protector*) patron/patroness
Ⓑ SM [1] (*Cos*) pattern; (*Téc*) standard, norm ► **patrón de distribución** distribution pattern ► **patrón oro** gold standard ► **patrón picado** stencilled pattern
[2] (*Bot*) stock (*for grafting*)
[3] (= *puntal*) prop, shore
Ⓒ ADJ INV (*gen*) standard, regular; (= *muestra*) sample *antes de s*

patronaje SM pattern designing

patronal Ⓐ ADJ [1] (*Com*) employers' *antes de s*; **sindicato ~** employers' association; **cierre ~** (management) lockout; **organización ~** employers' organization; **la clase ~** management, the managerial class; **cerrado por acto ~** closed by the owners *o* management
[2] (*Rel*) **fiesta ~** local holiday (*on the feast day of the local patron saint*)
Ⓑ SF employers' organization; (= *dirección*) management

patronato SM [1] [*de artes, causas benéficas*] patronage; (*Com*) sponsorship; **bajo el ~ de** under the patronage of, under the auspices of
[2] (*Com, Fin*) employers' association; (*Pol*) owners *pl*; **el ~ francés** French industrialists
[3] (= *junta*) board of management, board of trustees; **el ~ de turismo** the tourist board
[4] (= *fundación*) trust, foundation

patronear ▸conjug 1a◂ VT [+ *barco*] to skipper

patronímico ADJ, SM patronymic

patronista SMF pattern designer

patronizar ▸conjug 1f◂ VT to patronize

patrono/a SM/F [1] (*Com, Fin*) owner, employer
[2] (= *mecenas*) patron; (= *patrocinador*) sponsor; (= *protector*) protector, supporter
[3] (*Rel*) patron saint

patrulla SF patrol; **coche ~** patrol car ► **patrulla ciudadana** vigilante group

patrullaje SM patrolling; **bajo un fuerte ~ policial** under heavy police patrol

patrullar ▸conjug 1a◂ Ⓐ VT to patrol, police
Ⓑ VI to patrol

patrullera SF patrol boat

patrullero Ⓐ ADJ patrol *antes de s*
Ⓑ SM [1] (*Aut*) patrol car
[2] (*Náut*) patrol boat
[3] (*Méx*) (= *policía*) patrolman, policeman

patucho ADJ (*Andes*) short, squat

patucos SMPL [*de bebé*] bootees; (*) shoes

patudo Ⓐ ADJ (*Cono Sur*) rough, brash
Ⓑ SM (*Andes*) **el ~** the devil

patueco/a ADJ, SM/F (*CAm*) = **patojo**

patulea SF mob, rabble

patuleco/a ADJ, SM/F (*LAm*), **patulejo/a** ADJ, SM/F (*Cono Sur*), **patuleque** ADJ, SMF (*Caribe*) = **patojo**

patulenco* ADJ (*CAm*) clumsy, awkward

patullar ▸conjug 1a◂ VI [1] (= *pisar*) to trample about, stamp around
[2] (= *trajinar*) to bustle about
[3] (= *charlar*) to chat; (= *hacer ruido*) to talk noisily, make a lot of noise

paturro ADJ (*Andes, Cono Sur*) (= *rechoncho*) chubby, plump; (= *chaparro*) squat

paúl SM marsh

paular SM marshy ground

paulatinamente ADV gradually, slowly

paulatino ADJ gradual, slow

paulina* SF [1] (= *reprimenda*) telling-off*
[2] (= *carta*) poison-pen letter

Paulo SM Paul

pauperismo SM (*frm*) pauperism

pauperización SF (*frm*) impoverishment

paupérrimo ADJ very poor, poverty-stricken

pausa SF [1] (= *en programa, reunión*) break; (*al hablar, leer*) pause; (*Mús*) rest; **con ~** slowly, deliberately ► **pausa publicitaria** commercial break
[2] (*Téc*) (*en casette*) pause (button); (*en vídeo*) hold

pausadamente ADV slowly, deliberately

pausado ADJ slow, deliberate

pausar ▸conjug 1a◂ Ⓐ VT (= *retardar*) to slow down; (= *interrumpir*) to interrupt
Ⓑ VI to go slow

pauta SF [1] (= *modelo*) model; (= *guía*) guideline; (= *regla*) rule, guide; **marcar la ~** to set the standard; **París marca la ~ de la moda en todo el mundo** Paris sets the trend *o* the standard for fashion all over the world; **servir de ~ a** to act as a model for
[2] (*en papel*) lines *pl*

pautado Ⓐ ADJ **papel ~** ruled paper
Ⓑ SM (*Mús*) stave

pautar ▸conjug 1a◂ VT [1] (*Tip*) [+ *papel*] to rule
[2] (*esp CAm*) (= *marcar*) to mark, characterize; (= *reglar*) to establish a norm for, lay down a pattern for

pava SF [1] (*Orn*) turkey (hen); ✦*MODISMOS* **es una ~** (*Esp**) she's a complete bore; **echar la ~** (*Esp**) to puke up*, throw up; **pelar la ~** (*Esp**) to whisper sweet nothings ► **pava real**

peahen
2 (*Cono Sur*) (*para hervir*) kettle; (*para mate*) pot for making maté
3 (*Col, Ven*) (= *sombrero*) broad-brimmed straw hat
4 (*Andes, CAm*) (= *fleco*) fringe, bangs *pl* (*EEUU*)
5 (*Cono Sur, Méx*) (= *orinal*) chamber pot
6 (*Andes, Cono Sur*) (= *guasa*) coarse banter; (= *chiste*) tasteless joke; ✦*MODISMO* **hacer la ~ a algn*** to make sb look stupid
7 (*Andes, CAm**) (= *colilla*) cigarette-end, fag-end‡
8 (‡) (= *chica*) bird‡

pavada SF 1 (*esp Arg**) (= *tontería*) silly thing; **no digas ~s** don't talk rubbish
2 (*Orn*) flock of turkeys
3 (*Cono Sur*) (= *bagatela*) trivial thing; **cuesta una ~** it costs next to nothing
4 (*Caribe*) (= *mala suerte*) bit of bad luck

pavear ▸conjug 1a◂ Ⓐ VT 1 (*Andes*) (= *asesinar*) to kill treacherously
2 (*Andes, Cono Sur*) (= *burlarse de*) to play a joke on
Ⓑ VI 1 (*Cono Sur, Perú**) (= *hacer el tonto*) to act the fool, mess about
2 (*Cono Sur**) [*enamorados*] to whisper sweet nothings
3 (*Andes**) (= *hacer novillos*) to play truant, play hooky (*EEUU**)

pavería SF (*Cono Sur*) silliness, stupidity

pavero/a SM/F (*Andes, Cono Sur*) practical joker

pavesa SF piece of ash

pavimentación SF paving

pavimentar ▸conjug 1a◂ VT [+ *exteriores*] to pave; [+ *interiores*] to floor

pavimento SM 1 (*de asfalto*) roadway, road surface
2 (*de losas*) (*gen*) paving; (*en interior*) flooring

pavipollo SM 1 (*Orn*) young turkey
2 (*) (= *bobo*) twit*, idiot

pavisoso* ADJ dull, graceless

pavitonto* ADJ silly

pavo Ⓐ SM 1 (*Orn*) turkey; ✦*MODISMOS* **comer ~*** to be a wallflower (*at a dance*); (*LAm*) to be disappointed; **estar en la edad del ~** to be at an awkward age; **ir de ~** (*LAm**) to travel free, get a free ride; **tener mucho ~** to blush a lot; **tener un ~ encima**: **esta niña tiene un ~ encima que no se aclara** it looks like she'll never grow out of being a giggling teenager; **subírsele el ~ a algn**: **se le subió el ~** he went bright red ► **pavo real** peacock
2 (*Esp**) (= *tonto*) silly thing, idiot
3 (‡) (= *moneda*) five peseta coin
4 (*) (= *primo*) sucker‡
5 (*Chile**) (= *polizón*) stowaway
6 (*Andes*) (= *cometa*) large kite
7 (*Andes**) (= *espadón*) big shot*; (= *sospechoso*) evil-looking person
8 (*Caribe**) (= *reprimenda*) telling-off*
9 (‡) (= *hombre*) bloke‡; (*Caribe*‡) (= *joven*) youngster, kid*
10 (‡) (= *síndrome de abstinencia*) cold turkey*
Ⓑ ADJ (*) silly; **¡no seas ~!** don't be silly!

pavón SM 1 (*Orn*) peacock
2 (*Téc*) bluing, bronzing

pavonearse ▸conjug 1a◂ VPR (= *presumir*) (*gen*) to show off (**de** about); (*al hablar*) to brag (**de** about); (*al andar*) to swagger, strut

pavoneo SM (*gen*) showing-off; (*al hablar*) bragging; (*al andar*) swagger, strutting

pavor SM dread, terror

pavorosamente ADV terrifyingly

pavoroso ADJ terrifying

pavoso ADJ (*Caribe*) (= *desafortunado*) unlucky; (= *que trae mala suerte*) that brings bad luck

pay SM (*LAm*) pie

paya SF (*Cono Sur*) = **payada**

payacate SM (*Méx*) [*de bolsillo*] handkerchief; (= *prenda*) scarf, kerchief

payada SF (*Cono Sur*) *improvised gaucho folksong* ► **payada de contrapunto** *contest between two "payadores"*

payador SM (*Cono Sur*) gaucho minstrel

payar ▸conjug 1a◂ VI 1 (*Cono Sur*) (= *cantar*) *to improvise songs to a guitar accompaniment*
2 (*) (= *contar cuentos*) to talk big*, shoot a line*

payasada SF clownish trick, stunt; (*pey*) ridiculous thing (to do); **payasadas** clowning *sing*; (*Teat*) slapstick *sing*, knockabout humour *sing*, knockabout humor *sing* (*EEUU*)

payasear ▸conjug 1a◂ VI (*LAm*) to clown around

payaso/a SM/F clown (*tb fig*)

payés/esa SM/F (*Cataluña, Islas Baleares*) peasant farmer

payo/a Ⓐ ADJ 1 (*Arg*) (= *albino*) albino
2 (*Méx*) (= *simple*) rustic, simple
3 (*Méx*) [*ropa*] loud, flashy
Ⓑ SM/F (*para gitanos*) non-gipsy, non-gypsy (*EEUU*)

payuelas SFPL chickenpox *sing*

paz SF 1 (*gen*) peace; (= *tranquilidad*) peace and quiet, tranquillity, tranquility (*EEUU*); **¡a la ~ de Dios!** God be with you!; **en ~ y en guerra** in peace and war, in peacetime and wartime; **dejar a algn en ~** to leave sb alone, leave sb in peace; **¡déjame en ~!** leave me alone!; **descansar en ~** to rest in peace; **su madre, que en ~ descanse** her mother, God rest her soul; **estar en ~** (*gen*) to be at peace; (*fig*) to be even, be quits (**con** with); (*Méx*‡) to be high‡; **¡haya ~!** stop it!, that's enough!; **mantener la ~** to keep the peace; **perturbar la ~** to disturb the peace; ✦*MODISMOS* **no dar ~ a la lengua** to keep on and on; **¡... y en ~!, ¡aquí ~ y después gloria!** and that's that!, and Bob's your uncle!*
2 (= *tratado*) peace, peace treaty; **la ~ de los Pirineos** the Peace of the Pyrenees (*1659*); **firmar ~** to sign a peace treaty; **hacer las paces** (*gen*) to make peace; (*fig*) to make (it) up; **poner ~** to make peace
3 (*Rel*) kiss of peace, sign of peace

pazguato ADJ 1 (= *necio*) simple, stupid
2 (= *remilgado*) prudish

pazo SM (*Galicia*) country house

PC SM ABR 1 (= **personal computer**) PC
2 = **Partido Comunista**

p.c. ABR (= **por cien**) p.c.

PCB SM ABR (= **policlorobifenilo**) PCB

PCE SM ABR = **Partido Comunista Español**

PCN SM ABR (*El Salvador*) = **Partido de Conciliación Nacional**

PCUS SM ABR (*Pol, Hist*) = **Partido Comunista de la Unión Soviética**

PCV SM ABR (*Ven*) = **Partido Comunista Venezolano**

PD ABR, **P.D.** ABR (= **posdata**) PS

PDC SM ABR (*LAm*) = **Partido Demócrata Cristiano**

pdo. ABR (= **pasado**) ult.

Pdte. ABR (*Chile Prensa*) = **presidente**

pe SF *(name of the) letter P;* ✦*MODISMO* **de pe a pa*** from A to Z, from beginning to end

P.^e^ ABR (= **Padre**) F., Fr.

pea* SF **coger una ~** to get smashed*, get legless*

peaje SM toll; **autopista de ~** toll motorway, turnpike (*EEUU*)

peajista SMF collector of tolls

peal SM (*LAm*) lasso

pealar ▸conjug 1a◂ VT (*LAm*) to lasso

peana SF 1 (= *pedestal*) base, pedestal
2 (*Golf*) tee
3 (*) (= *pie*) foot

peatón SM pedestrian; **paso de peatones** pedestrian crossing, crosswalk (*EEUU*)

peatonal ADJ pedestrian *antes de s*; **calle ~** pedestrian precinct

peatonalización SF pedestrianization

peatonalizar ▸conjug 1f◂ VT to pedestrianize

pebete/a Ⓐ SM/F (*Arg, Uru**) (= *niño*) kid*; (= *persona baja*) short person
Ⓑ SM 1 (= *incienso*) joss stick
2 [*de cohete*] fuse
3 (= *olor*) stink
4 (*Cono Sur*) (= *panecillo*) roll

pebre SM (*esp Chile Culin*) *mild sauce made from vinegar, garlic, parsley and pepper*

peca SF freckle

pecado SM 1 (*Rel*) sin; **por mis ~s** for my sins; **un ~ de juventud** a youthful indiscretion, a sin of youth; **estar en ~** to be in a state of sin; ✦*MODISMO* **en el ~ llevas la penitencia** you've made your bed now lie in it ► **pecado capital** deadly sin ► **pecado de comisión** sin of commission ► **pecado nefando** sodomy ► **pecado original** original sin ► **pecado venial** venial sin
2 (= *cosa lamentable*) crime, sin; **sería un ~ no aprovecharlo** it would be a crime *o* sin not to make use of it; **¡es un ~ darle el filete al gato!** it's a crime to give steak to the cat!

pecador(a) Ⓐ ADJ sinful
Ⓑ SM/F sinner

pecaminosidad SF sinfulness

pecaminoso ADJ sinful

pecar ▸conjug 1g◂ VI 1 (*Rel*) to sin; (*fig*) to err; **si he pecado en esto, ha sido por ...** if I have been at fault in this, it has been because ...; **si me lo pones delante, acabaré pecando** if you put temptation in front of me, I shall fall
2 **~ de** + ADJ to be too + *adj*; **peca de generoso** he is too generous, he is generous to a fault; **peca por exceso de confianza** he is too confident

pécari SM (*LAm*), **pecarí** SM (*LAm*) peccary

peccata minuta SF **ser ~** to be no big deal, be unimportant

pecé* Ⓐ SM (*Esp*) (= *partido*) Communist Party
Ⓑ SMF (= *persona*) Communist

pecera SF (*redonda*) fishbowl; (*rectangular*) fish tank

pecero/a* SM/F (*Pol*) member of the Communist Party

pecha SF (*Cono Sur*) push, shove

pechada* SF [1] (= *hartazgo*) **llevamos una ~ de andar** that's more than enough walking (for one day), it's been a real slog*; **se dieron una ~ de trabajar** they really slogged their guts out*
[2] (*LAm*) (= *empujón*) push, shove
[3] (*LAm**) (= *sablazo*) scrounging*

pechador* ADJ (*Cono Sur*) demanding

pechar¹* ▸conjug 1a◂ (A) VT [1] (*LAm*) (= *empujar*) to push, shove
[2] (*Cono Sur*) (= *pedir dinero a*) to tap*, touch for
[3] (*Cono Sur*) (= *atrapar*) to collar*, grab
(B) VI **~ con** (*gen*) to put up with; [+ *cometido*] to shoulder, take on; [+ *problema*] to face up to

pechar² ▸conjug 1a◂ VT, VI to pay (as a tax)

pechazo* SM (*LAm*) [1] (= *empujón*) push, shove
[2] [*de dinero*] touch (for a loan)*

pechblenda SF pitchblende

peche⁑ (*CAm*) (A) ADJ skinny
(B) SM child

pechera SF [1] (*Cos*) [*de camisa*] shirt front; [*de vestido*] front; (*Mil*) chest protector
► **pechera postiza** dicky
[2] (*Anat** *hum*) big bosom

pechero¹/a SM/F (*Hist*) commoner, plebeian

pechero² SM (= *babero*) bib; [*de vestido*] front

pechicato ADJ (*Caribe*) = **pichicato**

pechina SF scallop

pecho¹ SM [1] (= *tórax*) chest; **le dieron una puñalada en el ~** he was stabbed in the chest; **tenía una herida en el ~** he had a chest injury; **estar de ~ sobre algo** to be leaning on sth; **estaba de ~ sobre la barandilla** he was leaning on the railing; **sacar ~** to stick one's chest out; **ponte firme y saca ~** stand up straight and stick your chest out; **el presidente ha sacado ~ ante las críticas** the president put on a brave face under the criticism; ✦***MODISMOS*** **abrir el ~ a algn** to confide in sb, open one's heart to sb; **no caberle a algn la alegría en el ~: no me/le cabía la alegría en el ~** I/he was bursting with happiness; **dar el ~** to face things squarely; **a ~ descubierto** (= *sin armas*) unarmed, defenceless, defenseless (*EEUU*); (= *francamente*) openly, frankly; **echarse entre ~ y espalda** [+ *comida*] to put away*; [+ *bebida*] to knock back*; **gritar a todo ~** (*Andes, Caribe*) to shout at the top of one's voice; **partirse el ~*** to bust a gut*; **quedarse con algo en el ~** to keep sth back; **tomarse algo a ~** to take sth to heart
[2] [*de mujer*] [2·1] (= *busto*) bust; **un sujetador que realza el ~** a bra which makes your bust look bigger; **de ~ plano** flat-chested; **tener mucho ~** to have a big bust; **tener poco ~** to be flat-chested
[2·2] (= *mama*) breast; **le han extirpado un ~** she had a breast removed; **dar el ~** to breast-feed; **un niño de ~** a baby at the breast
[3] (= *valor*) ✦***MODISMOS*** **¡~ al agua!** courage!; **a lo hecho, ~** we must make the best of it now
[4] (*Geog*) slope, gradient

pecho² SM (*Hist*) tax, tribute

pechoño ADJ (*Andes, Cono Sur*) sanctimonious

pechuga SF [1] (*Culin*) breast; (*) [*de mujer*] tits⁑ *pl*, bosom; (= *escote*) cleavage
► **pechuga de pollo** chicken breast
[2] (*Geog*) slope, hill
[3] (*LAm** *pey*) (= *descaro*) nerve, cheek*
[4] (*Andes, CAm**) (= *abuso de confianza*) abuse of trust
[5] (*CAm*) (= *molestia*) trouble, annoyance

pechugón/ona* (A) ADJ [1] (= *de mucho pecho*) busty*, big-bosomed
[2] (*LAm*) (= *descarado*) shameless; (= *franco*) outspoken; (= *chupón*) sponging; (= *egoísta*) selfish
[3] (*Cono Sur*) (= *resuelto*) single-minded
[4] (*) (= *atractivo*) dishy*
(B) SM/F (*LAm*) [1] (= *descarado*) shameless individual
[2] (= *gorrón*) sponger*

pechuguera SF (*Andes, Méx*) (= *ronquera*) hoarseness; (= *resfriado*) chest cold

pecio SM wrecked ship, shipwreck; **pecios** flotsam *sing*, wreckage *sing*

pecíolo SM, **peciolo** SM (leaf) stalk, petiole (*Téc*)

pécora SF (*tb* **mala ~**) (= *arpía*) bitch; (= *prostituta*) loose woman, whore

pecoso ADJ freckled

pecotra SF (*Cono Sur Anat*) bump, swelling; (*en madera*) knot

pectina SF pectin

pectoral (A) ADJ (*Anat*) pectoral; **pastillas ~es** cough drops
(B) SM [1] (*Rel*) pectoral cross
[2] **pectorales** (*Anat*) pectorals

pecuaca SF (*Andes, Caribe*) = **pecueca**

pecuario ADJ livestock *antes de s*

pecueca SF (*Andes, Caribe*) (= *pezuña*) hoof; (*hum*) (= *olor*) smell of feet

peculado SM embezzlement

peculiar ADJ [1] (= *particular, característico*) particular; **su ~ manera de ver las cosas** his particular way of seeing things, his own individual way of seeing things; **un rasgo ~ de su carácter** a particular *o* characteristic trait of his; **tiene un carácter muy ~** he's got a very individual personality; **una característica ~ del paisaje andaluz** a characteristic peculiar to the landscape of Andalusia
[2] (= *raro*) peculiar, unusual; **su comportamiento es un tanto ~** his behaviour is a bit peculiar *o* unusual

peculiaridad SF peculiarity, special characteristic; **cada país tiene sus ~es** each country has its own peculiarities

peculio SM (= *dinero*) one's own money; (= *ahorros*) modest savings *pl*; **de su ~** out of one's own pocket

pecunia* SF (= *dinero*) brass*; (*Caribe*) (= *moneda*) coin

pecuniario ADJ pecuniary, money *antes de s*; **pena pecuniaria** fine

pedagogía SF pedagogy

pedagógico ADJ pedagogic(al)

pedagogo/a SM/F (= *profesor*) teacher, educator; (= *teórico*) educationalist

pedal SM [1] [*de bicicleta, automóvil*] pedal
► **pedal de acelerador** accelerator (pedal)
► **pedal de(l) embrague** clutch (pedal)
► **pedal de freno** brake (pedal) ► **pedal dulce** (*Mús*) soft pedal ► **pedal fuerte** (*Mús*) loud pedal ► **pedal piano, pedal suave** (*Mús*) soft pedal
[2] (⁑) (= *borrachera*) **coger un ~** to get canned⁑

pedalear ▸conjug 1a◂ VI to pedal; **~ en agua** to tread water

pédalo SM pedal boat, pedalo

pedáneo ADJ **alcalde ~** mayor of a small town; **juez ~** local magistrate

pedanía SF district

pedante (A) ADJ (*gen*) pedantic; (= *pomposo*) pompous, conceited
(B) SMF pedant

pedantería SF (*gen*) pedantry; (= *pomposidad*) pomposity, conceit

pedantescamente ADV pedantically

pedantesco ADJ pedantic

pedazo SM [1] (= *trozo*) piece; **un ~ de papel** a piece of paper; **un ~ de pan** a piece of bread; **trabaja por un ~ de pan** he works for a mere pittance; **hacer algo a ~s** to do sth in pieces, do sth piecemeal; **caerse a ~s** to fall to bits; **hacer ~s** [+ *papel*] to rip, tear (up); [+ *vidrio, cristal*] to shatter, smash; [+ *persona*] to tear to shreds; **estoy hecho ~s** I'm worn out; **hacerse ~s** [*objeto*] to fall to pieces; [*vidrio, cristal*] to shatter, smash; ✦***MODISMO*** **ser un ~ de pan** to be a really nice person, be an angel
[2] (*con insultos*) **es un ~ de alcornoque** *o* **animal** *o* **bruto*** he's a blockhead*, he's an idiot
[3] (*con expresiones de cariño*) **¡~ de mi alma** *o* **mi corazón** *o* **mis entrañas!** my darling!

pederasta SMF pederast, paedophile, pedophile (*EEUU*)

pederastia SF pederasty, paedophilia, pedophilia (*EEUU*)

pedernal SM flint; **como un ~** of flint, flinty

pederse* ▸conjug 2a◂ VPR to fart⁑

pedestal SM pedestal, stand

pedestre ADJ [1] (= *a pie*) pedestrian; **carrera ~** walking race
[2] [*metáfora, arte, razón*] pedestrian

pedestrismo SM walking

pediatra SMF paediatrician, pediatrician (*EEUU*)

pediatría SF paediatrics *sing*, pediatrics *sing* (*EEUU*)

pediátrico ADJ paediatric, pediatric (*EEUU*)

pedicura SF chiropody, podiatry (*EEUU*)

pedicuro/a SM/F chiropodist, podiatrist (*EEUU*)

pedida SF (*Esp*) (*tb* **~ de mano**) engagement; *ver tb* **anillo, pulsera**

pedidera SF (*Andes, CAm, Caribe*) = **petición**

▼ **pedido** SM [1] (*Com*) order; **su ~ será atendido inmediatamente** your order will be dealt with immediately; **cursar** *o* **hacer un ~** to place an order; **servir un ~** (*Esp*) to deliver an order ► **pedido al contado** cash order ► **pedido atrasado** outstanding order ► **pedido de ensayo** trial order ► **pedido de repetición** repeat order ► **pedido pendiente** outstanding order ► **pedido por teléfono** telephone order; *ver tb* **cartera 6, hoja 2**
[2] (= *petición*) request; **a ~ de algn** at the request of sb; **hacer algo bajo** *o* **sobre ~** to make sth to order

pedigrí SM, **pedigree** [pedi'gri] SM pedigree

pedigüeño ADJ cadging, mooching (*EEUU**)

pedilón (A) ADJ (*LAm*) = **pedigüeño**
(B) SM (*LAm*) pest, nuisance

➤ LENGUA Y USO: **pedido 1** 47.2, 47.3, 47.4

pedimento SM (*gen*) petition; (*Jur*) claim, bill; (*Méx Com*) licence, license (*EEUU*), permit

pedir ▸conjug 3k◂ Ⓐ VT [1] (= *rogar, solicitar*) to ask for; **¿habéis pedido ya la cuenta?** have you asked for the bill yet?; **lo único que pido es que no llueva mañana** all I ask is that it doesn't rain tomorrow; **necesito ~te consejo** I need to ask your advice; **a ti nadie te ha pedido tu opinión** nobody asked your opinion; **estuve pidiendo auxilio durante un buen rato** I was calling for help for some time; **una manifestación pidiendo la libertad de los secuestrados** a demonstration calling for the release of the hostages; **llamé para ~ que me pusieran una canción** I phoned to request a song; **~ cuentas a algn** to demand an explanation from sb; **~ algo a Dios** to pray to God for sth; **~ disculpas** to apologize; **~ algo por favor**: **me pidió por favor que fuera discreto** he asked me to please keep it to myself; **te lo pido por favor, quédate conmigo** please stay with me; **~ hora** to make an appointment; **~ limosna** to beg; **~ la palabra** to ask for permission to speak; **pido la palabra, señoría** permission to speak, my lord; **~ perdón** (= *disculparse*) to apologize; (*suplicando*) to beg (for) forgiveness; **~ permiso** to ask (for) permission; ✦*MODISMOS* **te lo pido por Dios** I'm begging you; **¿qué más se puede ~?** what more can you ask (for)?
[2] (*Com*) (= *encargar*) to order; **he pedido unos zapatos por correo** I've ordered some shoes by post; **tengo pedidos varios libros** I've got some books on order
[3] (*en un restaurante*) to order; (*en un bar*) to ask for, order; **de primero hemos pedido sopa** we've ordered soup as a starter; **hemos pedido dos cafés y un té** we've asked for *o* ordered two coffees and a tea
[4] (*para casarse*) to propose to; **fue a su casa a ~la** he went to her house to propose to her; **mis dos hermanas ya están pedidas** my two sisters are already spoken for; **~ la mano de algn** to ask for sb's hand; **~ a algn en matrimonio** to ask for sb's hand in marriage
[5] (*Jur*) [+ *condena*] to ask for; **el fiscal pidió siete años de cárcel** the prosecution asked for a seven-year sentence
[6] (= *requerir*) to need; **esta planta pide mucho sol** this plant needs lots of sunlight; **ese sofá pide una cortina azul** that sofa needs a blue curtain to go with it; **~ algo a gritos** *o* **voces** to be crying out for sth; **la casa está pidiendo a voces que la pinten** the house is crying out to be painted
[7] (*tb* **~ prestado**) to borrow; **tengo que ~te unos libros** I need to borrow some books off you; **me pidió prestado el coche** he asked if he could borrow the car, he asked to borrow the car
Ⓑ VI [1] (= *rogar*) **este niño está todo el día pidiendo** that child is always asking for things; **~ por algn** (*Rel*) to pray for sb; **pido a Dios por los difuntos** I pray to God for the dead; ✦*MODISMO* **por ~ que no quede** there's no harm in asking
[2] (= *pedir dinero*) [*mendigo*] to beg; [*voluntario*] to collect money; **iba pidiendo por los vagones** he went begging from carriage to carriage; **piden para una buena causa** they are collecting money for a good cause
[3] (*en un bar, restaurante*) to order; **¿habéis pedido ya?** have you ordered yet?; *ver tb* **boca A3**
Ⓒ **pedirse** VPR (*) (= *elegir*) to bag*; **se pidió el mejor asiento** he bagged the best seat*; **yo me pido el de fresa** I bags the strawberry one*, bags I get the strawberry one*

> **PEDIR**
>
> **¿"Ask" o "Ask for"?**
>
> • La expresión **pedir algo** se traduce por **ask for something**:
>
> Pidieron muchas cosas diferentes
> ***They asked for many different things***
>
> **NOTA:** Si el verbo **pedir** lleva dos complementos, el complemento de persona siempre va delante:
>
> Pídele un lápiz a la profesora
> ***Ask the teacher for a pencil***
>
> • La estructura **pedir a alguien que haga algo**, se traduce al inglés por **ask** + **OBJETO** + **CONSTRUCCIÓN DE INFINITIVO**:
>
> Le pedí a mi hermana que me trajera una alfombra de Turquía
> ***I asked my sister to bring me a rug from Turkey***
>
> Le pediremos que nos haga un descuento
> ***We'll ask him to give us a discount***
>
> **NOTA:** si el contexto es más formal **pedir** también se puede traducir por **request**:
>
> Ambas partes en conflicto están pidiendo ayuda al extranjero
> ***Both sides are requesting help from abroad***
>
> *Para otros usos y ejemplos ver la entrada.*

pedo Ⓐ ADJ (‡) **estar ~** (= *borracho*) to be pissed**, be sloshed‡; (= *drogado*) to be high‡; **ponerse ~** (= *borracho*) to get pissed**, get sloshed‡; (= *drogado*) to get high‡
Ⓑ SM [1] (*) fart‡; **tirarse un ~** to fart‡
[2] (‡) [*de alcohol, drogas*] **agarrar** *o* **coger un ~** (= *emborracharse*) to get pissed**, get sloshed‡; (= *drogarse*) to get high‡; **estar en ~** (*Cono Sur*) to be pissed**, be sloshed‡; **¡estás en ~!** (*al hablar*) you must be kidding!; ✦*MODISMO* **al ~** (*Cono Sur*): **no me gusta trabajar al ~** I don't like working for the sake of it
[3] ► **pedo de lobo** (*Bot*) puffball
[4] ► **pedo de monja** (*Culin*) very light pastry

pedofilia SF paedophilia, pedophilia (*EEUU*)

pedófilo/a SM/F, **pedofílico/a** SM/F paedophile, pedophile (*EEUU*)

pedología SF pedology, study of soils

pedorrera‡ SF string of farts‡

pedorrero* ADJ given to farting‡, windy

pedorreta* SF raspberry*

pedorro/a* Ⓐ ADJ (= *tonto*) daft; (= *pelmazo*) annoying
Ⓑ SM/F (= *tonto*) twit*; (= *pelmazo*) pain*

pedrada SF [1] (= *acción*) throw of a stone; (= *golpe*) hit *o* blow from a stone; **matar a algn a ~s** to stone sb to death; **pegar una ~ a algn** to throw a stone at sb
[2] (= *comentario molesto*) snide remark, dig*
[3] ✦*MODISMOS* **sentar como una ~**: **la cosa le sentó como una ~** he took it very ill, the affair went down very badly with him; **me sienta como una ~ tener que irme** I hate having to go; **venir como ~ en ojo de boticario** to be just what the doctor ordered

pedrea SF [1] (= *combate*) stone-throwing, fight with stones
[2] (*Meteo*) hailstorm
[3] [*de lotería*] minor prizes *pl*

pedregal SM [*de piedras*] rocky ground, stony place; (*Méx*) [*de lava*] lava field

pedregón SM (*LAm*) rock, boulder

pedregoso ADJ stony, rocky

pedregullo SM (*Cono Sur*) gravel

pedrejón SM big stone, rock, boulder

pedrera SF quarry

pedrería SF precious stones *pl*, jewels *pl*

pedrero SM [1] (= *persona*) quarryman, stone cutter
[2] (*Andes, CAm, Cono Sur*) = **pedregal**

pedrisco SM [1] (= *granizo*) hail; (= *granizada*) hailstorm
[2] (= *montón*) heap of stones; (= *lluvia de piedras*) shower of stones

Pedro SM Peter; ✦*MODISMO* **entrar como ~ por su casa** to come in as if one owned the place

pedrusco SM [1] (= *piedra*) rough stone; (= *trozo de piedra*) piece of stone, lump of stone
[2] (*LAm*) = **pedregal**

peduncular ADJ stalk *antes de s*, peduncular (*Téc*)

pedúnculo SM stem, stalk

peerse* ▸conjug 2a◂ VPR = **pederse**

pega Ⓐ SF [1] (= *dificultad*) snag, problem; **todo son ~s** there's nothing but problems; **poner ~s** (= *objetar a algo*) to raise objections; (= *crear problemas*) to cause trouble
[2] **de ~** (*) (= *falso*) false, dud*; (= *de imitación*) fake, sham, bogus; **un billete de ~** a dud banknote*
[3] (= *acción*) sticking
[4] (= *chasco*) practical joke; (= *truco*) hoax, trick
[5] (= *paliza*) beating, beating-up*
[6] (*Caribe, Cono Sur, Méx*) (= *trabajo*) work
[7] (*Caribe*) (= *liga*) birdlime
[8] (*Cono Sur*) [*de enfermedad*] infectious period
[9] ✦*MODISMOS* **estar en la ~** (*Cono Sur*) to be at one's best; **jugar a la ~** (*Andes*) to play tag
Ⓑ SM ✦*MODISMO* **ser el ~*** to be the one who always sees problems

pegachento ADJ sticky

pegada SF [1] (*) (= *atractivo*) appeal; **un cantante con mucha ~** a singer with great appeal
[2] ► **pegada de carteles** (*Pol*) **dio comienzo la campaña con la tradicional ~ de carteles** the campaign began with the traditional sticking up of posters
[3] (*Cono Sur*) (= *mentira*) fib, lie
[4] (*Cono Sur*) (= *acierto*) **¡qué ~!** what a piece *o* stroke of luck!; **fue una ~ y por casualidad** it was a complete fluke
[5] **tiene una excelente ~** (*Boxeo*) he packs an excellent punch; (*Ftbl**) he has a good shot on him*

pegadillo SM (*Andes*) lace

pegadizo/a Ⓐ ADJ [1] (*Esp*) [*canción, melodía*] catchy
[2] [*risa, enfermedad*] contagious
[3] (= *pegajoso*) sticky
[4] (= *postizo*) false

5 (*Esp*) (= *gorrón*) sponging*
Ⓑ SM/F (*Esp*) sponger*

pegado Ⓐ ADJ 1 (= *adherido*) (*gen*) stuck; (*con pegamento*) glued; **me desperté con los ojos ~s** I woke up with my eyes stuck together; **¿está bien pegada la foto?** is the photo stuck on properly?; **el póster estaba ~ a la pared con chinchetas** the poster was stuck *o* fixed to the wall with drawing pins; *ver tb* **falda 1**
2 (= *junto*) **~ a algo**: **el estadio está ~ al río** the stadium is right beside the river; **íbamos muy ~s al coche de delante** we were right behind the car in front; **pon el piano ~ a la pared** put the piano right up *o* flush against the wall; **la lámpara estaba muy pegada al techo** the lamp was almost touching the ceiling; **los corredores iban muy ~s unos a otros** the runners were bunched together; **se tira las horas pegada al ordenador** she spends hours glued to the computer; **se pasan el día ~s a los libros** they spend all day with their noses stuck in books*; **está todo el día ~ a su madre** he's a real mother's boy
3 (= *quemado*) [*arroz, leche*] burnt, burned (EEUU); **oler a ~** to smell burnt; ✦MODISMO **quedarse ~*** to get an electric shock, get fried (EEUU*)
4 (*Esp*) (= *asombrado*) stunned; **me has dejado ~ con esa noticia** what you've just said has really stunned me *o* taken me aback, I'm really stunned by what you've just said
5 (*Esp‡*) **estar ~** to not have a clue*; **no me sé nada del examen, estoy ~** I haven't got a clue about the exam*
Ⓑ SM (*Med*) (= *parche*) sticking plaster, Band-Aid® (EEUU)

pegadura SF (*Andes*) practical joke

pegajoso ADJ 1 (= *que se adhiere*) [*superficie, suelo, manos*] sticky; [*miel*] sticky, gooey*; **la mesa está muy pegajosa** the table is all sticky; **hoy hace un calor ~** it's really sticky today
2 [*persona*] clingy*
3 (= *LAm*) [*canción, melodía*] catchy
4 (= *contagioso*) contagious

pegamento SM glue, adhesive ► **pegamento de caucho** (*Aut*) rubber solution ► **pegamento de contacto** contact adhesive

pegar ▸conjug 1h◂ Ⓐ VT 1 (= *adherir*) 1·1 (*gen*) to stick; (*con cola*) to glue, stick; [+ *cartel*] to stick up; [+ *dos piezas*] to fix together; (*Inform*) to paste; **tengo que ~ las fotos en el álbum** I have to stick the photos into the album; **~ un sello** to stick a stamp on; **lo puedes ~ con celo** you can stick it on with Sellotape®, you can sellotape it on; ✦MODISMO **no ~ sello*** not to lift a finger
1·2 (= *coser*) [+ *botón*] to sew on
2 (= *golpear*) (*gen*) to hit; (= *dar una torta a*) to smack; **Andrés me ha pegado** Andrés hit me; **hazlo o te pego** do it or I'll hit you; **es un crimen ~ a los niños** it's a crime to hit *o* smack children; **dicen que pega a su mujer** they say he beats his wife
3 (*) (= *dar*) **me pegó un golpe** he hit me; **~ un grito** to shout, cry out; **le han pegado un puntapié** they gave him a kick, they kicked him; **~ un salto** to jump (*with fright etc*); **~ un susto a algn** to scare sb, give sb a fright; **¡qué susto me has pegado!** what a fright you gave me!; **le ~on un tiro** they shot him; *ver tb* **fuego 1**
4 (= *arrimar*) **~ una silla a una pared** to move *o* put a chair up against a wall; **~ el oído a la puerta** to put one's ear to the door; ✦MODISMO **~ el oído *o* la oreja** to prick up one's ears
5 (*) (= *contagiar*) to give (**a** to); **me has pegado la gripe** you've given me the flu; **él me pegó la costumbre** I picked up the habit off him
6 ✦MODISMO **~la** (*Andes, Arg**) (= *tener suerte*) to be lucky; (= *lograrlo*) to manage it; (= *caer en gracia*) to have a hit (**con** with)
7 (*Méx*) (= *atar*) to tie, fasten (down); [+ *caballo*] to hitch up
8 (*Caribe*) [+ *trabajo*] to start
Ⓑ VI 1 (= *adherir*) to stick; (*Inform*) to paste
2 (= *agarrar*) [*planta*] to take (root); [*remedio*] to take; [*fuego*] to catch
3 **~ contra algo** to hit sth; **pegamos contra un muro** we hit a wall; **~ en algo** (= *dar*) to hit sth; (= *rozar*) to touch sth; **la flecha pegó en el blanco** the arrow hit the target; **la pelota pegó en el árbol** the ball hit the tree; **pegaba con un palo en la puerta** he was pounding on *o* hitting the door with a stick; **las ramas pegan en los cristales** the branches beat against the windows; **el sol pega en esta ventana** the sun beats down through this window; **el piano pega en la pared** the piano is touching the wall
4 (*) (= *armonizar*) to go well, fit; [*dos colores*] to match, go together; **es un ingrediente que no pega** it's an ingredient which does not go well with other dishes; **este sillón no pega aquí** this armchair doesn't look right here; **la cita no pega** the quotation is out of place; **~le a algn: no le pega nada actuar así** it's not like him to act like that; **~ con algo** to match sth, go with sth; **ese sombrero no pega con el abrigo** that hat doesn't match *o* go with the coat
5 (*) (= *ser fuerte*) to be strong; **este vino pega (mucho)** this wine is really strong *o* goes to your head; **a estas horas el sol pega fuerte** the sun is really hot at this time of day
6 (*) (= *tener éxito*) **ese autor está pegando** that author's a big hit; **esta canción está pegando muy fuerte** this song is rocketing up the charts; **los jóvenes vienen pegando (fuerte)** the younger generation's coming up fast
7 (*) (= *creer*) **me pega que ...: me pega que no vendrá** I have a hunch that he won't come
8 **~le a algo*** to be a great one for sth*; **~le a la bebida** to be a heavy drinker
9 (*Caribe, Méx**) (= *trabajar duro*) to slog away*
Ⓒ **pegarse** VPR 1 (= *adherirse*) to stick; **vigila o se ~á el arroz** be careful or the rice will stick
2 (= *pelearse*) to hit each other, fight
3 **~se a algn** (= *arrimarse*) to stay close to sb; (*Dep*) to stick close to sb; **pégate al grupo y no te perderás** stay close to the group and you won't get lost; **el niño se pegó a su madre** the boy clung to his mother; **si vamos a algún sitio siempre se nos pega** if we go anywhere he always latches on to us; **~se a una reunión** to gatecrash a meeting*; ✦MODISMO **~se a algn como una lapa** (*Esp*) to stick to sb like glue *o* a limpet
4 (*) (= *contagiarse*) (*lit*) to be catching; (*fig*) to be infectious, be catchy; **todo se pega (menos la hermosura)** everything's catching (except good looks); **se te ha pegado el acento andaluz** you've picked up an Andalusian accent
5 (*) (= *darse*) **~se un tiro** to shoot o.s.; **¡es para ~se un tiro!** it's enough to make you scream!; **~se un golpe** to hit o.s.; **me pegué un golpe en la cabeza** I hit my head; **se pega una vida padre** he lives the life of Riley; ✦MODISMOS **pegársela*** (= *fracasar*) to fail, come a cropper*; **pegársela a algn** (= *traicionar*) to double-cross sb; (= *ser infiel*) to cheat on sb

Pegaso SM Pegasus

pegatina SF sticker

pegativo ADJ (*CAm, Cono Sur*) sticky

pego* SM (*Esp*) ✦MODISMO **dar el ~**: **es una imitación barata pero da el ~** it's a cheap imitation but it looks like the real thing

pegón* ADJ 1 [*persona*] tough, hard, given to violence
2 [*vino*] strong

pegoste SM 1 (*LAm*) (= *esparadrapo*) surgical tape
2 (*Caribe**) (= *colado*) gatecrasher
3 (*CAm‡*) (= *parásito*) scrounger*

pegote* SM 1 (*Culin*) sticky mess
2 ✦MODISMOS **echarse un ~** ◊ **tirarse ~s*** to brag*, exaggerate, show off
3 (= *gorrón*) hanger-on
4 (*fig*) (= *chapuza*) botch; (= *parche*) patch

pegotear* ▸conjug 1a◂ VI to sponge*, cadge

pegujal SM 1 (*Fin*) wealth, money; (= *hacienda*) estate
2 (*Agr*) small plot, small private plot, smallholding

peina SF back comb, ornamental comb

peinada SF combing; **darse una ~** to comb one's hair

peinado Ⓐ ADJ 1 **bien ~** [*pelo*] well-combed; [*persona*] neat, well-groomed
2 (= *relamido*) [*persona*] foppish; [*estilo, ingenio*] affected
Ⓑ SM 1 [*de pelo*] hairdo, hairstyle ► **peinado de paje** pageboy hairstyle
2 (*) (= *investigación*) check, investigation; (= *redada*) sweep, raid; (= *casa por casa*) house-to-house search

peinador(a) Ⓐ SM/F (= *persona*) hairdresser
Ⓑ SM 1 (= *bata*) dressing gown, peignoir
2 (*LAm*) (= *tocador*) dressing table

peinadura SF 1 (= *acción*) combing
2 **peinaduras** (= *pelos*) combings

peinar ▸conjug 1a◂ Ⓐ VT 1 [+ *pelo*] (*con peine*) to comb; (*con cepillo*) to brush; **me peinan en Zoila's** I get my hair done at Zoila's
2 [+ *caballo*] to comb, curry
3 [+ *zona*] to comb
4 (*LAm*) [+ *roca*] to cut
5 (*Arg**) (= *adular*) to flatter
6 (*Dep**) [+ *balón*] to head
Ⓑ **peinarse** VPR to comb one's hair; **~se a la griega** to do one's hair in the Greek style

peine SM comb; ✦MODISMO **¡te vas a enterar de lo que vale un ~!** (*Esp**) now you'll find out what's what! ► **peine de púas** fine-toothed comb, nit comb

peinecillo SM fine comb

peineta SF back comb, ornamental comb

peinilla SF (*Andes, Caribe*) large machete

p.ej. ABR (= **por ejemplo**) e.g.

peje Ⓐ ADJ (*Méx*) stupid
Ⓑ SM [1] (*Zool*) fish ► **peje araña** weever ► **peje sapo** monkfish
[2] (*) (= *listillo*) twister, sharpie (*EEUU**)

pejiguera* SF bother, nuisance

Pekín SM Beijing, Peking

pela SF [1] (*Culin*) peeling
[2] (*Esp**) (= *peseta*) peseta; **~s** (= *dinero*) money *sing*; **unas buenas ~s** a good few bucks*; **mucha ~** *o* **~ larga** lots of dough‡; **mirar la ~** to be concerned only about money; ✦*MODISMO* **cambiar** *o* **echar la ~‡** to throw up*, puke (up)*
[3] (*LAm**) (= *zurra*) beating
[4] (*Méx**) [*de trabajo*] slog, hard work; (*CAm*) (= *fatiga*) exhaustion

pelada SF [1] (*LAm*) (= *corte de pelo*) haircut
[2] (*Cono Sur*) (= *calva*) bald head
[3] (*Andes, CAm, Caribe*) (= *error*) blunder
[4] **la Pelada** (*Andes, Caribe, Cono Sur*) (= *muerte*) Death

peladar SM (*Cono Sur*) arid plain

peladera SF [1] (*Med*) alopecia
[2] (*CAm, Méx*) (= *chismes*) gossip, backbiting
[3] (*Cono Sur*) (= *erial*) arid plain

peladero SM (*LAm*) = **pelador**

peladez* SF [1] (*Méx*) (= *vulgaridad*) vulgarity; (= *palabrota*) rude word, obscenity
[2] (*Andes*) (= *pobreza*) poverty

peladilla SF (*Esp*) sugared almond

pelado/a Ⓐ ADJ [1] (= *sin pelo*) **lleva la cabeza pelada** he has his head shaved
[2] (*por el sol*) **tengo la espalda pelada del sol** my back is peeling from being in the sun
[3] [*fruta, patata*] peeled; [*gamba*] shelled; **tomates ~s** peeled tomatoes; **sólo han dejado los huesos ~s** they left nothing but the bones
[4] [*terreno*] treeless, bare; [*paisaje*] bare; [*tronco*] bare, smooth; **una montaña pelada** a bare mountain
[5] (= *escueto*) bare; **cobra el sueldo ~** he gets just his bare salary; **he sacado un cinco ~** I just scraped a five
[6] (*) (= *sin dinero*) broke*, penniless
[7] (*Méx*) (= *grosero*) coarse, rude
[8] (*) [*número*] round; **el cinco mil ~** a round five thousand
[9] (*CAm, Caribe*) (= *descarado*) impudent
Ⓑ SM (*) (= *corte de pelo*) haircut
Ⓒ SM/F [1] (†) (= *pobre*) pauper
[2] (*Méx**) (= *obrero*) working-class person
[3] (*Andes, CAm**) (= *bebé*) baby

PELADO

A stock figure in Mexican theatre and film, the **pelado** *is a kind of rural anti-hero cum lovable rogue who survives by his quick wits in the foreign environment of the city. The Mexican actor and comedian Mario Moreno (1911-94) based the character* **Cantinflas** *on the* **pelado**, *for which he is famous all over the Spanish-speaking world. The* **pelado** *is closely related to the literary figure of the* **pícaro** *and forms part of a long line of anti-heroic characters in Hispanic literature.*
⇨ *See also* PÍCARO, CARPA

pelador SM (*Culin*) peeler

peladura SF [1] (= *acción*) peeling
[2] **peladuras** (= *mondaduras*) peel *sing*, peelings
[3] (= *calva*) bare patch

pelafustán/ana SM/F layabout, good-for-nothing

pelagatos SM INV, **pelagallos** SM INV nobody

pelágico ADJ pelagic, deep-sea *antes de s*

pelaje SM [1] (*Zool*) fur, coat
[2] (= *apariencia*) **tenía muy mal ~** he looked very suspicious *o* dodgy; **no me gusta nada el ~ de esa gente** I don't like the look of them at all; **¡qué ~ llevas! pareces un pedigüeño** just look at you! you look like a right tramp!; **y otros de ese ~** and others of that ilk; **de todo ~** of every kind
[3] (= *pelo*) (*) mop of hair*

pelambre SM [1] (*Zool*) skin, fleece (*cut from animal*)
[2] (*) [*de persona*] mop of hair*
[3] (*en cabeza, piel*) bare patch
[4] (*Cono Sur*) (= *murmullos*) gossip, slander

pelambrera * SF mop of hair*

pelanas SM INV nobody

pelandusca* SF (*Esp*) tart‡, slut‡

pelapatatas SM INV, **pelapapas** SM INV (*LAm*) potato peeler

pelar ▸conjug 1a◂ Ⓐ VT [1] (= *rapar*) **lo han pelado al cero** *o* **al rape** they've cropped his hair*, they've completely shaved his hair off
[2] [+ *fruta, patata*] to peel; [+ *habas, mariscos*] to shell
[3] (= *despellejar*) to skin; (= *desplumar*) to pluck
[4] (†) (= *criticar*) to flay, criticize
[5] (†) (= *quitar el dinero a*) to clean out*, fleece*
[6] (†) (= *matar*) to do in‡, bump off‡
[7] (*LAm*) (= *azotar*) to beat up*
[8] **~la** (*Andes**) (= *morir*) to kick the bucket‡, die
Ⓑ VI [1] (*Cono Sur*) (= *cotillear*) to gossip
[2] (*Esp**) **que pela: hace un frío que pela** it's bitterly cold; **la sopa está que pela** this soup is piping hot
Ⓒ **pelarse** VPR [1] (= *cortarse el pelo*) to get one's hair cut; **voy a ~me** I'm going to get my hair cut
[2] [*nariz, hombros*] to peel; **se me está pelando la espalda** my back is peeling
[3] ✦*MODISMOS* **pelársela**‡ (= *masturbarse*) to toss off‡; **pelársela*: se las peló en cuanto vio a su padre** he ran off as soon as he saw his dad; **me las pelo** I'm off*; **corre que se las pela** he runs like nobody's business*
[4] (*Méx*‡) (= *morir*) to kick the bucket‡

pelazón SF (*CAm, Méx*) [1] (= *chismes*) gossip, backbiting
[2] (= *pobreza*) chronic poverty

peldaño SM (*Arquit*) step, stair; [*de escalera portátil*] rung

pelea SF (*a golpes, patadas*) fight; (= *discusión, riña*) quarrel, row; **armar una ~** to start a fight; **gallo de ~** fighting cock, gamecock ► **pelea de gallos** cockfight

peleado ADJ **estoy peleada con dos amigas** I've fallen out with two friends; **María está peleada con su novio** María has broken up *o* split up with her boyfriend

peleador ADJ quarrelsome

pelear ▸conjug 1a◂ Ⓐ VI [1] (*físicamente*) to fight; **los dos púgiles ~án por el título mañana** the two boxers will fight for the title tomorrow; **los perros peleaban por un hueso** the dogs were fighting over a bone; **siempre me toca ~ con los niños a la hora del baño** I'm always the one who has to battle with the children at bathtime
[2] (= *esforzarse*) to struggle; **tuvo que ~ mucho para mantener a su familia** he had to struggle hard to support his family, it was a hard struggle for him to support his family
Ⓑ **pelearse** VPR [1] (*físicamente*) to fight; **dos niños se estaban peleando en el patio** there were two children fighting in the playground; **estaban peleándose a puñetazos** they were punching each other *o* laying into each other with their fists; **los hermanos se peleaban a patadas** the two brothers were kicking each other; **se estaban peleando por unos caramelos** they were fighting over some sweets; **~se con algn** to fight sb
[2] (= *discutir*) to argue, quarrel; **siempre nos peleamos cuando hablamos de política** we always end up arguing whenever we talk about politics
[3] (= *romper una relación*) [*dos amigos*] to fall out; [*novios*] to split up, break up; **se ha peleado con todas sus amigos** he's fallen out with all his friends; **se ha peleado con su novio** she has broken up *o* split up with her boyfriend

pelechar ▸conjug 1a◂ VI [1] (*Zool, Orn*) (= *perder pelo*) to moult, molt (*EEUU*); (= *criar pelo*) to grow new hair
[2] (= *recuperarse*) [*persona*] to be on the mend, regain one's strength; [*negocio*] to be turning the corner
[3] (*Cono Sur*) (= *enriquecerse*) prosper

pelecho SM (*Cono Sur, Méx*) [1] (= *pelo*) moulted fur; (= *piel*) sloughed skin
[2] (= *ropa*) old clothing

pelele SM [1] (= *figura*) guy, straw doll; (*fig*) tool, puppet
[2] (= *bobo*) simpleton
[3] [*de bebé*] Babygro®, rompers *pl*, creepers *pl* (*EEUU*)

pelendengue SM = **perendengue**

peleón ADJ [1] (= *belicoso*) aggressive
[2] (= *discutidor*) argumentative
[3] [*vino*] cheap, rough

peleona* SF (*gen*) row, set-to*; (*más violenta*) brawl

peleonero ADJ (*LAm*) = **peleón**

pelero SM [1] (*CAm, Cono Sur*) horse blanket
[2] (*Caribe*) = **pelambre**

pelés‡ SMPL (*Esp*) balls‡; ✦*MODISMO* **estar en ~** to be stark naked

pelete SM [1] = **pelado C1**
[2] **en ~** stark naked

peletería SF [1] (= *tienda*) furrier's, fur shop; (= *oficio*) furriery
[2] (*Caribe*) (= *zapatería*) shoe shop

peletero/a SM/F furrier

peli* SF = **película 1**

peliagudo ADJ [*tema*] tricky

pelicano[1] ADJ grey-haired

pelícano SM, **pelicano**[2] SM pelican

pelicorto ADJ short-haired

película SF [1] (*Cine*) film, movie (*EEUU*); **hoy echan** *o* **ponen una ~ de Hitchcock por la**

tele there's a Hitchcock film on TV tonight; **pasar una ~** to show a film; ✦*MODISMOS* **una cosa de ~** like something in the movies, an astonishing thing, something out of this world; **fue de ~** it was incredible; **¡allá ~s!*** it's nothing to do with me! ► **película de acción** action film ► **película de animación** cartoon ► **película de aventuras** adventure film ► **película de dibujos (animados)** cartoon ► **película de época** period film ► **película de gángsters** gangster film ► **película de la serie B** B film, B movie (*esp EEUU*) ► **película del Oeste** western ► **película de miedo** horror film ► **película de terror** horror film ► **película en color** colour film, color film (*EEUU*) ► **película muda** silent film ► **película S** porn film ► **película sonora** talkie ► **película (de) vídeo** video film

2 (*Fot*) film ► **película virgen** unexposed film

3 (*Téc*) film ► **película autoadherible** (*Méx*) Clingfilm®, Saran Wrap® (*EEUU*)

4 (*) (= *narración*) story, catalogue of events; (= *cuento*) tall story, tale; **¡cuánta ~!** what a load of rubbish!*

5 (*Caribe*) (= *disparate*) silly remark; (= *lío*) row, rumpus

peliculero* ADJ 1 (= *aficionado al cine*) fond of films *o* (*EEUU*) movies, fond of the cinema

2 (*) (= *afectado*) showy

peligrar ▸conjug 1a◂ VI to be in danger; **~ de hacer algo** to be in danger of doing sth

peligro SM (*gen*) danger, peril (*liter*); (= *riesgo*) risk; **en ~ de extinción** in danger of extinction; **no hay ~ de la vida de la madre** the mother's life is not in danger; **estos gases constituyen un ~ para la salud** these gases pose a risk to health, these gases pose a health hazard; **¡ese niño es un ~ andante!** (*hum*) that child is a walking disaster area!; **correr ~**: **corre el ~ de que lo descubran** he runs the risk of being found out; **bajo esta roca no corremos ~** we're in no danger under this rock, we're free from danger under this rock; **estar en ~** to be in danger; **está fuera de ~** he's out of danger; **poner en ~** to endanger, put at risk, jeopardize; **"peligro de incendio"** "fire risk", "fire hazard"; **"peligro de muerte"** "danger" ► **peligro amarillo** yellow peril

peligrosamente ADV (*gen*) dangerously; (= *arriesgadamente*) riskily

peligrosidad SF (*gen*) danger; (= *riesgo*) riskiness

peligroso ADJ (*gen*) dangerous; (= *arriesgado*) risky; [*herida*] ugly, nasty

pelilargo ADJ long-haired

pelillo* SM trifle, trivial thing; **no se para en ~s** he is not easily deterred; ✦*MODISMOS* **echar ~s a la mar** to bury the hatchet; **¡~s a la mar!** (*Esp*) let bygones be bygones!

pelín* Ⓐ SM bit, small amount; **un ~ de música** a bit of music

Ⓑ ADV a bit, just a bit; **es un ~ tacaño** he's just a bit mean; **te pasaste un ~** you went a bit too far

pelinegro ADJ black-haired

pelirrojo/a Ⓐ ADJ red-haired, red-headed

Ⓑ SM/F redhead; **la pequeña pelirroja** the little redhead

pelirrubio ADJ fair-haired

pella SF 1 (*gen*) ball, round mass; (*sin forma*) dollop; (*Culin*) lump of lard

2 [*de coliflor*] head

3 (*) (= *suma de dinero*) sum of money

4 ✦*MODISMO* **hacer ~s** to play truant*, play hooky (*EEUU**)

pelleja SF 1 (= *piel*) skin, hide

2 (*) (= *prostituta*) whore

3 (*) (= *mujer delgada*) thin woman

4 (*Esp*‡) (= *cartera*) wallet, billfold (*EEUU*)

pellejería SF 1 (= *pieles*) skins *pl*, hides *pl*

2 (= *curtiduría*) tannery

3 **pellejerías** (*Cono Sur*) (= *dificultades*) difficulties

pellejero/a‡ SM/F pickpocket

pellejo SM 1 [*de animal*] skin, hide; (*) [*de persona*] skin; [*de uva*] skin; ✦*MODISMOS* **no caber en el ~** to be bursting with pride; **estar en el ~ de algn**: **no quisiera estar en su ~** I wouldn't like to be in his shoes; **ponerse en el ~ de algn**: **ponte en su ~** put yourself in her shoes; **quitarle el ~ a algn** to flay sb, criticize sb harshly; **no tener más que el ~** to be all skin and bones

2 (*) (= *vida*) neck*; **arriesgar el ~** to risk one's neck*; **perder el ~** to snuff it*; **salvar el ~** to save one's skin *o* neck*

3 (= *odre*) wineskin

4 (*) (= *borracho*) drunk

5 (†) (= *mujeriego*) rake, womanizer

pellet SM (*pl* **pellets**) pellet

pellingajo SM (*Andes, Cono Sur*) 1 (= *trapo*) dishcloth

2 (= *objeto*) piece of junk

pelliza SF (*hecha de piel*) fur jacket; (*forrada de piel*) fur-lined jacket

pellizcar ▸conjug 1g◂ VT 1 [+ *persona, mejilla*] to pinch

2 [+ *comida*] to nibble, pick at

pellizco SM 1 (*en mejilla, brazo*) pinch

2 (= *cantidad pequeña*) small bit; **un ~ de sal** a pinch of salt; ✦*MODISMO* **un buen ~*** a tidy sum*

3 [*de sombrero*] pinch, dent

pellón SM (*LAm*) *sheepskin saddle blanket*

pelma Ⓐ SMF (*) bore; **¡no seas ~!** don't be such a bore!

Ⓑ SM lump, solid mass

pelmazamente* ADV boringly

pelmazo* Ⓐ ADJ boring

Ⓑ SMF bore

pelo SM 1 (= *filamento*) [*de persona, animal*] hair; [*de barba*] whisker; (*Téc*) fibre, fiber (*EEUU*), strand; **un ~ rubio** a blond hair

2 (*en conjunto*) [*de persona*] hair; (= *piel*) fur, coat; [*de fruta*] down; [*de jersey*] fluff; [*de tejido*] nap, pile; **tiene el ~ rubio** she has blond hair; **tiene el ~ rizado** he has curly hair; **tienes mucho ~** you have thick hair; **tiene poco ~** his hair is thin; **se me está cayendo el ~** I am losing my hair; **cortarse el ~** to have one's hair cut; **dos caballos del mismo ~** two horses of the same colour ► **pelo de camello** camel-hair, camel's hair (*EEUU*)

3 [*de reloj*] hairspring

4 [*de diamante*] flaw

5 (= *grieta*) hairline crack

6 (= *sierra*) hacksaw blade

7 ✦*MODISMOS* **a pelo***: **cabalgar** *o* **montar a ~** to ride bareback; **cantar a ~** to sing unaccompanied; **hacerlo a ~** (*sexualmente*) to have unprotected sex; **está más guapa a ~ que con maquillaje** she's prettier just as she is, without her make-up on; **ir a ~** (= *sin sombrero*) to go bareheaded; (= *desnudo*) to be stark naked; **pasar el mono a ~** (*de drogas*) to go through cold turkey; **agarrarse a un ~** to clutch at straws; **al ~***: **te queda al ~** it looks great on you, it fits like a glove; **este regalo me viene al ~** this present is just what I needed *o* wanted; **viene al ~ el comentario** that comment is spot on; **un tema que viene muy al ~ en esta discusión** a subject which is highly relevant to this debate; **caérsele el ~ a algn** (*esp Esp**) **¡se te va a caer el ~!** you're (in) for it now!; **cortar un ~ en el aire** to be pretty smart; **dar a algn para el ~*** (= *pegar*) to beat the living daylights out of sb*; (*en discusión*) to wipe the floor with sb*; (= *regañar*) to give sb a rollicking*; **con estos ~s***: **¡Juan viene a cenar y yo con estos ~s!** Juan is coming to dinner and look at the state I'm in!; **ser de dos ~s** (*Cono Sur*) to be two-faced; **echar el ~** (*Cono Sur**) to waste time, idle; **lucirle el ~ a algn***: **así nos luce el ~** and that's the awful state we're in, that's why we're so badly off; **de medio ~** (= *de baja calidad*) second-rate; (= *de baja categoría social*) of no social standing; **de ~ en pecho** manly; **un hombre de ~ en pecho** a real man; **hacer a ~ y pluma**‡ to be AC/DC‡; **por los ~s** by the skin of one's teeth; **pasó el examen por los ~s** he passed the exam by the skin of his teeth, he scraped through the exam; **parece traído por los ~s** it seems far-fetched; **con ~s y señales** in minute detail; **soltarse el ~*** to let one's hair down*; **tener el ~ de la dehesa** to be unable to hide one's rustic *o* humble origins; **no tener ~s en la lengua** not to mince one's words; **no tocar un ~ de la ropa a algn** not to lay a finger on sb; **tomar el ~ a algn** to pull sb's leg; **no ver el ~ a algn*** not to see hide nor hair of sb; **no se les ve el ~ desde hace mucho** there's been no sign of them for ages; *ver tb* **punta A2**

8 **un ~*** (= *un poco*) **no se mueve un ~ de aire** *o* **viento** there isn't a breath of wind stirring; **no me fío un ~ de ellos** I don't trust them an inch; **me temo que te pasas un ~** I am afraid you are going a bit too far; **no afloja un ~** (*Cono Sur*) he won't give an inch; **no tiene un ~ de tonto** he's no fool; **no perdí el avión por un ~** I only just caught the plane; **nos escapamos por un ~** we had a close shave

pelón Ⓐ ADJ 1 (= *calvo*) bald, hairless; (= *rapado*) with a crew-cut, close-cropped

2 (= *sin recursos*) broke*, penniless; (= *pobre*) poor

3 (= *tonto*) thick*, stupid

4 (*Andes*) (= *con mucho pelo*) hairy, long-haired

Ⓑ SM 1 (= *pobre diablo*) poor wretch

2 (*LAm*) (= *niño*) child, baby

3 (*Cono Sur*) (= *melocotón*) nectarine

4 (*Caribe**) (= *error*) blunder, boob*

pelona SF 1 (= *calvicie*) baldness

2 **la Pelona*** (= *muerte*) death

peloso ADJ hairy

pelota Ⓐ SF 1 (*Dep*) ball; **jugar a la ~** to play ball; ✦*MODISMOS* **devolver la ~ a algn** to turn the tables on sb; **hacer la ~ a algn*** to suck up to sb; **lanzar ~s fuera** to dodge the issue; **pasarse la ~** to pass the buck*; **la ~ si-**

gue en el tejado it's all still up in the air ► **pelota base** baseball ► **pelota de goma** (*Mil*) rubber bullet ► **pelota vasca** pelota
2 **pelotas**** (= *testículos*) balls**; **¿que te deje el coche? ¡las ~s!** you expect me to lend you the car? what a bloody cheek!*; **en ~s** (= *desnudo*) stark naked, starkers*; (= *sin dinero*) broke*; **coger** *o* **pillar a algn en ~s** to catch sb with their trousers down*; **dejar a algn en ~s** to strip sb clean *o* naked; (*en un juego*) to clean sb out*; ✦*MODISMOS* **hinchar las ~s a algn** to get on sb's tits*, bug sb*; **tener ~s** to have balls; **tocar las ~s a algn** to get on sb's tits*, bug sb*
3 (*) (= *cabeza*) nut*, noggin (*EEUU**), head
4 (*LAm**) [*de amigos*] bunch, gang
5 (*CAm, Caribe, Méx*) (= *pasión*) passion; **tener ~ por** to have a passion for
6 (*CAm, Caribe, Méx*) (= *amante*) girlfriend
7 (*en cárcel*) ✦*MODISMO* **estar en la ~*** to be in solitary*
Ⓑ SMF (*) creep*

pelotari (*Esp*) SMF pelota player

pelotazo SM 1 (*Esp**) drink; **pegarse un ~** to have a drink
2 (*Dep*) (*fuerte*) fierce shot; (*largo*) long ball

pelote* SM five-peseta coin

pelotear ▸conjug 1a◂ Ⓐ VT 1 (*Fin*) [+ *cuenta*] to audit
2 (*Andes**) **~ un asunto** to turn sth over in one's mind
3 (*LAm**) (= *captar*) to catch, pick up
Ⓑ VI 1 (*Dep*) to knock a ball about, kick a ball about; (*Tenis*) to knock up
2 (= *reñir*) to bicker, argue

peloteo SM 1 (*Tenis*) (*como entrenamiento*) knock-up; (= *tirada larga*) rally
2 (*Ftbl*) kick-about*; [*de entrada*] warm-up
3 (*) (= *adulación*) flattery
4 (= *intercambio*) exchange, sending back and forth; **hubo mucho ~ diplomático** there was a lot of diplomatic to-ing and fro-ing

pelotera* SF row, set-to*

pelotero/a Ⓐ ADJ (*) = **pelotillero A**
Ⓑ SM/F 1 (*LAm*) (= *jugador*) ball player; [*de fútbol*] footballer; [*de béisbol*] baseball player
2 (*) (= *lameculos*) creep*

pelotilla* SF 1 (= *adulación*) **hacer la ~ a algn** to suck up to sb*
2 [*de nariz*] bogey*; **hacer ~s** to pick one's nose

pelotilleo* SM crawling*, bootlicking*, brownnosing (*EEUU**)

pelotillero/a* Ⓐ ADJ crawling*, bootlicking*, brownnosing (*EEUU**)
Ⓑ SM/F crawler*, bootlicker*, brownnose (*EEUU**)

pelotón SM 1 [*de gente*] crowd; [*de atletas, ciclistas*] pack ► **pelotón de cabeza** leading group
2 (*Mil*) detachment, squad ► **pelotón de abordaje** boarding party ► **pelotón de demolición** demolition squad ► **pelotón de ejecución, pelotón de fusilamiento** firing squad
3 [*de hilos*] tangle, mat

pelotudez* SF (*LAm*) stupidity

pelotudo/a* Ⓐ ADJ 1 (= *valiente*) tough, gutsy
2 (*LAm*) (= *imbécil*) bloody stupid*; (= *inútil*) useless; (= *descuidado*) slack, sloppy
3 (*CAm**) [*salsa*] lumpy
Ⓑ SM/F (*LAm*) bloody fool*, jerk (*EEUU**)

pelpa* SF (*LAm*) joint*, reefer*

peltre SM pewter

peluca SF 1 (*para cabeza*) wig
2 (*) (= *rapapolvo*) dressing-down*

peluche SM felt, plush; *ver tb* **oso**

peluchento ADJ silky, smooth

peluco* SM clock, watch

pelucón/ona Ⓐ ADJ (*Andes*) long-haired
Ⓑ SM/F (*Cono Sur*†) (= *conservador*) conservative; (*Andes*) (= *de alta posición*) bigwig, big shot*

peludo Ⓐ ADJ 1 (= *con mucho pelo*) hairy, shaggy; (= *con pelo largo*) long-haired; [*animal*] furry, shaggy; [*barba*] bushy
2 (*CAm**) (= *difícil*) hard
Ⓑ SM 1 (= *felpudo*) round felt mat
2 (*Cono Sur Zool*) (species of) armadillo
3 (= *borrachera*) (*Cono Sur**) **agarrarse un ~** to get sloshed*

peluquearse ▸conjug 1a◂ VPR (*LAm*) to have a haircut

peluquería SF 1 (= *establecimiento*) [*de mujeres, hombres*] hairdresser's; [*de hombres sólo*] barber's (shop)
2 (= *oficio*) hairdressing

peluquero/a SM/F [*de mujeres, hombres*] hairdresser; [*de hombres sólo*] barber

peluquín SM toupée, hairpiece; ✦*MODISMO* **¡ni hablar del ~!*** no way!*

pelusa SF 1 (*Bot*) down; (*Cos*) fluff; (*en cara*) down, fuzz; (*bajo muebles*) fluff, dust
2 (*) (*entre niños*) envy, jealousy

pelusiento ADJ (*Andes, Caribe*) hairy, shaggy

peluso* SM (*Mil*) squaddie*, recruit

pélvico ADJ pelvic

pelvis SF INV pelvis

peme* SM military policeman

PEMEX SM ABR = **Petróleos Mexicanos**

PEN SM ABR 1 (*Esp*) = **Plan Energético Nacional**
2 (*Arg*) = **Poder Ejecutivo Nacional**

▼**pena** SF 1 (= *tristeza*) sorrow; **tenía mucha ~ después de la muerte de su hijo** she grieved a lot *o* was extremely upset after her son's death; **tengo una ~ muy grande porque no está con nosotros** I'm very sad that he is not here with us; **alma en ~** lost soul; **dar ~**: **da ~ verlos sufrir así** it's sad to see them suffer like that; **me daba ~ dejar España** I was sad *o* sorry to leave Spain; **Pepe me da mucha ~** I feel very sorry for Pepe; **morir de (la) ~** to die of a broken heart; ✦*MODISMO* **sin ~ ni gloria**: **ese año pasó sin ~ ni gloria** it was an uneventful sort of year; **la exposición pasó sin ~ ni gloria** the exhibition went almost unnoticed
2 (= *lástima*) shame, pity; **¿no podéis venir? ¡qué ~!** you can't come? what a shame *o* a pity!; **¡es una ~ que no tengamos más tiempo!** it's a shame *o* a pity that we haven't got more time!, it's too bad we haven't got more time! (*EEUU*); **mi habitación está que da ~ verla** my room is in a terrible state*; **de ~**: **la economía va de ~** the economy is in a terrible state; **el traje le quedaba de ~** the dress looked terrible on her; **estar hecho una ~** to be in a sorry state
3 **penas** (= *problemas*) **cuéntame tus ~s** tell me all your troubles; **logramos superarlo con muchas ~s** we had to struggle to overcome it; ✦*MODISMOS* **ahogar las ~s** to drown one's sorrows; **¡allá ~s!** I don't care!, that's not my problem!; **a duras ~s** with great difficulty; **a duras ~s consiguió alcanzar la orilla** he only managed to reach the shore with great difficulty; **a duras ~s llegamos a fin de mes** we can barely make ends meet
4 (= *esfuerzo*) **ahorrarse la ~** to save o.s. the trouble, save o.s. the bother*; **merecer** *o* **valer la ~** to be worth; **no merece la ~** it's not worth it; **una película que vale la ~ ver** a film that's worth seeing; **¿merece la ~ visitar la catedral?** is the cathedral worth a visit?; **no vale la ~ que perdamos el tiempo discutiendo eso** it's not worth wasting time arguing about it
5 (*Jur*) sentence; **el juez le impuso una ~ de tres años de prisión** the judge sentenced him to three years in prison; **bajo** *o* **so ~ de** [+ *castigo, multa, prisión*] on *o* under penalty of; **bajo ~ de muerte** on pain of death, on *o* under penalty of death; **tiene prohibido hacerlo, so ~ de ser expulsado** he is forbidden to do it, on *o* under penalty of expulsion ► **pena capital** capital punishment ► **pena de muerte** death penalty ► **pena máxima** maximum sentence; (*Ftbl*) penalty ► **pena pecuniaria** fine ► **pena privativa de libertad** custodial sentence
6 (*Méx, Andes*) (= *vergüenza*) embarrassment; **me da mucha ~** I'm very embarrassed; **¡qué ~!** how embarrassing!; **sentir** *o* **tener ~** to be *o* feel embarrassed, be *o* feel ill at ease
7 (*Andes*) (= *fantasma*) ghost

penable ADJ punishable

penacho SM 1 (*Orn*) tuft, crest
2 [*de casco, sombrero*] plume
3 (= *orgullo*) pride, arrogance
4 [*de humo*] plume

penado/a Ⓐ ADJ = **penoso 2**
Ⓑ SM/F convict

penal Ⓐ ADJ penal
Ⓑ SM 1 (= *prisión*) prison, (state) penitentiary (*EEUU*)
2 (*LAm Dep*) (= *penalty*) penalty (kick)

penales* SM INV police record *sing*

penalidad SF 1 **penalidades** (= *dificultades*) hardship *sing*
2 (*Jur*) penalty, punishment

penalista SMF expert in criminal law, penologist

penalización SF 1 (= *sanción*) penalty, penalization; **recorrido sin penalizaciones** (*Dep*) clear round
2 (*Jur*) criminalization

penalizar ▸conjug 1f◂ VT 1 (= *sancionar*) to penalize
2 (*Jur*) to criminalize

penalti (*pl* **penaltis**) SM, **penalty** (*pl* **penaltys, penalties**) SM (*Dep*) penalty (kick); **marcar de ~** to score from a penalty; **punto de ~** penalty spot; **pitar** *o* **señalar ~** to award a penalty; **transformar un ~** to convert a penalty, score a penalty; ✦*MODISMO* **casarse de ~*** to have a shotgun wedding

penar ▸conjug 1a◂ Ⓐ VT 1 (*Jur*) to punish; **la ley pena el asesinato** the law punishes murder; **un delito penado con diez años de cárcel** a crime punishable by ten years' imprisonment
2 (*Andes*) [*difunto*] to haunt

➤ LENGUA Y USO: **pena 2** 45.3

Ⓑ VI 1 (= *sufrir*) [*persona*] to suffer; [*alma*] to be in torment; **ha penado mucho con su hijo enfermo** she has suffered terribly with her sick child; **ella pena por todos** she takes everybody's sufferings upon herself; **~ de amores** (*liter*) to go through the pains of love (*liter*)
2 (= *desear*) **~ por algo** to pine for sth, long for sth; **~ por hacer algo** to pine to do sth, long to do sth
3 (*Andes*) [*difunto*] **en ese lugar penan** that place is haunted
Ⓒ **penarse** VPR to grieve, mourn

penca SF 1 (*Bot*) (= *hoja*) leaf; (= *nervio*) main rib; (= *chumbera*) prickly pear
2 (*Méx*) [*de cuchillo*] blade
3 ✦***MODISMOS*** **agarrar una ~** (*LAm**) to get sloshed*; **hacerse de ~s** to have to be coaxed into doing something
4 (*Andes*) **una ~ de casa** a great big house; **una ~ de hombre** a fine-looking man; **una ~ de mujer** a fine-looking woman
5 (*LAm***) (= *pene*) prick**

pencar‡ ▸conjug 1g◂ VI to slog away*, slave away*

pencazo* SM (*CAm*) (= *golpe*) smack; **cayó un ~ de agua** it pelted down*, the skies opened

penco Ⓐ ADJ (*CAm**) (= *trabajador*) hard-working
Ⓑ SM 1 (= *persona*) dimwit*, nitwit*
2 (= *caballo*) nag
3 (*Andes*) **un ~ de hombre** a fine-looking man
4 (*Caribe*‡) (= *homosexual*) poof‡, queer‡, fag (*EEUU*‡)

pendango ADJ (*Caribe*) (= *afeminado*) effeminate; (= *miedoso*) cowardly

pendejada* SF (*LAm*) 1 (= *tontería*) foolish thing
2 (= *acto cobarde*) cowardly act
3 (= *molestia*) curse, nuisance
4 (= *cualidad*) [*de necio*] foolishness, stupidity; [*del cobarde*] cowardliness

pendejear* ▸conjug 1a◂ VI (*Andes, Méx*) to act the fool

pendejeta* SMF (*Andes*) idiot

pendejo/a* Ⓐ ADJ 1 (*LAm*) (= *imbécil*) idiotic; (= *cobarde*) cowardly, yellow*
2 (*Andes*) (= *listo*) smart; (= *taimado*) cunning
3 (*Caribe, Méx*) (= *torpe*) ham-fisted
Ⓑ SM/F 1 (*LAm*) (= *imbécil*) fool, idiot; (= *cobarde*) coward
2 (*Cono Sur*) (= *muchacho*) kid*; (= *sabelotodo*) know-all
Ⓒ SM [*del pubis*] pubic hair, pube‡

pendencia SF (= *riña*) quarrel; (= *pelea*) fight, brawl; **armar ~** to stir up trouble

pendenciero/a Ⓐ ADJ quarrelsome, argumentative
Ⓑ SM/F troublemaker

pender ▸conjug 2a◂ VI 1 (= *colgar*) to hang (**de, en** from; **sobre** over); **la amenaza que pende sobre nosotros** the threat hanging over us
2 (*Jur*) to be pending
3 (= *depender*) to depend (**de** on)

pendiente Ⓐ ADJ 1 (= *a la expectativa*) **estar ~ de algo: estaban ~s de su llegada** they were waiting for him to arrive; **estamos ~s de lo que él decida** we are waiting to see what he decides; **quedamos ~s de sus órdenes** we await your instructions
2 (= *atento*) **estar ~ de algo/algn: está muy ~ de la salud de su madre** he always keeps an eye on his mother's health; **está demasiado ~ de su novio** she's too wrapped up in her boyfriend; **estaban muy ~s de lo que decía** they were listening to her intently
3 [*juicio, caso, pedido*] pending; **aún tenemos un par de asuntos ~s** we still have a couple of matters pending
4 [*cuenta*] outstanding, unpaid
5 [*asignatura*] **tengo las matemáticas ~s** I have to resit maths
6 (= *colgado*) hanging
Ⓑ SM (= *arete*) earring
Ⓒ SF [*de un terreno*] slope; [*de un tejado*] pitch; **subieron por una ~ muy pronunciada** they climbed up a steep slope; **en ~** sloping; ✦***MODISMO*** **estar en la ~ vital** to be over the hill*

pendil SM (woman's) cloak; ✦***MODISMO*** **tomar el ~*** to pack up*, clear out*

péndola SF 1 (= *pluma*) pen, quill
2 [*de puente*] suspension cable

pendolear ▸conjug 1a◂ VI 1 (*LAm*) (= *escribir mucho*) to write a lot; (*Cono Sur*) (= *tener buena letra*) to write neatly
2 (*Méx*) to be good in difficult situations, know how to manage people sensibly

pendolista SMF penman, calligrapher

pendón SM 1 (= *bandera*) banner, standard; [*de forma triangular*] pennant
2 (*) (= *vaga*) lazy woman; (= *mujer promiscua*) tart‡, slut‡
3 ✦***MODISMO*** **ser un ~**†* to be an awkward customer*

pendona* SF = **pendón 2**

pendonear* ▸conjug 1a◂ VI to loaf around*, hang out*

pendoneo* SM **irse de ~** to go out round the streets*

péndulo SM pendulum ► **péndulo de Foucault** Foucault's Pendulum

pene SM penis

Penélope SF Penelope

penene* SMF = **PNN A**

peneque Ⓐ ADJ (‡) (= *borracho*) **estar ~** to be pickled‡
Ⓑ SM (*Méx Culin*) stuffed tortilla

penetrable ADJ penetrable

penetración SF 1 (= *acción*) penetration
2 (= *agudeza*) sharpness, acuteness; (= *visión*) insight

penetrador ADJ = **penetrante 3**

penetrante ADJ 1 [*herida*] deep
2 [*arma*] sharp; [*frío, viento*] biting; [*sonido*] piercing; [*vista*] acute; [*aroma*] strong; [*mirada*] sharp, penetrating
3 [*genio, mente*] keen, sharp; [*ironía*] biting

penetrar ▸conjug 1a◂ Ⓐ VI 1 (= *entrar*) **~on a través de** *o* **por una claraboya** they entered through a skylight; **el humo penetraba a través de las rendijas** the smoke was filtering through the cracks; **el agua había penetrado a través de** *o* **por las paredes** the water had seeped into the walls; **~ en: penetramos en un túnel** we went into *o* entered a tunnel; **la luz apenas penetra en la habitación** hardly any light enters the room; **el cuchillo penetró en la carne** the knife went into *o* entered *o* penetrated the flesh; **ocho hombres armados ~on en la embajada** eight gunmen broke into the embassy; **penetramos poco en el mar** we did not go far out to sea; **su ingratitud penetró hondamente en mi corazón** her ingratitude pierced me to the bone
2 (*frm*) (= *descifrar*) to penetrate; **~ en el sentido de algo** to penetrate the meaning of sth
Ⓑ VT 1 (= *atravesar*) to go right through; **un frío glacial le penetró los huesos** an icy cold went right through to her bones
2 (*sexualmente*) to penetrate
3 (*frm*) (= *descubrir*) [+ *misterio*] to fathom; [+ *secreto*] to unlock; [+ *sentido*] to grasp; [+ *intención*] to see through, grasp
Ⓒ **penetrarse** VPR **~se de algo** (*frm*) (= *absorber*) to become imbued with sth; (*Esp*) (= *comprender*) to understand sth fully, become fully aware of (the significance of) sth

peneuvista (*Esp*) Ⓐ ADJ **política ~** policy of the PNV, PNV policy; *ver tb* **PNV**
Ⓑ SMF member of the PNV

penga SF (*Andes*) bunch of bananas

penicilina SF penicillin

península SF peninsula ► **la Península Ibérica** the Iberian Peninsula

peninsular Ⓐ ADJ peninsular
Ⓑ SMF **los ~es** peninsular Spaniards

penique SM penny; **~s** pence; **un ~** a penny, one penny

penitencia SF 1 (= *estado*) penitence
2 (= *castigo*) penance; **en ~** as a penance; **imponer una ~ a algn** to give sb a penance; **hacer ~** to do penance (**por** for)

penitenciado/a SM/F (*LAm*) convict

penitencial ADJ penitential

penitenciar ▸conjug 1b◂ VT to impose a penance on

penitenciaría SF prison, (state) penitentiary (*EEUU*)

penitenciario Ⓐ ADJ penitentiary, prison *antes de s*
Ⓑ SM confessor

penitente Ⓐ ADJ 1 (*Rel*) penitent
2 (*Andes*) (= *tonto*) silly
Ⓑ SMF (*Rel*) penitent; → SEMANA SANTA
Ⓒ SM (*Cono Sur*) 1 (= *pico*) rock pinnacle, isolated cone of rock
2 (= *figura de nieve*) snowman

penol SM yardarm

penosamente ADV arduously, laboriously, with great difficulty

penoso ADJ 1 (= *doloroso*) painful; **me veo en la penosa obligación de comunicarles que ...** I regret to have to inform you that ...
2 (= *difícil*) [*tarea*] arduous, laborious; [*viaje*] gruelling, grueling (*EEUU*)
3 (= *lamentable*) pitiful; **fue un espectáculo ~** it was a sorry *o* pitiful sight; **era ~ ver la casa en ese estado** the house was a sorry *o* pitiful sight, it was pitiful to see the house in such a state
4 (*Andes, Méx*) (= *tímido*) shy, timid
5 (*Andes, Méx*) (= *embarazoso*) embarrassing

penquista (*Chile*) Ⓐ ADJ of/from Concepción
Ⓑ SMF native/inhabitant of Concepción; **los ~s** the people of Concepción

▼ **pensado** ADJ **un proyecto poco ~** a badly-thought-out *o* an ill-thought-out scheme; **lo tengo bien ~** I have thought it over *o* out carefully; **tengo ~ hacerlo mañana** I mean *o*

➤ LENGUA Y USO: pensado 35.1

intend to do it tomorrow; **bien ~, creo que …** on reflection, I think that …; **en el momento menos ~** when you least expect it

pensador(a) SM/F thinker

pensamiento SM [1] (= *facultad*) thought; ✦*MODISMO* **como el ~** in a flash
[2] (= *mente*) mind; **acudir** *o* **venir al ~ de algn** to come to sb's mind; **no le pasó por el ~** it never occurred to him, it never entered his mind; **envenenar el ~ de algn** to poison sb's mind (**contra** against); **ni por ~** I wouldn't dream of it
[3] (= *cosa pensada*) thought; **mal ~** nasty thought; **el ~ de Quevedo** Quevedo's thought; **adivinar los ~s de algn** to read sb's thoughts, guess what sb is thinking; **nuestro ~ sobre este tema** our thinking on this subject ► **pensamiento único** (*Pol*) single system of values
[4] (= *propósito*) idea, intention; **mi ~ es hacer algo** my idea *o* intention is to do sth
[5] (*Bot*) pansy

pensante ADJ thinking

pensar ▸conjug 1j◂ Ⓐ VT [1] (= *opinar*) to think; **~ de**: **¿qué piensas de ella?** what do you think of her?; **¿qué piensas del aborto?** what do you think about abortion?; **~ que** to think that; **—¿piensas que van a venir? —pienso que sí** "do you think they'll come?" — "I think so"; **dice que las mujeres no tendrían que trabajar, yo pienso que sí** he says women shouldn't work, I think they should; **yo pienso que no** I don't think so
[2] (= *considerar*) to think about, think over; **lo ~é** I'll think about it, I'll think it over; **esto es para ~lo** this needs thinking about *o* careful consideration; **lo pensó mejor** she thought better of it; **me pongo triste sólo con ~lo** the mere thought of it makes me sad; **pensándolo bien …** on second thoughts …, on reflection …; **piénsalo bien antes de responder** think carefully before you answer; **¡ni ~lo!** no way!*
[3] (= *decidir*) **~ que** to decide that, come to the conclusion that …; **he pensado que no vale la pena** I've decided that it's not worth it, I've come to the conclusion that it's not worth it
[4] (= *tener la intención de*) **~ hacer algo** to intend to do sth; **pienso seguir insistiendo** I intend to keep on trying; **no pensaba salir** I wasn't intending *o* planning to go out; **no pienso volver a Cuba** I have no intention of going back to Cuba; **no pienso decir nada** I won't be saying anything
[5] (= *concebir*) to think up; **¿quién pensó este plan?** who thought this plan up?, whose idea was this plan?
[6] (= *esperar*) **cuando menos lo pienses** when you least expect it; **sin ~lo** unexpectedly
Ⓑ VI [1] (= *tener ideas*) to think; **eso me hace ~** that makes me think; **quieren imponer su forma de ~** they want to impose their way of thinking; **después de mucho ~ tuve una idea** after much thought I had an idea; **~ en algo/algn** to think about sth/sb; **¿en qué piensas?** what are you thinking about?; **estaba pensando en ir al cine esta tarde** I was thinking of going to the cinema this evening; **sólo piensa en pasarlo bien** all he thinks about is having a good time; **pienso mucho en ti** I think about you a lot; **~ para sí** to think to o.s.; **dar que ~**: **el hecho de que no llamara a la policía da que ~** the fact that she didn't call the police makes you think; **un reportaje que da que ~** a thought-provoking article; **dar que ~ a la gente** to set people thinking, arouse suspicions; **sin ~** without thinking; **~ sobre algo** to think about sth; ✦*MODISMO* **~ con los pies**: **estás pensando con los pies** you're not using your head
[2] **~ bien de algo/algn** to think well of sth/sb; **~ mal de algo/algn** to think ill of sth/sb; **¡no pienses mal!** don't be nasty!; **¡siempre pensando mal!** what a nasty mind you've got!; ✦*REFRÁN* **piensa mal y acertarás** you can't trust anybody
[3] (= *aspirar*) **~ en algo** to aim at sth; **piensa en una cátedra** he's aiming at a chair
Ⓒ **pensarse** VPR **piénsatelo** think it over; **tienes nueve días para pensártelo** you have nine days to think it over *o* to think about it; **sin pensárselo dos veces** without a second thought; **después de pensárselo mucho** after thinking about it long and hard, after much thought

pensativamente ADV pensively, thoughtfully

pensativo ADJ pensive, thoughtful

Pensilvania SF Pennsylvania

pensión SF [1] (*por vejez*) pension; (*por invalidez, de divorciada*) allowance; **cobrar la ~** to draw one's pension ► **pensión alimenticia** alimony, maintenance ► **pensión asistencial** state pension ► **pensión contributiva** contributory pension ► **pensión de invalidez, pensión de inválidos** disability allowance ► **pensión de jubilación, pensión de retiro** retirement pension ► **pensión de viudedad** widow's/widower's pension ► **pensión escalada** graduated pension ► **pensión vitalicia** annuity
[2] (= *casa de huéspedes*) boarding house, guest house; (*Univ*) lodgings *pl*; (*Andes*) (= *bar*) bar, café
[3] (= *precio*) board and lodging; **media ~** half board ► **pensión completa** full board
[4] (*Univ*) scholarship; [*de viaje*] travel grant
[5] (*Andes, Cono Sur*) (= *preocupación*) worry, anxiety; (= *remordimiento*) regret
[6] (†) (= *molestia*) drawback, snag

pensionado/a Ⓐ ADJ pensioned
Ⓑ SM/F (= *pensionista*) pensioner
Ⓒ SM (= *internado*) boarding school

pensionar ▸conjug 1a◂ VT [1] [+ *jubilado*] give a pension to; [+ *estudiante*] to give a grant to
[2] (*Andes, Cono Sur*) (= *molestar*) to bother; (= *preocupar*) to worry

pensionista SMF [1] (= *jubilado*) pensioner, old-age pensioner ► **pensionista por invalidez** recipient of disability allowance
[2] (= *huésped*) lodger, paying guest
[3] (*Escol*) boarder
[4] (*LAm*) (= *subscriptor*) subscriber

pentagonal ADJ pentagonal

pentágono SM pentagon; **el Pentágono** (*en EEUU*) the Pentagon

pentagrama SM stave, staff

pentámetro SM pentameter

Pentateuco SM Pentateuch

pentatlón SM pentathlon

pentatónico ADJ pentatonic

Pentecostés SM [1] (*cristiano*) Whitsun, Whitsuntide; **domingo de ~** Whit Sunday
[2] (*judío*) Pentecost

penúltima SF [1] (*Ling*) penult, penultima
[2] (*) (= *bebida*) **vamos a tomarnos la ~** let's have one for the road*

penúltimo/a ADJ, SM/F penultimate, last but one

penumbra SF half-light, semi-darkness; **sentado en la ~** seated in the shadows

penuria SF (= *pobreza*) poverty; (= *escasez*) shortage, dearth

peña SF [1] (*Geog*) crag
[2] (= *grupo*) group, circle; (*pey*) coterie, clique; (*LAm*) (= *club*) folk club; (= *fiesta*) party; **forma parte de la ~** he's a member of the circle; **hay ~ en el café los domingos** the group meets in the café on Sundays ► **peña deportiva** supporters' club ► **peña taurina** club of bullfighting enthusiasts
[3] (*) (= *gente*) crowd; **hay mucha ~** there's loads of people*
[4] (*Cono Sur*) (= *montepío*) pawnshop

peñascal SM (*gen*) rocky place; (= *colina*) rocky hill

peñasco SM [1] (= *piedra*) large rock, boulder
[2] (= *risco*) rock, crag; ✦*MODISMO* **no se me pasó por el ~*** it never occurred to me

peñascoso ADJ rocky, craggy

peñazo* Ⓐ ADJ **¡no seas tan ~!** don't be such a pain!*
Ⓑ SM pain (in the neck)*; **dar el ~** to be a pain*, be a bore*

peñista SMF (*Dep*) member of a supporters' club

peñón SM [1] (= *roca*) wall of rock, crag
[2] **el Peñón** the Rock (*of Gibraltar*)

peños‡ SMPL ivories*, teeth

peñusco* SM (*Caribe, Cono Sur*) crowd

peo‡ SM **¡vete al ~!** go to hell!*

peón SM [1] (*Téc*) labourer, laborer (*EEUU*); (*esp LAm Agr*) farm labourer, farmhand; (*Taur*) assistant; (*Méx*) (= *aprendiz*) apprentice; (= *ayudante*) assistant ► **peón caminero** navvy, roadmender ► **peón de albañil** bricklayer's mate
[2] (*Ajedrez*) pawn
[3] (*Mil, Hist*) infantryman, foot-soldier
[4] (= *peonza*) spinning top
[5] (*Mec*) spindle, shaft

peonada SF [1] (*Agr*) day's stint, day's shift
[2] (= *trabajadores*) gang of labourers, gang of laborers (*EEUU*)

peonaje SM (= *trabajadores*) group of labourers, group of laborers (*EEUU*); (*Taur*) assistants *pl*

peonar ▸conjug 1a◂ VI (*Cono Sur*) to work as a labourer

peoneta SM (*Chile Aut*) lorry driver's mate, truck driver's mate (*EEUU*)

peonía SF peony

peonza SF [1] (= *trompo*) (spinning) top
[2] (*) (= *persona*) busy bee*; **ser una ~** to be always on the go
[3] ✦*MODISMO* **ir a ~‡** to go on foot, hoof it*

peor Ⓐ ADJ [1] (*comparativo de malo*) [*producto, resultado, situación*] worse; [*oferta*] lower; [*calidad*] poorer; **la película era ~ de lo que yo pensaba** the film was worse than I thought; **su situación es ~ que la nuestra** their situation is worse than ours; **un vino de**

➤ LENGUA Y USO: **pensar A1** 33.1, 33.2, 53.6 **A3** 53.6 **A4** 35.1 **B1** 35.2

~ calidad an inferior wine; **ir a ~** to get worse; **la situación fue a ~** the situation got worse; **y lo que es ~** and what's worse; **~ es nada** (*LAm*) it's better than nothing; *ver tb* **tanto C2**
[2] (*superlativo de malo*) worst; **no se lo deseo ni a mi ~ enemigo** I wouldn't wish it on my worst enemy; **es el ~ de la clase** he is the worst in the class; **en el ~ de los casos** if the worst comes to the worst; **lo ~**: **lo ~ de todo es que no podemos hacer nada** the worst thing is that there is nothing we can do; **ponerse en lo ~** to imagine the worst; **la ~ parte** the worst part; **ya hemos hecho la ~ parte del trabajo** we have already done the worst part of the job; **te ha tocado la ~ parte en este asunto** you came off worst in this business
Ⓑ ADV [1] (*comparativo de mal*) worse; **ahora veo mucho ~** my sight is much worse now; **escribo cada vez ~** my handwriting is getting worse and worse; **hoy hemos jugado ~ que nunca** we played worse than ever today; **si no le gusta, ~ para él** if he doesn't like it, that's his loss *o* that's just too bad; *ver tb* **mal A6, mejor B1**
[2] (*superlativo de mal*) worst; **¿quién es el que lo hace ~ de los tres?** who does it worst out of the three?, which of the three does it worst?; **ésta es la carta ~ redactada que he leído nunca** this is the most badly *o* the worst written letter I've ever read

peoría SF worsening, deterioration

Pepa SF (*forma familiar*) *de* **Josefa, María José**; ✦*MODISMO* **¡viva la ~!** (*por despreocupación*) and to hell with everybody else!*; (*por regocijo*) jolly good!*

pepa SF [1] (*LAm*) (= *semilla*) [*de uva, tomate*] pip; [*de melocotón, dátil*] stone; ✦*MODISMO* **aflojar la ~*** to spill the beans*
[2] (*LAm*) (= *canica*) marble
[3] (*Andes**) (= *mentira*) lie
[4] (*Andes*) (= *pillo*) rogue

pepazo SM [1] (*LAm*) (= *tiro*) shot, hit; (= *pedrada*) throw
[2] (*Andes**) (= *mentira*) lie

Pepe SM (*forma familiar*) *de* **José**; ✦*MODISMO* **ponerse como un ~*** to have a great time*

pepe SM [1] (*Andes, Caribe**) (= *petimetre*) dandy
[2] (*CAm*) (= *biberón*) feeding bottle

pepenado/a SM/F (*CAm, Méx*) (= *huérfano*) orphan; (= *expósito*) foundling

pepenador(a) SM/F (*Méx*) scavenger (*on rubbish tip*)

pepenar ▸conjug 1a◂ Ⓐ VT [1] (*CAm, Méx*) (= *recoger*) to pick up; (*en la basura*) to search through; (= *escoger*) to choose; (= *obtener*) to get, obtain
[2] (*Méx*) (= *agarrar*) to grab hold of; (= *registrar*) to pick through, poke about in; (= *robar*) to steal
[3] (*Méx*) [+ *huérfano*] to take in, bring up
Ⓑ VI (*CAm, Méx*) to search through rubbish tips

pepián SM (*Andes, CAm, Méx*) (= *salsa*) *thick chili sauce*; (= *guiso*) *meat cooked in thick chili sauce*

pepinazo* SM [1] (= *explosión*) bang
[2] (*Ftbl*) screamer*, scorcher*
[3] (= *accidente*) smash

pepinillo SM gherkin

pepino SM [1] (*Bot*) cucumber; ✦*MODISMOS* **me importa un ~** ◊ **no se me da un ~*** I don't care two hoots*, I don't give a damn*
[2] (‡) (= *cabeza*) nut*, bonce*, noggin (*EEUU**)
[3] (**) (= *pene*) prick**

Pepita SF (*forma familiar*) *de* **Josefa**

pepita SF [1] (*Vet*) pip; ✦*MODISMO* **no tener ~ en la lengua** to be outspoken, not to mince one's words
[2] (*Bot*) pip
[3] (*Min*) nugget

Pepito SM (*forma familiar*) *de* **José**

pepito SM [1] (*Culin*) meat sandwich
[2] (*Andes, CAm, Caribe**) (= *petimetre*) dandy

pepitoria SF [1] (*Esp Culin*) **pollo en ~** chicken fricassée
[2] (*fig*) hotchpotch, hodgepodge (*EEUU*)
[3] (*CAm*) (= *semillas*) dried pumpkin seeds *pl*

pepón‡ ADJ (*Andes*) good-looking, dishy*

pepona SF large cardboard doll

pepsina SF pepsin

péptico ADJ peptic

peptona SF peptone

peque* SMF kid*, child

pequeñajo/a* Ⓐ ADJ little, tiny
Ⓑ SM/F little rascal, little devil

pequeñez SF [1] [*de tamaño*] smallness, small size; [*de altura*] shortness
[2] [*de miras*] pettiness, small-mindedness
[3] (= *nada*) trifle, trivial thing; **preocuparse por pequeñeces** to worry about trifles

pequeñín/ina Ⓐ ADJ tiny, little
Ⓑ SM/F little one

pequeño/a Ⓐ ADJ small, little; [*cifra*] small, low; (= *bajo*) short; **el hermano ~** the youngest brother; **un niño ~** a small child; **cuando era ~** ◊ **de ~** when I was a child, when I was little; **un castillo en ~** a miniature castle; **un negocio en ~** a small-scale business
Ⓑ SM/F child; **los ~s** the children, the little ones; **soy el ~** I'm the youngest

pequeñoburgués/esa Ⓐ ADJ petit bourgeois
Ⓑ SM/F petit bourgeois/petite bourgeoise

pequero* SM (*Cono Sur*) cardsharp

pequinés/esa Ⓐ ADJ of/from Peking
Ⓑ SM/F native/inhabitant of Peking; **los pequineses** the people of Peking
Ⓒ SM (= *perro*) Pekinese, Pekingese

pera[1] SF [1] (*Bot*) pear; ✦*MODISMOS* **eso es pedir ~s al olmo** that's asking the impossible; **esperar a ver de qué lado caen las ~s** to wait and see which way the cat will jump; **hacerse una ~**** to wank**; **partir ~s con algn** to fall out with sb; **poner a algn las ~s a cuarto** to tell sb a few home truths; **ser la ~*** to be the limit; **tirarse la ~** (*Andes**) to play truant, play hooky (*EEUU*); **tocarse la ~‡** to sit on one's backside (doing nothing)
[2] (= *barba*) goatee; (*Chile**) (= *barbilla*) chin
[3] [*de atomizador, bocina*] bulb
[4] (*Elec*) (= *bombilla*) bulb; (= *interruptor*) switch
[5] (‡) (= *cabeza*) nut*, bonce*, noggin (*EEUU**)
[6] **peras*** (= *pechos*) tits**
[7] (*) (= *empleo*) cushy job*
[8] (*LAm Dep*) punchball

pera[2]* ADJ INV (= *pijo*) posh*; **un barrio ~** a posh area; **fuimos a un restaurante muy ~** we went to a really swish *o* posh restaurant*; **niño** *o* **pollo ~** spoiled upper-class brat

pera[3]‡ SM fence*, receiver (of stolen goods)

peral SM pear tree

peraltado Ⓐ ADJ (*Arquit*) canted, sloping; [*curva, carretera*] banked, cambered
Ⓑ SM = **peralte**

peraltar ▸conjug 1a◂ VT [+ *curva, carretera*] to bank, camber

peralte SM (*Arquit*) cant, slope; [*de curva, carretera*] banking, camber

perca SF perch

percal SM, **percala** SF (*Andes, Méx*) [1] (= *tejido*) percale; ✦*MODISMO* **conocer el ~*** to know what the score is*
[2] (‡) (= *dinero*) dough‡, cash

percán SM (*Chile*) mould, mold (*EEUU*), mildew

percance SM [1] (*gen*) misfortune, mishap; (= *accidente*) accident; (*en plan*) setback, hitch; **sufrir** *o* **tener un ~** to suffer a mishap
[2] (*Fin*) perquisite, perk*

percanque SM (*Cono Sur*) mould, mold (*EEUU*), mildew

per cápita ADV per capita

percatarse ▸conjug 1a◂ VPR **~ de** (= *observar*) to notice; (= *comprender*) to realize; (= *hacer caso de*) to heed; (= *guardarse de*) to guard against

percebe SM [1] (*Zool*) barnacle
[2] (*) (= *tonto*) idiot, twit*

percentil SM percentile

percepción SF [1] (*facultad*) perception ► **percepción extrasensorial** extrasensory perception
[2] (= *idea*) perception, idea
[3] (*Com, Fin*) collection; (= *recibo*) receipt

perceptible ADJ [1] (= *visible*) perceptible, noticeable
[2] (*Com, Fin*) payable, receivable

perceptiblemente ADV perceptibly, noticeably

perceptivo ADJ perceptive

perceptor(a) SM/F (*gen*) recipient; [*de impuestos*] collector, receiver ► **perceptor(a) de subsidio de desempleo** *person who draws unemployment benefit*

percha SF [1] (*para ropa*) (clothes) hanger; (= *colgador*) clothes rack; (*para sombreros*) hat stand; **vestido de ~** ready-made dress, off-the-peg dress
[2] (*Téc*) rack ► **percha de herramientas** toolrack
[3] (*para pájaros*) perch
[4] (= *tronco*) pole
[5] (*) (= *tipo*) build, physique; [*de mujer*] figure
[6] (*Andes*) (= *ostentación*) showiness; **tener ~** (*Cono Sur*) to be smart
[7] (*Andes*) (= *ropa*) new clothes *pl*, smart clothing; (*Caribe*) (= *chaqueta*) jacket; (= *traje*) suit
[8] (*Cono Sur*) (= *montón*) pile
[9] (*Méx**) (= *grupo*) gang

perchero SM [*de pared*] clothes rack; [*de pie*] coat stand

perchudo ADJ (*Andes*) smart, elegant

percibir ▸conjug 3a◂ VT [1] (= *notar*) to perceive, notice; (= *ver*) to see, observe; [+ *peligro*] to sense, scent; **~ que …** to perceive that …, observe that …
[2] [+ *sueldo, subsidio*] to draw, receive

percollar ▸conjug 1a◂ VT (*Andes*) to monopolize

percuchante SM (*Andes*) fool

percudir ▸conjug 3a◂ VT (= *deslustrar*) to tarnish, dull; [+ *ropa*] to dirty, mess up; [+ *cutis*] to spoil

percusión SF percussion; **instrumento de ~** percussion instrument

percusionar ▸conjug 1a◂ VT to hit, strike

percusionista SMF percussionist

percusor SM (*Téc*) hammer; [*de arma*] firing pin

percutir ▸conjug 3a◂ VT to strike, tap

percutor SM = **percusor**

perdedor(a) Ⓐ ADJ [1] [*baza, equipo*] losing
[2] (= *olvidadizo*) forgetful, given to losing things
Ⓑ SM/F loser; **buen ~** good loser

perder ▸conjug 2g◂ Ⓐ VT [1] [+ *objeto, dinero, peso*] to lose; **he perdido el monedero** I've lost my purse; **a los seis años perdió a su padre** she lost her father when she was six; **he perdido cinco kilos** I've lost five kilos; **había perdido mucha sangre** she had lost a lot of blood; **ha perdido mucho dinero en la bolsa** she has lost a lot of money on the stock market; **no tienes nada que ~** you have nothing to lose; **~ el conocimiento** to lose consciousness; **~ la costumbre** to get out of the habit; **~ algo de vista** to lose sight of sth; **nunca pierde de vista el fin que persigue** he never loses sight of his goal; **no lo pierdas de vista** don't let him out of your sight; **conviene no ~ de vista que …** we mustn't forget that …, we mustn't lose sight of the fact that …
[2] [+ *tiempo*] to waste; **¡me estás haciendo ~ el tiempo!** you're wasting my time!; **sin ~ un momento** without wasting a moment
[3] [+ *aire, aceite*] to leak; **el vehículo pierde aceite** the car is leaking oil, the car has an oil leak; **la pelota perdió aire** the ball went flat
[4] (= *no coger*) [+ *tren, avión*] to miss; [+ *oportunidad*] to miss, lose; **no pierde detalle** he doesn't miss a thing
[5] (= *destruir*) to ruin; **ese vicio le ~á** that vice will ruin him, that vice will be his ruin; **ese error le perdió** that mistake was his undoing; **lo que le pierde es …** where he comes unstuck is …
[6] (*Jur*) to lose, forfeit
Ⓑ VI [1] (*en competición, disputa*) to lose; **el equipo perdió por 5-2** the team lost 5-2; **tienen** *o* **llevan todas las de ~** they look certain to lose; **saber ~** to be a good loser; **salir perdiendo**: **salí perdiendo en el negocio** I lost out on the deal; **salí perdiendo en la discusión** I came off worst in the argument
[2] (= *empeorar*) **era un buen cantante, pero ha perdido mucho** he was a good singer, but he's gone downhill; **era muy guapo, pero ha perdido bastante** he isn't nearly as good-looking as he used to be; **ha perdido mucho en mi estimación** he has gone down a lot in my estimation
[3] [*tela*] to fade
[4] **echar a ~** [+ *comida, sorpresa*] to ruin, spoil; [+ *oportunidad*] to waste; **echarse a ~** [*comida*] to go off; [*sorpresa*] to be ruined, be spoiled
Ⓒ **perderse** VPR [1] [*persona*] to get lost; **tenía miedo de ~me** I was afraid of getting lost *o* losing my way; **se perdieron en el bosque** they got lost in the wood; **se perdió en un mar de contradicciones** he got lost in a mass of contradictions; **¡piérdete!*** get lost!*
[2] [*objeto*] **se me han perdido las llaves** I've lost my keys; **¿qué se les ha perdido en Alemania?** what business have they in Germany?
[3] [+ *programa, fiesta*] to miss; **~se algo interesante** to miss something interesting; **¡no te lo pierdas!** don't miss it!; **no se pierde ni una** she doesn't miss a thing
[4] (= *desaparecer*) to disappear; **el tren se perdió en la niebla** the train disappeared into the fog; **el arroyo se pierde en la roca** the stream disappears into the rock
[5] (= *desperdiciarse*) to be wasted, go to waste; **se pierde mucho tiempo** a lot of time is wasted; **se pierden muchos talentos naturales** a lot of natural talent goes to waste; **nada se pierde con intentar** there's no harm in trying
[6] (= *arruinarse*) [*persona*] to lose one's way; [*cosecha*] to be ruined, get spoiled; **se perdió por el juego** gambling was his ruin *o* undoing; **con la lluvia se ha perdido la cosecha** the rain has ruined the crops
[7] **~se por algo/algn** to be mad about sth/sb; **~se por hacer algo** to be dying to do sth, long to do sth
[8] (*LAm*) (= *prostituirse*) to go on the streets

perdición SF (*Rel*) perdition; (*fig*) undoing, ruin; **fue su ~** it was his undoing; **será mi ~** it will be the ruin of me

perdida SF loose woman*; *ver tb* **perdido**

pérdida SF (*gen*) loss; (*Téc*) leakage, wastage; (*Jur*) forfeiture, loss; **~s** (*Fin, Mil etc*) losses; **es una ~ de tiempo** it's a waste of time; **¡no tiene ~!** you can't miss it!; **vender algo con ~** to sell sth at a loss; **a ~ de vista** as far as the eye can see; **entrar en ~** (*Aer*) to stall ► **pérdida contable** (*Com*) book loss ► **pérdida de conocimiento** loss of consciousness ► **pérdida efectiva** actual loss; *ver tb* **perdido**

perdidamente ADV **~ enamorado** hopelessly in love

perdidizo ADJ **hacer algo ~** to hide sth away, deliberately lose sth; **hacerse el ~** (*en juego*) to lose deliberately; (= *irse*) to make o.s. scarce, slip away

perdido/a Ⓐ ADJ [1] (= *extraviado*) lost; [*bala*] stray; **estaban ~s y tuvieron que preguntar el camino** they were lost and had to ask the way; **paraíso ~** paradise lost; **objetos ~s** lost property *sing*; **dar algo por ~** to give sth up for lost; **eso es tiempo ~** that's a waste of time; *ver tb* **rato 3**, **bala A1**
[2] (= *aislado*) remote, isolated; **un pueblo ~ en las montañas** a remote *o* isolated village in the mountains
[3] (= *sin remedio*) **estaba borracho ~** he was totally *o* dead* drunk; **está loco ~** he's raving mad; **es tonto ~** he's a complete idiot; **es un caso ~** he's a hopeless case; **¡estamos ~s!** we're done for!; ✦**MODISMO de ~s, al río** in for a penny, in for a pound
[4] (= *enamorado*) **estar ~ por algn** to be mad *o* crazy about sb
[5] (*) (= *sucio*) **ponerlo todo ~ de barro** to get everything covered in mud, get mud everywhere; **te has puesto ~ el pantalón** you've ruined your trousers
[6] (*LAm*) (= *vago*) idle; (= *pobre*) down and out
Ⓑ SM/F libertine; *ver tb* **perdida**

perdidoso ADJ [1] (= *que pierde*) losing
[2] (= *que se pierde fácilmente*) easily lost, easily mislaid

perdigar ▸conjug 1h◂ VT [+ *perdiz*] to singe

perdigón SM [1] (*Orn*) young partridge
[2] (= *bala*) pellet; **perdigones** shot *sing*, pellets ► **perdigón zorrero** buckshot

perdigonada SF [1] (= *disparo*) shot
[2] (= *herida*) shotgun wound

perdigonazo SM [1] (= *impacto*) blast of shot
[2] = **perdigonada 2**

perdiguero Ⓐ ADJ **perro ~** gundog
Ⓑ SM gundog

perdis* SM INV rake

perdiz SF partridge; ✦**MODISMO marear la ~** to mess about* ► **perdiz blanca**, **perdiz nival** ptarmigan

perdón SM [1] (= *acción*) [1·1] (*Rel*) forgiveness; **el ~ de los pecados** the forgiveness of sins
[1·2] (*Jur*) pardon; **el ~ del juez** the judge's pardon
[1·3] (*Econ*) write-off; **el ~ de la deuda externa** the write-off of the foreign debt
[1·4] (*locuciones*) **no cabe ~** it is inexcusable; **con ~** if you don't mind me saying so; **son todos unos imbéciles, con ~** they're all idiots, if you don't mind me saying so; **con ~ de la expresión** pardon my language, if you'll pardon the expression; **pedir ~ (a algn)** (*por algo leve*) to apologize (to sb); (*por algo grave*) to ask (sb's) forgiveness; **os pido ~ por el retraso** I'm sorry *o* I apologize for the delay; **le pido mil perdones por lo que le dije** I'm terribly sorry for what I said to you; **pido ~ a Dios** I ask God to forgive me, I ask God for forgiveness; **con ~ de los presentes** (= *con permiso*) if you'll permit me; (= *excepto*) present company excepted; ✦**MODISMO no tener ~**: **no tenéis ~ por lo que hicisteis** what you did was unforgivable, there's no excuse for what you did; **hace siglos que no voy al cine, no tengo ~ de Dios** (*hum*) I haven't been to the cinema for ages, I should be ashamed of myself (*hum*)
[2] (*independiente*) [2·1] **¡perdón!** (*disculpándose*) sorry!; (*tras eructar, toser*) excuse me!, pardon me!; (*llamando la atención*) excuse me!, pardon me! (*EEUU*); **~, ¿te ha dolido?** sorry, did I hurt you?; **~ ¿me puede indicar dónde está la estación?** excuse me, can you tell me where the station is?
[2·2] **¿perdón?** (*cuando no se ha entendido algo*) sorry?, pardon?, pardon me? (*EEUU*)

perdonable ADJ [*error, pecado*] forgivable, pardonable

perdonador ADJ forgiving

perdonar ▸conjug 1a◂ Ⓐ VT [1] (= *disculpar*) [1·1] [+ *falta, pecado*] to forgive; **es algo que no puedo ~ fácilmente** it's something I can't easily forgive; **perdona nuestras ofensas** (*Rel*) forgive us our trespasses; **perdona que te interrumpa** (I'm) sorry to interrupt; **perdona que te diga** if you don't mind me saying (so)
[1·2] **~ a algn** to forgive sb; **¿me perdonas?** do you forgive me?; **que Dios me perdone si me equivoco, pero …** may God forgive me if I'm wrong, but …
[2] (= *excusar*) [2·1] [+ *curiosidad, ignorancia*] to

pardon, excuse; **perdone mi ignorancia, pero ...** pardon *o* excuse my ignorance, but ...; **"perdonen las molestias"** "we apologize for any inconvenience"; **las plantas no perdonan la falta de luz** plants don't do well without light

2·2 **~ una obligación/una deuda a algn** to let sb off an obligation/a debt; **te perdono los 50 euros que me debes** I'll let you off the 50 euros you owe me; **le han perdonado la pena** he's been pardoned; **~ la vida a algn** to spare sb's life; (*Dep*) to let sb off the hook; **va con aires de ir perdonándole la vida a todo el mundo** he acts as if the world owes him a living

2·3 (*Econ*) [+ *deuda*] to write off

3 (= *perder*) [+ *detalle, ocasión*] to miss; **no perdona ni una sola ocasión de lucirse** he won't miss a single chance of showing off; ✦*MODISMO* **no perdona ni una*** he doesn't miss a trick*

Ⓑ VI (= *disculpar*) **¿perdona? ◊ ¿perdone?** (*cuando no se ha entendido algo*) sorry?, pardon?, pardon me? (*EEUU*); **¡perdona! ◊ ¡perdone!** (= *disculpándose*) (I'm) sorry!; (= *llamando la atención*) excuse me!, pardon me!; **¡ay, perdona, no te había visto!** oh, I'm sorry, I didn't see you there!; **perdone, ¿me podría decir el precio de este traje?** excuse me, could you tell me how much this suit is?; **perdona, pero yo iba primero** excuse me, but I was first; **los años no perdonan** time shows no mercy; **~ por algo**: **perdona por la interrupción, pero necesito hablar contigo** I'm sorry to interrupt, but I need to talk to you; **perdona por haberte ofendido** please forgive me if I have offended you, I'm sorry to have offended you

perdonavidas SMF INV 1 (= *matón*) bully, thug

2 (= *persona suficiente*) **es un ~** he's Mister High and Mighty

perdulario Ⓐ ADJ 1 (= *olvidadizo*) forgetful

2 (= *descuidado*) careless, sloppy

3 (= *vicioso*) dissolute

Ⓑ SM rake

perdurabilidad SF durability

perdurable ADJ (= *duradero*) lasting, abiding; (= *perpetuo*) everlasting

perdurar ▸conjug 1a◂ VI (= *durar*) to last, endure; (= *subsistir*) to remain, still exist

perecedero ADJ (*Com*) perishable; [*vida*] transitory; [*persona*] mortal; **géneros no ~s** non-perishable goods

perecer ▸conjug 2d◂ Ⓐ VI 1 [*persona*] to die, perish (*frm*); **~ ahogado** (*en agua*) to drown; (*por falta de oxígeno*) to suffocate

2 [*objeto*] to shatter

Ⓑ **perecerse** VPR (†) 1 **~se de risa** to die laughing; **~se de envidia** to be dying of jealousy

2 **~se por algo** to long for sth, be dying for sth; **~se por una mujer** to be crazy about a woman; **se perece por los calamares** he's crazy about squid; **~se por** + *INFIN* to long to + *infin*, be dying to + *infin*

peregrinación SF 1 (*Rel*) pilgrimage; **ir en ~** to make a pilgrimage, go on a pilgrimage (**a** to)

2 (= *viajes*) long tour, travels *pl*; (*hum*) peregrination

peregrinar ▸conjug 1a◂ VI 1 (*Rel*) to go on a pilgrimage, make a pilgrimage (**a** to)

2 (= *ir*) to go to and fro; (= *viajar*) to travel extensively

peregrino/a Ⓐ ADJ 1 (= *que viaja*) wandering, travelling, traveling (*EEUU*); (*Orn*) migratory

2 (= *exótico*) exotic; (= *extraño*) strange, odd; (= *singular*) rare, extraordinary; **ideas peregrinas** harebrained ideas

3 [*costumbre, planta*] alien, newly-introduced

Ⓑ SM/F pilgrim

perejil SM 1 (*Bot*) parsley

2 **perejiles** (*) (*Cos*) buttons and bows, trimmings; (= *títulos*) extra titles, handles (to one's name)*

3 ✦*MODISMO* **andar como ~** (*Cono Sur*) to be shabbily dressed

perendengue SM 1 (= *adorno*) trinket, cheap ornament

2 **perendengues*** (= *pegas*) snags, problems; **el problema tiene sus ~s** the question has its tricky points; **un proyecto de muchos ~s** a plan with a lot of snags

3 **perendengues*** (= *categoría*) (high) standing *sing*, importance *sing*; (= *valor*) spirit *sing*, guts

perengano/a SM/F somebody or other, someone or other

perenne ADJ (*gen*) perennial, constant; (*Bot*) perennial; **de hoja ~** evergreen

perennemente ADV constantly

perennidad SF (*gen*) perennial nature; (= *perpetuidad*) perpetuity

perentoriamente ADV (= *urgentemente*) urgently; (= *imperiosamente*) peremptorily

perentorio ADJ (= *urgente*) urgent; (= *imperioso*) peremptory; **plazo ~** final deadline

pereque* SM (*LAm*) nuisance, bore

perestroika SF perestroika

pereza SF laziness; **me da ~ ducharme** I can't be bothered to have a shower; **tener ~** to feel lazy; **¡qué ~!*** what a drag!*; **¡qué ~, tener que limpiar la casa!** what a drag, having to clean the house!*

perezosa SF (*Andes, Cono Sur*) deckchair

perezosamente ADV lazily

perezoso/a Ⓐ ADJ lazy

Ⓑ SM/F (= *vago*) idler, lazybones*

Ⓒ SM 1 (*Zool*) sloth

2 (*Caribe, Méx*) (= *imperdible*) safety pin

perfección SF 1 (= *cualidad*) perfection; **a la ~** to perfection

2 (= *acto*) completion

perfeccionamiento SM (= *proceso*) perfection; (= *mejora*) improvement

perfeccionar ▸conjug 1a◂ VT 1 (*gen*) to perfect; (= *mejorar*) to improve

2 (= *acabar*) to complete, finish

perfeccionismo SM perfectionism

perfeccionista SMF perfectionist

perfectamente ADV perfectly; **te entiendo ~** I perfectly understand what you mean, I know exactly what you mean; **—¿cómo está tu hermano? —¡perfectamente!** "how's your brother?" — "he's doing just fine"

perfectibilidad SF perfectibility

perfectible ADJ perfectible

▼ **perfecto** Ⓐ ADJ 1 (= *ideal*) perfect; **¡perfecto!** fine!; **me parece ~ que lo hagan** I think it quite right that they should do it

2 (= *completo*) complete; **un ~ imbécil** a complete idiot; **era un ~ desconocido** he was a complete *o* total stranger

Ⓑ SM (*Ling*) perfect, perfect tense

pérfidamente ADV perfidiously, treacherously

perfidia SF perfidy, treachery

pérfido ADJ perfidious, treacherous

perfil SM 1 (*gen*) profile (*tb fig*); (= *contorno*) silhouette, outline; (*Geol, Arquit*) section, cross section; (*Fot*) side view; **de ~** in profile, from the side; **ponerse de ~** to stand side on ► **perfil aerodinámico** streamlining ► **perfil bajo**: **neumáticos de ~ bajo** low-profile tyres *o* (*EEUU*) tires

2 (*profesional*) profile ► **perfil del cliente** (*Com*) customer profile ► **perfil psicológico** psychological profile

3 **perfiles** (= *rasgos*) features, characteristics; (= *cortesías*) social courtesies; (= *retoques*) finishing touches

perfilado ADJ 1 (*gen*) well-shaped, well-finished; [*rostro*] long; [*nariz*] well-formed, shapely

2 (*Aer*) streamlined

perfilador SM ► **perfilador de cejas** eyebrow pencil ► **perfilador de labios** lip-liner, lip pencil ► **perfilador de ojos** eye-liner

perfilar ▸conjug 1a◂ Ⓐ VT 1 (*gen*) to outline; (*fig*) to shape; **son los lectores los que perfilan los periódicos** it is the readers who shape their newspapers

2 (*Aer*) to streamline

3 (= *rematar*) to put the finishing touches to, round off

Ⓑ **perfilarse** VPR 1 [*modelo*] to show one's profile, stand sideways on; [*edificio*] to be silhouetted; (*Taur*) to prepare for the kill (**en** against)

2 (*fig*) to take shape; **el proyecto se va perfilando** the project is taking shape

3 (*LAm*) (= *adelgazar*) to slim, get slim

4 (*Cono Sur Dep*) to dribble and shoot

perforación SF 1 (= *orificio*) (*Tip*) perforation; (*Cine, Fot*) sprocket; (*Téc*) punch-hole; (*Min*) bore hole

2 (= *proceso*) (*gen*) piercing, perforation; (*Min*) drilling, boring; (*Tip*) punching, perforating

perforado Ⓐ ADJ [*papel*] holed; [*labios*] pierced

Ⓑ SM hole-punching

perforadora SF 1 (*Tip*) punch ► **perforadora de tarjetas** card punch

2 (*Téc*) drill ► **perforadora neumática** pneumatic drill

perforar ▸conjug 1a◂ Ⓐ VT (*gen*) to perforate, pierce; (*Min*) to drill, bore; [+ *tarjeta*] to punch, punch a hole in; [+ *ficha*] to punch; [+ *pozo*] to sink; (= *pinchar*) to puncture (*tb Med*)

Ⓑ VI (*Min*) to drill, bore

Ⓒ **perforarse** VPR [*úlcera*] to get perforated

perforista SMF (*Inform*) card puncher

performance [per'formans] SF performance

perfumado ADJ scented, perfumed

perfumador SM perfume spray

perfumar ▸conjug 1a◂ VT to perfume, scent

perfume SM perfume, scent

perfumería SF perfumery, perfume shop

perfumista Ⓐ ADJ [*empresa*] perfumery

Ⓑ SMF perfumer

➤ LENGUA Y USO: perfecto A1 40.2

pergamino SM parchment; **una familia de muchos ~s** a very blue-blooded family, a family of very noble lineage; **los ~s del mar Muerto** the Dead Sea scrolls

pergenio* SM (*Cono Sur hum*) bright boy, clever kid*

pergeñar ▸conjug 1a◂ VT 1 (= *tramar*) [+ *plan*] to sketch; [+ *asesinato*] to plot; [+ *texto*] to draft
2 (*) (= *arreglar*) [+ *cita*] to fix up, arrange
3 (*Cono Sur**) [+ *persona*] to eye from head to toe

pergeño SM aspect, appearance

pérgola SF pergola

peri... PREF peri...

perica SF 1 (*Andes, CAm*) (= *navaja*) razor, knife; (= *machete*) machete; (= *espada*) short sword
2 (= *borrachera*) (*Andes, CAm**) **agarrar una ~ to get sloshed***, get trashed (*EEUU*‡)
3 (‡) (= *chica*) bird‡, chick (*EEUU*‡); (= *puta*) tart‡, slut‡, whore
4 (‡) (= *droga*) snow‡, cocaine

pericia SF (= *habilidad*) skill; (= *experiencia*) expertise

pericial ADJ expert; **tasación ~** expert valuation; **testigo ~** expert witness

periclitar ▸conjug 1a◂ VI (*frm*) 1 (= *declinar*) to decay, decline; (= *quedar anticuado*) to become outmoded; **esos quedan ya periclitados** those are out of date now
2 (= *peligrar*) to be in danger

Perico SM (*forma familiar*) de **Pedro**; ✦*MODISMOS* **~ el de los palotes** (*Esp*) Mister So-and-So; **ser ~ entre ellas** to be a ladies' man

perico SM 1 (*Orn*) parakeet
2 (*Bot*) giant asparagus
3 (‡) (= *droga*) snow‡, cocaine
4 (*Col*) (= *café*) white coffee
5 (= *peluca*) wig, toupé
6 (*) (= *orinal*) chamberpot
7 (‡) (= *puta*) tart*, slut‡
8 **(huevos) ~s** (*Andes, Caribe*) *scrambled eggs with fried onions*

pericote SM (*Andes, Cono Sur*) 1 (= *ratón* large rat
2 (*) (= *niño*) kid*, nipper*

periferia SF 1 (*Mat*) periphery; (*Geog*) [*de población*] outskirts *pl*; **los que viven en la ~ social** those who live on the fringes of society
2 (*Inform*) peripherals *pl*

periférico Ⓐ ADJ peripheral; **barrio ~** outlying district; **unidad periférica** peripheral (unit); **carretera periférica** ring-road
Ⓑ SM 1 **periféricos** (*Inform*) peripherals
2 (*Méx Aut*) ring road, beltway (*EEUU*)

perifollo SM 1 (*Bot*) chervil
2 **perifollos** (= *adornos*) buttons and bows, trimmings

perífrasis SF INV periphrasis

perifrástico ADJ periphrastic

perilla SF 1 (= *barba*) goatee; ✦*MODISMO* **venir de ~(s)** to be more than welcome ▸ **perilla de la oreja** ear lobe
2 (= *joya*) pear-shaped ornament, drop
3 (*Elec*) switch ▸ **perilla del timbre** bellpush
4 (*Méx*) (= *manija*) handle
5 (= *tirador*) doorknob

perillán†* SM rogue, rascal; **¡perillán!** (*a un niño*) you little rascal!

perimetral ADJ perimeter *antes de s*; **vallado ~** perimeter fence

perímetro SM perimeter

perinatal ADJ perinatal

perinola Ⓐ SF teetotum
Ⓑ ADV **de ~** (*Caribe*) utterly, absolutely

periódicamente ADV periodically

periodicidad SF 1 [*de acción, evento*] regularity; [*de publicación*] frequency (*of publication*); **una revista de ~ mensual** a monthly magazine
2 (*Téc*) periodicity

periódico Ⓐ ADJ (*gen*) periodic(al); (*Mat*) recurrent
Ⓑ SM (= *diario*) newspaper, paper; (= *publicación periódica*) periodical ▸ **periódico de la tarde** evening newspaper, evening paper ▸ **periódico del domingo**, **periódico dominical** Sunday newspaper, Sunday paper ▸ **periódico mural** wall newspaper

periodicucho* SM (*pey*) rag*

periodismo SM journalism ▸ **periodismo amarillo** sensationalist journalism, ≈ tabloid journalism ▸ **periodismo deportivo** sports journalism ▸ **periodismo de investigación** investigative journalism ▸ **periodismo gráfico** photoreportage

periodista SMF journalist ▸ **periodista de radio** radio reporter ▸ **periodista de televisión** television reporter, TV reporter

periodístico ADJ journalistic; **estilo ~** journalistic style, journalese (*pey*); **el mundo ~** the newspaper world; **de interés ~** newsworthy

periodización SF periodization

periodo SM, **período** SM 1 [*de tiempo*] period ▸ **periodo contable** (*Com*) accounting period ▸ **período de incubación** incubation period
2 (= *menstruación*) period
3 (*Ling*) sentence, period

periodoncia SF periodontics *sing*, periodontology

peripatético ADJ peripatetic

peripecia SF 1 (= *incidente*) adventure, incident
2 (= *vicisitud*) vicissitude, sudden change

periplo SM (*gen*) (long) journey, tour; (*Náut*) (long) voyage; (*Hist*) periplus; (= *errabundeo*) wanderings *pl*; (*hum*) peregrination

peripuesto* ADJ (*gen*) dressed-up, smart; (*excesivamente*) overdressed; **tan ~** all dressed-up (to the nines)

periquear* ▸conjug 1a◂ (*Andes*) Ⓐ VI to get dressed up, get dolled up
Ⓑ **periquearse** VPR to get dressed up, get dolled up*

periquete SM **en un ~*** in a tick

periquito SM 1 (*Orn*) parakeet
2 (‡) (= *droga*) snow‡, cocaine

periscopio SM periscope

perista* SMF fence*, receiver of stolen goods

peristilo SM peristyle

perita[1]* ADJ = **pera**[2]

perita[2] SF ✦*MODISMO* **ser una ~ en dulce** to be gorgeous

peritaje SM 1 (= *informe*) specialist's report, expert's report; (= *trabajo*) expert work; (= *pericia*) expertise
2 (= *honorarios*) expert's fee
3 (= *estudios*) professional training

peritar ▸conjug 1a◂ VT to judge expertly, give an expert opinion on

perito/a Ⓐ ADJ (= *experto*) expert; (= *con experiencia*) experienced, seasoned; **ser ~ en** [+ *actividad*] to be expert at; [+ *materia*] to be an expert on
Ⓑ SM/F (*gen*) expert; (= *técnico*) technician; (= *ingeniero técnico*) technical engineer ▸ **perito/a agrónomo/a** agronomist ▸ **perito/a electricista** qualified electrician ▸ **perito/a en metales** metal expert, specialist in metals ▸ **perito/a testigo** (*Méx*) expert witness

peritoneo SM peritoneum

peritonitis SF INV peritonitis

perjudicar ▸conjug 1g◂ VT 1 (= *dañar*) to harm; **me perjudica que digan eso** their saying that is damaging to me
2 (†) (= *desfavorecer*) **ese sombrero la perjudica** that hat does not become her (*frm*), she doesn't look good in that hat
3 (*LAm*) (= *calumniar*) to malign, slander

perjudicial Ⓐ ADJ damaging, harmful, detrimental (*frm*)
Ⓑ SM (*Méx*‡) secret policeman

perjuicio SM damage, harm; **el escándalo ha reportado graves ~s al ministro** the scandal has done the minister serious damage *o* harm; **sufrir grandes ~s** to suffer great damage; **la crisis ha causado enormes ~s económicos** the crisis has caused severe financial damage; **en ~ de algo** to the detriment of sth, at the expense of sth; **han bajado los precios en ~ de la calidad** prices have fallen to the detriment *o* at the expense of quality; **redundar en ~ de algo** to be detrimental to sth, harm sth; **sin ~ de** (*Jur*) without prejudice to; **sin ~ de que luego me pueda arrepentir** even though I might change my mind later, in spite of the fact that I might change my mind later; *ver tb* **daño 1**

perjurar ▸conjug 1a◂ Ⓐ VI 1 (*Jur*) to perjure o.s., commit perjury
2 (= *jurar*) to swear a lot
Ⓑ **perjurarse** VPR to perjure o.s., commit perjury

perjurio SM perjury

perjuro/a Ⓐ ADJ perjured
Ⓑ SM/F perjurer

perla SF pearl; ✦*MODISMOS* **de ~s**: **me parece de ~s** it's absolutely splendid; **me viene de ~s** it suits me perfectly *o* just fine ▸ **perla cultivada** cultured pearl, cultivated pearl ▸ **perla negra** black pearl ▸ **perlas de imitación** imitation pearls

perlado ADJ pearly; **cebada perlada** pearl barley

perlático ADJ paralytic, palsied

perlesía SF paralysis, palsy

perlífero ADJ pearl-bearing; **ostra perlífera** pearl oyster

perlino ADJ pearly

permagel SM permafrost

permanecer ▸conjug 2d◂ VI 1 (*en un lugar*) to stay, remain; **¿cuánto tiempo vas a ~ en Toledo?** how long are you staying in Toledo?; **permaneció en cama durante toda la convalecencia** he stayed in bed throughout his

convalescence
2 (*en un estado*) to remain; **~ en silencio** to remain silent; **permanezcan sentados** (please) remain seated

permanencia SF 1 (= *continuidad*) **su ~ en el equipo depende de su rendimiento** his presence in the team will depend on his performance
2 (= *estancia*) stay; **escribió la novela durante su ~ en el sanatorio** he wrote the novel during his stay in the sanatorium ► **permanencia en filas** (period of) military service
3 **permanencias** [*de profesores*] obligatory administrative duties

permanente Ⓐ ADJ (*gen*) permanent; (= *constante*) constant; [*color*] fast; [*comisión*] standing
Ⓑ SF (*en pelo*) permanent wave, perm*; **hacerse una ~** to have one's hair permed

permanentemente ADV (= *perennemente*) permanently; (= *constantemente*) constantly

permanganato SM permanganate

permeabilidad SF permeability

permeable ADJ permeable (**a** to)

permisible ADJ permissible

permisionario/a SM/F (*LAm*) official agent, official agency, concessionaire

permisividad SF (*gen*) permissiveness; (*Fin*) liberal policies *pl*

permisivo ADJ permissive

permiso SM 1 (= *autorización*) permission; **solicitó ~ para abandonar la reunión** he asked for permission to leave the meeting; **¡permiso!** (*para pasar*) excuse me!; **con ~** (*pidiendo ver algo*) if I may; (*queriendo entrar, pasar*) (*esp LAm*) excuse me; **con ~ de ustedes me voy** excuse me but I must go; **con su ~, ¿se puede?** excuse me, may I come in?; **dar ~** to give permission; **no me dieron ~ para salir del cuartel** they didn't give me permission to leave the barracks; **¿me da ~ para salir hoy un poco antes?** will you let me leave a little earlier today?, could I leave a little earlier today?; **tener ~ para hacer algo** to have permission to do sth
2 (= *documento*) permit, licence, license (*EEUU*) ► **permiso de armas** gun licence, firearms certificate ► **permiso de circulación** registration document ► **permiso de conducción** (*Esp*), **permiso de conducir** (*Esp*) driving licence, driver's license (*EEUU*) ► **permiso de entrada** entry permit ► **permiso de exportación** export licence ► **permiso de importación** import licence ► **permiso de obras** planning permission, building permit ► **permiso de residencia** residence permit ► **permiso de salida** exit permit ► **permiso de trabajo** work permit, green card (*EEUU*)
3 (*para no trabajar*) leave; **ha pedido unos días de ~** he has asked for a few days' leave; **estar de ~** to be on leave ► **permiso por maternidad** maternity leave ► **permiso por paternidad** paternity leave

permitir ▸conjug 3a◂ Ⓐ VT 1 (= *autorizar*) 1·1 [+ *entrada, movimiento*] to allow, permit (*más frm*); **no permiten la entrada a menores de 18 años** under-18s are not allowed in; **—no puedo abrir la puerta —permítame** "I can't open the door" — "allow me"; **"no está permitido el uso de teléfonos móviles"** "the use of mobile phones is not permitted"; **si se me permite la expresión** *o* **la palabra** if you'll pardon the expression; **~ que**: **no le permitas que te hable así** don't allow her to talk to you like that; **permítame que la ayude, señora** please allow me to help you, madam
1·2 (*en preguntas*) **¿me permite?** (*al entrar*) may I (come in)?; (*al pasar al lado de algn*) excuse me, please; (*al ayudar a algn*) may I (help you)?; **¿me permite su pasaporte, por favor?** may I see your passport please?; **¿me permite que le diga una cosa?** may I say something to you?
2 (= *hacer posible*) to allow, permit (*más frm*); **las nuevas tecnologías ~án una mayor producción anual** the new technologies will allow *o* (*más frm*) permit a higher annual production; **este tejido permite el paso del aire** this material allows the air through; **si el tiempo lo permite** weather permitting; **~ (a algn) hacer algo** to allow (sb) to do sth; **la televisión nos permite llegar a más público** television lets us reach *o* allows us to reach a wider audience; **todos los datos permiten hablar de una epidemia** all the data points to *o* indicates an epidemic; **~ que** + SUBJUN to allow + *infin*; **un marco legal que permita que una persona decida libremente** a legal framework to allow people to choose freely; **el buen tiempo permitió que se celebrase el concierto al aire libre** the good weather allowed us to hold the concert outdoors
Ⓑ **permitirse** VPR 1 (= *atreverse a*) **se permite demasiadas libertades con su secretaria** he takes too many liberties with his secretary; **me permito recordarle que está prohibido fumar** (*frm*) may I remind you that smoking is forbidden (*frm*)
2 (= *concederse*) to allow o.s.; **me permito dos cigarrillos al día** I allow myself two cigarettes a day; **poder ~se (hacer) algo** to be able to afford (to do) sth; **no me puedo ~ más gastos este mes** I can't afford any more expense this month; **no puedo ~me comer fuera todos los días** I can't afford to eat out every day; **no podemos ~nos el lujo de ser ingenuos** we can't afford to be naive

permuta SF [*de bienes, mercancías*] exchange; [*de puesto de trabajo*] interchange

permutación SF 1 (*Mat*) permutation
2 = **permuta**

permutar ▸conjug 1a◂ VT 1 (*Mat*) to permute
2 [+ *puesto de trabajo*] to exchange, swap; [+ *acciones, edificios*] to switch, exchange; [+ *intervenciones, actuaciones*] to interchange; **~ algo con algn** to exchange sth with sb; **~ destinos con algn** to exchange *o* swap jobs with sb

pernada SF 1 **derecho de ~** (*Hist*) droit de seigneur
2 (= *coz*) kick; **dar ~s** to kick out

pernear ▸conjug 1a◂ VI 1 (= *agitar las piernas*) to kick one's legs, shake one's legs
2 (= *patear*) to stamp one's foot (with rage)
3 (*) (= *darse prisa*) to get cracking*

pernera SF trouser leg

perneta SF **en ~s** bare-legged, with bare legs

perniabierto ADJ bow-legged

perniche* SM blanket

pernicioso ADJ pernicious (*tb Med*); [*influencia, sustancia*] harmful; [*insecto*] injurious (**para** to); [*persona*] wicked, evil

pernicorto ADJ short-legged

pernigordo ADJ fat-legged

pernil SM 1 (*Zool*) upper leg, haunch; (*Culin*) leg; (*Caribe*) leg of pork, pork
2 (*Cos*) trouser leg

pernio SM hinge

perno SM bolt; ✦*MODISMO* **estar hasta el ~** (*Andes**) to be at the end of one's tether

pernocta SF **pase (de) ~** overnight pass

pernoctación SF overnight stay; **con tres pernoctaciones en hotel** with three nights in a hotel

pernoctar ▸conjug 1a◂ VI to spend the night, stay the night

pero[1] Ⓐ CONJ 1 but; **me gusta, ~ es muy caro** I like it, but it's very expensive; **yo no quería ir, ~ bueno …** I didn't want to go, but still …
2 (*al principio de frase*) **~, ¿dónde está Pedro?** where on earth is Pedro?; **~ bueno, ¿vienes o no?** now look, are you coming or not?; **~ vamos a ver** well let's see; **¡~ qué guapa estás!** you look great!; **¡~ si no tiene coche!** I tell you he hasn't got a car!
3 (*uso enfático*) **~ que muy: una chica guapa, ~ que muy guapa** what you call a really pretty girl, a pretty girl and no mistake; **hizo muy, ~ que muy mal** he was wrong, really, really wrong; **¡estoy ~ que muy harto!** I'm damn well fed up!*; **¡~ que muy bien!** well done!
Ⓑ SM 1 (= *falta, defecto*) snag; **el plan no tiene ~s** the plan hasn't any snags, there's nothing wrong with the plan
2 (= *pega*) objection; **encontrar** *o* **poner ~s a algo** to raise objections to sth, find fault with sth; **¡no hay ~ que valga!** there are no buts about it!

pero[2] SM (*Andes, Cono Sur*) pear tree

perogrullada SF platitude, truism

perogrullesco ADJ platitudinous

Perogrullo SM, **Pero Grullo** SM ✦*MODISMO* **verdad de ~** platitude, truism

perol SM 1 (= *cazuela*) (*grande*) pot; (*más pequeña*) saucepan
2 (*Caribe*) (= *utensilio*) kitchen utensil; (= *trasto*) piece of junk, worthless object

perola SF saucepan

perolero SM 1 (*Caribe*) (= *hojalatero*) tinsmith
2 (= *objetos*) pile of junk, collection of odds and ends

peronacho* SM (*Cono Sur pey*) Peronist

peroné SM fibula

peronismo SM Peronism

PERONISMO

General Juan Domingo Perón (1895-1974) came to power in Argentina in 1946, on a social justice platform known as **justicialismo**. *He aimed to break Argentina's dependence on exports by developing the domestic economy through state-led industrialization.* **Peronismo** *stood for nationalization of industry, trade unions, paid holidays, the welfare state, and the provision of affordable housing. Women were given the vote in 1947, a move championed by Perón's charismatic wife "Evita" (María Eva Duarte), who was extremely popular in certain circles and became a major public figure. Following her premature death from cancer in 1952, Perón's support began to crumble and*

➤ LENGUA Y USO: **permiso 1** 36.1, 36.2, 36.3 **permitir A1** 36.1, 36.3

he was driven into exile in 1955. His party was banned for almost a decade and did not regain power until 1973, when he was recalled from exile to become President. He died the following year and was succeeded by his second wife Isabel Martínez, who was ousted in a military coup in 1976. **Peronismo** *as a movement has survived, and the Peronist party returned to power in 1989 under Carlos Menem.*

peronista ADJ, SMF Peronist

peroración SF 1 (= *discurso*) peroration, speech; (= *perorata*) long-winded speech
2 (= *conclusión*) conclusion of a speech

perorar ▸conjug 1a◂ VI to make a speech; (*hum*) to spout

perorata SF (= *rollo*) long-winded speech; (= *soflama*) violent speech, harangue; **echar una ~** to rattle on* (**sobre** about)

peróxido SM peroxide ► **peróxido de hidrógeno** hydrogen peroxide

perpendicular Ⓐ ADJ perpendicular (**a** to); **el camino es ~ al río** the road is at right angles to the river
Ⓑ SF perpendicular; **salir de la ~** to be out of the perpendicular

perpendicularmente ADV perpendicularly

perpetración SF perpetration

perpetrador(a) SM/F perpetrator

perpetrar ▸conjug 1a◂ VT to perpetrate

perpetuación SF perpetuation

perpetuamente ADV perpetually

perpetuar ▸conjug 1e◂ VT to perpetuate

perpetuidad SF perpetuity; **a ~** in perpetuity, for ever; **condena a ~** life sentence; **le condenaron a prisión a ~** he was sentenced to life

perpetuo ADJ (*gen*) perpetual; [*condena, exilio*] life *antes de s*; (*Bot*) everlasting; **cadena perpetua** life imprisonment

Perpiñán SM Perpignan

perplejamente ADV perplexedly, in a puzzled way

perplejidad SF 1 (= *confusión*) perplexity, puzzlement
2 (= *indecisión*) hesitation
3 (= *situación perpleja*) perplexing situation

perplejo ADJ perplexed, puzzled; **me miró ~** he gave me a perplexed *o* puzzled look; **dejar a algn ~** to perplex sb, puzzle sb; **se quedó ~ un momento** he hesitated a moment, he looked perplexed for a moment

perra SF 1 (*Zool*) bitch
2 (*Esp**) (= *moneda*) copper, penny; **ahorró unas ~s** he saved a few coppers*; **no tener una ~*** to be broke*, be skint* ► **perra chica** (*Hist*) 5-céntimo coin ► **perra gorda** (*Hist*) 10-céntimo coin
3 (*) (= *rabieta*) tantrum; **el niño cogió una ~** the child had a tantrum
4 (*) (= *obsesión*) obsession, crazy idea; **está con la ~ de comprárselo** he's taken it into his head to buy it; **le cogió la ~ de ir a México** he got obsessed about going to Mexico*
5 (*Cono Sur*) (= *sombrero*) old hat
6 (*Cono Sur*) (= *cantimplora*) leather water bottle

perrada SF 1 (= *perros*) pack of dogs
2 (*) (= *acción*) dirty trick

perraje SM (*Andes*) 1 [*de perros*] pack of dogs
2 (*) [*de personas*] lower orders *pl*, lower ranks *pl*

perramus SM INV (*Arg*) raincoat

perrera SF 1 (*para perros callejeros*) dog pound; (*para perros con dueño*) kennels *pl*, kennel (*EEUU*)
2 (= *furgoneta*) dogcatcher's van
3 (*Chile**) (= *rabieta*) tantrum
4 (*Caribe*) (= *pelea*) row, shindy
5 (*en el trabajo*) grind; *ver tb* **perrero**

perrería SF 1 (= *perros*) pack of dogs; (*fig*) gang of villains
2 (*) (= *trampa*) dirty trick
3 (= *palabra*) harsh word, angry word; **decir ~s de algn** to say harsh things about sb

perrero/a SM/F dog catcher; *ver tb* **perrera**

perrillo SM 1 (*Zool*) puppy
2 (*Mil*) trigger

perrito/a Ⓐ SM/F puppy ► **perrito/a faldero/a** lapdog
Ⓑ SM ► **perrito caliente** hot dog

perro Ⓐ SM 1 (*Zool*) dog; **"cuidado con el perro"** "beware of the dog" ► **perro afgano** Afghan hound ► **perro antiexplosivos, perro buscadrogas** sniffer dog ► **perro callejero** stray (dog) ► **perro cobrador** retriever ► **perro dálmata** dalmatian ► **perro de agua** (*CAm*) coypu ► **perro de aguas** spaniel ► **perro de casta** pedigree dog ► **perro de caza** hunting dog ► **perro de ciego** guide dog ► **perro de lanas** poodle ► **perro de muestra** pointer ► **perro de presa** bulldog ► **perro de raza** pedigree dog ► **perro de San Bernardo** St Bernard ► **perro de Terranova** Newfoundland dog ► **perro de trineo** husky, sled dog ► **perro dogo** bulldog ► **perro esquimal** husky ► **perro faldero** lapdog ► **perro guardián** guard dog ► **perro guía** guide dog ► **perro lazarillo** guide dog ► **perro lebrel** whippet ► **perro lobo** alsatian, German shepherd ► **perro marino** dogfish ► **perro pastor** sheepdog ► **perro pequinés** Pekinese ► **perro policía** police dog ► **perro raposero** foxhound ► **perro rastreador, perro rastrero** tracker dog ► **perro salchicha*** sausage dog*, dachshund ► **perro vagabundo** stray (dog) ► **perro zorrero** foxhound
2 ✦*MODISMOS* **¡a otro ~ con ese hueso!** pull the other one, it has bells on it!*; **atar ~s con longaniza**: **se cree que allí atan los ~s con longaniza** he thinks it's the land of milk and honey; **de ~s** foul; **estaba de un humor de ~s** he was in a foul *o* stinking mood; **tiempo de ~s** foul *o* dirty weather; **echarle los ~s a algn*** to come down on sb like a ton of bricks*; **echar una hora a ~s** to waste a whole hour, get absolutely nothing done in an hour; **hacer ~ muerto** (*Chile, Perú**) to avoid paying; **heder a ~ muerto** to stink to high heaven; **meter los ~s en danza** to set the cat among the pigeons; **¿qué ~ te/le mordió?** (*Caribe**) what's up with you/him?*; **llevarse como (el) ~ y (el) gato** to fight like cat and dog; **ser como el ~ del hortelano** to be a dog in the manger; **ser ~ viejo** to be an old hand; **tratar a algn como a un ~** to treat sb like dirt; **vida de ~** dog's life; ✦*REFRANES* **a ~ flaco todo son pulgas** it never rains but it pours; **~ ladrador, poco mordedor** ◊ **~ que ladra no muerde** his bark is worse than his bite
3 (*Culin*) ► **perro caliente** hot dog
4 (* *pey*) (= *holgazán*) lazy sod**
5 (* *pey*) (= *persona despreciable*) swine*
6 (*Andes*) (= *modorra*) drowsiness
7 (*Cono Sur*) clothes peg, clothes pin (*EEUU*)
Ⓑ ADJ (*) rotten*; **¡qué perra suerte la mía!** what rotten luck I have!*; **esta perra vida** this wretched life; **¡qué perra vida!** life's a bitch!*; **he pasado una temporada perra** I've been through a rough patch*

perro-guía SM (*pl* **perros-guía**) guide dog

perrona† SF (= *moneda*) 10-céntimo coin; **de (a) ~*** cheapo*, cheap

perronero* ADJ cheapo*, cheap

perrucho SM (*pey*) hound, cur

perruna SF dog biscuit

perruno ADJ canine, dog *antes de s*; [*afecto, devoción*] doglike

persa Ⓐ ADJ, SMF Persian
Ⓑ SM (*Ling*) Persian
Ⓒ SF (*Cono Sur*) (= *mercado*) market, bazaar

per saecula saeculorum ADV (*frm*), **per secula seculorum** ADV for ever and ever

persecución SF 1 (= *acoso*) pursuit; **estar en plena ~** to be in full cry ► **persecución individual** (*Ciclismo*) individual pursuit ► **persecución sexual** sexual harassment
2 (*Pol, Rel*) persecution

persecutorio ADJ **manía persecutoria** persecution complex; **trato ~** cruel treatment

perseguible ADJ (*Jur*) [*delito*] indictable; [*persona*] liable to prosecution; **~ a instancia de parte** liable to private prosecution; **~ de oficio** liable to prosecution by the state

perseguidor(a) SM/F 1 (*gen*) pursuer
2 (*Rel, Pol*) persecutor

perseguimiento SM pursuit, hunt, chase; **en ~ de** in pursuit of

perseguir ▸conjug 3d, 3k◂ VT 1 [+ *presa, fugitivo*] (*gen*) to pursue, chase; (*por motivos ideológicos*) to persecute; (= *acosar*) to hunt down, hunt out
2 [+ *persona, empleo*] to chase after, go after; [+ *propósito, fin*] to pursue; **la persiguió durante dos años** he was after her for two years, he pursued her for two years; **me persiguieron hasta que dije que sí** they pestered me until I said yes; **lo persiguen los remordimientos** he is plagued by remorse; **lo persigue la mala suerte** he is dogged by ill luck

perseverancia SF perseverance, persistence

perseverante ADJ persevering, persistent

perseverantemente ADV perseveringly, persistently

perseverar ▸conjug 1a◂ VI to persevere, persist; **~ en** to persevere in, persist with

Persia SF Persia

persiana SF [*de lamas*] (Venetian) blind; [*de tablitas*] slatted shutter; (*enrollable*) roller blind; ✦*MODISMO* **enrollarse como una ~*** to go on and on

persignarse ▸conjug 1a◂ VPR to cross o.s.

persistencia SF persistence

persistente ADJ persistent

persistentemente ADV persistently

persistir ▸conjug 3a◂ VI to persist (**en** in)

persoga SF (*CAm, Méx*) halter (*of plaited vegetable fibre*)

persona SF 1 (= *individuo*) person; **es una ~ encantadora** he's a charming person; **20 ~s**

20 people; **aquellas ~s que lo deseen** those who wish; **es buena ~** he's a good sort; **en la ~ de** in the person of; **en ~** in person, in the flesh; **vendrá él en ~ a recoger los papeles** he will come and collect the papers in person; **vi al príncipe en ~** I saw the prince in the flesh *o* in person; **por ~** per person; **20 kilos por ~** 20 kilos per person; **tres caramelos por ~** three sweets per person *o* each; **dos dólares por ~** two dollars per person, two dollars a head; **tercera ~** third party; **sin inmiscuir a terceras ~s** without involving third parties ► **persona de edad** elderly person, senior citizen ► **persona de historia†** dubious individual ► **persona mayor** adult ► **persona no grata**, **persona non grata** persona non grata ► **personas reales** (*frm*) royalty *sing*, king and queen
2 (*Jur*) ► **persona física** natural person ► **persona jurídica** legal entity
3 (*Ling*) person; **la tercera ~ del singular** the third person singular
4 (*Rel*) **las tres ~s de la Santísima Trinidad** the three persons of the Holy Trinity

PERSONA

Mientras que **persona** en singular se traduce por **person**, el plural tiene dos traducciones: **people** y **persons**.
• **People** es la forma más utilizada, ya que **persons** se emplea solamente en el lenguaje formal o técnico. Las dos formas llevan el verbo en plural:
Acaban de llegar tres personas preguntando por un tal Sr. Oliva
Three people have just arrived asking for a Mr Oliva
"Peso máximo: 8 personas"
"Weight limit: 8 persons"
Para otros usos y ejemplos ver la entrada.

personaje SM 1 (= *sujeto notable*) personage, important person; (= *famoso*) celebrity, personality; **ser un ~** to be somebody, be important
2 (*Literat, Teat*) character

personajillo SM (*gen*) insignificant person; (*Literat, Teat*) minor character; (*hum*) minor celebrity

personal Ⓐ ADJ personal
Ⓑ SM 1 (= *plantilla*) staff, personnel; (*esp Mil*) force; (*Náut*) crew, complement; **estar falto de ~** to be shorthanded *o* shortstaffed ► **personal de cabina** cabin staff *o* crew ► **personal de exterior** surface workers *pl* ► **personal de interior** underground workers *pl* ► **personal de servicios** maintenance staff ► **personal de tierra** (*Aer*) ground crew, ground staff
2 (*) (= *gente*) people; **había mucho ~ en el cine** there was a big crowd in the cinema; ✦***MODISMO*** **quedarse con el ~*** to be a hit with people
Ⓒ SF (*Baloncesto*) personal foul

personalidad SF 1 (= *modo de ser*) personality; **doble ~** dual personality ► **personalidad desdoblada** split personality
2 (= *personaje público*) public figure; **~es** personalities, dignitaries
3 (*Jur*) legal entity

personalísimo ADJ intensely personal, highly individualistic

➤ LENGUA Y USO: **personalmente** 53.5

personalismo SM 1 (= *parcialidad*) partiality; **obrar sin ~s** to act impartially *o* without favouritism
2 (= *alusión personal*) personal reference; **tenemos que proceder sin ~s** we must carry on without getting personal
3 (= *egoísmo*) selfishness, egoism

personalizar ▸conjug 1f◂ Ⓐ VT (*gen*) to personalize; (= *personificar*) to embody, personify
Ⓑ VI 1 (= *nombrar en particular*) to name names
2 (= *hacer alusiones personales*) to get personal
Ⓒ **personalizarse** VPR to become personal

▼ **personalmente** ADV personally

personarse ▸conjug 1a◂ VPR to appear in person; **~ en** to present o.s. at, report to; **~ en forma** (*Jur*) to be officially represented; **el juez se personó en el lugar del accidente** the judge made an official visit to the scene of the accident

personería SF 1 (*Cono Sur*) (= *personalidad*) personality; (= *talento*) aptitude, talent
2 (*LAm Jur*) legal status

personero/a SM/F (*LAm Pol*) (= *representante*) (government) official; (= *portavoz*) spokesperson; (*Jur*) proxy

personificación SF 1 (= *representación*) personification, embodiment; **es la ~ de los celos** he is the embodiment of jealousy, he is jealousy personified
2 (*Literat*) personification

personificar ▸conjug 1g◂ VT 1 (= *encarnar*) to personify, embody; **es la codicia personificada** he is greed personified; **en esta mujer el autor personifica la maldad** the author makes this woman a personification of wickedness
2 (*en discurso*) to single out for special mention

perspectiva SF 1 (*Arte*) perspective; **en ~** in perspective; **le falta ~** he lacks a sense of perspective
2 (= *vista*) view, scene
3 (= *posibilidad*) prospect; **la ~ no es nada halagüeña** it's a most unwelcome prospect; **buenas ~s de mejora** good prospects for *o* of improvement; **se alegró con la ~ de pasar un día en el campo** he cheered up with the prospect of spending a day in the country; **encontrarse ante la ~ de hacer algo** to be faced with the prospect of doing sth; **tener algo en ~** to have sth in prospect; **las ~s de la cosecha son favorables** the harvest outlook is good

perspicacia SF 1 (= *agudeza mental*) perceptiveness, shrewdness
2 (= *agudeza visual*) keen-sightedness

perspicaz ADJ 1 (= *agudo, sagaz*) perceptive, shrewd
2 [*vista*] keen; [*persona*] keen-sighted

perspicuidad SF (*frm*) perspicuity (*frm*), clarity

perspicuo ADJ perspicuous (*frm*), clear

persuadir ▸conjug 3a◂ Ⓐ VT to persuade; **~ a algn de algo/para hacer algo** to persuade sb of sth/to do sth; **dejarse ~** to allow o.s. to be persuaded
Ⓑ **persuadirse** VPR to be persuaded

persuasión SF 1 (= *acción de persuadir*) persuasion
2 (= *convicción*) conviction; **tener la ~ de que …** to have the conviction that …, be convinced that …

persuasiva SF persuasiveness, power of persuasion

persuasivo ADJ [*vendedor, carácter*] persuasive; [*argumento, razones*] persuasive, convincing

pertenecer ▸conjug 2d◂ VI 1 (= *ser propiedad*) **~ a algn** to belong to sb; **los terrenos pertenecen al ayuntamiento** the land belongs to the council, the land is council property; **este diccionario te pertenece** this dictionary belongs to you
2 (= *formar parte*) **~ a algo** to belong to sth; **pertenecemos a un grupo pacifista** we belong to a pacifist group
3 (*frm*) (= *competer*) **~ a algn hacer algo** to be sb's responsibility to do sth; **le pertenece a él acabar el trabajo** it's his responsibility to finish the job, it's up to him to finish the job

perteneciente ADJ 1 (= *que pertenece*) belonging (**a** to); **los países ~s** the member countries; **las personas ~s al organismo** members of the organization
2 (= *relacionado*) **~ a** pertaining to

pertenencia SF 1 (= *posesión*) ownership; **las cosas de su ~** his possessions, his property
2 **pertenencias** (= *objetos personales*) personal belongings; [*de finca*] appurtenances, accessories
3 (*a club, asociación*) membership (**a** of)

pértica SF *land measure (= 2.70 metres)*

pértiga SF pole; **salto de ~** (*Dep*) pole vault ► **pértiga de trole** trolley pole

pertiguero SM verger

pertiguista SMF pole-vaulter

pertinacia SF 1 (= *persistencia*) persistence
2 (= *obstinación*) obstinacy

pertinaz ADJ 1 [*tos*] persistent; [*sequía*] long-lasting, prolonged
2 [*persona*] obstinate

pertinencia SF (= *relevancia*) relevance, pertinence; (= *idoneidad*) appropriateness

pertinente ADJ 1 (= *relevante*) relevant, pertinent; (= *adecuado*) appropriate; **no es ~ hacerlo ahora** this is not the appropriate time to do it
2 **~ a** concerning; **en lo ~ a libros** as regards books, as far as books are concerned

pertinentemente ADV (= *relevantemente*) relevantly, pertinently; (= *adecuadamente*) appropriately

pertrechar ▸conjug 1a◂ Ⓐ VT (*gen*) to supply (**con, de** with); (= *equipar*) to equip (**con, de** with); (*Mil*) to supply with ammunition and stores, equip
Ⓑ **pertrecharse** VPR **~se de algo** to provide o.s. with sth

pertrechos SMPL 1 (= *útiles*) gear *sing* ► **pertrechos de pesca** fishing tackle *sing*
2 (*Mil*) (*gen*) supplies and stores; (= *provisiones*) provisions; (= *munición*) munitions

perturbación SF 1 (*Meteo, Pol*) disturbance ► **perturbación del orden público** breach of the peace
2 (*Med*) upset, disturbance; (*mental*) mental disorder

perturbado/a Ⓐ ADJ mentally unbalanced
Ⓑ SM/F mentally unbalanced person

perturbador(a) Ⓐ ADJ 1 [*noticia*] disturbing, perturbing

2 [*conducta*] unruly, disorderly; [*movimiento*] subversive
Ⓑ SM/F disorderly element, unruly person

perturbadoramente ADV disturbingly

perturbar ▸conjug 1a◂ VT 1 (= *alterar*) [+ *orden*] to disturb; [+ *plan*] to upset; [+ *calma*] to disturb, ruffle
2 (*Med*) to disturb, mentally disturb

Perú SM Peru

peruanismo SM *word or phrase peculiar to Peru*

peruano/a Ⓐ ADJ Peruvian
Ⓑ SM/F Peruvian; **los ~s** the Peruvians

Perucho* SM (*Caribe*) ✦**MODISMO** **viven en plan de ~** they get on like a house on fire

peruétano* Ⓐ ADJ (*Andes, Caribe, Méx*) boring, tedious
Ⓑ SM (*Andes, Caribe, Méx*) (= *pelma*) bore; (= *necio*) dolt; **ese muchacho es un ~** (*Cono Sur*) (= *entrometido*) that lad is always sticking his nose where it doesn't belong

perversamente ADV wickedly

perversidad SF 1 (= *cualidad*) [*de depravado*] depravity; [= *de malvado*] wickedness
2 (= *acto*) evil deed

perversión SF 1 (= *depravación*) perversion ► **perversión sexual** sexual perversion
2 (= *maldad*) wickedness

perverso ADJ (= *depravado*) depraved; (= *malvado*) wicked

pervertido/a Ⓐ ADJ perverted, deviant
Ⓑ SM/F pervert, deviant

pervertidor(a) SM/F corruptor ► **pervertidor(a) de menores** child corruptor, corruptor of minors (*frm*)

pervertimiento SM perversion, corruption

pervertir ▸conjug 3i◂ Ⓐ VT [+ *persona*] to pervert; [+ *texto*] to distort, corrupt; [+ *gusto*] to corrupt
Ⓑ **pervertirse** VPR to become perverted

pervinca SF (*Bot*) periwinkle

pervivencia SF survival

pervivir ▸conjug 3a◂ VI to survive

pesa SF 1 (*Dep*) weight; **hacer ~s** to do weight training, do weights*; **levantamiento de ~s** weightlifting
2 [*de balanza, reloj*] weight
3 (*Andes, CAm, Caribe*) butcher's shop

pesabebés SM INV baby scales *pl*

pesadamente ADV 1 (= *con mucho peso*) heavily; **caer ~** to fall heavily
2 (= *lentamente*) slowly, sluggishly
3 (= *de manera aburrida*) boringly, tediously

pesadez SF 1 (= *peso*) weight
2 (= *lentitud*) slowness, sluggishness
3 (*Med*) (= *malestar*) heaviness; (= *somnolencia*) drowsiness ► **pesadez de estómago** bloated feeling in the stomach
4 (= *aburrimiento*) tediousness, boring nature; (= *molestia*) annoyance; **es una ~ tener que ...** it's a bore having to ...; **¡qué ~!** what a bore!

pesadilla SF 1 (= *mal sueño*) nightmare, bad dream; **una experiencia de ~** a nightmarish experience
2 (= *tormento*) nightmare; **ha sido la ~ de todos** it has been a nightmare for everybody; **ese equipo es nuestra ~** that is our bogey team

pesado/a Ⓐ ADJ 1 [*paquete, comida*] heavy; **industria pesada** heavy industry
2 (= *lento*) [*persona*] slow, sluggish; [*mecanismo*] stiff
3 (*Meteo*) heavy, sultry
4 [*sueño*] deep, heavy
5 (*Med*) heavy; **tengo la cabeza pesada** my head feels heavy; **tener el estómago ~** to feel bloated, feel full up
6 [*tarea*] (= *difícil*) tough, hard; (= *aburrido*) tedious, boring; (= *molesto*) annoying; [*lectura*] heavy, stodgy; **esto se hace ~** this is becoming tedious; **la lectura del libro resultó pesada** the book was heavy going; **es una persona de lo más ~** he's a terribly dull sort; **ése me cae ~** (*Caribe, Méx**) that chap gets on my nerves*; **es ~ tener que ...** it's such a bore having to ...; **¡no seas ~!** stop being such a pain!
Ⓑ SM/F 1 (= *aburrido*) bore; **es un ~** he's such a bore
2 (*Caribe**) (= *pez gordo*) big shot*
Ⓒ SM (= *acto*) weighing

pesador SM (*Andes, CAm, Caribe*) butcher

pesadumbre SF grief, sorrow

pesaje SM 1 (= *acción*) weighing
2 (*Dep*) weigh-in

pésame SM condolences *pl*; **dar el ~** to express one's condolences, send one's sympathy (**por** for, on); **mi más sentido ~** my deepest sympathy, my heartfelt condolences

pesantez SF weight, heaviness; (*Fís*) gravity

pesar ▸conjug 1a◂ Ⓐ VI 1 [*objeto, persona*]
1·1 (= *tener peso*) to weigh; (*Boxeo, Hípica*) to weigh in at; (*Inform*) to be; **pesa cinco kilos** it weighs five kilos; **¿cuánto pesas?** how much *o* what do you weigh?; **el boxeador pesó 90kg** the boxer weighed in at 90kg; **esta foto pesa 50k** this photo is 50k (in size)
1·2 (= *tener mucho peso*) to be heavy; **ese paquete no pesa** that parcel isn't heavy, that parcel hardly weighs anything; **¿pesa mucho?** is it heavy?; **¡cómo pesa esta bolsa!** this bag's really heavy!; **¡no pesa nada!** it's not heavy at all!; **~ como una losa** to weigh like a millstone round one's neck
2 (= *resultar pesado*) **~le a algn: le pesaba la mochila** his rucksack was weighing him down; **los pies me pesan, estoy muy cansado** I'm so tired, I can hardly lift my feet up any more
3 (= *afligir*) **me pesa mucho** I am very sorry about it *o* to hear it; **¡ya le ~á!** he'll be sorry!, he'll regret this!; **me pesa haberlo hecho** I regret having done it, I'm sorry I did it; **le pesa que no le hayan nombrado** he is hurt that he has not been appointed
4 (= *ser una carga*) **le pesa tanta responsabilidad** all that responsibility weighs heavily on him; **me pesan los años** I feel my age; **~ sobre** [*responsabilidad, preocupación*] to weigh heavily on; [*amenaza, acusación*] to hang over; **pesa sobre mi conciencia** it is weighing heavily on my conscience; **sobre ella pesan muchas obligaciones** she is burdened with many responsibilities; **las sospechas que pesan sobre Aguirre** the suspicions surrounding Aguirre; **pesa sobre ellos una orden de busca y captura** there is a warrant out for their arrest; **la hipoteca que pesa sobre el piso** the mortgage with which the flat is burdened; **la maldición que pesa sobre nuestra familia** the curse afflicting our family
5 (= *influir*) to carry weight; **sus opiniones no pesan en el partido** her opinions do not carry any weight in the party; **sus razones no han pesado en mi decisión** his arguments did not influence my decision
6 **pese a (que)** in spite of (the fact that), despite (the fact that); **pese a las dificultades** in spite of *o* despite the difficulties; **lo creo, pese a que ellos lo niegan** I believe it, even though they deny it, I believe it, in spite of *o* despite the fact that they deny it; **lo haré pese a quien pese** I'll do it whether people like it or not, I'll do it, no matter who I offend; *ver tb* **mal B**
7 (*Andes, CAm*) (= *vender carne*) to sell meat
Ⓑ VT 1 [+ *carta, fruta, etc*] to weigh
2 (= *sopesar*) to weigh up; **~ las posibilidades** to weigh up one's chances; **~ los pros y los contras** to weigh up the pros and cons
Ⓒ **pesarse** VPR to weigh o.s.; (*Boxeo, Hípica*) to weigh in; **tengo que ~me** I must weigh myself
Ⓓ SM 1 (= *aflicción*) sorrow; **la noticia le causó un hondo ~** the news caused him deep sorrow; **expresó su ~ a la familia de las víctimas** he expressed his sorrow to the families of the victims
2 (= *arrepentimiento*) regret; **expresó su ~ por el accidente** he expressed his regret at the accident; **a mi ~** to my regret; **con gran ~ mío** much to my regret; **sentir** *o* **tener ~ por no haber ...** to regret not having ...
3 **a pesar de** in spite of, despite; **a ~ de todo** in spite of *o* despite everything; **a ~ del mal tiempo** in spite of *o* despite the bad weather; **a ~ de que** even though; **a ~ de que no tiene dinero** even though he has no money, in spite of *o* despite the fact that he has no money; **a ~ de que la quiero** even though I love her; ✦**MODISMO** **a ~ de los ~es*** in spite of *o* despite everything

pesario SM pessary

pesaroso ADJ (= *arrepentido*) regretful; (= *afligido*) sorrowful, sad

pesca SF 1 (= *actividad*) fishing; **allí la ~ es muy buena** the fishing is very good there; **ir de ~** to go fishing; **andar a la ~ de** (*fig*) to fish for, angle for ► **pesca a caña** angling ► **pesca a mosca** fly-fishing ► **pesca de altura** deep sea fishing ► **pesca de bajura** coastal fishing, shallow water fishing ► **pesca de la ballena** whaling ► **pesca de perlas** pearl fishing ► **pesca submarina** underwater fishing
2 (= *lo pescado*) catch; **la ~ ha sido mala** it's been a poor catch; ✦**MODISMO** **... y toda la ~*** ... and all the rest of it, ... and whatnot*

pescada SF hake

pescadería SF (= *tienda*) fish shop, fishmonger's; (= *mercado*) fish market

pescadero/a SM/F fishmonger, fish merchant (*EEUU*)

pescadilla SF whiting, small hake

pescado SM 1 (*Culin*) fish; **quiero comprar ~** I want to buy some fish ► **pescado azul** blue fish
2 (*Andes, Cono Sur**) (= *policía*) secret police

pescador(a) Ⓐ ADJ fishing
Ⓑ SM/F fisherman/fisherwoman ► **pescador(a) a mosca** fly-fisherman/fly-fisherwoman ► **pescador(a) de caña** angler

pescante SM 1 [*de carruaje*] driver's seat, coachman's seat
2 (*Teat*) wire

➤ LENGUA Y USO: pésame 51.4

3 (*Téc*) jib
4 (*Náut*) davit

pescar ▸conjug 1g◂ Ⓐ VT 1 [+ *peces, mariscos*] to catch; **pescamos varias truchas** we caught several trout; **fuimos a ~ salmón** we went salmon-fishing
2 (*) (= *agarrar*) **lo ha pescado la policía** he's been caught *o* nabbed* by the police; **¡si no te abrigas vas a ~ una pulmonía!** if you don't wrap up you'll catch pneumonia!; **viene a ~ un marido** she's come to get *o* bag* a husband; **me ~on fumando** I got caught smoking; **¡te pesqué!** caught you!, got you!
3 (*) (= *entender*) to get; **¿aún no has pescado el chiste?** haven't you got the joke yet?; **en la clase de matemáticas no pesco nada** I don't understand a thing in maths
Ⓑ VI 1 [*pescador*] to fish; **ir a ~** to go fishing; **~ a mosca** to fish with a fly, flyfish; **~ a la rastra** ◊ **~ al arrastre** to trawl; ✦***MODISMO*** **~ en río revuelto** to fish in troubled waters
2 (*Andes, Cono Sur*) (= *dormitar*) to nod, doze
Ⓒ **pescarse** VPR ✦***MODISMO*** **no sabe lo que se pesca*** he hasn't a clue*, he has no idea

pescata SF catch, haul

pescocear ▸conjug 1a◂ VT (*LAm*) to grab by the scruff of the neck

pescozón SM slap on the neck

pescozudo ADJ thick-necked, fat in the neck

pescuezo SM 1 (*Zool*) neck; (*Anat*) scruff of the neck; **retorcer el ~ a una gallina** to wring a chicken's neck; **¡calla, o te retuerzo el ~!** shut up, or I'll wring your neck!
2 (†) (= *vanidad*) vanity; (= *altanería*) haughtiness, pride

pescuezón ADJ (*LAm*) 1 = **pescozudo**
2 (= *de cuello largo*) long-necked

pese PREP **~ a** despite, in spite of

pesebre SM 1 (*Agr*) manger
2 (*Rel*) nativity scene, crib

pesebrera SF (*Cono Sur, Méx*) = **pesebre 2**

pesera SF (*Méx*) = **pesero 1**

pesero SM 1 (*Méx*) (= *colectivo*) minibus
2 (*Andes, CAm, Caribe*) (= *carnicero*) butcher

peseta SF peseta; ✦***MODISMO*** **cambiar la ~*** to throw up

pesetada SF (*LAm*) joke, trick

pesetera SF (*CAm, Méx*) prostitute

pesetero ADJ 1 (= *avaro*) money-grabbing*, mercenary
2 (*Méx*) [*comerciante*] small-time
3 (*Andes, CAm, Caribe*) (= *gorrón*) sponging*

pésimamente ADV awfully, dreadfully

pesimismo SM pessimism

pesimista Ⓐ ADJ pessimistic
Ⓑ SMF pessimist

pésimo Ⓐ ADJ awful, dreadful
Ⓑ ADV (*Méx**) **lo hiciste ~** you did it awfully *o* dreadfully

peso SM 1 (*Fís, Téc*) weight; **no puedo levantar mucho ~** I can't lift much weight; **¿cuál es tu ~?** how much do you weigh?; **un vehículo de mucho/poco ~** a heavy/light vehicle; **las telas se venden al ~** the fabrics are sold by weight; **coger ~** (*Esp*) (= *engordar*) to put on weight; (= *levantar peso*) to lift weight; **no dar el ~** (*al pesarse*) [*boxeador*] not to make the weight; [*recién nacido*] to be below normal weight, be underweight; (*en una categoría*) not to make the grade, not come up to scratch; **ese escultor no da el ~** that sculptor doesn't make the grade *o* come up to scratch; **sostener algo en ~** to support the full weight of sth; **falto de ~** underweight; **ganar ~** to put on weight; **~s y medidas** weights and measures; **perder ~** to lose weight; ✦***MODISMOS*** **caer por su propio ~** (= *ser obvio*) to go without saying, be obvious; (= *no tener lógica*) not to stand up (to scrutiny); **valer su ~ en oro** to be worth one's weight in gold ► **peso atómico** atomic weight ► **peso bruto** gross weight ► **peso en vivo** live weight ► **peso escurrido** net weight ► **peso específico** (*lit*) specific gravity; (*fig*) influence ► **peso máximo autorizado** gross weight ► **peso molecular** (*Quím*) molecular weight ► **peso muerto** (*Náut, fig*) dead weight ► **peso neto** net weight
2 (= *acción*) **van a proceder al ~ de la fruta** they're going to weigh the fruit; **el ~ de la leña se hace en unas balanzas enormes** the firewood is weighed on enormous scales
3 [*de culpa, responsabilidad*] weight; **le cayó encima todo el ~ de la justicia** he felt the full weight of the law; **el delantero llevó todo el ~ del ataque** the forward carried the full weight of the attack; **el ~ de los años** the burden of old age; **quitarse un ~ de encima** to take a load *o* weight off one's mind; **me quitarías un buen ~ de encima** it would be a weight off my mind, you would take a weight off my mind
4 (= *importancia*) weight; **su opinión era la de mayor ~ en la reunión** his opinion carried the most weight at the meeting; **España tiene poco ~ en esa organización** Spain does not carry much weight in that organization; **de ~** [*persona*] influential; [*argumento*] weighty, forceful; **un argumento de poco ~** a lightweight argument; **razones de ~** good *o* sound reasons ► **peso político** political influence
5 (= *balanza*) scales *pl* ► **peso de baño** bathroom scales *pl* ► **peso de cocina** kitchen scales *pl* ► **peso de muelle** spring balance
6 (*Med*) heaviness; **noto un ~ muy grande en la cabeza** I can feel a great heaviness in my head
7 (*Dep*) 7·1 (*Esp*) (*Atletismo*) shot; **lanzamiento de ~** shot putting; **lanzar el ~** to put the shot
7·2 (*Halterofilia*) **levantamiento de ~s** weightlifting
7·3 (*Boxeo*) weight
► **peso completo** (*CAm, Méx, Ven*) heavyweight ► **peso gallo** bantamweight ► **peso ligero**, **peso liviano** (*Chile, Venezuela*) lightweight ► **peso medio** middleweight ► **peso medio fuerte** light heavyweight, cruiserweight ► **peso mosca** flyweight ► **peso pesado** heavyweight ► **peso pluma** featherweight ► **peso welter** welterweight
8 (*Fin*) peso; ✦***MODISMO*** **no valer un ~** to be no good

pesor SM (*CAm, Caribe*) weight, heaviness

pespunte SM (*Cos*) backstitch(ing)

pespuntear ▸conjug 1a◂ VT, VI to backstitch

pesquera SF 1 (= *zona*) fishing-ground, fishery
2 (= *presa*) weir

pesquería SF fishing ground, fishery

pesquero Ⓐ ADJ fishing *antes de s*
Ⓑ SM fishing boat

pesquis* SM (= *agudeza*) (*intelectual*) nous*; (*técnica*) know-how; **tener el ~ para hacer algo** to have the nous to do sth*

pesquisa Ⓐ SF (= *indagación*) investigation, inquiry; (= *búsqueda*) search
Ⓑ SM (*Andes, Cono Sur**) (= *policía*) secret police; (= *detective*) detective

pesquisador(a) SM/F (= *investigador*) investigator, inquirer; (= *detective*) detective; (*Andes, Cono Sur**) (= *policía*) member of the secret police

pesquisar ▸conjug 1a◂ VT to investigate, inquire into

pesquisidor(a)† SM/F investigator, inquirer

pestaña SF 1 [*de ojo*] eyelash; ✦***MODISMOS*** **no pegué ~*** I didn't get a wink of sleep; **quemarse las ~s** (= *excederse*) (*gen*) to burn one's fingers; (*estudiando*) to burn the midnight oil; **tener ~** to be pretty smart
2 (*Bot*) fringe
3 (= *saliente*) [*de caja*] flap; [*de neumático*] rim
4 (*Esp‡*) (= *policía*) **la ~** the fuzz‡, the cops* *pl*

pestañear ▸conjug 1a◂ VI, **pestañar** ▸conjug 1a◂ VI (*LAm*) to blink; **sin ~** without batting an eyelid

pestañeo SM blink(ing)

pestazo* SM stink, stench

peste SF 1 (*Med*) plague; **una ~ de ratones** a plague of mice; ✦***MODISMOS*** **huir de algo/algn como de la ~** to avoid sth/sb like the plague; **ser la ~*** to be a nuisance, be a pain* ► **peste aviar** fowl pest ► **peste bubónica** bubonic plague ► **peste negra** Black Death ► **peste porcina** swine fever
2 (= *mal olor*) stink, foul smell; **¡qué ~ hay aquí!** there's a real stink in here!
3 ✦***MODISMO*** **decir** *o* **echar ~s de algn** to slag sb off*; **siempre anda echando ~s de su jefe** she's always slagging off her boss*
4 (*Cono Sur*) (*gen*) infectious disease; (= *viruela*) smallpox
5 (*Andes*) (= *resfriado*) cold

pesticida SM pesticide

pestífero ADJ (= *dañino*) pestiferous; [*olor*] foul; [*influencia*] noxious, harmful

pestilencia SF 1 (= *plaga*) pestilence, plague
2 (= *mal olor*) stink, stench

pestilencial ADJ pestilential

pestilente ADJ 1 (= *dañino*) pestilent
2 (= *que huele mal*) smelly, foul

pestillo SM [*de puerta, ventana*] bolt; [*de cerradura*] latch; (*Cono Sur*) (= *picaporte*) door handle

pestiño SM (*Esp*) 1 (*Culin*) honey-coated fritter
2 (*) (= *lata*) bore, drag; **fue un ~** it was a real drag
3 (*) (= *chica*) plain girl

pestozos‡ SMPL socks

pesuña SF (*LAm*) = **pezuña**

peta[1]**‡** SF (*Esp*) peseta

peta[2]**‡** SM 1 (= *droga*) joint‡, reefer‡
2 (= *nombre*) name ► **peta chungo** false name
3 (= *documentación*) papers *pl*

petaca Ⓐ SF 1 [*de cigarrillos*] cigarette case; [*de puros*] cigar case; [*de pipa*] tobacco pouch; [*de alcohol*] flask; ✦***MODISMO*** **hacerle la ~ a algn** to make an apple-pie bed for sb
2 (*LAm*) (= *cesto*) wicker basket; (= *baúl*) leather-covered chest; (*Méx*) (= *maleta*) suit-

case; ✦*MODISMO* **se le fueron las ~s** (*Arg**) he lost his patience

3 (*CAm, Méx Anat*) hump

4 **petacas** (*Caribe, Méx*‡) (= *nalgas*) buttocks; (= *pechos*) big breasts

Ⓑ SMF (*Arg**) 1 (= *rechoncho*) short squat person

2 (= *vago*) lazy person

Ⓒ ADJ INV (*) 1 (*Chile*) (= *torpe*) slow, sluggish; (= *vago*) lazy, idle

2 (*Caribe*) (= *grosero*) coarse

petacho SM patch, mend

petacón* ADJ 1 (*Méx, Andes, Cono Sur*) (= *rechoncho*) plump, chubby

2 (*Méx*) (= *nalgudo*) fat-bottomed, broad in the beam*; **está petacona** she's rather broad in the beam*

petacudo* ADJ 1 (*Andes*) (= *grueso*) stout, fat

2 (*CAm*) (= *con joroba*) hunchbacked

3 (*Méx*) (= *nalgudo*) broad in the beam*

4 (*Col*) (= *lento*) slow, ponderous, sluggish

pétalo SM petal

petanca SF pétanque

petar* ▸conjug 1a◂ VI **no le peta trabajar en una oficina** he's not into working in an office; **ahora mismo no me peta** I don't feel like it now

petardazo SM 1 (= *fuegos artificiales*) firework display

2 (= *sonido*) crack, bang

3 (= *sorpresa*) shock result, upset

petardear ▸conjug 1a◂ Ⓐ VI (*Aut*) to backfire

Ⓑ VT (*) (= *estafar*) to cheat, swindle

petardista* SM/F 1 (*Méx*) (= *político*) crooked politician*

2 (*CAm*) (= *estafador*) cheat, swindler

petardo SM 1 (= *cohete*) banger, firecracker; (= *explosivo*) small explosive device; (*Mil*) petard

2 (*) (= *lo que aburre*) bore, drag; **ser un ~** to be dead boring*

3 (‡) (= *mujer fea*) hag‡, old hag‡

4 (‡) (= *droga*) joint‡

5 (*) (= *estafa*) fraud, swindle; **pegar un ~** pull a fast one (**a** on)

petate SM 1 (= *estera*) grass mat; (*esp LAm*) [*de palma*] mat of palm leaves; (*para dormir*) sleeping mat

2 (= *equipaje*) bundle of bedding and belongings; (*Mil*) kit bag; **liar el ~*** (*lit*) to pack; (= *irse*) to pack up and go, clear out*; (= *morir*) to kick the bucket*

3 (*) (= *estafador*) cheat, trickster

4 (*) (= *pobre hombre*) poor devil

5 ✦*MODISMO* **se descubrió el ~*** the fraud was uncovered

petatearse‡ ▸conjug 1a◂ VPR (*Méx*) to peg out‡, kick the bucket*

peteneras SFPL (*Esp*) ✦*MODISMO* **salir por ~** to say/do something quite inappropriate

petición SF 1 (= *solicitud*) (*gen*) request; (= *documento*) petition; **con referencia a su ~ del 20 de mayo** with reference to your request of May 20th; **vamos a oír las peticiones de los oyentes** we are going to hear the listeners' requests; **a ~ popular** by popular request; **a ~ de la familia** at the request of the family; **"consulta previa petición de cita"** "consultation by appointment"; **una ~ firmada por cinco mil personas** a petition signed by five thousand people ▸ **petición de divorcio** petition for divorce ▸ **petición de extradición** request for extradition ▸ **petición de indulto** appeal for a reprieve ▸ **petición de mano** proposal (of marriage) ▸ **petición de orden** (*Inform*) prompt

2 (*Jur*) (= *alegato*) plea; (= *reclamación*) claim; **una ~ de 12 años de condena** a recommendation to serve 12 years

peticionar ▸conjug 1a◂ VT (*LAm*) to petition

peticionario/a SM/F petitioner (*frm*), applicant

petimetre Ⓐ ADJ foppish

Ⓑ SM fop, dandy

petirrojo SM robin

petiso/a (*LAm*), **petizo/a** (*LAm*) Ⓐ ADJ (= *pequeño*) small, short; (= *rechoncho*) chubby

Ⓑ SM (= *caballo bajo*) small horse

Ⓒ SM/F (= *persona baja*) small person

petisú SM cream puff

petitorio ADJ **mesa petitoria** stall (*for charity collection*)

petizón ADJ (*Andes, Cono Sur*) = **petiso A**

peto SM [*de falda*] bodice; [*de pantalón*] bib; (*Mil*) breastplate; (*Taur*) horse's padding; **(pantalones con) ~** dungarees *pl*, overall (*EEUU*)

petral SM breast-strap (*of harness*)

Petrarca SM Petrarch

petrarquismo SM Petrarchism

petrarquista ADJ Petrarchan

petrel SM petrel

pétreo ADJ stony, rocky

petrificación SF petrifaction

petrificado ADJ petrified

petrificar ▸conjug 1g◂ Ⓐ VT (*lit, fig*) to petrify

Ⓑ **petrificarse** VPR (*lit*) to become petrified; (*fig*) to be petrified

petrodólar SM petrodollar

petróleo SM (*Min*) oil, petroleum; (*LAm*) (= *kerosene*) paraffin ▸ **petróleo combustible** fuel oil ▸ **petróleo crudo** crude oil ▸ **petróleo de alumbrado** paraffin (oil), kerosene (*EEUU*)

petrolero Ⓐ ADJ oil *antes de s*; **flota petrolera** oil tanker fleet; **industria petrolera** oil industry; **sindicato ~** oil workers' union

Ⓑ SM 1 (*Náut*) oil tanker

2 (*Com*) (*gen*) oil man; (= *obrero*) oil worker

3 (†) (= *incendiario*) arsonist, incendiary

petrolífero ADJ 1 (*Min*) oil-bearing

2 (*Com*) oil *antes de s*; **compañía petrolífera** oil company

petrología SF petrology

petroquímica SF (= *ciencia*) petrochemistry; (*Com*) petrochemical company; (= *fábrica*) petrochemical factory

petroquímico ADJ petrochemical

petulancia SF opinionated nature

petulante ADJ opinionated

petunia SF petunia

peuquino ADJ (*Cono Sur*) greyish, grayish (*EEUU*)

peyorativo ADJ pejorative

peyote SM (*LAm*) peyote cactus

pez[1] Ⓐ SM fish; **cogimos tres peces** we caught three fish; ✦*MODISMOS* **estar como el ~ en el agua** to feel completely at home, be in one's element; **ser un buen ~**†* to be a rogue, be a rascal; **quien quiera peces que se moje el culo*** if you want something, you have to go and get it ▸ **pez de colores** goldfish; ✦*MODISMO* **¡me río de los peces de colores!*** I couldn't care less! ▸ **pez espada** swordfish ▸ **pez gordo*** big shot* ▸ **pez martillo** hammerhead ▸ **pez mujer** manatee ▸ **pez sierra** sawfish ▸ **pez volador**, **pez volante** flying fish

Ⓑ ADJ (*) ✦*MODISMO* **estar ~ en algo** to know nothing at all about sth; **están algo peces en idiomas** they're pretty clueless about languages

pez[2] SF (= *brea*) pitch, tar

pezón SM 1 [*de persona*] nipple; [*de animal*] teat 2 (*Bot*) stalk 3 (*Mec*) ▸ **pezón de engrase** lubrication point, grease nipple

pezonera SF (*Cono Sur*) feeding bottle

pezuña SF 1 (*Zool*) hoof; (*) [*de persona*] hoof*, foot

2 (*Méx, Perú**) (= *olor*) smell of sweaty feet

PFCRN SM ABR (*Méx*) = **Partido del Frente Cardenista de Reconstrucción Nacional**

PGB SM ABR (*Chile*) (= **Producto Geográfico Bruto**) GDP

pgdo. ABR (= **pagado**) pd

PGP SM ABR (*Uru*) = **Partido por el Gobierno del Pueblo**

PGR SF ABR (*Méx*) = **Procuraduría General de la República**

phishing ['fiʃin] (*Internet*) phishing; **ataque ~** phishing attack

piada SF 1 (*Orn*) cheep, cheeping

2 (= *expresión copiada*) borrowed phrase

piadosamente ADV 1 (*Rel*) piously, devoutly

2 (= *bondadosamente*) kindly, mercifully

piadoso ADJ 1 (*Rel*) pious, devout

2 (= *bondadoso*) kind, merciful (**para, con** to); *ver tb* **mentira 1**

piafar ▸conjug 1a◂ VI [*caballo*] to paw the ground, stamp

pial SM lasso

pialar ▸conjug 1a◂ VT to lasso

Piamonte SM Piedmont

piamontés/esa Ⓐ ADJ of/from Piedmont

Ⓑ SM/F native/inhabitant of Piedmont; **los piamonteses** the people of Piedmont

pianista SMF pianist

pianístico ADJ piano *antes de s*

piano SM piano; **tocar el ~** (*lit*) to play the piano; (*) (= *fregar*) to do the washing-up; (*) (= *robar*) to rob, steal; (‡) (= *registrar huellas*) to have one's fingerprints taken, be fingerprinted; ✦*MODISMO* **como un ~** (*Esp**) huge, massive ▸ **piano de cola** grand piano ▸ **piano de media cola** baby grand ▸ **piano mecánico** pianola ▸ **piano recto**, **piano vertical** upright piano

piantado/a‡ (*Cono Sur*) Ⓐ ADJ nuts*, crazy

Ⓑ SM/F nutcase*

piantarse‡ ▸conjug 1a◂ VPR (*Cono Sur*) to escape, get out

piante* SMF **es un ~** he's a pain*

piar ▸conjug 1c◂ VI 1 [*ave*] to cheep

2 (*) (= *hablar*) to talk, chatter

3 (*) (= *quejarse*) to whine, grouse*; **~las*** to be forever whining o grousing*

4 (*) (= *soplar*) to spill the beans*; **¡no la píes!** don't let on!*

piara SF herd

piastra SF piastre, piaster (*EEUU*)

PIB SM ABR (= **producto interior bruto**) GDP

pibe/a* SM/F (*esp Arg*) (= *niño*) kid*; (= *muchacho*) boy/girl; (= *novio*) boyfriend/girlfriend

pibil SM (*Méx*) chili sauce

pica[1] SF (*Orn*) magpie

pica[2] SF (*Mil*) pike; (*Taur*) goad; (**) (= *pene*) prick**; ✦*MODISMO* **poner una ~ en Flandes** to bring off a real coup, achieve a signal success

pica[3] SF (*Andes Agr*) tapping (*of rubber trees*)

pica[4] SF 1 (*Andes*) (= *resentimiento*) pique, resentment
2 (*Cono Sur*) (= *mal humor*) annoyance, irritation; **sacar ~ a algn*** to annoy sb

pica[5]* SM/F [*de autobús*] inspector

pica[6] SF (*Andes, CAm, Caribe*) (= *camino*) forest trail, narrow path

picacera* SF (*Andes, Cono Sur*) irritation

picacho SM peak, summit

picada[1] SF 1 [*de abeja, avispa*] sting; [*de serpiente, mosquito*] bite; [*de ave*] peck
2 (*Cono Sur*) (= *mal humor*) bad temper, anger
3 **ir en ~** (*LAm lit*) to nose-dive; (*fig*) to plummet, take a nose-dive
4 (*Culin*) (= *salsa picante*) spicy sauce; (*Cono Sur*) (= *tapas*) snacks *pl*

picada[2] SF 1 (*LAm*) (= *senda*) forest trail, narrow path
2 (*Andes*) (= *vado*) ford

picada[3] SF (*Cono Sur*) small restaurant

picadero SM 1 (= *escuela*) riding school
2 (**) (= *apartamento*) bachelor pad*, *apartment used for sexual encounters*
3 (*LAm***) [*de drogas*] shooting gallery**
4 (*Andes*) (= *matadero*) slaughterhouse

picadillo SM [*de carne*] mince, ground meat (*EEUU*); **~ de cebolla** finely chopped onions *pl*; **los hizo ~** he made mincemeat out of them; ✦*MODISMO* **ser como el ~** (*Caribe**) to be boring

picado Ⓐ ADJ 1 (= *podrido*) [*diente*] rotten, decayed; [*fruta*] rotten; [*metal*] rusty, rusted; **tengo tres muelas picadas** I have three cavities
2 (*Culin*) [*ajo, cebolla, patata*] chopped; (*Esp, Cono Sur*) [*carne*] minced, ground (*EEUU*)
3 (= *triturado*) [*tabaco*] cut; [*hielo*] crushed
4 [*vino*] pricked, sour
5 [*mar*] choppy
6 **~ de viruelas** pockmarked
7 (*) (= *enfadado*) **estar ~** to be in a huff*; **están ~s desde hace muchos años** they fell out years ago
8 (*) (= *interesado*) **estar ~ con** *o* **por algo** to go for sth in a big way*; **está muy ~ con la lotería** he's really been bitten by the lottery bug*, he's gone for the lottery in a big way*
9 (= *borracho*) tipsy
10 (*Mús*) [*nota*] staccato
Ⓑ SM 1 (= *acción*) 1·1 (*Culin*) [*de ajo, cebolla, patata*] chopping; (*Esp, Cono Sur*) [*de carne*] mincing, grinding (*EEUU*)
1·2 [*de billete, boleto*] punching
1·3 (= *triturado*) [*de tabaco, de piedra*] cutting; [*de hielo*] crushing
2 (*Aer, Orn*) dive; **caer en ~** (*Esp Aer*) to plummet, nose-dive; [*precios, popularidad, producción*] to plummet, fall sharply
3 (*Mús*) staccato

picador SM 1 [*de caballos*] (*gen*) horse-trainer, horse-breaker; (*Taur*) picador
2 (*Min*) faceworker

picadora SF (*tb* **~ de carne**) mincer, mincing machine

picadura SF 1 (*gen*) prick; (= *pinchazo*) puncture; [*de abeja, avispa*] sting; [*de serpiente, mosquito*] bite
2 (= *tabaco picado*) cut tobacco

picaflor SM (*LAm*) 1 (*Orn*) hummingbird
2 (*) (= *tenorio*) ladykiller*, Don Juan; (= *mariposón*) flirt; (= *amante*) lover, boyfriend

picafuego SM poker

picahielos SM INV ice axe, ice ax (*EEUU*)

picajón* ADJ, **picajoso*** ADJ touchy

picamaderos SM INV woodpecker

picana SF (*LAm*) cattle prod, goad ► **picana eléctrica** electric prod (*esp for torture*)

picanear ▸conjug 1a◂ (*LAm*) VT (*gen*) to spur on, goad on; [+ *persona*] to torture with electric shocks

picante Ⓐ ADJ 1 (= *que pica*) [*comida, sabor*] hot, spicy; [*vino*] tart, sour
2 (= *malicioso*) [*comentario*] sharp, cutting; [*chiste*] dirty; [*comedia, película*] naughty, spicy; [*persona*] naughty
Ⓑ SM 1 (*Culin*) 1·1 (= *especia*) chilli; **esta salsa tiene mucho ~** this sauce is very hot *o* spicy
1·2 (*Andes, Cono Sur*) (= *guisado*) *meat stew with chilli sauce*
2 (= *picardía*) (*en persona*) zip, zest; (*en chiste, situación*) piquancy
3 **picantes** (*Esp***) (= *calcetines*) socks

picantería SF (*Andes, Cono Sur*) (cheap) restaurant (*specializing in spicy dishes*)

picantón SM spicy sauce

picapedrero SM stonecutter

picapica SF 1 (*Andes*) (= *serpentina*) streamer
2 **polvos de ~** itching powder

picapleitos SMF INV (*pey*) (= *pleitista*) litigious person; (= *abogado*) shark lawyer

picaporte SM (= *manija*) door handle; (= *pestillo*) latch; (= *aldaba*) doorknocker; (= *llave*) latchkey

picar ▸conjug 1g◂ Ⓐ VT 1 (*con el pico, la boca*) [*abeja, avispa*] to sting; [*mosquito, serpiente, pez*] to bite; [*ave*] to peck (at); **me ha picado un bicho en el cuello** an insect has bitten me on the neck; **los pájaros han picado toda la fruta** the birds have pecked holes in *o* pecked (at) all the fruit; **~ el anzuelo** (*lit*) to take *o* swallow the bait; (*fig*) to rise to the bait, fall for it*; ✦*MODISMO* **¿qué mosca le habrá picado?** what's got into her?, what's eating her? (*EEUU*)
2 (= *comer*) [*persona*] to nibble at; **he estado picando unos cacahuetes** I've been nibbling at some peanuts; **he picado algo antes de comer** I had a little nibble before lunch
3 (= *agujerear*) [+ *hoja, página*] to punch a hole/some holes in; [+ *billete, entrada*] to punch
4 (= *trocear*) 4·1 (*Culin*) [+ *ajo, cebolla, patata*] to chop; (*Esp, Cono Sur*) [+ *carne*] to mince, grind (*EEUU*); **pica la cebolla muy picadita** chop the onion very finely
4·2 [+ *tabaco*] to cut; [+ *hielo*] to crush
4·3 [+ *tierra*] to dig over, break up; [+ *piedra*] (*en trozos pequeños*) to chip at; (*en trozos grandes*) to break up; **acabó sus días picando piedra en una cantera** he ended his days breaking up stone in a quarry
5 (= *provocar*) [+ *persona*] to needle, goad; [+ *caballo*] to spur on; **estaba siempre picándome** he was always needling *o* goading me; **eso me picó la curiosidad** that aroused my curiosity; **lo que dijiste lo picó en su amor propio** what you said wounded *o* hurt his pride
6 (= *corroer*) [+ *diente, muela, madera*] to rot; [+ *hierro, metal*] to rust; [+ *cable*] to corrode; [+ *goma, neumático*] to perish; **las polillas han picado la lana** the moths have made holes in the wool
7 (*Inform*) [+ *texto*] to key in
8 (*Mús*) [+ *nota*] to play staccato
9 (*Taur*) [+ *toro*] to stick, prick (*with the goad*)
10 (*Mil*) [+ *enemigo*] to harass
11 (*Ven**) (= *sablear*) to scrounge*
12 (*Ven**) **~ el ojo a algn** to wink at sb
Ⓑ VI 1 (*con el pico, la boca*) [*abeja, avispa*] to sting; [*mosquito, serpiente*] to bite; [*ave*] to peck
2 (= *comer*) [*persona*] to nibble, snack; **llevo todo el día picando** I've been nibbling *o* snacking all day
3 (= *morder el cebo*) [*pez*] to bite; (*) [*persona*] to fall for it*; **hoy parece que no pican** it seems they aren't biting today; **ha picado mucha gente** a lot of people have fallen for it*; ✦*MODISMO* **~ muy alto** to aim too high, be over-ambitious
4 (= *ser picante*) [*comida*] to be hot, be spicy; **esta salsa sí que pica** this sauce is really hot *o* spicy
5 (= *causar picor*) [*herida, espalda*] to itch; **me pica la espalda** my back itches; **me pica por todo el cuerpo** I'm itching all over; **me pica la barba** I've got an itchy beard; **un jersey que pica** an itchy jumper; **¿le pica la garganta?** do you have a tickle in your throat?, do you have a tickly throat?; **me pican los ojos** my eyes are stinging *o* smarting; **el alcohol te va a ~ un poco** the alcohol is going to sting you a little; **¿qué te pica?** (*lit*) where does it itch?; (*fig*) what's got into you?, what's eating you? (*EEUU*); ✦*REFRÁN* **a quien le pique que se rasque** if you don't like it, you can lump it
6 [*sol*] to burn; **hoy sí que pica el sol** the sun is really burning today
7 (= *probar*) **~ en algo** to dabble in sth; **ha picado en todos los géneros literarios** he has dabbled in all the literary genres
8 (*Esp**) (= *llamar a la puerta*) to knock
9 (*Cono Sur**) (= *largarse*) to split**
10 (*Esp Aut*) to pink
11 **~le** (*Méx**) (= *darse prisa*) to hurry up
12 (*LAm*) [*pelota*] to bounce
Ⓒ **picarse** VPR 1 (= *corroerse*) [*diente, muela*] to rot, decay; [*hierro, metal*] to rust; [*goma, neumático*] to perish; [*cable*] to corrode; [*ropa*] to get moth-eaten; **se ha picado la chapa del coche** the bodywork has rusted
2 (*Culin*) [*fruta*] to go rotten; [*vino*] to go sour, turn sour
3 (*) 3·1 (= *enfadarse*) to get into a huff*; **¿no te habrás picado por lo que te he dicho?** you're not in a huff about what I said, are you?; ✦*REFRÁN* **el que se pica ajos come** if the cap fits, wear it
3·2 (= *sentirse provocado*) **se picó y pisó el acelerador** he rose to the challenge and stepped on the accelerator; **~se con algn** to

compete with sb; **siempre se están picando a ver quién es el primero** they're always competing to be the first
3·3 (= *aficionarse*) **~se con algo** to get hooked on sth*; **se ha picado con los videojuegos** he's got into video games in a big way*, he's got hooked on video games*
4 [*mar*] to get choppy
5 (*Caribe*) **~se de pecho** to become consumptive
6 (‡) (= *inyectarse droga*) to shoot up*; **ese tío se pica** that guy shoots up*; **~se heroína** to shoot heroin*

picarazado ADJ (*Caribe*) pockmarked

picardear ▸conjug 1a◂ Ⓐ VT **~ a algn** to get sb into bad habits, lead sb into evil ways
Ⓑ VI (= *jugar*) to play about; (= *dar guerra*) to play up, be mischievous
Ⓒ **picardearse** VPR to get into evil ways, go to the bad

Picardía SF Picardy

picardía SF 1 (= *cualidad*) (*del taimado*) slyness, craftiness; (*del travieso*) naughtiness
2 (= *acción*) prank, naughty thing (to do)
3 (= *grosería*) naughty thing (to say); (= *insulto*) insult; **le gusta decir ~s a la gente** he likes saying naughty things to people

picardías SM INV baby-doll pyjamas *pl*

picaresca SF 1 (*Literat*) (genre of the) picaresque novel
2 (= *astucia*) guile, chicanery (*liter*), subterfuge; **la ~ española** Spanish guile, Spanish wiliness
3 (= *hampa*) (criminal) underworld

picaresco ADJ 1 (= *travieso*) roguish, rascally
2 (*Literat*) picaresque

pícaro/a Ⓐ ADJ 1 (= *taimado*) sly, crafty; (= *travieso*) [*niño*] naughty, mischievous
2 (= *deshonesto*) crooked; (= *pillo*) roguish, knavish
3 (*hum*) naughty, wicked; **¡este ~ siglo!** what naughty times we live in!; **tiene inclinación a los ~s celos** she is prone to wicked jealousy
4 (= *precoz*) [*niño*] precocious, knowing (*esp sexually aware before the proper age*)
Ⓑ SM/F 1 (= *granuja*) rogue, scoundrel; (= *ladino*) sly sort; (= *niño*) rascal, scamp; **¡pícaro!** you rascal!
2 (*Literat*) rogue

PÍCARO

In Spanish literature, especially of the Golden Age, the **pícaro** *is a roguish character whose travels and adventures are used as a vehicle for social satire. The anonymous* **Lazarillo de Tormes** *(1554), which relates the life and adventures of one such character, is thought to be the first of the genre known as the picaresque novel, or* **novela picaresca**. *Other well-known picaresque novels were written by Cervantes (***Rinconete y Cortadillo***) and Francisco de Quevedo (***El Buscón***).*

picarón Ⓐ ADJ (*) naughty, roguish
Ⓑ SM (*LAm Culin*) fritter

picaruelo* ADJ roguish, naughty, sly; **me dio una mirada picaruela** she gave me a roguish look

picas SFPL (*Naipes*) spades

picatoste SM fried bread

picaza SF magpie

picazo SM (= *picotazo*) peck; (= *golpe*) jab, poke

picazón SF 1 (*Med*) (= *picor*) itch; (= *ardor*) sting, stinging feeling
2 (= *desazón*) uneasiness

píccolo SM piccolo

pícea SF spruce

picha[1] SF (*Méx*) 1 (= *manta*) blanket
2 (*hum*) (= *querida*) mistress

picha[2]** SF prick**

pichado ADJ (*Cono Sur*) easily embarrassed

pichana SF (*Andes, Cono Sur*) broom

pichanga SF 1 (*Andes*) (= *escoba*) broom
2 (*Cono Sur Dep*) friendly soccer match
3 (*Cono Sur Culin*) tray of cocktail snacks

pichango SM (*Cono Sur*) dog

piche SM 1 (*CAm*) (= *avaro*) miser, skinflint*
2 (*Andes, Cono Sur Zool*) *kind of armadillo*
3 (*Caribe, Cono Sur*) (= *miedo*) fright
4 (*Andes*) (= *empujón*) shove
5 (*Andes*) (= *suero*) whey
6 (*Andes*) (= *rojo*) red

pichel SM (= *vaso*) tankard, mug; (*Méx*) water jug

pichi[1]‡ Ⓐ ADJ (= *elegante*) smart, elegant
Ⓑ SM 1 (= *chulapo*) *Madrid man in traditional dress*
2 (*en oración directa*) mate*, man*, buddy (*EEUU**)

pichi[2]* SM **hacer ~** (*Andes, Cono Sur*) to have a pee*

pichi[3] SM (= *prenda*) pinafore dress

pichicata* SF (*LAm*) 1 (= *droga*) cocaine powder
2 (= *inyección*) shot*

pichicatero/a* SM/F (*LAm*) (= *adicto*) druggie*; (= *comerciante*) drug peddler

pichicato* ADJ (*LAm*) stingy

pichichi SM top goal-scorer

pichicote ADJ (*Andes*) mean, miserly

pichilingo SM (*Méx*) lad, kid*

pichincha* SF (*Andes, Cono Sur*) (= *ganga*) bargain; (= *precio*) bargain price; (= *trato*) good deal; (= *suerte*) lucky break

pichingo SM (*CAm*) jar, vessel; (*pey*) piece of junk

pichintún SM (*Cono Sur*) dash, smidgin*

pichirre* ADJ (*Andes, Caribe*) mean, stingy

picholear* ▸conjug 1a◂ VI 1 (*CAm, Cono Sur*) (= *jaranear*) to have a good time
2 (*CAm, Méx*) (= *apostar*) to have a flutter*

pichón SM 1 (= *paloma*) young pigeon; (*Culin*) pigeon ► **pichón de barro** clay pigeon
2 (*LAm*) (= *pollo*) chick
3 (*LAm**) (= *novato*) novice, greenhorn; (*Dep*) rookie
4 (*Cono Sur*) **un ~ de hombre** a well-bred man
5 (= *apelativo*) darling, dearest; **sí, ~** yes, darling *o* dearest

pichonear* ▸conjug 1a◂ Ⓐ VT 1 (*Méx*) (= *engañar*) to swindle, con*
2 (*Andes, CAm*) (= *pillar*) to catch out; (= *matar*) to kill, murder
3 (*Cono Sur*) = **pinchar**
4 (*Andes, CAm*) (= *tener prestado*) to borrow
Ⓑ VI (*Andes, Cono Sur, Méx*) to win an easy victory

pichoso ADJ (*Caribe*) dirty

pichula** SF (*Andes*) cock**, prick**

pichuleador* SM (*Cono Sur*) money-grubber

pichulear* ▸conjug 1a◂ VI 1 (*Cono Sur*) (= *negociar*) to be a smalltime businessman; (= *ser mercenario*) to be mercenary, be greedy for money
2 (*CAm, Méx*) (= *gastar poco*) to be careful with one's money

pichuleo* SM 1 (*Cono Sur*) (= *mezquindad*) meanness, stinginess*
2 (*CAm, Méx*) (= *negocio*) small business, retail business

pichulina‡ SF willy*, peter (*EEUU***)

picia* SF prank

pickles ['pikels] SMPL (*Cono Sur*) pickles

pick-up [pi'kap, pi'ku] SM 1 (†) (= *tocadiscos*) pickup
2 (*LAm*) (= *camioneta*) pickup (truck)

picnic SM 1 (= *excursión*) picnic
2 (= *cesta*) picnic basket, picnic set

pico SM 1 [*de ave*] beak, bill; [*de insecto*] beak
2 (= *punta*) corner, sharp point; **dobló el ~ de la página** he folded back the corner of the page; **el ~ de la plancha** the sharp point of the iron; **se sentó en el ~ de la cama** he sat on the edge *o* corner of the bed; **cuello de ~** V-neck; **sombrero de tres ~s** cocked hat, three-cornered hat; ✦*MODISMO* **irse de ~s pardos*** to go out on the town*, have a night on the town*
3 [*de jarra*] lip, spout
4 [*de montaña*] peak, summit; (*fig*) peak
5 (= *herramienta*) pick, pickaxe, pickax (*EEUU*)
6 [*de una cantidad*] **quédese con el ~** keep the change; **son las tres y ~** it's just after three; **tiene 50 libros y ~** he has 50-odd books *o* over 50 books; **tiene cuarenta y ~ años** she's forty-odd; **veinte euros y ~** just over twenty euros
7 (*) ✦*MODISMO* **costar un ~** to cost a fortune*
8 (*) (= *boca*) trap*; **¡cierra el ~!** shut your trap!*, shut up!*; ✦*MODISMOS* **darle al ~** to gab a lot*; **darse el ~** to kiss; **hincar el ~** (= *morir*) to peg out*; (= *ceder*) to give up, give in; **irse del ~** to gab a lot*; **ser un ~ de oro** ◊ **tener buen** *o* **mucho ~** to have the gift of the gab
9 (= *pájaro*) woodpecker
10 (*) [*de droga*] fix*, shot*
11 (*Naipes*) spade
12 (*Andes, Cono Sur***) (= *pene*) prick**

picolargo* ADJ (*Cono Sur*) (= *respondón*) pert, saucy, sassy (*EEUU**); (= *murmurador*) backbiting; (= *intrigante*) intriguing, scheming

picoleto‡ SM (*Esp*) Civil Guard

picón*/ona Ⓐ ADJ 1 (*Andes, Caribe*) (= *respondón*) cheeky*, sassy (*EEUU**)
2 (*Andes, Caribe*) (= *quisquilloso*) touchy
3 (*Caribe*) (= *burlón*) mocking
Ⓑ SM/F (*Andes*) gossip, telltale

picor SM = **picazón 1**

picoreto ADJ (*Andes, CAm, Caribe*) loose-tongued, indiscreet

picoso ADJ 1 (*LAm*) (= *picante*) very hot, spicy
2 (*de viruela*) pockmarked

picota SF 1 (*Arquit*) point, top; (*Geog*) peak
2 (*Bot*) bigarreau cherry
3 (*Hist*) pillory; ✦*MODISMO* **poner a algn en la ~** to pillory sb
4 (‡) (= *nariz*) hooter‡, conk‡

picotada SF, **picotazo** SM [*de pájaro*] peck; [*de abeja, avispa*] sting; [*de serpiente, mosquito*] bite; ✦*MODISMO* **tener mala ~** to be bad-tempered

picotear ▸conjug 1a◂ Ⓐ VT to peck (at)
Ⓑ VI 1 (*al comer*) to nibble
2 (*) (= *parlotear*) to gas*, gab*
Ⓒ **picotearse** VPR to squabble

picotero/a* Ⓐ ADJ chattering, gossipy, talkative
Ⓑ SM/F gossip, chatterer, gasbag*

picotón SM (*Andes, Cono Sur*) peck

picto/a Ⓐ ADJ Pictish
Ⓑ SM/F Pict; **los ~s** the Picts
Ⓒ SM (*Ling*) Pictish

pictograma SM pictogram

pictóricamente ADV pictorially

pictórico ADJ (*gen*) pictorial; [*paisaje*] worth painting; **tiene dotes pictóricas** she has a talent for painting

picú† SM record player, phonograph (*EEUU*)

picúa SF (*Caribe*) 1 (= *cometa*) small kite
2 (= *comerciante*) sharp businessman
3 (= *prostituta*) prostitute

picuda SF 1 (*Orn*) woodcock
2 (*Caribe*) (= *pez*) barracuda

picudo ADJ 1 (= *puntiagudo*) pointed; [*jarra*] with a spout; [*persona*] pointy-nosed
2 (*Méx**) (= *astuto*) crafty, clever
3 (*) = **picotero A**
4 (*Caribe*) = **cursi**

piculina‡ SF (*Esp*) tart‡, slut‡, whore

picup SM (*LAm*) pickup (truck)

picure SM 1 (*Andes*) (= *fugitivo*) fugitive; (= *gandul*) slacker
2 (*Caribe*) (= *salsa picante*) spicy sauce

picurearse* ▸conjug 1a◂ VPR (*Andes, Caribe*) to scarper‡

PID SM ABR (= **proceso integrado de datos**) IDP

pida, pido *etc ver* **pedir**

pídola SF leapfrog

pie SM 1 (*Anat*) foot; **levanta el ~ izquierdo** lift your left foot; **las plantas de los ~s** the soles of the feet; **no arrastres los ~s al andar** don't drag your feet while you walk; **con los ~s descalzos** barefoot; **se le fueron los ~s** he slipped; **poner el ~ en el acelerador** (*lit*) to step on the gas*; (*fig*) to speed things up, step up the pace; **volverse ~s atrás** to retrace one's steps ► **pie de atleta** athlete's foot ► **pie de cabra** crowbar ► **pie de rey** slide gauge ► **pies de barro** feet of clay ► **pies de cerdo** (*Culin*) (pig's) trotters ► **pies de gato** climbing boots ► **pies planos** flat feet
2 (*locuciones*) **a pie** on foot; **ir a ~** to go on foot, walk; **estar de ~** to be standing (up); **estaba de ~ junto a mi cama** he was standing next to my bed; **permanecieron mucho tiempo de ~** they were standing for a long time, they were on their feet a long time; **en ~**: **llevo en ~ desde las cuatro** I've been up since four; **mantenerse en ~** [*persona*] to stay standing *o* on one's feet; [*objeto*] to remain upright; **la oferta sigue en ~** the offer still stands; **ganado en ~** (*LAm*) cattle on the hoof; **a ~ enjuto**† (*lit*) dry-shod; (*fig*) without danger, without any risk; **a ~ firme**†: **permanecer a ~ firme** to remain steadfast; **ponerse de** *o* **en ~** to stand up; ✦*MODISMOS* **de a ~** common, ordinary; **gente de a ~** common *o* ordinary folk; **el hombre de a ~** the man in the street; **el español de a ~** the average Spaniard; **soldado de a ~** (*Hist*) foot-soldier; **andar con ~s de plomo** to tread carefully *o* warily; **de ~s a cabeza** from head to foot; **se mojó de ~s a cabeza** she got soaked from head to foot; **es un caballero de ~s a cabeza** he's a gentleman through and through; **caer de ~** to fall on one's feet; **cojear del mismo ~** to suffer from the same problem; **hacer algo con los ~s***: **han redactado este contrato con los ~s** they've made a mess of drawing up this contract; **estás pensando con los ~s** you're not using your head; **con los ~s por delante** feet first; **se lo llevaron con los ~s por delante** he left feet first, he left in a (wooden) box; **no dar ~ con bola*** to get everything wrong; **hoy no doy ~ con bola** I can't seem to get anything right today; **dale el ~ y se tomará la mano** give him an inch and he'll take a mile; **entrar con buen ~** *o* **con el ~ derecho** to get off to a good start; **estar con un ~ en el hoyo** to have one foot in the grave; **hacer ~** (*en el agua*) to touch the bottom; **no hacer ~** to be out of one's depth; **a ~s juntillas** blindly; **se lo creyeron a ~s juntillas** they blindly believed it; **levantarse con el ~ izquierdo** to get out of the wrong side of the bed; **nacer de ~** to be born lucky; **parar los ~s a algn** take sb down a peg or two; **perder el ~** to lose one's footing, slip; **poner el ~** *o* **los ~s en** to set foot in; **desde el pasado sábado, mi padre no ha puesto los ~s en casa** my father hasn't set foot in the house since last Saturday; **poner los ~s en el suelo** to put your feet firmly on the ground; **poner (los) ~s en polvorosa** to take to one's heels; **sacar los ~s del plato** *o* **tiesto** to kick over the traces; **salir por ~s*** to take to one's heels, leg it*; **sin ~s ni cabeza**: **un argumento sin ~s ni cabeza** an absurd argument; **el mensaje no tenía ni ~s ni cabeza** the message didn't make any sense at all, I couldn't make head or tail of the message; **el plan no tiene ni ~s ni cabeza** the plan is totally unworkable; *ver tb* **buscar 1.1**
3 (= *base*) [*de columna, estatua, lámpara*] base; [*de cama*] foot; [*de colina, escalera*] foot, bottom; [*de copa*] stem; [*de calcetín*] foot; **a los ~s de la cama** at the foot of the bed; **al ~ del monte** at the foot *o* bottom of the mountain; **al ~ de ese edificio** next to that building, right beside that building; **al ~ de fábrica** ex-works; **al ~ de la obra** (*Com*) including delivery charges; ✦*MODISMO* **al ~ del cañón**: **este fin de semana estará al ~ del cañón** he'll be hard at work this weekend; **ha cumplido 30 años al ~ del cañón** he spent 30 years on the job; **morir al ~ del cañón** to die in harness
4 [*de página*] foot, bottom; [*de foto*] caption; **notas a ~ de página** footnotes; ✦*MODISMO* **al ~ de la letra** [*citar*] literally, verbatim; [*copiar*] word for word; [*cumplir*] to the letter, down to the last detail ► **pie de imprenta** imprint
5 (*Bot*) [*de árbol*] trunk; [*de planta*] stem; [*de rosa*] stock
6 (= *unidad de medida*) foot; **tiene cuatro ~s de largo** it is four feet long ► **pie cuadrado** square foot
7 (*Teat*) cue
8 [*de vino*] sediment
9 (= *causa*) **dar ~ a** to give cause for; **dar ~ para que algn haga algo** to give sb cause to do sth
10 (= *posición*) **estar en ~ de igualdad** to be on an equal footing (**con** with); **estar en ~ de guerra** (*lit*) to be on a war footing, be ready to go to war; (*fig*) to be on the warpath; **poner a algn en ~ de guerra** to get sb up in arms
11 (*Literat*) foot
12 (*Cono Sur**) (= *pago*) deposit, down payment
13 ► **pie de vía** (*CAm Aut*) indicator, turn signal (*EEUU*)

piecería SF, **piecerío** SM (*Mec*) parts *pl*

piecero/a SM/F tailor's cutter, garment worker

piedad SF 1 (= *compasión, pena*) pity; **tuvo ~ del mendigo** he took pity on the beggar; **ten un poco de ~ con el pobrecillo** show some pity *o* sympathy for the poor boy; **¡por ~!** for pity's sake!; **mover a algn a ~** (*frm*) to move sb to pity, arouse compassion in sb
2 (= *clemencia*) mercy; **el rey tuvo ~ de sus súbditos** the king showed mercy to his subjects; **¡Dios, ten ~ de mí!** God, have mercy on me!
3 (*Rel*) piety
4 (†) (= *respeto*) respect ► **piedad filial** filial respect
5 (*Arte*) **la Piedad** the Pietà

piedra Ⓐ SF 1 (= *material*) stone; (= *trozo*) stone, rock (*EEUU*); **la ~ de la torre está gastada** the stone in the tower is ruined; **un puente de ~** a stone bridge; **nos tiraban ~s** they were throwing stones at us; **primera ~** foundation stone; **colocar la primera ~** to lay the foundation stone; **¿quién se atreve a lanzar la primera ~?** which of you shall cast the first stone?; ✦*MODISMOS* **no dejar ~ por mover** to leave no stone unturned; **no dejar ~ sobre ~** to raze to the ground; **hablar ~s** (*Andes*‡) to talk through the back of one's head*; **menos da una ~** it's better than nothing; **pasarse a algn por la ~**‡ to lay sb*; **no ser de ~**: **no soy de ~** I'm not made of stone, I do have feelings; **tener el corazón de ~** to be hard-hearted; **tirar la ~ y esconder la mano** to be a grass snake; **tirar ~s a** *o* **contra su propio tejado** to shoot o.s. in the foot ► **piedra angular** cornerstone ► **piedra arenisca** sandstone ► **piedra caliza** limestone ► **piedra de afilar, piedra de amolar** grindstone ► **piedra de cal** limestone ► **piedra de escándalo** source of scandal ► **piedra de molino** millstone ► **piedra de toque** touchstone ► **piedra filosofal** philosopher's stone ► **piedra fundamental** (*lit*) foundation stone; (*fig*) basis, cornerstone ► **piedra imán** lodestone ► **piedra poma** (*Méx*), **piedra pómez** pumice (stone) ► **piedra preciosa** precious stone; *ver tb* **tiro 1**
2 [*de mechero*] flint
3 (*Med*) stone
4 (*Meteo*) hailstone
5 **en ~** (*Cono Sur Culin*) with hot sauce
Ⓑ SMF (*Caribe*) (= *pesado*) bore

piel Ⓐ SF 1 [*de persona*] skin; **tiene la ~ grasa/seca** she has oily/dry skin; **estirarse la ~*** to have a facelift; ✦*MODISMOS* **dejarse la ~** to give one's all; **ponerse en la ~ de algn** to put o.s. in sb else's shoes; **se me/le puso la ~ de gallina** I/he came out in goose pim-

ples o goose flesh; ser de la ~ de Barrabás o del diablo* to be a little devil o monster ► piel de naranja (por celulitis) orange-peel skin
[2] [de animal] (gen) skin; [de vaca, búfalo, elefante] hide; [de foca, zorro, visón] fur; (= cuero) leather; abrigo de ~es fur coat; artículos de ~ leather goods; una maleta de ~ a leather suitcase; ✦MODISMO la ~ de toro Iberia ► piel de ante suede ► piel de becerro calf, calfskin ► piel de cabra goatskin ► piel de cerdo pigskin ► piel de ternera calfskin
[3] [de frutas] (gen) skin; [de naranja, limón] peel; [de manzana] skin, peel
Ⓑ SMF ► piel roja redskin; los ~es rojas the redskins

piélago SM (liter) [1] (= océano) ocean
[2] (fig) un ~ de dificultades a sea of difficulties

pienso^1 SM [1] (Agr) feed, fodder; ~s feeding stuffs
[2] (‡) (= comida) grub‡, chow (EEUU‡)

pienso^2†† SM thought; ✦MODISMO ¡ni por ~! never!, the very idea!

piercing ['pirsin] SM (pl piercings) piercing; lleva tres ~s en la oreja he's got three piercings in his ear; me voy a hacer un ~ en el ombligo I'm going to have my navel pierced

pierna SF [1] (Anat) leg; en ~s bare-legged; estirar las ~s to stretch one's legs; mañana iremos hasta el pueblo para hacer ~s we'll walk into the village tomorrow to get some exercise o for the exercise; ✦MODISMOS dormir a ~ suelta o tendida to sleep like a log*; salir por ~s* to take one's heels, leg it*
[2] (= muslo de animal) leg; ~ de cordero leg of lamb
[3] [de letra] stroke; (con pluma) downstroke
[4] (Cono Sur) player

piernas* SM INV twit*, idiot

piernicorto ADJ short-legged

pierrot [pie'ro] SM pierrot

pietista ADJ pietistic

pieza Ⓐ SF [1] (= componente) [1·1] [de rompecabezas, colección] piece; una vajilla de 60 ~s a 60-piece dinner service; un traje de baño de dos ~s a two-piece swimsuit; poco a poco fueron encajando todas las ~s del misterio little by little all the pieces of the mystery fell into place
[1·2] [de una exposición] exhibit; la colección expuesta consta de 30 ~s the collection on display includes 30 exhibits; una exposición de ~s de cerámica/orfebrería an exhibition of ceramics/silverware
[1·3] [de mecanismo, motor] part, component; las ~s del motor the engine parts o components
[1·4] de una ~: el capó estaba construido de una ~ the bonnet was made in one piece; un bañador de una ~ a one-piece swimsuit; un caballero de una ~ an upright gentleman; me dejas de una ~ con lo que me acabas de contar I'm astonished at what you've just told me; me quedé de una ~ I was totally dumbstruck o gobsmacked*; ✦MODISMO ser de una (sola) ~ (LAm) to be as straight as a die
► pieza arqueológica artefact ► pieza clave (lit) essential part; (fig) key element ► pieza de convicción (Jur) piece of evidence ► pieza de museo museum piece ► pieza de oro (= moneda) gold coin, gold piece; (= objeto) gold object ► pieza de recambio, pieza de repuesto spare (part), extra (EEUU)
[2] (= ejemplar) [2·1] [de carne, fruta] piece; dos ~s de fruta two pieces of fruit; vender algo por ~s to sell sth by the piece; sólo vendemos la carne por ~s enteras we only sell meat in whole cuts; "vendemos el queso por ~s" "we sell individual cheeses"
[2·2] (Arte) example; una ~ única del Románico a unique example of the Romanesque
[2·3] (tb ~ de caza) specimen; se cobró dos buenas ~s he shot two fine specimens
[3] (Ajedrez) piece
[4] (Cos) (= remiendo) patch; (= rollo de tela) roll
[5] (esp LAm) (= habitación) room ► pieza amueblada furnished room ► pieza de recibo reception room
[6] (= obra) (Mús) piece, composition; (Literat) work; (Teat) play ► pieza corta (Mús) short piece; (Teat) playlet ► pieza literaria literary work ► pieza musical piece of music, musical piece ► pieza oratoria speech
[7] (Mil) ► pieza de artillería artillery piece
[8] (Odontología) tooth ► pieza bucal, pieza dental, pieza dentaria tooth
[9] (*) (= persona) ¡buena ~ estás tú hecho! you're a fine one!; ✦MODISMOS ser una ~ para algo (Méx*) to be very good at sth; ser mucha ~ para algn (Méx*) to be in a different league from sb
Ⓑ SMF (‡) (= camello) pusher*

pífano SM fife

pifia SF [1] (Billar) miscue
[2] (*) (= error) blunder, bloomer*
[3] (Andes, Cono Sur) (= burla) mockery; (= chiste) joke; hacer ~ de (= burlarse) to mock, poke fun at; (= bromear) to make a joke of, joke about
[4] (Andes, Cono Sur) (= rechifla) hiss

pifiador ADJ (Andes, Cono Sur) joking, mocking

pifiar ▸conjug 1b◂ Ⓐ VT [1] (Andes, Arg) (= burlarse de) to joke about, mock; (= engañar) to play a trick on
[2] (Andes, Cono Sur) (= arruinar) to mess up, botch
[3] (Andes, Cono Sur) (= chiflar) to boo, hiss at
[4] (Méx‡) (= robar) to nick‡, lift*
[5] (*) ~la (= meter la pata) to blunder, make a bloomer*
Ⓑ VI [1] (Cono Sur) (= fracasar) to fail, come a cropper*; (en el juego) to mess up one's game
[2] (Andes, CAm) (= llevarse un chasco) to be disappointed, suffer a setback

pigmentación SF pigmentation

pigmentado/a Ⓐ ADJ (gen) pigmented; (euf) [persona] coloured, colored (EEUU)
Ⓑ SM/F (euf) coloured person, colored person (EEUU)

pigmento SM pigment

pigmeo/a ADJ, SM/F pigmy

pignorable ADJ objeto fácilmente ~ a thing which it is easy to pawn

pignorar ▸conjug 1a◂ VT to pawn

pigricia SF [1] (Andes) (= bagatela) trifle, bagatelle; (= pizca) small bit, pinch
[2] (= pereza) laziness

pija** SF prick**; ver tb pijo

pijada* SF [1] (= cosa absurda) eso es una ~ that's utter nonsense o rubbish
[2] (= cosa sin importancia) trifle
[3] (= capricho) expensive toy

pijama SM pyjamas pl, pajama (EEUU) ► pijama de playa beach pyjamas pl

pijar** ▸conjug 1a◂ VT to fuck**

pije SM (Chile) toff*, snob*

pijo/a Ⓐ ADJ (*) [1] [persona, ropa, discoteca] posh [2] (= tonto) stupid Ⓑ SM/F (*) [1] (= niño bien) spoilt brat, spoilt rich kid [2] (= tonto) berk*, twit*, jerk (EEUU*) Ⓒ SM [1] (Esp**) (= pene) prick** [2] (‡) ✦MODISMOS no te oyen ni ~ they can't hear you at all; ¡qué ~s! hell's bells!*; ¿qué ~s haces aquí? what in hell's name are you doing here?*; ver tb pija

pijolero/a* ADJ, SM/F = pijotero

pijotada* SF [1] = pijada
[2] (Méx) (= dinero) insignificant sum

pijotear* ▸conjug 1a◂ VI (Andes, Cono Sur, Méx) to haggle

pijotería* SF [1] (= esnobismo) snobbery, snobbishness [2] (= molestia) nuisance, annoying thing; (= petición) trifling request, silly demand
[3] (LAm) (= pequeña cantidad) insignificant sum, tiny amount; (= bagatela) trifle, small thing [4] (LAm) (= tacañería) stinginess*

pijotero/a* Ⓐ ADJ [1] (= molesto) tedious, annoying; (= condenado) bloody‡, bleeding‡
[2] (LAm) (= tacaño) mean, stingy*
[3] (Cono Sur) (= no fiable) untrustworthy
Ⓑ SM/F [1] (= persona molesta) pain*; ¡no seas ~! don't be such a pain!*
[2] (= tonto) berk‡, twit*

pijudo* ADJ [1] = pijotero A
[2] (CAm) (= muy bueno) great*, terrific*

pila^1 SF [1] [de libros, juguetes] pile, stack [2] (*) [de deberes, trabajo] heap; una ~ de heaps of, piles of; tengo una ~ de cosas que hacer I have heaps o piles of things to do; una ~ de años ages; una ~ de ladrones a bunch of thieves [3] (Arquit) pile

pila^2 SF [1] (= fregadero) sink; (= artesa) trough; (= abrevadero) drinking trough; [de fuente] basin; (LAm) (public) fountain ► pila de cocina kitchen sink
[2] (Rel) (tb ~ bautismal) font; nombre de ~ Christian name, first name; ✦MODISMO sacar de ~ a algn to act as godparent to sb ► pila de agua bendita holy water stoup
[3] (Elec) battery; aparato a ~s battery-run apparatus, battery-operated apparatus; ✦MODISMO cargar las ~s to recharge one's batteries ► pila alcalina alkaline battery, alkaline cell ► pila atómica atomic pile ► pila (de) botón watch battery, calculator battery ► pila seca dry cell ► pila solar solar battery
[4] ✦MODISMO ponerse las ~s* to get one's act together, put one's skates on
[5] (Caribe) (= grifo) tap, faucet (EEUU)

pilado‡ ADJ ✦MODISMO está ~ (Andes) (= seguro) it's a cert*; (= fácil) it's a cinch‡

pilar^1 SM [1] (= poste) post, pillar; (= mojón) milestone; [de puente] pier
[2] (fig) pillar, mainstay; un ~ de la monarquía a mainstay of the monarchy

pilar^2 SM [de fuente] basin, bowl

pilastra SF (gen) pilaster; (Cono Sur) [de puerta] frame

Pilatos SM Pilate

pilatuna* SF (*LAm*) dirty trick

pilatuno ADJ (*Andes*) manifestly unjust

pilcha* SF (*Cono Sur*) [1] (= *prenda*) [*de persona*] garment, article of clothing; [*de caballo*] harness
[2] **pilchas** (= *ropa vieja*) old clothes; (= *ropa elegante*) fine clothes
[3] (= *querida*) mistress

pilche SM (*LAm*) (coconut) gourd, calabash

píldora SF pill; **la ~ (anticonceptiva)** the (contraceptive) pill; ✦*MODISMOS* **dorar la ~** to sugar *o* sweeten the pill; **tragarse la ~** to be taken in ► **píldora abortiva** morning-after pill ► **píldora antibaby** contraceptive pill ► **píldora anticalvicie** anti-baldness pill ► **píldora anticonceptiva** contraceptive pill ► **píldora antifatiga** anti-fatigue pill, pep pill* ► **píldora del día después, píldora del día siguiente** morning-after pill

pildorazo* SM (*Mil*) burst of gunfire, salvo; (*Dep*) fierce shot

pildorita SF (*Cono Sur*) small cocktail sausage

pileta SF [1] (*gen*) basin, bowl; [*de cocina*] sink; (= *artesa*) trough
[2] (*LAm*) [*de baño*] wash basin ► **pileta de natación** swimming pool

pilgua SF (*Cono Sur*) wicker basket

pilier SM prop forward

piligüe Ⓐ ADJ (*CAm*) [*fruta*] shrivelled, empty
Ⓑ SMF (*CAm, Méx*) poor devil

pilila* SF willy*, peter (*EEUU***)

pililo SM (*Cono Sur*) tramp, hobo (*EEUU*)

pilintruca SF (*Cono Sur*) slut

pillada SF [1] (= *trampa*) dirty trick
[2] (*Cono Sur*) (= *sorpresa*) surprise revelation; (= *encuentro*) surprise encounter

pillaje SM pillage, plunder

pillar ▸conjug 1a◂ Ⓐ VT [1] (= *atrapar*) to catch; **nunca lo pillo en casa** I can never catch him at home; **lo pilló la policía** the police caught *o* nabbed* him; **el perro le pilló el pantalón** the dog caught his trouser leg; **me pilló el dedo con la puerta** he got my finger caught in the door; **¡como te pille ... !** if I get hold of you ... !
[2] (*) (= *tomar, coger*) to catch, get; **~ el autobús** to catch *o* get the bus; **píllame un asiento al lado tuyo** grab me a seat beside you*
[3] (= *sorprender*) to catch; **lo pillé fumando** I caught him smoking; **¡te he pillado!** caught *o* got you!
[4] (= *alcanzar*) to catch up with; **salí corriendo y la pillé a medio camino** I ran out and caught up with her on the way
[5] (= *atropellar*) to hit, run over; **la pilló una moto** she was hit by a motorbike
[6] [+ *resfriado, pulmonía*] to catch, get; **~ una borrachera** to get drunk
[7] (*) [+ *puesto*] to get, land
[8] [+ *broma, significado*] to get, catch on to
Ⓑ VI (*Esp**) **me pilla lejos** it's too far for me; **me pilla muy cerca** it's handy *o* near for me; **me pilla de camino** it's on my way
Ⓒ **pillarse** VPR to catch; **se pilló el dedo con la puerta** he caught his finger in the door

pillastre* SM/F scoundrel

pillería SF [1] (= *acción*) dirty trick
[2] [*de niños*] naughtiness; [*de adultos*] craftiness
[3] (= *pandilla*) gang of scoundrels

pillete SM rascal, scamp

pillín/ina SM/F rascal, scamp

pillo/a Ⓐ ADJ [*adulto*] sly, crafty; [*niño*] naughty
Ⓑ SM/F (= *adulto*) rogue, scoundrel; (= *niño*) rascal, scamp

pilluelo SM rascal, scamp

pilmama SF (*Méx*) (= *nodriza*) wet-nurse; (= *niñera*) nursemaid

pilme ADJ (*Cono Sur*) very thin

pilón[1] SM [1] (*gen*) pillar, post; (*Elec*) pylon
[2] (*Téc*) drop hammer
[3] [*de romana*] weight
[4] [*de azúcar*] sugar loaf
[5] (*Caribe Agr*) dump, store

pilón[2] SM [1] (= *abrevadero*) drinking trough; [*de fuente*] basin; (*Méx*) drinking fountain
[2] (= *mortero*) mortar
[3] (*Méx**) extra, bonus; (= *propina*) tip
[4] (*Cono Sur*) (= *capacho*) pannier

piloncillo SM (*Méx*) powdered brown sugar

pilongo ADJ [1] (= *flaco*) thin, emaciated
[2] [*castaña*] dried

pilosidad SF hairiness

piloso ADJ hairy

pilotaje SM (*Náut, Aer*) piloting; **fallo de ~** navigational error

pilotar ▸conjug 1a◂ VT [+ *avión*] to pilot; [+ *coche*] to drive; [+ *barco*] to steer, navigate

pilote SM [1] (*Arquit*) pile
[2] (*CAm**) (= *fiesta*) party

pilotear ▸conjug 1a◂ VT [1] = **pilotar**
[2] (*LAm*) (= *dirigir*) [+ *persona*] to guide, direct; [+ *negocio*] to run, manage
[3] (*Cono Sur*) [+ *persona*] to exploit

piloto Ⓐ SMF [1] (*Aer*) pilot; **segundo ~** co-pilot ► **piloto de caza** fighter pilot ► **piloto de pruebas** test pilot
[2] [*de coche*] driver, racing driver; [*de moto*] rider ► **piloto de pruebas** (*Aut*) test driver
[3] (*Náut*) navigator, navigation officer ► **piloto de puerto** harbour pilot
[4] (= *guía*) guide; (*en exploración*) pathfinder
Ⓑ SM [1] (= *aparato*) ► **piloto automático** automatic pilot ► **piloto de combate** fighter pilot
[2] (= *luz*) pilot, pilot light; (*Aut*) tail light, rear light ► **piloto de alarma** flashing light ► **piloto de niebla** fog light, fog lamp
Ⓒ ADJ INV pilot *antes de s*; **estudio ~** pilot study; **planta ~** pilot plant; **programa ~** pilot programme *o* (*EEUU*) program; **piso ~** show flat

pilpinto SM (*Andes, Cono Sur*) butterfly

pilsen SF, **pílsener** SF (*Chile*) beer

piltra* SF kip*

piltrafa SF [1] [*de carne*] poor quality meat; **~s** scraps
[2] (*fig*) (= *cosa*) worthless object; (= *persona*) wretch
[3] **piltrafas** (*LAm*) [*de ropa*] rags, old clothes
[4] (*Andes, Cono Sur*) (= *ganga*) bargain; (= *suerte*) piece of luck; (= *ganancia*) profit

piltrafiento ADJ [1] (*Cono Sur, Méx*) (= *harapiento*) ragged
[2] (*Cono Sur*) (= *marchito*) withered

piltrafoso ADJ (*Andes*) ragged

piltrafudo ADJ (*Andes*) weak, languid

piltre Ⓐ ADJ [1] (*Andes, Caribe*) (= *petimetre*) foppish
[2] (*Chile*) [*fruta*] (= *madura*) over-ripe; (= *seca*) shrivelled, dried up
Ⓑ SMF (*Andes**) snappy dresser*

pilucho (*Cono Sur*) Ⓐ ADJ (*) naked
Ⓑ SM [*de bebé*] cotton vest, dress

pimentero SM [1] (*Bot*) pepper plant
[2] (*Culin*) pepperpot, pepper shaker (*EEUU*)

pimentón SM [1] (= *especia*) (*tb* ~ **dulce**) paprika ► **pimentón picante** hot paprika, cayenne pepper
[2] (*LAm*) (= *fruto*) sweet pepper, capsicum

pimienta SF pepper ► **pimienta de cayena** cayenne pepper ► **pimienta inglesa** allspice ► **pimienta negra** black pepper

pimiento SM [1] (= *fruto*) pepper; ✦*MODISMO* **(no) me importa un ~** I don't care two hoots*; ► **pimiento del piquillo, pimiento morrón, pimiento rojo** red pepper ► **pimiento verde** green pepper
[2] (*Bot*) pepper plant

pimpampúm* SM [1] [*de ferias*] shooting gallery
[2] (= *ruido*) crash, bang, wallop

pimpante* ADJ [1] (= *acicalado*) smart, spruce
[2] (*tb* **tan ~**) (= *ufano*) smug, self-satisfied

pimpinela SF pimpernel

pimplar* ▸conjug 1a◂ Ⓐ VI to booze*
Ⓑ **pimplarse** VPR **~se una botella** to down a bottle*, quaff a bottle*

pimpollo SM [1] (*Bot*) (= *serpollo*) sucker, shoot; (= *brote*) sapling; (= *capullo*) bud
[2] (*) (= *niño*) bonny child; (= *mujer*) attractive woman; **hecho un ~** (= *elegante*) very smart; (= *joven*) very young for one's age

pimpón SM ping-pong

pimponista SMF ping-pong player

pin SM (*pl* **pins**) [1] (= *insignia*) badge
[2] (*Elec*) pin

pinabete SM fir, fir tree

pinacate SM (*Méx*) black beetle

pinacoteca SF art gallery

pináculo SM pinnacle

pinar SM pine grove

pinaza SF pinnace

pincel SM [1] (*para pintar*) paintbrush; [*de cocina*] brush; ✦*MODISMO* **estar hecho un ~** to be very smartly dressed
[2] (= *pintor*) painter

pincelada SF brushstroke; **última ~** (*fig*) finishing touch

pincha[1]* SF (*Caribe*) job, spot of work

pincha[2] SF (*Cono Sur*) hair-grip

pinchadiscos* SMF INV (*Esp*), **pincha[3]*** SMF INV (*Esp*) disc jockey, D.J.

pinchante ADJ [*grito*] piercing

pinchar ▸conjug 1a◂ Ⓐ VT [1] (= *reventar*) [+ *globo, pelota*] to burst; [+ *neumático, rueda*] to puncture; **me han pinchado las ruedas** my tyres have been slashed
[2] (= *picar*) [2·1] (*con algo punzante*) to prick; **le pinchó en el brazo con un alfiler** she pricked his arm with a pin
[2·2] (*Culin*) to test; **pincha la carne con el tenedor** test the meat with your fork, stick the fork in the meat; ✦*MODISMO* **ni ~ ni cortar*** to count for nothing
[3] (= *comer*) to nibble (at); **hemos pinchado unos taquitos de queso** we nibbled (at) a

few cubes of cheese

4 (*) (= *poner una inyección a*) to give a jab to*, give a shot to*; **tuvimos que ~lo para que se le calmase el dolor** we had to give him a jab *o* shot to ease the pain*; **me han pinchado un antibiótico** I got an antibiotic jab *o* a shot of antibiotics*

5 (*) (= *apuñalar*) to knife; **amenazó con ~lo si no le daba el dinero** he threatened to knife him if he didn't give him the money

6 (*) (= *presionar*) (*gen*) to prod; (*pey*) to pester; **hay que ~lo para que se mueva** he needs prodding to get him going; **no dejan de ~me para que me case** they keep getting on at me *o* pestering me to get married

7 (*) (= *provocar*) to wind sb up*; **siempre me está pinchando** he's always winding me up*

8 (*) [+ *línea, teléfono*] to tap, bug

9 (*Esp**) (*Mús*) **~ discos** to deejay*, be a disc jockey

Ⓑ VI 1 (= *hincarse*) [*espina*] to prick; [*clavo*] to stick; **ten cuidado con el rosal, que pincha** careful of the rosebush, it's prickly *o* it will prick you; **te pincha la barba** your beard is bristly *o* prickly

2 (= *tener un pinchazo*) to get a puncture; **pinchamos al salir de la curva** we got a puncture coming out of the bend

3 (*Esp**) (= *fracasar*) to come a cropper*; **hemos pinchado con este proyecto** we have come a cropper with this project*; **el Real Madrid ha pinchado en casa** Real Madrid have come a cropper at home*

4 (= *hacer clic*) to click (**en** on)

5 (*Chile**) (= *ligar*) **cuando era joven pinchaba harto** when he was young he had a lot of girlfriends; **~ con algn** to get off with sb*

Ⓒ **pincharse** VPR 1 (= *clavarse*) (*en dedo, brazo*) to prick o.s.; **me he pinchado con una aguja** I've pricked myself with a needle; **¿te has pinchado en el pie?** did you get something stuck in your foot?

2 (= *reventarse*) [*globo, pelota*] to burst; [*neumático, rueda*] to puncture; **se nos pinchó la rueda** we got a puncture; **tener un neumático pinchado** to have a puncture, have a flat tyre

3 (*Med*) [+ *antibiótico, insulina*] to inject o.s. with; **tengo que ~me insulina a diario** I have to inject myself with insulin every day; **hoy no tengo que ir a ~me** I don't have to go for an injection today

4 (⁑) (= *drogarse*) to shoot up*; **había un hombre pinchándose en el callejón** there was a man shooting up in the alley*; **se pincha heroína** he shoots heroin*

pinchazo SM 1 (*con objeto punzante*) prick; **me he metido un ~ cosiendo** I've pricked my finger *o* myself sewing

2 (*en neumático*) puncture; **tuvimos un ~** we got a puncture

3 (*) (= *inyección*) [*de antibiótico, insulina*] jab*, shot; [*de cocaína, heroína*] shot, fix⁑; **le encontraron varios ~s en el brazo** they found a number of needle marks on his arm

4 [*de dolor*] shooting pain, sharp pain

5 (*Telec**) tap*, bug*

6 (*Esp*) (= *fracaso*) fiasco; **las elecciones supusieron un gran ~ para el gobierno** the elections proved to be a disaster *o* fiasco for the government

pinche Ⓐ ADJ 1 (*Méx*⁑) (= *maldito*) bloody⁑, lousy⁑; **todo por unos ~s centavos** all for a few measly cents

2 (*CAm, Méx*) (= *miserable*) wretched

3 (*CAm**) (= *tacaño*) stingy, tight-fisted

Ⓑ SMF 1 [*de cocina*] kitchen hand, kitchen-boy

2 (*Cono Sur*) (= *oficinista*) minor office clerk; (= *criminal*) small-time criminal

3 (*Caribe, Méx*) (= *granuja*) rascal

Ⓒ SM 1 (*Andes*) (= *jamelgo*) nag

2 (*Cono Sur*) (= *horquilla*) hairpin, bobby pin (*EEUU*)

pinchito SM (*Esp*) tapa

pincho SM 1 (= *punta*) point; (= *varilla*) pointed stick, spike

2 [*de zarza, flor*] thorn, prickle; [*de cactus, animal*] spike, prickle

3 (⁑) (= *navaja*) knife

4 (*Culin*) tapa; **un ~ de tortilla** a small portion of omelette ► **pincho moruno** kebab

5 (**) (= *pene*) prick**

pinchota⁑ SMF *user of drugs by injection*

pinciano/a (*Esp*) Ⓐ ADJ of/from Valladolid

Ⓑ SM/F native/inhabitant of Valladolid; **los ~s** the people of Valladolid

pindárico ADJ Pindaric

Píndaro SM Pindar

pindonga* SF gadabout

pindonguear* ▸conjug 1a◂ VI to gad about

pindongueo* SM **ir de ~** to wander round, roam the streets

pinga SF 1 (*LAm***) (= *pene*) prick**

2 (*Caribe*) ✦**MODISMO de ~*** amazing, terrific*

pingajo SM rag, shred; **ir hecho un ~** to look a right mess*

pinganilla* SM 1 (*LAm*) (= *pretencioso*) sharp dresser

2 (*Méx*) **en ~s** (= *de puntillas*) on tiptoe; (= *en cuclillas*) squatting; (= *poco firme*) wobbly

pinganillo ADJ (*Andes*) chubby

pinganitos†* SMPL **estar en ~** to be well up, be well-placed socially; **poner a algn en ~** to give sb a leg up (socially)

pingo Ⓐ ADJ INV (* *pey*) loose*, promiscuous

Ⓑ SM 1 (= *harapo*) rag; (= *prenda*) old garment; **~s*** cheap women's clothes; **no tengo ni un ~ que ponerme*** I haven't a single thing I can wear; ✦**MODISMOS andar** *o* **ir de ~** to gad about; **poner a algn como un ~** to slag sb off*

2 (*) (= *callejeador*) gadabout; (*pey*) (= *mujer*) slut⁑

3 (*) (= *caballo*) (*Arg, Uru*) (*bueno*) good horse; (*Chile, Perú*) (*malo*) nag

4 (*Méx*) (= *niño*) scamp; **el ~** the devil

5 (*Cono Sur*) (= *niño*) lively child

pingonear* ▸conjug 1a◂ VI to gad about

pingorotear ▸conjug 1a◂ VI (*LAm*), **pingotear** ▸conjug 1a◂ VI (*LAm*) to skip about, jump

ping-pong ['pimpon] SM ping-pong

pinguchita* SF (*Cono Sur*) beanpole*, string bean (*EEUU**)

pingucho (*Cono Sur*) Ⓐ ADJ poor, wretched

Ⓑ SM urchin, ragamuffin

pingüe ADJ 1 (*gen*) abundant, copious; [*ganancias*] rich, fat; [*cosecha*] bumper; [*negocio*] lucrative

2 (= *grasiento*) greasy

pingui* SM swank

pingüinera SF penguin colony

pingüino SM penguin ► **pingüino de Humboldt** Humboldt's penguin

pinitos SMPL, **pininos** SMPL (*esp LAm*) **hacer sus ~** [*niño*] to toddle, take his/her first steps; [*novato*] to take his/her first steps; [*enfermo*] to start to get about again, get back on one's feet again; **hago mis ~ como pintor** I play *o* dabble at painting

pinja** SF (*Andes*) prick**

pino[1] SM 1 (*Bot*) pine, pine tree; ✦**MODISMOS ponerle ~** (*Cono Sur**) to make a great effort; **vivir en el quinto ~** to live at the back of beyond; **eso está en el quinto ~** that's miles away ► **pino albar** Scots pine ► **pino araucano** monkey-puzzle (tree) ► **pino bravo** cluster pine ► **pino de tea** pitch pine ► **pino marítimo**, **pino rodeno** cluster pine ► **pino silvestre** Scots pine

2 (*en gimnasia*) **hacer el ~** to do a handstand

3 **pinos** = **pinitos**

pino[2] ADJ steep; **en ~** (= *vertical*) upright, vertical; (= *de pie*) standing

pinocha SF pine needle

pinol SM (*CAm, Méx*), **pinole** SM (*CAm, Méx*) *drink made of roasted maize flour or* (*EEUU*) *roasted cornflour*

pinolero/a* (*CAm*) Ⓐ ADJ Nicaraguan

Ⓑ SM/F Nicaraguan; **los ~s** the Nicaraguans

pinrel* SM hoof*, foot

pinsapo SM (*Esp*) Spanish fir

pinta[1] SF 1 (= *lunar*) (*gen*) spot, dot; (*Zool*) spot, mark; **una tela a ~s azules** a cloth with blue spots

2 [*de líquidos*] drop, spot; [*de lluvia*] drop; (*) (= *bebida*) drop to drink; **una ~ de grasa** a grease spot

3 (*) (= *aspecto*) appearance; **por la ~** by the look of it; **tener buena ~** [*persona*] to look good, look well; [*comida*] to look good; **tener ~ de listo** to look clever; **tiene ~ de criminal** he looks like a criminal; **tiene ~ de español** he looks Spanish, he looks like a Spaniard; **¿qué ~ tiene?** what does he look like?; **con esa(s) ~(s) no puedes ir** you can't go looking like that; ✦**MODISMOS ¡a la ~!** (*Cono Sur*) perfect!, that's fine!; **estar a la ~** (*Cono Sur*) ◊ **tener ~** (*Cono Sur*) (= *atractivo*) to be attractive; (= *elegante*) to be smart, be well-dressed; **no se le vio ni ~** (*LAm**) there wasn't a sign *o* trace of him; **tirar ~*** to impress

4 (*LAm Zool*) (= *colorido*) colouring, coloring (*EEUU*), coloration; (= *característica*) family characteristic, distinguishing mark

5 (*CAm, Méx*) (= *pintada*) piece of graffiti

6 (*Naipes*) spot (*indicating suit*); **¿a qué ~?** what's trumps?, what suit are we in?

7 (*Andes, Cono Sur*) (= *juego*) draughts *pl*; (= *dados*) dice

8 (*Cono Sur Min*) high-grade ore

9 ✦**MODISMOS hacer ~** (*Méx*) ◊ **irse de ~** (*CAm*) to play truant; **ser de la ~** (*Caribe euf*) to be coloured

pinta[2] SF (= *medida inglesa*) pint

pinta[3]* SM rogue

pintada[1] SF (*Orn*) guinea-fowl

pintada[2] SF piece of graffiti; **~s** graffiti

pintado Ⓐ ADJ 1 (*Zool*) (= *moteado*) spotted; (= *pinto*) mottled, dappled

2 (*) (= *igual*) **~ a algn** exactly like sb, iden-

tical to sb; **el niño salió ~ al padre** the boy turned out exactly like his father *o* identical to his father

3 ✦*MODISMOS* **el más ~*** anybody; **eso podría pasarle al más ~** that could happen to anybody; **lo hace como el más ~** he does it as well as anybody; **sentar/venir que ni ~ a algn*** to suit sb down to the ground*

Ⓑ SM 1 (= *acción*) (*gen*) painting; (*Téc*) coating ► **pintado de campo** marking-out of the pitch

2 (*Esp*) *wine and vermouth cocktail*

pintalabios SM INV lipstick

pintamonas* SMF INV (*pey*) 1 (= *pintor*) dauber*

2 (= *don nadie*) **un ~** a nobody

pintar ▸conjug 1a◂ Ⓐ VT 1 (*Arte*) (*con óleo, acuarela*) to paint; (*con lápices, rotuladores*) (= *dibujar*) to draw; (= *colorear*) to colour, color (*EEUU*); **el primer cuadro que pintó** the first picture he painted; **~ algo al óleo/temple** to paint sth in oils/tempera; **píntame una casa** paint *o* draw me a house

2 (= *dar una capa de pintura a*) [+ *pared, habitación*] to paint; **hace falta ~ esta habitación** this room needs painting *o* decorating; **"recién pintado"** "wet paint"; **tengo que ~ el coche** the car needs a coat of paint *o* a re-spray; **~ algo de o en blanco/azul** to paint sth white/blue; **~ algo con pistola** to spray-paint sth

3 (= *describir*) to paint; **lo pinta todo muy negro** he paints it all very black; **tal como lo pintas, no parece que haya una solución fácil** the way you describe it *o* paint things , it seems there is no easy solution; *ver tb* **fiero A1**, **ocasión 2**

4 (*) (= *tener importancia*) **¿acaso tú pintas algo en esta cuestión?** what's this got to do with you?, what business is this of yours?; **¿pero qué pintamos aquí?** what on earth are we doing here?; **yo en esa fiesta no pinto nada** I'd be out of place at that party; **no pinta nada en la empresa** he's nobody important in the company; **antes me consultaban, pero ya no pinto nada** before I was consulted but my opinion counts for nothing now

Ⓑ VI 1 (*Arte*) to paint; **no pinto desde hace años** I haven't painted for years

2 (*para decorar*) to decorate; **cuando terminen la obra ~emos** when they finish the building work we'll decorate *o* do the decorating

3 (= *manchar*) (*de pintura, tinta*) **ten cuidado con ese banco, que pinta** be careful, that bench has wet paint on it; **"¡ojo, pinta!"** "wet paint"

4 (*) (= *escribir*) to write; **este boli ya no pinta** this biro doesn't work *o* write; **no pintéis en las mesas** don't write on the desks

5 (*Bot*) (= *madurar*) to ripen; **en agosto pintan las uvas** the grapes ripen in August

6 (*Naipes*) to be trumps; **¿qué pinta?** what's trumps?; **pintan corazones** hearts are trumps

7 (*LAm**) (= *mostrarse*) to look; **la situación pinta mejor** things are looking up; **no me gusta cómo pinta esto** I don't like the look of this

Ⓒ **pintarse** VPR 1 (= *maquillarse*) (*una vez*) to put one's make-up on, make o.s. up; (*con frecuencia*) to use make-up; **tardó una hora en ~se** she took an hour to put her make-up on *o* to make herself up; **no me gusta nada ir pintada** I don't like using make-up; **se ~on la cara para la fiesta de disfraces** they painted their faces for the fancy-dress party; **~se los labios** to put lipstick on; **~se los ojos**: **¿te has pintado los ojos?** have you got any eye make-up on?, did you put on your eye make-up?; **¿con qué te pintas los ojos?** what eye make-up do you use?; **~se las uñas** to paint one's nails; ✦*MODISMO* **pintárselas solo para algo*** to be an expert *o* a dab hand at sth; **se las pinta solo para conseguir lo que quiere** he's an expert *o* a dab hand at getting what he wants; **a la hora de meter la pata se las pinta solo** he's a specialist *o* an expert at putting his foot in it

2 (= *mancharse*) [+ *manos, ropa*] **te has pintado las manos de tinta** you've got ink on your hands

3 (= *notarse*) to show; **el cansancio se pintaba en su rostro** you could see the tiredness in her face, the tiredness showed on her face

4 (*Méx**) (= *largarse*) to beat it*

pintarrajear* ▸conjug 1a◂ VT, VI to daub

pintarrajo* SM daub

pintarroja SF dogfish

pintas* SMF INV scruff*, scruffily dressed person

pintear ▸conjug 1a◂ VI to drizzle, spot with rain

pintiparado ADJ 1 (= *idéntico*) identical (**a** to)

2 ✦*MODISMO* **me viene (que ni) ~** it suits me a treat

pintiparar ▸conjug 1a◂ VT to compare

Pinto SM ✦*MODISMO* **estar entre ~ y Valdemoro** (*Esp**) (= *indeciso*) to be in two minds; (= *borracho*) to be tipsy; **el examen está entre ~ y Valdemoro** the exam's a borderline case

pinto ADJ 1 (*LAm*) (= *con manchas*) spotted, dappled; (= *marcado*) marked (*esp in black and white*); (= *abigarrado*) motley, colourful, colorful (*EEUU*)

2 [*tez*] blotchy

3 (*Cuba*) (= *listo*) clever; (*pey*) sharp, shrewd

4 (*Caribe*) (= *borracho*) drunk

pintor(a) SM/F 1 painter ► **pintor(a) de brocha gorda** (*de paredes*) painter and decorator; (*de cuadros*) (*pey*) bad painter, dauber ► **pintor(a) decorador(a)** painter and decorator ► **pintor(a) de suelo** pavement artist

2 (*Cono Sur**) (= *fachendoso*) swank*

pintoresco ADJ picturesque

pintoresquismo SM picturesqueness

pintura SF 1 (= *forma artística, cuadro*) painting; ✦*MODISMO* **no lo podía ver ni en ~** she couldn't stand the sight of him ► **pintura a la acuarela**, **pintura a la aguada** watercolour, watercolor (*EEUU*) ► **pintura al óleo** oil painting ► **pintura al pastel** pastel drawing ► **pintura rupestre** cave painting

2 (= *descripción*) depiction

3 (= *material*) paint ► **pintura a la cola**, **pintura al temple** (*para paredes*) distemper; (*para cuadros*) tempera ► **pintura emulsionada** emulsion, emulsion paint

4 (= *lápiz de color*) crayon ► **pintura de cera** wax crayon

pinturero/a* Ⓐ ADJ swanky*

Ⓑ SM/F show-off*, swank*

pinza SF 1 [*de ropa*] clothes peg, clothespin (*EEUU*) ► **pinza de pelo** hairgrip

2 **pinzas** (*de depilar*) tweezers; (*para hielo, azúcar*) tongs; (*Med*) forceps; ✦*MODISMOS* **había que cogerlo con ~s** I had to take it very carefully; **no se lo sacan ni con ~s** wild horses won't drag it out of him

3 (*Cos*) pleat; **pantalones de ~s** trousers with waist pleats, pleated trousers

4 [*de cangrejo, langosta*] pincer, claw

pinzamiento SM ► **pinzamiento discal** slipped disc, slipped disk (*EEUU*)

pinzón SM (*Orn*) finch ► **pinzón real** bullfinch ► **pinzón vulgar** chaffinch

piña Ⓐ SF 1 [*de pino*] pine cone

2 (= *fruta*) pineapple ► **piña de América**, **piña de las Indias** pineapple

3 [*de personas*] (= *grupo*) group; (= *conjunto*) cluster, knot; (= *corrillo*) clique, closed circle; ✦*MODISMO* **como una piña: estaban unidos como una ~** they were a very close-knit group

4 (*Caribe, Méx*) [*de rueda*] hub

5 (*) (= *golpe*) punch, bash*; **darse una ~** to have a crash; **darse ~s** to fight, exchange blows

6 (*Méx*) [*de revólver*] chamber

7 (*Andes**) **¡qué ~!** bad luck!; **estar ~** to be unlucky

Ⓑ SM (*CAm**) poof*, faggot (*EEUU**)

piñal SM (*LAm*) pineapple plantation

piñar* SM (*Méx*) lie

piñata¹ SF (*en fiestas*) *container hung up at parties to be beaten with sticks until sweets or presents fall out*

piñata²* SF (= *dientes*) ivories* *pl*, teeth *pl*

piñata³ SF (*Cono Sur*) brawl, scrap*

piñatería SF (*Cono Sur*) armed hold-up

piño¹* SM (= *diente*) ivory*, tooth

piño²* SM (*Chile*) (= *reunión*) crowd, lot

piñón¹ SM (*Bot*) pine kernel; ✦*MODISMO* **estar o llevarse a partir un ~** to be the best of buddies, be bosom pals* (**con** with)

piñón² SM (*Orn, Téc*) pinion; ✦*MODISMOS* **seguir a ~ fijo*** (= *sin moverse*) to be rooted to the spot; (= *sin cambiar de idea*) to go on in the same old way, be stuck in one's old ways; **quedarse a ~ fijo*** to have a mental block

piñonate SM candied pine-nut

piñonear ▸conjug 1a◂ VI to click

piñoneo SM click

piñoso* ADJ (*Andes*) unlucky

Pío SM Pius

pío¹ ADJ [*caballo*] piebald, dappled

pío² ADJ 1 (*Rel*) pious, devout; (*pey*) sanctimonious

2 (= *compasivo*) merciful

pío³ SM 1 (*Orn*) cheep, chirp; ✦*MODISMO* **no decir ni ~** not to breathe a word; **¡de esto no digas ni ~!** don't you breathe a word!; **irse sin decir ni ~** to go off without a word

2 ✦*MODISMO* **tener el ~ de algo*** to long for sth

piocha Ⓐ SF 1 (*LAm*) (= *piqueta*) pickaxe, pickax (*EEUU*)

2 (*Chile*) (= *distintivo*) badge

3 (†) (= *joya*) jewel (worn on the head)

4 (*Méx*) (= *barba*) goatee

Ⓑ ADJ (*Méx*) nice

piojería SF 1 (= *lugar*) lousy place, verminous place

2 (= *pobreza*) poverty

3 (*) (= *miseria*) tiny amount, very small portion

piojo SM 1 (*Zool*) louse; ✦*MODISMOS* **dar el ~** (*Méx**) to show one's nasty side; **estar como ~s en costura** to be packed in like sardines ► **piojo resucitado*** jumped-up fellow, vulgar parvenu
2 (*Andes*) gambling den

piojoso ADJ 1 (= *con piojos*) lousy
2 (= *sucio*) filthy
3 (= *mezquino*) mean

piojuelo SM louse

piola Ⓐ SF 1 (*LAm*) (= *soga*) rope, tether
2 (*Andes, Caribe*) (= *cuerda*) cord, string; (= *maguey*) agave
3 (*Cono Sur***) (= *pene*) cock**
Ⓑ ADJ INV (*Arg**) (= *astuto*) smart, clever; (= *listo*) bright; (= *taimado*) sly; (= *servicial*) helpful; (= *bueno*) great*, terrific*; (= *elegante*) classy*

piolet [pio'le] SM (*pl* **piolets** [pio'les]) ice axe, ice ax (*EEUU*)

piolín SM (*LAm*) cord, twine

pionco ADJ 1 (*Cono Sur*) naked from the waist down
2 (*Méx*) (= *en cuclillas*) squatting
3 (*Méx*) [*caballo*] short-tailed

pionero/a Ⓐ ADJ pioneering
Ⓑ SM/F pioneer

pioneta SM (*Chile Aut*) lorry driver's mate, truck driver's mate (*EEUU*)

piorrea SF pyorrhoea

PIP SM ABR (*Puerto Rico*) = **Partido Independentista Puertorriqueño**

pipa[1] SF 1 (*de fumar*) pipe; **fumar en ~** ◊ **fumar una ~** to smoke a pipe
2 [*de vino*] (= *barril*) cask, barrel; (= *medida*) pipe
3 (*Bot*) (= *semilla*) pip, seed; [*de girasol*] (edible) sunflower seed; ✦*MODISMO* **no tener ni para ~s** to be broke, be skint*
4 (*Mús*) reed
5 (*LAm**) (= *barriga*) belly*; **tener ~** to be potbellied
6 (‡) (= *pistola*) rod‡, pistol; (= *ametralladora*) machine-gun
7 ✦*MODISMO* **pasarlo ~*** to have a great time*
8 (*Andes, CAm Bot*) green coconut

pipa[2]* SM 1 (*Mús*) assistant
2 (= *mozo de carga*) porter
3 (= *utillero*) boy, mate

pipear‡ ▸conjug 1a◂ Ⓐ VT to look at
Ⓑ VI to look

pipero[1]**/a** SM/F 1 (= *vendedor ambulante*) street vendor
2 (= *fumador*) pipe smoker

pipero[2] SM (= *estante*) pipe rack

pipeta SF pipette

pipi‡ SM 1 (*Mil*) squaddie*, recruit
2 (= *novato*) new boy

pipí* SM (= *orín*) pee*; (*entre niños*) wee wee*; **hacer ~** (*gen*) to do a wee wee*, have a pee*; **hacerse ~** to need a wee-wee; (*involuntariamente*) to wet oneself

pipián SM (*CAm, Méx*) (= *salsa*) thick chili sauce; (= *guiso*) *meat cooked in thick chili sauce*

pipiar ▸conjug 1c◂ VI to cheep, chirp

pipiciego ADJ (*Andes*) short-sighted, near-sighted (*EEUU*)

pipil* SM (*CAm hum*) Mexican

pipiolero* SM (*Méx*) crowd of kids*

pipiolo/a* SM/F 1 (= *joven*) youngster; (*LAm*) (= *chico*) little boy/little girl; (= *novato*) novice, greenhorn
2 (*Caribe, Cono Sur*) (= *tonto*) fool
3 **pipiolos** (*CAm*) (= *dinero*) money *sing*

pipirigallo SM sainfoin

pipiripao SM 1 (†*) (= *convite*) slap-up do*, beanfeast*
2 ✦*MODISMO* **de ~** (*LAm*) worthless

pipo Ⓐ ADJ (*Andes, Caribe*) potbellied; **estar ~** (*Caribe*) to be bloated
Ⓑ SM 1 (*Caribe*) (= *niño*) child
2 (*Andes, Caribe*) (= *empleado*) crooked employee*
3 (*Andes*) (= *golpe*) punch, bash*
4 (*Andes*) (= *licor*) contraband liquor

pipón* ADJ (*Andes, Caribe, Cono Sur*) (= *barrigón*) potbellied; (= *lleno de comida*) bloated

piporro SM 1 (= *instrumento*) bassoon
2 (= *persona*) bassoonist

pipote SM 1 (= *barril*) keg, cask
2 (*Ven*) (= *cubo de basura*) dustbin, trash can (*EEUU*)

pipudo‡ ADJ great*, super*

pique[1] SM 1 (= *resentimiento*) resentment, pique; (= *inquina*) grudge; (= *rivalidad*) rivalry, competition; **tener un ~ con algn** to have a grudge against sb; **tienen (un) ~ sobre sus coches** they're always trying to outdo one another with their cars; **estar de ~** to be at loggerheads
2 **echar a ~** [+ *barco*] to sink; [+ *futuro, carrera*] to wreck, ruin; **irse a ~** [*barco*] to sink; [*esperanza, familia*] to be ruined
3 **estar a ~ de hacer algo** (= *a punto de*) to be on the point of doing sth; (= *en peligro de*) to be in danger of doing sth
4 (*LAm Min*) (= *galería*) mine shaft; (*Méx*) (= *pozo*) drill, well
5 (*LAm*) (= *rebote*) bounce, rebound
6 (*CAm, Cono Sur*) (= *sendero*) trail, narrow path
7 (*Andes*) (= *insecto*) jigger flea

pique[2] SM (*Naipes*) spades

pique[3]‡ SM [*de droga*] fix‡, shot*

piquera SF 1 [*de tonel, colmena*] hole, vent
2 (*CAm, Méx**) (= *taberna*) dive*
3 (*Caribe*) [*de taxis*] taxi rank

piquero SM 1 (*Hist*) pikeman
2 (*Andes, Cono Sur*) (= *minero*) miner
3 (‡) (= *ratero*) pickpocket

piqueta SF (= *herramienta*) pick, pickaxe, pickax (*EEUU*); [*de tienda de campaña*] peg

piquetazo SM (*LAm*) 1 (= *tijeretazo*) snip, small cut
2 [*de pájaro*] peck

piquete SM 1 [*de personas*] (*Mil*) squad, party; (*en huelga*) picket ► **piquete de ejecución** firing squad ► **piquete informativo** picket ► **piquete móvil** flying picket ► **piquete secundario** secondary picket ► **piquete volante** flying picket
2 (*Arg*) (= *corral*) yard, small corral
3 (= *pinchazo*) prick, jab
4 (= *agujero*) small hole (*in clothing*)
5 (*Andes*) (= *merienda*) picnic
6 (*Caribe Mús*) street band

piquin SM 1 (*Andes*) (= *galán*) boyfriend

2 (*Cono Sur**) (= *pizca*) pinch, dash
3 (*Cono Sur*) (= *persona*) irritable sort

piquiña SF 1 (*Andes, Caribe*) = **picazón**
2 (*Caribe*) (= *envidia*) envy

pira[1] SF (= *hoguera*) pyre

pira[2]‡ SF ✦*MODISMOS* **hacer ~** ◊ **irse de ~** (= *largarse*) to clear off*; (*Escol*) to cut class*, play truant

pirado/a‡ Ⓐ ADJ (= *loco*) round the bend*, crazy; (= *drogado*) high‡, out of one's head‡
Ⓑ SM/F (= *majareta*) nutcase*; (= *drogado*) druggy‡

piragua SF canoe

piragüismo SM canoeing

piragüista SMF canoeist

piramidal ADJ 1 [*forma*] pyramidal
2 (*Andes**) terrific*, tremendous*

pirámide SF pyramid ► **pirámide de edad(es)** age pyramid

Píramo SM Pyramus

piraña SF piranha

pirarse* ▸conjug 1a◂ VPR (*tb* **pirárselas**) (= *largarse*) to beat it*, clear out*; (*Andes*) to escape from prison; (*Méx*) to peg out‡; **~ las clases** to cut class*

pirata Ⓐ SMF 1 (= *corsario*) pirate ► **pirata aéreo** hijacker
2 (*Inform*) ► **pirata informático/a** hacker
3 (*Literat**) plagiarist
4 (*) (= *granuja*) rogue, scoundrel
5 (*Com*) cowboy, shark
6 (†*) (= *persona cruel*) hard-hearted person
Ⓑ ADJ **barco ~** pirate ship; **disco ~** bootleg record; **edición ~** pirated edition; **emisora ~** pirate radio station

piratear ▸conjug 1a◂ Ⓐ VT (*Aer*) to hijack; (*Mús*) to pirate; (*Inform*) to hack into; [+ *libro*] to plagiarize
Ⓑ VI 1 [*barcos*] to buccaneer, practise piracy, practice piracy (*EEUU*)
2 (= *robar*) to steal

piratería SF, **pirateo** SM 1 [*de buque*] piracy ► **piratería aérea** highjacking
2 [*de disco, concierto, grabación*] bootlegging; **~ de vídeo** video piracy ► **piratería informática** hacking, software piracy
3 (= *robo*) theft, stealing
4 **piraterías** (= *estragos*) depredations

pirático ADJ piratical

piraya SF (*LAm*) piranha

pirca SF (*Andes, Chile*) dry-stone wall

pire‡ SM (= *drogas*) trip‡

pirenaico ADJ Pyrenean

pirético ADJ pyretic

piretro SM pyrethrum

pirgua SF (*Andes, Cono Sur*) shed, small barn

piri‡ SM grub‡, nosh‡, chow (*EEUU*‡)

piridina SF pyridine

pirineísta SMF mountaineer (who climbs in the Pyrenees)

Pirineo SM, **Pirineos** SMPL Pyrenees; **el ~ catalán** the Catalan (part of the) Pyrenees

pirineo ADJ Pyrenean

pirinola* SF (*Méx*) kid*, child

piripez†* SF **coger una ~** to get sozzled

piripi* ADJ **estar ~** to be sozzled*

pirita(s) SF pyrite, pyrites

pirlán SM (*Andes*) doorstep

piro* SM **darse el ~ de** to escape from; **darse el ~** to beat it*

piro... PREF pyro...

pirófago/a SM/F fire-eater

piromanía SF pyromania

pirómano/a SM/F pyromaniac

piropear ▸conjug 1a◂ VT to compliment, pay an amorous compliment to, make a flirtatious remark to

piropo SM [1] (= *cumplido*) flirtatious remark; (= *lisonja*) flattery; **echar ~s a** to make a flirtatious remark to
[2] (= *granate*) garnet; (= *rubí*) ruby
[3] (*Andes**) ticking-off*

piroso* ADJ lewd, dirty

pirotecnia SF (*gen*) pyrotechnics *pl*, fireworks *pl*; (= *fuegos artificiales*) firework display

pirotécnico ADJ pyrotechnic, firework *antes de s*

piroxidina SF pyridoxine

pirquén SM **mina al ~** (*Chile*) rented mine

pirrar* ▸conjug 1a◂, **pirriar** ▸conjug 1b◂ (A) VT **le pirraba el cine** he was really into the cinema*
(B) **pirr(i)arse** VPR **~se por** to be crazy about

pírrico ADJ **victoria pírrica** Pyrrhic victory

Pirro SM Pyrrhus

pirucho SM (*CAm*) (ice-cream) cone *o* cornet

pirueta SF (= *movimiento ágil*) pirouette; (= *cabriola*) caper; ✦**MODISMO hacer ~s** to perform a balancing act

piruetear ▸conjug 1a◂ VI (*gen*) to pirouette; (= *saltar*) to caper

pirula* SF [1] ✦**MODISMO hacer la ~ a*** (= *molestar*) to upset, annoy; (= *jugarla*) to play a dirty trick on; (= *embaucar*) to cheat
[2] (*Anat*) willy*, peter (*EEUU***); *ver tb* **pirulo**

piruleta SF lollipop

pirulí SM [1] (= *piruleta*) lollipop; ✦**MODISMO durar lo que un ~ a la puerta de un colegio** not to last five minutes
[2] (**) (= *pene*) prick**
[3] **el Pirulí*** Madrid television tower

pirulo[1] (*Cono Sur**) SM **tiene 40 ~s** he's the big four O, he's forty

pirulo[2]**/a** SM/F (= *niño*) slim child; *ver tb* **pirula**

pis* SM pee*; **hacer ~** to have a pee*, do a wee*; **hacerse ~ en la cama** to wet the *o* one's bed

Pisa SF Pisa

pisa SF [1] [*de uvas*] treading
[2] (*) (= *zurra*) beating

pisada SF (= *paso*) footstep; (= *huella*) footprint

pisadera SF (*Andes*) carpet

pisadero SM (*Méx*) brothel

pisado SM treading (of grapes)

pisano/a (A) ADJ Pisan
(B) SM/F native/inhabitant of Pisa; **los ~s** the people of Pisa

pisapapeles SM INV paperweight

pisar ▸conjug 1a◂ (A) VT [1] (= *andar sobre*) to walk on; **¿se puede ~ el suelo de la cocina?** can I walk on the kitchen floor?
[2] (= *poner el pie encima de*) to tread on, step on; **perdona, te he pisado** sorry, I trod *o* stepped on your foot; **vio una cucaracha y la pisó** she saw a cockroach and trod *o* stood on it; **~ el acelerador a fondo** to step on the accelerator, put one's foot down*; **"prohibido pisar el césped"** "keep off the grass"; ✦**MODISMOS ir pisando huevos** to tread carefully; **tiene un morro que se lo pisa*** he's a cheeky devil*
[3] (= *ir a*) to set foot in; **no volvimos a ~ ese sitio** we never set foot in that place again; **hace años que no pisa un bar** he hasn't been in a pub for years
[4] [+ *uvas*] to tread; [+ *tierra*] to tread down
[5] (= *avasallar*) to trample on, walk all over; **no se deja ~ por nadie** he doesn't let anybody trample on *o* walk all over him
[6] (*Mús*) [+ *tecla*] to strike, press; [+ *cuerda*] to hold down
[7] (*Andes*) [+ *hembra*] to cover; (*CAm***) to fuck**, screw**
[8] (*) (= *adelantarse a*) **otro le pisó el puesto** somebody got in first and collared the job; **el periódico le pisó la noticia** the newspaper got in first with the news; **~ una baza a algn** to trump sb's trick; *ver tb* **talón 1**
(B) VI (= *andar*) to tread; **hay que ~ con cuidado** you have to tread carefully; ✦**MODISMO ~ fuerte*** to make great strides; **entrar pisando fuerte** to burst onto the scene*

pisaverde† SMF toff*

pisca SF [1] (*Méx*) (= *cosecha*) maize harvest, corn harvest (*EEUU*)
[2] (*Andes*) (= *prostituta*) prostitute
[3] (= *parte*) = **pizca 1, 2**

piscador SM (*Méx*) harvester

piscar ▸conjug 1g◂ (*Méx*) VT to pinch, nip VI to harvest maize, harvest corn (*EEUU*)

piscicultor(a) SM/F fish farmer

piscicultura SF fish farming

piscifactoría SF fish farm

piscigranja SF (*LAm*) fish farm

piscina SF [1] (*Dep*) swimming pool ► **piscina climatizada** heated swimming pool ► **piscina cubierta** indoor swimming pool ► **piscina de saltos** diving pool ► **piscina olímpica** Olympic pool
[2] (= *estanque*) fishpond

Piscis SM Pisces

pisco[1] SM (*Andes*) [1] (= *pavo*) turkey
[2] (= *persona*) fellow, guy*

pisco[2] SM (*Andes, Chile*) strong grape liquor ► **pisco sauer** (*Andes*) pisco cocktail

piscoiro* SM, **piscoira** SF (*Cono Sur**) bright child

piscola SF (*Chile*) pisco and coca cola (drink)

piscolabis SM INV [1] (= *tentempié*) snack
[2] (*CAm, Méx*) money

pisicorre SM (*Caribe*) small bus

piso SM [1] (*esp LAm*) (= *suelo*) floor; (= *materiales para suelo*) flooring
[2] [*de edificio*] floor, storey, story (*EEUU*); [*de autobús, barco*] deck; [*de cohete*] stage; [*de pastel*] layer, tier; **primer ~** first floor, second floor (*EEUU*); **viven en el quinto ~** they live on the fifth floor; **un edificio de ocho ~s** an eight-storey building; **autobús de dos ~s** double-decker bus; **ir en el ~ de arriba** to travel on the top deck, travel upstairs ► **piso alto** top floor ► **piso bajo** ground floor, first floor (*EEUU*)
[3] (= *apartamento*) flat, apartment (*EEUU*); **poner un ~ a una** (*Esp*) to set a woman up in a flat ► **piso de seguridad, piso franco** (*Esp*) safe house ► **piso piloto** show flat
[4] (*Aut*) [*de neumático*] tread
[5] [*de zapato*] sole; **poner ~ a un zapato** to sole a shoe
[6] (*LAm*) (= *tapete*) table runner; (= *estera*) mat; (*Andes, Cono Sur*) (= *alfombra*) long narrow rug ► **piso de baño** bathmat
[7] (*Min*) set of workings; (*Geol*) layer, stratum
[8] (*Cono Sur*) (= *taburete*) stool; (= *banco*) bench

pisón SM [1] (*para aplastar tierra*) ram, rammer
[2] (*LAm*) = **pisotón 2**
[3] (*Cono Sur*) (= *mortero*) mortar

pisotear ▸conjug 1a◂ VT [1] (*gen*) to tread down, trample (underfoot); (= *hollar*) to stamp on
[2] (= *humillar*) to trample on; [+ *ley*] to abuse, disregard

pisoteo SM (*gen*) treading, trampling; (= *holladura*) stamping

pisotón SM [1] (*con el pie*) stamp; **me ha dado un ~** he trod on my foot
[2] (*Periodismo**) scoop

pispar* ▸conjug 1a◂ (A) VI (*Cono Sur*) (= *acechar*) to spy, keep watch
(B) VT (*) (= *robar*) to nick*

pis-pas* SM, **pispás*** SM **en un ~** in a flash, in no time at all

pisporra SF (*CAm*) wart

pista SF [1] (= *rastro*) track, trail; (*Inform*) track; **estar sobre la ~** to be on the scent; **estar sobre la ~ de algn** to be on sb's trail *o* track, be after sb; **seguir la ~ de algn** (*gen*) to be on sb's trail *o* track; [*de cerca*] to shadow sb
[2] (= *indicio*) clue; **dame una ~** give me a clue; **la policía tiene una ~ ya** the police already have a lead ► **pista falsa** (*gen*) false trail; (= *ardid*) red herring
[3] (*Dep*) [*de atletismo*] track; (= *cancha*) court; [*de circo*] ring; (*Aut*) carriageway; (*CAm*) (= *avenida*) avenue; **reunión de ~ cubierta** indoor athletics meeting; **atletismo en ~** track athletics ► **pista de aprendizaje** nursery slope ► **pista de aterrizaje** (*en aeropuerto*) runway; (*para aviones militares, privados*) landing strip ► **pista de atletismo** athletics track ► **pista de baile** dance floor ► **pista de bolos** bowling alley ► **pista de carreras** racetrack ► **pista de ceniza** dirt track ► **pista de esquí** piste, ski run ► **pista de hielo** ice rink ► **pista de hierba** grass court ► **pista de patinaje** skating rink ► **pista de squash** squash court ► **pista de tenis** tennis court ► **pista de tierra batida** clay court ► **pista dura** hard court ► **pista forestal** forest trail
[4] [*de cinta*] track

pistacho SM pistachio

pistero ADJ (*CAm*) mercenary, fond of money

pistilo SM (*Bot*) pistil

pisto SM [1] (*Esp Culin*) fried vegetable hash, ratatouille
[2] ✦**MODISMO darse ~*** to show off, swank*
[3] (= *revoltijo*) hotchpotch, hodgepodge (*EEUU*)
[4] (*LAm**) (= *dinero*) dough*
[5] (*Andes*) [*de revólver*] barrel
[6] (*Méx**) (= *trago*) shot of liquor*
[7] (†) (= *caldo de pollo*) chicken broth
[8] (†) ✦**MODISMO a ~s** (= *poco a poco*) little by little; (= *con escasez*) sparingly

pistola SF [1] (= *arma*) pistol, gun; (*Téc*) (*para pintar*) spray gun ► **pistola ametralladora** submachine-gun, tommy-gun ► **pistola de**

agua water pistol ► **pistola de engrase** grease gun ► **pistola de juguete** toy pistol ► **pistola de pintar** spray gun ► **pistola engrasadora** grease gun ► **pistola rociadora de pintura** spray gun
[2] (*Esp*) [*de pan*] French stick, baguette
[3] (**) (= *pene*) prick**

pistolera SF [1] (*para pistola*) holster; ✦*MODISMO* **salir de ~s** to get out of a tight spot
[2] **pistoleras** (*Anat**) flabby thighs

pistolerismo SM gun law, rule by terror

pistolero SM gunman ► **pistolero a sueldo** hired gunman

pistoleta SF (*Andes, Cono Sur*) small pistol

pistoletazo SM (= *disparo*) pistol shot; (*Dep*) (*tb* **~ de salida**) starting signal

pistolete SM pocket pistol

pistolo‡ SM soldier

pistón SM [1] (*Mec*) piston
[2] (*Mús*) key; (*Col*) (= *corneta*) bugle, cornet
[3] (*CAm, Méx*) (= *tortilla*) corn tortilla
[4] ✦*MODISMO* **de ~*** smashing*, terrific*

pistonudo* ADJ smashing*, terrific*

pistudo* ADJ (*CAm*) filthy rich*

pita SF [1] (= *planta*) agave, pita; (= *fibra*) pita fibre, pita thread; (*Chile, Perú*) (= *hilo*) string; ✦*MODISMO* **enredar la ~** (*LAm**) to stir things up
[2] **pitas** (*CAm*) (= *mentiras*) lies

pitada SF [1] (= *silbido*) whistle; (= *rechifla*) hiss
[2] (*LAm**) [*de cigarrillo*] puff, drag*
[3] (*) (= *salida inoportuna*) silly remark

pitador/a* SM/F (*LAm*) smoker

Pitágoras SM Pythagoras

pitagorín* SM brainbox*

pitandero/a* SM/F (*Cono Sur*) smoker

pitanza SF [1] (= *ración*) daily ration; (‡) grub‡, chow (*EEUU*‡)
[2] (*) (= *precio*) price
[3] (*Cono Sur*) (= *ganga*) bargain; (= *ventaja*) profit

pitar ▸conjug 1a◂ (A) VI [1] (= *sonar*) (*con silbato*) to blow one's whistle; (*con claxon*) to hoot, blow one's horn; **el policía nos pitó** the policeman blew his whistle at us; **el camionero me pitó** the lorry driver hooted at us, the lorry driver blew his horn at us
[2] (= *abuchear*) to whistle
[3] ✦*MODISMO* **ir** *o* **salir pitando***: **cuando la vio venir salió pitando** as soon as he saw her coming he was off like a shot*; **adiós, me tengo que ir pitando** bye, I must dash*; **vámonos pitando, que no llegamos** let's get a move on or we won't get there in time*
[4] (*LAm**) (= *fumar*) to smoke
[5] (†) (= *funcionar*) to work; **el negocio no pita** the business isn't going well
(B) VT [1] (*Dep*) **el árbitro pitó falta** the referee whistled *o* blew for a foul; **¿quién pita el partido?** who's refereeing the match?
[2] (*LAm**) (= *fumar*) to smoke

pitarra‡ SF grub‡, chow (*EEUU*‡), food

pitay SM (*Andes, Cono Sur*) rash

pitazo SM (*LAm*) whistle, hoot; ✦*MODISMO* **dar el ~ a algn** (*Caribe**) to tip sb the wink*

pítcher [pitʃer] SMF (*Béisbol*) pitcher

pitear ▸conjug 1a◂ VI (*LAm*) = **pitar A1**

pitido SM (= *silbido*) whistle; (= *sonido agudo*) beep; (= *sonido corto*) pip

pitilla SF (*Cono Sur*) string

pitillera SF cigarette case

pitillo SM [1] (*) (= *cigarrillo*) cigarette; **echarse un ~** to have a smoke
[2] (*Andes, Caribe*) (= *pajita*) drinking straw

pítima SF [1] (*Med*) poultice
[2] (= *borrachera*) **coger una ~*** to get plastered*

pitiminí SM ✦*MODISMO* **de ~** trifling, trivial

pitinsa* SF (*CAm*) overalls

pitiusa (A) ADJ of/from Ibiza *or* Formentera (*as opposed to the other Balearic islands*)
(B) SF **las Pitiusas** Ibiza and Formentera

pitiyanqui‡ SMF, **pitiyanki**‡ SMF (*Caribe*) Yankee-lover

pito SM [1] [*de coche, camión*] horn, hooter; [*de tren*] whistle, hooter; **el camionero tocó el ~** the lorry driver blew the horn *o* hooted
[2] (= *silbato*) whistle; **el arbitro tocó el ~** the referee blew his whistle; **tener voz de ~** to have a squeaky voice; ✦*MODISMOS* **cuando ~s, flautas*** it's always the same, one way or another it always happens; **cuando no es por ~s es por flautas*** if it isn't one thing it's another; **entre ~s y flautas*** what with one thing and another; **(no) importar un ~***: **no me importa un ~** I don't care two hoots*; **no tocar un ~ en algo***: **en este asunto no toca ~** he's got nothing to do with this matter; **tomar a algn por el ~ de un sereno***: **me tomaron por el ~ de un sereno** (*Esp**) they thought I was something the cat dragged in; **no vale un ~*** it's not worth tuppence
[3] (*) (= *cigarrillo*) fag*, ciggy*; (*LAm*) (= *pipa*) pipe
[4] (*) (= *pene*) willy*, peter (*EEUU***); ✦*MODISMO* **tocarse el ~**‡ to do damn-all‡, be bone-idle
[5] (*LAm*) ► **pito de ternera** steak sandwich
[6] (*Orn*) ► **pito real** green woodpecker; ✦*MODISMO* **~ ~ colorito** ≈ eeny meeny miney mo

pitón[1] SM (*Zool*) python

pitón[2] SM (= *cuerno*) horn; [*de jarra*] spout; (*LAm*) [*de manguera*] nozzle; (*Bot*) sprig, young shoot; (= *bulto*) bump, lump; **pitones**‡ (= *senos*) tits‡ ► **pitón de roca** sharp point of rock

pitonisa SF (= *adivinadora*) fortune teller; (= *hechicera*) witch, sorceress

pitopausia‡ SF male menopause

pitorrearse* ▸conjug 1a◂ VPR **~ de** to scoff at, make fun of

pitorreo* SM teasing, joking; **estar de ~** to be in a joking mood

pitorro SM spout

pitote* SM fuss, row

pitra SF (*Cono Sur*) rash

pituco/a* (*Andes, Cono Sur*) (A) ADJ posh*
(B) SM/F toff*, posh person*

pitufa‡ SF bird‡, chick (*EEUU**)

pitufo‡ SM [1] (*Pol*) career politician
[2] (*Méx*) (= *policía*) cop*, policeman

pituitario ADJ pituitary; **glándula pituitaria** pituitary (gland)

pituto* SM (*Cono Sur*) [1] (= *enchufe*) useful contact, connection
[2] (= *chapuza*) odd job

piuco ADJ (*Cono Sur*) timid, scared

piular ▸conjug 1a◂ VI to cheep, chirp

pívot SMF (*Dep*) pivot

pivotar ▸conjug 1a◂ VI [1] (*Dep*) to pivot
[2] (= *oscilar*) **~ alrededor de** to revolve around; **~ en política** to switch allegiances in politics

pivote (A) SMF (*Dep*) pivot
(B) SM pivot

píxel SM (*Inform*) pixel

píxide SF pyx

pixtón SM (*CAm*) thick tortilla

piyama SM (*LAm*) pyjamas *pl*, pajama (*EEUU*)

pizarra SF [1] (= *piedra*) slate; (= *esquisto*) shale
[2] (*Escol*) blackboard
[3] (*Cono Sur*) (= *tablero*) notice board, bulletin board (*EEUU*)
[4] (*LAm*) (= *marcador*) scoreboard

pizarral SM [1] (= *cantera*) slate quarry
[2] *ver* **pizarra 1**

pizarrín SM slate pencil

pizarrón SM (*LAm Escol*) blackboard; (*Dep*) scoreboard

pizarroso ADJ slaty

pizca SF [1] (= *partícula*) tiny bit; (= *migaja*) crumb; **una ~ de sal** a pinch of salt
[2] (= *rastro*) **ni ~** not a bit; **no tiene ni ~ de gracia** it's not funny at all; **no tiene ni ~ de verdad** there's not a shred of truth in it, it
[3] (*Méx Agr*) maize harvest

pizcar ▸conjug 1g◂ VT to pinch, nip

pizco SM pinch, nip

pizcucha SF (*CAm*) kite (*toy*)

pizote SM (*CAm*) coati(-mundi)

pizpireta* SF spirited girl, lively girl

pizpireto* ADJ flirty

pizza SF (*Culin*) pizza

pizzería [pitse'ria] SF pizzeria

PJ SM ABR (*Arg*) (= **Partido Justicialista**) *Peronist party*

p.j. SM ABR = **partido judicial**

PJF SF ABR (*Méx*) = **Policía Judicial Federal**

placa SF [1] (*gen*) plate; (= *lámina*) sheet; [*de cocina*] plate; (= *radiador*) radiator ► **placa conmemorativa** commemorative plaque ► **placa de hielo** icy patch ► **placa del nombre** nameplate ► **placa de matrícula** number plate, license plate (*EEUU*), registration plate ► **placa dental** (dental) plaque ► **placa de silicio** silicon chip ► **placa giratoria** (*Ferro*) turntable ► **placa madre** (*Inform*) motherboard ► **placa solar** (*en techo*) solar panel; (*en pared*) radiator; *ver tb* **vitrocerámica**
[2] (*Fot*) (*tb* **~ fotográfica**) plate ► **placa esmerilada** focusing screen
[3] (*LAm Mús*) gramophone record, phonograph record (*EEUU*)
[4] (= *distintivo*) badge, insignia
[5] (*LAm*) (= *erupción*) blotch, skin blemish

placaje SM (*Rugby*) tackle

placaminero SM persimmon

placar ▸conjug 1g◂ VT to tackle

placard SM (*Cono Sur*) built-in cupboard, (clothes) closet (*EEUU*)

placebo SM placebo; **efecto ~** placebo effect

pláceme SM (= *felicitación*) congratulations *pl*, message of congratulations; **dar el ~ a algn** to congratulate sb

placenta SF placenta, afterbirth

placentero ADJ pleasant, agreeable

placentino/a (*Esp*) Ⓐ ADJ of/from Plasencia
Ⓑ SM/F native/inhabitant of Plasencia; **los ~s** the people of Plasencia

placer¹ Ⓐ SM 1 (*gen*) pleasure; **es un ~ hacerlo** it is a pleasure to do it; **con mucho** *o* **sumo ~** with great pleasure; **tengo el ~ de presentarle a ...** it's my pleasure to introduce ...; **viaje de ~** pleasure trip; **a ~** as much as one wants ► **placer de dioses** heavenly delight
2 (= *deleite*) pleasure; **los ~es del ocio** the pleasures of idleness; **darse a los ~es** to give o.s. over to pleasure
Ⓑ ▸conjug 2w◂ VT (= *agradar*) to please; **me place poder hacerlo** I am glad to be able to do it

placer² SM 1 (*Geol, Min*) placer
2 (*Náut*) sandbank
3 (*Col*) (= *solar*) plot, patch; (*Agr*) *ground prepared for sowing*
4 (*Caribe*) field

placero/a SM/F 1 (= *vendedor*) stallholder, market trader
2 (*ocioso*) gossip

plácet SM blessing; **tiene el ~ de la dirección del partido** he has the blessing of the party leadership; **dar el ~ a algn** to give one's blessing to sb

placeta SF (*Cono Sur*) plateau

plácidamente ADV placidly

placidez SF placidity

plácido ADJ placid

pladur® SM plasterboard

plaf EXCL bang!, crash!

plafón SM 1 (*en el techo*) (= *rosetón*) ceiling rosette; (= *lámpara*) flush-fitting ceiling light
2 (*Arquit*) (= *panel*) soffit
3 (*LAm Constr*) ceiling

plaga SF 1 (*Agr, Zool*) pest; [*de langostas*] plague; (*Bot*) blight ► **plaga de la vid** grape vine blight ► **plaga del jardín** garden pest ► **plagas forestales** forest pests
2 (= *azote*) scourge; **aquí la sequía es una ~** drought is a scourge here; **una ~ de turistas** a plague of tourists
3 (= *exceso*) glut, abundance; **ha habido una ~ de lechugas** there has been a glut of lettuces
4 (= *aflicción*) affliction, grave illness

plagar ▸conjug 1h◂ Ⓐ VT (= *infestar*) to infest, plague; **han plagado la ciudad de carteles** they have covered *o* plastered the town with posters; **un texto plagado de errores** a text riddled with errors; **esta sección está plagada de minas** this part has mines everywhere
Ⓑ **plagarse** VPR **~se de** to become infested with

plagiar ▸conjug 1b◂ VT 1 (= *copiar*) to plagiarize; [+ *producto*] to pirate, copy illegally
2 (*Méx*) (= *secuestrar*) to kidnap

plagiario/a SM/F 1 (= *imitador*) plagiarist
2 (*Méx*) (= *secuestrador*) kidnapper

plagio SM 1 (= *copia*) plagiarism; [*de producto*] piracy, illegal copying
2 (*Méx*) (= *secuestro*) kidnap(ping)

plaguicida SM pest-control substance, insecticide

plan SM 1 (= *proyecto*) plan; (= *intención*) idea, intention; **¿qué ~es tienes para este verano?** what are your plans for the summer?; **no tengo ~es para el futuro** I have no plans for the future; **realizar su ~** to put one's plan into effect; **mi ~ era comprar otro nuevo** my idea *o* intention was to buy a new one; **tengo un ~ estupendo para mañana** I've got a splendid idea about what to do tomorrow ► **plan de choque** action plan, plan of action ► **plan de desarrollo** development plan ► **plan de incentivos** incentive scheme ► **plan de jubilación** retirement plan ► **plan de pensiones** pension plan ► **plan de vuelo** flight plan ► **plan quinquenal** five-year plan
2 [*de curso*] programme, program (*EEUU*) ► **plan de estudios** curriculum, syllabus
3 (*) (= *manera, actitud*) **este niño está en un ~ imposible** this child is really playing up; **si te pones en ese ~** if that's your attitude; **como sigas en ese ~** if you go on like that; **lo hizo en ~ bruto** he did it in a brutal way; **viajar en ~ económico** to travel cheap; **el negocio es en ~ timo** the deal is really a swindle; **chaparrones en ~ disperso** scattered showers; **viven en ~ pasota** they live like hippies; **en ~ de**: **lo dije en ~ de broma** I said it as a joke *o* for a laugh; **vamos en ~ de turismo** we're going as tourists; **salieron en ~ de divertirse** they went out looking for a good time; **está en ~ de rehusar** he's in a mood to refuse, he's likely to refuse at the moment
4 (*) ✦**MODISMOS eso no es ~** ◊ **tampoco es ~** that's not on*; **a todo ~**† sparing no expense; **no me hace ~**† + INFIN it doesn't suit me to + *infin*
5 (†*) (= *aventura*) date; (*pey*) fling*; **¿tienes ~ para esta noche?** have you got a date for tonight?; **buscar ~** to try to pick somebody up*; **tiene un ~ con la mujer del alcalde** he's having a fling with the mayor's wife*
6 (*Med*) course of treatment; **estar a ~** to be on a course of treatment
7 (*Topografía*) (= *nivel*) level; (= *altura*) height
8 (*Cono Sur, Méx*) [*de barco etc*] flat bottom
9 (*LAm*) (= *llano*) level ground; (*Cono Sur*) (= *falda de cerro*) foothills *pl*
10 (*Andes, CAm, Caribe*) [*de espada etc*] flat

plana SF 1 [*de hoja*] side, page; (*Tip*) page; (*Escol*) writing exercise, copywriting; **noticias de primera ~** front-page news; **en primera ~** on the front page; **escribir una ~ de castigo** to write lines as a punishment; ✦**MODISMO corregir** *o* **enmendar la ~ a algn** to put sb right; (*pey*) to find fault with sb, improve upon sb's efforts ► **plana de anuncios** advertisement page
2 ► **plana mayor** (*Mil*) staff; (*fig*) top brass*
3 (*Téc*) trowel; [*de tonelero*] cooper's plane

planazo SM 1 (*LAm**) **se dio un ~** he fell flat on his face
2 (*Caribe*) (= *trago*) shot of liquor

plancha SF 1 (= *lámina*) plate, sheet; (= *losa*) slab; (*Tip*) plate; (*Náut*) gangway; (*Med*) dental plate; **hacer la ~** [*bañista*] to float
2 (= *utensilio*) iron; (= *acción*) ironing; [*de traje*] pressing; (= *ropa para planchar*) ironing ► **plancha a** *o* **de vapor** steam iron ► **plancha eléctrica** electric iron
3 (*Culin*) grill; (*Cono Sur*) griddle pan; **a la ~** grilled; **pescado a la ~** grilled fish
4 (= *ejercicio*) press-up
5 (*) (= *error*) bloomer*; **hacer** *o* **tirarse una ~** to drop a clanger‡, put one's foot in it; ✦**MODISMOS pasar ~** (*Cono Sur*) to be embarrassed
6 (*Dep*) dive; **entrada en ~** sliding tackle; **lanzarse en ~** to dive (for the ball); **cabecear en ~** to do a diving header

planchada SF 1 (*para barcas*) landing stage
2 (*LAm*) = **plancha 5**

planchado Ⓐ ADJ 1 [+ *ropa*] ironed; [+ *traje*] pressed
2 (*CAm, Cono Sur*) (= *elegante*) very smart, dolled up*
3 (*LAm**) (= *sin dinero*) broke*
4 (*Culin*) pressed; **jamón ~** pressed ham
5 (*Méx*) (= *listo*) clever; (= *valiente*) brave
Ⓑ SM 1 (*a la ropa*) ironing; (*a un traje*) pressing; **una prenda que no necesita ~** a non-iron garment; **dar un ~ a** [+ *ropa*] to iron; [+ *traje*] to press
2 (*Andes, Cono Sur Aut*) panel beating

planchador(a) SM/F *person who does the ironing*

planchadora SF (= *máquina*) press, trouser press

planchar ▸conjug 1a◂ Ⓐ VT 1 [+ *ropa*] to iron; [+ *traje*] to press; **prenda de no ~** non-iron garment
2 (*LAm**) (= *adular*) to suck up to*
3 (*Méx**) (= *dejar plantado*) to stand up*
Ⓑ VI 1 (= *desarrugar*) to iron, do the ironing
2 (*LAm**) (= *no bailar*) to be a wallflower
3 (*Chile**) (= *meter la pata*) to drop a clanger‡; (= *parecer absurdo*) to look ridiculous

planchazo* SM = **plancha 5**

planchear ▸conjug 1a◂ VT to plate

plancheta SF 1 (*Agrimensura*) plane table
2 ✦**MODISMO echárselas de ~*** to show off, swank*

planchón SM (*Cono Sur*) (*en campo*) ice field; (*en montaña*) snowcap

plancton SM plankton

planeador SM glider

planeadora SF 1 (= *niveladora*) leveller, bulldozer
2 (*Náut*) speedboat, powerboat

planear ▸conjug 1a◂ Ⓐ VT (= *proyectar*) to plan; **~ hacer algo** to plan to do sth
Ⓑ VI (*Aer*) to glide; (*fig*) to hang, hover (**sobre** over)

planeo SM (*gen*) gliding; **un planeo** a glide

planeta SM planet; **el ~ rojo** the red planet, Mars

planetario Ⓐ ADJ planetary
Ⓑ SM planetarium

planicie SF (= *llanura*) plain; (= *llano*) flat area, level ground; (= *superficie plana*) flat surface

planificación SF (*gen*) planning; (*Inform*) scheduling ► **planificación corporativa** corporate planning ► **planificación familiar** family planning ► **planificación urbana** town planning

planificador(a) Ⓐ ADJ planning *antes de s*
Ⓑ SM/F planner

planificar ▸conjug 1g◂ VT to plan

planilla SF (*LAm*) 1 (= *lista*) list; (= *tabla*) table; (= *nómina*) payroll; (= *sujetapapeles*) clipboard; (= *papelito*) slip of paper
2 (*Ferro*) ticket
3 (*Andes, Cono Sur*) (= *formulario*) application form; (*Fin*) (= *cuenta*) account; [*de gastos*] expense account
4 (*Andes, Cono Sur*) (*para votar*) ballot paper, voting slip; (= *nómina de electores*) electoral roll *o* register; (= *candidatos*) ticket

planimetría SF surveying, planimetry

➤ LENGUA Y USO: **placer¹ A1** 36.2, 51.1, 52.1 **planear A** 35.2, 52.6

plan(n)ing ['planin] SM (*pl* **plan(n)ings** ['planin]) schedule, agenda

plano Ⓐ ADJ (= *llano*) flat, level; **tiene los pies ~s** he has flat feet; **es muy plana de pecho** she is very flat-chested

Ⓑ SM 1 (*Mat, Mec*) plane ► **plano focal** focal plane ► **plano inclinado** inclined plane

2 (= *posición, nivel*) plane; **están en un ~ distinto** they're on a different plane; **de distinto ~ social** of a different social plane *o* position

3 (*Cine, Fot*) shot; **unos preciosos ~s de elefantes** some beautiful elephant shots; **un primer ~** a close-up; **en primer ~** (*Cine, Fot*) in close-up; (*Arte*) in the foreground; **estar en (un) segundo ~** (*fig*) to be in the background ► **plano aéreo** aerial shot ► **plano corto** close-up ► **plano general** general view ► **plano largo** long shot

4 (*Aer*) ► **plano de cola** tailplane

5 (*Arquit, Mec*) plan; (*Geog*) map; [*de ciudad*] map, street plan; **levantar el ~ de** [+ *país*] to survey, make a map of; [+ *edificio*] to draw up the designs for ► **plano acotado** contour map

6 **de ~: caer de ~** to fall flat; **confesar de ~** to make a full confession; **le daba el sol de ~** the sun shone directly on it; **rechazar algo de ~** to turn sth down flat

7 [*de espada*] flat

planta[1] SF (*Bot*) plant ► **planta carnívora** carnivorous plant ► **planta de interior** indoor plant, houseplant ► **planta de Navidad** poinsettia

planta[2] SF 1 (= *piso*) floor; **vivo en la tercera ~** I live on the third floor; **un edificio de tres ~s** a three storey building ► **planta baja** ground *o* (*EEUU*) first floor ► **planta noble** function suite

2 (*Arquit*) (= *plano*) ground plan; **construir un edificio de (nueva) ~** to build a completely new building

3 (*tb* **~ del pie**) the sole of the foot; **asentar sus ~s en** (*iró*) to install o.s. in

4 (= *aspecto*) **de buena ~** fine-looking

5 (= *fábrica*) plant ► **planta de embotellado** bottling plant ► **planta de enlatado** canning factory ► **planta de ensamblaje** assembly plant ► **planta depuradora** water purification plant ► **planta de tratamiento térmico** (waste) incineration plant ► **planta piloto** pilot plant ► **planta potabilizadora** waterworks *sing*, water treatment plant

6 (*Baile, Esgrima*) position (of the feet)

7 (= *plan*) plan, programme, program (*EEUU*), scheme

plantación SF 1 (= *acción*) planting; **ha comenzado la ~ de pinos** they have started to plant pine trees

2 (= *terreno cultivado*) plantation; **una ~ de tabaco** a tobacco plantation

plantado ADJ 1 (*Bot*) planted (**de** with); **un campo ~ de viñedos** a field planted with vines

2 **dejar ~ a algn*** (*en una cita*) to stand sb up*; (*en una relación sentimental*) to dump sb*, ditch sb*; (*en una situación difícil*) to leave sb in the lurch*, leave sb high and dry; (*mientras se habla*) to leave sb in mid-sentence; **me dejó plantada el día de la boda** he stood me up *o* left me in the lurch on my wedding day*; **lo dejó todo ~ y se fue del país** he packed *o* chucked everything in and left the country*; (*con prisa*) he dumped everything and left the country*

3 (*) (= *de pie*) standing; **sigue ahí ~** he's still standing there

4 **bien ~*** (= *persona*) well-groomed; **un equipo muy bien ~ en el terreno de juego** a very well organized team on the pitch

plantador(a) Ⓐ SM/F (= *persona*) planter

Ⓑ SM (= *utensilio*) dibber, dibble

plantadora SF (*Agr*) (= *máquina*) planter, planting machine

plantaje* SM (*Andes, Caribe*) looks *pl*

plantar ▸conjug 1a◂ Ⓐ VT 1 (*Bot*) [+ *árbol, bulbo, jardín*] to plant; [+ *semilla*] to plant, sow; **plantó todo el jardín de flores** she planted the whole garden with flowers

2 (= *colocar*) [+ *estaca, poste*] to put, stick; **plantó el piano al lado de la ventana** he stuck the piano by the window; **le plantó sus cosas en mitad de la calle*** she dumped his things in the middle of the street*; ✦***MODISMO*** **~ el pie en algo** to set foot in sth; **no vuelvas a ~ el pie en mi casa** don't you ever set foot in my house again

3 (*) (= *dar*) [+ *beso*] to plant; [+ *insulto*] to hurl; **me plantó un beso en los labios** he planted a kiss on my lips; **~ una bofetada a algn** to slap sb*; ✦***MODISMOS*** **~ cara a** [+ *persona, críticas*] to stand up to; [+ *problema*] to face up to, confront; **no se atreven a ~le cara al jefe** they don't dare stand up to the boss; **durante seis años le estuvo plantando cara a la muerte** he held out against death for six years; **~ cuatro verdades a algn** to give sb a piece of one's mind*

4 (*) (= *abandonar*) (*en una cita*) to stand up*; [+ *novio*] to dump*, ditch*; [+ *actividad, estudios*] to pack in*, chuck in*; **plantó sus estudios y se marchó a Francia** he packed *o* chucked in his studies and went to France*

5 (*) (= *dar un corte*) **¿por qué no lo plantas de una vez?** why don't you tell him where to go once and for all?; **la planté para que no te insultara más** I cut her short before she insulted you any more

Ⓑ **plantarse** VPR 1 (= *colocarse*) to plant o.s., plonk o.s.*; **se nos plantó delante y no nos dejaba ver** he planted *o* plonked* himself in front of us so we couldn't see; **se plantó aquí con todas sus maletas** he planted *o* plonked* himself here with all his suitcases

2 (= *llegar*) **~se en** to get to, make it to; **en tres horas se plantó en Sevilla** he got to *o* made it to Seville in three hours; **se plantó sin esfuerzo en la final** he made it to the final easily

3 (= *mantenerse firme*) **~se en** to stick to; **se plantó en su decisión** she stuck to her decision; **debes ~te ahí y no dejarte influenciar** you should stick to that and not be swayed

4 (= *detenerse*) [*caballo*] to stop dead, pull up short

5 (*Naipes*) to stick; **me planto** I stick

6 (*Andes, CAm**) (= *arreglarse*) to doll o.s. up*

plante SM 1 (= *huelga*) stoppage, protest strike

2 (= *postura*) stand, agreed basis for resistance; (= *programa*) common programme of demands

▼ **planteamiento** SM 1 (= *exposición*) [*de novela, película*] first part, exposition (*frm*); **el ~ de la sinfonía** the way the symphony is structured; **el ~ del problema** (*Mat*) the way the problem is set out

2 (= *punto de vista*) approach; **el entrenador ha propuesto un ~ distinto del ataque** the coach has suggested a different approach in attack; **un ~ nuevo de la cuestión** a new way of looking at *o* approaching the issue; **sus ~s estéticos** his aesthetics

3 (= *idea*) plan; **yo me había hecho otro ~ de este fin de semana** I had made other plans for this weekend

4 (*Arquit*) (*tb* **~ urbanístico**) town planning

▼ **plantear** ▸conjug 1a◂ Ⓐ VT 1 (= *exponer*) 1·1 [+ *situación, problema*] to bring up, raise; **no me atrevo a ~les el tema a mis padres** I don't dare bring up *o* raise the issue with my parents; **planteáselo todo tal como es** explain *o* put the situation to him exactly as it is; **planteado el problema en estos términos ...** with the problem expressed *o* put in these terms ...

1·2 (*Mat*) [+ *ecuación, problema*] to set out

2 (= *proponer*) [+ *cambio, posibilidad*] to suggest; **he planteado la necesidad de un cambio** I have suggested that a change is necessary; **el futuro plantea un reto al que habrá que hacer frente** the future presents a challenge that will have to be met

3 (= *causar*) [+ *problema*] to pose, create; **esta decisión nos plantea un problema moral** this decision poses *o* creates a moral problem; **esta novela ~á problemas para adaptarla al cine** adapting this novel for the cinema will pose *o* create various problems

Ⓑ **plantearse** VPR 1 (= *cuestionarse*) to think about, consider; **ya es hora de que te plantees qué vas a hacer con tu vida** it's time you started thinking about *o* it's time you considered what you're going to do with your life; **yo no me planteo ese tipo de cosas** I don't think about that sort of thing; **me estoy planteando si merece la pena el esfuerzo** I'm thinking about *o* considering whether it is worth the effort

2 (= *considerar*) to see; **yo me planteo la vida como una lucha por sobrevivir** I see life as a struggle for survival; **en tu lugar, yo me lo ~ía de otro modo** if I were you, I would see things differently; **~se hacer algo** to think of doing sth, consider doing sth; **me estoy planteando seriamente dejar de fumar** I'm seriously thinking of *o* considering giving up smoking

3 (= *presentarse*) [*cuestión, problema*] to arise, come up; **esa cuestión volverá a ~se en el futuro** this question will arise *o* come up again in the future; **ahora se plantea el problema de la inflación** this raises the question of inflation, there arises the question of inflation (*frm*); **en el futuro se nos ~á el mismo dilema** we will be faced with the same dilemma in the future; **ahora se nos plantea la duda de qué hacer con todo este dinero** now we have the problem of what to do with all this money

plantel SM 1 (= *grupo*) **un ~ de jóvenes pintoras** a group of young painters; **un excelente ~ de actores** an excellent pool of actors; **un ~ de jugadores prometedores** an promising squad of players

2 (= *centro educativo*) training establishment

3 (*Bot*) nursery

4 (*LAm*) (= *escuela*) school

➤ LENGUA Y USO: **planteamiento 2** 53.3 **plantear A1** 53.2, 53.3, 53.6

plantificar ▸conjug 1g◂ Ⓐ VT (*) (= *colocar*) to plonk down, dump down*
Ⓑ **plantificarse** VPR [1] (*Caribe, Cono Sur, Méx**) (= *plantarse*) to plant o.s.; (= *no ceder*) to stand firm, stand one's ground; **se plantificó en la puerta** he planted himself in the doorway, he stood there in the doorway
[2] (*Méx*) (= *ataviarse*) to get dolled up*

plantilla SF [1] [*de zapato*] inner sole, insole; [*de media etc*] sole
[2] (*Téc*) pattern, template; (= *patrón*) stencil
[3] (= *personas*) staff, personnel; (*Dep*) playing staff; (= *lista*) list, roster; **estar de ~** to be on the payroll ► **plantilla de personal** staff

plantillada* SF (*Andes*) bragging

plantío SM [1] (= *acto*) planting
[2] (= *terreno*) bed, patch

plantista SM/F braggart

plantón SM [1] (*) (= *espera*) long wait; **dar (un) ~ a algn** to stand sb up*; **estar de ~** (*gen*) to be stuck, have to wait around; (*Mil*) to be on sentry duty; **tener a algn de ~** to keep sb waiting
[2] (*Bot*) (= *plántula*) seedling; (= *esqueje*) cutting

plántula SF seedling

plañidera SF (paid) mourner

plañidero ADJ mournful, plaintive

plañir ▸conjug 3h◂ VT to mourn, grieve over

plaqueta SF platelet

plas[1] EXCL = **plaf**

plas[2]**(a)**‡ SM/F brother/sister

plasma SM plasma ► **plasma sanguíneo** blood plasma

plasmación SF shape, form

plasmar ▸conjug 1a◂ Ⓐ VT [1] (= *dar forma a*) to embody; **sus ideas quedaron plasmadas en un manifiesto** his ideas were embodied in a manifesto
[2] (= *reflejar*) to capture, reflect; **la novela plasma perfectamente la angustia del autor** the novel captures *o* reflects the author's anguish perfectly
Ⓑ **plasmarse** VPR **~se en algo** to manifest itself in sth; **la indignación ciudadana se plasmó en revueltas callejeras** the anger among the population manifested itself in street riots

plasta Ⓐ SF [1] (*gen*) soft mass, lump; (= *cosa aplastada*) flattened mass
[2] (*) (= *desastre*) botch, mess; **es una ~ de edificio** it's a mess of a building; **el plan es una ~** the plan is one big mess, the plan is a complete botch
Ⓑ SMF (*) (= *pelmazo*) bore
Ⓒ ADJ INV boring

plástica SF plastic art, (art of) sculpture and modelling *o* (*EEUU*) modeling

plasticar ▸conjug 1g◂ VT (*LAm*) [+ *documento*] to cover with plastic, seal in plastic, laminate

plasticidad SF [1] [*de material*] plasticity
[2] (= *expresividad*) expressiveness; [*de descripción*] richness

plasticina® SF (*Cono Sur*) Plasticine®

plástico Ⓐ ADJ [1] (*gen*) plastic; **artes plásticas** plastic arts
[2] [*imagen*] expressive; [*descripción*] rich, evocative
[3] (*CAm**) **chico ~** young trendy
Ⓑ SM [1] (*gen*) plastic; **es de ~** (*fig*) it's fake, it's not real*
[2] (*) (= *disco*) record, disc; **pinchar un ~** spin a disc*
[3] (*Mil*) plastic explosive

plasticoso ADJ plastic, plasticky*

plastificación SF treatment with plastic, lamination

plastificado ADJ treated with plastic, laminated

plastificar ▸conjug 1g◂ VT [1] [+ *documento*] to cover with (laminated) plastic, laminate
[2] (*Mús*) to record, make a record of

plastilina® SF Plasticine®

plastrón SM (*LAm*) floppy tie, cravat

plata SF [1] (= *metal*) silver; (= *vajilla*) silverware; (*Fin*) silver; ✦**MODISMOS como una ~** bright as a pin; **hablar en ~** to speak bluntly, speak frankly
[2] (*esp LAm*) (= *dinero*) money; (= *riqueza*) wealth; **podrido en ~*** stinking rich*, rolling in it*
[3] **La Plata** (= *río*) the (River) Plate

platacho SM (*Cono Sur*) *dish of raw seafood*

platada SF (*LAm*) dish, plateful

plataforma SF [1] (*gen*) platform; (= *tablado*) stage; **zapatos de ~** platforms, platform shoes ► **plataforma continental** continental shelf ► **plataforma de carga** loading platform ► **plataforma de lanzamiento** launchpad, launching pad ► **plataforma de perforación** drilling rig, oil rig ► **plataforma espacial** space station ► **plataforma giratoria** turntable ► **plataforma petrolera, plataforma petrolífera** oil rig
[2] (*Pol*) (*tb* **~ electoral**) platform; (= *programa*) programme; [*de negociación*] package, set of proposals ► **plataforma reivindicativa** set of demands
[3] (*fig*) (*para lograr algo*) springboard

platal* SM (*LAm*) fortune

platanal SM, **platanar** SM (*Col*), **platanera** SF (*LAm*) banana plantation

platanero/a Ⓐ ADJ banana *antes de s*
Ⓑ SM/F (*LAm*) (= *cultivador*) banana grower; (*Com*) dealer in bananas

plátano SM [1] (= *fruta*) banana; (*para cocinar*) plantain; (= *árbol*) banana tree
[2] (= *árbol ornamental*) plane (tree)
[3] (‡) banana‡, prick**

platea SF (*Cine, Teat*) stalls *pl*, orchestra (section) (*EEUU*)

plateado Ⓐ ADJ [1] (= *de plata*) [*color, objeto*] silver; [*cabello*] silver, silvery; [*brillo*] silvery; (*Téc*) silver-plated
[2] (*Méx*) wealthy
Ⓑ SM silver-plating

platear ▸conjug 1a◂ Ⓐ VT [1] (*Téc*) to silver-plate, silver
[2] (*CAm, Méx*) to sell, turn into money
Ⓑ VI to turn silver

platense (*Arg*) Ⓐ ADJ [1] = **rioplatense A**
[2] (*de la ciudad de La Plata*) of/from La Plata
Ⓑ SMF [1] = **rioplatense B**
[2] native/inhabitant of La Plata; **los ~s** the people of La Plata

plateresco ADJ plateresque

platería SF [1] (= *arte*) silversmith's craft
[2] (= *tienda*) silversmith's
[3] (= *objetos*) silverware, silver

platero/a SM/F silversmith

plática SF (*esp Méx*) (= *charla*) talk, chat; (*Rel*) sermon; **estar de ~** to be chatting, be having a talk

platicador* ADJ (*Méx*) chatty, talkative

platicar ▸conjug 1g◂ Ⓐ VI (= *charlar*) to talk, chat
Ⓑ VT (*Méx*) (= *decir*) to tell

platija SF plaice, flounder

platilla SF (*Caribe*) water melon

platillo SM [1] (= *plato*) (*gen*) small plate; (*para taza*) saucer; [*de limosnas*] collecting bowl; [*de balanza*] pan; **pasar el ~** to pass the hat round ► **platillo volante, platillo volador** flying saucer
[2] **platillos** (*Mús*) cymbals
[3] (*CAm, Méx*) dish; **el tercer ~ de la comida** the third course of the meal

platina SF [1] [*de microscopio*] slide
[2] (*Mús*) [*de tocadiscos*] deck; [*de casete*] tape (deck); **doble ~** twin deck
[3] (*Tip*) platen

platino Ⓐ SM [1] (= *metal*) platinum
[2] **platinos** (*Aut*) contact points
Ⓑ ADJ **rubia ~** platinum blonde

plato SM [1] (= *recipiente*) (*para comer*) plate; (*de balanza*) pan; **fregar los ~s** to wash *o* do the dishes, wash up; ✦**MODISMOS pagar los ~s rotos** to carry the can*; **estar en el ~ y en la tajada** ◊ **estar al ~ y a las tajadas** to have one's cake and eat it; ✦**REFRÁN del ~ a la boca se pierde la sopa** there's many a slip 'twixt cup and lip ► **plato de postre** dessert plate ► **plato frutero** fruit dish ► **plato hondo** soup dish, soup plate ► **plato llano** dinner plate ► **plato sopero** soup dish, soup plate
[2] (= *contenido del plato*) plate, plateful; **un ~ de arroz** a plate *o* plateful of rice; ✦**MODISMO vender algo por un ~ de lentejas** to sell sth for a mess of pottage
[3] (*Culin*) (*en menú*) course; (= *guiso*) dish; **un menú de tres ~s** a three-course meal; **es un ~ típico español** it's a typical Spanish dish; **es mi ~ favorito** it's my favourite dish; ✦**MODISMOS no es ~ de mi gusto** it's not my cup of tea; **comen del mismo ~** they're great pals; **ser ~ de segunda mesa*** [*cosa*] to be second-best; [*persona*] play second fiddle ► **plato combinado** set main course ► **plato de fondo** main course ► **plato dulce** sweet course ► **plato fuerte** (= *comida principal*) main course; (= *abundante*) big meal; (= *tema principal*) main topic, central theme; (= *punto fuerte*) strong point ► **plato precocinado** pre-cooked meal ► **plato preparado** ready-to-serve meal ► **plato principal** main course
[4] [*de tocadiscos*] turntable ► **plato giradiscos, plato giratorio** turntable
[5] ► **plato de (la) ducha** shower tray
[6] (*Téc*) plate
[7] (*Dep*) **tiro al ~** clay pigeon shooting
[8] (*Cono Sur**) **es un ~** (= *guapo*) he's a dish*, he's very dishy*; **¡qué ~!** (= *divertido*) what a laugh!

plató SM set

Platón SM Plato

platón SM (*LAm*) [1] (*Culin*) (= *plato grande*) large dish; (*de servir*) serving dish
[2] (= *palangana*) washbasin, washbowl (*EEUU*)

platónicamente ADV platonically

platónico ADJ platonic

platonismo SM Platonism

platonista SMF Platonist

platudo* ADJ (*LAm*) rich, well-heeled*

plausible ADJ [1] [*argumento, motivo*] acceptable, admissible
[2] [*comportamiento, intento, esfuerzo*] commendable, praiseworthy

plausiblemente ADV [1] [*alegar*] reasonably, believably
[2] [*comportarse*] commendably, laudably

playa SF [1] (= *orilla del mar*) beach; **una ~ de arenas doradas** a beach with golden sands; **pasar el día en la ~** to spend the day at *o* on the beach; **pescar desde la ~** to fish from the beach *o* shore ► **Playa Girón** (*Caribe*) Bay of Pigs
[2] (= *costa*) seaside; **ir a veranear a la ~** to spend the summer at the seaside, go to the seaside for one's summer holidays
[3] (*LAm*) (= *llano*) flat open space ► **playa de carga y descarga** (*Ferro*) goods yard ► **playa de estacionamiento** car park, parking lot (*EEUU*) ► **playa de juegos** playground
[4] ✦*MODISMO* **una ~ de algo** (*Caribe**) loads of sth*

playera SF [1] (*CAm, Méx*) (= *camiseta*) T-shirt
[2] (= *zapatilla*) canvas shoe; [*de tenis*] tennis shoe

playero ADJ beach *antes de s*; **es muy ~** he loves going down the beach

playo ADJ (*Arg, Méx*) flat

play-off ['pleiof] SM (*pl* **play-offs**) (*Dep*) play-off

plaza SF [1] (*entre calles*) square; **la Plaza Roja** Red Square; ✦*MODISMOS* **abrir ~** (*Taur*) to open a bullfight; **regar la ~** (*Esp**) to have a beer (as a starter) ► **plaza de armas** parade ground ► **plaza de toros** bullring ► **plaza mayor** main square
[2] (= *mercado*) market, market place; **hacer la ~** to do the daily shopping
[3] (= *espacio*) (*gen*) room, space; [*de vehículo*] seat; **un vehículo de dos ~s** a two-seater vehicle; **el avión tiene 90 ~s** the plane carries 90 passengers; **reservar una ~** to book a seat; **"no hay ~s"** "no vacancies"; **abrir ~** to make way; **¡plaza!** make way! ► **plaza de atraque** berth, mooring ► **plaza de garaje** parking space (*in garage*) ► **plaza hotelera** hotel bed
[4] (= *puesto de trabajo*) (*gen*) post; (= *vacante*) vacancy; **cubrir una ~** to fill a vacancy *o* post *o* job; **sentar ~** (*Mil*) to enlist, sign on (**de** as)
[5] (†) (= *ciudad*) town, city
[6] (*tb* **~ fuerte**) (*Mil*) fortress, fortified town; (*Pol*) stronghold

▼ **plazo** SM [1] (= *período*) period; **dentro del ~ previsto** within the specified period; **en un ~ de diez días** within a period of ten days; **nos dan un ~ de ocho días para acabar el trabajo** they've given us eight days to finish the job; **¿cuándo vence el ~?** when is the deadline?; **a ~** (*Com*) on credit; **a ~ fijo** (*Com*) fixed-term; **a corto ~** (*adj*) short-term; (*adv*) in the short term; **a largo ~** (*adj*) long-term; (*adv*) in the long term; **es una tarea a largo ~** it's a long-term job; **veremos los resultados a largo ~** we'll see the results in the long term; **a medio ~** (*adj*) medium-term; (*adv*) in the medium term ► **plazo de entrega** delivery time, delivery date ► **plazo de prescripción** (*Jur*) time limit
[2] (= *pago*) instalment, installment (*EEUU*), payment; **no pagó el ~ de marzo** he didn't pay the March instalment; **a ~s** in instalments; **pagar algo a ~s** pay for sth in instalments

plazoleta SF, **plazuela** SF small square

pleamar SF high tide

plebe SF **la ~** (*gen*) the common people *pl*, the masses *pl*; (*pey*) the mob, the rabble, the plebs* *pl* (*pey*)

plebeyez SF plebeian nature; (*fig*) coarseness, commonness

plebeyo/a Ⓐ ADJ [1] (= *de la plebe*) plebeian
[2] (= *ordinario*) coarse, common
Ⓑ SM/F plebeian, commoner

plebiscito SM plebiscite

pleca SF (*Inform*) backslash

plectro SM plectrum

plegable ADJ [*mesa, cama*] folding, collapsible

plegadera SF paperknife

plegadizo ADJ = **plegable**

plegado SM [1] (= *acto*) [*de papel*] folding, creasing; [*de algo duro*] bending; [*de tela*] pleating
[2] (= *pliegue*) fold

plegamiento SM [1] (*Geol*) fold
[2] [*de camión*] jack-knifing

plegar ▸conjug 1h, 1j◂ Ⓐ VT [1] (= *doblar*) [+ *papel*] to fold; [+ *algo duro*] to bend
[2] (*Cos*) to pleat
Ⓑ VI to fold up
Ⓒ **plegarse** VPR [1] (= *someterse*) to yield, submit (**a** to)
[2] (= *doblarse*) [*algo duro*] to bend; [*mesa, cama*] to fold away, be collapsible

plegaria SF prayer

pleitear ▸conjug 1a◂ VI [1] (*Jur*) (= *litigar*) to go to court; **~ con** *o* **contra algn** to take sb to court
[2] (*esp LAm**) (= *reñir*) to argue

pleitesía SF **rendir ~ a algn** (= *respeto*) to show respect for sb, show sb courtesy; (= *homenaje*) to pay tribute to sb

pleitista Ⓐ ADJ [1] (*Jur*) litigious
[2] (= *reñidor*) quarrelsome, argumentative
Ⓑ SMF [1] (*Jur*) litigious person
[2] (*fig*) troublemaker
[3] (*LAm*) (= *peleón*) brawler

pleitisto ADJ (*LAm*) quarrelsome, argumentative

pleito SM [1] (*Jur*) lawsuit, case; **pleitos** litigation *sing*; **andar en ~s** to be engaged in lawsuits *o* litigation; **entablar ~** to bring an action, bring a lawsuit; **ganar el ~** to win one's case; **poner ~** to sue, bring an action; **poner ~ a algn** to bring an action against sb, take sb to court ► **pleito civil** civil action ► **pleito de acreedores** bankruptcy proceedings *pl*
[2] (= *litigio*) dispute
[3] (*esp LAm*) (= *discusión*) quarrel, argument; (= *pelea*) fight, brawl; **estar a ~ con algn** to be at odds with sb; **no quiero meterme en ~s** I don't want to get into an argument
[4] ► **pleito homenaje** homage

plenamente ADJ [*consciente, recuperado*] fully; [*satisfecho*] completely; **me satisface ~** it gives me complete satisfaction; **acertó ~** he was absolutely right; **vivir la vida ~** to live life to the full

plenaria SF plenary, plenary session

plenario ADJ plenary, full; *ver tb* **indulgencia 1**

plenilunio SM full moon

plenipotenciario/a ADJ, SM/F plenipotentiary

plenitud SF [1] (= *apogeo*) **en la ~ de sus poderes** at the height of his powers; **estaba en la ~ de la vida** he was in the prime of life
[2] (= *totalidad*) plenitude, fullness

pleno Ⓐ ADJ full; **~ empleo** full employment; **~s poderes** full powers; **en ~ día** ◊ **a plena luz del día** in broad daylight; **en ~ verano** in the middle of the summer; **vive en ~ centro de Bilbao** he lives right in the center of Bilbao; **le dio en plena cara** she hit him full in the face; **en plena vista** in full view
Ⓑ SM [1] (= *reunión*) plenary, plenary session
[2] (*en las quinielas*) *maximum number of points*
[3] **en ~: el gobierno en ~ asistió al funeral** the entire Cabinet attended the funeral; **ha dimitido la junta directiva en ~** the board of directors resigned en masse

pleonasmo SM pleonasm

pleonástico ADJ pleonastic

plepa SF [1] (= *persona enfermiza*) sickly person
[2] (*) (= *antipático*) unpleasant sort
[3] (*) (= *pesado*) pain*, nuisance

pletina SF = **platina**

plétora SF (*frm*) (= *abundancia*) plethora (*frm*), abundance; (= *exceso*) excess, surplus

pletórico ADJ **estar ~** [*jugador*] to be on top form; **~ de** [+ *fuerza, energía, entusiasmo*] full of, bursting with; [+ *vida, ilusiones*] full of; [+ *felicidad, salud*] bursting with; **el equipo está ~ de moral** the team's morale couldn't be higher

pleuresía SF pleurisy

plexiglás® SM Perspex®, Plexiglas® (*EEUU*)

plexo SM (*Anat*) ► **plexo solar** solar plexus

pléyade SF [1] (*Literat*) distinguished group *o* gathering
[2] **Pléyades** (*Mit*) Pleiades

plica SF (= *carta cerrada*) sealed envelope *o* document; (*en un concurso*) sealed entry; (*en concurso de obras*) sealed bid

pliego SM (= *hoja de papel*) sheet; (= *carpeta*) folder; (*Tip*) section, signature ► **pliego cerrado** (*Náut*) sealed orders *pl* ► **pliego de cargos** list of accusations ► **pliego de condiciones** specifications *pl* (of a tender) ► **pliego de descargo** evidence (for the defendant) ► **pliego de reivindicaciones**, **pliego petitorio** (*Cono Sur*) list of demands

pliegue SM [1] (= *doblez*) fold, crease
[2] (*Cos*) (*gen*) pleat; (= *alforza*) tuck
[3] (*Geol*) fold

plima SF **flor de la ~** (*Cono Sur*) wisteria

plin EXCL **¡a mí, ~!** I couldn't care less!

Plinio SM Pliny ► **Plinio el Joven** Pliny the Younger ► **Plinio el Viejo** Pliny the Elder

plinto SM plinth

plisado Ⓐ ADJ pleated
Ⓑ SM [1] (= *acción*) pleating
[2] (= *tablas*) pleats *pl*

plisar ▸conjug 1a◂ VT to pleat

PLN SM ABR (*Costa Rica*) = **Partido de Liberación Nacional**

plomada SF [1] (*Arquit*) plumb
[2] (*Náut*) lead
[3] (*Pesca*) weights *pl*, sinkers *pl*

plomar ▸conjug 1a◂ VT to seal with lead

plomazo SM [1] (*) (= *pelmazo*) bore
[2] (*CAm, Méx*) (= *tiro*) shot; (= *herida*) bullet wound

➤ LENGUA Y USO: **plazo 1** 47.2, 47.3, 47.5

plombagina SF plumbago

plomería SF [1] (*Arquit*) lead roofing
[2] (*LAm*) (= *sistema*) plumbing; (= *taller*) plumber's workshop

plomero/a SM/F (*esp LAm*) plumber

plomífero* ADJ deadly boring

plomizo ADJ (*de plomo*) grey, gray (*EEUU*); [*cielo*] leaden (*liter*), grey, gray (*EEUU*)

plomo Ⓐ SM [1] (= *metal*) lead; **~ derretido** molten lead; **gasolina con ~** leaded petrol; **gasolina sin ~** unleaded petrol; **soldadito de ~** tin soldier; ✦*MODISMO* **sacar ~ a algo** to make light of sth, play sth down
[2] (= *plomada*) plumb line; [*de pesca*] weight, sinker; **a ~** true, vertical(ly); (*fig*) (= *justo*) just right; **caer a ~** to fall heavily *o* flat
[3] (*Elec*) fuse; **se han fundido los ~s** the fuses have blown; **se le fundieron los ~s** (*Esp**) he blew his top*
[4] (*) (= *pesadez*) bore
[5] (*esp LAm*) (= *bala*) bullet
[6] (*Méx*) (= *tiroteo*) gunfight
Ⓑ ADJ [1] (*LAm*) (= *gris*) grey, gray (*EEUU*), lead-coloured, lead-colored (*EEUU*)
[2] **ponerse ~*** (= *enfadarse*) to dig one's heels in
[3] (*) (= *pesado*) boring, dull; **no seas ~** don't be such a bore

plomoso ADJ (*CAm*) boring

plotter ['ploter] SM (*pl* **plotters** ['ploter]) (*Inform*) plotter

plugo, pluguiere *etc ver* **placer**[1]

pluma Ⓐ SF [1] [*de ave*] feather; (*como adorno*) plume, feather; **colchón de ~s** feather bed; ✦*MODISMOS* **hacer a ~ y a pelo** to be versatile, be ready to undertake anything; **tener ~** (*Esp*) to be camp
[2] (*para escribir*) (*de metal, plástico*) pen; (*de ave*) quill; **y otras obras de su ~** and other works from his pen; **dejar correr la ~** to write spontaneously; ✦*MODISMO* **escribir algo a vuela ~** to scribble sth down ► **pluma atómica** (*Méx*) ballpoint pen ► **pluma electrónica** light pen ► **pluma esferográfica** (*LAm*) ballpoint pen ► **pluma estilográfica, pluma fuente** fountain pen
[3] (= *caligrafía*) penmanship, writing
[4] (*Bádminton*) (= *volante*) shuttlecock
[5] (*CAm*) (= *mentira*) fib, tale; (= *truco*) hoax
[6] (*Cono Sur**) (= *puta*) prostitute
[7] (*Andes, Caribe, Cono Sur*) (= *grifo*) tap, faucet (*EEUU*)
[8] (*Cono Sur*) (= *grúa*) crane, derrick
[9] (*Esp*‡) (= *peseta*) one peseta
[10] (*Esp***) (= *pene*) prick**
[11] (*Esp**) (= *periodista*) hack
Ⓑ SM (*Dep*) featherweight

plumada SF (= *plumazo*) stroke of the pen; (= *letra adornada*) flourish

plumado ADJ feathered

plumafuente SF (*LAm*) fountain pen

plumaje SM [1] (*Orn*) plumage, feathers *pl*
[2] (= *adorno*) plume, crest
[3] (= *penacho*) bunch of feathers

plumario/a SM/F (*CAm, Méx*) (= *periodista*) hack, journalist; (*) (= *funcionario*) penpusher, pencilpusher (*EEUU*)

plumazo SM [1] (= *trazo fuerte*) stroke of the pen; **de un ~** with one stroke of the pen; (*Caribe*) in a jiffy*; **es un cuento que escribió de un ~** it's a story which she dashed off
[2] (= *colchón*) feather mattress; (= *almohada*) feather pillow

plumbemia SF lead poisoning

plúmbeo ADJ [1] (= *de plomo*) lead *antes de s*, leaden (*liter*)
[2] (= *que pesa mucho*) weighty, heavy
[3] (= *aburrido*) boring, dull

plúmbico ADJ plumbic

plumear ▸conjug 1a◂ Ⓐ VT (*CAm, Méx**) to write, scribble
Ⓑ VI [1] [*ave*] to hatch
[2] (*Méx*‡) (= *ser prostituta*) to be on the game*

plumero Ⓐ SM [1] (*para limpiar*) feather duster
[2] (= *adorno*) plume
[3] (= *penacho*) bunch of feathers; ✦*MODISMO* **se le ve el ~*** you can see what his game is*
[4] (= *portaplumas*) penholder
[5] (= *estuche*) pencil case
[6] (*Andes*) (= *fontanero*) plumber
[7] (*Cono Sur*) (= *borla*) powder puff
Ⓑ ADJ (*) (= *homosexual*) camp

plumier(e) SM pencil case

plumífero[1] SM quilted anorak

plumífero[2]**/a** SM/F (*hum*) (= *escritor*) hack; (= *periodista*) hack

plumilla Ⓐ SF nib
Ⓑ SMF (= *periodista*) hack journalist

plumín SM nib

plumista SMF clerk, scrivener

plumón SM [1] (*Orn*) down
[2] (*para abrigar*) (= *abrigo*) quilted jacket; (= *edredón*) continental quilt, duvet, comforter (*EEUU*); (= *saco de dormir*) quilted sleeping bag
[3] (*LAm*) (= *rotulador*) felt-tip pen

plumoso ADJ feathery, downy

plural Ⓐ ADJ [1] (*Ling*) plural
[2] (*esp LAm*) (= *muchos*) many
Ⓑ SM plural; **en ~** in the plural

pluralidad SF [1] (= *diversidad*) plurality; **hay una alta ~ temática** there are many different themes
[2] **una ~ de** (= *varios*) a number of; **el asunto tiene ~ de aspectos** there are a number of sides to this question; **países con una ~ de culturas** countries with several cultures; **una ~ de ideas** diverse ideas, a variety of ideas
[3] ► **pluralidad de votos** majority of votes

pluralismo SM pluralism

pluralista Ⓐ ADJ [1] (= *abierto*) pluralist, pluralistic
[2] (= *polifacético*) many-sided, diverse
Ⓑ SMF pluralist

pluralización SF pluralization

pluralizar ▸conjug 1f◂ VT [1] (*Ling*) to pluralize
[2] (= *generalizar*) to generalize

pluri... PREF pluri..., many ..., multi...

plurianual ADJ (= *de varios años*) lasting for several years; (= *largo*) long-term

pluricelular ADJ multicellular

pluricultural ADJ multicultural

pluridimensional ADJ multidimensional, multifaceted, many-sided

pluridisciplinar ADJ multidisciplinary

pluriempleado/a Ⓐ ADJ having more than one job
Ⓑ SM/F person with more than one job, moonlighter*

pluriempleo SM having more than one job, moonlighting*

plurifamiliar ADJ **vivienda ~** multi-family housing unit

pluriforme ADJ very diverse, multifaceted

plurilingüe ADJ multilingual

plurilingüismo SM multilingualism

plurinacional ADJ **estado ~** state consisting of several nationalities

pluripartidismo SM multi-party system

pluripartidista ADJ **sistema ~** multi-party system

plurivalencia SF (= *valores*) many-sided value; (= *versatilidad*) versatility; (= *aplicaciones*) wide applicability

plurivalente ADJ (= *polivalente*) multivalent, having numerous values; (= *versátil*) versatile; (= *aplicable*) widely applicable

plus SM bonus; **con cinco dólares de ~** with a bonus of five dollars ► **plus de antigüedad** seniority bonus ► **plus de carestía de vida** cost-of-living bonus ► **plus de exclusividad** *bonus in return for working exclusively for one employer* ► **plus de nocturnidad** extra pay for unsocial hours ► **plus de peligrosidad** danger money ► **plus de productividad** productivity bonus ► **plus salarial** bonus

pluscafé SM (*LAm*) liqueur

pluscuamperfecto SM (*Ling*) pluperfect, past perfect

plusmarca SF record; **batir la ~** to break the record

plusmarquista SMF (= *poseedor*) record holder; (= *que mejora*) record-breaker; (= *ganador*) top scorer

plusvalía SF (*gen*) appreciation, added value; [*de capital*] capital gain; **impuesto sobre la ~** capital gains tax

Plutarco SM Plutarch

pluto‡ ADJ (*Andes*) drunk, sloshed*

plutocracia SF plutocracy

plutócrata SMF plutocrat

plutocrático ADJ plutocratic

Plutón SM Pluto

plutonio SM plutonium

pluvial ADJ rain *antes de s*

pluviometría SF rainfall, precipitation

pluviométrico ADJ rainfall *antes de s*; **media pluviométrica** average rainfall

pluviómetro SM rain gauge, pluviometer

pluviosidad SF rainfall

pluvioso ADJ rainy

pluviselva SF rain-forest

PM ABR (= **Policía Militar**) MP

p.m. ABR [1] (= **post meridiem**) pm
[2] = **por minuto**

pm. ABR = **próximo**

PMA SM ABR [1] (= **Programa Mundial de Alimentos**) WFP
[2] (*Aut*) = **peso máximo autorizado**

p/mes ABR (= **por mes**) pcm

PMM SM ABR (= **parque móvil de ministerios**) *official government cars*

PN SMF ABR (*Esp*) = **profesor numerario/profesora numeraria**

PNB SM ABR (= **producto nacional bruto**) GNP

P.N.D. SM ABR (*Educ*) (= **personal no docente**) *non-teaching staff*

PNN Ⓐ SMF ABR (*Educ*) = **profesor(a) no numerario/a**
Ⓑ SM ABR (*Econ*) (= **producto nacional neto**) NNP

PNP SM ABR (*Puerto Rico*) = **Partido Nuevo Progresista**

PNR SM ABR (*Méx Hist*) = **Partido Nacional Revolucionario**

PNUD SM ABR (= **Programa de las Naciones Unidas para el Desarrollo**) UNDP

PNV SM ABR (*Esp Pol*) = **Partido Nacionalista Vasco**

P.° ABR (= **Paseo**) Ave., Av.

p.o. ABR = **por orden**

poblacho SM, **poblachón** SM dump, one-horse town

población SF [1] (= *gente*) population
► **población activa** working population
► **población flotante** floating population
► **población marginada** marginalized sectors of society *pl*; **el aumento de la ~ marginada** the increasing marginalization of society
► **población ocupada** working population
► **población pasiva** non-working population
[2] (= *lugar habitado, ciudad*) town; (= *pueblo*) village; (*Cono Sur*) (= *caserío*) small hamlet
[3] (= *acción*) settlement
[4] (*Chile*) (*tb* ~ **callampa**) (= *suburbio*) shanty town; (= *barrio pobre*) slum area, poor quarter

poblacional ADJ population *antes de s*; **estudio ~** population study

poblada SF (*LAm*††) (= *revuelta*) rural revolt; (= *muchedumbre*) crowd

poblado Ⓐ ADJ [1] (= *habitado*) inhabited; **poco ~** sparsely populated; **densamente ~** densely populated; **la ciudad más poblada del país** the city with the largest population in the country
[2] **~ de** (= *habitado*) peopled *o* populated with; (= *lleno*) full of; (= *cubierto*) covered with
[3] [*barba, cejas*] bushy, thick
Ⓑ SM (= *pueblo*) village; (= *población*) town; (= *lugar habitado*) settlement; (*Aut*) built-up area
► **poblado de absorción, poblado dirigido** new town, satellite town

poblador(a) SM/F [1] (= *colonizador*) settler, colonist; (= *fundador*) founder; (= *habitante*) inhabitant; **los primeros ~es** the first settlers
[2] (*Chile*) slum dweller

poblano/a Ⓐ ADJ (*LAm*) village *antes de s*, town *antes de s*; (*Méx*) of/from Puebla
Ⓑ SM/F [1] (*LAm*) villager
[2] (*Méx*) native/inhabitant of Puebla

poblar ▸conjug 1l◂ Ⓐ VT [1] [*colonos, conquistadores*] to settle, populate
[2] [*animales, plantas*] inhabit; **los peces que pueblan las profundidades** the fish that inhabit the depths; **las estrellas que pueblan el espacio** the stars that fill space; **~ una colmena** (*Agr*) to stock a beehive;
[3] **~ de algo**: **han poblado el río con varias especies de peces** they have stocked the river with various species of fish; **~on el monte de abetos** they planted the trees with fir trees
Ⓑ **poblarse** VPR [1] (= *llenarse*) to fill (**de** with); **la región se pobló en pocos años** the area was settled *o* populated in the space of a few years; **el centro de la ciudad se pobló de gente** the city centre filled up with people
[2] (*Bot*) (= *cubrirse de hojas*) to come into leaf

pobo SM white poplar

pobre Ⓐ ADJ [1] [*persona, familia, barrio*] poor; **aquí vive gente muy ~** the people who live here are very poor
[2] (= *escaso*) poor; **sus conocimientos de inglés son muy ~s** his knowledge of English is very poor; **una dieta ~ en vitaminas** a diet poor in vitamins
[3] (*indicando compasión*) poor; **¡~ hombre!** poor man!, poor fellow!; **¡~ Francisco!** poor old Francisco!; **¡~ de mí!** poor me!; **¡~ de él!** poor man!, poor fellow!; **¡~ de ti si te pillo!** you'll be sorry if I catch you!; **~ diablo** poor wretch, poor devil
Ⓑ SMF [1] (= *necesitado*) poor person; (= *mendigo*) beggar; **un ~** a poor man; **los ~s** the poor, poor people; **un ~ pedía dinero** a beggar *o* poor man was asking for money
[2] (*indicando compasión*) poor thing; **la ~ estaba mojada** the poor thing was wet through

pobrecillo/a SM/F poor thing

pobremente ADV poorly

pobrería SF (*Cono Sur*), **pobrerío** SM (*Cono Sur*) the poor, poor people

pobrete/a Ⓐ SM/F poor thing, poor wretch
Ⓑ ADJ poor, wretched

pobretería SF [1] (= *los pobres*) the poor, poor people
[2] (= *pobreza*) poverty
[3] (= *tacañería*) miserliness, meanness

pobretón/ona Ⓐ ADJ very poor, terribly poor
Ⓑ SM/F poor man/woman

pobreza SF [1] (= *falta de dinero*) poverty; **vivían en la más absoluta ~** they lived in abject poverty; ✦**REFRÁN** **~ no es vileza** poverty is not a crime
[2] (= *escasez*) **nos sorprendió la ~ de su razonamiento** we were surprised by the poverty of his arguments; **~ de vocabulario** poverty of vocabulary
[3] (*Rel*) **voto de ~** vow of poverty

poca SM (*LAm*), **pócar** SM (*Méx*) poker

pocero SM well-digger

pocerón SM (*CAm, Méx*) large pool

pocha[1] SF (*Culin*) haricot bean

pocha[2] SF (*Cono Sur*) (= *mentira*) lie; (= *trampa*) trick

poch(e)ar ▸conjug 1a◂ VT (*Culin*) to poach

pochismo* SM (*Méx Ling*) *incorrect use of language caused by interference from American English*

pocho/a* Ⓐ ADJ [1] (= *estropeado*) [*flor*] withered; [*persona*] peaky*, off-colour*, off color (*EEUU**); [*fruta*] soft, overripe
[2] [*color*] faded
[3] (= *deprimido*) depressed, gloomy
[4] (*Cono Sur*) (= *gordito*) chubby; (= *bajo*) squat
Ⓑ SM/F (*Méx*) *United States national of Mexican origin*, Mexican-American

pochoclo SM (*Arg*) popcorn

pocholada* SF nice thing, pretty thing; **es una ~** it's lovely; **una ~ de niño** a sweet *o* cute little baby

pocholez* SF gem, treasure; **el vestido es una ~** it's a gorgeous dress

pocholo/a* Ⓐ ADJ nice, cute
Ⓑ SM/F pretty boy/pretty girl; (*en oración directa*) my little angel, my poppet

pocilga SF [1] (= *porqueriza*) pigsty, pigpen (*EEUU*)
[2] (= *lugar asqueroso*) pigsty, pigpen (*EEUU*)

pocillo SM [1] (= *tazón*) mug
[2] (= *cuenco*) (small) bowl, (small) dish
[3] (*LAm*) [*de café*] coffee cup
[4] (*Méx*) (= *jarra*) [*de cerveza*] tankard

pócima SF, **poción** SF [1] (*Farm*) potion, draught, draft (*EEUU*)
[2] (*Vet*) drench; (= *brebaje*) concoction

poco Ⓐ ADJ [1] (*en singular*) little, not much; **tenemos ~ tiempo** we have little time, we don't have much time; **hay muy ~ queso** there's very little cheese, there's hardly any cheese; **de ~ interés** of little interest; **con ~ respeto** with little respect, with scant respect; **el provecho es ~** the gain is small, there isn't much to gain; **poca cosa**: **no te preocupes por tan poca cosa** don't worry about such a little thing; **poca cosa se podría haber hecho** there wasn't much we could have done; **comemos, jugamos a cartas, leemos y poca cosa más** we eat, play cards, read and do little else *o* and that's about it; **es poca cosa** (= *no mucho*) it's not much; (= *no importante*) it's nothing much; **somos tan poca cosa** we're so insignificant; **es muy guapa pero poca cosa** she's very pretty, but there isn't much to her; **y por si fuera ~** and as if that weren't enough, and to cap it all
[2] (*en plural*) few, not many; **~s niños saben que ...** few *o* not many children know that ...; **tiene ~s amigos** he has few friends, he hasn't got many friends; **~s días después** a few days later; **compré unos ~s libros** I bought a few books; **me quedan pocas probabilidades** I don't have much chance; **todas las medidas son pocas** no measure will be enough
Ⓑ PRON [1] (*en singular*) [1·1] (= *poca cosa*) **la reforma servirá para ~** the reform won't do much good *o* won't be much use; **una hora da para ~** you can't get much done in an hour; **con lo ~ que me quedaba** with what little I had left; **ya sabes lo ~ que me interesa** you know how little it interests me
[1·2] **un ~** a bit, a little; **—¿tienes frío? —un ~** "are you cold?" — "a bit *o* a little"; **he bebido un ~, pero no estoy borracho** I've had a bit to drink, but I'm not drunk; **voy a dormir un ~** I am going to have a little sleep; **le conocía un ~** I knew him a bit *o* slightly; **necesito descansar un ~** I need to rest for a while; **espera un ~** wait a minute *o* moment; **estoy un ~ triste** I am rather *o* a little sad; **es un ~ lo que yo comentaba** that's more or less what I was saying; **un ~ como**: **es un ~ como su padre** he's rather *o* a bit like his father; **lo hice un ~ como protesta** I did it partly as a protest; **un ~ de**: **un ~ de dinero** a little money; **dame un ~ de vino** can I have some wine?; **¡un ~ de silencio!** let's have some quiet here!
[1·3] (*referido a tiempo*) not long; **tardaron ~ en hacerlo** it didn't take them long to do it, they didn't take long to do it; **lleva ~ trabajando aquí** he hasn't been working here long; **a ~ de** shortly after; **a ~ de haberlo firmado** shortly after signing it; **cada ~** every so often; **dentro de ~** shortly, soon; **~ después** shortly after; **hace ~** not long ago; **fuimos a verla hace ~** we visited her not long ago, we visited

her quite recently; **tu hermana ha llamado hace ~** your sister called a short while ago; **la conozco desde hace ~** I haven't known her long, I've only known her for a short while; **hasta hace ~** until recently
2 (*en plural*) few; **~s son los que ...** there are few who ...; **ya somos ~s los que nos sentimos así** there are now very few of us who feel this way; **~s de entre ellos** few of them; ✦*MODISMO* **como hay ~s**: **es tonto como hay ~s** he's as stupid as they come
Ⓒ ADV 1 (*con verbos*) not much, little; **cuesta ~** it doesn't cost much, it costs very little; **habla ~** he doesn't say much; **ahora trabaja ~** he doesn't work much now; **vamos ~ a Madrid** we don't go to Madrid much, we hardly ever go to Madrid; **lo estiman ~** they hardly value it at all, they value it very little
2 (*con adjetivos: se traduce a menudo por medio de un prefijo*) **~ dispuesto a ayudar** disinclined to help; **~ amable** unkind; **~ probable** unlikely; **~ inteligente** unintelligent, not very intelligent; **sus libros son ~ conocidos aquí** his books are not very well known here
3 (*otras locuciones*) **~ a ~** little by little; **¡~ a ~!** steady on!, easy does it!; **a ~** (*Méx**) **¿a ~?** never!, you don't say!; **¡a ~ no!** not much!*; **¿a ~ no?** (well) isn't it?; **¿a ~ crees que ...?** do you really imagine that ...?; **de a ~** (*LAm*) gradually; **tener en ~**: **tiene en ~ a su jefe** she doesn't think much of her boss; **tiene la vida en ~** he doesn't value his life; **~ más o menos** more or less; **por ~** almost, nearly; **por ~ me ahogo** I almost *o* nearly drowned; **a ~ que**: **a ~ que pueda** if at all possible; **a ~ que corras, lo alcanzas** if you run now you'll catch it

poda SF 1 (= *acto*) pruning
2 (= *temporada*) pruning season

podadera SF (= *cuchillo*) pruning knife, billhook; (= *tijera*) pruning shears *pl*; (*de tipo yunque*) secateurs *pl*

podadora SF (*Méx*) lawnmower

podar ▸conjug 1a◂ VT 1 [+ *árbol*] to lop, prune; [+ *rama*] to lop, trim, trim off; [+ *rosal*] to prune
2 (= *acortar*) [+ *texto*] to prune; [+ *pasaje, parte*] to cut out

podenco SM hound

▼**poder**

▸conjug 2s◂	C VERBO IMPERSONAL
A VERBO AUXILIAR	D SUSTANTIVO
B VERBO INTRANSITIVO	MASCULINO

Ⓐ VERBO AUXILIAR
1 = *tener la posibilidad o capacidad de* **yo puedo ayudarte** I can help you; **puedo hacerlo solo** I can do it on my own *o* by myself; **¿se puede llamar por teléfono desde aquí?** can you phone from here?; **no puede venir** he can't *o* cannot come; **llevo varios días sin ~ salir** I haven't been able to go out for several days; **no ha podido venir** he couldn't come, he was unable to come; **creo que mañana no voy a ~ ir** I don't think I'll be able to come tomorrow; **este agua no se puede beber** this water isn't fit to drink
2 = *tener permiso para* **puedes irte** you can *o* may go; **¿puedo usar tu teléfono?** can *o* may I use your phone?; **¿puedo abrir la ventana?** can *o* may I open the window?; **aquí no se puede fumar** you aren't allowed to smoke here, you can't smoke here
3 *en peticiones* **¿puedes/puede darme un vaso de agua?** can I/may I have a glass of water please?; **¿me puede usted decir cuándo sale el autobús?** can *o* could you tell me when the bus leaves?
4 *indicando eventualidad* **puede** *o* **podría estar en cualquier sitio** it could *o* might be anywhere; **¡cuidado, te puedes hacer daño!** careful, you could *o* might hurt yourself!; **podías haberte roto una pierna** you could *o* might have broken your leg; **puede haber salido** he may have gone out; **por lo que pueda pasar** just in case
5 *indicando obligación moral* **¡no pueden tratarnos así!** they can't treat us like this!; **bien podrían cuidarla un poco mejor** they really ought to take better care of her; **es lo menos que podemos hacer por ellos** it's the least we can do for them; **no podíamos dejarlo solo** we couldn't leave him alone
6 *en cálculos, aproximaciones* **¿qué edad puede tener?** I wonder what age he is?, how old do you reckon he is?; **puede costar unos cien euros** it could cost as much as a hundred euros
7 *en sugerencias* **podríamos ir al cine** we could go to the cinema; **siempre puedes volverlo a intentar** you can always try again later
8 *en reproches* **¡podías habérmelo dicho!** you could *o* might have told me!; **habría podido ser más amable** she could *o* might have been a bit nicer; **¡al menos podrías disculparte!** you could at least say sorry!
Ⓑ VERBO INTRANSITIVO
1 = *tener la posibilidad o capacidad* **no puedo** I can't; **lo haré si puedo** I'll do it if I can; **¡no puedo más!** (= *estoy agotado*) I can't go on!; (= *estoy desesperado*) I can't cope any more!; (= *he comido mucho*) I can't eat another thing!
2 = *tener permiso* **¿se puede?** may I come in?; **¿puedo?** may I?
3 = *tener dominio, influencia* **los que pueden** those who can, those who are able; **el dinero puede mucho** money can do almost anything, money talks; **la curiosidad pudo más que el temor** his curiosity got the better of his fear; **él puede mucho en el partido** he has a lot of influence in the party; **~ a algn: yo le puedo** I'm a match for him; (*entre niños*) I could have him*
◆ **poder con**: **¿puedes con la maleta?** can you manage the suitcase?; **no puedo con él** (= *no puedo controlarle*) I can't handle him; (= *pesa mucho*) he's too heavy for me; **no puedo con la hipocresía** I can't stand hypocrisy
4 *en locuciones* **a más no ~**: **es tonto a más no ~** he's as stupid as they come; **su actuación fue correcta a más no ~** he behaved entirely properly; **comió a más no ~** he ate until he couldn't eat any more; **no ~ por menos que**: **no pude por menos que decirle lo que pensaba de él** I just had to tell him what I thought of him
5 *CAm, Méx**: = *molestar* (*con irritación*) to annoy; (*con disgusto*) to upset; **su actitud me pudo** his attitude annoyed me *o* got on my nerves; **me pudo esa broma** that joke upset me
Ⓒ VERBO IMPERSONAL
◆ **puede (ser)** (= *es posible*) maybe, it may be so, perhaps; **¡no puede ser!** that can't be!, that's impossible!
◆ **puede (ser) que** + *SUBJUN*: **puede (ser) que esté en la biblioteca** he could *o* may be in the library, perhaps he's in the library; **puede (ser) que tenga uno ya** he may *o* might have one already; **puede (ser) que no venga** he may *o* might not come; **puede (ser) que tenga razón** she may *o* could be right; **puede (ser) que sí** maybe (so)
Ⓓ SUSTANTIVO MASCULINO
1 = *capacidad, facultad* power; **tiene un enorme ~ de concentración** she has tremendous powers of concentration; **afirma tener ~es mágicos** he claims to have magic powers ▸ **poder adquisitivo** purchasing power ▸ **poder de convocatoria**: **tienen un gran ~ de convocatoria** they really pull in the crowds, they're real crowd-pullers* ▸ **poder de negociación** bargaining power
2 = *autoridad, influencia* power; **ejercen un ~ enorme sobre la juventud** they have a lot of power *o* influence over young people; **en este país los militares tienen mucho ~** the military are very powerful in this country; **no tienen ~ para oponerse a estas medidas** they are not powerful enough to oppose these measures; **un partido jugado de ~ a ~** an evenly-matched game
3 *Pol* **el ~** power; **¡el pueblo al ~!** power to the people!; **¡Herrera al ~!** Herrera for leader!; **bajo el ~ de algn**: **estar en el ~** ◊ **ocupar el ~** to be in power; **subir al ~** to come to power; **el ~ central** central government; **el cuarto ~** the fourth estate; **el ~ establecido** the establishment; **los ~es fácticos** the powers that be; **los ~es públicos** the authorities ▸ **poder absoluto** absolute power ▸ **poder civil** civil power ▸ **poder ejecutivo** executive power ▸ **poder judicial** judiciary ▸ **poder legislativo** legislative power
4 = *fuerza, eficacia* **un detergente de gran ~ limpiador** a powerful detergent; **este medicamento no tiene ~ contra la tuberculosis** this drug is ineffective *o* isn't effective against tuberculosis
5 = *potestad* **poderes** powers; **les dieron amplios ~es para dirigir la empresa** they were given wide-ranging powers to run the company; **tiene plenos ~es para intervenir en el asunto** he has full authority to intervene in the matter
6 *Jur* **por ~es** *o* (*LAm*) **poder** by proxy; **casarse por ~es** to get married by proxy ▸ **poder notarial** power of attorney
7 = *posesión* possession; **tengo en mi ~ información confidencial** I am in possession of confidential information; **estar** *u* **obrar en ~ de algn** to be in sb's hands *o* possession; **esa información está** *u* **obra en ~ de la juez** that information is in the hands of the judge, that information is in the judge's possession; **pasar a ~ de algn** to pass to sb, pass into sb's possession
8 *Fís, Mec* power; **el ~ del motor** the power of the engine ▸ **poder calorífico** calorific value
9 *LAm*: = *persona* drug pusher

poderhabiente SMF proxy, attorney (*EEUU*)

poderío SM 1 (= *poder*) power; (= *fuerza*)

➤ LENGUA Y USO: **poder A1** 39.3, 42.4, 43.3, 43.4 **A2** 36.1, 36.2, 36.3, 37.4 **A3** 31, 42.3 **C** 39.3

might; (= *señorío*) authority, jurisdiction
[2] (*Fin*) wealth

poderosamente ADV powerfully

poderoso Ⓐ ADJ powerful; ✦*REFRÁN* **~ caballero es don dinero** money talks
Ⓑ SMPL **los ~s** (= *dirigentes*) the people in power; (= *ricos*) the rich and powerful

podiatría SF podiatry

podio SM (= *estrado*) podium; (*Méx*) rostrum; **subir al ~** (*Dep*) to mount the winners' podium; **estar en el ~ de la actualidad** to be in the limelight

pódium SM (*pl* **pódiums**) = **podio**

podología SF chiropody, podiatry (*EEUU*)

podólogo/a SM/F chiropodist, podiatrist (*EEUU*)

podómetro SM pedometer

podón SM billhook

podre SF pus

podredumbre SF [1] (= *cualidad*) rottenness, putrefaction; (= *parte podrida*) rot
[2] (= *corrupción*) rottenness, corruption
[3] (*Enología*) ► **podredumbre noble** noble rot
[4] (= *tristeza*) secret sorrow, secret sadness
[5] (*Med*) pus

podrida SF **armar la ~** (*Cono Sur**) to start a fight

podrido ADJ [1] (= *putrefacto*) rotten
[2] (= *corrupto*) rotten, corrupt; **el sistema está ~ por dentro** there is corruption inside the system; **están ~s de dinero*** they're filthy rich*
[3] (*Cono Sur**) (= *harto*) fed-up*

podrir ▸conjug 3a◂ = **pudrir**

poema SM poem; ✦*MODISMO* **ser todo un ~** to be quite a sight, be just like a fairy tale; (*pey*) to be a complete farce

poemario SM book of poems

poemático ADJ poetic

poesía SF [1] (= *arte*) poetry; **la ~ del Siglo de Oro** Golden Age poetry
[2] (= *poema*) poem
[3] (= *encanto*) poetry

poeta SMF [1] (= *compositor de versos*) poet
[2] (*LAm*) (= *escritor*) writer, author

poetastro SM poetaster

poética SF poetics *sing*, art of poetry

poéticamente ADV poetically

poético ADJ poetic, poetical

poetisa SF poetess, woman poet

poetizar ▸conjug 1f◂ Ⓐ VT [1] [+ *texto*] to poeticize, put into poetry
[2] (= *idealizar*) to idealize
Ⓑ VI to write poetry

pogrom SM, **pogromo** SM pogrom

póker SM poker

polaca SF (*Andes, Cono Sur*) (= *blusa*) smock

polaco[1]/a Ⓐ ADJ (= *de Polonia*) Polish
Ⓑ SM/F Pole
Ⓒ SM [1] (*Ling*) Polish
[2] (*CAm*) (= *policía*) cop*

polaco[2]/a (*pey*) ADJ, SM/F Catalan

polaina SF [1] (= *sobrecalza*) leggings *pl*
[2] (*Andes, CAm, Cono Sur*) (= *molestia*) nuisance; (= *chasco*) setback

polar ADJ polar

polaridad SF polarity

polarización SF polarization

polarizado Ⓐ ADJ polarized
Ⓑ SM polarizing

polarizar ▸conjug 1f◂ Ⓐ VT to polarize
Ⓑ **polarizarse** VPR to polarize, become polarized (**en torno a** around)

polca SF [1] (*Mús*) polka
[2] (*) (= *jaleo*) fuss, to-do*
[3] (*Andes*) (= *blusa*) blouse
[4] (*Andes, Cono Sur*) (= *chaqueta*) long jacket

polcata* SF row, shindy*

pólder SM (*pl* **pólders**) polder

polea SF pulley; (*Aut*) fan belt; (*Náut*) tackle, tackle block

poleada SF (*CAm*) *hot drink made of milk and flour*

polémica SF [1] (= *discusión*) controversy
[2] (= *género*) polemics *sing*

polémico ADJ controversial, polemical (*frm*)

polemista SMF polemicist; **un brillante ~** a brilliant polemicist

polemizar ▸conjug 1f◂ VI to argue (**en torno a** about); **se ha polemizado mucho en torno al tema** the matter has been the subject of much controversy; **no quiero ~** I have no wish to get involved in an argument; **~ con algn en la prensa** to have a debate with sb in the press

polemología SF war studies *pl*

polen SM pollen

polenta SF [1] (*Andes, Cono Sur*) (= *maicena*) cornflour, cornstarch (*EEUU*); (= *sémola de maíz*) ground maize, polenta
[2] **tener ~** (= *entusiasmo*) to be enthusiastic; (= *calidad*) to be first-rate

poleo SM pennyroyal

polera SF [1] (*Chile*) (= *camiseta*) T-shirt
[2] (*Cono Sur*) (= *jersey*) polo neck

poli* Ⓐ SM/F cop*
Ⓑ SF **la ~** the cops* *pl*

poli... PREF poly-

poliamida SM polyamide

poliandria SF polyandry

poliándrico ADJ polyandrous

polibán SM hip-bath

Polichinela SM Punch

policía Ⓐ SMF policeman/policewoman, police officer ► **policía de paisano** plain-clothes policeman ► **policía informático/a** *policeman specializing in computer crime* ► **policía local, policía municipal** local policeman/policewoman
Ⓑ SM ► **policía acostado** (*Ven Aut**) speed bump, sleeping policeman
Ⓒ SF (= *organización*) police; **¡llama a la ~!** call the police!; **Cuerpo Nacional de Policía** (*Esp*) ≈ the Police Force ► **policía antidisturbios** riot police ► **policía autonómica** *police force of a regional autonomy* ► **policía de barrio** community police ► **Policía de Tráfico** traffic police ► **Policía Local** Local Police ► **Policía Militar** military police ► **Policía Montada** mounted police ► **Policía Municipal** local police ► **Policía Nacional** national police ► **Policía Secreta** secret police

> **POLICÍA**
>
> *There are two types of* **policía** *in Spain, the* **policía nacional**, *in charge of national security and public order in general, and the* **policía municipal**, *with duties of regulating traffic and policing the local community. The Basque Country and Catalonia also have their own police forces, the* **Ertzaintza** *and the* **Mossos d'Esquadra** *respectively. In rural areas the* **Guardia Civil** *is responsible for policing duties.*
> ⇨ *See also* GUARDIA CIVIL, ERTZAINTZA

policiaco ADJ, **policíaco** ADJ police *antes de s*; **novela policíaca** detective story

policial Ⓐ ADJ police *antes de s*
Ⓑ SM (*CAm*) policeman

policivo ADJ (*Col*) police *antes de s*

policlínica SF, **policlínico** SM (*tb* **hospital policlínico**) general hospital

policromado Ⓐ ADJ polychrome
Ⓑ SM polychrome painting

policromo ADJ, **polícromo** ADJ polychromatic, polychrome

polideportivo SM sports centre, sports center (*EEUU*)

poliducto SM (*Perú, Ven*) oil pipeline

poliedro SM polyhedron

poliéster SM polyester

poliestireno SM polystyrene

polietileno SM polythene, polyethylene (*EEUU*)

polifacético ADJ multi-faceted, versatile

polifacetismo SM many-sidedness, versatility

Polifemo SM Polyphemus

polifonía SF polyphony

polifónico ADJ polyphonic

polifuncional ADJ multi-purpose, multi-functional

poligamia SF polygamy

polígamo Ⓐ ADJ polygamous
Ⓑ SM polygamist

poligénesis SF INV polygenesis

políglota ADJ, SMF, **poliglota** ADJ, SMF polyglot

polígloto/a ADJ, SM/F, **poligloto/a** ADJ, SM/F polyglot

poligonal ADJ polygonal

polígono SM [1] (*Mat*) polygon
[2] (= *terreno*) building lot ► **polígono de descongestión** overspill area ► **polígono de ensayos** test site, testing ground ► **polígono de tiro** shooting range; (*Mil*) firing range, artillery range ► **polígono industrial** industrial estate ► **polígono residencial** housing estate

polígrafo/a SM/F writer on a wide variety of subjects

poliinsaturado Ⓐ ADJ polyunsaturated
Ⓑ SM polyunsaturate

polilla SF (= *mariposa*) moth; (= *oruga*) grub; [*de la ropa*] clothes moth; [*de la madera*] woodworm; [*de libros*] bookworm

polímata SMF polymath

polimerización SF polymerization

polímero SM polymer

poli-mili SMF (*Esp Hist*) *member of the political-military wing of ETA*

polimorfismo SM polymorphism

polimorfo ADJ polymorphic

Polinesia SF Polynesia

polinesio/a ADJ, SM/F Polynesian

polínico ADJ pollen *antes de s*

polinización SF pollination ► **polinización cruzada** cross-pollination

polinizar ▸conjug 1f◂ VT to pollinate

polinosis SF INV hay fever

polio SF polio

poliomielitis SF INV poliomyelitis

polipiel® SF imitation leather

pólipo SM polyp, polypus

polipropileno SM polypropylene

Polisario SM ABR (*tb* **El Frente ~**) = **Frente Popular de Liberación del Sáhara y Río de Oro**

polisemia SF polysemy

polisémico ADJ polysemic

polisílabo Ⓐ ADJ polysyllabic Ⓑ SM polysyllable

polisón SM [1] (= *armazón*) bustle [2] (*) (= *trasero*) bottom

polista SMF polo player

politécnica SF ≈ technical college

politeísmo SM polytheism

politeísta ADJ polytheistic

politene SM, **politeno** SM polythene, polyethylene (*EEUU*)

política SF [1] (*Pol*) politics *sing*; **meterse en (la) ~** to get involved in politics; **la ~ en la posguerra** postwar politics ► **política de pasillo(s)** lobbying [2] (= *programa*) policy ► **política agraria** agricultural policy ► **política de cañonera** gunboat diplomacy ► **política de ingresos y precios, política de jornales y precios** prices and incomes policy ► **política de mano dura** strong-arm policy, tough policy ► **política de silla vacía** empty-chair policy, refusal to take one's seat (in parliament) ► **política de tierra quemada** scorched earth policy ► **política económica** economic policy ► **política exterior** foreign policy ► **política interior** [*de país*] domestic policy; [*de organización*] internal politics ► **política presupuestaria** budget policy ► **política salarial** incomes policy [3] (= *tacto*) tact, skill; (= *cortesía*) politeness, courtesy; (= *educación*) good manners *pl*

políticamente ADV politically; **~ correcto** politically correct

politicastro/a SM/F (*pey*) politico* (*pey*)

político/a Ⓐ ADJ [1] (*Pol*) political [2] [*persona*] (= *diplomático*) tactful; (= *hábil*) skilful, skillful (*EEUU*); (= *cortés*) polite, well-mannered; (= *reservado*) stiff, reserved [3] [*pariente*] **padre ~** father-in-law; **es tío ~ mío** he's an uncle of mine by marriage; **familia política** in-laws *pl* Ⓑ SM/F politician ► **político/a de café** armchair politician

politicón* ADJ [1] (*Pol*) strongly political, keenly interested in politics [2] (= *ceremonioso*) very ceremonious, obsequious

politiquear ▸conjug 1a◂ VI (= *actuar*) to play at politics, dabble in politics; (= *hablar*) to talk politics

politiqueo SM, **politiquería** SF (*pey*) political manoeuvring *o* (*EEUU*) maneuvering

politiquero/a SM/F (*pey*) political intriguer

politiqués SM political jargon

politiquillo/a SM/F minor politician

politización SF politicization

politizar ▸conjug 1f◂ VT to politicize

politología SF political science, study of politics

politólogo/a SM/F political scientist, political expert

politono SM (*Telec*) polyphonic ringtone, polytone

politoxicomanía SF multiple drug-addiction

politraumatismo SM multiple injuries *pl*

poliuretano SM polyurethane

polivalente ADJ [1] (*Quím, Med*) polyvalent [2] (= *versátil*) (*gen*) multi-purpose; [*avión*] multi-role [3] (= *con varios aspectos*) multi-faceted, many-sided

polivinilo SM polyvinyl

póliza SF [1] (*Com*) (= *certificado*) certificate, voucher; (= *giro*) draft; **pagar una ~** to pay out on an insurance policy ► **póliza de seguro(s)** insurance policy ► **póliza dotal** endowment policy [2] (= *impuesto*) tax stamp, fiscal stamp

polizón SM [1] (*Aer, Náut*) stowaway; **viajar de ~** to stow away (**en** on) [2] (= *vago*) tramp, vagrant, bum (*EEUU*)

polizonte⁑ SM cop*

polla SF [1] (*Orn*) pullet; (= *polluelo*) chick ► **polla de agua** moorhen [2] (⁑) (= *pene*) prick⁑; ✦**MODISMOS ¡una ~!** get away!*; **¡ni qué ~s!** no way!*; **¿qué ~s quieres?** what the hell do you want?*; **¡qué duquesa ni que ~s en vinagre!** duchess my arse!⁑; **dejarse de ~s** to stop farting about⁑ [3] (*LAm Naipes*) stakes *pl*, pool [4] (*Cono Sur*) (= *lotería*) lottery

pollaboba⁑ SM berk*, wimp*

pollada SF brood

pollastre* SM = **pollo 3**

pollastro* SM, **pollastrón*** SM sly fellow

pollera¹ SF [1] (*para pollos*) (= *criadero*) hencoop, chicken run; (= *cesto*) basket for chickens [2] (*LAm*) (= *falda*) skirt, overskirt [3] (*Cono Sur Rel*) soutane [4] (= *aparato*) walker; *ver tb* **pollero**

pollería SF poulterer's (shop)

pollero/a² SM/F [1] (= *criador*) chicken farmer; (= *vendedor*) poulterer [2] (*LAm*) (= *jugador*) gambler [3] (*Méx**) (= *guía*) *guide for illegal immigrants to USA*; *ver tb* **pollera**

pollerudo ADJ (*Cono Sur*) [1] (= *cobarde*) cowardly [2] (= *chismoso*) backbiting, gossipy [3] (= *santurrón*) self-righteous, sanctimonious

pollino/a SM/F [1] (= *burro*) donkey [2] (*) (= *persona*) ass*, idiot

pollita* SF [1] (= *gallina*) young pullet [2] (= *chica*) bird*, chick (*EEUU**); **ya está hecha una ~*** she's turned into quite a good-looking chick⁑ [3] ✦**MODISMO echar ~s** to tell lies

pollito SM [1] (*Orn*) chick ► **pollito de un día** day-old chick [2] (*) = **pollo 3**

pollo SM [1] (*Orn*) (= *adulto*) chicken; (= *cría*) chick; (*Culin*) chicken; **~ asado** *o* (*LAm*) **rostizado** roast chicken; ✦**MODISMOS echarse el ~** (*Cono Sur*) to pack up and go; **¡qué duquesa ni qué ~s en vinagre!*** duchess my foot!*; **¡ni eso ni ~s en vinagre!*** no way!*; **montar un ~** to make a fuss, make a scene ► **pollo de corral** free-range chicken ► **pollo de granja** broiler chicken [2] (*Pol*) *torture where the victim is suspended from a pole or spit* [3] (*) (= *joven*) young lad; **¿quién es ese ~?** who's that young lad?*; **es un ~ nada más** he's only a kid* ► **pollo pera*** (= *pijo*) rich kid; (= *chanchullero*) spiv*, flash Harry* [4] (*Esp*⁑) (= *esputo*) gob*; **soltar un ~** to gob* [5] (*Méx**) (= *emigrante*) *would-be immigrant to USA from Mexico*

polluelo SM chick

polo¹ SM [1] (*Geog*) pole; **de ~ a ~** from pole to pole ► **polo magnético** magnetic pole ► **Polo Norte** North Pole ► **Polo Sur** South Pole [2] (*Elec*) [*de imán*] pole; [*de enchufe*] pin; **una clavija de cuatro ~s** a four-pin plug ► **polo negativo** negative pole ► **polo positivo** positive pole [3] (= *centro*) centre, center (*EEUU*), focus ► **polo de atracción** centre *o* (*EEUU*) center of attraction ► **polo de desarrollo, polo de promoción** (*Com*) development area [4] (= *extremo*) **los dos generales son ~s opuestos** the two generals are poles apart; **esto es el ~ opuesto de lo que dijo antes** this is the exact opposite of what he said before ► **polo de referencia** point of reference [5] (*para comer*) ice lolly, Popsicle® (*EEUU*)

polo² SM (*Dep*) polo ► **polo acuático** water polo

polo³ SM (= *jersey*) polo-neck; (= *camisa*) polo shirt

polola¹ SF (*Cono Sur*) (= *coqueta*) flirt; (= *amiga*) girlfriend; *ver tb* **pololo**

pololear ▸conjug 1a◂ (*Chile**) Ⓐ VI [1] (= *salir*) to go out; **~ con algn** to be going out with sb, be dating sb* [2] (= *coquetear*) to flirt (**con** with) Ⓑ VT [1] (= *pretender*) to court [2] (= *coquetear con*) to flirt with

pololeo* SM (*Chile*) [1] [*de novios*] dating* [2] [*de pretendiente*] courting [3] (= *coqueteo*) flirting

pololito* SM (*Chile*) odd job, casual job

pololo/a² (*Chile*) Ⓐ SM/F (*) boyfriend/girlfriend; *ver tb* **polola** Ⓑ SM [1] (= *insecto*) moth [2] (= *pesado*) bore [3] (= *coqueto*) flirt [4] (= *pretendiente*) (persistent) suitor [5] (= *chulo*) pimp

polonesa SF polonaise

Polonia SF Poland

poltergeist SM INV poltergeist

poltrón ADJ idle, lazy

poltrona SF [1] (= *butaca*) easy chair [2] (*pey*) (= *cargo*) **abandonar la ~ ministerial** to resign one's post as minister; **pasó demasiado tiempo en la ~** he spent too long in power *o* office

poltronear ▸conjug 1a◂ VI (*Cono Sur, Méx*) to laze around, loaf around

polución SF [1] (= *contaminación*) pollution ► **polución ambiental** environmental pollution ► **polución de la atmósfera** air pollution [2] [*de semen*] ► **polución nocturna** nocturnal emission (*frm*), wet dream

polucionante ADJ polluting

polucionar ▸conjug 1a◂ VT to pollute

polvareda SF 1 (= *polvo*) cloud of dust
2 (= *jaleo*) fuss, rumpus*; **levantar una ~** to create a storm, cause a rumpus*, kick up a fuss*

polvera SF 1 (= *estuche*) powder compact
2 (*Méx*) cloud of dust

polvero SM 1 (*LAm*) cloud of dust
2 (*CAm*) (= *pañuelo*) handkerchief

polvete** SM = **polvo 5**

polvillo SM 1 (*LAm Agr*) blight
2 (*Andes, Cono Sur*) [*de tabaco*] *tobacco refuse*
3 (*CAm*) (= *cuero*) *leather for shoemaking*
4 (*Andes*) [*de arroz*] rice bran

polvo SM 1 (*en el aire*) dust; **lleno de ~** dusty; **limpiar** *o* **quitar el ~** to dust; **✦*MODISMOS*** **hacer algo ~*** to ruin sth; **hacer ~ a algn*** (= *agotar*) to wear sb out; (= *deprimir*) to depress sb; (*en discusión*) to wipe the floor with sb*; **hecho ~***: **estoy hecho ~** (= *cansado*) I'm shattered*, I'm knackered‡; (= *deprimido*) I feel really down; **el coche está hecho ~** the car is a wreck; **el libro está hecho ~** the book is falling to pieces; **limpio de ~ y paja**: **ganó 50 millones, limpios de ~ y paja** he won 50 million in his hand; **matar el ~** to lay the dust; **hacer morder el ~ a algn** to humiliate sb; **sacudir el ~ a algn** to thrash sb, beat sb up*; **✦*REFRÁN*** **aquellos ~s traen estos lodos** such are the consequences ► **polvo espacial** space dust
2 (*Quím, Culin, Med*) powder; [*de tocador*] face powder; **ponerse ~s** to powder one's face; **en ~** [*leche, canela, cocaína*] powdered; **sólo se encuentra en ~** it's only available in powdered form ► **polvos de arroz** rice powder *sing* ► **polvos de blanqueo** bleaching powder *sing* ► **polvos de chile** chili powder *sing* ► **polvo(s) de hornear, polvo(s) de levadura** baking powder *sing* ► **polvo dentífrico** tooth powder *sing* ► **polvos de picapica** itching powder *sing* ► **polvos de talco** talcum powder *sing* ► **polvos para dientes** tooth powder *sing*
3 (‡) (= *droga*) snow‡, coke*
4 (= *porción*) pinch; **un ~ de rapé** a pinch of snuff
5 (**) screw**, shag**; **echar un ~** to have a screw *o* shag**; **está para un buen ~** she's hot stuff‡

pólvora SF 1 (= *explosivo*) gunpowder; **✦*MODISMOS*** **no ha descubierto** *o* **inventado la ~** it's not as if he's done anything amazingly original; **gastar la ~ en salvas** (= *desperdiciar*) to waste time and energy; (= *hacer gestos inútiles*) to make empty gestures; (= *hacer aspavientos*) to make a great song and dance; **levantar ~** to create *o* make a stir; **oler a ~** to smell fishy*; **propagarse como la ~** to spread like wildfire ► **pólvora de algodón** guncotton
2 (= *fuegos artificiales*) fireworks *pl*
3 (= *mal genio*) bad temper, crossness
4 (= *viveza*) life, liveliness

polvorear ▸conjug 1a◂ VT to powder, sprinkle (**de** with)

polvoriento ADJ 1 [*superficie*] dusty
2 [*sustancia*] powdery

polvorilla* SMF **ser un(a) ~** (= *de genio vivo*) to be really touchy*; (= *inquieto*) to be a live wire

polvorín SM 1 (*Mil*) (= *almacén*) arsenal; (= *pólvora*) fine powder
2 (= *situación peligrosa*) powder keg
3 (*Cono Sur*) (= *insecto*) gnat
4 (*Cono Sur, Méx*) = **polvorilla**
5 (*Andes, Caribe*) (= *polvareda*) cloud of dust

polvorón SM *type of light, crumbly shortbread*

polvorosa SF **✦*MODISMO*** **poner pies en ~*** to beat it*, scarper*

polvoroso ADJ dusty

polvoso ADJ (*LAm*) dusty

pom SM (*CAm*) incense

poma SF 1 (= *manzana*) apple
2 (= *frasco*) scent bottle; (*Cono Sur*) small flask; (*Andes*) carafe
3 (*Méx*) (= *piedra*) pumice, pumice stone

pomada SF 1 (= *crema*) cream, ointment; **✦*MODISMOS*** **estar en la ~*** (= *metido*) to be mixed up in it, be involved; (= *al tanto*) to be in the know; **hacer algo ~** (*Cono Sur**) to break sth to bits, ruin sth
2 (= *gente*) **la ~‡** the cream, the top people

pomar SM apple orchard

pomelo SM grapefruit, pomelo (*EEUU*)

pómez SF **piedra ~** pumice (stone)

pomo SM 1 [*de puerta*] knob, handle; [*de espada*] pommel
2 (= *frasco*) scent bottle
3 (*Bot*) pome
4 (*Andes*) (= *borla*) powder puff

pompa SF 1 (= *burbuja*) bubble ► **pompa de jabón** soap bubble
2 (*Náut*) pump
3 (= *fasto*) pomp, splendour, splendor (*EEUU*); (= *ostentación*) show, display; (= *boato*) pageant, pageantry ► **pompas fúnebres** (= *ceremonia*) funeral *sing*; (= *cortejo*) funeral procession *sing* ► **"Pompas fúnebres"** (= *funeraria*) "Undertaker's" *sing*, "Funeral parlour" *sing*, "Funeral parlor" (*EEUU*) *sing*

Pompeya SF Pompeii

Pompeyo SM Pompey

pompis* SM INV bottom, behind*, butt (*EEUU*‡)

pompo ADJ (*Andes*) blunt

pompón SM pompom

pomposamente ADV (= *con esplendor*) splendidly, magnificently; (= *con majestuosidad*) majestically; (= *con ostentación*) pompously

pomposidad SF (= *esplendor*) splendour, splendor (*EEUU*), magnificence; (= *majestuosidad*) majesty; (*pey*) (= *ostentación*) pomposity, pompousness

pomposo ADJ (= *espléndido*) splendid, magnificent; (= *majestuoso*) majestic; (= *ostentoso*) pompous

pómulo SM (= *hueso*) cheekbone; (= *mejilla*) cheek

p.° n.° SM ABR (= **peso neto**) nt. wt.

ponchada[1] SF (*LAm*) 1 [*de poncho*] ponchoful
2 (= *mucho*) large quantity, large amount; **costó una ~** it cost a bomb*

ponchada[2] SF [*de ponche*] bowlful of punch

ponchada[3] SF (*Méx Aut*), **ponchadura** SF (*Méx Aut*) puncture, flat (*EEUU*)

ponchar ▸conjug 1a◂ Ⓐ VT (*Méx*) 1 [+ *neumático*] to puncture
2 [+ *billete*] to punch
Ⓑ VI (*LAm**) (= *resistir*) to champ at the bit

ponchazos* SMPL (*Arg*) **a los ~** with great difficulty

ponche SM punch

ponchera SF 1 (*para ponche*) punch bowl
2 (*Andes, Caribe, Méx*) (= *palangana*) washbasin, washbowl (*EEUU*); (*Andes*) (= *bañera*) bath
3 (*Cono Sur**) (= *barriga*) paunch, beer belly*, beer gut*

poncho[1] ADJ 1 (= *perezoso*) lazy, idle
2 (= *tranquilo*) quiet, peaceable
3 (*Andes*) (= *gordito*) chubby

poncho[2] SM (= *ropa*) poncho, cape; (= *manta*) blanket; **los de a ~** (*Andes**) the poor; **✦*MODISMOS*** **estar a ~** (*Andes**) to be in the dark; **arrastrar el ~** (*LAm**) to be looking o spoiling for a fight; **donde el diablo perdió el ~** (*Cono Sur**) at the back of beyond*; **pisarle el ~ a algn** (*Andes*) to humiliate sb; **pisarse el ~** (*Cono Sur**) to be mistaken

ponchura SF (*Ven*) wash basin

Poncio Pilato SM Pontius Pilate

ponderación SF 1 (*al decir algo*) (= *contrapeso*) weighing, consideration; (= *cuidado*) deliberation
2 (= *alabanza*) high praise; **está sobre toda ~** I can't praise it highly enough
3 [*de índice*] weighting
4 (= *equilibrio*) balance

ponderado ADJ 1 (= *alabado*) praised; **mi querido y nunca bien ~ amigo** my dear and unappreciated friend
2 (= *equilibrado*) balanced
3 (*Estadística*) weighted; **media ponderada** weighted average; **voto ~** proportional voting

ponderar ▸conjug 1a◂ VT 1 (= *alabar*) to praise highly, speak highly of; **~ algo a algn** to speak warmly of sth to sb, tell sb how good sth is; **le ponderan de inteligente** they speak highly of his intelligence
2 (= *considerar*) to weigh up, consider
3 (*Estadística*) to weight

pondré *etc ver* **poner**

ponedero SM nest, nesting box

ponedora ADJ **gallina ~** laying hen; **ser buena ~** to be a good layer

ponencia SF 1 (= *exposición*) paper, learned paper, communication; (= *informe*) report
2 (= *comisión*) committee, board

ponente SMF speaker (*at a conference*)

poner

▸conjug 2q◂
Ⓐ VERBO TRANSITIVO
Ⓑ VERBO INTRANSITIVO
Ⓒ VERBO PRONOMINAL

Para las expresiones ***poner cuidado, poner en duda, poner por las nubes, poner a parir, poner como un trapo, poner verde, poner de vuelta y media, poner por testigo, ponerse por delante****, ver la otra entrada.*

Ⓐ VERBO TRANSITIVO

1 ***= colocar, situar*** to put; **¿dónde pongo mis cosas?** where shall I put my things?; **pon los libros en la estantería** put the books on the shelf; **le puso la mano en el hombro** she put a hand on his shoulder; **me han puesto en la habitación de arriba** they've put me in the upstairs bedroom; **han puesto un anuncio en el periódico** they've put an advertisement in the paper; **voy a ~ las patatas** I'm going to put the potatoes on; **ponle un poco de mantequilla y verás qué bueno** put some butter in it and you'll see how

good it is; **~ algo aparte** to put sth aside, put sth to one side; **ponlo en su sitio** put it back

2 + *ropa, calzado* to put on; **le pusieron un vestido nuevo** they dressed her in a new dress; **ponle los zapatos** can you put his shoes on?

3 = *añadir* to add; **ponle más sal** add some salt, put some more salt in it; **pongo 20 más para llegar a 100** I'll add 20 more to make it 100

4 = *aplicar, administrar* to put; **le pusieron una tirita en la herida** they put a plaster on her wound; **ponle talco al cambiarle el pañal** put some talcum powder on him when you change his nappy; **le han puesto muchas inyecciones** she's been given a lot of injections

5 = *disponer, preparar* **pon cubiertos para 12 personas** set the table for 12 people; **~ la mesa** to lay *o* set the table

6 = *instalar* 6·1 [+ *teléfono, calefacción*] to put in; **queremos ~ moqueta** we want to have a carpet fitted

6·2 [+ *tienda*] to open; [+ *casa*] to furnish; **han puesto una tienda de muebles** they've opened a furniture shop; **han puesto la casa con todo lujo** they have furnished the house luxuriously

7 = *exponer* **ponlo al sol** leave *o* put it out in the sun; **~ algo a secar** to put sth out to dry

8 = *hacer funcionar* [+ *radio, televisión, calefacción*] to put on, turn on; [+ *disco*] to put on, play; **pon el radiador** put the radiator on; **¿pongo música?** shall I put some music on?

9 = *ajustar* [+ *despertador*] to set; **puse el despertador para las siete** I set the alarm for seven o'clock; **pon el horno al máximo** put the oven on maximum; **~ el reloj en hora** to put one's watch right; **ponlo más alto** turn it up

10 = *adoptar* **¿por qué pones esa voz tan tonta?** why are you speaking in that silly voice?; **puso acento francés al decirlo** she put on a French accent when she said it; **¡no pongas esa cara!** don't look at me like that!; **puso muy mala cara cuando se lo dije** he looked very annoyed when I told him; **puso cara de asombro** he looked surprised

11 = *volver* (+ *ADJ, ADV*) to make; **me pone furiosa** he makes me mad; **para no ~le de mal humor** so as not to make him cross, so as not to put him in a bad mood; **la has puesto colorada** you've made her blush; **la medicina lo puso bueno** the medicine made him better; **¡cómo te han puesto!** (= *te han manchado*) look what a mess you are!; (= *te han pegado*) they've given you a right thumping!

12 = *servir* **¿qué te pongo?** what can I get you?, what would you like?; **¿me pones más patatas?** could I have some more potatoes?

13 = *conectar por teléfono* to put through; **póngame con el conserje** put me through to the porter; **¿me pone con el Sr. García, por favor?** could you put me through to Mr García, please?; **le pongo en seguida** I'll put you through

14 = *exhibir* **¿qué ponen en el cine?** what's on at the cinema?; **¿ponen alguna película esta noche?** is there a film on tonight?

15 = *enviar* to send; **le puso un telegrama** he sent her a telegram

16 = *escribir* to put; **¿qué pongo en la carta?** what shall I put in the letter?; **¿te has acordado de ~ el remite?** did you remember to put the return address on it?

17 = *decir, estar escrito* to say; **¿qué pone aquí?** what does it say here?

18 = *imponer* [+ *examen, trabajo*] to give, set; **nos pone mucho trabajo** he gives *o* sets us a lot of work; **el ayuntamiento pone muchos impuestos** council taxes are very high; **me han puesto una multa** I've been fined, I've been given a fine

19 = *oponer* [+ *inconvenientes*] to raise; **nos han puesto muchos problemas** they've put a lot of obstacles in our way; **le pone peros a todo** he's always finding fault with everything

20 = *aportar, contribuir* [+ *dinero*] **he puesto 50 euros de mi bolsillo** I put in 50 euros out of my own pocket; **todos pusimos 10 euros para el regalo** we all put in 10 euros towards the present; **yo pongo el dinero pero ella escoge** I do the paying, but she does the choosing; **yo pongo la bebida y vosotros el postre** I'll get the drink and you can get the dessert

21 = *invertir* to put in; **hemos puesto más de cinco millones** we have put in over five million; **puso todos sus ahorros en aquel negocio** he put all his savings into that business

22 = *apostar* **pon tres fichas al rojo** put three chips on red; **pongo 1.000 pesetas a que mañana llueve** I bet 1,000 pesetas that it will rain tomorrow

23 = *llamar* to call; **¿qué nombre** *o* **cómo le van a ~?** what are they going to call him?, what name are they giving him?; **al niño le pusieron Luis** they called the child Luis

24 = *criticar, alabar* **te puso muy bien ante el jefe** she was very nice about you to the boss; **me han puesto muy bien esa película** I've heard that film is very good; **¡cómo te han puesto!** (= *te han criticado*) they had a real go at you!; (= *te han alabado*) they were really nice about you!; **tu cuñada te ha puesto muy mal** your sister-in-law was very nasty about you

25 = *tildar* **~ a algn de**: **la han puesto de idiota para arriba** they called her an idiot and worse

26 = *suponer* **pongamos 120** let's say 120; **pongamos que ganas la lotería** suppose *o* supposing you win the lottery; **poniendo que ...** supposing that ...

27 **~ a algn a** (+ *INFIN*): **nada más llegar nos pusieron a barrer** no sooner had we arrived than we were set to sweeping the floor; **puso a sus hijos a trabajar** she sent her children out to work

28 **~ a Juan bien con Pedro** to make things up between Juan and Pedro; **~ a Juan mal con Pedro** to make Juan fall out with Pedro, cause a rift between Juan and Pedro

29 *en trabajo* **~ a algn de**: **puso a su hija de sirvienta** she got her daughter a job as a servant; **lo han puesto de dependiente en una tienda** they got him a job as a shop assistant

30 ✦*MODISMO* **¡no pongo ni una!** (*Caribe**) I just can't get anything right!

31 *gallina* [+ *huevos*] to lay

Ⓑ VERBO INTRANSITIVO

1 *aves* to lay (eggs)

2 = *apostar* **no pongo a la lotería** I don't play the lottery

Ⓒ **ponerse** VERBO PRONOMINAL

1 = *colocarse, situarse* (*de pie*) to stand; (*sentado*) to sit; (*echado*) to lie; **se puso delante de la ventana** he stood in front of the window; **se ponía a mi lado en clase** he used to sit next to me in class; **póngase de lado** lie on your side; **~se cómodo** to make o.s. comfortable; **ponte en mi lugar** put yourself in my place; **todos se pusieron de** *o* **en pie** everyone stood up; **se puso de rodillas** she knelt down

2 + *ropa, calzado, joyas* to put on; **~se un traje** to put a suit on; **ponte las zapatillas** put your slippers on; **no sé qué ~me** I don't know what to wear

3 = *aplicarse, administrarse* **ponte más perfume** put some more perfume on; **te pones demasiado maquillaje** you wear too much make-up; **se puso un supositorio** he used a suppository

4 *sol* to set

5 = *volverse* (+ *ADJ, ADV*) **~se enfermo/gordo** to get ill/fat; **se puso hecho una furia** he got absolutely furious; **cuando se lo dije se puso muy triste** he was very sad when I told him; **¡no te pongas así!** don't be like that!; **¡qué guapa te has puesto!** you look lovely!; **en el agua se pone verde** it turns green in water

6 *al teléfono* **dile que se ponga** tell him to come to *o* on the phone; **no se quiere ~** she doesn't want to come on (the phone); **¿se puede ~ María, por favor?** could I speak to María, please?

7 = *empezar* **~se a hacer algo** to start *o* begin to do sth, start *o* begin doing sth; **se pusieron a gritar** they started *o* began shouting, they started *o* began to shout; **se va a ~ a llover** it's going to start raining; **si me pongo a pensar en lo que me espera ...** if I start thinking *o* to think about what awaits me ...; **~se con algo**: **ahora me pongo con los deberes** I'm going to start on my homework now

8 = *llenarse* **~se de algo**: **¡cómo te has puesto de barro!** you're all covered in mud!; **se puso perdida de alquitrán** she got covered in tar; **nos hemos puesto bien de comida** we ate our fill

9 = *llegar* **~se en** to get to, reach; **se puso en Madrid en dos horas** he got to *o* reached Madrid in two hours

10 = *emplearse* **me puse a servir** I went into service; **~se de conserje** to take a job as a porter

11 **~se a bien con algn** to get on good terms with sb; (*pey*) to get in with sb; **~se a mal con algn** to get on the wrong side of sb

12 ** = *drogarse* to get high*

13 = *parecerle* **se me pone que ...** (*LAm*) (= *me parece*) it seems to me that ...

14 ✦*MODISMO* **ponérselos a algn*** to cheat on sb

poney ['poni] SM (*pl* **poneys**) pony

ponga *etc ver* **poner**

pongaje SM (*Andes, Cono Sur*) = **pongueaje**

pongo[1] *ver* **poner**

pongo[2] SM orang-utan

pongo[3] SM (*Andes*) [1] (= *criado*) *(unpaid) Indian servant*; (= *inquilino*) *Indian tenant*
[2] (*Geog*) ravine
pongueaje SM (*Andes, Cono Sur*) (*esp Hist*) *domestic service which Indian tenants are obliged to give free*
poni SM pony
ponible ADJ wearable
poniente Ⓐ ADJ west, western
Ⓑ SM [1] (= *oeste*) west
[2] (= *viento*) west wind
ponja‡ ADJ, SMF (*Andes*) Jap**
pontaje SM, **pontazgo** SM toll
pontevedrés/esa (*Esp*) Ⓐ ADJ of/from Pontevedra
Ⓑ SM/F native/inhabitant of Pontevedra; **los pontevedreses** the people of Pontevedra
pontificado SM papacy, pontificate
pontifical ADJ papal, pontifical
pontificar ▸conjug 1g◂ VI to pontificate
pontífice SM pope, pontiff; **el Sumo Pontífice** the Supreme Pontiff
pontificio ADJ papal, pontifical
pontón SM [1] (= *barco*) pontoon; **puente de pontones** pontoon bridge
[2] (= *puente*) bridge of planks
[3] (*Aer*) [*de hidroavión*] float
[4] (= *buque viejo*) hulk
pony ['poni] SM (*pl* **ponys**) pony
ponzoña SF (= *tóxico*) poison, venom; (= *ideas*) poison
ponzoñoso ADJ [*ataque*] venomous, poisonous; [*propaganda*] poisonous; [*costumbre, idea*] pernicious
pool [pul] SM (*pl* **pools** [pul]) (*Fin*) consortium
pop Ⓐ ADJ pop
Ⓑ SM (*Mús*) pop, pop music
Ⓒ EXCL bingo!*
popa SF [1] (*Náut*) stern; **a ~** astern, abaft; **de proa a ~** fore and aft, from stem to stern; *ver tb* **viento 1**
[2] (= *culo*) rear*, backside, bottom
popar ▸conjug 1a◂ VT [1] (= *mimar*) to spoil, make a fuss of; (= *halagar*) flatter
[2] (= *mofarse de*) to scorn, jeer at
pope SM [1] (*Rel*) priest of the Orthodox Church
[2] (*) (= *líder*) guru, spiritual leader; (= *ídolo*) idol
popelín SM, **popelina** SF poplin
popería* SF pop fans *pl*
popero/a* Ⓐ ADJ **música popera** pop music
Ⓑ SM/F pop fan
popi* Ⓐ ADJ pop
Ⓑ SMF pop fan
popó‡ SM poo-poo‡; **hacer ~** to do a poo-poo‡
popof* ADJ INV, **popoff*** ADJ INV (*Méx*) posh*, society *antes de s*
poporo SM [1] (*Andes, Caribe*) (= *bulto*) bump, swelling
[2] (*Caribe*) (= *porra*) truncheon, nightstick (*EEUU*)
popote SM (*Méx*) (= *pajita*) drinking straw; (= *tallo*) long thin stem; (= *hierba*) *tough grass used for making brooms*
populachería SF cheap popularity, playing to the gallery
populachero ADJ [1] (= *plebeyo*) common, vulgar; (= *chabacano*) cheap
[2] [*discurso, política*] rabble-rousing; [*político*] demagogic (*frm*), who plays to the gallery
populacho SM (= *capa social*) plebs* (*pey*) *pl*; (= *multitud*) mob
popular ADJ [1] (= *del pueblo*) [*cultura, levantamiento*] popular; [*música*] popular, folk *antes de s*; [*tradiciones*] popular, folk *antes de s*; [*lenguaje*] popular, colloquial; **el tribunal ~** the people's court
[2] (= *de clase obrera*) **un barrio ~** a working-class neighbourhood *o* (*EEUU*) neighborhood
[3] (= *muy conocido*) popular; **es un actor muy ~** he is a very popular actor; **es la más ~ de su clase** she's the most popular child in her class
popularidad SF popularity
popularismo SM popularism
popularización SF popularization
popularizar ▸conjug 1f◂ Ⓐ VT to popularize
Ⓑ **popularizarse** VPR to become popular
populismo SM populism; (= *política*) populist policies *pl*
populista ADJ, SMF populist
populoso ADJ populous
popurrí SM potpourri
poquedad SF [1] (= *timidez*) timidity, pusillanimity (*frm*)
[2] (= *escasez*) scantiness; (= *pequeñez*) smallness
[3] **una ~** (= *algo pequeño*) a small thing; (= *nimiedad*) a trifle
póquer SM poker
poquísimo ADJ [1] (*con nombres incontables*) (*gen*) very little; (= *casi nada*) hardly any, almost no; **con ~ dinero** with very little money
[2] **poquísimos** very few
poquitín SM **un ~** a little bit
poquito SM [1] **un ~** a little bit (**de** of); (*como adv*) a little, a bit
[2] **a ~s** bit by bit, little by little; **¡~ a poco!** gently!, easy there!; **se añade la leche ~ a poco** the milk is added a little at a time *o* gradually

por PREPOSICIÓN
[1] *causa* [1·1] (+ *SUSTANTIVO*) because of; **tuvo que suspenderse ~ el mal tiempo** it had to be cancelled because of the weather; **no se realizó ~ escasez de fondos** it didn't go ahead because of a shortage of funding; **nos encontramos ~ casualidad** we met by chance; **lo hago ~ gusto** I do it because I like to; **fue ~ necesidad** it was out of necessity; **~ temor a** for fear of; **no se lo dijo ~ temor a ofenderla** he didn't tell her for fear of offending her
[1·2] (+ *INFIN*) **no aprobó ~ no haber estudiado** he didn't pass because he hadn't studied; **~ venir tarde se perdió la mitad** because he arrived late he missed half of it; **me castigaron ~ mentir** I was punished for lying
[1·3] (+ *ADJ*) **le expulsaron ~ revoltoso** they expelled him for being a troublemaker; **lo dejó ~ imposible** he gave it up as (being) impossible; **esto te pasa ~ tonto** this is what you get for being stupid
[2] *objetivo* [2·1] (+ *SUSTANTIVO*) for; **trabajar ~ dinero** to work for money; **daría lo que fuera ~ un poco de tranquilidad** I'd give anything for a bit of peace and quiet; **brindemos ~ nuestro futuro** let's drink to our future
[2·2] (+ *INFIN*) **lo hizo ~ complacerle** he did it to please her; **~ no llegar tarde** so as not to arrive late, in order not to be late; **hablar ~ hablar** to talk for the sake of talking
[3] *= en favor, defensa de* for; **lo hice ~ mis padres** I did it for my parents; **hazlo ~ mí** do it for me, do it for my sake; **luchar ~ la patria** to fight for one's country
[4] *elección* **su amor ~ la pintura** his love of painting; **está loca ~ ti** she's crazy about you; **no sabía ~ cuál decidirme** I couldn't decide which to choose
[5] *evidencia* judging by, judging from; **~ lo que dicen** judging by *o* from what they say; **~ la cara que pone no debe de gustarle** judging by *o* from his face I don't think he likes it; **~ las señas no piensa hacerlo** apparently he's not intending to do it, it doesn't seem like he's intending to do it
[6] *medio* **~ su propia mano** by his own hand; **lo obtuve ~ un amigo** I got it through a friend; **la conozco ~ mi hermano** I know her through my brother; **~ correo** by post; **~ mar** by sea; **hablar ~ señas** to use sign language
[7] *agente* by; **hecho ~ él** done by him; **"dirigido ~"** "directed by"; **fueron apresados ~ la policía** they were captured by the police
[8] *modo* by; **me agarró ~ el brazo** he grabbed me by the arm; **punto ~ punto** point by point; **buscaron casa ~ casa** they searched house by house; **están dispuestos ~ tamaños** they are arranged according to size *o* by size; **~ orden alfabético** in alphabetical order
[9] *lugar* **se va ~ ahí** it's that way; **¿~ dónde?** which way?; **ir a Bilbao ~ Santander** to go to Bilbao via Santander; **cruzar la frontera ~ Canfranc** to cross the border at Canfranc; **pasar ~ Madrid** to go through Madrid; **se asomaron ~ la ventana** they leaned out of the window; **iban cantando ~ la calle** they were walking along the street singing; **paseábamos ~ la playa** we were walking along the beach; **~ todas partes** everywhere; **~ todo el país** throughout the country; **viajar ~ el mundo** to travel (around) the world
[10] *aproximación* **busca ~ ahí** look over there; **viven ~ esta zona** they live around here; **~ aquí cerca** near *o* around here; **aquello ocurrió ~ abril** it happened around April; **~ la feria** round about *o* around carnival time; **está ~ el norte** it's somewhere up north
[11] *tiempo* **se levanta ~ la mañana temprano** she gets up early in the morning; **~ la mañana siempre tengo mucho trabajo** I always have a lot of work in *o* during the morning; **no sale ~ la noche** he doesn't go out at night
[12] *duración* for; **será ~ poco tiempo** it won't be for long; **se quedarán ~ 15 días** they will stay for a fortnight
[13] *sustitución, intercambio* (= *a cambio de*) for; (= *en lugar de*) instead of; **te doy éste ~ aquél** I'll swap you this one for that one; **le dieron uno nuevo ~ el viejo** they gave him a new one (in exchange) for the old one; **lo vendí ~ 15 dólares** I sold it for 15 dollars; **me dieron 13 francos ~ una libra** I got 13 francs to the pound; **hoy doy yo la clase ~ él** today I'm giving the class for him *o* in his place; **ha puesto B ~ V** he has put B instead of V

➤ LENGUA Y USO: **por 1** 44.1

14 *representación* **hablo ~ todos** I speak on behalf of *o* for everyone; **interceder ~ algn** to intercede on sb's behalf, intercede for sb; **diputado ~ Madrid** a member of parliament for Madrid; **vino ~ su jefe** he came instead of *o* in place of his boss

15 *distribución* **10 dólares ~ hora** 10 dollars an hour; **80km ~ hora** 80km per *o* an hour; **revoluciones ~ minuto** revolutions per minute; **tres dólares ~ persona** three dollars each, three dollars per person

16 *en multiplicaciones* **cinco ~ tres, quince** five times three is fifteen, five threes are fifteen; **mide 6 metros de alto ~ 4 de ancho** it is 6 metres high by 4 wide

17 *= en cuanto a* **~ mí no hay inconveniente** that's fine as *o* so far as I'm concerned; **~ mí, que se vaya** as *o* so far as I'm concerned he can go, for all I care he can go; **~ mí, como si quieres pasar una semana sin comer** I don't care if you want to go for a week without eating; **si ~ mi fuera, tú estarías trabajando** if it were *o* was down to me, you'd be working

18 *= como* **tomar a algn ~ esposo/esposa** to take sb to be one's husband/wife; **le dan ~ muerto** they have given him up for dead; **le tienen ~ tonto** they think he's stupid

19 *concesión* (+ *SUBJUN*) **~ (muy) difícil que sea** however hard it is *o* may be; **~ mucho que lo quisieran** however much they would like to, much as they would like to; **~ más que lo intente** no matter how *o* however hard I try, try as I might

20 *acción inacabada* (+ *INFIN*) **quedan platos ~ lavar** there are still some dishes to do; **aún me quedan tres páginas ~ traducir** I still have three pages left to translate

21

◆ **ir (a) por algo/algn** (= *en busca de*) to go and get sth/sb; **ha ido (a) ~ vino** she's gone to get some wine; **voy ~ el médico** I'll go and fetch *o* get the doctor; **voy a ~ él** (*a buscarle*) I'll go and get him; (*a atacarle*) I'm going to get him; **sólo van a ~ las pelas*** they're only in it for the money; **¡a ~ ellos!** get them!; ✦***MODISMO*** **ir a ~ todas** to really go for it

22 *en preguntas*

◆ **por qué** why; **¿~ qué no vienes conmigo?** why don't you come with me?; **no tengo ~ qué ir** there's no reason why I should go

◆ **¿por?** (*) why (do you ask)?

porcachón* ADJ = **porcallón**

porcada* SF = **porquería**

porcallón* ADJ filthy, dirty

porcelana SF (= *material*) porcelain; (= *loza*) china, chinaware, porcelain; **tienda de ~** china shop; **estantes llenos de ~s** shelves full of china *o* chinaware *o* porcelain

porcentaje SM percentage; **un elevado ~ de algo** a high percentage *o* proportion of sth; **el ~ de defunciones** the death rate; **trabajar a ~** to work on a percentage basis ► **porcentaje de accesos** (*Inform*) hit rate

porcentual ADJ percentage *antes de s*

porcentualmente ADV (= *en porcentaje*) in percentage terms, percentage-wise; (= *proporcionalmente*) proportionately

porche SM 1 [*de casa*] porch

2 (= *soportal*) arcade

Porcia SF Portia

porcino Ⓐ ADJ pig *antes de s*, porcine (*frm*); **ganado ~** pigs *pl*; *ver tb* **fiebre 2**, **peste 1**

Ⓑ SM 1 (= *animal*) pig, hog (*esp EEUU*); (= *lechón*) young pig; **carne de ~** pork

2 (*Med*) bump, swelling

porción SF 1 (= *parte*) (*gen*) portion; (*en un reparto*) share; (*en recetas*) quantity, amount; (*de chocolate, pastel*) piece; **una ~ de patatas fritas** a portion *o* helping of chips; **quesitos en porciones** cheese portions; **grandes porciones del presupuesto** large chunks of *o* a large proportion of the budget

2 (= *montón*) **una ~ de** a number of; **tengo una ~ de cosas que hacer** I have a number of things to do; **tuvimos una ~ de problemas** we had quite a few problems *o* a number of problems

porcuno ADJ pig *antes de s*

pordiosear ▸conjug 1a◂ VI to beg

pordiosero/a SM/F beggar

porende†† ADV hence, therefore

porfa* EXCL please

porfía SF 1 (= *cualidad*) (= *terquedad*) stubbornness, obstinacy; (= *persistencia*) persistence

2 (= *disputa*) dispute; (= *contienda*) continuous struggle, continuous competition

3 **a ~** in competition

porfiadamente ADV (= *tercamente*) stubbornly, obstinately; (= *con insistencia*) persistently

porfiado Ⓐ ADJ (= *terco*) stubborn, obstinate; (= *insistente*) persistent

Ⓑ SM (*LAm*) (= *muñeco*) roly-poly doll, tumbler, tumbler toy

porfiar ▸conjug 1c◂ VI 1 (= *persistir*) to persist, insist; **~ en algo** to persist in sth; **porfía en que es así** he insists that it is so, he will have it that it is so; **~ por hacer algo** to struggle obstinately to do sth; **porfían por escapar** they are bent on escaping

2 (= *disputar*) to argue stubbornly; **~ con algn** to argue with sb

pórfido SM porphyry

porfión ADJ dogged, stubborn

porfirismo SM porphyria

porfirista SMF (*Méx*) supporter of Porfirio Díaz

pormenor SM detail, particular

pormenorización SF **sin entrar en la ~** without going into detail

pormenorizadamente ADV in detail

pormenorizado ADJ detailed

pormenorizar ▸conjug 1f◂ Ⓐ VT 1 (= *describir*) to describe in detail

2 (= *detallar*) to detail, set out in detail

Ⓑ VI to go into detail

porno* Ⓐ ADJ INV porn*, porno*

Ⓑ SM porn* ► **porno blando** soft porn* ► **porno duro** hard porn*

pornografía SF pornography ► **pornografía dura** hard porn ► **pornografía infantil** child pornography

pornográfico ADJ pornographic

pornografista SMF pornographer

poro[1] SM (*Anat*) pore

poro[2] SM (*LAm*) (= *puerro*) leek

poronga** SF (*Cono Sur*) prick**, cock**

porongo SM (*LAm*) 1 (= *planta*) gourd, calabash, squash (*EEUU*)

2 (= *persona*) nobody

pororó SM (*Cono Sur*) popcorn

porosidad SF porousness, porosity

poroso ADJ porous

porotal SM (*LAm*) 1 (= *terreno*) beanfield, bean patch

2 **un ~ de*** a whole lot of, a whole heap of

poroto SM 1 (*Andes, Cono Sur*) (= *judía*) bean; **porotos*** grub* *sing*, chow *sing* (*EEUU**), food *sing*; ✦***MODISMOS*** **ganarse los ~s** to earn one's daily bread; **no valer un ~*** to be worthless ► **poroto verde** green bean, runner bean

2 (*Cono Sur Dep*) (*tb fig*) point; **anotarse un ~*** to score a point; **¡te anotaste un ~!** you made it!

3 (*Cono Sur**) (= *niño*) kid*; (= *alfeñique*) weakling

porpuesto SM (*Caribe*) minibus, taxi

porque CONJ 1 (= *por causa de que*) (+ *INDIC*) because; **no pudo ir ~ estaba enferma** she couldn't go because she was ill; **¿por qué no contestas? —~ no me da la gana** "why don't you answer?" — "because I don't feel like it"; **—¿por qué te vas? —porque sí** "why are you going?" — "just because"; **—¿por qué no puedo ir? —porque no** "why can't I go?" — "just because"

2 (= *para que*) (+ *SUBJUN*) so that, in order that; **elevó la voz ~ todos pudieran oírlo** he raised his voice so that everyone could hear him *o* in order that everyone might hear him; **recemos ~ vuelvan** let us pray that they may return

porqué SM 1 (= *motivo*) reason (**de** for); **me gustaría saber el ~ de su actitud** I'd like to know the reason for her attitude; **no me interesan los ~s** I'm not interested in the whys and wherefores; **el ~ de la revolución** the causes of the revolution

2 (†) (= *cantidad*) amount; **tiene mucho ~** he's got plenty of the ready*

porquería SF 1 (= *suciedad*) dirt, muck*; **¿qué es toda esta ~ que hay el suelo?** what's all this dirt *o* muck on the floor?; **estar hecho una ~** to be covered in dirt *o* muck*

2 (= *guarrada*) **no hagas ~s con la comida** don't make such a mess with your food

3 (= *indecencia*) **estas ~s no deberían salir por la tele** that filth *o* smut shouldn't be shown on TV; **decir ~s** to say filthy things

4 (= *cosa de poca calidad*) junk*, rubbish*, garbage (*EEUU**); **si comes tantas ~s, luego no vas a cenar** if you eat all that junk *o* rubbish now you won't want your dinner*; **en esta tienda sólo venden ~s** this shop only sells cheap rubbish*; **la novela es una ~** the novel is just rubbish*

5 (= *poco dinero*) pittance; **me han pagado una ~** they paid me a pittance; **lo vendieron por una ~** they sold it for next to nothing

6 (= *mala pasada*) **¡vaya ~ te han hecho despidiéndote así!** what a lousy thing they did to you, sacking you like that!*

7 **de ~** (*LAm**) (= *condenado*) lousy*

porqueriza SF pigsty, pigpen (*EEUU*)

porquerizo SM, **porquero** SM swineherd

porra SF 1 [*de policía*] truncheon, billyclub (*EEUU*)

2 (*Téc*) large hammer

3 (*Culin*) *large club-shaped fritter*

4 (*) (= *nariz*) conk*, hooter*, schnozzle (*esp EEUU**)

5 (= *juego*) sweep, sweepstake

[6] (*) (*exclamaciones*) **¡porras!** (= *¡maldición!*) damn!*; (= *¡mentira!*) rubbish!; **¡una ~!** no way!*; **¡a la ~!** get out!; **¡a la ~ el ministro!** the minister can go to hell!*; **mandar a algn a la ~** to tell sb to go to hell*, send sb packing; **¡vete a la ~!** go to hell!*; **¡qué coche ni que ~s!** car my foot!
[7] (*Méx Dep*) fans *pl*; (*Teat*) claque
[8] (*Andes, Cono Sur*) (= *mechón*) curl
[9] (*CAm, Méx Pol*) political gang
[10] (*CAm*) (= *olla*) metal cooking pot
[11] (**) (= *pene*) prick**
[12] (*) (= *pesado*) bore
[13] (*) (= *jactancia*) **gasta mucha ~** he's always boasting, he's always shooting his mouth off*

porracear* ▸conjug 1a◂ VT (*Caribe, Méx*) to beat up

porrada SF [1] (*) (= *montón*) **una ~ de** loads of*; **hace una ~ de tiempo** ages ago
[2] (= *porrazo*) thump, blow

porrata* SMF dope smoker*

porrazo SM [1] (= *golpe*) thump, blow; (= *caída*) bump; **le di un ~ con la silla** I whacked him with the chair; **me di un ~ contra la puerta** I banged myself on the door
[2] ✦**MODISMOS de ~** (*LAm*) in one go; **de golpe y ~** suddenly

porrear ▸conjug 1a◂ VI [1] (= *insistir*) to go on and on
[2] (= *drogarse*) to smoke dope*

porrería* SF [1] (= *petición*) annoying request
[2] (= *necedad*) stupidity

porrero/a* SM/F dope smoker*

porreta SF (*Bot*) green leaf; ✦**MODISMO en ~(s)*** stark naked, starkers*

porretada SF = **porrada 1**

porrillo*: **a ~** ADV loads of*, galore; **tiene ropa a ~** he's got loads of clothes*; **gana dinero a ~** he earns loads of money*

porro* Ⓐ SM [1] (*Esp*) (*de droga*) joint*
[2] (= *idiota*) idiot, oaf
[3] (*Andes, Caribe*) (= *baile*) *folk dance*
Ⓑ ADJ stupid, oafish

porrón[1] SM [1] (= *recipiente*) *jar with a long spout for drinking from*
[2] **un ~ de*** loads of*; **la película me gustó un ~*** the film is the business*; **esa tía me gusta un ~*** I fancy the pants off her*
[3] (*Arg*) [*de cerveza*] bottle of beer

porrón[2] ADJ (= *lerdo*) slow, stupid; (= *soso*) dull; (= *torpe*) sluggish

porrón[3] SM (*Orn*) pochard ► **porrón moñudo** tufted duck

porrudo ADJ [1] (= *abultado*) big, bulging
[2] (*Arg*) (= *melenudo*) long-haired
[3] (*Cono Sur*) (= *engreído*) big-headed, swollen-headed

porsiacaso SM (*Arg, Ven*) knapsack

port. ABR = **portugués**

porta SF port, porthole

portaaeronaves SM INV aircraft carrier

portaaviones SM INV aircraft carrier

portabebés SM INV baby carrier

portabilidad SF portability

portable Ⓐ ADJ portable
Ⓑ SM portable computer

portabotellas SM INV (= *botellero*) wine rack; (= *carrito*) bottle carrier; **carro ~** bottle carrier

portabultos SM INV carrier

portabusto(s) SM (*Méx*) brassiere (*frm*), bra

portacargas SM INV (= *caja*) crate; [*de bicicleta*] carrier

portacheques SM INV chequebook, checkbook (*EEUU*)

portación SF **~ de armas** carrying (of) a weapon

portacoches SM INV car transporter

portacontenedor SM, **portacontenedores** SM INV container ship

portacubiertos SM INV cutlery tray

portada SF [1] (= *primera plana*) [*de libro*] title page, frontispiece (*frm*); [*de periódico*] front page
[2] (= *cubierta*) [*de revista, libro*] cover; [*de disco*] sleeve, jacket (*EEUU*)
[3] (*Arquit*) (= *fachada*) façade; (= *pórtico*) porch, doorway; (= *portal*) carriage door, gateway

portadiscos SM INV record rack

portado ADJ **bien ~** (= *elegante*) well-dressed; (= *cortés*) well-behaved; (= *respetable*) respectable

portadocumentos Ⓐ SM INV document holder
Ⓑ ADJ INV **agenda ~** Filofax®; **cartera ~** briefcase

portador(a) SM/F [1] [*de cheque, carta*] bearer; **el ~ de esta carta** the bearer of this letter; **páguese al ~** pay the bearer
[2] (*Med*) [*de germen, virus*] carrier

portaequipajes SM INV [1] (*en un coche*) (= *maletero*) boot, trunk (*EEUU*); (= *baca*) roof-rack
[2] (*en tren, autocar*) luggage rack
[3] [*de bicicleta*] carrier

portaesquíes SM INV, **portaesquís** SM INV ski rack

portaestandarte SMF standard bearer

portafolio SM, **portafolios** SM INV briefcase, attaché case

portafotos SM INV locket

portafusil SM rifle sling

portahachón SM torchbearer

portal SM [1] [*de edificio*] (= *vestíbulo*) hallway; (= *puerta*) front door; **la llave del ~** the front door key; **un vecino de su ~** a neighbour who lives in the same block
[2] [*de casa*] hall, vestibule (*frm*)
[3] (*Rel*) ► **portal de Belén** (= *representación navideña*) Nativity scene; **el ~ de Belén** (*Biblia*) the stable at Bethlehem
[4] (*Dep*) goal
[5] [*de muralla*] gate
[6] (*Internet*) portal
[7] **portales** (= *soportales*) arcade *sing*

portalada SF = **portalón**

portalámparas SM INV (light)bulb socket

portalápices SM INV (= *estuche*) (*para llevar*) pencil case; (*para escritorio*) pencil holder, pen holder

portalibros SM INV book strap

portaligas SM INV suspender belt, garter belt (*EEUU*)

portalón SM [1] (*Arquit*) large gate, imposing entrance
[2] (*Náut*) gangway

portamaletas SM INV [1] (*Aut*) (= *baca*) roof rack; (*Chile*) (= *maletero*) boot, trunk (*EEUU*)
[2] (*en tren, autobús*) luggage rack

portamanteo SM (*Esp*) travelling bag

portaminas SM INV propelling pencil

portamisiles SM INV missile carrier

portamonedas SM INV purse, coin purse (*EEUU*)

portante SM ✦**MODISMO tomar el ~*** to clear off*

portañuela SF fly (*of trousers*)

portaobjeto SM, **portaobjetos** SM INV slide, microscope slide

portapapeles SM INV [1] (= *maletín*) briefcase
[2] (*Inform*) clipboard

portaplacas SM INV plate holder

portaplatos SM INV plate rack

portapliegos SM INV (*Andes*) office boy

portaplumas SM INV pen holder

portar ▸conjug 1a◂ Ⓐ VT [+ *bolsa, documentación*] to carry; [+ *arma*] to carry, bear (*frm*); [+ *gafas, ropa*] to wear
Ⓑ **portarse** VPR [1] (= *comportarse*) to behave, conduct o.s. (*frm*); **~se bien** to behave well; **~se mal** to misbehave, behave badly; **se portó muy bien conmigo** he treated me very well, he was very decent to me; **se ha portado como un cerdo** he has behaved like a swine
[2] (= *distinguirse*) to show up well, come through creditably
[3] (*LAm*) (= *comportarse bien*) to behave well

portarretratos SM INV photo frame, picture frame

portarrollos SM INV [*en baño*] toilet-roll holder; [*en cocina*] kitchen-roll holder

portasenos SM INV (*LAm*) brassiere (*frm*), bra

portátil Ⓐ ADJ portable
Ⓑ SM portable, portable computer

portatostadas SM INV toast rack

portatrajes SM INV suit bag

portavelas SM INV candle holder

portaviandas SM INV lunch box, dinner pail (*EEUU*)

portaviones SM INV aircraft carrier

portavocía SF office of spokesperson

portavoz Ⓐ SMF spokesman/spokeswoman, spokesperson
Ⓑ SM [1] (*pey*) (= *periódico, emisora*) mouthpiece
[2] (= *altavoz*) megaphone, loudhailer

portazgo SM toll

portazo SM slam; **cerrar la puerta de un ~** to slam the door (shut); **dar** *o* **pegar un ~** to slam the door

porte SM [1] (*Com*) (= *acto*) carriage, transport; (= *costos*) carriage; (*Correos*) postage ► **franco de porte** (*Com*) carriage paid; (*Correos*) post free ► **porte debido** (*Com*) freight C.O.D. ► **porte pagado** (*Com*) carriage paid; (*Correos*) post paid ► **porte por cobrar** freight forward
[2] (*esp Náut*) (= *tonelaje*) capacity
[3] (= *presencia*) bearing, demeanour, demeanor (*EEUU*); **de ~ distinguido** with a distinguished bearing *o* air
[4] (= *conducta*) behaviour, behavior (*EEUU*), conduct (*frm*)

porteador(a) SM/F (*en expedición*) porter; (*en la caza*) bearer; (*Com*) carrier

portear[1] ▸conjug 1a◂ VT to carry, transport

portear[2] ▸conjug 1a◂ VI [1] [*puerta*] to slam, bang
[2] (*Cono Sur*) to get out in a hurry

portento SM (= *prodigio*) marvel, wonder; (= *genio*) genius, wizard; **es un ~ de belleza** she is stunningly beautiful; **¡qué ~ de memoria!** what a prodigious memory!, what an amazing memory!

portentosamente ADV marvellously, marvelously (*EEUU*), extraordinarily

portentoso ADJ marvellous, marvelous (*EEUU*), extraordinary

porteño/a Ⓐ ADJ (*Arg*) of/from Buenos Aires; (*Chile*) of/from Valparaíso
Ⓑ SM/F (*Arg*) native/inhabitant of Buenos Aires; (*Chile*) native/inhabitant of Valparaíso; **los ~s** the people of Buenos Aires/Valparaíso

porteo SM carriage, conveyance

portería SF [1] (= *conserjería*) caretaker's office, concierge's office; (= *vivienda*) caretaker's flat, concierge's flat
[2] (*Dep*) (= *meta*) goal

portero/a Ⓐ SM/F [1] [*de edificio*] caretaker, concierge, (apartment house) manager (*EEUU*)
[2] (*en hotel, hospital*) porter
[3] (*Dep*) goalkeeper
Ⓑ SM ► **portero automático, portero eléctrico, portero electrónico** entry phone

portezuela SF [1] (= *puerta*) door ► **portezuela de la gasolina** fuel-filler flap
[2] (*Cos*) pocket flap

portezuelo SM (*Cono Sur*) pass

pórtico SM [1] [*de iglesia, monumento*] portico
[2] [*de tiendas*] arcade
[3] (= *entrada*) gateway

portilla SF porthole

portillo SM [1] (*en la pared*) (= *abertura*) gap, opening; (= *brecha*) breach; (= *puerta falsa*) side entrance
[2] (= *postigo*) wicket, wicket gate
[3] (*Geog*) narrow pass
[4] (*en objeto frágil*) (= *abolladura*) dent; (= *desportilladura*) chip
[5] (*para lograr algo*) (= *punto débil*) weak spot, vulnerable point; (*para solución*) opening

pórtland® SM (*LAm*) cement

portón SM [1] (= *puerta grande*) large door
[2] (= *puerta principal*) main door; (*LAm*) [*de casa*] front door
[3] (*en cerca*) gate
[4] (*Cono Sur*) (= *puerta trasera*) back door
[5] (*Aut*) (*tb* ~ **trasero**) hatch, hatchback, tailgate (*EEUU*)

portorriqueño/a ADJ, SM/F Puerto Rican

portuario ADJ (= *del puerto*) port *antes de s*, harbour *antes de s*, harbor *antes de s* (*EEUU*); (= *del muelle*) dock *antes de s*; **trabajador ~** docker

Portugal SM Portugal

portugués/esa Ⓐ ADJ, SM/F Portuguese
Ⓑ SM (*Ling*) Portuguese

portuguesismo SM portuguesism, *word/phrase etc borrowed from Portuguese*

porvenir SM future; **en el ~** in the future; **labrarse un ~** to carve out a future for o.s.; **un hombre sin ~** a man with no prospects *o* future; **le espera un brillante ~** he has a brilliant future ahead of him; **leer el ~ a algn** to tell sb's fortune

pos[1] SM **en ~ de** (*liter*) after, in pursuit of; **ir en ~ de algo/algn** to chase (after) sth/sb, pursue sth/sb; **va en ~ de triunfo** she's after success

pos[2]* CONJ (*esp LAm*) = **pues**

posada SF [1] (= *hospedaje*) shelter, lodging; **dar ~ a algn** to give shelter to sb, take sb in
[2] (= *lugar*) (*para comer*) inn; (*para dormir*) boarding house
[3] (= *morada*) house, dwelling
[4] (*CAm, Méx*) (= *fiesta*) Christmas party

posaderas* SFPL backside* *sing*, butt *sing* (*EEUU*‡), buttocks

posadero/a SM/F innkeeper

posar ▸conjug 1a◂ Ⓐ VT [+ *carga*] to lay down, put down; [+ *mano*] to place, lay; **posó la mirada en el horizonte** his gaze rested on the horizon, his eyes came to rest on the horizon
Ⓑ VI (*Arte*) to sit, pose
Ⓒ **posarse** VPR [1] (= *pararse en tierra*) [*pájaro*] to perch, sit, alight; [*insecto*] to alight; [*avión*] to land; **el avión se encontraba posado** the aircraft was on the ground
[2] [*líquido, polvo*] to settle

posas* SFPL backside* *sing*, butt *sing* (*EEUU*‡), buttocks

posavasos SM INV (*de corcho, madera*) coaster; (*de cartón*) beer mat

posbélico ADJ postwar *antes de s*

poscolonial ADJ post-colonial

poscombustión SF **dispositivo de ~** afterburner

posconciliar ADJ post-conciliar

posconcilio SM **los 20 años de ~** the 20 years following Vatican II

posdata SF postscript

posdoctoral ADJ post-doctoral

pose SF [1] (*para foto, cuadro*) pose; (*Fot*) exposure, time exposure
[2] (= *actitud*) attitude
[3] (*pey*) (= *afectación*) affectation, pose; (= *postura afectada*) affected pose
[4] (= *elegancia*) poise

poseedor(a) SM/F [1] (= *dueño*) owner, possessor (*frm*)
[2] [*de puesto, récord*] holder

poseer ▸conjug 2e◂ VT [1] (= *ser dueño de*) [+ *bienes*] to own; [+ *fortuna*] to own, have; [+ *talento, cultura*] to have; **poseía una inteligencia excepcional** he had an exceptional mind, he was exceptionally intelligent; **posee conocimientos de inglés** she has some knowledge of English; **lo poseyó un temblor convulso** he was overcome by *o* with a compulsive fit
[2] [+ *ventaja*] to have, enjoy; [+ *puesto, récord*] to hold
[3] (*sexualmente*) to possess, have

poseído/a Ⓐ ADJ [1] (= *poseso*) possessed (**por** by); (= *enloquecido*) maddened, crazed
[2] (= *engreído*) **estar muy ~ de algo** to be very vain about sth, have an excessively high opinion of sth
Ⓑ SM/F **gritar como un ~** to scream like one possessed

poselectoral ADJ post-electoral

posesión SF [1] (= *propiedad*) possession; [*de un puesto*] tenure, occupation; [*de lengua, tema*] complete knowledge, perfect mastery; **dar ~ a algn** to hand over to sb; **él está en ~ de las cartas** he is in possession of the letters; **está en ~ del récord** he holds the record; **tomar ~** to take over; **tomar ~ de algo** to take possession of sth, take sth over; **tomar ~ de un cargo** to take up a post
[2] (= *cosa poseída*) possession; (= *finca*) piece of property, estate; **huyen con sus escasas posesiones** they flee carrying their few possessions
[3] (*Chile Agr*) tenant's house and land
[4] (*Caribe*) ranch, estate

posesionar ▸conjug 1a◂ Ⓐ VT **~ a algn de algo** to hand sth over to sb
Ⓑ **posesionarse** VPR **~se de algo** to take possession of sth, take sth over

posesividad SF possessiveness

posesivo ADJ, SM possessive

poseso/a Ⓐ ADJ = **poseído A1**
Ⓑ SM/F = **poseído B**

posestructuralismo SM post-structuralism

posestructuralista ADJ, SMF post-structuralist

posfechar ▸conjug 1a◂ VT to postdate

posfranquismo SM *period after the death of Franco*

posfranquista ADJ **cultura ~** post-Franco culture, culture since Franco

posglacial ADJ post-glacial

posgrado SM **curso de ~** postgraduate course

posgraduado/a Ⓐ ADJ postgraduate
Ⓑ SM/F (= *persona*) graduate student, postgraduate
Ⓒ SM (= *título*) postgraduate degree

posgradual ADJ postgraduate

posguerra SF postwar period; **en la ~** in the postwar period, after the war; **los años de la ~** the postwar years

posibilidad SF [1] (= *oportunidad*) chance, possibility; **no existe ~ de que venga** there's no chance *o* possibility that he'll come; **no tenemos ninguna ~** we don't have the slightest chance, we don't stand a chance; **este chico tiene ~es** this boy has got potential; **la ~ de hacer algo** the chance of doing sth; **¿tienes ~ de aprobar el examen?** do you have any chance of passing the exam?; **tiene pocas ~es de ganar** he hasn't got much chance of winning; **me han dado la ~ de elegir** they have given me the choice *o* the chance to choose
[2] (= *alternativa*) possibility; **hemos descartado la ~ de una huelga** we've ruled out the possibility of a strike; **hay dos ~es: operación o radioterapia** there are two alternatives *o* possibilities: an operation or radiotherapy
[3] **posibilidades** (= *recursos*) means; **un deportivo no está dentro de mis ~es** a sports car is beyond my means *o* out of my price range; **vive por encima de sus ~es** he lives above his means

posibilista Ⓐ ADJ optimistic, positive
Ⓑ SMF optimist, positive thinker

posibilitar ▸conjug 1a◂ VT (= *hacer posible*) [+ *acuerdo, acceso*] to make possible; [+ *idea, plan*] to make feasible; **los satélites posibilitan las operaciones a gran distancia** satellites make long distance operations possible; **esto posibilita la realización del proyecto** this makes the project feasible; **~ que algn haga algo** to allow sb to do sth, make it possible for sb to do sth

posible Ⓐ ADJ [1] [*opción, solución*] possible; **un ~ comprador** a possible *o* potential buyer; **hemos hecho todas las concesiones ~s** we have made all possible concessions *o* all the concessions we can; **hay una ~ infección** there is a suspected *o* possible infection; hacer algo **~** to make sth possible; **su colaboración hizo ~ el acuerdo** her contribu-

➤ LENGUA Y USO: **posibilidad 1** 42.3, 43.3 **posible A1** 53.6

tion made the agreement possible; **entra dentro de lo ~** it is within the bounds of possibility; **en la medida de lo ~** as far as possible, insofar as possible (*frm*); **haremos todo lo ~ por evitarlo** we shall do everything possible *o* all we can to avoid it

2 **es ~** (= *probable, permitido*) it is possible; (= *realizable*) it is feasible; **—¿crees que vendrá? —es ~** "do you think he'll come?" — "possibly *o* he might *o* it's possible"; **¡eso no es ~!** it can't be!, that's not possible!; **esa propuesta es bastante ~** that proposal is quite feasible; **es ~ hacer algo** it is possible to do sth; **¿sería ~ comprar todavía las entradas?** would it still be possible to buy tickets?; **no me fue ~ llegar a tiempo** I was unable to get there in time; **es ~ que** (+ *SUBJUN*): **es ~ que no pueda ir** I might *o* may not be able to go; **es muy ~ que vuelva tarde** it's quite possible that I'll be back late, I may well be back late; **a** *o* **de ser ~** if possible; **si es ~** if possible; **si es ~, me gustaría verlo** I'd like to see him if possible; **le ruego que, si le es ~, acuda a la reunión** please come to the meeting if you possibly can; **si me fuera ~, te lo diría** if I could *o* if it were possible, I would tell you; ✦*MODISMO* **¿será ~?*** I can't believe it!; **¡pues sí que eres descarado! ¿será ~?** I can't believe you are so cheeky!; **¿será ~ que no haya venido?** I can't believe he hasn't come!

Ⓑ ADV **lo más ... ~** as ... as possible; **lo más pronto ~** as soon as possible; *ver tb* **mejor A2.3**

Ⓒ **posibles** SMPL (*Esp*) means; **una señora de ~s** a woman of means; **vive dentro de sus ~s** she lives within her means; **una familia de ~s** a well-to-do family

▼**posiblemente** ADV possibly; **~ el mejor vino del mundo** possibly the best wine in the world; **—¿crees que vendrá? —posiblemente** "do you think she'll come?" — "possibly *o* she might"; **~ tengamos que mudarnos** we might have to move, it's possible that we'll have to move

posición SF 1 (= *postura*) position; **mantener el frasco en ~ vertical** keep the bottle in an upright position; **estar en ~ de firme** (*Mil*) to be at attention; **estar en ~ de guardia** to be on guard ► **posición del misionero** missionary position

2 (= *lugar*) position; **la ~ de los jugadores en el terreno de juego** the position of the players on the pitch

3 (= *categoría*) position, standing; **disfrutan de una elevada ~ social** they enjoy a high social position

4 (= *punto de vista*) position, stance; **¿cuál es su ~ en este conflicto?** what's your position *o* stance on this dispute?

5 (*en competición, liga*) place, position; **ganó Alemania con Italia en segunda ~** Germany won, with Italy in second place *o* position; **terminó en primera ~** he finished first *o* in first place; **posiciones de honor** first three places, medal positions; **perder posiciones** (*en lucha, enfrentamiento*) to lose ground

6 (*LAm*) (= *puesto de trabajo*) position, post

posicionado SM positioning

posicionamiento SM (= *acción*) positioning; (= *postura*) stance, attitude

posicionar ►conjug 1a◄ Ⓐ VT to position

Ⓑ **posicionarse** VPR (= *tomar posición*) to adopt an attitude, take up a stance; (= *declarar su posición*) to define one's position, declare oneself

posimperial ADJ post-imperial

posimpresionismo SM post-impressionism

posimpresionista ADJ, SMF post-impressionist

posindustrial ADJ post-industrial

positiva SF (*Fot*) positive, print

positivado SM (*Fot*) printing

positivamente ADV positively

positivar ►conjug 1a◄ VT (*Fot*) (= *imprimir*) to print; (= *revelar*) to develop

positivismo SM positivism

positivista ADJ, SMF positivist

positivo Ⓐ ADJ 1 (= *afirmativo, beneficioso*) positive; **la prueba de embarazo dio ~** the pregnancy test was positive; **el atleta dio ~** the athlete tested positive; **el conductor dio ~** the driver tested positive

2 (*Mat*) positive, plus

3 [*idea*] constructive; **es ~ que ...** it is good that ..., it is encouraging that ...

Ⓑ SM 1 (*Ling*) positive

2 (*Fot*) positive, print

3 (*Dep*) point

pósito SM 1 (= *granero*) granary, public granary

2 (= *cooperativa*) cooperative; **~ de pescadores** fishing cooperative

positrón SM positron

posma* SMF bore, dull person

posmeridiano ADJ postmeridian, afternoon *antes de s*

posmodernidad SF post-modernity

posmodernismo SM postmodernism

posmoderno/a Ⓐ ADJ postmodern

Ⓑ SM/F postmodernist

posnatal ADJ postnatal

poso SM 1 (= *sedimento*) [*de mineral*] sediment, deposit; [*de vino*] sediment, dregs *pl*, lees *pl*; [*de café*] dregs *pl*, grounds *pl* ► **posos de té** tea leaves

2 (= *huella*) trace

posol SM (*CAm*) *maize drink*

posología SF dosage

posoperativo ADJ post-operative

posoperatorio Ⓐ ADJ post-operative

Ⓑ SM post-operative period, period of recovery after an operation

pososo ADJ (*CAm*) (= *poroso*) porous, permeable; (= *absorbente*) absorbent

posparto Ⓐ ADJ postnatal

Ⓑ SM postnatal period, postpartum (*frm*)

posponer ►conjug 2q◄ VT 1 (= *aplazar*) to postpone

2 (= *subordinar*) **~ la salud al trabajo** to put one's career before one's health; **~ el amor propio al interés general** to subordinate one's pride to the general interest; **~ a algn** to downgrade sb

posposición SF 1 (= *aplazamiento*) postponement

2 (*Ling*) postposition

3 (= *subordinación*) subordination

pospositivo ADJ postpositive

posproducción SF post-production

posquemador SM afterburner

post... PREF post...

posta Ⓐ SF 1 (†) (= *caballos*) relay, team; (= *tramo*) stage; (= *parada*) staging post; **por la ~** post-haste, as quickly as possible

2 ✦*MODISMO* **a ~** on purpose, deliberately

3 (*Caza*) (= *munición*) slug, pellet

4 (*Chile Med*) First Aid Post, First Aid Station

5 (*Naipes*) stake

6 (*Culin*) slice ► **posta de pierna** (*CAm*) leg of pork

Ⓑ SM courier

postal Ⓐ ADJ postal; **giro ~** postal order; *ver tb* **caja 2**, **código 2**

Ⓑ SF postcard ► **postal ilustrada** picture postcard

postcolonial ADJ post-colonial

postdata SF postscript

postdoctoral ADJ post-doctoral

poste SM (= *palo*) post, pole; (= *columna*) pillar; [*de ejecución*] stake; (*Dep*) post, upright; **el balón pasó entre los ~s** the ball went in between the posts; ✦*MODISMOS* **dar ~ a algn*** to keep sb hanging about; **mover los ~s** to move the goalposts; **oler el ~** (= *peligro*) to scent danger, see trouble ahead; (= *algo sospechoso*) to smell a rat* ► **poste de cerca** fence post ► **poste de llegada** winning post ► **poste del tendido eléctrico** electricity pylon ► **poste de portería** goalpost ► **poste de salida** starting post ► **poste indicador** signpost ► **poste telegráfico** telegraph pole

postelectoral ADJ post-electoral

postema SF 1 (*Med*) (= *absceso*) abscess

2 (*Méx*) (= *divieso*) boil; (= *pus*) pus

3 (*) (= *pelmazo*) bore, dull person

postemilla SF (*LAm*) gumboil

póster SM (*pl* **pósteres** *o* **pósters**) poster

postergación SF 1 [*de acto*] postponement

2 (= *relegación*) disregard, neglect; **ha sufrido una ~ en el trabajo** she has been passed over for promotion at work

postergar ►conjug 1h◄ VT 1 (= *aplazar*) to defer, postpone; (= *retrasar*) to delay

2 (= *relegar*) (*en el trato*) to disregard, neglect; (*en ascenso*) to pass over, ignore

posteridad SF 1 (= *futuro*) posterity

2 (*Esp**) (= *culo*) bottom, backside*

posterior ADJ 1 (= *trasero*) [*lugar*] back, rear; [*máquina, motor*] rear-mounted; **en la parte ~ del jardín** at the back of the garden

2 (*en tiempo*) later, subsequent; **ser ~ a algo** to be later than sth

3 (*en orden*) later, following

posteriori *ver* **a posteriori**

posterioridad SF **con ~** subsequently, later; **con ~ a algo** subsequent to sth, after sth

posteriormente ADV later, subsequently, afterwards

postgrado SM = **posgrado**

postgraduado/a ADJ, SM/F = **posgraduado**

postguerra SF = **posguerra**

postigo SM 1 (= *contraventana*) shutter

2 (†) (= *puerta chica en otra mayor*) wicket, wicket gate; (= *portillo*) postern; (= *puerta falsa*) side door, side gate

postillón SM postillion

postín* SM 1 (= *lujo*) elegance; **de ~** posh*

2 (= *jactancia*) **darse ~** to show off; **se da mucho ~ de que su padre es ministro** he boasts about his father being a minister

➤ LENGUA Y USO: **posiblemente A2** 31, 36.1, 42.3 **posiblemente** 53.6

postinear* ▸conjug 1a◂ VI to show off

postinero* ADJ 1 [*persona*] vain, conceited (**de** about)
2 [*traje*] posh*

postizas SFPL (*Esp*) *small castanets*

postizo Ⓐ ADJ [*dientes, sonrisa, bigote*] false; [*cuello de camisa*] detachable
Ⓑ SM [*de pelo*] hairpiece, switch

postnatal ADJ postnatal

postoperatorio ADJ, SM = **posoperatorio**

postor SM bidder; **al mejor ~** to the highest bidder

postparto ADJ, SM = **posparto**

postproducción SF post-production

postración SF prostration

postrado ADJ prostrate; **~ por el dolor** prostrate with grief

postrar ▸conjug 1a◂ Ⓐ VT 1 (*Med*) (= *debilitar*) to weaken, prostrate
2 (= *derribar*) to cast down, overthrow
Ⓑ **postrarse** VPR to prostrate o.s.

postre Ⓐ SM dessert, pudding; **¿qué hay de ~?** what's for dessert?; **de ~ tomé un helado** I had ice cream for dessert; **✦*MODISMOS*** **para ~** to cap it all, on top of everything; **y, para ~, vamos y nos perdemos** and to cap it all *o* on top of everything, we went and got lost; **llegar para los ~s** to come very late
Ⓑ SF **✦*MODISMO*** **a la ~** when all is said and done, at the end of the day; **a la ~, todos defendemos los mismos intereses** when all is said and done *o* at the end of the day, we all have the same interests

postremo ADJ = **postrero**

postrer ADJ = **postrero**

postrero ADJ (= *último*) last; (= *rezagado*) rear, hindmost; **palabras postreras** dying words

postrimerías SFPL 1 (= *final*) final stages, closing stages; **en las ~ del siglo** in the last few years of the century, at the end *o* close of the century
2 (= *agonía*) dying moments
3 (*Teología*) four last things

postulación SF 1 (= *proposición*) proposition, postulation
2 (*Rel*) postulancy
3 (= *colecta*) collection
4 (*LAm*) [*de candidato*] nomination, candidature

postulado SM (= *supuesto*) assumption, postulate (*frm*); (= *proposición*) proposition

postulante SMF 1 (*Rel*) postulant, candidate
2 (*en colecta*) collector
3 (*LAm*) [*de trabajo*] candidate

postular ▸conjug 1a◂ Ⓐ VT 1 (= *defender*) [+ *teoría*] to postulate
2 (= *pedir*) to demand, seek; **en el artículo postula la reforma de …** in the article he sets out demands for the reform of …
3 (*en colecta*) to collect (for charity)
4 (*LAm*) (= *proponer*) [+ *candidato*] to nominate
Ⓑ VI 1 (*en colecta*) to collect (for charity)
2 (*LAm*) to apply (**para** for)
Ⓒ **postularse** VPR (*LAm Pol*) to stand

póstumo ADJ posthumous

postura SF 1 [*del cuerpo*] position; **no sé cómo puedes estar en una ~ tan incómoda** I don't know how you can stand being in such an uncomfortable position ▸ **postura del loto** lotus position
2 (= *actitud*) stance, position; **adoptó una ~ poco razonable** he adopted an unreasonable stance *o* position; **tomar ~** to take a stand
3 (*en una subasta*) bid; **hacer ~** to make a bid
4 (*en juego de azar*) bet, stake
5 [*de ave*] (= *acción*) egg-laying; (= *conjunto de huevos*) eggs *pl*, eggs laid *pl*
6 (‡) (= *droga*) *1000-pesetas' worth of hashish*

postural ADJ postural

post-venta ADJ INV, **posventa** ADJ INV after-sales *antes de s*; **servicio** *o* **asistencia ~** after-sales service

pota SF 1 (= *calamar*) cuttlefish
2 **echar la(s) ~(s)‡** to puke‡, throw up*

potabilización SF purification

potabilizadora SF water-treatment plant, waterworks

potabilizar ▸conjug 1f◂ VT **~ el agua** to make the water drinkable

potable ADJ 1 drinkable; **agua ~** drinking water
2 (*) (= *aceptable*) good enough, passable

potaje SM 1 (*Culin*) *vegetable and pulse stew*
2 (= *revoltijo*) jumble

potar‡ ▸conjug 1a◂ VI to puke‡, throw up*

potasa SF potash

potasio SM potassium

pote SM 1 (= *tarro*) jar; (= *jarra*) jug; (= *vaso*) glass; (= *olla*) pot; (= *maceta*) flowerpot, pot; (*Ven*) (= *bote*) tin, can; (*Méx*) (= *vasija*) mug; (*Andes, Caribe*) (= *termo*) flask; **✦*MODISMOS*** **a ~** in plenty; **darse ~*** to show off
2 (*Culin*) stew ▸ **pote gallego** Galician stew
3 (*) (= *gesto*) pout, sulky look
4 (*) (= *trago*) drink; **tomar unos ~s** to have a few drinks

potear* ▸conjug 1a◂ VI to have a few drinks

potencia SF 1 (= *capacidad*) power ▸ **potencia de fuego** firepower ▸ **potencia electoral** voting power, power in terms of votes ▸ **potencia hidráulica** hydraulic power ▸ **potencia muscular** muscular power, muscular strength ▸ **potencia nuclear** nuclear power
2 (*Mec*) power ▸ **potencia (en caballos)** horsepower ▸ **potencia al freno** brake horsepower ▸ **potencia real** effective power
3 (*Pol*) power; **las grandes ~s** the great powers; **éramos una ~ naval** we used to be a naval power ▸ **potencia colonial** colonial power ▸ **potencia mundial** world power
4 (*Mat*) power; **elevado a la quinta ~** raised to the power of five
5 (*Rel*) (*tb* **~ del alma**) faculty
6 **en ~** potential, in the making; **es una guerra civil en ~** it is a civil war in the making

potenciación SF = **potenciamiento**

potenciador Ⓐ ADJ **ser ~ de algo** to stimulate sth
Ⓑ SM ▸ **potenciador del sabor** flavour enhancer

potencial Ⓐ ADJ potential
Ⓑ SM 1 (= *capacidad*) potential ▸ **potencial comercial** market potential ▸ **potencial de ventas** sales potential ▸ **potencial ganador** (*Fin*) earning potential; (*Dep*) potential to win
2 (*Ling*) conditional

potencialidad SF potentiality

potencialmente ADV potentially

potenciamiento SM 1 [*de turismo, artes, nuevo producto*] promotion
2 [*de economía, producción, cooperación*] boosting, strengthening

potenciar ▸conjug 1b◂ VT 1 [+ *turismo, artes, nuevo producto*] to favour, favor (*EEUU*), foster, promote; (= *desarrollar*) to develop; (= *mejorar*) to improve
2 (= *fortalecer*) to boost, strengthen
3 (*Inform*) to upgrade

potentado/a SM/F 1 (*en la industria*) tycoon, magnate; **un ~ de la construcción** a construction tycoon *o* magnate; **los ~s que veranean en Marbella** the idle rich who spend the summer in Marbella
2 (= *poderoso*) big shot*

potente ADJ 1 (= *poderoso*) powerful
2 (*) (= *grande*) mighty, big; **un grito ~** a great yell, an almighty shout*
3 (= *viril*) virile
4 (*Chile*) [*salsa*] hot

poteo* SM drinking; **ir de ~** to go for a few drinks

potestad SF authority, jurisdiction; **patria ~** paternal authority; **~ marital** husband's (legal) authority

potestativo ADJ (*Jur*) (= *optativo*) optional, facultative

potingue* SM 1 (= *brebaje*) concoction, brew
2 (= *crema*) face cream

potito SM 1 (*Esp*) (= *tarro*) jar of baby food
2 (*LAm**) (= *culo*) backside, bum‡, butt (*EEUU‡*)

poto* SM (*Andes, Cono Sur*) 1 (= *culo*) backside, bum‡, butt (*EEUU‡*)
2 (= *fondo*) lower end
3 (*Bot*) calabash
4 (= *vasija*) earthenware jug

potoco* ADJ (*Andes, Cono Sur*) squat

potón (*Cono Sur*) Ⓐ ADJ coarse
Ⓑ SM rustic, peasant

potosí SM fortune; **cuesta un ~** it costs the earth, it costs a fortune; **vale un ~** it's worth a fortune; **ella vale un ~** she's a treasure, she's worth her weight in gold; **en ese negocio tienen un ~** they've got a gold mine in that business

potra SF 1 (*Zool*) filly
2 (*) (= *suerte*) luck, jam*; **de ~** luckily, by luck; **tener ~** to be jammy*
3 (*Med*) (= *hernia*) rupture, hernia

potranco/a SM/F colt/filly, young horse/mare

potrear ▸conjug 1a◂ Ⓐ VT 1 (*Andes, CAm*) (= *zurrar*) to beat
2 (*Caribe, Méx*) [+ *caballo*] to break, tame
Ⓑ VI (*CAm, Cono Sur*) to caper about, chase around

potrero Ⓐ SM (*LAm*) 1 (= *pasto*) pasture; (= *cercado*) paddock
2 (= *finca*) [*de ganado*] cattle ranch; [*de cría*] stud farm
3 (*Cono Sur*) (= *parque*) playground
4 (*Méx*) (= *llanura*) open grassland
Ⓑ ADJ (‡) (= *afortunado*) lucky, jammy*

potrillo SM 1 (= *caballo*) colt
2 (*Chile*) (= *copa*) tall glass
3 (*Andes*) (= *canoa*) small canoe

potro SM 1 (*Zool*) colt

2 (Dep) (vaulting) horse
3 [de tortura] rack
4 [de herrar] shoeing frame
5 (LAm Med) hernia

potroso* ADJ jammy*, lucky

POUM SM ABR (Esp Hist) = **Partido Obrero de Unificación Marxista**

poyo SM (para sentarse) stone bench; (en cocina) stone kitchen top; (de ventana) stone ledge

poza SF 1 (= charca) (gen) puddle, pool; [de río] backwater, pool
2 (LAm*) (= escupitajo) gob* of spit

pozanco SM puddle, pool

pozo SM 1 [de agua] well; ✦MODISMOS **es un ~ de maldad** he is wicked through and through, he is rotten to the core; **ser un ~ de sabiduría** to be a fount of wisdom; **ser un ~ sin fondo** to be a bottomless pit; **caer en el ~** to fall into oblivion ► **pozo artesiano** artesian well ► **pozo ciego** cesspool ► **pozo de petróleo** oil well ► **pozo de riego** well used for irrigation ► **pozo negro** cesspool ► **pozo petrolífero** oil well ► **pozo séptico** septic tank
2 [de río] deep part
3 (Min) (= hueco) shaft; (= mina) pit, mine ► **pozo de aire** air shaft ► **pozo de registro, pozo de visita** manhole ► **pozo de ventilación** ventilation shaft
4 (Náut) hold
5 (LAm Astron) black hole

pozol SM (LAm) = **posol**

pozole SM (Méx Culin) maize stew

PP SM ABR (Esp Pol) = **Partido Popular**

PP. ABR (= **Padres**) Frs

pp. ABR (= **porte pagado**) CP, c/p

p.p. ABR (Jur) (= **por poder**) pp, per pro

p.p.m. ABR 1 (= **palabras por minuto**) wpm
2 (= **partes por millón**) ppm

p.p.p. ABR (= **puntos por pulgada**) d.p.i.

PR SM ABR = **Puerto Rico**

▼**práctica** SF 1 [de actividad] practice; **aprender con la ~** to learn by practice; **la ~ hace al maestro** practice makes perfect; **llevar algo a la ~** ◊ **poner algo en ~** to put sth into practice; **en la ~** in practice ► **práctica de riesgo** high-risk practice ► **práctica establecida** standard practice ► **prácticas restrictivas (de la competencia)** restrictive practices
2 **prácticas** (= aprendizaje) (gen) practice *sing*, training *sing*; [de profesor] teaching practice *sing*; [de laboratorio] experiments; **hacer ~s** to do one's training; **hacer ~s de clínica** to do one's hospital training; **contrato en ~s** work experience placement; **estudiantes en ~s** students doing work experience; **período de ~s** (practical) training period ► **prácticas de tiro** target practice ► **prácticas en empresa** work experience ► **prácticas profesionales** professional training, practical training (for a profession)

practicable ADJ 1 (= factible) practicable, workable, feasible
2 [camino] passable, usable
3 (Teat) [puerta] that opens, that is meant to open

prácticamente ADV practically; **está ~ terminado** it's practically finished, it's almost finished

practicante Ⓐ ADJ (Rel) practising, practicing (EEUU)
Ⓑ SMF (Med) (= ayudante) medical assistant, nurse (specializing in giving injections, taking blood pressure, etc); (Méx) (= estudiante) final year medical student

practicar ▸conjug 1g◂ Ⓐ VT 1 [+ habilidad, virtud] to practise, practice (EEUU), exercise
2 (= hacer prácticas de) [+ actividad, profesión] to practise, practice (EEUU); [+ deporte] to play; **le conviene ~ algún deporte** it would be good for him to play a sport *o* do some sport; **practica el francés con su profesor** she practises French with her teacher
3 (= ejecutar) [+ operación quirúrgica] to carry out, do, perform (frm); [+ detención] to make; [+ incisión] to make
4 [+ hoyo] to cut, make
Ⓑ VI (en deporte, juego) to practise, practice (EEUU); (en profesión) to do one's training *o* practice

practicidad SF (= viabilidad) practicality; (= resultado) effectiveness

practicismo SM down-to-earth attitude, sense of realism

práctico Ⓐ ADJ 1 (= útil) (gen) practical; [herramienta] handy; [ropa] sensible, practical; **no resultó ser muy ~** it turned out to be not very practical; **resulta ~ vivir tan cerca de la fábrica** it's convenient *o* handy to live so close to the factory
2 (= no teórico) [estudio, formación] practical; **conocimientos ~s de informática** practical experience of computers
3 (= pragmático) **sé ~ y búscate un trabajo que dé dinero** be practical *o* sensible and find a job with money
4 (frm) (= experto) **ser muy ~ en algo** to be very skilled at sth, be an expert at sth
Ⓑ SM 1 (Náut) pilot (in a port)
2 (Med) practitioner

pradera SF (= prado) meadow, meadowland; (de Canadá, EEUU) prairie; **unas extensas ~s** extensive grasslands

pradería SF meadowlands *pl*, grasslands *pl*

prado SM (= campo) meadow, field; (= parque) green grassy area; (= pastizal) pasture; (LAm) (= césped) grass, lawn

Praga SF Prague

pragmática SF 1 (Ling) pragmatics *sing*
2 (Hist) decree, proclamation

pragmático ADJ pragmatic

pragmatismo SM pragmatism

pragmatista SMF pragmatist

prángana* ADJ INV (Méx) poor

PRD SM ABR 1 (Méx) = **Partido de la Revolución Democrática**
2 (República Dominicana) = **Partido Revolucionario Dominicano**

pre... PREF pre...

preacordar ▸conjug 1l◂ VT to reach a preliminary agreement on, make a draft agreement on

preacuerdo SM preliminary agreement, outline *o* draft agreement

preadolescente Ⓐ ADJ pre-adolescent, prepubescent (pey)
Ⓑ SMF pre-adolescent boy/girl

prealarma SF early warning

prealerta SF standby, yellow alert; **en estado de ~** on standby, on yellow alert

preámbulo SM 1 (= introducción) [de libro, discurso] introduction; [de ley, constitución] preamble
2 (= rodeo) **andarse con ~s** ◊ **gastar ~s** to beat about the bush, avoid the issue; **sin más ~s** without further ado, without preamble
3 (= preliminar) prelude; **la visita del rey es el ~ de las conversaciones** the royal visit is a prelude to the negotiations

preautonómico ADJ (Esp Pol) *before the creation of the autonomous regional governments*

preaviso SM forewarning, early warning

prebélico ADJ prewar

prebenda SF 1 (Rel) (= renta) prebend
2 (= gaje) perk*; **las ~s del cargo** the perks of the job* ► **prebendas corporativas** business perks*

prebendado SM prebendary

preboste SM 1 (Hist) provost
2 (Pol) chief, leader

precalentamiento SM (Dep) warm-up; (Aut) warming up

precalentar ▸conjug 1j◂ Ⓐ VT to preheat; (Dep) to warm up
Ⓑ **precalentarse** VPR (Dep) to warm up

precampaña SF (tb **~ electoral**) run-up to the election campaign

precanceroso ADJ precancerous, pre-cancer

precandidato/a SM/F (esp Méx Pol) *official shortlisted Presidential candidate*

precariamente ADV precariously

precariedad SF 1 [de empleo, salud, situación] precariousness
2 [de recursos, medios] scarcity

precario Ⓐ ADJ [salud] precarious; [situación] precarious, difficult; [economía, democracia] unstable; [vivienda] poor, inferior; [medios] unpredictable, reduced
Ⓑ SM precarious state; **dejar a algn en ~** to leave sb in a difficult situation; **estamos en ~** we are in a difficult situation; **vivir en ~** to live from hand to mouth, scrape a living

precaución SF 1 (al hacer algo) (= cuidado) precaution; (= medida) preventive measure; **tomar precauciones** to take precautions; **extremar las precauciones** to be extra careful; **lo hicimos por ~** we did it to be on the safe side, we did it as a precautionary measure *o* as a precaution
2 (= previsión) foresight; (= cautela) caution; **ir con ~** to proceed with caution

precautorio ADJ precautionary

precaver ▸conjug 2a◂ Ⓐ VT (= prevenir) to try to prevent, guard against; (= anticipar) to forestall; (= evitar) to stave off
Ⓑ **precaverse** VPR to be on one's guard, take precautions (**contra** against); **~se de algo** to be on one's guard against sth, beware of sth

precavidamente ADV cautiously

precavido ADJ 1 (= cauteloso) cautious; ✦REFRÁN **hombre ~ vale por dos** forewarned is forearmed
2 (= preparado) prepared; **vengo ~** I came prepared

precedencia SF 1 (= prioridad) precedence, priority
2 (= preeminencia) greater importance, superiority

precedente Ⓐ ADJ preceding, previous, foregoing (frm); **cada uno mejor que el ~** each one better than the one before

➤ LENGUA Y USO: **práctica 2** 46.1

Ⓑ SM precedent; **de acuerdo con el ~** according to precedent; **establecer** *o* **sentar un ~** to set a precedent; **sin ~(s)** (= *sin antecedentes*) unprecedented, without precedent; (= *sin igual*) unparalleled; **sin que sirva de ~** just this once; **por primera vez y sin que sirva de ~, voy a seguir tu consejo** just this once, I'll follow your advice

precedentemente ADV earlier, at an earlier stage, previously

preceder ▸conjug 2a◂ Ⓐ VT [1] (= *anteceder*) **~ a algo/algn** to precede sth/sb; **le precedía un coche** he was preceded by a car; **los años que precedieron a la Guerra Civil** the years leading up to the Civil War, the years preceding the Civil War; **el título precede al nombre** the title goes before the name

[2] (= *tener prioridad*) **~ a algo/algn** to have priority over sth/sb, take precedence over sth/sb

Ⓑ VI to precede; **todo lo que precede** all the preceding (part), all that which comes before

preceptista SMF theorist

preceptiva SF precepts *pl*

preceptivo ADJ compulsory, obligatory, mandatory; **es ~ utilizar el formulario** the application form must be used

precepto SM (= *regla*) precept; (= *mandato*) order, rule; **día** *o* **fiesta de ~** (*Rel*) holy day of obligation

preceptor/a SM/F (*en colegio*) teacher; (*particular*) (private) tutor

preceptorado SM tutorship

preceptoral ADJ tutorial

preceptuar ▸conjug 1e◂ VT to lay down, establish

preces SFPL prayers, supplications

preciado ADJ [1] (= *estimado*) [*posesión*] prized; [*amigo*] valued, esteemed

[2] (= *presuntuoso*) presumptuous

preciarse ▸conjug 1b◂ VPR **~ de algo** to pride o.s. on sth; **~ de hacer algo** to pride o.s. on doing sth

precintado Ⓐ ADJ [*paquete*] sealed, presealed; [*calle, zona*] sealed off

Ⓑ SM [*de paquete*] sealing; [*de calle, zona*] sealing off

precintar ▸conjug 1a◂ VT [+ *paquete*] to seal, preseal; [+ *calle, zona*] to seal off

precinto SM [1] (*Com*) seal

[2] (= *acción*) [*de paquete*] sealing; [*de calle, zona*] sealing off

precio SM [1] (= *importe*) [*de producto*] price; [*de viaje*] fare; (*en hotel*) rate, charge; **han subido los ~s** prices have gone up; **¿qué ~ tiene?** how much is it?; **a ~ de saldo** at a knockdown price; **a** *o* **por un ~ simbólico** for a nominal *o* token sum; **"no importa precio"** "cost no object"; **"precio a discutir"** "offers"; **último ~** closing price; ✦*MODISMOS* **poner** *o* **señalar ~ a la cabeza de algn** to put a price on sb's head; **no tener ~** to be priceless; **este cuadro no tiene ~** this painting is priceless; **su lealtad no tiene ~** his loyalty is of enormous value ► **precio al contado** cash ► **precio al detalle, precio al por menor** retail price ► **precio de compra** purchase price ► **precio de coste, precio de costo** cost-price; **a ~ de coste** at cost price ► **precio de fábrica** ex works price; **a ~ de fábrica** at factory prices ► **precio de intervención** intervention price ► **precio de mercado** market price ► **precio de ocasión** bargain price ► **precio de oferta** offer price ► **precio de referencia** suggested price ► **precio de salida** starting price ► **precio de situación** (*LAm*) bargain price ► **precio de venta** sale price, selling price ► **precio de venta al público** retail price ► **precio de venta recomendado** recommended retail price ► **precio neto** net price ► **precio obsequio** giveaway price ► **precio orientativo** manufacturer's recommended price ► **precios al consumo** retail prices ► **precio tope** top price, ceiling price ► **precio unitario** unit price

[2] (= *coste, sacrificio*) **pagó un ~ muy alto por su libertad** he paid a very high price for his freedom; **lo hará a cualquier ~** he'll do it whatever the cost *o* at any price; **evítelo a cualquier ~** avoid it at all costs; **al ~ de** (*frm*) at the cost of; **ganó las elecciones, pero al ~ de su integridad** he won the election but at the cost *o* expense of his integrity

[3] (*frm*) (= *valor*) worth, value; **un hombre de gran ~** a man of great worth; **tengo en gran ~ su amistad** I value his friendship very highly

preciosamente ADV (= *maravillosamente*) beautifully; (= *con encanto*) charmingly

preciosidad SF [1] (*) (= *objeto*) (*bello*) beautiful thing; (*apreciado*) precious object; **es una ~** he's adorable; **¡oye, ~!** hey, beautiful!

[2] (*como cualidad*) (= *excelencia*) preciousness; (= *valor*) value, worth

[3] (*pey*) (= *afectación*) preciousness, preciosity

preciosismo SM preciosity

preciosista Ⓐ ADJ precious, affected

Ⓑ SMF affected writer, precious writer

precioso ADJ [1] (= *valioso*) precious, valuable; *ver tb* **piedra A1**

[2] (= *hermoso*) (*gen*) lovely, beautiful; (= *primoroso*) charming; **un vestido ~** a beautiful dress; **tienen un niño ~** they have a lovely child; **¿verdad que es ~?** isn't it lovely *o* beautiful?

preciosura SF = **preciosidad 1**

precipicio SM [1] (*en monte, peñasco*) cliff, precipice

[2] (= *situación arriesgada*) abyss; **un país al borde del ~** a country on the edge of the abyss, a country on the brink of disaster *o* ruin

precipitación SF [1] (*al hacer algo*) (= *prisa*) haste; (= *imprudencia*) rashness; **con ~** hastily, precipitately (*frm*)

[2] (*Meteo*) rainfall, precipitation (*frm*); **precipitaciones abundantes** heavy rainfall; **precipitaciones débiles** light rain; **abundantes precipitaciones de nieve** heavy snow

[3] (*Quím*) precipitation

precipitadamente ADV [*huir, lanzarse*] headlong; [*irse*] very suddenly; [*actuar*] rashly, precipitately (*frm*); **escribí una nota ~** I dashed off a note; **tuvieron que casarse ~** they had to get married in a hurry; **ha abandonado ~ el país** he left the country very suddenly

precipitado Ⓐ ADJ [*huida*] headlong; [*partida*] hasty, sudden; [*conducta*] hasty, rash

Ⓑ SM (*Quím*) precipitate

precipitador SM precipitant

precipitar ▸conjug 1a◂ Ⓐ VT [1] (= *arrojar*) to hurl down, throw (**desde** from)

[2] (= *apresurar*) hasten, to precipitate (*frm*); **aquello precipitó su salida** that affair hastened *o* (*frm*) precipitated his departure; **la dimisión precipitó la crisis** her resignation brought on *o* (*frm*) precipitated the crisis; **no precipitemos los acontecimientos** let's not rush things

[3] (*Quím*) to precipitate

Ⓑ **precipitarse** VPR [1] (= *arrojarse*) to throw o.s., hurl o.s. (**desde** from); **~se sobre algo** [*pájaro*] to swoop down on sth; [*animal*] to pounce on sth; **~se sobre algn** to throw *o* hurl o.s. on sb

[2] (= *correr*) to rush, dash; **~se a hacer algo** to rush to do sth; **~se hacia la salida** to rush towards the exit

[3] (= *actuar sin reflexión*) to act hastily; **se ha precipitado rehusándolo** he acted hastily in rejecting it, it was rash of him to refuse it; **no te precipites** don't rush into things

precipitoso ADJ [1] [*lugar*] precipitous, very steep

[2] [*huida, etc*] = **precipitado A**

precisa SF [1] (*CAm*) (= *urgencia*) urgency

[2] **tener la ~** (*Cono Sur**) to be on the ball

precisado ADJ **verse ~ a hacer algo** to be forced *o* obliged to do sth

precisamente ADV [1] (= *con precisión*) precisely

[2] (= *exactamente*) precisely, exactly; **¡precisamente!** exactly!, precisely!; **~ por eso** for that very reason, precisely because of that; **~ fue él quien lo dijo** as a matter of fact it was he who said it; **~ estamos hablando de eso** we're just talking about that; **llegó ~ cuando nos íbamos** he arrived just as we were leaving; **yo no soy un experto ~** I'm not exactly an expert; **no es eso ~** it's not quite that

precisar ▸conjug 1a◂ Ⓐ VT [1] (= *necesitar*) to need, require; **no precisa lavado** it needs no washing, it doesn't require washing; **el jefe precisa tu ayuda** the boss needs your help; **no precisamos que el candidato tenga experiencia** we do not require that the candidate should be experienced; **"se precisan mensajeros"** "messengers required", "messengers wanted"

[2] (= *especificar*) to specify; **no precisó a qué hora llegaría** he didn't specify when he would arrive; **aún no han precisado los detalles del contrato** they have not specified the details of the contract yet; **¿puedes ~ un poco más?** can you be a little more specific?; **precisó que no se trataba de un virus** he said specifically that it was not a virus

Ⓑ VI **~ de algo** to need *o* require sth; **no precisamos de sus servicios** we do not need *o* require your services

precisión SF [1] (= *exactitud*) precision, accuracy, preciseness; **instrumento de ~** precision instrument

[2] **hacer precisiones** to clarify matters

[3] (= *necesidad*) need, necessity; **tener ~ de algo** to need sth, be in need of sth; **verse en la ~ de hacer algo** to be forced *o* obliged to do sth

[4] (*Méx*) (= *urgencia*) urgency

▼ **preciso** ADJ [1] (= *exacto*) precise; **una descripción precisa** a precise description; **hemos recibido instrucciones precisas** we have received precise instructions; **un reloj**

➤ LENGUA Y USO: preciso 1 53.3

muy ~ a very precise *o* accurate watch
[2] (= *justo*) **en aquel ~ momento** at that precise *o* very moment; **tengo el tiempo ~ para comer y ducharme** I have just enough time to eat and shower
[3] (= *necesario*) necessary; **las cualidades precisas** the necessary qualities; **cuando sea ~** when it becomes necessary; **si es ~ iré yo mismo** I'll go by myself if necessary; **es ~ tener coche** it is essential to have a car; **es ~ que lo hagas** you must do it; **no es ~ que vengas** there's no need for you to come; ✦***MODISMO*** **ser un Don Preciso** (*Cono Sur*) to believe o.s. to be indispensable
[4] [*estilo, lenguaje*] concise
[5] (*Caribe*) [*persona*] conceited

precitado ADJ above-mentioned

preclaro ADJ illustrious

precocidad SF [1] (= *cualidad*) precociousness, precocity
[2] (*Bot*) earliness

precocinado ADJ pre-cooked; **platos ~s** ready meals, pre-cooked meals

precocinar ▸conjug 1a◂ VT to precook

precognición SF foreknowledge, precognition (*frm*)

precolombino ADJ pre-Columbian; **la América precolombina** America before Columbus

preconcebido ADJ preconceived; **idea preconcebida** preconceived idea, preconception

preconcepción SF preconception

preconciliar ADJ preconciliar, before Vatican II

precondición SF precondition

preconización SF [1] (= *recomendación*) recommendation
[2] (= *apoyo*) advocacy

preconizar ▸conjug 1f◂ VT [1] (= *elogiar*) to praise
[2] (= *recomendar*) to recommend, advise
[3] (= *apoyar*) to advocate

precontrato SM pre-contract

precordillera SF (*LAm*) Andean foothills *pl*

precoz ADJ [1] (= *prematuro*) [*envejecimiento, calvicie, eyaculación*] premature; [*diagnóstico, pronóstico*] early; [*niño*] precocious
[2] (*Bot*) early

precozmente ADV [1] (= *prematuramente*) [*envejecer, eyacular*] prematurely; [*diagnosticar, detectar*] early; **inició su actividad sexual ~** he became sexually active at an early age
[2] (*Bot*) early

precursor(a) SM/F precursor, forerunner

predación SF (*Biol*) predation; (*fig*) depredation, plundering

predador SM, **predator** SM predator

predecesor(a) SM/F predecessor

predecir ▸conjug 3o◂ VT to predict, forecast

predemocrático ADJ prior to the establishment of democracy

predestinación SF predestination

predestinado ADJ predestined; **estar ~ a hacer algo** to be predestined to do sth

predestinar ▸conjug 1a◂ VT to predestine

predeterminación SF predetermination

predeterminado ADJ predetermined

predeterminar ▸conjug 1a◂ VT to predetermine

prédica SF (= *sermón*) sermon; (= *arenga*) harangue; **~s** preaching

predicación SF preaching

predicado SM predicate

predicador/a SM/F preacher

predicamento SM [1] (= *prestigio*) standing, prestige; **no goza ahora de tanto ~** it has less prestige now, it is not so well thought of now
[2] (*LAm*) (= *situación difícil*) predicament

predicar ▸conjug 1g◂ VT, VI to preach; **~ con el ejemplo** to practise what one preaches

predicativo ADJ predicative

predicción SF [*de catástrofe, hecho futuro*] prediction; [*del tiempo*] forecast ► **predicción del tiempo** weather forecasting

predicho ADJ aforementioned

predigerido ADJ predigested

predilección SF predilection; **tener ~ por algo** to have a predilection for sth; **predilecciones y aversiones** likes and dislikes

predilecto ADJ favourite, favorite (*EEUU*); **fue nombrado hijo ~ de Madrid** he was named one of Madrid's honorary citizens

predio SM (= *finca*) property, estate; (*LAm*) (= *local*) premises *pl*; **~s** land *sing* ► **predio rústico** rural property, country estate ► **predio urbano** town property

predisponente ADJ [*factor, efecto*] underlying; **factores ~s de algo** the underlying factors of sth

predisponer ▸conjug 2q◂ VT to predispose; (*con prejuicios*) to prejudice, bias (**contra** against)

predisposición SF (= *tendencia*) predisposition; (= *prejuicio*) prejudice, bias (**contra** against); (*Med*) tendency, predisposition (**a** to)

predispuesto ADJ predisposed; **ser ~ a los catarros** to have a tendency to get colds; **es ~ al abatimiento** he tends to get depressed; **estar ~ contra algn** to be prejudiced against sb

predocumento SM draft, preliminary paper

predominante ADJ [1] (= *preponderante*) [*papel, poder*] predominant; [*opinión, ideología, viento*] prevailing
[2] (*Com*) [*interés*] controlling

predominantemente ADV predominantly

predominar ▸conjug 1a◂ Ⓐ VI [*papel, poder*] to predominate, dominate; [*opinión, ideología, viento*] to prevail
Ⓑ VT to dominate, predominate over

predominio SM predominance

preelectoral ADJ pre-election *antes de s*; **sondeo ~** pre-election survey

preeminencia SF pre-eminence

preeminente ADJ pre-eminent

preeminentemente ADV pre-eminently

preempción SF pre-emption

preenfriar ▸conjug 1c◂ VT to precool

preescoger ▸conjug 2c◂ VT [+ *jugadores*] to seed

preescolar Ⓐ ADJ preschool; **educación ~** preschool education, nursery education
Ⓑ SM (= *escuela*) nursery school, nursery
Ⓒ SMF (= *niño*) child of nursery school age

preestablecido ADJ pre-established

preestrenar ▸conjug 1a◂ VT to preview, give a preview of

preestreno SM preview, press view

preexistencia SF pre-existence

preexistente ADJ pre-existing, pre-existent

preexistir ▸conjug 3a◂ VI to pre-exist, exist before

prefabricado Ⓐ ADJ prefabricated
Ⓑ SM prefabricated building, prefab*

prefabricar ▸conjug 1g◂ VT to prefabricate

prefacio SM preface, foreword

prefecto SM prefect

prefectura SF prefecture

▼ **preferencia** SF [1] (= *prioridad*) preference; **tendrán ~ los que no lleguen al salario mínimo** preference will be given to those earning less than the minimum wage; **tienen ~ los vehículos que circulan por la derecha** vehicles coming from the right have priority; **localidad de ~** reserved seat; **tratamiento de ~** preferential treatment
[2] (= *predilección*) preference; **no tengo ninguna ~** I have no preference; **tiene una clara ~ por la hija mayor** he has a clear preference for his eldest daughter, his eldest daughter is his clear favourite

PREFERIR

Más verbo

• Cuando se habla de generalizaciones, **preferir** + **INFINITIVO** se traduce por **prefer** + **-ING**:
Prefiero nadar a correr
I prefer swimming to running
Juan siempre prefería leer a trabajar
Juan always preferred reading to working
• Cuando se habla de lo que se quiere hacer en una ocasión determinada, **prefiero/preferiría** se traducen por **would rather** + **INFINITIVO** *sin* **to** o, en un contexto más formal, por **would prefer** + **INFINITIVO** *con* **to**:
—¿Vamos al cine? —Preferiría quedarme en casa
"Shall we go to the cinema?" — "I'd rather stay *o* ***I'd prefer to stay at home"***
Prefiero quedarme en un hotel a alquilar un apartamento
I'd rather stay in a hotel than rent an apartment, I'd prefer to stay in a hotel rather than rent an apartment
NOTA: Como se puede ver en el ejemplo anterior, **would prefer to** se usa en correlación con **rather than** + **INFINITIVO** *sin* **to** y nunca con **than** solo.
• Cuando se trata de traducir estructuras como **preferiría que + ORACIÓN SUBORDINADA**, en inglés se emplea la siguiente estructura: **SUJETO DE LA ORACIÓN PRINCIPAL** + **would rather** + **SUJETO** + **VERBO EN PASADO**:
Preferiría que él me llamara
I'd rather he phoned me
—¿Te importa que hable con ella? —Preferiría que no lo hicieras
"Do you mind if I talk to her?" — "I'd rather you didn't"
NOTA: Otra posibilidad de expresar esta construcción en inglés sería: **would prefer it if** + **RESTO DE LA ORACIÓN** o **would prefer** + **OBJETO** + **CONSTRUCCIÓN DE INFINITIVO**:
Preferiría que él me llamara
I'd prefer it if he phoned me *o* ***I'd prefer him to phone me***
Para otros usos y ejemplos ver la entrada.

➤ LENGUA Y USO: **preferencia 2** 34.5

preferencial ADJ preferential

preferente ADJ 1 [*trato*] (= *especial*) preferential; (= *prioritario*) priority *antes de s*; [*lugar*] prominent; [*derecho*] prior; (*Fin*) [*acción*] preference *antes de s*
2 **clase ~** (*Aer*) club class

preferentemente ADV preferably

preferible ADJ preferable (**a** to)

preferiblemente ADV preferably

▼**preferido/a** Ⓐ ADJ favourite, favorite (*EEUU*); **es mi cantante ~** he's my favourite singer
Ⓑ SM/F favourite, favorite (*EEUU*); **yo era la preferida de mi madre** I was my mother's favourite

▼**preferir** ▸conjug 3i◂ VT to prefer; **~ el té al café** to prefer tea to coffee; **¿cuál prefieres?** which do you prefer?; **¿qué prefieres (tomar)?** what will you have?; **prefiero ir a pie** I prefer to walk, I'd rather walk

prefiguración SF foreshadowing, prefiguration

prefigurar ▸conjug 1a◂ VT to foreshadow, prefigure

prefijar ▸conjug 1a◂ VT 1 (= *predeterminar*) to fix beforehand, prearrange
2 (*Ling*) to prefix (**a** to)

▼**prefijo** SM 1 (*Ling*) prefix
2 (*Telec*) (dialling) code, STD code, area code (*EEUU*)

pregón SM (= *proclama*) proclamation, announcement (*by town crier*); (*Com*) street cry, vendor's cry ► **pregón de las fiestas** local festival opening speech

pregonar ▸conjug 1a◂ VT [+ *inocencia propia, interés*] to proclaim, announce; [+ *secreto*] to disclose, reveal; [+ *mercancía*] to hawk; [+ *méritos*] to proclaim (for all to hear); **no estaría bien que lo fueras pregonando por ahí** you shouldn't go spreading it around

pregonero/a SM/F 1 (*municipal*) town crier
2 [*de fiestas*] person who makes the opening speech
3 (*Méx*) (= *subastador*) auctioneer

pregrabado ADJ pre-recorded

pregrabar ▸conjug 1a◂ VT to pre-record

preguerra SF prewar period; **el nivel de la ~** the prewar level; **en la ~** in the prewar period, before the war

pregunta SF question; **contestar a una ~** to answer a question; **hacer una ~** to ask *o* put a question; **acosar a algn a ~s** to bombard sb with questions; **lo negó, a ~s de los periodistas** questioned by the press he denied it; **presentar una ~** (*Pol*) to put down a question, table a question; **"preguntas frecuentes"** "FAQs", "frequently asked questions"; ✦*MODISMO* **andar** *o* **estar a la cuarta ~** (*Esp**) to be broke* ► **pregunta capciosa** trick question ► **pregunta de elección múltiple** multiple-choice question ► **pregunta indiscreta** indiscreet question, tactless question ► **pregunta retórica** rhetorical question ► **pregunta sugestiva** (*Jur*) leading question ► **pregunta tipo test** multiple-choice question

preguntar ▸conjug 1a◂ Ⓐ VT to ask; **~ algo a algn** to ask sb sth; **siempre me preguntas lo mismo** you're always asking me the same question; **le pregunté la hora** I asked him the time; **pregúntale cómo se llama** ask her what her name is; **pregúntale si quiere venir** ask him if he wants to come, ask him whether he wants to come or not; **le fue preguntada su edad** (*frm*) he was asked his age
Ⓑ VI to ask, inquire; **~ por algn: si te preguntan por mí di que no he llegado** if they ask about me, tell them I haven't arrived; **cuando la vi ayer me preguntó por ti** she asked after you when I saw her yesterday; **hay alguien al teléfono que pregunta por el jefe** there's someone on the phone asking for the boss; **~ por la salud de algn** to ask after sb's health
Ⓒ **preguntarse** VPR to wonder; **me pregunto si vale la pena** I wonder if it's worthwhile

preguntón* ADJ inquisitive

prehispánico ADJ pre-Hispanic

prehistoria SF prehistory

prehistórico ADJ prehistoric

preignición SF pre-ignition

preimpositivo ADJ **beneficios ~s** pre-tax profits, profits before tax

preinforme SM preliminary report

preinscripción SF (*para cursar estudios*) pre-enrolment, pre-enrollment (*EEUU*); (*para congreso, cursillo*) provisional booking

preinstalación SF **~ de radio** radio fitted as standard; **~ de aire acondicionado** air conditioning pre-installed

preinstalado ADJ [*software*] pre-installed

prejubilación SF early retirement

prejubilado/a SM/F person who takes early retirement

prejuiciado ADJ (*LAm*) prejudiced (**contra** against)

prejuicio SM 1 (= *parcialidad*) prejudice, bias (**contra** against); **no tienen ~s contra los españoles** they are not prejudiced against Spaniards
2 (= *idea preconcebida*) preconception
3 (= *acto*) prejudgement

prejuzgar ▸conjug 1h◂ VT to prejudge

prelación SF precedence, priority; **tener ~ sobre algo** to have precedence *o* priority over sth

prelado SM prelate

prelatura SF prelature ► **prelatura personal** personal prelature

prelavado SM prewash

preliminar Ⓐ ADJ [*estudio, resultado*] preliminary; (*Dep*) **fase ~** qualifying round(s)
Ⓑ SM preliminary

preludiar ▸conjug 1b◂ Ⓐ VT to herald; **el calor que preludia la primavera** the warmth that heralds the coming of spring
Ⓑ VI (*Mús*) [*cantante*] to warm up; [*pianista*] to play a few scales; [*orquesta*] to tune up

preludio SM 1 (*Mús*) (= *comienzo*) prelude (**de** to); (= *ensayo*) warm-up
2 (= *comienzo*) prelude

premamá ADJ **vestido (de) ~** maternity dress

premarital ADJ premarital

prematrimonial ADJ premarital, before marriage; *ver tb* **relación 6**

prematuramente ADV prematurely

prematuro/a Ⓐ ADJ premature; **es ~ hablar de detalles** it's too early to talk about details, it would be rather premature to talk about details
Ⓑ SM/F premature baby

premedicación SF premedication

premeditación SF premeditation; **con ~** with premeditation, deliberately

premeditadamente ADV with premeditation, deliberately

premeditado ADJ [*acto, crimen, tiro*] premeditated; [*ironía*] deliberate; [*negligencia*] wilful; [*insulto*] calculated

premeditar ▸conjug 1a◂ VT (= *pensar*) to premeditate, think out (in advance); (= *planear*) [+ *crimen*] to premeditate, plan

premenstrual ADJ premenstrual; *ver tb* **síndrome**

premiado/a Ⓐ ADJ [*novela*] prizewinning; [*número, boleto*] winning; **tu billete resultó** *o* **salió ~ con 60 millones** your ticket won 60 million Ⓑ SM/F prizewinner

premiar ▸conjug 1b◂ VT 1 (= *dar un premio a*) to award a prize to; **el jurado ha premiado la película italiana** the jury awarded a prize to the Italian film; **fue premiado el director italiano** the Italian director received an award; **han premiado el documental** the documentary won an award
2 (= *recompensar*) to reward (**con** with); **han premiado su esfuerzo con un aumento de sueldo** they rewarded his efforts with a pay rise

premier [pre'mjer] SMF prime minister, premier

premiere [pre'mjer] SF premiere

premio Ⓐ SM 1 (*en competición*) prize; **Gran Premio de Fórmula Uno** Formula One Grand Prix; **llevarse un ~** to get a prize ► **premio de consolación** consolation prize ► **premio de fin de carrera** final-year prize ► **premio en metálico** cash prize ► **premio extraordinario** (*Univ*) award with special distinction ► **premio gordo** jackpot
2 (= *recompensa*) reward; **como ~ a sus servicios** as a reward for her services
3 (*Com, Fin*) (= *prima*) premium; **a ~** at a premium
Ⓑ SMF (= *persona galardonada*) **una entrevista con la ~ Nobel de la Paz** an interview with the winner of the Nobel Peace Prize; **intervendrá en el debate el actual ~ Cervantes** the current Cervantes Prize winner will take place in the debate

premioso ADJ 1 (= *apremiante*) pressing, urgent
2 [*orden*] strict
3 [*persona*] (*al hablar*) reticent, shy of speaking; (*al escribir*) slow (in writing); (*al moverse*) slow, awkward
4 [*estilo*] laboured, labored (*EEUU*)
5 [*vestido*] tight

premisa SF premise

premonición SF premonition

premonitoriamente ADV as a warning

premonitorio ADJ premonitory (*frm*), warning *antes de s*

premunirse ▸conjug 3a◂ VPR (*LAm*) = **precaver B**

premura SF 1 (= *prisa*) haste, urgency
2 (= *aprieto*) pressure; **con ~ de tiempo** under pressure of time, with very little time; **debido a ~ de espacio** because of pressure on space

prenatal ADJ antenatal, prenatal

prenavideño ADJ before Christmas, pre-Christmas *antes de s*

➤ LENGUA Y USO: **preferido A** 34.1, 34.3 **preferir** 34.1, 34.4, 35.5, 36.3 **prefijo** 27

prenda SF [1] (*tb* ~ **de vestir**) garment, article of clothing ► **prenda interior** undergarment, piece of underwear; **~s interiores** underwear *sing* ► **prendas de cama** bedclothes ► **prendas deportivas** sportswear *sing* ► **prendas de mesa** table linen *sing* ► **prendas de punto** knitwear *sing* ► **prendas de trabajo** work clothes
[2] (= *garantía*) pledge; **dejar algo en ~** (*por dinero*) to pawn sth; (*como garantía*) to leave sth as security; **en** *o* **como ~ de algo** as a token of sth; ✦*MODISMOS* **no soltar ~** to give nothing away; **no dolerle prendas a algn: a mí no me duelen ~s** I don't mind saying nice things about others, it doesn't worry me that I'm not as good as others; ✦*REFRÁN* **al buen pagador no le duelen ~s** a good payer is not afraid of giving guarantees
[3] **prendas** (= *cualidades*) talents, gifts; **buenas ~s** good qualities; **de todas ~s** first class, excellent
[4] (= *juego*) forfeit; **pagar ~** to pay a forfeit
[5] (*) (*en oración directa*) darling; **¡oye, ~!** hi, gorgeous!*
[6] **la ~** (*Cono Sur*) one's sweetheart, one's lover

prendar ▸conjug 1a◂ Ⓐ VT [1] [+ *persona*] (= *cautivar*) to captivate, enchant; (= *ganar la voluntad de*) to win over; **volvió prendado de la ciudad** by the time he came back he had fallen in love with the town
[2] (*Méx*) (= *empeñar*) to pawn
Ⓑ **prendarse** VPR **~se de algo** to be captivated by sth, be enchanted with sth; **~se de algn** to fall in love with sb

prendedera SF (*Andes*) waitress

prendedero SM, **prendedor** SM clasp, brooch, broach (*EEUU*)

prender ▸conjug 2a◂ Ⓐ VT [1] [+ *persona*] (= *capturar*) to catch, capture; (= *detener*) to arrest
[2] (*Cos*) (= *sujetar*) to fasten; (*con alfiler*) to pin, attach (**en** to); **~ el pelo con horquillas** to pin one's hair with grips
[3] (= *atar*) to tie, do up
[4] (*esp LAm*) [+ *fuego, horno, vela, cigarrillo*] to light; [+ *cerilla*] to strike; [+ *luz, TV*] to switch on; [+ *cuarto*] to light up
Ⓑ VI [1] [*fuego*] to catch; **sus ideas prendieron fácilmente en la juventud** his ideas soon caught on with the young
[2] (= *engancharse*) to catch, stick; **el ancla prendió en el fondo** the anchor buried itself in the seabed
[3] [*planta*] to take, take root
[4] [*vacuna*] to take
Ⓒ **prenderse** VPR [1] (= *encenderse*) to catch fire
[2] [*mujer*] to dress up
[3] (*Caribe*) (= *emborracharse*) to get drunk

prendería† SF [*de cosas usadas*] secondhand (clothes) shop; [*de baratijas*] junkshop; [*de empeños*] pawnbroker's (shop)

prendero/a† SM/F [1] [*de cosas usadas*] secondhand (clothes) dealer, junk dealer
[2] (= *prestamista*) pawnbroker

prendido Ⓐ ADJ [1] **quedar ~** (= *enganchado*) to be caught (fast), be stuck; (= *cautivado*) to be captivated
[2] (*Cono Sur Med*) constipated
[3] (*Méx*) (= *vestido*) dressed up
Ⓑ SM (= *adorno*) clip, brooch

prendimiento SM [1] (= *captura*) (*gen*) capture; [*de droga, contrabando*] seizure
[2] (= *detención*) arrest
[3] (*Cono Sur Med*) constipation

prensa SF [1] (= *publicaciones*) **la ~** the press, the (news)papers; **leer la ~** to read the (news)papers; **salir en la ~** to appear in the press *o* (news)papers; **tener mala ~** to have *o* get a bad press ► **la prensa amarilla** the gutter press ► **prensa del corazón** *periodicals specializing in real-life romance stories*
[2] (= *máquina*) (*Mec, Dep*) press; (*Tip*) printing press; [*de raqueta*] press; **aprobar un libro para la ~** to pass a book for the printers; **dar algo a la ~** to send sth to the printers; **entrar en ~** to go to press; **estar en ~** to be at the printers; **"libros en ~"** "forthcoming titles"

> **PRENSA DEL CORAZÓN**
>
> *The* **prensa del corazón** *is the generic term given in Spain to weekly or fortnightly magazines specializing in society gossip and the social lives of the rich and famous. The pioneer was* **¡Hola!** *which first appeared in 1944 (***Hello!** *magazine is the English-language version), while other popular titles include* **Pronto**, **Lecturas**, **Semana** *and* **Diez Minutos**. *They constitute a highly profitable sector of the market, occupying six of the top ten places in magazine sales.*

prensaajos SM INV garlic press

prensado Ⓐ ADJ compressed
Ⓑ SM [1] (= *acto*) pressing
[2] (= *lustre*) sheen, shine, gloss

prensador SM press, pressing machine ► **prensador de paja** straw baler

prensaestopas SM INV (*Náut*) stuffing box

prensaje SM (*Mús*) recording

prensalimones SM INV lemon-squeezer

prensar ▸conjug 1a◂ VT to press

prensil ADJ prehensile

preñado Ⓐ ADJ [1] [*mujer, animal*] pregnant; **está preñada de seis meses** she's six months pregnant
[2] **~ de algo** pregnant with sth, full of sth; **una situación preñada de peligros** a situation fraught with danger; **ojos ~s de lágrimas** eyes brimming with tears
[3] [*muro*] bulging, sagging
Ⓑ SM (= *embarazo*) pregnancy

preñar ▸conjug 1a◂ VT [1] (= *dejar embarazada*) to get pregnant; (*Zool*) to impregnate, fertilize
[2] (= *llenar*) to fill

preñez SF pregnancy

preocupación SF [1] (= *inquietud*) worry, concern; (= *miedo*) fear; **tiene la ~ de que su mujer le es infiel** he is worried that his wife is unfaithful to him
[2] (*LAm*) (= *preferencia*) special consideration, priority, preference

preocupado ADJ worried, concerned (**por** about)

preocupante ADJ worrying

preocupar ▸conjug 1a◂ Ⓐ VT (= *inquietar*) to worry; (= *molestar*) to bother; **esto me preocupa muchísimo** I'm extremely worried about this, this worries me very much; **me preocupa cómo decírselo** I'm worried about how to tell him; **no le preocupa el qué dirán** he's not bothered about what people may say
Ⓑ **preocuparse** VPR [1] (= *inquietarse*) to worry (**de, por** about); **¡no se preocupe!** (*para calmar a algn*) don't worry!; (*para que algn no haga algo*) don't bother!; **no te preocupes por eso** don't worry about that; **no se preocupa en lo más mínimo** he doesn't care in the least
[2] (= *ocuparse*) to concern o.s. (**de** about); **tú preocúpate de que todo esté listo** you see to it that everything is ready
[3] (= *dar prioridad*) **~se de algo** to give special attention to sth, give sth priority

preolímpico/a Ⓐ ADJ **torneo ~** Olympic qualifying tournament
Ⓑ SM (= *competición*) Olympic qualifying tournament *o* round
Ⓒ SM/F (= *clasificado*) Olympic qualifier; (= *participante*) *athlete etc taking part in an Olympic qualifying tournament*

preoperatorio Ⓐ ADJ pre-operative, pre-op*
Ⓑ SM pre-operative period

prepago SM prepayment; **tarjeta de ~** prepayment card

preparación SF [1] (= *realización*) preparation; **tiempo de ~: 30 minutos** preparation time: 30 minutes; **un plato de fácil ~** an easy dish to make; **estar en ~** to be in preparation; **tengo varios libros en ~** I have several books in preparation
[2] (*antes de hacer algo*) **¿cuánto tiempo dedicas a la ~ de un examen?** how long do you spend studying for *o* preparing an exam?; **la ~ de las vacaciones me llevó varias semanas** it took me weeks to prepare for the holidays; **clases de ~ al parto** ante-natal classes ► **preparación de datos** data preparation
[3] (= *formación*) (*de estudios*) education; (*profesional*) training; **salió de la universidad con una buena ~** he left university with a good education; **buscamos a alguien con una buena ~ informática** we're looking for someone with good computer training *o* with a good training in computers ► **preparación física** (= *entrenamiento*) training; (= *estado*) physical condition
[4] (*tb* **estado de ~**) preparedness, readiness; **~ militar** military preparedness
[5] (*Farm*) preparation

preparado Ⓐ ADJ [1] (= *dispuesto*) [*persona*] prepared, ready; **—¿te vas a presentar al examen? —no, todavía no estoy ~** "are you going to take the exam?" — "no, I'm not prepared *o* ready yet"; **¡~s, listos, ya!** (*gen*) ready, steady, go!; (*Dep*) on your marks, get set, go!; **no estoy ~ mentalmente para la entrevista** I am not mentally prepared for the interview
[2] (*Culin*) (= *listo para servir*) ready to serve; (= *precocinado*) ready cooked; *ver tb* **comida 1**
[3] (*Educ*) (*con estudios*) educated; (*profesional*) trained; (*con título*) qualified; **está muy bien ~ para este trabajo** he's very well trained for this job; **un candidato muy ~** a highly-qualified candidate
[4] (= *informado*) well-informed
Ⓑ SM (*Farm*) preparation

preparador(a) SM/F [1] (= *instructor*) [*de deportista*] trainer, coach; [*de opositor*] private tutor ► **preparador(a) físico/a** fitness trainer

2 [*de caballo*] trainer
3 (*en laboratorio*) assistant

preparar ▸conjug 1a◂ Ⓐ VT 1 (= *dejar listo*) [+ *comida*] to make, prepare; [+ *habitación, casa*] to prepare, get ready; [+ *compuesto, derivado*] (*Quím*) to prepare, make up; **estoy preparando la cena** I'm making *o* preparing dinner, I'm getting dinner ready; **¿te preparo un café?** shall I make you a coffee?; **¿me puedes ~ la cuenta, por favor?** can you make my bill up, please?; *ver tb* **terreno B4**
2 (= *organizar*) [+ *acción, viaje*] to prepare; [+ *ejemplar, revista*] to prepare, work on; **tardaron semanas en ~ el atraco** it took them weeks to set up *o* prepare the robbery; **tengo una sorpresa preparada para ti** I've got a surprise for you; **estamos preparando el siguiente número de la revista** we're working on *o* preparing the next issue of the magazine
3 (= *instruir*) (*para un partido*) to train, coach; (*para examen, oposición*) to coach, tutor; **lleva meses preparando al equipo** he has been training *o* coaching the team for months; **la están preparando en una academia** they are preparing *o* coaching her in a private school, she is being tutored in a private school; **~ a algn en algo** to coach sb in sth; **busco a alguien que me prepare en inglés** I'm looking for someone to coach me in English
4 [+ *examen, prueba*] to study for, prepare for; **llevo semanas preparando este examen** I have been studying *o* preparing for this exam for weeks
Ⓑ **prepararse** VPR 1 (= *disponerse*) to get ready; **venga, prepárate, que nos vamos** come on, get ready, we're going; **~se a hacer algo** to get ready to do sth; **se preparaba a salir de casa cuando sonó el teléfono** he was just about *o* getting ready to leave the house when the telephone rang; **prepárate a oír esto** get ready for this; **~se para** to get ready for, prepare for; **nos estamos preparando para las vacaciones** we are getting ready *o* preparing for the holidays
2 (= *estudiar*) [+ *discurso*] to prepare; [+ *examen*] to prepare for, study for; **lleva todo el día preparándose el discurso** she has been preparing her speech all day; **no me había preparado bien el examen** I hadn't done enough preparation for the exam, I hadn't prepared *o* studied properly for the exam
3 (= *formarse*) to prepare; **se están preparando para la prueba de acceso a la universidad** they are preparing for the university entrance exam; **me estoy preparando para el campeonato nacional** I'm preparing for the national championship
4 (= *aproximarse*) [*problemas, tormenta*] to loom; **vimos como se preparaba la tormenta** we saw how the storm was brewing *o* looming; **se prepara una reestructuración ministerial** a cabinet reshuffle is imminent *o* afoot *o* looming

preparativo Ⓐ ADJ preparatory, preliminary
Ⓑ **preparativos** SMPL preparations; **los ~s para la conferencia** the preparations for the conference; **hacer sus ~s** to make one's preparations, prepare

preparatoria SF (*CAm, Méx*) (= *colegio*) secondary school, high school (*EEUU*)

preparatorio ADJ [*curso, trabajo, material*] preparatory; [*diseño, dibujo, boceto*] preliminary; **ejercicios ~s** preliminary exercises, warm-up exercises

pre-Pirineo SM Pyrenean foothills

preponderancia SF (= *predominio*) preponderance; (= *superioridad*) superiority; **sus propuestas tienen ~ sobre las mías** his proposals carry more weight than mine

preponderante ADJ 1 (= *predominante*) predominant, preponderant (*frm*)
2 (= *superior*) superior

preponderar ▸conjug 1a◂ VI 1 (= *predominar*) to predominate, preponderate (*frm*)
2 (= *prevalecer*) to dominate, prevail

preponente ADJ (*Andes*) arrogant, self-important, conceited

preponer ▸conjug 2q◂ VT to place before

preposición SF preposition

preposicional ADJ prepositional

prepósito SM superior

prepotencia SF 1 (= *arrogancia*) high-handedness; **el incidente fue un ejemplo más de su ~** the incident was yet another example of his high-handedness; **nunca me habían tratado con tanta ~** I had never been treated in such a high-handed manner *o* with such arrogance
2 (= *poder*) power; **su ~ en el Congreso es absoluta** he has absolute power in Congress

prepotente ADJ 1 (= *arrogante*) high-handed; **actitud ~** high-handed attitude; **un ministro fatuo y ~** a conceited and arrogant minister
2 (= *poderoso*) powerful

preproducción SF pre-production

prepucio SM foreskin, prepuce (*frm*)

prerrequisito SM prerequisite

prerrogativa SF prerogative

prerrománico ADJ pre-romanesque

presa SF 1 (= *animal apresado*) (*por cazador*) catch; (*por otro animal*) prey; **ave de ~** bird of prey; **huyó ~ del pánico** he fled in panic; **hacer ~ en algo**: **la desesperación hizo ~ en los soldados** the soldiers were seized with despair; **ser ~ de algo** to be a prey to sth; **los ancianos son ~ fácil de los vendedores sin escrúpulos** old people are easy prey for unscrupulous salesmen
2 (*en un río*) (= *dique*) dam; (= *represa*) weir, barrage
3 (*Mil*) (= *botín*) spoils *pl*, booty; (*Náut*) prize
4 (*Agr*) ditch, channel
5 (= *colmillo*) tusk, fang; (*Orn*) claw
6 (*esp LAm*) [*de carne*] piece (of meat)

presagiador ADJ ominous

presagiar ▸conjug 1b◂ VT to betoken, forebode, presage

presagio SM omen, portent

presbicia SF long-sightedness

presbiopía SF presbyopia

présbita ADJ, **présbite** ADJ long-sighted

presbiteriano/a ADJ, SM/F Presbyterian

presbiterio SM presbytery, chancel

presbítero/a SM/F priest

presciencia SF prescience, foreknowledge

presciente ADJ prescient

prescindencia SF (*LAm*) (= *privación*) doing without, going without; (= *abstención*) non-participation, abstention

prescindente ADJ (*LAm*) non-participating

prescindible ADJ dispensable; **y cosas fácilmente ~s** and things we can easily do without

prescindir ▸conjug 3a◂ VI **~ de** 1 (= *renunciar a*) to do without, go without; **no puede ~ de su secretaria** he can't do without his secretary; **han prescindido del coche** they've given up their car
2 (= *ignorar*) to disregard; **no deberían ~ de su opinión** they shouldn't disregard *o* ignore her opinion
3 (= *omitir*) to dispense with; **prescindamos de los detalles inútiles** let's dispense with *o* skip the unnecessary details

prescribir ▸conjug 3a◂ (*pp* **prescrito**) Ⓐ VT to prescribe
Ⓑ VI [*plazo*] to expire, run out

prescripción SF 1 (*Med*) prescription ▸ **prescripción facultativa**, **prescripción médica** medical prescription; **por ~ facultativa** on the doctor's orders
2 (*Méx Jur*) legal principle

prescriptivo ADJ prescriptive

prescripto ADJ (*Arg*) prescribed

prescrito ADJ prescribed

presea SF 1 (*liter*) (= *joya*) jewel, gem; (= *cosa preciada*) treasure, precious thing
2 (*LAm*) (= *premio*) prize

preselección SF 1 (*Dep*) (= *acción*) seeding; (= *equipo*) squad, team
2 [*de candidatos, participantes*] shortlist, shortlisting; **hacer una ~** to draw up a shortlist

preseleccionado/a SM/F (*Dep*) squad member, member of the squad; (*en candidatura*) short-listed candidate; (*en concurso*) short-listed entry

preseleccionar ▸conjug 1a◂ VT 1 [+ *candidatos*] to shortlist
2 (*Dep*) to seed

presencia SF 1 (*al estar*) presence; **en ~ de algn** in the presence of sb, in sb's presence; **estamos en ~ de un gran escritor** we have here a great writer
2 (= *aspecto*) appearance; **buena ~** smart appearance; **tener buena ~** to look smart ▸ **presencia de ánimo** presence of mind

presencial ADJ **testigo ~** eyewitness

presenciar ▸conjug 1b◂ VT (= *asistir a*) to be present at, attend; (= *ver*) to witness, see

presentable ADJ presentable

presentación SF 1 (*entre personas*) introduction; **tras las oportunas presentaciones** after the appropriate introductions; *ver tb* **carta 1**, **tarjeta**
2 (= *introducción*) [*de personaje, proyecto*] presentation; [*de producto*] launch, presentation; [*de campaña*] launch; **el cantante llevó a cabo la ~ del acto** the singer presented *o* hosted the event; **texto de ~** introduction ▸ **presentación de modelos** fashion parade, fashion show ▸ **presentación editorial** (*dentro del libro*) publisher's foreword; (*en contraportada*) publisher's blurb ▸ **presentación en público** first public appearance, debut ▸ **presentación en sociedad** coming out, debut
3 (= *concurrencia*) **tras su ~ al concurso** after entering the competition; **¿cuáles son los motivos de su ~ a las elecciones?** what are your reasons for standing in these elections?

4 (= *llegada*) turning up; **su ~ en mitad de la reunión** her turning up in the middle of the meeting; **no entendemos el por qué de su ~ sin avisar** we don't understand why he turned up unannounced

5 (= *entrega*) submission; **la fecha de ~ del escrito** the date the document was submitted, the submission date of the document; **la ~ del trabajo tendrá que hacerse antes del día 31** the work must be submitted before the 31st; **el plazo de ~ de solicitudes está ya cerrado** applications are no longer being accepted, the closing date for applications is now past

6 (= *muestra*) presentation; **previa ~ de su carné de socio** on presentation of your membership card; **se requiere la ~ de la invitación** invitations must be presented *o* shown on request

7 (= *aspecto*) [*de persona*] appearance; [*de comida, producto, trabajo*] presentation; **se requiere buena ~ a los candidatos** candidates must be of good appearance

8 (*Chile*) (= *solicitud*) petition

presentador(a) SM/F 1 [*de acto*] host/hostess, presenter

2 (*TV, Radio*) [*de debate, documental, informativo*] presenter; [*de programa de variedades, concurso*] host/hostess, presenter

presentar ▸conjug 1a◂ Ⓐ VT 1 (= *enseñar, exponer*) (*gen*) to present; [+ *moción, candidato*] to propose, put forward; [+ *pruebas, informe*] to submit; [+ *documento, pasaporte*] to show; **~ una propuesta** to make *o* present a proposal; **~ algo al cobro** *o* **al pago** (*Com*) to present sth for payment

2 (= *entregar*) to hand in; **mañana tengo que ~ un trabajo** I have to hand in an essay tomorrow; **presentó la dimisión** he handed in his resignation, he resigned

3 (= *mostrar*) [+ *señal, síntoma*] to show; **presenta señales de deterioro** it is showing signs of wear

4 (= *exponer al público*) [+ *producto, disco, libro*] to launch; **presentó su obra en la Galería Mons** she showed her work at the Galería Mons

5 (*en espectáculo*) [+ *obra*] to perform; [+ *actor, actriz*] to present, feature; **el grupo presentó una obra en un solo acto** the group performed a one-act play

6 (= *ser presentador de*) [+ *programa televisivo*] to present, host; **J. Pérez presenta el programa** the programme is presented *o* hosted by J. Pérez; **¿quién presenta ahora las noticias de las nueve?** who presents *o* reads the nine o'clock news now?

7 (= *tener*) to have; **este año el examen presenta novedades** this year the exam has some new features; **el ferrocarril presenta ventajas evidentes** the train offers *o* has obvious advantages; **el cadáver presentaba varios impactos de bala** the body had several bullet wounds; **el coche presenta ciertas modificaciones** the car has had certain changes made to it

8 [+ *persona*] to introduce; **me presentó a sus padres** he introduced me to his parents; **permítanme ~les a don Narciso Gómez** allow me to introduce Mr Narciso Gómez (to you); **te presento a Carlos** this is Carlos; **a ver si te presento a mi amiga Jacinta** you must meet my friend Jacinta, I must introduce you to my friend Jacinta; **ser presentada en sociedad** to come out, make one's début

9 (= *ofrecer*) [+ *disculpa*] to offer, make; **presentó sus respetos** she paid her respects; **le presento mis consideraciones** (*en carta*) yours faithfully

10 (*Mil*) **~ armas** to present arms; **~ batalla** (*lit*) to draw up in battle array; (*fig*) to offer resistance

Ⓑ **presentarse** VPR 1 (= *aparecer*) to turn up; **se ~on sin avisar** they turned up unexpectedly; **se presentó en un estado lamentable** he turned up in a dreadful state

2 (= *comparecer*) **el atracador se presentó a la policía** the robber gave himself up to the police; **tengo que ~me ante el juez** I have to appear before the judge; **tendrá que ~se ante el juez cada semana** he'll have to report to the judge once a week; **hay que ~se el lunes por la mañana en la oficina del paro** we have to go to the Job Centre on Monday morning; **~se voluntario** to volunteer

3 (= *hacerse conocer*) to introduce o.s. (**a** to); **antes de nada, me voy a ~** first of all, let me introduce myself

4 [*candidato*] to run, stand; **~se a** [+ *puesto*] to apply for; [+ *examen*] to sit, enter for; [+ *concurso*] to enter; **he decidido no ~me a las elecciones** I've decided not to stand *o* run in the elections

5 (= *surgir*) [*problema*] to arise, come up; [*oportunidad*] to present itself, arise; **se presentó un caso singular** a strange case came up; **el futuro no se presenta optimista** the future isn't looking too good; **el día se presenta muy hermoso** it looks like it's going to be a lovely day

presente Ⓐ ADJ 1 (*en el espacio*) **el objeto del ~ trabajo** the purpose of this essay; **los firmantes del ~ escrito** we the undersigned; **el público ~** those present in the audience; **según uno de los testigos ~s** according to one of the witnesses; **—¡Miguel García! —¡presente!** "Miguel García!" — "here!"; **un problema siempre ~** an ever-present problem; estar **~** to be present; **¿estabas tú ~ en esa reunión?** were you present at that meeting?; **la mezcla de estilos está siempre ~ en sus películas** the mixing of styles is a permanent feature in his films; **esa posibilidad está siempre ~** there is always that possibility, that possibility always exists; hacerse **~** to manifest o.s.; **su espíritu se hizo ~ a través de la médium** his spirit manifested itself through the medium; tener **algo ~** to bear sth in mind; **hay que tener ~ esa posibilidad** we have to bear that possibility in mind; **te tendré ~ si me entero de algún trabajo** I will bear you in mind if I hear of any jobs; **siempre os tendré ~s en mis pensamientos** you will always be in my thoughts, I will never forget you; ✦*MODISMO* **mejorando lo ~** as you are yourself, just like you; **es muy buena actriz, mejorando lo ~** she's a very good actress, as you are yourself *o* just like you; *ver tb* **cuerpo 2**

2 (*en el tiempo*) [*año, mes, temporada*] current; [*momento*] present; **los acontecimientos ~s** current events; **en el ~ ejercicio fiscal** in the current tax year; **hasta el momento ~** up to the present time; **el día 28 del ~ mes** the 28th of this month

3 (*LAm*) (*en sobre*) **"presente"** "by hand"

Ⓑ SMF **los/las ~s** those present; **todos los allí ~s** all those present

Ⓒ SM 1 (*tb* **momento ~**) present; **hay que vivir el ~** you have to live in the present; **hasta el ~** up to the present

2 (*Ling*) present, present tense ▸ **presente de indicativo** present indicative ▸ **presente de subjuntivo** present subjunctive; *ver tb* **participio**

3 (= *regalo*) present, gift

Ⓓ SF (*frm*) **le comunico por la ~ que ...** I hereby inform you that ... (*frm*)

presentimiento SM premonition, presentiment; **tener un mal ~** to have a sense of foreboding

presentir ▸conjug 3i◂ VT to feel, be aware of; **presiento que ...** I have a feeling that ..., I feel that ...

preservación SF preservation, protection

preservante SM preservative

preservar ▸conjug 1a◂ VT 1 (= *proteger*) to protect, preserve (**contra** against; **de** from)

2 (*LAm*) (= *conservar*) to maintain, preserve

preservativo SM condom, contraceptive sheath (*frm*)

presi* SMF = **presidente**

presidencia SF 1 (= *gobierno*) [*de nación*] presidency; [*de comité*] chairmanship; **ocupar la ~ de** [+ *empresa*] to be the president of; [+ *comité*] to be the chairman of; **ocupar la ~ del gobierno** to be president; **España ocupa actualmente la ~ de la UE** Spain currently holds the presidency of the EU

2 **Presidencia** (= *oficina*) Prime Minister's office

presidenciable Ⓐ ADJ **ministro ~** minister who has the makings of a president

Ⓑ SMF possible candidate *o* contender for the presidency

presidencial ADJ presidential; **las (elecciones) ~es** the presidential elections

presidencialismo SM presidential rule

presidente/a SM/F (SF *tb* **presidente**) 1 (*Pol, Com*) [*de país, asociación*] president; [*de comité, reunión*] chair, chairperson, chairman/chairwoman; (*Esp Pol*) (*tb* **Presidente del Gobierno**) prime minister; [*de la cámara*] speaker; **candidato a ~** (*Pol*) presidential candidate; **es candidato a ~ de Cruz Roja/del Real Madrid** he is a candidate for the presidency of the Red Cross/he is a candidate to be chairman of the board of Real Madrid ▸ **presidente/a de honor** honorary president ▸ **presidente/a vitalicio/a** president for life

2 (*Jur*) (= *magistrado*) presiding magistrate; (= *juez*) presiding judge

3 (*LAm*) (= *alcalde*) mayor

PRESIDENTE DEL GOBIERNO

The head of the Spanish government, or **Presidente del Gobierno**, *is elected not just by the winning party but by the entire* **Congreso de los Diputados** *following a general election. The* **Presidente** *is appointed for a four-year term and called upon by the King to form a cabinet. As in Britain, he has the power to call an early election, and can be forced to do so by a censure motion in the* **Congreso**.

➤ LENGUA Y USO: **presentir** 33.2

presidiario/a SM/F convict

presidio SM 1 (= *cárcel*) prison, penitentiary (*EEUU*); **meter a algn en ~** to put sb in prison
2 (= *trabajos forzados*) hard labour, penal servitude
3 (*Pol*) praesidium, presidium
4 (*Mil*) (= *plaza fuerte*) garrison; (= *fortaleza*) fortress

presidir ▸conjug 3a◂ Ⓐ VT 1 (= *estar al frente de*) [+ *gobierno*] to preside over, be president of; [+ *reunión*] to chair, be chairman of
2 (= *dominar*) to dominate; **los temores presidieron la jornada de ayer** fear dominated *o* held sway the whole day yesterday; **la inoperancia y el recurso a medidas de emergencia presidieron su política** the predominant features of his policy were ineffectiveness and recourse to emergency measures
Ⓑ VI (*en gobierno*) to hold the presidency; (*en ceremonia*) to preside; (*en reunión*) to be the chair

presilla SF 1 (*para botón, corchete*) [*de hilo, tela*] loop; [*de metal*] eye
2 (= *cierre*) fastener, clip
3 (*LAm Mil*) shoulder badge, flash; (*Méx*) epaulette

presintonía SF presetting, preprogram(m)ing

presión SF 1 (*Meteo, Fís, Téc*) pressure; (*con la mano*) press, squeeze; **olla a ~** pressure cooker; **reactor de agua a ~** pressurized water reactor; **indicador/medidor de ~** pressure gauge; **tres atmósferas de ~** three atmospheres of pressure; **hacer ~ sobre algo** to press (on) sth ► **presión arterial** blood pressure ► **presión atmosférica** atmospheric pressure, air pressure ► **presión sanguínea** blood pressure
2 (= *influencia*) pressure; **ejercer** *o* **hacer ~ para que se haga algo** to press for sth to be done; (*Pol*) to lobby for sth to be done; **hay ~ dentro del partido** there are pressures within the party; **hacer algo bajo ~** to do sth under pressure ► **presión fiscal, presión impositiva** tax burden

presionar ▸conjug 1a◂ Ⓐ VT 1 [+ *botón, tecla*] to press
2 [+ *persona*] to pressure, pressurize, put pressure on; **~ a algn para que haga algo** to pressure *o* pressurize sb into doing sth, put pressure on sb to do sth; **el ministro, presionado por los fabricantes, accedió** the minister, under pressure from the manufacturers, agreed
Ⓑ VI to press; **~ para algo** to press for sth; **~ para que sea permitido algo** to press for sth to be allowed

preso/a Ⓐ ADJ **llevar ~ a algn** to take sb prisoner; **estuvo ~ durante tres años** he was in prison for three years; **la cárcel donde estuvo ~** the prison where he served his sentence; **estar ~ del pánico** to be panic-stricken; ✦*MODISMO* **~ por mil, ~ por mil quinientos** (*Esp*) in for a penny, in for a pound
Ⓑ SM/F (= *prisionero*) prisoner ► **preso/a común** ordinary prisoner ► **preso/a de conciencia** prisoner of conscience ► **preso/a de confianza** trusty ► **preso/a político/a** political prisoner ► **preso/a preventivo/a** remand prisoner

pressing ['presin] SM 1 (*Dep*) pressure
2 = **presión 2**

prestación SF 1 (= *subsidio*) benefit; (*Méx*) fringe benefit, perk* ► **prestación asistencial** social security benefit, welfare benefit (*EEUU*) ► **prestación por desempleo** unemployment benefit, unemployment compensation (*EEUU*) ► **prestación por jubilación** retirement benefit ► **prestaciones sociales** (= *dinero*) social security benefits; (= *servicios*) social services
2 (= *acción*) **se limitaron a la ~ de ayuda técnica** they limited themselves to giving technical aid; **le agradecemos la ~ de sus servicios** we are grateful for the services rendered ► **prestación de juramento** oath-taking, swearing in ► **prestación personal** obligatory service ► **prestaciones sanitarias** health services ► **prestación social sustitutoria** community service (*alternative to national service*)
3 (*Fin*) (= *préstamo*) lending, loan
4 **prestaciones** (*Téc, Inform*) features, facilities; (*Aut*) (= *equipamiento*) features; (= *rendimiento*) performance *sing*

PRESTACIÓN SOCIAL SUSTITUTORIA

The **Prestación Social Sustitutoria** (**PSS**) *is the non-military alternative to* **la mili** *for Spanish conscientious objectors. It involves a variety of largely unpaid community service ranging from social work to civil defence, to working on behalf of the local authority, the Red Cross or the Spanish equivalent of the Forestry Commission.*
⇨ *See also* MILI, INSUMISO

prestado ADJ (*gen*) borrowed; (*en biblioteca*) on loan; **llevaba un traje ~** he was wearing a borrowed suit; **de ~: fue a la boda de ~** he went to the wedding in borrowed clothes; **tuvo que vivir un tiempo de ~** he had to live at other people's expense for a while; **dejar algo ~** to lend sth; **pedir algo ~** (= *tomar prestado*) to borrow sth; (= *preguntar*) to ask to borrow sth; **tomar algo ~** to borrow sth

prestador(a) SM/F lender

prestamista SMF [*de dinero*] moneylender; [*de empeños*] pawnbroker

préstamo SM 1 (= *acción*) (*de prestar*) lending; (*de pedir prestado*) borrowing; **servicio de ~ de libros** book lending service; **buscamos una alternativa al ~ bancario** we are looking for an alternative to bank borrowing; **en ~** on loan ► **préstamo a domicilio** home lending ► **préstamo interbibliotecario** interlibrary loan
2 (= *dinero prestado*) loan; **necesitamos un ~ de cinco millones** we need a loan of five million; **conceder un ~** to grant a loan; **hacer un ~ a algn** to give sb a loan; **pedir un ~** to ask for a loan ► **préstamo bancario** bank loan ► **préstamo cobrable a la vista** call loan ► **préstamo colateral** collateral loan ► **préstamo con garantía** secured loan ► **préstamo hipotecario** mortgage (loan), real-estate loan (*EEUU*) ► **préstamo para la vivienda** home loan ► **préstamo personal** personal loan ► **préstamo pignoraticio** collateral loan ► **préstamo puente** bridging loan; *ver tb* **casa 8**
3 (*Ling*) loanword

prestancia SF (= *elegancia*) elegance, poise; (= *excelencia*) excellence, distinction

prestar ▸conjug 1a◂ Ⓐ VT 1 (= *dejar prestado*) to lend; **¿me puedes ~ el coche?** can I borrow your car?, can you lend me your car?; **prestó su imagen para un anuncio** he allowed his image to be used in an advertisement
2 (*LAm*) (= *pedir prestado*) to borrow (**a** from)
3 (= *dedicar*) [+ *esfuerzo*] to devote; [+ *apoyo, auxilio, ayuda*] to give; **le agradecemos los servicios prestados** we thank you for the services rendered; **la embajada también prestó su colaboración** the embassy also cooperated; **~ atención a algn/algo** to pay attention to sb/sth; **~ crédito a algo** to believe sth; **no podía ~ crédito a mis oídos** I couldn't believe my ears; **~ declaración** (*ante la policía*) to make a statement; (*en un juicio*) to give evidence, testify; **~ juramento** (*gen*) to take the oath, be sworn in; **prestó juramento sobre la Biblia** he swore on the Bible; **~ oídos a algo** to take notice of sth
4 (*frm*) (= *aportar*) **los jóvenes prestaban alegría a la fiesta** the young people brought good cheer to *o* brightened up the party; **el color azul le prestaba un encanto especial a la habitación** the blue colour gave *o* lent a special charm to the room
5 (*Ven*) **~ a algn** to do good to sb; **no le prestó el viaje** the trip didn't do him any good
Ⓑ VI 1 (= *dar de sí*) [*zapatos*] to give; [*cuerda*] to stretch
2 (= *servir*) **~ para algo** to be big enough for sth
Ⓒ **prestarse** VPR 1 **~se a** [*persona*] 1·1 (= *aceptar*) to accept; **yo nunca me ~ía a esa petición** I would never agree to that request; **no se ~á a participar en ese tipo de juego** he will never agree to be involved in that kind of game
1·2 (= *ofrecerse*) to volunteer to; **se prestó a echarnos una mano si hacía falta** he volunteered to give us a hand if we needed it
2 (= *dar lugar a*) **~se a algo: sus palabras se ~on a confusión** his words were misinterpreted; **la situación actual se presta a varias interpretaciones** the present situation could be interpreted in several ways; **ese argumento se presta a discusión** that argument is open to debate
3 (= *servir*) **~se para algo** to be suitable for sth; **se presta para cualquier uso** it is suitable for any purpose; **esta sala se presta muy bien para este tipo de concierto** this hall is perfectly suited to this type of concert
4 **~se de algo** (*Caribe*) to borrow sth

prestatario/a SM/F borrower

preste SM (*hum*) priest

presteza SF promptness, alacrity (*frm*); **con ~** speedily, promptly, with alacrity (*frm*)

prestidigitación SF (= *ilusionismo*) conjuring, sleight of hand, prestidigitation (*frm*); (= *malabarismo*) juggling

prestidigitador(a) SM/F (= *ilusionista*) conjurer, prestidigitator (*frm*); (= *malabarista*) juggler

prestigiado ADJ (*LAm*) (= *respetable*) worthy, estimable; (= *prestigioso*) prestigious

prestigiar ▸conjug 1b◂ VT (= *dar prestigio*) to give prestige to; (= *dar fama*) to make famous; (= *honrar*) to honour, honor (*EEUU*) (**con** with); (= *realzar*) to enhance

prestigio SM 1 (= *fama*) prestige; **de ~** prestigious
2 (= *ensalmo*) spell, magic spell
3 (= *truco*) trick

prestigioso ADJ prestigious, famous

presto Ⓐ ADJ 1 (= *rápido*) quick, prompt, swift
2 (= *listo*) ready (**para** for; **a** to)
3 (*Mús*) presto
Ⓑ ADV (= *rápidamente*) quickly, swiftly; (= *en seguida*) right away, at once

presumible ADJ presumable, probable; **es ~ que la cifra sea mucho más alta** we can assume that the figure is much higher, the figure is likely to be much higher, the figure is probably much higher; **es ~ la existencia de restos más antiguos** we can assume the existence of older remains, we can assume that older remains exist

presumiblemente ADJ presumably

presumido ADJ (= *creído*) conceited; (= *coqueto*) vain

presumir ▸conjug 3a◂ Ⓐ VI (= *alardear*) to give o.s. airs, show off; (= *envanecerse*) to be conceited; **lo hizo para ~ ante sus amistades** he did it to show off in front of his friends; **no presumas tanto** don't be so conceited; **~ de listo** to think o.s. very smart; **presume de experto** he likes to think he's an expert, he considers himself an expert; **~ demasiado de sus fuerzas** to overestimate one's strength
Ⓑ VT 1 (= *suponer*) to presume; **presumo que quedarán campeones de la liga** I presume that they will end up as league champions; **según cabe ~** as may be presumed, presumably; **es de ~ que** presumably, supposedly
2 (*Arg, Bol*) (= *pretender*) to court; (= *coquetear con*) to flirt with

presunción SF 1 [*de un conocimiento*] (= *conjetura*) supposition, presumption; (= *sospecha*) suspicion; **el principio de ~ de inocencia** the principle that one is presumed innocent until proven guilty
2 (= *vanidad*) conceit, presumptuousness

presuntamente ADV supposedly, allegedly; **un hombre ~ rico** a supposedly *o* an allegedly rich man; **~ causó la muerte de su hermano** he is alleged to have caused the death of his brother

presunto ADJ 1 (= *supuesto*) (*gen*) supposed, presumed; [*criminal*] suspected, alleged; **el ~ asesino** the alleged murderer; **Gómez, ~ implicado en …** Gómez, allegedly involved in …
2 [*heredero*] apparent, presumptive
3 (= *llamado*) so-called; **estos ~s expertos** these so-called experts

presuntuosamente ADV (= *con vanidad*) conceitedly, presumptuously; (= *con pretensión*) pretentiously

presuntuoso ADJ (= *vanidoso*) conceited, presumptuous; (= *pretencioso*) pretentious

presuponer ▸conjug 2q◂ VT to presuppose, assume

presuposición SF presupposition, assumption

presupuestal ADJ (*Méx*) = **presupuestario**

presupuestar ▸conjug 1a◂ VT [+ *gastos*] to budget for; **costó mucho más de lo presupuestado inicialmente** it cost much more than was initially budgeted for; **su costo está presupuestado en 16 millones** its cost is estimated at 16 million

presupuestario ADJ budget *antes de s*, budgetary

presupuestívoro/a SM/F (*LAm hum*) public employee

presupuesto SM 1 (*Fin*) budget; **~ de ventas** sales budget ► **los Presupuestos Generales (del Estado)** the national budget ► **presupuesto operante** operating budget
2 (*para obra, encargo, etc*) estimate; **pedir ~** to ask for an estimate; **"~ sin compromiso"** "free estimates — no obligation"
3 (= *supuesto*) premise, assumption

presurizado ADJ pressurized

presurosamente ADV (= *con rapidez*) quickly, promptly; (= *con prisa*) hastily

presuroso ADJ (= *rápido*) quick, speedy; (= *precipitado*) hasty; [*paso*] quick, brisk; **entró ~** he rushed in; **acudieron ~s a ayudarnos** they rushed to our aid

pretal SM (*esp LAm*) strap, girth

prêt-à-porter ADJ INV off-the-peg, ready-to-wear, off-the-rack (*EEUU*)

pretecnología SF (*Escol*) practical subjects *pl*

pretemporada SF (*Dep*) pre-season

pretenciosidad SF 1 (= *pretensiones*) pretentiousness; (= *fanfarronería*) showiness
2 (*LAm*) vanity, boastfulness

pretencioso ADJ 1 (= *vanidoso*) pretentious, presumptuous; (= *fanfarrón*) showy
2 (*LAm*) (= *presumido*) vain, stuck-up*

pretender ▸conjug 2a◂ VT 1 (= *aspirar a*) **¿qué pretende usted?** what are you after?, what do you hope to achieve?; **~ el trono** to pretend to the throne; **~ hacer algo**: **pretendió convencerme** he tried to convince me; **pretendo sacar algo de provecho** I intend to get something out of it; **¿qué pretende usted decir con eso?** what do you mean by that?; **no pretendo ser rico** I've no aspirations to be rich; **pretende llegar a ser médico** she hopes to become a doctor; **~ que** (+ *SUBJUN*) to expect that …; **¡no ~ás que te pague la comida!** you're not expecting me to pay for your meal, are you?
2 (*frm*) (= *afirmar*) to claim; **pretende que el coche le atropelló adrede** he claims that the car deliberately knocked him down
3 (†) (= *cortejar*) to woo, court

pretendidamente ADV supposedly, allegedly

pretendido ADJ supposed, alleged

pretendiente/a Ⓐ SM/F (= *aspirante*) (*a cargo*) candidate, applicant (**a** for); (*al trono*) pretender (**a** to)
Ⓑ SM [*de una mujer*] suitor

pretensado ADJ prestressed

pretensión SF 1 (= *intención*) aim; (= *aspiración*) aspiration; **un libro sin más ~ que divertir** a book which only aims to entertain; **tiene la ~ de que yo lo acompañe** he expects me to go with him
2 **pretensiones** (= *aspiraciones*) **tiene pretensiones de artista** she is an aspiring artist; **tiene pretensiones intelectuales** he likes to think of himself as an intellectual; **tiene pocas pretensiones** he doesn't aspire to much; **enviar historial profesional indicando pretensiones económicas** send curriculum vitae indicating desired salary; **una simple chaqueta sin pretensiones** a simple jacket, nothing fancy
3 (*LAm*) (= *vanidad*) vanity; (= *presunción*) presumption, arrogance

pretensioso ADJ (*LAm*) = **pretencioso 2**

pretensor SM **cinturón con ~** inertia-reel seatbelt

preterir ▸conjug 3a◂ VT to leave out, omit, pass over

pretérito Ⓐ ADJ 1 (*Ling*) past
2 (= *pasado*) past, former; **las glorias pretéritas del país** the country's former glories
Ⓑ SM (*Ling*) (*tb* **~ indefinido**) preterite, past historic ► **pretérito imperfecto** imperfect ► **pretérito perfecto** present perfect

preternatural ADJ preternatural

pretextar ▸conjug 1a◂ VT to use as an excuse; **~ que …** to claim that …, use as an excuse the fact that …

pretexto SM pretext; **vino con el ~ de ver al abuelo** he came on the pretext of visiting Granddad; **con el ~ de que …** on the pretext that …; **era sólo un ~ para no venir** it was only an excuse not to come; **bajo ningún ~** under no circumstances; **so ~ de** (*frm*) under pretext of; **tomar a ~** (*frm*) to use as an excuse

pretil SM 1 (*Constr*) (= *muro*) parapet; (= *barandilla*) handrail, railing
2 (*Andes*) [*de garaje, hotel*] forecourt
3 (*Caribe, Méx*) (= *banco*) bench
4 (*Méx*) (= *encintado*) kerb

pretina SF 1 (= *cinturilla*) waistband; (= *cinturón*) belt, girdle† (*liter*)
2 (*Andes, Cono Sur*) (= *correa*) leather strap
3 (*Caribe*) (= *bragueta*) flies *pl*, fly

pretor SM 1 (*Méx*) (= *juez*) lower-court judge, magistrate
2 (*Hist*) praetor

pretoriano ADJ **guardia pretoriana** praetorian guard

preu†* SM one-year pre-university course

preuniversitario/a† Ⓐ ADJ pre-university; **curso ~** one-year pre-university course
Ⓑ SM/F *student on a pre-university course*

prevalecer ▸conjug 2d◂ VI 1 (= *imponerse*) to prevail (**sobre** against, over)
2 (= *triunfar*) to triumph, win through
3 (*Bot*) (= *arraigar*) to take root and grow; (= *prosperar*) to thrive

prevaleciente ADJ prevailing, dominant

prevalerse ▸conjug 2q◂ VPR **~ de algo** (= *valerse*) to avail o.s. of sth; (= *aprovecharse*) to take advantage of sth

prevaricación SF, **prevaricato** SM (*Jur*) perversion of the course of justice, corrupt practice

prevaricar ▸conjug 1g◂ VI to pervert the course of justice, be guilty of corrupt practice

preve* SF = **prevención 6**

prevención SF 1 [*de accidente, enfermedad*] prevention; **en ~ de algo** in order to prevent sth; **medidas de ~** emergency measures, contingency plans
2 (= *medida*) precautionary measure, precaution; **hemos tomado ciertas prevenciones** we have taken certain precautionary measures *o* precautions

➤ LENGUA Y USO: **pretender 1** 35.2

3 (= *previsión*) foresight, forethought; **obrar con ~** to act with foresight
4 (= *prejuicio*) prejudice; **tener ~ contra algn** to be prejudiced against sb
5 (= *comisaría*) police-station
6 (*Mil*) guardroom, guardhouse

prevenido ADJ 1 **ser ~** (= *cuidadoso*) to be cautious; (= *previsor*) to be far-sighted
2 **estar ~** (= *preparado*) to be ready, be prepared; (= *advertido*) to be forewarned, be on one's guard (**contra** against); ✦*REFRÁN* **hombre ~ vale por dos** forewarned is forearmed

prevenir ▸conjug 3r◂ Ⓐ VT 1 (= *evitar*) to prevent; (= *prever*) to foresee, anticipate; **hay accidentes que no se pueden ~** some accidents cannot be prevented; ✦*REFRANES* **más vale ~ que curar** *o* **lamentar** prevention is better than cure, better safe than sorry
2 (= *advertir*) to warn; **~ a algn** to warn sb, put sb on his guard (**contra, de** against, about); **pudieron ~le a tiempo** they were able to warn him in time
3 (= *predisponer*) to prejudice, bias (**a favor de** in favour of; **en contra de** against)
4 (= *preparar*) to prepare, get ready (**para** for)
5 (= *proveer*) **~ a algn de algo** to provide sb with sth
Ⓑ **prevenirse** VPR 1 (= *prepararse*) to get ready, prepare; **~se para un viaje** to get ready for a trip; **~se contra algo** to take precautions against sth, prepare for sth
2 (= *proveerse*) **~se de ropa adecuada** to provide o.s. with suitable clothing
3 **~se en contra de algn** to set o.s. against sb

preventivo ADJ [*medida*] preventive, precautionary; (*Med*) preventive; *ver tb* **prisión 2**

▼ **prever** ▸conjug 2u◂ VT 1 (= *adivinar*) to foresee; (= *predecir*) to predict, forecast; **~ que ...** to anticipate that ..., expect that ...; **ya lo preveía** I expected as much; **se prevé un descenso de precios** a drop in prices is predicted *o* forecast; **si ganan como se prevé** if they win as expected *o* predicted
2 (= *proyectar*) to plan; **la elección está prevista para ...** the election is scheduled *o* planned for ...; **tenemos previsto atravesar el desierto** we are planning to cross the desert; **un embarazo no previsto** an unplanned pregnancy; **no teníamos previsto nada para eso** we had not made any allowance for that
3 (= *establecer*) to provide for, establish; **la ley prevé que ...** the law provides *o* stipulates that ...

previamente ADV previously

previo Ⓐ ADJ 1 (= *anterior*) [*experiencia, programa, conocimiento*] previous; [*examen*] preliminary; [*compromiso*] prior; **sin ~ aviso** without prior warning; **autorización previa** prior authorization, prior permission
2 **~ a** before, prior to
3 [*idea*] preconceived, received
Ⓑ PREP **~ acuerdo de todas las partes afectadas** subject to the agreement of all interested parties; **~ pago de los derechos** on payment of the fees; **"previa cita"** "by appointment only", "appointment required"
Ⓒ SM (*Cine*) playback

previsible ADJ foreseeable, predictable

previsiblemente ADV predictably

➤ LENGUA Y USO: **prever 2** 35.3

previsión SF 1 (*como cualidad*) (= *clarividencia*) foresight, far-sightedness; (= *prudencia*) caution
2 (= *acto*) precaution, precautionary measure; **en ~ de algo** (= *como precaución*) as a precaution against sth; (= *esperando*) in anticipation of sth
3 (= *pronóstico*) forecast; **previsiones económicas** economic forecast *sing*; **~ de ventas** sales forecast; **las previsiones del plan quinquenal** the forecasts of the five-year plan ► **previsión del tiempo, previsión meteorológica** weather forecast, weather forecasting
4 ► **previsión social** social security; (*Chile*) ≈ pension fund

previsional ADJ (*Cono Sur*) social security *antes de s*

previsivo ADJ (*Méx*) = **previsor**

previsor ADJ (= *precavido*) far-sighted; (= *prudente*) thoughtful, prudent

previsoramente ADV 1 (*previendo*) far-sightedly; (= *con prudencia*) prudently
2 (= *por si acaso*) just in case

previsto ADJ [*resultados*] predicted, anticipated; **la reunión prevista para el día 20** the meeting planned for the 20th; **empezó a la hora prevista** it started on time; **todo salió según lo ~** everything went as planned *o* (according) to plan

prez SM (†) honour, honor (*EEUU*), glory

PRI SM ABR (*Méx Pol*) = **Partido Revolucionario Institucional**

pribar* ▸conjug 1a◂ VT, VI = **privar**²

prieta SF (*Cono Sur*) black pudding

prieto Ⓐ ADJ 1 (= *apretado*) tight; **no hagas el nudo tan ~** don't tie the knot so tight; **de carnes prietas** firm-bodied; **un siglo ~ de historia** a century packed full of history, a century rich in history
2 (= *oscuro*) blackish, dark; (*esp Méx*) dark, swarthy
Ⓑ SM (*LAm*) (= *dado*) loaded dice

prietuzco ADJ (*CAm, Caribe, Méx*) blackish

priísta (*Méx Pol*) Ⓐ ADJ *of or pertaining to the PRI party*
Ⓑ SMF supporter of the PRI party

prima SF 1 [*de seguro*] premium
2 (= *gratificación*) bonus ► **prima a la producción, prima de incentivo** incentive bonus ► **prima de peligrosidad** danger money ► **prima de productividad** productivity bonus ► **prima por coste de la vida** cost of living bonus
3 (*Rel*) prime
4 (*Cono Sur*) **bajar la ~** to moderate one's language; **subir la ~** to use strong language; *ver tb* **primo**

primacía SF 1 (*como cualidad*) (= *superioridad*) primacy, first place; (= *supremacía*) supremacy; (= *prioridad*) priority; **tener la ~ sobre algo** to be superior to sth ► **primacía de paso** (*Aut*) priority, right of way
2 (*Rel*) primacy

primada* SF (= *estupidez*) piece of stupidity; (= *error*) silly mistake

primado SM (*Rel*) primate

primadona SF, **primadonna** SF prima donna

primal(a) Ⓐ ADJ yearling
Ⓑ SM/F yearling

primar ▸conjug 1a◂ Ⓐ VI (= *predominar*) **una zona en la que prima la actividad comercial** an area in which commercial activity predominates; **en el acuerdo bilateral prima la cooperación militar** military cooperation is key to the bilateral agreement; **en sus diseños prima la elegancia** elegance is the keynote in his designs; **~ sobre algo** to take precedence over sth, have priority over sth; **el materialismo prima sobre la espiritualidad** materialism takes precedence over spirituality
Ⓑ VT (*Dep*) to give a bonus to

primaria SF 1 (*Educ*) primary education
2 (*Pol*) (*tb* **~s**) primary election(s)

primariamente ADV primarily

primariedad SF primacy

primario ADJ [*color, sector*] primary; [*instinto, necesidad*] basic; **escuela primaria** primary school

primate Ⓐ SM 1 (*Zool*) primate
2 (= *prócer*) outstanding figure, important person
Ⓑ ADJ most important

primavera Ⓐ SF 1 (= *estación*) spring; **en ~** in spring, in springtime; ✦*REFRÁN* **la ~ la sangre altera** spring is in the air
2 (*liter*) (= *esplendor*) **está en la ~ de la vida** he is in the prime of life
3 **primaveras** (*liter*) (= *años*) summers (*liter*); **tenía quince ~s** she was a girl of fifteen summers (*liter*)
4 (*Orn*) blue tit
5 (*Bot*) primrose
Ⓑ SM **ser un ~** (*Esp**) to be a simple soul

primaveral ADJ spring *antes de s*, springlike

prime* ADJ = **primero**

primer ADJ *ver* **primero**

primera SF 1 (*Aut*) first gear, bottom gear; **meter (la) ~** to change into first gear; *ver tb* **bueno A9**
2 (*en viajes*) first class; **ir en ~** to go first class; **viajar en ~** to travel first class
3 **a la ~** (= *primera ocasión*) [*acertar*] first time; **las cosas no salen siempre a la ~** you don't always get it right first time; **saqué el carnet de conducir a la ~** I got my driving licence at the first attempt; **dijo sí a la ~** he said yes straight away
4 ✦*MODISMO* **de ~*** (= *excelente*) excellent, brilliant*; **el partido fue de ~** the match was excellent *o* brilliant*; **aquí vendemos un jamón de ~** here we sell the finest quality ham; **aquí se come de ~** you eat really well here, the food is excellent *o* brilliant* here; **hoy me encuentro de ~** I feel great today*; **esta cerveza me ha sentado de ~** this beer has gone down a treat*; **ese dinero me viene de ~** that money suits me down to the ground*; *ver tb* **clase A1.4**
5 (*Com*) ► **primera de cambio** first of exchange; ✦*MODISMO* **a la(s) ~(s) de cambio** (= *sin avisar*) without warning; (= *tras la primera dificultad*) at the first sign of trouble; *ver tb* **primero**

primeramente ADV (= *en primer lugar*) first, firstly; (= *principalmente*) chiefly

primerear ▸conjug 1a◂ VI (*Cono Sur*) to land the first blow, get in first

primerizo/a Ⓐ ADJ 1 (= *novato*) green, inexperienced
2 (= *primero*) first; **novela primeriza** first novel

Ⓑ SM/F (= *principiante*) beginner
Ⓒ SF (*Med*) first time mother

▼**primero/a** Ⓐ ADJ (*antes de sm sing* **primer**)
[1] (*en el espacio*) [*página, planta*] first; [*fila*] front, first; **vivo en el primer piso** I live on the first *o* (*EEUU*) second floor; **una foto en primera página** a front-page photo, a photo on the front page; **las primeras páginas del libro** the first few pages of the book; **un apartamento en primera línea de playa** an apartment right on the sea front; **estar ~** (*en una cola*) to be first; (*en importancia*) to come first; **perdone, pero yo estaba ~** excuse me, but I was first; **para mí ~ están mis estudios** my studies take priority *o* come first; **~ está la obligación y después la diversión** business before pleasure; *ver tb* **plana 1**, **plano B3**

[2] (*en el tiempo*) [*día, semana, fase*] first; [*época, poemas*] early; [*síntoma*] first, early; **la primera parte del partido** the first half of the match; **una novela escrita en primera persona** a novel written in the first person; **no es la primera vez** it is not the first time; **Juan Carlos Primero** Juan Carlos the First; **los ~s días estaba contento** I was happy for the first few days; **sus dos primeras novelas** his first two novels; **la primera época de Picasso** Picasso's early period; **en los ~s años del siglo** in the early years of the century; **a primera hora (de la mañana)** first thing in the morning; **mañana a primera hora** first thing tomorrow (morning); **a primeras horas de la tarde de ayer** early yesterday afternoon; **en primer lugar** (*dentro de un orden*) first of all; (*para dar énfasis*) in the first place; **en primer lugar vamos a visitar el Partenón** first of all we are going to visit the Parthenon; **en primer lugar, tú no deberías haber dicho nada** in the first place, you shouldn't have said anything; *ver tb* **hora 2.2**, **guerra 1**

[3] (= *principal*) [*deber, objetivo*] main, primary; **lo ~ es que te pongas bueno** the main thing is that you get well; **productos de primera calidad** top quality products; **artículos de primera necesidad** basic essentials, staple items; **primer actor** leading man; **primera actriz** leading lady; **~s auxilios** first aid; **el botiquín de ~s auxilios** the first-aid box; **de primera categoría** first-class; **un puerto de primera categoría** (*Ciclismo*) a first-category climb; **primer espada** (*Taur*) principal bullfighter; **primer violín** (= *concertino*) leader; (*de sección*) first violin; ✦**MODISMO lo ~ es lo ~** first things first; *ver tb* **bailarín**, **dama 1**, **mandatario 2**, **ministro**, **piedra A1**

Ⓑ SM/F first; **soy el ~ de la lista** I'm top of the list, I'm first on the list; **quedó entre los diez ~s** he was in *o* among the first ten; **es la primera de la clase** she is the best in the class, she is top of the class; **fui la primera en darme cuenta del fallo** I was the first to realize the mistake; **llegar el ~** to be the first to arrive; *ver tb* **bueno A9**, **vista A6.4**, **primera**

Ⓒ SM [1] **a ~s (de mes)** at the beginning of the month; **a ~s de junio** at the beginning of June
[2] (*tb* **primer plato**) starter, first course; **¿qué van a tomar de ~?** what will you have as a starter *o* for the first course?

Ⓓ ADV [1] (= *en primer lugar*) first; **~ iremos a comprar y luego al cine** first, we'll do the shopping and then go to the cinema

[2] (*indicando preferencia*) sooner, rather; **~ se queda en casa que pedir dinero** she'd sooner *o* rather stay at home than ask for money; **¡~ morir!** I'd rather die!

primicia SF [1] (= *novedad*) novelty; (= *estreno*) first appearance ► **primicia informativa** scoop
[2] **primicias** (= *primeros frutos*) first fruits

primigenio ADJ primitive, original

primípara SF first-time mother, primipara (*frm*)

primitiva SF **la ~*** = **lotería primitiva**; *ver* **lotería**

primitivamente ADV [1] (= *al principio*) at first
[2] (= *de un modo primitivo*) primitively, in a primitive way

primitivo ADJ [1] [*arte, pueblo*] primitive; (= *salvaje*) uncivilized; **en condiciones primitivas** in primitive conditions; **el hombre ~** primitive man
[2] (= *original*) first, original; **el texto ~** the original text; **quedan 200 de los ~s 850** there remain 200 from the original 850; **devolver algo a su estado ~** to restore sth to its original state; **es una obra primitiva** it is an early work
[3] [*color*] primary
[4] (*Fin*) [*acción*] ordinary

primo/a Ⓐ ADJ [1] [*número*] prime
[2] [*materia*] raw
Ⓑ SM/F [1] (= *pariente*) cousin; ✦**MODISMOS le vino el ~ de América**†* she started her period; **ser ~s hermanos** (*referido a cosas*) to be extraordinarily alike ► **primo/a carnal**, **primo/a hermano/a** first cousin
[2] (*) (= *incauto*) dupe, sucker*; ✦**MODISMOS hacer el ~** to be taken for a sucker*, be taken for a ride*; **tomar a algn por ~** to do sb down*, take sb in*; *ver tb* **prima**

primogénito/a ADJ, SM/F first-born

primogenitura SF [1] (*al nacer*) primogeniture
[2] (= *patrimonio*) birthright

primor SM [1] (= *delicadeza*) delicacy
[2] (= *maestría*) care, skill; **hecho con ~** done most skilfully, delicately made; **cose que es un ~** she sews beautifully
[3] (= *objeto primoroso*) fine thing, lovely thing; **hace ~es con la aguja** she makes lovely things with her needlework; **hijos que son un ~** delightful children, charming children

▼**primordial** ADJ fundamental, essential; **esto es ~** this is top priority; **es de interés ~** it is of fundamental concern; **es ~ saberlo** it is essential to know it; **ha desempeñado un papel de ~ importancia** it has played a crucial role

primordialidad SF (= *importancia*) overriding importance; (= *supremacía*) supremacy

primordialmente ADV basically, fundamentally

primorosamente ADV (= *con delicadeza*) exquisitely, delicately, elegantly; (= *con esmero*) neatly, skilfully, skillfully (*EEUU*)

primoroso ADJ (= *delicado*) exquisite, fine; (= *esmerado*) neat, skilful, skillful (*EEUU*)

prímula SF primrose

princesa SF princess ► **princesa real** ≈ Princess Royal

principado SM principality; **el Principado de Asturias** (the principality of) Asturias

▼**principal** Ⓐ ADJ [1] (= *más importante*) (*gen*) principal, main; [*crítico, adversario*] foremost; [*piso*] first, second (*EEUU*); **interpreta el papel ~** she plays the leading role; **lo ~ es que el problema se ha solucionado** the main thing is the problem has been solved
[2] [*persona, autoridad*] illustrious
Ⓑ SM [1] (= *persona*) head, chief, principal
[2] (*Fin*) principal, capital
[3] (*Teat*) dress circle
[4] (= *piso*) first floor, second floor (*EEUU*)

principalmente ADJ principally, chiefly, mainly

príncipe Ⓐ SM prince; **el ~ de Asturias** the heir to the Spanish throne ► **príncipe azul** Prince Charming, knight in shining armour ► **príncipe consorte** prince consort ► **príncipe de Gales** Prince of Wales ► **príncipe heredero** crown prince
Ⓑ ADJ INV **edición ~** first edition

principesco ADJ princely

principiante/a Ⓐ ADJ [*actor, fotógrafo, jugador*] inexperienced; **conductor ~** learner driver
Ⓑ SM/F (= *novato*) beginner, novice; (= *aprendiz*) learner; **cometen errores de ~** they make basic mistakes

principiar ▸conjug 1b◂ Ⓐ VT to begin
Ⓑ VI to begin; **~ a hacer algo** to begin to do sth, begin doing sth; **~ con algo** to begin with sth

▼**principio** SM [1] (= *comienzo*) beginning; **al ~** at first, in the beginning; **a ~s del verano** at the beginning of the summer, early in the summer; **desde el ~** from the first, from the outset; **desde el ~ hasta el fin** from start to finish, from beginning to end; **en un ~** at first, to start with; **dar ~ a algo** to start sth off; **tener ~ en algo** to start from sth, be based on sth
[2] **principios** (= *nociones*) rudiments, first notions; **"Principios de física"** "Introduction to Physics", "Outline of Physics"
[3] (= *norma*) principle; **persona de ~s** man of principles; **en ~** in principle; **por ~** on principle; **es inmoral por ~** it is immoral in principle; **sin ~s** unprincipled; **el ~ de la legalidad** the force of law, the rule of law
[4] (*Fil*) principle
[5] (*Quím*) element, constituent
[6] (*Culin*) entrée

principote* SM (= *jactancioso*) show-off*, swank*; (= *arribista*) parvenu, social climber

pringada SF *bread dipped in gravy etc*

pringado/a* SM/F [1] (= *víctima*) (innocent) victim; (= *sin suerte*) unlucky person; (= *infeliz*) poor devil, wretch; **el ~ del grupo** the odd man out, the loser
[2] (= *tonto*) fool, idiot; **¡no seas ~!** don't be an idiot!
[3] (= *gafe*) bringer of bad luck

pringao* SM = **pringado**

pringar ▸conjug 1h◂ Ⓐ VT [1] (*Culin*) [+ *pan*] to dip, dunk; [+ *asado*] to baste; **~ el pan en la sopa** to dip one's bread in the soup
[2] (= *ensuciar*) to dirty, soil (with grease); (*esp LAm*) to splash
[3] (*) (= *implicar*) **~ a algn en un asunto** to involve sb in a matter; **están pringadas en esto unas altas personalidades** some top people are mixed up in this
[4] (*) (= *herir*) **~ a algn** to wound sb, make sb bleed
[5] (*) (= *denigrar*) to blacken, run down*
[6] (*Cono Sur*) [+ *enfermedad*] to give

➤ LENGUA Y USO: **primero A3** 53.2 **primordial** 53.6 **principal A1** 53.2 **principio 3** 53.6

[7] (*Cono Sur**) [+ *mujer*] to put in the family way
[8] **~la**⁑ (= *meter la pata*) to drop a brick*, make a boob*; (*Med*) to get a dose of the clap⁑; **~la(s)**⁑ (= *morir*) to kick the bucket*, snuff it*
Ⓑ VI [1] (*) (= *perder*) to come a cropper*, take a beating; **hemos pringado** we're done for
[2] (= *trabajar*) to sweat one's guts out*, slog away*
[3] **~ en algo** (*superficialmente*) to dabble in sth; (*implicándose*) to take a hand in sth, get mixed up in sth
[4] (*) (= *morir*) to kick the bucket*, snuff it*
[5] (*CAm, Caribe, Méx*) (= *lloviznar*) to drizzle
Ⓒ **pringarse** VPR [1] (= *ensuciarse*) to get covered (**con, de** with, in)
[2] (*) (= *involucrarse*) to get mixed up (**en** in)
[3] (*) (= *comprometerse*) to get one's fingers burnt; **o nos pringamos todos, o ninguno** either we all carry the can or none of us does*
[4] (*) (= *ganar por medios dudosos*) to make money on the side; (= *sacar tajada*) to get a rake-off*; (= *enriquecerse*) to make a packet*

pringo SM (*LAm*) (= *gota*) drop; (= *pizca*) bit, pinch; **con un ~ de leche** with a drop of milk

pringón Ⓐ ADJ (= *sucio*) dirty, greasy
Ⓑ SM [1] (= *mancha*) grease stain, grease spot
[2] (⁑) (= *tajada*) rake-off*; (= *ganancias*) packet*

pringoso ADJ (= *grasiento*) greasy; (= *pegajoso*) sticky

pringue SM o SF [1] (= *grasa*) grease, dripping
[2] (= *mancha*) grease stain, grease spot; (= *suciedad*) dirt
[3] (*) (= *molestia*) nuisance; **es un ~ tener que …** it's a bind having to …*
[4] (*CAm, Méx*) (= *salpicadura*) splash (*of mud etc*)
[5] (*Andes*) (= *quemadura*) burn
[6] (⁑) (= *dinero*) dosh⁑, money
[7] (⁑) (= *policía*) Crime Squad

prior(a) SM/F prior/prioress

priorato SM (*Rel*) priory

priori *ver* **a priori**

prioridad SF (= *precedencia*) priority; (= *antigüedad*) seniority, greater age; (*Aut*) right of way, priority; **tener ~** to have *o* take priority (**sobre** over); (*Aut*) to have the right of way ► **prioridad de paso** (*Aut*) right of way

prioritariamente ADV (= *en primer lugar*) as a priority, first; (= *mayormente*) mainly, principally

prioritario ADJ (= *primero*) priority *antes de s*; (= *principal*) main, principal; (*Inform*) foreground *antes de s*; **un proyecto de carácter ~** a plan with top priority, a (top) priority plan; **lo ~ es …** the first thing (to do) is …

priorizar ▸conjug 1f◂ Ⓐ VT to give priority to, treat as a priority, prioritize
Ⓑ VI to determine priorities

prisa SF (= *prontitud*) hurry, haste; (= *premura*) urgency; **con las ~s me olvidé el paraguas** in the rush I forgot my umbrella; **voy con mucha ~** I'm in a great hurry; **a ~** quickly, hurriedly; **a toda ~** as quickly as possible; **correr ~** (*Esp*) to be urgent; **no corre ~** it's not urgent; **¿corren ~ estas cartas?** are these letters urgent?, is there any hurry for these letters?; **¿te corre ~?** are you in a hurry?; **darse ~** to hurry, hurry up; **¡date ~!** hurry (up)!, come along!; **de ~** quickly, hurriedly; **meter ~ a algn** to make sb get a move on, make sb hurry up; **tener ~** to be in a hurry; ✦*MODISMO* **sin ~ pero sin pausa** slow but steady

prisco Ⓐ ADJ (*LAm**) simple
Ⓑ SM (*esp Cono Sur*) (= *albaricoque*) apricot

prisión SF [1] (= *cárcel*) prison; **~ de alta** o **máxima seguridad** top-security prison
[2] (= *encarcelamiento*) imprisonment; **cinco años de ~** five years' imprisonment, prison sentence of five years ► **prisión domiciliaria** house-arrest ► **prisión mayor** *sentence of more than six years and a day* ► **prisión menor** *sentence of less than six years and a day* ► **prisión perpetua** life imprisonment ► **prisión preventiva** preventive detention; **el juez ha decretado la ~ preventiva** the judge remanded him in custody
[3] **prisiones** (= *grillos*) shackles, fetters

prisionero/a SM/F prisoner; **hacer ~ a algn** to take sb prisoner ► **prisionero/a de conciencia** prisoner of conscience ► **prisionero/a de guerra** prisoner of war ► **prisionero/a político/a** political prisoner

prisma SM [1] (*Fís, Ópt*) prism
[2] (= *punto de vista*) point of view, angle; **bajo** *o* **desde el ~ de** from the point of view of

prismático Ⓐ ADJ prismatic
Ⓑ **prismáticos** SMPL binoculars, field glasses

pristinidad SF pristine nature, original quality

prístino ADJ pristine, original

priva* SF (*Esp*) **la ~** the booze*, the drink

privacidad SF (= *intimidad*) privacy; (= *secreto*) secrecy

privación SF [1] (= *acto*) deprivation, deprival; **sufrir ~ de libertad** to suffer loss of liberty
[2] **privaciones** (= *miserias*) hardship *sing*, privations; **durante la guerra sufrimos muchas privaciones** we suffered a lot of hardship during the war

privada SF (*Méx*) private road

privadamente ADV privately

privado Ⓐ ADJ [1] [*club, colegio, avión*] private; **"~ y confidencial"** "private and confidential"
[2] (*LAm*) (= *alocado*) mad, senseless
[3] (*Caribe*) (= *débil*) weak, faint
Ⓑ SM [1] **en ~** privately, in private
[2] (*Pol*) (= *favorito*) favourite, favorite (*EEUU*), protégé; (*Hist*) royal favourite, chief minister

privanza SF favour; **durante la ~ de Lerma** when Lerma was royal favourite, when Lerma was chief minister

privar[1] ▸conjug 1a◂ Ⓐ VT [1] (= *despojar*) **~ a algn de algo** to deprive sb of sth, take sth away from sb; **~ a algn del conocimiento** to render sb unconscious; **lo ~on del carnet de conducir** they suspended his driving licence, they took away his driving licence; **quedaron privados de electricidad** they were without electricity; **nos vimos privados de su compañía** we found ourselves deprived of her company
[2] (= *prohibir*) **~ a algn de hacer algo** to forbid sb to do sth, prevent sb from doing sth; **no me prives de verte** don't forbid me to come to see you, don't tell me not to come again
[3] (= *impedir*) to prevent; **lo cual me privó de verlos** which prevented me from seeing them
[4] (= *extasiar*) to delight, overwhelm
Ⓑ VI [1] (*) (= *gustar mucho*) **las motos me privan** I'm mad about motorbikes*
[2] (*) (= *estar de moda*) to be in fashion, be the thing, be all the rage*; **en ese periodo privaba la minifalda** at that time miniskirts were in *o* were all the rage*; **la cualidad que más priva entre ellos** the quality which is most strongly present in them; **priva en algunos públicos** it's popular with some audiences
Ⓒ **privarse** VPR **~se de algo** (= *abstenerse*) to deprive o.s. of sth; (= *renunciar*) to give sth up, forgo sth; **no se privan de nada** they don't want for anything, they lack nothing

privar[2]* ▸conjug 1a◂ VT, VI (= *beber*) to booze*

privata⁑ SF = **priva**

privativo ADJ [1] (= *exclusivo*) exclusive; **esa función es privativa del presidente** that function is the president's alone; **el hecho no es ~ de España** it's not only *o* exclusively a Spanish phenomenon; **la planta es privativa del Brasil** the plant is peculiar *o* restricted to Brazil
[2] (*Jur*) **una pena privativa de libertad** a prison sentence

privatización SF privatization

privatizador ADJ [*proceso, política*] privatisation *antes de s*, of privatisation; **organismo ~** privatisation body

privatizar ▸conjug 1f◂ VT to privatize

prive⁑ SM = **priva**

privilegiado/a Ⓐ ADJ [*vida, posición, persona*] privileged; [*clima, inteligencia, memoria*] exceptional
Ⓑ SM/F privileged person; **los ~s** the privileged

privilegiar ▸conjug 1b◂ VT (= *favorecer*) to favour, favor (*EEUU*); (= *dar privilegio*) to grant a privilege to

privilegio SM privilege; **los ~s de la aristocracia** the privileges of the aristocracy; **tuve el ~ de conocerla en persona** I had the privilege of meeting her in person; **disfrutar** *o* **gozar de un ~** to enjoy a privilege; **conceder un ~** to grant a privilege ► **privilegio de invención** patent ► **privilegio fiscal** tax concession

privota⁑ SMF piss artist*⁑, boozer⁑

▼**pro** Ⓐ SM [1] (= *provecho*) profit, advantage; **en ~ de** (= *en nombre de*) on behalf of; (= *en favor de*) in favour of; **los ~s y los contras** the pros and cons, for and against; ✦*MODISMO* **buena ~ le haga** and much good may it do him
[2] **de ~** (= *bueno*) worthy; (= *verdadero*) real, true; **hombre de ~** worthy man, honest man; **para los cinéfilos de ~** for real film buffs
Ⓑ PREP (= *en favor de*) for, on behalf of; **asociación ~ ciegos** association for (aid to) the blind; **campaña ~ paz** peace campaign

pro- PREF pro-; **~norteamericano** pro-American; **gestoras ~amnistía** pro-amnesty lobby

pro… PREF pro-…; *p.ej.* **~árabe** pro-Arab

proa SF (*Náut*) bow, prow; (*Aer*) nose; **de ~** bow *antes de s*, fore; **de ~ a popa** from stem to stern; **en la ~** in the bows; **poner la ~ a** (*Náut*) to head for, set a course for; ✦*MODISMO* **poner la ~ a algn** to take a stand against sb, set o.s. against sb

➤ LENGUA Y USO: **pro A1** 53.4

proamnistía ADJ INV pro-amnesty; **gestora ~** (*Esp*) *organization calling for an amnesty for ETA prisoners*

▼**probabilidad** SF [1] (= *capacidad de suceder*) likelihood, probability; **según toda ~** in all probability; **nubes y claros con pocas ~es de lluvia** cloud and sunny periods with little likelihood of rain
[2] (= *oportunidad*) chance, prospect; **hay pocas ~es de que venga** there is little prospect of his coming; **tenemos grandes ~es de ganar** we've got a good chance of winning; **apenas tiene ~es** he hasn't much chance ► **probabilidades de vida** expectation of life, life expectancy

▼**probable** ADJ [1] (= *posible*) probable, likely; **es ~ que ...** it is probable that ..., it is likely that ...; **es ~ que no venga** he probably won't come
[2] (= *demostrable*) provable

▼**probablemente** ADV probably

probadamente ADV **un método ~ ineficaz** a method of proven inefficiency

probado ADJ [1] (= *demostrado*) proven; **un sistema de probada eficacia** a system of proven efficiency; **es un hecho ~ que ...** it has been proved that ...
[2] (= *analizado*) tested; **es un método ~ y eficaz** it is a tested, effective method; **productos de probada calidad** tried and tested products

probador SM [1] (*para cambiarse*) changing room, fitting room
[2] [*de perfume*] tester
[3] (*tb* **piloto ~**) test pilot

probanza SF proof, evidence

probar ▸conjug 1l◂ Ⓐ VT [1] (= *demostrar*) [+ *eficacia, inocencia, teoría*] to prove; **eso ~ía la existencia de vida en Marte** that would prove the existence of life on Mars; **~ que** to prove that; **¿cómo puedes ~ que no estabas allí?** how can you prove that you weren't there?; **el juez consideró probado que era culpable** the judge considered that he had been proved guilty
[2] (= *poner a prueba*) [+ *sustancia, vacuna, persona*] to test; [+ *método*] to try; [+ *aparato, arma*] to test, try out; [+ *actor, músico*] to audition; **hemos dejado dinero en el suelo para ~lo** we've left some money lying on the floor to test him; **prueben su puntería, señoras y señores** try your aim, ladies and gentlemen; **te dan diez días para ~ el vídeo** they give you a ten-day trial period for the video, they give you ten days to try out the video; **~on a muchos actores para el papel** they auditioned a lot of actors for the part; *ver tb* **fortuna 1**, **suerte 1**
[3] (= *catar*) to try, taste; **prueba un poco de este pescado** try *o* taste a bit of this fish; **el médico me ha prohibido que pruebe el marisco** the doctor says I'm not allowed (to eat) seafood; **yo el vino no lo pruebo** I never touch *o* drink wine; **llevamos horas sin ~ bocado** it's hours since we've had a bite to eat; ✦**REFRÁN al ~ se ve el mosto** the proof of the pudding is in the eating
[4] [+ *ropa*] (*hecha a medida*) to fit; (*de confección*) to try on; **¿puede venir mañana a que le pruebe el traje?** can you come tomorrow to have your suit fitted?; **tengo que ir a la modista a que me pruebe** I have to go to the dressmaker for a fitting; **te voy a ~ este abrigo a ver como te queda** I'm going to try this coat on you to see what it looks like
Ⓑ VI [1] (= *intentar*) to try, have a go; **déjame que pruebe yo** let me try, let me have a go; **¿has probado con este bolígrafo?** have you tried this pen?; **~ a hacer algo** to try doing sth; **he probado a hacerlo yo sola, pero no he podido** I tried doing it on my own but I couldn't; ✦**MODISMO con** *o* **por ~ nada se pierde** there's no harm in trying, nothing ventured, nothing gained
[2] (= *sentar*) [*actividad, ropa*] to suit; [*comida*] to agree with; **le probó mal ese oficio** that trade didn't suit him; **no me prueba bien el café** coffee doesn't agree with me
[3] **~ de algo** = A3
Ⓒ **probarse** VPR [+ *ropa, zapatos*] to try on; **¿me puedo ~ esta camisa?** can I try this shirt on?; **pruébate una talla más** try (on) a larger size

probatorio ADJ (*Jur*) [*dato, documento*] **un hecho de limitado valor ~** a fact of limited evidential value; **documentos ~s de su culpabilidad** documents in proof of his guilt, documents proving his guilt

probeta Ⓐ SF test tube
Ⓑ ADJ INV test-tube *antes de s*; **bebé ~** test-tube baby

probidad SF integrity, honesty

▼**problema** Ⓐ SM [1] (= *dificultad*) problem; **el ~ del paro** the problem of unemployment; **el ~ es que no tengo tiempo** the problem is I don't have time; **si hay algún ~ dímelo** let me know if there is any problem; **¿tienes ~s de dinero?** do you have any money worries *o* financial problems?; **este coche nunca me ha dado ~s** this car has never given me any trouble; **no quiero ~s** I don't want any trouble
[2] (*Mat*) problem
[3] (*Méx*) (= *accidente*) accident, mishap
Ⓑ ADJ INV (= *problemático*) problem *antes de s*; **niño ~** problem child

problemática SF problems *pl*, questions *pl*

problemático ADJ problematic

problematizar ▸conjug 1f◂ VT [+ *asunto*] to make problematic; [+ *persona*] to burden with problems

probo ADJ honest, upright

probóscide SF proboscis

procacidad SF [1] [*de persona*] (= *desvergüenza*) insolence, impudence; (= *descaro*) brazenness
[2] [*de comentario, chiste*] indecency, obscenity

procaz ADJ [1] [*persona*] (= *atrevido*) insolent, impudent; (= *descarado*) brazen
[2] [*comentario, chiste*] indecent, obscene

procedencia SF [1] (= *origen*) source, origin
[2] (= *lugar de salida*) [*de tren, avión*] point of departure; [*de barco*] port of origin
[3] (*Jur*) propriety, legitimacy
[4] (= *conveniencia*) properness

procedente ADJ [1] **~ de** from; **un queso ~ de Noruega** a Norwegian cheese, a cheese from Norway; **llegó a Madrid ~ de Colombia** he arrived in Madrid from Colombia; **el tren ~ de Sevilla** the train from Seville
[2] (= *conveniente*) proper, fitting
[3] (*Jur*) proper; **procedimiento ~** proper procedure

procedentemente ADV properly, in a right and proper fashion

proceder ▸conjug 2a◂ Ⓐ VI [1] (= *provenir*) **~ de** to come from, originate in; **procede de una familia rica** she comes from *o* belongs to a wealthy family; **todo esto procede de su negativa** all this springs from his refusal; **de donde procede que ...** (from) whence it happens that ... (*frm*)
[2] (*al actuar*) (= *obrar*) to act; (= *conducirse*) to proceed, behave; **ha procedido precipitadamente** he has acted hastily; **conviene ~ con cuidado** it is best to go carefully, it would be best to proceed with caution; **~ contra algn** (*Jur*) to take proceedings against sb
[3] (= *pasar*) to proceed; **~ a una elección** to proceed to an election; **procedieron a la detención de los sospechosos** they proceeded to arrest the suspects; **procedieron a despejar la carretera** they proceeded to clear the road
[4] (= *ser correcto*) to be right (and proper), be fitting; **no procede obrar así** it is not right to act like that; **si el caso procede** if the case warrants it; **luego, si procede, ...** then, if appropriate, ...; **táchese lo que no proceda** cross out what does not apply
[5] (*) (= *estar de moda*) to be in*, be in fashion
Ⓑ SM (= *conducta*) behaviour, behavior (*EEUU*); (= *línea de acción*) course of action

procedimental ADJ procedural; (*Jur*) legal

procedimiento SM (= *sistema*) process; (= *método*) means, method; (= *trámites*) procedure; (*Jur*) proceedings; **un ~ para abaratar el producto** a method of making the product cheaper; **por un ~ deductivo** by a deductive process; **los ~s establecidos en el Tratado** the procedures established by the Treaty

proceloso ADJ (*liter*) stormy, tempestuous

prócer SM [1] (= *persona eminente*) worthy, notable; (= *magnate*) important person; (*esp LAm Pol*) famous son, famous citizen; **~ de las letras** literary figure, eminent writer
[2] (= *líder*) great man, leader; (*LAm*) leader of the independence movement

procesado[1] Ⓐ ADJ [*alimento*] processed
Ⓑ SM (*Téc*) processing ► **procesado de aguas** water treatment ► **procesado de imágenes** image processing

procesado[2]**/a** ADJ, SM/F accused

procesador SM processor ► **procesador de datos** data processor ► **procesador de textos** word processor

procesadora SF (*LAm*) (*tb* **~ de alimentos**) food processor

procesal ADJ [*derecho, obligación*] procedural; [*gasto*] legal; **defecto ~** procedural technicality; **costas ~es** legal costs

procesamiento SM [1] (*Jur*) (*gen*) prosecution; (= *juicio*) trial; *ver tb* **auto**[2] **1**
[2] (*Inform*) processing ► **procesamiento concurrente** concurrent processing ► **procesamiento de datos** data processing ► **procesamiento de textos** word processing ► **procesamiento interactivo** interactive processing ► **procesamiento por lotes** batch processing ► **procesamiento simultáneo** simultaneous processing
[3] (*Téc*) processing

➤ LENGUA Y USO: **probabilidad 1** 42.2 **2** 42.2, 43.2 **probable 1** 42.2, 43.2 **probablemente** 53.6 **problema A1** 53.2, 53.3

procesar ▸conjug 1a◂ VT [1] (= *juzgar*) [*juez*] to try, put on trial; [*estado, acusación*] to prosecute, put on trial
[2] (= *demandar*) to sue, bring an action against
[3] (*Téc, Inform*) to process

procesión SF [1] (*Rel*) procession
[2] (= *hilera*) stream; **una ~ de mendigos/hormigas** a never-ending stream of beggars/ants; **una ~ de quejas** a never-ending series of complaints; ✦*MODISMO* **la ~ va por dentro** he keeps his troubles *o* problems to himself

procesional ADJ processional

procesionaria SF (= *mariposa*) processionary moth; (= *oruga*) processionary caterpillar

proceso SM [1] (= *desarrollo, tb Anat, Quím*) process; **el ~ de una enfermedad** the course *o* progress of a disease ► **proceso de paz** peace process; ► **proceso de selección** selection process ► **proceso mental** mental process
[2] (*Med*) **un ~ gastroenterítico** an attack of gastroenteritis; **un ~ gripal** a bout of flu ► **proceso infeccioso** infection ► **proceso pulmonar** lung disease
[3] (= *transcurso*) lapse of time; **en el ~ de un mes** in the course of a month
[4] (*Jur*) (= *juicio*) trial; (= *pleito*) lawsuit, proceedings *pl*; **abrir** *o* **entablar ~** to bring a suit (**a** against); ► **proceso verbal** (= *escrito*) record; (= *audiencia*) hearing
[5] (*Inform*) processing ► **proceso de imágenes** image processing ► **proceso de textos** word processing ► **proceso electrónico de datos** electronic data processing ► **proceso no prioritario** background processing ► **proceso por lotes** batch processing ► **proceso prioritario** foreground processing

procesual ADJ [1] (*Jur*) procedural
[2] (= *en progreso*) evolving

proclama SF [1] (*Pol*) (= *bando*) proclamation; (= *discurso*) address; (= *manifiesto*) manifesto
[2] **proclamas** (= *amonestaciones*) banns

proclamación SF proclamation

proclamar ▸conjug 1a◂ Ⓐ VT to proclaim; **~ a algn algo** to proclaim sb sth; ✦*MODISMO* **~ algo a los cuatro vientos** to shout sth from the rooftops
Ⓑ **proclamarse** VPR **~se campeón** to become champion, win the championship; **~se rey** to proclaim o.s. king

proclive ADJ inclined, prone (**a** to)

proclividad SF proclivity (*frm*), inclination

procónsul SM proconsul

procreación SF procreation (*frm*), breeding

procrear ▸conjug 1a◂ VT, VI to procreate (*frm*), breed

procura SF (*esp LAm*) obtaining, getting; **en ~ de** in search of; **andar en ~ de algo** to be trying to get sth

procuración SF (*Jur*) power of attorney, proxy

procurador(a) SM/F [1] (*Jur*) (= *abogado*) attorney, solicitor ► **procurador(a) general** attorney general
[2] (= *apoderado*) proxy
[3] (*tb* **~ en Cortes**) (*Pol, Hist*) deputy, *member of Spanish parliament under Franco*; (*actualmente*) *member of a regional parliament*

procuraduría SF [1] (= *despacho*) lawyer's office
[2] (*tb* **~ general**) (*Méx*) attorney general's office
[3] (= *costas*) legal costs *pl*, lawyers' fees *pl*

procurar ▸conjug 1a◂ Ⓐ VT [1] (= *intentar*) **~ hacer algo** to try to do sth, endeavour *o* (*EEUU*) endeavor to do sth; **procura conservar la calma** do try to keep calm; **procura que no te vean** don't let them see you, take care not to let them see you
[2] (= *conseguir*) to get, obtain; **~ un puesto a algn** to get sb a job, find a job for sb; **esto nos ~á grandes beneficios** this will bring us great benefits
[3] (= *lograr*) **~ hacer algo** to manage to do sth, succeed in doing sth; **por fin procuró dominarse** eventually he managed to control himself
Ⓑ **procurarse** VPR **~se algo** to secure sth

procurón* ADJ (*Méx*) interfering, nosey*

Procustes SM, **Procusto** SM Procrustes; **lecho de ~** Procrustes' bed

prodigalidad SF [1] (= *abundancia*) bounty, richness
[2] (= *liberalidad*) lavishness, generosity
[3] (= *despilfarro*) wastefulness, extravagance

pródigamente ADV [1] (= *abundantemente*) bountifully
[2] (= *generosamente*) lavishly
[3] (= *con prodigalidad*) prodigally
[4] (= *con despilfarro*) wastefully

prodigar ▸conjug 1h◂ Ⓐ VT (= *dar mucho*) to lavish, give lavishly; (= *despilfarrar*) to squander; **prodiga las alabanzas** he is lavish in his praise; **nos prodigó sus atenciones** he was very generous in his kindnesses to us; **~ algo a algn** to lavish sb with sth, lavish sth on sb
Ⓑ **prodigarse** VPR [1] (= *ser generoso*) to be generous (*with what one has*); **se ~on en alabanzas** they were lavish with *o* in their praise
[2] (= *dejarse ver*) to show o.s.; **no te prodigas mucho que digamos** we don't see much of you to say the least

prodigio Ⓐ SM [1] (= *cosa*) wonder; **los ~s de la tecnología moderna** the wonders of modern technology; **este nuevo chip es un ~ electrónico** this new chip is an electronic wonder *o* marvel
[2] (= *persona*) prodigy; **este niño es un auténtico ~** this child is a real prodigy
[3] (*Rel*) miracle
Ⓑ ADJ INV **niño ~** child prodigy

prodigiosamente ADV prodigiously, marvellously, marvelously (*EEUU*)

prodigioso ADJ prodigious, marvellous, marvelous (*EEUU*)

pródigo/a Ⓐ ADJ [1] (= *exuberante*) bountiful; **un discurso ~ en citas bíblicas** a discourse rich in biblical quotations; **fui tan ~ en los pormenores que ...** I was so lavish in *o* with details that ...; **la pródiga naturaleza** bountiful nature
[2] (= *generoso*) lavish, generous (**de** with); **ser ~ de sus talentos** to be generous in offering one's talents
[3] (= *derrochador*) prodigal, wasteful; **hijo ~** prodigal son
Ⓑ SM/F (= *derrochador*) spendthrift, prodigal

producción SF [1] (*Com*) (= *acción*) production; (= *cantidad*) output; **en fase de ~** in the production phase; **la ~ maderera de Brasil** Brazil's timber output ► **producción bruta** gross production ► **producción en cadena** production-line assembly ► **producción en serie** mass production
[2] (*Literat, Mús*) output; **la ~ poética de Lorca** Lorca's poetic output; **su abundante ~ operística** his prolific operatic work
[3] (*Cine, Teat*) production; **departamento de ~** production department; **una ~ italiana** an Italian production ► **producción propia** (*TV*) in-house production; **programas de ~ propia** in-house programmes

producir ▸conjug 3n◂ Ⓐ VT [1] [+ *cereales, fruta, petróleo*] to produce; **se producen miles de toneladas de aceitunas al año** thousands of tons of olives are produced each year; **este país produce buenos deportistas** this country produces good sportsmen
[2] (= *fabricar*) [+ *aceite, coche*] to produce, make; [+ *electricidad, energía*] to produce, generate; **esta factoría ha producido cinco mil vehículos en un mes** this factory has turned out *o* produced *o* made five thousand vehicles in a month; **~ algo en serie** to mass-produce sth
[3] [+ *cambio, efecto, herida, daños*] to cause; **el virus que produce la neumonía** the virus which causes pneumonia; **un fallo en los frenos produjo el accidente** the accident was caused by brake failure; **tanto ruido me produce dolor de cabeza** all this noise is giving me a headache; **el polvo me produce alergia** I'm allergic to dust; **¿qué impresión te produjo?** what impression did it make on you?; **~ alegría a algn** to make sb happy; **~ tristeza a algn** to make sb sad
[4] (*Fin*) [+ *interés*] to yield; [+ *beneficio*] to yield, generate; **mis ahorros me producen un interés anual del 5%** my savings yield an annual interest of 5%
[5] (= *crear*) [+ *novela, cuadro*] to produce; **llevo tiempo sin ~ nada** I haven't produced anything for some time
[6] (*Cine, TV*) to produce
Ⓑ **producirse** VPR [1] (= *ocurrir*) [*cambio, efecto*] to take place; [*accidente, explosión, terremoto*] to occur; [*guerra, incendio, revolución*] to break out; **a no ser que se produzca un cambio** unless there is a change, unless a change takes place; **el accidente se produjo al salir de la autopista** the accident occurred as they left the motorway; **se produjo un aumento sensible de la demanda de viviendas** there was a significant increase in the demand for houses; **se desconoce a qué hora se produjo la muerte** the time of death is unknown; **se ha producido una disminución de la inversión** investment has fallen
[2] (= *provocarse*) [+ *herida, fractura*] **se produjo varias heridas con una cuchilla** he inflicted wounds on himself with a razor blade; **al caerse se produjo una fractura en el pie** she fractured a bone in her foot when she fell; **él mismo se produjo la muerte** he caused his own death

productividad SF productivity

productivo ADJ [*tierra, fábrica, encuentro*] productive; [*negocio*] profitable; **~ de interés** [*bono*] interest-bearing

producto SM [1] (= *artículo*) product; **nuestra gama de ~s cosméticos** our range of cosmetic products; **~s de primera necesidad**

staple items, staple products, basic necessities; **"consuma ~s españoles"** "buy Spanish goods"; **los ~s del campo** country produce ► **productos agrícolas** agricultural produce *sing*, farm produce *sing* ► **productos alimenticios** foodstuffs ► **productos de belleza** beauty products ► **productos de consumo** consumer goods ► **productos de desecho** waste products ► **productos de limpieza** cleaning products ► **producto derivado** by-product; **~s derivados de la leche** dairy products, dairy produce *sing*; **~s derivados del petróleo** oil products ► **producto químico** chemical product, chemical ► **productos de marca** branded goods, brand name goods ► **producto secundario** by-product ► **productos estancados** goods sold by state monopoly ► **productos lácteos** dairy products, dairy produce *sing* ► **productos perecederos** perishable goods

2 (= *producción*) production; **ha aumentado el ~ de este año** production has increased this year

3 (= *resultado*) result, product; **la clonación es ~ de años de investigación** cloning is the result *o* product of years of research; **eso es ~ de tu imaginación** that is a figment of your imagination

4 (*Fin*) (= *beneficio*) yield, profit ► **producto interior bruto** gross domestic product ► **producto interno bruto** (*Arg*) gross domestic product ► **producto nacional bruto** gross national product

5 (*Mat*) product

productor(a)[1] Ⓐ ADJ 1 (*Com, Agr*) producing; **países ~es de petróleo** oil producing countries; **las naciones ~as** producer nations

2 (*Cine, TV, Mús*) production *antes de s*; **la compañía ~a** the production company

Ⓑ SM/F 1 (*Com*) producer; (*Agr*) producer, grower; **el principal ~ de refrescos del mundo** the largest producer of soft drinks in the world; **los ~es de aceite de oliva** olive oil producers; **los ~es de vino** wine producers *o* growers

2 (*Cine, TV*) producer ► **productor(a) asociado/a** associate producer ► **productor(a) ejecutivo/a** executive producer

3 (= *obrero*) labourer

productora[2] SF (= *empresa*) (*Com*) producer; (*Cine, TV*) production company; (*Mús*) record company

produje, **produzco** *etc ver* **producir**

proemio SM preface, introduction

proeza SF 1 (= *hazaña*) exploit, feat, heroic deed

2 (*LAm*) (= *alarde*) boast

Prof. ABR, **prof.** ABR (= **profesor**) Prof

Profa. ABR, **profa.** ABR (= **profesora**) Prof

profanación SF desecration

profanar ▸conjug 1a◂ VT [+ *tumba, templo*] to desecrate, defile; **~ la memoria de algn** to blacken the memory of sb

profano/a Ⓐ ADJ 1 (= *laico*) profane, secular

2 (= *irrespetuoso*) irreverent

3 (= *no experto*) lay, uninitiated; (= *ignorante*) ignorant; **soy ~ en la materia** I don't know anything about the subject; **soy ~ en música** I don't know anything about music, I'm a layman when it comes to music

4 (= *deshonesto*) indecent, immodest

Ⓑ SM/F (= *inexperto*) layman/laywoman; (= *ajeno*) outsider

profe* SM/F = **profesor(a)**

profecía SF prophecy

proferir ▸conjug 3i◂ VT [+ *palabra, sonido, maldición*] to utter; [+ *insinuación*] to drop, throw out; [+ *insulto*] to hurl, let fly (**contra** at); [+ *suspiro*] to fetch, heave

profesar ▸conjug 1a◂ Ⓐ VT 1 (*Rel*) [+ *religión*] to profess; [+ *admiración, creencia*] to profess, declare

2 [+ *profesión*] to practise, practice (*EEUU*)

3 [+ *materia*] to teach; (*Univ*) to hold a chair in

Ⓑ VI (*Rel*) to take vows

profesión SF 1 (= *ocupación*) profession; (*en formulario*) occupation; (= *vocación*) calling, vocation; **abogado de ~** ◊ **de ~ abogado** a lawyer by profession ► **profesión liberal** liberal profession

2 (*Rel*) [*de fe*] profession, declaration; (*en orden religiosa*) taking of vows

profesional Ⓐ ADJ professional; **no ~** non-professional

Ⓑ SMF professional; **un ~ del diseño** a professional designer; **esta gran ~ del cine** this great professional of the cinema ► **profesional del amor** prostitute ► **profesional del sexo** sex worker

profesionalidad SF 1 [*de asunto*] professional nature

2 (= *actitud*) professionalism, professional attitude

profesionalismo SM professionalism

profesionalización SF **la ~ del ejército** the professionalization of the army; **ingresar en la ~** to become a professional

profesionalizar ▸conjug 1f◂ Ⓐ VT to professionalize, make more professional

Ⓑ **profesionalizarse** VPR to become professional, turn professional

profesionalmente ADV professionally

profesionista SMF (*Méx*) professional

profeso ADJ (*Rel*) professed

profesor(a) SM/F 1 (= *enseñante*) (*gen*) teacher; (= *instructor*) instructor ► **profesor(a) de autoescuela** driving instructor ► **profesor(a) de canto** singing teacher, singing tutor ► **profesor(a) de educación física** P.E. teacher ► **profesor(a) de equitación** riding teacher ► **profesor(a) de esgrima** fencing master/mistress ► **profesor(a) de esquí** ski instructor, skiing instructor ► **profesor(a) de gimnasia** gym instructor ► **profesor(a) de natación** swimming instructor ► **profesor(a) de piano** piano teacher ► **profesor(a) particular** private tutor ► **profesor(a) robot** teaching machine

2 (*Escol*) teacher ► **profesor(a) de biología** biology teacher, biology master/mistress ► **profesor(a) de instituto** secondary teacher

3 (*Univ*) (= *titular*) lecturer, professor (*EEUU*); (= *catedrático*) professor; **es ~ de griego** he is a lecturer in Greek, he lectures in Greek; **nuestros ~es de la universidad** our university teachers *o* lecturers; **se reunieron los ~es** the staff met, the faculty met (*esp EEUU*) ► **profesor(a) adjunto/a** assistant lecturer, assistant professor (*EEUU*) ► **profesor(a) agregado/a** assistant lecturer, assistant professor (*EEUU*)

profesorado SM 1 (= *profesores*) teaching staff, faculty (*EEUU*)

2 (= *profesión*) teaching profession; (= *enseñanza*) teaching, lecturing

3 (= *cargo*) professorship

profesoral ADJ [*actitud, tono*] professorial; [*plantilla, materiales*] teaching *antes de s*

profesoril ADJ donnish

profeta SM prophet; ✦*MODISMO* **no ser ~ en su tierra** not to be a prophet in one's own land

proféticamente ADV prophetically

profético ADJ prophetic

profetisa SF prophetess

profetizar ▸conjug 1f◂ VT (= *predecir*) to prophesy; (= *adivinar*) to guess, conjecture

profiláctico Ⓐ ADJ prophylactic

Ⓑ SM (= *condón*) condom, sheath (*frm*), prophylactic (*frm*)

profilaxis SF INV prophylaxis

prófugo SM (= *fugitivo*) fugitive; (= *desertor*) deserter; **continúa ~** he is still at large *o* on the run ► **prófugo de la justicia** fugitive from justice

profundamente ADV 1 (*con verbos*) [*creer, meditar, desconfiar*] deeply, profoundly; [*dormir*] deeply, soundly

2 (*con adjetivos*) [*religioso, afectado*] deeply, profoundly; [*dividido*] deeply; [*conservador*] extremely

profundidad SF 1 (= *hondura*) depth; (*Mat*) depth, height; **tener una ~ de 30cm** to be 30cm deep; **¿qué ~ tiene?** how deep is it?; **la poca ~ del río** the shallowness of the river; **la ~ de la crisis** the severity of the crisis ► **profundidad de campo** (*Fot*) depth of field; *ver tb* **carga 4**

2 **las ~es del océano** the depths of the ocean

3 (= *meticulosidad*) depth, profundity; **investigación en ~** in-depth investigation; **reforma en ~** radical *o* far-reaching reform; **limpieza de cutis en ~** deep skin cleansing

profundímetro SM depth gauge

profundización SF [*de conocimientos, crisis*] deepening; **es necesaria una ~ de los conocimientos históricos** we need to deepen our awareness of historical knowledge; **hemos de avanzar en la ~ de la democracia** we must consolidate democracy

profundizar ▸conjug 1f◂ Ⓐ VI **~ en algo** to go more deeply into sth; **no voy a ~ en este tema** I'm not going to go any more deeply into this topic; **un libro que ayuda a ~ en el conocimiento de las culturas americanas** a book which helps us to understand American cultures more deeply

Ⓑ VT 1 [+ *hoyo, pozo*] to deepen, make deeper

2 (= *investigar*) [+ *asunto*] to study in depth, go deeply into; [+ *misterio*] to fathom, get to the bottom of

profundo ADJ 1 (= *hondo*) deep; **tener 20cm de ~** to be 20cm deep, be 20cm in depth; **¿cuánto tiene de ~?** how deep is it?; **poco ~** shallow

2 (= *intenso*) [*suspiro, voz, respiración*] deep; [*nota*] low, deep; [*sueño*] deep, sound; [*misterio, pensador*] profound; **siento un ~ respeto hacia él** I have great *o* a deep respect for him; **las imágenes le produjeron una profunda**

impresión the pictures made a profound impression on him; **conocedor ~ del arte** expert in the art; **en lo ~ del alma** in the depths of one's soul; **estaban inmersos en una profunda oscuridad** (*liter*) they were enveloped by a profound darkness (*liter*)
[3] **en la Francia profunda** in the French heartland; **en el Sussex ~** in deepest Sussex, deep in Sussex

profusamente ADV (= *con abundancia*) profusely; (= *con extravagancia*) lavishly, extravagantly

profusión SF [1] (= *abundancia*) profusion
[2] (= *prodigalidad*) wealth; **con ~ de detalles** with a wealth of detail

profuso ADJ (= *abundante*) profuse; (= *pródigo*) lavish, extravagant

progenie SF [1] (= *hijos*) progeny (*frm*), offspring, brood (*pey*)
[2] (= *ascendencia*) family, lineage

progenitor(a) SM/F (= *antepasado*) ancestor; (= *padre*) father/mother; **progenitores** (*hum*) parents

progenitura SF offspring

progesterona SF progesterone

programa SM [1] (*de curso, actividades, TV, Radio*) programme, program (*EEUU*); **~ de actividades** programme of activities; **~ de gimnasia** exercise plan *o* regime ► **programa coloquio** chat show ► **programa concurso** game show ► **programa debate** TV debate ► **programa de consumo** consumer affairs programme ► **programa de estudios** curriculum, syllabus ► **programa de fomento de empleo** job creation scheme ► **programa electoral** electoral programme, electoral program (*EEUU*), election manifesto ► **programa piloto** pilot scheme
[2] (*Cine*) ► **programa continuo** continuous showing ► **programa doble** double bill
[3] (*Inform*) program ► **programa de aplicación** application program ► **programa fuente** source program ► **programa objeto** object program ► **programa verificador de ortografía** spell checker
[4] (*Cono Sur**) (= *amorío*) love affair

programable ADJ that can be programmed, programmable

programación SF [1] (*Inform*) programming, programing (*EEUU*) ► **programación de ordenadores** computer programming *o* (*EEUU*) programing
[2] (*Radio, TV*) programme planning, program planning (*EEUU*); (*en periódico*) programme guide, viewing guide; **ha habido ciertos cambios en la ~** there have been a few changes to the schedule ► **programación abierta** uncoded programmes *pl*, non-scrambled programmes *pl* ► **programación codificada** scrambled programmes *pl*
[3] (*Ferro*) scheduling, timetabling

programado ADJ planned, scheduled

programador(a) SM/F programmer; (*Inform*) (computer) programmer ► **programador(a) de aplicaciones** applications programmer ► **programador(a) de sistemas** systems programmer

programar ▸conjug 1a◂ VT [1] [+ *actividades, vacaciones*] (= *planear*) to plan; (*detalladamente*) to draw up a programme *o* (*EEUU*) program for
[2] (*Inform*) [+ *ordenador*] to program; [+ *vídeo*] to programme, program (*EEUU*)
[3] (*TV, Radio*) to show
[4] (*Ferro*) to schedule, timetable
[5] [+ *futuro*] to shape, mould, mold (*EEUU*), determine

programático ADJ programmatical

programería SF (*Inform*) ► **programería fija** firmware

progre* Ⓐ ADJ (= *moderno*) (*gen*) trendy; (*en política*) leftish, liberal; (*en lo sexual*) liberal, permissive (*in outlook*)
Ⓑ SMF (= *moderno*) (*gen*) trendy; (*en política*) lefty*, liberal; (*en lo sexual*) sexual liberal

progresar ▸conjug 1a◂ VI to progress, make progress

progresía SF [1] **la ~** (= *personas*) [*de moda*] the trendies; (*en política*) the lefties*, the liberals; (*en lo sexual*) the sexual liberals
[2] (= *actitud*) (*gen*) trendiness; (*Pol*) leftish outlook

progresión SF progression ► **progresión aritmética** arithmetic progression ► **progresión geométrica** geometric progression

progresista ADJ, SMF progressive

progresivamente ADV progressively

progresividad SF progressiveness, progressive nature

progresivo ADJ (= *que avanza*) progressive; (= *paulatino*) gradual; (= *continuo*) continuous; (*Ling*) continuous

progreso SM (= *mejora*) progress; (= *avance*) advance; **progresos** progress *sing*; **hacer ~s** to progress, make progress, advance

progubernamental ADJ pro-government

prohibición SF [1] (= *veto*) ban (**de** on), prohibition (**de** of); **la ~ total de las pruebas nucleares** the total ban on *o* the total prohibition of nuclear testing; **la ~ de exportar cereales** the banning *o* prohibition of cereal exports, the ban on cereal exports; **levantar la ~ de algo** to remove *o* lift the ban on sth
[2] [*de exportaciones, venta*] embargo (**de** on)

prohibicionismo SM prohibitionism

prohibicionista ADJ, SMF prohibitionist

prohibir ▸conjug 3a◂ VT [1] (= *vedar*) [+ *venta, consumo, publicidad, prueba nuclear*] to ban, prohibit; **han prohibido la venta ambulante** street selling has been banned *o* prohibited; **la ley lo prohíbe** it is banned by law; **han prohibido la circulación de camiones este fin de semana** lorries have been banned from the roads this weekend; **quieren ~ la caza de ballenas** they want to put a ban on whaling, they want to ban whaling; **está totalmente prohibido hacer publicidad del tabaco** there is a total ban on tobacco advertising, tobacco advertising is completely banned *o* forbidden; **queda terminantemente prohibido** it is strictly forbidden
[2] (= *no permitir*) **~ algo a algn: prohibieron el acceso a la prensa** the press were banned; **el médico me ha prohibido los dulces** the doctor says I'm not allowed (to eat) sweet things, the doctor has banned me from eating sweet things; **~ a algn hacer algo: me prohibió entrar en su casa** he banned me from his house, he forbade me to enter his house; **la dirección nos prohibía usar maquillaje** the management prohibited us from wearing make-up, the management forbade us to wear make-up; **~ a algn que haga algo** to forbid sb to do sth; **te prohíbo que me hables así** I forbid you to talk to me like that; **tener algo prohibido: tengo prohibido el tabaco** I'm not allowed to smoke; **le tenían prohibido salir de casa** he was not allowed out; **me tienen prohibida la entrada** I'm banned, they have banned me; **me tienen prohibido hablar de política mientras comemos** I'm banned from talking politics at the dinner-table, I'm not allowed to talk politics at the dinner-table
[3] (*en letreros*) **"prohibida la caza"** "no hunting"; **"prohibida la entrada a menores de 18 años"** "no (admission to) under-18s"; **"prohibido el paso a toda persona ajena a la obra"** "no unauthorized entry", "authorized personnel only"; **"queda prohibido el consumo de alcohol en este local"** "no alcohol may be consumed on these premises"; **"prohibido fumar"** "no smoking"; **"prohibido jugar a la pelota"** "no ball games"; **"prohibido fijar carteles"** "stick no bills"

➤ LENGUA Y USO: **prohibir 1** 36.3, 37.4

prohibitivo ADJ [1] [*coste, precio*] prohibitive; **los precios del marisco son ~s** seafood is prohibitively expensive, the price of seafood is prohibitive
[2] [*ley, señal*] prohibitive

prohibitorio ADJ prohibitory

prohijar ▸conjug 1a◂ VT to adopt

prohombre SM (= *eminencia*) outstanding man, great man; (= *líder*) leader

prójima* SF [1] (= *fulana*) loose woman, woman of dubious character
[2] **la ~*** (= *esposa*) my old woman*, the wife*

projimidad SF (*Andes, Caribe, Cono Sur*) (= *compasión*) fellow feeling, compassion (for one's fellows); (= *solidaridad*) solidarity

prójimo SM [1] (= *semejante*) fellow man, fellow creature; (= *vecino*) neighbour, neighbor (*EEUU*); **el dinero del ~** other people's money; **meterse en los asuntos del ~** to meddle in other people's affairs; **amar al ~** to love one's neighbour
[2] (*) (= *tío*) so-and-so*, creature

prolapso SM prolapse

prole SF (= *descendencia*) offspring; (*pey, hum*) brood (*pey, hum*), spawn (*pey*); **padre de numerosa ~** father of a large family

prolegómeno SM preface, introduction; **los ~s del partido** (= *comienzo*) the early stages of the match; (= *ceremonias*) the pre-match ceremonies

proletariado SM proletariat

proletario/a Ⓐ ADJ proletarian
Ⓑ SM/F proletarian (*frm*), worker; **se negaron a disparar sobre sus hermanos ~s** they refused to shoot their fellow workers

proletarismo SM proletarianism

proletarizar ▸conjug 1f◂ VT to proletarianize

proliferación SF proliferation; **tratado de no ~ (de armas nucleares)** non-proliferation treaty (for nuclear weapons)

proliferar ▸conjug 1a◂ VI to proliferate

prolífico ADJ prolific (**en** of)

prolijamente ADV (= *interminablemente*) long-windedly; (= *con pesadez*) tediously; (= *con minuciosidad*) with an excess of detail

prolijidad SF (= *extensión*) long-windedness, prolixity (*frm*); (= *minuciosidad*) excess of detail

prolijo ADJ 1 (= *extenso*) prolix (*frm*); (= *largo*) long-winded; (= *pesado*) tedious; (= *muy minucioso*) excessively meticulous
2 (*Arg*) (= *pulcro*) smart, neat
3 (*Cono Sur*) (= *incansable*) untiring

prologar ▸conjug 1h◂ VT to preface, write an introduction to; **un libro prologado por Ortega** a book with a preface by Ortega

prólogo Ⓐ SM 1 [*de libro*] prologue, prolog (*EEUU*) (**de** to); **un texto con ~ y notas de García Márquez** a text edited by García Márquez
2 (= *principio*) prelude (**de** to)
Ⓑ ADJ INV **etapa ~** preliminary stage, preparatory stage

prologuista SMF prologue *o* (*EEUU*) prolog writer

prolongación SF 1 (= *acto*) prolongation, extension
2 [*de carretera*] extension; **por la ~ de la Castellana** along the new part of the Castellana, along the extension of the Castellana
3 (*Elec*) extension, flex

prolongado ADJ [*reunión, viaje*] lengthy; **no se recomienda su uso ~** not suitable for prolonged use

prolongar ▸conjug 1h◂ Ⓐ VT 1 (= *alargar*) (*gen*) to prolong, extend; [+ *tubo*] to make longer, extend; [+ *reunión*] to prolong
2 (*Mat*) [+ *línea*] to produce
Ⓑ **prolongarse** VPR (= *alargarse*) to extend, go on; **la carretera se prolonga más allá del bosque** the road goes on beyond the wood; **la sesión se prolongó bastante** the meeting went on quite a long time, it was a pretty long meeting; **la fiesta se prolongó hasta la madrugada** the party went on until the early hours

prom. ABR (= **promedio**) av

promedial ADJ average

promedialmente ADV on the average, as an average

promediar ▸conjug 1b◂ Ⓐ VT 1 (*Mat*) to work out the average of, average (out)
2 (= *tener un promedio de*) to average; **la producción promedia 100 barriles diarios** production averages 100 barrels a day
Ⓑ VI 1 (= *mediar*) to mediate (**entre** between)
2 **promediaba el mes** it was halfway through the month; **antes de ~ el mes** before the month is halfway through

promedio SM 1 (= *término medio*) average; **el ~ es de 35%** the average is 35%; **el ~ de asistencia diaria** the average daily attendance; **para aprobar hace falta sacar un cinco de ~** you need an average of five to pass
2 [*de distancia*] middle, mid-point

promesa Ⓐ SF 1 (= *ofrecimiento*) (*gen*) promise; (*con compromiso formal*) pledge; **absolver a algn de su ~** to release sb from his promise; **cumplir una ~** to keep a promise; **faltar a una ~** to break a promise, go back on one's word ► **promesa de matrimonio** promise of marriage
2 (= *persona*) **la joven ~ del deporte español** the bright hope of Spanish sport
Ⓑ ADJ INV **jugador ~** promising player

promesante SMF (*Cono Sur*), **promesero/a** SM/F (*Andes, Cono Sur*) pilgrim

prometedor ADJ, **prometente** ADJ promising

prometedoramente ADV promisingly

Prometeo SM Prometheus

prometer ▸conjug 2a◂ Ⓐ VT 1 (= *dar palabra*) to promise; **le han prometido unas vacaciones** they've promised her a holiday; **¡te lo prometo!** I promise!; **prometió llevarnos al cine** he promised to take us to the cinema
2 (*) (= *asegurar*) to assure; **te prometo que se acordará de mí** I can assure you he will remember me; **no me verás más, te lo prometo** you won't see me again, (that) I can assure you
3 (= *augurar*) to promise; **esto promete ser interesante** this promises to be interesting; **esto no nos promete nada bueno** this does not look at all hopeful for us, this promises to be pretty bad for us
4 (*Rel*) **~ hacer algo** to take a vow to do sth
Ⓑ VI (= *tener porvenir*) to have promise, show promise; **este jugador promete** this player has *o* shows promise
Ⓒ **prometerse** VPR 1 **~se algo** to expect sth, promise o.s. sth; **nos habíamos prometido algo mejor** we had expected sth better; ✦**MODISMO** **prometérselas muy felices** to have high hopes
2 [*novios*] to get engaged; **se prometió con él en abril** she got engaged to him in April

▼**prometido/a** Ⓐ ADJ 1 [*ayuda, favor*] promised; ✦**REFRÁN** **lo ~ es deuda** a promise is a promise, you can't break a promise; **la Tierra Prometida** the Promised Land
2 [*persona*] engaged; **estar ~ con algn** to be engaged to sb
Ⓑ SM/F (= *novio*) fiancé/fiancée
Ⓒ SM (= *promesa*) promise

prominencia SF 1 (= *abultamiento*) bump, protuberance (*tb Med*); (= *hinchazón*) swelling; [*del terreno*] rise
2 (*esp LAm*) (= *importancia*) prominence

prominente ADJ 1 [*mentón, tripa*] prominent
2 (= *importante*) prominent

promiscuidad SF 1 (*sexual*) promiscuity
2 (= *heterogeneidad*) mixture, confusion
3 (= *ambigüedad*) ambiguity

promiscuo ADJ 1 (*sexualmente*) promiscuous
2 (= *heterogéneo*) (*con intención*) mixed; (*por casualidad*) motley
3 [*sentido*] ambiguous

promisión SF **tierra de ~** land of promise, promised land

promisorio ADJ 1 [*futuro, artista*] promising
2 (*Jur*) promissory

promoción SF 1 (= *ascenso*) (*gen*) promotion, advancement; (*profesional*) promotion
2 [*de producto, oferta*] promotion ► **promoción de ventas** sales promotion ► **promoción por correspondencia directa** direct mail advertising
3 ► **promoción inmobiliaria** property development
4 (= *año*) class, year; **la ~ de 1975** the 1975 class; **estaba en mi ~** he was from my class *o* year, he was the same class *o* year as me
5 (= *ganga*) special offer; **está en ~** it's on (special) offer

promocional ADJ promotional

promocionar ▸conjug 1a◂ Ⓐ VT 1 [+ *producto, artista*] to promote
2 (+ *empleado*) to promote
Ⓑ **promocionarse** VPR to improve o.s., better o.s.

promontorio SM (= *altura*) promontory; (*en la costa*) promontory, headland

promotor(a) SM/F (*gen*) promoter; [*de disturbios*] instigator, prime mover; [*de ley*] sponsor; **el ~ de los disturbios** the instigator of the rioting ► **promotor(a) de ventas** sales promoter ► **promotor(a) inmobiliario/a** property developer

promotora SF property development company

promovedor(a) SM/F (*gen*) promoter; [*de disturbios etc*] instigator

promover ▸conjug 2h◂ VT 1 (= *impulsar*) [+ *proceso, plan, intereses, desarrollo*] to promote; [+ *ley*] to sponsor; [+ *debate, conflicto*] to provoke; **normas destinadas a ~ el libre comercio** regulations aimed at promoting free trade; **~ un pleito** to bring an action, file a suit
2 (= *provocar*) to cause; **su discurso promovió un enorme alboroto en la sala** his speech caused a tremendous uproar in the hall
3 (= *ascender*) [+ *persona, equipo*] to promote (**a** to)

promulgación SF 1 (= *anuncio solemne*) announcement
2 [*de ley*] enactment

promulgar ▸conjug 1h◂ VT 1 (= *anunciar solemnemente*) to announce
2 [+ *ley*] to enact, pass

pronombre SM pronoun ► **pronombre personal** personal pronoun ► **pronombre posesivo** possessive pronoun ► **pronombre reflexivo** reflexive pronoun

pronominal ADJ pronominal

pronominalización SF pronominalization

pronosticación SF prediction, forecasting, prognostication (*frm*)

pronosticador(a) SM/F (*gen*) forecaster; (*Carreras*) tipster

pronosticar ▸conjug 1g◂ VT to forecast; **han pronosticado nevadas** they are forecasting snow; **pronosticó un aumento de la inflación** he forecast *o* predicted an increase in inflation

pronóstico SM 1 (= *predicción*) (*gen*) prediction, forecast; (*en carreras*) tip; **~s para el año nuevo** predictions for the new year ► **pronóstico del tiempo** weather forecast
2 (*Med*) prognosis; **de ~ leve** slight, not serious; **su ~ es reservado** (*por falta de datos*) his condition is uncertain; (*por posibilidad de agravamiento*) his condition is unstable

prontamente ADV promptly

prontico* ADV, **prontito** ADV 1 (= *rápido*) double-quick; (= *enseguida*) right away
2 (= *temprano*) very early, nice and early

prontitud SF 1 (= *rapidez*) quickness, promptness; **respondió con ~** he replied promptly
2 (= *viveza*) quickness, sharpness

pronto Ⓐ ADV 1 (= *dentro de poco*) soon; **el tren estará ~ aquí** the train will be here soon; **~ hará diez años que nos casamos** it will soon be ten years since we got married; **todavía es ~ para salir** it's too soon *o* early to leave; **cuanto más ~ mejor** the sooner the better; **¡hasta ~!** see you soon!; **lo más ~ posible** as soon as possible

➤ LENGUA Y USO: **prometido A2** 51.2

2 (*Esp*) (= *temprano*) early; **hoy he comido un poco ~** I ate a bit early today; **acostarse ~** to go to bed early; **levantarse ~** to get up early
3 (= *rápidamente*) quickly; **se hizo famoso muy ~** he became famous very quickly; **¡venid aquí, ~!** come here, right now *o* quickly!; ✦*MODISMO* **se dice (muy) ~*** (*algo difícil*) it's easier said than done; (*algo sorprendente*) it's quite a thought
4 (*otras locuciones*) **al ~** at first; **de ~** (= *repentinamente*) suddenly; (= *inesperadamente*) unexpectedly; (*Col, Cono Sur*) (= *a lo mejor*) maybe, perhaps; **de ~ se cayó el cuadro de la pared** the picture suddenly fell off the wall; **se presentó de ~ en la casa** he turned up at the house unexpectedly; **de ~ no sabe** maybe *o* perhaps he doesn't know; **por de** *o* **lo ~** (= *por ahora*) for now, for the moment; (= *en primer lugar*) for a start, for one thing; **por lo ~ toma setenta euros, mañana te daré el resto** take seventy euros for now *o* for the moment, and I'll give you the rest tomorrow; **—¿por qué no viniste? —bueno, por lo ~ estaba demasiado cansado** "why didn't you come?" — "well, for a start *o* for one thing I was too tired"; **tan ~ se ríe, tan ~ llora** one minute he's laughing, the next he's crying; **tan ~ es amigo tuyo, como de repente ya no lo es** one minute he's your friend, the next he doesn't want to know; **tan ~ como** (+ *SUBJUN*) as soon as; **te llamaré tan ~ como sepa algo** I'll call you as soon as I hear anything
Ⓑ ADJ 1 (*frm*) (= *rápido*) [*regreso, solución, mejoría*] swift; [*respuesta*] prompt; [*servicio, persona*] quick; **le deseo una pronta recuperación** I wish you a swift recovery; **quedo a la espera de su pronta respuesta** I look forward to your prompt reply; **es ~ en las decisiones** he is quick about making decisions; **estuvo muy ~ para irse** he was very quick to leave
2 (*Cono Sur*) (= *preparado*) ready; **la comida está pronta** lunch is ready; **estar ~ para algo** to be ready for sth; **los republicanos estamos ~s para este desafío** we republicans are ready for this challenge; **estar ~ para hacer algo** to be ready to do sth
Ⓒ SM (*Esp**) (= *arrebato*) **le dio un ~ y se largó** he left on a sudden impulse; **tiene unos ~s muy malos** he gets ratty all of a sudden*; **le dio un ~ de enojo y me golpeó** she flew into a sudden rage and hit me

prontuario SM 1 (= *libro*) handbook, manual, compendium
2 (*Arg Jur*) criminal record

pronuncia SF (*Méx*) = **pronunciamiento**

pronunciación SF pronunciation

pronunciado ADJ [*acento*] pronounced, strong; [*curva*] sharp; [*facciones*] marked, noticeable; [*pendiente*] steep; [*tendencia*] marked, noticeable

pronunciamiento SM military revolt, military uprising

▼ **pronunciar** ▸conjug 1b◂ Ⓐ VT 1 (*Ling*) [+ *palabra, idioma*] to pronounce; [+ *sonido*] to make, utter
2 (= *decir*) [+ *discurso*] to make, deliver; [+ *brindis*] to propose; **~ unas palabras de elogio** to say a few words of tribute; **pronunció unas palabras en las que ...** she said that ...
3 (*Jur*) [+ *sentencia*] to pass, pronounce
Ⓑ **pronunciarse** VPR 1 to be pronounced; **no sé cómo se pronuncia esta palabra** I don't know how to pronounce this word
2 (= *expresarse*) to declare o.s., state one's opinion; **~se a favor de algo** to pronounce in favour of sth, declare o.s. in favour of sth; **~se sobre algo** to pronounce on sth, make a pronouncement about sth; **un 20% no se pronunció** 20% expressed no opinion
3 (*Pol, Mil*) (= *rebelarse*) to revolt, rise
4 (= *acentuarse*) to become (more) pronounced
5 (*) (= *apoquinar*) to cough up*, fork out*

pronuncio SM (*Andes*) = **pronunciamiento**

propagación SF 1 (= *extensión*) [*de enfermedad, infección, fuego*] spreading; [*de ruido*] spreading, diffusion (*frm*); [*de ideas*] spreading, dissemination (*frm*)
2 (*Biol*) propagation

propaganda SF 1 (*Pol*) propaganda ► **propaganda electoral** electoral propaganda
2 (*Com*) (= *publicidad*) advertising; **las revistas están llenas de ~** magazines are full of advertising; **hacer ~ de algo** to advertise sth; **han hecho mucha ~ del concierto** the concert has been well-advertised
3 (= *panfletos, octavillas*) advertising leaflets *pl*; **repartía ~ por la calle** he was handing out advertising leaflets in the street; **me han llenado el buzón de ~** I've been inundated with junk mail

propagandista SMF propagandist

propagandístico ADJ 1 (*Pol*) propaganda *antes de s*
2 (*Com*) advertising *antes de s*

propagar ▸conjug 1h◂ Ⓐ VT 1 (= *extender*) [+ *ideas*] to spread, disseminate; [+ *rumor, enfermedad, fuego*] spread
2 (*Biol*) to propagate
Ⓑ **propagarse** VPR 1 [*ideas, rumores, enfermedad, incendio*] to spread
2 (*Biol*) to propagate

propalación SF (= *divulgación*) disclosure; (= *diseminación*) dissemination

propalar ▸conjug 1a◂ VT (= *divulgar*) to divulge, disclose; (= *diseminar*) to disseminate; (= *publicar*) to publish an account of

propano SM propane

propasarse ▸conjug 1a◂ VPR (= *excederse*) to go too far, overstep the bounds; (*sexualmente*) to take liberties, overstep the bounds of propriety

propela SF (*Caribe, Méx*) (= *hélice*) propeller; (= *fuerabordo*) outboard motor

propelente SM propellent

propender ▸conjug 2a◂ VI **~ a algo** to tend towards sth, incline to sth; **~ a hacer algo** to tend to do sth, have a tendency to do sth

propensión SF inclination, tendency (**a** to); (*Med*) tendency

▼ **propenso** ADJ 1 **~ a** (= *predispuesto*) prone to, subject to; (*Med*) prone to; **es muy ~ a enfadarse** he has a tendency to get angry, he's prone to getting angry; **soy propensa a los resfriados** I am very prone to colds, I catch colds easily
2 (= *dispuesto*) inclined to; **ser ~ a hacer algo** to be *o* feel inclined to do sth

propi* SF = **propina**

propiamente ADV 1 (*tb* **~ dicho**) (*tb* **~ hablando**) strictly speaking; **éste es, ~, el centro del pueblo** this is, strictly speaking, the town centre; **~ hablando, esto no es un vaso, sino una taza** strictly speaking, that is a cup not a glass; **la ceremonia religiosa ~ dicha comenzará a las doce** the religious ceremony itself will begin at twelve
2 (= *auténticamente*) really, exactly; **la novela no es ~ autobiográfica** the novel is not really *o* exactly autobiographical

propiciación SF propitiation

propiciador(a) SM/F (*LAm*) sponsor

propiciar ▸conjug 1b◂ VT 1 [+ *cambio, revolución*] (= *favorecer*) to favour, favor (*EEUU*); (= *crear condiciones*) to create a favourable atmosphere for; (= *provocar*) to cause, give rise to; **tal secreto propicia muchas conjeturas** such secrecy gives rise to *o* causes a lot of speculation; **un hecho que propició que el fuego se extendiera** a fact which helped the fire to spread
2 (= *atraer*) to propitiate (*frm*), win over
3 (*LAm*) to sponsor

propiciatorio ADJ propitiatory; **víctima propiciatoria** scapegoat

propicio ADJ [*momento, condiciones*] favourable, favorable (*EEUU*); [*persona*] kind, well-disposed

propiedad SF 1 (= *pertenencia*) possession, ownership; **ser de la ~ de algn** to be the property of sb, belong to sb; **es ~ del municipio** it is the property of the town, it belongs to the council, it's council property; **una finca de la ~ del marqués** an estate belonging to the marquis; **en ~: tener un puesto de trabajo en ~** to have tenure; **tener un piso/una parcela en el cementerio en ~** to own a flat/a plot of land in the cemetery; **adquirir una vivienda/un terreno en ~** to purchase a home/a piece of land (*land or property*); **ceder algo a algn en ~** to transfer to sb the full rights (of ownership) over sth, transfer sth completely to sb ► **propiedad privada** private ownership; **"no pasar — ~ privada"** "no entry — private property" ► **propiedad pública** public ownership
2 (= *objeto poseído*) property; **una ~** a property, a piece of property; **este diamante es una de sus ~es más preciadas** this diamond is one of her most treasured possessions ► **propiedad particular** private property
3 (*Quím, Med*) property
4 (= *característica*) property, attribute
5 (= *adecuación*) propriety; **discutir la ~ de una palabra** to discuss the appropriateness of a word; **hablar con ~** to speak properly *o* correctly; **hablar español con ~** (= *expresarse bien*) to have a good command of Spanish; (= *hablar correctamente*) to speak Spanish correctly, speak correct Spanish
6 (= *exactitud*) accuracy; **lo reproduce con toda ~** he reproduces it faithfully
7 (*Com*) (= *derechos*) right, rights *pl*; **"es propiedad"** "copyright" ► **propiedad industrial** patent rights *pl* ► **propiedad intelectual, propiedad literaria** copyright

propietario/a Ⓐ ADJ **la inmobiliaria propietaria del piso** the property company which owns the flat
Ⓑ SM/F 1 (= *poseedor*) (*gen*) owner, proprietor/proprietress; [*de tierras*] landowner; **es ~ de una cadena de restauran-**

➤ LENGUA Y USO: pronunciar B2 33.3 propenso 1 53.1

tes he owns a chain of restaurants
2 (= *casero*) landlord/landlady

propina SF 1 (= *dinero extra*) (*en restaurante, bar*) tip, gratuity (*frm*); [*de los niños*] pocket money; **dar algo de ~** to give sth extra; **me dieron mil pesetas de ~** they gave me a thousand-peseta tip; **si compras seis te dan uno de ~** if you buy six you get one free
2 (*Mús*) encore

propinar ▸conjug 1a◂ Ⓐ VT 1 (= *dar*) [+ *golpe*] to strike, deal; [+ *azotes*] to give; **le propinó una buena paliza** he gave him a good thrashing; **le propinó una serie de consejos** he gave him a lot of advice, he made him listen to several bits of advice
2 (= *invitar*) **~ a algn** to buy sb a drink
Ⓑ **propinarse** VPR **~se algo** to treat o.s. to sth

propincuidad SF propinquity, nearness, proximity

propincuo ADJ near

propio Ⓐ ADJ 1 (*uso enfático*) 1·1 (*con posesivos*) own; **salió del hospital por su ~ pie** he left the hospital on his own two feet; **lo vi con mis ~s ojos** I saw it with my own eyes; ✦*MODISMO* **en mis propias narices** under my very nose
1·2 (= *mismo*) **me lo ha dicho el ~ ministro** the minister himself told me so; **la solicitud debe ser firmada por el ~ interesado** the application must be signed by the applicant himself; **hacer lo ~** to do the same, follow suit; **se marchó sin decir nada y pretendía que nosotros hiciéramos lo ~** he left without a word and wanted us to do the same *o* follow suit; **yo haría lo ~ que tú** I'd do the same as you; **al ~ tiempo** at the same time; **están subiendo los impuestos al ~ tiempo que baja la inflación** they are raising taxes at the same time as inflation is going down; **la novela es al ~ tiempo romántica y dinámica** the novel is both romantic and fast-moving at the same time
1·3 **al ~** (*CAm*) on purpose; **de ~** especially
2 (*indicando posesión*) own; **¿tiene coche ~?** do you have your own car?; **esos rizos parecen ~s** those curls look as if they are your own; **lo hizo en defensa propia** he did it in self-defence; **hablo en nombre ~ y en el de mis compañeros** I speak for myself and my colleagues
3 (= *característico*) **~ de algo/algn** typical of sth/sb; **una bebida propia del país** a drink typical of the country; **este sol es más ~ de un país mediterráneo** this sunshine is more typical of a Mediterranean country; **ese gesto era muy ~ de él** that gesture was very like him *o* very typical of him; **fruta propia del tiempo** seasonal fruit; **preguntas propias de un niño** questions that a child would ask
4 (= *inconfundible*) all (of) its own; **este perfume tiene un olor muy ~** this perfume has a scent all (of) its own
5 (= *adecuado*) suitable; **recibieron al rey con los honores que le son ~s** they received the king with the honours which are his due *o* with all suitable honours; **~ para algo** suitable for sth; **esa corbata no es muy propia para la ocasión** that tie is not very suitable for the occasion; **no es lugar ~ para este tipo de comportamiento** this is not the place for that sort of behaviour
6 (= *correcto*) strict, true; **utiliza las palabras en sentido ~** he uses the words in their strict *o* true sense
7 (*Esp**) (= *parecido*) **las manzanas están tan propias que dan ganas de comérselas** the apples look so real that you want to eat them; **has salido muy ~ en ese retrato** that portrait of you is a good likeness, that portrait looks really like you
8 (*esp Méx, CAm*) **—con su permiso —propio** "excuse me" — "certainly"
Ⓑ SM 1 (= *mensajero*) messenger
2 **~s y extraños** all and sundry; **su triunfo sorprendió a ~s y extraños** her victory surprised all and sundry

proponente SMF proposer

proponer ▸conjug 2q◂ (*pp* **propuesto**) Ⓐ VT
1 (= *sugerir*) [+ *idea, proyecto*] to suggest, propose; [+ *candidato*] to propose, put forward; [+ *brindis, moción de censura*] to propose; [+ *teoría*] to put forward, propound (*frm*); **hemos propuesto la creación de un centro de acogida** we have suggested *o* proposed the setting up of a reception centre; **el plan propuesto por el sindicato** the plan put forward *o* suggested *o* proposed by the union; **no creo que la solución sea ésa, como parece que algunos proponéis** I do not believe that is the solution, as some of you seem to suggest; **la cifra de ventas propuesta asciende a un millón de libras** the sales target comes to one million pounds; **te voy a ~ un trato** I'll make you a deal *o* a proposition; **~ a algn hacer algo** to suggest to sb that they should do sth; **fue ella quien me propuso hacer ese papel** it was her who suggested (to me) that I should play this part; **~ que** to suggest *o* propose that; **propongo que la reunión se aplace hasta mañana** I suggest *o* propose that the meeting be postponed till tomorrow, I suggest we put the meeting off till tomorrow; **yo propongo que lo paguemos a medias** I suggest we go halves on it; **le propuse que se casara conmigo** I proposed to her
2 (= *recomendar*) **~ a algn para** [+ *cargo*] to nominate sb for, propose sb as; [+ *premio*] to nominate sb for; **lo han propuesto para el cargo de secretario** they have nominated him for secretary, they have proposed him as secretary; **he sido propuesta para la beca de investigación** I've been nominated *o* proposed for the research scholarship; **la película ha sido propuesta como candidata para los Oscars** the film has been nominated for an Oscar
3 (= *plantear*) [+ *problema*] (*gen*) to pose; (*Mat*) to set
Ⓑ **proponerse** VPR **~se algo** to put one's mind to sth; **cuando me propongo algo seriamente, lo consigo** when I really set out to do something *o* put my mind to something, I get it done; **~se hacer algo** (*con intención*) to mean to do sth, intend to do sth; (*con empeño*) to be determined to do sth, be intent on doing sth; **me he propuesto dejar de fumar este año** I mean *o* intend to give up smoking this year; **no me había propuesto hacerte daño** I didn't mean *o* intend to hurt you; **me he propuesto terminar el libro hoy** I am determined to finish the book today, I am intent on finishing the book today; **~se que: ¿es que te has propuesto que lleguemos tarde?** you're determined to make us late, aren't you?, you're intent on making us late, aren't you?; **sin proponérselo** unintentionally; **y así, sin proponérmelo, me convertí en empresario** so, without exactly meaning to, I became a businessman, so I became a businessman unintentionally

proporción SF 1 (*gen*) proportion; (*Mat*) ratio; (= *relación*) relationship; (= *razón, porcentaje*) rate; **la ~ entre azules y verdes** the proportion of blues to greens; **está en ~ con los gastos** it is in proportion to the expenses; **ganaron la votación por una ~ de cinco a uno** they won the vote by a ratio of five to one; **esto no guarda ~ con lo otro** this is out of proportion to the rest; **guarda bien las proporciones** it remains in proportion
2 **proporciones** [*de objeto*] proportions; [*de plan, escándalo*] scope; **una máquina de proporciones gigantescas** a machine of huge size *o* proportions; **se desconocen las proporciones del desastre** the size *o* extent *o* scope of the disaster is unknown
3 (= *oportunidad*) chance, opportunity, right moment
4 **proporciones** (*Méx*) (= *riqueza*) wealth *sing*; **de proporciones** (*LAm*) (= *enorme*) huge, vast; (= *rico*) wealthy

proporcionadamente ADV proportionately, in proportion

proporcionado ADJ 1 **bien ~** [*persona, cara*] well-proportioned; [*talle*] shapely
2 (= *en proporción*) proportionate (**a** to)
3 (= *adecuado*) appropriate (**a** to); **de tamaño ~** of the appropriate size

proporcional ADJ proportional (**a** to)

proporcionalmente ADV proportionally

proporcionar ▸conjug 1a◂ VT 1 (= *dar*) to supply, provide; **~ dinero a algn** to supply sb with money; **esto le proporciona una renta anual de ...** this brings him in a yearly income of ...; **esto proporciona mucho encanto a la narración** this lends *o* gives great charm to the story; **su tío le proporcionó el puesto** his uncle found him the job, his uncle helped him into *o* helped him get the job
2 (= *adaptar*) to adjust, adapt (**a** to)

proposición SF 1 (= *sugerencia, oferta*) proposal; **aceptó nuestra ~ de vender la casa** he accepted our proposal to sell the house; **¿cuál es tu ~?** what do you propose?, what is your proposal *o* proposition? ► **proposición de ley** bill ► **proposición de matrimonio** marriage proposal, proposal of marriage ► **proposiciones deshonestas** indecent proposals, indecent suggestions ► **proposición no de ley** motion
2 (*Ling*) clause
3 (*Fil, Mat*) proposition

propósito SM 1 (= *intención*) purpose; **¿cuál es el ~ de su visita?** what is the purpose of his visit?; **para lograr este ~ se han desplazado a Madrid** with this in mind *o* for this purpose, they have gone to Madrid; **buenos ~s** (*para el futuro*) good intentions; (*para el año nuevo*) resolutions; **de ~** on purpose, deliberately; **fuera de ~** off the point; **hacer(se) (el) ~ de hacer algo** to resolve to do sth, decide to do sth; **los tres hicieron firme ~ de no atacar** the three of them resolved *o* decided not to attack; **nunca nos hemos hecho el ~ de gastar más dinero** it has never been our intention to spend more money; **sin ~** [*cami-*

➤ LENGUA Y USO: proponer A1 28.1 propósito 1 35.2 2 45.4

nar, moverse] aimlessly; [*actuar*] unintentionally; **tener (el) ~ de hacer algo** to intend *o* mean to do sth, be one's intention to do sth; **no tenía ~ ninguno de pelearme** I didn't intend *o* mean to get into a fight, it was not my intention to get into a fight; **tengo el firme ~ de irme de casa** I am determined to leave home, I am intent on leaving home ► **propósito de enmienda**: **no veo ~ de enmienda en su comportamiento** I don't see him mending his ways *o* turning over a new leaf
2 **a ~** 2·1 (*como adjetivo*) suitable, right (**para** for); **era la persona a ~ para el trabajo** he was very suitable for the job, he was the right person for the job; **hizo varios comentarios a ~** he made various comments on the matter
2·2 (*como adverbio*) on purpose, deliberately; **lo siento, no lo hice a ~** I'm sorry, I didn't do it on purpose *o* deliberately; **me he comprado un traje a ~ para la boda** I've bought a dress especially for the wedding; **venir a ~** (= *venir expresamente*) to come especially; (= *ser adecuado*) [*comentario, observación*] to be well-timed; [*dinero*] to come in handy; **he venido a ~ para verte** I have come especially to see you; **esa observación vino muy a ~** that was a timely remark, that remark was very well-timed; **el dinero que me diste me vino muy a ~** the money you gave me was just what I needed *o* came in very handy
2·3 (= *por cierto*) by the way; **a ~, ¿qué vais a hacer en Semana Santa?** by the way, what are you doing at Easter?
2·4 **a ~ de** (*después de verbo*) about; (*uso independiente*) talking of, à propos of; **estuvieron discutiendo a ~ de las elecciones** they were having a discussion about the election; **a ~ de Picasso, ¿has visto alguna vez el Guernica?** talking of *o* à propos of Picasso, have you ever seen Guernica?; **a ~ de dinero, ¿cuándo me vas a pagar?** now you mention it *o* talking of money, when are you going to pay me?; **¿a ~ de qué me dices eso ahora?** why do you say that now?

propuesta SF 1 (= *sugerencia*) proposal; **me hizo varias ~s de trabajo** he made me several work proposals; **a ~ de algn** at the proposal *o* suggestion of sb; **aprobar una ~** to approve a proposal; **desestimar una ~** to turn down *o* reject a proposal; **rechazar una ~** to reject a proposal, turn down a proposal ► **propuesta de ley** bill
2 (= *recomendación*) (*para un cargo*) candidature; (*para un premio*) nomination; **todos apoyaron su ~ como candidato** everyone supported his candidature; **la ~ de Elena como presidenta fue la más votada** Elena received most votes in the election for president
3 (= *proyecto*) design; **concurso de ~s** design competition

propuesto PP *de* **proponer**

propugnación SF advocacy

propugnar ▸conjug 1a◂ VT (= *proponer*) to advocate, propose, suggest; (= *apoyar*) to defend, support

propulsado ADJ **un avión ~ por tres motores** a plane driven by four engines; **el coche está ~ por un motor de ocho cilindros** the car has an eight-cylinder engine, the car runs on eight cylinders; **~ a chorro** jet-propelled

propulsante SM fuel, propellent

propulsar ▸conjug 1a◂ VT 1 (*Mec*) [+ *vehículo*] to drive, propel; [+ *avión, cohete*] to propel
2 [+ *actividad, cambio*] to promote, encourage

propulsión SF propulsion ► **propulsión a chorro** jet propulsion; **con ~ a chorro** jet-propelled ► **propulsión a cohete** rocket propulsion ► **propulsión por reacción** jet propulsion

propulsor(a) Ⓐ ADJ 1 [*motor*] jet *antes de s*
2 [*medidas*] driving
Ⓑ SM (*Téc*) (= *combustible*) propellent, fuel; (= *motor*) motor, engine
Ⓒ SM/F (= *persona*) promoter

propuse *etc ver* **proponer**

prorrata SF share, quota, prorate (*EEUU*); **a ~** proportionately, pro rata

prorratear ▸conjug 1a◂ VT to share out, distribute proportionately, prorate (*EEUU*); **~emos el dinero** we will share out the money pro rata; **los daños se ~án entre las cuatro aseguradoras** damages will be shared by the four insurers

prorrateo SM sharing (in proportion), apportionment; **a ~** pro rata, proportionately

prórroga SF (= *plazo extra*) extension; (*Dep*) extra time; (*Mil*) deferment; (*Jur*) stay (of execution), respite

prorrogable ADJ which can be extended

prorrogación SF deferment, prorogation (*frm*)

prorrogar ▸conjug 1h◂ VT [+ *período*] to extend; [+ *decisión*] to defer, postpone; [+ *sesión*] to prorogue, adjourn; (*Mil*) to defer; (*Jur*) to grant a stay of execution to; **prorrogamos una semana las vacaciones** we extended our holiday by a week; **no les ~on el contrato** their contract was not extended

prorrumpir ▸conjug 3a◂ VI to burst forth, break out; **la multitud prorrumpió en aplausos** the crowd burst (out) into applause; **~ en gritos** to start shouting; **~ en lágrimas** to burst into tears

prosa SF 1 (*Literat*) prose; **poema en ~** prose poem ► **prosa poética** prose poetry
2 (= *prosaísmo*) prosaic nature, ordinariness; **la ~ de la vida** the ordinariness of life
3 (*) (= *verborrea*) verbiage
4 (*Cono Sur*) (= *vanidad*) vanity, haughtiness
5 (*Andes, CAm*) (= *afectación*) pomposity, affectation

prosador(a) SM/F 1 (= *escritor*) prose writer
2 (*) (= *hablador*) chatterbox*, great talker

prosaicamente ADV prosaically

prosaico ADJ [*tono, lenguaje*] prosaic; [*explicación*] mundane, prosaic; [*ambición, objetivo*] mundane; **la realidad es mucho más prosaica** the truth is much more mundane

prosaísmo SM [*de lo cotidiano*] prosaic nature; (*Literat*) prosaicism

prosapia SF (= *alcurnia*) lineage, ancestry; **una familia de (mucha) ~** a (very) illustrious family; **es un liberal de ~** he comes from a long line of liberals

proscenio SM proscenium

proscribir ▸conjug 3a◂ VT 1 (= *prohibir*) (*gen*) to prohibit, ban; [+ *partido*] to proscribe, outlaw; [+ *criminal*] to outlaw; [+ *asunto*] to ban; **~ un tema de su conversación** to banish a topic from one's conversation
2 (= *desterrar*) to banish, exile

proscripción SF 1 (= *prohibición*) (*gen*) prohibition (*frm*) (**de** of), ban (**de** on); [*de partido*] proscription, outlawing
2 (= *destierro*) banishment

proscripto ADJ (*Arg*) = **proscrito**

proscrito/a Ⓐ PP *de* **proscribir**
Ⓑ ADJ 1 (= *prohibido*) (*gen*) banned, prohibited; [*actividad*] outlawed, proscribed; **un libro ~** a banned book
2 (= *desterrado*) exiled
Ⓒ SM/F (= *exiliado*) exile; (= *bandido*) outlaw

prosecución SF 1 (= *continuación*) continuation
2 [*de objetivo*] pursuit; [*de demanda*] pressing
3 (= *caza*) pursuit

proseguir ▸conjug 3d, 3k◂ Ⓐ VT (= *seguir*) [+ *charla, reunión*] to continue, carry on; [+ *demanda*] to go on with, press; [+ *investigación, estudio*] to pursue
Ⓑ VI 1 **~ en** *o* **con una actitud** to continue in one's attitude, maintain one's attitude
2 [*condición*] to continue, go on; **prosiguió con el cuento** he went on with the story; **¡por favor, prosiga!** please go on! *o* continue!; **prosigue el mal tiempo** the bad weather continues

proselitismo SM proselytism

proselitista ADJ proselytizing

prosélito/a SM/F convert, proselyte (*frm*); **hacer ~s** to win over converts

prosificación SF 1 (= *texto*) prose version
2 (= *acción*) rewriting as prose, turning into prose

prosificar ▸conjug 1g◂ VT to write a prose version of, rewrite as *o* in prose

prosista SMF prose writer

prosodia SF prosody

prosopopeya SF 1 (= *personificación*) personification, prosopopoeia (*frm*)
2 (= *pomposidad*) pomposity, affectation

prospección SF 1 (= *exploración*) exploration (**de** for); ► **prospección de mercados** market research
2 (*Min*) prospecting (**de** for); ► **prospección de petróleo** prospecting for oil, drilling for oil
3 (*Mil*) prospecting

prospeccionar ▸conjug 1a◂ VT to look to, examine

prospectar ▸conjug 1a◂ VT to survey

prospectiva SF futurology

prospectivo ADJ [*estudio, informe*] pilot; **análisis ~** forecast

prospecto SM 1 (= *folleto*) leaflet
2 (= *instrucciones*) (*gen*) sheet of instructions; [*de medicamento*] directions for use; [*de empresa, universidad*] prospectus

prospector(a) SM/F prospector ► **prospector(a) de mercados** market researcher

prósperamente ADV (= *con mejoras*) prosperously; (= *con éxito*) successfully

prosperar ▸conjug 1a◂ VI [*industria*] to prosper, thrive; [*idea, proyecto*] to prosper; (= *tener éxito*) to be successful; **la moción de censura no prosperó** the censure motion was unsuccessful *o* was defeated

prosperidad SF (= *bienestar*) prosperity; (= *éxito*) success; **en época de ~** in a period of prosperity, in good times; **desear a algn muchas ~es** to wish sb all success

próspero ADJ (= *floreciente*) prosperous, thriving; (= *venturoso*) successful; **feliz Navidad y ~ Año Nuevo** Happy Christmas and a prosperous new year; **con próspera fortuna** with good luck, favoured by fortune

próstata SF prostate

prosternarse ▸conjug 1a◂ VPR (= *postrarse*) to prostrate o.s.; (= *humillarse*) to bow low, bow humbly

prostético ADJ prosthetic

prostibulario ADJ brothel *antes de s*

prostíbulo SM brothel

prostitución SF prostitution; **casa de ~** brothel ▸ **prostitución infantil** child prostitution

prostituir ▸conjug 3g◂ Ⓐ VT [+ *persona*] to prostitute; [+ *ideales*] to prostitute
Ⓑ **prostituirse** VPR 1 (*en sentido sexual*) (*por primera vez*) to become a prostitute; (*como profesión*) to work as a prostitute
2 (= *corromperse*) to prostitute o.s.

prostituto/a SM/F male prostitute/prostitute

prosudo ADJ (*Andes, Cono Sur*) affected, pompous

protagónico ADJ leading, major

protagonismo SM 1 (= *papel*) leading role; (= *liderazgo*) leadership; **conceder el ~ al pueblo** to grant power to the people
2 (= *importancia*) prominence; (*en sociedad*) taking an active part, being socially active; **afán de ~** urge to be in the limelight; **tuvo poco ~** he made little showing; **el tema adquiere gran ~ en este texto** the theme takes on major importance in this text; **le gusta hacer las cosas sin ~s** he likes to do things without making a fuss
3 (= *defensa*) defence, defense (*EEUU*)
4 (= *apoyo*) support

protagonista Ⓐ ADJ central, leading; **tuvo un papel ~ en las negociaciones** she played a central *o* leading role in the negotiations
Ⓑ SMF 1 (*en hecho real*) main figure; **los ~s del conflicto** the main figures in the dispute
2 (= *personaje*) [*de obra literaria*] main character, protagonist (*frm*); [*de película, serie*] main character, lead; **el ~ no muere en la película** the main character *o* lead doesn't die in the film
3 (= *actor, actriz*) star; **la ~ de la película es Bette Davies** the star of the film is Bette Davies

protagonístico ADJ leading; **papel ~** leading role

protagonizar ▸conjug 1f◂ VT 1 (*Cine, Teat*) to play the lead in; **una película protagonizada por Greta Garbo** a film starring Greta Garbo
2 (= *formar parte de*) [+ *proceso, rebelión*] to lead; [+ *manifestación, protesta, accidente*] to be involved in; [+ *escándalo*] to be caught up in, be involved in; [+ *derrota, victoria*] to figure in, be involved in; **el mes ha estado protagonizado por ...** the month has been notable for ...; **un encuentro protagonizado por los dos actores principales** a meeting between the two main protagonists

proteaginosa SF protein product

protección SF protection ▸ **protección civil** civil defence *o* (*EEUU*) defense ▸ **protección de datos** data protection

proteccionismo SM protectionism

proteccionista Ⓐ ADJ [*medida*] protectionist; [*arancel*] protective
Ⓑ SMF protectionist

protector(a) Ⓐ ADJ 1 (= *defensivo*) protecting, protective; **cubierta ~a** protective cover; **medidas ~as de la industria** measures to protect industry, protective measures towards industry; **crema ~a** barrier cream
2 [*tono*] patronizing
Ⓑ SM/F (= *defensor*) (*gen*) protector; [*de artista*] patron; [*de la tradición*] guardian; **El Protector** (*LAm Hist Pol*) the Protector
Ⓒ SM 1 (*Inform*) ▸ **protector de pantalla** screen saver
2 ▸ **protector solar** sun protection
3 (*Boxeo*) ▸ **protector bucal** gum shield

protectorado SM protectorate

proteger ▸conjug 2c◂ Ⓐ VT 1 (= *resguardar*) to protect (**contra, de** against, from); **esta bufanda te ~á del frío** this scarf will protect you from the cold; **la policía protegió al árbitro de las iras del público** the police protected *o* shielded the referee from the wrath of the public; **sus padres la protegen demasiado** her parents are overprotective towards her; **protegemos los derechos de los trabajadores** we defend the rights of the workers; **~ contra grabación** *o* **escritura** (*Inform*) to write-protect
2 [+ *artista*] to act as patron to
Ⓑ **protegerse** VPR **~se de** *o* **contra algo** to protect o.s. from *o* against sth; **nos protegimos de** *o* **contra la lluvia en la cabaña** we sheltered from the rain in the hut; **se protegió del** *o* **contra el sol con una gorra** he wore a cap for protection against the sun; **~se de las miradas indiscretas** to shield o.s. from prying eyes

protegido/a Ⓐ ADJ 1 (= *resguardado*) protected; **especie protegida** protected species
2 [*vivienda*] subsidised
Ⓑ SM/F protégé, protégée

proteico ADJ 1 (= *cambiante*) protean
2 [*alimento, contenido*] protein *antes de s*

proteína SF protein

proteínico ADJ protein *antes de s*; **contenido ~** protein content

protervidad SF wickedness, perversity

protervo ADJ wicked, perverse

protésico/a Ⓐ ADJ prosthetic
Ⓑ SM/F prosthetist, limb-fitter ▸ **protésico/a dental** dental technician

prótesis SF INV (*Med*) (*gen*) prosthesis; (= *brazo, pierna*) artificial limb ▸ **prótesis de cadera** artificial hip ▸ **prótesis de mama** breast implant ▸ **prótesis dental** dental prosthesis ▸ **prótesis de silicona** silicone implant

protesta SF 1 (= *queja*) protest; **el ministro desoyó las ~s ciudadanas** the minister ignored the people's protests; **una manifestación de ~ contra la nueva ley** a protest demonstration against the new law; **los gritos de ~ fueron silenciados con aplausos** shouts of protest were drowned by the applause; **canción (de) ~** protest song; **déjate de ~s porque no pienso dejarte ir** you can stop protesting because I'm not going to let you go; **en señal de ~ contra** *o* **por algo** in protest against sth
2 (*frm*) (= *declaración*) protestation; **hacer ~s de lealtad** to protest one's loyalty

protestación SF protestation ▸ **protestación de fe** profession of faith ▸ **protestación de lealtad** protestation of loyalty, declaration of loyalty

protestante ADJ, SMF Protestant

protestantismo SM Protestantism

protestar ▸conjug 1a◂ Ⓐ VI 1 (= *quejarse*) to complain; **~on contra la subida de la gasolina** they complained *o* (*frm*) protested against the rise in the price of petrol; **protestó por lo mal que la habían tratado** she complained *o* (*frm*) protested about how badly she had been treated; **no protestes tanto y acábate la cena** stop complaining and finish your dinner
2 (*Jur*) **¡protesto, Su Señoría!** objection, Your Honour!; **¡protesto contra esa observación!** I resent that!, I object to that remark!
Ⓑ VT 1 [+ *letra, pagaré*] to protest, note; **un cheque protestado por falta de fondos** a cheque referred to drawer
2 (*frm*) (= *declarar*) to protest

protesto SM 1 [*de letra*] protest
2 (*LAm*) protest

protestón/ona* Ⓐ ADJ whingeing (*pey**), perpetually moaning
Ⓑ SM/F perpetual moaner, whinger (*pey**)

proto... PREF proto...

protocolario ADJ 1 (= *ceremonial*) required by protocol, established by protocol
2 (= *formulario*) ceremonial, formal

protocolo SM 1 (*Pol, Inform*) protocol
2 (= *reglas ceremoniales*) protocol, convention
3 (= *formalismo*) **sin ~s** informal(ly), without formalities
4 (*Med*) medical record

protón SM proton

protoplasma SM protoplasm

prototipo SM (= *arquetipo*) prototype; (= *modelo*) model

protuberancia SF 1 (= *bulto*) protuberance
2 (*en estadística*) bulge

protuberante ADJ protuberant

prov. ABR = **provincia**

provecho SM (= *ventaja*) advantage; (= *beneficio*) benefit; (*Fin*) (= *ganancia*) profit; **de ~** [*negocio*] profitable; [*actividad*] useful; [*persona*] worthy, honest; **¡buen ~!** enjoy your meal!; **¡buen ~ le haga!** and much good may it do him!; **en ~ de** to the benefit of; **un pueblo que lucha consigo mismo, en ~ de otros** a people who fight amongst themselves, to the benefit *o* advantage of others; **en ~ del prójimo** for the benefit of others; **en ~ propio** for one's own benefit, to one's own advantage; **sacar ~ de algo** to benefit from sth, profit by *o* from sth

provechosamente ADV advantageously, beneficially, profitably

provechoso ADJ (= *ventajoso*) advantageous; (= *beneficioso*) beneficial, useful; (= *rentable*) profitable

provecto ADJ aged, elderly; **de edad provecta** aged, elderly

proveedor(a) SM/F (= *abastecedor*) supplier, purveyor; (= *distribuidor*) dealer; **consulte a su ~ habitual** consult your usual dealer; **"Proveedores de la Casa Real"** "By appointment to His/Her Majesty" ▸ **proveedor de**

➤ LENGUA Y USO: **próspero** 50.2 **protestar A1** 41

servicios de Internet Internet Service Provider, ISP

proveeduría SF (*Cono Sur*) grocer's, grocery

proveer ▸conjug 2e◂ (*pp* **provisto y proveído**)
Ⓐ VT [1] (= *suministrar*) to supply, furnish (**de** with)
[2] (= *preparar*) to provide, get ready; **~ todo lo necesario** to provide all that is necessary (**para** for)
[3] [+ *vacante*] to fill
[4] [+ *negocio*] to transact, dispatch
[5] (*Jur*) to decree
Ⓑ VI **~ a** to provide for; **~ a las necesidades de algn** to provide for sb's needs; **~ a un vicio de algn** to pander to sb's vice
Ⓒ **proveerse** VPR **~se de algo** to provide o.s. with sth

proveniente ADJ **~ de** from; **gente ~ de diferentes países** people from different countries; **inversiones ~s de Japón** Japanese investment, investment from Japan

provenir ▸conjug 3r◂ VI **~ de** to come from; **la palabra "ruleta" proviene del francés** the word "roulette" comes from (the) French; **esto proviene de no haberlo curado antes** this stems from *o* comes from *o* is a result of not having treated it earlier

Provenza SF Provence

provenzal Ⓐ ADJ Provençal
Ⓑ SMF Provençal
Ⓒ SM (*Ling*) Provençal

proverbial ADJ proverbial

proverbialmente ADV proverbially

proverbio SM proverb

provida ADJ INV, **pro-vida** ADJ INV pro-life

próvidamente ADV providently

providencia SF [1] (*Rel*) **la (Divina) Providencia** (Divine) Providence
[2] **providencias** (= *precauciones*) measures, steps; **tomar las ~s necesarias para evitar accidentes** to take the steps necessary to avoid accidents
[3] (*Jur*) ruling, decision

providencial ADJ providential

providencialmente ADJ providentially

providente ADJ, **próvido** ADJ provident

provincia SF [1] (= *distrito*) province; (*Esp Admin*) ≈ county; **la capital de la ~** the provincial capital; **las Provincias Vascongadas** (*Hist*) the Basque Provinces, the Basque Country
[2] **de ~s: un pueblo de ~s** a country town, a provincial town; **lleva una vida de ~s** she lives a provincial life; **una gira por ~s** a tour of the provinces

> **PROVINCIA**
> *Spain is divided into 55 administrative* **provincias**, *including the islands and territories in North Africa. Each one has a* **capital de provincia** *which generally has the same name as the province itself.* **Provincias** *are grouped by geography, history and culture into* **comunidades autónomas.**
> ⇨ *See also* COMUNIDAD AUTÓNOMA

provincial¹ ADJ provincial, ≈ county *antes de s*

provincial²(a) SM/F (*Rel*) provincial

provincialismo SM [1] (= *cualidad*) provincialism
[2] (*Ling*) *dialect word, phrase etc*

provincianismo SM provincialism; **~ de cortas luces, ~ de vía estrecha** narrow provincialism, deadening provincialism

provinciano/a Ⓐ ADJ [1] (= *rural*) country *antes de s*
[2] (= *paleto*) provincial
[3] (†) (= *vasco*) Basque, of the Basque Provinces
Ⓑ SM/F [1] (= *de provincias*) provincial country dweller
[2] (†) (= *vasco*) Basque

proviniente ADJ = **proveniente**

provisión SF [1] (= *acto*) provision; **concurso para la ~ de 84 plazas de profesorado** competition to fill 84 teaching jobs
[2] (= *abastecimiento*) provision, supply
[3] **provisiones** (= *alimentos*) provisions, supplies
[4] (*Fin*) **cheque sin ~** bad cheque, bad check (*EEUU*) ► **provisión de fondos** financial cover
[5] (= *medida*) precautionary measure, step

provisional ADJ provisional

provisionalidad SF provisional nature, temporary character

provisionalmente ADV provisionally

provisionar ▸conjug 1a◂ VT to cover, make bad-debt provision for

provisorio ADJ (*esp LAm*) provisional

provista SF (*Cono Sur*) provisions *pl*, supplies *pl*

provisto PP *de* **proveer**; **~ de algo** [*persona*] provided with sth, supplied with sth; [*automóvil, máquina*] equipped with sth; **no iban ~s de suficiente comida** they didn't have enough food with them; **el televisor viene ~ de mando a distancia** the television comes with remote control included *o* complete with remote control

provocación SF provocation

provocador(a) Ⓐ ADJ provocative; **agente ~** agent provocateur
Ⓑ SM/F trouble-maker

▼ **provocar** ▸conjug 1g◂ Ⓐ VT [1] (= *causar*) [+ *protesta, explosión*] to cause, spark off; [+ *fuego*] to cause, start (deliberately); [+ *cambio*] to bring about, lead to; [+ *proceso*] to promote; **~ risa a algn** to make sb laugh; **incendio provocado** arson
[2] [+ *parto*] to induce, bring on
[3] [+ *persona*] (*gen*) to provoke; (= *incitar*) to rouse, stir up (to anger); (= *tentar*) to tempt, invite; **¡no me provoques!** don't start me!; **~ a algn a cólera** *o* **indignación** to rouse sb to fury; **~ a algn a lástima** to move sb to pity; **el mar provoca a bañarse** the sea invites one to go for a swim
[4] (*sexualmente*) to rouse
Ⓑ VI [1] (*LAm*) (= *gustar, apetecer*) **me provoca comer** I feel like eating; **¿te provoca un café?** would you like a coffee?, do you fancy a coffee?; **¿qué le provoca?** what would you like?, what do you fancy?; **no me provoca la idea** the idea doesn't appeal to me, I don't fancy the idea; **—¿por qué no vas? —no me provoca** "why aren't you going?" — "I don't feel like it"; **no me provoca estudiar hoy** I'm not in the mood for studying today, I don't feel like studying today
[2] (*) (= *vomitar*) to be sick, throw up*

provocativo ADJ [1] (= *incitante*) provocative
[2] (*sexualmente*) [*mirada, vestido*] provocative; [*risa, gesto*] inviting, provocative

proxeneta SMF pimp, procurer/procuress

proxenetismo SM procuring

próximamente ADV shortly, soon

proximidad SF nearness, closeness; **en las ~es de Madrid** in the vicinity of Madrid

próximo ADJ [1] (= *cercano*) near, close; [*pariente*] close; **un lugar ~ a la costa** a place near the coast; **vivimos muy ~s** we live very close by; **en fecha próxima** soon, at an early date; **estar ~ a algo** to be close to sth, be near sth; **estar ~ a hacer algo** to be on the point of doing sth, be about to do sth
[2] (= *siguiente*) next; **el mes ~** next month; **el ~ 5 de junio** on 5th June next; **se bajarán en la próxima parada** they will get off at the next stop

proyección SF [1] (= *acto*) [*de imagen*] projection; [*de luz*] casting, throwing
[2] (*Cine*) screening; **el tiempo de ~ es de 35 minutos** the film runs for 35 minutes, the screening lasts 35 minutes
[3] (= *diapositiva*) slide, transparency
[4] (= *alcance*) hold, influence; **la ~ de los periódicos sobre la sociedad** the hold of newspapers over society; **un intelectual con gran ~ social** a very influential intellectual; **un artista de una gran ~ internacional** an internationally renowned artist

proyeccionista SMF projectionist

proyectable ADJ **asiento ~** (*Aer*) ejector seat

proyectar ▸conjug 1a◂ VT [1] (= *planear*) **~ hacer algo** to plan to do sth; **tenía proyectado hablar con él** I was planning to speak to him
[2] (*Arquit*) to plan; (*Mec*) to design; **está proyectado para …** it is designed to …
[3] (*Cine, Fot*) to project, screen
[4] [+ *luz*] to cast, project; [+ *sombra*] to cast
[5] (= *dirigir*) [+ *objeto*] to hurl, throw; [+ *chorro, líquido*] to shoot out
[6] (*Mat*) to project

proyectil SM [1] (= *arma*) projectile, missile ► **proyectil balístico intercontinental** intercontinental ballistic missile ► **proyectil de iluminación** flare, rocket ► **proyectil (tele)dirigido** guided missile
[2] (*Mil*) (*de cañón*) shell; (*con cohete*) missile

proyectista SMF [1] (*Aer, Aut, Téc*) (= *diseñador*) designer; (= *delineante*) draughtsman, draftsman (*EEUU*) [2] (*Cine*) projectionist

proyecto SM [1] (= *intención*) plan; **cambiar de ~** to change one's plans; **está en ~ la publicación de los catálogos para el año que viene** the publication of the catalogues is planned for next year; **tener algo en ~** to be planning sth; **tener ~s para algo** to have plans for sth; **tener ~s sobre algo** to have designs on sth ► **proyecto piloto** pilot scheme
[2] (*Téc*) plan, design; (= *idea*) project
[3] (*Fin*) detailed estimate
[4] (*Pol*) ► **proyecto de declaración** draft declaration ► **proyecto de ley** bill
[5] (*Univ*) ► **proyecto de fin de carrera**, **proyecto final de carrera** (*práctico*) final-year project; (*teórico*) final-year dissertation

proyector SM [1] (*Cine*) projector ► **proyector de diapositivas** slide projector
[2] (= *foco de luz*) (*Teat*) spotlight; (*para*

➤ LENGUA Y USO: provocar A1 44.2

monumentos) floodlight; (*Mil*) (= *reflector*) searchlight ► **proyector antiniebla** foglamp

prudencia SF (= *cuidado*) care, caution; (= *cordura*) wisdom, prudence; (= *sensatez*) sound judgment, soundness; **actuar con ~** to be careful *o* cautious; **el problema debe ser analizado con ~** the problem must be carefully studied; **extremar la ~** to proceed with extreme caution

prudencial ADJ [1] (= *adecuado*) prudential; (= *sensato*) sensible; **tras un intervalo ~** after a decent interval, after a reasonable time [2] [*cantidad, distancia*] roughly correct

prudenciarse ►conjug 1b◄ VPR (*Andes, CAm, Méx*) (= *ser cauteloso*) to be cautious; (= *contenerse*) to hold back, control o.s.

▼**prudente** ADJ sensible, prudent; **lo más ~ sería ir ahora mismo al médico** the most sensible *o* prudent thing to do would be to go straight to the doctor; **es una conductora muy ~** she's a very careful driver; **manténgase a una distancia ~ del vehículo delantero** keep a safe distance from the car in front

prudentemente ADV (= *con sensatez*) sensibly, wisely, prudently; [*decidir*] judiciously, soundly; [*conducir*] carefully

prueba SF [1] (= *demostración*) proof; **esta es una ~ palpable de su incompetencia** this is clear proof of his incompetence; **¿tiene usted ~ de ello?** can you prove it?, do you have proof?; **eso es la ~ de que él lo hizo** this proves that he did it, this is the proof that he did it; **es ~ de que tiene buena salud** that proves *o* shows he's in good health; **sin dar la menor ~ de ello** without giving the faintest sign of it; **ser buena ~ de algo** to be clear proof of sth; **el resultado es buena ~ de su profesionalidad** the result is clear proof of her professionalism; **Alonso dio buena ~ de su calidad como orador** Alonso clearly demonstrated his quality as a speaker, Alonso gave clear proof of his quality as a speaker; **como** *o* **en ~ de** in proof of; **como** *o* **en ~ de lo cual** in proof of which; **me lo dio como** *o* **en ~ de amistad** he gave it to me as a token of friendship; **como** *o* **en ~ de que no es así te lo ofrezco gratis** to prove that that isn't the case, I'll give it to you for free; **a las ~s me remito** (I'll let) the facts speak for themselves
[2] (*Jur*) piece of evidence; **~s** evidence *sing*; **el fiscal presentó nuevas ~s** the prosecutor presented new evidence; **se encuentran en libertad por falta de ~s** they were released for lack of evidence ► **pruebas documentales** documentary evidence *sing* ► **pruebas indiciarias** circumstantial evidence *sing*
[3] (= *examen*) (*Escol, Univ, Med*) test; [*de actor*] (*Cine*) screen test; (*Teat*) audition; **la maestra nos hizo una ~ de vocabulario** our teacher gave us a vocabulary test; **el médico me hizo más ~s** the doctor did some more tests on me; **se tendrán que hacer la ~ del SIDA** they'll have to be tested for AIDS; ✦*MODISMO* **ser la ~ de fuego de algo** to be an acid test of sth ► **prueba de acceso** entrance test, entrance examination ► **prueba de alcoholemia** Breathalyzer® test ► **prueba de aptitud** aptitude test ► **prueba de capacitación** proficiency test ► **prueba de(l) embarazo** pregnancy test ► **prueba de inteligencia** intelligence test ► **prueba de nivel** placement test ► **prueba de paternidad** paternity test ► **prueba de selectividad** (*Univ*) entrance examination ► **prueba de tornasol** litmus test ► **prueba nuclear** nuclear test ► **prueba práctica** practical, practical test
[4] (= *ensayo*) [4·1] (*gen*) **haz la ~** try it; **período de ~** [*de persona*] probationary period; [*de producto*] trial period; **piloto de ~s** test pilot; **vuelo de ~s** test flight; **estar en (fase de) ~s** to be on trial; **emitir en ~s** (*TV*) to broadcast test transmissions
[4·2] **a prueba** (*Téc*) on trial; (*Com*) on approval, on trial; **el nuevo secretario está a ~ durante un mes** the new secretary is on trial for a month; **ingresar con un nombramiento a ~** to take up a post for a probationary period; **matrimonio a ~** trial marriage; **poner** *o* **someter a ~** to put to the test; **poner a ~ la paciencia de algn** to try sb's patience; **poner a ~ los nervios de algn** to test sb's nerves
[4·3] **a ~ de**: **a ~ de agua** waterproof; **a ~ de bala(s)** bulletproof; **a ~ de bomba(s)** (*lit*) bombproof, shellproof; **un método a ~ de bombas** a surefire method; **es de una honestidad a ~ de bomba** he's completely honest; **a ~ de choques** shockproof; **a ~ de ladrones** burglarproof; **a ~ de ruidos** soundproof
► **prueba clínica** clinical trial ► **prueba de campo** field trial ► **prueba en carretera** (*Aut*) test drive
[5] (*Dep*) (= *disciplina*) event; (= *carrera*) race; **la ~ de los cien metros lisos** the hundred metres; **la ~ de descenso** the downhill; **la ~ individual** (*Tenis*) the singles ► **prueba campo a través** (*Atletismo*) cross-country race; (*Hípica*) cross-country trial ► **prueba clasificatoria** heat ► **prueba contrarreloj** time trial ► **prueba de carretera** (*Ciclismo*) road trial ► **prueba de obstáculos** obstacle race ► **prueba de relevos** relay, relay race ► **prueba de resistencia** endurance test ► **prueba de vallas** hurdles, hurdles race ► **prueba eliminatoria** heat ► **prueba por equipos** (*Ciclismo*) team trial
[6] (*Cos*) fitting; **sala de ~s** fitting room
[7] (*Fot*) print ► **prueba negativa** negative ► **prueba positiva** print
[8] [*de comida*] (= *acto*) testing, sampling; (= *cantidad*) taste, sample
[9] (*LAm*) (*en el circo*) (= *número*) circus act; (*Andes*) (= *función*) circus show, performance
[10] **pruebas** (*Tip*) proofs; **primeras ~s** first proofs, galleys; **~s de planas** page proofs; **corrector de ~s** proofreader

pruebista SMF [1] (*LAm*) (= *acróbata*) acrobat; (= *funámbulo*) tightrope walker; (= *prestidigitador*) conjurer; (= *malabarista*) juggler; (= *contorsionista*) contortionist
[2] (*Cono Sur*) [*de libros*] proofreader

prurito SM [1] (*Med*) (= *picor*) itching, pruritus (*frm*)
[2] (= *anhelo*) itch, urge; **tener el ~ de hacer algo** to have the urge to do sth; **por un ~ de exactitud** out of an excessive desire for accuracy, because of his eagerness to get everything just right

Prusia SF Prussia

prusiano/a ADJ, SM/F Prussian

PS SM ABR (*Pol*) = **Partido Socialista**

pse... PREF, **psi...** PREF psy...; *all forms are pronounced with silent "p"*

PSE-EE SM ABR (*Esp*) = **Partido Socialista de Euskadi-Euskadiko Eskerra**

psefología SF psephology

psefólogo/a SM/F psephologist

pseudocientífico ADJ pseudo-scientific

psic... PREF psych...

psicoactivo ADJ psychoactive

psicoafectivo ADJ mental, psychological

psicoanálisis SM INV psychoanalysis

psicoanalista SMF psychoanalyst

psicoanalítico ADJ psychoanalytic, psychoanalytical; **diván ~** psychiatrist's couch

psicoanalizar ►conjug 1f◄ VT to psychoanalyse

psicocirugía SF psychosurgery

psicodélico ADJ psychedelic

psicodepresor SM depressant

psicodinámica SF psychodynamics *sing*

psicodrama SM psychodrama

psicoestimulante SM (mental) stimulant

psicofármaco SM psychotropic drug, mood-altering drug

psicolingüística SF psycholinguistics *sing*

psicolingüístico ADJ psycholinguistic

psicología SF psychology ► **psicología conductista** behavioural psychology, behavioral psychology (*EEUU*) ► **psicología de masas** mass psychology ► **psicología educativa** educational psychology ► **psicología femenina** feminine psychology, female psychology ► **psicología masculina** male psychology ► **psicología médica** medical psychology

psicológicamente ADV psychologically

psicológico ADJ psychological

psicólogo/a SM/F psychologist

psicomotricidad SF psychomotor activity

psiconeurosis SF INV psychoneurosis

psicópata SMF psychopath

psicopático ADJ psychopathic

psicopatología SF psychopathology

psicopedagogo/a SM/F educational psychologist

psicoquinesis SF INV psychokinesis

psicoquinético ADJ psychokinetic

psicosis SF INV psychosis

psicosomático ADJ psychosomatic

psicotécnico ADJ **test ~** ◊ **prueba psicotécnica** response test

psicoterapeuta SMF psychotherapist

psicoterapia SF psychotherapy

psicótico/a Ⓐ ADJ psychotic
Ⓑ SM/F psychotic

psicotrópico ADJ psychotropic, psychoactive

psiqu... PREF psych...

Psique SF Psyche

psique SF psyche

psiquiatra SMF psychiatrist

psiquiatría SF psychiatry

psiquiátrico Ⓐ ADJ psychiatric
Ⓑ SM mental hospital ► **psiquiátrico penitenciario** psychiatric prison

psíquico ADJ psychic, psychical; **enfermedades psíquicas** mental illnesses, psychological illnesses

psitacosis SF INV psittacosis

PSOE [pe'soe] SM ABR (*Esp*) = **Partido Socialista Obrero Español**

psoriasis SF INV psoriasis

➤ LENGUA Y USO: **prudente** 29.2

PSS SF ABR = **prestación social sustitutoria**; → INSUMISO, MILI, PRESTACIÓN SOCIAL SUSTITUTORIA

PSUM SM ABR (*Méx*) = **Partido Socialista Unificado de México**

pta ABR 1 (*Fin*) = **peseta**
2 = **presidenta**

Pta. ABR (*Geog*) (= **Punta**) Pt

ptas ABR = **pesetas**

PTB SM ABR (*Andes*) (= **Producto Territorial Bruto**) GDP

pte. ABR = **presidente**

pterodáctilo [tero'daktilo] SM pterodactyl

ptmo. ABR (*Com*) = **préstamo**

ptomaína [toma'ina] SF ptomaine

ptomaínico [toma'iniko] ADJ **envenenamiento ~** ptomaine poisoning

pts ABR = **pesetas**

púa SF 1 (= *pincho*) (*gen*) sharp point; (*Bot, Zool*) prickle, spine; [*de erizo*] quill; [*de peine*] tooth; [*de tenedor*] prong, tine; [*de alambre*] barb; (*LAm*) [*de gallo de pelea*] spur
2 (*Mús*) [*de guitarrista*] plectrum, pick; [*de tocadiscos*] gramophone needle, phonograph needle (*EEUU*)
3 (*Bot*) graft, cutting
4 (‡) one peseta

puaf* EXCL yuck!*

puazo* SM (*Arg*) slash

pub [pub, paβ] SM (*pl* **pubs** [pub, paβ]) *bar where music is played*

púber Ⓐ ADJ adolescent
Ⓑ SMF adolescent

pubertad SF puberty

pubescencia SF pubescence

pubescente ADJ pubescent

púbico ADJ pubic

pubis SM INV pubis

publicación SF publication

públicamente ADV publicly, in public; **lo admitió ~** he admitted it publicly *o* in public

publicar ▸conjug 1g◂ VT 1 (*Com*) [+ *libro, artículo*] to publish; [+ *disco, grabación*] to issue
2 (= *difundir*) (*gen*) to publicize; [+ *secreto*] to make public, divulge

publicidad SF 1 (*Com*) advertising; **hacer ~ de** to advertise; **se ha prohibido la ~ del tabaco** cigarette advertising has been banned ► **publicidad de lanzamiento** advertising campaign to launch a product, advance publicity ► **publicidad directa** direct advertising ► **publicidad en el punto de venta** point-of-sale advertising ► **publicidad estática** (advertising on) hoardings ► **publicidad gráfica** display advertising
2 (= *divulgación*) publicity; **dar ~ a algo** to give publicity to sth

publicista SMF publicist

publicitar ▸conjug 1a◂ Ⓐ VT 1 (*Com*) to advertise
2 (= *divulgar*) to publicize
Ⓑ **publicitarse** VPR to advertise

publicitario/a Ⓐ ADJ advertising *antes de s*, publicity *antes de s*; **campaña publicitaria** advertising campaign
Ⓑ SM/F advertising agent, advertising executive

público Ⓐ ADJ 1 (= *de los ciudadanos, del Estado*) [*transporte, teléfono, organismo, gasto*] public; **la gravedad de la situación es de dominio ~** the seriousness of the situation is public knowledge; **colegio ~** state school; **dinero ~** public money, government funds *pl*; **es un peligro ~ en la carretera** he is a danger to the public, he's a public menace on the roads*; **la vía pública** the street, the public highway (*frm*); *ver tb* **administración 1**, **deuda 2**, **opinión**, **sector**
2 (= *no íntimo*) [*acto, escándalo*] public; **los acusaron de escándalo ~** they were accused of public indecency; **se retiró de la vida pública** he retired from public life; **hacer algo ~** to make sth public; **en un comunicado de prensa hecho ~ ayer** in a press release issued yesterday; **su incompetencia fue pública y notoria** his incompetence was blatantly obvious *o* was plain for all to see; *ver tb* **relación 4**
Ⓑ SM 1 (= *audiencia*) (*Mús, Teat*) audience; (*Dep, Taur*) spectators *pl*, crowd; (*TV*) (*en el plató*) audience; (*en casa*) viewers *pl*, audience; **había poco ~ en la sala** there weren't many people in the audience; **"apta para todos los ~s"** "certificate U", "G movie" (*EEUU*); **el estadio estaba lleno de ~** the stadium was full of spectators, there was a big crowd in the stadium; **el ~ presente en el plató** the studio audience; **un programa con gran audiencia de ~** a programme with a large number of viewers *o* a large audience; **"aviso al público"** "public notice"; **en ~** [*actuar, hablar*] in public; [*actuación, presentación, aparición*] public; **el gran ~** (*gen*) the general public; **escribe para el gran ~** she writes for the average reader ► **público adulto** adult audience ► **público infantil** children's audience; **un programa de televisión dirigido al ~ infantil** a television programme for children *o* aimed at a children's audience ► **público objetivo** (*Com*) target customers *pl*; (*TV*) target audience
2 (= *seguidores*) 2·1 [*de periódico, escritor*] readers *pl*, readership; **no es lo que quiere nuestro ~** it's not what our readers want *o* our readership wants; **un diario para un ~ muy especializado** a newspaper for a very specialized readership
2·2 [*de cantante*] fans *pl*; **su ~ le sigue siendo fiel** her fans are still loyal to her
3 [*de oficina, banco, museo*] **nuestros precios están expuestos al ~** our prices are displayed publicly; **a las dos cerramos al ~** we close (to the public) at two o'clock; **"horario de atención al público"** (*en bancos*) "hours of business"; (*en tiendas*) "opening hours"

publirreportaje SM advertising feature

pucará SF 1 (*Arg, Andes Hist*) (= *fortaleza*) Indian fortress
2 (*LAm Arqueología*) (= *fuerte*) pre-Columbian fort; (= *tumba*) Indian burial mound

pucelano/a* Ⓐ ADJ of/from Valladolid
Ⓑ SM/F native/inhabitant of Valladolid; **los ~s** the people of Valladolid

pucha[1] SF 1 (*Cuba*) (= *ramo*) bouquet
2 (*Méx*) (= *pan*) ring-shaped loaf

pucha[2]* SF 1 (*LAm euf*) = **puta**
2 **¡(la) ~!** (*con sorpresa*) well I'm damned!; (*con irritación*) drat!

puchana SF (*Cono Sur*) broom

puchar‡ ▸conjug 1a◂ VT to speak, say

puchera SF stew

pucherazo* SM electoral fiddle*; **dar ~** to rig an election, fiddle the votes*

puchero SM 1 (= *olla*) cooking pot
2 (= *guiso*) stew
3 (= *sustento*) daily bread; **ganar(se) el ~*** to earn one's crust; **apenas gana para el ~** he hardly earns enough to live on
4 (*) (= *mueca*) pout; **hacer ~s** to pout, screw up one's face

puches SMPL porridge *sing*, gruel *sing*

puchica‡ EXCL (*Andes*) blast!*, damn!

puchito/a* SM/F (*Cono Sur*) youngest child

pucho SM 1 (*Cono Sur*) (= *colilla*) [*de cigarrillo*] fag end‡, dog end‡; [*de puro*] cigar stub
2 (*LAm*) (= *cigarrillo*) fag‡
3 (*LAm*) (= *resto*) (*gen*) scrap, left-over(s) *pl*; [*de bebida*] dregs *pl*; [*de tela*] remnant; (*Fin*) coppers *pl*, small change
4 (*LAm*) (= *nimiedad*) trifle, mere nothing; **a ~s** in dribs and drabs
5 (*Andes, Cono Sur*) (= *hijo*) youngest child

puco SM (*Andes, Cono Sur*) earthenware bowl

pude *etc ver* **poder**

pudendo Ⓐ ADJ **partes pudendas** private parts, pudenda (*frm*)
Ⓑ SM (= *pene*) penis

pudibundez SF (= *afectación*) false modesty; (= *remilgos*) excess of modesty

pudibundo ADJ (= *mojigato*) prudish; (= *vergonzoso*) bashful, modest; (= *tímido*) overshy

pudicicia SF (= *pudor*) modesty; (= *castidad*) chastity

púdico ADJ (= *recatado*) modest; (= *casto*) chaste

pudiendo *ver* **poder**

pudiente ADJ (= *rico*) wealthy, well-to-do; (= *poderoso*) powerful, influential; **las gentes menos ~s** the less well-off; **las clases ~s** the upper classes

pudín SM pudding

pudinga SF puddingstone

pudo *etc ver* **poder**

pudor SM 1 (= *recato*) modesty; (= *timidez*) shyness; (= *vergüenza*) (sense of) shame, (sense of) decency; **con ~** modestly, discreetly; **tenía ~ de confesarlo** he was ashamed to confess it; **alardea sin ~ de su riqueza** she boasts unashamedly *o* openly about her wealth; **lo dijo sin ningún ~** she said it without embarrassment
2 (= *castidad*) chastity, virtue; **atentado al ~** indecent assault

pudorosamente ADV (= *recatadamente*) modestly; (= *con timidez*) shyly; (= *castamente*) chastely, virtuously

pudoroso ADJ (= *recatado*) modest; (= *tímido*) shy; (= *casto*) chaste, virtuous

pudrición SF 1 (= *proceso*) rotting
2 (= *lo podrido*) rot ► **pudrición seca** dry rot

pudridero SM rubbish heap

pudrimiento SM 1 (= *proceso*) rotting
2 (= *lo podrido*) rot

pudrir ▸conjug 3a◂ Ⓐ VT 1 (= *descomponer*) to rot, decay
2 (*) (= *molestar*) to upset, vex
Ⓑ VI (*fig*) (= *haber muerto*) to rot, be dead and buried
Ⓒ **pudrirse** VPR 1 (= *corromperse*) [*comida*]

to rot, decay; [*valores*] to deteriorate
2 [*persona*] to rot, languish; **mientras se pudría en la cárcel** while he was languishing in jail; **te vas a ~ de aburrimiento** you'll die of boredom; **¡que se pudra!*** let him rot!; **¡ahí** *o* **así te pudras!*** get away!*, not on your nelly!‡

pueblada* SF 1 (*LAm*) (= *motín*) riot; (= *revuelta*) revolt, uprising
2 (*Cono Sur*) (= *multitud*) (*gen*) mob; [*de obreros*] gathering of workers

pueblerino/a Ⓐ ADJ [*carácter, ambiente*] small-town *antes de s*, countrified; [*persona*] rustic, provincial
Ⓑ SM/F (= *aldeano*) rustic, country person; (*pey*) country bumpkin*, hick (*EEUU**)

pueblero/a (*LAm*) Ⓐ ADJ town *antes de s*, city *antes de s*
Ⓑ SM/F townsman/townswoman, city dweller; (*pey*) city slicker

pueblito SM (*LAm*) little town; (*más pequeño*) little village

pueblo SM 1 (*Pol*) people, nation; **el ~ español** the Spanish people; **la voluntad del ~** the people's will; **hacer un llamamiento al ~** to call on the people ► **pueblo elegido** chosen people
2 (= *plebe*) common people *pl*, lower orders *pl*; **el ~ llano** the common people
3 (= *localidad pequeña*) (*gen*) small town; (*en el campo*) country town; (*de pocos habitantes*) village; **ser de ~** (*gen*) to be a country person, be from the countryside; (*pey*) to be a country bumpkin*, be a country hick (*EEUU**) ► **pueblo fantasma** ghost town ► **pueblo joven** (*Perú*) shanty town

puedo *etc ver* **poder**

puente Ⓐ SM 1 (*Arquit*) bridge; **sirven de ~ entre los refugiados y la Administración** they act as intermediaries *o* as a link between the refugees and the Government; ✦***MODISMOS*** **tender un ~** ◊ **tender ~s** to offer a compromise, go part-way to meet sb's wishes; **tender ~s de plata a algn** to make it as easy as possible for sb ► **puente aéreo** (*de servicio frecuente*) shuttle service; (*en crisis*) airlift ► **puente atirantado** suspension bridge ► **puente colgante** suspension bridge ► **puente de barcas** pontoon bridge ► **puente de peaje** toll bridge ► **puente de pontones** pontoon bridge ► **puente giratorio** swing bridge ► **puente grúa** bridge crane ► **puente levadizo** drawbridge ► **puente peatonal** footbridge ► **puente voladizo** cantilever bridge
2 [*de gafas, entre dientes*] bridge
3 (*Elec*) **hacer un ~ a un coche** to hot-wire a car
4 (*Náut*) (*tb* **~ de mando**) bridge; (= *cubierta*) deck ► **puente del timón** wheelhouse
5 (*entre fiestas*) long weekend; **hacer ~** to take a long weekend
6 (= *brecha*) gap; **habrá que salvar el ~ de una cosecha a otra** something will have to be done to fill *o* bridge the gap between one harvest and the next
7 (*Andes*) (= *clavícula*) collarbone
Ⓑ ADJ INV (= *temporal*) temporary; (= *de transición*) provisional, transitional; **crédito ~** bridging loan; **curso ~** intermediate course (*between two degrees*); **gabinete ~** caretaker government; **hombre ~** linkman, intermediary; **préstamo ~** bridging loan; **solución ~** temporary solution

> **HACER PUENTE**
>
> *When a public holiday in Spain falls on a Tuesday or Thursday it is common practice for employers to make the Monday or Friday a holiday as well and to give everyone a four-day weekend. This is known as* **hacer puente**. *When a named public holiday such as the* **Día de la Constitución** *falls on a Tuesday or a Thursday, people refer to the whole holiday period as e.g. the* **puente de la Constitución**.

puentear* ▸conjug 1a◂ Ⓐ VT 1 [+ *autoridad*] to bypass, pass over; **le ~on con el ascenso** they passed him over for the promotion
2 (*Fin*) to take out a bridging loan on sth
Ⓑ VI to jump a grade (in the hierarchy), go up to the grade next but one

puenting ['pwentin] SM bungee jumping (*from a bridge*)

puerca[1] SF 1 (*) (= *puta*) slut‡
2 (= *cochinilla*) woodlouse; *ver tb* **puerco**

puercada SF (*Andes, CAm, Caribe*) (= *acto*) dirty trick; (= *dicho*) obscene remark

puerco/a[2] Ⓐ SM/F 1 (= *cerdo*) pig/sow, hog/sow (*EEUU*) ► **puerco de mar** porpoise ► **puerco espín** porcupine ► **puerco jabalí** wild boar, wild pig ► **puerco marino** dolphin ► **puerco montés, puerco salvaje** wild boar, wild pig; *ver tb* **Martín**
2 (*) (= *sinvergüenza*) pig*; (= *canalla*) swine*, rotter*
Ⓑ ADJ 1 (= *asqueroso*) dirty, filthy
2 (= *repugnante*) nasty, disgusting
3 (= *grosero*) coarse
4 (= *mezquino*) rotten*, mean; *ver tb* **puerca**

puericia SF boyhood

puericultor(a) SM/F **médico ~** paediatrician, pediatrician (*EEUU*)

puericultura SF paediatrics *sing*, pediatrics *sing* (*EEUU*)

pueril ADJ 1 (*gen*) childish, child *antes de s*; **edad ~** childhood
2 (*pey*) puerile (*frm*), childish

puerilidad SF puerility (*frm*), childishness

puerperal ADJ puerperal; **fiebre ~** puerperal fever

puerqueza SF (*Cono Sur*) 1 (= *objeto*) dirty thing, filthy object
2 (= *trampa*) dirty trick
3 (*Zool*) bug, creepy-crawly*

puerro SM leek

puerta SF 1 (*para bloquear el paso*) [*de casa, vehículo, armario*] door; [*de jardín, ciudad*] gate; **llaman a la ~** there's somebody at the door; **espero no haberme equivocado de ~** I hope this is the right door; **un coche de dos ~s** a two-door car; **nos encontramos en la ~ del Ministerio** we met at the entrance to the Ministry; **le esperé a la ~ de la escuela** I waited for him outside the entrance to the school; **Susana me acompañó a la ~** Susana saw me out ► **puerta accesoria** side door ► **puerta acristalada** glass door ► **puerta corredera** sliding door ► **puerta cortafuegos** fire door ► **puerta de artistas** stage door ► **puerta de servicio** tradesman's entrance ► **puerta excusada** side door ► **puerta giratoria** revolving door ► **puerta oscilante** swing door ► **puerta principal** [*de una casa*] front door; [*de edificio público*] main entrance ► **puerta trasera** back door ► **puerta ventana, puerta vidriera** French window
2 (= *abertura en la pared*) doorway
3 (*locuciones*) **~ a ~**: **servicio ~ a ~** door-to-door service; **tardo tres horas de ~ a ~** it takes me three hours door-to-door; **hacer el ~ a ~** (*Pol*) to doorstep; **de ~s abiertas**: **jornada de ~s abiertas** open day; **política de ~s abiertas** open-door policy; **a ~ cerrada** (*gen*) behind closed doors; (*Jur*) in camera; **de ~ en ~** from door to door; **iban de ~ en ~ pidiendo firmas** they went from door to door collecting signatures; **vendedor de ~ en ~** door-to-door salesman; ✦***MODISMOS*** **a las ~s de**: **a las ~s de la muerte** at death's door; **ahora, a las ~s de la vejez, lo comprendo** now that I am approaching old age, I understand; **en septiembre, ya a las ~s del otoño** in September, with autumn just around the corner; **dejar la ~ abierta a algo** to leave the way open to sth; **dejar una ~ abierta a otras opciones** to leave the way open for other options; **abrir la ~ a algo** to open the door to sth; **de ~s adentro** behind closed doors, in private; **política de ~s adentro** domestic *o* home policy; **un sirviente de ~s adentro** (*LAm*) a live-in servant; **de ~s afuera**: **lo que pasa de ~s afuera** (= *fuera de casa*) what happens outside of this home; (= *en el extranjero*) what happens abroad; **de ~s afuera se dice que …** publicly it is being said that …; **la gente empieza a vivir menos de ~s afuera** people are starting to be less concerned about appearances; **cerrarle todas las ~s a algn** to close off all avenues to sb; **por la ~ chica**: **entrar por la ~ chica** to get in by the back door; **coger la ~*** to leave; **dar con la ~ en las narices a algn** to slam the door in sb's face; **dar ~ a algn*** to chuck sb out; **estar en ~s**: **el invierno está en ~s** winter is just around the corner; **estar en ~s de hacer algo** to be about to do sth; **enseñar la ~ a algn** to show sb the door; **equivocarse de ~**: **te has equivocado de ~** you've come to the wrong person; **franquear las ~s a algn** to welcome sb in; **por la ~ grande**: **entrar por la ~ grande** to make a grand entrance; **salir por la ~ grande** [*torero*] to make a triumphant exit; **si me voy, lo haré por la ~ grande** if I leave, I'll leave with my head held high; **quedarse a la ~** to fall at the last hurdle; **querer poner ~s al campo** to try to stem the tide; **salir por la ~ de los carros** (= *apurado*) to leave in a hurry; (= *destituido*) to leave in disgrace
4 (*Aer*) gate ► **puerta de embarque** boarding gate
5 (*Dep*) goal; **un disparo** *o* **remate a ~** a shot at goal; **sacar de ~** to take a goal kick
6 (*Inform*) port

puertaventana SF (= *puerta*) French window; (= *contraventana*) shutter

puertear ▸conjug 1a◂ VI (*Cono Sur*) to make a dash for the exit

puerto SM 1 (*para embarcaciones*) port, harbour, harbor (*EEUU*); **entrar a** *o* **tomar ~** to enter (into) port; ✦***MODISMO*** **llegar a buen ~** to get over a difficulty, come through safely ► **puerto comercial** trading port ► **puerto de contenedores** container port ► **puerto**

de entrada port of entry ► **puerto de escala** port of call ► **puerto de gran calado** deep-water port ► **puerto de mar** seaport ► **puerto de origen** home port ► **puerto deportivo** marina, yachting harbour ► **puerto franco, puerto libre** free port ► **puerto naval** naval port, naval harbour ► **puerto pesquero** fishing port
2 (*tb* ~ **de montaña**) pass
3 (*Inform*) port ► **puerto de expansión** expansion port ► **puerto de serie** serial port ► **puerto (de transmisión en) paralelo** parallel port ► **puerto (de transmisión en) serie, puerto en serie** serial port

Puerto Rico SM Puerto Rico

puertorriqueñismo SM word *o* phrase peculiar to Puerto Rico

puertorriqueño/a ADJ, SM/F Puerto Rican

▼ **pues** CONJ 1 (*con valor consecutivo*) then; — **tengo sueño —¡~ vete a la cama!** "I'm tired" — "then go to bed!"; **llegó, ~, con dos horas de retraso** so he arrived two hours late; **¿no vas con ella, ~?** aren't you going with her after all?
2 (*con valor enfático*) well; **~ no voy** well I'm not going; **~, como te iba contando ...** well, as I was saying ...; **¡~ no lo sabía!** well, I didn't know!; **¡~ claro!** yes, of course!; **~ sí** well, yes; (= *naturalmente*) certainly; **~ no** well, no; (= *de ningún modo*) not at all; **¡~ qué!** come now!, what else did you expect!
3 (*indicando duda*) **~, no sé** well, I don't know
4 (*frm*) (*con valor causal*) since, for; **cómpralo, ~ lo necesitas** buy it, since you need it

puesta SF 1 (= *acto*) ► **puesta a cero** (*Inform*) reset ► **puesta al día** updating ► **puesta a punto** fine tuning ► **puesta de largo** coming-out (in society) ► **puesta en antena** (*TV*) showing, screening ► **puesta en común** idea-sharing session ► **puesta en escena** staging ► **puesta en libertad** freeing, release ► **puesta en marcha** (= *acto*) starting; (= *dispositivo*) self-starter ► **puesta en práctica** putting into effect, implementation
2 (*Astron*) setting ► **puesta del sol** sunset
3 [*de huevos*] egg-laying; **una ~ anual de 300 huevos** an annual lay *o* output of 300 eggs
4 (*Naipes*) stake, bet
5 (*Cono Sur*) **¡puesta!** it's a tie!, it's a draw!; (*en carrera*) it's a dead heat!

puestero/a SM/F 1 (*esp LAm*) (*en mercado*) stallholder, market vendor
2 (*Cono Sur Agr*) (= *mayoral*) farm overseer, ranch caretaker; (= *agricultor*) small farmer, tenant farmer; (= *trabajador*) ranch hand

▼ **puesto** Ⓐ PP *de* **poner**
Ⓑ ADJ 1 **con el sombrero ~** with one's hat on, wearing a hat; **una mesa puesta para nueve** a table laid for nine; **salieron del país con lo ~** they left the country with nothing but the clothes they were wearing; ✦**MODISMO tenerlos bien ~s** (*Esp*✱) to be a real man
2 [*persona*] **bien ~** ◊ **muy ~** well dressed, smartly turned out
3 **ir ~*** (= *estar drogado*) to be high*; (= *estar borracho*) to be steaming*, be soused (*EEUU**)
4 **no está muy ~ en este tema** he's not very well up on this subject
Ⓒ SM 1 (= *lugar*) place; (= *posición*) position; **ocupa el tercer ~ en la liga** it is in third place in the league; **ceder el ~ a algn** to give up one's place to sb; **guardar** *o* **mantener su ~** to keep the proper distance; **sabe estar en su ~** he knows his place ► **puesto de amarre** berth, mooring ► **puesto de honor** leading position
2 (= *empleo*) post, position, job; **tiene un ~ de conserje** he works as a porter ► **puesto de decisión** position of power ► **puesto de trabajo** post, position, job; **se crearán 200 ~s de trabajo** 200 new jobs will be created
3 [*de vigilancia*] post ► **puesto de control** checkpoint ► **puesto de escucha** listening-post ► **puesto de observación** observation post ► **puesto de policía** police post ► **puesto de socorro** first-aid post ► **puesto de vigilancia** (= *garita*) guard post; (= *torre*) watchtower ► **puesto fronterizo** border post
4 (*Caza*) stand, place
5 (*Com*) (*en mercado*) stall; (*en feria de muestras*) stand, booth ► **puesto callejero** street stall ► **puesto de mercado** market stall ► **puesto de periódicos** newspaper stand
6 (*Cono Sur*) *land and house held by ranch caretaker*
Ⓓ **~ que** CONJ since, as

puf[1] EXCL ugh!

puf[2] SM (*pl* **pufs**) pouffe

pufo* SM 1 (= *trampa*) trick, swindle; **dar el ~ a algn** to swindle sb
2 (= *deuda*) debt
3 (= *persona*) con man*

púgil SM boxer

pugilato SM (= *boxeo*) boxing; (= *disputa*) conflict

pugilismo SM boxing

pugilista SM boxer

pugilístico ADJ boxing *antes de s*

pugío SM (*Andes, Cono Sur*) spring

pugna SF struggle, conflict; **entrar en ~ con algn** to clash with sb, come into conflict with sb; **estar en ~ con algn** to clash with sb, conflict with sb

pugnacidad SF pugnacity, aggressiveness

pugnar ▸conjug 1a◂ VI 1 (= *luchar*) to fight (**por** for); **~ en defensa de algo** to fight in defence of sth
2 (= *esforzarse*) to struggle, strive; **~ por hacer algo** to struggle *o* strive to do sth; **~ por no reírse** to struggle not to laugh
3 **~ con** [+ *opinión, idea*] to clash with, conflict with; [+ *persona*] to battle it out with

pugnaz ADJ pugnacious, aggressive

puja SF 1 (= *lucha*) struggle; **la ~ por el control de la empresa** the struggle for control of the firm
2 (*en una subasta*) bidding ► **puja de salida** opening bid
3 **sacar de la ~ a algn** (= *adelantarse*) to get ahead of sb; (= *sacar de apuro*) to get sb out of a jam*
4 (*Andes**) ticking-off*

pujante ADJ (= *fuerte*) strong, vigorous; (= *potente*) powerful; (= *enérgico*) forceful; (= *poderoso económicamente*) booming

pujanza SF [*de grupo, país*] power, strength; [*de idioma, industria, economía*] strength; [*de carácter*] forcefulness, drive

pujar ▸conjug 1a◂ VI 1 (*en subasta*) to bid, bid up; (*Naipes*) to bid; **~ en** *o* **sobre el precio** to bid the price up
2 (= *esforzarse*) to struggle, strain; **~ por hacer algo** to struggle to do sth
3 **~ para adentro** (*Méx**) to grin and bear it
4 (= *vacilar*) to falter, dither, hesitate
5 (= *no encontrar palabras*) to struggle for words, be at a loss for words
6 (= *hacer pucheros*) to be on the verge of tears
7 (*CAm*✱) (= *quejarse*) to moan, whinge*

puje* SM (*Andes*) ticking-off*

pujo SM 1 (*Med*) difficulty in relieving o.s., tenesmus (*frm*)
2 (= *ansia*) longing, strong urge; **sentir ~ de llorar** to be on the verge of tears; **sentir ~ de reírse** to have an uncontrollable urge to laugh
3 (= *intento*) attempt, try, shot; **tiene ~s de caballero** he has pretensions to being a gentleman

pulcramente ADV (= *con orden*) neatly, tidily, smartly; (= *con delicadeza*) exquisitely, delicately

pulcritud SF (= *orden*) neatness, tidiness; (= *delicadeza*) exquisiteness, delicacy

pulcro ADJ (= *ordenado*) neat, tidy; (= *elegante*) smartly dressed; (= *exquisito*) exquisite; (= *delicado*) dainty, delicate

pulga SF 1 (= *insecto*) flea; ✦**MODISMOS buscar las ~s a algn*** to tease sb, needle sb*; **no aguantar ~s*** to stand no nonsense; **tener malas ~s*** to be short-tempered, be bad-tempered; **un tío con muy malas ~s** a bad-tempered chap; **hacer de una ~ un elefante** *o* **un camello** (= *dar importancia*) to make a mountain out of a molehill; (= *buscar defectos*) to nit-pick
2 [*de juego*] tiddlywink; **juego de ~s** tiddlywinks
3 (*Inform*) bug

pulgada SF inch

pulgar SM thumb

pulgarada SF 1 (= *capirotazo*) flick, flip
2 [*de rapé*] pinch

Pulgarcito SM Tom Thumb

pulgón SM plant louse

pulgoso ADJ (*Andes*) flea-ridden, verminous

pulguero✱ SM 1 (*Esp*) (= *cama*) kip✱, bed
2 (*CAm, Caribe*) (= *cárcel*) jail

pulguiento ADJ (*Andes*) flea-ridden, verminous

pulidamente ADV 1 (= *con pulcritud*) neatly, tidily; (= *con esmero*) carefully; (= *refinadamente*) in a polished way; (*pey*) affectedly
2 (= *con cortesía*) courteously

pulido Ⓐ ADJ 1 [*madera, metal*] polished
2 [*estilo, lenguaje*] refined, polished
Ⓑ SM polish, polishing

pulidor(a) SM/F polisher

pulidora SF polishing machine

pulimentado SM polishing

pulimentar ▸conjug 1a◂ VT (= *pulir*) to polish; (= *dar lustre a algo*) to put a gloss on sth, put a shine on sth; (= *alisar*) to smooth

pulimento SM 1 (= *acto*) polishing
2 (= *brillo*) gloss
3 (= *sustancia*) polish

pulique SM (*CAm*) *dish of chillies and maize*

pulir ▸conjug 3a◂ Ⓐ VT 1 [+ *cristal, metal, suelo*] to polish
2 (= *perfeccionar*) to polish; **hace falta ~ esta traducción** this translation still needs

➤ LENGUA Y USO: **pues 4** 44.1 **puesto C2** 46.1, 46.5

polishing
[3] [+ *persona*] **nadie ha logrado ~lo** nobody has managed to polish his manners; **en este colegio ~án su educación** they will finish off *o* round off her education at this school
[4] (‡) (= *birlar*) to pinch*; **ya me han pulido el bolígrafo** they've gone and pinched my pen*
Ⓑ **pulirse** VPR [1] (= *refinarse*) to acquire polish
[2] (= *acicalarse*) to spruce o.s. up
[3] (*) (= *gastar*) to go through, get through

pull [pul] SM pullover

pulla SF [1] (= *insulto*) cutting remark, wounding remark; (= *mofa*) taunt; (= *indirecta*) dig
[2] (= *obscenidad*) obscene remark, rude word

pullman ['pulman] SM [1] (*Andes, Cono Sur Ferro*) sleeping car
[2] (*Chile*) (= *autobús*) long-distance coach

pullover [pul'oβer] SM pullover, jumper

pulmón SM (*Anat*) lung; **a pleno ~** [*respirar*] deeply; [*gritar*] at the top of one's lungs ► **pulmón de acero** iron lung

pulmonar ADJ pulmonary (*frm*), lung *antes de s*

pulmonía SF pneumonia ► **pulmonía doble** double pneumonia

pulmotor SM iron lung

pulóver SM pullover

pulpa SF [1] (*como resultado de machacar*) (*gen*) pulp; [*de fruta, planta*] flesh ► **pulpa de madera** wood pulp ► **pulpa dental**, **pulpa dentaria** pulp ► **pulpa de papel** paper pulp
[2] (= *pasta blanda*) soft mass
[3] (*Anat*) soft flesh
[4] (*LAm*) (= *carne*) meat off the bone, fillet

pulpejo SM fleshy part, soft part

pulpería SF (*LAm*) (= *tienda*) general store, food store; (= *taberna*) bar, tavern

pulpero/a SM/F (*LAm*) (= *comerciante*) storekeeper, grocer; (= *tabernero*) tavern keeper

púlpito SM pulpit

pulpo SM [1] (*Zool*) octopus; ✦***MODISMOS*** **estar más perdido que un ~ en un garaje*** not to have a clue; **ser como un ~** to be all arms
[2] (*Aut*) elastic strap

pulposo ADJ fleshy

pulque SM (*Méx*) pulque

> **PULQUE**
>
> ***Pulque** is a traditional alcoholic drink from Mexico. Thick, slightly sweet and milky, it is brewed from the juice of the agave plant, or **maguey**, and is roughly equivalent in strength to beer. It was the sacred drink of the Aztecs, who used it in offerings to the gods and also for medicinal purposes. In modern-day Mexico it is often given to children since it is rich in vitamins, and in the cities it is sold in special bars called **pulquerías**.*

pulquear ▸conjug 1a◂ (*Méx*) Ⓐ VI to drink pulque
Ⓑ **pulquearse** VPR to get drunk on pulque

pulquería SF (*Méx*) bar

pulquérrimo ADJ SUPERL *de* **pulcro**

pulsación SF [1] (= *latido*) beat
[2] [*de tecla*] (*Tip, Inform*) keystroke; **hace 200 pulsaciones por minuto** she does 200 keystrokes a minute ► **pulsación doble** (*Inform*) strikeover
[3] [*de pianista, mecanógrafo*] touch

pulsador SM (= *botón*) button, push-button; (= *interruptor*) switch

pulsar[1] ▸conjug 1a◂ Ⓐ VT [1] [+ *botón*] to press; [+ *tecla*] to strike, touch, tap; (*Mús*) to play
[2] [+ *opinión*] to sound out
[3] **~ a algn** (*Med*) to take sb's pulse, feel sb's pulse
Ⓑ VI to beat

pulsar[2] SM (= *estrella*) pulsar; (= *agujero negro*) black hole

pulsátil ADJ pulsating

pulseada SF (*Cono Sur*) arm-wrestling; (*fig*) intense competition; **hacer una ~** to arm-wrestle

pulsear ▸conjug 1a◂ VI (*Cono Sur*) [1] (= *echar un pulso*) to arm-wrestle
[2] (= *apuntar*) to take aim

pulsera SF bracelet, wristlet; **~ para reloj** watch strap; **reloj de ~** wristwatch ► **pulsera de pedida** (*Esp*) engagement bracelet

pulsión SF urge, drive, impulse

pulso SM [1] (*Anat*) pulse; **tomar el ~ a algn** to take sb's pulse, feel sb's pulse; ✦***MODISMOS*** **perder el ~ de algo: la Iglesia ha perdido el ~ de la sociedad** the church has lost touch with society; **tomar el ~ a algo: tomar el ~ a la opinión pública** to sound out public opinion; **tomar el ~ al mercado** to gauge the mood of the market
[2] (= *seguridad en la mano*) **tener buen ~** to have a steady hand; **tener mal ~** to have an unsteady hand; **tener ~** (*Cono Sur*) to have a good aim; **con ~ firme** with a firm hand; **le tiembla el ~** his hand is shaking
[3] **a~: levantar algo a ~** to lift sth with one hand; **levantar una silla a ~** to lift a chair with one hand; **tomar un mueble a ~** to lift a piece of furniture clean off the ground; **dibujo (hecho) a ~** freehand drawing; ✦***MODISMOS*** **ganar(se) algo a ~** (= *con esfuerzo*) to get sth through one's own hard work; (= *con dificultad*) to get sth the hard way; **hacer algo a ~** (= *sin ayuda*) to do sth without help from anyone; **a ~ sudando** by the sweat of one's brow
[4] (= *pelea*) **echar un ~** to arm-wrestle
[5] (= *contienda*) trial of strength, showdown; **el ~ entre el gobierno y la oposición** the confrontation *o* showdown between the government and the opposition; **echar un ~ a algn** (= *contender*) to have a trial of strength with sb; (= *desafiar*) to challenge sb
[6] (= *tacto*) tact; **con mucho ~** with great tact
[7] (*Col*) (= *pulsera*) bracelet; (= *reloj*) wristwatch

pulular ▸conjug 1a◂ Ⓐ VI [1] (= *bullir*) to swarm (**por** around); **los turistas pululan por el vestíbulo del hotel** the tourists are swarming around the hotel lobby, the hotel lobby is throbbing *o* swarming with tourists
[2] (= *abundar*) to swarm (**de** with); **aquí pululan los mosquitos** this place is teeming *o* swarming with mosquitoes
Ⓑ VT (*LAm*) to infest, overrun

pululo* ADJ (*CAm*) short and fat

pulverización SF [1] [*de sólidos*] pulverization
[2] [*de perfume, insecticida*] spraying

pulverizador SM [*de colonia, ambientador*] spray; [*de pintura*] spray gun ► **pulverizador nasal** nasal inhaler

pulverizar ▸conjug 1f◂ VT [1] [+ *sólido*] (*gen*) to pulverize; (= *reducir a polvo*) to powder, convert into powder
[2] [+ *líquido*] to spray
[3] (= *aniquilar*) [+ *enemigo, ciudad*] to pulverize, smash; [+ *rival, oponente*] to hammer, thrash; **pulverizó el récord** she smashed the record

pulverulento ADJ [1] [*sustancia*] powdered, powdery
[2] [*superficie*] dusty

pum EXCL (*en disparo*) bang!; (*en golpe*) thud!; ✦***MODISMO*** **ni ~** not a thing; **no entendí ni ~** I didn't understand a thing

puma SM puma

pumba EXCL (*imitando un golpe*) bang!, crash!; (*imitando una explosión*) boom!, bang!

puna SF (*Andes*) [1] (*Geog*) (= *altiplano*) puna; (= *páramo*) bleak upland
[2] (= *soroche*) mountain sickness
[3] (= *viento*) cold mountain wind

punch SM (*LAm*) [1] (= *puñetazo*) punch
[2] (*al hacer algo*) (= *empuje*) strength, punch; (= *agilidad*) agility
[3] **punches** (*CAm*) popcorn *sing*

punchar ▸conjug 1a◂ VT (*LAm*) to punch

punching ['punʃin] SM punchball

punching-ball ['punʃinbal] SM (*Boxeo*) punchball, whipping-boy

punción SF puncture ► **punción en la médula** lumbar puncture

pundonor SM (= *dignidad*) self-respect, amour propre; (= *honra*) honour, honor (*EEUU*); (= *desfachatez*) nerve, cheek*

pundonoroso ADJ (= *digno*) honourable, honorable (*EEUU*); (= *puntilloso*) punctilious, scrupulous

punga‡ Ⓐ SF (*Cono Sur*) thieving, nicking‡
Ⓑ SMF (*Cono Sur*) pickpocket, thief

pungir ▸conjug 3c◂ VT [1] (= *punzar*) to prick, puncture; (= *picar*) to sting
[2] (= *hacer sufrir*) to cause suffering to

punguista‡ SM/F (*Andes, Cono Sur*) (= *carterista*) pickpocket; (= *ladrón*) thief

punible ADJ punishable

punición SF punishment

púnico ADJ, SM (*Ling*) Punic

punitivo ADJ, **punitorio** ADJ punitive

punki, punkie ['punki] ADJ, SMF punk

punta Ⓐ SF [1] (= *extremo*) [*de dedo, lengua, pincel*] tip; [*de ciudad*] side; [*de mesa*] end; [*de pañuelo*] corner; **la ~ de los dedos** the fingertips, the tips of one's fingers; **colocad la ~ del pie hacia arriba** point your toes upwards; **vivimos en la otra ~ de Barcelona** we live on the other side of Barcelona; **se sentó en la otra ~ de la mesa** she sat at the other end of the table; **de ~ a <u>cabo</u>** *o* **de ~ a <u>punta</u>** from one end to the other; **nos recorrimos la ciudad de ~ a ~** we went from one end of the city to the other; **me leí el periódico de ~ a cabo** I read the paper from cover to cover; ✦***MODISMOS*** **la ~ del iceberg** the tip of the iceberg; **tener algo en la ~ de la lengua** to have sth on the tip of one's tongue
[2] (= *extremo puntiagudo*) [*de cuchillo, tijeras, lápiz*] point; [*de flecha*] tip; **un rotulador de ~ fina** a felt-tip pen with a fine point; **un cuchi-**

llo con ~ a pointed knife; una estrella de cinco ~s a five-pointed star; de ~: tenía todo el pelo de ~ her hair was all on end; las tijeras le cayeron de ~ en el pie the scissors fell point down *o* point first on his foot; unos zapatos de ~ a pair of pointed shoes; acabado en ~ pointed; a ~ de navaja at knife point; a ~ de pistola at gunpoint; sacar ~ a [+ *lápiz*] to sharpen; (*Esp*) [+ *comentario, opinión*] to twist; le saca ~ a todo lo que digo she twists everything I say; ✦MODISMOS a ~ de (*LAm**) salió adelante a ~ de esfuerzo he got ahead by sheer effort *o* by dint of hard work; va a entender a ~ de patadas he has to have sense beaten into him; vive a ~ de remedios he lives on medicines; estar de ~ [*persona*] to be irritable; estar de ~ con algn to be annoyed with sb; ponerse de ~ con algn to fall out with sb; ir de ~ en blanco to be all dressed up, be dressed up to the nines; ponerse de ~ en blanco to get all dressed up; poner a algn los pelos *o* el vello de ~ to make sb's hair stand on end; se me ponen los pelos de ~ de pensar en el miedo que pasamos my hair stands on end when I think of how scared we were; esas imágenes me pusieron el vello de ~ those images were really spine-chilling, those images made my hair stand on end; estar hasta la ~ de los pelos con *o* de algn* to be fed up to the back teeth with sb*; a ~ (de) pala (*Esp**) había gente a ~ pala there were loads of people*; tienen dinero a ~ pala they're loaded*, they've got loads of money* ► punta de diamante (= *cortador*) diamond glass cutter; (= *diseño*) diamond point; cristal tallado a ~ de diamante diamond-cut glass ► punta de lanza spearhead; son la ~ de lanza de nuestra ofensiva comercial they are spearheading our marketing campaign; *ver tb* nervio 2

3 (= *cantidad pequeña*) (*lit*) bit; (*fig*) touch; una puntita de sal a pinch of salt; tiene sus ~s de filósofo there's a touch of the philosopher about him; tiene una ~ de loco he has a streak of madness

4 (= *clavo*) tack

5 (*Geog*) (= *cabo*) point; (= *promontorio*) headland

6 (= *asta*) [*de toro*] horn; [*de ciervo*] point, tine

7 (*Ftbl*) juega en la ~ he plays up front

8 (= *colilla*) stub, butt

9 (*Cos*) (= *encaje*) dentelle

10 puntas 10·1 [*del pelo*] ends; tengo las ~s abiertas I have split ends; quiero cortarme las ~s I'd like a trim, I'd like to have my hair trimmed

10·2 (*Ballet*) points, ballet shoes

10·3 (*Culin*)

► puntas de espárrago asparagus tips

► puntas de solomillo *finest cuts of pork*

11 (*Cono Sur, Méx*) una ~ de algo a lot of sth; pagó una ~ de pesos por eso he paid a lot of money for that; son todos una ~ de ladrones they are all a bunch of thieves

12 (*Cuba*) [*de tabaco*] *leaf of best tobacco*

13 (*Bol*) *eight-hour shift of work*

14 (*Caribe*) (= *mofa*) taunt, snide remark

Ⓑ ADJ INV peak; horas ~ [*de electricidad, teléfono*] peak times; la hora ~ [*del tráfico*] the rush hour; el tráfico en la hora ~ rush-hour traffic; tecnología ~ latest technology, leading edge technology; velocidad ~ maximum speed, top speed

Ⓒ SMF (*Dep*) striker, forward; media ~ midfield player

puntada SF 1 (*Cos*) stitch; se ven las ~s you can see the stitching; dale unas puntaditas más a la manga put a few more stitches in the sleeves; ✦MODISMO no dar puntada: hoy no ha dado ~ he hasn't done a stroke all day; no ha dado ~ en el asunto he's done nothing at all about it ► puntada cruzada cross-stitch ► puntada invisible invisible mending

2 (*) (= *insinuación*) hint; pegar *o* soltar una ~ to drop a hint

3 (= *dolor*) stitch, sharp pain

4 (*Méx*) witty remark, witticism

puntaje SM (*LAm*) score

puntal SM 1 (= *soporte*) (*Arquit*) prop, support; (*Agr*) prop; (*Téc*) strut

2 (= *persona*) (*que sirve de apoyo*) chief supporter; (*que ayuda a resistir*) cornerstone; (*que está al frente*) leading light

3 (*LAm*) snack

puntapié SM kick; echar a algn a ~s to kick sb out; pegar un ~ a algn to give sb a kick ► puntapié colocado place kick ► puntapié de bote pronto drop kick ► puntapié de saque drop-out

puntazo SM 1 (*Taur*) jab (*with a horn*)

2 (*LAm*) (= *pinchazo*) jab, poke; (= *puñalada*) stab; (= *herida*) stab wound, knife wound

3 (*) fue un ~ it went down really well*; ¡qué ~ de fiesta! the party was just perfect!

punteado Ⓐ ADJ (= *moteado*) (*gen*) dotted, covered with dots; [*pintura*] stippled; [*diseño*] of dots; [*plumaje*] flecked

Ⓑ SM 1 (= *moteado*) (*en diseño*) series of dots, stippling; (*en plumaje*) flecking

2 (*Mús*) picking

puntear ►conjug 1a◄ Ⓐ VT 1 (*con puntos*) (= *motear*) to dot, cover *o* mark with dots; (= *pintar*) to stipple; (= *jaspear*) to fleck

2 (= *comprobar*) [+ *artículos*] to tick, put a mark against, check (*EEUU*); (*LAm*) [+ *lista*] to check off

3 (*Cos*) to stitch, stitch up

4 (*Mús*) [+ *guitarra*] to pluck; [+ *violín*] to play pizzicato

5 (*Cono Sur*) [+ *tierra*] to fork over

6 (*LAm*) [+ *desfile*] to head, lead

Ⓑ VI (*Náut*) to luff

punteo SM plucking

puntera SF 1 [*de zapato*] (= *punta*) toe; (= *refuerzo*) toecap

2 [*de lapicero*] pencil tip

3 (*) (= *puntapié*) kick

punterazo SM powerful shot, drive

puntería SF 1 (*al apuntar*) aim, aiming; enmendar *o* rectificar la ~ to correct one's aim; hacer la ~ de un cañón to aim a gun, sight a gun

2 (= *destreza*) marksmanship; tener buena ~ to be a good shot; tener mala ~ to be a bad shot

puntero Ⓐ ADJ (= *primero*) top, leading; (= *moderno*) up-to-date; más ~ (= *sobresaliente*) outstanding, furthest ahead; (= *último*) latest; empresa puntera leading company; equipo ~ top club; tecnología puntera the latest technology, state-of-the-art technology

Ⓑ SM 1 (*para señalar*) pointer ► puntero luminoso light pen

2 (= *cincel*) stonecutter's chisel

3 (= *persona que destaca*) outstanding individual; (= *líder*) leader, top man

4 (*LAm*) [*equipo*] leading team; [*de rebaño*] leading animal; [*de desfile*] leader

5 (*LAm*) [*de reloj*] hand

puntiagudo ADJ sharp, sharp-pointed

puntilla SF 1 (*Cos*) lace edging

2 (*Taur*) *short dagger for giving the coup de grâce*; ✦MODISMOS dar la ~ to finish off the bull, give the coup de grâce; dar la ~ a algo/algn to finish sth/sb off; aquello fue la ~ that was the last straw

3 de ~s on tiptoe; andar de ~s to walk on tiptoe

4 (*Téc*) tack

5 [*de pluma*] point, nib

puntillazo SM 1 (*Taur*) *the decisive, mortal blow in a bullfight*

2 dar el ~ a algo to put an end to sth

puntillismo SM pointillism

puntillo SM 1 (*pey*) (= *amor propio*) exaggerated sense of honour *o* (*EEUU*) honor, excessive amour propre, punctilio (*frm*)

2 (‡) coger *o* ligar un ~ (*con bebida*) to get merry*; (*con drogas*) to get high*; tener un ~ (*con bebida*) to be merry*; (*con drogas*) to be high*

puntilloso ADJ (= *detallista*) punctilious; (= *susceptible*) touchy, sensitive

▼**punto** SM 1 (= *topo*) (*en un diseño*) dot, spot; (*en plumaje*) spot, speckle; (*en carta, dominó*) spot, pip; aparecen en la piel unos ~s rojos red spots appear on the skin; línea de ~s dotted line ► punto negro (= *espinilla*) blackhead

2 (= *signo*) (*en la i*) dot; (*de puntuación*) full stop, period (*EEUU*); dos ~s colon; ✦MODISMOS con ~s y comas down to the last detail; les contó con ~s y comas lo que había pasado she told them what had happened down to the last detail; poner los ~s sobre las íes to dot the i's and cross the t's; le puso los ~s sobre las íes she corrected him, she drew attention to his inaccuracies; sin faltar ~ ni coma down to the last detail; y ~: ¡lo digo yo y ~! I'm telling you so and that's that! ► punto acápite (*LAm*) (*en dictado*) full stop, new paragraph, period, new paragraph (*EEUU*) ► punto final full stop, period (*EEUU*); (*fig*) end; poner ~ final a la discusión to put an end to the argument, draw a line under the argument ► puntos suspensivos (*gen*) suspension points; (*en dictado*) dot, dot, dot ► punto y aparte (*en dictado*) full stop, new paragraph, period, new paragraph (*EEUU*); esto marca un ~ y aparte en la historia del teatro this marks a break with tradition *o* the past in the theatre; este es un vino ~ y aparte this is an uncommonly good *o* exceptional wine ► punto y coma semicolon ► punto y seguido (*en dictado*) full stop (no new paragraph), period (no new paragraph) (*EEUU*)

3 (*Dep*) point; con ocho ~s a favor y tres en contra with eight points for and three against; los dos están empatados a ~s the two of them are level on points; ganar *o* vencer por ~s to win on points; perdieron por tres ~s they lost by three points; completó la ronda con cero ~s she had a clear round; ✦MODISMO perder (muchos) ~s to lose (a lot of) prestige; ¡qué ~ te has marcado con

➤ LENGUA Y USO: punto 4 53.1, 53.2 7 33.2

lo que has dicho!* what you said was spot-on*
4 (= *tema*) (*gen*) point; (*en programa de actividades*) item; **no quiero extenderme sobre ese ~** I don't wish to elaborate on that point; **los ~s en el orden del día son ...** the items on the agenda are ...; **contestar ~ por ~** to answer point by point ► **punto capital** crucial point ► **puntos a tratar** matters to be discussed ► **puntos de consulta** terms of reference
5 (= *labor*) knitting; (= *tejido*) knitted fabric, knit; **prendas de ~** knitwear *sing*; **falda de ~** knitted skirt; **chaqueta de ~** cardigan; **hacer ~** to knit ► **punto del derecho** plain knitting ► **punto del revés** purl ► **punto de media** plain knitting
6 (*Cos, Med*) (= *puntada*) stitch; [*de media*] loose stitch; **me tuvieron que dar cinco ~s** I had to have five stitches; **me van a quitar los ~s** I am having my stitches out; ✦***MODISMO*** **¡~ en boca!** mum's the word! ► **punto de costado** (= *dolor*) stitch; **tengo un ~ de costado** I've got a stitch, I've got a pain in my side ► **punto de cruz** cross stitch ► **punto de sutura** stitch
7 (= *lugar*) (*gen*) spot, place; (*Geog, Mat*) point; [*de proceso*] point, stage; (*en el tiempo*) point, moment; **al llegar a este ~** at this point *o* stage ► **punto cardinal** cardinal point; **los cuatro ~s cardinales** the four points of the compass ► **punto ciego** (*Anat*) blind spot ► **punto clave** key point; **el ~ clave de su razonamiento** the key point of her argument ► **punto crítico** critical point ► **punto culminante** high point; **llegar a su ~ culminante** to reach its climax ► **punto de asistencia** (*Aut*) checkpoint ► **punto débil** weak point *o* spot ► **punto de calor** heat source ► **punto de congelación** freezing-point ► **punto de contacto** point of contact ► **punto de control** checkpoint ► **punto de ebullición** boiling-point ► **punto de encuentro** meeting point ► **punto de equilibrio** (*Com*) break-even point ► **punto de fuga** vanishing point ► **punto de fusión** melting-point ► **punto de inflamación** flashpoint ► **punto de información** information centre ► **punto de mira** [*de rifle*] sight; (= *objetivo*) aim, objective; (= *punto de vista*) point of view; ✦***MODISMO*** **estar en el ~ de mira de algn**: **su comportamiento está en el ~ de mira de la prensa** his behaviour has come under scrutiny in the press; **el fraude fiscal está en el ~ de mira de Hacienda** the Treasury has targeted tax evasion; **Tokio está en el ~ de mira de sus misiles** their missiles are pointing towards Tokyo ► **punto de no retorno** point of no return ► **punto de partida** starting point ► **punto de penalti** penalty spot ► **punto de referencia** point of reference ► **punto de taxis** taxi stand, cab rank ► **punto de venta** point of sale; **terminales ~ de venta** point of sale terminals; **está presente en 3.000 ~s de venta** it's available at 3,000 outlets ► **punto de vista** point of view, viewpoint; **él lo mira desde otro ~ de vista** he sees it differently, he looks at it from another point of view ► **punto flaco** weak point, weak spot ► **punto muerto** (*Mec*) dead centre; (*Aut*) neutral (gear); (= *estancamiento*) deadlock, stalemate; **las negociaciones están en un ~ muerto** the negotiations are deadlocked, the talks have reached a stalemate ► **punto negro** (*Aut*) (accident) black spot; (*fig*) blemish ► **punto neurálgico** (*Anat*) nerve centre *o* (*EEUU*) center; (*fig*) key point ► **punto neutro** (*Mec*) dead centre; (*Aut*) neutral (gear)
8 (*otras locuciones*) **a punto** ready; **está a ~** it's ready; **con sus cámaras a ~ para disparar** with their cameras at the ready; **llegar a ~** to come just at the right moment; **poner un motor a ~** to tune an engine; **al ~** at once, immediately; **estar al ~** (*LAm**) to be high‡; **bajar de ~** to decline, fall off, fall away; **a ~ de**: **a ~ de caramelo** caramelized; **poner el azúcar a ~ de caramelo** to caramelize the sugar; **batir las claras a ~ de nieve** beat the egg whites until stiff *o* until they form stiff peaks; **estar a ~ de hacer algo** to be on the point of doing sth, be about to do sth; **estábamos a ~ de salir cuando llamaste** we were about to go out when you phoned; **estuve a ~ de llamarte** I almost called you; **estaba a ~ de llorar** he was on the verge of tears; **estuve a ~ de perder el tren** I very nearly missed the train; **en ~**: **a las siete en ~** at seven o'clock sharp *o* on the dot; **llegó en ~** he arrived right on time; **en su ~** [*carne*] done to a turn; [*fruta*] just ripe; **el arroz está en su ~** the rice is just right; **pongamos las cosas en su ~** let's be absolutely clear about this; **hasta cierto ~** up to a point, to some extent; **hasta tal ~ que ...** to such an extent that ...; **la tensión había llegado hasta tal ~ que ...** the tension had reached such a pitch that ...; **subir de ~** (= *aumentar*) to grow, increase; (= *empeorar*) to get worse; ✦***MODISMOS*** **coger** *o* **ligar** *o* **pillar un buen ~‡** (*con alcohol*) to get merry*; (*con drogas*) to get high*; **cogerle** *o* **pillarle el ~ a algn‡** to work sb out; **darle el ~ a algn‡**: **si me da el ~, voy** if I feel like it, I'll go; **si le da el ~ es capaz de cualquier cosa** if he gets it into his head he can do anything; **saber algo a ~ fijo** to know sth for sure; **de todo ~** completely, absolutely
9 (*Esp**) (= *hombre*) guy*; (*pey*) rogue; **¡vaya un ~!** ◊ **¡está hecho un ~ filipino!** he's a right rogue!*
10 (= *agujero*) hole; **darse dos ~s en el cinturón** to let one's belt out a couple of holes
11 (*Inform*) pixel ► **punto de parada** break-point ► **punto de referencia** benchmark

puntocom SF INV, ADJ INV dotcom, dot.com

puntuable ADJ **una prueba ~ para el campeonato** a race which counts towards *o* scores in the championship

puntuación SF 1 (*Ling, Tip*) punctuation
2 (= *puntos*) mark(s) (*pl*); (= *grado*) class, grade; (*Dep*) score
3 (= *acto*) (*Escol*) marking, grading (*EEUU*); (*Dep*) scoring; **sistema de ~** system of scoring

puntual Ⓐ ADJ 1 [*persona, llegada*] punctual
2 (= *detallado*) [*informe*] detailed; [*cálculo*] exact, accurate
3 (= *aislado*) **se trata de casos muy ~es** they are very isolated cases; **ha tenido unos cuantos éxitos ~es en su carrera** he's had the odd success in his career, he's had a few successes at odd times during his career
Ⓑ ADV (= *a tiempo*) **nunca llega ~** he's never on time

puntualidad SF 1 [*de llegada*] punctuality; **pagar con ~** to pay promptly
2 (= *exactitud*) exactness, accuracy
3 (= *fiabilidad*) reliability, conscientiousness

puntualización SF specification, detailed statement *o* explanation

puntualizador ADJ specific, detailed

puntualizar ▸conjug 1f◂ VT 1 [+ *detalles*] to specify 2 (= *recordar*) to fix in one's mind, fix in one's memory

puntualmente ADV 1 (= *con puntualidad*) [*llegar*] punctually; [*pagar*] promptly
2 (= *con exactitud*) precisely, exactly, accurately
3 (= *con fiabilidad*) reliably, conscientiously

puntuar ▸conjug 1e◂ Ⓐ VT 1 (*Ling, Tip*) to punctuate
2 (= *evaluar*) [+ *clase, estilo*] to evaluate, assess; [+ *examen*] to mark, grade (*EEUU*)
Ⓑ VI 1 (= *valer*) to count; **eso no puntúa** that doesn't count
2 (*Dep*) (= *marcar*) to score

puntudo ADJ (*LAm*) sharp

puntura SF puncture, prick

punzada SF 1 (= *puntura*) prick, jab
2 (*Med*) (= *punto*) stitch; (= *dolor*) twinge (of pain), shooting pain; (= *espasmo*) spasm
3 [*de pena, remordimiento*] pang, twinge
4 (*Caribe**) (= *insolencia*) cheek*, nerve

punzante ADJ 1 [*dolor*] shooting, stabbing
2 [*instrumento*] sharp
3 [*comentario*] biting, caustic

punzar ▸conjug 1f◂ VT 1 (= *pinchar*) (*gen*) to puncture, prick, pierce; (*Téc*) to punch; (= *perforar*) to perforate
2 (= *doler*) to hurt, grieve; **las sienes le punzaban** her temples were throbbing; **le punzan los remordimientos** he feels pangs of regret, his conscience pricks him

punzó ADJ (*Andes, Cono Sur*) bright red

punzón SM (*Téc*) punch; (*Tip*) bodkin

puñada SF punch, clout; **dar de ~s en** to punch, pound, beat on

puñado SM handful; **a ~s** by handfuls, in plenty; **me mola un ~*** I like it a lot, I love it

puñal SM dagger; ✦***MODISMO*** **poner un ~ al pecho a algn** to put sb on the spot

puñalada SF 1 (= *herida*) stab, wound, knife wound; **coser a ~s** to stab repeatedly, carve up*
2 (= *traición*) terrible blow ► **puñalada trapera** stab in the back

puñeta‡‡ Ⓐ SF 1 (*indicando enojo*) **¡no me vengas con ~s!** give me peace!, stop your whining!; **¡qué coche ni que ~s!** car my arse!‡‡; **tengo un catarro de la ~** I've got a hellish *o* a stinking cold*, I've got a bloody awful cold‡; ✦***MODISMO*** **irse a hacer ~s** to go to hell*; **¡vete a hacer ~s!** go to hell!*
2 **hacer la ~ a algn** to screw sb around‡‡
Ⓑ EXCL **¡~s!** ◊ **¡qué ~s!** (*indicando enojo*) shit!‡‡, hell!*; (*indicando asombro*) bugger me!‡‡, well I'm damned!

puñetazo SM punch; **a ~s** with one's fists; **dar a algn de ~s** to punch sb

puñetería‡ SF bore, drag

puñetero‡ ADJ (= *maldito*) damned*; (= *despreciable*) rotten

puño SM 1 (*Anat*) fist; **con el** *o* **a ~ cerrado** with one's clenched fist; **apretar los ~s** (*lit*) to clench one's fists; (*fig*) to struggle hard; ✦***MODISMOS*** **comerse los ~s** to be starving; **como un ~**: **su piso es como un ~** his flat is tiny *o* a matchbox; **es una verdad como un**

~ it's as plain as a pikestaff; **mentiras como ~s** whopping great lies*; **de mi/tu/su ~**: **de ~ y letra del poeta** in the poet's own handwriting; **ganar algo con los ~s** to get sth by sheer hard work; **tener a algn (metido) en un ~** to have sb under one's thumb ► **puño de hierro** knuckle-duster; *ver tb* **virgen B**
2 [*de camisa, chaqueta*] cuff
3 [*de espada*] hilt; [*de herramienta*] handle, haft, grip; [*de velero, vasija, puerta*] handle
4 (= *puñado*) handful, fistful

pupa Ⓐ SF 1 (*Med**) (= *ampolla*) blister; (*en los labios*) cold sore; (= *úlcera*) ulcer
2 (*) (*en lenguaje infantil*) pain; **hacer ~ a algn** to hurt sb; **hacerse ~** to get hurt
3 (*) (= *error*) gaffe, blunder
4 (*Entomología*) pupa
Ⓑ **pupas** SMF INV (*) unpredictable person; (= *gruñón*) moaner*

pupila SF 1 (*Anat*) pupil
2 (= *perspicacia*) sharpness, intelligence
3 (*Arg**) (= *prostituta*) prostitute, whore, hooker (*EEUU**)

pupilo/a SM/F 1 (*en pensión*) boarder; (*en un orfelinato*) inmate
2 (*Jur*) ward
3 (*Dep**) player

pupitre SM desk

pupo SM (*Andes, Cono Sur*) navel

pupón ADJ 1 (*Cono Sur, Méx**) (= *lleno*) stuffed, full, full up
2 (*Cono Sur*‡) (= *barrigón*) pot-bellied, paunchy

pupurrí SM pot-pourri

pupusa SF (*CAm Culin*) stuffed tortilla

pupusería SF (*CAm*) *shop selling stuffed tortillas*

puque ADJ (*Méx*) (= *podrido*) rotten, bad; (= *débil*) weak, sickly; (= *estéril*) sterile

puquío SM (*LAm*) spring, fountain

pura SF ✦**MODISMO por las ~s** (*Cono Sur**) just for the hell of it

puramente ADV purely, simply

purasangre SMF (*pl* **purasangres**) thoroughbred

puré SM (*Culin*) purée, (thick) soup; **~ de guisantes** (*lit*) pea soup; (*fig*) peasouper*, thick fog; **~ de patatas** mashed potatoes *pl*; **~ de tomate** tomato purée, tomato paste; **~ de verduras** thick vegetable soup; ✦**MODISMO estar hecho ~*** to be knackered*

purear ▸conjug 1a◂ VI (*Andes*) to drink one's liquor neat

pureta* Ⓐ ADJ old, elderly
Ⓑ SMF 1 (= *viejo*) old crock
2 (= *carca*) old square*

pureza SF purity

purga SF 1 (*Med*) purge, purgative
2 (*Pol*) purge
3 (= *drenaje*) venting, draining; **válvula de ~** vent

purgación SF 1 (= *acción*) purging; (= *medicina*) purgative
2 [*de mujer*] menstruation
3 **tener purgaciones*** to have the clap*

purgante SM, ADJ purgative

purgar ▸conjug 1h◂ Ⓐ VT 1 (*Med*) to purge, administer a purgative to
2 (*Pol*) (= *depurar*) to expel; **~ a los fascistas del partido** to purge the party of fascists, expel fascists from the party
3 (= *limpiar de*) [+ *pecado*] to purge, expiate; [+ *delito*] to pay for; [+ *pasiones*] to purge; **~ la religión de supersticiones** to purge *o* cleanse religion of superstition
4 (*Mec*) (= *drenar*) [+ *depósito, tubería*] to drain; [+ *radiador*] to bleed, drain; [+ *frenos*] to bleed
5 (= *purificar*) to purify, refine
Ⓑ **purgarse** VPR 1 (*Med*) to take a purge
2 (*fig*) **~se de algo** to purge o.s. of sth

purgativo ADJ purgative

purgatorio SM purgatory; **¡fue un ~!** it was purgatory!

puridad SF **en ~** (= *claramente*) plainly, directly; (= *estrictamente*) strictly speaking; (= *secretamente*) in secret

purificación SF purification ► **purificación étnica** ethnic cleansing

purificador Ⓐ ADJ purifying
Ⓑ SM ► **purificador de agua** water filter ► **purificador de aire** air purifier, air filter

purificante ADJ cleansing

purificar ▸conjug 1g◂ VT [+ *agua, raza*] to purify; [+ *metales*] to refine, purify; [+ *pulmones*] to cleanse

purili‡ SMF old geezer‡

Purísima ADJ SUPERL **la ~** the Virgin

purismo SM purism

purista SMF purist

puritanismo SM puritanism

puritano/a Ⓐ ADJ 1 (*Rel*) Puritan
2 [*actitud tradición*] puritanical, puritan
Ⓑ SM/F 1 (*Rel*) Puritan
2 (*fig*) puritan

puro Ⓐ ADJ 1 (= *sin mezcla*) [*color, lenguaje*] pure; [*aire*] clean; [*oro*] solid
2 (*con valor enfático*) pure, simple; **de ~ aburrimiento** out of sheer boredom; **por pura casualidad** by sheer chance; ✦**MODISMO ~ y duro***: **fue un timo ~ y duro** it was a straightforward *o* downright swindle; **es un reaccionario ~ y duro** he's an out-and-out reactionary
3 (= *casto*) pure, chaste
4 (*LAm*) (= *uno solo*) only, just; **me queda una pura porción** I have just one portion left
5 (*esp Andes, Caribe, Méx*) (= *idéntico*) identical; **el hijo es ~ el padre** the son is exactly like his father
Ⓑ ADV **de ~ bobo** out of sheer stupidity; **de ~ cansado** out of sheer tiredness; **no se le ve el color de ~ sucio** it's so dirty you can't tell what colour it is; **cosas que se olvidan de ~ sabidas** things which are so well known that they get overlooked
Ⓒ SM 1 (*tb* **cigarro ~**) cigar ► **puro habano** Havana cigar
2 ✦**MODISMO meter un ~ a algn*** (*gen*) to throw the book at sb*; (*Mil*) to put sb on a charge
3 **a ~ de**† by dint of, thanks only to

púrpura SF 1 (= *color*) purple
2 (= *cargo*) ► **púrpura cardenalicia** cardinal purple ► **la púrpura imperial** the mantel of emperor

purpurado SM (= *persona*) cardinal; (= *cargo*) purple

purpurar ▸conjug 1a◂ VT to dye purple

purpúreo ADJ purple

purpurina SF 1 (= *pintura*) (*gen*) metallic paint; (*para decoración, maquillaje*) glitter
2 (= *oropel*) glitz, tinsel

purpurino ADJ purple

purrela SF 1 (= *vino*) bad wine, cheap wine, plonk*
2 **una ~** a mere trifle, chicken feed (*pey*)

purrete* SM (*Cono Sur*) kid*, child

purulento ADJ purulent

pus SM pus

puse *etc ver* **poner**

pusilánime ADJ fainthearted, pusillanimous

pusilanimidad SF faintheartedness, pusillanimity

pústula SF pustule

put [pʌt] SM (*pl* **puts** [pʌt]) (*Golf*) putt

puta*‡ SF 1 (= *prostituta*) whore, prostitute; **casa de ~s** brothel; **¡la muy ~!** the slut!, the bitch!‡; **ir(se) de ~s** to go whoring ► **puta callejera** streetwalker
2 (*expresando fastidio*) **¡puta!** bloody hell!‡; **¡la ~!** (*expresando sorpresa*) well I'm damned!
3 (*Naipes*) jack, knave
4 **pasarlas ~s** to have a shitty time*, have a rotten time*; *ver tb* **puto**

putada*‡ SF (= *mala pasada*) dirty trick; **¡es una ~!** it's a real bugger!‡

putañear* ▸conjug 1a◂ VI to go whoring

putañero* Ⓐ ADJ 1 (= *que va de putas*) whoring
2 (= *cachondo*) randy, oversexed
Ⓑ SM whoremonger

putativo ADJ putative (*frm*), supposed

puteada* SF (*LAm*) (= *insultos*) shower of gross insults; (= *palabrota*) swearword

puteado*‡ ADJ 1 (= *fastidiado*) **nos tienen ~s** they're really screwing us around‡; **el ~ pueblo español** the long-suffering *o* hard done-by Spanish people
2 (= *harto*) fed up to the back teeth*, browned off*; **estar ~** to be fed up to the back teeth*, be browned off
3 (= *maleado*) corrupted, perverted

putear ▸conjug 1a◂ Ⓐ VT 1 (*‡) (= *fastidiar*) to bugger about‡, muck around
2 (*‡) (= *enfadar*) to upset, send up the wall*
3 (*LAm**) (= *insultar*) to swear at, curse
Ⓑ VI (*) 1 (= *ir de putas*) to go whoring
2 (= *ser prostituta*) to be on the game*
3 (*Cono Sur*) (= *jurar*) to swear, curse, eff and blind*

puteo* SM **ir de ~** (*Esp*) to go whoring

putería* SF 1 (*de putas*) (= *prostitución*) prostitution, whoring; (= *vida*) life of the prostitute
2 (= *prostitutas*) gathering of prostitutes
3 (= *prostíbulo*) brothel
4 (= *artimañas*) womanly wile(s)
5 (= *zalamería*) soft soap*

puterío* SM whoring, prostitution

puticlub* [putɪ'klu] SM (*hum*) pick up joint‡

putilla* SF scrubber‡

putiza‡ SF (*Méx*) brawl, set-to*

puto*‡ Ⓐ ADJ bloody*, bloody awful*; **no me hizo ni ~ caso** she completely bloody ignored me‡; **no tengo ni un ~ duro** I'm absolutely skint*; **¡ni puta idea!** I've no bloody idea!*; **por toda la puta calle** all along the bloody street‡; **¡qué puta suerte!** (= *mala*) what bloody awful luck!*; (= *buena*) what incredible luck!*; ✦**MODISMO de puta madre** (= *bueno*) terrific*, smashing*; (= *malo*) bloody awful‡; (*uso adverbial*) marvellously; **cocina de puta madre** she's a bloody marvellous

cook*; *ver tb* **puta 2**
Ⓑ SM [1] (= *prostituto*) male prostitute
[2] (= *insulto*) sod**

putrefacción SF rotting, putrefaction; **basura en ~** rotting rubbish; **alimentos sujetos a ~** perishable foods; **el cadáver estaba en avanzado estado de ~** the body was in an advanced estate of decomposition ► **putrefacción fungoide** dry rot ► **putrefacción política** political corruption

putrefacto ADJ (= *podrido*) rotten, putrid; (= *descompuesto*) decayed

putrescente ADJ rotting, putrefying

pútrido ADJ putrid, rotten

putt [pʌt] SM (*pl* **putts** [pʌt]) putt

putter ['pʌter] SM (*pl* **putters** ['pʌter]) putter

puya SF [1] (= *vara*) (*gen*) goad, pointed stick; (*Taur*) point of the picador's lance
[2] (= *sarcasmo*) gibe, barbed comment
[3] (*Caribe*) one cent

puyar ▸conjug 1a◂ Ⓐ VT [1] (*LAm*) to jab, prick
[2] (*Col**) (= *molestar*) to upset, needle*
Ⓑ VI (*Caribe*) [*planta*] to shoot, sprout

puyazo SM [1] (*Taur*) jab with the lance
[2] (= *palabras*) gibe, barbed comment

puyero SM (*Caribe*) pile of money; **divertirse un ~*** to have a great time*, have a whale of a time*

puyo SM (*Cono Sur*) coarse woollen poncho

puyón SM [1] (*Andes, Cono Sur*) (= *espolón*) cock's spur
[2] (*Méx*) (= *puya*) sharp point; (= *espina*) thorn, prickle
[3] (*Andes, CAm, Caribe*) (= *pinchazo*) jab, prick
[4] (*Andes, CAm, Méx*) (= *brote*) shoot, bud

puzcua SF (*Méx*) puffed maize

puz(z)le ['puθle] SM puzzle (*tb fig*)

PVC SM ABR (= **polyvinyl-chloride**) PVC

PVP SM ABR (= **precio de venta al público**) RRP

PYME SF ABR, **pyme** SF ABR = **Pequeña y Mediana Empresa**

PYRESA SF ABR = **Prensa y Radio Española, Sociedad Anónima**

Q q

Q, q [ku] SF (= *letra*) Q, q

Qatar SM Qatar

q.b.s.m. ABR (= **que besa su mano**) *courtesy formula*

q.b.s.p. ABR (= **que besa sus pies**) *courtesy formula*

q.D.g. ABR, **Q.D.G** ABR (= **que Dios guarde**) *courtesy formula*

QED ABR (= **quod erat demonstrandum**) QED

q.e.g.e. ABR (= **que en gloria esté**) ≈ RIP

q.e.p.d. ABR (= **que en paz descanse**) RIP

q.e.s.m. ABR (= **que estrecha su mano**) *courtesy formula*

QH SF ABR (= **quiniela hípica**) *horse-racing totalizator*

qm ABR = **quintal(es) métrico(s)**

qts. ABR (= **quilates**) c

Quáker® SM (*LAm*) porridge

quantum ['kwantum] SM (*pl* **quanta** ['kwanta]) (*Fís*) quantum

quark SM (*pl* **quarks**) quark

quásar SM quasar

quattrocentista ADJ quattrocento *antes de s*

que[1] PRON REL [1] (*refiriéndose a personas*) [1·1] (*como sujeto*) who, that; **el hombre ~ vino ayer** the man who *o* that came yesterday; **hable con alguien ~ entienda de esto** talk to someone who knows about this

[1·2] (*como complemento: a menudo se omite*) that; **el hombre ~ vi en la calle** the man (that) I saw in the street; **la chica ~ conoció durante las vacaciones** the girl (that) he met on holiday

[2] (*refiriéndose a cosas*) [2·1] (*como sujeto*) that, which; **la película ~ ganó el premio** the film that *o* which won the award

[2·2] (*como complemento: a menudo se omite*) that, which; **el coche ~ compré** the car (that *o* which) I bought; **el libro del ~ te hablé** the book (that *o* which) I spoke to you about; **el día ~ ella nació** the day (when *o* that) she was born; **la cama en ~ pasé la noche** the bed in which I spent the night, the bed I spent the night in

[3] **el/la/los/las ~** *ver* **el 8**

[4] **lo ~** *ver* **lo**[1] **3**

que[2] CONJ [1] (*en subordinada sustantiva: a menudo se omite*) [1·1] (+ *INDIC*) that; **creo ~ va a venir** I think (that) he will come; **dijo ~ vendría** he said (that) he'd come; **dile a Rosa ~ me llame** tell Rosa to call me; **estoy seguro de ~ lloverá** I am sure (that) it will rain; **aceptan la idea de ~ el diálogo es útil** they accept the idea that a dialogue is useful; **eso de ~ no lo sabía es un cuento** all that about him not knowing is pure fiction

[1·2] (+ *SUBJUN*) that; **no sabía ~ tuviera coche** I didn't know (that) he had a car; **me alegro de ~ hayan ganado** I am glad (that) they have won; **es una pena ~ no tengamos más tiempo** it's a pity (that) we haven't got more time; **no digo ~ sea un traidor** I'm not saying (that) he's a traitor; **espero ~ os sea útil** I hope you'll find it useful; **no creo ~ te sea difícil encontrarlo** I don't think you'll have any difficulty finding it; **quieren ~ les esperes** they want you to wait for them

[1·3] **decir ~ sí** to say yes; *ver tb* **claro B4**

[2] (*en comparaciones*) **eres <u>igual</u> ~ mi padre** you're just like my father; **<u>más</u> ~** more than; **ganas más ~ yo** you earn more than me; **es más alto ~ tú** he's taller than you; **más ~ nada** more than anything; **<u>menos</u> ~** less than; **<u>prefiero</u> estar aquí ~ en mi casa** I'd rather be here than at home; **prefiero las películas serias ~ las comedias** I prefer serious films to comedies; **<u>yo</u> ~ tú** if I were you; **yo ~ tú, iría** I'd go, if I were you

[3] (*expresando resultado*) [3·1] (*a menudo se omite*) that; **<u>tan</u> ... ~: es tan grande ~ no lo puedo levantar** it's so big (that) I can't lift it; **soplaba tan fuerte ~ no podíamos salir** it was blowing so hard (that) we couldn't go out; **<u>tanto</u> ... ~: las manos le temblaban tanto ~ apenas podía escribir** her hands were shaking so much (that) she could hardly write

[3·2] **tengo una sed ~ me muero** I'm dying of thirst; **huele ~ es un asco** it smells disgusting; *ver tb* **bendición 2, primor 2**

[4] (*expresando causa*) **llévate un paraguas, ~ está lloviendo** take an umbrella, it's raining; **no lo derroches, ~ es muy caro** don't waste it, it's very expensive; **¡vamos, ~ cierro!** come on now, I'm closing!; **¡cuidado, ~ te caes!** careful or you'll fall!, mind you don't fall!; **¡suélteme, ~ voy a gritar!** let go or I'll scream!

[5] (*expresando reiteración o insistencia*) **siguió toca ~ toca** he kept on playing; **estuvieron habla ~ habla toda la noche** they talked and talked all night; **¡~ <u>sí</u>!: —es verde —¡~ no! —¡~ sí!** "it's green" — "no it isn't!" — "yes it is!"; **—no funciona —~ sí, es ~ lo haces mal** "it doesn't work" — "yes it does, you're just doing it wrong"

[6] (*sin antecedente expreso*) [6·1] (*expresando mandato*) **¡~ lo haga él!** let him do it!, he can do it himself!; **¡~ entre!** send him in!, let him come in!

[6·2] (*expresando deseo*) **¡~ venga pronto!** let's hope he comes soon!; **¡~ te mejores!** get well soon!; **¡~ os guste la película!** enjoy the film!

[6·3] (*expresando sorpresa*) **¿~ no estabas allí?** (are you telling me) you weren't there?

[7] **<u>el</u> ~** (+ *SUBJUN*) (= *el hecho de que*) the fact that; **el ~ viva en Vitoria no es ningún problema** the fact that he lives in Vitoria isn't a problem; **el ~ quiera estar con su madre es natural** it is natural (that) he should want to be with his mother

qué Ⓐ PRON [1] (*interrogativo*) **¿qué?** what?; **¿~ has dicho?** what did you say?; **¿a ~ has venido?** why have you come?, what have you come for?; **¿con ~ lo vas a pagar?** how are you going to pay for it?, what are you going to pay with?; **¿de ~ lo conoces?** how do you know him?, where do you know him from?; **¿en ~ lo notas?** how can you tell?; **no sé ~ quiere decir** I don't know what it means; **¿~ tan grande es?** (*LAm*) how big is it?; **¿~ <u>más</u>?** (*gen*) what else?; (*en tienda*) anything else?; **¿<u>para</u> ~?: ¿para ~ lo quiere?** why does he want it?, what does he want it for?; **¿para ~, si nunca me hace caso?** what's the point? he never listens to me anyway; **¿<u>por</u> ~?** why?; **¿por ~ no se lo dices?** why don't you tell him?; **¿~ <u>tal</u>?** how are things?; **¿~ tal estás?** how are you?; **¿~ tal el trabajo?** how's work?; **¿~ <u>tanto</u>?** (*LAm*) (= *¿cuánto?*) how much?; **¿~ tanto lo quiere?** how much do you love him?; **¿<u>y</u> ~?** so what?; **no lo he hecho, ¿y ~?** so what if I haven't done it?; **¿y a mí ~?** so what?, what has that got to do with me?; ✦*MODISMOS* **ahí estaba el ~** that was the reason; **sin ~ ni para ~** without rhyme or reason

[2] (*exclamativo*) **¡~ <u>de</u> gente había!** what a lot of people there were!; **¡~ de cosas te diría!** what a lot I'd have to say to you!; **¡~ <u>va</u>!: ¡~ va!, no me parece caro** no, I don't think it's expensive at all!; **—es muy fea —¡~ va! a mí me parece monísima** "she's very ugly" — "you're joking, I think she's really pretty!"; **¿aquí, en España, corrupción? ¡~ va!** corruption, here in Spain? come off it!

Ⓑ ADJ [1] (*interrogativo*) **¿~ día del mes es hoy?** what's today's date?, what's the date today?; **¿~ camisa le regalarías?** which shirt would you give him?; **dime ~ libro buscas** tell me which book you are looking for; **—¿has encontrado mi lápiz? —¿~ lápiz?**

"have you found my pencil?" — "what pencil?"; **¡~ edad tiene?** how old is he?, what age is he?; **¿a ~ velocidad?** how fast?, at what speed?; **¿de ~ tamaño es?** how big is it?, what size is it?
[2] (*exclamativo*) **¡~ día más espléndido!** what a glorious day!; **¡~ casualidad!** what a coincidence!; **¡~ susto!** what a fright!; **¡~ asco!** how revolting!; **¡~ maravilla!** how wonderful!; **¡~ maravilla de casa!** what a wonderful house!
Ⓒ ADV **¡~ bonito!** isn't it pretty!, how pretty it is!; **¡~ boba eres!** you're so silly!; **¡~ mala eres!** you're awful!; **¡~ mala suerte!** what rotten luck!; **¡~ bien!** (= *estupendo*) great!, excellent!; (= *bravo*) well done!; **¡~ bien se vive solo!** it's great living on your own!; **¡~ bien canta!** she sings so well!, she's such a good singer!; **¡~ bien se oye!** you can hear so clearly!

quebracho SM [1] (= *árbol*) quebracho, quebracho tree; (= *madera*) break axe, break ax (*EEUU*)
[2] (*Téc*) *extract used in leather-tanning*

quebrada SF [1] (= *hondonada*) ravine, gorge; (= *puerto*) gap, pass
[2] (*LAm*) (= *arroyo*) brook, mountain stream

quebradero SM ► **quebradero de cabeza** headache, worry

quebradizo ADJ [1] (= *frágil*) (*gen*) fragile, brittle; [*hojaldre*] short; [*galleta*] crumbly; [*voz*] weak, faltering
[2] (= *enfermizo*) sickly, frail
[3] (= *muy sensible*) emotionally fragile, sensitive, easily upset
[4] (*moralmente*) weak, easily tempted

quebrado Ⓐ ADJ [1] (= *roto*) (*gen*) broken; [*terreno*] rough, uneven; [*línea*] irregular, zigzag
[2] **~ de color** [*rostro*] pale; [*tez*] pallid
[3] (*Med*) ruptured
[4] (*Fin*) bankrupt
Ⓑ SM [1] (*Mat*) fraction
[2] (*Fin*) bankrupt ► **quebrado no rehabilitado** undischarged bankrupt ► **quebrado rehabilitado** discharged bankrupt

quebradora SF (*CAm Med*) dengue fever

quebradura SF [1] (= *grieta*) fissure, crack
[2] (*Geog*) = **quebrada 1**
[3] (*Med*) rupture

quebraja SF fissure, slit, crack

quebrantadura SF, **quebrantamiento** SM
[1] (= *rotura*) (*gen*) breaking; (*al formarse una grieta*) cracking; [*de resistencia*] weakening; [*de cerradura*] forcing; [*de ley*] violation ► **quebrantadura de forma** (*Jur*) breach of normal procedure
[2] (= *estado*) exhaustion, exhausted state
[3] (= *mala salud*) broken health

quebrantahuesos SM INV bearded vulture

quebrantar ►conjug 1a◄ Ⓐ VT [1] (= *romper*) (*gen*) to break; (*haciendo grietas*) to crack; (*haciendo añicos*) to shatter
[2] (= *debilitar*) [+ *resistencia*] to weaken, break; [+ *salud, posición*] to destroy, undermine; [+ *persona*] to break; [+ *cimientos, furia, moral*] to weaken
[3] (= *abrir*) [+ *cerradura*] to force; [+ *caja fuerte, sello*] to break open; [+ *cárcel*] to break out of; [+ *recinto sagrado*] to break into, violate; [+ *terreno vedado*] to trespass on
[4] [+ *ley, promesa*] to break
[5] [+ *color*] to tone down
[6] (*LAm*) [+ *caballo*] to break in
Ⓑ **quebrantarse** VPR [*persona*] to be broken (in health *etc*)

quebranto SM [1] (= *perjuicio*) damage, harm
[2] [*de persona*] (= *agotamiento*) exhaustion; (= *depresión*) depression; (= *mala salud*) broken health
[3] (= *aflicción*) sorrow, affliction

quebrar ►conjug 1j◄ Ⓐ VT [1] (= *romper*) to break, smash
[2] (= *doblar*) (*gen*) to bend; [+ *cuerpo*] to bend (at the waist)
[3] (= *torcer*) to twist
[4] [+ *proceso*] (= *interrumpir*) to interrupt; (= *modificar*) to alter the course of, seriously interfere with
[5] [+ *color*] to tone down
[6] (*Méx**) (= *matar*) to bump off*, waste*
[7] = **quebrantar A2, 6**
Ⓑ VI [1] (*Fin*) to fail, go bankrupt
[2] (= *debilitarse*) to weaken
[3] **~ con algn** to break with sb
Ⓒ **quebrarse** VPR [1] to break, get broken, smash
[2] (*Med*) to rupture

quebraza SF [1] (= *grieta*) crack
[2] (*Med*) crack (*on the skin*), chap

quebrazón SF [1] (*LAm*) [*de vidrio*] smashing, shattering
[2] (*Cono Sur*) (= *contienda*) quarrel

quebroso ADJ (*Andes*) brittle, fragile

queche SM smack, ketch

quechua Ⓐ ADJ Quechua, Quechuan
Ⓑ SMF Quechua(n) Indian
Ⓒ SM (*Ling*) Quechua

> **QUECHUA**
>
> **Quechua**, *the language spoken by the Incas, is the most widely spoken indigenous language in South America, with some 13 million speakers in the Andean region. The first Quechua grammar was compiled by a Spanish missionary in 1560, as part of a linguistic policy intended to aid the process of evangelization. In 1975 Peru made Quechua an official state language. From Quechua come words such as "llama", "condor" and "puma".*

queda SF **toque de ~** curfew

quedada[1]†† SF (*CAm, Caribe, Méx*) spinster, old maid (*pey*)

quedada[2]* SF (= *broma*) joke, tease; (= *engaño*) hoax

quedado ADJ (*Cono Sur, Méx*) lazy

quedar

> ►conjug 1a◄
> [A] VERBO INTRANSITIVO [B] VERBO PRONOMINAL
> *Para expresiones como* ***quedarse tan ancho, quedarse con las ganas, quedársele grabado algn, quedarse helado, quedarse parado****, ver la otra entrada.*

Ⓐ VERBO INTRANSITIVO
[1] *indicando lugar* to be; **eso queda muy lejos** that's a long way away; **queda un poco más al oeste** it is a little further west; **queda a 6 km de aquí** it's 6 km from here; **queda hacia la derecha** it's over to the right; **¿por dónde queda Correos?** where's the post office?; **queda por aquí** it's around here somewhere; **esa cuestión queda fuera de nuestra responsabilidad** that matter lies outside our responsibility
[2] *indicando posición* **quedó el penúltimo** he was second last; **~ atrás**: **no quieren ~ atrás en la carrera espacial** they don't want to be left behind *o* fall behind in the space race; **la crisis ha quedado atrás** the crisis is behind us
[3] *indicando resultado* [3·1] (*con adjetivos, adverbios, locuciones preposicionales, participios*) **el autocar quedó destrozado** the coach was wrecked; **te ha quedado muy bonita la cocina** you've made a great job of the kitchen; **quedó paralítico tras el accidente** the accident left him paralysed; **la cara le ha quedado desfigurada** her face has been disfigured; **al final quedamos como amigos** we were still friends afterwards; **aún no han quedado definidos los criterios** the criteria still haven't been established; **la junta ha quedado constituida** the board has been elected; **~ ciego** to go blind; **~ huérfano** to be orphaned; **quedó huérfano de padre a los seis años** he lost his father when he was six years old; **~ viuda/viudo** to be widowed, lose one's husband/wife; ✦*MODISMO* **ahí quedó la cosa** that's how we left it
[3·2] **~ en algo**: **¿en qué quedó la conversación?** how did the conversation end?; **todas sus promesas ~on en nada** all her promises came to nothing; **al final todo quedó en un susto** it gave us a scare but it turned out all right in the end
[3·3] **~ sin**: **miles de personas han quedado sin hogar** thousands of people have been left homeless; **el proyecto quedó sin realizar** the project was never carried out; **la reconstrucción del puente ha quedado sin hacer por falta de presupuesto** the rebuilding of the bridge has been abandoned because of a shortage of funds
[4] *en el trato, al hablar* **ha quedado como un canalla** he has shown himself to be a rotter; **~ bien**: **regalando flores siempre queda uno bien** taking flowers always makes a good impression; **sólo lo ha hecho por ~ bien** he only did it to make himself look good; **~ bien con algn** to make a good impression on sb; **~ mal**: **nos hiciste ~ mal haciendo esas preguntas** you made us look bad by asking those questions; **no quiero ~ mal con ellos** I don't want to get on the wrong side of them; **por no ~ mal** so as not to cause any offence; **~ por algo** to be left looking like sth; **quedé por idiota** I was left looking like an idiot; **aunque fue idea de todos, yo quedé por el culpable** although everyone was to blame, it ended up looking as if it was my fault; **~ en ridículo**: **ha quedado en ridículo** he ended up looking a fool; **quería que su marido ~a en ridículo** she wanted to make her husband look a fool, she wanted to show her husband up
[5] *= permanecer* to stay; **~on allí una semana** they stayed there a week; **quedo a la espera de sus noticias** (*en carta*) I look forward to hearing from you
[6] *= haber todavía* to be left; **no queda ninguno** there are none left; **¿queda algo de la cena?** is there any dinner left?; **no quedan más que escombros** there is nothing left but rubble; **no quedaba nadie en el**

autobús there was nobody left on the bus; **de la ciudad sólo queda el castillo** all that remains *o* is left of the city is the castle; **no quedó ni un solo edificio en pie** not a single building was left standing; **se me cayó un poco de vino, pero no ha quedado ninguna mancha** I spilt some wine, but it didn't leave a stain; **si a 8 le quito 2, quedan 6** if I take 2 from 8, I'm left with *o* it leaves 6; **~le a algn**: **¿le quedan entradas para esta noche?** do you have any tickets left for tonight?; **me quedan cinco euros** I've got five euros left; **no nos queda mucho dinero** we don't have much money left; **~ a deber algo** to owe sth; **no tenía suficiente y tuve que ~le a deber** I didn't have enough money on me, so I had to owe him; **me quedó a deber 25 euros** he was left owing me 25 euros; **quedan pocos días para la fiesta** the party is only a few days away; **nos quedan 12 km para llegar a Badalona** we've still got 12 km to go to Badalona; **~ por hacer**: **nos queda por pagar la luz** we still have to pay the electricity bill; **queda por limpiar la cocina** the kitchen still needs cleaning; **eso queda todavía por estudiar** that remains to be studied; **no me queda más remedio** I have no alternative (left); ✦*MODISMO* **que no quede**: **por mí que no quede, yo he ayudado en lo que he podido** it won't be for want of trying on my part, I helped as much as I could; **por probar que no quede** there's no harm in trying; **tú por ser amable que no quede** nobody could accuse you of not being nice

7 ***Educ*** [*asignatura*] **me han quedado las matemáticas** I failed mathematics

8 ***ropa*** (= *ser la talla*) to fit; (= *sentar*) to suit; **¿qué tal (de grande) te queda el vestido?** does the dress fit you?; **me queda pequeño** it's too small for me; **no te queda bien ese vestido** that dress doesn't suit you; **te queda bien** it suits you; **no queda bien así/aquí** it doesn't look right like that/here

9 **~ en** (= *acordar*): **¿quedamos en eso, entonces?** we'll do that, then, all right?; **~ en** *o* (*LAm*) **de hacer algo** to agree to do sth; **~on en esperar unos días antes de tomar una decisión definitiva** they agreed to wait a few days before taking a final decision; **quedamos en vernos mañana** we arranged to meet tomorrow; **~ en que** to agree that; **quedamos en que cada uno traería una botella** we agreed that everyone would bring a bottle; **¿en qué quedamos? ¿lo compras o no?** so what's it to be then? are you going to buy it or not?

10 ***= citarse*** to arrange to meet; **hemos quedado en la puerta del cine** we've arranged to meet outside the cinema; **habíamos quedado, pero no se presentó** we had arranged to meet, but he didn't turn up; **¿quedamos a las cuatro?** shall we meet at four?; **¿cómo quedamos?** where shall we meet and what time?; **~ con algn** to arrange to meet sb; **¿quedamos con ella en la parada?** shall we meet her at the bus stop?

Ⓑ **quedarse** VERBO PRONOMINAL

1 ***= permanecer, estar*** 1·1 (*gen*) to stay; **ve tú, yo me quedo** you go, I'll stay; **se quedó toda la mañana en la cama** she stayed in bed all morning; **me quedé en casa** I stayed at home; **mis compañeros salieron de trabajar a las cinco, pero yo me quedé hasta las ocho** my colleagues all left work at five, but I stayed behind until eight; **sus preguntas se ~on sin respuesta** his questions remained *o* were left unanswered; **~se con unos amigos** to stay with some friends; **~se atrás** (= *atrasarse*) to fall behind, be left behind; (= *en posición retrasada*) to stay behind; **generalmente se queda atrás hasta la última vuelta** (*Dep*) he usually stays behind until the last lap

1·2 (+ *GERUND*) **me quedé estudiando hasta que cerraron la biblioteca** I carried on *o* stayed working in the library until it closed; **id vosotros, yo me quedo un rato más viendo el museo** you go, I want to stay and look round the museum a bit more; **me quedé viendo la tele hasta muy tarde** I stayed up late watching TV; **se nos quedó mirando asombrado** he stared at us in amazement; *ver tb* **A2**

2 ***indicando resultado*** 2·1 (*con adjetivos, locuciones preposicionales*) **me estoy quedando sordo** I'm going deaf; **se ha quedado viudo** he has been widowed, he has lost his wife; **~se en nada** to come to nothing; **se me ha quedado pequeña esta camisa** I've outgrown this shirt

2·2 **~se sin**: **nos hemos quedado sin café** we've run out of coffee; **~se sin empleo** to lose one's job; **al final nos quedamos sin ver el concierto** we didn't get to see the concert in the end; *ver tb* **A3**

3 ***= conservar*** (*gen*) to keep; (= *comprar*) to take; **quédatela como recuerdo** keep it as a memento; **me la quedo** I'll take it; **~se con** (= *retener*) to keep; (= *comprar*) to take; (= *preferir*) to go for, take; **quédese con la vuelta** keep the change; **se quedó con mi pluma** he kept my pen; **me quedo con este paraguas** I'll take this umbrella; **el vencedor se queda con todo** winner takes all; **entre A y B, me quedo con B** given a choice between A and B, I'd go for *o* take B; **así que me quedé con el más tonto de los tres** so I got (left with) the stupidest of the three; **~se con hambre** to be still hungry

4 ***= retener en la memoria*** **está muy mayor, no se le quedan las cosas** he's really old now, he can't remember things; **lo siento, no me quedé con su nombre** sorry, I can't quite remember your name; **tiene mucha facilidad para ~se con los números** she's very good at remembering numbers

5 (*Esp*) **~se con algn*** (= *engañar*) to con sb*; (= *tomar el pelo a*) to take the mickey out of sb*, pull sb's leg*; **¿te estás quedando conmigo?** are you trying to kid me?*

6 ***= calmarse*** [*viento*] to drop; [*mar*] to calm down

quedito ADV very softly, very gently

quedo Ⓐ ADJ 1 (= *inmóvil*) still

2 (= *tranquilo*) [*voz*] quiet, gentle; [*paso*] soft

Ⓑ ADV softly, gently; **¡quedo!** (= *con cuidado*) careful now!; (= *suave*) gently now!

quedón✱ ADJ (*Esp*) 1 (= *guasón*) jokey, waggish

2 (= *ligón*) flirtatious, fond of the men/the ladies

quehacer SM job, task; **~es domésticos** housework *sing*, household chores; **agobiado de ~** overburdened with work; **atender a sus ~es** to go about one's business; **tener mucho ~** to have a lot to do

queimada SF *traditional Galician hot drink made with flamed "orujo", sugar and lemon*

queja SF 1 (= *reclamación*) (*gen*) complaint; (*refunfuñando*) grumble, grouse*; (*con rencor*) grudge, resentment; **una ~ infundada** an unjustified complaint; **presentar una ~** to make *o* lodge a complaint; **tener ~ de algn** to have a complaint to make about sb; **tener motivo de ~** to have cause for complaint; **estoy harto de tus ~s** I'm tired of your complaining

2 (= *gemido*) moan, groan ► **queja de dolor** groan of pain

3 (*Jur*) protest

quejadera SF (*Andes, Méx*), **quejambre** SF (*Andes, Méx*) moaning

quejarse ▸conjug 1a◂ VPR 1 (= *reclamar*) (*gen*) to complain (**de** about, of); (*refunfuñando*) to grumble (**de** about, at); (*protestando*) to protest (**de** about, at); **~ a la dirección** to complain to the management; **~ de que** to complain (about the fact) that; **se quejó de que nadie lo escuchaba** he complained that nobody listened to him; **~ de vicio*** to be always complaining

2 (= *gemir*) (*gen*) to moan, groan; (*lloriqueando*) to whine

quejica Ⓐ ADJ moaning

Ⓑ SMF moaner, grumbler

quejido SM (= *gemido*) moan, groan; (= *lloriqueo*) whine; **dar ~s** (= *gemir*) to moan, groan; (= *lloriquear*) to whine

quejigal SM, **quejigar** SM gall-oak grove

quejigo SM gall-oak

quejón/ona* Ⓐ ADJ moaning, grumbling

Ⓑ SM/F moaner, grumbler

quejoso ADJ [*persona*] complaining; [*tono*] plaintive; **está ~ de mí** he is annoyed with me

quejumbre SF moan, groan

quejumbroso ADJ = **quejoso**

queli[1]✱ SM, **quel**✱ SF, **quela**✱ SF house; **irse a la ~** to go home

queli[2]✱ SM mate*, pal*, buddy (*EEUU**)

quelite SM (*CAm, Méx*) (= *verduras*) any green vegetable; (= *brote*) shoot, tip, green part; ✦*MODISMO* **poner a algn como un ~** (*Méx**) to make mincemeat of sb

quelonia SF (*Caribe*) turtle

quelonio SM chelonian

quelpo SM kelp

quema SF 1 (= *incendio*) fire; (= *combustión*) burning; (*LAm Agr*) burning-off (of scrub); ✦*MODISMO* **salvarse de la ~**: **fue el único atleta que se salvó de la ~** he was the only athlete to escape the carnage

2 (*Arg*) (= *vertedero*) rubbish dump

3 **hacer ~** (= *acertar*) to hit the target

4 (*Méx*) (= *peligro*) danger

quemable ADJ inflammable

quemado Ⓐ ADJ 1 (*por fuego, sol*) burned, burnt; **llegó muy ~ de la playa** he got back really burned *o* burnt from the beach; **esto sabe a ~** this tastes burned *o* burnt; **aquí huele a ~** there's a smell of burning in here

2 (= *desprestigiado*) **se le considera un político ya ~** he's regarded as a political has-been; **ya está ~ como futbolista** he's had it as a footballer*; **un artista ~ por salir demasiado en televisión** an artist who has become overexposed through being on television too much

[3] (*) (= *harto*) sick and tired*; **la vecina me tiene ~** I've had it up to here with the woman next door*, I'm sick and tired of the woman next door*; **estar ~ con algo** to be sick and tired of sth*
[4] (*LAm*) (= *bronceado*) tanned
[5] (*Chile**) (= *falto de suerte*) unlucky; **nací ~** I was born unlucky; **es tan ~ el pobre** he's such an unlucky guy*
Ⓑ SM [1] (= *acto*) burning; (*Med*) cauterization
[2] (*LAm*) burnt field
[3] **quemados** (= *heridos*) burn victims; **los ~s evolucionan favorablemente** the burn victims are making good progress; *ver tb* **unidad 3**

quemador SM burner ► **quemador de gas** gas burner

quemadura SF [1] (= *herida*) (*por fuego, sol*) burn; (*por líquido hirviendo*) scald; **una ~ de cigarro** a cigarette burn; **~ de primer/segundo grado** first-/second-degree burn ► **quemaduras de sol, quemaduras solares** sunburn *sing*
[2] [*de fusible*] blow-out
[3] (*Bot*) (*por helada*) cold blight; (= *tizón*) smut

quemar ▸conjug 1a◂ Ⓐ VT [1] (= *hacer arder*)
[1·1] [*fuego, sol*] [+ *papeles, mueble, arroz, patatas*] to burn; [+ *edificio*] to burn down; [+ *coche*] to set fire to; **lo ~on vivo** he was burned alive; **las ~on en la hoguera** they were burned at the stake; **tenía el rostro quemado por el sol** he had a sunburned face; **el incendio ha quemado varias hectáreas de bosque** the fire has destroyed *o* burned down several hectares of woodland; **he quemado la camisa con la plancha** I scorched *o* burned my shirt with the iron; **los guerrilleros ~on varias aldeas** the guerrillas set fire to *o* burned several villages; *ver tb* **nave 1**
[1·2] [*líquido hirviendo*] to scald; [*ácido, frío, helada*] to burn; **la pomada parece que te quema el brazo** the cream makes your arm burn
[2] (= *dar sensación de calor*) [*radiador, especia picante*] to burn; **el radiador me está quemando la espalda** the radiator is burning my back; **esta bebida te quema la garganta** this drink burns your throat
[3] [+ *fusible*] to blow
[4] (= *gastar*) [4·1] [+ *calorías*] to burn, burn up; [+ *energías*] to burn off
[4·2] [+ *fortuna*] to squander; [+ *dinero*] to blow*, squander; [+ *recursos*] to use up; **quemó su dinero en la lotería** he blew his money on the lottery*; ✦**MODISMO** **~ etapas** to rush ahead with things
[5] (*) (= *fastidiar*) to bug*, get*; **lo que más me quemó fue que me tratara como a un estúpido** what bugged* me *o* got* me most was the way he treated me as if I was stupid
[6] (= *desgastar*) [+ *político, gobierno*] to destroy, be the ruin of; **un escándalo sexual puede ~ a cualquier político** a sex scandal can destroy *o* can be the ruin of any politician; **tanto aparecer en televisión va a ~ su carrera** all these TV appearances will damage his career
[7] (*Com*) [+ *precios*] to slash, cut; [+ *géneros*] to sell off cheap
[8] (*Cuba*) (= *estafar*) to swindle
[9] (*CAm*) (= *denunciar*) to denounce, inform on
[10] (*Ven**) (*con arma de fuego*) to shoot
[11] (*Arg, Uru*) **~ a algn** to make a fool of sb
Ⓑ VI [1] (= *arder*) [*comida, líquido, metal*] to be boiling (hot); [*mejillas*] to be burning; **la sopa está quemando** the soup is boiling (hot); **ya no quema** it's not too hot now; **le quemaban las mejillas** her cheeks were burning; **¡cómo quema el sol!** the sun's really scorching (hot)!; **este sol no quema nada** (*LAm*) you won't get tanned in this sun
[2] (= *picar*) [*especia, picante*] to burn; **es una especia que quema en la lengua** this spice burns your tongue
Ⓒ **quemarse** VPR [1] [*persona*] (*con fuego*) to burn o.s.; (*con el sol*) to get burned; **se quemó con aceite hirviendo** he burned himself on hot oil; **me quemé la lengua con la sopa** I burned my tongue on the soup; **para no ~se con el sol** to avoid getting sunburnt; **~se a lo bonzo** to set fire to o.s.; *ver tb* **ceja 1**
[2] (= *arder*) [*cuadros, papeles*] to get burned; [*edificio*] to burn down; [*comida*] to burn; **se está quemando la cortina** the curtain is getting burned; **se me ha quemado la cena** I've burned the dinner, the dinner has burned; **se han quemado 100 hectáreas de pinares en el incendio** 100 hectares of pinewood have been destroyed in the fire; **no te acerques a la chimenea que se te va a ~ la ropa** don't go too close to the fire or you'll scorch *o* burn your clothes; **por el olor parece que algo se está quemando** it smells like something is burning
[3] (= *desprestigiarse*) **tantos años trabajando en esto y aún no se ha quemado** so many years working on this and he's still going strong; **quiere hacer menos en televisión para no ~se en poco tiempo** he wants to do less television to avoid overexposure *o* becoming overexposed; **te quemás si salís con él** (*Arg, Uru*) you'll look really bad if you go out with him
[4] (*en juego, adivinanzas*) **caliente, caliente ... ¡que te quemas!** (you're getting) warm, warmer ... you're really hot *o* you're boiling!
[5] (*Caribe*) (= *deprimirse*) to get depressed

quemarropa: **a ~** ADV point-blank

quemazón SF [1] (= *acción*) burning, combustion; (*CAm, Caribe, Méx*) fire
[2] (= *calor intenso*) intense heat
[3] (= *picazón*) (*Med*) burning sensation; (*fig*) itch
[4] (= *comentario*) cutting remark
[5] (= *resentimiento*) pique, resentment
[6] (*Com*) (= *saldo*) bargain sale, cut-price sale
[7] (*Cono Sur*) (= *espejismo*) mirage (*on the pampas*)

quemón[1]* SM (*Méx*) (= *chasco*) disappointment, let-down

quemón[2]/ona‡ SM/F (*Méx*) dope smoker*

quena SF (*Andes, Cono Sur*) Indian flute

queo[1]‡ SM (*Esp*) house

queo[2]* SM **dar el ~** to shout a warning

quepis SM INV (*esp LAm Mil*) kepi, *round military cap*

quepo *etc ver* **caber**

queque SM (*LAm*) cake (*of various kinds*)

queratina SF keratin

queratinizarse ▸conjug 1f◂ VPR to keratinize

querella SF [1] (*Jur*) (= *acusación*) charge, accusation; (= *proceso*) suit, case; **interponer** *o* **presentar una ~ contra algn** to bring a lawsuit *o* an action against sb ► **querella por difamación** action for libel *o* defamation ► **querella privada** action for damages
[2] (= *disputa*) dispute; **han olvidado sus viejas ~s** they have set aside their old disputes; **antiguas ~s familiares** old family feuds
[3] (†) (= *queja*) complaint

querellado/a SM/F defendant

querellante SMF (*Jur*) plaintiff; **la parte ~** the plaintiff

querellarse ▸conjug 1a◂ VPR [1] (= *quejarse*) to complain
[2] (*Jur*) to file a complaint, bring an action (**ante** before; **contra, de** against)

querencia SF [1] (*Zool*) (= *instinto*) homing instinct
[2] (*Zool*) (= *guarida*) lair, haunt
[3] (*Taur*) (bull's) favourite spot
[4] (= *terruño*) favourite haunt, home ground; **buscar la ~** to head for home
[5] (= *morriña*) homesickness, longing for home

querendón/ona* (*LAm*) Ⓐ ADJ affectionate, loving
Ⓑ SM/F (= *cariñoso*) loving *o* affectionate person; (= *favorito*) favourite, favorite (*EEUU*), pet; (= *amante*) lover

querer

▸conjug 2t◂

[A] VERBO TRANSITIVO	[C] VERBO PRONOMINAL
[B] VERBO INTRANSITIVO	[D] SUSTANTIVO MASCULINO

Para la expresión **querer decir**, *ver la otra entrada.*

Ⓐ VERBO TRANSITIVO
[1] ***a una persona*** (= *amar*) to love; (= *apreciar*) to like; **¡te quiero!** I love you!; **quiero mucho a mis abuelos** I love my grandparents very much; **no estoy enamorado, pero la quiero mucho** I'm not in love with her, but I'm very fond of her; **la quiero con locura** I'm madly in love with her; **me quiere ... no me quiere** (*deshojando una margarita*) she loves me ... she loves me not; **en la oficina lo quieren mucho** he is well liked at the office; **~ bien a algn** to want the best for sb; **hacerse ~ por algn** to endear o.s. to sb; **~ mal a algn** to wish sb ill; ✦**MODISMOS** **¡por lo que más quieras!** (*rogando*) by all that's sacred!; (*regañando*) for Heaven's sake!; **~ a algn como a la niña de sus ojos** to dote on sb; **la quiere como a la niña de sus ojos** she's the apple of his eye, he dotes on her
[2] ***= desear*** [2·1] [+ *objeto*] to want; **¿cuál quieres?** which one do you want?; **¿qué más quieres?** (*lit*) what else do you want?; (*iró*) what more do you want?; **hace lo que quiere** she does what she wants *o* as she pleases; **se lo di, pero no lo quiso** I gave it to him, but he didn't want (to take) it; **¡lo que quieras!** as you wish!, have it your own way!; **¿quieres un café?** would you like some coffee?; **~ pelea** to be looking for trouble; **todo lo que tú quieras**: **será muy feo y todo lo que tú quieras, pero es muy buena persona** he may be ugly and all that, but he's a very nice person
[2·2] (+ *INFIN*) to want; **~ hacer algo** to want to do sth; **quiere ser ingeniero** he wants to

➤ LENGUA Y USO: querer A2 35.4, 35.5, 36.3

be an engineer; **lleva días que no quiere comer** she's been off her food for several days; **¿qué quieres comer hoy?** what would you like for dinner today?; **no quiso pagar** he refused to pay, he wouldn't pay; **ha querido quedarse en casa** he preferred to stay at home

2·3 **~ que algn haga algo** to want sb to do sth; **no quiero que vayas** I don't want you to go; **el destino quiso que volvieran a verse** fate decreed that they should see each other again; **la tradición quiere que …** tradition has it that …; **éste quiere que le rompan la cabeza*** this guy is asking to get his head kicked in*; **¿quieres que me crea que tú solo te has bebido todo el whisky?** are you asking me to believe that you drank all the whisky by yourself?; **¿qué quieres que te diga?** what can I say?; **¿qué quieres que le haga?**: **si se va por ahí sin hacer caso, ¿qué quieres que le haga?** if he goes off without taking any notice, what am I supposed to do *o* what can I do about it?; **si estudio y no apruebo, ¿qué quieres que le haga?** if I study and still don't pass, what can I do?; **¡qué más quisiera yo!** if only I could!; **¿qué más quisiera yo que ver juntos a mis hijos?** what more could I wish for *o* want than to see my children together?

3 *= tener intención de* (+ *INFIN*) **no quería hacerte daño** I didn't mean to hurt you; **al ~ abrir la botella, saltó el tapón** the cork exploded while she was trying to open the bottle; **quiso hacerlo pero no pudo** he tried to do it but he couldn't

4 *pidiendo algo* **quería dos kilos de patatas, por favor** I'd like two kilos of potatoes, please, could I have two kilos of potatoes, please?; **¿quieres darme tu nueva dirección?** would *o* could you give me your new address?; **¿querría participar en nuestra oferta?** would you like to take advantage of our offer?; **¿cuánto quieren por el coche?** what are they asking for the car?, how much do they want for the car?

5 *= requerir* **¿para qué me querrá?** I wonder what he wants me for?, what can he want me for?; **el traje quiere un sombrero ancho** that dress needs a big hat to go with it

6 *uso impersonal* **quería amanecer** dawn was about to break; **quiere llover** it looks like rain

Ⓑ VERBO INTRANSITIVO

1 *= desear* **¿quieres?** (*ofreciendo algo*) do you want some?, would you like some?; **lo hago porque quiero** I do it because I want to; **—¿quieres casarte conmigo? —sí, quiero** "will you marry me?" — "yes, I will"; **—¿puedes enviar tú el correo? —como usted quiera** "could you take the post?" — "as you wish"; **mientras el jefe no quiera, no hay nada que hacer** as long as the boss is opposed, there's nothing to be done *o* nothing we can do about it; **ven cuando quieras** come whenever you like; ✦***MODISMOS*** **como quiere**: **¡está como quiere!** (*Esp*⁑) she's a bit of all right!⁑; **tiene tanto dinero que vive como quiere** he's so rich he can live as he pleases; **quiera o no** ◊ **quiera que no** whether he *etc* likes it or not; **quieras o no, eso cambiará nuestras vidas** whether you like it or not, that's going to change our lives; **con el cambio de trabajo, quieras que no, se ha animado un poco** you may agree or disagree, but the fact is he's perked up a bit since he changed jobs; ✦***REFRÁN*** **~ es poder** where there's a will there's a way

2 *= tener intención* **lo hizo queriendo** he did it deliberately *o* on purpose; **lo hizo sin ~** he didn't mean to do it, he did it inadvertently

3 **como quiera que** = **comoquiera**; **donde quiera que** = **dondequiera**

Ⓒ **quererse** VERBO PRONOMINAL

recíproco **nosotros nos queremos** we love each other; **se quieren como hermanos** they love each other like brothers

Ⓓ SUSTANTIVO MASCULINO

cosas del ~ affairs of the heart; **dimitieron por culpa de algún ~** they resigned because of love affairs; **tener ~ a** to be fond of

querida SF mistress

querido/a Ⓐ ADJ 1 (= *amado*) dear; **~s amigos, nos hemos reunido para …** dear friends, we are assembled here to …; **nuestra querida patria** our beloved country; **sus seres ~s** his loved ones; **~s hermanos** (*Rel*) dearly beloved; **un alcalde ~ por todos** a mayor who is well-liked in the community, a popular mayor

2 (*en cartas*) dear; **Queridos padres:** Dear parents,

3 (*Andes*) nice

Ⓑ SM/F 1 (*uso apelativo*) darling; **¡sí, ~!** yes, darling!

2 (= *amante*) lover

querindongo/a SM/F lover

quermes SF, **quermés** SF kermes

querosén SM, **querosene** SM (*LAm*), **queroseno** SM kerosene, paraffin

querúbico ADJ cherubic

querubín SM cherub

quesadilla SF 1 (= *pastel*) cheesecake

2 (*LAm*) pasty, folded tortilla

quesera SF cheese dish; *ver tb* **quesero**

quesería SF 1 (= *tienda*) cheese shop, dairy

2 (= *fábrica*) cheese factory

3 (= *quesos*) cheeses *pl*

4 (= *productos lácteos*) dairy products *pl*

quesero/a Ⓐ ADJ **la industria quesera** the cheese industry

Ⓑ SM/F cheesemaker; *ver tb* **quesera**

quesillo SM (*CAm*) *tortilla with cream cheese filling*

queso SM 1 (= *alimento*) cheese; **le huelen los pies a ~** he's got cheesy feet*; ✦***MODISMOS*** **dársela a algn con ~*** to take sb in*; **estar como un ~*** to be tasty *o* dishy* ► **queso azul** blue cheese ► **queso crema** (*LAm*) cream cheese ► **queso de bola** Edam ► **queso de nata** cream cheese ► **queso de oveja** sheep's cheese ► **queso de puerco** (*Méx*) jellied pork ► **queso de untar** cheese spread ► **queso fundido** processed cheese, process cheese (*EEUU*) ► **queso helado**† ice-cream brick ► **queso manchego** *sheep's milk cheese made in La Mancha* ► **queso parmesano** Parmesan cheese ► **queso rallado** grated cheese

2 **quesos**⁑ (= *pies*) plates*, feet

quetzal SM 1 (= *moneda*) *monetary unit of Guatemala*

2 (= *ave*) quetzal

quevedos SMPL pince-nez

quey SM (*Andes*) cake

quiá† EXCL never!, not on your life!

quíbole* EXCL (*Méx*) how's things?

quiche SM quiche

quichua Ⓐ ADJ Quechua, Quechuan

Ⓑ SMF Quechua(n) Indian

Ⓒ SM (*Ling*) Quechua

quichuismo SM Quechuan word *o* expression

quichuista SMF 1 (*LAm*) (= *especialista*) Quechua specialist

2 (*Andes, Cono Sur*) (= *hablante*) Quechua speaker

quicio SM doorjamb; ✦***MODISMOS*** **estar fuera de ~** to be out of joint; **sacar a algn de ~** to drive sb up the wall*, get on sb's nerves; **estas cosas me sacan de ~** these things make me see red *o* drive me mad

quico SM ✦***MODISMO*** **ponerse como el ~** (*Esp**) (= *comer mucho*) to stuff o.s.*; (= *engordar*) to get as fat as a pig

quid SM gist, crux; **dar en el ~** to hit the nail on the head; **he aquí el ~ de la cuestión** this is the crux of the matter

quídam SM 1 (= *alguien*) somebody (or other)

2 (= *don nadie*) nobody

quiebra SF 1 (*Fin*) bankruptcy; **ir a la ~** to go bankrupt ► **quiebra bancaria** bank failure ► **quiebra fraudulenta** fraudulent bankruptcy ► **quiebra voluntaria** voluntary bankruptcy

2 (= *deterioro*) breakdown; **la ~ de los valores tradicionales** the breakdown of traditional values

3 (†) (= *grieta*) crack, fissure

4 (†) (= *fracaso*) failure; **es algo que no tiene ~** it just can't go wrong

quiebre SM breaking, rupture

quiebro SM 1 (*Taur*) dodge, swerve; ✦***MODISMO*** **dar el ~ a algn** to dodge sb

2 (*Mús*) grace note(s), trill

quien PRON REL 1 (*con antecedente*) 1·1 (*como sujeto*) who; **hablé con mi abogado, ~ me dio la razón** I spoke to my solicitor, who said I was right; **él es ~ se ocupa de estos asuntos** he is the one who deals with these things; **el Ayuntamiento será ~ se haga cargo de eso** it'll be the Council that take care of that

1·2 (*como complemento*) who, whom (*frm*); **su profesor, a ~ está dedicado el libro, siempre lo apoyó** his teacher, who the book is dedicated to, always supported him, his teacher, to whom the book is dedicated, always supported him (*frm*); **el pintor a ~ describe en su libro** the painter he describes in his book, the painter whom he describes in his book (*frm*); **la señorita con ~ hablaba** the young lady I was talking to, the young lady to whom I was talking (*frm*)

2 (*como indefinido*) 2·1 (+ *SUBJUN*) **un libro muy interesante para ~ sepa poco del tema** a very interesting book for anyone who knows little about the subject; **~es no estén de acuerdo que se vayan** anyone who doesn't agree can leave; **pregúntale a ~ quieras** ask anyone *o* whoever you like; **"a ~ corresponda"** "to whom it may concern"

2·2 (+ *INDIC*) **~ más se quejaba era él** the person who complained most was him, he was the one that *o* who complained the most; **yo hablo con ~ quiero** I'll speak to who I like; **la tierra es para ~ la trabaja** the land belongs to he who works it; **lo dijo como ~ anuncia una gran noticia** he said it like someone announcing some really important news; **hay ~ no piensa lo mismo** there are some *o* those who do not think the same; **no hay ~ lo aguante** no one can stand him; **¡no hay ~ te entienda!** there's no understanding you!

[2·3] ✦*MODISMOS* **~ más, ~ menos**: **~ más, ~ menos tiene un amigo que ha estudiado en el extranjero** most of us have a friend who has studied abroad; **~ más, ~ menos, todos hemos tenido miedo a la oscuridad de pequeños** all of us, to some extent, have been afraid of the dark as children; **como ~ dice** so to speak; **nací en Navarra, a un paso, como ~ dice, de Francia** I was born in Navarre, just a stone's throw from France, so to speak; **como ~ no quiere la cosa**: **se acercó, como ~ no quiere la cosa, a enterarse de lo que decíamos** he casually moved closer to us to find out what we were saying; **era capaz de beberse una botella de vino, como ~ no quiere la cosa** he was quite capable of drinking a whole bottle of wine, just like that *o* as if it were nothing; **como ~ oye llover**: **estuve una hora intentando convencerlo, y él, como ~ oye llover** I spent an hour trying to persuade him but it was like water off a duck's back; **no ser ~**: **él no es quién para decirme lo que tengo que hacer** it's not for him to tell me what to do; **tú no eres ~ para decirme si tengo que llegar a casa antes de las diez** it's not for you to tell me whether I should come home before ten

quién PRON [1] (*interrogativo*) (*como sujeto*) who; (*como complemento*) whom; **no sé ~ lo dijo primero** I don't know who said it first; **¿~ es esa chica?** who's that girl?; **—te han llamado —¿~ era?** "somebody phoned you" — "who was it?"; **¿a ~ se lo diste?** who did you give it to?; **¿a ~ le toca?** whose turn is it?; **¿con ~ estabas anoche?** who were you with last night?; **¿de ~ es la bufanda esa?** whose scarf is that?; **¿~ de ustedes lo reconoce?** which of you recognizes it?

[2] (*exclamativo*) **¡~ sabe!** who knows!; **¡~ pudiese!** if only I could!; **¡~ lo hubiera dicho!** who would have thought it!

quienquiera PRON INDEF (*pl* **quienesquiera**) whoever; **le cazaremos ~ que sea** we'll catch him whoever he is; **~ que sea el responsable lo pagará** whoever is responsible will pay; **~ que críe un niño** whoever brings up a child, anybody who brings up a child; **dondequiera que estén y con ~ que estén** wherever and whoever they may be

quiera *etc ver* **querer**

quietismo SM quietism

quietista SMF quietist

quieto ADJ [1] [*animal, persona*] (= *parado*) still; (= *inmóvil*) motionless; **¡quieto!** (*al perro*) down boy!; (*a un niño*) keep still!, stop fidgeting!; (= *sé bueno*) behave yourself!; **dejar algo ~** to leave sth alone; **¡estáte ~!** keep still!; **estar ~ como un poste** *o* **una estatua** to stand stock-still, be as still as a statue

[2] [*carácter*] calm, placid

quietud SF [*de persona, noche*] stillness, quietude (*frm*); [*de situación*] calm

quif SM hashish

quihubo* EXCL (*Méx*) how's it going?

quijada SF jaw, jawbone

quijotada SF quixotic act

quijote SM quixotic person, dreamer, do-gooder*; (*pey*) well-meaning busybody; **Don Quijote** Don Quixote

quijotería SF [1] = **quijotismo**

[2] = **quijotada**

quijotescamente ADV quixotically

quijotesco ADJ quixotic

quijotismo SM quixotism

quil. ABR (= **quilates**) c

quilar** ▸conjug 1a◂ VT (*Esp*) to screw**

quilatar ▸conjug 1a◂ VT = **aquilatar**

quilate SM carat; **oro de 18 ~s** 18 carat gold; ✦*MODISMO* **de muchos ~s** high class, quality

quilco SM (*Chile*) large basket

quiligua SF (*Méx*) large basket

quilla[1] SF (*Náut*) keel; **colocar la ~ de un buque** to lay down a ship; **dar de ~** to keel over; ✦*MODISMO* **pasar a algn por la ~** to keelhaul sb

quilla[2] SF (*LAm*) (= *cojín*) cushion

quillango SM (*Cono Sur*) blanket of furs, fur blanket

quilo[1] SM kilogramme, kilogram (*EEUU*)

quilo[2] SM (*Anat*) chyle; ✦*MODISMO* **sudar el ~*** (= *sufrir*) to have a tough time; (= *trabajar*) to slave *o* slog away

quilo... PREF = **kilo...**

quilombear* ▸conjug 1a◂ VI (*Cono Sur*) to go whoring

quilombera* SF (*Cono Sur*) tart*, slut*, whore

quilombero* ADJ (*Cono Sur*) rowdy

quilombo SM (*Andes, Cono Sur*) [1] (= *burdel*) brothel

[2] (= *choza*) rustic hut, shack

[3] (*) (= *lío*) mess

quiltrear* ▸conjug 1a◂ VT (*Cono Sur*) to annoy

quiltro* SM (*Cono Sur*) [1] (= *perrito*) (*gen*) lapdog; (*callejero*) stray dog, mongrel

[2] (*) (= *tipo pesado*) pest, nuisance

quimba SF [1] (*Andes, Caribe*) (= *calzado*) sandal

[2] (*Andes*) (= *mueca*) grimace

[3] **quimbas** (*Andes*) (= *dificultades*) difficulties; (= *deudas*) debts

quimbo SM (*Caribe*) knife, machete

quimera SF [1] (*Mit*) (= *monstruo imaginario*) chimera

[2] (= *alucinación*) hallucination; (= *ilusión*) illusion, chimera; (= *noción*) fancy, fantastic idea; (= *sueño*) pipe dream

[3] (= *sospecha*) unfounded suspicion; **tener la ~ de que ...** to suspect quite wrongly that ...

[4] (= *riña*) quarrel

quimérico ADJ [*plan, proyecto, idea*] fanciful; [*esperanza*] impossible

quimerista Ⓐ ADJ [1] (= *soñador*) dreamy

[2] (= *pendenciero*) quarrelsome; (= *ruidoso*) rowdy

Ⓑ SMF [1] (= *soñador*) dreamer, visionary

[2] (= *pendenciero*) quarrelsome person; (= *ruidoso*) rowdy, brawler

quimerizar ▸conjug 1f◂ VI to indulge in fantasy *o* pipe dreams

química SF chemistry ► **química física** physical chemistry ► **química inorgánica** inorganic chemistry ► **química orgánica** organic chemistry

químico/a Ⓐ ADJ chemical

Ⓑ SM/F chemist

quimio* SF (= *quimioterapia*) chemo

quimioterapia SF chemotherapy

quimono SM kimono

quimoterapia SF chemotherapy

quina SF [1] (*Bot*) quinine, Peruvian bark; ✦*MODISMOS* **ser más malo que la ~*** to be a little horror; **tragar ~*** to have to put up with it

[2] (= *vino*) tonic wine

quinaquina SF (*Med*) quinine, cinchona bark

quincalla SF [1] (= *ferretería*) hardware, ironmongery

[2] (= *baratija*) trinket

quincallería SF ironmonger's (shop), hardware store (*EEUU*)

quincallero/a SM/F ironmonger, hardware dealer (*EEUU*)

quince Ⓐ ADJ INV, PRON (*gen*) fifteen; (*ordinal, en la fecha*) fifteenth; **le escribí el día ~** I wrote to him on the fifteenth; **~ días** a fortnight; ✦*MODISMO* **dar ~ y raya a algn** to be able to beat sb with one hand tied behind one's back; *ver tb* **seis**

Ⓑ SM (= *número*) fifteen; (= *fecha*) fifteenth; **los Quince** the 15 member nations (*of the EU*)

quinceañera SF (*Méx*) *coming-out ball for girls who have reached their 15th birthday*

quinceañero/a Ⓐ ADJ fifteen-year-old; (*en general*) teenage

Ⓑ SM/F fifteen-year-old; (*en general*) teenager

quinceavo ADJ, SM fifteenth

quincena SF [1] (= *quince días*) fortnight, two weeks; **la segunda ~ de enero** the second half of January, the last two weeks in January

[2] (= *condena*) fortnight's imprisonment

[3] (= *pago*) fortnightly pay

quincenal ADJ fortnightly, bimonthly (*EEUU*)

quincenalmente ADV fortnightly, once a fortnight, semimonthly (*EEUU*)

quinceno ADJ fifteenth

quincha SF (*LAm*) *wall or roof etc made of rushes and mud*

quinchar ▸conjug 1a◂ VI (*LAm*) to build walls *etc* of "quincha"

quincho SM (*Cono Sur*) (= *choza*) mud hut; (*Andes, Cono Sur*) (= *cerco*) mud wall; (*Cono Sur*) (= *restaurán*) steak restaurant

quincuagenario/a ADJ, SM/F fifty-year old

Quincuagésima SF Quinquagesima Sunday

quincuagésimo ADJ fiftieth; *ver tb* **sexto**

quindécimo ADJ fifteenth

quinfa SF (*Andes*) sandal

quingentésimo ADJ five-hundredth; *ver tb* **sexto**

quingo SM [1] (*Andes*) twist, turn

[2] **quingos** zigzag *sing*

quinguear ▸conjug 1a◂ VI (*Andes*) (= *girar*) to twist, turn; (= *zigzaguear*) to zigzag

quiniela SF [1] (= *boleto*) pools coupon; **echar la ~** to hand in one's coupon

[2] (= *juego*) football pool(s); **jugar a la ~** *o* **a las ~s** to do the (football) pools ► **quiniela hípica** horse-racing totalizator

QUINIELA

The **quiniela** *is the Spanish equivalent of the football pools and coupons are available from* **estancos**. *Players can predict a home win (1),*

a draw (X) or an away win (2) for most premier and first division matches. 12 or more correct forecasts wins a prize, the size of which varies from week to week depending on the takings or **recaudación**. *There is also a version for horse racing, the* **quiniela hípica**, *although most betting on horses is done at the racecourse.*
⇨ *See also* ESTANCO

quinielista SMF pools punter, participant in a football pool
quinielístico ADJ pools *antes de s*; **boleto ~** pools coupon; **peña quinielística** pools syndicate
quinientos/as ADJ, PRON, SMPL/FPL (*gen*) five hundred; (*ordinal*) five hundredth; **en el ~** in the sixteenth century; ✦*MODISMO* **volvió a las (mil) quinientas*** he got back at some ungodly hour; *ver tb* **seiscientos**
quinina SF quinine
quino SM (*LAm*) cinchona, cinchona tree
quinqué SM [1] (*para iluminar*) oil lamp
[2] (*) (= *astucia*) know-how, shrewdness; **tener mucho ~** to know what's what, know what the score is*
quinquenal ADJ quinquennial; **plan ~** five-year plan
quinquenalmente ADV every five years
quinquenio SM quinquennium, five-year period
quinqui* SM (= *delincuente*) small-time delinquent; (= *vendedor*) small-time dealer
quinta SF [1] (= *casa de campo*) villa, country house; (*LAm*) (= *chalet*) house; (= *finca*) *small estate on the outskirts of a town*
[2] (*Mil*) draft, call-up; **ser de la (misma) ~ de algn** to be the same age as sb; **la ~ de 1998** the 1998 call-up, the class called up in 1998; **entrar en ~s** (= *tener edad*) to reach the call-up age; (= *ser llamado*) to be called up
[3] (*Mús*) fifth
quintacolumnista SMF fifth columnist
quintada* SF joke, trick
quintaescencia SF, **quintaesencia** SF quintessence
quintaesencial ADJ quintessential
quintal SM [1] (= *medida*) 100lbs; **esto pesa un ~*** (*fig*) this weighs a ton* ► **quintal métrico** ≈ 100kg
[2] (*Castilla*) (= *peso*) ≈ 46kg
quintar ▸conjug 1a◂ VT (*Mil*) to call up, conscript, draft (*EEUU*)
quintería SF farmhouse
quintero SM (= *agricultor*) farmer; (= *bracero*) farmhand, labourer, laborer (*EEUU*)
quinteto SM quintet
quintilla SF (*Literat, Hist*) *five-line stanza*
quintillizo/a SM/F quintuplet
Quintín SM ✦*MODISMOS* **se armó la de San ~*** all hell broke loose*; **se va a armar la de San ~** there will be an almighty row*; **costó la de San ~*** it cost a bomb*
quinto Ⓐ ADJ fifth; **quinta columna** fifth column; *ver tb* **sexto**
Ⓑ SM [1] (*Mat*) fifth
[2] (*Mil*) conscript, draftee (*EEUU*), national serviceman
[3] (*) (= *juego*) bingo
[4] (*Méx*) (= *moneda*) nickel
[5] (= *botellín*) small bottle of beer

quíntral SM (*Andes, Cono Sur*) [1] (*Zool*) armadillo
[2] (*Mús*) ten-stringed guitar
quintuplicar ▸conjug 1g◂ Ⓐ VT to quintuple
Ⓑ **quintuplicarse** VPR to quintuple; **el número de casos se ha quintuplicado** the number of cases has increased fivefold, there has been a fivefold increase in the number of cases
quíntuplo Ⓐ ADJ quintuple, fivefold
Ⓑ SM quintuple; **25 es el ~ de 5** 25 is five times more than 5
quinzavo ADJ, SM = **quinceavo**
quiña SF (*Andes*), **quiñadura** SF (*Andes*) scratch
quiñar* ▸conjug 1a◂ VT (*Andes*) to scratch
quiñazo SM (*LAm*) smash, collision
quiño SM (*LAm*) (= *puñetazo*) punch
quiñón SM piece of land, plot of land
quiñonero SM part owner (of a piece of land)
quiosco SM [*de venta*] kiosk, stand, stall; (= *pabellón*) summerhouse, pavilion ► **quiosco de música** bandstand ► **quiosco de necesidad** public lavatory ► **quiosco de periódicos** news stand
quiosquero/a SM/F owner of a news-stand, newspaper seller
quipe SM (*Andes*) knapsack, rucksack, backpack (*EEUU*)
quipo SM, **quipos** SMPL (*Andes Hist*) quipu, *Inca system of recording information using knotted strings*
quipu SM = **quipo**
quique SM (*Chile*) grison
quiqui** SM screw**; **echar un ~** have a screw**, to play hide the sausage*
quiquiriquí SM cock-a-doodle-doo
quirico SM (*Caribe*) (= *criado*) servant; (= *mensajero*) messenger; (= *ladrón*) petty thief
quirófano SM operating theatre, operating room (*EEUU*); **pasar por la mesa del ~** to go under the knife*
quirógrafo SM (*Méx*) IOU
quirología SF palmistry, chiromancy
quiromancia SF palmistry
quiromántico/a SM/F palmist
quiromasaje SM massage
quiropedia SF, **quiropodia** SF chiropody, podiatry (*EEUU*)
quiropodista SMF chiropodist, podiatrist (*EEUU*)
quiropráctica SF osteopathy
quiropráctico/a SM/F chiropractor
quiroterapeuta SMF chiropractor
quirquincho SM (*Cono Sur*) *species of armadillo*
quirúrgicamente ADV surgically; **intervenir ~ a algn** to operate on sb
quirúrgico ADJ surgical; **se puede tratar sin intervención quirúrgica** it can be treated without surgery
quise *etc ver* **querer**
quisicosa* SF puzzle, conundrum
quisling ['kizlin] SM (*pl* **quislings** ['kizlin]) quisling
quisque* SM, **quisqui*** SM **cada** *o* **todo ~** (absolutely) everyone, every man-Jack; **como cada ~** like everyone else; **ni ~** not a living soul; **ser un ~** (*gen*) to be a fusspot*; (= *detallista*) to have a mania for details

quisquilla SF [1] (*Zool*) shrimp
[2] (= *nimiedad*) trifle, triviality
[3] (= *pega*) slight snag, minor problem
[4] **quisquillas** (= *sofisterías*) quibbles, quibbling, hair-splitting; **¡déjate de ~s!** (= *no seas quisquilloso*) stop fussing!; (= *no protestes*) stop quibbling!; **pararse en ~s** (= *reñir*) to bicker; (= *protestar*) to quibble
quisquilloso ADJ [1] (= *susceptible*) touchy, oversensitive; (= *irritable*) irritable; (= *perfeccionista*) pernickety*, persnickety (*EEUU**), choosy, fussy
[2] (= *preocupado por nimiedades*) too bothered about petty details
quiste SM cyst ► **quiste ovárico** ovarian cyst ► **quiste sebáceo** sebaceous cyst
quístico ADJ cystic; **fibrosis quística** cystic fibrosis
quisto ADJ **bien ~** = **bienquisto**; **mal ~** = **malquisto**
quita SF [1] [*de deuda*] release
[2] (*LAm*) (= *descuento*) rebate
[3] **de ~ y pon: un cuello de ~ y pon** a detachable collar; **una moda de ~ y pon** a passing fashion; **la actitud que adopta es de ~ y pon** he's just adopting that attitude because it's expedient
quitacutículas SM INV cuticle cream, cuticle conditioner
quitaesmalte SM, **quitaesmaltes** SM INV nail-polish *o* nail-varnish remover
quitagusto SM (*Andes*) intruder, gatecrasher
quitahielo SM windscreen scraper
quitaipón: **de ~** ADJ *ver* **quita 3**
quitalodos SM INV boot scraper
quitamanchas SM INV [1] (= *producto*) stain remover
[2] (†) (= *oficio*) dry cleaner; (= *tienda*) dry-cleaner's (shop)
quitamiedos SM INV (*Esp*) handrail
quitamotas* SM INV bootlicker*, toady
quitanieves SM INV snowplough, snowplow (*EEUU*)
quitapelillos* SM INV bootlicker*, toady
quitapenas SM INV [1] (‡) (= *pistola*) pistol, rod (*EEUU‡*); (= *navaja*) knife, chiv‡
[2] (= *consuelo*) comforter, solace
[3] (= *licor*) stiff drink
quitapesares SM INV comfort, distraction
quitapiedras SM INV (*Ferro*) cowcatcher
quitapintura SF paint remover, paint stripper
quitapón = **quitaipón**; *ver* **quita 3**
quitar ▸conjug 1a◂ Ⓐ VT [1] (= *sacar*) (*gen*) to remove; [+ *ropa, zapatos*] to take off; [+ *póster, estantes*] to take down; **le ~on las vendas** they took her bandages off, they removed her bandages; **tardaron dos días en ~ los escombros** it took two days to clear *o* remove the rubble; **~on las banderas de los balcones** they took the flags down from the balconies, they removed the flags from the balconies; **quita eso de allí** get that away from there; **querían ~le de su puesto** they wanted to remove him from his post; **~ la mesa** to clear the table; ✦*MODISMOS* **~ de en medio a algn** to get rid of sb; **no ~le ojo a algn** not to take one's eyes off sb
[2] (= *arrebatar*) (*gen*) to take away; (*para robar*) to take, steal; [+ *vida*] to take; **su hermana le quitó la pelota** his sister took the

ball away from him; **me ~on la licencia** I had my licence taken away; **le ~on la cartera en el tren** someone took his wallet on the train, he had his wallet stolen on the train; **me quitó la novia** he stole my girlfriend; **~ el sitio a algn** to steal sb's place

3 (= *eliminar*) [+ *mancha*] to remove, get rid of; [+ *dolor*] to relieve, stop; [+ *felicidad, ilusión, ganas*] to take away; [+ *preocupaciones, temores*] to allay; **me quitó las ganas de comer** it took my appetite away; **trataba de ~me esa idea de la cabeza** she tried to make me change my mind; **~ el hambre**: **un par de rodajas deben ~ el hambre** a couple of slices should stop you feeling hungry; **no alimenta mucho, pero quita el hambre** it's not very nutritious, but it's filling; **~ la sed** to quench one's thirst; **el vino no quita la sed** wine doesn't quench your thirst, wine isn't thirst-quenching; **~ el sueño**: **el café me quita el sueño** coffee stops me sleeping; **ese asunto no me quita el sueño** I'm not losing any sleep over that matter

4 (= *restar*) **no quita nada de su valor** it does not detract at all from its value; **no le quiero ~ méritos** I don't want to detract from him; **eso le quita la razón** that shows he's wrong, that proves him wrong; **quiero ~ unos cuantos centímetros a mi cintura** I want to lose a few centimetres from around the waist; **me quita mucho tiempo** it takes up a lot of my time; **~ extensión a un campo** to reduce the size of a field; **~ importancia a algo** to play sth down; **quitando el postre comimos bien** apart *o* aside from the dessert we had a good meal; **quitando tres o cuatro, van a ir todos** except for three or four (people), everybody is going

5 (= *impedir*) **~ a algn de hacer algo** to stop *o* prevent sb (from) doing sth

6 (*Mat*) to take away, subtract

7 [+ *golpe*] to ward off; (*Esgrima*) to parry

8 (*) [+ *dinero*] to make

Ⓑ VI **¡quita!, ¡quita de ahí!** (= *¡aparta!*) get out of the way!; (= *¡qué va!*) get away!, come off it!; ✦*MODISMOS* **eso no quita**: **eso no quita para que me ayudes** that doesn't stop *o* prevent you helping me, that doesn't mean you can't help me; **eso no quita que eche de menos a mi mujer** that doesn't mean I don't miss my wife; **ni quito ni pongo** I'm neutral, I'm not saying one thing or the other; *ver tb* **quita 3**

Ⓒ **quitarse** VPR 1 (= *apartarse*) **¡quítate de ahí!** ◊ **¡quítate de en medio!** get out of the way!; **¡quítate de mi vista!** get out of my sight!; **me quito** (*Andes**) I'm off, I must be going

2 (= *desaparecer*) [*dolor*] to go, go away; [*mancha*] come out; **esa mancha de vino no se quita** that wine stain won't come out

3 (= *acabarse*) **se me quitan las ganas de ir** I don't feel like going now; **se me ~on las ganas de viajar** I no longer felt like travelling

4 (= *sacarse*) 4·1 [+ *ropa, zapatos*] to take off; [+ *barba*] to shave; [+ *lentillas*] to take out; **~se años: te has quitado diez años (de encima)** you look ten years younger; **no te quites años** don't lie about your age; **~se la preocupación** to stop worrying; **~se una muela** to have a tooth out

4·2 **~se algo/a algn de encima** to get rid of sth/sb; **¡ya me he quitado de encima el coche viejo!** at last I've got rid of the old car!; **¡no me la puedo ~ de encima!** I can't get rid of her!; **¡qué peso nos hemos quitado de encima!** what a relief!, that's a real weight off our minds!

5 **~se de** (= *dejar*): **~se de un vicio** to give up a bad habit; **~se del tabaco** to give up smoking; **quitémonos de tonterías** let's stop being silly

quitasol SM sunshade, parasol

quitasueño SM worry, problem

quite SM 1 (= *acción*) removal

2 (= *movimiento*) (*gen*) dodge, sidestep; (*Esgrima*) parry; (*Taur*) distracting manoeuvre *o* (*EEUU*) maneuver; **estar al ~** to be always ready to help *o* be at hand; **hacer el ~ a algn** (*Cono Sur*) to avoid sb; **esto no tiene ~** there's no help for it

3 (*LAm Dep*) tackle

quiteño/a Ⓐ ADJ of *o* from Quito

Ⓑ SM/F native/inhabitant of Quito; **los ~s** the people of Quito

quitrín SM (*CAm, Caribe, Cono Sur*) (= *vehículo*) trap

▼**quizá** ADV, **quizás** ADV perhaps, maybe; **—¿vienes o no? —quizá** "are you coming?" — "perhaps"; **~ llegue mañana, si tenemos suerte** if we're lucky it may arrive tomorrow, perhaps it will arrive tomorrow; **~ no** maybe not

quórum ['kworum] SM (*pl* **quórums** ['kworum]) quorum; **constituir ~** to make up a quorum; **la reunión no pudo celebrarse por falta de ~** the meeting could not be held because there wasn't a quorum *o* because it was inquorate

➤ LENGUA Y USO: **quizá** 53.6

R r

R, r ['ere] SF (= *letra*) R, r

R. ABR 1 (*Rel*) (= **Reverendo**) Rev, Revd
2 (= **Real**) R
3 = **Rey, Reina**
4 = **remite; remitente**
5 (= **río**) R

rabada SF hindquarter, rump

rabadán SM head shepherd

rabadilla SF 1 (*Anat*) coccyx
2 (*Culin*) [*de pollo*] parson's nose*, pope's nose (*EEUU**)

rabanillo SM wild radish

rábano SM radish; ✦***MODISMOS*** **¡un ~!*** get away!; **me importa un ~*** I don't care *o* give two hoots*; **tomar el ~ por las hojas** to get the wrong end of the stick* ► **rábano picante** horseradish

rabear ▸conjug 1a◂ VI to wag its tail

rabelasiano ADJ Rabelaisian

rabí SM (*pl* **rabíes**) rabbi

rabia SF 1 (*Med*) rabies
2 (= *ira*) fury, anger; **me da ~** it makes me mad *o* infuriates me; **¡qué ~!** (= *ira*) isn't it infuriating!; (= *pena*) what a pity!; ✦***MODISMO*** **con ~: llueve con ~** it's raining with a vengeance; **es fea con ~** she's as ugly as sin*
3 (= *antipatía*) **tener ~ a algn** to have a grudge against sb, have it in for sb*; **el maestro le tiene ~** the teacher has it in for him*, the teacher doesn't like him; **tomar ~ a algn/algo** to take a dislike to sb/sth

rabiadero SM (*Andes*) fit of rage

rabiar ▸conjug 1b◂ VI 1 (*Med*) to have rabies, be rabid
2 (*) (= *sufrir*) (*de dolor*) to be in great pain; **estaba rabiando de dolor de muelas** she had a raging toothache
3 (*) (= *encolerizarse*) **hacer ~ a algn** to infuriate sb, make sb see red; **las cosas así le hacen ~** things like that infuriate him *o* make him see red; **¡para que rabies!** so there!; ✦***MODISMOS*** **a ~*: me gusta a ~** (= *muchísimo*) I just love it; **que rabia*: está que rabia** (= *furioso*) he's hopping mad*, he's furious; **esta sopa quema que rabia** this soup is hot enough to burn the roof of your mouth off*; **este cóctel está que rabia** (= *buenísimo*) this cocktail has a real kick to it*
4 (*) (= *anhelar*) **~ por algo** to long for sth, be dying for sth; **~ por hacer algo** to be dying to do sth

rabiasca SF (*Caribe*) fit of temper

rabieta SF tantrum; **coger(se) una ~** to throw a tantrum, fly into a rage

rabietas* SMF INV touchy sort, bad-tempered person

rabillo SM 1 (*Bot*) leaf stalk
2 (*Anat*) small tail
3 (= *punta*) tip; (= *parte delgada*) thin part; (= *tira*) thin strip of material; **mirar por el ~ del ojo** to look out of the corner of one's eye

rabimocho ADJ (*Andes, Caribe, Méx*) short-tailed

rabínico ADJ rabbinical

rabino SM rabbi; **gran ~** chief rabbi

rabión SM (*tb* **rabiones**) rapids *pl*

rabiosamente ADV 1 (= *furiosamente*) furiously, in a rage
2 [*doler*] terribly
3 (= *fanáticamente*) rabidly

rabioso ADJ 1 (*Med*) rabid; **perro ~** (*lit*) rabid dog; (*fig*) mad dog
2 (= *furioso*) [*persona*] furious; [*aficionado*] rabid, fervent; **poner ~ a algn** to enrage sb, make sb livid; **de rabiosa actualidad** highly topical
3 [*dolor*] terrible

rabo SM 1 (*Zool*) tail; ✦***MODISMOS*** **con el ~ entre las piernas** with one's tail between one's legs; **queda el ~ por desollar** the hardest part is still to come ► **rabo cortado** docked tail ► **rabo de buey** oxtail; *ver tb* **cabo 2**
2 (**) (= *pene*) cock**, dick** ► **rabo verde** (*CAm*) dirty old man*

rabón ADJ 1 [*animal*] (= *de rabo pequeño*) short-tailed; (= *sin rabo*) tailless
2 (*LAm*) (= *pequeño*) short, small
3 (*Cono Sur*) (= *desnudo*) stark naked
4 (*Caribe, Cono Sur*) [*cuchillo*] damaged
5 (*Méx*) (= *desgraciado*) down on one's luck

rabona SF 1 **hacer (la) ~** (*Escol*) to play truant, skip school, play hookey (*EEUU**)
2 (*LAm*) (= *prostituta*) camp follower

rabonear ▸conjug 1a◂ VI (*Cono Sur*) to play truant, skip school, play hookey (*EEUU**)

rabosear ▸conjug 1a◂ VT to mess up, rumple, crumple

rabotada SF rude remark

rabudo ADJ long-tailed

raca[1]* SF (*CAm*) (= *mamá*) mummy*

raca[2]*† SM (*Aut*) banger*

racanear* ▸conjug 1a◂ VI 1 (*con el dinero*) to be stingy*
2 (*en el trabajo*) to slack

racaneo* SM, **racanismo*** SM 1 (*con el dinero*) stinginess
2 (*en el trabajo*) slackness, idleness

rácano/a* Ⓐ ADJ 1 (= *tacaño*) stingy*, mean
2 (= *vago*) bone idle
3 (= *artero*) sly, cunning
Ⓑ SM/F 1 (= *tacaño*) mean devil, scrooge*
2 (= *vago*) slacker, idler; **hacer el ~** to slack

RACE SM ABR (= **Real Automóvil Club de España**) ≈ RAC, ≈ AA, ≈ AAA (*EEUU*)

racha SF 1 (*Meteo*) gust of wind
2 (= *periodo*) string, series; **buena ~** run of good luck; **mala ~** run of bad luck; ✦***MODISMOS*** **a ~s** by fits and starts; **estar de ~** (= *de suerte*) to be in luck; (*Dep*) (= *en forma*) to be in form

rache SM (*Caribe*) zip, zipper (*EEUU*)

racheado ADJ gusty, squally

rachi‡ SM night

rachir ▸conjug 3h◂ VT (*Cono Sur*) to scratch

rachoso ADJ (*Cono Sur*) ragged

racial ADJ racial, race *antes de s*; **odio ~** racial hatred, race hatred; **disturbios ~es** race riots

racimo SM 1 [*de uvas*] bunch, cluster
2 [*de flores*] (= *ramo*) bunch; (*Bot*) raceme

raciocinación SF ratiocination

raciocinar ▸conjug 1a◂ VI to reason

raciocinio SM 1 (= *facultad*) reason
2 (= *razonamiento*) reasoning

ración SF 1 (*Mat*) ratio
2 (= *porción*) portion, helping; (*Mil*) ration; **una ~ de jamón** a portion of ham; **una ~ de albóndigas** a portion *o* plate of meatballs; **darse una ~ de vista**† to have a good look ► **ración de campaña** ration (*for a soldier on active service*) ► **ración de hambre** starvation wage
3 (*Rel*) prebend

racional ADJ 1 (*Mat, Fil*) rational
2 (= *razonable*) reasonable, sensible

racionalidad SF rationality

racionalismo SM rationalism

racionalista ADJ, SMF rationalist

racionalización SF 1 (*Psic, Fil*) rationalization
2 (*Com*) streamlining, rationalization

racionalizador ADJ 1 (*Psic, Fil*) rationalizing
2 (*Com*) streamlining, rationalizing

racionalizar ▸conjug 1f◂ VT 1 (*Psic o Fil*) to rationalize
2 (*Com*) to streamline, rationalize

racionalmente ADV rationally, reasonably, sensibly

racionamiento SM rationing
racionar ▸conjug 1a◂ VT [1] (= *limitar*) to ration; **estar racionado** to be rationed
[2] (= *distribuir*) to ration out, share out
racionero SM (*Rel*) prebendary
racionista SMF [1] (= *que percibe pensión*) person living on an allowance
[2] (= *actor*) (*de papeles pequeños*) player of bit parts; (*de ínfima clase*) ham*, third-rate actor/actress
racismo SM racism, racialism
racista ADJ, SMF racist, racialist
raco* SM (*CAm*) (= *papá*) daddy*
rada SF (*Náut*) roads *pl*, roadstead
radar SM (= *sistema*) radar; (= *estación*) radar station
radárico ADJ radar *antes de s*
radiación SF [1] (*Fís*) radiation ► **radiación solar** solar radiation ► **radiación ultravioleta** ultraviolet radiation
[2] (*Radio*) broadcasting
radiactividad SF radioactivity; **detector de ~** Geiger counter
radiactivo ADJ radioactive
radiado ADJ [1] (*Radio*) radio *antes de s*; **en una entrevista radiada** in a radio interview
[2] (*Bot*) radiate
radiador SM radiator
radial ADJ [1] (*Mec*) radial
[2] (*LAm Radio*) radio *antes de s*; **comedia ~** radio play
[3] (*Aut*) **carretera ~** radial trunk road, *trunk road leading from periphery of a country to its centre*
radiante ADJ [1] (*Fís*) radiant
[2] [*persona*] radiant; **estaba ~** she was radiant (**de** with)
radiar¹ ▸conjug 1b◂ VT [1] (*Fís*) to radiate
[2] (*Radio*) to broadcast
[3] (*Med*) to treat with radiation
radiar² ▸conjug 1b◂ VT [1] (*LAm*) (= *borrar*) to delete, cross off; (= *suprimir*) to remove
[2] (= *expulsar*) to expel
radicado ADJ **~ en** based in
radical Ⓐ ADJ, SMF radical
Ⓑ SM [1] (*Ling*) root
[2] (*Mat*) square-root sign
[3] (*Quím*) radical
radicalidad SF (= *cualidad*) radical nature; (*Pol*) radicalism
radicalismo SM radicalism
radicalización SF [*de pensamiento*] increasing radicalism, radicalization (*frm*); [*de posturas, política*] toughening, radicalization (*frm*); [*de conflicto*] intensification
radicalizar ▸conjug 1f◂ Ⓐ VT to radicalize
Ⓑ **radicalizarse** VPR [1] (*Pol*) to become more radical, radicalize
[2] [*conflicto*] to intensify
radicalmente ADV radically
radicar ▸conjug 1g◂ Ⓐ VI [1] [*dificultad, problema*] **~ en** to lie in; **el problema no radicaba en la situación política** the (root) cause of the problem was not the political situation
[2] (*frm*) (= *localizarse*) to be, be situated, lie; **la sede principal radica en Barcelona** the headquarters are in Barcelona; **el centro de acogida radica dentro de la reserva natural** the reception centre is inside the nature reserve
[3] (*Bot*) to take root
Ⓑ **radicarse** VPR to establish o.s. (**en** in)
radicha* SMF (*Cono Sur*) radical
radicheta* SF (*Cono Sur hum*) radical
radícula SF radicle
radiestesia SF water divining, dowsing
radio¹ SM [1] (*Mat*) radius; **en un ~ de 10km** within a radius of 10km; **de corto ~** short-range *antes de s*; **de largo ~** long-range *antes de s* ► **radio de acción** [*de autoridad*] jurisdiction, extent of one's authority; (*Aer*) range; **un avión de largo ~ de acción** a long-range aircraft ► **radio de giro** turning circle
[2] [*de rueda*] spoke
[3] (*Quím*) radium
[4] (*Anat*) radius
[5] (= *mensaje*) wireless message
[6] (*LAm*) = **radio²**
radio² SF radio; **por ~** by radio, on the radio, over the radio; **hablar por ~** to talk on the radio ► **radio digital** digital radio ► **radio libre** pirate radio ► **radio macuto***: **enterarse de algo por ~ macuto** to hear sth on the grapevine ► **radio pirata** (= *sistema*) pirate radio; (= *emisora*) pirate radio station
radio... PREF radio...
radioactividad SF = **radiactividad**
radioactivo ADJ = **radiactivo**
radioaficionado/a SM/F radio ham*, amateur radio enthusiast
radioantena SF (*Radio*) antenna; (*Astron*) radio telescope
radioastronomía SF radio astronomy
radiobaliza SF radio beacon
radiobiología SF radiobiology
radiobúsqueda SF radiopaging
radiocaptar ▸conjug 1a◂ VT to listen in to, pick up
radiocarbono SM radiocarbon
radiocasete SM radio cassette, radio-cassette player
radiocomunicación SF radio contact, contact by radio
radiodespertador SM clock radio, radio alarm
radiodiagnóstico SM X-ray diagnosis
radiodifundir ▸conjug 3a◂ VT to broadcast
radiodifusión SF broadcasting
radiodifusora SF (*LAm*) radio station
radioemisora SF radio station
radioenlace SM radio link
radioescucha SMF listener
radioestesia SF water divining, dowsing
radiofaro SM radio beacon
radiofonía SF radiotelephony
radiofónico ADJ radio *antes de s*
radiogoniómetro SM direction finder
radiografía SF [1] (= *técnica*) radiography, X-ray photography
[2] **una ~** an X-ray, a radiograph (*frm*)
radiografiar ▸conjug 1c◂ VT [1] (*Med*) to X-ray
[2] (*Radio*) to radio, send by radio
radiográfico ADJ X-ray *antes de s*, radiographic (*frm*)
radiógrafo/a SM/F radiographer
radiograma SM radio message, radiogram
radiogramola† SF (*Esp*) radiogram
radioisótopo SM radioisotope
radiola SF (*Perú*) jukebox
radiólisis SF INV radiolysis
radiolocación SF radiolocation
radiología SF radiology
radiólogo/a SM/F radiologist
radiomensajería SF radiopaging
radionavegación SF radio navigation
radionovela SF radio serial
radiooperador(a) SM/F radio operator
radiopatrulla SM patrol car
radiorreceptor SM radio receiver, radio set ► **radiorreceptor de contrastación** monitor set
radioscopia SF radioscopy
radioso ADJ (*LAm*) radiant
radiotaxi SM radio cab, radio taxi
radiotécnica SF radio engineering
radiotécnico/a SM/F radio engineer
radiotelefonía SF radiotelephony
radiotelefonista SMF radiotelephonist
radioteléfono SM radiotelephone
radiotelegrafía SF radiotelegraphy
radiotelegrafiar ▸conjug 1c◂ VT to radiotelegraph
radiotelegrafista SMF radio operator
radiotelescopio SM radiotelescope
radioterapeuta SMF radiotherapist
radioterapia SF radiotherapy
radiotransmisión SF (= *acto*) transmission, broadcasting; (= *programa*) transmission, broadcast
radiotransmisor SM radio transmitter
radioyente SMF listener
radón SM radon
RAE SF ABR (*Esp*) = **Real Academia Española**

RAE

The **Real Academia Española de la Lengua** *was created in 1713 and given royal approval by Philip V in 1714 with the motto* **"limpia, fija y da esplendor"** *to protect the purity of the Spanish language. There are 46 members appointed for life from among Spain's most prestigious writers and linguists. Its first dictionary, the six-volume* **Diccionario de Autoridades**, *was published between 1726 and 1739. A condensed single-volume version was published in 1780, since when more than 20 new editions have appeared.*

raedera SF scraper
raedura SF [1] (= *acto*) scrape, scraping
[2] **raeduras** scrapings, filings
[3] (*Med*) abrasion, graze
raer ▸conjug 2y◂ Ⓐ VT [1] (= *rascar*) to scrape; (= *quitar*) to scrape off
[2] (*Med*) to graze, abrade (*frm*)
[3] [+ *contenido*] to level off, level with the brim
Ⓑ **raerse** VPR (= *excoriarse*) to chafe; [*paño*] to fray
raf SM rough
Rafael SM Raphael
ráfaga SF [1] (*Meteo*) gust
[2] [*de tiros*] burst
[3] [*de intuición, luz*] flash

[4] (*Andes, Cono Sur*) (= *racha*) run of luck; **estar de** *o* **en (mala) ~** to have a spell *o* run of bad luck, be going through a bad patch

rafaguear ▸conjug 1a◂ Ⓐ VT *to direct a burst of machine gun fire at*
Ⓑ VI *to fire a burst with a machine gun*

rafañoso* ADJ (*Cono Sur*) (= *sucio*) dirty; (= *ordinario*) coarse, common

rafia SF raffia

rafting ['raftin] SM white-water rafting

raglán ADJ INV **manga ~** raglan sleeve

RAH SF ABR (*Esp*) = **Real Academia de la Historia**

rai ADJ, SM rai

raicear ▸conjug 1a◂ VI (*LAm*) to take root

raicero SM (*LAm*) root system, roots *pl*

raid [raid] SM (*pl* **raids** [raid]) [1] (= *incursión*) [*de soldados*] raid; [*de policías*] police raid
[2] (= *plaga*) attack, infestation
[3] (*Aer*) long-distance flight; (*Aut*) rally drive
[4] (= *esfuerzo*) attempt, endeavour, endeavor (EEUU); (= *empresa*) enterprise; (= *hazaña*) heroic undertaking; (*Dep*) endurance test
[5] (*esp Méx Aut*) lift, ride (EEUU); **pedir ~** to hitch a lift

raído ADJ [1] [*paño*] frayed, threadbare; [*ropa, persona*] shabby
[2] (= *desvergonzado*) shameless

raigambre SF (*a veces* SM) [1] (*Bot*) root system, roots *pl*
[2] (= *tradición*) tradition; (= *antecedentes*) antecedents *pl*, history; **tienen ~ liberal** they have a liberal tradition; **una familia de fuerte ~ local** a family with deep roots in the area

raigón SM [1] (*Bot*) thick root, stump
[2] [*de diente*] root

rail SM, **raíl** SM rail ► **rail electrizado** electrified rail, live rail

Raimundo SM Raymond

▼**raíz** SF [1] [*de planta*] root; ✦**MODISMOS de ~: arrancar algo de ~** to root sth out completely; **cortar un problema de ~** to nip a problem in the bud; **echar raíces** [*planta*] to take root; [*persona*] to put down roots
[2] [*de diente, pelo*] root
[3] (*Mat*) ► **raíz cuadrada** square root ► **raíz cúbica** cube root
[4] (= *origen*) root; **ha vuelto a sus raíces** he has gone back to his roots; **hay que llegar a la ~ del problema** we have to get to the root of the problem; **la bebida fue la ~ de todos sus males** drink was the root cause *o* was at the root of all his troubles
[5] **a ~ de** as a result of; **a ~ de su depresión dejó el trabajo** as a result of his depression he gave up his job
[6] (*Ling*) root
[7] (*Inform*) root

raja SF [1] (= *hendidura*) (*en la piel*) gash; (*en muro*) chink; (*en porcelana, cristal, madera*) crack
[2] [*de melón, sandía*] slice
[3] (**) (= *vagina*) cunt**
[4] **sacar ~*** (= *sacar tajada*) to get a rake-off*, get one's cut*
[5] (*Caribe*) (= *sangre negra*) **tener ~** to have some black blood, be of African descent
[6] (*Andes*) ✦**MODISMO estar en la ~*** (= *sin dinero*) to be broke*
[7] **rajas** (*Méx Culin*) pickled green pepper

➤ LENGUA Y USO: **raíz 5** 44.1

rajá SM rajah

rajada* SF [1] (*Cono Sur*) (= *huida*) flight, hasty exit
[2] (*Méx*) (= *cobardía*) cowardly act

rajado/a* SM/F [1] (= *canalla*) swine*
[2] (= *cobarde*) coward, chicken*

rajador ADJ (*Cono Sur*) fast

rajadura SF = **raja 1**

rajamacana* SM (*Caribe*) [1] (= *trabajo duro*) tough job
[2] (= *persona*) (*duro*) tough character; (*terco*) stubborn person
[3] (= *experto*) expert
[4] **a ~** = **a rajatabla**; *ver* **rajatabla**

rajante* ADJ (*Cono Sur*) (= *perentorio*) peremptory, sharp; (= *inmediato*) immediate

rajar ▸conjug 1a◂ Ⓐ VT [1] [+ *papel, tejido*] to tear, rip; [+ *neumático, rueda*] to slash; [+ *vidrio, cerámica*] to crack; [+ *leña*] to chop up
[2] (*) (= *acuchillar*) to cut up*
[3] (*LAm*) (= *calumniar*) to slander, run down
[4] (*LAm**) [+ *examen*] to flunk*, fail
[5] (*Andes, Caribe*) (= *aplastar*) to crush, defeat; (= *arruinar*) to ruin; (= *fastidiar*) to annoy
[6] (*Cono Sur**) [+ *trabajador*] to fire*
Ⓑ VI [1] (*) (= *hablar mucho*) to natter*; **~ de algn*** (= *criticar*) to slag sb off*
[2] (*) (= *jactarse*) to brag
Ⓒ **rajarse** VPR [1] [*papel, tejido*] to tear, rip; [*vidrio, cerámica*] to crack; [*neumático*] to get ripped
[2] (*) (= *echarse atrás*) to back out*; **no te irás a ~ ahora que tenemos las entradas** you are not going to back out now we've got the tickets; **¡me rajé!** (*LAm*) that's enough for me!, I'm quitting!
[3] (*LAm*) (= *huir*) to run away

rajatabla: **a ~** ADV [1] (= *estrictamente*) strictly, rigorously; (= *exactamente*) exactly; **debéis seguir estas instrucciones a ~** you should follow these instructions exactly *o* to the letter; **cumplir las órdenes a ~** to carry out one's orders to the letter
[2] (*LAm*) **pagar a ~** to pay on the dot, pay promptly

rajatablas* SM INV (*Andes, Caribe*) ticking-off*, telling-off*

raje* SM (*Cono Sur*) [1] (= *despido*) firing*, sacking*; **dar el ~ a algn** (= *despedir*) to fire sb*, sack sb*
[2] (= *prisa*) **al ~** in a hurry; **tomar(se) el ~** to beat it*

rajita SF slice, thin slice

rajo SM (*LAm*) tear, rip

rajón/ona Ⓐ ADJ [1] (*LAm*) (= *liberal*) generous, lavish, free-spending
[2] (*CAm, Méx*) (= *cobarde*) cowardly
[3] (*CAm, Méx*) (= *pesimista*) readily disheartened
[4] (*Méx*) (= *de poca confianza*) unreliable
Ⓑ SM (*Andalucía, LAm*) (= *raja*) tear, rip
Ⓒ SM/F [1] (*CAm, Méx*) (= *remolón*) quitter
[2] (*CAm, Méx*) (= *matón*) bully; (= *jactancioso*) braggart
[3] (*Andes, Méx*) (= *chismoso*) gossip, telltale, tattletale (EEUU)

rajonada SF (*CAm*) [1] (= *baladronada*) boast, brag; (= *jactancia*) bragging
[2] (= *ostentación*) ostentation

rajuñar* ▸conjug 1a◂ VT (*Arg*) = **rasguñar**

rala SF (*Andes*) birdlime

rale SM (*Cono Sur*) wooden bowl, wooden dish

ralea SF (*pey*) kind, sort; **de esa ~** of that sort *o* (*liter*) ilk; **gente de baja ~** riffraff, common people

ralear ▸conjug 1a◂ VI to become thin, become sparse

ralentí SM [1] (*Cine*) slow motion; **al ~** in slow motion
[2] (*Aut*) **estar al ~** ◊ **funcionar al ~** to be ticking over

ralentización SF, **ralentizamiento** SM (= *desaceleración*) slowing down, deceleration; (*Econ*) slowing down

ralentizar ▸conjug 1f◂ VT, VI to slow down

rallado ADJ grated; *ver tb* **pan 1**

rallador SM grater

ralladura SF **~ de limón** grated lemon rind; **~s de patata/queso** grated potato/cheese *sing*

rallar ▸conjug 1a◂ VT [1] (*Culin*) to grate
[2] (*) (= *fastidiar*) to grate on; **me ralla esa actitud** that attitude grates on me
[3] (*Caribe*) (= *provocar*) to goad

rallo SM (*Culin*) grater; (*Téc*) file

rallón ADJ (*Andes*) bothersome, irritating

rally ['rrali] (*pl* **rallys**) SM, **rallye** SM ['rrali] [1] (*Aut*) rally ► **rally de coches de época** vintage car rally
[2] (*Fin*) rally

ralo Ⓐ ADJ [1] (= *claro*) [*pelo*] thin, sparse; [*bosque*] sparse; [*tela*] loosely woven; [*aire*] thin
[2] (*Cono Sur*) (= *insustancial*) insubstantial
Ⓑ ADV **ralo-~** (*Cono Sur*) sometimes

RAM SF ABR (= **Random Access Memory**) RAM

rama SF [1] [*de árbol*] branch; **en ~: algodón en ~** raw cotton; **canela en ~** cinnamon sticks *pl*; ✦**MODISMOS andarse** *o* **irse por las ~s** to beat about the bush; **poner algo en la última ~** to leave sth till last ► **rama de olivo** (*lit, fig*) olive branch ► **rama de perejil** sprig of parsley
[2] [*de ciencia, familia, organización*] branch; **Yolanda pertenece a la ~ materna de su familia** Yolanda is on his mother's side of the family
[3] (*Imprenta*) **en ~** unbound
[4] (*LAm**) (= *hachís*) pot*, hash*

ramada SF [1] (= *ramaje*) branches *pl*
[2] (*LAm*) (= *cobertizo*) *shelter or covering made of branches*

ramadán SM, **Ramadán** SM Ramadan

ramaje SM branches *pl*

ramal SM [1] (= *cabo*) strand; (*para el caballo*) halter
[2] (= *desvío*) (*Aut*) branch; (*Ferro*) branch line
[3] (= *derivación*) offshoot

ramalazo SM [1] (= *azote*) lash
[2] [*de depresión, locura*] fit; **me dio un ~ de dolor** I felt a sudden stab of pain; ✦**MODISMO tener ~** to be effeminate
[3] (= *ráfaga*) [*de viento*] gust; [*de lluvia*] blast

ramazón SF (*CAm, Cono Sur, Méx*) antler, horns *pl*

rambla SF [1] (= *avenida*) boulevard, avenue
[2] (= *arroyo*) watercourse
[3] (*LAm*) (= *paseo marítimo*) esplanade, promenade; (= *muelle*) quayside

ramera SF whore, prostitute

ramificación SF ramification

ramificarse ▸conjug 1g◂ VPR to branch, branch out, ramify (*frm*)
ramiforme ADJ ramiform
ramillete SM [1] [*de flores*] bouquet, bunch; (*de adorno*) corsage; (*Bot*) (= *inflorescencia*) cluster
[2] (= *conjunto selecto*) choice bunch, select group
ramita SF [*de árbol, planta*] twig, sprig; (= *ramo*) spray
ramo SM [1] [*de flores*] bouquet, bunch ► **ramo de novia** bride's bouquet
[2] [*de árbol*] branch
[3] (*Com*) (= *sector*) field, section, department; **es del ~ de la alimentación** he's in the food business; **el ministro del ~** the appropriate minister, the minister concerned with this; **es del ~*** (= *homosexual*) he's one of them*, he's a poof‡, he's a fag (*EEUU*‡)
[4] (*) (= *ramalazo*) (*tb* **~s**) **tiene ~s de loco** he has a streak of madness in him, he has a mad streak in him
ramojo SM brushwood
Ramón SM Raymond
ramonear ▸conjug 1a◂ VT [1] [+ *árboles*] to lop, lop the twigs of
[2] [*ovejas*] to browse on
rampa SF ramp ► **rampa de acceso** entrance ramp ► **rampa de desperdicios, rampa de la basura** refuse chute ► **rampa de lanzamiento** launch(ing) ramp ► **rampa de misiles** missile launcher ► **rampa móvil** mobile launch pad, mobile launching pad
rampante ADJ rampant
rampla SF (*Chile*) (truck) trailer
ramplón ADJ common, coarse
ramplonería SF commonness, coarseness
rana SF [1] (*Zool*) frog; ✦**MODISMOS** **cuando las ~s críen pelo** when pigs fly, when pigs learn to fly; **¡hasta que las ~s críen pelo!** if I never see you again it'll be too soon!; **pero salió ~*** but he turned out badly, but he was a big disappointment ► **rana toro** bullfrog
[2] (= *juego*) *game of throwing coins into the mouth of an iron frog*
ranchada SF [1] (*CAm*) (= *canoa*) canoe
[2] (*LAm*) (= *cobertizo*) shed, improvised hut
ranchar ▸conjug 1a◂ VI [1] (*Cono Sur, Méx*) (= *vagar*) to wander from farm to farm
[2] (*Andes, Caribe, Méx*) (= *pernoctar*) to spend the night; (= *establecerse*) to settle
[3] (*Caribe*) (= *obstinarse*) to persist
ranchear ▸conjug 1a◂ Ⓐ VT (*Caribe, Méx*) (= *saquear*) to loot, pillage; (= *robar*) to rob
Ⓑ VI [1] (*LAm*) (= *formar rancho*) to build a camp
[2] (*Andes, Cono Sur*) (= *comer*) to have a meal
ranchera SF [1] (*Méx Mús*) *Mexican folk song*
[2] (= *coche*) station wagon; *ver tb* **ranchero**
ranchería SF [1] (*LAm*) (*para trabajadores*) labourers' quarters, laborers' quarters (*EEUU*)
[2] (*LAm*) = **rancherío**
[3] (*Caribe*) (= *taberna*) poor country inn
[4] (*Caribe*) (= *chabolas*) shantytown
rancherío SM (*LAm*) settlement
ranchero/a Ⓐ ADJ (*Méx*) [1] (= *rudo*) uncouth; (= *ridículo*) ridiculous, silly
[2] (= *conocedor del campo*) **es muy ~** he's a real countryman *o* country person
[3] (*Culin*) **huevos ~s** *fried eggs in a hot chili and tomato sauce*
[4] (*Mús*) **música ranchera** ≈ country and western music
Ⓑ SM/F [1] (*LAm*) (= *jefe de rancho*) rancher
[2] (= *cocinero*) mess cook
[3] (*Méx*) peasant, country person; *ver tb* **ranchera**
ranchitos SMPL (*Ven*) shantytown *sing*
rancho SM [1] (*Méx*) (= *granja*) ranch, small farm
[2] (*LAm*) (= *choza*) hut, thatched hut; (*LAm*) (= *casa de campo*) country house, villa
[3] (*Caribe*) (= *chabola*) shanty, shack; **~s** (*Andes, Caribe*) shanty town
[4] (*Náut*) crew's quarters *pl*
[5] (= *campamento*) camp, settlement
[6] (*Mil*) mess, communal meal; (*pey*) (= *comida*) bad food, grub*; **asentar el ~** (= *preparar la comida*) to prepare a meal; (*fig*) (= *organizarse*) to settle in, get things organized; **hacer el ~** to have a meal; ✦**MODISMO** **hacer ~ aparte** to set up on one's own, go one's own way
[7] (*Cono Sur*) (= *sombrero*) straw hat
rancidez SF, **ranciedad** SF [1] [*de vino*] age, mellowness; [*de mantequilla, tocino*] staleness
[2] (= *antigüedad*) great age, antiquity; (*pey*) antiquatedness
rancio Ⓐ ADJ [1] [*vino*] old, mellow; [*mantequilla, tocino*] rancid
[2] [*linaje*] ancient; [*tradición*] very ancient, time-honoured, time-honored (*EEUU*); (*pey*) antiquated, old-fashioned; **esas dos son muy rancias** those two are a couple of old farts‡
Ⓑ SM = **rancidez**
rancontán ADV (*Andes, CAm, Caribe*) in cash
rand [ran] SM (*pl* **rands** [ran]) rand
randa¹ SF (*Cos*) lace, lace trimming
randa²* SM (= *ladrón*) pickpocket, petty thief; (= *sospechoso*) suspicious character, prowler
randar‡ ▸conjug 1a◂ VT to nick‡, rip off‡
randevú SM (*Cono Sur*) rendez-vous
randevuses SMPL (*Cono Sur*) courtesies
ranfaña* SM (*Andes, Cono Sur*) scruff*
ranfañoso* (*Andes, Cono Sur*) Ⓐ ADJ shabby, scruffy
Ⓑ SM scruff*
ranfla SF (*LAm*) ramp
ranga SF (*Andes*) nag, old horse
ranglán ADJ INV = **raglán**
rango¹ SM [1] (= *categoría*) rank; (= *prestigio*) standing, status; **de ~** of high standing, of some status; **de alto ~** of high standing, of some status
[2] (*LAm*) (= *lujo*) luxury; (= *pompa*) pomp, splendour, splendor (*EEUU*)
rango² SM (*Andes*) = **ranga**
rangosidad* SF (*Cono Sur*) generosity
rangoso* ADJ (*Cono Sur*) generous
Rangún SM Rangoon
ranita SM Baby-gro®, rompers *pl*, romper suit
ránking ['raŋkin] SM (*pl* **ránkings** ['raŋkin]) [1] (= *clasificación*) ranking
[2] (*Andes Mús*) top twenty, hit parade
rantifuso ADJ (*Cono Sur*) [1] (= *sucio*) dirty, grubby; (= *ordinario*) common
[2] (= *sospechoso*) suspicious
ranúnculo SM (*Bot*) ranunculus; (*esp Esp*) buttercup
ranura SF (= *hendedura*) groove; (*para monedas*) slot ► **ranura de expansión** (*Inform*) expansion slot
rap SM rap, rap music; **hacer ~** to rap
rapacidad SF rapacity
rapado/a Ⓐ ADJ [*pelo*] close-cropped
Ⓑ SM/F (= *persona*) skinhead
Ⓒ SM (= *corte de pelo*) **tiene un buen ~** he has his hair close shaven
rapadura SF (*LAm*) (= *azúcar*) brown sugar; (= *caramelo*) *sweet made of milk and syrup*
rapapolvo SM telling-off*, ticking-off*; **echar un ~ a algn** to give sb a telling-off *o* ticking-off*
rapar ▸conjug 1a◂ Ⓐ VT [1] [+ *pelo*] to crop; [+ *barba*] to shave
[2] (*) (= *arrebatar*) to snatch*, pinch*
Ⓑ **raparse** VPR **~se la cabeza** to shave one's head
rapaz¹ Ⓐ ADJ [1] (*Zool*) predatory; (*Orn*) of prey
[2] (= *avaricioso*) rapacious, greedy; (= *inclinado al robo*) thieving
Ⓑ SF (*Zool*) predatory animal; (*Orn*) bird of prey
rapaz²(a)†† SM/F (*Esp hum*) boy/girl, lad/lass
rape¹ SM [1] [*de barba*] quick shave; [*de pelo*] rough haircut; **al ~** cut close
[2] (*) (= *bronca*) ticking-off*, telling-off*
rape² SM (*Zool*) angler fish
rapé SM snuff
rapel SM, **rápel** SM = **rappel**
raper SMF (*pl* **rapers**) = **rapper**
rapero/a* Ⓐ ADJ rap *antes de s*
Ⓑ SM/F rapper
rápida SF (*Méx*) chute
rápidamente ADV fast, quickly
rapidez SF speed; **me sorprendió la ~ con que acabó el trabajo** the speed with which he finished the job surprised me, it surprised me how quickly he finished the job; **con ~** quickly; **se vistió con ~** she got dressed quickly
rápido Ⓐ ADJ [1] (= *veloz*) fast, quick; [*tren*] fast, express
[2] (*Andes, Caribe, Cono Sur*) [*campo, paisaje*] fallow
[3] (*Caribe*) [*tiempo*] clear
Ⓑ ADV quickly; **¡y ~, eh!** and make it snappy!*
Ⓒ SM [1] (*Ferro*) express
[2] (*Andes, Caribe, Cono Sur*) (= *campo*) open country
[3] **rápidos** (= *rabiones*) rapids
rapiña SF robbery, robbery with violence; *ver* **ave**
rapiñar ▸conjug 1a◂ VT to steal
raposa SF [1] (*Zool*) (= *zorro*) fox; (= *zorra*) vixen
[2] (*Caribe*) (= *bolsa*) carrier bag; *ver tb* **raposo**
raposera SF foxhole
raposero ADJ **perro ~** foxhound
raposo SM [1] (= *zorro*) fox
[2] (*Andes, Caribe*) (= *mocoso*) kid*; *ver tb* **raposa**
rappel SM abseiling; **a ~** by abseiling; **hacer ~** to abseil, abseil down
rappelar ▸conjug 1a◂ VI to abseil, abseil down
rapper SMF (*pl* **rappers**) rapper, rap artist
rapsodia SF rhapsody
rapsódico ADJ rhapsodic
raptar ▸conjug 1a◂ VT to kidnap, abduct

rapto SM [1] (= *secuestro*) kidnapping, kidnapping (*EEUU*), abduction
[2] (= *impulso*) sudden impulse; **en un ~ de celos** in a sudden fit of jealousy
[3] (= *éxtasis*) ecstasy, rapture

raptor(a) SM/F kidnapper

raque[1] SM beachcombing; **andar al ~** to beachcomb, go beachcombing

raque[2] SM (*Caribe*) bargain

raquear[1] ▸conjug 1a◂ VI to go beachcombing

raquear[2] ▸conjug 1a◂ VT (*Caribe*) to rob, hold up

Raquel SF Rachel

raquero/a SM/F beachcomber

raqueta SF [*de tenis, bádminton*] racket; [*de ping pong*] bat ► **raqueta de nieve** snowshoe

raquetazo SM shot, hit, stroke

raquítico ADJ [1] (*Med*) rachitic
[2] [*cantidad, sueldo*] paltry, miserly
[3] [*árbol*] stunted

raquitis SF INV, **raquitismo** SM rickets *pl*

raramente ADV rarely, seldom

rarefacción SF rarefaction

rareza SF [1] (= *calidad*) rarity
[2] (= *objeto*) rarity
[3] (= *rasgo singular*) oddity, peculiarity; **tiene sus ~s** he has his peculiarities, he has his little ways; **tiene alguna ~** there's something odd about him

raridad SF rarity

rarificar ▸conjug 1g◂ VT to rarefy

rarífico ADJ (*Cono Sur*) = **raro 1**

raro ADJ [1] (= *extraño*) strange, odd; **es un hombre muy ~** he's a very strange *o* odd man; **es ~ que no haya llamado** it's strange *o* odd that he hasn't called; **¡qué ~!** ◊ **¡qué cosa más rara!** how (very) strange!, how (very) odd!
[2] (= *poco común*) rare; **una especie muy rara** a very rare species; **con alguna rara excepción** with few *o* rare exceptions; **de rara perfección** of rare perfection, of remarkable perfection; **rara vez nos visita** ◊ **rara es la vez que nos visita** he rarely visits us
[3] (*Fís*) rare, rarefied

ras SM levelness, evenness; **a ~ de** level with, flush with; **volar a ~ de tierra** to fly (almost) at ground level; **~ con ~** level, on a level

rasado ADJ level; **cucharada rasada** level teaspoonful

rasante Ⓐ ADJ low; **tiro ~** low shot; **vuelo ~** low-level flight
Ⓑ SM slope; **cambio de ~** (*Aut*) brow of a hill

rasar ▸conjug 1a◂ Ⓐ VT [1] [+ *contenido*] to level, level with the brim
[2] (= *rozar*) to skim, graze; **la bala pasó rasando su sombrero** the bullet grazed his hat
[3] = **arrasar**
Ⓑ **rasarse** VPR [*cielo*] to clear

rasca[1]‡ SF [1] (*Esp*) (= *frío*) cold; **¿cómo se te ocurre salir con esta ~?** what do you think you're doing going out in this cold?; **¡menuda ~ hace!** it's freezing!
[2] (*Andes, CAm, Caribe*) (= *borrachera*) drunkenness

rasca[2]* ADJ (*Cono Sur*) (= *vulgar*) tacky*; (= *de mala calidad*) inferior

rascacielos SM INV skyscraper

rascacio SM scorpion fish

rascadera SF [1] (= *utensilio*) scraper
[2] (= *almohaza*) currycomb

rascado* ADJ [1] (*LAm*) (= *borracho*) drunk
[2] (*CAm*) (= *casquivano*) feather-brained

rascador SM [1] (= *utensilio*) scraper
[2] [*de pelo*] ornamental hairclasp

rascaespalda SM backscratcher

rascamoño SM [1] = **rascador 2**
[2] (*Bot*) zinnia

rascapies SM INV (*Andes*) firecracker

rascar ▸conjug 1g◂ Ⓐ VT [1] (*con uñas*) to scratch
[2] [+ *puerta, pared*] to scrape; [+ *pintura*] to scrape off
[3] (*hum*) [+ *instrumento*] to scrape, scratch *o* saw away at
Ⓑ VI (*LAm*) (= *picar*) to itch
Ⓒ **rascarse** VPR [1] (*con uñas*) to scratch, scratch o.s.; ✦**MODISMOS ~se la barriga** ◊ **~se la panza** to take it easy
[2] (*LAm*) (= *emborracharse*) to get drunk
[3] **~se juntos** (*CAm, Cono Sur*) to band together; ✦**MODISMO no ~se con algn** (*Andes*) not to hit it off with sb

rasca-rasca SM scratch-card game ► **tarjetas rasca-rasca** scratch cards

rascatripas* SMF INV fiddler, third-rate violinist

rasco* ADJ (*Chile*) common, ordinary

rascón[1] ADJ [1] (= *amargo*) sharp, sour (to taste)
[2] (*Méx*) (= *pendenciero*) quarrelsome

rascón[2] SM (*Orn*) water rail

rascuache ADJ (*CAm, Méx*) [1] (= *pobre*) poor, penniless
[2] (= *desgraciado*) wretched
[3] (= *ridículo*) ridiculous, in bad taste
[4] (= *grosero*) coarse, vulgar
[5] (= *tacaño*) mean, tightfisted

rascucho ADJ (*Cono Sur*) drunk

RASD SF ABR = **República Árabe Saharaui Democrática**

raseado ADJ level; **cucharada raseada** level spoonful

rasear ▸conjug 1a◂ VT [1] (= *rozar*) to skim, graze
[2] (= *nivelar*) to level, level off
[3] [+ *balón*] to play low, play along the ground

rasera SF fish slice

rasero SM strickle; **doble ~** double standards *pl*; ✦**MODISMO medir dos cosas con el mismo ~** to treat two things alike

rasete SM satinet, satinette

rasgado ADJ [1] [*ojos*] almond-shaped; [*boca*] wide, big
[2] [*ventana*] wide
[3] (*LAm*) (= *franco*) outspoken
[4] (*Andes*) (= *generoso*) generous

rasgadura SF tear, rip

rasgar ▸conjug 1h◂ VT [1] [+ *tejido, piel*] to tear, rip; [+ *papel*] to tear up, tear to pieces
[2] = **rasguear 1**

rasgo SM [1] (*Anat*) feature; **tiene unos ~s muy marcados** she has very pronounced (facial) features; **de ~s enérgicos** of energetic appearance
[2] (= *peculiaridad*) characteristic, feature ► **rasgos característicos** typical features ► **rasgos distintivos** distinctive features
[3] (*con pluma*) stroke, flourish; **~s** characteristics (*of one's handwriting*); ✦**MODISMO a grandes ~s** broadly speaking
[4] (= *acto*) ► **rasgo de generosidad** act of generosity; (= *acción noble*) noble gesture ► **rasgo de ingenio** flash of wit, stroke of genius
[5] (*LAm*) (= *acequia*) irrigation channel; (= *terreno*) plot, plot of land

rasgón SM tear, rip, rent (*liter*)

rasguear ▸conjug 1a◂ VT [1] (*Mús*) to strum
[2] (= *al escribir*) to write with a flourish; (*fig*) (= *escribir*) to write

rasguñadura SF (*LAm*) scratch

rasguñar ▸conjug 1a◂ VT [1] (= *rascar*) to scratch
[2] (*Arte*) to sketch, draw in outline

rasguño SM [1] (= *arañazo*) scratch; **salir sin un ~** to come out of it without a scratch
[2] (*Arte*) sketch, outline drawing

rasmillón SM (*Cono Sur*) scratch

raso Ⓐ ADJ [1] [*campo, terreno*] (= *llano*) flat, level; (= *sin árboles*) clear, open; (= *liso*) smooth
[2] [*asiento*] backless
[3] [*cielo*] clear; **está ~** the sky is clear
[4] [*contenido*] level, level with the brim; **una cucharada rasa** a level spoonful
[5] [*pelota, vuelo*] very low, almost at ground level; **marcó el gol por ~** he scored with a low shot
[6] (= *simple*) **soldado ~** private; **aprobado ~** bare pass, bare pass mark
Ⓑ ADV **tirar ~** (*Dep*) to shoot low
Ⓒ SM [1] (*Cos*) satin
[2] (= *campo llano*) flat country; (= *campo abierto*) open country; **dormir al ~** to sleep out in the open

raspa SF [1] (*Bot*) [*de cebada*] beard; [*de uva*] stalk
[2] [*de pez*] (= *espina*) fishbone; (= *espinazo*) backbone
[3] (*) (= *persona irritable*) grouch*
[4] (*) (= *persona delgada*) beanpole*, string bean (*EEUU**)
[5] (*LAm**) (= *reprimenda*) scolding, telling-off*, ticking-off*
[6] (*Caribe, Méx*) (= *azúcar*) brown sugar
[7] (*Cono Sur*) (= *herramienta*) rasp
[8] **ni de ~** (*Andes*) (= *de ninguna manera*) under no circumstances, no way*
[9] (*CAm, Méx*) (= *burla*) joke
[10] (*LAm*) (= *chusma*) riffraff

raspada* SF (*Caribe, Méx*) scolding, telling-off*, ticking-off*

raspado Ⓐ ADJ [1] (*CAm, Caribe*) shameless
[2] **un aprobado ~** a bare pass; **lo aprobé ~** I just scraped through
Ⓑ SM [1] (*Med*) D and C, dilation and curettage
[2] (*LAm*) (= *bebida*) water ice, sherbet (*EEUU*)

raspador SM [1] (= *herramienta*) scraper, rasp
[2] (*Méx Culin*) grater

raspadura SF [1] (= *acto*) scrape, scraping, rasping
[2] **raspaduras** [*de papel*] scrapings; [*de hierro*] filings
[3] (= *raya*) scratch, mark
[4] (= *borradura*) erasure
[5] (*LAm*) (= *azúcar*) brown sugar, brown sugar scrapings

raspante ADJ sharp, rough

raspar ▸conjug 1a◂ Ⓐ VT 1 [+ *pintura*] to scrape off; **raspó la pintura de la pared** he scraped the paint off the wall; **has raspado la pared con la bicicleta** you've scraped the wall with your bike; **tienes que ~ la puerta para quitarle el barniz** you have to sand the door to get the varnish off
2 [+ *piel*] to scratch; **este jersey me raspa el cuello** this jumper scratches my neck; **los socialistas quedaron raspando la mayoría absoluta** the Socialists were a whisker *o* an inch away from achieving an absolute majority, the Socialists were within a whisker *o* an inch of achieving an absolute majority
3 [*vino, licor*] to be rough on; **este vino raspa la garganta** this wine is rough on your throat
4 (*) (= *hurtar*) to pinch*, swipe*
5 (*Caribe**) (= *matar*) to kill
6 (*LAm**) (= *regañar*) to tick off*, tell off*, scold
7 (*Méx*) (= *injuriar*) to say unkind things to, make wounding remarks to
8 (*en un escrito*) to scratch out; **han raspado la firma** they have scratched out the signature
Ⓑ VI 1 [*manos, tejido, licor*] to be rough; **esta toalla raspa** this towel is rough
2 (*LAm**) (= *irse*) to leg it*; (= *morir*) to kick the bucket*

raspear* ▸conjug 1a◂ Ⓐ VT (*LAm*) to tick off*, tell off*, scold
Ⓑ VI [*pluma*] to scratch

raspón SM 1 (= *rasguño*) scratch, graze; (*LAm*) (= *abrasión*) abrasion; (= *cardenal*) bruise
2 (*LAm**) (= *regaño*) scolding, telling-off*, ticking-off*, scolding
3 (*Col*) (= *sombrero*) straw hat
4 (*Méx**) (= *comentario hiriente*) cutting remark

rasponear* ▸conjug 1a◂ VT (*Andes*) to scold, tick off*, tell off*

rasposo ADJ 1 [*sabor*] sharp, rough
2 (*LAm**) (= *tacaño*) stingy*
3 (*Cono Sur*) (= *raído*) scruffy, threadbare; (= *miserable*) wretched

rasqueta SF 1 (= *herramienta*) scraper, rasp
2 (*Cono Sur*) (= *almohaza*) horse brush, currycomb

rasquetear ▸conjug 1a◂ VT (*Cono Sur*) to brush down

rasquiña SF (*LAm*) itch

rasta ADJ, SMF Rasta

rastacuerismo* SM (*LAm*) (= *ambición social*) social climbing; (= *tren de vida*) rich living; (= *ostentación*) ostentation, display

rastacuero/a* ADJ, SM/F (*LAm*) nouveau riche

rastafario/a ADJ, SM/F Rastafarian

rastra SF 1 (*Agr*) (= *rastrillo*) rake; (= *grada*) harrow
2 **a ~s: tuvo que sacar al niño a ~s de la juguetería** she had to drag the child out of the toyshop; **llevaba la bolsa a ~s** she was dragging the bag along behind her; **el herido fue a ~s hasta la puerta** the injured man crawled to the door; **no voy al fútbol ni a ~s** wild horses wouldn't get me to a football match*; **desde hace años lleva este problema a ~s** she's been dogged by this problem for years; **con un sueldo tan bajo siempre vamos a ~s** with such a low salary we're always struggling (along)
3 (*Pesca*) trawl; **pescar a la ~** to trawl
4 (*para transportar*) trolley (*for moving heavy objects*), cart (*EEUU*)
5 (= *ristra*) string
6 (= *huella*) trail, track
7 (*Cono Sur*) (= *cinturón*) *metal ornament on gaucho's belt*
8 (†) (= *consecuencia*) unpleasant consequence, disagreeable result; (= *castigo*) punishment

rastreable ADJ traceable

rastreador(a) Ⓐ SM/F (= *persona*) tracker
Ⓑ SM (*Náut*) (*tb* **barco** ~) trawler ► **rastreador de minas** minesweeper

rastrear ▸conjug 1a◂ Ⓐ VT 1 (= *buscar*) to track, trail; [+ *satélite*] to track; [+ *río*] to drag; **~ el monte** to comb the woods; **~ los archivos** to trawl through the files
2 [+ *minas*] to sweep
3 (*Pesca*) to trawl
Ⓑ VI 1 (*Agr*) to rake, harrow
2 (*Pesca*) to trawl
3 (*Aer*) to skim the ground, fly very low

rastreo SM 1 (*en agua*) dredging, dragging; (*Pesca*) trawling
2 [*de satélite*] tracking

rastrerismo* SM (*LAm*) toadying, bootlicking*, brown-nosing (*EEUU*‡)

rastrero ADJ 1 (*Zool*) creeping, crawling; (*Bot*) creeping
2 [*vestido*] trailing
3 [*vuelo*] very low
4 [*conducta*] mean, despicable; [*persona*] cringing; [*método*] low; [*disculpa*] abject, humble

rastrillada SF (*Cono Sur*) track, trail

rastrillar ▸conjug 1a◂ Ⓐ VT 1 (*Agr*) to rake; (= *recoger*) to rake up; (= *alisar*) to rake smooth
2 (*LAm*) [+ *fusil*] to fire; [+ *fósforo*] to strike
3 (*CAm, Méx*) [+ *pies*] to drag
Ⓑ VI 1 (*Andes, Caribe, Cono Sur*) (= *errar el tiro*) to miss; (*Caribe, Cono Sur*) (= *disparar*) to fire, shoot
2 (*Cono Sur**) (= *robar*) to shoplift

rastrillazo SM (*CAm*) 1 (= *sueñecito*) light sleep
2 (= *piscolabis*) light meal, snack

rastrillero/a* SM/F (*Cono Sur*) shoplifter

rastrillo SM 1 (*Agr*) rake
2 (*Mil*) portcullis; (*Arquit*) spiked gate
3 (*Téc*) hackle, flax comb
4 [*de cerradura, llave*] ward
5 (*Ferro*) ► **rastrillo delantero** cowcatcher
6 (*Com*) (= *mercadillo*) jumble sale
7 (*Méx*) (= *cuchilla*) razor, safety razor

rastro SM 1 (= *pista*) trail; (= *olor*) scent; **la policía ha seguido el ~ a** *o* **de los atracadores** the police have followed the robbers' trail; **los perros le perdieron el ~** the dogs lost his scent
2 (= *señal*) trace; **quedaban ~s de sangre en el suelo** there were traces of blood on the floor; **desaparecer sin dejar ~** to vanish without trace; **ni ~: no ha quedado ni ~ del jamón** there isn't a scrap of ham left
3 (*Agr*) (= *rastrillo*) rake; (= *grada*) harrow
4 (= *mercadillo*) fleamarket; **el Rastro** *fleamarket in Madrid*
5 (†) (= *matadero*) slaughterhouse

rastrojear ▸conjug 1a◂ VI (*LAm*) (= *espigar*) to glean; [*animales*] to feed in the stubble

rastrojera SF stubble field

rastrojero SM 1 (*Cono Sur*) (= *campo*) stubble field
2 (*Cono Sur Aut*) jeep
3 (*Méx*) (= *maíz*) maize *o* (*EEUU*) corn stalks (*used as fodder*)

rastrojo SM 1 (*Agr*) (= *residuo*) [*de campo*] stubble; **campo de ~** stubble field
2 (*Cono Sur*) (= *terreno cultivado*) ploughed field, plowed field (*EEUU*)
3 **rastrojos** (*LAm*) (= *sobras*) waste *sing*, remains, leftovers

rasura SF 1 (= *llanura*) flatness, levelness; (= *lisura*) smoothness
2 (= *afeitado*) shave, shaving; (*Téc*) scrape, scraping
3 **rasuras** (= *raspaduras*) [*de papel*] scrapings; [*de hierro*] filings

rasurado SM shave

rasurador SM, **rasuradora** SF (*Méx*) electric shaver, electric razor

rasurar ▸conjug 1a◂ Ⓐ VT 1 (= *afeitar*) to shave
2 (*Téc*) to scrape
Ⓑ **rasurarse** VPR to shave

rata Ⓐ SF rat; ✦**MODISMO ser una ~ de biblioteca** to be a bookworm ► **rata común** house rat ► **rata gris** brown rat ► **rata negra** black rat, house rat
Ⓑ SMF (*) 1 (= *tacaño*) miser, mean devil, stingy devil*
2 (= *ladrón*) sneak thief

rataplán SM drumbeat, rub-a-dub

ratear ▸conjug 1a◂ Ⓐ VT 1 (= *hurtar*) to steal, pilfer
2 (= *repartir*) to share out
3 (= *reducir*) to reduce proportionately
Ⓑ VI (= *arrastrarse*) to crawl, creep

ratera SF (*Méx*) rat trap

ratería SF 1 (= *robo*) petty thieving; **una ~** a theft
2 (= *cualidad*) crookedness, dishonesty

raterismo SM (*LAm*) thieving

ratero/a Ⓐ ADJ 1 (= *que roba*) thieving, light-fingered
2 (= *despreciable*) despicable
Ⓑ SM/F (= *ladrón*) thief, petty thief; (= *carterista*) pickpocket; (*Méx*) [*de casas*] burglar

raticida SM rat poison

ratificación SF ratification

ratificar ▸conjug 1g◂ VT [+ *tratado*] to ratify; [+ *noticia*] to confirm; [+ *opinión*] to support; **~ que ...** to confirm that ...

rating ['ratin] SM (*pl* **ratings** ['ratin]) 1 (*Náut*) class
2 (*TV etc*) popularity rating

ratio SM (*a veces* SF) ratio

Ratisbona SF Regensburg, Ratisbon

rato SM 1 (= *espacio de tiempo*) 1·1 (*uso incontable*) **lleva bastante ~ hablando** he's been talking for quite a while *o* for quite some time; **hace ~** a while ago, some time ago; **hace ~ que se fue** he left a while ago, he left some time ago; **largo ~** a long time; **hablamos largo ~** we talked a long time; **más ~** (*Chile*) later; **déjalo para más ~** leave it for later; **nos vemos más ~** see you later; **mucho ~** a long time; **¿vas a tardar mucho ~?** will you be long?; ✦**MODISMO para ~: tenemos carretera para ~** we still have quite a way to go; **tenemos para ~ con este trabajo** we still have quite a lot to do to get this work finished, we're still a long way from finishing this work; **aún queda presidente para ~** the president will still be around for some time to come; *ver tb* **cuerda 2**

1·2 (*uso contable*) **durante el ~ que estuve esperando** during the short time I was waiting; **estoy encantada de haber tenido este ~ para charlar contigo** I'm delighted to have had this time to chat to you; **en esos ~s me olvido de todo** at such moments I forget about everything; **otro ~: ya lo llamaré otro ~** I'll call him back another time; **dile que se ponga otro ~ al teléfono** can you call her back to the phone for a minute?; **¡hasta otro ~!** so long!, I'll see you!; **todo el ~** the whole time, all the time

1·3 **un ~** a (short) while; **al cabo de un ~ dijo ...** after a (short) while he said ...; **dentro de un ~** in a (short) while; **sólo estuvo allí un ~** he was only there a (short) while; **todavía tardará un ~ en salir** it'll still be a while before he comes out; **me quedaré un ~ más** I'll stay a bit longer; **me tuvo esperando un buen ~** she kept me waiting a good while *o* quite some time; **escríbeme cuando tengas un ~** write to me when you have a spare moment; **no regresó hasta pasado un buen ~** he didn't come back for a while; **dar un mal ~ a algn** to give sb a hard time; **estos hijos no dan más que malos ~s** these children give you nothing but grief; **mujer, no te des mal ~** don't let yourself be upset; **pasar un buen/mal ~** to have a good/bad time; **me hizo pasar un mal ~** I had a terrible time because of him; **pasar el ~** to pass the time; **tener sus ~s** to have one's moments

► **ratos de ocio** leisure time ► **ratos libres** spare time, free time

2 (*otras expresiones temporales*) **al ~** shortly afterwards, shortly after, a short while later; **al poco ~ sonó el teléfono** shortly afterwards *o* shortly after *o* a short while later the phone rang; **llamaron al poco ~ de irte** they called a short while after *o* shortly after you left; **al ~ viene** (*Méx**) he'll be here soon *o* in a (short) while; **voy a comer al ~** (*Méx**) I'm going to eat soon *o* in a moment; **a cada ~** every other minute; **caminaba despacio, parándose a cada ~** she walked slowly, stopping all the time *o* every other minute; **de ~ en ~** every so often

3 **a ~s** at times; **a ~s, me parece sincero y a otros no** at times he seems sincere and at other times not; **el enfermo sólo se levanta a ~s** the patient only gets up from time to time *o* now and again; **de a ~s** (*Arg, Uru*) from time to time, now and again; **a ~s perdidos** in one's spare moments; **trabajo en el jardín a ~s perdidos** I work in the garden in my spare moments

4 (*) **un ~** (*Esp*) (*uso adverbial*) (= *bastante*) **es un ~ difícil** it's pretty tricky*; **es un ~ listo** he's pretty smart*; **pesan un ~** they weigh quite a bit, they're pretty heavy*; **sabe un ~ largo de matemáticas** she knows quite a bit of maths*

ratón SM 1 (*Zool, Inform*) mouse; ✦**MODISMO** **mandar a algn a capar ratones**‡ to tell sb to go to blazes* ► **ratón almizclero** muskrat ► **ratón de archivo, ratón de biblioteca** bookworm ► **ratón óptico** optical mouse

2 (*Caribe*) (= *petardo*) squib, cracker

3 (*Caribe**) (= *resaca*) hangover

4 (*) (= *pelusa*) ball of fluff

ratonar ▸conjug 1a◂ VT to gnaw, nibble

ratonera SF 1 (= *trampa*) mousetrap

2 (= *agujero*) mousehole

3 (*fig*) (= *trampa*) trap; **caer en la ~** to fall into the trap

4 (*Andes, Cono Sur**) (= *barrio bajo*) hovel, slum

5 (*Caribe*) (= *tienda*) ranch store

ratonero SM (*tb* **~ común**) buzzard

RAU SF ABR (= **República Árabe Unida**) UAR

raudal SM 1 (= *torrente*) torrent, flood

2 (= *abundancia*) plenty, abundance; **a ~es** in abundance, in great numbers; **entrar a ~es** to pour in, come flooding in

raudo ADJ (*frm*) (= *rápido*) swift

ravioles SMPL ravioli

raya[1] SF 1 (= *línea*) line; (*en mano*) line; (*en tela, diseño*) stripe; **a ~s** striped; ✦**MODISMOS** **hacer ~** to mark off; **mantener a ~ a algn** to keep sb at bay; **pasarse de la ~** to overstep the mark, go too far; **poner a ~** to check, hold back; **tener a ~** (= *impedir el avance*) to keep off, keep at bay; (= *controlar*) to keep in check, keep under control ► **raya diplomática** (*en tejido*) pinstripe ► **raya en negro** black line ► **raya magnética** magnetic stripe

2 (= *marca*) (*en una superficie*) scratch, mark

3 (*en el pelo*) parting, part (*EEUU*); **hacerse la ~** to part one's hair

4 (*en el pantalón*) crease

5 (*Tip*) line, dash; (*Telec*) dash

6 (‡) (= *droga*) fix*, dose

7 (*Méx††*) (= *sueldo*) pay, wages *pl*

raya[2] SF (= *pez*) ray, skate ► **raya manta** butterfly ray, California butterfly ray

rayadillo SM (*Cos*) [*de rayas*] striped material; [*de rayas azules y blancas*] blue-and-white striped material

rayado Ⓐ ADJ 1 [*papel*] ruled, lined; [*tela, diseño*] striped

2 [*disco, mueble*] scratched

3 [*cheque*] crossed

4 (*) (= *loco*) cracked*, crazy

5 (*Cono Sur*) (= *fanático*) extreme, fanatical

Ⓑ SM 1 (*en papel*) ruling, ruled lines *pl*; (*en tela, diseño*) stripes *pl*, striped pattern

2 (*Caribe Aut*) no parking area

rayador SM 1 (*Méx††*) (= *contador*) paymaster, accountant

2 (*Cono Sur*) (= *árbitro*) umpire

3 (*Cono Sur*) = **rallador**

rayadura SF scratch

rayajo* SM scrawl

rayano ADJ 1 (= *lindante*) adjacent, contiguous (*frm*); (= *fronterizo*) bordering

2 **~ en** bordering on

rayar ▸conjug 1a◂ Ⓐ VT 1 [+ *papel*] to rule, draw lines on

2 [+ *disco, mueble*] to scratch

3 [+ *cheque*] to cross

4 (= *garabatear*) to scribble on

5 [+ *caballo*] to spur on

6 (*Méx*) (= *pagar*) to pay, pay his wages to

7 (*Cono Sur*) = **rallar**

Ⓑ VI 1 **~ con** (= *lindar*) to be next to, be adjacent to

2 **~ en** (= *asemejarse*) to border on, verge on; **esto raya en lo increíble** this verges on the incredible; **raya en los cincuenta** he's pushing fifty*

3 (= *arañar*) to scratch; **este producto no raya al fregar** this product cleans without scratching

4 **al ~ el alba** at break of day, at first light

5 (*Méx*) (= *cobrar*) to draw one's wages

Ⓒ **rayarse** VPR 1 [*objeto*] to get scratched

2 (*Andes*) (= *ver realizados sus deseos*) to see one's dreams come true

3 (*Méx*) (= *enriquecerse*) to get rich

4 (*Andes, Cono Sur**) (= *enojarse*) to lose one's temper

5 (*Cono Sur*) (= *enloquecer*) to go crazy

rayero/a SM/F (*Cono Sur*) linesman, assistant referee

rayo[1] SM 1 [*de luz*] ray, beam ► **rayo de luna** moonbeam ► **rayo de la muerte** death ray ► **rayo de partículas** particle beam ► **rayo de sol** sunbeam, ray of sunlight ► **rayo láser** laser beam ► **rayos catódicos** cathode rays ► **rayos cósmicos** cosmic rays ► **rayos gamma** gamma rays ► **rayos infrarrojos** infrared rays ► **rayos luminosos** light rays ► **rayo solar** sunbeam, ray of sunlight ► **rayos ultravioleta** ultraviolet rays ► **rayos X** X-rays

2 [*de rueda*] spoke

3 (*Meteo*) lightning, flash of lightning; **cayó un ~ en la torre** the tower was struck by lightning; ✦**MODISMOS** **a ~s: huele a ~s*** it smells awful; **sabe a ~s*** it tastes awful; **como un ~** like lightning, like a shot; **la noticia le sentó como un ~** the news hit him like a bombshell; **entrar como un ~** to dash in; **salir como un ~** to dash out; **pasar como un ~** to rush past, flash past; **echar ~s y centellas** to rage, fume; **¡que le parta un ~!*** damn him!*; **¡que me parta un ~ si lo sé!** I'm damned if I know!*; **¡a los demás que les parta un ~!** and the rest of them can go to hell!*; **ser un ~** to be as sharp as they come

4 (*como exclamativo*) **¡~s!*** dammit!*; **¿qué ~s es eso?*** what in hell's name is that?*

rayo[2] *ver* **raer**

rayón SM rayon

rayuela SF (= *juego de adultos*) pitch-and-toss; (*Arg*) (= *juego de niños*) hopscotch

raza[1] SF 1 (= *grupo étnico*) race; [*de animal*] breed; **de ~** ◊ **de pura ~** [*caballo*] thoroughbred; [*perro*] pedigree ► **raza blanca** white race ► **raza humana** human race ► **raza negra** black race

2 (= *estirpe*) stock

raza[2] SF 1 (= *grieta*) crack, slit, fissure; (*en tela*) run

2 (= *rayo*) ray of light

3 (*Perú***) (= *descaro*) cheek*; **¡qué tal ~!** some cheek!*, what a cheek!*

razano ADJ (*Andes*) thoroughbred

razia SF raid

raziar ▸conjug 1b◂ VT to raid

razón SF 1 (= *facultad*) reason; **entrar en ~** to see sense, listen to reason; **hacer que algn entre en ~** to make sb see sense; **perder la ~** to go out of one's mind; **tener uso de ~: escribo desde que tengo uso de ~** I've been writing for as long as I can remember; **apenas tenían uso de ~ cuando ...** they were mere babes in arms when ...

2 (= *verdad*) **asistir la ~: le asiste la ~** he has right on his side; **cargarse de ~** to have

➤ LENGUA Y USO: **razón 2** 38.1, 40.3 **3** 44.1, 44.2, 53.2, 53.6

right fully on one's side; **quiero cargarme de ~ antes de ...** I want to be sure of my case before ...; **con ~ o sin ella** rightly or wrongly; **dar la ~ a algn** (= *estar de acuerdo*) to agree that sb is right; (= *apoyar*) to side with sb; **al final me dio la ~** in the end he agreed that I was right; **quitar la ~ a algn** to say sb is wrong; **tratar de quitar a algn la ~** to try to put sb in the wrong; **~ le sobra** she's only too right; **tener ~** to be right; **no tener ~** to be wrong; **tener parte de ~** to be partly right; **tienen toda la ~ (del mundo)** they're absolutely right

[3] (= *motivo*) reason; **¿cuál era la ~ de su visita?** what was the reason for his visit?; **la ~ por la que lo hizo** the reason why he did it, the reason for his doing it; **sus razones tendrá** he must have his reasons; **con ~** with good reason; **están hartos con toda la ~ (del mundo)** they're fed up and they have good reason to be, they're fed up and rightly so; **¡con ~!** naturally!; **~ de más: ~ de más para ayudarlas** all the more reason to help them; **en ~ a** *o* **de** (= *debido a*) owing to; (= *de acuerdo con*) according to; **no atender a razones: no atiende a razones** he won't listen to reason ► **razón de ser** raison d'être ► **razones de Estado** reasons of State

[4] (= *información*) **"razón: Princesa 4"** "inquiries to 4 Princesa Street", "for further details apply to 4 Princesa Street"; **dar ~ de algo/algn** to give information about sth/sb; **nadie me daba ~ de ella** nobody could tell me anything about her *o* give me any information about her; **nadie supo dar ~ de su paradero** no one knew *o* could tell us his whereabouts; **mandar a algn ~ de que haga algo**† to send word (to sb) to do sth

[5] (*Mat*) ratio; **en ~ directa con** in direct ratio to; **a ~ de: a ~ de cinco a siete** in the ratio of five to seven; **lo devolverán a ~ de mil dólares mensuales** they will pay it back at a rate of a thousand dollars a month; **abandonan el país a ~ de 800 cada año** they are leaving the country at the rate of 800 a year

[6] (*Com*) ► **razón social** trade name, firm's name

razonabilidad SF reasonableness

razonable ADJ reasonable

razonablemente ADV reasonably

razonado ADJ [1] (= *fundado en razones*) reasoned [2] [*cuenta*] itemized, detailed

razonamiento SM reasoning

razonar ▸conjug 1a◂ (A) VT [1] (= *argumentar*) to reason, argue [2] [+ *problema*] to reason out [3] [+ *cuenta*] to itemize (B) VI [1] (= *argumentar*) to reason, argue [2] (= *hablar*) to talk, talk together

razzia ['raθia] SF = **razia**

razziar ▸conjug 1b◂ VT = **raziar**

rbdo. ABR (*Com*) (= **recibido**) recd, rec'd

RCE SF ABR (*Esp*) = **Radio Cadena Española**

RCN SF ABR (*Méx, Col*) = **Radio Cadena Nacional**

RD ABR (*Esp*) = **Real Decreto**

RDA SF ABR (*Hist*) (= **República Democrática Alemana**) GDR

Rdo. ABR (= **Reverendo**) Rev, Revd

RDSI SF ABR (= **Red Digital de Servicios Integrados**) ISDN

re SM (*Mús*) D ► **re mayor** D major

re... PREF [1] (*esp LAm*) (*repetición*) re... [2] (*intensivo*) very; **refrío** very cold; **reguapa** really pretty; **¡rebomba!** (*Esp*†) that's amazing!; **¡rediez!** (*Esp*†) well I'm damned!*

reabastecer ▸conjug 2d◂ (A) VT [*de combustible, de gasolina*] to refuel (B) **reabastecerse** VPR to refuel

reabastecimiento SM refuelling, refueling (*EEUU*)

reabrir ▸conjug 3a◂ (*pp* **reabierto**) (A) VT to reopen; ✦***MODISMO*** **~ las heridas** to open old wounds (B) **reabrirse** VPR to reopen

reacción SF [1] (*Fís, Quím*) reaction (**a, ante** to); ► **reacción nuclear** nuclear reaction [2] (= *respuesta*) response (**a** to); **la ~ blanca** the white backlash ► **reacción en cadena** chain reaction [3] (*Téc*) **avión a** *o* **de ~** jet plane; **propulsión por ~** jet propulsion

reaccionar ▸conjug 1a◂ VI [1] (= *responder*) (*tb Fís, Quím*) to react (**a, ante** to; **contra** against; **sobre** on), respond (**a** to); **¿cómo reaccionó?** how did she react? [2] (= *sobreponerse*) to pull o.s. together

reaccionario/a ADJ, SM/F reactionary

reacio ADJ reluctant; **ser ~ a** to resist, resist the idea of; **ser ~ a hacer algo** to be reluctant *o* unwilling to do sth

reacondicionamiento SM [*de motor*] reconditioning; [*de empresa, organización*] reorganization, restructuring

reacondicionar ▸conjug 1a◂ VT [+ *motor*] to recondition; [+ *empresa, organización*] to reorganize, restructure

reactivación SF reactivating; **~ de la economía** economic recovery, economic upturn

reactivar ▸conjug 1a◂ VT to reactivate

reactividad SF reactivity

reactivo SM reagent

reactor SM [1] (*Fís*) reactor ► **reactor de agua a presión** pressurized water reactor ► **reactor enfriado por gas** gas-cooled reactor ► **reactor generador** breeder reactor ► **reactor nuclear** nuclear reactor ► **reactor reproductor** breeder reactor [2] (*Aer*) (= *motor*) jet engine; (= *avión*) jet plane ► **reactor ejecutivo** executive jet

readaptación SF readjustment ► **readaptación profesional** retraining ► **readaptación social** social rehabilitation

readaptar ▸conjug 1a◂ VT [1] [+ *datos*] to readjust, adapt [2] [+ *persona*] (*profesionalmente*) to retrain; (*socialmente*) to rehabilitate

readmisión SF readmission

readmitir ▸conjug 3a◂ VT to readmit

readquirir ▸conjug 3i◂ VT to recover

reafirmación SF reaffirmation

reafirmar ▸conjug 1a◂ VT to reaffirm, reassert

reagrupación SF regrouping

reagrupar ▸conjug 1a◂ (A) VT to regroup (B) **reagruparse** VPR to regroup

reagudizarse ▸conjug 1f◂ VPR [*problema*] to get worse again; [*enfermedad*] to get worse again, recrudesce

reaje‡ SM (*Cono Sur*) mob, rabble

reajustar ▸conjug 1a◂ (A) VT [1] (= *volver a ajustar*) to readjust [2] (*Pol*) to reshuffle [3] (= *subir*) [+ *precios*] to increase, put up (B) **reajustarse** VPR to readjust

reajuste SM [1] (= *acción*) readjustment; **un doloroso ~ de sus ideas** an agonizing reappraisal of his ideas [2] (*Pol*) reshuffle ► **reajuste ministerial** cabinet reshuffle [3] (*Econ*) ► **reajuste de precios** (= *subida*) price rise, price increase ► **reajuste salarial** (= *recorte*) wage cut

real¹ ADJ (= *verdadero*) real; **esta vez el dolor era ~** this time the pain was real; **en la vida ~** in real life; **la película está basada en hechos ~es** the film is based on real *o* actual events

real² (A) ADJ [1] (= *de la realeza*) royal; **la familia ~** the royal family; **porque no me da la ~ gana*** because I don't damn well feel like it* [2] (†) (= *espléndido*) grand, splendid; **una ~ hembra** (*hum*) a fine figure of a woman (B) SM [1] (*tb* **~ de la feria**) fairground [2] (*Hist*) army camp; ✦***MODISMO*** **asentar** *o* **sentar los ~es** (*Mil*) to set up camp; [*persona*] to install o.s.; **ha asentado sus ~es en mi casa y de aquí no lo sacas** he's installed himself in my house and you won't get him out of here [3] (*Hist, Fin*) *old Spanish coin of 25 céntimos, one quarter of a peseta*; **no tiene un ~*** he hasn't a bean*

reala SF (*CAm, Méx*) rope

realada SF (*Méx*) roundup, rodeo

realar ▸conjug 1a◂ VT (*Méx*) to round up

realce SM [1] (*Téc*) embossing [2] (*Arte*) highlight [3] (= *esplendor*) lustre, luster (*EEUU*), splendour, splendor (*EEUU*); (= *importancia*) importance, significance; **dar ~ a** (= *añadir esplendor*) to add lustre to, enhance; (= *destacar*) to highlight; **poner de ~** to emphasize

realengo ADJ [1] (*LAm*) [*animal*] ownerless [2] (*Méx, Caribe*) (= *ocioso*) idle; (= *libre*) free, unattached

realeza SF royalty

realidad SF reality; **la ~ de la política** the realities of politics; **la ~ siempre supera a la ficción** truth is stranger than fiction; **atengámonos a la ~** let's stick to the facts; **la dura ~** the harsh reality; **en ~** in fact, actually; **la ~ es que ...** the fact (of the matter) is that ... ► **realidad virtual** virtual reality

realimentación SF (*Radio, Inform*) feedback; (*Aer*) refuelling, refueling (*EEUU*)

realineamiento SM realignment

realinear ▸conjug 1a◂ VT to realign

realismo SM realism ► **realismo mágico** magical realism ► **realismo social** social realism ► **realismo sucio** dirty realism

REALISMO MÁGICO

***Realismo mágico**, which derives from a term coined by the Cuban writer Alejo Carpentier in 1949, **lo real maravilloso**, refers to a primarily Latin American literary genre in which the writer combines elements of the fantastic and realistic in a conscious effort to reconcile tradition with modernity and American-Indian and Black oral culture with European literary writing. Such writers felt that post-Enlightenment European culture had sacrificed imaginative experimentation and themes of in-*

➤ LENGUA Y USO: **razonable** 53.2 **realidad** 53.4, 53.6

stinct and desire to an intellectual rationalism which restricted their capacity to explore. The most celebrated magical realist writer is Colombian Nobel prize winner Gabriel García Márquez.

realista Ⓐ ADJ realistic
Ⓑ SMF realist

reality show [re'alitiʃow] SM (*pl* **reality shows**) real-life drama show, reality show (*EEUU*)

realizable ADJ [1] [*propósito*] attainable; [*proyecto*] practical, feasible
[2] (*Fin*) [*activo*] realizable

realización SF [1] [*de proyecto*] carrying out
[2] [*de promesa*] fulfilment, fulfillment (*EEUU*)
[3] [*de propósito*] achievement, realization
[4] [*de viaje, vuelo, visita, compra*] making; **tras la ~ de su primer vuelo** after making his first flight
[5] (*Fin*) realization; (= *venta*) sale, selling-up; (= *liquidación*) clearance sale ► **realización de beneficios, realización de plusvalías** profit taking
[6] (*Cine, TV*) production; (*Radio*) broadcast
[7] (*Ling*) performance

realizado ADJ **sentirse ~** to feel fulfilled

realizador(a) SM/F (*Cine, TV*) producer

realizar ▸conjug 1f◂ Ⓐ VT [1] [+ *propósito*] to achieve, realize; [+ *promesa*] to fulfil, fulfill (*EEUU*), carry out; [+ *proyecto*] to carry out, put into effect
[2] [+ *viaje, vuelo, visita, compra*] to make; [+ *expedición*] to carry out, go on
[3] (*Fin*) [+ *activo*] to realize; [+ *existencias*] to sell off, sell up; [+ *ganancias*] to take
Ⓑ **realizarse** VPR [1] [*sueño*] to come true; [*esperanzas*] to materialize; [*proyecto*] to be carried out
[2] [*persona*] to fulfil o.s., fulfill o.s. (*EEUU*); **~se como persona** to achieve personal fulfilment *o* (*EEUU*) fulfillment, fulfil *o* (*EEUU*) fulfill o.s. as a person

realmente[1] ADV [1] (= *verdaderamente*) really; **fue una época ~ difícil** it was a really difficult period
[2] (= *de hecho*) really, actually; **lo prometió, aunque ~ no pensaba hacerlo** she promised to do it although she didn't actually *o* really intend to; **nunca me creí que fuera él ~ el autor** I never really *o* actually believed that he was the author

realmente[2] ADV (*referente a la realeza*) royally

realojar ▸conjug 1a◂ VT to rehouse

realojo SM rehousing

realquilado/a Ⓐ ADJ sublet
Ⓑ SM/F sublessee

realquilar ▸conjug 1a◂ VT (= *subarrendar*) to sublet; (= *alquilar de nuevo*) to relet

realzar ▸conjug 1f◂ VT [1] (= *dar más importancia*) to enhance, heighten, add to
[2] (*Téc*) to emboss, raise
[3] (*Arte*) to highlight

reanimación SF (= *restablecimiento*) (*tb fig*) revival; [*de un enfermo, accidentado*] resuscitation

reanimar ▸conjug 1a◂ Ⓐ VT [1] (= *dar fuerzas*) to revive; **un té bien caliente te ~á** a nice hot cup of tea will revive you
[2] [+ *enfermo, accidentado*] to revive
[3] (= *dar ánimo*) to cheer up; **sus palabras de consuelo lograron ~la** his words of comfort cheered her up
Ⓑ **reanimarse** VPR to revive

reanudación SF renewal, resumption

reanudar ▸conjug 1a◂ Ⓐ VT [+ *diálogo, viaje*] to resume; **~on su amistad tras una larga separación** they resumed their friendship after a long separation, they took up their friendship again after a long separation; **han reanudado las negociaciones** they have resumed the talks
Ⓑ **reanudarse** VPR to resume; **las clases se ~án el lunes** classes will resume on Monday

reaparecer ▸conjug 2d◂ VI (= *volver a aparecer*) to reappear; [*síntomas*] to recur

reaparición SF (= *nueva aparición*) reappearance; [*de síntomas*] recurrence

reapertura SF reopening

reaplicar ▸conjug 1g◂ VT to reapply

reaprovisionamiento SM replenishment, restocking

reaprovisionar ▸conjug 1a◂ VT to replenish, restock

rearmar ▸conjug 1a◂ Ⓐ VT to rearm
Ⓑ **rearmarse** VPR to rearm

rearme SM rearmament

reasegurar ▸conjug 1a◂ VT to reinsure

reaseguro SM reinsurance

reasentar ▸conjug 1j◂ VT to resettle

reasfaltado SM resurfacing

reasfaltar ▸conjug 1a◂ VT to resurface

reasumir ▸conjug 3a◂ VT to resume, reassume

reata SF [1] (= *cuerda*) rope (*joining string of pack animals*); (*LAm*) (= *lazo*) rope, lasso; (*LAm*) (= *correa*) strap; (*Andes*) (= *tira de algodón*) strip of cotton cloth
[2] (= *caballos*) string, string of horses, pack train; **de ~** (= *en hilera*) in single file, one after the other; (= *sumisamente*) submissively
[3] (*Andes, Caribe, Méx*) [*de flores*] flowerbed, border
[4] (*Méx*) (= *enrejado*) bamboo screen
[5] (*Méx***) (= *pene*) prick**, cock**; **echar ~** to fuck**

reavivar ▸conjug 1a◂ VT to revive

rebaja SF [1] (= *descuento*) reduction, discount; **me hicieron una ~ de seis euros** they gave me a six-euro reduction *o* discount; **¿me puede hacer alguna ~?** could you give me a discount?; **no hacemos devolución en los artículos de ~** sales goods cannot be returned
[2] (= *reducción*) [*de impuestos, tarifas, condena*] reduction; **la empresa propone una ~ de los salarios de un 8%** the company is proposing an 8% wage cut *o* an 8% reduction in wages
[3] **rebajas** (*en comercios*) sales; **las ~s de marzo** the spring sales; **"rebajas"** "sale"; **"grandes rebajas"** "big reductions", "sale"; **están de ~s en Harrods** Harrods have a sale, Harrods are having a sale

rebajamiento SM [1] (= *humillación*) **nunca creí que llegara a tal ~** I never thought that he would lower himself *o* he would stoop so far; **~ de sí mismo** self-abasement
[2] (= *rebaje*) [*de puerta, salario, condena, nivel del agua*] lowering
[3] (= *reducción*) = **rebaja 2**

rebajar ▸conjug 1a◂ Ⓐ VT [1] (= *reducir*) [1·1] (*en dinero*) [+ *impuesto, coste, precio*] to reduce, cut, lower; **algunos bancos ~on ayer sus tipos de interés** some banks reduced *o* cut *o* lowered their interest rates yesterday; **le ~on el precio en un cinco por ciento** they reduced *o* cut the price by five per cent, they took five per cent off; **¿nos han rebajado algo?** have they taken something off?, have they given us a reduction *o* discount?; **hemos rebajado todos nuestros artículos** we have reduced all our stock
[1·2] (*en tiempo*) [+ *condena, castigo*] to reduce; [+ *edad, límite*] to lower; **le ~on la condena por buen comportamiento** his sentence was reduced for good behaviour; **han rebajado la edad penal a los 16 años** they have lowered the age of criminal responsibility to 16; **propusieron ~ la jornada de trabajo** they proposed shortening the working day; **rebajó la plusmarca mundial en 1,2 segundos** he took 1.2 seconds off the world record
[1·3] (*en cantidad*) [+ *nivel, temperatura*] to reduce, lower; [+ *luz, tensión, intensidad*] to reduce; [+ *peso*] to lose; [+ *dolor*] to ease, alleviate; **la OMS aconseja ~ el consumo de azúcar en la dieta** the WHO recommends reducing *o* lowering the sugar intake in one's diet; **quiere ~ cinco kilos** he wants to take off *o* lose five kilos; **el hotel rebajó su categoría de cinco a cuatro estrellas** the hotel reduced its rating from five-star to four-star
[2] (= *diluir*) [+ *líquido*] to dilute; [+ *pintura*] to thin; [+ *color*] to tone down; [+ *droga*] to cut, adulterate; **siempre rebaja el vino con gaseosa** he always dilutes his wine with soda water; **echa un poco más de agua al caldo para ~lo de sal** put a bit more water in the soup to make it less salty
[3] (= *bajar la altura de*) [+ *terreno*] to lower, lower the level of; [+ *tejado*] to lower; [+ *puerta*] to rabbet
[4] (= *humillar*) to humiliate, put down; **rebajó a su mujer delante de sus amigos** he put his wife down *o* humiliated his wife in front of their friends; **piensa que ese trabajo lo rebaja** he thinks that job is beneath him *o* is humiliating; **ese tipo de comportamiento te rebaja** that sort of behaviour does you no credit
[5] (*Mil*) (= *eximir*) to exempt (**de** from)
Ⓑ VI **~ de peso** (*Arg, Uru*) to slim, lose weight; **una dieta para ~ de peso** a diet to lose weight, a slimming diet
Ⓒ **rebajarse** VPR [1] **~se a hacer algo** to lower o.s. to do sth, stoop to do sth; **yo no me ~ía a hablar con él** I wouldn't lower myself *o* I wouldn't stoop to talk to him; **~se ante algn** to humble o.s. before sb; **es demasiado orgulloso para ~se ante ti** he's too proud to humble himself before you
[2] (*Arg, Uru*) **me rebajé el pelo** I had my hair cut in layers

rebaje SM [1] [*de terreno, nivel*] lowering
[2] (*Téc*) (*en madera*) rabbet
[3] (*Econ, Fin*) cut

rebajo SM (*Téc*) rabbet

rebalsa SF pool, puddle

rebalsar ▸conjug 1a◂ Ⓐ VT [1] [+ *agua*] to dam, dam up, block
[2] (*LAm*) [+ *orillas*] to burst, overflow
Ⓑ **rebalsarse** VPR to form a pool, form a lake, become dammed up

rebanada SF [1] (*Culin*) slice
[2] (*Méx*) (= *pestillo*) latch

rebanar ▸conjug 1a◂ VT [+ *pan*] to slice; [+ *árbol*] to slice through, slice down; (*) [+ *pierna*] to slice off

rebañar ▸conjug 1a◂ VT [+ *restos*] to scrape up; **rebañó la salsa (del plato) con pan** he wiped *o* mopped the sauce up (from the plate) with bread; **rebañó el plato de arroz** she mopped up the rice from the plate; **logró ~ ciertos fondos** he managed to scrape some money together

rebaño SM 1 [*de ovejas*] flock; [*de cabras*] herd
2 [*de personas*] (*tb Rel*) flock

rebasar ▸conjug 1a◂ VT 1 [+ *límite*] to pass; [+ *punto*] to pass, go beyond; [+ *límite de tiempo*] to exceed; (*en cualidad, cantidad*) to exceed, surpass; (*en carrera, progreso*) to overtake, leave behind; **han rebasado ya los límites razonables** they have already gone beyond all reasonable limits; **el inglés lo rebasó en la última vuelta** the Englishman overtook *o* passed him on the last lap; **nuestro sistema educativo ya ha rebasado al europeo** our education system has now overtaken the European one
2 (*esp Méx Aut*) to overtake, pass (*EEUU*); (*Náut*) to sail past

rebatible ADJ 1 [*argumento*] easily refuted
2 [*silla*] tip-up

rebatinga SF (*CAm, Méx*) = **rebatiña**

rebatiña SF (*LAm*) scramble, rush; **les echó caramelos a la ~** he threw sweets so that they could scramble for them; **andar a la ~ de algo** (= *pelear por algo*) to scramble for sth, fight over sth; (= *discutir por algo*) to argue fiercely over sth

rebatir ▸conjug 3a◂ VT 1 [+ *ataque*] to repel; [+ *golpe*] to parry, ward off
2 [+ *argumento*] to reject, refute; [+ *sugerencia*] to reject; [+ *tentación*] to resist
3 [+ *suma*] to reduce; [+ *descuento*] to deduct, knock off

rebato SM (= *alarma*) alarm; (*Mil*) surprise attack; **llamar** *o* (*frm*) **tañer** *o* **tocar a ~** to sound the alarm

rebautizar ▸conjug 1f◂ VT to rechristen

Rebeca SF Rebecca

rebeca SF cardigan

rebeco SM chamois, ibex

rebelarse ▸conjug 1a◂ VPR to rebel; **~ contra** to rebel against

rebelde Ⓐ ADJ 1 (= *que se rebela*) rebellious; **el gobierno ~** the rebel government; **ser ~ a algo** to rebel against sth
2 [*niño*] unruly; [*resfriado*] persistent; [*mancha*] stubborn; [*pelo*] wild; [*problema*] difficult; [*sustancia*] difficult to work with
3 (*Jur*) defaulting
Ⓑ SMF 1 (*Mil, Pol*) rebel
2 (*Jur*) defaulter

rebeldía SF 1 (= *cualidad*) rebelliousness; (= *desafío*) defiance, disobedience; **estar en plena ~** to be in open revolt
2 (*Jur*) default; **caer en ~** to be in default; **fue juzgado en ~** he was judged by *o* in default

rebelión SF rebellion

rebelón ADJ hard-mouthed

rebencudo ADJ (*Caribe*) stubborn

rebenque SM (*LAm*) whip, riding crop

rebenqueada* SF (*LAm*) whipping, lashing

rebenquear* ▸conjug 1a◂ VT (*LAm*) to whip, lash

reblandecer ▸conjug 2d◂ VT to soften

reblandecido* ADJ (*Andes*) (= *loco*) soft in the head; (= *senil*) senile

reblandecimiento SM softening; **~ cerebral** softening of the brain

reble‡ SM bum‡, ass (*EEUU***), bottom

rebobinado SM rewinding

rebobinar ▸conjug 1a◂ VT to rewind

rebojo SM crust, piece of bread

rebolichada SF (*Méx*) opportunity

rebolludo ADJ thickset, chunky*

reborde SM (= *saliente*) ledge; (*Téc*) flange, rim

rebosadero SM overflow

rebosante ADJ **~ de** (*lit, fig*) brimming with, overflowing with

rebosar ▸conjug 1a◂ Ⓐ VI 1 [*líquido, recipiente*] to overflow; **el café rebosa de la taza** the coffee cup is running over, the coffee is running *o* spilling over the edge of the cup; **la alegría le rebosa** he bubbles over with happiness; **les rebosa el dinero** they have pots of money; **el grupo llenó la sala a ~** the group filled the room to overflowing
2 **~ de algo** to overflow with sth, be brimming with sth; **~ de salud** to be radiant with health
3 (= *abundar*) to abound, be plentiful
Ⓑ VT to abound in; **su rostro rebosaba salud** he was the picture of health

reboso SM (*Caribe, Cono Sur*) driftwood

rebotado* SM (= *sacerdote*) ex-priest; (= *monje*) former monk

rebotar ▸conjug 1a◂ Ⓐ VT 1 [+ *pelota*] to bounce; [+ *ataque*] to repel, beat back; [+ *rayos*] to bounce back, cause to bounce off
2 [+ *clavo*] to clinch
3 (*) [+ *persona*] to annoy
4 (*Andes, Méx*) [+ *agua*] to muddy, stir up
Ⓑ VI [*pelota*] to bounce; [*bala*] to ricochet, glance (**de** off)
Ⓒ **rebotarse** VPR (*) to get cheesed off*; **~se con algn** to have a dig at sb*, have a go at sb*

rebote SM bounce, rebound; **de ~** (= *en el segundo bote*) on the rebound; (*fig*) (= *de rechazo*) indirectly

reboteador(a) SM/F rebounder

rebotear ▸conjug 1a◂ VI to get rebounds

rebotica SF back room

rebozado ADJ (*Culin*) fried in batter, fried in breadcrumbs

rebozar ▸conjug 1f◂ Ⓐ VT 1 (*Culin*) to roll in batter, roll in breadcrumbs
2 (*frm*) [+ *rostro*] to muffle up, cover
Ⓑ **rebozarse** VPR to muffle (o.s.) up

rebozo SM 1 (= *mantilla*) muffler, wrap; (*LAm*) (= *chal*) shawl
2 (*frm*) (= *ocultación*) dissimulation; **de ~** secretly; **sin ~** openly, frankly

rebrotar ▸conjug 1a◂ VI to break out again, reappear

rebrote SM new outbreak, reappearance

rebufar ▸conjug 1a◂ VI to snort loudly

rebufo SM loud snort

rebujo SM (= *maraña*) mass, knot, tangle; (= *paquete*) badly-wrapped parcel

rebullicio SM (= *bullicio*) hubbub, uproar; (= *agitación*) agitation

rebullir ▸conjug 3a◂ Ⓐ VT (*Méx*) to stir up
Ⓑ **rebullirse** VPR to stir, begin to move

rebultado ADJ bulky

rebumbio* SM (*Méx*) racket, din, hubbub

rebusca SF 1 (= *busca*) search
2 (*Agr*) gleaning
3 (= *restos*) leftovers *pl*, remains *pl*
4 (*Andes, Cono Sur*) (= *negocio*) small business; (*) (= *negocio ilegal*) shady dealing, illicit trading; (= *ganancia*) profit on the side

rebuscado ADJ 1 [*estilo*] affected; [*palabra*] recherché
2 (*LAm*) (= *afectado*) affected, stuck-up*

rebuscar ▸conjug 1g◂ Ⓐ VT 1 [+ *objeto*] to search carefully for; (*Agr*) to glean
2 [+ *lugar*] to search carefully; [+ *montón*] to search through, rummage in
Ⓑ VI (= *buscar minuciosamente*) to search carefully; (*Agr*) to glean; **estuve rebuscando en los armarios y no lo encontré** I was looking in the cupboards and I couldn't find it
Ⓒ **rebuscarse** VPR (*) 1 (*Andes, Cono Sur*) (= *buscar trabajo*) to look for work
2 (*Andes*) (= *ingeniárselas*) to get by

rebuznar ▸conjug 1a◂ VI to bray

rebuzno SM bray, braying

recabar ▸conjug 1a◂ VT 1 (= *obtener*) to manage to get (**de** from); **~ fondos** to raise funds
2 (= *reclamar*) to claim as of right, assert one's claim to
3 (= *solicitar*) to ask for, apply for; (= *exigir*) to demand, insist on

recadero/a SM/F (= *mensajero*) messenger; (= *repartidor*) errand boy/girl

recado SM 1 (= *mensaje*) message; **chico de los ~s** messenger, errand boy; **coger** *o* **tomar un ~** (*por teléfono*) to take a message; **dejar ~** to leave a message; **enviar a algn a un ~** to send sb on an errand; **mandar ~** to send word; **salir a un ~** ◊ **salir a hacer un ~** to go out on an errand
2 (= *provisión*) provisions *pl*, daily shopping
3 (= *equipo*) equipment, materials *pl* ► **recado de escribir** writing case, set of writing materials
4 (*LAm*) (= *montura*) saddle and trappings
5 (*Caribe*) (= *saludos*) greetings *pl*; **déle ~s a su familia** give my regards to his family
6 (††) (= *regalo*) gift, small present

recaer ▸conjug 2n◂ VI 1 (*Med*) to suffer a relapse, relapse
2 [*criminal etc*] to fall back, relapse (**en** into)
3 **~ en** *o* **sobre** [*elección*] to fall on, fall to; [*premio*] to go to; [*legado*] to pass to; [*deber*] to devolve upon; **las sospechas recayeron sobre el conserje** suspicion fell on the porter; **esta carga ~á más sobre los pobres** the poor will be the hardest hit by this burden; **la acusación recayó sobre él mismo** the charge came back on him
4 (*Arquit*) **~ a** to look out on, look over

recaída SF relapse (**en** into)

recalar ▸conjug 1a◂ Ⓐ VT to saturate, soak
Ⓑ VI 1 (*Náut*) to sight land, reach port
2 (*) (= *terminar en*) to end up (**en** at)
3 **~ a algn** (*LAm*) (= *recurrir*) to go to sb for help

▼ **recalcar** ▸conjug 1g◂ Ⓐ VT 1 (= *subrayar*) to stress, emphasize; **~ algo a algn** to stress the importance of sth to sb; **~ a algn que ...** to tell sb emphatically that ...; **~ cada sílaba** to stress every syllable

➤ LENGUA Y USO: **recalcar A1** 53.6

[2] [+ *contenido*] to press down, squeeze in; [+ *recipiente*] to cram, stuff (**de** with)
Ⓑ VI [1] (*Náut*) to list, heel
[2] (*esp LAm*) (= *terminar en*) to end up (**en** at, in)
Ⓒ **recalcarse** VPR **~se un hueso** (*LAm*) to dislocate a bone

recalcitrante ADJ recalcitrant

recalcitrar ▸conjug 1a◂ VI [1] (= *echarse atrás*) to take a step back
[2] (= *resistir*) to resist, be stubborn, refuse to take heed

recalentado ADJ warmed-up

recalentamiento SM [1] (= *calentamiento*) overheating ▸ **recalentamiento del planeta** global warming
[2] (*Culin*) warming-up, reheating

recalentar ▸conjug 1j◂ Ⓐ VT [1] (*demasiado*) to overheat
[2] [+ *comida*] to warm up, reheat
Ⓑ **recalentarse** VPR to get too hot

recalificación SF reassessment

recalificar ▸conjug 1g◂ VT to reassess

recalmón SM lull

recamado SM embroidery

recamar ▸conjug 1a◂ VT to embroider

recámara SF [1] (= *cuarto*) side room; (= *vestidor*) dressing room; (*esp Méx*) (= *dormitorio*) bedroom
[2] [*de fusil*] breech, chamber
[3] (= *cautela*) caution, wariness; **tener mucha ~** to be on the careful side, be naturally cautious

recamarera SF (*esp Méx*) chambermaid, maid

recambiar ▸conjug 1b◂ VT to change over

recambio SM (*Mec*) spare; [*de pluma*] refill; **neumático de ~** spare tyre, spare tire (*EEUU*); **piezas de ~** spares, spare parts

recañí: SF window

recapacitar ▸conjug 1a◂ Ⓐ VT to think over, reflect (up)on
Ⓑ VI to think things over, reflect

recapitulación SF recapitulation, summing-up

recapitular ▸conjug 1a◂ VT, VI to recapitulate, sum up

recargable ADJ rechargeable

recargado ADJ (= *sobrecargado*) overloaded; [*estilo, diseño*] overelaborate

recargar ▸conjug 1h◂ VT [1] [+ *encendedor, bolígrafo*] to refill; [+ *batería, pila*] to recharge; [+ *arma*] to reload
[2] (= *cargar demasiado*) to clutter; **han recargado la habitación con muebles** they have cluttered the room with furniture
[3] (*Fin*) **nos han recargado un 20%** we have to pay a 20% surcharge
[4] (*Jur*†) [+ *sentencia*] to increase

recargo SM [1] (*Fin*) extra charge, surcharge; (= *aumento*) increase
[2] (*Jur*) new charge, further charge
[3] (*Med*) rise in temperature
[4] (= *carga nueva*) new burden; (= *aumento de carga*) extra load, additional load

recatado ADJ [1] (= *modesto*) modest, shy, demure
[2] (= *prudente*) cautious, circumspect

recatar ▸conjug 1a◂ Ⓐ VT to hide
Ⓑ **recatarse** VPR [1] (= *ser discreto*) to act discreetly; **sin ~se** openly
[2] (= *ser prudente*) to be cautious; (= *vacilar*) to hesitate; **~se de algo** to fight shy of sth; **no se recata ante nada** nothing daunts her
[3] (= *ocultarse*) to hide o.s. away (**de** from)

recato SM [1] (= *modestia*) modesty, shyness
[2] (= *cautela*) caution, circumspection; (= *reserva*) reserve, restraint; **sin ~** openly, unreservedly

recatón SM (*Andes*) miner's pick

recauchado SM, **recauchaje** SM (*Chile*) retreading, remoulding, remolding (*EEUU*)

recauchar ▸conjug 1a◂ VT to retread, remould, remold (*EEUU*)

recauchutado SM [1] [*de neumático*] retread
[2] (= *proceso*) retreading, remoulding, remolding (*EEUU*)

recauchutar ▸conjug 1a◂ VT [+ *neumático*] to retread, remould, remold (*EEUU*)

recaudación SF [1] (= *acción*) collection ▸ **recaudación de fondos** fundraising
[2] (= *cantidad*) takings *pl*; (*Dep*) gate, gate money; → QUINIELA
[3] (†) (= *oficina*) tax office

recaudador(a) SM/F ▸ **recaudador(a) de impuestos** tax collector

recaudadora SF (*Andes*) tax office, Internal Revenue Service (*EEUU*)

recaudar ▸conjug 1a◂ VT [+ *impuestos*] to collect; [+ *dinero*] to raise; (*Com*) to take; [+ *fondos*] to raise; [+ *deuda*] to recover

recaudería SF (*Méx*) greengrocer's shop

recaudo SM [1] (*Fin*) collection
[2] (= *cuidado*) care, protection; (= *precaución*) precaution; **estar a buen ~** to be in a safe place; **poner algo a buen ~** to put sth in a safe place
[3] (*Jur*) surety, security
[4] (*CAm, Cono Sur, Méx*) (= *especias*) spices, condiments
[5] (*CAm, Cono Sur, Méx*) (= *legumbres*) *daily supply of fresh vegetables*

recebo SM gravel

recechar ▸conjug 1a◂ VT to stalk

rececho SM stalking; **cazar a** o **en ~** to stalk

recechor(a) SM/F stalker

recelar ▸conjug 1a◂ Ⓐ VT **~ que ...** to suspect that ..., fear that ...
Ⓑ VI **~ de** to be suspicious of; **~ de hacer algo** to be wary of doing sth

recelo SM (= *suspicacia*) suspicion; (= *temor*) misgiving, apprehension; (= *desconfianza*) distrust, mistrust

receloso ADJ (= *suspicaz*) suspicious; (= *desconfiado*) distrustful; (= *temeroso*) apprehensive

recensión SF review

recepción SF [1] (= *acto*) reception
[2] (*Radio*) reception
[3] (= *ceremonia*) reception
[4] (= *cuarto*) drawing room; [*de hotel*] reception, reception desk

recepcionar ▸conjug 1a◂ VT (*esp LAm*) to receive, accept

recepcionista SMF receptionist, hotel receptionist

receptación SF receiving, crime of receiving

receptáculo SM receptacle

receptar ▸conjug 1a◂ VT to receive

receptividad SF receptivity

receptivo ADJ receptive

receptor(a) Ⓐ SM (*Elec, Radio & TV*) receiver ▸ **receptor de televisión** television set
Ⓑ SM/F [1] (*Med*) recipient ▸ **receptor(a) universal** universal recipient
[2] (*Béisbol*) catcher; (*en fútbol americano*) receiver
[3] (*Ling*) recipient

recesar ▸conjug 1a◂ VI (*LAm Pol*) to recess, go into recess

recesión SF (*Com, Fin*) recession; [*de precios*] slide, fall

recesivo ADJ [1] (*Biol*) recessive
[2] (*Econ*) recession *antes de s*, recessionary

receso SM [1] (*LAm Parl*) recess
[2] (*Econ*) ▸ **receso económico** downturn in the economy

receta SF [1] (*Culin*) recipe (**de** for)
[2] (*Med*) prescription; **"con receta médica"** "available on prescription only"

recetar ▸conjug 1a◂ VT [1] (*Med*) to prescribe
[2] (*CAm, Méx*) [+ *golpe*] to deal

recetario SM collection of recipes, recipe book

rechace SM [1] (= *rechazo*) rejection
[2] (*Dep*) rebound

rechazamiento SM [1] [*de ataque, enemigo*] repelling, repulsion
[2] [*de acusación, idea*] rejection; [*de oferta*] refusal; [*de tentación*] resistance, rejection
[3] [*de luz*] reflection
[4] (*Med*) [*de órgano*] rejection

▼**rechazar** ▸conjug 1f◂ VT [1] [+ *persona*] to push away; [+ *ataque*] to repel, beat off; [+ *enemigo*] to drive back
[2] [+ *acusación, idea*] to reject; [+ *oferta*] to turn down, refuse; [+ *tentación*] to resist
[3] [+ *luz*] to reflect; [+ *agua*] to throw off
[4] (*Med*) [+ *órgano*] to reject

rechazo SM [1] (= *negativa*) refusal; **~ frontal** [*de propuesta*] outright rejection; [*de oferta*] flat refusal
[2] (*Med*) rejection
[3] (= *rebote*) bounce, rebound; **de ~** on the rebound
[4] (= *desaire*) rebuff
[5] [*de fusil*] recoil

rechifla SF [1] (= *silbido*) whistling; (= *abucheo*) booing; (*Teat*) catcall
[2] (= *burla*) mockery

rechiflar ▸conjug 1a◂ Ⓐ VT (= *silbar*) to whistle at; (= *abuchear*) to boo
Ⓑ VI (= *silbar*) to whistle; (= *abuchear*) boo
Ⓒ **rechiflarse** VPR [1] **~se de algn** to make a fool of sb
[2] (*Cono Sur*) (= *enojarse*) to get cross, lose one's temper

rechín SM (*Andes*) piece of burnt food; **huele a ~** I can smell food burning

rechinamiento SM [*de madera, puerta*] creak, creaking; [*de máquina*] clank, clanking; [*de metal seco*] grating; [*de motor*] grinding, whirr, whirring; [*de dientes*] grinding

rechinar ▸conjug 1a◂ Ⓐ VI [1] (= *chirriar*) [*madera, puerta*] to creak; [*máquina*] to clank; [*metal seco*] to grate; [*motor*] to grind, whirr; [*dientes*] to grind, gnash; **hacer ~ los dientes** to grind one's teeth
[2] (*Andes, Cono Sur, Méx**) (= *rabiar*) to rage, fume
[3] (*Caribe*) (= *quejarse*) to grumble; (= *contestar*) to answer back
Ⓑ VT (*CAm, Méx Culin*) to burn, overcook

➤ LENGUA Y USO: **rechazar 2** 39.1

Ⓒ **rechinarse** VPR [1] (*CAm, Méx*) (= *quemarse*) to burn, overcook
[2] (*Cono Sur**) (= *enojarse*) to get cross, lose one's temper

rechinido SM, **rechino** SM = **rechinamiento**

rechistar ▸conjug 1a◂ VI to complain; **se fue a la cama sin ~** he went to bed without complaint, he went to bed without a word of complaint; **nadie se atrevió a ~** nobody dared complain

rechonchez SF stockiness

rechoncho ADJ thickset, stocky

rechupete: **de ~*** Ⓐ ADJ (= *estupendo*) splendid, jolly good*; [*comida*] delicious, scrumptious*
Ⓑ ADV splendidly, jolly well*; **pasarlo de ~** to have a fantastic time*; **el examen me ha salido de ~** the exam went like a dream for me

recial SM rapids *pl*

reciamente ADV (= *fuertemente*) strongly; (= *con intensidad*) intensely

recibí SM "received with thanks"; **poner el ~ en algo** to sign for sth

recibidero ADJ receivable

recibido ADJ (*LAm*) qualified

recibidor[1] SM [*de casa*] hall

recibidor[2]**(a)** SM/F (= *persona*) recipient, receiver

recibimiento SM [1] (= *acogida*) welcome, reception; **dispensar a algn un ~ apoteósico** to give sb a tremendous *o* (*frm*) rapturous welcome *o* reception
[2] (†) (= *antesala*) anteroom, vestibule; (= *sala*) reception room; (= *vestíbulo*) hall

▼ **recibir** ▸conjug 3a◂ Ⓐ VT [1] (= *ser beneficiario de*) [1·1] [+ *dinero, apoyo, llamada, noticias*] to receive, get; [+ *ayuda, homenaje*] to receive; **~án una compensación económica** they'll get compensation, they will receive financial compensation (*más frm*); **he recibido del Sr Gómez la cantidad de ...** (*en recibo*) received from Sr Gómez the sum of ...; **¿recibiste mi carta?** did you get my letter?; **estamos a la espera de ~ más mercancía** we're waiting for some new stock to arrive; **recibió el premio a la mejor película extranjera** it won the prize for best foreign film; **recibió la orden de vender las acciones** he was instructed to sell the shares; **no reciben bien el Canal 8** the reception is not very good on Channel 8; **"mensaje recibido"** (*Radio*) "message received"; **~ asistencia médica** to receive medical assistance, be given medical assistance; **~ el calificativo de** to be labelled (as); **~ el nombre de** (*frm*) (= *llamarse*) to be called; (*al nacer*) to be named
[1·2] [*lago, río, mar*] **el río recibe las aguas de numerosos afluentes** a great many tributaries flow into the river
[2] (= *sufrir*) [+ *susto*] to get; **recibió un susto tremendo** she got a terrible shock; **~ un disparo** to be shot; **~ un golpe** to be hit, be struck
[3] [+ *persona*] [3·1] (= *acoger*) to welcome; **estaba en la puerta para ~ a los invitados** she was at the door to welcome the guests; **los recibieron muy mal** they were given a very poor welcome; **nos recibieron con gran alegría** they gave us a very warm welcome; **recibía a sus invitados en el salón** she entertained her guests in the drawing room; **ir a ~ a algn** to meet sb; **fueron a ~los a la estación** they went to meet them at the station; **salieron a ~los al jardín** they received them in the garden; ✦**MODISMO** **~ a algn con los brazos abiertos** to welcome sb with open arms
[3·2] (*para reunión, entrevista*) (*gen*) to see; (*formalmente*) to receive; **el doctor lo ~á enseguida** the doctor will see you in a moment; **el rey se negó a ~los** the king refused to receive them; **hoy no puede ~ visitas** she can't receive visitors today; **no se les permite ~ visitas de sus familiares** they are not allowed family visits
[3·3] (*en el matrimonio*) to take; **la recibió por esposa** he took her as *o* for his wife
[4] (*Taur*) **~ al toro** to meet the bull's charge
[5] (= *aceptar*) [+ *propuesta, sugerencia*] to receive; **la oferta fue mal recibida** the offer was badly received
[6] (*en correspondencia*) **recibe un fuerte abrazo de tus padres** lots of love from Mum and Dad; **reciba un saludo de ...** yours sincerely ...; **recibe mi más sincera felicitación** my sincerest congratulations
[7] (= *sostener*) [+ *peso*] to bear; **estas paredes reciben el peso de la casa** these are load-bearing walls
Ⓑ VI [1] (*frm*) (*en casa*) (= *tener invitados*) to entertain; (= *tener visitas*) to receive visitors; **reciben mucho en casa** they entertain a lot; **la baronesa sólo puede ~ los lunes** the baroness is only at home on Mondays, the baroness can only receive visitors on Mondays
[2] [*médico*] to see patients; **el dentista no recibe los viernes** the dentist doesn't see patients on Fridays
Ⓒ **recibirse** VPR (*LAm Univ*) to graduate; **aún no se ha recibido** he hasn't graduated yet; **me faltan dos años para ~me** I've got two years to go before I graduate; **~se de** to qualify as; **~se de abogado** to qualify as a lawyer; **~se de doctor** to get *o* (*frm*) take one's doctorate, receive one's doctor's degree

recibo SM [1] (= *factura*) bill, account; **~ de la luz** electricity bill
[2] [*de dinero*] receipt; **acusar ~ (de algo)** to acknowledge receipt (of sth)
[3] ✦**MODISMO** **ser de ~**: **no es de ~ que...** it is unacceptable that ...
[4] (*frm*) **estar de ~** [*persona*] to be at home, be at home to callers; [*traje, objeto*] to be ready for collection

reciclable ADJ recyclable

reciclado Ⓐ ADJ recycled
Ⓑ SM (*Téc*) recycling; [*de persona*] retraining

reciclador ADJ recycling

recicladora SF (= *planta*) recycling plant; (= *empresa*) recycling firm

reciclaje SM, **reciclamiento** SM [*de papel, vidrio*] recycling; [*de profesional*] retraining; [*de plan*] modification, adjustment

reciclar ▸conjug 1a◂ Ⓐ VT (*Téc*) to recycle; [+ *profesional*] to retrain; [+ *plan*] to modify, adjust
Ⓑ **reciclarse** VPR [*profesional*] to retrain

recidiva SF relapse

reciedumbre SF (= *fuerza*) strength; (= *vigor*) vigour, vigor (*EEUU*)

recién ADV [1] (*antepuesto a participio*) newly; **~ casado** newly married; **los ~ casados** the newlyweds; **~ hecho** newly-made; **~ llegado** newly arrived; **los ~ llegados** (*a un lugar*) the newcomers; (*a una reunión*) the latecomers; **el ~ nacido** the newborn; **un ~ nacido** a newborn child
[2] (*LAm*) (= *apenas*) just, recently; **~ llegó** he has only just arrived, he arrived only recently; **~ se acordó** he has just remembered it; **~ me lo acaban de decir** they've only just told me; **~ ahora** right now, this very moment; **~ aquí** right here, just here

reciente ADJ recent; **un descubrimiento muy ~** a very recent discovery; **su muerte está aún muy ~ en nuestra memoria** her death is still very fresh in our memory

recientemente ADV recently

Recife SM Recife; (††) Pernambuco

recinto SM (= *cercado*) enclosure; (= *área*) area, place; (= *zona delimitada*) precincts *pl*; **dentro del ~ universitario** on the university campus ► **recinto amurallado** walled enclosure ► **recinto ferial** exhibition site ► **recinto fortificado** fortified place ► **recinto penitenciario** prison grounds *pl*

recio Ⓐ ADJ [1] (= *fuerte*) [*persona*] strong, tough; [*cuerda*] thick, strong; [*prueba*] tough, demanding, severe; [*tierra*] solid
[2] [*voz*] loud
[3] [*tiempo*] harsh, severe
[4] (= *intenso*) **en lo más ~ del combate** in the thick of the fight; **en lo más ~ del invierno** in the depths of winter
Ⓑ ADV [*soplar, golpear*] hard; [*cantar, gritar*] loudly

recipiendario/a SM/F (*frm*) newly-elected member

recipiente Ⓐ SMF (= *persona*) recipient
Ⓑ SM (= *vaso*) container

reciprocación SF reciprocation

recíprocamente ADV reciprocally, mutually

reciprocar ▸conjug 1g◂ VT to reciprocate

reciprocidad SF reciprocity; **usar de ~** to reciprocate

recíproco ADJ (= *mutuo*) reciprocal; (= *inverso*) inverse; **a la recíproca** vice versa; **estar a la recíproca** to be ready to respond

recitación SF recitation

recitado SM (= *recitación*) recitation; (*Mús*) recitative

recital SM [*de música*] recital; [*de literatura*] reading; **dio todo un ~ del arte de torear** he gave a virtuoso demonstration of the bullfighter's art ► **recital de poesía** poetry reading

recitar ▸conjug 1a◂ VT to recite

recitativo SM recitative

reclamable ADJ reclaimable

reclamación SF [1] (= *queja*) complaint; **formular** *o* **presentar una ~** to make *o* lodge a complaint
[2] (= *reivindicación*) claim ► **reclamación salarial** wage claim

reclamar ▸conjug 1a◂ Ⓐ VT [1] [+ *herencia, tierras*] to claim; [+ *derechos*] to demand; **reclama su parte de los beneficios** he is claiming his share of the profits; **~ daños y perjuicios** to claim damages; **reclaman mejores condiciones de trabajo** they're demanding better working conditions; **~ una deuda** to demand payment of a debt; **~on su presencia ante el tribunal** they demanded him to appear before the court

➤ LENGUA Y USO: **recibir A1** 47.4

2 [+ *atención, solución*] to demand; **esto reclama toda nuestra atención** this demands our full attention
3 [+ *aves*] to call to
(B) VI (= *quejarse*) to complain; **fui a ~ al director** I went and complained to the manager; **~ contra algo** to complain about sth; **~ contra una sentencia** (*Jur*) to appeal against a sentence
(C) **reclamarse** VPR [*aves*] to call to one another

reclame SM o SF (*LAm*) advertisement; **mercadería de ~** loss leader

reclamo SM 1 (*Orn*) call; (*Caza*) decoy, lure
2 (= *llamada*) call; **acudir al ~** to answer the call
3 (= *anuncio*) advertisement; (= *slogan*) advertising slogan; (= *aliciente*) lure, attraction; (*Tip*) catchword ► **reclamo publicitario** advertising ploy
4 (*Jur*) claim
5 (= *afirmación*) claim, statement
6 (*LAm*) (= *protesta*) complaint

reclinable ADJ **asiento ~** reclining seat

reclinar ▸conjug 1a◂ (A) VT to lean, recline, rest (**contra** against; **sobre** on)
(B) **reclinarse** VPR to lean back

reclinatorio SM prie-dieu

recluir ▸conjug 3g◂ (A) VT (= *encerrar*) to shut away; (*Jur*) (= *encarcelar*) to imprison
(B) **recluirse** VPR to shut o.s. away

reclusión SF 1 (= *encarcelamiento*) imprisonment, confinement ► **reclusión mayor** imprisonment in conditions of maximum security ► **reclusión perpetua** life imprisonment
2 (= *cárcel*) prison
3 (= *encierro voluntario*) seclusion

recluso/a (A) ADJ imprisoned; **población reclusa** prison population
(B) SM/F 1 (*Jur*) inmate, prisoner ► **recluso/a de confianza** trusty ► **recluso/a preventivo/a** prisoner on remand, remand prisoner
2 (= *ermitaño*) recluse

reclusorio SM (*esp Méx*) prison

recluta (A) SMF (= *persona*) recruit
(B) SF (= *reclutamiento*) recruitment

reclutamiento SM recruitment

reclutar ▸conjug 1a◂ VT 1 [+ *soldados*] to recruit; [+ *trabajadores*] to contract, take on
2 (*Arg*) [+ *ganado*] to round up

recobrar ▸conjug 1a◂ (A) VT [+ *salud*] to recover, get back; [+ *ciudad, fugitivo*] to recapture; [+ *amistad*] to win back; **~ las fuerzas** to get one's strength back; **~ el conocimiento** to regain consciousness, come to; **sólo ha recobrado parte del dinero que le robaron** he has recovered only part of the money stolen from him; **el país ha recobrado la calma** the country is calm again, calm has returned to the country
(B) **recobrarse** VPR 1 (*Med*) (= *recuperarse*) to recover; **aún no se ha recobrado del accidente** he still hasn't recovered from the accident
2 (*frm*) (= *volver en sí*) to regain consciousness, come to
3 (*frm*) (= *serenarse*) to collect o.s.

recobro SM [*de salud*] recovery; [*de ciudad, fugitivo*] recapture; [*de dinero*] recovery, retrieval

➤ LENGUA Y USO: recomendación 1 46.5

recocer ▸conjug 2b, 2h◂ (A) VT 1 (= *calentar*) to warm up, heat up; (= *cocer demasiado*) to overcook
2 (*Metal*) to anneal
3 (*Cono Sur*) (= *cocer*) to cook
(B) **recocerse** VPR (*) (= *reconcomerse*) to be eaten up inside

recochinearse* ▸conjug 1a◂ VPR **~ de algn** (*Esp*) to take the mickey out of sb*

recochineo* SM mickey-taking*

recocina SF scullery

recodar ▸conjug 1a◂ VI to form a bend

recodo SM bend, turn

recogecables SM INV automatic cable retractor

recogedor SM (= *recipiente*) dustpan; (= *herramienta*) rake, scraper

recogepelotas SMF INV ball boy/ball girl

recoger ▸conjug 2c◂ (A) VT 1 (= *levantar*) [+ *objeto caído*] to pick up; [+ *objetos dispersos*] to gather (up), gather together; **se agachó para ~ la cuchara** he bent down to pick up the spoon; **recogí el papel del suelo** I picked the paper up off the floor; **recogió la ropa del suelo** she gathered the clothes up off the floor; **si tiras agua en el suelo recógela con la fregona** if you spill water on the floor mop it up
2 (= *recolectar*) [+ *datos, información*] to gather, collect; [+ *dinero, firmas*] to collect; [+ *correo, basura*] to collect, pick up; **¿a qué hora recogen el correo?** what time is the mail o post collected?, what time do they collect the mail o post?; **a las diez recogen la basura** the rubbish gets collected at ten o'clock
3 (= *ordenar*) [+ *objetos*] to clear up, clear away; [+ *casa, habitación*] to tidy up, straighten up; **recógelo todo antes de marcharte** clear up everything before you leave; **recogí los platos y los puse en el fregadero** I cleared away the plates and put them in the sink; **~ la mesa** to clear the table; **recoge tus cosas** get your things together, gather up your things
4 (= *guardar*) [+ *ropa lavada*] to take in, get in; [+ *herramientas*] to put away
5 (*Agr*) to harvest, gather in, take in; [+ *fruta, guisantes*] to pick; [+ *flores*] to pick, gather
6 (= *reducir, ajustar*) [+ *cuerda, vela*] to take in; [+ *alas*] to fold; [+ *cuernos*] to draw in; [+ *falda*] to gather up, lift up; [+ *mangas*] to roll up; (*Cos*) to take in, reduce, shorten
7 (= *almacenar*) [+ *polvo*] to gather; [+ *líquido*] to absorb, take up; (*en recipiente*) to collect
8 (= *ir a buscar*) [+ *persona*] to pick up, fetch, collect; [+ *billetes, paquete*] to collect, pick up; **te vendremos a ~ a las ocho** we'll come and pick you up o fetch you o collect you at eight o'clock, we'll come for you at eight o'clock
9 (= *mostrar*) to show; **la imagen recoge uno de los momentos más dramáticos** the picture shows o captures one of the most dramatic moments; **el informe recoge la situación** the situation is described in the report
10 (= *incluir*) to include; **el informe recoge diversas sugerencias** various suggestions are included in the report, the report includes various suggestions; **vocablos que no están recogidos en el diccionario** words not included in the dictionary
11 [+ *demandas, reivindicaciones*] to take into account; **el acuerdo recoge las demandas de los indígenas** the agreement takes into account the demands of the native people
12 (= *recibir*) **ahora empieza a ~ los frutos de su esfuerzo** she's beginning to reap the reward(s) of her efforts; **no recogió más que censuras** he received nothing but condemnation; **de todo esto van a ~ muy poco** they won't get much back out of all this, they will get very little return from all this
13 (= *retirar*) [+ *periódico, libro*] to seize; [+ *moneda*] to call in; **las autoridades recogieron todos los ejemplares** the authorities seized all the copies; **van a ~ las monedas antiguas** they are going to call in the old coins
14 (= *dar asilo*) to take in, shelter
(B) VI (= *ordenar*) to tidy up, straighten up; (*al cerrar, terminar*) to clear up
(C) **recogerse** VPR 1 (= *retirarse*) to withdraw, retire; (*a casa*) to go home; (= *acostarse*) to go to bed
2 (= *refugiarse*) to take shelter
3 [+ *falda*] to gather up, lift up; [+ *mangas, pantalones*] to roll up; **~se el pelo** to put one's hair up; **se recogió el pelo en un moño** she put her hair up in a bun; **se recogió el pelo en una coleta** he tied his hair back in a ponytail

recogida SF 1 [*de basura, correo*] collection; **hay seis ~s diarias** there are six collections a day ► **recogida de basuras** refuse collection, garbage collection (*EEUU*) ► **recogida de datos** (*Inform*) data capture ► **recogida de equipajes** (*Aer*) baggage reclaim
2 (*Agr*) harvest
3 (= *retiro*) withdrawal, retirement
4 (*Méx Agr*) round-up; (*Cono Sur*) [*de policía*] sweep, raid

recogido (A) ADJ 1 [*vida*] quiet; [*lugar*] secluded; [*persona*] reserved, retiring; **ella vive muy recogida** she lives very quietly
2 (= *apretado*) bunched up, tight
(B) SM tuck, gathering

recogimiento SM 1 (= *estado*) absorption; **vivir con ~** to live in seclusion, live in peace and quiet
2 (*Rel*) recollection
3 (= *retirada*) withdrawal

recolección SF 1 [*de dinero*] collection ► **recolección de basura** (*esp LAm*) refuse collection, garbage collection (*EEUU*)
2 (*Agr*) (= *acto*) harvesting; (= *época*) harvest time
3 (= *recopilación*) compilation; (= *resumen*) summary
4 (*Rel*) retreat

recolectar ▸conjug 1a◂ VT = **recoger A2**

recolector(a) SM/F (*Agr*) picker

recoleto ADJ 1 [*persona*] quiet, retiring
2 [*calle*] quiet

recolocación SF relocation

recolocar ▸conjug 1g◂ VT to relocate

recomendable ADJ recommendable; **poco ~** inadvisable; **es una persona muy poco ~** he's someone I wouldn't recommend

▼ **recomendación** SF 1 (= *consejo*) recommendation
2 (*para un trabajo*) **carta de ~** letter of introduction o recommendation (**para** to); **tiene buenas recomendaciones** he is strongly recommended

3 (*Rel*) ► **recomendación del alma** prayers *pl* for the dying

recomendado ADJ (*LAm*) registered

recomendar ▸conjug 1j◂ VT 1 (= *aconsejar*) to recommend; **~ a algn que haga algo** to recommend *o* advise sb to do sth; **le recomiendo esta novela** I recommend this novel to you

2 (*para un trabajo*) to recommend; **lo ~on para el puesto** he was recommended for the job

3 (*LAm Correos*) to register

recomendatorio ADJ recommendatory; **carta recomendatoria** letter of introduction (**para** to)

recomenzar ▸conjug 1f, 1j◂ VT, VI to begin again, recommence

recomerse ▸conjug 2a◂ VPR to bear a secret grudge, harbour *o* (*EEUU*) harbor resentment

recompensa SF 1 (*por un servicio*) reward, recompense; **como** *o* **en ~ por los servicios prestados** (in return) for services rendered

2 (*por daño, perjuicio*) (= *compensación*) compensation (**de** for)

recompensar ▸conjug 1a◂ VT 1 [+ *servicio*] to reward, recompense; **"se recompensará"** "reward offered"

2 [+ *daño, perjuicio*] to compensate

recomponer ▸conjug 2q◂ VT 1 (= *arreglar*) to mend, repair

2 (*Tip*) to reset

recompra SF repurchase, buying back

recomprar ▸conjug 1a◂ VT to repurchase, buy back

reconcentrar ▸conjug 1a◂ Ⓐ VT 1 (= *concentrar*) [+ *atención*] to concentrate, devote (**en** to)

2 (= *juntar*) to bring together

3 [+ *solución*] to make more concentrated

4 (= *disimular*) to hide

Ⓑ **reconcentrarse** VPR (= *concentrarse*) to concentrate hard, become totally absorbed

reconciliable ADJ reconcilable

reconciliación SF reconciliation

reconciliar ▸conjug 1b◂ Ⓐ VT to reconcile

Ⓑ **reconciliarse** VPR to become reconciled, be reconciled

reconcomerse ▸conjug 2a◂ VPR to bear a secret grudge, harbour *o* (*EEUU*) harbor resentment

reconcomio SM 1 (= *rencor*) grudge, resentment

2 (= *deseo*) urge, longing, itch

3 (= *sospecha*) suspicion

recóndito ADJ recondite; **en lo más ~ de** in the depths of; **en lo más ~ del corazón** in one's heart of hearts; **en lo más ~ de mi ser** deep down inside

reconducir ▸conjug 3n◂ VT 1 [+ *persona*] to take back, bring back (**a** to)

2 (*Jur*) to renew, extend

reconfortante Ⓐ ADJ (= *que conforta*) comforting; (= *que anima*) cheering

Ⓑ SM (*LAm*) tonic

reconfortar ▸conjug 1a◂ Ⓐ VT 1 (= *confortar*) to comfort; (= *animar*) to cheer, encourage

2 (*Med*) to strengthen

Ⓑ **reconfortarse** VPR **~se con** to fortify o.s. with

reconocer ▸conjug 2d◂ Ⓐ VT 1 (= *conocer*) to recognize; **no te he reconocido con ese sombrero** I didn't recognize you in that hat; **le reconocí por la voz** I knew *o* recognized him by his voice

2 (= *identificar*) to identify; **tuvo que ~ el cadáver de su hermano** he had to identify his brother's body

3 (= *considerar*) [+ *gobierno, hijo*] to recognize; **no le reconocieron como jefe** they did not recognize him as their leader

4 (= *admitir*) to admit; **reconócelo, ha sido culpa tuya** admit it, it was your fault; **hay que ~ que no es normal** you have to admit (that) it isn't normal; **reconozco que no existen pruebas** I admit that there is no evidence; **el acusado reconoció los hechos** the accused admitted what he had done; **me reconoció el mérito de haberlo hecho** he gave me the credit for doing it

5 (= *agradecer*) [+ *servicio*] to be grateful for

6 (*Med*) [+ *paciente*] to examine

7 [+ *terreno*] to survey; (*Mil*) to reconnoitre, spy out

8 (= *registrar*) to search

Ⓑ **reconocerse** VPR **se ha reconocido culpable** he has admitted his guilt

reconocible ADJ recognizable

reconocido ADJ 1 [*jefe*] recognized, accepted

2 (*frm*) (= *agradecido*) **estar** *o* **quedar ~** to be grateful

reconocimiento SM 1 (= *aprobación*) recognition; **en ~ a** ◊ **como ~ por** in recognition of

2 (= *registro*) search, searching; (= *inspección*) inspection, examination ► **reconocimiento de firma** (*Méx*) authentication of a signature

3 (*Mil*) reconnaissance; **vuelo de ~** reconnaissance flight

4 (*Med*) examination, checkup ► **reconocimiento físico** physical examination ► **reconocimiento médico** medical (examination)

5 (*Inform*) ► **reconocimiento de la voz** speech recognition ► **reconocimiento óptico de caracteres** optical character recognition

reconquista SF reconquest, recapture; **la Reconquista** the Reconquest (*of Spain*)

RECONQUISTA

The term **Reconquista** *refers to the eight centuries during which the Christian kings of the Spanish kingdoms gradually reclaimed their country from the Moors, who had invaded the Iberian Peninsula in 711. It is generally accepted that the reconquest began in 718 with the Christian victory at Covadonga in Asturias, and ended in 1492, when Ferdinand and Isabella, the* **Reyes Católicos**, *Catholic Monarchs, retook Granada, the last Muslim stronghold. In the intervening centuries there had been a great deal of contact and overlap between the two cultures. Christians living under Arab rule were called* **mozárabes**, *while* **mudéjares** *were practising Muslims living under Christian rule. In contrast with the pluralistic society that had existed under the Arabs, the final years of the* **Reconquista** *were a time of great intolerance with Arabs and Jews being forcibly converted to Christianity, after which they were known as* **conversos**. *Those refusing to be converted were expelled in 1492.*

reconquistar ▸conjug 1a◂ VT 1 (*Mil*) [+ *terreno*] to regain, reconquer; [+ *ciudad*] to recapture (**a** from)

2 (*fig*) [+ *estima*] to recover, win back

reconsideración SF reconsideration

reconsiderar ▸conjug 1a◂ VT to reconsider

reconstitución SF (= *acto*) reconstitution, reforming; [*de crimen, escena*] reconstruction

reconstituir ▸conjug 3g◂ VT (= *rehacer*) to reconstitute; [+ *crimen, escena*] to reconstruct

reconstituyente SM tonic

reconstrucción SF reconstruction

reconstruir ▸conjug 3g◂ VT to reconstruct

recontar ▸conjug 1l◂ VT 1 [+ *cantidad*] to recount, count again

2 [+ *cuento*] to retell, tell again

recontra* Ⓐ PREF (*LAm*) extremely, terribly; **~caro** terribly dear; **~bueno** really good; **estoy ~cansado** I'm terribly tired

Ⓑ EXCL well I'm ...!*

reconvención SF 1 (*frm*) (= *reprensión*) reprimand

2 (*Jur*) counterclaim

reconvenir ▸conjug 3r◂ VT 1 (= *reprender*) to reprimand

2 (*Jur*) to counterclaim

reconversión SF (= *reestructuración*) restructuring, reorganization ► **reconversión industrial** industrial rationalization ► **reconversión profesional** retraining

reconvertir ▸conjug 3i◂ VT 1 (= *transformar*) to reconvert (**en** to)

2 (= *reestructurar*) to restructure, reorganize; [+ *industria*] to rationalize; **~ profesionalmente** to retrain

recopa SF cup-winners' cup

recopilación SF 1 (= *recolección*) compilation; (= *resumen*) summary ► **recopilación de datos** (*Inform*) data collection

2 (*Jur*) code; **la Recopilación** *Spanish law code of 1567*; **la Nueva Recopilación** *Spanish law code of 1775*

recopilador(a) SM/F compiler

recopilar ▸conjug 1a◂ VT 1 (= *reunir*) to compile; (= *resumir*) to summarize

2 [+ *leyes*] to codify

recopilatorio Ⓐ ADJ compilation *antes de s*

Ⓑ SM compilation

récord, record ['rekor] Ⓐ ADJ INV record; **cifras ~** record numbers; **en un tiempo ~** in a record time

Ⓑ SM (*pl* **récords, records** ['rekor]) record; **batir el ~** to break the record

recordable ADJ memorable

recordación SF recollection; **digno de ~** memorable

recordar[1] ▸conjug 1l◂ Ⓐ VT 1 (= *acordarse de*) to remember; **prefieren no ~ aquellos tiempos** they prefer not to remember those times; **1999 será recordado como un año estupendo para todos** 1999 will be remembered as a great year for everybody; **recuerdo que un día se me acercó y me dijo ...** I remember that one day she came over to me and said ...; **no lo recuerdo** I can't remember, I don't remember; **creo ~ que ...** I seem to remember *o* recall that ...; **~ haber hecho algo** to remember doing *o* having done sth; **recuerda haberlo dicho** he remembers saying *o* having said it; **no recuerdo haberte dado permiso para salir** I don't remember *o*

recall giving o having given you permission to go out; **~ que** to remember that; **recuerdo que no llegó hasta por la noche** I remember that he didn't arrive until nighttime
2 (= *traer a la memoria*) to remind; **estas botas me recuerdan a las que llevábamos de pequeños** these boots remind me of the ones we used to wear as children; **¿a qué te recuerda esa foto?** what does that photo remind you of?; **el poema recuerda a García Lorca** the poem is reminiscent of García Lorca; **~ algo a algn** to remind sb of sth; **recuérdale que me debe 50 dólares** remind him that he owes me 50 dollars; **te recuerdo que son las tres** let me remind you that it's three o'clock; **me permito ~le que aún no hemos recibido el pago** I would remind you o may I remind you that we have not yet received payment; **~ a algn que haga algo** to remind sb to do sth; **recuérdame que ponga la lavadora** remind me to put the washing (machine) on
3 (*Méx**) (= *despertar*) to wake up
Ⓑ VI to remember; **no recuerdo** I can't o don't remember; **si mal no recuerdo** if my memory serves me right o correctly, if I remember rightly o correctly; **que yo recuerde** as far as I can remember, as I recall (*frm*)
Ⓒ **recordarse** VPR 1 (*Cono Sur, Méx**) (= *despertar*) to wake up
2 (*Andes, Caribe*) (= *volver en sí*) to come to, come round
3 (*Chile*) (= *acordarse*) **ahora que me estoy recordando, la conocí en Madrid** now that I remember, I met her in Madrid; **apenas me recuerdo de mi antigua casa** I (can) hardly remember my old house

recordar² ▸conjug 1l◂ VT (*CAm, Caribe, Méx*) [+ *voz*] to record

recordativo ADJ reminiscent; **carta recordativa** reminder

recordatorio SM 1 (= *tarjeta*) [*de fallecimiento*] in memoriam card; [*de primera comunión*] First Communion card
2 (= *aviso*) reminder; **esto te servirá de ~** let this be a reminder to you

recordman SM, **récordman** SM (*pl* **recordmans** o **récordmans**) record holder

recorrer ▸conjug 2a◂ VT 1 [+ *ciudad, país*] to travel around; **recorrimos Francia en moto** we travelled around France on a motorbike; **~ una ciudad a pie** to walk round a city, do a city on foot
2 [+ *trayecto*] to cover, do; **ese día recorrimos 100 kilómetros** we covered o did 100 kilometres that day; **aún nos quedan diez kilómetros por ~** we still have ten kilometres to go
3 (= *inspeccionar*) to go round; **he recorrido todas las librerías buscando esa novela** I've been round all the bookshops looking for that novel
4 (*Tip*) [+ *letras*] to take over
5 (†) (= *leer por encima*) **~ un escrito** to run one's eye over o look through a document
6 (†) (= *reparar*) to repair, mend

recorrido SM 1 (= *viaje*) run, journey; **hicimos un ~ por los pueblos de Andalucía** we travelled round the villages of Andalusia; **el ~ del primer día fue de 450km** we covered 450kms on the first day
2 (= *distancia*) **de corto ~** (*Aer*) short-haul; **de largo ~** (*Aer*) long-haul; **tren de largo ~** intercity train ► **recorrido de aterrizaje** (*Aer*) landing run
3 (= *ruta*) route; **este es el ~ más largo** this is the longest route o way
4 [*de émbolo*] stroke
5 (*Golf*) round; **un ~ en cinco bajo par** a round of five under par
6 (*Hípica*) **un ~ sin penalizaciones** a clear round
7 (*Mec*) repair

recortable SM cut-out

recortada SF sawn-off shotgun

recortado Ⓐ ADJ 1 [*borde*] uneven, irregular
2 (*CAm, Caribe*) (= *achaparrado*) short and stocky
3 (*CAm, Caribe**) (= *necesitado*) broke*
Ⓑ SM (*Andes, Caribe, Cono Sur*) sawn-off shotgun, pistol

recortar ▸conjug 1a◂ Ⓐ VT 1 [+ *pelo*] to trim; [+ *exceso, sobras*] to cut away, cut off
2 [+ *figura, diseño*] to cut out
3 [+ *escopeta*] to saw off
4 [+ *presupuesto*] to cut, reduce; [+ *plantilla*] to cut, cut back; [+ *víveres*] to cut down
5 (= *perfilar*) to draw in outline
Ⓑ **recortarse** VPR to stand out, be silhouetted (**en, sobre** against)

recorte SM 1 (= *acción*) cutting, trimming
2 [*del pelo*] trim
3 (*para economizar*) cut; **han anunciado un ~ de o en los gastos** they have announced a cut o cutback in spending ► **recorte presupuestario** spending cut ► **recorte salarial** wage cut ► **recortes de personal**, **recortes de plantilla** staff cutbacks
4 [*de periódico, revista*] cutting, clipping; **~s de periódico** newspaper cuttings o clippings; **el libro está hecho de ~s** the book is a scissors-and-paste job; **álbum de ~s** scrapbook
5 (*CAm**) (= *comentario*) nasty remark

recoser ▸conjug 2a◂ VT to patch up, darn

recosido SM patch, darn

recostable ADJ **asiento ~** reclining seat

recostado ADJ reclining; **estar ~** to be lying down

recostar ▸conjug 1l◂ Ⓐ VT to lean (**en** on)
Ⓑ **recostarse** VPR (= *reclinarse*) to lie back, recline (*frm*); (= *tumbarse*) to lie down

recotín* ADJ (*Cono Sur*) restless

recova SF 1 [*de aves*] (= *negocio*) poultry business, dealing in poultry; (= *mercado*) poultry market
2 (*Andes, Cono Sur*) (= *mercado*) food market; (*Andes*) (= *carnicería*) butcher's, butcher's shop
3 (*Cono Sur Arquit*) arcade, covered corridor (*along the front of a house*)

recoveco SM 1 [*de calle etc*] turn, bend
2 (*en casa*) nook, odd corner
3 **recovecos** (= *complejidades*) ins and outs; **el asunto tiene muchos ~s** it's a very complicated matter; **hablar sin ~s** to speak plainly o frankly

recovero/a SM/F poultry dealer

recreación SF (= *esparcimiento*) recreation; (= *diversión*) amusement

recrear ▸conjug 1a◂ Ⓐ VT 1 (= *crear de nuevo*) to recreate
2 (= *divertir*) to amuse, entertain
Ⓑ **recrearse** VPR to enjoy o.s.; **se recrea viendo los infortunios de otros** he takes pleasure in o gloats over others' misfortunes

recreativo ADJ Ⓐ ADJ recreational; **instalaciones recreativas** recreational facilities
Ⓑ SM games arcade

recrecer ▸conjug 2d◂ Ⓐ VT to increase
Ⓑ VI 1 (= *crecer*) to increase, grow
2 (= *volver a ocurrir*) to happen again
Ⓒ **recrecerse** VPR to cheer up, recover one's spirits

recreo SM 1 (= *esparcimiento*) recreation; (= *diversión*) amusement
2 (*Escol*) break, playtime, recess (*EEUU*)

recriminación SF 1 (= *reproches*) recrimination ► **recriminación mutua** mutual recrimination
2 (*Jur*) countercharge

recriminar ▸conjug 1a◂ Ⓐ VT 1 (= *reprochar*) to reproach
2 (*Jur*) to countercharge
Ⓑ VI to recriminate
Ⓒ **recriminarse** VPR to reproach each other

recrudecer ▸conjug 2d◂ Ⓐ VT to worsen
Ⓑ VI = C
Ⓒ **recrudecerse** VPR (= *intensificarse*) to intensify; (= *empeorar*) to intensify, worsen; (= *aumentar*) to recrudesce, break out again

recrudecimiento SM, **recrudescencia** SF new outbreak, flare-up

recrudescente ADJ recrudescent

recta SF 1 (= *línea*) straight line
2 (*Dep*) straight ► **recta de llegada**, **recta final** home straight
3 (= *última fase*) closing stages *pl*, final stage

rectal ADJ rectal

rectamente ADV 1 (= *correctamente*) [*comportarse, entender*] properly, correctly
2 (= *directamente*) straight; **mirar a algn ~ a los ojos** to look sb straight in the eyes

rectangular ADJ rectangular

rectángulo Ⓐ ADJ [*forma*] rectangular; [*triángulo*] right-angled
Ⓑ SM rectangle, oblong

rectificable ADJ rectifiable; **fácilmente ~** easily rectified

rectificación SF correction; **publicar una ~** to publish a correction

rectificador(a) SM/F rectifier

rectificar ▸conjug 1g◂ Ⓐ VT 1 (= *corregir*) to rectify, correct; [+ *cálculo*] to correct; [+ *conducta*] to change, reform
2 (= *enderezar*) to straighten, straighten out
3 (*Mec*) to rectify; [+ *cilindro*] to rectify, rebore
4 (*Culin*) to add; **~ de sal si hace falta** add salt to taste
Ⓑ VI to correct o.s.; **—no, eran cuatro, —rectificó** "no", he said, correcting himself, "there were four"; **rectifique, por favor** please see that this is put right

rectilíneo ADJ straight, rectilinear

rectitud SF 1 (= *calidad de justo*) rectitude, honesty
2 [*de una línea*] straightness

recto Ⓐ ADJ 1 (= *derecho*) straight; (= *vertical*) upright
2 **ángulo ~** right angle
3 [*persona*] (= *honrado*) honest, upright; (= *estricto*) strict; [*juez*] fair, impartial; [*juicio*] fair; [*intención*] honest
4 (= *literal*) [*sentido*] proper; **en el sentido ~**

de la palabra in the proper sense of the word
[5] (*Ling*) [*caso*] nominative
Ⓑ ADV **siga todo ~** go straight on; **la flecha fue recta al blanco** the arrow went straight to the target
Ⓒ SM (*Anat*) rectum

rector(a) Ⓐ ADJ [*entidad*] governing; [*idea, principio*] guiding, governing; **una figura ~a** an outstanding *o* leading figure; **los principios ~es del régimen** the régime's guiding principles
Ⓑ SM/F [1] (*Univ*) ≈ vice-chancellor, rector (*EEUU*), president (*EEUU*)
[2] [*de colegio*] principal

rectorado SM [1] (= *cargo*) ≈ vice-chancellorship, principalship, presidency (*EEUU*)
[2] (= *oficina*) ≈ vice-chancellor's office, president's office (*EEUU*)

rectorar ▸conjug 1a◂ VT (*CAm*) to rule, govern, direct

rectoría SF [1] = **rectorado**
[2] (*Rel*) rectory

recua SF mule train, train of pack animals; **una ~ de chiquillos** a bunch of kids

recuadro SM box

recubrir ▸conjug 3a◂ (*pp* **recubierto**) VT (= *cubrir*) to cover (**con, de** with); (= *pintar*) to coat (**con, de** with)

recuento SM (= *acto*) recount; (= *inventario*) inventory; **hacer el ~ de** to count up, reckon up ► **recuento de espermas** sperm count ► **recuento polínico** pollen count

▼ **recuerdo** Ⓐ ADJ (*Andes**) awake
Ⓑ SM [1] (= *memoria*) memory; **guardar un feliz ~ de algn** to have happy memories of sb; **contar los ~s** to reminisce; **"Recuerdos de la vida de hace 80 años"** "Reminiscences of life 80 years ago"; **entrar en el ~** ◊ **pasar al ~** (*euf*) to pass away
[2] (= *regalo*) souvenir, memento; **"~ de Mallorca"** "present from Majorca"; **toma esto como ~** take this as a keepsake ► **recuerdo de familia** family heirloom
[3] **recuerdos** (= *saludos*) regards; **¡~s a tu madre!** give my regards to your mother!; **os manda muchos ~s para todos** he sends you all his warmest regards

recuero SM muleteer

recuesto SM slope

reculada SF [1] (*con el cuerpo, vehículo*) backward movement
[2] (*del fusil*) recoil
[3] (*Méx Mil*) retreat

recular ▸conjug 1a◂ VI [1] (= *ir hacia atrás*) [*animal, vehículo*] to move backwards, go back; [*fusil*] to recoil
[2] (= *ceder*) to back down
[3] [*ejército*] to fall back, retreat

reculativa SF (*Méx*) = **reculada 3**

reculón SM [1] (*LAm*) = **reculada**
[2] **andar a reculones** to go backwards

recuperable ADJ [*dinero, pérdidas*] recoverable; [*envases*] returnable

▼ **recuperación** SF [1] (= *vuelta a la normalidad*) [*de economía, divisa*] recovery; [*de enfermo, paciente*] recovery, recuperation (*más frm*); **la lenta ~ del consumo privado** the slow recovery of consumer spending; **la pierna necesita un periodo de ~** your leg needs some time to recuperate
[2] (= *reutilización*) [2·1] [*de edificio*] restoration; [*de tierras*] reclamation; [*de chatarra, vidrio*] salvage; **un plan de ~ de edificios históricos de la ciudad** a restoration plan for historic buildings in the city
[2·2] [*de algo perdido, olvidado*] revival; **el movimiento de ~ de la música tradicional italiana** the movement for the revival of traditional Italian music
[3] [*de dinero, joyas*] recovery; (*Com*) [*de costes, pérdidas*] recovery, recoupment (*frm*)
[4] (*Esp Educ*) (= *examen*) resit; **examen de ~** resit; **tendrá que ir a clases de ~** he will have to do classes for the resits
[5] (*Inform*) retrieval

recuperar ▸conjug 1a◂ Ⓐ VT [1] (= *recobrar*)
[1·1] [+ *bienes*] to recover; [+ *costes, pérdidas, inversión*] to recoup, recover; **no recuperamos el dinero robado** we didn't get the stolen money back, we didn't recover the stolen money (*más frm*); **nunca ~ás lo que te gastas en lotería** you'll never get back what you spend on the lottery
[1·2] [+ *credibilidad, poder, libertad, control*] to regain; [+ *fuerzas*] to get back, regain; **ella ha hecho que recupere la confianza en la gente** she has made me regain my trust in people; **el jugador ha recuperado la forma física** the player has regained fitness; **el país comienza a ~ la normalidad** the country is beginning to return to normality; **al verte recuperó la sonrisa** the smile came back *o* returned to her face when she saw you; **el dólar recupera posiciones** the dollar is recovering; **nunca recuperó la memoria** she never got her memory back, she never regained *o* recovered her memory
[1·3] [+ *clase, día*] to make up; **ayer trabajaron el doble para ~ el tiempo perdido** they worked double time yesterday to make up the time lost; **esta clase tendremos que ~la** we'll have to make up this class
[1·4] (*Inform*) to retrieve
[2] (= *reutilizar*) [2·1] [+ *edificio*] to restore; [+ *tierras*] to reclaim; [+ *chatarra, vidrio*] to salvage
[2·2] (*del olvido*) [+ *artista, obra*] to revive; [+ *tradiciones*] to restore, revive; **esta exposición recupera a un gran pintor olvidado** this exhibition has revived a great but forgotten painter
[3] (*Educ*) to retake, resit; **tengo que ~ una asignatura** I have to retake *o* resit one subject
Ⓑ **recuperarse** VPR [1] [*enfermo*] to recover (**de** from); **la ciudad se recupera poco a poco tras la intensa nevada** the city is gradually recovering from the heavy blizzard; **~se de** [+ *operación, enfermedad, crisis, viaje*] to recover from
[2] (*Com*) [*economía, mercado, divisa*] to recover; **los mercados financieros parecen ~se** the money markets seem to be recovering

recuperativo ADJ recuperative

recurrencia SF [1] (= *repetición*) recurrence
[2] (= *apelación*) recourse, appeal

recurrente Ⓐ ADJ (= *repetitivo*) recurrent
Ⓑ SMF (*Jur*) appellant

recurrir ▸conjug 3a◂ Ⓐ VT (*Jur*) to appeal against
Ⓑ VI [1] **~ a** [+ *medio, violencia*] to resort to; [+ *persona*] to turn to
[2] (*Jur*) to appeal (**a** to; **contra** against)

recurso SM [1] (= *medio*) **es una mujer de ~s** she's a resourceful woman; **tiene infinidad de ~s** he's infinitely resourceful; **como último ~** as a last resort
[2] (*Jur*) appeal; **interponer ~ contra algn** to lodge an appeal against sb ► **recurso de apelación** appeal to the Supreme Court
[3] **recursos** (= *bienes*) resources; **la familia está sin ~s** the family has nothing to fall back on ► **recursos ajenos** borrowed capital ► **recursos económicos** economic resources ► **recursos energéticos** energy resources ► **recursos financieros** financial resources ► **recursos humanos** human resources ► **recursos naturales** natural resources ► **recursos no renovables** non-renewable resources

recusable ADJ objectionable

recusación SF [1] (= *rechazo*) rejection
[2] (*Jur*) challenge

recusante ADJ, SMF recusant

recusar ▸conjug 1a◂ VT [1] (= *rechazar*) to reject, refuse
[2] (*Jur*) to challenge, challenge the authority of

red SF [1] (*para pescar*) net; [*de portería*] net; [*del pelo*] hairnet; (= *malla*) mesh; (= *para equipajes*) (luggage) rack; (= *cerca*) fence; (= *enrejado*) grille ► **red barredera** trawl ► **red de alambre** wire mesh, wire netting ► **red de seguridad** safety net ► **red metálica** metal screen
[2] [*de cosas relacionadas*] network; [*de agua, suministro eléctrico*] mains, main (*EEUU*), supply system; [*de tiendas*] chain; **la Red** (*Internet*) the Net; **con agua de la ~** with mains water, with water from the mains ► **red de área extendida** wide area network ► **red de área local** local network, local area network ► **red de comunicaciones** communications network ► **red de conmutación de circuito** circuit switching network ► **red de distribución** distribution network ► **red de emisoras** radio network ► **red de espionaje** spy network ► **red de rastreo** tracking network ► **red de transmisión de datos** data network ► **Red Digital de Servicios Integrados** Integrated Services Digital Network ► **red ferroviaria** railway network, railway system ► **red informática** network ► **red local** (*Inform*) local network, local area network ► **red rastreadora** tracking network ► **red vascular** vascular system ► **red viaria** road network
[3] (= *trampa*) snare, trap; **aprisionar a algn en sus ~es** to have sb firmly in one's clutches, have sb well and truly snared; **caer en la ~** to fall into the trap; **tender una ~ para algn** to set a trap for sb

redacción SF [1] (= *acción*) writing; **la ~ del texto me llevó dos horas** it took me two hours to write the text
[2] (= *expresión*) wording; **dices cosas interesantes, pero tendrías que cuidar la ~** what you say is interesting, but you need to pay more attention to how you word it
[3] (*Escol*) essay, composition
[4] (= *oficina*) newspaper office; (= *personas*) editorial staff

redactar ▸conjug 1a◂ Ⓐ VT [1] [+ *carta, noticia, artículo*] to write; [+ *acuerdo, contrato*] to draw up; **un ensayo mal redactado** a badly written essay
[2] (*Prensa*) [+ *periódico*] to edit
Ⓑ VI to write; **redacta muy mal** he writes very badly

➤ LENGUA Y USO: recuerdo B3 48.2 recuperación 1 50.4

redactor(a) SM/F [1] (*en periódico*) editor
[2] (= *escritor*) writer, drafter

redada SF [1] [*de policía*] raid
[2] (*Pesca*) (= *acción*) cast, throw; (= *captura*) catch, haul

redaje SM (*Andes*) (= *red*) net; (= *maraña*) mess, tangle

redaño SM [1] (*Anat*) mesentery
[2] **redaños*** (= *valor*) guts*

redargüir ▸conjug 3g◂ Ⓐ VT [1] (*Jur*) to impugn, hold to be invalid
[2] (*frm*) **~ que …** to argue on the other hand that …
Ⓑ VI (*frm*) to turn an argument against its proposer

redecilla SF hairnet

rededor: **al ~** ◊ **en ~** = **alrededor**

redefinición SF redefinition

redefinir ▸conjug 3a◂ VT to redefine

redemocratización SF return to democracy, reestablishment of democracy

redención SF (*Rel*) redemption; (*Fin*) repayment, redemption (*frm*); (*Jur*) reduction in sentence

redentor(a) Ⓐ ADJ redeeming
Ⓑ SM/F redeemer; ✦*MODISMO* **meterse a ~** (*pey*) to stick one's oar in
Ⓒ SM **Redentor** Redeemer, Saviour, Savior (*EEUU*)

redescubrir ▸conjug 3a◂ (*pp* **redescubierto**) VT to rediscover

redesignar ▸conjug 1a◂ VT (*Inform*) to rename

redespachar ▸conjug 1a◂ VT (*Cono Sur Com*) to send on, forward, forward directly

redicho* ADJ affected

redil SM sheepfold

redimensionamiento SM (= *reestructuración*) remodelling, remodeling (*EEUU*); (*euf*) (= *racionalización*) racionalization

redimensionar ▸conjug 1a◂ VT (*Econ*) (= *reestructurar*) to remodel; (*euf*) (= *racionalizar*) to rationalize, streamline, cut back

redimible ADJ redeemable

redimir ▸conjug 3a◂ VT [1] (*Rel*) to redeem
[2] (*Fin*) to redeem (*frm*), repay
[3] (= *liberar*) [+ *cautivo*] to ransom, redeem (*frm*); [+ *esclavo*] to redeem (*frm*), purchase the freedom of

rediós* EXCL good God!

redistribución SF redistribution

redistribuir ▸conjug 3g◂ VT to redistribute

redistributivo ADJ redistributive; **programa ~** programme for the redistribution of wealth

rédito SM return, interest

redituable ADJ (*Cono Sur*) profitable

redituar ▸conjug 1e◂ VT to yield, produce, bear

redivivo ADJ revived, resuscitated

redoba SF (*Méx*) *wooden board hung round neck and used as a percussion instrument*

redoblado ADJ [1] (*Mec*) reinforced
[2] [*persona*] stocky, thickset
[3] [*paso*] double-quick
[4] [*fuerzas*] renewed; **volvió al ataque con fuerzas redobladas** he went back on the attack with renewed strength

redoblante SM side drum, long-framed side drum

redoblar ▸conjug 1a◂ Ⓐ VT [1] (= *aumentar*) to redouble
[2] (= *plegar*) [+ *papel etc*] to bend back; [+ *clavo*] to clinch
Ⓑ VI (*Mús*) to play a roll on the drum; [*trueno*] to roll, rumble

redoble SM [*de tambor*] drumroll; [*de trueno*] roll, rumble

redoma SF [1] (= *frasco*) flask, phial
[2] (*Cono Sur*) [*de pez*] fishbowl
[3] (*Caribe Aut*) roundabout, traffic circle (*EEUU*)

redomado ADJ [1] [*mentiroso, estafador*] inveterate
[2] (= *taimado*) sly, artful

redomón ADJ [1] (*LAm*) [*caballo*] (= *no domado por completo*) half-trained, not fully broken-in
[2] (*Méx*) [*caballo*] (= *salvaje*) wild, unbroken
[3] [*persona*] (= *inexperto*) untrained, unskilled; (= *torpe*) slow, dense
[4] (= *ordinario*) crude, rough

redonda SF [1] (*Mús*) semibreve, whole note (*EEUU*)
[2] (*Tip*) roman
[3] **a la ~**: **en muchas millas a la ~** for many miles around; **se olía a un kilómetro a la ~** you could smell it a mile off

redondear ▸conjug 1a◂ Ⓐ VT [1] (= *curvar*) to round off
[2] (= *completar*) to round off; **~ un negocio** to close a deal
[3] [+ *cifra*] (*tomando un valor superior*) to round up; (*tomando un valor inferior*) to round down
[4] (= *complementar*) to supplement, top up
Ⓑ **redondearse** VPR [1] (= *enriquecerse*) to become wealthy
[2] (= *librarse de deudas*) to get clear of debts

redondel SM [1] (= *círculo*) ring, circle ► **redondel de humo** smoke ring
[2] (*Taur*) bullring, arena
[3] (*Aut*) roundabout, traffic circle (*EEUU*)

redondez SF roundness; **en toda la ~ de la tierra** in the whole wide world

redondilla SF quatrain

redondo Ⓐ ADJ [1] [*forma*] round; **tiene la cara redonda** he has a round face; **tres metros en ~** three metres (a)round; ✦*MODISMO* **caer ~: le dispararon y cayó ~** he was shot and collapsed in a heap; **cayó ~ en la cama** he went out like a light as soon as he got into bed
[2] [*cantidad, cifra*] round; **en números ~s** in round numbers, in round figures
[3] (*) (= *completo*) complete, finished; **todo le ha salido ~** it all went well for him; **será un negocio ~** it will be a really good deal; **el negocio era ~** the business was really profitable; **triunfo ~** complete *o* resounding success
[4] (= *definitivo*) **dijo un no ~** he flatly refused
[5] (*Méx*) [*viaje*] round
[6] (*Méx**) (= *lerdo*) dense*, thick*; (= *débil*) weak
Ⓑ SM [1] **en ~**: **girar en ~** to turn right round; **negarse en ~** to refuse flatly
[2] (*Mús*†*) disc, record
[3] (*Culin*) rump steak

redopelo SM (*frm*) [1] (*) (= *riña*) scrap*, rough-and-tumble
[2] **a ~** = **a contrapelo**; **una lógica a ~** logic stood on its head, logic in reverse; **traer al ~ a algn** to treat sb very badly, ride roughshod over sb

redor SM **en ~** = **alrededor**

redro ADV behind

redrojo SM [1] (*Bot*) late fruit, withered fruit
[2] (*Cono Sur*) (= *exceso*) rest, remainder
[3] (*Méx**) (= *harapos*) rags *pl*

redropelo SM = **redopelo**

reducción SF [1] (= *disminución*) [1·1] [*de cantidad, precios, consumo, tamaño*] reduction; **una ~ del número de atentados** a reduction in the number of terrorist attacks; **una ~ del gasto público** a cut *o* reduction in public spending; **una ~ en el tamaño de los envases** a reduction in the size of containers; **estudian nuevas reducciones de personal** they are considering new staff cuts *o* reductions in staff
[1·2] [*de tiempo*] reduction; **la ~ a cinco años del mandato presidencial** the reduction of the presidential term to five years; **los sindicatos piden la ~ de la jornada laboral** they unions are calling for a shorter working day ► **reducción de jornada** reduction of working hours ► **reducción del activo** divestment ► **reducciones presupuestarias** budget cuts ► **reducciones salariales** wage cuts
[2] (*Mat*) (= *conversión*) [*de unidades, medidas*] conversion; [*de ecuaciones*] reduction
[3] [*de rebeldes*] defeat
[4] (*Med*) setting, reduction (*frm*)
[5] (*Chile*) [*de indígenas*] reservation (*of natives*)
[6] (*LAm Hist*) *settlement of Christianized Indians*

reduccionismo SM reductionism

reducible ADJ reducible

reducido ADJ [*grupo, número*] small; [*ingresos, recursos*] limited; [*tarifa, precio*] reduced; [*espacio*] confined; **una sala de dimensiones reducidas** a small-sized room; **personas con capacidad auditiva reducida** people with a hearing impairment; **a precios ~s** at reduced prices; **quedar ~ a** to be reduced to; **la plantilla quedó reducida a 70 personas** the staff was reduced to 70 people; **todo quedó ~ a un malentendido** everything boiled down to a misunderstanding

reducir ▸conjug 3n◂ Ⓐ VT [1] (= *disminuir*) [1·1] (*en cantidad*) [+ *gastos, inflación, precio*] to reduce, bring down, cut; [+ *tensión, ansiedad*] to reduce; [+ *riesgo*] to reduce, lessen; **medidas encaminadas a ~ el número de parados** measures designed to reduce *o* bring down *o* cut the number of unemployed; **han reducido las listas de espera en los hospitales** they have reduced *o* cut hospital waiting lists; **el autobús redujo su velocidad** the bus reduced speed, the bus slowed down; **conviene ~ el consumo de grasas** it is advisable to cut down on fatty foods; **el banco redujo su beneficio un 12%** the bank saw its profits fall by 12%; **un tratamiento para ~ la celulitis** a treatment to reduce cellulite; **~ algo <u>en</u> algo** to reduce sth by sth, cut sth by sth; **tenemos que ~ la producción en un 20%** we have to reduce *o* cut production by 20%; **~ a la mínima <u>expresión</u>** to reduce to the bare minimum; **~ algo al <u>mínimo</u>** to reduce *o* cut sth to the minimum; **~ algo a la <u>mitad</u>** to cut sth by half
[1·2] (*en tiempo*) [+ *jornada laboral*] to reduce, shorten; [+ *sentencia*] to reduce; **han reducido la mili a nueve meses** they have reduced *o* cut military service to nine months; **sus**

abogados consiguieron ~ la sentencia a dos meses his lawyers managed to get his sentence reduced to two months

1·3 (*en tamaño*) [+ *copia*] to reduce; [+ *discurso, artículo*] to cut down, shorten

2 **~ algo a algo** 2·1 (= *limitar*) to limit sth to sth; (= *simplificar*) to reduce sth to sth; **redujo su intervención a criticar al gobierno** her participation was limited to criticizing the government; **todo lo reduce a cosas materiales** he reduces everything to material terms

2·2 (= *convertir*) [+ *cantidad, medida*] to convert sth into sth; [+ *fracción, ecuación*] to reduce sth into sth; **~ un kilómetro a metros** to convert a kilometre into metres; **el techo fue reducido a cenizas por el fuego** the roof was reduced to ashes by fire; ✦*MODISMO* **~ algo al absurdo** to expose the absurdity of sth

3 (= *someter*) [+ *ladrón, fugitivo, loco*] to overpower; [+ *alborotadores*] to subdue; [+ *fortaleza*] to subdue, reduce (*frm*); **entre los tres lograron ~ al atracador** the three of them managed to overpower the robber; **~ a algn a la obediencia** to bring sb to heel; **~ a algn al silencio** (*por la fuerza, por miedo*) to silence sb; (*por vergüenza, humillación*) to reduce sb to silence

4 (*Med*) [+ *hueso, hernia*] to set, reduce (*frm*)

5 (*Quím*) to reduce

6 (*LAm*) (*en el mercado negro*) to get rid of*

Ⓑ VI (*Aut*) to change down; **reduce a segunda** change down to second gear

Ⓒ **reducirse** VPR 1 (= *disminuir*) [*inflación, población, beneficios*] to fall; [*calor*] to become less intense, decrease; [*salsa*] to reduce; **el número de accidentes se ha reducido en un 16,5%** the number of accidents has fallen by 16.5%; **sus gastos se redujeron a la mitad** their expenses were cut *o* reduced by half

2 (= *limitarse*) **~se a** 2·1 (*en cantidad*) **el mobiliario se reduce a unas pocas mesas y sillas** the furniture amounts to no more than *o* is simply a few tables and chairs; **sus ingresos se reducen a una pensión por invalidez de 56.000 pesetas** his income is limited to *o* consists only of a disability pension of 56.000 pesetas

2·2 (*en extensión*) **el consumo de heroína se ha ido reduciendo a la población más joven** heroin consumption has gradually been reduced to just the younger population; **el problema se reduce a una pura cuestión económica** the problem comes down to *o* boils down to simple economics, the problem is simply a question of economics; **la entrevista se redujo a un cuarto de hora escaso** the interview lasted barely a quarter of an hour; **el pensamiento del autor se puede ~ a lo siguiente** the author's thinking can be simplified *o* summarized as follows

2·3 [*persona*] to limit o.s. to; **en este ensayo nos ~emos a la situación en el siglo XVIII** in this essay we will limit ourselves to considering the situation in the 18th century; **se vieron reducidos a pedir limosna** they were reduced to begging for alms

reductible ADJ reducible

reductivo ADJ 1 (= *simplificador*) [*noción, enfoque*] reductive

2 [*régimen*] weight-losing; **mamoplastia reductiva** breast reduction

reducto SM [*de ideología, rebeldes*] stronghold, redoubt; **el último ~ del águila imperial** the last stronghold *o* redoubt of the imperial eagle; **el último ~ de los árabes en el reino de Castilla** the last Arab stronghold in the kingdom of Castile

reductor ADJ 1 (*Aut*) [*marcha*] reduction *antes de s*

2 (= *adelgazante*) [*crema*] slimming, reducing

3 (= *simplificador*) reductive

reductora SF (*Aut*) reduction gear

reduje *etc ver* **reducir**

redundancia SF redundancy; **valga la ~** forgive the repetition

redundante ADJ redundant, superfluous

redundar ▸conjug 1a◂ VI **~ en** to redound to (*frm*); **~ en beneficio de algn** to benefit sb, be to sb's advantage

reduplicación SF 1 (= *duplicación*) reduplication

2 [*de esfuerzos*] redoubling

3 (*Ling*) reduplication

reduplicar ▸conjug 1g◂ VT 1 (= *duplicar*) to reduplicate

2 [+ *esfuerzo*] to redouble

reedición SF reissue, reprint, reprinting

reedificación SF rebuilding

reedificar ▸conjug 1g◂ VT to rebuild

reeditar ▸conjug 1a◂ VT to reissue, republish, reprint

reeducación SF re-education ► **reeducación profesional** retraining

reeducar ▸conjug 1g◂ VT to re-educate; **~ profesionalmente** to give industrial retraining to

reelección SF re-election

reelecto ADJ (*LAm*) re-elected

reelectoral ADJ (*LAm*) re-electoral

reelegible ADJ eligible for re-election

reelegir ▸conjug 3c, 3k◂ VT to re-elect

reembalar ▸conjug 1a◂ VT to repack

reembolsable ADJ 1 [*gastos*] refundable, repayable

2 (*Com*) redeemable, refundable; **no ~** [*valores*] irredeemable; [*depósito*] non-returnable, non-refundable

reembolsar ▸conjug 1a◂ Ⓐ VT [+ *persona*] to reimburse; [+ *dinero*] to repay, pay back; [+ *depósito*] to refund, return

Ⓑ **reembolsarse** VPR to reimburse o.s.; **~se una cantidad** to recover a sum

reembolso SM [*de gastos*] reimbursement; [*de depósito*] refund; **enviar algo contra ~** to send sth cash on delivery ► **reembolso fiscal** tax rebate

reemisor SM booster station

reemplazable ADJ replaceable

reemplazante SMF (*esp LAm*) replacement, substitute

reemplazar ▸conjug 1f◂ VT 1 [+ *modelo, pieza*] to replace; **tenemos que encontrar la forma de ~ este sistema** we have to find a way of replacing this system; **~ a algo/algn** to replace sth/sb; **este motor ~á a los actuales de 11 litros** this engine will replace current 11 litre engines; **el nilón nunca podrá ~ al algodón** nylon will never be able to replace cotton; **~ algo con *o* por algo** to replace sth with sth; **van a ~ los discos duros por tarjetas de memoria RAM** hard disks will be replaced by RAM memory boards

2 [+ *persona*] 2·1 (= *ocupar el lugar de*) (*gen*) to replace; (*brevemente*) to stand in for; **durante la baja por maternidad mi ayudante me ~á** my assistant will take my place *o* will replace me while I am on maternity leave; **el subdirector lo reemplazó en la reunión** the assistant director stood in for him at the meeting; **tras el descanso, Pérez reemplazó a Carlos** Pérez came on for Carlos after half-time, Carlos was substituted by Pérez after half-time

2·2 (= *poner en lugar de*) to replace; **el entrenador no pretende ~ a ningún jugador** the coach does not intend to replace any player; **~ a algn con *o* por algn** to replace sb with sb; **los ~án por obreros extranjeros** they are going to be replaced by foreign workers, they will replace them with foreign workers

reemplazo Ⓐ SMF (= *persona sustituta*) replacement

Ⓑ SM 1 (= *sustitución*) replacement; **el coste del ~ de los productos sanguíneos sospechosos** the cost of replacing suspect blood products; **el entrenador decidió el ~ del portero** the coach decided to substitute the goalkeeper; **vino en ~ del profesor de física** he came to replace the physics teacher, he came as the replacement for the physics teacher

2 (*Esp Mil*) *intake of conscripts*; **los soldados pertenecientes al último ~ de 1994** soldiers recruited in the last call-up *o* draft of 1994; **soldados de ~** conscripts, draftees (*EEUU*)

reemprender ▸conjug 2a◂ VT to resume

reencarnación SF reincarnation

reencarnar ▸conjug 1a◂ Ⓐ VT to reincarnate

Ⓑ **reencarnarse** VPR to be reincarnated; **~se en algn/algo** to be reincarnated as sb/sth

reencauchado SM (*LAm*) retread, remould

reencauchar ▸conjug 1a◂ VT (*LAm*) to retread, remould

reencender ▸conjug 1j◂ VT to light again, rekindle

reencontrarse ▸conjug 1l◂ VPR to meet again

reencuadernar ▸conjug 1a◂ VT to rebind

reencuentro SM reunion

reengancharse ▸conjug 1a◂ VPR to re-enlist

reenganche SM (*Mil*) re-enlistment

reentrada SF re-entry

reenvasar ▸conjug 1a◂ VT to repack, rewrap

reenviar ▸conjug 1c◂ VT (*a nuevo domicilio*) to forward; (*a diferente dirección*) to redirect; (*al remitente*) to return

reenvío SM cross-reference

reequilibrar ▸conjug 1a◂ VT 1 (*Pol*) to restabilize

2 [+ *peso, carga*] to rebalance

reescribir ▸conjug 3a◂ VT to rewrite

reestatificación SF renationalization

reestatificar ▸conjug 1g◂ VT to renationalize

reestrenar ▸conjug 1a◂ VT (*Teat*) to revive, put on again; (*Cine*) to re-release

reestreno SM (*Teat*) revival; (*Cine*) re-release

reestructuración SF restructuring, reorganizing

reestructurar ▸conjug 1a◂ VT to restructure, reorganize

reevaluación SF reappraisal

reevaluar ▸conjug 1e◂ VT to reappraise

reexaminación SF re-examination

reexaminar ▸conjug 1a◂ VT to re-examine

reexpedir ▸conjug 3k◂ VT (*a nuevo domicilio*) to forward; (*a diferente dirección*) to redirect; (*al remitente*) to return

reexportación SF re-export

reexportar ▸conjug 1a◂ VT to re-export

REF SM ABR (*Esp Econ*) = **Régimen Económico Fiscal**

Ref.ª ABR (= **referencia**) ref

refacción SF [1] (*frm*) (= *colación*) light refreshment, collation (*frm*)
[2] (*LAm Mec*) repair; (*Arquit*) refurbishment, repair
[3] (*LAm Agr*) (= *gastos*) running costs *pl*
[4] (*Caribe, Méx*) (= *préstamo*) short-term loan; (= *subvención*) financial assistance
[5] **refacciones** (*Méx*) (= *repuestos*) spares, spare parts

refaccionar ▸conjug 1a◂ (*LAm*) VT [1] (*Mec*) to repair; (*Arquit*) to refurbish, repair
[2] (= *subvencionar*) to finance, subsidize

refaccionaria SF (*LAm*) repair shop

refajo† SM (= *enagua*) flannel underskirt; (= *combinación*) slip

refalar* ▸conjug 1a◂ (*Cono Sur*) Ⓐ VT [1] **~ algo a algn** (= *quitar*) to take sth from sb, take sth off sb
[2] (= *hurtar*) to steal
Ⓑ **refalarse** VPR (*) [1] (= *quitarse*) **~se los zapatos** to kick off one's shoes
[2] (= *huir*) to make off, beat it*
[3] (= *resbalar*) to slip

refalón* SM (*Cono Sur*) slip, fall

refaloso* ADJ (*Cono Sur*) [1] (= *resbaladizo*) slippery
[2] (= *tímido*) shy, timid

refanfinflar* ▸conjug 1a◂ VT **me la refanfinfla** I couldn't give a damn*

refectorio SM refectory

referencia SF [1] (= *mención*) reference; **con ~ a** with reference to; **hacer ~ a** to refer to, allude to ► **referencia comercial** trade reference ► **referencia cruzada** cross reference ► **referencia múltiple** general cross reference
[2] (= *informe*) account, report; **una ~ completa del suceso** a complete account of what took place; **me han dado buenas ~s de ella** I have had good reports of her ► **referencia bancaria** banker's reference

referenciar ▸conjug 1b◂ VT to index

referendo SM referendum

referéndum SM (*pl* **referéndums**) referendum

referente ADJ **~ a** relating to, about, concerning

referí SMF (*LAm*) referee, umpire

referible ADJ **~ a** referable to

referido ADJ [1] (= *antedicho*) above-mentioned
[2] (*Ling*) **discurso ~** reported speech

referir ▸conjug 3i◂ Ⓐ VT [1] (= *contar*) to tell, recount; **~ que ...** to say that ..., tell how ...
[2] (= *dirigir*) **~ al lector a un apéndice** to refer the reader to an appendix
[3] (= *relacionar*) to refer, relate; **todo lo refiere a su teoría favorita** he refers *o* relates everything to his favourite theory; **han referido el cuadro al siglo XVII** they have dated the picture as 17th-century
[4] **~ a** (*Fin*) to convert into
[5] (*CAm*) (= *insultar*) to abuse, insult
[6] **~ algo a algn en cara** (*Méx*) to throw sth in sb's face
Ⓑ **referirse** VPR **~se a** to refer to; **me refiero a lo de anoche** I refer to what happened last night; **¿a qué te refieres?** what exactly do you mean?; **por lo que se refiere a eso** as for that, as regards that, as far as that is concerned

refilón: **de ~** ADV obliquely, on the slant; **el sol da de ~** the sun falls on the slant, the sun comes slanting in; **mirar a algn de ~** to look out of the corner of one's eye at sb

refinación SF refining

refinado Ⓐ ADJ refined
Ⓑ SM refining

refinador(a) SM/F refiner

refinadura SF refining

refinamiento SM refinement; **con todos los ~s modernos** with all the modern refinements ► **refinamiento por pasos** (*Inform*) stepwise refinement

refinanciación SF refinancing

refinanciar ▸conjug 1b◂ VT to refinance

refinar ▸conjug 1a◂ VT [1] (*Téc*) to refine
[2] (= *perfeccionar*) [+ *sistema*] to refine, perfect; [+ *estilo*] to polish

refinería SF refinery ► **refinería de petróleo** oil refinery

refino Ⓐ ADJ extra fine, pure, refined
Ⓑ SM refining

refirmar ▸conjug 1a◂ VT (*LAm*) to reaffirm

refistolería SF [1] (*CAm*) (= *intriga*) scheming nature
[2] (*Méx*) (= *presunción*) vanity
[3] (*Caribe**) (= *zalamería*) boot-licking*

refistolero ADJ [1] (*CAm*) (= *intrigante*) intriguing, scheming
[2] (*Méx*) (= *presuntuoso*) vane
[3] (*Caribe*) (= *zalamero*) greasy, oily

reflación SF reflation

reflacionar ▸conjug 1a◂ VT to reflate

reflectante ADJ reflective

reflector SM [1] (= *cuerpo que refleja*) reflector ► **reflector posterior** (*Aut*) rear reflector
[2] (*Elec*) spotlight; (*Aer, Mil*) searchlight

reflejar ▸conjug 1a◂ Ⓐ VT [1] [+ *imagen, luz*] to reflect
[2] (= *manifestar*) to reflect; **la novela refleja la problemática social de la época** the novel reflects the social problems of the time; **su expresión reflejaba inquietud** you could see the worry in her face, she wore a worried expression (on her face)
Ⓑ **reflejarse** VPR [1] [*imagen, luz*] to be reflected
[2] (= *manifestarse*) **el temor se reflejaba en su rostro** fear was written on his face

reflejo Ⓐ ADJ [1] [*luz*] reflected
[2] [*movimiento*] reflex
[3] [*verbo*] reflexive
Ⓑ SM [1] (= *imagen*) reflection; **miraba su ~ en el agua** he was looking at his reflection in the water
[2] (= *índice*) reflection; **este es un ~ de la inquietud del pueblo** this reflects *o* is a reflection of people's unease
[3] (*Anat*) reflex; (= *acción*) reflex action; **tener buenos ~s** to have good reflexes; **perder ~s** (*fig*) to lose one's touch
[4] **reflejos** (= *brillo*) gleam *sing*, glint *sing*; **tiene ~s metálicos** it has a metallic glint
[5] **reflejos** (*en el pelo*) highlights; **tiene el pelo castaño con ~s rubios** she has chestnut hair with blond highlights
[6] (= *tinte para el pelo*) rinse; **darse un ~ azul** to have a blue rinse

reflejoterapia SF reflexology

reflex, **réflex** Ⓐ ADJ INV SLR, reflex
Ⓑ SF SLR camera

reflexión SF [1] (*Fís*) reflection
[2] (= *consideración*) reflection, thought; **con ~** on reflection; **sin ~** without thinking; **mis reflexiones sobre el problema** my reflections on the problem; **hacer reflexiones** to reflect

reflexionar ▸conjug 1a◂ Ⓐ VT to reflect on, think about, think over
Ⓑ VI (= *considerar*) to reflect (**sobre** on); (*antes de actuar*) to think, pause; **¡reflexione!** you think about it!, think for a moment!

reflexivamente ADV [1] (*Ling*) reflexively
[2] [*obrar*] thoughtfully, reflectively

reflexividad SF (*Ling*) reflexiveness

reflexivo ADJ [1] [*verbo*] reflexive
[2] [*persona*] thoughtful, reflective
[3] [*acto*] considered

reflexología SF reflexology

reflexoterapia SF reflex therapy

reflotar ▸conjug 1a◂ VT [+ *barco*] to refloat; [+ *empresa, negocio*] to relaunch, re-establish

refluir ▸conjug 3g◂ VI to flow back

reflujo SM ebb, ebb tide

refocilación SF, **refocilamiento** SM (= *placer*) huge enjoyment, great pleasure; (*pey*) (= *regodeo*) unhealthy pleasure, cruel pleasure

refocilar ▸conjug 1a◂ Ⓐ VT (= *encantar*) to delight; (= *divertir*) to amuse hugely; (= *alegrar*) to cheer up
Ⓑ VI (*Andes, Cono Sur*) [*rayo*] to flash
Ⓒ **refocilarse** VPR [1] (= *divertirse*) **~se con algo** to enjoy sth hugely, take great delight in sth; **se refocila viendo lo que sufre otro** he delights in *o* gloats over sb else's sufferings
[2] (= *alegrarse*) to cheer up no end

refocilo SM [1] = **refocilación**
[2] (*Andes*) (= *relámpago*) lightning

reforestación SF reforestation

reforestar ▸conjug 1a◂ VT to reforest

reforma SF [1] (= *modificación*) reform; **~s políticas** political reforms; **la Reforma** (*Rel*) the Reformation; (*Méx Pol*) *19th century reform movement* ► **reforma agraria** land reform ► **reforma educativa** education reform
[2] **reformas** (*en edificio, local*) alterations; **cerrado por ~s** closed for refurbishment, closed for alterations
[3] (*Cos*) alteration

reformación SF reform, reformation

reformado ADJ reformed

reformador(a) SM/F reformer

reformar ▸conjug 1a◂ Ⓐ VT [1] [+ *edificio*] to renovate; **van a ~ todas las casas del casco antiguo** they are going to renovate all the houses in the old quarter
[2] [+ *ley, sistema*] to reform; **han reformado los estatutos del partido** they have reformed the party statutes
[3] [+ *persona*] to reform; **su novia ha conseguido ~le y ya no bebe** his girlfriend has managed to reform him and he doesn't drink any more
[4] (*Cos*) to alter

5 (*frm*) (= *formar de otro modo*) to re-form
Ⓑ **reformarse** VPR [*persona*] to reform, mend one's ways

reformatear ▸conjug 1a◂ VT (*Inform*) to reformat

reformatorio SM reformatory ► **reformatorio de menores** remand home, reform school (*EEUU*)

reformismo SM reforming policy, reforming attitude

reformista Ⓐ ADJ reforming
Ⓑ SMF reformist, reformer

reforzado ADJ reinforced

reforzador SM (*Elec*) booster; (*Fot*) intensifier

reforzamiento SM reinforcement, strengthening

reforzar ▸conjug 1f, 1l◂ VT 1 (*Arquit, Carpintería*) to reinforce
2 (= *fortalecer*) to reinforce, strengthen; **debemos ~ nuestra estrategia de ventas** we must reinforce *o* strengthen our sales strategy
3 (*Mil*) to reinforce
4 [+ *dosis*] to increase
5 (*Fot*) to intensify

refracción SF refraction

refractante ADJ refractive

refractar ▸conjug 1a◂ VT to refract

refractario ADJ 1 (*Téc*) fireproof, heat-resistant; (*Culin*) ovenproof
2 **ser ~ a la reforma** to be resistant *o* opposed to reform; **ser ~ a las lenguas** to have no aptitude for languages, be hopeless where languages are concerned

refractivo ADJ refractive

refractor SM refractor

refrán SM proverb, saying; **como dice el ~** as the saying goes

refranero SM collection of proverbs

refraniento ADJ (*Cono Sur*) much given to quoting proverbs

refregar ▸conjug 1h, 1j◂ VT 1 (= *frotar*) to rub, rub hard; (= *limpiar*) to scrub
2 (*fig*) (= *restregar*) **~ algo a algn** *o* **en las narices de algn** to rub sth in to sb, harp on about sth to sb

refregón SM 1 (= *frotamiento*) (*sin darse cuenta*) rub, rubbing; (*limpiando*) scrub, scrubbing
2 (= *señal*) rub mark

refrenar ▸conjug 1a◂ VT 1 [+ *caballo*] to rein back
2 [+ *pasiones, ánimos*] to restrain, hold in check

refrendar ▸conjug 1a◂ VT 1 (= *dar validez a*) [+ *documento*] to countersign; [+ *decisión, nominación*] to endorse
2 [+ *pasaporte*] to stamp
3 (*) (= *repetir*) to do again, repeat; [+ *comida*] to order more of, have a second helping of

refrendo SM 1 (= *acto*) [*de documento*] countersigning; [*de decisión*] endorsement
2 (= *firma*) countersignature

refrescante ADJ refreshing, cooling

refrescar ▸conjug 1g◂ Ⓐ VT 1 (= *enfriar*) to cool, cool down
2 [+ *conocimiento*] to brush up, polish up; **~ la memoria** to refresh one's memory
3 [+ *acto*] to repeat; [+ *enemistad, interés*] to renew
Ⓑ VI 1 (*Meteo*) to get cooler, cool down; **en septiembre ya refresca** it starts to get cooler in September
2 [*bebida*] to be refreshing
3 (*Méx Med*) to get better
Ⓒ **refrescarse** VPR 1 (= *tomar el aire*) to go out for a breath of fresh air
2 (= *lavarse*) to freshen up
3 (= *beber*) to have a drink; (*Andes, esp Col*) (= *tomar té*) to have tea

refresco SM soft drink; **nos tomamos unos ~s** we had some soft drinks *o* refreshments; **después del concierto nos ofrecieron un ~** they laid on some refreshments for us after the concert ► **refresco de cola** cola

refresquería SF (*LAm*) refreshment stall

refri* SM (*Méx*) fridge*

refriega SF (*de poca importancia*) scuffle; (*violenta*) brawl

refrigeración SF [*de comida*] refrigeration; (*Mec*) cooling; [*de casa*] air conditioning ► **refrigeración por agua** water cooling ► **refrigeración por aire** air cooling

refrigerado ADJ [*comida*] chilled; [*sala*] air-conditioned; **~ por agua** water-cooled; **~ por aire** air-cooled

refrigerador Ⓐ ADJ cooling, refrigerating
Ⓑ SM 1 (= *frigorífico*) refrigerator, fridge
2 (*para el aire acondicionado*) cooling unit, cooling system

refrigeradora SF (*LAm*) refrigerator, fridge

refrigerante Ⓐ ADJ cooling, refrigerating
Ⓑ SM (*Quím*) refrigerant, coolant

refrigerar ▸conjug 1a◂ VT (= *enfriar*) to chill, refrigerate; (*Téc*) to refrigerate; (*Mec*) to cool; [+ *sala*] to air-condition

refrigerio SM 1 (= *piscolabis*) snack; (= *bebida*) cooling drink
2 (= *alivio*) relief

refrior SM chill, chill in the air

refrito Ⓐ ADJ 1 (*Culin*) refried
2 [*obra*] revised, rehashed
Ⓑ SM rehash, revised version

refucilar ▸conjug 1a◂ VI (*Andes, Cono Sur*) = **refocilar B**

refucilo SM (*Andes, Cono Sur*) lightning

refuerzo SM 1 (= *reforzamiento*) reinforcement
2 (*Téc*) support
3 **refuerzos** (*Mil*) reinforcements
4 (= *ayuda*) aid

refugiado/a ADJ, SM/F refugee

refugiarse ▸conjug 1b◂ VPR (= *acogerse a un refugio*) to take refuge; (= *cobijarse*) to shelter (**en** in); **se refugió en un país vecino** he fled to a neighbouring country

refugio SM 1 (= *sitio*) refuge, shelter; **acogerse a un ~** to take refuge, (take) shelter (**en** in); ► **refugio alpino** mountain hut ► **refugio antiaéreo** air-raid shelter ► **refugio antiatómico, refugio antinuclear, refugio atómico** fallout shelter ► **refugio de caza** hunting lodge ► **refugio de montaña** mountain hut ► **refugio fiscal** tax shelter ► **refugio nuclear** fallout shelter ► **refugio subterráneo** (*Mil*) underground shelter, dugout
2 (*Esp Aut*) street island

refulgencia SF (*frm*) brilliance, refulgence (*frm o liter*)

refulgente ADJ (*frm*) brilliant, refulgent (*frm o liter*)

refulgir ▸conjug 3c◂ VI (*frm*) to shine, shine brightly

refundar ▸conjug 1a◂ VT to relaunch

refundición SF 1 (*Téc*) recasting
2 [*de obra*] new version, adaptation

refundidor(a) SM/F reviser, adapter

refundir ▸conjug 3a◂ Ⓐ VT 1 (*Téc*) to recast
2 [+ *obra*] to adapt, rewrite
3 (*Andes, CAm, Méx*) (= *perder*) to lose, mislay
4 (*Cono Sur*) (= *arruinar*) to ruin, crush; (‡) [+ *candidato*] to plough‡, plow (*EEUU*)
5 (*CAm*) (= *guardar*) to keep carefully
Ⓑ **refundirse** VPR (*Andes, CAm, Méx*) to get lost, be mislaid

refunfuñar ▸conjug 1a◂ VI (= *gruñir*) to growl; (= *quejarse*) to grumble

refunfuño SM (= *gruñido*) growl, grunt; (= *queja*) grumble

refunfuñón/ona* Ⓐ ADJ grumpy
Ⓑ SM/F grouch*

refusilo SM (*Andes, Chile*) lightning

refutable ADJ refutable; **fácilmente ~** easily refuted

refutación SF refutation

refutar ▸conjug 1a◂ VT to refute

regada SF watering

regadera SF 1 (*Hort*) watering can; ✦**MODISMO estar como una ~** (*Esp**) to be crazy
2 (*Méx*) shower

regadío SM **de ~** irrigated; **tierra de ~** irrigated land; **cultivo de ~** crop that grows on irrigated land

regadizo ADJ irrigable

regador SM (*Cono Sur*) watering can

regadura SF (*en jardín*) sprinkling, watering; (*Agr*) irrigation

regala SF gunwale

regaladamente ADV [*vivir*] in luxury; **comer ~** to eat extremely well

regalado ADJ 1 (= *cómodo*) comfortable, pleasant; (*pey*) (= *fácil*) soft; ✦**MODISMO hace su regalada gana** (*LAm**) she does exactly what she likes *o* goes her own sweet way
2 (= *delicado*) dainty, delicate
3 (= *gratis*) free, given away; **me lo dio medio ~** he gave it to me for a song; **no lo quiero ni ~** I wouldn't have it at any price

regalar ▸conjug 1a◂ Ⓐ VT 1 (= *dar como regalo*) to give, give as a present; **~ algo a algn** to give sb sth, make sb a present of sth; **en su jubilación le ~on este reloj** they gave him this clock on his retirement, they presented him with this clock on his retirement; **están regalando plumas** they're giving pens away; **regaló el balón** (*Dep*) he gave the ball away
2 (*frm*) (= *agasajar*) **~ a algn con un banquete** to hold a dinner in sb's honour *o* (*EEUU*) honor; **le ~on con toda clase de atenciones** they lavished attention on him
Ⓑ **regalarse** VPR (= *darse gusto*) to indulge o.s., pamper o.s.

regalía SF 1 (= *privilegio*) privilege, prerogative
2 **regalías** [*del rey*] royal prerogatives; (*Com*) (= *bonificación*) bonus *sing*, perquisite *sing*; (= *derechos*) royalties *pl*; (= *adelanto*) advance payment *sing*

3 (*esp LAm*) (= *regalo*) gift, present
4 (*Caribe*) (= *excelencia*) excellence, goodness

regaliz SM, **regaliza** SF liquorice, licorice ► **regaliz de palo** stick of liquorice

regalo SM 1 (= *obsequio*) present, gift; **dar** *o* **hacer a algn un ~** to give sb a present *o* gift; **de ~: dan estos libros de ~** they're giving these books away; **entrada de ~** complimentary ticket; **estuche de ~** presentation case; **un libro de ~** a free book ► **regalo de boda** wedding present ► **regalo de Navidad**, **regalo de Reyes** Christmas present
2 (= *deleite, placer*) pleasure; [*de comida*] treat, delicacy; **es un ~ para el oído** it's a treat to listen to; **un ~ del cielo** a godsend
3 (††) (= *comodidad*) luxury, comfort

regalón ADJ 1 (= *comodón*) comfort-loving
2 [*vida*] (= *de lujo*) of luxury; (*pey*) (= *fácil*) soft, easy
3 (*LAm*) (= *predilecto*) **es el ~ de su padre** he's the apple of his father's eye, he's his daddy's pet
4 (*Andes*) (= *obsequioso*) fond of giving presents

regalonear ▸conjug 1a◂ (*Cono Sur*) Ⓐ VT (= *mimar*) to spoil, pamper
Ⓑ VI (= *dejarse mimar*) to allow o.s. to be pampered

regañada* SF (*CAm, Méx*) = **regaño**

regañadientes: **a ~** ADV unwillingly, reluctantly

regañado ADJ **estar ~ con algn** to be at odds with sb

regañar ▸conjug 1a◂ Ⓐ VT to scold, tell off*
Ⓑ VI 1 [*persona*] to grumble, grouse*
2 [*dos personas*] to fall out, quarrel
3 (††) [*perro*] to snarl, growl

regañina SF = **regaño 1**

regaño SM 1 (= *reprimenda*) scolding, telling-off*; **merecerse un ~** to get a telling off*
2 (= *gruñido*) snarl, growl; (= *mueca*) scowl; (= *queja*) grumble, grouse*

regañón ADJ (= *gruñón*) grumbling; [*mujer*] nagging

regar ▸conjug 1h, 1j◂ Ⓐ VT 1 [+ *planta, parterre*] to water; [+ *campo, terreno*] to irrigate; [+ *calle*] to hose down; **regó la carta con lágrimas** (*liter*) she cried all over the letter
2 (*Culin*) **~on la cena con Rioja** they washed the meal down with some Rioja; **durante la cocción se riega la carne con su jugo** whilst it is cooking, baste the meat in its own juice
3 (*Geog*) [*río*] to water; [*mar*] to wash; **una costa regada por un mar tranquilo** a coast washed by a calm sea
4 [+ *herida*] to wash, bathe (**con, de** with)
5 (= *esparcir*) to sprinkle, scatter; **iba regando monedas** he was dropping money all over the place
6 (*Andes, CAm**) (= *derramar*) to spill; (= *derribar*) to knock over, knock down
7 (*Caribe*) (= *pegar*) to hit
Ⓑ VI 1 (*Caribe**) (= *bromear*) to joke; **está regando** she's having us on*
2 (*Caribe*) (= *actuar sin pensar*) to act rashly
3 **~la** (*Méx*‡) (= *fracasar*) to screw it up‡, make a mess of it
Ⓒ **regarse** VPR 1 (*CAm, Méx*) (= *dispersarse*) to scatter, scatter in all directions
2 (*Caribe**) (= *enfadarse*) to get cross
3 (*LAm*) (= *ducharse*) to shower, take a shower

regata[1] SF (*Agr*) irrigation channel

regata[2] SF (*Náut*) (= *una carrera*) race, boat race; (= *varias carreras*) regatta

regate SM 1 (= *movimiento*) swerve, dodge; (*Dep*) dribble
2 (= *treta*) dodge, ruse

regatear[1] ▸conjug 1a◂ VI (*Náut*) to race

regatear[2] ▸conjug 1a◂ Ⓐ VT 1 (*Com*) [+ *objeto, precio*] to haggle over, bargain over
2 (= *economizar*) to be mean with, economize on; **aquí regatean el vino** they are mean with their wine here; **su padre no le regatea dinero** her father does not keep her short of money; **no hemos regateado esfuerzos para terminarlo** we have spared no effort to finish it
3 (*frm*) (= *negar*) to deny, refuse to allow; **no le regateo buenas cualidades** I don't deny his good qualities
Ⓑ VI 1 (*Com*) to haggle, bargain
2 (= *esquivar*) to swerve, dodge; (*Dep*) to dribble
Ⓒ **regatearse** VPR **~se algo** (*LAm*) to haggle over sth

regateo SM 1 (*Com*) haggling, bargaining
2 (*Dep*) dribbling

regatista SMF (= *participante*) competitor (*in yacht race*); (= *aficionado*) yachtsman/yachtswoman

regato SM pool

regatón[1] SM [*de bastón*] tip, ferrule

regatón[2] Ⓐ ADJ (*Com*) haggling
Ⓑ SM (*Caribe**) (= *restos*) dregs *pl*
Ⓒ SMF (*Méx**) (= *comerciante*) small-time dealer

regazo SM lap

regencia SF regency

regeneración SF regeneration

regenerado ADJ regenerate

regenerador ADJ regenerative

regeneramiento SM regeneration

regenerar ▸conjug 1a◂ VT to regenerate

regenta SF wife of the regent

regentar ▸conjug 1a◂ VT 1 (= *dirigir*) [+ *hotel, negocio*] to run, manage; [+ *destinos*] to guide, preside over
2 (= *ocupar*) [+ *puesto permanente*] to occupy, hold; [+ *puesto temporal*] to hold temporarily

regente Ⓐ ADJ 1 [*príncipe*] regent
2 [*director*] managing
Ⓑ SMF 1 (*Pol*) regent
2 [*de fábrica*] manager; (*Esp Farm*) chief pharmacist
Ⓒ SM (*Méx*) (= *alcalde*) mayor

reggae ['reɣe] SM reggae

regiamente ADV regally

regicida SMF regicide

regicidio SM regicide

regidor(a) Ⓐ ADJ [*principio*] governing, ruling
Ⓑ SM/F 1 (*Teat*) stage manager
2 (*TV*) floor manager
Ⓒ SM (*Hist*) alderman

regiego ADJ, SM = **rejego**

régimen SM (*pl* **regímenes**) 1 (*Pol*) régime; **antiguo ~** ancien régime; **bajo el ~ del dictador** under the dictator's régime *o* rule ► **régimen del terror** reign of terror
2 (*Med*) (*tb* **~ alimenticio**) diet; **estar a ~** to be on a diet; **poner a algn a ~** to put sb on a diet; **ponerse a ~** to go on a diet; **hacer ~** to be on a diet ► **régimen de adelgazamiento** diet, slimming diet ► **régimen lácteo** milk diet
3 (= *reglas*) rules *pl*, set of rules; **en ~ de franquicia** under franchise; **prisión de ~ abierto** open prison; **he cambiado de ~ de vida** I have changed my whole way of life; **alojamiento en ~ de pensión completa** full board; **viviendas en ~ de alquiler** homes for rent ► **régimen tributario** tax system

regimentación SF regimentation

regimiento SM 1 (*Mil*) regiment
2 (*) (= *multitud*) crowd

Reginaldo SM Reginald

regio Ⓐ ADJ 1 (= *real*) royal, regal
2 (= *suntuoso*) splendid, majestic
3 (*Andes, Cono Sur**) (= *genial*) great*, terrific*
Ⓑ EXCL (*Andes, Cono Sur**) great!*, fine!

regiomontano/a Ⓐ ADJ of/from Monterrey
Ⓑ SM/F native/inhabitant of Monterrey; **los ~s** the people of Monterrey

región SF 1 (*Geog, Pol*) region; (= *área*) area, part
2 (*Anat*) region

regional ADJ regional

regionalismo SM regionalism

regionalista ADJ, SMF regionalist

regionalización SF regionalization

regir ▸conjug 3c, 3k◂ Ⓐ VT 1 [+ *país*] to rule, govern; [+ *colegio*] to run; [+ *empresa*] to manage, run
2 (*Econ, Jur*) to govern; **según el reglamento que rige estos casos** according to the statute which governs these cases; **los factores que rigen los cambios del mercado** the factors which govern *o* control changes in the market
3 (*Ling*) to take; **ese verbo rige el dativo** that verb takes the dative
Ⓑ VI 1 (= *estar en vigor*) [*ley, precio*] to be in force; [*condición*] to prevail, obtain; **esa ley ya no rige** that law is no longer in force; **cuando estas condiciones ya no rijan** when these conditions no longer obtain
2 (*con mes, año*) **el mes que rige** the present month, the current month
3 (= *funcionar*) to work, go; **el timbre no rige** the bell doesn't work
4 (*) (= *estar cuerdo*) **no ~** to have a screw loose*, not be all there*
Ⓒ **regirse** VPR **~se por** to be ruled by, be guided by, go by

regista SMF producer

registrado ADJ 1 (= *anotado*) registered
2 (*Méx Correos*) (= *certificado*) registered

registrador(a) Ⓐ SM/F 1 (*Admin*) (= *persona*) recorder, registrar
2 ► **registrador(a) de sonido** (*TV*) sound recordist
Ⓑ SM ► **registrador de vuelo** flight recorder

registradora SF (*Com*) cash register

registrar ▸conjug 1a◂ Ⓐ VT 1 [+ *equipaje, lugar, persona*] to search; **lo hemos registrado todo de arriba abajo** we have searched the whole place from top to bottom; ✦***MODISMO*** **¡a mí que me registren!*** search me!*
2 (= *anotar*) to register, record; **han registra-**

do el nacimiento de su hijo they have registered the birth of their son

[3] [+ *temperatura, terremoto*] to record, register; [+ *terremoto, temblor*] to register; **el termómetro registró una mínima de diez grados** the thermometer recorded *o* registered a minimum temperature of ten degrees

[4] (*Mús*) to record; **~ la voz en una cinta** to record one's voice on tape

[5] (*Méx*) [+ *correo*] to register

[6] **~ un libro**† to mark one's place in a book

(B) **registrarse** VPR [1] (= *apuntarse*) to register; **tienes que ~te en el consulado** you have to register at the consulate; **me registré en el hotel** I checked into the hotel

[2] (= *ocurrir*) **hoy se han registrado las temperaturas más altas del año** the highest temperatures this year were recorded today; **se han registrado lluvias en toda la región** there was rain throughout the whole region; **se han registrado algunos casos de tifus** a few cases of typhus have been reported; **el cambio que se ha registrado en su actitud** the change which has occurred in his attitude

registro SM [1] (= *acción*) registration, recording

[2] (= *libro*) register; (*Inform*) record; **firmar el ~** to sign the register; **capacidad de ~** storage facility, recording capacity ► **registro catastral** land registry ► **registro de casamientos** register of marriages ► **registro de defunciones** register of deaths ► **registro de la propiedad inmobiliaria** land registry ► **registro de nacimientos** register of births ► **registro electoral** electoral register, electoral roll ► **registro lógico** logical record ► **registro mercantil** business register ► **registro parroquial** parish register

[3] (= *lista*) list, record; (= *apunte*) note ► **registro de erratas** list of errata

[4] (= *entrada*) entry

[5] (= *oficina*) registry, record office ► **registro civil** ≈ registry office, ≈ county clerk's office (EEUU) ► **registro de la propiedad** (= *oficina*) land registry, land registry office ► **registro de patentes y marcas** patent office

[6] (= *búsqueda*) search; (= *inspección*) inspection; **practicar un ~** to make a search (**en** of); **orden de ~** search warrant ► **registro domiciliario** house search ► **registro policíaco** police search

[7] (*Mús*) (= *grabación*) recording; **es un buen ~ de la sinfonía** it is a good recording of the symphony

[8] (*Mús*) (= *timbre*) [*de la voz*] register; [*del órgano*] stop; [*del piano*] pedal; ✦**MODISMOS adoptar un ~ muy raro** ◊ **salir por un ~ muy raro** to adopt a very odd tone; **mira por qué ~ nos sale ahora** look what he's coming out with now; **tocar todos los ~s** to pull out all the stops

[9] (*Téc*) manhole

[10] (*Ling*) register

[11] (*Dep*) (= *marca*) personal best; (= *récord*) record

[12] [*de reloj*] regulator

[13] (*Tip*) register; **estar en ~** to be in register

[14] (*Andes, Cono Sur*) (= *tienda*) wholesale textiles store

regla SF [1] (= *instrumento*) ruler ► **regla de cálculo** slide rule ► **regla de un pie** 12-inch rule ► **regla en T, regla T** T-square

[2] (= *norma*) rule; **las ~s del ajedrez** the rules of chess; **~s para utilizar una máquina** instructions for the use of a machine; **no hay ~ sin excepción** every rule has its exception; **las cuatro ~s** *addition, subtraction, multiplication and division*; **en ~** in order; **no tenía los papeles en ~** his papers were not in order; **todo está en ~** everything is in order; **poner algo en ~** to put sth straight; **por ~ general** generally, as a rule; **salir de ~** to overstep the mark; **en toda ~: hacer algo en toda ~** to do sth properly; **es un español en toda ~** he's a real Spaniard, he's a Spaniard through and through ► **reglas del juego** rules of the game ► **regla de tres** rule of three; **¿por qué ~ de tres ...?** (*Esp**) why on earth ...? ► **reglas de oro** golden rules

[3] (= *menstruación*) period

[4] (= *moderación*) moderation, restraint; **comer con ~** to eat in moderation

[5] (*Rel*) rule, order; **viven según la ~ benedictina** they live according to the Benedictine rule

reglable ADJ adjustable

reglaje SM [1] (*Mec*) adjustment ► **reglaje de neumáticos** wheel alignment

[2] (*Mil*) correction, correction of aim

reglamentación SF [1] (= *acción*) regulation

[2] (= *reglas*) regulations *pl*, rules *pl*

reglamentar ▸conjug 1a◂ VT to regulate

reglamentariamente ADV in due form, according to the rules

reglamentario ADJ [*uniforme*] regulation *antes de s*; **pistola reglamentaria** standard issue pistol; **en el traje ~** in the regulation dress; **en la forma reglamentaria** in the properly established way; **es ~** + INFIN the regulations stipulate that

reglamento SM (= *reglas*) rules *pl*, regulations *pl*; [*de reunión, sociedad*] standing order, standing orders *pl*; (*municipal*) by-law; [*de profesión*] code of conduct; **pistola de ~** standard issue pistol ► **reglamento de aduana** customs regulations *pl* ► **reglamento del tráfico** highway code

reglar ▸conjug 1a◂ (A) VT [1] [+ *papel*] to rule

[2] [+ *acciones*] to regulate

[3] (*Mec*) to check, overhaul

[4] (*Mil*) [+ *puntería*] to correct

(B) **reglarse** VPR **~se a** to abide by, conform to; **~se por** to be guided by

regleta SF space

regletear ▸conjug 1a◂ VT to space out

regocijadamente ADV merrily, joyfully

regocijado ADJ [1] [*carácter*] jolly, cheerful

[2] [*estado, humor*] merry, joyful

regocijar ▸conjug 1a◂ (A) VT to gladden, delight; **la noticia regocijó a la familia** the news delighted the family, the news filled the family with joy; **un chiste que regocijó a todos** a joke which made everyone laugh; **creó un personaje para ~ a los niños** she created a character to amuse children

(B) **regocijarse** VPR [1] (= *alegrarse*) to rejoice, be glad (**de, por** about, at); **se regocija de la mala suerte de otros** he delights in somebody else's misfortunes

[2] (= *reírse*) to laugh; **~se con un chiste** to laugh at a joke

[3] (= *pasarlo bien*) to have a good time

regocijo SM [1] (= *alegría*) joy, happiness; (= *júbilo*) delight, elation

[2] (††) (= *regodeo*) gloating (**por** over)

[3] **regocijos**†† (= *fiestas*) festivities, celebrations ► **regocijos navideños** Christmas festivities ► **regocijos públicos** public rejoicing

regodearse ▸conjug 1a◂ VPR [1] **~ con** *o* **en algo** to gloat over sth [2] (*LAm**) (= *ser exigente*) to be fussy, be hard to please

regodeo SM [1] (= *broma*) joking

[2] (= *deleite*) delight; (*pey*) (= *refocilo*) perverse pleasure *o* delight

regodeón (*LAm*) ADJ [1] (= *exigente*) fussy, hard to please [2] (= *egoísta*) self-indulgent

regodiente ADJ (*Andes*) fussy, hard to please

regojo SM [1] (= *pan*) piece of left-over bread

[2] (*) (= *persona*) tich*, titch*

regoldar* ▸conjug 1l◂ VI to belch

regordete ADJ [*persona*] chubby, plump; [*manos*] fat

regosto SM longing, craving (**de** for)

regrabadora SF rewriter ► **regrabadora de DVDs** DVD rewriter

regresar ▸conjug 1a◂ (A) VI (= *venir*) to return, come back; (= *irse*) to return, go back

(B) VT (*LAm*) to give back, return

(C) **regresarse** VPR (*LAm*) = **A**

regresión SF [1] (= *acción*) (*tb Psic*) regression

[2] (= *retroceso*) [*de productividad*] fall, decrease; [*de actividad cultural*] decline ► **regresión demográfica** population decline, fall in population

regresivo ADJ regressive, backward

regreso SM return; **viaje de ~** return trip; **emprender el ~ a** to return to, come/go back to; **estar de ~** to be back; **de ~** on the way back, on my/his/our *etc* way back; **de ~ a casa tuvimos una avería** the car broke down on the way home; **nos enteraremos al ~** we'll find out once we get back

regro ADJ (*Caribe*) great*, fabulous*

regto. ABR (= **regimiento**) Regt., Rgt

regüeldo SM (*frm*) belch, belching

reguera SF [1] (*Agr*) irrigation channel

[2] (*Náut*) cable, mooring rope, anchor chain

reguero SM [1] (= *señal*) track; [*de sangre*] trickle; [*de humo, pólvora*] trail; ✦**MODISMO propagarse como un ~ de pólvora** to spread like wildfire

[2] (*Agr*) irrigation ditch

reguío SM (*Andes*) = **riego**

regulable ADJ adjustable

regulación SF [1] (*con reglas*) regulation; (*Mec*) adjustment; (= *control*) control ► **regulación de la natalidad** birth control ► **regulación del tráfico** traffic control ► **regulación del volumen sonoro** (*Radio*) volume control

[2] (*euf*) (= *reducción*) reduction ► **regulación de empleo** redundancy ► **regulación de jornada** cut in working hours ► **regulación de plantilla** staff cut

regulador (A) ADJ regulating, regulatory

(B) SM (*Mec*) regulator, throttle; (*Radio*) control, button ► **regulador de intensidad (de luz)** dimmer, dimmer switch ► **regulador del volumen (sonoro)** volume control

regular[1] ADJ [1] (= *normal*) normal, usual

[2] (= *común*) ordinary; **por lo ~** as a rule, generally

[3] (= *uniforme*) regular; **a intervalos ~es** at regular intervals; **tiene un latido ~** it has a regular beat

4 (= *mediano*) medium, average; **de tamaño ~** medium-sized, average-sized
5 (= *no muy bueno*) so-so, not too bad; **es una novela ~** it's an average sort of novel; **—¿qué tal la fiesta? —regular** "what was the party like?" — "it was O.K. *o* all right *o* not too bad"; **—¿qué tal estás? —regular** "how are you?" — "so-so *o* all right *o* can't complain"
6 (*Rel, Mil*) regular

regular² ▸conjug 1a◂ VT 1 (= *ajustar*) to regulate, control; [*ley*] to govern; [+ *tráfico, precio*] to control
2 (*Mec*) to adjust, regulate; [+ *reloj*] to put right; [+ *despertador*] to set
3 (*Méx*) (= *calcular*) to calculate

regularcillo* ADJ = **regular¹ 5**

regularidad SF regularity; **con ~** regularly

regularización SF (= *legalización*) regularization; (= *acomodación*) standardization

regularizar ▸conjug 1f◂ VT (= *ajustar, legalizar*) to regularize; (= *acomodar*) to standardize, bring into line

regularmente ADV regularly

régulo SM (*frm*) kinglet, petty king

regurgitación SF regurgitation

regurgitar ▸conjug 1a◂ VT to regurgitate

regustado ADJ (*Caribe*) well-satisfied

regustar ▸conjug 1a◂ VT (*Caribe, Méx*) to taste, relish, savour, to savor (*EEUU*)

regusto SM aftertaste; **queda siempre el ~** it leaves a bad taste in the mouth

rehabilitación SF 1 [*de enfermo, delincuente*] rehabilitation
2 (*en cargo*) reinstatement
3 [*de edificio*] restoration
4 [*de una máquina*] overhaul

rehabilitar ▸conjug 1a◂ VT 1 [+ *persona*] to rehabilitate; (*en cargo*) to reinstate
2 (*Arquit*) to restore, renovate; (*Mec*) to overhaul

rehacer ▸conjug 2r◂ Ⓐ VT 1 (= *hacer de nuevo*) to do again, redo; **tengo que ~ toda la carta** I have to do the whole letter again, I have to redo the whole letter again
2 (= *recomponer*) **no ha podido ~ su vida** he hasn't been able to piece his life together again *o* rebuild his life
Ⓑ **rehacerse** VPR 1 (= *reponerse*) to recover; **~se de algo** to get over sth, recover from sth
2 (*Mil*) to re-form

rehecho ADJ 1 (= *robusto*) thickset, chunky
2 (= *descansado*) rested

rehén SMF hostage

rehenchir ▸conjug 3l◂ VT to fill, stuff, pack (**de** with)

rehilar ▸conjug 1a◂ VI 1 (= *temblar*) to quiver, shake 2 [*flecha*] to hum

rehilete SM 1 (= *flecha*) dart; (*Taur*) banderilla
2 (*Dep*) (= *volante*) shuttlecock
3 (= *comentario*) taunt

rehogar ▸conjug 1h◂ VT to sauté, toss in oil

rehostia** Ⓐ EXCL damn it!
Ⓑ SF **esto es la ~** this is the absolute limit; **se cree que es la ~** he thinks he's the best thing since sliced bread*

rehuir ▸conjug 3g◂ VT to avoid; **Juan me rehúye** Juan is avoiding me; **rehúye de las situaciones difíciles** she avoids *o* runs away from difficult situations

rehusar ▸conjug 1a◂ Ⓐ VT to refuse; **~ hacer algo** to refuse to do sth
Ⓑ VI to refuse

reidero* ADJ amusing, funny

reidor ADJ (*frm*) merry, laughing

reiki SM reiki

reilón ADJ (*Caribe*) (= *que se ríe*) given to laughing a lot, giggly; (= *alegre*) merry

reimplantar ▸conjug 1a◂ VT to re-establish, reintroduce

reimponer ▸conjug 2q◂ VT to reimpose

reimpresión SF reprint, reprinting

reimprimir ▸conjug 3a◂ VT to reprint

reina Ⓐ SF 1 (= *monarca*) queen ► **reina de (la) belleza** beauty queen ► **reina de la fiesta** carnival queen ► **reina madre** queen mother ► **reina mora** (= *juego*) hopscotch ► **reina viuda** dowager queen
2 (*Ajedrez*) queen
3 (*Entomología*) queen
4 (*Bot*) ► **reina claudia** greengage
5 (*) (= *droga*) pure heroin
Ⓑ ADJ INV **la prueba ~** the main event

reinado SM reign; **bajo el ~ de** in the reign of

Reinaldo SM Reginald

reinante ADJ 1 (= *soberano*) reigning
2 (*fig*) (= *que prevalece*) prevailing

reinar ▸conjug 1a◂ VI 1 [*rey, reina*] to reign, rule
2 [*caos, confusión, paz*] to reign; **reina una confusión total** total confusion reigns, there is total confusion; **entre la población reinaba el descontento** there was widespread discontent among the population; **reinan las bajas temperaturas** there are low temperatures everywhere, low temperatures prevail everywhere

reinauguración SF reinauguration

reinaugurar ▸conjug 1a◂ VT to reinaugurate

reincidencia SF 1 (= *acto*) relapse (**en** into)
2 (= *tendencia*) recidivism

reincidente SMF recidivist, persistent offender

reincidir ▸conjug 3a◂ VI (= *recaer*) to relapse (**en** into); [*criminal*] to reoffend; [*pecador*] to backslide

reincorporación SF 1 [*de trabajador*] (*tras descanso, vacaciones*) return; (*tras despido*) reinstatement
2 [*de colonia, territorio*] reincorporation

reincorporar ▸conjug 1a◂ Ⓐ VT 1 [+ *colonia, territorio*] to reincorporate
2 [+ *trabajador*] to reinstate
Ⓑ **reincorporarse** VPR **~se a algo** to rejoin sth; **~se al trabajo** (*tras vacaciones, descanso*) to return to work; (*tras despido*) to be reinstated

reindustrialización SF restructuring of industry

reineta Ⓐ ADJ **manzana ~** pippin
Ⓑ SF pippin

reingresar ▸conjug 1a◂ VI **~ en** to re-enter

reingreso SM re-entry (**en** into)

reinicializar ▸conjug 1f◂ VT (*Inform*) to reset, reboot

reiniciar ▸conjug 1b◂ VT to begin again

reinicio SM new beginning

reino SM kingdom ► **reino animal** animal kingdom ► **reino vegetal** plant kingdom; **el Reino Unido** the United Kingdom

reinona* SF (= *mariquita*) fairy*, fag (*EEUU**)

reinoso/a SM/F 1 (*Andes*) [*del interior*] inlander, inhabitant of the interior (*esp of the cold eastern upland*)
2 (*Caribe*) Colombian

reinserción SF ► **reinserción en la sociedad, reinserción social** social rehabilitation, assimilation into society

reinsertado/a SM/F (= *ex-terrorista*) reformed terrorist

reinsertar ▸conjug 1a◂ Ⓐ VT to rehabilitate, assimilate into society
Ⓑ **reinsertarse** VPR **~se en la sociedad** to resume an ordinary social life

reinstalar ▸conjug 1a◂ VT 1 [+ *aparato*] to reinstall
2 (*en un puesto*) to reinstate

reinstauración SF restoration

reinstaurar ▸conjug 1a◂ VT to restore

reintegrable ADJ returnable, refundable

reintegración SF 1 (*a cargo*) reinstatement (**a** in)
2 (*Fin*) refund, repayment
3 (= *vuelta*) return (**a** to)

reintegrar ▸conjug 1a◂ Ⓐ VT 1 (= *restituir, reconstituir*) to reintegrate
2 [+ *persona*] to reinstate (**a** in)
3 (*Fin*) [+ *dinero*] to pay back; **~ a algn una cantidad** to refund *o* pay back a sum to sb; **le han reintegrado todos sus gastos** he has been reimbursed for all his expenses
4 [+ *documento*] to attach a fiscal stamp to
Ⓑ **reintegrarse** VPR **~se a** to return to

reintegro SM 1 (*Fin*) refund, reimbursement; (*en banco*) withdrawal
2 [*de lotería*] return of one's stake
3 (= *sello*) fiscal stamp, cost of a fiscal stamp

reintroducción SF reintroduction

reintroducir ▸conjug 3n◂ VT to reintroduce

reinventar ▸conjug 1a◂ VT to reinvent

reinversión SF reinvestment

reinvertir ▸conjug 3i◂ VT to reinvest

reír ▸conjug 3l◂ Ⓐ VI 1 [*persona*] to laugh; **no me hagas ~** don't make me laugh; **echarse a ~** to burst out laughing; ✦***MODISMO*** **~ como un loco** to laugh one's head off; ✦***REFRÁN*** **el que ríe el último, ríe mejor** *o* **más fuerte** he who laughs last laughs longest
2 (*liter*) [*ojos*] to laugh (*liter*), sparkle; [*campo, mañana, naturaleza*] to sparkle, glow
Ⓑ VT to laugh at; **todos le ríen los chistes** everybody laughs at his jokes
Ⓒ **reírse** VPR 1 to laugh; **~se con algo/algn**: **todos se ríen con sus chistes** everybody laughs at his jokes; **siempre nos reímos con él** we always have a good laugh with him; **~se de algn/algo** to laugh at sb/sth; **se está riendo de mí** he's laughing at me; **¿de qué te ríes?** what are you laughing at?; ✦***MODISMO*** **¡déjame que me ría!** that's a good one!
2 (*) (= *estar roto*) **estos zapatos se ríen** these shoes are split wide open at the toes; **la chaqueta se me ríe por los codos** my jacket has worn through at the elbows

reiteración SF reiteration (*frm*), repetition; **llamada de ~** (*Com*) follow-up call; **visita de ~** (*Com*) follow-up visit

reiteradamente ADV repeatedly

reiterado ADJ repeated

reiterar ▸conjug 1a◂ VT to reiterate (*frm*), to repeat

reiterativo ADJ reiterative

reivindicable ADJ recoverable, recoverable at law

reivindicación SF 1 (= *reclamación*) demand; **el gobierno ha rechazado las reivindicaciones de los sindicatos** the government have rejected the union's demands ▸ **reivindicación salarial** pay claim, wage claim
2 [*de asesinato, crimen*] **se produjo la ~ del atentado** responsibility for the attack has been claimed
3 (= *desagravio*) **una lucha por la ~ de la memoria de Galileo** a fight to vindicate Galileo's memory; **era la justa ~ de los políticos de la República** it was a fair reappraisal of the politicians of the Republic
4 (*Jur*) recovery

reivindicar ▸conjug 1g◂ Ⓐ VT 1 (= *reclamar*) [+ *derechos, condiciones, independencia*] to demand; [+ *herencia*] to claim; **reivindican subidas salariales** they are demanding pay increases
2 [+ *asesinato, crimen*] to claim responsibility for; **han reivindicado la autoría del atentado** they have claimed responsibility for the attack
3 (= *desagraviar*) [+ *reputación*] to vindicate; **reivindican la memoria de los poetas asesinados** they're demanding a reappraisal of the murdered poets
4 (*Jur*) to recover
5 (*LAm**) (= *exigir*) to demand
Ⓑ **reivindicarse** VPR (*LAm*) to vindicate o.s.

reivindicativo ADJ, **reivindicatorio** ADJ [*movimiento, acto, plataforma*] protest *antes de s*; **adoptar una postura más reivindicativa** to be more aggressive in one's demands

reja SF 1 [*de ventana*] bars *pl*, grille; [*de cercado*] railing; ✦**MODISMO entre ~s**: **estar entre ~s** to be behind bars; **meter a algn entre ~s** to put sb behind bars
2 (*Rel*) screen
3 (*Agr*) ▸ **reja del arado** ploughshare, plowshare (*EEUU*)
4 (*LAm**) (= *cárcel*) prison, nick⁑
5 (*Méx Cos*) darn, darning
6 (*Cono Sur Agr*) cattle truck

rejado SM grille, grating

rejeada SF (*Andes, CAm*) thrashing

rejear ▸conjug 1a◂ VT (*CAm*) to jail, put in jail

rejego* Ⓐ ADJ (*Méx*) 1 (= *rebelde*) wild, rebellious
2 (= *lento*) slow, sluggish
Ⓑ SM (*CAm*) stud bull

rejiego ADJ (*Caribe, Méx*) = **rejego**

rejilla SF 1 [*de caño, alcantarilla*] grating, grille; [*de equipaje*] luggage rack; [*de horno*] shelf; [*de ventilador*] vent ▸ **rejilla de ventilación** ventilation grille
2 (= *muebles*) wickerwork; **silla de ~** wicker chair
3 (= *braserillo*) small stove, footwarmer
4 (*Cono Sur*) (= *fresquera*) meat safe, cooler (*EEUU*)

rejo SM 1 (= *punta*) spike, sharp point
2 [*de insecto*] sting
3 (*Bot*) radicle
4 (*fig*) (= *vigor*) strength, vigour, vigor (*EEUU*), toughness
5 (*LAm*) (= *látigo*) whip; (= *soga*) cattle rope
6 (*Caribe*) (= *tira*) strip of raw leather; (= *porra*) stick, club ▸ **rejo tieso** brave person
7 (*Andes*) (= *ordeño*) milking; (= *vacas*) herd of cows

rejón SM (= *barra de hierro*) pointed iron bar, spike; (*Taur*) lance

rejoneador(a) SM/F (*Taur*) *mounted bullfighter who uses the lance*

rejonear ▸conjug 1a◂ (*Taur*) Ⓐ VT [+ *toro*] to wound with the lance
Ⓑ VI to fight the bull on horseback with the lance

rejoya SF (*CAm Geog*) deep valley

rejudo ADJ (*Andes, Caribe*) (= *pegajoso*) sticky, viscous; (*Caribe*) [*líquido*] runny

rejugado ADJ 1 (*Andes, Caribe*) (= *astuto*) cunning, sharp
2 (*CAm*) (= *tímido*) shy

rejunta SF (*Cono Sur, Méx*) round-up, rodeo

rejuntar ▸conjug 1a◂ VT 1 (*esp Cono Sur*) (= *recoger*) to collect, gather in
2 (*Méx*) [+ *ganado*] to round up
3 (*Cono Sur*) [+ *suma*] to add up

rejuvenecedor ADJ rejuvenating

rejuvenecer ▸conjug 2d◂ Ⓐ VT to rejuvenate
Ⓑ **rejuvenecerse** VPR to be rejuvenated, become young again

rejuvenecimiento SM rejuvenation

relación SF 1 (= *vínculo*) connection; **no existe ninguna ~ entre los dos accidentes** there is no connection between the two accidents; **existe una ~ entre el tabaco y el cáncer** there is a connection *o* relation *o* relationship between cigarettes and cancer; **guardar ~ con algo** [*suceso*] to be connected with sth, be related to sth; [*persona*] to be connected with sth; **no guardar ~ (alguna) con algo** (= *no parecerse*) to bear no relation (whatsoever) to sth; (= *no estar relacionado*) to have no connection *o* relation (at all) with sth; **tener ~ con algo** = **guardar relación con algo** ▸ **relación calidad/precio** value for money; **tener buena ~ calidad/precio** to be good value for money ▸ **relación causa-efecto** cause and effect relationship ▸ **relación real de intercambio** terms of trade *pl*
2 **con** *o* **en ~**: **en ~ con** (= *comparado con*) compared to, compared with; (= *en lo referente a*) with regard to, in connection with; **un aumento del 3% con ~ al año anterior** an increase of 3% over *o* compared to *o* compared with the previous year; **con ~ a la encuesta publicada por este periódico** with regard to *o* in connection with the survey published by this newspaper; **fue interrogado en ~ con el secuestro** he was questioned in connection with the kidnapping
3 (= *entre personas*) 3·1 (*en el momento presente*) relations *pl*; **¿cómo es su ~** *o* **son sus relaciones con su jefe?** how are relations between you and your boss?; **estar en** *o* **mantener buenas relaciones con** [+ *persona*] to be on good terms with; [+ *organización*] to have good relations with; **romper las relaciones con** [+ *país, organización*] to break off relations with; [+ *familiar, amigo*] to break off all contact with
3·2 (*de larga duración*) relationship; **¿cómo eran las relaciones con su padre?** what was your relationship with your father like?; **tenía una ~ de amistad con algunos de sus alumnos** he had a friendly relationship with some of his students; **¿sigues manteniendo las relaciones con tus antiguos compañeros de universidad?** do you still keep in touch with people from your university days?
▸ **relaciones humanas** human relations
4 (*con empresa, organización*) connection; **¿tiene alguna ~ con esa empresa?** do you have any connection with that company?; **ha sido detenido por sus relaciones con la Mafia** he has been arrested because of his connections with the Mafia ▸ **relaciones comerciales** trade relations ▸ **relaciones diplomáticas** diplomatic relations ▸ **relaciones empresariales** business relations ▸ **relaciones laborales** labour relations, labor relations (*EEUU*) ▸ **relaciones públicas** (= *actividad*) public relations, PR; (= *profesional*) public relations officer, PR officer
5 (*tb* **~ amorosa**) relationship; **nuestra ~ duró hasta 1997** our relationship lasted until 1997; **no veían con buenos ojos sus relaciones con una extranjera** they did not view his relationship with a foreign woman favourably; **tu ~ de pareja** your relationship with your partner; **llevan varios meses de relaciones** they've been seeing each other for some months; **tienen una ~ formal desde hace un año** they've been formally going out for a year ▸ **relación sentimental** relationship
6 (*tb* **~ sexual**) (= *acto*) sex; (= *trato*) sexual relationship; **mantener** *o* **tener relaciones sexuales con algn** (*de forma esporádica*) to have sex with sb; (*de forma continuada*) to be in a sexual relationship with sb ▸ **relaciones carnales** carnal relations ▸ **relaciones extramatrimoniales** extra-marital relationships ▸ **relaciones ilícitas** illicit sexual relations ▸ **relaciones prematrimoniales** premarital sex, sex before marriage
7 (= *referencia*) **hacer ~ a algo** to refer to sth; **no hizo ~ a ese tema** she did not refer to that subject
8 **relaciones** (= *personas conocidas*) acquaintances; (= *enchufes*) contacts, connections; **tener (buenas) relaciones** to be well connected, have good contacts *o* connections
9 (*Mat*) (= *proporción*) ratio; **los superan numéricamente en una ~ 46-36%** they outnumber them by a ratio of 46-36% ▸ **relación de compresión** compression ratio
10 (*frm*) (= *narración*) account; **hacer una ~ de algo** to give an account of sth; **hizo una ~ detallada de lo que vio** she gave a detailed account of what she saw
11 (= *lista*) list; **la ~ de aprobados se publicará en marzo** the list of those who have passed will be issued in March; **el usuario dispone, junto a la factura telefónica, de una ~ de sus llamadas** the customer receives, together with the telephone bill, a breakdown of calls made
12 (*Jur*) (= *informe*) record, (official) return

relacionado ADJ 1 [*acontecimiento, tema, problema*] related; **las dos cuestiones están íntimamente relacionadas** the two matters are closely related; **~ con algo** related to sth; **delitos ~s con el narcotráfico** crimes related to drug trafficking; **actividades relacionadas con el teatro** theatre-related activities;

me interesa todo lo ~ con el tema I'm interested in everything to do with *o* connected with *o* related to the subject
2 [*persona*] **una persona bien relacionada** a well-connected person; **~ con algn/algo** connected with sb/sth, linked to sb/sth; **J.S. podría estar ~ con el atentado** J.S. could be connected with *o* linked to the bomb attack; **empresas relacionadas con la industria automovilística** companies connected with *o* linked to the car industry; **se le considera muy bien ~ con los servicios secretos** he is thought to have very close connections with the secret service

relacional ADJ 1 (*Inform, Mat*) relational
2 (*Sociol*) **estudio ~** study of (human) relationships

relacionar ▸conjug 1a◂ Ⓐ VT 1 (= *asociar*) to connect (**con** with); **ya hay tres documentos que lo relacionan con el caso** there are now three documents connecting him with *o* linking him to the case
2 (= *enumerar*) to list; **los ejemplos que se relacionan a continuación** the examples listed below
Ⓑ **relacionarse** VPR 1 [*persona*] **un hombre que sabe ~se** a man who mixes with the right people; **~se con algn** to mix with sb; **en el colegio no se relacionaba con nadie** he didn't mix with anybody at school; **se relacionaba poco con los vecinos** she had little contact with her neighbours
2 [*sucesos, temas*] to be connected, be related; **los dos hechos no se relacionan** the two events are not connected *o* related; **~se con algo** to be related to sth; **palabras que se relacionan con el mar** words related to the sea
3 (*frm*) (= *referirse*) **en lo que se relaciona a** as for, with regard to

relai [re'le] SM, **relais** [re'le] SM relay

relajación SF 1 (= *sosiego*) relaxation
2 (= *suavización*) slackening, loosening
3 (*moral*) laxity
4 (*Med*) hernia, rupture

relajado ADJ 1 (= *sosegado*) relaxed
2 (= *inmoral*) dissolute, loose
3 (*Med*) ruptured

relajadura SF (*Méx*) hernia, rupture

relajante Ⓐ ADJ 1 [*ejercicio, actividad*] relaxing
2 (*Med*) sedative
3 (*Cono Sur*) [*comida*] sickly, sweet and sticky
4 (= *repugnante*) revolting, disgusting
Ⓑ SM sedative

relajar ▸conjug 1a◂ Ⓐ VT 1 (= *sosegar*) to relax
2 (= *suavizar*) to slacken, loosen
3 (*moralmente*) to weaken, corrupt
4 (*LAm*) [*comida*] to cloy, sicken, disgust
5 (*Caribe*) (= *hacer mofa de*) to mock, deride; (= *escarnecer*) to poke fun at
Ⓑ **relajarse** VPR 1 (= *sosegarse*) to relax
2 (= *aflojarse*) to slacken off, loosen
3 (*moralmente*) [*persona*] to go off the straight and narrow, go to the bad; [*moralidad*] to become lax
4 (*Med*) **~se un tobillo** to sprain one's ankle; **~se un órgano** to rupture an organ

relajo SM (*LAm*) 1 (= *libertinaje*) laxity, dissipation, depravity; (= *indecencia*) lewdness
2 (= *acción inmoral*) immoral act; (= *acto indecente*) indecent act
3 (= *ruido*) row, din; (= *fiesta*) lewd party; (= *desorden*) commotion, disorder; (= *lío*) fuss, row; **¡qué ~!** what a row/mess!
4 (= *burla*) rude joke; (= *trastada*) practical joke; (= *escarnio*) derision; **echar algo a ~** to make fun of sth; **cuento de ~** blue joke
5 (*) (= *relajación*) relaxation; (= *descanso*) rest, break
6 (*Méx*) (= *opción fácil*) easy ride, soft option

relajón ADJ 1 (*Caribe*) (= *mofador*) mocking; (*) (= *obsceno*) dirty
2 (*Méx*) (= *depravado*) depraved, perverse

relamer ▸conjug 2a◂ Ⓐ VT to lick repeatedly
Ⓑ **relamerse** VPR 1 [*animal*] to lick its chops; [*persona*] (*tb* **~se los labios**) to lick one's lips
2 (*fig*) **~se con algo** to relish the prospect of sth; (*pey*) to gloat over the prospect of sth
3 (= *gloriarse*) to brag
4 (††) (= *maquillarse*) to paint one's face

relamido ADJ 1 (= *afectado*) affected
2 (= *acicalado*) overdressed
3 (= *remilgado*) prim and proper
4 (*CAm, Caribe**) (= *descarado*) shameless, cheeky*

relámpago Ⓐ SM (= *rayo*) flash of lightning; **vi un ~ en el horizonte** I saw a flash of lightning on the horizon; **ayer hubo ~s** there was lightning yesterday; ✦*MODISMO* **como un ~** as quick as lightning, in a flash ▸ **relámpago difuso** sheet lightning
Ⓑ ADJ INV **guerra ~** blitzkrieg; **visita ~** lightning visit; **viaje ~** lightning trip

relampagucear ▸conjug 1a◂ VI (*Caribe, Méx*) (= *parpadear*) to twinkle, flicker; (= *brillar*) to gleam

relampaguceo SM (*Caribe, Méx*) (= *parpadeo*) twinkle, flicker; (= *brillo*) gleam

relampagueante ADJ flashing

relampaguear ▸conjug 1a◂ VI 1 (*Met*) **relampagueó toda la noche** there was lightning all night
2 (= *arrojar luz*) to flash
3 (*Caribe*) (= *parpadear*) to twinkle, flicker; (= *brillar*) to gleam, shine

relampagueo SM 1 [*de luz*] flashing
2 (*Caribe*) (= *parpadeo*) twinkle, flicker; (= *brillo*) gleam, shine

relampuso ADJ (*Caribe*) shameless, brazen

relance SM (*Cono Sur*) 1 = **piropo 1**
2 **de ~** (= *al contado*) in cash

relanzamiento SM relaunch, relaunching

relanzar ▸conjug 1f◂ VT 1 [+ *plan*] to relaunch
2 [+ *ataque*] to repel, repulse

relatar ▸conjug 1a◂ VT to relate, tell

relativamente ADV relatively

relatividad SF relativity

relativismo SM relativism

relativista Ⓐ ADJ relativistic
Ⓑ SMF relativist

relativizar ▸conjug 1f◂ VT to play down, diminish the importance of

relativo Ⓐ ADJ 1 (= *no absoluto*) relative; **una humedad relativa del 60%** a relative humidity of 60%; **todo es ~** everything is relative; **un problema de una importancia muy relativa** a relatively unimportant problem; **fueron momentos de relativa riqueza** it was a time of relative prosperity; **sus conocimientos son muy ~s** his knowledge is very limited
2 (= *referente*) **~ a algo** relating to sth; **cuestiones relativas a la economía** matters relating to the economy; **en lo ~ a la educación ...** as regards education ..., with regard to education ...
3 (*Ling*) relative
Ⓑ SM relative

relato SM (= *narración*) story, tale; (= *informe*) account, report

relator(a) SM/F [*de cuentos*] teller, narrator; (*Jur*) court reporter

relatoría SF (*Jur*) post of court reporter

relauchar* ▸conjug 1a◂ VI (*Cono Sur*) to skive off*

relax [re'las] SM (*Esp*) 1 (= *sosiego*) relaxation, state of relaxation; **hacer ~** to relax; **vamos a hacer un poco de ~** let's take a break
2 **"relax"** (*euf*) (*anuncio*) "massage"

relé SM relay

releer ▸conjug 2e◂ VT to reread

relegación SF 1 (= *acción*) relegation
2 (*Hist*) (= *destierro*) exile, banishment

relegar ▸conjug 1h◂ VT 1 (= *apartar*) to relegate; **~ algo al olvido** to consign sth to oblivion
2 (*Hist*) (= *desterrar*) to exile, banish

relente SM night dew

releso ADJ (*Cono Sur*) stupid, thick*

relevación SF 1 (= *sustitución*) relief (*tb Mil*)
2 (*Jur*) [*de obligación*] exoneration; [*de contrato*] release

relevante ADJ 1 (= *destacado*) outstanding
2 (= *pertinente*) relevant

relevar ▸conjug 1a◂ VT 1 (*Mil*) [+ *guardia*] to relieve; [+ *colega*] to replace, substitute for; **~ la guardia** to relieve the guard
2 (= *destituir*) **~ a algn de un cargo** to remove sb from office; **ser relevado de su mando** to be relieved of one's command
3 (= *dispensar*) **~ a algn de una obligación** to relieve sb of a duty, free sb from an obligation; **~ a algn de hacer algo** to free sb from the obligation to do sth; **~ a algn de la culpa** to exonerate sb, free sb from blame
4 (*Téc*) to emboss

relevista SMF (= *corredor*) relay runner; (= *nadador*) relay swimmer

relevo SM 1 (= *acto*) relief, change; (= *personas*) relief; **tomar el ~** to take over; **~ de la guardia** changing of the guard; **~ de los tiros** change of horses
2 **relevos** (*Dep*) relay *sing*, relay race *sing*; **100 metros ~s** 100 metre relay ▸ **relevos femeninos** women's relay *sing* ▸ **relevos masculinos** men's relay *sing*

reliar ▸conjug 1c◂ VT to roll

relicario SM 1 (*Rel*) shrine, reliquary
2 (= *medallón*) locket

relieve SM 1 (*Arte, Téc*) relief; **alto ~** high relief; **bajo ~** bas-relief; **en ~** in relief; **estampar** *o* **grabar en ~** to emboss
2 (*Geog*) **un país de ~ montañoso** a mountainous country
3 (= *importancia*) importance; **un personaje de ~** an important *o* prominent figure; **dar ~ a algo** to lend importance to sth; **la asistencia del ministro dio ~ a la celebración** the minister's presence lent an added importance to the event; **poner algo de ~** to highlight sth; **el colapso circulatorio puso de ~ la**

falta de planificación the traffic chaos highlighted the lack of planning
[4] **relieves**†† (= *restos*) leftovers
religión SF (*Rel*) religion; **entrar en ~** to take vows, enter a religious order
religiosamente ADV religiously
religiosidad SF [1] (= *devoción*) piety, religiousness, religiosity
[2] (= *puntualidad*) religiousness
religioso/a Ⓐ ADJ religious
Ⓑ SM/F monk/nun, member of a religious order
relimpio* ADJ absolutely clean
relinchada SF (*Méx*) = **relincho**
relinchar ▸conjug 1a◂ VI to neigh, snort
relincho SM neigh, neighing, snort, snorting
reliquia SF [1] (*Rel*) relic
[2] **reliquias** (= *restos*) relics, remains; (= *vestigios*) traces, vestiges ► **reliquia de familia** family heirloom
[3] (*Med*) **reliquias** after effects
[4] (*Méx*) (= *exvoto*) offering, votive offering
rellano SM landing
rellena SF (*Col, Méx*) (= *morcilla*) black pudding, blood sausage (*EEUU*)
rellenable ADJ refillable, reusable
rellenado SM (= *llenado*) refill, replenishment; (*Aut*) refuelling, refueling (*EEUU*)
rellenar ▸conjug 1a◂ Ⓐ VT [1] (= *volver a llenar*) to refill, replenish; (*Aer*) to refuel
[2] (= *llenar hasta arriba*) to fill up
[3] [+ *formulario*] to fill in, fill out; [+ *espacios*] to fill in
[4] (*Culin*) to stuff (**de** with)
[5] (*Cos*) to pad
Ⓑ **rellenarse** VPR to stuff o.s. (**de** with)
rellenito ADJ plump
relleno Ⓐ ADJ [1] (= *lleno hasta arriba*) full up (**de** of)
[2] (*Culin*) stuffed (**de** with)
[3] (= *gordito*) [*persona*] plump; [*cara*] full
Ⓑ SM [1] (*Culin*) (*para dulces*) filling; (*para carnes*) stuffing
[2] [*de caramelo*] centre, center (*EEUU*) ► **relleno blando** soft centre ► **relleno duro** hard centre
[3] (*en un escrito*) **frases de ~** padding
[4] (*Arquit*) plaster filling
[5] (*Cos*) padding
[6] (*Mec*) packing
[7] (*Andes*) (= *vertedero*) tip, dump
reloj [re'lo] SM (*grande*) clock; [*de pulsera*] watch; **contra (el) ~** against the clock; ✦*MODISMO* **como un ~** like clockwork; **marchar como un ~** to go like clockwork ► **reloj automático** timer, timing mechanism ► **reloj biológico** biological clock ► **reloj de arena** hourglass, sandglass ► **reloj de bolsillo** pocket watch ► **reloj de caja** grandfather clock ► **reloj de carillón** chiming clock ► **reloj de cuco** cuckoo clock ► **reloj de estacionamiento** parking meter ► **reloj de fichar** time clock ► **reloj de la muerte** (*Entomología*) deathwatch beetle ► **reloj de pie** grandfather clock ► **reloj de pulsera** wristwatch ► **reloj de sol** sundial ► **reloj despertador** alarm clock ► **reloj digital** digital watch ► **reloj eléctrico** electric clock ► **reloj fichador** time clock ► **reloj parlante** talking clock ► **reloj registrador** time clock

relojear ▸conjug 1a◂ VT (*Cono Sur*) [1] [+ *carrera*] to time
[2] (*) (= *vigilar*) to spy on, keep tabs on; (= *controlar*) to check, keep a check on
relojería SF [1] (= *tienda*) watchmaker's, watchmaker's shop
[2] (= *arte*) watchmaking, clockmaking; **aparato de ~** clockwork; **bomba de ~** time bomb; **mecanismo de ~** timing device
relojero/a SM/F (= *fabricante*) (*de relojes de pulsera*) watchmaker; (*de relojes de pared*) clockmaker
reluciente ADJ [1] (= *brillante*) shining, brilliant; [*joyas*] glittering, sparkling
[2] [*persona*] (= *de buen aspecto*) healthy-looking; (= *gordo*) well-fed
relucir ▸conjug 3f◂ VI (= *brillar*) to shine; [*joyas*] to glitter, sparkle; ✦*MODISMO* **sacar algo a ~** [+ *tema*] to bring sth up, mention sth; **siempre saca a ~ sus éxitos** he's always going on about how successful he is
relujar ▸conjug 1a◂ VT (*CAm, Méx*) to shine
relumbrante ADJ (= *brillante*) brilliant, dazzling; (= *deslumbrante*) glaring
relumbrar ▸conjug 1a◂ VI (= *brillar*) to dazzle; (= *deslumbrar*) to glare
relumbrón SM [1] [*de luz*] flash
[2] (= *ostentación*) flashiness, ostentation; **vestirse de ~** to dress ostentatiously; **joyas de ~** flashy jewellery o (*EEUU*) jewelry
remachado ADJ (*Andes*) quiet, reserved
remachador(a) Ⓐ SM/F (= *persona*) riveter
Ⓑ SF (= *máquina*) riveting machine, riveter
remachar ▸conjug 1a◂ Ⓐ VT [1] (*Téc*) [+ *metales*] to rivet; [+ *clavo*] to clinch
[2] [+ *aspecto, asunto, punto*] **quisiera ~ este punto que considero de extrema importancia** I would like to stress this point, which I think is extremely important; **el político remachó ese punto recordándoles qué había pasado** the politician really hammered home the point by reminding them what had happened
[3] (= *finalizar*) to finish off
Ⓑ **remacharse** VPR (*Andes**) to remain stubbornly silent
remache SM [1] (*Téc*) rivet
[2] (= *acción*) [*de metal*] riveting; [*de clavo*] clinching
[3] (*Andes*) (= *terquedad*) stubbornness, obstinacy
remada SF stroke
remador(a) SM/F rower
remaduro ADJ (*LAm*) overripe
remake [ri'meik] SM remake
remalladora SF mender, darner
remallar ▸conjug 1a◂ VT to mend, darn
remalo* ADJ (*LAm*) really bad
remandingo SM (*Caribe*) row, uproar
remanente Ⓐ ADJ [1] (= *que queda*) remaining
[2] (*Com*) [*de producto*] surplus
[3] (*Fís*) remanent
Ⓑ SM (= *lo que queda*) remainder; (*Com*) [*de producto*] surplus
remangar ▸conjug 1h◂ VT = **arremangar**
remango* ADJ lively, energetic, vigorous
remangue* SM liveliness, energy, vigour, vigor (*EEUU*); **hacer algo con ~** to do sth energetically, tackle sth vigorously
remansarse ▸conjug 1a◂ VPR to form a pool

remanso SM [1] (*en río*) pool
[2] (= *lugar*) quiet place; **un ~ de paz** an oasis of peace
remaque SM remake
remar ▸conjug 1a◂ VI [1] (*Náut*) to row; **~ en seco** to go on a rowing machine
[2] (††) (= *pasar penurias*) to toil, struggle
remarcable ADJ (*esp LAm*) remarkable
remarcación SF mark-up
remarcar ▸conjug 1g◂ (*esp LAm*) VT [1] (= *observar*) to notice, observe
[2] (= *señalar*) to point out
[3] (= *subrayar*) to emphasize, underline
[4] [+ *precio*] to mark up
rematadamente ADV terribly, hopelessly; **~ mal** terribly o hopelessly bad; **es ~ tonto** he's utterly stupid
rematado ADJ [1] (= *total*) hopeless, complete; **es un loco ~** he's a raving lunatic; **es un tonto ~** he's an utter fool o a complete idiot
[2] (*Esp*†) [*niño*] very naughty
rematador(a) SM/F [1] (*Dep*) goal scorer
[2] (*Andes, Cono Sur*) auctioneer
rematadora SF auction house, auctioneer's
rematante SMF highest bidder
rematar ▸conjug 1a◂ Ⓐ VT [1] (= *matar*) to finish off
[2] (= *terminar*) [+ *discurso, actuación*] to round off, conclude; [+ *trabajo*] to finish off; [+ *bebida, comida*] to finish up, finish off; **remató el concierto cantando su último éxito** she rounded off the concert by singing her latest hit
[3] (*Tenis*) to smash; (*Ftbl*) (*con el pie*) to shoot; (*con la cabeza*) to head; **remató el centro (de cabeza)** he met the cross (with a header); **remató la jugada** he finished off the move
[4] (*Cos*) to cast off
[5] (*Arquit*) to top, crown
[6] (*LAm Com*) (= *subastar*) to auction; (= *liquidar*) to sell off cheap
[7] (*Cono Sur*) [+ *caballo*] to pull up
Ⓑ VI [1] (= *terminar*) to end, finish off; **remató con un par de chistes** he ended o finished off with a couple of jokes
[2] **~ en** to end in; **es del tipo que remata en punta** it's the sort which ends in a point; **fue una broma que remató en tragedia** it was a prank which ended in tragedy
[3] (*Tenis*) to smash; (*Ftbl*) (*con el pie*) to shoot; (*con la cabeza*) to head; **~ de cabeza** to head the ball towards goal
remate SM [1] (= *cabo*) end; (= *punta*) tip, point; [*de edificio, mueble*] ornamental top
[2] (= *toque final*) **como ~ al concierto hizo un bis** to round off the concert he played an encore; **poner ~ a algo** to cap sth; ✦*MODISMOS* **de ~***: **está loco de ~** he's stark raving mad*; **para ~*** to crown it all, to top it all; **para ~ va y me insulta** to crown o top it all he went and insulted me
[3] (*Ftbl*) (*con el pie*) shot; (*con la cabeza*) header; **un ~ de cabeza** a header; **un equipo sin ~** a team with no finishing power
[4] (*LAm Com*) (= *liquidación*) bargain sale; (= *subasta*) auction
[5] (*Bridge*) bidding
rematista SMF (*Andes, Caribe*) auctioneer
rembolsar *etc* ▸conjug 1a◂ VT = **reembolsar**
remecer ▸conjug 2d◂ Ⓐ VT (*LAm*) (*de lado a lado*) to shake; (= *agitar*) to wave

Ⓑ **remecerse** VPR to rock, swing, swing to and fro

remedar ▸conjug 1a◂ VT (= *imitar*) to imitate, copy; (*para burlarse*) to ape, mimic

remediable ADJ that can be remedied *o* put right; **fácilmente ~** easily remedied *o* put right

remediar ▸conjug 1b◂ VT 1 (= *solucionar*) to remedy; **no podemos ~ este problema** we cannot remedy this problem; **si el gobierno no lo remedia se perderán muchos puestos de trabajo** if the government does not remedy the situation a lot of jobs will be lost; **llorando no remedias nada** you're not going to solve anything by crying, crying won't solve anything
2 (= *evitar*) **no pudo ~ echarse a reír** she couldn't prevent herself from laughing; **es un mujeriego pero le quiero, no puedo ~lo** he's a womanizer but I love him, I can't help it
3 [+ *necesidades*] to meet, help with

➤**remedio** SM 1 (= *alternativa*) choice, alternative; **no tengo más ~ que ir** I've got no alternative *o* choice but to go; **—¿tienes que trabajar este sábado? —¡qué ~!** "are you working this Saturday?" — "I've got no choice!"; **¿qué ~ me queda?** what else can I do?, what choice have I got?; **no hay más ~ que operarle** there is nothing for it but to operate on him; **¡si no hay más ~, iré!** well, if I have to, I'll go!
2 (= *solución*) **Juan no tiene ~** Juan's a hopeless case, Juan's beyond redemption; **como último ~** as a last resort; **sin ~: tenemos que hacerlo hoy sin ~** we have to do it today without fail; **es un tonto sin ~** he's hopelessly stupid, he's so stupid he's beyond redemption; **poner ~ a algo** to remedy sth, correct sth
3 (*Med*) cure, remedy; **un buen ~ contra** *o* **para el resfriado** a good cure *o* remedy for colds; **un ~ contra** *o* **para la tos** a cough remedy; ✦*MODISMOS* **es peor el ~ que la enfermedad** the solution is worse than the problem; **¡ni por un ~!** not on your life!; **ni para un ~: no se le podía encontrar ni para un ~** it couldn't be had for love nor money; **no ha dejado leche ni para un ~** she hasn't left a single drop of milk ➤ **remedio casero** home remedy ➤ **remedio heroico** drastic action
4 (*frm*) (= *alivio*) relief, help; **es un ~ en su aflicción** it's a relief in her distress
5 (*Jur*) remedy, recourse

remedo SM (= *imitación*) imitation, copy; (*pey*) parody

rememorar ▸conjug 1a◂ VT to recall

remendar ▸conjug 1j◂ VT 1 [+ *ropa*] to darn, mend; (*con parche*) to patch
2 (*fig*) (= *corregir*) to correct

remendón/ona Ⓐ ADJ **zapatero ~** cobbler
Ⓑ SM/F cobbler

remera SF (*Arg*) (= *camiseta*) T-shirt

remero/a Ⓐ SM/F oarsman/oarswoman, rower
Ⓑ SM (= *máquina*) rowing machine

remesa SF [*de dinero*] remittance; [*de bienes*] shipment ➤ **remesa de fondos** (*Méx Com*) settlement, financial settlement

remesar ▸conjug 1a◂ VT [+ *dinero*] to remit, send; [+ *bienes*] to send, ship

remeter ▸conjug 2a◂ VPR (= *volver a meter*) to put back; [+ *camisa*] to tuck in

➤ LENGUA Y USO: **remedio 1** 37.1, 45.4

remezcla SF remix

remezón SM (*LAm*) earth tremor, slight earthquake

remiendo SM 1 [*de ropa*] mending; (*con parche*) patching
2 (= *arreglo*) mend, darn; (= *parche*) patch; **a ~s** piecemeal; **echar un ~ a algo** (= *coser*) to darn sth; (= *poner un parche*) to patch sth, put a patch on sth
3 (= *corrección*) correction
4 (*Med*) improvement
5 (*Zool*) spot, patch

remilgado ADJ 1 (= *melindroso*) finicky, fussy, particular
2 (= *mojigato*) prudish, prim
3 (= *afectado*) affected

remilgo SM 1 (= *melindre*) fussiness; **él no hace ~s a ninguna clase de trabajo** he won't turn up his nose at any kind of work
2 (= *mojigatería*) prudery, primness
3 (= *afectación*) affectation

remilgoso ADJ (*LAm*) = **remilgado**

reminiscencia SF reminiscence

remirado ADJ 1 (= *prudente*) cautious, circumspect, careful; (*pey*) overcautious
2 (*pey*) (= *gazmoño*) prudish; (= *afectado*) affected, over-nice; (= *melindroso*) fussy, pernickety*, persnickety (*EEUU*)*

remirar ▸conjug 1a◂ Ⓐ VT to look at again; **lo miraba y lo remiraba y aún no se lo creía** she stared and stared at it, but she still couldn't believe it
Ⓑ **remirarse** VPR to be extra careful (**en** about), take great pains (**en** over)

remise SM **auto de ~** (*Arg*) hire car

remisión SF 1 (= *envío*) sending; (*esp LAm Com*) shipment, consignment
2 (*al lector*) reference (**a** to)
3 (= *aplazamiento*) postponement
4 (= *disminución*) (*tb Med*) remission
5 (*Rel*) forgiveness, remission

remiso ADJ 1 [*persona*] **estar** *o* **mostrarse ~ a hacer algo** to be reluctant to do sth, be unwilling to do sth
2 [*movimiento*] slow, sluggish

remisor(a) SM/F (*LAm*) sender

remite SM sender

remitente SMF sender

remitido SM 1 (*en periódico*) paid insert
2 (*Méx*) (= *consignación*) shipment, consignment

remitir ▸conjug 3a◂ Ⓐ VT 1 (= *enviar*) to send; [+ *dinero*] to remit, send; (*Com*) to ship, send
2 [+ *lector*] to refer (**a** to)
3 (= *aplazar*) to postpone
4 **~ una decisión a algn** to refer a decision to sb
5 (*Rel*) to forgive, pardon
Ⓑ VI (= *disminuir*) to slacken, let up
Ⓒ **remitirse** VPR **a las pruebas me remito** the proof of the pudding is in the eating

remix SM remix

remo SM 1 (*Náut*) oar; **cruzar un río a ~** to row across a river; **pasaron los cañones a ~** they rowed the guns across; ✦*MODISMO* **a ~ y vela** speedily
2 (*Dep*) rowing; **practicar el ~** to row
3 (*Anat**) limb; [*de pájaro*] wing
4 (††) (= *penuria*) toils *pl*; **andar al ~** to be hard at it

remoción SF (*esp LAm*) (= *acción de remover*) removal; (= *cese*) dismissal

remodelación SF 1 (*Arquit*) remodelling, remodeling (*EEUU*)
2 (*Aut*) restyling
3 [*de organización*] restructuring; (*Pol*) reshuffle ➤ **remodelación de gobierno** government reshuffle ➤ **remodelación ministerial** cabinet reshuffle

remodelar ▸conjug 1a◂ VT (*Arquit*) to remodel; (*Aut*) to restyle; (*Pol*) to reshuffle; [+ *organización*] to restructure

remojar ▸conjug 1a◂ VT 1 [+ *legumbres, prenda*] to soak, steep (**en** in); [+ *galleta*] to dip (**en** in, into)
2 (*) (= *celebrar bebiendo*) **¡este triunfo habrá que ~lo!** this victory calls for a drink!
3 (*Méx**) (= *sobornar*) to bribe

remojo SM 1 **poner algo a** *o* **en ~** to leave sth to soak
2 (*LAm*) (= *regalo*) gift, present; (= *propina*) tip

remojón SM 1 (*en piscina, playa*) **darse un ~*** to go in for a dip
2 (*Culin*) piece of bread soaked in milk *etc*

remolacha SF beetroot, beet (*EEUU*) ➤ **remolacha azucarera** sugar beet ➤ **remolacha de mesa, remolacha roja** beetroot, beet (*EEUU*)

remolachero/a Ⓐ ADJ beet *antes de s*
Ⓑ SM/F beet farmer

remolcable ADJ that can be towed, towable

remolcador SM 1 (*Náut*) tug
2 (*Aut*) breakdown lorry, tow truck (*EEUU*)

remolcar ▸conjug 1g◂ VT 1 (*Náut*) to tug
2 (*Aut*) to tow

remoledor* ADJ (*Andes, Cono Sur*) roistering, party-going

remoler ▸conjug 2h◂ Ⓐ VT 1 (= *moler*) to grind up small
2 (*LAm**) (= *fastidiar*) to annoy, bug*
Ⓑ VI (*Cono Sur, Andes**) to live it up*

remolienda* SF (*Andes, Cono Sur*) party, wild time*

remolinar ▸conjug 1a◂ VI, **remolinear** ▸conjug 1a◂ VI = **arremolinarse**

remolino SM 1 [*de agua*] (*pequeño*) swirl, eddy; (*grande*) whirlpool
2 [*de aire*] (*pequeño*) eddy; (= *grande*) whirlwind; [*de humo, polvo*] whirl, cloud
3 [*de pelo*] cowlick
4 [*de gente*] crowd, throng
5 (= *conmoción*) commotion

remolón/ona* Ⓐ ADJ (= *vago*) lazy
Ⓑ SM/F 1 (= *vago*) slacker, shirker
2 (= *ignorante*) **hacerse el ~: le tocaba pagar pero se hizo el ~** it was his turn to pay, but made as if it wasn't

remolonear ▸conjug 1a◂ Ⓐ VI (= *vaguear*) to slack, shirk
Ⓑ **remolonearse** VPR **cuando llegó la hora de pagar empezó a ~se** when it came to paying, he started making as if it had nothing to do with him

remolque SM 1 (= *vehículo*) trailer; (= *caravana*) trailer, semitrailer (*EEUU*), caravan; (*Náut*) ship on tow
2 (= *acción*) towing; **a ~** on tow; **ir a ~** to be on tow; **llevar un coche a ~** to tow a car; **dar ~ a un coche** to tow a car; **ir a ~ de algn** to go along with sb (*in what they say or do*)
3 (= *cuerda*) towrope

remonda†* SF **¡es la ~!** this is the end!

remonta SF 1 (*Cos*) mending, repair
2 (*Mil*) remount, supply of cavalry horses

remontada SF recovery

▼ **remontar** ▸conjug 1a◂ Ⓐ VT 1 [+ *río*] to go up; [+ *obstáculo*] to negotiate, get over; *ver tb* **vuelo² 1**
2 [+ *zapato*] to mend, repair; [+ *media*] to mend, mend a ladder in
3 (*Mil*) [+ *caballo*] to remount
4 [+ *reloj*] to wind
5 (*Caza*) [+ *animales*] to frighten away
Ⓑ **remontarse** VPR 1 [*avión, pájaro*] to rise, soar; [*edificio*] to soar, tower; **~se en alas de la imaginación** (*liter*) to take flight on the wings of fantasy
2 (*Fin*) **~se a** to amount to
3 (*en tiempo*) **~se a** to go back to; **este texto se remonta al siglo XI** this text dates from *o* dates back to the 11th century; **sus recuerdos se remontan a la Guerra Civil** her memories go back to the Civil War; **tenemos que ~nos a los mismos orígenes** we must go back to the roots of this

remonte SM ski lift

remoquete SM 1 (= *apodo*) nickname; **poner ~ a algn** to give sb a nickname
2 (= *puñetazo*) punch
3 (= *comentario*) cutting remark, dig*
4 (*) (= *coqueteo*) flirting, spooning*; (= *pretendiente*) suitor

rémora SF 1 (*Zool*) remora
2 (= *obstáculo*) hindrance

remorder ▸conjug 2h◂ Ⓐ VI (= *reconcomer*) **me remuerde el haberle tratado así** I have a guilty conscience about treating him like that; **no me remuerde la conciencia** I don't have any qualms about it
Ⓑ **remorderse** VPR to feel/show remorse

remordimiento SM (*tb* **~s**) remorse, regret; **tener ~s** to feel remorse, suffer pangs of conscience

remotamente ADV 1 [*parecerse, recordar*] vaguely
2 [*pensar*] vaguely, tentatively

remotidad* SF (*CAm*) remote spot, distant place

▼ **remoto** ADJ 1 (*en el tiempo*) far-off, distant; **en épocas remotas** in far-off *o* distant times
2 (*en el espacio*) faraway, distant; **en un país ~** in a faraway *o* distant country
3 (= *poco probable*) remote; **existe la remota posibilidad de que venga** there is a remote possibility *o* a very slight chance he may come; **no tengo ni la más remota idea** I haven't the faintest *o* remotest idea; **no se me ocurriría insultarle ni por lo más ~** it would never enter my head to insult him; **—¿te enfrentarías a él? —¡ni por lo más ~!** "would you stand up to him?" — "no way *o* not on your life!"

remover ▸conjug 2h◂ VT 1 [+ *tierra*] to turn over, dig up; [+ *objetos*] to move round; [+ *fuego, brasas*] to poke, stir; [+ *sopa*] to stir; [+ *ensalada*] to toss; [+ *cóctel*] to shake; **~ el pasado** to stir up the past; **~ un asunto** to go into a matter; **~ un proyecto** to revive a scheme; ✦***MODISMOS*** **~ cielo y tierra** ◊ **~ Roma con Santiago** to move heaven and earth
2 (= *quitar*) to remove; (*Med*) to remove
3 (*esp LAm*) (= *cesar*) to dismiss

removimiento SM removal

remozado SM [*de persona*] rejuvenation; [*de edificio, fachada*] renovation

remozamiento SM [*de persona*] rejuvenation; [*de edificio, fachada*] renovation

remozar ▸conjug 1f◂ Ⓐ VT [+ *persona*] to rejuvenate; [+ *aspecto*] to brighten up; [+ *organización*] to give a new look to, give a face-lift to; [+ *edificio, fachada*] to renovate
Ⓑ **remozarse** VPR to be rejuvenated; **la encuentro muy remozada** she looks so much younger

remplazar ▸conjug 1f◂ VT = **reemplazar**

rempujar* ▸conjug 1a◂ VT to shove, push

rempujón* SM shove, push

remuda SF (= *cambio*) change, alteration; (= *reemplazo*) replacement; (*tb* **~ de ropa**) change of clothes, spare clothes *pl* ► **remuda de caballos** change of horses

remudar ▸conjug 1a◂ VT (= *cambiar*) to change, alter; (= *reemplazar*) to replace

remunerable ADJ remunerable

remuneración SF remuneration

remunerado ADJ **trabajo mal ~** badly-paid job

remunerador ADJ 1 (= *retribuido*) remunerative; **poco ~** unremunerative
2 (= *gratificante*) rewarding, worthwhile

remunerar ▸conjug 1a◂ VT (= *retribuir*) to remunerate; (= *premiar*) to reward

remunerativo ADJ remunerative

renacentista ADJ Renaissance *antes de s*

renacer ▸conjug 2d◂ VI 1 (= *volver a nacer*) to be reborn; (*Bot*) to reappear, come up again
2 (= *reavivar*) to revive; **hacer ~** to revive; **hoy me siento ~** today I feel like a new person *o* as if I've come to life again; **sentían ~ la esperanza** they felt new hope

renaciente ADJ renascent

renacimiento SM rebirth, revival; **el Renacimiento** the Renaissance

renacuajo SM 1 (*Zool*) tadpole
2 (*) (= *niño*) shrimp
3 (*pey*) (= *pequeñajo*) runt, little squirt*

renal ADJ renal, kidney *antes de s*

Renania SF Rhineland

renano ADJ Rhenish, Rhine *antes de s*

rencilla SF 1 (= *disputa*) quarrel; **~s** arguments, bickering *sing*
2 (= *rencor*) bad blood; **me tiene ~** he's got it in for me*, he bears me a grudge

rencilloso ADJ quarrelsome

renco ADJ lame

rencor SM (= *amargura*) rancour, rancor (*EEUU*), bitterness; (= *resentimiento*) ill feeling, resentment; (= *malicia*) spitefulness; **guardar ~** to bear malice, harbour *o* (*EEUU*) harbor a grudge (**a** against); **no le guardo ~** I bear him no malice

rencorosamente ADV 1 (= *con resentimiento*) resentfully; (= *con amargura*) bitterly
2 (= *con malicia*) spitefully, maliciously

rencoroso ADJ 1 [*ser*] spiteful, nasty
2 [*estar*] (= *resentido*) resentful; (= *amargado*) bitter

rendición SF 1 (*Mil*) surrender ► **rendición incondicional** unconditional surrender
2 (*Fin*) yield, profit, profits *pl*
3 (*Cono Sur Com, Fin*) trading balance; (*tb* **~ de cuentas**) balance

rendidamente ADV (= *sumisamente*) submissively; (= *servilmente*) obsequiously; (= *con devoción*) devotedly

rendido ADJ 1 (= *cansado*) exhausted, worn-out
2 (= *sumiso*) submissive; (= *servil*) obsequious; (= *enamorado*) devoted

rendidor ADJ (*LAm*) highly productive, highly profitable

rendija SF 1 (= *hendedura*) crack, cleft; (= *abertura*) aperture
2 (*en la ley*) loophole

rendimiento SM 1 [*de una máquina*] output; (= *capacidad*) capacity; (= *producción*) output; **aumentar el ~ de una máquina** to increase the output of a machine; **el ~ del motor** the performance of the engine; **funcionar a pleno ~** to work all-out, work at full throttle
2 [*de persona*] performance, achievement; **tiene muy bajo ~ escolar** he's not doing very well *o* achieving much academically; **Centro de Alto Rendimiento** *specialized sports training centre* ► **rendimiento académico** academic achievement ► **rendimiento laboral** performance at work
3 (*Fin*) yield, profit, profits *pl*; **ley del ~ decreciente** law of diminishing returns ► **rendimiento del capital** return on capital
4 (= *sumisión*) submissiveness; (= *servilismo*) obsequiousness; (= *devoción*) devotion; **su ~ total a la voluntad de ella** his complete submission to her will
5 (= *agotamiento*) exhaustion
6 (= *parte útil*) usable part, proportion of usable material

rendir ▸conjug 3k◂ Ⓐ VT 1 (= *producir*) to produce; [+ *beneficios etc*] to yield; [+ *producto, total etc*] to produce; [+ *interés*] to bear
2 (= *cansar*) to exhaust, tire out; **le rindió el sueño** he was overcome by sleep
3 **~ homenaje a** to pay tribute to; **~ culto a** to worship; **~ las gracias** (*frm*) to give thanks
4 (*Mil*) [+ *ciudad*] to surrender; [+ *fortaleza*] to take, capture; **~ la guardia** to hand over the guard
5 (*Mil*) [+ *bandera*] to dip; [+ *armas*] to lower, reverse
6 (*Esp*) (= *vomitar*) to vomit, bring up
7 (*Com*) [+ *factura*] to send
8 **~ examen** (*Cono Sur*) to sit *o* take an exam
9 (*frm*) (= *vencer*) [+ *país*] to conquer, subdue
10 (*frm*) (= *dominar*) to dominate; **logró ~ el albedrío de la joven** he came to dominate the young woman's will completely; **había que ~ su entereza** he had to overcome his moral objections
11 (*frm*) (= *devolver*) to give back, return; (= *entregar*) to hand over
Ⓑ VI 1 (= *producir*) to yield, produce; (= *dar resultados*) to give good results; **el negocio no rinde** the business is not profitable *o* doesn't pay; **la finca rinde para mantener a ocho familias** the estate produces enough to keep eight families; **este año ha rendido poco** it has done poorly this year; **trabajo, pero no rindo** I work hard but without much to show for it
2 [*arroz*] to swell up
3 (*LAm*) (= *durar*) to last longer, keep going
Ⓒ **rendirse** VPR 1 (= *ceder*) to yield (**a** to); (*Mil*) to surrender; (= *entregarse*) to give o.s. up; **~se a la razón** to yield to reason; **~se a la evidencia** to bow before the evidence; **~se**

➤ LENGUA Y USO: **remontar B3** 44.2 **remoto 3** 42.3

a la fuerza to yield to violence; **¡me rindo!** I give in!

2 (= *cansarse*) to wear o.s. out

renditivo ADJ (*Cono Sur*) productive

renegado/a Ⓐ ADJ 1 (= *traidor*) renegade; (*Rel*) apostate *antes de s*; (*Pol*) rebel *antes de s*

2 (*) (= *brusco*) gruff*; (= *malhumorado*) cantankerous, bad-tempered

Ⓑ SM/F (= *traidor*) renegade; (*Rel*) apostate; (*Pol*) rebel

renegar ▸conjug 1h, 1j◂ Ⓐ VI 1 **~ de: renegó de su fe** he renounced his faith; **ha renegado de su familia** she has disowned her own family

2 (= *maldecir*) to curse, swear; (= *blasfemar*) to blaspheme

3 (= *refunfuñar*) to complain (**de** about); **se pasa el día renegando de todo** she spends her time complaining about everything

4 (*Andes, Méx*) (= *enojarse*) to get angry, get upset

5 (*Andes, Méx*) (= *gritar*) to shout, rage

Ⓑ VT **negar y ~ algo** to deny sth vigorously; **niega y reniega haber provocado el incendio** he vigorously denies having started the fire

renegociación SF renegotiation

renegociar ▸conjug 1b◂ VT to renegotiate

renegón* ADJ grumbling, cantankerous, grouchy*

renegrido ADJ very black, very dark

RENFE SF ABR, **Renfe** SF ABR (*Ferro*) = **Red Nacional de los Ferrocarriles Españoles**

renglón SM 1 (= *línea*) line, line of writing; **escribir unos renglones** to write a few lines *o* words; **estos pobres renglones** (*liter*) these humble jottings; ✦***MODISMOS*** **a ~ seguido** immediately after; **leer entre renglones** to read between the lines

2 (*Com*) item of expenditure

3 (*LAm Com*) (= *género*) line of goods; (= *departamento*) department, area

rengo ADJ (*LAm*) lame, crippled

rengue‡ SM train

renguear ▸conjug 1a◂ VI 1 (*LAm*) (= *cojear*) to limp, hobble

2 (*Cono Sur*) (= *perseguir*) to pursue a woman

renguera SF (*LAm*) limp, limping

reniego SM 1 (= *juramento*) curse, oath; (*Rel*) blasphemy

2 (= *queja*) grumble, complaint

reno SM reindeer

renombrado ADJ renowned, famous

renombrar ▸conjug 1a◂ VT to rename

renombre SM (= *fama*) renown, fame; **de ~** renowned, famous

renovable ADJ renewable

renovación SF 1 [*de contrato, pasaporte, suscripción*] renewal

2 [*de edificio*] renovation; **han invertido 100 millones en la ~ del museo** they have invested 100 million in the renovation of the museum; **subvenciones para la ~ de los sistemas informáticos** subsidies for updating *o* upgrading computer systems

3 [*de partido, asamblea*] clearout; **el comité necesita una completa ~** the committee needs a complete clearout

4 (= *reanudación*) renewal; **la ~ de las hostilidades acabó con las esperanzas de paz** the renewal of hostilities scuppered hopes of peace

5 (*Rel*) ► **renovación espiritual** spiritual renewal

renovado ADJ renewed, redoubled; **con renovada energía** with renewed energy

renovador(a) (*Pol*) Ⓐ ADJ reformist

Ⓑ SM/F restorer; **~ de muebles** furniture restorer

renoval SM (*Cono Sur, Méx*) area of young trees

renovar ▸conjug 1l◂ Ⓐ VT 1 [+ *contrato, pasaporte, suscripción*] to renew

2 [+ *edificio*] to renovate; [+ *sistema informático*] to update, upgrade

3 [+ *muebles*] to change; **han renovado el mobiliario de la casa** they've changed the furniture in the house

4 [+ *partido, asamblea*] to clear out

5 (= *reanudar*) [+ *ataques*] to renew; [+ *conversaciones*] to resume

Ⓑ **renovarse** VPR 1 (= *reanudarse*) **se han renovado los ataques** there have been renewed attacks, the attacks have resumed

2 [*persona*] **~se o morir** adapt or perish

renquear ▸conjug 1a◂ VI 1 (= *cojear*) to limp, hobble

2 (*) (= *ir tirando*) to get by, just about manage

3 [*motor*] to splutter

4 (= *vacilar*) to dither

renqueo SM limp

renta SF 1 (= *ingresos*) income; (= *ganancia*) interest, return; **tiene ~s particulares** she has a private income; **vivir de (las) ~s** to live on one's private income; **política de ~s** incomes *o* (*EEUU*) income policy; **título de ~ fija** fixed-interest bond; **valores de ~ fija** fixed-yield securities ► **renta bruta nacional** gross national income ► **renta del trabajo** earned income ► **renta devengada** earned income ► **renta disponible** disposable income ► **renta gravable** taxable income ► **renta imponible** taxable income ► **renta nacional** national income ► **renta no salarial** unearned income ► **renta sobre el terreno** ground rent ► **rentas públicas** revenue *sing* ► **renta vitalicia** annuity

2 (= *deuda*) public debt, national debt

3 (*esp LAm*) (= *alquiler*) rent; **"casa de renta"** "house to let"

rentabilidad SF profitability

rentabilizar ▸conjug 1f◂ VT (= *hacer rentable*) to make profitable, make more profitable; (= *sacar provecho de*) to exploit to the full; (*pey*) to cash in on

rentable ADJ profitable; **no ~** unprofitable; **la línea ya no es ~** the line is no longer economic (to run)

rentado ADJ (*Cono Sur*) paid

rentar ▸conjug 1a◂ Ⓐ VT 1 (= *producir*) to produce, yield

2 (*LAm*) [+ *casa*] to let, rent out; **"rento casa"** "house to let"

Ⓑ **rentarse** VPR **"se renta"** (*Méx*) "to let"

rentero/a SM/F tenant farmer

rentista SMF 1 (= *accionista*) stockholder; (*que vive de sus rentas*) rentier

2 (= *especialista*) financial expert

rentístico ADJ financial

renuencia SF 1 [*de persona*] reluctance, unwillingness

2 [*de materia*] awkwardness

renuente ADJ 1 [*persona*] reluctant, unwilling

2 [*materia*] awkward, difficult

renuevo SM 1 (= *acto*) renewal

2 (*Bot*) shoot, sprout

renuncia SF 1 (*a derecho, trono*) renunciation; **la paz depende de una ~ total a la violencia** peace is dependent on a total renunciation of violence; **está considerando una posible ~ a sus derechos al trono** he is thinking of renouncing his rights to the throne; **han hecho pública la ~ a sus exigencias/planes** they announced that they have abandoned *o* dropped their claims/plans; **confirmó su ~ a participar en el proyecto** he confirmed his refusal to take part in the project

2 [*de empleado*] resignation; **presentó su ~** he tendered his resignation, he resigned

3 (= *abnegación*) renunciation; **una vida de ~ y sacrificio** a life of renunciation and sacrifice

renunciar ▸conjug 1b◂ VI 1 **~ a** [+ *derecho, trono*] to renounce; [+ *exigencia, plan*] to abandon, drop; **han renunciado a la violencia** they have renounced violence; **ha renunciado a su puesto de jefe de prensa** he has resigned his post as press officer; **tras su enfermedad renunció al tabaco** after his illness he gave up smoking; **¿renuncias a Satanás?** do you renounce Satan?

2 (= *dimitir*) to resign; **el ministro no ~á** the minister will not resign

3 (*Naipes*) to revoke

renuncio SM 1 (*Naipes*) revoke

2 (= *mentira*) **coger a algn en un ~** to catch sb in a fib, catch sb out

reñidamente ADV bitterly, hard, stubbornly

reñidero SM ► **reñidero de gallos** cockpit

reñido ADJ 1 [*batalla, concurso*] hard-fought, close; **un partido ~** a hard-fought *o* close game; **en lo más ~ de la batalla** in the thick of the fight

2 (= *enfadado*) **estar ~ con algn** to have fallen out with sb, be on bad terms with sb; **está ~ con su familia** he has fallen out with his family, he is on bad terms with his family

3 (= *en contradicción*) **estar ~ con algo: está ~ con el principio de igualdad** it goes against *o* is contrary to the principle of equality

reñidor ADJ quarrelsome

reñir ▸conjug 3h, 3k◂ Ⓐ VT 1 (= *regañar*) to scold; (= *reprender*) to tell off*, reprimand (**por** for)

2 [+ *batalla*] to fight, wage

Ⓑ VI (= *pelear*) to quarrel, fall out (**con** with); **ha reñido con su novio** she's fallen out *o* had a fight with her boyfriend; **se pasan la vida riñendo** they spend their whole time quarrelling; **riñeron por cuestión de dinero** they quarrelled about money, they quarrelled over money

reo¹ SMF 1 (= *delincuente*) culprit, offender; (*Jur*) accused, defendant ► **reo de Estado** person accused of a crime against the state ► **reo de muerte** person under sentence of death

2 (*Cono Sur*) (= *vagabundo*) tramp, bum (*EEUU**)

reo² SM (= *pez*) sea trout

reoca* SF **es la ~** (*Esp*) (= *bueno*) it's the tops*; (= *malo*) it's the pits*

reojo: **de ~** ADV **mirar a algn de ~** (= *disimuladamente*) to look at sb out of the corner of one's eye; (= *con recelo*) to look askance at sb

reorganización SF reorganization

reorganizar ▸conjug 1f◂ (A) VT to reorganize
(B) **reorganizarse** VPR to reorganize

reorientación SF [*de negocio, economía*] reorientation; [*de recursos*] redeployment

reorientar ▸conjug 1a◂ VT [+ *economía*] to reorientate; [+ *dirección, costumbre*] to change; [+ *recursos*] to redeploy

reóstato SM rheostat

Rep. ABR (= **República**) Rep

repanchigarse* ▸conjug 1h◂ VPR, **repantigarse*** ▸conjug 1h◂ VPR to lounge, sprawl, loll (back); **estar repanchigado en un sillón** to be sprawled *o* lolling (back) in a chair

repanocha* SF **¡eres la ~!** you're unbelievable!; **¡aquello fue la ~!** it was unbelievable!

reparable ADJ repairable

reparación SF [1] (= *acción*) repairing, mending
[2] (*Téc*) repair; **efectuar reparaciones en** to carry out repairs to *o* on; **"reparaciones en el acto"** "repairs while you wait"
[3] (= *desagravio*) reparation
[4] (*Jur*) redress

reparador(a) (A) ADJ [1] [*sueño*] refreshing; [*comida*] fortifying, restorative
[2] (*frm*) [*persona*] critical, faultfinding
(B) SM/F (= *criticón*) critic, faultfinder
(C) SM (*Téc*) repairer

reparadora SF ► **reparadora de calzados** (*Méx*) shoe repairer's

reparar ▸conjug 1a◂ (A) VT [1] (= *arreglar*) to repair, mend, fix
[2] [+ *energías*] to restore; [+ *fortunas*] to retrieve
[3] [+ *ofensa*] to make amends for; [+ *suerte*] to retrieve; [+ *daño, pérdida*] to make good; [+ *consecuencia*] to undo
[4] [+ *golpe*] to parry
[5] (= *observar*) to observe, notice
[6] (*Cono Sur*) (= *imitar*) to mimic, imitate
(B) VI [1] **~ en** (= *darse cuenta de*) to observe, notice; **no reparó en la diferencia** he didn't notice the difference; **sin ~ en que ya no funcionaba** without noticing it didn't work any more
[2] **~ en** (= *poner atención en*) to pay attention to, take heed of; (= *considerar*) to consider; **no ~ en las dificultades** not to consider the problems; **repara en lo que vas a hacer** consider what you are going to do, reflect on what you are going to do; **sin ~ en los gastos** regardless of the cost; **no ~ en nada** to stop at nothing
[3] (*LAm*) [*caballo*] to rear, buck
(C) **repararse** VPR [1] (= *controlarse*) to restrain o.s.
[2] (*CAm, Méx*) [*caballo*] to rear, buck

reparista ADJ (*Andes, CAm, Caribe*), **reparisto** ADJ (*CAm, Caribe*) = **reparón A**

▼**reparo** SM [1] (= *escrúpulo*) scruple, qualm; **no tuvo ~ en hacerlo** he had no qualms about doing it, he did not hesitate to do it
[2] (= *objeción*) objection; (= *crítica*) criticism; (= *duda*) doubt; **poner ~s** (= *oponerse*) to raise objections (**a** to); (= *criticar*) to criticize, express one's doubts
[3] (*frm*) (= *reparación*) repair; (*Arquit*) restoration
[4] (*Esgrima*) parry
[5] (= *protección*) defence, defense (*EEUU*), protection
[6] (*Med*) remedy
[7] (*CAm, Méx*) [*de caballo*] bucking, rearing; **tirar un ~** to rear, buck

reparón/ona (A) ADJ critical, faultfinding
(B) SM/F critic, faultfinder

repartición SF [1] (= *distribución*) distribution; (= *división*) sharing out, division
[2] (*Cono Sur Admin*) government department
[3] (*LAm Pol*) [*de tierras*] redistribution

repartida SF (*LAm*) = **repartición 1**

repartidor(a) SM/F (= *distribuidor*) distributor; (*Com*) deliveryman/deliverywoman ► **repartidor(a) de leche** milkman/milkwoman ► **repartidor(a) de periódicos** paperboy/papergirl ► **repartidor(a) de pizzas** pizza delivery boy/girl

repartija SF (*LAm pey*) share-out, carve-up*

repartimiento SM (= *distribución*) distribution; (= *división*) division

repartir ▸conjug 3a◂ (A) VT [1] (= *dividir entre varios*) to divide (up), share (out); **tendremos que ~ el pastel** we'll have to share (out) *o* divide (up) the cake; **~ dividendos** to share the profits; **los estudiantes están repartidos en cuatro grupos** the students are divided into four groups; **el premio está muy repartido** the prize is shared among many
[2] (= *distribuir, dar*) [+ *correo, periódicos*] to deliver; [+ *folletos, premios*] to give out, hand out; [+ *naipes*] to deal; **repartieron golpes a todo el que se les acercaba** they lashed out at anyone who came near them
[3] (= *esparcir*) **hay guarniciones repartidas por todo el país** there are garrisons dotted about *o* spread about *o* distributed all over the country
(B) **repartirse** VPR [1] (= *dividirse entre varios*) **se repartieron el botín** they divided (up) *o* shared (out) the spoils among themselves
[2] (= *distribuir*) **"se reparte a domicilio"** "home delivery (service)"

reparto SM [1] (= *partición*) sharing out; **el ~ de la herencia originó conflictos** the sharing out of the inheritance gave rise to disputes; **no existe un equilibrado ~ de la riqueza** there is not an even distribution of wealth, wealth is not evenly distributed ► **reparto de beneficios** profit sharing ► **reparto de dividendos** distribution of dividends
[2] (= *entrega*) [*de correo, periódicos*] delivery; **"reparto a domicilio"** "home delivery (service)"; **vamos a efectuar el ~ de premios** we are going to give out the prizes
[3] (*Cine, Teat*) cast; **un ~ estelar** a star cast
[4] (*LAm*) (= *solar*) building site; (= *barrio*) suburb

repasador SM (*Cono Sur*) dishcloth

repasar ▸conjug 1a◂ VT [1] [+ *cuenta*] to check; [+ *texto, lección*] to revise; [+ *apuntes*] to go over (again); [+ *publicación etc*] to put the finishing touches to, polish up
[2] (*Mec*) (= *arreglar*) to check, overhaul
[3] (*Cos*) **~ la plancha por una prenda** to iron a garment again, give a garment another iron
[4] (*Cos*) (= *coser*) to sew, sew up
[5] (*Cono Sur*) [+ *platos*] to wipe; [+ *mueble*] to dust, polish; [+ *ropa*] to brush, brush down
[6] [+ *lugar*] to pass again, pass by again; **pasar y ~ una calle** to go up and down a street

repaso SM [1] (= *revisión*) revision; **ejercicios de ~** revision exercises; **dale un ~ a esta lección** revise this lesson; **los técnicos daban el último ~ a la nave** the technicians were giving the ship a final check; **le di un último ~ a la carta antes de enviarla** I read through the letter again quickly before sending it; **un ~ de los temas tratados más importantes** a quick run-through *o* review of the main points I've dealt with; ✦**MODISMO dar** *o* **pegar un buen ~ a algn*** (= *regañar*) to give sb a proper ticking-off*; (= *ganar*) to thrash sb
[2] (*Cos*) (= *arreglo*) **tengo que darles un ~ a estos pantalones** I have to mend these trousers; **ropa de ~** mending, darning

repatear* ▸conjug 1a◂ VT (*Esp*) **ese tío me repatea** that guy gets on my wick‡ *o* turns me right off*

repatriación SF repatriation

repatriado/a (A) ADJ repatriated
(B) SM/F repatriate, repatriated person

repatriar ▸conjug 1b◂ (A) VT to repatriate; [+ *criminal*] to deport; **van a ~ el famoso monumento** they are going to send the famous monument back to its country of origin
(B) **repatriarse** VPR to return home, go back to one's own country

repe[1]* (A) ADJ repeated, duplicated; **este sello lo tengo ~** I've got this stamp twice
(B) SF (*TV*) repeat

repe[2] SM (*Andes*) mashed bananas with milk

repechar ▸conjug 1a◂ VI **~ contra** (*Méx*) to lean against, lean one's chest against

repecho SM [1] (= *vertiente*) sharp gradient, steep slope; **a ~** uphill
[2] (*Caribe, Méx*) (= *parapeto*) parapet
[3] (*Méx*) (= *refugio*) shelter, refuge

repela SF (*Andes, CAm*) gleaning, gleaning of coffee crop

repelar ▸conjug 1a◂ (A) VT [1] (= *pelar*) [+ *cabeza*] to leave completely bare, shear; [+ *persona*] to leave completely shaven, shear; [+ *hierba*] to nibble, crop; [+ *uñas*] to clip
[2] (= *arrancar pelo*) **~ a algn** to pull sb's hair
[3] (*Méx*) (= *criticar*) to raise objections to, call into question
[4] (*Méx*) (= *reprender*) to scold, tell off*
(B) **repelarse** VPR (*Cono Sur*) to feel remorse

repelencia SF (*esp LAm*) revulsion, disgust

repelente (A) ADJ [1] (= *repulsivo*) repellent, repulsive
[2] (*) (= *sabelotodo*) **es ~** he's a know-all
(B) SM repellent, insect repellent

repeler ▸conjug 2a◂ (A) VT [1] [+ *enemigo*] to repel, repulse, drive back
[2] (= *rechazar*) **el material repele el agua** the material is water-resistant; **la pared repele la pelota** the wall sends the ball back, the ball bounces off the wall
[3] [+ *idea, oferta*] to reject
[4] (= *repugnar*) to repel, disgust
(B) **repelerse** VPR **los dos se repelen** the two are incompatible, the two are mutually incompatible

➤ LENGUA Y USO: **reparo 2** 38.3

repellar ▸conjug 1a◂ VT 1 [+ *pared, muro*] to plaster, stucco
2 (*LAm*) (= *enjalbegar*) to whitewash
3 (*Caribe*) (= *menear*) to wriggle, wiggle

repello SM 1 (*en pared, muro*) **la pared tenía ~s** the cracks on the wall had been filled in with plaster
2 (*LAm*) (= *jalbegue*) whitewash, whitewashing
3 (*Caribe*) (*en baile*) wiggle, grind

repelo SM 1 (= *pelo*) hair out of place, hair that sticks up
2 (*en madera*) snag, knot
3 (*en la piel*) hangnail
4 (*) (= *riña*) tiff, slight argument
5 (= *aversión*) aversion
6 (*Andes, Méx*) (= *baratijas*) junk, bric-a-brac
7 (*Andes, Méx*) (= *trapo*) rag, tatter

repelón Ⓐ ADJ (*Méx*) grumbling, grumpy
Ⓑ SM 1 (= *tirón*) tug, tug at one's hair
2 (*Cos*) ruck, snag
3 (= *pedacito*) small bit, tag, pinch
4 [*de caballo*] dash, short run
5 (*Méx*) (= *reprimenda*) telling-off*, scolding

repelús* SM **me da ~** it gives me the willies* *o* shivers

repeluz SM **en un ~** (*Cono Sur*) in a flash, in an instant

repeluzno* SM nervous shiver, slight start of fear

repensar ▸conjug 1j◂ VT to rethink, reconsider

repente SM 1 (= *movimiento*) sudden movement, start; (*fig*) (= *impulso*) sudden impulse ► **repente de ira** fit of anger
2 **de ~** (= *de pronto*) suddenly; (= *inesperadamente*) unexpectedly
3 (*Méx Med*) (= *acceso*) fit; (= *desmayo*) fainting fit

repentinamente ADV **torcer ~** to turn sharply, make a sharp turn; *ver tb* **repente 2**

repentino ADJ 1 (= *súbito*) sudden; (= *imprevisto*) unexpected; [*curva, vuelta*] sharp
2 **tener repentina compasión** (*frm*) to be quick to pity

repentización SF (*Mús*) sight-reading; (= *improvisación*) ad-lib, improvisation

repentizar ▸conjug 1f◂ VI (*Mús*) to sight-read; (= *improvisar*) to ad-lib, improvise

repentón* SM violent start

repera* SF **es la ~** it's the tops*

repercusión SF 1 (= *consecuencia*) repercussion; **repercusiones** repercussions; **las repercusiones de esta decisión** the repercussions of this decision; **de amplia** *o* **de ancha ~** far-reaching, with profound effects; **tener ~** *o* **repercusiones en** to have repercussions on
2 [*de sonido*] repercussion; (= *reverberación*) reverberation, echo

repercutir ▸conjug 3a◂ Ⓐ VI 1 (= *influenciar*) **~ en** to have repercussions on, affect
2 (= *reverberar*) [*sonido*] to echo, reverberate
3 (= *rebotar*) to rebound, bounce off
4 (*Méx*) (= *oler mal*) to smell bad, stink
Ⓑ VT (*Andes*) to contradict
Ⓒ **repercutirse** VPR to reverberate

reperiquete SM (*Méx*) 1 (= *baratija*) cheap jewellery, cheap jewelery (*EEUU*)
2 (= *baladronada*) brag, boast

repertoriar ▸conjug 1b◂ VT to catalogue, catalog (*EEUU*), list

repertorio SM 1 (= *lista*) list, index; (= *catálogo*) catalogue, catalog (*EEUU*)
2 (*Teat*) repertoire
3 (*Inform*) repertoire

repesca SF 1 (*Escol*) repeat, repeat exam
2 (*Dep*) play-off, play-off for third place

repescar ▸conjug 1g◂ VT to give a second chance to

repeso SM (*Andes*) bonus, extra

repetición SF 1 (= *acción*) repetition; (= *reaparición*) recurrence
2 (*Teat*) encore
3 **fusil de ~** repeating rifle

repetidamente ADV repeatedly

repetido ADJ 1 (= *reiterado*) repeated; **el tan ~ aviso** the oft-repeated warning
2 (= *numeroso*) numerous; **en repetidas ocasiones** on numerous occasions; **repetidas veces** repeatedly, over and over again
3 [*sello*] duplicate

repetidor SM (*Radio, TV*) booster, booster station

repetidora SF repeater rifle

repetir ▸conjug 3k◂ Ⓐ VT (= *reiterar*) to repeat; (= *rehacer*) to do again; **le repito que es imposible** I repeat that it is impossible; **los niños repiten lo que hacen las personas mayores** children imitate adults; **~ el postre** to have a second helping *o* seconds* of dessert; **~ un curso** to repeat a year
Ⓑ VI 1 (= *servirse de nuevo*) to have a second helping; **se comió un buen plato y repitió** she ate a large plateful and then had a second helping
2 [*ajo, pepino, chorizo*] **el pepino repite mucho** cucumber keeps repeating on you; **las cebollas me repiten** onions repeat on me
Ⓒ **repetirse** VPR 1 [*persona*] to repeat o.s.
2 [*suceso*] to recur; **¡ojalá no se repita esto!** I hope this won't happen again!
3 [*comida*] **el ajo se me repite mucho** garlic repeats on me

repetitivo ADJ repetitive

repicado SM copying of tapes, copying of video tapes, video piracy

repicar ▸conjug 1g◂ Ⓐ VT 1 [+ *campanas*] to ring; ✦**MODISMO** **~ gordo un acontecimiento** to celebrate an event in style
2 [+ *carne*] to chop up finely
3 [+ *cinta*] to copy, pirate
Ⓑ **repicarse** VPR (†) to boast (**de** about, of)

repintar ▸conjug 1a◂ Ⓐ VT (= *volver a pintar*) to repaint; (= *pintar de prisa*) to paint hastily
Ⓑ **repintarse** VPR to pile the make-up on

repipi* ADJ (= *afectado*) affected; (= *esnob*) la-di-dah*; (= *engreído*) stuck-up*; **es una niña ~** she's a little madam

repique SM 1 [*de tambor*] beating
2 [*de campanas*] ringing, pealing
3 (*) (= *riña*) tiff, squabble

repiquete SM 1 [*de tambor*] beating; [*de campana*] pealing, ringing
2 (*Mil*) clash
3 (*Cono Sur Orn*) trill, song
4 (*Andes*) (= *resentimiento*) pique, resentment

repiquetear ▸conjug 1a◂ Ⓐ VT 1 [+ *campanas*] to ring
2 [+ *tambor*] to tap, beat rapidly
Ⓑ VI 1 (*Mús*) to peal, ring out
2 [*máquina*] to clatter
Ⓒ **repiquetearse** VPR (*) to squabble

repiqueteo SM 1 [*de tambor*] beating; [*de campana*] pealing, ringing
2 (*en mesa*) tapping
3 [*de máquina*] clatter

repisa SF (= *estante*) shelf; **la ~ de la chimenea** the mantelpiece; **la ~ de la ventana** the windowsill

replana SF (*Andes*) underworld slang

replantar ▸conjug 1a◂ VT to replant

replanteamiento SM rethink, reconsideration

replantear ▸conjug 1a◂ Ⓐ VT [+ *cuestión*] to raise again, reopen
Ⓑ **replantearse** VPR **~se algo** to rethink *o* reconsider sth, think again about sth; **me lo estoy replanteando** I'm thinking it over again

replantigarse* ▸conjug 1h◂ VPR (*LAm*) = **repanchigarse**

repleción SF repletion

replegable ADJ 1 (= *que se pliega*) folding, that folds, that folds up
2 (*Aer*) [*tren de aterrizaje*] retractable

replegar ▸conjug 1h, 1j◂ Ⓐ VT 1 (= *plegar*) to fold over; (*de nuevo*) to fold again, refold
2 [+ *tren de aterrizaje*] to retract, draw up
Ⓑ **replegarse** VPR (*Mil*) to withdraw, fall back

repletar ▸conjug 1a◂ (*frm*) Ⓐ VT to fill completely, stuff full, pack tight
Ⓑ **repletarse** VPR to stuff o.s., eat to repletion (*frm*)

repleto ADJ 1 (= *lleno*) full up; **~ de** full of, crammed with; **el cuarto estaba ~ de gente** the room was crammed with people; **una colección repleta de rarezas** a collection containing many rare pieces
2 **estar ~** [*persona*] to be full up (*with food*)
3 [*aspecto*] well-fed

réplica SF 1 (= *respuesta*) answer; (*Jur*) replication; **derecho de ~** right of reply; **~s** backchat *sing*; **dejar a algn sin ~s** to leave sb speechless
2 (*Arte*) replica, copy

replicar ▸conjug 1g◂ VI 1 (= *contestar*) to answer, retort
2 (= *objetar*) to argue, answer back; **¡no repliques!** don't answer back!

replicón* ADJ argumentative

repliegue SM 1 (= *pliegue*) fold, crease
2 (*Mil*) withdrawal, retreat ► **repliegue táctico** tactical withdrawal, tactical retreat

repoblación SF [*de personas*] repopulation; [*de peces*] restocking; [*de árboles*] reafforestation ► **repoblación forestal** reafforestation

repoblar ▸conjug 1l◂ VT [+ *país*] to repopulate; [+ *río*] to restock; (*con árboles*) to plant trees on

repollo SM cabbage

repollonco* ADJ (*Cono Sur*), **repolludo*** ADJ tubby*, chunky*

reponer ▸conjug 2q◂ (*pp* **repuesto**) Ⓐ VT 1 [+ *productos, surtido*] to replenish
2 (= *devolver*) [+ *objeto dañado*] to replace, pay for, pay for the replacement of; **~ el dinero robado** to pay back the stolen money
3 (*en un cargo*) to reinstate
4 (= *recuperar*) **~ fuerzas** to get one's strength back
5 (*Teat*) to revive, put on again; (*TV*) to repeat

6 (*frm*) (= *replicar*) to reply (**que** that)
Ⓑ **reponerse** VPR (= *recuperarse*) to recover; **~se de** to recover from, get over

repóquer SM (*tb* **~ de ases**) *four aces plus a wild card*

reportaje SM report, article ► **reportaje gráfico** illustrated report

reportar ▸conjug 1a◂ (*frm*) Ⓐ VT 1 (= *traer*) to bring, carry; (= *producir*) to give, bring; **esto le habrá reportado algún beneficio** this will have brought him some benefit; **la cosa no le reportó sino disgustos** the affair brought him nothing but trouble; **esto le habrá reportado dos millones** it must have landed him two million
2 (*LAm*) (= *informar*) to report; (= *denunciar*) to denounce, accuse; (= *notificar*) to notify, inform
Ⓑ VI (*LAm*) (*a cita*) to turn up (*for an appointment*)
Ⓒ **reportarse** VPR 1 (= *contenerse*) to control o.s.; (= *calmarse*) to calm down
2 (*Méx*) (= *presentarse*) to turn up

reporte SM (*esp CAm, Méx*) report, piece of news

reportear ▸conjug 1a◂ VT (*LAm*) 1 (= *fotografiar*) to photograph (*for the press*)
2 [+ *suceso*] to report, report on

repórter SMF = **reportero**

reportero/a SM/F reporter ► **reportero/a gráfico/a** news photographer, press photographer

reposabrazos SM INV armrest

reposacabezas SM INV headrest

reposacodos SM INV elbow rest

reposadamente ADV (= *con tranquilidad*) quietly; (= *descansadamente*) gently, restfully; (= *sin prisa*) unhurriedly, calmly

reposadera SF (*CAm*) drain, sewer

reposado ADJ (= *tranquilo*) quiet; (= *descansado*) gentle, restful; (= *lento*) unhurried, calm

reposapiés SM INV footrest

reposaplatos SM INV table mat, hot pad (*EEUU*)

reposar ▸conjug 1a◂ Ⓐ VI 1 (= *descansar*) to rest
2 (= *dormir*) to sleep
3 (= *apoyarse*) to lie, rest; **su mano reposaba sobre mi hombro** her hand lay *o* rested on my shoulder; **la columna reposa sobre una base circular** the column is resting *o* sitting on a circular base
4 [*restos mortales*] to lie, rest
5 (*Culin*) **dejar ~ algo** to let sth stand
Ⓑ VT 1 (= *apoyar*) to lay, rest; **reposó la cabeza sobre la almohada** she lay *o* rested her head on the pillow
2 **~ la comida** to let one's food settle *o* go down
Ⓒ **reposarse** VPR [*líquido*] to settle

reposera SF (*Cono Sur*) canvas chair, deck chair

reposición SF 1 (= *recambio*) replacement
2 (*Fin*) reinvestment
3 (*Teat*) revival; (*TV*) repeat
4 (*Med*) (*tb fig*) recovery

reposicionar ▸conjug 1a◂ VT to reposition

repositorio SM repository

reposo SM rest, repose (*frm o liter*); **estar en ~** to be resting; **guardar ~** (*Med*) to rest, stay in bed ► **reposo absoluto** (*Med*) complete rest

repostada SF (*LAm*) rude reply, sharp answer

repostadero SM refuelling stop, refueling stop (*EEUU*)

repostaje SM refuelling, refueling (*EEUU*), filling up

repostar ▸conjug 1a◂ Ⓐ VT [+ *surtido*] to replenish; **~ combustible** *o* **gasolina** (*Aer*) to refuel; (*Aut*) to fill up, fill up with petrol
Ⓑ VI to refuel
Ⓒ **repostarse** VPR to replenish stocks, take on supplies; **~se de combustible** to refuel

repostería SF 1 (= *tienda*) confectioner's, confectioner's shop, cake shop
2 (= *arte*) confectionery
3 (= *despensa*) larder, pantry

repostero/a Ⓐ SM/F confectioner, pastry cook
Ⓑ SM (*Andes, Chile*) (= *despensa*) pantry, larder; (= *estantería*) kitchen shelf unit

repostón* ADJ (*CAm, Méx*) rude, surly

repregunta SF (*Jur*) cross-examination, cross-questioning

repreguntar ▸conjug 1a◂ VT (*Jur*) to cross-examine, cross-question

reprender ▸conjug 2a◂ VT (= *amonestar*) to reprimand, tell off*; [+ *niño*] to scold; **~ algo a algn** to criticize sb for sth

reprensible ADJ reprehensible

reprensión SF (= *amonestación*) (*a un adulto*) reprimand, telling-off*; (*a un niño*) scolding

represa SF 1 (= *presa*) dam; (= *lago artificial*) lake, pool; (= *vertedero*) weir ► **represa de molino** millpond
2 (= *parada*) check, stoppage
3 (= *represión*) repression
4 (= *captura*) recapture

represalia SF reprisal; **como ~ por** in reprisal for; **tomar ~s** to retaliate, take reprisals (**contra** against)

represaliado/a SM/F victim of a reprisal

represaliar ▸conjug 1b◂ VT to take reprisals against

represar ▸conjug 1a◂ VT 1 (*Náut*) to recapture
2 (= *detener*) to check, put a stop to
3 (*Pol*) (= *reprimir*) to repress
4 [+ *agua*] to dam, dam up; (*fig*) to stem

representable ADJ 1 (= *ilustrable*) **es ~ en un gráfico** it can be represented in a graph
2 (*Teat*) **la obra no es ~** the play cannot be staged *o* performed

representación SF 1 [*de concepto, idea, imagen*] representation; **la ~ gráfica** the graphic representation; **en este cuadro el buitre es una ~ de la muerte** in this painting the vulture represents death
2 [*de país, pueblo, organización*] (= *acto*) representation; (= *delegación*) delegation; **partidos políticos con ~ parlamentaria** political parties represented in parliament; **en el congreso había una nutrida ~ de empresarios** there was a large representation of businessmen at the conference; **la ~ española en la feria** the Spanish delegation at the fair; **en ~ de**: **el abogado que actúa en ~ del banco** the lawyer representing the bank; **me invitaron a ir en ~ de la empresa** they invited me to go as a representative of the company, they invited me to go to represent the company; **habló en ~ de todos** she spoke on behalf of everyone ► **representación diplomática** (= *actividad*) diplomatic representation; (= *oficina*) embassy ► **representación legal** (= *acto*) legal representation; (= *abogado*) lawyer(s); **la ~ legal del acusado** (= *acto*) the defendant's legal representation; (= *abogado*) the lawyers representing the defendant, the defendant's lawyers ► **representación proporcional** proportional representation
3 (*Teat*) (= *función*) performance; (= *montaje*) production; **durante una ~ teatral** during a theatre performance; **una ~ financiada por el Patronato de Turismo** a production financed by the Tourist Board
4 (*Com*) representation; **ha conseguido la ~ de varias firmas farmacéuticas** he has managed to become an agent for various pharmaceutical companies, he has managed to obtain the representation of various pharmaceutical companies; **tener la ~ exclusiva de un producto** to be sole agent for a product, have sole agency of a product (*frm*)
5 (†) (= *súplica*) **hacer representaciones a algn** to make representations to sb (*frm*)
6 (††) (= *importancia*) standing; **un hombre de ~** a man of some standing

representado/a SM/F client

representante SMF 1 [*de organización, país, en parlamento*] representative; **la única ~ española en esta prueba** Spain's only representative in this event; **uno de los máximos ~s del surrealismo** one of the greatest exponents *o* representatives of surrealism ► **representante legal** legal representative ► **representante sindical** union representative
2 (*Com*) representative
3 [*de artista, deportista*] agent
4 (†) (= *actor*) performer, actor/actress

representar ▸conjug 1a◂ Ⓐ VT 1 (= *actuar en nombre de*) [+ *país, votantes*] to represent; [+ *cliente, acusado*] to act for, represent; **la cantante que ~á a España en el festival** the singer who will represent Spain at the festival; **el príncipe representó al rey en la ceremonia** the prince attended the ceremony on behalf of the king *o* representing the king
2 (= *simbolizar*) to symbolize, represent; **Don Quijote representa el idealismo** Don Quixote symbolizes *o* represents idealism; **cuando éramos pequeños nuestros padres representaban el modelo a seguir** when we were small our parents were our role models
3 (= *reproducir*) to depict; **este grabado representa a la amada del pintor** this engraving depicts the painter's lover; **nuevas formas de ~ el mundo** new ways of representing *o* portraying *o* depicting the world; **esta columna del gráfico representa los síes** this column of the graph shows *o* represents those in favour
4 (= *equivaler a*) [+ *porcentaje, mejora, peligro*] to represent; [+ *amenaza*] to pose, represent; **obtuvieron unos beneficios de 1,7 billones, lo que representa un incremento del 28% sobre el año pasado** they made profits of 1.7 billion, which represents an increase of 28% on last year; **los bantúes representan el 70% de los habitantes de Suráfrica** the Bantu account for *o* represent 70% of the inhabitants of South Africa; **la ofensiva de ayer representa una violación de la tregua** yesterday's offensive constitutes a violation of the truce; **no sabes lo mucho que representa este trabajo para él** you don't know how much this job means to him

5 (= *requerir*) [+ *trabajo, esfuerzo, sacrificio*] to involve; **representa mucho esfuerzo** it involves a great deal of effort
6 (*Teat*) [+ *obra*] to perform; [+ *papel*] to play; **el teatro donde se representa la obra** the theatre where the play is being performed; **en esta película represento el papel de un abogado** in this film I play the part of a lawyer; **¿quién va a ~ el papel que tenía antes la URSS?** who's going to play the part *o* role previously played by the USSR?
7 (= *aparentar*) [+ *edad*] to look; **no representa los años que tiene** she doesn't look her age; **representa unos 55 años** he looks about 55
8 (= *hacer imaginar*) to point out; **nos representó las dificultades con que nos podíamos encontrar** she pointed out the difficulties we might come up against
Ⓑ **representarse** VPR (= *imaginarse*) to imagine; **no puedo representármelo siendo fiel** I can't imagine him being faithful

representatividad SF **el sindicato con mayor ~ en la enseñanza** the union with the greatest representation in the teaching profession; **carece de la suficiente ~ para poder hablar en nombre del grupo** he is not representative enough of the group to speak on its behalf

representativo ADJ 1 (= *simbólico, característico*) representative; **estas cifras no son muy representativas** these figures are not very representative; **uno de los artistas más ~s de la época** one of the most representative artists of the age
2 (*Pol*) [*democracia, institución, organización*] representative; **organizaciones representativas de los indígenas** organizations representing the indigenous people

represión SF 1 [*de deseos, impulsos*] repression
2 (*Pol*) [*de rebelión*] suppression; **la brutal ~ de la rebelión por las tropas del gobierno** the brutal suppression of the rebellion by government troops; **la ~ es una realidad en China** repression is a fact of life in China

represivo ADJ, **represor** ADJ repressive

reprimenda SF reprimand, rebuke

reprimido/a Ⓐ ADJ repressed
Ⓑ SM/F repressed person

reprimir ▸conjug 3a◂ Ⓐ VT 1 [+ *deseos, impulsos*] to repress
2 [+ *rebelión*] to suppress
3 [+ *bostezo*] to suppress; [+ *risa*] to hold in, hold back
Ⓑ **reprimirse** VPR **~se de hacer algo** to stop o.s. (from) doing sth

reprisar ▸conjug 1a◂ VT (*CAm, Cono Sur, Méx*) to revive, put on again

reprise[1] SF (*esp LAm Teat*) revival

reprise[2] [re'pris] SM (*a veces* SF) (*Aut*) acceleration

repristinación SF (*frm*) restoration to its original state

repristinar ▸conjug 1a◂ VT (*frm*) to restore to its original state

reprivatización SF privatization, reprivatization

reprivatizar ▸conjug 1f◂ VT to privatize, reprivatize

reprobable ADJ reprehensible

reprobación SF (= *desaprobación*) reproval, reprobation; **escrito en ~ de ...** written in condemnation of ...

reprobador ADJ reproving, disapproving

reprobar ▸conjug 1l◂ VT 1 (= *desaprobar*) to reprove, condemn
2 (*LAm Escol*) (= *suspender*) to fail

reprobatorio ADJ = **reprobador**

réprobo ADJ damned

reprocesado SM, **reprocesamiento** SM reprocessing

reprocesar ▸conjug 1a◂ VT to reprocess

reprochable ADJ blameworthy, culpable

reprochar ▸conjug 1a◂ Ⓐ VT (= *reconvenir*) to reproach; **~ algo a algn** to reproach sb for sth; **le reprochan su descuido** they reproach him for his negligence
Ⓑ **reprocharse** VPR to reproach o.s.; **no tienes nada que ~te** you have nothing to reproach yourself for

reproche SM reproach (**a** for); **nos miró con ~** he looked at us reproachfully

reproducción SF reproduction ► **reproducción asexual** asexual reproduction ► **reproducción asistida** assisted reproduction

reproducir ▸conjug 3n◂ Ⓐ VT 1 (= *volver a producir*) to reproduce
2 (*Biol*) to reproduce, breed
3 (= *copiar*) to reproduce
Ⓑ **reproducirse** VPR 1 (*Biol*) to reproduce, breed
2 [*condiciones*] to be reproduced; [*suceso*] to happen again, recur; **se le han reproducido los síntomas** the symptoms have reappeared *o* recurred; **si se reproducen los desórdenes** if the disturbances happen again

reproductor Ⓐ ADJ [*yegua*] brood *antes de s*; [*órgano, sistema*] reproductive
Ⓑ SM ► **reproductor de CD** CD player ► **reproductor de compact disc, reproductor de discos compactos** compact disc player

reprografía SF reprography

reprogramar ▸conjug 1a◂ VT [+ *película*] to reprogramme, reprogram (*EEUU*); [+ *deuda*] to reschedule

reps SM INV rep

reptar ▸conjug 1a◂ VI to creep, crawl

reptil Ⓐ ADJ reptilian
Ⓑ SM reptile

república SF republic ► **república bananera** banana republic ► **República Dominicana** Dominican Republic ► **República Árabe Unida** United Arab Republic

republicanismo SM republicanism

republicano/a ADJ, SM/F republican

repudiación SF repudiation

repudiar ▸conjug 1b◂ VT 1 [+ *violencia*] to repudiate
2 (= *no reconocer*) to disown
3 (= *renunciar a*) to renounce

repudio SM repudiation

repudrir ▸conjug 3a◂ Ⓐ VT 1 (= *pudrir*) to rot
2 (*fig*) (= *consumir*) to gnaw at, eat up
Ⓑ **repudrirse** VPR to eat one's heart out, pine away

repuesto Ⓐ PP *de* **reponer**
Ⓑ SM 1 [*de pluma*] refill
2 (*Aut, Mec*) spare, spare part; **rueda de ~** spare wheel; **y llevamos otro de ~** and we have another as a spare *o* in reserve
3 (*Esp*) (= *mueble*) sideboard, buffet
4 (= *provisión*) stock, store; (= *abastecimiento*) supply

repugnancia SF 1 (= *asco*) disgust, repugnance; (= *aversión*) aversion (**hacia, por** to)
2 (= *desgana*) reluctance; **lo hizo con ~** he was loathe to do it
3 (*moral*) repugnance
4 (*Fil*) opposition, incompatibility

repugnante ADJ disgusting, revolting

repugnar ▸conjug 1a◂ Ⓐ VT 1 (= *causar asco*) to disgust, revolt; **ese olor me repugna** that smell is disgusting; **me repugna mirarlo** it disgusts *o* sickens me to watch it
2 (= *odiar*) to hate, loathe; **siempre ha repugnado el engaño** he's always hated deceit
3 (*Fil*) (= *contradecir*) to contradict
Ⓑ VI 1 (= *ser repugnante*) to be disgusting, be revolting
2 = **C**
Ⓒ **repugnarse** VPR (*Fil*) (= *ser opuestos*) to conflict, be in opposition; (= *contradecirse*) to contradict each other; **las dos teorías se repugnan** the two theories contradict each other

repujado ADJ embossed

repujar ▸conjug 1a◂ VT to emboss, work in relief

repulgado ADJ (*frm*) affected

repulgar ▸conjug 1h◂ VT 1 (*Cos*) to hem, edge
2 (*Culin*) to crimp

repulgo SM 1 (*Cos*) (= *dobladillo*) hem; (= *punto*) hemstitch
2 (*Culin*) crimping, fancy edging, decorated border ► **repulgos de empanada*** silly scruples

repulido ADJ 1 [*objeto*] polished
2 [*persona*] dressed up, dolled up*

repulir ▸conjug 3a◂ Ⓐ VT 1 [+ *objeto*] to polish up
2 [+ *persona*] to dress up
Ⓑ **repulirse** VPR (= *arreglarse*) to dress up, get dolled up*

repulsa SF 1 [*de oferta, persona*] rejection; [*de violencia*] **sufrir una ~** to meet with a rebuff
2 (*Mil*) check

repulsar ▸conjug 1a◂ VT (*frm*) 1 (= *rechazar*) [+ *solicitud*] to reject, refuse; [+ *oferta, persona*] to rebuff; [+ *violencia*] to condemn
2 (*Mil*) to repulse

repulsión SF 1 = **repulsa**
2 (= *aversión*) repulsion, disgust
3 (*Fís*) repulsion

repulsivo ADJ disgusting, revolting

repunta SF 1 (*Geog*) point, headland
2 (= *indicio*) sign, indication, hint
3 (= *resentimiento*) pique
4 (= *disgusto*) slight upset, tiff
5 (*LAm Agr*) round-up
6 (*Andes*) (= *riada*) sudden rise (*of a river*), flash flood

repuntar ▸conjug 1a◂ Ⓐ VT (*LAm*) [+ *ganado*] to round up
Ⓑ VI 1 [*marea*] to turn
2 (*LAm*) (= *manifestarse*) to begin to show; [*persona*] to turn up unexpectedly
3 (*LAm*) [*río*] to rise suddenly
Ⓒ **repuntarse** VPR 1 [*vino*] to begin to sour, turn

2 [*persona*] to get cross, get annoyed
3 [*dos personas*] to fall out, have a tiff

repunte SM 1 [*de mar*] turn of the tide; [*de río*] level
2 (= *mejora*) upturn, recovery; **ha habido un ~ económico** there has been an economic upturn *o* recovery
3 (*Andes Fin*) rise in share prices
4 (*LAm Agr*) round-up

reputación SF reputation

reputado ADJ (*frm*) **muy ~** highly reputed, reputable; **una colección reputada en mucho** a highly regarded collection

reputar ▸conjug 1a◂ VT (*frm*) (= *considerar*) to deem, consider; **~ a algn de** *o* **por inteligente** to consider sb intelligent; **le reputan no apto para el cargo** they consider him unsuitable for the post; **una colección reputada en mucho** a highly regarded collection

requebrar ▸conjug 1j◂ VT (*liter*) (= *halagar*) to flatter, compliment; (= *flirtear*) to flirt with

requemado ADJ [*objeto, terreno, planta*] scorched; [*comida*] overdone, overcooked

requemar ▸conjug 1a◂ Ⓐ VT (= *quemar*) to scorch; (*Culin*) to burn; ✦**MODISMO ~le la sangre a algn: todo esto me requema la sangre** the whole thing makes my blood boil
Ⓑ **requemarse** VPR 1 (= *quemarse*) to get scorched; (= *secarse*) to get parched, dry up; [*comida*] to burn; ✦**MODISMO ~se la lengua** to burn one's tongue
2 (= *guardar rencor*) to harbour a grudge, harbor a grudge (*EEUU*)

requenete ADJ (*Caribe*), **requeneto** ADJ (*Andes, Caribe*) = **rechoncho**

requerimiento SM 1 (= *petición*) request; **se personó en el juzgado a ~ del juez** she appeared in court after being summonsed by the judge
2 (= *notificación*) notification

requerir ▸conjug 3i◂ Ⓐ VT 1 (= *necesitar*) to need, require; **esto requiere cierto cuidado** this requires some care; **"se requiere dominio del inglés"** "fluent English required", "good command of English required"
2 (= *solicitar*) to request, ask; **~ a algn que haga algo** to request *o* ask sb to do sth; **el ministro requirió los documentos** the minister sent for his papers
3 (= *llamar*) to send for, summon (*frm*); **el juez le requirió para que lo explicara** the judge summonsed him to explain it
4 (††) (= *requebrar*) (*tb* **~ de amores**) to court, woo
Ⓑ VI **~ de** (*esp LAm*) to need, require

requesón SM cottage cheese

requeté SM 1 (*Hist*) Carlist militiaman
2 (†) (= *machote*) he-man*, tough guy*

requete...* PREF extremely ...; **una chica ~guapa** a really attractive girl; **me parece ~bién** it seems absolutely splendid to me; **lo tendré muy ~pensado** I'll think it over very thoroughly

requiebro SM (*liter*) compliment, flirtatious remark

réquiem SM (*pl* **réquiems**) requiem

requilorios SMPL (†) 1 (= *trámites*) tedious formalities, red tape *sing*
2 (= *adornos*) silly adornments, unnecessary frills
3 (= *preliminares*) time-wasting preliminaries; (= *rodeos*) roundabout way of saying something
4 (= *elementos dispersos*) bits and pieces

requintar ▸conjug 1a◂ Ⓐ VT 1 (*LAm*) (= *apretar*) to tighten
2 **~ a algn** (*Andes, Méx*) to impose one's will on sb, push sb around
3 (*Andes*) (= *insultar*) to abuse, swear at
Ⓑ VI (*Caribe*) (= *parecerse*) to resemble each other

requisa SF 1 (= *inspección*) survey, inspection
2 (*Mil*) requisition
3 (*esp LAm*) (= *confiscación*) seizure, confiscation

requisar ▸conjug 1a◂ VT 1 (= *confiscar*) to seize, confiscate
2 (*Mil*) to requisition
3 (*esp LAm*) (= *registrar*) to search

requisición SF 1 (= *confiscación*) seizure, confiscation
2 (*Mil*) requisition
3 (*esp LAm*) (= *inspección*) search

▼**requisito** SM requirement, requisite; **cumplir los ~s** to fulfil *o* (*EEUU*) fulfill the requirements; **cumplir los ~s para un cargo** to have the essential qualifications for a post
► **requisito previo** prerequisite

requisitoria SF 1 (*Jur*) (= *citación*) summons; (= *orden*) writ
2 (*LAm*) (= *interrogatorio*) examination, interrogation

res SF 1 (= *animal*) beast, animal; **100 ~es** 100 animals, 100 head of cattle ► **res lanar** sheep ► **res vacuna** (= *vaca*) cow; (= *toro*) bull; (= *buey*) ox
2 (*Méx*) (= *carne*) steak

resabiado ADJ [*persona*] knowing, crafty; [*caballo*] vicious

resabiarse ▸conjug 1b◂ VPR to acquire bad habits, get into bad habits

resabido ADJ 1 [*dato*] well known; **lo tengo sabido y ~** I know all that perfectly well
2 [*persona*] pretentious, pedantic

resabio SM 1 (= *gusto malo*) unpleasant aftertaste; **tener ~s de** (*fig*) to smack of
2 (= *mala costumbre*) [*de persona*] bad habit

resabioso ADJ (*Andes, Caribe*) = **resabiado**

resaca SF 1 [*de mar*] undertow, undercurrent
2 [*de borrachera*] hangover
3 (= *reacción*) reaction, backlash; **la ~ blanca** the white backlash
4 (*LAm**) (= *aguardiente*) high-quality liquor
5 (*Cono Sur*) (*en playa*) line of driftwood and rubbish (*left by the tide*)
6 (*Cono Sur**) (= *personas*) dregs *pl* of society
7 (*Caribe*) (= *paliza*) beating

resacado* Ⓐ ADJ (*Méx*) (= *tacaño*) mean, stingy; (= *débil*) weak; (= *estúpido*) stupid; **es lo ~** it's the worst of its kind
Ⓑ SM (*Andes*) liquor, contraband liquor

resacar ▸conjug 1g◂ VT (*LAm*) to distil

resacoso* ADJ hungover

resalado* ADJ (= *vivo*) lively

resaltable ADJ notable, noteworthy

resaltante ADJ (*LAm*) outstanding

resaltar ▸conjug 1a◂ Ⓐ VI 1 (= *destacarse*) to stand out; **lo escribí en mayúsculas para que ~a** I wrote it in capitals to make it stand out; **entre sus cualidades resalta su elegancia** her most striking quality is her elegance; **hacer ~ algo** to set sth off; (*fig*) to highlight sth; **este maquillaje hace ~ sus delicadas facciones** this makeup sets off her delicate features; **la encuesta hace ~ el descontento con el sistema educativo** the survey highlights the dissatisfaction with the education system
2 (= *sobresalir*) to jut out, project
Ⓑ VT (= *destacar*) to highlight; **el conferenciante resaltó el problema del paro** the speaker highlighted the problem of unemployment; **quiero ~ la dedicación de nuestros empleados** I would like to draw particular attention to the dedication of our staff

resalte SM, **resalto** SM 1 (= *saliente*) projection
2 (= *rebote*) bounce, rebound

resanar ▸conjug 1a◂ VT to restore, repair, make good

resaquero ADJ (*LAm*) = **remolón A**

resarcimiento SM (= *pago*) repayment; (= *compensación*) compensation

resarcir ▸conjug 3b◂ Ⓐ VT (= *pagar*) to repay; (= *compensar*) to indemnify, compensate; **~ a algn de una cantidad** to repay sb a sum; **~ a algn de una pérdida** to compensate sb for a loss
Ⓑ **resarcirse** VPR **~se de** to make up for

resbalada SF (*LAm*) slip

resbaladero SM 1 (= *lugar*) slippery place
2 (= *tobogán*) slide, chute

resbaladilla SF (*Méx*) slide, chute

resbaladizo ADJ slippery

resbalar ▸conjug 1a◂ Ⓐ VI 1 (*al andar*) to slip (**en, sobre** on); (*Aut*) to skid; **había llovido y resbaló** it had been raining and she slipped; **el coche resbaló y se dio contra el árbol** the car skidded into the tree; **le resbalaban las lágrimas por las mejillas** tears were trickling down her cheeks
2 (= *equivocarse*) to slip up, make a slip
3 (*) (= *ser indiferente*) **me resbala** it leaves me cold; **las críticas le resbalan** criticism runs off him like water off a duck's back
Ⓑ **resbalarse** VPR to slip; **se resbaló bajando la calle** she slipped walking down the street

resbalón SM 1 (= *acción*) slip; (*Aut*) skid
2 (= *equivocación*) slip, error; **dar** *o* **pegar un ~** to slip up

resbalosa SF *Peruvian dance*

resbaloso ADJ 1 (*LAm*) (= *resbaladizo*) slippery
2 (*Méx**) (= *coqueto*) flirtatious

rescatar ▸conjug 1a◂ Ⓐ VT 1 (= *salvar*) to save, rescue
2 [+ *cautivo*] to rescue, free; [+ *pueblo*] to recapture, recover
3 [+ *objeto empeñado*] to redeem
4 [+ *póliza*] to surrender
5 [+ *posesiones*] to get back, recover
6 [+ *tiempo perdido*] to make up
7 [+ *delitos*] to atone for, expiate (*frm*)
8 [+ *terreno*] to reclaim
9 (*LAm*) (= *revender*) to resell
Ⓑ VI (*Andes*) to peddle goods from village to village

rescate SM 1 (*en incendio, naufragio*) rescue; **operaciones de ~** rescue operations; **acudir al ~ de algn** to go to sb's rescue
2 [*de cautivo*] rescue, freeing; [*de pueblo*] recapture, recovery

➤ LENGUA Y USO: **requisito** 37.1

3 [*de algo empeñado*] redemption
4 (*en secuestro*) (= *dinero*) ransom
5 [*de posesiones*] recovery
6 [*de delitos*] atonement, expiation (*frm*)
7 ► **rescate de terrenos** land reclamation

rescindible ADJ **contrato ~ por ambas partes** contract that can be cancelled by either side

rescindir ▸conjug 3a◂ VT 1 [+ *contrato*] to cancel, rescind
2 [+ *privilegio*] to withdraw

rescisión SF 1 [*de contrato*] cancellation
2 [*de privilegio*] withdrawal

rescoldo SM 1 (= *brasa*) embers *pl*, hot ashes *pl*
2 (= *recelo*) doubt, scruple; ✦*MODISMO* **avivar el ~** to stir up the dying embers

rescontrar ▸conjug 1l◂ VT (*Com, Fin*) to offset, balance

resecación SF, **resecamiento** SM drying

resecar[1] ▸conjug 1g◂ Ⓐ VT (= *secar*) to dry off, dry thoroughly
Ⓑ **resecarse** VPR to dry up

resecar[2] ▸conjug 1g◂ VT (*Med*) (= *quitar*) to cut out, remove; (= *amputar*) to amputate

resección SF resection

reseco ADJ 1 (= *muy seco*) very dry, too dry
2 (= *flaco*) skinny, lean

reseda SF (*LAm*), **resedá** SF (*LAm*) mignonette

resellarse†* ▸conjug 1a◂ VPR to switch parties, change one's views

resembrado SM re-sowing, re-seeding

resembrar ▸conjug 1j◂ VT to re-sow, re-seed

resentido/a Ⓐ ADJ 1 (= *disgustado*) resentful; **aún está ~ porque no le felicitaste** he still feels resentful that you didn't congratulate him, he still resents the fact that you didn't congratulate him
2 (= *dolorido*) painful; **aún tiene la mano resentida por el golpe** his hand is still painful *o* hurting from the knock
Ⓑ SM/F **es un ~** he has a chip on his shoulder, he is resentful

resentimiento SM (= *rencor*) resentment; (= *amargura*) bitterness

resentirse ▸conjug 3i◂ VPR 1 (= *estar resentido*) **~ con** *o* **por algo** to resent sth, feel bitter about sth
2 (= *debilitarse*) to be weakened, suffer; **con los años se resintió su salud** his health suffered *o* was affected over the years; **los cimientos se resintieron con el terremoto** the foundations were weakened by the earthquake; **sin que se resienta el dólar** without the dollar being affected
3 (= *sentir*) **~ de** [+ *defecto*] to suffer from; **~ de las consecuencias de** to feel the effects of; **me resiento todavía del golpe** I can still feel the effects of the injury

reseña SF 1 (= *resumen*) outline, summary; [*de libro*] review
2 (= *descripción*) brief description
3 (*Mil*) review
4 (*Cono Sur, esp Chile*) (= *procesión*) procession held on Passion Sunday

reseñable ADJ 1 (= *destacado*) noteworthy, notable; (= *digno de mencionar*) worth mentioning
2 [*ofensa*] bookable

reseñante SMF reviewer

reseñar ▸conjug 1a◂ VT 1 (= *resumir*) to write up, write a summary of
2 [+ *libro*] to review
3 [+ *delincuente*] to book

reseñista SMF reviewer

resero/a (*LAm*) Ⓐ SM (= *vaquero*) cowboy, herdsman
Ⓑ SM/F (= *comerciante*) cattle dealer

▼ **reserva** Ⓐ SF 1 (= *provisiones*) [*de minerales, petróleo, armamentos, vitaminas*] reserve; [*de agua*] supply; [*de productos ya almacenados*] stock; **las ~s de agua están al mínimo** water supplies are at a minimum; **acumularon grandes ~s de carbón para el invierno** they built up large stocks of coal for the winter; **pasta, arroz, legumbres, tienen ~s de todo** pasta, rice, pulses, they have stocks of everything; **~s de víveres** food supplies; **estos chicos tienen grandes ~s de energía** these kids have endless amounts *o* reserves of energy; **de ~** [*precio, jugador, fondo*] reserve *antes de s*; [*zapatos, muda*] spare; **el equipo de ~** the reserve team
2 (*Econ*) reserve; **las ~s de divisas** currency reserves ► **reserva de caja** cash reserves *pl* ► **reserva en efectivo**, **reserva en metálico** cash reserves *pl* ► **reserva para amortización**, **reserva para depreciaciones** depreciation allowance ► **reservas de oro** gold reserves ► **reservas monetarias** [*de un país*] currency reserves ► **reservas ocultas** hidden reserves, secret reserves
3 (= *solicitud*) (*en hotel, avión*) reservation; (*en teatro, restaurante*) reservation, booking; **no se cobra por la ~ de asientos** there is no booking *o* reservation charge; **se pueden hacer ~s por teléfono** you can book by phone, you can make a telephone booking *o* reservation; **ya he hecho la ~ de plaza en la academia de baile** I've reserved *o* booked my place at the dance school
4 (= *territorio*) reserve ► **reserva biológica** wildlife sanctuary, wildlife reserve ► **reserva de caza** game reserve ► **reserva de indios** Indian reservation ► **reserva de pesca** protected fishing area, fishing preserve ► **reserva nacional** national park ► **reserva natural** nature reserve
5 (*Mil*) **nuestro ejército tiene una importante ~ de soldados** our army has significant reserves of soldiers; **pasar a la ~** to join the reserve ► **reserva activa** active reserve
6 (*Dep*) **estar en la ~** to be a reserve
7 (*Aut*) [*de gasolina*] reserve tank; **con la ~ tenemos para diez kilómetros** with the reserve tank we have enough to go ten kilometres
8 (= *recelo*) reservation; **el pacto será aprobado, aunque con algunas ~s** the agreement will be sanctioned, but with certain reservations; **contestó con ciertas ~s** she answered with some reservation; **nos apoyaron sin ~s** they gave us their unreserved support
9 [*de carácter*] (= *inhibición*) reserve; (= *discreción*) discretion; **confiamos en tu ~ al manejar este asunto** we are counting on your discretion in this matter
10 (= *secreto*) confidence; **se ruega absoluta ~** your strictest confidence is requested; **han mantenido la más absoluta ~ sobre este incidente** they have maintained the utmost confidence over this incident; **sus nombres se mantienen en ~ por razones de seguridad** their names have not been revealed for security reasons
11 **a ~ de** subject to; **a ~ de un estudio más detallado** subject to more detailed study; **a ~ de consultar antes con mis superiores** subject to prior consultation with my superiors; **a ~ de que …** unless …
Ⓑ SMF (*Dep*) reserve; **el banquillo de los ~s** the reserves' bench
Ⓒ SM (= *vino*) vintage wine (*that has been aged for a minimum of three years*)

> **RESERVA**
>
> *Quality Spanish wine is often graded* **Crianza**, **Reserva** *or* **Gran Reserva** *according to the length of bottle-ageing and barrel-ageing it has undergone. Red* **Reserva** *wines are at least three years old, having spent a minimum of one year in cask, and white* **Reserva** *wines are at least two years old with at least six months spent in cask. A* **Gran Reserva** *wine is a top-quality wine. A red must be aged for at least 2 years in an oak cask and 3 years in the bottle. White wine must be aged for 4 years, with at least 6 months in cask.*
>
> ⇨ *See also* CRIANZA

reservación SF (*LAm*) reservation

reservadamente ADV in confidence

reservado Ⓐ ADJ 1 [*actitud, persona*] (= *poco comunicativo*) reserved; (= *discreto*) discreet
2 (= *confidencial*) [*asunto, documento*] confidential; **estos documentos son materia reservada** these documents are confidential, these documents contain confidential material
Ⓑ SM 1 (= *habitación aparte*) (*en restaurante*) private room; (*en tren*) reserved compartment
2 (*Cono Sur*) (= *vino*) vintage wine

▼ **reservar** ▸conjug 1a◂ Ⓐ VT 1 [+ *asiento, habitación, mesa*] to reserve, book; [+ *billete, entrada*] to book; **~ en exceso** to overbook
2 (= *guardar*) to keep, keep in reserve, set aside; **lo reserva para el final** he's keeping it till last; **ha reservado lo mejor para sí** he has kept the best part for himself
Ⓑ **reservarse** VPR 1 (*para luego*) to save o.s. (**para** for); **no bebo porque me reservo para más tarde** I'm not drinking because I'm saving myself for later on
2 (= *encubrir*) to conceal; (= *callar*) to keep to o.s.; **prefiero ~me los detalles** I prefer not to reveal the details

reservista SMF reservist

reservón* ADJ excessively reserved

reservorio SM (*Med*) reservoir

resfriado Ⓐ ADJ 1 (= *acatarrado*) **estar ~** to have a cold
2 (*Arg**) (= *indiscreto*) indiscreet
Ⓑ SM cold; **coger un ~** to catch a cold

resfriar ▸conjug 1c◂ Ⓐ VT 1 (*Med*) **~ a algn** to give sb a cold
2 (= *enfriar*) to cool, chill
3 [+ *ardor*] to cool
Ⓑ VI (*Meteo*) to turn cold
Ⓒ **resfriarse** VPR 1 (*Med*) to catch a cold
2 [*relaciones*] to cool off

resfrío SM (*LAm*) cold

resguardar ▸conjug 1a◂ Ⓐ VT to protect, shield (**de** from)
Ⓑ **resguardarse** VPR 1 (= *protegerse*) to de-

➤ LENGUA Y USO:	reserva A3 48.4	A8 53.6	A10 46.5	reservar A1 48.3

fend o.s., protect o.s.
2 (= *obrar con cautela*) to proceed with caution

resguardo SM 1 [*de compra*] slip, receipt; [*de cheque*] stub ► **resguardo de consigna** cloakroom ticket, cloakroom check (*EEUU*)
2 (= *protección*) defence, defense (*EEUU*), protection; **servir de ~ a algn** to protect sb
3 (*Náut*) sea room

residencia SF 1 (= *casa*) residence; **la reunión tuvo lugar en la ~ del primer ministro** the meeting took place at the prime minister's residence; **segunda ~** second home ► **residencia canina** dogs' home, kennels *pl*, kennel (*EEUU*) ► **residencia de estudiantes** hall of residence ► **residencia oficial** official residence ► **residencia para ancianos, residencia para jubilados** residential home, old people's home ► **residencia sanitaria** hospital ► **residencia universitaria** hall of residence
2 (= *domicilio*) residence; **fijó su ~ en Barcelona** he took up residence in Barcelona; **con ~ en Bogotá** resident in Bogotá
3 (= *hotel*) guest house, boarding house
4 (= *estancia*) residence; **la conoció durante su ~ en Madrid** (*frm*) he got to know her during his residence *o* while he was living in Madrid; **permiso de ~** residence permit
5 (*Jur*) (= *investigación*) investigation, inquiry
6 (*Andes Jur*) ► **residencia vigilada** house arrest

residencial Ⓐ ADJ residential
Ⓑ SF (*Andes, Cono Sur*) boarding house, small hotel

residenciar ▸conjug 1b◂ Ⓐ VT (*Jur*) to investigate
Ⓑ **residenciarse** VPR (*frm*) to take up residence, establish o.s., settle

residente ADJ, SMF resident; **no ~** non-resident

residir ▸conjug 3a◂ VI 1 (= *vivir*) to reside, live
2 **~ en** (= *radicar en*) to reside in, lie in; (= *consistir en*) to consist in; **la dificultad reside en que ...** the difficulty resides in *o* lies in the fact that ...; **la autoridad reside en el gobernador** authority rests with the governor

residual ADJ residual, residuary; **aguas ~es** sewage *sing*

residuo SM 1 (= *parte que queda*) residue; (*Mat*) remainder; (*Quím*) residuum
2 **residuos** (= *restos*) remains; (= *basura*) refuse *sing*, waste *sing*; (*Téc*) waste products; **~s tóxicos** toxic waste *sing* ► **residuos atmosféricos** fallout *sing* ► **residuos nucleares** nuclear waste *sing* ► **residuos radiactivos** radioactive waste *sing* ► **residuos sólidos** solid waste *sing*

resignación SF resignation

resignadamente ADV resignedly, with resignation

resignado ADJ resigned

resignar ▸conjug 1a◂ Ⓐ VT (*frm*) [+ *puesto*] to resign; [+ *mando*] to hand over (**en** to)
Ⓑ **resignarse** VPR to resign o.s. (**a, con** to); **~se a hacer algo** to resign o.s. to doing sth

resina SF resin

resinoso ADJ resinous

resistencia SF 1 (= *oposición*) resistance; **la Resistencia** (*Hist*) the Resistance; **los acusaron de ~ a la autoridad** they were charged with resisting arrest; **ofrecer** *o* **oponer ~** to offer resistance, resist ► **resistencia pasiva** passive resistance
2 (= *aguante*) stamina; **los alpinistas necesitan mucha ~** mountaineers need lots of stamina; **el maratón es una carrera de ~** the marathon is an endurance race; **escribir una tesis es una prueba de ~** doing a thesis is a test of endurance; **carrera de ~** long-distance race
3 (*a la enfermedad, al frío*) resistance
4 [*de materiales*] strength; **este plástico es valorado por su ~** this plastic is valued for its strength
5 (*Elec*) (= *cualidad*) resistance; (= *componente de circuito*) resistor; [*de plancha, secador*] element

resistente Ⓐ ADJ (= *que ofrece resistencia*) resistant (**a** to); [*tela*] hard-wearing, tough; [*ropa*] strong; (*Bot*) hardy; **~ al calor** resistant to heat, heat-resistant; **~ al fuego** fireproof; **hacerse ~** (*Med*) to build up a resistance (**a** to)
Ⓑ SMF resistance fighter

resistible ADJ resistible

resistir ▸conjug 3a◂ Ⓐ VT 1 [+ *peso*] to bear, take, support; [+ *presión*] to take, withstand
2 [+ *ataque, tentación*] to resist; [+ *propuesta*] to resist, oppose, make a stand against; **resisto todo menos la tentación** I can resist anything but temptation
3 (= *tolerar*) to put up with, endure; **no puedo ~ este frío** I can't bear *o* stand this cold; **no lo resisto un momento más** I'm not putting up with this a moment longer
4 **~le la mirada a algn** to stare sb out
Ⓑ VI 1 (= *oponer resistencia*) to resist
2 (= *durar*) to last (out), hold out; **el equipo no puede ~ mucho tiempo más** the team can't last *o* hold out much longer; **el coche resiste todavía** the car is still holding out *o* going
3 (= *soportar peso*) **¿~á la silla?** will the chair take it?
Ⓒ **resistirse** VPR 1 = **B1**
2 (= *no estar dispuesto*) **~se a hacer algo** to be reluctant to do sth, resist doing sth; **no me resisto a citar algunos versos** I can't resist quoting a few lines; **me resisto a creerlo** I find it hard to believe
3 (= *encontrar difícil*) **se me resiste la química** I'm not very good at chemistry

resituar ▸conjug 1e◂ VT [+ *país*] to put back on track; [+ *debate, concepto*] to redefine

resma SF ream

resobado ADJ hackneyed, trite, well-worn

resobar ▸conjug 1a◂ VT 1 (= *manosear*) to finger, paw
2 [+ *tema*] to work to death

resobrino/a SM/F first cousin once removed

resol SM glare of the sun

resolana SF (*LAm*) (= *resol*) glare of the sun; (= *sitio*) sunspot, suntrap

resolano SM sunspot, suntrap

resollar ▸conjug 1l◂ VI 1 (= *respirar*) to breathe noisily; (= *jadear*) to puff and pant
2 (*fig*) **escuchar sin ~** to listen without saying a word in reply; **hace tiempo que no resuella** it's a long time since we heard from him

resoltarse ▸conjug 1l◂ VPR (*Andes*) to overstep the mark

resolución SF 1 (= *decisión*) decision; **tomar una ~** to take a decision ► **resolución fatal** decision to take one's own life
2 [*de problema*] (= *acción*) solving; (= *respuesta*) solution; **el problema no tiene ~** there is no solution to the problem
3 [*de conflicto*] resolution
4 (*Jur*) ► **resolución judicial** legal ruling
5 (= *determinación*) resolve, determination; **obrar con ~** to act with determination
6 (*frm*) (= *resumen*) **en ~** in a word, in short, to sum up
7 (*Inform*) **alta ~** high resolution; **baja ~** low resolution
8 (*Cono Sur*) (= *terminación*) finishing, completion

resolutivo ADJ decisive

resoluto ADJ = **resuelto B**

resolver ▸conjug 2h◂ (*pp* **resuelto**) Ⓐ VT 1 [+ *problema*] to solve; [+ *duda*] to settle; [+ *asunto*] to decide, settle; [+ *crimen*] to solve; **crimen sin ~** unsolved crime
2 (*Quím*) to dissolve
3 [+ *cuerpo de materiales*] to analyse, divide up, resolve (**en** into)
Ⓑ VI 1 (= *juzgar*) to rule, decide; **~ a favor de algn** to rule *o* decide in sb's favour
2 (= *decidirse por*) **~ hacer algo** to resolve to do sth
Ⓒ **resolverse** VPR 1 [*problema*] to resolve itself, work out
2 (= *decidir*) to decide, make up one's mind; **~se a hacer algo** to resolve to do sth; **~se por algo** to decide on sth; **hay que ~se por el uno o el otro** you'll have to make up your mind one way or the other
3 (*frm*) **~se en** to be transformed into; **todo se resolvió en una riña más** it all came down to one more quarrel

resonador SM resonator

resonancia SF 1 (= *reverberación*) resonance; (= *eco*) echo
2 (*Med*) (*tb* **~ magnética**) magnetic resonance scanning
3 (= *consecuencia*) wide impact, wide effect; **tener ~** to have repercussions, have a far-reaching effect

resonante ADJ 1 (= *que resuena*) resonant; (= *sonoro*) ringing, resounding
2 [*éxito*] tremendous, resounding

resonar ▸conjug 1l◂ VI to resound, ring (**de** with)

resondrar* ▸conjug 1a◂ VT (*Andes, Cono Sur*) to tell off, tick off*

resongar ▸conjug 1a◂ VT (*LAm*) = **rezongar**

resoplar ▸conjug 1a◂ VI 1 (*con ira*) to snort
2 (*por cansancio*) to puff

resoplido SM 1 (*de cansancio*) puff, puffing; (*de ira*) snort
2 (= *respiración fuerte*) **dar ~s** [*persona*] to breathe heavily, puff; [*motor*] to chug, puff
3 (= *exabrupto*) sharp answer

resorber ▸conjug 2a◂ VT to reabsorb

resorción SF resorption, reabsorption

resorte SM 1 (= *muelle*) spring
2 (= *medio*) means, expedient; (= *enchufe*) contact; (= *influencia*) influence; **tocar ~s** to pull strings; **tocar todos los ~s** to use all one's influence, pull all the strings one can
3 (*LAm**) (= *incumbencia*) concern; (= *competencia*) province; **no es de mi ~** it's not my concern *o* province

respaldar ▸conjug 1a◂ Ⓐ VT 1 [+ *documento*] to endorse
2 (= *apoyar*) to back, support
3 (*Inform*) to support
4 (= *garantizar*) to guarantee
Ⓑ **respaldarse** VPR 1 (= *apoyarse*) **~se con** *o* **en** to base one's arguments on
2 (= *reclinarse*) to lean back (**contra** against; **en** on)

respaldo SM 1 [*de silla*] back; [*de cama*] head
2 [*de documento*] (= *dorso*) back; (= *cosa escrita*) endorsement; **firmar al** *o* **en el ~** to sign on the back
3 (= *apoyo*) support, backing; (*LAm*) (= *ayuda*) help; (= *garantía*) guarantee; **operación de ~** back-up operation, support operation
4 (*Hort*) wall

respectar ▸conjug 1a◂ VT **por lo que respecta a** as for, with regard to

respectivamente ADV respectively

respectivo ADJ 1 (= *correspondiente*) respective
2 **en lo ~ a** as regards, with regard to

respecto SM **al ~** on this matter; **a ese ~** in that respect; **no sé nada al ~** I know nothing about it; **bajo ese ~** in that respect; **(con) ~ a** ◊ **~ de** with regard to, in relation to; **(con) ~ a mí** as for me

respetabilidad SF respectability

respetable Ⓐ ADJ respectable
Ⓑ SM **el ~** (*Teat*) the audience; (*hum*) the public

respetablemente ADV respectably

▼**respetar** ▸conjug 1a◂ Ⓐ VT 1 [+ *persona, derecho*] to respect; **respeto tu decisión** I respect your decision; **nunca ha respetado a sus padres** she has never respected *o* had any respect for her parents; **hacerse ~** to win respect, earn respect; **"respetad las plantas"** "be careful of the plants"
2 (= *obedecer*) to observe; **respeten las normas de seguridad** observe the safety regulations; **no respetan los semáforos** they ignore the traffic lights, they do not observe the traffic lights
3 (= *conservar*) to conserve; **al remodelar la zona ~on las murallas romanas** when they redeveloped the area they conserved the Roman walls
Ⓑ **respetarse** VPR (*reflexivo*) to have self-respect, respect o.s.; (*mutuo*) to respect each other; **no se respeta a sí misma** she has no self-respect; **un periodista que se respete no revela sus fuentes** no self-respecting journalist would reveal his sources

respeto SM 1 (= *consideración*) respect; **~ a la opinión ajena** respect for other people's opinion; **~ a las personas mayores** respect for one's elders; **con todos mis ~s, creo que se equivoca** with all due respect, I think you're wrong; **~ a** *o* **de sí mismo** self-respect; **¡un ~!** show some respect!; **faltar al ~ a algn** to be disrespectful to sb, be rude to sb; **guardar ~ a algn** to respect sb; **perder el ~ a algn** to lose one's respect for sb; **por ~ a algn** out of consideration for sb; **presentar sus ~s a algn** to pay one's respects to sb; **tener ~ a algn** to respect sb; ✦**MODISMO campar por sus ~s** to do as one pleases
2 (*) (= *miedo*) **volar me impone mucho ~** I'm very wary of flying; **le tengo mucho ~ a las tormentas** I'm fearful of thunderstorms
3 (†) **de ~** best, reserve *antes de s*; **cuarto de ~** best room; **estar de ~** to be dressed up

respetuosamente ADV respectfully

respetuosidad SF respectfulness

respetuoso ADJ respectful

réspice SM (*frm*) 1 (= *respuesta*) sharp answer, curt reply
2 (= *reprensión*) severe reprimand

respingado ADJ snub, turned-up

respingar ▸conjug 1h◂ VI 1 [*vestido*] to ride up
2 [*caballo*] to shy, balk
3 (= *mostrarse reticente*) to show o.s. unwilling, dig one's heels in

respingo SM 1 (= *sobresalto*) start, jump; **dar un ~** to start, jump
2 (*Cos*) **la chaqueta me hace un ~ aquí** the jacket rides up here
3 = **réspice**

respingón ADJ turned-up

respingona SF *traditional Castilian dance*

respirable ADJ breathable

respiración SF 1 [*de persona, animal*] breathing; **ejercicios de ~** breathing *o* (*más frm*) respiration exercises; **llegué sin ~** I arrived breathless *o* out of breath; **sus arriesgados saltos cortaban la ~** her dangerous leaps took your breath away; **contener la ~** to hold one's breath; **dejar a algn sin ~** to leave sb breathless, take sb's breath away; **quedarse sin ~** to be out of breath; **se quedó sin ~ después de correr tras el autobús** after running for the bus he was out of breath; **al ver aquello se quedó sin ~** the sight of it left him breathless *o* took his breath away ► **respiración artificial** artificial respiration ► **respiración asistida** artificial respiration (*by machine*); **está con ~ asistida** she is on a ventilator *o* respirator ► **respiración boca a boca** mouth-to-mouth resuscitation; **se le hizo la ~ boca a boca** he was given mouth-to-mouth resuscitation, he was given the kiss of life ► **respiración mecánica** = **respiración asistida**
2 [*de lugar cerrado*] ventilation

respiradero SM 1 (*Téc*) vent, valve
2 (*fig*) (= *respiro*) respite, breathing space

respirador SM (*tb* **~ artificial**) ventilator, (artificial) respirator

respirar ▸conjug 1a◂ Ⓐ VI 1 (= *tomar aire*) to breathe; **no respires por la boca** don't breathe through your mouth; **respire hondo** take a deep breath, breathe deeply; **~ con dificultad** to breathe with difficulty; **salí al balcón a ~ un poco** I went out to the balcony to get some air
2 (= *descansar*) **estos niños no me dejan ni tiempo para ~** these children don't give me time to breathe; **tengo tanto trabajo que no puedo ni ~** I'm up to my ears *o* eyes in work; **sin ~** without a break, without respite
3 (= *sentir alivio*) to breathe again; **¡respiro!** I can breathe again!, what a relief!; **~ aliviado** to breathe a sigh of relief; **~ tranquilo** to breathe easily *o* freely (again)
4 (= *hablar*) **no respiró en toda la reunión** he didn't utter a word in the whole meeting; **los niños lo miraban sin poder ~** the children watched him with bated breath
5 (= *ventilarse*) 5.1 [*fruta, vino*] to breathe
5.2 (*Aut*) **levanta el capó para que respire el motor** put the bonnet up to ventilate the engine
Ⓑ VT 1 [+ *aire, oxígeno*] to breathe; **necesito ~ un poco de aire fresco** I need to get some fresh air; **se podía ~ el aroma de las flores** you could breathe in the smell of the flowers; **se respiraba un aire cargado de humo** there was a smoke-filled atmosphere
2 (= *mostrar*) [+ *optimismo, felicidad*] to exude, radiate; **respira confianza** she exudes *o* radiates confidence
3 (= *notar*) **se respiraba un ambiente festivo en la manifestación** there was an air of festivity at the demonstration; **se respiraba ya un ambiente prebélico** there was a sense of war in the air; **¿cuál es el clima que se respira en el país tras el atentado?** what is the feeling in the country following the bomb attack?

respiratorio ADJ [*insuficiencia, sistema, vías*] respiratory; [*problemas, dificultades*] breathing *antes de s*, respiratory

respiro SM 1 (= *respiración*) breath; **dio un ~ hondo** he took a deep breath; **lanzó un ~ de alivio** she breathed a sigh of relief
2 (= *descanso*) [*de trabajo, esfuerzo*] break, rest; [*de ataque, preocupación*] respite; **llevas toda la semana trabajando, necesitas un ~** you've been working all week, you need a break *o* a rest; **los clientes no nos dan un momento de ~** the customers don't give us a moment's peace; **su rival no le concedió ningún ~** his rival gave him no respite; **trabajaba sin ~** she worked without respite; **tomarse un ~** to take a break, take a breather*
3 (= *alivio*) [*de enfermedad, preocupación*] relief; **las pastillas le dan algún que otro ~ del dolor** the pills ease the pain for a while, the pills give her some relief from the pain; **es un ~ saber que han encontrado trabajo** it's a relief to know that they have found work; **poder escaparse unos días a la playa es un ~** getting away to the beach for a few days is like a breath of fresh air
4 (= *prórroga*) extension; **los acreedores acordaron conceder un ~ de seis meses en el pago de la deuda** the creditors agreed to an extension of six months *o* agreed to grant six months' grace on the debt payment; **el gobierno necesita un ~ antes de las elecciones** the government needs a breathing space before the elections

respis SM = **réspice**

resplandecer ▸conjug 2d◂ VI 1 (= *relucir*) to shine; [*joyas*] to sparkle, glitter
2 (*de alegría*) to shine; **~ de felicidad** to be radiant *o* shine with happiness

resplandeciente ADJ 1 (= *brillante*) shining; [*joyas*] sparkling, glittering
2 (*de alegría*) radiant (**de** with)

resplandor SM 1 (= *brillantez*) brilliance, brightness; [*de joyas*] sparkle, glitter
2 (*Méx*) (= *luz del sol*) sunlight; (= *calor del sol*) warmth of the sun; (= *brillo*) glare

responder ▸conjug 2a◂ Ⓐ VI 1 (= *contestar*) (*a pregunta, llamada*) to answer; (*en diálogo, carta*) to reply; **la mayor parte de los encuestados respondió afirmativamente** the majority of people surveyed said yes *o* (*frm*) answered positively; **aunque llamen al timbre varias veces no respondas** even if they ring the bell a number of times don't answer; **respóndame lo antes posible** please reply as soon as possible; **respondió de forma**

➤ LENGUA Y USO: respetar A2 38.3

contundente he gave a forceful reply; **~ a** [+ *pregunta*] to answer; [+ *carta*] to reply to, answer; [+ *críticas, peticiones*] to respond to, answer; **la primera ministra eludió ~ a las acusaciones de la oposición** the prime minister avoided answering the opposition's accusations; **~ al nombre de** [*persona*] to go by the name of; [*animal*] to answer to the name of; **el detenido, cuyo nombre responde a las iniciales A. M., ...** the person under arrest, whose initials are A.M., ...

2 (= *replicar*) to answer back; **no me respondas** don't answer me back

3 (= *reaccionar*) to respond; **nunca se imaginó que la gente fuera a ~ tan bien** he never imagined that people would respond so well; **los frenos no respondieron** the brakes didn't respond; **si las abonas bien verás qué bien responden** if you feed them well you'll see how well they respond; **~ a: no respondió al tratamiento** he did not respond to the treatment; **el pueblo respondió a su llamada** the population answered his call *o* (*más frm*) responded to his call

4 (= *rendir*) [*negocio*] to do well; [*máquina*] to perform well; [*empleado*] to produce results; **debes preparar un equipo de profesionales que responda** you must train a team of professionals that can produce results *o* come up with the goods*

5 (= *satisfacer*) **~ a** [+ *exigencias, necesidades*] to meet; [+ *expectativas*] to come up to; **este tipo de productos no responde ya a las exigencias del mercado** this type of product no longer meets market demands; **el equipo italiano no ha respondido a las expectativas** the Italian team has not come up to expectations; **la construcción de esta nueva facultad responde a una necesidad social** this new faculty has been built in response to public need

6 (= *corresponder*) **~ a** [+ *idea, imagen, información*] to correspond to; [+ *descripción*] to answer, fit; **una imagen de fragilidad que no responde a la realidad** an image of fragility that does not correspond to reality; **uno de los detenidos responde a la descripción del sospechoso** one of those arrested answers *o* fits the description of the suspect

7 (= *responsabilizarse*) **yo ya te avisé, así que no respondo** I warned you before, I'm not responsible; **~ de** [+ *acto, consecuencia*] to answer for; [+ *seguridad, deuda*] to be responsible for; [+ *honestidad*] to vouch for; **cada cual debe ~ de sus actos** every person must answer for his or her actions; **tendrá que ~ de su gestión económica ante un tribunal** he will have to answer for his financial management in a court of law; **yo no respondo de lo que pueda pasar** I cannot answer for the consequences; **la empresa no responde de la seguridad del edificio** the company is not responsible for the security of the building

8 **~ por algn** to vouch for sb; **yo respondo por él** I can vouch for him

9 [*material*] to be workable, be easily worked

Ⓑ VT (= *contestar*) [+ *pregunta, llamada*] to answer; **responde algo, aunque sea al azar** give an answer *o* say something, even if it's a guess; **—no quiero —respondió** "I don't want to," he replied; **me respondió que no sabía** she told me that she didn't know, she replied that she didn't know; **le respondí que sí** I said yes

respondida SF (*LAm*) reply

respondón* ADJ cheeky, lippy*, mouthy*

responsabilidad SF responsibility; (*Jur*) liability; **hay que exigir ~es al gobierno por los hechos** the government must be held accountable *o* responsible for what happened; **bajo mi ~** under my responsibility; **cargo de ~** position of responsibility; **de ~ limitada** limited liability *antes de s* ► **responsabilidad civil** public liability, public liability insurance ► **responsabilidad contractual** contractual liability ► **responsabilidad ilimitada** (*Com*) unlimited liability ► **responsabilidad objetiva** (*Jur*) strict liability ► **responsabilidad solidaria** joint responsibility

responsabilizar ▸conjug 1f◂ Ⓐ VT to blame, hold responsible; **~ a algn de algo** to hold sb responsible for sth, place the blame for sth on sb

Ⓑ **responsabilizarse** VPR **no me responsabilizo de sus actos** I'm not responsible for her actions; **cada uno de nosotros debe ~se de sus actos** we must all accept responsibility for our actions; **~se de un atentado** to claim responsibility for an attack

responsable Ⓐ ADJ 1 (= *sensato*) responsible; **es un niño muy ~ para su edad** he is very a responsible boy for his age

2 (= *encargado*) responsible, in charge; **la persona ~ del departamento** the person in charge of the department, the person responsible for the department; **es ~ de la política municipal** she is responsible for *o* in charge of council policy

3 (= *culpable*) responsible; **el conductor ~ del accidente** the driver responsible for the accident; **cada cual es ~ de sus acciones** everybody is responsible for their own actions; **el fabricante es ~ de los daños causados** the manufacturer is liable for the damage caused; **ser ~ ante algn de algo** to be accountable *o* answerable to sb for sth; **hacer a algn ~ de algo** to hold sb responsible for sth; **hacerse ~ de algo** to take responsibility for sth; **no me hago ~ de lo que pueda pasar** I take no responsibility for what may happen

Ⓑ SMF 1 (= *culpable*) **tú eres la ~ de lo ocurrido** you're responsible for what happened; **la policía busca a los ~s** the police are looking for the culprits

2 (= *encargado*) **quiero hablar con el ~** I wish to speak to the person in charge; **Ramón es el ~ de la cocina** Ramón is in charge of the kitchen ► **responsable de prensa** press officer

responso SM prayer for the dead

responsorio SM response

▼**respuesta** SF 1 (= *contestación*) (*a pregunta, en examen, test*) answer; (*a carta, comentario*) reply; **preguntas y ~s** questions and answers; **demasiadas preguntas sin ~** too many unanswered questions; **su única ~ fue encogerse de hombros** his only reply was to shrug his shoulders

2 (= *reacción*) 2·1 (*ante un estímulo, ataque*) response; **la inflamación es una ~ defensiva del organismo** the inflammation is a defensive response of the body; **estoy satisfecho de la ~ positiva del público** I am satisfied with the positive response from the public

2·2 (*a problema*) answer; **la falta de ~ del gobierno a los problemas medioambientales** the government's failure to answer environmental problems

► **respuesta inmune, respuesta inmunitaria** immune response

resquebradura SF, **resquebrajadura** SF crack, split

resquebrajar ▸conjug 1a◂ Ⓐ VT to crack, split

Ⓑ **resquebrajarse** VPR to crack, split

resquebrar ▸conjug 1j◂ VI to begin to crack

resquemar ▸conjug 1a◂ VT 1 (= *quemar*) to burn slightly; (*Culin*) to scorch, burn; [+ *lengua*] to burn, sting; [+ *planta*] to parch, dry up

2 (= *amargar*) to cause bitterness to, upset

resquemor SM 1 (= *resentimiento*) resentment, bitterness

2 (= *sospecha*) secret suspicion

3 (= *sensación*) burn, sting; (*Culin*) burnt taste

resquicio SM 1 (= *abertura*) chink, crack

2 (= *oportunidad*) opening, opportunity; **un ~ de esperanza** a glimmer of hope ► **resquicio legal** legal loophole

3 (*LAm*) (= *vestigio*) sign, trace

4 (*Caribe*) (= *pedacito*) little bit, small piece

resta SF (*Mat*) 1 (= *sustracción*) subtraction

2 (= *residuo*) remainder

restablecer ▸conjug 2d◂ Ⓐ VT [+ *relaciones*] to re-establish; [+ *orden*] to restore

Ⓑ **restablecerse** VPR (*Med*) to recover

restablecimiento SM 1 [*de relaciones*] re-establishment; [*de orden*] restoration

2 (*Med*) recovery

restallar ▸conjug 1a◂ VI [*látigo*] to crack; [*papel*] to crackle; [*lengua*] to click

restallido SM [*de látigo*] crack; [*de papel*] crackle; [*de lengua*] click

restante ADJ remaining; **lo ~** the rest, the remainder; **los ~s** the rest

restañar ▸conjug 1a◂ VT to stanch, stop, stop the flow of; **~ las heridas** (*fig*) to heal the wounds

restañasangre SM bloodstone

restar ▸conjug 1a◂ Ⓐ VT 1 (*Mat*) to take away, subtract; **réstale 10 a 24** subtract 10 from 24, take away 10 from 24; **a esta cifra hay que ~le los gastos de comida** you have to deduct *o* subtract the meals allowance from this figure

2 [+ *autoridad, importancia*] **~ autoridad a algn** to take away authority from sb; **le restó importancia** he did not give it much importance

3 (*Dep*) [+ *pelota*] to return

Ⓑ VI (*frm*) to remain, be left; **restan tres días para terminarse el plazo** there are three days left before the closing date; **ahora sólo me resta hacerlo** it only remains for me now to do it, all I have to do now is do it

restauración SF 1 (= *acción*) restoration; **la Restauración** (*Esp*) *the restoration of the Spanish monarchy (1873)*

2 (= *hostelería*) **la ~** the restaurant industry; **la ~ rápida** the fast-food industry

restaurador(a) Ⓐ SM/F 1 (*Arte*) restorer

2 [*de hotel*] restaurateur, restaurant owner

Ⓑ SM ► **restaurador de cabello** hair restorer

➤ LENGUA Y USO: **respuesta 1** 46.1, 46.5, 47.1, 48.2

restaurán SM [resto'ran], **restaurant** SM = **restaurante**

restaurante SM restaurant

restaurar ▸conjug 1a◂ VT (*tb Inform*) to restore

restinga SF sandbar, shoal, mud bank

restitución SF 1 (= *devolución*) return
2 (= *restablecimiento*) restoration

restituir ▸conjug 3g◂ Ⓐ VT 1 (= *devolver*) to return, give back (**a** to)
2 (= *restablecer*) to restore
3 (*Arquit*) to restore
Ⓑ **restituirse** VPR (*frm*) **~se a** to return to, go back to

resto SM 1 (= *lo que queda*) rest; (*Mat*) remainder; **yo haré el ~** I'll do the rest; **no hace falta que te cuente el ~** I don't need to tell you the rest; ✦*MODISMO* **para los ~s***: **yo me quedo aquí para los ~s** I'm staying here for good
2 **restos** [*de edificio, muralla*] remains; [*de comida*] leftovers, scraps; [*de avión, naufragio*] wreckage *sing*; (= *escombros*) debris *sing*, rubble *sing* ▸ **restos de edición** remainders ▸ **restos de serie** leftovers, remainders ▸ **restos humanos** human remains ▸ **restos mortales** (mortal) remains
3 (*Dep*) (= *devolución de pelota*) return (of service); (= *jugador*) receiver; **estar al ~** to receive
4 (= *apuesta*) stake; **echar el ~*** (= *apostar*) to stake all one's money; (= *esforzarse al máximo*) to do one's utmost; **echar el ~ por hacer algo** to go all out to do sth, do one's utmost to do sth

restorán SM (*LAm*) restaurant

restregar ▸conjug 1h, 1j◂ VT (*con cepillo, estropajo*) to scrub; (*con trapo*) to rub, rub hard

restricción SF (= *limitación*) restriction, limitation; **sin ~ de** without restrictions as to; **hablar sin restricciones** to talk freely ▸ **restricciones eléctricas** electricity cuts, power cuts ▸ **restricción mental** mental reservations *pl* ▸ **restricciones presupuestarias** budgetary constraints ▸ **restricción salarial** wage restraint

restrictivo ADJ restrictive

restrillar ▸conjug 1a◂ Ⓐ VT (*Andes, Caribe*) [+ *látigo*] to crack
Ⓑ VI (*Caribe*) [*madera*] to crack, creak

restringido ADJ restricted, limited

restringir ▸conjug 3c◂ VT to restrict, limit (**a** to)

resucitación SF resuscitation

resucitador SM respirator

resucitar ▸conjug 1a◂ Ⓐ VT 1 (*Rel*) [+ *persona*] to raise from the dead; **podía ~ a los muertos** he could bring back the dead
2 [+ *ley*] to resurrect
Ⓑ VI to rise from the dead; **al tercer día resucitó** (*Biblia*) on the third day He rose again

resudar ▸conjug 1a◂ VT, VI 1 (= *sudar*) to sweat a little
2 [+ *recipiente*] to leak slightly

resuello SM 1 (= *aliento*) breath; (= *respiración*) breathing; **corto de ~** short of breath; **sin ~** out of breath, out of puff*; ✦*MODISMO* **sumir el ~ a algn** (*LAm**) to bump sb off*
2 (= *jadeo*) puff; (= *respiración ruidosa*) wheeze; ✦*MODISMO* **meter a algn el ~ en el cuerpo** to put the wind up sb*
3 (*LAm*) (= *respiro*) breathing space; (= *descanso*) rest; **tomar un ~** to take a breather
4 (*) (= *dinero*) bread*, money

resueltamente ADV (= *con determinación*) resolutely, with determination; (= *audazmente*) boldly; (= *firmemente*) steadfastly

▼ **resuelto** Ⓐ PP *de* **resolver**
Ⓑ ADJ (= *determinado*) resolute, resolved, determined; (= *audaz*) bold; (= *firme*) steadfast; **estar ~ a algo** to be set on sth; **estar ~ a hacer algo** to be determined to do sth

resulta SF result; **de ~s de** as a result of; **estar a ~s de** (*esp Esp*) to keep track of, keep up-to-date with

resultado SM 1 (= *dato resultante*) [*de elecciones, examen, competición, investigación*] result; [*de partido*] score, result; **la publicación de los ~s económicos de la empresa** the publication of the company's economic results; **el ~ fue de empate a dos** the result was a two-two draw; **los ~s de la jornada futbolística** the football scores
2 (= *efecto*) result; **el pacto fue el ~ de meses de trabajo** the pact was the result of months of work; **dar ~** [*plan, método*] to succeed, be successful; [*tratamiento*] to produce results; **la jugada no ha dado ~** the move didn't come off* *o* wasn't successful; **la prueba no siempre da ~s fiables** the test does not always give *o* provide reliable results; **las negociaciones están dando ~s positivos** the negotiations are proving positive
3 (*Mat*) result

resultante Ⓐ ADJ resulting *antes de s*, resultant (*frm*) *antes de s*; **~ de** resulting from
Ⓑ SF (*Fís*) resultant

▼ **resultar** ▸conjug 1a◂ VI 1 (= *tener como resultado*) 1·1 (+ *ADJ, SUSTANTIVO*) to be; **varias personas ~on heridas en el atentado** several people were wounded in the attack; **el conductor resultó muerto** the driver was killed; **resultó ganador un escritor desconocido** the winner was an unknown writer; **varios corredores han resultado positivos** a number of runners have tested positive; **la operación resultó un fracaso** the operation was a failure, the operation resulted in failure (*frm*)
1·2 (+ *INFIN*) **resultó no saber nada de aquel asunto** he turned out to know nothing about that matter, it turned out that he knew nothing about that matter; **~ ser** to turn out to be; **resultó ser el padre de mi amigo** he turned out to be my friend's father; **si resulta ser verdadero** if it proves (to be) true, if it turns out to be true; **el causante del incendio resultó ser un cable de la luz** the cause of the fire turned out *o* proved to be an electric cable
1·3 **resulta que** it turns out that; **ahora resulta que no vamos** now it turns out *o* now it seems (that) we're not going after all; **dijeron que lo había hecho él solo, cuando resulta que tenía varios cómplices** he was said to have done it on his own, when it turns out that he had several accomplices; **al final resultó que era inocente** he proved *o* he turned out to be innocent in the end, in the end it turned out that he was innocent; **me gustaría ir, pero resulta que no tengo dinero** I'd like to go, but the thing is *o* the fact is that I haven't got any money
2 (= *salir*) to turn out, work out; **todo resultó bien** everything turned out *o* worked out well; **aquello no resultó muy bien** that didn't turn out *o* work out very well; **no resultó** it didn't work
3 (*frm*) (= *ser*) (+ *ADJ*) 3·1 (*uso impersonal*) **resulta difícil decidir si …** it is hard to decide whether …; **su versión resulta difícil de creer** his story is hard to believe, it's hard to believe his story; **este trabajo está resultando un poco aburrido** this job is getting a bit boring; **resulta más barato hacerlo así** it works out cheaper to do it this way
3·2 (*con complemento de persona*) **me está resultando fácil** I'm finding it easy; **la casa nos resulta muy pequeña** the house is too small for us; **me resulta simpático** he seems like a nice guy to me
4 (*frm*) **~ de** to be the result of, result from; **la mayor parte de sus problemas resultan de su falta de diplomacia** most of his problems are the result of a lack of tact; **¿quién sabe lo que ~á de todo esto?** who knows what will come of all this?, who knows what the outcome of all this will be?
5 (*frm*) **~ en** to result in, lead to; **el latifundismo resulta en beneficios privados** large-scale landholding results in *o* leads to individual profits
6 (*Esp**) (= *agradar*) **tu prima no es una belleza, pero resulta** your cousin is no beauty, but she's got something (about her); **esa corbata no resulta con ese traje** that tie doesn't look right *o* go with that suit

resultón* ADJ attractive

▼ **resumen** Ⓐ SM summary, résumé; **hizo un ~ de lo que dijo** she gave a summary *o* résumé of what he said; **en ~** (= *en conclusión*) to sum up; (= *brevemente*) in short
Ⓑ ADJ INV **comparencia ~** brief concluding appearance; **exposición ~** summary; **programa ~** programme in summary form

resumidero SM (*LAm*) = **sumidero**

▼ **resumir** ▸conjug 3a◂ Ⓐ VT (= *recapitular*) to sum up; (= *condensar*) to summarize; (= *cortar*) to abridge, shorten
Ⓑ VI **bueno, resumiendo …** so, to sum up, …, so, in short, …
Ⓒ **resumirse** VPR 1 **la situación se resume en pocas palabras** the situation can be summed up in a few words
2 [*asunto*] **~se en** to boil *o* come down to; **todo se resumió en algunos porrazos** all it boiled *o* came down to was a few punches

resunta SF (*Andes*) summary

resurgimiento SM resurgence

resurgir ▸conjug 3c◂ VI 1 (= *reaparecer*) to reappear, revive
2 (*Med*) to recover

resurrección SF resurrection

retablo SM altarpiece

retacada SF foul stroke

retacado ADJ (*Méx*) full

retacarse ▸conjug 1g◂ VPR (*LAm*) to refuse to budge

retacear ▸conjug 1a◂ VT (*Andes, Cono Sur*) to give grudgingly

retachar ▸conjug 1a◂ VT, VI (*LAm*) to bounce

retacitos SMPL (*CAm*) confetti

retaco SM 1 (*) (= *persona*) midget
2 (*Billar*) short cue

retacón* ADJ (*esp Andes, Cono Sur*) short, squat

➤ LENGUA Y USO: **resuelto B** 35.2 **resultar 1** 41, 43.4, 53.1, 53.3, 53.6 **resumen A** 53.4 **resumir A** 53.1, 53.4

retador(a) Ⓐ ADJ challenging, defiant
Ⓑ SM/F (*LAm Dep*) challenger

retaguardia SF [1] (*Mil*) rearguard; **a ~** in the rear; **tres millas a ~** three miles to the rear, three miles further back; **estar** *o* **ir a** *o* **en ~** to bring up the rear
[2] (*) (= *culo*) rear*, posterior (*hum*)

retahíla SF (= *serie*) string, series; [*de injurias*] stream

retajado/a (*Cono Sur*) Ⓐ ADJ (*Zool*) castrated, gelded
Ⓑ SM/F (*‡*) wanker**

retajar ▸conjug 1a◂ VT [1] (= *cortar*) to cut out, cut round
[2] (*LAm*) (= *castrar*) to castrate, geld

retal SM remnant

retaliación SF (*LAm*) retaliation

retallones SMPL (*Caribe*) leftovers

retama SF, **retamo** SM (*LAm Bot*) broom

retar ▸conjug 1a◂ VT [1] (= *desafiar*) to challenge
[2] (*Arg**) (= *regañar*) to tell off, tick off*
[3] (*Cono Sur**) (= *insultar*) to insult, abuse; **~ a algn algo** to throw sth in sb's face

retardación SF (= *enlentecimiento*) retardation, slowing down; (= *retraso*) delaying; (*Mec*) deceleration

retardado ADJ **bomba de efecto ~** time bomb

retardar ▸conjug 1a◂ VT (= *frenar*) to slow down, slow up; [+ *marcha*] to hold up; [+ *tren*] to delay, make late

retardatriz ADJ delaying

retardo SM (*frm*) delay

retazar ▸conjug 1f◂ VT [1] (= *cortar*) to cut up, snip into pieces; [+ *leña*] to chop
[2] (= *dividir*) to divide up

retazo SM [1] (*Cos*) remnant, bit, piece; **retazos** snippets, bits and pieces; **a ~s** in bits
[2] (*Caribe*) bargain

RETD SF ABR (*Esp Telec*) = **Red Especial de Transmisión de Datos**

rete... PREF (*esp LAm*) very, extremely; **~bién** very well; **una persona ~fina** a really refined person*

retemblar ▸conjug 1j◂ VI to shudder, shake (**de** at, with)

retemplar ▸conjug 1a◂ VT (*Andes, CAm, Cono Sur*) to cheer up

retén SM [1] (*Téc*) stop, catch; (*Aut*) oil seal
[2] (= *reserva*) reserve, store; **tener algo de ~** to have sth in reserve
[3] (*Mil*) reserves *pl*, reinforcements *pl*; **hombre de ~** reserve; **estar de ~** to be on call
[4] (*LAm*) [*de policía*] roadblock, police roadblock
[5] (*Caribe*) (= *correccional*) remand home

retención SF [1] (= *contención*) retention ► **retención de tráfico** traffic delay, traffic hold-up
[2] (*Fin*) deduction, stoppage ► **retención a cuenta** deduction at source ► **retención fiscal** deduction for tax purposes
[3] (*Med*) retention
[4] (*Telec*) hold facility

retener ▸conjug 2k◂ Ⓐ VT [1] (= *no dejar marchar*) to keep; [*la policía*] to detain, hold; **lo retiene su familia** his family is what keeps him there; **no intentes ~me porque pienso ir** don't try and keep *o* stop me because I'm going; **retuvieron a los inmigrantes en la aduana** they held *o* detained the immigrants at customs; **una llamada de última hora me retuvo en la oficina** a last-minute phone call held me up *o* kept me back at the office; **~ a algn preso** to hold *o* keep sb prisoner
[2] (= *conservar*) [+ *datos, información*] to withhold; [+ *pasaporte*] to retain; **el Atlético ha conseguido ~ el título de Liga** Atlético managed to hold on to *o* keep *o* retain the league title
[3] (= *memorizar*) to retain; **es incapaz de ~ los nombres de la gente** he's incapable of retaining people's names
[4] (*Fin*) [+ *dinero*] to deduct
[5] [+ *calor*] to retain; [+ *líquido*] to hold; **no puede ~ la orina** he can't hold his water
[6] (*frm*) [+ *atención, interés*] to retain
[7] (*frm*) [+ *deseo, pasión*] to restrain; [+ *aliento*] to hold
Ⓑ **retenerse** VPR to restrain o.s.

retenida SF guy rope

retentiva SF memory

retentivo ADJ retentive

reteñir ▸conjug 3h y 3k◂ VT to redye

reticencia SF [1] (= *renuencia*) unwillingness, reluctance
[2] (= *reserva*) reticence, reserve
[3] (= *ironía*) irony, sarcasm

reticente ADJ [1] (= *reacio*) unwilling, reluctant; **estar** *o* **ser ~ a hacer algo** to be unwilling *o* reluctant to do sth; **se mostró ~ a aceptar** she was unwilling *o* reluctant to accept; **se declara ~ a meterse en política** he says he doesn't like the idea of getting involved in politics
[2] (= *con reserva*) reticent, reserved
[3] (= *irónico*) ironical, sarcastic

rético/a Ⓐ ADJ, SM/F Romansch
Ⓑ SM (*Ling*) Romansch

retícula SF [1] (*Ópt*) reticle
[2] (*Fot*) screen

reticular ADJ reticulated

retículo SM [1] (= *red*) reticle
[2] [*de medir*] grid

retina SF retina

retinol SM retinol

retintín SM [1] (= *tono sarcástico*) sarcastic tone; **decir algo con ~** to say sth sarcastically
[2] (= *tilín*) tinkle, tinkling; [*de llaves*] jingle, jangle; (*en el oído*) ringing

retinto ADJ (*esp LAm*) very dark

retiñir ▸conjug 3a◂ VI (= *resonar*) to tinkle; [*llaves*] to jingle, jangle; (*en el oído*) to go on ringing, go on ringing in one's ears

retirada SF [1] (*Mil*) retreat, withdrawal; **batirse en ~** ◊ **emprender la ~** to retreat, beat a retreat
[2] [*de dinero, embajador*] withdrawal
[3] [*de vehículo, objeto*] removal
[4] (††) (= *refugio*) safe place, place of refuge

retiradamente ADV [*vivir*] quietly, in seclusion

retirado ADJ [1] [*lugar*] remote
[2] [*vida*] quiet
[3] (= *jubilado*) retired
[4] (*Esp*††) **la tiene retirada** he keeps her as his mistress

retirar ▸conjug 1a◂ Ⓐ VT [1] [+ *acusación, apoyo, subvención*] to withdraw; [+ *demanda*] to withdraw, take back; **han retirado su apoyo al Gobierno** they have withdrawn their support for the Government; **les ~on las subvenciones** they had their subsidies taken away *o* withdrawn; **retiró su candidatura a la Presidencia** he stood down from the presidential election, he withdrew his candidacy for the presidency; **la mayoría del electorado le ha retirado la confianza** he has lost the confidence *o* trust of the majority of the electorate; **~ la palabra a algn** to stop speaking to sb; **~ el saludo a algn** to stop saying hello to sb
[2] [+ *moneda, sello*] to withdraw (from circulation); [+ *autobús, avión*] to withdraw (from service); **estos aviones serán retirados de** *o* **del servicio** these planes are to be withdrawn from service; **el producto fue retirado del mercado** the product was withdrawn from the market *o* taken off the market
[3] [+ *permiso, carnet, pasaporte*] to withdraw, take away; **le han retirado el permiso de conducir** he's had his driving licence taken away
[4] [+ *dinero*] to withdraw; **fui a ~ dinero de la cuenta** I went to withdraw some money from my account
[5] [+ *tropas*] to withdraw; [+ *embajador*] to recall, withdraw; [+ *atleta, caballo*] to withdraw, scratch
[6] (= *quitar*) to take away, remove; **la camarera retiró las copas** the waitress took the glasses away; **le ~on todos los objetos afilados de la celda** all sharp objects were removed from his cell
[7] [+ *cabeza, cara*] to pull back, pull away; [+ *mano*] to draw back, withdraw; [+ *tentáculo*] to draw in
[8] (= *jubilar*) to retire, pension off
Ⓑ **retirarse** VPR [1] (= *moverse*) to move back *o* away (**de** from); **retírate de la entrada para que pueda pasar la gente** move back *o* away from the door so that people can get through; **~se ante un peligro** to shrink back from a danger
[2] (= *irse*) **puede usted ~se** you may leave; **el testigo puede ~se** the witness may stand down; **se retiró enfadado a la cocina** he withdrew to the kitchen in a huff; **~se de las negociaciones** to withdraw from the negotiations; **se ~on del torneo** (*antes de su inicio*) they withdrew from *o* pulled out of the tournament; (*después de su inicio*) they retired from *o* pulled out of the tournament; **tuvo que ~se del terreno de juego** he had to leave the pitch
[3] **~se (a su habitación)** to retire (to one's room *o* to bed) (*frm, liter*)
[4] (*al teléfono*) **¡no se retire!** hold the line!
[5] (*Mil*) to withdraw, retreat
[6] (= *jubilarse*) to retire (**de** from); **mi padre se retira el año que viene** my father will be retiring next year; **cuando me retire de los negocios** when I retire from business; **se retiró anticipadamente** she took early retirement

retiro SM [1] (= *jubilación*) retirement; **un oficial en ~** a retired officer ► **retiro prematuro** early retirement
[2] (= *pensión*) retirement pension, pension
[3] (= *lugar*) quiet place, secluded spot; (*Rel*) retreat
[4] [*de dinero*] withdrawal

reto SM [1] (= *desafío*) challenge
[2] (*Cono Sur*) (= *reprimenda*) telling off, scold-

ing
3 (*Cono Sur*) (= *insulto*) insult

retobado ADJ 1 (*LAm*) [*animal*] (= *salvaje*) wild
2 (*LAm*) [*persona*] (= *taimado*) sly, crafty; (= *rebelde*) rebellious; (= *terco*) obstinate; (= *hosco*) sullen; (= *caprichoso*) unpredictable, capricious
3 (*Andes, CAm, Méx**) (= *gruñón*) grumbling; (= *descarado*) saucy, sassy (*EEUU*), cheeky*

retobar ▸conjug 1a◂ Ⓐ VT 1 (*Andes, Cono Sur*) (= *forrar*) to line with leather, line with sacking, line with oilcloth; (= *cubrir*) to cover with leather
2 (*Andes*) [+ *pieles*] to tan
Ⓑ VI = C
Ⓒ **retobarse** VPR (*LAm*) (= *obstinarse*) to be stubborn, dig one's heels in; (= *quejarse*) to grumble, protest

retobo SM 1 (*LAm*) (= *forro*) lining; (= *cubierta*) covering
2 (*Cono Sur*) (= *hule*) sacking, oilcloth
3 (*LAm*) (= *terquedad*) stubbornness; (= *protesta*) grumble, moan
4 (= *capricho*) whim
5 (*Andes, CAm Agr*) old stock, useless animals; (= *persona*) useless person; (= *objeto*) worthless object; (= *trastos*) junk, rubbish, garbage (*EEUU*)
6 (*LAm*) (= *resabio*) aftertaste

retobón ADJ (*Cono Sur*) = **retobado 1, 2**

retocar ▸conjug 1g◂ Ⓐ VT 1 [+ *dibujo, foto*] to touch up
2 [+ *grabación*] to play back
Ⓑ **retocarse** VPR (*Esp*) to freshen one's make-up

retomar ▸conjug 1a◂ VT to take up again

retoñar ▸conjug 1a◂ VT 1 (*Bot*) to sprout, shoot
2 (= *reaparecer*) to reappear, recur

retoño SM 1 (*Bot*) sprout, shoot
2 (*) (= *niño*) kid*

retoque SM 1 (= *acción*) touching-up; (= *último trazo*) finishing touch
2 (*Med*) symptom, sign, indication

retorcer ▸conjug 2b, 2h◂ Ⓐ VT 1 [+ *brazo*] to twist; [+ *manos, lavado*] to wring; [+ *hebras*] to twine, twine together; **~le el pescuezo a algn*** to wring sb's neck*
2 [+ *argumento*] to turn, twist; [+ *sentido*] to twist
Ⓑ **retorcerse** VPR 1 [*cordel*] to get into knots, get tangled (up) *o* twisted
2 [*persona*] to writhe, squirm; **~se de dolor** to writhe in pain; **~se de risa** to double up with laughter
3 **~ el bigote** to twirl one's moustache

retorcido ADJ 1 [*estilo*] involved
2 [*método, persona, mente*] devious

retorcijón SM (*LAm*) = **retortijón**

retorcimiento SM 1 [*de brazo*] twisting; [*de manos, ropa lavada*] wringing; [*de hebras*] entwining, twisting together
2 [*de estilo*] involved nature
3 [*de método, persona, mente*] deviousness

retórica SF 1 (*Literat*) rhetoric
2 **retóricas*** (= *palabrería*) hot air *sing*, mere words

retóricamente ADV rhetorically

retórico/a Ⓐ ADJ rhetorical
Ⓑ SM/F rhetorician

retornable ADJ returnable; **envase no ~** non-returnable container/bottle

retornar ▸conjug 1a◂ Ⓐ VI (= *venir*) to return, come back; (= *irse*) to return, go back
Ⓑ VT 1 (= *devolver*) to return, give back
2 (= *reponer*) to replace, put back
3 (= *mover*) to move back

retorno SM 1 (= *vuelta*) return; **viaje de ~** return journey; **operación ~** *traffic control operation for the mass return home after holidays or public holiday*
2 (*frm*) (= *recompensa*) reward; (= *pago*) repayment; (= *cambio*) exchange, barter; [*de regalo, servicio*] return
3 (*Elec*) ► **retorno terrestre** earth wire, ground wire (*EEUU*)
4 (*Inform*) ► **retorno del carro** (*tb Tip*) carriage return ► **retorno del carro automático** (*Inform*) word wrap, word wraparound
5 (*Méx Aut*) turning place; **"retorno prohibido"** "no U turns"

retorsión SF [*de brazo*] twisting; [*de manos, ropa mojada*] wringing

retorta SF retort

retortero* SM **andar al ~** to bustle about, have heaps of things to do; **andar al ~ por algo** to crave for sth; **andar al ~ por algn** to be madly in love with sb; **llevar** *o* **traer a algn al ~** to have sb under one's thumb

retortijón SM rapid twist ► **retortijón de tripas** stomach cramp

retostar ▸conjug 1l◂ VT to burn, overcook

retozar ▸conjug 1f◂ VI to romp, frolic, frisk about

retozo SM (= *holgorio*) romp, frolic; (= *jugueteo*) gambol; **~s** romping *sing*, frolics

retozón ADJ 1 (= *juguetón*) playful, frisky
2 [*risa*] bubbling

retracción SF retraction

retractable ADJ retractable

retractación SF retraction, recantation

retractar ▸conjug 1a◂ Ⓐ VT to retract, withdraw
Ⓑ **retractarse** VPR to retract, recant; **me retracto** I take that back; **me retracto de la acusación hecha** I withdraw the accusation

retráctil ADJ 1 (*Aer*) retractable
2 (*Biol*) retractile

retraer ▸conjug 2o◂ Ⓐ VT 1 [+ *uñas*] to draw in, retract
2 (= *volver a traer*) to bring back
3 (*frm*) (= *disuadir*) to dissuade
Ⓑ **retraerse** VPR 1 (= *retirarse*) **se retrajo a la aldea para su convalecencia** she withdrew to the village to convalesce
2 (= *intimidarse*) **se retrae cuando le preguntan algo** she goes into her shell when she's asked a question

retraído ADJ (= *tímido*) shy, reserved

retraimiento SM (= *timidez*) shyness, reserve

retranca SF (*LAm*) brake

retrancar ▸conjug 1g◂ Ⓐ VT (*LAm*) to brake
Ⓑ **retrancarse** VPR (*LAm*) (= *frenar*) to brake, apply the brakes

retransmisión SF (*TV, Radio*) **Canal Cinco realizará la ~ del partido** (*TV*) the match will be shown *o* broadcast on Channel Five; (*Radio*) the match will be broadcast on Channel Five; **durante la ~ no habrá cortes publicitarios** there will be no commercial breaks during the broadcast ► **retransmisión en diferido** delayed transmission ► **retransmisión en directo** live broadcast, live transmission

retransmitir ▸conjug 3a◂ VT 1 (*TV*) to show, broadcast; (*Radio*) to broadcast
2 (††) [+ *recado*] to relay, pass on

retrasado/a Ⓐ ADJ 1 (*en una actividad*) **estar** *o* **ir ~** to be behind; **va muy ~ en química** he is very behind in chemistry, he has a lot to make up in chemistry; **estar ~ en los pagos** to be behind in *o* with one's payments, be in arrears; **vamos ~s en la producción** we are lagging behind in the production
2 (*en el tiempo*) [*persona*] late; **llegó ~ a la reunión** he was late for the meeting, he got to the meeting late
3 (*en el desarrollo*) [*país, pueblo, sociedad*] backward; **nuestro sistema universitario va ~ respecto a otros países** our university system is very backward compared with *o* is behind that of other countries
4 (= *no actual*) [*ideas, estilo*] outdated, outmoded
5 [*reloj*] slow; **tengo el reloj ocho minutos ~** my watch is eight minutes slow
6 (*mentalmente*) mentally retarded
Ⓑ SM/F (*tb* **~/a mental**) (*pey*) mentally handicapped

retrasar ▸conjug 1a◂ Ⓐ VT 1 (= *aplazar*) [+ *suceso, acción*] to postpone, put off; [+ *fecha*] to put back; **retrasó en una hora su comparecencia ante la prensa** he postponed *o* put off his appearance before the press for an hour; **el sorteo ha sido retrasado una semana** the draw has been postponed for a week *o* put back a week; **han retrasado la fecha del examen** they've put back the date of the exam; **quieren ~ la edad de jubilación** they want to raise the retirement age
2 (= *retardar*) to delay, hold up; **varios problemas burocráticos ~on la salida del avión** a number of bureaucratic problems delayed *o* held up the departure of the plane; **la nieve está retrasando el tráfico** the snow is holding up *o* delaying traffic
3 [+ *reloj*] to put back; **esta noche tenemos que ~ los relojes** we have to put the clocks back tonight
Ⓑ VI [*reloj*] to be slow
Ⓒ **retrasarse** VPR 1 (*al llegar*) [*persona, tren*] to be late; **siento haberme retrasado** I'm sorry I'm late; **el avión se retrasó más de cuatro horas** the plane was more than four hours late
2 (*en una actividad*) to be late; **siempre se retrasaba en el cumplimiento de sus promesas** she was always late in fulfilling her promises; **se han retrasado en el pago de los sueldos este mes** they're late in paying the wages this month; **se han retrasado en el pago del alquiler** they're in arrears with the rent, they've fallen behind with the rent
3 [*acontecimiento, producción*] to be delayed, be held up; **el inicio del campeonato se retrasó por la lluvia** the start of the championship was delayed *o* held up by rain
4 (= *quedarse atrás*) (*en los estudios*) to get behind, fall behind; (*andando*) to lag behind; **empezó a ~se en los estudios cuando cayó enfermo** he began to fall *o* get behind in his studies when he fell ill
5 [*reloj*] to be slow

retraso SM [1] (*al llegar*) delay; **perdona el ~** sorry for the delay; **el ~ en la llegada de los bomberos** the delay in the arrival of the fire brigade; **nuestro vuelo ha sufrido un ~ de dos horas** our flight has been delayed by two hours; **ir con ~** to be running late; **llegar con ~** to be late, arrive late; **llegó con 25 minutos de ~** he was *o* arrived 25 minutes late
[2] (*en una actividad*) delay; **protestaron por el ~ en el cobro de sus salarios** they complained about the delay in the payment of their wages; **llevo un ~ de seis semanas en mi trabajo** I'm six weeks behind with my work; **las obras de la catedral se iniciaron con ~** the building work at the cathedral started late; **el mitin comenzó con una hora de ~** the rally began an hour late, the rally was delayed (by) an hour
[3] (*en país, investigación*) backwardness; **el ~ cultural del país con relación a los países vecinos** the cultural backwardness of the country compared to its neighbours; **llevamos años de ~ en la investigación espacial** we are years behind in space investigation
[4] ► **retraso mental** mental deficiency; **padece un leve ~ mental** he has mild learning difficulties, he's slightly retarded

retratar ▸conjug 1a◂ Ⓐ VT [1] (*Arte*) to paint the portrait of; (*Fot*) to photograph, take a picture of; **hacerse ~** (*en cuadro*) to have one's portrait painted; (*en fotografía*) to have one's photograph taken
[2] (= *representar*) to portray, depict, describe
Ⓑ **retratarse** VPR (*en cuadro*) to have one's portrait painted; (*en fotografía*) to have one's photograph taken

retratería SF (*LAm*) photographer's, photographer's studio

retratista SMF (*Arte*) portrait painter; (*Fot*) photographer

retrato SM [1] (*Arte*) portrait; (*Fot*) photograph, portrait; ✦*MODISMO* **ser el vivo ~ de algn** to be the spitting image of sb
[2] (= *descripción*) portrayal, depiction, description

retrato-robot SM (*pl* **retratos-robot**) Identikit picture

retrechería SF [1] (= *truco*) dodge*, wheeze*, crafty trick; (*hum*) rascally trick
[2] **retrecherías** (= *encantos*) winning ways, charming ways
[3] (= *atractivo*) charm, attractiveness

retrechero ADJ [1] (= *dado a trucos*) full of dodges*; (= *astuto*) wily, crafty; (*hum*) rascally
[2] (= *encantador*) winning, charming, attractive
[3] (*LAm*) (= *tacaño*) mean; (= *tramposo*) unreliable, deceitful; (= *sospechoso*) suspicious

retreparse ▸conjug 1a◂ VPR to lean back

retreta SF [1] (*Mil*) retreat; (= *exhibición*) tattoo, display
[2] (*LAm*) (= *concierto*) open-air band concert

retrete SM lavatory, bathroom (*EEUU*)

retribución SF [1] (= *pago*) pay, payment; (= *recompensa*) reward
[2] (*Téc*) compensation

retribuido ADJ [*esfuerzos*] rewarded; [*puesto*] salaried; **un puesto mal ~** a badly-paid post

retribuir ▸conjug 3g◂ VT [1] (= *pagar*) to pay; (= *recompensar*) to reward
[2] (*LAm*) [+ *favor*] to repay, return

retro* Ⓐ ADJ INV [1] [*moda*] backward-looking
[2] (*Pol*) reactionary
Ⓑ SM (*Pol*) reactionary

retro... PREF retro...

retroacción SF feedback

retroactivamente ADV retroactively, retrospectively

retroactividad SF [*de ley*] retroactivity, retrospective nature; **estas leyes carecen de ~** these laws do not have retroactive effect; **la ~ de los aumentos salariales no es negociable** backdating the wage increases is not negotiable

retroactivo ADJ retroactive, retrospective; **ley con** *o* **de efecto ~** retroactive *o* retrospective law; **un aumento ~ desde abril** a rise backdated to April; **dar efecto ~ a un pago** to backdate a payment

retroalimentación SF (*tb Inform*) feedback

retroalimentador ADJ feedback *antes de s*

retroalimentar ▸conjug 1a◂ VT to feed back

retrocarga SF **de ~** breechloading; **arma de ~** breechloader

retroceder ▸conjug 2a◂ VI [1] (= *moverse hacia atrás*) to move back, move backwards, go back, go backwards; [*ejército*] to fall back, retreat; [*aguas*] to go down; **retrocedió unos pasos** he went *o* moved back a few steps; **la policía hizo ~ a la multitud** the police made the crowd move back; **tienes que ~ a la primera casilla** you have to go back to the first square
[2] [*rifle*] to recoil
[3] (= *desistir*) to give up; (= *rajarse*) to back down; (*ante un peligro*) to flinch; **no ~** to stand firm

retroceso SM [1] (= *movimiento*) backward movement; (*Mil*) retreat
[2] [*de rifle*] recoil; **cañón sin ~** recoil-less gun
[3] (*Com*) (= *recesión*) recession, depression; [*de precio*] fall, drop
[4] (*Med*) new outbreak
[5] (*Tip*) backspace

retrocohete SM retrorocket

retrocuenta SF countdown

retrogradación SF retrogression

retrógrado ADJ [1] (*Pol*) reactionary
[2] (= *que retrocede*) retrograde, retrogressive

retrogresión SF retrogression

retronar ▸conjug 1l◂ VI = **retumbar**

retropropulsión SF jet propulsion

retroproyección SF (*con retroproyector*) overhead projection; (*Cine*) (= *efecto especial*) back projection

retroproyector SM overhead projector

retrospección SF retrospection

retrospectiva SF [1] (*Arte*) retrospective, retrospective exhibition
[2] **en ~** with hindsight

retrospectivamente ADV retrospectively; [*considerar*] in retrospect

retrospectivo ADJ retrospective; **escena retrospectiva** flashback; **mirada retrospectiva** backward glance, look back (**a** at)

retrotraer ▸conjug 2o◂ VT to carry back (in time), take back; **retrotrajo su relato a los tiempos del abuelo** he carried his tale back into his grandfather's day; **ahora podemos ~ su origen al siglo XI** now we can take its origin further back to the 11th century; **piensa ~ el problema a su origen** he hopes to trace the problem back to its origin

retroventa SF resale; **precio de ~** resale price

retrovírico ADJ retroviral

retrovirus SM INV retrovirus

retrovisión SF hindsight; (*Cine*) flashback, flashback technique

retrovisor SM (*tb* **espejo ~**) driving mirror, rear-view mirror

retrucar ▸conjug 1g◂ VI [1] [+ *argumento*] to turn against its user
[2] (*Cono Sur*) (= *replicar*) to retort; **le retruqué diciendo que ...** I retorted to him that ...
[3] (*Billar*) to kiss

retruécano SM pun, play on words

retruque SM [1] (*Andes, Cono Sur*) sharp retort
[2] **de ~** (*Cono Sur, Méx*) on the rebound

retumbante ADJ [1] (= *que retumba*) booming, rumbling; (= *sonoro*) resounding
[2] (= *enfático*) bombastic

retumbar ▸conjug 1a◂ VI [1] [*artillería*] to boom, thunder; [*trueno*] to roll, crash; **la cascada retumbaba a lo lejos** the waterfall roared in the distance
[2] [*voz, pasos*] to echo; **la caverna retumbaba con nuestros pasos** the cave echoed with our steps; **sus palabras retumban en mi cabeza** his words are still reverberating in my mind

retumbo SM [*de artillería*] boom, thunder; [*de trueno*] roll, rolling, crash, crashing; [*de voz*] boom, booming; [*de pasos*] echo

reubicación SF [*de trabajadores, empresas*] relocation; [*de comunidad, pueblo*] resettlement

reubicar ▸conjug 1g◂ VT [+ *trabajador, empresa*] to relocate; [+ *comunidad, pueblo*] to resettle

reuma SM, **reúma** SM rheumatism

reumático ADJ rheumatic

reumatismo SM rheumatism

reumatoide ADJ rheumatoid

reunido ADJ **está ~** (*Esp*) he's in a meeting; **el jefe está ~ con el director** the boss is in a meeting with his director

reunificación SF reunification

reunificar ▸conjug 1g◂ VT to reunify

reunión SF [1] (*de trabajo, deportiva*) meeting; (*social*) gathering; **¿irás a la ~ de padres?** are you going to the parents' meeting?; **no pudo ir a la ~ familiar** he couldn't go to the family gathering; **celebrar una ~** to hold a meeting; **convocar una ~** to call a meeting
► **reunión de trabajo** business meeting
► **reunión de ventas** sales meeting
► **reunión en la cumbre** summit (meeting)
► **reunión ilícita** unlawful assembly
► **reunión informativa** briefing ► **reunión plenaria** plenary session
[2] (= *gente reunida*) meeting; **el director se dirigió a la ~** the director addressed the meeting

reunir ▸conjug 3a◂ Ⓐ VT [1] (= *juntar*) to join, join together
[2] (= *recolectar*) [+ *cosas dispersas*] to gather, gather together, get together; [+ *datos*] to collect, gather; [+ *recursos*] to pool; [+ *colección*] to assemble, make; [+ *dinero*] to collect; [+ *fondos*] to raise; **la producción de los demás países reunidos no alcanzará al nuestro** the production of the other countries put together will not come up to ours; **los cuatro**

reunidos no valen lo que él he is better than the four of them put together; **~ esfuerzos** to join forces
[3] [*+ personas*] to bring together, get together; **reunió a sus amigos para discutirlo** he got his friends together to talk it over
[4] [*+ cualidades*] to combine; [*+ condiciones*] to have, possess; **la casa no reúne las condiciones** the house doesn't match up to requirements; **creo ~ todos los requisitos** I think I meet all the necessary requirements
Ⓑ **reunirse** VPR [1] (*= unirse*) to join together; (*de nuevo*) to reunite
[2] [*personas*] (*en asamblea*) to meet, gather; (*en casa*) to get together; **~se para hacer algo** to get together to do sth
[3] [*circunstancias*] to conspire (**para** to)

reutilizable ADJ reusable

reutilización SF reuse, recycling

reutilizar ▸conjug 1f◂ VT to reuse

reválida SF final examination

revalidar ▸conjug 1a◂ VT (*= ratificar*) to confirm, ratify; **~ un título** (*Dep*) to regain a title

revalorar ▸conjug 1a◂ VT = **revalorizar**

revalorización SF, **revaloración** SF [*de moneda*] revaluation; (*Fin*) reassessment

revalorizar ▸conjug 1f◂ Ⓐ VT [*+ moneda*] to revalue; (*Fin*) to reassess
Ⓑ **revalorizarse** VPR [*divisa*] to rise; [*mercancía*] to rise in value; **el euro se ha revalorizado frente a la libra** the euro has risen against the pound

revaluación SF revaluation

revaluar ▸conjug 1e◂ VT to revalue

revancha SF [1] (*= venganza*) revenge; **tomarse la ~** to get one's revenge, get one's own back
[2] (*Dep*) return match; (*Boxeo*) return fight

revanchismo SM revanchism

revanchista ADJ, SMF revanchist

revejido ADJ (*Andes*) weak, feeble

revelación Ⓐ SF revelation; [*de un secreto*] disclosure; **fue una ~ para mí** it was a revelation to me
Ⓑ ADJ INV **el coche ~ del año** the surprise car of the year; **el diputado ~ del año** the surprise of the year among MPs

revelado SM developing

▼ **revelador** Ⓐ ADJ [*información, documento*] revealing; (*= incriminador*) telltale
Ⓑ SM (*= sustancia*) developer

revelar ▸conjug 1a◂ Ⓐ VT [1] (*= descubrir*) to reveal; **reveló los nombres de sus cómplices** she revealed the names of her accomplices; **no quiso ~ su identidad** he did not want to reveal *o* disclose his identity, he did not want to identify himself; **~ un secreto** to reveal *o* give away a secret
[2] (*frm*) (*= evidenciar*) to reveal, show; **su expresión revelaba desprecio** his expression revealed *o* showed contempt
[3] (*Fot*) to develop; **todavía no hemos revelado las fotos** we haven't had the photos developed yet
Ⓑ **revelarse** VPR **~se como: se ha revelado como una gran pianista** she has turned out to be *o* shown herself to be a great pianist

revendedor(a) SM/F [1] [*de entradas*] ticket tout, scalper (*EEUU**)
[2] (*Com*) (*al por menor*) retailer

revender ▸conjug 2a◂ VT [1] [*+ entradas*] to tout, resell, scalp (*EEUU**)
[2] (*= vender*) to retail

revendón SM (*Andes*) middleman

revenido ADJ stale

revenirse ▸conjug 3r◂ VPR [1] [*pan, galletas, fritos*] to go stale; [*vino*] to go sour
[2] [*pintura, escayola*] to dry out
[3] (*= encogerse*) to shrink
[4] (*= ceder*) to give way

reventa Ⓐ SF [1] [*de entradas*] touting, scalping (*EEUU**)
[2] (*= venta al por menor*) resale; **precio de ~** resale price
Ⓑ SMF (*= persona*) ticket tout, scalper (*EEUU**)

reventadero SM [1] (*= trabajo*) tough job, heavy work, grind
[2] (*= terreno áspero*) rough ground; (*= terreno escarpado*) steep terrain
[3] (*Andes, Cono Sur, Méx*) (*= hervidero*) bubbling spring
[4] (*Cono Sur*) = **rompiente**

reventado* ADJ (*= cansado*) exhausted

reventador(a) SM/F [1] (*en mitín*) troublemaker, heckler
[2] (*= ladrón*) safe-breaker

reventar ▸conjug 1j◂ Ⓐ VT [1] (*por presión*) [*+ globo, neumático, tubería, ampolla*] to burst; [*+ espinilla*] to squeeze; **tengo una cubierta reventada** I've got a puncture, I have a flat tyre; **el ruido de las discotecas me revienta los oídos** I find the racket inside clubs deafening, the noise in clubs is enough to burst your eardrums; **"reventamos los precios"** "prices slashed"; **tanto alcohol le va a ~ el hígado** all this drink is going to do his liver in*
[2] (*por una explosión*) [*+ puente, vehículo*] to blow up; [*+ cristales*] to shatter, blow out; **la granada le reventó la mano** the grenade blew off his hand; **los ladrones ~on la caja fuerte** the robbers blew (open) the safe; **~on la puerta de un disparo** they shot open the door
[3] (*= estropear*) to ruin; **~ás la moto conduciendo así** you'll ruin the motorbike riding it like that
[4] (*= agotar*) [*+ caballo*] to ride into the ground
[5] (*) (*= golpear*) **lo ~on a palos** they beat the living daylights out of him*; **te voy a ~ a patadas** I'm going to kick your face in*; **si me desobedece lo reviento** if he doesn't obey me, I'll kill him*
[6] (*) (*= hacer fracasar*) [*+ plan, espectáculo*] to wreck; [*+ asamblea, mitin, ceremonia*] to disrupt; [*+ huelga*] to smash, quash; [*+ manifestación*] to break up; **le encanta ~ nuestros planes** he loves wrecking our plans; **un grupo de sindicalistas intentó ~ la intervención del conferenciante** a group of trade union members heckled the delegate's speech *o* tried to shout down the delegate during his speech
[7] (*) (*= fastidiar*) **le revienta tener que levantarse temprano** he can't stand having to get up early; **me revienta que nos traten así** being treated like that really bugs me*
Ⓑ VI [1] (*= explotar*) [*globo, tubería, depósito*] to burst; [*neumático*] to burst, blow out; [*granada, proyectil*] to blow up; [*cristal*] to break, shatter; **la presa reventó e inundó el valle** the dam burst, flooding the valley; **parecía que las venas del cuello le iban a ~** it looked as if the veins in his neck were about to burst; **le va a ~ el pantalón** his trousers are going to split; **hacer ~** [*+ neumático*] to burst; [*+ costuras*] to split; ✦**MODISMO a todo ~** (*Chile*) at the most; **es bastante joven, a todo ~ tiene 30 años** he's pretty young, 30 years old at the most; **no llegué tan tarde anoche, a todo ~ debían ser las once** I didn't get back so late last night, it must have been eleven at the latest
[2] [*persona*] [2·1] (*por estar lleno*) **no puedo comer más, voy a ~** I can't eat any more, I'm full to bursting; **necesito entrar al baño, voy a ~** I need to go to the toilet, I'm bursting*
[2·2] (*por enfado*) to explode; **cuando dijeron que no querían trabajar, reventé** when they told me they didn't want to work, I just exploded; **como esto dure un día más, creo que reviento** if this carries on one more day, I think I'll explode; **sus relaciones son tan tensas que van a ~ en cualquier momento** relations between them are so tense that things are going to blow up at any moment
[3] [*lugar*] **el teatro estaba a ~** the theatre was packed full, the theatre was full to bursting; **más de 20.000 personas llenaron la plaza de toros a ~** more than 20,000 people packed the bullring, the bullring was full to bursting with more than 20,000 people
[4] **~ de: reventaba de ganas de decirlo todo** I was dying *o* bursting to tell him all about it; **~ de cansancio** to be worn out, be shattered; **~ de indignación** to be bursting with indignation; **~ de ira** to be livid, be absolutely furious; **~ de risa** to kill o.s. laughing, split one's sides (laughing)
[5] **~ por** to be dying to, be bursting to; **reventaba por ver lo que pasaba** he was dying *o* bursting to see what was going on; **revienta por saber lo que dicen** she's dying *o* bursting to know what they're saying
[6] (*) (*= morir*) to drop dead*; **por mí como si revientas** you can drop dead for all I care*
[7] [*ola*] to break
Ⓒ **reventarse** VPR [1] (*= romperse*) [1·1] (*por presión*) [*tubería*] to burst; [*pantalón, vestido*] to split
[1·2] (*por explosión*) [*depósito, tanque*] to explode, blow up
[2] (*) (*= agotarse*) **se revienta a trabajar** he's slogging *o* sweating his guts out*, he's working his butt off (*EEUU**); **el toro se reventó corriendo** the bull ran itself into the ground
[3] (*Arg, Col, Uru**) to crash; **se reventó contra un poste** it crashed into a post
[4] (*Méx**) to have a great time; **nos reventamos en la boda de Rosa** we had a great time at Rosa's wedding

reventazón SF [1] (*Cono Sur*) (*= colina*) low ridge
[2] (*Méx*) [*de estómago*] flatulence
[3] (*Méx*) (*= fuente*) bubbling spring

reventón SM [1] (*= explosión*) [*de neumático*] blowout; [*de tubería*] burst
[2] (*= esfuerzo grande*) **le dio un ~ al caballo** he rode his horse into the ground; **darse** *o* **pegarse un ~*** to slog *o* sweat one's guts out*, work one's butt off (*EEUU**); **se da cada ~ de trabajar** he kills himself working
[3] (*Esp**) **dar un ~** (*= morirse*) to drop dead*
[4] (*= cuesta*) steep slope; (*= subida*) tough climb

➤ LENGUA Y USO: **revelador A** 53.6

[5] (= *apuro*) jam*, fix
[6] (*Méx**) (= *juerga*) rave-up*
[7] (*Cono Sur Min*) outcrop of ore
[8] (*CAm*) (= *empujón*) shove, push

rever ▸conjug 2u◂ (*pp* **revisto**) VT [1] (*Jur*) [+ *sentencia*] to review; [+ *pleito*] to retry
[2] (= *ver de nuevo*) to see again, look at again

reverberación SF reverberation

reverberador SM reverberator

reverberar ▸conjug 1a◂ VI [1] [*luz*] to play, be reflected; [*superficie*] to shimmer, shine; [*nieve*] to glare; **la luz reverberaba en el agua** the light played *o* danced on the water; **la luz del farol reverberaba en la calle** the lamplight was reflected on the street
[2] [*sonido*] to reverberate

reverbero SM [1] [*de luz*] play, reflection; [*de superficie*] shimmer, shine; [*de nieve*] glare; **el ~ de la nieve** the glare of the snow, the dazzle of the snow
[2] [*de sonido*] reverberation
[3] (= *reflector*) reflector
[4] (*LAm*) (= *cocinilla*) small spirit stove
[5] (*Caribe*) (= *licor*) cheap liquor

reverdecer ▸conjug 2d◂ Ⓐ VI [1] (*Bot*) to grow green again
[2] (= *renacer*) to come to life again, revive
Ⓑ VT (= *reavivar*) to revive, reawaken

reverencia SF [1] (= *inclinación*) bow; **hacer una ~** to bow
[2] (= *respeto*) reverence
[3] (*Rel*) **Reverencia** (*tb* **Su Reverencia, Vuestra Reverencia**) Your Reverence

reverencial ADJ reverential

reverenciar ▸conjug 1b◂ VT to revere, venerate

reverencioso ADJ reverent, respectful

reverendísimo ADJ Most Reverend

reverendo ADJ [1] (*Rel*) reverend; **el ~ padre Pabón** Reverend Father Pabón
[2] (= *estimado*) respected, revered
[3] (*) (= *solemne*) solemn
[4] (*LAm**) (= *inmenso*) big, awful; **un ~ imbécil** a complete idiot

reverente ADJ reverent

reverentemente ADV reverently

reversa SF (*LAm*) reverse

reversible ADJ reversible

reversión SF reversion

reversionario ADJ reversionary

reverso SM (= *revés*) back, other side; [*de moneda*] reverse; ✦***MODISMO*** **el ~ de la medalla** *o* **moneda** the other side of the coin

revertir ▸conjug 3i◂ VI [1] [*posesión*] to revert (**a** to)
[2] (= *volver*) **~ a su estado primitivo** to revert to its original state
[3] (= *venir a parar*) **~ en** to end up as; **~ en beneficio de** to benefit; **~ en perjuicio de** to be to the detriment of

revés SM [1] (= *lado contrario*) **el ~** [*de papel, sello, mano, tela*] the back; [*de prenda*] the inside; **siempre empieza las revistas por el ~** he always reads the magazines from the back; ✦***MODISMO*** **el ~ de la moneda** *o* **medalla** the other side of the coin
[2] **al** *o* **del ~** (*con sustantivo*) (= *lo de arriba abajo*) upside down; (= *lo de dentro fuera*) inside out; (= *lo de delante atrás*) back to front; **tienes el libro al ~** you are holding the book the wrong way round *o* upside down; **llevas los calcetines al ~** you've got your socks on inside out; **te has puesto la gorra del ~** you've put your cap on back to front; **has puesto los cables al ~** you've put the wires on the wrong way round; **llevas los zapatos al ~** you've got your shoes on the wrong feet; **volver al** *o* **del ~** [+ *prenda, objeto*] to turn the other way; [+ *argumento, situación*] to turn on its head
[3] **al ~** (*con verbo*) the other way round; (*como nexo*) on the contrary; **ponte al ~** turn the other way round; **Luis le dejó dinero a Gerardo, ¿o fue al ~?** Luis lent Gerardo some money, or was it the other way round?; **todo nos salió al ~** everything went wrong for us, nothing went right for us; **cuando tienes prisa lo haces todo al ~** when you're in a hurry you do everything wrong; **a mí no me produce ningún complejo, al ~, es un orgullo** I'm not embarrassed by it, on the contrary, I feel very proud; **al ~ de**: **fue al ~ de lo que dices** it was the opposite of what you say; **al ~ de lo que se cree, ...** contrary to popular belief, ...; **entender algo al ~** to get hold of the wrong end of the stick; **y al ~** and vice versa; **cuando yo quiero salir él quiere trabajar, y al ~** when I want to go out he wants to work, and vice versa
[4] (= *bofetada*) slap, backhand slap; **como me vuelvas a insultar te doy un ~** you insult me again and you'll get a slap *o* you'll feel the back of my hand
[5] (*Dep*) backhand; **un ~ a dos manos** a two-handed backhand; **un ~ cruzado** a cross-court backhand
[6] (= *contratiempo*) setback; **los reveses de la fortuna** changes in fortune; **sufrir un ~** to suffer a setback

revesado ADJ [1] [*asunto*] complicated, involved
[2] (= *rebelde*) [*niño*] unruly, uncontrollable

revesero ADJ (*Andes*) treacherous

revestimiento SM (*Téc*) coating, covering; (= *forro*) lining; [*de carretera*] surface; (*Mil*) revetment ► **revestimiento antiadherente** non-stick coating

revestir ▸conjug 3k◂ Ⓐ VT [1] (= *recubrir*) [+ *pared, suelo*] to cover (**de, con** with); [+ *tubo*] to sheathe (**de, con** in); [+ *fachada*] to face (**de, con** with, in); **revestimos el suelo con láminas de corcho** we covered the floor with cork tiles; **revistieron el techo con fibra de vidrio** they lined the ceiling with fibreglass; **un armazón de acero revestido de hormigón** a steel frame clad in concrete
[2] (*frm*) (= *presentar, tener*) to have, possess; **el acto revestía gran solemnidad** the ceremony was very solemn; **el asunto no reviste importancia** the matter is not important; **sus heridas no revisten importancia** his injuries are not serious
[3] (*frm*) (= *encubrir*) **revistió de ingenuidad sus comentarios maliciosos** he cloaked his barbed comments with apparent innocence
[4] (*frm*) [+ *lenguaje, texto*] to lard (**de** with); **revistió su discurso de frases grandilocuentes** he larded his speech with high-flown phrases
[5] [*sacerdote*] to put on, don
Ⓑ **revestirse** VPR [1] (*frm*) (= *recubrirse*) **~se de paciencia** to summon up all one's patience; **se revistió de valor y fue a hablarle** he summoned all his courage and went to speak to her; **está revestido de autoridad** he is invested with authority; **los árboles se revisten de hojas** the trees are coming into leaf
[2] [*sacerdote*] to put on one's vestments
[3] (*frm*) (= *apasionarse*) to get carried away

reviejo ADJ (= *muy viejo*) very old; [*niño*] wise beyond his years

revientapisos SMF INV burglar, housebreaker

revirado* ADJ (*Cono Sur*) [1] (= *de mal genio*) bad-tempered, irritable; (= *revoltoso*) unruly, wild
[2] (= *loco*) crazy

revirar ▸conjug 1a◂ Ⓐ VT to turn (round), twist (round)
Ⓑ **revirarse** VPR [1] (*Caribe, Cono Sur*) (= *rebelarse*) to rebel
[2] (*Cono Sur*) (= *enloquecer*) to go crazy
[3] **~se contra algn** (*Caribe, Cono Sur*) to turn on sb

revirón Ⓐ ADJ (*CAm, Caribe*) disobedient, rebellious, unruly
Ⓑ SM (*CAm, Caribe, Méx*) rebellion, revolt

revisación SF (*Cono Sur*), **revisada** SF (*LAm*) medical examination

revisar ▸conjug 1a◂ VT [1] [+ *texto*] to revise, look over, go through; [+ *edición*] to revise
[2] [+ *cuenta*] to check; (*Fin*) to audit
[3] (*Jur*) to review
[4] [+ *teoría*] to reexamine, review
[5] (*Mil*) to review
[6] (*Mec*) to check, overhaul; (*Aut*) to service

revisión SF [1] [*de cuenta*] check; [*de teoría, método*] review ► **revisión aduanera** customs inspection ► **revisión de cuentas** audit ► **revisión salarial** wage review
[2] (*Mec*) check, overhaul; (*Aut*) service

revisionismo SM revisionism

revisionista ADJ, SMF revisionist

revisor(a) Ⓐ SM/F [1] (*Ferro*) ticket collector, inspector
[2] (*Cine, TV*) ► **revisor(a) de guión** script editor
[3] (*Fin*) ► **revisor(a) de cuentas** auditor
Ⓑ SM ► **revisor ortográfico** spellchecker, spelling checker

revista SF [1] [*de información general*] magazine; (*especializada*) journal, review ► **revista científica** scientific journal ► **revista comercial** trade journal ► **revista de destape**† erotic magazine ► **revista de información general** current affairs magazine ► **revista del corazón** *magazine featuring celebrity gossip and real-life romance stories* ► **revista de moda** fashion magazine ► **revista gráfica**† illustrated magazine ► **revista juvenil** teenage magazine ► **revista literaria** literary review ► **revista semanal** weekly (magazine)
[2] (= *sección*) section ► **revista de libros** books section ► **revista de toros** bullfighting news
[3] (= *inspección*) inspection; (*Mil, Náut*) review, inspection; **pasar ~ a la tropa** to review *o* inspect the troops; **ahora pasaremos ~ a la actualidad deportiva** now we'll review today's sporting events; **¿ya has pasado ~ a todos los invitados?*** have you given all the guests the once-over, then?*
[4] (*Teat*) variety show, revue
[5] (*Jur*) retrial
[6] (*Andes*) [*del pelo*] trim

revistar ▸conjug 1a◂ VT (*Mil*) to review, inspect; (*Náut*) to review

revistero/a Ⓐ SM (= *mueble*) magazine rack
Ⓑ SM/F (*en periódico*) (= *crítico*) reviewer, critic; (= *escritor*) contributor ► **revistero/a deportivo/a** sports journalist ► **revistero/a literario/a** literary critic, book reviewer

revisto PP *de* **rever**

revitalización SF revitalization

revitalizador Ⓐ ADJ revitalizing
Ⓑ SM stimulant

revitalizante ADJ revitalizing, invigorating

revitalizar ▸conjug 1f◂ VT to revitalize

revival Ⓐ SM (*Mús*) revival; [*de persona*] comeback
Ⓑ ADJ INV **canción ~** hit song from the past

revivificar ▸conjug 1g◂ VT to revitalize

revivir ▸conjug 3a◂ Ⓐ VT [1] (= *recordar*) to revive memories of
[2] (= *vivir de nuevo*) to relive, live again
Ⓑ VI [1] (= *volver a vivir*) to revive, be revived
[2] (= *renacer*) to come to life again

revocación SF (*Jur*) revocation; (= *decisión contraria*) reversal

revocar ▸conjug 1g◂ VT [1] [+ *decisión*] to revoke, reverse; [+ *orden*] to cancel; [+ *persona*] to remove from his post, axe, ax (*EEUU*)
[2] [+ *humo*] to blow back
[3] (*Arquit*) (= *enlucir*) to plaster; (= *encalar*) to whitewash
[4] (= *disuadir*) to dissuade (**de** from)

revocatoria SF (*LAm*) revocation, repeal

revoco SM [1] (*Jur*) revocation; (= *decisión contraria*) reversal
[2] = **revoque**

revolar ▸conjug 1l◂ VI (= *alzar el vuelo*) to take to flight again; (= *revolotear*) to flutter about, fly around

revolcadero SM mudhole, mud bath

revolcar ▸conjug 1g, 1l◂ Ⓐ VT [1] [+ *persona*] to knock down, knock over; (*Taur*) to knock down and trample on
[2] (*) [+ *adversario*] to wipe the floor with*
[3] (= *humillar*) to bring down, deflate
Ⓑ **revolcarse** VPR [1] [*persona*] to roll about; [*animal*] to wallow; (*) [*amantes*] to have a romp in the hay*; **~se de dolor** to writhe in pain; ✦*MODISMOS* **~se en el vicio** to wallow in vice; **~se en la tumba** to turn in one's grave
[2] (= *obstinarse*) to dig one's heels in

revolcón* SM fall, tumble; **dar un ~ a algn** to wipe the floor with sb*; **darse un ~ con algn** to have a roll in the hay with sb*

revolear ▸conjug 1a◂ Ⓐ VT (*Cono Sur*) [+ *lazo*] to twirl, spin
Ⓑ VI to fly round

revolera SF whirl, twirl

revolica SF (*CAm*) confusion

revolotear ▸conjug 1a◂ VI [*pájaro*] to flutter, fly about; [*mariposa*] to flit (about)

revoloteo SM [*de pájaro*] fluttering; [*de mariposa*] flitting

revolqué *ver* **revolcar**

revoltijo SM, **revoltillo** SM (= *confusión*) jumble, confusion; (= *desorden*) mess ► **revoltijo de huevos** scrambled eggs *pl*

revoltoso/a Ⓐ ADJ (= *rebelde*) rebellious, unruly; [*niño*] naughty, unruly
Ⓑ SM/F (= *alborotador*) troublemaker, agitator

revoltura SF [1] (*LAm*) (= *confusión*) confusion, jumble
[2] (*Méx*) (= *mezcla*) mixture; (*Culin*) *scrambled eggs with vegetables*; (*Arquit*) mortar, cement

revolución SF [1] (*Téc*) revolution; **revoluciones por minuto** revolutions per minute
[2] (*Pol*) revolution ► **Revolución Cultural** Cultural Revolution ► **Revolución de Octubre** October Revolution ► **revolución de palacio** palace revolution ► **Revolución Industrial** Industrial Revolution ► **revolución islámica** Islamic revolution ► **Revolución Verde** Green Revolution

revolucionar ▸conjug 1a◂ VT [1] [+ *industria, moda*] to revolutionize
[2] (*Pol*) to stir up, sow discontent among
[3] [+ *persona*] to get excited

revolucionario/a ADJ, SM/F revolutionary

revoluta SF (*CAm*) revolution

revolvedora SF (*Cono Sur, Méx*) concrete mixer

revolver ▸conjug 2h◂ (*pp* **revuelto**) Ⓐ VT [1] [+ *líquido*] to stir
[2] [+ *papeles*] to look through
[3] [+ *tierra*] to turn over, turn up, dig over
[4] (= *enredar*) **¡deja de ~!** ◊ **¡no revuelvas!** (*a niño*) stop messing about with things!, stop fidgeting!; ✦*MODISMO* **~la** to mess everything up
[5] (= *desordenar*) to mix up, mess up; **han revuelto toda la casa** they've turned the whole house upside down
[6] [+ *asunto*] to go into, investigate; **~ algo en la cabeza** to turn sth over in one's mind
[7] (*Pol*) to stir up, cause unrest among; [+ *persona*] to provoke, rouse to anger
[8] **~ los ojos** to roll one's eyes; **~ el estómago** to turn one's stomach
[9] (= *envolver*) to wrap up
Ⓑ VI **~ en** to go through, rummage in, rummage about in; **~ en los bolsillos** to feel in one's pockets, fumble in one's pockets
Ⓒ **revolverse** VPR [1] (= *volver*) to turn round; (*en cama*) to toss and turn; **~se de dolor** to writhe in pain; **se revolvía en su silla** he was fidgeting about on his chair; **se me revuelve el estómago sólo de pensarlo** it turns my stomach just thinking about it; **~se al enemigo** to turn to face the enemy
[2] (= *enfrentarse*) **~se contra algn** to turn on *o* against sb
[3] [*sedimento*] to be stirred up; [*líquido*] to become cloudy
[4] (*Meteo*) to break, turn stormy
[5] (*Astron*) to revolve
[6] (*Andes**) (= *prosperar*) to get a lucky break, have a change of fortunes; (*pey*) to look after Number One

revólver SM revolver

revoque SM (*Arquit*) [1] (= *enlucimiento*) plastering; (= *encaladura*) whitewashing
[2] (= *enlucido*) plaster; (= *cal*) whitewash

revuelco SM fall, tumble

revuelo SM [1] [*de aves*] flutter, fluttering
[2] (= *conmoción*) stir, commotion; (= *jaleo*) row, rumpus; **de ~** incidentally, in passing; **armar** *o* **levantar un gran ~** to cause a great stir

revuelta SF [1] (*Pol*) disturbance, riot; **las ~s populares del siglo pasado** the civil disturbances of the last century; **la ~ militar acabó con la democracia** the military uprising put an end to democracy
[2] (= *agitación*) commotion, disturbance
[3] (= *curva*) bend, turn
[4] (= *vuelta*) turn; **dar vueltas y ~s a algo** to turn sth over and over in one's mind

revuelto Ⓐ PP *de* **revolver**
Ⓑ ADJ [1] [*objetos*] mixed up, in disorder; [*huevos*] scrambled; [*agua*] cloudy, turbid; [*mar*] rough; [*tiempo*] unsettled; **todo estaba ~** everything was in disorder *o* upside down; **los tiempos están ~s** these are troubled times; **tengo el pelo ~** my hair's all untidy *o* in a mess; **tener el estómago ~** to have an upset stomach, have a stomach upset
[2] (= *inquieto*) [*adulto*] restless, discontented; [*niño*] mischievous, naughty; [*población*] rebellious, mutinous; **la gente está revuelta por abusos como ese** people are up in arms about scandals like this
[3] [*asunto*] complicated, involved
Ⓒ SM [1] (*Culin*) *scrambled eggs with vegetables* ► **revuelto de gambas** scrambled eggs with prawns
[2] (*Andes*) (= *mosto*) must, grape juice

revulsar* ▸conjug 1a◂ VT (*Méx*) to vomit, throw up

revulsionar ▸conjug 1a◂ VT (*frm*) **~ a algn** to turn sb's stomach

revulsivo SM [1] (*Med*) enema, revulsive
[2] (= *acicate*) **el mal resultado electoral fue un ~ para la izquierda** the bad election results were a salutary lesson for the left

rey Ⓐ SM [1] (= *monarca*) king; **los Reyes inauguraron la exposición** the King and Queen opened the exhibition; **los Reyes Católicos** the Catholic Monarchs (*Ferdinand and Isabella of Aragon and Castile*); **el ~ de la selva** the king of the jungle; ✦*MODISMOS* **se cree el ~ del mambo** he really fancies himself*, he thinks he's the bee's knees*; **hablando del ~ de Roma (por la puerta asoma)** talk of the devil; **lo mismo me da ~ que roque** it's all the same to me, it's all one to me; **ni ~ ni roque** no-one at all, not a single living soul; ✦*REFRÁN* **a ~ muerto ~ puesto** off with the old, on with the new ► **rey de armas** (*Hist*) king of arms
[2] **Reyes** (= *fecha*) Epiphany; **los Reyes Magos** the Magi, the Three Kings, the Three Wise Men; **¿qué te han traído los Reyes?** ≈ what did Father Christmas bring you?
[3] (*en ajedrez, naipes*) king
[4] (*uso apelativo*) pet*; **anda, ~, cómetelo todo** come on, pet, eat it all up*
Ⓑ ADJ INV **el fútbol es el deporte ~** football is the king of sports

DÍA DE REYES

El Día de Reyes *or* **Día de los Reyes Magos**, *often shortened to* **Reyes**, *which is on 6 January (Epiphany), is the day when children and adults in Spain traditionally receive presents for the Christmas season. When children go to bed on the night of 5 January, they leave their shoes outside their bedroom doors or by their windows for the* **Reyes Magos** *to leave presents beside. They may already have written letters to* **SS.MM. los Reyes Magos de Oriente** *with a list of what they would like. For* **Reyes** *it is traditional to eat* **Roscón de Reyes**, *a ring-shaped cake studded with frosted fruits and containing a little trinket or coin.*

reyerta SF quarrel

reyezuelo SM 1 (= *monarca*) petty king, kinglet
2 (*Orn*) ~ **(sencillo)** goldcrest

rezaga SF (*LAm*) = **zaga**

rezagado/a Ⓐ ADJ **quedar ~** (= *quedar atrás*) to be left behind; (= *estar retrasado*) to be late, be behind; (*en pagos, progresos*) to fall behind; **carta rezagada** (*Andes, Méx*) (*sin reclamar*) unclaimed letter
Ⓑ SM/F (= *que llega tarde*) latecomer; (*Mil*) straggler

rezagamiento SM (= *atraso*) falling behind, lagging behind; (*en pagos, progresos*) backwardness

rezagar ▸conjug 1h◂ Ⓐ VT (= *dejar atrás*) to leave behind; (= *retrasar*) to delay, postpone
Ⓑ **rezagarse** VPR (= *atrasarse*) to fall behind; **nos rezagamos en la producción** we are falling behind in production

rezago SM 1 (= *material sobrante*) unused material, material which is left over
2 (*Cono Sur*) (= *mercancías*) unsold goods *pl*, remaindered goods *pl*; (= *ganado*) cattle rejected at the abattoir
3 (= *vacas dispersas*) group of straggling cattle
4 (*Andes, Méx Correos*) (= *cartas*) unclaimed letters *pl*

rezar ▸conjug 1f◂ Ⓐ VT [+ *oración*] to say
Ⓑ VI 1 (*Rel*) to pray (**a** to)
2 [*texto*] to read, go; **el anuncio reza así** the notice reads *o* goes as follows
3 **~ con** (= *tener que ver con*) to concern, have to do with; **eso no reza conmigo** that has nothing to do with me
4 (*) (= *quejarse*) to grumble

rezo SM 1 (= *oración*) prayer, prayers *pl*; **estar en el ~** to be at prayer
2 (= *acto*) praying

rezondrada* SF (*Andes*) scolding

rezondrar ▸conjug 1a◂ VT, VI (*Andes*) = **rezongar**

rezongador ADJ = **rezongón**

rezongar ▸conjug 1h◂ Ⓐ VT (*LAm*) (= *regañar*) to scold
Ⓑ VI (= *gruñir*) to grumble; (= *murmurar*) to mutter; (= *refunfuñar*) to growl

rezongo SM 1 (= *quejido*) grumble, moan
2 (*CAm*) (= *reprimenda*) reprimand; (= *regaño*) scolding

rezongón ADJ grumbling, grouchy*, cantankerous

rezumar ▸conjug 1a◂ Ⓐ VT to ooze, exude
Ⓑ VI 1 [*contenido*] to ooze (out), seep (out), leak (out); [*recipiente*] to ooze, leak
2 (= *transpirar*) to ooze; **le rezuma el orgullo** he oozes pride; **le rezuma el entusiasmo** he is bursting with enthusiasm
Ⓒ **rezumarse** VPR 1 = **B1**
2 (= *traslucirse un hecho*) to leak out, become known

RFA SF ABR (*Hist*) (= **República Federal Alemana**) FRG

RFE SF ABR = **Revista de Filología Española**

Rh ABR (= **Rhesus**) Rh; **soy Rh positivo** I'm rhesus positive

ría[1] SF estuary ► **Rías Altas** northern coast of Galicia ► **Rías Bajas** southern coast of Galicia

ría[2] *ver* **reír**

riachuelo SM brook, stream

Riad SM Riyadh

riada SF flood; ✦*MODISMO* **hasta aquí llegó la ~** that's how bad things were

ribazo SM steep slope, steep bank

ribeiro SM *young white wine from Galicia*

ribera SF 1 [*de río, lago*] bank; [*del mar*] beach, shore; (= *área*) riverside
2 (*Agr*) irrigated plain
3 (*Cono Sur, Méx*) [*de campo*] riverside community; (= *chabolas*) shanty town, slum quarter

riberano/a ADJ, SM/F (*LAm*) = **ribereño**

ribereño/a Ⓐ ADJ (= *de río*) riverside *antes de s*; (= *costero*) coastal
Ⓑ SM/F *person who lives near a river*, riverside dweller

ribete SM 1 (*Cos*) border
2 (= *adorno*) addition, adornment
3 **ribetes** (= *toques*): **tiene sus ~s de pintor** he's got a bit of the painter about him

ribetear ▸conjug 1a◂ VT to edge, border, trim (**de** with)

ribo SM (*Andes*) [*de río*] bank; [*de mar*] shore

riboflavina SF riboflavin

ricacho/a* SM/F, **ricachón/ona*** SM/F fabulously rich man/woman; (*pey*) well-heeled bourgeois*, dirty capitalist*

ricamente ADV 1 (= *lujosamente*) richly
2 (= *estupendamente*) **muy ~** very well; **viven muy ~ sin él** they manage very *o* perfectly well without him; **tan ~** very well; **he dormido tan ~** I've had such a good sleep; **comeremos tan ~** we'll have a really good meal

Ricardo SM Richard

ricino SM castor-oil plant; **aceite de ~** castor oil

ricito SM ringlet, kiss curl

rico/a Ⓐ ADJ 1 (= *adinerado*) rich, wealthy; ✦*REFRÁN* **llueva sobre el más ~** to he that has shall be given more
2 [*suelo*] rich; **~ de** *o* **en** rich in
3 (= *valioso*) valuable, precious; (= *lujoso*) luxurious, sumptuous, valuable; [*tela*] fine, rich, sumptuous
4 (= *sabroso*) delicious, tasty; **estos pasteles están muy ~s** these cakes are delicious
5 (*) (= *bonito*) cute, lovely; (*en oración directa*) **¡rico!** darling!; **¡oye, ~!** hey, watch it!*; **¡que no, ~!** (*Esp*) no way, mate!*; **¡qué ~ es el pequeño!** isn't he a lovely baby!; **está muy rica la tía** she's a bit of all right‡; **¡qué ~!** (*iró*) (isn't that just) great!
Ⓑ SM/F rich person; **nuevo ~** nouveau riche

rictus SM INV [*de desprecio*] sneer; [*de burla*] grin ► **rictus de amargura** bitter smile ► **rictus de dolor** wince of pain

ricura* SF 1 (= *sabrosura*) tastiness, delicious quality; **¡qué ~ de pastel!** isn't this cake delicious?
2 (= *hermosura*) **¡qué ~ de criatura!** what a gorgeous baby!
3 (= *chica*) **¡oye, ~!** hey, gorgeous!

ridi* Ⓐ ADJ ridiculous; **¡no seas ~!** don't be ridiculous!
Ⓑ SM **hacer el ~** to make a fool of o.s.

ridículamente ADV ridiculously, absurdly

ridiculez SF 1 (= *dicho absurdo*) **¡qué ~!** how ridiculous!; **no digas más ridiculeces** don't be so ridiculous
2 (= *insignificancia*) **¿y no os habláis por una ~ así?** (do) you mean you've stopped talking to each other because of a silly little thing like that?; **¿sólo vas a comer esta ~? ¡coge un poco más!** is that all you're eating? have a bit more!

ridiculización SF mockery

ridiculizador ADJ, **ridiculizante** ADJ mocking, derisive

ridiculizar ▸conjug 1f◂ VT to ridicule, deride; **~ a sus adversarios** to make one's opponents look silly

ridículo Ⓐ ADJ ridiculous; **¿a que suena ~?** doesn't it sound ridiculous?
Ⓑ SM **hiciste el ~** you made a fool of yourself; **puso a Ana en ~ delante de todos** he made a fool of Ana in front of everyone, he showed Ana up in front of everyone; **no te pongas en ~** don't make a fool of yourself, don't show yourself up; **no tiene sentido del ~** he isn't afraid of making a fool of himself; **exponerse al ~** (*frm*) to lay o.s. open to ridicule

riego SM 1 (= *aspersión*) watering; (= *irrigación*) irrigation; **la política de ~** irrigation policy ► **riego por aspersión** watering by spray, watering by sprinklers ► **riego por goteo** trickle irrigation
2 (*Anat*) ► **riego sanguíneo** blood flow, blood circulation

riel SM 1 (*Ferro*) rail; **~es** rails, track *sing*
2 (*Téc*) ingot

rielar ▸conjug 1a◂ VI (*poét*) to shimmer (*liter*)

rielazo* SM (*CAm*) blow, smack

rielero/a SM/F (*Méx*) railroad worker

ríen *etc ver* **reír**

rienda SF 1 (= *correa*) rein; ✦*MODISMOS* **aflojar las ~s** to let up; **empuñar las ~s** to take charge; **llevar las ~s** to be in charge, be in control; **soltar las ~s** to let go; **a ~ suelta** (= *con toda libertad*) without the least restraint; (= *con celeridad*) at top speed; **dar ~ suelta a** to give free rein to; **dar ~ suelta a los deseos** to really indulge o.s.; **dar ~ suelta a la imaginación** to let one's imagination run wild; **dar ~ suelta al llanto** to weep uncontrollably; **dar ~ suelta a algn** to give sb a free hand
2 (= *moderación*) restraint, moderating influence

riendo *ver* **reír**

riente ADJ (*liter*) 1 (= *risueño*) laughing, merry
2 [*paisaje*] bright, pleasant

riesgo SM risk (**de** of); **esta operación presenta mayores ~s** the risks are higher with this operation, this operation is riskier; **un ~ para la salud** a health hazard *o* risk; **factor de ~** risk factor; **grupos de ~** risk groups; **de alto ~** high-risk; **seguro a** *o* **contra todo ~** fully comprehensive insurance policy; **a ~ de**: **a ~ de que me expulsen** at the risk of being expelled; **correr ~s** to take risks; **no quiero correr ese ~** I'd rather not take that risk; **correr el ~ de hacer algo** to run the risk of doing sth; **corres el ~ de que te despidan** you run the risk of being dismissed; ✦*MODISMO* **por su cuenta y ~**: **los que se adentren en el bosque lo harán por su cuenta y ~** those who enter the forest do so at their own risk; **la compañía autorizó los pagos por su cuenta y ~, sin consultar** the company authorized the payments on their own behalf, without consulting ► **riesgo calculado** calculated risk ► **riesgo profesional** occupational hazard

riesgoso ADJ (*LAm*) risky, dangerous

Rif SM Rif, Riff

rifa SF [1] (= *lotería*) raffle
[2] (††) (= *riña*) quarrel, fight

rifar ▸conjug 1a◂ Ⓐ VT to raffle; **~ algo con fines benéficos** to raffle sth for charity
Ⓑ VI (††) to quarrel, fight
Ⓒ **rifarse** VPR [1] (*) (= *contender por*) **~se algo** to quarrel over sth, fight for sth; **~se el amor de algn** to vie for sb's love
[2] (*CAm*) (= *arriesgarse*) to take a risk

rifeño/a Ⓐ ADJ [*persona*] of/from Rif, of/from Riff; [*dialecto*] Riffian
Ⓑ SM/F Rif, Riff; **los ~s** the Rifs *o* Riffs, the Rif *o* Riff
Ⓒ SM (*Ling*) Riff

rifirrafe* SM, **rifirirafe*** SM shindy*, row

rifle SM (= *arma*) rifle; (*Dep*) sporting rifle; (*Caza*) hunting gun ► **rifle de repetición** repeating rifle

riflero/a Ⓐ ADJ (*Cono Sur, Méx*) [*tirador*] ace, crack
Ⓑ SM/F [1] (*Mil*) rifleman/riflewoman
[2] (*Cono Sur, Méx*) (= *tirador*) marksman/markswoman

rígidamente ADV [1] [*moverse*] rigidly, stiffly
[2] [*comportarse*] rigidly
[3] (= *estrictamente*) strictly, harshly
[4] (= *sin expresividad*) woodenly

rigidez SF [1] [*de material*] stiffness, rigidity; [*de pierna, tendón*] stiffness ► **rigidez cadavérica** rigor mortis
[2] (= *inflexibilidad*) [*de actitud*] inflexibility; [*de carácter*] strictness, inflexibility
[3] [*de expresión*] woodenness

rígido ADJ [1] (= *tieso*) rigid, stiff; **quedarse ~** (*gen*) to go rigid; (*de frío*) to get stiff, get stiff with cold
[2] [*actitud*] rigid, inflexible
[3] (*moralmente*) strict, harsh
[4] [*expresión*] wooden, expressionless

rigor SM [1] (= *severidad*) severity, harshness; (= *dureza*) toughness
[2] (*Meteo*) harshness, severity; **el ~ del verano** the hottest part of the summer; **los ~es del clima** the rigours *o* (*EEUU*) rigors of the climate
[3] (= *exactitud*) rigour, rigor (*EEUU*); **con todo ~ científico** with scientific precision; **una edición hecha con el mayor ~ crítico** an edition produced to rigorous critical standards
[4] **ser de ~** (= *esencial*) to be de rigueur, be absolutely essential; **después de los saludos de ~** after the usual *o* customary greetings; **me dio los consejos de ~** he gave me the advice you would have expected; **en ~** strictly speaking
[5] **un ~ de cosas** (*Andes*) (= *muchos*) a whole lot of things
[6] (*Cono Sur**) (= *paliza*) **dar un ~ a algn** to give sb a hiding*

rigorismo SM strictness, severity

rigorista Ⓐ ADJ strict
Ⓑ SMF strict disciplinarian

rigue SM (*CAm*) tortilla

rigurosamente ADV [1] (= *severamente*) severely, harshly
[2] (= *con exactitud*) rigorously
[3] (= *completamente*) **eso no es ~ exacto** that is not strictly accurate; **un estudio ~ científico** a thoroughly scientific study

rigurosidad SF rigour, rigor (*EEUU*), harshness, severity

riguroso ADJ [1] [*control, dieta, disciplina*] strict; [*actitud, castigo*] severe, harsh; [*medida*] tough; **es muy ~ con sus empleados** he's very strict with his employees; **iban de luto ~** they were wearing deep mourning; **exigen un cumplimiento ~ de los acuerdos** they're demanding strict compliance with the agreement; **en ~ orden alfabético** in strict alphabetical order
[2] [*invierno, clima*] harsh
[3] (= *concienzudo*) [*método, estudio*] rigorous; **es fruto de una investigación rigurosa** it's a product of rigorous research; **un trabajo poco ~** a sloppy piece of work
[4] (*liter*) cruel; **los hados ~s** cruel fate *sing*

rija SF quarrel, fight

rijio SM [1] (*CAm*) = **rijo**
[2] (*CAm, Méx*) (= *espíritu*) spirit, spirited temperament (*of a horse*)

rijioso ADJ (*CAm, Méx*) = **rijoso**

rijo SM lustfulness, sensuality

rijosidad SF [1] (= *susceptibilidad*) touchiness, susceptible nature
[2] (= *disposición para reñir*) quarrelsomeness
[3] (= *deseo sexual*) lustfulness, sensuality

rijoso ADJ [1] (= *susceptible*) sensitive, susceptible
[2] (= *peleador*) quarrelsome
[3] (= *sensual*) lustful, sensual
[4] [*caballo*] in rut

rila SF [1] (*Andes, Méx*) [*de carne*] gristle
[2] (*Andes*) (= *excremento*) bird droppings *pl*

rilarse‡ ▸conjug 1a◂ VI [1] (= *agotarse*) to knacker o.s.*, get shagged out‡
[2] (= *rajarse*) to back out, fall down on the job
[3] (= *asustarse*) to be dead scared
[4] (= *temblar*) to shiver
[5] (= *peerse*) to fart**

rima SF [1] (= *consonancia*) rhyme; **octava ~** ottava rima; **tercia ~** terza rima ► **rima imperfecta** assonance, half rhyme ► **rima interna** internal rhyme ► **rima perfecta** full rhyme
[2] (= *composición*) **rimas** verse *sing*, poetry *sing*

rimado ADJ rhymed, rhyming

rimador(a) SM/F rhymester

rimar ▸conjug 1a◂ VT, VI to rhyme (**con** with)

rimbombancia SF [1] (= *pomposidad*) pomposity, bombast
[2] (= *ostentosidad*) showiness, flashiness
[3] (= *resonancia*) resonance, echo

rimbombante ADJ [1] (= *pomposo*) pompous, bombastic
[2] (= *ostentoso*) showy, flashy
[3] (= *resonante*) resounding, echoing

rimbombar ▸conjug 1a◂ VI to resound, echo, boom

rímel SM, **rimmel** SM mascara

rimero SM stack, pile, heap

Rin SM Rhine

rin SM [1] (*Méx Aut*) rim, wheel rim
[2] (*Perú Telec*) metal phone token

rinche ADJ (*Andes, Cono Sur*) full to the brim, brimming over

rincón SM [1] (= *ángulo*) corner (*inside*)
[2] (= *escondrijo*) corner, nook; (= *retiro*) retreat; **en un ~ de mi mente** somewhere in the back of my mind
[3] (*esp LAm*) (= *terreno*) patch of ground

rinconada SF corner

rinconera SF [1] (= *mesita*) corner table, corner unit; (= *armario*) corner cupboard, dresser
[2] (*Arquit*) wall between corner and window

ring [rrin] SM (*esp LAm*) ring, boxing ring

ringla SF, **ringle** SM, **ringlera** SF row, line

ringlete (*Andes, Cono Sur*) Ⓐ ADJ fidgety*, restless
Ⓑ SMF fidget*, restless person

ringletear ▸conjug 1a◂ VI (*Cono Sur*) to fidget

ringorrango SM [1] (*en escritura*) flourish
[2] **ringorrangos** (= *adornos*) frills, buttons and bows, useless adornments

ringuelete Ⓐ SMF (*Cono Sur, Andes*) (= *inquieto*) rolling stone (*fig*)
Ⓑ SM (*Andes*) (= *rehilete*) dart; (= *molinillo*) toy windmill

ringueletear ▸conjug 1a◂ VI (*Andes, Cono Sur*) = **callejear**

rinitis SF INV ► **rinitis alérgica** hay fever

rinoceronte SM rhinoceros ► **rinoceronte blanco** white rhinoceros

rinoplastia SF rhinoplasty

rintoso‡ SM (*Caribe*) skiver‡, shirker

riña SF (= *discusión*) quarrel, argument; (= *lucha*) fight, brawl ► **riña de gallos** cockfight ► **riña de perros** dogfight, dogfighting

riñendo *etc ver* **reñir**

riñón SM [1] (*Anat*) (= *órgano*) kidney; **me duelen los riñones** my lower back hurts; ✦*MODISMOS* **me costó un ~*** it cost me a fortune, it cost the earth; **tener el ~ bien cubierto*** to be well off; **tener riñones*** to have guts, be tough ► **riñón artificial** artificial kidney
[2] (= *centro*) heart, core; **en el ~ de Castilla** in the very heart of Castile

riñonada* SF ✦*MODISMO* **me costó una ~** it cost the earth, it cost me a fortune

riñonera SF money belt, money pouch

riñonudo* ADJ tough

río[1] Ⓐ SM [1] (= *corriente de agua*) river; **es un ~ de oro** it's a gold mine; ✦*REFRANES* **a ~ revuelto, ganancia de pescadores** there is always somebody ready to take advantage of a chaotic situation; **cuando el ~ suena, agua lleva** ◊ **cuando el ~ suena, piedras trae** there's no smoke without fire ► **río abajo** downstream ► **río arriba** upstream
[2] (= *torrente*) stream, torrent; **un ~ de gente** a stream of people, a flood of people
Ⓑ ADJ INV (†) **novela ~** saga, roman fleuve; **programa ~** blockbuster of a programme; **serie ~** long-running series

río[2], rió *etc ver* **reír**

Río de Janeiro SM Rio de Janeiro

Río de la Plata SM River Plate

Rioja SF **La ~** La Rioja

rioja SM Rioja (wine)

riojano/a Ⓐ ADJ Riojan, of/from La Rioja
Ⓑ SM/F Riojan, native/inhabitant of La Rioja; **los ~s** the Riojans, the people of La Rioja
Ⓒ SM [1] (= *vino*) Rioja
[2] (*Ling*) Riojan dialect

riolada* SF flood, stream

rioplatense Ⓐ ADJ of/from the River Plate region
Ⓑ SMF native/inhabitant of the River Plate region; **los ~s** the people of the River Plate region

riostra SF brace, strut

ripiado ADJ 1 (*Andes*) (= *harapiento*) ragged
2 (*Caribe*) (= *pobre*) wretched, down-at-heel

ripiar ▸conjug 1b◂ VT 1 (*Arquit*) to fill with rubble
2 (*Andes, Caribe*) (= *cortar*) to shred, cut into shreds; (= *desmenuzar*) to crumble
3 (*Andes, Caribe*) (= *despilfarrar*) to squander
4 (*Andes*) [+ *persona*] to leave badly off; [+ *dos personas*] to mix up
5 (*Méx*) (= *espigar*) to glean
6 (*Caribe*) (= *pegar*) to hit

ripiería SF (*Andes*) mob, populace

ripio SM 1 (= *palabras inútiles*) padding, empty words *pl*; (*en poesía*) trite verse; ✦**MODISMO no perder ~** not to miss a trick
2 (= *residuo*) refuse, waste
3 (= *escombro*) rubble, debris
4 (*Chile*) (= *grava*) gravel

ripioso ADJ (*Andes, Caribe*) ragged

riqueza SF 1 (= *bienes*) wealth; **la distribución de la ~** the distribution of wealth; **no le importaba nada toda su ~** all her riches meant nothing to her; **vivir en la ~** to live in luxury ▸ **riqueza imponible** taxable assets *pl*
2 (= *abundancia*) richness; **su enorme ~ espiritual** his enormous spiritual wealth *o* richness of spirit; **tiene una gran ~ de vocabulario** she has a very extensive *o* rich vocabulary
3 (= *fertilidad*) richness; **la ~ del suelo** the richness of the soil

riquiña SF (*Caribe*) sewing basket

riquiñeque SM (*Andes*) quarrel

risa SF laugh; **el libro es una verdadera ~** the book is a real laugh; **hubo ~s** there was laughter; **causar ~ a algn** (*frm*) to make sb laugh; **dar ~: daba ~ la manera en que lo explicaba** it was so funny the way he told it; **me dio la ~** I got (a fit of) the giggles; **de ~: no es cosa de ~** it's no laughing matter; **le pagan un sueldo de ~** they pay him a pittance, what they pay him is a joke; **entrarle a algn la ~: me entró la ~** I got (a fit of) the giggles; **mover** *o* **provocar a algn a ~** (*frm*) to make sb laugh; **¡qué ~!: ¡qué ~! ¿cómo se llama este humorista?** he's hilarious *o* so funny! what's that comedian's name again?; **¡qué ~, casi se cae de culo!** what a laugh *o* it was so funny *o* it was such a laugh, she nearly fell on her backside!; **soltar la ~** to burst out laughing; **tomarse algo a ~** to treat sth as a joke; **no te tomes a ~ todo lo que te digo** don't treat everything I tell you as a joke; ✦**MODISMOS ahogarse de ~** to fall about laughing; **caerse de ~** to fall about laughing; **descoserse** *o* **desternillarse de (la) ~** to split one's sides laughing, laugh one's head off; **morirse de ~** to die laughing, kill o.s. laughing; **mondarse de ~** to split one's sides laughing, laugh one's head off; **muerto de ~: estaba muerto de ~ con la película** he was killing himself laughing at the film; **la bicicleta está muerta de ~ en el garaje** the bike is gathering dust in the garage; **partirse** *o* **troncharse de ~** to split one's sides laughing, laugh one's head off; ✦**REFRÁN la ~ va por barrios** every dog has his day ▸ **risa contagiosa** infectious laugh ▸ **risa de conejo** false laugh, affected laugh ▸ **risa floja, risa tonta: me dio** *o* **entró la ~ floja** *o* **tonta** I got (a fit of) the giggles ▸ **risas enlatadas** canned laughter *sing*

risco SM 1 (= *peñasco*) cliff, crag
2 **riscos** (= *terreno áspero*) rough parts

riscoso ADJ steep

risible ADJ ludicrous, laughable

risión SF derision, mockery; **ser un objeto de ~** to be a laughing stock

risotada SF guffaw, loud laugh

rispiar ▸conjug 1b◂ VI (*CAm*) to rush off

rispidez SF 1 (*esp LAm*) (= *mala educación*) coarseness, uncouthness
2 (= *aspereza*) roughness, sharpness

ríspido ADJ 1 (*esp LAm*) (= *maleducado*) rough, coarse
2 (= *áspero*) [*terreno*] rough, rocky

risquería SF (*Cono Sur*) craggy place

ristra SF string; **una ~ de ajos** a string of garlic

ristre SM **en ~** at the ready, all set; *ver tb* **lanza A1**

risueñamente ADV smilingly

risueño ADJ 1 [*cara*] smiling; **muy ~** with a big smile
2 [*temperamento*] cheerful
3 (*liter*) [*paisaje*] bright, pleasant
4 (*liter*) (= *favorable*) favourable, favorable (*EEUU*)

RITD SF ABR (*Telec*) = **Red Iberoamericana de Transmisión de Datos**

rítmico ADJ rhythmic, rhythmical

ritmo SM 1 (*Mús*) rhythm; **tiene mucho sentido del ~** she has a very good *o* strong sense of rhythm; **daban palmas al ~ de la música** they were clapping in time to the music; **marcar el ~: marcaba el ~ con el pie** he kept time with his foot; **París marca el ~ de la moda** Paris sets the fashion trends
2 (= *marcha*) pace; **el trabajo se mantiene a un ~ intenso** work is proceeding at a fast pace; **lo haré a mi ~** I'll do it at my own pace; **trabaja a ~ lento** she works slowly, she works at a slow pace; ✦**MODISMO a todo ~** flat out ▸ **ritmo cardíaco** heart rate ▸ **ritmo de crecimiento, ritmo de expansión** growth rate ▸ **ritmo de vida: el tranquilo ~ de vida de los pueblos** the quiet pace of life in the villages; **sin un sueldo no puedo llevar este ~ de vida** without a salary I can't keep up with this lifestyle ▸ **ritmo respiratorio** respiratory rate
3 (*frm*) (= *periodicidad*) rhythm; **de acuerdo con el ~ de las estaciones** in keeping with the rhythm of the seasons

rito SM rite ▸ **rito de iniciación** initiation rite ▸ **rito iniciático** initiation rite ▸ **ritos de paso** rites of passage

ritual Ⓐ ADJ ritual
Ⓑ SM ritual; **de ~** ritual, customary

ritualismo SM ritualism

ritualista Ⓐ ADJ ritualistic, ritual
Ⓑ SMF ritualist

ritualizado ADJ ritualized

rival Ⓐ ADJ rival, competing
Ⓑ SMF rival, competitor; **el eterno ~** the old enemy

rivalidad SF rivalry, competition

rivalizar ▸conjug 1f◂ VI to compete, contend; **~ con** to rival, compete with; **los dos rivalizan en habilidad** they rival each other in skill

rizado ADJ [*pelo*] curly; [*superficie*] ridged; [*terreno*] undulating; [*mar*] choppy

rizador SM curling iron, hair curler

rizadura SF ripple

rizapestañas SM INV eyelash curlers *pl*

rizar ▸conjug 1f◂ Ⓐ VT [+ *pelo*] to curl; [+ *superficie*] to ridge; [+ *mar*] to ripple, ruffle
Ⓑ **rizarse** VPR [*agua*] to ripple; **~se el pelo** to perm one's hair, have one's hair permed

rizo[1] Ⓐ ADJ curly
Ⓑ SM 1 [*de pelo*] curl; [*de superficie*] ridge; (*en agua*) ripple
2 (*Aer*) loop; **hacer el ~** (*Aer*) to loop the loop; ✦**MODISMO rizar el ~** (= *complicar*) to split hairs
3 (*Aer*) looping the loop

rizo[2] SM (*Náut*) reef

rizoma SM rhizome

R.M. ABR = **Reverenda Madre**

Rma. ABR (= **Reverendísima**) Rt Rev.

Rmo. ABR (= **Reverendísimo**) Rt Rev.

RNE SF ABR = **Radio Nacional de España**

R.O. ABR = **Real Orden**

roano Ⓐ ADJ roan
Ⓑ SM roan, roan horse

robacarros SMF INV (*LAm*) car thief

robacarteras SMF INV pickpocket

robagallinas* SMF INV petty thief

robalo SM, **róbalo** SM sea bass

robaperas* SMF INV petty thief

robar ▸conjug 1a◂ Ⓐ VT 1 [+ *objeto, dinero*] to steal; [+ *banco*] to rob; **¡nos han robado!** we've been robbed!; **~ algo a algn** to steal sth from sb; **les robaba dinero a sus compañeros de clase** he was stealing money from his classmates; **me han robado la cartera** my wallet has been stolen; **Ana le ha robado el novio** Ana has stolen her boyfriend; **el defensa le robó el balón** the defender stole the ball off him; **no quiero ~le su tiempo** I don't want to take up your time; **tuve que ~le horas al sueño para acabar el trabajo** I had to work into the night to finish the job; **~le el corazón a algn** (*liter*) to steal sb's heart
2 [+ *atención*] to steal, capture; [+ *paciencia*] to exhaust; [+ *tranquilidad*] to destroy, take away; [+ *vida*] to take, steal
3 (= *estafar*) to cheat, rob; **en ese negocio te han robado** you've been cheated *o* robbed in that deal
4 [+ *naipes*] to take, draw; **roba una carta de la baraja** take *o* draw a card from the deck
5 (*frm*) [*río, corriente*] to carry away
6 (††) (= *raptar*) to kidnap, abduct
Ⓑ VI 1 (= *sisar*) to steal; **lo cogieron robando** he was caught stealing; **no ~ás** (*Biblia*) thou shalt not steal; **entraron a ~ en mi casa** they broke into my house
2 (*Naipes*) to take a card, draw a card

Roberto SM Robert

robinsón SM castaway

roblar ▸conjug 1a◂ VT to rivet, clinch

roble SM oak, oak tree; **de ~** oak *antes de s*; **de ~ macizo** of solid oak, solid oak *antes de s*

robledal SM, **robledo** SM oakwood

roblón SM rivet

roblonar ▸conjug 1a◂ VT to rivet

robo SM [1] [*de dinero, objetos*] theft; (*en vivienda*) burglary; (*en tienda, banco*) robbery ► **robo a mano armada** armed robbery ► **robo con allanamiento** breaking and entering ► **robo con escalo** breaking and entering (*climbing over a wall*)
[2] (= *estafa*) **¡esto es un ~!** this is daylight robbery!; **¿cinco mil por una camiseta? ¡vaya ~!** five thousand for a T-shirt? what a rip-off!*
[3] (= *cosa robada*) stolen article; (= *cosas robadas*) stolen goods *pl*

robot [ro'βo] Ⓐ SM (*pl* **robots** [ro'βo]) robot
Ⓑ ADJ INV **retrato ~** Identikit picture

robótica SF robotics *sing*

robotización SF robotization

robotizar ▸conjug 1f◂ VT (= *automatizar*) to automate; (*fig*) [+ *persona*] to turn into a robot

robustecer ▸conjug 2d◂ Ⓐ VT to strengthen
Ⓑ **robustecerse** VPR to grow stronger

robustecimiento SM strengthening

robustez SF strength, toughness, robustness

robusto ADJ strong, tough, robust

ROC SM ABR (= **Reconocimiento Óptico de Caracteres**) OCR

Roca SF **la ~** the Rock, the Rock of Gibraltar

roca SF [1] (= *piedra*) rock; **en ~ viva** in(to) the living rock; ✦**MODISMO ser firme como una ~** to be as solid as a rock
[2] (‡) (= *droga*) crack

rocalla SF pebbles *pl*

rocalloso ADJ pebbly, stony

rocambolescamente ADV (= *extraordinariamente*) bizarrely, in a bizarre fashion; (= *recargadamente*) ornately, over-elaborately

rocambolesco ADJ (= *raro*) odd, bizarre; [*estilo*] ornate, over-elaborate

rocanola† SF jukebox

rocanrol SM rock-'n'-roll, rock and roll

rocanrolear* ▸conjug 1a◂ VI to rock and roll

roce SM [1] (= *acción*) rub, rubbing; (*Téc*) friction; (*Pol*) friction
[2] (= *herida*) graze
[3] (*) (= *contacto*) close contact; **tener ~ con algn** to be in close contact with sb, have a lot to do with sb
[4] (= *disgusto*) brush; **tuvo algún ~ con la autoridad** he had a few brushes with the law

rochabús* SM (*Perú*) water cannon truck, police water cannon truck

Rochela SF **La ~** La Rochelle

rochela* SF (*Andes, Caribe*) (= *fiesta*) rowdy party; (= *alboroto*) din, racket

rochelero* ADJ (*Andes, Caribe*) (= *ruidoso*) unruly, rowdy; (*Caribe*) (= *travieso*) mischievous, naughty

rociada SF [1] (= *aspersión*) shower, spray; (*en bebida*) dash, splash; (*Agr*) spray
[2] [*de piedras*] shower; [*de balas*] hail; [*de injurias*] hail, stream

rociadera SF watering can

rociado SM (= *aspersión*) sprinkling; (*Agr*) spraying

rociador SM (*para rociar*) spray; (*Agr*) sprinkler ► **rociador de moscas** fly spray

rociar ▸conjug 1c◂ Ⓐ VT [1] [+ *agua*] to sprinkle, spray; [+ *balas*] to spray
[2] (*Culin*) (= *acompañar*) **~ el plato con un vino de la tierra** to wash down the dish with a local wine
Ⓑ VI (*Meteo*) **empieza a ~** the dew is beginning to fall; **rocía esta mañana** there is a dew this morning

rocín SM [1] (= *caballo*) [*de trabajo*] hack, nag; (*Cono Sur*) [*de montar*] riding horse
[2] (*Andes*) (= *buey*) draught ox
[3] (*) (= *persona*) lout

rocinante SM broken-down old horse

rocío SM [1] (*Meteo*) dew
[2] (= *gotas*) sprinkling

rock ADJ, SM rock

rockero/a Ⓐ ADJ rock *antes de s*; **música rockera** rock music; **es muy ~** he's a real rock fan
Ⓑ SM/F (= *cantante*) rock singer; (= *músico*) rock musician; (= *aficionado*) rock fan

rococó ADJ, SM rococo

rocola SF jukebox

rocosidades SFPL rocky places

rocoso ADJ rocky

rocote SM (*LAm*), **rocoto** SM (*LAm*) large pepper, large chili

roda SF (*Náut*) stem

rodaballo SM turbot ► **rodaballo menor** brill

rodada SF [1] [*de rueda*] rut, track
[2] (*Cono Sur, Méx*) (= *caída*) fall (from a horse)

rodadero SM (*Andes*) cliff, precipice

rodado Ⓐ ADJ [1] [*tráfico*] vehicular
[2] [*piedra*] rounded; **canto ~** boulder; **salir** *o* **venir ~** to go smoothly
[3] [*caballo*] dappled
[4] [*estilo*] well-rounded, fluent
[5] (= *con experiencia*) experienced
Ⓑ SM (*Cono Sur*) vehicle, wheeled vehicle

rodadura SF [1] (*tb* **banda de ~**) [*de neumático*] tread
[2] (= *acto*) roll, rolling
[3] (= *rodada*) rut

rodaja SF [1] [*de pan, fruta*] slice; **limón en ~s** sliced lemon
[2] [*de mueble*] castor
[3] (= *ruedecilla*) small wheel
[4] (= *disco*) small disc

rodaje SM [1] (*Téc*) wheels *pl*, set of wheels
[2] (*Cine*) shooting, filming
[3] (*Aut*) running-in, breaking in (EEUU); **"en rodaje"** "running in"
[4] (= *inicio*) **período de ~** initial phase; **poner en ~** to launch
[5] (= *experiencia*) experience
[6] (*Andes*) (= *impuesto*) vehicle tax, road tax

rodamiento SM [1] ► **rodamiento a bolas, rodamiento de bolas** ball bearing
[2] (*tb* **banda de ~**) [*de neumático*] tread

Ródano SM Rhône

rodante ADJ rolling; **material ~** rolling stock

rodapié SM skirting board, baseboard (EEUU)

rodar ▸conjug 1l◂ Ⓐ VI [1] (= *dar vueltas*) [*pelota*] to roll; [*rueda*] to go round, turn; **la moneda fue rodando por el caño** the coin rolled down to the drain; **rodó escaleras abajo** he fell *o* rolled downstairs; **se oía el ~ de los carros** one could hear the sound of cartwheels; **~ de suelo** (*Aer*) to taxi; ✦**MODISMOS echarlo todo a ~** to mess it all up; **~ por algn** to be at sb's beck and call
[2] (*) (= *deambular*) **me han hecho ir rodando de acá para allá** they kept shunting me about from one place to another; **tienen al niño rodando de guardería en guardería** they keep moving *o* shifting the kid about from nursery to nursery
[3] (*Cine*) to shoot, film; **llevamos dos meses rodando en México** we've spent two months filming in Mexico
[4] (*) (= *existir todavía*) to be still going, still exist; **ese modelo rueda todavía por el mundo** that model is still about
[5] (*Méx, Arg*) [*caballo*] to stumble, fall forwards
Ⓑ VT [1] [+ *vehículo*] to wheel, wheel along; [+ *coche nuevo*] to run in
[2] (= *hacer rodar*) [+ *objeto*] to roll, roll along
[3] (*Cine*) to shoot, film
[4] (*Inform*) [+ *programa*] to run
[5] (*Caribe*) (= *agarrar*) to seize; (= *encarcelar*) to imprison
[6] (*LAm*) **~ (a patadas)** to knock over, kick over
[7] (*LAm*) [+ *ganado*] to round up

Rodas SF Rhodes

rodear ▸conjug 1a◂ Ⓐ VT [1] (= *poner alrededor de*) to encircle, enclose; **~on el terreno con alambre de púas** they surrounded the field with barbed wire, they put a barbed wire fence around the field; **le rodeó el cuello con los brazos** she threw her arms round his neck
[2] (= *ponerse alrededor de*) to surround; **los soldados ~on el edificio** the soldiers surrounded the building
[3] (*LAm*) [+ *ganado*] to round up
Ⓑ **rodearse** VPR [1] (= *volverse*) to turn round
[2] **~se de** to surround o.s. with; **se rodeó de gente importante** she surrounded herself with important people

rodela SF [1] (= *escudo*) buckler, round shield
[2] (*Cono Sur*) (= *rosca*) padded ring (*for carrying loads on one's head*)

rodenticida SM rat poison

rodeo SM [1] (= *ruta indirecta*) long way round, roundabout way; (= *desvío*) detour; **dar un ~** to make a detour
[2] (*en discurso*) circumlocution; **andarse con ~s** to beat about the bush; **no te andes con ~s** ◊ **déjate de ~s** stop beating about the bush; **hablar sin ~s** to speak plainly
[3] (*LAm Agr*) roundup
[4] (*Dep*) rodeo

rodera SF rut, wheel track

Rodesia SF (*Hist*) Rhodesia

rodesiano/a ADJ, SM/F (*Hist*) Rhodesian

rodete SM [1] [*de pelo*] coil, bun; [*de grasa*] roll; (*para llevar carga*) pad
[2] [*de cerradura*] ward

rodilla SF [1] (*Anat*) knee; **de ~s** kneeling; **doblar** *o* **hincar la ~** (= *arrodillarse*) to kneel down; (= *ser servil*) to bow, humble o.s. (**ante** to); **estar de ~s** to be kneeling, be kneeling down; **hincarse de** *o* **ponerse de ~s** to kneel, kneel down, get down on one's knees; **pusieron al país de ~s** they brought the country to its knees
[2] (*para llevar carga*) pad
[3] (= *paño*) floor cloth, mop

rodillazo SM push with the knee; **dar un ~ a** to knee

rodillera SF [1] (= *protección*) knee guard; (= *remiendo*) knee patch
[2] (= *abombamiento*) baggy part (*in knee of*

trousers)
[3] (*para llevar carga*) pad

rodillo SM (*Culin*) rolling pin; (*Tip*) ink roller; [*de máquina de escribir*] cylinder, roller; (*para pintura, césped*) roller; (= *exprimidor*) mangle; (*Agr*) roller ► **rodillo de pintura** paint roller ► **rodillo de vapor** steamroller ► **rodillo pastelero** rolling pin

rodillón/ona* SM/F (*Andes*) old geezer*/old bag*

rodio SM rhodium

rododendro SM rhododendron

Rodrigo SM Roderick; **~ el último godo** Roderick, the last of the Goths

rodrigón SM stake, prop, support

Rodríguez SM **estar de ~** (*Esp*) to be left on one's own

roedor Ⓐ ADJ [1] (*Zool*) gnawing
[2] (= *atormentador*) [*sensación, conciencia*] gnawing; [*duda, sospecha*] nagging
Ⓑ SM rodent

roer ▸conjug 2z◂ VT [1] [+ *comida*] to gnaw; (= *mordiscar*) to nibble at; [+ *hueso*] to gnaw, pick
[2] (= *corroer*) to corrode, eat away
[3] [+ *capital*] to eat into (bit by bit)
[4] [*conciencia*] to prick

rogación SF [1] (= *petición*) petition
[2] **rogaciones** (*Rel*) rogations

▼**rogar** ▸conjug 1h, 1l◂ Ⓐ VT (= *suplicar*) to beg; **démelo, se lo ruego** give it to me, I beg you; **ruegue a este señor que nos deje en paz** please ask this gentleman to leave us alone; **"se ruega no fumar"** "please do not smoke"
Ⓑ VI [1] (= *suplicar*) to beg, plead; **hacerse de ~** to play hard to get; **no se hace de ~** he doesn't have to be asked twice
[2] (*Rel*) to pray

rogativa SF (*Rel*) rogation

rogatoria SF (*LAm*) request, plea

rogatorio ADJ **comisión rogatoria** investigative commission, committee of inquiry

rojear ▸conjug 1a◂ VI [1] (= *volverse rojo*) to redden, turn red
[2] (= *tirar a rojo*) to be reddish

rojeras* SMF INV red, commie*

rojete SM rouge

rojez SF (= *cualidad*) redness; (*en la piel*) blotch

rojigualdo ADJ red-and-yellow (*colours of the Spanish flag*)

rojillo/a* ADJ, SM/F (= *izquierdista*) leftie*, pinko*

rojizo ADJ reddish

rojo/a Ⓐ ADJ [1] (*color*) red; **~ burdeos** maroon, dark red; **~ cereza** cherry red; **~ sangre** blood-red; **~ teja** brick-red; ✦***MODISMOS*** **poner ~ a algn** to make sb blush; **ponerse ~** to turn red, blush; **ponerse ~ de ira** to go purple with rage
[2] [*pelo*] red
[3] (*Pol*) red; (*Esp*) (*durante la Guerra Civil y con Franco*) Republican
Ⓑ SM [1] (= *color*) red, red colour *o* (*EEUU*) color; **calentar al ~ vivo** to make red-hot; **la atmósfera está al ~ vivo** the atmosphere is electric; **la emoción está al ~ vivo** excitement is at fever pitch; **un semáforo en ~** a red light
[2] (= *maquillaje*) ► **rojo de labios** lipstick
Ⓒ SM/F (*Pol*) (= *de izquierdas*) red; (= *republicano*) Republican

rojura SF redness

rol SM [1] (*Teat*) role, part; (*fig*) role; **juegos de ~** role-playing games; **desempeña un ~ importantísimo en la política municipal** she plays a very important role in local politics
[2] (*Méx*) (= *paseo*) **dar un ~** to take a walk
[3] (*Náut*) muster

rola* Ⓐ SF (*Caribe*) (= *comisaría*) police station
Ⓑ SMF (*Cono Sur*) (= *matón*) lout; (= *zonzo*) thickhead*, dope*

Rolando SM Roland

rolar ▸conjug 1a◂ Ⓐ VT [1] (*Andes, Cono Sur*) (= *mencionar*) to touch on, mention, mention in conversation; **la conversación roló la religión** the conversation touched on religion
[2] (*Méx*) (= *pasar*) to pass from hand to hand
Ⓑ VI [1] [*viento*] to veer round
[2] (*Cono Sur*) (= *ser arribista*) to be a social climber
[3] (*Andes, Cono Sur*) (= *hablar*) to talk, converse (**con** with)
[4] (*Andes, Cono Sur*) (= *alternar con*) to associate, be in contact (**con** with)

Roldán SM Roland

roldana SF pulley wheel

rollazo* Ⓐ ADJ dead boring*
Ⓑ SM real pain*

rollista* Ⓐ ADJ (*Esp*) **es muy ~** (= *pesado*) he's such a bore; (= *mentiroso*) he's such a storyteller *o* fibber*
Ⓑ SMF (*Esp*) (= *pesado*) bore; (= *mentiroso*) storyteller*, fibber*

rollito SM roll ► **rollito de primavera** spring roll

rollizo ADJ [1] (= *rechoncho*) plump; [*niño*] chubby; [*mujer*] plump, buxom
[2] (= *redondo*) round; (= *cilíndrico*) cylindrical

rollo Ⓐ SM [1] (= *cilindro*) [*de tela, papel, cuerda fina, cable fino*] roll; [*de cuerda gruesa, cable grueso*] coil; [*de película de cine*] reel; [*de pergamino*] scroll; **un ~ de papel higiénico** a roll of toilet paper; **regalamos un ~ color** we offer a free colour film; **papel en ~** rolled up paper; **los ~s del Mar Muerto** the Dead Sea Scrolls ► **rollo de pelo** (*Ven*) curler, hair curler, roller
[2] (*Culin*) [2·1] (*tb* **~ pastelero**) (*Esp*) rolling pin
[2·2] [*de masa, relleno*] (pastry) roll
► **rollo de primavera** spring roll
[3] (= *tronco*) log; **en ~** whole, uncut
[4] (*) (= *michelín*) roll of fat, spare tyre* (*hum*)
[5] (*Esp**) (*tb* **~ macabeo** *o* **patatero**) (= *explicación*) spiel*; (= *sermón*) lecture; (= *mentira*) yarn; **nos soltó el ~ de siempre** he gave us the usual spiel*; **¡menudo ~ nos contó tu padre!** what a lecture your dad gave us! (*iró*); **¡menudo ~ que tiene!** he's always waffling (on) about something!*; **nos vino con un ~ de su familia que no había quien se lo creyera** he spun us a yarn about his family that no one could possibly believe; **¡vaya ~ patatero que me estás contando!** you're talking a load of old tosh!*, you're talking a load of baloney! (*EEUU**); **perdona por el ~ que te he soltado** sorry if I have bored you to death with my story; ✦***MODISMOS*** **cortar el ~** to cut it short*, cut the crap**; **corta el ~ y dime exactamente lo que quieres** cut it short* *o* cut the crap** and tell me exactly what you want; **cinco minutos más y ya corto el ~** five minutes more and then I'll shut up*; **cortar el ~ a algn**: **mejor que le cortes el ~, que tenemos prisa** don't let him rattle on, we're in a hurry; **¡con lo bien que lo estábamos pasando! ¡nos has cortado el ~!** we were having a great time until you went and spoiled things!; **estar de ~** (*Esp, Méx*): **están de ~ desde hace dos horas** they've been rattling on for two hours now; **tirarse el ~** (*Esp, Méx*): **no te tires el ~ conmigo que te conozco** don't give me that spiel* — I know what you're like; **tírate el ~ e invítame a una copa** be a pal and get me a drink*
[6] (*) (= *aburrimiento*) **¡qué ~!** what a pain!*; **ser un ~** [*discurso, conferencia*] to be dead boring*; [*persona*] to be a bore*, be a pain*; **lo de las lentillas es un ~** contact lenses are a real pain*
[7] (*) (= *asunto*) thing; **está metido en muchos ~s** he's into all sorts of things; **no sabemos de qué va el ~** we don't know what it's all about *o* what's going on; **ir a su ~** to do one's own thing
[8] (*Esp**) (= *ambiente*) scene*; **no me va el ~ de esta gente** I'm not into their scene*
[9] (*) (= *sensación*) **buen/mal ~**: **en sus fiestas siempre hay buen ~** there's always a good atmosphere at his parties; **había muy buen ~ entre nosotros** we got on really well together; **¡qué mal ~!** what a pain!*; **me da buen/mal ~** I've got a good/nasty *o* bad feeling about it; **¡qué buen ~ me da ese tío!** that guy gives me really good vibes!*; **la película me dio tan mal ~ que me deprimí** the film was a real downer*; **tener un buen/mal ~ con algn** to get on well/badly with sb
[10] (*) (= *relación sentimental*) **tener un ~ (con algn)** to be involved (with sb)
Ⓑ ADJ INV (*Esp, Méx**) boring; **esa película es muy ~** that film's dead boring*; **no seas ~, Julián** don't be a bore* *o* pain*, Julián

rolo SM (*LAm*) stick, truncheon, billy (club) (*EEUU*)

ROM SF ABR (= **Read-Only Memory**) ROM

Roma SF Rome; ✦***MODISMOS*** **revolver ~ con Santiago** to leave no stone unturned; **~ no se construyó en un día** Rome was not built in a day; **por todas partes se va a ~** ◊ **todos los caminos llevan a ~** all roads lead to Rome

romadizo SM [1] (= *resfriado*) head cold; (= *catarro*) catarrh
[2] (*Caribe*) (= *reuma*) rheumatism

romana SF steelyard; ✦***MODISMO*** **cargar la ~** (*Cono Sur**) to heap the blame on somebody else; *ver tb* **romano**

romance Ⓐ ADJ [*idioma*] Romance
Ⓑ SM [1] (*Ling*) Romance language; (= *castellano*) Spanish, Spanish language; **hablar en ~** (= *con claridad*) to speak plainly
[2] (*Literat*) ballad
[3] (= *amorío*) romance, love affair; (= *amante*) lover

romancear ▸conjug 1a◂ Ⓐ VT (††) to translate into Spanish
Ⓑ VI (*Cono Sur*) [1] (= *charlar*) to waste time chatting
[2] (= *galantear*) to flirt

romancero SM collection of ballads; **el Romancero** the Spanish ballads

romancístico ADJ ballad *antes de s*

➤ LENGUA Y USO: **rogar A** 31, 45.1, 46.1, 46.4, 48.1

romaní Ⓐ ADJ Romany
Ⓑ SMF Romany
Ⓒ SM (*Ling*) Romany

Romania SF Romance countries *pl*, Romance-speaking regions *pl*

románico ADJ 1 [*idioma*] Romance
2 (*Arte, Arquit*) Romanesque; (*en Inglaterra*) Norman

romanizar ▸conjug 1f◂ Ⓐ VT to romanize
Ⓑ **romanizarse** VPR to become romanized

romano/a Ⓐ ADJ, SM/F Roman
Ⓑ SM (*Esp†*) cop*; *ver tb* **romana**

romanó SM (*Ling*) Romany

románticamente ADV romantically

romanticismo SM romanticism

romántico/a ADJ, SM/F romantic

romanticón* ADJ [*persona*] sentimental, soppy*; [*película, novela*] slushy*, soppy*

romaza SF dock, sorrel

rombal ADJ rhombic

rombo SM 1 (*Mat*) rhombus; (*en diseño*) diamond, diamond shape
2 (*TV†*) diamond (*warning of scenes with adult content*); **una película de dos ~s** an over-18 film

romboidal ADJ rhomboid

romboide SM rhomboid

Romeo SM Romeo

romereante SMF (*Andes, Caribe*) pilgrim

romería SF 1 (*Rel*) pilgrimage; **ir en ~** to go on a pilgrimage
2 (*Aut*) queue, tailback

> **ROMERÍA**
>
> *In Spain* **romerías** *are annual religious pilgrimages to chapels and shrines associated with particular saints or miracles of the Virgin. The pilgrims, called* **romeros**, *make their way on foot to the particular holy site, often covering long distances, and make offerings before gathering for a picnic. The day's festivities often include sports fixtures, fireworks and traditional music and dancing. Some* **romerías** *are large-scale events, one of the best known being the* **Romería de la Virgen del Rocío** *at Huelva in Andalusia, which involves spectacular processions of pilgrims in traditional Andalusian dress, some on horseback and some in brilliantly decorated wagons.*

romero[1]/a SM/F (= *peregrino*) pilgrim

romero[2] SM (*Bot*) rosemary

romo ADJ 1 (= *sin punta*) blunt; [*persona*] snub-nosed
2 (= *aburrido*) dull, lifeless

rompebolas** SMF INV (*Arg*) pain in the arse**

rompecabezas SM INV 1 (= *juego*) jigsaw, jigsaw puzzle
2 (= *algo complicado*) puzzle; (= *problema*) problem, headache

rompecojones** SMF INV pain in the arse**

rompecorazones SMF INV heartbreaker

rompedero Ⓐ SM ► **rompedero de cabeza** puzzle, brain teaser
Ⓑ ADJ (*frm*) breakable, delicate, fragile

rompedor ADJ [*obra, movimiento, ideas, artista*] ground-breaking

rompedora-cargadora SF power loader

rompehielos SM INV icebreaker

rompehuelgas SMF INV strikebreaker, blackleg

rompenueces SM INV nutcrackers *pl*, pair of nutcrackers

rompeolas SM INV breakwater

romper ▸conjug 2a◂ (*pp* **roto**) Ⓐ VT 1 (= *partir, destrozar*) 1·1 (*intencionadamente*) [+ *juguete, mueble, cuerda*] to break; [+ *rama*] to break, break off; [+ *vaso, jarrón, cristal*] to break, smash; **los ladrones entraron rompiendo la puerta a patadas** the burglars got in by kicking down the door; **la onda expansiva rompió los cristales** the shock wave broke *o* smashed the windows
1·2 (= *rasgar*) [+ *tela, vestido, papel*] to tear, rip; **¡cuidado, que vas a ~ las cortinas!** careful, you'll tear *o* rip the curtains!; **se disgustó tanto con la carta que la rompió en pedazos** he was so angry about the letter that he tore *o* ripped it up
1·3 (*por el uso*) [+ *zapatos, ropa*] to wear out
1·4 [+ *barrera*] (*lit*) to break down, break through; (*fig*) to break down; **tratan de ~ barreras en el campo de la informática** they are trying to break down barriers in the area of computing; **~ la barrera del sonido** to break the sound barrier
1·5 ✦**MODISMOS** **~ aguas**: **todavía no ha roto aguas** her waters haven't broken yet; **~ la cara a algn*** to smash sb's face in*; **~ el hielo** to break the ice; **~ una lanza en favor de algn/algo** to stick up for sb/sth; **no haber roto un plato**: **se comporta como si no hubiera roto un plato en su vida** he behaves as if butter wouldn't melt in his mouth; **de rompe y rasga**: **es una mujer de rompe y rasga** she's not someone to mess with; **quien rompe paga** one must pay the consequences for one's actions; *ver tb* **esquema 2**, **molde 1**
2 (= *terminar*) [+ *equilibrio, silencio, maleficio, contrato*] to break; [+ *relaciones, amistad*] to break off; **hagamos algo distinto que rompa la rutina** let's do something different to break the routine; **la patronal ha roto el pacto con los sindicatos** employers have broken the agreement with the unions; **~ la racha de algo** to break a run of sth; **~ el servicio a algn** (*Tenis*) to break sb's service
3 (*Mil*) [+ *línea, cerco*] to break, break through; **¡rompan filas!** fall out!; **~ (el) fuego** to open fire; **~ las hostilidades** to start hostilities
4 (*Agr*) [+ *tierra*] to break, break up
5 (*Arg, Uru***) (= *molestar*) to piss off**; **dejá de ~me** stop pissing me off**
Ⓑ VI 1 [*olas*] to break
2 (= *salir*) [*diente*] to come through; [*capullo, flor*] to come out; **~ entre algo** to break through sth, burst through sth; **los manifestantes rompieron entre el cordón de seguridad** the demonstrators broke *o* burst through the security cordon
3 [*alba, día*] to break; **al ~ el alba** at crack of dawn, at daybreak
4 (= *empezar*) **~ a hacer algo** to (suddenly) start doing sth, (suddenly) start to do sth; **rompió a proferir insultos contra todo el mundo** he suddenly started hurling *o* to hurl insults at everyone; **al verme rompió a llorar** when he saw me he burst into tears; **~ en llanto** to break down in tears; **cuando rompa el hervor** when it comes to the boil
5 (= *separarse*) [*pareja, novios*] to split up; **hace algún tiempo que rompieron** they split up some time ago; **~ con** [+ *novio, amante*] to split up with, break up with; [+ *amigo, familia*] to fall out with; [+ *aliado*] to break off relations with; [+ *tradición, costumbre, pasado*] to break with; [+ *imagen, tópico, leyenda*] to break away from; **ha roto con su novio** she has broken *o* split up with her boyfriend; **Albania rompió con China en 1978** Albania broke off relations with China in 1978; **han roto con una tradición de siglos** they have broken with a centuries-old tradition
Ⓒ **romperse** VPR 1 (= *partirse, destrozarse*) 1·1 [*juguete, mueble, cuerda*] to break; [*plato, cristal*] to break, smash; **la rama se ha roto con el viento** the branch broke (off) in the wind; **se me rompió un dedo en el accidente** my finger got broken in the accident, I broke a finger in the accident
1·2 (*uso enfático*) **me he roto la muñeca jugando al tenis** I broke my wrist playing tennis; **no te vayas a ~ de tanto trabajar** (*iró, hum*) don't strain yourself working so hard (*iró*); ✦**MODISMO** **~se la cabeza*** (= *pensar mucho*) to rack one's brains; (= *preocuparse*) to kill o.s. worrying; *ver tb* **cuerno 1**
2 (= *rasgarse*) [*tela, papel*] to tear, rip; **tiraron del gorro de papel hasta que se rompió** they pulled the paper hat till it tore *o* ripped; **se me han roto los pantalones** I've torn *o* ripped my trousers
3 (= *estropearse*) [*coche, motor*] to break down; [*televisor*] to break; **se ha roto la lavadora** the washing machine is broken, the washing machine has broken down
4 (= *gastarse*) [*ropa, zapatos*] to wear out; **se le han roto los pantalones por las rodillas** his trousers have worn (through) at the knees
5 (*Ciclismo*) [*pelotón*] to break up
6 (*Arg, Uru**) (= *esforzarse*) **no me rompí mucho, no valía la pena** I didn't go to a lot of trouble, it wasn't worth it; **el pobre se rompe tanto y saca malas notas** the poor guy works like crazy and gets really bad marks*; **así se lo agradecés a tu madre que se rompe todo por vos** that's how you thank your mother, who does all she can for you

rompiente SM 1 (= *escollo*) reef, shoal
2 **rompientes** (= *olas*) breakers, surf *sing*

rompimiento SM 1 [*de ladrillo, cristal, porcelana*] breaking, smashing; [*de muro*] breaking; [*de tela, papel*] tearing; **la tromba de agua causó el ~ del muro** the downpour caused the wall to break *o* collapse ► **rompimiento de aguas** downpour
2 [*de negociaciones, diálogo*] breaking-off; [*de récord*] breaking; **procederemos al ~ de contrato** we will break the contract forthwith (*frm*); **su ~ con el resto de las vanguardias europeas** his break with the rest of the European avant-garde ► **rompimiento de contacto** (*Mil*) disengagement
3 (= *abertura*) opening
4 (= *comienzo*) [*de hostilidades*] outbreak

romplón: **de ~** ADV (*LAm*) suddenly, unexpectedly

rompope SM (*CAm, Méx*) eggnog

Rómulo SM Romulus

ron SM rum

ronca SF 1 (*Zool*) (= *sonido*) roar (*of rutting stag*); (= *época*) rutting season

[2] (= *amenaza*) threat; **echar ~s** to bully, threaten

roncadoras SFPL (*LAm*) large spurs

roncar ▸conjug 1g◂ VI [1] (*cuando se duerme*) to snore
[2] [*ciervo, mar*] to roar
[3] (= *amenazar*) to threaten, bully
[4] (*Andes, Cono Sur**) (= *ser mandón*) to be bossy o domineering

roncear ▸conjug 1a◂ Ⓐ VT [1] (= *insistir*) to pester, keep on at
[2] (*LAm*) (= *espiar*) to keep watch on, spy on
[3] (*LAm*) = **ronzar[1]**
Ⓑ VI [1] (*Náut*) to move slowly
[2] (= *trabajar a desgana*) to work half-heartedly; (= *gandulear*) to slack, kill time

roncería SF [1] (= *desgana*) unwillingness
[2] (= *lisonja*) cajolery

roncero ADJ [1] (*Náut*) slow, slow-moving, sluggish
[2] (= *desganado*) unwilling; (= *gandul*) slack, slow; **estar ~** to find reasons for shirking work
[3] (= *gruñón*) grumpy, grouchy*
[4] (= *cobista*) smooth, smarmy*
[5] (*Andes, CAm, Cono Sur*) (= *taimado*) sly, sharp; (= *entrometido*) nosey*, meddling

roncha SF [1] (= *hinchazón*) swelling; ✦**MODISMOS hacer ~** (*Cono Sur**) to create an impression; **levantar ~** (*Caribe**) to pass a dud cheque*; **sacar ~*** to cause an upset
[2] (= *cardenal*) bruise
[3] (= *rodaja*) slice

ronco ADJ [*persona*] hoarse; [*voz*] husky; [*sonido*] harsh, raucous

roncón* ADJ (*Andes, Caribe*) boastful, bragging

ronda SF [1] [*de guardia*] beat; (= *personas*) watch, patrol, guard; **ir de ~** to do one's round ► **ronda nocturna** night patrol, night watch
[2] (*Mús*) group of serenaders
[3] [*de bebidas*] round; **pagar una ~** to pay for a round
[4] [*de negociaciones, elecciones*] round
[5] [*de cartas*] hand, game
[6] (*en competición, concurso*) round; (*Golf*) round
[7] (*Aut*) (*tb* **~ de circunvalación**) ring road, beltway (*EEUU*), bypass
[8] (*Mil*) sentry walk
[9] (*Cono Sur*) (= *juego*) ring-a-ring-a-roses; **en ~** in a ring, in a circle

rondalla SF [1] (*Mús*) band of street musicians
[2] (= *ficción*) fiction, invention

rondana SF (*LAm*) pulley

rondar ▸conjug 1a◂ Ⓐ VT [1] [*policía, soldado*] to patrol
[2] [+ *cifra, edad*] **el precio ronda los mil dólares** the price is in the region of a thousand dollars; **rondaba los 30 años** he was about 30
[3] (= *perseguir*) **la ronda a todas horas para que le preste dinero** he pesters her night and day to lend him money; **es una idea que me rondaba la cabeza desde hace tiempo** it's an idea which I've had going round in my head for quite a while; **me está rondando un catarro** I've got a cold hanging over me; **a estas horas siempre me ronda el sueño** I always start feeling sleepy around this time
[4] (†) (= *cortejar*) to court
Ⓑ VI [1] [*policía, soldado*] to (be on) patrol
[2] (= *deambular*) to prowl; **sospechan de un hombre que rondaba por allí** they suspect a man who was prowling around the area
[3] [*pensamiento, idea*] **debes rechazar las dudas que te rondan por la cabeza** you must dispel the doubts that are besetting you
[4] (†) [*enamorado, la tuna*] to serenade

rondeño/a Ⓐ ADJ of/from Ronda
Ⓑ SM/F native/inhabitant of Ronda; **los ~s** the people of Ronda

rondín[1] SM (*Andes, Cono Sur*) (= *vigilante*) night watchman

rondín[2] SM (*Andes Mús*) harmonica

rondó SM (*Literat*) rondeau; (*Mús*) rondo

rondón: **de ~** ADV unexpectedly; **entrar de ~** (= *sin aviso*) to rush in; (*en fiesta*) to gatecrash

ronquear ▸conjug 1a◂ VI to be hoarse

ronquedad SF, **ronquera** SF [1] [*de persona*] hoarseness
[2] [*de voz*] (*permanentemente*) huskiness; (*temporalmente*) hoarseness

ronquido SM snore, snoring

ronronear ▸conjug 1a◂ VI to purr

ronroneo SM purr

ronzal SM halter

ronzar[1] ▸conjug 1f◂ VT (*Náut*) to move with levers, lever along

ronzar[2] ▸conjug 1f◂ VT, VI (*al comer*) to munch, crunch

roña Ⓐ SF [1] (= *mugre*) dirt, grime; (*en metal*) rust
[2] (= *tacañería*) meanness, stinginess
[3] (*Vet*) mange
[4] (= *corteza*) pine bark
[5] (= *estratagema*) stratagem
[6] (*Caribe, Méx*) (= *envidia*) envy; (= *inquina*) grudge, ill will
[7] (*Andes Med*) feigned illness
[8] **jugar a la ~** to play for fun, play without money stakes
Ⓑ SMF (*) mean person, scrooge*

roñería SF meanness, stinginess

roñica* SMF skinflint

roñoso ADJ [1] (= *mugriento*) dirty, filthy; [*metal*] rusty
[2] (= *tacaño*) mean, stingy
[3] (= *inútil*) useless
[4] (*Vet*) mangy
[5] (*Andes*) (= *tramposo*) tricky, slippery
[6] (*Caribe, Méx*) (= *rencoroso*) bitter, resentful; (= *hostil*) hostile

ropa SF clothes *pl*; **¡quítate esa ~ tan sucia!** take those dirty clothes off!; **siempre lleva ~ pasada de moda** he always wears old-fashioned clothes; **voy a cambiarme de ~** I'm going to change (my clothes); **tender la ~** to hang out the washing; ✦**MODISMOS guardar la ~** to speak cautiously; **hay ~ tendida** the walls have ears; **nadar y guardar la ~** to cover one's back; **no tocar la ~ a algn** not to touch a hair of sb's head, keep one's hands off sb; ✦**REFRÁN la ~ sucia se lava en casa** don't wash your dirty linen in public ► **ropa blanca** (= *ropa interior*) underwear; (= *ropa de cama, manteles*) linen; (*para la lavadora*) whites *pl* ► **ropa de cama** bed linen ► **ropa de color** coloureds *pl*, coloreds *pl* (*EEUU*) ► **ropa de deporte** sportswear ► **ropa de mesa** table linen ► **ropa de trabajo** work clothes *pl* ► **ropa hecha** ready-made clothes *pl*, off-the-peg clothes *pl* ► **ropa interior** underwear ► **ropa íntima** (*LAm*) underwear ► **ropa para lavar, ropa sucia** dirty washing, dirty clothes *pl*, laundry ► **ropa usada** secondhand clothes *pl* ► **ropa vieja** (*esp Méx Culin*) meat stew

ropaje SM [1] (= *vestiduras*) gown, robes *pl*; **ropajes** (*Rel*) vestments *pl*
[2] (*Literat*) (= *adornos*) embellishments *pl*, rhetorical adornments *pl*

ropalócero SM butterfly

ropavejería SF old-clothes shop

ropavejero/a SM/F second-hand-clothes dealer

ropería SF [1] (= *tienda*) clothes shop
[2] (= *comercio*) clothing trade, garment industry (*EEUU*)

ropero Ⓐ ADJ for clothes, clothes *antes de s*; **armario ~** wardrobe
Ⓑ SM (= *guardarropa*) wardrobe; [*de ropa blanca*] linen cupboard

ropita SF baby clothes *pl*

ropón SM [1] [*de ceremonia*] long robe
[2] (= *bata*) loose coat, housecoat

roque[1] SM (*Ajedrez*) rook, castle

roque[2]* ADJ **estar ~** to be asleep; **quedarse ~** to fall asleep

roquedal SM rocky place

roqueño ADJ [1] (= *rocoso*) rocky
[2] (= *duro*) hard as rock, rock-like, flinty; (*fig*) rock-solid

roquero/a ADJ, SM/F = **rockero**

rorcual SM rorqual, finback, finback whale

ro-ro SM car ferry, roll-on/roll-off ferry

rorro SM [1] (*) (= *bebé*) baby
[2] (*Méx*) (= *persona*) fair blue-eyed person
[3] (*Méx*) (= *muñeca*) doll

Rosa SF Rose

rosa Ⓐ SF [1] (*Bot*) rose; **palo ~** rosewood; ✦**MODISMO como una ~**: **estar como una ~** to feel as fresh as a daisy; **un cutis como una ~** a skin as soft as silk; **estar como las propias ~s** to feel entirely at ease; **florecer como ~ en mayo** to bloom, flourish; ✦**REFRÁN no hay ~ sin espinas** there's no rose without a thorn ► **rosa almizcleña** musk rose ► **rosa laurel** rosebay, oleander
[2] **de color ~** ◊ **color de ~** pink; (*fig*) rosy; **vestidos color de ~** pink dresses; **verlo todo del color de ~** to see everything through rose-tinted spectacles o (*EEUU*) rose-colored glasses
[3] (*en la piel*) birthmark, red birthmark
[4] (*Arquit*) rose window
[5] ► **rosa de los vientos, rosa náutica** compass, compass card, compass rose
Ⓑ ADJ pink; **revista ~** magazine of sentimental stories; **Zona Rosa** (*Méx*) (= *barrio*) *elegant (tourist) quarter of Mexico City*

rosáceo ADJ = **rosado A**

rosacruciano ADJ Rosicrucian

rosado Ⓐ ADJ [1] [*color*] pink
[2] [*panorama*] rosy
Ⓑ SM (= *vino*) rosé

rosal SM [1] (= *planta*) rose bush, rose tree ► **rosal de China, rosal japonés** japonica ► **rosal silvestre** wild rose ► **rosal trepador** climbing rose, rambling rose
[2] (*Caribe, Cono Sur*) (= *rosaleda*) rose bed, rose garden

rosaleda SF rose bed, rose garden

rosario SM [1] (*Rel*) rosary; (= *sarta*) rosary beads *pl*, rosary; **rezar el ~** to say the rosary; ✦*REFRÁN* **acabar como el ~ de la aurora** *o* **del alba** to end up in confusion, end with everybody falling out
[2] (= *serie*) string, series; **un ~ de maldiciones** a string of curses
[3] (*Agr*) chain of buckets (*of a waterwheel*)
[4] (*Anat**) backbone
[5] (*Arquit*) beading

rosbif SM roast beef

rosca SF [1] [*de humo*] ring, spiral; **estaba hecho una ~** he was all curled up in a ball
[2] (*Culin*) ring-shaped roll, ring-shaped pastry, ≈ doughnut; ✦*MODISMOS* **hacer la ~ a algn*** to suck *o* (*EEUU*) kiss up to sb*; **no comerse una ~*** (= *no ligar*) to get absolutely nowhere
[3] [*de tornillo*] thread; [*de espiral*] turn; **pasarse de ~** [*tornillo*] to have a crossed thread; [*persona*] to go too far, overdo it
[4] (*Anat*) (= *hinchazón*) swelling; [*de grasa*] roll of fat
[5] (*Andes Pol*) ruling clique, oligarchy
[6] (*Cono Sur*) (*para llevar carga*) pad
[7] (*Cono Sur Naipes*) circle of card players
[8] (*Cono Sur*) (= *discusión*) noisy argument; (= *jaleo*) uproar, commotion; **se armó una ~** there was uproar

rosco[1] SM [1] (*Culin*) ring-shaped roll, ring-shaped pastry, ≈ doughnut; ✦*MODISMO* **no comerse un ~*** (= *no ligar*) to get absolutely nowhere (**con** with)
[2] (*) (= *nota*) zero, nought

rosco[2] SM (*LAm Com*) middleman

roscón SM (*tb* **~ de Reyes**) ring-shaped cake (*eaten on the 6th January*); → DÍA DE REYES

rosedal SM (*Cono Sur*) = **rosaleda**

Rosellón SM Roussillon

róseo ADJ (*liter*) rosy, roseate

roseta SF [1] (*Bot*) small rose
[2] (*Dep*) rosette
[3] [*de regadera*] rose, nozzle
[4] (*en la piel*) red spot
[5] (*Andes, Cono Sur*) [*de espuela*] rowel
[6] **rosetas** [*de maíz*] popcorn *sing*

rosetón SM [1] (*Arquit*) rose window
[2] (*Dep*) rosette
[3] (*Aut*) cloverleaf, cloverleaf junction

rosicler SM dawn pink, rosy tint of dawn

rosita SF [1] (*Bot*) small rose
[2] (*Cono Sur*) (= *pendiente*) earring
[3] **de ~** (*Méx*) (= *sin esfuerzo*) without effort; **andar de ~** (*LAm*) (*sin trabajo*) to be out of work
[4] **rositas** [*de maíz*] popcorn *sing*

rosquero* ADJ (*Cono Sur*) quarrelsome

rosquete‡ SM (*Andes*) queer‡, poof‡, fag (*EEUU‡*)

rosquetón‡ (*Perú*) Ⓐ ADJ effeminate
Ⓑ SM queer‡, fag (*EEUU‡*)

rosquilla SF [1] [*de humo*] ring
[2] (*Culin*) ring-shaped pastry, doughnut; ✦*MODISMO* **venderse como ~s** to sell like hot cakes
[3] (= *larva*) small caterpillar

rosticería SF (*Méx, Chile*) roast chicken shop

rostizado ADJ roast; **pollo ~** (*Méx*) roast chicken

rostizar ▸conjug 1a◂ VT to spit-roast

rostro SM [1] (= *semblante*) countenance; (= *cara*) face; **retrato de ~ entero** full-face portrait
[2] (*) (= *descaro*) nerve*, cheek*
[3] (*Náut*) beak
[4] (*Zool*) rostrum

rostropálido/a SM/F paleface

rotación SF [1] (= *giro*) rotation ► **rotación de la tierra** rotation of the earth
[2] (*Agr*) ► **rotación de cultivos** crop rotation
[3] (*Com*) [*de producción*] turnover ► **rotación de existencias** turnover of stock

rotacional ADJ rotational

rotaje* SM (*Chile*) plebs* *pl*

rotar ▸conjug 1a◂ VT to rotate

rotarianismo SM (*esp LAm*) Rotarianism

rotariano/a ADJ, SM/F (*LAm*) = **rotario**

rotario/a ADJ, SM/F (*esp LAm*) Rotarian

rotativamente ADV by turns

rotativo Ⓐ ADJ (= *que gira*) rotary, revolving; [*prensa*] rotary
Ⓑ SM [1] (*Tip*) rotary press
[2] (= *periódico*) newspaper
[3] (= *luz*) revolving light
[4] (*Cono Sur Cine*) continuous performance

rotatorio ADJ rotating; **la secretaría será rotatoria** the secretaryship will rotate

rotería SF [1] (*LAm*) (= *plebe*) common people *pl*, plebs* *pl*
[2] (*Cono Sur*) (= *truco*) dirty trick; (= *dicho*) coarse remark

rotisería SF (*Cono Sur*) delicatessen

roto/a Ⓐ PP *de* **romper**
Ⓑ ADJ [1] (= *partido, destrozado*) [*juguete, mueble, cristal, puerta*] broken; **tengo la pierna rota** I've broken my leg, I've got a broken leg
[2] (= *rasgado*) [*tela, papel*] torn; **la bolsa está rota** the bag is torn; **tienes rota la manga del vestido** the sleeve of your dress is ripped *o* torn; **la cuerda estaba rota por los extremos** the rope was frayed at the ends
[3] (= *estropeado*) [*lavadora, televisor*] broken; [*coche, motor*] broken down
[4] [*zapato*] worn, worn-out
[5] (= *destrozado*) [*persona*] broken; [*vida*] shattered; **estar ~ de cansancio** to be exhausted, be worn-out
[6] (††) (= *libertino*) debauched, dissipated
[7] (*Chile**) (= *de clase baja*) common, low-class; (= *maleducado*) rude
Ⓒ SM/F [1] (= *persona chilena*) [1·1] (*Perú, Bol**) Chilean, Chilean person
[1·2] (*Chile*) **el ~ chileno** the average Chilean
[2] (*Chile**) [2·1] (= *pobre*) pleb*
[2·2] (= *persona*) guy*/woman; **es una rota con suerte** she's a lucky woman; **el rotito quería que le pagáramos el viaje** the cheeky devil wanted us to pay for his trip*
[2·3] (= *maleducado*) **esta rota no sabe comportarse a la mesa** she's so rude *o* such a pig‡, she doesn't know how to behave at the dinner table
Ⓓ SM (= *agujero*) (*en pantalón, vestido*) hole; **te has hecho un ~ en la manga** you've got a hole in your sleeve; ✦*MODISMO* **valer** *o* **servir lo mismo para un ~ que para un descosido** to serve a multitude of purposes; ✦*REFRÁN* **nunca falta un ~ para un descosido** you can always find a companion in misfortune

rotograbado SM rotogravure

rotonda SF [1] (*Aut*) roundabout, traffic circle (*EEUU*)
[2] (*Arquit*) rotunda, circular gallery
[3] (*Ferro*) engine shed, roundhouse

rotor SM rotor

rotoso* ADJ [1] (*LAm*) (= *harapiento*) ragged, shabby
[2] (*Andes, Cono Sur**) (= *ordinario*) low-life, common

rótula SF [1] (*Anat*) kneecap
[2] (*Mec*) ball-and-socket joint

rotulación SF [1] (= *escritura*) labelling; (*en mapa etc*) lettering
[2] (= *profesión*) sign painting

rotulador SM felt tip pen

rotular ▸conjug 1a◂ VT [+ *objeto*] to label, put a label on; [+ *carta, documento*] to head, entitle; [+ *mapa*] to letter, inscribe

rotulata SF labels *pl*, inscriptions *pl* (*collectively*)

rotulista SMF sign painter

rótulo SM [1] (= *letrero*) sign, notice; (= *cartel*) placard, poster ► **rótulo de salida** (*TV*) credits *pl* ► **rótulo luminoso** illuminated sign
[2] (= *encabezamiento*) heading, title; (*en mapa*) lettering
[3] (= *etiqueta*) label, ticket

➤ **rotundamente** ADV [*negar*] flatly, roundly; [*afirmar, expresar acuerdo*] emphatically

rotundidad SF [1] [*de negativa*] flatness; [*de victoria*] clearness, convincing nature
[2] (= *redondez*) rotundity

rotundo ADJ [1] (= *terminante*) [*negativa*] flat; [*victoria*] clear, convincing; **me dio un "sí" ~** he gave me an emphatic "yes"
[2] (= *redondo*) round

rotura SF [1] [*de objeto*] **varios autobuses sufrieron la ~ de cristales** a number of buses had their windscreens smashed *o* broken; **el seguro del coche cubre la ~ de cristales** the car insurance covers window breakage; **la explosión causó la ~ de la presa** the explosion caused the dam to break *o* burst *o* collapse; **la casa está sin agua por una ~ en las tuberías** the house has no water because of a broken pipe; **en la fotografía puede apreciarse la ~ del muro** in the photograph you can see where the wall is broken *o* the break in the wall
[2] (*Med*) **la ~ del hueso se produjo en el momento de la caída** the bone broke at the moment of the fall; **ingresó por ~ de cadera** he was admitted for a broken hip; **ha sufrido una ~ de ligamentos** he has torn ligaments
[3] (*en tela*) tear, rip

roturación SF breaking-up, ploughing, plowing (*EEUU*)

roturar ▸conjug 1a◂ VT (*Agr*) to break up, plough, plow (*EEUU*)

rough [ruf] SM **el ~** (*Golf*) the rough

roulotte [ru'lo] SF caravan, trailer (*EEUU*)

round [raun] SM (*pl* **rounds**) round

roya SF rust, blight

royalty SM (*pl* **royalties**) royalty

roza SF [1] (*Arquit*) groove, hollow (*in a wall*)
[2] (*esp Cono Sur*) (= *hierbajos*) weeds *pl*
[3] (*Méx*) (= *matas*) brush, stubble
[4] (*Andes Agr*) planting in newly-broken ground
[5] (*CAm*) (= *tierra limpia*) cleared ground

rozado ADJ worn, grazed

➤ LENGUA Y USO: **rotundamente** 39.3

rozador SM (*Caribe*) machete

rozadura SF (= *marca*) mark of rubbing, chafing mark; (*en la piel*) abrasion, graze

rozagante ADJ (*liter*) [1] [*vestido*] showy; (= *llamativo*) striking
[2] (= *ufano*) proud

rozamiento SM [1] (= *fricción*) rubbing, chafing; (*Mec*) friction
[2] **tener un ~ con algn*** to have a slight disagreement with sb

rozar ▸conjug 1f◂ (A) VT [1] (= *tocar ligeramente*) **la rocé al pasar** I brushed past her; **estas botas me rozan los tobillos** these boots rub my ankles; **con esa falda vas rozando el suelo** your skirt is trailing on the floor; **la mesa ha rozado la pared** the table has scraped the wall; **la pelota rozó el poste** the ball shaved *o* grazed the post; **la flecha le rozó la oreja** the arrow grazed his ear; **la gaviota volaba rozando el mar** the seagull skimmed over the sea
[2] (= *acercarse a*) **debe estar rozando los 50** she must be getting on for 50; **su estilo de juego roza la perfección** his game is close to perfection; **es una cuestión que roza lo judicial** it's almost a judicial matter
[3] (*Arquit*) to make a groove *o* hollow in
[4] (*Agr*) [+ *hierba*] to graze; [+ *terreno*] to clear
(B) VI **~ con algo: eso roza con la codicia** that's bordering *o* verging on greed
(C) **rozarse** VPR [1] (= *tocarse ligeramente*) **se rozó conmigo al pasar** he brushed past me; **me rocé la rodilla con el muro** I grazed *o* scraped my knee on the wall
[2] (*) (= *tratarse*) **~se con algn** to hobnob with sb*, rub shoulders with sb
[3] (= *desgastarse*) [*cuello, puños*] to become frayed *o* worn
[4] (†) (= *tropezarse*) to trip over one's own feet; (*al hablar*) to get tongue-tied; **~se en un sonido** to stutter over a sound

roznar¹ ▸conjug 1a◂ VT, VI = **ronzar**

roznar² ▸conjug 1a◂ VI [*burro*] to bray

roznido SM bray, braying

R.P. ABR = **Reverendo Padre**

r.p.m. ABR (= **revoluciones por minuto**) rpm

RRPP ABR (= **relaciones públicas**) PR

Rte. ABR = **remite, remitente**

RTVE SF ABR = **Radiotelevisión Española**

rúa SF street

Ruán SM Rouen

ruana SF (*Andes, Caribe*) poncho, ruana

ruandés/esa ADJ, SM/F Rwandan

ruanetas SMF INV (*Col*) peasant

ruano ADJ, SM = **roano**

rubeola SF, **rubéola** SF German measles

rubí SM (= *piedra preciosa*) ruby; [*de reloj*] jewel

rubia SF [1] (*Esp*†*) (= *peseta*) peseta
[2] (*Aut*) estate car, station wagon (*EEUU*); *ver tb* **rubio**

rubiales* SMF INV blond/blonde, fair-haired person

rubiato/a (A) ADJ fair, blond/blonde
(B) SM/F fair-haired person, blond/blonde

Rubicón SM Rubicon; ✦***MODISMO*** **pasar el ~** to cross the Rubicon

rubicundo ADJ [1] [*cara*] ruddy; [*persona*] ruddy-faced
[2] (= *rojizo*) reddish

rubiez SF (*liter*) blondness

rubio/a (A) ADJ [1] [*persona*] fair-haired, blond/blonde; [*animal*] light-coloured, light-colored (*EEUU*), golden; **~ ceniza** ash-blond; **~ platino** platinum-blonde
[2] **tabaco ~** Virginia tobacco
(B) SM Virginia tobacco
(C) SM/F blond/blonde, fair-haired person ▸ **rubia ceniza** ash blonde ▸ **rubia de bote** peroxide blonde ▸ **rubia miel** honey blonde ▸ **rubia oxigenada** peroxide blonde ▸ **rubia platino** platinum blonde; *ver tb* **rubia**

rublo SM rouble

rubor SM [1] (*en cara*) blush, flush; **causar ~ a algn** to make sb blush
[2] (= *timidez*) bashfulness
[3] (= *color*) bright red

ruborizado ADJ (= *colorado*) blushing; (= *avergonzado*) ashamed

ruborizante ADJ blush-making

ruborizar ▸conjug 1f◂ (A) VT to cause to blush, make blush
(B) **ruborizarse** VPR to blush, redden (**de** at)

ruboroso ADJ (*frm*) [1] **ser ~** to blush easily
[2] **estar ~** (= *colorado*) to blush, be blushing; (= *avergonzado*) to feel bashful

rúbrica SF [1] (= *señal*) red mark
[2] [*de la firma*] flourish
[3] (= *título*) title, heading; **bajo la ~ de** under the heading of
[4] **de ~** customary, usual

rubricar ▸conjug 1g◂ VT [1] (= *firmar*) to sign with a flourish; [+ *documento*] to initial
[2] (= *concluir*) to sign and seal

rubro SM [1] (*LAm*) (= *título*) heading, title
[2] (*LAm Com*) ▸ **rubro social** trading name, firm's name
[3] (*LAm*) [*de cuenta*] heading

ruca SF [1] (*Cono Sur*) (= *cabina*) hut, Indian hut, cabin
[2] (*Méx*) (= *soltera*) old maid

rucho ADJ (*Andes*) [*fruta*] overripe

rucio/a (A) ADJ [1] [*caballo*] grey, gray (*EEUU*); [*persona*] grey-haired, gray-haired (*EEUU*)
[2] (*Chile**) (= *rubio*) fair, blond/blonde
(B) SM (= *caballo*) grey, gray (*EEUU*), grey horse, gray horse (*EEUU*)
(C) SM/F (*Chile**) (= *rubio*) blond/blonde, blond/blonde person

ruco ADJ [1] (*LAm*) (= *usado*) worn-out, useless; (= *agotado*) exhausted
[2] (*Andes, Méx*) (= *viejo*) old

ruda SF rue

rudamente ADV [1] (= *tosco*) coarsely
[2] (= *sencillamente*) simply, plainly

rudeza SF [1] (= *tosquedad*) coarseness ▸ **rudeza de entendimiento** stupidity
[2] (= *sencillez*) simplicity

rudimental ADJ, **rudimentario** ADJ rudimentary

rudimento SM [1] (*Anat*) rudiment
[2] **rudimentos** (= *lo básico*) rudiments

rudo ADJ [1] [*madera*] rough; (= *sin pulir*) unpolished
[2] (*Mec*) [*pieza*] stiff
[3] [*persona*] (= *sencillo*) simple
[4] (= *tosco*) coarse
[5] [*golpe*] hard; **fue un ~ golpe para mí** it was a terrible blow for me

rueca SF distaff

rueda SF [1] (*Mec*) wheel; (= *neumático*) tyre, tire (*EEUU*); [*de mueble*] roller, castor; ✦***MODISMOS*** **chupar ~** (*Ciclismo*) to tuck in; (= *aprovecharse*) to ride on sb's coattails; **ir sobre ~s*** (*en vehículo*) to go for a spin*; (= *marchar bien*) to go smoothly ▸ **rueda de agua** waterwheel ▸ **rueda de alfarero** potter's wheel ▸ **rueda de atrás** rear wheel, back wheel ▸ **rueda de cadena** sprocket wheel ▸ **rueda de la fortuna** wheel of fortune ▸ **rueda delantera** front wheel ▸ **rueda de molino** millwheel; ✦***MODISMO*** **comulga con ~s de molino** he'd swallow anything ▸ **rueda dentada** cog ▸ **rueda de paletas** paddle wheel ▸ **rueda de recambio** spare wheel ▸ **rueda de trinquete** ratchet wheel ▸ **rueda hidráulica** waterwheel ▸ **rueda impresora** (*Inform*) print wheel ▸ **rueda libre** freewheel ▸ **rueda motriz** driving wheel ▸ **ruedas de aterrizaje** (*Aer*) landing wheels
[2] (= *círculo*) circle, ring; **en ~** in a ring ▸ **rueda de identificación** identification parade ▸ **rueda de prensa** press conference ▸ **rueda de reconocimiento** identification parade ▸ **rueda informativa** press conference
[3] (= *rodaja*) slice, round
[4] (*en torneo*) round
[5] (*Hist*) rack
[6] (= *pez*) sunfish
[7] [*de pavón*] spread tail; **hacer la ~** to spread its tail; ✦***MODISMO*** **hacer la ~ a algn** to court sb; to play up to sb, ingratiate o.s. with sb
[8] **dar ~ (en)** (*Caribe Aut*) to drive (around)

ruedecilla SF (= *rueda pequeña*) small wheel; [*de mueble*] roller, castor

ruedero SM wheelwright

ruedo SM [1] (*Taur*) bullring, arena
[2] (*Pol*) ring
[3] (= *contorno*) edge, border; (= *circunferencia*) circumference; [*de vestido*] hem
[4] (= *esterilla*) mat, round mat
[5] (*Cono Sur*) (= *suerte*) luck, gambler's luck
[6] (= *rotación*) turn, rotation

ruega *etc ver* **rogar**

ruego SM request; **a ~ de** at the request of; **accediendo a los ~s de** in response to the requests of; **"~s y preguntas"** (*en una conferencia*) "any other business"

rufián SM [1] (= *gamberro*) hooligan; (= *canalla*) scoundrel
[2] (= *chulo*) pimp

rufianería SF, **rufianismo** SM [*de chulo*] pimping, procuring; (*Jur*) living off immoral earnings

rufianesca SF criminal underworld

rufo ADJ [1] (= *pelirrojo*) red-haired; (= *rizado*) curly-haired
[2] (*) (= *satisfecho*) smug, self-satisfied; (= *engreído*) cocky*, boastful

rugbista SMF rugby player

rugby ['rugbi] SM rugby

rugido SM roar ▸ **rugido de dolor** howl *o* roar of pain ▸ **rugido de tripas** stomach rumblings *pl*, collywobbles* *pl*

rugir ▸conjug 3c◂ VI [1] [*león etc*] to roar; [*toro*] to bellow; [*mar*] to roar; [*tormenta, viento*] to roar, howl, rage; [*estómago*] to rumble; [*persona*] to roar; **~ de dolor** to roar *o* howl with pain
[2] (‡) (= *oler mal*) to pong*, stink

rugosidad SF roughness

rugoso ADJ 1 (= *áspero*) rough
2 (= *arrugado*) wrinkled, creased

ruibarbo SM rhubarb

ruido SM 1 (= *sonido*) noise; **¿has oído ese ~?** did you hear that noise?; **no hagas tanto ~** don't make so much noise; **no hagas ~, que el niño está durmiendo** don't make a sound, the baby's sleeping; **me hace ~ el estómago*** my stomach is rumbling; **lejos del mundanal ~** (*hum o liter*) far from the madding crowd (*liter*); **sin ~** quietly; ✦***MODISMOS* mucho ~ y pocas nueces** much ado about nothing; **es más el ~ que las nueces: prometieron reformas para este año, pero era más el ~ que las nueces** they promised reforms for this year, but it was all hot air; **los grandes beneficios anunciados son más el ~ que las nueces** the large profits they announced are not all what they were cracked up to be ► **ruido blanco** white noise ► **ruido de fondo** background noise ► **ruido de sables: en los cuarteles se oye ~ de sables** there's talk of rebellion in the ranks
2 (= *escándalo*) **hacer** *o* **meter ~** to cause a stir; **quitarse de ~s** to keep out of trouble

ruidosamente ADV 1 (= *estrepitosamente*) noisily, loudly
2 (= *de manera sensacionalista*) sensationally

ruidoso ADJ 1 (= *estrepitoso*) noisy
2 [*noticia*] sensational

ruin ADJ 1 (= *vil*) [*persona*] contemptible, mean
2 [*trato*] (= *injusto*) mean, shabby; (= *cruel*) heartless, callous
3 (= *tacaño*) mean, stingy
4 (= *pequeño*) small, weak
5 [*animal*] vicious

ruina SF 1 (*Fin*) ruin; **estaba al borde de la ~** he was on the brink of (financial) ruin; **la empresa le llevó a la ~** the venture ruined him (financially); **estar en la ~** to be ruined; **tanto gastar en viajes va a ser mi ~** spending all this money on travel is going to cost me a fortune
2 [*de edificio*] collapse; **amenazar ~** to threaten to collapse, be about to fall down
3 [*de imperio*] fall, decline; [*de persona*] ruin, downfall; **el alcohol va a ser mi ~** alcohol will be the ruin of me, alcohol will be my downfall; **esto contribuyó a su ~ política** this contributed to his political downfall
4 (= *persona ajada*) **estar hecho una ~** to be a wreck, look a wreck
5 **ruinas** ruins; **han descubierto unas ~s romanas** they have discovered some Roman ruins; **el castillo está en ~s** the castle is in ruins
6 (*Jur*‡) bird‡, prison sentence

ruindad SF 1 (= *cualidad*) meanness, lowness
2 (= *acto*) low act, mean act

ruinoso ADJ 1 (*Arquit*) ruinous; (= *destartalado*) tumbledown
2 (*Fin*) ruinous, disastrous

ruiseñor SM nightingale

rula SF (*Andes, CAm*) hunting knife

rular‡ ▸conjug 1a◂ VT to pass round

rulemán SM (*Cono Sur*) ball-bearing, roller bearing

rulenco ADJ (*Cono Sur*), **rulengo** ADJ (*Cono Sur*) weak, underdeveloped

rulero SM (*Andes*) hair curler, roller

ruleta SF roulette ► **ruleta rusa** Russian roulette

ruletear ▸conjug 1a◂ VI (*CAm, Méx*) to drive a taxi, drive a cab

ruleteo SM (*CAm, Méx*) taxi driving, cab driving

ruletero SM (*CAm, Méx*) taxi driver, cab driver

rulo[1] SM 1 (= *rodillo*) roller; (*Culin*) rolling pin
2 [*de pelo*] curler
3 (= *pelota*) ball, round mass
4 (*Andes, Cono Sur*) (= *rizo*) natural curl

rulo[2] SM (*Cono Sur*) (= *terreno*) well-watered ground

rulota SF caravan, trailer (*EEUU*)

ruma SF (*LAm*) heap, pile

Rumanía SF, **Rumania** SF Romania

rumano/a Ⓐ ADJ, SM/F Rumanian, Romanian
Ⓑ SM (*Ling*) Rumanian, Romanian

rumba[1] SF 1 (*Mús*) rumba
2 (*LAm*) (= *fiesta*) party, celebration

rumba[2] SF (*Cono Sur*) = **ruma**

rumbar ▸conjug 1a◂ Ⓐ VT (*LAm*) to throw
Ⓑ VI 1 (*Andes*) (= *zumbar*) to buzz
2 (*Andes, Cono Sur*) (= *orientarse*) to get one's bearings
Ⓒ **rumbarse** VPR (*Andes*) to make off, go away

rumbeador SM (*Andes, Cono Sur*) pathfinder, tracker

rumbear ▸conjug 1a◂ VI 1 (*LAm Mús*) to dance the rumba
2 (*LAm*) (= *seguir*) to follow a direction; (= *orientarse*) to find one's way, get one's bearings
3 (*Cuba**) (= *ir de rumba*) to have a party
4 (*Méx*) (*en bosque*) to clear a path (through the undergrowth)

rumbero Ⓐ ADJ 1 (*Andes, Cono Sur*) (= *rumbeador*) tracking, pathfinding
2 (*Caribe*) [*juerguista*] party-going, fond of a good time
Ⓑ SM (*Andes*) (*en bosque*) pathfinder, guide; [*de río*] river pilot

rumbo[1] SM 1 (= *dirección*) (*Aer, Náut*) course; **corregir el ~** to correct one's course; **perder el ~** (*Aer, Náut*) to go off course; **poner ~ a** to set a course for; **con ~ a: acababa de despegar con ~ a Rumanía** it had just taken off for Romania; **zarparon con ~ sur** they set a southerly course; **sin ~ (fijo)** [*pasear*] aimlessly; [*viajar*] with no fixed destination; **una existencia sin ~** an aimless existence
2 (= *tendencia*) **los acontecimientos han tomado un nuevo ~** events have taken a new turn; **los nuevos ~s de la estrategia occidental** the new lines of western strategy
3 (= *generosidad*) generosity, lavishness; **de mucho ~** = **rumboso**; **viajar con ~** to travel in style
4 (*LAm*) (= *fiesta*) party
5 (*Cono Sur*) (= *herida*) cut (on the head)

rumbo[2] SM (*Andes Orn*) hummingbird

rumbón* ADJ = **rumboso**

rumbosidad SF lavishness

rumboso ADJ 1 [*persona*] (= *generoso*) generous; (= *espléndido*) big, splendid
2 [*regalo*] lavish; [*boda, fiesta*] big, showy

rumia SF, **rumiación** SF rumination

rumiante ADJ, SM ruminant

rumiar ▸conjug 1b◂ Ⓐ VI 1 [*rumiante*] to chew the cud
2 (= *considerar*) to ruminate, ponder; (*pey*) to take too long to make up one's mind
Ⓑ VT 1 (= *masticar*) to chew
2 [+ *asunto*] to chew over

rumor SM 1 (= *noticia vaga*) rumour, rumor (*EEUU*); **circula** *o* **corre el ~ de que ...** there's a rumour going round that ...
2 (= *murmullo*) murmur; [*de voces*] buzz

rumoreado ADJ rumoured, rumored (*EEUU*)

rumorearse ▸conjug 1a◂ VPR **se rumorea que** it is rumoured *o* (*EEUU*) rumored that

rumoreo SM murmur, murmuring

rumorología SF rumours *pl*, rumors *pl* (*EEUU*)

rumorólogo/a SM/F scandalmonger

rumorosidad SF noise level

rumoroso ADJ (*liter*) murmuring; [*arroyo*] babbling

runa[1] SF rune

runa[2] SM (*Andes, Cono Sur*) Indian, Indian man

runa simi SM (*Andes*) Quechua, Quechua language

runcho ADJ 1 (*Andes*) (= *ignorante*) ignorant; (= *obstinado*) stubborn
2 (*CAm*) (= *tacaño*) mean

rundir ▸conjug 3a◂ (*Méx*) Ⓐ VT (= *guardar*) to keep; (= *ocultar*) to hide, put away
Ⓑ VI to become drowsy
Ⓒ **rundirse** VPR to fall fast asleep

rundún SM (*Cono Sur*) hummingbird

runfla* SF (*LAm*), **runflada*** SF (*LAm*) (= *montón*) lot, heap; (= *multitud*) crowd; (= *pandilla*) gang, gang of kids*

rúnico ADJ runic

runrún SM 1 [*de voces*] murmur
2 (= *rumor*) rumour, rumor (*EEUU*), buzz*
3 [*de una máquina*] whirr

runrunearse ▸conjug 1a◂ VPR **se runrunea que ...** the rumour *o* (*EEUU*) rumor is that ...

runruneo SM = **runrún 1**

ruñir ▸conjug 3h◂ VT, VI (*Andes, Méx*) = **roer**; (*Caribe*) = **roer 1, 2**

rupestre ADJ rock *antes de s*; **pintura ~** cave painting; **planta ~** rock plant

rupia SF (= *moneda*) rupee

ruptor SM contact breaker

ruptura SF 1 [*de cable, cerco*] **tenemos que encontrar el punto de ~ del cable** we need to find the point where the cable broke; **la ofensiva de ~ del cerco de Sarajevo** the attack to break the siege of Sarajevo
2 (= *interrupción*) [*de pacto, contrato*] breaking; [*de relaciones, negociaciones*] breaking-off; **la construcción de la autopista puede llevar a la ~ del equilibrio ecológico** the construction of the motorway could upset the ecological balance; **el incidente causó la ~ de los lazos políticos entre ambos países** the incident led to the breaking-off of diplomatic ties between the two countries
3 (= *disolución*) break-up; **la ~ de la unidad familiar** the break-up of the family unit; **los motivos de su ~ matrimonial** the reasons for the break-up of their marriage; **la ~ de la coalición electoral** the break-up of the electoral coalition
4 (= *división*) split, rupture (*frm*); **las diferencias entre ambos líderes pueden provocar una ~ interna** the differences between the

two leaders could cause an internal split *o* (*frm*) a rupture within the party
[5] (*con el pasado*) break; **este cambio supone una ~ con todo lo anterior** this change means a break with everything that went before
[6] (*Tenis*) break; **seis puntos de ~** six break points ► **ruptura de servicio** break of service, service break

rural Ⓐ ADJ rural
Ⓑ SF (*Arg Aut*) estate car, station wagon (*EEUU*)
Ⓒ SM **los ~es** (*Méx Hist*) (= *la policía*) the rural police

Rusia SF Russia ► **Rusia Soviética** Soviet Russia

ruso/a Ⓐ ADJ Russian
Ⓑ SM/F [1] (= *de Rusia*) Russian; **los Rusos** the Russians, the people of Russia
[2] (*Arg**) Jew
Ⓒ SM (*Ling*) Russian

rústica SF **libro en ~** paperback (book); **edición (en) ~** paperback edition; *ver tb* **rústico**

rusticidad SF [1] (= *calidad*) rusticity, rural character
[2] (= *tosquedad*) coarseness, uncouthness; (= *grosería*) crudity; (= *descortesía*) bad manners *pl*, unmannerliness

rústico/a Ⓐ ADJ [1] (= *del campo*) rustic, rural, country *antes de s*
[2] (= *tosco*) coarse, uncouth; (= *grosero*) crude; (= *descortés*) unmannerly
Ⓑ SM/F peasant, yokel, hillbilly (*EEUU*); *ver tb* **rústica**

rustidera SF roasting tin

ruta SF [1] [*de un viaje*] route
[2] (= *camino*) ► **ruta aérea** air route, airway ► **ruta de la seda** silk route, silk road ► **Ruta Jacobea** Way of St James (*pilgrim road to Santiago de Compostela*)
[3] (*Cono Sur*) (= *carretera*) road

rutero/a Ⓐ ADJ road *antes de s*
Ⓑ SM/F [1] (= *camionero*) truck driver
[2] (*Esp*) (*de fin de semana*) raver

rutilancia SF sparkle

rutilante ADJ (*liter*) shining, sparkling, glowing

rutilar ▸conjug 1a◂ VI (*liter*) to shine, sparkle

rutina SF routine; **por ~** from force of habit ► **rutina diaria** daily routine

rutinariamente ADV (= *de manera rutinaria*) in a routine way; (= *sin imaginación*) unimaginatively

rutinario ADJ [1] [*procedimiento*] routine; (= *de cada día*) ordinary, everyday
[2] [*persona*] ordinary; (= *sin imaginación*) unimaginative; [*creencia*] unthinking, automatic

rutinizarse ▸conjug 1f◂ VPR to become routine, become normal

Rvdo. ABR (= **Reverendo**) Rev, Revd

S s

S, s ['ese] SF (= *letra*) S, s

S ABR [1] (= **sur**) S
[2] (= **septiembre**) Sept; **el 11-S** 9-11, Nine-Eleven
[3] (= **sobresaliente**) v.g.
[4] (*Cine*) **película S** pornographic film

S. ABR (*Rel*) (= **San, Santa, Santo**) St

s. ABR [1] (= **siglo**) c
[2] (= **siguiente**) foll.

s/ ABR (*Com*) (= **su, sus**) yr

S.ª ABR (= **Sierra**) Mts

S.A. ABR [1] (*Com*) (= **Sociedad Anónima**) Ltd, plc, Corp (*EEUU*), Inc (*EEUU*)
[2] (= **Su Alteza**) HH

sáb. ABR (= **sábado**) Sat

sábado SM [1] (= *día de la semana*) Saturday; **del ~ en ocho días** Saturday week, a week on Saturday, the Saturday after next; **el ~ pasado** last Saturday; **el ~ próximo** *o* **que viene** this *o* next Saturday; **el ~ por la mañana** (on) Saturday morning; **la noche del ~** (on) Saturday night; **un ~ sí y otro no** ◊ **cada dos ~s** every other *o* second Saturday; **no va al colegio los ~s** he doesn't go to school on Saturdays; **vendrá el ~ (25 de marzo)** he will come on Saturday (March 25th) ► **Sábado de Gloria**, **Sábado Santo** Easter Saturday
[2] (*Rel*) [*de los judíos*] Sabbath
[3] ✦**MODISMO** **hacer ~** to do the weekly clean

sábalo SM shad

sabana SF savannah

sábana SF [1] [*de cama*] sheet; **la Sábana Santa de Turín** the Holy Shroud of Turin; ✦**MODISMOS** **encontrar las ~s*** to hit the hay*; **se le pegan las ~s** he oversleeps; **ponerse en la ~** to strike it lucky ► **sábana de agua** sheet of rain
[2] (*Rel*) altar cloth
[3] (‡) (= *dinero*) 1000-peseta note; **media ~** 500-peseta note ► **sábana verde** 1000-peseta note

sabandija SF [1] (= *animal*) bug, creepy-crawly*; **~s** vermin *sing* [2] (*) (= *persona*) louse* [3] (*Arg**) (= *diablillo*) rascal

sabanear ▸conjug 1a◂ Ⓐ VT [1] (*CAm*) (= *agarrar*) to catch
[2] (*CAm*) (= *halagar*) to flatter
[3] (*CAm, Caribe*) (= *perseguir*) to pursue, chase
Ⓑ VI (*LAm*) (= *recorrer la sabana*) to travel across a plain; (= *reunir el ganado*) to round up cattle on the savannah, scour the plain for cattle

➤ LENGUA Y USO: **saber A4** 42.4, 43.4

sabanero/a (*LAm*) Ⓐ ADJ (= *de la sabana*) savannah *antes de s*, of/from the savannah
Ⓑ SM/F plainsman/plainswoman
Ⓒ SM (*CAm*) (= *matón*) bully, thug

sabanilla SF [1] (*Rel*) altar cloth
[2] (*Cono Sur*) (= *colcha*) bedspread

sabañón SM chilblain

sabara SF (*Caribe*) light mist, haze

sabatario/a ADJ, SM/F sabbatarian

sabateño SM (*Caribe*) boundary stone

sabático ADJ [1] (*Rel, Univ*) sabbatical
[2] (= *del sábado*) Saturday *antes de s*

sabatino ADJ Saturday *antes de s*

sabedor ADJ **ser ~ de algo** to know about sth

sabelotodo* SMF INV know-all*, know-it-all (*EEUU**)

▼ **saber** ▸conjug 2m◂ Ⓐ VT [1] (= *tener conocimiento de*) [1·1] [+ *dato, información*] to know; **no sabía que era tu cumpleaños** I didn't know it was your birthday; **sé que me has mentido** I know you've lied to me; **lo sé** I know; **sin ~lo yo** without my knowledge, without me knowing; **hacer ~ algo a algn** to inform sb of sth, let sb know about sth; **quiero hacerle ~ que ...** I would like to inform *o* advise you that ...; **el motivo de esta carta es hacerle ~ que ...** I am writing to inform *o* advise you that ...
[1·2] (*locuciones*) **a ~** namely; **dos planetas, a ~, Venus y la Tierra** two planets, namely Venus and Earth; **a ~ si realmente lo compró** I wonder whether he really did buy it; **a ~ dónde lo tiene guardado** I wonder where he has it hidden away; **anda a ~** (*LAm*) = **vete a saber**, **demasiado bien sé que ...** I know only too well that ...; **¡no lo sabes bien!*** not half!*; **cualquiera sabe si ...** it's anybody's guess whether ...; **¡de haberlo sabido!** if only I'd known!; **lo dudo, pero nunca se sabe** I doubt it, but you never know; **para que lo sepas** let me tell you, for your information; **que yo sepa** as far as I know; **que sepamos** as far as we know; **un no sé qué** a certain something; **un no sé qué de afectado** a certain (element of) affectation; **¡quién sabe!** who knows!; **¿quién sabe?** who knows?, who can tell?, who's to say?; **¡si lo sabré yo!** I should know!; **tú sabrás (lo que haces)** I suppose you know (what you're doing); **¿tú qué sabes?** what do you know about it?; **¡vete a ~!** God knows!; **¡vete a ~ de dónde ha venido!** goodness only knows where he came from!; **vete tú a ~** your guess is as good as mine; **ya lo sabía yo** I thought as much; **¡yo qué sé!, ¡qué sé yo!** how should I know!, search me!*; ✦**MODISMOS** **cada uno sabe dónde le aprieta el zapato** everyone knows their own weaknesses; **no sabía dónde meterse** he didn't know what to do with himself; **no ~ ni papa** not to know the first thing about sth; *ver tb* **Briján**
[2] (= *enterarse de*) to find out; **en cuanto lo supimos fuimos a ayudarle** as soon as we found out, we went to help him; **cuando lo supe** when I heard *o* found out about it; **lograron ~ el secreto** they managed to learn the secret
[3] (= *tener noticias*) to hear; **desde hace seis meses no sabemos nada de él** we haven't heard from him for six months
[4] (= *tener destreza en*) **¿sabes ruso?** do you speak Russian?, can you speak Russian?; **no sé nada de cocina** I don't know anything about cookery, I know nothing about cookery; **~ hacer algo**: **sabe cuidar de sí mismo** he can take care of himself, he knows how to take care of himself; **¿sabes nadar?** can you swim?; **saben tratar muy bien al forastero** they know how to look after visitors; **¿sabes ir?** do you know the way?; **todavía no sabe orientarse por la ciudad** he still doesn't know his way around town; **pocos campeones saben perder** few champions are good losers; **es una persona que sabe escuchar** she's a good listener
[5] (*LAm*) **~ hacer** to be in the habit of doing; **no sabe venir por aquí** he doesn't usually come this way, he's not in the habit of coming along here
Ⓑ VI [1] (= *tener conocimiento*) **~ de algo** to know of sth; **sabe mucho de ordenadores** he knows a lot about computers; **sé de un sitio muy bueno** I know of a very good place; **hace mucho que no sabemos de ella** it's quite a while since we heard from her, we haven't had any news from her for quite a while
[2] (= *estar enterado*) to know; **costó muy caro, ¿sabe usted?** it was very expensive, you know; **un 5% no sabe, no contesta** there were 5% "don't knows"
[3] (= *tener sabor*) to taste; **no sabe demasiado bien** it doesn't taste too good; **sabe un poco amargo** it tastes rather bitter; **~ a** to taste of; **esto sabe a queso** this tastes of cheese; **esto sabe a demonio(s)** this tastes awful; ✦**MODISMO** **~le mal a algn**: **me supo muy mal lo que hicieron** I didn't like what they did, I wasn't pleased *o* didn't feel good

about what they did; **no me sabe mal que un amigo me gaste bromas** I don't mind a friend playing jokes on me, it doesn't bother me having a friend play jokes on me

Ⓒ **saberse** VPR [1] (*uso enfático*) **eso ya me lo sabía yo** I already knew that; **se lo sabe de memoria** she knows it by heart; ✦*MODISMO* **se las sabe todas*** he knows every trick in the book*

[2] (*uso impersonal*) [2·1] (= *ser conocido*) **ya se sabe que ...** it is known that ..., we know that ...; **no se sabe** nobody knows, it's not known; **no se saben las causas** the causes are not known *o* are unknown; **¿se puede ~ si ...?** can you tell me if *o* whether ...?; **¿quién es usted, si se puede ~?** who are you, may I ask?; **sépase que ...** let it be known that ...; **nunca más se supo de ellos** they were never heard of again

[2·2] (= *ser descubierto*) **se supo que ...** it was learnt *o* discovered that ...; **por fin se supo el secreto** finally the secret was revealed

[3] (*de uno mismo*) **se saben héroes** they know they are heroes

Ⓓ SM knowledge, learning; **según mi leal ~ y entender** (*frm*) to the best of my knowledge ► **saber hacer** (*Téc*) know-how; (*Literat*) savoir-faire ► **saber popular** folk wisdom

> **SABER**
>
> Por regla general, si **saber** va seguido de un infinitivo, se traduce por **can** cuando indica una habilidad permanente y por **know how** cuando se trata de la capacidad de resolver un problema concreto. La construcción correspondiente habrá de ser **can** + INFINITIVO *sin* **to** *o* **know how** + INFINITIVO *con* **to**:
>
> Jaime sabe tocar el piano
> ***Jaime can play the piano***
> ¿Sabes cambiar una rueda?
> ***Do you know how to change a wheel?***
>
> **NOTA:** Hay que tener en cuenta que **know** (sin **how**) nunca puede ir seguido directamente de un infinitivo en inglés.
>
> *Para otros usos y ejemplos ver la entrada.*

sabiamente ADV [1] (= *eruditamente*) learnedly, expertly

[2] (= *prudentemente*) wisely, sensibly

sabichoso* ADJ (*Caribe*) = **sabihondo**

sabidillo/a* SM/F know-all*, know-it-all (*esp EEUU**)

sabido Ⓐ PP *de* **saber**; **es ~ que** it is well known that; **como es ~** as we all know

Ⓑ ADJ [1] (= *consabido*) well-known, familiar

[2] (*iró*) [*persona*] knowledgeable, learned

[3] **de ~** (= *por supuesto*) for sure, certainly

[4] (*Andes*) (= *travieso*) mischievous, saucy

sabiduría SF (= *saber*) wisdom; (= *instrucción*) learning ► **sabiduría popular** folklore

sabiendas: a ~ ADV (= *sabiendo*) knowingly; (= *a propósito*) deliberately; **a ~ de que ...** knowing full well that ...

sabihondo/a ADJ, SM/F know-all*, know-it-all (*esp EEUU**)

sabio/a Ⓐ ADJ [1] [*persona*] (= *docto*) learned; (= *juicioso*) [*persona*] wise, sensible; ✦*MODISMO* **más ~ que Salomón** wiser than Solomon

[2] [*acción, decisión*] wise, sensible

[3] [*animal*] trained

Ⓑ SM/F (= *docto*) learned man/learned woman; (= *experto*) scholar, expert; **¡hay que escuchar al ~!** (*iró*) just listen to the professor!; ✦*REFRÁN* **de ~s es rectificar** it takes a wise man to recognize that he was wrong

sabiondo/a ADJ, SM/F = **sabihondo**

sablazo SM [1] (= *herida*) sword wound; (= *golpe*) sabre slash, saber slash (*EEUU*)

[2] (*) (= *gorronería*) sponging*, scrounging*; **dar** *o* **pegar un ~ a algn** (*en tienda, restaurante*) to rip sb off*; (*al pedir dinero*) to touch sb for a loan*; **vivir de ~s** to live by sponging *o* scrounging*; **la cuenta fue un ~*** the bill was astronomical

sable[1] SM (= *arma*) sabre, cutlass, saber (*EEUU*)

sable[2] SM (*Heráldica*) sable

sablear* ▸conjug 1a◂ VT **~ dinero a algn** to scrounge money from *o* off sb*; **~ algo a algn** to scrounge sth from *o* off sb*

sablista* SMF sponger*, scrounger*

sabor SM taste, flavour, flavor (*EEUU*); **con ~ a queso** cheese-flavoured; **este caramelo tiene ~ a naranja** this sweet tastes of orange, this sweet's orange-flavoured; **con un ligero ~ arcaico** with a slightly archaic flavour (to it); **sin ~** tasteless; (*fig*) insipid; ✦*MODISMO* **le deja a uno mal/buen ~ de boca** it leaves a nasty/pleasant taste in the mouth ► **sabor local** local colour, local color (*EEUU*)

saborcillo SM slight taste

saborear ▸conjug 1a◂ Ⓐ VT [1] [+ *comida*] (*apreciando el sabor*) to savour, savor (*EEUU*); (= *probar*) to taste

[2] (= *dar sabor a*) to flavour, flavor (*EEUU*)

[3] (= *deleitarse con*) [+ *venganza, momento, triunfo, victoria*] to relish, savour, savor (*EEUU*); [+ *desgracia ajena*] to delight in

Ⓑ **saborearse** VPR to smack one's lips (in anticipation); **~se algo** (*fig*) to relish the thought of sth

saborete SM slight taste

saborizante SM flavouring, flavoring (*EEUU*)

sabotaje SM sabotage ► **sabotaje industrial** industrial sabotage

saboteador(a) SM/F saboteur

sabotear ▸conjug 1a◂ VT to sabotage

Saboya SF Savoy

saboyano/a Ⓐ ADJ of/from Savoy

Ⓑ SM/F native/inhabitant of Savoy; **los ~s** the people of Savoy

sabré *etc ver* **saber**

sabrosera SF (*LAm*) tasty thing, titbit

sabroso ADJ [1] [*comida*] tasty, delicious

[2] (= *agradable*) [*libro*] solid, meaty; [*oferta*] substantial; [*sueldo*] fat

[3] [*broma, historia*] racy, daring

[4] (*Andes, Caribe, Méx*) (= *ameno*) pleasant

[5] (*Andes, Caribe, Méx*) (= *parlanchín*) talkative

[6] (*Méx*) (= *fanfarrón*) bigheaded, stuck-up*

sabrosón* ADJ [1] (*LAm*) = **sabroso 1**

[2] (*Andes*) (= *parlanchín*) talkative, chatty

sabrosura SF (*LAm*) [1] [*de comida*] tastiness

[2] (= *lo agradable*) pleasantness, delightfulness, sweetness

[3] (= *placer*) delight, enjoyment

sabueso Ⓐ SM (*Zool*) bloodhound

Ⓑ SMF (= *detective*) sleuth*

saburra SF fur (*on tongue*)

saburroso ADJ coated, furred

saca[1] SF [1] (= *saco*) big sack ► **saca de correo**, **saca de correos** mailbag

[2] (*LAm*) [*de ganado*] herd of cattle, moving herd of cattle

saca[2] SF (= *acción*) (*gen*) taking out, withdrawal; (*Com*) export; **estar de ~** (*Com*) to be on sale; [*mujer*] to be of marriageable age ► **saca carcelaria** illegal removal of a prisoner from prison (for execution)

sacabocados SM INV punch (*for making holes*)

sacabotas SM INV bootjack

sacabuche SM sackbut

sacabullas* SM INV (*Méx*) bouncer*

sacaclavos SM INV nail-puller, pincers *pl*

sacacorchos SM INV corkscrew

sacacuartos SM INV = **sacadineros**

sacada SF (*Andes, Cono Sur*) = **sacadura**

sacadera SF landing-net

sacadineros* SM INV [1] (= *baratija*) cheap trinket

[2] (= *diversión*) *money-wasting spectacle, worthless sideshow etc*

[3] (= *persona*) cheat

sacador(a) SM/F server

sacadura SF (*Andes, Cono Sur*) extraction

sacafaltas SMF INV faultfinder

sacamuelas* SMF INV [1] (*hum*) (= *dentista*) tooth-puller

[2] (= *parlanchín*) chatterbox*

sacaniguas SM INV (*Andes*) squib, Chinese cracker

sacaperras* SMF INV con artist*

sacapuntas SM INV pencil sharpener

sacar

> ▸conjug 1g◂
> [A] VERBO TRANSITIVO [C] VERBO PRONOMINAL
> [B] VERBO INTRANSITIVO
>
> *Para las expresiones* ***sacar adelante, sacar brillo, sacar algo en claro, sacar los colores a algn, sacar faltas a algo, sacar algo en limpio, sacar provecho, sacar a relucir,*** *ver la otra entrada.*

Ⓐ VERBO TRANSITIVO

[1] [= *poner fuera*] to take out, get out; **sacó el revólver y disparó** he drew his revolver and fired, he took *o* got his revolver out and fired; **he sacado las toallas al sol** I've put the towels out to dry in the sun; **saca la basura, por favor** please put *o* take the rubbish out; **~on a los rehenes por la ventana** they got the hostages out through the window; **~ a algn a bailar** to get sb up for a dance; **~ algo/a algn de**: **sacó toda su ropa del armario** she took all his clothes out of the wardrobe, she removed all his clothes from the wardrobe; **sacó el regalo del paquete** he removed the present from its wrapping; **voy a ~ dinero del cajero** I'm going to take *o* get some money out of the machine; **quiero ~ un libro de la biblioteca** I want to get a book out of the library; **¡sacadme de aquí!** get me out of here!; **nunca saca a su mujer de casa** he never takes his wife out; **mañana sacan a dos terroristas de cárcel** tomorrow two terrorists will be released from jail; **~ a pasear a algn** to take sb (out) for a walk; **saqué al perro a pasear** I took the dog (out) for a walk; ✦*MODISMO* **~ a algn de sí** to drive sb mad

[2] [*de una persona*] [+ *diente*] to take out; **me han sacado una muela** I've had a tooth (tak-

en) out; **¡deja ese palo, que me vas a ~ un ojo!** stop playing with that stick, you're going to poke my eye out!; **~ sangre a algn** to take blood from sb
3 *con partes del cuerpo* to stick out; **saca la lengua** stick your tongue out; **~ la lengua a alguien** to stick one's tongue out at sb; **~ la barbilla** to stick one's chin out; **saca la mano si vas a aparcar** stick your hand out if you're going to park; *ver tb* **pecho[1] 1**
4 *= obtener* 4·1 [+ *notas, diputados*] to get; **siempre saca buenas notas** he always gets good marks; **han sacado 35 diputados** they have had 35 members (elected); **¿y tú qué sacas con denunciarlo a la policía?** and what do you get out of *o* gain from reporting him to the police?; **no consiguió ~ todos los exámenes en junio** (*Esp*) she didn't manage to pass *o* get all her exams in June; **sacó un seis** (*con dados*) he threw a six
4·2 [+ *dinero*] **lo hago para ~ unas pesetas** I do it to earn *o* make a bit of money; **sacó el premio gordo** he got *o* won the jackpot; **sacamos una ganancia de ...** we made a profit of ...
4·3 [+ *puesto*] to get; **sacó la plaza de enfermera** she got the nursing post
4·4 [+ *información*] to get; **los datos están sacados de dos libros** the statistics are taken *o* come from two books; **¿de dónde has sacado esa idea?** where did you get that idea?; **¿de dónde has sacado esa chica tan guapa?** where did you get *o* find such a beautiful girlfriend?
4·5 **~ algo de** [+ *fruto, material*] to extract sth from; **sacan aceite de las almendras** they extract oil from the almonds; **han sacado petróleo del desierto del Sáhara** they have extracted oil from the Sahara desert
4·6 **~ algo a algn** to get sth out of sb; **no conseguirán ~le nada** they won't get anything out of him; **le ~on millones a base de chantajes** they got millions out of him by blackmailing him; **le ~on toda la información que necesitaban** they got all the information they needed from *o* out of him
4·7 [+ *conclusión*] to draw; **¿qué conclusión se puede ~ de todo esto?** what can be concluded from all of this?, what conclusion can be drawn from all of this?; **lo que se saca de todo esto es que ...** the conclusion to be drawn from all this is that ...
4·8 [+ *característica*] **ha sacado el pelo rubio de su abuela** she gets her blonde hair from her grandmother
5 *= comprar* [+ *entradas*] to get; **yo ~é los billetes** I'll get the tickets
6 *= lanzar* [+ *modelo nuevo*] to bring out; [+ *libro*] to bring out, publish; [+ *disco*] to release; [+ *moda*] to create; **han sacado sus nuevos productos al mercado** they have brought out their new product range; **ya han sacado las nuevas monedas de una peseta** the new one-peseta coins are out
7 *= hacer* [+ *foto*] to take; [+ *copia*] to make; **te voy a ~ una foto** I'm going to take a photo of you; **esta cámara saca buenas fotos** this camera takes good photos
8 *= resolver* **no conseguí ~ el problema** I couldn't solve the problem
9 *= mostrar* **le han sacado en el periódico** he was in the paper; **los ~on en la tele** they were on TV; **no me sacó en la foto** he missed me out of the photo; **estamos sacando anuncios en TV** we're running some adverts on TV
10 *= mencionar* **no me saques ahora eso** don't come to me with that now
11 *esp LAm = quitar* [+ *ropa*] to take off; [+ *mancha*] to get out *o* off, remove (*frm*); **~ la funda a un fusil** to take the cover off a rifle
12 *= aventajar en* **al terminar la carrera le sacaba 10 metros al adversario** he finished the race 10 metres ahead of his rival; **le saca 10cm a su hermano** he is 10cm taller than his brother
13 *= salvar* to get out; **nos sacó de esa penosa situación** she got us out of that difficult situation; *ver tb* **apuro 1**
14 *= poner* [+ *apodo, mote*] to give
15 *Dep* 15·1 (*Tenis*) to serve
15·2 (*Ftbl*) **saca el balón Kiko** (*en saque de banda*) the throw-in is taken by Kiko; (*en falta*) Kiko takes the free kick; **~ una falta** to take a free kick
16 *Cos* [+ *prenda de vestir*] (= *ensanchar*) to let out; (= *alargar*) to let down
17 *Naipes* to play
Ⓑ VERBO INTRANSITIVO
1 *Tenis* to serve
2 *Ftbl* (*en córner, tiro libre*) to take the kick; (*en saque de banda*) to take the throw-in; **después de marcar un gol, saca el contrario** after a goal has been scored, the opposing team kicks off
Ⓒ **sacarse** VERBO PRONOMINAL
1 *= extraer* [+ *objeto*] to take out; [+ *diente*] to have out; **se sacó la mano del bolsillo** he took his hand out of his pocket; **casi me saco un ojo con la barra de hierro** I almost poked *o* took my eye out with the iron bar; **se tiene que ~ una muela** she has got to have a tooth out
2 *esp LAm = quitarse* **~se la ropa** to take one's clothes off
3 *= conseguir* to get; **~se unas pesetas** to get *o* make a few pesetas; **quiero ~me un doctorado** I want to get a PhD; **~se el carnet de conducir** to get one's driving licence, pass one's driving test; **~se el título de abogado** to qualify as a lawyer
4 *Méx = irse* to leave, go away; **¡sáquese de aquí!** get out of here!

sacarina SF saccharin, saccharine
sacarino ADJ saccharin, saccharine
sacatín SM (*Andes*) still
sacerdocio SM priesthood
sacerdotal ADJ priestly
sacerdote SM priest; **sumo ~** high priest ► **sacerdote obrero** worker priest
sacerdotisa SF priestess
sacha ADJ INV (*LAm*) 1 (= *fingido*) false, sham; **~ médico** quack
2 (= *desmañado*) bungling, unskilled; **~ carpintero** clumsy carpenter
sachadura SF weeding
sachar ▸conjug 1a◂ VT to weed
sacho SM weeding hoe
saciado ADJ **~ de** (*lit*) sated with; (*fig*) steeped in
saciar ▸conjug 1b◂ Ⓐ VT 1 [+ *hambre*] to satisfy; [+ *sed*] to quench
2 [+ *deseos, curiosidad*] to satisfy; [+ *ambición*] to fulfil, fulfill (*EEUU*)
Ⓑ **saciarse** VPR 1 (*de comida, bebida*) to sate *o* satiate o.s. (**con, de** with)
2 (= *satisfacerse*) to be satisfied (**con, de** with)
saciedad SF satiation, satiety; **comer hasta la ~** to eat one's fill; **repetir hasta la ~** to repeat ad nauseam
saco[1] SM 1 (= *costal*) (*referido al contenedor*) bag, sack; (*referido al contenido*) bagful; (*Mil*) kitbag; (*Dep*) punchball; ✦***MODISMOS*** **a ~s** by the ton; **por fin lo tenemos en el ~*** we've finally talked him round*; **no es** *o* **no parece ~ de paja** he can't be written off as unimportant; **caer en ~ roto** to fall on deaf ears; **no echar algo en ~ roto** to be careful not to forget sth; **dar a algn por ~**** to screw sb**; **mandar a algn a tomar por ~**** to tell sb to get stuffed**; **ser un ~ sin fondo** to spend money like water; **ser un ~ de huesos** to be a bag of bones ► **saco de arena** sandbag ► **saco de dormir** sleeping bag ► **saco postal** mailbag, postbag ► **saco terrero** sandbag
2 (*Anat*) sac ► **saco amniótico** amniotic sac
3 (= *gabán*) long coat, loose-fitting jacket; (*LAm*) (= *chaqueta*) jacket; (*Andes*) (= *jersey*) jumper
4 (‡) (= *cárcel*) nick‡, prison
saco[2] SM (*Mil*) sack; **entrar a ~ en** to sack
sacón/ona Ⓐ ADJ (*) 1 (*CAm*) [*soplón*] sneaky; [*cobista*] flattering, soapy*
2 (*LAm*) (= *entrometido*) nosey*, prying
Ⓑ SM/F (*) 1 (*CAm*) (= *zalamero*) flatterer, creep‡
2 (*LAm*) (= *entrometido*) nosey-parker*
Ⓒ SM (*Cono Sur*) woman's outdoor coat
saconear* ▸conjug 1a◂ VT (*CAm*) to soft-soap*
saconería* SF 1 (*CAm*) (= *zalamería*) flattery, soft soap*
2 (*LAm*) (= *curiosidad*) prying
SACRA SM ABR (*Arg*) = **Sindicato de Amas de Casa de la República Argentina**

SACRA

Founded in 1984, **SACRA**, *or the* **Sindicato de Amas de Casa de la República Argentina**, *was the world's first trade union for housewives. One of its main aims has been to redefine housework as employment and to obtain for its members the salaries, pensions and health benefits traditionally associated with union membership. It has developed an educational programme designed to improve women's job opportunities, organized cheap holidays for housewives and obtained free medical treatment for its members. While union membership has allowed thousands of women to take part in public affairs, critics believe that the idea that housewives should have salaries simply reaffirms the stereotypical view that women function best in the home and, in the long run, may encourage non-participation outside.*

sacral ADJ religious, sacral
sacralización SF consecration, canonization
sacralizar ▸conjug 1f◂ VT to consecrate
sacramental ADJ (*Rel*) [*rito*] sacramental; [*palabras*] ritual
sacramentar ▸conjug 1a◂ VT to administer the sacraments to

sacramento SM sacrament; **el Santísimo Sacramento** the Blessed Sacrament; **recibir los ~s** to receive the sacraments

sacrificado ADJ [1] [*profesión, vida*] demanding
[2] [*persona*] self-sacrificing

sacrificar ▸conjug 1g◂ Ⓐ VT [1] (*Rel*) to sacrifice (**a** to)
[2] (= *matar*) [+ *ganado*] to slaughter; [+ *animal doméstico*] to put to sleep
Ⓑ **sacrificarse** VPR to sacrifice o.s.

sacrificio SM [1] (*Rel*) sacrifice; **el ~ de la misa** the sacrifice of the mass
[2] [*de animal*] slaughter, slaughtering

sacrilegio SM sacrilege

sacrílego ADJ sacrilegious

sacristán SM verger, sexton, sacristan

sacristía SF [1] (*Rel*) vestry, sacristy
[2] (‡) (= *bragueta*) flies *pl*; (= *horcajadura*) crotch

sacro Ⓐ ADJ [*arte, música*] sacred; **Sacro Imperio Romano** Holy Roman Empire
Ⓑ SM (*Anat*) sacrum

sacrosanto ADJ sacrosanct

sacuara SF (*Andes*) bamboo plant

sacudida SF [1] (= *agitación*) shake, shaking; **dar una ~ a una alfombra** to beat a carpet; **avanzar dando ~s** to bump *o* jolt *o* lurch along
[2] (= *movimiento brusco*) [*de cuerpo, rodilla*] jerk; [*de cabeza*] toss
[3] [*de terremoto*] shock; [*de explosión*] blast; **la ~ de la bomba llegó hasta aquí** the bomb blast could be felt here ► **sacudida eléctrica** electric shock
[4] (= *alteración brusca*) [*de situación*] violent change; (*Pol*) upheaval; **hay que darle una ~** he needs a jolt

sacudido ADJ [1] (= *brusco*) ill-disposed, unpleasant
[2] (= *difícil*) intractable
[3] (= *resuelto*) determined

sacudidura SF, **sacudimiento** SM = **sacudida**

sacudir ▸conjug 3a◂ Ⓐ VT [1] (= *agitar*) [+ *árbol, edificio, cabeza*] to shake; [+ *ala*] to flap; [+ *alfombra*] to beat; [+ *colchón*] to shake, shake the dust out of
[2] (= *quitar*) [+ *tierra*] to shake off; [+ *cuerda*] to jerk, tug
[3] (= *conmover*) to shake; **una tremenda emoción sacudió a la multitud** a great wave of excitement ran through the crowd; **~ a algn de su depresión** to shake sb out of his depression; **~ los nervios a algn** to shatter sb's nerves
[4] (*) (= *pegar*) **~ a algn** to belt sb*
[5] **~ dinero a algn*** to screw money out of sb*
Ⓑ **sacudirse** VPR (*uno mismo*) to shake o.s.; [+ *brazo, pelo*] to shake; **el perro se sacudía el rabo** the dog was wagging its tail; **sacúdete la arena del pelo** shake the sand out of your hair; **salió del mar sacudiéndose el agua** he came out of the sea shaking the water off himself; **el caballo se sacudía las moscas con la cola** the horse brushed off the flies with its tail; **por fin se la han sacudido** they've finally got rid of her

sacudón SM (*LAm*) violent shake

S.A. de C.V. ABR (*Méx*) (= **Sociedad Anónima de Capital Variable**) Ltd, plc, Corp (*EEUU*), Inc (*EEUU*)

sádico/a Ⓐ ADJ sadistic
Ⓑ SM/F sadist

sadismo SM sadism

sadista SMF sadist

sado* ADJ = **sadomasoquista**

sadoca‡ SMF = **sadomasoquista**

sado-maso* SM S & M*

sadomasoquismo SM sadomasochism

sadomasoquista Ⓐ ADJ sadomasochistic
Ⓑ SMF sadomasochist

saeta SF [1] (*Mil*) arrow, dart
[2] (= *aguja*) [*de reloj*] hand; [*de brújula*] magnetic needle
[3] (*Mús*) *sacred song in flamenco style*
[4] (*Rel*) ejaculatory prayer

saetera SF loophole

saetín SM [1] [*de molino*] millrace
[2] (*Téc*) tack

safado* ADJ [1] (*LAm*) (= *loco*) mad, crazy
[2] (*Arg*) (= *despejado*) cute*, alert, bright

safagina SF (*Andes*), **safajina** SF (*Andes*) uproar, commotion

safari SM safari; **estar de ~** to be on safari; ✦***MODISMO*** **contar ~s*** to shoot a line*

safo‡ SM hankie*, handkerchief

saga SF [1] (*Literat*) saga
[2] (= *clan*) clan, dynasty

sagacidad SF (= *astucia*) shrewdness, cleverness; (= *perspicacia*) sagacity

sagaz ADJ [1] [*persona*] (= *astuto*) shrewd, clever; (= *perspicaz*) sagacious
[2] [*perro*] keen-scented

sagazmente ADV (= *con astucia*) shrewdly, cleverly; (= *con perspicacia*) sagaciously

Sagitario SM Sagittarius

sagrado Ⓐ ADJ [*lugar, libro*] holy, sacred; [*deber*] sacred; **Sagradas Escrituras** Holy Scriptures; **Sagrada Familia** Holy Family; *ver tb* **vaca 1**
Ⓑ SM sanctuary, asylum; **acogerse a ~** to seek sanctuary

sagrario SM sacrarium

sagú SM sago

Sahara [sa'ara] SM, **Sáhara** ['saxara] SM Sahara

saharaui [saxa'raui] Ⓐ ADJ Saharan
Ⓑ SMF native/inhabitant of the Sahara; **los ~s** the people of the Sahara

sahariana SF safari jacket

sahariano/a ADJ, SM/F = **saharaui**

Sahel SM Sahel

sahumadura SF = **sahumerio**

sahumar ▸conjug 1a◂ VT [1] (= *incensar*) to perfume, perfume with incense
[2] (= *fumigar*) to smoke, fumigate

sahumerio SM [1] (= *acto*) perfuming with incense
[2] (= *humo*) aromatic smoke
[3] (= *sustancia*) aromatic substance

S.A.I. ABR (= **Su Alteza Imperial**) HIH

saibó SM (*LAm*), **saibor** SM (*Andes, Caribe*) sideboard

saín SM [1] (= *grasa*) [*de animal*] animal fat; [*de pescado*] fish oil (*used for lighting*)
[2] (*en la ropa*) dirt, grease

sainete SM [1] (*Teat*) one-act farce, one-act comedy
[2] (*Culin*) (= *salsa*) seasoning, sauce; (= *bocadito*) titbit, delicacy

> **SAINETE**
>
> *A* ***sainete*** *is a humorous short, generally one-act, verse play sometimes performed as an interlude between the acts of a major play.* ***Sainetes*** *were developed in the 18th century by playwrights such as Ramón de la Cruz, and were largely based on satirical observations of ordinary people's lives and reflected this in the language they were written in. They were still being written by authors such as Carlos Arniches well into the 20th century.*
>
> ⇨ *See also* ENTREMÉS

sainetero/a SM/F, **sainetista** SMF writer of *sainetes*

sajar ▸conjug 1a◂ VT to cut open, lance

sajín* SM (*CAm*), **sajino*** SM (*CAm*) underarm odour, smelly armpits *pl*

sajón/ona ADJ, SM/F Saxon

Sajonia SF Saxony

sajornar ▸conjug 1a◂ VT (*Caribe*) to pester, harass

sal¹ SF [1] (*Culin, Quím*) salt ► **sal amoníaca** sal ammoniac ► **sal común** kitchen salt, cooking salt ► **sal de cocina** kitchen salt, cooking salt ► **sal de eno** (*CAm*) fruit salts, liver salts ► **sal de fruta(s)** fruit salts ► **sal de la Higuera** Epsom salts ► **sal de mesa** table salt ► **sal gema** rock salt ► **sales aromáticas** smelling salts ► **sales de baño** bath salts ► **sales minerales** mineral salts ► **sal gorda** kitchen salt, cooking salt ► **sal volátil** sal volatile
[2] [*de persona*] (= *gracia*) wit; (= *encanto*) charm; **tiene mucha ~** he's very amusing
[3] (*LAm*) (= *mala suerte*) misfortune, piece of bad luck

sal² *ver* **salir**

sala SF [1] (*en casa, tb* **~ de estar**) living room, sitting room, lounge; (= *cuarto grande*) hall; [*de castillo*] hall
[2] (= *local público*) (*Teat, Mús*) auditorium; (*Cine*) cinema, movie theater (*EEUU*); (*Jur*) court; (*Med*) ward; **deporte en ~** indoor sport; **un cine con diez ~s** a cinema with ten screens; **Titanic lo ponen en la ~ tres** Titanic is on screen three ► **sala capitular** chapterhouse, meeting room ► **sala cinematográfica** cinema, movie theater (*EEUU*) ► **sala de alumbramiento** delivery room ► **sala de autoridades** (*Aer*) VIP lounge ► **sala de banderas** guardroom ► **sala de cine** cinema, movie theater (*EEUU*) ► **sala de conciertos** concert hall ► **sala de conferencias** (*gen*) conference hall; (*Univ*) lecture hall, lecture theatre, lecture theater (*EEUU*) ► **sala de consejos** meeting room, conference room ► **sala de consulta** reading room ► **sala de embarque** departure lounge ► **sala de espera** (*Med, Ferro*) waiting room; (*Aer*) departure lounge ► **sala de fiestas** night club (*with cabaret*) ► **sala de grados** graduation hall ► **sala de juegos** (*en casino*) gaming room; (*en hotel, barco*) casino ► **sala de juntas** (*Com*) boardroom ► **sala de justicia** law court ► **sala de lectura** reading room ► **sala de lo civil** civil court ► **sala de lo criminal**, **sala de lo penal** criminal court

► **sala de máquinas** (*Náut*) engine room ► **sala de muestras** showroom ► **sala de operaciones** operating theatre, operating room (*EEUU*) ► **sala de partos** delivery room ► **sala de prensa** press room ► **sala de profesores** staffroom ► **sala de recibo** parlour ► **sala de salidas** departure lounge ► **sala de subastas** saleroom, auction room ► **sala de urgencias** accident and emergency department, casualty department ► **sala X** adult cinema
3 (= *muebles*) suite of living room furniture, lounge suite

salacidad SF salaciousness, prurience

sala-cuna SF (*pl* **salas-cuna**) (*Cono Sur*) day-nursery

saladar SM salt marsh

saladería SF (*Cono Sur*) meat-curing plant

saladito SM (*Cono Sur*) nibble, snack, bar snack

salado ADJ 1 (*Culin*) (= *con sal*) salt *antes de s*, salted; (= *con demasiada sal*) salty; (= *no dulce*) savoury; **agua salada** salt water; **está muy ~** it's very salty
2 (= *persona*) (= *gracioso*) amusing; (= *encantador*) charming; **¡qué ~!** (= *divertido*) how amusing!; (*iró*) very droll!; **es un tipo muy ~** he's a very amusing chap
3 [*lenguaje*] rich, racy
4 (*LAm*) (= *desgraciado*) unlucky, unfortunate
5 (*Cono Sur**) (= *caro*) [*objeto*] expensive; [*precio*] very high

SALADO

• **Salado** se traduce por **salt** al referirse al agua de mar (por oposición a agua dulce) o a un producto que ha sido curado con sal:

El Caspio es un lago de agua salada
The Caspian Sea is a salt lake
El bacalao salado se emplea mucho en la cocina española
Salt cod is used a great deal in Spanish cooking

• **Salado**, por oposición a dulce, se traduce por **savoury**:

...platos dulces y salados...
...sweet and savoury dishes...

• Si algo está **salado** porque sabe a sal o porque contiene demasiada sal, se debe traducir por **salty**:

Estas albóndigas están muy saladas
These meatballs are very salty

NOTA: **Salty** es la única de estas tres traducciones que se puede usar en grado superlativo o comparativo:

Esta carne está mucho más salada que la de ayer
This meat is much saltier than what we had yesterday

NOTA: Si nos referimos a almendras o cacahuetes salados se debe emplear **salted**.
Para otros usos y ejemplos ver la entrada.

Salamanca SF Salamanca

salamanca SF (*Cono Sur*) 1 (= *cueva*) cave, grotto
2 (= *lugar oscuro*) dark place
3 (= *brujería*) witchcraft, sorcery

salamandra SF salamander

salamanqués/esa ADJ, SM/F = **salmantino**

salamanquesa SF lizard, gecko

salame SM 1 (*Culin*) salami
2 (*Cono Sur**) idiot, thickhead*

salami SM salami

salar[1] SM (*Andes, Cono Sur*) (= *yacimiento*) salt flat, salt pan; (= *mina*) salt mine

salar[2] ▸conjug 1a◂ VT 1 (*Culin*) (*para poner salado*) to add salt to, put salt in; (*para conservar*) to salt
2 (*LAm*) (= *arruinar*) to ruin, spoil; (= *gafar*) to bring bad luck to, jinx*; (= *maldecir*) to curse, wish bad luck on
3 (*Andes*) [+ *ganado*] to feed salt to
4 (*CAm, Caribe*) (= *deshonrar*) to dishonour

salarial ADJ wage *antes de s*; **reclamación ~** wage claim

salario SM wage, wages *pl*, pay, salary ► **salario base** basic wage ► **salario de hambre**, **salario de miseria** starvation wage ► **salario inicial** starting salary ► **salario mínimo** minimum wage ► **salario mínimo interprofesional** guaranteed minimum wage

salaz ADJ salacious, prurient

salazón SF 1 (= *acto*) salting
2 (*Culin*) (= *carne*) salted meat; (= *pescado*) salted fish
3 (*CAm, Caribe, Méx*) (= *mala suerte*) bad luck

salazonera SF salting plant (*for salting fish*)

salbeque SM (*CAm*) knapsack, backpack (*esp EEUU*)

salbute SM (*Méx*) stuffed tortilla

salceda SF, **salcedo** SM willow plantation

salchicha SF sausage

salchichería SF pork butcher's (shop)

salchichón SM *salami-type sausage*

salchipapa SF (*Andes*) *kind of kebab*

salcochar ▸conjug 1a◂ VT to boil in salt water

saldar ▸conjug 1a◂ Ⓐ VT 1 (*Com*) [+ *cuenta*] to settle, pay; [+ *deuda*] to settle, pay off
2 [+ *diferencias*] to settle
3 (= *liquidar*) [+ *existencias*] to clear, sell off; [+ *libros*] to remainder
Ⓑ **saldarse** VPR **~se con algo** to result in sth; **el accidente se ha saldado con cuatro muertos** the accident resulted in four deaths, four people died in the accident

saldo SM 1 [*de cuenta*] balance; **comprobé el ~ de mi cuenta** I checked my account balance ► **saldo acreedor** credit balance ► **saldo activo** active balance ► **saldo a favor** credit balance ► **saldo anterior** balance brought forward ► **saldo comercial** trade balance ► **saldo deudor** debit balance ► **saldo en contra** debit balance, adverse balance ► **saldo final** final balance ► **saldo negativo** debit balance, adverse balance ► **saldo pasivo** debit balance ► **saldo positivo** credit balance ► **saldo vencido** balance due
2 (= *liquidación*) sale; **precio de ~** sale price; **un abrigo que compré en los ~s** a coat I bought in the sales
3 (= *pago*) settlement, payment
4 [*de móvil*] credit; **no me queda ~ en el móvil** I haven't any credit left on my mobile
5 (= *resultado final*) **la manifestación acabó con un ~ de 20 personas heridas** a total of 20 people were injured in the demonstration; **el ~ oficial es de 28 muertos** the official toll is 28 dead
6 **ser un ~*** [*cosa muy usada*] to have had it*; [*persona inútil*] to be hopeless, be a dead loss*; **cómprate otro abrigo, el que llevas es un auténtico ~** you should get yourself another coat, the one you're wearing has had it*; **eres un auténtico ~, no sabes ni freír un huevo** you're hopeless *o* you're a dead loss, you can't even boil an egg*

saledizo Ⓐ ADJ projecting
Ⓑ SM projection, overhang; **en ~** projecting, overhanging

salera SF (*Cono Sur*) = **salina**

salero SM 1 [*de mesa*] salt cellar, salt shaker (*EEUU*)
2 (= *almacén*) salt store
3 [*de persona*] (= *ingenio*) wit; (= *encanto*) charm; (= *atractivo*) sex appeal, allure
4 (*Agr*) salt lick
5 (*Cono Sur*) = **salina**

saleroso* ADJ = **salado 2**

saleta SF small room

salga *etc ver* **salir**

salida SF 1 [*de un lugar*] **le prohibieron la ~ del país** he was forbidden to leave the country; **exigen la ~ de las tropas extranjeras** they are demanding the withdrawal of foreign troops; **tras su ~ de la cárcel** when he came out of prison; **a la ~**: **te esperaremos a la ~** we'll wait for you on the way out; **a la ~ del cine fuimos a tomar una copa** after the cinema we went for a drink; **sondeos realizados a la ~ de las urnas** exit polls; **hubo ~ a hombros para el primero de los diestros** the first matador was carried out of the ring shoulder-high; **dar ~ a**: **el pasillo que da ~ a la pista de tenis** the passageway which leads out (on)to the tennis court; **necesitaba dar ~ a su creatividad** he needed to give expression to *o* find an outlet for his creativity; **dio ~ a su indignación** he gave vent to his anger; **puerta de ~** exit door; *ver tb* **visado**
2 (= *aparición*) **los fans esperaban su ~ al escenario** the fans were waiting for her to come (out) onto the stage; **tras la ~ de los futbolistas al terreno de juego** after the footballers came/went out onto the pitch; **la venda detuvo la ~ de sangre** the bandage stopped the flow of blood; **precio de ~** [*de objeto subastado*] starting price; [*de acciones*] offer price ► **salida del sol** sunrise
3 (= *lugar*) [*de edificio*] exit, way out; [*de autopista*] exit, turn-off; **¿dónde está la ~?** where's the exit *o* the way out?; **"salida"** (*encima de la puerta*) "exit"; (*en el pasillo*) "way out", "exit"; **una cueva sin ~** a cave with no way out; **el ejército controla las ~s de la ciudad** the army controls the roads out of the city; **tener ~ a algo**: **nuestro edificio tiene ~ a las dos calles** our building has access onto both streets; **un país que no tiene ~ al mar** a country with no access to the sea; **la sala tiene ~ al jardín** the living room opens on to the garden ► **salida de artistas** stage door ► **salida de emergencia** emergency exit ► **salida de incendios** fire exit; *ver tb* **callejón**
4 [*de avión, tren*] departure; **la hora de ~ del vuelo** the flight departure time; **"salidas internacionales"** "international departures"; **"salidas nacionales"** "domestic departures"; **el autobús efectuará su ~ desde el andén número cuatro** the bus will depart from bay number four; **después de la ~ del tren** after the train leaves, after the departure of the train
5 (= *escapada*) [*de viaje*] trip; [*de excursión*]

trip, outing; (*por la noche*) night out, evening out; **en mi primera ~ al extranjero** on my first trip abroad, on my first foreign trip; **me controlaban mucho las ~s por la noche** they kept tight control of my nights out *o* my going out at night; **es su primera ~ desde que dio a luz** it's the first time she's been out since she gave birth ► **salida al campo** field trip

6 (= *comienzo*) [*de carrera, desfile*] start; **fuimos a ver la ~ de la procesión** we went to see the start of the procession, we went to see the procession move off; **"salida"** "start"; **los corredores estaban preparados para la ~** the runners were ready for the start (of the race); **acudieron a los puestos de ~** they took their starting positions; **Palmer tuvo una mala ~ del tee** (*Golf*) Palmer played a poor tee shot; **dar la ~** to give the starting signal; **es el encargado de dar la ~ a la carrera** he is the one who starts the race *o* gives the starting signal for the race; **tomar la ~** (= *empezar*) to start the race; (= *participar*) to take part, compete ► **salida en falso, salida falsa** false start ► **salida lanzada** running start, flying start ► **salida nula** false start ► **salida parada** standing start; *ver tb* **parrilla 2**

7 (*Teat*) (*al entrar en escena*) appearance; (*para recibir aplausos*) curtain-call; **hago una sola ~ al principio de la obra** I only make one appearance at the beginning of the play; **hicieron tres ~s en los aplausos** they took three curtain calls

8 (= *solución*) solution; **buscan una ~ negociada al conflicto** they are seeking a negotiated solution to the conflict; **la única ~ está en la negociación** the only way out is through negotiation, the only solution is to negotiate; **buscan en la música una ~ a sus frustraciones** they try to find an outlet for their frustration in music; **no le quedaba otra ~ que la dimisión** she had no alternative *o* option but to resign

9 (*al hablar*) **¡qué buena ~!** that was a really witty comment!; **tiene unas ~s que te mueres de risa** some of the things he comes out with are just hilarious ► **salida de bombero** (*Esp hum*): **¡vaya ~s de bombero que tuvo!** he dropped some real clangers!* ► **salida de tono**: **fue una ~ de tono** it was inappropriate *o* uncalled-for

10 (*Com*) [*de producto*] launch; **dar ~ a**: **dar ~ a los excedentes agrícolas** to find an outlet for surplus produce; **dimos ~ a nuestras existencias en dos meses** we sold off our stock in two months; **tener ~** to sell well; **tener una ~ difícil** to be a hard sell; **tener una ~ fácil** to have a ready market, be a soft sell

11 (*Fin*) (= *cargo*) debit entry; **entradas y ~s** income and expenditure

12 **salidas** (*en el trabajo*) openings, job opportunities; **esa carrera no tiene apenas ~s** there are very few openings *o* job opportunities for someone with that degree ► **salidas profesionales** job opportunities

13 (*Téc*) [*de aire, gas, vapor*] vent; [*de agua*] outlet; **tiene ~s de aire caliente por los laterales** it has hot air vents on the sides; **los orificios de ~ de vapor** the steam vents; **apertura de ~ del agua** water outlet

14 (*Inform*) output ► **salida impresa** hard copy

15 (= *prenda*) ► **salida de baño** (*Cono Sur*) (*en casa*) bathrobe; (*en playa, piscina*) beach robe ► **salida de teatro** evening wrap

16 (*Arquit*) (= *saliente*) projection

17 (*Mil*) (*para el ataque*) sortie

18 (*Naipes*) lead

salido Ⓐ PP *de* **salir**

Ⓑ ADJ 1 (= *prominente*) [*rasgos*] prominent; [*ojos*] bulging; [*dientes*] protruding

2 (*Esp**) (= *cachondo*) randy*, horny*; **estar ~** [*animal*] to be on heat; [*persona*] to be in the mood, feel randy*, feel horny*

3 (*) (= *osado*) daring; (*pey*) rash, reckless

salidor ADJ 1 (*LAm*) (= *fiestero*) fond of going out a lot

2 (*Caribe*) (= *buscapleitos*) argumentative

saliente Ⓐ ADJ 1 (*Arquit*) projecting

2 [*rasgo*] prominent

3 (= *importante*) salient

4 [*sol*] rising

5 [*miembro*] outgoing, retiring

Ⓑ SM 1 (*Arquit*) projection

2 [*de carretera*] hard shoulder, verge, berm (*EEUU*)

3 (*Mil*) salient

salina SF 1 (= *mina*) salt mine

2 (= *depresión*) salt pan

3 **salinas** (= *fábrica*) saltworks; (= *saladar*) salt flats

salinera SF (*Andes, Caribe*) = **salina**

salinidad SF salinity, saltiness

salinización SF (= *acto*) salinization; (= *estado*) salinity

salinizar ▸conjug 1f◂ Ⓐ VT to salinize, make salty

Ⓑ **salinizarse** VPR to become salty

salino ADJ saline

salir

▸conjug 3q◂

A VERBO INTRANSITIVO B VERBO PRONOMINAL

Para las expresiones ***salir adelante, salir ganando, salir perdiendo, salir de viaje****, ver la otra entrada.*

Ⓐ VERBO INTRANSITIVO

1 = ***partir*** [*persona*] to leave; [*transportes*] to leave, depart (*frm*); (*Náut*) to leave, sail; **el autocar sale a las ocho** the coach leaves at eight; **sale un tren cada dos horas** there is a train every two hours; **~ de** to leave; **salimos de Madrid a las ocho** we left Madrid at eight; **saldremos del hotel temprano** we'll leave the hotel early; **quiere ~ del país** she wants to leave the country; **¿a qué hora sales de la oficina?** what time do you leave the office?; **salgo de clase a las cinco** I finish school at five; **~ para** to set off for; **después de comer salimos para Palencia** after we had eaten we set off for Palencia

2 = ***no entrar*** (= *ir fuera*) to go out; (= *venir fuera*) to come out; (*a divertirse*) to go out; **sal ahí fuera a recoger la pelota** go out there and get the ball back; **sal aquí al jardín con nosotros** come out into the garden with us; **salió a la calle a ver si venían** she went outside *o* she went out into the street to see if they were coming; **—¿está Juan? —no, ha salido** "is Juan in?" — "no, I'm afraid he's gone out"; **¿vas a ~ esta noche?** are you going out tonight?; **nunca he salido al extranjero** I've never been abroad; **la pelota salió fuera** (*Ftbl*) the ball went out (of play); **los rehenes salieron por la ventana** the hostages got out through the window; **salió corriendo (del cuarto)** he ran out (of the room); **~ de**: **nos la encontramos al ~ del cine** we bumped into her when we were coming out of the cinema; **¿de dónde has salido?** where did you appear *o* spring from?; **~ de un apuro** to get out of a jam; **~ del coma** to come out of a coma; **~ de paseo** to go out for a walk; ✦***MODISMOS*** **de esta no salimos*** we'll never get out of this one*; **~ de pobre**: **no salió nunca de pobre** he never stopped being poor

3 ***al mercado*** [*revista, libro, disco*] to come out; [*moda*] to come in; **el libro sale el mes que viene** the book comes out next month; **acaba de ~ un disco suyo** an album of his has just come out *o* been released

4 ***en medios de comunicación*** **la noticia salió en el periódico de ayer** the news was *o* appeared in yesterday's paper; **sus padres salieron en los periódicos** her parents were in the papers; **~ por la televisión** to be *o* appear on TV

5 = ***surgir*** to come up; **en el debate no salió el tema del aborto** the subject of abortion didn't come up in the debate; **si sale un puesto apropiado** if a suitable job comes up; **cuando salga la ocasión** when the opportunity comes up *o* arises; **¡ya salió aquello!** we know all about that!; **~le algo a algn: le ha salido novio/un trabajo** she's got herself a boyfriend/a job

6 = ***aparecer*** [*agua*] to come out; [*sol*] to come out; [*mancha*] to appear; **no sale agua del grifo** there's no water coming out of the tap; **ha salido una mancha en el techo** a damp patch has appeared on the ceiling; **me sale sangre** I'm bleeding

7 = ***nacer*** [*diente*] to come through; [*planta, sol*] to come up; [*pelo*] to grow; [*pollito*] to hatch; **me está saliendo una muela del juicio** one of my wisdom teeth is coming through; **ya le ha salido un diente al niño** the baby already has one tooth; **le han salido muchas espinillas** he's got a lot of blackheads; **nos levantamos antes de que saliera el sol** we got up before sunrise

8 = ***quitarse*** [*mancha*] to come out, come off; **el anillo no le sale del dedo** the ring won't come off her finger, she can't get the ring off her finger

9 = ***costar*** **la calefacción de gas saldría más barata** gas heating would work out cheaper; **~ a**: **sale a ocho euros el kilo** it works out at eight euros a kilo; **salimos a 10 libras por persona** it works out at £10 each; **~ por**: **me salió por 1.000 pesos** it cost me 1,000 pesos

10 = ***resultar*** **¿cómo salió la representación?** how did the performance go?; **espero que todo salga como habíamos planeado** I hope everything goes to plan; **la prueba salió positiva** the test was positive; **salió triunfador de las elecciones** he was victorious in the elections; **la secretaria salió muy trabajadora** the secretary turned out to be very hard-working; **¿qué número ha salido premiado en la lotería?** what was the winning number in the lottery?; **salió alcalde por tres votos** he was elected mayor by three votes; **tenemos que aceptarlo, salga lo que salga** we have to accept it, whatever happens; **~ bien**: **el plan salió bien** the plan worked out well; **espero que todo salga**

bien I hope everything works out all right; **¿salió bien la fiesta?** did the party go well?; **ha salido muy bien de la operación** she's come through the operation very well; **¿cómo te salió el examen?** how did your exam go?; **~ mal**: **salió muy mal del tratamiento** the treatment wasn't at all successful; **la celebración salió mal por la lluvia** the celebrations were spoiled by the rain; **les salió mal el proyecto** their plan didn't work out; **¡qué mal me ha salido el dibujo!** oh dear! my drawing hasn't come out very well!

11 **~le algo a algn** 11·1 (= *poder resolverse*) **he intentado resolver el problema pero no me sale** I've tried to solve the problem but I just can't do it; **este crucigrama no me sale** I can't do this crossword

11·2 (= *resultar natural*) **no me sale ser amable con ella** I find it difficult being nice to her

11·3 (= *poder recordarse*) **no me sale su apellido** I can't think of his name

12 **~ a** [*calle*] to come out in, lead to; **esta calle sale a la plaza** this street comes out in *o* leads to the square

13 **~ a algn** (= *parecerse*) to take after sb; **ha salido a su padre** he takes after his father

14 **~ con algn** to go out with sb; **está saliendo con un compañero de clase** she's going out with one of her classmates; **salen juntos desde hace dos años** they've been going out (together) for two years

15 **~ con algo** (*al hablar*) to come out with sth; **y ahora sale con esto** and now he comes out with this; **ahora me sale con que yo le debo dinero** and now he starts complaining that I owe him money

16 **~ de** [*proceder*] to come from; **el aceite que sale de la aceituna** oil which comes from olives

17 **~ por algn** (= *defender*) to come out in defence of sb, stick up for sb; (*económicamente*) to back sb financially; **cuando hubo problemas, salió por mí** when there were problems, she stuck up for me *o* came out in my defence

18 *Teat* to come on; **sale vestido de policía** he comes on dressed as a policeman; **"sale el rey"** (*acotación*) "enter the king"

19 *= empezar* (*Dep*) to start; (*Ajedrez*) to have first move; (*Naipes*) to lead; **~ con un as** to lead an ace; **~ de triunfo** to lead a trump

20 *Inform* to exit

21 *= sobresalir* to stick out; **el balcón sale unos dos metros** the balcony sticks out about two metres

22 *= pagar* **~ a los gastos de algn** to meet *o* pay sb's expenses

Ⓑ **salirse** VERBO PRONOMINAL

1 *= irse* to leave; **se salió del partido** he left the party; ✦**MODISMO ~se con la suya** to get one's way

2 *= escaparse* to escape (**de** from), get out (**de** of); **el tigre se salió de la jaula** the tiger escaped from the cage, the tiger got out of the cage

3 *= filtrarse* [*aire, líquido*] to leak (out); **la botella estaba rota y se salía el vinagre** the bottle was cracked and the vinegar was coming out *o* leaking (out); **se salía el aceite del motor** oil was leaking out of the engine; **el barril se sale** (*Esp*) the barrel is leaking

4 *= rebosar* to overflow; (*al hervir*) to boil over; **cierra el grifo antes de que se salga el agua** turn the tap off before the water overflows; **se ha salido la leche** the milk has boiled over; **el río se salió de su cauce** the river burst its banks; ✦**MODISMO ~se de madre** to lose one's self-control

5 *= desviarse* to come off; **nos salimos de la carretera** we came off the road; **~se de la vía** to jump the rails; **~se del tema** to get off the point

6 *= desconectarse* to come out; **se ha salido el enchufe** the plug has come out

7 *= excederse* **~se de lo normal** to go beyond what is normal; **~se de los límites** to go beyond the limits

SALIR

Para precisar la forma de salir

Aunque **salir (de)** se suele traducir por **come out (of)** o por **go out (of)** según la dirección del movimiento, cuando se quiere especificar la forma en que se realiza ese movimiento, estos verbos se pueden reemplazar por otros como **run out**, **rush out**, **jump out**, **tiptoe out**, **climb out**, *etc.*

Se vio a tres hombres enmascarados salir del banco corriendo

Three masked men were seen running out of the bank

Salió del coche con un salto

He jumped out of the car

Salió de puntillas de la habitación

He tiptoed out of the room

Para otros usos y ejemplos ver la entrada.

salita SF 1 (*en casa*) sitting room

2 (*Teat*) small auditorium

salitre SM 1 (= *sustancia salina*) saltpetre, saltpeter (*EEUU*), nitre

2 (*Chile*) (= *nitrato de Chile*) Chilean nitrate

salitrera SF (= *fábrica*) nitre works; (= *mina*) nitrate fields *pl*

saliva SF saliva; ✦**MODISMOS gastar ~** to waste one's breath (**en** on); **tragar ~** to swallow one's feelings

salivación SF salivation

salivadera SF spittoon, cuspidor (*EEUU*)

salival ADJ salivary

salivar ▸conjug 1a◂ VI 1 (= *segregar saliva*) to salivate

2 (*esp LAm*) (= *escupir*) to spit

salivazo SM gobbet of spit; **arrojar un ~** to spit

salivera SF (*Cono Sur*) spittoon, cuspidor (*EEUU*)

salmantino/a Ⓐ ADJ of/from Salamanca, Salamancan

Ⓑ SM/F native/inhabitant of Salamanca, Salamancan; **los ~s** the people of Salamanca, the Salamancans

salmear ▸conjug 1a◂ VI to sing psalms

salmo SM psalm

salmodia SF 1 (*Rel*) psalmody

2 (*) (= *canturreo*) drone

salmodiar ▸conjug 1b◂ VI 1 (*Rel*) to sing psalms

2 (*) (= *canturrear*) to drone

salmón SM salmon

salmonela SF salmonella

salmonelosis SF INV salmonellosis, salmonella food-poisoning

salmonero ADJ **río ~** salmon river

salmonete SM red mullet

salmuera SF pickle, brine

salobre ADJ salt, salty; **agua ~** brackish water

saloma SF 1 (*Náut*) sea shanty, sea song

2 [*de trabajo*] working song

Salomé SF Salome

Salomón SM Solomon

salomónicamente ADV with the wisdom of Solomon

salomónico ADJ **juicio ~** judgement of Solomon

salón SM 1 [*de casa*] living-room, lounge; **juego de ~** parlour game, parlor game (*EEUU*) ► **salón comedor** lounge-dining-room

2 [*de lugar público*] (*gen*) hall, assembly-room; [*de colegio*] common-room; (*Com*) show, trade fair, exhibition; (*Náut*) saloon; (*Chile Ferro*) first class ► **salón de actos** assembly room ► **salón de baile** ballroom ► **salón de belleza** beauty parlour, beauty parlor (*EEUU*) ► **salón de demostraciones** showroom ► **salón de fiestas** dance hall ► **salón de fumadores** smoking room ► **salón de juegos** (*en casino*) gaming room; (*en hotel, barco*) casino ► **salón del automóvil** motor show ► **salón de los pasos perdidos*** waiting room ► **salón de masaje** massage parlour, massage parlor (*EEUU*) ► **salón de pintura** art gallery ► **salón de plenos del Ayuntamiento** Council chamber ► **salón de reuniones** conference room ► **salón de sesiones** assembly hall ► **salón de té** tearoom ► **salón náutico** boat show

3 (= *muebles*) suite of living room furniture, lounge suite

saloncillo SM (*Teat*) private room

salonero SM (*Andes*) waiter

salpicadera SF (*Méx*) mudguard, fender (*EEUU*)

salpicadero SM dashboard

salpicado Ⓐ ADJ 1 **~ de** splashed *o* spattered with; **un diseño ~ de puntos rojos** a pattern with red spots in it; **una llanura salpicada de granjas** a plain with farms dotted about on it, a plain dotted with farms; **un discurso ~ de citas latinas** a speech sprinkled with Latin quotations, a speech full of Latin quotations

2 (*Cono Sur, Méx*) [*animal*] spotted, dappled

Ⓑ SM 1 (= *acto*) splashing

2 (= *diseño*) sprinkle

salpicadura SF 1 (= *acto*) splashing

2 (= *mancha*) splash

3 (*en conversación, discurso*) sprinkling

salpicar ▸conjug 1g◂ VT 1 (= *manchar*) (*de barro, pintura*) to splash (**de** with); (*de agua*) to sprinkle (**de** with); [+ *tela*] to dot, fleck (**de** with); **~ agua sobre el suelo** to sprinkle water on the floor; **la multitud de islas que salpican el océano** the host of islands dotted about the ocean; **este asunto salpica al gobierno** this affair hasn't left the government untouched, the government has been tainted by this affair

2 [+ *conversación, discurso*] to sprinkle (**de** with)

salpicón SM 1 = **salpicadura 1**

2 (*Culin*) ► **salpicón de marisco(s)** seafood salad

3 (*Andes*) (= *jugos mixtos*) cold mixed fruit juice

4 (*Andes, Cono Sur*) (= *ensalada*) raw vegetable salad

salpimentar ▸conjug 1a◂ VT 1 (*Culin*) to season, add salt and pepper to
2 (= *amenizar*) to spice up (**de** with)

salpiquear ▸conjug 1a◂ VT (*Andes, Caribe*) = **salpicar**

salpresar ▸conjug 1a◂ VT to salt, salt down

salpreso ADJ salted, salt

salpullido SM (= *erupción*) rash, skin eruption; (= *picadura*) fleabite; (= *hinchazón*) swelling (from a bite)

salsa¹ SF 1 (*Culin*) (*gen*) sauce; [*de carne*] gravy; (*para ensalada*) dressing; ✦*MODISMOS* **cocerse en su propia ~** to stew in one's own juice; **estar en su ~** to be in one's element; **es la ~ de la vida** it's the spice of life ► **salsa blanca** white sauce ► **salsa de ají** chili sauce ► **salsa de tomate** tomato sauce, ketchup ► **salsa holandesa** hollandaise sauce ► **salsa mahonesa, salsa mayonesa** mayonnaise ► **salsa tártara** tartar sauce
2 (✱) (= *ambiente*) scene*; **la ~ madrileña** the Madrid scene*

salsa² SF (*Mús*) salsa

salsera SF sauce boat

salsero/a Ⓐ ADJ (*Mús*) salsa-loving; **ritmo ~** salsa rhythm
Ⓑ SM/F salsa music player

salsifí SM salsify

saltabanco SM 1 (*Hist*) quack, mountebank
2 = **saltimbanqui**

saltado ADJ 1 [*loza*] chipped, damaged; **la corona tiene varias piedras saltadas** the crown has several stones missing
2 [*ojos*] bulging

saltador(a) Ⓐ SM/F (*Atletismo*) jumper; (*Natación*) diver ► **saltador(a) de altura** high-jumper ► **saltador(a) de longitud** long-jumper ► **saltador(a) de pértiga** pole-vaulter ► **saltador(a) de trampolín** trampolinist ► **saltador(a) de triple** triple jumper
Ⓑ SM (= *comba*) skipping rope

saltadura SF chip

saltamontes SM INV grasshopper

saltante ADJ (*Andes, Cono Sur*) outstanding, noteworthy

saltaperico SM (*Caribe*) squib, firecracker

saltar ▸conjug 1a◂ Ⓐ VI 1 [*persona, animal*] (= *dar un salto*) (*tb Atletismo*) to jump; (*más lejos*) leap; (*a la pata coja*) to hop; **~ de alegría** to jump with *o* for joy; **~ a la comba** to skip, jump rope (*EEUU*); **hacer ~ un caballo** to jump a horse, make a horse jump; ✦*MODISMO* **está a la que salta** (= *a la caza de una oportunidad*) he never misses a trick*; (= *al día*) he lives for the day
2 (= *lanzarse*) 2·1 (*lit*) **~ al campo** *o* **al césped** (*Dep*) to come out on to the pitch; **~ al agua** to jump *o* dive into the water; **~ de la cama** to leap out of bed; **~ en paracaídas** to parachute; **~ por una ventana** to jump *o* leap out of a window; **~ sobre algn** to jump *o* leap *o* pounce on sb; **~ a tierra** to leap ashore
2·2 (*fig*) **~ al mundo de la política** to go into politics, move into the political arena; **~ del último puesto al primero** to jump from last place to first; **~ a la fama** to win fame, be shot to fame
3 (= *salir disparado*) [*chispa*] to fly, fly out; [*líquido*] to shoot out, spurt out; [*corcho*] to pop out; [*resorte*] to break, go*; [*astilla*] to fly off; [*botón*] to come off; [*pelota*] to fly; **saltan chispas** sparks are flying; **está saltando el aceite** the oil is spitting; **la pelota saltó fuera del campo** the ball flew out of the ground; **el balón saltó por encima de la portería** the ball flew over the bar; **hacer ~ una trampa** to spring a trap; **el asunto ha saltado a la prensa** the affair has reached the newspapers; ✦*MODISMOS* **~ a la memoria** to leap to mind; **salta a la vista** it's patently obvious, it hits you in the eye
4 (= *estallar*) [*cristal*] to shatter; [*recipiente*] to crack; [*madera*] to crack, snap, break; **la bombilla saltó en pedazos** the light bulb was blown to bits; **hacer ~ un edificio** to blow a building up; **~ por los aires**: **el coche saltó por los aires** the car was blown up; **el acuerdo puede ~ por los aires** the agreement could be destroyed *o* go up in smoke; **hacer ~ algo por los aires** to blow sth up; *ver tb* **banca 2**
5 (*Elec*) [*alarma*] to go off; [*plomos*] to blow
6 (*al hablar*) 6·1 (*de forma inesperada*) to say, pipe up*; **—¡estupendo! —saltó uno de los chavales** "great!" piped up* *o* said one of the boys; **~ con una patochada** to come out with a ridiculous *o* foolish remark; **~ de una cosa a otra** to skip from one thing *o* subject to another, skip about
6·2 (*con ira*) to explode, blow up
7 (= *irse*) **~ de un puesto** to give up a job; **hacer ~ a algn de un puesto** to boot sb out of a job*
8 [*cantidad, cifra*] to shoot up, leap, leap up; **la mayoría ha saltado a 900 votos** the majority has shot up *o* leaped (up) to 900 votes
9 **~ atrás** (*Biol*) to revert
Ⓑ VT 1 [*+ muro, obstáculo*] (*por encima*) to jump over, jump; (*llegando más lejos*) to leap, leap over; (*apoyándose con las manos*) to vault; **el caballo saltó la valla** the horse jumped over *o* jumped the fence
2 (= *arrancar*) **le saltó tres dientes** he knocked out three of his teeth; **me has saltado un botón** you've torn off one of my buttons
3 (*con explosivos*) to blow up
Ⓒ **saltarse** VPR 1 (= *omitir*) to skip; **nos saltamos el desayuno** we skipped breakfast; **hoy me he saltado una clase** I skipped a class today; **~se un párrafo** to skip a paragraph, miss out a paragraph; **me he saltado un par de renglones** I've skipped a couple of lines
2 (= *no hacer caso de*) **~se un semáforo** to go through a red light, jump the lights, shoot the lights*; **~se un stop** to disobey a stop sign; **~se todas las reglas** to break all the rules; *ver tb* **torera**
3 (= *salirse*) [*pieza*] to come off, fly off; **se me ~on las lágrimas** I burst out crying

saltarín/ina Ⓐ ADJ 1 (= *que salta*) [*cabra, cordero, niño*] frolicking; [*rana, pulga*] jumping, leaping
2 (= *inquieto*) restless
Ⓑ SM/F dancer

salteado ADJ 1 (= *discontinuo*) **—¿has leído el libro? —sólo unas páginas salteadas** "have you read the book?" — "I just skipped through it"; **hizo unos cuantos ejercicios ~s y dejó el resto** he skipped through a couple of exercises and left the rest
2 (*Culin*) sauté, sautéed

salteador SM (*tb* **~ de caminos**) highwayman

salteamiento SM highway robbery, holdup

saltear ▸conjug 1a◂ Ⓐ VT 1 (*Culin*) to sauté
2 (= *atracar*) to hold up
3 (= *sorprender*) to take by surprise
Ⓑ VI (= *hacer discontinuamente*) (*al trabajar*) to do in fits and starts; (*al leer*) to skip (over) bits; **lo leyó salteando** he read bits of it here and there

salteña SF (*Andes*) meat pie

salterio SM 1 (*Rel*) (*gen*) psalter; (*en la Biblia*) Book of Psalms
2 (*Mús*) psaltery

saltimbanqui SM (= *malabarista*) juggler; (= *acróbata*) acrobat; (= *volatinero*) tightrope walker

salto SM 1 (= *acción*) (*gen*) jump; (*de mayor altura, distancia*) leap; (*al agua*) dive; **este invento es un gran ~ adelante en tecnología** this invention is a great leap forward in technology; **la novela está narrada con numerosos ~s atrás en el tiempo** the novel is told with a lot of flashbacks in time; **a ~s**: **cruzamos el río a ~s** we jumped across the river; **había que andar a ~s para no pisar los cristales** you had to hop about so as not to tread on the glass; **el pájaro avanzaba a saltitos** the bird hopped along; **dar un ~** [*persona, animal*] to jump; [*corazón*] to leap; **dio un ~ de dos metros** he jumped two metres; **cuando me enteré di un ~ de alegría** I jumped for joy when I found out; **al verla me dio un ~ el corazón** when I saw her my heart leapt; **empezó a dar ~s para calentarse** he started jumping about to warm up; **los niños les acompañaban dando ~s** the kids went with them, jumping *o* hopping about; **me daba ~s el corazón** my heart was pounding; **el progreso da ~s imprevisibles** progress makes unpredictable leaps; **al hablar da muchos ~s de un tema a otro** when he speaks, he jumps from *o* leaps around from one subject to the next; **de un ~**: **se puso en pie de un ~** he leapt *o* sprang to his feet; **de un ~ se encaramó a la rama de un árbol** he leapt up onto the branch of a tree; **subió/bajó de un ~** he jumped up/down; **el libro supuso su ~ a la fama** the book marked his leap to fame, the book was his springboard to fame; **pegar un ~** = **dar un salto**; ✦*MODISMOS* **a ~ de mata**: **vivir a ~ de mata** (= *sin organización*) to lead a haphazard life; (= *sin seguridad*) to live from hand to mouth; **estoy leyendo el libro a ~ de mata** I'm reading the book in dribs and drabs; **dar el ~** to make the leap *o* jump; **le gustaría dar el ~ al teatro profesional** he would like to make the leap *o* jump into professional theatre; **pegar el ~ a algn*** to cheat on sb*; **tirarse al ~** (*Chile**) to take a chance *o* risk ► **salto a ciegas, salto al vacío** leap in the dark
2 (*Atletismo*) jump; (*Natación*) dive; **un ~ de ocho metros** a jump of eight metres; **los participantes en las pruebas de ~s** the participants in the jump events; **triple ~** triple jump ► **salto alto** (*LAm*) high jump ► **salto con garrocha** (*LAm*), **salto con pértiga** pole vault ► **salto de altura** high jump ► **salto de ángel** swallow dive ► **salto de carpa** jack-knife dive ► **salto de esquí** ski-jump; **la Copa del Mundo de ~s de esquí** ski-jumping World Cup ► **salto de longitud** long jump ► **salto de palanca** high dive ► **salto de trampolín** springboard dive

► **salto en paracaídas** (= *salto*) parachute jump; (= *deporte*) parachuting ► **salto largo** (*LAm*) long jump ► **salto mortal** somersault ► **salto nulo** no-jump ► **saltos de obstáculos** hurdles
3 (= *diferencia*) gap; **entre los dos hermanos hay un ~ de nueve años** there is a gap of nine years between the two brothers; **hay un gran ~ entre su primer libro y éste último** there is a big leap between his first book and this latest one
4 (= *en texto*) **aquí hay un ~ de 50 versos** there's a gap of 50 lines here; **he dado un ~ de varias páginas** I've skipped several pages ► **salto de línea** (*Inform*) line break
5 (= *desnivel*) [*de agua*] waterfall; (*en el terreno*) fault ► **salto de agua** (*Geog*) waterfall; (*Téc*) chute
6 ► **salto de cama** negligee

saltón Ⓐ ADJ 1 (= *prominente*) [*ojos*] bulging; [*dientes*] protruding
2 (*LAm*) (= *poco hecho*) undercooked, half-cooked
Ⓑ SM grasshopper

saltona SF (*Cono Sur*) young locust

salubre ADJ healthy, salubrious (*frm*)

salubridad SF 1 (= *cualidad*) healthiness, salubriousness (*frm*)
2 (= *estadísticas*) health statistics

salud SF 1 (*Med*) health; **estar bien/mal de ~** to be in good/bad health; **mejorar de ~** to get better; **tener buena ~** ◊ **gozar de buena ~** to enjoy good health; **devolver la ~ a algn** to give sb back his health, restore sb to health; **¿cómo vamos de ~?** how are we today? ► **salud ambiental** environmental health ► **salud mental** mental health, mental wellbeing ► **salud ocupacional** occupational health ► **salud pública** public health
2 (= *bienestar*) welfare, wellbeing; **la ~ moral de la nación** the country's moral welfare; ✦***MODISMO*** **curarse en ~** to be prepared, take precautions
3 (*en brindis*) **¡a su ~!** ◊ **¡~ (y pesetas)!** cheers!, good health!; **beber a la ~ de algn** to drink to the health of sb
4 (*al estornudar*) **¡salud!** bless you!
5 (*Rel*) salvation

saludable ADJ 1 (*Med*) healthy
2 (= *provechoso*) good, beneficial; **un aviso ~** a salutary warning

saludador(a) SM/F quack doctor

▼**saludar** ▸conjug 1a◂ Ⓐ VT 1 (*al encontrarse con algn*) (*con palabras*) to say hello to, greet (*frm*); (*con gestos*) to wave at, wave to; **entré a ~la** I went in to say hello to her; **me saludó dándome un beso** he greeted me with a kiss; **nos saludó con la mano** she waved to us; **le saludé desde la otra acera** I waved to him from the other side of the street; **les saludaban desde el barco agitando pañuelos blancos** they waved white handkerchiefs at them from the ship; **la saludó con una leve inclinación de cabeza** he greeted her with a slight nod; **la compañía en pleno salió a ~ al público** the whole company came out to take a bow; **salude de mi parte a su marido** give my regards to your husband
2 (*en carta*) **le saluda atentamente** yours faithfully
3 (*Mil*) to salute
4 [+ *noticia, suceso*] to hail, welcome

➤ LENGUA Y USO: **saludar A1** 48.2

Ⓑ VI 1 (= *dirigir un saludo*) to say hello; **nunca saluda** she never says hello
2 (*Mil*) to salute
Ⓒ **saludarse** VPR **se ~on con un beso** they greeted each other with a kiss; **hace tiempo que no se saludan** they haven't been speaking for some time

saludo SM 1 (*al encontrarse con algn*) (= *palabra*) greeting; (= *gesto*) wave; **no contestó a mi ~** he didn't respond to my greeting; **nos dirigió un ~ con la mano** he gave us a wave, he waved to us; **~s** *o* **un ~ a Adela** regards to Adela; ✦***MODISMO*** **negar el ~ a algn** to cut sb dead, ignore sb, blank sb*
2 (*en carta*) **un ~ cariñoso a Gonzalo** warm regards to Gonzalo; **un ~ afectuoso** *o* **cordial** kind regards; **~s** best wishes; **¡~s a Teresa de mi parte!** give my best wishes to Teresa!, say hello to Teresa for me!; **os envía muchos ~s** he sends you warmest regards; **atentos ~s** yours sincerely, yours truly (*EEUU*); **~s cordiales** kind regards; **~s respetuosos**† respectfully yours
3 (*Mil*) salute

Salustio SM Sallust

salutación SF greeting, salutation

salva[1] SF 1 [*de aplausos*] storm
2 (*Mil*) salute, salvo ► **salva de advertencia** warning shots *pl*
3 (= *saludo*) greeting
4 (= *promesa*) oath, solemn promise

salva[2] SF (= *bandeja*) salver, tray

salvabarros SM INV mudguard, fender (*EEUU*)

salvación SF 1 (= *rescate*) rescue (**de** from)
2 (*Rel*) salvation ► **salvación eterna** eternal salvation

salvada SF (*LAm*) = **salvación 1**

salvado SM bran

Salvador SM 1 **el ~** (*Rel*) the Saviour, the Savior (*EEUU*)
2 **El ~** (*Geog*) El Salvador

salvador(a) SM/F 1 (= *que rescata*) rescuer, saviour, savior (*EEUU*)
2 [*de playa*] life-saver

salvadoreñismo SM *word or phrase etc peculiar to El Salvador*

salvadoreño/a ADJ, SM/F Salvadoran

salvaguarda SF safeguard

salvaguardar ▸conjug 1a◂ VT 1 (= *defender*) to safeguard 2 (*Inform*) to back up, make a backup copy of

salvaguardia SF 1 (= *defensa*) safeguard, defence, defense (*EEUU*)
2 (= *documento*) safe-conduct

salvajada SF savage deed, atrocity

salvaje Ⓐ ADJ 1 [*planta, animal, tierra*] wild
2 (= *no autorizado*) [*huelga*] unofficial, wildcat; [*construcción*] unauthorized
3 [*pueblo, tribu*] savage
4 (= *brutal*) savage, brutal; **un ~ asesinato** a brutal *o* savage murder
5 (*LAm**) (= *estupendo*) terrific*, smashing*
Ⓑ SMF (*lit, fig*) savage

salvajería SF = **salvajada**

salvajez SF = **salvajismo**

salvajino ADJ 1 (= *salvaje*) wild, savage
2 **carne salvajina** meat from a wild animal

salvajismo SM savagery

salvamanteles SM INV table mat, hot pad (*EEUU*)

salvamento SM 1 (= *acción*) (*gen*) rescue; [*de naufragio*] salvage; **de ~** rescue *antes de s*; **operaciones de ~** rescue operations; **bote de ~** lifeboat ► **salvamento y socorrismo** life-saving
2 (= *refugio*) place of safety, refuge

salvapantallas SM INV screensaver

salvaplatos SM INV table mat, hot pad (*EEUU*)

salvar ▸conjug 1a◂ Ⓐ VT 1 (*de un peligro*) to save; **me salvó la vida** he saved my life; **los bomberos nos ~on del fuego** the firemen saved us from the blaze; **apenas ~on nada del incendio** they hardly managed to salvage anything from the fire; **me has salvado de tener que sentarme con ese pesado** you saved me (from) having to sit next to that old bore
2 (*Rel*) to save
3 (*Inform*) to save
4 (= *evitar*) [+ *dificultad, obstáculo*] to get round, overcome; [+ *montaña, río, barrera*] to cross; [+ *rápidos*] to shoot
5 (*frm*) [+ *distancia*] to cover; **el tren salva la distancia en dos horas** the train covers *o* does the distance in two hours
6 (= *exceptuando*) **salvando: salvando algún detalle, la traducción está muy bien** apart from a few minor details, the translation is very good; *ver tb* **distancia 1**
7 (*frm*) [+ *altura*] to rise above
8 (*Cono Sur*) [+ *examen*] to pass
Ⓑ **salvarse** VPR 1 (*de un peligro*) to escape; **pocos se ~on del naufragio** few escaped from *o* survived the shipwreck; **¡sálvese quien pueda!** ◊ **¡sálvese el que pueda!** every man for himself!
2 (*) (= *librarse*) **considera incompetentes a todos los ministros, no se salva nadie** in his view all the ministers are, without exception, incompetent; **todos son antipáticos, Carlos es el único que se salva** they're an unfriendly lot, Carlos is the one exception
3 (*Rel*) to be saved

salvaslip SM (*pl* **salvaslips**) panty liner

salvataje SM (*Cono Sur*) rescue

salvavidas Ⓐ SM INV (= *flotador*) lifebelt, life preserver (*EEUU*); (= *chaleco*) life jacket
Ⓑ ADJ INV life-saving *antes de s*; **bote ~** lifeboat; **cinturón ~** lifebelt, life preserver (*EEUU*); **chaleco ~** life jacket

salvedad SF reservation, qualification; **con la ~ de que …** with the proviso that …; **me gustaría hacer una ~** I would like to qualify what you said *o* to make a qualification

Salvi SM (*forma familiar*) *de* **Salvador**

salvia SF sage

salvilla SF 1 (= *bandeja*) salver, tray
2 (*Cono Sur*) (= *vinagrera*) cruet

salvo Ⓐ ADJ safe; *ver tb* **sano 3**
Ⓑ PREP except, except for, save; **~ aquellos que ya contamos** except (for) those we have already counted; **de todos los países ~ de Italia** from all countries except Italy; **~ error u omisión** (*Com*) errors and omissions excepted
Ⓒ ADV **a ~** out of danger; **a ~ de** safe from; **nada ha quedado a ~ de sus ataques** nothing has been safe from *o* has escaped his attacks; **para dejar a ~ su reputación** in order to safeguard his reputation; **ponerse a ~** to reach safety; **en ~** out of danger, in a safe place

Ⓓ CONJ ~ **que** ◊ ~ **si** unless; **iré ~ que me avises al contrario** I'll go unless you tell me otherwise

salvoconducto SM safe-conduct

salvohonor SM (*hum*) backside

samaritano/a SM/F Samaritan; **buen ~** good Samaritan

samaruco SM (*Cono Sur*) hunter's pouch, gamebag

samba SF samba; *ver tb* **sambo**

sambenito SM [1] (= *deshonra*) **le colgaron el ~ de cobarde** they branded him a coward; **le colgaron el ~ de haberlo hecho** they put the blame for it on him; **echar el ~ a otro** to pin the blame on somebody else; **quedó con el ~ toda la vida** the stigma stayed with him for the rest of his life
[2] (*Hist*) sanbenito

sambo/a SM/F *offspring of black person and (American) Indian*

sambumbia SF [1] (*CAm, Caribe, Méx*) (= *bebida*) fruit drink
[2] (*Méx*) [*de ananás*] pineapple drink; (= *hordiate*) barley water drink
[3] (*Andes*) (= *trasto*) old thing, piece of junk; **volver algo ~** to smash sth to pieces

sambutir‡ ▸conjug 3a◂ (*Méx*) VT (= *meter a fuerza*) to stick in, stuff in*; (= *hundir*) to sink in, shove in

samotana* SF (*CAm*) row, uproar

samovar SM samovar

sampablera SF (*Caribe*) racket, row

sampán SM sampan

Samuel SM Samuel

samurear ▸conjug 1a◂ VI (*Caribe*) to walk with bowed head

San SM (*apócope de* **santo**) saint; **~ Juan** Saint John; **cerca de ~ Martín** near St Martin's (church); **se casarán por ~ Juan** (*en sentido extenso*) they'll get married sometime in midsummer; (*estrictamente*) they'll get married round about St John's Day; *ver tb* **santo, lunes**

sanable ADJ curable

sanaco ADJ (*Caribe*) silly

sanalotodo SM INV cure-all

sanamente ADV healthily

sananería SF (*Caribe*) stupid remark, silly comment

sanar ▸conjug 1a◂ Ⓐ VT [+ *herida*] to heal; [+ *persona*] to cure (**de** of)
Ⓑ VI [*herida*] to heal; [*persona*] to recover

sanativo ADJ healing, curative

sanatorio SM sanatorium, sanitarium (*EEUU*) ► **sanatorio mental** psychiatric clinic, psychiatric hospital

San Bernardo SM St Bernard

sancho SM [1] (= *cerdo*) pig, hog (*EEUU*)
[2] (*Méx*) (= *carnero*) ram; (= *cordero*) lamb; (= *macho cabrío*) billy goat; (= *animal abandonado*) orphan animal, suckling

sanción SF sanction; **sanciones comerciales** trade sanctions; **sanciones económicas** economic sanctions; **imponer sanciones** to impose sanctions; **levantar sanciones a algn** to lift sanctions against sb ► **sanción disciplinaria** punishment, disciplinary measure

sancionable ADJ punishable

sancionado/a SM/F guilty person; **los ~s** (*Pol*) those who have been punished for a political offence, those guilty of political crimes

sancionar ▸conjug 1a◂ VT [1] (= *castigar*) (*gen*) to sanction; (*Jur*) to penalize
[2] (= *permitir*) to sanction

sancionatorio ADJ (*Jur*) penal, penalty *antes de s*

sancochado SM (*Andes*) = **sancocho**

sancochar ▸conjug 1a◂ VT (*LAm*) to parboil

sancocho SM [1] (*Culin*) (= *comida mal guisada*) undercooked food; (= *carne*) parboiled meat
[2] (*LAm*) (= *guisado*) stew (of meat, yucca *etc*)
[3] (*CAm, Caribe, Méx*) (= *lío*) fuss
[4] (*Caribe*) (= *bazofia*) pigswill

San Cristóbal SM [1] (*Rel*) St Christopher
[2] (*Geog*) St Kitts

sandalia SF sandal

sándalo SM sandal, sandalwood

sandez SF [1] (= *cualidad*) foolishness
[2] (= *acción*) stupid thing; **decir sandeces** to talk nonsense; **fue una ~ obrar así** it was a stupid thing to do

sandía SF watermelon; *ver tb* **sandío**

sandinismo SM Sandinista movement

sandinista ADJ, SMF (*Nic*) Sandinista

sandío/a Ⓐ ADJ foolish, silly
Ⓑ SM/F fool; *ver tb* **sandía**

sánduche SM (*LAm*) sandwich

sandunga SF [1] (*) (= *encanto*) charm; (= *gracia*) wit
[2] (*LAm*) (= *juerga*) binge*, celebration

sandunguero ADJ (= *encantador*) charming; (= *gracioso*) witty

sándwich [saŋ'gwitʃ, sam'bitʃ] SM (*pl* **sándwichs, sándwiches**) sandwich

sandwichera SF toasted sandwich maker

sandwichería SF (*esp LAm*) sandwich bar

saneamiento SM [1] (= *limpieza*) [*de río, ciudad, alcantarillado*] clean-up; [*de terreno*] drainage; **pidió un préstamo para el ~ de la casa** she applied for a loan to upgrade the house; **materiales de ~** sanitary fittings
[2] [*de empresa*] restructuring; **invirtieron 100 millones en el ~ económico de la compañía** they invested 100 million in restructuring the company's finances; **el ~ de la economía** putting the economy back on a sound footing
[3] (*Fin*) [*de deuda*] write-off; [*de activo*] write-down
[4] (*Jur*) compensation, indemnification

sanear ▸conjug 1a◂ VT [1] (= *limpiar*) [+ *río, ciudad, alcantarillado*] to clean up; [+ *casa*] to upgrade
[2] [+ *empresa*] to restructure; **es preciso ~ la compañía** the company needs restructuring; **~ la economía** to put the economy back on a sound footing
[3] (*Fin*) [+ *deuda*] to write off; [+ *activo*] to write down
[4] (*Jur*) (= *compensar*) to compensate, indemnify

sanfasón* SF (*LAm*), **sanfazón** SF (*LAm*) cheek*; **a la ~** unceremoniously, informally; (*pey*) carelessly

sanfermines SMPL *festivities in celebration of San Fermín (Pamplona)*

> **SANFERMINES**
>
> *The* **Sanfermines** *is a week-long festival starting on July 7 in Pamplona (Navarre) to honour* **San Fermín**, *the town's patron saint. As with many other local Spanish festivities, one of the main events is bullfighting. In Pamplona, however, the bulls have to be led from their enclosure to the bullring early in the morning through the city's main streets. Young men, dressed in the traditional Navarrese attire of red berets, white shirts and trousers and red sashes round their waists, run through the streets leading the fast-moving bulls. This activity, known as the* **encierro**, *in which people risk serious injury and even death, was popularized by writers such as Ernest Hemingway and now attracts visitors from all over the world. The festivities start with the* **txupinazo**, *a large rocket fired from Pamplona's main square, and for a full week Pamplona becomes one large street party punctuated by the daily* **encierro**.

sanforizar ▸conjug 1f◂ VT to sanforize®

sango SM (*Andes*) *yucca and maize pudding*

sangradera SF [1] (*Med*) lancet
[2] [*de agua*] (= *acequia*) irrigation channel; (= *desagüe*) sluice, outflow

sangradura SF [1] (*Med*) (= *incisión*) cut made into a vein; (= *sangría*) bleeding, bloodletting
[2] (*Anat*) inner angle of the elbow
[3] (*Agr*) drainage channel

sangrante ADJ [1] [*encías, úlcera*] bleeding
[2] [*batalla, guerra*] bloody
[3] (= *indignante*) scandalous; **lo más ~ del caso es que la policía no hizo nada** the most scandalous aspect of the affair was that the police did nothing

sangrar ▸conjug 1a◂ Ⓐ VT [1] [+ *enfermo, vena*] to bleed
[2] (*Agr, Téc*) [+ *terreno*] to drain; [+ *agua*] to drain off; [+ *árbol, tubería, horno*] to tap
[3] [+ *texto, línea*] to indent
[4] (= *explotar*) **~ a algn** to bleed sb dry; **siempre está sangrando a sus padres** he is always bleeding his parents dry
[5] (*) (= *robar*) to filch
Ⓑ VI [1] [*persona, herida, encías*] to bleed; **me sangra la nariz** (*de forma espontánea*) I've got a nosebleed; (*a consecuencia de un golpe*) my nose is bleeding
[2] (*frm*) (= *doler*) to rankle; **aún le sangra la humillación** the humiliation still rankles
[3] (= *ser reciente*) **estar sangrando** to be still fresh

sangre Ⓐ SF [1] (*Biol*) blood; **tiene ~ de tipo O negativo** he's blood type O negative, his blood type is O negative; **las enfermedades de la ~** blood diseases; **la tela es de color rojo ~** the fabric is a blood-red colour; **chupar la ~ a algn** (*lit*) to suck sb's blood; (*fig*) (= *explotar*) to bleed sb dry; (*Méx*) (= *hacer pasar mal rato*) to give sb a hard time, make sb's life a misery; **dar ~** to give blood; **donar ~** to donate blood; **echar ~** to bleed; **estuvo echando ~ por la nariz** (*de forma natural*) he had a nosebleed; (*a consecuencia de un golpe*) his nose was bleeding, he was bleeding from the nose; **hacer ~ a algn** to make sb bleed; **me pegó y me hizo ~** he hit me and I started bleeding *o* to bleed, he hit me and made me bleed; **hacerse ~**: **¿te has hecho ~?** are you bleeding?; **me hice ~ en la rodilla** my knee started bleeding *o* to bleed; **salirle ~ a algn**: **me está saliendo ~ de la herida** my cut is bleeding ► **sangre caliente**: **a ~ caliente** in the heat of the moment; **por sus venas corre ~ caliente** he is very hot-blooded; **de ~ caliente** [*animal*] warm-blooded *antes de s*; [*persona*] hot-blooded *antes de s* ► **sangre fría** coolness, sang-froid (*frm*); **era el que tenía más ~ fría a la hora de tomar decisiones** he was the coolest when it came to taking decisions; **la ~ fría del asesino** the murderer's cold-blooded nature; **lo asesinaron a ~ fría** they killed him in cold blood; **de ~ fría** [*animal*] cold-blooded *antes de s*; [*persona*] coolheaded *antes de s*; **mantener la ~ fría** to keep calm, keep one's cool ► **sangre nueva** new blood; **los inmigrantes inyectaron ~ nueva en el país** the immigrants injected new blood into the country; *ver tb* **banco 3**, **baño 2**, **delito 1**

2 ✦*MODISMOS* **arderle la ~ a algn**: **me arde la ~ cada vez que me habla** each time he speaks to me it makes my blood boil; **beber la ~ a algn** (*Méx*) to give sb a hard time, make sb's life a misery; **bullirle la ~ a algn**: **me bulle la ~ ante tanto sufrimiento** seeing such suffering makes my blood boil; **son jóvenes y les bulle la ~ en las venas** they are young and bursting with energy; **hacer correr la ~** to shed blood; **no les importa hacer correr la ~ de sus compatriotas** they are unconcerned about shedding the blood of their fellow countrymen; **dar su ~ por algo** to give one's life for sth, shed one's blood for sth (*frm*); **dieron su ~ por sus ideales** they gave their lives for their beliefs; **encender la ~ a algn** to make sb's blood boil; **a ~ y fuego** ruthlessly, by fire and sword (*liter*); **la revuelta fue aplastada a ~ y fuego** the revolt was crushed ruthlessly *o* by fire and sword (*liter*); **hacerse mala ~** to get annoyed; **me hago muy mala ~ cuando me faltan al respeto** I get really annoyed when people are disrespectful to me; **helar la ~ a algn** to make sb's blood run cold; **sus gritos le helaban la ~ a cualquiera** her cries would make anyone's blood run cold; **hervirle la ~ a algn**: **me hierve la ~ cuando nos tratan así** it really makes me mad *o* it makes my blood boil when they treat us like this; **tener la ~ de horchata** *o* (*Méx*) **atole** to be cold-hearted; **ser de ~ ligera** (*Méx*) ◊ **ser liviano de ~** (*Chile*) to be easy-going *o* good-natured; **llegar a la ~** to come to blows; **andar con ~ en el ojo** (*Cono Sur**) to bear a grudge; **es de ~ pesada** (*Méx*) ◊ **es pesado de ~** (*Chile*) he's not a very nice person, he's not very good-natured; **quemar la ~ a algn** to make sb's blood boil; **me quema la ~ verlo sufrir** it makes my blood boil to see him suffer; **no llegar la ~ al río**: **discutimos un poco pero no llegó la ~ al río** we argued a bit but it didn't come *o* amount to much; **sudar ~** to sweat blood; **costar ~, sudor y lágrimas** to cost blood, sweat and tears; **no tener ~ en las venas** to be a cold fish

3 (= *linaje*) blood; **lleva ~ española en las venas** he has Spanish blood (in him); **somos hermanos de ~** we're blood brothers; **tenemos la misma ~** we are blood relations; ✦*MODISMOS* **llevar algo en la ~** to have sth in one's blood; **lleva la política en la ~** he's got politics in his blood; **la ~ tira (mucho)** blood is thicker than water ► **sangre azul** blue blood; **ser de ~ azul** to belong to the aristocracy

Ⓑ ► **pura sangre** SM INV (= *caballo*) thoroughbred

sangregorda* SMF bore

sangría SF 1 (*Med*) bleeding, bloodletting ► **sangría suelta** excessive flow of blood
2 [*de recursos*] outflow, drain
3 (*Anat*) inner angle of the elbow
4 (*Agr*) (= *acequia*) irrigation channel; (= *desagüe*) outlet, outflow; (= *zanja*) ditch; (= *drenaje*) drainage
5 [*de alto horno*] (= *acción*) tapping; (= *metal fundido*) stream of molten metal
6 (*Culin*) sangria
7 (*Tip, Inform*) indentation

sangrientamente ADV bloodily

sangriento ADJ 1 (= *con sangre*) [*herida*] bleeding; [*arma, manos*] bloody, bloodstained
2 [*batalla, guerra*] bloody
3 (= *cruel*) [*injusticia*] flagrant; [*broma*] cruel; [*insulto*] deadly
4 (*liter*) [*color*] blood-red

sangrigordo ADJ (*Caribe*) (= *aburrido*) tedious, boring; (= *insolente*) rude, insolent

sangriligero* ADJ (*LAm*), **sangriliviano** ADJ (*LAm*) pleasant, congenial

sangripesado* ADJ (*LAm**), **sangrón** ADJ (*Cuba, Méx*), **sangruno** ADJ (*Caribe*) (= *desagradable*) unpleasant, nasty; (= *aburrido*) boring, tiresome; (= *obstinado*) obstinate, pigheaded

sanguarañas* SFPL (*Andes*) circumlocutions, evasions

sánguche SM (*LAm*), **sanguchito** SM (*LAm*) sandwich

sangüich SM (*Esp*) sandwich

sanguijuela SF leech

sanguinario ADJ bloodthirsty, cruel

sanguíneo ADJ 1 (*Anat*) blood *antes de s*; **vaso ~** blood vessel
2 [*color*] blood-red

sanguinolento ADJ 1 (= *con sangre*) [*herida*] bleeding; [*flujo*] bloody; [*ojos*] bloodshot
2 (= *manchado de sangre*) bloodstained
3 [*color*] blood-red
4 (*Culin*) underdone, rare

sanidad SF 1 (= *cualidad*) health, healthiness
2 (*Admin*) health, public health; **(Ministerio de) Sanidad** Ministry of Health; **inspector de ~** health inspector ► **sanidad animal** animal welfare ► **sanidad pública** public health (department)

San Isidro SM Saint Isidore

> **SAN ISIDRO**
>
> **San Isidro** *is the patron saint of Madrid, and gives his name to the week-long festivities which take place round May 15. Originally an 18th-century trade fair, the* **San Isidro** *celebrations now include music, dance, a famous* **romería**, *theatre and bullfighting. The* **isidrada** *is in fact one of the most important dates in the bullfighting calendar.*
>
> ⇨ *See also* ROMERÍA

sanitaría SF (*Cono Sur*) plumber's, plumber's shop

sanitario/a Ⓐ ADJ [*condiciones*] sanitary; [*centro, medidas*] health *antes de s*; **política sanitaria** health policy; **control ~** public health inspection; **asistencia sanitaria** medical attention

Ⓑ **sanitarios** SMPL (= *aparatos de baño*) sanitary ware *sing*, bathroom fittings; (*Méx*) (= *wáter*) toilet *sing*, washroom *sing* (*EEUU*)

Ⓒ SM/F (*Med*) stretcher bearer

sanjacobo SM *escalope with cheese filling*

San Juan SM Saint John

> **SAN JUAN**
>
> *The* **Día de San Juan** *on June 24 fuses Christian tradition with ancient summer solstice celebrations. In many areas, particularly near the sea, it is customary to light large bonfires on open ground on the night of June 23 and to burn an effigy, normally a large rag doll, at the stake. These* **hogueras de San Juan**, *which are accompanied by fireworks and music, draw crowds of people wanting to dance or simply to enjoy the summer evening, until the fire dies out in the small hours. Some legends credit this night with magical qualities and talk of ghostly apparitions.*

San Lorenzo SM **el (Río) ~** the St Lawrence (River)

San Marino SM San Marino

sano ADJ 1 (= *con salud*) [*persona*] healthy; [*órgano*] sound; [*fruta*] unblemished; ✦*MODISMO* **cortar por lo ~** to take extreme measures, go right to the root of the problem
2 (= *beneficioso*) [*clima, dieta*] healthy; [*comida*] wholesome
3 (= *entero*) whole, intact; **~ y salvo** safe and sound; **no quedó plato ~ en toda la casa** there wasn't a plate in the house left unbroken; **esa silla no es muy sana** that chair is not too strong
4 (= *sin vicios*) [*persona*] healthy; [*enseñanza, idea*] sound; [*deseo*] earnest, sincere; [*objetivo*] worthy

sansalvadoreño/a Ⓐ ADJ of/from San Salvador
Ⓑ SM/F native/inhabitant of San Salvador; **los ~s** the people of San Salvador

sánscrito ADJ, SM Sanskrit

sanseacabó EXCL **y ~*** and that's the end of it

Sansón SM Samson; ✦*MODISMO* **es un ~** he's tremendously strong

Santa Bárbara SF Santa Barbara

santabárbara SF (*Náut*) magazine

santamente ADV **vivir ~** to live a saintly life

santanderino/a (*Esp*) Ⓐ ADJ of/from Santander
Ⓑ SM/F native/inhabitant of Santander; **los ~s** the people of Santander

santateresa SF praying mantis

santería SF 1 (*Cuba*) (= *tienda*) *shop selling religious images, prints, etc*; (= *brujería*) witchcraft
2 (*) = **santidad**
3 (*Caribe Rel*) *religion of African origin*

santero/a SM/F 1 (*Caribe*) *maker or seller of religious images, prints, etc*
2 (= *devoto*) *person excessively devoted to the saints*

Santiago SM St James ► **Santiago (de Chile)** Santiago (de Chile) ► **Santiago (de Compostela)** Santiago de Compostela

santiaguero/a* SM/F (*Cono Sur*) faith healer

santiagués/esa Ⓐ ADJ of/from Santiago de Compostela

Ⓑ SM/F native/inhabitant of Santiago de Compostela; **los santiagueses** the people of Santiago

santiaguino/a Ⓐ ADJ of/from Santiago (de Chile)
Ⓑ SM/F native/inhabitant of Santiago (de Chile); **los ~s** the people of Santiago (de Chile)

santiamén SM **en un ~** in no time at all, in a flash

santidad SF [*de lugar*] holiness, sanctity; [*de persona*] saintliness; **su Santidad** His Holiness

santificación SF sanctification

santificar ▸conjug 1g◂ VT [1] (*Rel*) [+ *persona*] to sanctify; [+ *lugar*] to consecrate; [+ *fiesta*] to keep; **santificado sea Tu Nombre** hallowed be Thy Name
[2] (*) (= *perdonar*) to forgive

santiguada SF (= *señal*) sign of the Cross; (= *acto*) act of crossing oneself

santiguar ▸conjug 1i◂ Ⓐ VT [1] (= *bendecir*) to make the sign of the cross over, bless
[2] (*) (= *pegar*) to slap, hit
[3] (*LAm*) (= *sanear*) to heal, heal by blessing
Ⓑ **santiguarse** VPR [1] (= *persignarse*) to cross o.s.
[2] (*) (= *exagerar*) to make a great fuss

santísimo Ⓐ ADJ SUPERL holy, most holy
Ⓑ SM **el Santísimo** the Holy Sacrament
Ⓒ SF ✦*MODISMO* **hacer la santísima a algn*** (= *jorobar*) to drive sb up the wall*; (= *perjudicar*) to do sb down*

santo/a Ⓐ ADJ [1] (*Rel*) [*vida, persona*] holy; [*tierra*] consecrated; [*persona*] saintly; [*mártir*] blessed; *ver tb* **semana**
[2] [*remedio*] wonderful, miraculous
[3] (*enfático*) blessed; **~ y bueno** well and good; **hacer su santa voluntad** to do as one jolly well pleases; **todo el ~ día** the whole blessed day; **y él con su santa calma** and he as cool as a cucumber
Ⓑ SM/F [1] (*Rel*) saint; **Santo Tomás** St Thomas ► **santo/a patrón/ona, santo/a titular** patron saint
[2] ✦*MODISMOS* **¿a ~ de qué?** why on earth?; **¿a qué ~?** what on earth for?; **¡por todos los ~s!** for pity's sake!; **no es ~ de mi devoción** he's not my cup of tea*; **alzarse con el ~ y la limosna*** to clear off with the whole lot*; **comerse los ~s*** to be terribly devout; **desnudar a un ~ para vestir otro** to rob Peter to pay Paul; **se le fue el ~ al cielo** he forgot what he was about to say; **¡que se te va el ~ al cielo!** you're miles away!; **llegar y besar el ~** to pull it off at the first attempt; **fue llegar y besar el ~** it was as easy as pie; **nacer con el ~ de espaldas** to be born unlucky; **poner a algn como un ~*** to give sb a telling-off*; **quedarse para vestir ~s** to be left on the shelf; **tener el ~ de cara*** to have the luck of the devil; **tener el ~ de espaldas*** to be cursed with bad luck
[3] (= *persona*) saint; **es un ~** he's a saint; **estaba hecho un ~** he was terribly sweet
Ⓒ SM [1] (= *onomástica*) saint's day; **mañana es mi ~** tomorrow is my name day *o* saint's day
[2] (*en libro*) picture
[3] ► **santo y seña** (*Mil*) password
[4] (*Cono Sur Cos*) patch, darn

> **SANTO**
>
> *As well as celebrating their birthday, many Spaniards celebrate their* **santo** *or* **onomástica**. *This is the day when the saint whose name they have is honoured in the Christian calendar. It used to be relatively common for newborn children to be called after the saint whose day they were born on. So a boy born on July 25 (Saint James's day) stood a good chance of being christened "Santiago". The tradition may be dying out now that parents are no longer restricted to names from the Christian calendar, as was the case in the past. As with birthdays, the person whose* **santo** *it is normally buys the drinks.*

Santo Domingo SM [1] (= *capital*) Santo Domingo
[2] (= *isla*) Hispaniola

santón* SM (*hum*) big shot*, big wheel*

santoral SM calendar of saints' days

santuario SM [1] (*Rel*) (= *templo*) sanctuary, shrine; (= *lugar sagrado*) sanctuary
[2] (*Andes, Caribe*) (= *ídolo*) native idol; (= *tesoro*) buried treasure

santulario ADJ (*Cono Sur*) = **santurrón A**

santurrón/ona Ⓐ ADJ (= *mojigato*) sanctimonious; (= *hipócrita*) hypocritical
Ⓑ SM/F (= *mojigato*) sanctimonious person; (= *hipócrita*) hypocrite

saña SF [1] (= *furor*) rage; (= *crueldad*) cruelty; **con ~** viciously
[2] (= *cartera*) wallet, billfold (*EEUU*)

sañero‡ SM (*Esp*) pickpocket

sañoso ADJ = **sañudo**

sañudamente ADV (= *furiosamente*) angrily, furiously; (= *con crueldad*) cruelly; (= *brutalmente*) viciously

sañudo ADJ [1] [*persona*] (= *furioso*) furious, enraged; (= *cruel*) cruel
[2] [*golpe*] vicious, cruel

sapaneco ADJ (*CAm*) plump, chubby

sáparo SM (*Andes*) wicker basket

sapiencia SF knowledge, wisdom

sapo[1] SM [1] (*Zool*) toad; ✦*MODISMO* **echar ~s y culebras** to turn the air blue
[2] (= *persona*) ugly creature
[3] (*LAm*) *game of throwing coins into the mouth of an iron toad*
[4] (*CAm, Caribe*) (= *soplón*) informer, grass*, fink (*EEUU**)
[5] (*Cono Sur*‡) (= *soldado*) soldier

sapo[2] ADJ [1] (*Andes, CAm, Cono Sur*) (= *astuto*) cunning, sly
[2] (*Cono Sur*) (= *hipócrita*) hypocritical, two-faced
[3] (*CAm, Caribe*) (= *chismoso*) gossipy

saporro ADJ (*Andes, CAm*) short and chubby

sapotear ▸conjug 1a◂ VT (*Andes*) to finger, handle

saprófago ADJ saprophagous

saprófito Ⓐ ADJ saprophytic
Ⓑ SM saprophyte

saque Ⓐ SM [1] (*Tenis*) service, serve; (*Rugby*) line-out; (*Ftbl*) (*para dar comienzo al partido*) kick-off ► **saque de banda** (*Ftbl*) throw-in ► **saque de castigo** penalty kick ► **saque de esquina** corner, corner kick ► **saque de falta** free kick ► **saque de honor** guest appearance ► **saque de mano** (*LAm*) throw-in ► **saque de portería, saque de puerta** goal kick ► **saque inicial** kick-off ► **saque lateral** throw-in ► **saque libre** free kick
[2] (= *apetito*) **tener buen ~** to have a hearty appetite
Ⓑ SMF (*Tenis*) server

saqué *etc ver* **sacar**

saqueador(a) SM/F looter

saquear ▸conjug 1a◂ VT [1] (*Mil*) to sack
[2] (= *robar*) to loot, plunder, pillage

saqueo SM [1] (*Mil*) sacking
[2] (= *robo*) looting, plundering, pillaging

saquito SM small bag ► **saquito de papel** paper bag

S.A.R. ABR (= **Su Alteza Real**) HRH

sarampión SM measles

sarao SM [1] (= *fiesta*) soirée, evening party
[2] (*) (= *lío*) fuss, to-do*

sarape SM (*Méx*) blanket

sarasa* SM pansy*, fairy*, fag (*EEUU*‡)

saraviado ADJ (*Andes*) [*objeto*] spotted, mottled; [*animal*] spotted; [*persona*] freckled

sarazo ADJ (*LAm*) = **zarazo**

sarazón ADJ (*Méx*) = **zarazo**

sarcasmo SM sarcasm; **es un ~ que …** it is ludicrous that …

sarcásticamente ADV sarcastically

sarcástico ADJ sarcastic

sarcófago SM sarcophagus

sarcoma SM sarcoma

sardana SF *Catalan dance and music*

sardina SF sardine; ✦*MODISMO* **como ~s en lata** like sardines ► **sardina arenque** herring ► **sardina noruega** brisling

sardinero ADJ sardine *antes de s*

sardo/a ADJ, SM/F Sardinian

sardónico ADJ sardonic, sarcastic

sargazo SM gulfweed

sargentear ▸conjug 1a◂ Ⓐ VT [1] (*Mil*) to command
[2] (*) (= *mandonear*) to boss about
Ⓑ VI (*) to be bossy, boss people about

sargento SMF [1] (*Mil*) sergeant ► **sargento de primera** [*de tierra*] staff sergeant; [*de aire*] flight sergeant
[2] (*pey*, *) (= *mandón*) bossy person

sargentona* SF tough mannish woman

sargo SM bream

sari SM sari

sarita SF (*Andes*) straw hat

sarmentoso ADJ [1] [*planta*] twining, climbing
[2] (*Anat*) [*manos*] gnarled; [*dedos*] long and thin

sarmiento SM vine shoot

sarna SF (*Med*) scabies; (*Vet*) mange

sarniento ADJ, **sarnoso** ADJ [1] (*Med*) scabious; (*Vet*) mangy
[2] (= *raquítico*) weak
[3] (*Andes, Cono Sur**) (= *despreciable*) lousy*, contemptible

sarong SM sarong

sarpullido SM [1] (*Med*) rash
[2] [*de pulga*] fleabite

sarraceno/a ADJ, SM/F Saracen

sarracina SF [1] (= *pelea*) brawl, free fight
[2] (= *matanza*) mass slaughter; **han hecho**

una ~ (*Educ*) they've ploughed almost everybody*

Sarre SM Saar

sarrio SM Pyrenean mountain goat

sarro SM [1] (= *depósito*) (*en los dientes*) tartar, plaque; (*en la lengua*) fur; (*en una caldera*) scale, fur
[2] (*Bot*) rust

sarroso ADJ [*dientes*] covered with tartar; [*caldera, lengua*] furred, furry

sarta SF, **sartalada** SF (*Cono Sur*) (= *serie*) string; (= *fila*) line, row; **una ~ de mentiras** a pack of lies

sartén SF (SM *en LAm*) frying pan; ✦*MODISMO* **coger la ~ por donde quema** to act rashly; **saltar de la ~ y dar en la brasa** to jump out of the frying pan into the fire; **tener la ~ por el mango** to have the upper hand

sarteneja SF (*Andes, Méx*) (= *marisma seca*) dried-out pool; (*Méx*) (= *bache*) pothole; (= *tierra seca*) cracked soil, parched soil

sasafrás SM sassafras

sastre/a Ⓐ SM/F tailor; (*Teat*) costumier; **hecho por ~** tailor-made ► **sastre de teatro** costumier
Ⓑ ADJ INV **traje ~** tailor-made suit

sastrería SF [1] (= *oficio*) tailor's trade, tailoring
[2] (= *tienda*) tailor's, tailor's shop

Satán SM, **Satanás** SM Satan

satánico ADJ (= *diabólico*) satanic; (= *malvado*) fiendish

satanismo SM Satanism, devil-worship

satanización SF demonizing

satanizar ▸conjug 1f◂ VT to demonize

satelitario ADJ satellite *antes de s*

satélite Ⓐ SM [1] (*Astron*) satellite; **transmisión vía ~** satellite broadcasting ► **satélite artificial** artificial satellite ► **satélite de comunicaciones** communications satellite ► **satélite espía** spy satellite ► **satélite meteorológico** weather satellite
[2] (= *persona*) (*gen*) satellite; (= *esbirro*) henchman; (= *compañero*) crony
Ⓑ ADJ INV satellite; **ciudad ~** satellite town; **país ~** satellite country

satén SM sateen

satín SM (*LAm*) sateen, satin

satinado Ⓐ ADJ glossy, shiny
Ⓑ SM gloss, shine

satinar ▸conjug 1a◂ VT to gloss, make glossy

sátira SF satire

satíricamente ADV satirically

satírico ADJ satiric, satirical

satirizar ▸conjug 1f◂ VT to satirize

sátiro SM [1] (*Literat*) satyr
[2] (= *hombre lascivo*) sex maniac

satisfacción SF [1] (= *placer*) satisfaction; **a ~ de** to the satisfaction of; **a su entera ~** to his complete satisfaction; **con ~ de todos** to everyone's satisfaction ► **satisfacción laboral, satisfacción profesional** job satisfaction
[2] [*de ofensa*] (= *compensación*) satisfaction, redress; (= *disculpa*) apology; **pedir una ~ a algn** to demand satisfaction from sb
[3] ► **satisfacción de sí mismo** self-satisfaction, smugness

satisfacer ▸conjug 2r◂ Ⓐ VT [1] [+ *persona*] to satisfy; **el resultado no me satisface** I'm not satisfied *o* happy with the result; **~ a algn de *o* por una ofensa** to give sb satisfaction for an offence
[2] (= *compensar*) [+ *gastos, demanda*] to meet; [+ *deuda*] to pay; [+ *éxito*] to gratify, please; [+ *necesidad, solicitud*] to meet, satisfy; (*Com*) [+ *letra de cambio*] to honour, honor (*EEUU*)
[3] [+ *culpa*] to expiate; [+ *pérdida*] to make good
Ⓑ **satisfacerse** VPR [1] (= *contentarse*) to satisfy o.s., be satisfied; **~se con muy poco** to be content with very little
[2] (= *vengarse*) to take revenge

satisfactoriamente ADV satisfactorily

satisfactorio ADJ satisfactory

satisfecho ADJ [1] (= *complacido*) satisfied; (= *contento*) content, contented; **darse por ~ con algo** to declare o.s. satisfied with sth; **dejar ~s a todos** to satisfy everybody
[2] (*después de comer*) **quedarse ~** to be full
[3] (*tb* **~ consigo mismo, ~ de sí mismo**) self-satisfied, smug; **nos miró ~** he looked at us smugly

sativa SF (*Cono Sur*) marijuana

satrústegui* EXCL well!, gee! (*EEUU*), well I'm blowed!*

satsuma SF satsuma

saturación SF saturation

saturado ADJ saturated

saturar ▸conjug 1a◂ VT (*Fís, Quím*) to saturate; **~ el mercado** to flood the market; **estos aeropuertos son los más saturados** those airports are the most crowded *o* stretched; **¡estoy saturado de tanta televisión!** I can't take any more television!

saturnales SFPL Saturnalia

saturnino ADJ saturnine

Saturno SM Saturn

sauce SM willow ► **sauce de Babilonia, sauce llorón** weeping willow

saucedal SM willow plantation

saúco SM elder

saudí ADJ, SMF, **saudita** ADJ, SMF Saudi

Saúl SM Saul

sauna SF (SM *en Cono Sur*) sauna

saurio SM saurian

savia SF sap

saxífraga SF saxifrage

saxo Ⓐ SM sax
Ⓑ SMF sax player

saxofón Ⓐ SM (= *instrumento*) saxophone
Ⓑ SMF (= *músico*) saxophonist

saxofonista SMF saxophonist

saxófono SMF = **saxofón A**

saya SF [1] (*para vestir*) (= *falda*) skirt; (= *enagua*) petticoat; (= *vestido*) dress
[2] (*Andes*) (= *mujer*) woman

sayal SM sackcloth

sayo SM (= *prenda*) smock, tunic; ✦*MODISMO* **cortar un ~ a algn** (*Esp*) to gossip about sb, talk behind sb's back; **¿qué ~ se me corta?** what are they saying about me?

sayón SM [1] (*Jur*) executioner
[2] (= *hombre peligroso*) ugly customer*

sayuela SF (*Caribe*) long shirt, smock

sazo* SM hankie*

sazón¹ SF [1] [*de fruta*] ripeness; **en ~** [*fruta*] ripe, ready (to eat); (= *oportunamente*) opportunely; **fuera de ~** [*fruta*] out of season; (= *inoportunamente*) inopportunely
[2] (*liter*) **a la ~** then, at that time
[3] (= *sabor*) flavour, flavor (*EEUU*)

sazón² ADJ (*Andes, CAm, Méx*) ripe

sazonado ADJ [1] [*fruta*] ripe
[2] [*plato*] seasoned
[3] **~ de** seasoned with, flavoured *o* (*EEUU*) flavored with
[4] (= *ingenioso*) witty

sazonar ▸conjug 1a◂ Ⓐ VT [1] [+ *fruta*] to ripen
[2] (*Culin*) to season (**de** with)
[3] (*Caribe*) (= *endulzar*) to sweeten
Ⓑ VI to ripen

s/c ABR (*Com*) [1] = **su casa**
[2] = **su cuenta**

scalextric® SM [1] Scalextric® (*model motor racing set*)
[2] (*Aut*) *complicated traffic interchange*, spaghetti junction*

schop [ʃop] SM (*Cono Sur*) (= *vaso*) mug, tankard; (= *cerveza*) beer, draught *o* (*EEUU*) draft beer

schopería [ʃope'ria] SF (*Cono Sur*) beer bar

scooter [es'kuter] SM motor scooter

Scotch® SM (*Andes, Méx*) Sellotape®, Scotch tape® (*EEUU*)

script [es'kri] SF (*pl* **scripts** [es'kri]) script-girl

Sdo. ABR (*Com*) (= **Saldo**) bal

SE ABR (= **sudeste**) SE

se¹ PRON PERS [1] (*complemento indirecto*) [1·1] (*a él*) him; (*a ella*) her; (*a ellos*) them; (*a usted, ustedes*) you; **voy a dárselo** I'll give it to him *o* her *o* them *o* you; **ya se lo dije** I (already) told him *o* her *o* them *o* you; **he hablado con mis padres y se lo he explicado** I've talked to my parents and explained it to them; **aquí tiene las flores, ¿se las envuelvo, señor?** here are your flowers, shall I wrap them for you, sir?; **no lo tenemos, pero se lo puedo encargar** we haven't got it, but I can order it for you
[1·2] (*con doble complemento indirecto*) **dáselo a Enrique** give it to Enrique; **¿se lo has preguntado a tus padres?** have you asked your parents about it?
[1·3] (*con partes del cuerpo, ropa*) **se rompió la pierna** he broke his leg; **Pablo se lavó los dientes** Pablo cleaned his teeth; **Carmen no podía abrocharse el vestido** Carmen couldn't do up her dress; **han prometido no cortarse la barba** they have sworn not to cut their beards; **tiene que cortarse el pelo** he must have a haircut
[1·4] (*uso enfático*) **se comió un pastel** he ate a cake; **no se esperaba eso** he didn't expect that
[2] (*uso reflexivo*) [2·1] (*masculino*) himself; (*femenino*) herself; (*plural*) themselves; (*de usted*) yourself; (*de ustedes*) yourselves; (*sujeto no humano*) itself; **Marcos se ha cortado con un cristal** Marcos cut himself on a piece of broken glass; **Margarita se estaba preparando para salir** Margarita was getting (herself) ready to go out; **¿se ha hecho usted daño?** have you hurt yourself?; **se tiraron al suelo** they threw themselves to the ground; **la calefacción se apaga sola** the heating turns itself off automatically; **se está afeitando** he's shaving; **¡siéntese!** sit down; **sírvase esperar un momento** please wait a moment; **vestirse** to get dressed
[2·2] (*indefinido*) oneself; **mirarse en el espejo** to look at oneself in the mirror

3 (*como parte de un verbo pronominal*) **se durmió** he fell asleep; **se enfadó** he got annoyed; **se marchó** he left; **mi hermana nunca se queja** my sister never complains; **se retira** he withdraws
4 (*uso recíproco*) each other, one another; **se escriben a menudo** they write to each other often; **se quieren** they love each other; **hace un año que no se ven** it's a year since they last saw each other; **procuran no encontrarse** they try not to meet each other; **se miraron todos** they all looked at one another; **no se hablan** they are not on speaking terms
5 (*uso impersonal*) 5·1 (*con sujeto indeterminado*) **se registraron nueve muertos** there were nine deaths, nine deaths were recorded; **se dice que es muy rico** he's said to be very rich; **no se sabe por qué** it is not known *o* people don't know why; **se compró hace tres años** it was bought three years ago; **en esa zona se habla galés** Welsh is spoken in that area, people speak Welsh in that area; **se cree que el tabaco produce cáncer** it is believed that smoking causes cancer
5·2 (*referido al hablante*) **no se oye bien** you can't hear very well; **es lo que pasa cuando se come tan deprisa** that's what happens when you eat so fast; **¿cómo se dice eso en inglés?** how do you say that in English?; **se está bien aquí** it's nice here; **se hace lo que se puede** we do what we can; **se admiten sugerencias** we welcome suggestions; **"véndese coche"** "car for sale"; **se avisa a los interesados que ...** those concerned are informed that ...
5·3 (*en recetas, instrucciones*) **se pelan las patatas** peel the potatoes; **"sírvase muy frío"** "serve chilled"; **"no se admiten visitas"** "no visitors"; **"se prohíbe fumar"** "no smoking"

sé *ver* **saber, ser**

S.E. ABR (= **Su Excelencia**) H.E.

SEA SM ABR (*Esp Agr*) = **Servicio de Extensión Agraria.**

sea [*etc*] *ver* **ser**

SEAT SF ABR, **Seat** SF ABR (*Esp*) = **Sociedad Española de Automóviles de Turismo**

sebáceo ADJ sebaceous

sebear ▸conjug 1a◂ VT (*Caribe*) to inspire love in

sebo SM 1 (= *grasa*) (*gen*) grease, fat; (*para velas*) tallow; (*Culin*) suet
2 (= *gordura*) fat

sebón ADJ (*Andes, CAm, Cono Sur*) idle, lazy

seboso ADJ (= *grasiento*) greasy; (= *mugriento*) grimy

Sec. ABR (= **secretario, secretaria**) sec

seca SF 1 (*Agr*) drought
2 (*Meteo*) dry season
3 (*Náut*) sandbank

secadero SM 1 (= *lugar*) drying place
2 (*Andes*) (= *terreno*) dry plain, scrubland

secado SM drying ► **secado a mano** blow-dry

secador SM drier, dryer ► **secador centrífugo** spin drier, spin dryer ► **secador de manos** hand drier, hand dryer ► **secador de pelo** hairdrier, hairdryer

secadora SF tumble drier, tumble dryer ► **secadora centrífuga** spin drier, spin dryer ► **secadora de cabello** (*CAm, Méx*) hairdrier, hairdryer

secamanos SM INV hand drier, hand dryer

secamente ADV [*contestar*] curtly; [*ordenar*] sharply; **—no sé nada —afirmó ~** "I don't know anything," he said curtly; **se comportó muy ~ con nosotros** he was very short *o* curt with us; **—ahora, ¡a dormir! —dijo ~** "now, off to sleep!," he said sharply

secano SM 1 (*Agr*) (*tb* **tierra de ~**) (= *sin lluvia*) dry land, dry region; (= *sin riego*) unirrigated land; **cultivo de ~** dry farming
2 (*Náut*) (= *banco de arena*) sandbank; (= *islote*) small sandy island

secante[1] Ⓐ ADJ 1 **papel ~** blotting paper
2 (*Andes, Cono Sur**) (= *latoso*) annoying
Ⓑ SM blotting paper, blotter

secante[2] SF (*Mat*) secant

secapelos SM INV hair-drier, hair-dryer

secar ▸conjug 1g◂ Ⓐ VT 1 (= *quitar la humedad*) (*con paño, toalla*) to dry; (*con fregona*) to mop up; (*con papel secante*) to blot; **me sequé las lágrimas** I dried my tears; **~ los platos** to dry the plates, dry up
2 (= *resecar*) [+ *planta, terreno*] to dry up; [+ *piel*] to dry out
3 (*Uru*) (= *fastidiar*) to annoy, vex
Ⓑ VI to dry; **lo he puesto a ~ cerca del radiador** I've left it to dry near the radiator
Ⓒ **secarse** VPR 1 (*uso reflexivo*) 1·1 [*persona*] to dry o.s., get dry; **me encanta ~me al sol** I love drying myself in the sun
1·2 [+ *manos, pelo*] to dry; [+ *lágrimas, sudor*] to dry, wipe; **~se la frente** to mop one's brow
2 (= *quedarse sin agua*) 2·1 [*ropa*] to dry, dry off; **no entres hasta que no se seque el suelo** don't come in until the floor is dry *o* has dried
2·2 [*arroz, pasta*] to go dry; [*garganta*] to get dry; [*río, pozo*] to dry up, run dry; [*hierba, terreno*] to dry up; [*planta*] to wither
3 [*herida*] to heal up
4 (*) (= *adelgazar*) to get thin
5 (*) (*tb* **~se de sed**) to be parched*

secarral SM dry plain, arid area

secarropa SM clothes-horse

sección SF 1 (*Arquit, Mat*) section ► **sección cónica** conic section ► **sección longitudinal** longitudinal section ► **sección transversal** cross section ► **sección vertical** vertical section
2 (= *parte*) (*gen*) section; [*de almacén, oficina*] department ► **sección de contactos** personal column (*containing offers of marriage etc*) ► **sección de cuerdas** string section ► **sección deportiva** sports page, sports section ► **sección económica** financial pages *pl*, city pages *pl* ► **sección fija** regular feature
3 (*Mil*) section, platoon

seccional Ⓐ ADJ sectional
Ⓑ SF 1 (*Cono Sur*) police station
2 (*Col*) branch office

seccionar ▸conjug 1a◂ VT (= *dividir*) to section, divide into sections; (= *cortar*) to cut, cut off; (= *disecar*) to dissect; **~ la garganta a algn** to cut sb's throat

secesión SF secession

secesionista ADJ, SMF secessionist

seco Ⓐ ADJ 1 (= *no húmedo*) dry; **tengo los labios ~s** my lips are dry; **las sábanas no están secas todavía** the sheets are still not dry; **es un calor ~** it's a dry heat; **en ~** (= *sin líquido*): **no me puedo tragar esto en ~** I can't swallow this without water; **"limpiar en seco"** "dry clean only"; *ver tb* **dique 1, ley 1**
2 (= *desecado*) [*higo, pescado*] dried; [*hojas*] dead, dried; [*árbol*] dead; **un cuadro de flores secas** a painting of dried flowers; **estaban ~s todos los geranios** all the geraniums had dried up; **dame una cerveza, que estoy ~*** give me a beer, I'm really parched*; *ver tb* **ciruela, fruto 1**
3 (= *no graso*) [*piel, pelo*] dry
4 (= *no dulce*) [*vino, licor*] dry; **un champán muy ~** a very dry champagne
5 (= *flaco*) thin, skinny*; ✦**MODISMO está ~ como un palo** he's (as) thin as a rake
6 (= *no amable*) [*persona, carácter, respuesta*] curt; [*orden*] sharp; [*estilo*] dry; **estuvo muy ~ conmigo por teléfono** he was very curt *o* short with me on the phone; **—no se puede —contestó muy ~** "can't be done," he replied curtly
7 (= *sin resonancia*) [*tos*] dry; [*ruido*] dull; [*impacto*] sharp; **oyó el golpe ~ de la puerta** he heard the dull thud of the door; **le dio un golpe ~ en la cabeza** he gave him a sharp bang on the head
8 **en ~** (= *bruscamente*): **frenar en ~** to brake sharply; **pararse en ~** to stop dead, stop suddenly; **parar a algn en ~** (*al hablar*) to cut sb short
9 (= *sin acompañamiento*) **sobrevivimos a base de pan ~** we survived on bread alone; **para vivir sólo tiene el sueldo ~** he has nothing but his salary to live on; *ver tb* **palo 5**
10 ✦**MODISMOS a secas**: **no existe la libertad a secas** there's no such thing as freedom pure and simple; **Gerardo García, Gerardo a secas para los amigos** Gerardo García, just Gerardo to his friends; **nos alimentamos de pan a secas** we survived on nothing but bread; **dejar ~ a algn*** (= *matar*) to kill sb stone dead*; **lo dejó ~ de un tiro** he blew him away*; **cuando me dijo el precio me dejó ~** I was stunned when he told me the price; **ser ~ para algo** (*Chile**) to be a great one for sth*; **tener ~ a algn** (*Col, Cono Sur*): **me tienen ~** I've had enough of them; **tomarse algo al ~** (*Chile*) to down sth in one; **a ver todos, ¿al ~?** come on everyone, (down) in one!
Ⓑ SM (*Col*) main course

secoya SF redwood, sequoia

secre* SMF = **secretario**

secreción SF secretion

secreta* Ⓐ SF secret police
Ⓑ SMF secret policeman/policewoman

secretamente ADV secretly

secretar ▸conjug 1a◂ VT to secrete

secretaría SF 1 (= *oficina*) secretary's office
2 (= *cargo*) secretaryship
3 **Secretaría** (*Méx*) (= *Ministerio*) Ministry

secretariado SM 1 (= *oficina*) secretariat
2 (= *cargo*) secretaryship
3 (= *curso*) secretarial course
4 (= *profesión*) profession of secretary

secretario/a SM/F 1 (= *administrativo*) secretary ► **secretario/a adjunto/a** assistant secretary ► **secretario/a de dirección** executive secretary ► **secretario/a de imagen** public relations officer ► **secretario/a de prensa** press secretary ► **secretario/a de rodaje** script clerk ► **secretario/a general** (*gen*) general secretary; (*Pol*) secretary general ► **secretario/a judicial** clerk of the court

► **secretario/a municipal** town clerk ► **secretario/a particular** private secretary
2 (*Méx Pol*) Minister, Minister of State, Secretary of State (*EEUU*) ► **secretario/a de Estado** (*Esp*) junior minister, undersecretary (*EEUU*)
secretear ▸conjug 1a◂ VI 1 (= *conversar*) to talk confidentially
2 (= *cuchichear*) to whisper (unnecessarily)
secreter SM writing desk
secretismo SM secrecy, excessive secrecy
secreto Ⓐ SM 1 (= *confidencia*) secret; **alto ~** top secret; **confiar** *o* **contar un ~ a algn** to tell sb a secret; **en ~** in secret, secretly; **estar en el ~** (*frm*) to be in on the secret; **guardar un ~** to keep a secret; **hacer ~ de algo** (*frm*) to be secretive about sth, keep sth secret ► **secreto a voces** open secret ► **secreto de confesión** (*Rel*) confessional secret ► **secreto de estado** state secret ► **secreto de Polichinela** (*frm*) open secret ► **secreto de sumario**, **secreto sumarial**: **debido al ~ del sumario** *o* **sumarial** because the matter is sub judice; **se ha levantado el ~ sumarial sobre el caso** reporting restrictions have been lifted; *ver tb* **mantener A2.2**
2 (= *clave*) secret; **el ~ está en la salsa** the secret is in the sauce; **¿cuál es el ~ de su éxito?** what is the secret of her success?
3 (= *reserva*) secrecy; **lo han hecho con mucho ~** they have done it in great secrecy
4 (= *cajón*) secret drawer
5 (= *combinación*) combination
Ⓑ ADJ secret; **todo es de lo más ~** it's all highly secret
secta SF sect
sectario/a Ⓐ ADJ sectarian; **no ~** (*Pol*) non-sectarian; (*Rel*) non-denominational
Ⓑ SM/F sectarian
sectarismo SM sectarianism
sector SM 1 (*Econ, Geom*) sector ► **sector privado** private sector ► **sector público** public sector ► **sector terciario** tertiary sector, service industries *pl*, service sector
2 (= *sección*) [*de opinión*] section; [*de ciudad*] area, sector
sectorial ADJ sectorial
sectorialmente ADV *in a way which relates to a particular sector o industry etc*
secuaz SMF (= *partidario*) (*gen*) follower, supporter; (*pey*) henchman
secuela SF 1 (= *consecuencia*) consequence
2 (*Méx Jur*) proceedings *pl*, prosecution
secuencia SF sequence ► **secuencia de arranque** (*Inform*) startup routine, startup sequence
secuenciación SF sequencing
secuencial ADJ sequential
secuencialmente ADV sequentially, in sequence
secuenciar ▸conjug 1b◂ VT to arrange in sequence
secuestración SF 1 (*Jur*) sequestration
2 = **secuestro**
secuestrador(a) SM/F 1 [*de persona*] kidnapper
2 [*de avión*] hijacker ► **secuestrador(a) aéreo/a** hijacker
secuestrar ▸conjug 1a◂ VT 1 [+ *persona*] to kidnap
2 [+ *avión*] to hijack
3 (*Jur*) to seize, confiscate
secuestro SM 1 [*de persona*] kidnapping, kidnaping (*EEUU*)
2 [*de avión*] hijack, hijacking ► **secuestro aéreo** hijack, hijacking
3 (*Jur*) [*de cargamento, contrabando*] seizure; [*de propiedad*] sequestration
secular ADJ 1 (*Rel*) secular, lay
2 (= *que dura 100 años*) century-old; (= *antiguo*) age-old, ancient; **una tradición ~** an age-old tradition
secularización SF secularization
secularizar ▸conjug 1f◂ VT to secularize
secundar ▸conjug 1a◂ VT 1 [+ *moción*] to second; [+ *huelga*] to take part in, join
2 [+ *persona*] (*en un proyecto*) to support; (*para la votación*) to second
secundario/a Ⓐ ADJ (= *no principal*) (*gen*) secondary; [*carretera, efectos*] side *antes de s*; (*Inform*) background *antes de s*; **actor ~** supporting actor; *ver tb* **educación 1**
Ⓑ SM/F supporting actor
secundinas SFPL afterbirth *sing*
secuoia SF (*LAm*), **secuoya** SF (*LAm*) = **secoya**
sed SF 1 (= *ganas de beber*) thirst; **apagar** *o* **saciar la ~** to quench one's thirst; **tener (mucha) ~** to be (very) thirsty; **~ inextinguible** *o* **insaciable** unquenchable thirst
2 (*Agr*) drought, dryness
3 (= *ansia*) thirst (**de** for), craving (**de** for); **tener ~ de** to thirst *o* be thirsty for, crave
seda SF 1 (= *hilo, tela*) silk; **de ~** silk *antes de s*; ✦*MODISMOS* **hacer ~**‡ to sleep, kip‡; **como la ~** (*adj*) as smooth as silk; (*adv*) smoothly; **ir como la ~** to go like clockwork ► **seda artificial** artificial silk ► **seda de coser** sewing silk ► **seda dental** dental floss ► **seda en rama** raw silk ► **seda hilada** spun silk ► **seda lavada** washed silk
2 (*Zool*) bristle
sedación SF sedation
sedal SM fishing line
sedán SM saloon, sedan (*EEUU*)
sedante Ⓐ ADJ 1 (*Med*) sedative
2 (= *relajante*) soothing, calming
Ⓑ SM sedative
sedar ▸conjug 1a◂ VT to sedate
sedativo ADJ sedative
sede SF 1 (= *lugar*) [*de gobierno*] seat; [*de organización*] headquarters *pl*, central office; (*Dep*) venue ► **sede diplomática** diplomatic quarter ► **sede social** head office, central office
2 (*Rel*) see; **Santa Sede** Holy See
sedentario ADJ sedentary
sedentarismo SM 1 (= *cualidad*) sedentary nature
2 (= *actitud*) sedentary lifestyle
sedente ADJ seated
sedeño ADJ 1 (= *sedoso*) silky, silken (*liter*)
2 (*Zool*) bristly
sedería SF 1 (*de seda*) (= *comercio*) silk trade; (= *manufactura*) silk manufacture, sericulture; (= *tienda*) silk shop
2 (= *géneros*) silk goods *pl*
sedero/a Ⓐ ADJ silk *antes de s*; **industria sedera** silk industry
Ⓑ SM/F silk dealer
SEDIC SF ABR = **Sociedad Española de Documentación e Información Científica**
sedicente ADJ self-styled, would-be
sedición SF sedition
sedicioso/a Ⓐ ADJ seditious
Ⓑ SM/F rebel
sediente ADJ **bienes ~s** real estate
sediento ADJ [*persona*] thirsty; [*campos*] parched; **~ de poder** power-hungry
sedimentación SF sedimentation
sedimentar ▸conjug 1a◂ Ⓐ VT 1 (= *depositar*) to deposit
2 (= *aquietar*) to settle, calm
Ⓑ **sedimentarse** VPR 1 (= *depositarse*) to settle
2 (= *aquietarse*) to calm down, settle down
sedimentario ADJ sedimentary
sedimento SM sediment, deposit
sedosidad SF silkiness
sedoso ADJ silky, silken
seducción SF 1 (= *acción*) seduction
2 (= *encanto*) seductiveness
seducir ▸conjug 3n◂ Ⓐ VT 1 (*en sentido sexual*) to seduce
2 (= *cautivar*) to charm, captivate; **seduce a todos con su simpatía** she captivates everyone with her charm; **la teoría ha seducido a muchos** the theory has attracted many people; **no me seduce la idea** I'm not taken with the idea
3 (*moralmente*) to lead astray
Ⓑ VI to be charming; **es una película que seduce** it's a captivating film
seductivo ADJ = **seductor A**
seductor(a) Ⓐ ADJ 1 (*sexualmente*) seductive
2 (= *cautivador*) [*persona*] charming; [*idea*] tempting
Ⓑ SM/F seducer/seductress
Sefarad SF 1 (*Hist*) Spain
2 (= *patria*) homeland
sefardí, **sefardita** Ⓐ ADJ Sephardic
Ⓑ SMF Sephardic Jew/Sephardic Jewess, Sephardi; **~es** ◊ **sefarditas** Sephardim
segable ADJ ready to cut
segadera SF sickle
segador(a) SM/F (= *persona*) harvester, reaper
segadora SF (*Mec*) harvester ► **segadora de césped** lawnmower
segadora-atadora SF binder
segadora-trilladora SF combine harvester
segar ▸conjug 1h, 1j◂ VT 1 (*Agr*) [+ *mies*] to reap, cut; [+ *hierba*] to mow, cut
2 (= *acabar con*) [+ *persona*] to cut off; [+ *esperanzas*] to ruin; **~ la juventud de algn** to cut sb off in his prime
seglar Ⓐ ADJ secular, lay
Ⓑ SMF layman/laywoman; **los ~es** the laity
segmentación SF segmentation
segmentar ▸conjug 1a◂ Ⓐ VT 1 (= *cortar*) to segment, cut into segments
2 (= *dividir*) to divide up, separate out
Ⓑ **segmentarse** VPR to fragment, divide up
segmento SM (*Mat, Zool*) segment; (*Com, Fin*) sector, group ► **segmento de émbolo** (*Aut*) piston ring
segoviano/a Ⓐ ADJ of/from Segovia
Ⓑ SM/F native/inhabitant of Segovia; **los ~s** the people of Segovia
segregación SF 1 (= *separación*) segregation ► **segregación racial** racial segregation
2 (*Anat*) secretion

segregacionista SMF segregationist, supporter of racial segregation

segregar ▸conjug 1h◂ VT [1] (= *separar*) to segregate

[2] (*Anat*) to secrete

seguida SF [1] **de ~** (= *sin parar*) without a break; (= *inmediatamente*) at once, immediately; **en ~** right away; **en ~ estoy con usted** I'll be with you right away; **en ~ voy** I'll be right there; **en ~ termino** I've nearly finished, I shan't be a minute; **en ~ tomó el avión para Madrid** he immediately caught the plane to Madrid

[2] ✦*MODISMO* **coger la ~** to get into the swing of it

seguidamente ADV [1] (= *sin parar*) continuously

[2] (= *inmediatamente después*) immediately after, next; **~ les ofrecemos ...** (*TV*) next ..., and next ...; **dijo ~ que ...** he went on at once to say that ...

seguidilla SF [1] (*Mús*) seguidilla (*dance and piece of music in a fast triple rhythm*)

[2] (*Literat*) seguidilla (*poem with four to seven lines used in popular songs*)

[3] **una ~ de protestas** a series of complaints

seguidista ADJ copycat *antes de s*

seguido Ⓐ ADJ [1] [*línea*] continuous, unbroken; **una fila seguida de casas** a row of terraced houses

[2] **~s: cinco días ~s** (= *ininterrumpidos*) five days running, five days in a row; **tres blancos ~s** three bull's-eyes in a row, three consecutive bull's-eyes; **llevo dos horas seguidas esperándote** I've been waiting for you for two whole *o* solid hours; **tuvo los niños muy ~s** she had all her children one after the other

[3] **~ de algo/algn** followed by sth/sb; **llegó el ministro ~ de sus colaboradores** the minister arrived, followed by his staff

Ⓑ ADV [1] (= *directo*) straight on; **vaya todo ~** just keep going straight on; **continúe por aquí ~** go straight on past here

[2] (= *detrás*) **ese coche iba primero y ~ el mío** that car was in front and mine was immediately behind it

[3] (*LAm*) (= *a menudo*) often; **le gusta visitarnos ~** she likes to visit us often

seguidor(a) SM/F (*gen*) follower; (*Dep*) supporter, fan*

seguimiento SM [1] (= *persecución*) pursuit; **ir en ~ de** to chase (after); **estación de ~** tracking station

[2] (= *continuación*) (*gen*) continuation; (*TV*) report, follow-up

[3] [*de proceso*] (*tb Med*) monitoring; **el secuestro ha tenido un gran ~ por todas las televisiones** the kidnapping received plenty of coverage on all channels; **el ~ de la huelga** the support for the strike

seguir ▸conjug 3d, 3k◂ Ⓐ VT [1] (= *perseguir*) [+ *persona, pista*] to follow; [+ *indicio*] to follow up; [+ *presa*] to chase, pursue; **tú ve primero que yo te sigo** you go first and I'll follow you; **ella llegó primero, seguida del embajador** she arrived first, followed by the ambassador; **nos están siguiendo** we're being followed; **seguía todos sus pasos** I followed his every step; **la seguía con la mirada** his eyes followed her; **me sigue como un perrito faldero** he's always tramping at my heels

[2] (= *estar atento a*) [+ *programa de TV*] to watch, follow; [+ *programa de radio*] to listen to, follow; [+ *proceso, progreso*] to monitor, follow up; [+ *satélite*] to track; **~ los acontecimientos de cerca** to monitor events closely; **estaba ocupada y no he seguido la conversación** I was busy and didn't follow the conversation; **esta exposición permite ~ paso a paso la evolución del artista** this exhibition allows the artist's development to be traced step by step

[3] (= *hacer caso de*) [+ *consejo*] to follow, take; [+ *instrucciones, doctrina, líder*] to follow; **siguió el ejemplo de su padre** he followed his father's example; **~ los pasos de algn** to follow in sb's footsteps; **sigue la tradición de la familia** he follows in the family tradition

[4] [+ *rumbo, dirección*] to follow; **seguimos el curso del río** we followed the course of the river; **siga la flecha** follow the arrow; **siga esta calle y al final gire a la derecha** carry on up *o* follow this street and turn right at the end; **~ su camino** to continue on one's way; **sigue su camino de cineasta independiente** he continues in his path of independent film-maker; **el mercado sigue su camino alcista** the market is continuing on its upward trend; **~ su curso: el proyecto sigue su curso** the project is still on course, the project continues on (its) course; **la enfermedad sigue su curso** the illness is taking *o* running its course; **que la justicia siga su curso** let justice take its course

[5] (= *entender*) [+ *razonamiento*] to follow; **es un razonamiento muy difícil de ~** it's an argument which is rather hard to follow; **¿me sigues?** are you with me?

[6] (*Educ*) [+ *curso*] to take, do

[7] (†) [+ *mujer*] to court†

Ⓑ VI [1] (= *continuar*) to go on, carry on; **¿quieres que sigamos?** shall we go on?; **¡siga!** (= *hable*) go on!, carry on; (*LAm*) (= *pase*) come in; **¡síguele!** (*Méx*) go on!; **"sigue"** (*en carta*) P.T.O.; (*en libro*) continued; **la carretera sigue hasta el pueblo** the road goes on as far as the town; **siga por la carretera hasta el cruce** follow the road up to the crossroads; **~ por este camino** to carry on along this path

[2] **~ adelante** [*persona*] to go on, carry on; [*acontecimiento*] to go ahead; **los Juegos Olímpicos siguieron (adelante) a pesar del atentado** the Olympics went ahead despite the attack; *ver tb* **adelante 1**

[3] (*en estado, situación*) to be still; **sigue enfermo** he's still ill; **sigue en Caracas** she's still in Caracas; **el ascensor sigue estropeado** the lift's still not working; **sigue soltero** he's still single; **¿cómo sigue?** how is he?; **que siga usted bien** keep well, look after yourself; **~ con una idea** to go on with an idea; **seguía en su error** he continued in his error; **seguimos sin teléfono** we still haven't got a phone; **sigo sin noticias** I still haven't heard anything; **sigo sin comprender** I still don't understand; **esas preguntas siguen sin respuesta** those questions remain unanswered

[4] **~ haciendo algo** to go on doing sth, carry on doing sth; **siguió mirándola** he went on *o* carried on looking at her; **siguió hablando con nosotros** he went on speaking to us; **el ordenador seguía funcionando** the computer carried on working, the computer was still working; **sigo pensando lo mismo** I still think the same; **sigue lloviendo** it's still raining

[5] (= *venir a continuación*) to follow, follow on; **como sigue** as follows; **lo que sigue es un resumen** what follows is a summary; **entre otros ejemplos destacan los que siguen** amongst other examples, the following stand out; **mencionaré varios casos en lo que sigue** I'll now move on to mention several cases; **~ a algo: las horas que siguieron a la tragedia** the hours following *o* that followed the tragedy; **a la conferencia siguió un debate** the lecture was followed by a discussion

Ⓒ **seguirse** VPR [1] (= *venir a continuación*) to follow; **una cosa se sigue a otra** one thing follows another; **después de aquello se siguió una época tranquila** after that there followed a quiet period

[2] (= *deducirse*) to follow; **de esto se sigue que ...** it follows from this that ...

▼**según** Ⓐ PREP [1] (= *de acuerdo con*) according to; **~ el jefe** according to the boss; **~ este mapa** according to this map; **obrar ~ las instrucciones** to act in accordance with one's instructions; **~ lo que dice** from what he says, going by what he says; **~ lo que se decida** according to what is decided; **~ parece** seemingly, apparently

[2] (= *depende de*) depending on; **~ tus circunstancias** depending on your circumstances; **~ el dinero que tengamos** depending on what money we have

Ⓑ CONJ [1] (= *depende de*) depending on; **~ esté el tiempo** depending on the weather; **~ (como) me encuentre** depending on how I feel; **~ (que) vengan tres o cuatro** depending on whether three or four come

[2] (*indicando manera*) as; **~ me consta** as I know for a fact; **está ~ lo dejaste** it's just as you left it; **~ están las cosas, es mejor no intervenir** the way things are, it's better not to get involved; **~ se entra, a la izquierda** to the left as you go in

[3] (*indicando simultaneidad*) as; **lo vi ~ salía** I saw him as I was going out; **~ íbamos entrando nos daban la información** they gave us the information as we went in

Ⓒ ADV (*) **—¿lo vas a comprar? —según** "are you going to buy it?" — "it all depends"; **~ y como** ◊ **~ y conforme** it all depends

segunda SF [1] (*Aut*) second gear

[2] (*Ferro*) second class; **viajar en ~** to travel second class

[3] (*Mús*) second

[4] **segundas** (= *doble sentido*) double meaning; **lo dijo con ~s** he really meant something else when he said it; *ver tb* **segundo**

segundar ▸conjug 1a◂ Ⓐ VT [1] (= *repetir*) to do again

[2] (*Cono Sur*) [+ *golpe*] to return

Ⓑ VI to come second, be in second place

segundero SM second hand (*of watch*)

segundo/a Ⓐ ADJ (*gen*) second; [*enseñanza*] secondary; [*intención*] double; **en ~ lugar** (*en clasificación*) in second place; (*en discurso*) secondly; *ver tb* **sexto A**

Ⓑ SM/F [1] (*en orden*) (*gen*) second; (*Admin, Mil*) second in command; **sin ~** unrivalled

► **segundo/a de a bordo** (*Náut*) first mate; (*fig*) second in command

[2] (*Mús*) alto

Ⓒ SM [1] (= *medida de tiempo*) second

➤ LENGUA Y USO: **según A1** 53.5

2 (= *piso*) second floor, third floor (*EEUU*)
3 (*Astron*) ► **segundos de arco** seconds of arc; *ver tb* **segunda**

segundón/ona Ⓐ SM second son, younger son
Ⓑ SM/F second-class citizen

segur SF (= *hoz*) sickle; (= *hacha*) axe, ax (*EEUU*)

seguramente ADV **—están llamando a la puerta —seguramente será el cartero** "there's someone at the door" — "it'll probably be the postman" *o* "I expect it'll be the postman"; **~ llegarán mañana** they'll probably arrive tomorrow, I expect they'll arrive tomorrow; **~ nos volveremos a ver** I'm sure *o* I expect we'll see each other again; **—¿lo va a comprar? —seguramente** "is he going to buy it?" — "I expect so"

seguridad SF **1** (= *falta de riesgo*) **1·1** (*ante accidente, peligro*) safety; (*ante delito, atentado*) security; **han aumentado la ~ en el circuito** they have increased safety on the circuit; **para mayor ~ recomendamos el uso de la mascarilla** for safety's sake we recommend that you use a mask; **han cuestionado la ~ del experimento** they have questioned the safety of the experiment; **cierre de ~** [*de pulsera, collar, arma*] safety catch; **cinturón de ~** safety belt; **empresa de ~** security company; **medidas de ~** (*ante accidente, incendio*) safety measures; (*ante delito, atentado*) security measures
1·2 (*económica*) security; **le preocupa la ~ de sus inversiones** he's worried about the security of his investments; **hasta que no tenga trabajo no tendrá ~ económica** until he has a job he won't have any financial security
1·3 (*Mil, Pol*) security; **consejo de ~** security council
► **seguridad ciudadana** *the security of the public from crime*; **nos preocupa mucho la ~ ciudadana** we are very concerned about crime ► **seguridad colectiva** collective security ► **seguridad contra incendios** fire precautions *pl* ► **seguridad del Estado** national security, state security; **las fuerzas de ~ del Estado** state security forces ► **seguridad en el trabajo** health and safety at work ► **seguridad en la carretera** road safety ► **seguridad social** (= *sistema de pensiones y paro*) social security, welfare (*EEUU*); (= *contribuciones*) national insurance; (= *sistema médico*) national health service, ≈ NHS ► **seguridad vial** road safety
2 (= *sensación*) (*de no tener peligro*) security; (*de confianza*) confidence, assurance; **la ~ que da tener unos buenos frenos** the security that good brakes give you; **habla con mucha ~** he speaks with great confidence *o* assurance; **quiere dar la impresión de ~** he wants to give a confident impression ► **seguridad en uno mismo** self-confidence, self-assurance
3 (= *certeza*) certainty; **no hay ninguna ~ de que vaya a ocurrir** there's no certainty that that will happen; **no puedo darle ~** I can't say for sure *o* for certain; **con ~**: **no lo sabemos con ~** we don't know for sure *o* for certain; **con toda ~, podemos decir que ...** with complete certainty, we can say that ...; **tener la ~ de que ...** to be sure *o* certain that ...; **tenía la ~ de que algo iba a pasar** he was sure *o* certain that something was going to happen; **tengan ustedes la ~ de que ...** (you may) rest assured that ... (*frm*)
4 (*Jur*) [*de fianza*] security, surety

seguro Ⓐ ADJ **1** (= *sin peligro*) **1·1** [*refugio, método, vehículo*] safe; **no te subas a esa escalera porque no es muy segura** don't go up that ladder, it's not very safe; **a causa de una práctica sexual poco segura** due to unsafe sex
1·2 [*persona, objetos de valor*] safe; **está más ~ en el banco** it's safer in the bank; **el bebé se siente ~ cerca de su madre** the baby feels safe *o* secure close to its mother
2 (= *sujeto, estable*) secure; **hay que atar mejor la carga porque no parece muy segura** the load needs to be fixed a bit better because it doesn't seem to be very securely attached *o* very secure; **su trabajo no es nada ~** his job is not at all secure
3 (= *definitivo*) [*fracaso, muerte*] certain; **su dimisión no es segura** her resignation is not certain; **aún no hay fecha segura** there's no definite date yet; **eso es lo más ~** that's the most likely thing; **lo más ~ es que no pueda ir** I almost certainly *o* most likely won't be able to go; **dar algo por ~**: **si yo fuera tú no daría la victoria por segura** if I were you I wouldn't be sure of victory; **se da por ~ que se trataba de un secuestro** there's little doubt that it was a kidnapping; **es ~ que ...**: **es ~ que ganaremos la copa** we're bound *o* sure *o* certain to win the cup; **lo que es ~ es que el congreso se celebrará en Barcelona** the conference is definitely going to be held in Barcelona
4 (= *convencido*) sure; **¿estás ~?** are you sure?; **sí, estoy completamente segura** yes, I'm absolutely sure *o* positive; **—¿estás ~ de que era él? —sí, segurísimo** "are you sure it was him?" — "yes, positive"; **—vamos a ganar —pues yo no estaría tan ~** "we're going to win" — "I wouldn't bet on it" *o* "I wouldn't be so sure"; **~ de algo** sure of sth; **nunca he visto un hombre tan ~ de sus opiniones** I've never seen a man so sure of his opinions; **no estoy ~ de poder ir** I'm not sure I'll be able to go; **no estés tan ~ de que vas a ganar** don't be so sure that you're going to win
5 (*de uno mismo*) confident; **se muestra cada vez más ~ en el escenario** he is more and more sure of himself *o* confident on stage; **me noto más segura al andar** I feel more steady on my feet, I feel more confident walking now; **~ de sí mismo** self-confident, self-assured
6 (= *fiable*) [*fuente, cálculo, método*] reliable; **no es un método muy ~** it's not a very reliable *o* sure method; **es la forma más segura de adelgazar** it's the surest way to lose weight
7 (*LAm*) (= *honesto*) trustworthy
Ⓑ ADV for sure, for certain; **no lo sabemos ~** we don't know for sure *o* certain; **—¿seguro que te interesa? —sí, seguro** "are you sure that you're interested?" — "yes, I'm sure"; **—estoy dispuesto a cambiar de actitud —sí, sí, ~** (*iró*) "I'm willing to change my attitude" — "yeah, yeah, sure!" (*iró*); **~ que algunos se alegrarán** some people will certainly be pleased, I'm sure that some people will be pleased; **~ que llueve mañana** it's sure to rain tomorrow; **a buen ~** ◊ **de ~** certainly; **a buen ~ o de ~ va a dar que hablar** it will certainly give people something to talk about; ✦**MODISMO** **ir** *o* **jugar sobre ~** to play (it) safe; **decidieron jugar sobre ~ contratando a un buen abogado** they decided to play (it) safe and hire a good lawyer
Ⓒ SM **1** (= *dispositivo*) **1·1** [*de puerta, lavadora*] lock; [*de arma de fuego*] safety catch; [*de pulsera*] clasp; **echa el ~, que van niños en el coche** lock the doors, there are children in the car
1·2 (*CAm, Méx*) (= *imperdible*) safety pin
2 (*Com, Fin*) insurance; **¿tienes el ~ del coche?** have you got your car insurance documents with you?; **hacerse un ~** to take out insurance ► **seguro a todo riesgo** comprehensive insurance ► **seguro contra terceros** third-party insurance ► **seguro de accidentes** accident insurance ► **seguro de crédito a la exportación** export credit guarantee ► **seguro de daños a terceros** third-party insurance ► **seguro de desempleo** unemployment benefit, unemployment compensation *o* insurance (*EEUU*) ► **seguro de enfermedad** health insurance ► **seguro de incendios** fire insurance ► **seguro de jubilación** retirement plan, pension plan, pension scheme ► **seguro de paro** (*Esp*) unemployment benefit, unemployment compensation *o* insurance (*EEUU*) ► **seguro de vida** life assurance, life insurance (*esp EEUU*) ► **seguro marítimo** marine insurance ► **seguro mixto** endowment assurance, endowment insurance (*esp EEUU*) ► **seguro multiriesgo** multirisk insurance ► **seguro mutuo** mutual insurance ► **seguro temporal** term insurance
3 (*) (= *sistema médico*) national health*; **los médicos de pago y los del ~** private doctors and national health *o* NHS ones ► **seguro social** (*LAm*) (= *sistema de pensiones y paro*) social security, welfare (*EEUU*); (= *contribuciones*) national insurance; (= *sistema médico*) national health service

seibó SM (*Andes, Caribe*) sideboard

seis Ⓐ ADJ INV, PRON (*gen*) six; (*ordinal, en la fecha*) sixth; **~ mil** six thousand; **tiene ~ años** she is six (years old); **un niño de ~ años** a six-year-old (child), a child of six; **son las ~** it's six o'clock; **son las cinco menos ~** it's six minutes to five; **nos fuimos los ~ al cine** all six of us went to the cinema; **somos ~ para comer** there are six of us for dinner; **unos ~** about six; **le escribí el día ~** I wrote to him on the sixth; **en la página ~** on page six
Ⓒ SM INV (= *número*) six; (= *fecha*) sixth; **dos más cuatro son ~** two plus four are six; **hoy es ~** today is the sixth; **llega el ~ de agosto** he arrives on the sixth of August *o* on August the sixth; **vive en el ~** he lives at number six; **el ~ de corazones** the six of hearts

seiscientos/as Ⓐ ADJ, PRON (*gen*) six hundred; (*ordinal*) six hundredth; **~ soldados** six hundred soldiers; **seiscientas botellas** six hundred bottles; **seiscientos treinta y dos euros** six hundred and thirty-two euros; **—¿cuántas habitaciones tiene el hotel? —seiscientas** "how many rooms does the hotel have?" — "six hundred"; **~ cuarenta** six hundred and forty; **el año ~** the year six hundred
Ⓑ SM **1** (= *número*) six hundred
2 (*) (*Aut*) *small, beetle-shaped 600cc car*

➤ LENGUA Y USO: **seguramente** 43.2 **seguridad 3** 42.1, 43.1, 53.6 **seguro A3** 42.1, 43.1, 52.6

manufactured by SEAT and highly popular in Spain during the sixties and seventies

seísmo SM earthquake

seisporocho SM (*Caribe*) *a Venezuelan folk dance*

SEL SF ABR = **Sociedad Española de Lingüística**

selección SF [1] (= *acción*) selection ► **selección biológica** natural selection ► **selección múltiple** multiple choice ► **selección natural** natural selection
[2] (*Dep*) ► **selección absoluta, selección nacional** national team, national side
[3] **selecciones** (*Literat, Mús*) selections

seleccionable ADJ eligible

seleccionado SM team

seleccionador(a) SM/F (*Dep*) manager, coach (*EEUU*)

seleccionar ▸conjug 1a◂ VT to select, pick, choose

selectividad SF [1] (= *cualidad*) selectivity
[2] (*Esp Univ*) entrance examination

selectivo ADJ selective

selecto ADJ [1] (= *exclusivo*) [*vino, producto*] select; [*club*] exclusive
[2] [*obras literarias*] selected

selector SM (*Téc*) selector ► **selector de programas** programme selector, program selector (*EEUU*)

selenizaje SM moon landing

selenizar ▸conjug 1f◂ VI to land on the moon

self-service SM self-service restaurant

sellado Ⓐ ADJ [*documento oficial*] sealed; [*pasaporte, visado*] stamped
Ⓑ SM [*de documento oficial*] sealing; [*de pasaporte, visado*] stamping

selladora SF primer, sealant

selladura SF (= *sello*) seal

sellar ▸conjug 1a◂ VT [1] (= *poner sello en*) [+ *documento oficial*] to seal; [+ *pasaporte, visado*] to stamp
[2] (= *marcar*) to brand
[3] (= *cerrar*) [+ *pacto, labios*] to seal; [+ *urna, entrada*] to seal up; [+ *calle*] to seal off

sello SM [1] (*Correos*) stamp; ✦***MODISMO*** **no pega ni un ~*** he's bone-idle* ► **sello aéreo** airmail stamp ► **sello conmemorativo** commemorative stamp ► **sello de correos** postage stamp ► **sello de urgencia** express-delivery stamp
[2] (= *estampación*) (*personal, de rey*) seal; (*administrativo*) stamp, official stamp; (*LAm*) (*en reverso de moneda*) tails ► **sello de caucho, sello de goma** rubber stamp ► **sello real** royal seal
[3] (*Com*) brand; (*Mús*) (*tb* ~ **discográfico**) record label; (*Literat*) publishing house; **lleva el ~ de esta oficina** it carries the stamp of this office ► **sello fiscal** revenue stamp ► **sellos de prima** (*Com*) trading stamps
[4] (*Med*) capsule, pill
[5] (= *marca*) (*tb* ~ **distintivo**) hallmark, stamp; **lleva el ~ de su genialidad** it carries the hallmark of his genius

seltz [selθ, sel] SM **agua (de)** ~ seltzer (water)

selva SF [1] (= *jungla*) jungle ► **selva tropical** rainforest, tropical rainforest
[2] (= *bosque*) forest ► **Selva Negra** Black Forest

selvático ADJ [1] (= *de la selva*) forest *antes de s*
[2] (= *de la jungla*) jungle *antes de s*
[3] (= *rústico*) rustic
[4] (*Bot*) wild

selvoso ADJ wooded, well-wooded

sem. ABR (= **semana**) wk

S.Em.ª ABR (= **Su Eminencia**) H.E.

semaforazo* SM *robbery (of occupants of a car) at traffic lights*

semáforo SM [1] (*Aut*) traffic lights *pl* ► **semáforo sonoro** pelican crossing
[2] (*Náut*) semaphore; (*Ferro*) signal

semana SF [1] (= *siete días*) week; **entre ~** during the week, in the week; **podemos vernos un día entre ~** we could see each other one day during the week; **vuelo de entre ~** mid-week flight; **días entre ~** weekdays ► **semana inglesa** five-day working week, five-day workweek (*EEUU*) ► **semana laboral** working week, workweek (*EEUU*) ► **Semana Santa** Holy Week
[2] (= *salario*) week's wages *pl*

> **SEMANA SANTA**
>
> *In Spain celebrations for* **Semana Santa** *(Holy Week) are often spectacular.* **Viernes Santo, Sábado Santo** *and* **Domingo de Resurrección** *(Good Friday, Holy Saturday, Easter Sunday) are all national public holidays, with additional days being given as local holidays. There are long processions through the streets with* **pasos** *- religious floats and sculptures. Religious statues are carried along on the shoulders of the* **cofrades***, members of the* **cofradías** *or lay brotherhoods that organize the processions. These are accompanied by* **penitentes** *and* **nazarenos** *generally wearing long hooded robes. Seville, Málaga and Valladolid are particularly well known for their spectacular Holy Week processions.*

semanal ADJ weekly

semanalmente ADV weekly, each week

semanario Ⓐ ADJ weekly
Ⓑ SM weekly, weekly magazine

semanero/a SM/F (*LAm*) weekly-paid worker

semántica SF semantics *sing*

semántico ADJ semantic

semblante SM (*liter*) (= *cara*) countenance (*liter*), face; (= *aspecto*) look; **alterar el ~ a algn** to upset sb; **componer el ~** to put on a serious *o* straight face; **mudar de ~** to change colour *o* (*EEUU*) color; **el caso lleva otro ~ ahora** things look different now; **tener buen ~** (*de salud*) to look well; (*de humor*) to be in a good mood

semblantear ▸conjug 1a◂ VT [1] (*CAm, Cono Sur, Méx*) (= *mirar a la cara*) **~ a algn** to look sb straight in the face, scrutinize sb's face
[2] (*CAm, Méx*) (= *examinar*) to study, examine, look at

semblanza SF biographical sketch

sembradera SF seed drill

sembradío SM = **sembrío**

sembrado SM sown field

sembrador(a) SM/F sower

sembradora SF (*Mec*) seed drill

sembradura SF sowing

sembrar ▸conjug 1j◂ VT [1] (*Agr*) to sow (**de** with); **~ un campo de nabos** to sow *o* plant a field with turnips; ✦***REFRÁN*** **el que siembra recoge** you reap what you sow
[2] [+ *superficie*] to strew (**de** with)
[3] (= *extender*) [+ *objetos*] to scatter, spread; [+ *noticia*] to spread; [+ *minas*] to lay; **~ minas en un estrecho** ◊ **~ un estrecho de minas** (*Náut*) to mine a strait, lay mines in a strait; **~ la discordia** to sow discord; **~ el pánico** to spread panic, sow panic (*liter*)
[4] (*Méx*) [+ *jinete*] to throw; (= *derribar*) to knock down

sembrío SM (*LAm*) sown field

semejante Ⓐ ADJ [1] (= *parecido*) similar; **ser ~s** to be alike *o* similar; **~ a** like; **es ~ a ella en el carácter** she is like her in character; **son muy ~s** they are very much alike *o* very similar; **dijo eso o algo ~** she said that or something similar *o* something like that
[2] (*Mat*) similar
[3] (*uso enfático*) such; **nunca hizo cosa ~** he never did any such thing *o* anything of the sort; **¿se ha visto frescura ~?** did you ever see such cheek?
[4] (*Cono Sur, Méx*) (= *enorme*) huge, enormous
Ⓑ SM [1] (= *prójimo*) fellow man, fellow creature; **nuestros ~s** our fellow men
[2] **no tiene ~** (= *equivalente*) it has no equal, there is nothing to equal it

▼ **semejanza** SF similarity, resemblance; **a ~ de** like, as; **tener ~ con** to look like, resemble ► **semejanza de familia** family likeness

semejar ▸conjug 1a◂ Ⓐ VI (= *parecerse a*) to look like, resemble
Ⓑ **semejarse** VPR to look alike, resemble each other; **~se a** to look like, resemble

semen SM semen

semental Ⓐ ADJ stud *antes de s*, breeding *antes de s*
Ⓑ SM [1] (*Zool*) stallion, stud horse
[2] (‡) (= *hombre*) stud‡

sementera SF [1] (= *acto*) sowing
[2] (= *temporada*) seedtime
[3] (= *tierra*) sown land
[4] (= *caldo de cultivo*) hotbed (**de** of), breeding ground (**de** for)

semestral ADJ [*reunión, examen, resultados*] half-yearly, six-monthly; [*informe, revista*] biannual

semestralmente ADV [*reunirse, examinarse*] half-yearly; [*publicarse*] biannually

semestre SM [1] (= *seis meses*) (*gen*) period of six months; (*Univ*) semester
[2] (*Fin*) half-yearly payment

semi... PREF semi..., half-

semiacabado ADJ half-finished

semialfabetizado ADJ semiliterate

semiamueblado ADJ semi-furnished

semiautomático ADJ semiautomatic

semibola SF small slam

semibreve SF semibreve, whole note (*EEUU*)

semicircular ADJ semicircular

semicírculo SM semicircle

semiconductor SM semiconductor

semiconsciente ADJ semi-conscious, half-conscious

semiconsonante SF semiconsonant

semicorchea SF semiquaver, sixteenth (note) (*EEUU*)

semicualificado ADJ semiskilled

➤ LENGUA Y USO: **semejanza** 32.1

semicultismo SM half-learned word

semiculto ADJ half-learned

semicupio SM (*CAm, Caribe*) hip bath

semiderruido ADJ half-ruined, half-collapsed

semidesconocido ADJ virtually unknown

semidescremado ADJ semi-skimmed

semidesértico ADJ semidesert *antes de s*

semidesierto ADJ half-empty

semidesnatado ADJ semi-skimmed

semidesnudo ADJ half-naked

semidiós SM demigod

semidormido ADJ half-asleep

semidúplex ADJ half duplex

semielaborado ADJ half-finished

semienterrado ADJ half-buried

semiexperto ADJ semiskilled

semifallo SM singleton (**a** in)

semifinal SF semifinal

semifinalista SMF semifinalist

semifondo SM middle-distance race

semifracaso SM partial failure, near failure

semiinconsciente ADJ semiconscious, half-conscious

semilla SF [1] (*Bot*) seed; **uvas sin ~s** seedless grapes ► **semilla de césped** grass seed
[2] (= *origen*) seed, source; **la ~ de la discordia** the seeds of discord
[3] (*Cono Sur*) (= *niño*) baby, small child; **la ~** the kids* (*collectively*)

semillero SM (= *terreno*) seedbed, nursery; (= *caja*) seed box; **un ~ de delincuencia** a hotbed of *o* a breeding ground for crime; **la decisión fue un ~ de disgustos** the decision caused a whole series of problems

semimedio SM welterweight

seminal ADJ seminal

seminario SM [1] (*Rel*) seminary
[2] (*Univ*) seminar
[3] (*Agr*) seedbed

seminarista SM seminarian

seminuevo ADJ (*Com*) nearly new, pre-owned (*EEUU*)

semioficial ADJ semi-official

semiología SF semiology

semiolvidado ADJ half-forgotten

semioruga SF (*tb* **camión ~**) half-track

semioscuridad SF half-darkness

semiótica SF semiotics *sing*

semiótico ADJ semiotic

semipesado ADJ light-heavyweight

semiprecioso ADJ semiprecious

semiprofesional ADJ, SMF semi-professional

semisalado ADJ brackish

semi-seco SM medium-dry

semiseparado ADJ semidetached

semisótano SM lower ground floor

semita Ⓐ ADJ Semitic
Ⓑ SMF Semite

semítico ADJ Semitic

semitono SM semitone

semivacío ADJ half-empty

semivocal SF semivowel

semivolea SF half-volley

sémola SF semolina

semoviente ADJ **bienes ~s** livestock

sempiterno ADJ (*lit*) eternal; (*fig*) never-ending

sen(a) SM/F senna

Sena SM Seine

senado SM [1] (*Pol*) senate
[2] (= *reunión*) assembly, gathering

> **SENADO**
>
> *The* **Senado** *is the Upper Chamber of the Spanish Parliament. Approximately 80% of its 256 members acquire their seats in the general elections while the remaining 20% are nominated by each of the Autonomous Regions (***Comunidades Autónomas***). Like the* **Congreso de los Diputados**, *the term of office for the* **Senado** *is no longer than four years.*
>
> ⇨ *See also* CONGRESO DE LOS DIPUTADOS

senador(a) SM/F senator

senatorial ADJ senatorial

sencillamente ADV simply; **es ~ imposible** it's simply impossible

sencillez SF [1] [*de costumbre, estilo, ropa*] simplicity; **se viste con mucha ~** she dresses very simply
[2] [*de tema, problema*] simplicity, straightforwardness; **no entendió nada pese a la ~ del asunto** she didn't understand a thing despite the simplicity *o* straightforwardness of the matter
[3] (= *naturalidad*) naturalness; **me gustó su ~ en el trato** I liked her naturalness
[4] (*LAm*) (= *necedad*) foolishness

sencillo Ⓐ ADJ [1] [*costumbre, estilo, ropa*] simple; **su forma de hablar es sencilla y directa** his manner of speaking is simple and direct
[2] [*asunto, problema*] simple, straightforward; **es un plato ~ de hacer pero apetitoso** it's a simple but tasty dish, the dish is straightforward to make, but tasty
[3] (= *no afectado*) natural, unaffected; **es muy rico pero muy ~ en el trato** he's very rich, but nevertheless very natural *o* unaffected
[4] [*billete*] single
[5] (*LAm*) (= *necio*) foolish
Ⓑ SM [1] (= *disco*) single
[2] (*LAm*) (= *cambio*) small change

senda SF [1] (= *sendero*) path, track
[2] (*para conseguir algo*) path
[3] (*Cono Sur Aut*) lane

senderismo SM rambling, hill walking

senderista[1] SMF (*Dep*) rambler, hill walker

senderista[2] (*Perú Pol*) Ⓐ ADJ *of or pertaining to the Sendero Luminoso guerrilla movement*
Ⓑ SMF member of Sendero Luminoso

sendero SM path, track ► **Sendero Luminoso** (*Perú Pol*) Shining Path guerrilla movement

sendos ADJ PL **les dio ~ golpes** he hit both of them, he gave each of them a beating; **recibieron ~ regalos** each one received a present; **con sendas peculiaridades** each with its own peculiarity

Séneca SM Seneca

senectud SF old age

Senegal SM (*tb* **El ~**) Senegal

senegalés/esa ADJ, SM/F Senegalese

senescencia SF ageing

senil ADJ senile

senilidad SF senility

senior, **sénior** Ⓐ ADJ INV [1] (*Dep*) senior
[2] (= *con experiencia*) senior
[3] (*acompañando a nombre propio*) senior
Ⓑ SMF (*pl* **seniors** *o* **séniors**) (*Dep*) senior

seno SM [1] (= *pecho*) breast; **una operación para reducir los ~s** a breast-reduction operation
[2] (= *centro*) **en el ~ de la familia** in the bosom of the family; **el ~ del movimiento** the heart *o* core of the movement ► **seno de Abraham** Abraham's bosom
[3] (*liter*) (= *útero*) **lleva un niño en su ~** she is with child (*liter*) ► **seno materno** womb
[4] (*Mat*) sine
[5] (*Anat*) ► **seno frontal** frontal sinus ► **seno maxilar** maxillary sinus
[6] (*Náut, Meteo*) trough
[7] (*Geog*) (= *ensenada*) small bay; (= *golfo*) gulf
[8] (*frm*) (= *hueco*) hollow; **un fregadero de dos ~s** a double sink

SENPA SM ABR (*Esp*) = **Servicio Nacional de Productos Agrarios**

sensación SF [1] (= *percepción*) feeling, sensation; **una ~ de placer** a feeling *o* sensation of pleasure; **tengo la ~ de que …** ◊ **me da la ~ de que …** I have a feeling that …
[2] (= *conmoción*) sensation; **causar** *o* **hacer ~** to cause a sensation

sensacional ADJ sensational

sensacionalismo SM sensationalism

sensacionalista Ⓐ ADJ sensationalist; **la prensa ~** the sensationalist press, the tabloid press
Ⓑ SMF sensationalist

sensacionalizar ▸conjug 1f◂ VT to sensationalize

sensatamente ADV sensibly

sensatez SF good sense; **con ~** sensibly

sensato ADJ sensible

sensibilidad SF [1] (*al dolor, al frío*) feeling; **no tiene ~ en las piernas** he has no feeling in his legs
[2] (= *emotividad*) sensitivity; **~ afectiva** emotional sensitivity
[3] (= *disposición*) feeling, sensitivity; **muestra una gran ~ para la música** she has a great feeling *o* sensitivity for music ► **sensibilidad artística** artistic feeling *o* sensitivity
[4] [*de aparato, máquina*] sensitivity; **una película de alta ~** a highly sensitive film

sensibilización SF sensitizing

sensibilizado ADJ [1] (= *alérgico*) sensitized
[2] (*Fot*) sensitive

sensibilizar ▸conjug 1f◂ VT [1] (= *concienciar*) to sensitize; **~ la opinión pública** to inform public opinion
[2] (*Fot*) to sensitize

sensible Ⓐ ADJ [1] (*al dolor, al frío*) sensitive; **tiene la piel muy ~** she has very sensitive skin; **~ a algo** sensitive to sth; **es muy ~ a los cambios de temperatura** it's very sensitive to changes in temperature; **los seres ~s** sentient beings
[2] (= *impresionable*) sensitive (**a** to); **es muy ~ y llora con facilidad** he is very sensitive and cries easily
[3] (= *perceptivo*) **~ a algo** sensitive to sth; **es muy ~ a los problemas de la población** he is very sensitive to people's problems; **Ana es muy ~ al arte** Ana has an artistic sensitivity
[4] (= *evidente*) [*cambio, diferencia*] appreciable, noticeable; [*pérdida*] considerable; **una ~ me-**

joría a noticeable improvement

5 (*Téc*) sensitive (**a** to); (*Fot*) sensitive; **un aparato muy ~** a very sensitive piece of equipment; **una placa ~ a la luz** a light-sensitive plate

6 (= *capaz*) **~ de** capable of; **~ de mejora** capable of improvement

Ⓑ SF (*Mús*) leading note

sensiblemente ADV perceptibly, appreciably, noticeably; **~ más** substantially more

sensiblería SF sentimentality

sensiblero ADJ sentimental, slushy*

sensitiva SF (*Bot*) mimosa

sensitivo ADJ 1 [*órgano*] sense *antes de s*

2 [*animal*] sentient, capable of feeling

sensomotor ADJ sensorimotor

sensor SM sensor ► **sensor de calor** heat sensor

sensorial ADJ, **sensorio** ADJ sensory

sensual ADJ sensual, sensuous

sensualidad SF sensuality, sensuousness

sensualismo SM sensualism

sensualista SMF sensualist

sentada SF 1 (= *tiempo que se está sentado*) sitting; **de** *o* **en una ~** at one sitting

2 (*Pol*) sit-in, sit-down protest; **hacer una ~** to organize a sit-in

sentadera SF 1 (*LAm*) (*para sentarse*) seat (*of a chair etc*)

2 **sentaderas** (*Méx**) (= *trasero*) backside* *sing*

sentadero SM seat

sentado ADJ 1 **estar ~** to be sitting, be seated; **estaba ~ a mi lado** he was sitting *o* seated next to me; **permanecer ~** to remain seated; ✦*MODISMO* **esperar ~***: **si crees que te lo devolverá ya puedes esperar ~** if you think he's going to give it back to you you've got another think coming* *o* you can think again

2 **dar por ~** to take for granted; **di por ~ que estabas de acuerdo** I took it for granted that you were in agreement, I assumed you were in agreement

3 **dejar ~**: **quiero dejar ~ que ...** I want to make it clear that ...

4 [*carácter, personalidad*] balanced

sentador ADJ (*Cono Sur*) smart, elegant

sentadura SF (*en piel*) sore; (*en fruta*) mark

sentar ▸conjug 1j◂ Ⓐ VT 1 [+ *persona*] to sit, seat

2 (= *colocar*) [+ *objeto*] to place, place firmly; **~ las costuras** to press the seams; **~ el último ladrillo** to tap the last brick into place; **~ las bases de algo** to lay the foundations for sth

3 (= *establecer*) [+ *base, principio*] to establish; [+ *precedente*] to set

4 **~ una suma en la cuenta de algn** (*Com*) to put a sum down to sb's account

5 (*Andes, Caribe*) [+ *persona*] to crush, squash

6 (*Andes*) [+ *caballo*] to rein in sharply, pull up sharply

Ⓑ VI 1 (*en el aspecto*) to suit; **ese peinado le sienta horriblemente** that hairstyle doesn't suit her at all, that hairstyle looks awful on her

2 **~ bien/mal a algn** [*comida*] to agree/disagree with sb; **no me sientan bien las gambas** prawns disagree with me; **unas vacaciones le ~ían bien** he could do with a holiday

3 (= *agradar*) **~ bien/mal** to go down well/badly; **le ha sentado mal que lo hayas hecho tú** he didn't like your doing it; ✦*MODISMO* **~ como un tiro**: **a mí me sienta como un tiro*** it suits me like a hole in the head*

Ⓒ **sentarse** VPR 1 [*persona*] to sit, sit down, seat o.s. (*frm*); **¡siéntese!** (do) sit down, take a seat; **sentémonos aquí** let's sit (down) here; **se sentó a comer** she sat down to eat

2 [*sedimento*] to settle

3 [*tiempo*] to settle, settle down, clear up

4 (*Arquit*) [*cimientos*] to settle

sentencia SF 1 (*Jur*) sentence; **dictar** *o* **pronunciar ~** to pronounce sentence; **visto para ~** ready for sentencing ► **sentencia de muerte** death sentence

2 (= *decisión*) decision, ruling; (= *opinión*) opinion

3 (*Literat*) maxim, saying

4 (*Inform*) statement

sentenciar ▸conjug 1b◂ Ⓐ VT 1 (*Jur*) to sentence (**a** to)

2 (*Dep*) [+ *partido*] to decide

3 (*LAm*) **~ a algn** to swear revenge on sb

Ⓑ VI 1 (= *dar su opinión*) to pronounce o.s., give one's opinion

2 (*Dep*) to decide the match

sentenciosamente ADV gravely, weightily

sentenciosidad SF 1 [*de refrán*] pithiness

2 [*de lenguaje*] sententiousness

sentencioso ADJ 1 [*refrán*] pithy

2 [*lenguaje*] sententious; [*carácter*] dogmatic

sentidamente ADV 1 (= *con sentimiento sincero*) sincerely, with great feeling

2 (= *con pesar*) regretfully

sentido Ⓐ ADJ 1 [*carta, declaración*] heartfelt; **pronunció unas sentidas palabras en su honor** he said some heartfelt words in his honour; **una pérdida muy sentida** a deeply felt loss; **mi más ~ pésame** my deepest sympathy, my heartfelt condolences

2 (= *dolido*) hurt; **estaba muy sentida con sus amigos** she was very hurt by her friends

3 [*carácter, persona*] sensitive

Ⓑ SM 1 (= *capacidad*) 1·1 (*para sentir*) sense; **ha perdido el ~ del gusto** he has lost his sense of taste; **los cinco ~s** the five senses; ✦*MODISMOS* **costar un ~** (*Esp*†*) to cost the earth; **poner los cinco ~s** to be on one's toes; **tener un sexto ~** to have a sixth sense

1·2 (*para percibir*) sense; **no tiene ~ del ritmo** he has no sense of rhythm; **tiene muy buen ~ del color** he has a very good sense of colour

► **sentido común** common sense ► **sentido de la orientación** sense of direction ► **sentido de la proporción** sense of proportion ► **sentido del humor** sense of humour ► **sentido de los negocios** business sense ► **sentido del ridículo**: **su ~ del ridículo le impidió hacerlo** he felt self-conscious *o* embarrassed so he didn't do it; **tiene un gran ~ del ridículo** she easily feels self-conscious *o* embarrassed ► **sentido práctico**: **tener ~ práctico** to be practical

2 (= *significado*) meaning; **ser madre le ha dado un nuevo ~ a su vida** being a mother has given a new meaning to her life; **¿cuál es el ~ literal de esta palabra?** what is the literal meaning of this word?; **la vida sin ti no tendría ~** without you life would have no meaning *o* would be meaningless; **doble ~** double meaning; **esa frase tenía doble ~** that sentence had a double meaning; **sin ~** [*palabras, comentario*] meaningless; **decía cosas sin ~** he was talking nonsense

3 (= *lógica*) sense; **no le veo ~ a esta discusión** I can't see any sense *o* point in this argument; **poco a poco, todo empieza a cobrar ~** everything is gradually beginning to make sense; **sin ~** [*crueldad, violencia*] senseless; **fue un debate sin ~** it was a pointless debate; **tener ~** to make sense; **sólo tiene ~ quejarse si así puedes conseguir lo que quieres** it only makes sense to complain if *o* the only point in complaining is if you can then get what you want; **no tiene ~ que te disculpes ahora** it's pointless (you) apologizing now, there's no sense *o* point in (you) apologizing now

4 (= *conciencia*) consciousness; **lo encontré en el suelo sin ~** I found him unconscious on the floor; **perder el ~** to lose consciousness; **recobrar el ~** to regain consciousness; ✦*MODISMO* **quitar el ~ a algn** to take sb's breath away

5 (= *dirección*) direction; **los dos avanzaban en el mismo ~** they were both moving forward in the same direction; **conducía en ~ contrario** he was driving in the opposite direction; **"sentido único"** "one way"; **en el ~ de las agujas del reloj** clockwise; **en ~ contrario al de las agujas del reloj** anticlockwise, counterclockwise (*EEUU*); *ver tb* **calle 1**

6 (*otras expresiones*) **en ~ amplio** in the broad sense; **en el buen ~ de la palabra** in the best *o* good sense of the word; **en cierto ~** in a sense; **en ese ~** (*con nombre*) to that effect; (*con verbo*) in that sense, in that respect; **ha habido rumores en ese ~** there have been rumours to that effect; **en ese ~ no sabemos qué hacer** in that sense *o* respect, we don't know what to do; **en ~ estricto** in the strict sense of the word *o* term; **no es, en ~ estricto, un pez de río** it's not a freshwater fish in the strict sense of the word *o* term, it's not strictly speaking a freshwater fish; **en ~ figurado** in the figurative sense, figuratively; **en ~ lato** in the broad sense; **tomar algo en el mal ~** to take sth the wrong way; **en tal ~** to that effect; **están dispuestos a dar testimonio en tal ~** they are prepared to testify to that effect; **un acuerdo en tal ~ sería interpretado como una privatización** such an agreement *o* an agreement to that effect would be interpreted as privatization

sentimental ADJ 1 (= *emotivo*) [*persona, objeto*] sentimental; [*mirada*] soulful; **ponerse ~** to get sentimental

2 [*asunto, vida*] love *antes de s*; **aventura ~** love affair

sentimentalismo SM sentimentality

sentimentalmente ADV sentimentally

sentimentaloide* ADJ sugary, over-sentimental

sentimentero ADJ (*Caribe, Méx*) = **sensiblero**

sentimiento SM 1 (= *emoción*) feeling; **pone mucho ~ cuando canta** he puts a lot of feeling into his singing; **despertó el ~ nacionalista del pueblo** it aroused the nationalistic feelings *o* sentiments of the people ► **sentimiento de culpa** feeling of guilt, guilty feeling ► **sentimiento del deber** sense of duty

[2] (= *pena*) sorrow; **lloraba con mucho ~** he cried with great sorrow; **le acompaño en el ~** please accept my condolences

[3] **sentimientos** (= *forma de sentir*) feelings; **has conseguido herir sus ~s** you've managed to hurt his feelings; **no deberías jugar con sus ~s** you shouldn't play with his emotions *o* feelings; **¿le has revelado ya tus ~s?** have you told her how you feel?; **es una persona de buenos ~s** she's a good-hearted person; **es cruel y no tiene ~s** he's cruel and unfeeling

sentina SF [1] (*Náut*) bilge

[2] (*en ciudad*) sewer, drain

▼**sentir** ▸conjug 3i◂ Ⓐ VT [1] [+ *emoción, sensación, dolor*] to feel; **de repente he sentido frío** I suddenly felt cold; **no siento la pierna** I can't feel my leg; **empezó a ~ los efectos del alcohol** he began to feel the effects of the alcohol; **sentí ganas de contárselo** I felt the urge to tell him about it; **dejarse ~** to be felt; **están empezando a dejarse ~ los efectos de la crisis** the effects of the crisis are beginning to be felt; **en octubre ya se deja ~ el frío** by October it's already starting to get cold; **~ hambre** to feel hungry; **~ pena por algn** to feel pity for sb, feel sorry for sb; **~ sed** to feel thirsty

[2] (= *percibir*) to sense; **sintió la presencia de alguien en la oscuridad** he sensed a presence in the darkness; **quizá sintió que no le estaba diciendo la verdad** maybe she sensed that I wasn't telling her the truth

[3] (*con otros sentidos*) [3·1] (= *oír*) to hear; **no la sentí entrar** I didn't hear her come in; **no se sentía el vuelo de una mosca** you could have heard a pin drop

[3·2] (*esp LAm*) [+ *olor*] to smell; [+ *sabor*] to taste; **¿sientes el olor a quemado?** can you smell burning?; **no le siento ningún gusto a esto** this doesn't taste of anything to me

[4] (= *presentir*) **siento que esto no acabará bien** I have a feeling that this isn't going to end well

[5] [+ *música, poesía*] to have a feeling for

[6] (= *lamentar*) to be sorry about, regret (*más frm*); **siento mucho lo que pasó** I'm really sorry about what happened; **siento no haber podido ir** I'm sorry I wasn't able to go; **siento informarle que no ha sido seleccionado** I'm sorry to tell you that you haven't been selected, I regret to inform you that you haven't been selected (*más frm*); **siento molestarlo, pero necesito su ayuda** I'm sorry to bother you, but I need your help; **lo siento** I'm sorry; **lo siento muchísimo** ◊ **¡cuánto lo siento!** I'm so sorry; **lo siento en el alma** I'm terribly sorry; **~ que ...** to be sorry that ...; **siento mucho que pienses de esa forma** I'm very sorry that you feel that way

Ⓑ VI to feel; **ni oía ni sentía nada** he could neither hear nor feel anything; **ama y siente como cualquier ser humano** he feels love and emotion like any human being; **el tiempo se me pasaba sin ~** I didn't notice the time passing

Ⓒ **sentirse** VPR [1] (*en estado, situación*) to feel; **¿cómo te sientes?** how do you feel?; **no me siento con ánimos para eso** I don't feel up to it; **podemos ~nos satisfechos con el resultado** we can feel satisfied with the result; **se sentía observada** she felt she was being watched; **se sintió herido en su orgullo** his pride had been wounded; **~se como en casa** to feel at home; **~se culpable** to feel guilty; **~se mal** to feel bad; **me sentí mal por lo que había dicho** I felt bad about what I had said; **me sentí mal y me fui directamente a casa** I felt ill *o* bad and went straight home

[2] (*Med*) **~se de algo**: **desde la operación se siente mucho de la espalda** she's had a lot of back pain since the operation; **ha vuelto a ~se del reúma** she has begun to suffer from rheumatism again

[3] (*LAm*) (= *ofenderse*) to take offence; **no te sientas con él, no se refería a ti** don't be annoyed with him *o* don't take offence, he wasn't talking about you

[4] (*Méx*) (= *resquebrajarse*) [*pared, hueso, vasija*] to crack

Ⓓ SM [1] (= *opinión*) feeling, opinion; **la decisión no refleja el ~ mayoritario** the decision does not reflect the feeling *o* opinion of the majority; **el ~ popular** popular feeling, popular opinion

[2] (= *sentimiento*) feelings *pl*; **no quiero herir tu ~** I don't want to hurt your feelings; **el resurgimiento del ~ religioso** the upsurge in religious sentiment *o* feeling

sentón SM (*CAm, Méx*) (= *caída*) heavy fall; **dar un ~** (*Méx*) (= *caerse*) to fall on one's backside; **dar un ~ a** (*Andes*) [+ *caballo*] to rein in suddenly

▼**seña** SF [1] (= *gesto*) sign; **hablar por ~s** (*gen*) to communicate using signs; [*sordos*] to use sign-language; **hacer una ~ a algn** to make a sign to sb, signal to sb; **le hizo una ~ para que fuera** he signalled to him to go

[2] **señas** (= *dirección*) address *sing*; **dar las ~s de algn** to give sb's address

[3] **señas** (= *indicios*): **dar ~s de algo** to show signs of sth; **daba ~s de cansancio** he showed signs of tiredness; **por las ~s, parece imposible conseguirlo** it seems it's impossible to get hold of it, it's apparently impossible to get hold of it; **las ~s son mortales**† the signs are unmistakable

[4] **señas** (= *detalles*): **con las ~s que me diste lo reconocí enseguida** I recognized him immediately thanks to your description; **por** *o* **para más ~s** to be precise; **es colombiana, de Cali para más ~s** she's Colombian, from Cali to be precise ► **señas de identidad** identifying marks, distinguishing marks ► **señas personales** (personal) description *sing*

[5] (*Mil*) **santo y ~** password

señá SF = señora

señal SF [1] [*de aviso*] (*gen*) signal; (= *letrero*) sign; **un silbido era la ~ para que se callaran** a whistle was the signal for them to keep quiet; **el avión esperaba la ~ para despegar** the plane was waiting for the signal to take off; **una ~ acordada con anterioridad** a prearranged signal; **han puesto una ~ al principio del camino** they have put up a sign at the start of the road; **dar la ~ de** *o* **para algo** to give the signal for sth; **hacer una ~ a algn** (*con un gesto cualquiera*) to gesture to sb; (*ya acordada*) to signal to sb; **me hizo una ~ para que me apartara** he gestured to me to move aside; **subieron a la azotea para hacer ~es al helicóptero** they went up to the roof to signal to the helicopter ► **señal de alarma** (*ante un peligro*) warning signal; (= *síntoma*) warning sign; **dieron la ~ de alarma** they gave the warning signal; **deberían interpretar esto como una ~ de alarma** they should interpret this as a warning sign; **la muerte de varias ovejas ha hecho sonar la ~ de alarma** the death of several sheep has set alarm bells ringing ► **señal de auxilio** distress signal ► **señales de humo** smoke signals ► **la señal de la cruz** the sign of the cross ► **señal de la victoria** victory sign, V-sign ► **señal de salida** (*Dep, Ferro*) starting signal; **dar la ~ de salida** to give the starting signal ► **señal de socorro** distress signal

[2] (*Aut*) sign; **la ~ de stop** the stop sign ► **señal de circulación** traffic sign, road sign ► **señal de peligro** warning sign ► **señal de preferencia** right of way sign ► **señal de tráfico** traffic sign, road sign ► **señal horizontal** road marking ► **señal vertical** road sign

[3] (= *indicio*) sign; **es ~ de que las cosas van mejorando** it is a sign that things are improving; **su cuerpo mostraba ~es de violencia** his body showed signs of violent treatment; **le contestó sin la menor ~ de sorpresa** she answered him without the slightest sign of surprise; **los ladrones no dejaron la más mínima ~** the robbers didn't leave the slightest trace; **es buena ~** it's a good sign; **dar ~es de algo** to show signs of sth; **no daba ~es de nerviosismo** he showed no signs of nervousness; **lleva más de un mes sin dar ~es de vida** there's been no sign of him for more than a month; **en ~ de algo** as a sign of sth; **se dieron la mano en ~ de amistad** they shook hands as a sign of friendship; **en ~ de respeto** as a mark *o* sign of respect

[4] (= *marca*) mark; **un vehículo sin ninguna ~ identificativa** a vehicle with no identifying marks; **haz una ~ en los paquetes urgentes** put a mark on the express parcels, mark the express parcels; **dejó una ~ en la esquina de la página** he marked the page; **la varicela le ha dejado la cara llena de ~es** her face has been left badly scarred *o* marked by chickenpox; **dejó ~es de dedos en el cristal** he left fingerprints on the glass

[5] (*Med*) (= *síntoma*) symptom

[6] (*Com, Fin*) (= *depósito*) deposit; **dejar una cantidad en ~** to leave a sum as a deposit

[7] (*Radio*) signal; **se ha ido la ~** the signal has gone ► **señal horaria** time signal

[8] (*Telec*) (*al teléfono*) tone; (*en contestador*) beep, tone; **deja tu mensaje tras oír la ~** leave your message after the beep *o* tone ► **señal de comunicando** engaged tone, busy signal (*EEUU*) ► **señal de llamada** dialling tone, ringing *o* (*EEUU*) ring tone ► **señal de ocupado** (*LAm*) engaged tone, busy signal (*EEUU*)

señala SF (*Cono Sur*) earmark

señaladamente ADV [1] (= *claramente*) clearly, distinctly; **mantiene una actitud ~ hostil** he maintains a clearly *o* distinctly hostile attitude

[2] (= *especialmente*) especially; **eso beneficiaría ~ a los que más tienen** that would especially benefit those who are better off

señalado ADJ [1] (= *especial*) [*día*] special; [*ocasión, acontecimiento*] special, momentous; **en**

➤ LENGUA Y USO: **sentir A6** 39.3, 45.1, 52.1, 52.5 **seña 2** 51.5

una fecha tan señalada como hoy on such a special *o* momentous day as today; **los rasgos más ~s de su poesía** the most notable features of his poetry

2 [*persona*] (*gen*) distinguished; (*pey*) notorious; **un político especialmente ~ por la calidad de sus discursos** a politician particularly distinguished by the quality of his speeches; **un ~ criminal** a notorious criminal

señalador SM (*tb* **~ de libros**) bookmark

señalar ▸conjug 1a◂ Ⓐ VT 1 (= *indicar*) (*gen*) to show; (*con el dedo*) to point; **me señaló el camino** he showed me the way; **como señala el informe** as shown in the report; **la aguja señala el nivel del aceite** the needle shows the oil level; **el termómetro señalaba 25 grados** the thermometer read 25 degrees; **es de mala educación ~ a la gente** it's rude to point (at people); **~ una falta** (*Dep*) to indicate a foul

2 (= *marcar*) to mark; **señala en rojo dónde están los fallos** mark the mistakes in red; **señaló las cajas con etiquetas** he labelled the boxes; **el acné le ha señalado la cara** his face has been marked *o* scarred by acne; **eso señaló el principio de la decadencia** that marked the start of the decline

3 (= *destacar*) to point out; **tenemos que ~ tres aspectos fundamentales** we have to point out three fundamental aspects; **tuve que ~le varios errores en el examen** I had to point out several mistakes in the exam to him; **~ que** to point out that

4 (= *designar*) [+ *fecha, precio*] to fix, settle; [+ *tarea*] to set; **en el momento señalado** at the given moment, at the appointed time; **todas las encuestas lo señalan como el candidato favorito** all the opinion polls point to him as the favourite candidate

5 (*Aut*) [+ *carretera, ruta*] to signpost

6 [+ *ganado*] to brand

Ⓑ **señalarse** VPR 1 (= *destacar*) to distinguish o.s. (**como** as); **se señaló como el mejor saltador de todos los tiempos** he established himself as the greatest jumper of all time; **se han señalado por su generosidad** they have distinguished themselves by their generosity

2 (= *llamar la atención*) to stand out; **viste sobriamente porque no le gusta ~se** she dresses plainly because she doesn't like to stand out; **se señaló por su actitud rebelde ante la prensa** she stood out for her defiant attitude towards the press

señalero SM (*Cono Sur*) signalman

señalización SF 1 (= *acto*) (*Aut*) signposting, signing (*EEUU*); (*Ferro*) signalling, signaling (*EEUU*)

2 (= *conjunto de señales*) (*en carretera*) road signs *pl*; (*en edificio*) signposting ► **señalización horizontal** markings *pl* on the road ► **señalización vertical** road signs *pl*

señalizador SM 1 (*tb* **~ vertical**) road sign

2 (*tb* **~ de viraje**) (*Cono Sur*) indicator, turn signal (*EEUU*)

señalizar ▸conjug 1f◂ Ⓐ VT 1 (*Aut*) [+ *ruta, carretera*] to signpost; **el desvío no estaba bien señalizado** the turn-off was not properly signposted; **un cartel señalizaba el área de servicio** a sign indicated the service area

2 (*Ferro*) to signal

Ⓑ VI (*con intermitente, con la mano*) to indicate, signal

señero ADJ 1 (= *sin par*) unequalled, unequaled (*EEUU*), outstanding

2 (= *solo*) alone, solitary

seño* SF (*Esp*) = **señorita B3**

señor(a) Ⓐ ADJ 1 (*) (*antes de sustantivo*) (*uso enfático*) great big*; **vive en una ~a casa** he lives in a great big house*; **eso es un ~ melón** that's some melon

2 (= *libre*) free, at liberty; **eres muy ~ de hacerlo si quieres** you're quite free *o* at liberty to do so if you want

Ⓑ SM/F 1 (= *persona madura*) man *o* (*más frm*) gentleman/lady; **ha venido un ~ preguntando por ti** there was a man *o* (*más frm*) a gentleman here asking for you; **le espera una ~a en su despacho** there's a lady waiting to see you in your office; **es todo un ~** he's a real gentleman; **lo he comprado en la planta de ~as** I bought it in ladieswear; ✦***MODISMO*** **dárselas de ~** to put on airs ► **señora de compañía** companion

2 (= *dueño*) [*de tierras*] owner; [*de criado, esclavo*] master/mistress; **el ~ no vendrá hoy a comer** the master will not be here for lunch today; **¿está la ~a?** is the lady of the house in?; **el ~ de la casa** the master of the house; **no es ~ de sus pasiones** he cannot control his passions

3 (*fórmula de tratamiento*) 3·1 (*con apellido*) Mr/Mrs; **es para el ~ Serrano** it's for Mr Serrano; **el ~ y la ~a Durán** Mr and Mrs Durán; **los ~es Centeno y Sánchez tuvieron que irse antes** (*frm*) Messrs Centeno and Sánchez had to leave early (*frm*); **los ~es (de) González** Mr and Mrs González

3·2 (*) (*con nombre de pila*) **buenos días, ~ Mariano** (*a Mariano Ruiz*) good morning, Mr Ruiz; **la ~a María es de mi pueblo** (*hablando de María Ruiz*) Mrs Ruiz is from my village

3·3 (*hablando directamente*) sir/madam; **no se preocupe ~** don't worry, sir; **¿qué desea la ~a?** (*en tienda*) can I help you, madam?; (*en restaurante*) what would you like, madam?; **¡oiga, ~a!** excuse me, madam!; **¡~as y ~es!** ladies and gentlemen!

3·4 (*con nombre de cargo o parentesco*) **el ~ alcalde** the mayor; **el ~ cura** the priest; **~ presidente** Mr President; **~ alcalde** Mr Mayor; **sí, ~ juez** yes, my Lord; **como diría tu ~a madre** as your mother would say

3·5 (*frm*) (*en correspondencia*) **muy ~ mío** Dear Sir; **muy ~a mía** Dear Madam; **muy ~es nuestros** Dear Sirs; **~ director** (*en carta a periódico*) Dear Sir

4 (*uso enfático*) **pues sí ~, así es como pasó** yes indeed, that's how it happened; **¡no ~, ahora no te vas!** oh no, you're not going anywhere yet!; *ver tb* **señora**

Ⓒ SM 1 (*Hist*) lord ► **señor de la guerra** warlord ► **señor feudal** feudal lord

2 (*Rel*) **el Señor** the Lord; **alabemos al Señor** let us praise the Lord; **Nuestro Señor** Our Lord; **Nuestro Señor Jesucristo** Our Lord Jesus Christ; **recibir al Señor** to take communion

señora SF 1 (= *esposa*) wife; **vino con su ~** he came with his wife; **la ~ de García** Mrs García; **mi ~** my wife

2 (*Rel*) **Nuestra Señora** Our Lady

señorear ▸conjug 1a◂ Ⓐ VT 1 (= *gobernar*) (*gen*) to rule; (*pey*) to domineer, lord it over

2 [+ *edificio*] to dominate, tower over

3 [+ *pasiones*] to master, control

Ⓑ **señorearse** VPR 1 (= *dominarse*) to control o.s.

2 (= *darse humos*) to adopt a lordly manner

3 **~se de** to seize, seize control of

señoría SF 1 **su** *o* **vuestra Señoría** your *o* his lordship/your *o* her ladyship

2 (= *dominio*) rule, sway

señorial ADJ noble, majestic, stately

señorío SM 1 (*Hist*) manor, feudal estate

2 (= *dominio*) rule, dominion (**sobre** over)

3 (= *cualidad*) majesty, stateliness

4 (*) (= *personas adineradas*) (*gen*) distinguished people; (*pey*) toffs*, nobs‡

señorita Ⓐ ADJ (= *de buenos modales*) (*Cono Sur*) polite

Ⓑ SF 1 (= *mujer soltera*) young lady; **una ~ ha llamado por teléfono** a young lady phoned; **ya estás hecha toda una ~** you've turned into a proper young lady; **la ~ no está contenta con nada** (*iró*) it would seem nothing pleases her ladyship; **residencia de ~s** hostel for young women ► **señorita de compañía** (*euf*) escort girl

2 (*fórmula de tratamiento*) 2·1 (*con apellido*) Miss; **~ Pérez** Miss Pérez; **¿es usted señora o ~?** is it Mrs or Miss?

2·2 (*con nombre de pila*) **buenos días, ~ Rosa** (*a Rosa Pérez*) good morning, Miss Pérez

2·3 (*hablando directamente*) **¿puedo ayudarla en algo, ~?** can I help you, madam?

2·4 (*usado por criados*) **la ~ no está en casa** (*referido a Rosa Pérez*) Miss Pérez is not at home; **¿a qué hora desea la ~ que la despierte?** what time would you like me to wake you, Miss?

2·5 (*en correspondencia*) **estimada ~** (*a Rosa Pérez*) Dear Miss Pérez, Dear Ms Pérez

3 (*) (= *maestra*) teacher; **mi ~ no nos ha mandado tarea** my teacher didn't give us any homework; **~, Luisa me ha quitado el bolígrafo** Miss, Luisa has taken my pen

señoritingo/a* SM/F spoilt brat*

señorito Ⓐ ADJ (*pey*) high and mighty*; **no le gusta trabajar, es muy señorita** she doesn't like working, she's too high and mighty*

Ⓑ SM 1 (= *hijo de señor*) young gentleman; (*en lenguaje de criados*) master, young master

2 (*pey*) rich kid*

señorón/ona* SM/F big shot*

señuelo SM 1 (*Caza*) decoy

2 (*fig*) (= *cebo*) bait, lure

3 (*Andes, Cono Sur*) (= *buey*) leading ox

seo SF (*Aragón*) cathedral

sep. ABR (= **septiembre**) Sept

sepa *etc ver* **saber**

separable Ⓐ ADJ 1 (= *distinguible*) separable; **el carácter no es totalmente ~ de la forma física** character is not totally separable from physical form; **la vida privada es muy difícilmente ~ de la pública** it is very difficult to keep your private life separate from your public life

2 (= *extraíble*) [*revista*] detachable; [*teclado*] removable

Ⓑ SM pull-out feature

separación SF 1 (= *división*) division; **la estantería sirve de ~ entre las dos zonas** the bookcase acts as a division between the two areas; **las tropas han cruzado la línea de ~** the troops have crossed the dividing line ► **separación de bienes** seperate estates ► **separación de poderes** separation of powers ► **separación racial** racial segregation

[2] (*entre cónyuges, amigos*) separation; **tras varios meses de ~** after several months of separation; **en el momento de la ~ de las dos compañías** at the moment when the two companies split ► **separación legal**, **separación matrimonial** legal separation

[3] (= *distancia*) gap, space; **deja un poco más de ~ entre los cuadros** leave a slightly bigger gap *o* space between the pictures

[4] [*de un cargo*] removal, dismissal; **tras su ~ del cargo** after his removal *o* dismissal from the post ► **separación del servicio** (*Mil*) discharge

separadamente ADV separately

separado/a Ⓐ ADJ [1] (= *independiente*) separate; **dormimos en camas separadas** we sleep in separate beds; **tiene los ojos muy ~s** his eyes are very far apart; **por ~** separately; **los trabajos se facturan por ~** each job is invoiced separately; **puede comprar los libros juntos o por ~** you can buy the books together or separately

[2] [*cónyuge*] separated; **está ~ de su mujer** he is separated from his wife; **es hija de padres ~s** her parents are separated

Ⓑ SM/F **los ~s con hijos** separated people with children

separador SM [1] (*en carpeta, maletín*) divider

[2] (*Téc*) separator

[3] (*Inform*) delimiter

[4] (*Col Aut*) central reservation, median strip (*EEUU*)

separadora SF burster

separar ▸conjug 1a◂ Ⓐ VT [1] (= *apartar*) to separate; **la maestra nos separó para que no habláramos** the teacher split us up *o* separated us so that we wouldn't talk; **si no los llegan a ~ se matan** if no one had pulled them apart *o* separated them, they would have killed each other; **separe la última sección del formulario** detach the bottom of the form; **~ algn/algo de algn/algo** to separate sb/sth from sb/sth; **al nacer los ~on de sus padres** they were taken (away) *o* separated from their parents at birth; **los ~on del resto de los pasajeros** they were split up *o* separated from the rest of the passengers; **separa el sofá de la pared** move the sofa away from the wall; **separe la cazuela de la lumbre** take the pot off the heat; ✦***MODISMO*** **~ el grano de la paja** to separate the wheat from the chaff

[2] (= *distanciar*) **nada conseguirá ~nos** nothing can come between us; **éramos buenos amigos, pero la política nos separó** we were good friends but politics came between us; **el trabajo la mantiene separada de su familia** work keeps her away from her family; **hasta que la muerte nos separe** till death us do part

[3] (= *existir entre*) **la distancia que separa Nueva York de Roma** the distance between New York and Rome; **el abismo que separa a los ricos de los pobres** the gulf between *o* separating (the) rich and (the) poor

[4] (= *deslindar*) **los Pirineos separan España de Francia** the Pyrenees separate Spain from France; **unas barreras de protección separaban el escenario de la plaza** there were crash barriers separating the stage from the rest of the square; **la frontera que separa realidad y ficción** the dividing line between reality and fiction, the line that separates reality from *o* and fiction

[5] (= *dividir*) to divide; **separa las palabras en sílabas** divide the words into syllables; **los separé en varios montones** I sorted them out into several piles

[6] (= *poner aparte*) **¿me puedes ~ un poco de tarta?** can you put aside some cake for me?

[7] (= *destituir*) (*de un cargo*) to remove, dismiss; **ser separado del servicio** (*Mil*) to be discharged

Ⓑ **separarse** VPR [1] (*en el espacio*) to part; **caminaron hasta la plaza, donde se ~on** they walked as far as the square, where they went their separate ways *o* where they parted; **al llegar a la juventud sus destinos parecen ~se** when they became teenagers they seemed to go their separate ways; **~se de algn/algo**: **no se separa de él ni un solo instante** she never leaves him *o* leaves his side for a moment; **no debí ~me de las maletas** I shouldn't have left the suitcases unattended; **no se separan ni un momento del televisor** they sit there glued to the television, they never take their eyes off the television; **consiguió ~se del pelotón** he managed to leave the pack behind; **no se separen del grupo hasta que estemos dentro de la catedral** stay with the group until we are in the cathedral; **no quiere ~se de sus libros** he doesn't want to part with his books; **se separó de la vida pública** she withdrew *o* retired from public life

[2] (*en una relación*) [*cónyuges*] to separate, split up; [*socios, pareja*] to split up; **sus padres se han separado** his parents have separated *o* split up; **¿en qué año se ~on los Beatles?** what year did the Beatles break up *o* split up?; **~se de** [+ *cónyuge*] to separate from, split up with; [+ *socio, pareja*] to split up with; **se separó de su marido** she separated from *o* split up with her husband; **se ha separado de todos sus amigos** he has cut himself off from all his friends; **piensa ~se de la empresa** he is thinking of leaving the company

[3] (= *desprenderse*) [*fragmento, trozo*] to detach itself (**de** from), come away; [*pedazos*] to come apart

[4] (*Pol, Rel*) to break away; **se separó de ellos para formar su propio partido** he broke away from them to form his own party; **cuando la Iglesia anglicana se separó de Roma** when the Anglican Church broke away *o* (*frm*) seceded from Rome

[5] (*Jur*) to withdraw (**de** from)

separata SF offprint

separatismo SM separatism

separatista ADJ, SMF separatist

separo SM (*Méx*) cell

sepelio SM burial, interment

sepia Ⓐ ADJ, SM INV (= *color*) sepia

Ⓑ SF [1] (= *pez*) cuttlefish

[2] (*Arte*) sepia

SEPLA SM ABR (= **Sindicato Español de Pilotos de Líneas Aéreas**) ≈ BALPA

sepsis SF INV sepsis

sept. ABR (= **septiembre**) Sept

septentrión SM (*liter*) north

septentrional ADJ north, northern

septeto SM septet

septicemia SF septicaemia, septicemia (*EEUU*)

séptico ADJ septic

septiembre SM September; **llegará el (día) 11 de ~** he will arrive on the 11th of September *o* on September the 11th; **en ~** in September; **en ~ del año pasado/que viene** last/next September; **a mediados de ~** in mid-September; **estamos a tres de ~** it's the third of September; **todos los años, en ~** every September

septillizo/a SM/F septuplet

séptimo ADJ, SM seventh; *ver tb* **sexto**

septuagenario/a Ⓐ ADJ septuagenarian, seventy-year-old

Ⓑ SM/F septuagenarian, person in his/her seventies, seventy-year-old

septuagésimo ADJ, SM seventieth

séptuplo ADJ sevenfold

sepulcral ADJ [1] (= *del sepulcro*) sepulchral; **la inscripción ~** the inscription on the tomb *o* grave

[2] (= *sombrío*) gloomy, dismal; **silencio ~** deathly silence

sepulcro SM (*esp Biblia*) tomb, grave, sepulchre, sepulcher (*EEUU*); **~ blanqueado** whited sepulchre

sepultación SF (*Cono Sur*) burial

sepultar ▸conjug 1a◂ VT [1] (= *enterrar*) (*gen*) to bury; (*en mina*) to trap, bury; **quedaron sepultados bajo la roca** they were buried under the rock

[2] (= *ocultar*) to hide away, conceal

sepultura SF [1] (= *acción*) burial; **dar ~ a** to bury; **dar cristiana ~ a algn** to give sb a Christian burial; **recibir ~** to be buried

[2] (= *tumba*) grave, tomb

sepulturero SM gravedigger

seque *etc ver* **secar**

sequedad SF [1] (= *falta de humedad*) dryness

[2] (*en contestación, carácter*) curtness

sequerío SM dry place, dry field

sequía SF [1] (= *falta de lluvias*) drought

[2] (= *temporada*) dry season

[3] (*Andes*) (= *sed*) thirst

sequiar ▸conjug 1c◂ VI (*Cono Sur*) to inhale

séquito SM [1] [*de rey, presidente*] retinue, entourage

[2] (*Pol*) followers *pl*

[3] [*de sucesos*] train, string; **con todo un ~ de calamidades** with a whole catalogue of disasters

SER SF ABR (*Esp*) (= **Sociedad Española de Radiodifusión**) *radio network*

ser

▸conjug 2v◂	[B] VERBO AUXILIAR
[A] VERBO INTRANSITIVO	[C] SUSTANTIVO MASCULINO

Ⓐ VERBO INTRANSITIVO

[1] ***con función copulativa*** [1·1] (+ *ADJ*) to be; **es difícil** it's difficult; **es muy alto** he's very tall; **soy casado/soltero/divorciado** I'm married/single/divorced; **compra uno que no sea caro** buy one that isn't too expensive; **es pesimista** he's a pessimist; **somos seis** there are six of us; **me es imposible asistir** I'm unable to attend, it's impossible for me to attend; **¡que seas feliz!** I wish you every happiness!; **—eres estúpida —no, no lo**

soy "you're stupid" — "no I'm not"; **¡~á posible!** I don't believe it!; **¡~ás burro!** you can be so stupid!

1·2 (+ *SUSTANTIVO, PRONOMBRE*) **el gran pintor que fue Goya** the great painter Goya; **hable con algún abogado que no sea Pérez** speak to some lawyer other than Pérez; **soy ingeniero** I'm an engineer; **con el tiempo fue ministro** he eventually became a minister; **yo era la reina, ¿vale?** suppose I were queen, right?; **presidente que fue de Francia** (*frm*) former president of France; **—¿dígame? —¡hola, soy Pedro!** "hello?" — "hello, it's Peter"; **—¿quién es? — soy yo** "who is it?" —"it's me"; **—¿quién ~á a estas horas? —~á tu hermano** "who can it be at this hour?" — "it must be your brother"; **—¿qué ha sido eso? —nada, la puerta ha dado un portazo** "what was that?" — "nothing, the door slammed shut"; **es él quien debiera hacerlo** he's the one who should do it

1·3 **~ de** (*indicando origen*) to be from; **ella es de Calatayud** she's from Calatayud; **estas naranjas son de España** these oranges are Spanish *o* from Spain; **¿de dónde es usted?** where are you from?

1·4 **~ de** (*indicando composición*) to be made of; **es de lana** it's made of wool, it's woollen; **es de piedra** it's made of stone

1·5 **~ de** (*indicando pertenencia*) to belong to; **el parque es del municipio** the park belongs to the town; **esta tapa es de otra caja** this lid belongs to another box; **¿de quién es este lápiz?** whose pencil is this?, who does this pencil belong to?; **éste es suyo** this one is his; **es de Joaquín** it's Joaquín's

1·6 + INFIN **es de creer que**: **continuó hablando, es de creer que sin interrupción** he went on talking, presumably without being interrupted; **si, como es de creer, ustedes también lo apoyan...** if, as may be supposed, you also support him...; **no es de creer que lo encarcelen, pero sí lo multarán** they probably won't put him in prison, but they are sure to fine him; **es de desear que ...** it is to be wished that ...; **es de esperar que ...** it is to be hoped that ...; **era de ver** it was worth seeing

2 **~ para** (*indicando dirección, finalidad*) **las flores son para ti** the flowers are for you; **el trofeo fue para Álvarez** the trophy went to Álvarez; **el sexto hoyo fue para García** García took the sixth hole; **este cuchillo es para cortar pan** this knife is for cutting bread; **ese coche no es para correr mucho** that car isn't made for going very fast; **esas finuras no son para mí** such niceties are not for me

3 *= existir* to be; **~ o no ~** to be or not to be; **Dios es** God exists; **érase que se era** ◊ **érase una vez** once upon a time

4 *= tener lugar* **la fiesta va a ~ en su casa** the party will be at her house; **el crimen fue en Agosto** the crime took place in August; ✦*MODISMO* **otra vez ~á**: **—no he podido ir a visitarla —bueno, otra vez ~á** "I wasn't able to visit her" — "never mind, you can do it some other time"; **—no he aprobado —¡otra vez ~á!** "I didn't pass" — "better luck next time!

5 *en preguntas retóricas* **¿qué ~á de mí?** what will become of me?; **¿qué habrá sido de él?** what can have become of him?, what can have happened to him?

6 *con horas del día, fecha, tiempo* to be; **es la una** it's one o'clock; **son las siete** it's seven o'clock; **~án las ocho** it must be about eight (o'clock); **~ían las nueve cuando llegó** it must have been about nine (o'clock) when he arrived; **hoy es cuatro de septiembre** today is the fourth of September; **es verano** it's summer; **era de noche** it was night time; *ver tb* **hora 2**

7 *= en cálculos* to be; **tres y dos son cinco** three plus two is five; **—¿cuánto es? —son dos euros** "how much is it?" — "two euros, please"

8 *locuciones en infinitivo* **a no ~**: **habríamos fracasado a no ~ por su apoyo** we would have failed had it not been for their help; **llegaremos tarde a no ~ que salgamos mañana** we'll be late unless we leave tomorrow; **como ha de** *o* **tiene que ~**: **es un hombre como tiene que ~** he's a real man; **se lo comió con cuchillo y tenedor, como ha de** *o* **tiene que ~** she ate it with a knife and fork, the way it's supposed to be eaten; **con ~** (= *a pesar de ser*): **con ~ ella su madre no le veo el parecido** she may well be his mother, but I can't see any resemblance; **de no ~**: **de no ~ esto cierto tendríamos que eliminarlo** if this weren't the case we'd have to get rid of him; **de no ~ por él me habría ahogado** if it hadn't been for him I'd have drowned; **no vaya a ~ que...**: **déjales tu teléfono, no vaya a ~ que se pierdan** give them your phone number in case they get lost; **anda despacio, no vaya a ~ que te caigas** walk slowly so you don't fall over

10 *locuciones en indicativo* **es más**: **creo que eso es así, es más, podría asegurártelo** I think that is the case, in fact I can assure you it is; **es que**: **—¿por qué no llamaste? —es que no pude** "why didn't you call?" — "because I couldn't"; **es que no quiero molestarle** it's just that I don't want to upset him; **¿es que no te enteras?** don't you understand, or what?; **¿cómo es que no llamaste?** how come you didn't call?

11 *locuciones en subjuntivo* **¡sea!** agreed!, all right!; **—compartiremos los gastos —¡sea!** "we'll share the cost" — "agreed!" *o* "all right!"; **(ya) sea ... (ya) sea**: **(ya) sea de izquierdas, (ya) sea de derechas yo no la voto** whether she's right-wing or left-wing, I'm not voting for her; **(ya) sea Juan o (ya) sea Antonio, alguien tiene que hacerlo** someone has to do it, (be it) either Juan or Antonio; **sea lo que sea**: **—¡pero si es economista! —sea lo que sea, yo no me fío de sus opiniones** "but he's an economist!" —"be that as it may *o* he may well be, but still I don't trust his opinions"; **o sea** that is; **mis compañeros, o sea, Juan y Pedro** my colleagues, that is, Juan and Pedro; **o sea, que no vienes** so you're not coming; **no sea que** in case; **llévate el móvil no sea que llamen** take your mobile phone with you in case they call; **pon aquí las llaves, no sea que las pierdas** put the keys here so you don't lose them

Ⓑ VERBO AUXILIAR

en formas pasivas to be; **fue construido** it was built; **~á fusilado** he will be shot; **está siendo estudiado** it is being studied; **ha sido asaltada una joyería** there has been a raid on a jeweller's

Ⓒ SUSTANTIVO MASCULINO

1 *= ente* being; **sus ~es queridos** her loved ones ► **ser humano** human being ► **Ser Supremo** Supreme Being ► **ser vivo** living creature

2 *= esencia, alma* being; **todo su ~ se conmovió ante tanta miseria** her whole being was moved by such poverty; **en lo más íntimo de su ~** deep within himself; **la quiero con todo mi ~** I love her with all my heart; **volver a su ~** to return *o* go back to normal

3 *existencia* life; **la mujer que le dio su ~** the woman who gave him (his) life, the woman who brought him into the world

> **SER**
>
> En español decimos **somos 15**, **son 28**, *etc.* Esta estructura se traduce al inglés por **there are/were/***etc* + **NÚMERO** + **of us/you/them**:
>
> Somos 50.
> ***There are 50 of us***
> Eran 38 en total
> ***There were 38 of them altogether***
>
> *Para otros usos y ejemplos ver la entrada.*

sera SF pannier, basket

seráficamente ADV angelically, like an angel

seráfico ADJ 1 (= *angélico*) angelic, seraphic
2 (*) (= *humilde*) poor and humble

serafín SM 1 (*Rel*) seraph; (*fig*) angel
2 (*Caribe*) (= *broche*) clip, fastener

serape SM (*Méx*) = **sarape**

serbal SM, **serbo** SM service tree, sorb

Serbia SF Serbia

serbio/a Ⓐ ADJ Serbian
Ⓑ SM/F Serb
Ⓒ SM (*Ling*) Serbian

serbobosnio/a ADJ, SM/F Bosnian Serb

serbocroata Ⓐ ADJ, SMF Serbo-Croatian
Ⓑ SM (*Ling*) Serbo-Croat

serenamente ADV 1 (= *con calma*) calmly, serenely
2 (= *tranquilamente*) peacefully, quietly

serenar ▸conjug 1a◂ Ⓐ VT (*frm*) 1 (= *calmar*) [+ *ánimo, mente*] to calm; [+ *discusión, pelea*] to calm down; [+ *problema*] to settle
2 [+ *líquido*] to clarify
Ⓑ VI (*Andes**) to drizzle
Ⓒ **serenarse** VPR 1 [*persona*] to calm down
2 (*Meteo*) [*mar*] to grow calm; [*tiempo*] to clear up, settle (down)
3 [*líquido*] to clear, settle

serenata SF serenade

serendipia SF serendipity

serenera SF (*Andes, CAm, Caribe*) cape, wrap

serenero SM (*Cono Sur*) (= *pañuelo*) headscarf; (= *chal*) wrap, cape

serenidad SF 1 (= *calma*) calmness, serenity
2 (= *tranquilidad*) peacefulness, quietness

serenísimo ADJ **su Alteza Serenísima** His/Her Serene Highness

sereno Ⓐ ADJ 1 (= *apacible*) [*persona*] calm, serene; [*cara, expresión*] serene
2 (*Meteo*) [*tiempo*] settled, fine; [*cielo*] cloudless, clear
3 (= *calmado*) [*ambiente*] calm, quiet; [*tarde, noche*] still, peaceful; [*aguas*] calm, still
4 (= *sobrio*) **estar ~** to be sober
Ⓑ SM 1 (= *humedad*) night dew; **dormir al ~**

to sleep out in the open; **le perjudica el ~** the night air is bad for her
2 (= *vigilante*) night watchman

sereta SF builder's bucket, basket

seriado ADJ mass-produced

serial SM (SF *en Cono Sur*) serial ► **serial radiofónico** radio serial

serialización SF serialization

serializar ►conjug 1f◄ VT to serialize

seriamente ADV seriously

seriar ►conjug 1b◄ VT 1 (= *poner en serie*) to arrange in series, arrange serially
2 (*TV, Radio*) to make a serial of, serialize
3 (= *producir*) to mass-produce

sericultura SF silk-raising, sericulture

serie SF 1 (= *sucesión*) (*tb Biol, Mat*) series; **ha escrito una ~ de artículos sobre la infancia** she has written a series of articles about childhood; **asesinatos en ~** serial killings; **asesino en ~** serial killer
2 (*Industria*) **de ~**: **tamaño de ~** standard size; **artículo de ~** mass-produced article; **equipamiento de ~** standard equipment; **modelo de ~** (*Aut*) standard model; **el aire acondicionado es de ~** air-conditioning comes as standard; **en ~**: **fabricación en ~** mass production; **fabricar** *o* **producir en ~** to mass-produce; **fuera de ~** (= *extraordinario*) special, out of the ordinary; **un fuera de ~** an extraordinary person, one of a kind; **artículos fuera de ~** (*Com*) goods left over, remainders
3 (*Elec*) **en ~** in series
4 (*Inform*) **impresora en ~** serial printer; **interface en ~** serial interface; **puerto (en) ~** serial port
5 (= *conjunto*) [*de monedas, sellos*] series; [*de inyecciones*] course
6 (*TV, Radio*) (*en episodios sueltos*) series; (*en historia continua*) serial
7 (*Cine*) **película de ~ B** B-movie
8 (*Dep*) qualifying heat

seriedad SF 1 (= *calidad personal*) seriousness; **hablar con ~** to speak seriously *o* in earnest
2 (= *responsabilidad*) responsibility, sense of responsibility; **falta de ~** lack of responsibility, irresponsibility
3 [*de enfermedad, crisis, problema*] seriousness
4 (= *fiabilidad*) reliability, trustworthiness

serigrafía SF silk-screen printing; **una ~** a silk-screen print

serigrafista SMF silk-screen printer

serimiri SM drizzle

serio ADJ 1 [*expresión, tono*] serious; **¿por qué estás hoy tan ~?** why are you (looking) so serious today?; **su padre es muy ~** his father's a very serious person; **se quedó mirándome muy ~** he looked at me very seriously, he stared gravely at me; **pareces muy ~** you're looking very serious; **ponerse ~**: **se puso seria al ver la foto** she went o became serious when she saw the photo; **me voy a poner seria contigo si no estudias** I'm going to get cross with you if you don't do some studying
2 **en ~** seriously; **tomar un asunto en ~** to take a matter seriously; **no hablaba en ~** I wasn't serious; **¿lo dices en ~?** are you serious?, do you really mean it?
3 [*problema, enfermedad, pérdida*] serious; **esto se pone ~** this is getting serious
4 (= *fiable*) [*persona*] reliable; [*trato*] straight, honest; **es una persona poco seria** he's not very reliable; **una empresa seria** a reliable firm; **no es ~ que ahora decidan echarse atrás** it's not very responsible of them to back out now
5 (= *severo*) **el negro es un color demasiado ~ para una niña** black is too serious *o* severe a colour for a young girl; **lleva un traje muy ~** he's wearing a very formal suit
6 [*estudio, libro*] serious

sermón SM 1 (*Rel*) sermon; **el Sermón de la Montaña** the Sermon on the Mount
2 (*) (= *regañina*) lecture*; **vaya ~ que nos soltó tu padre** what a lecture your dad gave us!

sermonear* ►conjug 1a◄ Ⓐ VT to lecture*
Ⓑ VI to sermonize

sermoneo* SM lecture*

sermonero* ADJ given to sermonizing

sernambí SM (*Andes, Caribe*) inferior rubber

serología SF serology

serón SM 1 (= *sera*) pannier, large basket
2 [*de bebé*] cot

seronegativo ADJ seronegative

seropositivo ADJ (*gen*) seropositive; (*con VIH*) HIV-positive

seroso ADJ serous

serotonina SF serotonin

serpa SF (*Bot*) runner

serpear ►conjug 1a◄ VI, **serpentear** ►conjug 1a◄ VI 1 (*Zool*) to wriggle, creep
2 [*camino*] to wind, twist and turn; [*río*] to wind, meander

serpenteante ADJ [*camino*] winding, twisting; [*río*] winding, meandering

serpenteo SM 1 (*Zool*) wriggling, creeping
2 [*de camino*] winding, twisting; [*de río*] winding, meandering

serpentín SM coil

serpentina SF 1 (*Min*) serpentine
2 (= *papel*) streamer

serpentino ADJ 1 (= *como serpiente*) snaky, sinuous
2 [*camino*] winding, meandering

serpiente SF snake, serpent; **la Serpiente** the (European monetary) Snake ► **serpiente boa** boa constrictor ► **serpiente de anteojos** cobra ► **serpiente de cascabel** rattlesnake, rattler (*EEUU**) ► **serpiente de mar** sea serpent ► **serpiente de verano** silly (season) story, non-story (*used to fill papers in the slack season*) ► **serpiente de vidrio** slow-worm ► **serpiente pitón** python

serpol SM wild thyme

serpollo SM sucker, shoot

serrado ADJ serrated, toothed

serraduras SFPL sawdust *sing*

serrallo SM harem

serrana SF = **serranilla;** *ver tb* **serrano**

serranía SF 1 (= *terreno montañoso*) mountains *pl*, mountainous area, hilly country
2 (*Méx*) (= *bosque*) wood, forest

serraniego ADJ = **serrano A**

serranilla SF *15th-century verse-form*

serrano/a Ⓐ ADJ 1 (*Geog*) mountain *antes de s*, hill *antes de s*
2 (= *tosco*) coarse, rustic
3 **partida serrana** (*Esp*) dirty trick
Ⓑ SM/F mountain-dweller, highlander; *ver tb* **serrana**

serrar ►conjug 1j◄ VT 1 [+ *madera*] to saw up
2 (= *separar*) to saw off

serrería SF sawmill

serrín SM sawdust

serrote SM (*Méx*) = **serrucho**

serruchar ►conjug 1a◄ VT (*esp LAm*) to saw (up); (= *separar*) to saw off

serrucho SM 1 (= *herramienta*) saw, handsaw
2 (*Caribe*) (= *prostituta*) whore
3 **hacer un ~** (*Andes, Caribe*) to split the cost

Servia SF = **Serbia**

servible ADJ serviceable, usable

servicial Ⓐ ADJ helpful, obliging
Ⓑ SM (*Andes*) servant

servicialidad SF helpfulness, obliging nature

servicio SM 1 (= *ayuda, atención*) 1·1 (*a empresa, país*) service; **lleva veinte años de ~ en la empresa** he has twenty years' service with the company; **no cobró nada por sus ~s** he didn't charge anything for his services; **al ~ de**: **un agente secreto al ~ de la Corona** a secret agent in the service of the Crown; **estar de ~** to be on duty; **estar de ~ de guardia** (*Mil*) to be on guard duty; **estar fuera** *o* **libre de ~** to be off duty; **un policía libre de ~** an off-duty policeman; **prestar ~** (*gen*) to work; (*Mil*) to serve; **ha prestado sus ~s en el hospital universitario** she has worked at the university hospital; **prestó sus ~s como teniente de la marina** he served as a lieutenant in the navy
1·2 (*a cliente*) service; **el ~ no está incluido** service is not included; **una empresa de ~s informáticos** a computing services company; **a su ~** at your service; **"servicio a domicilio"** "we deliver", "home delivery service"
1·3 [*de tren, autobús*] service; **el ~ a la costa ha quedado interrumpido** the service to the coast has been interrupted
► **servicio a bordo** (*en avión*) in-flight services *pl*; (*en barco, tren*) services on board *pl* ► **servicio comunitario** community service ► **servicio contra incendios** fire service ► **servicio de aduana** customs service ► **servicio de asesoramiento** advisory service ► **servicio de atención al cliente** customer service ► **servicio de bomberos** fire service ► **servicio de contraespionaje** secret service ► **servicio de entrega** delivery service ► **servicio de información**, **servicio de inteligencia** intelligence service ► **servicio de limpieza** cleaning services *pl* ► **servicio de megafonía** public address system ► **servicio de orden** (*en manifestación*) stewards *pl*, marshals *pl* ► **servicio de préstamo a domicilio** lending facility, home lending service ► **servicio de recogida de basura** refuse collection service ► **servicio de transportes** transport service ► **servicio de vigilancia aduanera** coastguard patrol ► **servicio médico** medical service ► **servicio permanente** round-the-clock service ► **servicio posventa** after-sales service ► **servicios de socorro** emergency services ► **servicio secreto** secret service ► **servicios informativos** broadcasting services ► **servicios mínimos** minimum service *sing*, skeleton service *sing* ► **servicio social (sustitutorio)** community service (*performed in place of military service*) ► **servicios postales** postal services ► **servicios sociales** social services; *ver tb* **estación 1**

2 (= *funcionamiento*) **estar en ~** to be in service; **entrar en ~** to come *o* go into service; **fuera de ~** out of service; **poner en ~** to put into service; **está previsto poner en ~ una segunda pista de aterrizaje** there are plans to open a second runway, there are plans to put a second runway into operation *o* service
3 (= *beneficio*) service; **hizo un gran ~ a su país** he did his country a great service; **es un abrigo viejo, pero me hace mucho ~** it's an old coat, but I get a lot of use out of it; **hacer un flaco ~ a algn** to do sb a disservice
4 (*Mil*) (*tb* **~ militar**) military service; **ser apto para el ~** to be fit for military service
► **servicio activo** active service
5 (*en un hospital*) department; **"servicio de pediatría"** "paediatric department" ► **servicio de urgencias** accident and emergency department, casualty department
6 **servicios** (*Econ*) public services; **el sector ~s** the public service sector
7 (= *retrete público*) toilet, washroom (*EEUU*), restroom (*EEUU*); **¿dónde están los ~s?** where are the toilets?
8 (*en la mesa*) 8·1 (*para cada comensal*) **un juego de café con seis ~s** a six-piece coffee set; **faltan dos ~s** we are two places *o* settings short
8·2 (= *juego*) set
► **servicio de café** coffee set, coffee service
► **servicio de mesa** dinner service
► **servicio de té** tea set, tea service
9 (= *servidumbre*) (*tb* **~ doméstico**) (= *personas*) servants *pl*; (= *actividad*) service, domestic service; **hay dos habitaciones para el ~** there are two rooms for the servants; **han mejorado las condiciones del ~** conditions of domestic service have improved; **escalera de ~** service staircase; **puerta de ~** tradesman's entrance
10 (*Tenis*) serve, service; **romper el ~ de algn** to break sb's serve *o* service
11 (*Rel*) service; **el ~ será oficiado por Monseñor Cipriá** Monsignor Cipriá will officiate at the service
12 (*Fin*) [*de una deuda*] servicing
13 (*LAm*) [*de un automóvil*] service; **le toca el ~ a los 3.000km** it's due (for) a service after 3000km

servidor(a) Ⓐ SM/F 1 (= *criado*) servant
2 (*como expresión cortés*) **—¿quién es la última de la cola? —~a** "who's last in the queue?" — "I am"; **—Francisco Ruiz —¡servidor!** (*frm*) "Francisco Ruiz" — "present! *o* at your service!" (*frm*); **¡~ de usted!** at your service!; **"su seguro ~"†** (*en cartas*) "yours faithfully" (*frm*), "yours truly" (*EEUU frm*); **un ~**: **al final un ~ tuvo que fregar todos los platos** (*hum*) in the end yours truly *o* muggins had to wash all the dishes*; **él y un ~ pasamos un buen rato** he and I had a good time
3 (*Cono Sur*) ► **servidor(a) del orden** police officer
Ⓑ SM (*Inform*) (= *empresa*) Internet Service Provider, ISP; (= *aparato*) server ► **servidor de red** network server

servidumbre SF 1 (= *conjunto de criados*) staff, servants *pl*
2 (= *condición*) [*de criado*] servitude; [*de esclavo*] slavery; **la ~ de los que trabajan para un jefe** the servitude of those who work for their boss; **el dinero se ha convertido en una forma de ~** money has turned into a form of slavery
3 (*Hist*) (*tb* **~ de la gleba**) serfdom
4 (*Jur*) ► **servidumbre de aguas** water rights *pl* ► **servidumbre de paso** rights *pl* of way

servil ADJ 1 (= *poco apreciado*) [*actitud, comportamiento*] servile, obsequious; [*trabajo*] menial
2 [*imitación, estilo*] slavish

servilismo SM servility, obsequiousness (*frm*)

servilla SF slipper, pump

servilleta SF serviette, napkin

servilletero SM serviette ring, napkin ring

➤ **servir** ▸conjug 3k◂ Ⓐ VT 1 [+ *persona, intereses, causa*] to serve; **seguiré sirviendo al pueblo** I will continue to serve the people; **están sirviendo a su interés personal** they are furthering *o* serving their own interests; **~ a Dios** to serve God; **~ a la patria** to serve one's country; **¿en qué puedo ~le?** how can I help you?; ✦**MODISMOS para ~le**† ◊ **para ~ a usted**† at your service; ✦**REFRÁN no se puede ~ a Dios y al diablo** no man can serve two masters
2 (*para comer*) 2·1 (*en la mesa*) [+ *comida*] to serve; [+ *bebida*] to serve, pour; **¿a qué hora sirven el desayuno?** what time is breakfast served?; **se negaron a ~nos** they refused to serve us; **¿me ayudas a ~ la mesa?** can you help me serve (the food)?; **la cena está servida** dinner's on the table, dinner is served (*frm*); **¿te sirvo un poco más?** would you like some more?, can I give you some more?; **había cinco criados para ~ la mesa** there were five servants waiting at *o* serving at table
2·2 (= *proporcionar*) to give, serve (*frm*); **ese día sirven una comida especial a la tropa** the troops are given *o* (*frm*) served a special meal that day; **sirvieron unos canapés tras la inauguración** after the opening ceremony there were canapés, canapés were served after the opening ceremony (*frm*)
3 (*Com*) [+ *pedido*] to process
4 (*Tenis*) to serve
5 (*Mec*) [+ *máquina, cañón*] to man
6 (*Naipes*) [+ *cartas*] to deal
Ⓑ VI 1 (= *ser útil*) to be useful; **todavía puede ~** it might still be useful; **este mismo me ~á** this one will do; **siempre que lo he necesitado me ha servido** whenever I've needed it, it's done the job; **eso no sirve** that's no good *o* use; **este sistema ya no sirve** this system is no good *o* use any more; **ya no me sirve** it's no good *o* use to me now; **la distinción entre derechas e izquierdas ya no sirve** the distinction between right and left is no longer valid; **~ para algo**: **puede ~ para limpiar el metal** it can be used for *o* it is suitable for cleaning metal; **¿para qué sirve?** what is it for?; **¿para qué sirve este aparato?** what's this gadget for?; **la nueva normativa sólo ha servido para crear polémica** the new regulation has only served to stir up controversy (*frm*), the only thing the new rule has done is to stir up controversy; **el acuerdo no ha servido para alcanzar la paz** the agreement has not succeeded in achieving peace; **esta huelga no está sirviendo para nada** this strike is not achieving anything; **no sirves para nada** you're completely useless; **yo no ~ía para médico** I'd be no good as a doctor
2 **~ de algo**: **la legislación italiana puede ~nos de guía** we can use Italian law as a guide, Italian law can serve a guide; **~ de ejemplo a algn** to be an example to sb; **esa experiencia le ha servido de lección** that experience taught him a lesson; **por si sirve de algo** in case that's any use; **no sirve de nada quejarse** it's no good *o* use complaining, there's no point in complaining; **no sirve de nada que vaya él** it's no good *o* use him going*, there's no point in him going; **¿de qué sirve mentir?** what's the good *o* use of lying?, what's the point in lying?; *ver tb* **precedente B**
3 (*en el servicio doméstico*) to work as a servant; **estuvo sirviendo en Madrid** she was a servant in Madrid; **ponerse a ~** to become a servant
4 [*camarero*] to serve; **vete a ~ en la barra** go and serve at the bar
5 (*Mil*) to serve (*frm*); **yo serví en la Marina** I was in the Navy, I served in the Navy (*frm*); **está sirviendo** he's doing his military service
6 (*Tenis*) to serve
7 (*Naipes*) (*tb* **~ del palo**) to follow suit
Ⓒ **servirse** VPR 1 (= *ponerse*) [+ *comida*] to help o.s. to; [+ *bebida*] to pour o.s., help o.s. to; **sírvete más ensalada** have some more salad, help yourself to more salad; **yo misma me ~é el café** I'll pour myself some coffee, I'll help myself to some coffee; **¿qué se van a ~?** (*LAm*) what will you have?
2 (= *utilizar*) **~se de** [+ *herramienta, objeto*] to use, make use of; [+ *amistad, influencia*] to use; **se han servido de su cargo para enriquecerse** they used their position to make money; **se sirvieron de la oscuridad para escapar** (*liter*) they availed themselves of the darkness to make good their escape (*liter*)
3 (*frm*) (= *hacer el favor de*) **~se hacer algo**: **sírvase volver por aquí mañana** (would you) please come back tomorrow; **le ruego que se sirva acompañarme** (would you) come with me, please; **si la señora se sirve pasar por aquí** if madam would care to come this way

servo SM servo

servo... PREF servo...

servoasistido ADJ servo-assisted

servodirección SF power steering

servofrenos SMPL power-assisted brakes

servomecanismo SM servo, servomechanism

sésamo SM sesame; **¡ábrete ~!** open sesame!

sesapil SM sex-appeal

sesear ▸conjug 1a◂ VT *to pronounce c (before e, i) and z as s (a feature of Andalusian and much LAm pronunciation)*

sesenta ADJ INV, PRON, SM sixty; (= *ordinal*) sixtieth; **los (años) ~** the sixties; *ver tb* **seis**

sesentañero/a SM/F man/woman of about sixty

sesentón/ona Ⓐ ADJ sixty-year-old, sixtyish
Ⓑ SM/F man/woman of about sixty, sixty-year-old

seseo SM *pronunciation of c (before e, i) and of z as s (a feature of Andalusian and much LAm pronunciation)*

sesera* SF brains *pl*

sesgado ADJ 1 (= *inclinado*) slanted, slanting, oblique
2 (= *ladeado*) awry, askew

➤ LENGUA Y USO: **servir B1** 43.4 **C3** 47.5, 48.3, 48.4

3 [*pelota*] swerving, sliced
4 [*opinión, reportaje*] bias(s)ed, slanted

sesgar ▸conjug 1h◂ VT 1 (= *inclinar*) to slant, place obliquely
2 (= *ladear*) to put askew, twist to one side
3 [+ *pelota*] to slice
4 (*Cos*) to cut on the bias
5 (*Téc*) to bevel
6 [+ *opinión, reportaje*] to bias, slant
7 [+ *vida*] to cut short

sesgo SM 1 (= *inclinación*) slant; **estar al ~** to be slanting
2 (= *torcimiento*) warp, twist
3 (*Cos*) bias; **cortar algo al ~** to cut sth on the bias
4 (*Téc*) bevel
5 (= *dirección*) direction; **ha tomado otro ~** it has taken a new turn
6 (*) (= *truco*) dodge*

sésil ADJ sessile

sesión SF 1 (*Admin*) session; **abrir/levantar la ~** to open/close *o* adjourn the session; **celebrar una ~** to hold a session ▸ **sesión de preguntas al gobierno** ≈ question time ▸ **sesión parlamentaria** parliamentary session ▸ **sesión secreta** secret session
2 (= *espacio de tiempo*) (*para retrato*) sitting; (*para tratamiento médico*) session ▸ **sesión de entrenamiento** training session ▸ **sesión de espiritismo** séance ▸ **sesión de lectura de poesías** poetry reading ▸ **sesión de prestidigitación** conjuring show ▸ **sesión fotográfica** photo session
3 (*Cine*) showing; (*Teat*) show, performance; **la segunda ~** the second showing; **hay tres sesiones diarias** there are three showings a day ▸ **sesión continua** continuous showing
4 (*Inform*) session

sesionar ▸conjug 1a◂ VI (= *estar en sesión*) to be in session; (= *celebrar sesión*) to hold a meeting

seso SM 1 (*Anat*) brain
2 (= *inteligencia*) brains *pl*, intelligence; ✦***MODISMOS*** **calentarse** *o* **devanarse los ~s** to rack one's brains; **eso le tiene sorbido el ~** he's crazy about it; **perder el ~** to go off one's head (**por** over)
3 **sesos** (*Culin*) brains

sesquicentenario SM 150th anniversary, sesquicentenary

sesquipedal ADJ sesquipedalian

sestear ▸conjug 1a◂ VI to take a siesta, have a nap

sesteo SM (*LAm*) siesta, nap

sesudamente ADV sensibly, wisely

sesudo ADJ 1 (= *sensato*) sensible, wise
2 (= *inteligente*) brainy
3 (*Cono Sur*) (= *terco*) stubborn, pig-headed

set SM (*pl* **set** *o* **sets**) (*Dep*) set

set. ABR (= **setiembre**) Sept

seta SF mushroom ▸ **seta venenosa** toadstool

setecientos/as ADJ, PRON, SM (*gen*) seven hundred; (*ordinal*) seven hundredth; **en el ~** in the eighteenth century; *ver tb* **seiscientos**

setenta ADJ INV, PRON, SM (*gen*) seventy; (*ordinal*) seventieth; **los (años) ~** the seventies; *ver tb* **seis**

setentañero/a SM/F man/woman of about seventy, seventy-year-old

setentón/ona Ⓐ ADJ seventy-year-old, seventyish Ⓑ SM/F man/woman of about seventy, seventy-year-old

setero/a Ⓐ ADJ mushroom *antes de s*
Ⓑ SM/F mushroom gatherer

setiembre SM = **septiembre**

seto SM 1 (= *cercado*) fence ▸ **seto vivo** hedge
2 (*Caribe*) (= *pared*) dividing wall, partition

setter SM (*pl* **setters** [se'ter]) setter

SEU SM ABR (*Hist*) = **Sindicato Español Universitario**

seudo... PREF pseudo...

seudohistoria SF pseudohistory

seudónimo Ⓐ ADJ pseudonymous
Ⓑ SM (= *nombre falso*) pseudonym; (= *nombre artístico*) pen name

Seúl SM Seoul

s.e.u.o. ABR (= **salvo error u omisión**) E & OE

severamente ADV 1 (= *con dureza*) severely
2 (= *con austeridad*) sternly

severidad SF 1 (*en el trato*) severity
2 (= *austeridad*) sternness

severo ADJ 1 (= *riguroso*) [*persona*] severe, harsh; [*padre, profesor, disciplina*] strict; [*castigo, crítica*] harsh; [*estipulaciones*] stringent; [*condiciones*] harsh, stringent; **ser ~ con algn** to treat sb harshly
2 (= *duro*) [*invierno*] severe, hard; [*frío*] bitter
3 (= *austero*) [*vestido, moda*] severe; [*actitud*] stern

seviche SM = **cebiche**

Sevilla SF Seville

sevillanas SFPL 1 (= *melodía*) *popular Sevillian tune*
2 (= *baile*) *typical Sevillian dance*

sevillano/a ADJ, SM/F Sevillian

sexagenario/a Ⓐ ADJ sexagenarian, sixty-year-old
Ⓑ SM/F sexagenarian, man/woman in his/her sixties, sixty-year-old

sexagésimo ADJ, SM sixtieth; *ver tb* **sexto 1**

sexar ▸conjug 1a◂ VT to sex

sexenio SM (*esp Méx*) *six-year Presidential term of office*

sexería SF sex shop

sexi = **sexy**

sexismo SM sexism

sexista ADJ, SMF sexist

sexo SM 1 (*Biol*) sex; **el bello ~** the fair sex; **el ~ débil** the weaker sex; **el ~ femenino/masculino** the female/male sex; **el ~ fuerte** the stronger sex; **el ~ opuesto** the opposite sex; **de ambos ~s** of both sexes; **sin ~** sexless; ✦***MODISMO*** **hablar del ~ de los ángeles** to indulge in pointless discussion; **sería como discutir sobre el ~ de los ángeles** it would be a totally pointless discussion ▸ **sexo en grupo** group sex ▸ **sexo oral** oral sex ▸ **sexo seguro** safe sex
2 (= *órgano sexual*) [*de hombre*] penis, sexual organs *pl* (*frm*); [*de mujer*] vagina, sexual organs *pl* (*frm*)

sexofobia SF aversion to sex

sexología SF sexology

sexólogo/a SM/F sexologist

sex shop [sek'ʃop] SF (*pl* **sex shops**) sex shop

sex symbol [sek'simβol] SMF (*pl* **sex symbols**) sex symbol

sexta SF (*Mús*) sixth; *ver tb* **sexto**

sextante SM sextant

sexteto SM sextet

sextillizo/a SM/F sextuplet

sexto Ⓐ ADJ sixth; **Juan ~** John the sixth; **en el ~ piso** on the sixth floor; **en ~ lugar** in sixth place, sixth; **vigésimo ~** twenty-sixth; **una sexta parte** a sixth
Ⓑ SM (= *parte*) sixth; **dos ~s** two sixths; *ver tb* **sexta**

séxtuplo ADJ sixfold

sexual ADJ sexual, sex *antes de s*; **vida ~** sex life

sexualidad SF 1 (= *opción sexual*) sexuality
2 (*Biol*) sex; **determinar la ~ de** to determine the sex of

sexualmente ADV sexually; **ser acosado ~** to be sexually harassed, suffer (from) sexual harassment

sexy Ⓐ ADJ [*persona*] sexy; [*libro, escena*] erotic, titillating
Ⓑ SM sexiness, sex appeal

s.f. ABR (= **sin fecha**) n.d.

s/f ABR (*Com*) = **su favor**

SGAE SF ABR = **Sociedad General de Autores de España**

SGEL SF ABR = **Sociedad Española General de Librería**

SGR SF ABR = **sociedad de garantía recíproca**

sgte. ABR (= **siguiente**) foll., f

sgtes. ABR (= **siguientes**) foll., ff

share [ʃear] SM (*TV*) audience share

shareware ['ʃerwer] SM INV (*Inform*) shareware

shiatsu ['sjatsu] SM shiatsu

shock [ʃok] SM (*pl* **shock** *o* **shocks** [ʃok]) shock

short [ʃor] SM, **shorts** [ʃor] SMPL shorts

show [tʃo, ʃou] SM 1 (*Teat*) show
2 (*Esp* *) (= *jaleo*) fuss, bother; **menudo ~ montó** he made a great song-and-dance about it
3 (= *farsa*) farce, masquerade

si[1] CONJ 1 (*uso condicional*) if; **si lo quieres, te lo doy** if you want it I'll give it to you; **si lo sé, no te lo digo** I wouldn't have told you, if I'd known; **si tuviera dinero, lo compraría** if I had any money I would buy it; **si me lo hubiese pedido, se lo habría** *o* **hubiera dado** if he had asked me for it I would have given it to him; **si no** (*condición negativa*) if not; (*indicando alternativa*) otherwise, or (else); **avisadme si no podéis venir** let me know if you can't come; **si no estudias, no aprobarás** you won't pass if you don't study, you won't pass unless you study; **ponte crema porque si no, te quemarás** put some cream on, otherwise *o* or (else) you'll get sunburned; **vete, si no, vas a llegar tarde** go, or (else) you'll be late; **llevo el paraguas por si (acaso) llueve** I've got my umbrella (just) in case it rains; **¿y si llueve?** what if it rains?; **¿y si se lo preguntamos?** why don't we ask her?
2 (*en interrogativas indirectas*) whether; **no sé si hacerlo o no** I don't know whether to do it or not; **no sabía si habías venido en avión o en tren** I didn't know whether *o* if you'd come by plane or train; **me pregunto si vale la pena** I wonder whether *o* if it's worth it; **no sé si será verdad** I don't know whether *o* if it's true; **¿sabes si nos han pagado ya?** do you know if we've been paid yet?
3 (*uso concesivo*) **no sé de qué te quejas, si**

eres una belleza I don't know what you're complaining about when you're so beautiful; **si bien** although; **si bien creó un amplio consenso político ...** although it is true *o* while it may be true that he created a broad political consensus ...
[4] (*uso desiderativo*) **¡si fuera verdad!** if only it were true!, I wish it were true!; **¡si viniese pronto!** I wish he'd come!, if only he'd come!
[5] (*indicando protesta*) but; **¡si no sabía que estabas allí!** but I didn't know you were there!; **¡si (es que) acabo de llamarte!** but I've only just phoned you!; **¡si tienes la tira de discos!** but you have loads of records!*
[6] (*uso enfático*) **¡si serán hipócritas!** they're such hypocrites!, they're so hypocritical!; **—es un pesado —¡si lo sabré yo!** "he's a pain" — "don't I know it!" *o* "you're telling me!"; **si lo sabré yo, que soy su mujer** I ought to know, I'm his wife; **que si engorda, que si perjudica a la salud ...** they say it's fattening and bad for your health; **que si lavar los platos, que si limpiar el suelo, que si ...** what with washing up and sweeping the floor and ...
[7] (*indicando sorpresa*) **¡pero si es el cartero!** why, it's the postman!; **¡pero si eres tú! no te había reconocido** oh, it's you, I didn't recognize you!

si[2] SM (*Mús*) B ► **si mayor** B major

sí[1] Ⓐ ADV [1] (*como respuesta*) yes; **—¿te gusta? —sí** "do you like it?" — "yes (I do)"; **un dedo en alto es que sí** if you put one finger up it means yes; **—¿sabes que me caso? —¿ah, sí?** "do you know I'm getting married?" — "really?"; **—el piso es bonito pero no tiene mucha luz —bueno, eso sí** "it's a nice flat but it's a bit dark" — "yes, that's true"; **sí pues** (*LAm*) of course
[2] (*uso enfático*) [2·1] (*en oposición a una negación*) **ellos no van pero nosotros sí** they're not going but we are; **él no quiere pero yo sí** he doesn't want to but I do; **no tiene hermanos, pero sí dos hermanas** he doesn't have any brothers but he does have two sisters; **—¿a que no eres capaz? —¿a que sí?** "I bet you can't" — "do you want a bet?"*; **—yo eso no me lo creo —¡que sí, hombre!** "I can't believe that" — "I'm telling you, it's true"; **un sábado sí y otro no** every other Saturday; ✦***MODISMOS*** **por sí o por no** in any case, just in case; **un sí es no es** somewhat; **resulta un sí es no es artificioso** it is somewhat contrived
[2·2] (*en oraciones afirmativas*) **vimos que sí, que era el mismo hombre** we saw that it was indeed the same man; **ahí sí me duele** it definitely hurts there, that's where it hurts; **apenas tienen para comer, pero eso sí, el tabaco no les falta** they hardly have enough money for food, but they're certainly never short of cigarettes; **ya llevamos aquí una semana, ¿a que sí, Luisa?** we've been here a week now, isn't that right, Luisa?; **ella sí vendrá** SHE'll certainly come; **sí que**: **pero nosotros sí que lo oímos** but WE certainly heard it; **sí que me lo dijo** (yes) he DID tell me; **¡pues sí que estoy yo para bromas!** (*iró*) this is a great time for jokes!; **eso sí que no**: **me piden que traicione a mis amigos y eso sí que no*** they're asking me to betray my friends and that's just not on*; **—¿puedo hacer unas fotos? —¡ah, no, eso sí que no!** "can I take some photos?" — "no, absolutely not!"; **eso sí que no se puede aguantar** that is just unbearable, I just can't stand that; ✦***MODISMO*** **porque sí**: **no se hacen ricos porque sí, sino a base de arriesgar mucho** they don't get rich just like that, they have to take a lot of risks; **no vamos a la huelga porque sí** we're not going on strike just for the sake of it; **—¿por qué yo? —pues porque sí** "why me?" — "(just) because!"
[3] (*en oraciones subordinadas*) **creo que sí** I think so; **—¿asistirá el presidente? —puede que sí** "will the president be there?" — "he might be"; **decir que sí** to say yes; **se lo pedimos y dijo que sí** we asked her and she agreed *o* she said yes; **dijo que sí con la cabeza** he nodded in agreement
Ⓑ SM [1] (= *consentimiento*) yes; **un sí rotundo** a definite yes; **todavía no tengo el sí por su parte** she hasn't said yes yet; **la propuesta obtuvo un sí abrumador** people voted overwhelmingly in favour of the proposal; **dar el sí** (*a una propuesta*) to say yes; (*en la boda*) to say "I do"; **le costó mucho dar el sí al proyecto** he found it hard to agree to the project; ✦***MODISMO*** **no tener ni un sí ni un no con algn**: **nunca hemos tenido ni un sí ni un no** we've never had a cross word *o* the slightest disagreement
[2] **síes** (= *votos*) votes in favour; **la mayoría necesaria era de 93 síes** a majority of 93 votes (in favour) was needed; **13 síes y 12 noes** 13 in favour and 12 against, 13 ayes and 12 noes

sí[2] PRON [1] (*uso reflexivo*) [1·1] (*de tercera persona*) (*referido a una persona*) himself/herself; (*referido a un objeto, concepto*) itself; (*en plural*) themselves; **no lo podrá hacer por sí solo** he won't be able to do it on his own *o* by himself; **sentía tras de sí los pasos de un hombre** she could hear the steps of a man following her; **tiene un currículum que para sí quisieran muchas actrices** she has a track record that many actresses would be envious of; **el producto en sí es inofensivo** the product itself is inoffensive; **sí mismo/a** (*referido a persona*) himself/herself; (*referido a objeto, concepto*) itself; (*uso impersonal*) yourself, oneself (*más frm*); **aquí el escritor habla de sí mismo** here the writer is talking about himself; **vivía muy encerrada en sí misma** she was very wrapped up in herself *o* wrapped up in her own world; **ha puesto lo mejor de sí mismo en ese proyecto** he has given his all to the project; **la tierra gira sobre sí misma** the earth turns on itself; **es mejor aprender las cosas por sí mismo** it's better to learn things by yourself *o* oneself (*más frm*); **sí mismos/as** themselves; **están muy seguros de sí mismos** they are very confident, they are very sure of themselves; **los datos hablan por sí mismos** the facts speak for themselves
[1·2] (*referido a usted*) (*en singular*) yourself; (*en plural*) yourselves; **sí mismo/a** yourself; **sí mismos/as** yourselves
[1·3] ✦***MODISMOS*** **de por sí**: **el problema ya es bastante difícil de por sí** the problem is difficult enough in itself *o* as it is; **él, de por sí, ya tiene mal carácter** he's got a really bad temper at the best of times; **estar en sí** to be in one's right mind; **estar fuera de sí** to be beside o.s.; **empezó a dar gritos fuera de sí** he started shouting hysterically; **estar sobre sí** to be on one's guard; *ver tb* **caber 1**, **volver B3**

> **SI**
>
> La conjunción **si** se puede traducir al inglés por **if** o **whether**; **si no** se traduce por **if not** o **unless**.
>
> **Si**
>
> • Por regla general, **si** se traduce al inglés por **if** en las oraciones condicionales y por **whether** o **if** en las dubitativas:
>
> Si me has mentido te arrepentirás
> ***If you have lied to me you'll regret it***
> Si tuviera mucho dinero me compraría un caballo
> ***If I had lots of money, I'd buy myself a horse***
> No sé si me dejará quedarme
> ***I don't know whether*** *o* ***if he'll let me stay***
>
> • **Si** se puede traducir sólo por **whether**, y nunca por **if**, cuando se presentan dos opciones a elegir, cuando va detrás de una preposición, delante de un infinitivo o de una oración interrogativa indirecta:
>
> No sé si ir a Canadá o a Estados Unidos
> ***I can't decide whether to go to Canada or the United States***
> Quiero que hablemos de si deberíamos mandar a los niños a un colegio interno
> ***I want to talk to you about whether we should send the children to boarding school***
> Todavía no tenemos muy claro si vamos a mudarnos o no
> ***We still haven't made up our minds about whether to move or not***
>
> **Si no**
>
> • **Si no** generalmente se traduce al inglés por **if not** aunque, cuando en español se puede reemplazar por **a no ser que**, se puede utilizar también **unless** y cuando equivale a **de lo contrario** se emplea preferentemente **otherwise** o **or else**:
>
> Iría al cine más a menudo si no fuera tan caro
> ***I would go to the cinema more often if it weren't so expensive***
> No te puedes quedar aquí si no pagas el alquiler
> ***You can't stay here unless you pay your rent*** *o* ***You can't stay here if you don't pay your rent***
> Tenemos que estar allí antes de las diez; si no, vamos a tener problemas
> ***We must be there by ten, otherwise*** *o* ***or else we'll be in trouble***
>
> NOTA: Las oraciones del tipo **si hubieras/si no hubieras hecho algo...** se pueden traducir, en un registro más culto, omitiendo la partícula **if** e invirtiendo el orden del sujeto y el verbo auxiliar:
>
> Si hubieras estado aquí esto no habría ocurrido
> ***Had you been here this would not have happened***
> Si no hubiese robado el dinero, ahora no estaría en la cárcel
> ***Had he not stolen the money, he wouldn't be in prison now***
>
> *Para otros usos y ejemplos ver la entrada.*

[2] **entre sí**: **son idénticos entre sí** they are

identical to each other; **se repartieron la herencia entre sí** they shared (out) the inheritance among themselves; **las dos soluciones son incompatibles entre sí** the two solutions are mutually incompatible; **las dos ciudades distan entre sí 45km** the two cities are 45km apart

Siam SM Siam

siamés/esa ADJ, SM/F Siamese

sibarita Ⓐ ADJ sybaritic, luxury-loving
Ⓑ SMF sybarite, lover of luxury

sibarítico ADJ sybaritic, luxury-loving

sibaritismo SM sybaritism, love of luxury

Siberia SF Siberia

siberiano/a ADJ, SM/F Siberian

sibil SM [1] (= *cueva*) cave
[2] (= *sótano*) vault, underground store
[3] [*de trigo*] corn-storage pit

Sibila SF Sibyl

sibila SF sibyl

sibilante ADJ, SF sibilant

sibilino ADJ sibylline

sic... PREF = **psic...**

sicalipsis SF INV (= *erotismo*) eroticism, suggestiveness; (= *pornografía*) pornography

sicalíptico ADJ (= *erótico*) erotic, suggestive; (= *pornográfico*) pornographic

sicario SM hired killer, hitman*

Sicilia SF Sicily

siciliano/a Ⓐ ADJ, SM/F Sicilian
Ⓑ SM (= *dialecto*) Sicilian

sico... PREF = **psico...**

sicofanta SM, **sicofante** SM sycophant

sicomoro SM, **sicómoro** SM sycamore

sicote* SM (*LAm*) foot odour

SIDA SM ABR, **sida** SM ABR (= **síndrome de inmunodeficiencia adquirida**) AIDS; **~ declarado** full-blown AIDS

sidatorio SM AIDS clinic

SIDE SF ABR (*Arg*) (= **Secretaría de Inteligencia del Estado**) *Peronist secret service*

sidecar SM sidecar

sideral ADJ [1] (*Astron*) (= *de los astros*) astral; (= *del espacio exterior*) space *antes de s*
[2] [*coste, precio*] astronomic

siderometalurgia SF iron and steel industry

siderometalúrgico ADJ iron and steel *antes de s*

siderurgia SF iron and steel industry

siderúrgica SF iron and steel works

siderúrgico ADJ iron and steel *antes de s*

sídico ADJ AIDS *antes de s*

sidoso/a Ⓐ ADJ AIDS *antes de s*
Ⓑ SM/F AIDS sufferer

sidra SF cider

sidrería SF cider bar

sidrero/a Ⓐ ADJ cider *antes de s*
Ⓑ SM/F cider maker

sidrina SF cider

siega SF [1] (= *acción*) (= *cosechar*) reaping, harvesting; (= *segar*) mowing
[2] (= *época*) harvest, harvest time

siembra SF [1] (= *acción*) sowing; **patata de ~** seed potato
[2] (= *época*) sowing time

siembre SM (*Caribe*) sowing

siempre Ⓐ ADV [1] (*indicando frecuencia*) always; **está ~ lloviendo** it's always raining; **una persona ~ dispuesta a ayudar** someone always ready to help; **como ~** as usual; **el día había empezado como ~** the day had begun as usual; **tú tan modesto como ~** (*iró*) modest as ever; **de ~** [*lugar, hora*] usual *antes de s*; **por favor, lo de ~** my usual, please; **protestan los de ~** it's the same people as usual protesting; **siguen con los mismos problemas de ~** they've still got the same old problems; **vino con el mismo cuento de ~** he came out with the same old story; **desde ~** always; **lo vienen haciendo así desde ~** they've always done it this way; **¡hasta ~!** farewell!; **para ~** forever, for good*; **se ha ido para ~** she has gone forever *o* for good*; **dijeron adiós para ~ a su país** they bade farewell to their country forever; **por ~** (*liter*) for ever; **por ~ jamás** for ever and ever
[2] (= *en todo caso*) always; **~ puedes decir que no lo sabías** you can always say you didn't know
[3] (*LAm**) (= *todavía*) still; **¿~ se va mañana?** are you still going tomorrow?
[4] (*esp Méx*) (= *definitivamente*) certainly, definitely; **~ no me caso este año** I'm certainly *o* definitely not getting married this year; **~ sí** certainly, of course
[5] (*Chile*) (= *de todas maneras*) still; **lo tenían completamente rodeado y ~ se escapó** they had him completely surrounded but he still escaped; **~ sí me voy** I'm going anyway
Ⓑ CONJ [1] **~ que** (= *cada vez*) whenever; (= *a condición de*) as long as, provided (that), providing (that); **voy ~ que puedo** I go whenever I can; **~ que salgo llueve** every time *o* whenever I go out it rains; **riéguelas ~ que sea necesario** water them whenever necessary; **~ que él esté de acuerdo** as long as he agrees, provided (that) *o* providing (that) he agrees
[2] **~ y cuando** as long as, provided (that), providing (that)

siempreverde ADJ evergreen

siempreviva SF houseleek

sien SF (*Anat*) temple

siena ADJ, SM INV (= *color*) sienna

siento *etc ver* **sentar, sentir**

sierpe SF snake, serpent

sierra SF [1] (= *herramienta*) saw ► **sierra circular** circular saw ► **sierra de arco** hacksaw ► **sierra de bastidor** frame saw, span saw ► **sierra de cadena** chainsaw ► **sierra de calados, sierra de calar** fretsaw ► **sierra de espigar** tenon saw ► **sierra de marquetería** fretsaw, coping saw ► **sierra de vaivén** jigsaw ► **sierra mecánica** power saw ► **sierra para metales** hacksaw
[2] (*Geog*) mountain range, sierra; **la ~** (= *zona*) the hills, the mountains; **van a la ~ a pasar el fin de semana** they're off to the mountains for the weekend
[3] (*Méx*) (= *pez*) swordfish

Sierra Leona SF Sierra Leone

siervo/a SM/F slave ► **siervo de Dios** servant of the Lord ► **siervo de la gleba** serf

siesta SF [1] (= *sueñecito*) siesta, nap; **la hora de la ~** siesta time (*after lunch*); **dormir la** *o* **echarse una ~** to have an afternoon nap
[2] (= *hora del día*) afternoon

siestecita SF nap, doze

siete[1] Ⓐ ADJ INV, PRON seven; (*ordinal, en la fecha*) seventh; **las ~** seven o'clock; **le escribí el día ~** I wrote to him on the seventh; ✦*MODISMO* **hablar más que ~** to talk nineteen to the dozen
Ⓑ SM [1] (= *número*) seven; *ver tb* **seis**
[2] (= *roto*) **hacerse un ~ en el pantalón** to tear one's trousers (*making an L-shaped tear*)
Ⓒ SF (*LAm**) **¡la gran ~!** wow!*, hell!*; **de la gran ~** terrible*, tremendous*; **hijo de la gran ~** bastard**, son of a bitch (*EEUU***)

siete[2]** SM (*LAm*) arsehole**, asshole (*EEUU***)

sietecueros SM INV (*LAm*) gumboil, whitlow

sietemesino/a Ⓐ ADJ [*niño*] two months premature
Ⓑ SM/F baby born two months premature

sífilis SF INV syphilis

sifilítico/a ADJ, SM/F syphilitic

sifón SM [1] (*Téc*) trap, U-bend
[2] [*de agua*] siphon, syphon; **whisky con ~** whisky and soda
[3] (*Geol*) flooded underground chamber
[4] (*Andes*) (= *cerveza*) beer, bottled beer

sifrino ADJ (*Caribe*) stuck-up*, full of airs and graces

sig. ABR (= **siguiente**) f

siga SF (*Cono Sur*) pursuit; **ir a la ~ de algo** to chase after sth

sigilo SM (= *silencio*) stealth; (= *secreto*) secrecy; **con mucho ~** [*entrar, caminar*] very stealthily; [*reunirse, negociar*] amid great secrecy, with great secrecy ► **sigilo sacramental** secrecy of the confessional

sigilosamente ADV (= *silenciosamente*) stealthily; (= *secretamente*) secretly

sigiloso ADJ (= *silencioso*) stealth; (= *secreto*) secret

sigla SF (= *símbolo*) symbol; **siglas** (*pronunciadas como una palabra*) acronym *sing*; (*pronunciadas individualmente*) abbreviation *sing*

siglo SM [1] (= *cien años*) century; **el jugador del ~** the player of the century; **los ~s medios** the Middle Ages; **por los ~s de los ~s** world without end, for ever and ever ► **Siglo de las Luces** Age of Enlightenment ► **siglo de oro** (*Mit*) golden age ► **Siglo de Oro** (*Literat*) Golden Age
[2] (= *largo tiempo*) **hace un ~** *o* **hace ~s que no le veo** I haven't seen him for ages
[3] (*Rel*) **el ~** the world; **retirarse del ~** to withdraw from the world

signar ▸conjug 1a◂ Ⓐ VT [1] (= *sellar*) to seal
[2] (= *marcar*) to put one's mark on
[3] (= *firmar*) to sign
[4] (*Rel*) to make the sign of the Cross over
Ⓑ **signarse** VPR to cross o.s.

signatario/a ADJ, SM/F signatory

signatura SF [1] (*Mús, Tip*) signature
[2] [*de biblioteca*] catalogue number, catalog number (*EEUU*), press mark

significación SF [1] (= *importancia*) significance
[2] (= *sentido*) meaning

significado Ⓐ ADJ well-known
Ⓑ SM [1] [*de palabra*] meaning; **su ~ principal es ...** its chief meaning is ...; **una palabra de ~ dudoso** a word of uncertain meaning
[2] (= *importancia*) significance

significante Ⓐ ADJ (*esp LAm*) significant
Ⓑ SM (*Ling*) signifier

significar ▸conjug 1g◂ Ⓐ VT [1] (= *querer decir*) [*palabra*] to mean; [*suceso*] to mean, signify; **¿qué significa "freelance"?** what does "freelance" mean?
[2] (= *representar*) **50 dólares significan muy poco para él** 50 dollars doesn't mean much to him; **él no significa nada para mí** he means nothing to me; **~á la ruina de la empresa** it will mean the end for the company; **él no significa gran cosa en estos asuntos** he doesn't count for much in these matters
[3] (= *expresar*) to make known, express (**a** to); **le significó la condolencia de la familia** he expressed *o* conveyed the family's sympathy
Ⓑ **significarse** VPR [1] (= *distinguirse*) to become known, distinguish o.s. (**como** as)
[2] (= *tomar partido*) to declare o.s., take sides; **no ~se** to refuse to take sides

significativamente ADV (= *considerablemente*) significantly; (= *expresivamente*) meaningfully

significativo ADJ [1] [*cambio, detalle, desarrollo*] significant; **es ~ que ...** it is significant that ...; **calcularlo a tres cifras significativas** to work it out to three significant figures
[2] [*mirada*] meaningful

signo SM [1] (= *señal*) (*gen*) sign; (*Mat*) sign, symbol; **ese apetito es ~ de buena salud** such an appetite is a sign of good health ► **signo de admiración** exclamation mark, exclamation point (*EEUU*) ► **signo de interrogación** question mark ► **signo de la cruz** sign of the Cross ► **signo de la victoria** victory sign, V-sign ► **signo de sumar** plus sign ► **signo igual** equals sign, equal sign (*EEUU*) ► **signo lingüístico** linguistic sign ► **signo más** plus sign ► **signo menos** minus sign ► **signo postal** postage stamp ► **signos de puntuación** punctuation marks
[2] (= *carácter*) **un ~ de los tiempos** a sign of the times; **una estrategia de ~ modernizador** a modernizing strategy; **invirtieron el ~ de la tendencia** they reversed the trend
[3] (*tb* **~ del zodíaco**) star sign; **¿de qué ~ es Carmen?** what (star) sign is Carmen?

sigo *etc ver* **seguir**

sigs. ABR (= **siguientes**) ff

siguiente ADJ next, following; **el ~ vuelo** the next flight; **¡que pase el ~, por favor!** next please!; **el** *o* **al día ~** the following *o* next day; **dijo lo ~** he said the following

sij ADJ, SMF (*pl* **sijs**) Sikh

sijolaj SM (*CAm Mús*) clay whistle, type of ocarina

sílaba SF syllable

silabario SM spelling book

silabear ▸conjug 1a◂ VT (= *dividir en sílabas*) to divide into syllables; (= *pronunciar*) to pronounce syllable by syllable

silabeo SM division into syllables

silábico ADJ syllabic

silba SF hissing, catcalls *pl*; **armar** *o* **dar una ~ (a)** to hiss

silbar ▸conjug 1a◂ Ⓐ VT [1] (*Mús*) [+ *melodía*] to whistle
[2] [+ *comedia, orador*] to hiss
Ⓑ VI [1] [*persona*] (*con los labios*) to whistle; (*al respirar*) to wheeze
[2] [*viento*] to whistle; [*bala, flecha*] to whistle, whizz
[3] (*Teat*) to hiss, boo

silbatina SF (*Andes, Cono Sur*) hissing, booing

silbato SM whistle

silbido SM, **silbo** SM [1] [*de persona*] (*con los labios*) whistle, whistling; (*al respirar*) wheezing
[2] (= *zumbido*) hum ► **silbido de oídos** ringing in the ears
[3] (= *abucheo*) hissing

silenciador SM silencer, muffler (*EEUU*)

silenciamiento SM [*de oposición*] silencing; [*de suceso*] hushing up

silenciar ▸conjug 1b◂ Ⓐ VT [1] [+ *suceso*] to hush up; [+ *hecho*] to keep silent about
[2] [+ *persona*] to silence
[3] (*Téc*) to silence
Ⓑ **silenciarse** VPR **se silenció el asunto** the matter was hushed up; **se silenció su labor** his work was kept secret

silencio Ⓐ SM [1] (= *falta de ruido*) silence; **¡silencio!** silence!, quiet!; **¡~ en la sala!** silence in court!; **nos escribió tras dos años de ~** after two years' silence she wrote to us; **un poco de ~, por favor** let's have a bit of quiet, please; **¡qué ~ hay aquí!** it's so quiet here!; **había un ~ sepulcral** it was deadly silent, there was a deathly silence; **en ~** in silence; **la casa estaba en ~** the house was silent; **en el ~ más absoluto** in dead silence; **guardar ~** to keep silent, keep quiet; **guardar un minuto de ~** to observe a one-minute *o* a minute's silence; **imponer ~ a algn** (*frm*) to make sb be quiet; **mantenerse en ~** to keep quiet, remain silent; **pasar una pena en ~** to suffer in silence; **reducir al ~** (*frm*) to silence, reduce to silence; **romper el ~** (*frm*) to break the silence ► **silencio administrativo** administrative silence
[2] (*Mús*) rest
Ⓑ ADJ (*Andes, CAm, Méx*) (= *silencioso*) silent, quiet; (= *tranquilo*) still

silenciosamente ADV silently, quietly, noiselessly

silencioso ADJ [*persona*] silent, quiet; [*máquina*] silent, noiseless

silense ADJ (*Esp*) of Silos, of Santo Domingo de Silos

silente ADJ silent, noiseless

sílex SM silex, flint

sílfide SF sylph

silfo SM sylph

silicato SM silicate

sílice SF silica

silíceo ADJ siliceous

silicio SM silicon

silicona SF silicone

silicosis SF INV silicosis

silla SF [1] (= *asiento*) seat, chair; **política de la ~ vacía** policy of the empty chair, policy of not taking one's seat (*in parliament etc*); ✦**MODISMO calentar la ~** to stay too long, outstay one's welcome ► **silla alta** high chair ► **silla de balanza**, **silla de hamaca** (*LAm*) rocking chair ► **silla de manos** sedan chair ► **silla de paseo** (*para bebé*) pushchair, stroller (*EEUU*) ► **silla de ruedas** wheelchair ► **silla de tijera** folding chair ► **silla eléctrica** electric chair ► **silla giratoria** swivel chair ► **silla plegable** folding chair
[2] (*tb* **~ de montar**) saddle

sillar SM block of stone, ashlar

sillería SF [1] (= *asientos*) chairs *pl*, set of chairs; (*Rel*) choir stalls *pl*; (*Teat*) seating
[2] (= *taller*) chair-maker's workshop
[3] (*Arquit*) masonry, ashlar work

sillero/a SM/F Ⓐ (= *artesano*) chair-maker
Ⓑ SM (*Cono Sur*) (= *caballo*) horse, mule

silleta SF [1] (= *silla pequeña*) small chair
[2] (*LAm*) (= *silla*) seat, chair; (= *taburete*) low stool
[3] (*Med*) bedpan

sillico SM chamber pot

sillín SM saddle

sillita SF small chair ► **sillita de niño** pushchair, stroller (*EEUU*)

sillón SM [1] (= *butaca*) armchair, easy chair; (*LAm*) (= *mecedora*) rocking chair ► **sillón de dentista** dentist's chair ► **sillón de hamaca** (*LAm*) rocking chair ► **sillón de lona** deck chair ► **sillón de orejas** wing chair ► **sillón de ruedas** wheelchair ► **sillón orejero** wing chair
[2] [*de montar*] sidesaddle

silo SM [1] (*Agr*) silo
[2] (*Mil*) silo, bunker
[3] (= *sótano*) underground store
[4] (= *depósito*) storage pit

silogismo SM syllogism

silogístico ADJ syllogistic

silueta SF [1] (= *contorno*) silhouette; **se adivinaba una ~ detrás de la cortina** you could make out a silhouette *o* figure behind the curtain; **la ~ del castillo se recortaba sobre el horizonte** the castle was silhouetted against the horizon
[2] (= *tipo*) figure; **un bañador que realza la ~** a swimsuit that shows off your figure
[3] (*Arte*) silhouette, outline drawing; **en ~** in silhouette

siluetear ▸conjug 1a◂ VT (*lit*) to outline; (*fig*) to shape, mould, mold (*EEUU*)

silvático ADJ = **selvático**

silvestre ADJ [1] (*Bot*) wild
[2] (= *agreste*) rustic, rural

silvicultor(a) SM/F forestry expert

silvicultura SF forestry

SIM SM ABR (*Esp*) = **Servicio de Investigación Militar**

sima SF [1] (= *abismo*) abyss, chasm
[2] (= *grieta*) deep fissure

Simbad SM Sinbad ► **Simbad el marino** Sinbad the sailor

simbiosis SF INV symbiosis

simbiótico ADJ symbiotic

simbólicamente ADV symbolically

simbólico ADJ [*momento, papel*] symbolic; [*cantidad, gesto, pago, huelga*] token

simbolismo SM symbolism

simbolista ADJ, SMF symbolist

simbolizar ▸conjug 1f◂ VT to symbolize

símbolo SM symbol ► **símbolo de la fe**, **símbolo de los apóstoles** Creed ► **símbolo de prestigio** status symbol ► **símbolo gráfico** (*Inform*) icon

simbología SF [1] (= *símbolos*) symbols *pl*, system of symbols
[2] (= *estudio*) study of symbols

simbombo ADJ (*Caribe*) cowardly

simetría SF [1] (= *igualdad*) symmetry
[2] (= *armonía*) harmony

simétricamente ADV [1] (= *con igualdad*) sym-

➤ LENGUA Y USO: significar A1 53.3

metrically
2 (= *con armonía*) harmoniously

simétrico ADJ 1 (= *igual*) symmetrical
2 (= *armonioso*) harmonious

simetrizar ▸conjug 1f◂ VT 1 [+ *forma*] to make symmetrical
2 (= *armonizar*) to bring into line, harmonize

símico ADJ = **simiesco**

simiente SF seed

simiesco ADJ simian

símil Ⓐ ADJ similar
Ⓑ SM 1 (= *comparación*) comparison
2 (*Literat*) simile

similar ADJ similar (**a** to)

similaridad SF = **similitud**

similitud SF similarity, resemblance

similor SM pinchbeck; **de ~** pinchbeck, showy but valueless

simiñaca SF (*Caribe*) tangle, mess

simio SM ape, simian (*frm*)

Simón SM Simon

simonía SF simony

simpatía SF 1 (= *afecto*) **son muestras de ~ hacia** *o* **por la víctima** it's a show of sympathy towards the victim; **coger ~ a algn** to take a liking to sb; **ganarse la ~ de todos** to win everybody's affection; **tener ~ a algn** ◊ **sentir ~ hacia** *o* **por algn** to like sb; **no le tenemos ~ en absoluto** we don't like him at all; **no tiene ~s en el colegio** nobody at school likes him; **~s y antipatías** likes and dislikes
2 (= *cordialidad*) friendly nature, friendliness; **su ~ nos cautivó** we were charmed by her friendly nature *o* friendliness; **la famosa ~ andaluza** that famous Andalusian friendliness; **tener (mucha) ~** to be (very) likeable *o* nice
3 **simpatías** (*Pol*) sympathies; **sus ~s se decantan por los socialistas** his sympathies lie with the socialists
4 (*Fís, Med*) sympathy; **explosión por ~** secondary explosion

simpático ADJ 1 (= *afectuoso*) [*persona*] nice, pleasant, likeable; [*ambiente*] congenial, pleasant; **¡qué policía más ~!** what a nice policeman!; **estuvo muy simpática con todos** she was very nice to everybody; **los cubanos son muy ~s** Cubans are very nice *o* friendly people; **no le hemos caído muy ~s** she didn't really take to us, she didn't really like us; **siempre procura hacerse el ~** he's always trying to ingratiate himself; **me cae ~** I think he's nice, I like him; **me es ~ ese muchacho** I like that lad
2 (*Anat, Med*) sympathetic

simpatiquísimo ADJ SUPERL *de* **simpático**

simpatizante SMF sympathizer (**de** with)

simpatizar ▸conjug 1f◂ VI 1 [*dos personas*] to get on, get on well together; **pronto ~on** they soon became friends
2 **~ con algn** to get on well with *o* take to sb

simplada SF (*Andes, CAm*) (= *cualidad*) simplicity, stupidity; (= *acto*) stupid thing, stupid thing to do *o* to say

simple Ⓐ ADJ 1 (= *sin adornos*) [*peinado, objeto*] simple; [*vestido, decoración*] plain
2 [*método*] simple, easy, straightforward
3 (*antes de sustantivo*) (= *mero*) mere; **por ~ descuido** through sheer carelessness; **es cosa de una ~ plumada** it's a matter of a mere stroke of the pen; **somos ~s aficionados** we're just amateurs
4 (*antes de sustantivo*) (= *corriente*) ordinary; **es un ~ abogado** he's only *o* just a solicitor; **un ~ soldado** an ordinary soldier
5 [*persona*] (= *sin complicaciones*) simple; (= *crédulo*) gullible; (*pey*) (= *de pocas luces*) simple-minded
6 (*Ling, Quím*) simple
7 (*Bot*) single
Ⓑ SMF (= *persona*) simpleton
Ⓒ SMPL **simples** (*Tenis*) singles; (*Bot*) simples

simplemente ADV simply, just; **~ tendrás que aceptarlo** you'll simply *o* just have to accept it; **~ pretendía ayudarte** I was only *o* just trying to help you; **~ te llamaba para confirmar la cita** I was just calling to confirm our date; **eso se arregla ~ diciéndole que no** the simple solution to that is to say no to him, that's easily solved by saying no to him

simpleza SF 1 [*de persona*] (= *cualidad mental*) simpleness; (= *credulidad*) gullibility; (= *necedad*) simple-mindedness
2 (= *acto*) silly thing, silly thing to do/say; **se contenta con cualquier ~** she's happy with any little thing; **se enojó por una ~** he got annoyed over nothing *o* over some silly little thing; **eso son ~s** that's nonsense

simplicidad SF simplicity, simpleness

simplificable ADJ simplifiable

simplificación SF simplification

simplificar ▸conjug 1g◂ VT to simplify

simplista ADJ simplistic

simplón/ona Ⓐ ADJ simple, gullible
Ⓑ SM/F simple soul, gullible person

simplote/a ADJ, SM/F = **simplón**

simposio SM symposium

simulación SF 1 (= *representación*) simulation
► **simulación por ordenador** computer simulation
2 (= *fingimiento*) pretence, pretense (*EEUU*)

simulacro SM 1 (= *fingimiento*) sham, pretence, pretense (*EEUU*; ► **simulacro de ataque** simulated attack, mock attack ► **simulacro de combate** mock battle ► **simulacro de incendio** fire practice, fire drill ► **simulacro de salvamento** (*Náut*) boat drill
2 (= *apariencia*) semblance

simulado ADJ (= *representado*) simulated; (= *fingido*) feigned

simulador SM ► **simulador de vuelo** flight simulator

simular ▸conjug 1a◂ VT 1 [+ *ataque, robo*] to simulate 2 (= *fingir*) to feign, sham; **simuló ser hermano del director** he pretended to be the director's brother

simultáneamente ADV simultaneously

simultanear ▸conjug 1a◂ VT **~ dos cosas** to do two things simultaneously; **~ A con B** to fit in A and B at the same time, combine A with B

simultaneidad SF simultaneousness

simultáneo ADJ simultaneous

simún SM simoom

sin Ⓐ PREP 1 (*seguido de sustantivo, pronombre*) without; **¿puedes abrirla ~ llave?** can you open it without a key?; **lo hice ~ la ayuda de nadie** I did it without anybody's help; **llevamos diez meses ~ noticias** it's been ten months since we've had any news, we've been ten months without news; **parejas jóvenes, ~ hijos** young couples with no children; **cerveza ~ alcohol** alcohol-free beer, non-alcoholic beer; **un producto ~ disolventes** a solvent-free product; **un vestido ~ tirantes** a strapless dress; **los ~ techo** the homeless; **un hombre ~ escrúpulos** an unscrupulous man; **agua mineral ~ gas** still mineral water; **estar ~ algo**: **estuvimos varias horas ~ luz** we had no electricity for several hours; **estoy ~ dinero** I've got no money; **quedarse ~ algo** (= *terminarse*) to run out of sth; (= *perder*) to lose sth; **me he quedado ~ cerillas** I've run out of matches; **se ha quedado ~ trabajo** he's lost his job
2 (= *no incluyendo*) not including, excluding; **ese es el precio de la bañera ~ los grifos** that is the price of the bath, excluding *o* not including the taps; **cuesta 550 euros, ~ IVA** it costs 550 euros, exclusive of VAT *o* not including VAT
3 + INFIN 3·1 (*indicando acción*) **se fueron ~ despedirse** they left without saying goodbye; **murió ~ haber hecho testamento** he died without having made a will; **nos despedimos, no ~ antes recordarles que ...** (*TV*) before saying goodnight we'd like to remind you that ...; **no me gusta estar ~ hacer nada** I don't like having nothing to do, I don't like doing nothing
3·2 (*indicando continuidad*) **son las doce y el cartero ~ venir** it's twelve o'clock and the postman still hasn't come; **llevan mucho tiempo ~ hablarse** they haven't spoken to each other for a long time; **llevamos dos meses ~ cobrar** we haven't been paid for two months; **seguir ~**: **las camas seguían ~ hacer** the beds still hadn't been made; **sigo ~ entender para qué sirven** I still don't understand what they are for
3·3 (*tras sustantivo pasivo*) **un montón de recibos ~ pagar** a pile of unpaid bills
4 **~ que** (+ *SUBJUN*) without; **salieron ~ que nadie se diera cuenta** they left without anyone realizing; **~ que él lo sepa** without him knowing, without his knowing; **no lo haré ~ que me lo pidan** I won't do it unless they ask me to
Ⓑ SF (*= *cervesa sin alcohol*) alcohol-free beer

sinagoga SF synagogue

Sinaí SM Sinai

sinalefa SF elision

sinalefar ▸conjug 1a◂ VT to elide

sinapismo SM 1 (*Med*) mustard plaster; **hay que ponerle un ~*** he needs gingering up
2 (= *persona*) (*aburrido*) bore; (*fastidioso*) nuisance, pest

sinarquismo SM (*Méx*) Sinarquism (*Mexican fascist movement of the 1930s*)

sinarquista SMF (*Méx*) Sinarquist

sinceramente ADV sincerely

sincerarse ▸conjug 1a◂ VPR (= *justificarse*) to vindicate o.s.; (= *decir la verdad*) to tell the truth, be honest; **~ a** *o* **con** to be honest with, level with; **~ ante el juez** to justify one's conduct to the judge; **~ de su conducta** to explain *o* justify one's conduct

sinceridad SF sincerity; **no pongo en duda su ~** I don't doubt her sincerity; **respóndeme con ~** please answer honestly; **dime con toda ~ lo que piensas de ella** tell me in all honesty what you think of her; **con toda ~,**

me parece un libro pésimo to be quite honest *o* in all sincerity, I think it's a terrible book

▼ **sincero** ADJ sincere; **es muy ~** he's very sincere; **ser ~ con algn** to be honest with sb; **si quieres que te sea ~, no estoy en absoluto de acuerdo** if you want my honest opinion, I don't agree at all; **reciba nuestro más ~ pésame** (*frm*) please accept our deepest sympathies *o* our heartfelt condolences

síncopa SF 1 (*Ling*) syncope
2 (*Mús*) syncopation

sincopar ▸conjug 1a◂ VT to syncopate

síncope SM 1 (*Ling*) syncope
2 (*Med*) syncope (*frm*); **casi le da un ~ cuando lo vio** she nearly fainted when she saw it

sincopizarse ▸conjug 1f◂ VPR to have a blackout

sincretismo SM syncretism

sincronía SF synchrony

sincrónico ADJ 1 (*Téc*) synchronized
2 [*sucesos*] simultaneous
3 (*Ling*) synchronic

sincronismo SM (= *correspondencia*) (*gen*) synchronism; [*de sucesos*] simultaneity; [*de fechas*] coincidence

sincronización SF synchronization

sincronizadamente ADV simultaneously

sincronizador SM timer

sincronizar ▸conjug 1f◂ VT to synchronize (**con** with)

síncrono ADJ synchronous

sincrotrón SM synchrotron

sindicación SF 1 [*de obreros*] unionization
2 (*Prensa*) syndication
3 (*LAm Jur*) charge, accusation

sindical ADJ union *antes de s*, trade-union *antes de s*

sindicalismo SM trade unionism, trades unionism

sindicalista Ⓐ ADJ union *antes de s*, trade-union *antes de s*
Ⓑ SMF trade unionist, trades unionist

sindicalizar ▸conjug 1f◂ Ⓐ VT to unionize
Ⓑ **sindicalizarse** VPR to form a union

sindicar ▸conjug 1g◂ Ⓐ VT 1 [+ *trabajadores*] to unionize
2 (*LAm*) to charge, accuse
Ⓑ **sindicarse** VPR [*trabajador*] to join a trade(s) union; [*trabajadores*] to form a trade(s) union

sindicato SM 1 [*de trabajadores*] trade union, trades union, labor union (*EEUU*) ► **sindicato amarillo** yellow union, *conservative union that is in the pocket of the management*; **el problema de los ~s amarillos** the problem of company unionism
2 [*de negociantes*] syndicate; ✦*MODISMO* **casarse por el ~*** to have a shotgun wedding

sindicatura SF syndicate

síndico SM [*de organización*] trustee; (*en caso de bancarrota*) receiver, official receiver

síndrome SM syndrome ► **síndrome de abstinencia** withdrawal symptoms *pl* ► **síndrome de Down** Down's syndrome ► **síndrome de Estocolmo** Stockholm syndrome ► **síndrome de fatiga crónica** chronic fatigue syndrome, ME ► **síndrome de la clase turista** economy-class syndrome ► **síndrome de Ménière** Ménière's syndrome, Ménière's disease ► **síndrome premenstrual** premenstrual syndrome, premenstrual tension ► **síndrome tóxico** poisoning

sinécdoque SF synecdoche

sinecura SF sinecure

sine die ADV sine die

sine qua non ADJ **condición ~** sine qua non

sinergía SF synergy

sinestesia SF synaesthesia, synesthesia (*EEUU*)

sinfín SM = **sinnúmero**

sinfonía SF symphony

sinfónico ADJ symphonic; **orquesta sinfónica** symphony orchestra

sinfonieta SF sinfonietta

sinfonola SF (*LAm*) jukebox

Singapur SM Singapore

singar ▸conjug 1h◂ Ⓐ VT (*Caribe**) to pester, annoy
Ⓑ VI (*CAm, Caribe***) to fuck**, screw**

singladura SF 1 (*Náut*) (= *recorrido*) day's run; (= *día*) nautical day
2 (*Pol*) course, direction

single SM 1 (*Mús*) single
2 **singles** (*Tenis*) singles

singlista SMF (*LAm*) singles player

singón SM (*Caribe, Méx*) womanizer, philanderer

singuisarra* SF (*Andes, Caribe*) row, racket

singular Ⓐ ADJ 1 (*Ling*) singular
2 **combate ~** single combat
3 (= *destacado*) outstanding, exceptional
4 (= *raro*) singular, odd
Ⓑ SM (*Ling*) singular; **en ~** (*lit*) in the singular; (*fig*) in particular; **se refiere a él en ~** it refers to him in particular; **que hable él en ~** let him speak for himself

singularidad SF singularity, peculiarity

singularizar ▸conjug 1f◂ Ⓐ VT to single out
Ⓑ **singularizarse** VPR (= *distinguirse*) to distinguish o.s., stand out; (= *llamar la atención*) to be conspicuous; **~se con algn** to single sb out for special treatment

singularmente ADV 1 (= *extrañamente*) singularly, peculiarly
2 (= *especialmente*) especially

sinhueso* SF tongue; ✦*MODISMO* **soltar la ~** to shoot one's mouth off*

siniestra SF left hand; **a mi ~** on my left

siniestrado/a Ⓐ ADJ damaged, wrecked, crashed; **la zona siniestrada** the affected area, the disaster zone
Ⓑ SM/F victim

siniestralidad SF accident rate

siniestro Ⓐ ADJ 1 (= *malintencionado*) [*intenciones, personaje*] sinister; [*mirada*] evil
2 (= *desgraciado*) [*día, viaje*] fateful; [*coincidencia*] unfortunate
3 (*liter*) (= *izquierdo*) left
Ⓑ SM (= *desastre natural*) disaster; (= *accidente*) accident ► **siniestro marítimo** disaster at sea ► **siniestro nuclear** nuclear disaster ► **siniestro total** total write-off; **fue declarado ~ total** it was declared a total write-off

sinnúmero SM **un ~ de** no end of, countless

sino[1] SM fate, destiny

sino[2] CONJ 1 (= *pero*) but; **no son ocho ~ nueve** there are not eight but nine; **no lo hace sólo para sí ~ para todos** he's not doing it only for himself but for everybody; **no sólo ..., sino ...** not only ..., but ...; **no cabe otra solución ~ que vaya él** the only answer is that he should go
2 (= *salvo*) except, save; **todos aplaudieron ~ él** everybody except him applauded; **no lo habría dicho ~ en broma** he could only have said it jokingly, he wouldn't have said it except as a joke
3 (= *únicamente*) only; **¿quién ~ él se habría atrevido?** only he would have dared!; **no te pido ~ una cosa** I ask only *o* but one thing of you

sino... PREF Chinese ..., Sino...

sínodo SM synod

sinología SF Sinology

sinólogo/a SM/F Sinologist

sinonimia SF synonymy

sinónimo Ⓐ ADJ synonymous (**de** with)
Ⓑ SM synonym

sinopsis SF INV synopsis

sinóptico ADJ synoptic, synoptical; **cuadro ~** diagram, chart

sinovitis SF INV ► **sinovitis del codo** tennis elbow

sinrazón SF wrong, injustice

sinsabor SM 1 (= *disgusto*) trouble, unpleasantness
2 (= *dolor*) sorrow
3 (= *preocupación*) uneasiness, worry

sinsentido SM absurdity

sinsilico* ADJ (*Méx*) stupid, thick*

sinsonte SM (*CAm, Méx*) mockingbird

sinsustancia* SMF idiot

sintáctico ADJ syntactic, syntactical

sintagma SM syntagma, syntagm

Sintasol® SM vinyl floor covering

sintaxis SF INV syntax

▼ **síntesis** SF INV 1 (= *resumen*) summary; **en ~** (*frm*) in short
2 (*Biol, Quím*) synthesis
3 (*Fil*) synthesis
4 (*Inform*) synthesis ► **síntesis del habla** voice synthesis, speech synthesis

sintéticamente ADV synthetically

sintético ADJ synthetic

sintetizador SM synthesizer ► **sintetizador de la voz humana, sintetizador de voz** voice synthesizer, speech synthesizer

sintetizar ▸conjug 1f◂ VT 1 (*Quím, Mús*) to synthesize 2 (= *resumir*) to summarize

sintiendo *etc ver* **sentir**

sintoísmo SM Shintoism

síntoma SM 1 (*Med*) symptom
2 (= *señal*) sign, indication

sintomático ADJ symptomatic

sintomatizar ▸conjug 1f◂ VT to typify, characterize, be symptomatic of

sintomatología SF symptomatology

sintonía SF 1 (*Radio*) [*del dial*] tuning
2 (*Radio*) (= *melodía*) signature tune; **estén atentos a nuestra ~** stay tuned
3 (*entre personas*) **estar en ~ con algn** to be in tune with sb

sintonización SF tuning

sintonizado SM tuning

sintonizador SM tuner

sintonizar ▸conjug 1f◂ Ⓐ VT 1 (*Radio*) [+ *estación, emisión*] to tune to, tune in to

➤ LENGUA Y USO: **sincero** 49 **síntesis** 53.4

[2] (*Cine*) to synchronize
[3] (*Elec*) to syntonize
Ⓑ VI **~ con** to be in tune with, be on the same wavelength as

sinuosidad SF [1] (= *cualidad*) sinuosity (*liter*), intricacy
[2] (= *curva*) curve; **las ~es del camino** the windings of the road, the twists and turns of the road
[3] [*de persona, actitud*] deviousness

sinuoso ADJ [1] (= *con curvas*) [*camino*] winding, sinuous; [*línea, raya*] wavy; [*rumbo*] devious
[2] [*persona, actitud*] devious

sinusitis SF INV sinusitis

sinvergonzón‡ SM rotter*, swine‡

sinvergüencería SF [1] (= *acción*) dirty trick*
[2] (= *descaro*) shamelessness

sinvergüenza Ⓐ ADJ (= *pillo*) rotten; (= *descarado*) brazen, shameless
Ⓑ SMF (= *pillo*) scoundrel, rogue; (= *canalla*) rotter*; (= *insolente*) cheeky devil; **¡sinvergüenza!** (*hum*) you villain!; **es una ~** she's a cheeky devil

sinvergüenzada* SF (*LAm*) rotten thing*, rotten thing to do*

sinvergüenzura SF (*LAm*) shamelessness

Sión SM Zion

sionismo SM Zionism

sionista ADJ, SMF Zionist

sipo ADJ (*Andes*) pockmarked

sipotazo SM (*CAm*) slap

siqu... *etc* PREF *ver* **psiqu...** (*p.ej.*) **siquiatría** *ver* **psiquiatría**

siquiera Ⓐ ADV [1] (= *al menos*) at least; **una vez ~** once at least, just once; **deja ~ trabajar a los demás** at least let the others work; **dame un abrazo ~** at least give me a hug; **~ come un poquito** at least eat a bit
[2] (*en frases negativas*) **ni ~ me dio las gracias** he didn't even say thank you, he didn't so much as say thank you; **ni me miró ~** ◊ **ni ~ me miró** she didn't even look at me; **ni él ~ vino** not even he came
Ⓑ CONJ [1] (= *aunque*) even if, even though; **ven ~ sea por pocos días** do come even if it's only for a few days
[2] **~ venga, ~ no venga** whether he comes or not

Siracusa SF Syracuse

sirena SF [1] (*Mit*) siren, mermaid ► **sirena de la playa** bathing beauty
[2] (= *bocina*) siren, hooter ► **sirena de buque** ship's siren ► **sirena de niebla** foghorn

sirga SF towrope

sirgar ▸conjug 1h◂ VT to tow

sirgo SM twisted silk, piece of twisted silk

Siria SF Syria

sirimba SF (*Caribe*) faint, fainting fit

sirimbo ADJ (*Caribe*) silly

sirimbombo ADJ (*Caribe*) (= *débil*) weak; (= *tímido*) timid

sirimiri SM drizzle

siringa SF [1] (*LAm*) rubber tree
[2] (*Andes*) panpipes *pl*

siringal SM (*LAm*) rubber plantation

Sirio SM Sirius

sirio/a ADJ, SM/F Syrian

sirla‡ SF [1] (= *arma*) chiv‡, knife
[2] (= *atraco*) holdup, stick-up‡

sirlero/a‡ SM/F mugger

siró SM (*Caribe*) syrup

siroco SM sirocco

sirope SM (*LAm*) syrup

sirsaca SF seersucker

sirte SF shoal, sandbank

sirviendo *etc ver* **servir**

sirviente/a SM/F servant

sisa SF [1] (= *robo*) (*gen*) petty theft; [*de criado*] dishonest profit (*made by a servant*); **~s** pilfering *sing*, petty thieving *sing*
[2] (= *tajada*) cut, percentage*
[3] (*Cos*) (*gen*) dart; (*para la manga*) armhole

sisal SM sisal

sisar ▸conjug 1a◂ VT [1] (= *robar*) to thieve, pilfer
[2] (= *engañar*) to cheat
[3] (*Cos*) to take in

sisear ▸conjug 1a◂ VT, VI to hiss

siseo SM hiss, hissing

Sísifo SM Sisyphus

sísmico ADJ seismic

sismo SM (*esp LAm*) = **seísmo**

sismografía SF seismography

sismógrafo SM seismograph

sismología SF seismology

sismólogo/a SM/F seismologist

sisón[1]/ona Ⓐ ADJ thieving, light-fingered
Ⓑ SM/F petty thief

sisón[2] SM (*Orn*) little bustard

sistema SM [1] (= *conjunto ordenado*) system ► **sistema binario** (*Inform*) binary system ► **sistema de alerta inmediata** early warning system ► **sistema de calefacción** heating, heating system ► **sistema de diagnosis** diagnostic system ► **sistema de facturación** invoicing system ► **sistema de fondo fijo** (*Com*) imprest system ► **sistema de gestión de base de datos** database management system ► **sistema de lógica compartida** shared logic system ► **sistema de seguridad** security system ► **sistema educativo** education system ► **sistema experto** expert system ► **sistema financiero** financial system ► **sistema frontal** (*Meteo*) front, frontal system ► **sistema impositivo** tax system ► **sistema inmunitario, sistema inmunológico** immune system ► **sistema métrico** metric system ► **Sistema Monetario Europeo** European Monetary System ► **sistema montañoso** mountain range ► **sistema nervioso** nervous system ► **sistema nervioso central** central nervous system ► **sistema operativo** operating system ► **sistema operativo en disco** disk operating system ► **sistema pedagógico** educational system ► **sistema rastreador** (*en investigaciones espaciales*) tracking system ► **sistema tributario** tax system
[2] (= *método*) method; **trabajar con ~** to work systematically *o* methodically; **yo por ~ lo hago así** I make it a rule to do it this way, I've got into the habit of doing it this way

sistemática SF systematics *sing*

sistemáticamente ADV systematically

sistematicidad SF systematicity

sistemático ADJ systematic

sistematización SF systematization

sistematizar ▸conjug 1f◂ VT to systematize

sitiador(a) SM/F besieger

sitial SM seat of honour

sitiar ▸conjug 1b◂ VT [1] (= *asediar*) to besiege, lay siege to
[2] (= *acorralar*) to corner, hem in

sitio SM [1] (= *lugar*) place; **un ~ tranquilo** a peaceful place *o* spot; **Real Sitio** royal country house; **cambiar algo de ~** to move sth; **cambiarse de ~ con algn** to change places with sb; **en cualquier ~** anywhere; **en ningún ~**: **no lo encuentro en ningún ~** I can't find it anywhere; **en ningún ~ se pasa tan bien como aquí** you'll enjoy yourself nowhere better than here, you won't enjoy yourself anywhere better than here; **en todos los ~s** everywhere; ✦*MODISMOS* **así no vas a ningún ~** you'll get nowhere like that; **dejar a algn en el ~** to kill sb on the spot; **poner a algn en su ~** to put sb firmly in his place; **quedarse en el ~** to die instantly, die on the spot
[2] (= *espacio*) room, space; **hay ~ de sobra** there's plenty of room *o* space; **¿hay ~?** is there any room?; **te he guardado un ~ a mi lado** I've saved you a place next to me; **¿has encontrado ~ para aparcar?** have you found somewhere to park *o* a parking space?; **¿tienes ~ para nosotros en tu casa?** do you have room for us in your house?; **hacer ~ a algn** to make room for sb; **te hemos hecho ~ en el coche** we've made room for you in the car
[3] (*Mil*) siege; **poner ~ a algo** to besiege sth; **levantar el ~** to raise the siege; *ver tb* **estado 1.2**
[4] (= *sitio web*) site ► **sitio web** website
[5] (*CAm, Cono Sur*) (= *solar*) building site, vacant lot (*EEUU*)
[6] (*Caribe, Méx Agr*) small farm, smallholding
[7] (*LAm*) (= *parada*) taxi rank, cab rank (*esp EEUU*); **carro de ~** taxi, cab (*esp EEUU*)

sito ADJ situated, located (**en** at, in)

situ: **in ~** ADV on the spot, in situ

situación SF [1] (= *circunstancias*) situation; **¿qué harías en una ~ así?** what would you do in a situation like that?; **me pones en una ~ muy difícil** you're putting me in a very difficult position; **no estoy en ~ de desmentirlo** I'm not in a position to deny it ► **situación jurídica** legal status ► **situación límite** extreme situation
[2] (= *emplazamiento*) situation, location; **la casa tiene una ~ inmejorable** the house is in a superb location, the house is superbly located *o* situated
[3] (*en la sociedad*) position, standing; **crearse una ~** to do well for o.s. ► **situación económica** financial position, financial situation
[4] (= *estado*) state; **la ~ del edificio es ruinosa** the building is in a state of ruin
[5] **precio de ~** (*LAm*) bargain price

situacional ADJ situational

situado ADJ [1] (= *colocado*) situated, placed; **está ~ en ...** it's situated in ...; **el piso no está muy bien ~** the flat isn't very well situated [2] (*Fin*) **estar (bien) ~** to be financially secure

situar ▸conjug 1e◂ Ⓐ VT [1] (= *colocar*) to place, put; (*Mil*) to post; **esto la sitúa entre los mejores** this places *o* puts her among the best; **van a ~ la estación en el centro de la**

ciudad the station is going to be located *o* sited in the city centre

[2] (= *señalar*) to find, locate; **no supo ~ Grecia en el mapa** he couldn't find *o* locate Greece on the map

[3] (†) [+ *dinero*] (= *invertir*) to place, invest; (= *depositar en banco*) to bank; **~ una pensión para algn** to settle an income on sb

Ⓑ **situarse** VPR [1] (= *colocarse*) to position o.s.; **los jugadores se ~on cerca de la portería** the players positioned themselves near the goal; **se ha situado muy bien en la empresa** he's got himself a very good position in the company; **se ha situado entre los tres países más ricos del mundo** it has become one of the three richest countries in the world

[2] [*novela, película*] to be set; **la acción se sitúa en Buenos Aires** the action is set in Buenos Aires

[3] (*en la sociedad*) to do well for o.s.; **se situó muy bien en la capital** she did really well for herself in the capital

siútico* ADJ (*Chile*) = **cursi**

siutiquería SF (*Cono Sur*) = **cursilería**

skay [es'kai] SM imitation leather

sketch [es'ketʃ] SM (*pl* **sketches** [es'ketʃ]) sketch

skin [es'kin] ADJ, SMF (*pl* **skins**), **skinhead** [es'kinxeð] ADJ, SMF (*pl* **skinheads**) skinhead

S.L. ABR [1] (*Com*) (= **Sociedad Limitada**) Ltd, Corp. (*EEUU*)

[2] = **Sus Labores**; *ver* **labor 1**

slalom [ez'lalom] SM slalom ► **slalom gigante** giant slalom

slam [ez'lam] SM (*Bridge*) slam; **gran ~** grand slam; **pequeño ~** little slam

slip [ez'lip] SM (*pl* **slips** [ez'lip]) [1] (= *calzoncillos*) underpants *pl*, briefs *pl*

[2] (= *bañador*) bathing trunks *pl*

s.l. ni f. ABR (= **sin lugar ni fecha**) n.p. or d.

slogan [ez'loɣan] SM (*pl* **slogans** [ez'loɣan]) slogan

slot [ez'lot] SM ► **slot de expansión** (*Inform*) expansion slot

S.M. ABR (*Esp*) [1] (*Rel*) = **Sociedad Marianista**

[2] (= **Su Majestad**) HM

smash [ez'mas] SM smash

SME SM ABR (= **Sistema Monetario Europeo**) EMS

SMI SM ABR = **salario mínimo interprofesional**

smiley SM smiley

smog [ez'smo] SM smog

smoking [ez'mokin] SM (*pl* **smokings** [ez'mokin]) dinner jacket, tuxedo (*EEUU*)

SMS SM (= *mensaje*) text (message), SMS (message)

s/n ABR = **sin número**

snack [ez'nak] SM (*pl* **snacks** [ez'nak]) [1] (= *merienda*) snack

[2] (= *cafetería*) snack bar

s.n.m. ABR = **sobre el nivel del mar**

snob [ez'noβ] = **esnob**

so¹ EXCL [1] (*para parar*) whoa!

[2] (*LAm*) (*¡silencio!*) quiet!, shut up!*

[3] (*Caribe*) (*a animal*) shoo!

so² EXCL (*como intensificador*) **¡so burro!** you idiot!, you great oaf!; **¡so indecente!** you swine!*

so³ PREP *ver* **pena 5, pretexto**

SO ABR (= **suroeste**) SW

s/o ABR (*Com*) = **su orden**

soasar ▸conjug 1a◂ VT to roast lightly

soba* SF [1] [*de tela, persona*] fingering

[2] (= *paliza*) hiding; (= *bofetada*) slap, punch; **dar una ~ a algn** to wallop sb*

sobacal ADJ underarm *antes de s*

sobaco SM [1] (*Anat*) armpit; ✦*MODISMO* **se lo pasó por el ~*** he dismissed it, he totally disregarded it [2] (*Cos*) armhole

sobada* SF [1] (= *manoseo*) feel, grope

[2] (= *dormida*) long sleep; **me voy a pegar una ~ de órdago** I'm going to sleep like a log

sobado ADJ [1] [*ropa*] (= *usado*) worn, shabby; (= *arrugado*) crumpled

[2] [*libro*] well-thumbed, dog-eared

[3] (= *trillado*) [*tema*] well-worn; [*chiste*] old, corny*

[4] (*Culin*) [*masa*] short, crumbly (*EEUU*)

[5] (*Cono Sur*) (= *enorme*) big, huge

sobador(a) SM/F [1] (*Andes, Méx Med*) (= *matasanos*) quack

[2] (*Andes, Caribe, Méx*) (= *lisonjero*) flatterer, smooth talker

sobajar ▸conjug 1a◂ VT [1] = **sobajear 1**

[2] (*Andes, Méx*) (= *humillar*) to humiliate

sobajear ▸conjug 1a◂ VT [1] (= *manosear*) to handle, finger

[2] (*LAm*) (= *apretar*) to squeeze, press; (= *desordenar*) to mess up

sobandero SM (*Andes*) (= *matasanos*) quack

sobao Ⓐ ADJ (*) **quedarse ~** to fall asleep; *ver tb* **sobado**

Ⓑ SM *sponge cake made with cream or lard*

sobaquera SF [1] (*Cos*) armhole

[2] (*) (= *mancha*) stain

[3] (= *pistolera*) shoulder holster

[4] (*CAm, Caribe*) (= *olor*) underarm odour, underarm odor (*EEUU*)

sobaquero ADJ **funda sobaquera** shoulder holster

sobaquina* SF underarm odour, underarm odor (*EEUU*)

sobar ▸conjug 1a◂ Ⓐ VT [1] (= *toquetear*) [+ *tela*] to finger, dirty (with one's fingers); [+ *ropa*] to rumple, mess up; [+ *masa*] to knead; [+ *músculo*] to massage, rub

[2] (*) (= *magrear*) to grope*, paw*

[3] (*) (= *pegar*) to wallop

[4] (*) (= *molestar*) to pester

[5] (*LAm*) [+ *huesos*] to set

[6] (*Andes*) (= *despellejar*) to skin, flay

[7] (*Andes, Caribe, Méx*) (= *lisonjear*) to flatter

[8] (*CAm, Méx*) (= *reprender*) to tell off*

Ⓑ VI (*) to kip*, sleep

Ⓒ **sobarse** VPR (*) [*enamorados*] to neck, make out (*EEUU**), have a grope

sobasquera SF (*CAm, Caribe, Méx*) = **sobaquina**

sobeo SM fondling

soberanamente ADV supremely

soberanía SF sovereignty ► **soberanía popular** popular sovereignty

soberano/a Ⓐ ADJ [1] (*Pol*) sovereign

[2] (= *supremo*) supreme

[3] (*) (= *tremendo*) real, really big; **una soberana paliza** a real walloping*

Ⓑ SM/F sovereign; **los ~s** the king and queen, the royal couple

soberbia SF [1] [*de persona*] (= *orgullo*) pride; (= *altanería*) haughtiness, arrogance

[2] (= *magnificencia*) magnificence

[3] (= *ira*) anger; (= *malhumor*) irritable nature

soberbio ADJ [1] [*persona*] (= *orgulloso*) proud; (= *altanero*) haughty, arrogant

[2] (= *magnífico*) magnificent, grand; **¡soberbio!** splendid!

[3] (= *enojado*) angry; (= *malhumorado*) irritable

[4] (*) = **soberano A3**

sobeta* ADJ INV **estar** *o* **quedarse ~** to be having a kip

sobijo SM [1] (*Andes, CAm*) = **soba**

[2] (*Andes*) (= *desolladura*) skinning, flaying

sobijón SM (*CAm*) = **sobijo**

sobón* ADJ [1] (= *que soba*) **es muy ~** his hands are everywhere; **¡no seas ~!** get your hands off me!, stop pawing me!*

[2] (= *gandul*) lazy, workshy

[3] (*Andes*) (= *adulón*) soapy*, greasy

sobornable ADJ bribable, venal

sobornar ▸conjug 1a◂ VT [1] (= *comprar*) to bribe

[2] (*hum*) (= *engatusar*) to get round

soborno SM [1] (= *pago*) bribe; **denunció un intento de ~** he reported an attempted bribe

[2] (= *delito*) bribery

[3] (*Andes, Cono Sur*) (= *sobrecarga*) extra load; (= *prima*) extra, bonus; **de ~** extra, in addition

➤ **sobra** SF [1] (= *excedente*) excess, surplus

[2] **sobras** [*de comida*] leftovers; (*Cos*) remnants

[3] **de ~** spare, extra; **aquí tengo de ~** I've more than enough here; **tenemos comida de ~** we've got more than enough food; **tengo tiempo de ~** I've got plenty of time; **tuvo motivos de ~** he was more than justified; **lo sé de ~** I know it only too well; **sabes de ~ que yo no he sido** you know full well that it wasn't me; **aquí estoy de ~** I'm not needed *o* I'm superfluous here; **es de ~ conocido** it's common knowledge

sobradamente ADV **lo conozco ~** I know him only too well; **con eso queda ~ satisfecho** he is more than satisfied with that; **es ~ sabido que ...** it is common knowledge that ...

sobradero SM overflow pipe

sobradillo SM penthouse

sobrado Ⓐ ADJ [1] [*cantidad, tiempo*] (= *más que suficiente*) more than enough; (= *superfluo*) superfluous, excessive; (= *sobreabundante*) superabundant; **hay tiempo ~** there's plenty of time; **motivo más que ~ para hacerlo** all the more reason to do it; **tuvo razones sobradas para ...** he had good reason to ...; **sobradas veces** repeatedly

[2] **estar ~ de algo** to have more than enough of sth

[3] (= *acaudalado*) wealthy; **no anda muy ~** he's not very well off

[4] (= *atrevido*) bold, forward

[5] (*Cono Sur*) (= *enorme*) colossal

[6] **darse de ~** (*Andes**) to be full of oneself

Ⓑ ADV too, exceedingly

Ⓒ SM [1] (= *desván*) attic, garret

[2] **sobrados** (*Andalucía, Cono Sur*) leftovers

sobrador* ADJ (*Cono Sur*) stuck-up*, conceited

sobrancero ADJ unemployed

sobrante Ⓐ ADJ (= *excedente*) spare; (= *restante*) remaining

Ⓑ SM [1] (= *lo que sobra*) (*gen*) surplus, remainder; (*Com, Fin*) surplus; (= *saldo activo*) balance in hand

➤ LENGUA Y USO: **sobra 3** 53.1

[2] **sobrantes** odds and ends
Ⓒ SMF redundant worker, laid-off worker (*EEUU*), person made redundant

sobrar ▸conjug 1a◂ Ⓐ VT to exceed, surpass
Ⓑ VI (= *quedar de más*) to remain, be left, be left over; (= *ser más que suficiente*) to be more than enough; (= *ser superfluo*) to be spare; **ha sobrado mucha comida** there's a lot of food left (over); **por este lado sobra** there's too much on this side; **sobra uno** there's one too many, there's one left; **con este dinero ~á** this money will be more than enough; **esta pieza sobra** this piece is spare; **este ejemplo sobra** this example is unnecessary; **no es que sobre talento** it's not that there's a surplus of talent; **todo lo que has dicho sobra** all that you've said is quite unnecessary; **nos sobra tiempo** we have plenty of time; **al terminar me sobraba medio metro** I had half a metre left over when I finished; **veo que aquí sobro** I see that I'm not needed *o* I'm superfluous here; ✦***REFRÁN*** **más vale que sobre que no que falte** better too much than too little

sobrasada SF Majorcan sausage

sobre[1] SM [1] (*para cartas*) envelope ► **sobre de paga**, **sobre de pago** pay packet ► **sobre de primer día (de circulación)** first-day cover ► **sobre de sellos** packet of stamps
[2] (*) (= *cama*) bed; **meterse en el ~** to hit the sack*, hit the hay*
[3] (*LAm*) (= *cartera*) handbag

sobre[2] PREP [1] (= *encima de*) on; **está ~ la mesa** it's on the table; **un puente ~ el río Ebro** a bridge across *o* over the river Ebro; **prestar juramento ~ la Biblia** to swear on the Bible; **la marcha ~ Roma** the march on Rome; **llevaba una chaqueta negra ~ camisa blanca** he wore a black jacket over a white shirt; **varios policías se abalanzaron ~ él** several policemen jumped on *o* fell upon him; **los insultos llovían ~ mí de todas partes** insults rained down on me from all sides; **la responsabilidad que recae ~ sus hombros** the responsibility which rests on *o* upon his shoulders; ✦***MODISMO*** **estar ~ algn** (= *vigilar*) to keep constant watch over sb; (= *acosar*) to keep on at sb; (= *dominar*) to control sb; **tengo que estar ~ él para que lo haga** I have to stand over him to make him do it, I have to keep a constant watch over him to make sure he does it; **quiere estar ~ todos** he wants to control everyone
[2] (= *por encima de*) [2·1] [+ *lugar*] over; **volamos ~ Cádiz** we're flying over Cadiz; **se inclinó ~ la mesa** she leant over the table
[2·2] (*con cantidades*) above; **500 metros ~ el nivel del mar** 500 metres *o* (*EEUU*) meters above sea level; **dos grados ~ cero** two degrees above cero; **diez dólares ~ lo estipulado** ten dollars over and above what was agreed
[3] (*indicando superioridad*) over; **tiene muchas ventajas ~ los métodos convencionales** it has many advantages over conventional methods; **están celebrando su victoria ~ el Atlético** they're celebrating their victory over Atlético; **amaba la belleza ~ todas las cosas** he loved beauty above all things
[4] (*indicando proporción*) out of, in; **tres ~ cien** three out of every hundred, three in a hundred; **cuatro personas ~ diez no votarían** four out of ten people would not vote, four in every ten people would not vote; **una puntuación de tres ~ cinco** three (marks) out of five
[5] (*Fin*) on; **un préstamo ~ una propiedad** a loan on a property; **un aumento ~ el año pasado** an increase on *o* over last year; **un impuesto ~ algo** a tax on sth
[6] (= *aproximadamente*) about; **~ las seis** at about six o'clock; **ocupa ~ 20 páginas** it fills about 20 pages, it occupies roughly 20 pages
[7] (= *acerca de*) about, on; **un libro ~ Tirso** a book about *o* on Tirso; **información ~ vuelos** information about flights; **hablar ~ algo** to talk about sth
[8] (= *además de*) in addition to, on top of; **~ todas mis obligaciones ahora tengo una nueva** on top of all my duties I now have a new one
[9] **~ todo** (= *en primer lugar*) above all; (= *especialmente*) especially; **~ todo, no perdamos la calma** above all, let's keep calm; **~ todo me gusta éste** I especially like this one

sobre... PREF super..., over...

sobreabundancia SF superabundance, overabundance

sobreabundante ADJ superabundant, overabundant

sobreabundar ▸conjug 1a◂ VI to be very abundant (**en** in, with)

sobreactuación SF overacting

sobreactuar ▸conjug 1e◂ VI to overact

sobrealimentación SF overfeeding

sobrealimentado ADJ supercharged

sobrealimentador SM supercharger

sobrealimentar ▸conjug 1a◂ VT [1] [+ *persona*] to overfeed
[2] (*Mec*) to supercharge

sobreañadido ADJ (= *extra*) additional; (= *superfluo*) superfluous

sobreañadir ▸conjug 3a◂ VT to give in addition, add, add as a bonus

sobrecalentamiento SM overheating

sobrecalentar ▸conjug 1j◂ VT to overheat

sobrecama SM *o* SF bedspread

sobrecaña SF splint

sobrecapacidad SF overcapacity, excess capacity

sobrecapitalización SF overcapitalization

sobrecapitalizar ▸conjug 1f◂ VT to overcapitalize

sobrecarga SF [1] (= *peso excesivo*) (*lit*) overload; (*fig*) extra burden
[2] (*Com*) surcharge ► **sobrecarga de importación** import surcharge
[3] (*Correos*) overprint, overprinting
[4] (= *cuerda*) rope

sobrecargar ▸conjug 1h◂ VT [1] (*con peso*) [+ *camión*] to overload; [+ *persona*] to weigh down, overburden (**de** with); **~ el mercado** (*Cono Sur*) to glut the market
[2] (*Com*) to surcharge
[3] (*Correos*) to surcharge, overprint (**de** with)
[4] (*Elec*) to overload

sobrecargo SMF [1] (*Náut*) purser
[2] (*Aer*) senior flight attendant

sobrecejo SM [1] (= *ceño*) frown
[2] (*Arquit*) lintel

sobreceño SM frown

sobrecito SM sachet

sobrecogedor ADJ [1] [*paisaje, silencio*] imposing, impressive
[2] (= *horrible*) horrific; **~as escenas de guerra** horrific scenes of war

sobrecoger ▸conjug 2c◂ Ⓐ VT (= *sobresaltar*) to startle, take by surprise; (= *asustar*) to scare, frighten
Ⓑ **sobrecogerse** VPR [1] (= *sobresaltarse*) to be startled, start; (= *asustarse*) to get scared, be frightened
[2] (= *quedar impresionado*) to be overawed (**de** by); **~se de emoción** to be overcome with emotion

sobrecontrata SF overbooking

sobrecontratar ▸conjug 1a◂ VT, VI to overbook

sobrecoste SM extra charges *pl*

sobrecubierta SF jacket, dust jacket

sobredicho ADJ aforementioned

sobredimensionado ADJ [1] (= *muy grande*) excessively large, oversized
[2] **estar ~ de** to have a surplus *o* excess of, have too much of

sobredimensionamiento SM [*de personal*] excessive number; [*de tamaño*] increase in size, expansion

sobredimensionar ▸conjug 1a◂ VT [1] [+ *beneficios, importancia, problema*] to inflate
[2] (*Téc, Aut*) to oversize

sobredorar ▸conjug 1a◂ VT [1] (= *dorar*) to gild
[2] (= *disimular*) to gloss over

sobredosis SF INV overdose

sobreentender ▸conjug 2g◂ Ⓐ VT (= *entender*) to understand; (= *adivinar*) to deduce, infer
Ⓑ **sobreentenderse** VPR **aquí se sobreentienden dos palabras** you can see that there should be two words here; **se sobreentiende que ...** it is implied that ..., it goes without saying that ...

sobreescribir ▸conjug 3a◂ VT to overwrite

sobreesfuerzo SM [1] (= *esfuerzo enorme*) superhuman effort
[2] (*Med*) overstrain

sobreestimación SF overestimate

sobreestimar ▸conjug 1a◂ VT to overestimate

sobreexcitación SF overexcitement

sobreexcitado ADJ overexcited

sobreexcitar ▸conjug 1a◂ Ⓐ VT to overexcite
Ⓑ **sobreexcitarse** VPR to get overexcited

sobreexplotación SF [*de recursos*] over-exploitation, draining; [*de trabajadores*] exploitation

sobreexplotar ▸conjug 1a◂ VT [+ *recursos*] to over-exploit, drain; [+ *trabajadores*] to exploit

sobreexponer ▸conjug 2q◂ VT to overexpose

sobreexposición SF overexposure

sobrefunda SF (*CAm*) pillowslip, pillowcase

sobregirar ▸conjug 1a◂ VT, VI to overdraw

sobregiro SM overdraft

sobrehilar ▸conjug 1a◂ VT to whipstitch, overcast

sobrehumano ADJ superhuman

sobreimpresión SF (*Correos*) overprint, overprinting

sobreimpresionado ADJ superimposed

sobreimpresionar ▸conjug 1a◂ VT to superimpose

sobreimpreso ADJ superimposed

sobreimprimir ▸conjug 3a◂ VT to overprint

sobrellevar ▸conjug 1a◂ VT [+ *peso*] to carry, help to carry; [+ *carga de otro*] to ease; [+ *desgracia, desastre, enfermedad*] to bear, endure; [+ *faltas ajenas*] to be tolerant towards

sobremanera ADV exceedingly; **me interesa ~** I'm most interested in it

sobremarca SF overbid

sobremarcha SF overdrive

sobremesa SF [1] (= *después de comer*) sitting on after a meal; **estar de ~** to sit round the table after lunch/dinner; **conversación de ~** table talk; **charla de ~** after-dinner speech; **orador de ~** after-dinner speaker; **programa de ~** (*TV*) afternoon programme; **un cigarro de ~** an after-lunch/dinner cigar; **hablaremos de eso en la ~** we'll talk about that after lunch/dinner
[2] **lámpara de ~** table lamp; **ordenador de ~** desktop computer
[3] (= *mantel*) table cover, tablecloth
[4] (= *postre*) dessert

SOBREMESA

After the main meal of the day, which usually takes place at around 2 or 3 p.m., the Spanish often linger on at table drinking coffee and/or liqueurs and chatting, playing cards or watching TV before returning to work later in the afternoon. While **estar de sobremesa** *is also occasionally applied to the period after the evening meal, it is more usually taken to mean after lunch, and the* **sobremesa** *time band used in TV programme listings applies only to between 2.00 and 5.00 p.m.*

sobremodo ADV very much, enormously

sobrenadar ▸conjug 1a◂ VI to float

sobrenatural ADJ [1] (= *inexplicable*) supernatural; **lo ~** the supernatural; **ciencias ~es** occult sciences; **vida ~** life after death
[2] (= *misterioso*) weird, unearthly

sobrenombre SM nickname

sobrentender ▸conjug 2g◂ VT = **sobreentender**

sobrepaga SF extra pay, bonus

sobreparto SM confinement (*after childbirth*); **dolores de ~** afterpains; **morir de ~** to die in childbirth

sobrepasar ▸conjug 1a◂ Ⓐ VT [+ *límite, esperanzas*] to exceed; [+ *rival, récord*] to beat; [+ *pista de aterrizaje*] to overshoot
Ⓑ **sobrepasarse** VPR = **propasarse**

sobrepelliz SF surplice

sobrepelo SM (*Cono Sur*) saddlecloth

sobrepesca SF over-fishing

sobrepeso SM [*de paquete, persona*] excess weight; [*de camión*] extra load

sobrepoblación SF overpopulation

sobreponer ▸conjug 2q◂ (*pp* **sobrepuesto**) Ⓐ VT [1] (= *poner encima de*) to put on top (**en** of), superimpose (**en** on)
[2] (= *añadir*) to add (**en** to)
[3] (= *anteponer*) **~ A a B** to give A preference over B
Ⓑ **sobreponerse** VPR [1] (= *recobrar la calma*) to control o.s., pull o.s. together
[2] (= *vencer dificultades*) to win through; **~se a una enfermedad** to pull through an illness; **~se a un enemigo** to overcome an enemy; **~se a un rival** to triumph over a rival; **~se a un susto** to get over a fright

sobreprecio SM (= *recargo*) surcharge; (= *aumento de precio*) increase in price

sobreprima SF extra premium

sobreproducción SF overproduction

sobreproducir ▸conjug 3n◂ VT to overproduce

sobreprotección SF over-protection

sobreprotector ADJ over-protective

sobreproteger ▸conjug 2c◂ VT to overprotect

sobrepuerta SF lintel

sobrepuesto Ⓐ PP *de* **sobreponer**
Ⓑ ADJ superimposed

sobrepujar ▸conjug 1a◂ VT [1] (*en subasta*) to outbid
[2] (= *superar*) to outdo, surpass; **sobrepuja a todos en talento** he outdoes all the rest in talent, he has more talent than all the rest

sobrereacción SF over-reaction

sobrereserva SF overbooking

sobrereservar ▸conjug 1a◂ VT, VI to overbook

sobrero Ⓐ ADJ extra, spare
Ⓑ SM (*Taur*) reserve bull

sobresaliente Ⓐ ADJ [1] (*Arquit*) projecting, overhanging
[2] (= *excelente*) outstanding
[3] (*Univ*) first class
Ⓑ SMF (*Teat*) understudy
Ⓒ SM (*Educ*) distinction

sobresalir ▸conjug 3q◂ VI [1] (*Arquit*) to project, overhang, jut out; (= *salirse de la línea*) to stick out
[2] (= *destacarse*) to stand out, excel

sobresaltar ▸conjug 1a◂ Ⓐ VT to startle, frighten
Ⓑ **sobresaltarse** VPR to start, be startled (**con, de** at)

sobresalto SM (= *sorpresa*) start; (= *susto*) fright, scare; (= *conmoción*) sudden shock; **de ~** suddenly

sobresanar ▸conjug 1a◂ VI [1] (*Med*) to heal superficially
[2] (= *ocultarse*) to conceal itself, hide its true nature

sobrescrito SM (= *señas*) address; (= *inscripción*) superscription

sobreseer ▸conjug 2e◂ VT [1] **~ una causa** (*Jur*) to dismiss a case
[2] **~ de algo** to desist from sth, give up sth

sobreseído ADJ **causa sobreseída** (*Jur*) case dismissed

sobreseimiento SM stay (of proceedings)

sobresello SM double seal

sobrestadía SF demurrage

sobrestante SM (= *capataz*) foreman, overseer; (= *gerente*) site manager

sobresueldo SM bonus, extra pay

sobretasa SF surcharge

sobretensión SF (*Elec*) surge

sobretiempo SM (*LAm*) overtime

sobretiro SM (*Méx*) offprint

sobretítulo SM (*Prensa*) general title, general heading

sobretodo SM overcoat

sobrevaloración SF [1] [*de dinero, moneda*] overvaluation
[2] (*en importancia*) overrating

sobrevalorado ADJ [1] [*dinero, moneda*] overvalued
[2] [*persona*] overrated

sobrevalorar ▸conjug 1a◂ VT [+ *dinero, moneda*] to overvalue; [+ *persona*] to overrate

sobrevaluado ADJ = **sobrevalorado**

sobrevender ▸conjug 2a◂ VT to overbook

sobrevenir ▸conjug 3r◂ VI (= *ocurrir*) to happen, happen unexpectedly; (= *resultar*) to follow, ensue

sobrevirar ▸conjug 1a◂ VI to oversteer

sobrevivencia SF survival

sobreviviente ADJ, SMF = **superviviente**

sobrevivir ▸conjug 3a◂ VI [1] (= *quedar vivo*) to survive; **sobrevivir a** [+ *accidente*] to survive; [+ *persona*] to survive, outlive
[2] (= *durar más tiempo que*) to outlast

sobrevolar ▸conjug 1l◂ VT to fly over

sobrevuelo SM overflying; **permiso de ~** permission to overfly

sobriedad SF [1] [*de estilo, color, decoración*] sobriety; **vestía con ~** he was soberly dressed
[2] (= *moderación*) moderation; **siempre come con ~** she always eats in moderation

sobrino/a SM/F nephew/niece; **mis ~s** (= *varones*) my nephews; **mis ~s** (= *varones y hembras*) my nieces and nephews

sobrinonieto/a SM/F great nephew/niece

sobrio ADJ [1] (= *no borracho*) sober
[2] [*color, estilo, decoración*] sober
[3] (= *moderado*) frugal; **llevan una vida muy sobria** they live a very frugal life; **ser ~ con la bebida** to drink in moderation; **es ~ de palabras** he's a man of few words
[4] (= *tranquilo*) restrained

sobros SMPL (*CAm*) leftovers, scraps

soca[1] SF [1] (*Andes*) [*de arroz*] young shoots of rice; [*de tabaco*] top leaf of tobacco plant, high-quality tobacco leaf
[2] (*CAm**) (= *embriaguez*) drunkenness

soca[2]* SM **hacerse el ~** to act dumb*

socaire SM [1] (*Náut*) lee; **al ~** to leeward
[2] **al ~ de algo** (= *al abrigo de*) under the protection of sth; (= *so pretexto de*) using sth as an excuse; **estar** o **ponerse al ~** to shirk

socaliña Ⓐ SF (= *astucia*) craft, cunning; (= *porfía*) clever persistence
Ⓑ SMF (*) twister, swindler

socaliñar ▸conjug 1a◂ VT to get by a swindle

socaliñero ADJ (= *astuto*) crafty, cunning; (= *porfiado*) persistent

socapa SF **a ~** surreptitiously

socapar* ▸conjug 1a◂ VT (*Andes, Méx*) **~ a algn** to cover up for sb

socar ▸conjug 1g◂ (*CAm*) Ⓐ VT [1] (= *comprimir*) to press down, squeeze, compress
[2] (*) (= *enojar*) to annoy, upset
Ⓑ VI to make an effort
Ⓒ **socarse** VPR [1] (= *emborracharse*) to get drunk
[2] **~se con algn** to fall out o squabble with sb

socarrar ▸conjug 1a◂ VT to scorch, singe

socarrón ADJ [1] (= *irónico*) [*persona, comentario, tono*] sarcastic, ironical; [*humor*] snide
[2] (= *astuto*) crafty, cunning, sly

socarronería SF [1] (= *ironía*) [*de persona, comentario, tono*] sarcasm, irony; [*de humor*] snide humour, snide humor (*EEUU*)
[2] (= *astucia*) craftiness, cunning, slyness

socava SF, **socavación** SF undermining

socavar ▸conjug 1a◂ VT [1] (= *minar*) to undermine
[2] (= *excavar*) [*persona*] to dig under; [*agua*] to hollow out
[3] (= *debilitar*) to sap, undermine

socavón SM [1] (*Min*) (= *galería*) gallery, tunnel; (= *hueco*) hollow; (= *cueva*) cavern; (*en la calle*) hole
[2] (*Arquit*) subsidence

soche SM (*Andes*) [*de oveja*] tanned sheepskin; [*de cabra*], tanned goatskin

socia* SF (*Esp*) whore

sociabilidad SF [*de persona*] sociability; [*de animal*] gregariousness; [*de reunión*] convivialitу

sociable ADJ [*persona*] sociable, friendly; [*animal*] social, gregarious; [*reunión*] convivial

sociablemente ADV sociably

social Ⓐ ADJ [1] (= *de la sociedad*) social
[2] (*Com, Fin*) company *antes de s*, company's; **acuerdo ~** ◊ **pacto ~** wages agreement; **paz ~** industrial harmony, agreement between employers and unions
Ⓑ **sociales** SMPL (*Escol**) social studies

socialdemocracia SF social democracy

socialdemócrata Ⓐ ADJ social democrat, social democratic
Ⓑ SMF social democrat

socialdemocrático ADJ social democratic

socialismo SM socialism

socialista Ⓐ ADJ socialist, socialistic
Ⓑ SMF socialist

socialización SF [*de país*] collectivization; [*de empresa*] nationalization

socializador ADJ, **socializante** ADJ [1] (= *que socializa*) socializing
[2] (*Pol*) [*reformas*] with Socialist leanings

socializar ▸conjug 1f◂ VT [+ *país*] to collectivize; [+ *empresa*] to nationalize

socialmente ADV socially

sociata‡ ADJ, SMF socialist

sociedad SF [1] (*Sociol*) society; **la ~ de consumo** the consumer society; **la ~ del ocio** the leisure society; **la ~ permisiva** the permissive society; **en la ~ actual** in contemporary society; **hacer ~** to join forces
[2] (= *asociación*) (*gen*) society, association; (*oficial*) body ► **sociedad científica** learned society ► **Sociedad de Jesús** Society of Jesus ► **Sociedad de Naciones** League of Nations ► **sociedad de socorros mutuos** friendly society, provident society ► **sociedad docta** learned society ► **sociedad gastronómica** dining club ► **sociedad inmobiliaria** building society ► **sociedad secreta** secret society
[3] (*Com, Fin*) (= *empresa*) (*gen*) company; [*de socios*] partnership ► **sociedad anónima** limited liability company, corporation (*EEUU*) ► **Sociedad Anónima** (*en nombres de empresa*) Limited, Incorporated (*EEUU*) ► **sociedad anónima laboral** workers' cooperative ► **sociedad comanditaria** limited partnership ► **sociedad conjunta** (*Com*) joint venture ► **sociedad de beneficencia** friendly society, benefit association (*EEUU*) ► **sociedad de cartera** holding company ► **sociedad de control** holding company ► **sociedad en comandita** limited partnership ► **sociedad instrumental, sociedad limitada** limited company, private limited company, corporation (*EEUU*) ► **sociedad mercantil** trading company ► **sociedad protectora de animales** society for the protection of animals
[4] **alta** *o* **buena ~** high society; **entrar en ~** ◊ **presentarse en (la) ~** to come out, make one's debut; **notas de ~** gossip column, society news column
[5] ► **sociedad conyugal** marriage partnership

societal ADJ societal

socio/a SM/F [1] (= *asociado*) [*de empresa*] associate; [*de club*] member; [*de sociedad docta*] fellow; **hacerse ~ de** to become a member of, join; **se ruega a los señores ~s ...** members are asked to ... ► **socio/a de honor** honorary member ► **socio/a de número** full member ► **socio/a honorario/a** honorary member ► **socio/a numerario/a** full member ► **socio/a vitalicio/a** life member
[2] (*Com, Fin*) partner ► **socio activo** active partner ► **socio capitalista, socio comanditario** sleeping partner, silent partner (*EEUU*)
[3] (*) (= *amigo*) buddy, mate*

socio... PREF socio...

sociobiología SF sociobiology

sociocultural ADJ sociocultural; **animador ~** [*de organización*] events organizer; [*de hotel*] entertainments manager

socioeconómico ADJ socioeconomic

sociolingüística SF sociolinguistics *sing*

sociolingüístico ADJ sociolinguistic

sociología SF sociology

sociológico ADJ sociological

sociólogo/a SM/F sociologist

sociopolítico ADJ sociopolitical

sociosanitario ADJ public health *antes de s*

soco Ⓐ ADJ [1] (*CAm*) (= *borracho*) drunk, tight*
[2] = **zoco[1] A2**
Ⓑ SM [1] (*Andes Anat, Bot*) stump
[2] (*Andes*) (= *cuchillo*) short blunt machete
[3] = **zoco[2]**

socola SF (*Andes, CAm*) clearing of land

socolar ▸conjug 1a◂ VT [1] (*Andes, CAm*) [+ *tierra*] to clear, clear of scrub
[2] (*Andes*) [+ *trabajo*] to bungle, do clumsily

socollón SM (*CAm, Caribe*) violent shaking

socollonear ▸conjug 1a◂ VT (*CAm*) to shake violently

socón‡ ADJ (*CAm*) studious, swotty*

soconusco SM [1] (= *chocolate*) fine chocolate
[2] (*Caribe**) (= *trato*) shady deal, dirty business

socorrer ▸conjug 2a◂ VT [+ *ciudad sitiada*] to relieve; [+ *expedición*] to bring aid to; **~ a algn** to help sb, come to sb's aid

socorrido ADJ [1] [*tienda*] well-stocked
[2] (= *útil*) handy; **un ~ primer plato** a common starter
[3] [*persona*] helpful, obliging
[4] [*ejemplo, método*] hackneyed, well-worn

socorrismo SM life-saving

socorrista SMF lifeguard, life-saver

socorro SM [1] (= *ayuda*) help, aid, assistance; (= *alivio*) relief; **¡socorro!** help!; **trabajos de ~** relief *o* aid work *sing*; **pedir ~** to ask for help; **acudió en su ~** she went to his aid ► **socorros mutuos** mutual aid *sing*
[2] (*Cono Sur*) (= *pago adelantado*) advance payment, sub*

socoyote SM (*Méx*) smallest child

Sócrates SM Socrates

socrático ADJ Socratic

socrocio SM plaster

socucha SF (*Cono Sur, Méx*), **socucho** SM (*Cono Sur, Méx*) (= *cuartito*) poky little room, den; (= *casucha*) hovel, slum

soda SF [1] (*Quím*) soda
[2] (= *bebida*) soda water

sódico ADJ sodium *antes de s*

sodio SM sodium

Sodoma SF Sodom

sodomía SF sodomy

sodomita SMF sodomite

sodomizar ▸conjug 1f◂ VT to sodomize

SOE SM ABR (*Esp*) = **Seguro Obligatorio de Enfermedad**

soez ADJ dirty, crude, coarse

sofá SM sofa, settee

sofá-cama SM (*pl* **sofás-cama**), **sofá-nido** SM (*pl* **sofás-nido**) sofa bed, studio couch

sofero ADJ (*Andes*) huge, enormous

Sofía[1] SF (= *nombre*) Sophia

Sofía[2] SF (*Geog*) Sofia

sofión SM (= *bufido*) angry snort; (= *reprimenda*) sharp rebuke; (= *réplica*) sharp retort

sofisma SM sophism

sofista SMF sophist

sofistería SF sophistry

sofisticación SF [1] [*de persona, gestos*] sophistication
[2] (= *afectación*) affectation

sofisticado ADJ [1] [*persona, gesto*] sophisticated
[2] (= *afectado*) (*pey*) affected

sofístico ADJ sophistic, sophistical

soflama SF [1] (= *fuego*) flicker, glow
[2] (= *sonrojo*) blush
[3] (= *arenga*) fiery speech, harangue
[4] (*) (= *engaño*) deceit; (= *halagos*) cajolery, blarney
[5] (*Méx*) (= *chisme*) piece of trivia, bit of gossip

soflamar ▸conjug 1a◂ VT [1] (= *quemar*) (*gen*) to scorch; (*Culin*) to singe
[2] (= *hacer sonrojar*) to make blush
[3] (*) (= *engañar*) to deceive; (= *halagar*) to cajole

sofocación SF [1] suffocation
[2] = **sofoco 2**

sofocado ADJ **estar ~** (= *sin aire*) to be out of breath; (= *ahogándose*) to feel stifled; (= *abochornado*) to be hot and bothered

sofocante ADJ stifling, suffocating

sofocar ▸conjug 1g◂ Ⓐ VT [1] (= *ahogar*) [*calor*] to stifle; [*fuego, humo*] to suffocate; **este tiempo tan húmedo me sofoca** I find this humid weather stifling
[2] (= *apagar*) [+ *incendio*] to smother, put out; [+ *rebelión*] to crush, put down; [+ *epidemia*] to stamp out
[3] (= *enojar*) to anger, upset
[4] (= *avergonzar*) to embarrass
[5] (= *sonrojar*) to make ... blush
Ⓑ **sofocarse** VPR [1] (= *ahogarse*) (*por el esfuerzo*) to get out of breath; (*por el calor*) to suffocate

2 (= *sonrojarse*) to blush
3 (= *avergonzarse*) to get embarrassed
4 (= *enojarse*) to get angry, get upset; **no vale la pena que te sofoques** it's not worth upsetting yourself about it
5 (*CAm, Méx*) (= *preocuparse*) to worry, be anxious

Sófocles SM Sophocles

sofoco SM 1 (*por el calor*) stifling sensation; (*por la menopausia*) hot flush, hot flash (*EEUU*)
2 (= *azoro*) embarrassment; **pasar un ~** to have an embarrassing time
3 (= *ira*) anger, indignation

sofocón* SM **llevarse un ~** to get upset

sofoquina* SF 1 (= *calor*) stifling heat; **hace una ~** it's stifling
2 = **sofocón**

sofreír ▸conjug 3l◂ (*pp* **sofrito**) VT to fry lightly

sofrenada SF 1 (*repentino*) sudden check, sudden jerk on the reins
2 (*) (= *bronca*) ticking-off*

sofrenar ▸conjug 1a◂ VT 1 [+ *caballo*] to rein back sharply
2 (= *controlar*) to restrain
3 (*) (= *echar una bronca a*) to tick off*

sofrito Ⓐ PP *de* **sofreír**
Ⓑ SM *fried onion, garlic and tomato used as a base for cooking sauces and dishes*

sofrología SF sleep therapy

software ['sofwer] SM software ► **software de aplicación** application software ► **software del sistema** system software ► **software del usuario** user software ► **software integrado** integrated software

soga SF (= *cuerda*) (*gen*) rope, cord; [*de animal*] halter; [*del verdugo*] hangman's rope; ✦***MODISMOS*** **hacer ~** to lag behind; **dar ~ a algn** to make fun of sb; **echar la ~ tras el caldero** to chuck it all up*, throw in one's hand; **estar con la ~ al cuello** to be in deep water; **hablar de la ~ en casa del ahorcado** to say the wrong thing

sogatira SM tug of war

soguear ▸conjug 1a◂ VT 1 (*Andes, CAm, Cono Sur*) (= *atar*) to tie with a rope
2 (*Caribe*) (= *lazar*) to lasso
3 (*Caribe*) (= *domesticar*) to tame
4 (*Andes**) (= *burlarse de*) to make fun of

soguero ADJ (*Caribe*) tame

sois *ver* **ser**

soja SF soya; **semilla de ~** soya bean

sojuzgar ▸conjug 1h◂ VT (= *vencer*) to conquer; (= *subyugar*) to subjugate

sol¹ SM 1 (= *astro*) sun; **al ponerse el ~** at sunset; **al salir el ~** at sunrise; **de ~ a ~** from dawn to dusk; ✦***MODISMOS*** **arrimarse al ~ que más calienta** to keep in with the right people; **como un ~** (= *brillante*) as bright as a new pin; **salga el ~ por donde quiera** come what may; **ser un ~: María es un ~, siempre tan agradable** María is a darling, she's always so pleasant; **el niño es un ~** he's a lovely child ► **sol naciente** rising sun ► **sol poniente** setting sun ► **sol y luna** (*Caribe**) machete, cane knife ► **sol y sombra** brandy and anisette
2 (= *luz solar*) sun, sunshine; **entra mucho ~ en el comedor** the dining room gets a lot of sun *o* sunshine; **ayer tuvimos nueve horas de ~** we had nine hours of sunshine yesterday; **hay** *o* **hace ~** it is sunny, the sun is shining; **un día de ~** a sunny day; **estar al ~** to be in the sun; **mirar algo a contra ~** to look at sth against the light; **tomar el ~** to sunbathe; **tumbarse al ~** to lie in the sun; ✦***MODISMOS*** **hacía un ~ de justicia** the sun was blazing down; **no me deja ni a ~ ni a sombra** he doesn't give me a moment's peace ► **sol artificial** sunlamp
3 (*uso apelativo*) **¡~ mío, ven con mamá!** come with Mummy, darling *o* pet!*
4 (*Taur*) **localidades de ~** *the cheapest seats in a bullring with no shade*
5 (*Perú Fin*) Sol, *former monetary unit of Peru*

sol² SM (*Mús*) G ► **sol mayor** G major

solada SF sediment

solado SM tiling, tiled floor

solamente ADV = **sólo**

solana SF 1 (= *lugar soleado*) sunny spot, suntrap
2 (= *solario*) sun lounge, solarium

solanas* ADJ INV alone, all on one's own

solanera SF 1 (= *sol*) scorching sunshine
2 (*Med*) (= *quemadura*) sunburn; (= *insolación*) sunstroke

solano SM east wind

solapa SF 1 [*de chaqueta*] lapel; [*de sobre, libro, bolsillo*] flap
2 (= *pretexto*) pretext

solapadamente ADV slyly, in an underhand way, sneakily

solapado ADJ (= *furtivo*) sly, underhand; (= *evasivo*) evasive; (= *secreto*) undercover

solapamiento SM overlapping

solapante ADJ overlapping

solapar ▸conjug 1a◂ Ⓐ VT 1 (= *cubrir parcialmente*) to overlap
2 (= *encubrir*) to cover up, keep dark
Ⓑ VI to overlap (**con** with)
Ⓒ **solaparse** VPR to overlap; **se ha solapado** it has got covered up, it has got hidden underneath

solapo SM 1 (*Cos*) lapel
2 **a ~*** = **solapadamente**

solar¹ SM 1 (= *terreno*) (*gen*) lot, piece of land, site; (*en obras*) building site
2 (= *casa solariega*) ancestral home, family seat
3 (= *linaje*) lineage

solar² ▸conjug 1l◂ VT [+ *suelo*] to tile; [+ *zapatos*] to sole

solar³ ADJ solar, sun *antes de s*; **rayos ~es** solar rays

solariego ADJ 1 **casa solariega** family seat, ancestral home
2 (*Hist*) [*ascendencia*] ancient and noble; [*títulos*] manorial; **tierras solariegas** ancestral lands

solario SM, **solárium** SM solarium

solas: a ~ ADV alone, by oneself; **finalmente se quedó a ~ en su despacho** at last she was alone *o* on her own in her office; **lo hizo a ~** he did it (all) by himself; **volar a ~** to fly solo; **vuelo a ~** solo flight

solateras* ADJ INV alone, all on one's own

solaz SM (= *descanso*) recreation, relaxation; (= *consuelo*) solace

solazar ▸conjug 1f◂ Ⓐ VT (= *divertir*) to amuse, provide relaxation for; (= *consolar*) to console, comfort; (= *alegrar*) to cheer
Ⓑ **solazarse** VPR to enjoy o.s., relax

solazo* SM scorching sun

solazoso ADJ (= *que descansa*) restful; (= *que entretiene*) recreational, relaxing

soldada SF pay; (*Mil*) service pay

soldadera SF (*Méx*) camp follower

soldadesca SF 1 (= *profesión*) military profession, military
2 (*pey*) (= *soldados*) army rabble

soldadesco ADJ soldierly

soldadito SM ► **soldadito de plomo** tin soldier

soldado¹ SMF soldier; **una joven ~** a young woman soldier; **la tumba del Soldado Desconocido** the tomb of the Unknown Soldier ► **soldado de infantería** infantryman ► **soldado de marina** marine ► **soldado de plomo** tin soldier ► **soldado de primera** lance corporal ► **soldado raso** private, private first class (*EEUU*)

soldado² ADJ [*junta*] welded; **totalmente ~** welded throughout

soldador(a) Ⓐ SM/F (= *persona*) welder
Ⓑ SM (*Téc*) soldering iron

soldadura SF 1 [*de materiales*] solder
2 (= *acción*) (*con estaño*) soldering; (*sin estaño*) welding ► **soldadura autógena** welding
3 (= *juntura*) welded seam, weld

soldar ▸conjug 1l◂ Ⓐ VT 1 (*Téc*) (*con estaño*) to solder; (*fundiendo*) to weld
2 (= *juntar*) to join, unite
3 [+ *disputa*] to patch up
Ⓑ **soldarse** VPR [*huesos*] to knit, knit together

soleado ADJ sunny

solear ▸conjug 1a◂ VT (= *dejar al sol*) to put *o* leave in the sun; (= *blanquear*) to bleach

solecismo SM solecism

soledad SF 1 (= *falta de compañía*) (*voluntaria*) solitude; (*involuntaria*) loneliness, lonesomeness (*EEUU*); **le gusta trabajar en la ~ de su habitación** he likes working in the solitude of his room; **tengo miedo a la ~** I have a fear of loneliness; **la ~ le deprime** being alone makes him feel depressed
2 **soledades** (*liter*) solitary place *sing*; **nadie habitaba aquellas ~es** no-one lived in that solitary place

solejar SM = **solana**

solemne ADJ 1 (= *serio*) solemn
2 (*) (= *enorme*) [*mentira*] downright; [*tontería*] utter; [*error*] complete, terrible

solemnemente ADV solemnly

solemnidad SF 1 [*de persona*] solemnity
2 [*de acontecimiento*] (= *majestuosidad*) impressiveness; (= *dignidad*) solemnity
3 (= *ceremonia*) solemn ceremony; **~es** solemnities
4 **solemnidades** (= *formalismos*) formalities, bureaucratic formalities
5 **pobre de ~** miserably poor, penniless

solemnización SF solemnization, celebration

solemnizar ▸conjug 1f◂ VT to solemnize, celebrate

solenoide SM solenoid

soler ▸conjug 2h; defectivo◂ VI 1 (= *acostumbrar*) 1·1 (*en presente*) **suele pasar por aquí** he usually comes this way; — **¿bebió alcohol? —pues no suele** "did he drink?" — "well, he doesn't usually"; **como se suele hacer por estas fechas** as is nor-

➤ LENGUA Y USO: **soler 1** 53.1

mal *o* customary at this time of the year
1·2 (*en pasado*) **solíamos ir todos los años a la playa** we used to go to the beach every year
2 (*Cono Sur*) (= *ocurrir*) to occur rarely, happen only occasionally; → ACOSTUMBRAR

solera SF 1 (= *tradición*) tradition; **éste es país de ~ celta** this is a country with a long-established Celtic tradition; **vino de ~** vintage wine; **es un barrio con ~** it is a typically Spanish *etc* quarter; **es de ~ de médicos** he comes from a line of doctors
2 (= *objeto*) (*de apoyo*) prop, support; (*para saltar*) plinth
3 [*de cuneta*] bottom
4 (= *piedra de molino*) lower millstone
5 (*Méx*) (= *baldosa*) flagstone
6 (*Cono Sur*) [*de acera*] kerb, curb (*EEUU*)

> **SOLERA**
> *Sherry does not have a specific vintage since it is a mixture of the vintages from different years; the* **solera** *method is used to ensure uniformity of quality. In the* **bodega** *(cellar) the casks are arranged in horizontal rows, with the bottom row, known as the* **solera**, *containing the oldest wine. When part of this is bottled, the casks are replenished with wine from the row immediately above, which in turn is refilled with wine from the next row, and so on.*
> ⇨ *See also* JEREZ

solería SF flooring
soleta SF 1 (*Cos*) patch, darn
2 (†) (= *mujer*) shameless woman
3 (*) **dar ~ a algn** to chuck sb out; **tomar ~** to beat it*; **dejar a algn en ~s** (*Andes*) to leave sb penniless
4 (*Méx Culin*) wafer, ladyfinger
solevantamiento SM 1 [*de objeto*] pushing up, raising
2 (*Pol*) rising
solevantar ▸conjug 1a◂ VT 1 [+ *objeto*] to push up, raise
2 (*Pol*) to rouse, stir up
solfa SF 1 (*Mús*) (= *solfeo*) sol-fa; (= *signos*) musical notation
2 (*) (= *paliza*) thrashing
3 ✦*MODISMO* **poner a algn en ~** to make sb look ridiculous
solfear ▸conjug 1a◂ VT 1 (*Mús*) to sol-fa
2 (*) (= *zurrar*) to thrash
3 (*) (= *echar una bronca a*) to tick off*
4 (†) (*Cono Sur*) (= *hurtar*) to nick‡, swipe‡
solfeo SM 1 (*Mús*) sol-fa, singing of scales, voice practice; **clase de ~** singing lesson
2 (*) (= *paliza*) thrashing; (= *reprensión*) ticking-off*
solicitación SF [*de beca, ayuda*] requesting; [*de votos*] canvassing
solicitado ADJ **estar muy ~** to be in great demand, be much sought after; **está muy solicitado por las chicas** all the girls are after him
solicitante SMF applicant
solicitar ▸conjug 1a◂ VT 1 (= *pedir*) [+ *permiso, apoyo*] to ask for, seek; [+ *visto bueno*] to seek; [+ *empleo, puesto*] to apply for; [+ *votos, opiniones*] to canvass; [+ *datos, información*] to ask for, request (*más frm*); **~ algo a algn** to ask sb for sth
2 [+ *atención, tb Fís*] to attract
3 (= *perseguir*) [+ *persona*] to pursue, try to attract; [+ *mujer*] to court
solícito ADJ (= *diligente*) solicitous (**por** about, for); (= *atento*) attentive; (= *servicial*) obliging
solicitud SF 1 (= *petición*) (*gen*) request; (*para puesto, beca, permiso*) application; **presenté** *o* **entregué la ~ para el trabajo** I submitted the application for the job; **denegar** *o* **rechazar una ~** to reject an application; **a ~** (*frm*) on request ► **solicitud de extradición** request *o* application for extradition ► **solicitud de pago** (*Com*) demand note
2 (= *impreso*) application form; **rellene la ~ en letra mayúscula** fill in the application (form) in block capitals
3 (*frm*) (= *atención*) **el recepcionista atendió con ~ nuestras reclamaciones** the receptionist was very solicitous in dealing with our complaints; **cuidaba con ~ a su nieto enfermo** she looked after her sick grandson with great devotion
sólidamente ADV solidly
solidariamente ADV jointly, mutually
solidaridad SF solidarity; **por ~ con** out of solidarity with
solidario ADJ 1 (= *humanitario*) caring; **Luis es muy ~** Luis is a very caring person; **vivimos en un mundo poco ~** we live in an uncaring world, we live in a world where it's every man for himself; **un acto ~** an act of solidarity; **~ con algo/algn**: **se ha mostrado muy ~ con nuestra causa** he has been very sympathetic to our cause, he has shown a lot of solidarity with our cause; **hacerse ~ con algo/algn** to declare one's solidarity with sth/sb; **~ de algo** (*frm*): **hacerse ~ de una opinión** to echo an opinion
2 (*Jur*) [*compromiso*] mutually binding, shared in common; [*participación*] joint, common; [*firmante, participante*] jointly liable; **responsabilidad solidaria** joint liability
solidarizarse ▸conjug 1f◂ VPR **~ con** to declare one's support for; **me solidarizo con esa opinión** I share that view
solideo SM calotte, skullcap
solidez SF (= *firmeza*) solidity; (= *dureza*) hardness
solidificación SF solidification, hardening
solidificar ▸conjug 1g◂ Ⓐ VT to solidify, harden
Ⓑ **solidificarse** VPR to solidify, harden
sólido Ⓐ ADJ 1 [*objeto*] (= *compacto*) solid; (= *duro*) hard
2 (*Téc*) (= *firme*) solidly made; (= *bien construido*) well built; [*zapatos*] stout, strong; [*color*] fast
3 (= *seguro*) [*argumento*] solid, sound; [*base, principio*] sound
Ⓑ SM solid
soliloquiar ▸conjug 1b◂ VI to soliloquize, talk to oneself
soliloquio SM soliloquy, monologue
solimán SM 1 (*Quím*) corrosive sublimate
2 (= *veneno*) poison
solio SM throne
solipsismo SM solipsism
solista SMF soloist
solitaria SF tapeworm
solitario/a Ⓐ ADJ 1 [*persona, vida*] solitary, lonely, lonesome (*EEUU*); **vivir ~** to live alone *o* on one's own
2 [*lugar*] lonely, desolate; **a esa hora la calle está solitaria** at that hour the street is deserted *o* empty
Ⓑ SM/F (= *recluso*) recluse; (= *ermitaño*) hermit
Ⓒ SM 1 (*Naipes*) solitaire
2 (= *diamante*) solitaire
3 **en ~** alone, on one's own; **vuelta al mundo en ~** solo trip around the world; **tocar en ~** to play solo
solito* ADJ **estar ~** to be all alone, be all on one's own
sólito ADJ usual, customary
soliviantado ADJ rebellious
soliviantar ▸conjug 1a◂ VT 1 (= *amotinar*) to stir up, rouse, rouse to revolt
2 (= *enojar*) to anger
3 (= *sacar de quicio*) to exasperate
4 (= *inquietar*) to worry; **le tienen soliviantado los celos** he is eaten up with jealousy
5 (= *hacer sentir ansias*) to fill with longing
6 (= *dar esperanzas a*) to buoy up with false hopes; **anda soliviantado con el proyecto** he has tremendous hopes for the scheme
soliviar ▸conjug 1b◂ Ⓐ VT to lift, push up
Ⓑ **soliviarse** VPR to half rise, partly get up
solla SF plaice
sollamar ▸conjug 1a◂ VT to scorch, singe
sollastre SM rogue, villain
sollo SM sturgeon
sollozar ▸conjug 1f◂ VI to sob
sollozo SM sob; **decir algo entre ~s** to sob sth
solo[1] Ⓐ ADJ 1 (= *sin compañía*) alone, on one's own; **pasa los días ~ en su cuarto** he spends the days alone *o* on his own in his room; **iré ~** I'll go alone *o* on my own; **dejar ~ a algn** to leave sb alone; **me quedé ~** I was left alone; **habla ~** he talks to himself; **se quedó ~ a los siete años** he was left an orphan *o* alone in the world at seven; ✦*MODISMOS* **estar más ~ que la una*** to be all on one's own; **es tonto como él ~** he's as stupid as they come; **lo hace como él ~** he does it as no one else can; **se queda ~ contando mentiras** he's as good a liar as you'll find; ✦*REFRÁN* **más vale estar ~ que mal acompañado** it's better to be on your own than in bad company
2 (= *solitario*) lonely; **me siento muy ~** I feel very lonely
3 (= *único*) **su sola preocupación es ganar dinero** his one *o* only concern is to make money; **con esta sola condición** on this one condition; **hay una sola dificultad** there is only *o* just one problem; **no hubo ni una sola objeción** there was not a single objection
4 (= *sin acompañamiento*) [*café, té*] black; [*whisky, vodka, ron*] straight, neat; **tendremos que comer pan ~** we shall have to eat plain bread
5 (*Mús*) solo; **cantar ~** to sing solo
Ⓑ SM 1 (*Mús*) solo; **un ~ de guitarra** a guitar solo; **un ~ para tenor** a tenor solo
2 (= *café*) black coffee
3 (*Naipes*) solitaire, patience
4 (*Cono Sur*) (= *lata*) tedious conversation
sólo ADV, **solo**[2] ADV (= *únicamente*) only; (= *exclusivamente*) solely, merely, just; **~ quiero verlo** I only *o* just want to see it; **es ~ un teniente** he's only a lieutenant, he's a mere lieutenant; **no ~ A sino también B** not only

A but also B; **~ con apretar un botón** at the touch of a button; **me parece bien ~ que no tengo tiempo** that's fine, only *o* but I don't have the time; **ven aunque ~ sea para media hora** come even if it's just for half an hour; **con ~ que sepas tocar algunas notas** even if you only know how to play a few notes; **~ con que estudies dos horas diarias** by studying for as little as two hours a day; **tan ~** only, just; **~ que ...** except that ...

solomillo SM sirloin steak

solón SM (*Caribe*) scorching heat, very strong sunlight

solsticio SM solstice ► **solsticio de invierno** winter solstice ► **solsticio de verano** summer solstice

soltar ▸conjug 1l◂ Ⓐ VT [1] (= *dejar de agarrar*) to let go of; (= *dejar caer*) to drop; **soltó mi mano** he let go of my hand; **¡suéltenme!** let go of me!, let me go!; **no sueltes la cuerda** don't let go of the rope; **el gato me soltó el ratón en los pies** the cat dropped the mouse at my feet; **dejó de escribir y soltó el bolígrafo** she stopped writing and put down her Biro
[2] [+ *amarras*] to cast off; [+ *nudo, cinturón*] (= *quitar*) to untie, undo; (= *aflojar*) to loosen; **ve soltando cuerda mientras bajas** pay the rope out gradually as you descend
[3] (*Aut*) [+ *embrague*] to let out, release, disengage (*frm*); [+ *freno*] to release
[4] (= *dejar libre*) [+ *preso, animal*] to release, set free; [+ *agua*] to let out, run off; **soltó una paloma blanca en señal de paz** he released a white dove as a token of peace
[5] (= *emitir*) [+ *gas, olor*] to give off; [+ *grito*] to let out; **suelta vapores peligrosos** it gives off dangerous fumes; **solté un suspiro de alivio** I let out *o* heaved a sigh of relief; **~ una carcajada** to burst out laughing; **~ un estornudo** to sneeze; **~ un suspiro** to sigh
[6] (= *asestar*) **~ un golpe** to deal a blow; **le soltó un puñetazo** she hit him
[7] (*al hablar*) [+ *noticia*] to break; [+ *indirecta*] to drop; [+ *blasfemia*] to come out with, let fly; **les volvió a ~ el mismo sermón** he gave them the lecture all over again; **¡suéltalo ya!** out with it!, spit it out!*; **soltó un par de palabrotas** he came out with a couple of rude words, he let fly a couple of obscenities; ✦***MODISMO*** **~ cuatro verdades a algn** to tell sb a few home truths
[8] (*) (= *perder*) [+ *puesto, privilegio*] to give up; [+ *dinero*] to cough up*; **no quiere ~ el puesto por nada del mundo** he won't give up the job for anything in the world
[9] [*serpiente*] [+ *piel*] to shed
[10] (= *resolver*) [+ *dificultad*] to solve; [+ *duda*] to resolve; [+ *objeción*] to satisfy, deal with
[11] (*Andes*) (= *ceder*) to cede, give, hand over
Ⓑ **soltarse** VPR [1] (= *liberarse*) **que no se vaya a ~ el perro** don't let the dog get out *o* get loose; **logró ~se y pedir ayuda** he managed to free himself *o* get free and call for help
[2] (= *desprenderse*) to come off; (= *aflojarse*) to come loose, work loose; **~se los botones** to undo one's buttons; **~se el pelo** to let one's hair down
[3] (= *deshacerse*) [*cordón, nudo*] to come undone, come untied; [*costura*] to come unstitched
[4] (= *desenvolverse*) (*con actividad*) to become expert; (*con idioma*) to become fluent; **~se a andar/hablar** to start walking/talking
[5] (= *independizarse*) to achieve one's independence, win freedom
[6] (= *desmandarse*) to lose control of o.s.; **~se a su gusto** to let off steam, let fly
[7] (*) **~se con**: **~se con una idea absurda** to come up with a silly idea; **~se con una contribución de 50 dólares** to come up with a 50-dollar contribution; **por fin se soltó con algunos peniques** he eventually parted with a few coppers

solterear ▸conjug 1a◂ VI (*Cono Sur*) to stay single

soltería SF (*gen*) single state, unmarried state; [*de hombre*] bachelorhood; [*de mujer*] spinsterhood; **está muy bien en su ~** she's perfectly happy being single

soltero/a Ⓐ ADJ single, unmarried; **está soltera** she's single, she's unmarried; **madre soltera** single *o* unmarried mother
Ⓑ SM/F single *o* unmarried man/woman, bachelor/spinster; **apellido de soltera** maiden name; **la señora de García, Rodríguez de soltera** Mrs García, née Rodríguez

solterón/ona SM/F (= *hombre*) confirmed bachelor; (= *mujer*) spinster; (*pey*) old maid; **tía ~** maiden aunt

soltura SF [1] (*al hablar*) fluency, ease; **habla árabe con ~** he speaks Arabic fluently
[2] (= *flojedad*) [*de cuerda*] slackness; [*de pieza, tornillo*] looseness; [*de brazos, piernas*] agility, nimbleness
[3] (*Med*) (*tb* **~ de vientre**) looseness of the bowels, diarrhoea, diarrhea (*EEUU*)
[4] (*pey*) (= *desvergüenza*) shamelessness

solubilidad SF solubility

soluble ADJ [1] (*Quím*) soluble; **~ en agua** water-soluble, soluble in water
[2] [*problema*] solvable, that can be solved

solución SF [1] (*Quím*) solution
[2] (= *respuesta*) [*de problema*] solution, answer (**a** to); [*de crucigrama, pregunta*] answer (**de** to); **esto no tiene ~** there's no answer to this, there's no solution to this one ► **solución final** final solution ► **solución salomónica** compromise solution
[3] (*Teat*) climax, dénouement
[4] ► **solución de continuidad** break in continuity, interruption

solucionar ▸conjug 1a◂ VT [1] [+ *problema*] to solve; **un problema sin ~** an unsolved problem
[2] (= *decidir*) to resolve, settle

solucionista SMF solver

solvencia SF [1] (*Fin*) (= *estado*) solvency; (= *acción*) settlement, payment
[2] (= *fiabilidad*) reliability; **de toda ~ moral** completely trustworthy; **fuentes de toda ~** completely reliable sources ► **solvencia moral** good character
[3] (= *reputación*) solid reputation
[4] (= *aptitud*) ability, competence

solventar ▸conjug 1a◂ VT [1] [+ *deuda*] to settle, pay
[2] (= *solucionar*) [+ *dificultad*] to resolve; [+ *asunto*] to settle

solvente Ⓐ ADJ [1] (*Fin*) solvent, free of debt
[2] (= *fiable*) [*persona*] reliable, trustworthy; [*fuente*] reliable
[3] (= *decente*) respectable, worthy
[4] (= *hábil*) able
Ⓑ SM (*Quím*) solvent

solysombra* SM brandy and anisette

somalí ADJ, SMF Somali

Somalia SF Somalia

somanta SF beating, thrashing

somantar ▸conjug 1a◂ VT to beat, thrash

somatada SF (*CAm*) blow, punch

somatar ▸conjug 1a◂ (*CAm*) Ⓐ VT [1] [+ *persona*] (= *zurrar*) to beat, thrash; (= *pegar*) to punch
[2] (= *vender*) to sell off cheap
Ⓑ **somatarse** VPR to fall and hurt o.s., knock o.s. about badly

somatén SM [1] (= *alarma*) alarm; **tocar a ~** to sound the alarm
[2] (*) (= *jaleo*) uproar, confusion

somático ADJ somatic

somatizar ▸conjug 1f◂ VT [1] (= *exteriorizar*) to externalize, express externally
[2] (= *caracterizar*) to characterize

somatón SM (*CAm*) = **somatada**

sombra SF [1] (*proyectada por un objeto*) shadow; **sólo vi una ~** I only saw a shadow; **Juan se ha convertido en tu ~** Juan follows you round like your shadow; **dar** *o* **hacer ~** to cast a shadow; **el ciprés da** *o* **hace una ~ alargada** cypress trees cast a long shadow; **un árbol que da** *o* **hace ~** a shady tree; **no quiere que otros le hagan ~** he doesn't want to be overshadowed by anybody else; ✦***MODISMO*** **no se fía ni de su ~** he doesn't trust a soul ► **sombra de ojos** eyeshadow ► **sombras chinescas** shadow play *sing*, pantomime *sing*
[2] (= *zona sin sol*) shade; **ven, siéntate aquí a la ~** come and sit here in the shade; **luz y ~** light and shade; **se sentó a la ~ del olivo** she sat in the shade of the olive tree; **medró a la ~ del presidente** she flourished under the protection of the president; ✦***MODISMOS*** **a la ~*** (= *en prisión*) in the clink*, inside*; **permanecer** *o* **quedarse en la ~** to stay in the background, remain on the sidelines
[3] (= *rastro*) shadow; **sin ~ de duda** without a shadow of a doubt; **no es ni ~ de lo que era** he's a shadow of his former self; **sin ~ de avaricia** without a trace of greed; **no tiene ni ~ de talento** he hasn't the least bit of talent; **tiene una ~ de parecido con su tío** he has a faint resemblance to his uncle
[4] (= *suerte*) luck; **¡qué mala ~!** how unlucky!, what bad luck!; **esta vez he tenido muy buena ~** I was very lucky this time
[5] (= *gracia*) **tiene muy buena ~ para contar chistes** he's got a knack *o* gift for telling jokes, he's very funny telling jokes; **tener mala ~** to have a bad sense of humour
[6] (= *mancha*) (*lit*) dark patch, stain; (*fig*) stain, blot; **es una ~ en su carácter** it is a stain *o* blot on his character
[7] (= *fantasma*) shade, ghost
[8] (*Arte*) shade
[9] (*Boxeo*) shadow-boxing; **hacer ~** to shadow-box
[10] (*CAm, Cono Sur*) (= *quitasol*) parasol, sunshade
[11] (*CAm, Méx*) (= *toldo*) awning; (= *pórtico*) porch
[12] (*CAm, Cono Sur*) (*para escribir*) guidelines *pl*
[13] (†) **sombras** (= *oscuridad*) darkness *sing*, obscurity *sing*; (= *ignorancia*) ignorance *sing*; (= *pesimismo*) sombreness *sing*

sombraje SM, **sombrajo** SM shelter from the sun; **hacer ~s** to get in the light

sombreado Ⓐ ADJ shady
Ⓑ SM (*Arte*) shading

sombreador SM ► **sombreador de ojos** eyeshadow

sombrear ▸conjug 1a◂ VT [1] (= *dar sombra*) to shade
[2] (*Arte*) to shade
[3] (= *maquillar*) to put eyeshadow on

sombrerera SF [1] (= *caja*) hatbox
[2] (*Andes, Caribe*) (= *perchero*) hat stand; *ver tb* **sombrerero**

sombrerería SF [1] (= *sombreros*) hats *pl*, millinery
[2] (= *tienda*) hat shop
[3] (= *fábrica*) hat factory

sombrerero/a Ⓐ SM/F (= *artesano*) (*para sombreros de hombre*) hatter; (*para sombreros de mujer*) milliner; *ver tb* **sombrerera**
Ⓑ SM (*Andes, Cono Sur*) (= *perchero*) hatstand

sombrerete SM [1] (= *sombrero*) little hat
[2] [*de seta*] cap
[3] (*Téc*) [*de carburador*] bonnet; (= *cubo de rueda*) cap; [*de chimenea*] cowl

sombrero SM [1] (= *gorro*) hat; ✦***MODISMO*** **quitarse el ~ ante algo** to take off one's hat to sth ► **sombrero apuntado** cocked hat ► **sombrero de ala ancha** wide-brimmed hat, broad-brimmed hat ► **sombrero de copa** top hat ► **sombrero de jipijapa** Panama hat ► **sombrero de paja** straw hat ► **sombrero de pelo** (*LAm*) top hat ► **sombrero de tres picos** cocked hat, three-cornered hat ► **sombrero flexible** soft hat, trilby, fedora (*EEUU*) ► **sombrero gacho** slouch hat ► **sombrero hongo** bowler, bowler hat, derby (*EEUU*) ► **sombrero safari** safari hat ► **sombrero tejano** stetson, ten-gallon hat
[2] (*Bot*) cap

sombríamente ADV sombrely, somberly (*EEUU*)

sombrilla SF parasol, sunshade; ✦***MODISMO*** **me vale ~** (*Méx**) I couldn't care less*

sombrío Ⓐ ADJ [1] (= *con sombra*) shaded
[2] (= *triste*) [*lugar*] sombre, somber (*EEUU*), gloomy, dismal; [*persona, perspectiva*] gloomy
Ⓑ SM (*Méx*) shady place

someramente ADV superficially

somero ADJ [1] (= *a poca profundidad*) shallow
[2] (= *poco detallado*) superficial, summary (*frm*)

someter ▸conjug 2a◂ Ⓐ VT [1] (= *dominar*) [+ *territorio, población*] to subjugate; [+ *rebeldes*] to subdue, put down; [+ *asaltante*] to overpower, overcome; **ni entre cuatro hombres lo pudieron ~** even four men were not enough to overpower *o* overcome him
[2] (= *subordinar*) **sometió sus intereses a los de su pueblo** he put the interests of the people before his own, he subordinated his interests to those of the people (*frm*); **~ su opinión a la de otros** to put the opinion of others above one's own
[3] **~ a** [3·1] (= *exponer*) [+ *represión, tortura, interrogatorio*] to subject to; **cuando se somete a elevadas temperaturas** when it is subjected to high temperatures; **hay que ~ a examen todas las ideas establecidas** all established ideas should be subjected to scrutiny; **lo tiene sometido a su entera voluntad** he is entirely subject to her will; **~án las propuestas a un amplio debate** the proposals will be widely debated; **han sometido a referéndum su ingreso en la UE** they have held a referendum on joining the EU; **~ algo/a algn a prueba** to put sth/sb to the test; **vamos a ~ nuestra hipótesis a prueba** we are going to put our hypothesis to the test; **la princesa sometió a sus pretendientes a una prueba** the princess made her suitors undergo a test; **~ algo a votación** to put sth to the vote
[3·2] (= *entregar*) to submit sth to; **~á el acuerdo a la aprobación de los ministros** he will submit the agreement for the approval of the ministers; **~ una obra a la censura** to submit a work to the censor
Ⓑ **someterse** VPR [1] (= *aceptar*) **~se a** [+ *disciplina, autoridad*] to submit to; [+ *normas*] to comply with; **me someto a la voluntad de Dios** I submit to God's will; **tienen que ~se a las normas urbanísticas** they must comply with urban development regulations; **~se a la mayoría** to give way to the majority; **~se a la opinión de algn** to bow to sb's opinion
[2] (= *exponerse*) **~se a** [+ *desprecio, humillación*] to subject o.s. to; [+ *operación, prueba, tratamiento*] to undergo; **me niego a ~me a tal suplicio** I refuse to subject myself to such an ordeal; **deberá ~se a un intenso entrenamiento** she will have to undergo intensive training

sometico ADJ (*Andes*), **sometido** ADJ (*Andes, CAm*) = **entrometido**

sometimiento SM [1] (= *dominación*) [*de un pueblo*] subjugation; **tras el ~ de los celtas, los romanos ...** after the subjugation of the Celts, the Romans ...; **han conseguido el ~ de los rebeldes** they have managed to subdue the rebels
[2] (= *sumisión*) [2·1] (*por la fuerza*) subjection (**a** to); **siglos de ~ al patriarcado** centuries of subjection to *o* being subject to patriarchy
[2·2] (*voluntariamente*) (*a la autoridad*) submission (**a** to); (*a la ley*) compliance (**a** with); **rechazan el ~ a la autoridad** they refuse to submit to *o* bow to authority
[3] (= *exposición*) **como consecuencia de su ~ a estímulos externos** as a result of being subjected to external stimuli
[4] (= *entrega*) [*de propuesta*] submission (**a** to); **tras pocos días de su ~ a la aprobación del pleno** a few days after its submission to the plenary session for approval; **tras el ~ de la propuesta a votación** after the proposal was put to the vote

somier [so'mjer] SM (*pl* **somiers, somieres** [so'mjer]) (*sin concretar tipo*) bed base; (*con muelles*) springs *pl*; (*con láminas de madera*) slats *pl*

somnambulismo SM sleepwalking, somnambulism (*frm*)

somnámbulo/a SM/F sleepwalker, somnambulist (*frm*)

somnífero Ⓐ ADJ sleep-inducing
Ⓑ SM sleeping pill

somnílocuo/a Ⓐ ADJ given to talking in one's sleep
Ⓑ SM/F person who talks in his *o* her sleep

somnolencia SF sleepiness, drowsiness

somnolento ADJ, **somnoliento** ADJ sleepy, drowsy

somorgujar ▸conjug 1a◂ Ⓐ VT to duck
Ⓑ **somorgujarse** VPR to dive, plunge (**en** into)

somormujo SM grebe ► **somormujo menor** dabchick

somos *ver* **ser**

sompopo SM (*El Salvador*) yellow ant

son[1] SM [1] (*Mús*) (= *sonido*) sound; (= *sonido agradable*) pleasant sound; **al ~ de** to the sound of; **a los ~es de la marcha nupcial** to the strains of the wedding march
[2] (= *rumor*) rumour, rumor (*EEUU*); **corre el ~ de que ...** there is a rumour *o* (*EEUU*) rumor going round that ...
[3] (= *estilo*) manner, style; **¿a qué ~?** ◊ **¿a ~ de qué?** why on earth?; **en ~ de** as, like; **en ~ de broma** as *o* for a joke; **en ~ de paz** in peace; **en ~ de guerra** in a warlike fashion; **no vienen en ~ de protesta** they haven't come with the idea of complaining; **por este ~** in this way; **sin ~** for no reason at all
[4] (*LAm*) *Afro-Cuban dance and tune* ► **son huasteco** (*Méx*) *folk song from Veracruz*; *ver* **bailar A1**

son[2] *ver* **ser**

sonado ADJ [1] (= *comentado*) [*éxito, noticia*] much talked-about; [*escándalo, estafa*] notorious; **ha sido un divorcio muy ~** their divorce has caused a great stir, it has been a much talked-about divorce; **el escándalo fue muy ~** the scandal was much talked about, it was a notorious scandal; **hacer una que sea sonada*** to kick up a stink*
[2] (*) (= *chiflado*) **estar ~** to be crazy; (*Boxeo*) to be punch drunk

sonaja SF [1] (= *campanilla*) little bell
[2] **sonajas** (*para niño*) rattle *sing*

sonajera SF (*Cono Sur*), **sonajero** SM rattle

sonambulismo SM sleepwalking, somnambulism (*frm*)

sonámbulo/a SM/F sleepwalker, somnambulist (*frm*)

sonanta‡ SF guitar

sonante ADJ *ver* **contante**

sonar[1] ▸conjug 1l◂ Ⓐ VI [1] (= *producir sonido*) [1·1] [*campana, teléfono, timbre*] to ring; [*aparato electrónico*] to beep, bleep; **este timbre no suena** this bell doesn't work *o* ring; **está sonando el busca** the pager is beeping *o* bleeping; **el reloj de la iglesia no sonó** the church clock did not chime; **acaban de ~ las diez** it has just struck ten; **hacer ~** [+ *alarma, sirena*] to sound; [+ *campanilla, timbre*] to ring; [+ *trompeta, flauta*] to play; **hace ~ su vieja gaita en las grandes ocasiones** he plays his old bagpipes on special occasions; **haz ~ el claxon** blow *o* beep the horn
[1·2] [*alarma, sirena*] to go off; **a las seis sonó el despertador** the alarm clock went off at six
[1·3] [*máquina, aparato*] to make a noise; [*música*] to play; **¡cómo suena este frigorífico!** what a noise this fridge makes!; **~on tres disparos** three shots were heard; **empezó a ~ el himno nacional** the national anthem started to play; **le sonaban las tripas** his stomach was rumbling; ✦***MODISMO*** **ni ~ ni tronar** not to count; *ver tb* **flauta A1**, **río A1**
[2] (*Ling*) [*fonema, letra*] to be pronounced; [*frase, palabra*] to sound; **la h de "hombre" no suena** the h in "hombre" is not pronounced *o* is silent; **escríbelo tal como sue-**

na write it as it sounds
[3] (= *parecer por el sonido*) to sound; **sonaba extraño viniendo de él** it sounded strange coming from him; **cantan en inglés y suenan muy bien** they sing in English and they sound very good; **ese título suena bien** that sounds like a good title; **~ a** to sound like; **suena a metálico** it sounds like metal; **eso me suena a excusa** that sounds like an excuse to me; **sus palabras sonaban a falso** his words rang *o* sounded false; **~ a hueco** to sound hollow; ✦***MODISMOS*** **así como suena** just like that; **le dijo que se fuera, así como suena** he told him to go, just like that; **se llama Anastasio, así como suena** he's called Anastasio, believe it or not; **me suena a chino** it sounds double Dutch to me
[4] (= *ser conocido*) to sound familiar, ring a bell*; **¿no te suena el nombre?** isn't the name familiar?, doesn't the name sound familiar *o* ring a bell?; **a mí su cara no me suena de nada** his face isn't at all familiar to me *o* doesn't look at all familiar to me
[5] (= *mencionarse*) **su nombre suena constantemente en relación con este asunto** her name is always coming up *o* being mentioned in connection with this affair; **no quiere que suene su nombre** he doesn't want his name mentioned
[6] (*Andes, Cono Sur**) (= *fracasar*) to come to grief*; **sonamos en la prueba de francés** we came to grief in the French test*; **ahora sí que sonamos** now we're really in trouble
[7] (*Cono Sur**) (= *morirse*) to kick the bucket*, peg out*
[8] (*Cono Sur**) (= *estropearse*) to pack up*
[9] **hacer ~** (*Cono Sur**) (*gen*) to wreck; [+ *dinero*] to blow*
[10] **hacer ~ a algn** (*Cono Sur**) (= *derrotar*) to thrash sb*; (= *castigar*) to do sb‡; (= *suspender*) to fail, flunk (*EEUU**); **lo van a hacer ~ si lo pillan** he'll get done for it if they catch him‡
Ⓑ VT [1] (= *hacer sonar*) [+ *campanilla*] to ring; [+ *trompeta*] to play; [+ *alarma, sirena*] to sound
[2] **~ la nariz a algn** to blow sb's nose
[3] (*Méx, Ven**) (= *pegar*) to clobber*
[4] (*Méx, Ven**) (= *ganar*) to thrash*
Ⓒ **sonarse** VPR (*tb* **~se los mocos** *o* **la nariz**) to blow one's nose

sonar² SM, **sónar** SM sonar

sonata SF sonata

sonda SF [1] (= *acción*) sounding
[2] (*Med*) probe
[3] (*Náut*) lead ► **sonda acústica** echo sounder ► **sonda espacial** space probe
[4] (*Téc*) bore, drill

sondaje SM (*Náut*) sounding; (*Téc*) boring, drilling; **conversaciones de ~** exploratory talks

sondar ▸conjug 1a◂ VT, **sondear** ▸conjug 1a◂ VT [1] (*Med*) to probe
[2] (*Náut*) to sound, take soundings of
[3] (*Téc*) to bore, bore into, drill
[4] (= *investigar*) [+ *misterio*] to fathom; [+ *persona, intenciones*] to sound out; **sondear a la opinión pública** to sound out public opinion; **sondear el terreno** to spy out the land, see how the land lies

sondeo SM [1] (*Med, Náut*) sounding
[2] (*Téc*) drilling
[3] (*Pol*) (= *encuesta*) poll; (= *contacto*) feeler, approach; **~ realizado a la salida de las urnas** exit poll ► **sondeo de audiencia** audience research ► **sondeo de la opinión pública** public opinion poll, Gallup Poll ► **sondeo de opinión** opinion poll ► **sondeo telefónico** telephone survey

sonería SF chimes *pl*

soneto SM sonnet

songa SF [1] (*Caribe*) (= *sarcasmo*) sarcasm, irony
[2] (*Méx*) (= *grosería*) dirty joke, vulgar remark
[3] **a la ~ (~)** (*Andes, CAm, Cono Sur**) slyly, underhandedly

songo Ⓐ ADJ (*Andes, Méx*) [1] (*) (= *estúpido*) stupid, thick*
[2] (*) (= *taimado*) sly, crafty
Ⓑ SM (*Andes*) buzz, hum

sónico ADJ sonic, sound *antes de s*

sonidista SMF sound engineer

sonido SM sound; **~ envolvente** surround sound

soniquete SM = **sonsonete 2**

sonista SMF sound engineer, sound recordist

sonitono SM (*Telec*) true tone

sonoboya SF sonar buoy

sonómetro SM sound level meter

sonoridad SF sonority

sonorización SF [1] [*de película*] adding of the soundtrack
[2] [*de local*] installation of a sound system
[3] (*Ling*) voicing

sonorizar ▸conjug 1f◂ Ⓐ VT [1] [+ *película*] to add the sound track to
[2] [+ *local*] to install a sound system in
[3] (*Ling*) to voice
Ⓑ **sonorizarse** VPR (*Ling*) to voice, become voiced

sonoro ADJ [1] (= *ruidoso*) [*cavidad*] resonant; [*voz*] rich, sonorous; [*poesía*] sonorous; [*cueva*] echoing; [*beso*] loud
[2] (*Ling*) voiced
[3] **banda sonora** sound track; **efectos ~s** sound effects

sonotone SM hearing aid

sonreír ▸conjug 3l◂ Ⓐ VI [1] [*persona*] to smile; **~ a algn** to smile at sb; **el chiste no le hizo ni ~** she didn't even smile at the joke; **~ forzadamente** to force a smile
[2] (= *favorecer*) **le sonríe la fortuna** fortune smiles (up)on him; **el porvenir le sonríe** he has a bright future ahead of him
Ⓑ **sonreírse** VPR to smile

sonría *etc ver* **sonreír**

sonriente ADJ smiling

sonrisa SF smile; **~ amarga** wry smile; **~ forzada** forced smile; **no perder la ~** to keep smiling; **una ~ de oreja a oreja** an ear-to-ear grin

sonrojante ADJ embarrassing

sonrojar ▸conjug 1a◂ Ⓐ VT **~ a algn** to make sb blush
Ⓑ **sonrojarse** VPR to blush (**de** at)

sonrojo SM [1] (= *rubor*) blush
[2] (= *improperio*) offensive word, embarrassing remark (*that brings a blush*)

sonrosado ADJ rosy, pink

sonrosarse ▸conjug 1a◂ VPR to turn pink

sonsacar ▸conjug 1g◂ VT to wheedle, coax; **~ a algn** to pump sb for information; **~ un secreto a algn** to worm a secret out of sb

sonsear ▸conjug 1a◂ VI (*Cono Sur*) = **zoncear**

sonsera SF (*LAm*), **sonsería** SF (*LAm*) = **zoncera**

sonso/a* ADJ, SM/F (*LAm*) = **zonzo**

sonsonete SM [1] (= *sonido*) [*de golpes*] tap, tapping; [*de traqueteo*] rattle; [*de cencerro*] jangling
[2] (= *voz monótona*) monotonous delivery, singsong, singsong voice
[3] (= *frase rimada*) jingle, rhyming phrase
[4] (= *tono mofador*) mocking undertone

sonsoniche SM (*Caribe*) = **sonsonete**

sonza SF [1] (*Caribe*) (= *astucia*) cunning, deceit
[2] (*Méx*) (= *sarcasmo*) sarcasm, mockery

soñación* SF **¡ni por ~!** not on your life!

soñado ADJ [1] (= *ideal*) dream *antes de s*; **¿cómo sería su casa soñada?** what would your dream home be like?
[2] (= *deseado*) dreamed-of; **llegó el ~ día del armisticio** the dreamed-of armistice day dawned
[3] (*Col, Cono Sur**) (= *divino*) gorgeous; **un traje de novia ~** a gorgeous wedding dress

soñador(a) Ⓐ ADJ [*ojos, mirada*] dreamy; **siempre he sido un poco ~a** I've always been a a bit of a dreamer; **la gente es menos ~a hoy día** nowadays people are less idealistic
Ⓑ SM/F dreamer

soñar ▸conjug 1l◂ Ⓐ VT [1] (*durmiendo*) [1·1] [+ *ensueño*] to dream; **no recuerdo lo que soñé anoche** I can't remember what I dreamed about last night; **soñé que me había perdido en la selva** I dreamed that I had got lost in the jungle
[1·2] (*LAm*) [+ *persona*] to dream about; **te soñé anoche** I dreamed about you last night
[2] (= *imaginar*) to dream; **han ganado más dinero del que jamás habían soñado** they have won more money than they ever dreamed of *o* dreamed possible; **nunca lo hubiera soñado** I'd never have dreamed it; ✦***MODISMOS*** **¡ni ~lo!***: **¿ir en avión? yo eso ¡ni ~lo!** me go by plane? no chance!*; **—¿me compras un abrigo de visón? —¡ni lo sueñes!** "will you buy me a mink coat?" — "in your dreams!" *o* "dream on!"*; **que ni soñado***: **fue un montaje teatral que ni soñado** the staging of the play was out of this world*; **me va que ni soñado** it suits me a treat*
Ⓑ VI [1] (*durmiendo*) to dream; **~ con algo** to dream about sth; **anoche soñé contigo** I dreamed *o* I had a dream about you last night; **"que sueñes con los angelitos"** "sweet dreams"; **~ en voz alta** to talk in one's sleep
[2] (= *fantasear*) to dream; **deja ya de ~ y ponte a trabajar** stop daydreaming *o* dreaming and get on with some work; **~ con algo** to dream of sth; **soñaban con la victoria** they dreamed of victory; **soñaba con una lavadora** she dreamed of (one day) having a washing machine; **~ con hacer algo** to dream of doing sth; **sueña con ser cantante** she dreams of being a singer; **no podemos ni ~ con comprarnos un coche** we can't even think of buying a car; **~ despierto** to daydream

soñarra SF, **soñera** SF [1] (= *modorra*) drowsiness, deep desire to sleep
[2] (= *sueño*) deep sleep

soñolencia SF = **somnolencia**

soñolientamente ADV sleepily, drowsily

soñoliento ADJ sleepy, drowsy

sopa SF 1 (= *caldo*) soup; ✦*MODISMOS* **hasta en la ~: los encontramos hasta en la ~** they're everywhere, they're ten a penny; **andar a** *o* **vivir a** *o* **comer la ~ boba** to scrounge one's meals*; **poner a algn como ~ de Pascua*** to give sb a ticking-off* ► **sopa chilena** (*Andes*) corn and potato soup ► **sopa de cebolla** onion soup ► **sopa de cola** (*CAm*) oxtail soup ► **sopa de fideos** noodle soup ► **sopa de sobre** packet soup ► **sopa de verduras, sopa juliana** vegetable soup
2 (= *pan mojado*) sop; **hacer ~s** to dunk*; ✦*MODISMOS* **estar hecho una ~** to be sopping wet, be soaked to the skin; **dar ~s con honda a algn** to be streets ahead of sb ► **sopas de leche** bread and milk
3 ► **sopa de letras** word search, word search game
4 (*Méx*) (*tb* **~ seca**) second course

sopaipilla SF (*Andes, Cono Sur*) fritter

sopapear ▸conjug 1a◂ VT 1 [+ *persona*] (= *golpear*) to slap, smack; (= *sacudir*) to shake violently
2 (= *maltratar*) to maltreat; (= *insultar*) to insult

sopapié SM (*Andes*) kick

sopapina SF series of punches, bashing*

sopapo SM slap, smack

sopar* ▸conjug 1a◂ (*Cono Sur*) Ⓐ VT [+ *pan*] to dip, dunk
Ⓑ VI to meddle

sopear ▸conjug 1a◂ VT (*LAm*) to soak

sopera SF soup tureen

sopero Ⓐ ADJ 1 [*plato, cuchara*] soup *antes de s*
2 (*Andes*) (= *curioso*) nosey*, gossipy
Ⓑ SM soup plate

▼ **sopesar** ▸conjug 1a◂ VT 1 (= *levantar*) to try the weight of
2 (= *evaluar*) [+ *situación*] to weigh up; [+ *palabras*] to weigh

sopetón SM 1 (= *golpe*) punch
2 **de ~** suddenly, unexpectedly; **entrar de ~** to pop in, drop in; **entrar de ~ en un cuarto** to burst into a room

sopimpa SF (*Caribe*) series of punches

soplacausas* SMF INV incompetent lawyer

soplado Ⓐ ADJ (*) 1 [*persona*] (= *borracho*) tight*; (= *limpio*) clean; (= *pulcro*) extra smart, overdressed; (= *afectado*) affected; (= *engreído*) stuck-up*
2 (*Cono Sur**) **ir ~** to drive very fast
Ⓑ SM (*tb* **~ de vidrio**) glass blowing

soplador(a) Ⓐ SM/F 1 [*de vidrio*] glass blower
2 (= *alborotador*) troublemaker
3 (*Andes, CAm Teat*) prompter
Ⓑ SM (= *ventilador*) fan, ventilator

soplagaitas* SMF INV idiot, twit*

soplamocos* SM INV 1 (= *puñetazo*) punch, slap
2 (*Méx*) (= *comentario*) put-down

soplapollas** SMF INV berk*, wanker**, prick**

soplar ▸conjug 1a◂ Ⓐ VT 1 (= *echar aire sobre*) [+ *polvo*] to blow away, blow off; [+ *superficie, sopa, fuego*] to blow on; [+ *vela*] to blow out; [+ *globo*] to blow up; [+ *vidrio*] to blow
2 (= *inspirar*) to inspire
3 (= *decir confidencialmente*) **~ la respuesta a algn** to whisper the answer to sb; **~ a algn** (= *ayudar a recordar*) to prompt sb; **~ a algn algo referente a otro** to tell sb something nasty about somebody
4 (*) (= *delatar*) to split on*
5 (*) (= *birlar*) to pinch*
6 (*) (= *cobrar*) to charge, sting*; **me han soplado ocho dólares** they stung me for eight dollars; **¿cuánto te ~on?** how much did they sting you for?
7 (*) [+ *golpe*] **le sopló un buen mamporro** she whacked *o* clouted him one*
Ⓑ VI 1 [*persona, viento*] to blow; **¡sopla!*** (*indicando sorpresa*) well I'm blowed!*
2 (*) (= *delatar*) to split*, squeal*
3 (*) [*beber*] to drink, booze
Ⓒ **soplarse** VPR 1 (*) (= *devorar*) **~se un pastel** to wolf (down) a cake; **se sopla un litro entero** he knocks back a whole litre*
2 (*) (= *delatar*) **~se de algn** to split on sb*, sneak on sb
3 (*) (= *engreírse*) to get conceited

soplete SM blowlamp, blowtorch ► **soplete oxiacetilénico** oxyacetylene burner ► **soplete soldador** welding torch

soplido SM strong puff, blast

soplo SM 1 [*de aire*] (*con la boca*) blow, puff; (*por el viento*) puff, gust; ✦*MODISMO* **en un ~: la semana pasó como** *o* **en un ~** the week flew by, the week was over in no time
2 (*Téc*) blast
3 (*) tip-off; **dar el ~** to squeal*; **ir con el ~ al director** to tell tales to the headmaster, go and tell the head*
4 (*) [*de policía*] informer, grass*, fink (*EEUU**)
5 ► **soplo cardíaco, soplo al corazón** heart murmur

soplón/ona* SM/F 1 [*de policía*] informer, grass*, fink (*EEUU**)
2 (*Méx*) (= *policía*) (*gen*) cop*; (*Andes*) [*de la policía secreta*] member of the secret police
3 (*CAm Teat*) prompter

sopón ADJ (*Caribe*) interfering

soponcio* SM **¡qué ~! me pillaron copiando en el examen** I nearly died! they caught me copying in the exam; **si no abres las ventanas nos va a dar un ~** if you don't open the windows we're all going to pass out; **al verlo con la cabeza rapada le dio un ~** she had a fit when she saw him with his head shaved

sopor SM 1 (*Med*) drowsiness
2 (= *letargo*) torpor

soporífero, soporífico Ⓐ ADJ 1 (*Med*) sleep-inducing
2 (= *aburrido*) soporific
Ⓑ SM 1 (= *pastilla*) sleeping pill
2 (= *bebida*) sleeping draught

soportable ADJ bearable

soportal SM 1 [*de casa*] porch
2 **soportales** (*en una calle*) arcade *sing*, colonnade *sing*

soportante ADJ supportive

▼ **soportar** ▸conjug 1a◂ Ⓐ VT 1 (= *resistir*) [+ *peso*] to support; [+ *presión*] to resist, withstand; **cuatro pilares soportan la bóveda** the vault is supported by four pillars; **las vigas soportan el peso del techo** the beams bear *o* carry the weight of the ceiling
2 (= *aguantar*) [+ *dolor, contratiempo, clima*] to bear; [+ *persona*] to put up with; **soportaba su enfermedad con resignación** she bore her illness with resignation; **soportó a su marido durante años** she put up with her husband for years; **soporta mal el dolor** she cannot stand pain; **no soporto a ese imbécil** I can't stand that idiot; **no soporta que la critiquen** she can't stand being criticized
Ⓑ **soportarse** VPR **Ruth y Blanca no se soportan** Ruth and Blanca can't stand each other

soporte SM 1 (= *apoyo*) [*de puente*] support; [*de repisa*] bracket
2 (= *pedestal*) base, stand
3 [*de persona*] support; **es un buen ~ para sus padres** she's a real support to her parents; **esto es un ~ para su opinión** this supports *o* backs up her opinion
4 (*Inform*) medium ► **soporte de entrada** input medium ► **soporte de salida** output medium ► **soporte físico** hardware ► **soporte lógico** software
5 (*Heráldica*) supporter

soprano SMF soprano

soquete SM (*LAm*) sock, ankle sock, anklet (*EEUU*)

sor SF Sister; **Sor María** Sister Mary; **una ~*** a nun

sorber ▸conjug 2a◂ VT 1 (= *beber*) (*poco a poco*) to sip; (*chupando*) to suck up; **~ por una paja** to drink through a straw; **~ por las narices** (*gen*) to sniff, sniff in, sniff up; (*Med*) to inhale
2 (= *absorber*) [*esponja, papel secante*] to soak up, absorb
3 (= *tragar*) [*mar*] to suck down, swallow up; [+ *palabras*] to drink in

sorbete SM 1 (= *postre*) sorbet, sherbet (*EEUU*)
2 (*Caribe, Cono Sur*) (= *pajita*) drinking straw
3 (*Méx*) (= *sombrero*) top hat

sorbetera SF ice-cream freezer

sorbetería SF (*CAm*) ice-cream parlour, ice-cream shop

sorbetón SM gulp, mouthful

sorbito SM sip

sorbo SM (*al beber*) (= *trago pequeño*) sip; (= *trago grande*) gulp, swallow; **un ~ de té** a sip of tea; **beber a ~s** to sip; **de un ~** in one gulp; **tomar de un ~** to down in one, drink in one gulp

sorche‡ SM, **sorchi**‡ SM soldier

sordamente ADV dully, in a muffled way

sordera SF deafness ► **sordera profunda** profound deafness

sordidez SF 1 (= *suciedad*) sordidness, squalor
2 (= *inmoralidad*) sordidness

sórdido ADJ 1 (= *sucio*) dirty, squalid
2 (= *inmoral*) sordid
3 [*palabra*] nasty, dirty

sordina SF 1 (*Mús*) mute
2 **con ~** on the quiet, surreptitiously

sordo/a Ⓐ ADJ 1 [*persona*] deaf; **quedarse ~** to go deaf; **mostrarse ~ a** ◊ **permanecer ~ a** to be deaf to; **se mostró ~ a sus súplicas** he was deaf to her entreaties, her entreaties fell on deaf ears; ✦*MODISMOS* **a la sorda** ◊ **a sordas** on the quiet, surreptitiously; **~ como una tapia** as deaf as a post
2 (= *insonoro*) [*ruido*] dull, muffled; [*dolor*] dull; [*emoción, ira*] suppressed
3 (*Ling*) voiceless

➤ LENGUA Y USO: **sopesar 2** 53.4 **soportar A2** 34.3, 41

Ⓑ SM/F deaf person; **hacerse el ~** to pretend not to hear, turn a deaf ear

sordociego/a Ⓐ ADJ blind and deaf
Ⓑ SM/F blind and deaf person

sordomudez SF deaf-muteness

sordomudo/a Ⓐ ADJ deaf and dumb
Ⓑ SM/F deaf-mute

sorgo SM sorghum

soriano/a (*Esp*) Ⓐ ADJ of/from Soria
Ⓑ SM/F native/inhabitant of Soria; **los ~s** the people of Soria

soriasis SF INV psoriasis

Sorlinga: **Islas ~** SFPL Scilly Isles

sorna SF 1 (= *malicia*) sarcasm
2 (= *tono burlón*) sarcastic tone; **con ~** sarcastically, mockingly
3 (= *lentitud*) slowness

sornar* ▸conjug 1a◂ VI to kip*, sleep

sorocharse ▸conjug 1a◂ VPR 1 (*LAm*) = **asorocharse**
2 (*Cono Sur*) (= *ponerse colorado*) to blush

soroche SM 1 (*LAm Med*) mountain sickness, altitude sickness
2 (*Cono Sur*) (= *rubor*) blush, blushing
3 (*Andes, Cono Sur Min*) galena, natural lead sulphide

sorprendente ADJ surprising; **no es ~ que ...** it is hardly surprising that ..., it is small wonder that ...

sorprender ▸conjug 2a◂ Ⓐ VT 1 (= *asombrar*) to surprise; **no me ~ía que ...** I wouldn't be surprised if ...
2 (= *coger desprevenido*) to catch; (*Mil*) to surprise; **lo sorprendieron robando** they caught him stealing
3 [+ *conversación*] to overhear; [+ *secreto*] to find out, discover; [+ *escondrijo*] to find
Ⓑ VI to be surprising; **sorprende observar cómo lo hace** it's surprising to see how he does it; **sorprende la delicadeza de su verso** the delicacy of her poetry is surprising
Ⓒ **sorprenderse** VPR to be surprised; **me sorprendí de la claridad de sus ideas** I was surprised at the clarity of his ideas; **no me sorprendí de que se enfadara** I wasn't surprised he got angry; **se sorprendió mucho** he was very surprised

sorprendido ADJ surprised

sorpresa Ⓐ SF 1 (= *asombro*) surprise; **¡qué** *o* **vaya ~!** what a surprise!; **fue una ~ verte allí** it was a surprise to see you there, I was surprised to see you there; **ante** *o* **para mi ~** to my surprise; **con gran ~ mía** much to my surprise; **causar ~ a algn** to surprise sb; **coger a algn de** *o* **por ~** to take sb by surprise; **dar una ~**: **Pablo quería darme una ~** Pablo wanted to take me by surprise *o* surprise me; **nunca ha llegado a la final, pero esta vez podría dar una** *o* **la ~** she has never reached the final before but this time she may cause an upset *o* she may surprise a few people; **llevarse una ~** to get a surprise; **producir ~ a algn** to surprise sb
2 (= *regalo*) surprise; **¿me has comprado alguna ~?** have you bought a surprise for me?
3 (*Mil*) surprise attack
Ⓑ ADJ INV surprise *antes de s*; **ataques ~** surprise attacks; **inspección ~** spot check; **resultado ~** surprise result; **sobres ~** lucky dip bags; **visita ~** unannounced visit, surprise visit

sorpresivamente ADV (= *asombrosamente*) surprisingly; (= *repentinamente*) suddenly, unexpectedly

sorpresivo ADJ (*esp LAm*) (= *asombroso*) surprising; (= *imprevisto*) sudden, unexpected

sorrajar ▸conjug 1a◂ VT (*Méx*) (= *golpear*) to hit; (= *herir*) to wound

sorrasear ▸conjug 1a◂ VT (*Méx*) to part-roast, grill

sorrongar ▸conjug 1h◂ VI (*Andes*) to grumble

sorrostrigar ▸conjug 1h◂ VT (*Andes*) to pester, annoy

sortario ADJ (*Caribe*) lucky, fortunate

sortear ▸conjug 1a◂ Ⓐ VT 1 (= *decidir al azar*) to draw lots for
2 (= *rifar*) (*gen*) to raffle; (*Dep*) to toss up for
3 (= *evitar*) [+ *obstáculo*] to dodge, avoid; **el torero sorteó al toro** the bullfighter dodged out of the bull's way; **el esquiador sorteó las banderas con habilidad** the skier swerved skilfully round the flags; **aquí hay que ~ el tráfico** you have to weave in and out of the traffic here
4 (= *librarse de*) [+ *dificultad*] to avoid, get round; [+ *pregunta*] to handle, deal with, deal with skilfully *o* (*EEUU*) skillfully
Ⓑ VI 1 (*en sorteo*) to draw lots
2 (*con moneda*) to toss, toss up

sorteo SM 1 (*en lotería*) draw; (= *rifa*) raffle; (*Dep*) toss; **ganar el ~** to win the toss; **el ganador se decidirá mediante ~** lots will be drawn to decide the winner ► **sorteo de regalos** prize draw; → LOTERÍA
2 (*al evitar algo*) dodging, avoidance

sortija SF 1 (= *anillo*) ring ► **sortija de compromiso**, **sortija de pedida** engagement ring ► **sortija de sello** signet ring
2 (= *bucle*) curl, ringlet

sortilegio SM 1 (= *hechizo*) spell, charm
2 (= *hechicería*) sorcery
3 (= *encanto*) charm

sos (*Arg*) = **sois**; *ver* **ser**

sosa SF soda ► **sosa cáustica** caustic soda

sosaina* Ⓐ ADJ dull, boring
Ⓑ SMF dull person, bore

sosco SM (*Andes*) bit, piece

sosegadamente ADV calmly, peacefully

sosegado ADJ 1 [*apariencia, vida*] calm, peaceful
2 [*persona*] calm, serene

sosegar ▸conjug 1h, 1j◂ Ⓐ VT 1 [+ *persona*] (= *calmar*) to calm; (= *aquietar*) to quieten, quiet (*EEUU*); (= *arrullar*) to lull
2 [+ *ánimo*] to calm
3 [+ *dudas, aprensiones*] to allay
Ⓑ VI to rest
Ⓒ **sosegarse** VPR (= *calmarse*) to calm down; (= *aquietarse*) to quieten down

soseras* ADJ = **soso 2**

sosería SF 1 (= *insulsez*) insipidness
2 (= *monotonía*) dullness; **es una ~** it's boring, it's terribly dull

sosia SM double

sosiego SM 1 [*de lugar, ambiente*] (= *tranquilidad*) calm, calmness, tranquility; (= *quietud*) peacefulness
2 [*de persona*] calmness, serenity, composure; **hacer algo con ~** to do sth calmly

soslayar ▸conjug 1a◂ VT 1 (= *poner ladeado*) to put sideways, place obliquely (*frm*)
2 (= *librarse de*) [+ *dificultad*] to get round; [+ *pregunta*] to avoid, dodge, sidestep; [+ *encuentro*] to avoid

soslayo: **al** *o* **de ~** ADV obliquely, sideways; **mirada de ~** sidelong glance; **mirar de ~** (*lit*) to look out of the corner of one's eye (at); (*fig*) to look askance (at)

soso ADJ 1 (*Culin*) (= *insípido*) tasteless, insipid; (= *sin sal*) unsalted; **estas patatas están sosas** these potatoes are unsalted *o* need more salt
2 (= *aburrido, inexpresivo*) dull, uninteresting

sospecha SF suspicion

sospechar ▸conjug 1a◂ Ⓐ VT to suspect; **sospecho que lo hizo él** I suspect (that) he did it; **—fue él el que lo robó —ya lo sospechaba** "it was he who stole it" — "I suspected as much"; **sospecho que no tardarán en llegar** I have a feeling they won't be long
Ⓑ VI **~ de algn** to suspect sb, be suspicious of sb; **la policía siempre sospechó del marido** the police always suspected the husband, the police were always suspicious of the husband

sospechosamente ADV suspiciously

sospechoso/a Ⓐ ADJ suspicious; **su comportamiento es muy ~** his behaviour is very suspicious; **el bar estaba lleno de tipos ~s** the bar was full of suspicious-looking types; **todos son ~s** everybody is under suspicion; **tiene amistades sospechosas** he has some dubious acquaintances; **es ~ de asesinato** he is suspected of murder
Ⓑ SM/F suspect

sosquín SM (*Caribe*) 1 (= *ángulo*) wide corner, obtuse angle
2 (= *golpe*) backhander, sweetener (*EEUU*), unexpected blow

sosquinar ▸conjug 1a◂ VT (*Caribe*) to hit unexpectedly, wound unexpectedly

sostén SM 1 (*Arquit*) support, prop
2 (= *prenda femenina*) bra, brassiere
3 (= *alimento*) sustenance
4 (= *apoyo*) support; **el único ~ de su familia** the sole support of his family; **el principal ~ del gobierno** the mainstay of the government

sostener ▸conjug 2k◂ Ⓐ VT 1 (= *sujetar*) 1·1 (*en las manos, los brazos*) to hold; **¡sostén esto un momentito!** hold this a minute!; **yo llevaba las cajas mientras él me sostenía la puerta** I carried the boxes while he held the door open for me
1·2 (*en pie*) [+ *construcción, edificio, techo*] to hold up, support; **los pilares que sostienen el puente** the pillars which hold up *o* support the bridge; **las piernas apenas me sostenían** my legs could barely hold me up *o* support me; **entró borracho, sostenido por dos amigos** he came in drunk, held up *o* supported by two friends
1·3 (= *soportar*) [+ *peso, carga*] to bear, carry, sustain (*frm*)
2 (= *proporcionar apoyo a*) 2·1 (*económicamente*) to support; **no gano suficiente para ~ a una familia** I don't earn enough to support a family; **algunas de las alternativas sugeridas para ~ al club** some of the alternatives suggested to keep the club going
2·2 (= *alimentar*) to support, sustain (*frm*); **la tierra no da para ~ a todo el mundo** the land does not provide enough to support *o* (*frm*) sustain everyone

➤ LENGUA Y USO: sorprender A1 42.2

2·3 (*moralmente*) to support; **la élite ha dejado de ~ al régimen** the elite has stopped supporting the regime; **una mayoría capaz de ~ al Gobierno** a majority large enough to keep *o* support the government in power; **sólo lo sostiene el cariño de sus hijos** the love of his children is all that keeps him going
3 (= *mantener*) 3·1 [+ *opinión*] to hold; **siempre he sostenido lo contrario** I've always held the opposite opinion; **sostiene un punto de vista muy diferente** he has *o* holds a very different point of view; **no tiene datos suficientes para ~ esa afirmación** she doesn't have enough information to back up *o* support that statement; **la investigación no ha terminado, como sostiene el juez** the investigation has not concluded, as the judge maintains *o* holds; **~ que** to maintain *o* hold that; **sigue sosteniendo que es inocente** she still maintains *o* holds that she is innocent
3·2 [+ *situación*] to maintain, keep up; **no podrán ~ su puesto en la clasificación** they won't be able to maintain *o* keep up their place in the ranking; **los campesinos han sostenido desde siempre una fuerte lucha con el medio** country people have always kept up *o* carried on a hard struggle against the environment; **~ la mirada de algn** to hold sb's gaze
4 (= *tener*) [+ *conversación, enfrentamiento, polémica*] to have; [+ *reunión, audiencia*] **sostuvo recientemente un enfrentamiento con el presidente** he recently had a clash with the president; **sostuvo un breve encuentro con sus ministros** he held a brief meeting with his ministers
5 (*Mús*) [+ *nota*] to hold, sustain
Ⓑ **sostenerse** VPR 1 (= *sujetarse*) to stand; **la escultura se sostiene sobre cuatro columnas** the sculpture stands on four columns; **un libro grueso que se sostiene de canto** a thick book which will stand up; **no se me sostiene el peinado** my hair won't stay up; **~se en pie** [*persona*] to stand upright, stand on one's feet; [*edificio*] to stand; **apenas podía ~me en pie** I could hardly stand upright, I could hardly stand on my feet; **la iglesia es lo único que se sostiene todavía en pie** only the church is still standing
2 (= *sustentarse*) 2·1 (*económicamente*) [*persona*] to support o.s.; [*empresa*] to keep going; **mientras pueda ~se con sus ingresos** as long as she can support herself on her income; **la minería se sostiene gracias a las subvenciones** the mining industry is kept going by subsidies
2·2 (*con alimentos*) **¿cómo puedes ~te sólo con un bocadillo?** how can you keep going on just a sandwich?; **~se a base de algo** to live on sth, survive on sth
3 (= *resistir*) **el mercado se sostiene firme** the market is holding firm; **~se en el poder** to maintain o.s. in power; **se sostiene en su negativa de no dejarlos participar** he persists in his refusal to let them take part

spammer [es'pamer] SMF (*pl* **spammers**) (*Internet*) spammer

sostenible ADJ [*desarrollo, crecimiento, recuperación*] sustainable; **la situación no parece ~ a largo plazo** the situation does not seem to be sustainable in the long term; **su postura resulta difícilmente ~** his position is difficult to sustain

sostenidamente ADV continuously

sostenido Ⓐ ADJ 1 (= *continuo*) sustained
2 (*Mús*) sharp; **do ~** C sharp
Ⓑ SM (*Mús*) sharp

sostenimiento SM 1 (= *sujeción*) support; **las vigas sirven de principal ~ al edificio** the girders act as the building's main support
2 (= *conservación*) **una política de ~ de precios** a policy of maintaining price levels; **medidas que contribuyen al ~ de la democracia** measures that contribute to the upholding *o* maintenance of democracy
3 (= *apoyo*) (*financiero*) maintenance; (*con alimentos*) sustenance; **para el ~ de la economía** for the maintenance of *o* to maintain the economy

sota¹ SF 1 (*Naipes*) jack, knave
2 (†) (= *descarada*) hussy, brazen woman; (= *puta*) whore

sota² SM (*Cono Sur**) overseer, foreman

sotabanco SM 1 (= *desván*) attic, garret
2 (*Cono Sur*) (= *cuartucho*) poky little room

sotabarba SF double chin, jowl

sotacura SM (*Andes, Cono Sur*) curate

sotana SF 1 (*Rel*) cassock, soutane
2 (*) (= *paliza*) hiding

sotanear* ▸conjug 1a◂ VT to tick off*

sótano SM 1 (*en casa*) (*habitable*) basement; (*como almacén*) cellar 2 (*en banco*) vault

Sotavento: **Islas ~** SFPL Leeward Isles

sotavento SM (*Náut*) lee, leeward; **a ~** to leeward; **de ~** leeward *antes de s*

sotechado SM shed

soterradamente ADV in an underhand way

soterrado ADJ buried, hidden

soterramiento SM excavation; **obras de ~** excavations, underground works

soterrar ▸conjug 1j◂ VT 1 (= *enterrar*) to bury
2 (= *esconder*) to hide away, bury

soto SM 1 (*Bot*) (= *matorral*) thicket; (= *arboleda*) grove, copse
2 (*Andes*) (*en la piel*) rough lump, bump; (= *nudo*) knot

sotobosque SM undergrowth

sotreta SF (*Andes, Cono Sur*) 1 (= *caballo*) horse; (= *caballo brioso*) frisky horse; (= *caballo viejo*) useless old nag
2 (= *persona*) loafer, idler, bum (*EEUU*)

soturno ADJ taciturn, silent

soufflé [su'fle] SM soufflé

soul ADJ INV, SM (*Mús*) soul

soutien [su'tjen] SM (*pl* **soutiens**) (*Arg*) bra, brassiere

souvenir [suβe'nir] SM (*pl* **souvenirs**) souvenir

soviet SM soviet

soviético/a Ⓐ ADJ Soviet *antes de s*
Ⓑ SM/F **los ~s** the Soviets, the Russians

soy *ver* **ser**

soya SF (*LAm*) soya, soy (*EEUU*)

S.P. ABR 1 (*Rel*) = **Santo Padre**
2 (*Esp Aut*) = **Servicio Público**
3 (*Admin*) = **Servicio Postal**

spaghetti(s) SMPL, **spaguetti(s)** SMPL [espa'ɣeti(s)] spaghetti *sing*

spárring [es'parin] SM sparring partner

speed* [es'pið] SM (= *droga*) speed

spi* [es'pi] SM spinnaker

spinning® [es'pinin] SM spinning®; **sesión de ~** spin® session, spinning® session

spleen [es'plin] SM = **esplín**

SPM SM ABR (= **síndrome premenstrual**) PMS

sponsor [espon'sor] SMF (*pl* **sponsors** [espon'sor]) sponsor

sport [es'por] SM sport; **chaqueta (de) ~** sports jacket, sports coat (*EEUU*); **ropa de ~** casual wear; **vestir de ~** to dress casually; **hacer algo por ~** to do sth (just) for fun

spot [es'pot] SM (*pl* **spots**) 1 (*TV*) ► **spot electoral** party political broadcast ► **spot publicitario** (*TV*) commercial, ad*
2 (*Cono Sur Elec*) spotlight

spray [es'prai] SM (*pl* **sprays**) spray, aerosol

sprint [es'prin] SM (*pl* **sprints** [es'prin]) 1 (*Dep*) sprint; **imponerse al ~** to win in a sprint finish; **tengo que hacer un ~** I must dash, I must get a move on 2 (*tb* **~ final**) (= *esfuerzo máximo*) final dash, last-minute rush

sprintar [esprin'tar] ▸conjug 1a◂ VI to sprint

sprínter [es'printer] SMF sprinter

squash [es'kwas] SM squash

Sr. ABR (= **Señor**) Mr; → DON/DOÑA

Sra. ABR (= **Señora**) Mrs; → DON/DOÑA

S.R.C. ABR (= **se ruega contestación**) RSVP

Sres. ABR (= **Señores**) Messrs

Sria. ABR (= **secretaria**) sec

Sri Lanka SM Sri Lanka

Srio. ABR (= **secretario**) sec

Srs. ABR (= **Señores**) Messrs

Srta. ABR (= **Señorita**) Miss, Ms; → DON/DOÑA

SS. ABR (= **Santos, Santas**) SS

ss. ABR 1 (= **siguientes**) following, foll.
2 (= **siglos**) cent.

S.S. ABR 1 (*Rel*) (= **Su Santidad**) HH
2 = **Seguridad Social**
3 = **Su Señoría**

s.s. ABR (= **seguro servidor**) *courtesy formula*

SSE ABR (= **sudsudeste**) SSE

SSI SM ABR (= **Servicio Social Internacional**) ISS

SS.MM. ABR = **Sus Majestades**

SSO ABR (= **sudsudoeste**) SSW

SSS SM ABR = **servicio social sustitutorio**

s.s.s. ABR (= **su seguro servidor**) *courtesy formula*

Sta. ABR (= **Santa**) St

staccato [esta'kato] ADV INV staccato

staff [es'taf] SM (*pl* **staffs** [es'taf]) 1 (= *equipo*) (*Mil*) staff, command; (*Pol*) ministerial team
2 (= *persona*) top executive
3 (*Cine, Mús*) credits *pl*, cast (and credits) (*EEUU*), credit titles *pl*

stage [es'teiʒ] SM period, phase

stagflación [estagfla'θjon] SF stagflation

Stalin [es'talin] SM Stalin

stand [es'tan] SM (*pl* **stands** [es'tan]) stand

standard ADJ, SM, **stándard** ADJ, SM [es'tandar] = **estándar**

standing [es'tandin] SM standing; **de alto ~** [*oficial*] high-ranking; [*ejecutivo*] top; [*piso*] luxury; **una mujer de alto ~** a woman of high standing

stárter [es'tarter] SM 1 (*Aut*) (= *aire*) choke; (*LAm*) (= *arranque*) self-starter, starter motor
2 (*LAm Equitación*) (= *persona*) starter; (= *puerta*) starting gate

statu quo SM status quo

status [es'tatus] SM INV status

Sto. ABR (= **Santo**) St

stock [es'tok] SM (*pl* **stocks** [es'tok]) stock, supply

stop [es'top] SM stop sign, halt sign

store [es'tor] SM sunblind, awning

stress [es'tres] SM stress

stretching [es'tretʃin] SM stretching

stripper [es'triper] SMF (*pl* **strippers**) stripper

strip-tease [es'triptis] SM, **striptease** [es'triptis] SM striptease

su ADJ POSES [1] (*sing*) (= *de él*) his; (= *de ella*) her; (= *de usted*) your; (= *de animal, cosa*) its; (*impersonal*) one's; **el chico perdió su juguete** the boy lost his toy; **María vino con su padre** María came with her father; **dígame su número de teléfono** give me your telephone number; **un oso y su cachorro** a bear and its cub; **uno tiene que mirar por su negocio** one has to look after one's own business
[2] (*pl*) (= *de ustedes*) your; (= *de ellos, de ellas*) their; **no olviden sus paraguas** don't forget your umbrellas; **las niñas se quedaron en su cuarto** the girls stayed in their room
[3] (*uso enfático*) **tendrá sus buenos 80 años** he must be a good 80 years old; **su dinero le habrá costado** it must have cost her a pretty penny; **una casa de muñecas con sus cortinitas y todo** a doll's house with little curtains and everything

suampo SM (*CAm*) swamp

suato* ADJ (*Méx*) silly

suave Ⓐ ADJ [1] (= *liso*) [*superficie*] smooth, even; [*piel, pasta*] smooth
[2] (= *no fuerte*) [*color, movimiento, brisa, reprimenda*] gentle; [*clima, sabor*] mild; [*trabajo*] easy; [*operación mecánica*] smooth, easy; [*melodía, voz*] soft, sweet; [*ruido*] low; [*olor*] slight; [*droga*] soft; ✦*MODISMO* **~ como el terciopelo** smooth as silk, like velvet
[3] [*persona, personalidad*] gentle, sweet; **estuvo muy ~ conmigo** he was very sweet to me, he behaved very nicely to me
[4] (*Chile, Méx**) (= *grande*) big, huge; (= *destacado*) outstanding
[5] (*Méx*⁑) (= *atractivo*) good-looking, fanciable*; (= *estupendo*) great*, fabulous*; **¡suave!** great idea!*, right on! (*EEUU**)
[6] **dar la ~** (*LAm*) (= *halagar*) to flatter
Ⓑ ADV [1] (*LAm*) [*sonar*] softly, quietly
[2] (*Méx*) **toca ~** she plays beautifully

suavemente ADV [*golpear, llover*] gently; [*entrar*] softly; [*mover, deslizar*] smoothly

suavidad SF [1] (= *lisura*) [*de superficie*] smoothness, evenness; [*de piel*] smoothness
[2] (= *falta de intensidad*) [*de color, movimiento, brisa, reprimenda*] gentleness; [*de clima, sabor, olor*] mildness; [*de trabajo*] easiness; [*de melodía, voz*] softness, sweetness; [*de ruido*] quietness

suavización SF [1] [*de superficie*] smoothing
[2] (= *ablandamiento*) [*de severidad, dureza*] softening, tempering; [*de medidas*] relaxation

suavizador SM razor strop

suavizante SM (*para ropa*) softener, fabric softener; (*para pelo*) conditioner

suavizar ▸conjug 1f◂ Ⓐ VT [1] (= *alisar*) to smooth out, smooth down
[2] (= *ablandar*) (*gen*) to soften; [+ *carácter*] to mellow; [+ *severidad, dureza*] to temper; [+ *medida*] to relax
[3] (= *quitar fuerza a*) [+ *navaja*] to strop; [+ *pendiente*] to ease, make more gentle; [+ *color*] to tone down; [+ *tono*] to soften
Ⓑ **suavizarse** VPR to soften

sub... PREF sub..., under...; **~empleo** underemployment; **~privilegiado** underprivileged; **~estimar** to underestimate; **~valorar** to undervalue; **la selección española ~-21** the Spanish under-21 team

suba SF (*CAm, Cono Sur*) rise, rise in prices

subacuático ADJ underwater

subalimentación SF undernourishment

subalimentado ADJ undernourished, underfed

subalpino ADJ subalpine

subalquilar ▸conjug 1a◂ VT to sublet

subalterno/a Ⓐ ADJ [*importancia*] secondary; [*personal*] auxiliary
Ⓑ SM/F [1] (= *subordinado*) subordinate
[2] (*Taur*) assistant bullfighter

subarbustivo ADJ shrubby

subarrendador(a) SM/F subtenant

subarrendar ▸conjug 1j◂ VT to sublet, sublease

subarrendatario/a SM/F subtenant

subarriendo SM subtenancy, sublease

subártico ADJ subarctic

subasta SF [1] (= *venta*) auction, sale by auction; **poner en** *o* **sacar a pública ~** to put up for auction, sell at auction ► **subasta a la baja, subasta a la rebaja** Dutch auction
[2] (= *contrato de obras*) tender, tendering
[3] (*Naipes*) auction

subastador(a) SM/F auctioneer

subastadora SF (= *casa*) auction house

subastar ▸conjug 1a◂ VT to auction, sell at auction

subatómico ADJ subatomic

subcampeón/ona SM/F runner-up

subcampeonato SM runner-up position, second place

subcomisario/a SM/F deputy superintendent

subcomisión SF subcommittee

subcomité SM subcommittee

subconjunto SM [1] (*Inform*) subset
[2] (*Pol*) subcommittee
[3] (*Zool*) subspecies

subconsciencia SF subconscious

subconsciente Ⓐ ADJ subconscious
Ⓑ SM **el ~** the subconscious; **en el ~** in one's subconscious ► **subconsciente colectivo** collective subconscious

subconscientemente ADV subconsciously

subcontinente SM subcontinent

subcontrata SF subcontract

subcontratación SF subcontracting

subcontratar ▸conjug 1a◂ VT to subcontract

subcontratista SMF subcontractor

subcontrato SM subcontract

subcultura SF subculture

subcutáneo ADJ subcutaneous

subdesarrollado ADJ underdeveloped

subdesarrollo SM underdevelopment

subdirección SF section, subdepartment

subdirector(a) SM/F [*de organización*] deputy director; [*de empresa*] assistant manager/manageress, deputy manager/manageress; [*de colegio*] deputy head ► **subdirector(a) de biblioteca** sub-librarian, deputy librarian

subdirectorio SM subdirectory

súbdito/a ADJ, SM/F subject

subdividir ▸conjug 3a◂ Ⓐ VT to subdivide
Ⓑ **subdividirse** VPR to subdivide

subdivisible ADJ subdivisible

subdivisión SF subdivision

sube SM (*LAm*) **dar un ~ a algn** to give sb a hard time ► **sube y baja** see-saw

subempleado ADJ underemployed

subempleo SM underemployment

subespecie SF subspecies

subestación SF substation

subestimación SF [*de capacidad, enemigo*] underestimation; [*de objeto, propiedad*] undervaluation; [*de argumento*] understatement

subestimar ▸conjug 1a◂ VT [+ *capacidad, enemigo*] to underestimate, underrate; [+ *objeto, propiedad*] to undervalue; [+ *argumento*] to understate

subexponer ▸conjug 2q◂ VT to underexpose

subexposición SF underexposure

subexpuesto ADJ underexposed

subfusil SM automatic rifle

subgénero SM [1] (*Literat*) minor genre
[2] (*Zool*) subspecies

subgerente SMF assistant director

subgrupo SM (*gen*) subgroup; (*Pol*) splinter group

subibaja SM seesaw, teeter-totter (*EEUU*)

subida SF [1] (= *ascensión*) [*de montaña, cuesta*] ascent; **dirigió la primera ~ al Kilimanjaro** he led the first ascent on Kilimanjaro; **es una ~ difícil** it's a tough ascent *o* climb; **una ~ en globo** a balloon ascent; **a la ~ tuvimos que parar varias veces** we had to stop several times on the way up
[2] (= *pendiente*) slope, hill
[3] (= *aumento*) rise, increase; **una ~ de los precios** a price rise *o* increase; **se espera una ~ de las temperaturas** temperatures are expected to rise ► **subida salarial** pay rise, wage increase
[4] (*) [*de drogas*] high*

subido ADJ [1] (= *intenso*) [*color*] bright, intense; [*olor*] strong; **un chiste ~ de tono** a risqué joke [2] [*precio*] high [3] (*) **hoy tienes el guapo ~** you're looking great today; **está de tonto ~** he's being really silly

subienda SF (*Andes*) shoal

subilla SF awl

subíndice SM subscript

subinquilino/a SM/F subtenant

subir ▸conjug 3a◂ Ⓐ VT [1] (= *levantar*) [+ *pierna, brazo, objeto*] to lift, lift up, raise; [+ *calcetines, pantalones, persianas*] to pull up; **sube los brazos** lift your arms (up), raise your arms
[2] (= *poner arriba*) (*llevando*) to take up; (*trayendo*) to bring up; **¿me puedes ayudar a ~ las maletas?** can you help me to take up the cases?; **voy a ~ esta caja arriba** I'll take this box upstairs; **¿puedes ~ ese cuadro de abajo?** could you bring that picture up from down there?; **lo subieron al portaequipajes** they put it up on the rack; **lo subimos a un taxi** we put him in a taxi
[3] (= *ascender*) [+ *calle, cuesta, escalera, montaña*] (= *ir arriba*) to go up; (= *venir arriba*) to come up; **subió las escaleras de dos en dos** she went up the stairs two at a time; **tenía problemas para ~ las escaleras** he had

difficulty getting up *o* climbing the stairs

[4] (= *aumentar*) [+ *precio, salario*] to put up, raise, increase; [+ *artículo en venta*] to put up the price of; **los taxistas han subido sus tarifas** taxi drivers have put their fares up *o* have raised their fares; **van a ~ la gasolina** they are going to put up *o* increase the price of petrol

[5] (= *elevar*) [+ *volumen, televisión, radio*] to turn up; [+ *voz*] to raise; **sube la radio, que no se oye** turn the radio up, I can't hear it

[6] (*en escalafón*) [+ *persona*] to promote

[7] (*Arquit*) to put up, build; **~ una pared** to put up *o* build a wall

[8] (*Mús*) to raise the pitch of

Ⓑ VI [1] (= *ir arriba*) to go up; (= *venir arriba*) to come up; (*en un monte, en el aire*) to climb; **suba al tercer piso** go up to the third floor; **sube, que te voy a enseñar unos discos** come up, I've got some records to show you; **seguimos subiendo hasta la cima** we went on climbing till we reached the summit; **estaba mirando como la mosca subía por la ventana** I watched the fly move slowly up the window; **tuvimos que ~ andando** we had to walk up

[2] (*Transportes*) (*en autobús, avión, tren, bicicleta, moto, caballo*) to get on; (*en coche, taxi*) to get in; **~ a un autobús/avión/tren** to get on(to) a bus/plane/train; **~ a un coche** to get in(to) a car; **~ a una bicicleta** to get on(to) a bike; **~ a un caballo** to mount a horse, get on(to) a horse; **~ a bordo** to go *o* get on board

[3] (*en el escalafón*) to be promoted (**a** to); **nuestro objetivo es ~ a primera división** our aim is to go up *o* be promoted to the First Division

[4] (= *aumentar*) [*precio, valor*] to go up, rise; [*temperatura*] to rise; **la gasolina ha vuelto a ~** (the price of) petrol has gone up again; **sigue subiendo la bolsa** share prices are still rising; **le ha subido la fiebre** her temperature has gone up *o* risen; *ver tb* **tono 2**

[5] (= *aumentar de nivel*) [*río, mercurio*] to rise; [*marea*] to come in

[6] [*cantidad*] **~ a** to come to, total

Ⓒ **subirse** VPR [1] (*Transportes*) (*en autobús, avión, tren*) to get on; (*en coche*) to get in; (*en bicicleta*) to get on, climb on; **~se a un autobús/avión/tren** to get on(to) a bus/plane/train; **~se a un coche** to get in(to) a car; **~se a una bicicleta** to get on(to) a bike; **~se a un caballo** to mount a horse, get on(to) a horse; **~se a bordo** to go *o* get on board

[2] (= *trepar*) (*a árbol, tejado*) to climb; **el niño se le subió a las rodillas** the child climbed (up) onto her knees; ✦***MODISMO* ~se por las paredes** to hit the roof; **están que se suben por las paredes** they're hopping mad; *ver tb* **barba A1, parra**

[3] (*con ropa*) **~se los calcetines/pantalones** to pull up one's socks/trousers; **~se la cremallera (de algo)** to zip (sth) up

[4] (*a la cabeza, cara*) **el vino se me sube a la cabeza** wine goes to my head; **el vino/el dinero se le ha subido a la cabeza** the wine/money has gone to his head; **se le subieron los colores a la cara** she blushed

[5] (*en comportamiento*) (= *engreírse*) to get conceited; (= *descararse*) to become bolder; (= *portarse mal*) to forget one's manners

[6] (*Bot*) to run to seed

SUBIR

Otros verbos de movimiento

• **Subir la cuesta/la escalera** *etc*, por regla general, se suele traducir por **to come up** o por **to go up**, según la dirección del movimiento (hacia o en sentido contrario al hablante), pero **come** y **go** se pueden reemplazar por otros verbos de movimiento si la oración española especifica la forma en que se sube mediante el uso de adverbios o construcciones adverbiales:

Tim subió las escaleras a gatas
Tim crept up the stairs
El mes pasado los precios subieron vertiginosamente
Prices shot up last month

Para otros usos y ejemplos ver la entrada.

súbitamente ADV (= *repentinamente*) suddenly; (= *de forma imprevista*) unexpectedly

súbito Ⓐ ADJ [1] [*cambio, acción*] (= *repentino*) sudden; (= *imprevisto*) unexpected; *ver tb* **muerte 1**

[2] (= *precipitado*) hasty, rash

[3] (*) (= *irritable*) irritable

Ⓑ ADV (*tb* **de ~**) suddenly, unexpectedly

subjefatura SF local headquarters, local police headquarters

subjetivamente ADV subjectively

subjetivar ▸conjug 1a◂ VT, **subjetivizar** ▸conjug 1f◂ VT to subjectivize, perceive in subjective terms

subjetividad SF subjectivity

subjetivismo SM subjectivism

subjetivo ADJ subjective

subjuntivo Ⓐ ADJ subjunctive

Ⓑ SM subjunctive, subjunctive mood

sublevación SF (= *motín*) [*de rebeldes, ciudadanos*] revolt, uprising; [*de militares*] mutiny; [*de presos*] riot

sublevar ▸conjug 1a◂ Ⓐ VT [1] (= *amotinar*) to rouse to revolt

[2] (= *indignar*) to infuriate

Ⓑ **sublevarse** VPR to revolt, rise, rise up

sublimación SF sublimation

sublimado SM sublimate

sublimar ▸conjug 1a◂ VT [1] [+ *persona*] to exalt

[2] [+ *deseos*] to sublimate

[3] (*Quím*) to sublimate

sublime ADJ [1] (= *excelso*) sublime; **lo ~** the sublime

[2] (*liter*) (= *alto*) high, lofty

sublimemente ADV sublimely

sublimidad SF sublimity

subliminal ADJ subliminal

subliteratura SF third-rate literature, pulp writing

submarinismo SM (*como deporte*) scuba diving; (*para pescar*) underwater fishing

submarinista Ⓐ ADJ **exploración ~** underwater exploration

Ⓑ SMF scuba diver

submarino Ⓐ ADJ underwater, submarine; **pesca submarina** underwater fishing

Ⓑ SM [1] (*Náut*) submarine

[2] (*Arg Culin*) *hot milk with piece of chocolate*

[3] (*Arg*) (= *tortura*) *repeated submersion of victim's head in water*

submundo SM underworld

subnormal Ⓐ ADJ [1] (*Med*) subnormal, mentally handicapped

[2] (**pey*) nuts*, mental*

Ⓑ SMF [1] (*Med*) subnormal person, mentally handicapped person

[2] (**pey*) nutcase*, blockhead*

subnormalidad SF subnormality, mental handicap

subocupación SF (*LAm*) underemployment

subocupado/a (*LAm*) Ⓐ ADJ underemployed

Ⓑ SM/F underemployed person; **los ~s** the underemployed

suboficial SMF non-commissioned officer, NCO

subordinación SF subordination

subordinado/a Ⓐ ADJ subordinate; **quedar ~ a algo** to be subordinate to sth

Ⓑ SM/F subordinate

subordinar ▸conjug 1a◂ Ⓐ VT to subordinate

Ⓑ **subordinarse** VPR **~se a** to subordinate o.s. to

subpárrafo SM subparagraph

subproducto SM by-product

subprograma SM subprogram

subrayable ADJ worth emphasizing; **el punto más ~** the point which should particularly be noted, the most important point

subrayado Ⓐ ADJ [1] (*con línea*) underlined

[2] (*en cursiva*) italicized, in italics

Ⓑ SM [1] (*con línea*) underlining

[2] (*en cursiva*) italics *pl*; **el ~ es mío** my italics, the italics are mine

subrayar ▸conjug 1a◂ VT [1] [+ *texto, frase*] (*con línea*) to underline; (*en cursiva*) to italicize, put in italics

[2] (= *recalcar*) to underline, emphasize

subrepticiamente ADV surreptitiously

subrepticio ADJ surreptitious

subrogación SF substitution, replacement

subrogante (*Chile*) Ⓐ ADJ acting

Ⓑ SMF substitute

subrogar ▸conjug 1h, 1l◂ VT to substitute, replace

subrutina SF subroutine

subsahariano ADJ sub-Saharan

subsanable ADJ (= *perdonable*) excusable; (= *reparable*) repairable; **un error fácilmente ~** an error which is easily put right *o* rectified; **un obstáculo difícilmente ~** an obstacle which is hard to overcome *o* get round

subsanar ▸conjug 1a◂ VT [+ *falta*] to overlook, excuse; [+ *perjuicio, defecto*] to repair, make good; [+ *error*] to rectify, put right; [+ *deficiencia*] to make up for; [+ *dificultad, obstáculo*] to get round, overcome

subscribir ▸conjug 3a◂ VT = **suscribir**

subsecretaría SF undersecretaryship

subsecretario/a SM/F undersecretary, assistant secretary

subsector SM subsection, subsector

subsecuente ADJ subsequent

subsede SF secondary venue

subsidiar ▸conjug 1b◂ VT to subsidize

subsidiariedad SF subordination, subsidiary nature

subsidiario ADJ subsidiary

subsidio SM [1] (*Fin*) (= *subvención*) subsidy, grant; (= *ayuda financiera*) aid ► **subsidio de desempleo** unemployment benefit, unem-

ployment compensation (*EEUU*) ► **subsidio de enfermedad** sick benefit, sick pay ► **subsidio de exportación** export subsidy ► **subsidio de huelga** strike pay ► **subsidio de natalidad** maternity benefit ► **subsidio de paro** unemployment benefit, unemployment compensation (*EEUU*) ► **subsidio de vejez** old age pension ► **subsidio familiar** ≈ family credit, ≈ welfare (*EEUU*)
[2] (*Andes*) (= *inquietud*) anxiety, worry

subsiguiente ADJ subsequent

subsistema SM subsystem

subsistencia SF (= *supervivencia*) subsistence; (= *sustento*) sustenance; **salario de ~** subsistence wage

subsistente ADJ (= *duradero*) lasting, enduring; (= *aún existente*) surviving; **una costumbre aún ~** a custom that still exists *o* survives

subsistir ▸conjug 3a◂ VI [1] (= *malvivir*) to subsist, live (**con, de** on); (= *perdurar*) to survive, endure; **todavía subsiste el edificio** the building is still standing; **es una creencia que subsiste** it is a belief which still exists; **sin ayuda económica no podrá ~ el colegio** the school will not be able to survive without financial aid
[2] (*Andes*) (= *vivir juntos*) to live together

subsónico ADJ subsonic

subsótano SM basement

subst... PREF = **sust...**

substituir ▸conjug 3g◂ VT = **sustituir**

subsuelo SM subsoil

subsumir ▸conjug 3a◂ VT to subsume

subte* SM (*Arg*) underground, tube*, subway (*EEUU*)

subteniente/a SM/F sub-lieutenant, second lieutenant

subterfugio SM subterfuge

subterráneo Ⓐ ADJ underground, subterranean
Ⓑ SM [1] (= *túnel*) underground passage
[2] (= *almacén bajo tierra*) underground store, cellar
[3] (*Arg*) (= *metro*) underground, subway (*EEUU*)

subtexto SM subtext

subtitulado SM subtitling

subtitular ▸conjug 1a◂ VT to subtitle

subtítulo SM subtitle, subheading; **~s** (*Cine, TV*) subtitles

subtotal SM subtotal

subtropical ADJ subtropical

suburbano Ⓐ ADJ suburban
Ⓑ SM (= *tren*) suburban train

suburbial ADJ suburban; (*pey*) slum *antes de s*

suburbio SM [1] (= *afueras*) suburb, outlying area
[2] (= *barrio bajo*) slum area, shantytown

subutilizado ADJ under-used, under-utilized

subvaloración SF undervaluing

subvalorar ▸conjug 1a◂ VT (= *no valorar*) to undervalue, underrate; (= *subestimar*) to underestimate

subvención SF subsidy, subvention, grant ► **subvenciones agrícolas** agricultural subsidies ► **subvención estatal** state subsidy ► **subvención para la inversión** (*Com*) investment grant

subvencionar ▸conjug 1a◂ VT to subsidize

subvenir ▸conjug 3r◂ VI **~ a** [+ *gastos*] to meet, defray; [+ *necesidades*] to provide for; **con eso subviene a sus vicios** he uses that to pay for his vices; **así subviene a la escasez de su sueldo** that's how he supplements his (low) salary

subversión SF [1] (= *acción*) subversion; **la ~ del orden establecido** the undermining of the established order
[2] (= *revolución*) revolution

subversivo ADJ subversive

subvertir ▸conjug 3i◂ VI [1] (= *alterar*) to subvert
[2] (= *derrocar*) to overthrow

subyacente ADJ underlying

subyacer ▸conjug 2x◂ VT to underlie

subyugación SF subjugation

subyugador ADJ, **subyugante** ADJ [1] (= *que domina*) dominating
[2] (= *que hechiza*) captivating, enchanting

subyugar ▸conjug 1h◂ VT [1] (= *dominar*) [+ *país*] to subjugate, subdue; [+ *enemigo*] to overpower; [+ *voluntad*] to dominate, gain control over
[2] (= *hechizar*) to captivate, charm

succión SF suction

succionar ▸conjug 1a◂ VT [1] (= *sorber*) to suck
[2] (*Téc*) to absorb, soak up

sucedáneo Ⓐ ADJ substitute
Ⓑ SM substitute

suceder ▸conjug 2a◂ Ⓐ VI [1] (= *ocurrir*) to happen; **pues sucede que no vamos** well it (so) happens we're not going; **no le había sucedido eso nunca** that had never happened to him before; **suceda lo que suceda** come what may, whatever happens; **¿qué sucede?** what's going on?; **lo que sucede es que ...** the fact *o* the trouble is that ...; **llevar algo por lo que pueda ~** to take sth just in case; **lo más que puede ~ es que ...** the worst that can happen is that ...; **lo mismo sucede con éste que con el otro** it's the same with this one as it is with the other
[2] (= *seguir*) **~ a algo** to follow sth; **al otoño sucede el invierno** winter follows autumn; **a este cuarto sucede otro mayor** a larger room leads off this one, a larger room lies beyond this one
Ⓑ VT [+ *persona*] to succeed; **~ a algn en un puesto** to succeed sb in a post; **si muere, ¿quién la ~á?** if she dies, who will succeed?
Ⓒ **sucederse** VPR to follow one another

sucesión SF [1] (*al trono, en un puesto*) succession (**a** to); **en la línea de ~ al trono** in line of succession to the throne ► **sucesión apostólica** apostolic succession
[2] (= *secuencia*) sequence, series; **una ~ de acontecimientos** a succession *o* series of events; **en rápida ~** in quick succession
[3] (= *herencia*) inheritance ► **derechos de sucesión** death duty
[4] (= *hijos*) issue, offspring; **morir sin ~** to die without issue

sucesivamente ADV successively, in succession; **y así ~** and so on

sucesivo ADJ (= *subsiguiente*) successive, following; (= *consecutivo*) consecutive; **tres días ~s** three days running, three consecutive days; **en lo ~** (= *en el futuro*) henceforth (*frm o liter*), in future; (= *desde entonces*) thereafter, thenceforth (*frm o liter*)

suceso SM [1] (= *acontecimiento*) event; (= *incidente*) incident; **sección de ~s** (*Prensa*) (section of) accident and crime reports
[2] (= *resultado*) issue, outcome; **buen ~** happy outcome

sucesor(a) SM/F [1] (*al trono, a un puesto*) successor
[2] (= *heredero*) heir/heiress

sucesorio ADJ [*lucha, derechos, crisis*] succession *antes de s*; [*impuesto*] inheritance *antes de s*; **tercero en la línea sucesoria** third in (the) line of succession

suche Ⓐ ADJ (*Caribe**) sharp, bitter
Ⓑ SM (*Cono Sur*) [1] (*) (= *grano*) pimple
[2] (*) (= *funcionario*) penpusher, pencil pusher (*EEUU*)
[3] (‡) (= *coime*) pimp

súchil SM (*LAm*) *an aromatic flowering tree*

sucho ADJ (*Andes*) maimed, crippled

suciamente ADV [1] (= *con suciedad*) dirtily, filthily
[2] (= *vilmente*) vilely, meanly
[3] (= *obscenamente*) obscenely

suciedad SF [1] (= *porquería*) dirt; **un detergente que elimina la ~** a detergent that banishes dirt
[2] (= *falta de limpieza*) dirtiness

sucintamente ADV succinctly, concisely

sucinto ADJ [1] [*discurso, texto*] succinct, concise
[2] [*prenda*] brief, scanty, skimpy*

sucio Ⓐ ADJ [1] (= *manchado*) [*cara, ropa, suelo*] dirty; **llevas los zapatos muy ~s** your shoes are very dirty; **tienes las manos sucísimas** your hands are filthy; **hazlo primero en ~** make a rough draft first, do it in rough first
[2] [*color*] dirty
[3] (= *fácil de manchar*) **los pantalones blancos son muy ~s** white trousers show the dirt, white trousers get dirty very easily
[4] (= *obsceno*) dirty, filthy; **palabras sucias** dirty words, filthy words
[5] (= *deshonesto*) [*jugada*] foul, dirty; [*táctica*] dirty; [*negocio*] shady
[6] [*conciencia*] bad
[7] [*lengua*] coated, furred
Ⓑ ADV **jugar ~** to play dirty
Ⓒ SM (*Andes*) bit of dirt

suco[1] ADJ (*Andes*) muddy, swampy

suco[2] ADJ (*Andes*) (= *rojizo*) bright red; (= *rubio*) blond, fair; (= *anaranjado*) orange

sucre SM sucre (*standard monetary unit of Ecuador*)

sucrosa SF sucrose

sucucho SM (*Caribe*) = **socucha**

suculencia SF (= *lo sabroso*) tastiness, richness; (= *jugosidad*) succulence

suculento ADJ (= *sabroso*) tasty, rich; (= *jugoso*) succulent

sucumbir ▸conjug 3a◂ VI to succumb (**a** to)

sucursal SF (= *oficina local*) branch, branch office; (= *filial*) subsidiary

sucusumuco ADV **a lo ~** (*Andes, Caribe*) pretending to be stupid, feigning stupidity

sud SM (*esp LAm*) south

sudaca* ADJ, SMF (*pey*) South American

sudadera SF sweatshirt

sudado Ⓐ ADJ sweaty
Ⓑ SM (*Perú*) stew

Sudáfrica SF South Africa

sudafricano/a ADJ, SM/F South African

Sudamérica SF South America

sudamericano/a ADJ, SM/F South American

Sudán SM Sudan

sudanés/esa ADJ, SM/F Sudanese

sudar ▸conjug 1a◂ Ⓐ VI 1 (= *transpirar*) to sweat; ✦*MODISMOS* **~ a chorros*** ◊ **~ a mares*** to sweat buckets*; **hacer ~ a algn** to make sb sweat

2 (= *exudar*) [*recipiente*] to ooze; [*pared*] to sweat

Ⓑ VT 1 (= *transpirar*) to sweat; ✦*MODISMO* **~ la gota gorda** to sweat buckets*; *ver tb* **sangre A2, tinta 1**

2 (= *mojar*) [+ *ropa, prenda*] to make sweaty; ✦*MODISMOS* **~ la camiseta** to sweat blood; **me la suda**‡: **es un asunto que me la suda** it bores the pants off me*

3 (*Bot*) (= *segregar*) to ooze, give out, give off

4 (*) (= *conseguir con esfuerzo*) **~lo** to sweat it out; **~ un aumento de sueldo** to sweat for a rise in pay; **ha sudado el premio** he really went flat out to get that prize

5 (*) [+ *dinero*] to cough up*, part with

sudario SM shroud

sudestada SF (*Cono Sur*) = **surestada**

sudeste SM = **sureste**

sudista Ⓐ ADJ southern

Ⓑ SMF Southerner

sudoeste = **suroeste**

sudón* ADJ (*LAm*) sweaty

sudor SM 1 (= *transpiración*) sweat; **con el ~ de su frente** by the sweat of one's brow; **estar bañado en ~** to be dripping with sweat

2 (*tb* **~es**) (= *esfuerzo*) toil *sing*, labour *sing*, labor *sing* (EEUU)

sudoración SF sweating

sudoroso ADJ, **sudoriento** ADJ, **sudoso** ADJ sweaty; **trabajo ~** thirsty work

Suecia SF Sweden

suecia SF suede

sueco/a Ⓐ ADJ Swedish

Ⓑ SM/F Swede; ✦*MODISMO* **hacerse el ~*** to act dumb

Ⓒ SM (*Ling*) Swedish

suegro/a SM/F father-in-law/mother-in-law; **suegros** parents-in-law, in-laws

suela SF 1 [*de zapato*] (= *base*) sole; (= *trozo de cuero*) piece of strong leather; **media ~** half sole; ✦*MODISMOS* **no llegarle a algn a la ~ del zapata: Juan no le llega a la ~ del zapato a Pablo** Juan can't hold a candle to Pablo; **duro como la ~ de un zapato** tough as leather, tough as old boots; **de siete ~s** utter, downright; **un pícaro de siete ~s** an utter *o* a downright *o* a proper rogue

2 (*Téc*) tap washer

3 **~s** (*Rel*) sandals

4 (= *pez*) sole

suelazo SM (*LAm*) (= *caída*) heavy fall, nasty bump; (= *golpe*) blow, punch

▼ **sueldo** SM (= *paga*) (*gen*) pay; (*mensual*) salary; (*semanal*) wages *pl*; **asesino a ~** hired killer, contract killer; **estar a ~** to be on a salary, earn a salary; **estar a ~ de una potencia extranjera** to be in the pay of a foreign power ▸ **sueldo atrasado** back pay ▸ **sueldo base** basic salary ▸ **sueldo en especie** payment in kind ▸ **sueldo fijo** regular salary ▸ **sueldo líquido** net salary

suelear* ▸conjug 1a◂ VT (*Cono Sur*) to throw, chuck

suelo SM 1 (*en el exterior*) (= *tierra*) ground; (= *superficie*) surface; **caer al ~** to fall to the ground, fall over; **echar al ~** [+ *edificio*] to demolish; [+ *esperanzas*] to dash; [+ *plan*] to ruin; **echarse al ~** (= *tirarse al suelo*) to hurl o.s. to the ground; (= *arrodillarse*) to fall on one's knees; ✦*MODISMOS* **por los ~s**: **los precios están por los ~s** prices are at rock bottom; **esos géneros están por los ~s** those goods are dirt cheap; **tengo el ánimo por los ~s** I feel really low; **arrastrar** *o* **poner** *o* **tirar por los ~s** [+ *persona*] to slate, slag off*; [+ *novela, película*] to pan, slam, rubbish*; **medir el ~** to measure one's length (on the ground); **tirarse por los ~s*** to roll in the aisles (with laughter)*; **venirse al ~** to fail, collapse, be ruined ▸ **suelo natal**, **suelo patrio** native land, native soil

2 (*en edificio*) (= *superficie*) floor; (= *solería*) flooring; **un ~ de mármol** a marble floor

3 (= *terreno*) soil, land ▸ **suelo edificable** building land ▸ **suelo empresarial** *space for office accommodation* ▸ **suelo vegetal** topsoil

4 [*de pan, vasija*] bottom

suelta SF **habrá una ~ de palomas** doves will be released

suelte *etc ver* **soltar**

sueltista SMF (*LAm*) freelance journalist

suelto Ⓐ ADJ 1 (= *libre*) (*gen*) free; [*criminal*] free, out; [*animal*] loose; **el bandido anda ~** the bandit's on the loose; **el perro anda ~** the dog is loose

2 (= *desatado*) [*cordones*] undone, untied; [*cabo, hoja, tornillo*] loose; **llevas ~s los cordones** your shoelaces are undone; **el libro tiene dos hojas sueltas** the book has two pages loose; **el arroz tiene que quedar ~** rice shouldn't stick together

3 **dinero ~** loose change

4 [*prenda de vestir*] loose, loose-fitting; **iba con el pelo ~** she had her hair down *o* loose

5 [*vientre*] loose

6 **~ de lengua** (= *parlanchín*) talkative; (= *respondón*) cheeky; (= *soplón*) blabbing; (= *obsceno*) foul-mouthed

7 (= *separado*) [*trozo, pieza*] separate, detached; [*ejemplar, volumen*] individual, odd; [*calcetín*] odd; **no se venden ~s** they are not sold singly *o* separately; **es un trozo ~ de la novela** it's a separate extract from the novel, it's an isolated passage from the novel; **son tres poesías sueltas** these are three separate poems; **hay un calcetín ~** there is one odd sock; **una mesa con números ~s de revistas** a table with odd copies of magazines

8 (*Com*) (= *no envasado*) loose

9 [*movimiento*] (= *libre*) free, easy; (= *ágil*) quick

10 (= *fluido*) [*estilo*] fluent; [*conversación*] easy, easy-flowing; **está muy ~ en inglés** he is very good at *o* fluent in English

11 (*moralmente*) free and easy

12 (*Literat*) [*verso*] blank

Ⓑ SM 1 (= *cambio*) loose change, small change

2 (= *artículo*) item, short article, short report

suene *etc ver* **sonar**

sueña *etc ver* **soñar**

sueñera SF (*LAm*) drowsiness, sleepiness

sueño SM 1 (= *estado*) sleep; **coger** *o* **conciliar el ~** to get to sleep; **echarse un ~** *o* **un sueñecito*** to have a nap, have a kip*; **en** *o* **entre ~s**: **me hablaste entre ~s** you talked to me but you were half asleep; **tener el ~ ligero** to be a light sleeper; **tener el ~ pesado** to be a heavy sleeper ▸ **sueño eterno** eternal rest ▸ **sueño invernal** (*Zool*) winter sleep ▸ **sueño paradójico** paradoxical sleep ▸ **sueño profundo** deep sleep ▸ **sueño REM** REM sleep; *ver tb* **dormir B2**

2 (= *ganas de dormir*) **tienes cara de ~** you look sleepy; **tengo ~ atrasado** I haven't caught up on sleep, I haven't had much sleep lately; **caerse de ~** to be asleep on one's feet; **dar ~**: **su conversación me da ~** his conversation sends me to sleep; **la televisión me da ~** television makes me sleepy; **morirse de ~** ◊ **estar muerto de ~** to be asleep on one's feet, be so tired one can hardly stand; **quitar el ~ a algn** to keep sb awake; **el café me quita el ~** coffee keeps me awake; **ya se me ha quitado el ~** I'm not sleepy any more; **tener ~** to be sleepy, be tired; ✦*MODISMO* **perder el ~ por algo** to lose sleep over sth; *ver tb* **vencer A3**

3 (= *imagen soñada*) dream; **anoche tuve un ~ espantoso** I had a horrible dream last night; **¿sabes interpretar los ~s?** do you know how to interpret dreams?; **¡que tengas dulces ~s!** sweet dreams!; ✦*MODISMO* **¡ni en ~s!*** no chance!*; **eso no te lo crees tú ni en ~s** don't give me that!‡; **no pienso volver a hablarle ni en ~s** there's no way I'd ever talk to him again* ▸ **sueño húmedo** wet dream

4 (= *ilusión*) dream; **por fin consiguió la casa de sus ~s** she finally got the house of her dreams *o* her dream home; **vive en un mundo de ~s** he lives in a dream world; **estas vacaciones son como un ~** these holidays are like a dream come true; **mi ~ dorado es vivir frente al mar** my greatest dream is to live by the sea ▸ **el sueño americano** the American Dream

suero SM 1 (*Med*) serum ▸ **suero fisiológico** saline solution

2 [*de leche*] whey ▸ **suero de leche** buttermilk

suertaza* SF great stroke of luck

▼ **suerte** SF 1 (= *fortuna*) luck; **con un poco de ~ podemos ganar** with a bit of luck we can win; **no me cupo tal ~** I had no such luck; **no nos acompañó mucho la ~** luck wasn't on our side; **¡suerte!** ◊ **¡buena suerte!** good luck!; **dar ~** to bring good luck; **el topacio da ~** topaz brings good luck; **este número me da ~** this is my lucky number; **día de ~** lucky day; **me considero un hombre de ~** I consider myself a lucky man; **estar de ~** to be in luck; **mala ~** bad luck; **la mala ~ está acompañando su gira** his tour is being dogged by bad luck; **¡siempre tengo tan mala ~ con los hombres!** I'm always so unlucky with men!, I always have such bad luck with men!; **¡qué mala ~!** how unlucky!, what bad luck!; **por ~** luckily, fortunately; **probar ~** to try one's luck; **tener ~** to be lucky; **¡que tengas ~!** good luck!, the best of luck!; **tuvo una ~ increíble** he was incredibly lucky; **tuvo la ~ de que el autobús saliera con retraso** he was lucky that the bus left late, luckily for him his bus left late; **tentar a la ~** to try one's

➤ LENGUA Y USO: **sueldo** 46.2 **suerte 1** 50.5

luck; **traer ~** to be lucky, bring good luck; **me trajo ~** it brought me good luck; **trae mala ~** it's bad luck, it's unlucky; ✦*MODISMO* **por ~ o por desgracia** for better or for worse; *ver tb* **golpe 11**

2 (= *destino*) fate; **la ~ que les espera** the fate which awaits them; **quiso la ~ que pasara por allí un médico** as luck *o* fate would have it a doctor was passing by; **estar resignado a su ~** to be resigned to one's fate; **los abandonaron a su ~** they left them to their fate; **no estaba contento con su ~** he wasn't happy with his lot; **correr la misma ~ que algn** to suffer the same fate as sb; **mejorar la ~ de algn** to improve sb's lot; **tentar a la ~** to tempt fate

3 (= *azar*) chance; **confiar algo a la ~** to leave sth to chance; **lo echaron a ~s** (*con cerillas, papeletas*) they drew lots; (*con moneda*) they tossed (a coin); ✦*MODISMOS* **caerle** *o* **tocarle en ~ a algn**: **al equipo español le tocó en ~ enfrentarse a Turquía** as chance had it, the Spanish team were drawn to play against Turkey; **¡vaya marido que me ha tocado en ~!** what a husband I ended up with!; **la ~ está echada** the die is cast

4 (= *clase*) sort, kind; **hubo toda ~ de comentarios** there were all sorts *o* kinds of remarks; **lo explicó con toda ~ de detalles** she explained it in great detail

5 (*frm*) (= *modo*) **de esta ~** in this way; **no podemos seguir de esta ~** we cannot go on in this way; **los molinos de agua pueden clasificarse de esta ~** water wheels can be classified in the following way *o* in this way; **de ~ que** in such a way that

6 (*Taur*) *stage of the bullfight* ➤ **suerte de banderillas** *the second stage of a bullfight, in which the "banderillas" are stuck into the bull's back* ➤ **suerte de capa** *stage of a bullfight where passes are made with the cape* ➤ **suerte de varas** *opening stage of a bullfight where the bull is weakened with the picador's lance* ➤ **suerte suprema** *final stage of a bullfight*

suertero ADJ (*LAm*), **suertudo** ADJ (*esp LAm*) lucky, jammy*

suertoso ADJ (*Andes*) lucky

suestada SF (*Arg*) southeast wind

sueste SM 1 (= *sombrero*) sou'wester
2 (*LAm*) (= *viento*) southeast wind

suéter SM sweater

Suetonio SM Suetonius

Suez SM Suez; **Canal de ~** Suez Canal

suficiencia SF 1 (= *cabida*) sufficiency; **con ~** sufficiently, adequately; **una ~ de …** enough …

2 (= *competencia*) competence; **demostrar su ~** to prove one's competence, show one's capabilities

3 (*Escol*) proficiency

4 (*pey*) (= *engreimiento*) self-importance; (= *satisfacción de sí mismo*) smugness, self-satisfaction

suficiente Ⓐ ADJ 1 (= *bastante*) enough; **ahora no llevo ~ dinero (como) para pagarte** I don't have enough money on me at the moment to pay you

2 (= *petulante*) smug, self-satisfied

Ⓑ SM (*Escol*) ≈ C, pass mark, passing grade (*EEUU*)

suficientemente ADV sufficiently, adequately; **no era ~ grande** it wasn't big enough *o* sufficiently big; **~ bueno** good enough

sufijo SM suffix

suflé SM soufflé

sufragáneo ADJ suffragan

sufragar ▸conjug 1h◂ Ⓐ VT 1 (= *ayudar*) to help, aid

2 (= *pagar*) [+ *gastos*] to meet, defray; [+ *proyecto*] to pay for, defray the costs of

Ⓑ VI (*LAm*) to vote (**por** for)

sufragio SM 1 (= *voto*) vote; **los ~s emitidos a favor del candidato** the votes cast for the candidate

2 (= *derecho al voto*) suffrage ➤ **sufragio universal** universal suffrage

3 (= *apoyo*) help, aid

4 (*Rel*) suffrage

sufragista Ⓐ ADJ, SMF suffragist

Ⓑ SF (*Hist*) suffragette

sufrible ADJ bearable

sufrido Ⓐ ADJ 1 [*persona*] (= *fuerte*) tough; (= *paciente*) long-suffering, patient

2 [*tela*] hard wearing, tough; [*color*] that does not show the dirt, that wears well

3 [*marido*] complaisant

Ⓑ SM complaisant husband

sufridor(a) Ⓐ ADJ suffering

Ⓑ SM/F (= *persona*) sufferer

Ⓒ SM (*Andes*) saddlecloth

sufrimiento SM 1 (= *padecimiento*) suffering; **una vida marcada por el ~** a life of suffering

2 (††) (= *paciencia*) patience; **tener ~ en las dificultades** to be patient in hard times, bear troubles patiently

sufrir ▸conjug 3a◂ Ⓐ VT 1 (= *tener*) [+ *accidente*] to have, suffer; [+ *consecuencias, revés*] to suffer; [+ *cambio*] to undergo; [+ *intervención quirúrgica*] to have, undergo; [+ *pérdida*] to suffer, sustain; **la ciudad sufrió un ataque** the city suffered *o* sustained an attack; **sufrió un ataque al corazón** he had a heart attack; **~ un colapso** to collapse

2 (= *soportar*) **Juan no puede ~ a su jefe** Juan can't bear *o* stand his boss; **no puede ~ que la imiten** she can't bear *o* stand people imitating her

3 [+ *examen, prueba*] to undergo

4 (*frm*) (= *sostener*) to hold up, support

Ⓑ VI to suffer; **sufría en silencio** she suffered in silence; **mi madre sufre mucho si llego tarde a casa** my mother gets terribly worried if I'm late home; **hacer ~ a algn** to make sb suffer; **~ de algo** to suffer from sth; **sufre de reumatismo** she suffers from rheumatism; **sufre mucho de los pies** she suffers a lot *o* has a lot of trouble with her feet

▼**sugerencia** SF suggestion; **hacer una ~** to make a suggestion; *ver tb* **buzón 1**

sugerente ADJ 1 (= *lleno de ideas*) [*exposición, obra*] thought-provoking; [*lenguaje*] evocative

2 (= *seductor*) [*mirada, gesto, voz*] suggestive; [*ropa, iluminación*] seductive; **con el ~ título de "Pasión tropical"** with the suggestive title of "Pasión tropical"

sugerible ADJ = **sugestionable**

sugerimiento SM suggestion

▼**sugerir** ▸conjug 3i◂ VT 1 (= *proponer*) to suggest; **¿tú qué me sugieres?** what do you suggest?; **nos sugirió la idea de grabar esa canción** he suggested the idea of recording that song to us; **~ hacer algo** to suggest doing sth; **yo sugiero empezar más temprano** I suggest that we begin earlier, I suggest beginning earlier; **~ a algn que** + *SUBJUN*: **me ha sugerido que escriba una novela** he has suggested that I write a novel *o* that I should write a novel

2 (= *insinuar*) to hint at, suggest; **sugirió la posibilidad de que el ministro dimitiera** he hinted at the possibility of the minister resigning, he suggested the possibility that the Minister would resign

3 (= *indicar*) to suggest; **los hallazgos arqueológicos sugieren la existencia de un asentamiento anterior** the archaeological finds suggest the existence of a previous settlement; **no es una novela histórica, como el título podría ~** it is not a historical novel, as the title might suggest

4 (= *evocar*) **la película me ha sugerido muchas cosas** the film was very thought-provoking, the film gave me much food for thought; **la idea que nos sugiere este nuevo producto** the idea conveyed by this new product, the image this new product calls to mind

sugestión SF 1 (= *convencimiento*) **sus problemas no son más que pura ~** his problems are all in his mind; **lo durmió gracias a sus poderes de ~** he made him go to sleep by his hypnotic powers

2 (= *insinuación*) suggestion; **nunca acepta las sugestiones de los demás** he never listens to anyone else's suggestions; **las sugestiones del demonio** the promptings of the devil

sugestionable ADJ (= *impresionable*) impressionable, suggestible; (= *influenciable*) readily influenced

sugestionar ▸conjug 1a◂ Ⓐ VT to influence; **es probable que se haya dejado ~ por …** he may have allowed himself to be influenced by …; **~ a algn para que haga algo** to influence sb to do sth

Ⓑ **sugestionarse** VPR to indulge in autosuggestion; **~se con algo** to talk o.s. into sth

sugestivo ADJ 1 (= *que invita a pensar*) stimulating, thought-provoking; (= *evocador*) evocative

2 (= *atractivo*) attractive

sugiera *etc ver* **sugerir**

suiche SM (*esp Méx*) 1 (*Elec*) switch

2 (*Aut*) ignition, ignition switch

suicida Ⓐ ADJ suicidal; **comando ~** suicide squad; **conductor ~** suicidal driver; **piloto ~** suicide pilot, kamikaze pilot

Ⓑ SMF (= *que ha intentado suicidarse*) suicidal case; (= *muerto*) suicide victim; **es un ~ conduciendo** he's a maniac behind the wheel

suicidado/a SM/F *person who commits suicide*

suicidar ▸conjug 1a◂ Ⓐ VT (*iró*) to murder, assassinate (*so as to convey an impression of suicide*), fake the suicide of

Ⓑ **suicidarse** VPR to commit suicide, kill o.s.

suicidario ADJ, **suicidiario** ADJ suicidal

suicidio SM suicide

sui géneris ADJ INV individual, idiosyncratic

suite [swit] SF 1 (*en hotel*) suite

2 (*Mús*) suite

Suiza SF Switzerland

suiza SF 1 (*CAm, Caribe*) (= *juego*) skipping,

➤ LENGUA Y USO: **sugerencia** 28.1 **sugerir 1** 28.1, 28.2, 53.6

jumping rope (*EEUU*), skipping game
[2] (*Andes, CAm*) (= *paliza*) beating

suizo¹/a ADJ, SM/F Swiss

suizo² SM (*Culin*) sugared bun

suje* SM bra

sujeción SF [1] (= *estado*) subjection
[2] (= *acción*) (*al cerrar*) fastening; (*al apoderarse de algo*) seizure
[3] (= *dominación*) subjection (**a** to); **con ~ a** subject to

sujetacorbata SM tiepin

sujetador SM [1] (= *prenda*) [*de ropa interior*] bra, brassiere (*frm*); [*del biquini*] top
[2] (*para pelo*) clip, hairgrip, bobby pin (*EEUU*)

sujetalibros SM INV book-end

sujetapapeles SM INV paper clip

sujetar ▸conjug 1a◂ Ⓐ VT [1] (= *agarrar*) to hold; **sujeta esto un momento** hold this a moment; **dos policías lo sujetaban contra la pared** two policemen pinned *o* held him against the wall; **lo tuvieron que ~ entre tres personas para que no huyera** he had to be held back *o* restrained by three people to stop him escaping
[2] (= *afianzar*) **lo sujeté con un esparadrapo** I fixed it with some sticking-plaster; **sujeta bien la ropa, que no se la lleve el viento** to peg the clothes (up) properly so the wind doesn't blow them away; **hay que ~ bien a los niños dentro del coche** children should be properly strapped in *o* properly secured when travelling by car; **~ algo a: se sujeta a la pared por medio de argollas** it is fixed *o* attached *o* secured to the wall through rings; **~ algo con: ~ algo con clavos** to nail sth down; **~ algo con grapas** to staple sth; **~ algo con tornillos** to screw sth down; **enrolló el mapa y lo sujetó con una goma** she rolled up the map and fastened *o* secured it with a rubber band; **sujetó las facturas con un clip** she clipped the invoices together
[3] (= *contener*) [+ *rebelde*] to subdue, conquer; [+ *rival, animal enfurecido*] to keep down; **es muy rebelde y sus padres no lo pueden ~** he's very rebellious — his parents can't control him; **lograron ~ las aspiraciones de los sindicatos** they succeeded in keeping the aspirations of the unions under control; **vive sin ataduras que la sujeten** she has nothing to tie her down, she has no ties to bind her; **mis deberes como político me sujetan aquí** my duties as a politician bind me here
Ⓑ **sujetarse** VPR [1] (= *agarrarse*) [1·1] [+ *pelo, sombrero*] to hold; **salió sujetándose los pantalones** he came out holding his trousers up; **¿tienes una goma para ~me el pelo?** have you got an elastic band to hold my hair up?; **inclinó la cabeza y se sujetó el sombrero** he tilted his head and held his hat on
[1·2] **~se a algo** to hold on to sth; **tuvo que ~se a la barandilla para no caerse** he had to hold on to the handrail so as not to fall over
[2] (= *someterse*) **~se a** [+ *normas, reglas*] to abide by; [+ *autoridad*] to submit to; **no quieren ~se a un horario fijo** they don't want to tie themselves down to fixed hours, they don't want to be bound by a fixed timetable

sujeto Ⓐ ADJ [1] (= *fijo*) fastened, secure; **¿está sujeta la cuerda?** is the rope fastened securely?, is the rope secure?; **las ruedas van sujetas por cuatro tuercas** the wheels are held on *o* secured by four nuts; **los espejos estaban ~s a la pared** the mirrors were fastened *o* fixed to the wall
[2] (= *pendiente*) **~ a algo** subject to sth; **vivimos ~s a las vicisitudes del destino** we are all subject to the vicissitudes of fate; **la programación podría estar sujeta a cambios** the programme could be subject to changes; **una suma de dinero no sujeta a impuestos** a non-taxable sum of money
Ⓑ SM [1] (*) (= *tipo*) character*; **un ~ sospechoso** a suspicious(-looking) character*
[2] (*Med, Fil*) subject; **todos los ~s estudiados** all the subjects studied
[3] (*Ling*) subject
[4] (*Fin*) ► **sujeto pasivo** taxpayer

sulfamida SF sulphonamide

sulfatar ▸conjug 1a◂ VT to fertilize, fertilize with sulphate

sulfato SM sulphate, sulfate (*EEUU*) ► **sulfato amónico** ammonium sulphate ► **sulfato de cobre** copper sulphate ► **sulfato de hierro** iron sulphate ► **sulfato magnésico** magnesium sulphate ► **sulfato potásico** potassium sulphate

sulfurado* ADJ cross, angry

sulfurar ▸conjug 1a◂ Ⓐ VT [1] (*Quím*) to sulphurate, sulfurate (*EEUU*)
[2] (*) (= *sacar de quicio a*) to rile*
Ⓑ **sulfurarse** VPR (*) (= *enojarse*) to get riled*, see red, blow up*

sulfúreo ADJ sulphurous, sulfurous (*EEUU*)

sulfúrico ADJ sulphuric, sulfuric (*EEUU*)

sulfuro SM sulphide, sulfide (*EEUU*)

sulfuroso ADJ sulphurous, sulfurous (*EEUU*)

sultán/ana SM/F sultan/sultana

sultanato SM sultanate

▼ **suma** Ⓐ SF [1] (*Mat*) (= *acción*) addition, adding, adding up; (= *cantidad*) total, sum; (= *dinero*) sum; **una ~ de dinero** a sum of money; **¿cuánto es la ~ de todos los gastos?** what are the total expenses?; **hacer ~s** to add up, do addition; **hizo la ~ de todo lo que habían gastado** he added up everything they had spent; **~ y sigue** (*Com*) "carried forward"; (*) and it's still going on ► **suma global** lump sum
[2] (= *resumen*) summary; **en ~** in short; **una ~ de perfecciones** perfection itself; **es la ~ y compendio de todas las virtudes** she is the personification of virtue
Ⓑ SM **un ~ y sigue de grandes aportaciones al mundo del automóvil** a whole host of great contributions to the motoring world; **su vida es un continuo ~ y sigue de tragedias** his life is one tragedy after another

sumador SM adder

sumadora SF adding machine

sumamente ADV extremely, exceedingly, highly

sumando SM addend

sumar ▸conjug 1a◂ Ⓐ VT [1] (*Mat*) to add (together); **suma estas dos cantidades** add these two amounts (together)
[2] (= *totalizar*) to add up to, come to; **la cuenta suma seis dólares** the bill adds up *o* comes to six dollars; **dos y dos suman cuatro** two and two are *o* make four
[3] (†) (= *resumir*) to summarize, sum up
Ⓑ VI to add up; **suma y sigue** (*Contabilidad*) carried forward
Ⓒ **sumarse** VPR **~se a algo** to join sth; **~se a un partido** to join a party; **~se a una protesta** to join in a protest

sumarial ADJ summary

sumariamente ADV summarily

sumario Ⓐ ADJ [1] (= *breve*) brief, concise
[2] (*Jur*) summary; **información sumaria** summary proceedings *pl*
Ⓑ SM [1] (= *resumen*) (*gen*) summary; (*en revista*) contents *pl*
[2] (*Jur*) indictment; **abrir** *o* **instruir un ~** to institute legal proceedings, present *o* issue an indictment (*esp EEUU*)

sumarísimo ADJ summary

Sumatra SF Sumatra

sumergible Ⓐ ADJ [*nave*] submersible; [*reloj*] waterproof
Ⓑ SM submarine

sumergido ADJ [1] (*en agua*) submerged, sunken
[2] (= *ilegal*) illegal, unauthorized; **economía sumergida** black economy; **tratos ~s** black-market deals

sumergimiento SM submersion, submergence

sumergir ▸conjug 3c◂ Ⓐ VT (*completamente*) to immerse; (*parcialmente*) to dip (**en** in); **~ la bolsa en agua hirviendo** put the bag into the boiling water
Ⓑ **sumergirse** VPR [1] (= *hundirse*) [*objeto, persona*] to sink beneath the surface; [*submarino*] to dive
[2] (*en un ambiente*) **~se en** to immerse o.s. in

sumersión SF [1] (= *inmersión*) submersion
[2] (= *absorción*) absorption (**en** in)

sumidero SM [1] (*en calle, azotea, patio*) drain
[2] (*Téc*) sump, oilpan (*EEUU*)
[3] (= *sangría*) drain; **es el gran ~ de las reservas** it is the chief drain on our reserves
[4] (*Andes, Caribe*) (= *pozo negro*) cesspool, cesspit
[5] (*Caribe*) (= *tremedal*) quagmire

sumido ADJ **~ en su trabajo** immersed *o* buried in one's work; **~ en mis pensamientos** lost in thought

sumiller SM wine waiter

suministrador(a) SM/F supplier

suministrar ▸conjug 1a◂ VT [+ *géneros, información*] to supply, provide; [+ *persona*] to supply; **me ha suministrado muchos datos** he has given me a lot of information, he has provided *o* supplied me with a lot of information

suministro SM [1] (= *provisión*) supply; **~s** (*Mil*) supplies ► **suministro de agua** water supply ► **suministro de gas** gas supply ► **suministros de combustible** fuel supply *sing*
[2] (= *acción*) supplying, provision

sumir ▸conjug 3a◂ Ⓐ VT [1] (= *hundir*) (*gen*) to sink, plunge; [*mar, olas*] to swallow up, suck down
[2] (= *abismar*) to plunge (**en** into); **el desastre lo sumió en la tristeza** the disaster filled him with sadness
[3] (*Andes, Cono Sur, Méx*) (= *abollar*) to dent
Ⓑ **sumirse** VPR [1] (= *hundirse*) to sink
[2] [*agua*] to run away
[3] **~se en el estudio** to throw o.s. into one's studies; **~se en la duda** to be seized by doubt; **~se en la tristeza** to be filled with sadness
[4] [*boca, pecho*] to sink, be sunken, become

➤ LENGUA Y USO: suma A1 53.4

hollow

5 (*LAm*) (= *encogerse*) to cower, cringe; (= *desanimarse*) to lose heart; (= *callar*) to fall silent from fear, clam up

6 **~se el sombrero** (*LAm*) to pull one's hat down over one's eyes

sumisamente ADV (= *dócilmente*) submissively, obediently; (= *sin resistir*) unresistingly; (= *sin quejarse*) uncomplainingly

sumisión SF 1 (= *acción*) submission

2 (= *docilidad*) submissiveness

sumiso ADJ (= *dócil*) submissive; (= *que no se resiste*) unresisting; (= *que no se queja*) uncomplaining

súmmum SM height

sumo[1] ADJ 1 (= *supremo*) great, supreme; **con suma dificultad** with the greatest *o* utmost difficulty; **con suma indiferencia** with supreme indifference; **con suma destreza** with consummate skill

2 [*rango*] high, highest; **~ sacerdote** high priest; **la suma autoridad** the supreme authority

3 **a lo ~** at (the) most

sumo[2] SM (*Dep*) sumo, sumo wrestling

sunco ADJ (*Andes*) = **manco A**

sungo ADJ (*Andes*) 1 (= *de raza negra*) (*gen*) black; (= *de piel lisa*) with a shiny skin

2 (= *tostado*) tanned

suní ADJ, SMF, **sunita** ADJ, SMF Sunni

suntuario ADJ sumptuary

suntuosamente ADJ (= *magníficamente*) sumptuously, magnificently; (= *pródigamente*) lavishly, richly

suntuosidad SF (= *magnificencia*) sumptuousness, magnificence; (= *prodigalidad*) lavishness

suntuoso ADJ (= *magnífico*) sumptuous, magnificent; (= *lujoso*) lavish, rich

sup. ABR (= **superior**) sup

supe *etc ver* **saber**

supeditar ▸conjug 1a◂ Ⓐ VT 1 (= *subordinar*) to subordinate (**a** to); **tendrá que ser supeditado a lo que decidan ellos** it will depend *o* be dependent on what they decide

2 (= *sojuzgar*) to subdue

3 (= *oprimir*) to oppress, crush

Ⓑ **supeditarse** VPR **~se a** (= *subordinarse*) to be subject to; (= *ceder*) to give in to; **no voy a ~me a sus caprichos** I am not going to give in to her whims

súper* Ⓐ ADJ super*

Ⓑ SM supermarket

Ⓒ SF (*Aut*) four-star petrol

Ⓓ ADV (*) **pasarlo ~** to have a great time*

super... PREF super..., over...; **~ambicioso** overambitious; **~atraco** major hold-up; **~caro*** dead expensive*; **~desarrollo** overdevelopment; **~famoso** really famous; **~reservado** excessively shy; **un texto ~comentado** a text which has so often been commented on

superable ADJ [*dificultad*] surmountable, that can be overcome; [*tarea*] that can be performed; **un obstáculo difícilmente ~** an obstacle not easily overcome

superabundancia SF superabundance, overabundance

superabundante ADJ superabundant

superación SF 1 (= *acto*) overcoming, surmounting

2 (= *mejora*) improvement; *ver tb* **afán 1**

superagente* SMF supercop*, super-sleuth*

superar ▸conjug 1a◂ Ⓐ VT 1 (= *aventajar*) [+ *contrincante, adversario*] to overcome; [+ *límite*] to go beyond; [+ *récord, marca*] to break; **fue incapaz de ~ al rival** he was unable to overcome his rival; **pronto superó al resto de los corredores** she soon overtook the other runners; **las ventas han superado con creces nuestras expectativas** sales have far exceeded our expectations; **las temperaturas han superado los 20 grados** temperatures have risen (to) above 20 degrees; **~ a algn en algo**: **superó al adversario en cuatro puntos** she beat her opponent by four points; **nos superaban en número** they outnumbered us; **nos supera a todos en inteligencia** she's cleverer than all of us

2 (= *pasar con éxito*) [+ *dificultad*] to overcome; [+ *enfermedad, crisis*] to get over; **ha tenido que ~ muchos obstáculos en su vida** she has had to overcome a lot of obstacles in her life; **aún no ha superado el divorcio de sus padres** he still hasn't got over his parents' divorce

3 [+ *etapa*] to get past; **el equipo francés no superó la primera ronda** the French team did not get past the first round; **ya hemos superado lo peor** we're over the worst now

4 [+ *prueba, examen*] to pass

Ⓑ **superarse** VPR to excel o.s.; **esta tortilla está buenísima, ¡te has superado!** this omelette is delicious, you've excelled yourself!; **un atleta que siempre intenta ~se** an athlete who is always trying to do better

superávit SM (*pl* **superávits**) surplus

superavitario ADJ surplus *antes de s*

superbombardero SM superbomber

supercarburante SM high-grade fuel

supercarretera SF superhighway

superchería SF fraud, trick, swindle

superchero ADJ fraudulent

superclase SMF (*Dep*) top-class sportsman/sportswoman

supercola SF superglue

superconductividad SF superconductivity

superconductor Ⓐ ADJ superconductive

Ⓑ SM superconductor

superconsumo SM overconsumption

supercopa SF cup-winners' cup

supercotizado ADJ in very great demand

supercuerda SF (*Fís*) superstring

superdirecta SF overdrive

superdotado/a Ⓐ ADJ extremely gifted

Ⓑ SM/F extremely gifted person

superego SM superego

superempleo SM overemployment

superentender ▸conjug 2g◂ VT to supervise, superintend

supererogación SF supererogation

superestrella SF superstar

superestructura SF superstructure

superferolítico* ADJ 1 (= *afectado*) affected

2 (= *muy refinado*) excessively refined

3 (= *delicado*) overnice, finicky, choosy*

superficial ADJ 1 [*herida*] superficial, skin *antes de s*

2 (= *poco perceptible*) [*interés*] superficial; [*mirada*] brief, perfunctory; [*carácter*] shallow; [*medidas*] surface *antes de s*

superficialidad SF 1 [*de herida*] superficiality

2 (= *frivolidad*) shallowness

superficialmente ADV superficially

superficie SF 1 [*de cuerpo, líquido*] surface; **la ~ terrestre** the earth's surface; **el submarino salió a la ~** the submarine surfaced, the submarine came to the surface; **ruta de ~** surface route ▸ **superficie de rodadura** (*Aut*) tread ▸ **superficie inferior** lower surface, underside

2 (*en medidas*) area; **en una extensa ~** over a wide area; **una ~ de 200 hectáreas** an area of 200 hectares ▸ **superficie útil** useful area, usable space

3 (= *aspecto externo*) surface; **es un comentario inofensivo en la ~** it's a harmless comment on the surface

4 (*Com*) **gran ~** (= *hipermercado*) hypermarket, superstore; **~ de venta(s)** sales area

superfino ADJ superfine

superfluamente ADV superfluously

superfluidad SF superfluity

superfluo ADJ superfluous

superfosfato SM superphosphate

superhéroe SM superhero

superhombre SM superman

superíndice SM superscript

superintendencia SF supervision

superintendente SMF (= *supervisor*) supervisor, superintendent; (= *capataz*) overseer; **~ de división** sectional head

▼**superior**[1] Ⓐ ADJ 1 (= *más alto*) [*estante, línea*] top *antes de s*; [*labio, mandíbula*] upper; **vive en el piso ~** he lives on the top floor; **en la parte ~ de la página** at the top of the page; **el cuadrante ~ izquierdo** the top left quadrant

2 (= *mejor*) superior, better; **ser ~ a algo** to be superior to sth, be better than sth; **sentirse ~ a algn** to feel superior to sb

3 (= *excelente*) **la orquesta estuvo ~** the orchestra was top-quality *o* top-class; **una moqueta de calidad ~** a superior quality *o* top-quality carpet

4 [*cantidad*] **cualquier número ~ a doce** any number above *o* higher than twelve; **nos son muy ~es en número** they greatly outnumber us

5 (*en categoría*) [*animal, especie*] higher; **una casta ~** a higher caste; **tiene un cargo ~ al tuyo** he has a higher-ranking post than yours

6 (*Educ*) [*curso, nivel*] advanced; [*enseñanza*] higher

Ⓑ SM (*en rango*) superior; **mis ~es** my superiors

superior[2]**/(a)** (*Rel*) Ⓐ ADJ superior

Ⓑ SM/F superior/mother superior

superioridad SF superiority; **con aire de ~** condescendingly, patronizingly

superitar ▸conjug 1a◂ VT (*Andes, Cono Sur*) 1 (= *superar*) to overcome

2 (= *aventajar*) to improve

superlativo ADJ, SM superlative

superlujo SM **hotel de ~** super-luxury hotel; **tiene categoría de ~** it is in the super-luxury class

supermercado SM supermarket

superministro/a SM/F minister with an overall responsibility, senior minister, overlord

supermoda SF **vestido de ~** high-fashion dress

➤ LENGUA Y USO: **superior**[1] **A2** 32.2

supermujer SF superwoman
supernova SF supernova
supernumerario/a ADJ, SM/F supernumerary
superordenador SM supercomputer
superpetrolero SM supertanker
superpoblación SF [*de país, región*] overpopulation; [*de barrio*] overcrowding
superpoblado ADJ [*país, región*] overpopulated; [*barrio*] overcrowded, congested
superponer ▸conjug 2q◂ VT 1 (= *colocar encima*) to superimpose, put on top
2 ~ **una cosa a otra** (*fig*) to give preference to one thing over another, put one thing before another
3 (*Inform*) to overstrike
superposición SF superposition
superpotencia SF superpower, great power
superpredador SM top predator, superpredator
superproducción SF overproduction
superprotector ADJ over-protective
supersecreto ADJ top secret
supersensible ADJ ultra-sensitive
supersimplificación SF oversimplification
supersónico ADJ supersonic
superstición SF superstition
supersticiosamente ADV superstitiously
supersticioso ADJ superstitious
supertalla SF outsize
supervalorar ▸conjug 1a◂ VT to overvalue
superventas* Ⓐ ADJ best-selling
Ⓑ SM INV best seller; **lista de ~** (*Mús*) charts *pl*
supervigilancia SF (*LAm*) supervision
supervisar ▸conjug 1a◂ VT to supervise
supervisión SF supervision
supervisor(a) SM/F supervisor
supervivencia SF survival ► **supervivencia de los más aptos, supervivencia de los mejor dotados** survival of the fittest
superviviente Ⓐ ADJ surviving
Ⓑ SMF survivor
supervivir ▸conjug 3a◂ VI to survive
superyo SM superego
supino ADJ, SM supine
súpito ADJ 1 = **súbito**
2 (*Andes*) (= *atónito*) dumbfounded
suplantación SF 1 (= *sustitución*) supplanting
2 (*al hacerse pasar por otro*) impersonation
3 (*Andes*) (= *falsificación*) forgery
suplantar ▸conjug 1a◂ VT 1 (= *sustituir*) to supplant, take the place of; (= *hacerse pasar por otro*) to impersonate
2 (*Andes*) (= *falsificar*) to falsify, forge
suplefaltas SMF INV 1 (= *chivo expiatorio*) scapegoat
2 (= *suplente*) substitute, stopgap, fill-in
suplemental ADJ supplementary
suplementario ADJ [*ingresos, vitaminas, información*] supplementary; **se cobra un precio ~** a supplement is charged; **empleo** *o* **negocio ~** sideline; **tren ~** extra *o* relief train; **tiempo ~** overtime
suplementero SM (*Cono Sur*) newsboy, news vendor
suplemento SM 1 (= *recargo*) (*al pagar*) supplement; (*Ferro*) excess fare ► **suplemento por habitación individual** single room supplement, single supplement
2 (= *revista*) supplement ► **suplemento a color** colour supplement ► **suplemento dominical** Sunday supplement ► **suplemento separable** pull-out supplement
suplencia SF (= *sustitución*) substitution, replacement; (= *etapa*) *period during which one deputizes etc*
suplente Ⓐ ADJ (= *sustituto*) substitute, deputy; (= *disponible*) reserve; **maestro ~** supply teacher
Ⓑ SMF (= *sustituto*) substitute, deputy; (= *reemplazo*) replacement; (= *jugador, deportista*) reserve; (= *profesor*) supply teacher; (= *médico*) locum; (*Teat*) understudy
supletorio Ⓐ ADJ [*cama, sillón*] extra; [*medida*] stopgap *antes de s*; **con la ventaja supletoria de que …** with the additional advantage that …; **llevar una lámpara supletoria** to take a spare bulb
Ⓑ SM (*Telec*) extension
súplica SF (= *ruego*) request; (= *petición*) supplication, entreaty, plea; (*Jur*) (= *instancia*) petition; **~s** entreaties, pleading *sing*; **acceder a las ~s de algn** to grant sb's request; **se publica a ~ de …** it is published at the request of …
suplicante Ⓐ ADJ [*tono de voz*] imploring, pleading
Ⓑ SMF petitioner, supplicant
suplicar ▸conjug 1g◂ VT 1 (= *rogar*) to beg, beg for, plead for, implore; **~ a algn no hacer algo** to beg *o* implore sb not to do sth; **te suplico que te quedes** I beg you to stay; **"se suplica cerrar la puerta"** "please shut the door"
2 (*Jur*) to appeal to, petition (**de** against)
suplicatorio SM 1 (*Pol*) *Supreme Court petition asking Parliament to overlook an MP's parliamentary immunity so that (s)he can be prosecuted*
2 (*Jur*) letter supplicatory
suplicio SM 1 (= *tortura*) torture; (*Hist*) (= *ejecución*) punishment, execution
2 (= *tormento*) torment, torture; **~ de Tántalo** ordeals of Tantalus; **es un ~ tener que escucharle** it's torture having to listen to him
suplir ▸conjug 3a◂ VT 1 (= *compensar*) [+ *necesidad*] to fulfil, fulfill (EEUU); [+ *omisión*] to make good; [+ *falta*] to make good, make up for; [+ *palabra que falta*] to supply
2 (= *sustituir*) to replace, substitute; **~ a uno con otro** to replace one with another, substitute one for another; **está supliendo al portero lesionado** he's replacing the injured goalkeeper; **suplen el aceite con grasa animal** they replace the oil with animal fat, they substitute animal fat for the oil
supo *etc ver* **saber**
supondré *etc ver* **suponer**
▼ **suponer** ▸conjug 2q◂ (*pp* **supuesto**) Ⓐ VT 1 (= *imaginar*) to imagine; **estoy muy satisfecho, como puedes ~** I'm very pleased, as you can imagine; **ya puedes ~ lo que pasó** you can guess *o* imagine what happened; **le pagaron, supongamos, diez millones** he was paid, say, ten million; **es de ~: es de ~ que haya protestas** I would imagine there will be protests, presumably there will be protests; **están muy apenados, como es de ~** they are very upset, as you would expect; **como era de ~, llegaron tarde** as was to be expected, they arrived late
2 **~ que** (*intentando adivinar*) to imagine that, suppose that, guess that*; (*como hipótesis*) to suppose that; (*dando por sentado*) to assume that, presume that; **supongo que necesitaréis unas vacaciones** I imagine *o* suppose you'll need a holiday, I guess you'll need a holiday*; **sí, supongo que tienes razón** yes, I suppose you're right, yes, I guess you're right*; **eso nos hace ~ que ha habido un cambio de actitud** this would suggest (to us) that there has been a change of attitude; **supón que tuvieras mucho dinero, ¿qué harías?** suppose *o* supposing you had a lot of money, what would you do?; **suponiendo que todo salga según lo previsto** assuming *o* presuming everything goes according to plan; **supongo que no: —¿crees que llegará tarde? —no lo sé, supongo que no** "do you think he'll be late?" — "I don't know, I don't suppose so"; **—no será fácil —no, supongo que no** "it won't be easy" — "no, I suppose not"; **supongo que no habrá problemas** I don't suppose there will be any problems; **supongo que sí** I suppose so, I imagine so, I guess so*
3 (= *atribuir*) (*con objeto indirecto de persona*) **os suponía informados de este asunto** I assumed *o* presumed you had been informed about this matter; **le suponía mucho más inteligente** I had imagined him to be more intelligent; **le supongo unos 60 años** I would say *o* guess he's about 60; **se le supone una gran antigüedad** it is thought *o* believed to be very old; **el equipo no mostró la calidad que se le suponía** the team did not show the talent expected of them *o* they had been credited with
4 (= *implicar*) to mean; **la mudanza no nos supondrá grandes gastos** the move won't mean *o* involve a lot of expense for us; **nuestra amistad supone mucho para mí** our friendship means a great deal to me; **el nuevo método supuso una auténtica revolución** the new method brought about a complete revolution
Ⓑ **suponerse** VPR to imagine; **el viaje resultó justo como me suponía** the trip turned out just as I had imagined; **ya me lo suponía** I thought so; **~se que: suponte que os pasa algo** suppose *o* supposing something happens to you; **me supongo que no irá** I suppose he won't go
Ⓒ SM **un ~: a ver, un ~, si tú fueras su marido, ¿qué harías?** OK, just supposing you were her husband, what would you do?; **si te ofrecen el puesto, es un ~, ¿lo aceptarías?** supposing *o* suppose they were to offer you the job, would you accept?; **supongamos, es sólo un ~, que eso sea verdad** let us suppose, for the sake of argument, that it is true
suponga *etc ver* **suponer**
suposición SF 1 (= *conjetura*) assumption
2 (= *calumnia*) slander
supositorio SM suppository
supra… PREF supra…
supradicho ADJ aforementioned
supranacional ADJ supranational
supremacía SF supremacy
supremo ADJ supreme; **jefe ~** commander-in-chief, supreme commander

➤ LENGUA Y USO: **suponer** A2 53.1, 53.2, 53.6

supresión SF [1] (= *acción*) [*de rebelión, crítica*] suppression; [*de costumbre, derecho, institución*] abolition; [*de dificultad, obstáculo*] removal, elimination; [*de restricción*] lifting; [*de detalle, pasaje*] deletion
[2] (= *prohibición*) banning

supresivo ADJ suppressive

supresor SM (*Elec*) suppressor

suprimido ADJ suppressed, banned

suprimir ▸conjug 3a◂ VT [+ *rebelión, crítica*] to suppress; [+ *costumbre, derecho, institución*] to abolish; [+ *dificultad, obstáculo*] to remove, eliminate; [+ *restricción*] to lift; [+ *detalle, pasaje*] to delete, cut out, omit; [+ *libro*] to suppress, ban; **~ la grasa de la dieta** to cut out *o* eliminate fat from one's diet

supuestamente ADV supposedly

▼**supuesto** Ⓐ PP *de* **suponer**
Ⓑ ADJ [1] (= *falso*) [*nombre*] assumed, false; **el ~ arquitecto resultó no tener título** the supposed architect proved not to be qualified
[2] (= *no demostrado*) supposed; **en el ~ informe policial** in the supposed police report
[3] **¡por ~!** of course!; **por ~ que iré** of course I'll go; **—¿puedo usar su teléfono? —¡por ~!** "can I use your phone?" — "of course (you can)!"
[4] **dar algo por ~** to take sth for granted; **dieron por ~ que estábamos interesados** they took it for granted that we were interested
[5] **~ que** (*frm*) (= *dando por sentado que*) assuming; (= *en caso de que*) in the event of; **~ que nuestra moneda no baje** (always) assuming our currency does not fall in value; **~ que las autoridades requieran una prueba** in the event of the authorities requiring proof
Ⓒ SM (= *hipótesis*) assumption; **partieron del ~ de que era verdad** they started from the assumption that it was true; **en el ~ de que no venga** assuming that he doesn't come
► **supuesto previo** prior assumption

supuración SF suppuration

supurar ▸conjug 1a◂ VI to suppurate, fester

supuse *etc ver* **suponer**

sur Ⓐ ADJ [*región*] southern; [*dirección*] southerly; [*viento*] south, southerly; **la zona ~ de la ciudad** the southern part of the city, the south of the city; **en la costa ~** on the south coast
Ⓑ SM [1] (= *punto cardinal*) south
[2] [*de región, país*] south; **el ~ del país** the south of the country; **al ~ de Jaén** (to the) south of Jaén; **eso cae más hacia el ~** that lies further (to the) south; **viajábamos hacia el ~** we were travelling south; **en la parte del ~** in the southern part; **las ciudades del ~** the southern cities, the cities of the south; **vientos del ~** south *o* southerly winds
[3] (= *viento*) south *o* southerly wind

sura SM sura

Suráfrica SF = **Sudáfrica**

surafricano/a ADJ, SM/F = **sudafricano**

Suramérica SF = **Sudamérica**

suramericano/a ADJ, SM/F = **sudamericano**

surazo SM (*Andes, Cono Sur*) strong southerly wind

surcar ▸conjug 1g◂ VT [+ *tierra*] to plough, plow (*EEUU*), plough through, plow through (*EEUU*), furrow; [+ *superficie*] to score, groove; **una superficie surcada de ...** a surface lined *o* criss-crossed with ...; **los barcos que surcan los mares** (*liter*) the ships which ply the seas; **las aves que surcan los aires** (*liter*) the birds which ride the winds

surco SM [1] (*Agr*) furrow; ✦**MODISMO echarse al ~** (*por pereza*) to sit down on the job; (= *terminar*) to knock off*, think one has done enough
[2] (= *ranura*) (*en metal*) groove, score; (*en disco*) groove
[3] (*Anat*) wrinkle
[4] (*en agua*) track, wake

surcoreano/a ADJ, SM/F South Korean

sureño/a Ⓐ ADJ southern
Ⓑ SM/F southerner

surero SM (*Andes*) cold southerly wind

surestada SF (*Cono Sur*) wet south-easterly wind

sureste Ⓐ ADJ [*parte*] southeast, southeastern; [*rumbo, viento*] southeasterly
Ⓑ SM [1] (*Geog*) southeast
[2] (= *viento*) southeast wind

surf SM surfing; **practicar el ~** to surf ► **surf a vela** windsurfing

surfero/a Ⓐ ADJ surfing
Ⓑ SM/F surfer

surfing SM **hacer ~** to surf, go surfing

surfista SMF surfer

surgencia SF, **surgimiento** SM emergence

surgir ▸conjug 3c◂ VI [1] (= *aparecer*) (*gen*) to arise, emerge, appear; [*líquido*] to spout, spout out, spurt; [*barco*] (*en la niebla*) to loom up; [*persona*] to appear unexpectedly; **la torre surge en medio del bosque** the tower rises up out of the woods
[2] [*dificultad*] to arise, come up, crop up; **han surgido varios problemas** several problems have come up *o* cropped up
[3] (*Náut*) to anchor

suriano ADJ (*Méx*) southern

surja *etc ver* **surgir**

surmenage SM, **surmenaje** SM (= *trabajo excesivo*) overwork; (= *estrés*) stress, mental fatigue; (= *crisis*) nervous breakdown

suroeste Ⓐ ADJ [*parte*] southwest, southwestern; [*rumbo, viento*] southwesterly
Ⓑ SM [1] (*Geog*) southwest
[2] (= *viento*) southwest wind

surrealismo SM surrealism

surrealista Ⓐ ADJ surrealist, surrealistic
Ⓑ SMF surrealist

surtido Ⓐ ADJ [1] (= *variado*) mixed, assorted, varied; **pasteles ~s** assorted cakes
[2] (= *provisto*) **estar bien ~ de** to be well supplied with, have good stocks of; **estar mal ~ de** to be badly off for
Ⓑ SM selection, assortment, range; **gran ~** large assortment, wide range; **artículo de ~** article from stock

surtidor SM [1] (= *chorro*) jet, spout; (= *fuente*) fountain
[2] ► **surtidor de gasolina** (= *aparato*) petrol pump, gas pump (*EEUU*); (= *lugar*) petrol station, gas station (*EEUU*)
[3] (*LAm*) [*de droga*] drug pusher

surtir ▸conjug 3a◂ Ⓐ VT [1] (= *suministrar*) to supply, furnish, provide; **~ a algn de combustible** to supply sb with fuel; **~ el mercado** to supply the market; **~ un pedido** to fill an order
[2] (= *tener*) *ver* **efecto 1**
Ⓑ VI (= *brotar*) to spout, spurt, spurt up, rise
Ⓒ **surtirse** VPR **~se de** to provide o.s. with

surto ADJ anchored

suruca SF (*Caribe*) [1] (= *algazara*) din, uproar
[2] (= *borrachera*) drunkenness

suruco** SM (*Cono Sur*) crap**, shit**

surumbático ADJ (*LAm*) = **zurumbático**

surumbo ADJ (*CAm*) = **zurumbo**

surumpe SM (*Andes*) inflammation of the eyes (*caused by snow glare*), snow blindness

surupa SF (*Caribe*) cockroach, roach (*EEUU*)

suruví SM (*Cono Sur*) catfish

survietnamita ADJ, SMF South Vietnamese

susceptibilidad SF [1] [*de persona*] susceptibility (**a** to)
[2] **susceptibilidades** (= *malentendidos*) sensibilities; **ofender las ~es de algn** to offend sb's sensibilities

susceptible ADJ [1] **~ de** capable of; **~ de mejora(r)** capable of improvement; **~ de sufrir daño** liable to suffer damage
[2] [*persona*] susceptible; **~ a las críticas** sensitive to criticism

suscitar ▸conjug 1a◂ VT [+ *rebelión*] to stir up; [+ *escándalo, conflicto*] to cause, provoke; [+ *discusión*] to start; [+ *duda, problema*] to raise; [+ *interés, sospechas*] to arouse; [+ *consecuencia*] to cause, give rise to, bring with it

▼**suscribir** ▸conjug 3a◂ (*pp* **suscrito**) Ⓐ VT [1] [+ *contrato, memoria*] to sign
[2] (= *reafirmar*) [+ *promesa*] to make; [+ *opinión*] to subscribe to, endorse
[3] (*Fin*) [+ *acciones*] to take out an option on; [+ *seguro*] to underwrite
[4] **~ a algn a una revista** to take out a subscription to a magazine for sb; **lo suscribió por 100 dólares** she put him down for a 100-dollar contribution
Ⓑ **suscribirse** VPR to subscribe (**a** to); **¿te vas a ~?** are you going to subscribe?; **~se a una revista** to take out a subscription for a magazine

suscripción SF subscription; **abrir una ~** to take out a subscription; **cerrar su ~** to cancel one's subscription; **por ~ popular** by public subscription

suscripto ADJ, PP (*Arg*) *de* **suscribir**

suscriptor(a) SM/F subscriber

suscrito PP *de* **suscribir**; **~ en exceso** oversubscribed

Suso SM *familiar form of Jesús*

susodicho ADJ above-mentioned

suspender ▸conjug 2a◂ Ⓐ VT [1] (= *colgar*) to hang, hang up, suspend (**de** from)
[2] (= *interrumpir*) [+ *pago, trabajo*] to stop, suspend; [+ *reunión, sesión*] to adjourn; [+ *línea, servicio*] to discontinue; [+ *procedimiento*] to interrupt; [+ *plan, viaje*] to call off, cancel; **~ hasta más tarde** to put off till later, postpone for a time; **~ a algn de empleo y sueldo** to suspend sb (from work) without pay; **~ la emisión de un programa** to cancel the showing of a programme; **ha suspendido su visita hasta la semana que viene** he's postponed his visit until next week; **el partido se suspendió a causa de la lluvia** the game was rained off; **han suspendido la boda** they've called the wedding off, they've cancelled the wedding
[3] (*Escol*) [+ *asignatura*] to fail; **he suspendido las matemáticas** I've failed maths; **lo han**

➤ LENGUA Y USO: supuesto B3 36.2, 40.2 suscribir A2 53.5

suspendido en química he's failed Chemistry

Ⓑ VI to fail

suspense SM suspense; **novela/película ~** thriller

suspensión SF [1] (*al colgar*) hanging, hanging up, suspension

[2] (*Aut, Mec*) suspension; **con ~ independiente** with independent suspension ► **suspensión hidráulica** hydraulic suspension

[3] (= *interrupción*) [*de campeonato*] stoppage, suspension; [*de sesión*] adjournment; [*de servicios*] stoppage ► **suspensión de empleo y sueldo** suspension without pay ► **suspensión de fuego** ceasefire ► **suspensión de hostilidades** cessation of hostilities ► **suspensión de pagos** suspension of payments

[4] (*Jur*) stay

suspensivo ADJ **puntos ~s** dots, suspension points

suspenso Ⓐ ADJ [1] (= *colgado*) hanging, suspended, hung (**de** from)

[2] (*Escol*) [*candidato*] failed

[3] **estar** *o* **quedarse ~** (= *pasmarse*) to be astonished, be amazed; (= *maravillarse*) to be filled with wonder; (= *aturdirse*) to be bewildered, be baffled

Ⓑ SM [1] (*Escol*) (= *asignatura*) fail, failure; **tengo un ~ en inglés** I failed English

[2] **estar en** *o* **quedar en ~**: **la reunión ha quedado en ~ hasta el jueves** they've adjourned the meeting until next Thursday; **el juicio está en ~ hasta que se encuentre un nuevo juez** the trial has been suspended until a new judge can be found

[3] (*LAm*) (= *misterio*) suspense; **una novela/película de ~** a thriller

suspensores SMPL [1] (*LAm*) (= *tirantes*) braces, suspenders (*EEUU*)

[2] (*Perú Dep*) athletic support *sing*, jockstrap *sing*

suspensorio Ⓐ ADJ suspensory

Ⓑ SM (= *prenda*) jockstrap; (*Med*) suspensory, suspensory bandage

suspicacia SF suspicion, mistrust

suspicaz ADJ suspicious, distrustful

suspirado ADJ longed-for, yearned for

suspirar ▸conjug 1a◂ VI to sigh; **~ por** (= *anhelar*) to long for

suspiro SM [1] (*lit, fig*) sigh; **deshacerse en ~s** to sigh deeply, heave a great sigh; **exhalar el último ~** to breathe one's last ► **suspiro de alivio** sigh of relief

[2] (*LAm Culin*) meringue

sustancia SF [1] (= *materia*) substance; **una ~ pegajosa** a sticky substance ► **sustancia blanca** (*Anat*) white matter ► **sustancia gris** (*Anat*) grey matter

[2] (= *esencia*) substance; **no has captado la ~ de su discurso** you haven't grasped the substance of his speech; **en ~** in substance, in essence; **sin ~** [*teoría, discurso*] lacking in substance; [*persona*] shallow, superficial

[3] (*Culin*) [*de alimento*] substance ► **sustancia de carne** meat stock

[4] (*Fil*) substance

sustancial ADJ [1] (= *importante*) substantial, significant; **no se han producido cambios ~es** there have been no substantial *o* significant changes

[2] (= *esencial*) substantial, fundamental

[3] = **sustancioso**

sustancialmente ADV (= *abundantemente*) substantially; (= *esencialmente*) essentially, vitally, fundamentally

sustancioso ADJ [*discurso*] that gives food for thought; [*comida*] solid, substantial; [*ganancias*] healthy, fat (*pey*)

sustantivación SF nominalization

sustantivar ▸conjug 1a◂ VT to nominalize

sustantivo Ⓐ ADJ substantive; (*Ling*) substantival, noun *antes de s*

Ⓑ SM noun, substantive ► **sustantivo colectivo** collective noun ► **sustantivo contable** count noun, countable noun ► **sustantivo no contable** uncount noun, uncountable noun

sustentabilidad SF viability

sustentable ADJ viable, sustainable

sustentación SF [1] (= *manutención*) maintenance

[2] (= *apoyo*) support

[3] (*Aer*) lift

sustentar ▸conjug 1a◂ Ⓐ VT [1] (= *sujetar*) to hold up, support, bear the weight of

[2] (= *alimentar*) to sustain, nourish

[3] [+ *familia, hijos*] to support, maintain

[4] [+ *esperanzas*] to sustain, keep alive

[5] [+ *idea, teoría*] to maintain, uphold

[6] (*Ecología*) to sustain

Ⓑ **sustentarse** VPR **~se con** to sustain o.s. with, subsist on; **~se de esperanzas** to live on hopes; **~se del aire** to live on air

sustento SM [1] (= *apoyo*) support

[2] (*para vivir*) (= *alimento*) sustenance; (= *manutención*) maintenance; **ganarse el ~** to earn one's living, earn a livelihood; **es el ~ principal de la institución** it is the lifeblood of the institution

sustitución SF substitution (**por** for), replacement (**por** by)

sustituible ADJ replaceable

sustituir ▸conjug 3g◂ VT [1] (= *poner en lugar de*) to replace, substitute; **~ A por B** to replace A by *o* with B, substitute B for A; **lo quieren ~** they want him replaced; **tendremos que ~ el neumático pinchado** we shall have to replace the flat tyre

[2] (= *tomar el lugar de*) (*gen*) to replace; (*temporalmente*) to stand in for; **los sellos azules sustituyen a los verdes** the blue stamps are replacing the green ones; **lo sustituí como secretario de la asociación** I replaced him as club secretary; **¿me puedes ~ un par de semanas?** can you stand in for me for a couple of weeks?; **me ~á mientras estoy fuera** he'll take my place *o* deputize for me while I'm away

sustitutivo Ⓐ ADJ substitute; **géneros propios ~s de los importados** home-produced goods in place of *o* to replace imported ones

Ⓑ SM substitute (**de** for)

sustituto/a SM/F (*temporal*) substitute, stand-in; (*para siempre*) replacement; **soy el ~ del profesor de inglés** I'm standing in for the English teacher

sustitutorio ADJ substitute, replacement *antes de s*; *ver tb* **servicio 1.3**

susto SM [1] (= *impresión repentina*) fright, scare; **¡qué ~!** what a fright!; **dar un ~ a algn** to give sb a fright *o* scare; **darse** *o* **pegarse un ~*** to have a fright, get scared (*EEUU*); **caerse del ~** to be frightened *o* scared to death; **meter un ~ a algn*** to put the wind up sb*; ✦***MODISMOS*** **no ganar para ~s***: **este año no ganamos para ~s** it's been one setback after another this year; **no pasó del ~** it was less serious than was at first thought

[2] (*Andes*) (= *crisis nerviosa*) nervous breakdown

[3] **el ~** (*hum*) (*en restaurante*) the bill

sustracción SF [1] (= *acto*) removal

[2] (*Mat*) (= *resta*) subtraction, taking away; (= *descuento*) deduction

[3] (= *hurto*) theft ► **sustracción de menores** child abduction

sustraer ▸conjug 2p◂ Ⓐ VT [1] (= *llevarse*) to remove, take away

[2] (*Mat*) (= *restar*) to subtract, take away; (= *descontar*) to deduct

[3] (= *robar*) [+ *dinero, cuadro*] to steal; [+ *persona*] to abduct

[4] [+ *agua*] to extract

Ⓑ **sustraerse** VPR **~se a** (= *evitar*) to avoid; (= *apartarse de*) to withdraw from, contract out of; **no pude ~me a la tentación** I could not resist the temptation

sustrato SM substratum

susurrante ADJ [*viento*] whispering; [*arroyo*] murmuring; [*follaje*] rustling

susurrar ▸conjug 1a◂ Ⓐ VT to whisper; **me susurró su nombre al oído** he whispered his name in my ear

Ⓑ VI [1] [*persona*] to whisper; **~ al oído de algn** to whisper to sb, whisper in sb's ear

[2] (= *sonar*) [*viento*] to whisper; [*arroyo*] to murmur; [*hojas*] to rustle; [*insecto*] to hum

Ⓒ **susurrarse** VPR **se susurra que …** it is being whispered that …, it is rumoured *o* (*EEUU*) rumored that …

susurro SM [1] (= *cuchicheo*) whisper

[2] (= *sonido*) [*de viento*] whisper; [*de arroyo*] murmur; [*de hojas*] rustle; [*de insecto*] hum, humming

sutién SM (*Arg*) bra, brassiere

sutil ADJ [1] [*diferencia*] subtle

[2] (= *perspicaz*) [*inteligencia, persona*] sharp, keen; [*comentario*] subtle

[3] (= *delicado*) [*hilo, hebra*] fine; [*tela*] delicate, thin, light; [*atmósfera*] thin; [*olor*] subtle, delicate; [*brisa*] gentle

sutileza SF [1] (= *delicadeza*) fineness, delicacy

[2] (= *perspicacia*) subtlety, subtleness; (= *agudeza*) sharpness, keenness

[3] (= *concepto sutil*) subtlety, fine distinction

[4] (*pey*) (= *maña*) artifice, artful deceit

sutilizar ▸conjug 1f◂ Ⓐ VT [1] [+ *objeto*] (= *reducir*) to thin down, fine down; (= *pulir*) to polish, perfect; (= *limar, mejorar*) to refine

[2] [+ *concepto*] (*pey*) to quibble about *o* over, split hairs about *o* over

Ⓑ VI (*pey*) (= *pararse en cosas nimias*) to quibble, split hairs

sutura SF suture

suturar ▸conjug 1a◂ VT to suture

suyo/a Ⓐ ADJ POSES [1] (= *de él*) his; (= *de ella*) her; (= *de ellos, ellas*) their; **la culpa es suya** it's his/her *etc* fault; **—permiso —es ~** (*Chile, Méx*) "excuse me" — "yes?"; **no es amigo ~** he is not a friend of his/hers *etc*; **no es culpa suya** it's not his/her *etc* fault, it's no fault of his/hers *etc*; **varios libros ~s** (= *de ellos*) several books of theirs, several of their books;

hacer algo ~: hizo suyas mis palabras he echoed my words; **eso es muy ~** that's just like him, that's typical of him; **él es un hombre muy ~** (= *reservado*) he's a man who keeps very much to himself; (= *quisquilloso*) he's a very fussy sort

2 (= *de usted, ustedes*) your; **¿es ~ esto?** is this yours?

Ⓑ PRON POSES (= *de él*) his; (= *de ella*) hers; (= *de usted, ustedes*) yours; (*de animal, cosa*) its; (= *de uno mismo*) one's own; (= *de ellos, ellas*) theirs; **este libro es el ~** this book is his/hers *etc*; **los ~s** (= *familia*) one's family *o* relations; (= *partidarios*) one's own people *o* supporters; **~ afectísimo** yours faithfully *o* sincerely, yours truly (*EEUU*); **de ~** in itself, intrinsically; **lo ~** (what is) his; (= *su parte*) his share, what he deserves; **aguantar lo ~** (= *su parte*) to do one's share; (= *mucho*) to put up with a lot; **él pesa lo ~** he's really heavy, he's a fair weight; ✦***MODISMOS*** **hacer de las suyas** to get up to one's old tricks; **ir a la suya** ◊ **ir a lo ~** to go one's own way; (*pey*) to go one's own sweet way, think only of o.s.; **salirse con la suya** to get one's own way; (*en una discusión*) to carry one's point; ✦***REFRÁN*** **cada cual a lo ~** it's best to mind one's own business

svástica [ez'bastika] SF swastika

swing [swin] SM 1 (*Mús*) swing
2 (*Golf*) swing

switch [switʃ] SM (*esp Méx*) 1 (*Elec*) switch
2 (*Aut*) ignition

T t

T¹, **t¹** [te] SF (= *letra*) T, t

T² ABR, **t²** ABR (= **tonelada**) t, ton

t. ABR (= **tomo(s)**) vol, vols

TA SF ABR (= **traducción automática**) AT

taba SF (= *hueso*) ankle bone; (= *juego*) jacks, knucklebones, jackstones (*EEUU*); ✦***MODISMO*** **menear las ~s*** (= *moverse con prisa*) to bustle about; (= *apresurarse*) to get cracking*

tabacal SM (= *plantación*) tobacco plantation; (= *terreno*) tobacco field

Tabacalera SF *Spanish state tobacco monopoly*; → ESTANCO

tabacalera SF (*Méx*) cigarette factory

tabacalero/a (A) ADJ tobacco *antes de s*
(B) SM/F (= *tendero*) tobacconist, tobacco dealer (*EEUU*); (= *cultivador*) tobacco grower; (= *mayorista*) tobacco merchant

tabaco (A) SM [1] (*para fumar*) [1·1] (= *producto*) tobacco; (= *planta*) tobacco plant; ✦***MODISMOS*** **se le acabó el ~** (*Cono Sur**) he ran out of dough*; **estar de mal ~** (*CAm**) to be in a bad mood; **estaba hecho ~*** [*persona*] he was all in; [*objeto*] it was all torn to pieces; **quitar el ~ a algn*** to do sb in*
[1·2] (= *cigarrillos*) cigarettes *pl*; **¿tienes ~?** have you any cigarettes?
[1·3] (*LAm*) (= *puro*) cigar
► **tabaco amarillo, tabaco americano** Virginia tobacco ► **tabaco de hebra** loose tobacco ► **tabaco de liar** rolling tobacco ► **tabaco de mascar** chewing tobacco ► **tabaco de pipa** pipe tobacco ► **tabaco en polvo** snuff ► **tabaco en rama** leaf tobacco ► **tabaco negro** dark tobacco ► **tabaco picado** shag, cut tobacco ► **tabaco rubio** Virginia tobacco ► **tabaco turco** Turkish tobacco
[2] (*LAm*) (= *droga*) reefer*, joint*
[3] (*Caribe**) (= *golpe*) slap, smack
(B) ADJ (*esp LAm*) dusty brown

tabacón‡ SM (*Méx*) marijuana, grass‡

tabalada SF bump, heavy fall

tabalear ▸conjug 1a◂ (A) VI (*con los dedos*) to drum, tap
(B) VT (= *balancear*) to rock, swing

tabaleo SM [1] (*con los dedos*) drumming, tapping
[2] (= *balanceo*) rocking, swinging

tabanco SM [1] (*CAm*) (= *desván*) attic
[2] (*Méx*) (= *puesto*) stall

tábano SM horsefly, gadfly

tabaqueada* SF (*Méx*) (= *paliza*) beating-up*; (= *pelea*) fist-fight

tabaquear ▸conjug 1a◂ VI (*Andes*) to smoke

tabaquera SF [1] (= *bolsa*) tobacco pouch
[2] (= *estuche*) (*para puros*) cigar case; (*para cigarrillos*) cigarette case; (*para rapé*) snuffbox
[3] (= *tarro*) tobacco jar
[4] [*de pipa*] bowl; *ver tb* **tabaquero**

tabaquería SF (*LAm*) [1] (= *tienda*) tobacconist's (shop), cigar store (*EEUU*)
[2] (= *fábrica*) cigar factory, tobacco factory

tabaquero/a (A) ADJ tobacco *antes de s*
(B) SM/F (= *tendero*) tobacconist, tobacco dealer (*EEUU*); (= *mayorista*) tobacco merchant; (= *cultivador*) tobacco grower; *ver tb* **tabaquera**

tabaquismo SM smoking habit
► **tabaquismo pasivo** passive smoking

tabaquito SM (*LAm*) small cigar

tabarra* SF nuisance, bore; **dar la ~** to be a nuisance, be a pain in the neck*; **dar la ~ a algn** to pester sb

tabasco® SM Tabasco®

tabear ▸conjug 1a◂ VI (*Cono Sur*) to gossip

taberna SF [1] (= *bar*) pub, bar; (*Hist*) tavern
[2] (*Caribe*) (= *tienda*) small grocery shop
[3] (*Cono Sur*) [*de juego*] gambling den

tabernáculo SM tabernacle

tabernario ADJ [*lenguaje*] rude, dirty, coarse, tavern *antes de s*

tabernero/a SM/F (= *dueño*) landlord/landlady, publican, bar manager; (= *camarero*) barman/barmaid, bartender

tabicar ▸conjug 1g◂ (A) VT [1] [+ *puerta, ventana*] (*con ladrillos*) to brick up; (*con madera*) to board up
[2] [+ *habitación*] to partition off
[3] [+ *nariz*] to block (up)
(B) **tabicarse** VPR [*nariz*] to get blocked up

tabicón SM (*Méx*) breeze block

tabique SM (= *pared*) thin wall; (*entre habitaciones*) partition, partition wall
► **tabique nasal** nasal septum

tabla (A) SF [1] (= *pieza*) [*de madera*] plank, board; [*de piedra*] slab; (*Arte*) panel; (= *estante*) shelf; (*Caribe*) (= *mostrador*) shop counter; ✦***MODISMOS*** **estar en las ~s** (*Caribe*) to be destitute; **escaparse en una ~** to have a narrow escape, have a close shave; **hacer ~ rasa** to make a clean sweep; **hacer ~ rasa de algo** to completely disregard sth, ride roughshod over sth; **salvarse en una ~** to have a narrow escape, have a close shave ► **tabla a vela** surfboard, windsurfing board ► **tabla de cocina** chopping board ► **tabla de dibujo** drawing board ► **tabla de esmeril** emery board ► **tabla de lavar** washboard ► **tabla del suelo** floorboard ► **tabla de picar** chopping board ► **tabla de planchar** ironing board ► **tabla de quesos** cheeseboard ► **tabla de salvación** (*fig*) last resort, only hope ► **tabla deslizadora, tabla de surf** surfboard ► **tabla de windsurf** windsurfing board
[2] **tablas** [2·1] (*Taur*) barrier *sing*
[2·2] (*Teat*) stage *sing*; **pisar las ~s** to tread the boards; **salir a las ~s** to go on the stage, become an actor/actress; ✦***MODISMOS*** **coger ~s** (*en teatro*) to gain acting experience; (*fig*) to get the hang of it; **tener (muchas) ~s** [*actor*] to have a good stage presence; [*político*] to be an old hand
[3] **tablas** (*Ajedrez*) draw *sing*; (*fig*) stalemate *sing*; **hacer ~s** ◊ **quedar en ~s** (*lit*) to draw; (*fig*) to reach stalemate, be deadlocked; **el partido quedó en ~s** the game was a draw, the game was drawn ► **tablas por ahogado** stalemate
[4] [*de falda*] box pleat, broad pleat
[5] (= *lista*) (*Mat*) table; (*en libro*) (= *índice*) table; (*Dep*) (*tb* **~ clasificatoria**) table, (league) table; (*Inform*) array ► **tabla de consulta** (*Inform*) lookup table ► **tabla de ejercicios, tabla de gimnasia** exercise routine, set of exercises ► **tabla de logaritmos** table of logarithms ► **tabla de mareas** tide table ► **tabla de materias** table of contents ► **tabla de multiplicar** multiplication table ► **tabla de valores** set of values ► **tabla salarial** wage scale ► **tabla trazadora** plotter
[6] (*Agr*) plot, patch
[7] (*Andes*) ✦***MODISMOS*** **cantarle las ~s a algn** to tell it to sb straight; **salir con las ~s** to fail
(B) SM (‡) queer‡, fairy‡, fag (*EEUU*‡)

tablada SF (*Cono Sur*) slaughterhouse

tablado SM [1] (= *plataforma*) stage
[2] (*Hist*) scaffold

tablaje SM, **tablazón** SF planks *pl*, planking, boards *pl*

tablao SM (= *espectáculo*) flamenco show; (= *escenario*) dance floor (*for flamenco dancing*); (= *local*) flamenco venue

tablear ▸conjug 1a◂ VT [1] [+ *madera*] to cut into boards *o* planks
[2] [+ *terreno*] (= *dividir*) to divide up into plots; (= *nivelar*) to level off
[3] (*Cos*) to pleat
[4] (*Cono Sur*) [+ *masa*] to roll out

tablero SM [1] (= *panel*) (*de madera*) board; (*para anuncios*) notice board, bulletin board

(*EEUU*); (= *pizarra*) blackboard; [*de mesa*] top; [*de mármol*] slab; (*Elec*) switchboard ► **tablero de dibujante, tablero de dibujo** drawing board ► **tablero de gráficos** (*Inform*) graph pad ► **tablero de instrumentos, tablero de mandos** instrument panel ► **tablero posterior** tailboard
[2] (*para juegos*) board ► **tablero de ajedrez** chessboard
[3] (= *garito*) gambling den

tableta SF [1] [*de chocolate*] bar, slab; (*Med*) tablet
[2] [*de madera*] (= *bloque*) block; (= *tablero*) board
[3] [*de escribir*] writing pad

tabletear ▸conjug 1a◂ VI to rattle

tableteo SM rattle

tablilla SF [1] (= *tabla*) small board; (*Med*) splint
[2] (*Méx*) [*de chocolate*] bar

tablista SMF windsurfer

tabloide SM tabloid

tablón SM [1] (= *tabla*) plank; (= *viga*) beam ► **tablón de anuncios** notice board, bulletin board (*EEUU*)
[2] (*) (= *borrachera*) **coger** *o* **pillar un ~** to get plastered*
[3] (*LAm Agr*) plot, bed

tablonazo SM (*Caribe*) trick, swindle

tabú Ⓐ ADJ INV taboo; **palabras ~** taboo words
Ⓑ SM (*pl* **tabús, tabúes**) taboo

tabuco SM (= *chabola*) slum, shack; (= *cuarto*) tiny room, poky little room

tabulación SF tabulation

tabulador SM tab, tabulator

tabular Ⓐ ▸conjug 1a◂ VT to tabulate
Ⓑ ADJ tabular

taburete SM stool

TAC SF/M ABR (= **tomografía axial computerizada**) CAT

tacada SF (*Billar*) stroke; (= *serie de puntos*) break; ✦***MODISMO*** **de una ~** all in one go

tacana SF [1] (*Andes, Cono Sur Agr*) cultivated hillside terrace
[2] (*Cono Sur, Méx*) [*de mortero*] pestle
[3] (*Cono Sur*) (= *policía*) fuzz‡, police

tacanear ▸conjug 1a◂ VT (*Cono Sur*) (= *apisonar*) to tread down; (= *machacar*) to pound, crush

tacañería SF [1] (= *mezquindad*) meanness, stinginess
[2] (= *astucia*) craftiness

tacaño ADJ [1] (= *avaro*) mean, stingy
[2] (= *astuto*) crafty

tacar ▸conjug 1g◂ VT (*Andes*) [1] (= *disparar*) to shoot at sb
[2] (= *llenar*) to fill, pack tightly (**de** with)

tacatá* SM, **tacataca** SM [*de bebé*] baby walker; [*de anciano*] walking frame, Zimmer frame®

tacha¹ SF [1] (*Téc*) large tack, stud
[2] (*LAm*) = **tacho**

tacha² SF blemish; **sin ~** [*vida, reputación*] unblemished; [*estilo, conducta*] faultless; [*lealtad*] absolute; **una persona sin ~** a person who is beyond reproach; **poner ~ a algo** to find fault with sth

tachadura SF (= *tachón*) crossing-out, erasure (*frm*); (= *corrección*) correction

tachar ▸conjug 1a◂ VT [1] (= *suprimir*) to cross out; (= *corregir*) to correct; **~ a algn de una lista** to cross *o* take sb off a list
[2] **~ a algn de** to brand sb (as); **lo ~on de colaboracionista** he was branded (as) a collaborator; **~ a algn de incapaz** to brand sb (as) incompetent; **tachó de inoportuna la invitación** he described the invitation as untimely; **me molesta que taches de tonterías lo que digo** I don't like the way you dismiss what I say as nonsense
[3] (*Jur*) [+ *testigo*] to challenge

tachero SM (*Cono Sur*) tinsmith

tachines‡ SMPL (*Esp*) (= *pies*) plates‡, feet; (= *zapatos*) shoes

tacho SM [1] (*LAm*) (= *cubo*) bucket, pail; (= *caldera*) boiler; (= *olla*) pan; (*para azúcar*) sugar pan, sugar evaporator; (= *arcón*) bin, container ► **tacho de la basura, tacho para la basura** (*Andes, Cono Sur*) dustbin, rubbish bin, trash *o* garbage can (*EEUU*) ► **tacho para lavar la ropa** clothes boiler
[2] (*Cono Sur*) (= *lavabo*) washbasin, bathroom sink *o* washbowl (*EEUU*); ✦***MODISMO*** **irse al ~*** to be ruined, fail

tachón¹ SM [1] (*Téc*) ornamental stud, boss
[2] (*Cos*) trimming

tachón² SM (= *tachadura*) crossing-out, deletion (*frm*); **escribe con letra clara y sin tachones** write clearly and avoid crossing things out

tachonado ADJ **~ de estrellas** star-studded, star-spangled; **candelabros ~s de diamantes** diamond-studded candelabras

tachonar ▸conjug 1a◂ VT to stud

tachoso ADJ defective, faulty

tachuela SF [1] (= *clavo*) (tin) tack; (*en cinturón, ropa*) stud; (*LAm*) (= *chincheta*) drawing pin
[2] (*Caribe*) (= *alfiler*) long pin
[3] (*Aut*) speed ramp, sleeping policeman
[4] (*LAm*) (= *recipiente*) metal pan; (= *cazo*) dipper; (= *taza*) metal cup
[5] (*LAm**) (= *persona*) short stocky person

tacita SF small cup; **la Tacita de Plata** Cadiz (*used affectionately*); ✦***MODISMO*** **como una ~ de plata** as bright as a new pin

tácitamente ADV tacitly

Tácito SM Tacitus

tácito ADJ [1] (*gen*) tacit; [*acuerdo*] unspoken, tacit; [*ley*] unwritten
[2] (*Ling*) understood

taciturnidad SF (= *reserva*) taciturnity, silent nature; (= *mal humor*) sullenness, moodiness; (= *tristeza*) glumness

taciturno ADJ (= *callado*) taciturn, silent; (= *malhumorado*) sullen, moody; (= *triste*) glum

tacizo SM [1] (*Andes, Caribe*) (= *hacha*) narrow-bladed axe
[2] (*Andes*) (= *celda*) small prison cell

taco SM [1] (= *pieza*) (*para tornillo*) Rawlplug®; (= *tapón*) plug, stopper; [*de bota de fútbol*] stud; (*para fusil*) wad, wadding; (= *tarugo*) wooden peg ► **taco de salida** (*Dep*) starting block
[2] (*Billar*) cue
[3] [*de papeles*] (*para escribir*) pad; [*de billetes, cupones*] book; [*de cheque*] stub; (= *calendario*) desk calendar
[4] [*de jamón, queso*] cube
[5] (*Esp**) (= *palabrota*) rude word, swearword; **soltar un ~** to swear; **dice muchos ~s** he swears a lot
[6] (*Esp‡*) (= *lío*) mess; **armarse** *o* **hacerse un ~** to get into a mess, get mixed *o* muddled up; **dejar a algn hecho un ~** to flatten sb (in an argument)
[7] (‡) (= *año*) year; **tener 16 ~s** to be 16 (years old); **cumple cinco ~s** (*en la cárcel*) he's doing five years' bird‡
[8] (*Mil, Hist*) ramrod
[9] (*LAm*) (= *tacón*) heel
[10] (*Méx Culin*) taco, filled rolled tortilla; (*) (= *bocado*) snack, bite; ✦***MODISMO*** **darse ~** (*CAm, Méx**) to give o.s. airs
[11] (*Chile*) (= *trago*) swig of wine*
[12] (*Cono Sur, Méx*) (= *obstáculo*) obstruction, blockage; (*Chile**) (= *atasco*) traffic jam
[13] (*aplicado a personas*) (*Cono Sur*) (= *chaparro*) short stocky person; (*Andes**) (= *personaje*) big shot*; (*CAm, Caribe, Méx*) fop, dandy
[14] (*CAm, Caribe*) (= *preocupación*) worry, anxiety; (= *miedo*) fear

tacógrafo SM tachograph, tacho*

tacómetro SM tachometer

tacón SM [1] [*de zapato*] heel; **tacones altos** high heels; **tacones bajos** low heels; **nunca llevo tacones** I never wear high heels; **zapatos de ~ (alto)** high-heeled shoes ► **tacón (de) aguja** stiletto heel ► **tacón de cuña** wedge heel
[2] (‡) (= *monedero*) purse, coin purse (*EEUU*)

taconazo SM (= *patada*) kick (*with one's heel*); (= *golpecito*) heel tap; **dar un ~** to click one's heels; **taconazos** (*Mil*) heel-clicking *pl*

taconear ▸conjug 1a◂ Ⓐ VI [1] (= *caminar*) to walk clicking *o* tapping one's heels
[2] (= *dar golpecitos*) to tap with one's heels; (*Mil*) to click one's heels
[3] (= *apresurarse*) to bustle about
Ⓑ VT (*Cono Sur*) to pack tight, fill right up

taconeo SM [1] (*al andar*) **podíamos oír el ~ de sus zapatos** we could hear her shoe heels clicking about
[2] (= *golpecitos*) tapping with one's heels; (*Mil*) heel-clicking

tacote‡ SM (*Méx*) marijuana, grass‡

táctica SF [1] (= *estrategia*) tactic; **una nueva ~** a new tactic, new tactics; **el equipo cambió de ~** the team changed tactics; **la ~ del avestruz** the head-in-the-sand approach ► **táctica de cerrojo** stonewalling, negative play
[2] (= *jugada*) move; (*fig*) gambit

tácticamente ADV tactically

táctico/a Ⓐ ADJ tactical
Ⓑ SM/F (= *experto*) tactician; (*Dep*) coach

táctil ADJ tactile

tacto SM [1] (= *sentido*) (sense of) touch; (= *acción*) touch; **ser áspero al ~** to be rough to the touch; **conoce las monedas por el ~** she identifies coins by touch
[2] (= *cualidad*) feel; **tiene un ~ viscoso** it has a sticky feel (to it)
[3] (= *diplomacia*) tact; **tener ~** to be tactful

tacuache SM (*Caribe*) fib, lie

tacuacín SM (*Méx*) sloth

tacuaco ADJ (*Cono Sur*) chubby

tacuche Ⓐ SM (*Méx*) bundle of rags
Ⓑ ADJ worthless

Tadjikstán SM, **Tadjikia** SF Tadjikistan

TAE SF ABR (= **tasa anual efectiva** o **equivalente**) APR

taekwondista SMF taekwondist

tae kwon do SM, **tae-kwon-do** SM taekwondo, tae-kwon-do

tafetán SM 1 (= *tela*) taffeta
2 (*tb* ~ **adhesivo,** ~ **inglés**) sticking plaster, Band-Aid® (*EEUU*)
3 **tafetanes** (= *banderas*) flags; (= *galas*) frills, buttons and bows

tafia SF (*LAm*) rum

tafilete SM morocco leather

tagalo/a Ⓐ ADJ, SM/F Tagalog
Ⓑ SM (*Ling*) Tagalog

tagarnia* SF **comer hasta la ~** (*Andes, CAm*) to stuff o.s.*

tagarnina SF 1 (= *puro*) (cheap) cigar
2 (*Méx*) (= *petaca*) leather tobacco pouch
3 (*Andes, CAm, Méx**) (= *borrachera*) **agarrar una ~*** to get tight*

tagarote* SM 1 (*Zool*) sparrowhawk
2 (*) (= *persona*) tall shabby person
3 (*) (= *empleadillo*) lawyer's clerk, pen-pusher, pencil pusher (*EEUU*)
4 (*CAm*) (= *personaje*) big shot*

tagua SF (*Andes*) ivory palm

tahalí SM swordbelt

Tahití SM Tahiti

tahona SF (= *panadería*) bakery, bakehouse; (= *molino*) flour mill

tahonero/a SM/F (= *panadero*) baker; (= *molinero*) miller

tahúr SMF (= *jugador*) gambler; (*pey*) cardsharp, cheat

taifa* SF gang, crew

taiga SF taiga

tailandés/esa Ⓐ ADJ, SM/F Thai
Ⓑ SM (*Ling*) Thai

Tailandia SF Thailand

taima SF 1 (= *astucia*) slyness, craftiness, slickness
2 (*Cono Sur**) (= *terquedad*) obstinacy, pigheadedness

taimadamente ADV craftily, cunningly

taimado ADJ 1 (= *astuto*) sly, crafty
2 (= *hosco*) sullen
3 (*Andes*) (= *perezoso*) lazy

taimarse ▸conjug 1a◂ VPR 1 (= *volverse taimado*) to get sly, adopt crafty tactics
2 (= *enfadarse*) to go into a huff, sulk; (= *obstinarse*) to be obstinate, dig one's heels in

taita* SM 1 (*Andes, Cono Sur*) (= *papá*) father, dad*, daddy*; (= *tío*) uncle
2 (*Cono Sur*) (*tratamiento*) *in direct address, term of respect used before a name*
3 (*Cono Sur*) (= *matón*) tough, bully; (= *pendenciero*) troublemaker
4 (††) (= *chulo*) pimp

Taiwán SM Taiwan

taiwanés/esa ADJ, SM/F Taiwanese

taja SF cut

tajada SF 1 (*Culin*) slice
2 (*) (= *beneficio*) rake-off*; **sacar ~** to get one's share, take one's cut*; **sacaron buena ~ de ello** they did well out of it
3 (= *raja*) cut, slash; **¡te haré ~s!** I'll have your guts for garters!*
4 (*) (= *borrachera*) **coger** o **pillar una ~** to get plastered*
5 (*Med*) hoarseness

tajadera SF 1 (= *hacha*) chopper; (= *cincel*) cold chisel
2 (= *tabla*) chopping block

tajadero SM chopping block

tajado ADJ sheer

tajador SM (*Andes*) pencil sharpener

tajalán/ana Ⓐ ADJ (*Caribe*) lazy
Ⓑ SM/F idler, layabout

tajaleo* SM (*Caribe*) 1 (= *comida*) food, grub‡, chow (*EEUU*‡)
2 (= *pelea*) row, brawl

tajaloseo* SM (*Caribe*) row

tajamar SM 1 (*Náut*) stem; [*de puente*] cutwater
2 (*CAm, Cono Sur*) (= *muelle*) mole; (*Andes, Cono Sur*) (= *presa*) dam, dike

tajante ADJ 1 (= *contundente*) [*negativa*] emphatic; [*órdenes*] strict; [*crítica, distinción*] sharp; [*comentario*] incisive; **contestó con un "no" ~** he answered with an emphatic "no"; **hacer afirmaciones ~s** to make categorical statements; **fueron ~s en su condena** they were categorical in their condemnation; **una crítica ~ del gobierno** some sharp criticism of the government; **es una persona ~** he calls a spade a spade
2 [*herramienta*] sharp, cutting

tajantemente ADV [*responder*] emphatically, sharply; **me niego ~** I categorically refuse; **la propuesta fue rechazada ~** the proposal was rejected outright

tajar ▸conjug 1a◂ VT to cut, slice, chop

tajarrazo SM (*CAm, Méx*) slash, wound; (*fig*) damage, harm

tajeadura SF (*Cono Sur*) long scar

tajear* ▸conjug 1a◂ VT (*LAm*) (= *cortar*) to cut (up), chop (up); (= *rajar*) to slash

Tajo SM Tagus

tajo SM 1 (= *corte*) cut, slash; **darse un ~ en el brazo** to cut one's arm; **cortar algo de un ~** to slice sth off; **tirar ~s a algn** to slash at sb
2 (*Geog*) (= *corte*) cut, cleft; (= *escarpa*) steep cliff, sheer drop
3 (*) (= *trabajo*) work; **todo el verano en el ~, sin vacaciones** I have to slog away all summer, without a holiday; **largarse al ~** to get off to work, get back on the job; **¡vamos al ~!** let's get on with it!
4 (*Culin*) (= *tabla*) chopping block
5 [*del verdugo*] executioner's block
6 (= *filo*) cutting edge
7 (= *taburete*) small three-legged stool

tajón SM (*Méx*) slaughterhouse

tal Ⓐ ADJ 1 (*en relación con algo ya mencionado*) such; **no existía ~ restaurante** no such restaurant existed; **nunca he hecho ~ cosa** I never did any such thing o anything of the sort; **en ~es casos es mejor consultar con un médico** in such cases it's better to consult a doctor; **nunca he visto a ~ persona** I've never seen any such person; **hace diez años, ~ día como hoy** on the same day ten years ago, ten years ago today; **el ~ cura resultó estar casado** this priest (we were talking about) o (*pey*) this priest person turned out to be married; *ver tb* **cosa 3, 4, 5, palo 1**
2 (*indicando extrañeza o exageración*) such; **con ~ atrevimiento** with such a cheek, so cheekily; **eran ~es sus deseos de venganza** her desire for revenge was so great; **¡había ~ confusión en el aeropuerto!** it was total chaos at the airport!; **~ era su fuerza que podía levantar a dos hombres** he was so strong that he could lift two men
3 (*indicando indeterminación*) **se aloja en ~ o cual hotel** he is staying at such-and-such a hotel; **~ día, a ~ hora** on such-and-such a day, at such-and-such a time; **vivía en la calle ~, en el número cual** she lived in such-and-such a street at such-and-such a number; **necesitaba un millón para ~ cosa y otro millón para ~ otra** he needed a million for one thing and another million for another; **un ~ García** one García, a man called García or something (*pey*)
Ⓑ PRON 1 (= *persona indeterminada*) **el ~** this man I mentioned; **ésa es una ~** (*pey*) she's a tart*; **me dijo que yo era un ~ o un cual** she called me all sorts of names; **es su padre, y como ~, es responsable de su hijo** he's his father, and as such he is responsible for his son; ✦***MODISMO*** **son ~ para cual** they're two of a kind; *ver tb* **fulano 1**
2 (= *cosa indeterminada*) **no haré ~** I won't do anything of the sort, I'll do no such thing; **y ~*: fuimos al cine y ~** we went to the pictures and stuff*; **había pinchos, bebidas y ~** there were snacks and drinks and things; **estábamos charlando y ~, y de pronto me dio un beso** we were just chatting and so on, when suddenly he kissed me; **~ y cual: teníamos prisa, pero entre ~ y cual tardamos una hora** we were in a hurry, but between one thing and another it took us an hour; **es muy simpática y ~ y cual, pero no me gusta** she's very nice and all that, but I don't like her; **me dijo que si ~ y que si cual, pero no pudo convencerme** he said this, that and the other, but he wasn't able to convince me
Ⓒ ADV 1 (*en comparaciones*) **~ como: estaba ~ como lo dejé** it was just as I had left it; **~ y como están las cosas, no creo que sea buena idea** as things are o given the current state of affairs, I don't think it would be a good idea; **~ y como están las cosas, es mejor que nos vayamos** under the circumstances, it would be better if we left; **~ cual: déjalo ~ cual** leave it just as it is; **después de tantos años sigue ~ cual** she hasn't changed after all these years; **se enteró de la noticia y se quedó ~ cual** when he heard the news he didn't bat an eyelid; **en la foto salió ~ cual es en realidad** it came out in the photo just like it is in real life; **~ la madre, cual la hija** like mother, like daughter; **~ que: tomaremos algo ligero ~ que una tortilla** we'll have something light such as o like an omelette
2 (*en preguntas*) **¿qué ~?** how's things?, how are you?; **¿qué ~ el partido?** what was the game like?, how was the game?; **¿qué ~ tu tío?** how's your uncle?; **¿qué ~ estás?** how are you?; **¿qué ~ estoy con este vestido?** how do I look in this dress?; **¿qué ~ has dormido?** how did you sleep?; **¿qué ~ es físicamente?** what does she look like?; **¿qué ~ si lo compramos?** why don't we buy it?, suppose we buy it?
3 **~ vez** perhaps, maybe; **son, ~ vez, las mejores canciones del disco** they are perhaps o maybe o possibly the best songs on the album; **—¿crees que ganarán? —tal vez** "do you think they'll win?" — "perhaps o maybe o they may do"; **~ vez me pase por tu**

casa mañana I may drop in at your place tomorrow

[4] **con ~ de**: **hace lo que sea con ~ de llamar la atención** he'll do anything to attract attention; **no importa el frío con ~ de ir bien abrigado** the cold doesn't matter as long as *o* if you're well wrapped up; **con ~ de que** provided (that), as long as; **con ~ de que no me engañes** provided (that) *o* as long as you don't deceive me; **con ~ de que regreséis antes de las once** provided (that) *o* as long as you get back before eleven

tala SF [1] *[de árboles]* felling, cutting down; (= *destrucción*) havoc

[2] (*Caribe*) (= *hacha*) axe, ax (*EEUU*)

[3] (*Caribe*) (= *huerto*) vegetable garden

[4] (*Cono Sur*) (= *pasto*) grazing

talabarte SM sword belt

talabartería SF [1] (= *taller*) saddlery, harness-maker's shop [2] (*LAm*) (= *tienda*) leather-goods shop

talabartero/a SM/F saddler, harness maker

talacha SF, **talache** SM (*Méx*) mattock

talado SM felling

taladradora SF pneumatic drill, jackhammer (*EEUU*)

taladrante ADJ piercing

taladrar ▸conjug 1a◂ VT [1] [+ *pared*] to drill a hole/holes in, drill; [+ *billete, documento*] to punch; **una bala le taladró el tobillo** a bullet pierced his ankle

[2] *[ruido, mirada, dolor]* to pierce; **un ruido que taladra los oídos** an ear-splitting noise; **me taladró con la mirada** she fixed me with a piercing gaze; **un llanto de bebé taladra el silencio** a baby's cry pierces the silence, the silence is shattered by a baby's cry

taladro SM [1] (= *herramienta*) drill ► **taladro mecánico** power drill ► **taladro neumático** pneumatic drill [2] (= *agujero*) drill hole

talaje SM [1] (*LAm*) (= *pasto*) pasture

[2] (*Cono Sur, Méx*) (= *pastoreo*) grazing, pasturage

tálamo SM marriage bed

talamoco ADJ (*Andes*) albino

talante SM [1] (= *carácter*) **un hombre de ~ liberal** a liberal-minded man

[2] (= *humor*) mood; **estar de buen ~** to be in a good mood; **estar de mal ~** to be in a bad mood; **responder de mal ~** to answer bad-temperedly

[3] (= *disposición*) **hacer algo de buen ~** to do sth willingly; **recibir a algn de buen ~** to give sb a warm welcome

talar ▸conjug 1a◂ VT [1] [+ *árbol*] to fell, cut down [2] (= *devastar*) to lay waste, devastate

[3] (= *podar*) to prune

talasoterapia SF thalassotherapy

talco SM (*Quím*) talc; (*tb* **polvos de ~**) talcum powder

talcualillo* ADJ so-so, middling, fair

talega SF [1] (= *bolsa*) sack, bag

[2] **talegas** [2·1] (= *dinero*) money *sing*

[2·2] (*Méx***) (= *testículos*) balls**

talegada SF, **talegazo** SM heavy fall

talego SM [1] (= *saco*) long sack, big sack

[2] (*) (= *persona*) lump*

[3] (‡) (= *cárcel*) nick*, jail, can (*EEUU*‡)

[4] (‡) (= *billete*) 1000 pesetas; **medio ~** 500 pesetas

[5] (‡) *[de hachís]* *small bar of hash*

taleguilla SF bullfighter's breeches *pl*

talejo SM (*Andes*) paper bag

talento SM [1] (= *inteligencia*) **una mujer de enorme ~** a woman of enormous talent

[2] (= *aptitud*) talent; **Ana tiene ~ para la música** Ana has a talent for music

[3] (= *prodigio*) talent; **su hijo es un auténtico ~** her son is a really gifted *o* talented boy

[4] (*Biblia*) talent

talentoso ADJ talented, gifted, exceptional (*EEUU*)

talero SM (*Cono Sur*) whip

Talgo SM ABR (*Esp*) (= **tren articulado ligero Goicoechea-Oriol**) *inter-city express train*

talibán/ana (*a veces invariable*) Ⓐ ADJ Taliban *antes de s*

Ⓑ SM/F (= *persona*) member of the Taliban; **los talibanes** the Taliban

talidomida SF thalidomide

talión SM **la ley del ~** an eye for an eye

talismán SM talisman

talla¹ SF [1] *[de ropa]* size; **camisas de todas las ~s** shirts in all sizes; **¿de qué ~ son estos pantalones?** what size are these trousers?

[2] (= *altura*) height; **dar la ~** (*lit*) to be tall enough; (*fig*) to measure up; **no ha dado la ~ para ingresar en el ejército** he wasn't tall enough to join the army, he didn't satisfy the minimum height requirement for joining the army; **no dio la ~ como solista** he didn't make the grade as a soloist, he didn't measure up as a soloist; **no dio la ~ en la disputa** he couldn't hold his own in the argument; **tener poca ~** to be short

[3] (= *categoría, nivel*) stature; **hay pocos políticos de la ~ de este ministro** there are few politicians of the stature of this minister

[4] (*Arte*) (= *escultura*) sculpture; *[de madera]* carving; (= *grabado*) engraving ► **talla en madera** woodwork, wood carving

[5] (= *vara*) measuring rod

[6] (*Naipes*) hand

[7] (*Med*†) gallstones operation

[8] (*Jur*†) reward (*for capture of a criminal*); **poner a algn a ~** to offer a reward for sb's capture

talla² SF [1] (*CAm*) (= *mentira*) fib, lie

[2] (*Cono Sur*) (= *chismes*) gossip, chitchat; (= *piropo*) compliment; **echar ~s a algn** to pay a compliment to a woman; ✦**MODISMO echar ~** to put on airs

[3] (*Andes*) (= *paliza*) beating

[4] (*Méx**) (= *pelea*) set-to*, squabble

tallado Ⓐ ADJ [1] *[madera]* carved; *[piedra]* sculpted; *[metal]* engraved

[2] **bien ~** shapely, well-formed; **mal ~** misshapen

Ⓑ SM (*en madera*) carving; (*en piedra*) sculpting; (= *grabado*) engraving ► **tallado en madera** woodcarving

tallador(a) SM/F [1] (= *persona*) *[de madera]* carver; *[de piedra]* sculptor; *[de diamantes]* cutter; *[de metal]* engraver ► **tallador(a) de madera** woodworker, wood carver

[2] (*LAm Naipes*) dealer, banker

tallar¹ ▸conjug 1a◂ Ⓐ VT [1] [+ *madera*] to carve, work; [+ *piedra*] to sculpt; [+ *diamante*] to cut; [+ *metal*] to engrave

[2] [+ *persona*] to measure (the height of)

[3] (*Naipes*) to deal

Ⓑ VI (*Naipes*) to deal, be banker

tallar²* ▸conjug 1a◂ Ⓐ VT [1] (*Andes*) (= *fastidiar*) to bother, annoy

[2] (*Andes*) (= *azotar*) to beat

Ⓑ VI (*Cono Sur*) (= *chismear*) to gossip; *[amantes]* to whisper sweet nothings

tallarín SM [1] (*Culin*) noodle

[2] (*Andes**) (= *galón*) stripe

talle SM [1] (= *cintura*) waist; **un vestido de ~ bajo** a dress with a low waist ► **talle de avispa** wasp waist

[2] (= *medidas*) waist and chest measurements *pl*; (= *talla*) size, fitting

[3] (= *tipo*) *[de mujer]* figure; *[de hombre]* build, physique; **de ~ esbelto** slim; **tiene buen ~** she has a good figure

[4] (= *aspecto*) look, appearance; (= *contorno*) outline

[5] (*CAm, Cono Sur*) (= *corpiño*) bodice

taller SM (*Téc, Educ, Teat*) workshop; (= *fábrica*) factory, mill; (*Aut*) garage, repair shop; (*Arte*) studio; (*Cos*) workroom; (*en lenguaje sindical*) shop ► **taller de coches** car repair shop, garage (*for repairs*) ► **taller de máquinas** machine shop ► **taller de montaje** assembly shop ► **taller de reparaciones** repair shop ► **taller de teatro** theatre workshop, drama workshop ► **taller de trabajo** (*en congreso etc*) workshop ► **talleres gráficos** printing works ► **taller mecánico** garage (*for repairs*) ► **taller ocupacional** occupational therapy workshop

tallero/a SM/F (*LAm*) [1] (= *verdulero*) vegetable merchant, produce dealer (*EEUU*)

[2] (= *embustero*) liar

tallista SMF wood carver

tallo SM [1] *[de flor]* stem, stalk; *[de hierba]* blade

[2] (*Andes*) (= *repollo*) cabbage

[3] **tallos** (*LAm*) (= *verdura*) vegetables, greens

[4] (= *fruta*) crystallized fruit

talludito* ADJ mature, middle-aged; **el actor es ~ ya para este papel** the actor is getting on a bit now for this role; **Sofía Loren, que está ya talludita** Sofia Loren, who is no longer as young as she was

talludo ADJ [1] *[planta]* tall; *[persona]* tall, lanky; *ver tb* **talludito**

[2] (*CAm, Méx*) *[fruta]* (= *duro*) tough; (= *correoso*) leathery; (= *difícil de pelar*) hard to peel

[3] (*CAm, Méx**) **es un viejo ~** he's old but there's life in him yet; **es una máquina talluda** it's an old machine but it still serves its purpose

talmente* ADV exactly, literally; **la casa es ~ una pocilga** the house is literally a pigsty

Talmud SM Talmud

talmúdico ADJ Talmudic

talón SM [1] *[del pie]* heel; *[de calcetín, zapato]* heel; ✦**MODISMO pisar los talones a algn** to be hard on sb's heels ► **talón de Aquiles** Achilles heel

[2] *[de neumático]* rim

[3] (= *cheque*) cheque, check (*EEUU*); (= *matriz*) stub, counterfoil; (*Ferro*) luggage receipt ► **talón al portador** bearer cheque, cheque payable to the bearer ► **talón en blanco** blank cheque ► **talón nominativo** non-negotiable cheque; **un ~ nominativo a favor de Luis González** a cheque made out to *o* made payable to Luis González ► **talón sin fondos** bad cheque

talonador(a) SM/F (*Rugby*) hooker
talonar ▸conjug 1a◂ VT (*Rugby*) to heel
talonario SM [*de cheques*] cheque book, check book (*EEUU*); [*de recibos*] receipt book; [*de billetes*] book of tickets; [*de recetas*] prescription pad
talonear ▸conjug 1a◂ Ⓐ VT 1 (*LAm*) [+ *caballo*] to spur along, dig one's heels into
2 (*Dep*) to heel
Ⓑ VI 1 (= *apresurarse*) to walk briskly, hurry along
2 (*Méx*) [*prostituta*] to walk the streets, ply her trade
talonera SF heel-pad; (*Andes*) heel
talquera SF talcum powder container; (*con borla*) compact
talquina* SF (*Cono Sur*) deceit, treachery
taltuza SF (*CAm*) raccoon
talud SM slope, bank; (*Geol*) talus
tamal SM (*LAm*) 1 (*Culin*) tamale
2 (= *trampa*) trick, fraud; (= *intriga*) intrigue; **hacer un ~** to set a trap
3 (*Méx*) pile, bundle
tamalero/a Ⓐ ADJ 1 fond of tamales
2 (= *intrigante*) scheming, fond of intrigue
Ⓑ SM/F (= *fabricante*) tamale maker; (= *vendedor*) tamale seller
tamango SM (*Cono Sur*) 1 (= *zapato*) sandal
2 (= *vendas*) bandages *pl*
tamañito ADJ **dejar a algn ~** (= *humillar*) to make sb feel very small; (*en debate*) to crush sb, flatten sb (in an argument); **me quedé ~** (= *achicado*) I felt about so high; (= *confuso*) I felt utterly bewildered
tamaño Ⓐ SM size; **son del mismo ~** ◊ **tienen el mismo ~** they are the same size; **¿de qué ~ es?** how big is it?, what size is it?; **un ordenador del ~ de un libro** a computer the size of a book; **una foto ~ carnet** a passport-size photo; **de ~ natural** full-size, life-size; **de ~ extra** o **extraordinario** outsize, extra large ► **tamaño de bolsillo** pocket-size ► **tamaño familiar** family-size ► **tamaño gigante** king-size
Ⓑ ADJ 1 (= *tan grande*) so big a, such a big; (= *tan pequeño*) so small a, such a small; **parece absurdo que cometiera ~ error** it seems absurd that he should make such a mistake
2 (*LAm*) (= *enorme*) huge, colossal
támara SF 1 (= *planta*) date-palm
2 **támaras** (= *dátiles*) dates, cluster *sing* of dates
tamarindo SM 1 (*Bot*) tamarind
2 (*Méx*‡) traffic policeman, traffic cop*
tamarisco SM, **tamariz** SM tamarisk
tambache SM (*Méx*) [*de ropa*] bundle of clothes; (= *bulto*) big package
tambaleante ADJ 1 [*persona*] staggering; [*paso*] unsteady; [*mueble*] unsteady, wobbly; [*vehículo*] swaying
2 [*economía, democracia*] shaky; [*régimen*] tottering
tambalear ▸conjug 1a◂ Ⓐ VT to shake, rock
Ⓑ **tambalearse** VPR 1 [*persona*] to stagger; [*vehículo*] to lurch, sway; [*mueble*] to wobble; **ir tambaleándose** to stagger along
2 [*gobierno*] to totter
tambaleo SM [*de persona*] staggering; [*de vehículo*] swaying; [*de mueble*] wobble
tambar ▸conjug 1a◂ VT (*Andes*) to swallow
tambarria* SF (*Andes, CAm*) binge*, booze-up*

tambero/a SM/F (*Andes Hist*) (= *mesonero*) innkeeper; (= *granjero*) dairy farmer
▼ **también** ADV 1 (= *además*) also, too, as well; **ha estado en China y ~ en Japón** he has been in China and also in Japan, he has been in China and in Japan too *o* as well; **hablaron ~ de otros temas** they also discussed other matters, they discussed other matters too *o* as well; **Isabel ~ sabe inglés** (*uso ambiguo*) Isabel knows English too *o* as well; (*también inglés*) Isabel also knows English, Isabel knows ENGLISH too *o* as well; (*también Isabel*) ISABEL knows English too *o* as well; **Italia tomará ~ parte en la competición** ITALY will take part in the competition too *o* as well; **~ los niños tienen derecho a dar su opinión** children have the right to give their opinion too *o* as well; **¿tú ~ tienes la gripe?** have YOU got the flu too *o* as well?; **si él no viene, ~ podemos ir nosotros** if he doesn't come, WE can always go; **—estoy cansado —yo ~** "I'm tired" — "so am I" *o* "me too*"; **—me gustó —a él ~** "I liked it" — "so did he"; **ácido ascórbico, ~ conocido como vitamina C** ascorbic acid, also known as vitamin C; **—¿y es guapa? —también** "and is she pretty?" — "yes, she is"
2 (*uso enfático*) **tuvimos mala suerte, aunque ~ es cierto que nos faltaba preparación** we were certainly unlucky but (then again) we were also underprepared *o* we were underprepared too *o* as well; **—me fui sin despedirme —¡pues anda que tú ~!** "I left without saying goodbye" —"what a thing to do!"
tambo SM 1 (*Andes Hist*) (= *taberna*) wayside inn, country inn
2 (*Andes, Cono Sur*) (= *granja*) (small) dairy (farm)
3 (*Cono Sur*) (= *corral*) milking yard
4 (*Cono Sur*) (= *burdel*) brothel
tambocha SF (*Col*) *highly poisonous red ant*
tambor SM 1 (*Mús*) (= *instrumento*) drum; (= *persona*) drummer; ✦*MODISMO* **venir** *o* **salir a ~ batiente** to come out with flying colours ► **tambor mayor** drum major
2 (*Téc*) drum; [*de lavadora*] drum ► **tambor del freno** brake drum
3 (*Anat*) ► **tambor del oído** eardrum
4 [*de detergente*] drum
5 ► **tambor magnético** (*Inform*) magnetic drum
6 (*Arquit*) [*de columna*] tambour
7 (*Cos*) (= *bastidor*) tambour
8 (*Caribe, Méx*) (= *tela*) burlap, sackcloth
tambora SF 1 (*Mús*) (= *tambor*) bass drum; (*Méx*) (= *banda*) brass band
2 (*Caribe**) (= *mentira*) lie, fib
tamboril SM small drum
tamborilada SF, **tamborilazo** SM (= *batacazo*) bump on one's bottom; (= *sacudida*) severe jolt; (= *espaldarazo*) slap on the shoulder
tamborilear ▸conjug 1a◂ Ⓐ VI 1 (*Mús*) to drum
2 (*con los dedos*) to drum
3 [*lluvia*] to patter, drum
Ⓑ VT (*) to praise up, boost
tamborileo SM 1 (*con los dedos*) drumming
2 [*de lluvia*] patter, pattering
tamborilero/a SM/F drummer
tambre SM (*Andes*) dam

tamegua SF (*CAm, Méx*) weeding, cleaning
tameguar ▸conjug 1d◂ VT (*CAm, Méx*) to weed, clean
Tamerlán SM Tamburlaine
Támesis SM Thames
tamil ADJ, SMF Tamil
tamiz SM sieve; ✦*MODISMO* **pasar algo por el ~** to go through sth with a fine-tooth comb, scrutinize sth
tamizado Ⓐ ADJ [*harina, información*] sifted; [*luz*] filtered
Ⓑ SM sifting
tamizar ▸conjug 1f◂ VT [+ *harina, azúcar*] to sift, sieve; [+ *datos, información*] to sift through; [+ *luz*] to filter; [+ *rayos*] to filter out
tamo SM (= *pelusa*) fluff, down; (*Agr*) dust; (= *paja*) chaff
tampa SF (*Cono Sur*) matted hair
támpax® SM INV Tampax®, tampon
tampiqueño/a Ⓐ ADJ of/from Tampico
Ⓑ SM/F native/inhabitant of Tampico; **los ~s** the people of Tampico
tampoco ADV 1 not...either, neither, nor; **yo no lo compré ~** I didn't buy it either; **~ lo sabe él** he doesn't know either; **ni Ana ni Cristóbal ~** neither Ana nor Cristóbal; **—yo no voy —yo ~** "I'm not going" — "nor am I *o* neither am I *o* me neither"; **—yo no fui —yo ~** "I didn't go" — "nor did I *o* neither did I *o* me neither"; **—nunca he estado en París —ni yo ~** "I've never been to Paris" — "neither have I *o* me neither"; **—¿lo sabes tú? —tampoco** "do you know?" — "no, I don't either"
2 (*uso enfático*) **~ nos vamos a enfadar ahora por eso** we're not going to fall out over that, are we?; **bueno, ~ es como para ponerse a llorar** it's not as if it's anything to cry about
tampón Ⓐ SM 1 (*Med*) tampon
2 (*para entintar*) ink pad
Ⓑ ADJ INV **parlamento ~** rubber-stamp parliament; **sistema ~** buffer system; **zona ~** buffer zone
tamuga SF 1 (*CAm*) (= *fardo*) bundle, pack; (= *mochila*) knapsack
2 (*LAm*‡) joint‡, reefer‡
▼ **tan** ADV 1 (*tras verbo*) so; **estaba ~ cansado que me quedé dormido** I was so tired I fell asleep; **no te esperaba ~ pronto** I wasn't expecting you so soon; **¡no es ~ difícil!** it's not so difficult!
2 (*tras sustantivo*) such; **¿para qué quieres un coche ~ grande?** what do you want such a big car for?; **no es una idea ~ buena** it's not such a good idea
3 (*en exclamaciones*) **¡qué idea ~ rara!** what an odd notion!; **¡qué regalo ~ bonito!** what a beautiful present!; **¡que cosa ~ rara!** how strange!
4 (*en comparaciones*) **es ~ feo como yo** he's as ugly as me; **~ es así que** so much so that
5 **~ sólo** only; **hace ~ sólo unas semanas** only a few weeks ago
6 **~ siquiera** = **siquiera A**
7 (*Méx*) **¿qué ~ grande es?** how big is it?; **¿qué ~ grave está el enfermo?** how ill is the patient?; **¿qué ~ lejos?** how far?
tanaca SF (*Andes*) slut
tanaceto SM tansy
tanaco ADJ (*Cono Sur*) foolish, silly

➤ LENGUA Y USO: **también 1** 53.5 **tan 4** 32.3

tanate SM (*CAm, Méx*) [1] (= *cesta*) basket, pannier
[2] **tanates** (= *trastos*) odds and ends, bits and pieces, gear *sing*

tanatorio SM funeral home (*EEUU*)

tanda SF [1] (= *grupo*) [*de cosas, personas*] batch; [*de golpes*] series; [*de huevos*] layer; [*de inyecciones*] course, series; [*de ladrillos*] course; **por ~s** in batches ► **tanda de penaltis** series of penalties, penalty shoot-out
[2] (= *turno*) [*de trabajo*] shift, turn; [*de riego*] turn (*to use water*) ► **tanda de noche** night shift
[3] (*Billar*) game; (*Béisbol*) innings *pl*
[4] (*LAm*) (= *espectáculo*) show, performance; (*Cono Sur*) (= *farsa*) farce; (*Cono Sur*) (= *musical*) musical; **primera ~** early performance, first show

tándem SM (= *bicicleta*) tandem; (*Pol*) duo, team; **en ~** (*Elec*) tandem; (*fig*) in tandem, jointly, in association

tanga SM tanga, G-string

tangada* SF trick, swindle

tangana SF (*Perú*) large oar

tanganear ►conjug 1a◄ VT (*Andes, Caribe*) to beat

tanganillas: **en ~** ADV (*lit*) unsteadily; (*fig*) uncertainly, dubiously

tanganillo SM prop, wedge, temporary support

tangar* ►conjug 1h◄ VT to swindle; **~ algo a algn** to do sb out of sth

tangencial ADJ tangential

tangencialmente ADV tangentially

tangente SF tangent; ✦*MODISMO* **salirse por la ~** (= *hacer una digresión*) to go off at a tangent; (= *esquivar una pregunta*) to dodge the issue

Tánger SM Tangier(s)

tangerino/a Ⓐ ADJ of/from Tangier(s)
Ⓑ SM/F native/inhabitant of Tangier(s); **los ~s** the people of Tangier(s)

tangibilidad SF tangibility

tangible ADJ (*lit*) tangible; (*fig*) tangible, concrete

tango SM tango

tanguear ►conjug 1a◄ VI [1] (*LAm*) (= *bailar*) to tango
[2] (*Andes*) [*borracho*] to reel drunkenly

tanguero/a SM/F, **tanguista** SMF tango dancer

tánico ADJ tannic; **ácido ~** tannic acid

tanino SM tannin

tano/a SM/F (*Cono Sur pey*) Italian, wop** (*pey*)

tanque SM [1] (= *depósito*) tank, reservoir; (*Aut*) tanker, tanker lorry ► **tanque de cerebros**, **tanque de ideas** think tank
[2] (*Mil*) tank
[3] (*Esp**) handbag, purse (*EEUU*)

tanquero SM (*Caribe Náut*) tanker; (*Aut*) tanker, tank wagon

tanqueta SF small tank, armoured *o* (*EEUU*) armored car

tanquista SMF member of a tank-crew

tanta SF (*Andes*) maize bread

tantán SM (= *tambor*) tomtom; (= *gong*) gong

tantarán SM, **tantarantán** SM [1] [*de tambor*] beat, rat-a-tat-tat
[2] (*) (= *golpe*) hefty punch; (= *sacudida*) violent shaking

tanteada SF [1] (*LAm*) = **tanteo**
[2] (*Méx*) (= *mala pasada*) dirty trick; (= *estafa*) hoax, swindle

tanteador(a) Ⓐ SM/F (= *persona*) scorer
Ⓑ SM (= *marcador*) scoreboard

tantear ►conjug 1a◄ Ⓐ VT [1] (*con la mano*) to feel; **tanteó la mesilla en busca del reloj** he felt for the watch on the bedside table
[2] (= *probar*) to test, try out; (= *sondear*) to probe; [+ *intenciones, persona*] to sound out; ✦*MODISMO* **~ el terreno** to test the water, get the lie of the land
[3] (= *calcular*) [+ *tela, cantidad*] to make a rough estimate of; [+ *peso*] to feel, get the feel of; [+ *situación*] to weigh up; [+ *problema*] to consider
[4] (*Arte*) to sketch in, draw the outline of
[5] (*Dep*) to keep the score of
[6] (*CAm, Méx*) (= *acechar*) to lie in wait for
[7] (*Méx*) (= *estafar*) to swindle; (= *burlarse*) to make a fool of, take for a ride*
Ⓑ VI [1] (*Dep*) to score, keep (the) score
[2] (*LAm*) (= *ir a tientas*) to grope, feel one's way; **¡tantee usted!** what do you think?

tanteo SM [1] (= *cálculo*) rough estimate; (= *consideración*) weighing up; **a** *o* **por ~** by guesswork
[2] (= *prueba*) test, testing, trial; [*de situación*] sounding out; **al ~** by trial and error; **conversaciones de ~** exploratory talks
[3] (*Dep*) score; **un ~ de 9-7** a score of 9-7

tantico* SM **un ~** (*esp LAm*) a bit, quite a bit; **es un ~ difícil** it's a bit awkward*

tantísimo ADJ so much; **~s** so many; **había tantísima gente** there was such a crowd

tantito* (*Méx*) Ⓐ ADJ a bit of, a little; **~ pulque** a little pulque
Ⓑ SM = **tantico**
Ⓒ ADV a bit, a little; **~ antes** a bit *o* little earlier

▼**tanto** Ⓐ ADJ [1] (*indicando gran cantidad*) (*en singular*) so much; (*en plural*) so many; **ahora no bebo tanta leche** I don't drink so *o* as much milk now; **tiene ~ dinero que no sabe qué hacer con él** he has so much money he doesn't know what to do with it; **¡tuve tanta suerte!** I was so lucky!; **¡tengo tantas cosas que hacer hoy!** I have so many things to do today!; **había ~s coches que no había donde aparcar** there were so many cars that there was nowhere to park; **~ ... como** (*en singular*) as much ... as; (*en plural*) as many ... as; **tiene ~ dinero como yo** he has as much money as I do; **no recibe tantas llamadas como yo** he doesn't get as many calls as I do; **~ gusto** how do you do?, pleased to meet you
[2] (*indicando cantidad indeterminada*) **había cuarenta y ~s invitados** there were forty-odd guests; **hay otros ~s candidatos** there are as many more candidates, there's the same number of candidates again; **se dividen el trabajo en otras tantas partes** they divide up the work into a like number of parts
Ⓑ PRON [1] (= *gran cantidad*) (*en singular*) so much; (*en plural*) so many; **gana ~** he earns so much; **no necesitamos tantas** we don't need so many; **vinieron ~s que no cabían en la sala** so many people came that they wouldn't all fit into the room; **~ como** (*en singular*) as much as; (*en plural*) as many as; **gano ~ como tú** I earn as much as you; **coge ~s como quieras** take as many as you like; **es uno de ~s** he's nothing special
[2] (= *cantidad indeterminada*) **nació en el mil novecientos cuarenta y ~s** she was born in nineteen forty-something *o* some time in the forties; **a ~s de marzo** on such and such a day in March; **yo no sé qué ~s de libros hay** I don't know how many books there are; ✦*MODISMO* **las tantas (de la madrugada** *o* **de la noche)**: **el tren llegó a las tantas** the train arrived really late *o* in the middle of the night; **estar fuera hasta las tantas** to stay out until all hours; **—¿qué hora es? —deben de ser las tantas** "what's the time?" — "it must be pretty late"
[3] (*otras locuciones*) **entre ~** meanwhile; **mientras ~** meanwhile; **no es para ~** (*al quejarse*) it's not as bad as all that; (*al enfadarse*) there's no need to get like that about it; **por lo ~** so, therefore; ✦*MODISMOS* **ni ~ así**: **no nos desviamos ni ~ así** we didn't deviate even by this much; **no le tengo ni ~ así de lástima** I haven't a scrap of pity for him; **¡y ~!**: **—¿necesitarás unas vacaciones? —¡y ~!** "do you need a holiday?" — "you bet I do!"
Ⓒ ADV [1] (*con verbos*) (*indicando duración, cantidad*) so much; (*indicando frecuencia*) so often; **se preocupa ~ que no puede dormir** he gets so worried that he can't sleep, he worries so much that he can't sleep; **estoy cansada de ~ andar** I'm tired after all this walking; **¡cuesta ~ comprar una casa!** buying a house is such hard work!; **no deberías trabajar ~** you shouldn't work so hard; **¡no corras ~!** don't run so fast!; **ya no vamos ~ al cine** we don't go to the cinema so *o* as much any more; **ahora no la veo ~** I don't see so *o* as much of her now, I don't see her so often now; **~ como**: **él gasta ~ como yo** he spends as much as I do *o* as me; **~ como corre, va a perder la carrera** he may be a fast runner, but he's still going to lose the race; **~ como habla no dice más que tonterías** all his talk is just hot air; **~ tú como yo** both you and I; **~ si viene como si no** whether he comes or not; **~ es así que** so much so that; *ver tb* **montar B3**
[2] (*con adjetivos, adverbios*) **los dos son ya mayores, aunque su mujer no ~** the two of them are elderly, although his wife less so; **~ como**: **es difícil, pero ~ como eso no creo** it's difficult, but not that difficult; **es un poco tacaño, pero ~ como estafador, no** he's a bit on the mean side, but I wouldn't go so far as to call him a swindler; **es ~ más difícil** it is all the more difficult; **es ~ más loable cuanto que …** it is all the more praiseworthy because …; **~ mejor** so much the better; **~ mejor para ti** so much the better for you; **~ peor** so much the worse; **~ peor para ti** it's your loss *o* that's just too bad; ✦*MODISMO* **¡ni ~ ni tan calvo!** there's no need to exaggerate!
[3] (*en locuciones conjuntivas*) **en ~** as (being); **estoy en contra de la leyes en ~ sistema represivo** I am against laws as (being) a repressive system; **en ~ que** (= *mientras que*) while; (= *como*) as; **no puede haber democracia en ~ que siga habiendo torturas** for as long as there is torture, there can never be democracy, there can not be democracy while there is torture; **la Iglesia en ~ que institución** the Church as an institution
Ⓓ SM [1] (= *cantidad*) **me paga un ~ fijo cada semana** he pays me a fixed amount

➤ LENGUA Y USO: tanto B3 44.1

each week; **cobra un ~ por página** he gets so much per page; **¿qué ~ será?** (*LAm*) how much (is it)?; **otro ~**: **las máquinas costaron otro ~** the machines cost as much again *o* the same again ► **tanto alzado** fixed price; **por un ~ alzado** for a fixed rate ► **tanto por ciento** percentage

[2] (= *punto*) (*Ftbl, Hockey*) goal; (*Baloncesto, Tenis*) point; **Juárez marcó el segundo ~** Juárez scored the second goal; **marcó dos ~s** he scored twice; **apuntar los ~s** to keep score ► **tanto a favor** goal for, point for ► **tanto del honor** consolation goal ► **tanto en contra** goal against, point against; *ver tb* **apuntar C3**

[3] **estar al ~** to be up to date; **estar al ~ de los acontecimientos** to be fully abreast of events; **mantener a algn al ~ de algo** to keep sb informed about sth; **poner a algn al ~ de algo** to put sb in the picture about sth

[4] **un ~** (*como adv*) rather; **estoy un ~ cansado** I'm rather tired

Tanzania SF Tanzania

tanzano/a ADJ, SM/F Tanzanian

tañar* ▸conjug 1a◂ VT to grasp, understand; **~ a algn** to twig what sb is saying*

tañedor(a) SM/F [*de instrumentos de cuerda*] player; [*de campanas*] bell-ringer

tañer ▸conjug 2f◂ VT [+ *instrumento de cuerda*] to play; [+ *campana*] to ring

tañido SM (*Mús*) sound; [*de campana*] ringing

TAO SF ABR (= **traducción asistida por ordenador**) CAT

tapa SF [1] [*de caja, olla, piano*] lid; [*de frasco*] top; [*de depósito de gasolina*] cap; ✦*MODISMO* **levantarse la ~ de los sesos** to blow one's brains out ► **tapa de registro** manhole cover, inspection cover

[2] [*de libro*] cover; **libro de ~s duras** hardback

[3] [*de zapato*] heelplate

[4] [*de canal*] sluicegate

[5] (= *ración de comida*) snack (*taken at the bar counter with drinks*); **ir de ~s** *ver* **tapeo**

[6] (= *pieza de carne*) flank

[7] (*Andes*) (= *bistec*) rump steak

[8] (*Méx Aut*) hubcap

[9] (*Caribe*) (= *comisión*) commission

tapaagujeros* SM INV, **tapagujeros*** SM INV [1] (*Arquit*) jerry-builder

[2] (= *sustituto*) stand-in, substitute

tapabarro SM (*Cono Sur*) mudguard, fender (*EEUU*)

tapaboca SF, **tapabocas** SM INV [1] (= *prenda*) muffler

[2] (= *manotada*) slap

tapaboquetes SM INV stopgap

tapacubos SM INV hubcap

tapada SF [1] **un gay de ~*** a closet gay*

[2] (= *mentira*) lie

tapadera SF [1] [*de olla*] lid; [*de tarro de plástico*] top, cap

[2] [*de organización*] cover, front, front organization (**de** for); [*de espía*] cover; **el restaurante es una ~ de la mafia** the restaurant is a cover *o* front for the mafia

tapadero SM stopper

tapadillo: **de ~** ADV secretly, stealthily

tapado/a Ⓐ ADJ [1] (*Chile*) [*animal*] *all one colour*

[2] (*Andes*) (= *vago*) lazy, slack; (= *ignorante*) ignorant

[3] (*Ven*) **ser ~ para algo** to be useless at sth

Ⓑ SM/F (*Méx Pol*) *potential PRI Presidential election candidate*

Ⓒ SM [1] (*Uru, Chile*) (= *abrigo*) coat

[2] (*Méx*) (= *chal*) shawl; (= *pañuelo*) headscarf

[3] (*Bol*) (= *tesoro*) buried treasure

[4] (*Andes, CAm Culin*) *dish of plantain and barbecued meat*

tapagrietas SM INV filler

tapalcate SM (*CAm, Méx*) (= *objeto*) piece of junk, useless object; (= *persona*) useless person

tapalodo SM (*Andes, Caribe*) mudguard

tapanca SF [1] (*LAm*) (= *gualdrapa*) saddle blanket; (*Andes, Cono Sur*) [*de caballo*] horse trappings *pl*

[2] (*Cono Sur*) (= *culo*) backside

tapaojo SM (*LAm*) (= *venda*) blindfold, bandage (over the eyes); (= *parche*) patch

tapaporos SM INV primer

tapar ▸conjug 1a◂ Ⓐ VT [1] (= *cubrir*) (*gen*) to cover; (*más deliberada o completamente*) to cover up; **un velo le tapaba parte de la cara** part of her face was covered by a veil; **le tapó la boca con la mano** she covered his mouth with her hand; **le ~on los ojos y se lo llevaron** he was blindfolded and taken away; **mandaron ~ los desnudos de la Capilla Sixtina** they ordered the nudes of the Sistine Chapel to be covered up

[2] (= *cerrar*) (*con tapadera*) [+ *olla, tarro*] to put the lid on; [+ *botella*] (*gen*) to put the top on; (*con corcho*) to put the cork on

[3] [+ *tubo, túnel, agujero, ranura*] (= *obstruir*) block up; (= *rellenar*) to fill, fill in

[4] (= *abrigar*) (*con ropa*) to wrap up; (*en la cama*) to cover up; **tapa bien al niño, que no se enfríe** wrap the child (up) well so that he doesn't catch cold

[5] (= *ocultar*) [+ *objeto*] to hide; [+ *vista*] to block; [+ *hecho, escándalo*] to cover up; **los arbustos tapaban el sendero** the bushes hid the path; **las nubes siguen tapando el sol** the clouds are still blocking the sun; **la madre le tapa las travesuras** when he does something naughty, his mother always covers up for him

[6] (*Chile, Méx, Andes*) [+ *diente*] to fill

[7] (*LAm*) [+ *cañería, excusado*] to block

[8] (*Andes*) (= *aplastar*) to crush, flatten; (= *chafar*) to crumple, rumple

[9] (*Andes*) (= *insultar*) to abuse, insult

Ⓑ **taparse** VPR [1] (= *cubrirse*) (*gen*) to cover o.s.; (= *envolverse*) to wrap (o.s.) up; **me tapé con la manta** I covered myself with the blanket; **tápate bien al salir** wrap yourself up well before going out

[2] **~se los oídos/ojos** to cover one's ears/eyes; **la peste le hizo ~se la nariz** the stench was so bad that he had to cover *o* hold his nose

[3] (= *atascarse*) [*oídos, nariz*] to get blocked, get blocked up; [*cañería, excusado*] (*LAm*) to get blocked; **al aterrizar se me ~on los oídos** my ears got blocked (up) when we landed; **tengo la nariz tapada** my nose is blocked (up), I have a blocked (up) nose

tapara SF (*Caribe*) calabash, gourd, squash (*EEUU*)

táparo SM (*Andes*) [1] (= *yescas*) tinderbox

[2] (= *tuerto*) one-eyed person; (*fig*) dolt

taparrabo SM, **taparrabos** SM INV loincloth

tapatío/a (*Méx*) Ⓐ ADJ of/from Guadalajara

Ⓑ SM/F native/inhabitant of Guadalajara; **los ~s** the people of Guadalajara

tapayagua SF (*CAm, Méx*), **tapayagüe** SM (*Méx*) (= *nubarrón*) storm cloud; (= *llovizna*) drizzle

tape* SM (*Caribe*) cover

tapear ▸conjug 1a◂ VI (*esp Esp*) *ver* **tapeo**

tapeo SM (*esp Esp*) **ir de ~** to go round the bars (*drinking and eating snacks*); **bar de ~** tapas bar

tapeque SM (*Andes*) equipment for a journey

tapera SF (*LAm*) [1] (= *casa*) ruined house

[2] (= *pueblo*) abandoned village

taperujarse* ▸conjug 1a◂ VPR to cover up one's face

tapesco SM (*CAm, Méx*) (= *armazón*) bedframe; (= *cama*) camp bed

tapete SM (= *mantel*) tablecloth (*usually lace or embroidered*); (= *paño*) runner; (= *alfombrita*) rug; (*tb* **~ verde**) (*Naipes*) card table; ✦*MODISMOS* **estar sobre el ~** to be under discussion; **poner un asunto sobre el ~** to put a matter up for discussion

tapetusa SF (*Andes*) contraband liquor

tapia SF [1] (= *muro*) (*gen*) wall; [*de jardín*] garden wall; [*de adobe*] mud wall, adobe wall; **saltar la ~** to climb over the wall; *ver tb* **sordo A1**

[2] (*) (= *compañero*) partner

tapial SM = **tapia**

tapialera SF (*Andes*) = **tapia**

tapiar ▸conjug 1b◂ VT [1] [+ *jardín, terreno*] to wall in

[2] [+ *puerta, ventana*] (*con ladrillos*) to brick up; (*con tablas*) to board up

tapicería SF [1] [*de coche, muebles*] upholstery; **tela de ~** upholstery fabric

[2] (= *tapiz*) tapestry

[3] (= *arte*) tapestry making

tapicero/a SM/F [*de muebles*] upholsterer

tapiñar* ▸conjug 1a◂ VT to scoff*, eat

tapioca SF tapioca

tapir SM tapir

tapisca SF (*CAm, Méx*) maize harvest, corn harvest (*EEUU*)

tapiscar ▸conjug 1g◂ VT (*CAm, Méx*) to harvest

tapita* COMO ADJ **estar ~** (*Caribe*) to be as deaf as a post

tapiz SM [*de pared*] tapestry; [*de suelo*] carpet ► **tapiz volador** magic carpet

tapizado SM [*de coche, mueble*] upholstery; [*de suelo*] carpeting; [*de pared*] tapestries *pl*

tapizar ▸conjug 1f◂ VT [1] [+ *muebles*] to upholster, cover; [+ *coche*] to upholster; [+ *suelo*] to carpet, cover; [+ *pared*] to hang with tapestries

[2] (*fig*) to carpet (**con, de** with)

tapón Ⓐ SM [1] [*de botella*] (*gen*) cap, top; [*de corcho*] cork; [*de vidrio*] stopper ► **tapón de corona, tapón de rosca** screw top

[2] (*en los oídos*) (*para el ruido*) earplug; [*de cera*] plug

[3] [*de lavabo*] plug

[4] (*Med*) tampon

[5] (*Baloncesto*) block

[6] (*Aut*) (= *atasco*) traffic jam

[7] (*) (= *persona*) chubby person

[8] (*Méx Elec*) fuse

[9] (= *estorbo*) obstacle, hindrance; (*Aut**)

slowcoach*
Ⓑ ADJ (*CAm, Cono Sur*) tailless

taponar ▸conjug 1a◂ Ⓐ VT [+ *tubería, puerta, carretera*] to block; [+ *agujero*] to plug, block; (*Dep*) to block, stop; (*Med*) to tampon
Ⓑ **taponarse** VPR [*nariz, oídos*] to get blocked up

taponazo SM pop

tapujar* ▸conjug 1a◂ Ⓐ VT to cheat, con*
Ⓑ **tapujarse** VPR to muffle o.s. up

tapujo* SM [1] (= *engaño*) deceit, dodge; (= *secreto*) secrecy; (= *subterfugio*) subterfuge, dodge*; **andar con ~s** to be involved in some shady business*; **llevan no sé qué ~ entre manos** they're up to something; **sin ~s** (= *claramente*) honestly, openly; (= *sin rodeos*) without beating about the bush
[2] (= *embozo*) muffler

taquear ▸conjug 1a◂ Ⓐ VT (*LAm*) [1] (= *llenar*) to fill right up, pack tight (**de** with)
[2] [+ *arma*] (= *cargar*) to tamp, ram; (= *disparar*) to fire
Ⓑ VI [1] (*LAm*) to play billiards *o* (*EEUU*) pool
[2] (*Méx*) (= *comer tacos*) to have a snack of tacos
[3] (*Caribe*) (= *vestirse*) to dress in style
Ⓒ **taquearse** VPR (*Andes*) to get rich

taquería SF [1] (*Méx*) taco stall, taco bar
[2] (*Caribe*) (= *descaro*) cheek

taquete SM (*Méx*) plug, bung

taquicardia SF abnormally rapid heartbeat, tachycardia

taquigrafía SF shorthand, stenography (*EEUU*)

taquigráficamente ADV in shorthand; **tomar un discurso ~** to take down a speech in shorthand

taquigráfico ADJ shorthand *antes de s*

taquígrafo/a SM/F shorthand writer, stenographer (*EEUU*); ✦***MODISMO*** **con luz y ~s** openly

taquilla SF [1] (*para billetes, entradas*) (= *sala*) booking office, ticket office; (= *ventanilla*) ticket window; [*de teatro, cine*] box office; **éxito de ~** box-office success, box-office hit
[2] (= *recaudación*) (*Teat*) takings *pl*, take (*EEUU*); (*Dep*) gate money, proceeds *pl*; **la ~ fue escasa** attendance was poor
[3] (= *armario*) locker; (= *archivador*) filing cabinet; (= *carpeta*) file
[4] (*CAm*) (= *bar*) bar; (= *tienda*) liquor store
[5] (*Andes, CAm, Cono Sur*) (= *clavo*) tack

taquillaje SM (*Teat etc*) takings *pl*, box-office receipts *pl*; (*Dep*) gate-money, gate

taquillero/a Ⓐ ADJ popular, successful (at the box office); **ser ~** to be good (for the) box office, be a draw, be popular; **función taquillera** box-office success, big draw; **el actor más ~ del año** the actor who has been the biggest box-office draw of the year
Ⓑ SM/F clerk, ticket clerk

taquimeca* SM/F shorthand typist, stenographer (*EEUU*)

taquimecanografía SF shorthand typing

taquimecanógrafo/a SM/F shorthand typist, stenographer (*EEUU*)

taquímetro SM tachymeter

taquito SM [*de jamón*] small cube

tara[1] SF [1] (= *peso*) tare
[2] (= *defecto*) defect, blemish

tara[2] SF tally stick

tarabilla Ⓐ SF [1] [*de ventana*] latch, catch
[2] (*) (= *charla*) chatter
Ⓑ SMF (*) [1] (= *hablador*) chatterbox*
[2] (= *casquivano*) featherbrained person; (= *inútil*) useless individual, dead loss*

tarabita SF [1] [*de cinturón*] tongue
[2] (*Andes*) (*en puente*) cable of a rope bridge (*with hanging basket for carrying passengers across ravines*)

taracea SF inlay, marquetry

taracear ▸conjug 1a◂ VT to inlay

tarado/a Ⓐ ADJ [1] (*Com*) defective, imperfect
[2] [*persona*] crippled
[3] (*) (= *idiota*) stupid; (= *loco*) crazy, nuts*
Ⓑ SM/F (*) (= *idiota*) cretin*, moron*

tarambana SMF, **tarambanas** SMF INV [1] (= *casquivano*) harebrained person; (= *estrafalario*) crackpot*; (= *no fiable*) fly-by-night
[2] (= *parlanchín*) chatterbox*

taranta SF [1] (*LAm*) (= *locura*) mental disturbance, madness; (*CAm*) (= *confusión*) bewilderment
[2] (*Méx*) (= *embriaguez*) drunkenness
[3] (*Andes, Cono Sur Zool*) tarantula

tarantear ▸conjug 1a◂ VI (*Cono Sur*) (= *hacer algo imprevisto*) to do sth unexpected; (= *cambiar*) to chop and change a lot; (= *hacer cosas raras*) to behave strangely, be eccentric

tarantela SF tarantella

tarantín SM [1] (*CAm, Caribe Culin*) kitchen utensil
[2] (*Caribe*) (= *patíbulo*) scaffold
[3] (*Caribe*) (= *puesto*) stall
[4] **tarantines** (*Caribe**) odds and ends

taranto ADJ (*Andes*) dazed, bewildered

tarántula SF tarantula

tarar ▸conjug 1a◂ VT (*Com*) to tare

tarareable ADJ **melodía ~** catchy tune, tune that you can hum

tararear ▸conjug 1a◂ VT, VI to hum

tararí* Ⓐ ADJ (*Esp*) crazy
Ⓑ EXCL no way!*, you must be joking!

tarasca SF [1] (= *monstruo*) carnival dragon, monster
[2] (= *comilón*) glutton; (= *sangría de recursos*) *person who is a drain on one's resources*
[3] (*) (= *mujer*) old hag, old bag*
[4] (*Andes, CAm, Cono Sur*) (= *boca*) big mouth

tarascada SF [1] (= *mordisco*) bite
[2] (*) (= *contestación*) tart reply, snappy answer

tarascar ▸conjug 1g◂ VT to bite

tarasco SM (*Andes*), **tarascón** SM (*LAm*) bite, nip

tarasquear ▸conjug 1a◂ VT (*CAm, Cono Sur, Méx*) (= *morder*) to bite; (= *cortar*) to bite off

tardanza SF [1] (= *demora*) delay
[2] (= *lentitud*) slowness

tardar ▸conjug 1a◂ Ⓐ VT **he tardado un poco debido a la lluvia** I'm a bit late because of the rain; **tardamos tres horas de Granada a Córdoba** we took three hours to get from Granada to Córdoba; **¿cuánto se tarda?** how long does it take?; **aquí tardan mucho en servirte** the service is very slow here, they take a long time to serve you here; **tardó tres horas en encontrarlo** he took three hours looking for it, it took him three hours to find it; **tardó mucho en repararlo** he took a long time to repair it
Ⓑ VI **vete a buscarlo, pero no tardes** go and fetch it, but don't be long; **te espero a las ocho, no tardes** I expect you at eight, don't be late; **~ en hacer algo**: **tardó en llegar** it was late in arriving; **tarda en hacer efecto** it takes a while to take effect, it doesn't take effect immediately; **no tarde usted en informarme** please tell me as soon as you know; **el público no tardó en reaccionar** the spectators were not slow *o* were quick to react; **a más ~** at the latest; **a las ocho a más ~** at eight o'clock at the latest; **sin ~** without delay; **a todo ~** at the latest
Ⓒ **tardarse** VPR (*Méx**) to be long, take a long time; **no me tardo** I won't be long, I won't take long

tarde Ⓐ ADV (*gen*) late; (= *demasiado tarde*) too late; **llegar ~** to be late, arrive late; **ya es ~ para quejarse** it's too late to complain now; **se hace ~** it's getting late; **se te hará ~ si no aligeras** you'll be late if you don't hurry up; **de ~ en ~** from time to time; **más ~** later; **un poco más ~** a bit later; **~ o temprano** sooner or later
Ⓑ SF (= *primeras horas*) afternoon; (= *últimas horas*) evening; **a las siete de la ~** at seven in the evening; **¡buenas ~s!** good afternoon!/good evening!; **tenlo listo a la ~** have it ready by the afternoon/evening; **en la ~ de hoy** this afternoon/evening; **en la ~ del lunes** on Monday afternoon/evening; **por la ~** in the afternoon/evening; **el domingo por la ~** on Sunday afternoon/evening; ✦***MODISMO*** **de la ~ a la mañana** overnight

tardecer ▸conjug 2d◂ VI = **atardecer**

tardecito ADV (*LAm*) rather late

tardíamente ADV (= *tarde*) late, belatedly; (= *demasiado tarde*) too late

tardío ADJ [*periodo, producto*] late; **el Renacimiento ~** the late Renaissance; **la medicina ha sido una vocación tardía** she came to medicine late in life; **tener un hijo ~** to have a child late in life; **el interés de los historiadores ha sido relativamente ~** historians have only relatively recently *o* lately taken an interest

tardo ADJ [1] (= *lento*) slow, sluggish
[2] (= *torpe*) dull, dense; **~ de oído** hard of hearing; **~ de reflejos** slow (to react)

tardo... PREF late; **~rromano** late Roman; **el ~franquismo** the last years of the Franco régime

tardón* ADJ [1] (= *lento*) slow
[2] (= *lerdo*) dim

tarea SF [1] (= *trabajo*) task, job; **una de sus ~s es repartir la correspondencia** one of his tasks *o* jobs is to hand out the mail; **es una ~ poco grata** it's a thankless task; **todavía me queda mucha ~** I've still got a lot left to do
► **tareas domésticas** housework *sing*, household chores
[2] [*de colegial*] **las ~s** homework *sing*
[3] (*Inform*) task

tareco SM (*Andes*) old thing, piece of junk

tarifa SF [1] (= *precio fijado*) [*de suministros*] rate; [*de transportes*] fare ► **tarifa apex** apex fare ► **tarifa bancaria** bank rate ► **tarifa de suscripción** subscription rate ► **tarifa nocturna** (*Telec*) cheap rate ► **tarifa postal** postal rate ► **tarifa reducida** (*Transportes*) reduced fare ► **tarifa turística** tourist rates
[2] (= *lista de precios*) price list

[3] (= *arancel*) tariff ► **tarifa aduanera** customs tariff

tarifar ▸conjug 1a◂ Ⓐ VT to price
Ⓑ VI to fall out, quarrel

tarifario ADJ **política tarifaria** pricing policy; **revisión tarifaria** revision of prices, revision of pricing; **la tendencia tarifaria será la de reducir precios** the tendency will be to reduce prices

tarificación SF metering

tarificar ▸conjug 1g◂ VT to meter

tarima SF [1] (= *plataforma*) platform; (= *estrado*) dais; (= *soporte*) stand
[2] (= *suelo*) flooring

tarimaco SM (*Caribe*) = **tareco**

tarja[1] SF (= *palo*) tally (stick)

tarja[2]* SF (= *golpe*) swipe, bash*

tarjar ▸conjug 1a◂ VT [1] (= *señalar*) to keep a tally of, notch up
[2] (*Andes, Cono Sur*) (= *tachar*) to cross out

tarjeta SF card; **dejar ~** to leave one's card; **pagar con ~** to pay by (credit) card; **pasar ~** to send in one's card ► **tarjeta amarilla** (*Dep*) yellow card ► **tarjeta bancaria** banker's card, bank card ► **tarjeta comercial** business card ► **tarjeta de banda magnética** swipe card ► **tarjeta de circuitos** (*Inform*) circuit board ► **tarjeta de crédito** credit card ► **tarjeta de embarque** boarding pass ► **tarjeta de expansión** expansion card ► **tarjeta de felicitación** greetings card, greeting card (*EEUU*) ► **tarjeta de fidelidad** loyalty card ► **tarjeta de gráficos** graphics card ► **tarjeta de identidad** identity card ► **tarjeta de lector** reader's ticket ► **tarjeta de memoria** memory card ► **tarjeta de multifunción** multifunction card ► **tarjeta de Navidad** Christmas card ► **tarjeta de periodista** press card ► **tarjeta de prepago** (*de móvil*) prepaid card ► **tarjeta de presentación** business card ► **tarjeta de respuesta** reply card ► **tarjeta de respuesta pagada** reply-paid postcard ► **tarjeta de saludo** greetings card, greeting card (*EEUU*) ► **tarjeta de sonido** sound card ► **tarjeta de vídeo** (*Esp*), **tarjeta de video** (*LAm*) video card ► **tarjeta de visita** business card, visiting card ► **tarjeta dinero** cash card ► **tarjeta gráfica** (*Inform*) graphics card ► **tarjeta inteligente** smart card ► **tarjeta monedero** electronic purse *o* wallet ► **tarjeta navideña** Christmas card ► **tarjeta perforada** punched card ► **tarjeta postal** postcard ► **tarjeta roja** (*Dep*) red card ► **tarjeta SIM** SIM card ► **tarjeta telefónica** phonecard ► **tarjeta verde** (*Méx*) (= *visado*) Green Card (*EEUU*)

tarjetear ▸conjug 1a◂ VT **~ a un jugador** to show a card to a player

tarjetero Ⓐ ADJ **el árbitro se mostró muy ~** (*Ftbl*) the referee was constantly reaching for his pocket, the referee booked a lot of players
Ⓑ SM (= *cartera*) credit card holder *o* wallet

tarot SM tarot

tarpón SM tarpon

tarquín SM mud, slime, ooze

tarra‡ SMF old geezer‡

tarraconense Ⓐ ADJ of/from Tarragona
Ⓑ SMF native/inhabitant of Tarragona; **los ~s** the people of Tarragona

Tarragona SF Tarragona

tarrajazo SM [1] (*Andes, Caribe*) (= *suceso*) unpleasant event
[2] (*CAm*) (= *golpe*) blow; (= *herida*) wound

tarramenta SF (*Caribe, Méx*) horns *pl*

tarrayazo SM [1] (*Andes, Caribe, Méx*) [*de red*] cast (of a net) [2] (*Caribe*) (= *golpe*) violent blow

tarrear ▸conjug 1a◂ VT (*Caribe*) to cuckold

tarrina SF [*de helado, margarina*] tub

tarro SM [1] (= *recipiente*) [*de vidrio*] jar; [*de porcelana*] pot
[2] (*Esp**) (= *cabeza*) nut*, noggin (*EEUU**); ✦**MODISMOS comer el ~ a algn** (= *engañar*) to put one over on sb*; (= *lavar el cerebro*) to brainwash sb; **comerse el ~** to rack one's brains, think hard
[3] (*esp LAm*) (= *lata*) tin, can; (= *bidón*) drum; ✦**MODISMO arrancarse con los ~s*** to run off with the loot*
[4] (*Andes*††) (= *chistera*) top hat
[5] (*Cono Sur*) (= *chiripa*) stroke of luck, fluke
[6] (*Caribe, Cono Sur*) (= *cuerno*) horn
[7] (*Caribe*) [*del marido*] cuckolding
[8] (*Caribe*) (= *asunto*) thorny question, complicated affair

tarsana SF (*LAm*) soapbark

tarso SM tarsus

tarta SF [1] (= *pastel*) cake; (*con base de hojaldre*) tart; ✦**MODISMO repartir la ~** to divide up the cake ► **tarta de bodas** wedding cake ► **tarta de cumpleaños** birthday cake ► **tarta de frutas** fruitcake ► **tarta de manzana** apple tart ► **tarta de queso** cheesecake ► **tarta nupcial** wedding cake
[2] (= *gráfico*) pie chart

tártago SM [1] (*Bot*) spurge
[2] (*) (= *desgracia*) mishap, misfortune
[3] (*) (= *trastada*) practical joke

tartaja* Ⓐ ADJ INV stammering, tongue-tied
Ⓑ SMF INV stammerer

tartajear ▸conjug 1a◂ VT to stammer

tartajeo SM stammer(ing)

tartajoso/a ADJ, SM/F = **tartaja**

tartalear ▸conjug 1a◂ VI [1] (*al andar*) (*aturdido*) to walk in a daze; (*tambaleándose*) to stagger, reel
[2] (*al hablar*) to stammer, be stuck for words

tartamudeante ADJ stuttering, stammering

tartamudear ▸conjug 1a◂ VI to stutter, stammer

tartamudeo SM stutter(ing), stammer(ing)

tartamudez SF stutter, stammer

tartamudo/a Ⓐ ADJ stuttering, stammering
Ⓑ SM/F stutterer, stammerer

tartán SM tartan

tartana SF [1] (= *carruaje*) trap, light carriage
[2] (*) (= *auto*) banger*, clunker (*EEUU**)

tartancho ADJ (*Andes, Cono Sur*) = **tartamudo**

Tartaria SF Tartary

tartárico ADJ tartaric; **ácido ~** tartaric acid

tártaro[1] SM (*Quím*) tartar; **salsa tártara** tartar sauce

tártaro[2]**/a** ADJ, SM/F Tartar

tartera SF (= *fiambrera*) lunch box; (*para horno*) cake tin

Tarteso SM Tartessus; (*Biblia*) Tarshish

tarugo Ⓐ ADJ [1] (*) (= *zoquete*) stupid
[2] (*Caribe*) (= *adulador*) fawning
Ⓑ SM [1] (= *pedazo de madera*) lump, chunk; (= *clavija*) wooden peg; (= *tapón*) plug, stopper; (= *adoquín*) wooden paving block
[2] (= *pan*) chunk of stale bread

[3] (*) (= *imbécil*) chump*, blockhead*
[4] (*Caribe**) (= *susto*) fright, scare
[5] (*Méx*) (= *miedo*) fear, anxiety
[6] (‡) (= *soborno*) backhander*

tarumba* ADJ **volver ~ a algn** (= *confundir*) to confuse sb, get sb all mixed up; (= *marear*) to make sb dizzy; **volverse ~** to get all mixed up, get completely confused; **esa chica me tiene ~** I'm crazy about that girl

tasa SF [1] (= *precio*) rate; **de cero ~** zero-rated ► **tasa básica** (*Com*) basic rate ► **tasa de aeropuerto** airport tax ► **tasa de basuras** refuse *o* (*EEUU*) garbage collection charge ► **tasa de cambio** exchange rate ► **tasa de descuento bancario** bank rate ► **tasa de instrucción** tuition fee ► **tasa de interés** interest rate ► **tasas académicas** tuition fees ► **tasas judiciales** legal fees ► **tasas locales, tasas municipales** local taxes
[2] (= *índice*) rate ► **tasa de crecimiento, tasa de desarrollo** growth rate ► **tasa de desempleo** level of unemployment, unemployment rate ► **tasa de mortalidad** death rate, mortality rate ► **tasa de nacimiento, tasa de natalidad** birth rate ► **tasa de paro** level of unemployment, unemployment rate ► **tasa de rendimiento** (*Com*) rate of return
[3] (= *tasación*) valuation, appraisal (*EEUU*)
[4] (= *medida, regla*) measure; **sin ~** boundless, limitless; **gastar sin ~** to spend like there's no tomorrow

tasable ADJ ratable

tasación SF valuation, appraisal (*EEUU*); **~ de un edificio** valuation of a building ► **tasación pericial** expert valuation

tasadamente ADV sparingly

tasador(a) SM/F valuer, appraiser (*EEUU*) ► **tasador(a) de averías** average adjuster ► **tasador(a) de impuestos** tax appraiser

tasajear ▸conjug 1a◂ VT (*LAm*) [1] (= *cortar*) to cut, slash [2] [+ *carne*] to jerk

tasajo SM [1] (= *cecina*) dried beef, jerked beef
[2] (*Andes*) (= *persona*) tall thin person

tasajudo ADJ (*LAm*) tall and thin

tasar ▸conjug 1a◂ VT [1] (= *valorar*) to value
[2] [+ *trabajo*] to rate (**en** at)
[3] (= *restringir*) to limit, put a limit on, restrict; (= *racionar*) to ration; (= *escatimar*) to be sparing with; (*pey*) to be mean with, stint; **les tasa a los niños hasta la leche** she even rations her children's milk

tasca SF pub, bar; **ir de ~s** to go on a pub crawl*

tascar ▸conjug 1g◂ VT [1] [+ *lino*] to swingle, beat [2] [+ *hierba*] to munch, champ; [+ *freno*] to champ at sth [3] (*Andes*) (= *masticar*) to chew, crunch

Tasmania SF Tasmania

tasquear* ▸conjug 1a◂ VI (*Esp*) to go drinking, go round the bars

tasqueo* SM **ir de ~** (*Esp*) = **tasquear**

tata* Ⓐ SM (*LAm*) (= *padre*) dad*, daddy*
Ⓑ SF (= *niñera*) nanny; (= *chacha*) maid; *ver tb* **tato**

tatarabuelo/a SM/F great-great-grandfather/-mother; **mis ~s** my great-great-grandparents

tataranieto/a SM/F great-great-grandson/-daughter; **sus ~s** his great-great-grandchildren

tatas: **a ~** ADV **andar a ~** (= *hacer pinitos*) to

toddle; (= *ir a gatas*) to crawl, get down on all fours

tate[1] EXCL (*sorpresa*) gosh!*, crumbs!*; (*al darse cuenta*) so that's it!, oh I see!; (*aviso*) look out!; (*admiración*) bravo!; (*ira*) come now!

tate[2]* SM (= *marihuana*) hash*, pot*

tato/a* Ⓐ SM/F (= *hermano*) brother/sister
Ⓑ SM (*LAm**) (= *padre*) dad(dy)*, pop (*EEUU**); *ver tb* **tata**

tatole* SM (*Méx*) plot

tatuaje SM [1] (= *dibujo*) tattoo
[2] (= *acto*) tattooing

tatuar ▸conjug 1d◂ VT to tattoo

tauca SF (*Andes*) [1] (= *objetos*) heap of things
[2] (= *bolsa*) large bag

taumaturgia SF miracle working, thaumaturgy

taumaturgo SM miracle worker

taurinamente ADV in bullfighting terms

taurino ADJ bullfighting *antes de s*; **el mundo ~** the bullfighting business; **una revista taurina** a bullfighting magazine

Tauro SM Taurus

taurofobia SF dislike of bullfighting

taurófobo/a SM/F opponent of bullfighting

taurómaco/a Ⓐ ADJ bullfighting *antes de s*
Ⓑ SM/F bullfighting expert

tauromaquia SF (art of) bullfighting, tauromachy (*frm*)

tauromáquico ADJ bullfighting *antes de s*

tautología SF tautology

tautológico ADJ tautological

TAV SM ABR (= **tren de alta velocidad**) HVT

taxativamente ADV [1] (= *específicamente*) specifically, in a restricted sense
[2] (= *tajantemente*) sharply, emphatically

taxativo ADJ [1] (= *restringido*) limited, restricted; [*sentido*] specific
[2] (= *tajante*) sharp, emphatic

taxi SM taxi, cab; **fuimos en ~** we went by taxi

taxidermia SF taxidermy

taxidermista SMF taxidermist

taximetrero/a SM/F (*Arg*), **taximetrista** SMF (*Arg*) taxi driver, cab driver

taxímetro SM [1] (= *aparato*) taximeter, clock
[2] (*Arg*) (= *vehículo*) taxi

taxista SMF taxi driver, cabby*, cab driver (*EEUU*)

taxonomía SF taxonomy

taxonomista SMF taxonomist

Tayikistán SM Tadzhikistan

taza SF [1] (= *recipiente*) cup; (= *contenido*) cupful ► **taza de café** (= *café*) cup of coffee; (= *recipiente*) coffee cup
[2] [*de fuente*] basin, bowl; [*de lavabo*] bowl; [*de retrete*] pan, bowl ► **taza del wáter** toilet bowl
[3] (*Cono Sur*) (= *palangana*) washbasin, bathroom sink (*EEUU*) ► **taza de noche** (*Cono Sur euf*) chamber pot

tazado ADJ [*ropa*] frayed, worn; [*persona*] shabby

tazar ▸conjug 1f◂ Ⓐ VT [1] (= *cortar*) to cut; (= *dividir*) to cut up, divide
[2] (= *desgastar*) to fray
Ⓑ **tazarse** VPR to fray

tazón SM (= *cuenco*) bowl; (= *taza*) large cup; (= *jarra*) mug

TBC SM ABR = **tren de bandas en caliente**

TC SM ABR = **Tribunal Constitucional**

TCI SF ABR (= **Tarjeta de Circuito Impreso**) PCB

TDV SF ABR (= **tabla deslizadora a vela**) windsurfing board

te[1] SF *name of the letter t*

te[2] PRON PERS [1] (*como complemento directo*) you; **te quiero mucho** I love you very much; **ayer te vi en el centro** I saw you in the city centre yesterday
[2] (*como complemento indirecto*) you; **te voy a dar un consejo** I'm going to give you some advice; **te he traído esto** I've brought you this, I've brought this for you; **me gustaría comprártelo para navidad** I'd like to buy it for you *o* buy you it for Christmas; **no te lo compro porque lo vendes muy caro** I'm not going to buy from you because you're charging too much for it; **¿te han arreglado el ordenador?** have they fixed your computer (for you)?
[3] (*con partes del cuerpo, ropa*) **¿te duelen los pies?** do your feet hurt?; **¿te has puesto el abrigo?** have you put your coat on?
[4] (*uso enfático*) **te lo comiste todo** you ate it all up; **se te ha caído el bolígrafo** you've dropped your pen; **se te ha parado el reloj** your watch has stopped
[5] (*uso reflexivo o pronominal*) **¿te has lavado?** have you washed?; **¡cálmate!** calm down!; **¿te levantas temprano?** do you get up early?; **tienes que defenderte** you have to defend yourself; **te vas a caer** you'll fall; **te equivocas** you're wrong; **¿te has hecho daño?** have you hurt yourself?
[6] (*uso impersonal*) **aquí siempre te intentan timar** they always try to cheat you here

té SM [1] (= *planta, bebida*) tea
[2] (= *reunión*) tea party; **dar un té** to give a tea party; ✦**MODISMO dar el té a algn*** to bore sb to tears

tea SF [1] (= *antorcha*) torch; (= *astilla*) firelighter; ✦**MODISMOS arder como una ~** ◊ **convertirse en una ~** to go up like a torch
[2] (*) (= *cuchillo*) knife

teatral ADJ [1] [*grupo, temporada*] theatre *antes de s*, theater *antes de s* (*EEUU*); [*asociación, formación*] dramatic; **obra ~** play
[2] (= *aparatoso*) (= *persona*) theatrical; [*gesto, palabras*] dramatic, theatrical; (*pey*) histrionic, stagey

teatralidad SF [1] (= *aparato*) theatricality; (= *drama*) drama; (*pey*) histrionics *pl*, staginess
[2] (= *sentido del teatro*) sense of theatre, stage sense; (*pey*) showmanship

teatralizar ▸conjug 1f◂ VT [+ *obra*] to stage; [+ *situación*] to dramatize

teatralmente ADV theatrically

teatrero/a* Ⓐ ADJ [1] (= *exagerado*) theatrical
[2] (= *aficionado*) **ser muy ~** to be a great theatre-goer
Ⓑ SM/F [1] (= *aficionado*) theatre-goer
[2] (= *profesional*) theatre-worker

teatro SM [1] (*gen*) theatre, theater (*EEUU*); (= *escenario*) stage; **escribir para el ~** to write for the stage; **en el ~ es una persona muy distinta** she's a very different person on the stage; **hacer que se venga abajo el ~** to bring the house down ► **teatro amateur, teatro de aficionados** amateur theatre, amateur dramatics ► **teatro de calle** street theatre ► **teatro del absurdo** theatre of the absurd ► **teatro de la ópera** opera house ► **teatro de repertorio** repertory theatre ► **teatro de títeres** puppet theatre ► **teatro de variedades** variety theatre, music hall, vaudeville theater (*EEUU*)
[2] (*Literat*) (= *género*) drama; (= *obras de teatro*) plays *pl*; **el ~ del siglo XVIII** 18th century theatre *o* drama; **el ~ de Cervantes** Cervantes's plays
[3] [*de suceso*] scene; (*Mil*) theatre, theater (*EEUU*) ► **teatro de guerra** theatre of war ► **teatro de operaciones** theatre of operations
[4] (= *exageración*) **hacer ~** (= *alborotar*) to make a fuss; (= *exagerar*) to exaggerate; **tiene mucho ~** he's always so melodramatic
[5] (*LAm*) (= *cine*) cinema, movies *pl*

Tebas SF Thebes

tebeo SM (children's) comic, comic book (*EEUU*); ✦**MODISMO está más visto que el ~** that's old hat ► **tebeo de terror** horror comic

tebeoteca SF collection of comics

teca SF teak

techado SM (= *tejado*) roof; (= *cubierta*) covering; **bajo ~** under cover, indoors

techar ▸conjug 1a◂ VT to roof (in *o* over)

techo SM [1] (*interior*) ceiling; (*exterior, Aut*) roof; **el ~ de mi cuarto está pintado de blanco** the ceiling in my room is painted white; **los ~s de las casas son de pizarra** the houses have slate roofs; **bajo ~** indoors; **tenis bajo ~** indoor tennis; **bajo el mismo ~** under the same roof; **un sin ~** a homeless person; **los sin ~** the homeless ► **techo corredizo, techo solar** (*Aut*) sunroof
[2] (= *límite, tope*) ceiling, limit; (*Fin*) ceiling; **ha tocado ~** it has reached its upper limit, it has peaked ► **techo de cristal** glass ceiling
[3] (*Aer*) ceiling

techumbre SF roof

tecito SM (*esp LAm*) cup of tea

tecla SF (*Inform, Mús, Tip*) key; ✦**MODISMOS dar en la ~*** (= *acertar*) to get it right; (= *aprender*) to get the hang of it; **dar en la ~ de hacer algo*** to fall into the habit of doing sth; **tocar ~s**: **no le queda ninguna otra ~ por tocar** there's nothing else left for him to try ► **tecla con flecha** arrow key ► **tecla de anulación** cancel key ► **tecla de borrado** delete key ► **tecla de cambio** shift key ► **tecla de control** control key ► **tecla de desplazamiento** scroll key ► **tecla de edición** edit key ► **tecla de función** function key ► **tecla de iniciación** booting-up switch ► **tecla del cursor** cursor key ► **tecla de retorno** return key ► **tecla de tabulación** tab key ► **tecla programable** user-defined key ► **teclas de control direccional del cursor** cursor control keys

teclado SM (*tb Inform*) keyboard, keys *pl*; [*de órgano*] keyboard, manual; **Gimbel a los ~s** Gimbel on keyboards; **marcación por ~** push-button dialling ► **teclado numérico** (*Inform*) numeric keypad

tecle ADJ (*Cono Sur*) weak, sickly

tecleado SM typing

teclear ▸conjug 1a◂ Ⓐ VT [1] (*gen*) to key in, type in; (*en cajero automático*) to enter
[2] (*) [+ *problema*] to approach from various angles
[3] (*LAm*) [+ *instrumento*] to play clumsily,

mess about on; [+ *máquina de escribir*] to mess about on

Ⓑ VI [1] (*en máquina de escribir, ordenador*) to type; (*en el piano*) to play

[2] (*) (= *tamborilear*) to drum, tap

[3] (*Cono Sur**) [*negocio*] to be going very badly; [*persona*] to be doing very badly; **ando tecleando** I'm doing very badly

tecleo SM [1] (= *tecleado*) typing, keying

[2] (*Mús*) playing

[3] (*) (= *tamborileo*) drumming, tapping

tecleteo SM = **tecleo**

teclista SMF (*Inform*) keyboard operator, keyboarder; (*Mús*) keyboard player

teclo/a Ⓐ ADJ (*Andes*) old

Ⓑ SM/F old man/woman

técnica SF [1] (= *método*) technique

[2] (= *tecnología*) technology; **los avances de la ~** advances in technology

[3] (= *destreza*) skill; *ver tb* **técnico**

técnicamente ADV technically

tecnicidad SF technicality, technical nature

tecnicismo SM [1] (= *carácter técnico*) technical nature

[2] (*Ling*) technical term, technicality

técnico/a Ⓐ ADJ technical

Ⓑ SM/F [1] (*en fábrica, laboratorio*) technician ► **técnico/a de laboratorio** laboratory technician, lab technician* ► **técnico/a de mantenimiento** maintenance engineer ► **técnico/a de sonido** sound engineer, sound technician ► **técnico/a de televisión** television engineer, television repairman ► **técnico/a informático/a** computer programmer

[2] (= *experto*) expert, specialist; **es un ~ en la materia** he's an expert on the subject

[3] (*Dep*) trainer, coach; *ver tb* **técnica**

tecnicolor® SM Technicolor®; **en ~** in Technicolor

tecnificar ▸conjug 1g◂ Ⓐ VT to make more technical Ⓑ **tecnificarse** VPR to become more technical

tecno Ⓐ ADJ [*música*] techno

Ⓑ SM (*Mús*) techno

tecno... PREF techno....

tecnocracia SF technocracy

tecnócrata SMF technocrat

tecnocrático ADJ technocratic

tecnología SF technology; **alta ~** high technology; **nuevas ~s** new technologies ► **tecnología Bluetooth**® Bluetooth® technology ► **tecnología de alimentos** food technology ► **tecnología de estado sólido** solid-state technology ► **tecnología de la información** information technology ► **tecnología inalámbrica** wireless technology ► **tecnología punta** leading-edge technology

tecnológico ADJ technological

tecnólogo/a SM/F technologist

teco* ADJ (*CAm, Méx*) drunk

tecolote Ⓐ SM [1] (*CAm, Méx*) (= *búho*) owl

[2] (*Méx**) (= *policía*) policeman, cop*

Ⓑ ADJ [1] (*CAm*) [*color*] reddish-brown

[2] (*CAm, Méx*) (= *borracho*) drunk

tecomate SM (*CAm, Méx*) [1] (= *calabaza*) gourd, calabash

[2] (= *recipiente*) earthenware bowl

tecorral SM (*Méx*) dry-stone wall

tectónica SF tectonics *sing*

tecuán Ⓐ ADJ (*CAm, Méx*) greedy, voracious

Ⓑ SM monster

tedio SM (= *aburrimiento*) boredom, tedium; (= *vaciedad*) sense of emptiness; **me produce ~** it just depresses me

tedioso ADJ tedious

tefe SM [1] (*Andes*) (= *cuero*) strip of leather; (= *tela*) strip of cloth

[2] (*Andes*) (= *cicatriz*) scar on the face

tegumento SM tegument

Teherán SM Teheran

tehuacán SM (*Méx*) mineral water

Teide SM **el (Pico de) ~** Teide, Teyde

teína SF theine

teísmo SM theism

teísta Ⓐ ADJ theistic Ⓑ SMF theist

teja[1] SF (roof) tile; **de color ~** brick red; ✦*MODISMOS* **pagar a toca ~*** to pay on the nail; **de ~s abajo** in this world, in the natural way of things; **de ~s arriba** in the next world; **por fin le cayó la ~** (*Cono Sur*) finally the penny dropped ► **tejas de pizarra** slates

teja[2] SF (*Bot*) lime (tree)

tejadillo SM top, cover

tejado SM (tiled) roof; ✦*MODISMO* **tiene el ~ de vidrio** people who live in glass houses shouldn't throw stones, it's the pot calling the kettle black

tejamaní SM (*LAm*), **tejamanil** SM (*LAm*) roofing board, shingle

tejano/a Ⓐ ADJ, SM/F Texan

Ⓑ **tejanos** SMPL (= *vaqueros*) jeans, denims

tejar[1] ▸conjug 1a◂ VT to tile, roof with tiles; **~ un techo** to tile a roof

tejar[2] SM tile factory

Tejas SM Texas

tejaván SM (*LAm*) (= *cobertizo*) shed; (= *galería*) gallery; (= *choza*) rustic dwelling

tejavana SF (= *cobertizo*) shed; (= *tejado*) shed roof, plain tile roof

tejedor(a) SM/F [1] (= *artesano*) weaver

[2] (*Andes, Cono Sur*) (= *intrigante*) schemer, meddler

tejedora SF (= *máquina*) (*de hacer punto*) knitting machine; (*de tejer*) loom

tejedura SF [1] (= *acto*) weaving

[2] (= *textura*) weave, texture

tejeduría SF [1] (= *arte*) (art of) weaving

[2] (= *fábrica*) textile mill

tejemaneje* SM [1] (= *intriga*) intrigue; (= *chanchullo*) shady deal*; **los políticos y sus ~s** politicians and their shady deals*

[2] (= *actividad*) bustle; (= *bulla*) fuss; **se trae un tremendo ~** he's making a tremendous fuss

tejer ▸conjug 2a◂ Ⓐ VT [1] [+ *tela*] to weave; [+ *tela de araña*] to spin, make; [+ *capullo*] to spin; **tejido a mano** hand-woven

[2] (= *hacer punto*) to knit; (= *hacer ganchillo*) to crochet; (= *coser*) to sew; **tejido a mano** hand-knitted

[3] [+ *complot*] to hatch; [+ *plan*] to devise; [+ *mentira*] to fabricate; [+ *cambio etc*] to bring about little by little

Ⓑ VI [1] (*en telar*) to weave; ✦*MODISMO* **~ y destejer** to chop and change, do and undo (*EEUU*)

[2] (= *hacer punto*) to knit; (= *hacer ganchillo*) to crochet; (= *coser*) to sew

tejerazo* SM (*Esp Hist*) **el ~** *the coup attempted by Col Tejero on 23 February 1981*

tejeringo SM fritter

tejido SM [1] (= *tela*) fabric, material; **el ~ social** the social fabric ► **tejido de punto** knitting, knitted fabric

[2] (= *trama*) weave; (= *textura*) texture; **un ~ de intrigas** a web of intrigue

[3] (*Anat*) tissue ► **tejido conjuntivo** connective tissue

tejo[1] SM [1] (= *aro*) ring, quoit; ✦*MODISMO* **echar** *o* **tirar los ~s a algn*** to make a play for sb

[2] (= *juego*) hopscotch

[3] (*Esp*†*) *5 peseta piece*

tejo[2] SM (*Bot*) yew (tree)

tejoleta SF shard

tejón SM badger

tejudo SM label (*on spine of book*)

tel. ABR (= **teléfono**) tel

tela SF [1] (= *tejido*) cloth, fabric; (= *trozo*) piece of cloth; **esta ~ es muy resistente** this cloth *o* fabric is very strong; **usó una ~ para hacer el remiendo** she used a piece of cloth as a patch; **un libro en ~** a clothbound book; ✦*MODISMO* **poner en ~ de juicio** to (call into) question, cast doubt on ► **tela asfáltica** roofing felt ► **tela cruzada** twill ► **tela de araña** spider's web ► **tela de saco** sackcloth ► **tela metálica** wire netting ► **tela mosquitera** mosquito net

[2] (*Arte*) (= *lienzo*) canvas, painting

[3] (*en líquido*) skin

[4] (*Anat*) membrane; ✦*MODISMO* **llegarle a algn a las ~s del corazón** to touch sb's heart

[5] (*Bot*) skin ► **tela de cebolla** onion skin

[6] (⁑) (= *dinero*) dough*, cash*; **sacudir** *o* **soltar la ~** to cough up*, fork out*

[7] (*Andes*) (= *tortilla*) thin maize pancake

[8] (*) (*tb* **~ marinera**) **el asunto tiene (mucha) ~** *o* **tiene ~ (marinera)** it's a complicated matter, there's a lot to it; **—ya va por el quinto marido —¡tiene ~ (marinera)!** "she's already on her fifth husband" — "that takes some beating!"*; **hay ~ para rato** there's lots to talk about

[9] (⁑) (*enfático*) **~ de: es ~ de guapa** she's dead *o* really gorgeous*

telabrejos SMPL (*LAm*) things, gear, odds and ends

telanda* SF brass*, money

telar SM [1] (= *máquina*) loom; **telares** (= *fábrica*) textile mill *sing*

[2] (*Teat*) gridiron

telaraña SF cobweb, spider's web

tele* SF telly*, TV; **mirar** *o* **ver la ~** to watch telly; **salir en** *o* **por la ~** to be on telly*, be on the box*

tele... PREF tele...

teleadicto/a* SM/F telly-addict*

telealarma SF alarm (system)

telebaby SM (*pl* **telebabys**) cable car

telebanco SM cash dispenser

telebasura* SF junk TV

telebrejos SMPL (*Méx*) = **telabrejos**

telecabina SF cable-car

telecámara SF television camera

telecargar ▸conjug 1h◂ VT (*Inform*) to download

telecomando SM remote control

telecomedia SF TV comedy show

telecompra SF TV shopping

telecomunicación SF telecommunication

teleconferencia SF (= *reunión*) teleconference; (= *sistema*) teleconferencing

telecontrol SM remote control

telecopia SF (= *sistema*) fax (system); (= *mensaje*) fax (message)

telecopiadora SF telecopier

telediario SM television news bulletin

teledifusión SF telecast

teledirigido ADJ remote-controlled, radio-controlled

telef. ABR (= **teléfono**) tel

telefacsímil SM, **telefax** SM (= *sistema*) fax (system); (= *mensaje*) fax (message)

teleférico SM cable railway, cableway, aerial tramway (*EEUU*); (*para esquiadores*) ski lift

telefilm SM, **telefilme** SM TV film

telefonazo* SM telephone call; **te daré un ~** I'll give you a ring *o* call

telefonear ▸conjug 1a◂ VT, VI to telephone, phone (up)

telefonema SM telephone message

telefonía SF telephony; **red de ~ móvil** mobile phone network; **servicios de ~ móvil** mobile phone services ► **telefonía celular** cellular telephone system

Telefónica SF **la ~** *former Spanish national telephone company*

telefónicamente ADV by telephone; **fue amenazado ~** he received threats by telephone

telefónico ADJ telephone *antes de s*, telephonic; **llamada telefónica** telephone call; **listín ~** telephone book; **marketing ~** telemarketing, telesales *pl*

telefonillo SM entry phone

telefonista SMF (telephone) operator, telephonist

▼ **teléfono** SM [1] (= *aparato*) telephone, phone; (= *número*) telephone number, phone number; **todas las habitaciones tienen ~** there are telephones in all the rooms; **¿tienes ~?** do you have a phone?, are you on the phone?; **apunta mi ~** write down my phone number; **coger el ~ ◊ contestar al ~** to answer the phone; **está hablando por ~** he's on the phone; **llamar a algn por ~** to phone sb (up), ring sb up; **te llaman por** *o* **al ~** there's someone on the phone for you ► **teléfono celular** cellphone, cellular phone ► **teléfono con cámara** camera phone ► **teléfono de la esperanza** ≈ Samaritans *pl* ► **teléfono de tarjeta** card phone ► **teléfono erótico** sex line; ► **teléfono gratuito** Freefone® ► **teléfono inalámbrico** cordless (tele)phone ► **teléfono inteligente** smart phone ► **teléfono móvil** mobile (phone) ► **teléfono móvil de coche** car phone ► **teléfono particular** home telephone number ► **teléfono rojo** (*Pol*) hotline ► **teléfono sin hilos** cordless (tele)phone; *ver tb* **colgar A3**
[2] [*de ducha*] shower head

telefotografía SF, **telefoto** SF telephoto

telefotográfico ADJ telephoto *antes de s*

telegenia SF telegenic quality

telegénico ADJ telegenic

telegrafía SF telegraphy

telegrafiar ▸conjug 1c◂ VT, VI to telegraph

telegráfico ADJ telegraphic, telegraph *antes de s*

telegrafista SMF telegraphist

telégrafo SM telegraph ► **telégrafo óptico** semaphore

telegrama SM telegram, wire (*EEUU*); **poner un ~ a algn** to send sb a telegram

teleimpresor SM, **teleimpresora** SF teleprinter

teleindicador SM TV monitor

teleinformático ADJ telematic

telele* SM fit, queer turn; **le dio un ~** it gave him quite a turn

telemandado ADJ remote-controlled

telemando SM remote control

telemanía SF TV addiction

telemarketing SM, **telemárketing** SM telesales *pl*

telemática SF data transmission, telematics *sing*

telemático ADJ telematic

telemedida SF telemetry

telemedir ▸conjug 3k◂ VT to telemeter

telémetro SM rangefinder

telengues SMPL (*CAm*) things, gear, odds and ends

telenoticias SFPL television news *sing*, TV news *sing*

telenovela SF soap (opera), TV serial

telenque ADJ (*Cono Sur*) weak, feeble

teleobjetivo SM telephoto lens, zoom lens

teleología SF teleology

teleoperador(a) SM/F telemarketing phone operator

telépata SMF telepathist

telepate SM (*CAm*) bedbug

telepatía SF telepathy

telepáticamente ADV telepathically

telepático ADJ telepathic

teleproceso SM teleprocessing

telequinesia SF telekinesis

telerrealidad SF reality TV

telerregulación SF adjustment by remote control

telescopar ▸conjug 1a◂ (A) VT to telescope (B) **telescoparse** VPR to telescope

telescópico ADJ telescopic

telescopio SM telescope

teleserie SF TV series

telesilla SM *o* SF chair lift, ski lift

telespectador(a) SM/F viewer

telesquí SM ski lift

teletaquilla SF pay-per-view television; **partidos de fútbol en ~** pay-per-view football matches

teletaxi SM radio cab, radio taxi

teletex SM, **teletexto** SM teletext

teletienda SF home shopping

teletipista SMF teletypist, teleprinter operator

teletipo SM teletype, teleprinter

teletrabajador(a) SM/F teleworker

teletrabajo SM teleworking

teletratamiento SM teleprocessing

teletubo SM cathode-ray tube, television tube

televendedor(a) SM/F telesales person

televenta SF, **televentas** SFPL telesales

televidente SMF viewer

televisar ▸conjug 1a◂ VT to televise

televisión SF television; **hacer ~** to work in television; **salir en** *o* **por la ~** to be on television; **ver la ~** to watch television ► **televisión comercial** commercial television ► **televisión de alta definición** high-definition television ► **televisión de circuito cerrado** closed-circuit television ► **televisión en color** colour *o* (*EEUU*) color television ► **televisión matinal** breakfast television ► **televisión pagada** pay-television, pay-TV ► **televisión por cable** cable television ► **televisión por satélite** satellite television

televisivo /a (A) ADJ [1] television *antes de s*; **serie televisiva** television series [2] (= *de interés televisivo*) televisual; [*persona*] telegenic (B) SM/F television personality

televisor SM television set

televisual ADJ television *antes de s*

télex SM INV telex

telón SM (*Teat*) curtain ► **telón de acero** (*Pol*) Iron Curtain ► **telón de boca** front curtain ► **telón de fondo, telón de foro** backcloth, backdrop ► **telón de seguridad** safety curtain ► **telón metálico** fire curtain

telonero/a (A) ADJ (*Mús*) [*grupo*] support *antes de s* (B) SM/F (*Mús*) support band, support act; (*Teat*) first turn, curtain-raiser

telúrico ADJ [1] (= *de la Tierra*) **movimiento ~** earthquake [2] [*fuerzas, corrientes*] telluric

▼ **tema** SM [1] (= *asunto*) subject; **luego hablaremos de ese ~** we'll talk about that subject later; **el ~ de su discurso** the subject *o* theme of his speech; **es un ~ muy manoseado** it's a hackneyed *o* well-worn theme; **es un ~ recurrente en su obra** it is a recurring theme in his work; **tienen ~ para rato** they have plenty to talk about; **cambiar de ~** to change the subject; **pasar del ~***: **—¿qué piensas de las elecciones? —paso del ~** "what do you think about the elections?" — "I couldn't care less about them"* ► **tema de actualidad** topical issue ► **tema de conversación** talking point ► **temas de actualidad** current affairs [2] (*Ling*) [*de palabra*] stem; [*de oración*] theme [3] (*Mús*) theme

temar ▸conjug 1a◂ VI (*Cono Sur*) [1] (= *tener idea fija*) to have a mania, be obsessed
[2] (= *tener inquina*) to bear ill will; **~ con algn** to have a grudge against sb

temario SM [1] (*Univ*) (= *temas*) list of topics; (= *programa*) programme, program (*EEUU*); (= *asignaturas*) syllabus
[2] [*de oposiciones*] set of topics
[3] [*de conferencia, reunión*] agenda

temascal SM (*CAm, Méx*) bathroom; (*fig*) hot place, oven

temática SF [1] (= *conjunto de temas*) subjects *pl*
[2] (= *tema*) [*de obra, película*] subject matter

temático ADJ [1] [*acuerdo, trato*] thematic; **las preguntas deben ordenarse por bloques ~s** questions must be grouped by *o* according to topic; **parque ~** theme park
[2] (*Ling*) stem *antes de s*
[3] (*Andes*) (= *poco prudente*) injudicious, tasteless

tembladera* SF [1] (= *tembleque*) violent shaking, trembling fit
[2] (*LAm*) quagmire

tembladeral SM (*Cono Sur, Méx*) quagmire

➤ LENGUA Y USO: **teléfono 1** 27 **tema 1** 53.1

temblar ▸conjug 1j◂ VI [1] [*persona*] [1·1] (*por miedo*) to tremble, shake; (*por frío*) to shiver; **me temblaba la mano** my hand was trembling *o* shaking; **~ de miedo** to tremble *o* shake with fright; **~ de frío** to shiver with cold; ✦*MODISMO* **~ como un azogado** to shake like a leaf, tremble all over
[1·2] (= *sentir miedo*) **echarse a ~** to get frightened; **tiemblo de pensar en lo que pueda ocurrir** I shudder to think what may happen; **~ ante la escena** to shudder at the sight; **~ por su vida** to fear for one's life
[2] [*edificio*] to shake, shudder; [*tierra*] to shake; ✦*MODISMO* **dejar una botella temblando*** to use most of a bottle

tembleque* SM [1] (= *temblor*) violent shaking, shaking fit; **le entró un ~** he got the shakes, he began to shake violently
[2] (*LAm*) (= *persona*) weakling

temblequeante* ADJ [*andar*] doddery, wobbly, tottering; [*voz*] quivering, tremulous

temblequear* ▸conjug 1a◂ VI (= *temblar*) to shake violently, be all of a quiver; (= *tambalearse*) to wobble

temblequera* SF [1] (= *temblor*) shaking; (= *tambaleo*) wobbling
[2] (*Andes, Caribe*) (= *miedo*) fear; (= *temblor*) trembling

temblón Ⓐ ADJ trembling, shaking; **álamo ~** aspen
Ⓑ SM aspen

temblor SM [1] [*de miedo*] trembling, shaking; [*de frío, fiebre*] shivering; **uno de los síntomas es un ligero ~ en las manos** one of the symptoms is a slight trembling *o* shaking of the hands; **cuando la vio le dio un ~** he trembled when he saw her; **le entró un ~ violento** he began to shake violently; **los ~es son síntomas de fiebre** shivering is a symptom of fever
[2] (*tb* **~ de tierra**) earthquake, (earth) tremor

tembloroso ADJ [1] [*persona*] (*por miedo*) shaking, trembling; (*por frío*) shivering; **con voz temblorosa** in a tremulous *o* shaky voice
[2] [*llama*] flickering

tembo ADJ (*Andes*) featherbrained, stupid

temer ▸conjug 2a◂ Ⓐ VT [+ *persona, castigo, consecuencias*] to be afraid of, fear; **teme al profesor** he's afraid *o* frightened of the teacher; **~ a Dios** to fear God; **~ hacer algo** to be afraid of doing sth; **temo ofenderles** I'm afraid of offending them; **~ que** to be afraid (that), fear (that); **teme que no vaya a volver** she's afraid *o* she fears (that) he might not come back
Ⓑ VI to be afraid; **no temas** don't be afraid; **~ por algo** to fear for sth; **~ por la seguridad de algn** to fear for sb's safety; **el equipo de rescate temía por nuestras vidas** the rescue team feared for our lives
Ⓒ **temerse** VPR **~se algo: ya me lo temía, es el carburador** it's the carburettor, I thought as much *o* I was afraid it might be; **—ha empezado a llover —me lo temía** "it has started raining" — "I was afraid it would"; **—no podré venir —me lo estaba temiendo** "I won't be able to come" — "I was afraid you wouldn't"; **se temen lo peor** they fear the worst; **~se que** to be afraid (that); **mucho me temo que ya no lo encontrarás** I'm very much afraid (that) you won't find it now, I very much suspect (that) you won't find it now; **me temo que no** I'm afraid not

temerariamente ADV (= *sin prudencia*) rashly, recklessly; (= *sin reflexión*) hastily; (= *con audacia*) boldly

temerario ADJ [1] [*persona, acto*] (= *imprudente*) rash, reckless; (= *audaz*) bold
[2] [*juicio*] hasty, rash

temeridad SF [1] (= *imprudencia*) rashness; (= *audacia*) boldness; (= *prisa*) hastiness
[2] (= *acto*) rash act, folly

temerón Ⓐ ADJ bullying, ranting, loud-mouthed
Ⓑ SM bully, ranter

temerosamente ADV fearfully

temeroso ADJ [1] (= *con temor*) fearful, frightened
[2] **~ de Dios** God-fearing, full of the fear of God
[3] (= *espantoso*) fearsome

temible ADJ fearsome, frightful; [*adversario*] fearsome, redoubtable

temor SM (= *miedo*) fear; **~ a** fear of; **por ~** from fear; **por ~ a** for fear of; **por ~ a equivocarme** for fear of making a mistake; **sin ~ a** without fear of ▸ **temor de Dios** fear of God

témpano SM [1] (*tb* **~ de hielo**) ice floe; ✦*MODISMO* **como un ~** as cold as ice, ice-cold; **quedarse como un ~*** to be chilled to the bone
[2] (= *tamboril*) small drum, kettledrum
[3] (= *parche*) drumhead
[4] (*Arquit*) tympan
[5] ▸ **témpano de tocino** (*Culin*) flitch of bacon

témpera SM tempera

temperadero SM (*LAm*) summer resort

temperado ADJ (*Andes*) = **templado**

temperamental ADJ temperamental

temperamento SM [1] (= *manera de ser*) temperament, nature; **tiene un ~ muy equilibrado** he has a very balanced temperament; **es una mujer de ~ emprendedor** she is a woman with an enterprising nature
[2] (= *genio*) temperament; **tener ~** to be temperamental

temperancia SF temperance

temperante (*LAm*) Ⓐ ADJ teetotal
Ⓑ SMF teetotaller, abstainer

temperar ▸conjug 1a◂ Ⓐ VT (= *moderar*) to temper; (= *calmar*) to calm; (= *aliviar*) to relieve
Ⓑ VI (*LAm*) (= *veranear*) to spend the summer, summer; (= *cambiar de aires*) to have a change of air, have a change of climate

temperatura SF temperature; **a ~ ambiente** at room temperature; **descenso/aumento de las ~s** fall/rise in temperature; **tomar la ~ a algn** to take sb's temperature

temperie SF (state of the) weather

tempestad SF storm; **levantar una ~ de protestas** to raise a storm of protest; **el libro ha cosechado una ~ de críticas** the book has provoked a storm of criticism; **"La Tempestad" de Shakespeare** Shakespeare's "Tempest" ▸ **tempestad de arena** sandstorm ▸ **tempestad de nieve** snowstorm ▸ **tempestad de polvo** dust storm

tempestivo ADJ timely

tempestuoso ADJ stormy

templado Ⓐ ADJ [1] [*líquido, comida*] lukewarm; [*clima*] mild, temperate; (*Geog*) [*zona*] temperate
[2] (= *moderado*) moderate, restrained; (*en comer*) frugal; (*en beber*) of sober habits, abstemious; **nervios ~s** nerves of steel
[3] (*Mús*) well-tuned
[4] (= *valiente*) brave, courageous; (= *franco*) bold, forthright
[5] (*) (= *listo*) bright, lively; (*CAm, Méx*) (= *hábil*) able, competent
[6] (*Andes*) (= *severo*) severe
[7] (*Andes, Caribe*) (= *borracho*) tipsy
[8] ✦*MODISMO* **estar ~** (*Andes, Cono Sur*) to be in love
Ⓑ SM (*Téc*) tempering, hardening

templanza SF [1] (= *virtud*) temperance
[2] (*Meteo*) mildness

templar ▸conjug 1a◂ Ⓐ VT [1] [+ *comida*] (= *calentar*) to warm up; (= *enfriar*) to cool down
[2] [+ *clima*] to make mild; [+ *calor*] to reduce
[3] (= *moderar*) to moderate; [+ *ánimos*] to calm; [+ *cólera*] to restrain, control
[4] (*Quím*) [+ *solución*] to dilute
[5] [+ *acero*] to temper, harden
[6] (*Mús*) to tune (up)
[7] (*Mec*) to adjust; [+ *tornillo*] to tighten up; [+ *resorte*] to set properly
[8] (*Arte*) [+ *colores*] to blend
[9] (*Andes*) (= *derribar*) to knock down; (*CAm*) (= *golpear*) to hit, beat up; (*Andes*) (= *matar*) to kill, bump off*
[10] (*Caribe***) to screw**, fuck**
Ⓑ VI [1] (*Meteo*) (= *refrescar*) to get cooler; (= *hacer más calor*) to get warmer, get milder
[2] (*Caribe*) (= *huir*) to flee
Ⓒ **templarse** VPR [1] [*agua, ambiente*] (= *calentarse*) to warm up, get warm; (= *enfriarse*) to cool down
[2] [*persona*] to be moderate, act with restraint; **~se en la comida** to eat frugally
[3] (*Andes, CAm*) (= *morir*) to die, kick the bucket*
[4] (*Caribe, Méx*) (= *huir*) to flee
[5] (*Andes, Caribe*) (= *emborracharse*) to get tipsy
[6] (*Cono Sur*) (= *enamorarse*) to fall in love
[7] (*Cono Sur*) (= *excederse*) to go too far, overstep the mark
[8] **templárselas** (*Andes*) to stand firm

templario SM Templar

temple SM [1] (*Téc*) (= *proceso*) tempering; (= *efecto*) temper
[2] (*Mús*) tuning
[3] (= *humor*) mood; **estar de mal ~** to be in a bad mood
[4] (= *coraje*) courage, boldness; (= *espíritu*) mettle, spirit
[5] (= *pintura*) distemper; (*Arte*) tempera; **pintar al ~** to distemper; (*Arte*) to paint in tempera
[6] (*Meteo*) state of the weather, temperature
[7] (*LAm*) (= *enamoramiento*) infatuation

templete SM [1] (*en parque*) pavilion, kiosk ▸ **templete de música** bandstand
[2] (= *templo*) small temple; (= *santuario*) shrine; (= *nicho*) niche

templo SM [1] (= *edificio de culto*) temple; **el ~ de Apolo** the Temple of Apollo; ✦*MODISMOS* **como un ~*** (= *enorme*) huge, enormous; (= *excelente*) first-rate, excellent; **una verdad como un ~** a glaring truth
[2] (= *iglesia*) church ▸ **templo metodista**

Methodist church *o* chapel ► **templo protestante** Protestant church

tempo SM tempo

temporada SF 1 (= *periodo determinado*) season; **los mejores goles de la ~** the best goals of the season; **en plena ~** at the height of the season; **estar fuera de ~** to be out of season ► **temporada alta** high season ► **temporada baja** low season ► **temporada de caza** open season ► **temporada de esquí** ski season ► **temporada de exámenes** examination period ► **temporada de fútbol** football season ► **temporada de ópera** opera season ► **temporada media** mid-season

2 (= *periodo indeterminado*) period; **pasa muchas ~s en el extranjero** she spends long periods abroad; **llevan una ~ de peleas continuas** they've been going through a phase *o* period of constant squabbling; **nos vamos a pasar una temporadita al campo** we're going to spend some time in the country; **a** *o* **por ~s** on and off; **—¿tienes mucho trabajo? —va a** *o* **por ~s** "have you got a lot of work?" — "it's a bit on and off *o* it goes in phases"*

temporadista SMF (*Caribe*) holiday-maker, vacationer (*EEUU*)

temporal Ⓐ ADJ 1 (= *provisional*) temporary; [*trabajo*] temporary, casual; (*en turismo, agricultura*) seasonal; **empresa de trabajo ~** temp recruitment agency

2 (*Rel*) temporal; **poder ~** temporal power

3 (*Anat*) temporal

Ⓑ SM 1 (= *tormenta*) storm; (= *mal tiempo*) spell of rough weather; ✦*MODISMO* **capear el ~** to weather the storm, ride out the storm ► **temporal de agua, temporal de lluvia** (= *tormenta*) rainstorm; (= *periodo lluvioso*) rainy weather, prolonged rain ► **temporal de nieve** (= *tormenta*) snowstorm; (= *período de nevadas*) snowy weather

2 (*Anat*) temporal bone

3 (*Caribe*) (= *persona*) shady character

temporalmente ADV temporarily

temporáneo ADJ temporary

temporario ADJ (*LAm*) temporary

témporas SFPL ember days; *ver tb* **culo 1**

temporero/a Ⓐ ADJ [*obrero*] (= *eventual*) temporary, casual; (= *de temporada*) seasonal

Ⓑ SM/F (= *eventual*) casual worker; (= *de temporada*) seasonal worker

temporizador Ⓐ ADJ **mecanismo ~** timing device

Ⓑ SM timer, timing device

temporizar ▸conjug 1f◂ VI to temporize

tempozonte ADJ (*Méx*) hunchbacked

tempranal ADJ early

tempranear ▸conjug 1a◂ VI 1 (*LAm*) to get up early

2 (*Cono Sur Agr*) to sow early

tempranero ADJ 1 [*fruta*] early

2 [*persona*] **ser ~** to be an early riser

temprano Ⓐ ADJ early; **a una edad temprana** at an early age

Ⓑ ADV early; **saldremos por la mañana ~** we shall be leaving early in the morning; **ayer me acosté ~** I went to bed early yesterday; **aún es ~ para conocer los resultados** it's too soon to know the results yet

ten *ver* **tener**

tenacidad SF 1 (= *perseverancia*) tenacity

2 (= *persistencia*) [*de dolor*] persistence; [*de mancha*] stubbornness; [*de creencia*] strength, stubbornness (*pey*); [*de resistencia*] tenacity

3 [*de material*] toughness, resilience

tenacillas SFPL (*para azúcar*) sugar tongs; (*para cabello*) curling tongs, curling iron *sing* (*EEUU*); (*Med*) tweezers, forceps; (*para velas*) snuffers

tenamaste Ⓐ ADJ (*CAm, Méx*) stubborn

Ⓑ SM 1 (*CAm, Méx*) (= *piedra*) cooking stone

2 (*CAm*) = **cachivache**

tenaz ADJ 1 [*persona*] (= *perseverante*) tenacious, persistent

2 (= *persistente*) [*dolor*] persistent; [*mancha*] stubborn; [*creencia*] firm, stubborn (*pey*); [*resistencia*] tenacious

3 [*material*] tough, durable, resistant

tenaza SF 1 (*Bridge*) squeeze (**a** in)

2 **tenazas** (*Téc*) pliers, pincers; [*de cocina, para el fuego*] tongs; (*Med*) forceps

tenazmente ADV (= *con perseverancia*) tenaciously; (= *con tozudez*) stubbornly

tenazón: **a** *o* **de ~** ADV (= *de pronto*) suddenly; [*disparar*] without taking aim

tenca[1] SF (= *pez*) tench

tenca[2] SF (*Cono Sur*) (= *engaño*) lie, swindle

tencal SM (*Méx*) wicker box, wicker poultry cage

tencel® SM Tencel®

tencha* SF (*CAm*) prison

tendajo SM = **tendejón**

tendal* SM 1 (*LAm*) (= *montón*) load*, heap*; **un ~ de** a load of*, a whole heap of*

2 (= *toldo*) awning

3 (*Agr*) (*para aceitunas*) *sheet spread to catch olives when shaken from the tree*

4 (*Cono Sur Agr*) (*para esquilar*) shearing shed; (*Andes, CAm*) (*para secar café*) *sunny place for drying coffee*

5 (*Andes*) (= *campo*) flat open field

6 (*Andes, Caribe*) (= *fábrica*) brickworks, tileworks

tendalada* SF (*LAm**) *a lot of scattered objects or people*; **una ~ de** a lot of, loads of*

tendear ▸conjug 1a◂ VI (*Méx*) to go window-shopping

tendedera SF 1 (*CAm, Caribe, Méx*) (= *cuerda*) clothes-line

2 (*Andes*) = **tendal**

tendedero SM (= *lugar*) drying place; (= *cuerda*) clothesline, washing line; (= *armazón*) clothes horse

tendejón SM (= *tienda*) small shop; (= *cobertizo*) stall, booth

▼ **tendencia** SF tendency, trend; **la ~ hacia el socialismo** the tendency *o* trend towards socialism; **una palabra con ~ a quedarse arcaica** a word which is tending to become archaic; **tener ~ a hacer algo** to have a tendency *o* to tend to do sth; **tengo ~ a engordar** I have a tendency *o* I tend to put on weight ► **tendencia a la baja** downward trend ► **tendencia al alza, tendencia alcista** upward trend ► **tendencia bajista** downward trend ► **tendencia imperante** dominant trend, prevailing tendency ► **tendencias del mercado** market trends

tendenciosidad SF tendentiousness

tendencioso ADJ tendentious

tendente ADJ **una actitud ~ al minimalismo** an attitude tending towards minimalism; **una medida ~ a mejorar los servicios** a measure designed to improve services

▼ **tender** ▸conjug 2g◂ Ⓐ VT 1 (= *extender*) [+ *herido, paciente*] to lay; [+ *mantel*] to spread; **lo tendieron en la cama** they laid him on the bed; **tendieron el cadáver sobre el suelo** they laid the corpse out on the floor; **tendí la toalla sobre la arena** I spread the towel (out) on the sand

2 (= *colgar*) [+ *ropa*] to hang out; [+ *cuerda*] to stretch

3 (= *alargar*) [+ *lápiz, libro*] to hold out; **me tendió la mano** he stretched *o* held out his hand to me

4 [+ *trampa*] to set, lay; **le tendieron una trampa** they set *o* laid a trap for him; **nos han tendido una emboscada** we've been ambushed

5 (= *construir*) [+ *puente, ferrocarril*] to build; [+ *cable, vía*] to lay

6 (*LAm*) **~ la cama** to make the bed; **~ la mesa** to lay the table, set the table

7 [+ *arco*] to draw

Ⓑ VI 1 **~ a hacer algo** to tend to do sth; **en octubre las temperaturas tienden a bajar** temperatures tend to fall in October; **las prendas de lana tienden a encoger** woollen clothes tend to shrink

2 **~ a algo** to tend to *o* towards sth; **tiende al egocentrismo** she tends to self-centredness; **la inflación tiende al alza** the trend is for inflation to go up; **el color tiende a verde** the colour is verging on *o* has a tendency towards green; **las plantas tienden a la luz** plants grow *o* turn towards the light

Ⓒ **tenderse** VPR 1 (= *acostarse*) to lie down, stretch (o.s.) out

2 [*caballo*] to run at full gallop

3 (*Naipes*) to lay down

4 (†) (= *despreocuparse*) to give up, let things go

ténder SM (*Ferro*) tender

tenderete SM 1 (*en mercado*) (= *puesto*) (market) stall; (= *carretón*) barrow; **montar un ~** to set up a stall

2 (= *géneros*) display of goods for sale

3 (*para ropa lavada*) = **tendedero**

tendero/a SM/F (*gen*) shopkeeper, storekeeper (*EEUU*); [*de comestibles*] grocer

tendida SF (*Cono Sur*) shy, start

tendido Ⓐ ADJ 1 [*persona*] lying, lying down; **estaba tendida en el suelo** she was lying on the ground

2 [*galope*] fast

Ⓑ SM 1 (= *ropa lavada*) (*tb* **~s**) washing, clothes *pl* (*hung out to dry*)

2 (*Taur*) front rows of seats

3 [*de cable, vía*] (*por tierra*) laying; (*por el aire*) hanging

4 (= *cables*) wires *pl* ► **tendido de alta tensión** high voltage power line ► **tendido eléctrico** power line, overhead cables *pl*, overhead lines *pl*

5 (*Culin*) batch of loaves

6 (*Arquit*) coat of plaster

7 (*Andes, Méx*) (= *ropa de cama*) bedclothes *pl*

8 (*CAm, Caribe*) (= *cuerda*) long tether, rope

9 (*Andes, Méx*) (= *puesto de mercado*) (market) stall

tendinitis SF INV tendinitis, tendonitis

tendinoso ADJ sinewy

➤ LENGUA Y USO: **tendencia** 53.1 **tender B1** 53.1

tendón SM tendon, sinew ► **tendón de Aquiles** Achilles' tendon

tendonitis SF INV tendinitis, tendonitis

tendré *etc ver* **tener**

tenducho* SM poky little shop

tenebrosidad SF [1] (*poét*) (= *oscuridad*) darkness, gloom(iness)
[2] [*de perspectiva*] gloominess, blackness
[3] [*de asunto, complot*] sinister nature
[4] [*de estilo*] obscurity

tenebroso ADJ [1] (= *oscuro*) dark, gloomy
[2] [*perspectiva*] gloomy, black
[3] (*pey*) [*complot, pasado*] sinister
[4] [*estilo*] obscure

tenedor(a) Ⓐ SM/F (*Com, Fin*) holder, bearer ► **tenedor(a) de acciones** shareholder ► **tenedor(a) de libros** book-keeper ► **tenedor(a) de obligaciones** bondholder ► **tenedor(a) de póliza** policyholder
Ⓑ SM [*de mesa*] fork; **restaurante de cinco ~es** ≈ five-star restaurant

teneduría SF ► **teneduría de libros** book-keeping

tenencia SF [1] (= *posesión*) [*de vivienda*] tenancy, occupancy; [*de propiedad*] possession; **~ de drogas** possession of drugs; **~ ilícita de armas** illegal possession of weapons
[2] [*de cargo*] tenure ► **tenencia asegurada** security of tenure
[3] (= *puesto*) **~ de alcaldía** post of deputy mayor
[4] (*Mil*) lieutenancy

▼tener

▸conjug 2k◂
[A] VERBO TRANSITIVO [C] VERBO PRONOMINAL
[B] VERBO AUXILIAR
Para las expresiones como ***tener cuidado, tener ganas, tener suerte, tener de particular, tener en cuenta****, ver la otra entrada.*

Ⓐ VERBO TRANSITIVO

El uso de **got** *con el verbo* **have** *es más frecuente en inglés británico, pero sólo se usa en el presente.*

[1] [*= poseer, disponer de*] to have, have got; **¿tienes dinero?** do you have *o* have you got any money?; **¿tienes un bolígrafo?** do you have *o* have you got a pen?; **¿tiene usted permiso para esto?** do you have *o* have you got permission for this?; **tiene un tío en Venezuela** he has an uncle in Venezuela, he's got an uncle in Venezuela; **ahora no tengo tiempo** I don't have *o* I haven't got time now

[2] [*referido a aspecto, carácter*] to have, have got; **tiene el pelo rubio** he has blond hair, he's got blond hair; **tenía una sonrisa preciosa** she had a lovely smile; **tiene la nariz aguileña** she has an aquiline nose, she's got an aquiline nose; **tenía el pelo mojado** his hair was wet

[3] [*referido a edad*] to be; **tiene siete años** he's seven (years old); **¿cuántos años tienes?** how old are you?; **al menos debe de ~ 55 años** she must be at least 55

[4] [*referido a ocupaciones*] to have, have got; **tenemos clase de inglés a las 11** we have an English class at 11, we've got an English class at 11; **el lunes tenemos una reunión** we're having a meeting on Monday, we've got a meeting on Monday; **mañana tengo una fiesta** I'm going to a party tomorrow

[5] [*= parir*] to have; **va a ~ un niño** she's going to have a baby

[6] [*= medir*] to be; **~ 5cm de ancho** to be 5cm wide

[7] [*= sentir*] (+ *SUSTANTIVO*) to be + *adj*; **~ hambre/sed/calor/frío** to be hungry/thirsty/hot/cold; **no tengas tantos celos** don't be so jealous; **hemos tenido mucho miedo** we have been very frightened; **le tengo mucho cariño** I'm very fond of him; **he tenido un presentimiento** I've had a premonition

[8] [*= padecer, sufrir*] to have; **han tenido un accidente** they have had an accident; **hemos tenido muchas dificultades** we have had a lot of difficulties; **Luis tiene la gripe** Luis has *o* has got flu; **tengo fiebre** I have *o* I've got a (high) temperature; **¿qué tienes?** what's the matter with you?, what's wrong with you?

[9] [*= sostener*] to hold; **tenía el pasaporte en la mano** he had his passport in his hand, he was holding his passport in his hand; **tenme el vaso un momento, por favor** hold my glass for me for a moment, please; **¡ten!** ◊ **¡aquí tienes!** here you are!

[10] [*= recibir*] to have; **aún no he tenido carta** I haven't had a letter yet; **¿has tenido noticias suyas?** have you heard from her?

[11] [*= pensar, considerar*] **~ a bien hacer algo** to see fit to do sth; **~ a algn en algo**: **te tendrán en más estima** they will hold you in higher esteem; **~ a algn por** (+ *ADJ*) to consider sb (to be) + *adj*; **le tengo por poco honrado** I consider him (to be) rather dishonest; **ten por seguro que ...** rest assured that ...

[12]

◆ **tener algo que** + *INFIN*: **tengo trabajo que hacer** I have *o* I've got work to do; **no tengo nada que hacer** I have *o* I've got nothing to do; **eso no tiene nada que ver** that has *o* that's got nothing to do with it

[13] [**locuciones**] **ya saben dónde me tienen** you always know where you can find me; **¡ahí lo tienes!** there you are!, there you have it!; **~ algo de** + ADJ: **de bueno no tiene nada** there's nothing good about it; **no tiene nada de particular** it's nothing special; **¿qué tiene de malo?** what's wrong with that?; **~lo difícil** to find it difficult; **~lo fácil** to have it easy; ✦***MODISMOS*** **¿(conque) ésas tenemos?** so that's the game, is it?, so it's like that, is it?; **no ~las todas consigo** (= *dudar*) to be dubious *o* unsure; (= *desconfiar*) to be uneasy, be wary; **no las tengo todas conmigo de que lo haga** I'm none too sure that he'll do it, I'm not entirely sure that he'll do it; **~ todas las de ganar** to hold all the winning cards, look like a winner; **~ todas las de perder** to be fighting a losing battle, look like losing; ✦***REFRÁN*** **quien tuvo retuvo** some things stay with you to the grave

Ⓑ VERBO AUXILIAR

[1]

◆ **tener que** + *INFIN* [1·1] (*indicando obligación*) **tengo que comprarlo** I have to *o* I've got to buy it, I must buy it; **tenemos que marcharnos** we have to *o* we've got to go, we must be going; **tienen que aumentarte el sueldo** they have to *o* they've got to give you a rise; **tuvo que devolver todo el dinero** he had to pay all the money back; **tiene que ser así** it has to be this way

[1·2] (*indicando suposición, probabilidad*) **¡tienes que estar cansadísima!** you must be really tired!; **tiene que dolerte mucho ¿no?** it must hurt a lot, doesn't it?; **tiene que estar en tu despacho** it must be in your office; **tiene que haberte dolido mucho** it must have hurt a lot

[1·3] (*en reproches*) **¡tendrías que haberlo dicho antes!** you should have said so before!; **¡tendría que darte vergüenza!** you should be ashamed of yourself!; **¡tú tenías que ser!** it would be you!, it had to be you!

[1·4] (*en sugerencias, recomendaciones*) **tendrías que comer más** you should eat more; **tendríamos que pedirle perdón** we should apologize to him

[2] (+ *PARTICIPIO*) **tenía puesto el sombrero** he had his hat on; **nos tenían preparada una sorpresa** they had prepared a surprise for us; **tenía pensado llamarte** I had been thinking of phoning you; **te lo tengo dicho muchas veces** I've told you hundreds of times; **yo no le tengo visto** I've never set eyes on him

[3] (+ *ADJ*) **procura ~ contentos a todos** he tries to keep everybody happy; **me tiene perplejo la falta de noticias** the lack of news is puzzling, I am puzzled by the lack of news

[4] [*esp Méx*: *= llevar*] **tienen tres meses de no cobrar** they haven't been paid for three months, it's three months since they've been paid; **tengo cuatro años aquí** I've been here for four years

Ⓒ **tenerse** VERBO PRONOMINAL

[1] [*= sostenerse*] **~se firme** (*lit*) to stand upright; (*fig*) to stand firm; **~se de** *o* **en pie** to stand up; **la muñeca se tiene de pie** the doll stands up; **no se puede ~ de pie** ◊ **no se tiene de pie** he can hardly stand; **estoy que no me tengo de sueño** I'm falling asleep on my feet, I'm about ready to drop

[2] [*= considerarse*] **~se en mucho** to have a high opinion of o.s.; **~se por**: **se tiene por muy listo** he thinks himself very clever, he thinks he's very clever

teneraje SM (*LAm*) calves *pl*

tenería SF tannery

Tenerife SM Tenerife

tenga, **tengo** *etc ver* **tener**

tenguerengue‡ SM (*Caribe*) hovel

tenia SF tapeworm

tenida SF [1] (*Cono Sur*) (= *traje*) suit, outfit; (= *uniforme*) uniform ► **tenida de gala** evening dress ► **tenida de luto** mourning ► **tenida de noche** evening dress
[2] (*LAm*) (= *reunión*) meeting, session; [*de masones*] meeting (*of a masonic lodge*)

tenienta SF (†) (= *esposa*) lieutenant's wife

teniente Ⓐ SMF (SF *a veces* **tenienta**) [1] (*Mil*) lieutenant, first lieutenant (*EEUU*) ► **teniente coronel** lieutenant colonel ► **teniente de navío** lieutenant ► **teniente general** lieutenant general
[2] (= *ayudante*) deputy, assistant ► **teniente de alcalde** deputy mayor ► **teniente fiscal** assistant prosecutor
Ⓑ ADJ **estar ~**‡ to be deaf

tenis SM INV [1] (= *deporte*) tennis ► **tenis de mesa** table tennis
[2] (= *zapato*) tennis shoe, plimsoll; ✦***MODISMO*** **colgar los ~**‡ to kick the bucket‡
[3] (= *pistas*) tennis courts *pl*; (= *club*) tennis club

tenista SMF tennis player

tenístico ADJ tennis *antes de s*

➤ LENGUA Y USO: **tener B1** 37.1, 37.2, 37.3, 45.2

tenor[1] SM (*Mús*) tenor

tenor[2] SM (= *sentido*) meaning, sense; **el ~ de esta declaración** the tenor of this statement; **a este ~** in this fashion, like this; **del siguiente ~** as follows; **a ~ de** (= *según*) according to; (*Jur*) in accordance with

tenorio* SM ladykiller, Don Juan

tensado SM [*de cable, cuerda*] tensioning, tightening; [*de arco*] drawing

tensamente ADV tensely

tensar ▸conjug 1a◂ Ⓐ VT [+ *cable, cuerda*] to tighten, tauten; [+ *músculo*] to tense; [+ *arco*] to draw; [+ *relaciones*] to strain

Ⓑ **tensarse** VPR [*relaciones*] to become strained

tensión SF [1] [*de cable, cuerda*] tension, tautness

[2] [*de músculos*] tension; **con los músculos en ~** with one's muscles all tensed up

[3] (*Med*) blood pressure; **tener la ~ alta** to have high blood pressure; **tomarse la ~** to have one's blood pressure taken ► **tensión arterial** blood pressure

[4] (*Elec*) (= *voltaje*) tension, voltage; **alta ~** high tension; **cable de alta ~** high-tension cable

[5] [*de gas*] pressure

[6] (= *estrés*) strain, stress; **estar en ~** to be tense ► **tensión excesiva** (over)strain ► **tensión nerviosa** nervous strain, nervous tension ► **tensión premenstrual** premenstrual tension, PMT

[7] (*en situación*) tension, tenseness; **hubo momentos de gran ~** there were some very tense moments; **la ~ de la situación política** the tenseness of the political situation ► **tensión racial** racial tension

tensionado ADJ tense, in a state of tension

tensional ADJ tense, full of tension

tensionar ▸conjug 1a◂ VT [1] [+ *músculo*] to tense

[2] [+ *adversario*] to put pressure on; [+ *relaciones*] to put a strain on

tenso ADJ [1] (= *tirante*) tense, taut

[2] [*persona, situación*] tense; [*relaciones*] strained; **es una situación muy tensa** it is a very tense situation; **las relaciones entre los dos están muy tensas** relations between the two are very strained

tensor Ⓐ SM (*Téc*) guy, strut; (*Anat*) tensor; [*de cuello*] stiffener; (*Dep*) chest expander

Ⓑ ADJ tensile

tentación SF [1] (= *impulso*) temptation; **resistir (a) la ~** to resist temptation; **no pude resistir la ~ de comprarlo** I couldn't resist the temptation to buy it; **vencer la ~** to overcome temptation

[2] (*) (= *cosa tentadora*) **las gambas son mi ~** I can't resist prawns; **¡eres mi ~!** you'll be the ruin of me!

tentacular ADJ tentacular; **la envergadura ~** the width of the tentacles

tentáculo SM tentacle; **la mafia va extendiendo sus ~s** the Mafia is gradually spreading its tentacles

tentado ADJ **estuve ~ de decírselo** I was tempted to tell him

tentador(a) Ⓐ ADJ tempting

Ⓑ SM/F tempter/temptress

tentar ▸conjug 1j◂ VT [1] (= *seducir*) to tempt; **me tentó con una copita de anís** she tempted me with a glass of anisette; **no me tienta nada la idea** I can't say I fancy the idea*; **~ a algn a hacer algo** to tempt sb to do sth

[2] (= *palpar*) to feel; (*Med*) to probe; **ir tentando el camino** to feel one's way

[3] (= *probar*) to test, try (out)

tentativa SF (= *intento*) attempt; (*Jur*) criminal attempt ► **tentativa de asesinato** attempted murder ► **tentativa de robo** attempted robbery ► **tentativa de suicidio** suicide attempt

tentativo ADJ tentative

tentebonete* SM (= *empleo*) cushy job*, plum; (= *gaje*) perk*

tentempié* SM snack, bite

tenue ADJ [1] [*tela, velo*] thin, fine

[2] [*olor, sonido, línea*] faint; [*neblina, lluvia*] light; [*aire*] thin

[3] [*razón*] tenuous, insubstantial; [*relación*] tenuous

[4] [*estilo*] simple, plain

tenuidad SF [1] [*de tela*] thinness, fineness

[2] [*de sonido*] faintness; [*de neblina, lluvia*] lightness; [*del aire*] thinness

[3] [*de razón, relación*] tenuousness

[4] [*de estilo*] simplicity

teñido SM dying

teñir ▸conjug 3h, 3k◂ Ⓐ VT [1] [+ *pelo, ropa*] to dye; **~ una prenda de azul** to dye a garment blue; **el jersey ha teñido los pañuelos** the colour of the jersey has come out on the handkerchiefs

[2] (= *manchar*) to stain; **teñido de sangre** stained with blood

[3] (= *matizar*) to tinge (**de** with); **un poema teñido de añoranza** a poem tinged with longing

[4] (*Arte*) [+ *color*] to darken

Ⓑ **teñirse** VPR [1] **~se el pelo** to dye one's hair

[2] **el mar se tiñó de negro** the sea darkened

teocali SM (*Méx*), **teocalli** SM (*Méx Hist*) Aztec temple

teocracia SF theocracy

teocrático ADJ theocratic

teodolito SM theodolite

teogonía SF theogony

teologal ADJ **las virtudes ~es** the three Christian virtues (*faith, hope and charity*)

teología SF theology

teológico ADJ theological

teólogo/a SM/F theologian, theologist

teorema SM theorem

teorético ADJ (*LAm*) theoretic(al)

▼ **teoría** SF theory; **en ~** in theory, theoretically ► **teoría atómica** atomic theory ► **teoría cuántica** quantum theory ► **teoría de conjuntos** set theory ► **teoría de la información** information theory ► **teoría de la relatividad** theory of relativity ► **teoría del caos** chaos theory

teóricamente ADV theoretically, in theory

teoricidad SF theoretical nature

teórico/a Ⓐ ADJ theoretic(al); **examen ~** theory (exam)

Ⓑ SM/F theoretician, theorist

teorización SF theorizing

teorizante SMF theoretician, theorist; (*pey*) theorizer

teorizar ▸conjug 1f◂ VI to theorize

teosofía SF theosophy

teosófico ADJ theosophical

teósofo/a SM/F theosophist

tepalcate SM (*CAm, Méx*) [1] (= *vasija*) earthenware jar; (= *fragmento*) fragment of pottery, shard

[2] (= *trasto*) piece of junk

tepalcatero/a SM/F (*Méx*) potter

tepe SM sod, turf, clod

tepetate SM (*CAm, Méx*) [1] (= *residuo*) slag

[2] (= *caliza*) limestone

tepocate SM (*CAm, Méx*) [1] (= *guijarro*) stone, pebble

[2] (*) (= *niño*) kid*

teporocho* ADJ (*Méx*) tight*, drunk

tequi* SM car

tequila SM tequila

tequilero* ADJ (*Méx*) tight*, drunk

tequío SM (*CAm, Méx*) (= *molestia*) trouble; (= *fardo*) burden; (= *daño*) harm, damage

tequioso ADJ (*CAm, Méx*) (= *molesto*) annoying; (= *gravoso*) burdensome; (= *dañino*) harmful

terapeuta SMF therapist

terapéutica SF therapeutics *sing*

terapéutico ADJ therapeutic(al)

terapia SF therapy ► **terapia aversiva** aversion therapy ► **terapia de choque** shock therapy ► **terapia de conducta** behavioural therapy, behavioral therapy (*EEUU*) ► **terapia de electrochoque** electroshock therapy ► **terapia de grupo** group therapy ► **terapia electroconvulsiva** electroconvulsive therapy ► **terapia génica** gene therapy ► **terapia laboral** occupational therapy ► **terapia lingüística** speech therapy ► **terapia ocupacional** occupational therapy ► **terapia por aversión** aversion therapy ► **terapia táctil** touch therapy

teratogénico ADJ teratogenic

tercamente ADV stubbornly, obstinately

tercena SF [1] (*Méx*) (= *almacén*) government warehouse

[2] (*Andes*) (= *carnicería*) butcher's (shop)

tercenista SMF (*Andes*) butcher

tercer ADJ *ver* **tercero**

tercera SF [1] (*Mús*) third

[2] (*Aut*) third (gear)

[3] (= *clase*) third class; **un hotel de ~** a third-rate hotel; *ver tb* **tercero**

tercería SF [1] (= *arbitración*) mediation, arbitration

[2] (*pey*) [*de alcahuete*] procuring

tercermundismo SM [1] (= *atraso*) backwardness, under-development

[2] (= *actitudes*) *attitudes or policies akin to those of a third-world country*

tercermundista Ⓐ ADJ third-world *antes de s*; (*pey*) (*fig*) backward

Ⓑ SM third-world country

tercero/a Ⓐ ADJ (*antes de sm sing* **tercer**) third; **la tercera vez** the third time; **terceras personas** third parties; **tercer grado (penitenciario)** *lowest category within the prison system which allows day release privileges*; **Tercer Mundo** Third World; ✦**MODISMO** **a la tercera va la vencida** third time lucky; *ver tb* **edad 1**, **sexto A**

Ⓑ SM/F [1] (= *árbitro*) mediator, arbitrator;

➤ LENGUA Y USO: **teoría** 53.2

(*Jur*) third party ► **tercero en discordia** third party
[2] (*pey*) (= *alcahuete*) procurer/procuress, go-between
Ⓒ SM (= *piso*) third floor; *ver tb* **tercera**

tercerola SF (*Caribe*) shotgun

terceto SM [1] (*Mús*) trio
[2] (*Literat*) tercet, triplet

terciada SF (*LAm*) plywood

terciado ADJ [1] (*en tamaño*) **una merluza terciada** a medium-sized hake
[2] (= *usado*) **está ~ ya** [*botella etc*] it's a third finished
[3] **azúcar terciada** brown sugar
[4] **llevar algo ~** [+ *bolso, arma*] to wear sth crosswise *o* across one's chest *etc*; **con el sombrero ~** with his hat at a rakish angle

terciana SF tertian (fever)

terciar ▸conjug 1b◂ Ⓐ VT [1] (*Mat*) (= *dividir en tres*) to divide into three
[2] (= *inclinar*) to slant, slope; [+ *arma*] to wear (diagonally) across one's chest; [+ *sombrero*] to tilt, wear on the slant
[3] (*Agr*) to plough a third time
[4] (*Andes, Cono Sur, Méx*) (*al hombro*) to hoist on to *o* carry on one's shoulder
[5] (*LAm*) [+ *vino*] to water down; (*Méx*) (= *mezclar*) to mix, blend
Ⓑ VI [1] (= *mediar*) to mediate; **~ entre dos rivales** to mediate between two rivals; **yo ~é con el jefe** I'll have a word with the boss
[2] (= *participar*) **~ en algo** to take part in sth, join in sth
[3] (= *completar el número*) to fill in, make up the numbers
Ⓒ **terciarse** VPR **si se tercia, él también sabe hacerlo** if it comes to that, he knows how to do it too; **si se tercia una buena oportunidad** if a good chance presents itself *o* comes up; **si se tercia alguna vez que yo pase por allí** if I should happen to go that way

terciario ADJ tertiary

tercio SM [1] (= *tercera parte*) third; **dos ~s** two thirds
[2] (*Taur*) stage, part (of the bullfight); **cambiar de ~** (*Taur*) to enter the next stage of the bullfight; (= *cambiar de tema*) to change the subject
[3] (*Mil, Hist*) regiment, corps ► **tercio de la guardia civil** division of the civil guard ► **tercio extranjero** foreign legion
[4] **hacer buen ~ a algn** (= *hacer favor*) to do sb a service; (= *ser útil*) to serve sb well, be useful to sb; **hacer mal ~ a algn** to do sb a bad turn; ✦***MODISMO*** **estar mejorado en ~ y quinto** to come out of it very well
[5] (*LAm*) (= *fardo*) pack, bale
[6] (*Caribe*) (= *hombre*) fellow, guy*

terciopelo SM velvet

terco ADJ [1] (= *obstinado*) stubborn, obstinate; ✦***MODISMO*** **~ como una mula** as stubborn as a mule
[2] (*Andes*) (= *severo*) harsh, unfeeling; (= *indiferente*) indifferent
[3] [*material*] hard, tough, hard to work

Tere SF (*forma familiar*) de **Teresa**

tere ADJ (*Andes*) [*niño*] weepy, tearful

terebrante ADJ [*dolor*] sharp, piercing

tereco SM (*Andes*) = **tereque**

Terencio SM Terence

tereque SM (*Andes, Caribe*) [1] = **cachivache**
[2] **tereques** things, gear* *sing*, odds and ends

Teresa SF T(h)eresa

teresiano ADJ **las obras teresianas** the works of Saint Teresa (of Ávila)

tergal® SM Terylene®, Dacron® (*EEUU*)

tergiversación SF distortion

tergiversar ▸conjug 1a◂ VT to distort, twist (the sense of)

terliz SM ticking

termal ADJ thermal

termalismo SM hydrotherapy, bathing at a spa

termalista Ⓐ ADJ spa *antes de s*
Ⓑ SMF *person who visits a spa*

termas SFPL (= *baños*) thermal baths; (= *manantiales*) thermal springs, hot springs

termes SM INV termite

termia SF (gas) therm

térmica[1] SF (= *corriente*) thermal, hot-air current

térmica[2] SF (*tb* **central ~**) power station

térmico ADJ thermic, heat *antes de s*; [*cristal*] heated; **baja térmica en el norte** a drop in temperature in the North

terminacho SM (= *palabra malsonante*) nasty word, rude word; (= *palabra fea*) ugly word; (= *palabra incorrecta*) incorrect word, malapropism, linguistic monstrosity

terminación SF [1] (= *finalización*) ending, termination; **la fecha prevista para la ~ de las obras** the date work was due to be finished
[2] (*Ling*) ending, termination
[3] (*Cono Sur Téc*) (= *acabado*) finish, finishing
[4] ► **terminaciones nerviosas** nerve endings

terminado Ⓐ SM (*Téc*) finish, finishing
Ⓑ ADJ (= *acabado*) finished; **bien ~** well finished

terminajo SM = **terminacho**

terminal Ⓐ ADJ [1] (= *final*) [*enfermedad, estación*] terminal; **un cáncer en fase ~** a terminal cancer; **un enfermo en fase ~** a terminal patient; **los enfermos ~es** the terminally ill; **el edificio ~ del aeropuerto** the airport terminal
[2] (*Bot*) [*hoja, rama*] terminal
Ⓑ SM (*a veces* SF) (*Elec, Inform*) terminal ► **terminal de computadora** computer terminal ► **terminal de vídeo** video terminal ► **terminal informático** computer terminal ► **terminal interactivo** interactive unit
Ⓒ SF (*a veces* SM) (*Aer, Náut*) terminal; [*de autobuses, trenes*] terminus ► **terminal de carga** freight terminal ► **terminal de contenedores** container terminal ► **terminal de pasajeros, terminal de viajeros** passenger terminal

terminante ADJ [*respuesta*] categorical, conclusive; [*negativa*] flat, outright; [*prohibición*] strict; [*decisión*] final

➤**terminantemente** ADV [*responder*] categorically, conclusively; [*negar*] flatly; [*prohibir*] strictly; **queda ~ prohibido fumar en clase** smoking during lectures is strictly forbidden

➤**terminar** ▸conjug 1a◂ Ⓐ VT to finish; **he terminado el libro** I've finished the book; **no me ha dado tiempo a ~ el vestido** I haven't had time to finish the dress; **quiso ~ sus días en Marbella** she wanted to end her days in Marbella
Ⓑ VI [1] [*persona*] [1·1] (*en una acción, un trabajo*) to finish; **¿todavía no has terminado?** haven't you finished yet?; **¿quieres dejar que termine?** would you mind letting me finish?; **~ de hacer algo** to finish doing sth, stop doing sth; **cuando termine de hablar** when he finishes *o* stops speaking; **terminó de llenar el vaso con helado** he topped *o* filled the glass up with ice-cream; **terminaba de salir del baño** she had just got out of the bath; **no termino de entender por qué lo hizo** I just can't understand why she did it; **no me cae mal, pero no termina de convencerme** I don't dislike him, but I'm not too sure about him
[1·2] (*de una forma determinada*) to end up; **terminé rendido** I ended up exhausted; **~on peleándose** they ended up fighting; **terminó mal** he ended up badly; **terminó diciendo que ...** he ended by saying that ...
[1·3] **~ con**: **han terminado con todas las provisiones** they've finished off all the supplies; **hace falta algo que termine con el problema del paro** we need something to put an end to the problem of unemployment; **un cáncer terminó con su vida** cancer killed him; **he terminado con Andrés** I've broken up with *o* finished with Andrés; **¡estos niños van a ~ conmigo!** these children will be the death of me!
[1·4] **~ por hacer algo** to end up doing sth; **seguro que ~á por dimitir** I bet he ends up resigning
[2] [*obra, acto*] to end; **¿cómo termina la película?** how does the film end?; **la ceremonia terminó con un baile** the ceremony ended with a dance; **esto va a ~ en tragedia** this will end in tragedy; **estoy deseando que termine este año** I can't wait for this year to be over *o* to end; **¿a qué hora termina la clase?** what time does the class finish *o* end?
[3] [*objeto, palabra*] **~ en algo** to end in sth; **termina en punta** it ends in a point; **termina en vocal** it ends in *o* with a vowel
[4] (*Inform*) to quit
Ⓒ **terminarse** VPR [1] [*obra, acto*] to end; **antes de que se termine el curso** before the year ends *o* finishes, before the year is over
[2] [*comida, gasolina, carrete*] to run out; **se nos ha terminado el café** we've run out of coffee
[3] [*persona*] to finish; **me terminé el libro en dos días** I finished the book in two days; **¡termínate toda la sopa!** finish (up) your soup!; **termínate la copa y vámonos** finish your drink and let's go, drink up and let's go

terminista SMF (*Cono Sur*) pedant

término SM [1] (= *fin*) end, conclusion (*frm*); **al ~ del partido/del debate** at the end *o* (*frm*) conclusion of the match/of the debate; **dar ~ a** [+ *situación*] to end; [+ *labor*] to complete; **dio ~ a la obra que su antecesor dejó sin concluir** he completed the work that his predecessor had left unfinished; **llegar a ~** [*negociación, proyecto*] to be completed, come to a conclusion; [*embarazo*] to go to (full) term; **las negociaciones llegaron a buen ~** the negotiations came to a successful conclusion; **llevar algo a ~** to bring sth to a conclusion; **llevar algo a buen** *o* **feliz ~** to bring sth to a successful conclusion; **llevar a ~ un embara-**

➤ LENGUA Y USO: **terminantemente** 36.3 **terminar A** 53.4

zo to go to (full) term, carry a pregnancy to full term; **poner ~ a algo** to put an end to sth; **tenemos que poner ~ a tales atrocidades** we must put an end to such atrocities

2 (= *lugar*) **primer ~** [*de imagen*] foreground; **en primer ~ podemos contemplar la torre** in the foreground, we can see the tower; **de ahí se deduce, en primer ~, que ...** thus we may deduce, firstly, that ...; **segundo ~** middle distance; **con la recesión el problema pasó a un segundo ~** with the recession the problem took second place; **en segundo ~** secondly; **en último ~** (= *en último lugar*) ultimately; (= *si no hay otro remedio*) as a last resort; **la decisión, en último ~, es suya** ultimately, the decision is his; **la causa fue, en último ~, la crisis económica de los 70** the cause was, in the final *o* last analysis, the economic crisis of the 70s; **en último ~ puedes dormir en el sofá** if the worst comes to the worst, you can always sleep on the sofa ► **término medio** (= *punto medio*) happy medium; (= *solución intermedia*) compromise, middle way; **ni mucho ni poco, queremos un ~ medio** neither too much nor too little, we want a happy medium; **tendrán que buscar un ~ medio** they will have to look for a compromise *o* middle way; **como** *o* **por ~ medio** on average

3 (*Ling*) (= *palabra, expresión*) term; **una lista de ~s médicos** a list of medical terms; **era una revolucionaria, en el buen sentido del ~** she was a revolutionary in the good sense of the word

4 **términos** 4·1 (= *palabras*) terms; **se expresó en ~s conciliatorios** he expressed himself in conciliatory terms; **han perdido unos 10.000 millones de dólares en ~s de productividad** they have lost some 10,000 million dollars in terms of productivity; **en ~s generales** in general terms, generally speaking; **(dicho) en otros ~s, ...** in other words ...; **en ~s reales** in real terms

4·2 (= *condiciones*) [*de contrato, acuerdo, tregua*] terms; **según los ~s del contrato** according to the terms of the contract; **los ~s del intercambio** the terms of trade; **estar en buenos ~s con algn** to be on good terms with sb

5 (*Mat, Fil*) [*de fracción, ecuación*] term; ✦**MODISMO invertir los ~s** to reverse the roles

6 (= *límite*) [*de terreno*] boundary, limit; (= *en carretera*) boundary stone ► **término municipal** municipal district, municipal area

7 (= *plazo*) period, term (*frm*); **en el ~ de diez días** within a period *o* (*frm*) term of ten days

8 (*Col, Méx*) (*en restaurante*) **—¿qué ~ quiere la carne? —término medio, por favor** "how would you like the meat?" — "medium, please"

9 (*Ferro*) terminus

terminología SF terminology

terminológico ADJ terminological

terminólogo/a SM/F terminologist

termita SF, **térmite** SF termite

termitero SM (= *montículo*) termite mound; (= *nido*) termite nest, termitarium (*frm*)

termo SM 1 (= *frasco*) Thermos flask®

2 (= *calentador*) water heater

termo... PREF thermo...

termoaislante ADJ heat-insulating

termodinámica SF thermodynamics *sing*

termodinámico ADJ thermodynamic

termoeléctrico ADJ thermoelectric

termoimpresora SF thermal printer

termoiónico ADJ thermionic

termómetro SM thermometer ► **termómetro clínico** clinical thermometer

termonuclear ADJ thermonuclear

termopar SM thermocouple

termopila SF thermopile

Termópilas SFPL **Las ~** Thermopylae

termostático ADJ thermostatic

termostato SM thermostat

termotanque SM (*Cono Sur*) immersion heater

terna SF short list (*of three candidates*)

ternario ADJ ternary

terne Ⓐ ADJ 1 (= *fuerte*) tough, strong, husky; (*pey*) bullying

2 (= *terco*) stubborn; **~ que ~** out of sheer stubbornness

Ⓑ SM 1 bully, tough*

2 (*Cono Sur*) rogue

ternejo ADJ (*Andes*) spirited, vigorous

ternera SF 1 (*Agr*) (heifer) calf

2 (*Culin*) veal

ternero SM (*Agr*) calf

ternerón ADJ 1 (*) (= *compasivo*) soft-hearted

2 (*Cono Sur, Méx*) [*mozo*] overgrown, big

terneza SF 1 (= *ternura*) tenderness

2 **ternezas*** (= *palabras tiernas*) sweet nothings, tender words

ternilla SF cartilage

ternilloso ADJ gristly, cartilaginous

terno SM 1 (= *grupo de tres*) set of three, group of three; (= *trío*) trio

2 (= *traje*) three-piece suit; (*LAm*) suit

3 (*Caribe*) (= *joyas*) necklace set

4 (*) (= *palabrota*) curse, swearword; **echar** *o* **soltar ~s** to curse, swear

ternura SF 1 (= *sentimiento*) tenderness; (= *cariño*) affection, fondness; **miró a los niños con ~** she looked fondly *o* tenderly at the children

2 (*) (= *palabra*) endearment

ternurismo SM sentimentality

ternurista ADJ sentimental, schmaltzy*

Terpsícore SF Terpsichore

terquedad SF 1 (= *obstinación*) stubbornness, obstinacy

2 (= *dureza*) hardness, toughness

3 (*Andes*) (= *severidad*) harshness, lack of feeling; (= *indiferencia*) indifference

terracota SF terracotta

terrado SM 1 (= *tejado*) flat roof; (= *terraza*) terrace

2 (*) (= *cabeza*) nut*, noggin (*EEUU**), bonce*

terraja SF diestock

terral Ⓐ SM (*LAm*) (= *polvareda*) cloud of dust

Ⓑ ADJ **viento ~** land breeze *o* wind

Terranova SF Newfoundland

terranova SM (= *perro*) Newfoundland dog

terraplén SM 1 (*en carretera, ferrocarril*) embankment

2 (*Agr*) terrace

3 (*Mil*) rampart, bank

4 (= *cuesta*) slope, gradient

terraplenar ▸conjug 1a◂ VT [+ *terreno*] (= *nivelar*) to (fill and) level (off); (= *elevar*) to bank up, raise; (*Agr*) to terrace; [+ *hoyo*] to fill in

terráqueo /a Ⓐ ADJ earth *antes de s*, terrestrial (*frm*); **globo ~** globe

Ⓑ SM/F earthling

terrario SM terrarium

terrateniente SMF landowner

terraza SF 1 (*Arquit*) (= *balcón*) balcony; (= *azotea*) flat roof, terrace

2 (= *café*) pavement café; **nos sentamos en la ~ de un café** we sat outside a cafe

3 (*Agr*) terrace

4 (*en jardín*) flowerbed, border

5 (*Culin*) (= *jarro*) two-handled glazed jar

6 (*) (= *cabeza*) nut*, noggin (*EEUU**), bonce*

terrazo SM terrazzo

terregal SM 1 (*LAm*) (= *terrón*) clod, hard lump of earth

2 (*Méx*) (= *tierra*) loose earth, dusty soil; (= *polvareda*) cloud of dust

terremoto SM earthquake

terrenal ADJ worldly; **la vida ~** worldly life, earthly life; *ver tb* **paraíso 1**

terreno Ⓐ ADJ 1 (*Rel*) [*bienes*] earthly; **esta vida terrena** this earthly life (*liter*)

2 (*Biol, Geol*) terrestrial

Ⓑ SM 1 (= *extensión de tierra*) (*gen*) land; (= *parcela*) piece of land, plot of land; **30 hectáreas de ~** 30 hectares of land; **es ~ municipal** it is council land; **los ~s pertenecientes al museo** the land belonging to the museum; **vender unos ~s** to sell some land; **nos hemos comprado un ~ en las afueras** we've bought a piece of land *o* plot of land *o* some land on the outskirts of the city; **el ~ que antes ocupaba la fábrica** the site the factory used to be on

2 (*explicando sus características*) (= *relieve*) ground, terrain; (= *composición*) soil, land; **los accidentes del ~** the unevenness of the ground *o* terrain; **un ~ pedregoso** stony ground *o* terrain; **estamos sobre un ~ arenoso** we're on sandy soil *o* land; **vehículos todo ~** all-terrain vehicles

3 (= *campo*) 3·1 [*de estudio*] field; **en el ~ de la química** in the field of chemistry; **ése no es mi ~** that's not my field

3·2 [*de actividad*] sphere, field; **el gobierno debe tomar medidas urgentes en el ~ económico** the government must take urgent measures in the economic sphere *o* field; **la competencia de las empresas extranjeras en todos los ~s** competition from foreign companies in all areas; **en cuanto a las pensiones, se ha avanzado poco en este ~** as for pensions, little progress has been made in this area; **este caso entra en el ~ militar** this case is a military matter

4 ✦**MODISMOS ceder ~** to give ground (**a, ante** to); **pisar ~ firme** to be on safe *o* firm *o* solid ground; **ganar ~** to gain ground; **perder ~** to lose ground; **saber** *o* **conocer el ~ que se pisa** to be on familiar ground; **preparar el ~** to pave the way; **vencer a algn en su propio ~** to defeat sb on his home *o* own ground; **recuperar ~** to recover lost ground; **sobre el ~** on the ground; **analizarán la situación sobre el ~** they will analyse the situation on the ground; **resolveremos el problema sobre el ~** we will solve the problem as we go along; **~**

abonado: **es ~ abonado para el vicio** it is a breeding ground for vice; **dichas tendencias han encontrado el ~ abonado entre la juventud** these trends have found a fertile breeding ground amongst the young; **este país es ~ abonado para las inversiones extranjeras** this country provides rich pickings for foreign investment; **llamar a algn a ~** to tell sb off, pull sb up* ► **terreno de pruebas** testing-ground
5 (*Dep*) **empataron en su ~** they drew at home; **perdieron en su propio ~** they lost on their home ground; **el equipo tuvo una nueva derrota fuera de su ~** the team suffered a fresh defeat away (from home) ► **terreno de juego** pitch, field

térreo ADJ (= *de tierra*) earthen; [*color*] earthy

terrero Ⓐ ADJ 1 (= *de la tierra*) earthy; *ver tb* **saco**[1] **1**
2 [*vuelo*] low, skimming
3 (= *humilde*) humble
Ⓑ SM pile, heap; (*Min*) dump

terrestre ADJ 1 (= *de la Tierra*) **la atmósfera ~** the earth's atmosphere; **la superficie ~** the surface of the earth, the earth's surface; **un observatorio que girará en órbita ~** an observatory that will orbit the earth; *ver tb* **corteza 1**
2 (= *ni de aire ni de agua*) [*fuerzas, tropas*] ground *antes de s*, land *antes de s*; [*minas, frontera*] land *antes de s*; [*transporte*] land *antes de s*, terrestrial (*frm*); [*ofensiva*] (= *no aérea*) ground *antes de s*; (= *no por mar*) land *antes de s*; **la distribución de alimentos por vía ~** distribution of food overland *o* by land
3 (*Téc, TV*) terrestrial
4 [*animal, vegetación*] land *antes de s*, terrestrial (*frm*)
5 (*Rel*) earthly

terrible ADJ terrible, awful

terriblemente ADV terribly, awfully

terrícola SMF earthling

terrier SM terrier

terrífico ADJ terrifying

terrina SF terrine

territorial ADJ (= *de territorio*) territorial; (= *de región*) regional

territorialidad SF territoriality

territorio SM territory; **en todo el ~ nacional** in the whole country ► **territorio bajo mandato** mandated territory

terrón SM 1 [*de tierra*] clod, lump
2 [*de azúcar*] lump; **azúcar en ~es** lump sugar
3 (= *terreno*) field, patch (of land); **destripar terrones** to work the land

terronera SF (*Andes*) terror, fright

terror SM terror; **película de ~** horror film; **me da ~ pensar que tengo que hablar con él** the thought of having to speak to him terrifies me, it terrifies me to think I have to speak to him ► **terrores nocturnos** nightmares

terrorífico ADJ terrifying, frightening

terrorismo SM terrorism ► **terrorismo de Estado** state terrorism

terrorista ADJ, SMF terrorist

terroso ADJ earthy

terruño SM 1 (= *parcela de tierra*) plot, piece of ground; (= *tierra nativa*) native soil, home (ground); **apego al ~** attachment to one's native soil
2 (= *terrón*) lump, clod

terso ADJ 1 (= *liso*) smooth; (= *brillante*) shiny, glossy; **piel tersa** smooth skin, soft skin
2 [*estilo*] polished, smooth

tersura SF 1 (= *suavidad*) smoothness; (= *brillo*) shine, glossiness
2 [*de estilo, lenguaje*] smoothness, flow

tertulia SF 1 (= *reunión*) social gathering, regular informal gathering; **la ~ del Café Gijón** the Cafe Gijón circle, the in-crowd at the Cafe Gijón; **estar de ~** to talk, sit around talking; **hacer ~** to get together, meet informally and talk; **hoy no hay ~** there's no meeting today, the group is not meeting today ► **tertulia literaria** literary circle, literary gathering ► **tertulia radiofónica** radio talk show ► **tertulia televisiva** talk show
2 (= *sala*) clubroom, games room
3 (*Cono Sur*) (= *galería*) gallery; (*Caribe*) (= *palcos*) boxes

> **TERTULIA**
>
> *The term* **tertulia** *is used for groups of people who meet informally on a regular basis to chat about current affairs, the Arts, etc and is also used to refer to the gathering itself. In early 20th Century Spain,* **tertulias literarias** *were much in vogue, and critics and writers would meet to discuss the literary issues of the day in places such as the famous Café Gijón. In more recent times, the term has been used to refer to the highly organized PR platforms in which writers of the moment engage in round-table discussions to promote their latest work.*

Tertuliano SM Tertullian

tertuliano/a SM/F 1 (= *contertulio*) member of a social gathering
2 (*Radio, TV*) talk show guest

tertuliar ▸conjug 1b◂ VI (*LAm*) (= *ir a una reunión*) to attend a social gathering; (= *reunirse*) to get together, meet informally and talk

Teruel SM Teruel

terylene® SM Terylene®, Dacron® (*EEUU*)

Tesalia SF Thessaly

tesar ▸conjug 1j◂ VT to tauten, tighten up

tesauro SM thesaurus

tescal SM (*Méx*) stony ground

tesela SF tessera

Teseo SM Theseus

tesina SF dissertation, minor thesis

▼**tesis** SF INV 1 (*Univ*) thesis ► **tesis doctoral** doctoral thesis, doctoral dissertation (*EEUU*), PhD thesis
2 (*Fil*) thesis
3 (= *teoría*) **su ~ es insostenible** his theory is untenable; **no podemos refutar las ~ de la defensa** we cannot refute the defence's arguments; **no comparto su ~** I don't share your opinion

tesitura SF 1 (= *mental*) attitude, frame of mind
2 (*Mús*) tessitura

teso Ⓐ ADJ (= *tenso*) tense
Ⓑ SM crest

tesón SM (= *tenacidad*) tenacity, persistence; (= *insistencia*) insistence; **resistir con ~** to resist tenaciously

tesonero ADJ (*LAm*) tenacious, persistent

tesorería SF 1 (= *cargo*) treasurership, office of treasurer
2 (= *oficina*) treasury
3 (= *activo disponible*) liquid assets *pl*

tesorero/a SM/F treasurer

tesoro SM 1 (*de mucho valor*) treasure; **valer un ~** to be worth a fortune; **tenemos una cocinera que es todo un ~** we have a cook who is a real treasure, we have a real gem of a cook; **el libro es un ~ de datos** the book is a mine of information; **es un ~ de recuerdos** it is a treasure-house of memories ► **tesoro escondido** buried treasure
2 (*en oración directa*) darling; **¡sí, ~!** yes, my darling!
3 (*Fin, Pol*) treasury ► **Tesoro público** Exchequer, Treasury
4 (= *pagaré*) treasury bond
5 (= *diccionario*) thesaurus

Tespis SM Thespis

test SM (*pl* **tests** [tes]) test; **examen tipo ~** multiple-choice exam ► **test de comprensión** comprehension test ► **test de embarazo** pregnancy test

testa SF 1 (= *cabeza*) head ► **testa coronada** crowned head
2 (*) (= *inteligencia*) brains *pl*; (= *sentido común*) gumption*

testador(a) SM/F testator/testatrix

testaduro ADJ (*Caribe*) = **testarudo**

testaferro SM front man

testamentaría SF 1 (= *acto*) execution of a will
2 (= *bienes*) estate

testamentario/a Ⓐ ADJ testamentary
Ⓑ SM/F executor/executrix

testamento SM 1 will, testament; **hacer ~** to make one's will
2 (*Biblia*) **Antiguo Testamento** Old Testament; **Nuevo Testamento** New Testament
3 (*) (= *escrito largo*) screed

testar[1] ▸conjug 1a◂ VI (= *hacer testamento*) to make a will

testar[2] ▸conjug 1a◂ VT (*Andes*) (= *subrayar*) to underline

testar[3] ▸conjug 1a◂ VT [+ *coche, producto*] to test

testarada* SF, **testarazo*** SM bump on the head; **darse una ~** to bump *o* bang one's head

testarudez SF stubbornness, pigheadedness

testarudo ADJ stubborn, pigheaded

testear ▸conjug 1a◂ (*LAm*) Ⓐ VT to test
Ⓑ VI to do a test, undergo a test

testera SF front, face; (*Zool*) forehead

testero SM 1 = **testera**
2 [*de cama*] bedhead
3 (*Arquit*) wall

testes SMPL testes

testiculamen‡ SM equipment*, balls‡ *pl*

testículo SM testicle

testificación SF 1 testification
2 = **testimonio**

testificar ▸conjug 1g◂ Ⓐ VT (= *atestiguar*) to attest; (*en juicio*) to testify to, give evidence of
Ⓑ VI (*en juicio*) to testify, give evidence; **~ de** (= *atestiguar*) to attest; (= *dar testimonio*) to testify to, give evidence of

testigo Ⓐ SMF 1 (*Jur*) witness; [*de boda, contrato*] witness; **citar a algn como ~** to call

➤ LENGUA Y USO: **tesis 3** 53.2

sb as a witness ► **testigo de cargo** witness for the prosecution ► **testigo de descargo** witness for the defence ► **testigo ocular** eyewitness ► **testigo pericial** expert witness ► **testigo presencial** eyewitness
[2] (= *espectador*) witness; **declaró un ~ del accidente** a person who had witnessed the accident gave evidence; **tú eres ~ de que nunca le he pegado** you can testify to *o* vouch for the fact that I have never hit him; **estas paredes han sido ~ de nuestro amor** these walls have witnessed *o* are the witness of our love; **pongo al cielo por ~** as God is my witness
[3] (*Rel*) ► **testigo de Jehová** Jehovah's witness
Ⓑ SM [1] (*Dep*) (*en relevos*) baton
[2] (*Aut*) ~ **luminoso** warning light
[3] (*en experimento*) control
[4] (*Geol*) sample core
Ⓒ ADJ INV **grupo ~** control group

testimonial ADJ token, nominal

testimonialmente ADV (= *como símbolo*) as a token gesture; (= *nominalmente*) nominally; (= *sin entusiasmo*) half-heartedly

testimoniar ▸conjug 1b◂ Ⓐ VT (= *testificar*) to testify to, bear witness to; (= *mostrar*) to show, demonstrate
Ⓑ VI to testify, bear witness

testimonio SM [1] (*Jur*) (= *declaración*) testimony, evidence; (= *afidávit*) affidavit; **dar ~** to testify (**de** to), give evidence (**de** of); **falso ~** perjury, false testimony
[2] (= *prueba*) proof; (= *indicación*) evidence; **~ de compra** proof of purchase; **los fósiles son ~ de ello** fossils are evidence of this; **las calles nos dan ~ de su pasado árabe** the streets bear witness to its Arab past; **como ~ de mi afecto** as a token *o* mark of my affection

testosterona SF testosterone

testuz SM [*de caballo*] forehead; [*de buey, toro*] nape (*of the neck*)

teta Ⓐ SF [1] (*) (= *mama*) breast, tit**, boob*; **dar (la) ~ a** to suckle, breast-feed; **quitar la ~ a** to wean; **niño de ~** baby at the breast; ✦*MODISMO* **mejor que ~ de monja*** really great*
[2] [*de biberón*] teat, nipple (*EEUU*)
Ⓑ ADJ INV **estar ~** (*Esp**) to be really great*

tetamen* SM big bust

tétano SM, **tétanos** SM INV tetanus

tete* SM (*Cono Sur*) mess, trouble

tetelque ADJ (*CAm, Méx*) sharp, bitter

tetera[1] SF (*para té*) teapot; (= *recipiente grande*) tea urn ► **tetera eléctrica** electric kettle

tetera[2] SF (*Méx*) (= *biberón*) feeding bottle; (= *vasija*) vessel with a spout

tetero SM (*Andes, Caribe*) feeding bottle

tetilla SF [1] [*de hombre*] nipple
[2] [*de biberón*] teat, nipple (*EEUU*)

tetina SF teat, nipple (*EEUU*)

Tetis SF Thetis

tetón[1] SM (*en neumático*) bubble, swelling

tetón[2]* ADJ (*Cono Sur*) stupid, thick*

tetona* ADJ busty*

tetrabrik® SM INV, **tetra brik®** SM INV Tetra-Pak®, carton

tetracilíndrico ADJ **motor ~** four-cylinder engine

tetracloruro SM tetrachloride ► **tetracloruro de carbono** carbon tetrachloride

tetraedro SM tetrahedron

tetrágono SM tetragon

tetrámetro SM tetrameter

tetramotor ADJ four-engined

tetrapak® SM INV, **tetra pak®** SM INV Tetra-Pak®

tetrarreactor SM four-engined jet plane

tetratlón SM tetrathlon

tétrico ADJ [*ambiente, habitación, lugar*] gloomy, dismal; [*humor, pensamiento, cuento, relato*] gloomy, pessimistic; [*luz*] dim, wan

tetuda* ADJ busty*

tetunte SM (*CAm*) bundle

teutón/ona Ⓐ ADJ Teutonic
Ⓑ SM/F Teuton

teutónico ADJ Teutonic

teveo SM = **tebeo**

textil Ⓐ ADJ [1] [*industria*] textile
[2] [*playa*] non-nudist
Ⓑ **textiles** SMPL (= *tejidos*) textiles
Ⓒ SF textile company

texto SM text; **libro de ~** textbook; **grabado fuera de ~** full-page illustration

textual ADJ [1] (= *de un texto*) textual; **cita ~** quotation
[2] (= *exacto*) exact; (= *literal*) literal; **son sus palabras ~es** those are his exact words

textualmente ADV [1] (*Literat*) textually
[2] (= *exactamente*) exactly; (= *literalmente*) literally, word for word; **dice ~ que ...** he says —and I quote— that ...

textura SF texture

tez SF (= *piel*) complexion, skin; (= *color*) colouring, coloring (*EEUU*); **de ~ morena** dark(-skinned), dusky (*liter*); **de ~ pálida** fair(-skinned)

tezontle SM (*Méx*) volcanic rock (*for building*)

Tfno. ABR, **tfno.** ABR (= **teléfono**) Tel, tel

TGV SM ABR (= **tren de gran velocidad**) ≈ APT

thriller SM (*pl* **thrillers**) thriller

ti PRON PERS you; **es para ti** it's for you; **ahora todo depende de ti** it all depends on you now; **esto no se refiere a ti** this doesn't refer to you; **¿a ti te gusta el jazz?** do you like jazz?; **¿a ti te han dicho algo?** have they said anything to you?; **sólo piensas en ti (mismo)** you only think of yourself; **no sabes defenderte por ti misma** you don't know how to stand up for yourself

tiamina SF thiamine

tiangue SM (*CAm*) (= *mercado*) small market; (= *puesto*) booth, stall

tianguis SM INV (*CAm, Méx*) (open-air) market

TIAR SM ABR = **Tratado Interamericano de Asistencia Recíproca**

tiara SF tiara

tiarrón/ona* SM/F big guy*/big girl

tibante ADJ (*Andes*) haughty

tibe SM (*Andes, Caribe*) whetstone

Tíber SM Tiber

Tiberio SM Tiberius

tiberio* Ⓐ ADJ (*CAm, Méx*) sloshed*
Ⓑ SM [1] (= *jaleo*) uproar, row; (= *pelea*) set-to*
[2] (*CAm, Méx*) binge*

Tíbet SM **El ~** Tibet

tibetano/a Ⓐ ADJ, SM/F Tibetan
Ⓑ SM (*Ling*) Tibetan

tibia SF tibia

tibiarse ▸conjug 1b◂ VPR (*CAm, Caribe*) to get cross

tibieza SF [1] [*de líquidos*] lukewarmness, tepidness
[2] [*de creencias*] half-heartedness; [*de persona*] lukewarmness, lack of enthusiasm

tibio ADJ [1] [*comida, líquido*] lukewarm, tepid
[2] [*creencia*] half-hearted; [*persona*] lukewarm; [*recibimiento*] cool, unenthusiastic; **estar ~ con algn** to be cool to sb, behave distantly towards sb; ✦*MODISMO* **poner ~ a algn*** (= *insultar*) to hurl abuse at sb, give sb a verbal battering; (*por detrás*) to say dreadful things about sb
[3] (*CAm, Caribe*) (= *enfadado*) cross, angry

tibor SM (= *jarro*) large earthenware jar; (*Caribe*) (= *orinal*) chamber pot; (*Méx*) (= *calabaza*) gourd, squash (*EEUU*)

tiburón SM [1] (*Zool*) shark ► **tiburón de río** pike
[2] (*) (= *persona sin escrúpulos*) shark*
[3] (*Bolsa*) raider
[4] (*Cono Sur*) wolf*, Don Juan

tiburoneo SM (*Bolsa*) share raiding

tic SM (*pl* **tics**) [1] (= *sonido*) click; [*de reloj*] tick
[2] (*Med*) tic ► **tic nervioso** nervous tic
[3] (= *costumbre*) habit

Ticiano SM Titian

tícket ['tike] SM (*pl* **tíckets** ['tike]) (= *billete*) ticket; [*de compra*] receipt

tico/a* ADJ, SM/F (*CAm*) Costa Rican

tictac SM [*de reloj*] tick, ticking; [*de corazón*] beat; **hacer ~** [*reloj*] to tick; [*corazón*] to beat

tiempecito SM (spell of) very bad weather

tiemple SM [1] (*Cono Sur*) (= *galanteo*) lovemaking, courting
[2] (*Cono Sur*) (= *amante*) lover
[3] (*LAm*) (= *enamoramiento*) infatuation

tiempo SM [1] (*indicando duración*) time; **no tengo ~** I haven't got time; **tenemos todo el ~ del mundo** we have all the time in the world; **el ~ pasa y no nos damos ni cuenta** time goes by *o* passes and we don't even realize it; **tómate el ~ que quieras** take as long as you want; **me llevó bastante ~** it took me quite a long time; **hace bastante ~ que lo compré** I bought it quite a while ago; **¿cuánto ~ se va a quedar?** how long is he staying for?; **¿cuánto ~ hace de eso?** how long ago was that?; **¿cuánto ~ hace que vives aquí?** how long have you been living here?; **¡cuánto ~ sin verte!** I haven't seen you for ages!; **más ~: necesito más ~ para pensármelo** I need more time *o* longer to think about it; **no puede quedarse más ~** he can't stay any longer; **mucho ~: una costumbre que viene de mucho ~ atrás** a long-standing custom; **has tardado mucho ~** you took a long time; **ocurrió hace mucho ~** it happened a long time ago; **hace mucho ~ que no la veo** I haven't seen her for a long time; **al poco ~ de** soon after; **al poco ~ de su muerte** soon after his death; **se acostumbró a la idea en muy poco ~** she soon got used to the idea, it didn't take her long to get used to the idea ► **tiempo de exposición** (*Fot*) exposure time ► **tiempo libre** spare time, free time

[2] (*otras locuciones*) **a tiempo** in time; **llegamos a ~ de ver la película** we got there in time to see the film; **todavía estáis a ~ de cambiar de idea** it's still not too late for you to change your minds; **el avión llegó a ~** the plane arrived on time; **cada cierto ~** every so often; **a ~ completo** full-time; **trabajar a ~ completo** to work full-time; **con ~**: **llegamos con ~ de darnos un paseo** we arrived in time to have a walk; **si me lo dices con ~** if you tell me beforehand; **con el ~** eventually; **con el ~ lo conseguiremos** we'll manage it eventually; **dar ~**: **no da ~ a terminarlo** there isn't enough time to finish it; **¿crees que te dará ~?** do you think you'll have (enough) time?; **dale ~** give him time; **fuera de ~** at the wrong time; **ganar ~** to save time; **hacer ~** to while away the time; **matar el ~** to kill time; **a ~ parcial** part-time; **trabajo a ~ parcial** part-time work; **trabajador a ~ parcial** part-timer; **de un** *o* **algún ~ a esta parte** for some time (past); **pasar el ~** to pass time; **no es más que una forma de pasar el ~** it just a way of passing time; **perder el ~** to waste time; **estás perdiendo el ~** you're wasting your time; **me estás haciendo perder el ~** you're wasting my time; **sería simplemente perder el ~** it would just be a waste of time; **¡rápido, no perdamos (el) ~!** quick, there's no time to lose!; **sin perder ~** without delay; **sacar ~ para hacer algo** to find the time to do sth; **tener ~ para algo** to have time for sth; ✦***MODISMOS*** **andando el ~** in due course, in time; **el ~ apremia** time presses; **dar ~ al ~** to let matters take their course; **de ~ en ~** from time to time; ✦***REFRANES*** **con el ~ y una caña (hasta las verdes caen)** all good things come to those who wait; **el ~ es oro** time is precious; **el ~ dirá** time will tell; **el ~ todo lo borra** ◊ **el ~ lo cura todo** time is a great healer

[3] (= *momento*) time; **al mismo ~** ◊ **a un ~** at the same time; **al (mismo) ~ que** at the (same) time as; **cada cosa a su ~** everything in good time; **llegamos antes de ~** we arrived early; **ha nacido antes de ~** he was born prematurely, he was premature; **a su debido ~** in due course

[4] (= *época*) time; **durante un ~ vivimos en Valencia** we lived in Valencia for a time *o* while; **en ~ de los griegos** in the days of the Greeks; **en mis ~s** in my day; **en ~s de mi abuelo** in my grandfather's day; **en los buenos ~s** in the good old days; **en estos ~s que corren** these days; **en otros ~s** formerly; **en los últimos ~s** recently, lately, in recent times; **a través de los ~s** through the ages; **los ~s están revueltos** these are troubled times; **hay que ir con los ~s** you have to move with the times; ✦***MODISMO*** **en ~s de Maricastaña**: **va vestida como en ~s de Maricastaña** her clothes went out with the ark, her clothes are really old-fashioned; **una receta del ~ de Maricastaña** an ancient *o* age-old recipe ► **tiempos modernos** modern times

[5] (= *edad*) age; **Ricardo y yo somos del mismo ~** Ricardo and I are the same age; **¿cuánto** *o* **qué ~ tiene el niño?** how old is the baby?

[6] (*Dep*) half; **primer ~** first half; **segundo ~** second half ► **tiempo muerto** (*lit*) time-out; (*fig*) breather

[7] (*Mús*) [*de compás*] tempo, time; [*de sinfonía*] movement

[8] (*Ling*) tense; **en ~ presente** in the present tense ► **tiempo compuesto** compound tense ► **tiempo simple** simple tense

[9] (*Meteo*) weather; **hace buen ~** the weather is good; **hace mal ~** the weather is bad; **¿qué ~ hace ahí?** what's the weather like there?; **si dura el mal ~** if the bad weather continues; **del ~**: **¿quiere el agua fría o del ~?** would you like the water chilled or at room temperature?; **prefiero la fruta del ~** I prefer fruit that's in season; ✦***REFRÁN*** **a mal ~, buena cara** one must try to put a brave face on it; *ver tb* **mapa**, **hombre A1**

[10] (*Inform*) time ► **tiempo compartido** time-sharing ► **tiempo de ejecución** run time ► **tiempo real** real time; **conversación en ~ real** real-time conversation; **cada jugador está conectado en ~ real** all the players are playing in real time

[11] (*Industria*) time ► **tiempo de paro**, **tiempo inactivo** downtime ► **tiempo preferencial** prime time

[12] (*Náut*) stormy weather

[13] (*Mec*) cycle; **motor de dos ~s** two-stroke engine

tienda SF [1] (*Com*) shop, store; **lo compré en esta ~** I bought it in this shop; **ir de ~s** to go shopping ► **tienda de comestibles** grocer's (shop), grocery (*EEUU*) ► **tienda de deportes** sports shop, sporting goods store (*EEUU*) ► **tienda de regalos** gift shop ► **tienda de ultramarinos** grocer's (shop), grocery (*EEUU*) ► **tienda libre de impuestos** duty-free shop ► **tienda por departamento** (*Caribe*) department store

[2] (*tb* **~ de campaña**) tent; **montar la ~** to pitch the tent; **desmontar la ~** to take down the tent

[3] (*Náut*) awning

[4] (*Med*) ► **tienda de oxígeno** oxygen tent

tienta SF [1] **a ~s** gropingly, blindly; **andar a ~s** to grope one's way along, feel one's way; (*fig*) to feel one's way; **buscar algo a ~s** to grope around for sth; **decir algo a ~s** to throw out a remark at random, say sth to see what effect it has

[2] (*Taur*) trial, test

[3] (*Med*) probe

tiento SM [1] (= *diplomacia*) tact; (= *prudencia*) care; (= *cautela*) wariness, circumspection; **ir con ~** to go carefully

[2] (= *toque*) feel(ing), touch; **a ~** (= *por el tacto*) by touch; (= *con inseguridad*) uncertainly; **perder el ~** to lose one's touch; **a 40 dólares nadie le echó un ~** at 40 dollars nobody was biting, at 40 dollars he didn't get a tickle*

[3] (*) (= *propuesta*) pass*; **echar un ~ a una chica** to make a pass at a girl, try it on with a girl*

[4] (= *buen pulso*) steadiness of hand, steady hand

[5] (*) (= *trago*) swig*; **dar un ~** to take a swig (**a** from)

[6] (*Zool*) feeler, tentacle

[7] (= *palo*) (*Circo*) balancing pole; [*de ciego*] blind man's stick

[8] (*) (= *puñetazo*) blow, punch; **dar ~s a algn** to hit sb

[9] (*Cono Sur*) (= *tira*) thong of raw leather, rawhide strap

tiernamente ADV tenderly

tierno ADJ [1] (= *blando*) [*carne*] tender; [*pan*] fresh

[2] [*brote*] tender

[3] (= *afectuoso*) [*persona*] tender, affectionate; [*mirada, sonrisa*] tender

[4] (= *joven*) tender; **a la tierna edad de cinco años** at the tender age of five; **en su más tierna infancia** in his tenderest youth

tierra SF [1] **la Tierra** the earth, the Earth

[2] (= *superficie*) [2·1] (*fuera del agua*) land; **¡~ a la vista!** land ahoy!; **permanecer en ~** to remain on land; **la industria pesquera genera unos 400.000 empleos en ~** the fishing industry provides 400,000 jobs on land; **saltar a ~** to leap ashore; **~ adentro** inland; **el desierto avanza ~ adentro** the desert is advancing inland; **soy de ~ adentro** I'm from inland; **por ~** overland, by land; **atravesar un país por ~** to go overland *o* by land across a country; **por ~ y por mar** by land and by sea; **tomar ~** to reach port, get in

[2·2] (= *no aire*) (*desde el aire*) ground; (*desde el espacio*) earth; **la explosión ocurrió cuando el avión cayó a ~** the explosion occurred when the aeroplane hit the ground; **un ataque por ~ y aire** a ground and air attack; **tocar ~** to touch down; **tomar ~** to land ► **tierra firme** (= *no aire*) solid ground; (= *no agua*) land

[3] (= *suelo*) ground; **estaba tirado en la ~** he was lying on the ground; **caer a ~** to fall down; **caer por ~** [*persona*] to fall to the ground; [*argumento, teoría*] to fall apart; **dar con algo en ~** to knock sth over; **echar a ~** [+ *construcción, rival*] to knock down; **echarse a ~** to throw o.s. on *o* to the ground; ✦***MODISMOS*** **besar la ~** to fall flat on one's face; **echar** *o* **tirar por ~** [+ *trabajo, organización*] to ruin, destroy; [+ *expectativas, sueños*] to shatter; [+ *teoría, tesis*] to demolish; **perder ~** (*antes de caerse*) to lose one's footing; (*en el agua*) to get out of one's depth; **poner ~ de por medio** to get away as quickly as possible; **venirse a** *o* **por ~** to collapse; **¡~, trágame!** I want to die! (*iró*)

[4] (= *material*) (*gen*) earth; (= *polvo*) dust; (= *barro*) mud; (*para jardinería, cultivo*) soil; **olía a ~ mojada** it smelled of wet earth; **se levantó mucha ~** a dust cloud blew up; **con los zapatos llenos de ~** (= *polvo*) with his shoes covered in dust; (= *barro*) with his shoes covered in mud; **viviendas con suelo de ~** houses with earth *o* dirt floors; **el avión aterrizó en una pequeña pista de ~** the aeroplane landed on a small dirt runway; **un camino de ~** a dirt road; **es muy buena ~ para las plantas** it's good soil for plants; **un saco de ~** a bag of soil; **jugarán en pistas de ~** they'll play on clay courts; **sacudir la ~** (*Cono Sur, Méx*) to dust; ✦***MODISMOS*** **estar bajo ~** to be dead and buried; **echar ~ a** *o* **sobre algo** (= *ocultar*) to hush up sth; (= *olvidar*) to put sth behind one; **acordaron echar ~ al incidente y seguir siendo amigos** they agreed to put the incident behind them and continue to be friends; **echar ~ a algn** (*Méx, Chile*) to sling *o* throw mud at sb; (*Col**) to make sb look bad; **le vienes a echar ~ a mi carro con tu descapotable** your convertible makes my car look ridiculous *o* really bad; **echarse ~ encima** to foul one's own nest ► **tierra caliente** (*LAm*) *land below 1000m. approximately* ► **tierra de batán** fuller's earth

► **tierra de brezo** peat ► **tierra fría** (*LAm*) *land above 2000m. approximately* ► **tierra quemada** (*Pol*) scorched earth ► **tierra templada** (*LAm*) *land between 1000m. and 2000m. approximately* ► **tierra vegetal** topsoil; *ver tb* **pista 3**, **política 2**
[5] (*Agr*) land; **trabajar la ~** to work the land; **las ~s de cereales** grain-growing land; **heredó unas ~s cerca del río** he inherited some land near the river; ✦*MODISMO* **en cualquier ~ de garbanzos** all over ► **tierra baldía** wasteland ► **tierra de cultivo** arable land ► **tierra de labor** agricultural land ► **tierra de pan llevar** grain-growing land ► **tierra de regadío** irrigated land ► **tierra de secano** dry land, unirrigated land
[6] (= *división territorial*) [6·1] (= *lugar de origen*) **en mi ~ no se usa esa expresión** we don't use that expression where I come from; **vamos a nuestra ~ a pasar las Navidades** we're going home for Christmas; **todo refugiado siente nostalgia de su ~** every refugee feels homesick for or misses his native land *o* homeland; **de la ~** [*vino, queso*] local, locally produced; [*fruta, verduras*] locally grown; **productos de la ~** local produce
[6·2] (*en plural*) **la expropiación de ~s palestinas** the expropriation of Palestinian land *o* lands; **sus viajes por ~s de Castilla** his travels through the lands of Castile; **su largo exilio en ~s australianas** her lengthy exile in Australia; **no es de estas ~s** he's not from these parts, he's not from this part of the world; ✦*MODISMO* **ver ~s**† to see the world ► **Tierra del Fuego** Tierra del Fuego ► **tierra de nadie** no-man's-land ► **tierra de promisión** promised land ► **tierra natal** native land ► **tierra prometida** promised land ► **Tierra Santa** Holy Land
[7] (*Elec*) earth, ground (*EEUU*); **conectar un aparato a ~** to earth *o* (*EEUU*) ground an appliance; *ver tb* **toma A1**

tierra-aire ADJ INV **misil ~** surface-to-air missile, ground-to-air missile

tierrafría SMF (*Andes*) highlander

tierral SM (*LAm*), **tierrazo** SM (*LAm*) = **terral**

tierra-tierra ADJ INV **misil ~** surface-to-surface missile

tierrero SM (*LAm*) cloud of dust

tierruca SF native land, native heath

tieso Ⓐ ADJ [1] (= *duro*) stiff; (= *rígido*) rigid; (= *erguido*) erect; (= *derecho*) straight; (= *tenso*) taut; **ponte tiesa** stand up straight; **con las orejas tiesas** with its ears pricked; ✦*MODISMOS* **dejar ~ a algn*** (= *matar*) to do sb in*; (= *sorprender*) to amaze sb, leave sb speechless; **quedarse ~*** (*de frío*) to be frozen stiff; (= *sorprenderse*) to be left speechless; (= *morirse*) to snuff it*, peg out*
[2] (= *sano*) fit; (= *vivo*) sprightly; (= *alegre*) chirpy*; **le encontré muy ~ a pesar de su enfermedad** I found him very chirpy in spite of his illness
[3] (= *poco amable*) (*en conducta*) stiff; (*en actitud*) rigid; **me recibió muy ~** he received me very coldly; ✦*MODISMO* **~ como un ajo** as stiff as a poker
[4] (= *orgulloso*) proud; (= *presumido*) conceited, stuck-up*; (= *pagado de sí mismo*) smug; **iba tan ~ con la novia al brazo** he was walking so proudly with his girl on his arm
[5] (= *terco*) stubborn; (= *firme*) firm, confident; **ponerse ~ con algn** to stand one's ground, insist on one's rights; (*pey*) to be stubborn with sb; **tenerlas tiesas con algn** to put up a firm resistance to sb, stand up for o.s.
[6] (*) (= *sin dinero*) (flat) broke*
Ⓑ ADV strongly, energetically, hard

tiesto SM [1] (= *maceta*) flowerpot
[2] (= *cascote*) shard, piece of pottery
[3] (*Cono Sur*) (= *vasija*) pot, vessel; (= *orinal*) chamber pot

tiesura SF [1] (= *rigidez*) stiffness
[2] (= *presunción*) conceit
[3] (= *terquedad*) stubbornness

tifiar‡ ▸conjug 1b◂ VT (*Caribe*) to nick‡, lift*

tifitifi* SM (*Caribe*) theft

tifo SM typhus ► **tifo asiático** cholera ► **tifo de América** yellow fever ► **tifo de Oriente** bubonic plague

tifoidea SF (*tb* **fiebre ~**) typhoid

tifón SM [1] (= *huracán*) typhoon
[2] (= *tromba*) waterspout
[3] (*Méx Min*) outcrop of ore

tifus SM INV [1] (*Med*) typhus ► **tifus exantemático** spotted fever ► **tifus icteroides** yellow fever
[2] (*Teat**) claque; **entrar de ~** to get in free

tigra SF (*LAm Zool*) female tiger; (= *jaguar*) female jaguar; ✦*MODISMO* **ponerse como una ~ parida** (*Andes, Cono Sur**) to fly off the handle*

tigre SM [1] (*Zool*) tiger; (*LAm*) jaguar ► **tigre de Bengala** Bengal tiger ► **tigre de colmillo de sable** sabre-toothed tiger ► **tigre de papel** paper tiger
[2] (*Andes*) (= *café*) *black coffee with a dash of milk*; (*Andes*) (= *combinado*) cocktail
[3] (‡) (= *wáter*) bog‡, loo*, john (*EEUU*‡); **esto huele a ~** this stinks, this smells foul

tigrero Ⓐ ADJ (*Cono Sur*) brave
Ⓑ SM (*LAm*) jaguar hunter

tigresa SF [1] (= *animal*) tigress
[2] (= *mujer cruel*) shrew; (= *mujer fatal*) vamp*

tigridia SF tiger lily

tigrillo SM (*LAm*) *member of the cat tribe, eg ocelot, lynx*

Tigris SM Tigris

tigrón* SM (*Caribe*) bully, braggart

tigüila SF (*Méx*) trick, swindle

tija SF (*Aut*) shank

tijera SF [1] (*tb* **~s**) scissors *pl*; (*para jardín*) shears *pl*, clippers *pl*; **unas ~s** a pair of scissors; **meter la ~ en algo** to cut into sth; **es un trabajo de ~** it's a scissors-and-paste job ► **tijeras de coser** sewing scissors ► **tijeras de podar** secateurs ► **tijeras para las uñas** nail scissors ► **tijeras podadoras** secateurs
[2] [*de bicicleta*] fork
[3] **de ~** folding; **silla de ~** (= *con respaldo*) folding chair; (= *banqueta*) folding stool, camp stool; **escalera de ~** steps, step-ladder
[4] (*LAm Zool*) claw, pincer
[5] (*) (= *persona*) gossip; **ser una buena ~** ◊ **tener buena ~** (= *chismoso*) to be a great gossip; (= *mordaz*) to have a sharp tongue; (= *criticón*) be a scandalmonger

tijeral SM (*Cono Sur*) stork

tijereta SF [1] (= *insecto*) earwig
[2] (*Bot*) vine tendril
[3] (*Dep*) scissor(s) kick, overhead kick

tijeretada SF, **tijeretazo** SM snip, snick

tijeretear ▸conjug 1a◂ Ⓐ VT to snip, snick
Ⓑ VI [1] (= *entrometerse*) to meddle
[2] (*CAm, Cono Sur, Méx*) (= *chismear*) to gossip, backbite

tijereteo SM [1] (*con tijeras*) snipping, snicking
[2] (= *entrometimiento*) meddling
[3] (*CAm, Cono Sur, Méx*) (= *chismes*) gossiping, backbiting

tila SF [1] (= *planta*) lime tree
[2] (= *infusión*) lime flower tea; ✦*MODISMO* **¡que te den ~!*** give me a break!*
[3] (‡) (= *droga*) hash*, pot*

tildar ▸conjug 1a◂ VT [1] (= *acusar*) **~ a algn de racista** to brand sb (as) a racist; **le ~on de vago** they dismissed him as lazy, they called him lazy
[2] (*Tip*) (*gen*) to put an accent on; (*sobre la n*) to put a tilde over

tilde SF [1] (*ortográfica*) (= *acento*) (*gen*) accent; (*sobre la n*) tilde
[2] (= *mancha*) blemish; (= *defecto*) defect, flaw
[3] (= *bagatela*) triviality; (= *pizca*) jot, bit; ✦*MODISMO* **en una ~*** in a jiffy*

tilichera SF (*CAm, Méx*) hawker's box, glass-covered box

tilichero/a SM/F (*CAm, Méx*) hawker, pedlar, peddler (*EEUU*)

tiliches* SMPL (*CAm, Méx*) (= *pertenencias*) belongings; (= *baratijas*) trinkets; (= *trastos*) junk *sing*

tilín SM [*de campanilla*] tinkle, ting-a-ling; ✦*MODISMOS* **hacer ~ a algn***: **me hace ~** [*persona*] I fancy him*; [*cosa*] I like it, I go for it*; **no me hace ~** [*cosa*] it doesn't do anything for me; **en un ~** (*Andes, Caribe, Cono Sur**) in a flash; **tener algo al ~** (*Caribe*) to have sth at one's fingertips

tilinches* SMPL (*Méx*) rags

tilingada* SF (*Cono Sur, Méx*) silly thing (to do *etc*)

tilingo/a* (*Andes, Cono Sur, Méx*) Ⓐ ADJ silly, stupid
Ⓑ SM/F fool

tilinguear* ▸conjug 1a◂ VI (*Andes, Cono Sur, Méx*) to act the fool

tilinguería* SF (*Andes, Cono Sur, Méx*) [1] (= *estupidez*) silliness, stupidity
[2] **tilinguerías** nonsense *sing*

tilintar ▸conjug 1a◂ VT (*CAm*) to stretch, tauten

tilinte ADJ (*CAm*) [1] (= *tenso*) tight, taut
[2] (= *elegante*) elegant
[3] (= *repleto*) replete

tilma SF (*Méx*) blanket, cape

tilo SM [1] (= *planta*) lime tree
[2] (*LAm*) (= *infusión*) lime flower tea

tiloso* ADJ (*CAm*) dirty, filthy

timador(a) SM/F swindler, trickster

timar ▸conjug 1a◂ Ⓐ VT to swindle, con*; **¡me han timado!** I've been conned!*; **le ~on la herencia** they swindled him out of his inheritance
Ⓑ **timarse** VPR (*) [*pareja*] to make eyes at each other; **~se con algn** (= *engatusar*) to play sb along, lead sb on; (*amorosamente*) to make eyes at sb, ogle sb

timba SF [1] (*en juego de azar*) hand
[2] (= *garito*) gambling den
[3] (*CAm, Caribe, Méx*) (= *tripa*) pot-belly
[4] ✦*MODISMO* **tener ~** (*Caribe*): **esto tiene ~** it's a sticky business

timbal SM 1 (*Mús*) small drum, kettledrum; **~es** timpani
2 (*Culin*) meat pie
3 **timbales**** (= *testículos*) balls**

timbembe* ADJ (*Cono Sur*) weak, trembling

timbero/a* (*Cono Sur*) Ⓐ ADJ given to gambling
Ⓑ SM/F gambler

timbiriche SM (*Caribe, Méx*) small shop

timbrado ADJ **voz bien timbrada** well-toned voice

timbrar ▸conjug 1a◂ VT 1 [+ *documento*] to stamp
2 [+ *carta*] to postmark, frank

timbrazo SM ring; **dar un ~** to ring the bell

timbre SM 1 (*Elec*) bell; **tocar el ~** to ring the bell ► **timbre de alarma** alarm bell
2 (*Mús*) timbre ► **timbre nasal** nasal timbre, twang
3 (*Com, Fin*) (= *sello*) fiscal stamp, revenue stamp; (= *renta*) stamp duty, revenue stamp (*EEUU*)
4 (*Méx*) [*de correos*] (postage) stamp
5 (*LAm*) (= *descripción*) [*de persona*] personal description; [*de géneros*] description of goods (*etc*)
6 ► **timbre de gloria** (= *señal*) mark of honour; (= *acto*) *action etc which is to one's credit*

timbrear ▸conjug 1a◂ VI to ring (the bell)

timbusca SF (*Andes*) (= *sopa*) thick soup; (= *plato rústico*) *spicy local dish*

tímidamente ADV shyly, timidly

timidez SF shyness, timidity

tímido ADJ shy, timid

timo SM swindle, con trick*; **dar un ~ a algn** to swindle sb, con sb*; **¡es un ~!** it's a rip-off!*

timón SM 1 (*Aer, Náut*) rudder; (= *mando, control*) helm; **poner el ~ a babor** to turn to port, port the helm; ✦**MODISMO coger** o **empuñar el ~** to take the helm, take charge ► **timón de deriva, timón de dirección** rudder ► **timón de profundidad** (*Aer*) elevator
2 [*de carruaje*] pole; [*de arado*] beam
3 (*Andes Aut*) steering wheel

timonear ▸conjug 1a◂ Ⓐ VT (*LAm*) (= *dirigir*) to direct, manage; (= *guiar*) to guide
Ⓑ VI to steer; (*Andes Aut*) to drive

timonel SMF (*Náut*) steersman/steerswoman, helmsman/helmswoman; (*en barca de remo*) cox

timonera SF wheelhouse

timonería SF (*Náut*) rudders *pl*, steering mechanisms *pl*; (*Ferro*) linkage

timonero SM = **timonel**

timorato ADJ 1 (= *tímido*) lily-livered, spineless
2 (= *mojigato*) sanctimonious, prudish
3 (= *que teme a Dios*) God-fearing

Timoteo SM Timothy

tímpano SM 1 (*Anat*) tympanum, eardrum
2 (*Arquit*) tympanum
3 (*Mús*) small drum, kettledrum; **tímpanos** (*en orquesta*) timpani

tina SF (= *recipiente*) tub, vat; (*para bañarse*) bath(tub) ► **tina de lavar** washtub

tinaco SM (*Méx*) (= *cisterna*) water tank; (*Andes, Méx*) (= *vasija*) tall earthenware jar

tinaja SF large earthenware jar

tinajero SM stone water filter

tinca SF 1 (*Cono Sur*) (= *capirotazo*) flip, flick
2 (*Andes*) bowls *pl*
3 (*Cono Sur*) (= *pálpito*) hunch

tincada SF (*Cono Sur*) hunch

tincanque SM (*Cono Sur*) = **tinca 1**

tincar* ▸conjug 1g◂ VI (*Chile*) 1 (= *presentir*) to have a hunch about; **me tinca que …** it seems to me that …, I have a feeling that…
2 (= *apetecer*) to like, fancy*; **me tinca** I like it; **no me tinca** I don't fancy the idea
3 (= *dar un capirotazo a*) to flip, flick

tincazo SM (*Cono Sur*) = **tinca 1**

tinctura SF tincture

tinerfeño/a Ⓐ ADJ of/from Tenerife
Ⓑ SM/F native/inhabitant of Tenerife; **los ~s** the people of Tenerife

tinga* SF (*Méx*) row, uproar

tingar ▸conjug 1h◂ VT (*Andes*) to flip, flick

tinglado SM 1 (= *tablado*) platform; (= *cobertizo*) shed
2 (*) (= *sistema*) set-up; **está metida en el ~ del espiritismo** she's into the spiritualism thing; **conocer el ~** to know the score*; **montar el ~** to get going, set up in business; **montar su ~** to do one's own thing*
3 (= *intriga*) plot, intrigue; (= *truco*) trick; **armar un ~** to hatch a plot
4 (= *follón*) mess

tingo SM (*Andes*), **tingue** SM (*Andes*) = **tinca 1**

tinieblas SFPL 1 (= *oscuridad*) dark(ness) *sing*; (= *sombras*) shadows; (= *tenebrosidad*) gloom *sing*
2 (= *confusión*) confusion *sing*; (= *ignorancia*) ignorance *sing*; **estamos en ~ sobre sus proyectos** we are in the dark about his plans

tino[1] SM 1 (= *habilidad*) skill, knack, feel; (= *seguridad*) (sureness of) touch; (= *conjeturas*) (good) guesswork; (*Mil*) (= *puntería*) (accurate) aim; **coger el ~** to get the feel o hang of it; **a ~** gropingly; **a buen ~** by guesswork
2 (= *tacto*) tact; (= *perspicacia*) insight, acumen; (= *juicio*) good judgement; **sin ~** foolishly; **obrar con mucho ~** to act very wisely; **perder el ~** to act foolishly, go off the rails; ✦**MODISMO sacar de ~ a algn** (= *enfadar*) to exasperate sb, infuriate sb; (= *confundir*) to confuse sb
3 (= *moderación*) moderation; **sin ~** immoderately; **comer sin ~** to eat to excess; **gastar sin ~** to spend recklessly

tino[2] SM 1 (= *tina*) vat; [*de piedra*] stone tank
2 (= *lagar*) winepress; [*de aceite*] olive press

tinoso ADJ (*Andes*) (= *hábil*) skilful, skillful (*EEUU*), clever; (= *juicioso*) sensible; (= *moderado*) moderate; (= *diplomático*) tactful

tinque SM (*Cono Sur*) = **tinca 1**

tinta SF 1 (*para escribir*) ink; **con ~** in ink; ✦**MODISMOS saber algo de buena ~** to know sth on good authority; **sudar ~*** to slog, slave one's guts out* ► **tinta china** Indian ink, India ink (*EEUU*) ► **tinta de imprenta** printing ink, printer's ink ► **tinta de marcar** marking ink ► **tinta indeleble** indelible ink ► **tinta invisible, tinta simpática** invisible ink
2 [*de pulpo, calamar*] ink; **calamares en su ~** squid in their own ink
3 (*Arte*) (= *color*) colour, color (*EEUU*); **tintas** (*liter*) shades, hues; **media ~** half-tone, tint; ✦**MODISMOS cargar las ~s** to exaggerate; **medias ~s** (= *medidas*) half measures; (= *ideas*) half-baked ideas; (= *respuestas*) inadequate answers
4 (= *tinte*) dye

tintar ▸conjug 1a◂ VT to dye

tinte SM 1 (= *acto*) dyeing
2 (= *producto*) dye, dyestuff; (*para madera*) stain
3 (= *tintorería*) dry cleaner's; (= *taller*) dyer's (shop)
4 (= *tendencia*) hint; **sin el menor ~ político** without the slightest hint of politics, with no political overtones whatsoever
5 (= *barniz*) veneer, gloss; **tiene cierto ~ de hombre de mundo** he has a slight touch of the man of the world about him

tinterillo SM 1 (= *empleado*) penpusher, pencil pusher (*EEUU*), small-time clerk
2 (*LAm*) (= *abogado*) shyster lawyer*

tintero SM 1 (= *recipiente*) inkpot, ink bottle (*EEUU*), inkwell; ✦**MODISMO dejarse algo en el ~** (= *olvidar*) to forget about sth; (= *no mencionar*) to leave sth unsaid; **no se deja nada en el ~** she leaves nothing unsaid
2 (*LAm*) (= *plumas*) desk set, writing set

tintillo SM (*Cono Sur*) red wine

tintín SM [*de campanilla*] tinkle, tinkling; [*de cadena, llaves*] jingle; [*de copas, tazas*] clink, chink

tintinear ▸conjug 1a◂ VI [*campanilla*] to tinkle; [*cadena, llaves*] to jingle; [*copas, tazas*] to clink, chink

tintineo SM = **tintín**

tinto Ⓐ ADJ 1 [*vino*] red
2 (= *teñido*) dyed; (= *manchado*) stained; **~ en sangre** stained with blood, bloodstained
Ⓑ SM 1 (= *vino*) red wine; **un ~** a (glass of) red wine
2 (*Col*) (= *café*) black coffee

tintorera SF (= *pez*) shark; (*Andes, CAm, Méx*) female shark; *ver tb* **tintorero**

tintorería SF 1 (= *tienda*) dry cleaner's
2 (= *actividad*) dyeing; (= *fábrica*) dyeworks; (= *establecimiento*) dyer's, dyer's shop

tintorero/a SM/F (= *que tiñe*) dyer; (= *que limpia en seco*) dry cleaner; *ver tb* **tintorera**

tintorro* SM plonk*, cheap red wine

tintura SF 1 (= *acto*) dyeing
2 (*Quím*) dye, dyestuff; (*Téc*) stain
3 (*Farm*) tincture ► **tintura de tornasol** litmus ► **tintura de yodo** (tincture of) iodine
4 (= *poquito*) smattering; (= *barniz*) thin veneer

tinturar ▸conjug 1a◂ VT 1 (= *teñir*) to dye
2 (= *instruir*) **~ a algn** to give sb a rudimentary knowledge, teach sb superficially

tiña SF 1 (*Med*) ringworm
2 (= *pobreza*) poverty
3 (= *tacañería*) meanness

tiñoso ADJ 1 (*Med*) scabby, mangy
2 (= *miserable*) poor, wretched
3 (= *tacaño*) mean

tío/a SM/F 1 (= *pariente*) uncle/aunt; **mi ~ Ignacio** my uncle Ignacio; **mis ~s** (= *sólo hombres*) my uncles; (= *hombres y mujeres*) my uncle(s) and aunt(s); **el ~ Sam** Uncle Sam; ✦**MODISMOS ¡no hay tu tía!*** nothing doing!; **¡cuéntaselo a tu tía!*** pull the other one!* ► **tío/a abuelo/a** great-uncle/great-aunt ► **tío/a carnal** blood uncle/aunt

[2] (*) (= *hombre*) guy*, bloke*; (= *mujer*) woman; (= *chica*) girl; **¿quién es ese ~?** who's that guy *o* bloke?*; **los ~s** guys*, blokes*; **las tías** women; **¡qué ~! ¡no ha perdido un solo partido!** the guy's incredible, he hasn't lost a single match!*; **¡qué ~! ¡nunca me deja en paz!** the guy's a real pain, he won't leave me alone!*; ♦*MODISMOS* **es un ~ grande** ◊ **es un ~ con toda la barba** he's a great guy *o* bloke* ► **tío/a bueno/a** hunk*/stunner*; **¡tía buena!** hello gorgeous!*
[3] (††) *title given to older people in traditional rural communities*; **ha muerto el ~ Francisco** old Francisco has died

tiovivo SM roundabout, carousel (*EEUU*), merry-go-round

tipa SF (*Andes, Cono Sur*) large wicker basket; *ver tb* **tipo**

tipazo* SM [1] (= *tipo*) [*de hombre*] build; [*de mujer*] figure; **¡qué ~ tiene Raquel!** what a figure Raquel's got!
[2] (= *hombre*) (*grande*) tall chap*, big guy*; (*arrogante*) arrogant fellow; (*Andes*) (= *importante*) bigwig*

tipear ▸conjug 1a◂ VT, VI (*LAm*) to type

tipejo/a* SM/F (*raro*) oddball*, queer fish*; (*despreciable*) nasty character

tiperrita SF (*Caribe*) typist

tipiadora† SF [1] (= *máquina*) typewriter
[2] (= *persona*) typist

típicamente ADV typically

tipicidad SF genuineness, authenticity

típico ADJ [1] (= *característico*) typical; **es muy ~ de él** it's typical of him; **¡lo ~!** typical!
[2] (= *pintoresco*) full of local colour *o* (*EEUU*) color; (= *tradicional*) traditional; (= *regional*) regional; [*costumbre*] typical; **es la taberna más típica de la ciudad** it's the most picturesque pub in town; **no hay que perderse tan típica fiesta** you shouldn't miss a festivity so full of local colour *o* tradition; **es un traje ~** it is a traditional costume; **baile ~** regional dance, national dance

tipificación SF classification

tipificar ▸conjug 1g◂ VT [1] (= *clasificar*) to class, consider (**como** as)
[2] (= *ser típico de*) to typify, characterize

tipismo SM (= *color*) local colour, local color (*EEUU*); (= *interés folklórico*) picturesqueness; (= *tradicionalismo*) traditionalism; (= *regionalismo*) regional character

tiple Ⓐ SM [1] (*Mús*) (= *persona*) treble, boy soprano
[2] (= *voz*) soprano
Ⓑ SF (*cantante*) soprano

tipo/a Ⓐ SM/F (*) (= *individuo*) (= *hombre*) guy*, bloke*; (= *mujer*) chick*, bird*, dame (*EEUU**); **¿quién es ese ~?** who's that guy *o* bloke?*; **dos ~s sospechosos** two suspicious characters*; *ver tb* **tipa**
Ⓑ SM [1] (= *clase*) type, kind, sort; **un coche de otro ~ pero del mismo precio** a different type *o* kind *o* sort of car but for the same price; **un nuevo ~ de bicicleta** a new type of bicycle; **no me gusta este ~ de fiestas** I don't like this kind of party; **todo ~ de ...** all sorts *o* kinds of ...; **tuvimos todo ~ de problemas** we had all sorts *o* kinds of problems
[2] (*Bot, Literat, Zool*) type
[3] (*Com, Fin*) rate ► **tipo a término** forward rate ► **tipo bancario**, **tipo base** base rate ► **tipo de cambio** exchange rate ► **tipo de descuento** discount rate ► **tipo de interés** interest rate ► **tipo impositivo** tax rate
[4] (= *figura, cuerpo*) [*de hombre*] build; [*de mujer*] figure; **tiene el ~ de su padre** he has his father's build; **tener buen ~** [*hombre*] to be well built; [*mujer*] to have a good figure; **Nuria tiene un ~ horrible** Nuria has a terrible figure; ♦*MODISMOS* **aguantar** *o* **mantener el ~** to keep one's composure; **jugarse el ~** to risk one's neck
[5] (*Tip*) type ► **tipo de letra** typeface ► **tipo gótico** Gothic type ► **tipo menudo** small type
Ⓒ ADJ INV [1] (= *similar a*) **un sombrero ~ Bogart** a Bogart-style hat; **una joven ~ Marilyn** a girl in the Marilyn mould; **una foto ~ carné** a passport-size photo; **un vehículo ~ jeep** a jeep-type vehicle
[2] (= *típico*) average, typical; **dos conductores ~** two average *o* typical drivers; **lengua ~** standard language

tipografía SF [1] (= *arte*) typography
[2] (= *taller*) printing works, printing press

tipográfico ADJ typographical, printing *antes de s*

tipógrafo/a SM/F printer

tipología SF typology

tiposo ADJ (*Andes*) ridiculous, eccentric

típula SF cranefly, daddy-long-legs

tique SM = **tíquet**

tiquear ▸conjug 1a◂ VT (*Cono Sur*) to punch

tíquet ['tike] SM (*pl* **tíquets** ['tike]) (= *billete*) ticket; (= *recibo de compra*) receipt; (*Andes*) (= *etiqueta*) label

tiquismiquis* Ⓐ SMF INV (= *persona*) fusspot*, fussbudget (*EEUU**)
Ⓑ SMPL [1] (= *escrúpulos*) silly scruples; (= *detalles*) fussy details; (= *quejas*) silly *o* trivial objections
[2] (= *cortesías*) affected courtesies, bowing and scraping
[3] (= *riñas*) bickering *sing*, squabbles
[4] (= *molestias*) minor irritations, pinpricks

tiquitique* SM **estar en el ~** to be gossiping

tira[1] Ⓐ SF [1] [*de tela*] strip; [*de zapato*] strap; **cortar algo en ~s** to cut sth into strips ► **tira cómica** comic strip ► **tira de películas** film strip ► **tira publicitaria** flysheet, advertising leaflet
[2] (*) ♦*MODISMO* **la ~*: me gusta la ~** I love it; **ganan la ~** they earn a packet*; **de eso hace la ~** that was ages ago; **la ~ de** loads of*, masses of; **estoy desde hace la ~ de tiempo** I've been here for absolutely ages
Ⓑ SM ► **tira y afloja** (= *negociaciones*) hard bargaining; (= *concesiones*) give and take, mutual concessions *pl*

tira[2] Ⓐ SF (*CAm, Méx**) police, cops* *pl*
Ⓑ SM (*Cono Sur**) (plainclothes) cop*, detective

tirabuzón SM [1] (= *rizo*) curl, ringlet
[2] (= *sacacorchos*) corkscrew; ♦*MODISMO* **sacar algo a algn con ~** to drag sth out of sb
[3] (*Natación*) twist, corkscrew

tirachinas SM INV catapult, slingshot (*EEUU*)

tirada SF [1] [*de dados, dardos*] throw; **en la primera ~ hizo diez puntos** he scored ten points in the first throw; **de una ~** in one go; **leyó la novela de una ~** he read the novel straight through in one go
[2] (= *distancia*) distance; **de aquí a Almería hay una ~ de 18kms** the distance from here to Almería is 18km; **aún nos queda una buena ~** we've still got a long way to go
[3] (*Tip*) (= *acto*) printing; (= *ejemplares impresos*) print run; (= *ejemplares vendidos*) circulation; **han hecho una ~ de 5.000 ejemplares** they have done a print run of 5,000 copies; **la revista tiene una ~ semanal de 200.000 ejemplares** the magazine has a weekly circulation of 200,000 copies ► **tirada aparte** offprint
[4] (= *retahíla*) string
[5] (*Cos*) length
[6] (*LAm*) (= *discurso*) boring speech
[7] (*Cono Sur*) (= *indirecta*) hint
[8] (*Caribe*) (= *mala pasada*) dirty trick

tiradera SF [1] (*CAm, Caribe, Cono Sur*) (= *faja*) sash; (= *correa*) belt, strap; (*Caribe*) [*de caballo*] harness strap, trace
[2] (*Andes, CAm**) (= *mofa*) taunt

tiradero SM (*Méx*) (= *vertedero*) tip, rubbish-dump; (= *suciedad, desorden*) mess; **esta casa es un ~** this house is a tip*

tirado/a Ⓐ ADJ [1] (= *tumbado*) **estar ~** to be lying; **siempre está ~ en el sofá** he's always lying on the sofa; **los juguetes estaban ~s por toda la habitación** the toys were lying *o* strewn all over the room
[2] (*) (= *barato*) **estar ~** to be dirt-cheap*
[3] (*) (= *fácil*) **estar ~** to be dead easy *o* a cinch*; **esa asignatura está tirada** that subject is dead easy*, that subject is a cinch*
[4] (*) **dejar ~ a algn** to leave sb in the lurch; **quedarse ~** to be left in the lurch
[5] (= *embarcación*) rakish
Ⓑ SM/F (*) (= *colgado*) no-hoper*

tirador(a) Ⓐ SM/F (= *persona*) marksman/markswoman, shooter; (*CAm, Méx*) (= *cazador*) hunter; **es un buen ~** he's a good shot ► **tirador(a) apostado/a** sniper ► **tirador(a) certero/a** sharpshooter
Ⓑ SM [1] [*de cajón*] handle; [*de puerta*] knob
[2] [*de campanilla*] bell pull
[3] (= *tirachinas*) catapult, slingshot (*EEUU*)
[4] (*Arte, Téc*) (= *pluma*) drawing pen
[5] (*Andes, Cono Sur*) (= *cinturón*) wide gaucho belt
[6] **tiradores** (*Cono Sur*) (= *tirantes*) braces, suspenders (*EEUU*)

tiragomas SM INV catapult, slingshot (*EEUU*)

tiraje SM [1] (*Tip*) (= *impresión*) printing; (= *cantidad*) print run
[2] (*CAm, Cono Sur, Méx*) [*de chimenea*] chimney flue

tiralevitas SMF INV bootlicker*

tiralíneas SM INV drawing pen, ruling pen

tiranía SF tyranny

tiránicamente ADV tyrannically

tiranicida SMF tyrannicide (*person*)

tiranicidio SM tyrannicide (*act*)

tiránico ADJ (*gen*) tyrannical; [*amor*] possessive, domineering; [*atracción*] irresistible, all-powerful

tiranizar ▸conjug 1f◂ VT (= *oprimir*) to tyrannize; (= *gobernar*) to rule despotically; (= *dominar*) to domineer

tirano/a Ⓐ ADJ (= *tiránico*) tyrannical, despotic; (= *dominante*) domineering
Ⓑ SM/F tyrant, despot
Ⓒ SM (*Méx**) (= *policía*) cop*

tirantas SFPL (*Andes, Méx*) braces, suspenders (*EEUU*)

tirante Ⓐ ADJ 1 [+ *soga*] tight, taut; (= *tensado*) tensed, drawn tight
2 [*relaciones, situación*] (= *tenso*) tense, strained; **estamos algo ~s** things are rather strained between us
3 (*Fin*) tight
Ⓑ SM 1 [*de vestido*] shoulder strap; **tirantes** [*de pantalones*] braces, suspenders (*EEUU*); **vestido sin ~s** strapless dress
2 (*Arquit*) crosspiece, brace; (*Mec*) strut, brace; [*de arreos*] trace

tirantear ▸conjug 1a◂ VT (*CAm, Cono Sur*) to stretch

tirantez SF 1 (*Téc etc*) tightness, tension
2 (*fig*) (= *tensión*) tension, strain; **la ~ de las relaciones con Eslobodia** the strained relations with Slobodia, the tense state of relations with Slobodia; **ha disminuido la ~** the tension has lessened
3 (*Fin*) tightness

tirar

▸conjug 1a◂ | B VERBO INTRANSITIVO
A VERBO TRANSITIVO | C VERBO PRONOMINAL

*Para las expresiones como **tirar de la lengua, tirar de la manta, tirar por la borda, tirar por tierra**, ver la otra entrada.*

Ⓐ VERBO TRANSITIVO

1 *= lanzar* to throw; **tiró un papel por la ventanilla** he threw a piece of paper out of the window; **~ algo a algn** (*para que lo coja*) to throw sth to sb; (*para hacer daño*) to throw sth at sb; **tírame la pelota** throw me the ball; **les tiraban piedras a los soldados** they were throwing stones at the soldiers; **me tiró un beso** she blew me a kiss

2 *= derribar* [+ *edificio*] to pull down; [+ *jarrón, silla, estatua*] to knock over; [+ *pared, verja*] to knock down; **van a ~ la casa** they are going to demolish *o* pull down the house; **la moto la tiró al suelo** the motorbike knocked her over; **el viento ha tirado la valla** the wind has knocked the fence down; **¡abre, o tiro la puerta abajo!** open up, or I'll break the door down!

3 *= dejar caer* to drop; **tropezó y tiró la bandeja** she tripped and dropped the tray; **han tirado muchas bombas en la capital** many bombs have been dropped on the capital

4 *= desechar* to throw away; **no tires las sobras, que se las voy a dar al perro** don't throw away the leftovers, I'll give them to the dog; **tira las sobras a la basura** throw the leftovers in the bin; **no tires el aceite por el sumidero** don't tip *o* pour the oil down the drain; **estos pantalones están para ~los** these trousers have had it, these trousers are about ready for the dustbin; **no hay que ~ la comida** you shouldn't waste food

5 *= malgastar* [+ *dinero*] to waste; [+ *fortuna*] to squander; **has tirado el dinero comprando eso** it was a waste of money buying that, you wasted your money buying that

6 *= disparar* [+ *tiro*] to fire; [+ *flecha*] to shoot; [+ *cohete*] to launch, fire; **el aparato tira el proyectil a 2.000m** the machine throws the projectile 2,000m

7 *+ foto* to take

8 *= dar, pegar* **deja ya de ~ patadas** stop kicking; **la mula le tiró una coz** the mule kicked him *o* gave him a kick; **¡mamá, Carlos me ha tirado un mordisco!** Carlos has bitten me, Mum!

9 *Tip* (= *imprimir*) to print, run off

10 *= trazar* [+ *línea*] to draw, trace

11 **: = suspender* **ya me han vuelto a ~ en química** I've failed chemistry again, I've flunked chemistry again (*esp EEUU**)

12 *Andes: = usar* to use; **~ brazo** to swim

13 *Andes, Caribe, Cono Sur: = acarrear* to cart, haul, transport

14 **~la de**† (= *dárselas de*) to fancy oneself as, pose as

Ⓑ VERBO INTRANSITIVO

1 *haciendo fuerza* 1·1 (= *traer hacia sí*) to pull; **¡tira un poco más fuerte!** pull a bit harder!; **~ de** [+ *soga, cuerda*] to pull; **tire de ese cabo** pull that end; **¡no le tires de la trenza a tu hermana!** don't pull your sister's pigtail!; **~ de la cadena (del wáter)** to flush the toilet, pull the chain; **~ de la manga a algn** to tug at sb's sleeve; **"tirar"** (*Esp*) (*en puerta etc*) "pull"; **"tire"** (*LAm*) (*en puerta etc*) "pull"

1·2 (= *llevar tras sí*) **~ de** to pull; **un burro tiraba de la carreta** a donkey was pulling the cart along, the cart was drawn by a donkey; **los niños tiraban del trineo** the children were pulling the sledge along

2 **: = atraer* **no le tira el estudio** studying does not appeal to him, studying holds no attraction for him; **la patria tira siempre** one's native land always exerts a powerful pull

3 *= estar tirante* [*ropa*] to be tight; **este vestido tira un poco de aquí** this dress is a bit tight here; **me tira de sisa** it's tight round my armpits

4 *= usar* **~ de** [+ *espada, navaja*] to draw; **~on de cuchillos** they drew their knives; **tiramos de diccionario y lo traducimos en un minuto*** if we use a dictionary it will just take a minute to translate

5 *= disparar* to shoot; **¡no tires!** don't shoot!; **~ con bala** to use live ammunition; **~ al blanco** to aim; **~ a matar** to shoot to kill; **los guardas tiraban a matar** the guards were shooting to kill; **mi jefa es de las que tiran a matar** my boss is the sort of person who goes for the kill

6 *Dep* (*con balón*) to shoot; (*con fichas, cartas etc*) to go, play; **¡tira!** shoot!; **tiró fuera de la portería** he shot wide of the goal; **tira tú ahora** it's your go now; **~ a puerta** (*Esp*) to shoot at goal

7 **: = arreglárselas* to get by; **podemos ~ con menos dinero** we can get by on less money; **ir tirando** to get by, manage; **—¿qué tal esa salud? —vamos tirando** "how's your health?" — "we're getting by"

8 *= funcionar* [*motor*] to pull; [*chimenea, puro*] to draw, pull; **el motor no tira** the engine isn't pulling; **esta moto no tira** there's no life in this motorbike

9 *= ir* to go; **tire usted adelante** go straight on; **¡tira de una vez!** get on with it!, go on, then!; **~ a la derecha** to turn right; **~ por una calle** to turn down a street, go off along a street

10 **: = durar* to last; **esos zapatos ~án todavía otro invierno** those shoes will last another winter yet

11 *seguido de preposición*

◆ **tirar a** (= *tender*) **tiene el pelo rubio tirando a rojizo** he has reddish blond hair; **es mediocre tirando a malo** it's middling to bad, it's mediocre verging on bad; **tira más bien a cuidadoso** he's on the careful side; **tira a su padre** he takes after his father

◆ **tirar para** (= *aspirar a ser*) **la pequeña tira para actriz** the little girl has ambitions of becoming an actress; **tira para médico** he's attracted towards a career in medicine

12 **✦MODISMO a todo ~** at the most; **nos queda gasolina para 20km a todo ~** we have only enough petrol for 20kms at the most *o* at the outside; **llegará el martes a todo ~** he'll arrive on Tuesday at the latest

13 *LAm**: sexualmente* to screw**

Ⓒ **tirarse** VERBO PRONOMINAL

1 *= lanzarse* to throw o.s.; **~se al suelo** to throw o.s. to the ground; **~se por una ventana** to jump from *o* out of a window, throw o.s. out of a window; **~se por un precipicio** to throw o.s. over a cliff; **~se al agua** (*gen*) to plunge into the water; (*de cabeza*) to dive *o* plunge into the water; **~se en la cama** to lie down in bed; **~se en paracaídas** to parachute (down); (*en emergencia*) to bale out; **~se sobre algn** to rush at sb, spring on sb

2 **: = pasar* to spend; **se tiró dos horas arreglándolo** he spent two hours fixing it; **me tiré mucho tiempo haciéndolo** I spent a lot of time doing it, it took me a long time to do it

3 *= expeler* **~se un eructo*** to burp*, belch, break wind; **~se un pedo*** to fart*

4 **~se a algn**** (*sexualmente*) to screw sb**, lay sb*

5 **: = irse* **~se a otra parte** to clear off somewhere else*

tirilla SF 1 (= *tira*) band, strip; (*Cos*) neckband
2 (*Cono Sur*) (= *ropa*) shabby dress, ragged garment

tirillas* SMF INV 1 (= *mequetrefe*) unimportant person, nobody; **¡vete, ~!** get along, little man!
2 (= *enclenque*) undersized individual, runt

tirillento ADJ (*LAm*) ragged, shabby

tirita SF 1 (*Med*) (sticking) plaster, Band-Aid® (*EEUU*)
2 (*Cos*) tag, tape (*for name on clothing*)

tiritaña* SF mere trifle

tiritar ▸conjug 1a◂ VI 1 (*de frío, miedo*) to shiver (**de** with)
2 (*) **✦MODISMO dejaron el pastel tiritando** they almost finished the cake off; **esta botella ha quedado tiritando** there isn't much left of this bottle

tiritón SM shiver

tiritona SF shivering (fit)

Tiro SM Tyre

tiro SM 1 (= *disparo*) shot; **oímos un ~** we heard a shot; **resultó herido con un ~ de bala en la pierna** he received a gunshot wound to the leg; **lo mataron de un ~** they shot him dead; **se oyeron varios ~s a lo lejos** gunfire was heard *o* shots were heard in the distance; **a tiros: liarse a ~s con algn** (*lit*) to have a gunfight with sb; (*fig*) to get involved in a slanging match with sb; **tendrán que decidirlo a ~s** they'll have to shoot it out; **ma-**

tar a algn a ~s to shoot sb (dead); **pegar un ~ a algn** to shoot sb; **le pegó un ~ a su amante** she shot her lover; **¡que le peguen cuatro ~s!** he ought to be shot!; **se pegó un ~** he shot himself; ✦*MODISMOS* **a ~ de piedra** a stone's throw away; **a ~ fijo*** for sure; **lo sé a ~ fijo** I know for sure; **esperar a ver por dónde van los ~s** to wait and see which way the wind is blowing; **creían que era un problema de trabajo, pero por ahí no iban los ~s** they thought the problem was work-related, but they were wide of the mark; **ir de ~s largos** to be all dressed up, wear one's Sunday best; **ni a ~s***: **no lo haría ni a ~s** I wouldn't do it for love or money; **salir el ~ por la culata**: **le salió el ~ por la culata** it backfired on him; **sentar como un ~***: **me sienta como un ~** [*obligación*] it's a real pain*; [*ropa, peinado*] it looks really awful *o* terrible on me*; [*comida*] it really doesn't agree with me; **me sentó como un ~ que no viniera a la cita** I was really miffed that she didn't turn up* ► **tiro al blanco** target practice ► **tiro al pichón** clay pigeon shooting ► **tiro al plato** trap shooting, clay pigeon shooting ► **tiro con arco** archery ► **tiro de escopeta** gunshot ► **tiro de gracia** coup de grâce ► **tiro de pichón** clay pigeon shooting; *ver tb* **campo 4, galería 1**

2 (= *alcance*) range; **estar a ~** to be within range; **cuando el jabalí estuvo a ~** once the boar was within range; **tenía varios ejemplares a ~** she had several copies to hand; **si se pone a ~, lo mato** if he comes near me, I'll kill him; **le pide dinero al primero que se le pone a ~** she's always asking the first person who comes along for money; **tener algo a ~** to be within one's reach, have within one's reach; **a ~ de fusil** within shooting distance

3 (*Dep*) (= *lanzamiento*) shot; **parar un ~** to stop a shot ► **tiro a gol** shot at goal ► **tiro de aproximación** (*Golf*) approach shot ► **tiro de revés** backhand (shot) ► **tiro libre** (*en fútbol*) free kick; (*en baloncesto*) free throw

4 [*de animales*] team; **animal de ~** draught animal; **caballo de ~** carthorse

5 [*de pantalón*] *distance between crotch and waist*; **el pantalón me va corto de ~** the trousers are too tight around my crotch

6 (*Arquit*) (*en escalera*) flight of stairs; [*de chimenea*] draught, draft (*EEUU*)

7 (*Min*) (= *pozo*) shaft ► **tiro de mina** mineshaft

8 (*para tirar*) (= *cuerda*) rope, cord; (= *cadena*) chain; [*de timbre*] bellpull; [*de arreos*] brace, strap

9 **tiros** (*Mil*) swordbelt *pl*; (*Cono Sur*) braces, suspenders (*EEUU*)

10 (*Méx**) (= *éxito*) hit*, success

11 (*LAm*) (*otras locuciones*) **a ~ de hacer algo** about to do sth, on the point of doing sth; ✦*MODISMOS* **al ~** (*esp Chile**) at once, right away; **de a ~** completely; **del ~** consequently; **hacer algo de un ~** to do sth in one go

12 (*Andes, Cono Sur, Méx*) (= *canica*) marble

13 (*Cono Sur*) (*en carreras*) distance, course

14 (*Méx*) (= *ejemplar*) issue; (= *edición*) edition

15 (*Cono Sur*) (= *indirecta*) hint

16 (*Caribe*) (= *astucia*) craftiness, cunning

tiroideo ADJ thyroid

tiroides Ⓐ ADJ INV thyroid

Ⓑ SM INV (*a veces* SF) thyroid (gland)

Tirol SM **El ~** the Tyrol

tirolés/esa ADJ, SM/F Tyrolean

tirón[1] SM 1 (= *acción*) pull, tug; **dar un ~ a algo** to give sth a pull *o* tug, pull *o* tug at sth; **me dio un ~ del jersey** she pulled *o* tugged at my jumper; **le dio un ~ de pelo** she pulled his hair; **dar un ~ de orejas a algn** (*lit*) to pull *o* tug sb's ear; (*fig*) to tell sb off; **me lo arrancó de un ~** she suddenly jerked it away from me; ✦*MODISMO* **aguantar el ~** to ride out *o* weather the storm

2 (*en músculo, tendón*) **sufrió un ~ en la pantorrilla** he pulled a calf muscle ► **tirón muscular** pulled muscle

3 (= *robo*) bag-snatching; **el ~ es el delito más común** bag-snatching is the most common crime; **intentó darle el ~** he tried to snatch her bag

4 (*de un coche, motor*) sudden jerk, sudden jolt

5 ✦*MODISMO* **de un ~**: **leyó la novela de un ~** he read the novel straight through in one go; **se lo bebió de un ~** he drank it down in one go; **trabajan diez horas de un ~** they work ten hours at a stretch; **he dormido toda la noche de un ~** I slept right through the night

tirón[2] SM (= *persona*) tyro, novice

tironear ▸conjug 1a◂ VT (*esp LAm*) = **tirar B1.1**

tironero SM/F, **tironista** SMF bag-snatcher

tirotear ▸conjug 1a◂ Ⓐ VT (= *disparar*) to shoot at, fire on; (= *matar*) to shoot, shoot down

Ⓑ **tirotearse** VPR to exchange shots

tiroteo SM (= *tiros*) shooting, exchange of shots; (= *escaramuza*) skirmish; (= *batalla*) gunfight; (*con policía*) shoot-out ► **tiroteo cruzado** crossfire

Tirreno ADJ **Mar ~** Tyrrhenian Sea

tirria* SF dislike; **tener ~ a algn** to dislike sb, have a grudge against sb

tisaje SM weaving

tisana SF tisane, herbal tea

tísico/a Ⓐ ADJ consumptive, tubercular

Ⓑ SM/F consumptive

tisiquento ADJ (*Cono Sur*), **tisiquiento** ADJ (*Cono Sur Med*) consumptive; (*de aspecto*) pale and thin

tisis SF INV consumption, tuberculosis

tisú SM (*pl* **tisús**) (= *tela*) lamé; (= *pañuelo*) tissue

tisular ADJ tissue *antes de s*

tít. ABR = **título**

Titán SM Titan

titán SM titan, giant; **una tarea de titanes** a titanic task; **un combate de titanes** a titanic struggle

titánico ADJ titanic

titanio SM titanium

titeador* ADJ (*Andes, Cono Sur*) mocking, derisive

titear* ▸conjug 1a◂ VT (*Andes, Cono Sur*) to mock, scoff at, to make fun of

titeo* SM (*Andes, Cono Sur*) mockery, scoffing; **tomar a algn para el ~** to scoff at sb, make fun of sb

títere Ⓐ SM 1 (= *marioneta*) puppet; ✦*MODISMO* **no dejar ~ con cabeza** (= *cambiar*) to turn everything upside down; (= *romper*) to break up everything in sight; (= *criticar*) to spare no one

2 **títeres** (= *espectáculo*) puppet show *sing*; (= *arte*) puppetry *sing*

3 (= *persona*) puppet, tool

Ⓑ ADJ INV **gobierno ~** puppet government

titi* SF bird*, chick*

tití SM (*LAm*) capuchin (monkey)

titilante ADJ twinkling

titilar ▸conjug 1a◂ VI [*luz, estrella*] to twinkle; [*párpado*] to flutter, tremble

titipuchal* SM (*Méx*) (noisy) crowd

titiritaña SF (*Méx*) 1 (= *espectáculo*) puppet show

2 (= *cosa insignificante*) piece of trivia; **de ~** sickly

titiritero/a SM/F 1 (= *que maneja marionetas*) puppeteer

2 (= *acróbata*) acrobat; (= *malabarista*) juggler; (= *artista de circo*) circus artist

tito/a* SM/F uncle/auntie*

Tito Livio SM Livy

titubeante ADJ 1 (= *que duda*) hesitant

2 (= *que balbucea*) stuttering

3 [*discurso, voz*] halting

titubear ▸conjug 1a◂ VI 1 (= *vacilar*) to hesitate, vacillate; **no ~ en hacer algo** not to hesitate to do sth; **respondió sin ~** he answered without hesitation

2 (= *balbucear*) to stutter

titubeo SM 1 (= *vacilación*) hesitation, vacillation; **proceder sin ~s** to act without hesitation, act resolutely

2 (= *balbuceo*) stuttering

▼ **titulación** SF (*Univ*) degrees and diplomas *pl*; **"se necesita ~ universitaria"** "university degree required"

titulado/a Ⓐ ADJ 1 [*libro*] entitled; **una obra titulada "Sotileza"** a book entitled "Sotileza"

2 [*persona*] with a degree, qualified; **~ en ingeniería** with a degree in engineering

Ⓑ SM/F graduate

titular Ⓐ ADJ **jugador ~** regular first-team player; **juez ~** *judge assigned to a particular court*; **médico ~** *doctor assigned to a particular post in the public health care system*; **profesor ~** *teacher assigned to a particular post in the state education system*

Ⓑ SMF 1 [*de puesto*] holder, incumbent; (*Rel*) incumbent

2 [*de cuenta, pasaporte*] holder; [*de coche, vivienda*] owner

3 (*Dep*) regular first-team player; (*LAm*) captain

Ⓒ SM (*Prensa*) headline; **los ~es** (*Radio, TV*) the (news) headlines

Ⓓ VT ▸conjug 1a◂ [+ *libro, película*] to title, entitle; **tituló la obra "Fiesta"** he (en)titled the play "Fiesta"; **¿cómo vas a ~ el trabajo?** what title are you going to give the essay?

Ⓔ **titularse** VPR 1 [*novela, poema*] **¿cómo se titula la película?** what's the title of the film?, what's the film called?; **la película se titula "Texas"** the film is called "Texas", the title of the film is "Texas"

2 (*Univ*) to graduate; **~se en algo** to graduate in sth

titularidad SF 1 (= *propiedad*) ownership; **empresa de ~ pública** publicly-owned company

➤ LENGUA Y USO: **titulación** 42.4

[2] (*de un cargo*) tenure; **durante la ~ de Bush** during Bush's period of office
[3] (*Dep*) first place, first-team place, top spot

titulillo SM (*Tip*) running title, page heading; (*Prensa*) subhead, section heading; ✦**MODISMO andar en ~s*** to watch out for every little thing

titulitis SF INV (*hum*) (*en una empresa etc*) *mania for employing graduate personnel*; (*en un estudiante*) *obsession with acquiring an academic degree*

titulización SF (*Fin*) securitization

titulizar ▸conjug 1f◂ VT (*Fin*) to securitize

título SM [1] [*de libro, película*] title; (*en periódico*) headline; (*Jur*) heading
[2] [*de campeón*] title
[3] (*Educ*) (= *diploma*) certificate; (= *licenciatura*) degree; (= *calificación*) qualification; (*Caribe Aut*) driving licence, driver's license (*EEUU*); **maestro sin ~** unqualified teacher; **títulos** qualifications; **tener los ~s para un puesto** to have the qualifications for a job ► **título universitario** university degree
[4] (= *dignidad*) title; (= *persona*) titled person; **casarse con un ~** to marry into the nobility, marry a titled person ► **título de nobleza** title of nobility
[5] (= *cualidad*) quality; **no es precisamente un ~ de gloria para él** it is not exactly a quality on which he can pride himself; **tiene varios ~s honrosos** he has several noble qualities, he has a number of worthy attributes
[6] (*en presupuesto*) item
[7] **a ~ de** (= *a modo de*) by way of; (= *en calidad de*) in the capacity of; **a ~ de ejemplo, ...** by way of example, ..., for example, ...; **el dinero fue a ~ de préstamo** the money was by way of (being) a loan; **a ~ de curiosidad** as a matter of interest; **ya ha comenzado a funcionar a ~ experimental** it is already being used on an experimental basis; **a ~ particular** *o* **personal** in a personal capacity, in an unofficial capacity; **a ~ póstumo** posthumously
[8] [*de bienes*] title ► **título de propiedad** title deed
[9] (*Fin*) (= *bono*) bond ► **título al portador** bearer bond ► **título de renta fija** fixed interest security ► **título de renta variable** variable yield security
[10] (= *derecho*) right; **con justo ~** rightly; **tener ~ de hacer algo** to be entitled to do sth

tiza SF (*para escribir, de billar*) chalk; **una ~** a piece of chalk

tizar ▸conjug 1f◂ VT [1] (*Cono Sur*) (= *planear*) to plan; (= *diseñar*) to design, model
[2] (*Andes*) [+ *traje*] to mark out for cutting

tizate SM (*CAm, Méx*) chalk

Tiziano SM Titian

tizna SF black, grime

tiznado/a‡ SM/F (*CAm, Méx*) bastard‡, son of a bitch (*EEUU*‡)

tiznajo* SM = **tiznón**

tiznar ▸conjug 1a◂ Ⓐ VT [1] (= *ennegrecer*) to blacken, black; (= *manchar*) to smudge, stain (**de** with)
[2] [+ *reputación*] to stain, tarnish; [+ *nombre, carácter*] to defame, blacken
Ⓑ **tiznarse** VPR [1] **~se la cara con hollín** to blacken one's face with soot
[2] (= *mancharse*) to get smudged, get soiled
[3] (*CAm, Cono Sur, Méx**) (= *emborracharse*) to get drunk

tizne SM (= *hollín*) soot; (= *mancha*) smut

tiznón SM [*de hollín*] speck of soot, smut; (= *mancha*) smudge

tizo SM firebrand

tizón SM [1] (= *madera*) firebrand; ✦**MODISMO negro como un ~** as black as coal
[2] (*Bot*) smut
[3] (= *deshonra*) stain, blemish

tizonazos SMPL pains of hell

tizonear ▸conjug 1a◂ VT [+ *fuego*] to poke, stir

tizos‡ SMPL dabs‡, fingers

tlacanear* ▸conjug 1a◂ VT (*Méx*) to feel up‡

tlachique SM (*Méx*) unfermented pulque

tlacote SM (*Méx*) growth, tumour, tumor (*EEUU*)

tlacual‡ SM (*Méx*) [1] (= *alimentos*) food; (= *comida, cena*) meal
[2] (= *olla*) cooking pot

tlapalería SF (*Méx*) (= *ferretería*) ironmonger's (shop), hardware store; (= *papelería*) stationer's

tlapiloya‡ SF (*Méx*) clink‡, jail

tlapisquera SF (*Méx*) shed, barn, granary

tlascal SM (*Méx*) tortilla

TLC SM ABR (= **Tratado de Libre Comercio**) NAFTA

tlecuil SM (*Méx*) brazier

Tm ABR, **tm** ABR (= **tonelada(s) métrica(s)**) tonne

TNT SM ABR (= **trinitrotolueno**) TNT

toa SF (*LAm*) hawser, rope, towrope

toalla SF towel; ✦**MODISMO arrojar** *o* **tirar la ~** to throw in the towel ► **toalla de baño** bath towel ► **toalla de mano** hand towel ► **toalla de playa** beach towel ► **toalla de rodillo** roller towel ► **toalla playera** beach towel

toallero SM towel rail

toba‡ SF [1] (= *colilla*) dog-end‡
[2] (= *puñetazo*) punch, bash*

tobar ▸conjug 1a◂ VT (*Andes*) to tow

tobera SF nozzle

tobillera SF [1] (*para tobillo*) ankle support
[2] (*) (= *chica*) teenager, bobbysoxer (*EEUU**)

tobillero Ⓐ ADJ [*falda*] ankle-length
Ⓑ SM (= *calcetín*) ankle-sock; (*Dep*) ankle-guard

tobillo SM ankle

tobo SM (*Caribe*) bucket

tobogán SM [1] (*en parque*) slide; (*en piscina*) chute, slide ► **tobogán acuático** water slide
[2] (*para nieve*) toboggan, sledge, sled (*EEUU*)
[3] [*de feria*] switchback ► **tobogán gigante** roller coaster

toc ADV **¡toc, toc!** (*en puerta*) rat-a-tat!, knock, knock!

toca[1] SF [1] [*de monja*] cornet, wimple
[2] (*Hist*) (= *tocado*) headdress; (= *sombrero sin ala*) toque; (= *gorrito*) bonnet ► **tocas de viuda** widow's weeds

toca[2] SMF (*LAm*) = **tocayo**

tocadiscos SM INV record player, phonograph (*EEUU*)

tocado[1] ADJ [1] [*fruta*] bad, rotten; [*carne etc*] tainted, bad; **estar ~** (*Dep*) to be injured; ✦**MODISMO estar ~ de la cabeza** to be weak in the head
[2] **una creencia tocada de heterodoxia** a somewhat unorthodox belief

tocado[2] Ⓐ ADJ **~ con un sombrero** wearing a hat
Ⓑ SM [1] (= *prenda*) headdress
[2] (= *peinado*) coiffure, hairdo
[3] (= *arreglo*) toilet, washroom (*EEUU*)

tocador[1] SM [1] (= *mueble*) dressing table; **jabón de ~** toilet soap; **juego de ~** toilet set
[2] (= *cuarto*) boudoir, dressing room ► **tocador de señoras** ladies' room
[3] (= *neceser*) toilet bag

tocador[2]**(a)** SM/F (*Mús*) player

tocadorista SMF dresser

tocamientos SMPL (sexual) molestation *sing*

tocante ADJ **~ a** regarding, with regard to, about; **en lo ~ a** so far as ... is concerned, as regards

tocar[1] ▸conjug 1g◂ Ⓐ VT [1] (*gen*) to touch; (*para examinar*) to feel; **si lo tocas te vas a quemar** if you touch it you'll burn yourself; **¡no me toques!** don't touch me!; **que nadie toque mis papeles** don't let anyone touch my papers; **no toques el dinero como no sea para una emergencia** don't touch the money unless it's an emergency; **tócalo, verás qué suave** feel it and see how soft it is; **tócale la frente, la tiene muy caliente** feel his forehead, it's very hot; **no toques la mercancía sin guantes** don't handle the goods without gloves; **el delantero tocó la pelota con la mano** the forward handled (the ball); ✦**MODISMO ~ madera** to touch wood, knock on wood (*EEUU*)
[2] (= *estar en contacto con*) to touch; **la mesa está tocando la pared** the table is touching the wall; **ponte ahí, tocando la pared** stand up against the wall over there; **~ tierra** to touch down, land
[3] (= *hacer sonar*) [+ *piano, violín, trompeta*] to play; [+ *campana, timbre*] to ring; [+ *tambor*] to beat; [+ *silbato*] to blow; [+ *disco*] to play; **el reloj de la iglesia ha tocado las diez** the church clock has just struck ten; **~ la bocina** *o* **el claxon** to hoot *o* sound one's horn; **~ la generala** (*Mil*) to sound the call to arms; **~ la retirada** to sound the retreat
[4] [+ *tema*] to refer to, touch on; **no tocó para nada esa cuestión** he didn't refer to *o* touch on that matter at all; **prefiero no ~ lo relacionado con el trabajo** I'd prefer not to talk about work
[5] (= *afectar*) to concern; **esa cuestión me toca de cerca** that issue closely concerns me; **por lo que a mí me toca** so far as I am concerned
[6] (= *estar emparentado con*) to be related to; **a mí Juan no me toca nada** Juan is not related to me in any way
[7] (= *conmover*) to touch; **las imágenes me ~on en lo más profundo** the pictures moved *o* touched me deeply; **el poema nos tocó el corazón** the poem touched our hearts; **me has tocado el amor propio** you've wounded my pride
[8] (*Dep*) to hit; **el balón tocó el palo** the ball hit the post
[9] (*Náut*) **hacía varios días que no tocábamos puerto** it was several days since we had called at *o* put in at a port; **en este crucero ~emos el puerto de Génova** on this cruise we will call *o* stop at Genoa

[10] (*Caza*) to hit
[11] (*Arte*) to touch up
Ⓑ VI [1] (*Mús*) to play; **toca en un grupo de rock** he's in *o* he plays in a rock group
[2] (= *sonar*) **en cuanto toque el timbre** when the bell rings; **tocan a misa** they are ringing the bell for mass; **~ a muerto** to toll the death knell
[3] (= *llamar*) **~ a una puerta** to knock on *o* at a door
[4] (= *corresponder*) **no toca hacerlo hasta el mes que viene** it's not due to be done until next month; **ahora toca torcer a la derecha** now you have to turn right; **~ a algn: les tocó un dólar a cada uno** they got a dollar each; **¿les ~á algo de herencia?** will they get anything under the will?; **me ha tocado el peor asiento** I ended up with *o* got the worst seat; **le tocó la lotería** he won the lottery; **¿a quién le toca?** whose turn is it?; **~ a algn hacer algo: te toca jugar** it's your turn (to play), it's your go; **nos toca pagar a nosotros** it's our turn to pay; **siempre me toca fregar a mí** I'm always the one who has to do the dishes; **a usted le toca reprenderle si lo cree conveniente** it is up to you to reprimand him if you see fit; ✦***MODISMO* ¡a pagar tocan!** it's time to pay up!
[5] (= *rayar*) **~ en algo** to border on sth, verge on sth; **esto toca en lo absurdo** this borders *o* verges on the ridiculous; **su conducta toca en locura** his behaviour borders *o* verges on madness
[6] (= *chocar*) **~ con algo** to touch sth
[7] **~ a su fin** to be drawing to a close; **el verano tocaba a su fin** summer was drawing to a close
Ⓒ **tocarse** VPR [1] (*uso reflexivo*) **no te toques los granos** don't pick your spots; **está todo el día tocándose la barba** he's always playing with his beard; **tocársela** (*Esp***) (= *masturbarse*) to jerk off**; (*fig*) to do bugger-all**; **está todo el día tocándosela** he does bugger-all all day**; ✦***MODISMO* tocárselas*** to beat it*
[2] (*uso recíproco*) to touch; **los cables no deben ~se** the wires should not be touching
[3] (*LAm**) (= *drogarse*) to be a junkie*

tocar² ▸conjug 1g◂ Ⓐ VT [+ *pelo*] to do, arrange, set
Ⓑ **tocarse** VPR to cover one's head, put on one's hat

tocata¹* SM record player, phonograph (*EEUU*)

tocata² SF (*Mús*) toccata

tocateja: **a ~*** ADV on the nail*

tocayo/a SM/F [1] namesake; **es mi ~** he's my namesake; **somos ~s** we have the same name
[2] (= *amigo*) friend

toche SM (*Méx*) hare

tochimbo SM (*Andes*) smelting furnace

tocho* SM big fat book, tome

tocineta SF (*Col*) bacon

tocinillo SM ► **tocinillo de cielo** *pudding made with egg yolk and syrup*

tocino SM [1] (= *grasa*) salted fresh lard; (*con vetas de carne*) salt pork; [*de panceta*] bacon ► **tocino entreverado, tocino veteado** streaky bacon
[2] ► **tocino de cielo** = **tocinillo de cielo**; *ver* **tocinillo**

toco¹/a SM/F (*CAm*) = **tocayo**

toco² SM (*Caribe*) = **tocón¹**

toco³* SM **costó un ~** (*Cono Sur*) it cost a hell of a lot*

tocoginecología SF obstetrics *sing*

tocoginecólogo/a SM/F obstetrician

tocología SF obstetrics *sing*

tocólogo/a SM/F obstetrician

tocolotear ▸conjug 1a◂ VI (*Caribe*) to shuffle (the cards)

TODAVÍA

Todavía se traduce principalmente al inglés por **still** o **yet**.

- Se traduce por **still** cuando nos referimos a una situación o acción que comenzó en el pasado y que todavía continúa. Generalmente **still** se coloca detrás de los verbos auxiliares o modales y delante de los demás verbos:

  Todavía tienen hambre
  They are still hungry
  Todavía toco el piano
  I still play the piano
  ¿Puedes verlos todavía?
  Can you still see them?

- También se puede traducir **todavía** por **still** para expresar insatisfacción o sorpresa en oraciones negativas. En este caso, **still** se coloca detrás del sujeto:

  Todavía no sé cómo ayudarle
  I still don't know how to help him
  Después de veinte años todavía no puede olvidarlo
  After twenty years she still can't forget him

- Se traduce generalmente por **yet** en frases negativas e interrogativas cuando nos referimos a una situación o acción que no ha tenido lugar todavía y que esperamos que ocurra. **Yet** va al final de la frase, aunque a veces puede ponerse delante del verbo principal en frases negativas:

  El doctor no ha llegado todavía
  The doctor hasn't arrived yet** o **hasn't yet arrived
  ¿Todavía no han llamado?
  Haven't they phoned yet?

NOTA: En lenguaje formal, se puede traducir **todavía** por **yet** en frases afirmativas para expresar que algo no se ha realizado. Para ello utilizamos la estructura **to have yet** + INFINITIVO *con* **to**:

  Todavía tienen que comunicarnos los resultados
  They have yet to tell us the results

- En oraciones comparativas **todavía** se traduce por **even**:

  Su prima es todavía más alta que ella
  Her cousin is even taller than she is

NOTA: El adverbio **aún** sigue las mismas pautas que **todavía**:

  Aún no sé cómo decírselo
  I still don't know how to tell him
  ¿Aún no has hablado con ella?
  Haven't you talked to her yet?
  Aún está trabajando para esa compañía de seguros
  She's still working for that insurance company
  Este pastel está aún mejor que el de la semana pasada
  This cake is even better than last week's

Para otros usos y ejemplos ver la entrada.

tocomocho* SM **el timo del ~** *confidence trick involving the sale of a worthless lottery ticket*

tocón¹ SM (*Bot*) stump

tocón²/ona* SM/F groper*; **es un ~** he's got wandering hands*

tocón³ ADJ (*Andes*) (= *sin rabo*) tailless; (*Caribe*) (= *sin cuernos*) hornless

tocuyo SM (*Andes, Cono Sur*) coarse cotton cloth

todavía ADV [1] (*temporal*) (*en oraciones afirmativas*) still; (*en oraciones negativas*) yet, still; **está nevando ~** it is still snowing; — **¿has acabado? —todavía no** "have you finished" — "not yet"; **~ no se ha ido** she hasn't gone yet, she still hasn't gone; **~ en 1970** as late as 1970
[2] (= *incluso, aun así*) even; **es ~ más inteligente que su hermano** he's even more intelligent than his brother, he's more intelligent still than his brother
[3] (*) (= *encima*) **has aprobado sin estudiar y ~ te quejas** you passed without doing any work and (yet) you're still complaining

toditito* ADJ (*LAm*), **todito** ADJ (absolutely) all

todo Ⓐ ADJ [1] (*en singular*) (= *en su totalidad*) all; **no han llamado en ~ el día** they haven't phoned all day; **no he dormido en toda la noche** I haven't slept all night; **lo golpeó con toda su fuerza** he hit him with all his might; **ha viajado por ~ el mundo** he has travelled throughout *o* all over the world; **lo sabe ~ Madrid** all Madrid knows it; **en toda España no hay más que cinco** there are only five in the whole of Spain; **recorrimos ~ el bosque** we searched the whole forest; **vino ~ el equipo** the whole team came; **el universo ~** the whole universe; **he limpiado toda la casa** I've cleaned the whole house; **puso una alfombra a ~ lo ancho de la habitación** she put a rug down right across the room; **en toda España no lo encuentras** you won't find it anywhere in Spain; **~ lo que usted necesite** everything *o* whatever you need; **con ~ lo listo que es, no es capaz de resolver esto** clever as he is *o* for all his intelligence, he can't solve this problem; **~ lo demás** all the rest; **a** *o* **con toda prisa** in all haste, with all speed; **a toda velocidad** at full speed; ✦***MODISMOS* a ~ esto** (= *entretanto*) meanwhile; (= *a propósito*) by the way; **a ~ esto, la orquesta siguió tocando** meanwhile, the band kept on playing; **a ~ esto, ¿os apetece ir al cine?** by the way, would you like to go to the cinema?; **a ~ esto, no nos olvidemos de llamarla** while we're on the subject, we mustn't forget to phone her; **¡toda la vida!** (*LAm**) yes, indeed!; *ver tb* **cuanto B1**, **mundo 1, 2, 6**
[2] (*en plural*) [2·1] (*en un conjunto*) all; **~s los libros** all the books; **~s vosotros** all of you
[2·2] (= *cada*) every; **~s los días** every day; **nos vemos todas las semanas** we see each other every week; **pararon a ~s los coches que pasaban** they stopped every car that went by; **habrá un turno para ~s y cada uno de los participantes** each and every one of the participants will have their turn; *ver tb* **forma 2**
[3] (*con valor enfático*) **es ~ un hombre** he's every inch a man, he's a real man; **es ~ un héroe** he's a real hero; **ese hombre es ~ ambición** that man is all ambition; **tiene toda la nariz de su abuela** her nose is exactly like her grandmother's; **el niño era ~ ojos** the

child was all eyes; **soy ~ oídos** I'm all ears; **puede ser ~ lo sencillo que usted quiera** it can be as simple as you wish; **dio un portazo por toda respuesta** his only response was to slam the door; **~ lo contrario** quite the opposite; *ver tb* **más A2.4**
[4] (= *del todo*) **lleva una falda toda rota** she's wearing a skirt that's all torn; **estaba ~ rendido** he was completely worn out; **vaya ~ seguido** go straight on *o* ahead
Ⓑ PRON [1] *(en singular)* **se lo comió ~** he ate it all; **cree que lo sabe ~** she thinks she knows it all; **lo han vendido ~** they've sold the lot, they've sold it all; **se enfada por ~** she gets angry about everything; **lo sabemos ~** we know everything; **~ cabe en él** he is capable of anything; **~ o nada** all or nothing; **~ son reveses** it's one setback after another; **y luego ~ son sonrisas** and then it's all smiles; **~ el que quiera ...** everyone *o* anyone who wants to ... ► **todo a cien** ≈ pound store, ≈ dollar store (EEUU), *shop selling everyday items at low prices*
[2] (*en plural*) (= *cosas*) all (of them); (= *personas*) everybody, everyone; **~s son caros** they're all expensive; **el más bonito de ~s** the prettiest of all; **~s estaban de acuerdo** everybody *o* everyone agreed; **~s los que quieran venir** all those who want to come, anyone who wants to come
[3] *(locuciones con preposición)* **ir a ~** to be prepared to do or die; **ante ~** first of all, in the first place; **con ~: con ~ y** in spite of; **el coche, con ~ y ser nuevo ...** the car, in spite of being new ..., despite the fact that the car was new ...; **con ~ (y con eso)** still, nevertheless; **con ~ y con eso llegamos una hora tarde** we still arrived an hour late, nevertheless we arrived an hour late; **de ~: lo llamaron de ~** they called him every name under the sun; **nos pasó de ~** everything possible happened to us, you name it, it happened to us; **del ~** wholly, entirely; **no es del ~ malo** it is not wholly *o* all bad; **no es del ~ verdad** it is not entirely true; **después de ~** after all; ✦*MODISMOS* **estar en ~** to be on the ball*; **de todas todas: ¡te digo que sí de todas todas!** I tell you it jolly well is!; **es verdad de todas todas** it's absolutely true; **ir a por todas** to give it one's all
Ⓒ SM **el ~** the whole; **como** *o* **en un ~** as a whole; ✦*MODISMO* **ser el ~*** to run the show; *ver tb* **jugar C1, C3.1**

todopoderoso Ⓐ ADJ almighty, all-powerful; **Dios Todopoderoso** Almighty God
Ⓑ SM **el Todopoderoso** the Almighty

todoterreno Ⓐ SM INV (*tb* **coche ~, vehículo ~**) four-wheel drive vehicle, all-terrain vehicle, SUV (*esp* EEUU)
Ⓑ ADJ INV [1] [*objeto, máquina*] (= *versátil*) multi-purpose; (= *adaptable*) adaptable
[2] [*persona*] versatile

tofo SM (*Cono Sur*) white clay

toga SF (*Hist*) toga; (*Jur*) robe, gown; (*Univ*) gown; **tomar la ~** to qualify as a lawyer

togado/a SM/F lawyer, attorney(-at-law) (EEUU)

Togo SM Togo

Togolandia SF Togoland

togolés/esa ADJ, SM/F Togolese

toilette [tua'le] SF (*Cono Sur*) toilet, lavatory, washroom (EEUU)

toisón SM (*tb* **~ de oro**) Golden Fleece

tojo[1] SM (*Bot*) gorse, furze

tojo[2] ADJ (*Andes*) (= *gemelo*) twin

Tokio SM Tokyo

> **TODO**
>
> • Para traducir el adjetivo **todo** con el sentido de **en su totalidad** se usa **all**, seguido del sustantivo en singular y sin determinante:
>
> Se pasó toda la tarde viendo la tele
> ***He spent all afternoon watching TV***
>
> • Con el mismo sentido anterior, también se puede traducir por **whole** o **entire**, éste último es más enfático. En este caso, el indefinido tiene que ir acompañado de un sustantivo contable en singular y precedido por un determinante:
>
> Se pasó toda la tarde viendo la tele
> ***He spent the whole** o **the entire afternoon watching TV***
>
> • **Todos** se traduce por **every** cuando se hace hincapié en todos y cada uno de los individuos de un grupo de personas o cosas y también cuando se habla de acciones repetidas:
>
> Todos los niños deben llevar el uniforme del colegio
> ***Every child must wear school uniform***
> Salimos a cenar todos los viernes
> ***We go out for dinner every Friday***
>
> **NOTA:** El sustantivo que sigue a **every** va en singular y nunca lleva determinante. El verbo va también en singular.
>
> • Cuando **todos** se emplea para generalizar, se traduce por **all**. En este caso el sustantivo que sigue a **all** no lleva determinante:
>
> Todos los alemanes saben hablar inglés
> ***All Germans can speak English***
>
> • **Todos** también se traduce por **all** para referirse al conjunto de individuos de un grupo pero, a diferencia de **every**, sin dar importancia a los elementos. En este caso el sustantivo lleva determinante y va en plural, como el verbo:
>
> Todos los libros de la biblioteca eran antiguos
> ***All the books in the library were old***
>
> *Para otros usos y ejemplos ver la entrada.*

tol SM (*CAm*) gourd, squash (EEUU)

tolda SF [1] (*LAm*) (= *tela*) canvas
[2] (*LAm*) (= *tienda de campaña*) tent; (= *refugio*) shelter; [*de barco*] awning
[3] (*Caribe*) (= *bolsa grande*) large sack
[4] (*Caribe*) (= *cielo nublado*) overcast sky
[5] (*Caribe Pol*) **es de la ~ Acción Democrática** he belongs to Acción Democrática

toldería SF (*Andes, Cono Sur*) Indian village, camp of Indian huts

toldillo SM (*Andes, Caribe*) mosquito net

toldo SM [1] (*en tienda, balcón*) awning; (*en la playa*) sunshade; (*para fiesta*) marquee, garden tent (EEUU); (*para tapar*) tarpaulin
[2] (*Méx Aut*) hood, top (EEUU)
[3] (*Andes, Cono Sur*) (= *choza*) Indian hut; (*Méx*) (= *tienda*) tent
[4] (*Andes, Caribe*) (= *mosquitera*) mosquito net

tole[1]* SM [1] (= *disturbio*) commotion, uproar; (= *protesta*) outcry; **levantar el ~** to kick up a fuss; **venir a algn con el ~** to pester *o* badger sb about sth, go on at sb about sth
[2] (= *chismes*) gossip, rumours *pl*
[3] ✦*MODISMO* **coger** *o* **tomar el ~** (= *irse*) to get out, pack up and go

tole[2] SM (*Andes*) track, trail

toledano/a Ⓐ ADJ Toledan, of/from Toledo; *ver tb* **noche 1**
Ⓑ SM/F Toledan, native/inhabitant of Toledo; **los ~s** the people of Toledo, the Toledans

tolempo SM (*Andes*) = **lempo**

tolerable ADJ tolerable

tolerado ADJ tolerated; **película tolerada (para menores)** a film suitable for children

tolerancia SF [1] (= *respeto*) tolerance; [*de ideas*] toleration ► **tolerancia cero** zero tolerance
[2] (*Med, Téc*) tolerance

tolerante ADJ tolerant

tolerantismo SM religious toleration

tolerar ▸conjug 1a◂ VT [1] (= *consentir*) to tolerate; **no se puede ~ esto** this cannot be tolerated; **no tolera que digan eso** he won't allow them to say that; **su madre le tolera demasiado** his mother lets him get away with too much
[2] (= *aguantar*) to bear, put up with; **su estómago no tolera los huevos** eggs don't agree with him; **el cosmonauta toleró muy bien esta situación difícil** the cosmonaut stood up very well to this awkward situation; **el puente no tolera el peso de los tanques** the bridge will not support the weight of the tanks
[3] (*Med, Téc*) to tolerate

tolete SM [1] (*Náut*) tholepin
[2] (*LAm*) (= *palo*) short club, stick, cudgel
[3] (*Andes, Caribe*) (= *pedazo*) piece, bit
[4] (*Andes*) (= *balsa*) raft

toletole SM [1] (*Andes, Cono Sur*) (= *alboroto*) row, uproar
[2] (*Andes*) (= *terquedad*) obstinacy
[3] (*Caribe**) (= *vida alegre*) high life; (= *vagabundeo*) roving life
[4] (= *chismes*) gossip, rumours *pl*

tolla SF [1] (= *pantano*) marsh, quagmire
[2] (*Caribe, Méx*) (= *abrevadero*) drinking trough

tollina* SF hiding*

Tolomeo SM Ptolemy

Tolón SM Toulon

toloncho SM (*Andes*) piece of wood

tolondro Ⓐ ADJ scatterbrained
Ⓑ SM (*Med*) (= *chichón*) bump, swelling

tolondrón ADJ, SM = **tolondro**

tolosarra Ⓐ ADJ of/from Tolosa
Ⓑ SMF native/inhabitant of Tolosa; **los ~s** the people of Tolosa

tolteca ADJ, SMF Toltec

tolva SF [1] (= *recipiente*) hopper; (= *vertedor*) chute
[2] (*Cono Sur, Méx Ferro*) hopper wagon, hopper car (EEUU)
[3] (*Méx Min*) shed for storing ore

tolvanera SF dustcloud

toma Ⓐ SF [1] (*Téc*) [*de agua, gas*] (= *entrada*) inlet; (= *salida*) outlet ► **toma de aire** air inlet, air intake ► **toma de antena** (*Radio, TV*) aerial socket ► **toma de corriente** power point ► **toma de tierra** earth (wire), ground (wire) (EEUU)
[2] (*Cine, TV*) shot; **la película empieza con una ~ aérea** the film begins with an aerial shot; **¡escena primera, tercera ~!** scene one, take three! ► **toma directa** live shot
[3] [*de jarabe, medicina*] dose; [*de bebé*] feed; **~ de rapé** pinch of snuff
[4] (*Mil*) (= *captura*) taking, capture; **la ~ de**

Granada the taking *o* capture of Granada; **la ~ de la Bastilla** the storming of the Bastille
5 (*LAm*) (= *acequia*) irrigation channel; (*CAm*) (= *arroyo*) brook
6 ► **toma de conciencia** realization ► **toma de contacto** initial contact ► **toma de decisiones** decision-making, decision-taking ► **toma de declaración** taking of evidence ► **toma de hábito** (*Rel*) taking of vows ► **toma de posesión**: **mañana tendrá lugar la ~ de posesión del nuevo presidente** the new president will take office tomorrow ► **toma de tierra** (*Aer*) landing, touchdown
Ⓑ SM ► **toma y daca** give and take

tomada SF (*LAm*) plug

tomadero SM 1 (= *asidero*) handle
2 (= *entrada*) inlet, intake; (= *grifo*) tap, faucet (*EEUU*)

tomado ADJ 1 [*voz*] hoarse
2 **estar ~** (*LAm**) (= *borracho*) to be drunk
3 (*tb* **~ de orín**) rusty

tomador(a) Ⓐ ADJ (*LAm**) (= *borracho*) drunken
Ⓑ SM/F 1 (*Com*) [*de bono, cheque*] drawee; [*de seguro*] policy holder
2 (*LAm**) (= *borracho*) drunkard
3 (†*) (= *ladrón*) thief

tomadura SF ► **tomadura de pelo** (= *guasa*) leg-pull*; (= *mofa*) mockery; (= *timo*) con*, rip-off*

tomaína SF ptomaine

tomante‡ SM queer‡, fag (*EEUU‡*)

---

tomar

▸conjug 1a◂
A VERBO TRANSITIVO C VERBO PRONOMINAL
B VERBO INTRANSITIVO
Para las expresiones ***tomar las aguas, tomar las armas, tomar la delantera, tomar impulso, tomar tierra,*** *ver la otra entrada.*

Ⓐ VERBO TRANSITIVO
1 **= coger** to take; **si no tienes bolígrafo toma éste** take this pen if you haven't got one; **la tomó de la mano** he took her by the hand; **lo toma o lo deja** take it or leave it; **¡toma!** here (you are)!; **vayan tomando asiento** please sit down, please be seated (*frm*); **~ la pluma** to pick *o* take up one's pen; ✦**MODISMO ~ las de Villadiego** to shift it*
2 **= ingerir, consumir** [+ *comida*] to eat, have; [+ *bebida*] to drink, have; [+ *medicina*] to take; **si tienes hambre podemos ~ algo** if you're hungry we can get something to eat; **tomas demasiado café** you drink too much coffee; **tomamos unas cervezas** we had a few beers; **¿qué quieres ~?** what would you like?, what will you have?; **tome una cucharada de jarabe cada ocho horas** take a spoonful of syrup every eight hours; **~ el pecho** to feed at the breast, breastfeed
3 **= viajar en** [+ *tren, avión, taxi*] to take; **vamos a ~ el autobús** let's take *o* get the bus; **cada día toma el tren de las nueve** he catches *o* takes the nine o'clock train every day
4 ***Cine, Fot, TV*** to take; **~ una foto de algn** to take a photo of sb, take sb's photo
5 **= apuntar** [+ *notas, apuntes*] to take; [+ *discurso*] to take down; **nunca toma apuntes en clase** he never takes notes in class; **tomo nota de todo lo que me has dicho** I have taken note of everything you have told me; **nos ~on declaración en comisaría** they took (down) our statements *o* they took statements from us at the police station; **~ por escrito** to write down
6 **= medir** [+ *temperatura, pulso*] to take; **tengo que ir a que me tomen la tensión** I have to go and have my blood pressure taken; **ven, que te tomo las medidas** let me take your measurements
7 **= adoptar** [+ *decisión, precauciones*] to take; **~emos medidas para que no vuelva a suceder** we will take steps to ensure that it does not happen again
8 **= adquirir** **la situación está tomando mal cariz** the situation is beginning to look ugly; **el proyecto ya está tomando forma** the project is taking shape; *ver tb* **color 2**, **conciencia 3**
9 **= empezar a sentir** **le han tomado mucho cariño** they have become very fond of him; **les tomé asco a los caracoles** I took a dislike to snails; ✦**MODISMO ~la *o* tenerla tomada con algn*** to have (got) it in for sb*; **la jefa la ha tomado *o* la tiene tomada conmigo** the boss has (got) it in for me
10 **= disfrutar de** [+ *baño, ducha*] to have, take; **~ el aire *o* el fresco** to get some fresh air; **~ el sol** to sunbathe
11 ***Mil*** (= *capturar*) to take, capture; (= *ocupar*) to occupy; **la policía tomó la fábrica** the police occupied the factory
12 **= contratar** [+ *empleado*] to take on, engage
13 **= ocupar** to take; **traducirlo me ha tomado tres horas** it took me three hours to translate it
14 **= entender, interpretar** to take; **tomó muy a mal que la suspendieran** she took it very badly when she failed; **lo tomó como una ofensa** he took offence at it, he was offended by it; **lo han tomado a broma** they haven't taken it seriously, they are treating it as a joke; **no lo tomes en serio** don't take it seriously
15
◆ **tomar a algn por** (= *confundir*) **~ a algn por policía** to take sb for a policeman, think that sb is a policeman; **~ a algn por loco** to think sb mad; **¿por quién me toma?** what do you take me for?, who do you think I am?
16 ***sexualmente*** to have
17 ***Andes***: **= molestar** to upset, annoy
Ⓑ VERBO INTRANSITIVO
1 ***Bot*** [*planta*] to take (root); [*injerto*] to take
2 ***LAm***: **= ir** **~ a la derecha** to turn right
3 ***LAm***: **= beber** to drink; **estaba tomando en varios bares** he was drinking in a number of bars
4 ***exlamaciones*** **¡toma! menuda suerte has tenido ...** well, of all the luck!, can you believe it? what luck!; **¡toma! pues yo también lo sé hacer** hey! I know how to do that too; **¡toma ya!**: **¡toma ya, vaya tío tan bueno!** wow, what an amazing guy!*; **¡toma ya, vaya golazo!** look at that, what a fantastic goal!
5 ***esp LAm**** **tomó y se fue** off he went, he upped and went; **tomó y lo rompió** he went and broke it
Ⓒ **tomarse** VERBO PRONOMINAL
1 **= cogerse** [+ *vacaciones*] to take; **me he tomado la libertad de leer tu informe** I have taken the liberty of reading your report; **no se ~on la molestia de informarnos** they didn't bother *o* take the trouble to let us know
2 **= ingerir** [+ *bebida*] to drink, have; [+ *comida*] to eat, have; [+ *medicina*] to take; **se tomó 13 cervezas** he drank *o* had 13 beers; **me tomé un bocadillo** I ate *o* had a sandwich; **tómate el yogur, verás qué bueno** eat up your yogurt, you'll like it
3 **= medirse** [+ *pulso, temperatura*] to take
4 **= entender, interpretar** to take; **no te lo tomes así** don't take it that way; **no te lo tomes tan a mal** don't take it so badly, don't take it so much to heart; **se lo sabe ~ bien** he knows how to take it, he can take it in his stride; **se lo toma todo muy en serio** he takes it all very seriously
5
◆ **tomarse por** (= *creerse*) to think o.s.; **¿por quién se toma ese ministro?** who does that minister think he is?
6 **= tomarse de orín** to get rusty

Tomás SM Thomas

tomatal SM 1 (= *terreno*) tomato bed, tomato field
2 (*LAm*) (= *planta*) tomato plant

tomatazo SM **recibió una lluvia de ~s** he was pelted with tomatoes; **lo echaron del escenario a ~s** they saw him offstage, throwing tomatoes

tomate SM 1 tomato; **salsa de ~** tomato sauce; ✦**MODISMO ponerse como un ~** to turn as red as a beetroot
2 (*) (*en calcetín, media*) hole
3 (*) (= *jaleo*) fuss, row; (= *pelea*) set-to*; **al final de la noche hubo ~** there was a fight at the end of the evening; **¡qué ~!** what a mess!; **esto tiene ~** this is tough, this is a tough one

tomatera SF 1 (= *planta*) tomato plant
2 (*Cono Sur**) (= *juerga*) drunken spree; (= *fiesta*) rowdy party

tomatero/a SM/F (= *cultivador*) tomato grower; (= *comerciante*) tomato dealer

tomavistas SM INV cine camera, movie camera (*EEUU*)

tombo‡ SM (*Andes*) fuzz‡, police

tómbola SF tombola

tomillo SM thyme ► **tomillo salsero** savory, garden thyme

tominero ADJ (*Méx*) mean

tomismo SM Thomism

tomista ADJ, SMF Thomist

tomiza SF esparto rope

tomo[1] SM volume; **en tres ~s** in three volumes

tomo[2] SM (= *bulto*) bulk, size; ✦**MODISMO de ~ y lomo*** utter, out-and-out; **un canalla de ~ y lomo** a real swine*

tomografía SF tomography

tomo-homenaje SM (*pl* **tomos-homenaje**) homage volume, Festschrift

tomón ADJ (*Andes*) teasing, jokey

tompiate SM (*Méx*) (= *canasta*) basket (*of woven palm leaves*); (= *bolsa*) pouch (*of woven palm leaves*)

ton SM ✦**MODISMO sin ~ ni son** (= *sin motivo*) for no particular reason; (= *sin lógica*) without rhyme or reason

tonada SF [1] (= *melodía*) tune; (= *canción*) song, air
[2] (*LAm*) (= *acento*) accent
[3] (*Caribe*) (= *embuste*) fib; (= *juego de palabras*) pun

tonadilla SF little tune, ditty

tonal ADJ tonal

tonalidad SF [1] (*Mús*) tonality; (*Radio*) tone; **control de ~** tone control ► **tonalidad mayor** major key ► **tonalidad menor** minor key [2] (*Arte*) (= *tono*) shade; (= *colores*) colour scheme, color scheme (*EEUU*); **una bella ~ de verde** a beautiful shade of green; **cambiar la ~ de un cuarto** to change the colour scheme of a room

tonel SM [1] (= *barril*) barrel, cask
[2] (*) (= *persona*) fat lump*

tonelada SF [1] (= *unidad*) ton ► **tonelada americana**, **tonelada corta** short ton ► **tonelada inglesa**, **tonelada larga** long ton, gross ton ► **tonelada métrica** metric ton, tonne
[2] (*Náut*) ► **tonelada de registro** register ton; **un buque de 30.000 ~s de registro bruto** a ship of 30,000 gross register tons

tonelaje SM tonnage

tonelería SF cooperage, barrel-making

tonelero/a SM/F cooper

tonelete SM [1] (= *tonel*) cask, keg
[2] (= *falda*) short skirt

Tonete SM (*forma familiar*) *de* **Antonio**

tonga SF [1] (= *capa*) layer, stratum; [*de ladrillos*] course
[2] (*Caribe, Méx*) (= *montón*) pile
[3] (*Andes, Aragón, Cono Sur*) (= *tarea*) job, task; (= *tanda*) spell of work
[4] (*Andes*) (= *siesta*) nap

tongada SF (= *capa*) layer; (= *revestimiento*) coat, covering

tongo[1] SM (*Dep*) (= *trampa*) fixing; **¡hay ~!** it's been fixed!, it's been rigged!; **hubo ~ en las elecciones** the elections were rigged

tongo[2] SM (*Andes, Chile*) [1] (= *bombín*) Indian woman's hat, bowler hat
[2] (= *bebida*) rum punch

tongonearse ▸conjug 1a◂ VPR (*LAm*) = **contonearse**

tongoneo SM (*LAm*) = **contoneo**

tongorí SM (*Andes, Cono Sur*) (= *hígado*) liver; (= *menudillos*) offal; (= *bofe*) lights *pl*

tongoy SM (*LAm*) bowler hat

Toni SM (*forma familiar*) *de* **Antonio**

tónica SF [1] (= *bebida*) tonic, tonic water
[2] (= *tendencia*) tone, trend, tendency; **es una de las ~s del estilo moderno** it is one of the keynotes of the modern style
[3] (*Mús*) tonic

tonicidad SF tonicity

tónico Ⓐ ADJ [1] (*Mús*) [+ *nota*] tonic; (*Ling*) [+ *sílaba*] tonic *antes de s*, stressed
[2] (*Med*) (= *estimulante*) tonic, stimulating
Ⓑ SM tonic

tonificador ADJ, **tonificante** ADJ invigorating, stimulating

tonificar ▸conjug 1g◂ VT [+ *músculos, piel*] to tone up; [+ *ánimo*] to invigorate

tonillo SM [1] (*especial*) (sarcastic) tone of voice
[2] (*monótono*) monotonous tone of voice, monotonous drone
[3] (*regional*) accent

tono SM [1] [*de sonido*] tone; **en ~ bajo** in low tones, in a low tone; **baja/sube un poco el ~ del televisor** turn down/up the television a little ► **tono de discado** (*Cono Sur*), **tono de marcar** (*Telec*) dialling tone, dial tone (*EEUU*) ► **tono de llamada** (*Telec*) ringtone ► **tono de voz** tone of voice; **lo noté por el ~ de su voz** I could tell from his tone of voice; **—ya me he dado cuenta —dijo, alzando el ~ de voz** "I can see that," he said, raising his voice
[2] [*de palabras, discusión, escrito*] tone; **le molestó el ~ de mi carta** she was upset by the tone of my letter; **¡cómo hablas en ese ~ a tu padre!** how dare you speak to your father in that tone (of voice)!; **esa expresión tiene un ~ despectivo** that expression sounds insulting; **contestó con ~ de enfado** she replied angrily; **intenté tratar la cuestión en ~ de broma** I tried to treat the whole matter lightheartedly; **nos habló con un ~ distante** her voice was rather distant as she spoke to us; **un disco de ~ más intimista** a record with a more intimate feel (to it); **bajar el ~** to soften one's tone; **bajar el ~ de algo** to soften the tone of sth, tone sth down; **cambiar de ~** to change one's tone; **cuando le dije eso se serenó y cambió de ~** when I told him that he calmed down and changed his tone *o* his tone changed; **fue él quien cambió el ~ de la conversación** it was him that changed the tone of the conversation; **la reunión cambió de ~ pasadas las nueve de la noche** the tone of the meeting changed after nine o'clock; **a este ~** in the same vein; **fuera de ~** [*respuesta, comentario, actitud*] uncalled for; **subir de ~** [*discusión, conversación*] to grow *o* become heated; [*conflicto*] to intensify; [*quejas*] to grow louder; **las voces empezaron a subir de ~** they began to raise their voices; **la oposición está subiendo el ~ de sus ataques al gobierno** the opposition is stepping up *o* intensifying its attacks on the government; **chistes subidos de ~** racy jokes
[3] **a ~** matching; **ropa náutica y accesorios a ~** sailing gear and matching accessories; **estar a ~ con algo** [*color*] to match sth; [*diseño, comentarios*] to be in keeping with sth; **una escena final divertida, muy a ~ con el resto de la película** an amusing final scene, very much in keeping with the rest of the film; **una ideología más a ~ con los tiempos** an ideology more in tune with the times; **ponerse a ~** (= *prepararse físicamente*) to get (o.s.) into shape; (= *animarse*) to perk o.s. up*; **voy a tomarme un whisky doble, a ver si me pongo a ~** I'm going to have a double whisky to perk myself up*
[4] (= *clase, distinción*) **una familia de ~** a good family; **eso no es de ~** that's just not done; **ser de buen/mal ~**: **ir a los balnearios era entonces una actividad de buen ~** visiting spas was quite the done thing then; **una fiesta de buen ~** a fashionable party; **es de mal ~ hablar de esos temas** it is bad form to talk about such matters, it's (simply) not done to talk about such things; ✦***MODISMO*** **darse ~** to put on airs
[5] [*de color*] shade, tone; **en ~s grises y azules** in shades of grey and blue, in grey and blue tones; **~s pastel** pastel shades, pastel tones
[6] (*Anat, Med*) tone ► **tono muscular** muscle tone
[7] (*Mús*) (= *intervalo*) tone; (= *tonalidad*) key; (= *altura*) pitch ► **tono mayor** major key ► **tono menor** minor key
[8] (*Mús*) (= *diapasón*) tuning fork; (= *corredera*) slide

tonsura SF tonsure

tonsurado ADJ tonsured

tonsurar ▸conjug 1a◂ VT [1] (*Rel*) to tonsure
[2] [+ *lana*] to clip, shear

tontada SF = **tontería 1, 2**

tontaina* SMF idiot, dimwit*

tontamente ADV stupidly; **sonreía ~ ante las cámaras** he grinned stupidly at the cameras; **se me olvidó llamar por teléfono ~** I stupidly forgot to phone; **tropezó ~** he tripped clumsily

tontear* ▸conjug 1a◂ VI [1] (= *hacer el tonto*) to fool about, act the fool
[2] (= *decir tonterías*) to talk nonsense
[3] (*amorosamente*) to flirt

tontera SF (*LAm*) = **tontería**

tontería SF [1] (= *dicho*) **eso son ~s** ◊ **eso es una ~** that's nonsense *o* rubbish *o* (*esp EEUU*) garbage; **decir ~s** to talk nonsense *o* rubbish *o* (*esp EEUU*) garbage; **¡qué ~ acabas de decir!** that was a silly thing to say!; **lo que has dicho no es ninguna ~** what you've just said isn't such a bad idea; **¡déjate de ~s!** don't be silly!, don't talk nonsense!; **dejémonos de ~s** let's be serious
[2] (= *acto*) **ha sido una ~ el negarte a verle** it was silly of you to refuse to see him; **hacer una ~** to do a silly thing *o* something silly; **no hace nada más que ~s** he's always doing silly things *o* being silly; **deja de hacer ~s** stop being silly
[3] (= *insignificancia*) silly little thing; **cualquier ~ le afecta** he gets upset over any silly little thing *o* the slightest thing; **lo vendió por una ~** he sold it for next to nothing
[4] (= *remilgo*) **Juanito tiene mucha ~ a la hora de comer** Juanito is so picky about his food
[5] (= *cualidad*) silliness, foolishness

tonto/a Ⓐ ADJ [1] [*persona*] [1·1] (= *bobo*) (*dicho con afecto*) silly; (*dicho con enfado*) stupid; **venga, vente con nosotros, ¡no seas ~!** come on, come with us, don't be silly!; **¡qué ~ soy!** how silly *o* stupid of me!; **fui tan ~ que me dejé engañar por ellos** I was silly enough to be taken in by them; **¿tú te has creído que yo soy ~?** ◊ **¿me tomas por ~?** do you think I'm stupid?; ✦***MODISMO*** **es ~ del bote** *o* **de capirote** *o* **de remate** he's a total *o* complete idiot*
[1·2] (*poco inteligente*) stupid; **¡y parecía ~!** and we thought he was stupid!; ✦***MODISMOS*** **a lo ~**: **¿para qué esforzarse a lo ~?** why go to all that trouble for nothing?; **y a lo ~, a lo ~, se le pasó la mitad del día** and before he knew it, half the day had slipped by; **es más ~ que Abundio** (*Esp**) he's as thick as two short planks*; **hacer ~ a algn** (*Chile**) to trick sb; **a tontas y a locas**: **piénsalo bien, no quiero que actúes/hables a tontas y a locas** think carefully, don't just do/say the first thing that comes into your head; **esos jóvenes sin seso que sólo hablan a tontas y a locas** these silly youngsters who chatter away

without even thinking what they're saying
1·3 (= *insolente*) silly; **¡si te pones ~ no te vuelvo a traer al cine!** if you start being silly I won't take you to the cinema again!
1·4 (= *torpe*) **me quedé como ~ después del golpe** I felt dazed after the knock; **hoy se me olvida todo, estoy como ~** I keep forgetting things today, I'm out of it*; **dejar a algn ~** (*Esp*) to leave sb speechless
1·5 (= *presumido*) stuck-up*; **pasaba muy ~ por delante de ella** he walked past her showing off; **está muy ~ desde que es médico** he's such a show-off since he became a doctor*
1·6 (*Med*) imbecile; *ver tb* **pelo 8**
2 [*risa, frase, accidente*] silly; **¡qué fallo más ~!** it was a really silly mistake!; **fue una respuesta tonta** that was a stupid answer; **me entró la risa tonta** I started giggling; **me pilló en una hora tonta y le presté el dinero** I wasn't thinking at that moment and I lent him the money; *ver tb* **caja 1**
Ⓑ SM/F 1 idiot; **soy un ~, ¡nunca debí haberla escuchado!** I'm such an idiot, I should never have listened to her!; **allí estaba, riéndome como una tonta** there I was, laughing like an idiot; **el ~ del pueblo** the village idiot; ✦*MODISMOS* **hacer el ~** (*a propósito*) to act the fool, play the fool; (*sin querer*) to be a fool; **has hecho el ~ no siguiendo sus consejos** you were a fool not to take her advice; **hacerse el ~** to act dumb ► **tonto útil** willing stooge
2 (*Med*) imbecile
Ⓒ SM 1 (*Circo, Teat*) clown, funny man
2 (*Andes, CAm*) (= *palanca*) jemmy

tontón¹/ona* SM/F = **tonto B**

tontón²* SM (= *vestido*) smock, maternity dress

tontorrón/ona* SM/F dimwit*

tontura SF = **tontería 5**

tontureco ADJ (*CAm*) = **tonto A**

tonudo* ADJ (*Cono Sur*) classy*

tony ['toni] SM (*LAm**) clown

toña‡ SF 1 (= *golpe*) (*con el puño*) bash*, punch; (*con el pie*) kick
2 (= *borrachera*) **pillarse una ~** (*Esp*) to get plastered‡

top* Ⓐ ADJ (= *mejor*) top, best; [*empresa, marca*] leading
Ⓑ SM INV 1 (= *prenda*) top
2 (= *persona*) top person, leading personality; **el ~ del ~** la crème de la crème; **el ~ de la gama** the best in its range

topacio SM topaz

topadora SF (*Cono Sur, Méx*) bulldozer

topar ▸conjug 1a◂ Ⓐ VI 1 (= *encontrar*) **~ con** [+ *persona*] to run into, come across, bump into; [+ *objeto*] to find, come across
2 (= *chocar*) **~ contra** to run into, hit; **~ con un obstáculo** to run into an obstacle, hit an obstacle
3 (= *consistir*) **la dificultad topa en eso** that's where the trouble lies, there's the rub
4 (*Méx*) (= *reñir*) to quarrel
Ⓑ VT 1 (*Zool*) to butt, horn
2 [+ *persona*] to run into, come across, bump into; [+ *objeto*] to find, come across; **le topé por casualidad en el museo** I happened to bump into him in the museum
3 (*Andes, Cono Sur, Méx*) (= *apostar*) to bet, stake
Ⓒ **toparse** VPR **~se con** [+ *persona*] to run into, come across, bump into; [+ *objeto*] to find, come across; **me topé con él hoy en el bar** I bumped into him in the bar today

tope¹ Ⓐ ADJ INV (= *máximo*) maximum, top; **la edad ~ para el puesto** the maximum age for the job; **fecha ~** closing date, deadline; **precio ~** top price; **sueldo ~** maximum salary
Ⓑ SM 1 (= *límite*) limit; ✦*MODISMOS* **estar a ~** *o* **hasta el ~** *o* **hasta los ~s***: **el teatro estaba (lleno) a ~** the theatre was packed out*; **el contenedor está hasta los ~s** the container is overloaded; **voy a estar a ~ de trabajo** I'm going to be up to my eyes *o* neck in work*; **ir a ~*** to go flat out*; **trabajar a ~*** to work flat out*; **vivir a ~*** to live life to the full ► **tope salarial** wage ceiling
2 (*Náut*) [*del mastelero*] masthead; (= *vigía*) lookout
3 (*Andes, Cono Sur*) (= *cumbre*) peak, summit
Ⓒ ADV (*Esp‡*) (= *muy*) **es ~ enrollada** she's mega-cool*; **es ~ guay** it's well cool*

tope² SM 1 (= *golpe*) (*gen*) bump, knock; (*con la cabeza*) butt
2 (= *riña*) quarrel; (= *pelea*) scuffle
3 (= *objeto*) stop, check; [*de tren*] buffer; [*de coche*] bumper, fender (*EEUU*); [*de puerta*] doorstop, wedge; [*de revólver*] catch; (*Méx*) (*en una carretera*) speed bump *o* hump ► **tope de tabulación** tab stop
4 (= *dificultad*) snag, problem; **ahí está el ~** that's the problem, that's just the trouble
5 (‡) (= *robo*) burglary

topera SF 1 (*Zool*) molehill
2 (‡) (= *metro*) tube*, subway (*EEUU*)

topero/a‡ SM/F burglar

toperol SM (*Cono Sur, Méx*) brass tack

topetada SF bump, bang

topetar ▸conjug 1a◂ VT 1 (= *golpear*) to butt, bump
2 (= *encontrarse*) to bump into

topetazo SM bump, bang

topetear ▸conjug 1a◂ VT (*Andes*) = **topetar**

topetón SM = **topetazo**

topicazo* Ⓐ ADJ corny, clichéd
Ⓑ SM cliché

▼ **tópico** Ⓐ ADJ 1 (*Med*) local; **de uso ~** for external use
2 (= *trillado*) commonplace, trite
Ⓑ SM 1 (= *lugar común*) commonplace, cliché
2 (*LAm*) (= *tema*) topic, subject

topillo¹ SM (*Méx*) (= *timo*) trick, swindle

topillo² SM (*Zool*) vole

topista‡ SMF burglar

top-less SM, **topless** SM (*en playa, piscina*) topless bathing; (*en club*) topless entertainment; **ir en** *o* **hacer ~** to go topless

top-model SMF (*pl* **top-models**) supermodel

topo¹ SM 1 (*Zool*) mole
2 (= *torpe*) clumsy person, blunderer
3 (= *espía*) mole
4 (*Esp*) (= *lunar*) polka dot
5 (*Mec*) mole, tunnelling machine

topo² SM 1 (*LAm*) (= *alfiler*) large pin
2 (*Andes*) (= *distancia*) *measurement of distance of 1.5 leagues*

topocho¹ ADJ (*Caribe*) (= *gordito*) plump, chubby

topocho² SM (*Caribe Bot*) plantain

topografía SF topography

topográfico ADJ topographic(al)

topógrafo/a SM/F topographer

topolino Ⓐ SM 1 (= *zapato*) wedge-heeled shoe
2 (= *coche*) small car (*Fiat 500 cc*)
Ⓑ SF (= *persona*) teenager, bobbysoxer (*EEUU*)

topón SM (*LAm*) = **topetada**

toponimia SF 1 (= *nombres*) toponymy (*frm*), place names *pl*
2 (= *estudio*) study of place names

toponímico ADJ toponymic

topónimo SM place name

toposo ADJ (*Caribe*) meddlesome

top-secret [top'sikret] ADJ, SM INV top secret

toque SM 1 (= *golpecito*) tap; **le dio un ~ en el hombro** he gave her a tap on the shoulder; **unos toquecitos con la varita y saldrá el conejo** a few taps of the magic wand and the rabbit will come out; ✦*MODISMOS* **dar un ~ de atención a algn** ◊ **dar un ~ a algn***: **el jefe tuvo que darle un ~ de atención por llegar tarde** the boss had to pull him up for being late; **te van a dar un ~ si sigues portándote mal** you'll get a telling-off if you keep behaving badly
2 (= *sonido*) [*de campana*] chime, ring; [*de reloj*] stroke; [*de timbre*] ring; [*de tambor*] beat; **al ~ de las doce** on the stroke of twelve; **dar un ~ a algn** (*por teléfono*) to give sb a bell* ► **toque de diana** reveille ► **toque de difuntos** death knell ► **toque de oración** call to prayer ► **toque de queda** curfew ► **toque de retreta** retreat ► **toque de silencio** lights out
3 (= *detalle*) touch; **el ~ personal** the personal touch; **faltan algunos ~s para completarlo** it still needs a few touches to finish it off; **dar el último ~** *o* **los últimos ~s a algo** to put the finishing touch *o* touches to sth
4 (*Arte*) [*de color, brillo*] touch ► **toque de luz** highlight
5 (*Quím*) test
6 (†) (= *quid*) crux, essence; **ahí está el ~** that's the crux of the matter
7 (*Andes*) (= *vuelta*) turn

toquetear* ▸conjug 1a◂ VT 1 (= *manosear*) to handle, finger
2 (*Mús*) to play idly, mess about on
3 (= *acariciar*) to fondle, feel up*, touch up*

toqueteo* SM 1 (= *manoseo*) handling, fingering
2 (= *caricias*) fondling, touching up*

toquido SM (*CAm, Méx*) = **toque**

toquilla SF 1 (= *chal*) knitted shawl; (*para la cabeza*) headscarf
2 (= *gorro*) woollen bonnet; (*Andes*) (= *sombrero*) straw hat

torácico ADJ thoracic

torada SF herd of bulls

tórax SM thorax; **radiografía de ~** chest X-ray

torbellino SM 1 [*de viento*] whirlwind; [*de polvo*] dust cloud
2 [*de cosas*] whirl
3 (= *persona*) whirlwind

torcaz ADJ **paloma ~** wood pigeon, ring dove

torcecuello SM (*Orn*) wryneck

torcedor SM 1 (*Téc*) spindle
2 (= *angustia*) torment, torture

torcedura SF 1 (*gen*) twist(ing); (*Med*)

➤ LENGUA Y USO: tópico B1 53.1

sprain, strain
[2] (= *vino*) weak wine

torcer ▸conjug 2b, 2h◂ Ⓐ VT [1] (= *retorcer*) [+ *dedo, muñeca, tronco*] to twist; [+ *tobillo*] to twist, sprain; [+ *madera*] to warp; [+ *soga*] to plait; (= *doblar*) to bend; **¡me torció el brazo!** he twisted my arm!; **le ha torcido el cuello** he's twisted his neck; **torció la cabeza para mirarla** he turned (his head) to look at her
[2] **~ el gesto** to scowl; **~ los ojos** *o* **la vista** to squint
[3] [+ *ropa*] to wring
[4] (= *cambiar*) [+ *rumbo*] to change; [+ *voluntad*] to bend; [+ *pensamientos*] to turn; [+ *significado*] to distort, twist; **el conflicto ha torcido el curso de los acontecimientos** the conflict has changed the course of events
[5] (= *pervertir*) [+ *persona*] to lead astray
Ⓑ VI (= *girar*) [*camino, vehículo, viajero*] to turn; **el coche torció a la izquierda** the car turned left; **al llegar allí tuerza usted a la derecha** when you get there turn right
Ⓒ **torcerse** VPR [1] (= *retorcerse*) to twist; (= *doblarse*) to bend; **me torcí el tobillo** I twisted *o* sprained my ankle
[2] (= *ladearse*) **gira el volante que te estás torciendo** turn the steering wheel, you're not driving straight; **usa papel rayado para no ~se escribiendo** use ruled paper so you write straight
[3] (= *ir por mal camino*) [*persona*] to go astray, go off the rails
[4] (= *ir mal*) [*proyecto*] to go off the rails; [*proceso, acontecimientos*] to take a strange turn
[5] (= *agriarse*) [*leche*] to turn, go off; [*vino*] to go sour

torcida SF wick

torcidamente ADV [1] (*lit*) in a twisted way, crookedly
[2] (*fig*) deviously, in a crooked way

torcido Ⓐ ADJ [1] (= *no derecho*) [*nariz, línea*] crooked; (= *doblado*) [*palo, alambre*] bent; **el cuadro está ~** the picture is not straight, the picture is crooked; **llevaba el sombrero algo ~** he had his hat on not quite straight
[2] (= *taimado*) devious, crooked
[3] (*Andes, CAm, Caribe*) (= *desgraciado*) unlucky
Ⓑ SM (= *acto*) [*de seda*] twist

torcijón SM [1] sudden twist
[2] = **retortijón**

torcimiento SM = **torcedura**

tordillo Ⓐ ADJ dappled, dapple-grey
Ⓑ SM dapple

tordo Ⓐ ADJ dappled, dapple-grey
Ⓑ SM (*Orn*) thrush

torear ▸conjug 1a◂ Ⓐ VT [1] [+ *toro*] to fight, play
[2] (= *evitar*) to dodge, avoid
[3] (= *acosar*) to plague; (= *burlarse*) to tease, draw on; (= *confundir*) to confuse; ✦**MODISMO** **¡a mí no me torea nadie!** nobody messes me around!*
[4] (= *mantener a raya*) to keep at bay; (= *dar largas a*) to put off, keep guessing
[5] (*CAm, Cono Sur*) [+ *animal*] to provoke, enrage; (*Cono Sur, Méx*) [+ *persona*] to infuriate
[6] (*Andes, Cono Sur*) [*perro*] to bark furiously at
Ⓑ VI [1] (*Taur*) to fight (bulls); **toreó bien Suárez** Suárez fought well; **no volverá a ~** he will never fight again; **el muchacho quiere ~** the boy wants to be a bullfighter
[2] (*) (= *dar largas*) to spin it out, procrastinate
[3] (*Andes, Cono Sur*) (= *ladrar*) to bark furiously

toreo SM (art of) bullfighting

torera SF (= *chaqueta*) short tight jacket; ✦**MODISMOS** **saltarse un deber a la ~** to neglect one's duty; **saltarse una ley a la ~** to flout a law; *ver tb* **torero**

torería SF [1] (= *toreros*) bullfighters *pl*; (= *mundo del toreo*) bullfighting world
[2] (*Caribe, CAm*) (= *broma*) prank

torero/a SM/F bullfighter; ✦**MODISMO** **hacer una de ~*** to say sth completely off the point; *ver tb* **torera**

torete SM [1] (= *toro*) (*pequeño*) small bull; (*joven*) young bull
[2] (= *niño*) (*fuerte*) strong child, robust child; (*travieso*) mischievous child; (*de mal genio*) bad-tempered child

toril SM bullpen

torio SM thorium

torito* SM (*Andes Entomología*) bluebottle

tormenta SF [1] (*Meteo*) storm; ✦**MODISMO** **una ~ en un vaso de agua** a storm in a teacup, a tempest in a teapot (*EEUU*) ► **tormenta de arena** sandstorm ► **tormenta de nieve** snowstorm ► **tormenta de polvo** dust storm
[2] (= *discusión etc*) storm; (= *trastorno*) upheaval, turmoil; **desencadenó una ~ de pasiones** it unleashed a storm of passions; **sufrió una ~ de celos** she was eaten up with jealousy ► **tormenta de cerebros** brainstorm, brainstorming

tormento SM (= *tortura*) torture; (*fig*) torture, torment; (= *angustia*) anguish, agony; **dar ~ a** to torment; (*fig*) to torment, plague; **darse ~** to torment o.s.; **estos zapatos son un ~** these shoes are agony; **sus dos hijos son un ~ perpetuo** her two sons are a constant trial *o* torment to her

tormentoso ADJ stormy

tormo SM lump, mass

torna SF (= *vuelta*) return; ✦**MODISMOS** **cambiar las ~s** to turn the tables; **volver las ~s a algn** to turn the tables on sb; **se han vuelto las ~s** now the boot's on the other foot, it's a different story now

tornada SF return

tornadera SF pitchfork, winnowing fork

tornadizo/a Ⓐ ADJ (= *cambiadizo*) changeable; (= *caprichoso*) fickle
Ⓑ SM/F (*Hist*) renegade

tornado SM tornado

tornar ▸conjug 1a◂ Ⓐ VT [1] (= *devolver*) to give back, return
[2] (= *cambiar*) to change (**en** into), alter
Ⓑ VI [1] (= *volver*) to return, go back
[2] **~ a hacer algo** to do sth again; **tornó a llover** it began to rain again; **tornó a estudiar el problema** he studied the problem again
[3] **~ en sí** to regain consciousness, come to
Ⓒ **tornarse** VPR [1] (= *regresar*) to return
[2] (= *volverse*) to become, turn

tornasol SM [1] (*Bot*) sunflower
[2] (*Quím*) litmus; **papel de ~** litmus paper
[3] (*fig*) sheen, iridescence

tornasolado ADJ (*gen*) iridescent, sheeny; [*seda*] shot

tornasolar ▸conjug 1a◂ Ⓐ VT to make iridescent, put a sheen on
Ⓑ **tornasolarse** VPR to be *o* become iridescent, show different lights

tornavía SF turntable

tornavoz SF [*de instrumento musical*] sounding board; [*de púlpito*] sounding board, canopy; **hacer ~** to cup one's hands to one's mouth

torneado Ⓐ ADJ [1] (*Téc*) turned (*on a lathe*)
[2] [*brazo*] shapely, delicately curved; [*figura*] pleasingly rounded
Ⓑ SM turning

tornear ▸conjug 1a◂ VT to turn (*on a lathe*)

torneo SM [1] (*Dep*) tournament, competition ► **torneo de tenis** tennis tournament ► **torneo por equipos** team tournament
[2] (*Hist*) (= *justa*) joust

tornero/a SM/F machinist, turner

tornillería SF (= *tornillos*) screws *pl*; (*sin especificar*) nuts and bolts *pl*

tornillo SM [1] (*en punta*) screw; (*para tuerca*) bolt; ✦**MODISMOS** **apretar los ~s a algn** to apply pressure on sb, put the screws on sb*; **le falta un ~*** he has a screw loose*; **hacer ~** (*Mil*) to desert ► **tornillo de banco** vice, vise (*EEUU*), clamp ► **tornillo sin fin** worm gear
[2] (*Cono Sur**) (= *frío*) bitter cold

torniquete SM [1] (= *barra giratoria*) turnstile
[2] (*Med*) tourniquet

torniscón SM [1] (= *apretón*) pinch, squeeze
[2] (= *manotazo*) (*en la cara*) slap on the face; (*en la cabeza*) smack on the head, cuff

torno SM [1] (*para levantar pesos*) winch, windlass; (*para tensar*) winding drum
[2] (*para tornear*) lathe; **labrar a ~** to turn on the lathe ► **torno de alfarero** potter's wheel ► **torno de asador** spit ► **torno de banco** vice, vise (*EEUU*), clamp ► **torno de hilar** spinning wheel ► **torno de tornero** turning lathe
[3] [*de río*] (= *recodo*) bend; (= *rabiones*) race, rapids *pl*
[4] **en ~ a: se reunieron en ~ a él** they gathered round him; **la conversación giraba en ~ a las elecciones** the conversation revolved *o* centred around the election; **polemizar en ~ a un texto** to argue about a text; **todo estaba inundado en muchos kilómetros en ~** everything was flooded for miles around

toro SM [1] (*Zool*) bull; ✦**MODISMOS** **coger el ~ por los cuernos** ◊ **irse a la cabeza del ~** to take the bull by the horns; **echar el ~ a algn*** to give sb a severe dressing-down*; **hacer un ~*** (*Teat*) to stand in for somebody; **a ~ pasado** with hindsight, in retrospect; **soltar el ~ a algn*** to give sb a severe dressing-down* ► **toro bravo, toro de lidia** fighting bull
[2] (= *hombre*) strong man, he-man*, tough guy*; ✦**MODISMO** **ser ~ corrido** to be an old hand at it, be an old fox
[3] **los ~s** (= *corrida*) bullfight *sing*; (= *toreo*) bullfighting; **ir a los ~s** to go to the bullfight; **este año no habrá ~s** there will be no bullfight this year; **no me gustan los ~s** I don't like bullfighting; ✦**MODISMOS** **ciertos son los ~s** it turns out that it's true; **ver los ~s desde la barrera** to stand on the sidelines, remain uncommitted
[4] ✦**MODISMO** **hacer ~s*** to play truant, cut

class
[5] **Toro** (*Zodíaco*) Taurus

torombolo* ADJ (*Caribe*) (= *gordito*) plump; (= *barrigón*) pot-bellied

toronja SF grapefruit, pomelo (*EEUU*)

toronjil SM lemon balm

toronjo SM grapefruit tree

torpe ADJ [1] (= *poco ágil*) [*persona*] clumsy; [*movimiento*] ungainly; **¡qué ~ eres, ya me has vuelto a pisar!** you're so clumsy, you've trodden on my foot again!; **un hombre de ~s andares** a man with an ungainly walk
[2] (= *necio*) dim, slow; **soy muy ~ para la informática** I'm very dim *o* slow when it comes to computers; **es bastante ~ y nunca entiende las lecciones** he's a bit dim *o* slow, he never understands the lessons
[3] (= *sin tacto*) clumsy; **¡qué ~ soy! me temo que la he ofendido** how clumsy *o* stupid of me! I'm afraid I've offended her

torpear ▸conjug 1a◂ VI (*Cono Sur*) to be dishonest, behave dishonourably

torpedear ▸conjug 1a◂ VT (*Mil*) to torpedo; [+ *proyecto*] to torpedo; **~ a algn con preguntas** to bombard sb with questions

torpedeo SM bombardment

torpedero SM torpedo boat

torpedo SM torpedo

torpemente ADV [1] (= *sin destreza*) clumsily, awkwardly
[2] (= *neciamente*) slow-wittedly

torpeza SF [1] (= *falta de agilidad*) [*de persona*] clumsiness; [*de movimientos*] ungainliness
[2] (= *falta de inteligencia*) dimness, slowness
[3] (= *falta de tacto*) **¡menuda ~ la tuya! has ofendido a toda la familia** that was really tactless *o* clumsy of you, you've offended the whole family!; **fue una ~ por mi parte decírselo** it was stupid *o* clumsy of me to tell him
[4] (= *tontería*) **cometer una ~** to do sth stupid

torpón ADJ (*Cono Sur*) = **torpe**

torpor SM torpor

torrado SM [1] (‡) (= *cabeza*) bonce‡, head
[2] **torrados** (*Culin*) toasted chickpeas

torrar ▸conjug 1a◂ Ⓐ VT [1] (*Culin*) to toast, roast
[2] (‡) (= *robar*) to pinch*, nick*
Ⓑ **torrarse** VPR [1] (= *asarse*) to roast
[2] (*) (= *dormirse*) to go off to sleep

torre SF [1] (*Arquit*) tower; [*de oficinas, viviendas*] tower block; (*Radio*) mast, tower; [*de electricidad*] pylon; [*de pozo de petróleo*] derrick ► **torre de alta tensión, torre de conducción eléctrica** electricity pylon ► **Torre de Babel** Tower of Babel ► **torre de marfil** ivory tower ► **torre de música** hi-fi
[2] (*Ajedrez*) rook, castle
[3] (*Aer, Mil, Náut*) turret; (*Mil*) watchtower ► **torre de control** (*Aer*) control tower ► **torre de lanzamiento** launch tower ► **torre del homenaje** keep ► **torre de mando** [*de submarino*] conning tower ► **torre de observación** observation tower, watchtower ► **torre de perforación** drilling rig ► **torre de refrigeración** cooling tower ► **torre (de) vigía** (*Náut*) crow's nest; [*de submarino*] conning tower ► **torre de vigilancia** watchtower
[4] (*Caribe, Méx*) (= *chimenea*) factory chimney
[5] ✦**MODISMO dar en la ~** (*Méx*) to hit where it hurts most

torrefacción SF toasting, roasting

torrefacto ADJ high roast

torreja SF [1] (*LAm*) *(fried) slices of fruit and vegetables*
[2] (*Cono Sur*) slice of fruit

torrencial ADJ torrential

torrencialidad SF torrential nature

torrencialmente ADV torrentially

torrente SM [1] (= *río*) torrent; **llover a ~s** to rain cats and dogs, rain in torrents ► **torrente de sangre, torrente sanguíneo** bloodstream
[2] [*de palabras*] torrent, rush; [*de insultos*] stream, torrent; [*de lágrimas*] flood; [*de gente*] stream ► **torrente de voz** powerful voice

torrentera SF gully, watercourse

torrentoso ADJ (*LAm*) [*río*] torrential, rushing; [*lluvia*] torrential

torreón SM [*de castillo*] tower; [*de casa*] turret

torrero SM lighthouse keeper

torreta SF [1] (*Aer, Mil, Náut*) turret; [*de submarino*] conning tower ► **torreta de observación, torreta de vigilancia** watchtower
[2] (*Elec*) pylon, mast

torrezno SM rasher, slice of bacon

tórrido ADJ torrid

torrificar ▸conjug 1g◂ VT (*Méx*) [+ *café*] to toast, roast

torrija SF *bread soaked in milk and fried in batter with honey or sugar and wine, eaten especially at Easter*

torsión SF [1] (= *torcedura*) twist, twisting
[2] (*Mec*) torsion, torque

torsional ADJ torsional

torso SM (*Anat*) torso; (*Arte*) head and shoulders

torta SF [1] (*) (= *bofetada*) thump; (= *puñetazo*) punch, sock*; (= *caída*) fall; (= *choque*) crash; **liarse a ~s** to get involved in a punch-up
[2] (= *pastel*) cake; (*con base de masa quebrada*) tart, flan; (= *crepe*) pancake; (*Méx*) sandwich; ✦**MODISMOS la ~ costó un pan** it worked out dearer than expected, it was more trouble than it was worth; **eso es ~s y pan pintado** it's child's play, it's a cinch‡; **¡ni ~!*** I haven't a clue!, not the foggiest!; **no entendió ni ~** he didn't understand a word of it; **nos queda la ~** there's a lot left over
[3] (*CAm, Méx*) (= *tortilla*) ► **torta de huevos** omelet(te)
[4] (*Esp*‡) (= *borrachera*) **agarrar una ~** to get plastered*
[5] (*Tip*) font

tortazo* SM (= *bofetada*) slap, sock*; (= *golpe*) thump; **pegarse un ~** to get a knock

tortear ▸conjug 1a◂ Ⓐ VT (*Cono Sur*) [+ *masa*] to flatten, roll; (*CAm, Méx*) [+ *tortilla*] to shape *(with the palms of one's hands)*
Ⓑ VI (*Méx*) (= *aplaudir*) to clap, applaud

tortero ADJ (*Andes*) round and flat, disc-shaped

tortícolis SF INV stiff neck; **me levanté con ~** I got up with a stiff neck *o* a crick in my neck

tortilla SF [1] [*de huevo*] omelette; ✦**MODISMOS hacer algo una ~** to smash sth up; **van a hacer el negocio una ~** they're sure to mess the deal up; **hacer a algn una ~*** to beat sb up*; **dar la vuelta a la ~** to turn the tables; **volverse la ~**: **se ha vuelto la ~** now the boot is on the other foot, it's a different story now; **se le volvió la ~** it came out all wrong for him, it all blew up in his face ► **tortilla de patatas, tortilla española** Spanish potato omelette ► **tortilla francesa** plain omelette
[2] (*CAm, Méx*) [*de maíz*] flat maize pancake, tortilla
[3] (‡) (= *lesbianismo*) lesbian sex

tortillera SF [1] (*CAm, Méx*) (= *vendedora*) seller of maize pancakes
[2] (**‡) (= *lesbiana*) dyke**‡, lesbian

tortita SF pancake

tórtola SF turtledove

tortoleo SM (*Méx*) billing and cooing

tórtolo SM [1] (= *ave*) (male) turtledove
[2] (*) (= *amante*) lovebird, loverboy; **tórtolos** pair of lovers, lovebirds

tortuga SF [*de tierra*] tortoise; (*tb* **~ marina**) turtle; ✦**MODISMO a paso de ~** at a snail's pace

tortuguismo SM (*Méx*) go-slow, slowdown (*EEUU*)

tortuoso ADJ [1] [*camino*] winding, full of twists and turns
[2] [*conducta*] devious

tortura SF torture

torturado/a SM/F torture victim

torturar ▸conjug 1a◂ VT to torture

toruno SM [1] (*CAm*) (= *semental*) stud bull; (*Cono Sur*) (= *toro viejo*) old bull; (*Cono Sur*) (= *buey*) ox
[2] (*Cono Sur*) (= *hombre*) fit old man

torvisca SF, **torvisco** SM spurge flax

torvo ADJ grim, fierce; **una mirada torva** a fierce look

torzal SM [1] (= *hilo*) cord, twist
[2] (*Cono Sur*) (= *lazo*) plaited rope, lasso

tos SF cough; **acceso de ~** coughing fit; **tiene ~** he's got a cough ► **tos convulsa, tos ferina** whooping cough

toscamente ADV roughly, crudely

Toscana SF **La ~** Tuscany

toscano/a Ⓐ ADJ, SM/F Tuscan
Ⓑ SM [1] (*Ling*) Tuscan; (*Hist*) Italian
[2] (= *puro*) (a kind of) cigar

tosco ADJ coarse, rough, crude

tosedera SF (*LAm*) nagging cough

toser ▸conjug 2a◂ Ⓐ VI to cough
Ⓑ VT ✦**MODISMO no hay quien le tosa** he's in a class by himself; **no hay quien le tosa a la hora de cocinar** he's in a class by himself when it comes to cooking; **cuando se pone así no hay quien le tosa** no one gets in his way when he's in that mood

tosido SM (*CAm, Cono Sur, Méx*) cough

tósigo SM poison

tosquedad SF coarseness, roughness, crudeness

tostada SF [1] [*de pan*] piece of toast; **~s** toast *sing*; ✦**MODISMO olerse la ~** to smell a rat
[2] **una ~ de*** a load of*, masses of; **hace una ~ de años** ages ago
[3] (*Méx*) (= *tortilla*) fried tortilla; (*CAm*) (= *plátano*) toasted slice of banana
[4] (*Cono Sur*) (= *conversación*) long boring conversation

tostado Ⓐ ADJ [1] (*Culin*) toasted
[2] [*color*] dark brown, ochre; [*persona*] tanned

Ⓑ SM [1] (= *acción*) [*de pan*] toasting; [*de café*] roasting
[2] (= *bronceado*) tan

tostador SM [*de pan*] toaster; [*de café*] roaster ► **tostador de pan** electric toaster

tostadora SF toaster

tostadura SF [*de café*] roasting

tostar ▸conjug 1l◂ Ⓐ VT [1] [+ *pan*] to toast; [+ *café*] to roast; [+ *carne*] to brown
[2] (= *broncear*) to tan
[3] (*Caribe, Cono Sur**) (= *pegar*) **~ a algn** to tan sb's hide*
[4] (*Méx*) (= *ofender*) to offend; (= *perjudicar*) to harm, hurt; (= *matar*) to kill
[5] (*Caribe, Cono Sur*) (= *proseguir*) to push on with
Ⓑ **tostarse** VPR (*tb* **~se al sol**) to tan, get brown

tostelería SF (*CAm*) cake shop

tostón SM [1] (*) (= *lata*) bore, nuisance; (= *discurso*) long boring speech; (= *cuento*) tedious tale; **dar el ~** (= *aburrir*) to be a bore; (= *fastidiar*) to be a nuisance
[2] (*Culin*) (= *cubito*) crouton; (= *tostada*) piece of toast dipped in oil; (= *tostada quemada*) *piece of bread toasted too much*; (= *garbanzo*) toasted chickpea
[3] (= *lechón*) roast sucking pig
[4] (*Caribe*) (= *banana*) slice of fried green banana
[5] (*Méx**) (= *moneda*) 50-cent piece

tostonear* ▸conjug 1a◂ VT, VI (*Méx*) to sell at bargain prices

total Ⓐ ADJ [1] (= *absoluto*) [*éxito, fracaso*] total; **una revisión ~ de su teoría** a complete revision of his theory; **una calamidad ~** a total disaster
[2] (= *global*) [*importe, suma*] total
[3] (*) (= *excelente*) smashing, brilliant; **es un libro ~** it's a brilliant book
Ⓑ ADV [1] (= *resumiendo*) in short, all in all; (= *así que*) so; **~ que** to cut a long story short, the upshot of it all was that ...; **~, que no fuimos** so we didn't go after all; **~, que vas a hacer lo que quieras** basically then you're going to do as you please
[2] (= *al fin y al cabo*) at the end of the day; **~, ¿qué más te da?** at the end of the day, what do you care?; **~, usted manda** well, you're the boss after all
Ⓒ SM (= *suma total*) total; (= *totalidad*) whole; **el ~ son 50 pesos** the total is 50 pesos; **el ~ de la población** the whole (of the) population; **en ~** in all; **en ~ éramos catorce** there were fourteen of us altogether ► **total debe** debit total ► **total de comprobación** hash total ► **total haber** assets total

totalidad SF whole; **la ~ de la población** the whole (of the) population; **la práctica ~ de los votantes** nearly all the voters; **quieren publicar el informe en su ~** they want to publish the report in its entirety; **la aseguradora cubrirá los gastos en su ~** the insurer will cover all expenses

totalitario ADJ totalitarian

totalitarismo SM totalitarianism

totalizador Ⓐ ADJ all-embracing, all-encompassing
Ⓑ SM totalizator

totalizar ▸conjug 1f◂ Ⓐ VT to totalize, add up
Ⓑ VI to add up to, total

➤ LENGUA Y USO: **totalmente** 38.1, 39.2, 40.1, 53.6

▼**totalmente** ADV totally, completely; **Mario es ~ distinto a Luis** Mario is totally *o* completely different from Luis; **estoy ~ de acuerdo** I totally *o* completely agree; **—¿estás seguro? —totalmente** "are you sure?" — "absolutely"

totazo SM [1] (*Andes*) (= *explosión*) bursting, explosion
[2] (*Andes, Caribe*) (= *golpe*) bang on the head

totear ▸conjug 1a◂ (*Andes, Caribe*) Ⓐ VI to burst, explode
Ⓑ **totearse** VPR (= *reventar*) to burst; (= *agrietarse*) to crack, split

tótem SM (*pl* **tótems**) totem, totem pole

totémico ADJ totemic

totemismo SM totemism

totopo SM (*CAm, Méx*), **totoposte** SM (*CAm, Méx*) crisp tortilla

totora SF (*Andes*) large reed

totoral SM (*LAm*) reed bed

totoreco* ADJ (*CAm*) thick*, stupid

totovía SF woodlark

totuma SF [1] (*Andes, Caribe Bot*) gourd, squash (*EEUU*), calabash
[2] (*Cono Sur*) (= *cardenal*) bruise; (= *chichón*) bump, lump
[3] (*Andes, Caribe, Cono Sur*) (= *cabeza*) nut*, head; **cortarse ~** (*Caribe*) to get one's hair cut

totumo SM [1] (*LAm*) (= *árbol*) calabash tree
[2] (*Cono Sur*) (= *chichón*) bump on the head

touroperador(a) SM/F tour operator

toxicidad SF toxicity

tóxico Ⓐ ADJ toxic, poisonous
Ⓑ SM poison, toxin

toxicodependencia SF drug-addiction

toxicodependiente SMF drug-addict

toxicología SF toxicology

toxicológico ADJ toxicological

toxicólogo/a SM/F toxicologist

toxicomanía SF drug-addiction

toxicómano/a Ⓐ ADJ addicted to drugs
Ⓑ SM/F drug addict

toximia SF toxaemia, toxemia (*EEUU*)

toxina SF toxin

toxinfección SF poisoning ► **toxinfección alimentaria** food poisoning

tozudez SF stubbornness, obstinacy

tozudo ADJ stubborn, obstinate

traba SF [1] (= *unión*) bond, tie; (*Mec*) clasp, clamp; [*de caballo*] hobble; (*Cono Sur*) hair slide
[2] **trabas** [*de prisionero*] shackles
[3] (= *estorbo*) obstacle, hindrance; **sin ~s** unrestrained, free; **poner ~s a** to restrain, obstruct; **ponerse ~s** to make difficulties for o.s.
[4] (*Caribe, Méx*) [*de gallos*] (= *pelea*) cockfight; (= *lugar*) cockpit

trabacuenta SM mistake, miscalculation; **andar con ~s** to be engaged in endless controversies

trabado ADJ [1] (= *unido*) joined; [*discurso*] coherent, well constructed
[2] (= *fuerte*) tough, strong
[3] (*LAm*) (*al hablar*) stammering
[4] (*Andes*) (= *bizco*) cross-eyed

trabajado ADJ [1] (= *elaborado*) carefully worked; **bien ~** well made, elaborately fashioned
[2] (*pey*) forced, strained, artificial
[3] [*persona*] (= *cansado*) worn out, weary from overwork

trabajador(a) Ⓐ ADJ hard-working, industrious
Ⓑ SM/F worker, labourer, laborer (*EEUU*); (*Pol*) worker ► **trabajador(a) autónomo/a** self-employed person ► **trabajador(a) eventual** casual worker ► **trabajador(a) por cuenta ajena** employee, employed person ► **trabajador(a) por cuenta propia** self-employed person ► **trabajador(a) portuario/a** docker ► **trabajador(a) social** social worker

trabajar ▸conjug 1a◂ Ⓐ VI [1] [*persona*] to work; **trabaja en las afueras** she works on the outskirts of town; **no trabajes tanto** don't work so hard; **ahora trabajo más que antes** I work harder now than I used to; **se mata trabajando para alimentar a su familia** he works himself to death to feed his family; **llevo una semana sin ~** I haven't done any work for a week; **ese actor trabaja muy bien** that actor's very good; **~ de algo** to work as sth; **trabajo de camarero** I work as a waiter; **~ en algo**: **¿en qué trabajas?** what's your job?; **¿ha trabajado antes en diseño gráfico?** do you have any previous work experience in graphic design?; **trabajan en una compañía aérea** they work for an airline; **~ por horas** to work by the hour; **~ jornada completa** to work full-time; **~ media jornada** to work half-days; **~ por hacer algo**: **estamos trabajando por conseguir nuestros derechos** we are working towards getting our rights; **~ a tiempo parcial** to work part-time; ✦***MODISMOS*** **~ como un buey** *o* **como una mula** to work like a Trojan; **~ como un condenado** *o* **un negro** to work like a slave
[2] (= *funcionar*) [*fábrica*] to work; [*máquina*] to run, work; **la fábrica trabaja día y noche** the factory works day and night; **para que el cerebro trabaje** for the brain to work (properly); **el sistema inmunitario trabaja para vencer las infecciones** the immune system works to overcome infections; **el tiempo trabaja a nuestro favor** time is on our side; **hacer ~**: **si quiere hacer trabar su dinero llámenos** if you want to make your money work for you, give us a call
[3] [*tierra, árbol*] to bear, yield
Ⓑ VT [1] [+ *tierra, cuero, madera*] to work; [+ *masa*] to knead; [+ *ingredientes*] to mix in
[2] [+ *detalle, proyecto*] to work on; [+ *mente*] to exercise; **hay que ~ un poco más los números musicales** we need to do a bit more work on the musical numbers; **el pintor ha trabajado muy bien los árboles** the painter has put a lot of work into the trees
[3] (*Com*) (= *vender*) to sell; **es mi colega quien trabaja ese género** it is my colleague who sells *o* handles that line; **nosotros no trabajamos esa marca** we don't sell *o* stock that brand
[4] [+ *caballo*] to train
Ⓒ **trabajarse** VPR [1] [+ *persona*] to work on; **se está trabajando a su tía para sacarle los ahorros** he's working on his aunt in order to get hold of her savings
[2] [+ *asunto*] to work on; **tienes que ~te el ascenso un poco más** you need to work a bit harder on getting that promotion; **tienes que ~te un poco más el alemán** you've got

to work on your German a bit; **quien no se lo trabaja no consigue nada** you won't get anything if you don't work for it

trabajo SM [1] (= *labor*) work; **tengo mucho ~** I have a lot of work; **me queda ~ para una hora** I have an hour's work left; **¡buen ~!** good work!; **en reconocimiento a su ~ como actor** in recognition of his work as an actor; **tiene una enorme capacidad de ~** she's a very willing worker; **planchar la ropa es el ~ que menos me gusta** the ironing is the job I like least; **a veces le sale algún que otro trabajillo** he gets odd jobs now and then; **el ~ de la casa** the housework; **ropa de ~** work clothes; **estar sin ~** to be unemployed; **los que están sin ~** the unemployed; **quedarse sin ~** to find o.s. out of work, lose one's job; ✦*MODISMO* **¡esto es un ~ de chinos!** this is really painstaking work! ► **trabajo a destajo** piecework ► **trabajo de campo, trabajo en el terreno** fieldwork ► **trabajo en equipo** teamwork ► **trabajo intelectual** brainwork ► **trabajo manual** manual labour, manual labor (*EEUU*) ► **trabajo nocturno** night work ► **trabajo por turnos** shiftwork ► **trabajos forzados** hard labour *sing*, hard labor (*EEUU*) *sing* ► **trabajos manuales** (*Escol*) handicrafts ► **trabajo social** social work ► **trabajo sucio** dirty work

[2] (*tb* **puesto de ~**) job; **le han ofrecido un ~ en el banco** he's been offered a job at the bank; **tengo un ~ de media jornada** I have a job working half-days; **no encuentro ~** I can't find work *o* a job ► **trabajo eventual** temporary job ► **trabajo fijo** permanent job

[3] (*tb* **lugar de ~**) work; **vivo cerca de mi ~** I live near work *o* near my workplace; **está en el ~** she's at work; **me puedes llamar al ~** you can call me at work; **ir al ~** to go to work

[4] (= *esfuerzo*) **lo hizo con mucho ~** it cost him a lot of effort to do it; **han sido muchos años de ~ para ganar el pleito** it has taken many years' hard work to win the lawsuit; **ahorrarse el ~** to save o.s. the trouble; **costar ~**: **le cuesta ~ hacerlo** he finds it hard to do; **me cuesta ~ decir que no** I find it hard to say no; **dar ~**: **reparar la casa nos ha dado mucho ~** it was hard work *o* a real job repairing the house; **los niños pequeños dan mucho ~** small children are a lot of work; **tomarse el ~ de hacer algo** to take the trouble to do sth; ✦*REFRÁN* **~ te doy, ~ te mando** it's no easy task, it's a tough job

[5] (= *obra*) (*Arte, Literat*) work; (*Educ*) essay; [*de investigación*] study; **uno de los mejores ~s del arquitecto** one of the architect's greatest works; **tengo que entregar dos ~s mañana** I have to hand in two essays tomorrow

[6] (*Econ*) [6·1] (= *mano de obra*) labour, labor (*EEUU*)

[6·2] (*tb* **Ministerio de Trabajo**) ≈ Department of Employment, ≈ Department of Labor (*EEUU*)

trabajoadicto/a SM/F workaholic

trabajosamente ADV (= *con trabajo*) laboriously; (= *dolorosamente*) painfully

trabajoso ADJ [1] (= *difícil*) hard, laborious; (= *doloroso*) painful

[2] (*Med*) pale, sickly

[3] (*Cono Sur*) (= *exigente*) exacting, demanding; (= *astuto*) wily

[4] (*Andes*) (= *poco amable*) unhelpful; (= *malhumorado*) bad-tempered, tetchy

[5] (*Cono Sur*) (= *molesto*) annoying

trabalenguas SM INV tongue twister

trabar ▸conjug 1a◂ Ⓐ VT [1] [+ *puerta, ventana*] (*para que quede cerrada*) to wedge shut; (*para que quede abierta*) to wedge open; **trabó la puerta con una silla para que no entrara** he wedged the door shut with a chair to stop her getting in; **trabó la pata de la mesa con una madera** she wedged a piece of wood under the table leg

[2] [+ *salsa, líquido*] to thicken

[3] (*Carpintería*) to join; (*Constr*) to point

[4] (= *comenzar*) [+ *conversación, debate*] to start (up), strike up; [+ *batalla*] to join; **~ amistad** to strike up a friendship

[5] (= *enlazar*) **una serie de razonamientos muy bien trabados** a tightly woven *o* very well constructed argument

[6] (= *obstaculizar*) to hold back; **la falta de recursos ha trabado el desarrollo de la investigación** research has been held back by the lack of funds

[7] [+ *caballo*] to hobble

[8] [+ *sierra*] to set

[9] (*CAm, Caribe*) (= *engañar*) to deceive

Ⓑ VI [1] [*planta*] to take

[2] [*ancla, garfio*] to grip

Ⓒ **trabarse** VPR [1] (= *enredarse*) to get tangled up; **me trabé en un matorral y no podía salir** I got tangled up in a thicket and couldn't get free; **se le traba la lengua** he gets tongue-tied; (*Caribe*) he loses the thread (of what he is saying)

[2] (= *atascarse*) [*cajón, puerta, mecanismo*] to jam, get jammed

[3] (= *involucrarse*) **~se en una discusión** to get involved in an argument

trabazón SF [1] (*Téc*) joining, assembly

[2] [*de líquido*] consistency

[3] (= *coherencia*) coherence

trabilla SF (= *tira*) small strap; (= *broche*) clasp; [*de cinturón*] belt loop; (= *puntada*) dropped stitch

trabucar ▸conjug 1g◂ Ⓐ VT (= *confundir*) to confuse; (= *desordenar*) to mix up, mess up; [+ *palabras, sonidos*] to mix up, confuse

Ⓑ **trabucarse** VPR to get all mixed up

trabuco SM [1] (*tb* **~ naranjero**) blunderbuss; (= *juguete*) popgun

[2] (**) (= *pene*) prick**

traca SF [1] [*de fuegos artificiales*] string of fireworks; (= *ruido fuerte*) row, racket

[2] **es de ~*** it's killingly funny

trácala SF [1] (*Andes*) (= *gentío*) crowd, mob

[2] (*Caribe, Méx*) (= *trampa*) trick, ruse

[3] (*Méx*) (= *tramposo*) trickster

tracalada* SF [1] (*LAm*) (= *gentío*) crowd; **una ~ de** a load of*; **a ~s** by the hundred

[2] (*Méx*) (= *trampa*) trick, ruse

tracalero/a* (*Méx, Caribe*) Ⓐ ADJ (= *astuto*) crafty; (*tramposo*) sly, deceitful

Ⓑ SM/F cheat, trickster

tracamundana* SF [1] (= *jaleo*) row, rumpus

[2] (= *cambio*) swap, exchange

tracatrá* EXCL no way!*, get away!*

tracción SF traction, drive ► **tracción a las cuatro ruedas** four-wheel drive ► **tracción delantera** front-wheel drive ► **tracción integral, tracción total** four-wheel drive ► **tracción trasera** rear-wheel drive

tracería SF tracery

tracoma SM trachoma

tractivo ADJ tractive

tractor Ⓐ SM tractor ► **tractor agrícola** agricultural tractor, farm tractor ► **tractor de oruga** caterpillar tractor

Ⓑ ADJ **rueda ~a** drive wheel

tractorada SF *demonstration where farmers block the streets with their tractors*

tractorista SMF tractor driver

trad. ABR (= **traducido**) trans

tradición SF tradition

tradicional ADJ traditional

tradicionalidad SF traditionality, traditional character

tradicionalismo SM traditionalism

tradicionalista ADJ, SMF traditionalist

tradicionalmente ADV traditionally

tráding ['tradin] Ⓐ ADJ **empresa ~** trading company

Ⓑ SF trading company

traducción SF translation (**a** into; **de** from); ► **traducción asistida por ordenador** computer-assisted translation ► **traducción automática, traducción automatizada** automatic translation, machine translation ► **traducción directa** *translation into one's own language* ► **traducción simultánea** simultaneous translation

traducible ADJ translatable

traducir ▸conjug 3n◂ Ⓐ VT to translate (**a** into; **de** from)

Ⓑ **traducirse** VPR **~se en** (= *significar*) to mean in practice; (= *suponer*) to entail, result in

traductor(a) SM/F translator ► **traductor(a) jurado/a** official translator

traer ▸conjug 2o◂ Ⓐ VT [1] (= *transportar*) to bring; **¿has traído el dinero?** have you brought the money?; **¿me traes un vaso de agua?** can you bring *o* fetch *o* get me a glass of water?; **el muchacho que trae los periódicos** the lad who delivers *o* brings the newspapers; **¿nos trae la cuenta, por favor?** can we have the bill, please?; **trae, ya lo arreglo yo** give it to me, I'll fix it; **¿me puedes ~ mañana a la oficina?** can you bring me to work *o* give me a lift to work tomorrow?; **¿qué la trae por aquí?** what brings you here?; **~ un hijo al mundo** to bring a child into the world; **~ buenas/malas notas** to get good/bad marks *o* grades (*EEUU*); ✦*MODISMO* **como su madre** *o* **como Dios lo trajo al mundo** as naked as the day he was born, in his birthday suit; *ver tb* **memoria 1**

[2] (= *llevar encima*) [+ *ropa*] to wear; [+ *objeto*] to carry; **traía unos zapatos muy bonitos** she was wearing some very nice shoes; **¿qué traes en esa bolsa?** what have you got in that bag?, what are you carrying in that bag?

[3] [*periódico, revista*] **el periódico no trae nada sobre eso** there's nothing about it in the newspaper; **¿trae alguna noticia interesante?** is there any interesting news?

[4] (= *causar*) [+ *suerte, paz, beneficios*] to bring; [+ *recuerdos*] to bring back; [+ *consecuencias*] to have; **te ~á buena suerte** it'll bring you good luck; **el embargo trajo como consecuencia la ruina económica** the embargo brought

about *o* resulted in the economic ruin; ~ **consigo** to bring about; **la recesión trajo consigo un aumento del paro** the recession brought with it *o* brought about an increase in unemployment; *ver tb* **colación 1**, **cuento[1] 3**

[5] (= *tener*) (+ *ADJ*) **la ausencia de noticias me trae muy inquieto** the lack of news is making me very anxious; **el juego lo trae perdido** gambling is his ruin; *ver tb* **loco A1**

[6] ✦*MODISMOS* **me trae sin cuidado** ◊ **me trae al fresco*** I couldn't care less*; **me la trae floja‡** I couldn't give a damn‡; ~ **de cabeza a algn**: **el caso trae de cabeza a la policía local** this case is proving to be a headache for local police; **el horario comercial trae de cabeza a los consumidores** shopping hours are a headache for consumers; **~la con algn** (*Méx*) to have it in for sb*; **llevar** *o* **~ a mal ~ a algn** [*persona*] to give sb nothing but trouble; [*problema*] to be the bane of sb's life; **¡este hijo mío me trae a mal ~!** this son of mine is really giving me a hard time!, this son of mine is (giving me) nothing but trouble!; **~ y llevar a algn** (= *molestar*) to pester sb; (= *chismorrear*) to gossip about sb; *ver tb* **traído**

[7] (= *atraer*) [+ *imán*] to draw, attract

Ⓑ **traerse** VPR [1] (= *tramar*) to be up to; **estoy seguro de que esos dos se traen algún manejo sucio** I'm sure the two of them are up to something shady; *ver tb* **mano 2**

[2] (*uso enfático*) to bring; **me he traído la cámara** I've brought the camera, I've brought the camera with me; **no se trajo al novio** she didn't bring her boyfriend

[3] (*) ✦*MODISMO* **se las trae**: **es un problema que se las trae** it's a real nightmare of a problem; **tiene un padre que se las trae** her father is impossible, her father is a real nightmare

[4] (*Esp††*) **~se bien** (= *vestirse*) to dress well; (= *comportarse*) to behave properly; **~se mal** (= *vestirse*) to dress shabbily; (= *comportarse*) to behave badly

trafagar ▸conjug 1h◂ VI to bustle about

tráfago SM [1] (= *ajetreo*) bustle, hustle

[2] (*Com*) traffic, trade

[3] (= *trabajo*) (*pesado*) drudgery, toil; (*rutinario*) routine job

trafaguear ▸conjug 1a◂ VI (*Méx*) to bustle about, keep on the go

traficante SMF dealer (**en** in); ► **traficante de armas** arms dealer ► **traficante de drogas** drug dealer ► **traficante de esclavos** slave trader

traficar ▸conjug 1g◂ VI [1] (= *negociar*) to deal (**con** with; **en** in); (*pey*) to traffic (**en** in)

[2] (†) (= *moverse*) to keep on the go, be on the move; (= *viajar*) to travel a lot

tráfico SM [1] (*Aut, Ferro*) traffic; **accidente de ~** road accident, traffic accident; **cortar el ~** to interrupt traffic ► **tráfico de carga** (*LAm*), **tráfico de mercancías** goods traffic ► **tráfico por ferrocarril** rail traffic ► **tráfico rodado** road traffic, vehicular traffic

[2] (*tb* **Dirección General de Tráfico**) *public department in charge of controlling traffic*

[3] (= *negocio*) trade; (*pey*) traffic (**en** in); ► **tráfico de drogas**, **tráfico de estupefacientes** drug traffic ► **tráfico de influencias** peddling of political favours *o* (*EEUU*) favors

[4] (*LAm*) (= *tránsito*) transit, passage

tragabalas SM INV (*Méx*) bully, braggart

tragadera‡ SF (*LAm*) slap-up do*, blow-out‡, chow-down (*EEUU‡*)

tragaderas SFPL [1] (= *garganta*) throat *sing*, gullet *sing*

[2] (= *credulidad*) gullibility *sing*; (= *tolerancia*) tolerance *sing*; **tener buenas ~** (= *ser crédulo*) to be gullible; (= *ser permisivo*) to be very easy-going, be prepared to put up with a lot

tragadero SM throat, gullet; **la comida fue un ~** (*Méx**) we stuffed ourselves*

tragador(a) SM/F glutton

tragafuegos SMF INV fire eater

trágala* Ⓐ SMF (= *glotón*) glutton

Ⓑ SM ✦*MODISMOS* **cantar el ~ a algn** to laugh in sb's face; **es el país del ~** it's the country where you accept something whether you like it or not

tragaldabas* SMF INV glutton, pig*, hog (*EEUU*)

tragaleguas* SMF INV great walker

tragalibros SMF INV (= *lector*) bookworm; (= *empollón*) swot*, grind (*EEUU*)

tragallón ADJ (*Cono Sur*) greedy

tragaluz SM skylight

tragamonedas SM INV = **tragaperras**

traganíqueles* SM INV (*CAm*) = **tragaperras**

tragantada* SF swig*, mouthful

tragantón* ADJ greedy

tragantona* SF [1] (*) (= *comilona*) slap-up meal, blow-out*, chow-down (*EEUU‡*)

[2] (= *trago*) gulp

[3] (= *acto*) (act of) swallowing hard

tragaperras SF INV (*gen*) slot machine; (*en bar*) fruit-machine, one-armed bandit; *ver tb* **máquina 1**

tragar ▸conjug 1h◂ Ⓐ VT [1] [+ *comida, bebida*] to swallow; **un poco de agua te ayudará a ~ la pastilla** the tablet will be easier to swallow with a little water; **nunca he visto a nadie ~ tanta comida*** I've never seen anyone put away so much food*; **le molesta la garganta al ~ saliva** her throat bothers her when she swallows hard; **me insultó, pero tragué saliva por respeto a su padre** he insulted me, but I bit my tongue out of respect for his father

[2] (= *absorber*) to soak up; **esta tierra traga el agua rápidamente** this ground soaks the water up very quickly

[3] (*) (= *gastar*) to use; **este coche traga mucha gasolina** this car uses a lot of petrol *o* guzzles* petrol

[4] (*) (= *aguantar*) [+ *insultos, reprimenda*] to put up with; **le ha hecho ~ mucho a su mujer** his wife has had to put up with a lot; **no puedo ~ a tu hermano** I can't stand your brother

[5] (*) (= *creer*) to swallow*, fall for*; **nadie se va a ~ esa historia** nobody is going to swallow *o* fall for that story*

Ⓑ VI [1] (*) (= *engullir*) **tu hijo traga que da gusto** your son really enjoys *o* loves his food

[2] (*) (= *creer*) to swallow*, fall for*; **—¿han tragado? —no, no se han creído nada** "did they swallow it *o* fall for it?" — "no, they didn't believe a word"*

Ⓒ **tragarse** VPR [1] [+ *comida, bebida*] to swallow; **se lo tragó entero** he swallowed it whole; **el perro se ha tragado un hueso** the dog has swallowed a bone; **eso me lo trago en dos minutos*** I could put that away in no time*

[2] (= *absorber*) [*arena, tierra*] to soak up; [*mar, abismo*] to swallow up, engulf

[3] [*teléfono, máquina*] to swallow; **la máquina del café se me ha tragado todas las monedas** the coffee machine has swallowed all my change

[4] (= *aguantar*) [+ *insultos, reprimenda*] to put up with; **tuvo que ~se las amenazas de su jefe** he had to put up with his boss's threats; **siempre tengo que ~me los problemas de los demás** I always have to sit and listen to other people's problems; **pone la tele y se traga todo lo que le echen** he puts the TV on and watches anything that's on

[5] (*) (= *creer*) to swallow*, fall for*; **se ~á todo lo que se le diga** he'll swallow *o* fall for whatever he's told*

[6] (= *reprimir*) **~se las lágrimas** to hold back one's tears; **~se el orgullo** to swallow one's pride

tragasables SMF INV sword-swallower

tragasantos SMF INV excessively pious person

tragavenado SM (*Andes, Caribe*) boa constrictor

tragedia SF tragedy; **monta una ~ de cualquier tontería** he makes a drama out of every little thing

trágicamente ADV tragically

trágico Ⓐ ADJ tragic(al); **lo ~ es que ...** the tragedy of it is that ..., the tragic thing about it is that ...

Ⓑ SM tragedian

tragicomedia SF tragicomedy

tragicómico ADJ tragicomic

trago SM [1] (*de un líquido*) drink; **un traguito de agua** a sip of water; **no vendría mal un ~ de vino** a drop of wine would not come amiss; **echar un ~** to have a drink, have a swig*; **beber algo de un ~** to drink sth in one gulp; ✦*MODISMOS* **el ~ del estribo** one for the road; **brindar el ~ a algn** (*LAm*) to stand sb a drink

[2] (= *bebida alcohólica*) drink; (*LAm*) (= *licor*) hard liquor; **¡échame un ~!** give me a drink!; **ser demasiado aficionado al ~** to be too fond of the drink

[3] (= *experiencia*) **mal ~** ◊ **~ amargo** (= *momento difícil*) hard time, rough time; (= *golpe*) blow; (= *desgracia*) misfortune, calamity; **fue un ~ amargo** it was a cruel blow; **nos quedaba todavía el ~ más amargo** the worst of it was still to come

[4] **a ~s: hacer algo a ~s** to do sth bit by bit

tragón/ona Ⓐ ADJ greedy

Ⓑ SM/F glutton; **es un ~** he is very greedy, he's a greedy pig*

traguear* ▸conjug 1a◂ Ⓐ VT, VI (*CAm*) (= *beber*) to drink; (*Caribe*) (= *emborracharse*) to get sloshed*

Ⓑ **traguearse** VPR (*Andes, CAm, Méx*) to get sloshed*

trai SM (*Cono Sur Rugby*) try

traición SF [1] (= *deslealtad*) betrayal; (= *alevosía*) treachery; **una ~** a betrayal; **cometer una ~ contra algn** to betray sb; **matar a algn a ~** to kill sb treacherously

[2] (*Jur*) treason; **alta ~** high treason

traicionar ▸conjug 1a◂ VT to betray

traicionero ADJ treacherous

traída SF carrying, bringing ► **traída de aguas** water supply

traído Ⓐ ADJ (†) worn, threadbare; ✦MODISMO **~ y llevado**: **el tan ~ y llevado tema del papel de la familia hoy día** the overworked *o* time-worn subject of the role of the family today; **el tan ~ y llevado oro de Moscú** the much talked-about Moscow gold
Ⓑ **traídos** SMPL (*Col*) presents, gifts

traidor(a) Ⓐ ADJ [*persona*] treacherous; [*acto*] treasonable
Ⓑ SM/F traitor/traitress; (*Teat*) villain

traidoramente ADV treacherously, traitorously

traiga *etc ver* **traer**

trailer SM (*pl* **trailers**), **tráiler** SM (*pl* **tráilers**)
1 (*Cine*) trailer
2 (= *caravana*) caravan, trailer (*EEUU*); [*de camión*] trailer, trailer unit

traílla SF 1 (*Téc*) scraper, leveller; (*Agr*) harrow 2 [*de perro*] lead, leash 3 (= *conjunto de perros*) team of dogs

traillar ▸conjug 1a◂ VT (= *rascar*) to scrape; (= *allanar*) to level; (*Agr*) to harrow

traína SF, **traiña** SF sardine-fishing net, dragnet

trainera SF [*de pesca*] small fishing boat (*used for trawling*); [*de remo*] *rowing boat used for racing*

training ['treinin] SM (*pl* **trainings**) 1 (= *entrenamiento*) training 2 (= *curso*) training course

Trajano SM Trajan

traje[1] *ver* **traer**

traje[2] SM (*de dos piezas*) suit; (= *vestido*) dress; (*típico*) dress, costume; (*fig*) garb, guise; **~ hecho** off-the-peg suit; **~ hecho a la medida** made-to-measure suit; **un policía en ~ de calle** a plain-clothes policeman; ✦MODISMOS **cortar un ~ a algn** to gossip about sb; **en ~ de Eva** in her birthday suit ► **traje de agua** wet suit ► **traje de baño** bathing costume, swimsuit, swimming costume ► **traje de campaña** battledress ► **traje de ceremonia** full dress ► **traje de chaqueta** suit ► **traje de cóctel** cocktail dress ► **traje de cuartel** (*Mil*) undress ► **traje de época** period costume ► **traje de etiqueta** dress suit, dinner dress ► **traje de luces** bullfighter's costume ► **traje de noche** evening dress ► **traje de novia** wedding dress, bridal gown ► **traje de oficina** business suit ► **traje de paisano** (*Esp*) civilian clothes; (*de policía*) plain clothes ► **traje de playa** sunsuit ► **traje espacial** spacesuit ► **traje isotérmico** wet suit ► **traje largo** evening gown ► **traje pantalón** trouser suit ► **traje regional** regional costume, regional dress ► **traje serio** business suit

trajeado ADJ **ir bien ~** to be well dressed, be well turned out; **estar ~ de** to be dressed in; (*hum*) to be got up in, be rigged out in; **estar bien ~ para la temporada** to have the right clothes for the weather *o* season

trajear ▸conjug 1a◂ Ⓐ VT (= *vestir*) to clothe, dress (**de** in); (*hum*) to get up, rig out (**de** in)
Ⓑ **trajearse** VPR (= *vestirse*) to dress up; (= *adquirir*) to provide o.s. with clothes

trajelarse⁑ ▸conjug 1a◂ VPR **~ una botella** to knock a bottle back*

traje-pantalón SM (*pl* **trajes-pantalón**) trouser suit

trajera *etc ver* **traer**

traje-sastre SM (*pl* **trajes-sastre**) suit, tailor-made suit

trajín SM 1 (*) (= *ajetreo*) coming and going, bustle, commotion; (= *jaleo*) fuss
2 (= *transporte*) haulage, transport
3 **trajines*** (= *actividades*) affairs, goings-on; **trajines de la casa** household chores

trajinado ADJ [*tema*] well-worked, overworked, trite

trajinar ▸conjug 1a◂ Ⓐ VI (= *ajetrearse*) to bustle about; (= *viajar*) to travel around a lot; (= *moverse mucho*) to be on the go, keep on the move
Ⓑ VT 1 (= *transportar*) to carry, transport
2 (*Cono Sur*) (= *estafar*) to swindle, deceive
3 (*Cono Sur*) (= *registrar*) to search
4 (**) (*sexualmente*) to lay⁑

trajinería SF carriage, haulage

trajinista SMF (*Caribe, Cono Sur*) busybody, snooper

tralla SF (= *cuerda*) whipcord, whiplash; (= *látigo*) lash, whip

trallazo SM 1 [*de látigo*] (= *ruido*) crack of a whip; (= *golpe*) lash
2 (*) (= *bronca*) telling-off*
3 (*Dep*) fierce shot, hard shot

trama SF 1 [*de un tejido*] weft, woof
2 [*de historia*] plot
3 (= *conjura*) plot, scheme, intrigue
4 (= *vínculo*) connection, link; (= *correlación*) correlation
5 (*Tip*) shaded area

tramar ▸conjug 1a◂ Ⓐ VT 1 (= *tejer*) to weave
2 [+ *engaño, enredo*] to plan, plot; [+ *complot*] to lay, hatch; **están tramando algo** they're up to sth; **¿qué estarán tramando?** I wonder what they're up to?
Ⓑ **tramarse** VPR **algo se está tramando** there's something going on, there's sth afoot

trambucar ▸conjug 1g◂ VI 1 (*Andes, Caribe*) (= *naufragar*) to be shipwrecked
2 (*Caribe*) (= *enloquecer*) to go out of one's mind, lose one's marbles⁑

trambuque SM (*Andes*) shipwreck

trámil ADJ (*Cono Sur*) awkward, clumsy

tramitación SF **~ de divorcio** divorce proceedings *pl*; **~ de visado** visa application; **~ de subvención** grant application procedure

tramitar ▸conjug 1a◂ VT (= *gestionar*) [+ *pasaporte, permiso*] to process; [+ *crédito*] to negotiate; **el consulado le está tramitando el pasaporte** the consulate is processing his passport application; **vamos a empezar a ~ el permiso de obras** we're going to apply for planning permission; **estoy tramitando un préstamo con el banco** I'm negotiating a loan with the bank; **ya están tramitando su divorcio** they have started divorce proceedings

trámite SM 1 (= *fase*) step, stage; **obtener un visado implica toda una serie de ~s** there are a number of steps *o* stages involved in obtaining a visa; **tuvimos que hacer muchos ~s antes de abrir el negocio** we had a lot of paperwork to do before we could start the business; **estoy harto de tantos ~s** I'm fed up with all this red tape *o* form-filling
2 (= *formalidad*) formality; **este examen es puro ~, ya tienes el puesto asegurado** this exam is purely a formality, you've already got the job
3 (= *proceso*) procedure; **para acortar los ~s lo hacemos así** to make the procedure shorter we do it this way; **de ~**: **el gobierno se limita a resolver asuntos de ~** the government is dealing only with routine business matters; **en ~** in hand; **lo tenemos en ~** we have the matter in hand, we are pursuing the matter; **el proyecto de ley está en ~ parlamentario** the bill is going through parliament; **"patente en trámite"** "patent pending", "patent applied for" ► **trámites judiciales** court proceedings

tramo SM 1 [*de carretera*] section, stretch; [*de puente*] span; [*de escalera*] flight ► **tramo cronometrado** time trial
2 [*de tiempo*] period; **el ~ final de las rebajas** the last few days of the sale
3 (= *terreno*) plot
4 (*Fin*) [*de préstamo*] tranche; [*de impuestos*] band

tramontana SF 1 (= *viento*) north wind; (= *dirección*) north; ✦MODISMO **perder la ~*** to lose one's head
2 (= *soberbia*) pride, conceit; (= *lujo*) luxury

tramontar ▸conjug 1a◂ Ⓐ VI [*sol*] to sink behind the mountains
Ⓑ **tramontarse** VPR to escape over the mountains

tramoya SF 1 (*Teat*) piece of stage machinery
2 (= *enredo*) plot, scheme; (= *estafa*) trick, swindle; (= *parte oculta*) secret part (of a deal)

tramoyar ▸conjug 1a◂ VT (*Andes, Caribe*) to swindle

tramoyero ADJ (*CAm, Caribe*) tricky, sharp

tramoyista SMF 1 (*Teat*) stagehand, scene shifter
2 (= *estafador*) swindler, trickster; (= *farsante*) humbug; (= *impostor*) impostor; (= *intrigante*) schemer

trampa SF 1 (*para cazar*) trap; (= *lazo*) snare ► **trampa explosiva** (*Mil*) booby trap ► **trampa mortal** death trap ► **trampa para ratas** rat trap
2 (= *engaño*) trap; **no vayas, es una ~** don't go, it's a trap; **esto tiene ~** ◊ **aquí hay ~** there's a catch here; **caer en la ~** to fall into the trap; **coger a algn en la ~** to catch sb lying; **tender una ~ a algn** to set *o* lay a trap for sb; ✦MODISMO **ni ~ ni cartón**: **este contrato no tiene ni ~ ni cartón** there's no hidden catch in this contract
3 (*en el juego*) **¡eso es ~!** that's cheating!; **hacer ~(s)** to cheat
4 (= *puerta*) trapdoor; [*de mostrador*] hatch
5 (*Golf*) bunker, sand trap (*EEUU*)
6 (*Com*) bad debt
7 (†) (= *bragueta*) fly

trampantojo* SM (= *juego de manos*) sleight of hand, trick; (= *chanchullo*) fiddle*, cheat; (= *método poco limpio*) underhand method

trampear ▸conjug 1a◂ Ⓐ VT (*en el juego*) to cheat
Ⓑ VI 1 (= *hacer trampa*) to cheat; (= *conseguir dinero*) to get money by false pretences
2 (= *ir tirando*) to manage, get by
3 [*vestido, zapatos etc*] to last out

trampería SF = **tramposería**

trampero Ⓐ ADJ (*CAm, Cono Sur, Méx*) = **tramposo A**
Ⓑ SM 1 (= *cazador*) trapper
2 (*Cono Sur*) (= *trampa*) trap for birds

trampilla SF [1] (= *escotilla*) trap, hatchway ► **trampilla de carburante** filler cap, fuel (tank) cap
[2] (= *mirilla*) peephole
[3] (= *bragueta*) fly

trampista SMF = **tramposo B**

trampolín SM [1] (*Dep*) (*en piscina*) springboard, diving board; (*en gimnasia*) trampoline; [*de esquí*] ski-jump
[2] (*para conseguir algo*) springboard

trampón* ADJ crooked*

tramposería SF crookedness

tramposo/a Ⓐ ADJ crooked, tricky; **ser ~** to be a cheat
Ⓑ SM/F [1] (*en el juego*) cheat; (= *estafador*) crook*, shyster (*EEUU*), swindler; (= *tahúr*) cardsharp
[2] (*Fin*) bad payer

tranca SF [1] [*de puerta, ventana*] bar; ✦***MODISMO*** **a ~s y barrancas** with great difficulty, overcoming many obstacles
[2] (= *garrote*) cudgel, club
[3] (*esp LAm**) (= *borrachera*) **tener una ~** to be drunk
[4] **trancas** (*Méx**) (= *piernas*) legs; ✦***MODISMO*** **saltar las ~s** (*Méx*) (= *rebelarse*) to rebel; (= *perder la paciencia*) to lose one's patience
[5] (*Cono Sur*) [*de escopeta*] safety catch
[6] (*Caribe*) dollar, peso
[7] (*Caribe Aut*) traffic jam
[8] (*Cono Sur**) (= *complejo*) complex, neurosis

trancada SF (= *paso*) stride; **en dos ~s** (*lit*) in a couple of strides; (*fig*) in a couple of ticks

trancantrulla SF (*Cono Sur*) trick, fraud

trancaperros SM INV (*Caribe*) row, scrap

trancar ▸conjug 1g◂ Ⓐ VT [1] [+ *puerta, ventana*] to bar
[2] (*Caribe Aut*) to box in, block in, shut in
Ⓑ VI (*al caminar*) to stride along
Ⓒ **trancarse** VPR [1] (*LAm*) (= *estar estreñido*) to be constipated
[2] (*Caribe**) to get drunk

trancazo SM [1] (= *golpe*) blow, bang (with a stick)
[2] (*) (= *gripe*) flu

trance SM [1] (= *momento difícil*) **estamos pasando por un mal ~** we're going through a difficult period *o* patch; **aún no ha logrado superar el ~** he still hasn't managed to get over what he's been through; **puesto en tal ~** placed in such a predicament; **estar en ~ de muerte** to be at death's door; **estar en ~ de hacer algo** to be on the point of doing sth; **último ~** last *o* dying moments; **a todo ~** at all costs ► **trance mortal** last *o* dying moments *pl*
[2] [*de médium*] trance; (*Rel*) trance, ecstasy; **entrar en ~** to fall *o* go into a trance; **estar en ~** to be in a trance

tranco SM [1] (= *paso*) stride, big step; **andar a ~s** to walk with long strides, take big steps; **en dos ~s** (*lit*) in a couple of strides; (*fig*) in a couple of ticks
[2] (*Arquit*) threshold

trancón SM (*Col Aut*) traffic jam

tranque SM (*Cono Sur*) (= *presa*) dam; (= *embalse*) reservoir

tranquera SF [1] (= *cercado*) palisade, fence
[2] (*LAm*) (*para ganado*) cattle gate

tranquero SM (*Andes, Caribe, Cono Sur*) cattle gate

tranqui* Ⓐ EXCL cool it!*, calm down!
Ⓑ ADJ = **tranquilo**

tranquilamente ADV [1] (= *plácidamente*) peacefully; **el bebé dormía ~ en su cuna** the baby was sleeping peacefully in its cot
[2] (= *sin prisa*) **fuimos paseando ~ hasta el pueblo** we took a leisurely stroll into the village; **piénsalo ~ antes de responder** take your time and think about it before you answer
[3] (= *con aplomo*) calmly; **háblale ~** speak to him calmly
[4] (= *sin preocupación*) **le puedo contar todos mis secretos ~** I can tell her all my secrets with no worries
[5] (= *con descaro*) **y se fue ~ sin pagar** and he went off, cool as you please *o* like, without paying
[6] (= *fácilmente*) **se puede ver ~ tres películas seguidas** he's quite capable of watching three films in a row

tranquilidad SF [1] (= *placidez*) peace; **¡qué ~ se respira en el campo!** the countryside is so peaceful!; **si no hay ~ no puedo estudiar** I can't study without peace and quiet; **con tres hijos no tengo ni un momento de ~** with three children I never get a moment's peace
[2] (= *falta de prisa*) **llévatelo a casa y léelo con ~** take it home and read it at your leisure
[3] (= *aplomo*) calm; **respondió con ~** he answered calmly
[4] (= *falta de preocupación*) **para mayor ~ llama a tus padres** call your parents, to put your mind at rest; **¡qué ~! ya se han acabado los exámenes** what a relief, the exams are over at last!; **puedes decírmelo con total ~, no se lo contaré a nadie** you're quite safe telling me, I won't tell anyone; **perder la ~** to lose patience
[5] (= *descaro*) **dijo con toda ~ que no pensaba pagar** she said quite calmly *o* as cool as you please *o* like that she didn't intend to pay

tranquilino/a SM/F (*LAm*) drunkard

tranquilizador ADJ [*música*] soothing; [*hecho*] reassuring

tranquilizadoramente ADV (*calmando*) soothingly; (*quitando ansiedad*) reassuringly

tranquilizante Ⓐ ADJ = **tranquilizador**
Ⓑ SM (*Med*) tranquillizer, tranquilizer (*EEUU*)

tranquilizar ▸conjug 1f◂ Ⓐ VT to calm down; **un brandy te ~á** a brandy will calm you down; **el árbitro intentó ~ a los jugadores** the referee tried to calm the players down; **las palabras del médico me ~on** the doctor's words reassured me; **¿por qué no llamas a tu madre para ~la?** why don't you call your mother to put her mind at rest?
Ⓑ **tranquilizarse** VPR to calm down; **¡tranquilícese!** calm down!; **se tranquilizó al saber que habían llegado bien** she stopped worrying when she found out that they had arrived safely

tranquilla SF [1] (= *pasador*) latch, pin
[2] (*en conversación*) trap, catch
[3] (*Andes*) (= *obstáculo*) hindrance, obstacle

tranquillo* SM knack; **coger el ~ a algo** to get the hang of sth, get the knack of sth

tranquilo/a Ⓐ ADJ [1] (= *plácido*) [*sitio, momento*] quiet, peaceful; [*mar*] calm; **se fueron a vivir a un pueblecito ~** they went to live in a quiet *o* peaceful little village; **una tarde tranquila** a quiet *o* peaceful afternoon
[2] (= *sosegado*) calm; **es una persona muy tranquila** she's a very calm person; **el día del examen estaba bastante ~** the day of the exam I was quite calm; **contestó muy ~ a todas las preguntas** he answered all the questions calmly
[3] (= *sin preocupación*) **¡estad ~s que yo me encargo de todo** don't worry, I'll look after everything; **tú estáte ~ hasta que yo vuelva** you stay put till I come back; **¡deja ya ~ al pobre chico!** leave the poor boy alone!; **¡~, no merece la pena enfadarse!** calm down! there's no point getting annoyed; **¡eh, ~, sin empujar!** hey, easy does it! no pushing!; **tener la conciencia tranquila** to have a clear conscience
[4] (= *descarado*) **¡mira que es tranquila! todos esperando y ella como si nada** nothing seems to bother her! everyone's waiting and she couldn't care less; **se quedó tan ~** he didn't bat an eyelid; **lo ha suspendido todo y él tan ~** he's failed the lot, but it doesn't seem to worry him
Ⓑ SM/F **¡es una tranquila de cuidado! aún no ha acabado los deberes** she's not bothered about anything, that one — she still hasn't finished her homework!

tranquis* ADJ **hacer algo en plan ~** to take one's time to do sth

tranquiza SF (*Andes, Méx*) beating

Trans. ABR (*Com*) = **transferencia**

trans... PREF trans...; *ver tb* **tras...**

transacción SF [1] (*Com*) transaction; (= *acuerdo*) deal, bargain ► **transacción comercial** business deal
[2] (*Jur*) (*para evitar un pleito*) compromise, compromise settlement; **llegar a una ~** to reach a compromise

transandino ADJ trans-Andean

transar[1] ▸conjug 1a◂ Ⓐ VT (*Cono Sur*) (= *comerciar*) to trade
Ⓑ VI (*LAm*) = **transigir A**

transar[2] ▸conjug 1a◂ VT (*Méx*) (= *defraudar*) to cheat, swindle, defraud

transatlántico Ⓐ ADJ transatlantic; [*travesía*] Atlantic; **los países ~s** the countries on the other side of the Atlantic
Ⓑ SM (= *barco*) (ocean) liner

transbordador Ⓐ SM (*Náut*) ferry; (*Aer*) shuttle ► **transbordador espacial** space shuttle ► **transbordador funicular** cable railway ► **transbordador para coches** car ferry
Ⓑ ADJ **puente ~** transporter bridge

transbordar ▸conjug 1a◂ Ⓐ VT (*gen*) to transfer; (*Náut*) to transship
Ⓑ VI (*Ferro*) to change

transbordo SM [1] (*Ferro*) [*de pasajeros*] change; **hacer ~** to change (**en** at)
[2] [*de equipajes*] transfer

transcender ▸conjug 2g◂ VT = **trascender**

transceptor SM transceiver

transcribir ▸conjug 3a◂ (*pp* **transcrito**) VT (= *copiar*) to transcribe; (*de alfabeto distinto*) to transliterate

transcripción SF (= *copia*) transcription; [*de alfabeto distinto*] transliteration

transcrito PP *de* **transcribir**

transcultural ADJ cross-cultural

transculturización SF transculturation

transcurrir ▸conjug 3a◂ VI [1] [*tiempo*] to pass, elapse; **han transcurrido siete años** seven years have passed
[2] [*acto, celebración*] to pass, go; **la manifestación transcurrió sin incidentes** the demonstration passed without incident; **todo transcurrió normalmente** everything went normally

transcurso SM passing, lapse, course; **~ del tiempo** course of time, passing of time; **en el ~ de ocho días** in the course o space of a week; **en el ~ de los años** over the years

transecto SM transect

transepto SM transept

transeúnte Ⓐ ADJ (= *no residente*) transient, transitory; [*miembro*] temporary
Ⓑ SMF [1] (*en la calle*) passer-by; **~s** passers-by
[2] (= *no residente*) non-resident; (*euf*) (= *mendigo*) vagrant

transexual ADJ, SMF transsexual

transexualidad SF transsexuality

transexualismo SM transsexualism

transferencia SF [1] (*Jur, Dep*) transfer ► **transferencia bancaria** banker's order, bank transfer ► **transferencia cablegráfica** cable transfer ► **transferencia de crédito** credit transfer ► **transferencia electrónica de fondos** electronic funds transfer ► **transferencia por cable** cable transfer
[2] (*Psic*) transference

transferible ADJ transferable

transferir ▸conjug 3i◂ VT to transfer

transfiguración SF transfiguration

transfigurar ▸conjug 1a◂ VT to transfigure (**en** into)

transformable ADJ transformable; (*Aut*) convertible

transformación SF [1] (= *cambio*) transformation, change (**en** into; **en** into)
[2] (*Culin*) processing
[3] (*Rugby*) conversion

transformacional ADJ transformational

transformador SM (*Elec*) transformer

transformar ▸conjug 1a◂ Ⓐ VT [1] (= *convertir*) **~ algo en algo** to turn sth into sth; **han transformado el palacio en museo** they have turned o converted the palace into a museum; **pretendía ~ el plomo en oro** he aimed to turn lead into gold
[2] (= *cambiar*) to transform; **su novia lo ha transformado** his girlfriend has transformed him; **las nuevas tecnologías han transformado el mundo de la comunicación** new technology has transformed the world of communications
[3] (*Rugby*) to convert
Ⓑ **transformarse** VPR [1] (= *convertirse*) **~se en algo** to turn into sth; **al hervir, el agua se transforma en vapor** water turns o is converted into steam when it boils; **la rana se transformó en príncipe** the frog turned into a prince
[2] (= *cambiar*) **cuando sonríe se le transforma la cara** her face is transformed when she smiles; **desde que dejó de beber se ha transformado** since he stopped drinking he's a changed man

transformismo SM [1] (*Biol*) evolution, transmutation
[2] (*sexual*) transvestism

transformista SMF [1] (*Teat*) quick-change artist(e)
[2] (*sexual*) transvestite

transfronterizo ADJ cross-border *antes de s*; **seguridad transfronteriza** cross-border security

tránsfuga SMF (*Pol*) [*de partido*] turncoat; [*de nación*] defector

transfuguismo SM tendency to defect

transfundir ▸conjug 3a◂ VT [1] [+ *líquidos*] to transfuse
[2] [+ *noticias*] to tell, spread

transfusión SF transfusion ► **transfusión de sangre, transfusión sanguínea** blood transfusion; **hacer una ~ de sangre a algn** to give sb a blood transfusion

transgenia SF genetic modification

transgénico ADJ genetically modified, GM *antes de s*

transgredir ▸conjug 3a◂ VT, VI to transgress

transgresión SF transgression

transgresor(a) SM/F transgressor

transiberiano ADJ trans-Siberian

transición SF transition (**a** to; **de** from); **período de ~** transitional period; **la ~** (*Esp Pol*) the transition (*to democracy after Franco's death*)

LA TRANSICIÓN

The death of General Franco on 20 November 1975 ushered in a period of transition to democracy in Spain which was to end with the democratic transfer of power to the **PSOE** *(Spanish Socialist Party) on November 28, 1982.*
On 22 November 1975 Juan Carlos I was proclaimed king. Though initially handicapped by a constitutional system devised by Franco, the King was able to appoint the **aperturista** *Adolfo Suárez as Prime Minister in July 1976. Within three months Suárez rushed through a political reform bill introducing universal suffrage and a two-chamber parliament which was put to a referendum and endorsed by 94.2% of the electorate. Political parties were legalized and elections were held on 15 June 1977. Suárez and his party, the newly-formed* **UCD** *(***Unión de Centro Democrático***), won without gaining an overall majority. Through accords with the other parties — the* **Pactos de la Moncloa** *- they were able to manage the transitional process, which included the drafting and endorsement of the 1978 Constitution.*
The **UCD** *went on to win the next general election in 1979 by an even tighter margin. Splits within the party finally led to Suárez's resignation in 1981, which was seized upon by sections of the military as the opportunity for a coup. Early general elections in November 1982 led to a landslide victory for the Socialists.*
⇨ *See also* APERTURISMO, 23-F

transicional ADJ transitional

transido ADJ **~ de angustia** beset with anxiety; **~ de dolor** racked with pain; **~ de frío** frozen to the marrow; **~ de hambre** fainting with hunger

transigencia SF [1] (= *avenencia*) compromise; (*cediendo*) yielding
[2] (= *actitud*) spirit of compromise, accommodating attitude

transigente ADJ [1] (= *que cede*) accommodating
[2] (= *tolerante*) tolerant

transigir ▸conjug 3c◂ Ⓐ VI [1] (= *ceder*) to give way, make concessions; **hemos transigido con la demanda popular** we have bowed to popular demand
[2] (= *tolerar*) **~ con algo** to tolerate sth; **yo no transijo con tales abusos** I cannot tolerate this sort of outrage
Ⓑ VT **~ un pleito** (*Jur*) to settle (a suit) out of court

Transilvania SF Transylvania

transistor SM transistor

transistorizado ADJ transistorized

transitable ADJ passable

transitar ▸conjug 1a◂ VI [*vehículo*] to travel; [*peatón*] to go, walk; **calle transitada** busy street; **~ por** to go along, pass along

transitivamente ADV transitively

transitivo ADJ transitive

tránsito SM [1] (= *paso*) transit, passage, movement; **"se prohíbe el ~"** "no thoroughfare"; **el ~ de este camino presenta dificultades** the going on this road is not easy; **estar de ~** to be in transit, be passing through; **en ~** in transit
[2] (= *tráfico*) movement, traffic; **calle de mucho ~** busy street; **horas de máximo ~** rush hour *sing*, peak (traffic) hours ► **tránsito rodado** vehicular traffic
[3] [*de puesto*] transfer, move
[4] (= *muerte*) passing, death
[5] (= *parada*) [*de transporte público*] stop; [*de turismos*] stopping place; **hacer ~** to make a stop
[6] (= *pasillo*) passageway

transitoriedad SF transience

transitorio ADJ [1] (= *provisional*) [*medida*] provisional, temporary; [*período*] transitional, of transition
[2] (= *pasajero*) transitory

transliteración SF transliteration

transliterar ▸conjug 1a◂ VT to transliterate

translucidez SF translucence

translúcido ADJ translucent

transmarino ADJ overseas

transmigración SF migration, transmigration

transmigrar ▸conjug 1a◂ VI to migrate, transmigrate

transmisibilidad SF (*Med*) contagiousness, ability to be transmitted

transmisible ADJ transmissible; (*Med*) contagious

transmisión SF [1] (= *acto*) transmission; (*Jur*) transfer ► **transmisión de dominio** transfer of ownership
[2] (*Mec*) transmission
[3] (*Elec*) transmission; (*Radio, TV*) transmission, broadcast(ing) ► **transmisión en circuito** hookup ► **transmisión en diferido** recorded programme o (*EEUU*) program, repeat broadcast ► **transmisión en directo** live broadcast ► **transmisión exterior** outside broadcast ► **transmisión por satélite** satellite broadcasting
[4] **transmisiones** (*Mil*) signals (corps)

5 (*Inform*) **media ~ bidireccional** half duplex; **plena ~ bidireccional** full duplex ► **transmisión de datos** data transmission ► **transmisión de datos en paralelo** parallel data transmission ► **transmisión de datos en serie** serial data transmission

transmisor Ⓐ ADJ transmitting; **aparato ~** ◊ **estación ~a** transmitter
Ⓑ SM transmitter

transmisora SF transmitter, radio relay station

transmisor-receptor SM transceiver; (*portátil*) walkie-talkie

▼ **transmitir** ▸conjug 3a◂ Ⓐ VT 1 (*Radio, TV*) [+ *señal, sonido*] to transmit; [+ *programa*] to broadcast
2 [+ *bienes, saludos, recados*] to pass on
3 [+ *enfermedad, gérmenes*] to give, pass on
4 (*Jur*) to transfer (**a** to)
Ⓑ VI (*Radio, TV*) to broadcast

transmutable ADJ transmutable

transmutación SF transmutation

transmutar ▸conjug 1a◂ VT to transmute (**en** into)

transnacional Ⓐ ADJ transnational, international
Ⓑ SF transnational (company), multinational (company)

transoceánico ADJ transoceanic

transparencia SF 1 [*de cristal, agua*] transparency
2 (= *claridad*) openness, transparency; **el nuevo Ejecutivo se caracteriza por su ~** the new Government is characterized by its policy of openness; **todos los partidos prometen ~ en su financiación** all the parties are promising to be open about their sources of finance, all the parties are promising financial transparency ► **transparencia fiscal** fiscal *o* tax transparency ► **transparencia informativa** information transparency *o* disclosure
3 (*Fot*) slide, transparency

transparentar ▸conjug 1a◂ Ⓐ VT (= *dejar ver*) to reveal, allow to be seen; [+ *emoción*] to reveal, betray
Ⓑ VI [*ser transparente*] to be transparent; (= *dejarse ver*) to show through
Ⓒ **transparentarse** VPR 1 [*vidrio, agua*] to be transparent, be clear; [*objeto, ropa*] to show through; **se te transparenta el sujetador** your bra is showing through, you can see your bra through that
2 (*) [*ropa gastada*] to become threadbare; [*persona*] to be dreadfully thin
3 (= *insinuarse*) to show clearly, become perceptible; **se transparentaba su verdadera intención** his real intention became clear

transparente Ⓐ ADJ 1 [*agua, cristal*] transparent, clear; [*aire*] clear; [*vestido*] see-through
2 [*persona*] transparent; [*intenciones, motivos*] clear, transparent
3 [*gestión, contabilidad*] open, transparent; **el Presidente ha prometido una gestión ~** the President has promised open *o* transparent government
Ⓑ SM (= *pantalla*) blind, shade

transpiración SF 1 (= *sudor*) perspiration
2 (*Bot*) transpiration

transpirar ▸conjug 1a◂ VI 1 (= *sudar*) to perspire
2 [*líquido*] to seep through, ooze out; (*Bot*) to transpire
3 (= *revelarse*) to transpire, become known

transpirenaico ADJ [*ruta*] trans-Pyrenean; [*tráfico*] passing through *o* over the Pyrenees

transplantar ▸conjug 1a◂ VT = **trasplantar**

transpondedor SM transponder

transponer ▸conjug 2q◂ (*pp* **transpuesto**) Ⓐ VT 1 (*gen*) to transpose; (= *cambiar de sitio*) to switch over, move about
2 (= *trasplantar*) to transplant
3 **~ la esquina** to disappear round the corner
Ⓑ VI (= *desaparecer*) to disappear from view; (= *ir más allá*) to go beyond, get past; [*sol*] to go down
Ⓒ **transponerse** VPR 1 (= *cambiarse*) to change places
2 (= *esconderse*) to hide (behind); [*sol*] to go down
3 (= *dormirse*) to doze (off)

transportable ADJ transportable; **fácilmente ~** easily carried, easily transported

transportación SF transportation

transportador SM 1 (*Mec*) conveyor, transporter ► **transportador de banda**, **transportador de correa** conveyor belt
2 (*Mat*) protractor

transportar ▸conjug 1a◂ Ⓐ VT 1 [+ *tropas, mercancías*] (*gen*) to transport; (*en barco*) to ship; **transportan el ganado por ferrocarril** the livestock is transported by rail; **el camión transportaba medicamentos** the lorry was carrying medicines; **el avión podrá ~ 100 pasajeros** the plane will be able to carry 100 passengers; **aquella música la transportaba a su adolescencia** that music took her back *o* transported her to when she was a teenager
2 (*Elec*) [+ *corriente*] to transmit
3 (*Mús*) to transpose
Ⓑ **transportarse** VPR (= *extasiarse*) to be transported, be enraptured

transporte SM 1 [*de pasajeros, tropas*] transport, transportation (*EEUU*); [*de mercancías*] transport, transportation (*EEUU*), carriage; **se me va el sueldo en ~** all my wages go on transport; **¿cuál es su medio de ~ habitual?** what is your usual means of transport?; **Ministerio de Transportes** Ministry of Transport, Department of Transportation (*EEUU*) ► **transporte colectivo** public transport, public transportation (*EEUU*) ► **transporte de mercancías** goods transport ► **transporte escolar** school buses *pl* ► **transporte por carretera** road transport, haulage ► **transporte público** public transport, public transportation (*EEUU*)
2 (*Náut*) transport, troopship
3 (= *éxtasis*) transport
4 (*Méx**) vehicle

transportista Ⓐ SMF (*Aut*) haulier, haulage contractor
Ⓑ SM (*Aer*) carrier

transposición SF transposition

transpuesto ADJ **quedarse ~** to doze off

transustanciación SF transubstantiation

transustanciar ▸conjug 1b◂ VT to transubstantiate

transvasar ▸conjug 1a◂ VT = **trasvasar**

transversal Ⓐ ADJ transverse, cross; (= *oblicuo*) oblique; **calle ~** cross street; **otra calle ~ de la calle mayor** another street which crosses the high street
Ⓑ SF **una ~ de la Gran Vía** a street crossing *o* which cuts across the Gran Vía

transversalmente ADV (= *cruzando*) transversely, across; (= *oblicuamente*) obliquely

transverso ADJ = **transversal A**

transvestido/a ADJ, SM/F transvestite

transvestismo SM transvestism

tranvía SM (= *coche*) tram(car), streetcar (*EEUU*); (= *sistema*) tramway; (*Ferro*) local train

trapacear* ▸conjug 1a◂ VI (= *trampear*) to cheat, be on the fiddle*; (= *causar líos*) to make mischief

trapacería* SF 1 (= *trampa*) racket, fiddle*
2 (= *chisme*) piece of gossip, malicious rumour *o* (*EEUU*) rumor

trapacero/a* Ⓐ ADJ (= *tramposo*) dishonest, swindling
Ⓑ SM/F 1 (= *tramposo*) cheat, swindler
2 (= *chismoso*) gossip, mischief-maker

trapacista SMF = **trapacero B**

trapajoso ADJ 1 (= *andrajoso*) shabby, ragged
2 [*pronunciación*] defective, incorrect; [*persona*] (*que habla mal*) who talks incorrectly; (*con defecto*) who has a speech defect

trápala Ⓐ SF 1 [*de caballo*] clatter, clip-clop
2 (*) (= *jaleo*) row, uproar, shindy*; (= *parloteo*) talkativeness
3 (= *trampa*) swindle, trick
Ⓑ SMF 1 (*) (= *hablador*) chatterbox*
2 (*) (= *tramposo*) swindler, cheat

trapalear ▸conjug 1a◂ VI 1 [*caballo*] to clatter, beat its hooves, clip-clop; [*persona*] to clatter, go clattering along
2 (*) (= *parlotear*) to chatter, jabber
3 (= *mentir*) to fib, lie; (= *trampear*) to be on the fiddle*

trapalero* ADJ (*Caribe*) = **trapalón**

trapalón* ADJ (= *mentiroso*) lying; (= *tramposo*) dishonest, swindling

trapalonear ▸conjug 1a◂ VI (*Cono Sur*) = **trapalear 3**

trapatiesta* SF (= *jaleo*) commotion, uproar, shindy*; (= *pelea*) fight, brawl

trapaza SF = **trapacería**

trapeador SM (*LAm*) floor mop

trapear ▸conjug 1a◂ VT 1 (*LAm*) [+ *suelo*] to mop
2 (*CAm**) (= *pegar*) to beat, tan*; (= *insultar*) to insult; (= *regañar*) to tick off*

trapecio SM 1 (*en gimnasia, circo*) trapeze
2 (*Mat*) trapezium, trapezoid (*EEUU*)

trapecista SMF trapeze artist(e)

trapería SF 1 (= *trapos*) rags *pl*; (= *ropa vieja*) old clothes *pl*
2 (= *tienda*) [*de ropa*] second-hand clothes shop; [*de cacharros*] junk shop

trapero/a Ⓐ ADJ *ver* **puñalada**
Ⓑ SM/F ragman/ragwoman

trapezoide SM trapezoid

trapicar ▸conjug 1g◂ VI (*Cono Sur*) [*comida*] to taste very hot; [*herida*] to sting, smart

trapichar ▸conjug 1a◂ VT (*Andes, Méx*) to smuggle (in); (*Caribe*) to deal in

trapiche SM 1 (*para aceite de oliva*) olive-oil press; (*para azúcar*) sugar mill
2 (*Andes, Cono Sur Min*) ore crusher

trapichear* ▸conjug 1a◂ Ⓐ VI 1 (= *hacer trampa*) to be on the fiddle*; (= *tramar*) to plot, scheme; (= *andar en malos pasos*) to be

➤ LENGUA Y USO: **transmitir A2** 49

mixed up in something shady*
2 (*Cono Sur*) (= *comerciar*) to scrape a living by buying and selling
Ⓑ VT to deal in, trade in

trapicheo* SM fiddle*, shady deal*; **trapicheos** (= *trampas*) fiddles*, shady dealing* *sing*; (= *intrigas*) plots, schemes, tricks

trapichero/a* SM/F 1 (= *negociante*) small-time dealer
2 (*Andes, Caribe*) (= *entrometido*) busybody

trapiento ADJ ragged, tattered

trapillo SM **estar** *o* **ir de ~** to be dressed in ordinary clothes, be informally dressed

trapío* SM 1 (= *encanto*) charm; (= *garbo*) elegance, graceful way of moving; **tener buen ~** to have a fine presence, carry o.s. elegantly, move well *o* gracefully; (*fig*) to have real class
2 [*de toro*] fine appearance

trapisonda SF 1 (= *pelea*) row, brawl; (= *jaleo*) row, commotion, shindy*
2 (*) (= *trampa*) swindle, fiddle*; (= *asunto sucio*) monkey business*, shady affair*, fiddle*; (= *intriga*) intrigue

trapisondear ▸conjug 1a◂ VI (= *intrigar*) to scheme, plot, intrigue; (= *hacer trampa*) to fiddle*, wangle*

trapisondeo* SM, **trapisondería*** SF (= *intriga*) scheming, plotting, intrigues; (= *trampa*) fiddling*, wangling*

trapisondista* SMF (= *conspirador*) schemer, intriguer; (= *tramposo*) fiddler*, wangler*

trapito* SM **cada día se pone un ~ distinto** she puts on some different garb every day, she's in some different get-up every day*; **siempre se está comprando ~s** she's always buying herself clothes; ✦*MODISMO* **sacar los ~s al sol** (*LAm*) to rake up the past ► **trapitos de cristianar**† Sunday best, glad rags*

trapo SM 1 (= *paño para limpiar*) (*gen*) cloth; (*usado, raído*) rag; **un ~ húmedo** a damp cloth; **pasar un ~ por** [+ *suelo*] to give a wipe over *o* down; [+ *muebles*] to dust ► **trapo de cocina** (*para secar los platos*) tea towel, dish towel (*EEUU*); (*para limpiar*) dish cloth ► **trapo del polvo** duster, dust cloth (*EEUU*)
2 (= *trozo de tela*) (*gen*) piece of material; (*usado, raído*) rag, piece of rag; **un dragón de cartón y ~** a dragon made of cardboard and rags; ✦*MODISMO* **tener manos de ~** to have butterfingers; *ver tb* **muñeca 2**
3 **trapos*** (= *ropa*) clothes; **gasta una barbaridad en ~s** she spends a fortune on clothes
4 (*Náut*) (= *vela*) canvas, sails *pl*; **a todo ~** under full sail
5 (*Taur**) cape
6 ✦*MODISMOS* **como un ~***: **dejar a algn como un ~*** to tear sb to shreds*; **estar como un ~*** to be like a limp rag*; **poner a algn como un ~*** to lay into sb*, slag sb off‡; **entrar a** *o* **al ~** to go on the attack; **no pudo aguantar más críticas y entró al ~** he couldn't stand being criticized any longer and went on the attack; **hecho un ~*** = **como un trapo**; **soltar el ~** (*al llorar*) to burst into tears; (*al reír*) to burst out laughing; **a todo ~*** (= *muy rápido*) at full speed, flat out*; (= *a toda potencia*) full blast, at full blast; (*LAm*) (= *a todo lujo*) in style; **iban a todo ~** they were going at full speed *o* flat out*; **tenían la música puesta a todo ~** they had the music on (at) full blast; **celebraron la boda a todo ~** they celebrated the wedding in style; **llorar a todo ~** to cry one's eyes out ► **trapos sucios**: **no quieren que salgan a la luz los ~s sucios** they don't want the skeletons in the cupboard to come out; **lavar los ~s sucios en casa** not to wash one's dirty linen in public; **en la cena sacaron los ~s sucios (a relucir** *o* (*Esp*) **a la luz)** everyone at the dinner party washed their dirty linen in public; **le sacaron los ~s sucios a relucir** they were raking up his past

traposiento ADJ (*Andes*) ragged

traposo ADJ 1 (*Andes, Caribe, Cono Sur*) (= *harapiento*) ragged
2 (*Cono Sur*) = **trapajoso 2**
3 (*Cono Sur*) [*carne*] tough, stringy

trapujear ▸conjug 1a◂ VI (*CAm*) to smuggle

trapujero SM (*CAm*) smuggler

traque SM 1 (= *ruido*) crack, bang
2 (‡) (= *pedo*) noisy fart‡

tráquea SF trachea, windpipe

traquear ▸conjug 1a◂ Ⓐ VT 1 (*CAm, Cono Sur, Méx*) (= *dejar huella*) to make deep tracks on
2 (*Caribe*) [+ *persona*] to take about from place to place; (*Cono Sur*) [+ *ganado*] to switch from place to place
3 (*Caribe*) (= *probar*) to test, try out; (= *entrenar*) to train
Ⓑ VI 1 (*con ruido*) = **traquetear B**
2 (*Cono Sur*) (= *frecuentar*) to frequent a place
3 (*Caribe*) (= *beber*) to drink
Ⓒ **traquearse** VPR (*Caribe*) to go out of one's mind

traqueo SM = **traqueteo**

traqueotomía SF tracheotomy, tracheostomy

traqueteado ADJ hectic, busy

traquetear ▸conjug 1a◂ Ⓐ VT [+ *recipiente*] to shake; [+ *sillas etc*] to rattle, bang about, make a lot of noise with, muck about with
Ⓑ VI 1 (*con ruido*) [*vehículo*] to rattle, jolt; [*cohete*] to crackle, bang; [*ametralladora*] to rattle, clatter
2 (*Cono Sur, Méx*) (= *apresurarse*) to bustle about, go to and fro a lot; (*Cono Sur*) (= *cansarse*) to tire o.s. out at work

traqueteo SM 1 (= *acción*) [*de vehículo*] rattle, rattling, jolting; [*de cohete*] crackle, bang; [*de ametralladora*] rattle
2 (*Andes, Caribe, Méx*) (= *ruido*) row, din; (= *movimiento*) hustle and bustle, coming and going

traquidazo SM (*Méx*) = **traquido**

traquido SM [*de látigo*] crack; [*de disparo*] crack, bang, report

traquinar ▸conjug 1a◂ VI (*Caribe*) = **trajinar A**

tras¹ Ⓐ PREP 1 (= *después de*) after; **~ unos días de vacaciones volvió a su trabajo** after a few days' holiday she went back to work; **~ perder las elecciones se retiró de la política** after losing the election he retired from politics; **día ~ día** day after day; **uno ~ otro** one after another *o* the other
2 (= *por detrás de*) behind; **estaba oculto ~ las cortinas** he was hidden behind the curtains; **¿qué escondes ~ esa mirada inocente?** what are you hiding behind that innocent face?; **andar** *o* **estar ~ algo** to be after sth; **anda ~ un puesto en la administración pública** he's after a job in the civil service; **correr** *o* **ir ~ algn** to chase (after) sb
3 **~ (de)**: **~ (de) abollarme el coche va y se enfada** he dents my car and on top of that *o* then he gets angry
Ⓑ SM (†*) (= *trasero*) behind, rump

tras² EXCL **¡tras, tras!** tap, tap!; (*llamando*) knock, knock!

tras... PREF *ver* **trans...**

trasalcoba SF dressing room

trasaltar SM retrochoir

trasbocar* ▸conjug 1g◂ VT, VI (*Andes, Cono Sur*) to vomit, throw up

trasbucar ▸conjug 1g◂ VT (*Caribe, Cono Sur*) to upset, overturn

trasbuscar ▸conjug 1g◂ VT (*Cono Sur*) to search carefully

trascendencia SF 1 (= *importancia*) importance, significance; (= *consecuencias*) implications *pl*, consequences *pl*; **una discusión sin ~** a discussion of no particular significance; **un encuentro sin ~** an inconsequential meeting; **la matanza no ha tenido ~ informativa** the killing did not make the headlines
2 (*Fil*) transcendence

trascendental ADJ 1 (= *importante*) significant, important; (= *esencial*) vital
2 (*Fil*) transcendental

trascendente ADJ = **trascendental**

trascender ▸conjug 2g◂ Ⓐ VI 1 (= *conocerse*) to leak out, get out; **por fin ha trascendido la noticia** the news has leaked *o* got out at last; **no queremos que sus comentarios trasciendan** we do not want her remarks to leak out *o* to get out
2 (= *propagarse*) **~ a algo** to extend to sth; **su influencia trasciende a los países más remotos** his influence extends to the most remote countries
3 (= *ir más allá*) **~ de algo** to transcend sth, go beyond sth; **una cuestión que trasciende de los intereses nacionales** a matter that transcends *o* goes beyond national interests; **el debate ha trascendido de los círculos académicos** the debate has gone beyond academic circles
4 (*Fil*) to transcend
5 (†) (= *oler*) to smell (**a** of); (= *heder*) to reek (**a** of)
Ⓑ VT to transcend, go beyond; **esto trasciende los confines de la razón** it transcends *o* goes beyond the boundaries of reason

trascocina SF scullery

trascolar ▸conjug 1l◂ VT to strain

trasconejarse* ▸conjug 1a◂ VPR to get lost, be misplaced

trascordarse ▸conjug 1l◂ VPR **~ algo** to forget sth, lose all memory of sth; **estar trascordado** to be completely forgotten

trascoro SM retrochoir

trascorral SM 1 (= *corral*) inner yard
2 (*) (= *culo*) bottom

trascuarto SM back room

trasegar ▸conjug 1h, 1j◂ Ⓐ VT 1 (= *cambiar de sitio*) to move about, switch round; [+ *puestos*] to reshuffle
2 [+ *vino*] (*para la mesa*) to decant; (*en bodega*) to rack, pour into another container *o* bottle
3 (*) [+ *bebida*] to knock back*
4 (= *trastornar*) to upset
Ⓑ VI (*) to drink, booze*

trasera SF back, rear

trasero Ⓐ ADJ [*puerta*] back; [*asiento*] back, rear; **la parte trasera del edificio** the back *o* rear of the building; **motor ~** rear-mounted engine; **rueda trasera** back wheel, rear wheel
Ⓑ SM 1 (*euf*) (= *culo*) bottom, behind; ✦*MODISMO* **quedar(se) con el ~ al aire*** to be caught with one's pants down*
2 (*Zool*) hindquarters *pl*
3 (††) **traseros** (= *antepasados*) ancestors

trasfondo SM (*gen*) background; [*de crítica*] undertone, undercurrent

trasgo SM 1 (= *duende*) goblin, imp
2 (= *niño*) imp

trasgredir ▸conjug 3a◂ VT = **transgredir**

trashojar ▸conjug 1a◂ VT to leaf through, glance through

trashumancia SF, **trashumación** SF seasonal migration, transhumance (*frm*)

trashumante ADJ migrating, on the move to new pastures

trashumar ▸conjug 1a◂ VI to make the seasonal migration, move to new pastures

trasiego SM 1 (= *cambio de sitio*) move, switch; [*de puestos*] reshuffle; [*de vino*] (*para la mesa*) decanting; (*en bodega*) racking
2 (= *trastorno*) upset
3 (= *ir y venir*) coming and going

trasigar ▸conjug 1h◂ VT (*Andes*) to upset, turn upside down

trasijado ADJ skinny

traslación SF 1 (*Astron*) movement, passage
2 (= *copia*) copy; (= *acción*) copy(ing)
3 (= *metáfora*) metaphor; (= *uso figurado*) figurative use

trasladar ▸conjug 1a◂ Ⓐ VT 1 [+ *empleado, preso*] to transfer, move; [+ *muebles, tienda, oficina*] to move; **la han trasladado de sección** she has been transferred *o* moved to another department; **ayúdame a ~ estos archivadores al otro despacho** help me move these filing cabinets into the other office; **han trasladado la oficina a otra ciudad** they have moved the office to another city, they have relocated to another city
2 (= *copiar*) [+ *carta, informe*] to copy
3 (= *aplazar*) [+ *evento*] to postpone (**a** until); [+ *reunión*] to adjourn (**a** until)
4 (= *traducir*) to translate (**a** into); **trasladó su pensamiento al papel** she transferred her thoughts onto paper; **~ una novela a la pantalla** to transfer a novel to the screen
Ⓑ **trasladarse** VPR 1 (= *desplazarse*) to travel; **los que se trasladan al trabajo en coche** those who travel to work by car; **después de la ceremonia nos trasladamos al hotel** after the ceremony we moved on *o* went to the hotel
2 (= *mudarse*) to move (**a** to); **nos hemos trasladado a un local más céntrico** we've moved to more central premises; **~se a otro puesto** to move to a new job

traslado SM 1 [*de muebles*] removal; [*de oficina, residencia*] move; **mi cuñado nos ayudó con el ~** my brother-in-law helped us with the move
2 [*de empleado, preso*] transfer; **le han denegado el ~ a Madrid** they refused him his transfer to Madrid; **el preso se fugó durante su ~ a otro centro penitenciario** the prisoner escaped while he was being transferred *o* moved to another prison
3 ► **traslado de bloque** (*Inform*) cut-and-paste operation
4 (= *copia*) copy
5 (*Jur*) notification; **dar ~ a algn de una orden** to give sb a copy of an order

traslapar ▸conjug 1a◂ Ⓐ VT to overlap
Ⓑ **traslaparse** VPR to overlap

traslapo SM overlap, overlay

traslaticiamente ADV figuratively

traslaticio ADJ figurative

traslucir ▸conjug 3f◂ Ⓐ VT (= *mostrar*) to show; (= *revelar*) to reveal, betray
Ⓑ VI **dejar ~ algo** to suggest sth
Ⓒ **traslucirse** VPR 1 (= *ser transparente*) to be translucent, be transparent
2 (= *ser visible*) to show through
3 (= *inferirse*) to reveal itself, be revealed; (= *ser obvio*) to be plain to see; **en su cara se traslucía cierto pesimismo** his expression revealed *o* showed a certain pessimism
4 (= *saberse*) to leak out, come to light

traslumbrar ▸conjug 1a◂ Ⓐ VT to dazzle
Ⓑ **traslumbrarse** VPR 1 (= *ser deslumbrado*) to be dazzled
2 (= *ir y venir*) to appear and disappear suddenly, come and go unexpectedly; (= *pasar rápidamente*) to flash across

trasluz SM 1 **al ~: mirar algo al ~** to look at sth against the light
2 (= *luz difusa*) diffused light; (= *luz reflejada*) reflected light, gleam
3 (*Caribe*) (= *semblanza*) resemblance

trasmano SM 1 **a ~** (= *apartado*) out of the way; **me pilla a ~** it's out of my way, it's not on my way
2 (*Andes*) **por ~** (= *secretamente*) secretly, in an underhand way

trasminante ADJ (*Cono Sur*) [*frío*] bitter, piercing

trasminarse ▸conjug 1a◂ VPR to filter through, pass through

trasmundo SM hidden world, secret world

trasnochada SF 1 (= *vigilia*) vigil, watch; (= *noche sin dormir*) sleepless night
2 (*Mil*) night attack
3 (= *noche anterior*) last night, the night before

trasnochado ADJ 1 (= *obsoleto*) outmoded
2 (= *ojeroso*) haggard, run-down

trasnochador/a Ⓐ ADJ **son muy ~es** they go to bed very late, they keep very late hours
Ⓑ SM/F night bird, night owl

trasnochar ▸conjug 1a◂ Ⓐ VI 1 (= *acostarse tarde*) to stay up late, go to bed late; (= *no acostarse*) to stay up all night; (= *ir de juerga*) to have a night out, have a night on the tiles
2 **~ en un sitio** to spend the night in a place
Ⓑ VT [+ *problema*] to sleep on
Ⓒ **trasnocharse** VPR (*Méx**) = **trasnochar A**

trasoír ▸conjug 3p◂ VT, VI to mishear

trasojado ADJ haggard, hollow-eyed

traspaís SM interior, hinterland

traspalar ▸conjug 1a◂ VT to shovel about, move with a shovel

traspapelar ▸conjug 1a◂ Ⓐ VT to lose, mislay
Ⓑ **traspapelarse** VPR to get mislaid

traspapeleo SM misplacement

traspar ▸conjug 1a◂ VI (*Méx*) to move house

traspasar ▸conjug 1a◂ Ⓐ VT 1 (= *penetrar*) to pierce, go through, penetrate; [*líquido*] to go/come through, soak through; **la bala le traspasó el pulmón** the bullet pierced his lung; **~ a algn con una espada** to run sb through with a sword
2 [*dolor*] to pierce, go right through; **un ruido que traspasa el oído** an ear-splitting noise; **el grito me traspasó** the yell went right through me; **la escena me traspasó el corazón** the scene pierced me to the core
3 [+ *calle*] to cross over
4 [+ *límites*] to go beyond, overstep; **esto traspasa los límites de lo aceptable** this goes beyond what is acceptable; **~ la barrera del sonido** to break the sound barrier
5 [+ *ley, norma*] to break, infringe
6 [+ *propiedad*] (= *transferir*) to transfer; (= *vender*) to sell, make over; (*Jur*) to convey; **"se traspasa negocio"** "business for sale"
7 (*Dep*) [+ *jugador*] to transfer
8 (*Pol*) [+ *poderes, competencias*] to devolve
Ⓑ **traspasarse** VPR to go too far, overstep the mark

traspaso SM 1 (= *venta*) transfer, sale; (*Jur*) conveyance
2 (= *propiedad*) property transferred; (*Jur*) property being conveyed
3 (*Dep*) (= *acción*) transfer; (= *pago*) transfer fee
4 (*Esp Pol*) ► **traspaso de competencias** transfer of powers
5 [*de ley*] infringement
6 (= *pena*) anguish, pain, grief

traspatio SM (*LAm*) backyard

traspié SM 1 (= *tropezón*) trip, stumble; **dar un ~** to trip, stumble
2 (= *error*) blunder, slip

traspintarse ▸conjug 1a◂ VPR 1 (*en papel*) to come through, show through
2 (*) (= *acabar mal*) to backfire, turn out all wrong

trasplantado/a SM/F transplant patient

trasplantar ▸conjug 1a◂ Ⓐ VT to transplant
Ⓑ **trasplantarse** VPR to emigrate, uproot o.s.

trasplante SM 1 (*Med*) transplant, transplantation ► **trasplante de corazón** heart transplant ► **trasplante de órganos** organ transplant ► **trasplante hepático** liver transplant
2 (*Bot*) transplanting

trasponer ▸conjug 2q◂ VT = **transponer**

traspontín SM = **traspuntín**

traspuesta SF 1 (= *transposición*) transposition; (= *cambio*) switching, changing over
2 (*Geog*) rise
3 (= *huida*) flight, escape; (= *acto de esconderse*) hiding
4 (= *patio*) backyard; (= *dependencias*) outbuildings *pl*

traspuesto ADJ **quedarse ~** to doze off

traspunte SMF prompt, prompter

traspuntín SM 1 (= *asiento*) tip-up seat, folding seat
2 (*) (= *culo*) backside*, bottom

trasque CONJ (*LAm*) in addition to the fact that …, besides being …

trasquiladura SF shearing

trasquilar ▸conjug 1a◂ VT 1 [+ *oveja*] to shear; [+ *pelo, persona*] to crop; ✦*MODISMO* **ir por lana y volver trasquilado** to get more than you bargained for
2 (*) (= *cortar*) to cut (down)

trasquilón SM **¡menudo ~ que le han dado!** what a mess they've made of his hair!; **cortado a trasquilones** unevenly cut

trastabillar ▸conjug 1a◂ VI (*esp LAm*) to stagger, stumble

trastabillón SM (*LAm*) stumble, trip

trastada* SF 1 (= *travesura*) prank, mischief
2 (= *mala pasada*) dirty trick; **hacer una ~ a algn** to play a dirty trick on sb

trastajo* SM piece of junk

trastazo* SM bump, bang, thump; **darse** *o* **pegarse un ~** (*lit*) to get a knock; (*fig*) to come a cropper*

traste[1] SM 1 (*Mús*) [*de guitarra*] fret
2 ✦**MODISMOS dar al ~ con algo** to spoil sth, mess sth up; **dar al ~ con una fortuna** to squander a fortune; **dar al ~ con los planes** to ruin one's plans; **esto ha dado al ~ con mi paciencia** this has exhausted my patience; **irse al ~** to fall through, be ruined

traste[2] SM 1 (*LAm*) = **trasto**
2 (*Cono Sur**) bottom, backside*

trastear ▸conjug 1a◂ Ⓐ VT 1 (*Mús*) (= *tocar*) to play (well)
2 [+ *objetos*] (= *mover*) to move around; (= *revolver*) to disarrange, mess up
3 (*Taur*) to play with the cape
4 [+ *persona*] (= *manipular*) to twist around one's little finger, lead by the nose; (= *hacer esperar*) to keep waiting, keep hanging on
5 (*Méx*‡) (= *acariciar*) to feel up*, touch up*
Ⓑ VI 1 (= *mover objetos*) to move things around; **~ con** *o* **en** (= *buscar*) to rummage among; (= *manosear*) to fiddle with; (= *desordenar*) to mess up, disarrange
2 (*Andes, CAm*) (= *mudarse*) to move house
Ⓒ **trastearse** VPR (*Andes, Cono Sur*) to move house

trastera SF 1 (= *cuarto*) lumber room
2 (*Méx*) (= *armario*) cupboard
3 (*Caribe*) (= *trastos*) heap of junk

trastería SF 1 (= *trastos*) lumber, junk
2 (= *tienda*) junkshop
3 = **trastada**

trastero SM 1 (= *cuarto*) lumber room
2 (*Méx*) (= *armario*) cupboard, closet (*EEUU*)
3 (*Méx*‡) (= *culo*) backside*
4 (*CAm, Méx*) (*para platos*) dishrack

trastienda SF 1 [*de tienda*] back room; ✦**MODISMO obtener algo por la ~** to get sth under the counter
2 (*) (= *astucia*) cunning; **tiene mucha ~** he's a sly one
3 (*Cono Sur, Méx**) (= *culo*) backside*

trasto SM 1 (= *cosa inútil*) piece of junk; ✦**MODISMO tirarse los ~s a la cabeza** to have a blazing row ► **trastos viejos** junk *sing*, rubbish *sing*, garbage *sing* (*EEUU*)
2 **trastos*** gear *sing*, tackle *sing*; **liar los ~s** to pack up and go ► **trastos de matar** weapons ► **trastos de pescar** fishing tackle *sing*
3 **trastos** (*Teat*) (= *decorado*) scenery *sing*; (= *accesorios*) stage furniture *sing*, properties
4 (*) (= *persona inútil*) good-for-nothing, dead loss*
5 (*) (= *niño*) little rascal

trastocamiento SM disruption

trastocar ▸conjug 1g, 1l◂ VT = **trastrocar**

trastornado ADJ [*persona*] disturbed; [*mente*] disturbed, unhinged

trastornar ▸conjug 1a◂ Ⓐ VT 1 (= *perturbar*) [+ *mente*] to disturb, unhinge; [+ *persona*] to drive crazy, mentally disturb; **esa chica le ha trastornado** that girl is driving him crazy, he's lost his head over that girl
2 (*) (= *encantar*) to delight; **le trastornan las joyas** she's crazy about jewels, she just lives for jewels
3 (= *alterar*) [+ *persona*] to upset, trouble, disturb; [+ *ideas*] to confuse, upset; [+ *proyecto*] to upset; [+ *vida*] to mess up; [+ *sentidos*] to daze, mess up; [+ *nervios*] to shatter; [+ *orden público*] to disturb; [+ *objetos*] to mix up, turn upside down
Ⓑ **trastornarse** VPR 1 [*persona*] to go out of one's mind, become deranged *o* disturbed
2 [*proyectos*] to fall through, be ruined

trastorno SM 1 (= *molestia*) inconvenience, trouble; **tener que esperar es un ~** it's a real nuisance having to wait
2 (*Pol*) disturbance, upheaval; **los ~s políticos** the political disturbances
3 (*Med*) upset, disorder ► **trastorno de personalidad** personality disorder ► **trastorno digestivo**, **trastorno estomacal** stomach upset ► **trastorno mental** mental disorder

trastrabillar ▸conjug 1a◂ VI 1 (= *tropezar*) to trip, stumble
2 (= *tambalearse*) to totter, reel, stagger
3 (= *tartamudear*) to stammer, stutter

trastrocar ▸conjug 1g, 1l◂ VT 1 [+ *objetos*] to switch over, change round; [+ *orden*] to reverse, invert
2 [+ *palabras*] to change, transform

trastrueco SM, **trastrueque** SM 1 (= *cambio*) [*de objetos*] switch, changeover; [*de orden*] reversal, switch
2 (= *transformación*) change, transformation

trastumbar ▸conjug 1a◂ VT **~ la esquina** (*Méx*) to disappear round the corner, turn the corner

trasudar ▸conjug 1a◂ VI [*atleta*] to sweat lightly; [*cosa*] to seep

trasudor SM slight sweat

trasuntar ▸conjug 1a◂ VT 1 (= *copiar*) to copy, transcribe
2 (= *resumir*) to summarize
3 (= *mostrar*) to show, exude; **su cara trasuntaba serenidad** his face exuded calm

trasunto SM 1 (= *copia*) copy, transcription
2 (= *semejanza*) image, likeness; (= *copia exacta*) carbon copy; **fiel ~** exact likeness; **esto es un ~ en menor escala de lo que ocurrió** this is a repetition on a smaller scale of what happened

trasvasable ADJ transferable

trasvasar ▸conjug 1a◂ VT 1 [+ *líquido*] to pour into another container, transfer; [+ *vino*] to decant
2 [+ *río*] to divert

trasvase SM 1 (= *paso*) [*de vino*] pouring, decanting; [*de río*] diversion
2 (= *fuga*) drain

trasvasijar ▸conjug 1a◂ VT (*Cono Sur*) = **trasvasar**

trasvolar ▸conjug 1l◂ VT to fly over, cross in an aeroplane

trata SF ► **trata de blancas** white slave trade ► **trata de esclavos** slave trade

tratable ADJ 1 (= *amable*) friendly, sociable
2 [*enfermedad*] treatable
3 (*Cono Sur*) passable

tratadista SMF writer (of a treatise)

tratado SM 1 (*Com*) agreement; (*Pol*) treaty, pact ► **Tratado de Adhesión** Treaty of Accession (*to EU*) ► **tratado de paz** peace treaty ► **Tratado de Roma** Treaty of Rome ► **Tratado de Utrecht** Treaty of Utrecht
2 (= *libro*) treatise; **un ~ de física** a treatise on physics

tratamiento SM 1 [*de objeto, material, tema*] treatment; [*de problema*] handling, treatment
2 (*Med*) treatment ► **tratamiento ambulatorio** out-patient treatment ► **tratamiento con rayos X** X-ray treatment ► **tratamiento de choque** shock treatment ► **tratamiento médico** medical treatment
3 (*Inform*) processing ► **tratamiento de datos** data processing ► **tratamiento de gráficos** graphics processing ► **tratamiento de la información** information processing ► **tratamiento de márgenes** margin settings ► **tratamiento de textos** word processing ► **tratamiento por lotes** batch processing
4 [*de persona*] treatment; **el ~ que recibí** the way I was treated, the treatment I received
5 (= *título*) title, style (*of address*); **dar ~ a algn** to give sb his full title; ✦**MODISMO apear el ~ a algn** to drop sb's title, address sb without formality

tratante SMF dealer, trader (**en** in)

tratar ▸conjug 1a◂ Ⓐ VT 1 [+ *persona, animal, objeto*] to treat; **su novio la trata muy mal** her boyfriend treats her very badly; **hay que ~ a los animales con cariño** animals should be given plenty of affection, animals should be treated lovingly; **te dejo la cámara, pero trátala bien** I'll let you have the camera, but be careful with it *o* treat it carefully; **la vida la ha tratado muy bien** life has been very kind to her, life has treated her very well; **este asunto debe ser tratado con cuidado** this matter should be handled carefully; **~ a algn de loco** to treat sb like a madman; ✦**MODISMO ~ a algn a patadas** to treat sb like dirt
2 (= *llamar*) **¿cómo le tenemos que ~ cuando nos hable?** how should we address him when he speaks to us?; **~ a algn de algo** to call sb sth; **~ a algn de vago** to call sb a layabout; **~ a algn de tú/usted** to address sb as "tú"/"usted"
3 (= *relacionarse con*) **~ a algn: ya no lo trato** I no longer have any dealings with him; **lo trato sólo desde hace seis meses** I have only known him for six months; **me cae bien, pero no la he tratado mucho** I like her, but I haven't had a lot to do with her
4 (*Med*) [+ *paciente, enfermedad*] to treat; **me están tratando con un nuevo fármaco** I'm being treated with a new drug; **le ~on la neumonía con antibióticos** they treated the pneumonia with antibiotics; **¿qué médico te está tratando?** which doctor is giving you treatment?
5 [+ *tejido, madera, residuos*] to treat; **el agua se ha tratado con cloro** the water has been treated with chlorine
6 (= *discutir*) [+ *tema*] to deal with; [+ *acuerdo, paz*] to negotiate; **~emos este tema en la reunión** we'll deal with this subject in the meeting; **este asunto tiene que ~lo direc-**

tamente con el director you'll have to speak directly with the manager about this matter

7 (*Inform*) to process

Ⓑ VI 1 **~ de** [*libro*] to be about, deal with; [*personas*] to talk about, discuss; **la película trata de un adolescente en Nueva York** the film is about a teenager in New York; **ahora van a ~ del programa** they're going to talk about *o* discuss the programme now

2 (= *intentar*) **~ de hacer algo** to try to do sth; **~é de llegar pronto** I'll try to arrive early; **trata de no ser demasiado estricto con él** try not to be too strict with him; **~ de que**: **~é de que ésta sea la última vez** I'll try to make sure that this is the last time; **trata por todos los medios de que el trabajo esté acabado para mañana** try and do whatever you can to make sure that the job is done by tomorrow

3 (= *relacionarse*) **~ con algn**: **trato con todo tipo de gente** I deal with all sorts of people; **no tratamos con traidores** we don't have dealings with traitors; **no había tratado con personas de esa clase** I had not previously come into contact with people like that; **para ~ con animales hay que tener mucha paciencia** you have to be very patient when dealing with animals; **es muy difícil ~ con el enemigo** it is not at all easy to have dealings with the enemy

4 (*Com*) **~ con** *o* **en algo** to deal in sth; **trataban con** *o* **en pieles** they dealt in furs, they were involved in the fur trade

Ⓒ **tratarse** VPR 1 (= *cuidarse*) to look after o.s.; **ahora se trata con mucho cuidado** he looks after himself very carefully now; **no se trata nada mal el chico** (*iró*) he certainly looks after himself all right

2 (= *relacionarse*) **~se con algn** to have dealings with sb; **hace tiempo que no me trato con ellos** it is a while since I've had any dealings *o* had anything to do with them; **se trató con gente rica** she mixed with wealthy people

3 (= *hablarse*) to address each other; **¿cómo nos tenemos que ~?** how should we address each other?; **no se tratan desde hace tiempo** they haven't been speaking (to each other) for some time; **~se de**: **se tratan de usted** they address each other as "usted"; **¿aquí nos tratamos de tú o de usted?** are we on "tú" or "usted" terms here?

4 **~se de algo** 4·1 (= *ser acerca de*) to be about sth; **se trata de la nueva piscina** it's about the new pool; **¿de qué se trata?** what's it about?

4·2 (= *ser cuestión de*) **se trata de aplazarlo un mes** it's a question of putting it off for a month; **se trata sencillamente de que rellenéis este formulario** all you have to do is fill in this form

4·3 (= *ser*) **ahora bien, tratándose de ti ...** now, seeing as it's you ...; **si no se trata más que de eso** if there's no more to it than that, if that's all it is; **se ~á de su primera visita a Colombia** it will be her first visit to Colombia

tratativas SFPL (*Cono Sur*) (= *negociaciones*) negotiations; (= *medidas*) steps, measures

trato SM 1 (= *acuerdo*) deal; **¡~ hecho!** it's a deal!; **cerrar un ~** to close *o* clinch a deal; **hacer un ~** to do a deal; **hacer buenos ~s a algn†** to offer sb advantageous terms ► **trato comercial** business deal

2 (= *relación*) **ya no tengo ~ con ella** I don't have anything to do with her any more; **no quiero ~ con él** I want nothing to do with him; **romper el ~ con algn** to break off relations with sb ► **trato carnal**, **trato sexual**: **tener ~ carnal** *o* **sexual con algn** to have sexual relations with sb

3 **tratos** (= *negociaciones*) negotiations; **entrar en ~s con algn** to enter into negotiations *o* discussions with sb; **estar en ~s con algn** to be in negotiations with sb, be negotiating with sb

4 (= *tratamiento*) treatment; **daba muy mal ~ a sus empleados** he treated his employees very badly; **malos ~s** physical abuse *sing*; **malos ~s a menores** child abuse *sing* ► **trato de favor**, **trato preferente** preferential treatment

5 (= *manera de ser*) manner; **es una persona de ~ agradable** he has a pleasant manner; **de fácil ~** easy to get on with

6 (*forma de cortesía*) **no sé qué ~ darle, si de tú o de usted** I don't know whether to address him as "tú" or as "usted"; **dar a algn el ~ debido** to give sb his proper title

7 (*Méx*) (= *puesto*) market stall; (= *negocio*) small business

trauma SM 1 (= *shock*) trauma

2 (= *lesión*) injury

3 (*Med*) = **traumatología**

traumar ▸conjug 1a◂ VT to traumatize

traumático ADJ traumatic

traumatismo SM traumatism

traumatizante ADJ traumatic

traumatizar ▸conjug 1f◂ VT (*Med, Psic*) to traumatize; (*fig*) to shock, affect profoundly

traumatología SF orthopedic surgery

traumatólogo/a SM/F traumatologist

trauque SM (*Cono Sur*) friend

travelling SM (*pl* **travelling(s)** ['traβelin]), **travelín** SM (*Cine*) (= *aparato*) dolly, travelling platform; (= *movimiento*) tracking shot

través SM 1 (*Arquit*) (= *viga*) crossbeam

2 (*Mil*) traverse; (= *muro*) protective wall

3 (= *curva*) bend, turn; (= *inclinación*) slant; (= *sesgo*) bias; (= *deformación*) warp

4 (= *contratiempo*) reverse, misfortune; (= *trastorno*) upset

5 **a ~ de** across; (= *por medio de*) through; **fuimos a ~ del bosque** we went through the woods; **un árbol caído a ~ de los carriles** a tree fallen across the lines; **lo sé a ~ de un amigo** I heard about it through a friend

6 **al ~** across, crossways; **de ~** across, crossways; (= *oblicuamente*) obliquely; (= *de lado*) sideways; **hubo que introducirlo de ~** it had to be squeezed in sideways; **con el sombrero puesto de ~** with his hat on crooked *o* askew; **ir de ~** (*Náut*) to drift/be blown off course; **mirar de ~** to squint; **mirar a algn de ~** (*lit*) to look sideways at sb; (*fig*) to look askance at sb

travesaño SM 1 (*Arquit*) crossbeam; (*Dep*) crossbar

2 [*de cama*] bolster

3 (*CAm, Caribe, Méx Ferro*) sleeper, tie (*EEUU*)

travesear ▸conjug 1a◂ VI 1 (= *jugar*) to play around; (= *ser travieso*) to play up, be mischievous, be naughty; (*pey*) to live a dissipated life

2 (= *hablar*) to talk wittily, sparkle

3 (*Méx*) [*jinete*] to show off one's horsemanship

traveseo SM (*Méx*) display of horsemanship

travesera SF (*Mús*) flute

travesero Ⓐ ADJ cross *antes de s*, slanting, oblique; **flauta travesera** flute

Ⓑ SM bolster

travesía SF 1 (= *calle*) side street; [*de pueblo*] *road that passes through a village*

2 (= *viaje*) (*Náut*) crossing, voyage; (*Aer*) crossing; (= *distancia*) distance travelled, distance to be crossed ► **travesía del desierto** (*fig*) period in the wilderness

3 (= *viento*) crosswind; (*Cono Sur*) west wind

4 (*en el juego*) (= *ganancias*) amount won; (= *pérdidas*) amount lost

5 (*Andes, Cono Sur*) (= *desierto*) arid plain, desert region

travesti SMF, **travestí** SMF transvestite; (= *artista*) drag artist

travestido/a Ⓐ ADJ disguised, in disguise

Ⓑ SM/F = **travesti**

travestirse ▸conjug 3k◂ VPR to cross-dress

travestismo SM transvestism

travesura SF 1 (= *broma*) prank, lark; **son ~s de niños** they're just childish pranks; **las ~s de su juventud** the wild doings of his youth, the waywardness of his young days

2 (= *mala pasada*) sly trick

3 (= *gracia*) wit, sparkle

traviesa SF 1 (*Arquit*) (= *viga*) crossbeam

2 (*Ferro*) sleeper, tie (*EEUU*)

3 (*Min*) cross gallery

4 **fuimos (a) campo ~** we went across country

travieso ADJ 1 [*niño*] naughty, mischievous

2 [*adulto*] (= *inquieto*) restless; (= *vivo*) lively; (= *vicioso*) dissolute; (= *listo*) bright, clever, shrewd; (= *gracioso*) witty

trayecto SM 1 (= *distancia*) distance; **recorrió el ~ en cinco horas** she covered the distance in five hours

2 (= *viaje*) journey; **comeremos durante el ~** we'll eat during the journey *o* on the way; **también puedes hacer el ~ en autobús** you can also do the journey by bus; **final del ~** end of the line

3 [*de bala*] trajectory

trayectoria SF 1 (= *camino*) trajectory, path ► **trayectoria de vuelo** flight path

2 (= *desarrollo*) development, path; **la ~ actual del partido** the party's present line; **la ~ poética de Garcilaso** Garcilaso's poetic development ► **trayectoria profesional** career

trayendo *etc ver* **traer**

traza SF 1 (= *aspecto*) appearance; **este hombre tiene mala ~** this man has an unpleasant appearance; **nunca conseguirás trabajo con esas ~s** you'll never get a job looking like that; **por** *o* **según las ~s** judging by appearances; **esto lleva** *o* **tiene ~s de no acabar nunca** this looks as though it will never end

2 [*de edificio*] plan, design; [*de ciudad*] layout

3 (= *habilidad*) skill, ability; **darse** *o* **tener ~ para hacer algo** to be skilful *o* clever at doing sth; **para pianista tiene poca ~** she's not much of a pianist

4 (*Inform*) trace

5 (*Cono Sur*) (= *huella*) track, trail

trazable ADJ traceable

trazada SF line, course, direction; **cortar la ~ a algn** (*Aut*) to cut in on sb

trazado SM 1 [*de carretera*] route
2 [*de edificio*] plan, design; [*de ciudad*] layout
3 (*Andes*) (= *cuchillo*) machete

trazador(a) Ⓐ ADJ (*Mil, Fís*) tracer *antes de s*; **bala ~a** tracer bullet; **elemento ~** tracer element
Ⓑ SM/F (= *persona*) planner, designer
Ⓒ SM 1 (*Fís*) tracer
2 (*Inform*) ► **trazador de gráficos, trazador gráfico** plotter ► **trazador plano** flatbed plotter

trazadora SF tracer, tracer bullet

trazar ▸conjug 1f◂ VT 1 (= *dibujar*) [+ *línea*] to draw, trace; (*Arte*) to sketch, outline; (*Arquit, Téc*) to plan, design
2 [+ *fronteras, límites*] to mark out; [+ *itinerario*] to plot; [+ *desarrollo, política*] to lay down, mark out
3 (= *explicar*) to outline, describe

trazo SM 1 (= *línea*) stroke, line ► **trazo de lápiz** pencil line, pencil stroke ► **trazo discontinuo** broken line
2 (= *esbozo*) sketch, outline
3 **trazos** [*de cara*] lines, features; **de ~s enérgicos** vigorous-looking; **de ~s indecisos** with an indecisive look about him
4 [*de ropaje*] fold

TRB SFPL ABR (= **toneladas de registro bruto**) GRT

TRC SM ABR (= **tubo de rayos catódicos**) CRT

trébedes SFPL trivet *sing*

trebejos SMPL 1 (= *utensilios*) equipment *sing*, things ► **trebejos de cocina** kitchen utensils, kitchen things
2 (*Ajedrez*) chessmen

trébol SM 1 (*Bot*) clover
2 (*Arquit*) trefoil
3 **tréboles** (*Naipes*) clubs

trebolar SM (*Cono Sur*) clover field, field covered in clover

trece ADJ INV, PRON, SM (*gen*) thirteen; (*ordinal, en la fecha*) thirteenth; **le escribí el día ~** I wrote to him on the thirteenth; ✦*MODISMO* **mantenerse en sus ~** to stand one's ground, stick to one's guns; *ver* **seis**

treceavo Ⓐ ADJ thirteenth
Ⓑ SM **el ~** the thirteenth; **un ~** a thirteenth, a thirteenth part

trecho SM 1 (= *tramo*) stretch; (= *distancia*) way, distance; (= *tiempo*) while; **andar un buen ~** to walk a good way; **a ~s** (= *en parte*) in parts, here and there; (= *cada tanto*) intermittently, by fits and starts; **de ~ en ~** every so often, at intervals; **muy de ~ en ~** very occasionally, only once in a while
2 (*Agr*) (= *parcela*) plot, patch
3 (*) (= *trozo*) bit, part; **queda un buen ~ que hacer** there's still quite a bit to do; **he terminado ese ~** I've finished that bit

trefilar ▸conjug 1a◂ VT [+ *alambre*] to draw (out)

tregua SF 1 (*Mil*) truce
2 (= *descanso*) lull, respite; **sin ~** without respite; **no dar ~** to give no respite; **dar ~s** [*dolor*] to come and go, let up from time to time; [*asunto*] not to be urgent

treinta ADJ thirty; [*fecha*] thirtieth; *ver tb* **seis**

treintañero/a Ⓐ ADJ thirtysomething*
Ⓑ SM/F thirtysomething*

treintena SF (about) thirty

treintón/ona Ⓐ ADJ thirtysomething*
Ⓑ SM/F thirtysomething*

trekking SM trekking

trematodo SM (*Zool*) fluke

tremebundo ADJ (= *terrible*) terrible, frightening; (= *amenazador*) threatening; (= *violento*) fierce, savage

tremedal SM quaking bog

tremenda SF **tomarse algo a la ~** to make a great fuss about sth, take sth too seriously

tremendamente ADV tremendously

tremendismo SM 1 [*de noticia*] stark reality
2 (*Arte*) use of realism to shock

tremendista Ⓐ ADJ crude, coarsely realistic
Ⓑ SMF 1 (= *alarmista*) alarmist
2 (= *escritor*) *coarsely realistic writer, writer who shocks by his realism*

tremendo ADJ 1 (*) (= *grandísimo*) tremendous; **hay unas diferencias tremendas entre los dos** there are tremendous differences between the two of them; **le dio una paliza tremenda** he gave him a tremendous beating; **un error ~** a terrible mistake; **me llevé un disgusto ~** I was terribly upset; **una roca tremenda de alta** a terrifically high rock*
2 (= *terrible*) terrible, horrific; **hemos presenciado escenas tremendas** we witnessed terrible *o* horrific scenes
3 (*) (= *divertido*) **es ~, ¿eh?** he's something else, isn't he?*
4 (*) (= *travieso*) **esta niña es tremenda** this girl is a (little) terror

trementina SF turpentine

tremolar ▸conjug 1a◂ Ⓐ VT 1 [+ *bandera*] to wave
2 (*fig*) to show off, flaunt
Ⓑ VI to wave, flutter

tremolina* SF row, fuss, commotion, shindy*; **armar una ~** to start a row, make a fuss, to kick up a shindy*

tremotiles SMPL (*Andes, Caribe*) tools, tackle *sing*

trémulamente ADV tremulously

trémulo ADJ [*voz*] tremulous, shaky, quavering; [*mano*] trembling; [*luz*] flickering; **le contestó trémula de emoción** she answered him, trembling *o* quivering with emotion

tren SM 1 (*Ferro*) train; **cambiar de ~** to change trains, change train; **subirse a** *o* **tomar** *o* **coger un ~** to catch a train; **ir en ~** to go by train; ✦*MODISMOS* **dejar el ~ a algn** (*Chile, Ven**) to be left on the shelf; **tiene miedo de que la deje el ~** she's scared of being left on the shelf; **estar como un ~** (*Esp**) to be hot stuff*, be a bit of alright*; **llevarse el ~ a algn** (*Méx**) (= *morirse*) to kick the bucket*; (= *estar furioso*) to be in a rage, be incensed; **para parar un ~***: **tenemos libros para parar un ~** we've got books coming out of our ears*; **recibimos cartas para parar un ~** we got more letters than you could possibly imagine; **perder el ~ de algo**: **perdimos el ~ de la revolución científica** when it came to the scientific revolution, we missed the boat; **este país no puede perder una vez más el ~ del cambio** this country mustn't get left behind on the road to change; **subirse al ~ de algo**: **no han sabido subirse al ~ de la reconversión económica** they failed to take the road to economic restructuring; **no era de ésos que se empeñaban en subirse al ~ de la unión europea** he was not one of those determined to jump on *o* climb on the European bandwagon ► **tren ascendente**† up train ► **tren botijo**†* excursion train ► **tren correo** mail train ► **tren cremallera** cog railway ► **tren de alta velocidad** high-speed train ► **tren de carga** goods train, freight train (*EEUU*) ► **tren de cercanías** suburban train, local train ► **tren de contenedores** container train ► **tren de la bruja** ghost train ► **tren de largo recorrido** long-distance train ► **tren de mercancías** goods train, freight train (*EEUU*) ► **tren de pasajeros** passenger train ► **tren descendente**† down train ► **tren directo** through train ► **tren expreso** express, express train ► **tren mixto** passenger and goods train ► **tren ómnibus**† stopping train, local train, accommodation train (*EEUU*) ► **tren postal** mail train ► **tren rápido** express, express train ► **tren suplementario** relief train
2 (= *ritmo*) **ir a buen ~** to go at a good speed; **forzar el ~** to force the pace; **a fuerte ~** fast; ✦*MODISMO* **vivir a todo ~** to live in style ► **tren de vida** lifestyle; **no pudo sostener ese ~ de vida** he could not keep up that lifestyle
3 (*Mec*) set (*of gears, wheels*) ► **tren de aterrizaje** (*Aer*) undercarriage, landing gear ► **tren de bandas en caliente** hot-strip mill ► **tren de laminación** rolling-mill ► **tren delantero** (*Aut*) front wheel assembly ► **tren de lavado** (*Aut*) car wash ► **tren trasero** (*Aut*) rear wheel assembly
4 (*en viajes*) (= *equipaje*) luggage; (= *equipo*) equipment ► **tren de viaje** equipment for a journey
5 (*Mil*) convoy
6 **en ~ de** (*LAm*) in the process of; **estamos en ~ de realizarlo** we are in the process of doing it; **estar en ~ de recuperación** to be on the road to recovery
7 (*Caribe*) (= *taller*) workshop; (= *empresa*) firm, company ► **tren de lavado** laundry ► **tren de mudadas** removal company
8 (*CAm*) 8·1 (= *trajín*) coming and going
8·2 **trenes** shady dealings
9 (*Méx*) (= *tranvía*) tram, streetcar (*EEUU*)
10 (*Caribe*) (= *majadería*) cheeky remark

trena‡ SF clink‡, prison, can (*EEUU*‡)

trenca SF duffle-coat

trencilla SF, **trencillo** SM braid

tren-cremallera SM (*pl* **trenes-cremallera**) funicular (railway)

trenista SMF 1 (*Caribe*) (= *patrón*) owner of a workshop; (= *gerente*) company manager
2 (*Méx Ferro*) railway worker, railroad worker (*EEUU*)

Trento SM Trent; **Concilio de ~** Council of Trent

trenza SF 1 [*de pelo*] plait, braid (*EEUU*); (*Cos*) braid; [*de pajas, cintas*] plait; [*de hilos*] twist; ✦*MODISMO* **encontrar a una mujer en ~** to find a woman with her hair down ► **trenza postiza** hairpiece
2 (*LAm*) [*de cebollas*] string
3 **trenzas** (*Caribe*) [*de zapatos*] shoelaces
4 (*Culin*) plait
5 (*Cono Sur*) (= *recomendación*) recommendation, suggestion
6 (*Cono Sur*) (= *pelea*) hand-to-hand fight

trenzado Ⓐ ADJ [*pelo*] plaited, braided (*EEUU*); (*Cos*) braided; (= *entrelazado*) intertwined, twisted together
Ⓑ SM [1] [*de pelo*] plaiting, braiding (*EEUU*); [*de pajas, cintas*] plaiting
[2] (*Ballet*) entrechat

trenzar ▸conjug 1f◂ Ⓐ VT [+ *cabello*] to plait, braid (*EEUU*); [+ *pajas, cintas*] to plait; (*Cos*) to braid; [+ *hilo*] to weave, twist (together)
Ⓑ VI [*bailarines*] to weave in and out; [*caballo*] to caper
Ⓒ **trenzarse** VPR (*LAm*) [1] (*) (= *pelear*) to come to blows
[2] **~se en una discusión** to get involved in an argument

trepa[1] Ⓐ SF [1] (= *subida*) climb, climbing
[2] (= *voltereta*) somersault
[3] (= *ardid*) trick, ruse
[4] (*Caza*) hide, blind (*EEUU*)
[5] (*) (= *paliza*) tanning*
Ⓑ SMF (*) (= *arribista*) social climber; (= *cobista*) creep*

trepa[2] SF [1] (*Téc*) (*con taladro*) drilling, boring
[2] (*Cos*) (= *guarnición*) trimming
[3] [*de madera*] grain

trepada SF climb; (*fig*) rise, ascent

trepaderas SFPL (*Caribe, Méx*) climbing irons

trepado SM [1] (*Téc*) drilling, boring
[2] [*de sello*] perforation

trepador(a) Ⓐ ADJ [1] [*planta*] climbing; [*rosa*] rambling
[2] **este vino es bien ~** (*Andes**) this wine goes straight to your head
Ⓑ SM/F (*) (= *persona*) social climber
Ⓒ SM [1] (*Bot*) climber; (= *rosa*) rambler
[2] (*Orn*) nuthatch
[3] **trepadores** (= *garfios*) climbing irons

trepadora SF (*Bot*) climber, rambler

trepanación SF trepanation

trepanar ▸conjug 1a◂ VT to trepan

trepar[1] ▸conjug 1a◂ Ⓐ VI [1] [*persona, animal*] to climb; **~ a un árbol** to climb (up) a tree
[2] (*Bot*) to climb (**por** up)
Ⓑ VT **~ puestos** to climb the ladder

trepar[2] ▸conjug 1a◂ VT [1] (*Téc*) (= *taladrar*) to drill, bore [2] (*Cos*) to trim

trepe* SM telling-off*; **echar un ~ a algn** to tell sb off*

trepetera* SF (*Caribe*) hubbub, din

trepidación SF vibration, shaking

trepidante ADJ [*ritmo*] frenetic, frantic; [*ruido*] intolerable, ear-splitting; [*frío*] extreme

trepidar ▸conjug 1a◂ VI [1] (= *temblar*) to shake, vibrate
[2] (*LAm*) (= *vacilar*) to hesitate, waver; **~ en hacer algo** to hesitate to do sth

treque ADJ (*Caribe*) witty, funny

tres Ⓐ ADJ INV, PRON (*gen*) three; (*ordinal, en la fecha*) third; **las ~** three o'clock; **le escribí el día ~** I wrote to him on the third; ✦***MODISMOS*** **de ~ al cuarto** cheap, poor quality; **como ~ y dos son cinco** as sure as sure can be, as sure as eggs is eggs; **ni a la de ~** on no account, not by a long shot; **no ver ~ en un burro** to be as blind as a bat
Ⓑ SM (= *número*) three; (= *fecha*) third ► **tres en raya** (= *juego*) noughts and crosses, tic tac toe (*EEUU*); *ver tb* **seis**

trescientos/as ADJ, PRON, SM (*gen*) three hundred; (*ordinal*) three hundredth; *ver tb* **seiscientos**

tresillo SM [1] [*de muebles*] three-piece suite
[2] (*Mús*) triplet

tresnal SM (*Agr*) shock, stook

treso ADJ (*Méx*) dirty

treta SF [1] (= *truco*) trick; (= *ardid*) ruse, stratagem; (*Com*) stunt, gimmick ► **treta publicitaria** advertising gimmick
[2] (*Esgrima*) feint

tri... PREF tri..., three-

tríada SF triad

trial Ⓐ SM (*Dep*) trial
Ⓑ SF trial motorcycle

triangulación SF triangulation

triangular Ⓐ ADJ triangular
Ⓑ ▸conjug 1a◂ VT to triangulate

triángulo SM triangle ► **triángulo amoroso** love triangle ► **triángulo de aviso** warning triangle ► **triángulo de las Bermudas** Bermuda Triangle

triates SMPL (*Méx*) triplets

triatlón SM triathlon

tribal ADJ tribal

tribalismo SM tribalism

tribu SF tribe

tribulación SF tribulation

tribulete* SM trainee journalist

tribuna SF [1] [*de orador*] platform, rostrum; (*en mitin*) platform ► **tribuna libre**, **tribuna pública** (= *debate*) open forum, forum for debate
[2] (*Dep*) stand, grandstand ► **tribuna cubierta** covered stand ► **tribuna de invitados** visitors gallery ► **tribuna de prensa** (*Dep*) press box; (*Parl*) press gallery
[3] (*Rel*) gallery ► **tribuna del órgano** organ loft
[4] (*Jur*) ► **tribuna del acusado** dock ► **tribuna del jurado** jury box

tribunal SM [1] (*Jur*) (= *lugar*) court; (= *conjunto de jueces*) court, bench; **en pleno ~** in open court; **llevar a algn ante los ~es** to take sb to court; **sus actos serán juzgados por el ~ de la opinión pública** public opinion will be the judge of his actions ► **Tribunal Constitucional** constitutional court ► **Tribunal de Justicia de las Comunidades Europeas**, **Tribunal de Justicia de la Unión Europea** European Court of Justice ► **Tribunal de la Haya** International Court of Justice ► **tribunal de primera instancia** court of first instance ► **Tribunal Internacional de Justicia** International Court of Justice ► **tribunal popular** jury ► **Tribunal Supremo** High Court, Supreme Court (*EEUU*) ► **tribunal (tutelar) de menores** juvenile court
[2] (*Univ*) (= *examinadores*) board of examiners
[3] (*Pol*) (= *comisión investigadora*) tribunal
[4] (*Cono Sur Mil*) court martial

TRIBUNAL CONSTITUCIONAL

The role of the Spanish **Tribunal Constitucional** *is to see that the 1978 Constitution is adhered to by the organs of government. It has jurisdiction in conflicts of power between the Spanish State and the* **Comunidades Autónomas** *and between the Autonomous Communities themselves, and it also has powers to safeguard the basic rights of citizens. It consists of 12 members, 4 nominated by Congress and by Senate, 2 by the Government and 2 by the governing body of the Spanish judiciary, the* **Consejo General del Poder Judicial**.
⇨ *See also* LA CONSTITUCIÓN ESPAÑOLA

tribuno SM tribune

tributación SF [1] (= *pago*) payment
[2] (= *impuesto*) taxation ► **tributación directa** direct taxation

tributar ▸conjug 1a◂ Ⓐ VT [1] (*Fin*) to pay
[2] [+ *homenaje, respeto etc*] to pay; [+ *gracias, recibimiento*] to give; [+ *afecto etc*] to have, show (**a** for)
Ⓑ VI (= *pagar impuestos*) to pay taxes

tributario Ⓐ ADJ [1] (*Geog, Pol*) tributary *antes de s*
[2] (*Fin*) tax, taxation *antes de s*; **sistema ~** tax system; **privilegio ~** tax concession
Ⓑ SM tributary

tributo SM [1] (= *homenaje*) tribute; **rendir ~** to pay tribute
[2] (*Fin*) (= *impuesto*) tax

tricampeón/ona SM/F triple champion, three-times champion

tricentenario SM tercentenary

tricentésimo ADJ three hundredth

trichina SF (*LAm*) trichina

triciclo SM tricycle

tricófero SM (*Andes, Cono Sur, Méx*) hair restorer

tricola SF (*Cono Sur*) knitted waistcoat

tricolor Ⓐ ADJ tricolour, tricolor (*EEUU*), three-coloured, three-colored (*EEUU*); **bandera ~** tricolour
Ⓑ SF tricolour

tricornio SM three-cornered hat

tricota SF (*LAm*) heavy knitted sweater

tricotar ▸conjug 1a◂ Ⓐ VT to knit; **tricotado a mano** hand-knitted
Ⓑ VI to knit

tricotosa SF knitting machine

tridente SM trident

tridentino ADJ Tridentine, of Trent; **Concilio Tridentino** Council of Trent; **misa tridentina** Tridentine Mass

tridimensional ADJ three-dimensional

trienal ADJ triennial

trienalmente ADV triennially

trienio SM [1] (= *periodo*) period of three years, triennium (*frm*)
[2] (= *pago*) *monthly bonus for each three-year period worked with the same employer*

trifásico Ⓐ ADJ (*Elec*) three-phase, triphase
Ⓑ SM **tener ~*** to have pull, have influence

triforio SM (*Rel*) triforium, clerestory

trifulca* SF row, shindy*

trifulquero* ADJ rowdy, trouble-making

trifurcación SF trifurcation

trifurcarse ▸conjug 1g◂ VPR to divide into three

trigal SM wheat field

trigésimo ADJ thirtieth; *ver tb* **sexto A**

trigo SM [1] (= *cereal*) wheat; **de ~ entero** wholemeal; ✦***MODISMO*** **no ser ~ limpio** to be dishonest; **no todo era ~ limpio** it wasn't completely above board, it was a bit fishy* ► **trigo blando** soft wheat ► **trigo candeal** bread wheat ► **trigo duro** hard wheat, durum wheat ► **trigo sarraceno** buckwheat
[2] **trigos** (= *campo*) wheat *sing*, wheat field(s); ✦***MODISMO*** **meterse en ~s ajenos** to

meddle in somebody else's affairs
[3] (‡) (= *dinero*) dough*, money

trigonometría SF trigonometry

trigonométrico ADJ trigonometric(al)

trigueño/a ADJ [*cabello*] dark blond, corn-coloured; [*rostro*] olive-skinned, golden-brown; (*LAm euf*) dark-skinned

triguero/a Ⓐ ADJ wheat *antes de s*; *ver tb* **espárrago**
Ⓑ SM/F (= *comerciante*) corn merchant
Ⓒ SM (= *tamiz*) corn sieve

trila SF, **triles** SMPL (game of) "find the lady"

trilateral ADJ, **trilátero** ADJ trilateral, three-sided

trilero SM card-sharp

trilingüe ADJ trilingual

trilita SF trinitrotoluene

trilla SF [1] (*Agr*) threshing
[2] (*Caribe, Cono Sur*) (= *paliza*) thrashing, beating
[3] (*Méx*) (= *senda*) track
[4] (*Caribe*) (= *atajo*) short cut

trillado Ⓐ ADJ [1] (*Agr*) threshed
[2] [*camino*] well-trodden
[3] [*tema*] (= *gastado*) well-worn, hackneyed; (= *conocido*) well-known
Ⓑ SM [1] (= *investigación*) thorough investigation
[2] (*Caribe*) (= *sendero*) path, track

trillador SM thresher

trilladora SF threshing machine

trilladura SF threshing

trillar ▸conjug 1a◂ VT [1] (*Agr*) to thresh
[2] [+ *tema etc*] to overuse

trillizo/a SM/F triplet

trillo SM [1] (= *máquina*) threshing machine
[2] (*CAm, Caribe*) (= *sendero*) path, track

trillón SM trillion, quintillion (*EEUU*)

trilogía SF trilogy

trimarán SM trimaran

trimestral ADJ quarterly, three-monthly; (*Univ*) term *antes de s*

trimestralmente ADV quarterly, every three months

trimestre SM [1] (= *periodo*) (*gen*) quarter, period of three months; (*Univ*) term
[2] (*Fin*) (= *pago*) quarterly payment; (= *alquiler*) quarter's rent

trinado SM (*Orn*) song, warble; (*Mús*) trill

trinar ▸conjug 1a◂ VI [1] (*Orn*) to sing, warble, trill; (*Mús*) to trill
[2] (*) (= *enfadarse*) to fume, be angry; (*Cono Sur*) (= *gritar*) to shout; **está que trina** he's hopping mad*

trinca SF [1] (= *tres*) group of three, set of three, threesome
[2] (*Andes, Cono Sur*) (= *pandilla*) band, gang; (= *facción*) faction; (= *complot*) plot, conspiracy
[3] (*Cono Sur*) (= *canicas*) marbles *pl*
[4] (*Caribe, Méx*) (= *embriaguez*) drunkenness; *ver tb* **trinco**

trincar[1] ▸conjug 1g◂ Ⓐ VT [1] (= *atar*) to tie up, bind; (*Náut*) to lash
[2] (= *inmovilizar*) to pinion, hold by the arms
[3] (*) (= *detener*) to nick*
[4] (‡) (= *matar*) to do in*
[5] (**) (= *copular*) to screw**
[6] (*CAm, Cono Sur, Méx*) (= *exprimir*) to squeeze, press
[7] (*Cono Sur**) **me trinca que ...** I have a hunch that ...
Ⓑ **trincarse** VPR (*CAm, Méx*) **~se a hacer algo** to start to do sth *o* doing sth, set about doing sth

trincar[2] ▸conjug 1g◂ VT [1] (= *romper*) to break up
[2] (= *cortar*) [+ *carne*] to chop up; [+ *papel*] to tear up

trincar[3]* ▸conjug 1g◂ Ⓐ VT, VI (= *beber*) to drink
Ⓑ **trincarse** VPR (*Caribe, Méx*) to get drunk

trinchador SM carving knife, carver

trinchante SM [1] (= *cuchillo*) carving knife, carver; (= *tenedor*) meat fork, carving-fork
[2] (= *mueble*) side table; (*Cono Sur*) sideboard

trinchar ▸conjug 1a◂ VT [1] (= *cortar*) to carve, cut up
[2] (‡) (= *matar*) to do in*

trinche Ⓐ SM [1] (*LAm*) (= *tenedor*) fork
[2] (*Andes, Cono Sur, Méx*) (= *mueble*) side table
[3] (*Méx Agr*) pitchfork
Ⓑ ADJ **pelo ~** (*Andes*) frizzy hair

trinchera SF [1] (= *zanja*) ditch; (*Mil*) trench; (*Ferro*) cutting; **guerra de ~s** trench warfare
[2] (= *abrigo*) trench coat
[3] (*LAm*) (= *cercado*) fence, stockade
[4] (*Méx*) (= *cuchillo*) curved knife

trinchete SM shoemaker's knife; (*Andes*) table knife

trincho SM (*Andes*) (= *parapeto*) parapet; (= *zanja*) trench, ditch

trinco/a SM/F (*Caribe, Méx*) drunkard; *ver tb* **trinca**

trincón‡ ADJ murderous

trineo SM (*pequeño*) sledge, sled (*EEUU*); (*grande*) sleigh ▸ **trineo de balancín** bobsleigh ▸ **trineo de perros** dog sleigh

Trini SF (*forma familiar*) *de* **Trinidad**

Trinidad SF [1] (*Rel*) Trinity
[2] (*Geog*) Trinidad

trinidad SF trio, set of three

trinitaria SF [*de jardín*] pansy; (*silvestre*) heart's-ease

trinitrotolueno SM trinitrotoluene

trino SM (*Orn*) warble, trill; (*Mús*) trill

trinomio ADJ, SM trinomial

trinque* SM liquor, booze*

trinquetada SF (*Caribe*) period of danger; (*Andes, Méx*) hard times

trinquete[1] SM (*Mec*) pawl, catch; [*de rueda dentada*] ratchet

trinquete[2] SM [1] (*Náut*) (= *palo*) foremast; (= *vela*) foresail
[2] (*Dep*) pelota court

trinquete[3] SM (*Méx*) [1] (= *soborno*) bribe; (= *asunto turbio*) shady deal*, corrupt affair
[2] **es un ~ de hombre*** he really is a tough customer
[3] (*Andes*) (= *habitación*) small room

trinquis* Ⓐ SM INV drink, swig*
Ⓑ ADJ (*Méx*) drunk, sloshed*

trío SM trio

tripa SF, **tripas** SFPL [1] (= *intestino*) intestine, gut; (= *vísceras*) guts*, insides*, innards*; **me duele la ~** I have a stomach ache; **quitar las ~s a un pez** to gut a fish; **le gruñían las ~s** his tummy was rumbling*; ✦*MODISMOS* **hacer de ~s corazón** to pluck up courage; **echar las ~s** (= *vomitar*) to retch, vomit violently; **tener malas ~s** to be cruel; **revolver las ~s algn** to turn sb's stomach; **¡te sacaré las ~s!** I'll rip you apart!, I'll tear your guts out!‡
[2] (*) (= *barriga*) [2.1] (*gen*) belly, tummy*; **echar ~** to put on weight, start to get a paunch; **tener mucha ~** to be fat, have a paunch; **llenar la ~ a costa de otro** to eat well at somebody else's expense
[2.2] (*Esp*) [*de mujer encinta*] bulge; **dejar a una chica con ~†** to get a girl in the family way; **estar con ~** to be in the family way
[3] [*de fruta*] core, seeds *pl*
[4] **las ~s*** (= *mecanismo*) the insides*, the works; (= *piezas*) the parts; **sacar las ~s de un reloj** to take out the works of a watch
[5] [*de vasija*] belly, bulge
[6] (*Com, Jur etc*) (= *expediente*) file, dossier
[7] (*Caribe*) [*de neumático*] inner tube

tripartito ADJ tripartite

tripe SM shag

tripear* ▸conjug 1a◂ VI to stuff o.s.*, scoff*

triperío SM (*Andes, Méx*) guts *pl*, entrails *pl*

tripero* ADJ greedy

tripi‡ SM LSD, dose of LSD

tripicallos SMPL (*Esp Culin*) tripe *sing*

tripitir ▸conjug 3a◂ VT to repeat again, do a third time

triple Ⓐ ADJ triple; (*de tres capas*) with three layers; **~ salto** triple jump
Ⓑ SM [1] **el ~: es el ~ de lo que era** it is three times what it was *o* as big as it was; **su casa es el ~ de grande que la nuestra** their house is three times bigger than *o* as big as ours
[2] (*Dep*) (= *salto*) triple jump; (*en baloncesto*) three-point basket
Ⓒ SF ▸ **triple vírica** triple vaccine
Ⓓ ADV (*) **esta cuerda es ~ gruesa que ésa** this string is three times thicker than that bit

tripleta SF trio, threesome

triplicado ADJ triplicate; **por ~** in triplicate

triplicar ▸conjug 1g◂ Ⓐ VT to treble, triple; **las pérdidas triplican las ganancias** losses are three times bigger *o* more than the profits
Ⓑ **triplicarse** VPR to treble, triple

triplo SM = **triple B1**

trípode SM tripod

Trípoli SM Tripoli

tripón/ona* Ⓐ ADJ fat, potbellied
Ⓑ SM/F (*Méx*) little boy, little girl; **los tripones** the kids*

tríptico SM [1] (*Arte*) triptych
[2] (= *formulario*) form in three parts; (= *documento*) three-part document; (= *folleto*) three-page leaflet

triptongo SM triphthong

tripudo ADJ fat, potbellied

tripulación SF crew

tripulado ADJ **vuelo ~** manned flight; **vuelo no ~** unmanned flight; **~ por** manned by, crewed by

tripulante SMF [*de barco, avión*] crew member; **tripulantes** crew *sing*

tripular ▸conjug 1a◂ VT [1] [+ *barco, avión*] to crew
[2] (*Aut etc*) to drive
[3] (*Cono Sur*) to mix (up)

tripulina* SF (*Cono Sur*) row, brawl

trique SM [1] (= *ruido*) crack, sharp noise, swish

[2] **a cada ~** at every moment, repeatedly
[3] (*Andes, Méx*) (= *truco*) trick, dodge
[4] **triques** (*Méx**) things, gear *sing*, odds and ends; (*Andes, CAm*) (= *juego*) noughts and crosses, tic tac toe (*EEUU*)

triquina SF trichina
triquinosis SF INV trichinosis
triquiñuela SF trick, dodge; **saber las ~s del oficio** to know the tricks of the trade, know all the dodges; **es un tío ~s*** he's an artful old cuss*
triquis SMPL (*Méx*) = **trique 4**
triquitraque SM string of fire crackers
trirreactor SM tri-jet
trirreme SM trireme
tris SM INV [1] (= *estallido*) crack; (*al rasgarse*) rip, tearing noise
[2] ✦*MODISMOS* **en un ~** in a trice; **recogimos la mesa en un ~** we cleared the table in no time; **está en un ~** it's touch and go; **estar en un ~ de hacer algo** to be within an inch of doing sth; **estuvo en un ~ que lo perdiera** he very nearly lost it, he was within an inch of losing it; **por un ~**: **los dos coches evitaron el choque por un ~** the two cars avoided a collision by a hair's breadth
[3] (*LAm*) (= *juego*) noughts and crosses *pl*, tic tac toe (*EEUU*)
trisar ▸conjug 1a◂ VT (*Andes, Cono Sur*) (= *rajar*) to crack; (= *desportillar*) to chip
trisca SF [1] (= *crujido*) crunch, crushing noise
[2] (= *bulla*) uproar; (*) rumpus, row
[3] (*Caribe*) (= *mofa*) mockery; (= *chiste*) private joke
triscar ▸conjug 1g◂ Ⓐ VT [1] (= *enredar*) to mix, mingle; (= *confundir*) to mix up
[2] [+ *sierra*] to set
[3] (*Andes, Caribe*) (= *mofar*) to mock, joke about; (= *tomar el pelo*) to tease
Ⓑ VI [1] (= *patalear*) to stamp one's feet about
[2] [*corderos etc*] to gambol, frisk about; [*personas*] to romp, play about
triscón ADJ (*Andes*) hypercritical, overcritical
trisecar ▸conjug 1g◂ VT to trisect
trisemanal ADJ triweekly
trisemanalmente ADV triweekly, thrice weekly
trisilábico ADJ trisyllabic, three-syllabled
trisílabo Ⓐ ADJ trisyllabic, three-syllabled
Ⓑ SM trisyllable
trisito SM (*Andes*) (= *pizca*) pinch; (= *pedacito*) scrap, piece
trismo SM lockjaw
Tristán SM Tristram, Tristan
triste Ⓐ ADJ [1] (= *entristecido*) [*persona*] sad; (= *desgraciado*) miserable; [*carácter*] gloomy, melancholy; **poner ~ a algn** to make sb sad, make sb unhappy, make sb miserable; **me puse muy ~ cuando me enteré de la noticia** I was very sad when I heard the news
[2] (= *entristecedor*) [*noticia, canción*] sad; [*paisaje*] dismal, desolate; [*cuarto*] gloomy
[3] (*) (= *mustio*) [*flor*] withered
[4] (= *lamentable*) sad, sorry; **es ~ verle así** it is sad to see him like that; **es ~ no poder ir** it's a pity *o* shame we can't go; **hizo un ~ papel** he cut a sorry figure; **la ~ verdad es que …** the sad truth is that …
[5] (= *insignificante*) miserable; **no queda sino un ~ penique** there's just one miserable penny left; **me dieron un ~ trozo de pan para comer** they gave me a miserable piece of bread for lunch
[6] (*Andes*) (= *tímido*) shy, timid
Ⓑ SM (*LAm*) (= *canción*) sad love song
tristemente ADV sadly; **el ~ famoso lugar** the sadly notorious *o* well-known place
tristeza SF [1] [*de persona*] sadness, sorrow
[2] (*Bot*) *tree virus*
[3] **tristezas** (= *sucesos*) unhappy events; (= *noticias*) sad news *sing*
tristón ADJ (= *triste*) sad, downhearted; (= *pesimista*) pessimistic, gloomy; (= *depresivo*) given to melancholy
tristura SF (*esp LAm*) = **tristeza**
Tritón SM Triton
tritón SM (*Zool*) newt
trituración SF, **triturado** SM grinding, crushing, trituration (*frm*)
triturador SM, **trituradora** SF (*Téc*) grinder, crushing machine; (*Culin*) mincer, mincing machine ▸ **triturador de basuras** waste-disposal unit ▸ **triturador (de papel)** shredder
triturar ▸conjug 1a◂ VT to grind, crush, triturate (*frm*)
triunfador(a) Ⓐ ADJ [*ejército*] triumphant, victorious; [*equipo, concursante*] winning, victorious
Ⓑ SM/F winner; **es un ~ nato** he's a born winner
triunfal ADJ [1] [*arco, marcha*] triumphal
[2] [*grito, sonrisa, recibimiento*] triumphant; **el presidente hizo su entrada ~** the President made his triumphant entrance; **el equipo hizo su entrada ~ en la ciudad** the team entered the city in triumph
triunfalismo SM [1] [*de persona*] (= *optimismo*) euphoria, excessive optimism; (= *petulancia*) smugness, over-confidence, triumphalism; **lo digo sin ~s** I say it without wishing to gloat
[2] [*de país*] jingoism
triunfalista ADJ [1] [*persona*] (= *optimista*) euphoric, excessively optimistic; (= *petulante*) smug, over-confident, triumphalist
[2] [*país, declaraciones*] jingoistic
triunfalmente ADV triumphantly
triunfante ADJ [1] (= *victorioso*) triumphant; **salir ~** to come out the winner, emerge victorious
[2] (= *jubiloso*) jubilant, exultant
triunfar ▸conjug 1a◂ VI [1] (= *ganar, vencer*) to triumph, win; **los socialistas ~on en las elecciones** the socialists triumphed in *o* won the elections; **~ en un concurso** to win a competition; **~ sobre los enemigos** to triumph over one's enemies; **la razón ha triunfado sobre la ignorancia** reason has triumphed over ignorance; **al final triunfó el amor** in the end love conquered all
[2] (= *tener éxito*) to be successful, succeed; **ha triunfado en su profesión** she has been successful in her profession; **~ en la vida** to succeed *o* be successful in life
[3] (*Naipes*) [*jugador*] to play a trump; **triunfan corazones** hearts are trumps
triunfo SM [1] (= *victoria*) win, victory; (= *éxito*) victory, success; **fue el sexto ~ consecutivo del equipo** it was the team's sixth consecutive win *o* victory; **ha sido un verdadero ~** it has been a real triumph *o* victory; **adjudicarse el ~** to win; ✦*MODISMO* **costar un ~** to be a huge effort; **sacarme la carrera me ha costado un ~** getting a degree has been a huge effort
[2] (*Naipes*) trump; **seis sin ~s** six no-trumps; **palo del ~** trump suit; ✦*MODISMO* **tener todos los ~s en la mano** to hold all the trump-cards
[3] (= *trofeo*) trophy
triunvirato SM triumvirate
trivial ADJ trivial, trite
trivialidad SF [1] (= *cualidad*) triviality, triteness
[2] (= *asunto*) trivial matter; (= *dicho*) trite remark; **~es** trivia, trivialities; **decir ~es** to talk in platitudes
trivialización SF trivializing, minimizing (the importance of), playing-down
trivializar ▸conjug 1f◂ VT to trivialize, minimize (the importance of), play down
trivialmente ADV trivially, tritely
triza SF bit, shred; **hacer algo ~s** (= *rasgar*) to tear sth to shreds; (= *hacer pedazos*) to smash sth to bits; **los críticos hicieron ~s la obra** the critics pulled the play to pieces, the critics tore the play to shreds; **hacer ~s a algn** (= *cansar*) to wear sb out; (= *aplastar*) to flatten sb, crush sb; **estar hecho ~s** [*persona*] to be shattered*
trizar ▸conjug 1f◂ VT (= *rasgar*) to tear to shreds; (= *hacer pedazos*) to smash to bits
troca SF (*Méx*) lorry, truck
trocaico ADJ trochaic
trocar ▸conjug 1g, 1l◂ Ⓐ VT [1] (= *canjear*) barter, to exchange
[2] (= *cambiar*) to change; **~ la alegría en tristeza** to change gaiety into sadness
[3] (*Cono Sur*) (= *vender*) to sell; (*Andes*) (= *comprar*) to buy
[4] (= *confundir*) to mix up, confuse
[5] [+ *comida*] to vomit
Ⓑ **trocarse** VPR [1] (= *transformarse*) **~se en** become, turn into; **las víctimas se ~on en verdugos** the victims became executioners
[2] (= *confundirse*) to get mixed up
trocear ▸conjug 1a◂ VT to cut up, cut into pieces
trocha SF [1] (= *senda*) narrow path; (= *atajo*) short cut
[2] (*LAm Ferro*) gauge, gage (*EEUU*) ▸ **trocha normal** standard gauge
[3] (*Cono Sur Aut*) (= *carril*) lane
[4] (*Andes*) (= *trote*) trot
[5] (*Andes*) (= *porción*) portion, helping (*of meat*)
trochar ▸conjug 1a◂ VI (*Andes*) to trot
troche: **a ~ y moche** ADV [*correr*] helter-skelter, pell-mell; [*desparramar*] all over the place; [*distribuir*] haphazardly; **gastar dinero a ~ y moche** to spend money like water
trochemoche: **a ~** ADV *ver* **troche**
trofeo SM [1] (= *copa*) trophy
[2] (= *victoria*) victory, triumph
troglodita SMF [1] (= *cavernícola*) cave dweller, troglodyte
[2] (= *bruto*) brute, oaf; (= *huraño*) unsociable individual, recluse
[3] (*) (= *glotón*) glutton
troica SF troika
troja SF (*LAm*) granary, barn
troje SF, **troj** SF granary, barn
trola[1]* SF fib, lie

trola[2] SF (*Andes*) (= *jamón*) slice of ham; (= *cuero*) piece of raw hide; (= *corteza*) piece of loose bark

trole SM [1] (*Elec*) trolley, cart (*EEUU*), trolley pole
[2] (†*) (= *autobús*) trolley bus

trolebús SM trolley bus

trolero/a* SM/F fibber, liar

tromba SF whirlwind; **pasar como una ~** to go by like a whirlwind; **entrar en ~** to come in in a torrent, come rushing in ► **tromba de agua** violent downpour ► **tromba de polvo** column of dust ► **tromba marina** waterspout ► **tromba terrestre** whirlwind, tornado

trombo SM clot, thrombus (*frm*)

trombón Ⓐ SM (= *instrumento*) trombone ► **trombón de varas** slide trombone
Ⓑ SMF (= *músico*) trombonist

trombonista SMF trombonist

trombosis SF INV thrombosis ► **trombosis cerebral** brain haemorrhage, cerebral haemorrhage

trome* ADJ (*Andes*) bright, smart

trompa Ⓐ SF [1] (*Mús*) horn; ✦***MODISMO*** **sonar la ~ marcial** to sound a warlike note ► **trompa de caza** hunting horn
[2] (= *juguete*) spinning top
[3] (*Zool*) [*de elefante*] trunk; [*de insecto*] proboscis
[4] (*) (= *nariz*) snout‡, hooter‡; (*LAm*) (= *labios*) thick lips *pl*, blubber lips *pl*; **¡cierra la ~!** (*CAm, Méx*‡) shut your trap!‡
[5] (*Anat*) tube, duct; **ligadura de ~s** tubal ligation ► **trompa de Eustaquio** Eustachian tube ► **trompa de Falopio** Fallopian tube
[6] (*Meteo*) = **tromba**
[7] (*) (= *borrachera*) **cogerse** *o* **agarrarse una ~** to get tight*
[8] (*Méx Ferro*) cowcatcher
Ⓑ SMF [1] (*Mús*) horn player
[2] (*Cono Sur**) (= *patrón*) boss, chief
Ⓒ ADJ (*) **estar ~** to be tight*

trompazo SM, **trompada** SF [1] (= *choque*) bump, bang
[2] (= *puñetazo*) punch, swipe
[3] (*Méx*) (= *zurra*) thrashing, beating-up*

trompeadura SF (*LAm*) [1] (= *choques*) bumping, banging
[2] (= *puñetazos*) series of punches; (= *paliza*) beating-up*

trompear ▸conjug 1a◂ (*LAm*) Ⓐ VT to punch, thump
Ⓑ **trompearse** VPR to fight

trompeta Ⓐ SF [1] (*Mús*) (= *instrumento*) trumpet; (*fig*) clarion
[2] (‡) (= *droga*) reefer*, joint*
[3] (*Cono Sur Bot*) daffodil
Ⓑ SMF (*Mús*) trumper player; (*Mil*) trumpeter
Ⓒ SM (= *imbécil*) twit*; (= *borracho*) drunk*, old soak*
Ⓓ ADJ (*Méx**) (= *borracho*) sloshed*, tight*

trompetazo SM (*Mús*) trumpet blast; (*fig*) blast, blare

trompetear ▸conjug 1a◂ VI to play the trumpet

trompeteo SM sound of trumpets

trompetero/a SM/F [*de orquesta*] trumpet player; (*Mil*) trumpeter

trompetilla SF [1] (*tb* **~ acústica**) ear trumpet
[2] (*Caribe**) (= *ruido*) raspberry*

trompetista SMF trumpet player

trompeto* ADJ (*Méx*) drunk

trompezar ▸conjug 1f◂ VI (*LAm*) = **tropezar**

trompezón SM (*LAm*) = **tropezón**

trompicar ▸conjug 1g◂ Ⓐ VT (= *hacer tropezar*) to trip up
Ⓑ VI (= *tropezarse*) to trip

trompicón SM [1] (= *tropiezo*) trip, stumble; ✦***MODISMO*** **a trompicones** in fits and starts
[2] (*Caribe*) (= *puñetazo*) blow, punch

trompis* SM INV punch, bash*

trompiza* SF (*Andes, Méx*) punch-up‡

trompo SM [1] (= *juguete*) spinning top; ✦***MODISMO*** **ponerse como un ~*** to stuff o.s.*, eat to bursting point ► **trompo de música** humming top
[2] (*Aut*) *180 degree turn or skid*
[3] (*Dep*) spin
[4] (*LAm*) (= *desmañado*) clumsy person; (= *bailador*) rotten dancer*
[5] (*Esp*‡) (= *dinero*) 1000-peseta note

trompón SM [1] (*) (= *choque*) bump, bang
[2] (= *puñetazo*) hefty punch, vicious swipe
[3] (*Bot*) (*tb* **narciso ~**) daffodil

trompudo ADJ (*LAm*) thick-lipped, blubber-lipped

tron‡ SM = **tronco**[2]

trona SF high chair

tronada SF, **tronadera** SF (*Méx*) thunderstorm

tronado ADJ [1] (= *viejo*) old, useless
[2] (*) **estar ~** (= *loco*) to be potty*; (*LAm*) (= *drogado*) to be high (on drugs)*; (*CAm*) (= *sin dinero*) to be broke*

tronadura SF (*Chile Min*) blasting

tronamenta SF (*Andes, Méx*) thunderstorm

tronar ▸conjug 1l◂ Ⓐ VI [1] (*Meteo*) to thunder; ✦***MODISMO*** **por lo que pueda ~** just in case, to be on the safe side
[2] [*cañones etc*] to boom, thunder
[3] (*) (= *enfurecerse*) to rave, rage; **~ contra** to spout forth against, rage *o* thunder against
[4] (*) (= *reñir*) **~ con algn** to fall out with sb
[5] (*) (= *arruinarse*) to go broke*; (= *fracasar*) to fail, be ruined
Ⓑ VT [1] (*CAm, Méx**) (= *fusilar*) to shoot
[2] **la tronó** (*Méx**) he blew it‡, he messed it up
Ⓒ **tronarse** VPR (*) [1] (*CAm, Méx*) (= *matarse*) to shoot o.s., blow one's brains out
[2] (*LAm*) (= *drogarse*) to take drugs

tronazón SF (*CAm, Méx*) thunderstorm

troncal ADJ **línea ~** main (trunk) line; **materia ~** core subject

troncar ▸conjug 1g◂ VT = **truncar**

troncha SF [1] (*LAm**) (= *tajada*) slice; (= *pedazo*) piece, chunk
[2] (*LAm**) (= *prebenda*) sinecure, soft job
[3] (*Méx*) (= *comida*) [*de soldado*] soldier's rations *pl*; (*escasa*) meagre meal

tronchacadenas SM INV chain cutters *pl*

tronchado* Ⓐ SM (*Méx*) (= *buen negocio*) gold mine; (= *negocio próspero*) prosperous business
Ⓑ ADJ (*Andes*) (= *lisiado*) maimed, crippled

tronchante* ADJ hilarious, killingly funny

tronchar ▸conjug 1a◂ Ⓐ VT [1] (= *talar*) to fell, chop down; (= *cortar*) to cut up, cut off; (= *hender*) to split, crack, shatter
[2] [+ *vida*] to cut short; [+ *esperanzas*] to dash
[3] (*) (= *cansar*) to tire out
Ⓑ **troncharse** VPR [1] (*) (tb **~se de risa**) to split one's sides laughing
[2] *árbol*] to fall down, split
[3] (*) (= *cansarse*) to tire o.s. out

troncho Ⓐ SM [1] (*Bot*) stem, stalk
[2] (*Cono Sur*) (= *trozo*) piece, chunk
[3] (*Andes*) (= *enredo*) knot, tangle
[4] (**) (= *pene*) prick**
Ⓑ ADJ (*Cono Sur*) maimed, crippled

tronco[1] SM [1] [*de árbol*] trunk; (= *leño*) log; ✦***MODISMO*** **dormir como un ~** to sleep like a log ► **tronco de Navidad** (*Culin*) yule log
[2] (*Anat*) trunk
[3] (= *estirpe*) stock
[4] (*Ferro*) main line, trunk line
[5] (**) (= *pene*) prick**

tronco[2]**/a**‡ SM/F [1] (= *tío*) bloke*/bird*; **María y su ~** María and her bloke*
[2] (= *amigo*) (*en oración directa*) mate*, pal*; **—oye, ~** "hey, man"*

tronera Ⓐ SF [1] (*Mil*) (= *aspillera*) loophole, embrasure; (*Arquit*) small window
[2] (*Billar*) pocket
[3] (*Méx*) (= *chimenea*) chimney, flue
Ⓑ SMF (*) (= *tarambana*) harebrained person
Ⓒ SM (*) (= *libertino*) rake, libertine

tronido SM [1] (*Meteo*) thunderclap; **~s** thunder *sing*, booming *sing*
[2] (= *explosión*) loud report, bang, detonation

tronío SM lavish expenditure, extravagance

trono SM [1] [*de monarca*] (= *asiento*) throne; (= *símbolo*) crown; **heredar el ~** to inherit the crown; **nuestra lealtad al ~** our loyalty to the crown; **subir al ~** to ascend the throne, come to the throne
[2] [*de campeón*] crown

tronquista SMF (*LAm*) lorry driver, truck driver (*EEUU*)

tronzar ▸conjug 1f◂ VT [1] (= *cortar*) to cut up; (= *romper*) to split, rend, smash
[2] (*Cos*) to pleat
[3] (*) [+ *persona*] to tire out

tropa SF [1] (*Mil*) (= *soldados rasos*) rank and file, ordinary soldiers *pl*; (= *ejército*) army; **las ~s** the troops; **ser de ~** to be in the army ► **tropas de asalto**, **tropa de choque** storm troops
[2] (= *multitud*) crowd, troop; (*pey*) mob, troop
[3] (*LAm Agr*) flock, herd
[4] (*Cono Sur*) (= *vehículos*) stream of vehicles; (= *coches*) line of cars; (= *carros*) line of carts
[5] (*Méx*) (= *maleducado*) rude person; (*Caribe**) (= *tonto*) dope*

tropear ▸conjug 1a◂ VT (*Arg*) to herd

tropecientos* ADJ PL umpteen*

tropel SM [1] (= *gentío*) mob, crowd; **acudir en ~** to crowd in, come en masse
[2] (= *revoltijo*) mess, jumble
[3] (= *prisa*) rush, haste

tropelía SF outrage, violent act; **cometer una ~** to commit an outrage

tropero SM [1] (*Arg Agr*) cowboy, cattle drover
[2] (*Méx*) boor

tropezar ▸conjug 1f, 1j◂ Ⓐ VI [1] (*con los pies*) to trip, stumble; **tropezó y por poco se cae** he tripped *o* stumbled and nearly fell; **¡cuidado, no tropieces!** mind you don't trip up!; **ha tropezado con una piedra** she tripped on a stone; **he tropezado con el escalón** I tripped on the step
[2] (= *chocar*) **~ con** *o* **contra algo** to bump into sth; **~ con** *o* **contra un árbol** to bump

into a tree

3 (= *enfrentarse*) **~ con algo** to run into sth, encounter sth; **tropezamos con una dificultad** we ran into *o* encountered a difficulty; **tropezó con muchos obstáculos durante su carrera política** she came up against *o* encountered numerous obstacles in her political career

4 (= *encontrarse*) **~ con algn** to bump into sb, run into sb; **he tropezado con María en la facultad** I bumped *o* ran into María in the department

5 (= *reñir*) **~ con algn** to have an argument with sb

6 (= *cometer un error*) to err, make a mistake; **ha tropezado muchas veces en la vida** she has erred many times *o* made many mistakes in her life

Ⓑ **tropezarse** VPR [*dos personas*] to bump *o* run into each other; **nos tropezamos casi cada día por la calle** we bump *o* run into each other practically every day in the street; **~se con algn** to bump *o* run into sb; **me tropecé con Juan en el banco** I bumped *o* ran into Juan at the bank

tropezón SM **1** (= *traspié*) trip, stumble; **dar un ~** to trip, stumble; **hablar a tropezones** to speak jerkily, speak falteringly; **proceder a ~es** to proceed by fits and starts

2 (= *equivocación*) slip, blunder; (*moral*) lapse

3 **tropezones** (*Culin*) *small pieces of food added to soup*

tropical ADJ **1** (= *del trópico*) tropical

2 (*Cono Sur*) (= *melodramático*) rhetorical, melodramatic, highly-coloured

tropicalismo SM (*Cono Sur*) rhetoric, melodramatic style, excessive colourfulness

trópico SM **1** (*Geog*) tropic; **los ~s** the tropics ► **trópico de Cáncer** Tropic of Cancer ► **trópico de Capricornio** Tropic of Capricorn

2 **trópicos** (*Caribe*) (= *dificultades*) hardships, difficulties; ✦*MODISMO* **pasar los ~s** to suffer hardships, have a hard time

tropiezo SM **1** (= *error*) slip, blunder; (*moral*) moral lapse

2 (= *revés*) (*gen*) setback; (*en el amor*) disappointment in love

3 (= *desgracia*) misfortune, mishap

4 (= *disputa*) argument, quarrel

tropilla SF (*Cono Sur*) drove, team

tropo SM trope

troquel SM die

troquelado SM die cut

troquelar ▸conjug 1a◂ VT **1** [+ *cuero, cartón*] to die-cut; [+ *moneda, medalla*] to strike; [+ *metal*] to die-cast

2 (= *perforar*) to punch

troqueo SM trochee

trosco/a* SM/F Trot*, Trotskyist

trotacalles* SMF INV bum*

trotaconventos SF INV go-between, procuress

trotamundos SMF INV globetrotter

trotar ▸conjug 1a◂ VI **1** [*caballo*] to trot

2 (*) (= *viajar*) to travel about, chase around here and there

trote SM **1** [*de caballo*] trot; **ir al ~** to trot, go at a trot; **irse al ~** to go off in a hurry; **tomar el ~** to dash off

2 (*) (= *uso*) **de mucho ~** hard-wearing, tough; **chaqueta para todo ~** a jacket for everyday wear

3 (*) (= *ajetreo*) bustle; **el abuelo ya no está para esos ~s** grandad is not up to that sort of thing any more

trotskismo SM Trotskyism

trotskista ADJ, SMF Trotskyist

trova SF ballad

trovador SM troubadour

Troya SF Troy; ✦*MODISMOS* **¡aquí fue ~!** you should have heard the fuss!; **¡arda ~!** press on regardless!, never mind the consequences!

troyano/a Ⓐ ADJ, SM/F Trojan

Ⓑ SM (*Inform*) Trojan horse

troza SF log

trozo SM **1** (= *pedazo*) piece, bit; **un ~ de madera** a piece of wood; **a ~s** in bits; **cortado a ~s** cut into pieces; **vi la película a ~s** I only saw bits of the film; ✦*MODISMO* **es un ~ de pan*** he's a dear, he's a sweetie*

2 (*Literat, Mús*) passage; **~s escogidos** selected passages, selections

trucaje SM **1** (*Cine*) trick photography

2 (*en el juego*) rigging, fixing

trucar* ▸conjug 1g◂ Ⓐ VT **1** [+ *resultado*] to fix, rig; [+ *baraja*] to tamper with; **las cartas estaban trucadas** (*fig*) the dice were loaded against us

2 (*Aut*) [+ *motor*] to soup up*

Ⓑ VI (*Billar*) to pot the ball, pot

trucha[1] SF **1** (= *pez*) trout ► **trucha arco iris** rainbow trout ► **trucha marina** sea trout

2 (*Téc*) crane, derrick

trucha[2] SF (*CAm Com*) (= *puesto*) stall, booth

trucha[3]* SMF (= *persona*) (= *taimado*) tricky individual, wily bird; (= *tramposo*) cheat

truche‡ SM (*Andes*) snappy dresser*, dude (*EEUU**)

truchero[1]**/a** SM/F (*CAm*) hawker, vendor

truchero[2] ADJ trout *antes de s*; **río ~** trout river

truchimán SM **1** (*Hist*) interpreter

2 (*) rogue, villain

trucho ADJ (*Andes*) sharp, rascally

truco SM **1** (= *ardid*) trick, dodge; (*Cine*) trick effect, piece of trick photography; **el tío tiene muchos ~s** the fellow is up to all the tricks in the book; **coger el ~ a algn** to see how sb works a trick, catch on to sb's little game; **arte de los ~s** conjuring ► **truco de naipes** card trick ► **truco publicitario** advertising gimmick

2 (= *habilidad*) knack; **coger el ~** to get the knack, get the hang of it, catch on

3 (*Andes, Cono Sur*) (= *puñetazo*) punch, bash*

4 (*Cono Sur Naipes*) *popular card game*

5 **trucos** (*Billar*) billiards *sing*, pool *sing*

truculencia SF gruesomeness

truculento ADJ gruesome, horrifying

trueco SM = **trueque**

trueno SM **1** (*Meteo*) **un ~** a clap of thunder, a thunderclap; **~s** thunder *sing*

2 (= *ruido*) [*de cañón*] boom, thundering ► **trueno gordo*** (*lit*) finale (*of firework display*); (*fig*) big row, major scandal

3 (*) (= *tarambana*) wild youth, madcap; (= *libertino*) rake

4 (*Caribe*) (= *juerga*) binge*, noisy party

5 **truenos** (*Caribe*) (= *zapatos*) stout shoes

trueque SM **1** (= *cambio*) exchange; (*Com*) barter; **a ~ de** in exchange for; **aun a ~ de perderlo** even if it means losing it

2 **trueques** (*Andes Fin*) change *sing*

trufa SF **1** (*Bot*) truffle

2 (*) (= *mentira*) fib, story

trufado ADJ stuffed with truffles

trufar ▸conjug 1a◂ Ⓐ VT **1** (*Culin*) to stuff with truffles

2 (*) (= *estafar*) to take in*, swindle

Ⓑ VI (*) (= *mentir*) to fib, tell stories

trufi* SM (*Andes*) taxi

truhán SM **1** (= *pillo*) rogue, crook*, shyster (*EEUU*); (= *estafador*) swindler; (= *charlatán*) mountebank

2 (*Hist*) jester, buffoon

truhanería SF **1** (= *picardía*) roguery; (= *estafa*) swindling **2** (*Hist*) buffoonery

truhanesco ADJ **1** (= *tramposo*) dishonest, crooked*

2 (*Hist*) buffoonish

truísmo SM truism

truja‡ SM fag‡, gasper‡

trujal SM [*de vino*] winepress; [*de aceite*] olive-oil press

trujimán SM = **truchimán**

trujis‡ SM INV fag‡, gasper‡

trulla SF **1** (= *bullicio*) bustle; (= *disturbio*) commotion; (= *ruido*) noise

2 (= *multitud*) crowd, throng

3 (*Andes*) (= *broma*) practical joke

trullada SF (*Caribe*) crowd, throng

trullo‡ SM nick‡, jail, can (*EEUU*‡)

truncado ADJ (= *reducido*) truncated, shortened; (= *incompleto*) incomplete

truncamiento SM truncation, shortening

truncar ▸conjug 1g◂ VT **1** (= *acortar*) [+ *texto*] to truncate, shorten; [+ *cita*] to mutilate

2 [+ *carrera, vida*] to cut short; [+ *esperanzas*] to dash; [+ *proyecto*] to ruin; [+ *desarrollo*] to stunt, check

trunco ADJ (= *reducido*) truncated, shortened; (= *incompleto*) incomplete

truquero/a (*LAm*) Ⓐ ADJ tricky gimmicky

Ⓑ SM/F trickster

truqui* SM = **truco 1, 2**

trusa SF **1** (*Caribe*) (= *bañador*) bathing trunks *pl*

2 (*Andes, Méx*) (= *calzoncillos*) underpants *pl*; (= *bragas*) knickers *pl*, panties *pl* (*EEUU*); [*de bebé*] pants *pl*

trust [trus] SM (*pl* **trusts** [trus]) (*Fin*) trust, cartel

tsunami SM (*pl* **tsunamis** *o* **tsunami**) tsunami

Tte. ABR (= **teniente**) Lieut, Lt

TU SM ABR (= **tiempo universal**) U.T.

tu ADJ POSES your; **han venido tu tía y tus primos** your aunt and your cousins have come; **hágase tu voluntad** (*Rel*) thy will be done

tú PRON PERS **1** you; **cuando tú quieras** whenever you like; **que esto quede entre tú y yo** this is between you and me; **¿yo, gordo? ¿y tú qué?** fat? me? what about you?; **llegamos antes que tú** we arrived before you (did); **es mucho más alto que tú** he is much taller than you (are); **en el partido se mantuvo el tú a tú** the game was between equals, the game was an equal struggle; **hablar** *o* **llamar** *o* **tratar a algn de tú** to use the "tú" form of address; **nos tratamos de tú** we address each other as tú; **háblame de tú, que ahora**

somos familia you can address me as "tú", we're family now

[2] (*) (*uso vocativo*) **¡tú! ven aquí** you! come here; **¡oye tú, que me voy a tener que enfadar!** listen, you, I'm going to have to get cross!; **¡tú cállate!** shut up, you!

tualé (*LAm*) Ⓐ SM toilet, bathroom (*EEUU*), lavatory
Ⓑ SF toilet

tuareg ADJ, SMF (*pl* **tuareg** o **tuaregs**) Tuareg

tubercular ADJ tubercular

tubérculo SM [1] (*Bot*) tuber; (= *patata*) potato
[2] (*Anat, Med*) tubercle

tuberculosis SF tuberculosis

tuberculoso/a Ⓐ ADJ tuberculous, tubercular; **estar ~** to suffer from tuberculosis, have tuberculosis
Ⓑ SM/F tuberculosis patient

tubería SF [1] (= *tubo*) pipe
[2] (= *conjunto de tubos*) pipes *pl*, piping

Tubinga SF Tübingen

tubo SM [1] (= *recipiente*) tube; ✦**MODISMO pasar por el ~*** to knuckle under ► **tubo acústico** speaking-tube ► **tubo capilar** capillary ► **tubo de chimenea** chimneypot ► **tubo de desagüe** (*interior*) waste pipe; (*exterior*) drainpipe ► **tubo de ensayo** test tube ► **tubo de escape** exhaust (pipe) ► **tubo de humo** chimney, flue ► **tubo de imagen** television tube ► **tubo de lámpara** lamp glass ► **tubo de órgano** organ pipe ► **tubo de radio** wireless valve, tube (*EEUU*) ► **tubo de rayos catódicos** cathode-ray tube ► **tubo de respiración** breathing-tube ► **tubo de vacío** valve, vacuum tube (*EEUU*) ► **tubo digestivo** alimentary canal ► **tubo fluorescente** fluorescent tube ► **tubo lanzatorpedos** torpedo tube
[2] (= *tubería*) pipe
[3] ✦**MODISMO por un ~*** loads*; **gastó por un ~** he spent a fortune*; **lo vendió por un ~*** he sold it for a fantastic price*
[4] (*LAm*) [*de teléfono*] handset, earpiece
[5] (‡) (= *cárcel*) nick‡, can (*EEUU*‡)

tubular Ⓐ ADJ tubular
Ⓑ SM (= *prenda*) roll-on

tucán SM, **tucano** SM (*LAm*) toucan

Tucídides SM Thucydides

tuco¹/a Ⓐ ADJ [1] (*LAm*) (= *mutilado*) maimed, limbless; (= *manco*) with a finger/hand missing
[2] (*CAm**) (= *achaparrado*) squat
Ⓑ SM/F (= *persona*) cripple*
Ⓒ SM (*LAm Anat*) stump

tuco² SM (*Cono Sur*) (= *salsa*) pasta sauce; [*de tomate*] tomato sauce

tuco³ SM (*Andes, Cono Sur Entomología*) glow-worm

tuco⁴/a SM/F (*CAm*) (= *tocayo*) namesake

tucura SF [1] (*Cono Sur*) (= *langosta*) locust
[2] (*Andes*) (= *libélula*) dragonfly; (= *mantis*) praying mantis; (= *saltamontes*) grasshopper
[3] (= *sacerdote*) corrupt priest

tucuso SM (*Caribe*) hummingbird

tudesco/a ADJ, SM/F German

tuerca SF nut; ✦**MODISMO apretar las ~s a algn** to tighten the screws on sb ► **tuerca mariposa** wing nut

tuerce‡ SM (*CAm*) misfortune, setback

tuerto/a Ⓐ ADJ [1] (= *con un ojo*) one-eyed; (= *ciego en un ojo*) blind in one eye
[2] (= *torcido*) twisted, bent, crooked
[3] **a tuertas** (= *invertido*) upside-down; (= *al revés*) back to front; ✦**MODISMO a tuertas o a derechas** (= *con razón o sin ella*) rightly or wrongly; (= *sea como sea*) by hook or by crook; (= *sin pensar*) thoughtlessly, hastily
Ⓑ SM/F (= *persona*) (= *con un ojo*) one-eyed person; (= *ciego en un ojo*) person who is blind in one eye
Ⓒ SM (= *injusticia*) wrong, injustice

tuesta* SF (*Caribe*) binge*

tueste SM roasting

tuétano SM [1] (= *médula*) marrow, squash (*EEUU*); ✦**MODISMO hasta los ~s** through and through, utterly; **mojarse hasta los ~s** to get soaked to the skin; **enamorado hasta los ~s** head over heels in love
[2] (= *meollo*) core, essence

tufarada SF (= *olor*) bad smell, foul smell; (= *racha de aire*) gust

tufillas* SMF INV bad-tempered person

tufillo SM slight smell (**a** of)

tufo¹ SM [1] (= *emanación*) fumes *pl*
[2] (= *hedor*) (*gen*) stink; [*de cuarto*] fug; ✦**MODISMO se le subió el ~ a las narices** he got very cross
[3] **tufos*** (= *vanidad*) swank* *sing*, conceit *sing*; **tener ~s** to be swanky*, be conceited

tufo² SM (= *rizo*) curl, sidelock

tugurio SM [1] (= *cafetucho*) den, joint‡; (= *chabola*) hovel, slum, shack; (= *cuartucho*) poky little room; (*Agr*) shepherd's hut
[2] **tugurios** (*Andes*) shanty town *sing*

tuja SF (*Andes*) hide-and-seek

tul SM tulle, net

tulenco ADJ (*CAm*) splay-footed

tulipa SF lampshade

tulipán SM tulip; (*Andes, Caribe, Méx*) hibiscus

tulipanero SM, **tulipero** SM tulip-tree

tulis SM INV (*Méx*) highway robber, brigand

tullida SF (*Caribe*) (= *truco*) dirty trick

tullido/a Ⓐ ADJ (= *lisiado*) crippled; (= *paralizado*) paralysed
Ⓑ SM/F cripple

tullir ►conjug 3h◄ VT [1] (= *lisiar*) to cripple, maim; (= *paralizar*) to paralyse
[2] (= *cansar*) to wear out, exhaust
[3] (= *maltratar*) to abuse, maltreat

tumba¹ SF (= *sepultura*) tomb, grave; ✦**MODISMOS hablar a ~ abierta** to speak openly; **llevar a algn a la ~** to carry sb off; **ser (como) una ~** to keep one's mouth shut, not breathe a word to anyone

tumba² SF [1] (*LAm*) (= *tala*) felling of timber, clearing of ground; (= *tierra*) ground cleared for sowing; (= *claro*) forest clearing
[2] (= *sacudida*) shake, jolt
[3] (= *voltereta*) somersault
[4] (*Cono Sur*) (= *carne*) *boiled meat of poor quality*

tumba³ SF (*Caribe, Cono Sur*) (= *tambor*) African drum

tumbacuartillos* SM INV old soak‡

tumbacuatro SM (*Caribe*) braggart

tumbadero SM (*Caribe, Méx*) [1] (*Agr*) ground cleared for sowing
[2] (*) (= *burdel*) brothel

tumbadora SF (*Caribe*) large conga drum

tumbar ►conjug 1a◄ Ⓐ VT [1] (= *derribar*) [+ *persona*] to knock down, knock over; [+ *puerta*] (*a golpes*) to batter down; (*a patadas*) to kick down o in; [*viento*] to blow down; **tanto alcohol acabó tumbándolo** all that alcohol ended up laying him out; **lo ~on a golpes** they punched him to the ground
[2] (‡) (= *matar*) to do in‡
[3] (*) [*olor*] to knock back*; **un olor que te tumba*** an overpowering smell, a smell which knocks you back*
[4] (= *impresionar*) to amaze, overwhelm; **el espectáculo me dejó tumbado** the sight overwhelmed me; **su presunción tumbó a todos** his conceit amazed everybody, his conceit knocked everybody sideways
[5] (**‡) (= *copular*) to lay‡, screw**‡
[6] (*) (= *suspender*) to fail, flunk (*EEUU*)
[7] (*LAm*) [+ *árbol*] to fell; [+ *tierra*] to clear
Ⓑ VI [1] (= *caerse*) to fall down
[2] (*Náut*) to capsize
[3] (*) (= *impresionar*) **tiene una desfachatez que tumba de espaldas** his cheek is enough to take your breath away*
Ⓒ **tumbarse** VPR [1] (= *acostarse*) to lie down; **estar tumbado** to lie, be lying down
[2] [*trigo*] to go flat
[3] (= *relajarse*) to decide to take it easy; (= *abandonarse*) to give up (on things), let o.s. go (*after achieving a success etc*)

tumbilla SF (*CAm*) wicker suitcase

tumbo¹ SM [1] (= *sacudida*) shake, jolt; ✦**MODISMO dando ~s** with all sorts of difficulties
[2] (= *caída*) fall, tumble; **dar un ~** to fall, shake

tumbo² SM (*Hist*) monastic cartulary

tumbón* ADJ lazy, bone idle

tumbona SF (= *butaca*) easy chair; [*de playa*] deckchair, beach chair (*EEUU*)

tumefacción SF swelling

tumefacto ADJ swollen

tumescente ADJ tumescent

tumido ADJ swollen, tumid (*frm*)

tumor SM tumour, tumor (*EEUU*), growth ► **tumor cerebral** brain tumour ► **tumor benigno** benign tumour ► **tumor maligno** malignant growth

túmulo SM [1] (= *sepultura*) tumulus, burial mound
[2] (*Geog*) mound

tumulto SM turmoil, tumult; (*Pol*) (= *motín*) riot, disturbance ► **tumulto popular** popular rising

tumultuario ADJ = **tumultuoso**

tumultuosamente ADV tumultuously; (*pey*) riotously

tumultuoso ADJ tumultuous; (*pey*) riotous, disorderly

tuna¹ SF (*Bot*) prickly pear

tuna² SF [1] (*Esp Mús*) ► **tuna estudiantina** student music group
[2] (= *vida picaresca*) rogue's life, vagabond life; (*fig*) merry life; **correr la ~** to have a good time, live it up*
[3] (*CAm*) (= *embriaguez*) drunkenness

TUNA

***Tunas**, also known as **estudiantinas** are groups of students dressed in 17th century costumes who play guitars, lutes and tambourines and go serenading through the streets. They also make impromptu appearances at wed-*

dings and parties singing traditional Spanish songs, often of a bawdy nature, in exchange for drinks or some money.

tunantada SF dirty trick

tunante SM rogue, villain; **¡~!** you villain!; (*a un niño*) you young scamp!

tunantear ▸conjug 1a◂ VI to live a rogue's life, be a crook*

tunantería SF [1] (= *vileza*) crookedness, villainy [2] (= *engaño*) dirty trick, villainy

tunar ▸conjug 1a◂ VI to loaf, idle, bum around (*EEUU*)

tunco/a (*CAm, Méx*) Ⓐ ADJ (= *lisiado*) maimed, crippled; (= *manco*) one-armed
Ⓑ SM/F (= *persona*) cripple
Ⓒ SM (*Zool*) pig, hog (*EEUU*)

tunda[1] SF (= *esquileo*) shearing

tunda[2] SF [1] (= *paliza*) beating, thrashing
[2] **darse una ~** to wear o.s. out

tundir[1] ▸conjug 3a◂ VT [+ *pieles*] to shear; [+ *hierba*] to mow, cut

tundir[2] ▸conjug 3a◂ VT [1] (= *golpear*) to beat, thrash [2] (= *cansar*) to exhaust, tire out

tundra SF tundra

tunear ▸conjug 1a◂ VI [1] (= *vivir como pícaro*) to live a rogue's life
[2] (= *gandulear*) to loaf, idle; (= *divertirse*) to have a good time

tunecino/a ADJ, SM/F Tunisian

túnel SM [1] (= *paso*) tunnel ► **túnel aerodinámico** wind tunnel ► **túnel de lavado** car wash ► **túnel del Canal de la Mancha** Channel Tunnel ► **túnel del tiempo** time warp ► **túnel de pruebas aerodinámicas** wind tunnel ► **túnel de vestuarios** tunnel leading to the changing-rooms ► **túnel de viento** wind tunnel
[2] (= *crisis*) bad time
[3] (*Dep*) nutmeg

tuneladora SF tunnelling machine

tunelar ▸conjug 1a◂ VI to tunnel

tunes SMPL (*Andes, CAm*) first steps (*of a child*); **hacer ~** to toddle, start to walk, take one's first steps

Túnez SM (= *país*) Tunisia; (= *ciudad*) Tunis

tungo Ⓐ ADJ (*Andes*) short, shortened, blunt
Ⓑ SM [1] (*Andes*) (= *trozo*) bit, chunk
[2] (*Cono Sur Anat*) (= *cuello*) neck

tungsteno SM tungsten

túnica SF [1] (*Hist*) tunic; [*de monje*] robe
[2] (*Anat, Bot*) tunic

Tunicia SF Tunisia

túnico SM (*LAm*) shift, long undergarment

túnido SM tuna (fish)

tuning ['tunin] SM car styling, *accessorizing and styling cars*

tuno/a Ⓐ SM/F (= *pícaro*) rogue, villain; **el muy ~** the old rogue
Ⓑ SM (*Mús*) *member of a student music group*; → TUNA

tunoso ADJ (*Andes*) prickly

tuntún: **al ~** ADV thoughtlessly, any old how; **juzgar al buen ~** to judge hastily, jump to conclusions

tuntuneco* ADJ (*CAm, Caribe*) stupid, dense*

tuñeco ADJ (*Caribe*) maimed, crippled

tupamaro/a (*Cono Sur Hist, Pol*) Ⓐ ADJ Tupamaro *antes de s*, urban guerrilla *antes de s*
Ⓑ SM/F Tupamaro, urban guerrilla

tupé SM [1] (= *mechón*) quiff
[2] (= *peluca*) toupée, hairpiece
[3] (*) (= *caradura*) nerve*, cheek*

tupí Ⓐ SMF [1] Tupi (Indian)
[2] (*esp Par*) = **tupí-guaraní**
Ⓑ SM (*Ling*) Tupi

tupia SF (*Andes*) dam

tupiar ▸conjug 1b◂ VT (*Andes*) to dam up

tupición SF [1] (*LAm*) (= *obstrucción*) blockage, obstruction; (*Med*) catarrh
[2] (*LAm*) (= *multitud*) dense crowd, throng
[3] (*Andes, Méx*) (= *vegetación*) dense vegetation
[4] (*Cono Sur**) **una ~ de cosas** a lot of things
[5] (*LAm*) (= *confusión*) bewilderment, confusion

tupido Ⓐ ADJ [1] (= *denso*) thick; (= *impenetrable*) impenetrable; [*tela*] close-woven
[2] (*LAm*) (= *obstruido*) blocked up, obstructed
[3] (= *torpe*) dim*, dense*
[4] (*Méx*) (= *frecuente*) common, frequent
Ⓑ ADV (*Méx*) (= *con tesón*) persistently, steadily; (= *a menudo*) often, frequently

tupí-guaraní Ⓐ ADJ Tupi-Guarani
Ⓑ SMF Tupi-Guarani (Indian)
Ⓒ SM (*Ling*) Tupi-Guarani

tupinambo SM Jerusalem artichoke

tupir ▸conjug 3a◂ Ⓐ VT [1] (= *apretar*) to pack tight, press down, compact
[2] (*LAm*) (= *obstruir*) to block, stop up, obstruct
Ⓑ **tupirse** VPR [1] (*) (= *comer mucho*) to stuff oneself*
[2] (*LAm*) (= *desconcertarse*) to feel silly, get embarrassed

turba[1] SF (= *combustible*) peat

turba[2] SF (= *muchedumbre*) crowd, throng; (*en movimiento*) swarm; (*pey*) mob

turbación SF [1] (= *alteración*) disturbance
[2] (= *inquietud*) alarm, worry; (= *perplejidad*) bewilderment, confusion; (= *agitación*) trepidation
[3] (= *vergüenza*) embarrassment

turbado ADJ [1] (= *alterado*) disturbed
[2] (= *inquieto*) alarmed, worried; (= *perplejo*) bewildered
[3] (= *avergonzado*) embarrassed

turbador ADJ (= *inquietante*) disturbing, alarming; (= *vergonzoso*) embarrassing

turbal SM peat bog

turbamulta SF mob, rabble

turbante SM [1] (= *prenda*) turban
[2] (*Méx Bot*) gourd, calabash, squash (*EEUU*)

turbar ▸conjug 1a◂ Ⓐ VT [1] [+ *silencio, reposo, orden*] to disturb; **el ruido turbó su sueño** the noise disturbed her sleep; **nada turbó la buena marcha de las negociaciones** nothing hindered *o* disturbed the smooth progress of the negotiations
[2] [+ *agua*] to disturb, stir up
[3] (= *alterar*) **la noticia turbó su ánimo** the news troubled his mind, the news perturbed him; **su llegada inesperada la turbó visiblemente** his unexpected arrival visibly disturbed her
[4] (= *avergonzar*) to embarrass; **sus palabras de amor la ~on** his words of love embarrassed her
Ⓑ **turbarse** VPR [1] (= *alterarse*) **al reconocer a su agresor se turbó enormemente** she was deeply disturbed when she recognized her attacker; **se turbó de tal modo que no pudo responder** he was so disturbed he couldn't reply
[2] (= *avergonzarse*) to get embarrassed; **se turbó al ver que ella lo miraba fijamente** when he realized she was staring at him he came over *o* got all embarrassed

turbera SF peat bog

turbiedad SF [1] [*de líquidos*] cloudiness
[2] (= *opacidad*) opacity; (= *confusión*) confusion
[3] (= *turbulencia*) turbulence

turbina SF turbine ► **turbina a** *o* **de vapor** steam engine ► **turbina de gas** gas turbine ► **turbina eólica** wind turbine

turbio Ⓐ ADJ [1] [*agua*] cloudy, muddy, turbid (*frm*)
[2] [*vista*] dim, blurred; [*mente, pensamientos*] disturbed; [*tema*] unclear, confused
[3] [*período*] turbulent, unsettled
[4] [*negocio*] shady*; [*método*] dubious
Ⓑ ADV **ver ~** not to see clearly, to have blurred vision
Ⓒ **turbios** SMPL sediment *sing*

turbión SM [1] (*Meteo*) (= *aguacero*) heavy shower, downpour
[2] (= *aluvión*) shower, torrent

turbo Ⓐ SM (*Mec*) turbo, turbocharger; (= *coche*) turbocharged car
Ⓑ ADJ INV turbo *antes de s*

turbo... PREF turbo...

turboalimentado ADJ turbocharged

turbocompresor SM turbo-compressor; (= *diesel*) turbo-supercharger

turbodiesel ADJ INV, SM turbo diesel

turbohélice Ⓐ SM turboprop, turboprop aeroplane
Ⓑ ADJ INV turboprop *antes de s*

turbonada SF (*Cono Sur*) sudden storm, squall

turbopropulsado ADJ turboprop *antes de s*

turbopropulsor, **turborreactor** Ⓐ SM turbojet (aeroplane)
Ⓑ ADJ INV turbojet *antes de s*

turbulencia SF [1] (*Meteo*) turbulence
[2] [*de río, aguas*] turbulence
[3] (= *desorden*) [*de época*] turbulence; [*de reunión*] storminess
[4] (= *inquietud*) restlessness

turbulento ADJ [1] [*río, aguas*] turbulent
[2] [*período*] troubled, turbulent; [*reunión*] stormy
[3] [*carácter*] restless

turca‡ SF piss-up‡, binge*; **coger** *o* **pillar una ~** to get sozzled*, get pissed‡

turco/a Ⓐ ADJ Turkish
Ⓑ SM/F [1] (= *de Turquía*) Turk; **joven ~** (*Pol*) young Turk
[2] (*LAm pey*) *immigrant from the Middle East*
[3] (*LAm*) (= *buhonero*) pedlar, peddler (*EEUU*), hawker
Ⓒ SM (*Ling*) Turkish

turcochipriota ADJ, SMF Turkish-Cypriot

túrdiga SF thong, strip of leather

Turena SF Touraine

turf SM [1] (= *deporte*) **el ~** the turf, horse-racing
[2] (= *pista*) racetrack

turfista Ⓐ ADJ fond of horse-racing
Ⓑ SM/F racegoer

turgencia SF turgidity

turgente ADJ, **túrgido** ADJ turgid, swollen

Turín SM Turin

Turingia SF Thuringia

turismo SM [1] (= *actividad*) tourism; (= *industria*) tourist industry *o* trade; **el ~ constituye su mayor industria** tourism is their biggest industry; **se ha desarrollado mucho el ~ en el norte** tourism has been greatly developed in the north; **ahora se hace más ~ que nunca** numbers of tourists are greater now than ever ► **turismo blanco** winter holidays *pl*, skiing holidays *pl* ► **turismo cultural** cultural tourism ► **turismo de calidad** quality tourism ► **turismo ecológico** eco-tourism ► **turismo interior** domestic tourism ► **turismo rural** country holidays *pl*, green tourism; **promover el ~ rural** to promote tourism in rural areas; **casas de ~ rural** ≈ holiday cottages ► **turismo sexual** sex tourism
[2] (*Aut*) car, private car

turista SMF (*gen*) tourist; (= *visitante*) sightseer; **clase ~** economy class, tourist class

turístico ADJ tourist *antes de s*

turistizado ADJ touristy

Turkmenistán SM Turkmenistan

turma SF [1] (*Anat*) testicle
[2] (*Bot*) truffle; (*Andes*) potato

túrmix® SM *o* SF mixer, blender

turnar ▸conjug 1a◂ Ⓐ VI to take turns
Ⓑ **turnarse** VPR to take turns; **se turnan para usarlo** they take it in turns to use it

turné SM tour, trip

turno SM [1] (= *vez*) turn; (*en juegos*) turn, go; **es tu ~** it's your turn; **cuando te llegue el ~** when your turn comes; **espere su ~** wait your turn; **por ~s** in turns, by turns; **estuvo con su querida de ~** he was with his lover of the moment; **el tonto de ~** the inevitable idiot ► **turno de preguntas** round of questions
[2] [*de trabajo*] shift; **hago el ~ de tarde** I do the afternoon shift; **estar de ~** to be on duty; **farmacia de ~** duty chemist; **médico de ~** duty doctor, doctor on duty; **trabajo por ~s** shiftwork; **trabajar por ~s** to work shifts, do shiftwork ► **turno de día** day shift ► **turno de noche** night shift ► **turno de oficio** spell of court duty ► **turno rotativo** rotating shift

turolense Ⓐ ADJ of/from Teruel
Ⓑ SMF native/inhabitant of Teruel; **los ~s** people of Teruel

turón SM polecat

turqueo* SM (*CAm*) fight

turquesa Ⓐ ADJ, SM (= *color*) turquoise
Ⓑ SF turquoise

turquesco ADJ Turkish

turquí ADJ **color ~** indigo, deep blue

Turquía SF Turkey

turra‡ SF (*Cono Sur*) whore, prostitute

turrón SM [1] (= *dulce*) nougat
[2] (*) (= *cargo*) cushy job, sinecure

> **TURRÓN**
>
> *Turrón is a type of Spanish sweet rather like nougat which is eaten particularly around Christmas. It has Arabic origins and is made of honey, egg whites, almonds and hazelnuts. There are two traditional varieties:* **alicante**, *which is hard and contains whole almonds, and* **jijona**, *which is soft and made from crushed almonds.*

turulato* ADJ stunned, flabbergasted; **se quedó ~ con la noticia** he was stunned by the news

tururú* Ⓐ ADJ (= *loco*) **estar ~** to be crazy
Ⓑ EXCL no way!*, you're joking!

tus[1] EXCL (*a un perro*) good dog!, here boy!

tus[2]* SM ✦**MODISMO no decir ~ ni mus** to remain silent, say nothing; **sin decir ~ ni mus** without saying a word

tusa SF [1] (*Andes, CAm, Caribe*) [*de maíz*] (= *mazorca*) cob of maize, corncob; (*sin grano*) corn husk, maize husk; (*Caribe*) (= *cigarro*) *cigar rolled in a maize leaf*; (*Cono Sur*) (= *seda*) corn silk
[2] (*Cono Sur*) (= *crin*) horse's mane
[3] (*Cono Sur*) (= *esquileo*) clipping, shearing
[4] (*Andes*) [*de viruela*] pockmark
[5] (*Andes**) (= *susto*) fright; (= *inquietud*) anxiety
[6] (*CAm, Caribe*) (= *mujerzuela*) whore
[7] ✦**MODISMO no vale ni una ~** (*CAm, Caribe**) it's worthless

tusar ▸conjug 1a◂ VT (*LAm*) (= *esquilar*) to cut, clip, shear; (= *cortar*) to cut roughly, cut badly

tuse SM (*Cono Sur*) = **tusa**

tuso ADJ [1] (*Andes, Caribe*) (= *esquilado*) cropped, shorn
[2] (*Caribe*) (= *rabón*) docked, tailless
[3] (*Andes, Caribe*) (= *picado de viruelas*) pockmarked

tútano SM (*LAm*) = **tuétano**

tute SM *card game similar to bezique*; ✦**MODISMO darse un ~** to work extra hard

tutear ▸conjug 1a◂ Ⓐ VT **~ a algn** (*lit*) to address sb as "tú" (*2nd person sing*); (*fig*) to be on familiar terms with sb
Ⓑ **tutearse** VPR **se tutean desde siempre** they have always addressed each other as "tú", they have always been on familiar terms

tutela SF [1] (*Jur*) guardianship; **bajo ~** in ward; **estar bajo ~ jurídica** [*niño*] to be a ward of court
[2] (= *protección*) tutelage, protection; **estar bajo la ~ de** (= *amparo*) to be under the protection of; (= *auspicios*) to be under the auspices of

tutelaje SM (*LAm*) = **tutela**

tutelar Ⓐ ADJ tutelary; **ángel ~** guardian angel
Ⓑ ▸conjug 1a◂ VT (= *proteger*) to protect, guard; (= *guiar*) to advise, guide; (= *vigilar*) to supervise, oversee

tuteo SM use of (the familiar) "tú", addressing a person as "tú"; **se ha extendido mucho el ~** the use of "tú" has greatly increased

tutilimundi* SM (*LAm*) everybody

tutiplén†*: **a ~** ADV [*dar*] freely; [*repartir*] haphazardly, indiscriminately; [*comer*] hugely, to excess

tutor(a) Ⓐ SM/F [1] (*Jur*) guardian
[2] (*Univ*) tutor ► **tutor(a) de curso** (*Escol*) form master/mistress
Ⓑ SM (*Agr*) prop, stake

tutoría SF [1] (*Jur*) guardianship
[2] (*Univ*) tutorial (class), section (of a course) (*EEUU*)

tutorial ADJ tutorial

tutorizar ▸conjug 1f◂ VT = **tutelar B**

tutú SM tutu

tutuma SF (*Andes, Cono Sur*) [1] (‡) (= *cabeza*) nut‡, noggin (*EEUU**), head; (= *bollo*) bump; (= *joroba*) hump; (= *cardenal*) bruise
[2] (= *fruta*) *type of cucumber*

tutumito SM (*Andes, CAm*) idiot

tuturuto Ⓐ ADJ [1] (*CAm, Caribe, Méx*) (= *borracho*) drunk
[2] (*Andes, CAm, Caribe*) (= *tonto*) stupid; (= *aturdido*) dumbfounded, stunned
Ⓑ SM (*Cono Sur*) (= *chulo*) pimp

tuve *etc ver* **tener**

tuyo/a Ⓐ ADJ POS yours; **¿es ~ este abrigo?** is this coat yours?; **cualquier amigo ~** any friend of yours
Ⓑ PRON POS [1] (*gen*) yours; **este es el ~** this one's yours; **la tuya está en el armario** yours is in the cupboard; **mis amigos y los ~s** my friends and yours; **¡adelante, ésta es la tuya!** go on, now's your chance!; **¿ya estás haciendo de las tuyas?** are you up to your tricks again?; **lo ~: todo lo ~ me pertenece a mi también** everything that is yours also belongs to me; **he puesto lo ~ en esta caja** I've put your things in this box; **sé que lo ~ con Ana acabó hace tiempo** I know that you and Ana finished a while ago; **la informática no es lo ~** computers are not your thing
[2] **los ~s** (= *tus familiares*) your folks*, your family; **¿echas de menos a los ~s?** do you miss your folks?

tuza SF (*LAm Zool*) mole

TV SF ABR (= **televisión**) TV

TVE SF ABR = **Televisión Española**

tweed [twi] SM tweed

txistu SM (Basque) flute

txistulari SM (Basque) flute player

U u

U, **u¹** [u] SF (= *letra*) U, u; **doble U** (*Méx*) W; **curva en U** hairpin bend

u² CONJ (*used instead of "o" before o-, ho-*) or; **siete u ocho** seven or eight

U. ABR (= **Universidad**) Univ., U

ualabi SM wallaby

UAM SF ABR [1] (*Esp*) = **Universidad Autónoma de Madrid**
[2] (*Méx*) = **Universidad Autónoma Metropolitana**

ubérrimo ADJ exceptionally fertile

ubicación SF [1] (*esp LAm*) (= *posición*) situation, location
[2] (= *empleo*) job, position

ubicado ADJ [1] (*esp LAm*) (= *situado*) situated, located; **una tienda ubicada en la calle Lagasca** a shop in Lagasca street; **bien ~** ◊ **ubicadísimo** (*Méx*) well situated *o* located, in a desirable location
[2] (*en un trabajo*) working

ubicar ▸conjug 1g◂ Ⓐ VT [1] (*esp LAm*) (= *colocar*) to place, locate; [+ *edificio*] to site
[2] (= *encontrar*) [2·1] **~ algo** to find sth, locate sth; **no supo ~ Madrid en el mapa** he was unable to find *o* locate Madrid on the map
[2·2] (*LAm*) **~ a algn** to find sb, locate sb; **no hemos podido ~ al jefe** we have been unable to find *o* locate the boss, we have been unable to track down the boss
Ⓑ **ubicarse** VPR [1] (= *estar situado*) **el museo se ubica en el centro de la ciudad** the museum is located o situated in the city centre
[2] (= *orientarse*) to find one's way around; **a pesar del mapa no consigo ~me** even though I have a map I can't find my way around; **este es el museo, ¿te ubicas ahora?** this is the museum, have you got your bearings now?
[3] (*LAm**) (= *colocarse*) to get a job

ubicuidad SF ubiquity; **el don de la ~** the gift for being everywhere at once

ubicuo ADJ ubiquitous

ubre SF udder

ubrera SF (*Med*) thrush

UCD SF ABR (*Esp*) = **Unión de Centro Democrático**; → LA TRANSICIÓN

UCE SF ABR [1] (*Fin*) (= **Unidad de Cuenta Europea**) ECU
[2] (*Esp*) = **Unión de Consumidores de España**

ucedista (*Esp*) Ⓐ ADJ **política ~** policy of UCD, UCD policy
Ⓑ SMF member of UCD

-ucho, **-ucha** *ver* **Aspects of Word Formation in Spanish 2**

uchuvito* ADJ (*Andes*) drunk, tight*

UCI SF ABR (= **Unidad de Cuidados Intensivos**) ICU

UCM SF ABR (*Esp*) = **Universidad Complutense de Madrid**

-uco, -uca *ver* **Aspects of Word Formation in Spanish 2**

UCP SF ABR (= **unidad central de proceso**) CPU

UCR SF ABR (*Arg*) = **Unión Cívica Radical**

Ucrania SF Ukraine

ucraniano/a ADJ, SM/F, **ucranio/a** ADJ, SM/F Ukrainian

ucronía SF uchronia, imaginary time

ucrónico ADJ uchronic, imaginary

Ud. PRON ABR = **usted**

-udo *ver* **Aspects of Word Formation in Spanish 2**

Uds. PRON ABR = **ustedes**

UDV SF ABR (= **unidad de despliegue visual**) VDU

UE SF ABR (= **Unión Europea**) EU

UEFA SF ABR (= **Unión Europea de Fútbol Asociación**) UEFA

UEI SF ABR (= **Unidad Especial de Intervención**) *special force of the Guardia Civil*

-uelo, -uela *ver* **Aspects of Word Formation in Spanish 2**

UEM SF ABR (= **unión económica y monetaria**) EMU

UEO SF ABR (= **Unión Europea Occidental**) WEU

UEP SF ABR (= **Unión Europea de Pagos**) EPU

UEPS ABR (= **último en entrar, primero en salir**) LIFO

UER SF ABR (= **Unión Europea de Radiodifusión**) EBU

UF SF ABR (*Chile*) (= **Unidad de Fomento**) *changing monetary unit in a fixed dollar system*

uf EXCL (*cansancio*) phew!; (*repugnancia*) ugh!

ufanamente ADV (= *con orgullo*) proudly; (= *con jactancia*) boastfully; (= *con satisfacción*) smugly

ufanarse ▸conjug 1a◂ VPR to boast; **~ con** *o* **de algo** to boast of sth, pride o.s. on sth

ufanía SF [1] (= *orgullo*) pride; (= *jactancia*) boastfulness; (= *satisfacción*) smugness
[2] (*Bot*) = **lozanía 1**

ufano ADJ [1] (= *orgulloso*) proud; (= *jactancioso*) boastful; (= *satisfecho*) smug; **iba muy ~ en el nuevo coche** he was going along so proudly in his new car; **está muy ~ porque le han dado el premio** he is very proud that they have awarded him the prize
[2] (*Bot*) = **lozano 1**

ufología SF ufology, study of unidentified flying objects

ufólogo/a SM/F ufologist

Uganda SF Uganda

ugandés/esa ADJ, SM/F Ugandan

ugetista (*Esp*) Ⓐ ADJ **política ~** policy of the UGT, UGT policy
Ⓑ SMF member of the UGT

UGT SF ABR (*Esp*) = **Unión General de Trabajadores**

UIT SF ABR (= **Unión Internacional para las Telecomunicaciones**) ITU

ujier SM (*en un tribunal*) usher; (= *conserje*) doorkeeper, attendant

-ujo, -uja *ver* **Aspects of Word Formation in Spanish 2**

újule EXCL (*Méx*) (*para indicar desprecio*) huh!; (*para indicar sorpresa*) wow!, phew!

úlcera SF [1] (*Med*) ulcer, sore ► **úlcera de decúbito** bedsore ► **úlcera duodenal** duodenal ulcer ► **úlcera gástrica** gastric ulcer
[2] (*Bot*) rot

ulceración SF ulceration

ulcerar ▸conjug 1a◂ Ⓐ VT to make sore, ulcerate
Ⓑ **ulcerarse** VPR to ulcerate

ulceroso ADJ ulcerous

ule SM (*CAm, Méx*) = **hule¹ 1**

ulerear ▸conjug 1a◂ VT (*Cono Sur*) to roll out

ulero SM (*Cono Sur*) rolling pin

Ulises SM Ulysses

ulluco SM (*Andes, Cono Sur*) manioc

ulpo SM (*Chile, Perú*) maize gruel

ulterior ADJ [1] [*sitio*] farther, further
[2] [*tiempo*] later, subsequent

ulteriormente ADV later, subsequently

ultimación SF completion, conclusion

ultimador(a) SM/F (*LAm*) killer, murderer

últimamente ADV [1] (= *recientemente*) lately, recently; **no lo he visto ~** I haven't seen him lately o recently
[2] (= *por último*) lastly, finally
[3] (= *en último caso*) as a last resort
[4] **¡últimamente!** (*LAm*) well, I'll be damned!, that's the absolute end!

ultimar ▸conjug 1a◂ VT [1] (= *terminar*) [+ *detalles, acuerdo*] to finalize; [+ *proyecto, obra*] to put the finishing *o* final touches to; **el tratado que ultiman estos días ambos gobiernos** the treaty which the two governments have been finalizing over the last few days; **están ultimando la nueva edición del libro** they are putting the finishing *o* final touches to the new edition of the book; **están ultimando los preparativos para la boda** they are making the final preparations for the wedding

2 (*LAm frm*) (= *matar*) to kill, murder

ultimato SM, **ultimátum** SM (*pl* **ultimátums**) ultimatum

ultimizar ▸conjug 1f◂ VT = **ultimar**

▼**último/a** Ⓐ ADJ 1 (= *final*) last; **el ~ día del mes** the last day of the month; **la última película que hizo Orson Wells** the last film Orson Wells made; **las últimas Navidades que pasamos allí** the last Christmas we spent there; **la Última Cena** (*Rel*) the Last Supper; **a lo ~*** in the end; **¿y qué ocurre a lo ~?** and what happens in the end?; **estoy a lo ~ del libro** I've nearly finished the book; **por ~** finally, lastly; **por ~, el conferenciante hizo referencia a ...** finally *o* lastly, the speaker mentioned ...; **por última vez** for the last time

2 (= *más reciente*) 2·1 (*en una serie*) [*ejemplar, moda, novedad*] latest; [*elecciones, periodo*] last; **este coche es el ~ modelo** this car is the latest model; **¿has leído el ~ número de la revista?** have you read the latest issue of the magazine?; **las últimas noticias** the latest news; **las últimas novedades musicales** the latest music releases; **los dos ~s cuadros que ha hecho no son tan innovadores** his two latest *o* his latest two paintings are not so innovative; **durante la última década** in *o* over the last decade; **en las últimas horas ha aparecido otro posible comprador** in the last few hours another possible buyer has emerged; **volvió a salir elegido en las últimas elecciones** he was reelected at the last election; **la última película que he visto** the last film I saw; **las últimas películas que he visto** the last few films I have seen; **ahora ~** (*Chile*) recently; **su malhumor no es de ahora ~** his bad mood is not a recent thing; **ha estado estudiando más ahora ~** he's been studying more recently; **en los ~s años** in *o* over the last few years, in recent years; **en los ~s tiempos** lately

2·2 (*entre dos*) latter; **de los dos, éste ~ es el mejor** of the two, the latter is the best; *ver tb* **hora 2.2**

3 (*en el espacio*) 3·1 (= *más al fondo*) back; **un asiento en la última fila** a seat in the back row

3·2 (= *más alto*) top; **viven en el ~ piso** they live on the top floor

3·3 (= *más bajo*) bottom, last; **el ~ escalón** the bottom *o* last step; **el equipo en última posición** the team in last *o* bottom place; **ocupan el ~ lugar en el índice de audiencia** they have the lowest viewing figures

3·4 (= *más lejano*) most remote, furthest; **las noticias llegan hasta el ~ rincón del país** news gets to the most remote *o* the furthest parts of the country

4 (= *extremo*) **sólo lo aceptaremos como ~ recurso** we will only accept it as a last resort; **en ~ caso, iría yo** as a last resort *o* if all else fails, I would go; **esta medida tiene como fin ~ reducir el nivel de contaminación** the ultimate aim of this measure is to reduce pollution levels; *ver tb* **extremo² A2**, **instancia 3**, **remedio 2**

5 (= *definitivo*) **es mi última oferta** that's my final offer; **dígame cuál es el ~ precio** tell me what your lowest price is; ✦**MODISMO decir la última palabra** to have the last word

6 **lo ~*** 6·1 (= *lo más moderno*) the latest thing; **lo ~ en pantalones** the latest thing in trousers; **lo ~ en tecnología ofimática** the latest (in) office technology

6·2 (= *lo peor*) the limit; **pedirme eso encima ya es lo ~** for him to ask that of me as well really is the limit

Ⓑ SM/F 1 **el ~** the last, the last one; **el ~ de la lista** the last (one) on the list; **¿quién es la última?** who's the last in the queue?; **hablar el ~** to speak last; **llegó la última** she arrived last; **ser el ~ en hacer algo** to be the last (one) to do sth; **el ~ en salir que apague la luz** the last one to leave, turn the light off; ✦**MODISMOS reírse el ~** to have the last laugh; **a la última**: **estar a la última** to be bang up-to-date*; **siempre va vestida a la última** she's always wearing the latest thing; **zapatos a la última** the latest thing in shoes; **estar en las últimas*** (= *a punto de morir*) to be at death's door, be on one's last legs*; (= *sin dinero*) to be down to one's last penny *o* (*EEUU*) cent; **en últimas** (*Col*) as a last resort; *ver tb* **vestir B1**

2 (*) **¿a qué no sabes la última de Irene?** do you know the latest about Irene?

3 (*Esp*) **a últimos de mes** towards the end of the month

Ⓒ ADV (*Cono Sur*) in the last position, in the last place

ultra Ⓐ ADJ INV extreme right-wing

Ⓑ SMF neo-fascist

ultra... PREF ultra..., extra...

ultracongelación SF (*Esp*) (deep-)freezing

ultracongelado ADJ (*Esp*) deep-frozen

ultracongelador SM (*Esp*) deep-freeze, freezer

ultracongelar ▸conjug 1a◂ VT (*Esp*) to deep-freeze

ultraconservador(a) ADJ, SM/F ultra-conservative

ultracorrección SF hypercorrection

ultracorto ADJ ultra-short

ultraderecha SF extreme right, extreme right-wing

ultraderechista Ⓐ ADJ extreme right(-wing)

Ⓑ SMF extreme right-winger

ultrafino ADJ ultrafine

ultraísmo SM *revolutionary poetic movement of the 1920s (imagist, surrealist etc)*

ultraizquierda SF extreme left(-wing)

ultraizquierdista Ⓐ ADJ extreme left(-wing)

Ⓑ SMF extreme left-winger

ultrajador ADJ, **ultrajante** ADJ (= *ofensivo*) offensive; (= *injurioso*) insulting; (= *descomedido*) outrageous

ultrajar ▸conjug 1a◂ VT 1 (= *ofender*) to offend; (= *injuriar*) to insult, abuse

2 (*liter*) (= *estropear*) to spoil, crumple, disarrange

ultraje SM (= *injuria*) insult; (= *atrocidad*) outrage

ultrajoso ADJ = **ultrajador**

ultraligero Ⓐ ADJ microlight

Ⓑ SM microlight, microlight aircraft

ultramar SM **de** *o* **en ~** overseas, abroad; **los países de ~** foreign countries; **productos venidos de ~** goods from abroad; **pasó ocho años en ~** he spent eight years overseas

ultramarino Ⓐ ADJ 1 (= *extranjero*) overseas, foreign

2 (*Com*) (= *importado*) imported

Ⓑ **ultramarinos** SM INV (*tb* **tienda de ~s**) grocer's (shop), grocery (*EEUU*)

Ⓒ **ultramarinos** SMPL (= *comestibles*) groceries, foodstuffs

ultramoderno ADJ ultramodern

ultramontanismo SM ultramontanism

ultramontano ADJ, SM ultramontane

ultranza SF **a ~** 1 (*como adjetivo*) (*Pol etc*) out-and-out, extreme; **un nacionalista a ~** a rabid nationalist; **paz a ~** peace at any price

2 (*como adverbio*) **luchar a ~** to fight to the death; **lo quiere hacer a ~** he wants to do it at all costs

ultrapotente ADJ extra powerful

ultrarrápido ADJ extra fast

ultrarrojo ADJ = **infrarrojo**

ultrasecreto ADJ top secret

ultrasensitivo ADJ ultrasensitive

ultrasofisticado ADJ highly sophisticated

ultrasónico ADJ ultrasonic

ultrasonido SM ultrasound

ultrasur SMF INV *extremist fan of Real Madrid FC*

ultratumba SF **la vida de ~** life beyond the grave, life after death; **una voz de ~** a ghostly voice

ultravioleta ADJ INV ultraviolet; **rayos ~** ultraviolet rays

ulular ▸conjug 1a◂ VI [*animal, viento*] to howl, shriek; [*búho*] to hoot, screech

ululato SM [*de animal*] howl, shriek; [*de búho*] hoot, screech

UM SF ABR (*Esp*) = **Unión Mallorquina**

umbilical ADJ umbilical; **cordón ~** umbilical cord

umbral SM 1 [*de entrada*] threshold; **pasar** *o* **traspasar el ~ de algn** to set foot in sb's house; **en los ~es de la muerte** at death's door

2 (= *comienzo*) **estar en los ~es de algo** to be on the threshold *o* verge of sth; **eso está en los ~es de lo imposible** that borders *o* verges on the impossible

3 (*Com*) ► **umbral de la pobreza** poverty line ► **umbral de rentabilidad** break-even point

umbralada SF (*Andes, Cono Sur*), **umbralado** SM (*Andes, Cono Sur*), **umbraladura** SF (*Andes*) threshold

umbrío ADJ, **umbroso** ADJ shady

UME SF ABR (= **Unión Monetaria Europea**) EMU

UMI SF ABR (= **unidad de medicina intensiva**) ICU

un(a) Ⓐ ART INDEF 1 (*en singular*) (*refiriéndose a algo no conocido o de forma imprecisa*) a; (*antes de vocal o de h*) an; (*dando mayor énfasis, con expresiones temporales*) one; **una silla** a chair; **un paraguas** an umbrella; **hacía una mañana espléndida** it was a lovely morning; **hay una cosa que me gustaría saber** there is one

➤ LENGUA Y USO: **último A1** 53.5

thing I would like to know; **una mañana me llamó** he called me one morning

2 (*en plural*) 2·1 (*uso indefinido*) (= *algunos*) some; (= *pocos*) a few; **fui con unos amigos** I went with some friends; **hay unas cervezas en la nevera** there are a few *o* some beers in the fridge; **unas horas más tarde** a few hours later

2·2 (*con partes del cuerpo*) **tiene unas piernas muy largas** she has very long legs

2·3 (*con objetos a pares*) some; **me he comprado unos zapatos de tacón** I've bought some high-heels; **necesito unas tijeras** I need a pair of scissors

2·4 (*con cantidades, cifras*) about, around; **había unas 20 personas** there were about *o* around 20 people, there were some 20 people; **unos 80 dólares** about *o* around 80 dollars, some 80 dollars; **hacía unos 30 grados** it was about 30 degrees

3 (*enfático*) **¡se dio un golpe ...!** he banged himself really hard!; **¡había una gente más rara ...!** there were some real weirdos there!*; **¡sois unos vagos!** you're so lazy!

Ⓑ ADJ (*numeral*) one; **sólo quiero una hoja** I only want one sheet; **una excursión de un día** a one-day trip, a day trip; **tardamos una mañana entera** it took us a whole morning; *ver tb* **uno**

una PRON 1 **es la ~** (= *hora*) it's one o'clock; **¡a la ~, a las dos, a las tres!** (*antes de empezar algo*) one, two, three!; (*en subasta*) going, going, gone!; (*Dep*) ready, steady, go!; ✦***MODISMOS*** **~ de dos** either one thing or the other; **todos a ~** all together

2 (*enfático*) 2·1 (= *pelea, paliza*) **armar ~** to kick up a fuss; **te voy a dar ~ que verás** I'm going to give you what for; ✦***MODISMO*** **no dar ~** not to get a single thing right

2·2 (= *mala pasada*) **hacerle ~ a algn** to play a dirty trick on sb

3 (*enfático*) **¡había ~ de gente!** what a crowd there was!

U.N.A.M. SF ABR (*Méx*) = **Universidad Nacional Autónoma de México**

unánime ADJ unanimous

unánimemente ADV unanimously

unanimidad SF unanimity; **por ~** unanimously

uncial ADJ, SF uncial

unción SF 1 (*Med*) anointing

2 (*Rel*) (*tb fig*) unction

uncir ▸conjug 3b◂ VT to yoke

undécimo ADJ, SM eleventh; *ver tb* **sexto A**

UNED SF ABR (*Esp*) (= **Universidad Nacional de Educación a Distancia**) ≈ OU

UNESCO SF ABR (= **United Nations Educational, Scientific and Cultural Organization**) UNESCO

ungido ADJ anointed; **el Ungido del Señor** the Lord's Anointed

ungir ▸conjug 3c◂ VT 1 (*Med*) to put ointment on, rub with ointment

2 (*Rel*) to anoint

ungüento SM 1 (= *sustancia*) ointment, unguent

2 (= *remedio*) salve, balm

ungulado Ⓐ ADJ ungulate, hoofed

Ⓑ SM ungulate, hoofed animal

uni... PREF uni..., one-..., single-...

únicamente ADV only, solely

unicameral ADJ (*Pol*) single-chamber

unicameralismo SM system of single-chamber government

unicato* SM (*Méx*) sole rule, power monopoly

UNICEF SF ABR (= **United Nations International Children's Emergency Fund**) UNICEF

unicelular ADJ unicellular, single-cell

unicidad SF uniqueness

único ADJ 1 (= *solo*) only; **es el ~ ejemplar que existe** it is the only copy in existence; **fue el ~ sobreviviente** he was the sole *o* only survivor; **hijo ~** only child; **sistema de partido ~** one-party *o* single-party system; **la única dificultad es que ...** the only difficulty is that ...; **es lo ~ que nos faltaba** (*iró*) that's all we needed

2 (= *singular*) unique; **este ejemplar es ~** this specimen is unique; **como pianista es única** as a pianist she is in a class of her own; **¡eres ~! sólo a ti se te podía ocurrir algo así** you're amazing! only you could think of something like that

unicolor ADJ one-colour, all one colour

unicornio SM unicorn

unidad SF 1 (= *cohesión*) unity; **defienden la ~ del Estado** they defend the unity of the State; **falta de ~ en la familia** lack of family unity ▸ **unidad de acción** (*Literat*) unity of action; [*de partido, movimiento*] unity ▸ **unidad de lugar** (*Literat*) unity of place ▸ **unidad de tiempo** (*Literat*) unity of time

2 (*Com, Mat*) unit; **precio por ~** unit price; **—¿cuánto es? —un euro la ~** "how much is it?" — "one euro each"; **se venden en cajas de seis ~es** they are sold in boxes of six ▸ **unidad de cuenta europea** European currency unit ▸ **unidad de medida** unit of measurement ▸ **unidad monetaria** monetary unit

3 (*Med*) (= *pabellón, sala*) unit ▸ **unidad coronaria** coronary unit ▸ **unidad de cuidados intensivos** intensive care unit ▸ **unidad de quemados** burns unit ▸ **unidad de vigilancia intensiva** intensive care unit

4 (*Radio, TV*) ▸ **unidad móvil** outside broadcast unit

5 (*Inform*) ▸ **unidad central** mainframe computer ▸ **unidad de control** control unit ▸ **unidad de disco fijo** hard (disk) drive ▸ **unidad de visualización** visual display unit ▸ **unidad periférica** peripheral device

6 (*Ferro*) (= *vagón*) coach, wagon, freight car (*EEUU*)

7 (*Aer*) (= *avión*) aircraft ▸ **unidad de cola** tail unit

8 (*Mil*) unit ▸ **unidad de combate** combat unit ▸ **unidad militar** military unit

unidimensional ADJ one-dimensional

unidireccional ADJ **calle ~** one-way street

unido ADJ [*amigos, familiares*] close; **una familia muy unida** a very close *o* very close-knit family; **está muy unida a su madre** she's very close to her mother; **mantenerse ~s** to keep together, stick together, stay together

unifamiliar ADJ single-family

unificación SF unification

unificador ADJ unifying, uniting

unificar ▸conjug 1g◂ VT 1 (= *unir*) to unite, unify

2 (= *hacer uniforme*) to standardize

uniformado/a Ⓐ ADJ uniformed

Ⓑ SM/F (*gen*) man/woman in uniform; (= *policía*) policeman/policewoman

uniformar ▸conjug 1a◂ VT 1 (= *hacer uniforme*) to make uniform; (*Téc*) to standardize

2 [+ *persona*] to put into uniform, provide with a uniform

uniforme Ⓐ ADJ [*movimiento, sistema*] uniform; [*superficie*] level, even, smooth; [*velocidad*] steady, uniform

Ⓑ SM uniform ▸ **uniforme de campaña**, **uniforme de combate** battledress ▸ **uniforme de gala** full-dress uniform

uniformemente ADV uniformly

uniformidad SF (*gen*) uniformity; [*de acabado*] evenness, smoothness; [*de velocidad*] steadiness

uniformización SF standardization

uniformizar ▸conjug 1f◂ VT = **uniformar**

Unigénito SM **el ~** the Only Begotten Son

unilateral ADJ unilateral, one-sided

unilateralismo SM unilateralism

unilateralmente ADV unilaterally

unión SF 1 (= *acción*) 1·1 [*de puntos, extremos*] joining together; [*de empresas*] merger; **la operación consiste en la ~ de los extremos del hueso fracturado** the operation consists of joining together the two ends of the fractured bone; **crearon el nombre de la empresa mediante la ~ de sus apellidos** the name of the company was created by joining together *o* combining their surnames; **solicitaron su ~ a la OTAN en 1993** they applied to join NATO in 1993

1·2 **en ~ con** *o* **de** (= *acompañado de*) together with, along with; (= *en asociación con*) in association with, together with; **viajó a París en ~ de sus colegas** he travelled to Paris together with *o* along with his associates; **la construcción del centro fue concedida a Unitex, en ~ con otra empresa** the contract to build the centre was awarded to Unitex, in association with another firm

2 (= *cualidad*) unity; **hemos fracasado por falta de ~** we have failed through lack of unity; **la ~ de los cristianos está muy lejana todavía** Christian unity is still a long way off; ✦***REFRÁN*** **la ~ hace la fuerza** united we stand

3 (= *organización*) ▸ **unión aduanera** customs union ▸ **Unión Europea** European Union ▸ **Unión General de Trabajadores** (*Esp*) *socialist union confederation* ▸ **Unión Monetaria (Europea)** (European) Monetary Union ▸ **Unión Panamericana** Pan-American Union ▸ **Unión Soviética** (*Hist*) Soviet Union

4 [*de pareja*] (= *matrimonio*) union; **su ~ en santo matrimonio** their union in holy matrimony ▸ **unión consensual** common-law marriage ▸ **unión libre** cohabitation

5 (*Mec*) joint; **punto de ~** junction (**entre** between)

unipartidario ADJ one-party

unipartidismo SM one-party system

unipersonal ADJ single, individual

unir ▸conjug 3a◂ Ⓐ VT 1 (= *acercar*) 1·1 [+ *grupos, tendencias, pueblos*] to unite; **es la persona perfecta para ~ al partido** he is the ideal person to unite the party

1·2 [*sentimientos*] to unite; **los une el mismo amor a la verdad** they are united in their love of the truth; **a nuestros dos países los unen muchas más cosas de las que los dividen** there are far more things that unite our two countries than divide them; **nos une el interés por la ciencia** we share an interest in science; **me une a él una estrecha amistad** I have a very close friendship with him

1·3 [*lazos*] to link, bind; **los lazos que unen ambos países** the ties that bind *o* link both countries

2 (= *atar*) [*contrato*] to bind; **con el periódico me unía un mero contrato** I was bound to the newspaper by nothing more than a simple contract; **el jugador ha rescindido el contrato que lo unía al club** the player has terminated the contract binding him to the club; **~ a dos personas en matrimonio** to join together two people in matrimony

3 (= *asociar, agrupar*) to combine; **uniendo los dos nombres resulta un nuevo concepto** a new concept is created by combining the two nouns; **el esquí de fondo une dos actividades: montañismo y esquí** cross-country skiing combines two activities: mountaineering and skiing; **decidieron ~ sus fuerzas para luchar contra el crimen** they decided to join forces in the fight against crime; **ha logrado ~ su nombre al de los grandes deportistas de este siglo** he has won a place among the great sporting names of this century

4 (= *conectar*) [*carretera, vuelo, ferrocarril*] to link (**con** with); **la autopista une las dos poblaciones** the motorway links the two towns

5 [+ *objetos, piezas*] (*gen*) to join, join together; (*con pegamento, celo*) to stick together; (*con clavos, puntas*) to fasten together; **~ los bordes con cinta adhesiva** stick the edges together with adhesive tape; **van a tirar el tabique para ~ el salón a la cocina** they are going to knock together the lounge and the kitchen

6 (*Culin*) [+ *líquidos*] to mix; [+ *salsa*] to blend

7 (*Com*) [+ *compañías, intereses*] to merge

Ⓑ **unirse** VPR 1 (= *cooperar*) (*para proyectos importantes*) to join together, come together, unite; (*en problemas puntuales*) to join forces; **los sindicatos se han unido en la lucha contra el paro** the trade unions have joined together *o* come together *o* united in the fight against unemployment; **si nos unimos todos, seremos más fuertes** if we all join together *o* come together *o* unite, we will be stronger; **ambas empresas se han unido para distribuir sus productos en Asia** the two companies have joined forces to distribute their products in Asia; **todos los partidos se unieron para mostrar su rechazo a la violencia** all the parties joined together *o* were united in their rejection of violence

2 (= *formar una unidad*) [*empresas, instituciones*] to merge; **tres cajas de ahorro se unen para crear un nuevo banco** three savings banks are merging to make a new bank; **~se en matrimonio** to be joined in matrimony (*frm*), marry

3 **~se a** 3·1 [+ *movimiento, organización, expedición*] to join; **se unieron al resto del grupo en París** they joined the rest of the group in Paris; **los taxistas se han unido a la huelga de camioneros** the taxi drivers have joined the lorry drivers' strike

3·2 [*problemas, características, estilos*] **a este atraso económico se une un paro estructural** this economic underdevelopment is compounded by structural unemployment; **a la maravillosa cocina se une un servicio muy eficiente** the wonderful cooking is complemented by very efficient service

3·3 [+ *propuesta, iniciativa*] to support; **me uno a esta propuesta** I support this proposal

4 **~se con** to join together with, combine with; **se unieron con los demócratas para formar una coalición** they joined together *o* combined with the democrats to form a coalition

5 [*líneas, caminos*] to meet; **se unen las ramas por encima** the branches meet overhead

unisex ADJ INV unisex

unísono Ⓐ ADJ unisonous, unison

Ⓑ SM **al ~** (*lit*) in unison; (*fig*) in unison, with one voice; **al ~ con** in tune *o* harmony with

unitario/a Ⓐ ADJ 1 (*Pol*) unitary

2 (*Rel*) Unitarian

Ⓑ SM/F 1 (*Arg Hist*) centralist

2 (*Rel*) Unitarian

unitarismo SM Unitarianism

univalente ADJ univalent

univalvo ADJ univalve

universal ADJ (= *general*) universal; (= *mundial*) world, world-wide; **historia ~** world history; **de fama ~** internationally *o* world famous; **una especie de distribución ~** a species with a world-wide distribution *o* found all over the world

universalidad SF universality

universalizar ▸conjug 1f◂ Ⓐ VT (= *hacer universal*) to universalize; (= *generalizar*) to bring into general use

Ⓑ **universalizarse** VPR to become widespread

universalmente ADV (= *generalmente*) universally; (= *mundialmente*) all over the world

universiada SF university games *pl*, student games *pl*

universidad SF university ▸ **Universidad a Distancia** ≈ Open University ▸ **universidad laboral** polytechnic, technical school *o* institute (*EEUU*) ▸ **Universidad Nacional de Educación a Distancia** ≈ Open University ▸ **universidad popular** extramural classes *pl*, extension courses *pl*

universitario/a Ⓐ ADJ university *antes de s*

Ⓑ SM/F (= *estudiante*) (university) student; (= *licenciado*) university graduate

universo SM 1 (= *cosmos*) universe

2 (= *conjunto*) world; **el ~ poético de Lorca** Lorca's poetic world; **todo un ~ de regalos** a whole world of gifts

unívoco ADJ [*palabra, término*] univocal, monosemous; [*correspondencia*] one-to-one

UNO SF ABR (*Nic*) = **Unión Nacional Opositora**

uno/a Ⓐ PRON 1 (*uso como numeral*) one; **queda sólo ~** there's only one left; **trece votos a favor y ~ en contra** thirteen votes in favour and one against; **voy a hacer café, ¿quieres ~?** I'm going to make some coffee, do you want one?; **dos maletas grandes y una más pequeña** two large suitcases and a smaller one; **~ es joven y el otro viejo** one (of them) is young and the other is old; **~ a ~** one by one; **cada ~**: **había tres manzanas para cada ~** there were three apples each; **cada ~ a lo suyo** everyone should mind their own business; **de ~ en ~** one by one; **Dios es ~** God is one; **la verdad es una** there is only one truth; **~ y otro** both; **el ~ y el otro están locos** they're both mad; **el ~ le dijo al otro** one said to the other; **~ con otro salen a diez dólares** they average out at ten dollars each; **~ tras otro** one after another, one after the other; **~ por ~** one by one; ✦***MODISMOS*** **una y no más** that's the last time I'm doing that; **lo ~ por lo otro** what you lose on the swings you gain on the roundabouts; **es todo ~** ◊ **es ~ y lo mismo** it's all the same; **comer y sentirse mal fue todo ~** no sooner had she eaten than she fell ill

2 (*uso indefinido*) (= *persona*) 2·1 (*en singular*) somebody, someone; **~ dijo hace poco que debería estar prohibido** somebody *o* someone said recently that it should be banned; **ha venido una que dice que te conoce** somebody *o* someone came who says she knows you; **más de ~**: **no gustará a más de ~** there are quite a few (people) who won't like this; **más de ~ estaría encantado con esto** most people would be more than happy with this; **para mí es ~ de tantos** as far as I'm concerned he's just one of many *o* a very ordinary sort

2·2 (*en plural*) **llegaron ~s y se sentaron** some people arrived and sat down; **~s que estaban allí protestaron** some (of those) who were there protested; **~s me gustan y otros no** some I like, some *o* others I don't; **admirado por ~s y odiado por otros** admired by some and hated by others; **los ~s dicen que sí y los otros que no** some say yes and some *o* others say no; **~s y otros** all of them

3 (*uso impersonal*) you, one (*frm*); **~ puede equivocarse** you *o* (*frm*) one can make a mistake; **~ nunca sabe qué hacer** you never know *o* (*frm*) one never knows what to do; **~ no es perfecto** I'm not perfect, one isn't perfect (*frm*); **~ mismo** yourself, oneself; **es mejor hacerlo ~ mismo** it's better to do it yourself *o* oneself; **reírse de ~ mismo** to laugh at yourself *o* oneself; **tener confianza en ~ mismo** to be self-confident

4 (*uso recíproco*) **el ~ al otro** each other; **se miraban fijamente el ~ al otro** they stared at each other; **se interrumpen el ~ al otro** they interrupt each other; **~s a otros** each other, one another; **se detestan ~s a otros** they hate each other *o* one another

Ⓑ SM (*gen*) one; (*ordinal*) first; **el ~ es mi número de la suerte** one is my lucky number; **ciento ~** a hundred and one; **el ~ de mayo** the first of May, May the first; **planta ~** first floor; **la fila ~** the first row, the front row; **número ~** number one; **este disco ha llegado al número ~** this record has reached number one; **el enemigo público número ~** public enemy number one; **el paro es el problema número ~** unemployment is the number one problem; **es la número ~ del tenis mundial** she's the number one tennis player in the world; *ver tb* **un, seis**

untadura SF 1 (= *acto*) (= *cubrimiento*) smearing, rubbing; (= *engrase*) greasing

2 (= *producto*) (*Med*) ointment; (*Mec etc*) grease, oil

3 (= *mancha*) mark, smear

untar ▸conjug 1a◂ Ⓐ VT [1] (= *cubrir*) to smear, rub (**con, de** with); (*Med*) to anoint, rub (**con, de** with); (*Mec etc*) to grease, oil; **~ su pan en la salsa** to dip *o* soak one's bread in the gravy; **~ el pan con mantequilla** to spread butter on one's bread; **~ los dedos de tinta** to smear ink on one's fingers, smear one's fingers with ink
[2] (*) (= *sobornar*) to bribe, grease the palm of
Ⓑ **untarse** VPR [1] (= *ensuciarse*) **~se con** *o* **de** to smear o.s. with
[2] (*) (*fraudulentamente*) to have sticky fingers*

unto SM [1] (= *ungüento*) ointment
[2] (= *grasa*) grease, animal fat
[3] (*Cono Sur*) (= *betún*) shoe polish

untuosidad SF greasiness, oiliness

untuoso ADJ (= *graso*) greasy, oily

untura SF = **untadura**

uña SF [1] (*Anat*) [*de la mano*] nail, fingernail; [*del pie*] toenail; (*Zool*) claw; **comerse las ~s** (*lit*) to bite one's nails; (*fig*) to get very impatient; (*LAm*) (= *ser pobre*) to be really poor; **hacerse las ~s** to have one's nails done, do one's nails; ✦*MODISMOS* **tener las ~s afiladas** to be light-fingered; **ser ~ y carne** to be inseparable; **estar de ~s con algn** to be at daggers drawn with sb; **defender algo con ~s y dientes** to defend sth tooth and nail; **dejarse las ~s: se dejó las ~s en ese trabajo** he wore his fingers to the bone at that job; **enseñar las ~s** to show one's claws; **tener las ~s largas** to be light-fingered; **mostrar** *o* **sacar las ~s** to show one's claws ► **uña encarnada** ingrowing toenail
[2] (= *pezuña*) hoof ► **uña de caballo** (*Bot*) coltsfoot; ✦*MODISMO* **escapar a ~ de caballo** to ride off at full speed ► **uña de vaca** (*Culin*) cow heel
[3] [*del alacrán*] sting
[4] (*Téc*) claw, nail puller (*EEUU*)
[5] [*de ancla*] fluke

uñada SF scratch

uñalarga SMF (*LAm*) thief

uñarada SF = **uñada**

uñero SM [1] (= *panadizo*) whitlow
[2] (= *uña encarnada*) ingrowing toenail
[3] [*de libro*] thumb notch; **dos tomos con ~** two volumes with thumb index

uñeta SF (*Chile*) plectrum

uñetas* SMF INV (*LAm*) thief

uñetear ▸conjug 1a◂ VT (*Cono Sur*) to steal

uñilargo SM, **uñón** SM (*Perú*) thief

UOE SF ABR (*Esp Mil*) = **Unidad de Operaciones Especiales**

UP SF ABR [1] (*Chile*) = **Unidad Popular**
[2] (*Col*) = **Unión Patriótica**
[3] (*Perú*) = **Unión Popular**

upa[1] SM (*Andes*) idiot

upa[2] EXCL up, up!

UPA SF ABR (= **Unión Panamericana**) PAU

UPAE SF ABR = **Unión Postal de las Américas y España**

upar* ▸conjug 1a◂ VT = **aupar**

UPC SF ABR (= **unidad de procesamiento central**) CPU

uperización SF UHT treatment

uperizado ADJ **leche uperizada** UHT milk

UPN SF ABR (*Esp*) (= **Unión del Pueblo Navarro**) *Navarrese nationalist party*

UPU SF ABR (= **Unión Postal Universal**) UPU

Urales SMPL (*tb* **Montes ~**) Urals

uralita® SF *corrugated asbestos and cement roofing material*

uranio SM uranium ► **uranio enriquecido** enriched uranium

Urano SM Uranus

urbanícola SMF city dweller

urbanidad SF courtesy, politeness, urbanity (*frm*)

urbanificar ▸conjug 1g◂ VT = **urbanizar**

urbanismo SM [1] (= *planificación*) town planning; (= *desarrollo*) urban development
[2] (*Caribe*) real-estate development

urbanista SMF town planner

urbanístico ADJ [*problemas*] town-planning *antes de s*; [*plan, entorno*] urban, city *antes de s*

urbanita SMF city dweller, urbanite (*EEUU*)

urbanizable ADJ **terreno ~** building land; **zona no ~** green belt, land designated as not for building

urbanización SF [1] (= *acto*) urbanization
[2] (= *colonia, barrio*) housing development, housing estate

urbanizado ADJ built-up

urbanizadora SF property development company

urbanizar ▸conjug 1f◂ VT [1] [+ *terreno*] to develop, build on, urbanize
[2] [+ *persona*] to civilize

urbano ADJ [1] (= *de la ciudad*) urban, town *antes de s*, city *antes de s*
[2] (= *educado*) courteous, polite, urbane (*frm*)

urbe SF large city, metropolis; (= *capital*) capital city; **La Urbe** (*Esp*) Madrid, the Capital

urbícola SMF city dweller

urco SM (*Andes, Cono Sur*) (*gen*) ram; (= *alpaca*) alpaca

urdimbre SF [1] [*de tela*] warp
[2] (= *intriga*) scheme, intrigue

urdir ▸conjug 3a◂ VT [1] [+ *tela*] to warp
[2] (= *tramar*) to plot

urdu SM (*Ling*) Urdu

urea SF urea

urente ADJ burning, stinging

uréter SM ureter

uretra SF urethra

urgencia SF [1] (= *apresuramiento*) urgency; **con toda ~** with the utmost urgency; **pedir algo con ~** to request sth urgently; **trataron varios asuntos de ~** they dealt with a number of urgent *o* pressing matters
[2] (= *emergencia*) emergency; **en caso de ~** in case of (an) emergency, in an emergency; **medida de ~** emergency measure; **déjame entrar en el baño, por favor, que tengo una ~** let me in to the bathroom, please, it's an emergency; **procedimiento de ~** (*Admin*) emergency procedure
[3] (*Med*) emergency; **el doctor se ocupará primero de las ~s** the doctor will deal with the emergencies *o* emergency cases first; **servicios de ~** emergency services; **la operaron de ~** she underwent emergency surgery; **"urgencias"** "accident & emergency"; **tuvimos que ir a ~s** we had to go to casualty

urgente ADJ [*mensaje, trabajo*] urgent; [*asunto*] urgent, pressing; **carta ~** special delivery letter; **pedido ~** rush order

urgentemente ADV urgently

urgir ▸conjug 3c◂ VI to be urgent *o* pressing; **urge el dinero** the money is urgently needed; **me urge la respuesta** I need a reply urgently *o* as soon as possible; **el tiempo urge** time presses, time is short; **me urge terminarlo** I must finish it as soon as I can; **me urge partir** I have to leave at once; **"úrgeme vender: dos gatos ..."** "must be sold: two cats ..."

úrico ADJ uric

urinario Ⓐ ADJ urinary
Ⓑ SM urinal, public lavatory

urna SF (= *vasija*) urn; [*de cristal*] glass case; (*Pol*) (*tb* **~ electoral**) ballot box; **acudir a las ~s** to vote, go to the polls

URNG SF ABR (*Guat*) = **Unidad Revolucionaria Nacional Guatemalteca**

uro SM aurochs

urogallo SM capercaillie

urogenital ADJ urogenital

urología SF urology

urólogo/a SM/F urologist

urpo SM (*Cono Sur*) = **ulpo**

urraca SF [1] (= *ave*) magpie
[2] (*) (= *habladora*) chatterbox*; (= *chismosa*) gossip

URSS [urs] SF ABR (*Hist*) (= **Unión de Repúblicas Socialistas Soviéticas**) USSR

ursulina SF [1] (*Rel*) Ursuline nun
[2] (*Esp**) goody-goody*

urta SF sea bream

urticaria SF urticaria, nettle rash

urubú SM (*Cono Sur*) black vulture

Uruguay SM (*tb* **el ~**) Uruguay

uruguayismo SM *word or phrase peculiar to Uruguay*

uruguayo/a ADJ, SM/F Uruguayan

USA ADJ INV United States *antes de s*, American; **dos aviones ~** two US planes

usado ADJ [1] (= *no nuevo*) [*coche*] second-hand, used; [*televisor, ropa*] second-hand; [*sello, billete*] used
[2] (= *gastado*) [*pila*] flat; [*ropa, disco*] worn-out; **un diccionario muy ~** a well-thumbed dictionary

usagre SM (*Med*) impetigo; (*Vet*) mange

usanza SF usage, custom; **a ~ india** ◊ **a ~ de los indios** according to Indian custom

usar ▸conjug 1a◂ Ⓐ VT [1] (= *utilizar*) [+ *aparato, transporte, sustancia, expresión*] to use; **sólo usan el coche cuando salen al campo** they only use the car when they go to the country; **están dispuestos a ~ la violencia para defender sus ideas** they are prepared to use *o* resort to violence to defend their ideas; **la maleta está sin ~** the suitcase has never been used; **esta herramienta ha de ~se con sumo cuidado** this tool must be used with great care; **no sé ~ este teléfono** I don't know how to use this telephone; **no olvide ~ el cinturón de seguridad** don't forget to wear your seat belt; **~ algo/a algn como** to use sth/sb as; **lo ~on como conejillo de indias** they used him as a guinea pig; **de ~ y tirar** [*envase, producto*] disposable; **literatura que algunos llaman de "~ y tirar"** so-called "pulp fiction"
[2] (= *llevar*) [+ *ropa, perfume*] to wear; **el pañuelo que usan los palestinos** the scarf worn by the Palestinians; **esos pantalones**

están sin ~ these trousers have not been worn; **¿qué número usa?** what size do you take?
3 (= *soler*) **~ hacer algo** to be in the habit of doing sth
Ⓑ VI **~ de** [+ *derecho, poder*] to exercise; **~ del derecho al voto** to exercise one's right to vote, use one's vote
Ⓒ **usarse** VPR to be worn; **la chistera ya no se usa** top hats are not worn nowadays, no one wears top hats nowadays

Usbekia SF, **Usbiekistán** SM Uzbekistan

usía PRON PERS Your Lordship/Your Ladyship

usina SF 1 (*LAm*) factory, plant
2 (*Cono Sur*) [*de electricidad*] power plant; [*de gas*] gasworks; [*de tranvías*] tram depot

uslero SM (*Chile*) rolling pin

USO SF ABR (*Esp*) = **Unión Sindical Obrera**

uso SM 1 (= *utilización*) use; **los médicos desaconsejan el ~ indiscriminado de antibióticos** doctors advise against the indiscriminate use of antibiotics; **un mango de plata gastado por el ~** a silver handle worn through use; **una base de datos para ~ exclusivo de los científicos** a database for the use of scientists only, a database exclusively for scientists' use; **el ~ correcto del pronombre "le"** the correct use of the pronoun "le"; **el ~ de la bicicleta no está permitido en autopistas** bicycles are not allowed *o* permitted on motorways; **no está permitido el ~ del claxon en las proximidades de un hospital** you cannot hoot your horn in the vicinity of a hospital; **el ~ y abuso de un producto/una expresión** the excessive use of a product/an expression; **términos de ~ común** terms in common use *o* usage; **un analgésico de ~ corriente** a commonly used painkiller; **aparatos de ~ doméstico** domestic appliances; **"de uso externo"** (*Med*) "for external use"; **objeto de ~ personal** article for personal use, personal item; **jeringuillas de un solo ~** disposable syringes; **estar en ~** to be in use; **tratamientos médicos actualmente en ~** medical treatments currently being used *o* currently in use; **un termino aún hoy en ~** a term still used today; **estar en buen ~** to be in good condition; **está fuera de ~** (= *no se usa*) it is not in use; (= *no funciona*) it is out of order; **hacer ~ de** [+ *derecho, privilegio, poder*] to exercise; [+ *armas, fuerza*] to use; **estar en el ~ de la palabra** to be speaking, have the floor (*frm*); **hacer ~ de la palabra** to speak ► **uso de razón**: **desde que tuvo ~ de razón** (*lit*) since he reached the age of reason; (*fig*) for as long as he could remember
2 (= *aplicación*) use; **el mercurio tiene innumerables ~s industriales** mercury has countless uses in industry; **esta calculadora tiene varios ~s** this calculator has several uses
3 (= *costumbre*) custom; **los ~s sociales de nuestro tiempo** the social customs of our time; **los ~s más tradicionales de la región** the most traditional customs of the region
4 **al ~**: **los tópicos al ~** the usual clichés; **ésta no es una guía de turismo al ~** this is not the usual sort of travel guide, this is not a travel guide in the usual sense of the word; **por emplear el tecnicismo al ~** to use the current technical jargon; **las ideas posmodernistas tan al ~ en los últimos años** the post-modernist ideas so fashionable in recent years

usted PRON PERS 1 (*en singular*) you (*polite or formal address*); **esto es para ~** this is for you; **lo haremos sin ~** we'll do it without you; **—muchas gracias —a ~** "thank you very much" — "thank YOU"; **el coche de ~** your car; **mi coche y el de ~** my car and yours; **hablar** *o* **llamar** *o* **tratar de ~ a algn** to use the "usted" form with sb, address sb using the "usted" form; **no me hables de ~, que no soy tan vieja** you needn't use the "usted" form with me — I'm not that old
2 **ustedes** you (*polite or formal address in most of Spain and replaces vosotros in Latin America*); **gracias a todos ~es podremos pagarlo** thanks to all of you we shall be able to pay it; **pasen ~es, por favor** please come in; **a ver, niños ¿~es qué quieren para cenar?** (*esp LAm*) right, what do you children want for tea?

usual ADJ usual, customary

usualmente ADV usually

usuario/a SM/F user; **~ de la vía pública** road user; **~ final** (*Inform*) end user

usufructo SM usufruct, use ► **usufructo vitalicio** life interest (**de** in)

usufructuario/a SM/F usufructuary

usura SF usury

usurario ADJ usurious, extortionate

usurear ▸conjug 1a◂ VI (= *prestar*) *to lend money at an exorbitant rate of interest*

usurero/a SM/F usurer

usurpación SF [*de poder, trono*] usurpation; [*de tierras*] seizure

usurpador(a) SM/F usurper

usurpar ▸conjug 1a◂ VT [+ *poder, trono*] to usurp; [+ *tierras*] to seize

usuta SF (*Arg, Perú*) = **ojota 1**

utensilio SM (= *herramienta*) tool, implement; (*Culin*) utensil; **con los ~s de su oficio** with the tools of his trade ► **utensilios de cirujano** surgeon's instruments ► **utensilios de pintor** artist's materials ► **utensilios para escribir** writing materials ► **utensilios para pescar** fishing tackle

uterino ADJ uterine; **hermanos ~s** children born of the same mother; *ver tb* **furor**

útero SM womb, uterus ► **útero alquilado**, **útero de alquiler** surrogate motherhood

útil Ⓐ ADJ 1 (= *de utilidad*) useful; (= *servible*) usable, serviceable; **es muy ~ saber conducir** it is very useful to be able to drive; **las plantas ~es para el hombre** plants which are useful to man; **el coche es viejo pero todavía está ~** the car is old but it is still serviceable; **es muy ~ tenerlo aquí cerca** it's very handy having it close by here; **¿en qué puedo serle ~?** can I help you?, what can I do for you?
2 **día ~** (= *hábil*) working day, weekday
3 (*Mil*) **~ para el servicio** [*persona*] fit for military service; [*vehículo*] operational
Ⓑ **útiles** SMPL tools, equipment *sing* ► **útiles de chimenea** fire irons ► **útiles de labranza** agricultural implements ► **útiles de pesca** fishing tackle

utilería SF (*LAm*) props *pl*

utilero/a SM/F (*LAm Teat*) property manager, props man

utilidad SF 1 (*gen*) usefulness; **no pongo en duda la ~ de tu invento** I'm not questioning the usefulness of your invention; **un método de gran ~ para aprender inglés** a very useful method for learning English; **no lo tires, ya le encontraremos alguna ~** don't throw it away, we'll find some use for it; **un servicio de ~ pública** a public service; **sacar la máxima ~ a algo** to use sth to the full, make full use of sth
2 (*LAm Com, Fin*) profit ► **utilidades ocasionales** windfall profits
3 (*Inform*) utility

utilitario Ⓐ ADJ 1 [*persona*] utilitarian
2 [*coche, ropa*] utility *antes de s*
Ⓑ SM (*Aut*) small car, compact car

utilitarismo SM utilitarianism

utilitarista SMF utilitarian

utilizable ADJ 1 (= *que puede usarse*) usable, serviceable; (= *disponible*) available for use, ready to use
2 (*Téc*) reclaimable

utilización SF 1 (= *uso*) use, utilization (*frm*)
2 (*Téc*) reclamation

utilizar ▸conjug 1f◂ VT 1 (= *usar*) to use, make use of, utilize (*frm*); **¿qué medio de transporte utilizas?** which means of transport do you use?; **me dejó ~ su ordenador** she let me use her computer
2 (= *explotar*) [+ *recursos*] to harness; [+ *desperdicios*] to reclaim

utillaje SM tools *pl*, equipment

utillero SM 1 (= *ayudante*) plumber's mate
2 (*Ftbl*) kit man

útilmente ADV usefully

utopía SF, **utopia** SF Utopia

utópico ADJ Utopian

utopista ADJ, SMF Utopian

utrículo SM utricle

UV Ⓐ ABR (= **ultravioleta**) UV
Ⓑ SF ABR (*Esp Pol*) = **Unió(n) Valenciana**

UVA ABR (= **ultravioleta**) UV

uva SF 1 grape; **las doce ~s** ◊ **las ~s de la suerte** *twelve grapes eaten at midnight on New-Year's Eve*; ✦**MODISMOS de ~s a peras** once in a blue moon; **ir de ~s a peras** to change the subject for no reason; **entrar a por ~s** to take the plunge; **estar de mala ~** (*Esp**) to be in a bad mood; **tener muy mala ~** to be a nasty piece of work*; **estar hecho una ~** to be as drunk as a lord ► **uva blanca** green grape, white grape ► **uva crespa** gooseberry ► **uva de Corinto** currant ► **uva de gato** (*Bot*) stonecrop ► **uva espina** gooseberry ► **uva moscatel** muscatel grape ► **uva negra** black grape ► **uva pasa** raisin ► **uvas de mesa** dessert grapes ► **uvas verdes** (*fig*) sour grapes
2 (*) (= *vino*) wine; (= *bebida*) drink (*in general*)
3 (*Cono Sur*) (= *beso*) kiss

uve SF (name of the letter) V; **en forma de ~** V-shaped; **escote en ~** V-neck ► **uve doble** (name of the letter) W

UVI SF ABR (= **unidad de vigilancia intensiva**) ICU ► **UVI móvil** mobile intensive care unit

úvula SF uvula

uvular ADJ uvular

uxoricida SM uxoricide, wife-killer

uxoricidio SM uxoricide

-uzo, -uza *ver* **Aspects of Word Formation in Spanish 2**

V v

V, **v** ['uβe, be'korta (*LAm*)] SF (= *letra*) V, v; **en (forma de) V** V-shaped; **escote en V** V-neck ► **V chica** (*LAm**), **V corta** (*LAm**) (the letter) V ► **V de la victoria** (*gen*) V for victory; (= *signo*) victory sign, V-sign ► **V doble** (*Esp*), **doble V** (*LAm*) (the letter) W

V ABR (*Elec*) (= **voltio(s)**) v

V. ABR [1] = **Usted**
[2] = **Véase**
[3] (= **Visto**) OK

v. ABR [1] = **ver, véase**
[2] (*Literat*) (= **verso**) v

va *ver* **ir**

V.A. ABR = **Vuestra Alteza**

vaca SF [1] (*Zool*) cow; **el mal** *o* **la enfermedad de las ~s locas** mad cow disease; ✦*MODISMOS* **(los años de) las ~s flacas** the lean years; **(los años de) las ~s gordas** the fat years, the boom years; **pasar las ~s gordas** to have a grand time of it*; **ponerse como una ~*** to get as fat as a pig* ► **vaca de leche** (*lit*) dairy cow; (*LAm*) (*fig*) good business, profitable deal ► **vaca de San Antón** ladybird, ladybug (*EEUU*) ► **vaca lechera** dairy cow ► **vaca marina** sea cow, manatee ► **vaca sagrada** (*tb fig*) sacred cow
[2] (*Culin*) beef
[3] (= *cuero*) cowhide
[4] (*LAm Com*) *enterprise with profits on a pro rata basis*
[5] ✦*MODISMO* **hacer(se) la ~** (*Andes*) to play truant, play hooky (*EEUU*)

vacaburra‡ SF boor; **¡vacaburra!** animal!‡

vacación SF, **vacaciones** SFPL holiday(s), vacation *sing* (*EEUU*); **estar de vacaciones** to be (away) on holiday; **irse** *o* **marcharse de vacaciones** to go (away) on holiday, go off on holiday; **hacer vacaciones** to take a day off ► **vacaciones escolares** school holidays ► **vacaciones pagadas**, **vacaciones retribuidas** holidays with pay

vacacional ADJ holiday *antes de s*, vacation *antes de s*; **período ~** holiday period

vacacionista SMF holidaymaker, vacationer (*EEUU*)

vacada SF herd of cows

vacaje SM [1] (*Cono Sur*) (= *vacada*) cows *pl*, cattle *pl*; (= *manada*) herd of cows
[2] (*Méx*) herd of beef cows

vacante Ⓐ ADJ (*gen*) vacant; [*silla*] empty, unoccupied; [*puesto*] unfilled
Ⓑ SF [1] (= *puesto*) vacancy, (unfilled) post; **hay una ~ en la oficina** there is a vacancy in the office; **proveer una ~** to fill a post
[2] (*LAm*) (= *asiento*) empty seat

VACACIONES

¿"Holiday" o "holidays"?

- En inglés británico, **vacaciones** se puede traducir tanto por **holiday** como por **holidays** cuando hablamos de un periodo de tiempo sin colegio o trabajo:

  ¿Dónde pasaste las vacaciones?
  Where did you spend your holiday(s)?
  Larry fue a Londres un par de días durante las vacaciones
  Larry went to London for a couple of days during the holiday(s)

- **Vacaciones** se traduce por **holiday** cuando se habla de un viaje en particular:

  El año pasado pasamos unas vacaciones maravillosas en Mallorca
  We had a lovely holiday in Majorca last year
  ¿Te lo has pasado bien en las vacaciones?
  Did you have a good holiday?

NOTA: Aquí **holiday** funciona como un sustantivo contable normal; se añade una "s" cuando se trata de más de un viaje.

- **Estar de vacaciones** se traduce por **to be on holiday**. En este caso **holiday** no acepta el plural:

  Estaré de vacaciones dos semanas
  I'll be on holiday for a fortnight

Para otros usos y ejemplos ver la entrada.

---

vacar ▸conjug 1g◂ VI [1] (*gen*) to fall vacant, become vacant; [*puesto*] to remain unfilled
[2] (†) [*persona*] (= *cesar*) to cease work; (= *estar inactivo*) to be idle
[3] (†) **~ a** *o* **en** to engage in, devote o.s. to
[4] (†) **~ de** to lack, be without

vacarí ADJ cowhide *antes de s*

vaccinio SM (*Esp*) bilberry, blueberry (*EEUU*)

vaciadero† SM [1] (= *conducto*) drain
[2] (= *vertedero*) rubbish tip, garbage dump (*EEUU*)

vaciado Ⓐ ADJ [1] [*estatua*] cast in a mould, cast in a mold (*EEUU*); [*útiles*] hollow-ground
[2] (*Méx*) (= *estupendo*) great*, terrific*
Ⓑ SM [1] [*de objeto*] cast, mould(ing), mold(ing) (*EEUU*) ► **vaciado a troquel** diecast ► **vaciado de yeso** plaster cast
[2] (= *acto de vaciar*) [*de madera, piedra*] hollowing out; (= *excavación*) excavation; [*de piscina, estanque*] emptying
[3] [*de cuchillo*] sharpening
[4] (*Aer*) ► **vaciado rápido** jettisoning

vaciapatatas SM INV potato scoop

vaciar ▸conjug 1c◂ Ⓐ VT [1] [+ *recipiente, contenido*] to empty; [+ *radiador*] to drain; (= *beber*) to drink up; (*Aer*) to jettison; (*Inform*) to dump; **vacié la nevera para limpiarla** I emptied the fridge to clean it; **vació los bolsillos en la mesa** he emptied out his pockets on to the table; **vació la leche en un vaso** he poured the milk into a glass; **lo vació todo sobre su cabeza** he poured the lot over his head
[2] [+ *madera, piedra*] to hollow out; [+ *estatua*] to cast
[3] [+ *cuchillo*] to sharpen, grind
[4] [+ *tema, teoría*] to expound at length
[5] [+ *texto*] to copy out
[6] (*) (= *hacer una histerectomía a*) to give a hysterectomy to
Ⓑ VI [*río*] to flow, empty (**en** into)
Ⓒ **vaciarse** VPR [1] [*bañera, depósito*] to empty
[2] (*) (*tb* **~se por la lengua**) to blab*, spill the beans*

vaciedad SF [1] (= *estado*) emptiness
[2] (= *necedad*) (piece of) nonsense; **~es** nonsense *sing*, rubbish *sing*, garbage *sing* (*EEUU*)

vacila* SM tease, joker

vacilación SF hesitation, vacillation; **sin vacilaciones** unhesitatingly

vacilada SF [1] (*esp CAm, Méx**) (= *broma*) mickey-taking‡; (= *chiste*) joke; (= *chiste verde*) dirty joke; **de ~** as a joke, for a laugh*
[2] (*Méx**) (= *borrachera*) binge*, spree
[3] (= *truco*) trick

vacilante ADJ [1] [*mano, paso*] unsteady; [*voz*] faltering, halting; [*memoria*] uncertain; [*mueble*] wobbly, tottery
[2] [*persona*] (= *inseguro*) hesitant, uncertain; (= *indeciso*) indecisive
[3] [*luz*] flickering

vacilar ▸conjug 1a◂ Ⓐ VI [1] (= *dudar*) to hesitate, waver; (= *ser indeciso*) to vacillate; (= *esperar*) to hold back from doing sth; **sin ~** unhesitatingly; **~ en hacer algo** to hesitate to do sth; **~ entre dos posibilidades** to hesitate between two possibilities; **es un hombre que vacila mucho** he is a very indecisive man, he is a man who dithers a lot; **no vaciles en decírmelo** don't hesitate to tell me about it
[2] (*por falta de estabilidad*) [*mueble*] to be unsteady, wobble; [*persona*] (*al andar*) to totter, reel; (*al hablar*) to falter; [*memoria*] to fail; [*moralidad*] to be collapsing
[3] [*luz*] to flicker

4 (= *variar*) **un sabor que vacila entre agradable y desagradable** a taste which varies *o* ranges between nice and nasty
5 (*) (= *guasearse*) **~ con algn** to tease sb, take the mickey out of sb‡
6 (*Méx**) (= *divertirse*) to have fun, lark about*; (= *ir de juerga*) to go on a spree
7 (*) (= *presumir*) to talk big*, show off, swank*
Ⓑ VT 1 (= *burlarse de*) to take the mickey out of‡, make fun of; **¡no me vaciles!** stop messing me about!*
2 (*CAm**) (= *engañar*) to trick

vacile SM 1 (*) (= *guasa*) teasing; **estar de ~** to tease
2 (= *duda*) hesitation

vacilón/ona* Ⓐ ADJ 1 (= *guasón*) teasing, jokey; **estar ~** to be in a jokey mood
2 (*CAm, Méx*) (= *juerguista*) fun-loving
3 (= *presumido*) swanky*, stuck-up*
Ⓑ SM/F 1 (= *bromista*) tease, joker
2 (*CAm, Méx*) (= *juerguista*) party-goer, reveller
3 (= *presumido*) poser*, show-off*
Ⓒ SM (*CAm, Méx*) (= *juerga*) party; (= *diversión*) fun; **andar de ~** to be out on the town

vacío Ⓐ ADJ 1 (*gen*) empty; [*puesto, local*] vacant, empty; **el teatro estaba medio ~** the theatre was half empty; **nunca bebo cerveza con el estómago ~** I never drink beer on an empty stomach; **he alquilado un piso ~ porque sale más barato** I've rented an unfurnished flat because it's cheaper; **Madrid queda ~ en agosto** Madrid is empty *o* deserted in August; **de ~: el camión volvió de ~** the lorry came back empty; **lo pedí pero tuve que marcharme de ~** I asked for it but had to go away empty-handed; ✦**MODISMO irse con las manos vacías** to leave empty-handed
2 (= *superficial*) [*persona*] shallow; [*conversación*] meaningless; **un discurso ~ de contenido** a speech empty *o* devoid of any content
3 (= *sin sentido*) [*existencia*] empty, meaningless
4 (= *vano*) [*esfuerzo*] vain; [*promesa*] empty, hollow
5 **pan ~** (*Andes, CAm, Caribe*) dry bread
Ⓑ SM 1 (*Fís*) vacuum; **envasar al ~** to vacuum-pack; **envasado al ~** vacuum-packed
2 (= *hueco*) (empty) space, gap; **han dejado un ~ para el nombre** they have left a space for the name; **tener un ~ en el estómago** to have an empty stomach; ✦**MODISMO hacer el ~ a algn** to send sb to Coventry
3 (= *abismo*) **el ~** the void, space; **saltó al ~ desde lo alto del acantilado** he jumped from the top of the cliff into space *o* the void; **se arrojó al ~ desde un quinto piso** he threw himself out of a fifth-floor window; ✦**MODISMO caer en el ~** to fall on deaf ears
4 (= *falta de sentido*) void; **el ~ existencial** the existential void; **su muerte dejó un ~ en nuestras vidas** his death left a void in our lives; **una sensación de ~** a feeling of emptiness
5 (*Jur, Pol*) ► **vacío de poder** power vacuum ► **vacío legislativo** gap in the legislation ► **vacío político** political vacuum
6 (*Mec*) **marchar en ~** to tick over
7 (*Anat*) side, flank

vacuidad SF (*frm*) vacuity (*frm*), vacuousness (*frm*)

vacuna SF 1 (= *sustancia*) vaccine; **la ~ de la hepatitis** the hepatitis vaccine; **ponerle una ~ a algn** to vaccinate sb ► **vacuna antigripal** flu vaccine
2 (*esp LAm*) (= *acto*) vaccination

vacunación SF vaccination

vacunar ▸conjug 1a◂ Ⓐ VT 1 (*Med*) to vaccinate (**contra** against)
2 (*ante adversidad, dolor*) (= *preparar*) to prepare; (= *habituar*) to inure; (= *prevenir*) to forearm
Ⓑ **vacunarse** VPR to be *o* get vaccinated

vacuno Ⓐ ADJ bovine, cow *antes de s*; **ganado ~** cattle
Ⓑ SM (= *ganado*) cattle *pl*; **carne de ~** beef ► **vacuno de carne** beef cattle ► **vacuno de leche, vacuno lechero** dairy cattle

vacuo ADJ 1 (= *vacío*) empty
2 [*comentario, comportamiento*] vacuous (*frm*), frivolous

vade† SM = **vademécum 2**

vadeable ADJ 1 [*río*] fordable, crossable
2 [*problema*] not impossible, not insuperable

vadear ▸conjug 1a◂ Ⓐ VT 1 [+ *río*] (= *atravesar*) to ford; (*a pie*) to wade across; [+ *agua*] to wade through
2 [+ *dificultad*] to surmount, overcome
3 [+ *persona*] to sound out
Ⓑ VI to wade; **cruzar un río vadeando** to wade across a river; **llegar a tierra vadeando** to wade ashore

vademécum SM (*pl* **vademécums**) 1 (= *libro*) vade mecum
2 (*Escol*) satchel, schoolbag

vadera SF wide ford

vade retro EXCL (*hum*) go away!; **¡~, Satanás!** get thee behind me (Satan)!

vado SM 1 [*de río*] ford
2 (*Esp Aut*) garage entrance; **"vado permanente"** "garage entrance", "keep clear"
3 (†) (*fig*) (= *salida*) way out, solution; **no hallar ~** to see no way out, find no solution; **tentar el ~** to look into possible solutions
4 (†) (*fig*) (= *descanso*) respite

vagabundaje SM vagrancy

vagabundear ▸conjug 1a◂ VI 1 (= *andar sin rumbo*) to wander, rove
2 (*pey*) [*pordiosero*] to be a tramp, be a bum (*EEUU*)
3 (= *gandulear*) to loaf, idle

vagabundeo SM 1 (*sin rumbo*) wandering, roving
2 [*de pordiosero*] tramp's life, bumming (*EEUU*); (*pey*) vagrancy
3 (= *ganduleo*) loafing, idling

vagabundo/a Ⓐ ADJ 1 (= *errante*) [*persona*] wandering, roving; [*perro*] stray
2 (= *pordiosero*) vagabond (*frm*); (*pey*) vagrant
Ⓑ SM/F 1 (= *persona errante*) wanderer, rover
2 (= *pordiosero*) vagabond (*frm*), tramp, bum (*EEUU*); (*pey*) vagrant

vagación SF (*Mec*) free play

vagamente ADV vaguely

vagamundería SF (*LAm*) idleness, laziness

vagamundero ADJ (*LAm*) idle, lazy

vagancia SF 1 (= *pereza*) laziness, idleness
2 (= *vagabundeo*) vagrancy

vagante ADJ 1 (*liter*) (= *sin rumbo*) wandering
2 (*Mec*) (= *suelto*) free, loose

vagar ▸conjug 1h◂ Ⓐ VI 1 (= *errar*) to wander (about), roam; (= *rondar*) to prowl about; (= *pasear*) to saunter up and down, wander about the streets; (= *entretenerse*) to loiter; (= *gandulear*) to idle, loaf; **~ como alma en pena** to wander about like a lost soul
2 (*Mec*) to be loose, move about
Ⓑ SM (= *tiempo libre*) leisure, free time; (= *pereza*) idleness; (= *calma*) lack of anxiety, freedom from worry; **andar de ~** to be at leisure

vagido SM cry (*of new-born baby*)

vagina SF vagina

vaginal ADJ vaginal

vaginitis SF INV vaginitis

vago/a Ⓐ ADJ 1 (*gen*) vague; (*Arte, Fot*) blurred, ill-defined; (= *indeterminado*) indeterminate
2 [*persona*] (= *perezoso*) lazy, slack; (= *poco fiable*) unreliable; (= *ocioso*) idle, unemployed; ✦**MODISMO ser más ~ que la chaqueta de un guardia*** to be a lazy devil*
3 [*ojo*] lazy; [*objeto*] idle, unused; [*espacio*] empty
4 (= *errante*) roving, wandering
5 (†) **en ~** [*mantenerse*] unsteadily; [*esforzarse*] in vain; **dar golpes en ~** to flail about, beat the air
Ⓑ SM/F 1 (= *holgazán*) idler, lazybones*; (= *inútil*) useless individual, dead loss; **hacer el ~** to loaf around
2 (= *vagabundo*) tramp, vagrant, bum (*EEUU*); (= *pobre*) down-and-out

vagón SM (*Ferro*) [*de pasajeros*] coach, carriage, passenger car (*EEUU*); [*de mercancías*] goods *o* freight van, goods *o* freight wagon, freight car (*EEUU*) ► **vagón cama** sleeping car ► **vagón cisterna** tanker, tank wagon ► **vagón de cola** (*lit*) guard's van, caboose (*EEUU*); (*fig*) rear, tail end ► **vagón de equipajes** luggage van ► **vagón de ganado, vagón de hacienda** (*Cono Sur*) cattle truck, stock car (*EEUU*) ► **vagón de primera** first-class carriage ► **vagón de reja** (*Cono Sur*) cattle truck, stock car (*EEUU*) ► **vagón de segunda** second-class carriage ► **vagón directo** through carriage ► **vagón mirador** observation car ► **vagón postal** mailcoach, mailcar (*EEUU*) ► **vagón restaurante** dining car ► **vagón tanque** tanker, tank wagon ► **vagón tolva** hopper

vagonada SF truckload, wagonload

vagoneta SF light truck

vaguada SF watercourse, stream bed

vaguear ▸conjug 1a◂ VI to laze around

vaguedad SF 1 (= *ambigüedad*) vagueness
2 (= *una vaguedad*) vague remark; **hablar sin ~es** to get straight to the point

vaguería SF, **vaguitis*** SF INV (*Esp*) laziness, idleness, slackness

vaharada SF 1 [*de aliento*] puff of breath
2 (= *olor*) smell; (= *ráfaga de olor*) whiff; (= *tufo*) reek

vahear ▸conjug 1a◂ VI 1 (= *echar vapor*) to steam
2 (= *humear*) to fume, give off fumes, smoke
3 (= *oler*) smell; (= *atufar*) to reek

vahído SM dizzy spell

vaho SM 1 (= *vapor*) steam, vapour, vapor (*EEUU*); (*en cristal*) mist, condensation; (= *aliento*) breath; (= *ráfaga de olor*) whiff
2 **vahos** (*Med*) inhalation *sing*

vaina Ⓐ SF [1] [*de espada*] sheath, scabbard; [*de útil*] sheath, case; [*de cartucho*] case
[2] (*Bot*) [*de garbanzo, guisante*] pod; [*de nuez*] husk, shell
[3] **vainas** (= *judías*) green beans
[4] (= *pega*) problem, snag; (*LAm**) (= *molestia*) nuisance, bore; (= *cosa*) thing; **¡qué ~!** what a nuisance!
[5] (*Andes*) (= *chiripa*) fluke, piece of luck
[6] (*Cono Sur*) (= *estafa*) swindle
[7] ✦***MODISMO*** **echar ~** (*Caribe***) to screw**, fuck**
Ⓑ SMF (*) (= *persona inútil*) twit*, nitwit*, dork (*esp EEUU**)
Ⓒ ADJ (*LAm*) (= *enojoso*) annoying

vainica SF (*Cos*) hemstitch

vainilla SF vanilla

vainillina SF vanillin

vainita SF (*LAm*) green bean

vais *ver* **ir**

vaivén SM [1] (= *balanceo*) swaying; (= *acción de mecerse*) rocking; [*de columpio*] swinging; (= *ir y venir*) to-ing and fro-ing; [*de pistón*] backward and forward motion; (= *sacudidas*) lurching
[2] [*de tráfico, circulación*] constant movement
[3] [*de la suerte*] change of fortune
[4] (*Pol*) swing, seesaw, teeter-totter (*EEUU*)
[5] **vaivenes** (= *altibajos*) ups and downs, vicissitudes (*frm*)

vaivenear† ▸conjug 1a◂ VT (*gen*) to oscillate; (= *mecer*) to rock; (*adelante y atrás*) to move backwards and forwards; (= *balancear*) to swing, sway

vajear ▸conjug 1a◂ VT (*CAm, Caribe, Méx*) [+ *culebra*] to fascinate, hypnotize; (= *hechizar*) to bewitch; (= *seducir*) to win over by flattery, seduce

vajilla SF (*gen*) crockery, dishes *pl*; (= *una vajilla*) service, set; **lavar la ~** to wash up ► **vajilla de oro** gold plate ► **vajilla de porcelana** chinaware

valdiviano/a Ⓐ ADJ of/from Valdivia
Ⓑ SM/F native/inhabitant of Valdivia; **los ~s** the people of Valdivia
Ⓒ SM *typical Chilean dish of dried meat and vegetables*

valdré *etc ver* **valer**

vale[1] SM (*Fin*) (= *pagaré*) promissory note (*frm*), IOU*; (= *recibo*) receipt; (= *cuenta*) bill, check (*EEUU*); (= *cupón*) voucher, chit ► **vale de comida** luncheon voucher ► **vale de correo** money order ► **vale de descuento** discount voucher ► **vale de regalo** gift voucher, gift certificate (*EEUU*) ► **vale (de) restaurante** luncheon voucher ► **vale postal** money order

vale[2]* EXCL (*Esp*) OK, sure; *ver tb* **valer B8**

vale[3]* SM (*LAm*) (= *amigo*) pal*, chum, buddy (*EEUU*); **ser ~ con algn** (*Andes*) to be pals with sb* ► **vale corrido** (*Caribe*) old crony

valedero ADJ (= *válido*) valid; (*Jur*) binding; **~ para seis meses** valid for six months; **~ hasta el día 16** valid until the 16th

valedor(a) SM/F [1] (= *protector*) protector, guardian
[2] (*LAm*) = **vale**[3]

valedura SF [1] (*Méx*) (= *ayuda*) help; (= *protección*) protection; (= *favor*) favour, favor (*EEUU*)

➤ LENGUA Y USO: **valer B5** 28.1, 29.2

[2] (*Andes, Caribe*) (= *propina*) *gift made by a gambler out of his winnings*

valemadrista* (*Méx*) Ⓐ ADJ [1] (= *apático*) indifferent, laid-back*
[2] (= *cínico*) cynical
Ⓑ SMF [1] (= *apático*) indifferent person
[2] (= *cínico*) cynic

Valencia SF Valencia

valencia SF (*Quím*) valency, valence (*EEUU*)

valenciana SF (*Méx*) trouser turn-up, trouser cuff (*EEUU*); *ver tb* **valenciano**

valencianismo SM [1] (*Ling*) *word/phrase etc peculiar to Valencia*
[2] (*culturalmente*) *sense of the differentness of Valencia*; (*Pol*) *doctrine of or belief in Valencian autonomy*

valenciano/a Ⓐ ADJ of/from Valencia
Ⓑ SM/F native/inhabitant of Valencia; **los ~s** the people of Valencia; *ver tb* **valenciana**

valentía SF [1] (= *valor*) bravery, courage; (= *atrevimiento*) boldness; (= *resolución*) resoluteness
[2] (= *jactancia*) boastfulness
[3] (= *acto de valor*) brave deed, heroic exploit
[4] (*pey*) (= *dicho*) boast, brag

valentón/ona Ⓐ ADJ (= *fanfarrón*) boastful; (= *arrogante*) arrogant; (= *matón*) bullying
Ⓑ SM/F (= *fanfarrón*) braggart; (= *matón*) bully

valentonada SF (= *dicho*) boast, brag; (= *acto*) arrogant act

▼valer

▸conjug 2p◂
[A] VERBO TRANSITIVO
[B] VERBO INTRANSITIVO
[C] VERBO PRONOMINAL
Para la frase ***valer la pena****, ver la otra entrada.*

Ⓐ VERBO TRANSITIVO
[1] [= ***costar***] to cost; **sólo el vuelo ya vale 8000 euros** the flight alone costs 8000 euros; **este libro vale cinco dólares** this book costs five dollars; **¿cuánto vale?** ◊ **¿qué vale?** how much is it?, how much does it cost?; **ésas valen (a) dos euros el kilo** those are two euros a kilo
[2] [= ***tener un valor de***] to be worth; **el terreno vale más que la casa** the land is worth more than the house; ✦***MODISMOS*** **no vale un higo** *o* **un pimiento** (*Esp**) it's not worth a brass farthing; **vale lo que pesa (en oro)** it's worth its weight in gold
[3] [= ***ser causa de***] [+ *premio*] to win; [+ *críticas, amenazas*] to earn; **la final histórica que le valió a Brasil la copa del mundo** the famous final in which Brazil won the world cup; **son las cualidades que le valieron el premio** these are the qualities which won him the prize; **esa tontería le valió un rapapolvo** that piece of stupidity got *o* earned him a telling-off; **su ausencia le valió la pérdida del contrato** his absence lost *o* cost him the contract
[4] [***Mat***] (= *equivaler a*) to equal; **en ese caso X vale 9** in that case X equals 9; **el ángulo B vale 38 grados** angle B is 38 degrees
[5] [= ***proteger***] **¡válgame (Dios)!** oh, my God!, God help me!
Ⓑ VERBO INTRANSITIVO
[1] [= ***costar***] **este coche vale muy caro** this car is very expensive *o* costs a lot of money; **¿vale mucho?** is it very expensive?
[2] [= ***tener valía***] **vale mucho como intérprete** he's an excellent *o* first-rate interpreter; **Juan vale más que su hermano** Juan is a better person than his brother; **su última película no vale gran cosa** his latest film is not up to much *o* is not much good; **este coche no vale nada** this car is useless; **hacer ~**: **hizo ~ su derecho al veto** he exercised his veto; **hizo ~ sus derechos** he asserted his rights; **hizo ~ sus argumentos en la reunión** she got her arguments across during the meeting; **hacerse ~** to assert o.s.; **~ por** (= *equivaler a*) to be worth; **cada cupón vale por un paquete de azúcar** each coupon is worth *o* can be exchanged for one bag of sugar; **cuatro fichas azules valen por una negra** four blue counters equal *o* are worth one black one
[3] [= ***servir***] [3·1] [*herramienta, objeto*] to be useful; **todavía puede ~** it might still be useful; **este mismo valdrá** this one will do; **eso no vale** that's no good *o* use; **hay que tirar todo lo que no vale** we must throw out everything that is no use; **ya no me vale** it's no good *o* use to me now; **este destornillador no me vale porque es pequeño** this screwdriver is no good to me, it's too small; **~ para algo**: **es viejo, pero vale para la lluvia** it's old, but it'll do for when it rains; **este trozo no me vale para hacer la cortina** this piece won't do to make the curtain; **este cuchillo no vale para nada** this knife is useless
[3·2] [*ropa*] **este sombrero me vale aún** I can still wear *o* use this hat; **me vale la ropa de mi hermana** my sister's clothes do for* *o* fit me as well; **a mi hijo no le vale la ropa del año pasado** the clothes my son wore last year are too small for him now
[3·3] [*situación*] **no le vale ser hijo del ministro** being the minister's son is no use to him; **su situación privilegiada no le valió** his privileged position was no help *o* use to him; **no le valdrán excusas** excuses won't help him *o* do him any good
[3·4] [*persona*] **yo no valdría para enfermera** I'd be no good as a nurse; **el chico no vale para el trabajo** the boy is no good *o* not right for the job; **no vales para nada** you're hopeless *o* useless, you're a dead loss*
[4] [= ***ser válido***] [*documento*] to be valid; [*moneda, billete*] to be legal tender; **este tipo de pasaporte no vale desde hace un mes** they stopped using this type of passport a month ago; **estos billetes ya no valen** these banknotes are no longer legal tender; **es una teoría que no vale ya** it is a theory which no longer holds; **valga la expresión** for want of a better way of putting it; **está un poco chiflado, valga la expresión** he's a bit cracked, for want of a better way of putting it, he's a bit cracked, so to speak; ✦***MODISMO*** **¡no hay ... que valga!**: **—¡pero querido! —¡no hay querido que valga!** "but darling!" — "don't darling me!"*; *ver tb* **pero B2**, **redundancia**
[5] **más vale**: **más vale así** it's better this way; **más vale no hacerlo** it would be better not to do it; **más vale mantener esto en secreto** it would be best to keep this quiet; **—mañana te devuelvo el dinero —más te vale** "I'll give you the money back tomorrow" — "you'd better!"; **más vale que me vaya** I'd *o* I had better go; **más vale que te lleves el abrigo** you'd *o* you had better take your coat; **más vale que vayas tú** it would be better if YOU went; ✦***REFRÁN*** **más vale tarde que**

nunca better late than never

6 *Esp = ser suficiente* to be enough; **dos terrones valen para endulzarlo** two lumps are enough to sweeten it; **vale ya, que habéis estado gritando toda la tarde** that's enough! you've been shouting all afternoon; **¡vale, vale!, no me eches más azúcar** OK! that's enough! don't put any more sugar in; **—¿subo más la persiana? —no, así ya vale** "shall I put the blind up a bit more?" — "no, it's OK like that"

7 ** = estar permitido* to be allowed; **—¿puedo darle con la mano? —no, eso no vale** "can I hit it with my hand?" — "no, that's not allowed"; **no vale intentarlo dos veces** you're not allowed to have two goes; **no vale empujar** no pushing!, pushing's not allowed; **—le han dado el trabajo al hijo del jefe —¡pues, eso no vale!** "they've given the job to the boss's son" — "that's not on!"* *o* "they can't do that!"

8

◆ **vale** (*Esp**) (= *de acuerdo*) all right, OK*; **—¿vamos a tomar algo? —¡vale!** "shall we go for a drink?" — "OK!" *o* "all right!"; **pásate por mi casa esta tarde, ¿vale?** drop by my house this afternoon, OK?; **vale que discutan, pero que se peguen es imperdonable** having an argument is one thing but hitting each other is another matter entirely *o* is inexcusable

9 ✦***MODISMO*** **me vale madre** *o* **sombrilla** (*Méx**) I couldn't care less*, I don't give a damn!*

Ⓒ **valerse** VERBO PRONOMINAL

1 **~se de** (= *utilizar*) [+ *herramienta, objeto*] to use, make use of; (= *aprovecharse de*) [+ *amistad, influencia*] to use; **se valió de un bastón para cruzar el río** he used a cane to get across the river; **se valió del derecho al veto para frenar el acuerdo** he made use of *o* exercised his veto to put a stop to the agreement; **se valió de su cargo para conseguir la información** she used her position to obtain the information

2 *= arreglárselas* **es muy mayor, pero todavía se vale** she is very old, but she can still do things for herself; **no se vale solo** ◊ **no puede ~se por sí mismo** he can't look after himself *o* manage on his own

valeriana SF valerian

valerosamente ADV bravely, valiantly

valeroso ADJ brave, valiant

valet [ba'le] SM (*pl* **valets** [ba'le]) (*Naipes*) jack, knave

valetudinario/a ADJ, SM/F valetudinarian

valga *etc ver* **valer**

Valhala SM Valhalla

valía SF 1 (= *valor*) worth, value; **de gran ~** [*objeto*] very valuable, of great worth; [*persona*] worthy, estimable

2 (= *influencia*) influence

validación SF (*gen*) validation; (*Pol*) ratification

validar ▸conjug 1a◂ VT (*gen*) to validate; (*Pol*) to ratify

validez SF validity; **dar ~ a** (*gen*) to validate; (*Pol*) to ratify

valido SM (*Hist*) (royal) favourite, (royal) favorite (*EEUU*)

válido ADJ 1 [*billete, respuesta*] valid (**hasta** until; **para** for)

2 (*Med*) (= *fuerte*) strong, robust; (= *sano*) fit

valiente Ⓐ ADJ 1 [*persona, acción, decisión*] brave, courageous, valiant (*liter*); **no te las des de ~ porque sé que tienes miedo** don't pretend to be brave because I know you're frightened

2 (*iró*) (*antes de s*) fine; **¡~ amigo estás tú hecho!** a fine friend *o* some friend you are!*; **¡~ gobierno!** some government!*, what a government!*

Ⓑ SMF brave man/woman; **se hace el ~ porque le están mirando todos** he's pretending to be brave because everyone's looking at him

valientemente ADV bravely, courageously, valiantly (*liter*)

valija SF 1 (= *maleta*) case; (*LAm*) suitcase; (= *portamantas*) valise; (= *cartera*) satchel

2 (*Correos*) mailbag; (= *correspondencia*) mail, post ► **valija diplomática** diplomatic bag, diplomatic pouch (*EEUU*)

valijería SF (*Cono Sur*) travel-goods shop

valimiento SM 1 (= *valor*) value; (= *beneficio*) benefit

2 (*Pol*) favour, favor (*EEUU*), protection; (*Hist*) position of royal favourite, status of the royal favourite; **~ con algn** ◊ **~ cerca de algn** influence with sb

valioso ADJ 1 (= *de valor*) valuable; (= *útil*) useful, beneficial; (= *estimable*) estimable (*frm*)

2 (†) (= *rico*) wealthy; (= *poderoso*) powerful

valisoletano/a ADJ, SM/F = **vallisoletano**

valkiria SF Valkyrie

valla SF 1 (= *cercado*) fence; (*Mil*) barricade; (= *empalizada*) palisade, stockade; (*Dep*) hurdle; **400 metros ~s** 400 metres hurdles ► **valla de contención** crush barrier ► **valla de protección, valla de seguridad** barrier ► **valla electrificada** electric fence ► **valla publicitaria** hoarding, billboard (*EEUU*)

2 (*fig*) (= *barrera*) barrier; (= *límite*) limit; (= *estorbo*) obstacle, hindrance; **romper** *o* **saltar(se) las ~s** to disregard social conventions

3 (*Andes, Caribe, Méx*) [*de gallos*] cockpit

4 (*Andes*) (= *zanja*) ditch

valladar SM 1 = **valla 1**

2 (= *defensa*) defence, defense (*EEUU*), barrier

vallado Ⓐ ADJ (= *cercado*) fenced

Ⓑ SM 1 = **valla 1**

2 (*Mil*) defensive wall, rampart

3 (*Méx*) (= *zanja*) deep ditch

Valladolid SM Valladolid

vallar ▸conjug 1a◂ VT to fence in, put (up) a fence round

valle SM 1 (*Geog*) valley ► **valle de lágrimas** (*liter*) vale of tears (*liter*)

2 **energía de ~** off-peak power demand/supply; **horas de ~** off-peak hours

vallero/a (*Méx*) Ⓐ ADJ valley *antes de s*

Ⓑ SM/F valley dweller

vallino ADJ (*Andes*) valley *antes de s*

vallisoletano/a Ⓐ ADJ of/from Valladolid

Ⓑ SM/F native/inhabitant of Valladolid; **los ~s** the people of Valladolid

vallista SMF hurdler

vallisto ADJ (*Cono Sur, Méx*) valley *antes de s*

vallunco ADJ (*CAm*) rustic, peasant *antes de s*

valón/ona Ⓐ ADJ Walloon

Ⓑ SM/F Walloon; **los valones** the Walloons

Ⓒ SM (*Ling*) Walloon

valona SF 1 (*Andes, Caribe*) [*de caballo*] *artistically trimmed mane*; **hacer la ~** (*Caribe*) to shave

2 (*Méx*) = **valedura 1**

valonar ▸conjug 1a◂ VT (*Andes*) to shear

valonearse ▸conjug 1a◂ VPR (*CAm*) to lean from the saddle

valor SM 1 (*Com, Fin*) value; **¿cuál es el ~ real de ese cuadro?** what's this painting worth in real terms?, what's the real value of this painting?; **un documento de gran ~** a very valuable document, a document of great value; **objetos de incalculable ~** priceless objects; **billetes de pequeño ~** small-denomination notes; **el contrato fue declarado nulo y sin ~** the contract was declared null and void; **el ~ del cheque no es correcto** the amount on the cheque is not correct; **de ~** [*joya, obra*] valuable; **objetos de ~** valuables; **por ~ de** to the value of; **importaciones por ~ de un millón de dólares** imports to the value of one million dollars; **un cheque por ~ de 500 euros** a cheque for the sum of *o* to the value of 500 euros; **ha habido pérdidas por ~ de diez millones de euros** there have been losses of ten million euros ► **valor adquisitivo** purchasing power ► **valor a la par** par value ► **valor añadido** added value ► **valor catastral** rateable value ► **valor comercial** commercial value ► **valor contable** asset value ► **valor de cambio** exchange value ► **valor de compra** purchasing power ► **valor de desecho** salvage value ► **valor de escasez** scarcity value ► **valor de mercado** market value ► **valor de rescate** surrender value ► **valor desglosado** break-up value ► **valor de sustitución** replacement value ► **valor de uso** use value ► **valor en bolsa** stock market value ► **valor en libros** book value ► **valor estrella** blue-chip stock, blue-chip share ► **valor facial** face value, denomination ► **valor nominal** nominal value ► **valor por defecto** default value ► **valor según balance** book value

2 (= *importancia*) value; **una composición de indudable ~ musical** a composition of undoubted musical value; **una pintura de gran ~ artístico** a painting of great artistic merit *o* value; **este anillo tiene un gran ~ para mí** this ring means a great deal to me, this ring is very valuable to me; **dar ~ a algo**: **lo que le da ~ musical a este trabajo es su originalidad** it is the originality of this work that gives it its musical worth *o* value; **no dábamos ~ a nuestro patrimonio** we didn't value our heritage highly enough; **no le di ~ a sus palabras** I didn't attach any importance to what he said; **quitar ~ a algo** to minimize the importance of sth ► **valor alimenticio** nutritional value, food value ► **valor calorífico** calorific value ► **valor nutritivo** nutritional value ► **valor sentimental** sentimental value

3 **valores** 3·1 (= *principios*) values; **los ~es morales de la sociedad occidental** the moral values of Western society; *ver tb* **escala 1, juicio 3**

3·2 (*Fin*) (= *títulos*) securities, stocks, bonds ► **valores de renta fija** fixed-interest securities ► **valores de renta variable** variable-yield securities ► **valores en cartera** holdings ► **valores fiduciarios** fiduciary issue

sing, banknotes ► **valores habidos** investments ► **valores inmuebles** real estate *sing*
4 (= *persona famosa*) star; **uno de los nuevos ~es del cine español** one of the rising stars of Spanish cinema
5 (= *validez*) validity; **tener ~** to be valid; **este documento ya no tiene ~** this document is no longer valid
6 (*en una escala*) level; **las temperaturas han alcanzado ~es superiores a los normales** temperatures have reached higher than normal levels; **se han medido ~es de 80 litros por metro cúbico** levels of 80 litres per cubic metre have been recorded
7 (*Mat*) value ► **valor absoluto** absolute value
8 (*Mús*) value; **el ~ de una blanca es de dos negras** a minim is worth two crotchets
9 (= *coraje*) bravery, courage; **el ~ de los soldados** the bravery *o* courage of the soldiers; **le dieron una medalla al ~** he was awarded a medal for bravery; **no tuve ~ para decírselo** I didn't have the courage to tell her; **armarse de ~** to pluck up (the) courage ► **valor cívico** (sense of) civic duty
10 (*) (= *descaro*) nerve*; **¿cómo puedes tener el ~ de negarlo?** how do you have the nerve to deny it?*

valoración SF 1 (= *tasación*) 1·1 [*de joya, obra de arte*] valuation; **hacer una ~ de algo** to value sth, give a valuation of sth; **la ~ social del trabajo doméstico** the value that society places on housework, how much society values housework
1·2 [*de daños, pérdidas*] (= *acción*) assessment; (= *resultado*) estimate; **hacer una ~ de algo** to assess sth, give an assessment of sth
2 [*de actuación, situación*] assessment; **¿cuál es su ~ de lo que ha pasado?** what's your assessment of what happened?; **en su ~ de los datos** in assessing the facts, in his assessment of the facts; **hacer una ~ de algo** to make an assessment of sth, assess sth; **no quisieron hacer ninguna ~ de los resultados electorales** they declined to make any assessment of the election results
3 (*Quím*) titration

valorar ▸conjug 1a◂ VT 1 (= *tasar*) [+ *joya, obra de arte*] to value (**en** at); [+ *daños, pérdidas*] to assess (**en** at); **un cuadro valorado en dos millones** a painting valued at two million; **las pérdidas han sido valoradas en miles de millones** the damage has been estimated *o* assessed at thousands of millions
2 (= *apreciar*) [+ *cualidad*] to value, appreciate; **no sabes ~ la amistad** you don't value *o* appreciate friendship; **un trabajo no valorado por la sociedad** it is a job which is not valued *o* appreciated by society; **valoro mucho la sinceridad** I value honesty highly; **los resultados han sido valorados negativamente** the results were judged negatively; **los jóvenes valoran muy poco a los políticos** young people have a very poor opinion of politicians; **"se ~án los conocimientos de inglés"** "knowledge of English an advantage"
3 (= *revalorizar*) to raise the value of
4 (*Quím*) to titrate

valorización SF 1 (= *tasación*) = **valoración 1**
2 (*LAm*) (= *aumento*) increase in value

valorizar ▸conjug 1f◂ Ⓐ VT 1 (= *tasar*) = **valorar 1**
2 (*LAm*) (= *aumentar*) to raise the value of
Ⓑ **valorizarse** VPR (*LAm*) to increase in value

Valquiria SF Valkyrie

vals (*pl* **valses**) SM waltz

valsar ▸conjug 1a◂ VI to waltz

valse SM 1 (*LAm*) (= *vals*) waltz
2 (*Caribe*) *Venezuelan folk dance*

valsear ▸conjug 1a◂ VI (*LAm*) to waltz

valuable ADJ (*LAm*) 1 (= *valioso*) valuable
2 (= *calculable*) calculable

valuación SF = **valoración 1**

valuador(a) SM/F (*LAm*) valuer

valuar ▸conjug 1e◂ VT = **valorar**

valumen SM 1 (*Cono Sur*) [*de plantas*] luxuriance, rankness
2 (*Méx*) (= *lío*) bundle; (= *masa*) mass, bulk

valumoso ADJ 1 (*CAm, Cono Sur*) [*planta*] luxuriant, rank
2 (*Andes, CAm, Méx*) (= *voluminoso*) bulky
3 (*Caribe*) (= *vanidoso*) vain, conceited

valva SF (*Bot, Zool*) valve

válvula SF valve ► **válvula de admisión** inlet valve ► **válvula de escape** (*Mec*) exhaust valve; (*fig*) safety valve ► **válvula de purga** vent ► **válvula de seguridad** safety valve

vamos *ver* **ir**

vampi* SF = **vampiresa**

vampiresa SF (*Cine*) vamp, femme fatale

vampirizar ▸conjug 1f◂ VT to sap, milk, bleed dry

vampiro SM 1 (*Zool, Mit*) vampire
2 (= *explotador*) vampire, bloodsucker

van *ver* **ir**

vanagloria SF vainglory

vanagloriarse ▸conjug 1b◂ VPR 1 (= *jactarse*) to boast (**de** of); **~ de hacer algo** to boast of doing sth
2 (= *envanecerse*) to be vain, be arrogant

vanaglorioso ADJ (= *ostentoso*) vainglorious; (= *vano*) vain, boastful, arrogant

vanamente ADV 1 (= *inútilmente*) in vain
2 (= *con vanidad*) vainly

vanarse ▸conjug 1a◂ VPR (*Andes, Caribe, Cono Sur*) [*fruto*] to shrivel up; [*negocio*] to fall through, come to nothing, produce no results

vandálico ADJ 1 [*acto, comportamiento*] loutish
2 (*Hist*) Vandal, Vandalic

vandalismo SM vandalism

vándalo/a Ⓐ ADJ loutish
Ⓑ SM/F 1 (= *salvaje*) vandal
2 (*Hist*) Vandal

vanguardia SF (*Mil*) (*fig*) vanguard; **de ~** (*Arte*) avant-garde; (*Pol*) vanguard *antes de s*; **un pintor de ~** an avant-garde painter; **estar en la ~ del progreso** to be in the vanguard of progress; **ir a la** *o* **en ~** (*lit*) to be in the vanguard; (*fig*) to be at the forefront

vanguardismo SM (*Arte, Literat*) avant-garde movement; (= *estilo*) ultramodern manner

vanguardista Ⓐ ADJ [*moda, estilo*] avant-garde; [*tecnología*] revolutionary; **un coche de tecnología ~** a car at the cutting edge of technology
Ⓑ SMF avant-garde artist

vanidad SF 1 (= *presunción*) vanity; **por pura ~** out of sheer vanity; **halagar la ~ de algn** to play up to sb's vanity
2 (= *irrealidad*) unreality; (= *inutilidad*) uselessness, futility; (= *superficialidad*) shallowness
3 (*Rel*) vanity; **~ de ~es** (*Biblia*) vanity of vanities

vanidoso ADJ vain, conceited

vano Ⓐ ADJ 1 (= *infundado*) [*ilusión, esperanza*] empty, vain; [*temor, sospecha*] groundless; [*superstición*] foolish
2 (= *inútil*) [*intento*] vain, futile; **~s esfuerzos** vain *o* futile efforts; **sus esfuerzos fueron ~s** their efforts were in vain; **en ~** in vain; **no en ~ se le considera el mejor nadador** not for nothing is he held to be the best swimmer
3 (= *vacío*) [*promesa, excusa*] empty; **no son más que palabras vanas** they are just empty words
4 [*persona*] (= *superficial*) shallow; (= *vanidoso*) vain
5 [*cáscara*] empty, hollow
Ⓑ SM (*Arquit*) space, opening

vapor SM 1 (*gen*) vapour, vapor (*EEUU*); (*Téc*) [*de agua*] steam; [*de gas*] fumes *pl*; (*Meteo*) mist, haze; **verduras al ~** steamed vegetables; **a todo ~** (*lit, fig*) at full steam; **de ~** steam *antes de s*; **acumular ~** to get steam up; **echar ~** to give off steam, steam ► **vapor de agua** water vapour
2 (*Náut*) steamship, steamer ► **vapor correo** mail boat ► **vapor de paletas, vapor de ruedas** paddle steamer ► **vapor volandero** tramp steamer
3 (*Med*) vertigo, giddiness
4 **vapores**† (= *accesos histéricos*) vapours, vapors (*EEUU*)

vapora SF 1 (= *barco*) steam launch
2 (*Caribe Ferro*) steam engine

vaporar ▸conjug 1a◂ VT, VI = **vaporear**

vaporear ▸conjug 1a◂ Ⓐ VT to evaporate
Ⓑ VI to give off vapour
Ⓒ **vaporearse** VPR to evaporate

vaporización SF vaporization

vaporizador SM (*para agua*) vaporizer; (= *pulverizador*) spray

vaporizar ▸conjug 1f◂ Ⓐ VT (*gen*) [+ *agua*] to vaporize; [+ *perfume*] to spray
Ⓑ **vaporizarse** VPR to vaporize

vaporizo SM (*Caribe, Méx*) 1 (= *calor*) strong heat, steamy heat
2 (*Med*) inhalation

vaporoso ADJ 1 [*tela*] sheer, diaphanous
2 (*de vapor*) vaporous; (= *brumoso*) misty; (= *lleno de vapor*) steamy, steaming

vapulear ▸conjug 1a◂ VT 1 [+ *alfombra, persona*] to beat; (= *azotar*) to beat up*, thrash; (*con látigo*) flog
2 (= *regañar*) to slate*

vapuleo SM 1 (= *paliza*) beating, thrashing; (*con látigo*) flogging
2 (= *regañina*) slating*

vaquerear ▸conjug 1a◂ VI (*Andes*) to play truant

vaquería SF 1 (= *lechería*) dairy
2 (*LAm*) (= *arte del vaquero*) craft of the cowboy; (= *cuidado de ganado*) cattle farming
3 (*Andes, Caribe*) (= *cubo*) milking pail; (= *establo*) milking shed
4 (*Caribe*) (= *ganado*) herd of dairy cows
5 (*Caribe*) (= *caza*) hunting with a lasso
6 (*Méx*) (= *baile*) barn dance, country dance

vaqueriza SF (= *establo*) cowshed; (= *corral*) cattle yard

vaquerizo/a Ⓐ ADJ cattle *antes de s*
Ⓑ SM/F cowherd

vaquero/a Ⓐ ADJ (= *de los pastores*) cowboy *antes de s*; [*tela, falda*] denim *antes de s*; **pantalones ~s** jeans
Ⓑ SM/F [1] [*de ganado*] cowherd, cowboy/cowgirl
[2] (*LAm*) (= *lechero*) milkman/milkwoman
[3] (*Andes*) (= *ausente*) truant
Ⓒ SM [1] (*Caribe*) (= *látigo*) rawhide whip
[2] **vaqueros** (= *pantalones*) jeans

vaqueta Ⓐ SF [1] (= *cuero*) cowhide, leather
[2] (*para afilar*) razor strop
Ⓑ SM (*Caribe*) shifty sort*

vaquetón ADJ [1] (*Caribe*) (= *poco fiable*) unreliable, shifty
[2] (*Méx*) (= *lerdo*) dim-witted; (= *flemático*) phlegmatic, slow
[3] (*Méx*) (= *descarado*) barefaced, brazen

vaquetudo ADJ (*Caribe, Méx*) = **vaquetón**

vaquilla SF [1] (= *ternera*) heifer
[2] **vaquillas** (= *reses*) young calves; (= *fiesta*) (*tb* **corrida de ~s**) *bullfight with young bulls*

vaquillona SF (*LAm*) heifer

V.A.R. ABR (= **Vuestra Alteza Real**) HRH

vara SF [1] (= *palo*) stick, pole; (*Mec*) rod, bar; [*de carro, carroza*] shaft; (*Bot*) branch (*stripped of its leaves*); [*de flor*] central stem, main stalk ► **vara de las virtudes** magic wand ► **vara de medir** yardstick, measuring rod ► **vara de oro** goldenrod ► **vara de pescar** fishing rod ► **vara de San José** goldenrod ► **vara mágica** magic wand
[2] (*Pol*) (= *insignia*) staff of office; **doblar la ~ de la justicia** to pervert (the course of) justice; **empuñar la ~** to take over, take (up) office (*as mayor etc*); ✦*MODISMO* **medir las cosas con la misma ~** to judge things by the same standards ► **vara alta** (= *autoridad*) authority, power; (= *peso*) influence; (= *dominio*) dominance; **tener mucha ~ alta** to have great influence, be influential ► **vara consistorial** staff of office
[3] (*esp LAm Mat*) ≈ yard (= *.836 metres, = 2.8 feet*)
[4] (*Taur*) (= *lanza*) lance, pike; (= *herida*) wound with the lance; **poner ~s al toro** to wound the bull with the lance
[5] ✦*MODISMO* **dar la ~ a*** to annoy, bother
[6] (†*) (= *revés*) blow; (= *disgusto*) upset, setback

varada SF [1] (*Náut*) beaching
[2] (= *lanzamiento*) launching

varadero SM dry dock

varado Ⓐ ADJ [1] (*Náut*) **estar ~** (*en la playa*) to be beached; (*en un banco de arena*) to be grounded
[2] (*LAm**) ✦*MODISMO* **estar ~** (*Cono Sur*) (= *sin trabajo*) to be without regular work; (*CAm, Cono Sur, Méx*) (= *sin dinero*) to be broke*
Ⓑ SM (*Cono Sur*) *man without a regular job*

varadura SF stranding, running aground

varajillo SM (*Caribe*) liqueur coffee

varal SM [1] (= *palo*) long pole; [*de carro, carroza*] shaft; (*Teat*) batten; (= *armazón*) framework of poles; (= *puntal*) strut, support
[2] (*) (= *persona*) beanpole*

varapalear ▸conjug 1a◂ VT to slate, tear to pieces

varapalo SM [1] (= *palo*) long pole
[2] (= *golpe*) blow with a stick; (= *paliza*) beating
[3] (= *regañina*) dressing-down*
[4] (= *disgusto*) disappointment, blow

varar ▸conjug 1a◂ Ⓐ VT [1] (= *llevar a la playa*) to beach, run aground
[2] (= *botar*) to launch
Ⓑ VI, **vararse** VPR [1] (*Náut*) to run aground
[2] [*negocio, asunto*] to get bogged down

varayoc SM (*Andes*) Indian chief

varazo SM blow with a stick

varazón SF (*Andes, Caribe, Méx*) sticks *pl*, bunch of sticks

vardasca SF green twig, switch

varé†* SM (*Esp*) 100 pesetas

vareador(a) SM/F olive picker, olive harvester

varear ▸conjug 1a◂ VT [1] [+ *persona*] to beat, hit; [+ *frutas*] to knock down (*with poles*); [+ *alfombra*] to beat; (*Taur*) goad (*with the lance*)
[2] (*Com*) [+ *paño*] to sell by the yard
[3] (*Cono Sur*) [+ *caballo*] to exercise, train

varec SM kelp, wrack

varejón SM (*Cono Sur*) [1] = **vardasca**
[2] (= *palo*) stick, straight branch (*stripped of leaves*)

vareta SF [1] (= *ramita*) twig, small stick; (*con liga*) *lime twig for catching birds*
[2] (*Cos*) stripe
[3] (= *indirecta*) insinuation; (= *pulla*) taunt; **echar ~s** to make insinuations
[4] ✦*MODISMOS* **estar de ~** ◊ **irse de ~** to have diarrhoea

varetazo SM (*Taur*) *sideways thrust with the horn*

varga SF *steepest part of a slope*

variabilidad SF variability

variable Ⓐ ADJ (*gen*) variable, changeable; (*Mat, Inform*) variable
Ⓑ SF (*Mat, Inform*) variable

variación SF (*gen, Mús*) variation; (*Meteo*) change; **sin ~** unchanged

variado ADJ (*gen*) varied; (= *diverso*) mixed; (= *surtido*) assorted; [*superficie, color*] variegated

variante Ⓐ ADJ variant
Ⓑ SF [1] [*de palabra, texto*] variant ► **variante dialectal** dialectal variant ► **variante fonética** phonetic variant, alternative pronunciation ► **variante ortográfica** spelling variant, alternative spelling
[2] (*Aut*) diversion
[3] (*en quiniela*) *draw or away win*
Ⓒ SM [1] **variantes** (*Esp Culin*) pickled vegetables (*as hors d'oeuvres*)
[2] (*Andes*) (= *senda*) path; (= *atajo*) short cut

variar ▸conjug 1c◂ Ⓐ VT [1] (= *cambiar*) to change, alter; **han variado el enfoque de la revista** they have changed *o* altered the magazine's focus
[2] (= *dar variedad a*) to vary; **intento ~ el menú** I try to vary the menu
Ⓑ VI [1] (= *cambiar*) to vary; **los precios varían según el tamaño** prices vary according to size; **~ de opinión** to change one's mind; **~ de precio** to vary in price; **~ de tamaño** to vary in size; **para ~** (*iró*) (just) for a change; **hoy hemos comido sopa, para ~** we had soup today, (just) for a change
[2] (= *ser diferente*) to be different, differ; **esto varía de lo que dijo antes** this is different *o* this differs from what he said earlier

varicela SF chickenpox

varicoso ADJ [1] [*pierna*] varicose
[2] [*persona*] *suffering from varicose veins*

variedad SF [1] (= *diversidad*) variety
[2] (*Biol*) variety
[3] **variedades** (*Teat*) variety show *sing*; **teatro de ~es** variety theatre, music hall, vaudeville theater (*EEUU*)

varietés SMPL (*Teat*) = **variedad 3**

varilla SF [1] [*de metal*] (*Mec*) rod, bar; [*de faja, abanico, paraguas*] rib; [*de rueda*] spoke; [*de corsé*] rib, stay; [*de gafas*] sidepiece, earpiece ► **varilla del aceite** dipstick ► **varilla de zahorí** divining rod
[2] (*Anat*) jawbone
[3] (*Méx*) (= *baratijas*) cheap wares *pl*, trinkets *pl*
[4] (*Caribe*) (= *vaina*) nuisance, bother

varillaje SM [*de abanico, paraguas*] ribs *pl*, ribbing; (*Mec*) rods *pl*, links *pl*

varillar ▸conjug 1a◂ VT (*Caribe*) [+ *caballo*] to try out, train

vario Ⓐ ADJ [1] (= *variado*) varied; [*color*] variegated, motley
[2] (= *cambiable*) varying, changeable; [*persona*] fickle
[3] **varios** (= *muchos*) several, a number of; **hay varias posibilidades** there are several *o* a number of *o* various possibilities; **en ~s libros que he visto** in a number of books which I have seen; **los inconvenientes son ~s** there are several drawbacks; **asuntos ~s** (any) other business
Ⓑ **varios** PRON (= *unos*) some; **~s piensan que** ... some (people) think that ...

varioloso ADJ pockmarked

variopinto ADJ [1] (= *de distintos colores*) multicoloured, multi-colored (*EEUU*), colourful, colorful (*EEUU*)
[2] (= *diverso*) [*objetos, regalos*] diverse, miscellaneous; [*gente, público*] very mixed

varita SF wand ► **varita de las virtudes**, **varita mágica** magic wand

variz (*pl* **varices** *o* **várices**) SF (*Med*) varix; **tener varices** to have varicose veins

varón Ⓐ ADJ male; **hijo ~** son, boy
Ⓑ SM [1] (= *niño*) boy; (= *hombre*) man, male; (= *gran hombre*) great man, worthy man; **tuvo cuatro hijos, todos varones** she had four children, all boys; **es un santo ~** (= *hombre bondadoso*) he's a saint; (= *hombre simple*) he's a simple fellow ► **varón de Dios** saintly man
[2] (*Andes*) (= *marido*) husband
[3] (*Cono Sur, Méx*) (= *vigas*) beams *pl*, timber

varona SF, **varonesa** SF mannish woman

varonil ADJ [1] (= *viril*) manly, virile; (= *enérgico*) vigorous
[2] (*Biol*) male
[3] (*pey*) [*mujer*] mannish; **una mujer de aspecto ~** a woman of mannish appearance

Varsovia SF Warsaw

vas *etc ver* **ir**

vasallaje SM (*Hist*) vassalage; (*pey*) (= *sumisión*) subjection, serfdom

vasallo SM vassal

vasar SM kitchen dresser, kitchen cabinet (*EEUU*)

vasco/a Ⓐ ADJ Basque
Ⓑ SM/F Basque; **los ~s** the Basques
Ⓒ SM (*Ling*) Basque

vascófilo/a SM/F expert in Basque studies

vascófono/a Ⓐ ADJ Basque-speaking
Ⓑ SM/F Basque speaker

vascofrancés/esa Ⓐ ADJ **País Vascofrancés** French Basque Country
Ⓑ SM/F French Basque

vascohablante Ⓐ ADJ Basque-speaking
Ⓑ SMF Basque speaker

Vascongadas SFPL **las ~** the Basque Provinces

vascongado/a ADJ, SM/F = **vasco**

vascuence SM (*Ling*) Basque

vascular ADJ vascular

vase†† *ver* **ir**

vasectomía SF vasectomy

vaselina SF Vaseline®, petroleum jelly; ✦*MODISMOS* **hacer una ~** (*Fbtl*) to ease the ball in over the goalie's head; **poner ~*** to calm things down, make things go smoothly

vasera SF kitchen shelf, rack

vasija SF (*Hist*) vessel; (*Culin*) pot, dish

vaso SM 1 (*para beber*) (*gen*) glass; (*para whisky*) tumbler; (*Andes*) small cup; ✦*MODISMO* **ahogarse en un ~ de agua** to make a mountain out of a molehill ► **vaso alto** tall glass ► **vaso de vino** (= *recipiente*) wineglass; (= *contenido*) glass of wine
2 (= *cantidad*) glass, glassful
3 (= *recipiente*) (*para flores*) vase; [*de pila*] cell; (*liter*) vase, urn; (*Andes Aut*) hubcap ► **vaso de engrase** (*Mec*) grease cup ► **vaso litúrgico, vaso sagrado** liturgical vessel ► **vasos comunicantes** communicating vessels
4 (*Anat*) vessel; (= *canal*) duct, tube ► **vaso capilar** capillary ► **vaso sanguíneo** blood vessel
5 (*Náut*) (= *barco*) boat, ship; (= *casco*) hull
6 (*Zool*) hoof
7 (= *orinal*) (*tb* **~ de noche**†) chamber pot

vasoconstrictor Ⓐ ADJ vasoconstrictor *antes de s*, vasoconstrictive
Ⓑ SM vasoconstrictor, vasoconstrictive substance

vasodilatador Ⓐ ADJ vasodilator *antes de s*, vasodilating
Ⓑ SM vasodilator

vasquismo SM (*culturalmente*) *sense of the differentness of the Basque Country*; (*Pol*) *doctrine of or belief in Basque autonomy*

vasquista Ⓐ ADJ that supports *etc* Basque autonomy; **el movimiento ~** the movement for Basque autonomy; **la familia es muy ~** the family strongly supports Basque autonomy
Ⓑ SMF supporter *etc* of Basque autonomy

vástago SM 1 (*Bot*) shoot
2 (*Mec*) rod ► **vástago de émbolo** piston rod
3 (= *hijo, descendiente*) offspring, descendant
4 (*Andes, CAm, Caribe*) (= *tronco*) trunk of the banana tree

vastedad SF vastness, immensity

vasto ADJ vast, huge

vataje SM wattage

vate SM 1 (*Hist*) seer, prophet
2 (*Literat*) poet, bard

váter SM lavatory, W.C., restroom (*EEUU*)

Vaticano SM Vatican; **la Ciudad del ~** Vatican City

vaticano ADJ (*gen*) Vatican; (= *papal*) papal

vaticinador SM (= *profeta*) seer, prophet; [*del tiempo, economía*] forecaster

vaticinar ▸conjug 1a◂ VT (= *predecir*) to predict; (= *pronosticar*) to forecast

vaticinio SM (= *predicción*) prediction; (= *pronóstico*) to forecast

vatio SM watt

vaya *etc ver* **ir**

VCL SM ABR (= **visualizador cristal líquido**) LCD

Vd. ABR = **usted**

Vda. ABR = **viuda**

Vds. ABR = **ustedes**

ve[1] *ver* **ir**, **ver**

ve[2] SF (*LAm*) ► **ve chica, ve corta** *name of the letter V* ► **ve doble** *name of the letter W*

V.E. ABR = **Vuestra Excelencia**

vea *etc ver* **ver**

vecinal ADJ 1 [*camino*] local; [*impuesto*] local, municipal; **padrón ~** list of residents
2 (*LAm*) (= *vecino*) neighbouring, neighboring (*EEUU*), adjacent

vecindad SF 1 (= *barrio*) neighbourhood, neighborhood (*EEUU*); (= *cercanía*) vicinity; (*LAm*) (= *barrio pobre*) inner-city slum
2 (= *vecinos*) neighbours *pl*, neighbors (*EEUU*) *pl*, neighbourhood; (= *comunidad local*) local community; (= *residentes*) residents *pl*
3 (*Jur*) residence, abode; **declarar su ~** to state where one lives, give one's place of residence

vecindario SM (= *barrio*) neighbourhood, neighborhood (*EEUU*); (= *población*) population, residents *pl*; (= *comunidad local*) local community

vecino/a Ⓐ ADJ 1 (= *cercano*) neighbouring, neighboring (*EEUU*); **se fue a vivir a un pueblo ~** he went to live in a neighbouring *o* nearby village
2 (= *contiguo*) **vive en el edificio ~** he lives in the house next door; **el garaje ~ al mío** the garage next to mine; **las dos fincas son vecinas** the two properties adjoin
3 (*frm*) (= *parecido*) similar; **suertes vecinas** similar fates
Ⓑ SM/F 1 [*de edificio, calle*] neighbour, neighbor (*EEUU*); **somos ~s** we are neighbours; **el ~ de al lado** the next-door neighbour ► **vecino/a de rellano** next-door neighbour (*in a block of flats*)
2 (= *habitante*) [*de un pueblo*] inhabitant; [*de un barrio*] resident; **un pueblo de 800 ~s** a village of 800 inhabitants; **un ~ de la calle Corredera** a resident of *o* a person who lives in Corredera street; **asociación de ~s** residents' association

vector SM vector

Veda SM Veda

veda SF 1 (= *prohibición*) prohibition
2 (= *temporada*) close season, closed season (*EEUU*)

vedado SM private preserve; **cazar/pescar en ~** to poach, hunt/fish illegally ► **vedado de caza** game reserve

vedar ▸conjug 1a◂ VT (= *prohibir*) to prohibit, ban; (= *impedir*) to stop, prevent; [+ *idea, plan*] to veto; **~ a algn hacer algo** to forbid sb to do sth

vedeta SF = **vedette**

vedetismo SM (= *protagonismo*) insistence on being in the forefront, insistence on playing the star role; (= *estrellato*) stardom

vedette [be'ðet] SF 1 [*de revista musical*] (= *artista principal*) star; (*de menor importancia*) starlet
2 [*de fiesta, equipo, acontecimiento*] star
3 (*Méx*) (= *corista*) chorus girl

védico ADJ Vedic

vedija SF 1 (= *lana*) tuft of wool
2 (= *greña*) mat of hair, matted hair

vega SF 1 (= *terreno bajo*) fertile plain, rich lowland area; (= *prado*) water meadows *pl*; (*Andes*) *stretch of alluvial soil*
2 (*Caribe*) (= *tabacal*) tobacco plantation

vegetación SF 1 (= *plantas*) vegetation
2 (*Med*) ► **vegetaciones adenoideas** adenoids

vegetal Ⓐ ADJ [*aceite, productos*] vegetable *antes de s*; **patología ~** plant pathology
Ⓑ SM 1 (= *planta*) plant, vegetable
2 **vegetales** (*CAm, Méx*) (= *verduras*) vegetables
3 (= *persona*) vegetable

vegetar ▸conjug 1a◂ VI 1 (*Bot*) to grow
2 (*fig*) [*persona*] to vegetate; [*negocio*] to stagnate

vegetarianismo SM vegetarianism

vegetariano/a ADJ, SM/F vegetarian

vegetativo ADJ vegetative; **sistema nervioso ~** vegetative nervous system; **vida vegetativa** vegetative life

vegoso ADJ (*Cono Sur*) [*tierra*] soggy, damp

veguero Ⓐ ADJ lowland *antes de s*, low-lying
Ⓑ SM 1 (= *agricultor*) lowland farmer
2 (*Caribe*) [*de tabaco*] tobacco planter
3 (= *cigarro puro*) coarse cigar; (*Cono Sur*) (= *tabaco cubano*) good-quality Cuban tobacco, good cigar

vehemencia SF vehemence

vehemente ADJ vehement

vehicular† ▸conjug 1a◂ VT (*gen*) to transport; (= *transmitir*) to transmit, convey

vehiculizar ▸conjug 1f◂ VT = **vehicular**

vehículo SM 1 (*Aut*) vehicle ► **vehículo a motor** motor vehicle ► **vehículo astral** spacecraft ► **vehículo automóvil** motor vehicle ► **vehículo carretero** road vehicle ► **vehículo cósmico** spacecraft ► **vehículo de carga** goods vehicle ► **vehículo de la empresa** company car ► **vehículo de motor** motor vehicle ► **vehículo de transporte** goods vehicle ► **vehículo espacial** spacecraft ► **vehículo industrial** commercial vehicle ► **vehículo privado** private vehicle ► **vehículo utilitario** commercial vehicle
2 [*de modas, ideas*] vehicle (**de** for)
3 (*Med*) carrier, transmitter (**de** of)

veinte ADJ INV, PRON, SM (*gen*) twenty; (*ordinal, en la fecha*) twentieth; **el siglo ~** the twentieth century; **le escribí el día ~** I wrote to him on the twentieth; **los (años) ~** the twenties; *ver tb* **seis**

veinteañero/a, veintiañero/a Ⓐ ADJ twentyish, about twenty
Ⓑ SM/F person of about twenty, person in his/her twenties

veintena SF **una ~** about twenty

veintipocos ADJ PL twenty-odd

veintitantos ADJ PL twenty-odd; **tiene ~ años** he's in his twenties, he's twenty-something*, he's twenty-odd*

veintiuna SF (*Naipes*) pontoon, twenty-one (*EEUU*)

vejación SF (= *humillación*) humiliation; (= *maltrato*) ill-treatment; **sufrir vejaciones** to suffer humiliation

vejamen SM [1] = **vejación**
[2] (= *pasquín*) satire, lampoon; (= *pulla*) shaft, taunt

vejaminoso ADJ (*Andes, Caribe*) irritating, annoying

vejancón/ona* Ⓐ ADJ, **vejarrón/ona*** ADJ ancient*, doddery*, decrepit
Ⓑ SM/F old chap/dear*, old dodderer*

vejar ▸conjug 1a◂ VT (= *molestar*) to vex, annoy; (= *humillar*) to humiliate; (= *mofarse de*) to scoff at; (= *atormentar*) to harass

vejarano ADJ (*LAm**) ancient*, doddery*, decrepit

vejatorio ADJ (= *molesto*) annoying, vexatious; (= *humillante*) humiliating, degrading; [*comentarios*] hurtful, offensive; **es ~ para él tener que pedirlo** it is humiliating for him to have to beg for it

vejestorio SM (*pey*) old dodderer*, old crock*

vejete* SM old boy*

vejez SF [1] (= *senectud*) old age; ✦*MODISMO* **¡a la ~, viruelas!** fancy that happening at his *etc* age!*
[2] (†) (= *cuento*) old story; (= *noticia*) piece of stale news
[3] **vejeces** (= *achaques*) ills of old age; (= *manías, chocheces*) grouchiness *sing*, grumpiness *sing*

vejiga SF [1] (*Anat*) bladder ► **vejiga de la bilis** gallbladder ► **vejiga natatoria** air bladder, swim bladder
[2] (*Med*) blister
[3] (*en pintura*) blister

vela¹ SF [1] [*de cera*] candle; ✦*MODISMOS* **estar a dos ~s*** (= *sin enterarse*) to be in the dark; (= *sin dinero*) to be broke*; **encender** *o* **poner una ~ a Dios y otra al diablo** to have it both ways; **¿quién te dio ~ en este entierro?** who asked you to butt in? ► **vela de sebo** tallow candle
[2] (= *vigilia*) **estar en ~** to be unable to get to sleep; **pasar la noche en ~** to have a sleepless night
[3] (*) (= *moco*) bogey*
[4] (*Taur**) horn
[5] (= *trabajo nocturno*) night work; (*Mil*) (period of) sentry duty
[6] (*LAm*) (= *velorio*) wake
[7] (*Cono Sur*) (= *molestia*) nuisance; **¡qué ~!** what a nuisance!; ✦*MODISMO* **aguantar la ~** (= *soportar*) to put up with it; (= *plantar cara*) to face the music*
[8] (*Caribe, Méx*) (= *bronca*) telling-off*

vela² SF (*Náut*) sail; (= *deporte*) sailing; **barco de ~** sailing ship; **darse** *o* **hacerse a la ~** ◊ **largar las ~s** to set sail, get under way; **hacer ~** to go sailing; **a toda ~** ◊ **a ~s desplegadas** (*lit*) under full sail; (*fig*) vigorously, energetically; ✦*MODISMOS* **arriar** *o* **recoger ~s** (= *retractarse*) to back down; (= *abandonar*) to give up, chuck it in*; **estar a dos ~s*** to be broke*, be skint‡; **estar entre dos ~s*** ◊ **ir a la ~*** to be half-seas over‡; **ir como las ~s** (*Cono Sur*) to drive very fast; **plegar ~s** to slow down ► **vela balón** spinnaker ► **vela mayor** mainsail

velación SF wake, vigil

velada SF (evening) party, soirée ► **velada de boxeo** fight night ► **velada musical** musical evening

veladamente ADV in a veiled way

velado ADJ (*gen, tb fig*) veiled; (*Fot*) fogged, blurred; [*sonido*] muffled

velador SM [1] (= *mesa*) pedestal table; (*LAm*) (= *mesita*) bedside table, night table (*EEUU*)
[2] (*para velas*) candlestick
[3] (*Cono Sur*) (= *lámpara*) night light
[4] (*Méx*) (= *pantalla*) lampshade
[5] (= *vigilante*) watchman, caretaker; (*Hist*) sentinel

veladora SF [1] (*Méx*) (= *lámpara*) table lamp, bedside lamp
[2] (*LAm*) (= *vela*) candle; (*Rel*) paraffin lamp

velamen SM sails *pl*, canvas

velar¹ ▸conjug 1a◂ Ⓐ VT [1] [+ *enfermo*] to sit up with; [+ *muerto*] to keep vigil over
[2] (*Mil*) to watch, keep watch over
[3] (*LAm*) (= *codiciar*) to look covetously at
Ⓑ VI [1] (†) (= *permanecer despierto*) to stay awake, go without sleep
[2] **~ por algo/algn** (= *cuidar*) to look after sth/sb; **velaba por la salud de sus hijos** she looked after her children's health; **nadie vela por mis intereses** nobody watches over my interests; **tendremos que ~ por que esto no se repita** we'll have to see to it *o* ensure that this doesn't happen again
[3] (*Rel*) to keep vigil
[4] [*arrecife*] to appear

velar² ▸conjug 1a◂ Ⓐ VT [1] (*Fot*) to fog
[2] (*liter*) (= *cubrir con un velo*) to veil
[3] (*liter*) (= *ocultar*) to conceal
Ⓑ **velarse** VPR [1] (*Fot*) to fog
[2] (*liter*) (= *cubrirse con un velo*) to veil o.s.

velar³ ADJ (*Ling*) velar

velarizar ▸conjug 1f◂ VT to velarize

velarte SM (*Hist*) broadcloth

velatorio SM wake

Velázquez SM Velázquez, Velasquez

veleidad SF [1] (= *volubilidad, inconstancia*) fickleness, capriciousness
[2] (= *capricho*) whim; [*de humor*] unpredictable mood

veleidoso ADJ fickle, capricious

velero Ⓐ ADJ [*barco*] manoeuvrable, maneuverable (*EEUU*)
Ⓑ SM [1] (*Náut*) (*grande*) sailing ship; (*pequeño*) sailing boat, sailboat (*EEUU*)
[2] (*Aer*) glider
[3] (= *persona*) sailmaker

veleta Ⓐ SF [1] [*de edificio*] weather vane, weathercock
[2] (*Pesca*) float
Ⓑ SMF (= *persona*) fickle person, weathercock

veletería SF (*Cono Sur*) chopping and changing, fickleness

velís SM (*Méx*) (= *maleta*) suitcase; (= *bolso*) valise, overnight bag

veliz SM (*Méx*) = **velís**

vello SM (*Anat*) fuzz, soft hair; (*Bot*) down; (*en frutas*) bloom; (*en cuerna*) velvet ► **vello facial** facial hair

vellocino SM fleece ► **Vellocino de Oro** Golden Fleece

vellón¹ SM [1] (= *lana*) fleece; (= *piel*) sheepskin
[2] (= *mechón*) tuft of wool

vellón² SM [1] (*Téc*) copper and silver alloy
[2] (*CAm, Caribe*) (= *moneda*) five-cent coin

vellonera SF (*Caribe*) jukebox

vellosidad SF (= *pelusa*) downiness; (= *pelo fuerte*) hairiness; (= *lanosidad*) fluffiness

velloso ADJ (= *con pelusa*) downy; (*más fuerte*) hairy; (= *lanoso*) fluffy

velludo Ⓐ ADJ hairy
Ⓑ SM plush, velvet

velo SM [1] [*de tul, gasa*] veil; **tomar el ~** to take the veil; **corramos un tupido ~ sobre esto** let us draw a discreet veil over this
[2] (*fig*) (= *cobertura*) veil, light covering; (*Fot*) fog; (*en cristal*) mist; [*de silencio, misterio*] shroud
[3] (= *pretexto*) pretext, cloak
[4] (= *confusión*) confusion, mental fog
[5] (*Anat*) ► **velo de paladar** soft palate, velum

velocidad SF [1] (*gen*) speed; (*Téc*) velocity; (*fig*) swiftness, speediness; **de alta ~** high-speed; **a gran ~** at high speed; **a máxima** *o* **toda ~** at full speed, at top speed; **¿a qué ~?** how fast?, at what speed?; **¿a qué ~ ibas?** what speed were you doing?; **cobrar ~** to pick up *o* gather speed; **disminuir** *o* **moderar la ~** ◊ **perder ~** to slow down; **exceder la ~ permitida** to speed, exceed the speed limit; ✦*MODISMO* **confundir la ~ con el tocino*** to get things mixed up ► **velocidad adquirida** momentum ► **velocidad de crucero** cruising speed ► **velocidad de despegue** takeoff speed ► **velocidad del sonido** speed of sound ► **velocidad de obturación, velocidad de obturador** shutter speed ► **velocidad de transferencia** transfer rate ► **velocidad económica** cruising speed ► **velocidad máxima** maximum speed, top speed ► **velocidad máxima de impresión** (*Inform*) maximum print speed ► **velocidad punta** maximum speed, top speed
[2] (*Mec*) gear, speed; **primera ~** ◊ **~ corta** low gear, bottom gear, first gear; **segunda/tercera/cuarta ~** second/third/top gear; **meter la segunda ~** to change into second gear; **cuatro ~es hacia adelante** four forward gears ► **velocidades de avance** forward gears

velocímetro SM speedometer

velocípedo SM velocipede

velocista SMF sprinter

velódromo SM cycle track

velomotor SM moped

velón SM [1] (= *lámpara*) oil lamp
[2] (*Andes, Cono Sur, Méx*) (= *vela*) thick tallow candle
[3] (*CAm*) (= *parásito*) sponger*, parasite
[4] (*Andes, Caribe*) *person who casts covetous glances*

velorio¹ SM [1] (= *fiesta*) party, celebration; (*Andes, Caribe, Cono Sur*) dull party, flat affair
[2] (*esp LAm*) (= *velatorio*) funeral wake, vigil for the dead ► **velorio del angelito** *wake for a dead child*

velorio² SM (*Rel*) *ceremony of taking the veil*

veloz ADJ [*tren, coche, barco*] fast; [*movimiento*] quick, swift; **~ como un relámpago** as quick as lightning

velozmente ADV fast, quickly, swiftly

ven *ver* **venir**

vena SF [1] (*Anat*) vein; **abrirse** *o* **cortarse las ~s** to slit one's wrists; **inyectar en ~** to inject into a vein ► **vena yugular** jugular vein
[2] (*Min*) vein, seam
[3] (*en piedra, madera*) grain
[4] (*Bot*) vein, rib
[5] [*de humor, ánimo*] mood; **le dio la ~ por hacer eso** he had a notion to do that; **coger a algn de** *o* **en ~** to catch sb in the right mood; **estar de** *o* **en ~** (= *tener ganas*) to be in the mood (**para** for); (= *estar en forma*) to be in good form ► **vena de locura** streak of madness
[6] (= *talento*) talent, promise; **tiene ~ de pintor** he has the makings of a painter, he shows a talent for painting
[7] (*Geog*) underground stream

venablo SM dart; ✦*MODISMO* **echar ~s** to burst out angrily

venado SM [1] (= *ciervo*) deer; (*macho*) stag
[2] (*Culin*) venison
[3] (*Caribe*) (= *piel*) deerskin
[4] (*Caribe*) (= *prostituta*) whore
[5] (*Andes*) (= *contrabando*) contraband
[6] ✦*MODISMO* **correr** *o* **pintar el ~** (*CAm, Méx*) to play truant, play hookey (*EEUU*)

venal[1] ADJ (*Anat*) venous

venal[2] ADJ (*frm*) [1] (= *vendible*) vendible (*frm*), saleable, salable (*EEUU*)
[2] (*pey*) (= *sobornable*) venal (*frm*), corrupt

venalidad SF venality, corruptness

venático ADJ crazy, mad

venatorio ADJ hunting *antes de s*

vencedor(a) Ⓐ ADJ [*equipo, partido*] winning, victorious (*frm*); [*general, país*] victorious
Ⓑ SM/F (= *ganador*) [*de una competición, elecciones*] winner; [*de una guerra*] victor; **una guerra sin ~es ni vencidos** a war with neither victor nor vanquished

vencejo[1] SM (*Orn*) swift

vencejo[2] SM (*Agr*) straw plait, string (*used in binding sheaves*)

vencer ▸conjug 2b◂ Ⓐ VT [1] (= *derrotar*) [+ *enemigo, rival*] to defeat, beat; [+ *enfermedad, dolor*] to beat, overcome; **vencieron al equipo visitante por 3 a 2** they defeated *o* beat the visiting team 3-2; **nuestro sistema inmunológico es capaz de ~ al virus** our immune system is capable of beating *o* overcoming the virus; **a decir tonterías nadie le vence** when it comes to talking rubbish he's in a class of his own, no one beats him when it comes to talking rubbish; **vence a todos en elegancia** he outdoes them all in style, he beats them all for style
[2] (= *controlar*) [+ *miedo, tentación*] to overcome; [+ *pasión*] to control; **consiguió ~ la tentación de fumar** he managed to overcome the temptation to smoke
[3] (= *prevalecer*) [*miedo, sueño*] to overcome; **por fin lo venció el sueño** sleep finally overcame him; **me venció el pánico cuando tuve que hablarle** panic got the better of me *o* I was overcome with panic when I had to speak to him
[4] (*Dep*) [+ *obstáculo*] to overcome; [+ *prueba*] to complete; [+ *distancia*] to do, complete; [+ *montaña*] to conquer; **vencieron los 15km en dos horas** they did *o* completed the 15km in two hours; **no consiguió ~ todas las pruebas** he didn't manage to complete all the heats
[5] (= *hacer ceder*) [+ *soporte, rama*] to break; **el peso de los libros ha vencido el estante** the shelf gave way under the weight of the books, the weight of the books broke the shelf; **conseguimos ~ la puerta** we managed to break the door down
Ⓑ VI [1] (*en batalla, partido, elecciones*) to win; **hemos vencido por dos a cero** we won two nil; **¡~emos!** we shall win *o* overcome!; **dejarse ~ (por)** to give in (to); **no te dejes ~ y sigue adelante** keep going and don't give in; **por fin se dejó ~ por la curiosidad** he finally gave in to his curiosity, he finally let (his) curiosity get the better of him; **no te dejes ~ por las dificultades** don't give up in the face of difficulties, don't let difficulties get the better of you
[2] (*liter*) [*amor, pasión*] to triumph, be triumphant
[3] (*Com*) [*documento, póliza, pasaporte*] to expire; [*inversión*] to mature; **su contrato vence a final de año** his contract runs out *o* expires at the end of the year; **el plazo para pagar el alquiler vence mañana** the deadline for paying the rent is tomorrow, the rent is due tomorrow; **el plazo para la entrega de solicitudes vence mañana** the closing date for applications is tomorrow; **la semana que viene me vence el primer plazo del ordenador** I have to pay my first instalment on the computer next week, my first instalment on the computer is due next week
Ⓒ **vencerse** VPR [1] (= *ceder*) [*muelle, estante, soporte*] to give way; **la cama se venció con tanto peso** the bed gave way under the weight; **la mesa se vence hacia un lado** the table leans to one side; **la cabeza se le vencía hacia un lado** his head hung *o* leaned to one side
[2] (*LAm*) [*pasaporte, permiso*] to expire; **cómetelo antes de que se venza** eat it before the use-by date; **se venció el plazo** the time's up
[3] (*Cono Sur, Méx*) [*elástico, resorte*] to wear out; [*costura*] to come apart
[4] (= *dominarse*) [*persona*] to control o.s.

vencido/a Ⓐ ADJ [1] (= *derrotado*) [*ejército, general*] defeated; [*equipo, jugador*] losing; **darse por ~** to give up, give in; **ir de ~** [*persona*] to be all in, be on one's last legs; **la enfermedad va de vencida** the illness is past its worst; **la tormenta va de vencida** the worst of the storm is over
[2] (= *combado*) [*tabla, viga de madera*] sagging; **la estantería estaba vencida con tanto peso** the shelves were sagging under the weight
[3] (*Com*) [*intereses, deuda*] due, payable; **con los intereses ~s** with the interest which is due *o* payable; **le pagan por meses ~s** he is paid at the end of the month
[4] (*LAm*) [*boleto, permiso*] out of date; [*medicamento, alimento*] past its use-by date
[5] (*Cono Sur, Méx*) [*elástico, resorte*] worn out
Ⓑ SM/F (*Dep*) loser; **los ~s** (*Dep*) the losers; (*Mil*) the defeated, the vanquished (*frm*); *ver tb* **tercero A**, **vencedor B**
Ⓒ ADV **pagar ~** to pay in arrears

vencimiento SM [1] (*Com*) [*de plazo, contrato*] expiry, expiration (*frm*); [*de inversión, préstamo*] expiry date, date of expiration (*frm*); [*de deuda*] maturity; **al ~ del título** on expiry of the title *o* when the title expires; **con ~ el 1 de marzo** expiring on 1st March
[2] [*de estantería, viga*] (*al combarse*) sagging; (*al romperse*) collapse
[3] [*de dificultad*] **tras el ~ de los primeros obstáculos** after overcoming the first few obstacles

venda SF bandage ► **venda elástica** elastic bandage

vendaje[1] SM (*Med*) dressing, bandaging ► **vendaje compresivo** support bandage ► **vendaje provisional** first-aid bandage

vendaje[2] SM [1] (*Com*) commission
[2] (*LAm*) (= *plus*) bonus, perk*

vendar ▸conjug 1a◂ VT [1] [+ *herida*] to bandage, dress; [+ *ojos*] to cover, blindfold
[2] (*fig*) (= *enceguecer*) to blind; ✦*MODISMO* **~ los ojos a algn** to hoodwink sb

vendaval SM (= *ventarrón*) gale, strong wind; (*fig*) storm

vendedor(a) Ⓐ ADJ selling; (*Fin*) **corriente ~a** selling tendency, tendency to sell
Ⓑ SM/F (*gen*) seller, vendor; (*en tienda*) shop assistant, sales assistant, sales clerk (*EEUU*); (= *minorista*) retailer; [*de empresa*] sales representative, salesman/saleswoman ► **vendedor(a) a domicilio** door-to-door salesman/saleswoman ► **vendedor(a) ambulante** hawker, pedlar, peddler (*EEUU*) ► **vendedor(a) de seguros** insurance salesman/saleswoman

vendeja† SF [1] (= *venta*) public sale
[2] (= *géneros*) *collection of goods offered for sale*

vendepatrias SMF INV traitor

vender ▸conjug 2a◂ Ⓐ VT [1] [+ *producto*] to sell; **venden la bicicleta a mitad de precio** they are selling the bicycle at half price; **lo vendieron por 50 euros** they sold it for 50 euros; **~le algo a algn** to sell sb sth, sell sth to sb; **me ha vendido un ordenador** he sold me a computer; **~ al contado** to sell for cash; **~ al por mayor** to sell wholesale; **~ al por menor** to sell retail; **este coche está sin ~** this car remains unsold; ✦*MODISMO* **¡a mí que las vendo!** I'm not falling for that one!
[2] (= *traicionar*) [+ *amigo*] to betray, sell out*; [+ *cómplice*] to shop*
Ⓑ VI to sell; **los buenos productos siempre venden** a good product will always sell; **vendemos a precios inmejorables** our prices are unbeatable
Ⓒ **venderse** VPR [1] [*producto*] to sell, be sold; **este artículo se vende muy bien** this item is selling very well; **se vende en farmacias** it is sold in chemists'; **el cuadro se vendió por cuatro millones** the painting sold *o* was sold for four million; **se vendían a diez euros en el mercado** they were selling at *o* for ten euros in the market; **es buen político, pero no sabe ~se** he's a good politician but he doesn't know how to sell himself; **"se vende"** "for sale"; **"se vende coche"** "car for sale"; ✦*MODISMO* **~se caro** to play hard to get
[2] (= *dejarse corromper*) to sell out; (= *dejarse sobornar*) to accept a bribe; **le acusaron de ~se a las multinacionales** they accused him of selling out to the multinationals; **el árbitro se vendió** the referee accepted a bribe
[3] (= *traicionarse*) to give o.s. away

vendetta [ben'ðeta] SF vendetta

vendí SM certificate of sale

vendibilidad SF (*gen*) saleability; (*Com*) marketability

vendible ADJ (*gen*) saleable; (*Com*) marketable

vendido ADJ ✦*MODISMO* **ir** *o* **estar ~ a algo/algn*** to be at the mercy of sth/sb

vendimia SF [1] [*de uvas*] grape harvest, wine harvest; (*relativo a calidad, año*) year; **la ~ de 1985** the 1985 vintage
[2] (= *provecho*) big profit, killing

vendimiador(a) SM/F vintager

vendimiar ▸conjug 1b◂ VT [1] [+ *uvas*] to harvest, pick
[2] (*fig*) to squeeze a profit out of, make a killing out of*
[3] (†*) (= *matar*) to bump off*

vendré *etc ver* **venir**

venduta SF [1] (*LAm*) (= *subasta*) auction, public sale
[2] (*Caribe*) (= *frutería*) greengrocer's (shop), fruiterer's (shop); (= *abacería*) small grocery store
[3] (*Caribe*) (= *estafa*) swindle

vendutero SM [1] (*LAm*) (*en subasta*) auctioneer
[2] (*Caribe*) (= *comerciante*) greengrocer, produce dealer (*EEUU*)

Venecia SF Venice

veneciano/a Ⓐ ADJ of/from Venice
Ⓑ SM/F native/inhabitant of Venice; **los ~s** the people of Venice

veneno SM (*gen*) poison; [*de serpiente*] venom

venenoso ADJ [*animal*] poisonous, venomous; [*planta, sustancia*] poisonous; [*palabras, lengua*] venomous

venera SF (*Zool*) scallop; (= *concha*) scallop shell; → CAMINO DE SANTIAGO

venerable ADJ venerable

veneración SF (*gen*) worship; (*Rel*) veneration

venerando ADJ venerable

venerar ▸conjug 1a◂ VT (*gen*) to worship, revere; (*Rel*) to venerate

venéreo ADJ venereal; **enfermedad venérea** venereal disease

venero SM [1] (*Min*) lode, seam
[2] (= *fuente*) spring
[3] (*fig*) source, origin ► **venero de datos** mine of information

venezolanismo SM *word or phrase peculiar to Venezuela*

venezolano/a Ⓐ ADJ Venezuelan
Ⓑ SM/F Venezuelan; **los ~s** the Venezuelans

Venezuela SF Venezuela

venga *etc ver* **venir**

vengador(a) Ⓐ ADJ avenging
Ⓑ SM/F avenger

venganza SF revenge, vengeance; **lo hizo con espíritu de ~** he did it in a spirit of revenge *o* vengeance; **mintió por** *o* **como ~** she lied out of revenge *o* vengeance; **jurar ~ a algn** to swear vengeance on sb; **clamar ~** (*frm*) to cry for vengeance (*frm*)

vengar ▸conjug 1h◂ Ⓐ VT to avenge
Ⓑ **vengarse** VPR to take revenge, get one's revenge; **~se de algn** to take revenge on sb; **~se de una ofensa** to take revenge for an offence

vengativo ADJ [*persona, espíritu*] vengeful, vindictive; [*acto*] retaliatory

vengo *etc ver* **venir**

venia SF [1] (= *perdón*) pardon, forgiveness
[2] (= *permiso*) permission, consent; **con su ~** by your leave, with your permission; **casarse sin la ~ de sus padres** to marry without the consent of one's parents
[3] (*LAm Mil*) salute

venial ADJ venial

venialidad SF veniality

venida SF [1] (*gen*) coming; (= *llegada*) arrival; (= *vuelta*) return
[2] (†) (= *ímpetu*) impetuosity, rashness

venidero ADJ coming, future; **en lo ~** in (the) future; **los ~s** posterity, future generations

venir

▸conjug 3r◂
[A] VERBO INTRANSITIVO [B] VERBO PRONOMINAL
Para las expresiones ***venir al caso, venir de lejos, venir a las manos, venir a menos, venir a pelo, venir de perlas, venirse abajo, venirse encima****, ver la otra entrada.*

Ⓐ VERBO INTRANSITIVO

[1] [a un lugar] to come; **vino a Córdoba desde Barcelona** he came to Córdoba from Barcelona; **¡ven acá** *or* **aquí!** come (over) here!; **vino en taxi** he came by taxi; **~ a** + INFIN: **vinieron a verme al hospital** they came to see me in hospital; **me vienen a recoger en coche** they're coming to pick me up in the car; **¿y todo esto a qué viene?** what's all this in aid of?; **¿a qué vienen tantos llantos?** what's all this crying about?; **¿y ahora a qué vienes?** what do you want now?; **hacer ~ a algn**: **le hicieron ~ desde Londres** they had him come (all the way) from London; **hicieron ~ al médico** they sent for the doctor, they called out the doctor; **~ (a) por algn/algo** to come for sb/sth; **vinieron (a) por el enfermo** they came to pick up the patient, they came for the patient; **han venido (a) por el coche** they've come to pick up the car, they've come for the car; ✦*MODISMO* **~le a algn con**: **no me vengas con historias** don't give me any of your stories

[2] [= volver] **¡enseguida** *o* **ahora vengo!** I'll be right back!*; **cuando vinimos de las vacaciones todo estaba sucio** when we got back from our holiday everything was dirty

[3] [= estar] to be; **la noticia venía en el periódico** the news was in the paper; **viene en la página 47** it's on page 47; **esta palabra no viene en el diccionario** this word isn't in the dictionary; **el texto viene en castellano** the text is (written) in Spanish; **viene en varios colores** it comes in several colours

[4] [= ocurrir] to come; **la guerra y todo lo que vino después** the war and everything that happened *o* came afterwards; **ahora viene lo mejor de la película** this is the best bit in the film, the best bit in the film is coming up now; **lo veía ~** I could see it coming; ✦*MODISMOS* **(estar) a verlas ~** to wait and see what happens; **venga lo que venga** come what may; **~ rodado** to go smoothly; ✦*REFRÁN* **las desgracias nunca vienen solas** it never rains but it pours

[5]
◆ **venir de** (= *provenir*) to come from; **esta palabra viene del árabe** this word comes from the Arabic; **esta especia viene de oriente** this spice comes from the East; **la fortuna le viene de su padre** his fortune comes from his father; **de ahí vienen muchos problemas** it is the cause of many problems; **la honestidad le viene de familia** honesty runs in her family

[6] [= sobrevenir] **de repente le vinieron muchos problemas** a lot of problems suddenly cropped up; **le vino un gran dolor de cabeza** he got a terrible headache; **le vino la idea de salir** he had the idea of going out; **me vinieron ganas de llorar** I felt like crying; ✦*MODISMO* **como te** *o* **le venga en gana** just as you wish

[7] [= quedar] **la falda me viene ancha** the skirt is too loose (for me); **el abrigo te viene algo pequeño** the coat is rather small on *o* for you; **te viene estrecho en la espalda** it's too tight round your shoulders; **este puesto de trabajo me viene grande** *o* **ancho** this job is beyond me, this job is too much for me; **~ bien**: **¿te viene bien el sábado?** is Saturday all right for you?; **hoy no me viene bien** today is not convenient for me; **eso vendrá bien para el invierno** that will come in handy for the winter*; **me vendría bien una copita** I could do with a drink*; **~ mal**: **mañana me viene mal** tomorrow is inconvenient; **no me vendría mal un descanso** I could do with a rest

[8]
◆ **por venir** (= *futuro*) **las generaciones por ~** future generations, generations to come; **lo peor está por ~** the worst is yet *o* still to come
◆ **que viene** (= *próximo*) next; **el mes que viene** next month; **lo estudiaremos el curso que viene** we'll be studying it next year
◆ **venga a** (*con sentido reiterativo*) **yo estoy nerviosísimo y ella venga a mirarme** I'm really nervous and she won't stop staring at me; **yo no tenía dinero y el niño venga a pedir chucherías** I didn't have any money and my boy was always *o* forever asking for little treats; **tenía mucha prisa y los periodistas venga a preguntas** I was in a real hurry and the journalists wouldn't stop asking questions

[9] [como auxiliar] [9·1] **~ a** + INFIN: **el desastre vino a turbar nuestra tranquilidad** the disaster upset our peaceful existence; **viene a llenar un gran vacío** it fills a big gap; **vino a parar** *o* **dar a la cárcel** he ended up in jail; **~ a ser**: **viene a ser 84 en total** it comes to 84 all together; **viene a ser lo mismo** it comes to *o* amounts to the same thing
[9·2] (+ GERUND) **eso lo vengo diciendo desde hace tiempo** that's what I've been saying all along
[9·3] (+ PARTICIPIO) **vengo cansado** I'm tired; **venía hecho polvo*** he was shattered*

[10]
◆ **¡venga!** (*Esp**) **¡venga, vámonos!** come on, let's go!; **¡venga, una canción!** let's have a song!; **préstame cinco euros, venga** go on, lend me five euros; **—¿quieres que lo hagamos juntos? —¡venga!** "shall we do it together?" — "come on, then"; **—¡hasta luego! —¡venga!** "see you later!" — "O.K.!" *o* "right!"; **¡venga ya, no seas pesado!** come on, don't be such a bore!; **—me ha tocado la lotería —¡venga ya!** "I've won the lottery" — "you're kidding!*"

Ⓑ **venirse** VERBO PRONOMINAL

[1] [= llegar] to come; **el niño se vino solo**

➤ LENGUA Y USO: venir A7 31

the child came here all on his own
[2] [= volver] to come back; **se vino de la fiesta porque estaba aburrido** he came back from the party because he was bored
[3] [= fermentar] [*vino*] to ferment; [*masa*] to prove
[4] [= convenirse] **lo que se ha venido en llamar ...** what we have come to call ...
[5] [CAm**: sexualmente] to come**

VENIR

Aunque **venir** y **come** generalmente dan una idea de movimiento en dirección al hablante, e **ir** y **go** implican que hay un movimiento en dirección opuesta al hablante, tenemos que distinguir algunos casos en los que hay diferencias entre los dos idiomas.

• En español no solemos describir el movimiento de una acción desde el punto de vista de la otra persona, mientras que en inglés sí. Por ejemplo, si alguien nos llama, respondemos:

Ya voy
I'm coming

• Si estamos organizando algo por teléfono, por carta, o en una conversación:

Iré a recogerte a las cuatro
I'll come and pick you up at four
¿Voy contigo?
Shall I come with you?

• Por lo tanto, tenemos que traducir **ir** por **come** cuando, si vamos a algún sitio, nos unimos a alguien o a un grupo que va o ya está en ese sitio.

Para otros usos y ejemplos ver la entrada.

venoso ADJ [1] [*sangre*] venous
[2] [*hoja*] veined, ribbed

venpermutar ▸conjug 1a◂ VT (*Col*) to offer for sale or exchange

venta SF [1] (*Com*) sale; **han prohibido la ~ de armas** the sale of arms has been banned; **a la ~** on sale; **estar a la ~** to be on sale; **poner algo a la ~** to put sth on *o* up for sale; **salir a la ~** to go on sale; **de ~: de ~ únicamente en farmacias** available only at chemists'; **en ~: estar en ~** to be (up) for sale, be on the market; **"en venta"** "on sale" ► **venta a domicilio** door-to-door selling ► **venta al contado** cash sale ► **venta al detalle** retail ► **venta al por mayor** wholesale ► **venta al por menor** retail ► **venta a plazos** hire purchase, installment plan (*EEUU*) ► **venta callejera** peddling, hawking ► **venta de liquidación** clearance sale ► **venta directa** direct selling ► **venta piramidal** pyramid selling ► **venta por balance** stocktaking sale ► **venta por catálogo** mail-order selling ► **venta por correo** mail-order selling ► **venta por cuotas** hire purchase, installment plan (*EEUU*) ► **venta por inercia** inertia selling ► **venta posbalance** stocktaking sale ► **venta pública** public sale, auction ► **ventas a término** forward sales ► **ventas brutas** gross sales ► **ventas de exportación** export sales ► **ventas por teléfono** telephone sales
[2] (†) (= *posada*) country inn
[3] (*Caribe, Méx*) (= *tienda*) small shop, stall; (*Cono Sur*) [*de feria, exposición*] stall, booth

ventada SF gust of wind

ventaja SF [1] (= *beneficio*) advantage; **tiene la ~ de que está cerca de casa** it has the advantage of being close to home; **es un plan que tiene muchas ~s** it is a plan that has many advantages; **llevar ~ a algn** to have the advantage over sb, be ahead of sb, be one up on sb; **la ~ que A le lleva a B es grande** A has a big advantage over B; **sacar ~ de algo** (= *aprovechar*) to derive profit from sth; (*pey*) to use sth to one's own advantage
[2] (*Dep*) (*en carrera*) start, advantage; (*Tenis*) advantage; (*en las apuestas*) odds *pl*; **me dio una ~ de cuatro metros ◊ me dio cuatro metros de ~** he gave me a four metre start; **me dio una ~ de 20 puntos** he gave me an advantage of 20 points; **llevar ~** (*en carrera*) to be leading *o* ahead; **llevaba una ~ de varios segundos sobre su rival** he was several seconds ahead of his rival; **llevan una ~ de 1-0** they are 1-0 up *o* ahead
[3] **ventajas** (*en empleo*) extras, perks* ► **ventajas supletorias** fringe benefits

ventajear ▸conjug 1a◂ VT (*Andes, CAm*) [1] (= *rebasar*) to outstrip, surpass; (= *llevar ventaja a*) to get the advantage of
[2] (= *mejorar*) to better, improve on
[3] (= *preferir*) to prefer, give preference to
[4] **~ a algn** (*pey*) to beat sb to it, get the jump on sb*

ventajero/a ADJ, SM/F (*LAm*) = **ventajista**

ventajismo SM [1] (= *oportunismo*) opportunism
[2] (*LAm*) cheek*, nerve*

ventajista Ⓐ ADJ (= *poco escrupuloso*) unscrupulous; (= *egoísta*) self-seeking, grasping; (= *taimado*) sly, treacherous
Ⓑ SMF (= *oportunista*) opportunist

ventajosamente ADV (*gen*) advantageously; (*Fin*) profitably; **estar ~ colocado** to be well placed

ventajoso ADJ [1] (*gen*) advantageous; (*Fin*) profitable
[2] (*LAm*) = **ventajista A**

ventana SF [1] (*Constr*) window; **doble ~** double-glazed window; **tirar algo por la ~** (*lit*) to throw sth out of the window; (*fig*) to throw sth away, fail to make any use of sth ► **ventana aislante** double-glazed window ► **ventana de guillotina** sash window ► **ventana salediza** bay window ► **ventana vidriera** picture window ► **ventanas dobles** double glazing *sing*
[2] [*de nariz*] nostril
[3] (*Inform*) window ► **ventana emergente** (*Inform*) pop-up (window)
[4] (*Andes*) (= *claro de bosque*) forest clearing, glade

ventanaje SM windows *pl*

ventanal SM large window

ventanear ▸conjug 1a◂ VI to be always at the window, be forever peeping out

ventanilla SF [1] [*de vehículo*] window; **si tienes calor baja la ~** open the window if you're hot
[2] (*en cine, teatro*) box office; (*en oficina*) window; **recoja sus entradas en la ~** pick your tickets up at the box office; **para abonar en cuenta pase por ~** please make deposits at the cash desk; **me tuvieron todo el día de ~ en ~** they gave me the runaround all day*; **programa de ~ única** *programme to simplify bureaucratic procedures*
[3] [*de sobre*] window
[4] (*Anat*) (*tb* **~ de la nariz**) nostril

ventanillero/a SM/F counter-clerk

ventanillo SM (= *ventana*) small window; (= *mirilla*) peephole

ventarrón SM (= *viento*) gale, strong wind; (= *ráfaga*) blast

ventear ▸conjug 1a◂ Ⓐ VT [1] [*perro*] to sniff
[2] [+ *ropa*] (= *airear*) to air; (= *secar*) to put out to dry
[3] (*LAm*) [+ *animal*] to brand
[4] (*LAm*) (= *abanicar*) to fan
[5] (*Cono Sur*) [+ *adversario*] to get far ahead of, leave far behind
[6] (*LAm Agr*) to winnow
Ⓑ VI (= *curiosear*) to snoop, pry; (= *investigar*) to inquire, investigate
Ⓒ **ventearse** VPR [1] (= *henderse*) to split, crack; (= *ampollarse*) to blister; (= *secarse*) to get too dry, spoil
[2] (= *ventosear*) to break wind
[3] (*Andes, Caribe, Cono Sur*) (= *estar mucho fuera*) to be outdoors a great deal
[4] (*Andes, Caribe*) (= *engreírse*) to get conceited

ventero/a SM/F innkeeper

ventilación SF [1] [*de habitación, edificio*] ventilation; (= *abertura*) opening for ventilation; **sin ~** unventilated ► **ventilación mecánica** artificial respiration
[2] (= *corriente*) draught, draft (*EEUU*)
[3] [*de problema, asunto*] airing

ventilado ADJ draughty, drafty (*EEUU*), breezy

ventilador SM [1] (*gen, de coche*) fan
[2] (= *abertura*) air vent, ventilator
[3] (*Med*) ventilator

ventilar ▸conjug 1a◂ Ⓐ VT [1] (= *airear*) [+ *cuarto*] to air, ventilate; [+ *ropa*] to air
[2] (*) (= *resolver*) to sort (out)*; **han ventilado el problema en dos horas** they sorted (out) the problem in two hours*
[3] (= *hacer público*) [+ *intimidades, secreto*] to air; **ha estado ventilando los detalles íntimos de su relación** he's been airing the intimate details of their relationship
Ⓑ **ventilarse** VPR [1] (= *airearse*) [*ropa*] to air; **abre la ventana para que se ventile la habitación** open the window to air *o* ventilate the room
[2] (*frm*) (= *tomar aire*) [*persona*] to get some (fresh) air
[3] (*) [+ *comida, bebida, trabajo*] to polish off*; **se ventiló la botella de whisky en un día** he polished off the bottle of whisky in one day*
[4] (*) (= *matar*) **~se a algn** to do sb in*
[5] (*Esp***) **~se a algn** (= *copular con*) to shag sb**, screw sb**

ventisca SF blizzard, snowstorm

ventiscar ▸conjug 1g◂ VI, **ventisquear** ▸conjug 1a◂ VI (= *nevar*) to blow a blizzard, snow with a strong wind; [*nieve*] to drift

ventisquero SM [1] (= *tormenta*) blizzard, snowstorm
[2] (= *montículo*) snowdrift; (= *barranco*) *gully/slope where the snow lies*

vento: SM (*Cono Sur*) dough‡

ventolada SF (*LAm*) strong wind, gale

ventolera SF [1] (= *ráfaga*) gust of wind, blast
[2] (= *juguete*) windmill
[3] (*) (= *capricho*) whim, wild idea; **le dio la**

~ de comprarlo he had a sudden notion to buy it
4 (= *vanidad*) vanity, conceit; (= *satisfacción*) smugness; (= *arrogancia*) arrogance; (= *jactancia*) boastfulness; **tiene mucha ~** she's terribly big-headed*

ventolina SF 1 (*LAm*) (= *ráfaga*) sudden gust of wind
2 (*Náut*) light wind

ventorrillo SM 1 (= *taberna*) small inn, roadhouse
2 (*Caribe, Méx*) (= *tienda*) small shop

ventosa SF 1 (= *agujero*) vent, air hole
2 (*Zool*) sucker
3 (*Med*) cupping glass
4 (*Téc*) suction pad

ventosear ▸conjug 1a◂ VI to break wind

ventosidad SF wind, flatulence (*frm*)

ventoso Ⓐ ADJ 1 (*Meteo*) windy
2 (= *flatulento*) windy, flatulent (*frm*)
Ⓑ SM (*Esp*‡) (= *ladrón*) burglar

ventral ADJ ventral

ventregada SF brood, litter

ventrículo SM ventricle

ventrílocuo/a SM/F ventriloquist

ventriloquia SF ventriloquism

ventrudo ADJ potbellied

ventura SF 1 (= *dicha*) happiness
2 (= *suerte*) luck, (good) fortune; (= *casualidad*) chance; **mala ~** bad luck; **por su mala ~** as bad luck would have it; **por ~** (*frm*) (= *por suerte*) fortunately; (= *por casualidad*) by (any) chance; **¿piensas ir, por ~?** are you by any chance thinking of going?; **echar la buena ~ a algn** to tell sb's fortune; **probar ~** to try one's luck; **~ te dé Dios** I wish you luck; ✦*MODISMO* **a la ~** at random; **ir a la ~** to go haphazardly, go without a fixed plan; **vivir a la ~** to live in a disorganized way; **todo lo hace a la ~** he does it all in a hit-or-miss fashion; ✦*REFRÁN* **viene la ~ a quien la procura** God helps those who help themselves

venturero ADJ (*Méx*) 1 [*cosecha*] out of season
2 [*trabajo*] temporary, casual

venturoso ADJ 1 (= *afortunado*) lucky, fortunate; (= *exitoso*) successful
2 (= *dichoso*) happy

Venus Ⓐ SF (*Mit*) Venus
Ⓑ SM (*Astron*) Venus

venus SF (= *mujer*) goddess

venusiano/a ADJ, SM/F Venusian

veo-veo SM (= *juego*) I spy (with my little eye)

ver

▸conjug 2u◂
A VERBO TRANSITIVO
B VERBO INTRANSITIVO
C VERBO PRONOMINAL
D SUSTANTIVO MASCULINO
*Para las expresiones **ver visiones, no ver tres en un burro**, ver el sustantivo.*

Ⓐ VERBO TRANSITIVO
1 *= percibir* 1·1 [+ *persona, objeto*] to see; **te vi en el parque** I saw you in the park; **desde aquí lo ~ás mejor** you can see it better from here; **lo he visto con mis propios ojos** I saw it with my own eyes; **me acuerdo como si lo estuviera viendo** I remember it as if I were seeing it now, I remember it as if it were yesterday; **¡vieran qué casa!** (*Méx*) ◊ **¡hubieran visto qué casa!** (*Méx*) you should have seen the house!; **dejarse ~: este año Pedro no se ha dejado ~ por aquí** we haven't seen much of Pedro this year; ✦*MODISMOS* **no veo ni jota** I can't see a thing; **si te he visto no me acuerdo: le pedí que me ayudara, pero si te he visto no me acuerdo** I asked him to help me but he (just) didn't want to know; **~ algn/algo venir: —¿que ha dimitido? —eso ya lo veía venir** "he's resigned?" — "well, you could see it coming"; **ya te veo venir, ¿a que quieres que te preste el coche?** I know what you're after, you want to borrow the car, don't you?
1·2 (+ *GERUND*) **los vi paseando por el parque** I saw them walking in the park
1·3 + *INFIN* **la vi bajar la escalera** I saw her come downstairs; **eso lo he visto hacer aquí muchas veces** I have often seen that done here
1·4 (+ *ADJ*) **te veo muy triste** you look very sad; **esta casa la veo pequeña para tanta gente** I think this house is too small for so many people
2 *= mirar* [+ *televisión, programa, partido*] to watch; **anoche vi una película en la tele** I saw *o* watched a film on TV last night; **es (digno) de ~** it's worth seeing; ✦*MODISMO* **no poder (ni) ~ a algn: no lo puedo (ni) ~** I can't stand him
3 *en saludos* **¡cuánto tiempo sin ~te!** I haven't seen you for ages!; **¡hasta más ~!** see you again!
4 *= visitar* to see; **ayer fui a ~ a tu hermano** I went to see your brother yesterday; **tendré que ir a ~ al abogado** I shall have to go to *o* and see my solicitor; **el médico todavía no la ha visto** the doctor hasn't seen her yet
5 *= imaginar* to see, imagine; **lo estoy viendo de almirante** I can just see *o* imagine him as an admiral
6 *= vivir* to live through; **yo he visto dos guerras mundiales** I have lived through two world wars; ✦*MODISMOS* **y usted que lo vea** ◊ **y tú que lo veas: —¡a celebrarlo con salud el año próximo! — ¡y usted que lo vea!** "many happy returns!" — "thank you!"
7 *= examinar* to look at; **este tema lo ~emos en la próxima clase** we'll be looking at this subject in the next lesson
8 *= comprobar* to see; **¡~ás como al final te caerás!** you'll fall, you just wait and see!; **ya ~ás como al final tengo que hacerlo yo** I'll end up doing it myself, you'll see; **habrá que ~: habrá que ~ lo que les habrá contado** we'll have to see what he's told them; **voy a ~ si está en su despacho** I'll see if he's in his office
9 *= notar* to see; **no veo la diferencia entre uno y otro** I can't see the difference between them; **ya veo que tendré que hacerlo yo solo** I can see I'll have to do it myself; **—¿ves que no son iguales? —pues, no lo veo** "can't you see they're not the same?" — "no, I can't"; **—gana más de cien mil al mes —¡ya ves!** "she earns more than 100,000 a month" — "well, there you go!"; **dejarse ~: los efectos de la crisis se dejaron ~ meses después** the effects of the crisis were felt months later; **la preocupación se dejaba ~ en su cara** the worry showed in his face; **echar de ~ algo** to notice sth; **por lo que veo** from what I can see
10 *= entender* to see; **ahora veo la importancia del problema** I see how serious the problem is now; **¿no ves que ...?** don't *o* can't you see that ...?; **no veo muy claro para qué lo quiere** I can't really see what he wants it for; **hacer ~ algo a algn** to point sth out to sb
11 *= encontrar* to see; **no veo nada en contra de eso** I see nothing against it; **no le veo solución al conflicto** I can't see a solution to the conflict **yo este tema no lo veo así** I don't see this issue that way
12 *Jur* [*pleito*] to hear, try; **el proceso se ~á en mayo** the case will be heard in May
13
◆ **tener que ver: —es demasiado pequeño —¿y eso qué tiene que ~?** "it's too small" — "what's that got to do with it?"; **esto tiene que ~ con lo que estudiamos ayer** this has to do with what we were looking at yesterday; **yo no tuve nada que ~ en la venta del terreno** I had nothing to do with the sale of the land
14
◆ **a ver: a ~ niños, ¿cuál es la capital de Francia?** now, children, what is the capital of France?; **—mira, tú sales en la foto —¿a ~?** "look, you're in the photo" — "let's have a look" *o* "let's see"; **a ~ ese niño, que no se quede solo** don't leave that child on his own; **a ~ qué dicen las noticias sobre el robo** let's see if there's anything about the robbery on the news; **a ~ qué está pasando** let's see what's happening; **—estás estudiando mucho —¡a ~, no queda más remedio!** "you're doing a lot of studying" — "well, I haven't got much choice!"; **¡a ~, cállate ya!** shut up, will you!; **¿a ~?** (*Andes Telec*) hello?; **a ~ si ...: a ~ si acabas pronto** see if you can finish this off quickly; **¡a ~ si te crees que no lo sé!** surely you don't think I don't know about it!

Ⓑ VERBO INTRANSITIVO
1 *= percibir* to see; **no veo muy bien con el ojo derecho** I can't see very well with my right eye; **como vimos ayer en la conferencia** as we saw in the lecture yesterday; **como ~emos más adelante** as we shall see later; **eso está por ~** that remains to be seen; ✦*MODISMOS* **que no veo***: **tengo un hambre que no veo** I'm famished!; **que no veas***: **hay un ruido que no veas** there's a hell of a racket!*; **un coche que no veas** an amazing car; **~ y callar: no digas nada, tú sólo ~ y callar** you'd better keep your mouth shut about this; **~ para creer** seeing is believing
2 *= comprobar* to see; **según voy viendo...** as I am beginning to see...; **—¿quién ha venido? —no sé, voy a ~** "who is it?" —"I don't know, I'll go and see"; **—al final siempre me toca hacerlo a mi —ya veo** "in the end it's always me that has to do it" — "so I see"
3 *= entender* to see; **¿ves?, así es mucho más fácil** you see? it's much easier like this; **a mi modo de ~** as I see it, the way I see it; **¿viste?** (*Cono Sur*) right?, are you with me?
4 **~ de hacer algo** to see about doing sth, try to do sth; **tenemos que ~ de solucionar este problema** we must try to *o* and find a solution to this problem; **~emos de salir temprano** we'll see if we can leave early, we'll try to *o* and leave early

5 *otras locuciones* **¡hay que ~!**: **¡hay que ~ lo que te pareces a tu madre!** gosh! how like your mother you are *o* look!; **¡hay que ~ lo que ha cambiado la ciudad!** it's incredible *o* you wouldn't believe how much the town has changed!; **¡para que veas!**: **ha aprobado todo las asignaturas, ¡para que veas!** she passed all her exams, how about that!; **no sólo no perdí, sino que arrasé, ¡para que veas!** not only did I not lose, but I won by a mile, so there!; **lo dijo por ~** (*Caribe*) ◊ **lo dijo de por ~** (*Cono Sur*) he was just trying it on*; **quedar en ~emos** (*LAm*): **todo quedó en ~emos** it was all left in the air; **eso está** *o* **queda en ~emos** it's not certain yet; **vamos a ~** let's see …, let me see …; **—¿esto tiene arreglo? —no sé, vamos a ~** "can this be repaired?" — "I don't know, let's see *o* let me see"; **¿por qué no me llamaste, vamos a ~?** why didn't you call me, I'd like to know?; **ya veremos** we'll see; **—¿podré ir a la fiesta? —ya ~emos** "can I go to the party?" — "we'll see"

Ⓒ **verse** VERBO PRONOMINAL

1 *reflexivo* to see o.s.; **no quiere ~se en el espejo** she doesn't want to see herself in the mirror; **se vio reflejado en el espejo** he saw his reflection in the mirror

2 *recíproco* (= *saludarse, visitarse*) to see each other; (= *citarse*) to meet; **ahora apenas nos vemos** we hardly see (anything of) each other nowadays; **¡luego nos vemos!** see you later!; **¡nos estamos viendo!** (*LAm*) see you (later)!; **quedamos en ~nos en la estación** we arranged to meet at the station; **~se con algn** to see sb

3 *= percibirse* **desde aquí no se ve** you can't see it from here; **se le veía mucho en el parque** he was often to be seen in the park; **se le veían las bragas** you could see her knickers; **no se ha visto un lío parecido** you never saw such a mess; **¿cuándo se vio nada igual?** have you ever seen anything like it!; **es digno de ~se** it's worth seeing; **¡habráse visto!*** of all the cheek!*, well I like that!; **eso ya se ~á** that remains to be seen

4 *= mirar* **véase la página 9** see page 9

5 *= notarse* **—ahora estoy muy feliz —ya se ve** "I'm very happy now" — "I can see that"; **se ve que no tiene idea de informática** he obviously hasn't got a clue about computers; **se ve que sí** so it seems; **¡qué se vean los forzudos!** let's see how tough you are!

6 *= imaginarse* to see o.s., imagine o.s.; **yo ya me veía en la cárcel** I could see myself going to jail

7 *LAm* = parecer* to look; **te ves divina** you look wonderful; **te ves cansado** you look tired; **te vas a ~ precioso así** you'll look lovely like that

8 *= estar, encontrarse* to find o.s., be; **~se en un apuro** to find o.s. *o* be in a jam*; **se veía en la cumbre de la fama** he was at the height of his fame

9

◆ **vérselas**: **me las vi y me las deseé para hacerlo*** it was a real sweat to get it done*, it was a tough job to get it done*; **vérselas con algn**: **tendrá que vérselas con mi abogado** he'll have my solicitor to deal with

Ⓓ SUSTANTIVO MASCULINO

1 *= aspecto* **de buen ~** good-looking; **tener buen ~** to be good-looking

2 *= opinión* **a mi ~** as I see it, the way I see it

➤ LENGUA Y USO: **verdad 1** 38.1 **2** 45.1

vera SF (*gen*) edge, verge, berm (*EEUU*); [*de río*] bank; **a la ~ de** (*poét*) near, next to; **a la ~ del camino** beside the road, at the roadside; **se sentó a mi ~** he sat down beside me

veracidad SF truthfulness, veracity (*frm*)

veracruzano/a Ⓐ ADJ of/from Veracruz
Ⓑ SM/F native/inhabitant of Veracruz; **los ~s** the people of Veracruz

veragua SF (*CAm*) mildew (*on cloth*)

veranda SF veranda(h)

veraneante SMF holidaymaker, (summer) vacationer (*EEUU*)

veranear ▸conjug 1a◂ VI to spend the summer (holiday), spend the summer vacation (*EEUU*), holiday; **veranean en Jaca** they go to Jaca for the summer; **es un buen sitio para ~** it's a nice place for a summer holiday

veraneo SM summer holiday, summer vacation (*EEUU*); **lugar de ~** summer resort, holiday resort; **estar de ~** to be away on (one's summer) holiday; **ir de ~ a la montaña** to go off to spend one's summer holidays in the mountains

veraniego ADJ 1 (= *del verano*) summer *antes de s*
2 (*fig*) trivial

veranillo SM 1 ► **veranillo de San Martín** (*en noviembre*) Indian summer ► **veranillo de San Miguel** (*en septiembre*) Indian summer
2 (*CAm*) dry spell (*in the rainy season*) ► **veranillo de San Juan** (*Cono Sur*) (*en junio*) ≈ Indian summer

verano SM 1 (= *estación calurosa*) summer
2 (*en regiones equatoriales*) dry season

veranoso ADJ (*LAm*) dry

veras SFPL 1 (= *cosas serias*) serious things; **entre burlas y ~** half jokingly
2 **de ~** (= *de verdad*) really, truly; (= *sinceramente*) sincerely; (= *con empeño*) in earnest; **¿de ~?** really?, is that so?; **lo siento de ~** I am truly sorry; **esto va de ~** this is serious; **ahora va de ~ que lo hago** now I really am going to do it; **ahora me duele de ~** now it really does hurt; **esta vez va de ~** this time it's the real thing*

veraz ADJ truthful

verbal ADJ (*gen*) verbal; [*mensaje*] oral

verbalizar ▸conjug 1f◂ VT to verbalize, express

verbalmente ADV [*acordar*] verbally; [*comunicar*] orally

verbena SF 1 (= *fiesta*) fair; [*de santo*] *open-air celebration on the eve of a saint's day*; (= *baile*) open-air dance
2 (*Bot*) verbena

verbenero ADJ of *o* relating to a *verbena*; **persona verbenera** party animal*; **alegría verbenera** fun of the fair; **música verbenera** fairground music

verbigracia ADV for example, e.g.

verbo SM 1 (*Ling*) verb ► **verbo activo** active verb ► **verbo auxiliar** auxiliary verb ► **verbo defectivo** defective verb ► **verbo deponente** deponent verb ► **verbo finito** finite verb ► **verbo intransitivo**, **verbo neutro** intransitive verb ► **verbo reflexivo** reflexive verb ► **verbo transitivo** transitive verb
2 (*Literat*) language, diction; **de ~ elegante** elegant in style
3 (= *juramento*) curse, oath; **echar ~s** to swear, curse
4 **el Verbo** (*Rel*) the Word

verborrea SF, **verborragia** SF verbosity, verbal diarrhoea *o* (*EEUU*) diarrhea*

verborreico ADJ verbose, wordy

verbosidad SF verbosity, wordiness

verboso ADJ verbose, wordy

▼**verdad** SF 1 (= *veracidad*) truth; **la pura ~** the plain truth; **no pudo esclarecer la ~ de los hechos** he couldn't establish the truth about what happened; **hay una parte de ~ en todo esto** there is some truth *o* an element of truth in all this; **nadie está en posesión de la ~** no one has an exclusive right to the truth; **decir la ~** to tell the truth; **a decir ~** ◊ **si te digo la ~** to be honest, to tell you the truth; **la ~ sea dicha** if (the) truth be known; **en ~** to be honest, really; **en ~ no sé qué contestarte** to be honest I don't know what to say to you, I really don't know what to say to you; **en ~ os digo que seréis recompensados** (*Biblia*) verily I say unto you, you shall be rewarded; **faltar a la ~** to be untruthful, be economical with the truth (*euf*); **en honor a la ~** to be perfectly honest, in all honesty; ✦*MODISMO* **ir con la ~ por delante** to be completely open about things; *ver tb* **hora 2.2**
2 **de ~** (*como adj*) real; (*como adv*) really; **¿son de ~ estas balas?** are those real bullets?; **ése sí que es un torero de ~** he's what I call a real bullfighter; **—mañana vendré a ayudarte —¿de ~?** "I'll come and help you tomorrow" — "really?" *o* "will you?"; **la quiero de ~** I really love her; **esta vez me voy a enfadar de ~** this time I really am going to get angry; **de ~ que no me importa ir** I really don't mind going, I don't mind going, honestly *o* really
3 **es ~** it's true; **eso no es ~** that's not true; **¿es ~ que a Diego le ha tocado la lotería?** is it true that Diego has won the lottery?; **bien es ~ que** of course; **bien es ~ que es aún pronto para juzgar los resultados** of course, it's too soon to make any judgement about the results; **si bien es ~ que** although, even though; **si bien es ~ que llevamos poco tiempo aquí, ya puedo decir que …** although *o* even though we haven't been here long, I can already say that …
4 (*) (*para enfatizar*) **pues la ~, no sé** to be honest I don't know, I don't really know; **la ~ es que no me gusta mucho** to be honest I don't like it much, I don't really like it much
5 (*para corroborar algo*) **estás cansado ¿verdad?** *o* **¿no es ~?** you're tired, aren't you?; **hace frío ¿verdad?** *o* **¿no es ~?** it's cold, isn't it?; **no os gustó ¿verdad?** you didn't like it, did you?; **¿~ que sí fuimos?** we went, didn't we?, we did go, didn't we?; **¿~ que has sido tú?** it was you, wasn't it?
6 (= *afirmación verdadera*) truth; **no me gustan las ~es a medias** I don't like half-truths; **lo que acabas de decir es una gran ~** you couldn't have spoken a truer word; **~ científica** scientific truth; **~ objetiva** objective truth; ✦*MODISMOS* **ser una ~ de Perogrullo** to be patently obvious; **ser una ~ como un puño*** to be the bitter *o* painful truth; **ser una ~ como un templo** to be the

plain truth; **las ~es del barquero** the plain truths, the simple truths; **decirle cuatro ~es a algn** to give sb a piece of one's mind*

verdaderamente ADV [1] (= *de verdad*) really; **es ~ una pena** it really is a shame
[2] (*con adjetivo*) really, truly; **es ~ triste** it's really *o* truly sad; **un hombre ~ bueno** a really *o* truly good man
[3] (*para confirmar*) indeed; **y ~, el sitio no es nada especial** and indeed, the place is nothing special

verdadero ADJ [1] (= *auténtico*) [*caso, joya, motivo, nombre*] real; [*historia, versión*] true; [*testimonio*] truthful; **no creo que sea ésa la verdadera razón** I don't think that's the real reason; **¿cuál es tu ~ nombre?** what's your real name?; **es un ~ amigo** he's a true friend
[2] (*para enfatizar*) real; **es un ~ héroe** he's a real hero; **fue un ~ desastre** it was a real *o* (*frm*) veritable disaster; **es el ~ retrato de su madre** he's the spitting image of his mother
[3] (= *sincero*) [*persona*] truthful

verde (A) ADJ [1] (*color*) green; ✦*MODISMOS* **estar ~ de envidia** to be green with envy; **poner ~ a algn*** to run sb down*, slag sb off‡; **siempre ponen ~ al jefe** they're always running down* *o* slagging off‡ the boss; **me llamó y me puso ~ por no haberla ayudado** she called me and gave me a piece of her mind for not helping her*
[2] [*árbol, planta*] green; [*fruta, verdura*] green, unripe; [*legumbres*] green; [*madera*] unseasoned
[3] [*zona, espacio*] green; **faltan zonas ~s en esta ciudad** there are not enough green spaces in this city
[4] (*) [*plan, proyecto*] **el proyecto está muy ~** the project is at a very early stage
[5] (*) (= *sin experiencia*) green*; **está muy ~*** he's very green*, he doesn't know a thing
[6] (*) [*chiste, canción*] smutty*, blue*, dirty; **viejo ~** dirty old man*
[7] (*Pol*) Green
(B) SM [1] (= *color*) green ► **verde botella** bottle green ► **verde esmeralda** emerald green ► **verde lima** lime green ► **verde manzana** apple green ► **verde oliva** olive green ► **verde pistacho** pistachio green
[2] (= *hierba*) grass; (= *follaje*) foliage, greenery; (= *forraje*) green fodder; **sentarse en el ~** to sit on the grass; **segar la hierba en ~** to cut the grass while it is still green
[3] (*) (= *billete*) [*de mil pesetas*] 1,000-peseta note; [*de un dólar*] dollar bill, buck (*EEUU**), greenback (*EEUU**)
[4] ✦*MODISMO* **darse un ~ de algo**† to have one's fill of sth
[5] (*Cono Sur*) (= *mate*) maté
[6] (*Cono Sur*) (= *pasto*) grass, pasture
[7] (*Cono Sur*) (= *ensalada*) salad
[8] (*Andes*) (= *plátano*) plantain
[9] (*Caribe, Méx*) (= *campo*) country, countryside
[10] (*Caribe**) (= *policía*) cop*
(C) SMF (*Pol*) Green; **los Verdes** the Greens, the Green Party

verdear ▸conjug 1a◂ VI [1] (= *tener color*) to look green; (= *tirar a verde*) to be greenish
[2] (= *volverse verde*) to go green, turn green
[3] (*Cono Sur*) (= *beber mate*) to drink maté
[4] (*Cono Sur Agr*) to graze

verdecer ▸conjug 2d◂ VI [*objeto*] to turn green, grow green; [*persona*] to go green

verdegay ADJ, SM light green

verdemar ADJ, SM sea-green

verde-oliva ADJ INV olive green

verderón SM [1] (*Orn*) greenfinch
[2] (*Esp*‡) 1,000-peseta note

verdete SM verdigris

verdiazul ADJ greenish-blue

verdiblanco ADJ light green

verdín SM [1] (= *color*) fresh green
[2] (*Bot*) (= *verdete*) verdigris; (= *capa*) scum; (= *musgo*) moss
[3] (*en la ropa*) green stain

verdinegro ADJ dark green

verdino ADJ bright green

verdirrojo ADJ green and red

verdolaga SF **crecer como la ~** (*CAm*) to spread like wildfire

verdón (A) ADJ (*Cono Sur*) [1] (= *verdino*) bright green
[2] [*fruta*] slow to ripen
(B) SM [1] (*Orn*) = **verderón 1**
[2] (*Cono Sur*) (= *cardenal*) bruise, welt

verdor SM [1] (= *color*) greenness
[2] (*Bot*) verdure
[3] (†) (= *juventud*) youth

verdoso ADJ greenish

verdugo SM [1] (= *ejecutor*) executioner; (*en la horca*) hangman
[2] (= *tirano*) cruel master, tyrant; (= *atormentador*) tormentor
[3] (= *látigo*) lash
[4] (= *tormento*) torment
[5] (= *cardenal*) welt, weal
[6] (*Bot*) shoot
[7] (= *estoque*) rapier
[8] (= *pasamontañas*) balaclava

verdugón SM [1] (= *cardenal*) weal, welt
[2] (*Bot*) twig, shoot, sprout
[3] (*Andes*) (= *rasgón*) rent, rip

verdulera SF (*pey*) fishwife, coarse woman; *ver tb* **verdulero**

verdulería SF greengrocer's (shop)

verdulero/a SM/F greengrocer, vegetable merchant (*EEUU*); *ver tb* **verdulera**

verdura SF [1] (*Culin*) greens *pl*, (green) vegetables *pl*; **sopa de ~(s)** vegetable soup
[2] (= *color*) greenness; (= *follaje*) greenery, verdure (*liter*)
[3] (†) (= *obscenidad*) smuttiness*, scabrous nature

verdusco ADJ dark green, dirty green

vereco* ADJ (*CAm*) cross-eyed

verecundia SF bashfulness, sensitivity, shyness

verecundo ADJ bashful, sensitive, shy

vereda SF [1] (= *senda*) path, lane; ✦*MODISMOS* **entrar en ~** [*persona*] to toe the line; [*elemento*] to fall into place, fit into the normal pattern; **hacer entrar en ~ a algn** ◊ **meter en ~ a algn** to bring sb into line, make sb toe the line; **ir por la ~** to do the right thing, keep to the straight and narrow
[2] (*LAm*) (= *acera*) pavement, sidewalk (*EEUU*)
[3] (*Andes*) (= *pueblo*) village, settlement; (= *zona*) *section of a village*
[4] (*Méx*) (= *raya*) parting, part (*EEUU*)

veredicto SM verdict; **emitir ~** to issue *o* give a verdict ► **veredicto de culpabilidad** verdict of guilty, guilty verdict ► **veredicto de inculpabilidad** verdict of not guilty, not guilty verdict

veredón SM (*Cono Sur*) broad pavement, broad sidewalk (*EEUU*)

verga SF [1] (= *vara*) rod, stick; (*Náut*) yard(arm), spar
[2] (*Zool*) penis; (**) [*de hombre*] prick**, cock**; ✦*MODISMOS* **me vale ~**** I don't give a toss‡; **¡ni ~!**** you must be joking!*, no bloody way !**
[3] (*CAm**) ✦*MODISMOS* **a ~** by hook or by crook; **por la ~ grande** at the back of beyond*

vergajo SM [1] [*de toro*] pizzle; (**) [*de hombre*] prick**, cock**; **dar un ~**** to have a screw**
[2] (= *látigo*) lash, whip
[3] (*Andes**) (= *canalla*) swine*, rat*

vergazo SM **un ~ de** (*CAm**) lots of*, loads of*

vergel SM (*liter*) (= *jardín*) garden, yard (*EEUU*); (= *huerto*) orchard

vergonzante ADJ [1] (= *que tiene vergüenza*) shamefaced; (= *tímido*) bashful; **pobre ~** *poor but too ashamed to beg openly*
[2] (= *que produce vergüenza*) shameful, shaming

vergonzosamente ADV [1] (= *con timidez*) bashfully, shyly; (= *con modestia*) modestly
[2] (= *deshonrosamente*) shamefully, disgracefully

vergonzoso ADJ [1] [*persona*] (= *tímido*) bashful, shy; (= *modesto*) modest
[2] [*acto*] shameful, disgraceful; **es ~ que ...** it is disgraceful that ...
[3] **partes vergonzosas** (*euf*) (*Anat*) private parts

vergüenza SF [1] (= *azoramiento*) embarrassment; **casi me muero de ~** I almost died of embarrassment; **¡qué ~!** how embarrassing!; **me da ~ decírselo** I feel too embarrassed to tell him; **sentir ~ ajena** to feel embarrassed for sb
[2] (= *dignidad*) shame, sense of shame; **si tuviera ~ no lo haría** if he had any (sense of) shame he wouldn't do it; **¡~ debería darte!** you should be ashamed!, shame on you!; **¡vaya manera de tratar a tu abuela, qué ~!** what a way to treat your grandmother, you should be ashamed *o* shame on you!; **¡qué poca ~ tienes!** you've got no shame!, you're utterly shameless; **perder la ~** to lose all sense of shame; **sacar a algn a la ~**†† (*lit*) to make a public display of sb; (*fig*) to hold sb up to shame
[3] (= *escándalo*) disgrace; **el hijo es la ~ de su familia** the son is a disgrace to his family; **es una ~ que esté tan sucio** it's a disgrace *o* it's disgraceful that it should be so dirty
[4] **vergüenzas*** (*euf*) (= *genitales*) privates (*euf*), naughty bits* (*hum*); **con las ~s al aire** fully exposed (*hum*)

vericuetos SMPL [1] (= *terreno escarpado*) rough track *sing*
[2] (= *complejidades*) **los ~ del sistema fiscal** the intricacies of the tax system

verídico ADJ truthful, true

verificabilidad SF verifiability

verificable ADJ verifiable

verificación SF [1] (= *inspección*) inspection, check; (*Mec*) testing; [*de resultados*] verification; [*de testamento*] proving ► **verificación médica** checkup
[2] (= *cumplimiento*) fulfilment, fulfillment (*EEUU*)
[3] [*de profecía*] realization

verificar ▸conjug 1a◂ Ⓐ VT 1 (= *inspeccionar*) to inspect, check; (*Mec*) to test; [+ *resultados*] to check; [+ *hechos*] to verify, establish; [+ *testamento*] to prove
2 (= *realizar*) [+ *inspección*] to carry out; [+ *ceremonia*] to perform; [+ *elección*] to hold
Ⓑ **verificarse** VPR 1 [*acontecimiento*] to occur, happen; [*mitin*] to be held, take place
2 [*profecía*] to come true

verija SF 1 (*Anat*) groin, genital region
2 (*LAm*) [*de caballo*] flank

verijón* ADJ (*Méx*) idle, lazy

veringo ADJ (*Andes*) nude, naked

veringuearse ▸conjug 1a◂ VPR (*Andes*) to undress

verismo SM (= *realismo*) realism, truthfulness; (*Arte, Literat*) verism

verista ADJ (*Arte, Literat*) veristic

verja SF (= *puerta*) iron gate; (= *cerca*) railings *pl*; (= *reja*) grating, grille

vermicida SM vermicide

vermicular ADJ vermicular

vermífugo SM vermifuge

verminoso ADJ infected, wormy

vermú SM (*pl* **vermús** [ber'mu]) = **vermut**

vermut [ber'mu] SM (*pl* **vermuts** [ber'mus]) 1 (= *bebida*) vermouth
2 (*Andes, Cono Sur Cine*) (early evening) cinema matinee

vernáculo ADJ vernacular; **lengua vernácula** vernacular

vernal ADJ (*poét*) vernal (*poét*), spring *antes de s*

Verónica SF Veronica

verónica SF 1 (*Bot*) veronica, speedwell
2 (*Taur*) *a kind of pass with the cape*

verosímil ADJ (= *probable*) likely, probable; (= *creíble*) credible

verosimilitud SF 1 (= *probabilidad*) likelihood, probability; (= *credibilidad*) credibility
2 (*Literat*) verisimilitude

verosímilmente ADV (= *de modo probable*) in a likely way; (= *de modo creíble*) credibly

verraco SM 1 (= *cerdo*) boar, male pig
2 (*Andes*) (= *carnero*) ram
3 (*Caribe*) (= *jabalí*) wild boar

verraquear ▸conjug 1a◂ VI 1 (= *gruñir*) to grunt
2 [*niño*] to wail, howl with rage

verraquera SF 1 (= *enfado*) fit of rage, tantrum; (= *lloro*) crying spell
2 (*Caribe*) (= *borrachera*) drunken spell

verruga SF 1 (*en cara, espalda*) wart; (*en manos, pies*) verruca
2 (*Bot*) wart
3 (= *latoso*) pest, nuisance
4 (*) (= *defecto*) fault

verrugoso ADJ warty, covered in warts

versación SF (*Cono Sur, Méx*) expertise, skill

versada SF (*LAm*) long tedious poem

versado ADJ **~ en** (= *conocedor*) versed in, conversant with; (= *experto*) expert in, skilled in

versal (*Tip*) Ⓐ ADJ capital
Ⓑ SF capital (letter)

versalitas SFPL (*Tip*) small capitals

Versalles SM Versailles

versallesco ADJ 1 (*Arte, Hist*) Versailles *antes de s*
2 [*lenguaje, modales*] extremely refined

versar ▸conjug 1a◂ VI 1 **~ sobre** (= *tratar*) to deal with, be about
2 (= *girar*) to go round, turn
3 (*Caribe*) (= *versificar*) to versify, improvise verses
4 (*Caribe*) (= *charlar*) to chat, talk
5 (*Méx**) (= *guasearse*) to tease, crack jokes

versátil ADJ 1 (= *adaptable*) versatile
2 (*pey*) (= *inconstante*) fickle, changeable
3 (*Anat*) mobile, loose

versatilidad SF 1 (= *adaptabilidad*) versatility
2 (*pey*) (= *inconstancia*) fickleness
3 (*Anat*) mobility, ease of movement

versículo SM verse

versificación SF versification

versificador(a) SM/F versifier

versificar ▸conjug 1g◂ Ⓐ VT to versify, put into verse
Ⓑ VI to write verses, versify

versión SF (*gen*) version; (= *traducción*) translation; (= *adaptación*) adaptation; **película en ~ original** original version; **película en ~ española** Spanish-language version; **~ (de) concierto** concert performance

versionar ▸conjug 1a◂ VT (= *adaptar*) to adapt, make a new version of; (*Mús*) to adapt; (= *grabar*) record a version of; (= *traducir*) to translate

vers.° ABR (*Rel*) (= **versículo**) v

verso SM 1 (= *género*) verse; (= *línea*) line, verse line; (= *poema*) poem; **teatro en ~** verse drama; **en el segundo ~ del poema** in the second line of the poem; **hacer ~s** to write poetry ► **verso libre** free verse ► **verso suelto** blank verse
2 **echar ~** (*Caribe, Méx**) to rabbit on*

versolari SM (*País Vasco, Aragón*) *improviser of verse*

versus PREP versus, against

vértebra SF vertebra

vertebración SF 1 (= *apoyo*) support
2 (= *estructuración*) structuring, essential structure

vertebrado ADJ, SM vertebrate

vertebrador ADJ **fuerza ~a** unifying force, force making for cohesion; **columna ~a** central column; **soporte ~** principal support

vertebral ADJ vertebral; **columna ~** spinal column, spine

vertebrar ▸conjug 1a◂ VT 1 (= *apoyar*) to hold up, support
2 (= *estructurar*) to provide the backbone of, be the essential structure of

vertedero SM 1 [*de basura*] rubbish tip, garbage dump (*EEUU*)
2 = **vertedor**
3 (*Cono Sur*) (= *pendiente*) slope, hillside

vertedor SM 1 (= *desagüe*) drain, outlet; [*de presa*] spillway
2 (*Náut*) scoop, bailer
3 (= *cuchara, pala*) scoop, small shovel

verter ▸conjug 2g◂ Ⓐ VT 1 [+ *contenido*] to pour (out), empty (out); (*sin querer*) to spill, pour; [+ *lágrimas, luz, sangre*] to shed; [+ *basura, residuos*] to dump, tip; **vertió el contenido de la bolsa encima de la mesa** she poured the contents of the bag onto the table; **he vertido el café sobre el mantel** I've spilled my coffee on the tablecloth
2 [+ *recipiente*] (= *vaciar*) to empty (out); (= *invertir*) to tip up; (*sin querer*) to upset
3 (*Ling*) to translate (**a** into)
Ⓑ VI [*río*] to flow, run (**a** into); [*declive*] to fall (**a** towards)

vertical Ⓐ ADJ [*línea, plano*] vertical; [*postura, piano*] upright; **despegue ~** (*Aer*) vertical take-off; **ponlo ~** put it upright
Ⓑ SF 1 (*Téc, Mat*) vertical line, vertical; **descender en ~** to descend vertically; **elevarse en ~** to rise vertically
2 (*Dep*) **hacer la ~** to do a handstand
Ⓒ SM (*Astron*) vertical circle

verticalidad SF (= *posición*) vertical position; (= *dirección*) vertical direction

verticalmente ADJ vertically

vértice SM 1 [*de cono, pirámide*] apex, vertex; [*de ángulo*] vertex ► **vértice geodésico** bench mark, survey point
2 (*Anat*) crown (of the head)

verticilo SM whorl

vertido SM 1 (= *acto*) (*accidental*) spillage; (*deliberado*) dumping; [*de líquido*] pouring; **el ~ de residuos nucleares** the dumping of nuclear waste
2 **vertidos** (= *residuos*) waste *sing*; **~s tóxicos** toxic waste *sing*

vertiente SF 1 [*de montaña, tejado*] slope
2 (= *aspecto*) side, aspect; **sin considerar la ~ ética de la cuestión** without considering the ethical side *o* aspect of the issue; **la ~ humanística del movimiento** the humanistic side of the movement; **el curso tiene una ~ filosófica** the course has a philosophical dimension
3 (*LAm*) (= *manantial*) spring

vertiginosamente ADV 1 (= *de manera vertiginosa*) giddily, dizzily, vertiginously (*frm*)
2 (*fig*) (= *excesivamente*) dizzily, excessively; (= *rápidamente*) very rapidly; **los precios suben ~** prices are rising rapidly, prices are spiralling up

vertiginoso ADJ 1 (= *que causa vértigo*) giddy, dizzy, vertiginous (*frm*)
2 [*velocidad*] dizzy, excessive; [*alza*] very rapid

vértigo SM 1 (*por la altura*) **mirar hacia abajo me da ~** looking down makes me (feel) dizzy; **no subo porque tengo ~** I'm not going up because I'm afraid of heights
2 (*Med*) vertigo; **tiene ~** he suffers from *o* has vertigo; **las pastillas pueden provocar ~(s)** these tablets may cause giddiness
3 (= *frenesí*) frenzy; **el ~ de la vida en la ciudad** the frenzy of city life; **el ~ de los negocios** the frenzied rush of business; **el ~ de los placeres** the whirl of pleasures
4 (*) **de ~: iban a una velocidad de ~** they were going at breakneck speed; **tiene un talento de ~** he has a breathtaking talent; **es de ~ cómo crece la ciudad** it's astonishing how quickly the city is growing

vesania SF rage, fury; (*Med*) insanity

vesánico ADJ raging, furious; (*Med*) insane

vesícula SF (*Anat*) vesicle; (= *ampolla*) blister ► **vesícula biliar** gall-bladder

vespa® SF Vespa®, scooter, motor-scooter

vespertino Ⓐ ADJ evening *antes de s*; **periódico ~** evening paper
Ⓑ SM evening paper

vespino SM small motorcycle

vesre* SM (*Arg*), **vesrre*** SM (*Arg*) back slang

vestal ADJ, SF vestal

veste SF (*liter*) garb (*liter*)

vestíbulo SM [*de casa, hotel*] vestibule (*frm*), lobby, hall; (*Teat*) foyer

vestiditos SMPL baby clothes

vestido Ⓐ ADJ dressed; **era la mejor vestida de la fiesta** she was the best dressed woman at the party; **me gusta ir bien ~** I like to be well-dressed; **¿cómo iba vestida la novia?** what was the bride wearing?; **~ con algo** wearing sth, dressed in sth; **va ~ con un traje azul** he's wearing a blue suit, he's dressed in a blue suit; **~ de algo** wearing sth, dressed in sth; **siempre va ~ de negro** he always wears black; **mi mayor ilusión es verte vestida de blanco** my greatest wish is to see you all in white; **¡en marzo y ya vas vestida de verano!** it's only March and you're wearing summer clothes already!
Ⓑ SM 1 (= *prenda*) [*de mujer*] dress; (*Col*) [*de hombre*] suit ► **vestido de debajo**† undergarment (*frm*) ► **vestido de encima**† outer garment (*frm*) ► **vestido de fiesta** party dress ► **vestido de noche** evening dress ► **vestido de novia** wedding dress, bridal gown ► **vestido isotérmico** wet suit
2 (= *vestimenta*) clothes *pl*; **la historia del ~** the history of costume

vestidor SM dressing room

vestidura SF 1 (*liter*) clothing, apparel
2 **vestiduras** (= *ropa*) clothes; ✦*MODISMO* **rasgarse las ~s** to tear one's hair
3 **vestiduras** (*Rel*) vestments ► **vestiduras sacerdotales** priestly vestments

vestigial ADJ vestigial

vestigio SM 1 (= *señal*) trace, vestige; **no quedaba el menor ~ de ello** there was not the slightest trace of it
2 **vestigios** (= *ruinas*) remains, relics

vestimenta SF 1 (= *ropa*) clothing; (*pey*) gear‡, stuff*
2 **vestimentas** (*Rel*) vestments

vestir ▸conjug 3k◂ Ⓐ VT 1 (= *poner la ropa a*) [+ *niño , muñeca*] to dress; **su madre la vistió de novia** her mother helped her dress for the wedding; ✦*REFRÁN* **vísteme despacio, que tengo prisa** more haste less speed; *ver tb* **santo B2**
2 (= *disfrazar*) to dress up; **¿de qué lo vas a ~?** what are you going to dress him up as?
3 (= *hacer la ropa a*) **lo viste un buen sastre** he has his clothes made at a good tailor's; **la modista que la viste cobra muy barato** the dressmaker who makes her clothes is very cheap
4 (= *proporcionar la ropa*) [*persona*] to clothe; [*institución, Estado*] to pay for one's clothing; **tengo una familia que ~ y alimentar** I have a family to feed and clothe; **~ al desnudo** (*Biblia*) to clothe the naked; **lo viste el Ayuntamiento** the Council pays for his clothing
5 (= *llevar puesto*) to wear; **la modelo viste un traje de noche con sombrero** the model is wearing an evening dress with a hat
6 (= *revestir*) [+ *sillón*] to cover, upholster; [+ *pared*] to cover, decorate
7 (*liter*) (= *disfrazar*) [+ *defecto*] to conceal; **viste de prudencia su cobardía** he conceals his cowardice behind a pretence of discretion; **vistió de gravedad su rostro** he assumed *o* adopted a serious expression
Ⓑ VI 1 (= *llevar ropa*) to dress; **siempre viste a la última moda** she always dresses in *o* wears the latest fashions; **abrió la puerta a medio ~** he opened the door only half-dressed; **¿todavía estás sin ~?** aren't you dressed yet?, haven't you got dressed yet?; **~ bien** to dress well; **~ mal** to dress badly; **~ de**: **le gusta ~ de gris** he likes to wear grey; **~ de paisano** [*policía*] to be in plain clothes; [*soldado*] to be in civilian clothes *o* in civvies* *o* in mufti*; **~ de sport** to dress casually; **~ de uniforme** [*policía, soldado*] to wear a uniform, be in uniform; [*alumno*] to wear a uniform; ✦*MODISMO* **el mismo que viste y calza**† the very same
2 (= *ser elegante*) [*traje, color*] to be elegant; **el negro viste mucho** black is very elegant; **tener un coche así sí que viste*** owning a car like that is really flashy*; **ahora lo que viste es viajar al Caribe*** the Caribbean is the trendy *o* the in place to go these days*; **de ~** [*ropa, zapatos*] smart; [*traje*] formal; **necesito algo un poco más de ~** I need something a bit smarter *o* more formal; **ese traje es de mucho ~** that suit's too dressy* *o* formal; **saber ~** to know how to dress, have good dress sense
Ⓒ **vestirse** VPR 1 (= *ponerse la ropa*) to get dressed; **no tardo nada en ~me** I get dressed in no time; **me vestí con lo primero que encontré** I put on the first thing I picked up; **¿cómo te vas a ~ para la fiesta?** what are you going to wear to the party?; **~se de algo** to wear sth; **voy a empezar a ~me de verano** I'm going to start wearing my summer clothes; **~se de fiesta** *o* **de gala** [*persona*] to get (all) dressed up; [*ciudad*] to be (all) decked out; **~se de largo** (*para fiesta, recepción*) to wear an evening dress; *ver tb* **mona 1**
2 (= *disfrazarse*) **~se de algo** to dress up as sth; **¿de qué te vas a ~?** what are you going to dress up as?; **me vestí de marinero** I dressed up as a sailor
3 (= *comprar la ropa*) to buy one's clothes; **se viste en las mejores tiendas** she buys her clothes in the best shops
4 (*liter*) (= *cubrirse*) **~se de algo** to be covered in sth; **toda la ciudad amaneció vestida de blanco** day dawned on a city entirely covered in white; **el cielo se vistió de nubes** the sky clouded over; **su rostro se vistió de severidad** his face took on a serious expression
5 (*tras enfermedad*) to get up again
Ⓓ SM (= *forma de vestir*) **su elegancia en el ~** the smart way she dresses

vestón SM (*Chile*) jacket

vestuario SM 1 (*gen*) clothes *pl*, wardrobe; (*Teat*) wardrobe, costumes *pl*; (*Mil*) uniform
2 (= *cuarto*) (*Teat*) [*de actor*] dressing room; (= *área*) backstage area; (*Dep*) (*en club*) changing room
3 (*Teat*) (= *guardarropa*) cloakroom

Vesubio SM Vesuvius

veta SF (*Min*) seam, vein; [*de madera*] grain; (*en piedra, carne*) streak, stripe

vetar ▸conjug 1a◂ VT (*gen*) to veto; [+ *socio*] to blackball

vetazo SM (*Andes*) lash

veteada SF (*Andes*) flogging, beating

veteado Ⓐ ADJ [*mármol*] veined; [*madera*] grained; [*carne*] streaked (**de** with); [*tocino*] streaky
Ⓑ SM [*del mármol*] veining; [*de la madera*] graining; [*de la carne*] streaks *pl*

vetear ▸conjug 1a◂ VT 1 (*gen*) to grain; [+ *carne*] to streak
2 (*Andes*) (= *azotar*) to flog, beat

veteranía SF (= *estatus*) status *o* dignity *etc* of being a veteran; (= *servicio*) long service; (= *antigüedad*) seniority

veterano/a Ⓐ ADJ (*Mil*) veteran; **es veterana en el oficio** she's an old hand*
Ⓑ SM/F (*Mil*) veteran; (*fig*) old hand*, old stager*

veterinaria SF veterinary medicine, veterinary science

veterinario/a SM/F veterinary surgeon, vet, veterinarian (EEUU)

vetevé SM (*Andes*) sofa

veto SM veto; **poner el ~ a algo** to veto sth; **tener ~** to have a veto

vetulio SM (*Andes*) old man

vetustez SF (*liter*) great age, antiquity; (*iró*) hoariness

vetusto ADJ ancient, very old; (*iró*) hoary

➤ **vez** SF 1 (= *ocasión*) time; **aquella ~** that time; **por esta ~** this time, this once; **la próxima ~** next time; **a la ~**: **hablaban todos a la ~** they were all talking at once *o* at the same time; **canta a la ~ que toca** she sings and plays at the same time, she sings while she plays; **me fascina a la ~ que me repele** I find it both fascinating and revolting at the same time; **¿has estado alguna ~ en ...?** have you ever been to ...?; **alguna que otra ~** occasionally, now and again; **las más de las veces** mostly, in most cases; **por primera ~** for the first time; **la primera ~ que lo vi** the first time I saw him; **toda ~ que ...** since ..., given that ...; **por última ~** for the last time; **¿cuándo lo viste por última ~?** when was the last time you saw him?, when did you see him last?; *ver tb* **tal C3**
2 (*indicando frecuencia*) **lo he hecho cien veces** I've done it hundreds *o* lots of times*; **¿cuántas veces al año?** how many times a year?; **tres veces** three times; **es cinco veces más caro** it's five times more expensive, it costs five times as much; **a veces** ◊ **algunas veces** sometimes, at times; **contadas veces** seldom; **de ~ en cuando** now and again, from time to time, occasionally; **¿cuántas veces?** how often?, how many times?; **dos veces** twice; **a una velocidad dos veces superior a la del sonido** at twice the speed of sound; **en ... veces**: **se fríen las patatas en dos veces** fry the potatoes in two batches; **por enésima ~** for the umpteenth time*; **muchas veces** often; **otra ~** again; **pocas veces** seldom, rarely; **rara ~** ◊ **raras veces** seldom, rarely; **repetidas veces** again and again, over and over again; **una ~** once; **la veo una ~ a la semana** I see her once a week; **una ~ dice que sí y otra que no** first he says yes and then he says no, one time he says yes, the next he says no; **más de una ~** more than once; **érase** *o* **había una ~ una princesa ...** once upon a time there was a princess ...; **"una ~ al año no hace daño"** once in a while can't hurt; **una y otra ~** time and (time) again; **varias veces** several times; *ver tb* **cada 2, 3**
3 (*otras expresiones*) **de una ~** (= *en una sola ocasión*) in one go; (= *definitivamente*) once and

➤ LENGUA Y USO: **vez 2** 53.1

for all*; **las derribó todas de una ~** she knocked them all down in one go; **¡acabemos de una ~!** let's get it over with (once and for all)!*; **¡cállate de una ~!** for the last time, shut up!*; **¡dilo de una ~!** just say it!; **en ~ de** instead of; **hacer las veces de** to serve as; **un vestíbulo que hacía las veces de vestuario** a hall that served as a changing room; **hizo las veces de musa y amante del poeta** she was a muse and lover to the poet; **una ~ que** once; **una ~ que me lo dijo se fue** once he had told me, he left; **una ~ que se hayan marchado todos me iré yo** once they've all left, I'll go too; **de una ~ para siempre** ◊ **de una ~ por todas** once and for all*, for good

[4] (= *turno*) turn, go; **a su ~** in turn; **cuando le llegue la ~** when his turn comes; **ceder la ~** (*gen*) to give up one's turn; (*en cola*) to give up one's place; **pedir la ~** to ask who's last in the queue; **quitar la ~ a algn** to push in in front of sb

[5] (*Mat*) **siete veces nueve** seven times nine

veza SF vetch

v.g. ABR, **v.gr.** ABR (= **verbigracia**) viz

vía Ⓐ SF [1] (= *calle*) road; (*en autopista*) lane; **¡por favor, dejen la ~ libre!** please make way! ► **vía de abastecimiento** supply route ► **vía de acceso** access road ► **vía de agua** leak; **se abrió una ~ de agua en el barco** the boat sprang a leak ► **vía de circunvalación** bypass, ring road, beltway (*EEUU*) ► **vía de dirección única** one-way street *o* road ► **vía de escape** escape route, way out ► **Vía Láctea** Milky Way ► **vía libre**: **el gobierno ha dado** *o* **dejado ~ libre al proyecto** the government has given the go-ahead to the project; **eso es dar** *o* **dejar la ~ libre a la corrupción** that's leaving the way open for corruption ► **vía pecuaria** cattle route ► **vía pública** public highway, thoroughfare ► **vía romana** Roman road

[2] (*Ferro*) (= *raíl*) track, line; (= *andén*) platform; **fue arrollado cuando cruzaba la ~** he was run over when he was crossing the track *o* line; **el tren está estacionado en la ~ ocho** the train is (standing) at platform eight ► **vía ancha** broad gauge; **de ~ ancha** broad-gauge *antes de s* ► **vía doble** double track ► **vía estrecha** narrow gauge; **de ~ estrecha** narrow-gauge *antes de s* ► **vía férrea** railway, railroad (*EEUU*) ► **vía muerta** (*Ferro*) siding; **el proceso ha entrado en una ~ muerta** the process has come to a dead end ► **vía única** single track; **de ~ única** single-track *antes de s*

[3] (*Transportes, Correos*) ► **vía aérea** airway; **por ~ aérea** [*viaje*] by air; [*envío postal*] (by) airmail ► **vía de comunicación** communication route ► **vía fluvial** waterway ► **vía marítima** sea route, seaway; **por ~ marítima** by sea ► **vía terrestre** overland route; **por ~ terrestre** [*viaje*] overland, by land; [*envío postal*] (by) surface mail

[4] (*Anat*) tract ► **vías digestivas** digestive tract *sing* ► **vías respiratorias** respiratory tract *sing* ► **vías urinarias** urinary tract *sing*

[5] (= *medio, canal*) **no conseguirán nada por la ~ de la violencia** they won't achieve anything through violence *o* by using violence; **por ~ arbitral** by (process of) arbitration; **por ~ oficial** through official channels; **tercera ~** middle way, compromise ► **vía judicial**: **recurrir a la ~ judicial** to go to the courts, have recourse to the law ► **vías de hecho** (*euf*) physical violence *sing*, assault and battery *sing*

[6] (*Med*) **por ~ oral** *o* **bucal** orally; **por ~ tópica** topically, externally; **por ~ interna** internally; **por ~ intravenosa** intravenously

[7] **en ~s de: un país en ~s de desarrollo** a developing country; **una especie en ~s de extinción** an endangered species; **el asunto está en ~s de solución** the matter is on its way to being solved

[8] (*Rel*) way ► **Vía Crucis** Way of the Cross, Stations of the Cross *pl*

[9] (*Quím*) process

Ⓑ PREP via; **un vuelo a Nueva York ~ Londres** a flight to New York via London; **retransmisión ~ satélite** satellite broadcast

viabilidad SF [1] [*de un plan*] viability, feasibility

[2] (*Aut*) road conditions *pl*

viabilizar ▸conjug 1f◂ VT to make viable

viable ADJ viable, feasible

viacrucis SM INV [1] (*Rel*) Way of the Cross, Stations of the Cross *pl*; ✦*MODISMO* **hacer el ~**⁑ to go on a pub-crawl*

[2] (= *problemas*) load of disasters, heap of troubles

viada SF (*Andes*) speed

viaducto SM viaduct

viajado ADJ **ser muy ~** to be well-travelled

viajante SMF ► **viajante (de comercio)** commercial traveller, traveling salesman (*EEUU*) ► **viajante en jabones** traveller in soap, soap salesman

viajar ▸conjug 1a◂ VI [1] (= *hacer viajes*) to travel; **ha viajado mucho** he has travelled a lot; **~ en coche/autobús** to go by car/bus; **~ por** to travel around, tour

[2] (⁑) (= *flipar*) to trip⁑

viajazo SM [1] (*Méx*) (= *empujón*) push, shove

[2] (*Caribe*) (= *azote*) lash

[3] (*CAm*) (= *bronca*) telling-off*

viaje[1] SM [1] (= *desplazamiento*) (*gen*) trip; (*por mar, el espacio*) voyage; **es su primer ~ al extranjero** it's her first trip abroad; **¡buen ~!** have a good trip!; **un ~ en barco** a boat trip; **los ~s** (= *actividad*) travelling, traveling (*EEUU*), travel; **tras dos años de ~s por África** after two years travel in Africa; **agencia de ~s** travel agent's, travel agency; **estar de ~** to be away; **salir de ~** to go away; **se fue de ~ a Perú** she went on a trip to Peru ► **viaje de buena voluntad** goodwill trip, goodwill mission ► **viaje de Estado** state visit ► **viaje de estudios** field trip ► **viaje de fin de curso** end-of-year trip ► **viaje de ida** outward journey ► **viaje de ida y vuelta**, **viaje redondo** (*LAm*) return trip, round trip ► **viaje de negocios** business trip ► **viaje de novios** honeymoon ► **viaje de recreo** pleasure trip ► **viaje organizado** package tour ► **viaje relámpago** lightning visit, flying visit

[2] (= *trayecto*) journey; **es un ~ muy largo** it's a very long journey

[3] (= *carga*) load; **un ~ de leña** a load of wood

[4] (*) [*de droga*] trip*; **tuvo un mal ~** she had a bad trip*

[5] (*esp Caribe*) (= *vez*) time; **de un ~** all in one go, at one blow; **lo repitió varios ~s** he repeated it several times

[6] ✦*MODISMO* **echar un ~ a algn** (*CAm*) to give sb a telling-off*

VIAJE

¿"Journey", "voyage", "trip" o "travel"?

• **Viaje** se traduce por **journey** cuando se refiere a un **viaje** en particular, tanto por aire como por tierra:

El viaje de Londres a Madrid dura unas dos horas

The journey from London to Madrid takes about two hours

• Un largo **viaje** por mar se traduce por **voyage**:

Muchos marineros murieron en el primer viaje de Colón a América

Many sailors died on Columbus's first voyage to America

• Cuando **viaje** hace referencia no sólo al trayecto de ida y vuelta, sino también a la estancia en un lugar, se suele traducir por **trip**. Normalmente se trata de un viaje con un fin concreto o de un viaje corto:

Fui a Alemania en viaje de negocios

I went to Germany on a business trip

• Como sustantivo incontable, **travel** se utiliza sólo en lugar de **travelling** para traducir la actividad de viajar; también, en muy contadas ocasiones, puede usarse en plural referido a viajes concretos:

No le gusta nada viajar en barco

He hates travelling by sea o ***He hates sea travel***

Colecciona recuerdos en sus viajes al extranjero

He collects souvenirs on his travels abroad

Para otros usos y ejemplos ver la entrada.

viaje[2]* SM (= *tajada*) slash (*with a razor*); (= *golpe*) bash*; (= *puñalada*) stab; **tirar un ~ a algn** to take a slash at sb

viajero/a Ⓐ ADJ travelling, traveling (*EEUU*); (*Zool*) migratory

Ⓑ SM/F (*gen*) traveller, traveler (*EEUU*); (= *pasajero*) passenger; **¡señores ~s, al tren!** will passengers kindly board the train!, all aboard!

vial Ⓐ ADJ (*gen*) road *antes de s*; (*de la circulación*) traffic *antes de s*; **circulación ~** road traffic; **fluidez ~** free movement of traffic; **reglamento ~** (= *control*) traffic control; (= *código*) rules *pl* of the road, highway code; **seguridad ~** road safety, safety on the road(s)

Ⓑ SM road

vialidad SF highway administration

vianda SF (*tb* **~s**) [1] (= *comida*) food

[2] (*Caribe*) (= *verduras*) vegetables *pl*

[3] (*Andes, Cono Sur*) (= *fiambrera*) lunch box, dinner pail (*EEUU*)

viandante SMF (= *peatón*) pedestrian; (= *paseante*) passer-by; (= *viajero*) traveller, traveler (*EEUU*)

viaraza SF (*LAm*) [1] (= *enojo*) fit of anger, fit of temper; **estar con la ~** to be in a bad mood

[2] (= *idea*) bright idea

viario ADJ road *antes de s*; **red viaria** road network; **sistema ~** transport system, system of communications

viático SM [1] (*Rel*) viaticum

[2] (*Hist*) (= *comida*) *food for a journey*

3 **viáticos** (= *estipendio*) travelling *o* (*EEUU*) traveling expenses, travel allowance *sing*

víbora SF 1 (*Zool*) viper; **tener lengua de ~** to have a sharp tongue
2 (*Méx*) (= *cartera*) money belt

viborear ▸conjug 1a◂ VI 1 (*Cono Sur*) (= *serpentear*) to twist and turn, snake along
2 (*Caribe Naipes*) to mark the cards

vibración SF 1 (= *temblor*) vibration
2 (*Ling*) roll, trill
3 **vibraciones*** (= *sentimientos*) vibrations, vibes*; **vibraciones negativas** bad vibes*

vibracional ADJ vibratory

vibrador SM vibrator

vibráfono SM vibraphone

vibrante Ⓐ ADJ 1 (= *que vibra*) vibrating
2 (*Ling*) rolled, trilled
3 [*voz*] ringing; [*reunión*] exciting, lively; **~ de** ringing with, vibrant with
Ⓑ SF (*Ling*) vibrant

vibrar ▸conjug 1a◂ Ⓐ VI 1 (= *moverse*) to vibrate; (= *agitarse*) to shake, rattle; (= *pulsar*) to throb, beat, pulsate; [*voz*] to quiver
2 (*Ling*) **hacer ~ las erres** to roll *o* trill one's r's
Ⓑ VT (= *hacer mover*) to vibrate; (= *agitar*) to shake, rattle

vibratorio ADJ vibratory

viburno SM viburnum

vicaria SF woman priest

vicaría SF vicarage; **pasar por la ~*** to tie the knot*, get hitched‡

vicario SM (*Rel*) curate ► **Vicario de Cristo** Vicar of Christ (*the Pope*) ► **vicario general** vicar general

vice* SMF vice-president

vice... PREF vice…

vicealcalde/esa SM/F deputy mayor

vicealmirante SMF vice-admiral

vicecampeón/ona SM/F runner-up

vicecanciller SMF 1 (*Univ*) vice-chancellor
2 (*en Alemania, Austria*) vice-chancellor
3 (*LAm*) deputy foreign minister, assistant secretary of state (*EEUU*)

viceconsejero/a SM/F *deputy minister in a regional government*

vicecónsul SMF vice-consul

vicedecanato SM vice-deanship

vicedecano/a SM/F vice-dean

vicedirector(a) SM/F [*de empresa, organismo*] deputy director; (*Escol*) deputy headmaster, deputy headmistress; (*Prensa*) deputy editor

vicegerente SM assistant manager

vicelendakari SMF, **vicelehendakari** SMF *vice-president of the Basque autonomous government*

vicelíder SMF deputy leader

viceministro/a SM/F deputy minister

Vicente SM Vincent

vicepresidencia SF (*Pol*) vice-presidency; [*de empresa, comité*] vice-chairmanship

vicepresidente/a SM/F (*Pol*) vice-president; [*de comité, empresa*] vice-chairman

vicetiple SF chorus-girl

viceversa ADV vice versa

vichadero SM (*Cono Sur*) = **bichadero**

vichear ▸conjug 1a◂ VT (*Cono Sur*), **vichar** ▸conjug 1a◂ VT (*Cono Sur*) = **bichear**

viciado ADJ 1 [*aire*] foul, stale
2 [*costumbres, texto*] corrupt
3 [*comida*] contaminated

viciar ▸conjug 1b◂ Ⓐ VT 1 (= *corromper*) to corrupt, pervert
2 (*Jur*) to nullify, invalidate
3 [+ *texto*] (= *alterar*) to corrupt; (= *interpretar mal*) to interpret erroneously
4 [+ *droga, producto*] to adulterate; [+ *aire*] to pollute; [+ *comida*] to spoil, contaminate
5 [+ *objeto*] to bend, twist; [+ *madera*] to warp
Ⓑ **viciarse** VPR 1 (= *corromperse*) become corrupted; *ver tb* **enviciar B**
2 [*objeto*] to warp, lose its shape
3 [*comida*] to be/become contaminated
4 [*aire, agua*] to be/become polluted

vicio SM 1 (= *corrupción*) vice
2 (= *mala costumbre*) bad habit, vice; **no le podemos quitar el ~** we can't get him out of the habit; **tiene el ~ de no contestar las cartas** he has the bad habit of not answering letters; **de** *o* **por ~** out of sheer habit; **quejarse de ~** to complain for no reason at all; **hablar de ~** to chatter away; **eso tiene mucho ~*** that's very habit-forming* *o* addictive ► **vicio inveterado**, **vicio de origen** ingrained bad habit
3 (= *adicción*) **el ~** the drug habit, drug addiction; **darse al ~** to take to drugs
4 (= *defecto*) defect, blemish; (*Jur*) error; (*Ling*) mistake, incorrect form; **adolece de ciertos ~s** it has a number of defects
5 [*de superficie*] warp; [*de línea*] twist, bend
6 (*con niño*) excessive indulgence
7 (*Bot*) rankness
8 **de ~*** (= *estupendo*) great, super*
9 **estar de ~** (*LAm*) (= *sin trabajar*) to be idle

viciosamente ADV 1 (= *depravadamente*) dissolutely
2 (*Bot*) rankly, luxuriantly

vicioso/a Ⓐ ADJ 1 (= *depravado*) dissolute, depraved
2 (= *mimado*) spoiled
3 (*Mec*) faulty, defective
4 (*Bot*) rank
Ⓑ SM/F 1 (= *depravado*) dissolute person, depraved person
2 (= *adicto*) addict; **soy un ~ del fútbol** I am hooked on football*, I am a football fanatic *o* addict*

vicisitud SF 1 (= *suceso*) vicissitude (*liter*); (= *desgracia*) accident, mishap; (= *cambio*) sudden change
2 **vicisitudes** (= *alternancia*) vicissitudes (*liter*)

víctima SF 1 (*gen*) victim; (*Zool*) prey; [*de accidente*] casualty; **fue ~ de una estafa** she was the victim of a swindle; **no hay que lamentar ~s del accidente** there were no casualties in the accident; **hay pocas ~s mortales** there are not many dead; **falleció ~ de un ataque cardiaco** he died of *o* from a heart attack; **es ~ de alguna neurosis** he is a prey to some neurosis
2 (*Hist*) sacrifice

victimar ▸conjug 1a◂ VT (*LAm*) (= *herir*) to wound; (= *matar*) to kill

victimario/a SM/F 1 (*Hist*) *person who helped the priest during human sacrifices*
2 (*LAm*) (= *asesino*) killer, murderer

victimismo SM *tendency to see oneself as being victimized*; **reaccionó con ~** he claimed he was being victimized

victimizar ▸conjug 1f◂ VT to victimize

Victoria SF Victoria

victoria SF victory; (*Dep*) win, victory; **la ~ del partido conservador** the conservative party's victory; **su primera ~ fuera de casa** (*Dep*) their first away win *o* victory; ✦*MODISMO* **cantar ~** to claim victory; **no podemos cantar ~ hasta que acabe el recuento de votos** we can't claim victory until all the votes have been counted ► **victoria pírrica** Pyrrhic victory ► **victoria por puntos** (*Boxeo*) points victory

victoriano ADJ Victorian

victoriosamente ADV victoriously

victorioso ADJ victorious

victrola SF (*LAm*) gramophone, phonograph (*EEUU*)

vicuña SF vicuna

vid SF vine

vid. ABR (= **vide, ver**) v

vida SF 1 (= *existencia*) life; **he vivido aquí toda mi ~** I've lived here all my life; **está escribiendo la ~ de Quevedo** he is writing the life *o* a life *o* a biography of Quevedo; **¿qué es de tu ~?** what's new?, how's life?; **le va la ~ en ello** his life depends on it; **con ~** alive; **estar con ~** to be still alive; **escapar** *o* **salir con ~** to escape *o* come out alive; **en ~ de**: **en ~ de mi marido** when my husband was alive, during my husband's lifetime; **¡en la** *o* **mi ~!** never (in all my life)!; **en mi ~ he visto semejante cosa** I've never seen such a thing (in all my life); **~ o muerte**: **una operación a ~ o muerte** a life-or-death operation; **es una cuestión de ~ o muerte** it's a matter of life and death; **estar entre la ~ y la muerte** to be at death's door; **debatirse entre la ~ y la muerte** to be fighting for one's life; **la otra ~** the next life; **perder la ~** to lose one's life; **de por ~** for life; **quitar la ~ a algn** to take sb's life; **quitarse la ~** to take one's own life; **rehacer la ~** to start a new life; **sin ~** lifeless; **encontró en el suelo el cuerpo sin ~ de su marido** she found her husband's lifeless body on the floor; **fue hallado sin ~** he was found dead; **un cuerpo sin ~** a (dead) body, a corpse; **toda la ~**: **un amigo de toda la ~** a lifelong friend; **ya no hay trabajos para toda la ~** there are no jobs for life nowadays ► **vida eterna** everlasting life ► **vida íntima** private life ► **vida nocturna** nightlife ► **vida privada** private life ► **vida sentimental** love-life; *ver tb* **esperanza**
2 (= *forma de vivir*) life; **llevan una ~ muy tranquila** they lead a very quiet life; **la ~ airada** (= *modo de vida*) the criminal life; (= *hampa*) the underworld; **de ~ airada** loose-living, immoral; **mujer de ~ alegre** loose woman; **~ arrastrada** wretched life; **la ~ cotidiana** everyday life; **doble ~** double life; **llevar una doble ~** to lead *o* live a double life; **hacer ~ marital** to live together (as man and wife); **hacer una ~ normal** to lead a normal life; **no hacer ~ social** to have no social life; **hay que dejarles hacer su ~** you must let them live their own life; **mala ~**: **echarse a la mala ~** to go astray; **llevar mala ~** to have a dissolute lifestyle; **mujer de mala ~** loose woman ► **vida de perros**, **vida perra** dog's

life, wretched life

3 (= *sustento*) **la ~ está muy cara** the cost of living is very high; **tienen la ~ resuelta** they are set up for life; **coste de la ~** cost of living; **ganarse la ~** to earn *o* make one's living; **se gana la ~ haciendo traducciones** he earns *o* makes his living doing translations; **nivel de ~** standard of living; *ver tb* **buscar C1**

4 [*de objeto*] **la ~ de estos edificios es breve** the life of these buildings is short; **la media de ~ de un televisor** the average lifespan of a television set ► **vida útil** (*Com*) lifespan; (*Téc*) useful life

5 ✦*MODISMOS* **amargar la ~ a algn** to make sb's life a misery; **así es la ~** that's life, such is life; **¡por ~ del chápiro verde!*** I'll be darned!*; **complicarse la ~** to make life difficult for o.s.; **contar la ~**: **¡no me cuentes tu ~!** I don't want your life story!; **costarle la ~ a algn**: **le costó la ~** it cost him his life; **dar ~ a algn**: **la mujer que me dio la ~** the woman who brought me into the world; **dar ~ a un personaje** to play a part; **darse buena ~** *o* **la ~ padre** to live the life of Riley*; **estar encantado de la ~** to be delighted; **acepté encantada de la ~** I was delighted to accept; **enterrarse en ~** to cut o.s. off from the world; **¡esto es ~!** this is the life!; **hacer por la ~*** to eat; **dar mala ~ a algn** to ill-treat sb, make sb's life a misery; **meterse en ~s ajenas** to pry into other people's affairs, meddle in other people's affairs; **¡hijo de mi ~!** my dear child!; **la ~ y milagros de algn** sb's life story; **cuéntame tu ~ y milagros** tell me all about yourself; **pasarse la ~**: **se pasa la ~ quejándose** he's forever complaining; **pasar la ~ a tragos*** to have a miserable life; **pasar a mejor ~** (*euf*) to pass away, go to a better place; **pegarse la gran ~** *o* **la ~ padre** to live the life of Riley‡; **tener siete ~s como los gatos** (*hum*) to have nine lives; **vender cara la ~** to sell one's life dearly; *ver tb* **vivir B1**

6 (= *vitalidad*) **lleno de ~** [*ojos*] lively; [*persona*] full of life; **sus ojos sin ~** his lifeless eyes; **este sol es la ~** this sunshine is a real tonic; **dar ~ a**: **la música le da ~ a estas imágenes** the music brings these images to life; **dar ~ a una fiesta** to liven up a party

7 (*apelativo cariñoso*) **¡vida!** ◊ **¡~ mía!** my love!, my darling!

8 (*euf*) (= *prostitución*) **una mujer de la ~** a loose woman; **echarse a la ~** to go on the game*; **hacer la ~** to be on the game*

videncia SF clairvoyance

vidente Ⓐ ADJ sighted

Ⓑ SMF 1 (= *no ciego*) sighted person

2 (= *clarividente*) clairvoyant(e); (= *profeta*) seer

3 (*TV*) viewer

vídeo SM (= *sistema*) video; (= *aparato*) video (recorder); (= *cinta*) video, videotape; **cinta de ~** videotape; **película de ~** video film; **registrar** *o* **grabar en ~** to video, (video)tape ► **vídeo compuesto** (*Inform*) composite video ► **vídeo comunitario** community video ► **vídeo doméstico** home video ► **vídeo inverso** (*Inform*) reverse video ► **vídeo musical** music video ► **vídeo promocional** promotional video

vídeo... PREF video ...

videoadicción SF video addiction*

videoadicto/a SM/F video addict*

videoaficionado/a SM/F video fan

videocámara SF video camera

videocasete SM video cassette

videocasetera SF video cassette recorder

videocassette SF video cassette

videocine SM video films *pl*

videocinta SF videotape

videoclip SM (*pl* **videoclips**) videoclip, video

videoclub SM (*pl* **videoclubs** *o* **videoclubes**) video shop, video store

videoconferencia SF videoconference, teleconference

videoconsola SF (video) games console

videocopia SF pirate video

videodisco SM video disc o (*EEUU*) disk

videoedición SF video editing

videofilm SM, **videofilme** SM videofilm

videófono SM videophone

videofrecuencia SF video frequency

videograbación SF (= *acto*) videotaping, taping; (= *programa registrado*) recording

videograbador SM (*Arg*) video recorder, video

videograbadora SF video recorder, video

videograbar ▸conjug 1a◂ VT to video, videotape

videográfico ADJ video *antes de s*

videograma SM video recording, videogram, video

videojuego SM video game

videolibro SM video book

videollamada SF video call

videomarcador SM electronic scoreboard

videopiratería SF video piracy

videopresentación SF video-presentation

videoproyección SF video-screening; **pantalla de ~** video-screen

videoproyector SM video projector

videorregistrador SM video (tape-)recorder

videorrevista SF video magazine

videoteca SF video library

videotelefonía SF videotelephony

videoteléfono SM videophone

videoterminal SM video terminal, visual display unit, VDU

videotex SM Videotex®

videotexto SM videotext

vidilla* SF **dar ~ a algo** to spice sth up, liven sth up; **dar ~ a algn** to liven sb up

vidorra* SF good life, easy life; **pegarse la ~** to live it up*

vidorria SF 1 (*Arg**) (= *vida alegre*) gay life, easy life

2 (*Andes, Caribe*) (= *vida triste*) miserable life

vidriado Ⓐ ADJ glazed

Ⓑ SM 1 (= *barniz*) glaze, glazing

2 (= *loza*) glazed earthenware

vidriar ▸conjug 1b◂ Ⓐ VT to glaze

Ⓑ **vidriarse** VPR [*objeto*] to become glazed; [*ojos*] to glaze over

vidriera SF 1 (= *puerta*) glass door; (= *ventana*) glass window ► **vidriera (de colores)** stained glass window

2 (*LAm*) (= *escaparate*) shop window; (= *vitrina*) showcase

3 (*Caribe*) (= *puesto*) tobacco stall, tobacco kiosk

vidriería SF 1 (= *fábrica*) glassworks

2 (= *objetos*) glassware

vidriero SM glazier

vidrio SM 1 (= *material*) glass; (*esp LAm*) (= *ventana*) window; **bajo ~** under glass; **~s rotos** broken glass *sing*; ✦*MODISMOS* **pagar los ~s rotos** to carry the can*; **soplar ~*** to booze* ► **vidrio cilindrado** plate glass ► **vidrio coloreado**, **vidrio de colores** stained glass ► **vidrio deslustrado**, **vidrio esmerilado** frosted glass, ground glass ► **vidrio inastillable** laminated glass, splinter-proof glass ► **vidrio pintado** stained glass ► **vidrio plano** sheet glass ► **vidrio polarizado** polarized glass ► **vidrio tallado** cut glass

2 (*) (= *vaso*) glass; **tomar unos ~s** to have a few drinks

3 (*Cono Sur*) (= *botella*) bottle of liquor

4 (*LAm*) (= *ventanilla*) window

vidrioso ADJ 1 (*gen*) glassy; (= *frágil*) brittle, fragile; (= *como vidrio*) glass-like

2 [*ojo*] glassy; [*expresión*] glazed; [*superficie*] slippery

3 [*persona*] touchy, sensitive

4 [*asunto*] delicate

vidurria SF (*Andes, Caribe, Cono Sur*) = **vidorria**

vieira SF scallop

vieja SF 1 (= *anciana*) old woman

2 (*) **la ~** (= *madre*) my mum*; (= *esposa*) my old woman*

3 (*Cono Sur*) (= *petardo*) cracker, squib

4 (*Méx*) [*de cigarro*] cigar stub

viejada SF (*Cono Sur*) group of old people

viejales* SM INV old chap*

viejera SF 1 (*Caribe*) (= *vejez*) old age

2 (*Caribe*) (= *trasto*) bit of old junk

viejito/a* SM/F (*LAm*) 1 (= *anciano*) old person

2 (= *amigo*) friend

viejo/a Ⓐ ADJ 1 (= *de mucha edad*) old; **hacerse** *o* **ponerse ~** to grow old, get old; **de ~ me gustaría vivir junto al mar** when I'm old, I'd like to live by the sea; ✦*MODISMOS* **~ como el mundo** as old as the hills; **más ~ que el cagar**‡ bloody ancient‡

2 (= *envejecido*) old; **está muy ~ para la edad que tiene** he looks very old for his age

3 (= *usado*) old; **tiraré todos los zapatos ~s** I'll throw all my old shoes away; **ropa vieja** old clothes *pl*; (= *de segunda mano*) secondhand clothes *pl*; **librería de ~** secondhand bookshop; **zapatero de ~** cobbler; ✦*MODISMO* **se cae de ~** it's falling to bits o pieces

4 (= *antiguo*) old; **un ~ amigo** an old friend; **viejas costumbres** old customs; **mi padre es de la vieja escuela** my father is of the old school

5 **Plinio el Viejo** Pliny the Elder

Ⓑ SM/F 1 (= *persona mayor*) old man/old woman; **los ~s** the elderly, old people; **el Viejo de Pascua** (*LAm*) Father Christmas; *ver tb* **verde A6**

2 (*LAm**) **mi ~** (= *padre, esposo*) my old man*; **mi vieja** (= *madre, esposa*) my old woman*; **mis ~s** (*esp LAm*) (= *padres*) my parents, my folks*

3 (*LAm**) (*en oración directa*) (= *querido*) darling

4 (*LAm**) (= *chica*) **las viejas** the chicks*, the birds*

5 (*) (*como excl*) (= *tío, colega*) mate*, pal*, buddy (*EEUU**)

viejón ADJ (*Andes, Cono Sur*) elderly

Viena SF Vienna

viene *etc ver* **venir**

vienés/esa ADJ, SM/F Viennese

viento SM [1] (*Meteo*) wind; (*ligero*) breeze; **corre** *o* **hay** *o* **hace** *o* **sopla (mucho) ~** it is (very) windy; **~ en popa** following wind; **✦*MODISMOS* beber los ~s por algn** to be crazy about sb; **como el ~** like the wind; **correr malos ~s para algo** to be the wrong moment for sth; **contra ~ y marea** at all costs, come what may; **gritar algo a los cuatro ~s** to shout sth from the rooftops, tell all and sundry about sth; **echar a algn con ~ fresco*** to chuck sb out*; **¡vete con ~ fresco!** go to blazes!*; **lo mandé a tomar ~*** I sent him packing; **ir ~ en popa** to go splendidly, go great guns*; [*negocio*] to prosper; **sorber los ~s por algn** to be crazy about sb; **✦*REFRÁN* quien siembra ~s recoge tempestades** sow the wind and reap the whirlwind ► **viento a favor** tailwind ► **viento ascendente** (*Aer*) upcurrent ► **viento colado** draught, draft (*EEUU*) ► **viento contrario** headwind ► **viento de cara** headwind ► **viento de cola** tailwind ► **viento de costado** crosswind, side wind ► **viento de espalda** tailwind ► **viento de la hélice** slipstream ► **viento de proa** headwind ► **viento en contra** headwind ► **viento favorable** lead wind; (*en atletismo*) wind assistance ► **viento huracanado** hurricane force wind, violent wind ► **viento lateral** side wind ► **viento portante** prevailing wind ► **viento racheado** gusty wind, squally wind ► **vientos alisios** trade winds ► **vientos nuevos** (*fig*) winds of change ► **viento terral** land breeze ► **viento trasero** tailwind
[2] (*Mús*) wind instruments *pl*, wind section
[3] (*Camping*) guy rope, guy
[4] (= *ventosidad*) wind, flatulence (*frm*)
[5] (*Caza*) scent
[6] [*de perro*] sense of smell, keen scent
[7] (= *vanidad*) conceit, vanity; **estar lleno de ~** to be puffed up (with conceit)
[8] (*Andes*) [*de cometa*] strings *pl* (*of a kite*)
[9] (*CAm*) (= *reuma*) rheumatism

vientre SM [1] (= *estómago*) belly; **bajo ~** lower abdomen
[2] (= *matriz*) womb; **llevar un hijo en su ~** to carry a child in one's womb
[3] (= *intestino*) bowels *pl*; **hacer de ~** ◊ **descargar el ~** ◊ **exonerar el ~** to have a bowel movement, move one's bowels ► **vientre flojo** looseness of the bowels
[4] [*de animal muerto*] guts *pl*, entrails *pl*
[5] (*Zool*) foetus, fetus (*EEUU*)
[6] [*de recipiente*] belly, wide part

vier. ABR (= **viernes**) Fri

viernes SM INV Friday ► **Viernes Santo** Good Friday; *ver tb* **sábado**

Vietnam SM Vietnam ► **Vietnam del Norte** North Vietnam ► **Vietnam del Sur** South Vietnam

vietnamita[1] Ⓐ ADJ, SMF Vietnamese
Ⓑ SM (*Ling*) Vietnamese

vietnamita[2] SF (= *máquina*) duplicator

viga SF (= *madera*) balk, timber, lumber (*EEUU*); (*Arquit*) [*de madera*] beam, rafter; [*de metal*] girder; **✦*MODISMO* estar contando las ~s** to be gazing vacantly at the ceiling ► **viga maestra** main beam ► **viga transversal** crossbeam

vigencia SF [1] (= *validez*) validity, applicability; [*de contrato*] term, life; [*de ley, reglamento*] operation; **entrar en ~** to come into effect, take effect; **estar en ~** to be in force, be valid; **perder ~** to go out of use, be no longer applicable; **tener ~** to be valid, apply
[2] (= *norma social*) social convention, norm of society

vigente ADJ [*ley, reglamento*] current, in force; [*tarifa*] current; **según la normativa ~** according to the regulations currently in force; **una costumbre aún ~ en nuestro siglo** a custom which still prevails in our own century

vigésimo ADJ, SM twentieth; *ver tb* **sexto A**

vigía Ⓐ SMF lookout, watchman; **los ~s** (*Náut*) the watch
Ⓑ SF [1] (*Mil*) watchtower
[2] (*Geog*) reef, rock

vigilancia SF [1] (= *custodia*) vigilance; **los niños pequeños requieren ~ constante** small children require constant vigilance; **burlaron la ~ de sus guardianes** they evaded the watchful eye of their guards; **tener bajo ~** [+ *paciente*] to keep under observation; [+ *prisionero*] to keep under surveillance ► **vigilancia intensiva** (*Med*) intensive care
[2] (= *servicio*) security; **la ~ del hotel es excelente** security at the hotel is excellent

vigilante Ⓐ ADJ (*gen*) vigilant, watchful; (= *alerta*) alert
Ⓑ SMF [1] (*en cárcel*) warder, guard (*EEUU*); [*de trabajo*] supervisor; (*en tienda*) store detective; [*de museo*] keeper; (*en piscina*) attendant ► **vigilante de noche, vigilante nocturno** night watchman ► **vigilante jurado** armed security guard
[2] (*Cono Sur*) (= *policía*) policeman

vigilantemente ADV vigilantly, watchfully

vigilar ▸conjug 1a◂ Ⓐ VT [1] [+ *niño, enfermo, equipaje, máquina*] to keep an eye on, watch; **vigila a los niños para que no se hagan daño** keep an eye on *o* watch the children to see they don't get hurt; **vigila el arroz para que no se pegue** keep an eye on the rice to make sure it doesn't stick
[2] [+ *trabajo*] to supervise
[3] [+ *presos*] to guard; [+ *frontera*] to guard, police; **vigilaban de cerca al sospechoso** they kept a close watch on the suspect
Ⓑ VI to keep watch; **tú vigila fuera mientras yo me escondo** you keep a lookout *o* keep watch outside while I hide; **~ por algo** to watch over sth; **su misión es ~ por la seguridad del Estado** his task is to watch over national security

vigilia SF [1] (= *vela*) wakefulness; (= *vigilancia*) watchfulness; **pasar la noche de ~** to stay awake all night
[2] (= *trabajo*) night work, late work; (= *estudio*) night-time study
[3] (*Rel*) vigil; (= *víspera*) eve; (= *abstinencia*) abstinence; (= *ayuno*) fast; **día de ~** day of abstinence; **comer de ~** abstain from meat; **potaje de ~** vegetable stew

vigor SM [1] (= *fuerza*) vigour, vigor (*EEUU*); (= *vitalidad*) vitality; (= *resistencia*) toughness, hardiness; (= *empuje*) drive; **con ~** vigorously
[2] (= *vigencia*) **en ~** [*norma*] in force; [*tarifa, horario*] valid, applicable; **entrar en ~** to take effect, come into force; **poner en ~** to put into effect, put into operation; *ver tb* **mantenerse B2**

vigorización SF (= *refuerzo*) strengthening; (= *estímulo*) encouragement, stimulation; (= *vitalidad*) revitalization

vigorizador ADJ, **vigorizante** ADJ (*gen*) invigorating; [*frío, viento*] bracing; [*ducha, bebida*] revitalizing; [*medicina*] tonic

vigorizar ▸conjug 1f◂ VT to invigorate; (= *animar, alentar*) to encourage, stimulate; (= *dar fuerza a*) to strengthen; (= *revitalizar*) to revitalize

vigorosamente ADV (*gen*) vigorously; (= *con fuerza*) strongly, forcefully; (= *con dificultad*) strenuously

vigoroso ADJ (*gen*) vigorous; (= *fuerte*) strong, tough; [*esfuerzo*] strenuous; [*protesta*] vigorous, forceful; [*niño*] sturdy

viguería SF (= *vigas*) beams *pl*, rafters *pl*; [*de metal*] girders *pl*, metal framework

vigués/esa Ⓐ ADJ of Vigo
Ⓑ SM/F native/inhabitant of Vigo; **los vigueses** the people of Vigo

vigueta SF joist, small beam

VIH SM ABR (= **virus de la inmunodeficiencia humana**) HIV

vihuela SF (*Hist*) *early form of the guitar*

vihuelista SMF (*Hist*) *vihuela player*

vijúa SF (*Andes*) rock salt

vikingo/a SM/F Viking

vil ADJ [*persona*] low, villainous; [*acto*] vile, rotten; [*conducta*] despicable, mean; [*trato*] unjust, shabby; **el ~ metal** filthy lucre

vileza SF [1] (= *cualidad*) vileness, foulness; (= *carácter*) meanness; (= *injusticia*) injustice
[2] (= *acción*) vile act, base deed

vilipendiar ▸conjug 1b◂ VT [1] (= *denunciar*) to vilify, revile
[2] (= *despreciar*) to despise, scorn

vilipendio SM [1] (= *denuncia*) vilification, abuse
[2] (= *desprecio*) contempt, scorn; (= *humillación*) humiliation

vilipendioso ADJ (= *despreciable*) contemptible; (= *humillante*) humiliating

villa SF [1] (= *pueblo*) small town; (*Pol*) borough, municipality; **la Villa (y Corte)** (*Esp*) Madrid ► **villa de emergencia** (*Arg*), **villa miseria** (*Arg*), **villa precaria** (*Arg*) shantytown, slum quarter ► **villa olímpica** Olympic village
[2] (= *casa*) villa

Villadiego SM **tomar las de ~*** to beat it quick*

villanaje SM [1] (= *estatus*) humble status, peasant condition
[2] (= *personas*) peasantry, villagers *pl*

villancico SM (Christmas) carol

villanesco ADJ (= *de campesinos*) peasant *antes de s*; (= *de pueblo*) village *antes de s*, rustic

villanía SF [1] (= *cualidad*) villainy, baseness
[2] (= *acción*) = **vileza 2**
[3] (= *dicho*) obscene expression, filthy remark
[4] (*Hist*) humble birth, lowly status

villano/a Ⓐ ADJ [1] (*Hist*) (= *campesino*) peasant *antes de s*; (= *rústico*) rustic
[2] (= *grosero*) coarse
[3] (= *vil*) villainous, base
Ⓑ SM/F [1] (*Hist*) serf, villein; (= *campesino*) peasant, rustic

[2] (= *canalla*) rotter*, rat*; (*Cine*) villain
[3] (*LAm*) villain

villista SMF (*Méx Pol*) supporter of Pancho Villa

villorrio SM one-horse town, dump*; (*LAm*) shantytown

vilmente ADV (= *con vileza*) vilely, foully; (= *despreciablemente*) despicably; (= *injustamente*) unjustly

vilo ADV [1] **en ~** (= *levantado*) into the air; (= *suspenso*) suspended, unsupported; **sostener algo en ~** to hold sth up
[2] **en ~** (= *intranquilo*) on tenterhooks; **estar** *o* **quedar en ~** ◊ **estar con el alma en ~** to be left in suspense, be on tenterhooks; **tener a algn en ~** to keep sb in suspense, keep sb waiting

vilote SM (*LAm*) coward

vinagre SM vinegar ► **vinagre de sidra** cider vinegar ► **vinagre de vino** wine vinegar

vinagrera SF [1] (= *botella*) vinegar bottle
[2] **vinagreras** (= *juego*) cruet stand *sing*
[3] (*LAm Med*) heartburn, acidity

vinagreta SF (*tb* **salsa ~**) vinaigrette, French dressing

vinagroso ADJ [1] (= *ácido*) vinegary, tart
[2] [*persona*] bad-tempered, sour

vinatería SF [1] (= *tienda*) wine shop
[2] (= *comercio*) wine trade

vinatero/a SM/F wine merchant, vintner

vinaza SF nasty wine, wine from the dregs

vinazo SM strong wine

vincha SF (*Andes, Cono Sur*) hairband, headband

vinculación SF [1] (= *relación*) linking, binding; (*fig*) bond, link
[2] (*Jur*) entail

vinculante ADJ binding (**para** on)

vincular ▸conjug 1a◂ Ⓐ VT [1] (= *relacionar*) to link, bind (**a** to); **~ sus esperanzas a algo** to base one's hopes on sth; **~ su suerte a la de otro** to make one's fate dependent on sb else's; **están estrechamente vinculados entre sí** they are closely bound together
[2] (*Jur*) to entail
Ⓑ **vincularse** VPR to be linked, link o.s. (**a** to)

vínculo SM [1] (= *relación, lazo*) link, bond; **los ~s de la amistad** the bonds of friendship; **hay un fuerte ~ histórico** there is a strong historical link ► **vínculo de parentesco** family ties *pl*, ties *pl* of blood
[2] (*Jur*) entail

vindicación SF [1] (= *defensa*) vindication
[2] (= *venganza*) revenge, vengeance

vindicar ▸conjug 1g◂ Ⓐ VT [1] [+ *persona, reputación*] to vindicate; [+ *derecho*] to regain, win back
[2] (= *vengar*) to avenge
Ⓑ **vindicarse** VPR [1] (= *vengarse*) to avenge o.s.
[2] (= *justificarse*) to vindicate o.s.

vine *etc ver* **venir**

vineo* SM **ir de ~** to go boozing*

vinería SF (*LAm*) wine shop

vínico ADJ wine *antes de s*

vinícola ADJ [*industria*] wine *antes de s*; [*región*] wine-growing *antes de s*, wine-making *antes de s*

vinicultor(a) SM/F wine grower

vinicultura SF wine growing, wine production

vinificable ADJ that can be made into wine, suitable for wine-making

vinificación SF fermentation

vinílico ADJ vinyl *antes de s*

vinillo SM thin wine, weak wine

vinilo SM vinyl

vino SM [1] (= *bebida*) wine; **aguar** *o* **bautizar el ~** to water the wine; ✦***MODISMOS*** **dormir el ~** to sleep off a hangover; **echar agua al ~** to water down a statement; **tener buen ~** to be able to handle one's drink; **tener mal ~** to get wild after a few drinks ► **vino añejo** mature wine ► **vino blanco** white wine ► **vino corriente** ordinary wine ► **vino de aguja** sparkling wine ► **vino de Jerez** sherry ► **vino de la casa** house wine ► **vino del año** new wine, wine for early drinking ► **vino de Málaga** Malaga (wine) ► **vino de mesa** table wine ► **vino de Oporto** port (wine) ► **vino de pasto** ordinary wine ► **vino de postre** dessert wine ► **vino de reserva** reserve ► **vino de solera** vintage wine ► **vino espumoso** sparkling wine ► **vino peleón** cheap wine, plonk* ► **vino rosado** rosé (wine) ► **vino tinto** red wine ► **vino tranquilo** non-sparkling wine
[2] (= *recepción*) drinks *pl*, reception; **después de la conferencia hubo un ~** there were drinks after the lecture ► **vino de honor** official reception; (*Cono Sur*) special wine

vinolento ADJ boozy*, fond of the bottle

vinoso ADJ [*sabor*] like wine, vinous (*frm*); [*color*] wine-coloured, wine-colored (*EEUU*)

vinoteca SF collection of wines

vinotería SF (*Méx*) wine-shop

viña SF [1] (= *planta*) vine; (= *lugar*) vineyard
[2] (*Méx*) (= *vertedero*) rubbish dump, garbage dump (*EEUU*)

viñador(a) SM/F (= *propietario*) wine grower; (= *trabajador*) vineyard worker

viñal SM (*Cono Sur*) vineyard

viñatero/a SM/F (*Andes, Cono Sur*) wine grower

viñedo SM vineyard

viñeta SF (*Arte, fig*) vignette; (*Prensa*) cartoon, sketch, drawing; (= *emblema*) emblem, device

viola Ⓐ SF [1] (*Bot*) viola
[2] (*Mús*) viola; (*Hist*) viol ► **viola de gamba** viola da gamba
Ⓑ SMF viola player

violáceo ADJ violet

violación SF [1] (*sexual*) rape
[2] [*de ley*] infringement; [*de acuerdo, principio*] violation, breach; [*de derecho, territorio*] violation ► **violación de contrato** breach of contract ► **violación de domicilio** housebreaking
[3] (= *profanación*) violation

violado ADJ, SM violet

violador(a) Ⓐ SM rapist
Ⓑ SM/F violator, offender (**de** against)

violar ▸conjug 1a◂ VT [1] [+ *persona*] to rape
[2] [+ *ley*] to break, infringe (*frm*); [+ *acuerdo, principio*] to violate, breach; [+ *derecho, territorio*] to violate; [+ *domicilio*] to break into, force entry into
[3] (= *profanar*) to violate

violatorio ADJ **ser ~ de** to be in breach *o* violation of

violencia SF [1] (*gen*) violence; (= *fuerza*) force; (*Jur*) assault, violence; (*Pol*) rule by force; **no ~** non-violence; **hacer algo con ~** to do sth violently; **usar ~ para abrir una caja** to force open a box; **no se consigue nada con él usando la ~** you will not achieve anything with him by using force, you won't get anywhere with him if you use force; **amenazar ~** to threaten violence; [*turba*] to turn ugly; **apelar a la ~** to resort to violence, use force; **hacer ~ a** = **violentar A2** ► **violencia doméstica** domestic violence
[2] (= *vergüenza*) embarrassment; (= *situación*) embarrassing situation; **si eso te causa ~** if that makes you feel awkward *o* uncomfortable, if that embarrasses you; **estar con ~** to be *o* feel awkward
[3] **una ~** a damaging act; (= *atrocidad*) an outrage
[4] (*Col Hist, Pol*) **la Violencia** *long period of civil disturbances and killings beginning in 1948*

violentamente ADV [1] (= *con violencia*) violently; (= *con furia*) furiously, wildly
[2] (*LAm*) (= *rápidamente*) quickly

violentar ▸conjug 1a◂ Ⓐ VT [1] [+ *puerta, cerradura*] to force; [+ *rama*] to bend, twist (out of shape); [+ *casa*] to break into
[2] [+ *persona*] (= *avergonzar*) to embarrass; (= *forzar*) to force, persuade forcibly; (= *maltratar*) to subject to violence; (*Jur*) to assault
[3] [+ *principio*] to violate, outrage; [+ *sentido*] to distort, twist
Ⓑ **violentarse** VPR (= *avergonzarse*) to get embarrassed; (= *forzarse*) to force o.s.

violentismo SM (*Chile*) social agitation

violentista ADJ, SMF (*Chile Pol*) subversive

violento ADJ [1] [*acto, deporte, persona*] violent; **se produjo una violenta explosión** there was a violent explosion; **murió de muerte violenta** he suffered a violent death
[2] (= *incómodo*) awkward, uncomfortable; **me fue muy ~ verlo llorar** seeing him cry made me feel very awkward *o* uncomfortable; **me encuentro ~ estando con ellos** I feel awkward *o* I don't feel at ease when I'm with them
[3] [*postura*] awkward
[4] [*interpretación*] forced
[5] (*LAm*) (= *repentino*) quick; **tuvo que hacer un viaje ~** she had to make a sudden trip

violeta Ⓐ SF violet; **conservador a la ~** dyed-in-the-wool conservative ► **violeta africana** African violet ► **violeta de genciana** gentian violet
Ⓑ ADJ INV violet
Ⓒ SM violet

violín Ⓐ SM [1] (= *instrumento*) violin
[2] ► **violín de Ingres** *spare-time occupation, art, hobby etc at which one shines*
[3] (*Caribe*) (= *mal aliento*) bad breath
[4] **de ~** (*Méx**) gratis, free
[5] ✦***MODISMOS*** **embolsar el ~** (*LAm*) to get egg on one's face*; **meter ~ en bolsa** (*Cono Sur**) to be embarrassed; **pintar un ~** (*Méx**) to make a rude sign; **tocar ~** (*Andes**) to play gooseberry, be a third wheel (*EEUU*)
Ⓑ SMF (= *persona*) violinist; **primer ~** ◊ **~ primero** (= *concertino*) leader; [*de sección*] first violin; **segundo ~** second violin

violinista SMF violinist, fiddler*

violón Ⓐ SM double bass; ✦***MODISMO*** **tocar el ~*** to talk rot
Ⓑ SMF (= *persona*) double bass player

violoncelista SMF cellist

violoncelo SM cello
violonchelista SMF cellist
violonchelo SM cello
vip* SM (*pl* **vips**) VIP
viperino ADJ viperish; **lengua viperina** wicked tongue
vira[1] SF (*Mil*) dart
vira[2] SF [*de zapato*] welt
viracho ADJ (*Cono Sur*) cross-eyed
Viracocha SM 1 (*Andes, Cono Sur Hist*) *Inca god*
2 (*Andes Hist**) (= *título*) *name given by Incas to the Spanish Conquistadors*
virada SF (*Náut*) tack, tacking
virador SM (*Fot*) toner
virago SF mannish woman
viraje SM 1 (*Náut*) tack; [*de coche*] turn; (*repentino*) swerve; (*en carretera*) bend, curve ► **viraje en horquilla** hairpin bend
2 (*fig*) change of direction; (*Pol*) abrupt switch, volte-face; [*de votos*] swing
3 (*Fot*) toning
virar ▸conjug 1a◂ Ⓐ VT 1 (*Náut*) to put about, turn
2 (*Fot*) to tone
3 (*LAm*) (= *dar vuelta a*) to turn (round); (= *invertir*) to turn over, turn upside down
4 (*Caribe*) (= *azotar*) to whip
Ⓑ VI 1 (= *cambiar de dirección*) to change direction, turn; (*Náut*) to tack, go about; [*vehículo*] to turn; (*con violencia*) to swerve; **tuve que ~ a la izquierda para no atropellarle** I had to swerve left to avoid hitting him; **~ en redondo** to turn round completely; **~ a estribor** to turn to starboard; **~ hacia el sur** to turn towards the south
2 (= *cambiar de parecer*) to change one's views; [*voto*] to swing; **el país ha virado a la derecha** the country has swung (to the) right; **~ en redondo** to swing round completely, make a complete volte-face
Ⓒ **virarse** VPR (*Caribe*‡) (= *morirse*) to kick the bucket‡
virgen (*pl* **vírgenes**) Ⓐ ADJ [*persona*] virgin; [*cinta*] blank; [*película*] unexposed
Ⓑ SMF virgin; (*Rel*) **la Virgen** the Virgin; **la Virgen de las Angustias** Our Lady of Sorrows; **la Santísima Virgen** the Blessed Virgin; **¡Santísima Virgen!** by all that's holy!; **✦*MODISMOS*** **aparecérsele la Virgen a algn***: **se le apareció la Virgen** he got his big chance, he struck lucky*; **ser (devoto) de la Virgen del Puño*** to be very tight-fisted; **ser un viva la Virgen***: **es un viva la Virgen** he doesn't give a damn‡, he doesn't care one bit*
virgencita SF small picture of the Virgin
Vírgenes SFPL **Islas ~** Virgin Islands
virgiliano ADJ Virgilian
Virgilio SM Virgil
virginal ADJ 1 [*cuerpo, doncella*] virginal
2 (*Rel*) *of or relating to the Virgin*
virginidad SF virginity
Virgo SM Virgo
virgo SM virginity
virguería SF 1 (= *adorno*) silly adornment, frill; (= *objeto delicado*) pretty thing, delicately made object
2 (= *maravilla*) wonder, marvel; **es una ~** it's wonderful; **hacer ~s** (*fig*) to work wonders, do clever things; **hacer ~s con algo** to be clever enough to handle sth well
virguero* ADJ 1 (= *bueno*) super*, smashing*
2 (= *elegante*) smart, nattily dressed; (= *exquisito*) pretty, delicately made
3 (= *hábil*) clever, smart
viricida Ⓐ ADJ viricidal
Ⓑ SM viricide
vírico ADJ viral, virus *antes de s*; **enfermedad vírica** viral illness
viril ADJ virile, manly; **la edad ~** the prime of life; *ver tb* **miembro A1**
virilidad SF 1 (= *cualidad*) virility, manliness
2 (= *estado*) manhood
virilizar ▸conjug 1f◂ Ⓐ VT to make like a man, induce male characteristics in
Ⓑ **virilizarse** VPR to become like a man, acquire male characteristics
viringo ADJ (*Andes*) 1 (= *desnudo*) bare, naked
2 (= *despellejado*) skinned, skinless
viroca SF (*Cono Sur*) serious mistake
virola SF 1 (= *regatón*) metal tip, ferrule; [*de herramienta, lanza*] collar
2 (*Cono Sur, Méx*) (= *argolla*) silver ring; (= *disco*) metal disc (*fixed to harness etc as an adornment*)
virolento ADJ pockmarked
virolo ADJ (*Andes*) cross-eyed
virología SF virology
virólogo/a SM/F virologist
virote SM 1 (= *flecha*) arrow
2 (*Méx**) (= *pan*) bread roll
3 (†) (= *señorito*) hooray Henry*
4 (*Andes, Méx*) (= *tonto*) simpleton
virreinato SM viceroyalty
virrey SM viceroy
virriondo‡ ADJ (*Méx*) 1 [*animal*] (*hembra*) on heat; (*macho*) in rut
2 [*persona*] randy*, horny‡
virtual ADJ 1 (= *potencial*) potential; **el ~ candidato a la presidencia** the potential candidate for president; **tras el partido de hoy son ya los ~es campeones** after today's match they are virtually assured of the championship
2 (*Inform, Fís*) virtual; **memoria ~** virtual memory; **realidad ~** virtual reality
virtualidad SF potentiality; **tiene ciertas ~es** it has certain potentialities
virtualmente ADJ virtually
▼ **virtud** SF 1 (= *calidad*) virtue; **~ cardinal** cardinal virtue
2 (= *capacidad*) ability, power; (= *eficacia*) efficacy; **en ~ de** by virtue of, by reason of; **tener la ~ de ...** + INFIN to have the virtue of ... + *ger*, have the power to ... + *infin*; **una planta que tiene ~ contra varias enfermedades** a plant which is effective against certain diseases; **~es curativas** healing power *sing*, healing properties
3 (*Caribe***) (= *pene*) prick**; (= *vagina*) cunt**
virtuosamente ADV virtuously
virtuosismo SM virtuosity
virtuosista ADJ virtuoso
virtuoso/a Ⓐ ADJ virtuous
Ⓑ SM/F virtuoso
viruela SF 1 (= *enfermedad*) smallpox
2 **viruelas** (= *marcas*) pockmarks; **picado de ~s** pockmarked ► **viruelas locas** chickenpox *sing*
virulé: **a la ~*** ADJ 1 (= *estropeado*) damaged; (= *torcido*) bent, twisted; (= *viejo*) old; (= *raído*) shabby; **ojo a la ~** shiner*
2 [*persona*] cracked, potty*
virulencia SF virulence
virulento ADJ virulent
virus SM INV virus; **enfermedad por ~** viral illness ► **virus atenuado** attenuated virus ► **virus de inmunodeficiencia humana** human immunodeficiency virus ► **virus gripal** flu virus ► **virus informático** computer virus
viruta Ⓐ SF 1 [*de madera, metal*] shaving ► **virutas de acero** steel wool *sing*
2 (‡) (= *dinero*) bread‡, money
Ⓑ SM, **virutas** SM INV carpenter
vis SF **~ cómica** sense of comedy; **tener ~ cómica** to be witty
visa SF (*LAm*) visa ► **visa de permanencia** residence permit ► **visa de tránsito** transit visa
visado SM visa ► **visado de entrada** entry visa ► **visado de salida** exit visa ► **visado de tránsito** transit visa ► **visado de turista**, **visado turístico** tourist visa
visaje SM (wry) face, grimace; **hacer ~s** to pull faces, grimace
visar ▸conjug 1a◂ VT 1 [+ *pasaporte*] to visa
2 [+ *documento*] to endorse, approve
vis a vis Ⓐ ADV face to face
Ⓑ SM (= *reunión*) face to face (meeting); (*en la cárcel*) private visit
visceral ADJ 1 (*Anat*) visceral
2 (= *profundo*) visceral, deep-rooted; **aversión/reacción ~** gut aversion/reaction; **sentimientos ~es** gut feelings
visceralmente ADV deeply, viscerally (*frm*)
vísceras SFPL (*Anat*) viscera *pl*, entrails; (*fig*) guts, bowels
visco SM birdlime
viscosa SF viscose
viscosidad SF 1 (= *cualidad*) viscosity; [*de líquido*] thickness
2 (*Bot, Zool*) (= *sustancia*) slime; (= *secreción*) sticky secretion
viscoso ADJ (*gen*) viscous; [*líquido*] thick; [*secreción*] slimy
visera SF (*Mil*) visor; [*de gorra*] peak; [*de jockey, tenista*] eyeshade; (*Caribe*) [*de caballo*] (horse's) blinkers *pl*; [*de estadio*] canopy ► **visera de béisbol** baseball cap
visibilidad SF visibility; **la ~ es de 200m** there is a visibility of 200m; **la ~ queda reducida a cero** visibility is down to zero; **una curva de escasa ~** (*Aut*) a bend with poor visibility ► **visibilidad cero** zero visibility
visible ADJ 1 (= *que se ve*) visible; **es ~ a simple vista** it's visible to the naked eye, it can be seen with the naked eye; **ponlo donde esté bien ~** put it where it can be easily seen, put it where it's clearly visible
2 (= *evidente*) **dio muestras de ~ disgusto** he was visibly upset; **la miró con ~ enojo** he looked at her, visibly annoyed
3 (= *decente*) decent, presentable; **¿estás ~?** are you decent *o* presentable?
visiblemente ADV visibly
visigodo/a Ⓐ ADJ Visigothic
Ⓑ SM/F Visigoth

➤ LENGUA Y USO: **virtud 2** 44.1

visigótico ADJ Visigothic

visillo SM [1] (= *cortina*) lace curtain, net curtain
[2] (*en butaca*) antimacassar

visión SF [1] (*Anat*) vision, (eye)sight; **perder la ~ de un ojo** to lose the sight in *o* of one eye ► **visión borrosa** blurred vision ► **visión de túnel** tunnel vision ► **visión doble** double vision ► **visión reducida** impaired vision
[2] (*Rel*) vision; (= *fantasía*) fantasy; (= *ilusión*) illusion; **ver visiones** to be seeing things, suffer delusions; **se le apareció en ~** it came to him in a vision
[3] (= *vista*) view; **un político con ~ de futuro** a farsighted politician ► **visión de conjunto** complete picture, overall view
[4] (= *punto de vista*) view, point of view; **su ~ del problema** his view of the problem
[5] (*pey*) scarecrow, fright*; **ella iba hecha una ~** she looked a real sight*; **han comprado una ~ de cuadro** they've bought an absolutely ghastly picture

visionado SM [1] (= *acción*) viewing, inspection [2] (*TV*) viewing-room

visionadora SF (*Fot*) viewer

visionar ▸conjug 1a◂ VT [1] (*TV*) to view, see; (*por adelantado*) to preview; (*Fot*) to view, have a viewing of
[2] (= *entrever*) to glimpse; (= *prever*) to foresee
[3] (= *presenciar*) to witness

visionario/a Ⓐ ADJ visionary; (*pey*) deluded, subject to hallucinations
Ⓑ SM/F visionary; (*pey*) deluded person; (= *loco*) lunatic, crazy individual

visir SM vizier; **gran ~** grand vizier

visita SF [1] (= *acción*) visit; (*breve*) call; **horas de ~** visiting hours; **tarjeta de ~** business card, visiting card; **estar de ~ en un lugar** to be on a visit to a place; **ir de ~** to go visiting; **devolver** *o* **pagar una ~** to return a visit; **hacer una ~ a** to visit, pay a visit to ► **visita conyugal** conjugal visit ► **visita de cortesía, visita de cumplido** formal visit, courtesy call ► **visita de despedida** farewell visit ► **visita de Estado** state visit ► **visita de intercambio** exchange visit ► **visita de médico*** very short call, brief visit ► **visita de pésame** *visit to express one's condolences* ► **visita en grupo** group visit ► **visita íntima** conjugal visit ► **visita oficial** official visit ► **visita relámpago** flying visit
[2] (= *persona*) visitor, caller; **hoy tenemos ~** we have visitors today; **"no se admiten ~s"** "no visitors"
[3] (*en la aduana*) search; **derecho de ~** right to search
[4] (*Internet*) hit
[5] (*Caribe Med*) enema

visitación SF (*Rel*) visitation

visitador(a) Ⓐ SM/F [1] (= *visitante*) frequent visitor
[2] (= *inspector*) inspector
[3] (*Com, Med*) drug company salesman
Ⓑ SF (*LAm*) [1] (= *jeringa*) syringe
[2] (= *enema*) enema

visitante Ⓐ ADJ visiting
Ⓑ SMF visitor

visitar ▸conjug 1a◂ Ⓐ VT (*gen*) to visit; (*brevemente*) to call on; **fuimos a ~ a mis tíos** we went to visit my aunt and uncle; **5.000 personas han visitado ya la exposición** 5,000 people have already visited the exhibition
Ⓑ VI **el médico está visitando** the doctor is holding his surgery
Ⓒ **visitarse** VPR [1] [*personas*] to visit each other
[2] (*Med*) to attend the doctor's surgery

visiteo SM frequent visiting, constant calling

visitero/a Ⓐ ADJ fond of visiting, much given to calling
Ⓑ SM/F frequent visitor, constant caller

visitón* SM long and boring visit, visitation (*hum*)

vislumbrar ▸conjug 1a◂ VT [1] [+ *paisaje, figura*] to glimpse, catch a glimpse of
[2] [+ *solución*] to glimpse, begin to see; [+ *futuro*] to get a slight idea of; [+ *hecho desconocido*] to surmise

vislumbre SF [1] (= *vista*) glimpse, brief view
[2] (= *brillo*) gleam, glimmer
[3] (= *posibilidad*) glimmer, slight possibility; (= *conjetura*) conjecture; (= *noción*) vague idea; **tener ~s de** to get an inkling of, get a vague idea of

viso SM [1] [*de metal*] gleam, glint
[2] (= *aspecto*) **hay un ~ de verdad en esto** there is an element of truth in this; **tenía ~s de nunca acabar** it seemed that it was never going to finish; **tiene ~s de ser puro cuento** it looks like being just a story; ✦***MODISMOS*** **a dos ~s** ◊ **de dos ~s** with a double purpose, two-edged
[3] (= *ropa*) slip
[4] ✦***MODISMO*** **ser persona de ~** to be somebody, be important
[5] (*Geog*) viewpoint, vantage point
[6] **visos** [*de tela*] sheen *sing*, gloss *sing*; **negro con ~s azules** black with a bluish sheen, black with bluish lights in it; **hacer ~s** to shimmer

visón SM mink

visor SM [1] (*Aer*) bombsight; (*Mil*) sight ► **visor nocturno** night sight ► **visor telescópico** telescopic sight
[2] (*Fot*) (*tb* **~ de imagen**) viewfinder

víspera SF eve, day before; **la ~ de** ◊ **en ~s de** on the eve of (*tb fig*); **estar en ~s de hacer algo** to be on the point *o* verge of doing sth ► **víspera de Navidad** Christmas Eve

▼**vista** Ⓐ SF [1] (= *visión*) sight, eyesight; **hasta donde alcanza la ~** as far as the eye can see; **el coche desapareció de mi ~** the car disappeared from sight; **nublarse la ~: se me nubló la ~** my eyes clouded over; **perder la ~** to lose one's sight; **tener buena/mala ~** to have good/bad eyesight; ✦***MODISMO*** **hacer la ~ gorda** to turn a blind eye, pretend not to notice ► **vista cansada** (*por defecto*) longsightedness; (*por agotamiento*) eyestrain ► **vista corta** short sight ► **vista de águila, vista de lince** eagle eye; **tener ~ de águila** *o* **de lince** to have eagle eyes, to have eyes like a hawk *o* a lynx
[2] (= *ojos*) [2·1] (= *órgano*) eyes *pl*; **tiene un problema en la ~** she has something wrong with her eyes; **a la altura de la ~** at eye level; **una luz que hiere la ~** a dazzling light, a light that hurts one's eyes; **torcer la ~** to squint
[2·2] (= *mirada*) **¡~ a la derecha!** (*Mil*) eyes right!; **aguzar la ~** (*para ver a lo lejos*) to screw one's eyes up; (*para descubrir algo*) to look sharp; **alzar la ~** to look up; **apartar la ~** to look away; **no apartar la ~ de algo** to keep one's eyes glued to sth; **bajar la ~** to look down, lower one's gaze; **buscar algo con la ~** to look around for sth; **clavar la ~ en algn/algo** to stare at sb/sth, fix one's eyes on sb/sth; **dirigir la ~ a algn/algo** to look towards sb/sth, turn one's gaze on sb/sth; **echar una ~ a algn/algo** to take a look at sb/sth; **fijar la ~ en algn/algo** to stare at sb/sth, fix one's eyes on sb/sth; **medir a algn con la ~** to size sb up; **pasar la ~ por algo** to look over sth, glance quickly at sth; **con la ~ puesta en la pared** with his eyes fixed on the wall; **con la ~ puesta en las elecciones** with a view to the elections; **con la ~ puesta en la futura legislación medioambiental, la compañía ha sacado un nuevo modelo** in the light of the forthcoming environmental legislation, the company has launched a new model; **¡quítate de mi ~!** get out of my sight!; **recorrer algo con la ~** to run one's eye over sth; **seguir algo con la ~** to follow sth with one's eyes; **volver la ~** to look away; **volver la ~ atrás** to look back; ✦***MODISMOS*** **comerse** *o* **devorar a algn con la ~** (*con deseo*) to devour sb with one's eyes; (*con ira*) to look daggers at sb*; **perder algo de ~** to lose sight of sth; **no perder a algn de ~** to keep sb in sight; **saltar a la ~: su inteligencia salta a la ~** she is strikingly intelligent; **una cosa que salta a la ~ es ...** one thing that immediately hits *o* strikes you is ...; **salta a la ~ que ...** it's blindingly obvious that ...
[3] (= *perspicacia*) foresight; **tuvieron ~ para comprar las acciones** they showed foresight in buying the shares, it was shrewd of them to buy the shares; **ha tenido mucha ~ con el piso** he was very far-sighted about the flat; **tener ~ para los negocios** to have good business acumen
[4] (= *panorama*) view; **la ~ desde el castillo** the view from the castle; **con ~s a: con ~s a la montaña** with a view of the mountains; **una habitación con ~s al mar** a room with a sea view, a room overlooking the sea; **con ~s al oeste** facing west ► **vista anterior, vista frontal** front view
[5] (*Fot*) (= *imagen*) view; **una tarjeta con una ~ de Venecia** a card with a view of Venice ► **vista de pájaro** bird's-eye view; **observar algo a ~ de pájaro** to get a bird's-eye view of sth ► **vista fija** still ► **vista frontal** front view
[6] (*otras expresiones*) [6·1] **a la ~** in sight *o* view; **la parte que quedaba a la ~** the part that was visible *o* in view; **no es muy agradable a la ~** it's not a pretty sight, it's not very pleasant to look at; **cuenta a la ~** (*Fin*) instant access account; **a la ~ está (que ...)** it's obvious (that ...), you can see for yourself (that ...); **no tengo ningún proyecto a la ~** I have no plans in sight; **estaré a la ~ de lo que pase** I will keep an eye on developments; **yo me quedo a la ~ del fuego** I'll keep an eye on the fire; **a la ~, no son pobres** from what you can tell, they're not poor; **a la ~ de todos** in full view (of everyone); **los resultados están a la ~ de todos** the results are there for everyone to see; **lo fríen a la ~ del cliente** it's fried in front of the customer; **a la ~ de tal espectáculo** at the sight of such a scene; **a la ~ de sus informes** in

➤ LENGUA Y USO: vista A6 35.2, 44.1

the light of *o* in view of his reports; **poner algo a la ~** to put sth on view

6·2 **a ... años/días ~**: **pagadero a 30 días ~** payable within 30 days; **a un año ~ de las elecciones** (= *antes*) a year before the elections; **a cinco años ~** (= *después*) five years from then; **a dos años ~ de la exposición** two years after the exhibition

6·3 **con ~s a** with a view to; **con ~s a una solución del problema** with a view to solving the problem; **han modernizado el estadio con ~s al Mundial** they have modernized the stadium ahead of the World Cup; **una medida con ~s al futuro** a measure taken with the future in mind

6·4 **de ~** by sight; **conocer a algn de ~** to know sb by sight; **en ~ de** in view of; **en ~ de que ...** in view of the fact that ...; **¡hasta la ~!** see you!, so long!; **a primera ~** at first sight, on the face of it; **a simple ~** (= *sin ayuda de aparatos*) to the naked eye; (= *por la primera impresión*) at first sight

7 (= *aspecto*) appearance, looks *pl*; **esos plátanos no tienen muy buena ~** those bananas don't look too good; **un coche con una ~ estupenda** a wonderful-looking car; **de ~ poco agradable** not very nice to look at, unprepossessing

8 (*Jur*) hearing; **~ de una causa** hearing of a case ▸ **vista oral** first hearing

9 **vistas** (*Hist*) meeting *sing*, conference *sing*

Ⓑ SMF (*tb* **~ de aduana**) customs official

vistar* ▸conjug 1a◂ VT (*LAm*) to have a look at, look over, look round

vistazo SM look, glance; **de un ~** at a glance; **echar** *o* **pegar un ~ a*** to glance at, have a (quick) look at

vistillas SFPL viewpoint *sing*

visto[1] *ver* **vestir**

visto[2] Ⓐ PP *de* **ver**

Ⓑ ADJ 1 (= *conocido*) **no, ésa chaqueta no, que la tengo muy vista** no, not that jacket, I wear it all the time; **ese color está muy ~** you see that colour all over the place, everyone is wearing that colour; **no quisiera hacerme demasiado ~ en este bar** I don't want to be seen too much in this bar; **ese chiste ya está más que ~** that joke is as old as the hills; **ser lo nunca ~** to be unheard of; **tres derrotas consecutivas es lo nunca ~ en este estadio** three defeats in a row is unheard of *o* has never happened before in this stadium; **el ministro, cosa nunca vista, hizo unas declaraciones en contra del presidente** the minister spoke out against the president, something which is unheard of; ✦**MODISMO más ~ que el tebeo** (*Esp*) as old as the hills

2 (= *considerado*) **estar bien/mal ~** [*comportamiento*] to be the done thing/be frowned upon; [*persona*] to be well/badly thought of; [*iniciativa, propuesta*] to be welcomed/not welcomed; **lo que está bien ~** the done thing; **estaba mal ~ que una mujer saliera sola** it was not the done thing for a woman to go out alone, it was frowned upon for a woman to go out alone; **no está bien ~ dentro del sindicato** he's not very well thought of *o* highly regarded in the union

3 (= *expuesto*) [*ladrillo*] bare, exposed; [*viga*] exposed; **un edificio de ladrillo ~** a building of bare *o* exposed brick

4 (*Jur*) **¡visto!** case adjourned; **~ para sentencia** adjourned for sentencing

5 (*en locuciones*) **está ~ que ...** it is clear *o* obvious that ...; **está ~ que el problema no tiene solución** it is clear *o* obvious that there is no solution to the problem; **estaba ~ que la historia terminaría en boda** you could tell that they would end up getting married, it was clear *o* obvious that they would end up getting married; **por lo ~** apparently; **por lo ~, no les interesa** apparently *o* from what I can see, they are not interested; **—¿no ha venido el cartero todavía? —por lo ~ no** "hasn't the postman come yet?" — "apparently not" *o* "it would appear not"; ✦**MODISMOS ni ~ ni oído** like lightning; **~ y no ~**: **cogió el bolso y salió corriendo, fue ~ y no ~** he grabbed the bag and ran out, one minute he was there and the next minute he was gone; **lo fusilaron ~ y no ~** they shot him just like that; **en un ~ y no ~** in a flash; **en un ~ y no ~ el conejo desapareció de ante nuestros ojos** in a flash the rabbit disappeared before our very eyes

6 **~ que** since; **~ que no nos hacían caso nos fuimos** since they took no notice of us we left

Ⓒ SM ▸ **visto bueno** approval, go-ahead*; **vuestra propuesta no ha recibido el ~ bueno** your proposal has not been approved *o* didn't get the go-ahead*; **dar el ~ bueno a algo** to give sth one's approval, give sth the go-ahead*; **el juez ha dado el ~ bueno para que se investigue el caso** the judge has given his approval *o* given the go-ahead for the case to be investigated*; **dar el ~ bueno a algn para que haga algo** to give one's approval for sb to do sth, give sb the go-ahead to do sth*

vistosamente ADV (*gen*) brightly, colourfully, colorfully (*EEUU*); (*pey*) gaudily

vistosidad SF (*gen*) brightness, colourfulness, colorfulness (*EEUU*); (*pey*) gaudiness; [*de feria, ballet*] spectacular nature

vistoso ADJ [*ropa*] bright, colourful, colorful (*EEUU*); (*pey*) gaudy; [*partido*] spectacular

Vístula SM Vistula

visual Ⓐ ADJ visual; **campo ~** field of vision; **memoria ~** visual memory

Ⓑ SF 1 (= *línea*) line of sight

2 (*) (= *vistazo*) look, glance; **echar una ~** to take a look (**a** at)

visualización SF 1 (= *representación*) visualization

2 (*Inform*) display(ing); **pantalla de ~** display screen, VDU

3 ▸ **visualización radiográfica** (*Med*) scanning

visualizador SM (*Inform*) display screen, VDU

visualizar ▸conjug 1f◂ VT 1 (= *imaginarse*) to visualize

2 (= *hacer visible*) to visualize

3 (*Inform*) to display

4 (*LAm*) (= *divisar*) to see, make out

5 **~ radiográficamente** (*Med*) to scan

visualmente ADV visually

vital ADJ 1 (= *de la vida*) life *antes de s*; **fuerza ~** life force; **espacio ~** living space

2 (= *fundamental*) vital; **es ~ que haya unidad en el partido** party unity is vital; **de importancia ~** vitally important

3 (= *enérgico*) vital, full of vitality

4 (*Anat*) vital; **órganos ~es** vital organs

vitaliciamente ADV for life

vitalicio Ⓐ ADJ life *antes de s*, for life; **cargo ~** post held for life; **pensión vitalicia** life pension

Ⓑ SM life annuity

vitalidad SF vitality

vitalismo SM 1 (*Fil*) vitalism

2 [*de persona*] vitality

vitalista Ⓐ ADJ 1 (*Fil*) vitalist

2 [*persona*] vital, full of life

Ⓑ SMF (*Fil*) vitalist

vitalización SF vitalization

vitalizador ADJ **acción ~a** ◊ **efecto ~** revitalizing effect

vitalizante ADJ revitalizing

vitalizar ▸conjug 1f◂ VT (*esp LAm*) to vitalize

vitamina SF vitamin

vitaminado ADJ with added vitamins

vitaminar ▸conjug 1a◂ VT to add vitamins to

vitamínico ADJ vitamin *antes de s*

vitaminizado ADJ with added vitamins

vitando (*frm*) ADJ (*gen*) to be avoided; [*crimen*] heinous

vitela SF vellum

vitícola ADJ [*industria*] grape *antes de s*, vine *antes de s*; [*región*] grape-producing, vine-producing

viticultor(a) SM/F (= *cultivador*) vine grower; (= *dueño*) proprietor of a vineyard

viticultura SF vine growing, viticulture (*frm*)

vitíligo SM vitiligo

vitivinicultura SF grape and wine-growing

vitoco* ADJ (*Caribe*) vain, stuck-up*

vitola SF 1 [*de cigarro*] cigar band

2 (= *aspecto*) appearance, looks *pl*

3 (*Mec*) calibrator

vitoquear* ▸conjug 1a◂ VI (*Caribe*) to be conceited, swank*

vítor Ⓐ EXCL hurrah!

Ⓑ SM cheer; **entre los ~es de la multitud** among the cheers of the crowd; **dar ~es a** to cheer (on)

vitorear ▸conjug 1a◂ VT to cheer, acclaim

Vitoria SF Vitoria

vitoriano/a Ⓐ ADJ of/from Vitoria

Ⓑ SM/F native/inhabitant of Vitoria; **los ~s** the people of Vitoria

vitral SM stained-glass window

vítreo ADJ 1 [*ojos*] glassy

2 (*Geol, Min*) vitreous

3 (*Anat*) vitreous; **humor ~** vitreous humour, vitreous humor (*EEUU*); **membrana vítrea** vitreous membrane

vitrificación SF vitrification

vitrificar ▸conjug 1g◂ Ⓐ VT to vitrify

Ⓑ **vitrificarse** VPR to vitrify

vitrina SF 1 [*de tienda*] glass case, showcase; (*en casa*) display cabinet

2 (*LAm*) (= *escaparate*) shop window

vitriolo SM vitriol

vitro ADJ, ADV *ver* **in vitro**

vitrocerámica SF **placa de ~** glass-ceramic hob

vitrocerámico ADJ glass-ceramic

vitrola SF (*LAm*) gramophone, phonograph (*EEUU*)

vitualla SF, **vituallas** SFPL provisions *pl*, victuals *pl*

vituperable ADJ reprehensible

vituperación SF condemnation, censure, vituperation (*frm*)

vituperar ▸conjug 1a◂ VT to condemn, censure, vituperate against (*frm*)

vituperio SM [1] (= *condena*) condemnation, censure, vituperation (*frm*)
[2] (= *deshonra*) shame, disgrace
[3] **vituperios** (= *insultos*) abuse *sing*, insults

vituperioso ADJ (*frm*) vituperative (*frm*), abusive

viuda SF [1] ▸ **viuda negra** (= *araña*) black widow (spider)
[2] (*Andes, Cono Sur*) (= *fantasma*) ghost
[3] (*Andes Culin*) fish stew
[4] (*Caribe*) (= *cometa*) large kite; *ver tb* **viudo**

viudedad SF [1] (= *viudez*) [*de mujer*] widowhood; [*de hombre*] widowerhood
[2] (*Fin*) widow's pension

viudez SF [*de mujer*] widowhood; [*de hombre*] widowerhood

viudo/a Ⓐ ADJ [1] [*persona*] widowed; **estar viuda*** (= *sola*) to be a grass widow
[2] (*Culin**) **garbanzos ~s** chickpeas by themselves
Ⓑ SM/F widower/widow; *ver tb* **viuda**

viva SM cheer; **dar un ~** to give a cheer; **prorrumpir en ~s** to burst out cheering, start to cheer

vivac SM (*pl* **vivacs**) bivouac

vivacidad SF [1] (= *vigor*) vigour, vigor (*EEUU*)
[2] (= *personalidad*) liveliness, vivacity; (= *inteligencia*) sharpness
[3] [*de colores*] brightness

vivalavirgen* Ⓐ ADJ INV happy-go-lucky*
Ⓑ SMF INV happy-go-lucky person*

vivales* SM INV wide boy*, punk (*EEUU**), smooth operator

vivamente ADV (*gen*) in lively fashion; [*describir, recordar*] vividly; [*protestar*] sharply, strongly; [*sentir*] acutely, intensely; **lo siento ~** I am deeply sorry, I sincerely regret it; **se lo deseo ~** I sincerely hope he gets it

vivaque SM bivouac

vivaquear ▸conjug 1a◂ VI to bivouac

vivar[1] SM [1] (*Zool*) warren
[2] (*para peces*) (= *estanque*) fishpond; (*industrial*) fish farm

vivar[2] ▸conjug 1a◂ VT (*LAm*) (= *vitorear*) to cheer

vivaracho ADJ [1] [*persona*] (= *vivo*) jaunty; (= *vivaz*) vivacious
[2] [*ojos*] bright, lively, twinkling
[3] (*Méx*) sharp, sly

vivaz ADJ [1] [*niño, persona*] (= *vivo*) lively; (= *listo*) keen, sharp
[2] (= *de larga vida*) long-lived; (= *duradero*) enduring, lasting; (*Bot*) perennial
[3] (= *vigoroso*) vigorous

vivencia SF experience

vivencial ADJ existential

vivenciar ▸conjug 1b◂ VT to experience

víveres SMPL provisions; (*esp Mil*) stores, supplies

vivero SM [1] [*de plantas*] nursery; (= *semillero*) seedbed; [*de árboles*] tree nursery
[2] (*para peces*) (= *estanque*) fishpond; (*Com*) fish farm; (*Zool*) vivarium ▸ **vivero de ostras** oyster bed
[3] (*fig*) breeding ground; (*pey*) hotbed; **es un ~ de discordias** it's a hotbed of discord

viveza SF [*de ritmo*] liveliness; [*de imagen*] vividness; [*de luz, color*] brightness; [*de mente, movimiento*] sharpness, quickness; [*de sensación*] intensity, acuteness; [*de emoción*] strength, depth; **contestar con ~** to answer with spirit; **la ~ de su inteligencia** the sharpness of his mind; **la ~ de sus sentimientos** the strength of his feelings

vividero ADJ habitable, inhabitable, that can be lived in

vivido ADJ [1] (= *experimentado*) **los años ~s en Brasil** the years we lived in Brazil; **la crisis vivida por el gobierno** the crisis the government went through *o* experienced; **un episodio ~ por el autor** an episode which the author himself experienced
[2] (= *habitado*) lived-in; **la zona más vivida del palacio** the most lived-in part of the palace

vívido ADJ vivid, graphic

vividor(a) Ⓐ ADJ opportunistic
Ⓑ SM (= *aprovechado*) hustler, wide boy*, punk (*EEUU**)
Ⓒ SM/F opportunist

vivienda SF [1] (= *alojamiento*) housing; **el problema de la ~** the housing problem; **la escasez de (la) ~** the housing shortage
[2] (= *casa*) house, home; (= *piso*) flat, apartment (*EEUU*); **segunda ~** second home; **bloque de ~s** block of flats, apartment block (*EEUU*) ▸ **vivienda de renta limitada** *controlled rent housing* ▸ **vivienda en alquiler** (= *casa*) house to let *o* rent; (= *piso*) flat to let *o* rent ▸ **viviendas de protección oficial** *state-subsidized housing*

viviente ADJ living; **los ~s** the living

vivificador ADJ (*gen*) life-giving; (*fig*) revitalizing

vivificante ADJ = **vivificador**

vivificar ▸conjug 1g◂ VT [1] [+ *persona*] to give life to, invigorate
[2] [+ *industria*] to revitalize, bring new life to
[3] [+ *situación, suceso*] to enliven

vivillo ADJ, SM (*Cono Sur*) = **vividor**

vivíparo ADJ viviparous

vivir ▸conjug 3a◂ Ⓐ VI [1] (= *estar vivo*) to live; **los elefantes viven muchos años** elephants live long lives, elephants live for many years; **mientras yo viva** as long as I live; **todavía vive** he's still alive
[2] (= *pasar la vida*) to live; **sólo vive para la música** music is her whole life, she only lives for music; **siempre he vivido honradamente** I have always lived an honest life; **ahora ya puedes ~ tranquila** now you can relax; **desde que me subieron el sueldo no vivo tan mal** since I had a pay rise I haven't been that badly off; **vivieron felices y comieron perdices** they lived happily ever after; **~ bien** to live well; **en este país se vive bien** people live well in this country, people have a good life in this country; ✦**MODISMOS ~ del cuento** to live on *o* by one's wits; **~ para ver** you live and learn; *ver tb* **cuerpo 1**, **Dios 2**
[3] (= *disfrutar de la vida*) **no vivo de la intranquilidad que tengo** I'm worried to death; **no podía ~ de la vergüenza** the shame of it was killing him; **no dejar ~ a algn**: **su marido no la deja ~** her husband is always on at her*, her husband doesn't give her a moment's peace; **los dolores no me dejan ~** the pain never lets up; **los celos no la dejan ~** she is eaten up with jealousy; **saber ~** to know how to live; **tú sí que sabes ~** you really know how to live
[4] (= *habitar*) to live; **en esa casa no vive nadie** nobody lives in that house; **estuve viviendo un año en Londres** I lived in London for a year; **¿vives sola?** do you live on your own?; **viven juntos** (*como pareja*) they live together; (*compartiendo casa*) they live together, they share a house (together)
[5] (= *subsistir*) **con lo que gano no me llega para ~** what I earn is not enough to live on; **la fotografía no me da para ~** I can't make *o* earn a living from photography, photography doesn't give me enough to live on; **viven por encima de sus posibilidades** they live beyond their means; **~ de algo** to live on sth; **vive de la caridad** he lives on charity; **yo vivo de mi trabajo** I work for a living; **vive de ilusiones** he lives in a dream world; **~ al día** to live from day to day; **~ de la pluma** to live by one's pen; **~ de las rentas** (*lit*) to have a private income; **publicó un libro hace años y desde entonces vive de las rentas** years ago he published a book and he's lived off it *o* lived on the strength of it ever since; *ver tb* **aire 1**
[6] (= *durar*) [*recuerdo*] to live, live on; [*prenda, objeto*] to last; **su recuerdo siempre ~á en nuestra memoria** his memory will always be with us, his memory will live on in our minds; **esa chaqueta ya no ~á mucho tiempo** that jacket won't last much longer
[7] (*Mil*) **¿quién vive?** who goes there?; **pedir el quién vive a algn** to challenge sb
[8] (*como exclamación*) **¡viva!** hurray!; **¡viva el rey!** long live the king!; **¡vivan los novios!** (here's) to the bride and groom!
Ⓑ VT [1] (= *experimentar*) [+ *guerra, periodo difícil*] to live through, go through; **nosotros no vivimos la época del comunismo** we didn't live through the communist era; **la época que nos ha tocado ~** the age in which we happen to live; **ha vivido momentos de verdadera angustia** she went through moments of real agony; **tú dedícate a ~ la vida** go ahead and live life to the full *o* get the most out of life
[2] (= *sentir*) to experience; **yo vivo la música de una forma distinta** I experience music in a different way; **parece que estoy viviendo ese momento otra vez** it's as if I were *o* was experiencing that moment all over again
Ⓒ SM (= *forma de vida*) (way of) life; **el buen ~** the good life; **de mal ~**: **una mujer de mal ~** a loose woman; **gente de mal ~** undesirable people

vivisección SF vivisection

vivisector(a) SM/F vivisectionist

vivito ADJ **estar ~ y coleando** to be alive and kicking

vivo/a Ⓐ ADJ [1] (= *con vida*) [1·1] [*persona, animal*] (*tras sustantivo*) living; (*tras verbo*) alive; **los seres ~s** living beings; **lo quemaron ~** he was burned alive; **"se busca vivo o muerto"** "wanted, dead or alive"; **venden los cebos ~s** they sell live bait
[1·2] [*piel*] raw; **tenía la piel en carne viva** his skin was raw; **me dio** *o* **hirió en lo más ~** it cut me to the quick; ✦**MODISMO a lo ~**: **le quitó la muela a lo ~** he just pulled the tooth clean out; **lo explica a lo ~** he explains it very expressively; **describir algo a lo ~** to

describe sth very realistically; *ver tb* **cal**, **fuerza 5**, **lágrima**, **lengua 4**
[2] (*TV, Radio*) **en ~** (= *en directo*) live; (= *en persona*) in person; **una transmisión en ~ desde el estadio** a live broadcast from the stadium; **un espectáculo con música en ~** a live music show, a show with live music; **¿has visto en ~ a algún famoso?** have you ever seen anyone famous in the flesh?
[3] (= *intenso*) [*descripción*] vivid, graphic; [*imaginación, mirada, ritmo*] lively; [*movimiento, paso*] quick, lively; [*color*] bright; [*sensación*] acute; [*genio*] fiery; [*ingenio*] ready; [*inteligencia*] sharp, keen; [*filo*] sharp; **su recuerdo siempre seguirá ~ entre nosotros** her memory will always be with us, her memory will live on in our minds; ♦*MODISMO* **ser la viva imagen** *o* **el ~ retrato de algn** to be the spitting image of sb; *ver tb* **rojo B1**, **voz 1**
[4] [*persona*] (= *listo*) clever; (= *astuto*) sharp; (= *animado*) lively; **pasarse de ~** to be too clever by half*
Ⓑ SM/F [1] (*) (= *aprovechado*) **es un ~** he's a clever one*, he's a sly one*
[2] **los ~s** the living
Ⓒ SM (*Cos*) edging, border

vizacha SF (*LAm Zool*) viscacha

vizcaíno/a Ⓐ ADJ of/from Biscay
Ⓑ SM/F native/inhabitant of Biscay; **los ~s** the people of Biscay

Vizcaya SF Biscay (*Spanish province*); **el Golfo de ~** the Bay of Biscay

vizcondado SM viscounty

vizconde SM viscount

vizcondesa SF viscountess

V.M. ABR = **Vuestra Majestad**

v.m.†† ABR (= **vuesa merced**) *courtesy formula*

V.O. ABR (*Cine*) = **versión original**

Vº.Bº. ABR (= **visto bueno**) OK

vocablo SM (*frm*) word, term; **jugar del ~** to pun, play on words

vocabulario SM vocabulary

vocación SF vocation, calling; **errar la ~** to miss one's vocation; **tener ~ por** to have a vocation for

vocacional Ⓐ ADJ vocational
Ⓑ SF (*Méx Educ*) technical college

vocal Ⓐ ADJ [*cuerdas*] vocal
Ⓑ SMF [*de comité, tribunal*] member; (= *director*) director, member of the board of directors; (= *portavoz*) chairperson
Ⓒ SF (*Ling*) vowel

vocalía SF committee

vocálico ADJ vocalic, vowel *antes de s*

vocalismo SM vowel system

vocalista SMF vocalist, singer

vocalizar ▸conjug 1f◂ Ⓐ VI [1] (= *pronunciar*) to vocalize
[2] (*Mús*) (= *canturrear*) to hum; (= *hacer prácticas*) to sing scales, practise, practice (*EEUU*)
Ⓑ **vocalizarse** VPR to vocalize

vocalmente ADV vocally

vocativo SM vocative

voceado ADJ vaunted, much-trumpeted

voceador Ⓐ ADJ loud, loud-mouthed
Ⓑ SM [1] (= *pregonero*) town crier
[2] (*LAm*) [*de periódicos*] news vendor, newspaper seller

vocear ▸conjug 1a◂ Ⓐ VT [1] [+ *mercancías*] to cry
[2] (= *llamar*) to call loudly to, shout to
[3] (= *dar vivas a*) to cheer, acclaim
[4] [+ *secreto*] to shout to all and sundry, shout from the rooftops
[5] (= *manifestar*) to proclaim; **su cara voceaba su culpabilidad** his face proclaimed his guilt
[6] (*) (= *jactarse*) to boast about, lay public claim to
Ⓑ VI to yell, bawl

vocejón SM loud voice, big voice

voceo SM shouting, yelling, bawling

voceras‡ SM INV loudmouth

vocería SF [1] (= *griterío*) shouting, yelling; (= *escándalo*) hullabaloo*, uproar
[2] (*esp LAm*) (= *cargo*) position of spokesperson

vocerío SM = **vocería**

vocero/a SM/F (*esp LAm*) spokesman/spokeswoman, spokesperson

vociferación SF shouting

vociferador ADJ loud, loud-mouthed

vociferar ▸conjug 1a◂ Ⓐ VT [1] (= *gritar*) to yell, shout
[2] (= *jactarse*) to proclaim boastfully
Ⓑ VI to yell, shout, vociferate (*frm*)

vocinglería SF [1] (= *griterío*) shouting; (= *escándalo*) hubbub, uproar
[2] (= *cualidad*) [*del vociferador*] loudness, noisiness; [*del hablador*] garrulousness

vocinglero ADJ [1] (= *vociferador*) loud-mouthed
[2] (= *hablador*) garrulous

vodevil SM music hall, variety show *o* theatre, vaudeville (*EEUU*)

vodevilesco ADJ music-hall *antes de s*, vaudeville *antes de s* (*EEUU*)

vodka SM vodka

vodú SM (*LAm*) voodoo

voduísmo SM (*LAm*) voodooism

vol. ABR (= **volumen**) vol.

volada SF [1] (= *vuelo*) short flight, single flight
[2] (*LAm*) (*diversos sentidos*) = **bolada**

voladizo ADJ (*Arquit*) projecting

volado Ⓐ ADJ [1] (*Tip*) superior, raised; **letra volada** *o* **voladita** superscript
[2] **estar ~*** (= *loco*) to be crazy*; (= *intranquilo*) to be worried; (= *drogado*) to be high*; (*Méx, Caribe*) (= *soñando*) to be in a dreamy state
[3] (*Chile**) (= *despistado*) absent-minded
[4] (*LAm**) (*de genio*) quick-tempered
[5] (*Arquit*) [*balcón, cornisa*] projecting
Ⓑ SM [1] (*Méx*) (*con una moneda*) **echar un ~** to toss a coin
[2] (*Méx*) (= *aventura*) affair
[3] (*CAm*) (= *mentira*) fib, lie
[4] (*Caribe, Cono Sur Cos*) flounce
Ⓒ ADV (*Andes, CAm, Méx*) in a rush, hastily; **ir ~** to go off in a hurry

volador Ⓐ ADJ flying *antes de s*
Ⓑ SM [1] (= *pez*) flying fish; (= *calamar*) *species of squid*
[2] (= *cohete*) rocket
[3] (*Andes, CAm*) (= *molinillo*) toy windmill
[4] (*Caribe*) (= *cometa*) kite

voladura SF [1] (= *derribo*) blowing up; (*Min*) blasting ► **voladura controlada** controlled explosion
[2] (*Cos*) flounce, ruffle

volandas ADV [1] **en ~** (= *por el aire*) through the air; **¡voy en ~!** (*hum*) I must fly!*
[2] (*) **en ~** (= *con rapidez*) like lightning

volandera SF [1] (= *piedra*) millstone, grindstone
[2] (*Mec*) washer
[3] (*) (= *mentira*) fib

volandero ADJ [1] [*pieza*] loose, shifting; [*cuerda, hoja*] loose; [*dolor*] that moves about
[2] (= *al azar*) random, casual; (= *imprevisto*) unexpected
[3] (*Orn*) fledged, ready to fly; [*persona*] restless

volanta SF [1] (*Andes, Caribe*) (= *rueda*) large wheel
[2] (*Caribe*) (= *carro*) break

volantazo SM (*Aut*) sharp turn; (*fig*) sudden switch, sudden change of direction

volante Ⓐ ADJ [1] (= *volador*) flying
[2] (= *itinerante*) [*estudio, sede*] travelling, traveling (*EEUU*); *ver tb* **meta A1**
[3] (= *inquieto*) [*persona*] unsettled
Ⓑ SM [1] (*Aut*) steering wheel; **se puso un rato al ~** she took the wheel for a while; **ir al ~** to be at the wheel, be driving
[2] (*Téc*) (*en motor*) flywheel; (*en reloj*) balance wheel
[3] (*tb* **papel ~**) (= *nota*) note; (*LAm*) [*de propaganda*] pamphlet; *ver tb* **hoja 2**
[4] (*Esp Med*) referral note; **me dieron un ~ para el oftalmólogo** I was referred to *o* I was given a referral to the ophthalmologist
[5] (*Bádminton*) (= *pelota*) shuttlecock; (= *juego*) badminton
[6] (*Cos*) flounce
Ⓒ SMF (*Chile*) [1] (*Ftbl*) (= *jugador*) winger
[2] (= *conductor*) driver; [*de carreras*] racing driver

volantín Ⓐ ADJ loose, unattached
Ⓑ SM [1] (= *sedal*) fishing line
[2] (*LAm*) (= *cometa*) kite
[3] (*Andes*) (= *cohete*) rocket
[4] (*LAm*) (= *voltereta*) somersault

volantista SM (*Aut*) driver; [*de carreras*] (racing) driver; (*pey*) road hog

volantón Ⓐ ADJ fledged, ready to fly
Ⓑ SM fledgling

volantusa SF (*LAm*) prostitute

volantuzo* SM (*Andes*) snappy dresser*

volapié SM (*Taur*) wounding thrust; **a ~** [*ave*] half walking and half flying; ♦*MODISMO* **de ~*** in a split second

volar ▸conjug 1l◂ Ⓐ VI [1] (= *en el aire*) [*avión, pájaro, persona*] to fly; **nunca he volado en helicóptero** I've never flown in *o* been in a helicopter; **¿a qué hora vuelas mañana?** what time is your flight tomorrow?, what time do you fly tomorrow?; **los papeles salieron volando por la ventana** the papers blew out of the window; **el balón pasó volando por encima de nosotros** the ball flew over our heads; **"vuela con Iberia"** "fly (with) Iberia"; **echar a ~** [+ *pájaro*] to set free, let go; [+ *globo, cometa*] to fly; [+ *noticia*] to spread; **echarse a ~** [*pájaro*] (*por primera vez*) to (begin to) fly; (= *levantar el vuelo*) to take off; **~ en globo** to balloon; **dejar ~ la imaginación** to let one's imagination run riot; ♦*MODISMOS* **~ alto**: **este joven escritor ~á alto** this young writer will go far; **ese político quiere ~ de-**

masiado alto that politician is too ambitious; **en su última novela vuela alto** in his latest novel he reaches new heights; **~ solo** to go it alone; **un sindicato que hoy vuela solo** a trade union which nowadays is going it alone; **empezó a ~ solo en su último libro** in his latest book he branched out on his own; **desde pequeño se le notaban las ganas de ~ solo** since he was a child you could see how much he wanted to do things his own way; *ver tb* **burro B1**
[2] **hacer ~ algo/a algn** to blow sth/sb up; **una bomba hizo ~ el automóvil** a bomb blew up the car; **el choque le hizo ~ por los aires a más de dos metros de la carretera** he was thrown more than two metres from the road by the impact; **hacer ~ algo en pedazos** to blow sth to pieces *o* to smithereens
[3] **volando: ¡venga, volando, que nos vamos!** come on, get a move on, we're going!*; **¡voy para allá volando!** I'll be right there!*; **me preparó la cena volando** he made my dinner in double-quick time*; **hice las maletas volando y me fui** I packed my bags as quick as I could and left*; **pasó volando en la moto** he whizzed *o* sped past on his motorbike; **el deportivo iba volando por la autopista** the sports car sped down the motorway; **~ a hacer algo** to rush to do sth; **voló a decírselo a todo el mundo** he rushed to tell everybody; **me voy volando a echar esta carta** I must rush to post this letter
[4] (= *pasar rápido*) [*noticia*] to travel fast; [*tiempo*] to fly; [*días, semanas, meses*] to fly by; **las buenas noticias vuelan** good news travels fast; **¡cómo vuela el tiempo!** (how) time flies!; **los meses vuelan y pronto llegará el verano** the months are flying by and summer will soon be here
[5] (*) (= *desaparecer*) [*objeto, persona*] to go, disappear; **cuando me di cuenta, el bolso ya había volado** before I knew it, the bag was gone *o* had gone *o* had disappeared; **en una semana ~on las diez botellas** the ten bottles went *o* disappeared in the space of a week; **cuando llegó la policía los ladrones ya habían volado** when the police arrived the robbers had vanished *o* disappeared; **el tabaco parece que vuela en esta casa** cigarettes seem to sprout legs in this house*
[6] (*Arquit*) to stick out
[7] (*Méx**) [*alcohol, diluyente*] to evaporate
[8] (*) (*con drogas*) to trip*, get high*
Ⓑ VT [1] (= *hacer volar*) [+ *cometa, globo*] to fly; (*Caza*) [+ *pájaro*] to flush out; **se pasa el día volando aviones de papel** he spends the day flying paper aeroplanes
[2] (= *hacer explotar*) [+ *edificio, vehículo*] to blow up; [+ *caja fuerte*] to blow (open); **~on la entrada de la mina** they blasted open the entrance to the mine; **le ~on la cabeza de un disparo** they blew his head off with one shot
[3] (*Tip*) [+ *letra, número*] to put in superscript
[4] (*Chile, Méx, Ven**) (= *robar*) to pinch*, nick*
[5] (*LAm**) (= *irritar*) [+ *persona*] to irritate
[6] (*CAm*) ✦**MODISMOS ~ diente** to eat; **~ lengua** to talk, speak; **~ máquina** to type; **~ pata** to walk
Ⓒ **volarse** VPR [1] (= *irse por el aire*) [*papel, paraguas*] to blow away; [*globo*] to fly away, fly off; [*sombrero*] to blow off; **se me ~on todos los papeles** all my papers blew away; **con el viento se me ha volado el paraguas** the wind has blown my umbrella away; **se le voló el sombrero** his hat blew off
[2] (*) (= *escaparse*) [*persona*] to run off; **el marido se voló con su amante** the husband ran off with his lover
[3] (*LAm**) (= *desaparecer*) to go, disappear
[4] (*LAm**) (= *enfadarse*) to lose one's temper, blow up*

volate SM [1] (*Andes*) (= *confusión*) confusion, mess
[2] (*Andes*) (= *objetos*) lot of odd things
[3] **echar ~** (*Caribe**) (= *desesperarse*) to throw up one's hands in despair

volatería SF [1] (= *cetrería*) hawking, falconry
[2] (*Orn*) (= *pájaros*) birds *pl*, flock of birds; (= *aves*) fowls *pl*
[3] (= *pensamientos*) random thoughts *pl*, formless collection of ideas
[4] (*Andes*) (= *fuegos artificiales*) fireworks *pl*

volatero SM (*Andes*) rocket

volátil ADJ [1] (*Quím*) volatile
[2] [*carácter, situación*] volatile, changeable

volatilidad SF [1] (*Quím*) volatility, volatile nature
[2] [*de carácter, situación*] volatility, changeableness

volatilizar ▸conjug 1f◂ Ⓐ VT (*Quím*) to volatilize
Ⓑ **volatilizarse** VPR [1] (*Quím*) to volatilize
[2] (= *esfumarse*) to vanish into thin air; **¡volatilízate!**‡ get lost!‡

volatín SM [1] (= *acrobacia*) acrobatics *pl*
[2] = **volatinero**

volatinero/a SM/F tightrope walker

volcado SM ► **volcado de memoria** (*Inform*) dump

volcán SM [1] (*Geog*) volcano; ✦**MODISMO estar sobre un ~** to be sitting on top of a powder keg ► **volcán apagado** extinct volcano ► **volcán de lodo** mud volcano ► **volcán inactivo** dormant volcano
[2] (*Andes, Cono Sur*) (= *torrente*) summer torrent; (= *avalancha*) avalanche
[3] (*CAm*) (= *montón*) pile, heap; **un ~ de cosas** a lot of things, a whole heap of things
[4] (*Caribe*) (= *estrépito*) deafening noise; (= *confusión*) confusion, hubbub

volcanada SF (*Cono Sur*) whiff

volcanarse ▸conjug 1a◂ VPR (*Andes*) to break down

volcánico ADJ volcanic

volcar ▸conjug 1g, 1l◂ Ⓐ VT [1] (= *tirar*) [+ *vaso*] to upset, knock over; [+ *contenido*] to empty out, tip out; [+ *carga*] to dump; [+ *coche, camión*] to overturn; [+ *barco*] to overturn, capsize
[2] **estar volcado a un cometido** to be dedicated to a task
[3] **~ a algn**† (= *marear*) to make sb dizzy, make sb's head swim; (= *convencer*) to force sb to change his mind
[4] (†) (= *irritar*) to irritate, exasperate; (= *desconcertar*) to upset; (= *embromar*) to tease
Ⓑ VI [*coche, camión*] to overturn
Ⓒ **volcarse** VPR [1] (= *voltearse*) [*recipiente*] to be upset, get overturned; [*contenido*] to tip over; [*coche, camión*] to overturn; [*barco*] to capsize
[2] (= *desvivirse*) to bend over backwards*, to go out of one's way; **~se para** *o* **por conseguir algo** to do one's utmost to get sth; **~se por complacer a algn** to bend over backwards to satisfy sb*
[3] (= *entregarse*) **~se en una actividad** to throw o.s. into an activity

volea SF volley; **media ~** half volley

volear ▸conjug 1a◂ VT, VI to volley; **~ por alto** to lob

voleibol SM volleyball

voleiplaya SM beach ball, beach volleyball

voleo SM [1] (= *volea*) volley; ✦**MODISMOS de un ~** ◊ **del primer ~** (= *rápidamente*) quickly; (= *bruscamente*) brusquely, suddenly; (= *de un golpe*) at one blow; **sembrar a** *o* **al ~** to scatter the seed; **repartir algo a** *o* **al ~** to distribute sth haphazardly
[2] (*) (= *golpe*) punch, bash*

volframio SM wolfram

Volga SM Volga

volibol SM volleyball

volición SF volition

volido SM (*LAm*) flight; **de un ~** quickly, at once

volitivo ADJ volitional, volitive; **capacidad volitiva** willpower

volován SM vol-au-vent

volqueta SF, **volquete** SM (*Aut*) dumper, dumping lorry, dump truck (*EEUU*); (= *carro*) tipcart

voltaico ADJ voltaic

voltaje SM voltage

voltario ADJ (*Cono Sur*) [1] (= *cambiable*) fickle, changeable
[2] (= *voluntarioso*) wilful, headstrong
[3] (= *pulcro*) spruce, dapper

volteada SF [1] (*Cono Sur Agr*) roundup
[2] (*CAm, Cono Sur, Méx Pol*) defection

volteado SM [1] (= *volcado*) turn-over, turning over
[2] (*Andes Mil*) deserter; (*Pol*) turncoat

volteador(a) SM/F acrobat

voltear ▸conjug 1a◂ Ⓐ VT [1] (*esp LAm*) (= *volver al revés*) to turn over, turn upside down; (= *dar la vuelta a*) to turn round; (= *lanzar al aire*) to toss
[2] **~ la espalda** (*LAm*) (= *dar la espalda*) to turn one's back
[3] (*esp Cono Sur, Méx*) (= *volcar*) to knock, knock over
[4] [+ *campanas*] to peal
[5] (*esp LAm*) [+ *lazo*] to whirl, twirl
[6] **~ a algn** (*Andes, Caribe*) to force sb to change his mind
[7] (*Caribe*) (= *buscar*) to search all over for
Ⓑ VI [1] (= *dar vueltas*) to roll over, go rolling over and over; (= *dar una voltereta*) to somersault
[2] (*LAm*) (= *torcer*) to turn; **~ a la derecha** to turn right; (= *volverse*) to turn round
[3] (*LAm*) **~ a hacer algo** to do sth again; **volteó a decirlo** he said it again
[4] (*Caribe*‡) **volteó con mi amiga** he went off with my girlfriend
Ⓒ **voltearse** VPR (*LAm*) [1] (= *dar la vuelta*) to turn round; (*Pol*) (= *cambiar de lado*) to change one's allegiance, go over to the other side
[2] (= *volcarse*) to overturn, tip over

voltereta SF (= *de acróbata, gimnasta*) (*hacia delante*) somersault; (*hacia los lados*) cartwheel; (*por caída*) roll, tumble; **dar ~s** (*hacia delante*) to turn somersaults; (*hacia los lados*) to do cartwheels ► **voltereta lateral** cartwheel ► **voltereta sobre las manos** handspring

voltímetro SM voltmeter

voltio SM 1 (*Fís*) volt
 2 (*) (= *vuelta, paseo*) stroll; **darse un ~** to go for *o* take a stroll

volubilidad SF (= *inconstancia*) fickleness, changeableness; (= *imprevisibilidad*) unpredictability; (= *inestabilidad*) instability

voluble ADJ 1 [*persona*] (= *inconstante*) fickle, changeable; (= *imprevisible*) erratic, unpredictable; (= *inestable*) unstable
 2 (*Bot*) twining, climbing

volumen SM (*pl* **volúmenes**) 1 [*de cuerpo*] volume; **el ~ de un líquido** the volume of a liquid; **cajas de gran ~** large *o* bulky boxes ► **volumen atómico** atomic volume ► **volumen molecular** molecular volume
 2 [*de sonido*] volume; **bajar el ~** to turn the volume down; **subir el ~** to turn the volume up; **puso la radio a todo ~** he turned the radio full up
 3 (*Com*) volume; **el ~ de las exportaciones** the volume of exports ► **volumen de contratación** trading volume ► **volumen de negocios**, **volumen de operaciones** turnover
 4 (= *tomo*) volume
 5 [*de cabello*] body; **esta espuma da ~ y brillo a su cabello** this foam gives your hair body and shine

volumétrico ADJ volumetric

voluminoso ADJ (*gen*) voluminous; [*paquete*] bulky

voluntad SF 1 (= *capacidad decisoria*) will; **no tiene ~ propia** he has no will of his own; **por ~ propia** of one's own volition *o* free will
 2 (= *deseo*) wish; **su ~ es hacerse misionero** his wish is to become a missionary; **no lo dije con ~ de ofenderle** I did not say it with any wish to offend you, I had no desire to offend you; **última ~** last wish; (*Jur*) last will and testament; **lo hizo contra mi ~** he did it against my will; **tienen ~ de ganar** they have the will to win; **hágase tu ~** (*Rel*) Thy will be done; **por causas ajenas a mi ~** for reasons beyond my control; **hace siempre su santa ~** he always does exactly as he pleases ► **voluntad divina** divine will ► **voluntad popular** will of the people
 3 (= *determinación*) (*tb* **fuerza de ~**) willpower; **le cuesta, pero tiene mucha ~** it's difficult for him, but he has a lot of willpower *o* a strong will; **no tiene ~ para dejar de beber** he hasn't the willpower to give up drinking; **es una chica con mucha ~** she's a very strong-willed girl; **hace falta ~ para escucharlo hasta el final** you need a strong will to listen to it right through ► **voluntad débil** weak will ► **voluntad de hierro**, **voluntad férrea** iron will
 4 (= *disposición*) will; **buena ~**: **lo solucionaremos con un poco de buena ~** with a bit of good will we'll find a solution; **lo sugerí con buena ~** I suggested it with the best of intentions, I suggested it in good faith; **los hombres de buena ~** (*Rel*) men of goodwill; **mala ~**: **hay muy mala ~ contra el presidente** there is a lot of ill will against the president; ✦MODISMO **ganar(se) la ~ de algn** to win sb over
 5 **a ~** at will; **se abre a ~** it opens at will; **se puede beber a ~** you can drink as much as you like
 6 **la ~** (= *dinero*): **un mendigo le pidió la ~** a beggar asked him if he could spare some money; **cada uno da la ~ para contribuir al regalo** everyone is free to contribute what they want towards the present; **—¿cuánto es? —la ~** "how much is it?" — "as much as you think it's worth"
 7 (†) (= *afecto*) fondness, affection; **tener ~ a algn** to be fond of sb, feel affection for sb

voluntariado SM (= *trabajo*) voluntary work; (= *trabajadores*) voluntary workers *pl*

voluntariamente ADV voluntarily

voluntariedad SF wilfulness, unreasonableness

voluntario/a Ⓐ ADJ 1 (= *no obligado*) voluntary
 2 (*Mil*) voluntary; [*fuerza*] volunteer *antes de s*
 Ⓑ SM/F volunteer; **alistarse** *u* **ofrecerse ~** to volunteer (**para** for)

voluntariosamente ADV 1 (= *con buenas intenciones*) dedicatedly, in a well-intentioned way
 2 (= *tercamente*) wilfully

voluntarioso ADJ 1 (= *dedicado*) dedicated, willing
 2 (= *terco*) headstrong, wilful, willful (*EEUU*)

voluntarismo SM (= *terquedad*) headstrong nature, wilfulness; (= *arbitrariedad*) arbitrariness

voluntarista ADJ (= *terco*) headstrong, wilful; (= *arbitrario*) arbitrary

voluptuosamente ADV voluptuously

voluptuosidad SF voluptuousness

voluptuoso/a Ⓐ ADJ voluptuous
 Ⓑ SM/F voluptuary

voluta SF 1 (*Arquit*) scroll, volute
 2 [*de humo*] spiral, column

volvedor Ⓐ ADJ (*Andes, Caribe*) **este caballo es ~** this horse always finds its way home
 Ⓑ SM 1 (= *llave inglesa*) wrench; (= *destornillador*) screwdriver
 2 (*Andes*) (= *plus*) bonus, extra

volver ▸conjug 2h◂ (*pp* **vuelto**) Ⓐ VT 1 (= *dar la vuelta a*) [+ *cabeza*] to turn; [+ *colchón, tortilla, enfermo*] to turn over; [+ *jersey, calcetín*] to turn inside out; [+ *página*] to turn, turn over; **~ la espalda** to turn away; **me volvió la espalda** he turned his back on me; **~ la esquina** to go round *o* turn the corner; ✦MODISMO **tener a algn vuelto como un calcetín** *o* **una media** to have sb wrapped round one's little finger
 2 (= *cambiar la orientación de*) to turn; **volvió el arma contra sí mismo** he turned the gun on himself; **~ la vista atrás** to look back; **~ los ojos al pasado** to look back; **volvieron los ojos a épocas más recientes** they looked to more recent times; **vuelve sus ojos ahora hacia uno de sus grandes compositores** she now turns to one of her favourite composers; **~ el pensamiento a Dios** to turn one's thoughts to God; **~ la proa al viento** to turn the bow into the wind
 3 (*) (= *devolver*) [+ *compra*] to return; [+ *comida*] to bring up; [+ *imagen*] to reflect; [+ *objeto lanzado*] to send back, return; [+ *visita*] to return; **~ algo a su lugar** to return sth to its place, put sth back (in its place); **~ la casa a su estado original** to return *o* restore the house to its original condition; **~ bien por mal** to return good for evil
 4 (= *enrollar*) [+ *manga*] to roll up
 5 (+ *ADJ*) to make; **el accidente lo volvió inservible** the accident left it useless; **el ácido lo vuelve azul** the acid turns it blue, the acid makes it go blue; **vuelve fieras a los hombres** it turns men into wild beasts; **~ loco a algn** to drive sb mad
 6 (*Ling*) to translate (**a** into)
 Ⓑ VI 1 (= *regresar*) (*a donde se está*) to come back, return; (*a donde se estaba*) to go back, return (**a** to; **de** from); **déjalas aquí y luego vuelves a por ellas** leave them here and come back for them later; **~ victorioso** to come back victorious, return in triumph; **no he vuelto por allí** I've never gone back there; **volvió muy cansado** he got back very tired; **volviendo a lo que decía …** going back *o* returning to what I was saying …; **~ atrás** to go back, turn back; **~ a una costumbre** to revert to a habit
 2 **~ a hacer algo** to do sth again; **~ a empezar** to start (over) again; **me he vuelto a equivocar** I've made a mistake again, I've made another mistake; **he vuelto a salir con ella** I've started going out with her again; **volvió a casarse** she remarried, she (got) married again; **volví a poner en marcha el motor** I restarted the engine; **~ a hacerlo** to redo it; **~ a pintar algo** to repaint sth
 3 **~ en sí** to come to, come round; **~ sobre sí** to change one's mind
 4 [*camino*] to turn (**a** to)
 Ⓒ **volverse** VPR 1 1 (= *darse la vuelta*) 1·1 [*persona*] to turn, turn round; **se volvió a mí** he turned to me; **se volvió para mirarlo** he turned (round) to look at it; **~se atrás** (*en camino*) to turn back; (*en decisión*) to back out; (*en negociaciones*) to withdraw; **a última hora se han vuelto atrás** they pulled out *o* backed out at the last minute; **si pudiese ~me atrás en el tiempo …** if I could go back in time …
 1·2 [*objeto*] (*boca abajo*) to turn upside down; (*de dentro a fuera*) to turn inside out; **se le volvió el paraguas** his umbrella turned inside out; ✦MODISMO **~se (en) contra (de) algn** to turn against sb; **todo se le vuelve en contra** everything is turning against him; **todo se le vuelven dificultades** troubles come thick and fast for him
 2 (= *regresar*) to turn back, go back; **empezó a llover y nos volvimos** it started to rain and we turned back; **vuélvete a buscarlo** go back and look for it
 3 (+ *ADJ*) **se ha vuelto muy cariñoso** he's become very affectionate; **en el ácido se vuelve más oscuro** it turns *o* goes darker in the acid; **~se loco** to go mad
 4 [*leche*] to go off, turn sour

vomitado ADJ [*persona*] sickly

vomitar ▸conjug 1a◂ Ⓐ VT 1 (= *devolver*) to vomit, bring up; **~ sangre** to spit blood
 2 [+ *humo, llamas*] to belch, belch forth; [+ *lava*] spew; [+ *injurias*] to hurl (**contra** at)
 3 [+ *secreto*] to tell reluctantly, finally come out with; [+ *ganancias*] to disgorge, shed
 Ⓑ VI 1 (= *devolver*) to vomit, be sick
 2 (*fig*) **eso me da ganas de ~** that makes me sick, that makes me want to puke*

vomitera SF, **vomitina** SF vomiting, retching

vomitivo Ⓐ ADJ [1] (*Med*) emetic
[2] (*fig*) disgusting; [*chiste*] sick-making, repulsive
Ⓑ SM [1] (*Med*) emetic
[2] (*Cono Sur*) (= *fastidio*) nuisance, bore

vómito SM [1] (= *acto*) vomiting, being sick ► **vómito de sangre** spitting of blood
[2] (= *materia*) vomit, sick
[3] (*LAm*) ► **vómito negro** yellow fever

vomitona* SF bad turn*

vomitorio SM vomitorium, vomitory

voquible SM (*hum*) word

voracear ▸conjug 1a◂ VT (*Cono Sur*) to challenge in a loud voice

voracidad SF voracity, voraciousness

vorágine SF [*de mar, río*] whirlpool, vortex, maelstrom (*frm*); [*de odio, destrucción, confusión*] maelstrom; [*de actividad, publicidad*] whirl

voraz ADJ [1] (= *devorador*) voracious, ravenous; (*pey*) greedy
[2] [*fuego*] raging, fierce
[3] (*Méx*) (= *audaz*) bold

vorazmente ADV (*gen*) voraciously, ravenously; (*pey*) greedily

vórtice SM [1] (= *remolino*) [*de agua*] whirlpool, vortex; [*de viento*] whirlwind
[2] [*de ciclón*] eye

vos PRON PERS [1] (*esp Cono Sur**) you *sing*
[2] (††) you, ye††

vosear* ▸conjug 1a◂ VT (*esp Cono Sur*) to address as "vos"

voseo* SM (*esp Cono Sur*) *addressing a person as "vos", the familiar usage*

Vosgos SMPL Vosges

vosotros/as PRON (*esp Esp*) [1] (*sujeto*) you (*familiar form of address*); **~ vendréis conmigo** you'll come with me; **hacedlo ~ mismos** do it yourselves
[2] (*después de prep, en comparaciones*) you; **lo he comprado para ~** I've bought it for you; **¿no pedís nada para ~?** aren't you going to ask for anything for yourselves?; **lo han hecho mejor que vosotras** they've done it better than you; **irán sin ~** they'll go without you

votación SF (= *acto*) voting; (= *votos*) ballot, vote; **por ~ popular** by popular vote; **por ~ secreta** by secret ballot; **someter algo a ~** to put sth to the vote, take a vote on sth; **la ~ ha sido nutrida** voting has been busy ► **votación a mano alzada** show of hands ► **votación por poder** voting by proxy ► **votación táctica** tactical voting ► **votación unánime** unanimous vote

votante Ⓐ ADJ voting
Ⓑ SMF voter

votar ▸conjug 1a◂ Ⓐ VT [1] (*Pol*) [+ *candidato, partido*] to vote for; [+ *moción, proyecto de ley*] to pass, approve (by vote); **Pérez fue el más votado** Pérez received the highest number of votes, Pérez got most votes
[2] (*Rel*) to vow, promise (**a** to)
Ⓑ VI [1] (*Pol*) to vote (**por** for)
[2] (*Rel*) to vow, take a vow
[3] (= *echar pestes*) to curse, swear

votivo ADJ votive

voto SM [1] (*Pol*) vote; **dar su ~** to cast one's vote, give one's vote (**a** for); **emitir su ~** to cast one's vote; **ganar por siete ~s** to win by seven votes; **hubo 13 ~s a favor y 11 en contra** there were 13 votes for and 11 against; **tener ~** to have a vote ► **voto afirmativo** vote in favour ► **voto bloque** block vote ► **voto cautivo** captive vote ► **voto de calidad** casting vote ► **voto de castigo** protest vote ► **voto de censura** vote of censure, vote of no confidence ► **voto decisivo** casting vote ► **voto de conciencia** free vote ► **voto de confianza** vote of confidence ► **voto de desconfianza** vote of no confidence ► **voto de gracias** vote of thanks ► **voto de los indecisos** floating vote ► **voto en blanco** blank vote ► **voto fluctuante** floating vote ► **voto grupo** card vote ► **voto nulo** spoiled ballot paper ► **voto por correo** postal vote ► **voto secreto** secret vote, secret ballot
[2] (*Rel*) (= *promesa*) vow; (= *ofrenda*) ex voto; **hacer ~ de** + INFIN to take a vow to + *infin* ► **voto de castidad** vow of chastity ► **voto de obediencia** vow of obedience ► **voto de pobreza** vow of poverty ► **voto de silencio** vow of silence ► **votos monásticos** monastic vows
[3] (= *juramento*) oath, curse; (= *palabrota*) swearword
[4] **votos** (= *deseos*) wishes, good wishes; **hacer ~s por el restablecimiento de algn** to wish sb a quick recovery, hope that sb will get well soon; **hago ~s para que se remedie pronto** I pray that it will be speedily put right, I earnestly hope that something will soon be done about it; **mis mejores ~s por su éxito** my best wishes for its success

vox populi ADJ vox populi; **ser ~** to become common knowledge

voy *ver* **ir**

voyeur [bo'jer] SM voyeur

voyeurismo [boje'rismo] SM voyeurism

vóytelas EXCL (*Méx*) wow!*

voz SF [1] (= *sonido humano*) voice; **con la ~ entrecortada** *o* **empañada** in a voice choked with emotion; **me temblaba la ~** my voice was trembling *o* shaking; **aclararse la ~** to clear one's throat; **ahuecar la ~** to deepen one's voice; **en ~ alta** (= *de forma audible*) aloud, out loud; (= *con tono potente*) loudly; **leyó el poema en ~ alta** he read the poem aloud *o* out loud; **soñar en ~ alta** to think aloud *o* out loud; **¿me lo puedes repetir en ~ alta?** can you say that again louder?; **en ~ baja** in a low voice, in a whisper; **me lo dijo en ~ baja** she whispered it to me, she told me in a whisper *o* in a low voice; **algunos comentaban, en ~ baja, que sería mejor que dimitiera** some were whispering that it would be best if he resigned; **le canta en ~ baja para que se duerma** he sings softly to her to put her to sleep; **está empezando a cambiar la ~** his voice is beginning to break; **forzar la ~** to strain one's voice; **a media ~** in a whisper; **estábamos hablando a media ~ en la oscuridad** we were whispering in the dark; **mudar la ~** = **cambiar la voz**; **perder la ~** ◊ **quedarse sin ~** (*temporalmente*) to lose one's voice; (*definitivamente*) to lose the power of speech; **tener la ~ tomada** to be hoarse; **a una ~** with one voice; **de viva ~** aloud; **la votación se realizó de viva ~** people voted aloud; **me lo dijo de viva ~** he told me himself *o* personally *o* in person; ✦***MODISMOS* decir algo a ~ en cuello** *o* **a ~ en grito** to shout sth at the top of one's voice; **ser la ~ de su amo** to speak with one's master's voice ► **voz argentina** silvery voice ► **voz en off** (*TV, Cine*) voice-over ► **voz humana** human voice; *ver tb* **anudar B3**, **desanudar**, **levantar A7**, **torrente 2**
[2] (*Mús*) [2·1] (= *sonido*) [*de instrumento*] sound; **la ~ del órgano** the sound *o* (*liter*) the strains of the organ
[2·2] (= *persona*) voice; **canción a cuatro voces** song for four voices, four-part song; **cantar a dos voces** to sing a duet; **llevar la ~ cantante** (*en un grupo de pop, rock*) to be the lead singer; (*en un concierto clásico*) to be the lead soprano/tenor *etc*; (*fig*) to call the tune
[2·3] (= *habilidad para el canto*) voice; **tiene muy buena ~** she has a very good voice; **estar en ~** to be in good voice
[3] (= *aviso*) voice; **la ~ de la conciencia** the promptings *o* voice of conscience; **hay que escuchar también la ~ del corazón** you must listen to your heart as well; **dar la ~ de alarma** to raise the alarm; **los consumidores han dado la ~ de alarma** consumers have raised the alarm; **dar una ~ a algn** to give sb a shout; **cuando hayas terminado, dame una ~** give me a shout when you've finished* ► **voz de mando** (*Mil*) command; **formaron a la ~ de mando** they lined up at the command; **Patricia parece llevar la ~ de mando en este asunto** Patricia is the boss when it comes to this matter
[4] (= *rumor*) rumour, rumor (EEUU); **circula** *o* **corre la ~ de que …** there is a rumour going round that …, the word is that …; **hacer circular** *o* **correr la ~ de que …** to spread the rumour *o* word that … ► **voz común** hearsay, gossip
[5] (*Pol*) (= *opinión*) voice; **la ~ del pueblo** the voice of the people; **tener ~ y voto** to have full voting rights; **miembro con ~ y voto** full member; **nosotros no tenemos ni ~ ni voto en este asunto** we have no say whatsoever in this matter; ✦***MODISMO* no tener ~ en capítulo** to have no say in a matter ► **voz pública** public opinion; **sus equivocaciones no suelen salir a la ~ pública** their mistakes are never made public
[6] **voces** (= *gritos*) shouting *sing*; **se oían voces a lo lejos** there was shouting in the distance; **a voces**: **discutir a voces** to argue noisily *o* loudly; **estuve llamando a voces pero no me abrieron la puerta** I called out *o* shouted but they didn't open the door; **su boda es un secreto a voces** their marriage is a well-known secret; **dar** *o* **pegar voces** to shout; ✦***MODISMO* dar cuatro voces a algn** to take sb to task; *ver tb* **pedir A6**
[7] (*en el juego*) call
[8] (*Ling*) [8·1] (= *vocablo*) word; **una ~ de origen árabe** a word of Arabic origin
[8·2] [*del verbo*] voice
► **voz activa** active voice ► **voz media** middle voice ► **voz pasiva** passive voice

vozarrón SM booming voice

VP ABR (= **Vice-Presidente**) V.P.

VPO SF ABR = **vivienda de protección oficial**

vra. ABR = **vuestra**

vro. ABR = **vuestro**

vs. ABR (= **versus**) vs

vto. ABR (*Com*) = **vencimiento**

vudú SM voodoo

vuduismo SM voodooism

vuela *etc ver* **volar**

vuelapluma: **a ~** ADV quickly, without much thought

vuelco SM [1] (= *acción*) upset, spill; **dar un ~** [*coche*] to overturn; [*barco*] to capsize
[2] **mi corazón dio un ~** my heart missed a beat
[3] (*fig*) catastrophe; **este negocio va a dar un ~** this business is heading for catastrophe

vuelillo SM lace adornment, frill

vuelo[1] *ver* **volar**

vuelo[2] SM [1] [*de ave, avión*] flight; **se servirá un desayuno durante el ~** breakfast will be served during the flight; **alzar** *o* **levantar el ~** (= *echar a volar*) to fly off; (= *marcharse*) to dash off; (= *independizarse*) to leave the nest; **remontar el ~: la cigüeña remontó el ~** the stork soared (up) into the sky, the stork took the sky; **la economía empieza a remontar el ~** the economy is beginning to take off; ✦*MODISMOS* **captar** *o* **cazar** *o* **coger algo al ~** to be quick to understand sth; **cazarlas al ~** to be quick on the uptake*; **de** *o* **en un ~** rapidly; **no se oía ni el ~ de una mosca** you could have heard a pin drop; **tomar ~** to grow, develop ► **vuelo a baja cota** low-level flying ► **vuelo a vela** gliding ► **vuelo chárter** charter flight ► **vuelo con ala delta** hang-gliding ► **vuelo con motor** powered flight ► **vuelo de demostración** demonstration flight ► **vuelo de instrucción** training flight ► **vuelo de órbita** orbital flight ► **vuelo de prueba(s)** test flight ► **vuelo de reconocimiento** reconnaissance flight ► **vuelo directo** direct flight, non-stop flight ► **vuelo en picado** dive ► **vuelo espacial** space flight ► **vuelo interior** internal flight, domestic flight ► **vuelo libre** hang-gliding ► **vuelo nacional** domestic flight ► **vuelo rasante** low-level flying ► **vuelo regular** scheduled flight ► **vuelo sin escalas, vuelo sin etapas** non-stop flight ► **vuelo sin motor** gliding
[2] (*Orn*) (= *plumas*) flight feathers *pl*; (= *alas*) wings *pl*; **tirar al ~** to shoot at birds on the wing; ✦*MODISMOS* **cortar los ~s a algn** to clip sb's wings; **de altos ~s** [*plan*] important; [*ejecutivo*] high-flying
[3] [*de falda, capa*] **el ~ de la falda** the spread *o* swirl of the skirt; **falda de mucho ~** full *o* wide skirt
[4] (*Arquit*) projection

vuelta SUSTANTIVO FEMENINO
[1] [= **giro**] **una ~ de la tierra** one revolution of the earth; **el documento dio la ~ por toda la oficina** the document went all round the office; **¡media ~!** (*Mil*) about turn!, about face! (*EEUU*); **los soldados dieron media ~** the soldiers did an about-turn *o* (*EEUU*) an about-face; **estaba cerrado y tuvimos que darnos media ~** it was closed so we had to turn round and go back; **la ~ al mundo** (= *viaje*) a round-the-world trip; **quiere dar la ~ al mundo** she wants to go round the world ► **vuelta al ruedo** (*Taur*) *circuit of the ring made by a triumphant bullfighter*; **dar la ~ al ruedo** to go round the ring ► **vuelta atrás** backward step ► **vuelta de campana**: **el coche dio una ~ de campana en el aire** the car turned right over in mid-air ► **vuelta de tuerca** turn of the screw ► **vuelta en redondo** complete turn
◆ **dar la vuelta** (= *volverse*) to turn round; **al final del callejón tienes que dar la ~** you'll have to turn round at the end of the street; **dar la ~ a** [+ *llave, manivela*] to turn; [+ *página*] to turn (over)
◆ **dar vueltas**: **el camión dio dos ~s y cayó boca abajo** the lorry turned over twice and landed upside down; **dar ~s sobre un eje** to turn on *o* spin round an axis; **he estado dando ~s en la cama toda la noche** I've been tossing and turning (in bed) all night; **el avión dio ~s y más ~s antes de aterrizar** the plane circled round and round before landing; **he tenido que dar muchas ~s para encontrarlo** I had to go all over the place to find it; **dar ~s alrededor de un planeta** to go *o* revolve round a planet
◆ **dar vueltas a algo**: **el cinturón le daba dos ~s a la cintura** the belt went twice round her waist; **le dimos tres ~s al parque corriendo** we ran three times round the park
◆ **darle vueltas a algn**: **me da ~s la cabeza** my head is spinning; **estaba mareado y todo me daba ~s** I was dizzy and everything was going *o* spinning round
◆ **darse la vuelta** (*de pie*) to turn round; (*tumbado*) to turn over; **date la ~ para que te pueda peinar** turn round so I can do your hair; **me di la ~ porque me estaba quemando la espalda** I turned over because my back was getting burnt
[2] [= **otro lado**] [*de hoja*] back, other side; [*de tela*] wrong side; **a la ~ de la página** on the next page, overleaf; **lo escribió a la ~ del sobre** he wrote it on the back of the envelope; **dar la ~ a** [+ *disco*] to turn over; **dale la ~ al jersey** (= *ponlo del derecho*) turn the jumper the right way out; (= *ponlo del revés*) turn the jumper inside out; **dale la ~ al vaso** (= *ponlo boca arriba*) turn the glass the right way up; (= *ponlo boca abajo*) turn the glass upside down; **a la ~ de la esquina** around the corner; **la tienda está a la ~ de la esquina** the shop is just around the corner; **las elecciones están ya a la ~ de la esquina** the elections are almost upon us *o* just around the corner
[3] [= **regreso**] [3·1] (= *acción*) **¿para cuándo tenéis prevista la ~?** when do you expect to be back?; **¡hasta la ~!** see you when I/you get back; **este acuerdo supone una ~ a la normalidad** the agreement means that things should get back to normal; **la ~ al colegio** (*en septiembre*) the new school year; **"~ al colegio"** "back to school"; **a ~ de correo** by return (of post); **de ~** on the way back; **de ~, iremos a verlos** we'll go and see them on the way back; **de ~ al trabajo** back to work; **estar de ~** (*lit*) to be back; **estaremos de ~ el domingo** we'll be back on Sunday; **¿meterme en política? a mi edad uno ya está de ~ de todo** go into politics? I'm too old for that sort of thing; **el público ya está de ~ de todo** the public has seen it all before
[3·2] (*en transportes*) **si cierras la ~ el billete sale más barato** the ticket is cheaper if you specify the return date; **billete de ida y ~** return ticket; **el viaje de ~** the return journey
[4] [= **paseo**] (*a pie*) stroll; (*en coche, bicicleta*) ride; **dar una ~**: **dimos una ~ por el parque** we went for a stroll in the park; **después de estudiar me voy a dar una ~** I'm going out for a bit when I've finished studying; **salieron a dar una ~ en la bici** they went out for a ride on their bikes; **nos dio una ~ en su coche** he gave us a ride in his car, he took us for a spin in his car*; **si quieres ver pobreza date una ~ por esta zona** if you want to see poverty take a walk round here
[5] [*en camino, ruta*] **una carretera con muchas ~s** a road with lots of bends *o* twists and turns in it; **el camino da muchas ~s hasta llegar a la cima** the road twists and turns up to the summit; **por este camino se da mucha más ~** it's much further this way, this is a much longer way round
[6] [*a un circuito, pista*] lap; (*Golf*) round; **di tres ~s a la pista** I did three laps of the track ► **vuelta de honor** lap of honour
[7] [*Ciclismo*] tour ► **vuelta ciclista** cycle tour; **la ~ ciclista a España** the Tour of Spain
[8] [= **ronda**] [*de elección, torneo, bebidas*] round; **el presidente ganó en la segunda ~** the president won in the second round; **la segunda ~ de la competición** the second round of the competition; **partido de ~** return match; **me tocó pagar la primera ~** I had to pay the first round
[9] [= **dinero suelto**] change; **quédese con la ~** keep the change
[10] [= **cambio**] **las ~s de la vida** the ups and downs of life; **este acontecimiento dio la ~ a las negociaciones** this event changed the direction of the talks completely
[11] [= **cabo, fin**] **a la ~ de tres años** after three years
[12] [*de cuerda*] loop ► **vuelta de cabo** (*Náut*) hitch
[13] [*Cos*] [*de puntos*] row; [*de pantalón*] turn-up, cuff (*EEUU*)
[14] ✦*MODISMOS* **a ~s con algo**: **¡ya estamos otra vez a ~s con la guerra!** not the war again!; **siempre están a ~s con lo mismo** they're always going on about the same thing; **buscar las ~s a algn** to try to catch sb out; **dar cien (mil) ~s a algn***: **te da cien (mil) ~s** she can run rings round you, she's miles better than you; **dar la ~ a algn** (*CAm**) to con sb*; **darle ~s a algo**: **darle ~s a un asunto** to think a matter over; **no le des más ~s a lo que dijo** stop worrying about what he said; **no tiene ~ de hoja**: **esto es así y no tiene más ~ de hoja** that's how it is and that's all there is to it; **tenemos que hacerlo ya y no hay más ~ de hoja** we've got to do it now, there are no two ways about it *o* there's no alternative; **poner a algn de ~ y media*** (= *insultar*) to lay into sb; (= *reprender*) to give sb a dressing-down*; **sacar la ~ a algn** (*Andes*) to cuckold sb; **dar la ~ a la tortilla** to change things completely

vueltero ADJ (*Cono Sur*) [*persona*] difficult

vueltita* SF (*LAm*) (short) stroll *o* walk; (*en coche*) (short) drive

vuelto Ⓐ PP *de* **volver**
Ⓑ SM (*LAm*) = **vuelta 9**

vuelva *etc ver* **volver**

vuestro/a (*esp Esp*) Ⓐ ADJ POSES your (*familiar form of address*); (*después de sustantivo*) of yours; **~ perro** your dog; **~s hijos** your children; **una idea vuestra** an idea of yours, one of your ideas; **un amigo ~** a friend of yours
Ⓑ PRON POSES yours (*familiar form of address*); **—¿de quién es esto? —es ~** "whose is this?" — "it's yours"; **éste es el ~** this one's yours; **la vuestra está en el jardín** yours is in

➤ LENGUA Y USO: **vuelta 14** 35.2

the garden; **mis amigos y los ~s** my friends and yours; **¡ánimo, ésta es la vuestra!** come on, this is your big chance!; **lo ~: lo ~ también le pertenece a ella** what is yours also belongs to her; **he puesto lo ~ en la caja** I have put your things in the box; **¿ya se han enterado de lo ~?** do they know about you two yet?; **lo ~ es jugar al fútbol** playing football is your thing*; **los ~s** (= *vuestra familia*) your folks*; (= *vuestro equipo*) your lot*, your side; **es (uno) de los ~s** he's one of you

vulcanita SF vulcanite

vulcanización SF vulcanization

vulcanizar ▸conjug 1f◂ VT to vulcanize

Vulcano SM Vulcan

vulcanología SF vulcanology

vulcanólogo/a SM/F vulcanologist

vulgar ADJ [1] (= *no refinado*) [*lengua, gusto, vestido*] vulgar; [*modales, rasgos*] coarse
[2] (= *común, corriente*) [*persona, físico*] ordinary, common; [*suceso, vida*] ordinary, everyday; **~ y corriente** ordinary; **el hombre ~** the ordinary man, the common man
[3] (= *no técnico*) common; **"glóbulo blanco" es el nombre ~ del leucocito** "white blood cell" is the common name for leucocyte

vulgaridad SF [1] (= *cualidad*) vulgarity, coarseness
[2] (= *frase*) vulgar *o* coarse expression
[3] **vulgaridades** (= *trivialidades*) banalities, platitudes; (= *necedades*) inanities

vulgarismo SM vulgarism

vulgarización SF [1] (= *popularización*) popularization; **obra de ~** popular work
[2] (*Ling*) translation into the vernacular

vulgarizar ▸conjug 1f◂ VT [1] (= *hacer popular*) to popularize
[2] (*Ling*) to translate into the vernacular

vulgarmente ADV commonly, ordinarily; (*pey*) vulgarly; **los nevus, ~ llamados "lunares"** naevi, commonly *o* popularly known as "moles"

Vulgata SF Vulgate

vulgo Ⓐ SM common people; (*pey*) lower orders *pl*, common herd
Ⓑ ADV **el mingitorio, ~ "meadero"** the urinal, commonly *o* popularly known as the "bog"

vulnerabilidad SF vulnerability

vulnerable ADJ vulnerable (**a** to)

vulneración SF infringement, contravention

vulnerar ▸conjug 1a◂ VT [1] (= *perjudicar*) [+ *fama*] to damage, harm; [+ *costumbre, derechos*] to interfere with, affect seriously
[2] (*Jur, Com*) to violate, break

vulpeja SF vixen

vulpino ADJ (*Zool*) vulpine; (*fig*) foxy

vulva SF vulva

W w

W, **w** ['uβe 'doβle, (*LAm*) 'doβle be] SF (= *letra*) W, w

W ABR, **W** ABR (= **vatio**) w

wachimán SM (*LAm*) = **guachimán**

walkie ['walki] SM, **walky** ['walki] SM walkie-talkie

walki-talki [walki'talki] SM walkie-talkie

Walkman® ['walkman] SM Walkman®

walquiria [bal'kirja] SF Valkyrie

wamba® ['bamba] SF plimsoll, sneaker (*EEUU*)

WAP Ⓐ ADJ WAP
Ⓑ SM WAP ► **teléfono WAP** WAP phone

wat SM, **watt** SM [bat, wat] (*pl* **wats**, **watts**) watt

wáter ['bater] SM toilet, lavatory

waterpolista SMF water polo player

waterpolo SM water polo

web SM *o* SF (= *página*) web page; (= *red*) (World Wide) Web ► **web site** website

webcam [web'kam] SF webcam

weblog ['weblog] SM (*pl* **weblogs**) (*Internet*) weblog

webmaster ['webmaster, web'master] SMF webmaster

wedge [weʒ] SM wedge

welter SM, **wélter** SM ['belter] welterweight

western SM western

whiskería SF, **wisquería** SF bar (*specializing in whisky*)

whisky SM, **whiskey** SM ['wiski, 'gwiski] whisky, whiskey ► **whisky de malta** malt whisky

wikén SM (*Chile*) weekend

Winchester SM **disco ~** Winchester disk

windsurf ['winsurf] SM windsurfing; **hacer ~** to go windsurfing

windsurfista [winsur'fista] SMF windsurfer

wolfram ['bolfram] SM, **wolframio** [bol'framjo] SM wolfram

wonderbra® SM, **wonderbrá** SM Wonderbra®

X x

X, x ['ekis] SF (= *letra*) X, x
xantofila SF xanthophyll
XDG SF ABR (*Esp Pol*) = **Xunta Democrática de Galicia**
xeno SM xenon
xenofilia SF xenophilia
xenófilo/a Ⓐ ADJ xenophilic Ⓑ SM/F xenophile
xenofobia SF xenophobia
xenófobo/a Ⓐ ADJ xenophobic Ⓑ SM/F xenophobe
xenón SM xenon
xenotransplante SM xenograft, xenotransplant
xerocopia SF photocopy
xerocopiar ▸conjug 1b◂ VT to photocopy
xerófito ADJ xerophytic
xerografía SF xerography
xerografiar ▸conjug 1b◂ VT to xerograph
xilófono SM xylophone
xilografía SF [1] (= *arte*) xylography [2] (= *impresión*) xylograph, wood engraving
xilográfico ADJ xylographic
Xto. ABR = **Cristo**
Xunta SF *Galician autonomous government*

Y y

Y, y [i'ɣrjeɣa] SF (= *letra*) Y, y

y CONJ 1 (*uso copulativo*) and; **fuimos a Málaga y a Granada** we went to Malaga and Granada; **una isla exótica y de gran belleza** an exotic, tremendously beautiful island; **treinta y uno** thirty-one; **un kilo y cuarto** one and a quarter kilos
2 (*al comienzo de una pregunta*) **—ya ha llegado el primer grupo —¿y los demás?** "the first group has already arrived" — "(and) what about the others?"; **a mí no me apetece ir, ¿y a ti?** I don't feel like going, what about you?; **—id vosotros —¿y tú, qué vas a hacer?** "you go" — "but what are you going to do?"; **¿y Max? no lo veo por ninguna parte** where's Max? I can't see him anywhere; **—he decidido dejar de estudiar —¿y eso?** "I've decided to stop studying" — "why's that then?"; **¿y qué?** (*con desinterés, desprecio*) so (what)?; (*con interés*) and?; **no, no me han aceptado, ¿y qué?** they haven't accepted me, who cares *o* so what?; **—ya tengo las notas —¿y qué?, ¿has aprobado?** "I've just got the marks" — "and, did you pass?"
3 (*uso adversativo*) **¡él viviendo en una mansión y su hermano en la calle!** he's living in a mansion while his brother's on the streets!; **¿dices que no quieres tarta y te la comes entera?** you say you don't want any cake and then you eat a whole one?
4 (*esp LAm*) (*en repetición*) **estuvo llora y llora** he was crying and crying
5 (*esp Arg, Uru*) (*en respuestas*) **—lo lamento mucho —y bueno, habrá que aceptarlo** "I'm very sorry" — "well, we just have to accept it"

▼**ya** Ⓐ ADV 1 (*con acción pasada*) already; **lo hemos visto ya** we've seen it already; **ya han dado las diez** it's past ten already; **¿ya has terminado?** have you finished already?; **¿ya habías estado antes en Valencia?** had you been to Valencia before?; **ya me lo suponía** I thought as much; **ya se acabó** it's all over now; **ya en el siglo X** as early as the tenth century
2 (*con verbo en presente*) 2·1 (*con una acción esperada*) **ya es la hora** time's up; **ya es hora de irnos** it's time for us to go now; **ya está aquí** he's here already; **ya viene el autobús** here's the bus; **ya puedes irte** you can go now; **ya podéis ir pasando al comedor** you can start going through into the dining room now; **estos zapatos ya me están pequeños** these shoes are too small for me now; **¿ya anda?** is she walking yet?
2·2 (*expresando sorpresa*) **¿ya te vas?** are you leaving already?
2·3 (= *ahora*) now; **lo quiero ya** I want it (right) now; **¡cállate ya!** oh, shut up!; **¡ya voy!** coming!; **desde ya (mismo)** (*Esp*): **lo que quiero es empezar desde ya** I want to start right now *o* away; **una estrategia que empiezo a poner en marcha desde ya mismo** a strategy which I will start to adopt as of now *o* as of this very moment; **ya mismo** (*esp Cono Sur**) (= *en seguida*) at once; (= *claro*) of course, naturally
3 (*con acción futura*) **ya te llegará el turno a ti** you'll get your turn; **ya lo arreglarán** it'll get fixed sometime; **ya iré cuando pueda** I'll try and make it when I can; **ya verás como todo se arregla** it'll all work out, don't you worry; **ya veremos** we'll see (about that)
4 **ya no** not any more, no longer; **ya no vive aquí** he doesn't live here any more, he no longer lives here; **ya no viene a visitarnos** he doesn't come to see us any more, he no longer comes to see us; **ya no quiero más** I don't want any more; **ya no lo volverás a ver** you won't see it any more; **Javier ya no es tan alto como su hermano** Javier isn't as tall as his brother any more, Javier is no longer as tall as his brother
5 (*expresando que se ha entendido o se recuerda algo*) **ya entiendo** I see; **¡ya lo sé!** I know!; **—¿no te acuerdas de ella? es la hija de Ricardo —¡ah, ya!** "don't you remember her? she's Ricardo's daughter" — "oh yes, of course!"
6 (*expresando acuerdo o incredulidad*) **ya, pero …** yes, but …; **¡ya, ya!** (*iró*) yes, yes!, oh, yes!, oh, sure!; **ya, y luego viste un burro volando ¿no?** (*iró*) sure, and pigs might fly!; **esto ya es un robo** this really is robbery
7 (*con valor enfático*) **pues ya gasta ¿eh?** he really does spend a lot, doesn't he?; **¿una hora tardas en llegar al trabajo? pues ya está lejos ¿eh?** it takes you an hour to get to work? it must be quite some way away! **ya lo creo que estuvimos allí** you bet we were there; **¿que no se ha casado? ya lo creo que sí** you say she hasn't got married? I think you'll find she has; **es más pobre que Haití, que ya es decir** it's poorer than Haiti, and that's saying something; **¡murió con 104 años, que ya es decir!** she was 104 when she died, which is no mean achievement!; **pues si él no viene, ya me dirás qué hacemos** you tell me what we'll do if he doesn't come; **¡ya está!** that's it!; **rellena el impreso y ya está** fill in the form and that's it; **¡ya está bien!** that's (quite) enough!; **¡ya me gustaría a mí poder viajar!** I wouldn't mind being able to travel either!; **¡ya era hora!** about time too!; **¡ya podían haber avisado de que venían!** they could have said they were coming!; **¡ya puedes ir preparando el dinero!** you'd better start getting the money ready!
Ⓑ CONJ 1 (*uso distributivo*) **ya por una razón, ya por otra** whether for one reason or another; **ya te vayas, ya te quedes, me es igual** whether you go or stay is all the same to me; **ya dice que sí, ya dice que no** first he says yes, then he says no, one minute he says yes, the next he says no; **no ya** not only; **no ya aquí, sino en todas partes** not only here, but everywhere; **debes hacerlo, no ya por los demás, sino por ti mismo también** you should do it, not just for everyone else's sake but for your own sake too
2 **ya que** (seeing) as, since; **ya que no viene, iremos nosotros** (seeing) as *o* since she's not coming, we'll go; **ya que ha dejado de llover, ¿por qué no salimos a dar una vuelta?** (seeing) as *o* since it's stopped raining, why don't we go for a walk?; **ya que no estudia, por lo menos podía ponerse a trabajar** seeing as she isn't studying, the least she could do is get a job

yac [jak] SM (*pl* **yacs**) yak

yacaré SM (*LAm*) alligator

yacente ADJ reclining, recumbent

yacer ▸conjug 2x◂ VI 1 (= *estar tendido*) to lie; **los heridos yacían sobre el asfalto** the injured were lying on the tarmac; **libros y papeles yacían en confuso montón** books and papers lay in a confused heap
2 (= *estar enterrado*) to lie; **aquí yace Pedro Núñez** here lies Pedro Núñez
3 (††) (= *fornicar*) **~ con** to lie with (*liter*)

yacija SF 1 (= *cama*) bed; (*mala*) rough bed; **ser de mala ~** (= *dormir mal*) to sleep badly, be a restless sleeper; (*fig*) be a ne'er-do-well
2 (= *sepultura*) grave, tomb

yacimiento SM (*Geol*) bed, deposit; (*arqueológico*) site ► **yacimiento petrolífero** oilfield

yacuzzi® [ja'kusi] SM (*pl* **yacuzzis**) Jacuzzi®

yagua SF (*Ven*) (= *palma*) royal palm; (= *tejido*) *fibrous tissue from the wood of the royal palm*

yagual SM (*CAm, Méx*) padded ring (*for carrying loads on the head*)

yaguar SM (*LAm*) jaguar

➤ LENGUA Y USO: ya B2 44.1

yaguareté SM (*Andes, Cono Sur*) jaguar

yaguré SM (*LAm*) skunk

yaíta ADV (*LAm*) = **ya**

yak [jak] SM (*pl* **yaks**) yak

Yakarta SF Jakarta

yámbico ADJ iambic

yana ADJ (*Andes*) black

yanacón/ona SM/F (*Andes, Cono Sur Hist*) (= *aparcero*) Indian tenant farmer, Indian sharecropper; (= *criado*) Indian servant

yancófilo ADJ (*LAm*) pro-American, pro-United States

yanomami ADJ, SMF Yanomami

yanqui* Ⓐ ADJ Yankee*
Ⓑ SMF Yank*, Yankee*

yanquilandia SF (*LAm pey*) the USA

yantar†† ▸conjug 1a◂ Ⓐ VT to eat
Ⓑ VI to have lunch
Ⓒ SM food

yapa* SF [1] (*LAm*) (= *plus*) extra bit; (= *trago*) one for the road, last drink; **dar algo de ~** (*lit*) to throw in a bit extra for free; (*fig*) to add sth for good measure
[2] (*Caribe, Méx*) (= *propina*) tip
[3] (*Cono Sur Mec*) attachment, end piece

yapada SF (*LAm*) extra bit

yapar ▸conjug 1a◂ Ⓐ VT (*LAm*) [1] (= *dar de más*) to throw in as an extra
[2] (= *extender*) to stretch; (= *alargar*) to add a bit to, lengthen
Ⓑ VI to throw in an extra bit

yarará SF (*Andes, Cono Sur*) rattlesnake

yaraví SM (*Andes, Arg*) plaintive Indian song

yarda SF yard

yate SM [*de vela*] yacht; [*de motor*] pleasure cruiser, motor cruiser

yatista SMF yachtsman/yachtswoman

yaya[1]* SF nan, nana

yaya[2] SM [1] (*LAm*) (= *herida*) minor wound; (= *cicatriz*) scar; (= *dolor*) slight pain
[2] (*Caribe*) (= *bastón*) stick, walking stick

yaz SM jazz

yazca *etc ver* **yacer**

yda ABR (= **yarda**) yd

ye... (*para ciertas palabras*) *ver* **hie...** *p. ej.* **yerra**

yedra SF ivy

yegua Ⓐ SF [1] (= *animal*) mare ▸ **yegua de cría** brood mare
[2] (*Andes, Cono Sur** *pey*) old bag*; (= *puta*) whore (*pey*)
[3] (*Andes, CAm*) [*de cigarro*] cigar stub
Ⓑ ADJ [1] (*CAm, Caribe*) (= *tonto*) stupid; (= *ordinario*) rough, coarse
[2] (*Cono Sur*) (= *grande*) big, huge

yeguada SF [1] (= *rebaño*) herd of horses; (= *caballeriza*) stud; (*Cono Sur*) (= *yeguas*) group of breeding mares
[2] (*CAm, Caribe*) (= *burrada*) stupid thing, foolish act

yeguarizo SM (*Cono Sur*) [1] [*de cría*] stud, group of breeding mares
[2] (= *caballos*) horses *pl*

yegüerío SM (*CAm, Caribe*) = **yeguarizo 1**

yeísmo SM *pronunciation of Spanish "ll" as "y"*

yelmo SM helmet

yema SF [1] [*del huevo*] yolk; (*LAm*) (= *huevo*) egg ▸ **yema mejida** egg flip
[2] (*Bot*) leaf bud
[3] (*Anat*) ▸ **yema del dedo** fingertip
[4] (*Culin*) *sweet made with egg yolk and sugar*
[5] (= *lo mejor*) best part
[6] (= *medio*) middle; **dar en la ~** to hit the nail on the head; **en la ~ del invierno** in the middle of winter
[7] (= *dificultad*) snag

Yemen SM Yemen

yemení ADJ, SMF, **yemenita** ADJ, SMF Yemeni

yen SM (*pl* **yens** *o* **yenes**) yen

yendo *ver* **ir**

yerba SF [1] = **hierba**
[2] **~ (de) mate** maté
[3] (*) (= *marihuana*) grass‡

yerbabuena SF (*LAm*) mint

yerbal SM (*Cono Sur*), **yerbatal** SM (*Andes*) maté plantation

yerbatero/a (*LAm*) Ⓐ ADJ of *o* pertaining to maté
Ⓑ SM/F [1] (= *herbolario*) herbalist; (= *curandero*) quack doctor
[2] (= *comerciante*) maté dealer; (= *cultivador*) maté grower

yerbear ▸conjug 1a◂ VI (*Cono Sur*) to drink maté

yerbera SF (*Cono Sur*) maté (leaves) container

yerbero/a SM/F (*LAm*) = **yerbatero B**

yerga *etc ver* **erguir**

yermar ▸conjug 1a◂ VT to lay waste

yermo Ⓐ ADJ (= *inhabitado*) uninhabited; (= *estéril*) barren
Ⓑ SM wasteland

yerna* SF (*Andes, Caribe*) daughter-in-law

yerno SM son-in-law

yernocracia* SF nepotism

yeros SMPL lentils

yerre *etc ver* **errar**

yerro SM error, mistake

yersey SM (*LAm*), **yersi** SM (*LAm*) jersey

yerto ADJ stiff, rigid; **~ de frío** frozen stiff*

yesca SF [1] (= *materia inflamable*) tinder; (*Cono Sur*) (= *piedra*) flint; **caja de ~** tinderbox; **arder como si fuera ~** to burn like tinder
[2] (*fig*) (= *pábulo*) fuel; (= *situación*) inflammable situation; (= *grupo*) group which is easily inflamed
[3] (*fig*) (*Culin*) thirst-making food
[4] (*Andes Fin*) debt

yesería SF plastering, plasterwork

yesero SM plasterer

yeso SM [1] (*Geol*) gypsum
[2] (*Arquit*) plaster; **dar de ~ a una pared** to plaster a wall ▸ **yeso mate** plaster of Paris
[3] (*Med*) (= *material*) plaster; (= *molde*) plaster cast
[4] (*Arte*) plaster cast
[5] (= *tiza*) chalk

yesquero SM (*LAm*) cigarette lighter

yeta* SF (*LAm*) bad luck

yetar* ▸conjug 1a◂ VT (*Cono Sur*) to put a jinx on*, jinx*

yeti SM yeti

ye-yé†* Ⓐ ADJ groovy*, trendy; **música ~** sixties pop music
Ⓑ SMF groover*, trendy

yídish SM, **yíddish** SM ['jidiʃ] Yiddish

yihad [ji'ad] SM jihad

yip SM (*LAm*) jeep

yirante* SF (*Cono Sur*) streetwalker

yo Ⓐ PRON PERS [1] (*sujeto*) I; **Carlos y yo no fuimos** Carlos and I didn't go; **yo no soy de los que exageran** I'm not one to exaggerate; **¡y yo que confiaba en ti!** and to think that I trusted you!; **yo que tú** if I were you; **—¿quién es? —soy yo** "who is it?" — "it's me"; **—¿quién lo dijo? —yo no** "who said that?" — "not me"; **lo hice yo misma** I did it myself
[2] (*en comparaciones, después de prep*) me; **es más delgada que yo** she is slimmer than me *o* than I am; **que esto quede entre tú y yo** this is between you and me; **nos lo comeremos entre tú y yo** we'll eat it between us
Ⓑ SM (*Psic*) **el yo** the self, the ego

yod SF yod

yodado ADJ iodized, with added iodine; **sal yodada** iodized salt

yodo SM iodine

yodoformo SM iodoform

yoga[1] SM yoga

yoga[2] SF (*Méx*) (= *daga*) dagger

yogui SM yogi

yogur SM [1] (= *alimento*) yoghurt; **mal ~** (*euf*) = **mala leche** ▸ **yogur descremado**, **yogur desnatado** low-fat yoghurt
[2] (*Esp*‡) (= *coche de policía*) police car, squad car

yogurtera SF [1] (= *electrodoméstico*) yoghurt-maker
[2] (*Esp*‡) (= *coche*) police car, squad car

yol SM yawl

yola SF yawl; (= *yate*) sailing boat; [*de carreras*] (racing) shell

yonqui* SMF junkie*

yoquei SM = **yóquey**

yoquepierdismo* SM (*CAm*) self-interest, I'm-all-right-Jack attitude*

yóquey SMF (*pl* **yóqueis**) jockey

yoyó SM (*pl* **yoyós**), **yo-yo** SM (*pl* **yo-yos**) yo-yo

YPF SMPL ABR (*Arg*) = **Yacimientos Petrolíferos Fiscales**

YPFB SMPL ABR (*Bol*) = **Yacimientos Petrolíferos Fiscales Bolivianos**

yuca Ⓐ SF [1] (*Bot*) yucca; (*LAm*) manioc root, cassava
[2] (*Caribe*) (= *pobreza*) poverty; **pasar ~** to be poor
[3] (*Andes*) (= *comida*) food
[4] (*Andes*) (= *pierna*) leg
[5] (*Andes, CAm*) (= *mentira*) lie
Ⓑ ADJ (*CAm*‡) (= *difícil*) tough, hard

yucateco/a Ⓐ ADJ of/from Yucatan
Ⓑ SM/F native/inhabitant of Yucatan; **los ~s** the people of Yucatan

yudo SM judo

yugar* ▸conjug 1a◂ VI (*CAm*) to slog away*

yugo SM yoke; **sacudir el ~** (*fig*) to throw off the yoke ▸ **yugo del matrimonio** marriage tie

Yugoslavia SF, **Yugoeslavia** SF (*Hist*) Yugoslavia

yugoslavo/a, **yugoeslavo/a** (*Hist*) Ⓐ ADJ Yugoslavian
Ⓑ SM/F Yugoslav

yuguero SM ploughman, plowman (*EEUU*)

yugular ADJ jugular; ✦*MODISMOS* **encontrar la ~ de algn** to find sb's weak spot; **lanzarse a la ~** to go for the jugular

yuju EXCL yipee!

yungas SFPL (*Andes, Cono Sur Geog*) *hot tropical valleys*

yungla SF jungle

yunque SM [1] [*de metal*] anvil; ✦MODISMO **hacer** *o* **servir de ~** to have to put up with hardships *o* abuse
[2] (*Anat*) anvil
[3] (= *persona*) (*paciente*) stoical person; (*trabajador*) tireless worker

yunta SF [1] [*de bueyes*] yoke, team (of oxen)
[2] (*Chile*) [*de personas*] couple, pair
[3] **yuntas** (*LAm*) (= *botones*) cufflinks

yuntero SM ploughman, plowman (*EEUU*)

yuppie ['jupi] ADJ, SMF yuppie

yuta SF [1] (*Cono Sur Bio*) slug
[2] **hacer la ~** (*Andes, Cono Sur*) to play truant

yute SM jute

yuxtaponer ▸conjug 2q◂ VT to juxtapose

yuxtaposición SF juxtaposition

yuxtapuesto PP *de* **yuxtaponer**

yuyal SM (*Cono Sur*) scrub(land)

yuyerío SM (*Andes, Cono Sur*) (= *malas hierbas*) weeds *pl*; (= *plantas silvestres*) wild plants *pl*

yuyero/a SM/F (*Cono Sur*) herbalist

yuyo (*LAm*) SM [1] (= *planta silvestre*) weed; (= *planta medicinal*) herb, medicinal plant; (= *condimento*) herb flavouring *o* (*EEUU*) flavoring; (*Andes*) cooking herb; ✦MODISMO **estar como un ~** (*Cono Sur*) to be wet*
[2] (*Andes*) (= *emplasto*) herbal poultice
[3] **yuyos** (*CAm*) (= *ampollas*) blisters on the feet

Zz

Z, z ['θeta, *(esp LAm)* 'seta] SF (= *letra*) Z, z
zabordar ▸conjug 1a◂ VI to run aground
zabullir ▸conjug 3h◂ VT = **zambullir**
zacapela SF, **zacapella** SF rumpus*, row
zacatal SM *(CAm)* pasture
zacate SM [1] *(CAm)* (= *hierba*) grass; (= *heno*) hay, fodder; *(CAm, Méx)* (= *paja*) straw, thatch
[2] *(Méx)* (= *trapo*) dishcloth
zacatear ▸conjug 1a◂ *(CAm)* (A) VT to beat
(B) VI to graze
zacatera SF *(CAm)* (= *pasto*) pasture; (= *almiar*) haystack
zafacoca* SF [1] *(LAm)* (= *pelea*) brawl
[2] *(Méx)* (= *paliza*) beating
[3] *(Caribe)* (= *disturbio*) riot
zafacón SM *(Ant, Caribe)* wastepaper basket, waste basket *(EEUU)*
zafado* ADJ *(LAm)* [1] (= *loco*) mad, crazy
[2] (= *descarado*) cheeky*, cute *(EEUU*)*
zafadura SF *(LAm)* dislocation
zafaduría* SF *(LAm)* [1] (= *descaro*) cheek*, nerve*
[2] (= *acción*) bit of cheek*
zafante PREP *(Caribe)* except (for)
zafar ▸conjug 1a◂ (A) VT [1] (= *soltar*) to untie
[2] (= *desembarazar*) [+ *barco*] to lighten; [+ *superficie*] to clear, free
[3] *(LAm)* (= *excluir*) to exclude
(B) **zafarse** VPR [1] (= *escaparse*) to escape, run away; (= *irse*) to slip away; (= *soltarse*) to break loose; (= *ocultarse*) to hide o.s. away
[2] *(Téc)* to slip off, come off
[3] **~se de** [+ *persona*] to get away from; [+ *trabajo*] to get out of; [+ *dificultad*] to get round; [+ *acuerdo*] to get out of, wriggle out of
[4] (*) **~se con algo** (= *robar*) to pinch sth*; (= *librarse*) to get away with sth
[5] *(LAm)* **~se un brazo** to dislocate one's arm
[6] *(CAm, Cono Sur)* (= *esquivar*) to dodge
[7] *(Andes)* (= *volverse loco*) to go a bit crazy, lose one's marbles*
zafarrancho SM [1] *(Náut)* clearing for action
► **zafarrancho de combate** call to action stations
[2] (= *desastre*) havoc; **hacer un ~** to cause havoc
[3] (*) (= *riña*) fracas, row
zafio ADJ coarse, uncouth
zafiro SM sapphire
zafo (A) ADJ [1] *(Náut)* clear
[2] (= *ileso*) unharmed; (= *intacto*) undamaged, intact; **salir ~ de algo** to come out of sth unscathed
[3] *(LAm)* (= *libre*) free
(B) PREP *(CAm)* (= *excepto*) except (for)
zafón SM *(Andes)* slip, error
zafra[1] SF oil jar, oil container
zafra[2] SF *(LAm)* (= *cosecha*) sugar harvest; (= *fabricación*) sugar making
zaga SF [1] (= *parte trasera*) rear; **a la ~** behind, in the rear; **A ha quedado muy a la ~ de B** A is well behind B; **A no le va a la ~ a B** A is every bit as good as B; **no le va a la ~ a nadie** he is second to none; **dejar en ~** to leave behind
[2] *(Dep)* defence, defense *(EEUU)*
zagal(a) SM/F (= *muchacho*) boy/girl, lad/lass; *(Agr)* shepherd/shepherdess
zagalejo/a SM/F (= *muchacho*) lad/lass; *(Agr)* shepherd boy/girl
zagalón/ona SM/F strapping young lad/lass
zagual SM paddle
zaguán SM [1] (= *entrada*) hallway, entrance hall
[2] *(CAm)* (= *garaje*) garage
zaguero/a (A) ADJ [1] (= *trasero*) rear, back *antes de s*; **equipo ~** bottom team
[2] [*carro*] *too heavily laden at the back*
[3] (= *retrasado*) slow
(B) SM/F *(Ftbl)* defender; *(Rugby)* full back
zahareño ADJ [1] (= *salvaje*) wild
[2] (= *arisco*) unsociable
zaherimiento SM (= *crítica*) criticism; (= *reprimenda*) reprimand
zaherir ▸conjug 3i◂ VT (= *criticar*) to criticize sharply, attack; (= *herir*) to wound, hurt; (= *reprender*) to upbraid, reprimand
zahiriente ADJ wounding, hurtful
zahones SMPL chaps
zahorí SMF [1] (= *vidente*) clairvoyant; (*que busca agua*) water diviner
[2] (= *persona perspicaz*) highly perceptive person
zahúrda SF [1] *(Agr)* pigsty
[2] (*) (= *tugurio*) hovel, shack
zahurra SF *(Andes)* din, hullabaloo*
zaino[1] ADJ [*caballo*] chestnut; [*vaca*] black
zaino[2] ADJ (= *pérfido*) treacherous; [*animal*] vicious; **mirar a lo** *o* **de ~** to look sideways
zainoso ADJ *(Cono Sur)* treacherous
Zaire SM Zaire
zaireño/a ADJ, SM/F Zairean
zalagarda SF [1] *(Mil)* ambush, trap; *(Caza)* trap; (= *escaramuza*) skirmish; (= *ardid*) ruse
[2] (= *alboroto*) row, din; (= *riña*) noisy quarrel; (= *jaleo*) shindy*
zalamerear ▸conjug 1a◂ VI *(Andes)* to flatter
zalamería SF (*tb* **~s**) flattery; **no me vengas con ~s** stop trying to butter me up*
zalamero/a (A) ADJ (= *lisonjero*) flattering; (= *relamido*) suave; *(pey)* slimy
(B) SM/F flatterer; *(pey)* slimeball*
zalea SF sheepskin
zalema SF [1] (= *reverencia*) salaam, deep bow
[2] = **zalamería**
zalenco ADJ *(Caribe)* lame
zalenquear ▸conjug 1a◂ VI *(Andes)* to limp
zamacuco/a SM/F crafty person
zamarra SF (= *piel*) sheepskin; (= *chaqueta*) sheepskin jacket
zamarrazo SM (= *golpe*) blow; (= *revés*) setback
zamarrear ▸conjug 1a◂ VT [1] [*perro*] to shake
[2] (= *sacudir*) to shake; (= *empujar*) to shove around
[3] (*) (*en discusión*) to corner*
zamarro SM [1] (= *piel*) sheepskin; (= *chaqueta*) sheepskin jacket
[2] **zamarros** *(Andes)* (= *pantalones*) chaps
[3] (*) (= *rústico*) boor, yokel; (= *taimado*) sly person
zamba SF *Argentinian handkerchief dance*; *ver tb* **zambo**
zambada SF *(Andes)* group of half-breeds
zambardo *(Cono Sur)* SM [1] (= *desmañado*) clumsy person
[2] (= *desmaña*) clumsiness; (= *daño*) damage, breakage
[3] (= *chiripa*) fluke
zambeque *(Caribe)* (A) ADJ silly
(B) SM [1] (= *idiota*) idiot
[2] (= *jaleo*) uproar, hullabaloo*
zambequería SF *(Caribe)* silliness
zamberío SM *(Andes)* half-breeds *pl**
Zambeze SM Zambesi
Zambia SF Zambia
zambiano/a ADJ, SM/F Zambian
zambo/a (A) ADJ (*) knock-kneed
(B) SM/F *(LAm)* person of mixed race (*esp of black and Indian parentage*); *ver tb* **zamba**
zambomba SF [1] (= *tambor*) *kind of rustic drum*
[2] (*como excl*) **¡zambomba!*** wow!
zambombazo SM [1] (= *estallido*) bang, explosion
[2] (= *golpe*) blow, punch
zambombo SM boor, yokel

zambra SF **1** (= *baile*) gipsy *o* (*EEUU*) gypsy dance
2 (*) (= *alboroto*) uproar

zambrate SM (*CAm*), **zambrera** SF (*Caribe*) row, commotion

zambucar ▸conjug 1g◂ VT to hide, tuck away

zambuir ▸conjug 3g◂ VI (*Andes*) = **zambullir**

zambullida SF dive, plunge

zambullir ▸conjug 3h◂ (A) VT (*en el agua*) to plunge (**en** into); (*debajo del agua*) to duck (**en** under)
(B) **zambullirse** VPR **1** (*en el agua*) to dive (**en** into); (*debajo del agua*) to duck (**en** under)
2 (= *ocultarse*) to hide

zambullón SM (*Andes*) = **zambullida**

Zamora SF Zamora

zamorano/a (A) ADJ of/from Zamora
(B) SM/F native/inhabitant of Zamora; **los ~s** the people of Zamora

zampa SF (*Arquit*) pile

zampabollos* SMF INV **1** (= *glotón*) greedy pig*, glutton
2 (= *grosero*) coarse individual

zampar* ▸conjug 1a◂ (A) VT **1** (= *esconder*) to put away hurriedly (**en** in)
2 (= *sumergir*) to plunge (**en** into)
3 (= *arrojar*) to hurl, dash (**en** against, to); **lo zampó en el suelo** he hurled *o* dashed it to the floor
4 (= *comer*) to wolf down
5 (*LAm*) **~ una torta a algn** to wallop sb*
(B) VI to gobble
(C) **zamparse** VPR **1** (= *lanzarse*) to bump, crash; **se zampó en medio del corro** he thrust himself roughly into the circle
2 (*en fiesta, reunión*) to gatecrash, go along uninvited
3 **~se en** to dart into, shoot into; **se zampó en el cine** he shot into the cinema
4 (= *comerse*) **~se algo** to wolf sth down; **se zampó cuatro porciones enteras** he wolfed down four whole helpings

zampatortas* SMF INV = **zampabollos**

zampón* ADJ greedy

zampoña SF shepherd's pipes *pl*, rustic flute

zampuzar ▸conjug 1f◂ VT **1** = **zambullir**
2 = **zampar**

zamuro SM (*Ven*) turkey vulture, turkey buzzard (*EEUU*)

zanahoria (A) SF carrot; *ver tb* **palo 1**
(B) SMF (*Cono Sur**) (= *imbécil*) idiot, nitwit*; (= *desmañado*) clumsy oaf; (= *pobre*) poor wretch

zanate SM (*CAm, Méx*) rook

zanca SF **1** [*de ave*] shank
2 [*de persona*] (*hum*) shank

zancada SF stride; **alejarse a grandes ~s** to stride away; **en dos ~s** (= *rápidamente*) in a couple of ticks; (= *fácilmente*) very easily

zancadilla SF (*para derribar a algn*) trip; (= *trampa*) trick; **echar la ~ a algn** (*lit*) to trip sb up; (*fig*) to put the skids under sb*

zancadillear ▸conjug 1a◂ VT (*lit*) to trip (up); (*fig*) to put the skids under*

zancajear ▸conjug 1a◂ VI to rush around

zancajo SM **1** (= *talón*) heel; **A no le llega los ~s a B** A can't hold a candle to B
2 (*) (= *persona*) dwarf, runt

zancajón ADJ (*Méx*) **1** (= *alto*) tall, lanky
2 (= *torpe*) clumsy

zancarrón SM **1** [*de la pierna*] leg bone
2 (†*) (= *viejo*) old bag of bones
3 (†*) (= *profesor*) poor teacher

zanco SM stilt; ✦**MODISMO** **estar en ~s** to be high up

zancón ADJ **1** (= *de piernas largas*) long-legged
2 (*CAm*) (= *alto*) lanky
3 (*LAm*) [*vestido*] too short

zancudero SM (*CAm, Caribe*) swarm of mosquitoes

zancudo (A) ADJ long-legged; *ver tb* **ave**
(B) SM (*LAm*) mosquito

zanfona SF hurdy-gurdy

zangamanga* SF trick

zanganada SF stupid remark, silly thing (to say)

zanganear* ▸conjug 1a◂ VI **1** (= *gandulear*) to idle, loaf about; (= *hacer el tonto*) to fool around
2 (= *decir disparates*) to make stupid remarks

zángano/a (A) SM/F **1** (*) (= *holgazán*) idler, slacker
2 (*) (= *pícaro*) rogue
3 (*) (= *pesado*) bore
(B) SM (= *insecto*) drone

zangarriana SF **1** (*Med*) (= *jaqueca*) severe headache, migraine; (= *trastorno leve*) minor upset
2 (= *abatimiento*) blues *pl*, depression

zangolotear ▸conjug 1a◂ (A) VT to shake
(B) VI to buzz about uselessly
(C) **zangolotearse** VPR **1** [*ventana*] to rattle, shake
2 [*persona*] to fidget

zangoloteo SM (= *sacudida*) shaking; [*de persona*] fidgeting; [*de ventana*] rattling

zangolotino ADJ **niño ~** (= *infantil*) big kid*; (= *tonto*) silly child

zangón SM big lazybones, lazy lump*

zanguanga* SF fictitious illness; **hacer la ~** to swing the lead*, malinger

zanguango/a* (A) ADJ idle, slack
(B) SM/F slacker, shirker

zanja SF **1** (= *fosa*) ditch; (= *hoyo*) pit; (= *tumba*) grave; **abrir las ~s** (*Arquit*) to lay the foundations (**de** for)
2 (*LAm*) (= *barranco*) gully, watercourse
3 (*Andes*) (= *límite*) fence, low wall

zanjar ▸conjug 1a◂ VT **1** (= *abrir una zanja*) to dig a trench in
2 (= *acabar*) [+ *dificultad*] to get around; [+ *conflicto*] to resolve, clear up; [+ *discusión*] to settle

zanjón SM **1** (= *zanja profunda*) deep ditch
2 (*Caribe, Cono Sur*) (= *risco*) cliff; (= *barranco*) gully, ravine

zanquear ▸conjug 1a◂ (A) VT (*CAm, Caribe, Méx*) to hunt for
(B) VI **1** (= *andar mal*) to waddle
2 (= *ir rápidamente*) to stride along
3 (= *trajinar*) to rush about, bustle about

zanquilargo ADJ long-legged, leggy

zanquivano ADJ spindly-legged

Zanzíbar SM Zanzibar

zapa[1] SF **1** (= *pala*) spade
2 (*Mil*) sap, trench

zapa[2] SF sharkskin, shagreen

zapador SM sapper

zapallada SF **1** (*Cono Sur*) (= *chiripa*) fluke; (= *suerte*) lucky break; (= *conjetura*) lucky guess
2 (*Andes*) (= *comentario*) silly remark

zapallito SM (*Cono Sur*) courgette, zucchini (*EEUU*)

zapallo SM **1** (*LAm*) (= *calabaza*) gourd, pumpkin
2 (*Cono Sur*) = **zapallada 1**
3 (*Andes*) (= *gordo*) fat person
4 (*Andes, CAm*) (= *tonto*) dope*, fool
5 (*Cono Sur‡*) (= *cabeza*) nut‡

zapallón* ADJ (*Andes, Cono Sur*) chubby, fat

zapapico SM pick, pickaxe, pickax (*EEUU*)

zapar ▸conjug 1a◂ VT, VI to sap, mine

zaparrazo SM scratch

zapata SF **1** (= *calzado*) half-boot
2 (*Mec*) shoe ► **zapata de freno, zapata de frenos** brake shoe

zapatazo SM **1** (= *golpe dado con zapato*) blow with a shoe; (= *caída, ruido*) thud; **tratar a algn a ~s*** to ride roughshod over sb
2 (*Dep*) fierce kick, hard shot
3 (*Náut*) violent flap of a sail

zapateado SM **1** (= *claqué*) tap dance
2 (= *baile típico español*) zapateado

zapatear ▸conjug 1a◂ (A) VI **1** (= *dar golpecitos*) to tap one's feet; (= *bailar*) to tap-dance
2 [*conejo*] to thump
3 [*vela*] to flap violently
(B) VT **1** (= *dar golpecitos en*) to tap with one's foot
2 (= *patear*) to boot*
3 (= *maltratar*) to ill-treat, treat roughly

zapateo SM tapping

zapatería SF **1** (= *tienda*) shoeshop; (= *fábrica*) shoe factory, footwear factory
2 (= *oficio*) shoemaking

zapatero/a (A) ADJ **1** [*industria*] shoemaking *antes de s*
2 [*legumbres, patatas*] hard, undercooked
(B) SM/F shoemaker; ✦**REFRÁN ~, a tus zapatos** the cobbler should stick to his last ► **zapatero de viejo, zapatero remendón** cobbler
(C) SM (= *mueble*) shoe rack

zapatiesta* SF set-to*, shindy*

zapatilla SF **1** (*para casa*) slipper; (*Dep*) training shoe ► **zapatillas de ballet** ballet shoes ► **zapatillas de clavos** running shoes, spikes ► **zapatillas de deporte** sports shoes, trainers, sneakers (*EEUU*) ► **zapatillas de tenis** tennis shoes
2 (*Mec*) washer

zapatista ADJ, SMF Zapatista

zapato SM shoe; ✦**MODISMOS** **estaban como tres en un ~** they were packed in like sardines; **meter a algn en un ~** to bring sb to heel; **saber dónde aprieta el ~** to know the score* ► **zapato náutico** boat shoe ► **zapatos de cordones** lace-up shoes ► **zapatos de golf** golf shoes ► **zapatos de goma** (*LAm*), **zapatos de hule** (*Méx*) tennis shoes ► **zapatos de plataforma** platform shoes ► **zapatos de salón** court shoes, pumps (*EEUU*) ► **zapatos de tacón, zapato[s] de tacones altos** high-heeled s[hoes] ► **zapatos de tacón de aguja** stil[etto heels] *tb* **niño B1**; → PANTALONES, ZAPAT[OS]

zapatón SM (*LAm*) overshoe

zape EXCL **1** (*a animal*) ...
2 (*sorpresa*) good ...

zapear ▸conjug 1a◂ (A) VI (*TV*) to channel-hop
(B) VT [1] [+ *gato*] to shoo, scare away; [+ *persona*] to shoo away, get rid of
[2] (*Andes, CAm*) (= *espiar*) to spy on, watch

zapeo SM channel-hopping

zaperoco* SM (*Caribe*) muddle, mess

zapote SM (*CAm, Méx*) (= *planta*) sapodilla, sapota; (= *fruta*) sapodilla plum, sapota

zapoteca ADJ, SMF Zapotec

zapping ['θapin] SM channel-hopping; **hacer ~** to channel-hop

zaque SM [1] [*de vino*] wineskin
[2] (‡) (= *borracho*) boozer‡, old soak‡

zaquizamí SM [1] (= *buhardilla*) attic, garret
[2] (= *cuartucho*) poky little room, hole; (= *tugurio*) hovel

zar SM tsar, czar (*esp EEUU*)

zarabanda SF [1] (*Hist*) sarabande
[2] (= *movimiento*) rush, whirl
[3] (*Méx*) (= *paliza*) beating

zaragata SM [1] (*) (= *ajetreo*) bustle; (= *jaleo*) hullabaloo*; (= *riña*) row, set-to*
[2] **zaragatas** (*Caribe*) (= *zalamerías*) flattery *sing*

zaragate* SM [1] (*LAm*) (= *malvado*) rogue, rascal; (= *entrometido*) busybody
[2] (*Caribe*) (= *zalamero*) flatterer, creep‡

zaragatero* (A) ADJ (= *bullicioso*) rowdy, noisy; (= *peleador*) quarrelsome
(B) SM rowdy, hooligan

Zaragoza SF Saragossa

zaragozano/a (A) ADJ of/from Saragossa
(B) SM/F native/inhabitant of Saragossa; **los ~s** the people of Saragossa

zaragüelles SMPL *baggy trousers that form part of the traditional dress of Valencia and Murcia*

zaramullo (A) ADJ [1] (*Andes, CAm, Caribe*) (= *afectado*) affected; (= *engreído*) conceited; (= *delicado*) finicky
[2] (*Andes, Caribe*) (= *divertido*) amusing, witty
(B) SM (*Andes*) [1] (= *tontería*) silly thing
[2] (= *entrometido*) busybody; (= *tonto*) fool

zaranda SF [1] (= *tamiz*) sieve
[2] (*Méx*) (= *carrito*) wheel barrow
[3] (*Caribe*) (= *juguete*) spinning top; (*Mús*) horn

zarandajas* SFPL trifles, odds and ends, little things

zarandear ▸conjug 1a◂ (A) VT [1] (= *sacudir*) to shake vigorously; (= *empujar*) to jostle, push around
[2] (*) (= *dar prisa a*) to keep on the go
[3] (= *cribar*) to sieve, sift
[4] (*LAm*) (= *balancear*) to swing, push to and fro
[5] (= *insultar*) to abuse publicly
(B) **zarandearse** VPR [1] (*esp LAm*) (= *pavonearse*) to strut about
[2] (= *ir y venir*) to keep on the go

zarandeo SM [1] (= *sacudida*) shaking
[2] (*por el tamiz*) sieving

zarandillo SM (= *persona enérgica*) active person; (= *persona inquieta*) fidget; ✦***MODISMO*** **llevar a algn como un ~** to keep sb on the go

zarapito SM (*tb* **~ real**) curlew

zaraza SF chintz, printed cotton cloth

zarazas SFPL rat poison *sing*

... ADJ (*LAm*) [1] [*fruta*] underripe
...*ido*) tipsy, tight*

zarcillo SM [1] (= *pendiente*) earring
[2] (*Bot*) tendril
[3] (*Cono Sur, Méx Agr*) earmark

zarco ADJ light blue

zarigüeya SF opossum, possum

zarina SF tsarina, czarina (*esp EEUU*)

zarista ADJ, SMF tsarist, czarist (*esp EEUU*)

zaroche SM (*LAm*) = **soroche**

zarpa SF [1] [*de león, tigre*] paw; (*) [*de persona*] paw, mitt; **echar la ~ a algo** to get one's hands on sth
[2] [*de barro*] splash of mud

zarpada SF = **zarpazo**

zarpar ▸conjug 1a◂ VI to weigh anchor, set sail

zarpazo SM [1] [*de animal*] **el gato me dio un ~** the cat scratched me; **el oso me dio un ~** the bear hit me with its paw
[2] (= *desgracia*) blow

zarpear ▸conjug 1a◂ VT (*CAm, Méx*) to splash with mud

zarrapastroso ADJ, **zarrapastrón** ADJ [*persona*] scruffy; [*ropa*] shabby

zarria SF [1] (= *salpicadura*) splash of mud
[2] (= *harapo*) rag, tatter

zarza SF bramble, blackberry (bush)

zarzal SM bramble patch

zarzamora SF blackberry

zarzaparrilla SF sarsaparilla

zarzo SM [1] (*Agr*) hurdle; (*para construir*) wattle
[2] (*Andes*) (= *buhardilla*) attic

zarzuela [1] SF *Spanish light opera*
[2] ► **zarzuela de mariscos** (*Esp*) seafood casserole
[3] **(Palacio de) la Zarzuela** *royal palace in Madrid*

> **ZARZUELA**
>
> ***Zarzuelas**, named after the Zarzuela Palace where they were first performed in the 17th century for the entertainment of Philip IV, are a kind of Spanish comic folk opera. They are usually in three acts, and their chief ingredients include stock characters, traditional scenes and a mixture of dialogue, music and traditional song. After a decline in popularity in the 18th century, interest in this very Spanish genre was rekindled as part of the 19th century revival of Spanish nationalism.*

zarzuelista SMF *composer of Spanish light opera*

zas EXCL bang!, crash!; **le pegó un porrazo ... ¡zas! ... que ...** he gave him a swipe ... bang! ... which ...; **apenas habíamos puesto la radio y ... ¡zas! ... se cortó la corriente** we had only just switched on the radio when "click!" and off went the current; **cayó ¡zas! al agua** she fell into the water with a big splash

zasca EXCL [1] bang!, crash!
[2] (*como adv*) all of a sudden

zascandil* SM ne'er-do-well

zascandilear ▸conjug 1a◂ VI to buzz about uselessly, fuss around

zaya SF (*Caribe*) whip

zeda SF (name of the) letter z

zen ADJ INV, SM Zen

Zenón SM Zeno

zenzontle SM (*CAm, Méx*) mockingbird

zepelín SM zeppelin

zeta (A) SF the (name of the) letter z
(B) SM (*Aut*) Z-car, police car

Zetlandia SF **Islas de ~** Shetland Isles *o* Islands, Shetland

zigoto SM zygote

zigzag SM (*pl* **zigzagues** *o* **zigzags**) zigzag; **relámpago en ~** forked lightning

zigzagueante ADJ zigzag *antes de s*

zigzaguear ▸conjug 1a◂ VI to zigzag

zigzagueo SM zigzagging

Zimbabue SM, **Zimbabwe** SM Zimbabwe

zimbabuo/a ADJ, SM/F Zimbabwean

zinc SM zinc

zíngaro/a ADJ, SM/F = **cíngaro**

zíper SM (*Méx*) zip, zipper (*EEUU*)

zipizape* SM set-to*, rumpus*; **armar un ~** to start a rumpus; **los dos están siempre de ~** the two of them are always squabbling

zócalo SM [1] (*Arquit*) (= *pedestal*) plinth, base
[2] [*de pared*] skirting board, baseboard (*EEUU*)
[3] (*Méx*) (= *plaza*) main square; (= *bulevar*) walk, boulevard; (= *parque*) park

zocato/a (A) ADJ [1] [*fruta, legumbre*] hard
[2] [*persona*] left-handed
(B) SM/F left-handed person
(C) SM (*Andes*) (= *pan*) stale bread

zoclo SM = **zueco**

zoco¹/a (A) ADJ [1] (= *zurdo*) left-handed
[2] (*Andes*) (= *manco*) one-armed; (*Andes, Caribe, Cono Sur*) (= *mutilado*) maimed
(B) SM/F [1] (= *zurdo*) left-handed person
[2] (*Caribe*) (= *tonto*) fool
(C) SM (*Cono Sur*) (= *puñetazo*) hefty punch

zoco² SM (Arab) market, souk

zocotroco SM (*Andes, Cono Sur*) chunk, big lump; **~ de hombre*** hefty man*

zodiaco SM, **zodíaco** SM zodiac

zollenco ADJ (*Méx*) big and tough

zollipar* ▸conjug 1a◂ VI to sob

zombi SMF zombie

zona SF [1] (*en país, región*) area; **las ~s afectadas por las inundaciones** the areas affected by flooding; **las ~s más ricas/remotas/deprimidas del país** the richest/remotest/most depressed areas *o* parts of the country; **la ~ norte/sur/este/oeste de la isla** the northern/southern/eastern/western part of the island; **comimos en uno de los restaurantes típicos de la ~** we ate in a restaurant typical of the area, we ate in a typical local restaurant; **~s costeras** coastal areas; **~ montañosa** *o* **de montaña** mountainous area, mountainous region; **~s rurales** rural areas; **~s turísticas** tourist areas; **~s urbanas** urban areas ► **zona catastrófica** disaster area ► **zona de combate** combat zone ► **zona de conflicto** (*Mil*) conflict zone ► **zona de desarrollo** development area ► **zona de exclusión (aérea)** (air) exclusion zone ► **zona de guerra** war zone ► **zona de influencia** area of influence ► **zona de libre comercio** free-trade zone, free-trade area ► **zona de peligro** danger zone, danger area ► **zona de picnic** picnic area ► **zona de seguridad** security zone ► **zona desnuclearizada** nuclear-free zone ► **zona euro** Eurozone; **los países de la ~ euro** the Eurozone countries ► **zona franca** duty-free zone ► **zona fronteriza** (*gen*) border area; (*Mil*) border zone ► **zona húmeda** wetland

► **zona industrial** industrial area ► **zona militar** military zone, military area ► **zona roja** (*Esp*) Republican territory ► **zona segura** safe zone
[2] (*en ciudad*) area ► **zona azul** (*Esp Aut*) ≈ pay-and-display area ► **zona centro** centre; **los aparcamientos de la ~ centro** city centre car parks ► **zona cero** Ground Zero ► **zona comercial** (*para negocios en general*) commercial district; (*sólo de tiendas*) shopping area ► **zona de copas**: **¿dónde está la ~ de copas?** where do people go out to drink? ► **zona de ensanche** development area ► **zona edificada** built-up area ► **zona marginada** (*CAm*) slum area ► **zona peatonal** pedestrian precinct ► **zona residencial** residential area ► **zona roja** (*LAm*) red-light district ► **zona rosa** (*Méx*) *partly pedestrianized zone, so called because of its pink paving stones* ► **zona verde** green space
[3] (*en edificio, recinto*) area; **las ~s comunes de la prisión** the communal areas of the prison; **~ de no fumadores** no smoking area ► **zona ancha** (*Dep*) midfield ► **zona de castigo** (*Dep*) sin bin ► **zona de penumbra**, **zona de sombra** (*lit*) shaded area; (*fig*) area of secrecy ► **zona oscura**: **las ~s oscuras de la personalidad** the hidden areas of the personality; **las ~s oscuras de la política** the shady *o* murky areas of politics
[4] (*Geog*) zone ► **zona glacial** glacial zone ► **zona templada** temperate zone ► **zona tórrida** torrid zone
[5] (*Anat, Med*) area; **las ~s próximas a la columna vertebral** the areas around the spinal column; **sentí un dolor por la ~ del hombro** I felt a pain around my shoulder; ► **zona erógena** erogenous zone; ► **zona lumbar** lumbar region
[6] (*Baloncesto*) free-zone lane

zonación SF zoning

zonal ADJ zonal

zoncear ▸conjug 1a◂ VI (*LAm*) to behave stupidly

zoncera SF, **zoncería** SF [1] (*LAm*) (= *cualidad*) silliness, stupidity
[2] (*Cono Sur*) mere trifle; **costar una ~** to cost next to nothing; **comer una ~** to have a bite to eat

zonchiche SM (*CAm, Méx*) buzzard

zonda SF (*Arg*) hot northerly wind

zonificar ▸conjug 1g◂ VT to zone, divide into zones

zonzo/a Ⓐ ADJ [1] (*LAm*) (= *tonto*) silly, stupid; (= *pesado*) boring
[2] (*Méx*) (= *aturdido*) dazed
Ⓑ SM/F (*LAm*) (= *tonto*) idiot; (= *pesado*) bore

zonzoneco ADJ (*CAm*), **zonzoreco** ADJ (*CAm*), **zonzoreno** ADJ (*CAm*) stupid

zoo SM zoo

zoo... PREF zoo...

zoología SF zoology

zoológico Ⓐ ADJ zoological
Ⓑ SM zoo

zoólogo/a SM/F zoologist

zoom [θum] SM (= *objetivo*) zoom lens; (= *toma*) zoom shot

zoomórfico ADJ zoomorphic

zoomorfo SM zoomorph

zooplancton SM zooplankton

zoo-safari SM safari park

zope SM (*CAm*) vulture

zopenco/a* Ⓐ ADJ dull, stupid
Ⓑ SM/F clot*, nitwit*

zopilote SM (*CAm, Méx*) [1] (= *ave*) vulture
[2] (*) (= *ladrón*) thief

zopilotear* ▸conjug 1a◂ VT (*CAm, Méx*) [1] (= *comer*) to wolf down
[2] (= *robar*) to pinch*, nick*

zopo ADJ crippled, maimed

zoquetada SF (*LAm*) stupidity

zoquetazo SM (*Cono Sur, Méx*) swipe, punch

zoquete Ⓐ SMF (*) (= *zopenco*) blockhead; (= *patán*) lout, oaf
Ⓑ SM [1] [*de madera*] block
[2] [*de pan*] crust
[3] (*LAm*) (= *suciedad*) body dirt, human dirt
[4] (*Caribe, Méx*) (= *puñetazo*) punch; (= *trompada*) smack in the face

zoquetillo SM shuttlecock

zorenco ADJ (*CAm*) stupid

Zoroastro SM Zoroaster

zorongo SM (*Mús*) *popular song and dance of Andalusia*

zorra Ⓐ SF [1] (= *animal*) vixen
[2] (‡) (= *prostituta*) whore (*pey*), tart‡, slut‡; **¡zorra!** you slut!‡
[3] (*) (= *borrachera*) **pillar una ~** to get sloshed*
Ⓑ ADJ (‡) (= *puñetero*) bloody‡; **no tengo ni ~ idea** I haven't a bloody clue‡; **toda la ~ noche** the whole bloody night‡; *ver tb* **zorro**

zorral ADJ [1] (*Andes, CAm*) (= *molesto*) annoying
[2] (*Andes*) (= *obstinado*) obstinate

zorrear* ▸conjug 1a◂ VI to be up to one's tricks again, be up to no good

zorrera SF [1] (= *madriguera*) foxhole; (*fig*) smoky room
[2] (= *turbación*) worry, anxiety
[3] (= *modorra*) drowsiness

zorrería SF [1] (= *astucia*) foxiness, craftiness
[2] (= *acción*) sly trick

zorrero ADJ foxy, crafty

zorrillo SM (*Cono Sur*), **zorrino** SM (*Cono Sur*) skunk

zorro Ⓐ ADJ foxy, crafty
Ⓑ SM [1] (= *animal*) fox ► **zorro gris** grey fox
[2] (= *piel*) fox fur, fox skin ► **zorro plateado** silver fox (fur)
[3] (= *persona*) (= *taimado*) crafty old fox; (= *gandúl*) slacker, shirker; ✦**MODISMOS estar hecho un ~** to be very drowsy; **estar hecho unos ~s*** [*habitación*] to be in an awful state; [*persona*] to be all in; *ver tb* **zorra**

zorrón* ADJ sluttish

zorruno ADJ foxy, fox-like

zorrupia‡ SF tart‡, whore (*pey*)

zorzal SM [1] (= *ave*) thrush
[2] (= *hombre listo*) shrewd man; (= *hombre taimado*) sly fellow
[3] (*Cono Sur*) (= *tonto*) simpleton; (= *inocente*) dupe, naïve person

zorzalear* ▸conjug 1a◂ VI (*Cono Sur*) to sponge*

zorzalero* ADJ (*Cono Sur*) sponging*, parasitical

zorzalino* ADJ **la vida zorzalina** the easy life

zosco SM (*Caribe*) idiot

zotal® SM disinfectant

zote* Ⓐ ADJ dim, stupid
Ⓑ SMF dimwit*

zozobra SF [1] (*Náut*) capsizing, overturning
[2] (= *inquietud*) worry, anxiety; (= *nerviosismo*) jumpiness

zozobrar ▸conjug 1a◂ VI [1] [*barco*] (= *hundirse*) to founder, sink; (= *volcar*) to capsize, overturn; (= *peligrar*) to be in danger
[2] (= *fracasar*) [*plan*] to fail, founder; [*negocio*] to be ruined
[3] [*persona*] to be anxious, worry

zueco SM clog, wooden shoe

zulla* SF human excrement

zullarse* ▸conjug 1a◂ VPR (= *ensuciarse*) to dirty o.s.; (= *ventosear*) to fart‡, break wind

zullón* SM fart‡

zulo SM [*de armas*] cache; [*de documentos*] hiding place

zulú Ⓐ ADJ [1] Zulu
[2] († *pey*) brutish
Ⓑ SMF [1] Zulu
[2] († *pey*) brute

Zululandia SF Zululand

zumaque SM sumac(h)

zumba SF [1] (= *burla*) teasing; **dar** *o* **hacer ~ a algn** to tease sb
[2] (*LAm**) (= *paliza*) beating
[3] (*Méx*) drunkenness

zumbado* ADJ **estar ~** to be crazy, be off one's head*

zumbador SM [1] (*Elec*) buzzer
[2] (*Caribe, Méx*) (= *ave*) hummingbird

zumbar ▸conjug 1a◂ Ⓐ VI [1] (= *sonar*) [*insecto*] to buzz; [*máquina*] to hum, whirr; [*oídos*] to ring, buzz; **~le a algn los oídos: me zumban los oídos** my ears are ringing, I have a buzzing in my ears; **le estarán zumbando los oídos** his ears must be burning
[2] ✦**MODISMO salir zumbando*** to shoot off*; **salió zumbando cuando vio a la policía** he shot off as soon as he caught sight of the police*; **tengo que salir zumbando para no perder el tren** I must rush so I don't miss the train
[3] (*) (= *quedar cerca*) to be very close; **no está en peligro ahora, pero le zumba** he's not actually in danger now but it's not far away
Ⓑ VT [1] (= *burlar*) to tease
[2] (= *golpear*) to beat, hit
[3] (*LAm**) (= *tirar*) chuck*
[4] (‡) (= *robar*) to nick‡
[5] (‡*) (= *copular con*) to fuck‡*
Ⓒ **zumbarse** VPR [1] (= *burlarse*) **~se de algn** to tease sb, poke fun at sb
[2] (*Andes, Caribe*) (= *marcharse*) to clear off*
[3] (*Caribe*) (= *pasarse*) to overstep the mark
[4] (= *copular con*) **~se a algn**‡* to fuck sb‡*
[5] (= *masturbarse*) **zumbársela**‡* to wank‡*

zumbido SM [1] [*de insecto*] buzz(ing); [*de máquina*] hum(ming), whirr(ing) ► **zumbido de oídos** buzzing in the ears, ringing in the ears [2] (*) (= *puñetazo*) punch, biff*

zumbo¹ SM (*Andes, CAm*) gourd, calabash

zumbo² SM = **zumbido 1**

zumbón/ona Ⓐ ADJ [*persona*] waggish, funny; [*tono*] teasing; (*pey*) sarcastic
Ⓑ SM/F joker, tease

zumiento ADJ juicy

zumo SM [1] [*de frutas, verduras*] juice ► **zumo de naranja** orange juice

2 (= *provecho*) **sacar el ~ a algo** to get the most out of sth

zumoso ADJ juicy

zuncho SM metal band, metal hoop

zupia SF 1 (= *heces*) dregs *pl*; (= *vino*) muddy wine; (= *brebaje*) nasty drink, evil-tasting liquid
2 (= *gentuza*) dregs *pl*
3 (*Andes*) (= *aguardiente*) rough liquor

zurcido SM 1 (= *acto*) darning, mending
2 (= *remiendo*) darn, mend

zurcidura SF = **zurcido**

zurcir ▸conjug 3b◂ VT 1 (= *coser*) to darn, mend
2 (= *juntar*) to join, put together; [+ *mentiras*] to concoct, think up
3 ✦**MODISMOS ¡que las zurzan!*** to hell with them!*; **¡que te zurzan!*** get lost!*

zurdazo SM (= *golpe*) left-handed punch; (= *tiro*) left-footed shot

zurdear ▸conjug 1a◂ VT (*LAm*) to do with the left hand

zurdo/a Ⓐ ADJ [*mano*] left; [*persona*] left-handed; **a zurdas** (*lit*) with the left hand; (*fig*) the wrong way, clumsily; ✦**MODISMO no es ~** he's no fool
Ⓑ SM/F 1 (= *persona*) (*gen*) left-handed person; (*Tenis*) left-hander
2 (*Cono Sur Pol pey*) lefty*, left-winger

zurear ▸conjug 1a◂ VI to coo

zureo SM coo, cooing

zuri‡ SM **darse el ~** to clear out*

zurito SM small glass (*of beer*)

zuro SM cob, corncob

zurra SF 1 (*) (= *paliza*) hiding*
2 (*) (= *trabajo*) hard grind*, drudgery
3 (*) (= *pelea*) roughhouse*
4 [*de pieles*] dressing

zurrador SM dresser

zurrapa SF 1 (= *mancha*) smudge, smear; (*en calzoncillos, bragas*) skidmark*; (= *hilo*) thread, stream (*of dirt*); **zurrapas** (= *posos*) dregs
2 (= *cosa despreciable*) trash, rubbish

zurraposo ADJ full of dregs, muddy

zurrar ▸conjug 1a◂ VT 1 (*) (= *pegar*) to wallop*, give a hiding*
2 (*) (*en discusión*) to flatten
3 (*) (= *criticar*) to lash out at, lay into*
4 [+ *pieles*] to dress

zurria* SF 1 (*Andes, CAm*) (= *paliza*) hiding*
2 (*Andes*) (= *multitud*) lot, crowd

zurriaga SF whip, lash

zurriagar ▸conjug 1h◂ VT to whip, lash

zurriagazo SM 1 (= *azote*) lash, stroke
2 (= *desgracia*) stroke of bad luck; (= *revés*) severe blow; (= *mal trato*) piece of unjust o harsh treatment

zurriago SM whip, lash

zurribanda* SF = **zurra 1, 3**

zurriburri* SM 1 (= *confusión*) turmoil, confusion; (= *lío*) mess, mix-up; (= *ruido*) hubbub
2 (= *persona despreciable*) worthless individual
3 (= *pandilla*) gang; (= *turba*) rabble

zurrón SM pouch, bag

zurullo SM, **zurullón** SM 1 (*en líquido*) lump
2 (**) (= *excremento*) turd**
3 (‡) (= *persona*) lout, hooligan

zurumato ADJ (*Méx*) (= *turulato*) light-headed, woozy*; (= *estúpido*) stupid

zurumbanco ADJ (*CAm, Méx*) 1 = **zurumato**
2 (*) (= *medio borracho*) half-drunk, half cut*

zurumbático ADJ **estar ~** to be stunned, be dazed

zurumbo ADJ (*CAm*) 1 = **zurumato**
2 (*) (= *medio borracho*) half-drunk, half cut*

zutano/a SM/F (Mr *etc*) So-and-so; **si se casa fulano con zutana** if Mr X marries Miss Y; *ver tb* **fulano 1**

Language in Use
Lengua y Uso

by

Beryl T. Atkins and Hélène M. A. Lewis

Teresa Álvarez García   Diana Feri   José Miguel Galván Déniz   Cordelia Lilly

Language in Use

Contents

Spanish-English

		Page
	Introduction	5
1	Suggestions	6
2	Advice	6
3	Offers	7
4	Requests	7
5	Comparisons	8
6	Opinions	9
7	Likes, dislikes and preferences	10
8	Intentions and desires	10
9	Permission	11
10	Obligation	12
11	Agreement	13
12	Disagreement	13
13	Approval	14
14	Disapproval	15
15	Certainty, probability, possibility and capability	15
16	Doubt, improbability, impossibility and incapability	16
17	Explanations	17
18	Apologies	18
19	Job applications	18
20	Commercial correspondence	20
21	General correspondence	22
22	Thanks	24
23	Best wishes	24
24	Announcements	24
25	Invitations	26
26	Essay writing	27
27	The telephone	33
27a	E-mail	35

Lengua y Uso

Índice de materias

Inglés-Español

		Página
	Introducción	5
27	El teléfono	35
27a	Correo electrónico	36
28	Sugerencias	37
29	Consejos	37
30	Propuestas	38
31	Peticiones	38
32	Comparaciones	39
33	Opiniones	40
34	Gustos y preferencias	40
35	Intenciones y deseos	41
36	Permiso	42
37	Obligación	43
38	Acuerdo	44
39	Desacuerdo	44
40	Aprobación	45
41	Desaprobación	46
42	Certeza, probabilidad, posibilidad y capacidad	46
43	Incertidumbre, improbabilidad, imposibilidad e incapacidad	47
44	Explicaciones	48
45	Disculpas	49
46	Solicitudes de trabajo	49
47	Correspondencia comercial	51
48	Correspondencia de carácter general	53
49	Agradecimientos	56
50	Saludos de cortesía y felicitaciones	56
51	Notas y avisos de sociedad	56
52	Invitaciones	57
53	Redacción	58

Corpus Acknowledgements

We would like to acknowledge the assistance of the many hundreds of individuals and companies who have kindly given permission for copyright material to be used in The Bank of English. The written sources include many national and regional newspapers in Britain and overseas; magazine and periodical publishers in Britain, the United States and Australia. Extensive spoken data has been provided by radio and television broadcasting companies; research workers at many universities and other institutions; and individual numerous contributors. We are grateful to them all.

Agradecimientos

Agradecemos especialmente la valiosa colaboración de los periódicos EL MUNDO y ABC, así como del Laboratorio de Lingüística Informática de la Universidad Autónoma de Madrid, en el que se realizó el 'Corpus de Referencia de la Lengua Española Contemporánea: corpus oral centro-peninsular' dirigido por el Prof. Dr. Francisco A. Marcos-Marín.

Introduction to Language in Use – New Edition

Our aim in writing **Language in Use** has been to help non-native speakers find fluent, natural ways of expressing themselves in the foreign language, without risk of the native-language distortion that sometimes results from literal translation.

To achieve this, we have identified a number of essential language functions, such as *agreement, suggestions* and *apologies,* and provided a wealth of examples to show typical ways of expressing them. Users can select phrases to meet their needs using either their knowledge of the foreign language alone or by looking at the translations of the key elements.

In this completely revised and updated edition of **Language in Use**, the authentic examples are taken from Collins vast computerized databases of modern English and Spanish. These databases consist of around 400 million English and Spanish words from a variety of modern written and spoken sources: literature, magazines, newspapers, letters, radio and television.

The fresh new colour layout is designed to make consultation even easier. Clear headings and subdivisions enable you to find the topic of your choice at a glance. We have given style guidance, where appropriate, so that you can be confident that the phrase you have chosen is as assertive, tentative, direct or indirect as you want it to be.

The main dictionary text is linked to the **Language in Use** section. Certain words, *suggestion,* for example, have been marked in the main dictionary to show that additional material is given in Language in Use. In these cases, an arrow symbol appears in the margin beside the headword, and a footnote (**suggestion 1** 1.1, 1.2) tells you which **Language in Use** section(s) to go to – in this case, sections 1.1 and 1.2 for examples relating to category 1. As all cross-referred words are underlined in the relevant **Language in Use** section, you will quickly be able to locate them there.

Since Spanish forms of address corresponding to the English *you* vary according to the formality of the relationship, we have tried to reflect this in a consistent manner. As a general rule, *tú/te* has been shown in everyday one-to-one situations where there is no evidence of formality. Where the situation or language suggests a more formal relationship, *usted/le* has been used. Where more than one person is addressed, *vosotros/as* and *ustedes/les* have been used in a similar way. Nevertheless, as usage of *tú/usted* and *vosotros/ustedes* varies depending on which variety of Spanish is being spoken and the age of the speakers, you should be prepared to make adjustments accordingly.

Lengua y Uso – Introducción a la nueva edición

Nuestro objetivo al escribir este suplemento de **Lengua y Uso** ha sido ayudar a los estudiantes de ambas lenguas a encontrar formas de expresarse con naturalidad en el idioma extranjero y evitar así las distorsiones que a veces resultan de una traducción literal.

Para ello, se ha analizado el acto de la comunicación partiendo de ciertas funciones del tipo *consejos, permiso* o *posibilidad,* para agrupar toda una serie de frases y expresiones bajo las secciones correspondientes. De esta manera el lector puede seleccionar la frase que le hace falta gracias tanto a sus conocimientos pasivos del idioma extranjero como a la traducción dada a su propia lengua de dichas frases.

En esta nueva edición, totalmente revisada y actualizada, hemos hecho uso de ejemplos de la lengua hablada y escrita tomados de la base de datos electrónica de la que dispone Collins para su labor lexicográfica: más de 400 millones de palabras en inglés y español, recogidas de libros, revistas, periódicos, cartas, programas de radio y televisión.

La nueva presentación gráfica, ahora en color, tiene como objetivo facilitar aún más la labor de consulta. La claridad de los encabezamientos y subdivisiones permite encontrar en un momento el tema buscado. Además, se da una orientación de estilo en los casos apropiados para que pueda saberse con seguridad si la frase se usa de forma más o menos directa, o en un contexto más o menos familiar etc.

El texto central de diccionario enlaza con este suplemento. En algunas entradas (como *recomendar,* por ejemplo), hay una llamada que indica que podrán verse más ejemplos relacionados con ellas en la sección correspondiente de **Lengua y Uso**. En estos casos, al lado de la palabra cabeza de artículo aparece una flecha, además de una nota a pie de página (**recomendar 1** 28.1, 29.1, 40.4, 46.5) que indica en qué sección pueden encontrarse dichos ejemplos. En el caso de *recomendar,* se verán ejemplos relacionados con la acepción 1 en las secciones 28.1, 29.1, 40.4, 46.5. Como además todas las palabras remitidas a este suplemento vienen subrayadas en el mismo, se las puede localizar rápidamente.

En cuanto al tratamiento de *tú* o *usted* en las frases en español y en las traducciones de este suplemento, se ha decidido usar como norma general el *tuteo,* excepto en los ejemplos de situaciones que requieren un trato más formal y por lo tanto el uso de *usted.*

1 SUGGESTIONS

1.1 Making suggestions

Using direct questions

- **¿Quieres que** ponga la maceta en la ventana?
  = *would you like me to*
- **¿Te apetece que** vayamos a verle esta tarde?
  = *do you fancy going*
- **¿Por qué no** lo dejas hasta que volvamos a casa?
  = *why don't you*
- **¿Y si** organizáramos una fiesta para darle una sorpresa?
  = *what if we*
- **¿Te parece bien** que la invitemos a la fiesta?
  = *do you think we should*
- **¿Qué te parece** decírselo por carta?
  = *what do you think about*
- **¿No se te ha ocurrido que** el mejor regalo no es siempre el más caro?
  = *hasn't it ever occurred to you that*
- **¿No cree que sería mejor** hacerlo ahora?
  = *mightn't it be better to*
- **¿Puedo hacerle una propuesta** que quizá le parezca interesante?
  = *may I make a suggestion*

Assertively

- **Yo que tú** no haría nada por ahora
  = *if I were you*
- **Lo que sugiero es lo siguiente**: por ahora no cambiemos los planes
  = *what I suggest is that*
- **Lo que deberíamos hacer es no** preocuparnos demasiado de los demás
  = *what we should not do is*
- **Propongo que** busquemos ayuda profesional
  = *I suggest that*
- **Lo mejor sería no** involucrarse en un conflicto en el que no tenemos ni arte ni parte
  = *it would be best not to*
- **No se olvide de** avisarme en cuanto llegue
  = *don't forget to*
- **Yo propondría que** la actual reforma de la ley se negocie buscando el consenso de todos
  = *I would suggest that*
- **Les sugeriría que** llamaran antes por teléfono
  = *I would advise you to*
- **Quisiera hacer una propuesta para** mejorar el servicio
  = *I should like to make a suggestion to*
- **Si se me permite una sugerencia,** yo creo que debemos trazar un plan de actuación detallado
  = *if I may make a suggestion*

Tentatively

- **Sería cuestión de** hacer una prueba para ver si funciona
  = *we/you would have to*
- **Si le parece bien, podemos** enviárselo por correo urgente
  = *if you agree, we could*
- **Lo que podríamos hacer es** hablar con él antes de que se marche a Italia
  = *what we could do is*
- **Sería mejor que** el ganador del premio fuera un escritor novel
  = *it would be best if*
- **Sería buena idea** aprovechar la atención que va a atraer el acontecimiento
  = *it would be a good idea to*
- **No sería mala idea** levantarse un poco más temprano
  = *it mightn't be a bad idea to*
- **Quizás habría que** ser un poco más firmes con ellos
  = *perhaps you/we should*
- En estas circunstancias **sería muy poco aconsejable** enviar más tropas a la zona
  = *it would be very inadvisable to*
- **Sería preferible** tener mejor calidad de vida para nuestra población
  = *it would be preferable to*
- **Convendría** encontrar una alternativa más sencilla
  = *it would be advisable to*
- **Convendría que** recurriera a los servicios de un especialista
  = *you would do well to*
- **Sería conveniente que** acudieran a un abogado con la documentación
  = *it would be advisable for ... to*

1.2 Asking for suggestions

- **¿Alguna idea**?
  = *any ideas?*
- **¿Tú qué dices**?
  = *what do you think?*
- **¿Cómo lo ves**?
  = *what do you think?*
- **¿Tú qué harías**?
  = *what would you do?*
- **¿Qué hacemos ahora**?
  = *what shall we do now?*
- **¿A tí qué te parece que podemos** hacer ahora?
  = *what do you think we can*
- **Si se le ocurre algo** ...
  = *if you have any ideas*
- **¿Qué haría usted en mi lugar**?
  = *what would you do if you were me?*
- **¿Tiene usted alguna sugerencia** al respecto?
  = *have you any suggestions?*

2 ADVICE

2.1 Asking for advice

- **¿Tú qué me aconsejas**?
  = *what would you advise me to do?*
- **¿Tú qué harías (si estuvieras) en mi lugar**?
  = *what would you do if you were me?*
- **¿Te puedo pedir un consejo**?
  = *can I ask your advice about something?*
- **¿Tú crees que a estas alturas sirve de algo que** desconvoquen la huelga?
  = *do you think there is any point in ...at this late stage?*
- **Necesito que alguien me aconseje**
  = *I need some advice*
- **¿Qué es lo más recomendable** en esta situación?
  = *what would be advisable*
- **Quería pedirle un consejo**
  = *I'd like to ask your advice about something*
- **¿Usted qué me aconsejaría que** hiciera?
  = *what would you advise me to*
- **Le agradecería que me asesorase sobre** ese asunto
  = *I would be grateful for your advice on*

2.2 Giving advice

- **Yo que tú** no haría nada por ahora
  = *if I were you*
- **Yo en tu lugar** no lo dudaría
  = *if I were you*

- **Hay que** tomarse las cosas con más calma
  = *you must*
- **Te interesa más** comprar acciones de la otra empresa
  = *you would be better to*
- **Deberías** mostrarte más abierto y sincero en tu relación
  = *you should*
- **Lo que ella debería hacer es** cambiar su imagen ligeramente
  = *what she should do is*
- **Harías bien en** visitar a un especialista
  = *you would do well to*
- **Más vale no** decir nada por el momento
  = *it would be better or best not to*
- **Mi consejo es que** te sinceres con ellos y les digas la verdad
  = *my advice would be to*
- **Habría que** sopesar los pros y los contras antes de tomar una decisión definitiva
  = *we/you ought to*
- **Lo que habría que hacer es** consultarlo con quien sepa sobre el tema
  = *what we/you ought to do is*
- **Lo que haría falta es que** instalaran un nuevo sistema de refrigeración
  = *what they should do is*
- **Lo mejor que puede hacer es** dirigirse a la oficina central
  = *the best thing you can do is*
- **Le recomiendo que** abandone el hábito del cigarrillo si quiere mejorar su estado de salud
  = *I would advise you to*
- **Sería totalmente desaconsejable** intervenir ahora
  = *it would be extremely inadvisable to*
- **Permítanme ustedes que insista en la necesidad de** presionar a la compañía
  = *I'd like to emphasize the need to*
- **Me permito sugerirle que** corrija dichos errores, para mejorar aún más si cabe la calidad de su periódico
  = *I should like to suggest that you*

More tentatively

- **¿Y si** fueras a verle y le pidieras perdón?
  = *what if you*
- **Yo te aconsejaría** un cambio de aires
  = *I'd recommend*
- **Quizás habría que** preparar unos planes más detallados
  = *perhaps we should*
- **Yo le diría que** fuera prudente a la hora de tomar una decisión
  = *I would advise you to*
- **No sería mala idea** enviarlo todo exprés
  = *it wouldn't be a bad idea to*
- **Sería prudente** llamar antes por teléfono, por si acaso está fuera
  = *it would be wise to*

2.3 Warnings

- **Os advierto que** no vamos a dar ninguna información
  = *I should warn you that*
- **Debo advertirle que** esa agencia no es de fiar
  = *I must warn you that*
- **Si no** pides disculpas ahora, **deberás atenerte a las consecuencias**
  = *if you don't ... you must accept the consequences*
- **Corremos el riesgo de** perder toda credibilidad
  = *we run the risk of*
- **Que sirva de advertencia:** si continuáis con esa actitud, las consecuencias pueden ser nefastas
  = *be warned:*
- **Sería cosa de locos** *or* **una locura** proseguir en estas pésimas condiciones
  = *it would be madness to*

- **Es necesario** cambiar de rumbo **antes de que sea demasiado tarde**
  = *we need to ... before it is too late*
- **Es absolutamente indispensable que** modifiquemos nuestra política de ventas
  = *it is absolutely vital that*

3 OFFERS

3.1 Using direct questions

- ¿**Te ayudo**?
  = *can I help (you)?*
- ¿**Cierro** la ventana?
  = *shall I close*
- ¿**Quieres que** vaya a recoger al niño al colegio?
  = *would you like me to*
- ¿**Necesitas ayuda**?
  = *do you need any help?*
- ¿**Me dejas que te eche una mano con** los preparativos?
  = *can I lend (you) a hand with*
- ¿**Puedo ayudarle en algo**?
  = *can I do anything to help?*
- ¿**Me permite que le ofrezca mi colaboración** de cara al proyecto?
  = *perhaps you will allow me to offer some help*

3.2 Direct offers

- No te preocupes, **ya lo hacemos nosotros**
  = *we'll do it*
- **Si quieres** te acompaño
  = *... if you like*
- **Puedo ir yo si** no hay nadie disponible
  = *I could go if*
- **Déjeme que le ayude**
  = *let me help you*
- **Estoy para lo que haga falta**
  = *I'm ready and willing to do whatever's needed*
- **Estoy dispuesto a** hacer todo lo que sea necesario
  = *I'm prepared to*
- **No dude en venir a mí si** le surge algún problema
  = *don't hesitate to come back to me if*
- **Permítame usted por lo menos que** le lleve a la estación
  = *at least let me*
- **Me tiene a su entera disposición** para todo lo que necesite
  = *I'm entirely at your disposal*
- **Sería un placer** poder servirle en todo lo que haga falta
  = *it would be a pleasure to*

4 REQUESTS

4.1 Using direct questions

- ¿**Me traes** un vaso de agua?
  = *would you fetch me*
- ¿**Me dejas** tu chaqueta?
  = *can I borrow*
- ¿**Quieres** cambiarme el turno?
  = *would you mind*
- ¿**Te importa** echar esta carta al correo?
  = *would you mind*
- ¿**Te puedo pedir un favor**?
  = *would you do me a favour?*
- ¿**Podría decirme** qué pone en ese cartel, **por favor**?
  = *could you tell me ..., please?*

- **¿Le importaría** cerrar un poco la ventana?
  = would you mind
- **¿Sería tan amable de** enseñármelo usted mismo?
  = would you be so kind as to
- **¿Podría** aclararme unas dudas sobre su patrimonio, **si tiene la bondad**?
  = would you mind

Assertively

- **Déjame el coche, anda**, sólo por una noche
  = *lend me the car, won't you*
- **Por favor, házmelo** cuanto antes
  = *please can you do it for me*
- **Sólo te pido que** bajes un poco la voz
  = *I'm only asking you to*
- **Alcánzame** las gafas, **si me haces el favor**
  = *pass me ..., will you?*
- **Haga el favor de no** poner los pies en el asiento
  = *please don't*
- Vuelva a llamar en cinco minutos, **si es tan amable**
  = *if you don't mind*
- **Le ruego que** se apresure en responder
  = *please*

More tentatively

- **Si no es mucho pedir**, mándame un listado de direcciones
  = *please ..., if it isn't too much trouble*
- **Nos vendría bien** saberlo mañana, antes de la reunión
  = *it would be good if we could*
- **Preferiría que no** lo utilizara a partir de las ocho
  = *I would rather you didn't*
- **Si no es demasiada molestia, ¿podrías** comentarnos cómo es el panorama musical en tu ciudad?
  = *if it isn't too much trouble, could you*
- **Le agradecería que** me ayudara a resolver el problema
  = *I'd be grateful if you would*

In writing

- **Tenga la amabilidad de** presentarse en nuestras oficinas en horario laboral
  = *please*
- **Agradeceríamos su colaboración en** cualquier aspecto de nuestra investigación
  = *we should be grateful if you would help us in*
- **Les quedaríamos muy agradecidos si** se pudieran poner en contacto con nuestros representantes
  = *we should be very grateful if*
- **Tengan a bien** comunicarnos la respuesta por télex
  = *please*

5 COMPARISONS

5.1 Constrasting facts

- Las carreteras están **relativamente** tranquilas para esta época del año
  = *comparatively*
- Las nuestras son producciones modestas, **comparadas con** las más "aparatosas" de otros teatros
  = *compared with*
- **En comparación con** el interior del país, el clima en la costa **no es tan** extremo
  = *in comparison with ... is not so*
- **Si comparamos** el actual estado del río **y** *or* **con** el anterior, podemos observar un aumento en el grado de contaminación
  = *if we compare ... and or with*
- Los países desarrollados consumen en exceso, **mientras que** los del Tercer Mundo no llegan a cubrir las necesidades básicas
  = *while*

5.2 Comparing similar things

- Estos dos cuadros **son igualitos**
  = *are just the same*
- Su programa político **es igual que** el de la oposición
  = *is the same as*
- En nuestras carreteras se producen **casi tantos** accidentes **como** en las de Grecia y Portugal
  = *almost as many ... as*
- El paisaje es **tan** bello **como** lo describió el poeta
  = *as ... as*
- García Márquez se limita a transcribir la realidad **tal como es**
  = *just as or like it is*
- Ambos coches valen **exactamente lo mismo**
  = *exactly the same*
- Ha vuelto a suceder **lo mismo que** hace unos años
  = *the same thing as*
- **Al igual que sucede** en el reino animal, las plantas también luchan por su supervivencia
  = *just as happens*
- Los dos hermanos **se parecen mucho** físicamente
  = *are very alike*
- Las temperaturas aquí **son muy parecidas** *or* **similares a** las de mi tierra
  = *are very similar to*
- Esto **equivale a** veinte horas de trabajo
  = *is equivalent to*

5.3 Comparing dissimilar things

- Los pros **son (muchos) más que** los contras
  = *there are (far) more ... than*
- En su tierra se le aprecia **(muchísimo) menos que** en el extranjero
  = *far less than*
- Es aún **(mucho) más** nacionalista **que** su hermano
  = *far more ... than*
- Un coche nuevo contamina **bastante menos que** uno viejo
  = *considerably less than*
- Al contribuyente se le cobra **mucho menos de lo que** cuestan los servicios
  = *much less than*
- Lo que diga una revista del corazón **no es lo mismo que** las manifestaciones públicas de un presidente
  = *is not the same as*
- Esa canción ya **no** suena **tanto como** el año pasado
  = *not ... as much as*
- **No se parece en nada a** su padre
  = *he is not at all like*
- **¡Hay diferencia entre** este vino y el otro ...!
  = *there's quite some difference between*
- Un modelo **se diferencia** *or* **distingue del** otro en el número de extras que lleva incorporados
  = *the difference between ... and ... lies in*
- La realidad **es muy diferente** *or* **distinta de** lo que teníamos creído
  = *is very different from*

5.4 Comparing favourably

- Me encuentro **muchísimo mejor** ahora que me han operado
  = *much better*
- Este vino **es muy superior** al otro
  = *is vastly superior to*

5.5 Comparing unfavourably

- Para muchos perder su cargo público resulta **mucho peor que**

perder la dignidad
= *much worse than*

- Las posibilidades que ofrece una máquina de escribir **no tienen (ni punto de) comparación con** las prestaciones de un procesador de textos
  = *between ... and*

- Este premio **no es tan** importante **como** el que consiguió hace unos años
  = *is not as ... as*

- Como deportista, Juan **no le llega ni a la suela de los zapatos**
  = *isn't a patch on him*

5.6 Increasing and decreasing

- Estos juegos **tienen cada vez más aceptación entre** los estudiantes
  = *are becoming more and more popular with*

- Las desigualdades **son cada vez mayores**
  = *are becoming greater and greater*

- A decir verdad, yo escribo **cada vez menos**, y acabaré sin duda por dejar de escribir
  = *less and less*

- **Son cada vez menos los que** se casan antes de los 29 años
  = *fewer and fewer people*

- **Cuanto más** madura un vino, **más** añejo es su sabor
  = *the more ..., the more*

6 OPINIONS

6.1 Asking for someone's opinion

- ¿**Qué piensas de** su actitud?
  = *what do you think of*

- ¿**Qué te parece** mi trabajo?
  = *what do you think of*

- ¿**Crees que** le gustará el regalo?
  = *do you think that*

- ¿**Piensas que** se puede estudiar en estas condiciones?
  = *do you think that*

- ¿**Qué opina usted de** la exportación de animales vivos?
  = *what do you think of or about*

- ¿**Qué opinión tiene usted de** sus compatriotas?
  = *what is your opinion of*

- ¿**Qué opinión le merece** la subida del precio de los carburantes?
  = *what is your opinion of*

- ¿**Nos puede ofrecer su opinión sobre** la liberalización del mercado?
  = *could you give us your opinion on*

- **Quisiera saber lo que opina sobre** el informe publicado en la prensa
  = *I should like to know what you think about*

- **Me interesaría conocer su opinión en torno a** la nueva política exterior del gobierno
  = *I should be interested to know your opinion of*

6.2 Expressing your opinion

- **Creo que** le va a encantar tu visita
  = *I think that*

- **Me parece que** le has caído muy bien a todos
  = *I think that*

- **Para ser sincero**, su obra no me apasiona
  = *to be honest*

- **En mi opinión**, fue un error no haberle contratado antes
  = *in my opinion*

- **A mi parecer** *or* **A mi manera de ver**, las cosas se deberían hacer de otro modo
  = *in my view*

- **Mi opinión personal es que** se debería nombrar un comité al respecto
  = *my personal opinion is that*

- **Yo considero que** eso no es perjudicial para el sistema democrático
  = *it is my belief that*

- **Personalmente, creo que** es un gasto innecesario
  = *personally, I think that*

- **Debo reconocer** *or* **admitir que** nuestra posición se ha visto debilitada
  = *I must admit that*

- **Mi posición al respecto** difiere de la suya
  = *my position on the matter*

- **En mi calidad de** *or* **Como** Premio Nobel de la Paz, **quiero reafirmar** mi apoyo inequívoco a una solución pacífica y negociada
  = *as ..., I should like to reaffirm*

- **Si me permite que le dé mi opinión, me parece que** esa oferta es un engaño
  = *if I may be allowed to offer my opinion, I think that*

With more conviction

- **Lo que es yo**, no lo veo necesario
  = *personally*

- **Si quieres mi opinión**, déjame que te diga que no tienes de qué quejarte
  = *if you want my opinion*

- **Si quieren que les dé mi opinión**, hay necesidades más importantes en las que gastar el dinero
  = *if you want my opinion*

- **Tengo que decir que** no me gusta nada
  = *I must say that*

- **Estoy totalmente seguro de que** nos lo van a devolver
  = *I'm quite sure that*

- **Estoy convencida de que** no cuentan con fondos suficientes
  = *I'm convinced that*

- **No puedo menos que pensar que** es un acto deliberado
  = *I can't help thinking that*

More tentatively

- **Me da que** no va a venir
  = *I suspect that*

- **Me da la sensación de que** no va a dar resultado
  = *I have a (funny) feeling that*

- **Tengo la impresión de que** algo marcha mal
  = *I have the impression that*

- **Supongo que** es una posibilidad tan buena como cualquier otra
  = *I suppose that*

- Los padres, **imagino que** también tendrán que contribuir a ello
  = *I suppose that*

- **Con el debido respeto, debo decirle que** eso no es así
  = *with all due respect, I have to tell you that*

6.3 Replying without giving an opinion

- **No sabría decir**
  = *I couldn't say*

- **Preferiría reservarme la opinión**
  = *I would rather reserve judgement*

- **Es difícil dar una opinión** sin conocer las circunstancias
  = *it's difficult to give an opinion*

- **No puedo opinar sobre** un tema del que no tengo conocimiento
  = *I can't express an opinion on*

- **No deseamos ofrecer ninguna opinión hasta que** la situación se haya aclarado
  = *we would rather not express an opinion until*

- **No estoy en posición de hacer declaraciones** al respecto
  = *I'm not in a position to make a statement*

- **No puedo pronunciarme a favor de** ninguna de las opciones
  = *I cannot say I am in favour of*
- **No me es posible emitir una opinión objetiva sobre** este asunto
  = *I cannot give an objective opinion on*

7 LIKES, DISLIKES AND PREFERENCES

7.1 Asking people what they like

- ¿**Te gusta** el yogur de fresa?
  = *do you like*
- ¿**Cuál de** las tres camisas **te gusta más**?
  = *which of ... do you like best?*
- ¿**Le gustaría** viajar a otra época?
  = *would you like to*
- De las dos posibilidades, ¿**cuál prefiere**?
  = *which do you prefer?*
- **Quería saber si prefieren** salir ahora **o** después de comer
  = *I wanted to know if you would prefer to ... or*
- ¿**Podrían darme su parecer sobre** el nuevo programa?
  = *could you give me your opinion on*

7.2 Saying what you like

- **Me agrada que** hayan venido a verme desde tan lejos
  = *it was good of them to*
- **A todos nos gusta que** nos reconozcan un trabajo bien hecho
  = *we all like it when*
- **Me ha gustado mucho el regalo** que me has enviado
  = *I was delighted with the present*
- A mí los turistas que vienen por aquí **me caen (muy) bien**
  = *I (really) like ...*
- **Lo que más me gusta es** observar a la gente
  = *what I like (doing) best is*
- **Disfruto** charlando con los niños
  = *I enjoy*
- **Disfruto con** sus atrevidos comentarios en televisión
  = *I enjoy*
- **Me seduce la idea de** viajar a Finlandia, no sé por qué
  = *the idea of ... really appeals to me*
- Para muchos ver la televisión **es su pasatiempo favorito**
  = *is their favourite pastime*
- **Soy muy aficionado a** la danza contemporánea
  = *I'm very keen on*
- **Me encanta** el mar y navegar a vela
  = *I love*
- **Me fascina observar** el firmamento en una noche clara
  = *I love watching*
- **Me apasiona** la luminosidad del paisaje mediterráneo
  = *I love*
- **Siento verdadera debilidad por** los postres cremosos
  = *I have a weakness for*

7.3 Saying what you dislike

- **No me gusta** comer fuera de casa
  = *I don't like*
- Sus canciones **no son nada del otro mundo**
  = *aren't anything to write home about*
- **Me cuesta tener que** criticarle en público
  = *I find it hard to have to*
- **No me gusta nada que** me mientan
  = *I don't like ... at all*
- **No me resulta nada agradable** ir a trabajar a estas horas de la noche
  = *I'm not at all keen on*
- **Me molesta** el olor de las sardinas asadas
  = *I find ... very unpleasant*
- Mis nuevos vecinos **me caen muy mal** *or* **no me caen nada bien**
  = *I don't like ... at all*
- **Le he cogido manía a** ese chico
  = *I've really taken a dislike to*
- **No soporto que** me hagan esperar
  = *I can't stand*
- **Lo que más me fastidia es que** suban tanto el volumen
  = *what really annoys me is when*
- **Si hay algo que no aguanto es que** cambien la programación sin avisar
  = *if there's one thing I can't bear, it's when*
- **Detesto** cualquier tipo de violencia
  = *I hate*
- **Me horrorizan** las corridas de toros
  = *I really hate*

7.4 Saying what you prefer

- **Prefiero la** lectura **a la** televisión
  = *I prefer ... to*
- **Prefiero que** llegues tarde **a que** no vengas
  = *I'd rather you ... than*
- **Es mejor** *or* **preferible** hablar en el idioma del cliente
  = *it's better to*
- **Preferiría que** nadie me acompañara
  = *I would rather*
- **Nos vendría mejor** *or* **Nos convendría más** salir antes para evitar la hora de más tráfico
  = *we would do better to*
- **Tengo especial predilección por** la música de Falla
  = *I am particularly fond of*

7.5 Expressing indifference

- Vamos a esperar hasta encontrar la persona idónea, **no pasa nada porque** no haya titular durante un tiempo
  = *it doesn't matter if*
- **Me da igual** *or* **Me da lo mismo** vivir aquí **que** allí
  = *it's all the same to me whether ... or*
- **Me es (completamente) indiferente** que salga de presidente uno **u** otro
  = *it makes (absolutely) no difference to me whether ... or*
- **Si** no le veo hoy **no importa**
  = *it doesn't matter if*
- **No tiene (la mayor) importancia que** se demoren unos minutos
  = *it doesn't matter (in the slightest) if*

8 INTENTIONS AND DESIRES

8.1 Asking what someone intends or plans to do

- ¿**Qué piensas hacer**?
  = *what do you intend to do?*
- ¿**Qué vas a hacer** con las plantas estas vacaciones?
  = *what are you going to do?*
- ¿**Qué planes tienes** para la familia?
  = *what plans have you got?*
- ¿**Qué intentas hacer**?
  = *what are you trying to do?*
- ¿**Qué esperan ustedes conseguir con** esta propuesta?
  = *what do you hope to achieve with?*
- **Quisiera saber cómo piensa** actuar en lo referente al tema que nos ocupa
  = *I'd like to know how you intend to*

8.2 Talking about intentions

- **Voy a** tomar el tren de las siete
  = *I'm going to*

- **Pienso** marcharme cuando me haya recuperado por completo
  = *I intend to*
- **Haremos** los preparativos para la fiesta la noche antes
  = *we shall*
- **Tengo la intención de** empezar una serie de conciertos para niños
  = *I plan or intend to*
- **Mi intención no es otra que** explicar que la promoción de la salud es el objetivo principal de la salud pública
  = *my sole aim is to*
- **Me propongo** alcanzar la cima en un tiempo récord
  = *my aim is to*
- **Tienen previsto** casarse coincidiendo con las vacaciones
  = *they are planning to*
- Los vecinos **tienen pensado** denunciar la situación a las autoridades
  = *are planning to*
- **El objetivo de** la directiva **es** remodelar los estatutos del partido
  = *the aim of ... is to*
- El médico **está decidido a** salvar la vida del niño como sea
  = *is determined to*
- **Está resuelta a no** dejarlo hasta que acabe
  = *she is determined not to*
- La presidencia alemana **se ha planteado unos objetivos muy ambiciosos**
  = *has set itself some very ambitious goals*
- **Desconozco sus intenciones**
  = *I don't know what he is intending to do*

8.3 Saying what you would like

- **Me gustaría** saber qué se propone hacer como nuevo director
  = *I'd like to*
- **Me gustaría que** el partido tuviera una actitud más realista
  = *I'd like ... to*
- **Me único deseo es** volver a mi hogar
  = *all I want is to*
- **Nuestro deseo es que**, de una vez por todas, se nos tome en serio
  = *what we want is for ... to*
- Como actriz, **me encantaría poder** trabajar con un director como él
  = *I'd love to be able to*
- **Ojalá no lloviera** tanto para poder salir más a menudo
  = *if only it didn't rain*
- **Esperemos que** todo salga bien
  = *let's hope that*
- **Es de esperar que** las negociaciones lleguen a buen puerto
  = *it's to be hoped that*
- **Quisiera** dedicar una canción a mi hija Gemma, que cumple mañana 12 años
  = *I should like to*
- **Querría que** mis cuadros estuviesen colgados junto a los de los grandes maestros
  = *I'd like ... to*
- **Desearía que** se le prestara mayor atención a los desamparados
  = *I should like ... to*
- **Sueña con** llegar a ser modelo
  = *her dream is to*

8.4 Saying what you don't intend or don't want to do

- **No quiero que vayan** a pensar otra cosa
  = *I don't want you to*
- Por ahora **no me planteo** hacer una película sobre temas tan delicados
  = *I'm not considering*
- Convocar elecciones anticipadas **no entraba en nuestros planes**
  = *was not on our agenda*
- **No se trata de** hablar otra vez con ellos, sino de que acepten lo que hemos propuesto ya varias veces
  = *it's not a question of*
- **No desearíamos** causarles molestias
  = *we would not wish to*

With more determination

- **No pienso** hacerle caso
  = *I do not intend to*
- **No tenía la más mínima intención de** dimitir
  = *he didn't have the slightest intention of*
- **Jamás haría** una cosa así
  = *I would never do*
- **Me niego (rotundamente) a** entrar en la polémica
  = *I (categorically) refuse to*

9 PERMISSION

9.1 Asking for permission

- ¿**Puedo** pasar?
  = *may I*
- ¿**Me dejas que** lo use yo antes?
  = *will you let me ... please?*
- ¿**Se puede** aparcar aquí?
  = *can I*
- ¿**Te importa si** subo la tele un poco?
  = *do you mind if I*
- ¿**Podría** hacerle unas preguntas?
  = *could I*
- ¿**Le importaría que** me sentara?
  = *would you mind if I*
- ¿**Les molesta que** abra la ventana?
  = *do you mind if I*
- **Con su permiso** vamos a cerrar el tema de una vez
  = *... if you don't mind*
- ¿**Sería mucha molestia** dejarlo para más tarde?
  = *would it be an awful nuisance if*
- ¿**Me permite** usar su teléfono?
  = *may I*
- ¿**Tendrían inconveniente en que** tomáramos unas fotografías?
  = *would you mind if*
- **Espero que no les importe que** hagamos uso de esta información
  = *I hope you don't mind if*

9.2 Giving permission

- ¡**Naturalmente que** puedes ir!
  = *of course*
- **Puede** escoger otro modelo, si le conviene más
  = *you can (always)*
- **Les autorizamos a que** actúen como estimen más conveniente
  = *you have our permission to*
- **Tiene mi autorización para** llevar a cabo el proyecto
  = *you have my authorization to*
- **No tengo ningún inconveniente en** responder a sus preguntas
  = *I don't have any objection to*

9.3 Refusing permission

- ¿Es que piensas que te voy a dejar el coche? **¡Ni pensarlo**!
  = *no way!*
- **No puedo dejarte** ir de excursión con el tiempo tan malo que hace
  = *I can't let you*
- ¡**No consiento** ese tipo de lenguage en esta casa!
  = *I will not tolerate*
- **No se puede** fumar aquí
  = *you can't*
- **Me opongo a que se les permita** acudir a la reunión
  = *I am opposed to their being allowed to*

- **Eso es imposible, porque no lo permite** el decreto de 1983
  = *that's impossible because ... doesn't allow it*
- **Lo siento, pero no está permitido** entrar si no se pertenece a la organización
  = *I'm sorry, but you aren't allowed to*
- **Le prohíbo (terminantemente) que** se dirija a mí de esa manera
  = *I absolutely forbid you to*

9.4 Saying that permission is granted

- **Le dejan** acostarse a la hora que quiera
  = *he's allowed to*
- **Me dijo que podía** venir cuando quisiera
  = *she said I could*
- Nuestros padres **nos dieron permiso para** organizar una fiesta
  = *gave us permission to*
- **Nos han concedido** la licencia de importación
  = *we have been granted*
- El alcohol es la única droga cuyo consumo público **está permitido**
  = *is allowed*
- **Tengo autorización para** firmar en nombre del Consejo de Administración
  = *I am authorized to*

9.5 Saying that permission is refused

- **No me dejan** participar en la carrera por problemas de salud
  = *I'm not allowed to*
- **Me han denegado** la beca de estudios que necesitaba
  = *I've been refused*
- **No nos han otorgado la autorización necesaria**
  = *we haven't been given the necessary authorization*
- **No nos está permitido** hablar del tema con la prensa
  = *we aren't allowed to*
- **No estoy autorizado para** hacer declaraciones de ningún tipo
  = *I'm not authorized to*
- **No tengo autorización para** darles acceso a las instalaciones
  = *I'm not authorized to*
- El médico **me ha prohibido** fumar
  = *has forbidden me to*
- **Tengo totalmente prohibido** el alcohol, a causa de problemas hepáticos
  = *I'm not allowed*

10 OBLIGATION

10.1 Saying what someone must do

- **Tenemos que** levantarnos a primera hora de la mañana
  = *we have to*
- Hagas lo que hagas, **no te olvides de** avisarme si tienes problemas
  = *don't forget to*
- **No le queda más remedio que** *or* **No tiene más remedio que** soportar la afrenta con dignidad
  = *he has no option but to*
- **Me han encargado que** realice esta inspección
  = *I've been given the job of*
- En nombre del gobierno **debo** hacer la siguiente declaración: ...
  = *I must*
- Las circunstancias políticas **me obligaron a** salir de mi país
  = *forced me to*
- Todos **estamos obligados a** *or* **tenemos la obligación de** actuar con un gran sentido de la responsabilidad
  = *have a duty to*
- Por razones de seguridad a bordo **nos vemos obligados a** limitar el equipaje de mano de nuestros pasajeros
  = *we are obliged to*
- **Tengo el deber de informarles de que** su petición ha sido rechazada
  = *it is my duty to inform you that*
- Aquí **hace falta que alguien** ponga un poco de orden
  = *what we need is someone to*
- En verano **hay que** proteger la piel contra las radiaciones solares
  = *you must*
- Para viajar a Copiapó **es preciso** atravesar desiertos de arena y riscos áridos
  = *you have to*
- **Es obligatorio que** figure en el envase la fecha de elaboración
  = *it is compulsory for ... to*
- **Es esencial** *or* **imprescindible** *or* **indispensable** devolver el agua al medio natural sin contaminaciones
  = *it is essential to*
- **Para que sea** válida la renuncia al puesto **se requiere que** esté hecha libremente
  = *in order to be ... must*
- La ley **estipula que hay que** superar los dieciséis años para solicitar una licencia
  = *stipulates that you have to*
- Es un país donde **se exige que** los automóviles lleven un nivel de equipamiento y automatización muy alto
  = *are required to*
- **Se exige** experiencia en ventas
  = *... required*
- **Es requisito indispensable tener** cumplido el servicio militar
  = *it is essential to have*

10.2 Enquiring if someone is obliged to do something

- ¿**De verdad tengo que** pagar para entrar?
  = *do I really have to*
- ¿**Qué debo hacer para** empezar a escribir novelas?
  = *what must I do in order to*
- ¿**Se necesita** carnet de conducir?
  = *do I need*
- ¿**Estoy obligada a** atenerme a estas normas?
  = *do I have to*
- ¿**Tiene** un ciudadano **la obligación de** demostrar su identidad si así lo requiere la policía?
  = *is ... obliged to*

10.3 Saying what someone is not obliged to do

- **No vale** *or* **merece la pena que** te molestes en acompañarme
  =*there's no need for ... to*
- Los ciudadanos europeos **no necesitan** pedir un permiso de trabajo
  = *do not need to*
- **No hace falta que** tomen las comidas en el hotel **si no quieren**
  = *you needn't ... if you don't want to*
- **No está obligada a** contestar si no quiere
  = *you're not obliged to*
- **No tiene por qué** aceptar una oferta que no le interesa
  = *there is no reason why you should*
- **No es obligatorio** llevar el pasaporte
  = *it is not compulsory to*
- **No es necesario** hacer trasbordo para ir a Barcelona
  = *you don't need to*
- Los militares de reemplazo **no tendrán obligación de** obedecer órdenes si no están de servicio
  = *will not be under any obligation to*
- **No es indispensable que** lleguemos antes de las ocho
  = *we don't absolutely have to*
- **No se sientan obligados a** aceptar la propuesta de la Delegación del Gobierno
  = *don't feel obliged to*

10.4 Saying what someone must not do

- **No puedes** presentarte a votar en nombre de otra persona
  = *you cannot*
- **No se puede** solicitar permiso de residencia **hasta que** no se tenga un contrato de trabajo
  = *you cannot ... until you have*
- **No me hable** más del tema
  = *would you mind not saying*
- **No le permito que** hable a los clientes de ese modo
  = *I won't have you*
- **No tiene usted derecho a** tratarme como si fuera un esclavo
  = *you have no right to*
- **Le prohíbo** nombrar al director para nada
  = *I forbid you to*
- **Está prohibido** pisar el césped en los parques
  = *you are not allowed to*
- El régimen ha advertido que **no tolerará que critiquen** abiertamente al Gobierno
  = *it will not tolerate any ... criticism*

11 AGREEMENT

11.1 Agreeing with a statement

- **Claro que** la colección más importante de bonsais es la del Palacio Imperial Japonés
  = *of course*
- ¡**Exacto**! Ahí está la raíz del problema
  = *exactly*
- **Naturalmente**. Esa es la única forma de acabar con la corrupción política
  = *of course*
- **Yo también pienso lo mismo**. Nuestro equipo no tiene posibilidades en el campeonato
  = *I agree*
- **Estoy de acuerdo contigo en lo que dices del** machismo
  = *I agree with what you say about*
- **Por supuesto que** no hay derecho a que nos traten así
  = *of course*
- Todo el pueblo cree todavía hoy que está vivo. **Y puede que tengan razón**
  = *they may be right*
- **En eso tienes** *or* **te doy toda la razón**, el emigrante trabaja mucho y nunca se queja
  = *you are quite right there*
- **Te entiendo perfectamente**: yo he pasado por lo mismo hace años
  = *I know exactly what you mean*
- Mi maestra **tenía razón** al decir que para ser bailarín profesional hay que ser bueno
  = *was right*
- **Es cierto que** es un tema que nunca se ha tratado en serio
  = *it is true that*
- **Comprendo muy bien que** es un asunto muy delicado
  = *I quite understand that*
- **Admito que** estaba equivocado
  = *I admit that*
- Los dos **somos del mismo parecer** *or* **de la misma opinión**
  = *are of the same opinion*
- **Compartimos la misma opinión** *or* **el mismo punto de vista**
  = *we share the same view*
- **En eso coincido totalmente con** usted
  = *I entirely agree with ... on that*
- **Estamos en completo acuerdo**
  = *we are in complete agreement*
- **Ningún experto podrá refutar** dicho principio
  = *no one could argue with*

11.2 Agreeing to a proposal

- ¡**Me apunto**!
  = *count me in!*
- ¡**Claro**! Podéis venir cuando queráis
  = *of course*
- ¡**Vale**! Nos vemos a las cuatro
  = *fine*
- **De acuerdo**: publicaremos el artículo en el próximo número de la revista
  = *agreed*
- **Perfecto**. Allí estaremos
  = *fine*
- **Me parece bien que** le invites a cenar
  = *I think it's a good idea (for you) to*
- **Me parece una idea estupenda**
  = *I think it's a great idea*
- **Tengo que reconocer** *or* **admitir que la idea me gusta**
  = *I must admit that I like the idea*
- **Estamos conformes con** el precio que piden
  = *we agree to*
- **Apoyaremos su propuesta** ante el consejo ejecutivo
  = *we will back your proposal*
- **Acepto con mucho gusto** su invitación a visitarle en México
  = *I am very pleased to accept*
- El parlamento **está dispuesto a aceptar** la nueva ley reguladora
  = *is willing to accept*
- La asamblea de accionistas **aprobó el plan** presentado por la junta directiva
  = *approved the plan*
- **Tendré en cuenta sus consejos** a la hora de firmar el acuerdo
  = *I'll bear your advice in mind*
- **Quiero expresarle mi total conformidad con** su plan de actuación para los próximas meses
  = *I should like to say that I wholeheartedly endorse*

11.3 Agreeing to a request

- ¡**Claro, hombre**! ¡**Para eso están los amigos**!
  = *of course! That's what friends are for!*
- ¿Que si puedo echar una mano mañana? ¡**Por supuesto que sí**!
  = *of course I will*
- **Sí**, mujer, **faltaría más**, úsalo cuando quieras
  = *but of course*
- **Bueno**. Mañana estaré libre si me necesitas
  = *fine*
- Las fechas que propones **me vienen bien**
  = *are fine for me*
- **Si me necesitas, no tienes más que avisarme**
  = *if you need me, just let me know*
- **Puedes contar con** nuestro apoyo
  = *you can count on*
- **Estaré encantado de** participar en ese intercambio
  = *I'll be delighted to*
- El famoso cantante **accedió a que** la prensa estuviera presente
  = *agreed to*
- **No tengo ningún inconveniente en** que se haga público el informe judicial
  = *I have no objection to*

12 DISAGREEMENT

12.1 Disagreeing with what someone has said

- ¿5.000? No, ¡**qué va**!, 10.000 por lo menos
  = *no way!*

- ¿Madridista yo? ¡**Pero que dices, hombre**! Yo del Real Betis y nadie más
  = *you must be joking!*
- **Yo no lo veo así**
  = *that's not how I see it*
- ¿**No lo dirás en serio**?
  = *you can't be serious*
- **En eso te equivocas** *or* **estás equivocado**
  = *you're wrong there*
- **No estoy de acuerdo contigo en** ese punto
  = *I disagree with you on*
- **Estamos en contra de** toda clase de extremismos
  = *we are against*
- **No entiendo tu actitud** ante el problema
  = *I can't understand your attitude*
- **No se trata de** *or* **No es cuestión de** hacer nuevas leyes, **sino de** poner en práctica las que ya existen
  = *it's not a question of ... but of*
- **Yo personalmente me inclino por** la segunda opción
  = *personally, I favour*
- Sus críticas **no tienen justificación alguna**
  = *there is absolutely no justification for*
- **Deseo expresar mi total disconformidad con** esta medida
  = *I should like to express my total disagreement with*

More tentatively

- **Yo opino de manera distinta**
  = *I see it differently*
- En lo que se refiere al tema de la seguridad social tengo **una opinión muy distinta** a la suya
  = *I take a very different view*
- **Siento (tener que) contradecirte** *or* **llevarte la contraria, pero** las cosas son como son
  = *I'm sorry to (have to) contradict you, but*
- **No comparto tu opinión** al respecto
  = *I do not share your view*
- **No coincidimos con** su planteamiento
  = *we do not agree with*

12.2 Disagreeing with what someone proposes

- ¡**Vaya ocurrencia**!
  = *what a ridiculous idea!*
- **Me parece una idea descabellada** el cambiar ahora de táctica
  = *I think it would be madness to*
- **No estamos dispuestos a aceptar** sus planteamientos
  = *we are not prepared to accept*
- **Resulta (más que) discutible que** sea la única solución
  = *it's (highly) debatable whether*
- **Me niego a** votar sin estar debidamente informado
  = *I refuse to*
- **No podemos adherirnos a la propuesta del** portavoz de la oposición
  = *we cannot agree to the proposal made by*
- **No podemos suscribir** el ultimátum dado por la OTAN
  = *we cannot support*

More tentatively

- **No lo veo muy claro**
  = *I'm not sure*
- **No me hace mucha gracia** levantarme tan temprano
  = *I'm not keen on (the idea of)*
- **Lo de** introducirnos en el mercado extranjero **no nos convence**
  = *we're not keen on the idea of*
- **Me es imposible apoyar** su solicitud
  = *I cannot give you my support for*
- Su plan **no nos parece factible**
  = *does not seem feasible to us*
- **Me temo que no me será posible** aceptar su proyecto
  = *I'm afraid I shall not be able to*

12.3 Refusing a request

- ¡**Ni pensarlo**!
  = *it's out of the question*
- **No puede ser**. Ya no hay tiempo para cambiar el procedimiento
  = *it's impossible*
- **Lo siento, pero no estamos en condiciones de** aceptar su propuesta en este momento
  = *I'm sorry, but we are not in a position to*
- **Es totalmente imposible** reducir el personal de la empresa
  = ... *is out of the question*
- **No accederemos jamás a** introducir la semana de 32 horas
  = *we shall never agree to*

More tentatively

- **Me gustaría, pero no voy a poder**
  I'd like to, but I can't
- **Lo sentimos, pero no podemos atender su petición**
  we regret that we cannot grant your request
- **Por desgracia** *or* **Desgraciadamente, su demanda no puede ser atendida**
  unfortunately, your request cannot be granted
- **Aun sintiéndolo mucho, he de negarme a** hacer lo que nos piden
  I'm very sorry, but I must refuse to
- **Lamentamos comunicarle que** su petición ha sido denegada
  we are sorry to have to inform you that

13 APPROVAL

- Y si se quieren casar, **pues muy bien**, que se casen
  fine
- ¡**Así se hace**!
  = *well done!*
- ¡**Estupendo**!, por mi ahora mismo
  = *great!*
- **Me parece perfecto**. Podemos empezar cuando queráis
  = *that seems fine to me*
- ¡**Buena idea**! Yo también me voy a bañar
  = *good idea!*
- **No hay problema**. Dame tu dirección y te lo mando por correo urgente
  = *no problem*
- **Conforme**: No tomaremos ninguna medida hasta previo aviso
  = *agreed*
- **Trato hecho**
  = *it's a deal*
- **Sigue así** *or* **por ese camino**
  = *carry on just as you are doing*
- **Has hecho bien en** decírmelo
  = *you were right to*
- **Me parece muy bien que** te estés tomando las cosas con tranquilidad
  = *I think it's great that*
- **Me alegro mucho de que** tomes un paso tan importante
  = *I'm so pleased that*
- **Estoy muy contento con** el rendimiento de los jugadores
  = *I'm very pleased with*
- Todos **han dado por bueno** el resultado del referéndum que se convocó el pasado mes de diciembre
  = *has welcomed*

More formally

- **Estoy satisfecho con** la decisión del organismo mundial
  = *I am* *<u>satisfied</u> with*
- **Nos parece una idea excelente que** haya decidido usted encargarse del asunto
  = *we think it is <u>excellent</u> that*
- Cualquier propuesta **será bien recibida**
  = *will be <u>welcomed</u>*
- **Celebro que** se hayan desmentido los rumores
  = *I am <u>delighted</u> that*
- **Será un placer** colaborar con ustedes
  = *I shall be <u>delighted</u> to*

14 DISAPPROVAL

- Pero **¿qué dices**, Pedro Morán el mejor corredor del mundo?
  = *what are you on about?*
- **Sólo a tí se te ocurre una cosa así**
  = *trust you to come up with something like that!*
- **¡Menuda ocurrencia**!
  = *what a <u>ridiculous</u> idea!*
- **¿Cómo voy a aprobar su conducta si** va en contra de mis principios?
  = *how could I possibly <u>approve of</u> such behaviour when*
- **Me parece fatal que** la gente fume en los vagones de no fumadores
  = *I think it's <u>awful</u> that*
- **Lo que me parece mal es que** se hagan inversiones desmesuradas a costa de otras zonas mucho más necesitadas
  = *what I think is <u>wrong</u> is that*
- **De ninguna manera** deben paralizarse las obras
  = *under no <u>circumstances</u>*
- Hay capítulos que **no deberían haber sido** publicados
  = *<u>should</u> not have been*
- Muchos de los encuestados **no están nada contentos con** el rumbo actual de la economía
  = *are <u>unhappy</u> with*
- **¿Con qué derecho se atreven a** prohibirme que hable?
  = *who do they think they are to*
- **¡Eso no se puede tolerar**!
  = *this cannot be <u>tolerated</u>*
- **No estoy dispuesto a tolerar** tales afirmaciones
  = *I am not prepared to <u>put up with</u>*
- **Es intolerable que** no se haya llegado a un acuerdo definitivo todavía
  = *it is <u>intolerable</u> that*
- **Es inconcebible que** en los albores del siglo XXI se sigan produciendo este tipo de intoxicaciones
  = *it is <u>unbelievable</u> that*
- Todas las instituciones democráticas **condenan** la violencia
  = *<u>condemn</u>*
- **Deseamos protestar contra** la severidad de la pena impuesta por el juez
  = *we should like to <u>protest</u> against*
- El gobierno **expresó su más enérgica repulsa por** el atentado cometido ayer
  = *expressed its strongest <u>condemnation</u> of*

More tentatively

- **No estamos conformes con** el tono en que se expuso el informe
  = *we are not <u>happy</u> about*
- Los profesores universitarios **están poco satisfechos con** las instituciones para las que trabajan
  = *are <u>unhappy</u> with*
- **Me decepciona que** no haya conseguido su objetivo todavía
  = *I am <u>disappointed</u> that*
- **Nos disgusta** el tratamiento que algunas tertulias radiofónicas dan a Cataluña y el catalán
  = *we are <u>unhappy</u> about*
- **Es deplorable que** ocurran cosas de esta naturaleza
  = *it is <u>deplorable</u> that*

15 CERTAINTY, PROBABILITY, POSSIBILITY AND CAPABILITY

15.1 Expressing certainty

- **Seguro que** no está en casa
  = *I'm <u>sure</u>*
- **Está claro que** lo que pretende la publicidad de estos productos es satisfacer el deseo de muchos de perder unos kilos
  = *it is <u>obvious</u> that*
- **Salta a la vista que** no son del lugar ... por la vestimenta, digo
  = *it's patently <u>obvious</u> that*
- **Estoy segura de que** ésa es la fecha exacta de su nacimiento
  = *I'm <u>sure</u> that*
- **Estamos convencidos de que** los coches se roban para venderlos
  = *we are <u>convinced</u> that*
- **Es obvio que** *or* **Es evidente que** se va a convertir en el principal tema de conversación en los próximos días
  = *it is <u>clear</u> that*
- **Por supuesto que** siempre va a haber alguien que se crea eso
  = *of <u>course</u>*
- La fecha de inicio **será, casi con toda** *or* **total seguridad**, el primer domingo de septiembre
  = *will almost <u>certainly</u> be*
- **Se tiene la certeza de que** los secuestradores fueron como máximo tres
  = *we know for <u>certain</u> that*
- **Sin lugar a dudas** *or* **Sin duda alguna**, esta nueva victoria es un gran aliciente para el equipo
  = *without a <u>doubt</u>*
- **No cabe la menor duda de que** sus condiciones de vida eran infrahumanas
  = *there can't be the slightest <u>doubt</u> that*
- **Es innegable que** determinadas melodías perdurarán siempre
  = *it is <u>undeniable</u> that*

15.2 Expressing probability

- Aquí en este barrio **es fácil que** te atraquen
  = *you are quite <u>likely</u> to be*
- **Ya verás como** todo sale bien
  = *you'll see how*
- **Seguramente** se ha retrasado por el camino
  = *... <u>probably</u> ...*
- **Debe (de) haberse** olvidado de su compromiso
  = *he <u>must</u> have*
- **Lo más seguro** *or* **probable es que** esa no fuera su verdadera intención
  = *... <u>probably</u> ...*
- **Es muy posible** *or* **probable que** lleguemos a nuestro destino dentro del horario previsto
  = *it seems very <u>likely</u> that*
- **(Muy) posiblemente** *or* **probablemente** se trate de una falsa alarma
  = *... (very) <u>probably</u> ...*
- **Parece ser que** la autoridad monetaria podría tomar la decisión de subir los tipos de interés el próximo día 23
  = *it <u>seems</u> that*
- **No sería de extrañar que** *or* **No sería extraño que** los animales fueran al final los más perjudicados
  = *it wouldn't be <u>surprising</u> if*
- **No me sorprendería que** el ciclista francés ganara la etapa de hoy
  = *I shouldn't be <u>surprised</u> if*

- Según la agencia meteorológica, **hay muchas** *or* **grandes posibilidades de que** se produzcan nuevas erupciones
  = *it is very likely that*
- **Todavía tiene mucha** *or* **una buena chance de** ganar la carrera (*LAm*)
  = *he still has a good chance of*
- **Todo lleva a suponer** *or* **Todo parece indicar que** las rupturas matrimoniales seguirán en aumento
  = *all the indications are that*

15.3 Expressing possibility

- **Igual** no tengo suerte y suspendo
  = *I may*
- **A lo mejor** hago escala en Tenerife de camino a Montevideo
  = *maybe*
- **Quizá(s)** tengamos que volver antes de lo previsto
  = *perhaps*
- **Tal vez** nuestras sospechas son infundadas
  = *perhaps*
- **Puede que** la situación se convierta en irreversible
  = *... may*
- Dicho comando **podría ser** el autor de diversos atentados terroristas cometidos en la región desde octubre
  = *could be*
- **Siempre existe la posibilidad de que** el nivel de precios aumente
  = *there's always the possibility that*
- **Cabe la posibilidad de que** los afectados hayan bebido agua contaminada
  = *it is possible that*
- **Cabe pensar que** el error haya sido a propósito
  = *it is possible that*

15.4 Expressing capability

- ¿**Sabes** escribir a máquina?
  = *can you*
- ¿**Sabes** usar el nuevo procesador de textos?
  = *do you know how to*
- **Hablo** francés y **entiendo** el italiano
  = *I can speak ... I can understand*
- **Puedo** invertir hasta trece millones en las obras
  = *I can*
- Se exigen **conocimientos básicos de** mecánica
  = *a basic knowledge of*
- El niño **tiene aptitudes para** la física y las matemáticas
  = *has an aptitude for*
- El ser humano **tiene la capacidad del** raciocinio
  = *has the capacity for*

16 DOUBT, IMPROBABILITY, IMPOSSIBILITY AND INCAPABILITY

16.1 Expressing doubt

- **No sé si** debemos discutir ese tema ahora
  = *I don't know whether*
- **No estoy seguro de cuáles son** sus condiciones
  = *I'm not sure what ... are*
- **No es seguro que** el viaje de vuelta sea en el mismo tren
  = *it isn't certain that*
- **No está claro quién** va a salir más perjudicado de la situación
  = *it isn't clear who*
- **No tengo muy claro que** sirva de algo el que vayamos a la huelga
  = *I'm not very sure that*
- **Me pregunto si** realmente merece la pena trabajar fuera
  = *I wonder whether*
- **No estoy (plenamente) convencido de que** su propuesta sea la solución más acertada
  = *I'm not (entirely) convinced that*
- **Dudo que** vuelva a haber otra oferta similar
  = *I doubt whether*
- **Todavía quedan dudas sobre** las circunstancias en que acontecieron los hechos
  = *doubts still remain about*
- **No hay ninguna seguridad de que** el proyecto esté finalizado el mes que viene
  = *we cannot be certain that*
- **Ya veremos si** conviene o no meterse en ese tipo de aventuras
  = *we shall see in due course whether*
- **No se sabe con certeza si** es una enfermedad hereditaria
  = *no one knows for certain whether*

16.2 Expressing improbability

- **Es difícil que** el número uno español participe en el campeonato el próximo año
  = *... is unlikely to*
- **Dudo mucho que** el cambio se traduzca en una mejora de la calidad
  = *I very much doubt whether*
- **Es bastante dudoso que** se convoque el referéndum
  = *it is rather doubtful whether*
- **No parece que** vaya a hacer buen tiempo
  = *it doesn't look as if*
- **Me extrañaría** *or* **Me sorprendería (mucho) que** la fruta madurara en esas condiciones
  = *I should be (very) surprised if*
- **Es (muy) poco probable que** una subida de las multas se traduzca en un descenso del número de infracciones
  = *... is (very) unlikely to*
- **No parece muy probable que** se logre desarrollar una vacuna eficaz
  = *it doesn't seem very likely that*
- **Es (muy/bastante) improbable que** ocurra un accidente en una central nuclear moderna
  = *... is (very/pretty) unlikely to*
- Quien pierde su empleo **cada vez tiene menos probabilidades de** encontrar uno nuevo a corto plazo
  = *has less and less chance of*

16.3 Expressing impossibility

- No, no estuve en París. ¡**Qué más quisiera yo**!
  = *chance would be a fine thing!*
- A estas horas **no puede ser** el cartero
  = *it can't be*
- **No es posible que se trate** de la misma persona
  = *it can't be*
- **Es totalmente** *or* **completamente imposible que** la vegetación crezca en unas condiciones tan adversas
  = *... can't possibly*
- **Me resulta (materialmente) imposible** despedirme de todos en persona
  = *it would be (physically) impossible for me to*
- El camino de la negociación **tiene escasas posibilidades de** éxito
  = *has very little chance of*
- **No hay** *or* **No existe ninguna posibilidad de que** los sindicatos lleguen a un acuerdo con el gobierno en tan poco tiempo
  = *there isn't the slightest chance of*
- **Me es imposible** llamarle hasta mañana
  = *I can't*
- **No parece factible que** el delantero uruguayo vaya a fichar por el Barcelona
  = *it doesn't seem feasible that*

- Se ha demostrado que el plan de regulación del tráfico **es poco viable**
  = *is not very practicable*

16.4 Expressing incapability

- **No veo nada** desde aquí
  = *I can't see anything*
- **No sé cómo explicar** lo que vi
  = *I can't explain*
- **Apenas se podía uno** mover de la cantidad de gente que había
  = *one could hardly*
- Muchos industriales de nuestro país **no se sienten capaces de** competir de igual a igual con los extranjeros
  = *feel incapable of*
- **Yo soy (totalmente) incapaz de** montar escenas en público porque soy muy pudorosa
  = *I am (quite) incapable of*
- Este chico **no sirve para** este trabajo
  = *is no good at*
- **Carece de las aptitudes necesarias para** una misión de tal envergadura
  = *he hasn't the necessary aptitude for*
- Muy a menudo la policía **se ve imposibilitada para** actuar con una mayor efectividad
  = *find themselves unable to*

17 EXPLANATIONS

17.1 Emphasizing the reason for something

- Tuvimos que marcharnos **porque** se puso a llover
  = *because*
- **Como** tardabas en llegar, decidimos irnos
  = *as*
- Las plantas se han marchitado **por** exceso de riego
  = *due to*
- Tiene 10.000 acciones **gracias a** los ahorros de toda la vida
  = *thanks to*
- **Con** la nevada que ha caído no hay correo
  = *what with*
- **Es que** llevamos tanto tiempo agarrados al kalashnikov que no podemos soltarlo fácilmente
  = *it's just that*
- Ha tenido muy mala suerte. **Por eso** le tengo tanta lástima
  = *that's why*
- Habla tan bajo que a menudo parece que susurrara. **Por eso mismo** le aconsejaron que interviniera lo menos posible en mítines populares
  = *that's why*
- El fenómeno **tiene muchísimo que ver con** las nuevas formas de vida que aíslan cada vez más al hombre de la ciudad
  = *has a great deal to do with*
- No toleraba flores junto a ella **por miedo a que** la intoxicaran
  = *for fear that*
- **No es** la religión **la causa de** tanta guerra
  = *it is not ... that causes*
- **En vista de que** el fuego había provocado una densa humareda, se decidió la evacuación del recinto
  = *seeing that*

More formally

- El problema es grave, **ya que** el consumo anual es mayor que la producción
  = *for*
- Se recomienda ir pronto, **puesto que** se forman colas importantes
  = *since*
- La cuantía de las donaciones no era demasiado elevada, **pues** únicamente había monedas de bajo valor
  = *as*
- La evacuación del edificio se vio dificultada **a causa del** bloqueo de una de las salidas de emergencia
  = *because of*
- En todo el mundo se ha desencadenado una gran competencia por las áreas de pesca. **Por este motivo** han surgido grandes problemas
  = *for this reason*
- El absentismo entre los eurodiputados es muy preocupante, **dado que** el Parlamento europeo toma cada vez más decisiones
  = *given that*
- **Por razones de seguridad**, aparcamos el automóvil lejos de la casa
  = *for ... reasons*
- **Sus motivos para** abrir una nueva oficina **son** de orden económico
  = *his reasons for ... are*
- La capital se hallaba ayer prácticamente paralizada **a consecuencia de** la huelga general
  = *as a result of*
- **Como consecuencia de** la crisis económica, las ventas se redujeron en un porcentaje considerable
  = *as a result of*
- **Como resultado de** las acciones emprendidas, los trabajadores lograron parte de sus reivindicaciones
  = *as a result of*
- **Debido a** condiciones meteorológicas adversas, nos vemos obligados a suspender la celebración anunciada
  = *owing to*
- Los problemas de suciedad en la zona **se deben a** una mala gestión municipal
  = *are due to*
- La falta de lluvias **ha ocasionado** una grave sequía al sur del país
  = *has caused*
- Su especial percepción de la atmósfera parisina **arranca de** una infancia llena de vivencias
  = *dates back to*
- Dicha teoría sostiene que la evolución **resulta de** una interacción entre la variación y la selección
  = *is a result of*
- El descenso de la competitividad **procede principalmente de** los elevados costes y del declive de la productividad
  = *is mainly due to*
- La fuerza de esta poesía **radica en** su brillante capacidad verbal
  = *lies in*
- **Ocurre que** a veces a algunos les da por hablar en un tono ofensivo
  = *what happens is that*
- La explosión, **provocada por** una bomba, ha causado un alto número de heridos
  = *which was caused by*
- Yo personalmente **lo atribuyo a** un error del conductor
  = *I attribute it to*

17.2 Emphasizing the result of something

- No quería ir con el estómago vacío, **así que** me preparé un sandwich previo
  = *so*
- Me atrae **tanto** lo que hago **que** no me merece la pena restarle tiempo para dedicarlo a otras cosas
  = *so much that*
- Salieron temprano, **de modo que** cuando él llegó se encontró la casa vacía
  = *so that*
- El recuerdo del hambre infantil le marcó **de tal manera que** siempre devoraba grandes cantidades de pan
  = *in such a way that*

- No fabrican anticuerpos **y por lo tanto** no pueden inmunizarse contra los parásitos y los virus
  = *and therefore*

18 APOLOGIES

18.1 Apologizing

- **Perdona**, me había olvidado de tí
  = *I'm sorry*
- **Perdona que** no avisara con tiempo suficiente
  = *I'm sorry*
- No consigo acordarme del autor. **Lo siento**
  = *I'm sorry*
- **Siento mucho no haber podido** conseguir la información
  = *I'm so sorry that I wasn't able to*
- **Pido perdón a** la familia **por** lo que hicimos
  = *I ask ... to forgive*
- Cualquiera que se atreva a hacer una cosa así es, **con perdón**, un perfecto imbécil
  = *if you'll forgive me for saying so*
- **Lo lamento**. A veces me cuesta reprimirme
  = *I am very sorry*

More formally

- El escritor **pidió disculpas por** su ausencia en el acto inaugural
  = *apologized for*
- En cualquier caso **acepte mis disculpas, por favor**
  = *please accept my apologies*
- **Disculpen si** les he causado alguna molestia
  = *I apologize if*
- **Rogamos disculpen las molestias que** esta deficiencia pueda causarles
  = *we apologize for any inconvenience that*
- **Espero que** el avisado lector **excuse** estas generalidades que seguramente conoce
  = *I hope that ... will excuse*
- **Espero dispensen lo ocurrido**
  = *I hope you'll forgive us/me for this unfortunate incident*
- **Lamentamos profundamente que** haya ocurrido este incidente
  = *we are very sorry that*

18.2 Apologizing for being unable to do something

- **Por desgracia** la empresa **no puede** atender su petición en estos instantes
  = *unfortunately* or *I'm afraid ... is unable to*
- **Sentimos comunicarle que** a partir de la fecha dejaremos de abonar el importe correspondiente al seguro de las pólizas
  = *we regret to inform you that*
- **Desgraciadamente** *or* **Lamentablemente, nos es imposible** aceptar su propuesta
  = *unfortunately, we are unable to*
- **Muy a nuestro pesar nos vemos obligados a** prescindir de sus servicios a partir de hoy
  = *we very much regret that we areobliged to*

18.3 Admitting responsibility

- **Es culpa mía**. Me lo he buscado
  = *it's my fault*
- **Reconozco que estaba equivocado**
  = *I admit I was wrong*
- **Sé que** mis palabras de anoche **no tienen perdón**
  = *I know that ... was unforgivable*
- **Debo confesar que** el error **fue culpa mía**
  = *I must confess that ... was my fault*
- **Me responsabilizo plenamente de** lo ocurrido
  = *I take full responsibility for*
- **Admitimos que** existen defectos en la organización
  = *we admit that*
- **Asumimos plenamente nuestra responsabilidad**
  = *we fully accept our responsibility*

18.4 Disclaiming responsibility

- De verdad que **no lo hice a posta**
  = *I didn't do it on purpose*
- **Ha sido sin querer**
  = *it was an accident*
- **Lo dijeron sin mala intención**
  = *they didn't mean any harm*
- **No era mi intención ofenderle**: hablaba en broma
  = *I didn't mean to offend you*
- **Pensé que hacía bien en** dirigirme a ellos directamente
  = *I thought I was doing the right thing in*
- **Teníamos entendido que** ellos estaban de acuerdo
  = *we thought that*
- Habría querido actuar de otro modo, **pero no tenía otra salida**
  = *but I had no alternative*
- **Espero que comprenda usted** lo difícil de nuestra situación
  = *I hope you will understand*

18.5 Replying to an apology

- **No pasa nada**, hombre: si se ha roto me compro otro y ya está
  = *don't worry about it*
- **No te preocupes**. ¿Qué culpa tienes tú?
  = *don't worry*
- Fue un lapsus: **no se hable más**
  = *we won't say any more about it*
- **No importa**, ya lo sabíamos
  = *it doesn't matter*
- **No te guardo (ningún) rencor**
  = *I don't bear you any grudge*
- **No es ninguna molestia**
  = *it's no trouble*
- El retraso **no tiene (ninguna) importancia**
  = *is of no importance*
- **Aceptamos de buen grado sus disculpas**
  = *we are happy to accept your apologies*

19 JOB APPLICATIONS

19.1 Starting your letter

- **En referencia al anuncio publicado en** la edición de hoy de La Gaceta, **le agradecería que me enviara los datos y la documentación pertinente** al puesto anunciado
  = *with reference to your advertisement in ..., I should be grateful if you would send me details of*
- **En respuesta a su anuncio de hoy en** Noticias, **les agradecería que me considerasen para el puesto de** jefe de ventas
  = *in response to your advertisement in today's ..., I should be grateful if you would consider me for the position of*
- **Me permito enviarles mis detalles para que los tomen en consideración** en el caso de que necesiten los servicios de alguien con mis cualificaciones/mi experiencia
  = *I am writing to you with my particulars in the hope that you may consider them*

19.2 Detailing your experience and giving your reasons for applying

- **Soy licenciado en Ciencias de la Información y llevo seis meses trabajando en** la redacción de un periódico local, **donde estoy al**

Julia Guedes Tola
Paseo Buenos Aires 141, 5° A
07052 Alicante

12 de julio, 2004

Sr. Director Gerente
INFOCOMP, Sistemas informáticos
C/ Primero de Mayo 73, 1°
46002 VALENCIA

Muy Señor mío:

Me dirijo a usted para solicitar el puesto de Director de ventas anunciado en EL PAIS el día 9 de este mes.

Como podrá ver en la copia del currículum vitae que adjunto, tengo considerable experiencia en el sector comercial, además de numerosas relaciones con empresas de la zona, sin duda de gran utilidad para un puesto como el que solicito.

Adjunto también toda la documentación justificativa que se exige.

Quedo a su disposición para cualquier aclaración que necesite y le agradezco la atención prestada.

Atentamente,

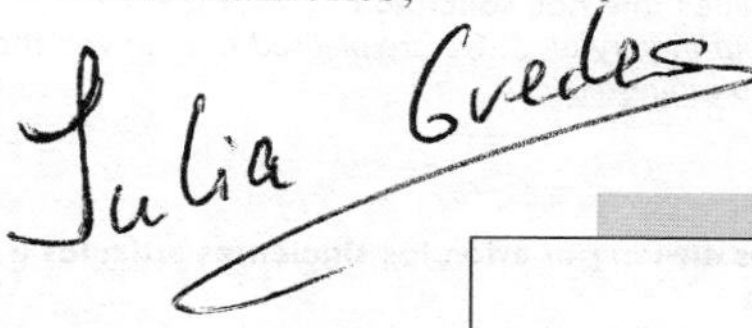

CURRICULUM VITAE

NOMBRE Y APELLIDOS	**Julia Guedes Tola**
DOMICILIO	Paseo Buenos Aires 141, 5° A 07052 Alicante
TELÉFONO	(965) 93 15 58
FECHA DE NACIMIENTO	5 de septiembre de 1970
ESTADO CIVIL	soltera

ESTUDIOS [1]

1988-93 :	Licenciatura en Ciencias Empresariales, Universidad de Valencia
1992 marzo-junio :	Universidad de Dublín, intercambio Erasmus
1987-88 :	COU, Instituto Salzillo, Murcia

EXPERIENCIA PROFESIONAL

Desde mayo 1998 :	Directora de Ventas, ELECTRÓNICA COSTA BLANCA, Alicante
Febrero 1994 - marzo 1998 :	Encargada de Administración, Agencia de Publicidad PLENA PLANA, Castellón
Veranos 1992 y 1993 :	Profesora de matemáticas, Academia ESTUDIOS, Alcoy
Enero - marzo 1993 :	Prácticas laborales en INTER-CHIP, Valencia

INFORMACIÓN COMPLEMENTARIA

Idiomas: inglés, uso habitual en el entorno laboral. Numerosos contactos empresariales en toda la Costa Blanca. Asesoramiento empresarial ofrecido con regularidad a pequeñas y medianas empresas de la industria turística. Destreza en el uso y aprovechamiento de recursos informáticos en la empresa.

[1] People with British, American or other qualifications applying for jobs in Spanish-speaking countries might use some form of wording to explain their qualifications such as *"equivalente al bachillerato superior español/mejicano"* etc. (3 A-levels), *"equivalente a una licenciatura en Letras/Ciencias"* etc. (B.A. B.Sc. etc) etc. Alternatively, *"Licenciado en Lenguas Clásicas"* etc. might be used.

cargo de la sección de sucesos
= *I have a degree in Media Studies and for the last six months have been working on ... where I am in charge of*

- **Tengo dos años de experiencia como** auxiliar administrativo **en** una empresa de importación-exportación
= *I have two years' experience as ... in*
- Además del inglés, mi lengua materna, **hablo español con fluidez** *or* **soltura, tengo conocimientos de francés y entiendo el italiano escrito**
= *I speak Spanish fluently, have a working knowledge of French, and can understand written Italian*
- **Aunque no tengo experiencia previa en** este tipo de trabajo, **he desempeñado otros trabajos eventuales durante las vacaciones de verano**. Si lo desean, puedo darles los nombres de las entidades en las que he estado empleado
= *although I have no previous experience of ..., I have had other holiday jobs*
- **Mi sueldo actual es de** ... ptas **al año, e incluye cuatro semanas de vacaciones remuneradas**
= *my current salary is ... a year, with four weeks paid holiday*
- **Desearía trabajar en su país** durante algún tiempo **con objeto de perfeccionar mis conocimientos de español y adquirir experiencia en** el sector hotelero
= *I should like to work in your country ... so as to improve my Spanish and gain experience in*
- He terminado recientemente mis estudios de Filología Hispánica y **estoy muy interesado en usar mis conocimientos de español dentro de un entorno laboral**
= *I am very keen to use my Spanish in a work environment*
- **Tengo extremo interés en trabajar con** una empresa de su prestigio
= *I should very much like to work for*

19.3 Closing the letter

- **Estoy a su entera disposición para ofrecerles cualquier información complementaria que necesiten**
= *I should be happy to supply any further information that you may need*
- **Podría incorporarme a su empresa a partir de** primeros de junio
= *I would be available for work from*
- **Tendré mucho gusto en entrevistarme con ustedes** cuando lo consideren conveniente
= *I should be delighted to attend for interview*
- **Le agradezco la atención prestada y quedo a la espera de su respuesta**
= *thanking you for your kind attention, I look forward to hearing from you*

19.4 Asking for and giving references

- **Le ruego se sirva comunicarnos** cuánto tiempo lleva trabajando la Sra. Fernández en su empresa, cuáles eran sus responsabilidades **y qué opinión le merece su capacidad profesional para el puesto que solicita. Trataremos su respuesta con la mayor reserva y confidencialidad**
= *please would you let us know ... what you think of her suitability for the post that she has applied for. We shall treat your reply in the strictest confidence*
- **Durante los cinco años que** la Sra. Díaz **ha trabajado en nuestra empresa, siempre ha demostrado** gran constancia, sentido de la responsabilidad ycapacidad de organización. **No dudo en recomendarla para el puesto mencionado**
= *in the five years ... has worked for us, she has shown ... I have no hesitation in recommending her for the post in question*

19.5 Accepting and refusing

- **Acudiré con mucho gusto a sus oficinas** de la calle Rato **para una entrevista** el próximo día 15 de octubre a las 10 de la mañana
= *I shall be delighted to attend for interview at your offices*
- **Deseo confirmar mi aceptación del puesto** que me han ofrecido y la fecha de mi incorporación al mismo
= *I am writing to confirm my acceptance of the post*
- **Antes de tomar una decisión, les agradecería que discutiéramos algunos puntos** de su oferta
= *before coming to a decision, I should be grateful if we could discuss a few points*
- **Tras considerarla detenidamente, lamento tener que rechazar** su oferta de trabajo
= *after much consideration, I am sorry to have to decline*

20 COMMERCIAL CORRESPONDENCE

20.1 Enquiries

- **Hemos visto en el último número de** nuestro boletín industrial **su oferta especial en** artículos de oficina
= *having seen your special offer on ... in the last issue of*
- **Les agradeceríamos que nos enviaran información más detallada sobre** los productos que anuncian, **incluyendo descuentos por pedidos al por mayor, forma de pago y fechas de entrega**
= *we should be grateful if you would send us details of ..., including wholesale discounts, payment terms and delivery times*

20.2 ... and replies

- **Acusamos recibo de su carta con fecha de** 10 de febrero, **interesándose por** nuestros equipos. **Adjunto encontrará** nuestro catálogo general y lista de precios en vigor
= *thank you for your letter of ..., inquiring about .... Please find enclosed*
- **En respuesta a su consulta del** 20 del corriente, **nos complace enviarle los detalles que nos solicitaba**
= *in reply to your inquiry of ..., we are pleased to send you the information you requested*

20.3 Orders

- **Les rogamos nos envíen por avión los siguientes artículos a la mayor brevedad**
= *please send us the following items by airmail as soon as possible*
- **Les agradeceríamos que tomaran nota de nuestro pedido** núm. 1.443 **y nos confirmen su aceptación a vuelta de correo**
= *we should be grateful if you would note our order ... and confirm acceptance by return of post*
- **Adjunta le remitimos nota de pedido núm.** 8.493, **que esperamos se sirva cumplimentar con la mayor urgencia**
= *please find enclosed order no ..., which we hope can be executed with all possible speed*
- **Tengan la amabilidad de efectuar la entrega dentro del plazo especificado. De no ser así nos reservamos el derecho a rechazar la mercancía**
= *please ensure that delivery is within the specified time. Otherwise, we must reserve the right to refuse the merchandise*

20.4 ... and replies

- **Acusamos recibo de su pedido núm**. 7721
= *we acknowledge receipt of your order no.*
- **Le agradecemos su pedido con fecha del** 3 de septiembre, **al que daremos salida** tan pronto como nos sea posible
= *thank you for your order of ..., which we will dispatch*
- **La entrega se efectuará en un plazo no superior** a veinte días
= *you should allow 20 days for delivery*

20.5 Deliveries

- **Efectuaremos entrega de los productos en cuanto** recibamos sus instrucciones
= *orders will be dispatched as soon as*
- **No nos responsabilizamos de los daños que la mercancía pueda sufrir en tránsito**
= *we cannot accept responsibility for goods damaged in transit*
- **Sírvanse enviar acuse de recibo**
= *please confirm receipt*

TODOLIBRO S.A.

EDITORES – DISTRIBUIDORES

Av. del Guadalquivir, 144 - 41005 Sevilla
Tel (954) 34 34 90 - Fax (954) 34 00 39

West Distribution Services Ltd
14 St David's Place
Birmingham B12 5TS

Sevilla, 12 de octubre de 2004

Estimados señores:

Acusamos recibo de su carta del 20 de septiembre, en la que nos sugieren la posibilidad de que su representante el Sr. John Kirk nos visite en Sevilla aprovechando su próximo viaje por España, al objeto de establecer una relación más estrecha entre nuestras respectivas casas.

Tendremos, naturalmente, mucho gusto en recibirle y en principio sugerimos la fecha del lunes 23 de octubre para nuestro primer contacto, que podría tener lugar en nuestras oficinas a las 10 de la mañana.

Sin otro particular, quedamos a la espera de sus noticias.

Atentamente,

J. J. Rodriguez

Juan José Rodriguez
Director Comercial

Calzados la Mallorquina

Casa fundada en 1928

Carretera de la Finca, s/n - 07034 Palma de Mallorca - Teléfono (971) 100303

Palma, 2 de marzo de 2004

Dña Ana Hernández
Import-Export. S.A.
Mellado 38
28034 Madrid

Estimada Sra. Hernández:

Con referencia a su carta del 20-2-04, sobre la liquidación de nuestra factura núm 86-109876, le informo que aún existe un saldo pendiente de 800 euros, debido al parecer a que han deducido una nota de crédito por dicha cantidad de la que no tenemos conocimiento.

Sin duda se trata de un error fácilmente subsanable, por lo que le rogamos que revisen sus cálculos con el fin de aclarar su cuenta y podamos continuar nuestras transacciones como de costumbre.

Reciba un atento saludo,

Andrés Carbonell

Andrés Carbonell
Jefe de Ventas

- Le informamos que **la mercancía ha sido despachada según lo acordado**
  = *the goods were dispatched as agreed*

20.6 Payments

- Cumpliendo su encargo, **le remitimos adjunta factura por valor de** 35.000 ptas, **con vencimiento a** diez días **vista**
  = *please find enclosed our invoice for the sum of .... Payment is due within ... of receipt*
- **El importe total se eleva a** 320.700 ptas
  = *the final total amounts to*
- **Sírvase remitirnos el pago a vuelta de correo**
  = *please send payment by return*
- **Adjuntamos cheque por valor de** 356.000 ptas **en liquidación de su factura**
  = *please find enclosed our cheque for the sum of ... in settlement of your invoice*

20.7 Complaints

- **Les comunicamos que no hemos recibido nuestro pedido del 4 de julio dentro del plazo acordado.** Les rogamos que hagan las indagaciones pertinentes
  = *please note that we have not received our order of ... within the agreed time*
- **Nos permitimos recordarle que estamos a la espera del pago de nuestra factura** núm. 43.809, **cuyo plazo venció** el 2 del corriente. Le rogamos se ponga en contacto con nosotros a la mayor brevedad
  = *we should like to remind you that we are awaiting payment for invoice no. ... which fell due on*
- **Hemos apreciado un error de suma en su factura** núm. 7.787, por lo que les rogamos se sirvan remitirnos rectificación
  = *we have found an addition error in invoice*

21 GENERAL CORRESPONDENCE

21.1 Starting a letter

To a friend or acquaintance

- **Como hace tanto tiempo que no sé de tí me he decidido a** mandarte unas líneas ...
  = *as it's been so long since I had news of you, I decided to*
- **Me alegró mucho recibir noticias tuyas**, después de tanto tiempo
  = *it was lovely to hear from you*
- **Gracias por la amable carta** que me enviaste
  = *thank you for the very nice letter*
- **Perdona que no te haya escrito antes pero** mis ocupaciones profesionales me dejan poco tiempo para más
  = *please forgive me for not having written before but*

In formal correspondence

- **Me dirijo a ustedes para solicitar mayor información sobre** los cursos de verano organizados por su entidad
  = *I am writing to ask for further information on*
- **Les ruego que me envíen** los números de abril y mayo pasados de su revista. Adjunto el cupón con detalles de mi tarjeta de crédito
  = *please send me*
- **Le agradecería que me informara si** han encontrado una chaqueta negra que creo haber olvidado en la habitación que ocupamos en su hotel
  = *I should be grateful if you would let me know if*

... and replies

- **En contestación a su carta del** 19 de noviembre, **he de informarle que** no hemos encontrado los documentos por los que se interesa
  = *in answer to your letter of ..., I regret to inform you that*
- **Acusamos recibo de su carta, en la que pregunta por** nuestros cursos de verano
  = *thank you for your letter inquiring about*
- **He recibido su carta en la que solicita** autorización para reproducir uno de mis cuadros en la portada de su revista
  = *I have received your letter asking for*
- **Gracias por su carta del** 29 de enero y disculpe la tardanza en responder
  = *thank you for your letter of*
- **En referencia a su petición para que** se reforme el reglamento del club, **tengo el gusto de comunicarle que** ya ha sido remitida a órgano de dirección
  = *with reference to your request for ..., I am pleased to advise you that*

21.2 Ending a letter

- **Espero que tardes menos en escribirme esta vez**
  = *I hope that this time you won't take so long to write to me*
- **No te olvides de darle mis recuerdos a** todos por ahí
  = *do give my best wishes to*
- **A ver si podemos vernos** pronto
  = *let's see if we can get together*
- **Recuerdos de parte de** mi madre
  = *... sends her best wishes*

In formal correspondence

- **Quedo a la espera de sus noticias**
  = *I look forward to hearing from you*
- **No dude en ponerse en contacto con nosotros si requiere más información**
  = *don't hesitate to contact us if you need further information*
- **Muchas gracias de antemano por su colaboración**
  = *thanking you in advance for your help*

21.3 Travel plans

- **¿Disponen ustedes de un listado de cámpings de** la región?
  = *do you have a list of campsites for*
- **Sírvanse enviarme su guía de actividades deportivas** y lista de precios
  = *please would you send me your guide to sports activities*
- **¿Podría decirme si quedan plazas para** el viaje por el Marruecos interior que anuncian en el número de este mes de su revista?
  = *please could you tell me if there are any places left for*

21.4 Bookings

- Me han recomendado encarecidamente su hotel, por lo que **les agradeceré que me reserven** dos **habitaciones individuales con cuarto de baño** para la primera semana de junio
  = *I should be grateful if you would reserve me ... single rooms with en suite bathroom ...*
- **Deseo confirmar mi reserva. Tenga la amabilidad de decirme si requiere el pago por adelantado**
  = *I should like to confirm my booking. Please would you let me know if you require payment in advance*
- Por circunstancias ajenas a mi voluntad, **me veo obligado a cancelar la reserva hecha** la semana pasada
  = *I am obliged to cancel the booking I made*

Santander, 10 de marzo de 2004

Querido César:

Recibí la carta que nos escribiste hace unos meses. Siento no haberte contestado hasta ahora, aunque ya te imaginarás que no se debe a que no nos hayamos acordado de tí, simplemente hemos estado demasiado ocupados con el traslado.

Tanto Rosa como yo tenemos recuerdos muy agradables de la temporada que pasamos en tu casa de Puebla. En realidad, el objeto principal de esta carta es invitarte a pasar unas semanas con nosotros este verano. Sabemos lo mucho que te gustaría visitar nuestra tierra y en estas fechas nosotros vamos a poder respirar por fin tras unos meses de intensa actividad.

Espero que te encuentres bien y que podamos verte pronto.

Un saludo muy afectuoso de Rosa y un abrazo de

José

Liverpool, 5 de noviembre de 2004

Sra. Dña. Agustina Martos
Dpto de Historia Moderna
Facultad de Filosofía y Letras
Universidad de Salamanca
C/ Fray Luís de León
37002 SALAMANCA
Spain

Estimada señora:

Me dirijo a usted para solicitarle su inestimable colaboración sobre un tema del que tengo entendido que es una gran experta.

Estoy realizando una investigación sobre el comercio durante el reinado de los Reyes Católicos para una futura tesis doctoral y tenía pensado pasar unos meses en España para estudiar el asunto con detenimiento a partir de las fuentes. Un amigo me recomendó que me pusiera en contacto con usted, de ahí esta carta.

En principio mi idea era visitar el Archivo de Simancas, pero antes quisiera saber su opinión; si me aconseja que empiece mis investigaciones en otros archivos o bibliotecas y si debería realizar algún trámite previo para acceder a los mismos.

A pesar de llevar poco tiempo estudiando este periodo de la historia, ha llegado ya a apasionarme y, si no es inconveniente, le estaría inmensamente agradecido si me permitiera visitarla en algún momento de mi viaje a España.

Una vez más, le agradezco de antemano cualquier ayuda que pueda prestarme.

Atentamente,

J. Hamilton

Standard opening and closing formulae

When the person is known to you

OPENING FORMULAE	CLOSING FORMULAE
(fairly formal)	
Estimado señor (García):[1]	Reciba un cordial saludo de
Estimada señorita (González):[1]	
Estimado colega:	Un cordial saludo
Estimada Carmen:	
[1] *the forms Sr., Sra., Srta. can be used before the surname*	
(fairly informal)	
Mi apreciado amigo:	Afectuosamente
Mi apreciada amiga:	
Mi querido amigo:	Un afectuoso saludo de
Mi querida amiga:	

Writing to a firm or an institution (see also 20)

OPENING FORMULAE	CLOSING FORMULAE
Muy señor mío:[1] *(esp Sp)*	Le saluda atentamente
Muy señores míos:[2]	Les saluda atentamente
Estimados señores:[2]	Atentamente
De nuestra consideración: *(LAm)*	
[1] *if the addressee's job title etc is given*	
[2] *if not naming individual addressee*	

When the recipient is not personally known to you

OPENING FORMULAE	CLOSING FORMULAE
Muy señor mío: *(esp Sp)*	Reciba un respetuoso saludo de
Distinguido señor:	
Distinguida señora:	
More formal	
Estimado señor:	Atentamente
Estimada señora:	Le saluda(n[1]) atentamente
	[1] *if the signatory is more than one person*

To close friends and family

OPENING FORMULAE	CLOSING FORMULAE
Querido Juan:	Recibe un fuerte abrazo de
Querida Elvira:	Muchos besos y abrazos de
Mi querido Pepe:	Tu amigo que no te olvida
Mis queridos primos:	
Queridísima Julia:	Con mucho cariño

To a person in an important position

OPENING FORMULAE	CLOSING FORMULAE
Señor Director:	Respetuosamente le saluda
Señor Secretario General:	

22 THANKS

- **Gracias por todo**
  = *thank you for everything*
- **Te escribo esta nota para darte las gracias por** haber ayudado tanto a mi hija a superar sus problemas
  = *I am writing to thank you for*
- **Te agradezco mucho** las molestias que te has tomado
  = *I am very grateful to you for*
- **Te estoy muy agradecido por** el interés que has demostrado
  = *I am very grateful to you for*
- **Ha sido muy amable de su parte** acompañarme durante tan grata visita
  = *it was very kind of you to*
- **Le estamos profundamente agradecidos por** las atenciones que ha mostrado con nosotros
  = *we are very grateful to you for*
- **Quisiera expresarles mi más sincero agradecimiento por** la inestimable ayuda que nos han prestado
  = *I should like to express my heartfelt gratitude for*
- **Le ruego que transmita a** sus colegas **nuestro reconocimiento por** el interés que mostraron en nuestras propuestas
  = *please would you convey our thanks to ... for*

23 BEST WISHES

23.1 For any occasion

- **Les deseamos un feliz** fin de semana
  = *have a good*
- **Le deseo una feliz** estancia en nuestra compañía
  = *I wish you a happy*
- **Le deseamos lo mejor en** estas fechas tan señaladas
  = *all best wishes on*
- **Un cariñoso saludo de** todos nosotros
  = *very best wishes from*
- **Espero que se encuentren todos bien y que podamos tener el placer de volver a verlos pronto**
  = *I hope you are all well and that we shall have the pleasure of seeing you again soon*
- **Transmita mis mejores deseos al** Sr. Giménez **por** su candidatura
  = *please convey my best wishes to ... for*

23.2 Season's greetings

- **Feliz Navidad y Próspero Año Nuevo**
  = *Merry Christmas and a Happy New Year*
- **Felices Pascuas**
  = *Happy Christmas*
- **Les deseamos unas Felices Navidades y lo mejor para el año entrante**
  = *best wishes for a Merry Christmas and a Happy, Prosperous New Year*
- **Felices Fiestas** a todos
  = *Happy Christmas to you all*

23.3 Birthdays and saint's day

- **¡Felicidades!**
  = *Happy Birthday!*
- **¡Feliz cumpleaños!/¡Feliz aniversario!** (*CAm*)
  = *Happy Birthday!*
- **Te deseamos muchas felicidades** y que cumplas muchos más
  = *Happy Birthday and Many Happy Returns of the Day*
- **Muchísimas felicidades en el día de tu santo**
  = *With All Best Wishes on your Saint's Day*
- ¡Feliz **onomástico**! (*LAm*)
  = *Happy Saint's Day!*

23.4 Get well wishes

- **Que te mejores pronto**
  = *get well soon*
- **Espero que te pongas bien cuanto antes**
  = *I hope that you'll be better soon*
- **Le deseamos una pronta recuperación**
  = *we hope that you'll soon be better*

23.5 Wishing someone luck

- **¡Suerte!**
  = *good luck!*
- **¡Buena suerte con** tu nuevo trabajo!
  = *good luck with*
- Adiós y **muchísima suerte**
  = *the best of luck*
- **Te deseo toda la suerte del mundo** en el examen
  = *the very best of luck*
- **Espero que te salga todo bien**
  = *I hope that everything goes well for you*
- **Os deseamos mucho éxito para** el estreno de la obra
  = *we wish you every possible success for*

23.6 Congratulations

- **Felicidades por tu reciente paternidad**, Antonio
  = *congratulations on becoming a father*
- **¡Enhorabuena** (*Sp*) por la noticia!
  = *congratulations!*
- **Mi más cordial** *or* **calurosa enhorabuena** (*Sp*)
  = *many congratulations*
- Ha estado usted inmejorable. **¡Le felicito!**
  = *congratulations!*
- **Reciba mis más sinceras felicitaciones por** el premio
  = *warmest congratulations on*

NB: In Spain and South America, births, engagements and marriages are not usually announced in the formal way that they are in English-speaking countries

24 ANNOUNCEMENTS

24.1 Announcing a birth and responding

- El matrimonio Rodríguez García **se complace en anunciar el nacimiento de su hijo** Guillermo el 10 de julio de 2000 en Edimburgo
  = *are pleased to announce the birth of their son*
- **Me alegra comunicarte que** Lola y Fernán **han sido padres de una niña**, que nació el 25 de septiembre y que recibirá el nombre de Emma. Tanto la madre como la niña se encuentran en perfecto estado de salud
  = *I am very glad to tell you that ... have had a daughter*
- **Nuestra más cordial felicitación por el nacimiento de su hijo**, con nuestro deseo de una vida llena de salud y prosperidad
  = *warmest congratulations on the birth of your son*
- **Nos ha dado una gran alegría recibir las noticias del nacimiento de** Ana y les felicitamos de todo corazón
  = *we were delighted to learn of the birth of ...*

24.2 Announcing an engagement and responding

- Los señores de Ramírez López y Ortega de los Ríos **se complacen en anunciarel compromiso matrimonial de** sus hijos Roberto y María José
  = *are happy to announce the engagement of*
- **Deseamos participarte que** Ana y Manolo **se han prometido**. Como es natural, **nos alegramos mucho de que** hayan tomado esta decisión
  = *we wanted to let you know that ... have got engaged .... We are delighted that*

- Hemos sabido que se ha anunciado su compromiso matrimonial con la Srta Gil de la Casa y **aprovechamos esta oportunidad para darle la enhorabuena** (*Sp*) *or* **felicitarle** en tan dichosa ocasión
  = *we should like to take this opportunity to offer you our very best wishes and congratulations*
- Me he enterado de que se ha formalizado el compromiso de boda. **Me alegro enormemente y les deseo lo mejor** a los novios
  = *it is splendid news and I should like to send ... my very best wishes*

24.3 Announcing a change of address

- **Deseamos comunicarles nuestra nueva dirección a partir del** 1 de marzo: Fernández de la Hoz, 25, 2° derecha, 28010 Madrid. Teléfono 543 43 43
  = *please be advised that from ... our address will be*

24.4 Announcing a wedding

See also **INVITATIONS**

- Helena Pérez Cantillosa y Antonio Fayos de la Cuadra **tienen el placer de anunciar el próximo enlace matrimonial de su hija** María de los Angeles **con** Pedro Carbonell i Trueta, **que se celebrará** en la parroquia de Santa María la Grande el próximo día 3 de mayo a las doce del mediodía
  = *are pleased to announce the forthcoming marriage of their daughter ... and ... which will take place*
- **Me alegra comunicarles que la boda de** mi hijo Juan y Carmen **se celebró** el pasado día 4 en el Juzgado Municipal (*Sp*) *or* Registro Civil (*LAm*)
  = *I am pleased to be able to tell you that ... were married on*

24.5 Announcing a death and responding

- Dña Juana Gómez Rivero, viuda de Tomás Alvarez Ramajo, **falleció en el día de ayer a la edad de 72 años después de recibir los Santos Sacramentos** y la bendición apostólica. **D.E.P.** Sus hijos, hermanos, y demás familia **ruegan** a sus amistades y personas piadosas **una oración por su alma. El funeral por su eterno descanso tendrá lugar mañana** a las diez de la mañana en la Iglesia de Nuestra Señora de los Remedios
  = *... passed away yesterday aged 72, having received the Holy Sacrament. R.I.P. ... would ask ... to pray for her .... the funeral will take place tomorrow*
- **Con gran dolor anunciamos que** nuestro querido padre, D. Carlos Delgado, ha fallecido en la madrugada del día 10. Rogamos una oración por su alma
  = *it is with deepest sorrow that we have to announce that*
- **Deseamos expresarle nuestro más sentido pésame por tan dolorosa pérdida, y hacemos votos para que logren hacer frente a estos difíciles momentos con la mayor entereza**
  = *we should like to extend our deepest sympathy to you on your sad loss and to say that we very much hope you will be able to find the strength to bear up in this sad time*
- **Me he enterado con gran tristeza de la muerte de** tu hermano Carlos. De verdad **lo siento en el alma. Comprendo que estas palabras no te servirán de consuelo, pero ya sabes que puedes contar conmigo para lo que necesites....**
  = *I was very sad to learn of the death of I am so very sorry. Words are of little comfort, but you know you can count on me if there is anything you need*

25 INVITATIONS

25.1 Marriages

- Las familias Herrera Martínez y Gil Pérez **tienen el placer de comunicarles el próximo enlace matrimonial de** sus hijos Cristina y Andrés. **La ceremonia religiosa tendrá lugar el** 5 de junio en la Iglesia de San Francisco de Villalta, a la una de la tarde **y a continuación se dará un almuerzo en** el hotel Las Encinas
  = *... are pleased to announce the marriage of .... The ceremony will take place on ... and there will be a reception afterwards at*

... and replies

- **Tenemos sumo gusto en aceptar su amable invitación a** la boda de su hija. **Aprovechamos la ocasión para felicitar sinceramente a los novios**
  = *we are delighted to accept your kind invitation to ..., and we should like to offer our warmest congratulations to the happy couple*

25.2 Other formal receptions

- María Luisa Gómez y Roberto Espinedo **tienen el gusto de invitarles al bautizo de su hija** Leticia, **que se celebrará** el domingo día 3 a las once de la mañana en la Iglesia parroquial de S. Marcos. **La recepción tendrá lugar en** el restaurante "Los Molinos", Calle de S. Juan 27
  = *request the pleasure of your company at the christening of their daughter ...,which will take place .... A reception will be held afterwards at*
- A la atención de la Srta. Marta Goikoetxea: El Decano de la Facultad de Estudios Empresariales de la Universidad de Donosti **se complace en invitarla a la cena que tendrá lugar el** 3 de julio **con motivo del** décimo aniversario de su incorporación a nuestra facultad. **S.R.C.**
  = *requests the pleasure of your company at a dinner on ... to celebrate the ... R.S.V.P.*
- En Ediciones Frontera **celebramos** el lanzamiento de nuestra nueva colección "Letras históricas" **con un cóctel en** la Galería de Arte de Carmen Villarroel el martes a las ocho de la tarde. **Esperamos que le sea posible acudir** al mismo
  = *we are having a cocktail party to celebrate .... We hope you will be able to attend*

... and replies

- **Agradecemos su amable invitación, que aceptamos con mucho gusto**
  = *thank you very much for your kind invitation, which we are delighted to accept*
- **Gracias por su invitación a** la cena de homenaje del Presidente de la Asociación, **a la que acudiré encantada**
  = *thank you for your invitation to .... shall be delighted to attend*
- **He recibido su invitación, pero lamento no poder asistir, como hubiera sido mi deseo, por tener un compromiso previo**
  = *thank you for your invitation. I greatly regret that, owing to a prior engagement, I shall not be able to attend*

25.3 Less formal invitations

- **Quisiéramos corresponder de alguna forma a su amabilidad al** tener en su casa a nuestra hija el verano pasado, **por lo que hemos pensado que podrían pasar con nosotros** las vacaciones de Semana Santa, si les viene bien
  = *we should like to do something to show our appreciation for your kindness in ... and we wondered if you would be able to spend ... with us*
- **Nos gustaría mucho que** María Teresa y tú **vinierais a cenar con nosotros** el viernes por la noche
  = *we should be so glad if ... would come to dinner*
- **Quedas invitado a una fiesta que damos** el sábado a las nueve de la noche **y a la que esperamos que puedas venir**
  = *you are invited to a party ... and we very much hope you can come*
- **Vamos a reunirnos unos cuantos amigos** en casa el sábado por la tarde para tomar unas copas y picar algo **y nos encantaría que pudieras venir tú también**, sola o acompañada, como prefieras
  = *we are having a little gathering with some friends ... and we should be delighted if you could come too*
- Pascual y yo normalmente pasamos todo el mes de agosto en el apartamento de Gandía, pero en julio **lo tienes a tu disposición. No tienes más que avisar si quieres** pasar allí una temporada
  = *you would be very welcome to use it. Just let us know if you would like to*

... and replies

- **Le agradezco enormemente su amabilidad al invitarme a** pasar unos días conustedes. **Estoy deseando que lleguen** las vacaciones para ponerme en marcha
  = *it was extremely kind of you to invite me to .... I'm so much looking forward to*
- **Muchas gracias por tu invitación** para el viernes. María Teresa y yo **acudiremos con mucho gusto**
  = *thank you very much for your invitation .... would be delighted to come*
- **Lo siento en el alma pero no me es posible** cenar contigo el domingo
  = *I am extremely sorry but I am unable to*

26 ESSAY WRITING

26.1 The broad outline of the essay

Introductory remarks

- **Hoy es un hecho bien sabido que** ciertas corrientes vanguardistas de la Europa de entreguerras tuvieron especial eco en Canarias
  = *nowadays, it is a well-known fact that*
- **La historia ha sido testigo en repetidas ocasiones de** la ambición de las naciones dominantes
  = *throughout history there have been repeated examples of*
- **Una actitud muy extendida hoy día es la de considerar que** nada tiene valor permanente
  = *the attitude that ... is very widespread these days*
- **Hoy en día todo el mundo está de acuerdo en que** el progreso significa un aumento del nivel de vida. **Sin embargo, cabe preguntarse si** esta mejora repercute por igual en todos los sectores de la población
  = *nowadays, everyone agrees that .... However, we should perhaps ask ourselves whether*
- **Normalmente, al hablar de** "cultura", **nos referimos al** sentido antropológico de la palabra
  = *when we talk about ..., we usually mean*
- **Se suele afirmar que** la televisión tiene una influencia excesiva en elcomportamiento de los más jóvenes. **Convendría analizar esta afirmación a la luz de** nuevas investigaciones psicológicas
  = *it is often said that .... This statement needs to be examined in the light of*
- **Uno de los temas que más preocupa a la opinión pública es el de** la seguridad ciudadana
  = *one of the issues which the public is particularly concerned about is*
- **Existe una gran divergencia de opiniones sobre** la dirección que ha de tomar la reforma educativa
  = *there are many different opinions about*
- **Un tema que se ha planteado reiteradamente es el de** la presencia de la mujer en el mundo empresarial
  = *one issue which has often been raised is*
- **Se debate con frecuencia en nuestros días el problema de** los cambios estructurales en la familia
  = *a problem which is often discussed these days is*

Explaining the aim of the essay

- **En el presente informe vamos a abordar** la influencia que el turismo puede haber ejercido en el desarrollo de la España contemporánea
  = *in this paper we shall examine*
- **En este trabajo trataremos de averiguar si** las bacterias deberían incluirse en el reino animal o vegetal
  = *in this essay we shall try to establish whether*
- **Este ensayo es un intento de dar respuesta a una pregunta de crucial importancia**: ¿a qué se debe que la industria de la defensa sea la única que no esté recorrida por los aires desreguladores del liberalismo?
  = *this essay is an attempt to answer a fundamental question*
- **Nuestro propósito es** hacer justicia a la obra de España en América, tantas veces criticada entre nosotros
  = *our aim is to*
- **Este trabajo tiene como objetivo** aclarar las circunstancias que llevaron a este pueblo a ser una fuerza invasora
  = *the aim of this essay is to*
- **Con objeto de** profundizar el papel que ciertos productos tienen en el desarrollo de las alergias, se ha llevado a cabo un estudio en dos escuelas de la ciudad
  = *with the aim of*

Developing the argument

- **Empecemos diciendo que** ninguna filosofía se puede considerar la panacea de todos los problemas
  = *let us begin by saying that*
- **Para comenzar, debemos hacer hincapié en** la diferencia entre adictos y consumidores ocasionales de drogas
  = *first of all, ... must be emphasized*
- **Damos por sentado que** la situación económica del país en el siglo pasado dificultaba la adopción de las nuevas tendencias artísticas
  = *we are assuming that*
- **Centrémonos primero en el problema de** la congestión en el centro de las grandes ciudades
  = *first, let us concentrate on the problem of*
- **En primer lugar conviene examinar si** existe algún uso o costumbre que no permita la agrupación de accionistas
  = *first, we need to consider whether*
- **Como punto de partida hemos tomado** la situación inmediatamente anterior al estallido del conflicto
  = *we have taken as a starting-point*
- **Si partimos del principio del** equilibrio del ecosistema, **podremos comprender cómo** muchas de nuestras actividades lo rompen constantemente
  = *if we start from the principle of ..., we shall be able to see how*
- Los que abogan por una disminución de la actividad pesquera esgrimen varios argumentos de peso. **El primero que vamos a analizar es** la reducción acelerada de los bancos de pesca
  = *the first ... that we shall examine is*

Connecting elements

- **Pero debemos concentrar la atención en** el aspecto realmente importante del problema
  = *however, we should now focus our attention on*
- **Pasemos ahora a considerar otro aspecto del** tema que nos ocupa
  = *let us move on to another aspect of*
- **Dirijamos la atención al segundo aspecto que** apuntábamos
  = *let us turn our attention to the second point that*
- **A continuación trataremos un punto estrechamente relacionado**
  = *next, we shall look at another closely related issue*
- **Nos ocupamos seguidamente de** los detalles que muchos críticos han ignorado
  = *next, we shall consider*
- **Continuemos con** una mención detallada de los distintos apartados de la declaración
  = *let us now move on to*
- **Pero volvamos de nuevo al asunto** que nos ocupa
  = *but, to return to the issue*
- **Examinemos con más detalle** los orígenes de la situación
  = *let us look in greater detail at*

The other side of the argument

- **Pero pasemos al segundo argumento planteado, según el cual** tener el dinero inutilizado en una cuenta corriente perjudica al

Tesoro, pero beneficia al banco emisor
= *now let us move on to the second <u>argument</u>, according to which*

- **Consideremos ahora lo que ocurriría si** contáramos con un aparato que pudiese grabar cada acto de nuestra existencia de manera que tuviéramos un rápido acceso a todo lo que nos ha sucedido
  = *now let us <u>consider</u> what would happen if*
- **Pero existe otro factor sin el cual no se puede comprender la importancia de** la ingeniería genética para la naciente bioindustria
  = *but there is another <u>factor</u> that should be taken into account if we are to understand the <u>importance</u> of*
- **Un segundo enfoque consiste en decidir si** las limitaciones impuestas a los extranjeros que quieran participar en las empresas privatizadas se adapta a la normativa comunitaria
  = *a second <u>approach</u> would be to decide whether*
- **Sin embargo, también merece atención el planteamiento de quienes aseguran que** el transporte es un servicio social subvencionado
  = *however, it is also <u>worthwhile</u> <u>considering</u> the <u>view</u> of those who <u>maintain</u> that*
- **Es preciso advertir, no obstante, que** esta biografía es muy elemental y está orientada a lectores con mínimos conocimientos sobre el asunto
  = *it should be <u>pointed</u> <u>out</u>, <u>however</u>, that*
- **Lo que digo sobre** la poesía oriental **puede ser aplicado igualmente a** la poesía occidental, tanto la europea como la americana
  = *my <u>comments</u> on ... can <u>equally</u> well be applied to*
- **En contrapartida, la creencia de que** es bueno romper estereotipos hace que nuestro estilo de diálogo aparente ser más violento que en otras culturas
  = *on the other hand, the <u>belief</u> that*
- **Ante tal afirmación se puede objetar que** uno debe votar a aquéllos ante los cuales se siente más representado
  = *such an <u>assertion</u> can be countered with the <u>argument</u> that*

In conclusion

- **En resumen**, los servicios ferroviarios del país necesitan una planificación seria y a largo plazo
  = *in <u>short</u>*
- **En definitiva**, la búsqueda de lo absoluto es esencial en su obra
  = *in the final <u>analysis</u>*
- **Se trata, en suma, de** desarrollar un método de diseño que permita que la arquitectura aproveche las posibilidades tecnológicas en beneficio de todos
  = *in <u>short</u>, it is a <u>question</u> of*
- **Todos los argumentos vistos aquí llevan a la misma conclusión**: se tardarán tantos años en recuperar la biodiversidad perdida que es importante que empecemos a conservarla ya
  = *all the <u>arguments</u> set out here lead to the same <u>conclusion</u>*
- **De todo lo que antecede se deduce que** durante algunos años al menos, no se puede esperar llegar a un acuerdo sobre este tema a nivel universal
  = *from what has been said, it can be seen that*
- **Todo ello demuestra** la inviabilidad de los sistemas de reparto del trabajo como método de reducir el paro
  = *all of this demonstrates*
- **Llegamos así a la conclusión de que** la responsabilidad recae en los países desarrollados
  = *we are <u>therefore</u> drawn to the <u>conclusion</u> that*
- **En conclusión**, existe un grave problema de vivienda en la ciudad, que debemos intentar resolver cuanto antes
  = *in <u>conclusion</u>*
- **Para concluir, diremos que** los argumentos con los que nos hallamos más de acuerdo son aquellos refrendados por la investigación científica
  = *let us <u>conclude</u> by saying that*
- **Como colofón, hagamos mención de** lo que decía el dramaturgo: "Y los sueños, sueños son"
  = *<u>finally</u>, let us <u>remember</u>*

26.2 Constructing a paragraph

Ordering elements

- **Ante todo**, entendemos por escalada libre la progresión por una pared sin emplear más que la roca, los pies y las manos
  = *<u>first</u> and <u>foremost</u>*
- En esta discusión median poderosas razones políticas; **primero**, porque el tradicional apoyo a la iniciativa privada del Gobierno de Estados Unidos influye también en las actividades culturales; **en segundo lugar**, porque la cultura europea ha estado siempre sujeta al Estado y no es fácil separarlas de repente
  = *<u>firstly</u> ...; <u>secondly</u>*
- **Pero antes de examinar esta cuestión, veamos primeramente** cuáles son las enfermedades hereditarias que podrían beneficiarse de esta terapia y cuáles son los equipos que trabajan en este campo
  = *before <u>examining</u> this <u>question</u> in <u>detail</u>, let us look at*
- **Finalmente**, habría que pedir con urgencia a todos los responsables públicos que se comiencen a discutir los temas de bioética con la mayor transparencia
  = *<u>finally</u>*
- **Por último**, hay que resaltar que la obra hace gala de un estilo que rebasa la simple eficacia
  = *<u>lastly</u>*

Connecting elements

- La tendencia de las sociedades humanas es a endiosar mitos y anatemizar diablos. De **los primeros** se esperan milagrosas salvaciones; contra **los segundos** se descargan las miserias
  = *the <u>former</u> ... the <u>latter</u>*
- **No sólo** *or* **solamente** se ha creado la esperanza de una paz duradera **sino que también** *or* **además** se han sentado las bases para que así ocurra
  = *not only ... but <u>also</u>*
- **En relación con** *or* **En conexión con** lo expuesto anteriormente, hemos de añadir la falta de previsión
  = *in connection with*
- **A este respecto hay que destacar que** las enfermedades de transmisión sexual están más extendidas entre los hombres que entre las mujeres
  = *in this <u>regard</u> we should <u>point out</u> that*
- **Tanto** la forma **como** el contenido muestran una estructura simétrica
  = *both ... and*
- El estudio determina, **por otra parte**, la relación de causa-efecto que se da en la construcción española entre la crisis que padece y su efecto multiplicador
  = *<u>moreover</u>*
- El libro tiene dos virtudes. **Por una parte**, reúne toda la información sobre los maltratos a menores **y por otra**, pone sobre la mesa lo que está pasando
  = *on the one hand ... and on the other*
- **Si por un lado** en sus mejores obras consigue una trascendentalización del arte, **por otro**, en las más repetitivas, se reduce a una mera manifestación convencional
  = *while on the one hand ..., on the other*
- Las operaciones se llevaron a cabo, **bien** por negligencia de los supervisores, **bien** por astucia del perpetrante
  = *<u>either</u> ... <u>or</u>*
- **Ni** sus colegas **ni** sus ayudantes, **ni siquiera** los más allegados, tenían idea de lo que el artista se proponía lograr
  = *<u>neither</u> ... <u>nor</u> ... nor even*

Adding elements

- Un ajuste de tal magnitud afectaría, **además**, a otras empresas estatales
  = *<u>moreover</u>*
- **Además de** los instrumentos señalados para el fomento de la investigación científica por parte de la Administración, **existen** otras

medidas indirectas que pueden tomar diferentes Ministerios
= *in addition to ..., there are*

- **Otro dato a tener en cuenta es** la aprobación de un comunicado conjunto
  = *another factor to take into account is*
- **Otro acontecimiento que tuvo también gran importancia fue** la firma de un acuerdo de cooperación entre ambos países
  = *another very important event was*
- **Y no sólo eso** *or* **eso no es todo**: tales medidas no compensan a los afectados de ninguna manera
  = *and that is not all*
- Todo ejercicio aeróbico estresa el sistema central. **Es más**, el corazón no puede saber qué ejercicio está realizando
  = *moreover*
- **Cabe destacar igualmente** que la transferencia genética se ha empleado con éxito en células de mamífero
  = *it should also be noted that*
- **Por lo que respecta a** las novedades de producto, la gama todo terreno se ha ampliado con la llegada de tres nuevas versiones
  = *as far as ... are concerned*
- **En cuanto a** las tendencias para los 12 meses siguientes, el gasto en software se incrementará en el 59,9% de las empresas
  = *as for*

Introducing one's own point of view

- **Soy de la opinión de que** es mejor que los medios de comunicación estén en manos de los propietarios de la edición y de la comunicación que controlados por los propietarios de entes financieros
  = *I am of the opinion that*
- La exposición más destacada del pintor aragonés fue, **a mi criterio**, la exhibida en el Casón del Buen Retiro a principios de los sesenta
  = *to my mind*
- Para muchos la diferencia es simplemente administrativa, **y yo lo suscribo totalmente**
  = *and I would agree wholeheartedly*
- Hasta cierto punto **comparto esta opinión**
  I share that view
- **Nuestra hipótesis es que** el pintor busca plasmar la fugacidad, aunque tal vez nos equivoquemos
  = *our hypothesis is that*
- **Podemos afirmar que** las raíces del levantamiento armado hay que buscarlas en las condiciones de vida de la población indígena
  = *it is true to say that*
- **Vaya por delante mi firme convicción de que**, en un tiempo razonable, vamos a ser capaces de relanzar el arte de nuestra tierra hasta volverle a situar en lugar destacado dentro de Europa
  = *first and foremost I am convinced that*
- El problema, **desde mi punto de vista**, reside en que aún no se ha conseguido sintetizar culturalmente una nueva idea de España, como comunidad de pueblos o nación de naciones
  = *as I see it*
- **Basta** comenzar a leer la obra **para sentirse** transportado a la época
  = *you only need to ... to feel*

Introducing someone else's point of view

- Tras ellos el arte posmodernista **- según concluye el autor -** ha terminado por ser un barrio de Disneylandia, un paraíso de masas
  = *as the author concludes*
- Esta y otras consideraciones, **como señala el autor**, deben estimular a nuevas y específicas investigaciones y debates
  = *as the author points out*
- **Como afirmó Platón**, ningún hombre puede aspirar al conocimiento total de la verdad absoluta
  = *as Plato stated*
- Parece que fue una clara agresión, **a juzgar por los comentarios de** la prensa y de algunas personas
  = *judging by the comments of*
- La comisión que investiga el caso **mantiene la teoría de** la existencia de "un poder político paralelo sin cuyo concurso no hubiera sido posible el fraude masivo detectado"
  = *the theory supported by ... is that*
- El proponente **reiteró su tesis sobre** la inadmisibilidad de la tortura en ningún supuesto
  = *repeated his argument about*
- El museo **asegura que** la retirada del logotipo había sido decidida en la etapa del ministro anterior
  = *maintains that*

Introducing an example

- **Sirva de ejemplo** la situación descrita por uno de los viajeros
  = *as an example, let us take*
- **Y mencionaré como ejemplo de ello** el episodio independiente compuesto por unas jornadas de cacería en las que el protagonista participa
  = *and I shall take as an example*
- **Podemos hacer uso de un ejemplo gráfico**
  = *to give a graphic example:*
- **Pongamos por caso** *or* **Supongamos que** uno de los rivales decide retirarse
  = *let us suppose that*
- **Procederé a ilustrar con algunos ejemplos** la idea de que se ha producido un desfase entre la ciencia económica y la sociedad
  = *with the help of some examples, I shall move on to*
- Las autoridades arguyen que la medida supone un importante ahorro de energía, pero yo disiento. **Veamos un ejemplo**
  = *let us look at an example*

Introducing a quotation or source

- **Ya lo dice el refrán**, "Dime con quién andas y te diré quién eres"
  = *as the saying goes*
- Tal convicción animó al Realismo decimonónico, **que, en palabras de** Clarín, exigía del novelista la facultad de "saber ver y copiar"
  = *which, in the words of*
- **Según la frase atribuida al** famoso pintor, "Yo no busco, encuentro"
  = *as ... is supposed to have said*
- **Ya dice** d'Ors **que** el dandismo de Valle-Inclán "no es sino el uniforme de los estudiantes de Coimbra y Santiago, perpetuado toda una vida"
  = *as ... says*
- **Podemos citar un pasaje que ilustra** esta posibilidad
  = *let us take a passage which illustrates*
- **Tomemos como referencia el momento en que** todo se descubre
  = *let us take as our point of reference the moment when*

26.3 The mechanics of the argument

Stating facts

- **La característica más destacada del problema es** su universalidad
  = *the most notable aspect of the problem is*
- **A medida que se avanza** en la lectura de la obra, **se abren nuevas perspectivas**
  = *as one progresses ..., new perspectives open up*
- **Podemos observar que**, en estos momentos, **existe** una clara tendencia común en los ejecutivos europeos
  = *it can be seen that ... there is*
- **Se puede constatar que** hay un gran índice del alcoholismo en la isla
  = *it can be seen that*
- **Es un hecho que** la industria está demostrando interés por este

tipo de buques ya que se han hecho varios pedidos de barcos porta-barcazas
= *it is a* *fact* *that*

- **Si partimos de la base de que** las corrientes que se engloban bajo el título de "Nuevas tecnologías" nunca han tenido un especial prestigio en este país ...
  = *if we start from the premise that*

Making a supposition

- Por los documentos que existen **podemos suponer que** Ferri sea valenciano, descendiente tal vez de Féliz Ferri, pintor levantino del siglo XVIII
  = *it can be assumed that*
- Esta novedad **permite pensar que** será posible un tratamiento de afecciones neuromusculares humanas en un futuro próximo
  = *leads us to believe that*
- La ruptura entre ambos **podría interpretarse como** una celosa competencia de naturaleza literaria
  = *could be interpreted as*
- **Me atrevo a pensar que** aquellos años fueron los más felices en su matrimonio, como así lo pude constatar en dos ocasiones en que fui a visitarle
  = *I would venture to suggest that*
- **Podría quizá pensarse que** la física da una respuesta clara al problema de la naturaleza del tiempo, pero nada más alejado de la verdad, como observan los dos libros objeto del presente comentario
  = *one might (be tempted to) think that*
- La simplicidad del método **hace suponer que** se continuará empleando en el futuro
  = *suggests that*
- **Especulemos con la hipótesis de** un descenso acelerado de la temperatura del planeta
  = *let us take the hypothetical situation in which there is*

Expressing a certainty

- **Lo cierto es que** los mecanismos de lucha contra el terrorismo no sólo no han mejorado, sino que se encuentran en uno de sus peores momentos
  = *one thing is certain:*
- La salida de presos preventivos produce una sensación de inseguridad en los ciudadanos, pero **está claro que** la justicia debe predominar sobre todo
  = *it is clear that*
- **Es indudable que** Chigorin fue un precursor del nuevo ajedrez, que sería creado en el primer cuarto de este siglo por la llamada escuela hipermoderna
  = *without a doubt*
- **No hay duda de que** esta nueva medida del gobierno supone un peligro para la libertad de expresión
  = *there can be no doubt that*
- **No se puede negar que** el yogur es el derivado lácteo preferido por los españoles
  = *it cannot be denied that*
- **Todos coinciden en que** hay argumentos de peso para defender la filosofía como pilar básico de la formación académica
  = *everyone agrees that*
- **Es evidente que** si la informática y las telecomunicaciones no pudiesen ser utilizadas para reforzar el poder existente, habrían sido dejadas totalmente de lado
  = *it is clear that*
- Más allá de la guerra de cifras, **es incontestable que** la convocatoria de huelga tuvo un seguimiento mayoritario en el sector industrial
  = *unquestionably*
- Un político dimite - **como es obvio en cualquier democracia** - por sentido de la responsabilidad y no por disciplina de partido
  = *as is the case in any normal democracy*

Expressing doubt

- **Es improbable que** un académico empleara la forma "andase"
  = *it is unlikely that*
- **Resulta difícil creer que** una obra de tal celebridad pueda ser vendida en el mercado secreto del arte robado
  = *it is hard to believe that*
- Y aún **cabría preguntarse si** la auténtica literatura no ha sido siempre la manifestación de lo individual e incluso de lo íntimo
  = *the question arises as to whether*
- **Todavía está por ver**, sin embargo, cuáles van a ser las tendencias en las subastas de arte cuando cese la actual recesión
  = *it still remains to be seen*
- Su parecido físico con el autor del crimen, **introduce un elemento de duda** en la identificación
  = *introduces an element of doubt*
- Un nuevo atraco **pone en cuestión** la seguridad de los furgones blindados
  = *raises doubts about*

Conceding a point

- España, que debe considerarse un país desarrollado en el conjunto occidental, no tiene, **sin embargo**, una política medioambiental integral
  = *nevertheless*
- Todavía no estamos en situación de valorar su trabajo, **aunque** sí creemos que es un autor con mucho que decir
  = *although*
- Asegura que lo que le interesa es la felicidad. Habría que saber, **no obstante**, en qué consiste para ella ese concepto tan abstracto
  = *however*
- **Aunque** hayan surgido escépticos por todas partes, el acuerdo de paz entre ambos países se irá construyendo poco a poco
  = *even if*
- Es la operación más importante que haya pactado nunca una empresa española quisiera aclarar en el exterior. **Pero** amenaza también con convertirse en la más controvertida
  = *however*
- **A pesar de que** la obre carece de la unidad que poseen otras "semióperas" de Purcell, el conjunto es de una frescura, una variedad y un encanto admirables
  = *in spite of the fact that*
- **Por mucho que se complique** el lenguaje de la clase política, existe una gran masa de población capaz de descifrarlo
  = *however complicated ... becomes*
- El hombre es capaz de mantener su temperatura corporal en unos límites muy estrechos, **sea cual sea** la temperatura ambiental
  = *whatever ... is*
- Estos viajes cuasidiplomáticos al extranjero por parte de un candidato de la oposición durante el año electoral son, **como mínimo**, insólitos
  = *to say the least*
- No se puede caer en la tentación, comprensible **hasta cierto punto**, de disminuir los precios de los productos petrolíferos a los usuarios
  = *up to a point*
- En el plano social, **hay que reconocer que** los resultados obtenidos a lo largo de más de una década de aplicación de esta ley son, en términos generales, muy satisfactorios
  = *it must be recognized that*
- **Hemos de admitir que** el turismo también ha afectado negativamente a la zona
  = *it must be admitted that*

Emphasizing particular points

- **Ante todo debemos subrayar que** esta obra es muy superior a las anteriores
  = *first and foremost, it should be stressed that*

- **Conviene también precisar que** el hecho de pasar unas vacaciones en la nieve no tiene por qué suponer obligatoriamente pasarse el día exclusivamente esquiando
  = *it should also be pointed out that*
- De todos modos, es evidente que fue un pionero, **no sólo** en lo ideológico, **sino también** en lo que se refiere a la acción social
  = *not only ... but also*
- La gente no le ha apoyado en parte por las sospechas que levanta su personalidad. **Pero un factor aún más importante es** que su discurso democrático hace temblar a una región poco democrática
  = *but an even more important factor is*
- En cuanto al tema de la corrupción, **sería preciso matizar que** no son sólo los cargos públicos los culpables, ya que también se han beneficiado individuos de la sociedad civil
  = *it should be pointed out that*
- **La cuestión fundamental es que** la lucha de los ecologistas no está únicamente encaminada a salvar a tal o cual animal, sino a recuperar el equilibrio entre el hombre y la Tierra
  = *the fact is that*
- La poesía explica el tiempo, y **yo diría incluso que** la poesía no tiene tiempo, que la poesía "es" el tiempo
  = *I would go as far as to say that*
- **Es precisamente** la teoría cuántica, aun con sus paradojas, la que hace posible la creación de una máquina del tiempo
  = *it is precisely ...*

Moderating a statement

- **Sería deseable** la implantación de un impuesto verde que gravase las energías contaminantes
  = *... would be desirable*
- Quizás muchos tan sólo relacionen al director con aquellos años de apertura erótica, **pero sería injusto** condicionar toda su obra a esa etapa transitoria
  = *but it would be unfair to*
- Probablemente por ello se han vertido inexactitudes que, **sin ánimo polémico**, quisiera aclarar
  = *without wishing to be controversial*
- **La cuestión no tendría más importancia si no fuera porque** ese dinero procede de los fondos de ayuda al desarrollo teóricamente destinados a financiar proyectos en países del Tercer Mundo
  = *this would not be particularly important were it not for the fact that*
- **A pesar de ser** una tesis bien construida, **se hace necesario en cierta medida cuestionarse** su validez en el mundo de hoy
  = *although it is ..., should perhaps be questioned*

Indicating agreement

- Por lo que conocemos del autor, bastantes de los episodios aquí narrados son, **efectivamente**, autobiográficos
  = *in fact*
- **Nada más cierto que** la afirmación que la autora hace al final del libro: "Saber dialogar es una asignatura pendiente en la sociedad democrática"
  = *... is absolutely right*
- Debido a la actual necesidad de prudencia, **sí parece justificada** la lentitud del Consejo en la toma de decisiones
  = *does indeed seem justified*
- **Es cierto que** el poder consultar los microfilmes indexados por temas y fechas ayuda considerablemente al historiador
  = *it is true that*
- **Soy partidario del** acuerdo, porque el diálogo y la concordia son siempre armas justas
  = *I am in favour of*
- Como reacción contra ese concepto de realismo, que el autor da **justamente** como extinguido, se alzó el contrario
  = *rightly*
- La exposición del problema que realizó el nuevo presidente de la organización parece **razonable y convincente**
  = *reasonable and convincing*

Indicating disagreement

- En cambio, lo que sí **resulta altamente discutible** es la atención morbosa con que los medios de comunicación han seguido el caso
  = *is highly questionable*
- El resultado de sus obras **es poco convincente**
  = *is not very impressive*
- Pero el trabajo tiene inconvenientes metodológicos que **lo ponen en tela de juicio**
  = *raise doubts about it*
- Con la debida humildad, **expreso mis reservas sobre** lo radical de dicha revisión
  = *I should like to express my doubts about*
- Esas interpretaciones **carecen de base sólida**
  = *there are no real grounds for ...*
- Las soluciones por ellos aportadas **distan mucho de ser indiscutibles**
  = *are questionable, to say the least*
- **Pecaríamos de ingenuos si creyéramos que** ése es el único argumento válido
  = *it would be extremely naïve to believe that*
- El punto de vista antropocentrista que pretende que somos los únicos hombres del universo **es** hoy día **totalmente inaceptable**
  = *is totally unacceptable*
- **Sería un grave error** acabar con el cinturón de dunas en el que se ubicaría la urbanización
  = *it would be a serious mistake to*
- **Es de todo punto absurdo mantener que** los acontecimientos del este de Europa no han repercutido sobre los nacionalismos de los países occidentales
  = *it is completely absurd to suggest that*

Making a correction

- El segundo lienzo de la subasta estaba valorado en 4-6 millones y fue vendido por 3.500.000; **en realidad**, 3.920.000
  = *or, to be precise*
- La idea de este proyecto es difundir el conocimiento de las Reales Academias. **No se trata propiamente de** una historia de las Academias, **sino de** una presentación de las mismas
  = *it is not really ..., but rather*
- Si rechazan escribir sobre literatura **no es porque** tengan mucho que ocultar sobre el proceso de la escritura. **Me parece más bien que** carecen de una sólida cultura literaria
  = *it is not because ..., but rather, it seems to me, because*
- **Tal vez sería más adecuado hablar de** problemas por resolver **que de** inconvenientes, dado que con el ritmo de desarrollo actual los problemas analizados a continuación tendrán solución a corto o medio plazo
  = *perhaps it would be better to talk about ... rather than*
- La transexualidad **tiene más de** conflicto **que de** la perversión sexual que muchos le atribuyen
  = *is more a question of ... than of*

Indicating the reason for something

- La tierra está agotada **debido a** la agricultura y a la ganadería intensiva que practicó la cooperativa durante años
  = *owing to*
- En estas tierras habría habido una ruptura total con el pasado anterior, **lo cual explica** la inexistencia de siervos y libertos y el clima de libertad personal de la época medieval
  = *which explains*
- El descubrimiento fue posible **gracias a** los grandes progresos técnicos que pusieron el radiotelescopio a disposición de los astrónomos
  = *thanks to*

- Y si quienes conocían el manuscrito no concedieron importancia a esas disquisiciones, **es, sin duda, porque** nada en ellas les resultaba digno de especial mención
  = *it is doubtless because*
- Ambas pinturas necesitan ser restauradas, **dado que** su estado de conservación no es bueno
  = *since*
- En la semiótica de entrada cabe todo, **puesto que** todo es signo, o signo de un signo
  = *since*
- El estudio ha demostrado que esta enfermedad **es el motivo de** baja laboral de un 8%
  = *is responsible for*
- **Si** no se observan distorsiones, **es porque** los rayos viajan una distancia corta y bajo un ángulo demasiado empinado para que se curven apreciablemente
  = *if ..., it is because*

Indicating the consequences of something

- El informe prevé una reactivación en la demanda de pisos, **lo que llevará a** un ligero aumento de los precios
  = *which will lead to*
- La enmienda fue aprobada por unanimidad, **lo que significa** que irá directamente al Congreso Federal del partido sin que sea debatida por el pleno
  = *which means that*
- Las galas televisivas recaudan centenares de millones, **por lo que** la ayuda final superará fácilmente los mil millones de pesetas
  = *for which reason*
- La industria auxiliar de la automoción atraviesa una fuerte crisis **como consecuencia de** la recesión en las ventas de automóviles
  = *as a result of*
- El carácter documental de sus libros, unido a la técnica literaria de los mismos, **daba como resultado** una fórmula muy bien acogida por la industria editorial y su público
  = *resulted in*
- El uso de la mitad del arsenal atómico mundial existente **provocaría** en el hemisferio Norte un largo invierno nuclear y la desaparición de la vida humana
  = *would cause*
- Este insecto-palo, carece de alas y es idéntico a una ramita seca. **De ahí que** resulte tan difícil distinguirlo entre la maleza
  = *that is why*
- Tendrán que perfeccionar su producto y seguir las tendencias del mercado, **lo que implica** producir coches para todos los niveles adquisitivos
  = *which involves*

Contrasting or comparing

- Las ciencias sociales se verán severamente afectadas con la reforma universitaria, **por el contrario** las ciencias aplicadas y las carreras técnicas serán muy favorecidas
  = *whereas*
- Las causas clásicas de mortalidad tienden a disminuir en los países desarrollados, **en cambio**, las enfermedades hereditarias toman cada vez mayor relieve
  = *whereas*
- El olfato humano está muy poco desarrollado **en comparación con** el de algunos animales
  = *in comparison with*
- La exportación mantuvo ritmos positivos de crecimiento, **en contraste con** el comportamiento medio de los países de la OCDE
  = *in contrast with*
- **En contraposición al** descenso que se observa en la venta de libros a Europa,las exportaciones a otros países han experimentado un aumento respecto al año anterior
  = *unlike*
- En *La Riqueza de las Naciones*, de Adam Smith, se puede ver **la diferencia entre** la tradición liberal **y** el neoliberalismo actual
  = *the difference between ... and*
- Esta zona posee la mayoría de los yacimientos de crudo **mientras que** en Esmeralda está la principal refinería y puerto de exportación del crudo
  = *while*
- La organización se ha gastado una suma **muy superior a** la prevista
  = *far higher ... than*
- Este material se compone de microfibras con un diámetro **diez veces inferior al de** las fibras de poliéster corriente
  = *ten times smaller than*

27 EL TELÉFONO

Para obtener un número

Could you get me 043 65 27 82, please?
(o-four-three six-five two-seven eight-two)

Could you give me directory enquiries *(Brit)* *o* directory assistance *(EEUU)* please?

Can you give me the number of Europost of 54 Broad Street, Newham?

It's not in the book

What is the code for Exeter?

How do I make an outside call?

You omit the '0' when dialling England from Spain

Diferentes tipos de llamadas

It's a local call

It's a long-distance call

I want to make an international call

I want to make a reverse charge call to a London number *(Brit)* *o* I want to call a London number collect *(EEUU)*

I'd like an alarm call for 7.30 tomorrow morning

Habla el telefonista

What number do you want? *o* What number are you calling?

Where are you calling from?

You can dial the number direct

Replace the receiver and dial again

There's a Mr Campbell calling you from Canberra and wishes you to pay for the call. Will you accept it?

Go ahead, caller

(Información) There's nothing listed under that name

There's no reply from 45 77 57 84

Hold the line, please

All lines are engaged - please try later

I'm trying it for you now

It's ringing for you now

The line is engaged *(Brit)* *o* busy *(EEUU)*

Cuando contestan

Could I have extension 516? *o* Can you give me extension 516?

Is that Mr Lambert's phone?

Could I speak to Mr Swinton, please? *o* Is Mr Swinton there?

Who's speaking?

I'll call back in half an hour

I'm ringing from a callbox *(Brit)* *o* I'm calling from a pay station *o* payphone *(EEUU)*

Could you ask him to ring me when he gets back?

Could you tell him I called?

27 THE TELEPHONE

Getting a number

¿Por favor, me puede poner con el 043 65 27 82?
(cero cuarenta y tres, sesenta y cinco, veintisiete, ochenta y dos)

¿Me pone con Información (Urbana/Interurbana), por favor?

¿Me puede decir el número de Europost? La dirección es Plaza Mayor, 34, Carmona, provincia de Sevilla

No está en la guía

¿Cuál es el prefijo de León?

¿Qué hay que hacer para obtener línea?

No marque el cero del prefijo cuando llame a Londres desde España

Different types of call

Es una llamada local *or* urbana

Es una llamada interurbana

Deseo llamar al extranjero

Quisiera hacer una llamada a cobro revertido a Londres

Por favor, ¿me podrían avisar por teléfono mañana por la mañana a las siete y media?

The operator speaks

¿Con qué número desea comunicar?

¿Desde dónde llama usted?

Puede marcar el número directamente

Cuelgue y vuelva a marcar

Hay una llamada para usted del Sr. Lopez, que telefonea desde Bilbao y desea hacerlo a cobro revertido. ¿Acepta usted la llamada?

Ya puede hablar, señor/señora/señorita or ¡Hable(, por favor)!

(Directory Enquiries) Ese nombre no figura en la guía

El 45 77 57 84 no contesta

No se retire(, señor/señora/señorita)

Las líneas están saturadas; llame más tarde, por favor

Le pongo *(Sp)* *or* Le estoy conectando *(LAm)*

Está sonando *or* llamando

Está comunicando

When your number answers

¿Me da la extensión *or* el interno *(S. Cone)* 516?

¿Es éste el número del señor Lambert?

Por favor, ¿podría hablar con Carlos García? *or* Quisiera hablar con Carlos García, por favor *or* ¿Está Carlos García?

¿De parte de quién? *or* ¿Quién le/la llama?*or* ¿Quién habla?

Llamaré otra vez dentro de media hora

Llamo desde una cabina (telefónica)

¿Puede decirle que me llame cuando vuelva?

¿Podría decirle que llamé?

Contesta la centralita *o* el conmutador (*LAm*)

Queen's Hotel, can I help you?
Who is calling, please?
Do you know his extension number?
I am connecting you now *o* I'm putting you through now
I have a call from Tokyo for Mrs Thomas
Sorry to keep you waiting
There's no reply
You're through
Would you like to leave a message?

Para contestar

Hello?

Hello, this is Anne speaking
(Is that Anne?) Speaking
Would you like to leave a message?
Put the phone down and I'll call you back
This is a recorded message
Please speak after the tone

En caso de dificultad

I can't get through
The number is not ringing
I'm getting 'number unobtainable'
Their phone is out of order
We were cut off
I must have dialled the wrong number
We've got a crossed line
I got the wrong extension
This is a very bad line

The switchboard operator speaks

Hotel Castellana, ¿dígame?
¿Me puede decir quién llama?
¿Sabe usted qué extensión *or* interno *(S. Cone)* es?
Le pongo *(Sp) or* Le conecto *or* Le paso
Hay una llamada de Tokio para la Sra. Martínez
Perdone la demora, pero no se retire
No contesta
Ya tiene línea
¿Quiere dejar un recado?

Answering the telephone

¿Diga? *or* ¿Dígame? *or* ¿Aló? *(LAm) or* ¿Bueno? *(Mex) or* ¿Hola? *(S. Cone)*
Sí, soy Ana, ¿dígame?
(¿Es Ana?) Si, soy yo *or* Sí, aquí Ana *or* Al aparato
¿Quiere dejar un recado?
Cuelgue y le llamaré yo
Este es el contestador automático de ...
Deje su mensaje después de la señal

In case of difficulty

No consigo comunicar
El teléfono no suena
Me sale la señal de línea desconectada
Ese teléfono está estropeado
Nos han cortado (la comunicación)
Debo de haberme equivocado de número
Hay un cruce de líneas
Me han dado una extensión que no era la que yo quería
Se oye muy mal *or* La línea está muy mal

27a E-MAIL

Sending messages

Nuevo mensaje

Archivo Edición Ver Herramientas **Correo** Ayuda Enviar

Correo menu:
- Nuevo mensaje
- Responder al autor
- Responder a todos
- Reenviar
- Archivo adjunto

A: glopez@infotec.es
CC: cperez@infotec.es
Copia oculta:
Asunto: Reunión

Necesitaríamos reunirnos para discutir el asunto de la remodelación de la oficina y la contratación de un nuevo servicio de limpieza. Se me ocurre que podría ser el próximo lunes. Pensáoslo y dadme una respuesta.

Un saludo.

Pedro.

Archivo	File
Edición	Edit
Ver	View
Herramientas	Tools
Correo	Compose
Ayuda	Help
Enviar	Send
Nuevo mensaje	New
Responder al autor	Reply to Sender

Receiving messages

Reunión

Archivo Edición Ver Herramientas Correo Ayuda

De: Gloria López (glopez@infotec.es)
Fecha: 20 de enero de 2005 11:38
A: psierra@infotec.es
CC: cperez@infotec.es
Asunto: Re: Reunión

In Spanish, when telling someone your e-mail address you say : **"glopez arroba infotec punto es"**.

A mí me parece bien el lunes. Propongo que lo hagamos a primera hora; por ejemplo a las nueve en la sala de reuniones. Espero respuesta.

Un saludo.

Gloria.

Responder a todos	Reply to all
Reenviar	Forward
Archivo adjunto	Attachment
A	To
CC	CC
Copia oculta	BCC (blind carbon copy)
Asunto	Subject
De	From
Fecha	Sent

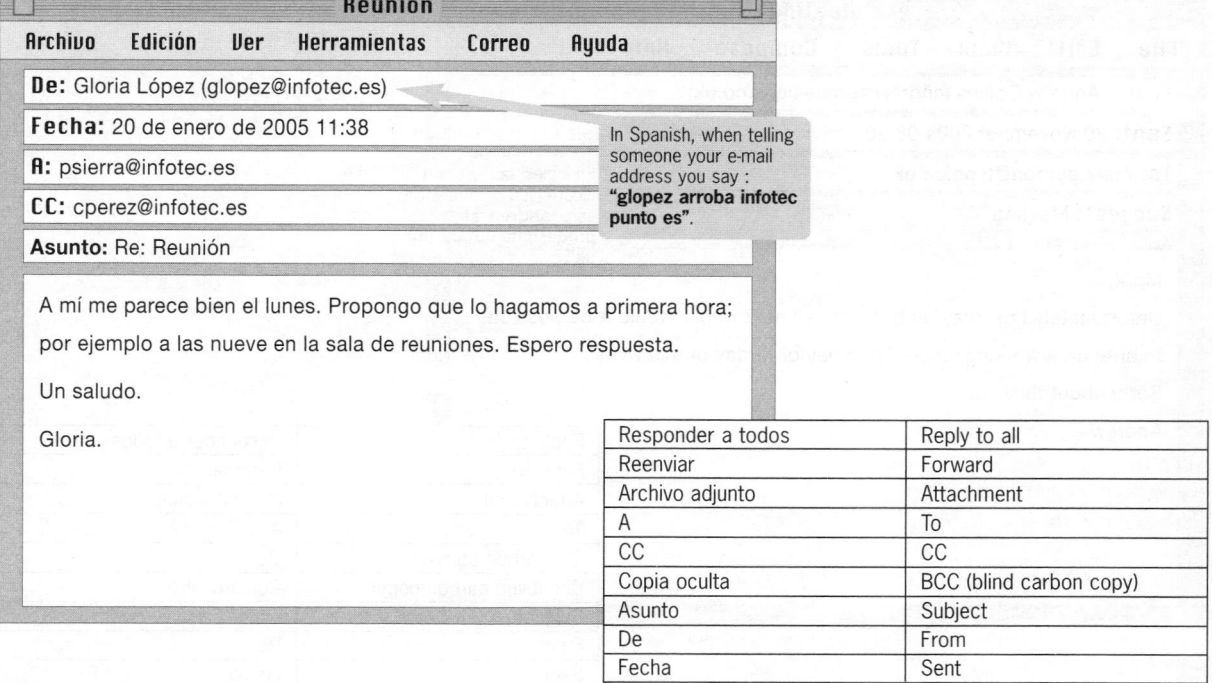

27a CORREO ELECTRÓNICO

Enviar mensajes

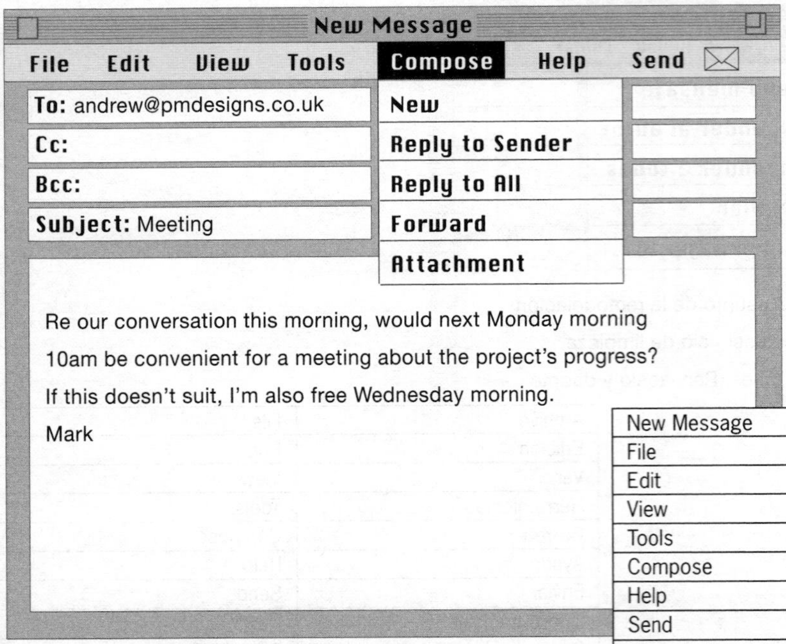
New Message
File
Edit
View
Tools
Compose
Help
Send
To: andrew@pmdesigns.co.uk
Cc:
Bcc:
Subject: Meeting
New
Reply to Sender
Reply to All
Forward
Attachment
Re our conversation this morning, would next Monday morning
10am be convenient for a meeting about the project's progress?
If this doesn't suit, I'm also free Wednesday morning.
Mark

New Message	Nuevo mensaje
File	Archivo
Edit	Edición
View	Ver
Tools	Herramientas
Compose	Correo
Help	Ayuda
Send	Enviar
New	Nuevo mensaje
Reply to Sender	Responder al autor

Recibir mensajes

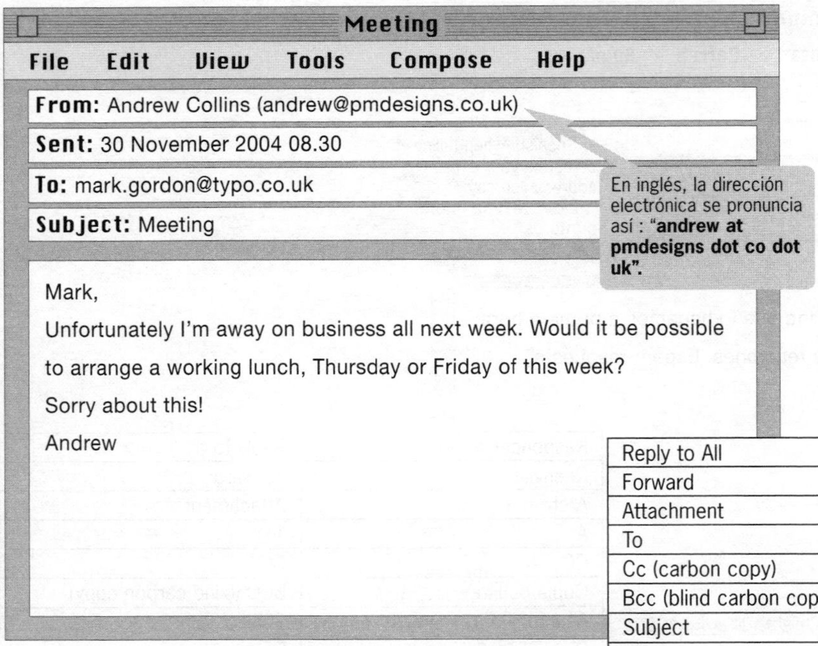
Meeting
File
Edit
View
Tools
Compose
Help
From: Andrew Collins (andrew@pmdesigns.co.uk)
Sent: 30 November 2004 08.30
To: mark.gordon@typo.co.uk
Subject: Meeting
Mark,
Unfortunately I'm away on business all next week. Would it be possible
to arrange a working lunch, Thursday or Friday of this week?
Sorry about this!
Andrew
En inglés, la dirección electrónica se pronuncia así : "andrew at pmdesigns dot co dot uk".

Reply to All	Responder a todos
Forward	Reenviar
Attachment	Archivo adjunto
To	A
Cc (carbon copy)	CC
Bcc (blind carbon copy)	Copia oculta
Subject	Asunto
From	De
Sent	Fecha

28 SUGERENCIAS

28.1 Para hacer sugerencias

- **You might like to** think it over before giving me your decision
  = *tal vez quiera*
- **If you were to** give me the negative, **I could** get copies made
  = *si me diera ... yo podría*
- **You could** help me clear out my office, **if you don't mind**
  = *podría ... si no le importa*
- **We could** stop off in Venice for a day or two, **if you like**
  = *podríamos ... si te apetece*
- I've got an idea - **let's organize** a surprise birthday party for Megan!
  = *vamos a organizar*
- **If you've no objection(s), I'll** speak to them personally
  = *si no tienes inconveniente, hablaré*
- **If I were you, I'd** go
  = *yo que tú, iría*
- **If you ask me, you'd better** take some extra cash
  = *en mi opinión, más vale que*
- **I'd be very careful not to** commit myself at this stage
  = *tendría cuidado de no*
- **I would recommend (that) you** discuss it with him before making a decision
  = *te recomendaría que*
- **It could be in your interest to** have a word with the owner first
  = *te convendría*
- **There's a lot to be said for** living alone
  = *... tiene muchas ventajas*
- Go and see Pompeii - **it's a must!**
  = *no dejes de ir a ver*

Más directamente

- **I suggest that you** go to bed and try to sleep
  = *te sugiero que*
- **I'd like to suggest that you** seriously consider taking a long holiday
  = *te sugeriría*
- **We propose that** half the fee be paid in advance, and half on completion
  = *proponemos que*
- **It is very important that** you take an interest in what he is trying to do
  = *es muy importante que*
- **I am convinced that** this would be a dangerous step to take
  = *estoy convencido de que*
- I cannot put it too strongly: **you really must** see a doctor
  = *de verdad, tienes que*

Menos directamente

- **Say you were to** approach the problem from a different angle
  = *y si*
- In these circumstances, **it might be better to** wait
  = *quizás sería mejor*
- **It might be a good thing** *o* **a good idea to** warn her about this
  = *estaría bien*
- **Perhaps it would be as well to** change the locks
  = *quizás convendría*
- **Perhaps you should** take up a sport
  = *tal vez deberías*
- **If I may make a suggestion,** a longer hemline might suit you better
  = *si me permite una sugerencia*
- **Might I be allowed to offer a little advice?** - talk it over with a solicitor before you go any further
  = *¿me permite que le dé un pequeño consejo?*
- **If I might be permitted to suggest something,** installing bigger windows would make the office much brighter
  = *si se me permite hacer una sugerencia*

Haciendo una pregunta

- **How do you fancy** a holiday in Australia?
  = *¿te apetece ...?*
- I was thinking of going for a drink later. **How about it?**
  = *¿qué te parece?*
- **What would you say to** a trip up to town next week?
  = *¿qué te parecería ...?*
- **Would you like to** stay in Paris for a couple of nights?
  = *¿te gustaría ...?*
- **What if** you try ignoring her and see if that stops her complaining?
  = *¿y si ...?*
- What you need is a change of scene. **Why not** go on a cruise?
  = *¿por qué no ...?*
- **Suppose** *o* **Supposing** you left the kids with your mother for a few days?
  = *¿y si ...?*
- **How would you feel about** taking calcium supplements?
  = *¿qué te parecería ...?*
- **Have you ever thought of** starting up a magazine of your own?
  = *¿no se te ha ocurrido ...?*
- **Would you care to** have lunch with me?
  = *¿querría ...?*

28.2 Para pedir sugerencias

- **What would you do if you were me?**
  = *¿qué harías tú en mi lugar?*
- **Have you any idea how I should** go about it to get the best results?
  = *¿tienes idea cómo debería ...?*
- I've no idea what to call our new puppy: **have you any suggestions?**
  = *¿se te ocurre algo?*
- I can only afford to buy one of them: **which do you suggest?**
  = *¿cuál me aconsejas?*
- **I wonder if you could suggest** where we might go for a few days?
  = *¿podría sugerirnos ...?*
- **I'm a bit doubtful about** where to start
  = *no estoy muy seguro de*

29 CONSEJOS

29.1 Para pedir consejo

- What would you do **if you were me?**
  = *en mi lugar*
- Would a pear tree grow in this spot? If not, **what would you recommend?**
  = *qué recomendaría usted*
- **Do you think I ought to** tell the truth if he asks me where I've been?
  = *crees que debería*
- **What would you advise me to do** in the circumstances?
  = *¿qué me aconsejaría que hiciera?*
- **Would you advise me to** seek promotion within this firm or apply for another job?
  = *¿me aconsejaría usted que ...?*
- **I'd like** *o* **I'd appreciate your advice on** personal pensions
  = *me gustaría que me aconsejara sobre*
- **I'd be grateful if you could advise me on** how to treat this problem
  = *le agradecería que me aconsejara sobre*

29.2 Para aconsejar

De manera impersonal

- **It might be wise** *o* **sensible to** consult a specialist
  = *quizás sería prudente*
- **It might be a good idea to** seek professional advice
  = *quizás sería buena idea*
- **It might be better to** think the whole thing over before taking any decisions
  = *sería mejor*
- **You'd be as well to** state your position at the outset, so there is no mistake
  = *más te valdría*
- **You would be well-advised to** invest in a pair of sunglasses if you're going to Spain
  = *haría bien en*
- **You'd be ill-advised to** have any dealings with this firm
  = *sería poco aconsejable que*
- **t would certainly be advisable to** book a table
  = *se aconseja*
- **It is in your interest** *o* **your best interests to** keep your dog under control if you don't want it to be reported
  = *le conviene*
- **Do be sure to** read the small print before you sign anything
  = *asegúrate de*
- **Try to avoid** upsetting her; she'll only make your life a misery
  = *intenta evitar*
- **Whatever you do, don't** drink the local schnapps
  = *no se te ocurra*

De manera más personal

- **If you ask me, you'd better** take some extra cash
  = *para mí que es mejor que lleves*
- **If you want my advice, you should** steer well clear of them
  = *si quieres un consejo, aléjate*
- **If you want my opinion, I'd** go by air to save time
  = *si quieres mi opinión, yo iría*
- **In your shoes** *o* **If I were you, I'd** be thinking about moving on
  = *yo que tú, me pondría a pensar*
- **Take my advice** and don't rush into anything
  = *hazme caso*
- **I'd be very careful not to** commit myself at this stage
  = *yo tendría mucho cuidado de no*
- **I think you ought to** *o* **should** seek professional advice
  = *creo que deberías*
- **My advice would be to** have nothing to do with them
  = *yo te aconsejaría que*
- **I would advise you to** pay up promptly before they take you to court
  = *yo te aconsejaría que*
- **I would advise against** calling in the police unless he threatens you
  = *yo aconsejaría no*
- **I would strongly advise you to** reconsider this decision
  = *yo le aconsejo que*
- **I would urge you to** reconsider selling the property
  = *le ruego encarecidamente que*
- **Might I be allowed to offer a little advice?** - talk it over with a solicitor before going any further
  = *¿me permite que le dé un consejo?*

29.3 Para hacer una advertencia

- It's really none of my business but **I don't think you should** get involved
  = *creo que no deberías*
- **A word of caution:** watch what you say to him if you want it to remain a secret
  = *una advertencia:*
- **I should warn you that** he's not an easy customer to deal with
  = *te advierto que*
- **Take care not to** lose the vaccination certificate
  = *ten cuidado de no*
- **Watch you don't** trip over your shoelaces
  = *cuidado no*
- **Make sure that** *o* **Mind that** *o* **See that you don't** say anything they might find offensive
  = *ten cuidado de no*
- **I'd think twice about** sharing a flat with him
  = *me lo pensaría dos veces antes de*
- **It would be sheer madness to** attempt to drive without your glasses
  = *sería una auténtica locura*
- **You risk** a long delay in Amsterdam **if** you come back by that route
  = *corre el riesgo de ... si*

30 PROPUESTAS

De manera directa

- **I would be delighted to** help out, if I may
  = *me encantaría*
- **It would give me great pleasure to** show you round the city
  = *sería un placer*
- **We would like to offer you** the post of Sales Director
  = *quisiéramos ofrecerle*
- **I hope you will not be offended if I offer** a contribution towards your expenses
  = *espero que no se ofenda si le ofrezco*
- **Do let me know if I can** help in any way
  = *avísame si puedo*
- **If we can** be of any further assistance, **please do not hesitate to** contact us
  = *si podemos ... no dude en*

Haciendo una pregunta

- **Say we were to** offer you a 5% rise, **how would that sound?**
  = *¿qué le parecería si le ofreciéramos ...?*
- **What if I were to** call for you in the car?
  = *¿y si yo ...?*
- **Could I** give you a hand with your luggage?
  = *¿puedo ...?*
- **Shall I** do the photocopies for you?
  = *¿te hago ...?*
- **Is there anything I can do to** help you find suitable accommodation?
  = *¿puedo hacer algo para ...?*
- **May** *o* **Can I offer you** a drink?
  = *¿le pongo ...?*
- **Would you like me to** find out more about it for you?
  = *¿quieres que ...?*
- **Would you allow me to** pay for dinner, at least?
  = *¿me deja que ...?*
- **You will let me** show you around Glasgow, **won't you?**
  = *¿me dejarás que ... ¿no?*

31 PETICIONES

- **Please would you** drop by on your way home and pick up the papers you left here?
  = *¿puedes ...?*
- **Would you please** try to keep the noise down while I'm studying?
  = *haced el favor de*

- **Would you mind** looking after Hannah for a couple of hours tomorrow?
  = *¿te importaría ...?*
- **Could I ask you to** watch out for anything suspicious in my absence?
  = *¿podrías ...?*

Por escrito

- **I should be grateful if you could** confirm whether it would be possible to increase my credit limit to £5000
  = *le agradecería que confirmara*
- **We would ask you not to** use the telephone for long-distance calls
  = *le pedimos que no*
- **You are requested to** park at the rear of the building
  = *se ruega*
- **We look forward to** receiv**ing** confirmation of your order within 14 days
  = *quedamos a la espera de*
- **Kindly inform us if** you require alternative arrangements to be made
  = *tenga la amabilidad de comunicarnos si*

De manera más indirecta

- **I would rather you didn't** breathe a word to anyone about this
  = *preferiría que no*
- **I would appreciate it if you could** let me have copies of the best photos
  = *te agradecería que*
- **I was hoping that you might** have time to visit your grandmother
  = *esperaba que tendrías*
- **I wonder whether you could** spare a few pounds till I get to the bank?
  = *¿te sería posible ...?*
- **I hope you don't mind if I** borrow your exercise bike for half an hour
  = *espero que no te importe que ...*
- **It would be very helpful** *o* **useful if you could** have everything ready beforehand
  = *nos vendría muy bien si*
- **If it's not too much trouble, would you** pop my suit into the dry cleaners on your way past?
  = *si no es mucha molestia, podrías*
- **You won't forget** to lock up before you leave, **will you?**
  = *no te olvidarás de ..., ¿no?*

32 COMPARACIONES

32.1 Objetivas

- The streets, though wide for China, are narrow **compared with** English ones
  = *comparadas con*
- The bomb used to blow the car up was small **in** *o* **by comparison with** those often used nowadays
  = *en comparación con*
- **f you compare** the facilities we have here **with** those in other towns, you soon realize how lucky we are
  = *si se comparan ... con*
- It is interesting to note **the similarities and the differences between** the two approaches
  = *las semejanzas y las diferencias entre*
- **In contrast to** the opulence of the Kirov, the Northern Ballet Theatre is a modest company
  = *en contraste con*
- Only 30% of the females died **as opposed to** 57% of the males
  = *frente a*
- **Unlike** other loan repayments, those to the IMF cannot simply be rescheduled
  = *a diferencia de*
- The quality of the paintings is disappointing **beside** that of the sculpture section
  = *al lado de*
- **Whereas** burglars often used to make off only with video recorders, they now also tend to empty the fridge
  = *mientras que*
- **What differentiates these wines from** a good champagne is their price
  = *lo que diferencia ... de*

32.2 Comparaciones favorables

- Orwell was, indeed, **far superior to** him intellectually
  = *muy superior a*
- Personally I think high-speed trains **have the edge over** both cars and aircraft for sheer convenience
  = *aventajan a*
- Michaela was astute beyond her years and altogether **in a class of her own**
  = *única en su género*

32.3 Comparaciones desfavorables

- Matthew's piano playing **is not a patch on** his sister's
  = *no le llega a la suela del zapato a*
- My old chair **was nowhere near as** comfortable **as** my new one
  = *no era ni mucho menos tan ... como*
- The parliamentary opposition **is no match for** the government, which has a massive majority
  = *no puede con*
- Commercially-made ice-cream **is far inferior to** the home-made variety
  = *es muy inferior a*
- The sad truth was that **he was never in the same class as** his friend
  = *no estaba a la misma altura que*
- Ella doesn't rate anything **that doesn't measure up to** Shakespeare
  = *que no esté al nivel de*
- Her brash charms **don't bear comparison with** Marlene's sultry sex appeal
  = *no tienen comparación con*
- The Australians are far bigger and stronger than us - **we can't compete with** their robot-like style of play
  = *no podemos competir con*

32.4 Para destacar el parecido

- The new computerized system costs **much the same as** a more conventional one
  = *prácticamente lo mismo que*
- When it comes to performance, **there's not much to choose between** them
  = *no hay mucha diferencia entre*
- The impact was **equivalent to** 250 hydrogen bombs exploding
  = *equivalente a*
- English literature written by people of the ex-colonies **is** clearly **on a par with** the writings of native-born British people
  = *está al mismo nivel que*
- In Kleinian analysis, the psychoanalyst's role **corresponds to** that of mother
  = *corresponde a*
- The immune system **can be likened to** *o* **compared to** a complicated electronic network
  = *se le puede comparar con*
- **There was a close resemblance between** her **and** her son
  = *había un gran parecido entre ... y*
- **It's swings and roundabouts** - what you win in one round, you lose in another
  = *al final viene a ser lo mismo*

32.5 **Para destacar el contraste**

- **You cannot compare** a small local library **with** a large city one
  = *no se puede comparar con*
- Homemade clothes **just cannot compare with** bought ones
  = *no se pueden comparar con*
- **There's no comparison between** the sort of photos I take **and** those a professional could give you
  = *no hay comparación entre ... y*
- His books **have little in common with** those approved by the Party
  = *tienen poco en común con*
- We might be twins, but **we have nothing in common**
  = *no tenemos nada en común*
- The modern army **bears little resemblance to** the army of 1940
  = *se parece poco a*

33 OPINIONES

33.1 **Para pedir la opinión de alguien**

- **What do you think of** the new Managing Director?
  = *¿qué piensas de ...?*
- **What is your opinion on** women's rights?
  = *¿qué opinas sobre ...?*
- **What are your thoughts on** the way forward?
  = *¿cuál es su opinión sobre ...?*
- **What is your attitude to** people who say there is no such thing as sexual inequality?
  = *¿cuál es su actitud hacia ...?*
- **What are your own feelings about** the way the case was handled?
  = *¿qué opina usted acerca de ...?*
- **How do you see** the next stage **developing**?
  = *¿cómo ve el desarrollo de ...?*
- **How do you view** an event like the Birmingham show in terms of the cultural life of the city?
  = *¿cóme ve ...?*
- **I would value your opinion on** how best to set this all up
  = *apreciaría su opinión sobre*
- **I'd be interested to know what your reaction is to** the latest report on food additives
  = *me interesaría conocer su reacción ante*

33.2 **Para expresar la opinión propia**

- **In my opinion,** eight years as President is quite enough for anyone
  = *en mi opinión*
- **As I see it,** everything depended on Karlov being permitted to go to Finland
  = *según lo veo yo*
- **I feel that** there is an epidemic of fear about cancer which is not helped by all the publicity about the people who die of it
  = *pienso que*
- **Personally, I believe** the best way to change a government is through the electoral process
  = *personalmente, creo que*
- **It seems to me that** the successful designer leads the public
  = *a mi parecer*
- **I am under the impression that** he is essentially a man of peace
  = *mi impresión es que*
- **I have an idea that** you are going to be very successful
  = *presiento que*
- **I am of the opinion that** the rules should be looked at and refined
  = *soy de la opinión de que*
- **I'm convinced that** we all need a new vision of the future
  = *estoy convencido de que*
- **I daresay** there are so many names that you get them mixed up once in a while
  = *me figuro que*
- We're prepared to prosecute the company, which **to my mind** has committed a criminal offence
  = *a mi parecer*
- **From my point of view** activities like these should not be illegal
  = *desde mi punto de vista*
- **As far as I'm concerned,** Barnes had it coming to him
  = *en lo que a mí respecta*
- It's a matter of common sense, nothing more. **That's my view of the matter**
  = *Esa es mi opinión sobre el tema*
- **It is our belief that** to be proactive is more positive than being reactive
  = *nosotros creemos que*
- **If you ask me,** there's something a bit strange going on
  = *para mí que*
- **If you want my opinion,** if you don't do it soon you'll lose the opportunity altogether
  = *si quiere mi opinión*

33.3 **Para responder sin expresar una opinión**

- Would I say she had been a help? **It depends what you mean by** help
  = *depende de lo que quiera decir con*
- It could be seen as a triumph for capitalism but **it depends on your point of view**
  = *depende de su punto de vista*
- **It's hard** *o* **difficult to say whether** she has benefited from the treatment or not
  = *resulta difícil decir si*
- **I'm not in a position to comment on whether** the director's accusations are well-founded
  = *no estoy en situación de comentar si*
- **I'd prefer not to comment on** operational decisions taken by the service in the past
  = *preferiría no pronunciarme sobre*
- **I'd rather not commit myself** at this stage
  = *preferiría no comprometerme*
- **I don't have any strong feelings about which of the two** companies we decide to use for the job
  = *no tengo una opinión firme sobre cuál de las dos compañías*
- **This isn't something I've given much thought to**
  = *es algo en lo que no me he parado a pensar*
- **I know nothing about** fine wine
  = *no sé nada sobre*

34 GUSTOS Y PREFERENCIAS

34.1 **Para preguntarle a alguien sus preferencias**

- **Would you like to** visit the castle, while you are here?
  = *¿te gustaría ...?*
- **How would you feel about** Simon joining us?
  = *¿qué te parecería si ...?*
- **What do you like** doing **best** when you're on holiday?
  = *¿qué es lo que más te gusta hacer ...?*
- **What's your favourite** film?
  = *¿cuál es tu ... preferida?*
- **Which of the two** proposed options **do you prefer?**
  = *¿cuál de las dos ... prefiere?*
- We could either go to Rome or stay in Florence - **which would you rather** do?
  = *¿qué preferirías ...?*

34.2 **Para expresar gustos**

- **I'm very keen on** gardening
  = *me gusta mucho*

- **I'm very fond of** white geraniums and blue petunias
  = *me gustan mucho*
- **I really enjoy** a good game of squash after work
  = *disfruto con*
- **There's nothing I like more than** a quiet night in with a good book
  = *no hay nada que me guste más que*
- **I have a weakness for** rich chocolate gateaux
  siento debilidad por
- **I've always had a soft spot for** the Dutch
  = *siempre he sentido debilidad por*

34.3 Para decir lo que a uno no le gusta

- Acting **isn't really my thing** - I'm better at singing
  = *no es lo mío*
- Watching football on television **isn't my favourite** pastime
  = *no es mi ... preferido*
- Some people might find it funny but **it's not my kind of** humour
  = *no es mi tipo de*
- I enjoy playing golf, although this type of course **is not my cup of tea**
  = *no es plato de mi gusto*
- Sitting for hours on motorways **is not my idea of fun**
  = *no es lo que yo llamo divertirse*
- The idea of walking home at 10 or 11 o'clock at night **doesn't appeal to me**
  = *no me resulta nada atractiva*
- **I've gone off the idea of** cycling round Holland
  = *se me han quitado las ganas de*
- **I can't stand** *o* **can't bear** the thought of seeing him
  = *no soporto*
- **I am not enthusiastic about** shopping in large supermarkets
  = *no me entusiasma*
- **I'm not keen on** seafood
  = *no me entusiasma*
- **I don't like the fact that** he always gets away with not helping out in the kitchen
  = *no me gusta que*
- **What I hate most is** waiting in queues for buses
  = *lo que más detesto es*
- **I dislike** laziness since I'm such an energetic person myself
  = *me desagrada*
- **There's nothing I dislike more than** having to go to work in the dark
  = *no hay nada que me guste menos que*
- **I have a particular aversion to** the religious indoctrination of schoolchildren
  = *siento una aversión especial por*
- **I find it intolerable that** people like him should have so much power
  = *me resulta intolerable que*

34.4 Para decir lo que uno prefiere

- **I'd prefer to** *o* **I'd rather** wait until I have enough money to go by air
  = *preferiría*
- **I'd prefer not to** *o* **I'd rather not** talk about it just now
  = *prefiero no*
- **I'd prefer you to** give *o* **I'd rather you** gave me your comments in writing
  = *prefiero que*
- **I'd prefer you not to** *o* **I'd rather you didn't** invite him
  = *prefiero que no lo invites*
- **I like** the blue curtains **better than** the red ones
  = *... me gustan más que ...*
- **I prefer** red wine **to** white wine
  = *prefiero ... a*

34.5 Para expresar indiferencia

- **It makes no odds whether you have** a million pounds or nothing, we won't judge you on your wealth
  = *da lo mismo que tengas*
- **I really don't care what** you tell her as long as you tell her something
  = *me trae sin cuidado lo que*
- **It's all the same to me whether** he comes **or** not
  = *me da igual que ... o que*
- **I don't mind at all** - let's do whatever is easiest
  = *me da exactamente lo mismo*
- **It doesn't matter which** method you choose to use
  = *no importa qué*
- **I don't feel strongly about** the issue of privatization
  = *no tengo una opinión definida sobre*
- **I have no particular preference**
  = *no tengo preferencias*

35 INTENCIONES Y DESEOS

35.1 Para preguntar a alguien lo que piensa hacer

- **Will you** take the job?
  = *¿vas a ...?*
- **What do you intend to do?**
  = *¿qué piensas hacer?*
- **Did you mean to** *o* **intend to** tell him about it, or did it just slip out?
  = *¿tenías intención de ...?*
- **What do you propose to do** with the money?
  = *¿qué piensas hacer ...?*
- **What did you have in mind for** the rest of the programme?
  = *¿qué tenías pensado ...?*
- **Have you anyone in mind for** the job?
  = *¿tienes a alguien pensado para ...?*

35.2 Para expresar las propias intenciones

- **We're toying with the idea of** releasing a compilation album
  = *le estamos dando vueltas a la posibilidad de*
- **I'm thinking of** retiring next year
  = *estoy pensando en*
- **I'm hoping to** go and see her when I'm in Paris
  = *espero*
- I studied history, **with a view to** becoming a politician
  = *con vistas a*
- We bought the land **in order to** farm it
  = *para*
- We do not penetrate foreign companies **for the purpose of** collecting business information
  = *con el fin de*
- **We plan to** move *o* **We are planning on** moving next year
  = *estamos planeando*
- **Our aim** *o* **Our object in** buying the company **is to** provide work for the villagers
  = *nuestro propósito al ... es*
- **I aim to** reach Africa in three months
  = *pretendo*

Con mayor convicción

- **I am going to** sell the car as soon as possible
  = *voy a*
- **I intend to** put the house on the market
  = *tengo la intención de*
- **I have made up my mind to** *o* **I have decided to** go to Japan
  = *he decidido*

- I went to Rome **with the intention of** visit**ing** her, but she had gone away
  = *con intención de*
- **We have every intention of** winn**ing** a sixth successive championship
  = *estamos decididos a*
- **I have set my sights on** recaptur**ing** the title
  = *mi objetivo es volver a ganar*
- **My overriding ambition is to** get into politics
  = *mi gran ambición es*
- **I resolve to** do everything in my power to help you
  = *estoy resuelto a*

35.3 Para expresar lo que no se piensa hacer

- **I don't mean to** offend you, but I think you're wrong
  = *no es mi intención*
- **I don't intend to** pay unless he completes the job
  = *no es mi intención*
- **I have no intention of** accept**ing** the post
  = *no tengo intención de*
- **We are not thinking of** tak**ing** on more staff
  = *no tenemos previsto*
- **We do not envisage** mak**ing** changes at this late stage
  = *no contemplamos*

35.4 Para expresar lo que se desea hacer

- **I'd like to** see the Sistine Chapel some day
  = *me gustaría*
- **I want to** work abroad when I leave college
  = *quiero*
- **We want her to** be an architect when she grows up
  = *queremos que sea*
- **I'm keen to** develop the business
  = *tengo mucho interés en*

Con gran entusiasmo

- **I'm dying to** leave home
  = *me muero de ganas de*
- **My ambition is to** become an opera singer
  = *lo que ambiciono es*
- **I long to** go to Australia but I can't afford it
  = *tengo el anhelo de*
- **I insist on** speak**ing** to the manager
  = *insisto en*

35.5 Para expresar lo que no se quiere hacer

- **I would prefer not to** *o* **I would rather not** have to speak to her about this
  = *preferiría no*
- **I wouldn't want to** have to change my plans just because of her
  = *no quisiera*
- **I don't want to** take the credit for something I didn't do
  = *no quiero*
- **I have no wish** *o* **desire to** become rich and famous
  = *no tengo ningún deseo de*
- **I refuse to** be patronized by the likes of her
  = *me niego a*

36 PERMISO

36.1 Para pedir permiso

- **Can I** *o* **Could I borrow** your car this afternoon?
  = *¿me dejas ...?*
- **Can I** use the telephone, please?
  = *¿puedo ...?*
- **Can I have the go-ahead to** order the supplies?
  = *¿me das luz verde para ...?*
- **Are we allowed to** say what we're up to or is it top secret at the moment?
  = *¿podemos ...?*
- **Would it be all right if** I arrived on Monday instead of Tuesday?
  = *¿te importaría que ...?*
- **Would it be possible for us to** leave the car in your garage for a week?
  = *¿nos sería posible dejar ...?*
- We leave tomorrow. **Is that all right by you**?
  = *¿te parece bien?*
- **Do you mind if** I come to the meeting next week?
  = *¿te importa que ...?*
- **Would it bother you if** I invited him?
  = *¿te molestaría que lo invitara ...?*
- **Would you let me** come into partnership with you?
  = *¿me dejaría ...?*
- **Would you have any objection to** sail**ing** at once?
  = *¿tiene algún inconveniente en ...?*
- **With your permission, I'd like to** ask some questions
  = *con su permiso, quisiera*

Con más cautela

- **Is there any chance of** borrow**ing** your boat while we're at the lake?
  = *¿nos sería posible ...?*
- **I wonder if I could possibly** use your telephone?
  = *¿podría ...?*
- **Might I be permitted to** suggest the following ideas?
  = *¿me permitirían que ...?*
- **May I be allowed to** set the record straight?
  = *¿me dejan que ...?*

36.2 Para dar permiso

- **You can** have anything you want
  = *puedes*
- **You are allowed to** visit the museum, as long as you apply in writing to the Curator first
  = *puedes*
- **It's all right by me if** you want to skip the Cathedral visit
  = *por mí puedes ... si*
- **You have my permission to** be absent for that week
  = *te doy permiso para*
- **I've nothing against her** go**ing** there with us
  = *no me opongo a que*
- The Crown **was agreeable to** hav**ing** the case called on March 23
  = *dio su consentimiento para que*
- **I do not mind if** my letter is forwarded to the lady concerned
  = *no veo inconveniente en que*
- **You have been authorized to** use all necessary force to protect relief supply routes
  = *está autorizado a*
- **We should be happy to allow you to** inspect the papers here
  = *no tenemos inconveniente en que*

Con más insistencia

- If you need to keep your secret, **of course you must keep it**
  = *guárdalo, claro*
- **By all means** charge a reasonable consultation fee
  = *por supuesto*
- **I have no objection at all to your** quot**ing** me in your article
  = *no tengo ningún inconveniente en que*

- **We would be delighted to** have you
  = sería un _placer_

36.3 Para denegar permiso

- **You can't** *o* **you mustn't** go anywhere near the research lab
  = no _puedes_
- **I don't want you to** see that man again
  = no _quiero_ que
- **I'd rather you didn't** give them my name
  = _preferiría_ que no
- **You're not allowed to** leave the ship until relieved
  = no tienes _permiso_ para
- **I've been forbidden to** swim for the moment
  = me han _prohibido_ que
- **I've been forbidden** alcohol **by** my doctor
  = ... me ha _prohibido_
- **I couldn't possibly allow you to** pay for all this
  = ¿cómo te voy a _dejar_ ...?
- **You must not** enter the premises without the owners' authority
  = no se le _autoriza_ a
- **We cannot allow** the marriage **to** take place
  = no podemos _permitir_ que

Con más insistencia

- **I absolutely forbid you to** take part in any further search
  = te _prohíbo terminantemente_
- **You are forbidden to** contact my children
  = tienes _prohibido_
- Smoking **is strictly forbidden** at all times
  = está _terminantemente prohibido_
- **It is strictly forbidden to** carry weapons in this country
  = está _terminantemente prohibido_
- **We regret that it is not possible for you to** visit the castle at the moment, owing to the building works (*por escrito*)
  = _lamentamos_ informarle que no se _puede_

37 OBLIGACIÓN

37.1 Para explicar lo que se está obligado a hacer

- **You've got to** *o* **You have to** be back before midnight
  = _tienes_ que
- **You must** have an address in Prague before you can apply for the job
  = _tienes_ que
- **You need to** have a valid passport if you want to leave the country
  = _hay_ que
- I have no choice: this is how **I must** live and I cannot do otherwise
  = _debo_
- **He was forced to** ask his family for a loan
  = se vio _obligado_ a
- Jews **are obliged to** accept the divine origin of the Law
  = están _obligados_ a
- A degree **is indispensable** for future entrants to the profession
  = es _indispensable_
- Party membership **is an essential prerequisite of** a successful career
  = es un _requisito indispensable_ para
- **It is essential to** know what the career options are before choosing a course of study
  = es esencial
- Wearing the kilt **is compulsory for** all those taking part
  = es _obligatorio_ para
- One cannot admit defeat, **one is driven to** keep on trying
  = algo te empuja a
- **We have no alternative but to** fight
  = no nos queda otro _remedio_ más que
- Three passport photos **are required**
  = se _necesitan_
- Club members **must not fail to** observe the regulations about proper behaviour
  = _han_ de
- **You will** go directly to the headmaster's office and wait for me there
  = vete

37.2 Para saber si se está obligado a hacer algo

- **Do I have to** *o* **Have I got to** be home by midnight?
  = ¿_tengo_ que ...?
- **Does one have** to *o* **need to** book in advance?
  = ¿_hay_ que ...?
- **Is it necessary to** go into so much detail?
  = ¿es _necesario_ ...?
- **Ought I to** tell my colleagues?
  = ¿_debería_ ...?
- **Should I** call the police?
  = ¿_debería_ ...?
- **Am I meant to** *o* **Am I expected to** *o* **Am I supposed to** fill in this bit of the form?
  = ¿_tengo_ que ...?

37.3 Para explicar lo que no se está obligado a hacer

- **I don't have to** *o* **I haven't got to** be home so early now the nights are lighter
  = no _tengo_ que
- **You don't have to** *o* **You needn't** go there if you don't want to
  = no hace _falta_ que
- **You are not obliged to** *o* **You are under no obligation to** invite him
  = no estás _obligado_
- **It is not compulsory** *o* **obligatory to** have a letter of acceptance but it does help
  = no es _obligatorio_
- The Council **does not expect you to** pay all of your bill at once
  = no espera que

37.4 Para explicar lo que no se debe hacer

- **On no account must you** be persuaded to give up the cause
  = no _debes_ de ninguna manera
- **You are not allowed to** sit the exam more than three times
  = no _puedes_
- Smoking **is not allowed** in the dining room
  = no se _puede_
- **You mustn't** show this document to any unauthorized person
  = no _debe_
- These are tasks **you cannot** ignore, delegate or bungle
  = no _puedes_
- **You're not supposed to** *o* **meant to** use this room unless you are a club member
  = no _puede_
- **I forbid you to** return there
  = te _prohíbo_ que

De forma menos directa

- **It is forbidden to** bring cameras into the gallery
  = está _prohibido_
- **You are forbidden to** talk to anyone while the case is being heard
  = le está _prohibido_
- Smoking **is prohibited** *o* **is not permitted** in the dining room
  = está _prohibido_

38 ACUERDO

38.1 Para expresar acuerdo con lo que se dice

- **I fully agree with you** *o* **I totally agree with you** on this point
  = *estoy totalmente de acuerdo contigo*
- **We are in complete agreement** on this
  = *estamos totalmente de acuerdo*
- **I entirely take your point about** the extra vehicles needed
  = *tienes toda la razón en que*
- I think **we see completely eye to eye** on this issue
  = *pensamos exactamente lo mismo*
- I talked it over with the chairman and **we are both of the same mind**
  = *ambos somos de la misma opinión*
- **You're quite right in** pointing at distribution as the main problem
  = *tienes razón en*
- **We share your views** on the proposed expansion of the site
  = *compartimos su opinión*
- **My own experience** certainly **bears out** *o* **confirms** what you say
  = *mi experiencia personal confirma*
- **It's true that** you had the original idea but many other people worked on it
  = *es verdad que*
- **As you have quite rightly pointed out**, this will not be easy
  = *como bien dijo usted*
- **I have to concede that** the results are quite eye-catching
  = *he de reconocer que*
- **I have no objection to** this being done
  = *no tengo inconveniente en que*
- **I agree in theory**, but in practice it's never quite that simple
  = *en principio estoy de acuerdo*
- **I agree up to a point**
  = *estoy de acuerdo hasta cierto punto*

De forma más familiar

- Go for a drink instead of working late? **Sounds good to me!**
  = *me parece estupendo*
- **That's a lovely idea**
  = *¡qué buena idea!*
- **I'm all for** encouraging a youth section in video clubs such as ours
  = *soy partidario de*
- **I couldn't agree with you more**
  = *estoy totalmente de acuerdo contigo*

De forma menos directa

- **I am delighted to wholeheartedly endorse** your campaign
  = *me complace dar mi incondicional apoyo a*
- **Our conclusions are entirely consistent with** your findings
  = *nuestras conclusiones confirman ... totalmente*
- Independent statistics **corroborate** those of your researcher
  = *corroboran*
- **We applaud** the group's decision to stand firm on this point
  = *celebramos*

38.2 Para expresar acuerdo con lo propuesto

- This certainly **seems the right way to go about it**
  = *parece ser la forma correcta de proceder*
- **I will certainly give my backing to** such a scheme
  = *cuenta con todo mi apoyo*
- **It makes sense to** enlist helping hands for the final stages
  = *tiene sentido*
- **We certainly welcome** this development
  = *nos alegra*

De forma más familiar

- **It's a great idea**
  = *es una idea estupenda*
- Cruise control? **I like the sound of that**
  = *suena bien*
- **I'll go along with** Ted's proposal that we open the club up to women
  = *apoyo*

De forma menos directa

- This solution **is most acceptable** to us
  = *nos parece muy aceptable*
- The proposed scheme **meets with our approval**
  = *aprobamos*
- This is a proposal which **deserves our wholehearted support**
  = *merece nuestro apoyo incondicional*
- I shall do my best to **fall in with** her wishes
  = *acceder a*

38.3 Para expresar acuerdo con lo que pide alguien

- Of course **I'll be happy to** organize it for you
  = *estaré encantado de*
- **I'll do as you suggest** and send him the documents
  = *seguiré tu consejo*
- **There's no problem about** getting tickets for him
  = *podemos/puedo ... sin problema*

De forma menos directa

- Reputable builders **will not object to** this reasonable request
  = *no podrán reparos a*
- **We should be delighted to** cooperate with you in this enterprise
  = *con mucho gusto*
- An army statement said it **would comply with** the ceasefire
  = *respetaría*
- **I consent to** the performance of such procedures as are considered necessary
  = *accedo a*

39 DESACUERDO

39.1 Para mostrarse en desacuerdo con lo que se ha dicho

- There must be some mistake - **it can't possibly** cost as much as that
  = *no es posible que*
- I'm afraid he **is quite wrong** if he has told you that
  = *se equivoca*
- **You're wrong in thinking that** I haven't understood
  = *te equivocas al pensar que*
- The article **is mistaken in** claiming that debating the subject is a waste of public money
  = *comete un error al*
- Surveys **do not bear out** Mrs Fraser's assumption that these people will return to church at a later date
  = *no confirman*
- **I cannot agree with you** on this point
  = *no estoy de acuerdo contigo*
- **We cannot accept the view that** the lack of research and development explains the decline of Britain
  = *no aceptamos la opinión de que*
- To say we should forget about it, no **I cannot go along with that**
  = *no puedo aceptar eso*
- **We must agree to differ on this one**
  = *habrá que aceptar que nunca nos pondremos de acuerdo en este punto*

Con más insistencia

- **This is most emphatically not the case**
  = *insisto en que no es así*
- **I entirely reject** his contentions
  = *rechazo totalmente*
- **I totally disagree with** the previous two callers
  = *no estoy en absoluto de acuerdo con*
- his is your view of the events: **it is certainly not mine**
  = *yo desde luego no lo veo así*
- **I cannot support you** on this matter
  = *no puedo apoyarte*
- **Surely you can't believe that** he'd do such a thing?
  = *¿no creerás que ...?*

39.2 Para mostrarse en desacuerdo con lo que se ha propuesto

Con decisión

- **I'm dead against** this idea
  = *estoy totalmente en contra de*
- **Right idea, wrong approach**
  = *es una buena idea, pero mal enfocado*
- **I will not hear of** such a thing
  = *no quiero ni oír hablar de*
- **It is not feasible to** change the schedule at this late stage
  = *no es viable*
- This **is not a viable alternative**
  = *no es una alternativa viable*
- Trade sanctions will have an immediate effect but it **is the wrong approach**
  = *no es forma de hacer las cosas*

Con menos insistencia

- **I'm not too keen on** this idea
  = *no me convence mucho*
- **I don't think much of** this idea
  = *no me convence mucho*
- **This doesn't seem to be the right way of** dealing with the problem
  = *esta no parece la mejor forma de*
- While we are grateful for the suggestion, **we are unfortunately unable to** implement this change
  = *por desgracia nos es imposible*
- **I regret that I am not in a position to** accept your kind offer
  = *lamento no hallarme en condiciones de*

39.3 Para mostrarse en desacuerdo con lo que se ha pedido

- **I wouldn't dream of** doing a thing like that
  = *no se me ocurriría*
- I'm sorry but **I just can't** do it
  = *es que no puedo*
- **I cannot in all conscience** leave those kids in that atmosphere
  = *en conciencia no puedo*

Con más decisión

- **This is quite out of the question** for the time being
  = *no puede ser*
- **I won't agree to** any plan that involves your brother
  = *no voy a apoyar*
- **I refuse point blank to** have anything to do with this affair
  = *me niego rotundamente*

De forma menos directa

- **I am afraid I must refuse**
  = *lo siento pero he de negarme*
- **I cannot possibly comply with** this request
  = *me es imposible acceder a*
- **It is unfortunately impracticable for us to** commit ourselves at this stage
  = *nos es, por desgracia, imposible*
- In view of the proposed timescale, **I must reluctantly decline to** take part
  = *aun sintiéndolo, me veo obligado a declinar*

40 APROBACIÓN

40.1 Para aprobar lo que se ha dicho

- **I couldn't agree** (with you) **more**
  = *Estoy totalmente de acuerdo (contigo)*
- **I couldn't have put it better myself**
  = *tal y como lo hubiera dicho yo mismo*
- We must oppose terrorism, whatever its source. - **Hear, hear!**
  = *¡sí, señor!*
- **I endorse** his feelings regarding the condition of the Simpson memorial
  = *suscribo*

40.2 Para aprobar una propuesta

- **It's just the job!**
  = *¡perfecto!*
- **This is just the sort of thing I wanted**
  = *es justo lo que quería*
- **This is exactly what I had in mind**
  = *es justo lo que yo tenía pensado*
- Thank you for sending the draft agenda: **I like the look of it very much**
  = *me ha causado muy buena impresión*
- **We are all very enthusiastic about** *o* **very keen on** his latest set of proposals
  = *estamos todos entusiasmados con*
- **I shall certainly give it my backing**
  = *por supuesto que lo voy a apoyar*
- Any game which is as clearly enjoyable as this **meets with my approval**
  = *tiene mi aprobación*
- Skinner's plan **deserves our total support** *o* **our wholehearted approval**
  = *merece todo nuestro apoyo*
- **There are considerable advantages** in the alternative method you propose
  = *... comporta numerosas ventajas*
- **We recognize the merits** of this scheme
  = *reconocemos los méritos de*
- **We view** your proposal to extend the site **favourably**
  = *... nos merece una opinión favorable*
- This project **is worthy of our attention**
  = *merece de nuestra atención*

40.3 Para aprobar una idea

- **You're quite right to** wait before making such an important decision
  = *tienes toda la razón al*
- **I entirely approve of** the idea
  = *apruebo totalmente*
- **I'd certainly go along with that!**
  = *estoy totalmente de acuerdo*
- **I'm very much in favour of** that sort of thing
  = *soy muy partidario de*
- **What an excellent idea!**
  = *¡Qué idea tan estupenda!*

40.4 Para aprobar una acción

- **I applaud** Noble's perceptive analysis of the problems
  = ... *merece un aplauso*
- **I have a very high opinion of** their new teaching methods
  = *tengo muy buena opinión de*
- **I have a very high regard for** the work of the Crown Prosecution Service
  = *tengo muy buen concepto de*
- **I think very highly of** the people who have been leading thus far
  = ... *me merecen muy buena opinión*
- **I certainly admire** his courage in telling her what he thought of her
  = *siento gran admiración por*
- **I must congratulate you on** the professional way you handled the situation
  = *debo felicitarle por*
- **I greatly appreciated** the enormous risk that they had all taken
  = *les agradecí mucho*
- **I can thoroughly recommend** the event to field sports enthusiasts
  = *recomiendo plenamente*

41 DESAPROBACIÓN

- **This doesn't seem to be the right way of** going about it
  no parece ésta la mejor manera de
- **I don't think much of** what this government has done so far
  no tengo muy buena opinión de
- **I can't say I'm pleased about** what has happened
  no es que esté muy contento con
- The police **took a dim view of** her attempt to help her son break out of jail
  veía ... con malos ojos
- **We have a low** *o* **poor opinion of** opportunists like him
  sentimos poca estima por
- They **should not have refused to** give her the money
  no deberían haberse negado a

Más directamente

- **I'm fed up with** having to wait so long for payments to be made
  = *estoy hasta la coronilla de*
- **I've had (just) about enough of** this whole supermodel thing
  = ... *(ya) me tiene harto*
- **I can't bear** *o* **stand** people who smoke in restaurants
  = *no soporto*
- **How dare he** say that!
  = *¡cómo se atreve a ...!*
- **He was quite wrong to** repeat what I said about her
  = *hizo muy mal en*
- **I cannot approve of** *o* **support** any sort of testing on live animals
  = *me resulta inaceptable*
- **We are opposed to** all forms of professional malpractice
  = *nos oponemos a*
- **We condemn** any intervention which could damage race relations
  = *condenamos*
- **I must object to** the tag "soft porn actress"
  = *tengo que protestar contra*
- **I'm very unhappy about** your (idea of) going off to Turkey on your own
  = *me hace muy poca gracia*
- **I strongly disapprove of** such behaviour
  = *desapruebo totalmente*

42 CERTEZA, PROBABILIDAD, POSIBILIDAD Y CAPACIDAD

42.1 Certeza

- **She was bound to** discover that you and I had talked
  = *era de esperar que*
- **It is inevitable that they will** get to know of our meeting
  = *es inevitable que se enteren*
- **I'm sure** *o* **certain (that)** he'll keep his word
  = *estoy seguro de que*
- **I'm positive** *o* **convinced (that)** it was your mother I saw
  = *estoy convencido de que*
- **We now know for certain** *o* **for sure that** the exam papers were seen by several students before the day of the exam
  = *sabemos ya con seguridad*
- **I made sure** *o* **certain that** no one was listening to our conversation
  = *me aseguré de que*
- From all the evidence **it is clear that** they were planning to sell up
  = *está claro que*
- **What is indisputable is that** a diet of fruit and vegetables is healthier
  = *lo que es indiscutible es que*
- **It is undeniable that** racial tensions in Britain have been increasing
  = *no se puede negar que*
- **There is no doubt that** the talks will be long and difficult
  = *no hay ninguna duda de que*
- **There can be no doubt about** the objective of the animal liberationists
  = *no cabe ninguna duda acerca de*
- This crisis has demonstrated **beyond all (possible) doubt** that effective political control must be in place before the creation of such structures
  = *sin lugar a dudas*
- Her pedigree **is beyond dispute** *o* **question**
  = *está fuera de dudas*
- **You have my absolute assurance that** this is the case
  = *tiene mi garantía absoluta de que*
- **I can assure you that** I have had nothing to do with any dishonest trading
  = *puedo asegurarle que*
- **Make no mistake about it** - I will return when I have proof of your involvement
  = *que quede bien claro*

42.2 Probabilidad

- **There is a good** *o* **strong chance that** they will agree to the deal
  = *hay bastantes probabilidades de que*
- **It seems highly likely that** it was Bert who told Peter what had happened
  = *parece muy probable que*
- **The chances** *o* **the odds are that** he will play safe in the short term
  = *lo más probable es que*
- **The probability is that** your investment will be worth more in two years time
  = *lo más probable es que*
- The child's hearing will, **in all probability,** be severely affected
  = *con toda probabilidad*
- You will **very probably** be met at the airport by one of our men
  = *es muy probable que*
- **It is highly probable that** American companies will face retaliation abroad
  = *es muy probable que*
- **It is quite likely that** you will get withdrawal symptoms at first
  = *es bastante probable que*

- **The likelihood is that** the mood of mistrust and recrimination will intensify
  = *lo más probable es que*
- The person indicted is, **in all likelihood**, going to be guilty as charged
  = *con toda probabilidad*
- **There is reason to believe that** the books were stolen from the library
  = *hay motivo para creer que*
- **He must** know of the paintings' existence
  = *debe de*
- The talks **could very well** spill over into tomorrow
  = *podrían muy bien*
- The cheque **should** reach you by Saturday
  = *debería*
- **It wouldn't surprise me** *o* **I wouldn't be surprised if** he was working for the Americans
  = *no me sorprendería que*

42.3 Posibilidad

- The situation **could** change from day to day
  = *podría*
- Britain **could perhaps** play a more positive role in developing policy
  = *podría quizá*
- **I venture to suggest (that)** a lot of it is to do with his political ambitions
  = *me atrevería a sugerir que*
- **It is possible that** psychological factors play some unknown role in the healing process
  = *es posible que*
- **It is conceivable that** the economy is already in recession
  = *cabe la posibilidad de que*
- **It is well within the bounds of possibility that** England could be beaten
  = *no se puede descartar la posibilidad de que*
- **It may be that** the whole battle will have to be fought over again
  = *puede ser que*
- **It may be (the case) that** they got your name from the voters' roll
  = *puede ser que*
- **There is an outside chance that** the locomotive may appear in the Gala
  = *hay una remota posibilidad de que*
- **There is a small chance that** your body could reject the implants
  = *existe una pequeña posibilidad de que*

42.4 Para expresar lo que alguien es capaz de hacer

- Our Design and Print Service **can** supply envelopes and package your existing literature
  = *pueden*
- Applicants must **be able to** use a word processor
  = *saber*
- **He is qualified to** teach physics
  = *tiene titulación para*

43 INCERTIDUMBRE, IMPROBABILIDAD, IMPOSIBILIDAD E INCAPACIDAD

43.1 Incertidumbre

- **I doubt if** *o* **It is doubtful whether** he knows where it came from
  = *dudo que*
- **There is still some doubt surrounding** his exact whereabouts
  = *sigue habiendo dudas acerca de*
- **I have my doubts about** replacing private donations with taxpayers' cash
  = *tengo mis dudas sobre la sustitución de*
- **It isn't known for sure** *o* **It isn't certain** where she is
  = *no se sabe con certeza*
- **No one can say for sure** how any child will develop
  = *no se puede decir con seguridad*
- It's all still up in the air - **we won't know for certain** until next week
  = *no lo sabremos con seguridad*
- You're asking why I should do such an extraordinary thing and **I'm not sure** *o* **certain that** I really know the answer
  = *no estoy seguro de*
- **I'm not convinced that** you can really teach people who don't want to learn
  = *no estoy convencido de que*
- **We are still in the dark about** where the letter came from
  = *seguimos sin saber*
- How long this muddle can last **is anyone's guess**
  = *cualquiera sabe*
- Sterling is going to come under further pressure. **It is touch and go whether** base rates will have to go up
  = *está por ver si*
- **I'm wondering if** I should offer to help?
  = *no sé*

43.2 Improbabilidad

- You have **probably not** yet seen the document I am referring to
  = *seguramente no*
- **It is highly improbable that** there will be a challenge for the party leadership in the near future
  = *hay poquísimas probabilidades de que*
- **It is very doubtful whether** the expedition will reach the summit
  = *es muy dudoso que*
- **In the unlikely event that** the room was bugged, the music would drown out their conversation
  = *si se diera el caso poco probable de que*
- **It was hardly to be expected that** democratization would be easy
  = *apenas cabía esperar que*

43.3 Imposibilidad

- **There can be no** changes in the schedule
  = *no puede haber*
- Nowadays Carnival **cannot** happen **without** the police telling us where to walk and what direction to walk in
  = *no puede ... sin que*
- People said prices would inevitably rise; **this cannot be the case**
  = *esto es imposible*
- **I couldn't possibly** invite George and not his wife
  = *¿cómo voy a ...?*
- The report **rules out any possibility of** exceptions, and amounts to little more than a statement of the obvious
  = *descarta cualquier posibilidad de*
- **There is no question of** us getting this finished on time
  = *es imposible que*
- A West German spokesman said **it was out of the question that** these weapons would be based in Germany
  = *que ... de ninguna manera*
- **There is not (even) the remotest chance that** *o* **There is absolutely no chance that** he will succeed
  = *no existe la más remota posibilidad de que*
- The idea of trying to govern twelve nations from one centre **is unthinkable**
  = *es impensable*
- Since we had over 500 applicants, **it would be quite impossible to** interview them all
  = *sería del todo imposible*

43.4 Para expresar lo que uno es incapaz de hacer

- **I can't** drive, I'm afraid
  = *no sé*

- **I don't know how to** use a word processor
  = no sé
- The army **has been unable to** suppress the political violence in the area
  = no ha podido
- The congress had shown itself **incapable of** real reform
  = incapaz de
- His fellow-directors **were not up** to running the business without him
  = no eran capaces de
- We hoped the sales team would be able to think up new marketing strategies, but they **were** unfortunately **not equal to the task**
  = no fueron capaces de hacerlo
- I'm afraid the task **proved** (to be) **beyond his capabilities**
  = resultó demasiado para él
- I'd like to leave him but sometimes I feel that such a step **is beyond me**
  = es superior a mis fuerzas
- **He simply couldn't cope with** the stresses of family life
  = es que no podía con
- Far too many women accept that they're **hopeless at** *o* **no good at** managing money
  = no sirven para controlar
- **I'm not in a position to** say now how much substance there is in the reports
  = no estoy en situación de
- **It is quite impossible for me to** describe the confusion and horror of the scene
  = me resulta casi imposible

44 EXPLICACIONES

44.1 Para dar las razones de algo

- He was sacked **for the simple reason that** he just wasn't up to it any more
  = por la sencilla razón de que
- **The reason that** we admire him is that he knows what he is doing
  = la razón de que
- He said he could not be more specific **for** security **reasons**
  = por razones de
- The students were arrested **because of** suspected dissident activities
  = por
- Parliament has prevaricated, **largely because of** the unwillingness of the main opposition party to support the changes
  = sobre todo a causa de
- Teachers in the eastern part of Germany are assailed by fears of mass unemployment **on account of** their communist past
  = a causa de
- Morocco has announced details of the austerity package it is adopting **as a result of** pressure from the International Monetary Fund
  = como consecuencia de
- They are facing higher costs **owing to** rising inflation
  = debido a
- The full effects will be delayed **due to** factors beyond our control
  = debido a
- **Thanks to** their generosity, the charity can afford to buy new equipment
  = gracias a
- What also had to go was the notion that some people were born superior to others **by virtue of** their skin colour
  = en virtud de
- Both companies became profitable again **by means of** severe cost-cutting
  = mediante
- He shot to fame **on the strength of** a letter he had written to the papers
  = a raíz de
- The King and Queen's defence of old-fashioned family values has acquired a poignancy **in view of** their inability to have children
  = en vista de
- The police have put considerable pressure on the Government to toughen its stance **in the light of** recent events
  = a la luz de
- **In the face of** this continued disagreement, the parties have asked for the polling to be postponed
  = ante
- His soldiers had been restraining themselves **for fear of** harming civilians
  = por temor a herir
- A survey by the World Health Organization says that two out of every five people are dying prematurely **for lack of** food or health care
  = por falta de
- **Babies have died for want of** *o* **for lack of** proper medical attention
  = por falta de
- I refused her a divorce, **out of** spite I suppose
  = por
- The warder was freed unharmed **in exchange for** the release of a colleague
  = a cambio de
- The court had ordered his release, **on the grounds that** he had already been acquitted of most of the charges against him
  = basándose en que
- I am absolutely in favour of civil disobedience **on** moral **grounds**
  = por motivos
- It is unclear why they initiated this week's attack, **given that** negotiations were underway
  = dado que
- **Seeing that** he had a police escort, the only time he could have switched containers was on the way to the airport
  = dado que
- **As** he had been up since 4 a.m., he was doubtless very tired
  = como
- International intervention was appropriate **since** tensions had reached the point where there was talk of war
  = ya que
- She could not have been deaf, **for** she started at the sound of a bell (*literario*)
  = pues
- I cannot accept this decision. **So** I confirm it is my intention to appeal to a higher authority
  = así que
- What the Party said was taken to be right, **therefore** anyone who disagreed must be wrong
  = por lo tanto
- **Following** last weekend's rioting in central London, Conservatives say some left-wing Labour MPs were partly to blame
  = tras
- **The thing is that** once you've retired there's no going back
  = lo que pasa es que

44.2 Para explicar la causa o el origen de algo

- The serious dangers to your health **caused by** *o* **brought about by** cigarettes are now better understood
  = provocados por
- When the picture was published recently, **it gave rise to** *o* **led to** speculation that the three were still alive and being held captive
  = dio lugar a
- The army argues that security concerns **necessitated** the demolitions
  = hacían necesarias

- This lack of recognition **was at the root of** the dispute
  = *fue la razón fundamental de*
- **I attribute** all this mismanagement **to** the fact that the General Staff in London is practically non-existent
  = *atribuyo ... a*
- This unrest **dates from** colonial times
  = *data de*
- The custom **goes back to** pre-Christian days
  = *se remonta a*

45 DISCULPAS

45.1 Para disculparse

- **I'm really sorry**, Steve, **but** we won't be able to come on Saturday
  = *de verdad lo siento ... pero*
- **I'm sorry that** your time has been wasted
  = *siento que*
- **I am sorry to have to** say this to you but you're no good
  = *siento tener que*
- **Apologies if** I wasn't very good company last night
  = *disculpa si*
- **I must apologize for** what happened. Quite unforgivable, and the man responsible has been disciplined
  = *le ruego disculpe*
- **I owe you an apology**. I didn't think you knew what you were talking about
  = *te debo una disculpa*
- The general back-pedalled, saying that **he had not meant to** offend the German government
  = *no había sido su intención ofender*
- **Do forgive me for** being a little abrupt
  = *le ruego me perdone que haya sido*
- **Please forgive me for** behaving so badly
  = *perdóname por haberme comportado*
- **Please accept our apologies** if this has caused you any inconvenience
  = *les rogamos acepten nuestras disculpas*

45.2 Para aceptar responsabilidad de algo

- **I admit** I overreacted, but someone needed to speak out against her
  = *admito que*
- **I have no excuse for** what happened
  = *no tengo excusa para explicar*
- **It is my fault that** our marriage is on the rocks
  = *es culpa mía que*
- The Government **is not entirely to blame for** the crisis
  = *no tiene toda la culpa de*
- **I should never have** let him rush out of the house in anger
  = *no tenía que haber*
- Oh, but **if only I hadn't** lost the keys
  = *ojalá no hubiera*
- I hate to admit that the old man was right, but **I made a stupid mistake**
  = *fue un fallo tonto*
- **My mistake was in** failing to push my concerns and convictions as hard as I could have done
  = *mi error fue no conseguir*
- **My mistake was to** arrive wearing a jacket and polo-neck jumper
  = *cometí el error de*
- In December and January the markets raced ahead, and I missed out on that. **That was my mistake**
  = *ese fue mi error*

45.3 Para expresar lo que se lamenta

- **I'm very upset about** her decision but I accept she needs to move on to new challenges
  = *estoy muy disgustado por*
- **It's a shame that** the press gives so little coverage to these events
  = *es una pena que*
- **I feel awful about** saying this but you really ought to spend more time with your children
  = *me sabe mal*
- **I'm afraid I can't** help you very much
  = *(me temo que) no puedo*
- **It is a pity that** my profession can make a lot of money out of the misfortunes of others
  = *es una lástima que*
- **It is unfortunate that** the matter should have come to a head just now
  = *es de lamentar que*
- David and I **very much regret that** we have been unable to reach an agreement
  = *lamentamos mucho*
- The accused **bitterly regrets** this incident and it won't happen again
  = *lamenta de corazón*
- **We regret to inform you that** the post of Editor has now been filled
  = *lamentamos tener que informarle que*

45.4 Para rechazar toda responsabilidad

- **I didn't do it on purpose**, it just happened
  = *no lo hice a propósito*
- Sorry, Nanna. **I didn't mean to** upset you
  = *no era mi intención*
- Sorry about not coming to the meeting **I was under the impression that** it was just for managers
  = *tenía idea de que*
- **We are simply trying to** protect the interests of local householders
  = *intentamos sencillamente*
- I know how this hurt you but **I had no choice**. I had to put David's life above all else
  = *no me quedaba otro remedio*
- **We were obliged to** accept their conditions
  = *nos vimos obligados a*
- We are unhappy with 1.5%, but under the circumstances **we have no alternative but to** accept
  = *no nos queda otra alternativa que*
- **I had nothing to do with** the placing of any advertisement
  = *no tuve nada que ver con*
- A spokesman for the club assured supporters that **it was a genuine error** and **there was no intention to** mislead them
  = *se trataba de un error auténtico y que no hubo intención de*

46 SOLICITUDES DE TRABAJO

46.1 Para empezar la carta

- **In reply to your advertisement** for a Trainee Manager in today's *Guardian*, I would be grateful if you would send me further details of the post
  = *en respuesta a su anuncio*
- **I wish to apply for the post of** bilingual correspondent, as advertised in this week's
  = *desearía que se me considerara para Euronews el puesto de*
- **I am writing to ask if there is any possibility of work in your company**
  = *le ruego me informe si existe alguna posibilidad de empleo dentro de su empresa*

89 Short Street
Glossop
Derby SK13 4AP

The Personnel Director
Norton Manufacturing Ltd
Sandy Lodge Industrial Estate
Northants NN10 8QT

3 February 2005

Dear Sir or Madam[1]

With reference to your advertisement in the Guardian of 2 February 2005, I wish to apply for the post of Export Manager in your company.

I am currently employed as Export Sales Executive for United Engineering Ltd. My main role is to develop our European business by establishing contact with potential new distributors and conducting market research both at home and abroad.

I believe I could successfully apply my sales and marketing skills to this post and therefore enclose my curriculum vitae for your consideration. Please do not hesitate to contact me if you require further details. I am available for interview at any time.

I look forward to hearing from you.

Yours faithfully

Janet Lilly

[1] Cuando no se sabe si el destinatario es hombre o mujer, se debe usar esta fórmula. Por otra parte, si se conoce la identidad del destinatario se puede utilizar una de estas formas al escribir el nombre y dirección:

Mr Derek Balder
Mrs Una Claridge
Ms Nicola Stokes
O
Personnel Director
Messrs. J.M. Kenyon Ltd. *etc.*

En el encabezamiento de la carta, las fórmulas correspondientes serían: "Dear Mr Balder", "Dear Mrs Claridge" etc, "Dear Sir/ Madam" (según corresponda, si se sabe si es hombre o mujer), "Dear Sir or Madam" (si no se sabe).

Las cartas que comienzan con el nombre de la persona en el encabezamiento (e.g. "Dear Mr Balder") pueden terminar con la fórmula de despedida "Yours sincerely"; las que empiezan con "Dear Sir/ Madam" normalmente acaban con "Yours faithfully", seguido de la firma. Véanse más detalles en las páginas 822-825.

[2] Si se solicita un puesto en el extranjero se puede emplear una frase que explique el título académico que se posee, p.ej. "Spanish/Mexican etc. equivalent of A-Levels (bachillerato superior)", "equivalent to a degree in English Studies etc. (licenciatura en Filología Inglesa etc)".

CURRICULUM VITAE

Name: Margaret Sinclair

Address: 12 Poplar Avenue, Leeds LS12 9DT, England

Telephone: 0113 246 6648

Date of Birth: 2.2.75

Marital Status: Single

Nationality: British

Qualifications[2]: Diploma in Business Management, Liverpool College of Business Studies (1999)
B.A. Honours in French with Hispanic Studies (Upper 2nd class), University of York (1998)
A-Levels: English (B), French (A), Spanish (A), Geography (C) (1993)
O-Levels: in 8 subjects (1991)

Employment History: Assistant Manager, Biblio Bookshop, York (October 1999 to present)
Sales Assistant, Langs Bookshop, York (summer 1999)
English Assistant, Lycée Victor Hugo, Nîmes, France (1996-97)
Campsite courier, Peñíscola, Spain (summer 1994)

Other Information: I enjoy reading, the cinema, skiing and amateur dramatics. I hold a clean driving licence and am a non-smoker.

References:

Mr John Jeffries
Manager
Biblio Bookshop
York
YT5 2PS

Ms Teresa González
Department of Spanish
University of York
York
YT4 3DE

- **I am writing to enquire about the possibility of joining your company on work placement** for a period of 3 months
  = *le agradecería me informara sobre la posibilidad de efectuar prácticas de trabajo en su empresa*

46.2 Para hablar de la experiencia profesional propia

- **I have** three **years' experience of** office work
  = *tengo ... años de experiencia en*
- **I am familiar with word processors**
  = *tengo experiencia en proceso de textos*
- **As well as speaking fluent** English, **I have a working knowledge of** German
  = *además de hablar ... con fluidez, tengo buenos conocimientos de*
- **As you will see from my CV,** I have worked in Belgium before
  = *como verá en mi currículum*
- **Although I have no experience of** this type of work, I have had other holiday jobs and can supply references from my employers, if you wish
  = *a pesar de carecer de experiencia en*
- **My current salary is** ... per annum and I have four weeks' paid leave
  = *mi sueldo actual es de*

46.3 Para exponer las motivaciones propias

- **I would like to make better use of my languages**
  = *quisiera hacer más uso de los idiomas que conozco*
- **I am keen to work in** public relations
  = *tengo mucho interés en trabajar en*

46.4 Para terminar la carta

- **I will be available from** the end of April
  = *estaré libre a partir de*
- **I am available for interview** at any time
  = *me tendrá a su disposición para una entrevista personal*
- **Please do not hesitate to contact me** for further information
  = *no dude en ponerse en contacto conmigo*
- **Please do not contact my current employers**
  = *le rogaría que no se comunicara con mi empresa*
- **I enclose** a stamped addressed envelope for your reply
  = *adjunto*

46.5 Como pedir y redactar referencias

- In my application for the position of lecturer, I have been asked to provide the names of two referees and **I wondered whether you would mind if I gave your name** as one of them
  = *le agradecería me permitiera dar su nombre*
- Ms Lee has applied for the post of Marketing Executive with our company and has given us your name as a reference. **We would be grateful if you would let us know whether you would recommend her for this position**
  = *le agradeceríamos nos informase si merece su recomendación para tal puesto*
- **Your reply will be treated in the strictest confidence**
  = *su respuesta será tratada con absoluta reserva*
- I have known Mr Chambers for four years in his capacity as Sales Manager and **can warmly recommend him for the position**
  = *me complace recomendarlo para el puesto*

46.6 Para aceptar o rechazar una propuesta de empleo

- Thank you for your letter of 20 March. **I will be pleased to attend for interview** at your Manchester offices on Thursday 7 April at 10am
  = *con mucho gusto me presentaré a la entrevista personal que me solicitan*
- **I would like to confirm my acceptance of** the post of Marketing Executive
  = *deseo confirmar que acepto*
- **I would be delighted to accept this post. However,** would it be possible to postpone my starting date until 8 May?
  = *aceptaría encantado el puesto. Sin embargo,*
- **I would be glad to accept your offer; however,** the salary stated is somewhat lower than what I had hoped for
  = *aceptaría con mucho gusto su oferta; sin embargo*
- Having given your offer careful thought, **I regret that I am unable to accept**
  = *lamento no poder aceptarla*

47 CORRESPONDENCIA COMERCIAL

47.1 Peticiones de información

- **We see from** your advertisement in the Healthy Holiday Guide that you are offering cut-price holidays in Scotland, and **would be grateful if you would send us** details
  = *hemos visto ... Les agradeceríamos que nos enviaran*
- I read about the Happy Pet Society in the NCT newsletter and would be very interested to learn more about it. **Please send me details of** membership
  = *les agradecería que me enviaran información detallada sobre*

... y cómo responder

- **In response to your enquiry of** 8 March, **we have pleasure in enclosing** full details on our activity holidays in Cumbria, **together with** our price list, valid until October 2000
  = *en respuesta a su consulta del ... adjuntamos ... acompañados de*
- **Thank you for your enquiry about** the Society for Wildlife Protection. **I enclose** a leaflet explaining our beliefs and the issues we campaign on. **Should you wish** to join, a membership application form is also enclosed
  = *le agradecemos el interés mostrado por ... Le envío ... Si se decidiera a*

47.2 Pedidos y cómo responder

- **We would like to place an order for** the following items, in the sizes and quantities specified below
  = *desearíamos hacer un pedido de*
- **Please find enclosed our order no.** 3011 for ...
  = *adjunto encontrará nuestro pedido n°*
- **The enclosed order** is based on your current price list, assuming our usual discount
  = *el pedido adjunto*
- **I wish to order** a can of "Buzz off!" wasp repellent, as advertised in the July issue of Gardeners' Monthly, **and enclose a cheque for** £2.50
  = *desearía encargar ... para lo que adjunto un cheque por valor de*
- **Thank you for your order of** 3 May, which will be dispatched within 30 days
  = *le agradecemos su pedido de fecha*
- **We acknowledge receipt of your order no.** 3570 and advise that the goods will be dispatched within 7 working days
  = *acusamos recibo de su pedido n°*
- **We regret that the goods you ordered are temporarily out of stock**
  = *lamentamos tener que informarle que los artículos solicitados se hallan agotados temporalmente*
- **Please allow** 28 days **for delivery**
  = *la entrega se efectuará en un plazo de*

47.3 Entregas

- **Our delivery time is** 60 days from receipt of order
  = *nuestro plazo de entrega es de*
- **We await confirmation of your order**
  = *quedamos a la espera de confirmación de su pedido*

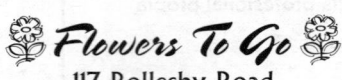

Flowers To Go
117 Rollesby Road
Beccles NR6 9DL
☎ 61 654 31 71

Ms Sharon McNeillie
41 Courthill Street
Beccles NR14 8TR

18 January 2004

Dear Ms McNeillie

Special Offer! 5% discount on orders received in January!

Thank you for your recent enquiry. We can deliver fresh flowers anywhere in the country at very reasonable prices. Our bouquets come beautifully wrapped, with satin ribbons, attractive foil backing, a sachet of plant food and, of course, your own personalized message. For that special occasion, we can even deliver arrangements with a musical greeting, the ideal surprise gift for birthdays, weddings or Christmas!

Whatever the occasion, you will find just what you need to make it special in our latest brochure, which I have pleasure in enclosing, along with our current price list. All prices include delivery within the UK.

During the promotion, a discount of 5% will apply on all orders received before the end of January, so hurry!

We look forward to hearing from you.

Yours sincerely

Daisy Duckworth

Daisy Duckworth
Promotions Assistant

Carrick Foods Ltd
Springwood Industrial Estate
Alexandra Road
Sheffield S11 5GF

Ms J Birkett
Department of English
Holyrood High School
Mirlees Road
Sheffield S19 7KL

14 April 2004

Dear Ms Birkett

Thank you for your letter of 7 April enquiring if it would be possible to arrange a group visit to our factory. We would of course be delighted to invite you and your pupils to take part in a guided factory tour. You will be able to observe the process from preparation through to canning, labelling and packaging of the final product ready for dispatch. Our factory manager will be available to answer pupils' questions at the end of the tour.

I would be grateful if you could confirm the date of your proposed visit, as well as the number of pupils and teachers in the party, at your earliest convenience.

Thank you once again for your interest in our company. I look forward to meeting you.

Yours sincerely

George Whyte

- **We confirm that the goods were dispatched on** 4 September
  = *confirmamos que el envío de la mercancía tuvo lugar el*
- **We cannot accept responsibility for** goods damaged in transit
  = *lamentamos no poder responsabilizarnos de*

47.4 Para hacer una reclamación

- **We have not yet received** the items ordered on 6 May (ref. order no. 541)
  = *no hemos recibido aún*
- **Unfortunately**, the goods were damaged in transit
  = *desgraciadamente*
- **The goods received differ significantly from the description** in your catalogue.
  = *los artículos recibidos difieren sustancialmente de los descritos*
- If the goods are not received by 20 October, **we shall have to cancel our order**nos
  = *veremos obligados a anular nuestro pedido*

47.5 Pagos

- **The total amount outstanding is ...**
  = *el importe pendiente se eleva a*
- **We would be grateful if you would attend to this account** immediately
  = *les agradeceríamos que nos enviaran liquidación de esta cuenta*
- **Please remit payment by return**
  = *sírvase remitirnos el pago a vuelta de correo*
- Full payment **is due within** 14 working days from receipt of goods
  = *vence en un plazo de*
- **We enclose** a cheque for ... **in settlement of your invoice no.** 2003L/58
  = *adjuntamos ... como liquidación de su factura n°*
- We must point out an error in your account and **would be grateful if you would adjust your invoice** accordingly
  = *les agradeceríamos que rectificaran su factura*
- This mistake was due to an accounting error, and **we enclose a credit note for** the sum involved
  = *abonamos*
- **Thank you for your cheque for** ... in settlement of our invoice
  = *le agradecemos su cheque por valor de*
- **We look forward to doing further business with you** in the near future
  = *Esperamos poder volver a servirles*

48 CORRESPONDENCIA DE CARÁCTER GENERAL

48.1 Para comenzar una carta

Para escribir a alguien que se conoce

- **Thank you** o **Thanks for your letter** which arrived yesterday
  = *gracias por tu carta*
- **It was good** o **nice** o **lovely to hear from you**
  = *me alegró recibir noticias tuyas*
- It's such a long time since we were last in touch that **I felt I must write a few lines** just to say hello
  = *pensé que tenía que escribirte unas líneas*
- **I'm sorry I haven't written for so long**, and hope you'll forgive me; I've had a lot of work recently and ...
  = *perdona que no te haya escrito desde hace tanto tiempo*

Para escribir a una organización

- **I am writing to ask whether** you have in stock a book entitled ...
  = *el motivo de mi carta es preguntarles si*
- **Please send me** ... I enclose a cheque for ...
  = *les ruego me envíen*
- When I left your hotel last week, I think I may have left a red coat in my room. **Would you be so kind as to** let me know whether it has been found?
  = *si fueran tan amables, ¿podrían ...?*
- **I** have seen the details of your summer courses, and **wish to know whether** you still have any vacancies on the Beginners' Swedish course
  = *desearía saber si*

48.2 Para terminar el cuerpo de la carta (antes de la despedida)

A un conocido

- **Gerald joins me in sending very best wishes to you all**
  = *Gerald y yo os deseamos lo mejor a todos*
- **Please remember me to** your wife - I hope she is well
  = *dele mis recuerdos a*
- **I look forward to hearing from you**
  = *quedo a la espera de tu respuesta*

A un amigo

- **Say hello to Martin for me**
  = *saluda a Martin de mi parte*
- **Give my warmest regards to Vincent**
  = *un abrazo para Vincent*
- **Do write** when you have a minute
  = *escríbeme*
- **Hoping to hear from you before too long**
  = *esperando recibir noticias tuyas pronto*

A amigos íntimos

- Rhona **sends her love**/Ray **sends his love**
  = *abrazos/besos de parte de*
- **Give my love to** Daniel and Laura, and tell them how much I miss them
  = *abrazos/besos a*
- Jodie and Carla **send you a big hug**
  = *te mandan un muy fuerte abrazo*

48.3 Preparativos de viaje

Para reservar una habitación

- **Please send me details of** your prices
  = *sírvanse enviarme información detallada sobre*
- **Please let me know by return of post if** you have one single room with bath, half board, for the week commencing 3 October
  = *sírvanse informarme a vuelta de correo si*
- **I would like to book** bed-and-breakfast accommodation with you
  = *desearía reservar*

48.4 Para confirmar o anular una reserva

- **Please consider this a firm booking** and hold the room until I arrive, however late in the evening
  = *le ruego considere esta como una reserva en firme*
- **Please confirm the following by fax**: one single room with shower for the nights of 20-23 April 2000
  = *sírvanse confirmarme por fax los siguientes datos*
- **We expect to arrive** in the early evening, unless something unforeseen happens
  = *esperamos llegar*
- **I am afraid I must ask you to alter my booking from** 25 August **to** 3 September. I hope this will not cause too much inconvenience
  = *me veo obligado a solicitarle que cambie mi reserva del ... al*
- Owing to unforseen circumstances, **I am afraid (that) I must cancel the booking** made with you for the week beginning 5 September
  = *lamento tener que anular la reserva*

226 Wilton Street
Leicester LE8 7SP

20th November 2004

Dear Hannah,

Sorry I haven't been in touch for a while. It's been hectic since we moved house and we're still unpacking! Anyway, it's Leah's first birthday on the 30th and I wondered if you and the kids would like to come to her party that afternoon. We were planning to start around 4 o'clock and finish around 5.30 or so. I've invited a clown and a children's conjurer, mainly for the entertainment of the older ones. With a bit of luck, you and I might get a chance to catch up on all our news!

Drop me a line or give me a ring if you think you'll be able to make it over on the 30th. It would be lovely if you could all come!

Hoping to hear from you soon. Say hello to Danny, Paul and Jonathan for me.

Love,

Jackie

---

14 Apsley Grove
Aberdeen AB4 7LP
Scotland

14th April 2004

Dear Paloma and Paco,

How are you? I hope you and the children enjoyed Montse's birthday party yesterday. I wish I could have been there too.

My flight from Madrid was delayed, so we didn't reach Gatwick till after midnight last night. I am a bit tired, but at least I have the weekend ahead to recover before going back to work on Monday!

You were so kind to me and I can't thank you enough for all your warmth and hospitality. It was a truly unforgettable stay. I took lots of photographs, as you know, and I intend to have them developed as soon as possible so I can look at them and think of you all. I shall, of course, send you copies of the best ones.

Remember that you are only too welcome to come and stay with me any time. It would be lovely to see you both and to have the opportunity to do something for you at last.

Keep in touch and take care!

With love from

Sandra

Fórmulas de saludo y de despedida

El esquema siguiente proporciona ejemplos de fórmulas de saludo y de despedida que se usan a menudo en la correspondencia. Dentro de cada sección son posibles las permutaciones:

A alguien conocido personalmente

FÓRMULAS DE SALUDO	FÓRMULAS DE DESPEDIDA
Dear Mr Brown Dear Mrs Drake Dear Mr & Mrs Charlton Dear Miss Baker Dear Ms Black Dear Dr Armstrong Dear Professor Lyons Dear Sir Gerald Dear Lady MacLeod Dear Andrew Dear Margaret	Yours sincerely With all good wishes, Yours sincerely[1] With kindest regards, Yours sincerely[1] *[1] tratamiento más cordial*

A un(a) amigo(a), a un pariente

FÓRMULAS DE SALUDO	FÓRMULAS DE DESPEDIDA
Dear Victoria	With love from
Dear Aunt Eleanor	Love from
Dear Granny and Grandad	Love to all[1]
Dear Mum and Dad	Love from us all[1]
My dear Elizabeth	Yours[1]
My dear Albert	All the best[1]
Dearest Norman	With much love from[2]
My dearest Mother	Lots of love from[2]
My dearest Lucy	Much love, as always[2]
My darling Peter	All my love[2]
	[1] tratamiento familiar *[2] tratamiento afectuoso*

A un conocido o un(a) amigo(a)

FÓRMULAS DE SALUDO	FÓRMULAS DE DESPEDIDA
Dear Alison Dear Annie and George Dear Uncle Eric Dear Mrs Newman Dear Mr and Mrs Jones My dear Miss Armitage	Yours sincerely With best wishes, Yours sincerely[1] With kindest regards, Yours sincerely[1] All good wishes, Yours sincerely[1] With best wishes, *(etc)* Yours ever[2] Kindest regards,[2] Best wishes[2] With best wishes, As always[2] *[1] tratamiento más cordial* *[2] tratamiento familiar*

Cartas comerciales (véase también 47)

FÓRMULAS DE SALUDO	FÓRMULAS DE DESPEDIDA
Dear Sirs[1] Dear Sir[2] Dear Madam[3] Dear Sir or Madam[4] *[1] para dirigirse a una empresa* *[2] para dirigirse a un hombre* *[3] para dirigirse a una mujer* *[4] cuando no se sabe si se dirige uno a un hombre o una mujer*	Yours faithfully

49 AGRADECIMIENTOS

- **Just a line to say thanks for** the lovely book which arrived today
  = *sólo unas letras para darle las gracias por*
- **I can't thank you enough for** finding my watch
  = *no se cómo darle las gracias por*
- **(Would you) please thank him from me**
  = *dele las gracias de mi parte*
- **We greatly appreciated** your support during our recent difficulties
  = *agradecemos enormemente*
- Your advice and understanding **were much appreciated**
  = *le quedamos muy reconocidos por*
- **I am writing to thank you** *o* **to say thank you for** allowing me to quote your experience in my article on multiple births
  = *me dirijo a usted para darle las gracias por permitirme*
- **Please accept our sincere thanks for** all your help and support
  = *le damos nuestro más sincero agradecimiento por*
- **A big thank you to everyone** involved in the show this year
  = *muchísimas gracias a todos*
- **We would like to express our appreciation to** the University of Durham Research Committee for providing a grant
  = *queremos expresar nuestro reconocimiento a*

De parte de un grupo

- **Thank you on behalf of** the Manx Operatic Society **for** all your support
  = *gracias en nombre de ... por*
- **I am instructed by** our committee **to convey our sincere thanks for** your assistance at our recent Valentine Social
  = *... me ha encomendado que les transmitiera nuestro sincero agradecimiento por*

50 SALUDOS DE CORTESÍA Y FELICITACIONES

50.1 Expresiones para cualquier ocasión

- **I hope you have** a lovely holiday
  = *espero que tengas*
- **With love and best wishes for** your wedding anniversary
  = *os deseo un feliz*
- **(Do) give my best wishes to** your mother **for** a happy and healthy retirement
  = *dile a ... que le deseo lo mejor en*
- Len **joins me in sending you our very best wishes for** your future career
  = *... y yo te deseamos lo mejor en*

50.2 En Navidad y Año Nuevo

- **Merry Christmas and a happy New Year**
  = *Feliz Navidad y Próspero Año Nuevo*
- **With season's greetings and very best wishes from** (+ *firma*)
  = *les deseamos unas felices fiestas*
- **May I send you all our very best wishes for** 2000
  = *quisiera desearles a todos un feliz*

50.3 Para un cumpleaños

- **All our love and best wishes on your** 21st **birthday**, from Simon, Liz, Kerry and the cats
  = *te deseamos muchísimas felicidades en tu 21 cumpleaños. Con todo nuestro cariño*
- I am writing to wish you **many happy returns (of the day)**. Hope your birthday brings you everything you wished for
  = *muchas felicidades (en el día de tu cumpleaños)*

50.4 Para desear una pronta recuperación

- Sorry (to hear) you're ill - **get well soon!**
  = *que te mejores pronto*
- I was very sorry to learn that you were ill, and **send you my best wishes for a speedy recovery**
  = *le deseo una pronta recuperación*

50.5 Para desear buena suerte

- **Good luck in your** driving test. I hope things go well for you on Friday
  = *buena suerte en el*
- Sorry to hear you didn't get the job - **better luck next time!**
  = *¡que haya más suerte la próxima vez!*
- **We all wish you the best of luck in** your new job
  = *te deseamos mucha suerte con*

50.6 Para felicitar a alguien

- You're expecting a baby? **Congratulations!** When is the baby due? (*hablado*)
  = *¡enhorabuena! (esp Sp), ¡felicitaciones! (esp LAm)*
- You've finished the job already? **Well done!** (*hablado*)
  = *¡muy bien!*
- **We all send you our love and congratulations on** such an excellent result (*escrito*)
  = *enhorabuena de parte de todos por*
- **This is to send you our warmest congratulations and best wishes on** your engagement (*escrito*)
  = *recibe nuestra más cordial enhorabuena por*

51 NOTAS Y AVISOS DE SOCIEDAD

51.1 Para anunciar un nacimiento

- Julia Archer **gave birth to** a 6lb 5oz **baby son**, Andrew, last Monday. **Mother and baby are doing well**
  = *... dio a luz un niño. Tanto la madre como el niño se encuentran en perfecto estado*
- Ian and Zoë Pitt **are delighted to announce the birth of a daughter**, Laura, on 1st May, 2000, at Minehead Hospital (*en una carta o periódico*)
  = *se complacen en anunciar el nacimiento de su hija*
- At the Southern General Hospital, on 1st December, 1999, **to Paul and Diane Kelly (née Smith) a son, John Alexander,** a brother for Helen (*en un periódico*)
  = *Paul y Diane Kelly tienen el placer de anunciar el nacimiento de su hijo, John Alexander*

... y para responder

- **Congratulations on the birth of** your son
  = *enhorabuena por el nacimiento de*
- **We were delighted to hear about the birth of** Stephanie, and send our very best wishes to all of you
  = *nos alegró mucho saber del nacimiento de*

51.2 Para anunciar un compromiso matrimonial

- I'm sure you'll be pleased to hear that Jim and I **got engaged** yesterday
  = *estamos prometidos desde*
- **It is with much pleasure that the engagement is announced between** Michael, younger son of Professor and Mrs Perkins, York, **and** Jennifer, only daughter of Dr and Mrs Campbell, Hucknall (*en un periódico*)
  = *nos complace anunciar el compromiso matrimonial entre ... y*

... y para responder

- **Congratulations to you both on your engagement**, and very best wishes for a long and happy life together
  = *enhorabuena a los dos por vuestro compromiso*
- **I was delighted to hear of your engagement**, and wish you both all the best for your future together
  = *me ha alegrado mucho saber de su compromiso*

51.3 Para anunciar una boda

- **I'm getting married** in June, to a wonderful man named Lester Thompson
  = *me caso el 1 de junio de 2000 tuvo*
- At Jurby Church, on 1st June, 2000, Eve, daughter of Ian and Mary Jones, Jurby,to John, son of Ray and Myra Watt, Ayr (*en un periódico*)
  = *lugar el enlace matrimonial de Eve Jones, hija de Ian y Mary Jones, vecinos de Jurby, con John Watt, hijo de Ray y Myra Watt de Ayr. La ceremonia fue celebrada en la Iglesia de Jurby*

... y para responder

- **Congratulations on your marriage, and best wishes to you both for your future happiness**
  = *enhorabuena por vuestra boda. Os deseamos lo mejor para el futuro*
- **We were delighted to hear about your daughter's marriage to** Iain, and wish them both all the best for their future life together
  = *nos hemos alegrado mucho de saber de la boda de su hija con*

51.4 Para anunciar un fallecimiento

- My husband **died suddenly** in March
  = *murió de repente*
- **It is with great sadness that I have to tell you that** Joe's father **passed away** three weeks ago
  = *con gran dolor tengo que comunicarte el fallecimiento*
- **Suddenly**, at home, in Newcastle-upon-Tyne, on Saturday 2nd July, 2000, Alan, aged 77 years, **the beloved husband of** Helen and **loving father of** Matthew (*en un periódico*)
  = *... falleció repentinamente ... dejando a su desconsolada esposa ... e hijo*

... y para responder

- My husband and I **were greatly saddened to learn of the passing of** Dr Smith, and send (*o* offer) you and your family our most sincere condolences
  = *nos entristeció enormemente enterarnos del fallecimiento de*
- **We wish to extend our deepest sympathy for your sad loss to you and your wife**
  = *queremos expresarle nuestro más sentido pésame a su mujer y a usted por su dolorosa pérdida*

51.5 Para anunciar el cambio de dirección

- We are moving house next week. **Our new address** as of 4 May 2000 **will be ...**
  = *las nuevas señas ... son*

52 INVITACIONES

52.1 Invitaciones oficiales

- Mr and Mrs James Waller **request the pleasure of your company at the marriage of** their daughter Mary Elizabeth to Mr Richard Hanbury at St Mary's Church, Frampton on Saturday, 21st August, 2000 at 2 o'clock and afterwards at Moor House, Frampton
  = *tienen el placer de invitarles al enlace de*
- The Chairman and Governors of Hertford College, Oxford **request the pleasure of the company of** Miss Charlotte Young and partner **at a dinner** to mark the anniversary of the founding of the College
  = *tienen el placer de invitar a ... a la cena*

... y para responder

- **We thank you for your kind invitation to** the marriage of your daughter Annabel on 20th November, **and have much pleasure in accepting**
  = *gracias por su amable invitación a ..., que aceptamos con mucho gusto*
- Mr and Mrs Ian Low **thank** Dr and Mrs Green for **their kind invitation to** the marriage of their daughter Ann on 21st July **and are delighted to accept**
  = *agradecen su amable invitación a ... y aceptan encantados*
- **We regret that we are unable to accept your invitation to** the marriage of your daughter on 6th May
  = *sentimos no poder aceptar su invitación a*

52.2 Invitaciones a fiestas

- **We are celebrating Rosemary's engagement to David** by holding a dinner dance at the Central Hotel on Friday 11th February, 2000, **and very much hope that you will be able to join us**
  = *celebramos el compromiso matrimonial de Rosemary y David ... y esperamos que podáis acompañarnos*
- **We are giving a dinner party** next Saturday, **and would be delighted if you and your wife could come**
  = *damos una cena ... y nos encantaría que vinierais tu mujer y tú*
- **I'm having a party** next week for my 18th - **come along, and bring a friend**
  = *voy a hacer una fiesta ... te espero. Y puedes traer a un amigo*

52.3 Para quedar con alguien

- **Would you and Gordon like to come** to dinner next Saturday?
  = *¿os gustaría venir a tí y a Gordon ...?*
- **Would you be free for** lunch next Tuesday?
  = *¿tienes tiempo para ...?*
- **Perhaps we could** meet for coffee some time next week?
  = *podíamos*

52.4 Para aceptar una invitación

- **Yes, I'd love to meet up with you** tomorrow
  = *sí, me encantaría verte*
- **It was good of you to invite me**, I've been longing to do something like this for ages
  = *me alegro de que me hayas invitado*
- **Thank you for your invitation to** dinner - **I look forward to it very much**
  = *gracias por su invitación a ... iré con mucho gusto*

52.5 Para declinar una invitación

- **I'd love to come, but I'm afraid** I'm already going out that night
  = *me encantaría ir, pero*
- **I wish I could come, but unfortunately** I have something else on
  = *ojalá pudiera ir, pero por desgracia*
- It was very kind of you to invite me to your dinner party next Saturday. **Unfortunately I will not be able to accept**
  = *desgraciadamente no voy a poder aceptar*
- **Much to our regret, we are unable to accept**
  = *sentimos tener que decirle que nos es imposible aceptar*

52.6 Sin dar una respuesta concreta

- **I'm not sure** what I'm doing that night, but I'll let you know later
  = *no estoy seguro de*
- **It all depends on whether** I can get a sitter for Rosie at short notice
  = *depende de si*
- **I'm afraid I can't really make any definite plans** until I know when Alex will be able to take her holidays
  = *el problema es que no puedo planear nada definitivamente*

53 REDACCIÓN

53.1 El argumento en líneas generales

Para introducir un tema

De manera impersonal

- **It is often said** *o* **claimed that** teenagers get pregnant in order to get council accommodation
  = *se suele afirmar que*
- **It is a cliché** *o* **a commonplace (to say) that** American accents are infinitely more glamorous than their British counterparts
  = *es un tópico (decir) que*
- **It is undeniably true that** Gormley helped to turn his union members into far more sophisticated workers
  = *es innegable que*
- **It is a well-known fact that** in this age of technology, it is computer screens which are responsible for many illnesses
  = *es un hecho de sobra conocido que*
- **It is sometimes forgotten that** much Christian doctrine comes from Judaism
  = *a veces se olvida que*
- **It would be naïve to suppose that** in a radically changing world these 50-year-old arrangements can survive
  = *sería ingenuo suponer que*
- **It would hardly be an exaggeration to say that** the friendship of both of them with Britten was among the most creative in the composer's life
  = *se puede decir sin temor a exagerar que*
- **It is hard to open a newspaper nowadays without reading that** TV is going to destroy reading and that electronic technology has made the written word obsolete
  = *hoy en día resulta difícil abrir un periódico en el que no leamos que*
- **First of all, it is important to try to understand** some of the systems and processes involved in order to create a healthier body
  = *en primer lugar, es importante intentar comprender*
- **It is in the nature of** sociological theory **to** make broad generalizations about such things as the evolution of society
  = *es un rasgo característico de*
- **It is often the case that** early interests lead on to a career
  = *suele suceder que*

De manera personal

- **By way of introduction, let me** summarize the background to this question
  = *a modo de introducción, voy a*
- **I would like to start with** a very sweeping statement which can be easily challenged
  = *comenzaré con*
- **Before going specifically into the issue of** criminal law, **I wish first to summarize** how Gewirth derives his principles of morality and justice
  = *antes de entrar en el tema concreto de ... quisiera resumir*
- **Let us look at** what self-respect in your job actually means
  = *examinemos*
- **We commonly think of** people **as** isolated individuals but, in fact, few of us ever spend more than an hour or two of our waking hours alone
  = *normalmente consideramos a ... como*
- **What we are mainly concerned with here is** the conflict between what the hero says and what he actually does
  = *nuestra principal preocupación aquí es*
- **We live in a world in which** the word "equality" is liberally bandied about
  = *en el mundo en que vivimos*

Para incluir conceptos y problemas

- **The concept of** controlling harmful insects by genetic means isn't new
  = *el concepto de*
- **The idea of** getting rich without too much effort has universal appeal
  = *la idea de*
- **The question of whether** Hamlet was really insane has long occupied critics
  = *que ... es una cuestión que*
- Why they were successful where their predecessors had failed **is a question that has been much debated**
  = *es una cuestión muy debatida*
- **One of the most striking aspects of this issue is** the way (in which) it arouses strong emotions
  = *uno de los aspectos más notables de este tema*
- **There are a number of issues** on which China and Britain openly disagree
  = *hay una serie de puntos*

Para hacer generalizaciones

- **People who** work outside the home **tend to believe that** parenting is an easy option
  = *la gente que ... tiende a creer que*
- **There's** always **a tendency for people to** exaggerate their place in the world
  = *hay una tendencia entre la gente a*
- Many gardeners **have a tendency to** treat plants like humans
  = *tienen tendencia a*
- Viewed psychologically, it would seem that **we all have the propensity for** such traits
  = *todos somos propensos a*
- **For the (vast) majority of people**, literature is a subject which is studied at school but which has no relevance to life as they know it
  = *para la (inmensa) mayoría de la gente*
- **For most of us**, housework is a necessary but boring task
  = *para la mayoría de nosotros*
- History **provides numerous examples** *o* **instances of** misguided national heroes who did more harm than good in the long run
  = *aporta numerosos ejemplos*

Para ser más preciso

- The impact of these theories on the social sciences, and economics **in particular**, was extremely significant
  = *en concreto*
- **One particular issue** raised by Butt was, suppose Hughes at the time of his conviction had been old enough to be hanged, what would have happened?
  = *un punto en concreto*
- **A more specific point** relates to using this insight as a way of challenging our hidden assumptions about reality
  = *un aspecto más concreto*
- **More specifically**, he accuses Western governments of continuing to supply weapons and training to the rebels
  = *más en concreto*

53.2 Para presentar una tesis

Para introducirla

- **First of all, let us consider** the advantages of urban life
  = *en primer lugar, consideremos*
- **Let us begin with an examination of** the social aspects of this question
  = *comencemos con un examen de*
- **The first thing that needs to be said is that** the author is presenting a one-sided view
  = *lo primero que hay que decir es que*

- **What should be established at the very outset is that** we are dealing here with a practical issue rather than a philosophical one
  = *antes de nada debemos dejar claro que*

Para delimitar el debate

- **In the next section, I will pursue the question of** whether the expansion of the Dutch prison system can be explained by Box's theory
  = *en la próxima sección me centraré en la cuestión de*
- **I will then deal with the question of** whether or not the requirements for practical discourse are compatible with criminal procedure
  = *a continuación me ocuparé de la cuestión de*
- We must distinguish between the psychic and the spiritual, and **we shall see how** the subtle level of consciousness is the basis for the spiritual level
  = *veremos cómo*
- **I will confine myself to** giving an account of certain decisive facts in my militant career with Sartre
  = *me limitaré a*
- In this chapter, **I shall largely confine myself to** a consideration of those therapeutic methods that use visualization as a part of their procedures
  = *me limitaré en gran medida a*
- **We will not concern ourselves here with** the Christian legend of St James
  = *no nos vamos a ocupar aquí de*
- **Let us now consider** to what extent the present municipal tribunals differ from the former popular tribunals in the above-mentioned points
  = *pasemos a considerar ahora*
- **Let us now look at** the ideal types of corporatism that neo-corporatist theorists developed to clarify the concept
  = *pasemos a examinar*

Para exponer los puntos

- **The main issue under discussion is** how the party should re-define itself if it is to play any future role in Hungarian politics
  = *el principal punto de debate es*
- **A second, related problem is** that business ethics has mostly concerned itself with grand theorizing
  = *otro problema relacionado con esto es*
- **The basic issue at stake is this**: is research to be judged by its value in generating new ideas?
  = *el punto básico en cuestión es éste:*
- **An important aspect of** Milton's imagery **is** the play of light and shade
  = *un aspecto importante de ... es*
- **It is worth mentioning here that** when this was first translated, the opening reference to Heidegger was entirely deleted
  = *cabe mencionar aquí que*
- **Finally, there is the argument that** watching too much television may stunt a child's imagination
  = *por último, está el argumento de que*

Para poner un argumento en duda

- World leaders appear to be taking a tough stand, but **is there any real substance in what's been agreed**?
  = *¿se ha decidido algo concreto?*
- This is a question which **merits close(r) examination**
  = *merece un estudio (más) detallado*
- The unity of the two separate German states **has raised fundamental questions** for Germany's neighbours
  = *ha planteado interrogantes fundamentales para*
- The failure to protect our fellow Europeans in Bosnia **raises fundamental questions on** the role of the armed forces
  = *plantea problemas fundamentales sobre*

- **This raises once again the question of** whether a government's right to secrecy should override the public's right to know
  = *... lo que plantea, una vez más, la cuestión de*
- **This poses the question of** whether these measures are really helping the people they were intended to help
  = *la cuestión que esto plantea es*

Para ofrecer un análisis de la cuestión

- **It is interesting to consider why** this scheme has been so successful
  = *es interesante examinar porqué*
- **On the question of** whether civil disobedience is likely to help end the war, Chomsky is deliberately diffident
  = *en lo que concierne a*
- **We are often faced with the choice between** our sense of duty **and** our own personal inclinations
  = *solemos vernos ante la necesidad de escoger entre ... y*
- **When we speak of** realism in music, **we do not at all have in mind** the illustrative bases of music
  = *al hablar de ..., no tenemos presente en absoluto*
- **It is reasonable to assume that** most people living in industrialized societies are to some extent contaminated by environmental poisons
  = *está dentro de lo razonable suponer que*

Para aportar un argumento

- **An argument in support of** this approach **is that** it produces ...
  = *un argumento a favor de ... es que*
- **In support of his theory,** Dr Gold notes that most oil contains higher-than-atmospheric concentrations of helium-3
  = *para apoyar su teoría*
- **This is the most telling argument in favour of** an extension of the right to vote
  = *éste es el argumento más convincente a favor de*
- **The second reason for advocating** this course of action **is that** it benefits the community at large
  = *la segunda razón para mostrarse partidario de ... es que*
- **The third, more fundamental, reason for** looking to the future **is that** even the angriest investors realize they need a successful market
  = *la tercera razón, más fundamental, para ... es que*
- Despite communism's demise, confidence in capitalism seems to be at an all-time low. **The fundamental reason for** this contradiction seems to me quite simple
  = *la razón fundamental de*

53.3 Para presentar una antítesis

Para criticar u oponerse a algo

- **In actual fact, the idea of** there being a rupture between a so-called old criminology and an emergent new criminology **is somewhat misleading**
  = *de hecho, la idea de ... es en cierto modo engañoso*
- In order to argue this, **I will show that** Wyeth's **position is**, in actual fact, **untenable**
  = *voy a demostrar que la postura de ... es ... insostenible*
- **It is claimed, however,** that the strict Leboyer method is not essential for a less traumatic birth experience
  = *se afirma, sin embargo,*
- **This need not mean that** we are destined to suffer for ever. **Indeed, the opposite may be true**
  = *esto no significa que .... De hecho quizá sea lo contrario*
- Many observers, though, **find it difficult to share his opinion that** it could mean the end of the Tamil Tigers
  = *les resulta difícil compartir su opinión de que*
- **On the other hand**, there are more important factors that should be taken into consideration
  = *por otra parte*

- The judgement made **may well be true but** the evidence given to sustain it is unlikely to convince the sceptical
  = *bien puede ser cierto pero*
- Reform **is all very well, but** it is pointless if the rules are not enforced
  = *está muy bien, pero*
- The case against the use of drugs in sport rests primarily on the argument that .... **This argument is weak,** for two reasons
  = *este argumento carece de solidez*
- According to one theory, the ancestors of vampire bats were fruit-eating bats. But **this idea does not hold water**
  = *esta idea no se sostiene*
- Their claim to be a separate race **does not stand up to** historical scrutiny
  = *no resiste*
- **This view does not stand up** if we examine the known facts about John
  = *esta opinión no se sostiene*
- **The trouble with this idea is not that** it is wrong, **but rather that** it is uninformative
  = *el problema no es que esta idea ... sino que*
- **The difficulty with this view is that** he bases the principle on a false premise
  = *el problema que plantea esta opinión radica en que*
- **The snag with** such speculations **is that** too much turns on one man or event
  = *la pega de ... es que*
- But removing healthy ovaries **is entirely unjustified in my opinion**
  no tiene, en mi opinión, justificación alguna

Para proponer una alternativa

- **Another approach may be to** develop substances capable of blocking the effects of the insect's immune system
  = *otro planteamiento posible es*
- **Another way to** reduce failure is to improve vocational education
  = *otra forma de*
- **However, the other side of the coin is** the fact that an improved self-image really can lead to prosperity
  = *sin embargo, la otra cara de la moneda es*
- **It is more accurate to speak of** a plurality of new criminologies rather than of a single new criminology
  = *es más preciso hablar de*
- **Paradoxical as it may seem**, computer models of mind can be positively humanizing
  = *aunque parezca paradójico*

53.4 Para presentar la síntesis argumental

Para evaluar los argumentos expuestos

- **How can we reconcile** these two apparently contradictory viewpoints?
  = *¿cómo reconciliar ...?*
- **On balance**, making money honestly is more profitable than making it dishonestly
  = *al fin y al cabo*
- Since such vitamins are more expensive, **one has to weigh up the pros and cons**
  = *hay que sopesar los pros y los contras*
- **We need to look at the pros and cons of** normative theory as employed by Gewirth and Phillips
  = *es necesario examinar los pros y contras de*
- **The benefits of** partnership in a giant trading market **will** almost certainly **outweigh the disadvantages**
  = *los beneficios de ... pesarán más que los inconvenientes*
- **The two perspectives are not mutually exclusive**
  = *las dos perspectivas no se excluyen mutuamente*

Para decantarse por uno de los argumentos

- Dr Meaden's theory **is the most convincing explanation**
  = *es la explicación más convincente*
- **The truth** *o* **fact of the matter is that** in a free society you can't turn every home into a fortress
  = *lo cierto es que*
- But **the truth is that** Father Christmas has a rather mixed origin
  = *lo cierto es que*
- Although this operation sounds extremely dangerous, **in actual fact** it is extremely safe
  = *en realidad*
- **When all is said and done, it must be acknowledged that** a purely theoretical approach to social issues is sterile
  = *a fin de cuentas, se debe reconocer que*

Para resumir los argumentos

- In this chapter, **I have demonstrated** *o* **shown that** the Cuban alternative has been undergoing considerable transformations
  = *he demostrado que*
- **This shows how**, in the final analysis, adhering to a particular theory on crime is at best a matter of reasoned choice
  = *esto demuestra cómo*
- **The overall picture shows that** prison sentences were relatively frequent, but not particularly severe
  = *la visión de conjunto demuestra que*
- **To recap** *o* **To sum up, then, (we may conclude that)** there are in effect two possible solutions to this problem
  = *en resumen, (se puede concluir que)*
- **To sum up this chapter** I will offer two examples ...
  = *para resumir este capítulo*
- **To summarize**, we have seen that the old staple industries in Britain had been hit after the First World War by a deteriorating international competitive position
  = *en resumen*
- Habermas's argument, **in a nutshell**, is as follows
  = *en suma*
- But **the key to the whole argument is** a single extraordinary paragraph
  = *la clave del problema ... se encuentra en*
- **To round off this section on** slugs, gardeners may be interested to hear that there are three species of predatory slugs in the British Isles
  = *para terminar esta sección sobre*

Para extraer conclusiones

- **From all this, it follows that** it is impossible to extend those kinds of security measures to all potential targets of terrorism
  = *de todo esto se deduce que*
- This, of course, **leads to the logical conclusion that** those who actually produce do have a claim to the results of their efforts
  = *nos lleva a la conclusión lógica de que*
- **There is only one logical conclusion we can reach**, which is that we ask our customers what is the Strategic Reality that they perceive in our marketing programme
  = *sólo podemos llegar a una conclusión lógica*
- **The inescapable conclusion is that** the criminal justice system does not simply reflect the reality of crime; it helps create it
  = *la conclusión ineludible es que*
- **We must conclude that** there is no solution to the problem of defining crime
  = *debemos decir, a modo de conclusión, que*
- **In conclusion**, because interpersonal relationships are so complex, there can be no easy way of preventing conflict
  = *en conclusión*
- **The upshot of all this is that** treatment is unlikely to be available
  la consecuencia de todo esto es que

- **So it would appear that** butter is not significantly associated with heart disease after all
  = *parece, pues, que*
- **This only goes to show that** a good man is hard to find
  = *esto demuestra*
- **The lesson to be learned** from this **is that** you cannot hope to please everyone all of the time
  = *la lección que se puede aprender es*
- **At the end of the day**, the only way the drug problem will be beaten is when people are encouraged not to take them
  = *al fin y al cabo*
- **Ultimately, then**, while we may have some sympathy for these young criminals, we must do our utmost to protect society from them
  = *en definitiva*

53.5 La estructura del párrafo

Para añadir información

- **In addition**, the author does not really empathize with his hero
  = *además*
- This award-winning writer, **in addition to** being a critic, biographer and poet, has written 26 crime novels
  = *además de ser*
- But this is only part of the picture. **Added to this are** fears that a major price increase would cause riots
  = *hay que añadir*
- **An added** complication **is** that the characters are not aware of their relationship to one another
  = *una ... más es*
- **Also**, there is the question of language
  = *además*
- **The question also arises as to** how this idea can be put into practice
  = *también se plantea la cuestión de*
- Politicians, **as well as** academics and educationalists, tend to feel strongly about the way history is taught
  = *al igual que*
- But, **over and above that**, each list contains fictitious names and addresses
  = *además de eso*
- **Furthermore**, ozone is, like carbon dioxide, a greenhouse gas
  = *además*

Para comparar

- **Compared with** the heroine, Alison is an insipid character
  = *comparada con*
- **In comparison with** the Czech Republic, the culture of Bulgaria is less westernized
  = *en comparación con*
- This is a high percentage for the English Midlands but low **by comparison with** some other parts of Britain
  = *si se compara con*
- **On the one hand**, there is no longer a Warsaw Pact threat. **On the other (hand)**, the positive changes could have negative side-effects
  = *por una parte ... por otra*
- **Similarly**, a good historian is not obsessed by dates
  = *del mismo modo*
- There can only be one total at the bottom of a column of figures and **likewise** only one solution to any problem
  = *del mismo modo*
- What others say of us will translate into reality. **Equally**, what we affirm as true of ourselves will likewise come true
  = *de igual manera*
- There will now be a change in the way we are regarded by our partners, and, **by the same token**, the way we regard them
  = *del mismo modo*
- **There is a fundamental difference between** adequate nutrient intake **and** optimum nutrient intake
  = *hay una diferencia fundamental entre ... y*

Para unir dos elementos

- **First of all** *o* **Firstly**, I would like to outline the benefits of the system
  = *en primer lugar*
- In music we are concerned **first and foremost** with the practical application of controlled sounds relating to the human psyche
  = *ante todo*
- **In order to understand** the conflict between the two nations, **it is first of all necessary to** know something of the history of the area
  = *para comprender ... es necesario ante todo*
- **Secondly**, it might be simpler to develop chemical or even nuclear warheads for a large shell than for a missile
  = *en segundo lugar*
- **In the first/second/third place**, the objectives of privatization were contradictory
  = *en primer/segundo/tercer lugar*
- **Finally**, there is the argument that watching too much television may stunt a child's imagination
  = *por último*

Para expresar una opinión personal

- **In my opinion**, the government is underestimating the scale of the epidemic
  = *en mi opinión*
- **My personal opinion is that** the argument lacks depth
  = *mi opinión personal es que*
- This is a popular viewpoint, but **speaking personally**, I cannot understand it
  = *yo personalmente*
- **Personally**, I think that no one can appreciate ethnicity more than black or African people themselves
  = *yo personalmente*
- **For my part**, I cannot agree with the leadership on this question
  = *por mi parte*
- **My own view is that** what largely determines the use of non-national workers are economic factors rather than political ones
  = *mi opinión personal es que*
- **In my view**, it only perpetuates the very problem that it sets out to address
  = *a mi parecer*
- Although the author argues the case for patriotism, **I feel that** he does not do it with any great personal conviction
  = *creo que*
- **I believe that** people do understand that there can be no quick fix for Britain's economic problems
  = *yo creo que*
- **It seems to me that** what we have is a political problem that needs to be solved at a political level
  = *a mi parecer*
- **I would maintain that** we have made a significant effort to ensure that the results are made public
  = *yo afirmaría que*

Para expresar la opinión de otra persona

- **He claims** *o* **maintains that** intelligence is conditioned by upbringing
  = *mantiene que*
- Bukharin **asserts that** all great revolutions are accompanied by destructive internal conflict
  = *afirma que*
- The communiqué **states that** some form of nuclear deterrent will continue to be needed for the foreseeable future
  = *manifiesta que*

- **What he is saying is that** the time of the old, highly structured political party is over
  = *lo que dice es que*
- His admirers **would have us believe that** watching this film is more like attending a church service than having a night at the pictures
  = *quieren hacernos creer*
- **According to** the report, poverty creates a climate favourable to violence
  = *según*

Para dar un ejemplo

- **To take another example**: many thousands of people have been condemned to a life of sickness and pain because ...
  = *para poner otro ejemplo*
- Let us consider, **for example** *o* **for instance**, the problems faced by immigrants arriving in a strange country
  = *por ejemplo*
- His meteoric rise **is the most striking example yet of** voters' disillusionment with the record of the previous government
  = *es el ejemplo más claro de ... hasta ahora*
- The case of Henry Howey Robson **serves to illustrate** the courage exhibited by young men in the face of battle
  = *sirve para ilustrar*
- Just consider, **by way of illustration**, the difference in amounts accumulated if interest is paid gross, rather than having tax deducted
  = *a modo de ejemplo*
- **A case in point is** the decision to lift the ban on contacts with the republic
  = *un ejemplo que viene al caso es*
- **Take the case of** the soldier returning from war
  = *tomemos el caso de*
- **As** the Prime Minister **remarked** recently, the Channel Tunnel will greatly benefit the whole of the European Community
  = *tal y como ha señalado ...*

53.6 Los mecanismos del debate

Para presentar una suposición

- They have telephoned the president to put pressure on him. **And that could be interpreted as** trying to gain an unconstitutional political advantage
  = *y eso se podría interpretar como*
- Retail sales rose sharply last month. This was higher than expected and **could be taken to mean that** inflationary pressures remain strong
  = *podría hacernos suponer*
- In such circumstances, **it might well be prudent** to diversify your investments
  = *quizá sería prudente*
- These substances do not remain effective for very long. **This is possibly because** they work against the insects' natural instinct to feed
  = *posiblemente se deba a que*
- His wife had become an embarrassment to him and therefore **it is not beyond the bounds of possibility that** he may have contemplated murdering her
  = *no está fuera de lo posible que*
- Mr Fraser's assertion **leads one to suppose that** he is in full agreement with Catholic teaching as regards marriage
  = *nos lleva a suponer*
- **It is probably the case that** all long heavy ships are vulnerable
  = *probablemente*
- After hearing nothing from the taxman for so long, most people **might reasonably assume that** their tax affairs were in order
  = *podría suponerse lógicamente que*
- **One could be forgiven for thinking that** because the substances are chemicals they'd be easy to study
  = *es comprensible que se piense que*
- **I venture to suggest that** very often when people like him talk about love, they actually mean lust
  = *me atrevo a sugerir que*

Para expresar certeza

Véase también la sección 42 CERTEZA

- **It is clear that** any risk to the human foetus is very low
  = *está claro que*
- Benn is **indisputably** a fine orator, one of the most compelling speakers in politics today
  = *indiscutiblemente*
- British universities are **undeniably** good, but they are not turning out enough top scientists
  = *no se puede negar que*
- **There can be no doubt that** the Earth underwent a dramatic cooling which destroyed the environment and life style of these creatures
  = *no cabe duda alguna de que*
- **It is undoubtedly true that** over the years there has been a much greater emphasis on safer sex
  = *es indudable que*
- **As we all know**, adultery is far from uncommon, particularly in springtime
  = *como todos sabemos*
- **One thing is certain**: the party is far from united
  = *lo que es cierto es que*
- **It is (quite) certain that** unless peace can be brought to this troubled land no amount of aid will solve the long-term problems of the people
  = *está (muy) claro que*

Para expresar dudas

Véase también la sección 43 DUDAS

- **It is doubtful whether**, in the present repressive climate, anyone would be brave or foolish enough to demonstrate publicly
  = *es dudoso que*
- **It remains to be seen whether** the security forces will try to intervene
  = *queda por ver si*
- **I have a few reservations about** the book
  = *tengo ciertas reservas acerca de*
- The judges are expected to endorse the recommendation, but **it is by no means certain that** they will make up their minds today
  = *no hay ninguna seguridad de que*
- **It is questionable whether** media coverage of terrorist organizations actually affects terrorism
  = *es discutible que*
- **This raises the whole question of** exactly when men and women should retire
  = *esto plantea la cuestión de*
- The crisis **puts a question mark against** the Prime Minister's stated commitment to intervention
  = *abre un interrogante acerca de*
- **Both these claims are true up to a point** and they need to be made. But they are limited in their significance
  = *ambas afirmaciones son ciertas hasta cierto punto*

Para mostrarse de acuerdo

Véase también la sección 38 ACUERDO

- **I agree wholeheartedly with** the opinion that smacking should be outlawed
  = *coincido totalmente con*
- **One must acknowledge that** their history will make change more painful
  = *hay que reconocer que*

- **It cannot be denied that** there are similarities between the two approaches
  = *no se puede negar que*
- Courtney - **rightly in my view** - is strongly critical of the snobbery and élitism that is all too evident in these circles
  = *pienso que con toda la razón*
- Preaching was considered an important activity, **and rightly so** in a country with a high illiteracy rate
  = *y con mayor razón*
- You may dispute the Pope's right to tell people how to live their lives, **but it is hard to disagree with** his picture of modern society
  = *pero es difícil no coincidir con*

Para mostrarse en desacuerdo

Véase también la sección 39 DESACUERDO

- **I must disagree with** Gordon's article on criminality: it is dangerous to suggest that to be a criminal one must look like a criminal
  = *debo mostrar mi desacuerdo con*
- As a former teacher **I find it hard to believe that** there is no link at all between screen violence and violence on the streets
  = *me cuesta creer que*
- The strength of their feelings **is scarcely credible**
  = *es poco verosímil*
- Her claim to have been the first to discover the phenomenon **lacks credibility**
  = *carece de toda credibilidad*
- Nevertheless, **I remain unconvinced by** Milton
  = *... sigue sin convencerme*
- Many do not believe that water contains anything remotely dangerous. Sadly, **this is far from the truth**
  = *dista mucho de ser cierto*
- To say that everyone requires the same amount of a vitamin is as stupid as saying we all have blonde hair and blue eyes. **It simply isn't true**
  = *sencillamente no es cierto*
- His remarks **were** not only highly offensive to black and other ethnic minorities but **totally inaccurate**
  = *totalmente erróneos*
- Stomach ulcers are often associated with good living and a fast-moving lifestyle. **(But) in reality** there is no evidence to support this theory
  = *pero en realidad*
- This version of a political economy **does not stand up to close scrutiny**
  = *no resiste un análisis pormenorizado*

Para resaltar uno de los argumentos

- Nowadays, **there is clearly** less stigma attached to unmarried mothers
  = *está claro que hay*
- Evidence shows that ..., so once again **the facts speak for themselves**
  = *los hechos hablan por sí solos*
- **Few will argue with the principle that** such a fund should be set up
  = *apenas hay quien discuta el principio*
- Hyams **supports this claim** by looking at sentences produced by young children learning German
  = *apoya esta afirmación*
- **The most important thing is to** reach agreement from all sides
  = *lo más importante es*
- Perhaps **the most important aspect of** cognition is the ability to manipulate symbols
  = *el aspecto más importante de*

Para destacar un punto en concreto

- **It would be impossible to exaggerate the importance of** these two volumes for anyone with a serious interest in the development of black gospel music
  = *no se puede exagerar la importancia de*
- The symbolic importance of Jerusalem for both Palestinians and Jews **is almost impossible to overemphasize**
  = *nunca se insistirá demasiado en*
- **It is important to be clear that** Jesus does not identify himself with Yahweh
  = *es importante dejar claro que*
- **It is significant that** Mandalay seems to have become the central focus in this debate
  = *resulta revelador que*
- **It should not be forgotten that** many of those now in exile were close to the centre of power until only one year ago
  = *no hay que olvidar que*
- **It should be stressed that** the only way pet owners could possibly contract such a condition from their pets is by eating them
  = *habría que recalcar que*
- **There is a very important point here and that is that** the accused claims that he was with Ms Martins all evening on the night of the crime
  = *lo que resulta importante aquí es que*
- At the beginning of his book Mr Stone **makes a telling point**. The Balkan peoples, he notes, are for the first time ...
  = *hace un comentario revelador*
- Suspicion is **the chief feature of** Britain's attitude to European theatre
  = *el rasgo primordial de*
- **In order to focus attention on** Hobson's distinctive contributions to macroeconomics, these wider issues are neglected here
  = *con objeto de centrarnos en*
- **These statements are interesting in that** they illustrate different views
  = *estas afirmaciones son interesantes porque*

ENGLISH~SPANISH DICTIONARY

DICCIONARIO INGLÉS~ESPAÑOL

A a

A, a[1] [eɪ] Ⓐ N [1] (= *letter*) A, a *f*; **A for Andrew** A de Antonio; **to get from A to B** ir de A a B; **No. 32A** (= *house*) núm. 32 bis, núm. 32 duplicado; **the A-Z of Management Techniques** el manual básico de Técnicas de Gestión, Técnicas de Gestión de la A a la Z; ✦***IDIOM*** **to know sth from A to Z** conocer algo de pe a pa *or* de cabo a rabo
[2] (*Mus*) **A** la *m*; **A major/minor** la mayor/menor; **A sharp/flat** la sostenido/bemol
[3] (*Scol*) sobresaliente *m*
Ⓑ CPD ► **A level** N ABBR (*Brit Scol*) (= **Advanced level**) ≈ bachillerato *m*; **to take three A levels** presentarse como candidato en tres asignaturas de *A level*; **she has an A level in chemistry** tiene un título de *A level* en química ► **A road** N (*Brit*) ≈ carretera *f* nacional ► **"A" shares** NPL acciones *fpl* de clase A ► **A side** N [*of record*] cara *f* A ► **A to Z**® N (= *map book*) callejero *m*

A LEVELS

Al terminar la educación secundaria obligatoria, los estudiantes de Inglaterra, Gales e Irlanda del Norte pueden estudiar otros dos años para preparar dos o tres asignaturas más y examinarse de ellas a los 18 años. Estos exámenes se conocen con el nombre de ***A levels*** *o* ***Advanced levels****. Cada universidad determina el número de* ***A levels*** *y la calificación necesaria para acceder a ella.*
En Escocia los exámenes equivalentes son los ***Highers*** *o* ***Higher Grades****, que se hacen de unas cinco asignaturas tras un año de estudios. Después se puede optar entre entrar en la universidad directamente o estudiar otro año más, bien para hacer el mismo examen de otras asignaturas, o para sacar los* ***CSYS****, abreviatura de* ***Certificate of Sixth Year Studies****.*
⇨ *Ver tb* GCSE

a[2] [eɪ, ə] INDEF ART (*before vowel or silent h* **an** [æn, ən, n]) [1] un(a) *m/f*; (+ *fem noun starting with stressed* **a** *or* **ha**) un; **a book** un libro; **an apple** una manzana; **a soul** un alma; **an eagle** un águila; **an axe** un hacha
[2] (*article often omitted in translation*) [2·1] (*with professions*) **he is an engineer** es ingeniero; **I am not a doctor** yo no soy médico; BUT **he's a brilliant scientist** es un excelente científico; **that child's a thief!** ¡ese niño es un ladrón!
[2·2] (*after* **tener/buscar** *if singular object the norm*) **I have a wife and six children** tengo mujer y seis hijos; **have you got a passport?** ¿tiene usted pasaporte?; **I haven't got a car** no tengo coche; **she's looking for a secretary** busca secretaria; BUT **she has a daughter** tiene una hija; **they have a lovely house** tienen una casa preciosa; → LOOK FOR
[2·3] (*after negatives*) **you don't stand a chance** no tienes posibilidad alguna; **without a doubt** sin duda; **without saying a word** sin decir palabra
[2·4] (*in expressions*) **half an hour** media hora; **a fine excuse!** ¡bonita disculpa!; **what an idiot!** ¡qué idiota!; **a hundred pounds** cien libras; **a drink would be nice** me gustaría algo de beber
[2·5] (*apposition*) **Patrick, a lecturer at Glasgow University, says that ...** Patrick, profesor de la Universidad de Glasgow, dice que ...; BUT **the Duero, a Spanish river** el Duero, un río español
[3] (= *a certain*) un(a) tal; **a Mr Smith called to see you** vino a verte un tal señor Smith
[4] (= *each, per*) por; **two apples a head** dos manzanas por persona; **£80 a week** 80 libras por semana; **50 kilometres an hour** 50 kilómetros por hora; BUT **30 pence a kilo** 30 peniques el kilo; **once a week/three times a month** una vez a la semana/tres veces al mes

A. ABBR (= **answer**) R

a. ABBR = **acre**

a... PREFIX a...; **atonal** atonal; **atypical** atípico

a- PREFIX (†† *or dial*) **everyone came a-running** todos acudieron corriendo; **it was a-snowing hard** estaba nevando mucho

A1 [ˈeɪˈwʌn] ADJ de primera clase, de primera categoría; **to feel A1** estar muy bien

A3 [ˈeɪˈθriː] ADJ **A3 paper** ◊ **A3-size paper** papel *m* tamaño A3, doble folio *m*

A4 [ˈeɪˈfɔː] ADJ **A4 paper** ◊ **A4-size paper** papel *m* tamaño A4, papel *m* tamaño folio, folios *mpl*

AA N ABBR [1] (= **Alcoholics Anonymous**) A.A.
[2] (*Brit*) (= **Automobile Association**) ≈ RACE *m*
[3] (*US Univ*) = **Associate in Arts**
[4] (*Mil*) = **anti-aircraft**

AAA N ABBR [1] = **Amateur Athletics Association**
[2] (*US*) (= **American Automobile Association**) ≈ RACE *m*

Aachen [ˈɑːxən] N Aquisgrán *m*

AAF N ABBR = **American Air Force**

AAIB N ABBR (*Brit*) = **Air Accident Investigation Branch**

AAM N ABBR = **air-to-air missile**

A&E [ˌeɪənˈdiː] N ABBR (= **Accident and Emergency**) ≈ Urgencias *fpl*

AAR ABBR = **against all risks**

aardvark [ˈɑːdvɑːk] N (*Zool*) cerdo *m* hormiguero

Aaron [ˈɛərən] N Aarón

AAU N ABBR (*US*) = **Amateur Athletic Union**

AAUP N ABBR (*US Univ*) = **American Association of University Professors**

AB ABBR [1] (*Naut*) = **able(-bodied) seaman**
[2] (*US Univ*) (= **Bachelor of Arts**) Lic. en Fil. y Let.
[3] (*Canada*) = **Alberta**

ABA N ABBR [1] = **Amateur Boxing Association**
[2] (*US*) = **American Bankers Association**
[3] (*US*) = **American Bar Association**

aback [əˈbæk] ADV **to take ~** desconcertar, sorprender; **to be taken ~** quedarse desconcertado, sorprenderse; **I was quite taken ~ by the news** la noticia me causó gran sorpresa, la noticia me dejó desconcertado

abacus [ˈæbəkəs] N (*pl* **abacuses, abaci** [ˈæbəsaɪ]) ábaco *m*

abaft [əˈbɑːft] (*Naut*) Ⓐ ADV a popa, en popa
Ⓑ PREP detrás de

abalone [ˌæbəˈləʊnɪ] N oreja *f* marina

abandon [əˈbændən] Ⓐ VT [1] (= *desert*) [+ *car, family*] abandonar, dejar; **to ~ sb to his fate** abandonar a algn a su suerte; **~ ship!** ¡evacuar el barco!
[2] (= *give up*) [+ *plan, attempt*] renunciar a; [+ *game*] anular; **the game was ~ed after 20 minutes' play** después de 20 minutos de juego se anuló el partido; **~ all hope ye who ...** abandonad toda esperanza aquellos que ...; **to ~ o.s. to sth** entregarse *or* abandonarse a algo
Ⓑ N **to dance with wild ~** bailar desenfrenadamente; *see also* **gay A3**

abandoned [əˈbændənd] ADJ [1] (= *deserted*) [*house, building*] abandonado, desierto; [*child*] abandonado, desamparado; [*vehicle, pet*] abandonado
[2] (= *unrestrained*) [*manner*] desinhibido, desenfrenado; **in an ~ fashion** con abandono, desenfrenadamente
[3] (†) (= *dissolute*) **an ~ woman** una mujer perdida *or* de conducta dudosa

abandonment [əˈbændənmənt] N [1] (= *state*) abandono *m*; (= *act*) acto *m* de desamparar, el abandonar
[2] (*moral*) = **abandon B**

abase [əˈbeɪs] VT [+ *person*] humillar, rebajar; **to ~ o.s. (so far as to** + INFIN**)** rebajarse (hasta el punto de + *infin*)

abasement [əˈbeɪsmənt] N (= *humiliation*) humillación *f*, degradación *f*; (= *moral decay*) depravación *f*, envilecimiento *m*

abashed [əˈbæʃt] ADJ (= *shy*) tímido, retraído; (= *ashamed*) avergonzado; **to be ~ at sth** avergonzarse de algo; **he carried on not a bit ~** siguió como si tal cosa

abate [əˈbeɪt] Ⓐ VI [*wind, storm*] amainar; [*fever*] bajar; [*flood*] retirarse, bajar; [*noise*] disminuir; [*anger*] aplacarse; [*pain, symptoms*] remi-

tir; [*enthusiasm*] moderarse; **inflationary pressures are abating** ceden *or* remiten las presiones inflacionistas
Ⓑ VT (*Jur*) [+ *noise, pollution*] (= *eliminate*) eliminar; (= *reduce*) disminuir

abatement [ə'beɪtmənt] N [1] (= *reduction*) [*of wind, storm*] amaine *m*; [*of fever, flood*] bajada *f*; [*of anger*] aplacamiento *m*; [*of enthusiasm*] moderación *f*; [*of pain, symptoms*] remisión *f*
[2] (*Jur*) [*of noise, pollution*] (= *elimination*) eliminación *f*; (= *reduction*) disminución *f*, moderación *f*

abattoir ['æbətwɑːʳ] N matadero *m*

abbacy ['æbəsɪ] N abadía *f*

abbé ['æbeɪ] N abate *m*

abbess ['æbɪs] N abadesa *f*

abbey ['æbɪ] Ⓐ N abadía *f*; **Westminster Abbey** la Abadía de Westminster
Ⓑ CPD ► **abbey church** N iglesia *f* abacial, iglesia *f* de abadía

abbot ['æbət] N abad *m*

abbr., **abbrev.** ABBR = **abbreviation, abbreviated**

abbreviate [ə'briːvɪeɪt] VT abreviar

abbreviation [ə,briːvɪ'eɪʃən] N [1] (= *short form*) abreviatura *f*
[2] (= *act of shortening*) abreviación *f*

ABC ['eɪbiː'siː] N ABBR [1] (= *alphabet*) abecé *m*; **it's as easy** *or* **simple as ~*** es coser y cantar*, es facilísimo; **the ~ of Politics** (*as title*) el Abecé de la Política
[2] (*US*) = **American Broadcasting Company**
[3] (*Australia*) = **Australian Broadcasting Commission**

abdicate ['æbdɪkeɪt] Ⓐ VT [1] [+ *throne*] abdicar
[2] [+ *responsibility, right*] renunciar a
Ⓑ VI abdicar (**in favour of** en, en favor de)

abdication [,æbdɪ'keɪʃən] N [1] [*of monarch*] abdicación *f*
[2] [*of responsibility, right*] renuncia *f* (**of** a)

abdomen ['æbdəmen, (*Med*) æb'dəʊmen] N (*Anat*) abdomen *m*, vientre *m*; [*of insect*] abdomen *m*

abdominal [æb'dɒmɪnl] Ⓐ ADJ abdominal
Ⓑ N **abdominals** (= *muscles*) abdominales *mpl*

abducent [æb'djuːsənt] ADJ abductor

abduct [æb'dʌkt] VT raptar, secuestrar

abduction [æb'dʌkʃən] N rapto *m*, secuestro *m*

abductor [æb'dʌktəʳ] N raptor(a) *m/f*, secuestrador(a) *m/f*

abed†† [ə'bed] ADV en cama, acostado

Aberdonian [,æbə'dəʊnɪən] Ⓐ ADJ de Aberdeen
Ⓑ N nativo/a *m/f* de Aberdeen, habitante *mf* de Aberdeen

aberrant [ə'berənt] ADJ (*Bio*) aberrante; [*behaviour*] anormal

aberration [,æbe'reɪʃən] N aberración *f*; **mental ~** enajenación *f* mental

abet [ə'bet] VT [+ *criminal*] incitar; [+ *crime*] instigar; **to ~ sb in a crime** ser cómplice de algn en un delito; *see also* **aid 2**

abetment [ə'betmənt] N incitación *f*, instigación *f*; (*Jur*) complicidad *f*

abetter, **abettor** [ə'betəʳ] N instigador(a) *m/f*, fautor(a) *m/f*; (*esp Jur*) cómplice *mf*

abeyance [ə'beɪəns] N **to be in ~** estar en desuso; **to fall into ~** caer en desuso

abhor [əb'hɔːʳ] VT aborrecer, abominar

abhorrence [əb'hɒrəns] N [1] (= *feeling*) aborrecimiento *m*, repugnancia *f*; **violence fills me with ~** aborrezco la violencia; **to hold in ~** aborrecer, detestar
[2] (= *object*) abominación *f*

abhorrent [əb'hɒrənt] ADJ aborrecible, detestable; **it's totally ~ to me** lo detesto totalmente

abide [ə'baɪd] (*pt, pp* **abode** *or* **abided**) Ⓐ VT (*neg only*) aguantar, soportar; **I can't ~ him** no lo aguanto *or* soporto, no lo puedo ver; **I can't ~ a coward** aborrezco los cobardes; **I can't ~ tea** me da asco el té
Ⓑ VI (†) (= *dwell*) morar; (= *stay*) permanecer, continuar

►**abide by** VI + PREP [+ *rules*] atenerse a, obrar de acuerdo con; [+ *promise*] cumplir con; [+ *decision*] respetar, atenerse a; [+ *rules of competition*] ajustarse a, aceptar

abiding [ə'baɪdɪŋ] ADJ (*liter*) permanente, perdurable

ability [ə'bɪlɪtɪ] N [1] (= *capacity*) aptitud *f*, capacidad *f*; **~ to pay** solvencia *f*, recursos *mpl*; **his ~ in French** su aptitud para el francés; **to the best of my ~** lo mejor que pueda *or* sepa; **my ~ to do it depends on ...** el que yo lo haga depende de ...
[2] (= *talent*) **a boy of ~** un chico de talento; **he has great ~** tiene un gran talento (**for** para); **abilities** talento *m*, dotes *fpl*

ab initio [,æbɪ'nɪʃɪəʊ] Ⓐ ADV ab initio, desde el principio
Ⓑ ADJ **~ learner** principiante *mf*

abiotic [,eɪbaɪ'ɒtɪk] ADJ abiótico

abject ['æbdʒekt] ADJ [1] (= *wretched*) [*condition*] deplorable; [*state*] lamentable; **England's ~ performance in the World Cup** la pésima actuación de Inglaterra en el Mundial
[2] (= *grovelling*) sumiso; **an ~ slave to fashion** un esclavo sumiso de la moda; **he sounded ~** su tono era sumiso y arrepentido; **we received an ~ apology from the travel company** recibimos una carta de la agencia de viajes deshaciéndose en disculpas
[3] (*as intensifier*) [*misery, failure*] absoluto; [*stupidity*] supino; [*cowardice*] abyecto, vil (*liter*); [*surrender*] indigno; **to live in ~ poverty** vivir en la miseria más absoluta

abjectly ['æbdʒektlɪ] ADV [*fail*] de la forma más indigna, miserablemente; **he apologized ~** se deshizo en disculpas; **~ miserable** sumamente desgraciado; **to be ~ poor** vivir en la miseria más absoluta

abjectness ['æbdʒektnɪs] N [1] (= *wretchedness*) [*of conditions*] lo miserable; [*of position*] lo indigno; **the ~ of the conditions in which they live** lo miserable de las condiciones en que viven; **we were shocked at the ~ of their performance** nos dejo horrorizados lo mal que lo hicieron
[2] (= *grovelling quality*) **the ~ of his apology** el tono sumiso y arrepentido de su disculpa

abjure [əb'dʒʊəʳ] VT (*frm*) renunciar a, abjurar de

Abkhaz [æb'kɑːz], **Abkhazi** [æb'kɑːzɪ], **Abkhazian** [æb'kɑːzɪən] Ⓐ ADJ abjasio
Ⓑ N (*pl* **Abkhaz**) [1] (= *person*) abjasio/a *m/f*
[2] (*Ling*) abjasio *m*

Abkhazia [æb'kɑːzɪə] N Abjazia *f*

ablative ['æblətɪv] (*Ling*) Ⓐ ADJ ablativo
Ⓑ N (*also* **~ case**) ablativo *m*; **in the ~** en ablativo
Ⓒ CPD ► **ablative absolute** N ablativo *m* absoluto

ablaze [ə'bleɪz] ADV [1] (= *on fire*) en llamas, ardiendo; **the cinema was ~ in five minutes** en cinco minutos el cine estaba en llamas *or* ardiendo; **to set sth ~** prender fuego a algo
[2] (*fig*) **the house was ~ with light** la casa resplandecía de luz; **the garden was ~ with colour** el jardín resplandecía de color; **to be ~ with indignation** estar indignadísimo *or* encolerizado

able ['eɪbl] Ⓐ ADJ [1] **to be ~ to do sth** (*of acquired skills*) saber hacer algo; (*other contexts*) poder hacer algo; **the child isn't ~ to walk (yet)** el niño no sabe andar (todavía); **he's not ~ to walk** no puede andar; **come as soon as you are ~** ven en cuanto puedas; **I was eventually ~ to escape** por fin pude escaparme, por fin logré escaparme; **~ to pay** solvente
[2] (= *capable*) [*person*] capaz; [*piece of work*] sólido; **she is one of our ~st pupils** es una de nuestras alumnas más capaces
Ⓑ CPD ► **able seaman** N marinero *m* de primera *or* patentado

ABLE, CAN

Poder and **saber** can both translate **to be able to**, **can** and **could**.

Skills

- Use **saber** when **to be able to**, **can** and **could** mean "know how to":
  Can you type?
  ¿Sabes escribir a máquina?
  His wife couldn't drive
  Su mujer no sabía conducir

Other contexts

- Generally, use **poder**:
  He can stay here
  Puede quedarse aquí
  We have not been able to persuade them
  No hemos podido convencerlos

NOTE: When **can** and **could** are followed by **find** or a verb of perception - **see**, **hear**, **feel**, **taste** or **smell** - they are usually not translated:
  I can't find it
  No lo encuentro
  What can you see?
  ¿Qué ves?

Alternatives to "poder"

- When **to be able** means "to be capable of", you can often use **ser capaz de** as an alternative to **poder**:
  I don't think he'll be able to resist it
  No creo que sea capaz de *or* ***pueda resistirlo***

For further uses and examples, see main entries at ***able*** *and* ***can.***

...able SUFFIX ...able

able-bodied ['eɪbl'bɒdɪd] Ⓐ ADJ sano
Ⓑ CPD ► **able-bodied seaman** N marinero *m* de primera, marinero *m* patentado

ablution [ə'bluːʃən] N [1] (*Rel*) ablución *f*; **to perform one's ~s** (*hum*) lavarse; **to be at one's ~s** (*hum*) estar en el lavabo
[2] **ablutions** (*Mil**) servicios *mpl*

ably ['eɪblɪ] ADV hábilmente, con mucha habilidad; **~ assisted by** hábilmente ayudado por, con la experta colaboración de

ABM N ABBR = **anti-ballistic missile**

abnegate ['aebnɪgeɪt] VT (*frm*) [+ *responsibility*] eludir, rehuir; [+ *one's religion*] abjurar; **to ~ one's rights** renunciar a sus derechos

abnegation [,æbnɪ'geɪʃən] N (*frm*) abnegación *f*

abnormal [æb'nɔːməl] ADJ anormal; [*shape*] irregular

abnormality [,æbnɔː'mælɪtɪ] N (= *condition*) anormalidad *f*; (= *instance*) anormalidad *f*, desviación *f*

abnormally [æbˈnɔːməlɪ] ADV 1 irregularmente; **an ~ formed bone** un hueso de formación anormal
2 (= *exceptionally*) de modo anormal, anormalmente; **an ~ large sum** una cantidad descomunal

Abo** [ˈæbəʊ] N (*Australia pej*) = **aborigine**

aboard [əˈbɔːd] Ⓐ ADV (*Naut*) a bordo; **to go ~** embarcar, subir a bordo; **to take ~** embarcar, cargar; **all ~!** (*Rail*) ¡viajeros, al tren!; **life ~ is pleasant** es agradable la vida de a bordo
Ⓑ PREP **~ the ship** a bordo del barco; **~ the train** en el tren

abode [əˈbəʊd] Ⓐ PT, PP *of* **abide**
Ⓑ N (*esp Jur*) morada *f*, domicilio *m*; **place of ~** domicilio *m*; **right of ~** derecho *m* a domiciliarse; **of no fixed ~** sin domicilio fijo; **to take up one's ~** domiciliarse, establecerse

abolish [əˈbɒlɪʃ] VT abolir, suprimir

abolishment [əˈbɒlɪʃmənt] N = **abolition**

abolition [ˌæbəʊˈlɪʃən] N abolición *f*, supresión *f*

abolitionist [ˌæbəʊˈlɪʃənɪst] N (*Hist*) abolicionista *mf*

A-bomb [ˈeɪbɒm] N ABBR (= **atom(ic) bomb**) bomba *f* atómica

abominable [əˈbɒmɪnəbl] Ⓐ ADJ abominable, detestable; [*taste, workmanship*] detestable, pésimo
Ⓑ CPD ► **the abominable snowman** N el abominable hombre de las nieves

abominably [əˈbɒmɪnəblɪ] ADV abominablemente, pésimamente; **to behave ~** comportarse abominablemente *or* pésimamente; **he writes ~** escribe pésimamente; **to be ~ rude to sb** ser terriblemente grosero con algn

abominate [əˈbɒmɪneɪt] VT (*frm*) abominar (de), detestar

abomination [əˌbɒmɪˈneɪʃən] N 1 (= *feeling*) aversión *f*
2 (= *detestable act, thing*) escándalo *m*

aboriginal [ˌæbəˈrɪdʒənl] Ⓐ ADJ aborigen, indígena
Ⓑ N aborigen *mf*, indígena *mf*

aborigine [ˌæbəˈrɪdʒɪnɪ] N aborigen *mf* australiano/a

abort [əˈbɔːt] Ⓐ VI 1 (*Med*) abortar
2 (*Comput*) abandonar
3 (= *fail*) [*plan, project, negotiations*] fracasar, malograrse
Ⓑ VT 1 (*Med*) abortar; **~ed foetuses** *or* (*US*) **fetuses** fetos *mpl* de abortos
2 (= *abandon*) [+ *mission, operation*] suspender; [+ *deal, agreement*] anular; [+ *plan*] abandonar; [+ *landing, takeoff*] abortar
3 (= *cause to fail*) malograr; **the bad weather ~ed plans for an air display** el mal tiempo malogró los planes de llevar a cabo una exhibición aérea
4 (*Comput*) abandonar

abortifacient [əˌbɔːtɪˈfeɪʃənt] Ⓐ ADJ abortivo
Ⓑ N abortivo *m*

abortion [əˈbɔːʃən] Ⓐ N 1 (*Med*) 1·1 (= *termination*) aborto *m* (provocado); **illegal ~** aborto *m* ilegal; **to have an ~** hacerse un aborto, abortar (*no de forma espontánea*); **to perform** *or* **carry out an ~** practicar un aborto
1·2 (*frm*) (*also* **spontaneous ~**) aborto *m* (espontáneo)
2 (*) (= *failure*) fracaso *m*, malogro *m*
Ⓑ CPD ► **abortion clinic** N clínica *f* donde se practican abortos ► **abortion law** N ley *f* del aborto ► **abortion pill** N píldora *f* abortiva

abortionist [əˈbɔːʃənɪst] N abortista *mf*

abortive [əˈbɔːtɪv] ADJ 1 (= *failed*) [*attempt, plan*] fracasado, frustrado
2 (*Med*) [*method, medicine*] abortivo

abortively [əˈbɔːtɪvlɪ] ADV [*try, attempt*] en vano; **the negotiations ended ~** las negociaciones fracasaron

abound [əˈbaʊnd] VI (= *exist in great quantity*) abundar; **to ~ in** *or* **with** (= *have in great quantity*) estar lleno de, abundar en

about [əˈbaʊt]

*When **about** is an element in a phrasal verb, eg **bring about, come about, turn about, wander about**, look up the verb.*

Ⓐ ADV 1 (= *approximately*) más o menos, aproximadamente, alrededor de; **~ £20** unas 20 libras, 20 libras más o menos; **there were ~ 25 guests** había unos 25 invitados, había como 25 invitados (*esp LAm*); **~ seven years ago** hace unos siete años; **at ~ two o'clock** a eso de las dos, sobre las dos; **it's ~ two o'clock** son las dos, más o menos; **he must be ~ 40** tendrá alrededor de 40 años; **that's ~ all I could find** eso es más o menos todo lo que podía encontrar; **that's ~ it** eso es(, más o menos); **it's just ~ finished** está casi terminado; **that's ~ right** eso es(, más o menos); **he's ~ the same** sigue más o menos igual; **it's ~ time you stopped** ya es hora de que lo dejes
2 (*place*) **is anyone ~?** ¿hay alguien?; **is Mr Brown ~?** ¿está por aquí el Sr. Brown?; **to be ~ again** (*after illness*) estar levantado; **we were ~ early** nos levantamos temprano; **all ~** (= *everywhere*) por todas partes; **there's a lot of measles ~** hay mucho sarampión, está dando el sarampión; **there isn't much money ~** hay poco dinero, la gente tiene poco dinero; **to run ~** correr por todas partes; **he must be ~ somewhere** debe de andar por aquí; **there's a thief ~** por aquí anda un ladrón; **to walk ~** pasearse
3 **to be ~ to do sth** estar a punto de *or* (*LAm*) por hacer algo; **nobody is ~ to sell it** nadie tiene la más mínima intención de venderlo; **I'm not ~ to do all that for nothing** no pienso hacer todo eso gratis
Ⓑ PREP 1 (= *relating to*) de, acerca de, sobre; **a book ~ gardening** un libro de jardinería, un libro sobre la jardinería; **I can tell you nothing ~ him** no le puedo decir nada acerca de él; **I'm phoning ~ tomorrow's meeting** llamo por la reunión de mañana; **they fell out ~ money** riñeron por cuestión de dinero; **~ the other night, I didn't mean what I said** respecto a la otra noche, no iba en serio cuando dije esas cosas; **do something ~ it!** ¡haz algo!; **there's nothing I can do ~ it** no puedo hacer nada al respecto; **how** *or* **what ~ this one?** ¿qué te parece éste?; **he was chosen out of 200, how** *or* **what ~ that!** entre 200 lo eligieron a él, ¡quién lo diria! *or* ¡fijate!; **how** *or* **what ~ coming with us?** ¿por qué no vienes con nosotros?; **how** *or* **what ~ a drink?** ¿vamos a tomar una copa?; **how** *or* **what ~ a song?** ¿por qué no nos cantas algo?; **how** *or* **what ~ it?** (= *what do you say?*) ¿qué te parece?; (= *what of it?*) ¿y qué?; **how** *or* **what ~ me?** y yo, ¿qué?; **what's that book ~?** ¿de qué trata ese libro?; **what did she talk ~?** ¿de qué habló?; **what's all this noise ~?** ¿a qué se debe todo este ruido?; **"I want to talk to you" — "what ~?"** — quiero hablar contigo —¿acerca de qué?
2 (= *particular to*) **there's something ~ him (that I like)** tiene un no sé qué (que me gusta); **there's something ~ a soldier** los soldados tienen un no sé qué; **he had a mysterious air ~ him** tenía un cierto aire misterioso; **there's something odd ~ it** aquí hay algo raro
3 (= *doing*) **while you're ~ it can you get me a beer?** ya que estás en ello ¿me traes una cerveza?; **and while I'm ~ it I'll talk to your father** y de paso hablaré con tu padre; **you've been a long time ~ it** has tardado bastante en hacerlo; *see also* **go about**
4 (= *intending*) **I can't imagine what he was ~ when he did that** no entiendo lo que pretendía con eso
5 (= *around*) **to do jobs ~ the house** (= *repairs*) hacer arreglos en la casa; **I had no money ~ me** no llevaba dinero encima; **he looked ~ him** miró a su alrededor; **somewhere ~ here** por aquí cerca; **to wander ~ the town** deambular por la ciudad

about-face [əˌbaʊtˈfeɪs] N, VI = **about-turn**

about-turn [əˌbaʊtˈtɜːn] Ⓐ N 1 (*Mil*) media vuelta *f*
2 (*fig*) cambio *m* radical de postura, giro *m* (brusco)
Ⓑ VI 1 (*Mil*) dar media vuelta
2 (*fig*) cambiar radicalmente de postura

above [əˈbʌv]

*When **above** is an element in a phrasal verb, eg **get above**, look up the verb.*

Ⓐ ADV 1 (= *overhead*) arriba; **seen from ~** visto desde arriba; **the flat ~** el piso de arriba
2 (*referring to heaven*) **from ~** del cielo, de lo alto; **God, who is in heaven ~** Dios en las alturas, Dios que vive en el reino de los cielos; **the gods ~** los dioses en las alturas
3 (*in status*) de más categoría; **those ~** los de más categoría; **orders from ~** órdenes *fpl* superiores *or* de arriba
4 (*in text*) arriba, más arriba; **see ~** véase (más) arriba; **as set out ~** según lo arriba expuesto; **as I said ~** como ya he dicho
5 (= *more*) **boys of five and ~** los niños mayores de cinco años; **seats are available at £5 and ~** las entradas cuestan a partir de 5 libras
Ⓑ PREP 1 (= *higher than, over*) encima de; **there was a picture ~ the fireplace** había un cuadro encima de la chimenea; **~ the clouds** encima de las nubes; **~ ground: they were trapped 150ft ~ ground** estaban atrapados a una altura de 150 pies sobre el nivel del suelo; **vegetables that grow ~ ground** las verduras que crecen en la superficie; **2,000 metres ~ sea level** 2.000 metros sobre el nivel del mar; **I couldn't hear ~ the din** no podía oír con tanto ruido
2 (= *upstream of*) **the Thames ~ London** el Támesis más arriba de Londres
3 (*of rank*) **he is ~ me in rank** tiene una categoría superior a la mía, tiene un rango superior al mío; *see also* **station A4**; (*of priority*) **~ all** sobre todo; **he values honesty ~ all else** ante todo valora la honestidad; **he was, ~ all else, a musician** era, ante todo, un músico
4 (= *morally superior*) **he's ~ that sort of thing** está muy por encima de esas cosas; **he's not ~ a bit of blackmail** es capaz hasta del chantaje; **to get ~ o.s.** pasarse (de listo)
5 (= *beyond*) **it's ~ me** es demasiado complicado para mí
6 (*numbers*) más de, superior a; **there were not ~ 40 people** no había más de 40 personas; **any number ~ 12** cualquier número superior a 12; **she can't count ~ ten** no sabe contar más allá de diez; **children ~ seven years of age** los niños mayores de siete años; **temperatures ~ 40 degrees** temperaturas *fpl* por encima de los 40 grados; **temperatures well ~ normal** temperaturas *fpl* muy

superiores a las normales; **wage rises of 3% ~ inflation** aumentos *mpl* de sueldo de un 3% por encima del nivel de inflación; *see also* **average B**
Ⓒ ADJ [*fact, place*] sobredicho, arriba mencionado; [*photo, illustration*] de arriba
Ⓓ N **the ~ is a photo of ...** lo anterior *or* lo que se ve arriba es una foto de ...; **please translate the ~** por favor traduzca lo anterior

above-board [ə'bʌv'bɔːd] Ⓐ ADV abiertamente, sin rebozo
Ⓑ ADJ legítimo, honrado

above-mentioned [ə'bʌv'menʃənd] ADJ [*fact, point, place*] sobredicho, arriba mencionado; [*person*] susodicho

above-named [ə'bʌv'neɪmd] ADJ = **above-mentioned**

Abp ABBR (= **Archbishop**) Arz., Arzpo.

abracadabra [ˌabrəkə'dæbrə] N abracadabra *m*

abrade [ə'breɪd] VT (*frm*) raer, raspar

Abraham ['eɪbrəhæm] N Abrahán, Abraham

abrasion [ə'breɪʒən] N (= *act, injury*) abrasión *f*, escoriación *f*

abrasive [ə'breɪsɪv] Ⓐ ADJ 1 [*substance, surface*] abrasivo
2 (*fig*) [*personality*] desabrido, brusco; [*tone*] áspero, desabrido
Ⓑ N abrasivo *m*

abrasively [ə'breɪsɪvlɪ] ADV [*say, reply*] ásperamente, con tono áspero *or* desabrido

abrasiveness [ə'breɪsɪvnɪs] N 1 [*of surface, substance*] lo abrasivo
2 (*fig*) [*of person, tone*] torpeza *f*, desabrimiento *m*

abreaction [ˌæbrɪ'ækʃən] N (*Psych*) abreacción *f*

abreast [ə'brest] ADV 1 (= *side by side*) **to march four ~** marchar en columna de cuatro en fondo; **streets so narrow that two can barely walk ~** calles tan estrechas que dos personas difícilmente pueden andar hombro con hombro; **to come ~ of sth/sb** llegar a la altura de algo/algn
2 (= *aware of*) **to be/keep ~ of sth** estar/mantenerse al corriente de algo; **to keep ~ of the news** mantenerse al día *or* al corriente

abridge [ə'brɪdʒ] VT [+ *book*] resumir, compendiar; (= *cut short*) abreviar, acortar

abridged [ə'brɪdʒd] ADJ [*book*] resumido, compendiado

abridgement [ə'brɪdʒmənt] N 1 (= *shortened version*) resumen *m*, compendio *m*
2 (= *act*) abreviación *f*

abroad [ə'brɔːd] ADV 1 (= *in foreign country*) en el extranjero; **to live ~** vivir en el extranjero; **to go ~** ir al extranjero; **he had to go ~** (*fleeing*) tuvo que salir del país; **when the minister is ~** cuando el ministro está fuera del país; **our army ~** nuestro ejército en el extranjero; **our debts ~** nuestras deudas en el exterior; **troops brought in from ~** tropas traídas del extranjero
2 (*frm*) (= *about*) **there is a rumour ~ that ...** corre el rumor de que ...; **how did the news get ~?** ¿cómo se divulgó la noticia?
3 (†) (= *outside*) fuera; **there were not many ~ at that hour** había poca gente por las calles a aquella hora

abrogate ['æbrəʊgeɪt] VT (*frm*) abrogar

abrogation [ˌæbrəʊ'geɪʃən] N (*frm*) abrogación *f*

abrupt [ə'brʌpt] ADJ 1 (= *sudden*) [*change, rise*] brusco; [*departure*] repentino; [*resignation, dismissal*] repentino, súbito; **to come to an ~ end** terminar de repente; **to come to an ~ halt** *or* **stop** (*lit*) pararse bruscamente *or* en seco; (*fig*) terminarse de repente
2 (= *brusque*) [*person*] brusco, cortante; [*question*] brusco; [*comment, reply*] cortante; **he was ~ to the point of rudeness** estuvo tan brusco *or* cortante que resultaba hasta grosero; **he was very ~ with me** estuvo muy brusco *or* cortante conmigo; **I was taken aback by her ~ manner** me chocó su brusquedad
3 (= *steep*) [*hillside, precipice*] abrupto, escarpado

abruptly [ə'brʌptlɪ] ADV 1 (= *suddenly*) [*stop, end, leave*] bruscamente, repentinamente; [*brake*] bruscamente
2 (= *brusquely*) [*say, ask*] bruscamente
3 (= *steeply*) abruptamente; **a cliff rose ~ before them** frente a ellos se alzaba abruptamente un acantilado

abruptness [ə'brʌptnɪs] N 1 (= *suddenness*) lo repentino; **we were taken aback by the ~ of his departure** nos sorprendió lo repentino de su marcha; **we were shocked by the ~ of his dismissal** nos dejó horrorizados que lo despidieran tan de repente
2 (= *brusqueness*) brusquedad *f*
3 (= *steepness*) lo escarpado

ABS N ABBR (= **antilock braking system**) ABS *m*

abscess ['æbsɪs] N absceso *m*

abscond [əb'skɒnd] VI fugarse; (*with funds*) huir

absconder [əb'skɒndəʳ] N (*from prison*) fugitivo/a *m/f*, evadido/a *m/f*

absconding [əb'skɒndɪŋ] ADJ en fuga

abseil ['æbsaɪl] VI (*Brit Sport*) (*also* **~ down**) hacer rappel, bajar en la cuerda; **he ~ed down the rock** hizo rappel roca abajo

abseiling ['æbsaɪlɪŋ] N (*Brit Sport*) rappel *m*

absence ['æbsəns] N [*of person*] ausencia *f*; [*of thing*] falta *f*; **in the ~ of** [+ *person*] en ausencia de; [+ *thing*] a falta de; **after an ~ of three months** tras una ausencia de tres meses; **to be sentenced in one's ~** ser condenado en ausencia; **~ of mind** distracción *f*, despiste *m*; ✦*PROV* **~ makes the heart grow fonder** la ausencia es al amor lo que el viento al aire, que apaga el pequeño y aviva el grande

absent Ⓐ ['æbsənt] ADJ 1 (= *not present*) [*person, thing*] ausente; **"to ~ friends!"** (*toast*) "¡por los amigos ausentes!"; **to be ~** faltar (**from** a); **to be ~ from school** faltar al colegio; **he has been ~ from his desk for two weeks** lleva dos semanas sin aparecer por el despacho; **~ without leave** (*Mil*) ausente sin permiso; **to go ~ without leave** ausentarse sin permiso
2 (= *absent-minded*) ausente, distraído; **she was ~, preoccupied** estaba ausente *or* distraída, preocupada; **an ~ stare** una mirada ausente *or* distraída
3 (= *lacking*) **a spirit of compromise was noticeably ~ from the meeting** en la reunión la voluntad de llegar a un acuerdo brilló por su ausencia
Ⓑ [æb'sent] VT **to ~ o.s.** ausentarse (**from** de)

absentee [ˌæbsən'tiː] Ⓐ N (*from school, work*) ausente *mf*
Ⓑ CPD ► **absentee ballot** N (*US*) voto *m* por correo ► **absentee landlord** N propietario/a *m/f* absentista ► **absentee rate** N nivel *m* de absentismo

absenteeism [ˌæbsən'tiːɪzəm] N absentismo *m*

absently ['æbsəntlɪ] ADV distraídamente

absent-minded ['æbsənt'maɪndɪd] ADJ (*momentarily*) distraído, ausente; (*habitually*) despistado, distraído; **an ~ professor** un profesor despistado *or* distraído

absent-mindedly ['æbsənt'maɪndɪdlɪ] ADV distraídamente

absent-mindedness ['æbsənt'maɪndɪdnɪs] N (*momentary*) distracción *f*; (*habitual*) despiste *m*

absinth(e) ['æbsɪnθ] N 1 (= *drink*) absenta *f*
2 (*Bot*) ajenjo *m*

absolute ['æbsəluːt] Ⓐ ADJ 1 (= *complete, unqualified*) [*certainty, confidence, majority, need*] absoluto; [*support*] incondicional, total; [*refusal*] rotundo; [*prohibition, command*] terminante; [*proof*] irrefutable; [*denial*] rotundo, categórico; [*right*] incuestionable; **he's an ~ beginner** es un auténtico principiante; **it's an ~ fact that ...** es indiscutible el hecho de que ...; **the divorce was made ~** concedieron el divorcio por sentencia firme; **~ monopoly** monopolio *m* total; **it was the ~ truth, I promise** era la pura verdad, se lo prometo; **~ veto** veto *m* total
2 (= *unlimited*) [*power, monarch*] absoluto
3 (= *not relative*) [*value*] absoluto; **in ~ terms** en términos absolutos; **the quest for ~ truth** la búsqueda de la verdad absoluta
4 (*as intensifier*) [*liar, villain*] redomado; **the party was an ~ disaster** la fiesta fue un completo desastre; **it's an ~ disgrace** es una auténtica vergüenza; **it's the ~ end!** ¡es el colmo!; **she wore an expression of ~ hatred** la expresión de su cara estaba llena de odio; **the man's an ~ idiot** es completamente idiota; **it's ~ rubbish!** ¡es puro disparate!
5 (*Gram*) absoluto
Ⓑ N (*Philos*) **the ~** lo absoluto
Ⓒ CPD ► **absolute alcohol** N alcohol *m* puro ► **absolute liability** N (*Fin, Jur*) responsabilidad *f* total ► **absolute pitch** N (*Mus*) oído *m* absoluto; **to have ~ pitch** tener oído absoluto ► **absolute temperature** N temperatura *f* absoluta ► **absolute zero** N cero *m* absoluto

absolutely ['æbsəluːtlɪ] ADV 1 (= *completely*) [*clear, impossible, alone, untrue*] completamente, totalmente; [*hilarious, beautiful, wonderful*] realmente; [*exhausted, horrible*] totalmente; [*necessary*] absolutamente; **it's ~ boiling in here!** ¡aquí dentro hace un calor infernal!; **he's ~ delighted at being a father again** está contentísimo de volver a ser padre; **the food was ~ disgusting** la comida era verdaderamente asquerosa; **punctuality is ~ essential** la puntualidad es de vital importancia; **~ everybody** absolutamente todo el mundo; **~ everything** absolutamente todo; **I've looked ~ everywhere for it** lo he buscado absolutamente por todas partes; **your hands are ~ filthy** tienes las manos sucísimas *or* verdaderamente sucias; **it is ~ forbidden to** + INFIN queda terminantemente prohibido + *infin*; **it's ~ freezing in here!** ¡aquí dentro hace un frío que pela!; **it makes ~ no difference** no cambia nada en absoluto; **~ nobody/nothing** nadie/nada en absoluto; **to be ~ right** tener toda la razón; **to lie ~ still** permanecer tumbado completamente quieto; **are you ~ sure?** ¿estás completamente seguro?; **it's ~ true** es la pura verdad, es totalmente cierto
2 (= *unconditionally*) [*refuse, deny*] rotundamente; [*believe*] firmemente; **I agree ~** estoy totalmente de acuerdo
3 (*) (= *certainly*) desde luego; **"it's worrying, isn't it?" — "absolutely"** —es preocupante ¿verdad? —desde luego; **~ not!** ¡de ninguna manera!; **"does this affect your attitude to your work?" — "~ not"** —¿afecta esto a su actitud hacia su trabajo? —no, en absoluto

[4] (*Gram*) **adverbs used ~** adverbios de uso absoluto

absolution [ˌæbsəˈluːʃən] N (*Rel*) absolución *f*; **to give ~ to sb** dar la absolución a algn, absolver a algn

absolutism [ˈæbsəluːtɪzəm] N absolutismo *m*

absolutist [ˈæbsəluːtɪst] Ⓐ ADJ absolutista
Ⓑ N absolutista *mf*

absolve [əbˈzɒlv] VT (= *free*) absolver (**from** de)

absorb [əbˈzɔːb] VT [1] [+ *liquid*] absorber; [+ *heat, sound, shock, vibrations, radiation*] amortiguar
[2] (*fig*) [+ *information*] asimilar; [+ *time, energy*] ocupar, absorber; **the business ~s most of his time** el negocio absorbe *or* le lleva la mayor parte de su tiempo; **the parent company ~s the losses made by the subsidiary** la empresa matriz absorbe las pérdidas de la filial; **the country ~ed 1,000 refugees** el país dio entrada a *or* acogió a 1.000 refugiados
[3] (= *engross*) **to be ~ed in** estar absorto en, estar ensimismado con; **she was ~ed in a book** estaba absorta en *or* ensimismada con un libro; **to get ~ed in** centrarse *or* meterse de lleno en

absorbable [əbˈzɔːbəbl] ADJ absorbible

absorbency [əbˈzɔːbənsɪ] N absorbencia *f*

absorbent [əbˈzɔːbənt] Ⓐ ADJ absorbente
Ⓑ CPD ► **absorbent cotton** N (*US*) algodón *m* hidrófilo

absorbing [əbˈzɔːbɪŋ] ADJ [*study etc*] (= *fascinating*) apasionante; (= *engrossing*) absorbente; **I find history very ~** me apasiona la historia, encuentro la historia apasionante

absorption [əbˈzɔːpʃən] Ⓐ N (*Comm, fig*) absorción *f*
Ⓑ CPD ► **absorption costing** N cálculo *m* del costo de absorción

abstain [əbˈsteɪn] VI [1] (= *refrain*) abstenerse (**from** de); **to ~ from comment** no ofrecer comentario
[2] (= *not vote*) abstenerse
[3] (= *not drink*) abstenerse de las bebidas alcohólicas

abstainer [əbˈsteɪnəʳ] N [1] (= *non-voter*) abstencionista *mf*
[2] (= *teetotaller*) (*also* **total ~**) abstemio/a *m/f*

abstemious [əbˈstiːmɪəs] ADJ [*person*] abstemio; [*meal*] sin alcohol

abstemiousness [əbˈstiːmɪəsnɪs] N sobriedad *f*, moderación *f*

abstention [əbˈstenʃən] N abstención *f*; **there were 20 ~s** hubo 20 abstenciones

abstinence [ˈæbstɪnəns] Ⓐ N abstinencia *f* (**from** de); **total ~** abstinencia *f* total (*esp* de bebidas alcohólicas)
Ⓑ CPD ► **abstinence syndrome** N síndrome *m* de abstinencia

abstinent [ˈæbstɪnənt] ADJ abstinente

abstract Ⓐ [ˈæbstrækt] ADJ abstracto
Ⓑ [ˈæbstrækt] N [1] (= *summary*) resumen *m*, sumario *m*
[2] (*Art*) pintura *f* abstracta
[3] **in the ~** en abstracto
Ⓒ [æbˈstrækt] VT [1] (= *remove*) quitar; (*Chem*) extraer
[2] (= *steal*) sustraer, robar
[3] (= *summarize*) [+ *book, article*] resumir
[4] **to ~ o.s.** abstraerse (**from** de), ensimismarse
Ⓓ [ˈæbstrækt] CPD ► **abstract art** N arte *m* abstracto ► **abstract expressionism** N expresionismo *m* abstracto ► **abstract noun** N nombre *m* abstracto

abstracted [æbˈstræktɪd] ADJ distraído, ensimismado

abstractedly [æbˈstræktɪdlɪ] ADV **she listened ~** escuchaba distraída

abstraction [æbˈstrækʃən] N [1] (= *act*) abstracción *f*
[2] (= *absent-mindedness*) distraimiento *m*, ensimismamiento *m*

abstruse [æbˈstruːs] ADJ recóndito, abstruso

abstruseness [æbˈstruːsnɪs] N lo recóndito, carácter *m* abstruso

▼**absurd** [əbˈsɜːd] Ⓐ ADJ [*idea, plan*] absurdo; [*appearance*] ridículo; **don't be ~!** ¡no digas tonterías!; **how ~!** ¡qué ridículo!; **you look ~ in that hat** con ese sombrero estás ridículo
Ⓑ N **the ~** el absurdo; **the theatre of the ~** el teatro del absurdo

absurdist [əbˈsɜːdɪst] ADJ [*play, novel*] del absurdo

absurdity [əbˈsɜːdɪtɪ] N [1] (= *quality*) lo absurdo
[2] (= *act of madness*) locura *f*, disparate *m*; **it would be an ~ to try** sería una locura *or* un disparate intentarlo; **it would be an ~ to say that** sería absurdo decir eso

absurdly [əbˈsɜːdlɪ] ADV [*long, complicated*] absurdamente, ridículamente; **they were all laughing ~** todos se estaban riendo de una forma ridícula

ABTA [ˈæbtə] N ABBR (= **Association of British Travel Agents**) ≈ AEDAVE *f*

Abu Dhabi [ˌæbʊˈdɑːbɪ] N Abu Dhabi *m*

abulia [əˈbuːlɪə] N (*Psych*) abulia *f*

abundance [əˈbʌndəns] N abundancia *f*; **in ~** en abundancia, en cantidad, en grandes cantidades; **we have a great ~ of plums** tenemos ciruelas en abundancia; **we had an ~ of rain** llovió copiosamente

abundant [əˈbʌndənt] ADJ abundante; **a country ~ in minerals** un país rico en minerales

abundantly [əˈbʌndəntlɪ] ADV abundantemente; **he made it ~ clear to me that ...** me dejó meridianamente claro que ...

abuse Ⓐ [əˈbjuːs] N [1] (= *insults*) insultos *mpl*, improperios *mpl* (*more frm*); **to heap ~ on sb** ◊ **hurl ~ at sb** llenar a algn de improperios
[2] (= *misuse*) abuso *m*; **~ of trust/power** abuso de confianza/poder; **open to ~** abierto al abuso; *see also* **child B**, **drug C**, **sexual B**
Ⓑ [əˈbjuːz] VT [1] (= *insult*) insultar, injuriar; **he roundly ~d the government** dijo mil improperios contra el gobierno
[2] (= *mistreat*) [+ *child*] (*physically*) maltratar; (*sexually*) abusar de
[3] (= *misuse*) [+ *position, privilege*] abusar de

abuser [əˈbjuːzəʳ] N (*physical*) *culpable de malos tratos*; (*sexual*) *culpable de abusos deshonestos*; **she killed her ~** mató al que la abusaba; *see also* **child B**, **drug C**

Abu Simbel [ˌæbʊˈsɪmbl] N Abu Simbel *m*

abusive [əbˈjuːsɪv] ADJ [1] (= *offensive*) ofensivo, insultante; [*language*] lleno de insultos, injurioso; **to be ~ to sb** ser grosero a algn, decir cosas injuriosas a algn (*more frm*); **to become ~** ponerse grosero
[2] (*physically*) [*person*] que maltrata; [*relationship*] de malos tratos
[3] (*sexually*) [*person*] que abusa (sexualmente); [*relationship*] de abuso sexual
[4] [*practice*] abusivo

abusively [əbˈjuːsɪvlɪ] ADV [*speak, refer*] de manera insultante *or* desconsiderada

abut [əˈbʌt] Ⓐ VI **to ~ on sth** [*land*] lindar con algo, confinar con algo; [*house, building*] estar contiguo con algo, colindar con algo
Ⓑ VT **to ~ sth** = **to abut on sth**

abutment [əˈbʌtmənt] N (*Archit*) estribo *m*, contrafuerte *m*; (*Carpentry*) empotramiento *m*

abutting [əˈbʌtɪŋ] ADJ contiguo, colindante

abuzz [əˈbʌz] ADJ **the whole office was ~ with the news** toda la oficina comentaba la noticia

abysmal [əˈbɪzməl] ADJ [1] (= *very bad*) [*result, performance*] pésimo; **the play was ~** la representación fue pésima
[2] (= *very great*) [*ignorance*] abismal; **to live in ~ poverty** vivir en la mayor miseria

abysmally [əˈbɪzməlɪ] ADV [*play, sing*] pésimamente; [*bad, low*] terriblemente; [*fail*] rotundamente

abyss [əˈbɪs] N (*lit*) abismo *m*, sima *f*; (*fig*) abismo *m*

Abyssinia [ˌæbɪˈsɪnɪə] N Abisinia *f*

Abyssinian [ˌæbɪˈsɪnɪən] Ⓐ ADJ abisinio
Ⓑ N abisinio/a *m/f*

AC N ABBR [1] (*Elec*) (= **alternating current**) C.A. *f*
[2] (*Aer*) = **aircraftman**
[3] (*US Sport*) (= **Athletic Club**) C.A. *m*

a/c ABBR [1] (= **account**) c/, c.ta
[2] (*US*) (= **account current**) c/c

acacia [əˈkeɪʃə] N acacia *f*

Acad ABBR = **academy, academic**

academe [ˈækədiːm], **academia** [ˌækəˈdiːmɪə] N (*liter*) mundo *m* académico

academic [ˌækəˈdemɪk] Ⓐ ADJ [1] (*Scol, Univ*) [*ability, qualifications, achievement*] académico; **~ standards were high** los niveles académicos eran buenos; **in ~ circles** en círculos universitarios; **~ freedom** libertad *f* de cátedra; **~ journal** revista *f* dirigida a académicos; **~ staff** profesorado *m*, personal *m* docente; **the ~ world** el mundo académico
[2] (= *scholarly*) intelectualmente dotado; **an exam for ~ children** un examen para niños intelectualmente dotados
[3] (= *theoretical*) [*question*] (puramente) teórico, sin interés práctico; [*debate*] (puramente) teórico; **that's all quite ~** eso no tiene ninguna trascendencia; **it is of ~ interest only** sólo tiene interés teórico
Ⓑ N académico/a *m/f*, profesor(a) *m/f* universitario/a
Ⓒ CPD ► **academic advisor** N (*US*) jefe *mf* de estudios ► **academic dean** N (*US*) decano/a *m/f* ► **academic dress** N vestidura *f* universitaria ► **academic gown** N toga *f* ► **academic officers** NPL (*US*) personal *m* docente ► **academic rank** N (*US*) rango *m* académico ► **academic year** N (*Univ*) año *m* académico; (*Scol*) año *m* escolar

academically [ˌækəˈdemɪkəlɪ] ADV [1] (*Scol, Univ*) **an ~ gifted child** un niño con grandes dotes intelectuales; **~, the boy is below average** en los estudios el chico está por debajo del promedio; **she's outstanding ~** es muy brillante desde el punto de vista académico; **an ~ renowned professor** un catedrático de renombre en círculos universitarios; **an ~ sound argument** un argumento sólido desde el punto de vista intelectual
[2] (= *theoretically*) **to argue ~** dar razones puramente teóricas

academicals [ˌækəˈdemɪkəlz] NPL vestidura *fsing* universitaria

academician [əˌkædəˈmɪʃən] N académico/a *m/f*

academy [əˈkædəmɪ] Ⓐ N [1] (= *private college*) academia *f*; (*Scot*) instituto *m* (de segunda enseñanza), colegio *m*; **~ of music** conservatorio *m*; **~ for young ladies** colegio *m* para señoritas; *see also* **military, naval**
[2] (= *learned society*) academia *f*; **the Spanish**

➤ LANGUAGE IN USE: **absurd** A 26.3

Academy la Real Academia Española; *see also* **royal**
Ⓑ CPD ► **Academy Award** N (*Cine*) galardón *m* de la Academia de Hollywood, Oscar *m*

acanthus [əˈkænθəs] N (*pl* **acanthuses, acanthi**) acanto *m*

ACAS [ˈeɪkæs] N ABBR (*Brit*) (= **Advisory Conciliation and Arbitration Service**) ≈ IMAC *m*

acc. ABBR [1] (*Fin*) (= **account**) c/, c.ta
[2] (*Ling*) = **accusative**

accede [ækˈsiːd] VI **to ~ to** [1] (= *assent to*) [+ *request*] acceder a; [+ *suggestion*] aceptar
[2] (= *gain, enter into*) [+ *office, post*] tomar posesión de; [+ *party*] adherirse a; [+ *throne*] acceder a, subir a; [+ *treaty*] adherirse a

accelerate [ækˈseləreɪt] Ⓐ VT acelerar, apresurar; **~d depreciation** depreciación *f* acelerada; **~d program** (*US Univ*) curso *m* intensivo
Ⓑ VI (*esp Aut*) acelerar

acceleration [ækˌseləˈreɪʃən] Ⓐ N (*esp Aut*) aceleración *f*
Ⓑ CPD ► **acceleration clause** N (*Fin*) provisión *f* para el vencimiento anticipado de una deuda

accelerator [ækˈseləreɪtəʳ] N (*Aut*) acelerador *m*; **to step on the ~** pisar el acelerador

accent Ⓐ [ˈæksənt] N [1] (*written*) acento *m*; **put an ~ on the "o"** pon un acento sobre la "o"; **acute ~** acento *m* agudo; **written ~** acento *m* ortográfico
[2] (= *pronunciation*) acento *m*; **he has a French ~** tiene acento francés; **with a strong Andalusian ~** con (un) fuerte acento andaluz
[3] (= *emphasis*) (*fig*) **to put the ~ on** subrayar (la importancia de), recalcar; **the minister put the ~ on exports** el ministro recalcó la importancia de la exportación; **this year the ~ is on bright colours** (*Fashion*) este año están de moda los colores vivos
[4] (*liter*) (= *tone*) **in ~s of some surprise** en cierto tono de asombro
Ⓑ [ækˈsent] VT [1] [+ *syllable, word*] acentuar
[2] [+ *need, difference*] recalcar, subrayar
[3] [+ *colour, feature*] realzar
Ⓒ [ˈæksənt] CPD ► **accent mark** N acento *m* ortográfico

accented [ækˈsentɪd] ADJ [*syllable*] acentuado; [*voice*] con acento

accentual [ækˈsentjʊəl] ADJ acentual

accentuate [ækˈsentjʊeɪt] VT [1] (*lit*) [+ *syllable, word*] acentuar
[2] (*fig*) [+ *need, difference etc*] recalcar, subrayar; [+ *colour, feature*] realzar

accentuation [ækˌsentjʊˈeɪʃən] N acentuación *f*

▼ **accept** [əkˈsept] Ⓐ VT [1] [+ *gift, invitation, apology, offer*] aceptar; [+ *report*] aprobar; (*Med*) [+ *transplant*] tolerar; **the Academy ~ed the word in 1970** la Academia admitió la palabra en 1970
[2] [*machine*] [+ *coin*] admitir
[3] (*Comm*) [+ *cheque, orders*] aceptar
[4] (= *acknowledge*) reconocer, admitir; [+ *person*] admitir, acoger; **it is ~ed that …** se reconoce *or* admite que …; **I do not ~ that way of doing it** no apruebo ese modo de hacerlo; **to ~ responsibility for sth** asumir la responsabilidad de algo; **he was ~ed as one of us** se lo admitió *or* acogió como a uno de nosotros
Ⓑ VI aceptar, asentir

acceptability [əkˌseptəˈbɪlətɪ] N aceptabilidad *f*

acceptable [əkˈseptəbl] ADJ [*behaviour, plan, offer*] aceptable; [*gift*] grato; **that would not be ~ to the government** eso no le resultaría aceptable al gobierno; **that kind of behaviour is not socially ~** ese tipo de comportamiento no es socialmente aceptable

acceptably [əkˈseptəblɪ] ADV [1] (= *in the accepted manner*) [*behave, phrase*] de manera aceptable
[2] (= *satisfactorily*) [*play, sing*] razonablemente bien; **inflation is now ~ low** la inflación es ahora lo suficientemente baja

▼ **acceptance** [əkˈseptəns] Ⓐ N [1] [*of gift, invitation, apology, offer, cheque*] aceptación *f*
[2] (= *approval*) aprobación *f*, acogida *f*; **to meet with general ~** tener una buena acogida general; **to win ~** lograr la aprobación
Ⓑ CPD ► **acceptance credit** N crédito *m* de aceptación

acceptation [ˌæksepˈteɪʃən] N acepción *f*

accepted [əkˈseptɪd] ADJ [*fact, idea, practice*] reconocido, establecido; **it's the ~ thing** es lo establecido, es la norma; **he's an ~ expert** es un experto reconocido (como tal); **it is not a socially ~ habit** es una costumbre que no es socialmente aceptable

acceptor [əkˈseptəʳ] N aceptador(a) *m/f*; (*Comm*) aceptante *mf*

access [ˈækses] Ⓐ N [1] (= *entry etc*) acceso *m*; **a road was built to improve ~ to the property** se construyó una carretera para facilitar el acceso a la propiedad; **of easy ~** de fácil acceso; **to gain ~ (to)** (*lit*) lograr entrar (en); **to gain ~ to sb** conseguir libre acceso a algn; **to give ~ to a room** comunicar con *or* dar acceso a una habitación; **this gives ~ to the garden** por aquí se sale al jardín; **to have ~ to sb** tener libre acceso a algn; **the house has ~ onto the park** la casa tiene salida al parque; **he had ~ to the family papers** tuvo acceso a los papeles de la familia, se le facilitaron los papeles de la familia; **to obtain legal ~ to a property** conseguir una autorización legal para entrar en una propiedad
[2] (*Jur*) (*in divorce*) derecho *m* de visita
[3] (*Comput*) acceso *m*
[4] (= *sudden outburst*) acceso *m*, arrebato *m*; **he had a sudden ~ of generosity** tuvo un repentino acceso *or* arrebato de generosidad; **in an ~ of rage** en un arrebato *or* acceso de cólera
Ⓑ VT (*Comput*) [+ *file*] conseguir acceso a
Ⓒ CPD ► **access code** N código *m* de acceso ► **access course** N (*Brit*) curso *m* de acceso ► **access road** N vía *f* de acceso ► **access time** N (*Comput*) tiempo *m* de acceso

accessibility [ækˌsesɪˈbɪlɪtɪ] N [*of place*] facilidad *f* de acceso; [*of person*] lo asequible, carácter *m* abordable; [*of art, language*] accesibilidad *f*; **they want to increase the ~ of art to ordinary people** quieren hacer que el arte sea más accesible al ciudadano medio

accessible [ækˈsesəbl] ADJ [1] [*place*] accesible
[2] (= *approachable*) [*person*] accesible, asequible
[3] (= *understandable*) [*art, language*] accesible (**to** para)
[4] (= *able to be influenced*) **he is not ~ to reason** no escucha la razón, hace oídos sordos a la razón

accession [ækˈseʃən] N (*frm*) [1] (= *elevation*) (*to office, post*) entrada *f* en posesión (**to** de); [*of king, queen*] subida *f*, ascenso *m* (**to the throne** al trono); **~ to power** subida *f or* ascenso *m* al poder
[2] (= *consent*) (*to treaty*) accesión *f*, adherencia *f* (**to** a)
[3] (= *entry, admission*) entrada *f* (**to** en)
[4] (= *increase*) aumento
[5] (*in library, museum*) (= *acquisition*) (nueva) adquisición *f*

accessorize [əkˈsesəˌraɪz] VT (*US*) [*dress*] comprar el bolso y los zapatos a juego con

accessory [ækˈsesərɪ] Ⓐ ADJ [1] (= *additional*) accesorio, secundario
[2] (*Jur*) **to be ~ to** ser cómplice de
Ⓑ N [1] **accessories** (*Aut etc*) accesorios *mpl*; (*to outfit*) complementos *mpl*, accesorios *mpl*; **kitchen/bathroom accessories** accesorios *or* artículos *mpl* de cocina/baño
[2] (*Jur*) cómplice *mf* (**to** de); **~ after the fact** cómplice *mf* encubridor(a); **~ before the fact** cómplice *mf*

accidence [ˈæksɪdəns] N accidentes *mpl*

▼ **accident** [ˈæksɪdənt] Ⓐ N [1] (= *mishap*) accidente *m*; **to meet with** *or* **have an ~** tener *or* sufrir un accidente; ✦**IDIOM it's an ~ waiting to happen** es un peligro en potencia; ✦**PROV ~s will happen** son cosas que pasan; *see also* **road B**
[2] (= *unforeseen event*) casualidad *f*; **by ~** (= *by chance*) por *or* de casualidad; (= *unintentionally*) sin querer, involuntariamente; **by some ~ I found myself there** me encontré allí por accidente; **more by ~ than design** más por casualidad que por intención; **I'm sorry, it was an ~** lo siento, lo hice sin querer; **it's no ~ that …** no es casualidad *or* casual que …
[3] (*Geol, Philos*) accidente *m*
Ⓑ CPD ► **Accident and Emergency Department** N (*in hospital*) Urgencias *fpl* ► **(road) accident figures** NPL cifras *fpl* de accidentes (en carretera) ► **accident insurance** N seguro *m* contra accidentes ► **accident prevention** N prevención *f* de accidentes ► **(road) accident statistics** NPL estadísticas *fpl* de accidentes (en carretera)

accidental [ˌæksɪˈdentl] Ⓐ ADJ [1] (= *by chance*) casual, fortuito; **~ death** muerte *f* por accidente
[2] (= *unintentional*) imprevisto; **I didn't do it deliberately, it was ~** no lo hice adrede, fue sin querer
Ⓑ N (*Mus*) accidente *m*

accidentally [ˌæksɪˈdentəlɪ] ADV [1] (= *by chance*) por casualidad; **we met quite ~** nos encontramos por pura casualidad
[2] (= *unintentionally*) sin querer, involuntariamente; **he was ~ killed** fue muerto por accidente; **the liquids were ~ mixed** los líquidos se mezclaron por descuido; ✦**IDIOM ~ on purpose*** sin querer y no tan sin querer

accident-prone [ˈæksɪdəntˌprəʊn] ADJ susceptible a los accidentes

acclaim [əˈkleɪm] Ⓐ VT [1] (= *praise*) aclamar, alabar; **the play was ~ed** la obra fue aclamada
[2] (= *proclaim*) aclamar; **he was ~ed king** lo aclamaron rey
Ⓑ N (= *praise*) alabanza *f*, aclamación *f*; (= *applause*) aplausos *mpl*; **the book met with great ~** el libro tuvo una extraordinaria acogida, el libro recibió encendidos elogios

acclamation [ˌækləˈmeɪʃən] N [1] (= *approval*) aclamación *f*
[2] (= *applause*) aplausos *mpl*, vítores *mpl* (*more frm*); **amid the ~s of the crowd** entre los aplausos *or* (*more frm*) vítores de la multitud; **to be chosen by ~** ser elegido por aclamación

acclimate [əˈklaɪmət] VT, VI (*US*) = **acclimatize**

acclimation [ˌæklaɪˈmeɪʃən] N (*US*) = **acclimatization**

acclimatization [əˌklaɪmətaɪˈzeɪʃən], **acclimation** (*US*) [ˌæklaɪˈmeɪʃən] N aclimatación *f*

➤ LANGUAGE IN USE: **accept A** 11.2, 25.2 **acceptance A1** 19.5, 20.3 **accident A2** 18.4

acclimatize [ə'klaɪmətaɪz], **acclimate** (*US*) [ə'klaɪmət] Ⓐ VT aclimatar (**to** a); **to ~ o.s.** aclimatarse (**to** a)
Ⓑ VI aclimatarse (**to** a)

acclivity [ə'klɪvɪtɪ] N subida *f*, cuesta *f*

accolade ['ækəʊleɪd] N 1 (= *praise*) elogio *m* entusiasta; (= *honour*) honor *m*; (= *award*) galardón *m*, premio *m*
2 (*Hist*) acolada *f*, espaldarazo *m*

accommodate [ə'kɒmədeɪt] Ⓐ VT 1 (= *lodge, put up*) [+ *person*] alojar, hospedar; **can you ~ four people in July?** ¿tiene usted habitaciones para cuatro personas en julio?
2 (= *have space for*) tener cabida para; **this car ~s six** este coche tiene cabida *or* asientos para seis personas; **can you ~ two more in your car?** ¿caben dos más en tu coche?
3 (= *reconcile*) [+ *differences*] acomodar, concertar; [+ *quarrel*] poner fin a; [+ *quarrellers*] reconciliar
4 (= *adapt*) acomodar, adaptar (**to** a)
5 (= *supply*) proveer (**with** de); **to ~ sb with a loan** facilitar un préstamo a algn
6 (= *oblige*) complacer, hacer un favor a
Ⓑ VI [*eye*] adaptarse (**to** a)

accommodating [ə'kɒmədeɪtɪŋ] ADJ (= *helpful*) servicial, complaciente; (= *easy to deal with*) acomodadizo, acomodaticio

accommodation [ə,kɒmə'deɪʃən] Ⓐ N 1 (*also US* **~s**) (= *lodging*) alojamiento *m*; (= *rooms*) habitaciones *fpl*; **have you any ~ available?** ¿tiene usted habitaciones disponibles?; **to book ~ in a hotel** reservar una habitación en un hotel; **"accommodation to let"** "se alquilan habitaciones"
2 (= *space*) lugar *m*, cabida *f*; **there is ~ for 20 passengers** hay lugar para 20 pasajeros; **there is standing ~ only** hay sitio solamente para estar de pie; **the plane has limited ~** el avión tiene un número limitado de plazas
3 (= *agreement*) acuerdo *m*; **to reach an ~ with creditors** llegar a un acuerdo con los acreedores
4 (= *adaptation*) acomodación *f*, adaptación *f*
5 (= *loan*) crédito *m*, préstamo *m*
Ⓑ CPD ► **accommodation address** N domicilio *f* postal ► **accommodation bill** N (*Comm*) pagaré *m* de favor ► **accommodation bureau** N oficina *f* de hospedaje ► **accommodation note** N = **accommodation bill** ► **accommodation train** N (*US*) tren *m* de cercanías

accompaniment [ə'kʌmpənɪmənt] N (*also Mus*) acompañamiento *m*; **they marched to the ~ of a military band** desfilaban al compás de una banda militar

accompanist [ə'kʌmpənɪst] N (*Mus*) acompañante/a *m/f*

accompany [ə'kʌmpənɪ] VT 1 (= *escort*) acompañar; **to be accompanied by sb** ir acompañado de algn
2 (*fig*) acompañar; **accompanied by** acompañado de; **he accompanied this with a grimace** esto lo dijo acompañado de una mueca, al decir esto hizo una mueca; **~ing letter** carta *f* adjunta
3 (*Mus*) acompañar (**on the violin/piano** con el violín/al piano); **to ~ o.s. on the piano** acompañarse al piano

accomplice [ə'kʌmplɪs] N cómplice *mf*

accomplish [ə'kʌmplɪʃ] VT 1 (= *achieve*) efectuar, lograr; [+ *task, mission*] llevar a cabo; [+ *purpose, one's design*] realizar
2 (= *finish*) terminar, concluir

accomplished [ə'kʌmplɪʃt] ADJ 1 [*pianist etc*] experto, consumado; [*performance*] logrado
2 [*fact*] consumado

accomplishment [ə'kʌmplɪʃmənt] N 1 (= *achievement*) logro *m*; **a great ~** un gran logro; **it's quite an ~ to** + INFIN exige mucho talento + *infin*; **her ~ in finishing the film although ill** su logro de terminar la película a pesar de estar enferma
2 (= *completion, fulfilment*) realización *f*; **difficult of ~** de difícil consecución
3 (= *skill*) talento *m*; **accomplishments** talento *m*, dotes *fpl*

accord [ə'kɔːd] Ⓐ N 1 (= *harmony*) acuerdo *m*, armonía *f*; **with one ~** de *or* por común acuerdo; **to be in ~** estar de acuerdo (**with** con), estar en armonía (**with** con); **of his/her own ~** espontáneamente, (de) motu proprio
2 (= *treaty*) acuerdo *m*
Ⓑ VT [+ *welcome, praise*] dar (**to** a); [+ *honour*] conceder (**to** a)
Ⓒ VI concordar, armonizar (**with** con)

accordance [ə'kɔːdəns] N **in ~ with** conforme a, de acuerdo con

according [ə'kɔːdɪŋ] ADV 1 **~ to** según; (= *in accordance with*) conforme a, de acuerdo con; **~ to him …** según él …; **~ to what he told me** según me dijo; **it went ~ to plan** salió conforme a *or* de acuerdo con nuestros *etc* planes; **classified ~ to size** clasificado por *or* según tamaños; **to play the game ~ to the rules** jugar siguiendo las reglas
2 **~ as** según que, a medida que

accordingly [ə'kɔːdɪŋlɪ] ADV 1 (= *correspondingly*) **it is a difficult job and he should be paid ~** es un trabajo difícil y debería recibir un pago acorde; **to act ~** actuar en consecuencia
2 (= *therefore*) por consiguiente, por lo tanto; **the text was too long and the editor ~ cut it by 20%** el texto era demasiado largo y por consiguiente *or* por lo tanto el editor lo acortó un 20%

accordion [ə'kɔːdɪən] N acordeón *m*

accordionist [ə'kɔːdɪənɪst] N acordeonista *mf*

accost [ə'kɒst] VT abordar; **he ~ed me in the street** me abordó en la calle, se dirigió a mí en la calle; **he ~ed me for a light** se acercó a mí para pedir fuego

accouchement [ə'kuːʃmɑ̃ːŋ] N (*frm*) parto *m*

➤**account** [ə'kaʊnt] Ⓐ N 1 (*Comm, Fin*) (*at shop*) cuenta *f*; (= *invoice*) factura *f*; (= *bank account*) cuenta *f* (bancaria); **they have the Blotto ~** (*Advertising*) ellos hacen la publicidad de Blotto; **cash or ~?** ¿en metálico o a cuenta?; **to charge sth to sb's ~** cargar algo en cuenta a algn; **to close an ~** liquidar una cuenta; **payment on ~** pago *m* a cuenta; **to get £50 on ~** recibir 50 libras anticipadas; **to put £50 down on ~** cargar 50 libras a la cuenta; **to buy sth on ~** comprar algo a cuenta; **to open an ~** abrir una cuenta; **~ payable** cuenta *f* por pagar; **"account payee only"** "únicamente en cuenta del beneficiario"; **~ receivable** cuenta *f* por cobrar; **to render an ~** pasar factura; **~ rendered** cuenta *f* pasada; **to settle an ~** liquidar una cuenta; **to settle ~s (with)** (*fig*) ajustar cuentas (con); **statement of ~** estado *m* de cuenta; **the Account** (*St Ex*) periodo *m* (de 15 días) al fin del cual se ajustan las cuentas; *see also* **current, deposit C, joint D**
2 **accounts** (*Comm*) (= *calculations*) cuentas *fpl*; (= *department*) (sección *f* de) contabilidad *f*; **to keep the ~s** llevar las cuentas
3 (= *report*) informe *m*; **by all ~s** a decir de todos, según se dice; **by** *or* **according to her own ~** por lo que dice ella; **to give an ~ of** dar cuenta de, informar sobre; **to keep an ~ of** [+ *events*] guardar relación de; [+ *amounts*] llevar cuentas de
4 (= *consideration*) consideración *f*; **on no ~** ◊ **not on any ~** de ninguna manera, bajo ningún concepto; **on that ~** por eso; **on his ~** por él, en su nombre; **on his own ~** por cuenta propia; **on ~ of** (= *because of*) a causa de; (*esp US**) (= *because*) porque, debido a que; **I couldn't do it on ~ of my back's sore*** no he podido hacerlo porque me duele la espalda; **to leave sth out of ~** no tomar algo en consideración *or* cuenta; **to take ~ of sth** ◊ **take sth into ~** tener algo en cuenta *or* consideración, tener algo presente; **to take no ~ of** no tomar *or* no tener en cuenta
5 (= *importance*) importancia *f*; **of no** *or* **little** *or* **small ~** de poca importancia; **of some ~** de cierta importancia, de alguna consideración
6 (= *explanation*) **to bring** *or* **call sb to ~** pedir cuentas a algn; **to give an ~ of o.s.** justificar su conducta; **to give a good ~ of oneself** (= *perform well*) tener una buena actuación; (= *make good impression*) causar buena impresión; **to be held to ~ for sth** ser obligado a rendir cuentas por algo
7 (= *benefit*) **to put** *or* **turn sth to (good) ~** aprovechar algo, sacar provecho de algo
Ⓑ VT (*frm*) considerar, creer; **I ~ him a fool** lo considero un tonto; **I ~ myself lucky** me considero afortunado; **he is ~ed an expert** se le considera un experto; **I should ~ it a favour if …** agradecería que …
Ⓒ CPD ► **account balance** N saldo *m* de la cuenta ► **account book** N libro *m* de cuentas ► **account day** N día *m* de liquidación ► **account number** N (*at bank etc*) número *m* de cuenta ► **accounts department** N sección *f* de contabilidad

►**account for** VI + PREP 1 (= *explain*) explicar, justificar; **how do you ~ for it?** ¿cómo lo explica *or* justifica usted?; **I cannot ~ for it** no me lo explico; **that ~s for it** ésa es la razón *or* la explicación; ✦*IDIOM* **there's no ~ing for taste(s)** sobre gustos no hay nada escrito
2 (= *give reckoning of*) [+ *actions, expenditure*] dar cuenta de, responder de; **everything is now ~ed for** ya se ha dado cuenta de todo, todo está completo ya; **many are still not ~ed for** aún se desconoce la suerte que han corrido muchas personas
3 (= *represent*) representar, suponer; **children ~ for 5% of the audience** los niños representan *or* suponen el 5 por ciento de la audiencia
4 (= *destroy, kill*) acabar con; **one bomb ~ed for the power station** una bomba acabó con la central eléctrica; **they ~ed for three stags** mataron tres ciervos; **the ship ~ed for three enemy aircraft** el barco derribó tres aviones enemigos

accountability [ə,kaʊntə'bɪlətɪ] N responsabilidad *f*

accountable [ə'kaʊntəbl] ADJ responsable (**for** de; **to** ante); **not ~ for one's actions** no responsable de los propios actos; **he is ~ only to himself** sólo se da cuentas a sí mismo, sólo se siente responsable ante sí mismo

accountancy [ə'kaʊntənsɪ] N contabilidad *f*

accountant [ə'kaʊntənt] N contable *mf*, contador(a) *m/f* (*LAm*); (*in bank etc*) economista *mf*; **~'s office** contaduría *f*; *see also* **chartered**

accounting [ə'kaʊntɪŋ] Ⓐ N contabilidad *f*
Ⓑ CPD ► **accounting period** N periodo *m* contable, ejercicio *m* financiero

accoutred, accoutered (*US*) [ə'kuːtəd] PP, ADJ (*frm or liter*) equipado (**with** de)

➤ LANGUAGE IN USE: **account** A4 26.2

accoutrements [əˈkuːtrəmənts], **accouterments** (*US*) [əˈkuːtəmənts] NPL (*frm*) equipo *msing*, avíos *mpl*

accredit [əˈkredɪt] VT [1] (= *credit*) atribuir (**to** a); **to ~ a quality to sb** ◊ **~ sb with a quality** atribuir una cualidad a algn
[2] (= *recognize*) [+ *qualification*] reconocer (oficialmente); [+ *representative, body*] autorizar, acreditar
[3] (= *appoint*) acreditar; **to ~ an ambassador to** acreditar a algn como embajador en

accreditation [əˌkredɪˈteɪʃən] Ⓐ N reconocimiento *m* (oficial); (*US Scol, Univ*) habilitación *f* de enseñanza
Ⓑ CPD ► **accreditation officer** N (*US Scol*) inspector(a) *m/f* de enseñanza

accredited [əˈkredɪtɪd] ADJ [*source, supplier, agent*] autorizado

accretion [əˈkriːʃən] N aumento *m*, acrecentamiento *m*

accrual [əˈkrʊəl] N (*frm*) acumulación *f*

accrue [əˈkruː] (*frm*) Ⓐ VI (= *mount up*) acumularse (*also Fin*); **to ~ from** proceder de; **to ~ to** corresponder a; **some benefit will ~ to you from this** de esto resultará algo a beneficio de usted
Ⓑ CPD ► **accrued charges** NPL gastos *mpl* vencidos ► **accrued income** N renta *f* acumulada ► **accrued interest** N interés *m* acumulado

acct ABBR (= **account**) c/, c.[ta]

acculturate [əˈkʌltʃəˌreɪt] VT (*frm*) aculturar

acculturation [əˌkʌltʃəˈreɪʃən] N (*frm*) aculturación *f*

accumulate [əˈkjuːmjʊleɪt] Ⓐ VT acumular
Ⓑ VI acumularse
Ⓒ CPD ► **accumulated depreciation** N depreciación *f* acumulada

accumulation [əˌkjuːmjʊˈleɪʃən] N [1] (= *amassing*) acumulación *f*, acopio *m*
[2] (= *mass*) montón *m*

accumulative [əˈkjuːmjʊlətɪv] ADJ acumulativo

accumulator [əˈkjuːmjʊleɪtəʳ] N [1] (*Elec, Comput*) acumulador *m*
[2] (*Brit*) (= *bet*) apuesta *f* múltiple acumulativa

accuracy [ˈækjʊrəsɪ] N [*of measurement, figures, clock*] exactitud *f*; [*of instrument*] precisión *f*; [*of translation, copy, words, description*] fidelidad *f*, exactitud *f*; [*of forecast*] lo acertado; [*of aim, shot*] lo certero; **~ is very important for a good typist** no cometer errores es muy importante para un buen mecanógrafo; **they were impressed by the typist's ~** estaban impresionados por la falta de errores en el trabajo del mecanógrafo

accurate [ˈækjʊrɪt] ADJ [*number, measurement, figure, calculation*] exacto; [*instrument, scales*] preciso; [*translation, copy, information, description, memory*] fiel, exacto; [*observation, answer, forecast*] acertado; [*instructions*] preciso; [*shot, aim*] certero; [*missile*] de gran precisión; [*typist*] que no comete errores; **is that clock ~?** ¿tiene ese reloj la hora exacta?; **~ spelling is important** escribir sin faltas es muy importante; **it was his father or, to be ~, his stepfather** era su padre o, para ser exacto, su padrastro; **to be strictly ~ …** para ser más preciso *or* exacto …; **the newspaper has been ~ in its reports** el periódico ha informado fielmente de los hechos en sus reportajes; **the tests are 90% ~ in identifying future victims** los análisis aciertan al detectar futuras víctimas en un 90 por ciento de los casos; **clocks that are ~ to one second in 40 million years** relojes que no pierden ni ganan más de un segundo en 40 millones de años; **the scales are ~ to half a gram** la balanza tiene un margen de error de sólo medio gramo

accurately [ˈækjʊrɪtlɪ] ADV [*measure*] con exactitud; [*calculate*] exactamente; [*reflect, translate, copy, draw*] fielmente, exactamente; [*inform, describe*] fielmente con exactitud; [*predict*] con exactitud; [*shoot, aim*] certeramente

accursed†, **accurst**† [əˈkɜːst] ADJ (*liter*) maldito; (= *ill-fated*) infausto, desventurado; **~ be he who …!** ¡maldito sea quien …!, ¡mal haya quien …!

accusal [əˈkjuːzl] N (*Jur*) acusación *f*

accusation [ˌækjʊˈzeɪʃən] N (= *charge*) acusación *f*

accusative [əˈkjuːzətɪv] (*Ling*) Ⓐ ADJ acusativo
Ⓑ N (*also* **~ case**) acusativo *m*; **in the ~** en acusativo

accusatorial [əˌkjuːzəˈtɔːrɪəl] ADJ = **accusatory**

accusatory [əˈkjuːzətərɪ] ADJ [*remark*] acusatorio; [*glance, gesture, manner*] acusador

accuse [əˈkjuːz] VT **to ~ sb (of)** acusar a algn (de); **he stands ~d of …** se le acusa de …

accused [əˈkjuːzd] N **the ~** (*Jur*) (*sing*) el/la acusado/a; (*pl*) los/las acusados/as

accuser [əˈkjuːzəʳ] N acusador(a) *m/f*

accusing [əˈkjuːzɪŋ] ADJ [*look, eyes*] acusador; **in an ~ voice** en tono acusador; **to point an ~ finger at sb** (*lit*) señalar a algn con un dedo acusador; (*fig*) acusar a algn

accusingly [əˈkjuːzɪŋlɪ] ADV [*say*] en tono acusador; **she looked at me ~** me lanzó una mirada acusadora; **she pointed at Derek ~** señaló a Derek con un dedo acusador

accustom [əˈkʌstəm] VT acostumbrar, habituar (**to** a); **to ~ sb to (doing) sth** acostumbrar a algn a (hacer) algo; **to ~ o.s. to (doing) sth** acostumbrarse a (hacer) algo; **to be ~ed to (doing) sth** estar acostumbrado a (hacer) algo; **to get ~ed to (doing) sth** acostumbrarse a (hacer) algo

accustomed [əˈkʌstəmd] ADJ acostumbrado, usual

AC/DC [ˌeɪsiːˈdiːsiː] Ⓐ N ABBR = **alternating current/direct current**
Ⓑ ADJ **he's ~**‡ es bisexual

ACE N ABBR (*US*) = **American Council on Education**

ace [eɪs] Ⓐ N [1] (*Cards*) as *m*; ♦**IDIOMS to be within an ~ of** estar a punto *or* a dos dedos de; **to keep an ~ up one's sleeve** ◊ **have an ~ in the hole** (*US**) guardar un triunfo en la mano, guardarse un as en la manga; **to play one's ~** jugar su triunfo; **to hold all the ~s** tener la sartén por el mango
[2] (*Tennis*) ace *m*
[3] (= *pilot, racing driver etc*) as *m*; **he's ~s** (*US**) es fenomenal*
Ⓑ ADJ (*) estupendo*, de aúpa*; **~ player** as *m*
Ⓒ CPD ► **Ace bandage**® N (*US*) venda *f* elástica

acephalous [əˈsefələs] ADJ acéfalo

acerbic [əˈsɜːbɪk] ADJ [1] [*taste*] acre, acerbo
[2] (*fig*) mordaz, cáustico

acerbity [əˈsɜːbɪtɪ] N [1] [*of taste*] acritud *f*, aspereza *f*
[2] (*fig*) mordacidad *f*

acetate [ˈæsɪteɪt] N acetato *m*

acetic [əˈsiːtɪk] Ⓐ ADJ acético
Ⓑ CPD ► **acetic acid** N ácido *m* acético

acetone [ˈæsɪtəʊn] N acetona *f*

acetylene [əˈsetɪliːn] Ⓐ N acetileno *m*
Ⓑ CPD ► **acetylene burner** N soplete *m* oxiacetilénico ► **acetylene lamp** N lámpara *f* de acetileno ► **acetylene torch** N soplete *m* oxiacetilénico ► **acetylene welding** N soldadura *f* oxiacetilénica

ache [eɪk] Ⓐ N (= *pain*) dolor *m*; **I have an ~ in my side** me duele el costado; **full of ~s and pains** lleno de achaques *or* goteras*; ♦**IDIOM with an ~ in one's heart** con mucho pesar
Ⓑ VI [1] (= *hurt*) doler; **my head ~s** me duele la cabeza; **it makes my head ~** me da dolor de cabeza; **I'm aching all over** me duele todo
[2] (*fig*) **it was enough to make your heart ~** era para romperle a uno el alma; **my heart ~s for you** lo siento en el alma
[3] (= *yearn*) desear, suspirar (**for** por); **I am aching for you** suspiro por ti; **I am aching to see you again** me muero por volver a verte; **I ~d to help** me moría por ayudar

achievable [əˈtʃiːvəbl] ADJ alcanzable; **an aim readily ~** un propósito fácil de alcanzar

➤**achieve** [əˈtʃiːv] Ⓐ VT (= *reach*) conseguir, alcanzar; (= *complete*) llevar a cabo; (= *accomplish*) realizar; **he will never ~ anything** él no hará nunca nada; **what do you hope to ~ by that?** ¿qué esperas lograr con eso?
Ⓑ VI (= *be successful*) avanzar, hacer progresos; **the children are not achieving as they should** los niños no avanzan *or* hacen los progresos que debieran

achievement [əˈtʃiːvmənt] N [1] (= *act*) realización *f*, consecución *f*
[2] (= *thing achieved*) logro *m*, éxito *m*; **that's quite an ~** es todo un logro *or* éxito, es toda una hazaña; **among his many ~s** entre los muchos éxitos *or* las muchas hazañas en su haber
[3] (*Scol*) **the level of ~** el nivel de rendimiento escolar; *see also* **record A5.1**

achiever [əˈtʃiːvəʳ] N (*also* **high ~**) *persona que realiza su potencial or que llega muy alto*

Achilles [əˈkɪliːz] Ⓐ N Aquiles
Ⓑ CPD ► **Achilles heel** N talón *m* de Aquiles ► **Achilles tendon** N tendón *m* de Aquiles

aching [ˈeɪkɪŋ] Ⓐ ADJ [1] [*tooth, feet*] dolorido, que duele
[2] (*fig*) **with an ~ heart** con mucho pesar
Ⓑ N dolor *m*

achromatic [ˌækrəʊˈmætɪk] ADJ acromático

achy* [ˈeɪkɪ] ADJ dolorido; **to feel ~** sentirse dolorido; **I feel ~ all over** me duele todo

acid [ˈæsɪd] Ⓐ N [1] (*Chem*) ácido *m*
[2] (‡) (= *drug*) ácido* *m*; **to drop ~** consumir ácido
Ⓑ ADJ [1] (= *not alkaline*) [*soil, food, conditions*] ácido
[2] (= *sharp, bitter*) [*fruit, taste*] ácido
[3] (*fig*) [*remark, tone*] mordaz; [*voice*] agrio, mordaz; **to have an ~ tongue** tener la lengua viperina
Ⓒ CPD ► **acid drops** NPL (*Brit*) caramelos *mpl* ácidos ► **acid green** N verde *m* limón ► **acid head**‡ N (*Drugs*) adicto/a *m/f* al ácido ► **acid house (music)** N música *f* acid ► **acid house party** N fiesta *f* acid ► **acid rain** N lluvia *f* ácida ► **acid rock** N (*Mus*) rock *m* acid ► **the acid test** N (*fig*) la prueba de fuego, la prueba decisiva ► **acid yellow** N amarillo *m* limón

acidic [əˈsɪdɪk] ADJ ácido

acidifier [əˈsɪdɪfaɪəʳ] N acidulante *m*

acidify [əˈsɪdɪfaɪ] Ⓐ VT acidificar
Ⓑ VI acidificarse

acidity [əˈsɪdɪtɪ] N acidez *f*

acidly [ˈæsɪdlɪ] ADV [*comment, reply*] mordazmente

acidophilous [ˌæsɪˈdɒfɪləs] ADJ acidófilo

➤ LANGUAGE IN USE: achieve A 8.1

acid-proof ['æsɪdpru:f], **acid-resisting** ['æsɪdrɪ'zɪstɪŋ] ADJ a prueba de ácidos

acidulant [ə'sɪdjʊlənt] N acidulante *m*

acidulous [ə'sɪdjʊləs] ADJ acídulo

ack-ack* ['æk'æk] Ⓐ N (= *gunfire*) fuego *m* antiaéreo; (= *guns*) artillería *f* antiaérea
Ⓑ CPD ► **ack-ack fire** N fuego *m* antiaéreo
► **ack-ack gun** N cañón *m* antiaéreo

▼**acknowledge** [ək'nɒlɪdʒ] VT [1] (= *admit*) reconocer; [+ *claim, truth*] admitir; [+ *crime*] confesarse culpable de; **I ~ that ...** reconozco que ...; **to ~ defeat** darse por vencido; **to ~ that sb is superior** ◊ **~ sb as superior** reconocer que algn es mejor; **to ~ sb as leader** reconocer a algn como jefe; **I ~ myself the loser** reconozco que he perdido; **she ~d herself in the wrong** reconoció que estaba equivocada
[2] (= *thank for*) [+ *favour, gift*] agradecer, dar las gracias por
[3] (*also* ~ **receipt of**) [+ *letter*] acusar recibo de
[4] (= *greet*) [+ *person*] saludar; (= *reply to*) [+ *greeting*] contestar a

acknowledged [ək'nɒlɪdʒd] ADJ **an ~ expert** un experto reconocido como tal; **a generally ~ fact** un hecho generalmente reconocido

acknowledgement [ək'nɒlɪdʒmənt] N [1] (= *admission*) admisión *f*; (= *recognition*) reconocimiento *m*; **in ~ of** en reconocimiento de, en agradecimiento a; **I wish to make public ~ of the help** quiero agradecer públicamente la ayuda; **to make ~s** expresar su agradecimiento
[2] (*Comm*) [*of letter etc*] acuse *m* de recibo
[3] [*of greeting*] contestación *f*
[4] **to quote sb without ~** citar a algn sin mencionar la fuente; **acknowledgements** (*in book*) menciones *fpl*

ACLU N ABBR = **American Civil Liberties Union**

> **ACLU**
>
> *La **American Civil Liberties Union** o **ACLU** es una organización no partidista que se fundó en 1920 para proteger los derechos de los ciudadanos estadounidenses tal y como lo establece la Constitución. La **ACLU** presta su apoyo en los tribunales cuando se trata de casos de violación de las libertades del ciudadano, especialmente en circunstancias de discriminación por motivos de religión, raza, color o sexo, o en casos relacionados con la libertad de expresión. Esta organización jugó un papel importante en la lucha contra la segregación racial. Sin embargo, debido a su defensa de la libertad total, también ha apoyado marchas del Partido Nazi Americano y del Ku Klux Klan, decisiones que han creado mucha polémica.*

acme ['ækmɪ] N colmo *m*, cima *f*; **the ~ of perfection** la suma perfección, el colmo de la perfección; **he is the ~ of good taste** es el buen gusto en persona

acne ['æknɪ] N acné *m or f*

acolyte ['ækəʊlaɪt] N [1] (*Rel*) acólito *m*, monaguillo *m*
[2] (*fig*) acólito/a *m/f*

aconite ['ækənaɪt] N acónito *m*

acorn ['eɪkɔ:n] N bellota *f*

acoustic [ə'ku:stɪk] Ⓐ ADJ acústico
Ⓑ CPD ► **acoustic coupler** N acoplador *m* acústico ► **acoustic guitar** N guitarra *f* acústica ► **acoustic nerve** N nervio *m* auditivo ► **acoustic screen** N panel *m* acústico ► **acoustic shock** N (*Telec*) choque *m or* shock *m* acústico

acoustically [ə'ku:stɪklɪ] ADV [*poor, perfect*] desde el punto de vista acústico; [*record*] acústicamente

acoustics [ə'ku:stɪks] N [1] (*with sing vb*) (*Phys*) acústica *f*
[2] (*with pl vb*) [*of hall etc*] acústica *f*

ACPO ['ækpəʊ] N ABBR (*Brit*) = **Association of Chief Police Officers**

acquaint [ə'kweɪnt] VT [1] (= *inform*) **to ~ sb with sth** informar a algn de *or* sobre algo; **to ~ o.s. with sth** informarse sobre algo
[2] (= *know*) **to be ~ed** conocerse; **to be ~ed with** [+ *person*] conocer; [+ *fact*] saber; [+ *situation*] estar enterado *or* al corriente de; **to become ~ed with** [+ *person*] (llegar a) conocer; [+ *fact*] saber; [+ *situation*] ponerse al tanto de

acquaintance [ə'kweɪntəns] N [1] (*with person*) relación *f*; (*with subject etc*) conocimiento *m*; **to make sb's ~** conocer a algn; **I am very glad to make your ~** tengo mucho gusto en conocerlo; **a plumber of my ~** un fontanero que conozco; **I don't have the honour of her ~** no tengo el honor de conocerla; **it improves on ~** mejora a medida que lo vas conociendo; **on closer** *or* **further ~ it seems less attractive** al conocerlo mejor tiene menos atracción; **to renew (one's) ~ with sb** reanudar la amistad con algn; *see also* **nod C4**
[2] (= *person*) conocido/a *m/f*; **an ~ of mine** un conocido mío; **we're just ~s** nos conocemos ligeramente nada más; **we're old ~s** nos conocemos desde hace tiempo; **to have a wide circle of ~s** conocer a muchas personas

acquaintanceship [ə'kweɪntənsʃɪp] N [1] (*between two people*) relaciones *fpl*
[2] (= *knowledge*) conocimiento *m* (**with** de), familiaridad *f* (**with** con)

acquiesce [,ækwɪ'es] VI (= *agree*) consentir (**in** en), conformarse (**in** con); (*unwillingly*) someterse, doblegarse

acquiescence [,ækwɪ'esns] N aquiescencia *f* (**in** a, en), consentimiento *m* (**in** para)

acquiescent [,ækwɪ'esnt] ADJ conforme, aquiescente; **he was perfectly ~** se mostró completamente conforme; **he is ~ by nature** por su naturaleza se conforma con todo

acquire [ə'kwaɪəʳ] VT [+ *possessions*] (= *get*) adquirir, obtener; (= *manage to get*) conseguir; [+ *habit, reputation, native language*] adquirir; [+ *foreign language*] aprender; [+ *territory*] tomar posesión de; [+ *colour, tint*] adquirir, tomar; **where did you ~ that?** ¿dónde conseguiste eso?; **I seem to have ~d a strange umbrella** parece que he tomado el paraguas de otro; **to ~ a name for honesty** ganarse fama de honrado; *see also* **taste A5**

acquired [ə'kwaɪəd] ADJ adquirido; **an ~ taste** un gusto adquirido

acquirement [ə'kwaɪəmənt] N [1] [*of possessions*] adquisición *f*, obtención *f*
[2] **acquirements** (*frm*) (= *skills*) conocimientos *mpl*

acquirer [ə'kwaɪərəʳ] N (*Comm, Fin*) adquirente *mf*

acquisition [,ækwɪ'zɪʃən] N [1] (= *act, purchased object*) adquisición *f*
[2] (*Comm*) [*of company*] absorción *f*

acquisitive [ə'kwɪzɪtɪv] ADJ codicioso; **the ~ society** la sociedad de consumo

acquisitiveness [ə'kwɪzɪtɪvnɪs] N codicia *f*

acquit [ə'kwɪt] VT [1] (*Jur*) **to ~ sb (of)** absolver *or* exculpar a algn (de); **he was ~ted on all charges** lo absolvieron de todas las acusaciones
[2] **to ~ o.s.: how did he ~ himself?** ¿cómo se desenvolvió?; **to ~ o.s. well** defenderse bien; **to ~ o.s. of** [+ *duty*] desempeñar

acquittal [ə'kwɪtl] N (*Jur*) absolución *f*, exculpación *f*

acre ['eɪkəʳ] N acre *m* (*4.047 metros cuadrados*); **the family's broad** *or* **rolling ~s** las extensas fincas de la familia; **there are ~s of space for you to play in*** hay la mar de espacio para que juguéis*; **I've got ~s of weeds*** tengo un montón de malas hierbas*

acreage ['eɪkərɪdʒ] N superficie *f* medida en acres, extensión *f* medida en acres; **the 1990 wheat ~** el área sembrada de trigo en 1990; **what ~ do you have here?** ¿cuánto miden estos terrenos?, ¿qué extensión tiene esta tierra?; **they farm a large ~** cultivan unos terrenos muy extensos

acrid ['ækrɪd] ADJ [1] (*lit*) [*smell, taste*] acre, punzante
[2] (*fig*) áspero, mordaz

Acrilan® ['ækrɪlæn] N acrilán® *m*

acrimonious [,ækrɪ'məʊnɪəs] ADJ [*argument*] reñido, enconado; [*debate, meeting, exchange*] reñido; [*divorce, break-up*] amargo; [*remark*] mordaz, cáustico

acrimoniously [,ækrɪ'məʊnɪəslɪ] ADV [*argue*] enconadamente; [*end, break up*] amargamente; [*say*] mordazmente

acrimony ['ækrɪmənɪ] N acritud *f*, acrimonia *f*; **there has been no ~ between us** no ha habido acritud *or* acrimonia entre nosotros; **their first meeting ended in ~** su primera reunión acabó en una disputa enconada

acrobat ['ækrəbæt] N acróbata *mf*

acrobatic [,ækrəʊ'bætɪk] ADJ acrobático

acrobatics [,ækrəʊ'bætɪks] NPL acrobacia *fsing*; (*as profession*) acrobacia *fsing*, acrobatismo *msing*; (*Aer*) vuelo *msing* acrobático; **mental/verbal ~** malabarismos *mpl* mentales/verbales

acronym ['ækrənɪm] N sigla(s) *f(pl)*, acrónimo *m*

acropolis [ə'krɒpəlɪs] N acrópolis *f*

across [ə'krɒs]

> *When **across** is an element in a phrasal verb, eg **come across, run across**, look up the verb.*

Ⓐ PREP [1] (= *from one side to other of*) a través de; **a tree had fallen ~ the road** había caído un árbol a través de la carretera; **to go ~ a bridge** atravesar *or* cruzar un puente; **to run ~ a road** cruzar una calle corriendo; **the bridge ~ the Tagus** el puente sobre el Tajo; **with arms folded ~ his chest** con los brazos cruzados sobre el pecho
[2] (= *on the other side of*) al otro lado de; **~ the street from our house** al otro lado de la calle enfrente de nuestra casa; **the lands ~ the sea** las tierras más allá del mar; **from ~ the sea** desde más allá del mar
[3] (*in measurements*) **it is 12km ~ the strait** el estrecho tiene 12km de ancho
[4] (= *crosswise over*) a través de; *see also* **board A1**
Ⓑ ADV [1] (= *from one side to the other*) a través, al través; **don't go around, go ~** no des la vuelta, ve al través; **shall I go ~ first?** ¿paso yo el primero?; **to run ~** (*over bridge*) atravesar *or* cruzar corriendo; **to swim ~** atravesar a nado; **to cut sth ~** cortar algo por (el) medio; **a plank had been laid ~** habían colocado una tabla encima; **he helped an old lady ~** ayudó a una señora mayor a cruzar la calle
[2] (= *on opposite side*) **it's ~ from the Post Office** está enfrente de Correos; **he sat down ~ from her** se sentó frente a ella
[3] (*in measurements*) **the lake is 12km ~** el

➤ LANGUAGE IN USE: acknowledge 3 20.4

lago tiene 12km de ancho; **the plate is 30cm ~** el plato tiene un diámetro de 30cm; **how far is it ~?** (*river*) ¿cuántos metros tiene de ancho?

[4] (= *crossways*) a través, en cruz, transversalmente

across-the-board [əˈkrɒsðəˈbɔːd] ADJ [*increase*] global, general

acrostic [əˈkrɒstɪk] N acróstico *m*

acrylic [əˈkrɪlɪk] (A) ADJ acrílico
(B) CPD ► **acrylic fibre** N fibra *f* acrílica

acrylonitrile [ˌækrɪləʊˈnaɪtraɪl] N acrilonitrilo *m*

ACT N ABBR (*US*) (= **American College Test**) *examen que se hace al término de los estudios secundarios*

act [ækt] (A) N [1] (= *deed*) acto *m*, acción *f*; **to catch sb in the ~** sorprender a algn en el acto; **I was in the ~ of writing to him** justamente le estaba escribiendo
[2] (*Parl*) ley *f*
[3] (*Theat*) (= *division*) acto *m*; (= *performance*) número *m*; ✦**IDIOMS** **it's a hard** *or* **tough ~ to follow** es muy difícil de igualar; **to get into** *or* **in on the ~*** introducirse en el asunto, lograr tomar parte; **to get one's ~ together*** organizarse, arreglárselas
[4] (*fig*) (= *pretence*) cuento *m*, teatro *m*; **to put on an ~** fingir, hacer teatro*
(B) VT (*Theat*) [+ *play*] representar; **to ~ the part of** (*lit*) hacer el papel de; **he really ~ed the part** (*fig*) la verdad es que daba el papel; ✦**IDIOM** **to ~ the fool** hacerse el tonto
(C) VI [1] (= *perform*) (*Theat*) hacer teatro; (*Cine*) hacer cine; **I ~ed in my youth** de joven fui actor; **she's away ~ing in the provinces** está actuando en provincias; **to ~ in a film** tener un papel en una película; **have you ever ~ed?** ¿has actuado alguna vez?, ¿tienes experiencia como actor?; **who's ~ing in it?** ¿quién actúa?
[2] (= *pretend*) **he's only ~ing** lo está fingiendo (nada más); **to ~ ill** fingirse enfermo; *see also* **stupid**
[3] (= *behave*) actuar, comportarse; **he is ~ing strangely** está actuando *or* se está comportando de una manera rara; **she ~ed as if she was unwell** actuaba *or* se comportaba como si estuviera enferma
[4] (= *take action*) obrar, tomar medidas; **to ~ with caution** obrar con precaución; **he ~ed to stop it** tomó medidas para impedirlo; **now is the time to ~** hay que ponerse en acción ahora mismo; **he declined to ~** se negó a actuar; **he ~ed for the best** hizo lo que mejor le parecía
[5] (= *work*) **he was ~ing as ambassador** hacía de embajador; **~ing in my capacity as chairman** en mi calidad de presidente; **to ~ for sb** representar a algn
[6] (= *function*) [*thing*] funcionar; **to ~ as sth** servir de algo; **it ~s as a deterrent** sirve para disuadir, sirve de disuasión; **it ~s as a safety valve** funciona como válvula de seguridad
[7] (= *take effect*) [*drug*] surtir efecto, actuar; **the medicine is slow to ~** la medicina tarda en surtir efecto *or* actuar; **it ~s by stimulating the immune system** actúa estimulando el sistema inmunológico
(D) CPD ► **act of contrition** N acto *m* de contrición ► **act of faith** N acto *m* de fe ► **act of folly** N locura *f* ► **act of God** N (caso *m* de) fuerza *f* mayor; **we're not insured against ~s of God** no estamos asegurados en casos de fuerza mayor *or* no estamos asegurados contra fuerzas mayores ► **act of justice** N acto *m* de justicia ► **Act of Parliament** N ley *f* (*aprobada por el Parlamento*) ► **act of treason** N traición *f*; **an ~ of treason** una traición ► **act of war** N acción *f* de guerra ► **the Acts of the Apostles** NPL los Hechos de los Apóstoles

►**act on** VI + PREP = **act upon**

►**act out** VT + ADV representar; **to ~ out a macabre drama** (*fig*) representar (hasta el final) un drama macabro; **she is given to ~ing out her fantasies** tiene tendencia a hacer vivir sus fantasías en la realidad

►**act up*** VI + ADV [*person*] portarse mal; [*knee, back, injury*] molestar, doler; [*machine*] fallar, estropearse

►**act upon** VI + PREP [1] [+ *advice, suggestion*] seguir; [+ *order*] obedecer; **to ~ upon the evidence** obrar de acuerdo con los hechos
[2] (= *affect*) afectar (a); **the drug ~s upon the brain** la droga afecta al cerebro

> **ACT OF PARLIAMENT**
>
> *A una ley ya aprobada por el Parlamento británico se la denomina* **Act of Parliament**. *Antes, cuando todavía es un proyecto de ley (***bill***), puede ser modificado tanto por la Cámara de los Comunes como por la de los Lores. Si ambas cámaras lo aprueban, se envía al monarca para que dé su aprobación (***Royal Assent***), aunque esto es una mera formalidad. Tras ello la ley ya es oficialmente un* **Act of Parliament**, *y pasa a formar parte de la legislación británica, reemplazando cualquier ley consuetudinaria (***common law***) que hubiera sobre ese asunto.*
>
> ⇨ *Ver tb* COMMON LAW

actable [ˈæktəbl] ADJ representable

acting [ˈæktɪŋ] (A) ADJ [*headmaster, president etc*] interino, suplente
(B) N (*Theat*) (= *performance*) interpretación *f*, actuación *f*; (= *profession*) profesión *f* de actor, teatro *m*; **what was his ~ like?** ¿qué tal hizo el papel?; **this is ~ as it should be** esto se llama realmente ser actor *or* actriz, así es el teatro de verdad; **~ is not in my line** yo no soy actor; **she has done some ~** tiene alguna experiencia como actriz; **to go in for ~** hacerse actor

actinic [ækˈtɪnɪk] ADJ actínico

actinium [ækˈtɪnɪəm] N actinio *m*

action [ˈækʃən] (A) N [1] (= *activity*) **the time has come for ~** ha llegado el momento de hacer algo *or* de actuar; **when shall we get some ~ on this?** ¿cuándo se va a hacer algo al respecto?; **into ~**: **they went into ~ to rescue the climbers** intervinieron para rescatar a los alpinistas; **to put a plan into ~** poner un plan en práctica *or* en marcha; **emergency procedures will be put into ~** las medidas de emergencia serán puestas en marcha; **a man of ~** un hombre de acción; **to be out of ~** [*machinery*] no funcionar, estar averiado; **the lifts are out of ~** los ascensores no funcionan *or* están averiados; **"out of action"** "no funciona", "fuera de servicio"; **he was out of ~ for months** estuvo sin poder hacer nada durante meses; **the illness put him out of ~ for six months** la enfermedad lo dejó seis meses fuera de combate; **~ stations!** ¡a sus puestos!; *see also* **disciplinary, freedom, industrial**
[2] (= *steps*) medidas *fpl*; **emergency ~** medidas *fpl* de emergencia; **to take ~ against sb/sth** tomar medidas contra algn/algo; **their advice is to take no ~** aconsejan no hacer nada
[3] (= *deed*) acto *m*; **he wasn't responsible for his ~s** no era responsable de sus actos; **to judge sb by his ~s** juzgar a algn por sus actos *or* acciones; ✦**IDIOM** **to suit the ~ to the word** unir la acción a la palabra; ✦**PROV** **~s speak louder than words** obras son amores, que no buenas razones
[4] (*) (= *excitement*) animación *f*, marcha* *f*; **they were hoping to find some ~** esperaban encontrar algo de animación, esperaban encontrar algo de marcha*; **where's the ~ in this town?** ¿dónde está la marcha en este pueblo?*; **he likes to be where the ~ is** le gusta estar en medio del meollo*; ✦**IDIOM** **a piece** *or* **slice of the ~*** una tajada*, una parte de los dividendos
[5] (*Mil*) (= *intervention*) intervención *f*; (= *engagement*) contienda *f*, enfrentamiento *m*; **we are trying to avoid military ~** estamos tratando de evitar la intervención militar; **we didn't know how many men we had lost until the ~ was over** no supimos cuántos hombres habíamos perdido hasta que terminó la contienda *or* el enfrentamiento; **to go into ~** [*person, unit*] entrar en acción *or* en combate; [*army, battleship*] entrar en acción; **wounded/killed in ~** herido/muerto en acción (de guerra) *or* en combate; **to see ~** luchar
[6] (= *mechanism*) [*of piano*] transmisión *f*; [*of clock*] mecanismo *m*
[7] (= *motion*) (*gen*) movimiento *m*; [*of horse*] marcha *f*
[8] (= *effect, operation*) [*of acid, drug, elements*] efecto *m*; **stones worn smooth by the ~ of water** piedras *fpl* erosionadas por efecto del agua
[9] (*Jur*) (= *measures*) acción *f* judicial; (= *lawsuit*) proceso *m* judicial; **the police are not taking any ~** la policía no va a emprender ninguna acción judicial; **to bring an ~ against sb** comenzar un proceso judicial contra algn; **~ for damages** demanda *f* por daños y perjuicios; *see also* **court D, legal A1, libel**
[10] (*Theat, Cine*) [*of play*] acción *f*; **the ~ (of the play) takes place in Greece** la acción (de la obra) se desarrolla en Grecia; **~!** (*Cine*) ¡acción!
[11] (*Phys*) acción *f*
(B) VT poner en práctica, poner en marcha
(C) CPD ► **action committee** N comité *m* de acción ► **action film** N película *f* de acción ► **action group** N grupo *m* de acción ► **action man** N (*esp hum*) hombre *m* de acción ► **action movie** N (*US*) = **action film** ► **action painting** N tachismo *m* ► **action point** N punto *m* a seguir, acción *f* a tomar ► **action replay** N (*TV*) repetición *f* (de la jugada); (*fig*) repetición *f*

actionable [ˈækʃnəbl] ADJ (*Jur*) justiciable, procesable

action-packed [ˈækʃnpækt] ADJ [*film, book*] lleno de acción; [*holiday, life*] muy movido

activate [ˈæktɪveɪt] VT activar

activator [ˈæktɪˌveɪtəʳ] N activador *m*

active [ˈæktɪv] (A) ADJ [1] (= *lively*) [*person, brain*] activo; [*imagination*] vivo; **he has an ~ mind** tiene una mente muy activa
[2] (= *busy*) [*life, day, period*] de mucha actividad, muy movido
[3] (= *not passive*) [*member, population*] activo; **guerrilla groups are ~ in the province** grupos de guerrilleros están luchando en la provincia; **animals which are ~ at night** los animales que desarrollan su actividad por la noche; **we are giving it ~ consideration** lo estamos estudiando en serio; **to take an ~ interest in sth** interesarse vivamente por algo; **after 17 years' ~ involvement in the party**

después de 17 años de militar activamente en el partido; **to play** *or* **take an ~ part in sth** participar activamente en algo; **he withdrew from ~ participation in the project** dejó de participar activamente en el proyecto; **to be politically ~** ◊ **to be ~ in politics** militar políticamente; **he played an ~ role in bringing about a ceasefire** desempeñó un papel activo a la hora de conseguir el alto al fuego; **to be sexually ~** tener relaciones sexuales; **the government must take ~ steps to bring down inflation** el gobierno debe tomar medidas directas para bajar la inflación
4 (= *not extinct*) [*volcano*] en actividad
5 (*Chem, Physics, Electronics*) activo; **the ~ ingredient** el ingrediente activo
6 (*Fin, Comm*) [*trading, market*] activo; **~ assets** activo *msing* productivo; **~ balance** saldo *m* activo; **~ money** dinero *m* activo, dinero *m* disponible; **~ partner** socio/a *m/f* activo/a; **~ trade balance** balanza *f* comercial favorable, balanza *f* comercial acreedora
7 (*Mil*) **~ service** *or* (*US*) **duty** servicio *m* activo; **to be on ~ service** *or* **duty** estar en activo; **to die on ~ service** morir en acto de servicio; **he saw ~ service in Italy and Germany** estuvo en servicio activo en Italia y Alemania
8 (*Ling, Gram*) **~ vocabulary** vocabulario *m* activo; **the ~ voice** la voz activa; **in the ~ voice** en voz activa
Ⓑ N (*Gram*) **the ~** la voz activa
Ⓒ CPD ► **active birth** N (*Med*) parto *m* natural ► **active file** N (*Comput*) fichero *m* activo ► **the active list** N la reserva activa; **to be on the ~ list** estar en la reserva activa ► **active suspension** N (*Aut*) suspensión *f* activa

actively ['æktɪvlɪ] ADV [*encourage, promote, campaign, support,*] enérgicamente; [*seek, consider*] seriamente; **to be ~ involved in sth** tomar parte activa en algo, participar activamente en algo

activism ['æktɪvɪzəm] N activismo *m*

activist ['æktɪvɪst] N activista *mf*

activity [æk'tɪvɪtɪ] Ⓐ N [*of person*] actividad *f*; (*in port, town*) movimiento *m*, actividad *f*; **business activities** actividades *fpl* comerciales; **leisure activities** pasatiempos *mpl*; **social activities** actividades *fpl* sociales; **terrorist activities** actividades *fpl* terroristas
Ⓑ CPD ► **activity book** N (*accompanying text book*) libro *m* de actividades, cuaderno *m* de actividades; (= *book of games*) libro *m* de pasatiempos ► **activity holiday** N *vacaciones con actividades ya programadas*

actor ['æktəʳ] N actor *m*

actress ['æktrɪs] N actriz *f*

actual ['æktjʊəl] Ⓐ ADJ 1 (= *real*) real; **the ~ number is much higher than that** el número real es mucho más alto; **the film was based on ~ events** la película estaba basada en hechos reales; **let's take an ~ case/example** tomemos un caso/ejemplo concreto; **there is no ~ contract** no hay contrato propiamente dicho; **you met an ~ film star?** ¿has conocido a una estrella de cine de verdad?; **in ~ fact** en realidad; **~ size** tamaño *m* real
2 (= *precise*) [*amount, figure*] exacto; [*words*] exacto, textual; **I don't remember the ~ figures** no recuerdo las cifras exactas; **what were his ~ words?** ¿cuáles fueron sus palabras exactas *or* textuales?
3 (= *very*) **they couldn't find the ~ gun that was used** no encontraron el arma que se utilizó; **the film used the ~ people involved as actors** la película utilizó como actores a los implicados
4 (= *proper*) **the ~ wedding procession starts at eleven** el desfile de boda propiamente dicho empieza a las once; **on the ~ day somebody will carry that for you** ese día alguien lo llevará por ti
Ⓑ CPD ► **actual bodily harm** N (*Jur*) daños *mpl* físicos, lesiones *fpl* corporales ► **actual loss** N (*Comm*) pérdida *f* efectiva

actuality [,æktjʊ'ælɪtɪ] N realidad *f*; **in ~** en realidad

actualize ['æktjʊəlaɪz] VT 1 (= *make real*) realizar
2 (= *represent*) representar de manera realista, describir con realismo

actually ['æktjʊəlɪ] ADV 1 (= *really*) en realidad, realmente; **she didn't ~ see the accident** en realidad no vio el accidente, no vio el accidente realmente; **no one ~ died** en realidad no murió nadie; **can computers ~ create language?** ¿pueden realmente crear un idioma los ordenadores?; **inflation has ~ fallen** la inflación de hecho ha bajado; **I never thought you'd ~ do it!** ¡jamás pensé que lo harías de verdad!
2 (*correcting, clarifying*) **that's not true, ~** bueno, eso no es cierto; **~, I don't know him at all** pues la verdad, no lo conozco de nada; **~, you were quite right** pues mira, de hecho tenías razón; **"he earns £30,000 a year" — "£30,500, actually"** —gana 30.000 libras al año —30.500 libras para ser exactos; **~, I didn't come here just to help you** en realidad, no he venido sólo para ayudarte
3 (= *exactly*) exactamente; **what did he ~ say?** ¿qué es lo que dijo exactamente?
4 (*for emphasis*) **we ~ caught a fish!** ¡incluso *or* hasta pescamos un pez!; **I was so bored I ~ fell asleep!** ¡me aburría tanto que de hecho me quedé dormido!; **you only pay for the electricity you ~ use** sólo pagas la electricidad que consumes

actuarial [,æktjʊ'ɛərɪəl] Ⓐ ADJ actuarial
Ⓑ CPD ► **actuarial tables** NPL tablas *fpl* actuariales

actuary ['æktjʊərɪ] N actuario/a *m/f* de seguros

actuate ['æktjʊeɪt] VT 1 [+ *person*] mover, motivar; **he was ~d by envy** estaba movido *or* motivado por la envidia; **a statement ~d by malice** una declaración movida *or* motivada por el rencor
2 (*Mech*) impulsar, accionar

acuity [ə'kjuːɪtɪ] N acuidad *f*, agudeza *f*

acumen ['ækjʊmen] N perspicacia *f*, tino *m*, agudeza *f*

acupressure [ækjə,preʃəʳ] N acupresión *f*, digitopuntura *f*

acupuncture ['ækjʊpʌŋktʃəʳ] N acupuntura *f*

acupuncturist [,ækjʊ'pʌŋktʃərɪst] N acupuntor(a) *m/f*, acupunturista *mf*

acute [ə'kjuːt] ADJ 1 (= *intense*) [*crisis, shortage, problem*] grave; [*anxiety, joy*] profundo, intenso; [*pain*] agudo; [*discomfort*] fuerte; **the report has caused the government ~ embarrassment** el informe ha puesto en una situación de lo más embarazosa al gobierno; **to become ~** [*shortage, problem*] agravarse
2 (= *keen*) [*hearing*] fino, agudo; [*sense of smell*] fino; **to have ~ powers of observation** tener agudas *or* grandes dotes de observación
3 (= *shrewd*) [*person, mind, comment*] agudo, perspicaz; **that was very ~ of you!** ¡qué perspicaz!, ¡eres un lince!
4 (*Med*) [*illness, case, appendicitis*] agudo
5 (*Geom*) [*angle*] agudo
6 (*Ling*) [*accent*] agudo; **e ~** e con acento agudo

acutely [ə'kjuːtlɪ] ADV 1 (= *intensely*) [*feel, suffer*] intensamente; [*embarrassing, uncomfortable*] sumamente; **I am ~ aware that …** me doy perfecta cuenta de que …, me doy cuenta perfectamente de que …, soy perfectamente consciente de que …; **they were ~ aware of the difficulties involved** tenían plena consciencia de todas las dificultades que suponía
2 (= *shrewdly*) perspicazmente

acuteness [ə'kjuːtnɪs] N 1 (= *keenness*) [*of vision, hearing, observation, analysis*] agudeza *f*
2 (= *shrewdness*) perspicacia *f*, agudeza *f*
3 (*Med*) gravedad *f*

AD Ⓐ ADV ABBR (= **Anno Domini**) d. de C., d.C.
Ⓑ N ABBR (*US Mil*) = **active duty**

ad* [æd] N ABBR = **advertisement**

a.d. ABBR = **after date**

A/D ABBR = **analogue-digital**

adage ['ædɪdʒ] N adagio *m*, refrán *m*

adagio [ə'dɑːdʒɪəʊ] N adagio *m*

Adam ['ædəm] Ⓐ N Adán; ✦***IDIOMS*** **I don't know him from ~*** no lo conozco en absoluto; **to be as old as ~** ser de tiempos de Maricastaña, ser más viejo que el mundo
Ⓑ CPD ► **Adam's ale** N agua *f* ► **Adam's apple** N nuez *f* (de la garganta)

adamant ['ædəmənt] ADJ (*fig*) firme, inflexible; **he was ~ in his refusal** se mantuvo firme *or* inflexible en su negativa

adamantine [,ædə'mæntaɪn] ADJ adamantino

adamantly ['ædəməntlɪ] ADV [*refuse*] rotundamente, terminantemente; **to be ~ opposed to sth** oponerse terminantemente *or* firmemente a algo

adapt [ə'dæpt] Ⓐ VT 1 [+ *machine*] ajustar, adaptar; [+ *building*] remodelar; **it is perfectly ~ed to its environment** está adaptado perfectamente a su ambiente; **to ~ o.s. to sth** adaptarse a algo, ajustarse a algo
2 [+ *text*] adaptar; **~ed from the Spanish** adaptado del español; **~ed for the screen** adaptado para el cine *or* la pantalla; **his novel was ~ed for television** su novela fue adaptada para la televisión; **a novel ~ed by H. Campbell** una novela en versión de H. Campbell
Ⓑ VI adaptarse

adaptability [ə,dæptə'bɪlɪtɪ] N adaptabilidad *f*, capacidad *f* para adaptarse *or* acomodarse

adaptable [ə'dæptəbl] ADJ [*vehicle etc*] adaptable; [*person*] capaz de acomodarse, adaptable; **he's very ~** se adapta *or* se acomoda con facilidad a las circunstancias

adaptation [,ædæp'teɪʃən] N (*Bio*) adaptación *f*; [*of text*] versión *f*

adapter, adaptor [ə'dæptəʳ] N (*gen*) adaptador *m*; (*Brit Elec*) enchufe *m* múltiple, ladrón *m*

adaption [æ'dæpʃən] N = **adaptation**

adaptive [ə'dæptɪv] ADJ **the human body is remarkably ~** el cuerpo humano tiene una gran adaptabilidad *or* una gran capacidad de adaptación; **an ~ reaction to an intolerable situation** una reacción de adaptación a una situación intolerable

ADC N ABBR 1 = **aide-de-camp**
2 (*US*) = **Aid to Dependent Children**
3 = **analogue-digital converter**

ADD N ABBR = **attention deficit disorder**

add [æd] Ⓐ VT 1 (*Math*) sumar
2 (= *join*) añadir, agregar (*esp LAm*) (**to** a); **there is nothing ~ed** no hay nada añadido; **"add salt to taste"** "añadir sal al gusto";

✦*IDIOM* **to ~ insult to injury** para colmo de males

3 (= *say further*) añadir, agregar; **he ~ed that …** añadió que …, agregó que …; **there's nothing to ~** no hay nada que añadir, no hay nada más que decir

Ⓑ VI (= *count*) sumar

►**add in** VT + ADV añadir, incluir

►**add on** VT + ADV añadir; **we ~ed two rooms on** hicimos construir *or* añadimos dos habitaciones más; **you have to ~ 15 dollars on for service** hay que añadir 15 dólares por el servicio

►**add to** VI + PREP aumentar, acrecentar; **it only ~ed to our problems** no hizo sino aumentar nuestros problemas; **then, to ~ to our troubles …** luego, para colmo de desgracias …, luego, para más desgracias …

►**add together** VT + ADV sumar

►**add up** Ⓐ VT + ADV 1 [+ *figures*] sumar

2 [+ *benefits, advantages*] calcular

Ⓑ VI + ADV 1 [*figures*] sumar; **it doesn't ~ up** (*Math*) no cuadra

2 (*fig*) (= *make sense*) tener sentido; **it all ~s up** es lógico, tiene sentido; **it's all beginning to ~ up** la cosa empieza a aclararse; **it just doesn't ~ up** no tiene sentido

►**add up to** VI + PREP 1 (*Math*) sumar, ascender a; **it ~s up to 25** suma 25, asciende a 25

2 (*fig*) (= *mean*) querer decir, venir a ser; **what all this ~s up to is …** lo que quiere decir *or* significa todo esto es que …; **it doesn't ~ up to much** es poca cosa, no tiene gran importancia

added ['ædɪd] Ⓐ ADJ añadido, adicional; **with ~ emphasis** con mayor énfasis, con más énfasis aún; **it's an ~ problem** es un problema más; **~ to which …** y además …, por si fuera poco …

Ⓑ CPD ► **added value** N valor *m* añadido

addendum [ə'dendəm] N (*pl* **addenda** [ə'dendə]) ad(d)enda *f*, adición *f*, artículo *m* suplementario

adder ['ædəʳ] N víbora *f*

addict ['ædɪkt] N 1 (*addicted to drugs etc*) adicto/a *m/f*

2 (*) (= *enthusiast*) entusiasta *mf*; **I'm a detective story ~*** yo soy un entusiasta de la novela policíaca; **a telly ~*** un(a) teleadicto/a

addicted [ə'dɪktɪd] ADJ (*lit*) adicto; **to be ~ to sth** ser adicto a algo (*also fig*); **I'm ~ to chocolate** soy adicto al chocolate; **to be ~ to drugs** ser drogadicto; **to be ~ to heroin** ser heroinómano; **I went through four years of being ~ to video games** pasé cuatro años enganchado a los videojuegos; **to become ~ to** [+ *drugs etc*] enviciarse con; **she had become ~ to golf** se envició con el golf, se convirtió en una adicta al golf, se había vuelto una apasionada del golf

addiction [ə'dɪkʃən] N 1 (*to drugs, alcohol*) adicción *f*, dependencia *f*; **his ~ to drugs** su adicción a *or* dependencia de las drogas, su drogodependencia; **heroin ~** adicción *f* a *or* dependencia *f* de la heroína, heroinomanía *f*

2 (*fig*) adicción *f*; **his ~ to TV soaps** su adicción a las telenovelas

addictive [ə'dɪktɪv] ADJ 1 (*lit*) [*drug*] que crea adicción, adictivo; [*personality*] propenso a las adicciones; **cigarettes are highly ~** los cigarros son muy adictivos *or* crean una fuerte adicción; **an ~ habit** un vicio que crea adicción

2 (*fig*) **to be ~** ser como una droga, ser adictivo, ser un vicio*; **rock climbing is ~** el alpinismo es como una droga, el alpinismo es adictivo, el alpinismo es un vicio*; **movie-making can quickly become ~** el hacer películas puede convertirse pronto en una adicción

adding machine ['ædɪŋmə,ʃiːn] N sumadora *f*

Addis Ababa ['ædɪs'æbəbə] N Addis Abeba *m*

▼**addition** [ə'dɪʃən] Ⓐ N 1 (*Math*) adición *f*, suma *f*; **if my ~ is correct** si he sumado bien; **to do ~** hacer sumas

2 (= *act*) adición *f*; **in ~** además; **in ~ to** además de; **with the ~ of a cardigan, it makes the perfect summer outfit** añadiendo una chaqueta, es el conjunto perfecto para el verano

3 (= *thing added*) **these are our new ~s** éstas son nuestras nuevas adquisiciones; **this is a welcome ~ to our books on agriculture** éste aumenta valiosamente nuestra colección de libros sobre agricultura; **we made ~s to our stocks** aumentamos nuestras existencias; **an ~ to the family** un nuevo miembro de la familia

Ⓑ CPD ► **addition sign** N signo *m* de sumar

additional [ə'dɪʃənl] ADJ [*cost, payment*] adicional, extra; [*troops, men*] más; **the US is sending ~ troops to the region** los Estados Unidos van a mandar más tropas a la región; **it is an ~ reason to** + INFIN es razón de más para + *infin*; **this gave him ~ confidence** esto aumentó su confianza; **~ charge** cargo *m* adicional

additionality [ə,dɪʃə'nælɪtɪ] N adicionalidad *f*

additionally [ə'dɪʃənlɪ] ADV 1 (= *even more*) [*worry*] aún más; **this makes it ~ difficult for me** esto me lo hace aún más difícil, esto aumenta (aún más) mis dificultades

2 (= *moreover*) además

additive ['ædɪtɪv] N aditivo *m*

additive-free ['ædɪtɪv'friː] ADJ sin aditivos

addled ['ædld] ADJ 1 (= *rotten*) huero, podrido

2 (= *confused*) [*brain*] confuso, débil

add-on ['ædɒn] Ⓐ N (*Comput*) componente *m* *or* dispositivo *m* adicional

Ⓑ ADJ [*product, part*] adicional

▼**address** [ə'dres] Ⓐ N 1 [*of house etc*] dirección *f*, señas *fpl*; **she isn't at this ~ any more** ya no vive en esta casa; *see also* **business B, forwarding, home D**

2 (= *speech*) discurso *m*; (= *lecture*) conferencia *f*; **election ~** (= *speech*) discurso *m* electoral; (= *leaflet*) carta *f* de propaganda electoral; *see also* **public**

3 (*Parl etc*) petición *f*, memorial *m*

4 (= *title*) **form of ~** tratamiento *m*

5 (*Comput*) dirección *f*; **absolute/relative ~** dirección *f* absoluta/relativa

6 (†) (= *skill*) destreza *f*, habilidad *f*

7 (††) (= *manners*) modales *mpl*; (= *behaviour*) conducta *f*, comportamiento *m*

8 **to pay one's ~es to**† hacer la corte a, pretender a

Ⓑ VT 1 [+ *letter*] (= *direct*) dirigir (**to** a); (= *put address on*) poner la dirección en; **the letter was ~ed to the editor** la carta iba dirigida al director; **I ~ed it to your home** lo mandé a tu casa; **this is ~ed to you** esto viene con *or* a su nombre; **this letter is wrongly ~ed** esta carta lleva la dirección equivocada; **I haven't ~ed it yet** todavía no le he puesto la dirección

2 [+ *person*] 2·1 (= *speak to*) dirigirse a; **are you ~ing me?** ¿se está usted dirigiendo a mí?; **the judge ~ed the jury** el juez se dirigió al jurado

2·2 (= *make a speech to*) [*audience*] pronunciar un discurso ante; **to ~ the House** (*Parl*) pronunciar un discurso en el Parlamento

2·3 **to ~ sb as "tú"** tratar a algn de "tú", tutear a algn; **to ~ sb by his proper title** dar el debido tratamiento a algn

2·4 **to ~ o.s. to** [+ *person*] dirigirse a; [+ *problem, task*] aplicarse a

3 [+ *remarks*] dirigir; **please ~ your complaints to the manager** se ruega dirijan sus reclamaciones al director

4 [+ *problem*] abordar

Ⓒ CPD ► **address book** N librito *m* de direcciones, agenda *f* ► **address commission** N (*Comm*) *comisión que se paga al agente fletador por su tarea de embarque* ► **address label** N etiqueta *f* para la dirección

addressee [,ædre'siː] N destinatario/a *m/f*; (*Comm*) consignatario/a *m/f*; **"postage to be paid by the ~"** "a franquear en destino"

addressing [ə'dresɪŋ] Ⓐ N (*Comput*) direccionamiento *m*

Ⓑ CPD ► **addressing machine** N máquina *f* de direcciones

Addressograph® [ə'dresəʊgrɑːf] N máquina *f* de direcciones *or* para dirigir sobres

adduce [ə'djuːs] VT (*frm*) alegar, aducir

adductor [ə'dʌktəʳ] N (*Anat*) aductor *m*

Adelaide ['ædəleɪd] N Adelaida *f*

Aden ['eɪdn] N Adén *m*; **Gulf of ~** Golfo *m* de Adén

adenoidal ['ædɪnɔɪdl] ADJ adenoideo; **he has an ~ tone** tiene una voz gangosa

adenoids ['ædɪnɔɪdz] NPL vegetaciones *fpl* adenoideas

adept Ⓐ [ə'dept] ADJ experto, hábil, ducho (**at, in** en)

Ⓑ ['ædept] N experto/a *m/f*, maestro/a *m/f*; **to be an ~ at sth/at doing sth** ser experto *or* maestro en algo/en hacer algo

adeptly [ə'deptlɪ] ADV con acierto *or* habilidad

adequacy ['ædɪkwəsɪ] N [*of income, explanation, facilities*] lo aceptable; [*of punishment, reward, diet*] lo apropiado; [*of person*] capacidad *f*, competencia *f*

adequate ['ædɪkwɪt] ADJ 1 (= *sufficient*) [*funds*] suficiente; **an ~ supply of food** suficientes alimentos; **one teaspoonful should be ~** una cucharadita bastará *or* será suficiente; **I didn't think the sentence was ~** la sentencia no me pareció correcta

2 (= *satisfactory*) [*diet*] equilibrado, apropiado; [*income, standard*] aceptable; [*housing, facilities*] adecuado, apropiado; **he failed to provide an ~ explanation for the delay** no fue capaz de dar una explicación convincente de su retraso; **there are no words ~ to express my gratitude** no hay palabras que expresen adecuadamente mi gratitud; **to be ~ for sb** [*housing*] ser adecuado para algn; **my income is quite ~ for my needs** mis ingresos cubren bien mis necesidades; **this saw should be ~ for the job** este serrucho valdrá para ese trabajo; **this typewriter is perfectly ~** esta máquina de escribir me sirve perfectamente; **to feel ~ to a task** sentirse capacitado para una tarea

3 (*pej*) (= *passable*) [*performance, essay*] aceptable, pasable; **the pay was ~ but hardly out of this world** el sueldo era aceptable *or* pasable, pero desde luego, nada del otro mundo

adequately ['ædɪkwɪtlɪ] ADV [*prepared, trained, protected*] suficientemente; [*punish*] de forma apropiada; [*respond*] apropiadamente; [*perform*] de forma aceptable; **this has never been ~ explained** esto nunca se ha explicado con claridad; **he speaks the language ~** habla el idioma de forma aceptable

ADHD N ABBR = **attention deficit hyperactivity disorder**

➤ LANGUAGE IN USE: **addition A2** 26.2 **address A1** 24.3

adhere [əd'hɪəʳ] VI (= *stick*) adherirse, pegarse (**to** a)

►**adhere to** VI + PREP (= *observe*) [+ *party, policy*] adherirse a; [+ *rule*] observar; (= *stand by*) [+ *belief*] aferrarse a; (= *fulfil*) [+ *promise*] cumplir

adherence [əd'hɪərəns] N 1 (*lit*) adherencia *f* (**to** a)
2 (*fig*) (*to policy*) adhesión *f*; (*to rule*) observancia *f* (**to** de)

adherent [əd'hɪərənt] Ⓐ ADJ adhesivo, adherente
Ⓑ N (= *person*) partidario/a *m/f*

adhesion [əd'hi:ʒən] N = **adherence**

adhesive [əd'hi:zɪv] Ⓐ ADJ adhesivo
Ⓑ N adhesivo *m*, pegamento *m*
Ⓒ CPD ► **adhesive plaster** N esparadrapo *m*
► **adhesive tape** N (= *stationery*) cinta *f* adhesiva, Scotch® *m*, celo *m*; (*Med*) esparadrapo *m*

ad hoc [,æd'hɒk] ADJ [*decision*] para el caso; [*committee*] formado con fines específicos

adieu [ə'dju:] Ⓐ EXCL ¡adiós!
Ⓑ N (*pl* **adieus** *or* **adieux** [ə'dju:z]) (*frm*) adiós *m*; **to bid ~ to** [+ *person*] despedirse de; [+ *thing*] renunciar a, abandonar; **to say one's adieus** *or* **adieux** despedirse

ad infinitum [,ædɪnfɪ'naɪtəm] ADV hasta el infinito, ad infinitum; **and so on ~** y así hasta el infinito *or* ad infinitum; **it just carries on ~** es inacabable, es cosa de nunca acabar; **it varies ~** tiene un sinfín de variaciones

ad interim ['æd'ɪntərɪm] Ⓐ ADV en el ínterin, interinamente
Ⓑ ADJ interino

adipose ['ædɪpəʊs] ADJ adiposo

adiposity [,ædɪ'pɒsɪtɪ] N adiposidad *f*

adjacent [ə'dʒeɪsənt] ADJ contiguo; [*angle*] adyacente; **~ to** contiguo a

adjectival [,ædʒek'taɪvəl] ADJ adjetivo, adjetival

adjectivally [,ædʒek'taɪvəlɪ] ADV adjetivamente

adjective ['ædʒektɪv] N adjetivo *m*

adjoin [ə'dʒɔɪn] Ⓐ VT estar contiguo a, lindar con, colindar con
Ⓑ VI estar contiguo, colindar

adjoining [ə'dʒɔɪnɪŋ] ADJ contiguo, colindante (*more frm*); **the ~ house** la casa contigua, la casa de al lado, la casa colindante (*more frm*); **two ~ countries** dos países vecinos, dos países colindantes (*more frm*); **in an ~ room** en un cuarto contiguo

adjourn [ə'dʒɜ:n] Ⓐ VT 1 (= *suspend*) suspender; (= *postpone*) aplazar; **to ~ a discussion for a week** aplazar un debate por una semana; **I declare the meeting ~ed** se levanta la sesión; **to stand ~ed** estar en suspenso
2 (*Jur*) **the court is ~ed** se levanta la sesión
Ⓑ VI 1 [*meeting*] aplazarse; (*Parl*) disolverse; **the court then ~ed** entonces el tribunal levantó la sesión
2 (= *move*) (*frm or hum*) **to ~ to** [+ *sitting-room, verandah*] pasar a; **they ~ed to the pub** se trasladaron al bar

adjournment [ə'dʒɜ:nmənt] N (= *period*) suspensión *f*; (= *postponement*) aplazamiento *m*

Adjt. ABBR = **adjutant**

adjudge [ə'dʒʌdz] VT 1 (= *pronounce, declare*) declarar; **he was ~d the winner** se lo declaró ganador, se le concedió la victoria; **to ~ that …** estimar que …, considerar que …
2 (*Jur*) [+ *costs, damages*] adjudicar; **to ~ sb guilty** declarar culpable a algn

adjudicate [ə'dʒu:dɪkeɪt] Ⓐ VT [+ *contest*] arbitrar, hacer de árbitro en; [+ *claim*] decidir sobre
Ⓑ VI arbitrar; **to ~ on a matter** arbitrar en un asunto

adjudication [ə,dʒu:dɪ'keɪʃən] Ⓐ N adjudicación *f*; **~ of bankruptcy** (*Jur*) adjudicación *f* de quiebra
Ⓑ CPD ► **adjudication order** N (*Jur*) orden *f* de adjudicación

adjudicator [ə'dʒu:dɪkeɪtəʳ] N juez *mf*, árbitro *mf*

adjunct ['ædʒʌŋkt] N adjunto/a *m/f*, accesorio/a *m/f*

adjure [ə'dʒʊəʳ] VT (*frm*) **to ~ sb to do sth** (= *order*) ordenar solemnemente a algn que haga algo; (= *implore*) suplicar *or* implorar a algn que haga algo

adjust [ə'dʒʌst] Ⓐ VT 1 (= *regulate*) [+ *height, temperature, speed, knob, dial*] regular; [+ *machine, engine, brakes*] ajustar; **she ~ed her wing mirror** ajustó el retrovisor exterior; **this chair can be ~ed** esta silla se puede regular; **"do not adjust your set"** "no modifique los controles de su aparato"
2 (= *correct*) [+ *figures*] ajustar; [+ *salaries, wages, prices*] reajustar; **~ed gross income** ingresos *mpl* brutos ajustados; **the seasonally ~ed unemployment total** la tasa de desempleo desestacionalizada; **we have ~ed all salaries upwards/downwards** hemos hecho un reajuste de todos los salarios al alza/a la baja
3 (= *change, adapt*) [+ *terms*] modificar; **I tried to ~ my eyes to the darkness** intenté que los ojos se me acostumbrasen a la oscuridad; **to ~ o.s. to a new situation** adaptarse a una nueva situación
4 (= *arrange*) [+ *hat, tie, clothes*] arreglar; [+ *straps*] ajustar; **she ~ed her head scarf** se arregló la pañoleta
5 (*Insurance*) [+ *claim*] liquidar, tasar
Ⓑ VI [*person*] adaptarse; [*machine, device*] ajustarse; **the boy is having trouble in ~ing** el niño está teniendo dificultades para adaptarse; **to ~ to sth** [*person*] acostumbrarse a algo, adaptarse a algo; [*eyes, body*] acostumbrarse a algo; **the seat ~s to various heights** el asiento se puede regular a distintas alturas

adjustability [ə,dʒʌstə'bɪlɪtɪ] N adaptabilidad *f*

adjustable [ə'dʒʌstəbl] Ⓐ ADJ ajustable, regulable; **the date is ~** podemos cambiar la fecha
Ⓑ CPD ► **adjustable spanner** N llave *f* inglesa

adjuster [ə'dʒʌstəʳ] N 1 (= *device*) ajustador *m*, tensor *m*
2 *see* **loss B**

adjustment [ə'dʒʌstmənt] N 1 (= *regulation*) [*of temperature, height, knob, dial*] regulación *f*; [*of machine, engine, brakes*] ajuste *m*
2 (= *rearrangement*) [*of clothing*] arreglo *m*
3 (= *alteration*) modificación *f*, cambio *m*; **we can always make an ~** siempre podemos cambiarlo; **to make an ~ to one's plans** modificar sus planes
4 (= *adaptation*) [*of person*] adaptación *f*; **social ~** adaptación *f* social
5 (*Econ*) ajuste *m*, reajuste *m*; **~ of prices** ajuste *m* de precios; **~ of wages** reajuste *m* salarial; **after ~ for inflation** después de los ajustes *or* reajustes debidos a la inflación
6 (*Insurance*) [*of claim*] liquidación *f*, tasación *f*

adjutant ['ædʒətənt] Ⓐ N ayudante *mf*
Ⓑ CPD ► **Adjutant General** N *general responsable del aparato administrativo*

Adlerian [,æd'lɪərɪən] ADJ (*Psych*) adleriano

ad lib [æd'lɪb] Ⓐ ADV [*perform, speak*] improvisando; [*continue*] a voluntad, a discreción
Ⓑ ADJ [*production, performance, speech*] improvisado
Ⓒ VT [+ *music, words etc*] improvisar
Ⓓ VI [*actor, speaker etc*] improvisar

Adm. ABBR 1 = **Admiral**
2 = **Admiralty**

adman* ['ædmæn] N (*pl* **admen**) profesional *m* de la publicidad, publicista *m*

admass ['ædmæs] N *la masa influenciable por la publicidad*

admin* ['ædmɪn] N ABBR (*Brit*) (= **administration**) administración *f*

administer [əd'mɪnɪstəʳ] VT 1 (= *manage*) [+ *company, estate, funds, finances*] administrar; [+ *country*] gobernar
2 (= *dispense*) [+ *medicine, sacrament*] administrar; [+ *justice, laws, punishment*] administrar, aplicar; **to ~ an oath to sb** tomar juramento a algn

administered [əd'mɪnɪstəd] CPD ► **administered price** N precio *m* fijado por el fabricante (*y que no puede ser variado por el detallista*)

administrate [əd'mɪnɪstreɪt] VT administrar, dirigir

administration [əd,mɪnɪs'treɪʃən] N 1 [*of company, estate, finances*] administración *f*; [*of country*] gobierno *m*; **a lot of time is spent on ~** se emplea mucho tiempo en la administración; **the job involves a lot of routine ~** el trabajo comprende bastantes tareas rutinarias de administración; **business ~** administración *f* de empresas
2 [*of medicine, sacrament*] administración *f*, dispensa *f*; [*of justice, punishment*] administración *f*, aplicación *f*; **~ of an oath** toma *f* de juramento
3 (= *governing body*) [*of company, institution*] administración *f*; **the college ~** la administración del colegio
4 (*esp US Pol*) (= *government*) gobierno *m*, administración *f*; **the Reagan ~** el gobierno de Reagan, la administración de Reagan

administrative [əd'mɪnɪstrətɪv] ADJ 1 [*work, officer, system*] administrativo; [*costs, expenses*] de administración, administrativo; **~ assistant** ayudante *mf* administrativo/a; **~ law** derecho *m* administrativo; **~ skills** dotes *fpl* administrativas; **~ staff** personal *m* de administración
2 (*US Jur*) **~ court** tribunal *m* administrativo; **~ machinery** maquinaria *f* administrativa, aparato *m* administrativo

administratively [əd'mɪnɪstrətɪvlɪ] ADV desde el punto de vista administrativo

administrator [əd'mɪnɪstreɪtəʳ] N administrador(a) *m/f*; (*Jur*) albacea *mf*

admirable ['ædmərəbl] ADJ admirable, digno de admiración

admirably ['ædmərəblɪ] ADV admirablemente, de una manera digna de admiración

admiral ['ædmərəl] N almirante *mf*

Admiralty ['ædmərəltɪ] Ⓐ N (*Brit*) Ministerio *m* de Marina, Almirantazgo *m*; **First Lord of the ~** Ministro *m* de Marina
Ⓑ CPD ► **Admiralty court** N (*US*) tribunal *m* marítimo

admiration [,ædmə'reɪʃən] N admiración *f*

admire [əd'maɪəʳ] VT (*gen*) admirar; (= *express admiration for*) elogiar; **she was admiring herself in the mirror** se estaba admirando en el espejo

admirer [əd'maɪərəʳ] N admirador(a) *m/f*

admiring [əd'maɪərɪŋ] ADJ [*look, glance, tone, voice*] (lleno) de admiración, admirativo; **his ~ fans** sus admiradores

admiringly [əd'maɪərɪŋlɪ] ADV [*say, describe*] con admiración; **to speak ~ of sb** hablar con admiración de algn; **he looked at her ~** le lanzó una mirada (llena) de admiración, le lanzó una mirada admirativa

admissibility [əd,mɪsə'bɪlɪtɪ] N admisibilidad *f*

admissible [əd'mɪsəbl] ADJ admisible, aceptable

admission [əd'mɪʃən] Ⓐ N 1 (*to building*) entrada *f*; **~ is free on Sundays** la entrada es gratuita los domingos; **"admission free"** "entrada gratis"; **"no admission"** "prohibida la entrada", "se prohíbe la entrada"; **we gained ~ by a window** logramos entrar por una ventana
2 (*to institution as member*) ingreso *m* (**to** en)
3 (= *acknowledgement*) confesión *f*, reconocimiento *m*; **it would be an ~ of defeat** sería un reconocimiento de la derrota, sería reconocer la derrota; **by** *or* **on his own ~** él mismo lo reconoce; **he made an ~ of guilt** hizo una confesión de culpabilidad, se confesó culpable
Ⓑ CPD ► **admission fee** N cuota *f* de entrada ► **admissions form** N (*US Univ*) impreso *m* de matrícula ► **admissions office** N (*US Univ*) secretaría *f*

▼ **admit** [əd'mɪt] VT 1 (= *allow to enter*) [+ *person*] dejar entrar; [+ *patient*] (*to hospital*) ingresar; [+ *air, light*] dejar pasar, dejar entrar; **"children not admitted"** "se prohíbe la entrada a los menores de edad"; **"this ticket admits two"** "entrada para dos personas"; **to be ~ted to the Academy** ingresar en la Academia; **to be ~ted to hospital** ingresar en el hospital; **~ting office** (*US Med*) oficina *f* de ingresos
2 (= *acknowledge*) reconocer; [+ *crime*] confesar; [+ *error*] reconocer; **it is hard, I ~** es difícil, lo reconozco; **it must be ~ted that ...** hay que reconocer que ...; **I ~ nothing!** ¡no tengo nada que confesar!

► **admit of** VI + PREP (*frm*) admitir; **it ~s of no other explanation** no cabe otra explicación

► **admit to** VI + PREP [+ *crime*] confesarse culpable de; **she ~s to doing it** confiesa haberlo hecho; **I ~ to feeling a bit ill** confieso que me siento algo mal

admittance [əd'mɪtəns] N entrada *f*; **to gain ~** conseguir entrar; **he was refused ~** se le negó la entrada; **"no admittance"** "se prohíbe la entrada", "prohibida la entrada"

admittedly [əd'mɪtɪdlɪ] ADV **it's only a theory, admittedly, but ...** reconozco que sólo es una teoría, pero ..., es verdad que *or* de acuerdo que sólo es una teoría, pero ...; **admittedly, economists often disagree among themselves** hay que reconocer que *or* hay que admitir que *or* es verdad que los economistas a menudo no están de acuerdo entre ellos

admixture [əd'mɪkstʃəʳ] N mezcla *f*, adición *f*; (*fig*) dosis *f inv*

admonish [əd'mɒnɪʃ] VT (*frm*) 1 (= *reprimand*) reprender, amonestar (**for** por)
2 (= *warn*) advertir, prevenir
3 (= *advise*) aconsejar (**to do** hacer)

admonishment [əd'mɒnɪʃmənt] N = **admonition**

admonition [,ædməʊ'nɪʃən] N (*frm*) (= *reproof*) reprensión *f*; (= *warning*) amonestación *f*, advertencia *f*; (= *advice*) consejo *m*, recomendación *f*

admonitory [əd'mɒnɪtərɪ] ADJ (*frm*) admonitorio

ad nauseam [,æd'nɔːsɪæm] ADV hasta la saciedad

adnominal [,aed'nɒmɪnəl] Ⓐ ADJ adnominal
Ⓑ N adnominal *m*

ado [ə'duː] N **without further** *or* **more ~** sin más (ni más); ✦**IDIOM much ~ about nothing** mucho ruido y pocas nueces

adobe [ə'dəʊbɪ] N adobe *m*

adolescence [,ædəʊ'lesns] N adolescencia *f*

adolescent [,ædəʊ'lesnt] Ⓐ ADJ adolescente
Ⓑ N adolescente *mf*

Adolf ['ædɒlf], **Adolphus** [ə'dɒlfəs] N Adolfo

Adonis [ə'dəʊnɪs] N Adonis

adopt [ə'dɒpt] VT 1 [+ *child*] adoptar
2 [+ *report*] aprobar; [+ *suggestion*] seguir, aceptar; (*Pol*) [+ *candidate*] elegir

adopted [ə'dɒptɪd] ADJ [*child*] adoptivo, adoptado (*Mex*)

adoption [ə'dɒpʃən] N adopción *f*; **they have two children by ~** tienen dos hijos adoptivos; **country of ~** patria *f* adoptiva

adoptive [ə'dɒptɪv] ADJ adoptivo

adorable [ə'dɔːrəbl] ADJ adorable, encantador

adorably [ə'dɔːrəblɪ] ADV de manera adorable *or* encantadora

adoration [,ædɔː'reɪʃən] N adoración *f*

adore [ə'dɔːʳ] VT (= *love*) adorar; **I ~ your new flat** me encanta tu nuevo piso

adoring [ə'dɔːrɪŋ] ADJ [*look*] lleno de adoración; [*parent etc*] cariñoso

adoringly [ə'dɔːrɪŋlɪ] ADV con adoración

adorn [ə'dɔːn] VT adornar, embellecer

adornment [ə'dɔːnmənt] N 1 (= *act*) [*of body, person*] adorno *m*, embellecimiento *m*; [*of building, room*] decoración *f*
2 (= *object*) adorno *m*

ADP N ABBR = **Automatic Data Processing**

adrenal [ə'driːnl] Ⓐ ADJ suprarrenal
Ⓑ CPD ► **adrenal gland** N glándula *f* suprarrenal

adrenalin(e) [ə'drenəlɪn] N adrenalina *f*; **I feel the ~ rising** (*fig*) siento que me sube la adrenalina

Adriatic [,eɪdrɪ'ætɪk] Ⓐ ADJ adriático
Ⓑ N **the ~ (Sea)** el (Mar) Adriático

adrift [ə'drɪft] ADV 1 (*esp Naut*) a la deriva; **to be cast ~** (*lit*) (*accidentally*) irse a la deriva; (*deliberately, also fig*) ser arrojado a la deriva; **to come ~** [*boat*] soltarse, irse a la deriva; [*wire, rope*] soltarse, desprenderse; **to be cut ~** ser soltado a la deriva; **to be set ~** ser dejado a la deriva
2 (= *directionless*) perdido; **she felt ~ and isolated** se sentía perdida y aislada
3 (= *awry*) **profits can be as much as £5m ~** los beneficios pueden estar hasta 5 millones de libras por debajo de lo esperado; **to go ~** [*plan, scheme*] fallar, irse al garete*
4 (*Sport*) **to be five points/seconds ~ of** estar a cinco puntos/segundos de, ir cinco puntos/segundos a la zaga de

adroit [ə'drɔɪt] ADJ diestro, hábil

adroitly [ə'drɔɪtlɪ] ADV diestramente, hábilmente

adroitness [ə'drɔɪtnɪs] N destreza *f*, habilidad *f*

ADT N ABBR (*US, Canada*) = **Atlantic Daylight Time**

adulate ['ædjʊleɪt] VT adular

adulation [,ædjʊ'leɪʃən] N adulación *f*

adulatory [,ædjʊ'leɪtərɪ, (*US*) 'ædʒələtɔːrɪ] ADJ adulador

adult ['ædʌlt] Ⓐ ADJ 1 [*person*] adulto, mayor; [*animal*] adulto
2 (= *explicit*) [*film, book*] para adultos
3 (= *mature*) maduro, adulto; **to be ~ about sth** comportarse como una persona adulta/como personas adultas con respecto a algo
Ⓑ N adulto/a *m/f*; **"adults only"** (*Cine*) "autorizado para mayores de 18 años"
Ⓒ CPD ► **adult education** N educación *f* para adultos

adulterate [ə'dʌltəreɪt] VT adulterar

adulteration [ə,dʌltə'reɪʃən] N adulteración *f*

adulterer [ə'dʌltərəʳ] N adúltero *m*

adulteress [ə'dʌltərɪs] N adúltera *f*

adulterous [ə'dʌltərəs] ADJ adúltero

adultery [ə'dʌltərɪ] N adulterio *m*

adulthood ['ædʌlthʊd] N adultez *f*, mayoría *f* de edad, edad *f* adulta

adumbrate ['ædʌmbreɪt] VT (*frm*) bosquejar; (= *foreshadow*) presagiar, anunciar

adumbration [,ædʌm'breɪʃən] N (*frm*) bosquejo *m*; (= *foreshadowing*) presagio *m*, anuncio *m*

ad val. ADJ, ADV ABBR (*Comm*) = **ad valorem**

ad valorem [ædvə'lɔːrəm] Ⓐ ADV conforme a su valor, por avalúo
Ⓑ CPD ► **ad valorem tax** N impuesto *m* según valor

▼ **advance** [əd'vɑːns] Ⓐ N 1 (= *forward movement*) avance *m*; **the rapid ~ of the Russian army** el rápido avance de las tropas rusas
2 (= *progress*) (*in science, technology*) avance *m*, adelanto *m*; [*of disease*] avance *m*; **an important scientific ~** un importante avance *or* adelanto científico; **the rapid ~ of modern industrial society** el vertiginoso desarrollo de la sociedad industrial moderna; **with the ~ of old age** según se va/iba envejeciendo
3 [*of money*] 3·1 (= *initial payment*) anticipo *m*, adelanto *m*; **she was paid a £530,000 ~ for her next novel** le dieron un anticipo *or* adelanto de 530.000 libras por su próxima novela
3·2 (*on salary*) **could you give me an ~?** ¿me podría dar un anticipo?; **she got an ~ on her salary** consiguió que le anticiparan parte del sueldo
3·3 (= *loan*) préstamo *m*
4 (= *rise*) (*in prices*) alza *f*, aumento *m*; **any ~ on £15?** (*in auction*) ¿alguien ofrece más de 15 libras?, 15 libras ¿alguien da más?
5 **advances** (*amorous*) insinuaciones *fpl*; (*Pol*) intentos *mpl* de acercamiento; **to make ~s to** *or* **toward(s) sb** (*amorous*) insinuarse a algn, hacer insinuaciones a algn; **she accused him of making unwanted sexual ~s** lo acusó de insinuaciones sexuales indebidas; **she rejected his ~s** no hizo caso de sus insinuaciones
6 **in ~: to let sb know a week in ~** avisar a algn con ocho días de antelación; **to book in ~** reservar con antelación; **the dish may be made in ~** el plato puede prepararse con anterioridad; **in ~ of: to arrive in ~ of sb** llegar antes que algn; **to be in ~ of one's time** adelantarse a su época, estar por delante de su época; **to pay in ~** pagar por adelantado; **to send sb on in ~** mandar a algn por delante; **thanking you in ~** agradeciéndole de antemano
Ⓑ VT 1 (= *move forward*) [+ *time, date, clock*] adelantar; (*Mil*) [+ *troops*] avanzar; **it ~s the ageing process** acelera el envejecimiento
2 (= *further*) [+ *plan, knowledge*] potenciar; [+ *interests*] promover, fomentar; [+ *career*] promocionar; [+ *cause, claim*] promover; [+ *person*] (*in career*) ascender (**to** a); **he has done much to ~ our understanding of music** ha contribuido mucho a potenciar nuestros conocimientos musicales
3 (= *put forward*) [+ *idea, opinion, theory*] pro-

➤ LANGUAGE IN USE: **admit** 2 6.2, 11.1, 11.2, 18.3, 26.3 **advance** A6 21.4

poner, sugerir; [+ *suggestion*] hacer; [+ *proposal*] presentar; [+ *opinion*] expresar; **he ~d the theory that ...** propuso *or* sugirió la teoría de que ...

4 (= *hand over*) [+ *money*] (*as initial fee*) adelantar, anticipar; (*as early wages*) adelantar; (*as loan*) prestar

Ⓒ VI 1 (= *move forward*) avanzar; **the advancing enemy army** el ejército enemigo que avanza; **she ~d across the room** avanzó hacia el otro lado de la habitación; **to ~ on sth/sb** (*gen*) acercarse a algo/algn, avanzar hacia algo/algn; **to ~ on sth** (*Mil*) avanzar sobre algo

2 (= *progress*) [*science, technology*] progresar, adelantarse; [*work, society*] avanzar; [*career*] progresar; [*person, pupil*] hacer progresos, progresar; (*in rank*) ascender (**to** a); **her film career was advancing nicely** su carrera cinematográfica progresaba bien *or* iba por muy buen camino; **despite his advancing years he was a good player** a pesar de su edad (avanzada) era un buen jugador; **with advancing years one forgets** con el paso de los años uno se olvida

3 (*Fin*) (= *rise*) [*price*] subir

Ⓓ CPD ► **advance booking** N reserva *f* anticipada, reserva *f* por anticipado; **"advance booking advisable"** "se recomienda que reserven por adelantado" ► **advance booking office** N (*Brit*) taquilla *f* (de reservas *or* venta anticipada) ► **advance copy** N [*of book*] ejemplar *m* de muestra; [*of speech*] copia *f* (del discurso) ► **advance guard** N (= *reconnaissance group*) avanzada *f*; (= *lookouts*) avanzadilla *f*; (= *mobile unit*) brigada *f* móvil ► **advance man** N (*US Pol*) *responsable de una campaña política* ► **advance notice** N aviso *m* previo; **meals can be provided with ~ notice** con aviso previo, se preparan comidas ► **advance party** N (= *reconnaissance group*) avanzada *f*; (= *lookouts*) avanzadilla *f* ► **advance payment** N anticipo *m* ► **advance publicity** N promoción *f* (antes del estreno, lanzamiento, etc) ► **advance warning** N aviso *m* previo

advanced [əd'vɑːnst] Ⓐ ADJ 1 (= *developed*) [*civilization, society*] avanzado

2 (= *not elementary*) [*course, level, studies*] avanzado, superior; [*student*] (de nivel) avanzado; **~ mathematics** matemáticas *fpl* avanzadas *or* superiores

3 (= *precocious*) adelantado; **her youngest child is very ~ for his age** su hijo menor es muy adelantado para su edad

4 (= *modern*) [*ideas*] avanzado

5 (*in time*) [*stage*] avanzado; [*disease*] de grado avanzado; **the talks are at an ~ stage** las negociaciones están muy avanzadas; **women in ~ stages of pregnancy** mujeres *fpl* en los últimos meses del embarazo; **the research is well ~** la investigación está muy adelantada; **patients with ~ cancer** los pacientes con cáncer de grado avanzado; **she became a mother at the ~ age of 44** tuvo su primer hijo a la avanzada edad de 44 años; **a man of ~ years** un hombre entrado en años, un hombre de edad avanzada; **to be ~ in years** estar entrado en años

Ⓑ CPD ► **advanced gas-cooled reactor** N reactor *m* avanzado refrigerado por gas ► **Advanced Level** N (*Brit Scol frm*) ≈ bachillerato *m*; **she has an Advanced level in chemistry** tiene un título de *Advanced Level* en química; → A LEVELS

advancement [əd'vɑːnsmənt] N 1 (= *furthering*) fomento *m*

2 (= *improvement*) progreso *m*

3 (*in rank*) ascenso *m*

advantage [əd'vɑːntɪdʒ] N 1 ventaja *f*; **it's no ~ to play first** el jugar primero no es una ventaja; **"languages and shorthand an ~"** (*in job advert*) "serán méritos *or* se valorarán idiomas y taquigrafía"; **to have an ~ over sb** llevar ventaja a algn; **I'm sorry, you have the ~ of me** (*fig*) lo siento, pero no recuerdo su nombre; **to have an ~ in numbers** llevar ventaja en cuanto al número; **he has the ~ of youth** tiene la ventaja de ser joven; **the plan has many ~s** el proyecto tiene muchas ventajas; **to show sth off to best ~** hacer que algo se vea bajo la luz más favorable; **to take ~ of sb** (*unfairly*) aprovecharse de algn, sacar partido de algn; (*sexually*) abusar de algn; **to take ~ of an opportunity** aprovechar una oportunidad; **it's to our ~** es ventajoso para nosotros; **to turn sth to (one's) ~** sacar buen partido de algo

2 (*Sport*) **~ González** (*Tennis*) ventaja González

advantaged [əd'vɑːntɪdʒd] NPL **the ~** los privilegiados, los favorecidos

advantageous [,ædvən'teɪdʒəs] ADJ [*offer, position*] ventajoso, provechoso; **to be ~ to sb** ser ventajoso *or* provechoso para algn, beneficiar a algn

advantageously [,ædvən'teɪdʒəslɪ] ADV ventajosamente, provechosamente

advent ['ædvənt] Ⓐ N 1 (= *arrival*) advenimiento *m*

2 (*Rel*) **Advent** Adviento *m*

Ⓑ CPD ► **Advent calendar** N calendario *m* de Adviento ► **Advent Sunday** N domingo *m* de Adviento

adventitious [,ædven'tɪʃəs] ADJ (*frm*) adventicio

adventure [əd'ventʃəʳ] Ⓐ N aventura *f*; **the spirit of ~** el espíritu de aventura, el espíritu aventurero

Ⓑ CPD ► **adventure playground** N (*Brit*) parque *m* infantil ► **adventure story** N novela *f* de aventuras

adventurer [əd'ventʃərəʳ] N 1 (= *explorer*) aventurero/a *m/f*

2 (*pej*) (= *opportunist*) desaprensivo/a *m/f*

adventuress [əd'ventʃərɪs] N aventurera *f*

adventurism [əd'ventʃərɪzm] N aventurismo *m*

adventurist [əd'ventʃərɪst] Ⓐ ADJ aventurista

Ⓑ N aventurista *mf*

adventurous [əd'ventʃərəs] ADJ [*person*] aventurero; [*enterprise*] peligroso, arriesgado; [*style*] innovador, atrevido; [*journey*] (= *intrepid*) intrépido; (= *eventful*) lleno de incidentes; **we had a very ~ time getting here** el viaje para llegar aquí ha estado repleto de incidentes; **we need a more ~ slogan** necesitamos un eslogan más llamativo

adventurously [əd'ventʃərəslɪ] ADV (= *intrepidly*) con espíritu aventurero *or* emprendedor; (= *boldly*) atrevidamente

adverb ['ædvɜːb] N adverbio *m*

adverbial [əd'vɜːbɪəl] ADJ adverbial

adversarial [,ædvɜː'sɛərɪəl] Ⓐ ADJ [*role*] de antagonista; [*relationship*] de enfrentamiento, conflictivo

Ⓑ CPD ► **adversarial procedure** N procedimiento *m* de confrontación ► **the adversarial system** N (*Jur*) el sistema acusatorio

adversary ['ædvəsərɪ] N adversario/a *m/f*, contrario/a *m/f*

adverse ['ædvɜːs] ADJ [*criticism, decision, effect, wind*] adverso, contrario; [*conditions*] adverso, desfavorable; **to be ~ to** ser contrario a, estar en contra de

adversely ['ædvɜːslɪ] ADV desfavorablemente, negativamente; **to affect ~** perjudicar

adversity [əd'vɜːsɪtɪ] N infortunio *m*, desgracia *f*; **in times of ~** en tiempos difíciles; **he knew ~ in his youth** de joven conoció la miseria; **companion in ~** compañero *m* de desgracias

advert[1] [əd'vɜːt] VI (*frm*) **to ~ to** referirse a

advert[2]* ['ædvɜːt] N ABBR (*Brit*) = **advertisement**

advertise ['ædvətaɪz] Ⓐ VT 1 (*Comm etc*) anunciar; **"as ~d on TV"** "anunciado en TV"

2 (= *draw attention to*) [+ *weakness etc*] exponer, revelar públicamente

Ⓑ VI [*company*] hacer publicidad, hacer propaganda; (*in newspaper etc*) poner un anuncio; (*on TV*) hacer publicidad; **it pays to ~** la publicidad siempre rinde; **to ~ for** buscar por medio de anuncios

advertisement [əd'vɜːtɪsmənt] Ⓐ N anuncio *m* (**for** de); **to put an ~ in a newspaper** poner un anuncio en un periódico; **it's not much of an ~ for the place*** no dice mucho en favor de la ciudad/del hotel *etc*

Ⓑ CPD ► **advertisement column** N (*Brit*) columna *f* or sección *f* de anuncios ► **advertisement rates** NPL tarifas *fpl* de anuncios

advertiser ['ædvətaɪzəʳ] N anunciante *mf*

advertising ['ædvətaɪzɪŋ] Ⓐ N 1 (= *business*) publicidad *f*; **my brother's in ~** mi hermano se dedica a la publicidad

2 (= *advertisements collectively*) anuncios *mpl*

Ⓑ CPD ► **advertising agency** N agencia *f* de publicidad ► **advertising campaign** N campaña *f* publicitaria ► **advertising manager** N jefe/a *m/f* de publicidad ► **advertising medium** N medio *m* de publicidad ► **advertising rates** NPL tarifa *fsing* de anuncios

advertorial [,ædvə'tɔːrɪəl] N (*Press*) publirreportaje *m*

▼ **advice** [əd'vaɪs] Ⓐ N 1 (*gen*) consejos *mpl*; **he ignored my ~** ignoró mis consejos; **it was good ~** *or* **a good piece of ~** fue un buen consejo; **her doctor's ~ was to rest** el médico le aconsejó descansar; **he did it against the ~ of friends** lo hizo en contra de lo que le aconsejaron sus amigos; **to follow sb's ~** seguir el consejo *or* los consejos de algn; **let me give you some ~** permíteme que te dé un consejo, permíteme que te aconseje; **if you want my ~ ...** si quieres (seguir) mi consejo ...; **my ~ to you is not to say anything** te aconsejo no decir nada, mi consejo es que no digas nada; **I need your ~** necesito que me aconsejes; **on the ~ of sb** siguiendo el consejo *or* los consejos de algn; **a piece of ~** un consejo; **to take sb's ~** seguir el consejo *or* los consejos de algn, hacer caso a algn; **take my ~ and stay away from him!** ¡sigue mi consejo y no te metas con él!, ¡hazme caso y no te metas con él!; **when I want your ~ I'll ask for it** cuando quiera que me aconsejes te lo pediré, cuando quiera tu consejo te lo pediré

2 (= *professional help, information*) asesoramiento *m*; **you need expert ~** necesitas el asesoramiento de un experto, necesitas hacerte asesorar por un experto; **the tourist office will give us ~ on places to visit** la oficina de turismo nos asesorará sobre qué lugares visitar; **to seek sb's ~** consultar a algn, hacerse asesorar por algn; **to seek professional/medical ~** consultar a *or* hacerse asesorar por un profesional/médico; **to take legal ~** con-

➤ LANGUAGE IN USE: advice A1 2.1, 2.2

sultar a un abogado, asesorarse con un abogado

[3] (*Comm*) aviso *m*, notificación *f*

Ⓑ CPD ► **advice column** N (*gen*) consultorio *m*; (= *agony aunt*) consultorio *m* sentimental ► **advice note** N nota *f* de aviso ► **advice service** N servicio *m* de asesoramiento

advisability [əd,vaɪzə'bɪlɪtɪ] N conveniencia *f*, prudencia *f*

▼ **advisable** [əd'vaɪzəbl] ADJ aconsejable, conveniente; **it would be ~ to** + INFIN sería aconsejable + *infin*, sería conveniente + *infin*; **if you think it ~** si le parece bien

▼ **advise** [əd'vaɪz] Ⓐ VT [1] (= *recommend*) [+ *action*] aconsejar, recomendar; **he ~s caution** aconseja *or* recomienda prudencia; **I'd ~ leaving the car here** aconsejaría que dejáramos el coche aquí; **to ~ sb to do sth** aconsejar a algn que haga algo; **what would you ~ me to do?** ¿qué me aconsejas (que haga)?; **you would be ill ~d to go** no sería prudente que fueras, harías mal yendo *or* en ir; **you would be well ~d to go** sería prudente que fueras, harías bien yendo *or* en ir; *see also* **ill-advised**

[2] (= *give advice to*) aconsejar; (= *help and inform professionally*) asesorar; **can you ~ me on the best route?** ¿me puede aconsejar cuál es la mejor ruta?; **he ~s them on investment** les asesora en sus inversiones; **she will ~ you what to do** ella te dirá lo que tienes que hacer

[3] (*frm*) (= *inform*) informar; (*officially*) notificar; **to ~ sb of sth** informar a algn de algo; (*officially*) notificar algo a algn; **he wrote to ~ me of his decision** me escribió para informarme de *or* notificarme su decisión; **please ~ us of a convenient date** le ruego nos notifique una fecha conveniente; **to keep sb ~d of** *or* **about sth** mantener a algn al corriente *or* informado de algo

[4] (= *warn*) advertir; **they were ~d that it would look bad** les advirtieron (de) que causaría una mala impresión; **to ~ sb against doing sth** aconsejar a algn que no haga algo; **they ~d me against selling the house** me aconsejaron que no vendiera la casa; **the doctor ~d me against it** el médico me lo desaconsejó; **no one had ~d him of the possible consequences** nadie lo había advertido de las posibles consecuencias

Ⓑ VI (= *make recommendations*) dar consejos; **I would ~ against it** yo te lo desaconsejaría, yo no te lo aconsejaría; **he ~d against going** nos aconsejó que no fuéramos; **to ~ on sth** (= *give information on*) informar *or* dar información sobre algo; [*lawyer, accountant*] asesorar sobre algo; **job centres will ~ on training courses** en las oficinas de empleo informan *or* dan información sobre cursillos de formación

advisedly [əd'vaɪzɪdlɪ] ADV deliberadamente; **to speak ~** hablar con conocimiento de causa; **I say so ~** lo digo después de pensarlo bien

advisement [əd'vaɪzmənt] (*US*) Ⓐ N consulta *f*, deliberación *f*; **to take sth under ~** (= *think over*) estudiar algo; (= *get expert advice on*) consultar algo con expertos, someter algo a la deliberación de expertos

Ⓑ CPD ► **advisement counseling** N guía *f* vocacional

adviser, **advisor** [əd'vaɪzəʳ] N (*in business, politics etc*) asesor(a) *m/f*, consejero/a *m/f*; **legal ~** abogado/a *m/f*, asesor(a) *m/f* jurídico/a; **spiritual ~** consejero *m* espiritual

advisory [əd'vaɪzərɪ] Ⓐ ADJ [*body*] consultivo; **in an ~ capacity** como asesor(a)

Ⓑ N (*esp US*) nota *f* oficial, anuncio *m* público

Ⓒ CPD ► **advisory board** N junta *f* consultiva ► **advisory committee** N (*US Pol*) comité *m* consultivo ► **advisory opinion** N (*US Jur*) opinión *f* consultiva *or* asesora ► **advisory service** N servicio *m* consultivo

advocacy ['ædvəkəsɪ] N [1] (= *support*) apoyo *m* (activo)

[2] (*Jur*) defensa *f*

advocate Ⓐ ['ædvəkeɪt] VT (= *be in favour of*) abogar por, ser partidario de; **what do you ~?** ¿qué nos aconsejas?; **I ~ doing nothing** yo recomiendo no hacer nada

Ⓑ ['ædvəkɪt] N defensor(a) *m/f*, partidario/a *m/f*; (*Scot Jur*) abogado/a *m/f*; *see also* **devil**; → LAWYERS, QC/KC

advt ABBR = **advertisement**

adze, **adz** (*US*) [ædz] N azuela *f*

AEA N ABBR [1] (*Brit*) (= **Atomic Energy Authority**) ≈ JEN *f* (*Sp*)

[2] (= **Association of European Airlines**) AAE *f*

AEC N ABBR (*US*) (= **Atomic Energy Commission**) ≈ JEN *f* (*Sp*)

AEEU N ABBR (*Brit*) = **Amalgamated Engineering and Electrical Union**

AEF N ABBR (*US*) = **American Expeditionary Forces**

Aegean [iː'dʒiːən] N **the ~ (Sea)** el (Mar) Egeo

aegis, **egis** (*US*) ['iːdʒɪs] N **under the ~ of** (= *protection*) bajo la tutela de; (= *patronage*) patrocinado por, bajo los auspicios *or* (*frm*) la égida de

aegrotat [iː'grəʊtæt] N (*Brit*) *título universitario que se concede al candidato que por enfermedad no ha podido presentarse a los exámenes*

Aeneas [iː'niːəs] N Eneas

Aeneid ['iːnɪɪd] N Eneida *f*

aeon ['iːən] N [1] (*Astron*) eón *m*

[2] (*fig*) eternidad *f*

aerate ['ɛəreɪt] VT [+ *liquid*] gasificar; [+ *blood*] oxigenar; **~d water** agua *f* con gas

aeration [ɛə'reɪʃən] N aireación *f*

aerial ['ɛərɪəl] Ⓐ ADJ aéreo

Ⓑ N (*Brit Rad, TV*) antena *f*; (*also* **~ mast**) torre *f* de antena; **indoor ~** antena *f* interior

Ⓒ CPD ► **aerial input*** N (*US*) mensaje *m* recibido por antena ► **aerial ladder** N (*US*) escalera *f* de bomberos ► **aerial photograph** N aerofoto *f*, fotografía *f* aérea ► **aerial photography** N fotografía *f* aérea ► **aerial railway** N teleférico *m* ► **aerial survey** N reconocimiento *m* aéreo ► **aerial tanker** N transportador *m* aéreo

aerie ['ɛərɪ] N (*US*) = **eyrie**

aero... ['ɛərəʊ] PREFIX aero...

aerobatic [,ɛərəʊ'bætɪk] ADJ [*display*] de acrobacia aérea

aerobatics [,ɛərəʊ'bætɪks] NPL acrobacia *fsing* aérea

aerobic [ɛə'rəʊbɪk] ADJ [*shoes, dance*] de *or* para aerobic; [*exercise*] aeróbico

aerobics [ɛə'rəʊbɪks] NPL aerobic *msing*; **I do ~** hago aerobic

aerodrome ['ɛərədrəʊm] N (*esp Brit*) aeródromo *m*

aerodynamic ['ɛərəʊdaɪ'næmɪk] ADJ aerodinámico

aerodynamically ['ɛərəʊdaɪ'næmɪklɪ] ADV desde el punto de vista aerodinámico, aerodinámicamente

aerodynamics ['ɛərəʊdaɪ'næmɪks] N aerodinámica *fsing*

aero-engine ['ɛərəʊ,endʒɪn] N motor *m* de aviación

aerofoil ['ɛərəʊfɔɪl], **airfoil** (*US*) ['ɛə,fɔɪl] N plano *m* aerodinámico

aerogram(me) ['ɛərəʊgræm] N [1] (= *air-letter*) aerograma *m*

[2] (= *radio message*) radiograma *m*

aerolite ['ɛərəlaɪt] N aerolito *m*

aeromodelling ['ɛərəʊ'mɒdlɪŋ] N aeromodelismo *m*

aeronaut ['ɛərənɔːt] N aeronauta *mf*

aeronautic [,ɛərə'nɔːtɪk] ADJ = **aeronautical**

aeronautical [,ɛərə'nɔːtɪk] ADJ aeronáutico

aeronautics [,ɛərə'nɔːtɪks] N aeronáutica *fsing*

aeroplane ['ɛərəpleɪn] N (*Brit*) avión *m*; *see also* **model B1**

aerosol ['ɛərəsɒl] N aerosol *m*, atomizador *m*

aerospace ['ɛərəʊspeɪs] ADJ aeroespacial; **the ~ industry** la industria aeroespacial

Aertex® ['ɛəteks] N *tejido ligero de algodón usado esp. para prendas deportivas*

Aeschylus ['iːskɪləs] N Esquilo

Aesop ['iːsɒp] N Esopo; **~'s Fables** Fábulas *fpl* de Esopo

aesthete, **esthete** (*US*) ['iːsθiːt] N esteta *mf*

aesthetic, **esthetic** (*US*) [iːs'θetɪk] ADJ estético

aesthetical, **esthetical** (*US*) [iːs'θetɪkəl] ADJ = **aesthetic**

aesthetically, **esthetically** (*US*) [iːs'θetɪkəlɪ] ADV estéticamente

aestheticism, **estheticism** (*US*) [iːs'θetɪsɪzəm] N esteticismo *m*

aesthetics, **esthetics** (*US*) [iːs'θetɪks] N estética *fsing*

AEU N ABBR (*Brit*) (*formerly*) = **Amalgamated Engineering Union**

a.f. N ABBR [1] = **audio frequency**

[2] (*Comm*) = **advance freight**

AFA N ABBR (*Brit*) = **Amateur Football Association**

afar [ə'fɑːʳ] ADV (*liter*) lejos; **from ~** desde lejos; **~ off** a lo lejos, en lontananza (*liter*)

AFB N ABBR (*US Mil*) = **Air Force Base**

AFC N ABBR [1] (*Brit*) = **Amateur Football Club**

[2] (*Brit*) = **Association Football Club**

[3] = **automatic frequency control**

AFDC N ABBR (*US Admin*) = **Aid to Families with Dependent Children**

affability [,æfə'bɪlɪtɪ] N afabilidad *f*

affable ['æfəbl] ADJ [*person, mood*] afable

affably ['æfəblɪ] ADV afablemente

affair [ə'fɛəʳ] N [1] (= *business*) asunto *m*; **the government has mishandled the ~** el gobierno ha llevado mal el asunto

[2] **affairs** (= *matters*) asuntos *mpl*; **you will have to put your ~s in order** tendrás que aclarar tus asuntos; **she runs my business ~s** ella se encarga de lo relacionado con mis negocios; **~s of the heart** asuntos *mpl* del corazón; **a man of ~s** un hombre de negocios; **~s of state** asuntos *mpl* de estado

[3] (= *event*) ocasión *f*; **it will be a big ~** será una ocasión importante, será todo un acontecimiento; **the minister's visit will be a purely private ~** la visita del ministro tendrá un carácter puramente privado; **dinner was a gloomy ~** la cena no fue una ocasión muy alegre

[4] (= *case*) caso *m*, asunto *m*; **the Watergate ~** el caso Watergate, el asunto (de) Watergate

[5] (= *concern*) asunto *m*; **that's my ~** eso es asunto mío *or* cosa mía, eso sólo me concierne a mí; **if he wants to make a fool of him-**

➤ LANGUAGE IN USE: **advisable** 1.1, 2.1 **advise A1, 2** 1.1, 2.1, 2.2 **A1, 23** 21.1

self, that's his ~ si quiere hacer el ridículo, es asunto suyo *or* allá él
[6] (= *love affair*) aventura *f* (amorosa), affaire *m*, lío *m* (amoroso)*; **he had an ~ with a French girl** tuvo una aventura *or* un affaire con una chica francesa, tuvo un lío *or* estuvo liado con una chica francesa*; **they're having an ~** están liados
[7] (*) (= *thing*) **the bed was an iron ~ with brass knobs** la cama era un trasto de hierro con adornos de bronce; **the house was a ramshackle, wooden ~** la casa era un destartalado cobertizo de madera

affect [əˈfekt] Ⓐ VT [1] (= *have effect on*) afectar, influir en; **it did not ~ my decision** no influyó en mi decisión
[2] (= *concern*) afectar, tener que ver con; **this will ~ everybody** esto afectará a todos
[3] (= *harm*) perjudicar
[4] (*Med*) **a wound ~ing the right leg** una herida que afecta a la pierna derecha; **his whole left side was ~ed** tenía todo el costado izquierdo afectado
[5] (= *move emotionally*) conmover, afectar; **he seemed much ~ed** parecía muy conmovido *or* afectado
[6] (= *feign*) **he ~ed indifference** afectó *or* aparentó indiferencia, fingió ser indiferente; **she ~ed to cry** ella fingió llorar
[7] (†† *or frm*) (= *like*) **she ~s bright colours** a ella le gustan los colores claros
Ⓑ N (*Psych*) afecto *m*, estado *m* afectivo

affectation [ˌæfekˈteɪʃən] N afectación *f*, falta *f* de naturalidad; **affectations** afectación *fsing*

affected [əˈfektɪd] ADJ [1] (= *pretentious*) [*person, manner, accent*] afectado
[2] (= *feigned*) [*remorse, enthusiasm*] fingido
[3] (= *suffering effects*) [*area, region, part of body*] afectado; **the worst ~ areas of Central China** las zonas peor afectadas de China Central

affectedly [əˈfektɪdlɪ] ADV de manera afectada, con afectación

affecting [əˈfektɪŋ] ADJ conmovedor, enternecedor

affection [əˈfekʃən] N afecto *m* (**for** a; **towards** hacia), cariño *m*; **to transfer one's ~s** dar su amor a otro/a

affectionate [əˈfekʃənɪt] ADJ [1] cariñoso, afectuoso
[2] (*in letter endings*) **with ~ greetings** cariñosamente, afectuosamente; **your ~ nephew** con abrazos de tu sobrino

affectionately [əˈfekʃənɪtlɪ] ADV [1] afectuosamente, cariñosamente
[2] (*in letter endings*) **~ yours** ◊ **yours ~** un abrazo cariñoso

affective [əˈfektɪv] ADJ afectivo

affectivity [ˌæfekˈtɪvətɪ] N afectividad *f*

affiance [əˈfaɪəns] VT (*frm*) prometer en matrimonio (**to** a); **to be ~d** estar prometido (**to** a); **to ~ o.s. to** prometerse a

affidavit [ˌæfɪˈdeɪvɪt] N (*Jur*) declaración *f* jurada, afidávit *m*; **to swear an ~ (to the effect that)** hacer una declaración jurada (que)

affiliate Ⓐ [əˈfɪlɪeɪt] VI **to ~ to** ◊ **~ with** afiliarse a
Ⓑ [əˈfɪlɪɪt] N (= *organization*) filial *f*; (= *person*) afiliado/a *m/f*

affiliated [əˈfɪlɪeɪtɪd] ADJ [*member, society*] afiliado (**to, with** a); **~ company** empresa *f* filial *or* subsidiaria

affiliation [əˌfɪlɪˈeɪʃən] Ⓐ N [1] (= *connection*) afiliación *f*; **political ~s** filiación *fsing* política
[2] (*Jur*) paternidad *f*
Ⓑ CPD ► **affiliation order** N decreto *m* relativo a la paternidad ► **affiliation proceedings** NPL proceso *m* para determinar la paternidad

affinity [əˈfɪnɪtɪ] N [1] (= *similarity, relationship*) afinidad *f*; **A has certain affinities with B** entre A y B existe cierta afinidad
[2] (= *liking*) simpatía *f*; **I feel no ~ whatsoever with** *or* **for him** no siento ninguna simpatía por él

affirm [əˈfɜːm] VT (= *state*) afirmar, aseverar; (= *confirm*) confirmar

affirmation [ˌæfəˈmeɪʃən] N afirmación *f*, aseveración *f*

affirmative [əˈfɜːmətɪv] Ⓐ ADJ afirmativo
Ⓑ N **to answer in the ~** dar una respuesta afirmativa, contestar afirmativamente
Ⓒ CPD ► **affirmative action** N (*US Pol*) medidas *fpl* a favor de las minorías

AFFIRMATIVE ACTION

Affirmative action *es el término estadounidense que hace referencia al tratamiento privilegiado que reciben las minorías étnicas y las mujeres en lo que concierne al empleo o la educación. La administración del presidente Kennedy puso en marcha esta política en los años sesenta, estableciendo cuotas para asegurar más puestos de trabajo y plazas universitarias a aquellos colectivos con baja representación, lo cual se garantizó gracias a la Ley de Igualdad de Oportunidades Laborales (***Equal Employment Opportunities Act***), de 1972. Esta discriminación positiva fue para muchos la causa de que fueran a su vez discriminados los colectivos no minoritarios, por ejemplo, los hombres de raza blanca, por lo que la aplicación estricta de los cupos se ha relajado un tanto desde entonces.*

affirmatively [əˈfɜːmətɪvlɪ] ADV afirmativamente

affix Ⓐ [əˈfɪks] VT [+ *signature*] poner, añadir; [+ *stamp*] poner, pegar; [+ *seal*] imprimir; **to ~ a notice to the wall** pegar un anuncio en la pared
Ⓑ N [ˈæfɪks] (*Ling*) afijo *m*

afflict [əˈflɪkt] VT afligir; **the ~ed** los afligidos; **to be ~ed with** *or* **by** sufrir de, estar aquejado de

affliction [əˈflɪkʃən] N [1] (= *suffering*) aflicción *f*, congoja *f*
[2] (*bodily*) mal *m*; **the ~s of old age** los achaques de la vejez
[3] (= *misfortune*) desgracia *f*, infortunio *m*; **it's a terrible ~** es una desgracia tremenda

affluence [ˈæfluəns] N riqueza *f*, opulencia *f*; **to live in ~** vivir con lujo

affluent [ˈæfluənt] Ⓐ ADJ acaudalado, rico; **the ~ society** la sociedad de la abundancia
Ⓑ N [1] **the ~** los ricos
[2] (*Geog*) afluente *m*

afflux [ˈæflʌks] N afluencia *f*; (*Med*) aflujo *m*

afford [əˈfɔːd] VT [1] (= *pay for*) **we can ~ it** podemos permitírnoslo; **we can't ~ such things** no podemos permitirnos tales cosas, tales cosas no están a nuestro alcance; **we can't ~ to go on holiday** no podemos permitirnos el lujo de ir de vacaciones; **how much can you ~?** ¿cuánto puedes gastar?
[2] (= *spare, risk*) **I can't ~ the time** no tengo tiempo; **I can't ~ to be idle** no puedo permitirme el lujo de no hacer nada; **I can't ~ not to do it** no puedo permitirme el lujo de no hacerlo; **we can ~ to wait** nos podemos permitir esperar; **an opportunity you cannot ~ to miss** una ocasión que no puedes desperdiciar; **can we ~ the risk?** ¿podemos arriesgarnos?
[3] (*frm*) (= *provide*) [+ *opportunity*] proporcionar, dar; **it ~s shade** da sombra; **that ~ed me some relief** eso me proporcionó cierto alivio; **this ~s me a chance to speak** esto me da la oportunidad de hablar

affordable [əˈfɔːdəbl] ADJ [*price*] razonable; [*purchase*] posible

afforest [æˈfɒrɪst] VT poblar de árboles, poblar con árboles

afforestation [æˌfɒrɪsˈteɪʃən] N forestación *f*

afforested [æˈfɒrɪstɪd] ADJ [*land*] poblado de árboles

affray [əˈfreɪ] N (*frm*) refriega *f*, reyerta *f*

affreightment [əˈfreɪtmənt] N fletamento *m*

affricate [ˈæfrɪkət] Ⓐ ADJ africado
Ⓑ N africada *f*

affright†† [əˈfraɪt] VT (*poet*) asustar, espantar

affront [əˈfrʌnt] Ⓐ N afrenta *f*, ofensa *f*; **to be an ~ to** afrentar a
Ⓑ VT ofender, afrentar; **to be ~ed** ofenderse

Afghan [ˈæfgæn] Ⓐ ADJ afgano
Ⓑ N [1] (= *person*) afgano/a *m/f*
[2] (*Ling*) afgano *m*
[3] (= *dog*) perro/a *m/f* afgano/a

Afghanistan [æfˈgænɪstæn] N Afganistán *m*

aficionado [əˌfɪsjəˈnɑːdəʊ] N aficionado/a *m/f*

afield [əˈfiːld] ADV **far ~** muy lejos; **countries further ~** países más lejanos; **you'll have to go further ~ for that** para eso hará falta buscar más lejos

afire [əˈfaɪəʳ] ADJ (*liter*) **to be ~** arder, estar en llamas; **to be ~ to help** anhelar ardientemente ayudar

aflame [əˈfleɪm] ADJ (*liter*) en llamas

AFL-CIO N ABBR (*US*) = **American Federation of Labor and Congress of Industrial Organizations**

afloat [əˈfləʊt] ADJ a flote; **the oldest ship ~** el barco más viejo que sigue a flote; **by a miracle we were still ~** quedamos a flote de milagro; **the largest navy ~** la mayor marina del mundo; **to spend one's life ~** pasar toda la vida a bordo; **to keep sth ~** (*lit, fig*) mantener algo a flote; **to stay** *or* **keep ~** (*lit, fig*) mantenerse a flote; **to get a business ~** lanzar un negocio

aflutter [əˈflʌtəʳ] ADJ **to set sb's heart ~** hacer que el corazón de algn se acelere

afoot [əˈfʊt] ADV **there is something ~** algo se está tramando; **there is a plan ~ to remove him** existe un plan para apearlo; **to set a scheme ~** poner un proyecto en marcha, poner una idea en movimiento

afore [əˈfɔːʳ] CONJ (†† *or dial*) (*esp Scot*) antes (de) que

aforementioned [əˌfɔːˈmenʃənd], **aforenamed** [əˈfɔːneɪmd], **aforesaid** [əˈfɔːsed] ADJ susodicho, mencionado

aforethought [əˈfɔːθɔːt] ADJ **with malice ~** con premeditación

afoul [əˈfaʊl] ADV [1] **to run ~ of sb** ponerse a malas *or* indisponerse con algn
[2] **to run ~ of a ship** chocar con un barco

AFP, afp N ABBR (= **alpha-fetoprotein**) AFP *f*

▼**afraid** [əˈfreɪd] ADJ [1] (= *frightened*) **to be ~** tener miedo; **don't be ~** no tengas miedo; **I was ~ that nobody would believe me** tenía miedo de que nadie me creyera, temía que nadie me creyera; **I was ~ to ask** me daba miedo preguntar, tenía miedo de preguntar; **to be ~ for sb** temer por algn; **to be ~ for sb's**

➤ LANGUAGE IN USE: **afraid 2** 18.2

life temer por la vida de algn; **she suddenly looked ~** de repente parecía asustada; **to be ~ of sth/sb** tener miedo de algo/a algn, temer algo/a algn (*more frm*); **they're ~ of you** te tienen miedo; **he was ~ of losing his job** tenía miedo de perder su trabajo, temía perder su trabajo (*more frm*); **she's ~ of flying** le da miedo volar; **I'm ~ of dogs** los perros me dan miedo, les tengo miedo a los perros; **you have nothing to be ~ of** no tienes nada que temer; **he's not ~ of hard work** el trabajo duro no le asusta; **I was ~ of that** me lo temía; **✦IDIOM to be ~ of one's own shadow** tener miedo hasta de su propia sombra
[2] (= *sorry*) **I'm ~ he's out** lo siento, pero no está; **it's a bit stuffy in here, I'm ~** me temo que el aire aquí dentro está muy cargado; **I'm ~ not** me temo que no *or* no, lo siento; **I'm ~ so** me temo que sí *or* sí, lo siento

afresh [ə'freʃ] ADV de nuevo, otra vez; **to do sth ~** volver a hacer algo; **to start ~** volver a empezar

Africa ['æfrɪkə] N África *f*

African ['æfrɪkən] (A) ADJ africano
(B) N africano/a *m/f*

African-American [ˌæfrɪkənə'merɪkən] (A) ADJ afroamericano
(B) N afroamericano/a *m/f*

Afrikaans [ˌæfrɪ'kɑːns] N afrikaans *m*

Afrikaner [ˌæfrɪ'kɑːnəʳ] (A) ADJ afrikaner
(B) N afrikaner *mf*

Afro ['æfrəʊ] N (*also* ~ **hairstyle**) peinado *m* afro

Afro... ['æfrəʊ] PREFIX afro...

Afro-American [ˌæfrəʊə'merɪkən] (A) ADJ afroamericano
(B) N afroamericano/a *m/f*

Afro-Asian [ˌæfrəʊ'eɪʃən] (A) ADJ afroasiático
(B) N afroasiático/a *m/f*

Afro-Caribbean [ˌæfrəʊkærɪ'biːən] (A) ADJ afrocaribeño
(B) N afrocaribeño/a *m/f*

AFT N ABBR (*US*) = **American Federation of Teachers**

aft [ɑːft] ADV (*Naut*) en popa; **to go ~** ir a popa

after ['ɑːftəʳ]

When **after** *is an element in a phrasal verb, eg* **ask after, look after, take after,** *look up the verb.*

(A) PREP [1] (*in time*) después de; **soon ~ eating it** poco después de comerlo; **I'll have a shower ~ you** me ducharé después que tú; **it was twenty ~ three** (*US*) eran las tres y veinte
[2] (*in position, order*) detrás de, tras; **day ~ day** día tras día; **one ~ the other** uno tras otro; **excuse ~ excuse ◊ one excuse ~ another** excusas y más excusas; **~ you!** ¡pase usted!, ¡usted primero!; **~ you with the salt** pásame la sal cuando acabes; **our biggest customer ~ the US** nuestro mayor cliente después de Estados Unidos
[3] (= *behind*) **close the door ~ you** cierra la puerta al salir *or* cuando salgas; **I'm tired of cleaning up ~ you** estoy cansado de ir detrás de ti limpiándolo todo; **he ran ~ me with my umbrella** corrió tras de mí con mi paraguas
[4] (= *seeking*) **the police are ~ him** la policía lo está buscando *or* está detrás de él; **I have been ~ that for years** eso lo busco desde hace años; **she's ~ a special dress** busca un vestido especial; **she's ~ a husband** va en pos de un marido; **they're all ~ the same thing** todos van a por lo mismo; **what is he ~?** ¿qué pretende?; **I see what you're ~** ya caigo, ya comprendo lo que quieres decir; (*hostile*) ya te he calado
[5] (= *in the manner of*) **this is ~ Goya** esto se pintó según el estilo de Goya; **~ the English fashion** a la (manera) inglesa; *see also* **heart A2**
[6] (= *in honour of*) **he is named ~ Churchill** se le llamó así por Churchill
[7] (= *in view of*) después de; **~ all I've done for you** después de *or* con todo lo que he hecho por ti; **he can't go back ~ what he's done** después de lo que ha hecho no puede volver; **~ all** después de todo
(B) ADV [1] (= *afterward*) después; **for weeks ~** durante varias semanas después; **long ~** mucho tiempo después; **soon ~** poco después
[2] (= *behind*) detrás
(C) CONJ después de que, después que*; **we ate ~ they'd gone** comimos después de que ellos se marcharon; **I went out ~ I'd eaten** salí después de comer; **we'll eat ~ you've gone** comeremos cuando te hayas ido
(D) ADJ [1] **in ~ years** (*frm*) en los años siguientes, años después
[2] (*Naut*) de popa

afterbirth ['ɑːftəbɜːθ] N secundinas *fpl*, placenta *f*

afterburner ['ɑːftəˌbɜːnəʳ] N dispositivo *m* de poscombustión

aftercare ['ɑːftəkɛəʳ] N (*Med*) asistencia *f* postoperatoria; [*of prisoners*] asistencia *f* (para expresioneros)

afterdeck ['ɑːftədek] N cubierta *f* de popa

after-dinner ['ɑːftə'dɪnəʳ] ADJ de sobremesa; **~ speech** discurso *m* de sobremesa; **~ drink** copa *f* de después de la cena

after-effect ['ɑːftərɪfekt] N consecuencia *f*; **after-effects** [*of treatment*] efectos *mpl* secundarios; [*of illness, operation, accident*] secuelas *fpl*

afterglow ['ɑːftəgləʊ] N [1] (*in sky*) arrebol *m*, resplandor *m* crepuscular
[2] (*bodily*) sensación *f* de bienestar

after-hours ['ɑːftə'aʊəz] (A) ADV fuera de horas
(B) ADJ **~ dealings** transacciones *fpl* fuera de horas

afterlife ['ɑːftəlaɪf] N vida *f* de ultratumba

aftermath ['ɑːftəmæθ] N consecuencias *fpl*, secuelas *fpl*; **in the ~ of the war** en el periodo de posguerra

afternoon ['ɑːftə'nuːn] (A) N tarde *f*; **good ~!** ¡buenas tardes!; **in the ~** por la tarde; **(in the) ~s he's generally out** por las tardes en general no está
(B) CPD ► **afternoon performance** N función *f* de la tarde ► **afternoon tea** N (*Brit*) ≈ merienda *f*

afterpains ['ɑːftəˌpeɪnz] NPL dolores *mpl* de posparto

afters* ['ɑːftəz] NPL (*Brit*) postre *msing*; **what's for ~?** ¿qué hay de postre?

after-sales ['ɑːftəseɪlz] CPD ► **after-sales service, after-sales support** N servicio *m* posventa, asistencia *f* posventa

aftershave ['ɑːftəʃeɪv] N (*also* ~ **lotion**) aftershave *m inv*, loción *f* para después del afeitado

aftershock ['ɑːftəʃɒk] N [*of earthquake*] réplica *f*

aftertaste ['ɑːftəteɪst] N (*lit, fig*) regusto *m*, dejo *m*

after-tax ['ɑːftə'tæks] (A) ADJ después de impuestos
(B) CPD ► **after-tax profits** N beneficios *mpl* postimpositivos

AFTER

Time

Preposition

- You can usually translate **after** referring to a point in time using **después de**:

Please ring after six
Por favor, llama después de las seis
I'll phone you after the match
Te llamaré después del partido
...Francoism after Franco...
...el franquismo después de Franco...

- To translate **after** + PERIOD OF TIME, you can also use **al cabo de** in more formal Spanish:

After a year in the army, he had had enough
Después de (estar) un año en el ejército *or* ***Al cabo de un año en el ejército, no lo soportaba más***

! Use **más tarde *que*** or **después *que*** with names of people and personal pronouns when they stand in for a verb:

He got there half an hour after us *or* after we did
Llegó allí media hora más tarde que nosotros *or* ***después que nosotros***

- Translate **after** + **-ING** using **después de** + INFINITIVE:

Don't go swimming immediately after eating
No te bañes justo después de comer

Conjunction

- When the action in the **after** clause has already happened, and the subjects of the two clauses are different, you can generally translate **after** using **después de que**. This can be followed either by the *indicative* or, especially in formal or literary Spanish, by the *subjunctive*:

I met her after she had left the company
La conocí después de que dejó *or* ***dejara la empresa***

- When the action in the **after** clause has not happened yet or had not happened at the time of speaking, **cuando** is more common than **después de que**, though both translations are possible. In both cases, use the *subjunctive*:

We'll test the brakes after you've done another thousand miles
Comprobaremos los frenos cuando *or* ***después de que haya recorrido mil millas más***

- If the subject of both clauses is the same, **después de** + INFINITIVE is usually used rather than **después de que**:

He wrote to me again after he retired
Me volvió a escribir después de jubilarse

NOTE: This construction is also sometimes used in colloquial Spanish even when the subjects are different:

After you left, the party ended
Después de irte tú, se terminó la fiesta

For further uses and examples, see main entry.

afterthought ['ɑːftəθɔːt] N ocurrencia *f* tardía, idea *f* adicional; **as an ~** por si acaso

after-treatment ['ɑːftətriːtmənt] N tratamiento *m* postoperatorio

afterward ['ɑːftəwəd], **afterwards** ['ɑːftəwədz] (*esp Brit*) ADV después, más tarde; **~ we all helped with the washing up** después *or* luego *or* más tarde todos ayudamos a fregar los platos; **I realized ~ that he was right** después *or* luego me di cuenta de que él tenía razón; **immediately ~** inmediatamente después, acto seguido; **long ~** mucho tiempo después; **shortly** *or* **soon ~** poco después, al poco rato; **I didn't remember until ~** no lo recordé hasta después *or* hasta más tarde

afterword ['ɑftə'wɜːd] N epílogo *m*

afterworld [ˈɑːftəwɜːld] N mundo *m* más allá

AG ABBR 1 = **Adjutant General**
2 = **Attorney General**; *see* **attorney**

again [əˈgen] ADV 1 (= *once more*) otra vez, de nuevo; (*often translated by "volver a" + infin*) **try ~** inténtalo otra vez *or* de nuevo, vuelve a intentarlo; **he climbed up ~** volvió a subir; **would you do it all ~?** ¿lo volverías a hacer?; **come ~ soon** vuelve pronto; **what was that joke ~?** ¿cómo era el chiste aquel (que contaste)?; **what, you ~?** ¿tú otra vez (por aquí)?; **~ and ~** una y otra vez, vez tras vez; **I've told you ~ and ~** te lo he dicho una y otra vez *or* mil veces; **I won't do it ever ~** no lo haré nunca más; **as many ~** otros tantos; **as much ~** otro tanto; **never ~!** ¡nunca más!; **oh no, not ~!** ¡Dios mío, otra vez!; **now and ~** de vez en cuando; **he is as old ~ as I am** me dobla la edad
2 (= *besides, moreover*) **and again ...** ◊ **then again ...** (= *on the other hand*) por otra parte ...; (= *moreover*) además ...; **~, we just don't know** por otra parte, realmente no sabemos; **~, it may not be true** por otra parte, puede no ser verdad; **these are different ~** también éstos son distintos

▼**against** [əˈgenst]

*When **against** is an element in a phrasal verb, eg **go against, run up against**, look up the verb.*

Ⓐ PREP 1 (= *in opposition to*) [+ *person*] contra, en contra de; [+ *plan*] en contra de; **what have you got ~ me?** ¿qué tiene usted en contra de mí?, ¿qué tiene usted contra mí?; **I spoke ~ the plan** hablé en contra del proyecto; **I see nothing ~ it** no veo nada en contra; **he was ~ it** estaba en contra, se opuso a ello; **he was ~ going** estaba en contra de ir; **it's ~ the law** la ley lo prohíbe, es ilegal; **it's ~ the rules** no lo permiten las reglas; **conditions are ~ us** las condiciones nos son desfavorables; **luck was ~ him** la suerte le era contraria; **to stand** *or* **run ~ sb** (*Pol*) presentarse en contra de algn; ✦*IDIOM* **to be up ~ it** estar en un aprieto; **now we're really up ~ it!** ¡ahora sí tenemos problemas!; *see also* **tide 2**
2 (= *in contact with*) contra; **he hit his head ~ the wall** se dio con la cabeza contra la pared; **he leant the ladder ~ the wall** apoyó la escalera contra la pared
3 (= *in front of*) contra; **~ the light** contra la luz, a contrasol; **the hills stood out ~ the sunset** las colinas se destacaban sobre la puesta del sol
4 (*in comparisons*) **(as) ~** contra, en contraste con; **six today, as ~ seven yesterday** seis hoy, en comparación con siete ayer
5 (= *for*) **refund available ~ this voucher** se devuelve el precio al presentar este comprobante; **everything was ready ~ his arrival** todo estaba listo para su llegada
Ⓑ ADV en contra; **well, I'm ~** bueno, yo estoy en contra; **there were 20 votes ~** hubo 20 votos en contra

Agamemnon [ˌægəˈmemnən] N Agamenón

agape [əˈgeɪp] ADJ, ADV boquiabierto

agar-agar [ˌeɪgəˈeɪgəʳ] N gelatina *f*, agar-agar *m*

agate [ˈægət] N ágata *f*

agave [əˈgeɪvɪ] N agave *f*, pita *f*, maguey *m* (*LAm*)

age [eɪdʒ] Ⓐ N 1 [*of person, animal, building*] edad *f*; **what ~ is she?** ¿qué edad tiene?, ¿cuántos años tiene?; **when I was your ~** cuando tenía tu edad; **I have a daughter your ~** *or* **the same ~ as you** tengo una hija de tu edad *or* de tu misma edad; **he's twice your ~** te dobla la edad; **he's half your ~** lo doblas en edad; **act your ~!** ¡compórtate de acuerdo con tu edad!, ¡no seas niño!; **people of all ~s** gente de todas las edades; **at my ~** a mi edad; **at the ~ of 11** a los 11 años, a la edad de 11 años; **from an early ~** desde muy pequeño; **to feel one's ~** sentirse viejo; **she looks/doesn't look her ~** aparenta/no aparenta la edad que tiene; **60 is no ~ at all** 60 años no son nada; **he is five years of ~** tiene cinco años (de edad); **they are both of an ~** los dos tienen la misma edad; **to be of an ~ to do sth** tener edad suficiente para hacer algo
2 (= *adulthood*) **to be of ~** ser mayor de edad; **to come of ~** (*lit, fig*) llegar a *or* alcanzar la mayoría de edad; **to be under ~** ser menor de edad
3 (= *old age*) **~ is beginning to tell on him** los años empiezan a pesar sobre él; **wine improves with ~** el vino mejora con el paso del tiempo
4 (= *era*) era *f*; **this is the ~ of the car** ésta es la era del automóvil; **the ~ we live in** los tiempos que vivimos, los tiempos que corren; **in the ~ of steam** en la era de las locomotoras de vapor; *see also* **enlightenment, nuclear, reason A3**
5 (*) (= *long time*) **we waited an ~** *or* **for ~s** esperamos una eternidad; **it's ~s** *or* **an ~ since I saw him** hace siglos *or* un siglo que no lo veo; **you took ~s** has tardado una eternidad *or* un siglo
Ⓑ VT [+ *person*] envejecer; [+ *wine*] envejecer, criar, añejar; **the experience had ~d her terribly** esa experiencia la había envejecido tremendamente
Ⓒ VI [*person*] envejecer; [*wine*] madurar, añejarse; **he has ~d a lot** ha envejecido mucho; **she seems to have ~d ten years in the last month** parece haber envejecido diez años en el último mes; **to ~ well** [*wine*] mejorar con los años; **she has ~d well** se conserva bien para la edad que tiene, le sientan bien los años
Ⓓ CPD ► **age bracket** N grupo *m* de edad, grupo *m* etario (*more frm*) ► **age difference** N diferencia *f* de edad ► **age discrimination** N discriminación *f* por razón de edad ► **age group** N grupo *m* de edad, grupo *m* etario (*more frm*); **the 40 to 50 ~ group** el grupo que comprende los de 40 a 50 años, el grupo de edad de 40 a 50; **children of the same ~ group** niños de la misma edad ► **age limit** N límite *m* de edad, edad *f* mínima/máxima; **there is no upper ~ limit** no hay un límite máximo de edad ► **age range** N escala *f* de edad; **children in the ~ range from 12 to 14** niños que van de los 12 a los 14 años

aged Ⓐ [ˈeɪdʒɪd] ADJ 1 (= *old*) viejo, anciano
2 [eɪdʒd] **~ 15** de 15 años (de edad), que tiene 15 años
Ⓑ [ˈeɪdʒɪd] NPL **the ~** los ancianos *mpl*

ageing [ˈeɪdʒɪŋ] Ⓐ ADJ [*person*] anciano, envejecido; [*machinery, vehicle*] anticuado, viejo
Ⓑ N envejecimiento *m*, el envejecer, senescencia *f*; **the ~ process** el proceso de envejecer

ageism [ˈeɪdʒɪzəm] N discriminación *f* por razón de edad

ageist [ˈeɪdʒɪst] Ⓐ ADJ (= *discriminatory*) [*policy*] que discrimina en razón de la edad; (= *prejudiced*) [*person*] *con prejuicios por razón de edad*
Ⓑ N *persona con prejuicios por razón de edad*

ageless [ˈeɪdʒlɪs] ADJ (= *eternal*) eterno; (= *always young*) siempre joven

age-long [ˈeɪdʒlɒŋ] ADJ multisecular

agency [ˈeɪdʒənsɪ] Ⓐ N 1 (= *office*) agencia *f*; *see also* **advertising, travel D**
2 (= *branch*) delegación *f*
3 (= *institution*) organismo *m*; **International Atomic Energy Agency** Organismo *m* Internacional de Energía Atómica
4 (= *mediation*) **through the ~ of** por medio de, por la mediación de
Ⓑ CPD ► **Agency for International Development** N (*US*) Agencia *f* para el Desarrollo Internacional

agenda [əˈdʒendə] N 1 (*at meeting*) orden *m* del día; **on the ~** en el orden del día
2 (*fig*) **environmental issues are high on the party's ~** los asuntos medioambientales ocupan un lugar prominente en el programa político del partido; **to have one's own ~** tener sus propias prioridades; **to set the ~** marcar la pauta

agent [ˈeɪdʒənt] N 1 (*for company, sports personality, actor*) agente *mf*, representante *mf*; (*Jur*) apoderado/a *m/f*; (*Pol*) delegado/a *m/f*; (*undercover*) agente *mf*; **his father acts as his ~** su padre actúa como su representante; *see also* **free E, literary, sole**[3]
2 (*US*) (= *station master*) jefe/a *m/f* de estación
3 (*Chem*) agente *m*; **chemical ~** agente *m* químico
4 (= *catalyst*) **she has portrayed herself as an ~ of change** se ha descrito a sí misma como agente *or* propulsora *or* motor del cambio

agentive [ˈeɪdʒəntɪv] N (*Gram*) agentivo *m*

agent provocateur [ˈæʒɑ̃ːprɒvɒkəˈtɜːʳ] N agente *mf* provocador(a)

age-old [ˈeɪdʒəʊld] ADJ multisecular, antiquísimo

agglomeration [əˌglɒməˈreɪʃən] N aglomeración *f*

agglutinate [əˈgluːtɪneɪt] Ⓐ VT aglutinar
Ⓑ VI aglutinarse

agglutination [əˌgluːtɪˈneɪʃən] N aglutinación *f*

agglutinative [əˈgluːtɪnətɪv] ADJ aglutinante

aggrandize [əˈgrændaɪz] VT (= *increase stature of*) [+ *person*] engrandecer; (= *exaggerate*) agrandar, exagerar; **to ~ o.s.** darse aires (de grandeza)

aggrandizement [əˈgrændɪzmənt] N [*of person*] engrandecimiento *m*; *see also* **self-aggrandizement**

aggravate [ˈægrəveɪt] VT 1 (= *make worse*) agravar
2 (*) (= *annoy*) irritar, sacar de quicio

aggravating [ˈægrəveɪtɪŋ] ADJ 1 (*Jur*) agravante
2 (*) (= *annoying*) molesto; **he's an ~ child** es un niño molesto; **it's very ~** es para volverse loco

aggravation [ˌægrəˈveɪʃən] N 1 (= *exacerbation*) [*of problem, situation, illness*] agravación *f*, empeoramiento *m*
2 (*) (= *annoyance*) irritación *f*
3 (*Jur*) circunstancia *f* agravante; **robbery with ~** robo *m* agravado

aggregate Ⓐ [ˈægrɪgɪt] N 1 (= *total*) conjunto *m*; **on ~** en conjunto; **Scotland won 5-4 on ~** ganó Escocia por 5 a 4 en conjunto; **in the ~** en conjunto, en total
2 (*Geol, Constr*) agregado *m*
Ⓑ [ˈægrɪgɪt] ADJ total, global
Ⓒ [ˈægrɪgeɪt] VT juntar, sumar

aggression [əˈgreʃən] N 1 (= *behaviour*) agresión *f*; **an act of ~** un acto de agresión
2 (= *feeling*) agresividad *f*; **~ is not a solely**

➤ LANGUAGE IN USE: **against A1** 12.1

masculine trait la agresividad no es una característica únicamente masculina

aggressive [ə'gresɪv] ADJ 1 (= *belligerent*) [*person, animal, behaviour*] agresivo; **he was in a very ~ mood** estaba muy agresivo
2 (= *assertive*) [*salesman, company*] enérgico, agresivo; [*player*] agresivo; **~ marketing techniques** técnicas *fpl* de marketing agresivas

aggressively [ə'gresɪvlɪ] ADV 1 (= *belligerently*) [*behave, react*] agresivamente, de manera agresiva; [*say*] con mucha agresividad
2 (= *assertively*) [*trade, sell*] enérgicamente, con empuje; [*play*] agresivamente

aggressiveness [ə'gresɪvnɪs] N 1 (= *belligerence*) agresividad *f*
2 (= *assertiveness*) empuje *m*

aggressor [ə'gresəʳ] N agresor(a) *m/f*

aggrieved [ə'griːvd] Ⓐ ADJ ofendido; **the ~ husband** el marido ofendido; **in an ~ tone** en un tono de queja; **he was much ~** se ofendió mucho; **to feel ~** ofenderse, resentirse (**at** por)
Ⓑ CPD ► **the aggrieved party** N la parte perjudicada *or* agraviada

aggro* ['ægrəʊ] N (*Brit*) 1 (= *violence*) agresividad *f*, violencia *f*; **the crowd was looking for ~** la gente buscaba camorra*
2 (= *hassle*) líos *mpl*, problemas *mpl*; **I'm not going, it's too much ~** no voy, es mucha lata*

aghast [ə'gɑːst] ADJ horrorizado, pasmado (**at** ante); **to be ~ at** horrorizarse *or* pasmarse ante

agile ['ædʒaɪl] ADJ ágil

agility [ə'dʒɪlɪtɪ] N agilidad *f*

agin [ə'gɪn] PREP (*Scot, also hum*) = **against**; **to be** *or* **take ~ sth** oponerse a algo

aging ['eɪdʒɪŋ] ADJ, N = **ageing**

agitate ['ædʒɪteɪt] Ⓐ VT 1 (= *excite, upset*) inquietar, perturbar
2 (= *shake*) agitar
Ⓑ VI (*Pol*) **to ~ for sth** hacer campaña en pro de algo; **to ~ against sth** hacer campaña en contra de algo

agitated ['ædʒɪteɪtɪd] ADJ inquieto, perturbado; **in an ~ tone** en tono inquieto; **to be very ~** estar muy inquieto (**about** por)

agitation [,ædʒɪ'teɪʃən] N 1 (*mental*) inquietud *f*, perturbación *f*
2 (= *shaking*) agitación *f*
3 (*Pol*) agitación *f*

agitator ['ædʒɪteɪtəʳ] N 1 (*Pol*) agitador(a) *m/f*
2 (*Chem*) agitador *m*

agitprop ['ædʒɪt,prɒp] N propaganda *f* política (*esp de izquierdas*)

aglow [ə'gləʊ] ADJ radiante, brillante; **to be ~ with** brillar de; **to be ~ with happiness** irradiar felicidad

AGM N ABBR (= **annual general meeting**) junta *f* anual

Agnes ['ægnɪs] N Inés

agnostic [æg'nɒstɪk] Ⓐ ADJ agnóstico
Ⓑ N agnóstico/a *m/f*

agnosticism [æg'nɒstɪsɪzəm] N agnosticismo *m*

ago [ə'gəʊ] ADV **long ~** hace mucho tiempo; **not long ~** no hace mucho (tiempo); **how long ~ was it?** ¿hace cuánto tiempo?, ¿cuánto tiempo hace?; **as long ~ as 1978** ya en 1978; **no longer ~ than yesterday** ayer solamente, ayer nada más; **a week ~** hace una semana; **a little while ~** hace poco; **just a moment ~** hace un momento nada más

agog [ə'gɒg] ADJ **the country was ~** el país estaba emocionadísimo; **he was ~ to hear the news** tenía enorme curiosidad por saber las noticias; **to set ~** emocionar, crear gran curiosidad a

agonize ['ægənaɪz] VI atormentarse; **to ~ over a decision** dudar antes de tomar una decisión

agonized ['ægənaɪzd] ADJ angustioso

agonizing ['ægənaɪzɪŋ] ADJ [*pain*] atroz, muy agudo; [*indecision, suspense*] angustioso; [*moment*] de angustia; [*reappraisal*] agonizante, doloroso

agonizingly ['ægənaɪzɪŋlɪ] ADV (= *painfully*) dolorosamente; **it was ~ painful** era atrozmente doloroso; **~ close** angustiosamente cerca; **~ slow** terriblemente *or* desesperantemente lento

agony ['ægənɪ] Ⓐ N 1 (*physical*) dolor *m* agudo; **I was in ~** sufría dolores horrorosos
2 (*mental*) angustia *f*; **to suffer agonies of doubt** estar atormentado por las dudas; **to be in an ~ of impatience** impacientarse mucho; **it was ~!*** ¡fue fatal!*; **the play was sheer ~*** la obra era una birria*; *see also* **pile on B**
3 (= *final agony, death agony*) agonía *f*; **he was in his final** *or* **death ~** estaba agonizando
Ⓑ CPD ► **agony aunt*** N (*Brit*) columnista *f* del consultorio sentimental ► **agony column*** N (*Brit*) consultorio *m* sentimental ► **agony uncle*** N (*Brit*) columnista *m* del consultorio sentimental

agoraphobe ['ægərəfəʊb] N agorafóbico/a *m/f*

agoraphobia [,ægərə'fəʊbɪə] N agorafobia *f*

agoraphobic [,ægərə'fəʊbɪk] Ⓐ ADJ agorafóbico
Ⓑ N agorafóbico/a *m/f*

AGR N ABBR = **Advanced Gas-Cooled Reactor**

agrammatical [,eɪgrə'mætɪkəl] ADJ agramatical

agrarian [ə'greərɪən] Ⓐ ADJ agrario
Ⓑ CPD ► **agrarian reform** N reforma *f* agraria ► **agrarian revolution** N revolución *f* agraria

agrarianism [ə'greərɪənɪzəm] N agrarismo *m*

▼**agree** [ə'griː] Ⓐ VI 1 (= *consent*) consentir; **eventually he ~d** por fin consintió; **you'll never get him to ~** no lograrás nunca su consentimiento; **to ~ to sth** consentir en *or* aceptar algo; **he'll ~ to anything** se aviene a todo; **I ~ to your marrying my niece** acepto que usted se case con mi sobrina
2 (= *be in agreement*) estar de acuerdo; (= *come to an agreement*) ponerse de acuerdo; **I ~** estoy de acuerdo, estoy conforme; **I quite ~** estoy completamente de acuerdo; **don't you ~?** ¿no está de acuerdo?, ¿no le parece?; **to ~ about** *or* **on sth** (= *be in agreement*) estar de acuerdo sobre algo; (= *come to an agreement*) ponerse de acuerdo sobre algo; **I don't ~ about trying again tomorrow** no estoy de acuerdo con lo de volverlo a intentar mañana; **to ~ with** [+ *person*] estar de acuerdo *or* coincidir con; [+ *policy*] estar de acuerdo con, aprobar
3 (= *accord, coincide*) concordar; **these statements do not ~ (with each other)** estas declaraciones no concuerdan; **his reasoning ~s with mine** su razonamiento concuerda con el mío
4 (= *get on together*) [*people*] congeniar; **we simply don't ~** simplemente no congeniamos
5 **to ~ with** 5·1 (= *approve of*) aprobar; **I don't ~ with women playing football** no apruebo que las mujeres jueguen al fútbol
5·2 (= *be beneficial to*) [*food, climate*] **garlic/this heat doesn't ~ with me** el ajo/este calor no me sienta bien
6 (*Gram*) concordar (**with** con)
Ⓑ VT 1 (= *consent*) **to ~ to do sth** consentir en *or* aceptar hacer algo
2 (= *be in agreement, come to an agreement*) **"it's impossible," she ~d** —es imposible —asintió; **to ~ that** estar de acuerdo en que; **everyone ~s that it is so** todos están de acuerdo en que es así; **it was ~d that ...** se acordó que ...; **it is ~d that ...** (*on legal contracts*) se acuerda que ...; **they ~d among themselves to do it** (todos) se pusieron de acuerdo para hacerlo; **it was ~d to** + INFIN se acordó + *infin*; **we ~d to meet up later** quedamos en vernos después; **to ~ to disagree** *or* **differ** estar en desacuerdo amistoso
3 (= *admit*) reconocer; **I ~ that I was too hasty** reconozco que lo hice con precipitación; **I ~ that it was foolish** reconozco que era insensato
4 [+ *plan, statement etc*] aceptar, llegar a un acuerdo sobre; [+ *price*] convenir; **the plan was speedily ~d** el proyecto fue aceptado sin demora; **"salary to be agreed"** "sueldo a convenir"; **at a date to be ~d** en una fecha (que queda) por determinar *or* concertar

agreeable [ə'griːəbl] ADJ 1 (= *pleasing*) [*sensation, pastime, surprise*] agradable; [*person*] agradable, simpático; **it was ~ having her in the office** era agradable tenerla en la oficina; **she made a point of being ~ to them** se esforzó por ser agradable *or* simpática con ellos
2 (*frm*) (= *acceptable*) **is that ~ to you?** ¿está de acuerdo?, ¿está conforme?; **a solution that would be ~ to all** una solución satisfactoria para todos
3 (*frm*) (= *willing*) **get your secretary to do it if she is ~** dáselo a tu secretaria para que lo haga si a ella no le importa; **she is ~ to making the arrangements** no le importa encargarse de los preparativos

agreeably [ə'griəblɪ] ADV [*chat, reply*] agradablemente; **they were ~ surprised to discover that ...** se llevaron una agradable sorpresa al descubrir que ...

▼**agreed** [ə'griːd] ADJ [*time, plan*] convenido; **as ~** según lo convenido; **are we all ~?** ¿estamos todos de acuerdo?; **~!** ¡de acuerdo!, ¡conforme(s)!

▼**agreement** [ə'griːmənt] N 1 (= *understanding, arrangement*) acuerdo *m*; (= *consent*) consentimiento *m*; (= *treaty etc*) acuerdo *m*, pacto *m*; (*Comm*) contrato *m*; **to come to** *or* **reach an ~** llegar a un acuerdo; **to enter into an ~** firmar un contrato; **to enter into an ~ to do sth** firmar un contrato para hacer algo; **by mutual ~** por acuerdo mutuo, de común acuerdo; *see also* **gentleman**
2 (= *shared opinion*) acuerdo *m*; **he nodded in ~** ◊ **he nodded his ~** asintió con la cabeza; **to be in ~ on a plan** estar conformes en un proyecto; **to be in ~ with** [+ *person*] estar de acuerdo con; [+ *decision*] estar de acuerdo con, estar conforme con; (= *consistent with*) concordar con, estar en concordancia con
3 (*Gram*) concordancia *f*

agribusiness ['ægrɪ,bɪznɪs] N agroindustria *f*, industria *f* agropecuaria

agricultural [,ægrɪ'kʌltʃərəl] Ⓐ ADJ agrícola
Ⓑ CPD ► **agricultural college** N escuela *f* de agricultura ► **agricultural expert** N perito/a *m/f* agrónomo/a ► **agricultural show** N feria *f* agrícola *or* de campo ► **agricultural subsidy** N subvención *f* agrícola

agriculturalist [,ægrɪ'kʌltʃərəlɪst] N 1 (= *farmer*) agricultor(a) *m/f*
2 (= *professional expert*) perito/a *m/f* agrónomo/a

agriculture ['ægrɪkʌltʃəʳ] N agricultura *f*; **Ministry of Agriculture, Fisheries and Food**

➤ LANGUAGE IN USE: **agree A1** 11.2, 11.3, 12.2, 12.3 **A2** 11.1, 26.1, 26.2, 26.3 **agreed** 11.2, 13 **agreement 2** 11.1

(*Brit*) ≈ Ministerio *m* de Agricultura, Pesca y Alimentación (*Sp*)

agriculturist [ˌægrɪˈkʌltʃərɪst] N = **agriculturalist**

agrobiologist [ˌægrəʊbaɪˈɒlədʒɪst] N agrobiólogo/a *m/f*

agrobiology [ˌægrəʊbaɪˈɒlədʒɪ] N agrobiología *f*

agrochemical [ˌægrəʊˈkemɪkəl] Ⓐ ADJ agroquímico
Ⓑ N (producto *m*) agroquímico *m*

agronomist [əˈgrɒnəmɪst] N agrónomo/a *m/f*

agronomy [əˈgrɒnəmɪ] N agronomía *f*

agroproduct [ˌægrəʊˈprɒdʌkt] N agroproducto *m*

aground [əˈgraʊnd] ADV (*Naut*) **to be ~** estar encallado *or* varado; **to run ~** encallar; **to run a ship ~** varar un barco, hacer que encalle un barco

agt ABBR (*Comm*) = **agent**

ague†† [ˈeɪgjuː] N fiebre *f* intermitente

AH ABBR = **anno Hegirae** (= *from the year of the Hegira*) a.h.

ah [ɑː] EXCL ¡ah!

aha [ɑːˈhɑː] EXCL ¡ajá!

ahead [əˈhed] ADV

When ***ahead*** *is an element in a phrasal verb, eg* ***draw ahead, go ahead****, look up the verb.*

1 (*in space, order*) delante; **to be ~** (*in race*) llevar la delantera, ir (por) delante, ir ganando; (*fig*) llevar la ventaja, ir a la cabeza; **to go on ~** ir adelante; **this put Barcelona three points ~** esto dio al Barcelona tres puntos de ventaja; **to send sb ~** enviar a algn por delante; *see also* **straight B1**
2 (*in time*) antes; [*book*] con anticipación; **there's trouble ~** han de sobrevenir disgustos, ya se prevén dificultades; **there's a busy time ~** tendremos mucha tarea; **to look ~** (*fig*) anticipar; **to plan ~** planificar por adelantado *or* con anticipación; **to think ~** pensar en el futuro
3 **~ of** 3·1 (*in space, order*) delante de; **there were three people ~ of us** había tres personas delante de nosotros; **to be ~ of sb** (*in race, competition*) llevar ventaja a; **to get ~ of sb** (*lit, fig*) adelantarse a algn
3·2 (*in time*) **you'll get there ~ of us** llegarás antes que nosotros; **he's two hours ~ of the next competitor** lleva dos horas de ventaja sobre el rival más próximo; **share prices rose ~ of the annual report** la cotización subió en anticipación del informe anual; **we are three months ~ of schedule** llevamos tres meses de adelanto sobre la fecha prevista; **to arrive ~ of time** llegar antes de la hora prevista; **to be ~ of one's time** anticiparse a su época; **Wagner was two centuries ~ of his time** Wagner se anticipó en dos siglos a su época; **the plane is ~ of its time** el avión va por delante de su tiempo

ahem [əˈhem] EXCL ¡ejem!

ahold [əˈhəʊld] N (*esp US*) 1 **to get ~ of sb** (= *get in touch with*) contactar con algn; (= *find*) localizar a algn; **to get ~ of sth** (= *obtain*) conseguir *or* obtener algo
2 **to get ~ of o.s.** (*fig*) controlarse

ahoy [əˈhɔɪ] EXCL **ship ~!** ¡barco a la vista!; **~ there!** ¡ah del barco!

AHQ N ABBR = **Army Headquarters**

AI N ABBR 1 (= **Amnesty International**) AI *f*
2 (= **artificial intelligence**) IA *f*
3 = **artificial insemination**

AID N ABBR 1 = **artificial insemination by donor**
2 (*US*) (= **Agency for International Development**) AID *f*
3 (*US Admin*) = **Aid to Families with Dependent Children**

aid [eɪd] Ⓐ N 1 (= *assistance*) ayuda *f*; **to come/go to sb's ~** (*lit*) acudir en ayuda *or* (*more frm*) en auxilio de algn; (*in argument*) salir en defensa de algn; **a neighbour rushed to his ~** un vecino corrió en su ayuda *or* (*more frm*) en su auxilio; **a charity performance in ~ of the blind** una representación benéfica a beneficio de los ciegos; **what's all this in ~ of?*** ¿a qué viene todo esto?; **with the ~ of** con la ayuda de; **she could only walk with the ~ of crutches** sólo podía andar con la ayuda *or* ayudándose de unas muletas; **the star can be seen without the ~ of a telescope** la estrella se puede ver sin necesidad *or* ayuda de un telescopio
2 (*economic, medical*) ayuda *f*; **to give ~** prestar ayuda; *see also* **food B, legal B**
3 (= *book, tool*) ayuda *f*; **the book is an invaluable ~ to teachers** el libro es una ayuda valiosísima para los profesores; *see also* **audiovisual, deaf C, hearing B, teaching B, visual**
4 (= *person*) asistente *mf*
Ⓑ VT 1 [+ *progress, process, recovery*] (= *speed up*) acelerar; (= *contribute to*) contribuir a
2 [+ *person*] ayudar; **to ~ sb to do sth** ayudar a algn a hacer algo; **to ~ one another** ayudarse mutuamente; **to ~ and abet sb** ser cómplice de algn; (*Jur*) instigar y secundar a algn
Ⓒ VI ayudar; **it ~s in the prevention of tooth decay** ayuda a prevenir la caries
Ⓓ CPD ► **aid agency** N organismo *m* de ayuda ► **aid package** N dotación *f* de ayuda ► **aid programme, aid program** (*US*) N programa *m* de ayuda ► **aid station** N (*US*) puesto *m* de socorro ► **aid worker** N cooperante *mf*

aide [eɪd] N 1 (*Mil*) edecán *m*
2 (*Pol*) ayudante *mf*

-aided [ˈeɪdɪd] ADJ (*ending in compounds*) **state~ schools** escuelas *fpl* subvencionadas por el estado; **grant~ factories** fábricas *fpl* subvencionadas; **computer~ design** diseño *m* asistido por ordenador *or* (*esp LAm*) computador

aide-de-camp [ˌeɪddəˈkɑ̃ːŋ] N (*pl* **aides-de-camp**) edecán *m*

aide-mémoire [ˈeɪdmeɪˈmwɑː] N (*pl* **aides-mémoire, aide-mémoires**) memorándum *m*

AIDS, Aids [eɪdz] Ⓐ N ABBR (= **Acquired Immune Deficiency Syndrome**) SIDA *m*, sida *m*
Ⓑ CPD ► **AIDS campaign** N campaña *f* antisida ► **AIDS clinic** N sidatorio *m* ► **AIDS sufferer** N enfermo/a *m/f* del sida ► **AIDS test** N prueba *f* del sida ► **AIDS victim** N víctima *f* del sida

AIDS-related [ˈeɪdzrɪˌleɪtɪd] ADJ relacionado con el SIDA

AIH N ABBR = **artificial insemination by husband**

ail [eɪl] Ⓐ VT (†) afligir; **what ~s you?** ¿qué tienes?, ¿qué te pasa?
Ⓑ VI (*also* **to be ~ing**) estar enfermo, estar sufriendo

aileron [ˈeɪlərɒn] N alerón *m*

ailing [ˈeɪlɪŋ] ADJ [*person*] enfermo, achacoso; [*industry, economy*] debilitado

ailment [ˈeɪlmənt] N enfermedad *f*, achaque *m*

AIM N ABBR (*Brit St Ex*) (= **Alternative Investment Market**) segundo mercado *m*, mercado *m* de títulos no cotizados

aim [eɪm] Ⓐ N 1 (= *purpose, object*) objetivo *m*, propósito *m*; **his one ~ was to escape** su único objetivo *or* propósito era escaparse; **to achieve one's ~s** conseguir sus propósitos *or* lo que se propone; **I achieved the ~ I set myself** conseguí mi propósito, conseguí lo que me había propuesto; **to have no ~ in life** no tener un norte *or* una meta en la vida; **with the ~ of doing sth** con miras a hacer algo, con la intención de hacer algo
2 (*with gun, arrow*) puntería *f*; **to have a good/poor ~** tener buena/mala puntería; **to miss one's ~** fallar *or* errar el tiro; **to take ~ (at sth/sb)** apuntar (a algo/algn); **he took careful ~** apuntó con cuidado
Ⓑ VT [+ *gun*] apuntar; [+ *camera*] dirigir, enfocar; [+ *blow*] lanzar, intentar dar; [+ *remark, criticism*] dirigir; **he ~ed the pistol at me** me apuntó con la pistola; **missiles ~ed at the capital** misiles apuntando a la capital; **he ~ed a kick at my shins** me lanzó una patada a las canillas, intentó darme una patada en las canillas; **this advertising is ~ed at children** esta campaña va dirigida a los niños; **talks ~ed at ending the war** conversaciones *fpl* *or* negociaciones *fpl* encaminadas a la finalización de la guerra
Ⓒ VI 1 (*with weapon*) apuntar; **I ~ed at his forehead** le apunté a *or* en la frente; **~ for the centre of the green** intenta lanzar la pelota al centro del green
2 (= *aspire*) **to ~ to do sth** ponerse como objetivo hacer algo; **~ to drink five glasses of water a day** póngase como objetivo beber cinco vasos de agua al día; **we must ~ at reducing inflation** debemos aspirar a *or* dirigir nuestros esfuerzos a reducir la inflación; **to ~ for sth** aspirar a algo; **it will give you something to ~ for** así tendrás algo a lo que aspirar; ♦***IDIOM*** **to ~ high** picar muy alto, aspirar a mucho
3 (= *intend*) **to ~ to do sth** [*person*] proponerse *or* pretender hacer algo; **I ~ to finish it today** me he propuesto *or* me propongo terminarlo hoy, pretendo terminarlo hoy; **the book ~s to answer these questions** el libro tiene como objetivo *or* pretende contestar estas preguntas

aimless [ˈeɪmlɪs] ADJ [*way of life, pursuit*] sin sentido, sin propósito; [*person*] sin objeto, sin propósito; **after hours of ~ wandering he went home** tras pasar horas deambulando sin rumbo (fijo), se fue a casa

aimlessly [ˈeɪmlɪslɪ] ADV [*wander, drift, walk*] sin rumbo (fijo); [*chat, talk*] por hablar; [*live*] sin propósito

aimlessness [ˈeɪmlɪsnɪs] N [*of wandering*] falta *f* de rumbo; [*of life*] falta *f* de sentido, falta *f* de propósito; [*of conversation*] falta *f* de objeto

ain't‡ [eɪnt] (*dial*) = **am not, is not, are not, has not, have not**; *see* **be, have**

air [ɛəʳ] Ⓐ N 1 (*lit*) aire *m*; **I need some ~!** ¡necesito un poco de aire!; **by ~** [*travel*] en avión; [*send*] por avión, por vía aérea; **(seen) from the ~** desde el aire; **to get some fresh ~** tomar un poco el aire; **to throw sth (up) in** *or* **into the ~** lanzar algo al aire; **the balloon rose (up) in** *or* **into the ~** el globo se elevó en el aire; **we let the ~ out of his tyres** le desinflamos las ruedas; **one can't live on ~** no se puede vivir del aire; **the cold night ~** el aire frío de la noche; **in the open ~** al aire libre; **the ~ rang with their laughter** su risa resonaba en el aire; **the sea ~** el aire del mar; **spring is in the ~** ya se siente la primavera; **to take the ~**† tomar el fresco, airearse; **to take to the ~** [*bird*] alzar *or* levantar el vuelo; [*plane*] despegar; **to fly through the ~** vo-

➤ LANGUAGE IN USE: **aim A1** 8.2, 26.1

lar por el aire *or* por los aires; ♦*IDIOMS* **to be in the ~**: **it's still very much in the ~** está todavía en el aire, todavía no es seguro; **there's something in the ~** se respira algo; **to leave sth (hanging) in the ~** dejar algo en el aire *or* pendiente; **our plans are up in the ~** nuestros planes están en el aire; **to be walking** *or* **floating on ~** no caber en sí de alegría; *see also* **breath A2**, **change A1**, **clear D1**, **hot D**, **thin A9**

2 (*Rad, TV*) **off ~** fuera de antena; **the argument continued off ~** la discusión continuó fuera de antena; **to go off (the) ~** [*broadcaster, station*] cerrar la emisión; [*programme*] finalizar; **to be on (the) ~** [*programme, person*] estar en el aire; [*station*] emitir, estar en el aire; **we are on (the) ~ from six to seven** emitimos de seis a siete, estamos en el aire de seis a siete; **the programme could be on (the) ~ within a year** el programa podría emitirse dentro de un año; **you're on (the) ~** estás en el aire, estamos emitiendo; **would you be prepared to talk about it on (the) ~?** ¿estaría dispuesto a hablar de ello durante la emisión del programa?, ¿estaría dispuesto a hablar de ello una vez estemos en el aire?; **to go on (the) ~** salir al aire

3 (= *appearance, manner*) aire *m*; **he looked at me with an ~ of surprise** me miró con aire de sorpresa, me miró algo sorprendido; **he has an ~ of importance** tiene cierto aire de importancia; **to give o.s. ~s** ◊ **put on ~s** darse aires (de importancia); **~s and graces** afectación *fsing*

4 (*Mus*) aire *m*

5 (†) (= *breeze*) brisa *f*

Ⓑ VT 1 (= *ventilate*) [+ *room*] ventilar, airear; [+ *clothes, bed*] airear, orear

2 (= *make public*) [+ *idea, grievance*] airear, hacer público; **it gives them a chance to ~ their views** les da la oportunidad de airear *or* hacer públicos sus puntos de vista; **he always has to ~ his knowledge in front of me** siempre tiene que hacer alarde de *or* lucir lo que sabe delante de mí

3 (*US Rad, TV*) [+ *programme*] emitir

4 (*US*) (= *transport*) transportar por avión, aerotransportar

Ⓒ VI 1 [*clothes*] airearse, orearse; **I hung the blankets out to ~** colgué las mantas fuera para que se aireasen *or* se oreasen

2 (*US TV, Rad*) [*programme*] emitirse

Ⓓ CPD ► **air alert** N alerta *f* aérea ► **air ambulance** N (= *plane*) avión *m* sanitario, avión *m* ambulancia; (= *helicopter*) helicóptero *m* sanitario, helicóptero *m* ambulancia ► **air attack** N ataque *m* aéreo ► **air bag** N airbag *m*, bolsa *f* de aire ► **air base** N base *f* aérea ► **air bed** N colchón *m* inflable ► **air bladder** N (*Zool*) vejiga *f* natatoria ► **air brake** N (*Aut, Rail*) freno *m* neumático *or* de aire; (*Aer*) freno *m* aerodinámico ► **air brick** N ladrillo *m* de ventilación ► **air bridge** N puente *m* aéreo ► **air bubble** N burbuja *f* de aire ► **air burst** N explosión *f* en el aire ► **air cargo** N carga *f* aérea ► **air carrier** N aerolínea *f* ► **air chamber** N cámara *f* de aire ► **air chief marshal** N (*Brit*) comandante *m* supremo de las Fuerzas Aéreas ► **air commodore** N (*Brit*) general *m* de brigada aérea ► **air conditioner** N acondicionador *m* de aire ► **air conditioning** N aire *m* acondicionado, climatización *f*; **a cinema with ~ conditioning** un cine climatizado ► **air corridor** N pasillo *m* aéreo, corredor *m* aéreo ► **air cover** N (*Mil*) cobertura *f* aérea ► **air current** N corriente *f* de aire ► **air cushion** N (= *inflatable cushion*) almohada *f* inflable; (*Aer*) colchón *m* de aire ► **air cylinder** N bombona *f* de aire ► **air disaster** N catástrofe *f* aérea ► **air duct** N tubo *m* de aire, tubo *m* de ventilación ► **air express** N (*US*) avión *m* de carga ► **air fare** N tarifa *f* aérea, precio *m* del billete de avión; **a 10% reduction in ~ fares** un descuento del 10% en las tarifas aéreas *or* los precios de los billetes de avión; **I'll pay for the ~ fare** yo pagaré el billete de avión ► **air ferry** N transbordador *m* aéreo ► **air filter** N filtro *m* de aire ► **air force** N fuerzas *fpl* aéreas, ejército *m* del aire ► **air force base** N (*esp US*) base *f* aérea ► **Air Force One** N (*US*) avión *m* presidencial ► **air freight** N (= *transport, charge*) flete *m* aéreo; (= *goods*) carga *f* aérea; **to send sth by ~ freight** transportar algo por avión ► **air freight terminal** N terminal *f* de mercancías (*transportadas por aire*) ► **air freshener** N ambientador *m* ► **air guitar** N guitarra *f* imaginaria ► **air gun** N (= *pistol*) pistola *f* de aire (comprimido); (= *rifle*) escopeta *f* de aire (comprimido) ► **air hole** N respiradero *m* ► **air hostess** N (*Brit*) azafata *f*, aeromoza *f* (*LAm*), cabinera *f* (*Col*) ► **air intake** N (*on aircraft*) toma *f* de aire; (*when breathing*) aire *m* inhalado, capacidad *f* pulmonar ► **air lane** N pasillo *m* aéreo, corredor *m* aéreo ► **air letter** N aerograma *m* ► **air marshal** N (*Brit*) mariscal *m* del aire ► **air mass** N masa *f* de aire ► **air mattress** N colchón *m* inflable ► **air miles** NPL puntos *mpl* (acumulables para viajar) ► **air miss** N air-miss *m*, aproximación *f* peligrosa entre dos aviones ► **air pocket** N bolsa *f* de aire ► **air pollutant** N contaminante *m* atmosférico ► **air pollution** N contaminación *f* del aire, contaminación *f* atmosférica ► **air power** N fuerza *f* aérea; **the use of ~ power** el uso de la fuerza aérea ► **air pressure** N presión *f* atmosférica ► **air pump** N bomba *f* de aire ► **air purifier** N purificador *m* de aire ► **air rage** N síndrome *m* del pasajero alborotador ► **air raid** N ataque *m* aéreo; *see also* **air-raid** ► **air rifle** N escopeta *f* de aire (comprimido) ► **air shaft** N pozo *m* de ventilación ► **air show** N (*commercial*) feria *f* de la aeronáutica; (= *air display*) exhibición *f* de acrobacia aérea ► **air shuttle** N puente *m* aéreo ► **air sock** N manga *f* (de viento) ► **air space** N espacio *m* aéreo ► **air steward** N auxiliar *m* de vuelo ► **air stewardess** N auxiliar *f* de vuelo, azafata *f* ► **air strike** N ataque *m* aéreo ► **air superiority** N supremacía *f* aérea ► **air suspension** N (*Aut*) suspensión *f* neumática ► **air taxi** N aerotaxi *m* ► **air terminal** N terminal *f* (de aeropuerto) ► **air ticket** N billete *m* de avión ► **air time** N (*Rad, TV*) tiempo *m* en antena ► **air traffic** N tráfico *m* aéreo; *see also* **air-traffic** ► **air travel** N viajes *mpl* en avión ► **air valve** N respiradero *m* ► **air vent** N (*in building*) respiradero *m*; (*in clothing*) abertura *f* (*en prenda de ropa*); (*on dryer*) tobera *f* de aire caliente ► **air vice-marshall** N (*Brit*) general *m* de división de las Fuerzas Aéreas ► **air waybill** N hoja *f* de ruta aérea

airborne [ˈɛəbɔːn] ADJ 1 [*aircraft*] volando, en el aire; **to become ~** elevarse en los aires, subir; **we shall soon be ~** el avión despegará pronto; **suddenly we were ~** de repente nos vimos en el aire; **we were ~ for eight hours** volamos durante ocho horas

2 (*Mil*) aerotransportado; **~ troops** tropas *fpl* aerotransportadas

3 [*virus, germ, bacteria*] transmitido por el aire; [*seed*] llevado por el aire

airbrush [ˈɛəbrʌʃ] Ⓐ N aerógrafo *m*

Ⓑ VT pintar con aerógrafo

airbus [ˈɛəbʌs] Ⓐ N aerobús *m*

Ⓑ CPD ► **airbus service** N puente *m* aéreo

air-condition [ˈɛəkən,dɪʃən] VT climatizar, refrigerar

air-conditioned [ˈɛəkən,dɪʃənd] ADJ [*room, hotel*] climatizado, con aire acondicionado

air-cooled [ˈɛəkuːld] ADJ refrigerado por aire

aircraft [ˈɛəkrɑːft] Ⓐ N (*pl inv*) avión *m*; **the ~ industry** la industria aeronáutica

Ⓑ CPD ► **aircraft carrier** N porta(a)viones *m*

aircraftman [ˈɛəkrɑːftmən] N (*pl* **aircraftmen**) (*Brit*) cabo *m* segundo (de las fuerzas aéreas)

aircrew [ˈɛəkruː] N tripulación *f* de avión

airdrome [ˈɛə,drəʊm] N (*US*) = **aerodrome**

airdrop [ˈɛədrɒp] Ⓐ N entrega *f* por paracaídas

Ⓑ VT entregar por paracaídas, lanzar desde el aire

Airedale [ˈɛədeɪl] N (*also* **~ dog**) perro *m* Airedale

airfield [ˈɛəfiːld] N campo *m* de aviación

airflow [ˈɛəfləʊ] N corriente *f* de aire, flujo *m* de aire

airfoil [ˈɛə,fɔɪl] N (*US*) = **aerofoil**

airframe [ˈɛəfreɪm] N armazón *m or f* (*de avión*)

airhead* [ˈɛəhed] N cabeza *f* de serrín*, chorlito* *m*

airily [ˈɛərɪlɪ] ADV [*say*] sin darle importancia; [*dismiss*] muy a la ligera; [*wave, gesture*] despreocupadamente

airiness [ˈɛərɪnɪs] N 1 [*of room, building*] (= *spaciousness*) lo espacioso, lo amplio; (= *ventilation*) buena ventilación *f*

2 [*of manner*] ligereza *f*

airing [ˈɛərɪŋ] Ⓐ N **to give sth an ~** [+ *linen, room*] ventilar algo; [+ *idea*] airear algo, someter algo a la discusión; [+ *issue, matter*] ventilar algo; [+ *film on TV*] dar algo, pasar algo, proyectar algo; [+ *play*] poner en escena algo

Ⓑ CPD ► **airing cupboard** N (*Brit*) armario *m* para oreo

airless [ˈɛəlɪs] ADJ [*room*] mal ventilado; [*day*] sin viento; **it's very ~ in here** aquí dentro falta aire

airlift [ˈɛəlɪft] Ⓐ N puente *m* aéreo

Ⓑ VT aerotransportar, transportar por avión

airline [ˈɛəlaɪn] Ⓐ N línea *f* aérea

Ⓑ CPD ► **airline pilot** N piloto *mf* de compañía aérea

airliner [ˈɛəlaɪnəʳ] N avión *m* de pasajeros

airlock [ˈɛəlɒk] N (*in pipe*) burbuja *f* de aire; (*in spacecraft etc*) cámara *f* estanca, compartimento *m* estanco; (*accidental*) bolsa *f* de aire

▼ **airmail** [ˈɛəmeɪl] Ⓐ N correo *m* aéreo; **to send a letter (by) ~** mandar una carta por correo aéreo *or* por avión

Ⓑ CPD ► **airmail edition** N (*Press*) edición *f* aérea ► **airmail letter** N carta *f* por correo aéreo ► **airmail paper** N papel *m* para avión ► **airmail sticker** N etiqueta *f* de correo aéreo

Ⓒ VT mandar por correo aéreo *or* por avión

airman [ˈɛəmən] N (*pl* **airmen**) aviador *m*, piloto *m*

airplane [ˈɛəpleɪn] N (*US*) = **aeroplane**

airplay [ˈɛəpleɪ] N (*Rad*) cobertura *f* radiofónica

airport [ˈɛəpɔːt] Ⓐ N aeropuerto *m*

Ⓑ CPD ► **airport tax** N impuestos *mpl* de aeropuerto

airproof [ˈɛəpruːf] ADJ hermético

air-raid [ˈɛəreɪd] CPD ► **air-raid precautions** NPL precauciones *fpl* a tomar en caso de ataque aéreo ► **air-raid shelter** N refugio *m* antiaéreo ► **air-raid warden** N vigilante *mf* que se encarga de dar la voz de alarma en caso de ataque aéreo ► **air-raid warning** N alarma *f* antiaérea; *see also* **air D**

airscrew [ˈɛəskruː] N (*Brit*) hélice *f* de avión

➤ LANGUAGE IN USE: airmail A 20.3

air-sea [ɛə'siː] CPD ► **air-sea base** N base *f* aeronaval ► **air-sea rescue** N rescate *m* aeronaval

airship ['ɛəʃɪp] N aeronave *f*

airsick ['ɛəsɪk] ADJ mareado (en avión); **to be ~** estar mareado (en avión); **to get ~** marearse (en avión)

airsickness ['ɛəsɪknɪs] N mareo *m* (en avión)

airspeed ['ɛəspiːd] Ⓐ N velocidad *f* aérea
Ⓑ CPD ► **airspeed indicator** N anemómetro *m*

airstream ['ɛəstriːm] N corriente *f* de aire

airstrip ['ɛəstrɪp] N pista *f* de aterrizaje

airtight ['ɛətaɪt] ADJ [1] (*lit*) [*container, seal*] hermético
[2] (= *not open to question*) [*case, argument*] sin fisuras, irrefutable

air-to-air [ˌɛətə'ɛəʳ] ADJ [*missile*] aire-aire

air-to-ground [ˌɛətə'graʊnd] ADJ [*missile*] aire-tierra, aire-superficie

air-to-sea [ˌɛətə'siː] ADJ [*missile*] aire-mar

air-to-surface [ˌɛətə'sɜːfɪs] ADJ [*missile*] aire-superficie, aire-tierra

air-traffic ['ɛətræfɪk] CPD ► **air-traffic control** N control *m* del tráfico aéreo ► **air-traffic controller** N controlador(a) *m/f* aéreo/a; *see also* **air D**

airwaves ['ɛəweɪvz] NPL (*Rad, TV*) (= *radio waves*) ondas *fpl* hertzianas; (= *programmes*) programación *f*; **over the ~** a través de las ondas, por los medios de comunicación audiovisuales

airway ['ɛəweɪ] N [1] (*Aer*) (= *company*) línea *f* aérea, aerolínea *f*; (= *route*) ruta *f* aérea
[2] (*Anat*) vía *f* respiratoria
[3] (= *ventilator shaft*) conducto *m* de ventilación

airwoman ['ɛəˌwʊmən] N (*pl* **airwomen**) aviadora *f*

airworthiness ['ɛəˌwɜːðɪnɪs] N buenas condiciones *fpl* para el vuelo

airworthy ['ɛəwɜːðɪ] ADJ en condiciones de volar, en condiciones de vuelo

airy ['ɛərɪ] ADJ (*compar* **airier**; *superl* **airiest**) [1] [*room, building*] (= *spacious*) espacioso, amplio; (= *well ventilated*) bien ventilado
[2] [*fabric, clothing*] (= *lightweight*) ligero; (= *unsubstantial*) etéreo
[3] (= *careless, light*) [*remark*] hecho a la ligera; [*gesture, wave*] despreocupado
[4] (= *empty*) [*idea, generalization*] ligero; **he's always full of ~ promises** siempre hace promesas a la ligera

airy-fairy* [ˌɛərɪ'fɛərɪ] ADJ (*Brit*) [*ideas, principles*] superficial, vacío; [*plan, promises*] vano, fantasioso; [*person*] insustancial

aisle [aɪl] N (*Rel*) nave *f* (lateral); (*in theatre, plane, train, coach, supermarket*) pasillo *m*; **~ seat** asiento *m* de pasillo; ✦***IDIOMS*** **to walk up** *or* **down the ~ with sb†** llevar al altar a algn; **it had them rolling in the ~s** los tuvo muertos de (la) risa

AISP N ABBR (= **Agricultural Income Subsidies Programme**) PARA *m*

aitch [eɪtʃ] N *nombre de la h inglesa*; **to drop one's ~es** no pronunciar las haches (*indicio clasista o de habla dialectal*)

Aix-la-Chapelle ['eɪkslæʃə'pel] N Aquisgrán *m*

Ajaccio [ə'ʒætʃɪəʊ] N Ajaccio *m*

ajar [ə'dʒɑːʳ] ADV entreabierto; **to leave the door ~** dejar entreabierta la puerta, no cerrar completamente la puerta, entrecerrar la puerta (*Mex*)

Ajax ['eɪdʒæks] N Áyax

AK ABBR (*US Post*) = **Alaska**

AKA, aka ABBR (= **also known as**) alias

akimbo [ə'kɪmbəʊ] ADV **with arms ~** en jarras

akin [ə'kɪn] ADJ [1] parecido (**to** a), semejante (**to** a)
[2] (*frm*) (= *related by blood*) consanguíneo; **they are not ~** no tienen parentesco consanguíneo

AL ABBR (*US*) = **Alabama**

ALA N ABBR (*US*) = **American Library Association**

Ala. ABBR (*US*) = **Alabama**

alabaster ['æləbɑːstəʳ] Ⓐ N alabastro *m*
Ⓑ ADJ alabastrino

alabastrine [ˌælə'bæstraɪn] ADJ alabastrino

à la carte [ælæ'kɑːt] ADV a la carta

alacrity [ə'lækrɪtɪ] N prontitud *f*, presteza *f*; **with ~** con prontitud *or* presteza

Aladdin [ə'lædɪn] Ⓐ N Aladino
Ⓑ CPD ► **Aladdin's cave** N (*fig*) cueva *f* de ricos tesoros ► **Aladdin's lamp** N lámpara *f* de Aladino

Alans ['ælənz] NPL alanos *mpl*

Alaric ['ælərɪk] N Alarico

alarm [ə'lɑːm] Ⓐ N [1] (= *warning, bell*) alarma *f*; (= *signal*) señal *f* de alarma; **to raise** *or* **sound the ~** dar la alarma; *see also* **false B, fire D**
[2] (= *fear*) alarma *f*, sobresalto *m*; **there was general ~** cundió la alarma general; **there was some ~ at this** esto produjo cierta inquietud; **to cry out in ~** gritar alarmado; **to cause ~** causar alarma; **~ and despondency** inquietud y desconcierto
[3] (*also* **~ clock**) despertador *m*
Ⓑ VT alarmar; **to be ~ed at** asustarse de; **don't be ~ed** no te asustes, no te inquietes
Ⓒ CPD ► **alarm bell** N timbre *m* de alarma; **the court's decision has set ~ bells ringing in government** la decisión del tribunal ha hecho cundir la alarma entre el gobierno ► **alarm call** N (= *wake-up call*) llamada *f* de aviso (para despertar); **I'd like an ~ call for six a.m., please** llámenme *or* despiértenme a las seis, por favor ► **alarm clock** N despertador *m* ► **alarm signal** N señal *f* de alarma ► **alarm system** N sistema *m* de alarma

alarmed [ə'lɑːmd] ADJ [*voice*] sobresaltado, asustado; *see also* **alarm B**

alarming [ə'lɑːmɪŋ] ADJ alarmante

alarmingly [ə'lɑːmɪŋlɪ] ADV de modo alarmante; **~ high numbers** cifras *fpl* alarmantes

alarmist [ə'lɑːmɪst] Ⓐ ADJ alarmista
Ⓑ N alarmista *mf*

alarum [ə'lærəm] N (†† *or hum*) = **alarm A1**

alas [ə'læs] EXCL († *or liter*) ¡ay (de mí)!; **~, it is not so** desafortunadamente, no es así; **I must tell you, ~, that …** tengo que decirte, y lo siento, que …; **I have no money, ~** no tengo dinero, y esto es triste; **~ for Poland!** ¡ay de Polonia!

Alas. ABBR (*US*) = **Alaska**

Alaska [ə'læskə] Ⓐ N Alaska *f*
Ⓑ CPD ► **Alaska Highway** N carretera *f* de Alaska ► **Alaska Range** N Cordillera *f* de Alaska

Alaskan [ə'læskən] Ⓐ ADJ de Alaska
Ⓑ N nativo/a *m/f* de Alaska, habitante *mf* de Alaska

alb [ælb] N (*Rel*) alba *f*

Albania [æl'beɪnɪə] N Albania *f*

Albanian [æl'beɪnɪən] Ⓐ ADJ albanés
Ⓑ N [1] (= *person*) albanés/esa *m/f*
[2] (*Ling*) albanés *m*

albatross ['ælbətrɒs] N [1] (*Orn*) albatros *m inv*
[2] (*fig*) (= *burden*) rémora *f*; ✦***IDIOM*** **to be an ~ around sb's neck** suponer una rémora para algn
[3] (*Golf*) albatros *m inv*, menos tres *m*

albeit [ɔːl'biːɪt] CONJ aunque

Albert ['ælbət] N Alberto

Albigenses [ˌælbɪ'dʒensiːz] NPL albigenses *mpl*

Albigensian [ˌælbɪ'dʒensɪən] ADJ albigense

albinism ['ælbɪnɪzəm] N albinismo *m*

albino [æl'biːnəʊ] Ⓐ ADJ albino
Ⓑ N albino/a *m/f*

Albion ['ælbɪən] N Albión *f*

album ['ælbəm] Ⓐ N (= *book, record, CD*) álbum *m*; **autograph/photograph ~** álbum *m* de autógrafos/fotografías
Ⓑ CPD ► **album cover** N portada *f* de disco

albumen, albumin ['ælbjʊmɪn] N (= *egg white*) clara *f* de huevo; (*Bot*) albumen *m*; (*Chem*) albúmina *f*

albuminous [æl'bjuːmɪnəs] ADJ albuminoso

alchemical [æl'kemɪkəl] ADJ alquímico, de alquimia

alchemist ['ælkɪmɪst] N alquimista *mf*

alchemy ['ælkɪmɪ] N (= *ancient chemistry*) alquimia *f*; (*fig*) (= *mysterious power*) poder *m* mágico

alcohol ['ælkəhɒl] N (= *drink*) alcohol *m* (*also Chem*); **I never touch ~** no pruebo el alcohol, soy abstemio

alcohol-free ['ælkəhɒlˌfriː] ADJ sin alcohol

alcoholic [ˌælkə'hɒlɪk] Ⓐ ADJ alcohólico; **~ drinks** bebidas *fpl* alcohólicas
Ⓑ N alcohólico/a *m/f*, alcoholizado/a *m/f*

alcoholism ['ælkəhɒlɪzəm] N alcoholismo *m*; **to die of ~** morir alcoholizado

alcopop ['ælkəʊpɒp] N (*Brit*) *combinado de refresco y alcohol que se vende ya embotellado*

alcove ['ælkəʊv] N nicho *m*, hueco *m*

Ald. ABBR = **alderman**

alder ['ɔːldəʳ] N aliso *m*

alderman ['ɔːldəmən] N (*pl* **aldermen**) concejal(a) *m/f* (*de categoría superior*)

aldosterone [æl'dɒstəˌrəʊn] N aldosterona *f*

aldrin ['ɔːldrɪn] N aldrina *f*

ale [eɪl] N cerveza *f*; *see also* **brown E, light² D, pale¹ C**

aleatoric [ˌeɪlɪə'tɒrɪk], **aleatory** ['eɪlɪətərɪ] ADJ aleatorio

Alec ['ælɪk] N (*familiar form*) of **Alexander**

alehouse† ['eɪlˌhaʊs] N taberna *f*

alert [ə'lɜːt] Ⓐ ADJ [1] (= *mentally acute*) [*person*] espabilado, despierto; [*expression*] vivo; **they were ~** eran espabilados, tenían la mente despierta; **he's a very ~ baby** es un bebé muy despierto
[2] (= *vigilant*) alerta *inv*, atento; **we must stay ~** hay que estar atentos
[3] (= *aware*) **to be ~ to sth** ser consciente *or* al tanto de algo
Ⓑ N alerta *f*; **to be on the ~** estar alerta; **to put** *or* **place troops on (the) ~** poner a las tropas sobre aviso *or* en situación de alerta; *see also* **red C**
Ⓒ VT alertar, poner sobre aviso; **to ~ sb to sth** alertar a algn de algo, poner a algn sobre aviso de algo; **we are now ~ed to the dangers** ahora estamos sobre aviso en cuanto a los peligros

alertness [ə'lɜːtnɪs] N (= *mental acuteness*) lo espabilado, lo despierto; (= *vigilance*) vigilancia *f*

Aleutian [ə'luːʃən] ADJ **the ~ Islands** ◊ **the ~s** las Islas Aleutianas

A-level ['eɪˌlevl] N ABBR (*Brit Scol*) *see* **A**

Alex ['ælɪks] N (*familiar form*) of **Alexander**

Alexander [ˌælɪg'zɑːndəʳ] N Alejandro; **~ the Great** Alejandro Magno

Alexandria [ˌælɪg'zɑːndrɪə] N Alejandría *f*

alexandrine [ˌælɪg'zændraɪn] N alejandrino *m*

ALF N ABBR (*Brit*) (= **Animal Liberation Front**) *movimiento reivindicativo de los derechos de los animales*

Alf [ælf] N (*familiar form*) of **Alfred**

alfalfa [æl'fælfə] N alfalfa *f*

Alfred ['ælfrɪd] N Alfredo

alfresco [æl'freskəʊ] Ⓐ ADJ al aire libre
Ⓑ ADV al aire libre

alga ['ælgə] N (*pl* **algae** ['ældʒiː]) alga *f*

algal ['ælgəl] ADJ de algas

Algarve [æl'gɑːv] N **the ~** el Algarve

algebra ['ældʒɪbrə] N álgebra *f*

algebraic [ˌældʒɪ'breɪɪk] ADJ algebraico

Algeria [æl'dʒɪərɪə] N Argelia *f*

Algerian [æl'dʒɪərɪən] Ⓐ ADJ argelino
Ⓑ N argelino/a *m/f*

algicide ['ældʒɪsaɪd] N algicida *m*

Algiers [æl'dʒɪəz] N Argel *m*

algorithm ['ælgəˌrɪðəm] N algoritmo *m*

algorithmic [ˌælgə'rɪðmɪk] ADJ algorítmico

alias ['eɪlɪəs] Ⓐ N alias *m inv*
Ⓑ ADV **Smith ~ Stevens** Smith alias Stevens

alibi ['ælɪbaɪ] Ⓐ N (*in relation to crime*) coartada *f*; (*) (= *excuse*) excusa *f*, pretexto *m*
Ⓑ VT **to ~ sb** (*US**) proveer de una coartada a algn
Ⓒ VI (*US**) buscar excusas (**for doing sth** por haber hecho algo)

Alice ['ælɪs] Ⓐ N Alicia; **~ in Wonderland** Alicia en el país de las maravillas; **~ through the Looking-Glass** Alicia en el país del espejo
Ⓑ CPD ► **Alice band** N (*Brit*) diadema *f*

alien ['eɪlɪən] Ⓐ ADJ 1 (= *foreign*) extranjero
2 (= *unfamiliar*) extraño, ajeno; **~ to** ajeno a
3 (= *extraterrestrial*) alienígena, extraterrestre; **~ being** alienígena *mf*, extraterrestre *mf*
Ⓑ N 1 (= *foreigner*) extranjero/a *m/f*
2 (= *extraterrestrial*) alienígena *mf*, extraterrestre *mf*

alienate ['eɪlɪəneɪt] VT 1 (= *offend*) [+ *person*] ofender; [+ *sb's sympathies*] perder, enajenar (*frm*); **to ~ o.s. from sb** alejarse *or* apartarse de algn
2 (*Pol, Philos*) alienar, enajenar
3 (*Jur*) enajenar

alienated ['eɪlɪəneɪtɪd] ADJ alienado

alienation [ˌeɪlɪə'neɪʃən] N 1 (*Pol, Philos*) alienación *f*, enajenación *f*; **feelings of ~ (from society)** sentimientos *mpl* de alienación *or* enajenación (social)
2 (= *estrangement*) [*of friend*] alejamiento *m*
3 (*Jur*) enajenación *f*, traspaso *m*
4 (*Med*) enajenación *f* mental

alienist ['eɪljənɪst] N (*US*) alienista *mf*

alight[1] [ə'laɪt] ADJ 1 (*lit*) **to be ~** [*fire*] estar ardiendo; [*lamp*] estar encendido *or* (*LAm*) prendido; **to keep a fire ~** mantener un fuego ardiendo; **to set ~** pegar fuego a, incendiar
2 (*fig*) **~ with** [+ *happiness, enthusiasm*] resplandeciente de

alight[2] [ə'laɪt] VI 1 (*from vehicle*) bajar, apearse (**from** de)
2 (*on branch, etc*) [*bird, insect*] posarse (**on** sobre)

►**alight on** VI + PREP [+ *fact, idea*] caer en la cuenta de, darse cuenta de

align [ə'laɪn] VT alinear; **to ~ o.s. with** (*Pol, fig*) ponerse del lado de

alignment [ə'laɪnmənt] N (*lit, fig*) alineación *f*; **to be in ~** estar alineados, estar en línea recta; **to be out of ~ (with)** no estar alineado (con)

▼**alike** [ə'laɪk] Ⓐ ADJ **they are very ~** son muy parecidos, se parecen mucho; **you're all ~!** ¡sois todos iguales!, ¡todos son iguales! (*esp LAm*); **to look ~** parecerse; **they all look ~ to me** yo no veo diferencia entre ellos, para mí todos son iguales
Ⓑ ADV 1 (= *in the same way*) del mismo modo, igual; **to think/dress ~** pensar/vestir del mismo modo *or* igual
2 (= *both, equally*) **men and women ~** tanto los hombres como las mujeres

alimentary [ˌælɪ'mentərɪ] Ⓐ ADJ alimenticio
Ⓑ CPD ► **alimentary canal** N tubo *m* digestivo

alimony ['ælɪmənɪ] N (*Jur*) pensión *f* alimenticia

A-line ['eɪlaɪn] ADJ [*dress*] de línea trapezoide

alive [ə'laɪv] ADJ 1 vivo; **to be ~** estar vivo, vivir; **it's good to be ~!** ¡qué bueno es vivir!; **to be still ~** vivir todavía; [*dying person*] estar todavía con vida; **while ~ he did no harm** en vida no hizo daño a nadie; **she plays as well as any pianist ~** toca tan bien como cualquier pianista del mundo; **he's the best footballer ~** es el mejor futbolista del mundo; **to bring a story ~** dar vida a una historia, animar una historia; **to be buried ~** ser enterrado vivo; **to burn sb ~** quemar a algn vivo; **the scene came ~ as she described it** la escena se animaba *or* vivificaba al describirla ella; **we were being eaten ~ by mosquitoes** los mosquitos nos comían vivos; **to keep sb ~** conservar a algn con vida; **to keep a memory ~** guardar vivo *or* fresco un recuerdo, hacer perdurar una memoria; **to keep a tradition ~** mantener viva una tradición; **man ~!**† ¡hombre!; **no man ~ could do better** no lo podría hacer mejor nadie; **he managed to stay ~ on fruit** logró sobrevivir comiendo frutas; **the prisoner must be taken ~** hay que capturar vivo *or* con vida al prisionero; *see also* **dead A1**
2 (*fig*) (= *lively*) activo, enérgico; **look ~!**†* (= *hurry*) ¡date prisa!, ¡apúrate! (*LAm*); ✦*IDIOM* **~ and kicking*** vivito y coleando
3 **~ with** [+ *insects*] lleno de, hormigueante en; **a book ~ with interest** un libro lleno de interés
4 (*frm*) **~ to** (= *aware of*) consciente de; **I am ~ to the danger** estoy consciente del peligro, me doy cuenta del peligro; **I am fully ~ to the fact that ...** soy consciente de que ..., no ignoro que ...; **I am fully ~ to the honour you do me** soy plenamente consciente del honor que se me hace

alkali ['ælkəlaɪ] N (*pl* **alkalis, alkalies**) álcali *m*

alkaline ['ælkəlaɪn] ADJ alcalino

alkalinity [ˌælkə'lɪnɪtɪ] N alcalinidad *f*

alkaloid ['ælkəlɔɪd] Ⓐ ADJ alcaloideo
Ⓑ N alcaloide *m*

alkie‡, **alky**‡ ['ælkɪ] N ABBR (= **alcoholic**) borrachín/ina *m/f*

all [ɔːl]

A ADJECTIVE	D NOUN
B PRONOUN	E COMPOUNDS
C ADVERB	

When ***all*** *is part of a set combination, eg* ***in all seriousness/probability****, look up the noun. Note that* ***all right*** *has an entry to itself.*

Ⓐ ADJECTIVE
1 todo; **~ my life** toda mi vida; **~ my friends** todos mis amigos; **~ men** todos los hombres; **they drank ~ the beer** se bebieron toda la cerveza; **~ the others went home** todos los demás se fueron a casa; **it rained ~ day** llovió todo el día, llovió el día entero; **she hasn't been in ~ day** no ha estado en todo el día; *BUT* **~ three (of them) were found guilty** los tres fueron declarados culpables; **I'll take ~ three (of them)** me llevo los tres; **40% of ~ marriages end in divorce** el 40% de los matrimonios terminan en divorcio; **it would have to rain today, of ~ days!** ¡tenía que llover hoy justamente!; **for ~ their efforts, they didn't manage to score** a pesar de todos sus esfuerzos, no lograron marcar un tanto; **they chose him, of ~ people!** lo eligieron a él, como si no hubiera otros; **~ those who disobey will be punished** todos aquéllos que desobedezcan serán castigados

◆ **all that**: **it's not as bad as ~ that** no es para tanto; **~ that is irrelevant now** todo eso ya no importa

◆ **and all that** y cosas así, y otras cosas por el estilo; **he went on about loyalty and ~ that** habló sin parar sobre la lealtad y cosas así; **sorry and ~ that, but that's the way it is** disculpas y todo lo demás, pero así son las cosas

◆ **of all the ...**: **of ~ the luck!** ¡vaya suerte!; **of ~ the tactless things to say!** ¡qué falta de tacto!; *see also* **best, four B2**

2 = *any* **it has been proved beyond ~ doubt** se ha probado sin que quepa la menor duda; **the town had changed beyond ~ recognition** la ciudad había cambiado hasta hacerse irreconocible

Ⓑ PRONOUN
1 *singular* 1·1 (= *everything*) todo; **it's ~ done** está todo hecho; **we did ~ we could to stop him** hicimos todo lo posible para detenerlo; **it was ~ I could do not to laugh** apenas pude contener la risa; **~ is not lost** (*liter or hum*) aún quedan esperanzas; **~ of it** todo; **I didn't read ~ of it** no lo leí todo *or* entero; **not ~ of it was true** no todo era cierto; **you can't see ~ of Madrid in a day** no puedes ver todo Madrid *or* Madrid entero en un día; **I do ~ of the work** yo hago todo el trabajo; **I do ~ of the cooking** siempre cocino yo; **it took him ~ of three hours** (= *at least*) le llevó tres horas enteras; (*iro*) (= *only*) le llevó ni más ni menos que tres horas; **she must be ~ of 16** (*iro*) debe de tener al menos 16 años; **is that ~?** ◊ **will that be ~?** ¿es eso todo?, ¿nada más?; **six o'clock? is that ~?** ¿las seis? ¿nada más?; **that's ~** eso es todo, nada más; **~ is well** todo está bien; ✦*IDIOM* **when ~ is said and done** a fin de cuentas; ✦*PROV* **~'s well that ends well** bien está lo que bien acaba; *see also* **best, once A1, tell**
1·2 (= *the only thing*) **~ I can tell you is ...** todo lo que puedo decirte es ..., lo único que puedo decirte es ...; **~ I want is to sleep** lo único que quiero es dormir; **that was ~ that we managed to salvage from the fire** eso fue todo lo que conseguimos rescatar del incendio; **~ that matters is that you're safe** lo único que importa es que estás a salvo; **~ that he did was laugh** lo único que hizo fue reírse
2 *plural* todos *mpl*, todas *fpl*; **they ~ came with their husbands** todas vinieron con sus maridos; **this concerns ~ of you** esto os afecta a todos (vosotros); **his was the worst performance of ~** la suya fue la peor actuación de todas; **they ~ say that** todos dicen lo mismo; **~ who knew him loved him** todos los que le conocieron le querían
3 *in scores* **the score is two ~** van empatados a dos, el marcador es de empate a dos; **to draw two ~** empatar a dos; **it's 30 ~** (*Ten-*

➤ LANGUAGE IN USE: **alike A** 5.2

nis) treinta iguales

4 *in set structures*

◆ **above all** sobre todo
◆ **after all** después de todo
◆ **all but**: **~ but seven/twenty** todos menos siete/veinte
◆ **all for nothing**: **I rushed to get there, ~ for nothing** fui a toda prisa, todo para nada, fui a toda prisa, y total para nada
◆ **all in all** en general; **~ in ~, things turned out quite well** en general, las cosas salieron bastante bien; **we thought, ~ in ~, it wasn't a bad idea** pensamos que, mirándolo bien, no era una mala idea
◆ **and all**: **what with the rain and ~** con la lluvia y todo lo demás; **the dog ate the sausage, mustard and ~** el perro se comió la salchicha, mostaza incluida
◆ **for all I care**: **you can go right now for ~ I care** por mí como si te vas ahora mismo
◆ **for all I know**: **for ~ I know he could be dead** puede que hasta esté muerto, no lo sé; **for ~ I know, he could be right** igual hasta tiene razón, no lo sé
◆ **if (...) at all**: **I'll go tomorrow if I go at ~** si es que voy, iré mañana; **it rarely rains here, if at ~** aquí rara vez llueve, si es que llueve; **I'd like to see him today, if (it's) at ~ possible** me gustaría verlo hoy, si es del todo posible; **they won't attempt it, if they have any sense at ~** si tienen el más mínimo sentido común, no lo intentarán
◆ **in all**: **50 men in ~** 50 hombres en total
◆ **it all**: **he ate it ~** se lo comió todo; **it ~ happened so quickly** sucedió todo tan rápido; **she seemed to have it ~: a good job, a happy marriage** parecía tenerlo todo: un buen trabajo, un matrimonio feliz
◆ **it's all or nothing** es todo o nada
◆ **most of all** sobre todo, más que nada
◆ **no ... at all**: **I have no regrets at ~** no me arrepiento en absoluto; **it makes no difference at ~** da exactamente igual
◆ **not ... at all**: **I don't feel at ~ well** no me siento nada bien; **she wasn't at ~ apologetic** no se disculpó para nada; **I'm not at ~ tired** no estoy cansado en lo más mínimo *or* en absoluto; **it was not at ~ nice** no fue nada agradable; **you mean he didn't cry at ~?** ¿quieres decir que no lloró nada?; **did you mention me at ~?** ¿mencionaste mi nombre por casualidad?
◆ **not at all!** (*answer to thanks*) ¡de nada!, ¡no hay de qué!; **"are you disappointed?" — "not at ~!"** —¿estás defraudado? —en absoluto

Ⓒ ADVERB

1 *= entirely* todo

Make **todo** *agree with the person or thing described:*

she went ~ red se puso toda colorada; **you're ~ wet** estás todo mojado; **it's ~ dirty** está todo sucio; **the children were ~ alone** los niños estaban completamente solos; **there were insects ~ around us** había insectos por todas partes; **I did it ~ by myself** lo hice completamente solo; **he was ~ covered in blood** estaba completamente cubierto de sangre; **she was dressed ~ in black** iba vestida completamente de negro; **we shook hands ~ round** nos estrechamos todos las manos

2 *in set structures*

◆ **all along**: **~ along the street** a lo largo de toda la calle, por toda la calle; **this is what I feared ~ along** esto es lo que estaba temiendo desde el primer momento *or* el principio
◆ **all but** (*= nearly*) casi; **he ~ but died** casi se muere, por poco se muere; **he's ~ but forgotten now** ya casi no se le recuerda
◆ **all for sth**: **to be ~ for sth** estar completamente a favor de algo; **I'm ~ for it** estoy completamente a favor; **I'm ~ for giving children their independence** estoy completamente a favor de *or* apoyo completamente la idea de dar independencia a los niños
◆ **all in** (*= all inclusive*) (*Brit*) todo incluido; (*) (*= exhausted*) hecho polvo*; **the trip cost £200 ~ in** el viaje costó 200 libras, todo incluido; **after a day's skiing I was ~ in** después de un día esquiando, estaba hecho polvo* *or* rendido; **you look ~ in** se te ve rendido, ¡vaya cara de estar hecho polvo!*
◆ **all out**: **to go ~ out** (*= spare no expense*) tirar la casa por la ventana; (*Sport*) emplearse a fondo; **to go ~ out for the prize** volcarse por conseguir el premio; **we must go ~ out to ensure it** hemos de desplegar todos nuestros medios para asegurarlo
◆ **all over**: **~ over the world you'll find ...** en *or* por todo el mundo encontrarás ...; **he's travelled ~ over the world** ha viajado por todo el mundo; **you've got mud ~ over your shoes** tienes los zapatos cubiertos de barro; **I spilled coffee ~ over my shirt** se me cayó el café encima y me manché toda la camisa; **they were ~ over him*** le recibieron con el mayor entusiasmo; **I ache ~ over** me duele (por) todo el cuerpo; **I looked ~ over for you** te busqué por *or* en todas partes; **it happens ~ over** ocurre en todas partes; **that's him ~ over*** eso es muy típico de él
◆ **all the more ...**: **considering his age, it's ~ the more remarkable that he succeeded** teniendo en cuenta su edad, es aún más extraordinario que lo haya logrado; **she valued her freedom, ~ the more so because she had fought so hard for it** valoraba mucho su libertad, tanto más cuanto que había luchado tanto por conseguirla
◆ **all too ...**: **it's ~ too true** lamentablemente es cierto; **~ too soon, the holiday was over** cuando quisimos darnos cuenta las vacaciones habían terminado; **the evening passed ~ too quickly** la tarde pasó demasiado rápido
◆ **all up with**: **it's ~ up with him** está acabado
◆ **all very ...**: **that's ~ very well but ...** todo eso está muy bien, pero ...
◆ **not all there**: **he isn't ~ there*** no tiene todos los tornillos bien*, le falta algún tornillo*
◆ **not all that ...**: **it isn't ~ that far** no está tan lejos; **it shouldn't be ~ that difficult** no debería resultar tan difícil

see also **all-out, better B**

Ⓓ NOUN

= utmost **he had given her his ~** (*= affection*) se había entregado completamente a ella; (*= possessions*) le había dado todo lo que tenía; **I really didn't give it my ~** no di todo lo que podía dar de mí; **I decided to give it my ~** decidí echarle el resto; **he puts his ~ into every game** se da completamente en cada partido, siempre da todo lo que puede de sí en cada partido

Ⓔ COMPOUNDS ► **the all clear** N (*= signal*) el cese de la alarma, el fin de la alarma; (*fig*) el visto bueno, luz verde; **~ clear!** ¡fin de la alerta!; **to be given the ~ clear** (*to do sth*) recibir el visto bueno, recibir luz verde; (*by doctor*) recibir el alta médica *or* definitiva ► **All Fools' Day** N ≈ día *m* de los (Santos) Inocentes ► **All Hallows' (Day)** N día *m* de Todos los Santos ► **All Saints' Day** N día *m* de Todos los Santos ► **All Souls' Day** N día *m* de (los) Difuntos (*Sp*), día *m* de (los) Muertos (*LAm*)

all- [ɔːl] PREFIX **~American** típicamente americano, americano cien por cien; **~leather** todo cuero; **with an ~Chinese cast** con un reparto totalmente chino; **there will be an ~Spanish final** en la final figurarán únicamente españoles; **it's an ~woman show** es un espectáculo enteramente femenino

ALL-AMERICAN

El término **all-American** *se usa para referirse a los deportistas universitarios que son seleccionados por su habilidad en un deporte determinado para formar parte de un equipo nacional, equipo que no compite como tal, ya que es sólo un título honorífico. De estos equipos, el que recibe mayor publicidad es el de fútbol americano.*

Este término se usa también para hacer referencia a una persona que representa el ideal de la clase media norteamericana, como cuando se dice, por ejemplo: **he is a fine, upstanding all-American boy**.

Allah [ˈælə] N Alá *m*

all-around [ˈɔːləˈraʊnd] ADJ (*US*) = **all-round**

allay [əˈleɪ] VT [+ *fears*] aquietar, calmar; [+ *doubts*] despejar; [+ *pain*] aliviar

all-consuming [ˈɔːlkənˈsjuːmɪŋ] ADJ [*passion, interest*] absorbente

allegation [ˌælɪˈɡeɪʃən] N alegato *m*

allege [əˈledʒ] VT 1 (*with verb/clause*) afirmar (**that** que); **she is ~d to have stolen money from a cash box** se afirma que robó dinero del que había en una caja; **he is ~d to be wealthy** según se dice es rico; **he is ~d to be the leader** según se dice él es el jefe

2 (*with noun*) alegar; **he absented himself alleging illness** se ausentó alegando estar enfermo

alleged [əˈledʒd] ADJ [*crime, thief, victim, author*] presunto; [*fact, reason*] supuesto; **~ police brutality** presunta brutalidad policial; **his ~ involvement in the scandal** su presunta *or* supuesta relación con el escándalo

allegedly [əˈledʒɪdlɪ] ADV presuntamente, supuestamente; **the crimes he had ~ committed** los crímenes que presuntamente *or* supuestamente había cometido; **his van ~ struck two people** según se afirma *or* supuestamente, su furgoneta atropelló a dos personas; **~ illegal immigrants** inmigrantes presuntamente ilegales; **his ~ beautiful wife** su esposa, que según se dice es muy bella

allegiance [əˈliːdʒəns] N lealtad *f*; **to owe ~ to** deber lealtad a; **to pledge** *or* **swear ~ to** jurar lealtad a; **oath of ~** (*Brit*) juramento *m* de lealtad *or* fidelidad

allegoric [ˌælɪˈɡɒrɪk] ADJ = **allegorical**

allegorical [ˌælɪˈɡɒrɪkəl] ADJ alegórico

allegorically [ˌælɪˈɡɒrɪkəlɪ] ADV alegóricamente

allegorize [ˈælɪɡəraɪz] VT alegorizar

allegory [ˈælɪɡərɪ] N alegoría *f*

allegro [əˈleɡrəʊ] N alegro *m*

alleluia [ˌælɪˈluːjə] N aleluya *f*

all-embracing [ˈɔːlɪmˈbreɪsɪŋ] ADJ [*survey, study, work, knowledge*] exhaustivo, global; [*hospitality*] generalizado, sin distingos

Allen key [ˈælən,kiː], **Allen wrench** (*US*) [ˈælən,rentʃ] N llave *f* (de) Allen

allergen [ˈælədʒən] N alérgeno *m*

allergenic [ˌæləˈdʒenɪk] ADJ alergénico

allergic [əˈlɜːdʒɪk] ADJ alérgico; **to be ~ to** (*Med, hum*) ser alérgico a

allergist [ˈælədʒɪst] N alergista *mf*, alergólogo/a *m/f*

allergy ['ælədʒɪ] Ⓐ N alergia *f* (**to** a); **total ~ syndrome** síndrome *m* de alergia total
Ⓑ CPD ► **allergy clinic** N clínica *f* de alergias

alleviate [ə'li:vɪeɪt] VT aliviar, mitigar

alleviation [ə,li:vɪ'eɪʃən] N alivio *m*, mitigación *f*

alley ['ælɪ] Ⓐ N [1] (*between buildings*) callejón *m*, callejuela *f*; (*in garden, park*) paseo *m*; ✦*IDIOM* **this is right up my ~*** esto es lo que me va, esto es lo mío
[2] (*US Tennis*) banda *f* lateral para dobles; *see also* **blind E**, **bowling B**
Ⓑ CPD ► **alley cat** N (*also fig*) gato/a *m/f* callejero/a

alleyway ['ælɪweɪ] N = **alley A1**

all-fired* ['ɔ:lfaɪəd] (*US*) Ⓐ ADJ excesivo; **in an ~ hurry** con muchísima prisa
Ⓑ ADV a más no poder

alliance [ə'laɪəns] N alianza *f*; **to enter into an ~ with** aliarse con

allied ['ælaɪd] Ⓐ ADJ [1] (*Mil, Pol*) [1·1] (= *united, in league*) [*troops, countries, parties*] aliado; **~ against sb/sth** aliado en contra de algn/algo; **a group closely ~ to General Pera's faction** un grupo estrechamente ligado a la facción del General Pera; **~ with sth/sb** aliado con algo/algn
[1·2] **Allied** (*Hist*) [*nations, tanks, operation, casualties*] aliado; **the Allied forces** las fuerzas aliadas
[2] (= *associated*) [*subjects, products, industries*] relacionado, afín; **~ to sth** relacionado con algo, afín a algo; **lectures on subjects ~ to health** conferencias sobre temas relacionados con *or* afines a la salud
[3] (= *coupled*) **~ to** *or* **with sth** combinado con algo; **his sense of humour ~ to** *or* **with his clean-cut looks** su sentido del humor combinado con su cuidado aspecto
Ⓑ CPD ► **allied health professional** N (*US*) *profesional de la medicina o la enfermería que trabaja para una mutua*

alligator ['ælɪgeɪtəʳ] N caimán *m*

all-important ['ɔ:lɪm'pɔ:tənt] ADJ de primera *or* de suma importancia

all-in ['ɔ:lɪn] Ⓐ ADJ (*Brit*) [*price*] global, con todo incluido; [*insurance policy*] contra todo riesgo
Ⓑ CPD ► **all-in wrestling** N lucha *f* libre

all-inclusive ['ɔ:lɪn'klu:sɪv] ADJ [*price*] con todo incluido; **~ insurance policy** póliza *f* de seguro contra todo riesgo

alliteration [ə,lɪtə'reɪʃən] N aliteración *f*

alliterative [ə'lɪtərətɪv] ADJ aliterado

all-metal ['ɔ:l'metl] ADJ enteramente metálico

all-night ['ɔ:l'naɪt] Ⓐ ADJ [*café, garage*] abierto toda la noche; [*vigil, party*] que dura toda la noche
Ⓑ CPD ► **all-night pass** N (*Mil*) permiso *m* de pernocta ► **all-night service** N servicio *m* nocturno ► **all-night showing** N (*Cine*) sesión *f* continua nocturna

all-nighter* ['ɔ:l'naɪtəʳ] N *espectáculo o fiesta etc que dura hasta la madrugada*

allocate ['æləʊkeɪt] VT [1] (= *allot*) asignar (**to** a); **to ~ funds for a purpose** asignar *or* destinar fondos para un propósito
[2] (= *distribute*) repartir (**among** entre)

allocation [,æləʊ'keɪʃən] N [1] (= *allotting*) (*also Comput*) asignación *f*
[2] (= *distribution*) reparto *m*
[3] (= *share, amount*) ración *f*, cuota *f*

allomorph ['æləʊmɔ:f] N alomorfo *m*

allopathic [,æləʊ'pæθɪk] ADJ alopático

allopathy [æ'lɒpəθɪ] N alopatía *f*

allophone ['æləʊfəʊn] N alófono *m*

allot [ə'lɒt] VT [1] (= *assign*) [+ *task, share, time*] asignar (**to** a); **the space ~ted to each contributor** el espacio asignado a cada colaborador; **we finished in the time ~ted** terminamos en el tiempo previsto; **he was ~ted the role of villain** le dieron el papel de malo
[2] (= *distribute*) repartir, distribuir

allotment [ə'lɒtmənt] N [1] (= *distribution*) reparto *m*, distribución *f*
[2] (= *quota*) asignación *f*, cuota *f*
[3] (*Brit*) (= *land*) parcela *f*

all-out ['ɔ:l'aʊt] Ⓐ ADJ [*effort*] supremo; [*attack*] con máxima fuerza; **~ strike** huelga *f* general; **~ war** (*Mil*) guerra *f* total, conflicto *m* bélico generalizado; (*fig*) guerra *f* total
Ⓑ **all out** ADV *see* **all C2**

all-over ['ɔ:l'əʊvəʳ] ADJ [*pattern*] repetido sobre toda la superficie; [*suntan*] completo, integral

▼**allow** [ə'laʊ] VT [1] (= *permit*) [1·1] permitir; **smoking is not ~ed** no está permitido fumar; **"no dogs allowed"** "no se admiten perros"; **~ me!** ¡permítame!; **he can't have sweets, he's not ~ed** no puede comer caramelos, no se lo permiten *or* no lo dejan; **to ~ sb to do sth** dejar *or* (*more frm*) permitir a algn hacer algo, dejar *or* (*more frm*) permitir que algn haga algo; **nobody was ~ed to leave** no dejaron *or* permitieron marcharse a nadie, no dejaron *or* permitieron que nadie se marchara; **~ me to introduce you to Dr Amberg** permítame que le presente al Dr Amberg; **we cannot ~ this to happen** no podemos permitir que esto ocurra; **~ the mixture to cool** deje enfriar la mezcla; **he was ~ed home after hospital treatment** le permitieron *or* le dejaron irse a casa tras recibir tratamiento en el hospital; **he is not ~ed visitors** no le permiten visitas
[1·2] **to ~ sb in/out/past** permitir *or* dejar a algn entrar/salir/pasar, permitir *or* dejar a algn que entre/salga/pase; **he's not ~ed out on his own** no le dejan salir *or* que salga solo a la calle, no le permiten salir *or* que salga solo a la calle; **they made holes in the box to ~ air in** hicieron unos agujeros en la caja para que entrara el aire
[2] **to ~ o.s.**: **to ~ o.s. to be persuaded** dejarse convencer; **he won't ~ himself to fail** hará lo imposible por evitar el fracaso; **she ~ed herself a smile** dejó escapar una sonrisa
[3] (= *reckon on*) dejar; **~ 5cms for shrinkage** dejar 5cms por si encoge; **~ (yourself) three hours for the journey** deja *or* calcula tres horas para el viaje; **how much should I ~ for expenses?** ¿cuánto debo prever para los gastos?; **please ~ 28 days for delivery** lo recibirá en su casa en un plazo de 28 días
[4] (= *grant*) [+ *money*] asignar; [+ *time*] dar; **the time ~ed has been extended to 28 days** el plazo establecido ha sido ampliado a 28 días; **the judge ~ed him £1,000 costs** el juez le asignó 1.000 libras en concepto de costes; **to ~ sb a discount** aplicar *or* hacer un descuento a algn; **the extra income will ~ me more freedom** el ingreso extra me dará más libertad
[5] (*Jur*) (= *admit*) [+ *claim, appeal*] admitir, aceptar; (*Sport*) [+ *goal*] conceder; **to ~ that** reconocer que; **I had to ~ that she was discreet** tuve que reconocer que era discreta

►**allow for** VI + PREP tener en cuenta; **after ~ing for his costs** después de haber tenido en cuenta sus gastos; **~ for delays on some roads** tengan en cuenta que puede haber retenciones en algunas carreteras; **we have to ~ for that possibility** debemos tener presente esa posibilidad; **we must ~ for the cost of the wood** tenemos que dejar un margen para el coste de la madera

►**allow of** VI + PREP admitir; **a question that ~s of only one reply** una pregunta que sólo admite una respuesta

allowable [ə'laʊəbl] ADJ [1] (= *permissible*) permisible, admisible
[2] [*expense*] deducible; **~ against tax** desgravable

allowance [ə'laʊəns] N [1] (= *payment*) (*from state*) prestación *f*; (*from ex-husband, benefactor*) pensión *f*; (*from parents*) dinero mensual/semanal/*etc*; (= *allocated from fund*) asignación *f*; (*esp US*) (= *pocket money*) dinero *m* de bolsillo; **he makes his mother an ~** le concede una pensión a su madre; **he has an ~ of £100 a month** tiene una asignación de 100 libras mensuales; *see also* **family B**
[2] (= *discount*) descuento *m*, rebaja *f*; (*Tax*) desgravación *f*; **tax ~** desgravación *f* fiscal
[3] (= *concession*) concesión *f*; **one must make ~s** hay que hacer concesiones; **to make ~(s) for sb** ser comprensivo con algn, disculpar a algn; **to make ~(s) for the weather** tener en cuenta el tiempo
[4] (*Mech*) tolerancia *f*
[5] (= *volume, weight*) margen *m*

alloy ['ælɔɪ] Ⓐ N (= *metal*) aleación *f*; (*fig*) mezcla *f*
Ⓑ ['ælɔɪ] CPD ► **alloy wheels** NPL llantas *fpl* de aleación
Ⓒ [ə'lɔɪ] VT alear, ligar

all-party ['ɔ:l'pɑ:tɪ] ADJ [*group, talks*] multipartidista

all-pervading [,ɔ:lpə'veɪdɪŋ], **all-pervasive** [,ɔ:lpə'veɪsɪv] ADJ omnipresente

all-points bulletin [,ɔ:lpɔɪnts'bʊlɪtɪn] N (*US*) *boletín difundido por la policía para la búsqueda y captura de un sospechoso*

all-powerful ['ɔ:l'paʊəfʊl] ADJ omnipotente, todopoderoso

all-purpose ['ɔ:l'pɜ:pəs] ADJ [*tool, cleaner*] multiuso *inv*, universal; [*vehicle, flour, wine*] para todo uso

all right [,ɔ:l'raɪt] Ⓐ ADJ [1] (= *satisfactory*) **it's ~** (= *it's fine*) todo está bien; (= *passable*) no está mal; (= *don't worry*) no te preocupes; **the film was ~** la película no estuvo mal; **yes, that's ~** sí, de acuerdo *or* vale; **are you ~?** ¿estás bien?; **well, he's ~** (= *not bad*) bueno, es regular; **he's ~ as a goalkeeper** como portero vale; **it's ~ by me** yo, de acuerdo, lo que es por mí, no hay problema; **it's ~ for you!** a ti ¿qué te puede importar?; **it's ~ for some!** (*iro*) ¡los hay con suerte!; **it's ~ for you to smile** tú bien puedes sonreír; **is it ~ for me to go at four?** ¿me da permiso para *or* puedo marcharme a las cuatro?; **is it ~ for me to take the dog?** ¿se me permite llevar al perro?; **is that ~ with you?** ¿te parece bien?; **it's ~ with me** yo, de acuerdo, lo que es por mí, no hay problema; **is he ~ with the girls?** ¿se comporta bien con las chicas?; ✦*IDIOMS* **it'll be ~ on the night** todo estará listo para el estreno; **she's a bit of ~**‡ ¡está buenísima!*
[2] (= *safe, well*) bien; **I'm/I feel ~ now** ya estoy bien; **it's ~, you can come out again now** está bien, puedes salir ya; **do you think the car will be ~ there overnight?** ¿tú crees que le pasará algo al coche allí toda la noche?; **she's ~ again now** está mejor, se ha repuesto ya
[3] (= *well-provided*) **we're ~ for the rest of our lives** no tendremos problemas económicos en el resto de la vida; **are you ~ for cigarettes?** ¿tienes suficiente tabaco?; ✦*IDIOM*

➤ LANGUAGE IN USE: **allow 1** 9.3, 9.4, 9.5, 10.4 **2** 20.4

I'm ~, Jack (*Brit**) mientras yo esté bien, a los demás que los zurzan*
[4] (= *available*) **are you ~ for Tuesday?** ¿te viene bien el martes?
Ⓑ ADV [1] (= *satisfactorily, without difficulty*) bien; **everything turned out ~** todo salió bien; **I can see ~, thanks** veo bien, gracias; **he's doing ~ for himself*** no le van nada mal las cosas
[2] (*) (= *without doubt*) **he complained ~!** ¡ya lo creo que se quejó!; **you'll get your money back ~** se te devolverá tu dinero, eso es seguro
Ⓒ EXCL (*in approval*) ¡bueno!, ¡muy bien!; (*in agreement*) ¡de acuerdo!, ¡vale!, ¡okey!; (*introducing a new subject*) bueno; (*in exasperation*) ¡se acabó!; (*esp US*) (*in triumph*) ¡olé!, ¡sí señor!; **~, let's get started** bueno, vamos a empezar; **~, who's in charge here?** muy bien ¿quién manda aquí?; **"we'll talk about it later" — "all ~"** —lo hablamos después —vale

all-risks ['ɔːl'rɪsks] CPD ► **all-risks insurance** N seguro *m* contra todo riesgo

all-round ['ɔːl'raʊnd] ADJ [*success etc*] completo; [*improvement*] general, en todos los aspectos; [*view*] amplio; [*person*] completo, con capacidad para todo

all-rounder ['ɔːl'raʊndəʳ] N persona *f* con capacidad para todo

allspice ['ɔːlspaɪs] N pimienta *f* inglesa, pimienta *f* de Jamaica

all-star ['ɔːl'stɑː] ADJ [*cast*] todo estelar; **~ performance** ◊ **show with an ~ cast** función *f* de primeras figuras, función *f* estelar

all-terrain vehicle [,ɔːltə,reɪn'viːɪkl] N vehículo *m* todo terreno

all-the-year-round [,ɔːlðə,jɪə'raʊnd] ADJ [*sport*] que se practica todo el año; [*resort*] abierto todo el año

all-time ['ɔːl'taɪm] ADJ de todos los tiempos; **an ~ record** un récord nunca igualado; **exports have reached an ~ high** las exportaciones han alcanzado cifras nunca conocidas antes; **the pound is at an ~ low** la libra ha caído a su punto más bajo

allude [ə'luːd] VI **to ~ to** aludir a, referirse a

allure [ə'ljʊəʳ] Ⓐ N atractivo *m*, encanto *m*
Ⓑ VT (*liter*) atraer, cautivar

alluring [ə'ljʊərɪŋ] ADJ seductor, atrayente

alluringly [ə'ljʊərɪŋlɪ] ADV de manera seductora, de manera atrayente

allusion [ə'luːʒən] N alusión *f*, referencia *f*

allusive [ə'luːsɪv] ADJ lleno de alusiones, lleno de referencias

alluvial [ə'luːvɪəl] ADJ aluvial

alluvium [ə'luːvɪəm] N (*pl* **alluviums, alluvia**) aluvión *m*, depósito *m* aluvial

all-weather ['ɔːl'weðəʳ] ADJ para todo tiempo

ally ['ælaɪ] Ⓐ N aliado/a *m/f*; **the Allies** los Aliados
Ⓑ [ə'laɪ] VT **to ~ o.s. with** aliarse con, hacer alianza con

all-year-round [,ɔːl,jɪə'raʊnd] ADJ [*sport*] que se practica todo el año; [*resort*] abierto todo el año

alma mater ['ælmə'meɪtəʳ] N alma máter *f*

almanac ['ɔːlmənæk] N almanaque *m*

almighty [ɔːl'maɪtɪ] Ⓐ ADJ [1] (= *omnipotent*) todopoderoso; **Almighty God** ◊ **God Almighty** Dios Todopoderoso; **the ~ dollar** el todopoderoso dólar
[2] (*) (= *tremendous*) tremendo, de mil demonios*; **an ~ din** un ruido tremendo *or* de mil demonios; **I foresee ~ problems** preveo unos enormes problemas; **he's an ~ fool if he believes that!** ¡vaya tonto si cree eso!
Ⓑ N **the Almighty** el Todopoderoso
Ⓒ ADV (*) terriblemente, la mar de*; **an ~ loud bang** un estallido terriblemente fuerte

almond ['ɑːmənd] Ⓐ N (= *nut*) almendra *f*; (= *tree*) almendro *m*
Ⓑ ADJ **an ~ taste** un sabor a almendra
Ⓒ CPD [*essence, extract*] de almendra(s)
► **almond oil** N aceite *m* de almendra
► **almond paste** N pasta *f* de almendras
► **almond tree** N almendro *m*

almond-eyed ['ɑːmənd'aɪd] ADJ de ojos almendrados

almond-shaped ['ɑːmənd,ʃeɪpt] ADJ almendrado

almoner† ['ɑːmənəʳ] N [1] (*Hist*) limosnero *m*
[2] (*Brit Med*) oficial *mf* de asistencia social (adscrito a un hospital)

almost ['ɔːlməʊst] ADV casi; **it's ~ finished/ready** casi está terminado/listo; **it's ~ midnight** ya es casi medianoche; **he ~ certainly will win** casi seguro que gana; **he ~ fell** casi se cae, por poco no se cae; **I had ~ forgotten about it** casi lo olvido, por poco no lo olvido; **we're ~ there** estamos a punto de llegar, ya nos falta poco para llegar; **"have you finished?" — "almost"** —¿has acabado? —casi

alms [ɑːmz] NPL limosna *fsing*

almsbox ['ɑːmzbɒks] N cepillo *m* para los pobres

almshouse ['ɑːmzhaʊs] N (*pl* **almshouses**) hospicio *m*, casa *f* de beneficencia

aloe ['æləʊ] Ⓐ N aloe *m*, agave *f*
Ⓑ CPD ► **aloe vera** N aloe *m* vera

aloft [ə'lɒft] ADV (*liter*) (= *above*) arriba; (= *upward*) hacia arriba; (*Naut*) en *or* a la arboladura

alone [ə'ləʊn] Ⓐ ADJ [1] (= *by oneself*) solo; **she lives ~** vive sola; **to be ~** estar solo *or* a solas; **I was left to bring up my two children ~** me quedé solo teniendo que criar a mis dos hijos; **all ~** (completamente) solo; **I feel so ~** me siento tan solo; **am I ~ in thinking so?** ¿soy yo el único que lo cree?; **they are not ~ in their belief** no son los únicos que lo creen, no son ellos solos los que lo creen; **to leave sb ~** dejar solo a algn; **I only left him ~ for a moment** no lo dejé solo más que un momento; **don't leave them ~ together** no los dejes solos a los dos; **I won't leave you ~ with him** no te dejaré solo con él; **we spent some time ~ together** pasamos algún tiempo juntos los dos solos; **I was ~ with my thoughts** estaba a solas con mis pensamientos
[2] (= *undisturbed*) [2·1] **to leave or let sb ~** dejar a algn en paz; **leave** *or* **let me ~!** ¡déjame en paz!, ¡déjame estar! (*LAm*)
[2·2] **to leave** *or* **let sth ~** no tocar algo; **leave** *or* **let it ~!** ¡déjalo!, ¡no lo toques!; **why can't he leave** *or* **let things ~?** (*fig*) ¿por qué no puede dejar las cosas como están?; **to leave** *or* **let well ~**: **you'd better leave** *or* **let well ~** mejor no te metas en ese asunto; **don't interfere, just leave** *or* **let well ~** no te entrometas, déjalo estar; **the article doesn't look bad as it is, I would leave** *or* **let well ~** el artículo no está mal tal y como está, yo no lo tocaría
[3] (*as conj*) **let ~**: **I wouldn't allow her to go with her sister, let ~ by herself** no la dejaría ir con su hermana, y aún menos sola; **he can't read, let ~ write** no sabe leer y aún menos escribir; **he can't change a light bulb, let ~ rewire the house!** no puede ni cambiar una bombilla, ¿cómo va a renovar toda la instalación eléctrica de la casa?
Ⓑ ADV solamente, sólo; **you and you ~ can make that decision** tú y solamente *or* sólo tú puedes tomar esa decisión, eres el único que puede tomar esa decisión; **the travel ~ cost £600** solamente *or* sólo el viaje costó 600 libras; **she spends more money on hats ~ than I do on my entire wardrobe** sólo en sombreros se gasta más de lo que yo gasto en ropa, se gasta más en sombreros nomás que lo que yo gasto en toda mi ropa (*LAm*); **a charm which is hers ~** un encanto que es muy suyo; **to go it alone***: **I decided to go it ~** (= *do it unaided*) decidí hacerlo solo, decidí hacerlo por mi cuenta; (= *start a company*) decidí establecerme por mi cuenta; **the US is prepared to go it ~ as the only nation not to sign the treaty** EEUU está dispuesto a quedarse solo siendo el único país que no firme el tratado; ✦**PROV man cannot live by bread ~** no sólo de pan vive el hombre

along [ə'lɒŋ]

When ***along*** *is an element in a phrasal verb, eg* ***get along, play along, string along****, look up the verb.*

Ⓐ ADV [1] (= *forward*) **move ~ there!** ¡circulen, por favor!; **she walked ~** siguió andando
[2] (= *with you, us etc*) **bring him ~ if you like** tráelo, si quieres; **are you coming ~?** ¿tú vienes también?
[3] (= *here, there*) **I'll be ~ in a moment** ahora voy; **she'll be ~ tomorrow** vendrá mañana
[4] (*in set expressions*) **all ~** desde el principio; **he was lying to me all ~** me había mentido desde el principio; **~ with** junto con; **he came, ~ with his friend** él vino, junto con su amigo
Ⓑ PREP por, a lo largo de; **to walk ~ the street** andar por la calle; **the trees ~ the path** los árboles a lo largo del camino; **all ~ the street** todo lo largo de la calle; **the shop is ~ here** la tienda está por aquí; **we acted ~ the lines suggested** hemos obrado de acuerdo con las indicaciones que nos hicieron; **somewhere ~ the way it fell off** en alguna parte del camino se cayó; **somewhere ~ the way** *or* **the line someone made a mistake** (*fig*) en un momento determinado alguien cometió un error

alongside [ə'lɒŋ'saɪd] Ⓐ PREP [1] (= *next to*) al lado de; **there's a stream ~ the garden** hay un arroyo al lado del jardín; **the car stopped ~ me** el coche se paró a mi lado; **they have to work ~ each other** tienen que trabajar juntos; **how can these systems work ~ each other?** ¿cómo estos sistemas pueden funcionar en colaboración?
[2] (*Naut*) al costado de; **to come ~ a ship** atracarse al costado de un buque
Ⓑ ADV (*Naut*) de costado; **to bring a ship ~** acostar un buque; **to come ~** atracar

aloof [ə'luːf] ADJ [1] (= *standoffish*) [*person, manner*] distante; **he was very ~ with me** conmigo se mostró muy distante; **she has always been somewhat ~** ella siempre ha guardado las distancias
[2] (= *uninvolved*) **to hold o.s.** *or* **remain** *or* **stand ~ from sb** guardar *or* mantener las distancias con algn, mantenerse apartado de algn; **to hold o.s.** *or* **remain** *or* **stand ~ from sth** mantenerse al margen de algo

aloofness [ə'luːfnɪs] N actitud *f* distante

alopecia [,æləʊ'piːʃə] N alopecia *f*

aloud [ə'laʊd] ADV en voz alta; **to think ~** pensar en voz alta

alpaca [æl'pækə] N alpaca *f*

alpenhorn ['ælpənhɔːn] N trompa *f* de los Alpes

alpenstock ['ælpɪnstɒk] N alpenstock *m*, bastón *m* montañero

alpha ['ælfə] Ⓐ N (= *letter*) alfa *f*; (*Brit Scol, Univ*) sobresaliente *m*
Ⓑ CPD ► **alpha particle** N (*Phys*) partícula *f* alfa ► **alpha rhythm, alpha wave** N (*Physiol*) ritmo *m* alfa

alphabet ['ælfəbet] N alfabeto *m*

alphabetic [,ælfə'betɪk] ADJ = **alphabetical**

alphabetical [,ælfə'betɪkəl] ADJ alfabético; **in ~ order** en *or* por orden alfabético

alphabetically [,ælfə'betɪkəlɪ] ADV alfabéticamente, en *or* por orden alfabético

alphabetize ['ælfəbətaɪz] VT alfabetizar, poner en orden alfabético

alphanumeric [,ælfənjuː'merɪk] Ⓐ ADJ alfanumérico
Ⓑ CPD ► **alphanumeric character** N carácter *m* alfanumérico ► **alphanumeric field** N campo *m* alfanumérico

Alphonso [æl'fɒnsəʊ] N Alfonso

alpine ['ælpaɪn] Ⓐ ADJ alpino
Ⓑ N planta *f* alpestre

alpinist ['ælpɪnɪst] N alpinista *mf*

Alps [ælps] NPL **the ~** los Alpes

al Qaeda [,ælkaɪ'iːdə] N Al Qaeda *m o f*

already [ɔːl'redɪ] ADV ya; **Liz had ~ gone** Liz ya se había ido; **is it finished ~?** ¿ya está terminado?; **that's enough ~!** (*US**) ¡basta!, ¡ya está bien!

alright [,ɔːl'raɪt] = **all right**

Alsace ['ælsæs] N Alsacia *f*

Alsace-Lorraine ['ælsæslə'reɪn] N Alsacia-Lorena *f*

Alsatian [æl'seɪʃən] Ⓐ ADJ alsaciano
Ⓑ N 1 (= *person*) alsaciano/a *m/f*
2 (*Brit*) (*also* **~ dog**) (perro *m*) pastor *m* alemán, perro *m* lobo

▼**also** ['ɔːlsəʊ] ADV 1 (*gen*) también; **her cousin ~ came** su primo también vino
2 (*as linker*) además; **~, I must explain that ...** además debo aclarar que ...

also-ran ['ɔːlsəʊræn] N 1 (*Sport*) caballo *m* perdedor
2 (*) (= *person*) nulidad *f*

alt. ABBR (= **altitude**) alt.

Alta ABBR (*Canada*) = **Alberta**

Altamira [,æltə'miːrə] N **the ~ caves** las cuevas de Altamira

altar ['ɒltər] Ⓐ N altar *m*; **high ~** altar *m* mayor; ✦**IDIOMS he sacrificed all on the ~ of his ambition** lo sacrificó todo en aras de su ambición; **to lead a girl to the ~** conducir a una chica al altar
Ⓑ CPD ► **altar boy** N acólito *m*, monaguillo *m* ► **altar cloth** N sabanilla *f*, paño *m* de altar ► **altar rail** N comulgatorio *m*

altarpiece ['ɒltəpiːs] N retablo *m*

alter ['ɒltər] Ⓐ VT 1 (= *change*) [+ *text*] modificar, cambiar; (*esp for the worse*) alterar; [+ *painting, speech*] retocar; [+ *opinion, course*] cambiar de; (*Archit*) reformar; (*Sew*) arreglar; **then that ~s things** entonces la cosa cambia; **it has ~ed things for the better** ha cambiado las cosas para mejor, ha mejorado las cosas; **circumstances ~ cases** el caso depende de las circunstancias; **I see no need to ~ my view** no veo ninguna necesidad de cambiar mi opinión
2 (= *falsify*) [+ *evidence*] falsificar; [+ *document*] alterar
3 (*US*) (= *castrate*) castrar
Ⓑ VI [*person, place*] cambiar; **I find him much ~ed** le veo muy cambiado; **to ~ for the better** mejorar, cambiar para mejor; **to ~ for the worse** empeorar, cambiar para peor

alteration [,ɒltə'reɪʃən] N 1 (= *change*) (*to text*) modificación *f*, cambio *m*; (*esp for the worse*) alteración *f* (**in, to** de); (*to painting, speech etc*) retoque *m*; (*Sew*) arreglo *m*; **to make ~s to** [+ *building, text*] hacer modificaciones en; [+ *dress*] hacer arreglos a
2 **alterations** (*Archit*) reformas *fpl*

altercation [,ɒltə'keɪʃən] N altercado *m*

alter ego ['æltər'iːgəʊ] N álter ego *m*

alternate Ⓐ [ɒl'tɜːnɪt] ADJ 1 (= *alternating*) alterno; **~ layers of cheese and potatoes** capas alternas de queso y patatas; **we had a week of ~ rain and sunshine** tuvimos una semana en la que se alternaron el sol y las lluvias; **let's read ~ lines** vamos a leer cada uno un renglón
2 (= *every second*) **on ~ days** cada dos días, un día sí y otro no; **he lives ~ months in Brussels and London** vive un mes en Bruselas y uno en Londres; **to write on ~ lines** escribir en renglones alternos
3 (*Bot, Math*) alterno
4 (*US*) = **alternative A**
Ⓑ [ɒl'tɜːnɪt] N (*US Sport*) (*at conference*) suplente *mf*
Ⓒ ['ɒltɜːneɪt] VI alternar; **an annual cycle of drought alternating with floods** un ciclo anual de sequías alternando con inundaciones; **the temperatures ~ between very hot and extremely cold** las temperaturas oscilan entre un calor y un frío intensos; **he ~s between euphoria and depression** pasa de la euforia a la depresión y vice versa; **they ~ between avoiding us and ignoring us** unas veces nos evitan y otras nos ignoran
Ⓓ ['ɒltɜːneɪt] VT alternar

alternately [ɒl'tɜːnɪtlɪ] ADV **the meetings took place ~ in France and Germany** las reuniones se celebraron una vez en Francia y la siguiente en Alemania; **he could ~ bully and charm people** un momento podía intimidar a la gente y al siguiente embelesarles; **I lived ~ with my mother and my grandmother** vivía unas veces con mi madre y otras con mi abuela; **she became ~ angry and calm** su ánimo iba de la ira a la calma y vice versa; **we have Mondays off ~** nos turnamos para librar el lunes

alternating ['ɒltɜːneɪtɪŋ] Ⓐ ADJ alterno
Ⓑ CPD ► **alternating current** N (*Elec*) corriente *f* alterna

alternation [,ɒltɜː'neɪʃən] N alternación *f*; **in ~** alternativamente

▼**alternative** [ɒl'tɜːnətɪv] Ⓐ ADJ 1 [*plan, route*] alternativo, otro; **the only ~ system** el único sistema alternativo; **do you have an ~ candidate?** ¿tienes otro candidato?
2 (= *non-traditional*) alternativo; **the ~ society** la sociedad alternativa
Ⓑ N alternativa *f*; **there are several ~s** hay varias alternativas *or* posibilidades; **what ~s are there?** ¿qué alternativas *or* opciones hay?; **I have no ~** no tengo más remedio, no me queda otra alternativa *or* opción; **there is no ~** no hay otro remedio, no queda otra (*LAm*); **you have no ~ but to go** no tienes más alternativa *or* opción *or* remedio que ir; **fruit is a healthy ~ to chocolate** la fruta es una opción más sana que el chocolate
Ⓒ CPD ► **alternative comedian** N humorista *mf* alternativo/a ► **alternative comedy** N humorismo *m* alternativo ► **alternative energy** N energías *fpl* alternativas ► **alternative medicine** N medicina *f* alternativa ► **alternative school** N (*US*) *colegio para niños que requieren una atención diferenciada*

alternatively [ɒl'tɜːnətɪvlɪ] ADV **~, you can use household bleach** si no, puede usar lejía doméstica; **we could go on to the next village, or, ~, we could camp here** podemos ir hasta el siguiente pueblo, o podemos acampar aquí

alternator ['ɒltɜːneɪtər] N (*Aut, Elec*) alternador *m*

▼**although** [ɔːl'ðəʊ] CONJ aunque; **~ it's raining, there are 20 people here already** aunque está lloviendo, ya hay aquí 20 personas; **~ poor, they were honest** aunque eran pobres, eran honrados

altimeter ['æltɪmiːtər] N altímetro *m*

altitude ['æltɪtjuːd] Ⓐ N altitud *f*, altura *f*; **at these ~s** a estas altitudes
Ⓑ CPD ► **altitude sickness** N mal *m* de altura, soroche *m* (*LAm*)

alto ['æltəʊ] Ⓐ N (= *instrument, male singer*) alto *m*; (= *female singer*) contralto *f*
Ⓑ ADJ alto
Ⓒ CPD ► **alto saxophone** N saxofón *m* alto

altocumulus [,æltəʊ'kjuːmjʊləs] N (*pl* **altocumuli** [,æltəʊ'kjuːmjʊlaɪ]) altocúmulo *m*

altogether [,ɔːltə'geðər] Ⓐ ADV 1 (= *in all*) en total; **~, he played in 40 matches** en total, participó en 40 partidos; **how much is that ~?** ¿cuánto es en total?; **~ it was rather unpleasant** en general fue muy desagradable
2 (= *entirely*) [*stop, disappear*] por completo, del todo; [*different, impossible*] totalmente; [*wonderful*] realmente; **he abandoned his work ~** dejó de trabajar por completo *or* del todo; **she looked ~ lovely** estaba realmente encantadora; **I'm not ~ happy with your work** no estoy del todo satisfecho con tu trabajo; **Asia was another matter ~** lo de Asia era un tema totalmente diferente; **"do you believe him?" — "not ~"** —¿le crees? —no del todo; **it's ~ out of the question** es totalmente imposible; **I'm not ~ sure** no estoy del todo seguro, no estoy totalmente seguro; **it's ~ too complicated** es realmente demasiado complicado
Ⓑ N **in the ~*** (= *naked*) en cueros*

altoist ['æltəʊɪst] N (= *saxophone player*) saxo *m* alto, saxofonista *mf* alto

altostratus [,æltəʊ'streɪtəs] N (*pl* **altostrati** [,æltəʊ'streɪtaɪ]) altostrato *m*

altruism ['æltrʊɪzəm] N altruismo *m*

altruist ['æltrʊɪst] N altruista *mf*

altruistic [,æltrʊ'ɪstɪk] ADJ altruista

ALU N ABBR (= **Arithmetical Logic Unit**) ULP *f*

alum ['æləm] N alumbre *m*

aluminium [,æljʊ'mɪnɪəm], **aluminum** (*US*) [ə'luːmɪnəm] Ⓐ N aluminio *m*
Ⓑ CPD ► **aluminium foil** N papel *m* de aluminio, aluminio *m* doméstico

alumnus [ə'lʌmnəs] N (*pl* **alumni** [ə'lʌmnaɪ]), **alumna** [ə'lʌmnə] N (*pl* **alumnae** [ə'lʌmniː]) (*esp US*) graduado/a *m/f*; **~ association** asociación *f* de graduados

alveolar [æl'vɪələr] ADJ alveolar

alveolus [æl'vɪələs] N (*pl* **alveoli** [æl'vɪəlaɪ]) alvéolo *m*, alveolo *m*

always ['ɔːlweɪz] ADV siempre; **as ~** como siempre; **nearly ~** casi siempre; **he's ~ late** siempre llega tarde; **he's ~ moaning** siempre está quejándose; **you can ~ go by train** también puedes ir en tren

Alzheimer's (disease) ['æltshaɪməz(dɪ,ziːz)] N (enfermedad *f* de) Alzheimer *m*

► LANGUAGE IN USE: **also 1** 26.2, 26.3 **alternative B** 18.4 **although** 26.3

AM N ABBR [1] (= **amplitude modulation**) A.M. *f*
[2] (*US*) = **Artium Magister, Master of Arts**; *see* **MA**
[3] (*Welsh Pol*) (= **Assembly Member**) parlamentario/a *m/f*

Am ABBR [1] = **America**
[2] = **American**

am [æm] 1ST PERS SING PRESENT *of* **be**

a.m. ADV ABBR (= **ante meridiem**) a.m.; **at four ~** a las cuatro de la mañana

AMA N ABBR (*US*) = **American Medical Association**

amalgam [əˈmælgəm] N amalgama *f* (**of** de)

amalgamate [əˈmælgəmeɪt] Ⓐ VT [+ *texts*] amalgamar; [+ *companies*] fusionar
Ⓑ VI [*organizations*] amalgamarse, unirse; [*companies*] fusionarse

amalgamation [əˌmælgəˈmeɪʃən] N amalgamiento *m*; (*Comm*) fusión *f*

amanita [ˌæməˈnaɪtə] N amanita *f*

amanuensis [əˌmænjʊˈensɪs] N (*pl* **amanuenses** [əˌmænjuˈensiːz]) amanuense *mf*

Amaryllis [ˌæməˈrɪlɪs] N Amarilis

amaryllis [ˌæməˈrɪlɪs] N amarilis *f inv*

amass [əˈmæs] VT [+ *wealth, information*] acumular

amateur [ˈæmətəʳ] Ⓐ N [1] (*lit*) (= *non-professional*) amateur *mf*; (= *hobbyist*) aficionado/a *m/f*; **he boxed first as an ~ then as a professional** boxeó primero como amateur y después como profesional; **an enthusiastic ~** un amateur entusiasta; **I love gardening but I'm just an ~** me encanta la jardinería, pero no soy más que un aficionado
[2] (*pej*) chapucero/a *m/f*; **those guys are ~s!*** ¡esos tipos son unos chapuceros!
Ⓑ ADJ [1] (= *not professional*) [*athlete, actor, production*] amateur; [*club, competition*] para amateurs, para aficionados; **~ athletics/photography** atletismo/fotografía para amateurs; **an ~ photographer** un aficionado a la fotografía, un fotógrafo aficionado; **an ~ detective** un detective aficionado; **I have an ~ interest in pottery** me interesa la cerámica como aficionado; **~ status** condición *f* de amateur
[2] (*pej*) [*production, performance*] de aficionados, chapucero; **it was a very ~ performance** fue una actuación de aficionados *or* muy chapucera
Ⓒ CPD ► **amateur dramatics** NSING teatro *m* amateur, teatro *m* de aficionados

amateurish [ˈæmətərɪʃ] ADJ (*pej*) poco profesional, inexperto

amateurishly [ˈæmətərɪʃlɪ] ADV (*pej*) de manera poco profesional

amateurism [ˈæmətərɪzəm] N [1] (= *amateur status*) lo amateur
[2] (*pej*) falta *f* de profesionalidad

amatory [ˈæmətərɪ] ADJ (*frm, liter*) amatorio, erótico

amaze [əˈmeɪz] VT pasmar, asombrar; **to be ~d (at)** quedar pasmado (de); **I was ~d that I managed to do it** estaba asombrado de haberlo conseguido; **you ~ me!** ¡me admiras!, ¡me dejas patidifuso!*

amazed [əˈmeɪzd] ADJ [*glance, expression*] asombrado, lleno de estupor

amazement [əˈmeɪzmənt] N asombro *m*; **the news caused general ~** la noticia causó sorpresa generalizada *or* un asombro general; **they looked on in ~** miraron asombrados; **to my ~** para mi gran asombro *or* sorpresa

amazing [əˈmeɪzɪŋ] ADJ [1] (= *astonishing*) asombroso; **that's ~ news!** ¡es una noticia asombrosa!
[2] (= *wonderful*) extraordinario; **Kay's an ~ cook** Kay es una cocinera extraordinaria

amazingly [əˈmeɪzɪŋlɪ] ADV [1] (= *astonishingly*) asombrosamente; **it was ~ easy** asombraba lo fácil que era, era asombrosamente fácil; **~ enough** por increíble que parezca, aunque parece mentira; **~, nobody was killed** por milagro, no hubo víctimas
[2] (= *wonderfully*) extraordinariamente; **she is ~ generous** es extraordinariamente generosa; **he is ~ fit for his age** su estado físico es extraordinario para un hombre de su edad; **he did ~ well** tuvo un éxito formidable

Amazon [ˈæməzən] Ⓐ N [1] (*Geog*) Amazonas *m*
[2] (*Myth*) amazona *f*; (*fig, also* **amazon**) amazona *f*; (*US pej*) marimacho *m*
Ⓑ CPD ► **Amazon basin** N cuenca *f* del Amazonas ► **Amazon jungle** N selva *f* de Amazonas

Amazonia [ˌæməˈzəʊnɪə] N Amazonia *f*

Amazonian [ˌæməˈzəʊnɪən] ADJ amazónico

ambassador [æmˈbæsədəʳ] N embajador(a) *m/f*; (*fig*) embajador(a) *m/f*, representante *mf* (**for** de); **the Spanish ~** el embajador de España

ambassadorial [æmˌbæsəˈdɔːrɪəl] ADJ de embajador

ambassadorship [æmˈbæsədəʃɪp] N embajada *f*

ambassadress† [æmˈbæsədrɪs] N embajadora *f*

amber [ˈæmbəʳ] Ⓐ N ámbar *m*; **at** *or* **on ~** (*Brit Aut*) en ámbar
Ⓑ ADJ [1] [*jewellery*] de ámbar; [*colour*] ambarino
[2] (*Brit Aut*) **~ light** luz *f* ámbar

ambergris [ˈæmbəgriːs] N ámbar *m* gris

ambi... [ˈæmbɪ] PREFIX ambi...

ambiance [ˈæmbɪəns] = **ambience**

ambidextrous [ˌæmbɪˈdekstrəs] ADJ ambidiestro, ambidextro

ambience [ˈæmbɪəns] N ambiente *m*, atmósfera *f*

ambient [ˈæmbɪənt] Ⓐ ADJ ambiental
Ⓑ CPD ► **ambient music** N música *f* ambiental

ambiguity [ˌæmbɪˈgjʊɪtɪ] N (= *lack of clarity*) ambigüedad *f*; [*of meaning*] doble sentido *m*

ambiguous [æmˈbɪgjʊəs] ADJ [*remark, meaning*] ambiguo

ambiguously [æmˈbɪgjʊəslɪ] ADV ambiguamente, de forma ambigua

ambiguousness [æmˈbɪgjʊəsnɪs] N ambigüedad *f*

ambit [ˈæmbɪt] N ámbito *m*; **within the ~ of** dentro del *or* en el ámbito de

ambition [æmˈbɪʃən] N ambición *f*; **to achieve one's ~** realizar su ambición; **he has no ~** no tiene ambición; **to have an ~ to be a doctor** ambicionar ser médico; **his ~ is to ...** ambiciona ...

ambitious [æmˈbɪʃəs] ADJ [*person, plan, goal*] ambicioso; **he was not an ~ man** no era un hombre ambicioso; **perhaps you're being too ~** quizá estés intentando abarcar demasiado; **if you feel a bit more ~ you could try this recipe** si te sientes con ganas de probar algo más difícil, puedes intentar esta receta; **to be ~ for** *or* **of sth** (*frm*) ambicionar algo; **to be ~ for sb** ambicionar grandes cosas para algn; **he was ~ to be the boss** aspiraba a *or* ambicionaba ser el jefe; **his ~ reform programme** su ambicioso programa de reforma; **that's rather ~, isn't it?** eso es bastante ambicioso, ¿no?; **starting with this could be a little ~** empezar con eso podría ser querer abarcar demasiado *or* podría ser un poco ambicioso

ambitiously [æmˈbɪʃəslɪ] ADV ambiciosamente; **a book ~ titled ...** un libro con el ambicioso título de ...; **next Keith will ~ attempt to name all Shakespeare's plays in two minutes** ahora Keith llevará a cabo su ambicioso intento de nombrar todas las obras de Shakespeare en dos minutos; **he decided, perhaps rather ~, to build the extension himself** decidió, quizás sobrevalorando sus posibilidades *or* intentando abarcar demasiado, construir la extensión él mismo; **he had ~ hoped to finish the job in a month** había esperado poder terminar el trabajo en un mes, lo que era mucho esperar

ambivalence [æmˈbɪvələns] N ambivalencia *f*

ambivalent [æmˈbɪvələnt] ADJ ambivalente

amble [ˈæmbl] Ⓐ VI [*person*] andar sin prisa; [*horse*] amblar, ir a paso de andadura; **to ~ along** andar sin prisa, pasearse despacio; **the bus ~s along at 40kph** el autobús va tranquilamente a 40kph; **he ~d into my office at ten o'clock** entró tranquilamente en mi oficina a las diez; **he ~d up to me** se me acercó a paso lento
Ⓑ N [*of horse*] ambladura *f*, paso *m* de andadura; **to walk at an ~** [*person*] andar sin prisa, pasearse despacio

Ambrose [ˈæmbrəʊz] N Ambrosio

ambrosia [æmˈbrəʊzɪə] N ambrosía *f*

ambulance [ˈæmbjʊləns] Ⓐ N ambulancia *f*
Ⓑ CPD ► **ambulance chaser*** N (*esp US pej*) *abogado sin escrúpulos a la caza de personas accidentadas cuyos casos reporten jugosos beneficios* ► **ambulance driver** N conductor/a *m/f* de ambulancia, ambulanciero *m* ► **ambulance man** N ambulanciero *m*

ambulatory [ˌæmbjʊˈleɪtərɪ] ADJ (*US Med*) no encamado

ambush [ˈæmbʊʃ] Ⓐ N emboscada *f*; **to set** *or* **lay an ~ for** tender una emboscada a; **to lie in ~** estar emboscado (**for** para coger)
Ⓑ VT cazar por sorpresa, agarrar por sorpresa (*LAm*); **to be ~ed** caer en una emboscada, ser cazado por sorpresa

ameba [əˈmiːbə] N (*US*) = **amoeba**

ameliorate [əˈmiːlɪəreɪt] (*frm*) Ⓐ VT mejorar
Ⓑ VI mejorar, mejorarse

amelioration [əˌmiːlɪəˈreɪʃən] N (*frm*) mejora *f*, mejoramiento *m*

amen [ˈɑːˈmen] Ⓐ EXCL amén; **~ to that** así sea, ojalá sea así
Ⓑ N amén *m*

amenable [əˈmiːnəbl] ADJ [1] (= *responsive*) **~ to argument** flexible, que se deja convencer; **~ to discipline** sumiso, dispuesto a dejarse disciplinar; **~ to reason** dispuesto a entrar en razón; **~ to treatment** susceptible de ser curado, curable; **I'd like to visit you at home if you're ~** me gustaría hacerle una visita en su casa, si le parece bien
[2] (*Jur*) responsable (**for** de)

amend [əˈmend] VT [+ *law*] enmendar; [+ *text, wording*] corregir

amendment [əˈmendmənt] N [1] (*to law*) enmienda *f* (**to** a); **the Fifth Amendment** (*US*) la Quinta Enmienda (*a la Constitución de los Estados Unidos*); **to invoke** *or* **plead** *or* **take the Fifth (Amendment)** (*US*) acogerse a la quinta, negarse a dar testimonio bajo la protección de la Quinta Enmienda (*relativa a la*

autoincriminación)
2 (*to text*) corrección *f*

FIFTH AMENDMENT

La Quinta Enmienda a la Constitución de los Estados Unidos establece varios principios legales fundamentales que protegen al ciudadano frente al poder del Estado. Entre estos derechos están el de que una persona no sea encarcelada o sus bienes sean embargados sin juicio previo, así como el derecho a no ser procesada dos veces por el mismo delito, o a no ser obligada a aportar pruebas contra sí misma. Al hecho de negarse a aportar pruebas autoincriminatorias se le conoce como **taking the fifth** *(acogerse a la quinta) y, durante las investigaciones anticomunistas que el senador McCarthy realizó en la década de los años 50, aquéllos que se acogían a esta quinta enmienda eran generalmente acusados de llevar a cabo actividades antiamericanas.*

amends [əˈmendz] NPL **to make ~ (to sb) for sth** (= *apologize*) dar satisfacción (a algn) por algo; (= *compensate*) compensar (a algn) por algo; **I'll try to make ~ in future** trataré de dar satisfacción en el futuro

amenity [əˈmiːnɪtɪ] Ⓐ N 1 (= *quality*) amenidad *f*
2 (= *thing*) (*gen pl*) **amenities** comodidades *fpl*; **the amenities of life** las cosas agradables de la vida; **a house with all amenities** una casa con todas las comodidades *or* todo confort; **the hotel has very good amenities** el hotel tiene excelentes servicios e instalaciones; **the town has many amenities** la ciudad ofrece gran variedad de servicios; **we are trying to improve the city's amenities** nos esforzamos por mejorar las instalaciones de la ciudad
Ⓑ CPD ► **amenity bed** N (*Brit Med*) habitación *f* privada ► **amenity society** N (*Brit*) asociación *f* para la conservación del medio ambiente

amenorrhoea, **amenorrhea** (*US*) [eɪˌmenəˈrɪə] N amenorrea *f*

America [əˈmerɪkə] N (= *continent*) América *f*; (= *USA*) Estados *mpl* Unidos

American [əˈmerɪkən] Ⓐ ADJ (= *of USA*) norteamericano, estadounidense; [*continent*] americano; **the ~ dream** el sueño americano; ✦**IDIOM as ~ as apple pie** genuinamente americano
Ⓑ N 1 (= *person*) (*from USA*) norteamericano/a *m/f*, americano/a *m/f*; (*from continent*) americano/a *m/f*
2 (*Ling**) inglés *m* americano
Ⓒ CPD ► **American English** N inglés *m* americano ► **American football** N fútbol *m* americano ► **American Indian** N amerindio/a *m/f* ► **American leather** N cuero *m* artificial ► **American Legion** N *organización de veteranos de las dos guerras mundiales*; → LEGION; ► **American plan** N (*US*) (*in hotel*) (habitación *f* con) pensión *f* completa ► **American Spanish** N español *m* de América

AMERICAN DREAM

El término **American Dream**, *(el sueño americano), se refiere a los valores y creencias que para muchos estadounidenses son característicos de su modo de entender la vida como nación y que encuentran su materialización en la Declaración de Independencia de 1776. Con este término se pone especial énfasis en el individualismo, la importancia de trabajar duro, el hecho de que todos podemos mejorar y que la libertad y la justicia han de ser universales. Para muchos el "sueño americano" era una oportunidad para hacer fortuna.*
El término también se usa de forma irónica para referirse al contraste entre estos ideales y las actitudes materialistas que caracterizan a la sociedad estadounidense actual.

Americana [əˌmerɪˈkɑːnə] N *objetos, documentos etc pertenecientes a la herencia cultural norteamericana*

Americanism [əˈmerɪkənɪzəm] N americanismo *m*

Americanization [əˌmerɪkənaɪˈzeɪʃən] N americanización *f*

Americanize [əˈmerɪkənaɪz] VT americanizar; **to become ~d** americanizarse

americium [ˌæməˈrɪsɪəm] N americio *m*

Amerind [ˌæmərɪnd] N amerindio/a *m/f*

Amerindian [ˌæməˈrɪndɪən] Ⓐ ADJ amerindio
Ⓑ N amerindio/a *m/f*

amethyst [ˈæmɪθɪst] N amatista *f*

Amex [ˈæmeks] N ABBR (*US*) 1 ® (= **American Express**®) ~ **card** tarjeta *f* de American Express
2 (*US*) = **American Stock Exchange**

amiability [ˌeɪmɪəˈbɪlɪtɪ] N amabilidad *f*, afabilidad *f*

amiable [ˈeɪmɪəbl] ADJ amable, afable

amiably [ˈeɪmɪəblɪ] ADV amablemente, afablemente

amicable [ˈæmɪkəbl] ADJ amistoso, amigable; **to reach an ~ settlement** llegar a un acuerdo amistoso

amicably [ˈæmɪkəblɪ] ADV amistosamente, amigablemente

amid [əˈmɪd] PREP en medio de, entre

amidships [əˈmɪdʃɪps] ADV en medio del barco

amidst [əˈmɪdst] PREP (*frm*) en medio de, entre

amino-acid [əˈmiːnəʊˌæsɪd] N aminoácido *m*

Amish [ˈɑːmɪʃ] N **the ~** los amish (*secta religiosa menonita*)

amiss [əˈmɪs] Ⓐ ADJ **there's something ~** pasa algo; **something is ~ in your calculations** algo falla en tus cálculos; **have I said something ~?** ¿he dicho algo inoportuno?; **there was nothing ~ that I could see** por lo que vi, todo estaba bien
Ⓑ ADV **don't take it ~, will you?** no lo tomes a mal, no te vayas a ofender; **a lick of paint wouldn't go** *or* **come ~** una mano de pintura no vendría mal; **a little politeness wouldn't go** *or* **come ~** un poco de educación no estaría de más, no vendría mal un poco de educación

amity [ˈæmɪtɪ] N (*frm*) concordia *f*, amistad *f*

AMM N ABBR = **antimissile missile**

Amman [əˈmɑːn] N Ammán *m*

ammeter [ˈæmɪtəʳ] N amperímetro *m*

ammo* [ˈæməʊ] N ABBR = **ammunition**

ammonal [ˈæmənəl] N amonal *m*

ammonia [əˈməʊnɪə] N amoníaco *m*; **liquid ~** amoníaco *m* líquido

ammonium [əˈməʊnɪəm] Ⓐ N amonio *m*
Ⓑ CPD ► **ammonium hydroxide** N hidróxido *m* amónico ► **ammonium sulphate** N sulfato *m* amónico

ammunition [ˌæmjʊˈnɪʃən] Ⓐ N 1 (*lit*) munición *f*
2 (*fig*) argumentos *mpl*
Ⓑ CPD ► **ammunition belt** N cartuchera *f*, canana *f* ► **ammunition dump** N depósito *m* de municiones ► **ammunition pouch** N cartuchera *f* ► **ammunition store** N depósito *m* de municiones

amnesia [æmˈniːzɪə] N amnesia *f*

amnesiac [æmˈniːzɪæk] Ⓐ ADJ amnésico
Ⓑ N amnésico/a *m/f*

amnesty [ˈæmnɪstɪ] Ⓐ N amnistía *f*; **to grant an ~ to** amnistiar (a), conceder una amnistía a
Ⓑ VT amnistiar

Amnesty International [ˌæmnɪstɪɪntəˈnæʃnəl] N Amnistía *f* Internacional

amnio* [ˈæmnɪəʊ] N = **amniocentesis**

amniocentesis [ˌæmnɪəʊsenˈtiːsɪs] N (*pl* **amniocenteses** [ˌæmnɪəʊsənˈtiːsiːz]) amniocentesis *f*

amniotic [ˌæmnɪˈɒtɪk] ADJ amniótico; **~ fluid** líquido *m* amniótico; **~ sac** saco *m* amniótico

amoeba [əˈmiːbə] N (*pl* **amoebas**, **amoebae** [əˈmiːbiː]) ameba *f*, amiba *f*

amoebic [əˈmiːbɪk] Ⓐ ADJ amébico
Ⓑ CPD ► **amoebic dysentery** N disentería *f* amébica

amok [əˈmɒk] ADV **to run ~** enloquecerse, desbocarse

among(st) [əˈmʌŋ(st)] PREP entre, en medio de; **from ~** de entre; **~ the Yanomami it is deemed a virtue** entre los yanomami se considera una virtud; **he is ~ those who ...** es de los que ...; **it is not ~ the names I have** no figura entre los nombres que tengo; **this is ~ the possibilities** ésa es una de las posibilidades; **they quarrelled ~ themselves** riñeron entre sí; **one can say that ~ friends** eso se puede decir entre amigos; **share it ~ yourselves** repartíoslo entre vosotros

amoral [eɪˈmɒrəl] ADJ amoral

amorality [ˌeɪmɒˈrælɪtɪ] N amoralidad *f*

amorous [ˈæmərəs] ADJ [*person, look*] apasionado; **to feel ~** sentirse apasionado; **he made ~ advances to his secretary** se le insinuó a su secretaria

amorously [ˈæmərəslɪ] ADV [*look, embrace*] apasionadamente

amorphous [əˈmɔːfəs] ADJ amorfo

amortizable [əˈmɔːtɪzəbl] Ⓐ ADJ amortizable
Ⓑ CPD ► **amortizable loan** N préstamo *m* amortizable

amortization [əˌmɔːtɪˈzeɪʃən] N amortización *f*

amortize [əˈmɔːtaɪz] VT amortizar

amount [əˈmaʊnt] N 1 (= *quantity*) cantidad *f*; **a huge ~ of rice** una cantidad enorme de arroz; **there is quite an ~ left** queda bastante; **any ~ of** cualquier cantidad de; **I have any ~ of time** tengo mucho tiempo; **we have had any ~ of trouble** hemos tenido un sinnúmero de problemas; **no ~ of arguing will help** es totalmente inútil discutir; **in small ~s** en pequeñas cantidades; **the total ~** el total, la cantidad total
2 (= *sum of money*) cantidad *f*, suma *f*; **a large ~ of money** una gran cantidad *or* suma de dinero
3 (= *total value*) valor *m*; **a bill for the ~ of** una cuenta por importe *or* valor de; **check in the ~ of $50** (*US*) cheque *m* por valor de 50 dólares; **to the ~ of** por valor de; **debts to the ~ of £100** deudas *fpl* por valor de 100 libras

▼► **amount to** VI + PREP 1 (= *add up to*) [*sums, figures, debts*] sumar, ascender a
2 (= *be equivalent to*) equivaler a, significar; **it ~s to the same thing** es igual, viene a ser lo mismo; **this ~s to a refusal** esto equivale a

➤ LANGUAGE IN USE: **amount to** 20.6

una negativa
[3] (= *be worth*) **it doesn't ~ to much** apenas es significativo, viene a ser poca cosa; **he'll never ~ to much** nunca dejará de ser nadie

amour† [ə'mʊəʳ] N (*liter*) amorío *m*, aventura *f* amorosa

amour-propre ['æmʊə'prɒpr] N amor *m* propio

amp [æmp] N [1] (*also* **ampere**) amperio *m*; **a 13-~ plug** un enchufe de 13 amperios
[2] (*) (*also* **amplifier**) ampli* *m*, amplificador *m*

amperage ['æmpərɪdʒ] N amperaje *m*

ampere, ampère ['æmpɛəʳ] Ⓐ N amperio *m*
Ⓑ CPD ► **ampere-hour** N amperio-hora *m*

ampersand ['æmpəsænd] N el signo & (= *and*)

amphetamine [æm'fetəmi:n] N anfetamina *f*

amphibia [æm'fɪbɪə] NPL anfibios *mpl*

amphibian [æm'fɪbɪən] Ⓐ N anfibio *m*
Ⓑ ADJ anfibio

amphibious [æm'fɪbɪəs] ADJ [*animal, vehicle*] anfibio

amphitheatre, amphitheater (*US*) ['æmfɪ,θɪətəʳ] N anfiteatro *m*

Amphitryon [æm'fɪtrɪən] N Anfitrión

amphora ['æmfərə] N (*pl* **amphoras, amphorae** ['æmfə,ri:]) ánfora *f*

ample ['æmpl] ADJ (*compar* **ampler**, *superl* **amplest**) [1] (= *plentiful, more than sufficient*) [1·1] (*before noun*) [*evidence, proof, resources*] abundante; [*time, space*] de sobra; **to have ~ time (to do sth)** tener tiempo de sobra (para hacer algo); **there is ~ space for a desk in this room** hay sitio de sobra para un escritorio en esta habitación; **she has ~ means** tiene medios más que suficientes; **there'll be ~ opportunity to relax** habrá oportunidades de sobra para relajarse; **an ~ supply of jars** una abundante cantidad de tarros; **there was an ~ supply of food** había comida en abundancia; **to make ~ use of sth** usar algo en abundancia; **she was given ~ warning that ...** se le avisó con tiempo de sobra de que ...
[1·2] **to be ~** ser más que suficiente; **eight hours' sleep should be ~** ocho horas de sueño deberían ser más que suficientes; **one cupful of rice is ~ for two people** una taza de arroz es más que suficiente para dos personas; **thanks, I have ~** gracias, tengo bastante
[2] (= *generous*) [*garment*] amplio, grande; [*waist*] ancho, generoso; [*portion, bosom*] generoso; **his ~ stomach** su enorme *or* prominente barriga; **his ~ chin** su papada

amplification [,æmplɪfɪ'keɪʃən] N [1] [*of sound*] amplificación *f*
[2] (*fig*) (= *elaboration*) desarrollo *m*, explicación *f*

amplifier ['æmplɪfaɪəʳ] N amplificador *m*

amplify ['æmplɪfaɪ] VT [1] [+ *sound*] amplificar; (*also Rad*) aumentar
[2] (*fig*) [+ *statement etc*] desarrollar; **he refused to ~ his remarks** se negó a hacer más comentarios

amplitude ['æmplɪtju:d] N amplitud *f*

amply ['æmplɪ] ADV [1] (= *sufficiently*) [*demonstrate, illustrate*] ampliamente, suficientemente; **we were ~ rewarded** fuimos ampliamente recompensados; **we were ~ justified** estuvimos plenamente justificados
[2] (= *generously*) **she is ~ proportioned** es de proporciones generosas

ampoule, ampule (*US*) ['æmpu:l] N ampolla *f*

amputate ['æmpjʊteɪt] VT amputar

amputation [,æmpjʊ'teɪʃən] N amputación *f*

amputee [,æmpjʊ'ti:] N *persona cuya pierna o cuyo brazo ha sido amputada/o*

Amsterdam [,æmstə'dæm] N Amsterdam *m*

amt ABBR (= **amount**) impte

Amtrak ['æmtræk] N (*US*) *empresa nacional de ferrocarriles de los EEUU*

amuck [ə'mʌk] ADV = **amok**

amulet ['æmjʊlɪt] N amuleto *m*

amuse [ə'mju:z] VT [1] (= *cause mirth to*) divertir; **the thought seemed to ~ him** la idea parecía divertirle; **this ~d everybody** divirtió *or* hizo reír a todos; **we are not ~d** (*hum*) no nos hace gracia; **to be ~d at** *or* **by** divertirse con; **with an ~d expression** con una mirada risueña
[2] (= *entertain*) distraer, entretener; **to keep sb ~d** entretener a algn; **this should keep them ~d for years** esto deberá ocupar su atención por muchos años; **to ~ o.s.** distraerse; **run along and ~ yourselves** marchaos y a pasarlo bien

amusement [ə'mju:zmənt] Ⓐ N [1] (= *mirth*) **with a look of ~** con mirada risueña; **there was general ~ at this** al oír esto se rieron todos; **much to my ~** con gran regocijo mío; **to conceal one's ~** ocultar sus ganas de reír, aguantarse la risa
[2] (= *entertainment*) distracción *f*, diversión *f*; **they do it for ~ only** para ellos es un pasatiempo nada más
[3] **amusements** (= *pastimes*) diversiones *fpl*, distracciones *fpl*; (*Brit*) (*in fairground*) atracciones *f*; (*in amusement arcade*) máquinas *fpl* electrónicas, máquinas *fpl* tragaperras; **a town with plenty of ~s** una ciudad que ofrece muchas diversiones
Ⓑ CPD ► **amusement arcade** N (*Brit*) sala *f* de juegos recreativos ► **amusement park** N (*esp US*) parque *m* de atracciones

amusing [ə'mju:zɪŋ] ADJ [1] (= *funny*) gracioso, divertido; **I found it ~** me pareció gracioso *or* divertido; **I didn't find it ~** no le vi la gracia
[2] (= *entertaining*) entretenido

amusingly [ə'mju:zɪŋlɪ] ADV [1] (= *funnily*) de forma divertida; **~ written** escrito con gracia
[2] (= *entertainingly*) de forma entretenida

an [æn, ən, n] INDEF ART *see* **a**

ANA N ABBR (*US*) [1] = **American Newspaper Association**
[2] = **American Nurses' Association**

anabolic [,ænə'bɒlɪk] ADJ anabólico; **~ steroid** esteroide *m* anabolizante

anachronism [ə'nækrənɪzəm] N anacronismo *m*

anachronistic [ə,nækrə'nɪstɪk] ADJ anacrónico

anacoluthon [,ænəkə'lu:θɒn] N (*pl* **anacolutha** [,ænəkə'lu:θə]) anacoluto *m*

anaconda [,ænə'kɒndə] N anaconda *f*

Anacreon [ə'nækrɪən] N Anacreonte

anaemia, anemia (*US*) [ə'ni:mɪə] N anemia *f*

anaemic, anemic (*US*) [ə'ni:mɪk] ADJ (*Med*) anémico; (*fig*) (= *weak*) débil

anaerobic [,ænɛə'rəʊbɪk] ADJ anaerobio

anaesthesia, anesthesia (*US*) [,ænɪs'θi:zɪə] N anestesia *f*

anaesthetic, anesthetic (*US*) [,ænɪs'θetɪk] Ⓐ N anestésico *m*; **local/general ~** anestesia *f* local/total; **to be under (an) ~** estar anestesiado; **to give sb an ~** ◊ **put sb under (an) ~** anestesiar a algn
Ⓑ ADJ anestésico

anaesthetist, anesthetist (*US*) [æ'ni:sθɪtɪst] N anestesista *mf*

anaesthetize, anesthetize (*US*) [æ'ni:sθɪtaɪz] VT anestesiar

anagram ['ænəgræm] N anagrama *m*

anal ['eɪnəl] Ⓐ ADJ anal
Ⓑ CPD ► **anal retentive** N (*Psych*) persona estancada en la fase anal; (*) quisquilloso/a *m/f*, puñetero/a *m/f* ► **anal sex** N sexo *m* anal

analgesia [,ænæl'dʒi:zɪə] N analgesia *f*

analgesic [,ænæl'dʒi:sɪk] Ⓐ ADJ analgésico
Ⓑ N analgésico *m*

analog ['ænəlɒg] N (*US*) = **analogue**

analogical [,ænə'lɒdʒɪkəl] ADJ analógico

analogous [ə'næləgəs] ADJ análogo (**to, with** a)

analogue ['ænəlɒg] Ⓐ N análogo *m*
Ⓑ CPD analógico ► **analogue computer** N ordenador *m* analógico

analogy [ə'nælədʒɪ] N analogía *f*; (= *similarity*) semejanza *f*; **by ~ with** ◊ **on the ~ of** por analogía con; **to argue from** *or* **by ~** razonar por analogía; **to draw an ~ between** señalar una semejanza entre

analysand [ə'nælɪ,sænd] N (*Psych*) sujeto *m* analizado, analizando *m*

analyse, analyze (*US*) ['ænəlaɪz] VT [1] (= *study*) analizar
[2] (*Psych*) psicoanalizar

analyser, analyzer (*US*) ['ænəlaɪzəʳ] N (*Tech*) analizador *m*

▼ **analysis** [ə'nælɪsɪs] N (*pl* **analyses** [ə'nælɪsi:z]) [1] (= *study*) análisis *m inv*; **in the final** *or* **last** *or* **ultimate ~** a fin de cuentas
[2] (*Psych*) psicoanálisis *m*

analyst ['ænəlɪst] N [1] (*Chem etc*) analista *mf*
[2] (*Psych*) psicoanalista *mf*

analytic [,ænə'lɪtɪk] ADJ = **analytical**

analytical [,ænə'lɪtɪkəl] Ⓐ ADJ analítico; **an ~ mind** una mente analítica
Ⓑ CPD ► **analytical psychology** N psicología *f* analítica

analyze ['ænəlaɪz] VT (*US*) = **analyse**

analyzer ['ænəlaɪzəʳ] N (*US*) = **analyser**

anapaest, anapest ['ænəpi:st] N anapesto *m*

anaphoric [,ænə'fɒrɪk] ADJ anafórico

anarchic [æ'nɑ:kɪk] ADJ anárquico

anarchical [æ'nɑ:kɪkəl] ADJ = **anarchic**

anarchism ['ænəkɪzəm] N anarquismo *m*

anarchist ['ænəkɪst] Ⓐ N anarquista *mf*
Ⓑ ADJ anarquista

anarchistic [,ænə'kɪstɪk] ADJ anarquista

anarcho-syndicalism [,ænəkəʊ'sɪndɪkəlɪzəm] N anarcosindicalismo *m*

anarchy ['ænəkɪ] N [1] (*Pol*) anarquía *f*
[2] (*) (= *chaos*) anarquía *f*

anathema [ə'næθɪmə] N [1] (*Rel*) anatema *m*
[2] (*fig*) **he is ~ to me** no lo puedo ver, para mí es inaguantable; **the idea is ~ to her** para ella la idea es una abominación, la idea le resulta odiosa

anathematize [ə'næθɪmətaɪz] VT anatematizar

anatomical [,ænə'tɒmɪkəl] ADJ anatómico

anatomist [ə'nætəmɪst] N anatomista *mf*

anatomize [ə'nætəmaɪz] VT (*Bio*) anatomizar; (*fig*) analizar minuciosamente, diseccionar

anatomy [ə'nætəmɪ] N [1] (*Med*) anatomía *f*
[2] (*hum*) (= *body*) anatomía *f*
[3] (*frm*) (= *analysis*) análisis *m inv* minucioso, disección *f*

ANC N ABBR (= **African National Congress**) CNA *m*

ancestor ['ænsɪstəʳ] N [1] (= *person*) antepasado/a *m/f*
[2] (*fig*) [*of machine, idea, organization*] antecesor(a) *m/f*, predecesor(a) *m/f*

ancestral [æn'sestrəl] Ⓐ ADJ ancestral
Ⓑ CPD ► **ancestral home** N casa *f* solariega

➤ LANGUAGE IN USE: **analysis 1** 26.1

ancestress† ['ænsɪstrɪs] N antepasada *f*

ancestry ['ænsɪstrɪ] N (= *lineage*) ascendencia *f*, linaje *m*; (= *noble birth*) abolengo *m*

anchor ['æŋkəʳ] Ⓐ N [1] (*Naut*) ancla *f*; **to be** *or* **lie** *or* **ride at ~** estar al ancla, estar anclado; **to cast** *or* **drop ~** echar anclas; **~s aweigh!** ¡leven anclas!; *see also* **weigh A3**
[2] (*fig*) seguridad *f*, sostén *m*; (= *person*) pilar *m*
[3] = **anchorman, anchorwoman**
Ⓑ VT [1] (*Naut*) anclar
[2] (*fig*) sujetar (**to** a), afianzar (**to** en)
[3] (*esp US TV, Rad*) presentar
Ⓒ VI (*Naut*) anclar

anchorage ['æŋkərɪdʒ] Ⓐ N ancladero *m*, fondeadero *m*
Ⓑ CPD ► **anchorage dues**, NPL **anchorage fee** N anclaje *m*

anchorite ['æŋkəraɪt] N anacoreta *mf*

anchorman ['æŋkəmæn] N (*pl* **anchormen**) (*TV, Rad*) presentador *m*; (*fig*) hombre clave

anchorwoman ['æŋkə,wʊmən] N (*pl* **anchorwomen**) (*TV, Rad*) presentadora *f*

anchovy ['æntʃəvɪ] N (*live, fresh*) boquerón *m*; (*salted, tinned*) anchoa *f*

ancient ['eɪnʃənt] ADJ [1] (= *old, classical*) antiguo; **~ Greek** griego *m* antiguo; **~ history** historia *f* antigua; **that's ~ history!*** ¡eso pertenece a la historia!; **in ~ days** en la antigüedad, hace muchísimo tiempo; **~ monument** (*Brit*) monumento *m* histórico; **~ Rome** la Roma antigua; **remains of ~ times** restos *mpl* de la antigüedad
[2] (* *hum*) [*person*] viejo, anciano; [*clothing, object*] antiquísimo, de los tiempos de Maricastaña*; **we went in his ~ car** fuimos en su antiquísimo coche; **he's getting pretty ~** va para viejo; → [OLD]

ancients ['eɪnʃənts] NPL **the ~** los antiguos

ancillary [æn'sɪlərɪ] ADJ [1] (= *secondary*) subordinado (**to** a)
[2] (= *supporting*) [*staff, workers*] auxiliar; [*services*] complementario
[3] (= *additional*) [*charges, costs*] adicional

and [ænd, ənd, nd, ən] CONJ [1] y; (*before i-, hi- but not hie-*) e; **you ~ me** tú y yo; **French ~ English** francés e inglés; **and?** ¿y?, ¿y qué más?; **~ how!*** ¡y (no veas) cómo!; **~/or** y/o
[2] (*with compar adj*) **better ~ better** cada vez mejor; **more ~ more** cada vez más; **more ~ more difficult** cada vez más difícil
[3] (*in numbers*) **one ~ a half** uno y medio; **a hundred ~ one** ciento uno; **two hundred ~ ten** doscientos diez; **five hours ~ 20 minutes** cinco horas y 20 minutos; **ten dollars ~ 50 cents** diez dólares y *or* con 50 centavos
[4] (*negative sense*) ni; **without shoes ~ socks** sin zapatos ni calcetines; **you can't buy ~ sell here** aquí no se permite comprar ni vender
[5] (*repetition, continuation*) **she cried ~ cried** no dejaba de llorar, lloraba sin parar; **I rang ~ rang** llamé muchas veces; **he talked ~ talked** habló sin parar *or* (*LAm*) cesar
[6] (*before infin*) **try ~ do it** trata de hacerlo; **please try ~ come!** ¡procura venir!; **wait ~ see** espera y verás; **come ~ see me** ven a verme
[7] (*implying a distinction*) **there are lawyers ~ lawyers!** hay abogados y abogados
[8] (*implying a conditional*) **one move ~ you're dead!** ¡como te muevas disparo!, ¡un solo movimiento y disparo!

Andalusia [,ændə'lu:zɪə] N Andalucía *f*

Andalusian [,ændə'lu:zɪən] Ⓐ ADJ andaluz
Ⓑ N [1] (= *person*) andaluz(a) *m/f*
[2] (*Ling*) andaluz *m*

> **AND**
>
> In order to avoid two "i" sounds coming together, **and** is translated by **e** not **y** before words beginning with **i** and **hi** and before the letter **y** used on its own:
> ...Spain and Italy...
> ***...España e Italia...***
> ...grapes and figs...
> ***...uvas e higos...***
> ...words ending in S and Y...
> ***...palabras terminadas en S e Y...***
> **NOTE:** Words beginning with **hie** are preceded by **y**, since **hie** is not pronounced "i":
> ...coal and iron mines...
> ***...minas de carbón y hierro...***

Andean ['ændɪən] Ⓐ ADJ andino
Ⓑ CPD ► **Andean high plateau** N altiplanicie *f* andina, altiplano *m* (*LAm*) andino

Andes ['ændi:z] NPL **the ~** los Andes

andiron ['ændaɪən] N morillo *m*

Andorra [,æn'dɔ:rə] N Andorra *f*

Andorran [,æn'dɔ:rən] Ⓐ ADJ andorrano
Ⓑ N andorrano/a *m/f*

Andrew ['ændru:] N Andrés

androcentric [,ændrəʊ'sentrik] ADJ androcéntrico

androcentricity [,ændrəʊsen'trɪsɪtɪ] N androcentrismo *m*

androgen ['ændrədʒən] N andrógeno *m*

androgenic ['ændrə'dʒenɪk] ADJ androgénico

androgynous [æn'drɒdʒɪnəs] ADJ andrógino

androgyny [æn'drɒdʒɪnɪ] N androginia *f*

android ['ændrɔɪd] N androide *m*

Andromache [æn'drɒməkɪ] N Andrómaca

Andromeda [æn'drɒmɪdə] N Andrómeda

androsterone [æn'drɒstə,rəʊn] N androsterona *f*

Andy ['ændɪ] N (*familiar form*) *of* **Andrew**

anecdotal [,ænɪk'dəʊtəl] ADJ anecdótico

anecdote ['ænɪkdəʊt] N anécdota *f*

anemia [ə'ni:mɪə] N (*US*) = **anaemia**

anemic [ə'ni:mɪk] ADJ (*US*) = **anaemic**

anemone [ə'nemənɪ] N (*Bot*) anémona *f*, anemone *f*; (= *sea anemone*) anémona *f*

aneroid ['ænərɔɪd] Ⓐ ADJ aneroide
Ⓑ CPD ► **aneroid barometer** N barómetro *m* aneroide

anesthesia [,ænɪs'θi:zɪə] N (*US*) = **anaesthesia**

anesthesiologist [,ænɪs,θi:zɪ'ɒlədʒɪst] N (*US*) anestesista *mf*

anesthetic [,ænɪs'θetɪk] ADJ, N (*US*) = **anaesthetic**

anesthetist [æ'ni:sθɪtɪst] N (*US*) = **anaesthetist**

anesthetize [æ'ni:sθɪtaɪz] VT (*US*) = **anaesthetize**

aneurism, aneurysm ['ænjə,rɪzəm] N aneurisma *m*

anew [ə'nju:] ADV (*liter*) de nuevo, otra vez; **to begin ~** comenzar de nuevo, volver a empezar

angel ['eɪndʒəl] Ⓐ N [1] (*Rel*) ángel *m*; **Angel of Darkness** ángel *m* de las tinieblas; **the Angel of Death** el ángel exterminador; ✦***IDIOMS*** **I'm on the side of the ~s** yo estoy de parte de los ángeles; **speak** *or* **talk of ~s!** hablando del ruin de Roma (por la puerta asoma); **to rush in where ~s fear to tread** meterse en la boca del lobo; *see also* **fool A1, guardian**
[2] (*) (= *person*) **she's an ~** es un ángel; **be an ~ and give me a cigarette** ¿me das un pitillo, amor?
[3] (*esp Theat**) caballo *m* blanco*, promotor(a) *m/f*
Ⓑ CPD ► **angel dust*** N (*Drugs*) polvo *m* de ángel ► **angel food cake** (*US*) N *bizcocho muy esponjoso hecho sin las yemas de huevo* ► **angels on horseback** NPL (*Brit Culin*) *rollitos de beicon rellenos de ostras y servidos sobre pan tostado*

Angeleno [,ændʒə'li:nəʊ] N habitante *mf* de Los Angeles

angelfish ['eɪndʒəlfɪʃ] N (*pl* **angelfish**) angelote *m*, pez *m* ángel

angelic [æn'dʒelɪk] ADJ angélico

angelica [æn'dʒelɪkə] N angélica *f*

angelical [æn'dʒelɪkəl] ADJ = **angelic**

angelically [æn'dʒelɪklɪ] ADV angelicalmente, como los ángeles

angelus ['ændʒɪləs] N ángelus *m*

anger ['æŋgəʳ] Ⓐ N ira *f*; **red with ~** rojo de ira; **to move** *or* **rouse sb to ~** provocar la ira de algn; **to speak in ~** hablar indignado; **words spoken in ~** palabras pronunciadas en un momento de enfado (*Sp*), palabras pronunciadas en un momento de enojo (*LAm*)
Ⓑ VT enfadar (*Sp*), enojar (*LAm*); **to be easily ~ed** enfadarse fácilmente (*Sp*), enojarse fácilmente (*LAm*)

angina [æn'dʒaɪnə] N (*Med*) (*also* **~ pectoris**) angina *f* (de pecho)

angiogram ['ændʒɪəʊgræm] N angiograma *m*

angiosperm ['ændʒɪə,spɜ:m] N angiosperma *f*

angle[1] [æŋgl] Ⓐ N [1] (*Math, Geom, etc*) ángulo *m*; **at an ~ of 80 degrees** ◊ **at an 80 degree ~** con un ángulo de 80 grados; **an iron bar stuck out at an ~** una barra de hierro sobresalía formando un ángulo; **he wore his hat at an ~** llevaba el sombrero ladeado, llevaba el sombrero hacía un lado; **hold the knife at an ~** coge el cuchillo inclinado; **cut the bread at an ~** corte el pan en diagonal; **to be at an ~ to sth** formar ángulo con algo; **to look at a building from a different ~** contemplar un edificio desde otro ángulo; **photographed from a low ~** fotografiado desde un ángulo inferior; **a high-/low-~ shot** (*Phot*) una toma desde un ángulo superior/inferior; **~ of approach** (*Aer*) ángulo *m* de aterrizaje; **~ of climb** (*Aer*) ángulo *m* de subida; *see also* **right E**
[2] (*fig*) [2·1] (= *point of view*) punto *m* de vista; **what's your ~ on this?** ¿cuál es tu punto de vista al respecto?, ¿tú qué opinas de esto?; **from the parents' ~** desde el punto de vista *or* la perspectiva de los padres
[2·2] (= *aspect*) componente *m*; **the director decided to play down the love ~** el director decidió restar importancia al componente amoroso
[2·3] (= *focus*) perspectiva *f*, ángulo *m*; **to look at sth from a different ~** enfocar algo desde otra perspectiva *or* desde otro ángulo; **to look at a problem from all ~s** estudiar un problema desde todas las perspectivas, estudiar un problema desde todos los ángulos *or* puntos de vista; **this article gives a new ~ on the question** este artículo da un nuevo enfoque a la cuestión
Ⓑ VT [1] [+ *object*] orientar; (*Sport*) [+ *shot*] sesgar, ladear; **he ~d the lamp towards his desk** orientó la luz de la lámpara hacia la mesa; **an ~d header** un cabezazo sesgado *or* ladeado *or* de lado
[2] (*fig*) [2·1] (= *aim*) dirigir; **this article is ~d towards non-specialists** este artículo va dirigido al lector no especializado
[2·2] (= *bias*) sesgar; **the report was ~d so as**

to present them in a bad light el informe estaba sesgado de forma que daba una mala impresión de ellos
Ⓒ VI (= *turn*) desviarse, torcerse; **the path ~d sharply to the left** el camino se desviaba *or* torcía de pronto hacia la izquierda
Ⓓ CPD ► **angle bracket** N (= *support*) escuadra *f*; (*Typ*) corchete *m* agudo ► **angle iron** N (*Constr*) hierro *m* angular

angle² [æŋgl] VI [1] (= *fish*) pescar (con caña); **to ~ for trout** pescar truchas
[2] (*fig*) **to ~ for sth** (*gen*) andar buscando algo; (*for votes, for job*) andar a la caza de algo; **he's just angling for sympathy** sólo anda buscando compasión

Angle ['æŋgl] N anglo/a *m/f*

Anglepoise® ['æŋglpɔɪz] N (*Brit*) (*also* **~ lamp**) lámpara *f* de estudio

angler ['æŋglər] N pescador(a) *m/f* (de caña)

anglerfish ['æŋgləfɪʃ] N rape *m*

Angles ['æŋglz] NPL anglos *mpl*

Anglican ['æŋglɪkən] Ⓐ ADJ anglicano
Ⓑ N anglicano/a *m/f*

Anglicanism ['æŋglɪkənɪzəm] N anglicanismo *m*

anglicism ['æŋglɪsɪzəm] N anglicismo *m*, inglesismo *m*

anglicist ['æŋglɪsɪst] N anglicista *mf*

anglicize ['æŋglɪsaɪz] VT dar forma inglesa a, anglicanizar

angling ['æŋglɪŋ] N pesca *f* con caña

Anglo* ['æŋgləʊ] N blanco/a *m/f*, americano/a *m/f* (de origen no hispano)

Anglo- ['æŋgləʊ] PREFIX anglo…; **~Spanish** angloespañol; **an ~French project** un proyecto anglofrancés

Anglo-American ['æŋgləʊə'merɪkən] Ⓐ ADJ angloamericano
Ⓑ N angloamericano/a *m/f*

Anglo-Asian ['æŋgləʊ'eɪʃn] Ⓐ ADJ angloasiático
Ⓑ N angloasiático/a *m/f*

Anglo-Catholic ['ænglәʊ'kæθɪk] Ⓐ ADJ anglocatólico
Ⓑ N anglocatólico/a *m/f*

Anglo-Catholicism ['æŋgləʊkə'θɒlɪsɪzəm] N anglocatolicismo *m*

Anglo-Indian ['æŋgləʊ'ɪndɪən] Ⓐ ADJ angloindio
Ⓑ N angloindio/a *m/f*

Anglo-Irish ['æŋgləʊ'aɪərɪʃ] Ⓐ ADJ angloirlandés
Ⓑ N angloirlandés/esa *m/f*

Anglo-Norman [,æŋgləʊ'nɔːmən] Ⓐ ADJ anglonormando
Ⓑ N [1] (= *person*) anglonormando/a *m/f*
[2] (*Ling*) anglonormando *m*

anglophile ['æŋgləʊfaɪl] N anglófilo/a *m/f*

anglophobe ['æŋgləʊfəʊb] N anglófobo/a *m/f*

anglophobia [,æŋgləʊ'fəʊbjə] N anglofobia *f*

anglophone ['æŋgləʊfəʊn] Ⓐ ADJ anglófono
Ⓑ N anglófono/a *m/f*

Anglo-Saxon ['æŋgləʊ'sæksən] Ⓐ ADJ anglosajón
Ⓑ N [1] (= *person*) anglosajón/ona *m/f*
[2] (*Ling*) anglosajón *m*

ANGLO-SAXON

La lengua anglosajona, **Anglo-Saxon**, *también llamada* **Old English**, *se extendió en Inglaterra tras las invasiones de pueblos germánicos en el siglo V y continuó usándose hasta la conquista normanda de la isla. Hoy en día sigue siendo una parte importante del idioma inglés. Como ejemplos de palabras de origen anglosajón que aún se usan tenemos* **man**, **child**, **eat**, **love** *o* **harvest**.
El término se usa también para describir el mundo angloparlante, sobre todo si tiene su origen o está muy influido por costumbres inglesas, si bien hay personas de origen escocés, irlandés, galés o minorías étnicas que prefieren no usarlo.

Angola [æŋ'gəʊlə] N Angola *f*

Angolan [æŋ'gəʊlən] Ⓐ ADJ angoleño
Ⓑ N angoleño/a *m/f*

angora [æŋ'gɔːrə] N angora *f*; **an ~ sweater** un jersey *or* suéter de angora

angostura [,æŋgə'stjʊərə] Ⓐ N angostura *f*
Ⓑ CPD ► **angostura bitters**® NPL bíter *msing* de angostura

Angoulême [ɑːŋgʊ'lɛm] N Angulema *f*

angrily ['æŋgrɪlɪ] ADV [*react, speak*] con ira; **"I tried!" he said ~** —¡lo intenté! —dijo enfadado *or* (*LAm*) enojado; **he protested ~** protestó airadamente

angry ['æŋgrɪ] ADJ (*compar* **angrier**; *superl* **angriest**) [1] (= *cross*) [*person*] enfadado (*Sp*), enojado (*LAm*); [*voice*] de enfado (*Sp*), de enojo (*LAm*); [*letter, reply*] airado; **to be ~** estar enfadado (**with** con); **he was very ~** estaba muy enfadado; **you won't be ~, will you?** no te vas a enfadar *or* (*LAm*) enojar ¿verdad?; **to be ~ about** *or* **at sth** estar enfadado por algo; **he was very ~ about** *or* **at being dismissed** estaba furioso porque lo habían despedido; **to get ~** enfadarse (*Sp*), enojarse (*LAm*); **she gave me an ~ look** me miró enfadada; **your father looks very ~** tu padre parece estar muy enfadado; **this sort of thing makes me ~** estas cosas me sacan de quicio*; **don't make me ~!** ¡no me hagas enfadar!; **there were ~ scenes when it was announced that …** hubo escenas airadas cuando se anunció que …; **~ young man** (*Brit*) joven *m* airado
[2] (*liter*) [*sky*] tormentoso, borrascoso; [*sea*] bravo
[3] (*Med*) [*wound, rash*] inflamado; **the blow left an ~ mark on his forehead** el golpe dejó una marca de un rojo encendido en su frente

angst [æŋst] N angustia *f*

angstrom ['æŋstrʌm] N angstrom *m*

anguish ['æŋgwɪʃ] N (*physical*) tormentos *mpl*; (*mental*) angustia *f*; **to be in ~** (*physically*) padecer tormentos, sufrir lo indecible; (*mentally*) estar angustiado

anguished ['æŋgwɪʃt] ADJ (*physically*) atormentado de dolor; (*mentally*) angustiado

angular ['æŋgjʊlər] ADJ [*shape, lines*] angular; [*face, features*] anguloso

angularity [,æŋgjʊ'lærətɪ] N [*of shape, lines*] angularidad *f*; [*of face, features*] angulosidad *f*

aniline ['ænɪliːn] Ⓐ N anilina *f*
Ⓑ CPD ► **aniline dye** NPL colorante *m* de anilina

anima ['ænɪmə] N (*Psych*) ánima *f*, alma *f*

animal ['ænɪməl] Ⓐ N [1] (= *not plant*) animal *m*; **man is a political ~** el hombre es un animal político
[2] (*fig*) (= *thing*) cosa *f*; **there's no such ~** no existe tal cosa; **they are two different ~s** son cosas bien distintas
[3] (* *pej*) (= *person*) animal* *mf*, bestia* *mf*; **you ~!** ¡animal!*, ¡bestia!*
Ⓑ ADJ animal
Ⓒ CPD ► **animal cracker** N (*US*) galletita *f* de animales ► **animal fats** NPL grasas *fpl* de animal ► **animal husbandry** N cría *f* de animales ► **animal instinct** N instinto *m* animal ► **the animal kingdom** N el reino animal ► **Animal Liberation Front** N (*Brit*) Frente *m* de Liberación de los Animales ► **animal liberationist** N miembro *mf* del Frente de Liberación de los Animales ► **animal lover** N amante *mf* de los animales ► **animal magnetism** N [*of person*] atracción *f* animal, magnetismo *m* salvaje ► **animal rights movement** N movimiento *m* pro derechos de los animales ► **animal sanctuary** N centro *m* de acogida para animales ► **animal spirits** NPL vitalidad *f* ► **animal testing** N pruebas *fpl* de laboratorio con animales

animalcule [,ænɪ'mælkjuːl] N (*frm*) animálculo *m*

animality [,ænɪ'mælətɪ] N animalidad *f*

animate Ⓐ ['ænɪmɪt] ADJ vivo
Ⓑ ['ænɪmeɪt] VT animar, estimular

animated ['ænɪmeɪtɪd] ADJ [1] (= *lively*) [*person, discussion*] animado; **to become ~** animarse
[2] (*Cine*) **~ cartoon** dibujos *mpl* animados

animatedly ['ænɪmeɪtɪdlɪ] ADV [*talk, behave*] animadamente

animation [,ænɪ'meɪʃən] N [1] (= *liveliness*) vivacidad *f*, animación *f*
[2] (*Cine*) (= *process*) animación *f*; (= *film*) película *f* de animación, dibujos *mpl* animados

animator ['ænɪmeɪtər] N (*Cine*) animador(a) *m/f*

animatronics [,ænɪmə'trɒnɪks] N (*Cine*) animación *f* por ordenador

animism ['ænɪmɪzəm] N animismo *m*

animist ['ænɪmɪst] Ⓐ ADJ animista
Ⓑ N animista *mf*

animosity [,ænɪ'mɒsɪtɪ] N animosidad *f*, rencor *m*

animus ['ænɪməs] N [1] (= *animosity*) odio *m*
[2] (*Psych*) animus *m*, alma *f*

anise ['ænɪs] N anís *m*

aniseed ['ænɪsiːd] Ⓐ N (= *flavour*) anís *m*; (= *seed*) grano *m* de anís
Ⓑ CPD ► **aniseed ball** N bolita *f* de anís

anisette [,ænɪ'zet] N anisete *m*, anís *m*

Anjou [ɑːŋ'ʒuː] N Anjeo *m*

Ankara ['æŋkərə] N Ankara *f*

ankle ['æŋkl] Ⓐ N tobillo *m*; **I've twisted my ~** me he torcido el tobillo
Ⓑ CPD ► **ankle joint** N articulación *f* del tobillo ► **ankle sock** N (*Brit*) calcetín *m* tobillero ► **ankle strap** N tirita *f* tobillera

anklebone ['æŋklbəʊn] N hueso *m* del tobillo

ankle-deep ['æŋkl'diːp] ADV **to be ~ in water** estar metido hasta los tobillos en el agua; **the water is only ~** el agua llega a los tobillos nada más

anklet ['æŋklɪt] N brazalete *m* para el tobillo, ajorca *f* para el pie; (*US*) calcetín *m* corto

ankylosis [,æŋkɪ'ləʊsɪs] N anquilosis *f*

Ann [æn] N Ana; **~ Boleyn** Ana Bolena

ann ABBR [1] = **annual**
[2] (*Fin*) = **annuity**

annalist ['ænəlɪst] N analista *mf*, cronista *mf*

annals ['ænəlz] NPL anales *mpl*; **in all the ~ of crime** en toda la historia del crimen; **never in the ~ of human endeavour** nunca en la historia de los esfuerzos humanos

Anne [æn] N Ana

anneal [ə'niːl] VT templar

annex [ə'neks] Ⓐ VT [1] [+ *territory*] anexar, anexionar (**to** a)
[2] [+ *document*] adjuntar, añadir (**to** a)
Ⓑ ['æneks] N (*US*) = **annexe**

annexation [,ænek'seɪʃən] N anexión *f*

annexe ['æneks] N 1 (= *building*) edificio *m* anexo
2 (= *document*) anexo *m*

annihilate [ə'naɪəleɪt] VT aniquilar

annihilation [ə,naɪə'leɪʃən] N aniquilación *f*, aniquilamiento *m*

anniversary [,ænɪ'vɜːsərɪ] N aniversario *m*; **wedding ~** aniversario *m* de bodas; **golden/silver wedding ~** bodas *fpl* de oro/plata; **the Góngora ~ dinner** el banquete para festejar el aniversario de Góngora

Anno Domini ['ænəʊ'dɒmɪnaɪ] N (*frm*) **~ 43** el año 43 después de Jesucristo; **the third century ~** el siglo tercero de Cristo

annotate ['ænəʊteɪt] VT anotar, comentar

annotation [,ænəʊ'teɪʃən] N (= *act*) anotación *f*; (= *instance*) anotación *f*, apunte *m*

▼**announce** [ə'naʊns] VT 1 (*gen*) anunciar; **we regret to ~ the death of ...** lamentamos tener que anunciar la muerte de ...
2 (= *inform*) comunicar, hacer saber; **it is ~d from London that ...** se comunica desde Londres que ...
3 (= *declare*) declarar; **he ~d that he wasn't going** declaró que no iba

announcement [ə'naʊnsmənt] N (*gen*) anuncio *m*; (= *declaration*) declaración *f*; **~ of birth** (aviso *m*) natalicio *m*; **~ of death** (nota *f*) necrológica *f*; **I'd like to make an ~** tengo algo que anunciar

announcer [ə'naʊnsər] N 1 (*TV, Rad*) locutor(a) *m/f*
2 (*at airport etc*) el *or* la que hace anuncios

▼**annoy** [ə'nɔɪ] VT molestar, fastidiar; **he's just trying to ~ you** lo que quiere es molestarte *or* fastidiarte; **is this man ~ing you, madam?** ¿le está molestando este hombre, señora?; **don't be ~ed if I can't come** no te enfades si no puedo venir; **to be ~ed about** *or* **at sth** estar enfadado *or* molesto por algo; **to be ~ed with sb** estar enfadado *or* molesto con algn; **to get ~ed** enfadarse; **it's no good getting ~ed with me** de nada sirve enfadarte conmigo

annoyance [ə'nɔɪəns] N 1 (= *displeasure*) irritación *f*; (= *anger*) enfado *m*, enojo *m* (*LAm*); **to my ~ I find that ...** con gran disgusto mío descubro que ...
2 (= *annoying thing*) molestia *f*

annoying [ə'nɔɪɪŋ] ADJ [*habit, noise*] molesto, irritante; [*person*] irritante, pesado; **the ~ thing about it is that ...** lo que más me fastidia del asunto es que ...; **how ~!** ¡qué fastidio!; **it's ~ to have to wait** es un fastidio tener que esperar; **he's such an ~ person!** ¡qué hombre más irritante *or* pesado!; **I find her very ~** me resulta muy pesada; **I find it very ~** me molesta mucho

annoyingly [ə'nɔɪɪŋlɪ] ADV [*behave, act*] de modo irritante; **and then, ~ enough, she wasn't at home** y encima no estaba en casa, lo que me fastidió mucho; **~, I shan't be able to be there** me da mucha rabia, pero no voy a poder ir; **the radio was ~ loud** la radio estaba tan alta que molestaba; **she was ~ vague** era tan distraída que sacaba de quicio*; **he has an ~ loud voice** tiene un vozarrón de lo más irritante

annual ['ænjʊəl] (A) ADJ anual
(B) N 1 (= *publication*) anuario *m*; (= *children's comic book*) *cómic para niños que se publica en forma de libro normalmente por Navidad*
2 (*Bot*) planta *f* anual
(C) CPD ► **annual general meeting** N (*Brit*) junta *f* general anual ► **annual income** N ingresos *mpl* anuales ► **annual report** N informe *m* anual

annually ['ænjʊəlɪ] ADV anualmente, cada año; **£500 ~** 500 libras al año

annuity [ə'njuːɪtɪ] N renta *f* vitalicia

annul [ə'nʌl] VT [+ *judgment, contract, marriage*] anular; [+ *law*] revocar, abrogar

annulment [ə'nʌlmənt] N [*of marriage*] anulación *f*; [*of law*] revocación *f*, abrogación *f*

annum ['ænəm] N *see* **per**

Annunciation [ə,nʌnsɪ'eɪʃən] N Anunciación *f*

anode ['ænəʊd] N ánodo *m*

anodize ['ænədaɪz] VT anodizar

anodyne ['ænəʊdaɪn] (A) ADJ (*Med*) analgésico; (*fig*) anodino
(B) N (*Med*) analgésico *m*; (*fig*) remedio *m*

anoint [ə'nɔɪnt] VT 1 (*with oil etc*) ungir (**with** de)
2 (*fig*) (= *nominate*) designar, nombrar

anointing [ə'nɔɪntɪŋ] N unción *f*; **~ of the sick** (*Rel*) unción *f* de los enfermos

anomalous [ə'nɒmələs] ADJ anómalo

anomaly [ə'nɒməlɪ] N anomalía *f*

anon[1] [ə'nɒn] ADV 1 luego, dentro de poco; **I'll see you ~** nos veremos luego
2 (††) **ever and ~** de vez en cuando

anon[2] [ə'nɒn] ABBR = **anonymous**

anonymity [,ænə'nɪmɪtɪ] N anonimato *m*; **to preserve one's ~** permanecer en el anonimato; **the ~ of rented rooms** lo anónimo de las habitaciones de alquiler

anonymous [ə'nɒnɪməs] ADJ 1 (= *unnamed*) [*caller, writer, phone call, poem*] anónimo; [*ballot*] secreto; **he received an ~ letter** recibió un anónimo; **Alcoholics Anonymous** Alcohólicos *mpl* Anónimos; **he wishes to remain ~** quiere permanecer en el anonimato
2 (= *unmemorable*) [*place, room*] anónimo, sin ninguna seña de identidad; **~-looking people** gente de apariencia anónima

anonymously [ə'nɒnɪməslɪ] ADV [*send, give, speak*] anónimamente, de manera anónima; [*live*] en el anonimato; [*publish*] de forma anónima, sin el nombre del autor; **the book came out ~** el libro salió de forma anónima *or* sin el nombre del autor

anorak ['ænəræk] N 1 (*esp Brit*) (= *coat*) anorak *m*
2 (*Brit* pej*) (= *person*) pelmazo/a *m/f*, petardo/a *m/f*

anorectic [,ænə'rektɪk] = **anorexic**

anorexia [,ænə'reksɪə] (A) N (*Med*) anorexia *f*
(B) CPD ► **anorexia nervosa** N anorexia *f* nerviosa

anorexic [,ænə'reksɪk] (A) ADJ anoréxico
(B) N anoréxico/a *m/f*

▼**another** [ə'nʌðər] (A) ADJ 1 (= *additional*) otro; **would you like ~ beer?** ¿quieres otra cerveza?; **have ~ one** toma *or* coge otro; **we need ~ two men** necesitamos dos hombres más, necesitamos otros dos hombres; **not ~ minute!** ¡ni un minuto más!; **there are ~ two months to go** faltan otros dos meses *or* dos meses más; **~ two kilometres** dos kilómetros más; **without ~ word** sin decir ni una palabra más; **there's not ~ painting like it** no existe otro cuadro como éste; **I don't think he'll be ~ Mozart** no creo que llegue a ser otro Mozart; **I've discovered yet ~ problem** he descubierto otro problema más; **take ~ five** coge cinco más *or* otros cinco, toma cinco más *or* otros cinco (*LAm*)
2 (= *different*) otro; **do it ~ time** hazlo en otra ocasión; **that's quite ~ matter** eso es otra cosa totalmente distinta, eso es otro cantar
(B) PRON otro/a *m/f*; **help yourself to ~** sírvete otro; **in one form or ~** de una forma u otra; **what with one thing and ~** entre una cosa u otra; **if not this time then ~** si no esta vez, pues otra; *see also* **one C5**

A.N. Other [,eɪ,en'ʌðər] N fulano* *m*, un tipo cualquiera*; **"A.N. Other"** (*on list*) "a concretar"

anoxia [ə'nɒksɪə] N anoxia *f*

anoxic [ə'nɒksɪk] ADJ anóxico

Ansaphone® ['ɑːnsəfəʊn] N = **answerphone**

ANSI N ABBR (*US*) = **American National Standards Institute**

▼**answer** ['ɑːnsər] (A) N 1 (= *reply*) respuesta *f*, contestación *f*; **he has an ~ for everything** tiene respuesta *or* contestación para todo; **I never got an ~ to my question** nunca me respondieron *or* contestaron (a) la pregunta; **he smiled in ~** como respuesta esbozó una sonrisa; **in ~ to your letter** en respuesta a su carta; **in ~ to your question** en *or* como respuesta a su pregunta, para responder *or* contestar (a) su pregunta; **there's no ~** (*Telec*) no contestan; **I knocked but there was no ~** llamé a la puerta pero no hubo respuesta *or* no abrieron; **there's no ~ to that** no existe una respuesta para eso; **I made no ~** no respondí; **her only ~ was to smile** respondió simplemente con una sonrisa, como respuesta se limitó a sonreír; **it was the ~ to my prayers** fue la solución a todos mis problemas; ✦**IDIOMS to know all the ~s** tener respuesta para todo, saberlo todo; **he's not exactly the ~ to a maiden's prayer** no es precisamente un príncipe azul
2 (= *solution*) solución *f*; **we have the ~ to your problem** tenemos la solución a su problema; **prison is not the ~** la cárcel no es solución; **there is no easy ~** no hay una solución fácil
3 (= *equivalent*) **cachaça is Brazil's ~ to tequila** la cachaça es el tequila brasileño; **Belgium's ~ to Sylvester Stallone** el Sylvester Stallone belga
4 (*in exam, quiz*) 4·1 (= *correct response*) (*to question*) respuesta *f*; (*to problem*) solución *f*
4·2 (= *individual response*) respuesta *f*; **write your ~s on the sheets provided** escriba las respuestas en las hojas que se le han proporcionado
5 (*Jur*) contestación *f* a la demanda, réplica *f*
(B) VT 1 (= *reply to*) [+ *person*] contestar a, responder a; [+ *question*] contestar (a), responder (a); [+ *letter*] contestar (a); [+ *criticism*] responder a; **~ me** contéstame, respóndeme; **to ~ your question, I did see him** contestando *or* respondiendo a tu pregunta, (te diré que) sí lo vi; **she never ~ed my letters** nunca contestaba (a) mis cartas; **he ~ed not a word** no dijo (ni una) palabra; **to ~ that ...** responder que ..., contestar que ...; **"not yet," he ~ed** —aún no —respondió; **to ~ a call for help** acudir a una llamada de socorro; **to ~ the door** (ir a) abrir la puerta, atender la puerta (*LAm*); **our prayers have been ~ed** nuestras súplicas han sido escuchadas; **to ~ the telephone** contestar el teléfono
2 (= *fulfil*) [+ *needs*] satisfacer; [+ *description*] responder a; **two men ~ing the description of the suspects** dos hombres que respondían a la descripción de los sospechosos; **it ~s the purpose** sirve para su propósito, cumple su cometido
3 (*Jur*) **to ~ a charge** responder a una acusación, responder a un cargo
4 (*Naut*) **to ~ the helm** obedecer al timón
(C) VI contestar, responder; **she didn't ~ im-**

➤ LANGUAGE IN USE: **announce 1** 24.1, 24.2, 24.4, 24.5 **annoy** 7.3 **another A1** 26.2 **answer A1** 21.1 **B1** 26.1

mediately tardó en contestar *or* responder; **if the phone rings, let someone else ~** si suena el teléfono, deja que conteste otro; **the doorbell rang but I didn't ~** sonó el timbre pero no abrí
Ⓓ CPD ► **answer paper** N hoja *f* de respuestas
►**answer back** VI + ADV [1] (= *be cheeky*) (*on one occasion*) replicar, contestar; (*habitually*) ser respondón/ona; **don't ~ back!** ¡no repliques!
[2] (= *defend o.s.*) defenderse (*contra las críticas*)
►**answer for** VI + PREP [1] (= *take responsibility for*) [+ *actions*] responder de; **I'll not ~ for the consequences** no respondo de las consecuencias, no me responsabilizo de las consecuencias; **to ~ for the truth of sth** responder de la veracidad de algo; **to ~ for sb's safety** responder de la seguridad de algn; **he's got a lot to ~ for** tiene la culpa de muchas cosas; **he must be made to ~ for his crimes** le tienen que hacer pagar por sus crímenes
[2] (= *reply for*) responder por; **I can't ~ for the others, but ...** no puedo responder por los demás, pero ...; **can't she ~ for herself?** ¿no sabe responder ella sola?
[3] (= *serve as*) servir de
►**answer to** VI + PREP [1] (= *be accountable to*) **to ~ to sb** responder ante algn; **I ~ to nobody** no tengo que darle cuentas a nadie
[2] (= *respond to*) **the steering ~s to the slightest touch** la dirección responde *or* es sensible al más mínimo roce
[3] (= *be called*) **the dog ~s to the name of Kim** el perro atiende por Kim
[4] (= *fit*) [+ *description*] responder a; **he ~s to the description circulated by police** responde a la descripción que ha hecho circular la policía

answerable ['ɑːnsərəbl] ADJ [1] (= *accountable*) responsable; **to be ~ to sb (for sth)** ser responsable ante algn (de algo); **he's not ~ to anyone** no tiene que dar cuentas a nadie
[2] [*question*] que tiene respuesta; **the question is not readily ~** la pregunta no tiene respuesta fácil

answering ['ɑːnsərɪŋ] CPD ► **answering machine** N contestador *m* (automático) ► **answering service** N (*live*) servicio *m* telefónico de contestación; (*with answerphone*) servicio *m* de contestador automático

answerphone ['ɑːnsəˌfəʊn] N contestador *m* (automático)

ant [ænt] N hormiga *f*; ✦***IDIOM*** **to have ~s in one's pants*** tener avispas en el culo*

ANTA N ABBR (*US*) = **American National Theater and Academy**

antacid ['ænt'æsɪd] Ⓐ ADJ antiácido
Ⓑ N antiácido *m*

antagonism [æn'tægənɪzəm] N (*towards sb*) hostilidad *f*; (*between people*) rivalidad *f*, antagonismo *m*

antagonist [æn'tægənɪst] N antagonista *mf*, adversario/a *m/f*

antagonistic [ænˌtægə'nɪstɪk] ADJ [1] (= *hostile*) [*person, attitude*] hostil, antagonista
[2] (= *opposed*) [*ideas, views*] antagónico, opuesto; **I am not in the least ~ to the idea** yo no me opongo en lo más mínimo a la idea

antagonize [æn'tægənaɪz] VT **I don't want to ~ him** no quiero contrariarle; **he managed to ~ everybody** logró ponerse a malas con todos, logró suscitar el antagonismo de todos

Antarctic [ænt'ɑːktɪk] Ⓐ ADJ antártico
Ⓑ N **the ~** el Antártico
Ⓒ CPD ► **the Antarctic Circle** N el círculo Polar Antártico ► **the Antarctic Ocean** N el Océano Antártico

Antarctica [ænt'ɑːktɪkə] N Antártida *f*

ante ['æntɪ] (*esp US*) Ⓐ N (*Cards*) apuesta *f*; ✦***IDIOM*** **to raise** *or* **up the ~*** (*Cards*) subir la apuesta; (*fig*) elevar las demandas
Ⓑ VT apostar
Ⓒ VI poner su apuesta
►**ante up*** VI + ADV (*US*) pagar, apoquinar*

ante... ['æntɪ] PREFIX ante...

anteater ['æntˌiːtəʳ] N (*Zool*) oso *m* hormiguero

antebellum ['æntɪ'beləm] ADJ prebélico (*particularmente referido a la guerra civil norteamericana*)

antecedent [ˌæntɪ'siːdənt] Ⓐ N antecedente *m*; **antecedents** (= *past history*) antecedentes *mpl*; (= *ancestors*) antepasados *mpl*
Ⓑ ADJ precedente, que precede (**to** a)

antechamber ['æntɪˌtʃeɪmbəʳ] N antecámara *f*, antesala *f*

antedate ['æntɪ'deɪt] VT [1] (= *precede*) preceder, ser anterior a; **text A ~s B by 50 years** el texto A es anterior a B en 50 años; **this building ~s the Norman conquest** este edificio data de antes de *or* es anterior a la conquista normanda
[2] [+ *cheque*] antedatar

antediluvian ['æntɪdɪ'luːvɪən] ADJ (*Rel, fig*) antediluviano

antelope ['æntɪləʊp] N (*pl* **antelope, antelopes**) antílope *m*

antenatal ['æntɪ'neɪtl] Ⓐ ADJ prenatal; **~ exercises** ejercicios *mpl* para mujeres embarazadas
Ⓑ N = **antenatal examination**
Ⓒ CPD ► **antenatal care** N asistencia *f* prenatal ► **antenatal clinic** N clínica *f* prenatal ► **antenatal examination** N reconocimiento *m* prenatal

antenna [æn'tenə] N (*pl* **antennas** *or* **antennae** [æn'teniː]) [1] [*of insect, animal*] antena *f*
[2] (*TV*) antena *f*

antepenult [ˌæntipɪ'nʌlt] N sílaba *f* antepenúltima

antepenultimate ['æntɪpɪ'nʌltɪmɪt] ADJ antepenúltimo

anterior [æn'tɪərɪəʳ] ADJ anterior (**to** a)

anteroom ['æntɪrʊm] N antesala *f*

anthem ['ænθəm] N himno *m*; (*Rel*) antífona *f*; *see also* **national C**

anther ['ænθəʳ] N antera *f*

anthill ['ænthɪl] N hormiguero *m*

anthologist [æn'θɒlədʒɪst] N antologista *mf*

anthologize [æn'θɒlədʒaɪz] VT [+ *works*] hacer una antología de; [+ *poem, author*] incluir en una antología

anthology [æn'θɒlədʒɪ] N antología *f*

Anthony ['æntənɪ] N Antonio

anthracite ['ænθrəsaɪt] N antracita *f*

anthrax ['ænθræks] N ántrax *m*

anthropo... [ˌænθrəʊpɒ] PREFIX antropo...

anthropocentric [ˌænθrəʊpəʊ'sentrɪk] ADJ antropocéntrico

anthropoid ['ænθrəʊpɔɪd] Ⓐ ADJ antropoide
Ⓑ N antropoide *mf*

anthropological [ˌænθrəpə'lɒdʒɪkəl] ADJ antropológico

anthropologist [ˌænθrə'pɒlədʒɪst] N antropólogo/a *m/f*

anthropology [ˌænθrə'pɒlədʒɪ] N antropología *f*

anthropometry [ˌænθrə'pɒmɪtrɪ] N antropometría *f*

anthropomorphic [ˌænθrəpəʊ'mɔːfɪk] ADJ antropomórfico

anthropomorphism [ˌænθrəʊpə'mɔːfɪzəm] N antropomorfismo *m*

anthropomorphist [ˌænθrəpəʊ'mɔːfɪst] Ⓐ ADJ antropomorfista
Ⓑ N antropomorfista *mf*

anthropomorphous [ˌænθrəʊpə'mɔːfəs] ADJ antropomorfo

anthropophagi [ˌænθrəʊ'pɒfəgaɪ] NPL antropófagos *mpl*

anthropophagous [ˌænθrəʊ'pɒfəgəs] ADJ antropófago

anthropophagy [ˌænθrəʊ'pɒfədʒɪ] N antropofagia *f*

anti ['æntɪ] Ⓐ PREP **she is ~ the whole idea*** ella está completamente en contra de la idea
Ⓑ ADJ **he's rather ~*** está más bien opuesto

anti... ['æntɪ] PREFIX anti...

anti-abortion [ˌæntɪə'bɔːʃən] ADJ **~ campaign** campaña *f* en contra del aborto, campaña *f* antiabortista

anti-abortionist [ˌæntɪə'bɔːʃənɪst] N antiabortista *mf*

anti-aircraft ['æntɪ'ɛəkrɑːft] ADJ [*gun*] antiaéreo

anti-apartheid ['æntɪə'pɑːteɪt] ADJ antiapartheid

anti-authority ['æntɪɔː'θɒrɪtɪ] ADJ [*speeches, attitude*] antiautoritario, contestatario

anti-bacterial ['æntɪbæk'tɪərɪəl] ADJ bactericida

anti-ballistic ['æntɪbə'lɪstɪk] ADJ antibalístico; **~ missile** misil *m* antibalístico

antibiotic ['æntɪbaɪ'ɒtɪk] Ⓐ N antibiótico *m*
Ⓑ ADJ antibiótico

antibody ['æntɪˌbɒdɪ] N anticuerpo *m*

antic ['æntɪk] N *see* **antics**

Antichrist ['æntɪkraɪst] N Anticristo *m*

anticipate [æn'tɪsɪpeɪt] Ⓐ VT [1] (= *expect*) [+ *trouble, pleasure*] esperar, contar con; **this is worse than I ~d** esto es peor de lo que esperaba; **the police ~d trouble** la policía esperaba disturbios, la policía contaba con que hubiera disturbios; **I ~ seeing him tomorrow** espero *or* cuento con verlo mañana; **as ~d** según se esperaba, como esperábamos; **the ~d audience did not materialize** no apareció el público que se esperaba *or* con que se había contado; **an eagerly-~d event** un acontecimiento muy esperado; **to ~ that ...** prever que ..., calcular que ...; **do you ~ that this will be easy?** ¿crees que esto va a resultar fácil?; **we ~ that he will come in spite of everything** contamos con que *or* esperamos que venga a pesar de todo
[2] (= *foresee*) [+ *event*] prever; [+ *question, objection, wishes*] anticipar; **~d cost** (*Comm*) coste *m* previsto; **~d profit** beneficios *mpl* previstos
[3] (= *forestall*) [+ *person*] anticiparse a, adelantarse a; [+ *event*] anticiparse a, prevenir; **you have ~d my wishes** usted se ha anticipado *or* adelantado a mis deseos; **you have ~d my orders** (*wrongly*) usted ha actuado sin esperar mis órdenes
Ⓑ VI (= *act too soon*) anticiparse

anticipation [ænˌtɪsɪ'peɪʃən] N [1] (= *expectation*) expectativa *f*; **in ~** (= *ahead of time*) de antemano; **in ~ of a fine week** esperando una semana de buen tiempo; **I bought it in ~ of her visit** lo compré en previsión de su visita; **thanking you in ~** en espera de sus noticias
[2] (= *excitement*) ilusión *f*; **we waited in**

great ~ esperábamos con gran ilusión
[3] (= *foresight*) previsión *f*, anticipación *f*; **to act with ~** obrar con previsión
[4] (= *foretaste*) anticipo *m*, adelanto *m*

anticipatory [æn'tɪsɪpeɪtərɪ] ADJ anticipador; **~ breach of contract** violación *f* anticipadora de contrato

anticlerical ['æntɪ'klerɪkl] Ⓐ ADJ anticlerical
Ⓑ N anticlerical *mf*

anticlericalism ['æntɪ'klerɪklɪzəm] N anticlericalismo *m*

anticlimactic ['æntɪklaɪ'mæktɪk] ADJ decepcionante

anticlimax ['æntɪ'klaɪmæks] N [1] (= *disappointment*) decepción *f*; **what an ~!** ¡qué decepción!; **the book ends in ~** la novela termina de modo decepcionante; **the game came as an ~** el partido no correspondió con lo que se esperaba
[2] (*Rhetoric*) anticlímax *m inv*

anticlockwise ['æntɪ'klɒkwaɪz] (*Brit*) Ⓐ ADJ en sentido contrario al de las agujas del reloj
Ⓑ ADV en sentido contrario al de las agujas del reloj

anticoagulant ['æntɪkəʊ'ægjʊlənt] Ⓐ ADJ anticoagulante
Ⓑ N anticoagulante *m*

anticorrosive ['æntɪkə'rəʊzɪv] ADJ anticorrosivo

antics ['æntɪks] NPL [*of clown etc*] payasadas *fpl*; [*of child, animal etc*] gracias *fpl*; (= *pranks*) travesuras *fpl*; **he's up to his old ~ again** (*pej*) ya está haciendo de las suyas otra vez

anticyclone ['æntɪ'saɪkləʊn] N anticiclón *m*

anticyclonic [,æntɪsaɪ'klɒnɪk] ADJ anticiclónico, anticiclonal

anti-dandruff [,æntɪ'dændrəf] ADJ anticaspa *inv*

antidazzle ['æntɪ'dæzl] ADJ antideslumbrante

antidepressant [,æntɪdɪ'presnt] Ⓐ ADJ antidepresivo
Ⓑ N antidepresivo *m*

antidote ['æntɪdəʊt] N (*Med*) antídoto *m* (**for, to** contra); (*fig*) remedio *m* (**for, to** contra, para)

anti-dumping ['æntɪ'dʌmpɪŋ] ADJ [*duty, measures*] anti-dumping *inv*

anti-Establishment ['æntɪɪs'tæblɪʃmənt] ADJ en contra del sistema

antifeminism [,æntɪ'femɪnɪzəm] N antifeminismo *m*

antifeminist [,æntɪ'femɪnɪst] Ⓐ ADJ antifeminista Ⓑ N antifeminista *mf*

antifreeze ['æntɪ'fri:z] N anticongelante *m*

anti-friction ['æntɪ'frɪkʃən] ADJ antifriccional, contrafricción *inv*

antigen ['æntɪdʒən] N antígeno *m*

anti-glare ['æntɪ'gleər] ADJ antideslumbrante

anti-globalization ['æntɪ,gləʊbəlaɪ'zeɪʃən] N antiglobalización *f*; **~ protesters** manifestantes *mfpl* antiglobalización

Antigone [æn'tɪgənɪ] N Antígona

Antigua [æn'ti:gə] N Antigua *f*

anti-hero ['æntɪ,hɪərəʊ] N antihéroe *m*

anti-heroine ['æntɪ'herəʊɪn] N antiheroína *f*

antihistamine [,æntɪ'hɪstəmɪn] Ⓐ ADJ antihistamínico Ⓑ N antihistamínico *m*

anti-inflammatory ['æntɪɪn'flæmətərɪ] Ⓐ ADJ antiinflamatorio
Ⓑ N antiinflamatorio *m*

anti-inflationary [,æntɪɪn'fleɪʃnərɪ] ADJ antiinflacionista

anti-knock ['æntɪ'nɒk] ADJ antidetonante

Antilles [æn'tɪli:z] NPL Antillas *fpl*

anti-lock ['æntɪ'lɒk] ADJ [*device, brakes*] antibloque *inv*

antilogarithm [,æntɪ'lɒgərɪðəm] N antilogaritmo *m*

antimacassar ['æntɪmə'kæsər] N antimacasar *m*

antimagnetic [,æntɪmæg'netɪk] ADJ antimagnético

antimalarial [,æntɪmə'lɛərɪəl] ADJ antipalúdico

anti-marketeer ['æntɪ,mɑ:kə'tɪər] N (*Brit Pol*) persona *f* contraria al Mercado Común

antimatter ['æntɪ,mætər] N antimateria *f*

antimissile ['æntɪ'mɪsaɪl] ADJ antimisil

antimony ['æntɪmənɪ] N antimonio *m*

anti-motion sickness [,æntɪ'məʊʃən,sɪknɪs] ADJ [*pill*] contra el mareo

antinomy [æn'tɪnəmɪ] N antinomia *f*

antinuclear ['æntɪ'nju:klɪər] ADJ antinuclear

antinuke* [,æntɪ'nju:k] ADJ antinuclear

Antioch ['æntɪɒk] N Antioquía *f*

antioxidant ['æntɪ'ɒ:ksədənt] N antioxidante *m*

antiparasitic [,æntɪ,paerə'sɪtɪk] ADJ antiparasitario

antipathetic [,æntɪpə'θetɪk] ADJ hostil (**to** a)

antipathy [æn'tɪpəθɪ] N (*between people*) antipatía *f* (**between** entre; **towards, to** hacia); (*to thing*) aversión *f* (**towards, to** hacia, por)

antipersonnel ['æntɪpɜ:sə'nel] ADJ (*Mil*) destinado a causar bajas

antiperspirant [,æntɪ'pɜ:spərənt] Ⓐ ADJ antitranspirante
Ⓑ N antitranspirante *m*

antiphon ['æntɪfən] N antífona *f*

antiphony [æn'tɪfənɪ] N canto *m* antifonal

Antipodean, antipodean [æn,tɪpə'di:ən] Ⓐ ADJ de las antípodas; (*Brit hum*) (= *Australian*) australiano
Ⓑ N habitante *mf* de las antípodas; (*Brit hum*) (= *Australian*) australiano/a *m/f*

antipodes [æn'tɪpədi:z] NPL antípodas *fpl*; **the Antipodes** (*Brit esp hum*) Australia *f* (y Nueva Zelanda *f*)

antipope ['æntɪpəʊp] N antipapa *m*

antiprotectionist [,æntɪprə'tekʃənɪst] ADJ antiproteccionista

antiquarian [,æntɪ'kwɛərɪən] Ⓐ ADJ anticuario
Ⓑ N (= *collector*) coleccionista *mf* de antigüedades; (= *dealer*) anticuario/a *m/f*
Ⓒ CPD ► **antiquarian bookseller** N librero/a *m/f* de viejo ► **antiquarian bookshop** N librería *f* de viejo ► **antiquarian collection** N colección *f* de antigüedades

antiquary ['æntɪkwərɪ] N = **antiquarian B**

antiquated ['æntɪkweɪtɪd] ADJ (*pej*) anticuado

antique [æn'ti:k] Ⓐ ADJ [1] [*furniture, vase*] de época; [*bracelet*] antiguo
[2] (= *ancient*) antiguo, de la antigüedad; (*pej*) anticuado
Ⓑ N antigüedad *f*
Ⓒ CPD ► **antique dealer** N anticuario/a *m/f* ► **antique shop** N tienda *f* de antigüedades

antiqued [æn'ti:kt] ADJ [*furniture*] envejecido

antiquity [æn'tɪkwɪtɪ] N [1] (= *age, ancient times*) antigüedad *f*; **of great ~** muy antiguo; **high ~** remota antigüedad; **in ~** en la antigüedad, en el mundo antiguo
[2] **antiquities** antigüedades *fpl*

anti-racism ['æntɪ'reɪsɪzəm] N antirracismo *m*

anti-racist ['æntɪ'reɪsɪst] Ⓐ ADJ antirracista
Ⓑ N antirracista *mf*

anti-religious ['æntɪrɪ'lɪdʒəs] ADJ antirreligioso

anti-riot ['æntɪ'raɪət] ADJ [*police, troops*] antidisturbios

anti-roll ['æntɪ'rəʊl] CPD ► **anti-roll bar** N barra *f* estabilizadora, barra *f* antivuelco ► **anti-roll device** N estabilizador *m*

antirrhinum [,æntɪ'raɪnəm] N antirrino *m*

anti-rust ['æntɪ'rʌst] ADJ antioxidante

anti-segregationist ['æntɪsegrə'geɪʃənɪst] ADJ antisegregacionista

anti-semite ['æntɪ'si:maɪt] N antisemita *mf*

anti-semitic ['æntɪsɪ'mɪtɪk] ADJ antisemita

anti-semitism ['æntɪ'semɪtɪzəm] N antisemitismo *m*

antiseptic [,æntɪ'septɪk] Ⓐ ADJ antiséptico
Ⓑ N antiséptico *m*

anti-skid ['æntɪ'skɪd] ADJ antideslizante

anti-slavery ['æntɪ'sleɪvərɪ] ADJ en contra de la esclavitud

anti-smoking ['æntɪ'sməʊkɪŋ] ADJ antitabaco

antisocial ['æntɪ'səʊʃəl] ADJ [1] (= *offensive*) [*behaviour, tendency*] antisocial
[2] (= *unsociable*) insociable

antistatic ['æntɪ'stætɪk] ADJ antiestático

anti-strike ['æntɪ'straɪk] ADJ antihuelga

anti-submarine ['æntɪsʌbmə'ri:n] ADJ antisubmarino

anti-tank ['æntɪ'tæŋk] ADJ antitanque

anti-terrorist ['æntɪ'terərɪst] ADJ antiterrorista

anti-theft [,æntɪ'θeft] CPD ► **anti-theft device** N sistema *m* antirrobo

antithesis [æn'tɪθɪsɪs] N (*pl* **antitheses** [æn'tɪθɪsi:z]) antítesis *f inv*

antithetic [,æntɪ'θetɪk] ADJ = **antithetical**

antithetical [,æntɪ'θetɪkəl] ADJ antitético

antithetically [,æntɪ'θetɪkəlɪ] ADV por antítesis

antitoxic ['æntɪ'tɒksɪk] ADJ antitóxico

antitoxin ['æntɪ'tɒksɪn] N antitoxina *f*

anti-trust ['æntɪ'trʌst] Ⓐ ADJ (*US*) antimonopolista
Ⓑ CPD ► **anti-trust law** N ley *f* antimonopolios ► **anti-trust legislation** N legislación *f* antimonopolios

antivirus [,æntɪ'vaɪərəs] ADJ [*program, software, company*] antivirus *inv*

antivivisection ['æntɪ,vɪvɪ'sekʃən] Ⓐ N antiviviseccionismo *m*
Ⓑ CPD ► **antivivisection movement** N movimiento *m* antiviviseccionista

antivivisectionism ['æntɪ,vɪvɪ'sekʃənɪzəm] N antiviviseccionismo *m*

antivivisectionist ['æntɪ,vɪvɪ'sekʃənɪst] N antiviviseccionista *mf*

anti-war [,æntɪ'wɔ:r] ADJ antibelicista, pacifista

anti-wrinkle ['æntɪ'rɪŋkl] ADJ antiarrugas

antler ['æntlər] N cuerna *f*, asta *f*; **antlers** cornamenta *fsing*

Antony ['æntənɪ] N Antonio

antonym ['æntənɪm] N antónimo *m*

antonymy [æn'tɒnɪmɪ] N antonimia *f*

antsy‡ ['æntsɪ] ADJ (*US*) nervioso, inquieto

Antwerp ['æntwɜ:p] N Amberes *m*

anus ['eɪnəs] N ano *m*

anvil ['ænvɪl] N yunque *m*

anxiety [æŋ'zaɪətɪ] Ⓐ N [1] (= *concern*) preocupación *f*, inquietud *f*; **he expressed his anxieties about the future** expresó su preocupación *or* inquietud por el futuro; **we've had a lot of ~ over the children's health** hemos estado muy preocupados por la salud de los niños; **it is a great ~ to me** me preocupa mucho
[2] (= *keenness*) ansia *f*, afán *m*; **~ to do sth** ansia *or* afán de hacer algo; **in his ~ to leave, he forgot his case** estaba tan ansioso por irse que olvidó su maleta

[3] (*Med, Psych*) ansiedad *f*, angustia *f*
(B) CPD ► **anxiety attack** N ataque *m* de ansiedad ► **anxiety neurosis** N neurosis *f inv* de ansiedad

anxious ['æŋkʃəs] ADJ [1] (= *worried*) [*person*] preocupado, inquieto; [*expression*] de preocupación, de inquietud; [*face, eyes*] angustiado; **you'd better go home, your mother will be ~** es mejor que te vayas a casa, tu madre estará preocupada *or* inquieta; **to be ~ about sth** estar preocupado por algo; **he was ~ about starting his new job** le preocupaba empezar en el nuevo trabajo; **I'm very ~ about you** me tienes muy preocupado; **to become** *or* **get ~** ponerse nervioso; **to feel ~** estar preocupado, estar inquieto; **with an ~ glance** con una mirada llena de preocupación *or* inquietud; **in an ~ voice** en un tono angustiado
[2] (= *worrying*) [*situation, wait*] angustioso; [*hours, days*] lleno de ansiedad, angustioso; **it's been a very ~ time for me** ha sido un periodo muy angustioso para mí, he pasado un periodo lleno de ansiedad; **it was an ~ moment** fue un momento angustioso
[3] (= *keen*) **he's ~ that nothing should go wrong** no quiere que exista el más mínimo riesgo de que algo salga mal, no quiere de ninguna manera que nada vaya mal; **I am very ~ that he should go** quiero que vaya a toda costa; **she is ~ to see you before you go** tiene muchas ganas de verte antes de que te vayas; **I'm not very ~ to go** tengo pocas ganas de ir; **~ to please her mother, she cleaned the house** deseosa de *or* deseando agradar a su madre, limpió la casa; **to be ~ for reform** desear *or* ansiar una reforma; **he is ~ for results** está deseoso de *or* ansioso por ver resultados; **to be ~ for promotion/success** ansiar *or* ambicionar un ascenso/el éxito; **he was ~ for her to leave** estaba impaciente por que ella se marchara, tenía muchas ganas de que ella se marchara
[4] (*Med, Psych*) [*feeling*] de angustia; [*person*] que padece de ansiedad; **to be ~** padecer ansiedad

anxiously ['æŋkʃəslɪ] ADV [1] (= *worriedly*) [*look, wait*] con preocupación, con inquietud; **"am I boring you?" she said, ~** —¿te aburro? —dijo con ansiedad
[2] (= *keenly, eagerly*) ansiosamente, con ansiedad

anxiousness ['æŋkʃəsnɪs] N [1] (= *concern*) preocupación *f*, inquietud *f*; (= *fear*) (*also Med, Psych*) ansiedad *f*, angustia *f*
[2] (= *keenness*) ansia *f*, afán *m*; **~ to do sth** ansia *or* afán de hacer algo

any ['enɪ]

[A] ADJECTIVE	[C] ADVERB
[B] PRONOUN	

(A) ADJECTIVE

[1] ***in questions***

When **any** *modifies an uncountable noun in questions it is usually not translated:*

have you got ~ money? ¿tienes dinero?; **is there ~ sugar?** ¿hay azúcar?

When **any** *modifies a plural noun in questions it is often not translated. However, if a low number is expected in response,* **algún/alguna** *+ singular noun is used:*

are there ~ tickets left? ¿quedan entradas?; **did they find ~ survivors?** ¿hubo supervivientes?; **do you speak ~ foreign languages?** ¿hablas algún idioma extranjero?; **do you have ~ questions?** ¿alguna pregunta?

[2] ***with negative, implied negative***

When **any** *modifies an uncountable noun it is usually not translated:*

I haven't ~ money no tengo dinero; **I have hardly ~ money left** casi no me queda dinero

When the translation is countable, **ningún/ninguna** *+ singular noun can be used:*

you haven't ~ excuse no tienes ninguna excusa; **she accepted without ~ hesitation** aceptó sin ninguna duda; **we got him home without ~ problem** lo llevamos a casa sin ningún problema

When **any** *modifies a plural noun, it is either left untranslated or, for greater emphasis, translated using* **ningún/ninguna** *+ singular noun:*

he hasn't got ~ friends no tiene amigos; **I can't see ~ cows** no veo ninguna vaca; **I won't do ~ such thing!** ¡no voy a hacer una cosa semejante!

[3] ***in conditional constructions***

Any *+ plural noun is often translated using* **algún/alguna** *+ a singular noun:*

if there are ~ problems let me know si hay algún problema, me lo dices; **if there are ~ tickets left** si queda alguna entrada; [BUT] **if he had ~ decency he would apologize** si tuviera un poco de decencia, se disculparía; **if it is in ~ way inconvenient to you ...** si por cualquier razón le resultara inconveniente ...

[4] ***= no matter which*** cualquier; **~ teacher will tell you** te lo dirá cualquier profesor; **bring me ~ (old) book** tráeme un libro cualquiera; **buy ~ two tins of soup and get one free** por cada dos latas de sopa cualesquiera que compre le regalamos otra; **wear ~ hat (you like)** ponte el sombrero que quieras; **he's not just ~ violinist** no es un violinista cualquiera; **take ~ one you like** tome cualquiera, tome el que quiera; **it could have happened to ~ one of us** le podría haber pasado a cualquiera de nosotros; **it's much like ~ other seaside resort** es muy parecido a cualquier otro sitio costero; **come at ~ time** ven cuando quieras; **we can cater for up to 300 guests at ~ one time** podemos proveer hasta a 300 invitados en cada ocasión; **~ person who** *or* **that breaks the rules will be punished** se castigará a toda persona que no acate las reglas; *see also* **day A1, minute 1, moment 1, case A3, rate A2**

[5] ***in set expressions*** **~ amount of: they'll spend ~ amount of money to get it** se gastarán lo que haga falta para conseguirlo; **~ number of: there must be ~ number of people in my position** debe haber gran cantidad de personas en mi situación; **I've told you ~ number of times** te lo he dicho montones de veces

(B) PRONOUN

[1] ***in questions***

When **any** *refers to an uncountable noun in questions it is usually not translated:*

I fancy some soup, have we got ~? me apetece sopa, ¿tenemos?; **is there ~ milk left?** ¿queda (algo de) leche?

When **any** *refers to a plural noun in questions it is often translated using* **alguno/alguna** *in the singular:*

I need a stamp, have you got ~? necesito un sello, ¿tienes alguno?; **do ~ of you know the answer?** ¿sabe alguno (de vosotros) la respuesta?; **have ~ of them arrived?** ¿ha llegado alguno (de ellos)?

[2] ***with negative, implied negative***

When **any** *refers to an uncountable noun it is usually not translated:*

"can I have some bread?" — "we haven't ~" —¿hay pan? —no nos queda nada *or* no tenemos

When **any** *refers to a plural noun, it is either left untranslated or, for greater emphasis, translated using* **ningún/ninguna** *in the singular:*

"did you buy the oranges?" — "no, there weren't ~" ¿compraste (las) naranjas? —no, no había *or* no tenían; **she has two brothers but I haven't got ~** tiene dos hermanos pero yo no tengo ninguno; **I don't like ~ of them** no me gusta ninguno; **I don't believe ~ of them has done it** no creo que lo haya hecho ninguno de ellos; [BUT] **he hasn't done ~ of his homework** no ha hecho nada de deberes

[3] ***in conditional constructions*** **if ~ of you knows how to drive** si alguno de vosotros sabe conducir; **few, if ~, survived** pocos, si alguno, sobrevivió

[4] ***= no matter which*** cualquiera; **~ of those books will do** cualquiera de esos libros servirá; **it's better than ~ of his other films** es mejor que cualquiera de sus otras películas

(C) ADVERB

[1] ***in questions*** **would you like ~ more soup?** ¿quieres más sopa?; **is he ~ better?** ¿está (algo) mejor?

[2] ***with negative*** **don't wait ~ longer** no esperes más (tiempo); **I don't love him ~ more** ya no le quiero; **I couldn't do that ~ more than I could fly** yo puedo hacer eso tanto como volar; **the room didn't look ~ too clean** la habitación no parecía muy limpia

[3] ***esp US* = at all*** **it doesn't help us ~** eso no nos ayuda para nada; **does she sing ~?** ¿sabe cantar de una forma u otra?

anybody ['enɪbɒdɪ] PRON [1] (*in questions, conditional constructions*) alguien; **did you see ~?** ¿viste a alguien?; **has ~ got a pen?** ¿tiene alguien un bolígrafo?; **is this ~'s seat?** ¿es de alguien *or* alguno este asiento?, ¿está *or* hay alguien sentado aquí?; **is there ~ else I can talk to?** ¿hay alguien más con quien pueda hablar?; **if ~ calls, I'm not in** si llama alguien, no estoy; **if ~ can do it, he can** si alguien lo puede hacer, es él
[2] (*with negative, implied negative*) nadie; **I can't see ~** no veo a nadie; **she doesn't like ~ contradicting her** no le gusta que nadie la contradiga; **I didn't ask ~ else** no se le pregunté a nadie más; **hardly ~ came** apenas vino nadie; **there was hardly ~ there** casi no había nadie
[3] (= *no matter who*) cualquiera; **I need a volunteer, ~ will do** necesito un voluntario, cualquier persona *or* cualquiera sirve; **~ will tell you the same** cualquiera te diría lo mismo, todos te dirán lo mismo; **~ would have thought he had lost!** cualquiera habría pensado que había perdido!; **it's ~'s race** esta carrera la podría ganar cualquiera; **it would have defeated ~ but Jane** habría desanimado a cualquiera *or* a todos menos a Jane; **~ else would have laughed** cualquier otro se hubiera reído; **that's ~'s guess** ¡quién sabe!; **it's not available to just ~** no está a disposición de cualquier persona *or* cualquiera; **I'm not going to marry just ~** yo no me caso con cualquiera; **he's not just ~, he's the boss** no es cualquiera, es el jefe; **bring ~ you like** trae a quien quieras; **~ who** *or* **that wants to go back should go now** si alguno quiere volver, que lo haga ahora; **I'll shoot ~**

who *or* **that moves** al primero que se mueva le disparo; **~ who** *or* **that invests in this** todo el que invierta en esto; **~ with any sense would know that!** ¡cualquiera con (algo de) sentido común sabría eso!

4 (= *person of importance*) alguien; **she knows everybody who's ~** conoce a todo el mundo que es alguien *or* importante

anyhow ['enɪhaʊ] ADV 1 = **anyway**

2 (*) (= *carelessly, haphazardly*) de cualquier modo, de cualquier manera; **he leaves things just ~** deja las cosas de cualquier modo *or* manera; **the books were all ~, on the floor** los libros estaban por el suelo de cualquier modo *or* manera; **I came in late and finished my essay off ~** volví tarde y terminé mi ensayo sin pensarlo mucho

anymore [,enɪ'mɔːʳ] ADV *see* **any C1, C2**

anyone ['enɪwʌn] PRON = **anybody**

anyplace* ['enɪpleɪs] PRON (*US*) = **anywhere**

anyroad‡ ['enɪrəʊd] ADV (*Brit*) = **anyway 1**

anything ['enɪθɪŋ] PRON 1 (*in questions, conditional constructions*) algo, alguna cosa; **do you need ~?** ¿necesitas algo *or* alguna cosa?; **would you like ~ to eat?** ¿quieres algo *or* alguna cosa de comer?; **is there ~ inside?** ¿hay algo *or* alguna cosa dentro?; **can ~ be done?** ¿se puede hacer algo *or* alguna cosa?; **are you doing ~ tonight?** ¿haces algo *or* alguna cosa esta noche?, ¿tienes algún plan para esta noche?; **is there ~ more boring than ...?** ¿puede haber algo más aburrido que ...?; **did you see ~ interesting?** ¿viste algo de interés?; **if ~ should happen to me** si algo me ocurriera; **if I hear ~ I'll tell you** si oigo algo, te lo diré; BUT **think before you say ~** piensa antes de decir nada; **~ else?** (*in shop etc*) ¿algo más?, ¿alguna cosa más?; **if ~ it's much better** es mucho mejor si cabe; **if ~ it's larger** si acaso, es algo más grande; **is there ~ in what he says?** ¿hay algo de verdad en lo que dice?; **have you heard ~ of them?** ¿tienes alguna noticia de ellos?

2 (*with negative, implied negative*) nada; **I can't see ~** no veo nada; **you haven't seen ~ yet** todavía no has visto nada; **can't ~ be done?** ¿no se puede hacer nada?; **I didn't see ~ interesting** no vi nada de interés; **we can't do ~ else** no podemos hacer otra cosa, no podemos hacer nada más; **hardly ~** casi nada; **I don't think there's ~ more annoying than ...** no creo que haya nada más irritante que ...; ✦**IDIOM not for ~ in the world** por nada del mundo

3 (*no matter what*) cualquier cosa; **~ could happen** puede pasar cualquier cosa; **they'll eat ~** comen de todo, comen cualquier cosa (*pej*); BUT **he will give you ~ (that) you ask for** te dará lo que pidas; **~ but that** todo menos eso; **"was she apologetic?" — "~ but!"** —¿se disculpó? —¡nada de eso!; **it was ~ but pleasant** fue cualquier cosa menos agradable, era de todo menos agradable; **their friendship was more important than ~ else** su amistad era más importante que todo lo demás; **~ else would be considered unacceptable** todo lo demás se consideraría inaceptable; **she wanted more than ~ else to be an actress** ella quería ser actriz por encima de todo; **he did it more out of pity than ~ else** más que nada lo hizo por compasión; **I'm not buying just ~** yo no compro cualquier cosa; **sing ~ you like** canta lo que quieras, canta cualquier cosa; **it could take ~ up to three months** podría llevar hasta tres meses; ✦**IDIOM I'd give ~ to know** daría cualquier cosa por saberlo

4 (*in guesses, estimates*) **he must have ~ between 15 and 20 apple trees** debe de tener entre 15 y 20 manzanos

5 (*in set expressions*) **as ~***: **she was as white as ~** estaba más pálida que todo, estaba de lo más pálida; **it's as clear as ~ what they want** lo que quieren está tan claro como el agua*, está muy claro lo que quieren; **as much as ~**: **I'm in it for the publicity as much as ~** más que nada estoy en esto por la publicidad; **it was a matter of principle as much as ~** era una cuestión de principios más que nada; **he ran like ~*** corrió hasta más no poder, corrió como loco*; **she cried like ~*** lloró como una descosida*; **or ~** (= *or anything like it*): **did she say who she was or ~?** ¿dijo quién era ella o algo por el estilo?; **he's not a minister or ~** no es ministro ni nada por el estilo; **he's not ugly or ~, just strange** no es feo ni nada por el estilo, sólo raro

anytime ['enɪtaɪm] ADV *see* **time A4**

anyway ['enɪweɪ], **anyways*** ['enɪweɪz] (*US*) ADV 1 (= *in any event*) de todas formas, de todos modos; **~, you're here** de todas formas *or* de todos modos, estás aquí; **~, it's not my fault** de todas formas *or* de todos modos, yo no tengo la culpa; **he doesn't want to go out and ~ he's not allowed** no quiere salir y de todas formas *or* de todos modos no le dejan; **whose money is this ~?** de todas formas *or* de todos modos, ¿de quién es el dinero?; **who needs men ~?** de todas formas *or* de todos modos, ¿quién necesita a los hombres?; **~, why invite somebody you never speak to?** de todas formas *or* de todos modos ¿por qué invitar a alguien con quien nunca hablas?

2 (= *regardless*) de todas formas, de todos modos; **I shall go ~** iré de todas formas *or* de todos modos; **he's not supposed to drink but he does ~** se supone que no debe beber, pero lo hace de todas formas *or* de todos modos

3 (= *at least*) al menos; **it's not a good idea, I don't think so ~** no es buena idea, al menos eso es lo que yo pienso

4 (= *incidentally*) por cierto; **why are you going ~?** por cierto ¿por qué te vas?

5 (*continuing what has been said*) en fin; **~, as I was saying ...** en fin, como decía antes ...; **so ~, this policeman came up to me and said ...** en fin, este policía se me acercó y dijo ...

anywhere ['enɪwɛəʳ] Ⓐ ADV 1 (*in questions*) (*location*) en alguna parte, en algún lugar *or* sitio; (*direction*) a alguna parte, a algún lugar *or* sitio; **have you seen my coat ~?** ¿has visto mi abrigo en *or* por alguna parte?, ¿has visto mi abrigo por algún sitio?; **can you see him ~?** ¿le ves por alguna parte *or* por algún sitio?; **did you visit ~ else?** ¿visitasteis algún otro sitio?

2 (*with negatives, implied negatives*) (*location*) por *or* en ninguna parte, por *or* en ningún sitio; (*direction*) a ninguna parte, a ningún sitio; **I can't find it ~** no lo encuentro por *or* en ninguna parte, no lo encuentro por *or* en ningún sitio; **I'm not going ~** no voy a ninguna parte, no voy a ningún sitio; **we didn't go ~ special** no fuimos a ningún sitio especial; **he was first and the rest didn't come ~** él se clasificó primero y los demás quedaron muy por debajo; **it's not available ~ else** no lo tienen en ningún otro sitio, no lo tienen en ninguna otra parte; **I wouldn't live ~ else** no viviría en ninguna otra parte, no viviría en ningún otro sitio; **I'm not going to live just ~** yo no voy a vivir en cualquier sitio; **it isn't ~ near Castroforte** está bastante lejos de Castroforte; **the house isn't ~ near big enough*** la casa no es ni por asomo lo bastante grande; **it isn't ~ near enough*** (*sum of money*) con eso no hay suficiente ni mucho menos; ✦**IDIOM that won't get you ~*** así no conseguirás nada

3 (*in affirmative sentences*) en cualquier parte; **put the books down ~** pon los libros en cualquier parte *or* donde sea; **~ you go you'll see the same** dondequiera que vayas verás lo mismo, verás lo mismo en cualquier parte a donde vayas; **sit ~ you like** siéntate donde quieras; **she leaves her things just ~** deja sus cosas en cualquier parte; **you can buy stamps almost ~** se pueden comprar sellos casi en cualquier sitio; **she could have been ~ between 30 and 50 years old** podría haber tenido desde 30 hasta 50 años; **it would be the same ~ else** sería lo mismo en cualquier otra parte; **~ from 200 to 300** (*US*) entre 200 y 300; **~ in the world** en cualquier parte del mundo

Ⓑ PRON **we haven't found ~ else to live** no hemos encontrado ningún otro sitio para vivir; **it's miles from ~** está completamente aislado; **a plane ticket to ~ in the world** un billete de avión a cualquier parte del mundo

Anzac ['ænzæk] N ABBR = **Australia-New Zealand Army Corps**

AOB ABBR (= **any other business**) ruegos *mpl* y preguntas

AOCB ABBR (= **any other competent business**) ruegos *mpl* y preguntas

AONB N ABBR (*Brit*) (= **Area of Outstanding Natural Beauty**) ≈ Paraje *m* Natural

aorist ['ɛərɪst] N aoristo *m*

aorta [eɪ'ɔːtə] N (*pl* **aortas, aortae** [eɪ'ɔːtiː]) aorta *f*

aortic [eɪ'ɔːtɪk] ADJ aórtico

AP N ABBR = **Associated Press**

apace [ə'peɪs] ADV (*frm*) aprisa, rápidamente

apache [ə'pætʃɪ] N apache *m*

apart [ə'pɑːt]

When **apart** *is an element in a phrasal verb, eg* **fall apart, tear apart**, *look up the verb.*

ADV 1 (= *separated*) **it was the first time we had been ~** era la primera vez que estábamos separados; **with one's feet ~** con los pies apartados; **the two towns are 10km ~** los dos pueblos están a 10km el uno del otro; **their birthdays are two days ~** sus cumpleaños se separan por dos días; **posts set equally ~** postes espaciados con regularidad *or* colocados a intervalos iguales; **to hold o.s. ~** mantenerse aparte; **to keep ~** separar, mantener aislado (**from** de); **he lives ~ from his wife** vive separado de su mujer; **they have lived ~ for six months** viven separados desde hace seis meses; **we live three doors ~** vivimos a tres puertas de ellos; **the house stands somewhat ~** la casa está algo aislada; **they stood a long way ~** estaban muy apartados (el uno del otro); **he stood ~ from the others** se mantuvo apartado de los otros; **I can't tell them ~** no puedo distinguir el uno del otro; *see also* **set apart**

2 (= *in pieces*) **to come** *or* **fall ~** romperse, deshacerse; **to take sth ~** desmontar algo; *see also* **fall apart, take apart, tear apart**

3 (= *aside*) **joking ~ ...** en serio ...; **these problems ~ ...** aparte de estos problemas ..., estos problemas aparte ...

4 **~ from** 4·1 (= *excluding*) aparte de; **~ from the fact that ...** aparte del hecho de que ...; **but quite ~ from that ...** pero aparte de eso ...

4·2 (= *except for*) **he ate everything ~ from the meat** comió todo menos *or* excepto la carne; **they all voted against ~ from John** todos votaron en contra aparte de John

apartheid [ə'pɑːteɪt] N apartheid *m*

aparthotel [ə'pɑːthəʊ,tel] N aparthotel *m*

apartment [ə'pɑːtmənt] Ⓐ N 1 (*US*) (= *flat*) piso *m*, departamento *m* (*LAm*)
2 (*Brit*) (= *room*) cuarto *m*, aposento *m* (*liter*); *see also* **state**
Ⓑ CPD ► **apartment hotel** N (*US*) aparthotel *m* ► **apartment house** N (*US*) casa *f* de apartamentos

apathetic [,æpə'θetɪk] ADJ apático; **to be ~ towards sth** ser indiferente hacia algo, no mostrar interés alguno en algo

apathetically [,æpə'θetɪkəlɪ] ADV con apatía, con indiferencia

apathy ['æpəθɪ] N apatía *f*, indiferencia *f*; **~ towards sth** indiferencia hacia algo, falta *f* de interés en algo

APB N ABBR (*US*) (= **all points bulletin**) *frase usada por la policía por "descubrir y aprehender"*

APC N ABBR = **armo(u)red personnel carrier**

ape [eɪp] Ⓐ N 1 (*Zool*) mono *m*, simio *m*, antropoide *mf*; ✦*IDIOM* **to go ~** (*US*‡) (= *lose one's temper*) ponerse como un energúmeno*, ponerse hecho una fiera*; (= *go crazy*) ponerse como una moto‡
2 (* *pej*) (= *person*) **you (great) ~!** ¡bestia!*
Ⓑ VT imitar, remedar

APEC ['eɪpek] N ABBR = **Asia Pacific Economic Co-operation**

Apennines ['æpɪnaɪnz] NPL Apeninos *mpl*

aperient [ə'pɪərɪənt] Ⓐ ADJ laxante
Ⓑ N laxante *m*

aperitif [ə,perɪ'tiːf] N aperitivo *m*

aperture ['æpətʃjʊəʳ] N 1 (= *crack*) rendija *f*, resquicio *m*
2 (*Phot*) abertura *f*

apeshit** ['eɪpʃɪt] ADJ (*esp US*) ✦*IDIOM* **to go ~** (= *lose one's temper*) ponerse como un energúmeno*, ponerse hecho una fiera*; (= *go crazy*) ponerse como una moto‡

APEX ['eɪpeks] N ABBR 1 (*Brit*) = **Association of Professional, Executive, Clerical and Computer Staff**
2 (*also* **apex**) = **Advance Purchase Excursion**; **~ fare** precio *m* APEX; **~ ticket** billete *m* APEX

apex ['eɪpeks] N (*pl* **apexes, apices** ['eɪpɪsiːz])
1 (*Math*) vértice *m*
2 (*fig*) cumbre *f*, cima *f*

aphasia [æ'feɪzɪə] N afasia *f*

aphid ['eɪfɪd] N áfido *m*

aphis ['eɪfɪs] N (*pl* **aphides** ['eɪfɪdiːz]) áfido *m*

aphonic [,eɪ'fɒnɪk] ADJ afónico

aphorism ['æfərɪzəm] N aforismo *m*

aphoristic [,æfə'rɪstɪk] ADJ aforístico

aphrodisiac [,æfrəʊ'dɪzɪæk] Ⓐ ADJ afrodisiaco
Ⓑ N afrodisiaco *m*

Aphrodite [,æfrəʊ'daɪtɪ] N Afrodita

API N ABBR (*US*) = **American Press Institute**

apiarist ['eɪpɪərɪst] N apicultor(a) *m/f*

apiary ['eɪpɪərɪ] N colmenar *m*

apiculture ['eɪpɪkʌltʃəʳ] N apicultura *f*

apiece [ə'piːs] ADV (= *for each person*) cada uno/a; (= *for each thing*) cada uno/a; **they had a gun ~** tenía cada uno un revólver; **he gave them an apple ~** dio una manzana a cada uno; **the rule is a dollar ~** la regla es un dólar por cabeza *or* persona

aplastic anaemia, **aplastic anemia** (*US*) [eɪ'plæstɪkə'niːmɪə] N anemia *f* aplástica

aplenty [ə'plentɪ] ADV (*liter*) **there was food ~** había comida abundante, había abundancia de comida

aplomb [ə'plɒm] N (*liter*) aplomo *m*; **with great ~** con gran aplomo *or* serenidad

APO N ABBR (*US*) = **Army Post Office**

Apocalypse [ə'pɒkəlɪps] N Apocalipsis *m*

apocalyptic [ə,pɒkə'lɪptɪk] ADJ apocalíptico

apocopate [ə'pɒkəpeɪt] VT apocopar

apocope [ə'pɒkəpɪ] N apócope *f*

Apocrypha [ə'pɒkrɪfə] NPL libros *mpl* apócrifos de la Biblia, Apócrifos *mpl*

apocryphal [ə'pɒkrɪfəl] ADJ apócrifo

apodosis [ə'pɒdəsɪs] N apódosis *f*

apogee ['æpədʒiː] N apogeo *m*

apolitical [,eɪpə'lɪtɪkəl] ADJ apolítico

Apollo [ə'pɒləʊ] N Apolo

apologetic [ə,pɒlə'dʒetɪk] ADJ [*look, smile, letter, tone*] de disculpa; **he came in with an ~ air** entró como pidiendo disculpas; **he didn't seem in the least ~** no parecía sentirlo en absoluto; **"oh, I'm sorry," said the girl, immediately ~** —ay, lo siento —dijo la niña disculpándose rápidamente; **twenty minutes late, a profusely ~ Mrs Perks arrived** la Sra. Perks llegó con veinte minutos de retraso disculpándose profusamente; **he was very ~** se deshizo en disculpas; **to be ~ about sth** disculparse por algo

apologetically [ə,pɒlə'dʒetɪkəlɪ] ADV **he smiled ~** sonrió como pidiendo disculpas; **"it's my fault," he said ~** —es culpa mía —dijo en tono de disculpa; **he came in ~** entró como pidiendo perdón

apologetics [ə,pɒlə'dʒetɪks] NSING apologética *f*

apologia [,æpə'ləʊdʒɪə] N apología *f*

apologist [ə'pɒlədʒɪst] N apologista *mf*

▼ **apologize** [ə'pɒlədʒaɪz] VI disculparse, pedir perdón; (*for absence etc*) presentar las excusas; **there's no need to ~** no hay de qué disculparse; **I ~!** ¡lo siento!; **to ~ to sb (for sth)** disculparse con algn (por algo); **he ~d for being late** se disculpó por llegar tarde; **to ~ for sb** disculparse *or* pedir perdón por algn; **never ~!** disculpas, ¡nunca!

apologue ['æpəlɒg] N apólogo *m*

▼ **apology** [ə'pɒlədʒɪ] N 1 (= *expression of regret*) disculpa *f*; **letter of ~** carta *f* de disculpa; **I demand an ~** exijo una disculpa; **to make** *or* **offer an ~** disculparse, presentar sus excusas (**for** por); **to make no ~** *or* **apologies for sth** no tener reparo en algo; **I make no apologies for being blunt** no tengo ningún reparo en serle franco; **please accept my apologies** le ruego me disculpe; **I owe you an ~** te debo una disculpa; **to send an ~** (*at meeting*) presentar sus excusas; **there are apologies from Gerry and Jane** se han excusado Gerry y Jane
2 (*Literat*) apología *f*
3 (*pej*) **an ~ for a stew** una birria de guisado; **this ~ for a letter** ésta que apenas se puede llamar carta

apophthegm ['æpəθem] N apotegma *m*

apoplectic [,æpə'plektɪk] ADJ 1 (*Med*) apoplético
2 (*) (= *very angry*) furioso; **to get ~** enfurecerse

apoplexy ['æpəpleksɪ] N 1 (*Med*†) apoplejía *f*
2 (= *rage*) cólera *f*, ira *f*

apostasy [ə'pɒstəsɪ] N apostasía *f*

apostate [ə'pɒstɪt] N apóstata *mf*

apostatize [ə'pɒstətaɪz] VI apostatar (**from** de)

a posteriori ['eɪpɒs,terɪ'ɔːraɪ] ADJ, ADV a posteriori

apostle [ə'pɒsl] N 1 (*Rel*) apóstol *m*
2 (*fig*) apóstol *m*, paladín *m*

apostolate [ə'pɒstəlɪt] N apostolado *m*

apostolic [,æpəs'tɒlɪk] Ⓐ ADJ apostólico; **the ~ coalition** la coalición apostólica
Ⓑ CPD ► **apostolic succession** N sucesión *f* apostólica

apostrophe [ə'pɒstrəfɪ] N 1 (*Ling*) apóstrofo *m*
2 (= *address*) apóstrofe *m*

apostrophize [ə'pɒstrəfaɪz] VT apostrofar

apothecary† [ə'pɒθɪkərɪ] N boticario *m*

apotheosis [ə,pɒθɪ'əʊsɪs] N (*pl* **apotheoses** [ə,pɒθɪ'əʊsiːz]) apoteosis *f*

appal, **appall** (*US*) [ə'pɔːl] VT horrorizar; **everyone was ~led** se horrorizaron todos, todos quedaron consternados; **I was ~led by the news** me horrorizó la noticia

Appalachia [,æpə'leɪtʃɪə] N *región de los (montes) Apalaches*

Appalachians [,æpə'leɪtʃənz] NPL (montes *mpl*) Apalaches *mpl*

appalling [ə'pɔːlɪŋ] ADJ [*sight, behaviour, weather, destruction*] espantoso, horroroso; [*suffering, crime, conditions*] atroz, espantoso; [*spelling, mistake, headache, smell*] espantoso; **he has ~ taste in clothes** tiene un gusto pésimo para la ropa; **her first novel was ~** su primera novela fue un horror

appallingly [ə'pɔːlɪŋlɪ] ADV 1 (= *badly*) [*sing, play*] pésimamente; [*treat*] espantosamente mal, terriblemente mal; [*suffer*] horriblemente, terriblemente; **he had behaved ~** se había portado fatal *or* terriblemente mal; **the situation has deteriorated ~** la situación ha empeorado de forma terrible
2 (= *extremely*) [*difficult, selfish, ignorant*] terriblemente; **the film was ~ bad** la película era pésima

apparatchik [,æpə'rættʃɪk] N 1 (*in Communist country*) miembro *m* del aparato del partido comunista, apparatchik *m*
2 (*in organization*) funcionario/a *m/f*, burócrata *mf*

apparatus [,æpə'reɪtəs] (*pl* **apparatus, apparatuses**) N 1 (*Anat, Mech*) aparato *m*; (= *set of instruments*) equipo *m*
2 (*fig*) (= *system*) sistema *m*, aparato *m*

apparel [ə'pærəl] Ⓐ N 1 (*Brit*†) atuendo *m*; (*hum*) atavío *m*
2 (*US*) ropa *f*
Ⓑ VT vestir (**in** de); (*hum*) trajear, ataviar (**in** de)

apparent [ə'pærənt] ADJ 1 (= *clear*) claro; **to be ~ that** estar claro que; **it was ~ that there were problems** estaba claro que había problemas; **it was immediately ~ that he was lying** enseguida se vio claramente que mentía; **to become ~** hacerse patente; **it became ~ that he was not coming** se hizo patente que no venía; **it is becoming ~ that we will have to find larger premises** ya se está viendo que vamos a tener que encontrar un local más grande; **this attitude is ~ in some of the things they say** esta actitud queda patente *or* se ve claramente en algunas de las cosas que dicen; **for no ~ reason** sin motivo aparente; **it was ~ to me that there were problems** veía claro *or* me resultaba obvio que había problemas
2 (= *seeming*) [*success, contradiction, interest*] aparente; **more ~ than real** más aparente que real
3 *see* **heir**

apparently [ə'pærəntlɪ] ADV 1 (= *it appears*) por lo visto, según parece; **~, they're getting**

➤ LANGUAGE IN USE: **apologize** 18.1 **apology 1** 18.1, 18.5

a divorce por lo visto *or* según parece, se van a divorciar; **"is she the new teacher?" — "apparently"** —¿es ella la nueva profesora? —por lo visto *or* eso parece; **"I thought they were coming" — "apparently not"** —pensé que venían —por lo visto no *or* parece que no
2 (= *seemingly, on the surface*) aparentemente; **to be ~ calm** estar aparentemente tranquilo; **an ~ harmless question** una pregunta aparentemente inocente; **the murders follow an ~ random pattern** los asesinatos parecen seguir un esquema aleatorio

apparition [ˌæpəˈrɪʃən] N 1 (= *ghost*) aparecido *m*, fantasma *m*
2 (= *appearance*) aparición *f*

▼**appeal** [əˈpiːl] Ⓐ N 1 (*requesting sth*) 1·1 (= *call*) llamamiento *m*, llamado *m* (*LAm*); (= *request*) petición *f*, solicitud *f*; **he made an ~ for calm** hizo un llamamiento a la calma; **to issue an ~ for aid for sb** hacer un llamamiento solicitando ayuda para algn; **the police repeated their ~ for witnesses to contact them** la policía volvió a hacer un llamamiento a posibles testigos del hecho para que se pusieran en contacto con ellos; **an ~ to arms/reason** un llamamiento a las armas/la cordura; **our ~ for volunteers** la petición *or* solicitud que hicimos de voluntarios
1·2 (= *entreaty*) súplica *f*; **he was deaf to all ~s** hacía oídos sordos a todas las súplicas
1·3 (= *campaign for donations*) **they launched a £5 million ~ for cancer research** realizaron una campaña para la recaudación de 5 millones de libras para la lucha contra el cáncer; **an ~ on behalf of a mental health charity** una petición de ayuda para una organización benéfica de salud mental
1·4 (*Jur*) apelación *f*, recurso *m* (de apelación); **his ~ was successful** su apelación *or* recurso (de apelación) dio resultado; **there is no ~ against his decision** su fallo es inapelable; **she won/lost the case on ~** ganó/perdió el caso en la apelación *or* en segunda instancia; **right of** *or* **to ~** derecho *m* de apelación, derecho *m* a apelar; **their lands were forfeit without ~** sus tierras fueron confiscadas sin posibilidad de apelación; *see also* **court**
2 (= *attraction*) atractivo *m*, encanto *m*; **the party's new name was meant to give it greater public ~** el nuevo nombre del partido tenía como objetivo atraer a más público; **the idea held little ~** la idea no le resultaba muy atrayente; *see* **sex**
Ⓑ VI 1 **to ~ for** (= *call publicly for*) [+ *peace, tolerance, unity*] hacer un llamamiento a; (= *request*) solicitar, pedir; **the authorities ~ed for calm** las autoridades hicieron un llamamiento a la calma; **the police have ~ed to the public for information** la policía ha hecho un llamamiento al público pidiendo información; **to ~ for funds** solicitar *or* pedir fondos; **he ~ed for silence** rogó silencio
2 (= *call upon*) **to ~ to sb's finer feelings/sb's generosity** apelar a los sentimientos nobles/la generosidad de algn; **to ~ to the country** (*Pol*) recurrir al arbitrio de las urnas
3 (*Jur*) apelar; **to ~ against** [+ *sentence, ruling*] apelar contra *or* de, recurrir (contra); **they have ~ed to the Supreme Court to stop her extradition** han apelado *or* recurrido al Tribunal Supremo para detener su proceso de extradición
4 (= *be attractive*) **that sort of comedy doesn't ~ any more** ese tipo de humor ya no gusta; **to ~ to sb** [*idea, activity*] atraer a algn, resultar atrayente a algn; **I don't think this will ~ to the public** no creo que esto le atraiga al público, no creo que esto le resulte atrayente al público; **it ~s to the child in everyone** hace salir al niño que llevamos dentro
Ⓒ VT (*US Jur*) **to ~ a decision/verdict** apelar contra *or* de una decisión/un veredicto, recurrir (contra) una decisión/un veredicto
Ⓓ CPD ► **appeal(s) committee** N comité *m* de apelación ► **appeal court** N tribunal *m* de apelación ► **appeal judge** N juez *mf* de apelación, jueza *f* de apelación ► **appeal(s) procedure** N procedimiento *m* de apelación ► **appeal(s) process** N proceso *m* de apelación

appealing [əˈpiːlɪŋ] ADJ 1 (= *attractive*) [*idea*] atractivo, atrayente; **the idea would be very ~ to Britain** la idea resultaría muy atractiva *or* atrayente para Gran Bretaña; **the book is especially ~ to the younger reader** el libro es de especial interés para el lector joven; **they are trying to make the party more ~ to younger voters** intentan hacer que el partido atraiga al electorado joven
2 (= *beseeching*) [*look, eyes*] suplicante

appealingly [əˈpiːlɪŋlɪ] ADV 1 (= *attractively*) **a lock of hair fell ~ across his forehead** un mechón de pelo le caía sobre la frente de modo que resultaba muy atractivo *or* atrayente; **he found her ~ stubborn** su terquedad le resultaba atractiva *or* atrayente
2 (= *beseechingly*) de modo suplicante

appear [əˈpɪəʳ] VI 1 (= *arrive, become visible*) [*person, graffiti*] aparecer; [*ghost*] aparecerse; [*spot, stain, crack*] aparecer, salir; [*symptom*] aparecer, presentarse; **Trudy ~ed at last** por fin apareció Trudy; **he ~ed briefly to address his supporters** hizo una breve aparición para dirigirse a sus seguidores; **he ~ed without a tie** se presentó sin corbata; **he ~ed from nowhere** salió *or* apareció de la nada; **where did you ~ from?** ¿de dónde has salido?; **the sun ~ed from behind a cloud** el sol salió de detrás de una nube; **to ~ in public** aparecer en público; **to ~ to sb** (*as vision*) aparecerse a algn; **he ~ed to me in a dream** se me apareció en sueños
2 (*Theat, TV*) salir; **she ~ed in "Fuenteovejuna"** salió *or* hizo un papel en "Fuenteovejuna"; **she ~ed as Ophelia** hizo (el papel) de Ofelia; **to ~ on stage** aparecer en escena; **to ~ on television** salir en *or* por televisión
3 (*Jur*) 3·1 [*defendant*] comparecer; **to ~ before sb** comparecer ante algn; **to ~ in court** comparecer ante el tribunal *or* los tribunales; **to ~ on a charge of murder** comparecer acusado de homicidio
3·2 [*lawyer*] **to ~ for** *or* **on behalf of sb** representar a algn; **to ~ for the defence/the prosecution** representar a la defensa/la acusación
4 (= *be published*) salir, publicarse; **the book ~ed in 1960** el libro salió *or* se publicó en 1960; **the term first ~ed in print in 1530** el primer testimonio escrito del término se remonta a 1530; **it was her life's ambition to ~ in print** la ilusión de su vida era ver su nombre impreso
5 (= *seem*) parecer; **he ~s tired** parece cansado; **how does it ~ to you?** ¿qué impresión le da?; **it ~s to me that they are mistaken** me da la impresión de que *or* me parece que están equivocados; **they ~ not to like each other** parece que no se gustan, no parece que se gusten; **there ~s to be a mistake** parece que hay un error; **she ~ed not to notice** no pareció darse cuenta; **we must ~ to be fair** debemos dar la impresión de ser justos; **it ~s not** ◊ **it would ~ not** parece que no; **"he came then?" — "so it would ~"** —¿entonces él ha venido? —eso parece; **she got the job, or so it would ~** le dieron el trabajo, según parece
6 (= *become apparent*) **as will ~ in due course** según se verá a su debido tiempo

appearance [əˈpɪərəns] Ⓐ N 1 (= *act of showing o.s.*) aparición *f*; **to make an ~** aparecer, dejarse ver; **to make a personal ~** aparecer en persona; **to put in an ~** hacer acto de presencia
2 (*Theat, TV*) aparición *f*; **to make one's first ~** hacer su primera aparición, debutar; **his ~ as Don Mendo** su actuación en el papel de Don Mendo; **his ~ in "Don Mendo"** su actuación en "Don Mendo"; **cast in order of ~** personajes *mpl* en orden de aparición en escena
3 (*Jur*) comparecencia *f*; **to make an ~ in court** comparecer ante el tribunal
4 [*of book etc*] publicación *f*
5 (= *look*) aspecto *m*; **she takes great care over her ~** cuida mucho su aspecto; **at first ~** a primera vista; **to have a dignified ~** tener aspecto solemne; **he had the ~ of an executive** parecía ejecutivo, tenía aspecto de ejecutivo; **in ~** de aspecto
6 **appearances** apariencias *fpl*; **~s can be deceptive** las apariencias engañan; **to** *or* **by all ~s** al parecer; **contrary to all ~s** en contra de las apariencias; **you shouldn't go by ~s** no hay que fiarse de las apariencias; **to judge by ~s, …** a juzgar por las apariencias, …; **to keep up ~s** guardar las apariencias; **for the sake of ~s** ◊ **for ~s' sake** para guardar las apariencias
Ⓑ CPD ► **appearance money** N remuneración *f* por hacer acto de presencia

appease [əˈpiːz] VT 1 (= *pacify*) [+ *person*] apaciguar, calmar; [+ *anger*] aplacar
2 (= *satisfy*) [+ *person*] satisfacer; [+ *hunger*] saciar; [+ *curiosity*] satisfacer, saciar
3 (*Pol*) apaciguar, contemporizar con

appeasement [əˈpiːzmənt] N 1 (= *pacification*) [*of person*] apaciguamiento *m*; [*of anger*] aplacamiento *m*
2 (*Pol*) contemporización *f*, entreguismo *m*

appellant [əˈpelənt] N apelante *mf*

appellate [əˈpelɪt] ADJ **~ court** (*US Jur*) tribunal *m* de apelación

appellation [ˌæpeˈleɪʃən] N (= *name*) nombre *m*; (= *title*) título *m*; [*of wine*] denominación *f* de origen

append [əˈpend] (*frm*) VT 1 (= *add*) [+ *signature*] añadir; [+ *note*] agregar, añadir
2 (= *attach*) adjuntar
3 (*Comput*) anexionar (al final)

appendage [əˈpendɪdʒ] N 1 (*frm*) (= *adjunct*) apéndice *m*
2 (*fig*) pegote* *m*

appendectomy [ˌæpenˈdektəmɪ] N apendectomía *f*

appendicitis [əˌpendɪˈsaɪtɪs] N apendicitis *f inv*; **to have ~** tener apendicitis; **acute ~** apendicitis *f* aguda

appendix [əˈpendɪks] N (*pl* **appendixes**, **appendices** [əˈpendɪsiːz]) 1 (*Anat*) apéndice *m*; **to have one's ~ out** hacerse extirpar el apéndice
2 [*of book*] apéndice *m*

apperception [ˌæpəˈsepʃən] Ⓐ N (*frm*) percepción *f*
Ⓑ CPD ► **apperception test** N (*US*) test *m* de percepción

appertain [ˌæpəˈteɪn] VI **to ~ to** relacionarse con, tener que ver con

➤ LANGUAGE IN USE: **appeal** B4 7.2

appetite ['æpɪtaɪt] N [1] (*for food*) apetito *m*; **to eat with an ~** comer con buen apetito *or* con ganas; **to have a good ~** tener buen apetito; **to have no ~** no tener apetito; *see also* **suppressant**
[2] (*fig*) deseo *m*, anhelo *m* (**for** de); **they had no ~ for further fighting** ya no les apetecía seguir luchando, no tenían más ganas de luchar; **it spoiled their ~ for going abroad** eso les quitó las ganas de ir al extranjero

appetizer ['æpɪtaɪzəʳ] N (= *drink*) aperitivo *m*; (= *food*) aperitivo *m*, tapas *fpl* (*Sp*), botanas *fpl* (*Mex*), bocaditos *mpl* (*Peru*)

appetizing ['æpɪtaɪzɪŋ] ADJ apetitoso

Appian Way ['æpɪən'weɪ] N Vía *f* Apia

applaud [ə'plɔ:d] Ⓐ VT [1] [*audience, spectators*] aplaudir
[2] (*fig*) [+ *decision, efforts*] aplaudir
Ⓑ VI aplaudir

applause [ə'plɔ:z] N [1] (= *clapping*) aplausos *mpl*; **a round of ~ for Peter!** ¡un aplauso para Peter!; **there was loud ~** sonaron fuertes aplausos
[2] (= *approval*) aprobación *f*; (= *praise*) alabanza *f*, aplauso *m*; **to win the ~ of** ganarse la aprobación de

apple ['æpl] Ⓐ N (= *fruit*) manzana *f*; (= *tree*) manzano *m*; **~ of discord** manzana *f* de la discordia; ✦*IDIOMS* **~s and pears** (*Brit*‡) (= *stairs*) escalera *f*; **the Big Apple** (*US**) la Gran Manzana, Nueva York *f*; → CITY NICKNAMES; **the ~ of one's eye** la niña de los ojos de algn; **one bad** *or* **rotten ~ can spoil the whole barrel** manzana podrida echa ciento a perder
Ⓑ CPD ► **apple blossom** N flor *f* del manzano ► **apple brandy** N licor *m* de manzana ► **apple core** N corazón *m* de manzana ► **apple dumpling** N *postre a base de manzana asada y masa* ► **apple fritter** N manzana *f* rebozada ► **apple orchard** N manzanar *m*, manzanal *m* ► **apple pie** N pastel *m* de manzana, pay *m* de manzana (*LAm*); *see also* **apple-pie** ► **apple sauce** N (*Culin*) compota *f* de manzana; (*US**) (= *hokum*) tonterías *fpl* ► **apple tart** N tarta *f* de manzana ► **apple tree** N manzano *m*

applecart ['æplkɑ:t] N ✦*IDIOM* **to upset** *or* **overturn the ~** echarlo todo a rodar, desbaratar los planes

apple-green ['æplgri:n] Ⓐ ADJ verde manzana *inv*
Ⓑ N verde *m* manzana

applejack ['æpldʒæk] N (*US*) licor *m* de manzana

apple-pie ['æpl'paɪ] ADJ **in ~ order** en perfecto orden; **to make sb an ~ bed** (*Brit*) hacerle la petaca a algn; *see also* **apple**

applet [æplɪt] N applet *m*

appliance [ə'plaɪəns] N [1] (= *device*) aparato *m*; **electrical ~** (aparato *m*) electrodoméstico *m*
[2] (= *application*) [*of skill, knowledge*] aplicación *f*
[3] (*Brit*) (*also* **fire ~**) coche *m* de bomberos

applicability [,æplɪkə'bɪlɪtɪ] N aplicabilidad *f*

applicable [ə'plɪkəbl] ADJ aplicable, pertinente (**to** a); **delete what is not ~** táchese lo que no proceda; **this law is also ~ to foreigners** esta ley es aplicable *or* se refiere también a los extranjeros; **a rule ~ to all** una regla que se extiende a todos

applicant ['æplɪkənt] N [1] (*for job etc*) aspirante *mf*, candidato/a *m/f* (**for** a)
[2] (*for money, assistance*) solicitante *mf*
[3] (*Jur*) suplicante *mf*

application [,æplɪ'keɪʃən] Ⓐ N [1] [*of ointment etc*] aplicación *f*; **"for external application only"** "para uso externo"
[2] (= *request*) solicitud *f*, petición *f* (**for** de); **~ for shares** solicitud *f* de acciones; **~s in triplicate** las solicitudes por triplicado; **to make an ~ for** solicitar; **to make an ~ to** dirigirse a; **prices on ~** los precios, a solicitud; **details may be had on ~ to the office** los detalles pueden obtenerse mediante solicitud a nuestra oficina; **are you going to put in an ~?** ¿te vas a presentar?; **to submit one's ~** presentar su solicitud
[3] (= *diligence*) aplicación *f*; **he lacks ~** le falta aplicación
Ⓑ CPD ► **application form** N solicitud *f* ► **applications package** N (*Comput*) paquete *m* de programas de aplicación ► **application(s) program** N (*Comput*) programa *m* de aplicación *or* aplicaciones ► **application(s) software** N (*Comput*) paquete *m* de aplicación *or* aplicaciones

applicator ['æplɪkeɪtəʳ] N aplicador *m*

applied [ə'plaɪd] ADJ aplicado; **~ linguistics** lingüística *fsing* aplicada; **~ mathematics** matemáticas *fpl* aplicadas; **~ science** ciencias *fpl* aplicadas

appliqué [æ'pli:keɪ] N (*also* **~ lace, ~ work**) encaje *m* de aplicación

▼**apply** [ə'plaɪ] Ⓐ VT [1] [+ *ointment, paint etc*] aplicar (**to** a); **to ~ heat to a surface** (*Tech*) exponer una superficie al calor; (*Med*) calentar una superficie; **to ~ a match to sth** prender fuego a algo con una cerilla
[2] (= *impose*) [+ *rule, law*] aplicar, emplear
[3] (= *use*) **to ~ the brakes** frenar; **to ~ pressure on sth** ejercer presión sobre algo; **to ~ pressure on sb** (*fig*) presionar a algn
[4] (= *dedicate*) **to ~ one's mind to a problem** dedicarse a resolver un problema; **to ~ o.s. to a task** dedicarse *or* aplicarse a una tarea
Ⓑ VI [1] (= *be relevant*) ser aplicable, ser pertinente; **cross out what does not ~** táchese lo que no proceda; **to ~ to** (= *be applicable to*) ser aplicable a, referirse a; **the law applies to everybody** la ley es aplicable a *or* de obligado cumplimiento para todos; **this rule doesn't ~ to us** esta norma no nos afecta
[2] (*for job, audition*) presentarse; **are you ~ing?** ¿te vas a presentar?; **"please apply at the office"** "diríjanse a la oficina"; **to ~ to sb** dirigirse a algn, acudir a algn; **to ~ for** [+ *scholarship, grant, assistance*] solicitar, pedir; [+ *job*] solicitar, presentarse a; **"patent applied for"** "patente en trámite"; **to ~ to sb for sth** solicitar algo a algn; *see also* **within**

appoggiatura [ə,pɒdʒə'tʊərə] N (*pl* **appoggiaturas, appoggiature** [ə,pɒdʒə'tʊəre]) apoyatura *f*

appoint [ə'pɔɪnt] VT [1] (= *nominate*) nombrar (**to** a); **they ~ed him chairman** le nombraron presidente; **they ~ed him to do it** le nombraron para hacerlo
[2] (*frm*) [+ *time, place*] fijar, señalar (**for** para); **at the ~ed time** a la hora señalada

appointee [əpɔɪn'ti:] N persona *f* nombrada

appointive [ə'pɔɪntɪv] ADJ **~ position** (*US*) *puesto que se cubre por nombramiento*

appointment [ə'pɔɪntmənt] Ⓐ N [1] (= *arrangement to meet*) [1·1] (*with client, bank manager etc*) cita *f*; **to meet sb by ~** reunirse con algn mediante cita previa; **I have an ~ at ten** tengo cita a las diez; **do you have an ~?** (*to caller*) ¿tiene usted cita?; **to keep an ~** acudir a una cita; **to make an ~ (with sb)** concertar una cita (con algn); **to make an ~ for three o'clock** pedir (una) cita para las tres
[1·2] (*with dentist, doctor, hairdresser etc*) hora *f*; **I have an ~ at ten** tengo hora a las diez; **do you have an ~?** ¿tiene usted hora?; **to make an ~ (with sb)** pedir hora (con algn); **to make an ~ for three o'clock** pedir hora para las tres
[2] (*to a job*) nombramiento *m* (**to** para); (= *job*) puesto *m*, empleo *m*; **there are still several ~s to be made** todavía hay varios nombramientos por hacer; **"by appointment to HRH"** "proveedores oficiales de S.A.R."; **"appointments (vacant)"** (*Press*) "oferta de empleo"
[3] **appointments** (*frm*) (= *furniture etc*) mobiliario *msing*
Ⓑ CPD ► **appointments board, appointments service** N (*Univ etc*) oficina *f* de colocación ► **appointments bureau** N agencia *f* de colocaciones

apportion [ə'pɔ:ʃən] VT [+ *resources etc*] repartir, distribuir; [+ *blame*] asignar; **the blame is to be ~ed equally** todos tienen la culpa por partes iguales

apportionment [ə'pɔ:ʃənmənt] N [1] [*of resources etc*] reparto *m*, distribución *f*
[2] (*US Pol*) delimitación *f* de distritos *or* condados

apposite ['æpəzɪt] ADJ apropiado (**to** para)

apposition [,æpə'zɪʃən] N [1] [*of position*] yuxtaposición *f*
[2] (*Gram*) aposición *f*; **in ~** en aposición

appositional [,æpə'zɪʃənl] ADJ aposicional

appraisal [ə'preɪzəl] N [1] (= *valuation*) tasación *f*, valoración *f*
[2] [*of worth, importance*] estimación *f*, apreciación *f*; [*of situation, employee*] evaluación *f*

appraise [ə'preɪz] VT [1] (= *value*) [+ *property, jewellery*] tasar, valorar
[2] (= *assess*) [+ *worth, importance*] estimar, apreciar; [+ *situation*] evaluar; [+ *staff*] evaluar
[3] (*US*) (= *price*) tasar

appraiser [ə'preɪzəʳ] N (*US Comm, Fin*) tasador(a) *m/f*

appraising [ə'preɪzɪŋ] ADJ [*look etc*] apreciativo

appreciable [ə'pri:ʃəbl] ADJ [1] (= *noticeable*) apreciable; **an ~ difference** una diferencia apreciable
[2] (= *large*) importante, considerable; **an ~ sum** una cantidad importante *or* considerable

appreciably [ə'pri:ʃəblɪ] ADV [*change, grow*] sensiblemente, perceptiblemente; **he is ~ older than his brother** es considerablemente mayor que su hermano; **the weather had turned ~ colder** el tiempo se había vuelto bastante más frío

appreciate [ə'pri:ʃɪeɪt] Ⓐ VT [1] (= *be grateful for*) agradecer; **I ~d your help** agradecí tu ayuda; **I ~ the gesture** agradezco el detalle; **we should much ~ it if ...** agradeceríamos mucho que + *subjun*
[2] (= *value, esteem*) apreciar, valorar; **he does not ~ music** no sabe apreciar *or* valorar la música; **I am not ~d here** aquí no se me aprecia *or* valora; **we much ~ your work** tenemos un alto concepto de su trabajo
[3] (= *understand*) [+ *problem, difference*] comprender; **I ~ your wishes** comprendo sus deseos; **yes, I ~ that** sí, lo comprendo; **to ~ that ...** comprender que ...; **we fully ~ that ...** comprendemos perfectamente que ...
[4] (= *be sensitive to*) percibir; **the smallest change can be ~d on this machine** en esta máquina se percibe el más leve cambio
Ⓑ VI [*property etc*] revalorizarse, aumentar(se) en valor

➤ LANGUAGE IN USE: **apply B2** 19.4

appreciation [əˌpriːʃɪ'eɪʃən] N [1] (= *understanding*) comprensión *f*; [*of art etc*] aprecio *m*; **he showed no ~ of my difficulties** no reconoció mis dificultades; **you have no ~ of art** no sabes apreciar el arte, no entiendes de arte
[2] (= *gratitude*) gratitud *f*, agradecimiento *m*; (= *recognition*) apreciación *f*, reconocimiento *m*; **as a token of my ~** en señal de mi gratitud *or* agradecimiento; **she smiled her ~** sonrió agradecida
[3] (= *report*) informe *m*; (= *obituary*) nota *f* necrológica, necrológica *f*; (*Literat*) crítica *f*, comentario *m*
[4] (= *rise in value*) revalorización *f*, aumento *m* en valor

appreciative [ə'priːʃɪətɪv] ADJ [1] (= *grateful*) [*person*] agradecido; [*smile*] de agradecimiento; [*look*] lleno de agradecimiento; **to be ~ of** [+ *kindness, efforts*] mostrarse agradecido por, agradecer; **he was very ~ of what I had done** se mostró muy agradecido por lo que yo había hecho, agradeció mucho lo que yo había hecho
[2] (= *admiring*) [*person*] apreciativo; [*comment*] elogioso; [*look, whistle*] de admiración; **it's rewarding to act before an ~ audience** es gratificante actuar ante un público que sabe apreciar la calidad de lo que ve *or* ante un público apreciativo; **to be ~ of** [+ *art, music, good food*] saber apreciar
[3] (= *aware*) **to be ~ of** [+ *danger, risk*] ser capaz de apreciar; **they were not fully ~ of the danger that lay ahead** no eran capaces de apreciar del todo el peligro que les acechaba

appreciatively [ə'priːʃɪətɪvlɪ] ADV **he accepted the gift ~** aceptó el regalo agradecido; **the audience clapped** *or* **applauded ~** el público aplaudió agradecido; **she smiled ~** sonrió con admiración, sonrió agradecida

apprehend [ˌæprɪ'hend] (*frm*) VT [1] (= *arrest*) detener, aprehender
[2] (= *understand*) comprender
[3] (= *fear*) recelar, recelar de

apprehension [ˌæprɪ'henʃən] N [1] (= *fear*) aprensión *f*, temor *m*; **she was filled with ~ at the prospect** le invadía el temor ante esa perspectiva; **my chief ~ is that ...** mi mayor temor es que + *subjun*
[2] (*frm*) (= *awareness*) comprensión *f*
[3] (*frm*) (= *arrest*) detención *f*

apprehensive [ˌæprɪ'hensɪv] ADJ inquieto; **I was feeling a little ~** sentía cierta aprensión, me sentía inquieto; **he is ~ that he might fail the exam** teme *or* le preocupa suspender el examen; **she is ~ that some accident might befall her children** teme que *or* le preocupa que sus hijos puedan tener un accidente; **to be ~ about sth** estar inquieto por algo; **everyone is ~ about the ordeals to come** todos están inquietos por los terribles momentos que puedan avecinarse; **I'm a bit ~ about the trip** el viaje me tiene inquieto; **they're a little ~ about coming** les inquieta un poco la idea de venir; **we were both ~ about the reaction of the other players** ambos temíamos la reacción de los otros jugadores; **to grow ~** inquietarse; **he gave her an ~ look** la miró aprensivo *or* inquieto, le dirigió una mirada de aprensión *or* inquietud

apprehensively [ˌæprɪ'hensɪvlɪ] ADV con aprensión, con temor

apprentice [ə'prentɪs] Ⓐ N [1] (= *learner*) aprendiz(a) *m/f*
[2] (= *beginner*) principiante *mf*
Ⓑ VT **to ~ sb to** colocar a algn de aprendiz con; **to be ~d to** estar de aprendiz con
Ⓒ CPD ► **apprentice electrician** N aprendiz(a) *m/f* de electricista

apprenticeship [ə'prentɪʃɪp] N aprendizaje *m*; **to serve one's ~** hacer el aprendizaje

apprise [ə'praɪz] VT (*frm*) informar; **to ~ sb of sth** informar a algn de algo; **to be ~d of** estar al corriente de; **I was never ~d of your decision** no se me comunicó su decisión, no me informaron de su decisión

appro* ['æprəʊ] ABBR (*Comm*) = **approval**; **on ~** a prueba

approach [ə'prəʊtʃ] Ⓐ VT [1] (= *come near*) [+ *place*] acercarse a, aproximarse a; [+ *person*] abordar, dirigirse a; **he ~ed the house** se acercó *or* aproximó a la casa; **a man ~ed me in the street** un hombre me abordó en la calle
[2] (*with request etc*) dirigirse a; (= *speak to*) hablar con; **have you tried ~ing the mayor?** ¿has probado a dirigirte al alcalde?; **have you ~ed your bank manager about the loan?** ¿has hablado con el gerente del banco sobre el préstamo?; **he is difficult to ~** no es fácil abordarle
[3] (= *tackle*) [+ *subject, problem, job*] abordar; **we must ~ the matter with care** tenemos que abordar el asunto con mucho cuidado; **I ~ it with an open mind** me lo planteo sin ningún prejuicio; **it all depends on how we ~ it** depende de cómo lo enfoquemos
[4] (= *approximate to*) (*in quality*) aproximarse a; (*in appearance*) parecerse a; **here the colour ~es blue** aquí el color tira a azul; **it was ~ing midnight** era casi medianoche; **the performance ~ed perfection** la interpretación rayaba en la perfección; **he's ~ing 50** se acerca a los 50; **no other painter ~es him** (*fig*) no hay otro pintor que se le pueda comparar
Ⓑ VI acercarse
Ⓒ N [1] (= *act*) acercamiento *m*, aproximación *f*; **at the ~ of the enemy** al acercarse *or* aproximarse el enemigo; **at the ~ of Easter** al acercarse la Pascua; **at the ~ of night** al caer la noche; **we observed his ~** lo vimos acercarse
[2] (*to problem, subject*) enfoque *m*, planteamiento *m*; **a new ~ to maths** un nuevo enfoque *or* planteamiento sobre las matemáticas; **I don't like your ~ to this matter** no me gusta tu modo de enfocar esta cuestión; **we must think of a new ~** tenemos que idear otro método
[3] (= *offer*) oferta *f*, propuesta *f*; (= *proposal*) proposición *f*, propuesta *f*; **to make ~es to sb** dirigirse a algn; **to make amorous ~es to sb** (*liter*) requerir de amores a algn
[4] (= *access*) acceso *m* (**to** a); (= *road*) vía *f* de acceso, camino *m* de acceso; **~es** accesos *mpl*; (*Mil*) aproches *mpl*; **the northern ~es of the city** los accesos *or* las vías de acceso a la ciudad por el norte
[5] (*Golf*) aproximación *f*, golpe *m* de aproximación
Ⓓ CPD ► **approach light** N (*Aer*) baliza *f* de aproximación ► **approach road** N vía *f* de acceso, entrada *f* ► **approach shot** N (*Golf*) golpe *m* de aproximación

approachable [ə'prəʊtʃəbl] ADJ [*person*] accesible, abordable; [*place*] accesible; [*text, idea, work*] asequible

approaching [ə'prəʊtʃɪŋ] ADJ próximo, venidero; [*car, vehicle*] que se acerca en dirección opuesta, que viene en dirección contraria; **the ~ elections** las próximas elecciones

approbation [ˌæprə'beɪʃən] N aprobación *f*

appropriate Ⓐ [ə'prəʊprɪɪt] ADJ [*time, place, method, response*] apropiado, adecuado; [*moment*] oportuno, apropiado, adecuado; [*authority, department*] competente, correspondiente; **it is ~ that ...** resulta apropiado *or* adecuado que ...; **it may be ~ to discuss this with your solicitor** quizá sería conveniente que discutiera esto con su abogado; **she's the most ~ person to present the award** es la persona más indicada *or* más adecuada para presentar el premio; **to take ~ action** tomar las medidas apropiadas *or* adecuadas *or* pertinentes; **choose A, B or C as ~** elija A, B o C según corresponda; **this treatment was very ~ for our son** este tratamiento resultó ser muy apropiado *or* adecuado para nuestro hijo; **it would not be ~ for me to discuss individual cases** no sería apropiado que comentara casos concretos; **to take ~ precautions** tomar las debidas precauciones; **it seemed ~ to end with a joke** parecía apropiado terminar con un chiste; **words ~ to the occasion** palabras apropiadas *or* adecuadas para la ocasión; **a job ~ to his talents** un trabajo que se adecúa a sus aptitudes; **A, and where ~, B** A, y en su caso, B; **you will be answering queries, and, where ~, demonstrating our software** dará información a quien la pida y, si se presta, hará demostraciones de nuestro software
Ⓑ [ə'prəʊprɪeɪt] VT [1] (= *steal*) apropiarse de
[2] (= *set aside*) [+ *funds*] asignar, destinar (**for** a)

appropriately [ə'prəʊprɪɪtlɪ] ADV [*dress*] apropiadamente; [*respond*] apropiadamente, adecuadamente; [*act*] debidamente; **~ dressed for the occasion** vestido apropiadamente para la ocasión, vestido acorde con la ocasión; **it's entitled, ~ enough, "Art for the Nation"** se titula, muy apropiadamente, "Arte para la Nación"; **they have committed a crime and they must be punished ~** han cometido un crimen y deben recibir el correspondiente castigo

appropriateness [ə'prəʊprɪɪtnɪs] N lo apropiado

appropriation [əˌprəʊprɪ'eɪʃən] Ⓐ N [1] (= *confiscation*) apropiación *f*; **illegal ~** apropiación *f* indebida
[2] (= *allocation*) asignación *f*
[3] (= *funds assigned*) fondos *mpl*; (*US*) crédito *m*
Ⓑ CPD ► **appropriation account** N cuenta *f* de asignación ► **appropriation bill** N (*US Pol*) proyecto *m* de ley de presupuestos ► **Appropriation Committee** N (*US Pol*) Comisión *f* de gastos de la Cámara de Representantes ► **appropriation fund** N fondo *m* de asignación

approval [ə'pruːvəl] N (= *consent*) aprobación *f*, visto *m* bueno; **does this have your ~?** ¿le da usted su aprobación *or* visto bueno a esto?; **to meet with sb's ~** obtener la aprobación de algn; **a look of ~** una mirada de aprobación; **on ~** (*Comm*) a prueba; **he nodded his ~** asintió con la cabeza

approve [ə'pruːv] Ⓐ VT [+ *plan, decision, legislation, expenditure, minutes*] aprobar; [+ *drug, medicine, method*] autorizar; **the council has ~d the construction of a hotel** el ayuntamiento ha dado su aprobación para *or* ha aprobado la construcción de un hotel
Ⓑ VI [1] (= *be in favour*) **I think she'll ~** creo que estará de acuerdo, creo que le parecerá bien; **he's not allowed sweets, his mother doesn't ~** no le dejan comer caramelos, a su madre no le gusta
[2] (= *give authorization*) dar su aprobación; **if**

► LANGUAGE IN USE: approach C2 26.1 approve A 11.2

Congress ~s, the project will go ahead next year si el Congreso da su aprobación *or* lo aprueba, el proyecto se llevará a cabo el año que viene

▼ ► **approve of** VI + PREP [1] **to ~ of sth: not everyone ~s of the festival** no todo el mundo está de acuerdo con la celebración del festival; **he doesn't ~ of drinking** no le parece bien *or* no le gusta que se beba alcohol; **I don't ~ of her going** no me parece bien *or* no me gusta que vaya
[2] **to ~ of sb: they don't ~ of my fiancé** no les parece bien mi novio

approved Ⓐ ADJ (= *accredited*) acreditado; **the ~ method of cleaning** el método de limpieza aconsejado por las autoridades
Ⓑ CPD ► **approved school** N (*Brit*) correccional *m*, reformatorio *m*

approving [ə'pru:vɪŋ] ADJ [*words, look*] aprobatorio, de aprobación; **several people gave her ~ glances** varias personas le lanzaron miradas aprobatorias *or* de aprobación

approvingly [ə'pru:vɪŋlɪ] ADV con aprobación; **he looked at her ~** la miró con aprobación; **he nodded ~** hizo un gesto de aprobación con la cabeza

approx [ə'prɒks] ABBR (= **approximately**) aprox.

approximate Ⓐ [ə'prɒksɪmɪt] ADJ aproximado
Ⓑ [ə'prɒksɪmeɪt] VI **to ~ to** aproximarse a, acercarse a

approximately [ə'prɒksɪmɪtlɪ] ADV aproximadamente, más o menos; **the film lasts three hours ~** la película dura aproximadamente tres horas, la película dura tres horas (poco) más o menos

approximation [ə,prɒksɪ'meɪʃən] N aproximación *f*

appt. ABBR (*US*) = **appointment**

appurtenance [ə'pɜ:tɪnəns] N (= *appendage*) dependencia *f*; (= *accessory*) accesorio *m*; **the house and its ~s** la casa con sus dependencias

APR, apr N ABBR (= **annual(ized) percentage rate**) TAE *f*

Apr. ABBR (= **April**) ab., abr.

après-ski [,æpreɪ'ski:] Ⓐ N après-ski *m*
Ⓑ ADJ de après-ski

apricot ['eɪprɪkɒt] N [1] (= *fruit*) albaricoque *m*, chabacano *m* (*Mex*), damasco *m* (*LAm*)
[2] (= *tree*) albaricoquero *m*, chabacano *m* (*Mex*), damasco *m* (*LAm*)

April ['eɪprəl] Ⓐ N abril *m*; *see* **July** *for usage*
Ⓑ CPD ► **April Fool** N (= *trick*) ≈ inocentada *f*; **~ Fool!** ≈ ¡inocente! ► **April Fools' Day** N ≈ día *m* de los (Santos) Inocentes (*en el Reino Unido y los EEUU, el 1 abril*) ► **April showers** NPL lluvias *fpl* de abril

> **APRIL FOOLS' DAY**
> *El 1 de abril es* **April Fools' Day** *en la tradición anglosajona. En ese día se les gastan bromas a los desprevenidos, quienes reciben la denominación de* **April Fool** *(inocente), y tanto la prensa escrita como la televisión difunden alguna historia falsa con la que sumarse al espíritu del día.*

a priori [eɪpraɪ'ɔ:raɪ] Ⓐ ADV a priori
Ⓑ ADJ apriorístico

apron ['eɪprən] Ⓐ N [1] (= *garment*) delantal *m*; (*workman's, mason's etc*) mandil *m*
[2] (*Aer*) plataforma *f* de estacionamiento
[3] (*Theat*) proscenio *m*
Ⓑ CPD ► **apron stage** N (*Theat*) escena *f* saliente ► **apron strings** NPL (*fig*) **he's tied to his mother's/wife's ~ strings** está pegado a las faldas de su madre/esposa

apropos [,æprə'pəʊ] Ⓐ ADV a propósito
Ⓑ PREP **~ of** a propósito de
Ⓒ ADJ oportuno

apse [æps] N ábside *m*

APT N ABBR (*Brit*) (*formerly*) (= **Advanced Passenger Train**) ≈ TGV *m*, ≈ AVE *m* (*Sp*)

apt [æpt] ADJ (*compar* **apter**; *superl* **aptest**) [1] (= *suitable*) [*name, title*] acertado, apropiado; [*description*] acertado, atinado; [*remark*] acertado, oportuno; **how ~ that he should have been jailed on the anniversary of his crime!** ¡qué oportuno que lo hayan encerrado en el aniversario de su delito!
[2] (= *liable*) **to be ~ to do sth** tener tendencia a hacer algo, tender a hacer algo; **we are ~ to forget that ...** nos olvidamos fácilmente de que ..., tenemos tendencia *or* tendemos *or* somos propensos a olvidarnos de que ...; **he's ~ to be late** tiene tendencia a *or* tiende a *or* suele llegar tarde; **I am ~ to be out on Mondays** los lunes no suelo estar; **this is ~ to occur** esto tiene tendencia *or* tiende a ocurrir, hay propensión a que esto ocurra
[3] (= *clever*) capaz; **he has proved himself an ~ pupil** ha demostrado ser un alumno capaz

apt. ABBR (= **apartment**) apto.

▼ **aptitude** ['æptɪtju:d] Ⓐ N (= *ability*) aptitud *f*, talento *m*; (= *tendency*) inclinación *f*; **to have an ~ for sth** tener aptitud(es) *or* talento para algo
Ⓑ CPD ► **aptitude test** N prueba *f* de aptitud

aptly ['æptlɪ] ADV [*describe, remark*] acertadamente; **he was ~ described by his biographer as ...** fue descrito acertadamente por su biógrafo como ...; **an ~ named plant** una planta con un nombre muy acertado *or* apropiado; **I always felt he had been ~ named** siempre me pareció que su nombre era muy acertado *or* apropiado

aptness ['æptnɪs] N [*of name, description*] lo acertado, lo apropiado; [*of remark*] lo acertado, lo oportuno

Apuleius [,æpjə'lɪəs] N Apuleyo

aqua-aerobics ['ækwəeə'rəʊbɪks] N aerobic *msing* acuático

aquafarming ['ækwə,fɑ:mɪŋ] N piscicultura *f*

aqualung ['ækwəlʌŋ] N escafandra *f* autónoma

aquamarine [,ækwəmə'ri:n] Ⓐ ADJ (de color) verde mar *inv*
Ⓑ N aguamarina *f*

aquanaut ['ækwənɔ:t] N submarinista *mf*

aquaplane ['ækwəpleɪn] Ⓐ N tabla *f* de esquí acuático
Ⓑ VI (*Brit Aut*) patinar

Aquarian [ə'kweərɪən] N acuario *mf*

aquarium [ə'kweərɪəm] N (*pl* **aquariums** *or* **aquaria** [ə'kweərɪə]) (= *tank, building*) acuario *m*

Aquarius [ə'kweərɪəs] N [1] (= *sign, constellation*) Acuario *m*
[2] (= *person*) acuario *mf*; **she's (an) ~** es acuario

aquatic [ə'kwætɪk] Ⓐ ADJ acuático
Ⓑ N [1] (*Bot*) planta *f* acuática
[2] (*Zool*) animal *m* acuático

aquatics [ə'kwætɪks] N (*Sport*) deportes *mpl* acuáticos

aquatint ['ækwətɪnt] N acuatinta *f*

aqueduct ['ækwɪdʌkt] N acueducto *m*

aqueous ['eɪkwɪəs] ADJ acuoso, ácueo (*frm*)

aquifer ['ækwɪfə^r] N acuífero *m*

aquiferous [ə'kwɪfərəs] ADJ acuífero

aquiline ['ækwɪlaɪn] ADJ **an ~ nose** una nariz aguileña *or* aquilina

Aquinas [ə'kwaɪnəs] N Aquino; **St Thomas ~** Santo Tomás de Aquino

AR ABBR [1] (*Comm*) = **account rendered**
[2] (*for tax*) = **annual return**
[3] (*report*) = **annual return**
[4] (*US*) = **Arkansas**

A/R ABBR = **against all risks**

ARA N ABBR (*Brit*) = **Associate of the Royal Academy**

Arab ['ærəb] Ⓐ ADJ árabe
Ⓑ N [1] (= *person*) árabe *mf*
[2] (= *horse*) caballo *m* árabe

arabesque [,ærə'besk] N (*Ballet etc*) arabesco *m*

Arabia [ə'reɪbɪə] N Arabia *f*

Arabian [ə'reɪbɪən] Ⓐ ADJ árabe, arábigo; **the ~ Desert** el desierto Arábigo; **the ~ Gulf** el golfo Arábigo; **the ~ Sea** el mar de Omán; **The ~ Nights** Las mil y una noches
Ⓑ N árabe *mf*

Arabic ['ærəbɪk] Ⓐ ADJ árabe
Ⓑ N (*Ling*) árabe *m*
Ⓒ CPD ► **Arabic numerals** NPL numeración *fsing* arábiga

Arabist ['ærəbɪst] N arabista *mf*

arabization [,ærəbaɪ'zeɪʃən] N arabización *f*

arabize ['ærəbaɪz] VT arabizar

arable ['ærəbl] Ⓐ ADJ cultivable, arable (*esp LAm*); **~ farm** granja *f* agrícola; **~ farming** agricultura *f*; **~ land** tierra *f* de cultivo *or* cultivable
Ⓑ N tierra *f* de cultivo, tierra *f* cultivable

arachnid [ə'ræknɪd] N arácnido *m*

Aragon ['ærəgən] N Aragón *m*

Aragonese [,ærəgə'ni:z] Ⓐ ADJ aragonés
Ⓑ N [1] (= *person*) aragonés/esa *m/f*
[2] (*Ling*) aragonés *m*

ARAM N ABBR (*Brit*) = **Associate of the Royal Academy of Music**

Aramaic [,ærə'meɪɪk] N arameo *m*

arbiter ['ɑ:bɪtə^r] N [1] (= *adjudicator*) árbitro/a *m/f*
[2] (*fig*) **to be an ~ of taste/style** ser un árbitro del buen gusto/de la moda

arbitrage [,ɑ:bɪ'trɑ:ʒ] N arbitraje *m*

arbitrageur [,ɑ:bɪtræ'ʒɜ:] N arbitrajista *mf*

arbitrarily ['ɑ:bɪtrərɪlɪ] ADV arbitrariamente

arbitrariness ['ɑ:bɪtrərɪnɪs] N arbitrariedad *f*

arbitrary ['ɑ:bɪtrərɪ] ADJ arbitrario

arbitrate ['ɑ:bɪtreɪt] Ⓐ VT resolver, juzgar
Ⓑ VI arbitrar, mediar (**between** entre)

arbitration [,ɑ:bɪ'treɪʃən] N arbitraje *m*; **they went to ~** recurrieron al arbitraje; **the question was referred to ~** se confió el asunto a un tribunal de arbitraje

arbitrator ['ɑ:bɪtreɪtə^r] N árbitro/a *m/f*, mediador(a) *m/f*

arbor ['ɑ:bə^r] N (*US*) = **arbour**

arboreal [ɑ:'bɔ:rɪəl] ADJ arbóreo

arboretum [,ɑ:bə'ri:təm] N (*pl* **arboretums, arboreta** [,ɑ:bə'ri:tə]) arboreto *m*, jardín *m* botánico arbóreo

arboriculture ['ɑ:bərɪ,kʌltʃə^r] N arboricultura *f*

arbour, arbor (*US*) ['ɑ:bə^r] N cenador *m*, pérgola *f*

arbutus [ɑ:'bju:təs] N madroño *m*

ARC N ABBR [1] (*Med*) = **AIDS-related complex**
[2] = **American Red Cross**

arc [ɑ:k] Ⓐ N arco *m*
Ⓑ VI arquearse, formar un arco

➤ LANGUAGE IN USE: **approve of 1** 14 **aptitude A** 15.4, 16.4

Ⓒ CPD ► **arc lamp** N lámpara *f* de arco; (*in welding*) arco *m* voltaico ► **arc welding** N soldadura *f* por arco

arcade [ɑːˈkeɪd] Ⓐ N [1] (= *shopping precinct*) galería *f* comercial; (*round public square*) soportales *mpl*, pórtico *m*; (*in building*) galería *f* interior; (*in church*) claustro *m*
[2] (*Brit*) (*also* **amusement ~**) sala *f* de juegos, salón *m* de juegos
[3] (*Archit*) (= *arch*) bóveda *f*; (= *passage*) arcada *f*
Ⓑ CPD ► **arcade game** N videojuego *m*

Arcadia [ɑːˈkeɪdɪə] N Arcadia *f*

Arcadian [ɑːˈkeɪdɪən] Ⓐ ADJ árcade, arcádico
Ⓑ N árcade *mf*, arcadio/a *m/f*

Arcady [ˈɑːkədɪ] N Arcadia *f*

arcane [ɑːˈkeɪn] ADJ arcano

arch¹ [ɑːtʃ] Ⓐ N [1] (*Archit*) arco *m*; (= *vault*) bóveda *f*
[2] [*of foot*] puente *m*; **fallen ~es** pies *mpl* planos
[3] (*dental*) arcada *f*, arco *m*
Ⓑ VT [+ *back, body etc*] arquear; **to ~ one's eyebrows** arquear las cejas
Ⓒ VI [1] arquearse, formar un arco
[2] **to ~ over** (*Archit*) abovedar

arch² [ɑːtʃ] ADJ [1] (= *superior*) [*look*] de superioridad; [*remark*] en tono de superioridad
[2] (= *mischievous*) malicioso
[3] (= *cunning*) [*glance, person*] astuto

arch³ [ɑːtʃ] ADJ (= *great*) **an ~ criminal** un consumado delincuente; **an ~ hypocrite** un consumado hipócrita, un hipócrita de primer orden; *see also* **arch-enemy**

archaeological, **archeological** (*esp US*) [ˌɑːkɪəˈlɒdʒɪkəl] ADJ arqueológico

archaeologist, **archeologist** (*esp US*) [ˌɑːkɪˈɒlədʒɪst] N arqueólogo/a *m/f*

archaeology, **archeology** (*esp US*) [ˌɑːkɪˈɒlədʒɪ] N arqueología *f*

archaic [ɑːˈkeɪɪk] ADJ arcaico

archaism [ˈɑːkeɪɪzəm] N arcaísmo *m*

archangel [ˈɑːkˌeɪndʒəl] N arcángel *m*

archbishop [ˈɑːtʃˈbɪʃəp] N arzobispo *m*; **the Archbishop of Canterbury** el Arzobispo de Canterbury

> **ARCHBISHOP**
>
> *En la Iglesia anglicana (***Church of England***) existen dos arzobispos:* **Archbishop of York** *y* **Archbishop of Canterbury***, siendo éste el jefe espiritual de la Iglesia. Ambos arzobispos, que ocupan un escaño en la Cámara de los Lores, son nombrados por el monarca con el asesoramiento del Primer Ministro y los representantes de la Iglesia anglicana. El Arzobispo de Canterbury es quien corona al nuevo monarca británico en la ceremonia de la coronación (***Coronation Ceremony***) y oficia en las bodas reales. Los dos arzobispos ejercen autoridad administrativa sobre el clero en sus respectivos arzobispados (***provinces***).*
>
> ⇨ *Ver tb* CHURCHES OF ENGLAND/SCOTLAND

archbishopric [ɑːtʃˈbɪʃəprɪk] N arzobispado *m*

archdeacon [ˈɑːtʃˈdiːkən] N arcediano *m*

archdiocese [ˈɑːtʃˈdaɪəsɪs] N archidiócesis *f inv*

archduke [ˈɑːtʃˈdjuːk] N archiduque *m*

arched [ɑːtʃt] ADJ [*roof, window, doorway*] abovedado; [*bridge*] con arcos, con arcadas; [*brow*] arqueado

arch-enemy [ˈɑːtʃˈenɪmɪ] N archienemigo/a *m/f*

archeological [ˌɑːkɪəˈlɒdʒɪkəl] ADJ (*esp US*) = **archaeological**

archeologist [ˌɑːkɪˈɒlədʒɪst] N (*esp US*) = **archaeologist**

archeology [ˌɑːkɪˈɒlədʒɪ] N (*esp US*) = **archaeology**

archer [ˈɑːtʃəʳ] N arquero/a *m/f*

archery [ˈɑːtʃərɪ] N tiro *m* con arco

archetypal [ɑːkɪˈtaɪpl] ADJ arquetípico

archetypally [ˌɑːkɪˈtaɪpəlɪ] ADV arquetípicamente

archetype [ˈɑːkɪtaɪp] N [1] (= *original*) arquetipo *m*
[2] (= *epitome*) modelo *m*, arquetipo *m*

archetypical [ˌɑːkɪˈtɪpɪkəl] ADJ = **archetypal**

Archimedes [ˌɑːkɪˈmiːdiːz] N Arquímedes; **~' screw** rosca *f* de Arquímedes

archipelago [ˌɑːkɪˈpelɪgəʊ] N (*pl* **archipelagos, archipelagoes**) archipiélago *m*

archiphoneme [ˈɑːkɪˌfəʊniːm] N archifonema *m*

architect [ˈɑːkɪtekt] N [1] (= *professional*) arquitecto/a *m/f*
[2] (*fig*) artífice *mf*; **the ~ of victory** el artífice de la victoria

architectonic [ˌɑːkɪtekˈtɒnɪk] ADJ arquitectónico

architectural [ˌɑːkɪˈtektʃərəl] ADJ arquitectónico

architecturally [ˌɑːkɪˈtektʃərəlɪ] ADV arquitectónicamente; **an ~ striking building** un edificio impresionante desde el punto de vista arquitectónico

architecture [ˈɑːkɪtektʃəʳ] N arquitectura *f*

architrave [ˈɑːkɪtreɪv] N arquitrabe *m*

archive [ˈɑːkaɪv] Ⓐ N (*gen*) archivo *m*; (*Comput*) archivo *m*, fichero *m*
Ⓑ VT archivar
Ⓒ CPD ► **archive file** N (*Comput*) fichero *m* archivado ► **archive film** N imágenes *fpl* de archivo ► **archive material** N material *m* de archivo

archivist [ˈɑːkɪvɪst] N archivero/a *m/f*, archivista *mf* (*LAm*)

archly [ˈɑːtʃlɪ] ADV [1] (= *in a superior way*) con aire de superioridad
[2] (= *mischievously*) maliciosamente
[3] (= *cunningly*) con astucia

archness [ˈɑːtʃnɪs] N [1] (= *air of superiority*) aire *m* de superioridad
[2] (= *mischievousness*) malicia *f*
[3] (= *cunning*) astucia *f*

archpriest [ˈɑːtʃˈpriːst] N arcipreste *m*

archway [ˈɑːtʃweɪ] N (= *passage*) pasaje *m* abovedado; (= *arch*) arco *m*

ARCM N ABBR (*Brit*) = **Associate of the Royal College of Music**

arctic [ˈɑːktɪk] Ⓐ ADJ [1] (*Geog*) ártico
[2] (*fig*) (= *cold*) glacial, gélido
Ⓑ N **the Arctic** el Ártico
Ⓒ CPD ► **Arctic Circle** N Círculo *m* Polar Ártico ► **arctic fox** N zorro *m* polar ► **Arctic Ocean** N Océano *m* Ártico

ARD N ABBR (*US*) = **acute respiratory disease**

Ardennes [ɑːˈdənz] NPL Ardenas *fpl*

ardent [ˈɑːdənt] ADJ [1] (= *enthusiastic*) [*supporter, admirer, opponent*] apasionado, ferviente; [*feminist, nationalist*] acérrimo; [*desire*] ardiente, ferviente; [*belief, plea*] ferviente; **she is ~ in her opposition to the proposals** se opone ardientemente a las propuestas
[2] (= *passionate*) [*lover, lovemaking*] apasionado

ardently [ˈɑːdəntlɪ] ADV [1] (= *enthusiastically*) [*support, defend, desire*] ardientemente, fervientemente; [*speak*] con vehemencia
[2] (= *passionately*) [*kiss*] apasionadamente

ardour, **ardor** (*US*) [ˈɑːdəʳ] N [1] (*for sth*) (= *love*) pasión *f*; (= *fervour, eagerness*) fervor *m*, ardor *m*
[2] (*romantic*) ardor *m*, pasión *f*

arduous [ˈɑːdjʊəs] ADJ [*work, task*] arduo; [*climb, journey*] arduo, penoso; [*conditions*] riguroso, duro

arduously [ˈɑːdjʊəslɪ] ADV [*work*] arduamente; [*climb*] con dificultad, penosamente

arduousness [ˈɑːdjʊəsnɪs] N [*of work, task*] lo arduo; [*of climb, journey*] lo arduo, lo penoso; [*of conditions*] lo riguroso, lo duro

are [ɑːʳ] PRESENT (*2nd pers sing, 1st, 2nd, 3rd pers pl*) *of* **be**

area [ˈɛərɪə] Ⓐ N [1] (= *surface measure*) superficie *f*, extensión *f*, área *f*; **the lake is 130 square miles in ~** el lago tiene 130 millas cuadradas de superficie *or* de extensión, el lago se extiende sobre una superficie *or* área de 130 millas cuadradas; *see also* **surface**
[2] (= *region*) [*of country*] zona *f*, región *f*; [*of city*] zona *f*; (*Admin, Pol*) zona *f*, área *f*; **in mountainous ~s of Europe and Asia** en las zonas *or* regiones montañosas de Europa y Asia; **an ~ of outstanding natural beauty** una zona de una belleza natural excepcional; **an ~ of high unemployment** una zona con un alto índice de desempleo; **the London ~** la zona *or* el área de Londres; **rural/urban ~s** zonas *fpl* rurales/urbanas; *see also* **catchment**, **disaster**, **sterling**
[3] (= *extent, patch*) zona *f*; **the blast caused damage over a wide ~** la explosión causó daños en una extensa zona; **there is an ~ of wasteland behind the houses** hay un terreno baldío detrás de las casas; **when applying the cream avoid the ~ around the eyes** evite aplicarse la crema en la zona que rodea los ojos
[4] (= *space*) zona *f*; **communal ~** zona *f* comunitaria; **dining ~** comedor *m*; **picnic ~** merendero *m*; **play ~** zona *f* recreativa; **reception ~** recepción *f*; **slum ~** barrio *m* bajo; **smoking ~s are provided** se han habilitado zonas para fumadores; **waiting ~** zona *f* de espera
[5] (*Sport*) (*also* **penalty ~**) área *f* de penalti, área *f* de castigo; *see also* **goal**
[6] (*Brit*) (= *basement courtyard*) patio *m*
[7] (= *sphere*) [*of knowledge*] campo *m*, terreno *m*; [*of responsibility*] esfera *f*; **I am not a specialist in this ~** no soy especialista en este campo *or* terreno; **~ of study** campo *m* de estudio; **that is not my ~ of competence** eso no es competencia mía; **it affects all ~s of our lives** afecta a todos los sectores de nuestra vida; **it's a potential ~ of concern** puede llegar a ser motivo de preocupación; **there are still some ~s of disagreement** aún existen discrepancias sobre algunos puntos; **one of the problem ~s is lax security** una cuestión problemática es la falta de seguridad; *see also* **grey**
Ⓑ CPD ► **area code** N (*US Telec*) prefijo *m* (local), código *m* territorial ► **area manager** N jefe/a *m/f* de zona ► **area office** N oficina *f* regional ► **area representative** N representante *mf* de zona

arena [əˈriːnə] N [1] (= *stadium*) estadio *m*
[2] (= *circus*) pista *f*
[3] (*Bullfighting*) (= *building*) plaza *f*; (= *pit*) ruedo *m*
[4] (*fig*) (= *stage*) palestra *f*; **the political ~** el ruedo político

aren't [ɑːnt] = **are not**

areola [əˈrɪələ] N (*pl* **areolas** *or* **areolae**) aureola *f*, areola *f*

Argentina [ˌɑːdʒənˈtiːnə] N Argentina *f*

Argentine [ˈɑːdʒəntaɪn] Ⓐ ADJ argentino
Ⓑ N [1] (= *person*) argentino/a *m/f*
[2] **the ~** la Argentina

Argentinian [ˌɑːdʒənˈtɪnɪən] Ⓐ ADJ argentino
Ⓑ N argentino/a *m/f*

Argie* [ˈɑːdʒɪ] N (*pej*) = **Argentinian**

argon [ˈɑːgɒn] N argón *m*

Argonaut [ˈɑːgənɔːt] N argonauta *m*

argot [ˈɑːgəʊ] N argot *m*

arguable [ˈɑːgjʊəbl] ADJ discutible; **it is ~ whether ...** no está probado que ...; **it is ~ that ...** se puede decir que ...

arguably [ˈɑːgjʊəblɪ] ADV **he is ~ the best player in the world** se podría mantener que es el mejor jugador del mundo

▼**argue** [ˈɑːgjuː] Ⓐ VI [1] (= *disagree*) discutir; (= *fight*) pelearse; **his parents were always arguing** sus padres estaban siempre discutiendo *or* peleándose; **he started arguing with the referee** empezó a discutir con el árbitro; **to ~ (with sb) about** *or* **over sth** discutir *or* pelearse (con algn) por algo; **they were arguing about what to do next** estaban discutiendo sobre qué hacer después; **she achieved it, you can't ~ with that** lo logró, eso es indiscutible; **I didn't dare ~** no me atreví a llevar la contraria; **just get in and don't ~ (with me)!** ¡entra y no (me) discutas!
[2] (= *reason*) **he ~s well** presenta sus argumentos de modo convincente, razona bien; **to ~ against sth** dar razones en contra de algo; **to ~ against doing sth** dar razones para que no se haga algo; **to ~ for sth** abogar por algo; **he ~d for the president's powers to be restricted** abogó en favor de que se limitaran los poderes del presidente; **he ~s from a deeply religious conviction** sus argumentos parten de una profunda convicción religiosa
[3] (= *indicate*) **his lack of experience ~s against him** su falta de experiencia es un factor en su contra; **it ~s well for him** es un elemento a su favor
Ⓑ VT [1] (= *debate*) discutir; **I won't ~ that point** no voy a discutir ese punto; *see also* **toss A3**
[2] (= *persuade*) **he ~d me into/out of going** me convenció de que fuera/no fuera; **he ~d his way out of getting the sack** consiguió que no lo despidieran con buenos razonamientos
[3] (= *maintain*) sostener; **to ~ that** sostener que; **he ~d that it couldn't be done** sostenía que no se podía hacer; **it could be ~d that we are not doing enough** se podría decir que no estamos haciendo lo suficiente
[4] (= *cite, claim*) (*esp Jur*) alegar; **the defence ~d diminished responsibility** la defensa alegó un atenuante de responsabilidad
[5] **to ~ a case** [5·1] (*Jur*) presentar un pleito, exponer un pleito
[5·2] (*fig*) **a well ~d case** un argumento bien expuesto; **to ~ the case for sth** abogar en favor de algo
[6] (= *suggest*) indicar; **it ~s a certain lack of feeling** indica cierta falta de sentimientos
►**argue out** VT + ADV [+ *problem*] discutir a fondo; **they ~d the whole thing out over dinner** discutieron a fondo todo el asunto durante la cena

▼**argument** [ˈɑːgjʊmənt] N [1] (= *disagreement*) discusión *f*; (= *fight*) pelea *f*; **I don't want any ~ (about it)** no quiero discutir, no hay discusión que valga; **to get into an ~ (with sb)** empezar a discutir (con algn); **to have an ~ (with sb)** discutir (con algn); (*more heatedly*) pelearse (con algn); **we had an ~ about money** tuvimos una discusión *or* discutimos por razones de dinero; **let's not have an ~ about it** no discutamos; **there was an ~ over the missing plate** hubo una discusión sobre el plato que faltaba; **you've only heard one side of the ~** tú sólo conoces una cara del asunto; ✦*IDIOM* **he had an ~ with a wall** (*hum*) se dio contra la pared
[2] (= *debate*) polémica *f*; **there is some ~ as to whether or not it's possible** hay bastante polémica sobre si es posible o no; **she is open to ~** está dispuesta a discutirlo; **the conclusion is open to ~** la conclusión se presta a discusión *or* es discutible; **to win/lose an ~** ganar/perder (en) un enfrentamiento; *see also* **sake**
[3] (= *case*) argumento *m*, razones *fpl*; **there is a strong ~ for** *or* **in favour of doing nothing** existen argumentos *or* razones de peso para *or* en favor de no hacer nada; **an ~ could be made for government intervention** se podrían alegar razones para la intervención del gobierno
[4] (= *reasoning*) razonamiento *m*; **if you take this ~ one step further** si llevas el razonamiento un poco más allá; **his ~ is that ...** él sostiene que ...; *see also* **line**[1] **A11**
[5] (= *synopsis*) argumento *m*, resumen *m*
[6] (*Jur*) **opening ~** exposición *f* inicial; **closing ~** conclusiones *fpl* finales

argumentation [ˌɑːgjʊmənˈteɪʃən] N argumentación *f*, argumentos *mpl*

argumentative [ˌɑːgjʊˈmentətɪv] ADJ [*person*] amigo de las discusiones, discutidor

Argus [ˈɑːgəs] N Argos

argy-bargy* [ˈɑːdʒɪˈbɑːdʒɪ] N (*Brit*) pelotera* *f*, altercado *m*

aria [ˈɑːrɪə] N aria *f*

Arian [ˈɛərɪən] Ⓐ ADJ arriano
Ⓑ N arriano/a *m/f*

Arianism [ˈɛərɪənɪzəm] N arrianismo *m*

ARIBA [əˈriːbə] N ABBR (*Brit*) = **Associate of the Royal Institute of British Architects**

arid [ˈærɪd] ADJ (*lit, fig*) árido

aridity [əˈrɪdɪtɪ] N (*lit, fig*) aridez *f*

Aries [ˈɛəriːz] N [1] (= *sign, constellation*) Aries *m*
[2] (= *person*) aries *mf*; **I'm (an) ~** soy aries

aright [əˈraɪt] ADV correctamente, acertadamente; **if I heard you ~** si le oí bien; **if I understand you ~** si le entiendo correctamente; **to set ~** rectificar

arise [əˈraɪz] (*pt* **arose**; *pp* **arisen** [əˈrɪzn]) VI [1] (= *occur*) surgir, presentarse; **difficulties have ~n** han surgido *or* se han presentado dificultades; **a storm arose** (*liter*) se levantó una tormenta; **a great clamour arose** (*liter*) se produjo un tremendo clamor; **should the need ~** de ser necesario; **should the occasion ~** si se presenta la ocasión; **the question does not ~** no hay tal problema, la cuestión no viene al caso; **the question ~s whether ...** se plantea el problema de si ...
[2] (= *result*) surgir; **there are problems arising from his attitude** surgen problemas a raíz de su actitud; **matters arising (from the last meeting)** asuntos pendientes (de la última reunión); **arising from this, can you say ...?** partiendo de esta base, ¿puede usted decir ...?
[3] (†) (= *get up*) levantarse, alzarse; **arise!** (*slogan*) ¡arriba!

arisen [əˈrɪzn] PP of **arise**

aristo* [ˈærɪstəʊ] N (*Brit*) aristócrata *mf*

aristocracy [ˌærɪsˈtɒkrəsɪ] N (= *nobility*) aristocracia *f*

aristocrat [ˈærɪstəkræt] N aristócrata *mf*

aristocratic [ˌærɪstəˈkrætɪk] ADJ aristocrático

Aristophanes [ˌærɪsˈtɒfəniːz] N Aristófanes

Aristotelian [ˌærɪstəˈtiːlɪən] ADJ aristotélico

Aristotelianism [ˌærɪstəˈtiːlɪənɪzəm] N aristotelismo *m*

Aristotle [ˈærɪstɒtl] N Aristóteles

arithmetic Ⓐ [əˈrɪθmətɪk] N aritmética *f*; *see also* **mental**
Ⓑ [ˌærɪθˈmetɪk] ADJ aritmético; **~ progression** progresión *f* aritmética
Ⓒ [ˌærɪθˈmetɪk] CPD ► **arithmetic mean** N media *f* aritmética

arithmetical [ˌærɪθˈmetɪkəl] ADJ = **arithmetic B**

arithmetician [əˌrɪθməˈtɪʃən] N aritmético/a *m/f*

Ariz. ABBR (*US*) = **Arizona**

ark [ɑːk] N arca *f*; **Noah's Ark** el Arca *f* de Noé; **Ark of the Covenant** Arca *f* de la Alianza; ✦*IDIOM* **it's out of the Ark*** viene del año de la nana*

Ark. ABBR (*US*) = **Arkansas**

arm[1] [ɑːm] N [1] (*Anat*) brazo *m*; **with one's ~s folded** con los brazos cruzados; **to give sb one's ~** dar el brazo a algn; **to hold sth/sb in one's ~s** coger algo/a algn en brazos; **arm in arm**: **he walked ~ in ~ with his wife** iba cogido del brazo de su mujer; **they were walking along ~ in ~** iban cogidos del brazo; **they rushed into each other's ~s** corrieron a echarse uno en brazos del otro; **this pushed them into the ~s of the French** esto les obligó a buscar el apoyo de los franceses; **he held it at ~'s length** (*lit*) lo sujetaba con el brazo extendido; *see also* **to keep sb at ~'s length**; **she came in on her father's ~** entró del brazo de su padre; **with his coat over his ~** con el abrigo sobre el brazo; **to put one's ~(s) round sb** abrazar a algn; **within ~'s reach** al alcance de la mano; **to take sb's ~** coger a algn del brazo; **to take sb in one's ~s** tomar a algn en sus brazos; **to throw one's ~s round sb's neck** echar los brazos al cuello a algn; **he had a parcel under his ~** llevaba un paquete debajo del brazo *or* bajo el brazo; ✦*IDIOMS* **to cost an ~ and a leg*** costar un ojo de la cara*; **to keep sb at ~'s length** (*fig*) mantener las distancias con algn; **a list as long as your ~** una lista kilométrica; **the (long** *or* **strong) ~ of the law** el brazo de la ley; **to welcome sth/sb with open ~s** recibir algo/a algn con los brazos abiertos; **to put the ~ on sb** (*US**) presionar a algn; **I'd give my right ~ to own it** daría mi brazo derecho por que fuera mío; *see also* **babe, chance B1, fold**[2]**, twist B2**
[2] (= *part*) [2·1] [*of chair, river, crane, pick-up*] brazo *m*; [*of spectacles*] patilla *f*; [*of coat*] manga *f*; **~ of the sea** brazo *m* de mar
[2·2] [*of organization, company, also Mil*] (= *division*) división *f*; (= *section*) sección *f*; (*Pol*) brazo *m*; **the military ~ of the Western alliance** el brazo armado de la alianza occidental; **the political ~ of a terrorist group** el brazo político de un grupo terrorista; *see also* **fleet**

arm[2] [ɑːm] Ⓐ N [1] (= *weapon*) arma *f*; **to bear ~s** portar armas; **to lay down one's ~s** deponer *or* rendir las armas; **order ~s!** ¡descansen armas!; **present ~s!** ¡presenten armas!; **shoulder ~s!** ◊ **slope ~s!** ¡sobre el hombro, armas!; **to take up ~s (against sth/sb)** tomar las armas (contra algo/algn); **by 1809 Britain had 817,000 men under ~s** en 1809

➤ LANGUAGE IN USE: **argue A1** 11.1 **argument 3, 4** 26.1, 26.2

Gran Bretaña tenía 817.000 hombres en sus filas *or* en las fuerzas armadas; ✦*IDIOM* **to be up in ~s about sth**: **environment groups are up in ~s about the plan** los grupos ecologistas están oponiéndose al plan enfurecidamente; **no need to get up in ~s over such a small thing** no hace falta poner el grito en el cielo *or* ponerse así por una cosa tan insignificante; *see also* **rise B9**
2 **arms** (= *coat of arms*) escudo *msing* de armas, blasón *msing*
Ⓑ VT [+ *person, ship, nation*] armar, proveer de armas; [+ *missile*] equipar; **to ~ sb with sth** (*lit*) armar a algn de *or* con algo; (*fig*) proveer a algn de algo; **to ~ o.s. with sth** (*lit*) armarse de *or* con algo; (*fig*) armarse de algo; **she had ~ed herself with a rifle** se había armado de *or* con un rifle; **I ~ed myself with all the information I would need** me armé de toda la información que necesitaría
Ⓒ VI armarse (**against** contra)
Ⓓ CPD ► **arms control** N control *m* de armamento(s) ► **arms dealer** N traficante *mf* de armas ► **arms embargo** N embargo *m* de armas ► **arms factory** N fábrica *f* de armas ► **arms limitation** N límite *m* armamentístico ► **arms manufacturer** N fabricante *mf* de armas ► **the arms race** N la carrera armamentística, la carrera de armamentos ► **arms reduction** N reducción *f* de armas ► **arms trade** N tráfico *m* de armas

armada [ɑːˈmɑːdə] N flota *f*, armada *f*; **the Armada** (*Hist*) la (Armada) Invencible

armadillo [ˌɑːməˈdɪləʊ] N armadillo *m*

Armageddon [ˌɑːməˈgedn] N (*Bible*) la batalla de Armagedón; (*fig*) la guerra del fin del mundo

armament [ˈɑːməmənt] Ⓐ N armamento *m*; **~s** (= *weapons*) armamento *msing*
Ⓑ CPD ► **the armaments industry** N la industria de armamento, la industria armamentista *or* armamentística

armature [ˈɑːmətjʊəʳ] N 1 (*Bot, Elec, Zool*) armadura *f*; [*of dynamo*] inducido *m*
2 (= *supporting framework*) armazón *f*

armband [ˈɑːmbænd] N brazalete *m*

armchair [ˈɑːmtʃɛəʳ] Ⓐ N sillón *m*
Ⓑ CPD ► **armchair general** N general *mf* de salón ► **armchair strategist** N estratega *mf* de salón, estratega *mf* de café

armed [ɑːmd] Ⓐ ADJ [*conflict, struggle, resistance*] armado; **their men were not ~** sus hombres no iban armados; **their men were heavily ~** sus hombres iban bien provistos de armas; **~ guards** guardias *mpl* armados; **the ~ forces** las fuerzas armadas; **~ robbery** robo *m* a mano armada; **~ with sth** (*lit, fig*) armado de *or* con algo; **they were ~ with machine guns** iban armados de *or* con ametralladoras; **she came ~ with reams of statistics** vino armada de *or* con páginas y páginas de estadísticas; **the missile was ~ with a conventional warhead** el misil estaba equipado de *or* con una cabeza convencional; ✦*IDIOM* **~ to the teeth** armado hasta los dientes
Ⓑ PT, PP *of* **arm**²

-armed [ɑːmd] ADJ (*ending in compounds*) de brazos ...; **strong-armed** de brazos fuertes; **one-armed** manco

Armenia [ɑːˈmiːnɪə] N Armenia *f*

Armenian [ɑːˈmiːnɪən] Ⓐ ADJ armenio
Ⓑ N 1 (= *person*) armenio/a *m/f*
2 (*Ling*) armenio *m*

armful [ˈɑːmfʊl] N brazada *f*

armhole [ˈɑːmhəʊl] N sobaquera *f*, sisa *f*

armistice [ˈɑːmɪstɪs] N armisticio *m*

armlet [ˈɑːmlɪt] N brazal *m*

armlock [ˈɑːmˈlɒk] N llave *f* de brazo; **to hold sb in an ~** inmovilizar a algn con una llave

armor [ˈɑːməʳ] N (*US*) = **armour**

armored [ˈɑːməd] ADJ (*US*) = **armoured**

armorer [ˈɑːmərəʳ] N (*US*) = **armourer**

armorial [ɑːˈmɔːrɪəl] ADJ heráldico; **~ bearings** escudo *m* de armas

armor-piercing [ˈɑːməˌpɪəsɪŋ] ADJ (*US*) = **armour-piercing**

armor-plated [ˈɑːməˈpleɪtɪd] ADJ (*US*) = **armour-plated**

armory [ˈɑːmərɪ] N (*US*) = **armoury**

armour, **armor** (*US*) [ˈɑːməʳ] Ⓐ N 1 (*Mil, Zool, fig*) armadura *f*; (= *steel plates*) blindaje *m*
2 (= *tank forces*) divisiones *fpl* acorazadas, fuerzas *fpl* blindadas
Ⓑ VT blindar, acorazar
Ⓒ CPD ► **armour plate** N blindaje *m* ► **armour plating** N = **armour plate**

armour-clad [ˈɑːməklæd] ADJ = **armoured**

armoured, **armored** (*US*) [ˈɑːməd] ADJ acorazado, blindado; **~ car** carro *m* blindado; **~ column** columna *f* blindada; **~ personnel carrier** vehículo *m* blindado para el transporte de tropas

armourer, **armorer** (*US*) [ˈɑːmərəʳ] N armero *m*

armour-piercing, **armor-piercing** (*US*) [ˈɑːməˌpɪəsɪŋ] ADJ [*shell*] perforante

armour-plated, **armor-plated** (*US*) [ˈɑːməˈpleɪtɪd] ADJ = **armoured**

armoury, **armory** (*US*) [ˈɑːmərɪ] N 1 (*lit, fig*) (= *arsenal*) arsenal *m*
2 (*US*) (= *arms factory*) fábrica *f* de armas

armpit [ˈɑːmpɪt] N 1 (*Anat*) sobaco *m*, axila *f*
2 (*) (= *unpleasant place*) cloaca *f*

armrest [ˈɑːmrest] N [*of chair*] brazo *m*; (*in bus, plane, etc*) apoyo *m* para el brazo, apoyabrazos *m inv*

arm-twisting* [ˈɑːmˌtwɪstɪŋ] N presión *f*

arm-wrestling [ˈɑːmˌreslɪŋ] N pulso *m*, pulseada *f* (*S. Cone*)

army [ˈɑːmɪ] Ⓐ N 1 (*Mil*) ejército *m*; **to be in the ~** ser militar; **to join the ~** alistarse
2 (*fig*) ejército *m*, multitud *f*
Ⓑ CPD ► **army chaplain** N capellán *m* castrense ► **army corps** N cuerpo *m* del ejército ► **army doctor** N médico/a *m/f* militar ► **army life** N vida *f* militar ► **Army list** N lista *f* de oficiales del ejército ► **army of occupation** N ejército *m* de ocupación ► **army slang** N argot *m* militar ► **army surplus** N excedentes *mpl* del ejército

army-issue [ˈɑːmɪˌɪʃuː] ADJ del ejército, proporcionado por el ejército

arnica [ˈɑːnɪkə] N árnica *f*

aroma [əˈrəʊmə] N aroma *m* (**of** de, a)

aromatherapist [əˈrəʊməˈθerəpɪst] N aromaterapeuta *mf*

aromatherapy [əˈrəʊməˈθerəpɪ] N aromaterapia *f*

aromatic [ˌærəʊˈmætɪk] ADJ aromático

arose [əˈrəʊz] PT *of* **arise**

around [əˈraʊnd]

> *When* **around** *is an element in a phrasal verb, eg* **look around, move around, potter around,** *look up the verb.*

Ⓐ ADV alrededor, en los alrededores; **is he ~?** ¿está por aquí?; **there's a lot of flu ~** hay mucha gripe por ahí; **all ~** por todos lados; **she's been ~*** (= *travelled*) ha viajado mucho, ha visto mucho mundo; (*pej*) (= *experienced*) se las sabe todas; **~ here** por aquí; **is there a chemist's ~ here?** ¿hay alguna farmacia por aquí?; **we're looking ~ for a house** estamos buscando casa; **for miles ~** en muchas millas a la redonda; **he must be somewhere ~** debe de estar por aquí
Ⓑ PREP 1 alrededor de; **she wore a scarf ~ her neck** llevaba una bufanda alrededor del cuello; **she ignored the people ~ her** ignoró a la gente que estaba a su alrededor; **to wander ~ the town** pasearse por la ciudad; **there were books all ~ the house** había libros en todas partes de la casa *or* por toda la casa; **to go ~ the world** dar la vuelta al mundo; *see also* **round**, **corner**
2 (= *approximately*) aproximadamente, alrededor de; **it costs ~ £100** cuesta alrededor de *or* aproximadamente 100 libras; **~ 50** 50 más o menos; **he must be ~ 50** debe de tener unos 50 años; **~ 1950** alrededor de 1950, hacia 1950; **~ two o'clock** a eso de las dos

arousal [əˈraʊzəl] N (*sexual*) excitación *f* (sexual)

arouse [əˈraʊz] VT 1 (*frm*) (= *awaken from sleep*) despertar
2 (= *stimulate*) [+ *suspicion, curiosity*] despertar, suscitar; **it ~d great interest** despertó *or* suscitó mucho interés; **to ~ the appetite** abrir el apetito; **it should ~ you to greater efforts** debería incitarte a esforzarte más
3 (*sexually*) excitar

ARP NPL ABBR = **air-raid precautions**

arpeggio [ɑːˈpedʒɪəʊ] N arpegio *m*

arr. ABBR 1 (*on timetable*) = **arrives, arrival**
2 (*Mus*) (= **arranged**) *adaptación de*

arrack [ˈærək] N arac *m*, aguardiente *m* de palma *or* caña *etc*

arraign [əˈreɪn] VT procesar, acusar (**before** ante)

arraignment [əˈreɪnmənt] N (*Jur*) ≈ lectura *f* del acta de acusación

arrange [əˈreɪndʒ] Ⓐ VT 1 (= *put into order*) [+ *books, thoughts*] ordenar; [+ *hair, flowers*] arreglar; **to ~ one's affairs** poner sus asuntos en orden; **how did we ~ matters last time?** ¿cómo lo organizamos la última vez?
2 (= *place*) [+ *furniture, chairs*] disponer, colocar; **how is the room ~d?** ¿qué disposición tienen los muebles?
3 (= *plan*) planear, fijar; [+ *meeting*] organizar; [+ *schedule, programme*] acordar; **to ~ a party** organizar una fiesta; **everything is ~d** todo está arreglado; **"to be ~d"** "por determinar"; **it was ~d that ...** se quedó en que ...; **have you anything ~d for tomorrow?** ¿tienes planes para mañana?, ¿tienes algún compromiso mañana?; **a marriage has been ~d between ...** se ha concertado la boda de ...; **I've ~d a surprise for tonight** he preparado una sorpresa para esta noche; **to ~ a time for** fijar una hora para; **what did you ~ with him?** ¿en qué quedaste con él?
4 (*Mus*) adaptar, hacer los arreglos de
Ⓑ VI **to ~ to do sth** quedar en hacer algo; **I ~d to meet him at the cafe** quedé en verlo *or* quedé con él en el café; **I have ~d to see him tonight** quedamos en vernos esta noche, he quedado con él esta noche; **to ~ with sb to** + *INFIN* ponerse de acuerdo con algn para que + *subjun*; **to ~ with sb that** convenir con algn en que + *subjun*; **I have ~d for you to go** lo he arreglado para que vayas; **can you ~ for my luggage to be sent up?** por favor, (haga) que me suban el equipaje; **can you ~ for him to replace you?** ¿puedes arreglarlo para que te sustituya?

arranged [əˈreɪndʒd] ADJ [*marriage*] concertado (por los padres)

arrangement [ə'reɪndʒmənt] N [1] (= *order*) orden *m*
[2] (*Mus*) arreglo *m*
[3] (= *agreement*) acuerdo *m*; **prices by ~** precios a convenir; **larger orders by ~** los pedidos de mayor cantidad previo acuerdo; **by ~ with Covent Garden** con permiso de Covent Garden; **to come to an ~ (with sb)** llegar a un acuerdo (con algn); **we have an ~ with them** tenemos un acuerdo con ellos; **he has an ~ with his secretary** (*amorous*) se entiende con su secretaria
[4] (= *plan*) plan *m*; **if this ~ doesn't suit you** si este plan no le viene bien
[5] **arrangements** (= *plans*) planes *mpl*; (= *preparations*) preparativos *mpl*; **what are the ~s for your holiday?** ¿qué plan *or* planes tienes para las vacaciones?; **we must make ~s to help** debemos ver cómo podemos ayudar; **to make one's own ~s** obrar por cuenta propia; **if she doesn't like the idea she must make her own ~s** si no le gusta la idea que se las arregle sola; **all the ~s are made** todo está arreglado; **Pamela is in charge of the travel ~s** Pamela se encarga de los preparativos para el viaje

arranger [ə'reɪndʒə^r] N [1] (*Mus*) arreglista *mf*
[2] (= *organizer*) organizador(a) *m/f*

arrant ['ærənt] ADJ (*frm*) [*knave, liar etc*] consumado; **~ nonsense** puro disparate *m*

array [ə'reɪ] (A) N [1] (*Mil*) formación *f*, orden *m*; **in battle ~** en orden *or* formación de batalla; **in close ~** en filas apretadas
[2] (= *collection*) colección *f*; (= *series*) serie *f*; **a fine ~ of flowers** un bello conjunto de flores; **a great ~ of hats** una magnífica colección de sombreros
[3] (= *dress*) atavío *m*
[4] (*Comput*) matriz *f*, tabla *f*
(B) VT (*frm*) [1] (= *arrange, display*) disponer
[2] (= *line up*) formar (**against** contra)
[3] (= *dress*) ataviar, engalanar (**in** con, de)

arrears [ə'rɪəz] NPL [1] [*of money*] atrasos *mpl*; **rent ~** atrasos *mpl* de alquiler; **to be in ~** (*with rent*) ir atrasado en los pagos; **to get into ~** atrasarse en los pagos; **to pay one month in ~** pagar con un mes de retraso *or* a mes vencido; **to be in ~ with one's correspondence** tener correspondencia atrasada
[2] (*Sport*) **to be in ~** ir retrasado

arrest [ə'rest] (A) N [*of person*] detención *f*; [*of goods*] secuestro *m*; **to make an ~** hacer una detención; **to be under ~** estar detenido; **you're under ~** queda usted detenido; **to put** *or* **place sb under ~** detener *or* arrestar a algn
(B) VT [1] [+ *criminal*] detener
[2] [+ *attention*] atraer
[3] [+ *progress, decay etc*] (= *halt*) detener, parar; (= *hinder*) obstaculizar; **measures to ~ inflation** medidas para detener la inflación
(C) CPD ► **arrest warrant** N orden *f* de detención

arrested development [əˌrestɪddɪ'veləpmənt] N atrofia *f*, desarrollo *m* atrofiado

arresting [ə'restɪŋ] ADJ llamativo, que llama la atención

arrival [ə'raɪvəl] (A) N [1] [*of person, letter etc*] llegada *f*, arribo *m* (*esp LAm*); **"Arrivals"** (*Aer*) "Llegadas"; **on ~** al llegar; **dead on ~** ingresó cadáver
[2] (= *person*) persona *f* que llega; **Jim was the first ~ at the party** Jim fue el primero en llegar a la fiesta; **a new ~** (= *newcomer*) un recién llegado; (= *baby*) un recién nacido
(B) CPD ► **arrivals hall** N (*Aer*) sala *f* de llegadas

arrive [ə'raɪv] VI [1] [*person, taxi, letter, meal etc*] llegar, arribar (*esp LAm*); [*time, winter, event etc*] llegar; **to ~ (up)on the scene** entrar en escena
[2] [*baby*] nacer, llegar
[3] (*) (= *succeed in business etc*) triunfar, alcanzar el éxito
►**arrive at** VI + PREP [+ *decision, solution*] llegar a; [+ *perfection*] lograr, alcanzar; **we finally ~d at a price** por fin convenimos (en) un precio; **they finally ~d at the idea of doing …** finalmente llegaron a la conclusión de hacer …; **how did you ~ at this figure?** ¿cómo has llegado a esta cifra?

arriviste [ˌæri'vi:st] N arribista *mf*

arrogance ['ærəgəns] N arrogancia *f*, prepotencia *f* (*esp LAm*)

arrogant ['ærəgənt] ADJ arrogante, prepotente (*esp LAm*)

arrogantly ['ærəgəntlɪ] ADV con arrogancia, con prepotencia (*esp LAm*)

arrogate ['ærəʊgeɪt] VT **to ~ sth to o.s.** arrogarse algo

arrow ['ærəʊ] N (= *weapon, sign*) flecha *f*

arrowhead ['ærəʊhed] N punta *f* de flecha

arrowroot ['ærəʊru:t] N arrurruz *m*

arse** [ɑ:s] (*Brit*) (A) N culo‡ *m*; **get (up) off your ~!** ¡mueve el culo!‡; **move** *or* **shift your ~!** (= *move over*) córrete para allá; (= *hurry up*) ¡mueve el culo!‡; ✦*IDIOM* **he can't tell his ~ from his elbow** no tiene ni puñetera *or* puta idea‡, confunde la velocidad con el tocino*
(B) VT **I can't be ~d** no me apetece un huevo‡
►**arse about****, **arse around**** VI + ADV hacer el ganso *or* idiota*

arsehole** ['ɑ:sheʊl] N (*Brit*) [1] (= *person*) gilipollas** *mf inv*, pendejo/a *m/f* (*LAm**), huevón/ona *m/f* (*S. Cone**)
[2] (*Anat*) culo‡ *m*

arsenal ['ɑ:sɪnl] N arsenal *m*

arsenic ['ɑ:snɪk] N arsénico *m*

arsenical [ɑ:'senɪkl] ADJ arsénico, arsenical

arson ['ɑ:sn] N incendio *m* premeditado

arsonist ['ɑ:sənɪst] N incendiario/a *m/f*, pirómano/a *m/f*

art[1] [ɑ:t] (A) N [1] (= *painting etc*) arte *m*; **the ~s** las bellas artes; **art for ~'s sake** el arte por el arte; **work of ~** obra *f* de arte
[2] (= *skill*) arte *m*, habilidad *f*, destreza *f*; (= *technique*) técnica *f*; (= *knack*) maña *f*; (= *gift*) don *m*, facilidad *f*; **the ~ of embroidery** el arte del bordado; **the ~ of persuasion/seduction** el arte de la persuasión/la seducción; *see also* **fine**[1]
[3] (*Univ*) **Arts** Filosofía *f* y Letras; **Faculty of Arts** Facultad *f* de Filosofía y Letras; *see also* **bachelor, master**
[4] (= *cunning*) arte *m*
(B) CPD ► **art collection** N colección *f* de arte ► **art college** N escuela *f* de Bellas Artes ► **art dealer** N marchante *mf* ► **art deco** N art decó *m* ► **art exhibition** N exposición *f* de arte ► **art form** N medio *m* de expresión artística ► **art gallery** N (*state-owned*) museo *m* (de arte); (*private*) galería *f* de arte ► **art lover** N aficionado/a *m/f* al arte ► **art nouveau** N modernismo *m* ► **art paper** N papel *m* cuché ► **arts and crafts** NPL artesanías *fpl* ► **art school** N escuela *f* de Bellas Artes ► **Arts Council** N (*Brit*) *institución pública encargada de la promoción de la cultura y de las actividades artísticas* ► **Arts degree** N licenciatura *f* en Letras ► **Arts student** N estudiante *mf* de Letras ► **art student** N estudiante *mf* de Bellas Artes; *see also* **performance**

art[2]†† [ɑ:t] PRESENT (*thou form*) *of* **be**

artefact ['ɑ:tɪfækt] N [1] (= *object*) artefacto *m*
[2] (*fig*) (= *product*) producto *m*; (= *accident*) accidente *m*

arterial [ɑ:'tɪərɪəl] ADJ [*blood*] arterial; **~ road** arteria *f*

arteriosclerosis [ɑ:'tɪərɪəʊsklɪə'rəʊsɪs] N arteriosclerosis *f inv*

artery ['ɑ:tərɪ] N [1] (*Anat*) arteria *f*
[2] (= *road*) arteria *f*

artesian [ɑ:'ti:zɪən] ADJ **~ well** pozo *m* artesiano

artful [ɑ:tfʊl] ADJ [1] (= *cunning*) [*person, trick*] astuto, taimado, ladino (*esp LAm*)
[2] (= *skilful*) ingenioso; **an ~ way of doing sth** una forma ingeniosa de hacer algo

artfully ['ɑ:tfəlɪ] ADV [1] (= *cunningly*) con mucha maña, astutamente
[2] (= *skilfully*) [*arranged, constructed, designed*] ingeniosamente

artfulness ['ɑ:tfʊlnɪs] N [1] (= *cunning*) maña *f*, astucia *f*
[2] (= *skill*) ingenio *m*

art-house ['ɑ:thaʊs] ADJ [*film*] de autor, de arte y ensayo; **~ cinema** (= *films*) cine *m* de autor, cine *m* de arte y ensayo; (= *place*) cine *m* de arte y ensayo

arthritic [ɑ:'θrɪtɪk] ADJ artrítico

arthritis [ɑ:'θraɪtɪs] N artritis *f inv*

arthropod ['ɑ:θrəpɒd] N artrópodo *m*

Arthur ['ɑ:θə^r] N Arturo; **King ~** el Rey Arturo

Arthurian [ɑ:'θjʊərɪən] ADJ artúrico

artic* [ɑ:'tɪk] N (*Brit Aut*) = **articulated lorry**

artichoke ['ɑ:tɪtʃəʊk] N [1] (= *globe artichoke*) alcachofa *f*, alcaucil *m*
[2] (= *Jerusalem artichoke*) aguaturma *f*, cotufa *f* (*LAm*)

article ['ɑ:tɪkl] (A) N [1] (= *item, product*) artículo *m*; (= *object*) objeto *m*, cosa *f*; **~s of value** objetos *mpl* de valor; **~s of clothing** prendas *fpl* de vestir
[2] (*in newspaper etc*) artículo *m*; *see also* **leading**
[3] (*Ling*) artículo *m*; **definite/indefinite ~** artículo *m* definido/indefinido, artículo *m* determinado/indeterminado
[4] (*Admin, Jur*) artículo *m*, cláusula *f*
(B) VT (*Brit*) **to be ~d to sb** estar de aprendiz con algn
(C) CPD ► **article of faith** N artículo *m* de fe ► **article of partnership** N contrato *m* de asociación ► **articles of apprenticeship** NPL (*Brit*) contrato *msing* de aprendizaje ► **articles of association** NPL (*Comm*) estatutos *mpl* sociales ► **articles of war** NPL (*US Mil Hist*) código *msing* militar

articled clerk ['ɑ:tɪkld'klɑ:k] N (*Brit*) pasante *mf*

articulate (A) [ɑ:'tɪkjʊlɪt] ADJ [1] [*speech, account*] articulado; [*person*] que se expresa bien; **she's very** *or* **highly ~** se expresa muy bien; **he's not very ~** le cuesta expresarse
[2] (*Anat*) articulado
(B) [ɑ:'tɪkjʊleɪt] VT [1] (= *express*) [+ *thoughts, feelings*] expresar
[2] (= *pronounce*) [+ *word, sentence*] articular

articulated [ɑ:'tɪkjʊleɪtɪd] ADJ **~ lorry** camión *m* articulado

articulately [ɑ:'tɪkjʊlɪtlɪ] ADV [*speak, express o.s.*] con facilidad, fluidamente; [*pronounce*] articulando bien

articulation [ɑ:ˌtɪkjʊ'leɪʃən] N [1] (= *expression*) [*of thoughts, feelings*] expresión *f*
[2] (= *pronunciation*) [*of word, sentence*] articulación *f*
[3] (*Anat*) articulación *f*

articulatory [ɑːˈtɪkjʊlətərɪ] ADJ articulatorio

artifact [ˈɑːtɪfækt] N (*esp US*) = **artefact**

artifice [ˈɑːtɪfɪs] N 1 (= *cunning*) habilidad *f*, ingenio *m*

2 (= *trick*) artificio *m*, ardid *m*; (= *stratagem*) estratagema *f*

artificial [ˌɑːtɪˈfɪʃəl] Ⓐ ADJ 1 (= *synthetic*) [*light, flower, lake, leg, limb*] artificial; [*leather*] sintético; [*jewel*] de imitación; [*hair*] postizo

2 (*fig*) [*person, manner*] artificial, afectado; [*smile*] forzado; [*situation*] artificial

Ⓑ CPD ► **artificial horizon** N horizonte *m* artificial ► **artificial insemination** N inseminación *f* artificial ► **artificial intelligence** N inteligencia *f* artificial ► **artificial manure** N abono *m* químico ► **artificial respiration** N respiración *f* artificial ► **artificial silk** N seda *f* artificial, rayón *m* ► **artificial sweetener** N edulcorante *m*

artificiality [ˌɑːtɪfɪʃɪˈælɪtɪ] N 1 (*lit*) (= *synthetic nature*) artificialidad *f*

2 (*fig*) [*of person, manner*] artificialidad *f*, afectación *f*, falta *f* de naturalidad

artificially [ˌɑːtɪˈfɪʃəlɪ] ADV 1 (= *by synthetic means*) artificialmente

2 (*fig*) con afectación

artillery [ɑːˈtɪlərɪ] N (= *guns, troops etc*) artillería *f*

artilleryman [ɑːˈtɪlərɪmən] N (*pl* **artillerymen**) artillero *m*

artisan [ˈɑːtɪzæn] N artesano/a *m/f*

artisanal [ɑːˈtɪzənəl] ADJ [*skills, groups, clothes*] artesanal

artist [ˈɑːtɪst] N artista *mf*

artiste [ɑːˈtiːst] N (*esp Brit Theat*) artista *mf* (del espectáculo); (*Mus*) intérprete *mf*

artistic [ɑːˈtɪstɪk] Ⓐ ADJ [*ability, design, temperament, freedom*] artístico; **to be ~** [*person*] tener dotes artísticas; **an ~ flower arrangement** un arreglo floral muy artístico

Ⓑ CPD ► **artistic director** N director(a) *m/f* artístico/a

artistically [ɑːˈtɪstɪkəlɪ] ADV [*arranged, presented*] con mucho arte, artísticamente; **~ gifted children** niños con dotes artísticas; **to be ~ inclined** tener dotes artísticas; **~, the photographs are stunning** desde el punto de vista artístico, las fotografías son sensacionales

artistry [ˈɑːtɪstrɪ] N (= *skill*) arte *m*, habilidad *f*

artless [ˈɑːtlɪs] ADJ 1 (= *straightforward*) [*beauty*] natural; [*person, smile, comment*] ingenuo, sin malicia; [*book, story, film*] sencillo, sin artificios

2 (= *naïve*) simple

3 (= *clumsy*) torpe

artlessly [ˈɑːtlɪslɪ] ADV 1 (= *innocently*) ingenuamente

2 (= *clumsily*) torpemente

artlessness [ˈɑːtlɪsnɪs] N 1 (= *straightforwardness*) [*of beauty*] naturalidad *f*; [*of person, behaviour, comment*] ingenuidad *f*, falta *f* de malicia

2 (= *clumsiness*) torpeza *f*

artsy* [ˈɑːtsɪ] (*esp US*) = **arty**

artsy-craftsy* [ˈɑːtsɪˈkrɑːftsɪ] ADJ (*US*) = **arty-crafty**

artsy-fartsy‡ [ˈɑːtsɪˈfɑːtsɪ] ADJ (*US*) = **arty-farty**

artwork [ˈɑːtwɜːk] N material *m* gráfico

arty* [ˈɑːtɪ] ADJ [*style*] con pretensiones artísticas, seudoartístico; [*clothing*] afectado, extravagante; [*person*] de gusto muy afectado, que se las da de muy artista; **she looks ~** ◊ **she is ~-looking** tiene pinta de cultureta

arty-crafty* [ˈɑːtɪˈkrɑːftɪ], **artsy-craftsy*** (*US*) [ˈɑːtsɪˈkrɑːftsɪ] ADJ [*style*] con pretensiones artísticas; [*person*] (= *creative*) con inclinación por las manualidades, muy manitas *inv*; (= *keen on craftware*) metido a artesano, enamorado de la artesanía

arty-farty‡ [ˈɑːtɪˈfɑːtɪ], **artsy-fartsy*** (*US*) [ˈɑːtsɪˈfɑːtsɪ] ADJ pretencioso, con pretensiones artísticas

ARV N ABBR (*US*) (= **American Revised Version**) *versión norteamericana de la Biblia*

arvee* [ɑːˈviː] N (*US*) = **recreational vehicle**

Aryan [ˈɛərɪən] Ⓐ ADJ ario

Ⓑ N ario/a *m/f*

AS ABBR (*US*) 1 = **Associate in Sciences**

2 = **American Samoa**

▼**as** [æz, əz]

A CONJUNCTION	C ADVERB
B PREPOSITION	

For set combinations in which **as** *is not the first word, eg* **such ... as, the same ... as, dressed as, acknowledge as,** *look up the other word.*

Ⓐ CONJUNCTION

1 ***in time clauses***

You can usually use **cuando** *when the* **as** *clause simply tells you* **when** *an event happened:*

cuando; **as I was passing the house** cuando pasaba por delante de la casa; **he came in as I was leaving** entró cuando yo salía

Alternatively, use **al** + INFINITIVE:

he came in as I was leaving entró al salir yo; **he tripped as he was coming out of the bank** tropezó al salir *or* cuando salía del banco; **as the car drew level with us, I realized Isabel was driving** al llegar el coche a nuestra altura *or* cuando el coche llegó a nuestra altura, me di cuenta de que lo conducía Isabel

Translate **as** *using* **mientras** *for longer actions which are happening at the same time:*

(= *while*) mientras; **as we walked, we talked about the future** mientras caminábamos, hablábamos del futuro

In the context of two closely linked actions involving parallel development, translate **as** *using* **a medida que** *or* **conforme**. *Alternatively, use* **según va** *etc* + GERUND:

as one gets older, life gets more and more difficult a medida que se envejece *or* conforme se envejece *or* según va uno envejeciendo, la vida se hace cada vez más difícil; **as he got older he got deafer** a medida que *or* conforme envejeció se fue volviendo más sordo, según fue envejeciendo se fue volviendo más sordo

2 ***in reason clauses***

When **as** *means "since" or "because", you can generally use* **como**, *provided you put it at the beginning of the sentence. Alternatively, use the more formal* **puesto que** *either at the beginning of the sentence or between the clauses or* **ya que** *especially between the clauses.*

como; (*more frm*) puesto que, ya que; **as you're here, I'll tell you** como estás aquí *or* puesto que estás aquí, te lo diré; **he didn't mention it as he didn't want to worry you** como no quería preocuparte, no lo mencionó, no lo mencionó puesto que no quería preocuparte; **he couldn't come as he had an appointment** no pudo asistir porque *or* puesto que *or* ya que tenía un compromiso; **patient as she is, she'll probably put up with it** con lo paciente que es, seguramente lo soportará

3 ***describing way, manner*** como; **leave things as they are** dejad las cosas como están; **I'm okay as I am** estoy bien tal como estoy; **knowing him as I do, I'm sure he'll refuse** conociéndolo como lo conozco, estoy seguro de que no aceptará; **the village, situated as it is near a motorway, ...** el pueblo, situado como está cerca de una autopista, ...; **as I've said before ...** como he dicho antes ...; **as I was saying ...** como iba diciendo ...; **her door is the first as you go up** su puerta es la primera según se sube; **she is very gifted, as is her brother** tiene mucho talento, al igual que su hermano; **you'll have it by noon as agreed** lo tendrá antes del mediodía, tal como acordamos; **it's not bad, as hotels go** no está mal, en comparación con otros hoteles; **as in all good detective stories** como en toda buena novela policíaca; **as you know** como sabe; **Arsenal are playing as never before!** ¡Arsenal está jugando mejor que nunca!; **as often happens** como suele ocurrir; **he performed brilliantly, as only he can** actuó de maravilla, como sólo él sabe hacerlo; **as you were!** (*Mil*) ¡descansen!; **do as you wish** haga lo que quiera

4 **= *though*** aunque; **tired as he was, he went to the party** aunque estaba cansado, asistió a la fiesta; **interesting as the book is, I don't think it will sell very well** el libro es interesante, pero aún así no creo que se venda bien, aunque el libro es interesante, no creo que se venda bien; **try as she would** *or* **might, she couldn't lift it** por más que se esforzó no pudo levantarlo; **unlikely as it may seem ...** por imposible que parezca ...

5 ***in set structures***

♦ **as if** *or* **as though** como si; **it was as if** *or* **as though he were still alive** era como si estuviera todavía vivo; **he looked as if** *or* **as though he was ill** parecía como si estuviera enfermo; **it isn't as if** *or* **as though he were poor** no es que sea pobre, que digamos; **as if she knew!** ¡como si ella lo supiera!

♦ **as if to**: **the little dog nodded his head, as if to agree** el perrito movió la cabeza, como asintiendo

♦ **as in**: **it's spelled with V as in Valencia** se escribe con V de Valencia

♦ **as it is**: **as it is, it doesn't make much difference** en realidad, casi da lo mismo; **as it is we can do nothing** en la práctica *or* tal y como están las cosas no podemos hacer nada; **I've got quite enough to do as it is** tengo ya bastante trabajo

♦ **as it were**: **I'd understood the words, but I hadn't understood the question, as it were** había entendido las palabras, pero no había comprendido la pregunta, por así decirlo; **I have become, as it were, two people** me he convertido como en dos personas; **he was as it were tired and emotional** estaba de alguna forma cansado y con los nervios a flor de piel

♦ **as was**: **that's the headmistress, the deputy as was** esa es la directora, que antes era la subdirectora

Ⓑ PREPOSITION

1 **= *while*** **she was often ill as a child** de pequeña se ponía enferma con frecuencia

2 **= *in the capacity of*** como; **he succeeded as a politician** tuvo éxito como político; **I don't think much of him as an actor** como actor, no me gusta mucho; **she treats me as her equal** me trata de igual a igual; **we're going as tourists** vamos en plan de turismo; **he was there as adviser** estaba allí en calidad de asesor; **Gibson as Hamlet** (*Theat*) Gibson en el papel de Hamlet; **he works as a waiter** trabaja de camarero; *see also* **such C**

Ⓒ ADVERB

1 ***in comparisons***

♦ **as ... as** tan ... como; **I am as tall as him** soy

➤ LANGUAGE IN USE: **as A2** 17.1 **A3** 5.2 **C1** 5.2, 5.3, 5.5

tan alto como él; **this tree can grow as tall as 50 feet** este árbol puede llegar a medir 50 pies de alto; **as big as a house** (tan) grande como una casa; **she hit him as hard as she could** lo golpeó lo más fuerte que pudo, lo golpeó tan fuerte como pudo; **he was writing as long ago as 1945** en 1945 ya escribía; **she doesn't walk as quickly** *or* **as fast as me** no camina tan rápido como yo; **walk as quickly** *or* **as fast as you can** camina lo más rápido que puedas; **he ate as quickly as possible** comió lo más rápido posible; **it was still being done by hand as recently as 1960** en 1960 todavía seguía haciéndose a mano; **the fresh snow was as white as white could be** la nieve fresca era todo lo blanca que podía ser; **is it as far as that?** ¿tan lejos está?; **is it as big as all that?** ¿es de verdad tan grande?

♦ **as little as**: **by saving as little as ten pounds a month** ahorrando tan sólo diez libras al mes

♦ **as many ... as** tantos/as ... como; **I haven't got as many pairs of shoes as you** no tengo tantos pares de zapatos como tú; **I've got a lot of tapes but I haven't got as many as him** *or* **as he has** tengo muchas cintas, pero no tantas como él; **she gets as many as eight thousand letters a month** llega a recibir hasta ocho mil cartas al mes

♦ **as much**: **she thought he was an idiot, and said as much** pensaba que era un idiota, y así lo expresó

♦ **as much ... as** tanto/a ... como; **I haven't got as much energy as you** no tengo tanta energía como tú; **you've got as much as she has** tienes tanto como ella; **you spend as much as me** *or* **as I do** tú gastas tanto como yo; **it didn't cost as much as I had expected** no costó tanto como yo me esperaba; **it can cost as much as $2,000** puede llegar a costar 2.000 dólares

♦ **as one**: **they all stood up as one** se levantaron todos a la vez

♦ **half/twice/three times as ...**: **it's half as expensive** es la mitad de caro; **it's twice as expensive** es el doble de caro; **it's three times as expensive** es tres veces más caro; **she's twice as nice as her sister** es el doble de simpática que su hermana; **her coat cost twice as much as mine** su abrigo costó el doble que el mío

♦ **without as** *or* **so much as**: **she gave me back the book without as much as an apology** me devolvió el libro sin pedirme siquiera una disculpa

[2] *in set structures*

♦ **as for**: **as for the children, they were exhausted** en cuanto a los niños, estaban rendidos, los niños, por su parte, estaban rendidos; **as for that ...** en cuanto a esto ...

♦ **as from**: **as from tomorrow** a partir de mañana

♦ **as of**: **as of yesterday/now** a partir de ayer/ahora

♦ **as to**: **as to that I can't say** en lo que a eso se refiere, no lo sé; **as to her mother ...** en cuanto a su madre ...; **to question sb as to his intentions** preguntar a algn sus intenciones; **they make decisions as to whether students need help** deciden si los alumnos necesitan ayuda; **he inquired as to what the problem was** preguntó cuál era el problema

♦ **as yet** hasta ahora, hasta el momento; *see also* **regard B4**

ASA N ABBR [1] (*Brit*) = **Advertising Standards Authority**
[2] (*Brit*) = **Amateur Swimming Association**
[3] (*US*) = **American Standards Association**

ASA/BS ABBR = **American Standards Association/British Standard**

a.s.a.p.* ADV ABBR (= **as soon as possible**) lo antes posible, lo más pronto posible

asbestos [æz'bestəs] N amianto *m*, asbesto *m*

asbestosis [,æzbes'təusɪs] N asbestosis *f inv*

ascend [ə'send] Ⓐ VT (*frm*) [+ *stairs*] subir; [+ *mountain*] subir a; [+ *throne*] ascender a, subir a
Ⓑ VI (= *rise*) subir, ascender; (= *slope up*) elevarse

ascendancy [ə'sendənsɪ] N ascendiente *m*, dominio *m*

ascendant [ə'sendənt] N **to be in the ~** estar en auge, ir ganando predominio

ascending [ə'sendɪŋ] ADJ ascendente; **in ~ order** en orden ascendente

ascension [ə'senʃən] Ⓐ N ascensión *f*
Ⓑ CPD ► **Ascension Day** N día *m* de la Ascensión ► **Ascension Island** N Isla *f* Ascensión

ascent [ə'sent] N [1] (= *climb, way up*) subida *f*; (*in plane*) ascenso *m*
[2] (= *slope*) pendiente *f*, cuesta *f*
[3] (*fig*) ascenso *m*

ascertain [,æsə'teɪn] VT determinar, establecer (**that** que)

ascertainable [,æsə'teɪnəbl] ADJ determinable

ascertainment [,æsə'teɪnmənt] N determinación *f*

ascetic [ə'setɪk] Ⓐ ADJ ascético
Ⓑ N asceta *mf*

asceticism [ə'setɪsɪzəm] N ascetismo *m*

ASCII ['æskiː] Ⓐ N ABBR (= **American Standard Code for Information Interchange**) ASCII *m*
Ⓑ CPD ► **ASCII file** N fichero *m* ASCII

ascorbic [ə'skɔːbɪk] ADJ **~ acid** ácido *m* ascórbico

> **ASCOT**
>
> ***Ascot*** *o* ***Royal Ascot*** *es una competición de carreras de caballos que dura cuatro días y se celebra en junio en el hipódromo de Ascot, cerca del castillo de Windsor, en el sur de Inglaterra. Es uno de los acontecimientos más importantes en el calendario hípico británico, y también lo es a nivel social, pues a él acuden miembros de la realeza y la clase alta británica. La familia real hace acto de presencia en carruajes, y sigue las carreras desde una zona reservada llamada* ***Royal Enclosure****. Se considera un gran honor ser invitado a ella y los invitados han de observar estrictas normas de etiqueta. En el día conocido como* ***Ladies Day*** *(el Día de las Damas), es tradicional que las mujeres vayan a las carreras luciendo sombreros y vestidos espectaculares.*

ascribable [əs'kraɪbəbl] ADJ atribuible (**to** a)

ascribe [ə'skraɪb] VT **to ~ sth to sb/sth** atribuir algo a algn/algo

ascription [ə'skrɪpʃən] N atribución *f*

ASCU N ABBR (*US*) = **Association of State Colleges and Universities**

ASE N ABBR (*US*) = **American Stock Exchange**

ASEAN N ABBR = **Association of South-East Asian Nations**

aseptic [eɪ'septɪk] ADJ aséptico

asexual [eɪ'seksjʊəl] ADJ asexual

asexually [eɪ'seksjʊəlɪ] ADV de forma asexual

ASH [æʃ] N ABBR (*Brit*) = **Action on Smoking and Health**

ash¹ [æʃ] Ⓐ N [1] (*also* **~ tree**) fresno *m*
[2] (= *wood*) (madera *f* de) fresno *m*
Ⓑ ADJ de madera de fresno; **a black ~ table** una mesa negra (de madera) de fresno

ash² [æʃ] Ⓐ N (*from fire, cigarette*) ceniza *f*; **~es** (*gen, mortal remains*) cenizas *fpl*; **to burn** *or* **reduce sth to ~es** reducir algo a cenizas; **~es to ~es, dust to dust** (*Rel*) las cenizas a las cenizas, el polvo al polvo; **the Ashes** (*Cricket*) *trofeo de los partidos de críquet Australia-Inglaterra*; ♦***IDIOM*** **to rise out of the ~es of sth** surgir de las cenizas de algo
Ⓑ CPD ► **ash bin**, **ash can** (*US*) N cubo *m or* (*LAm*) bote *m or* (*LAm*) tarro *m* de la basura ► **Ash Wednesday** N miércoles *m inv* de Ceniza; *see also* **ash blond(e)**

ashamed [ə'ʃeɪmd] ADJ [1] (= *remorseful*) avergonzado, apenado (*LAm*); **he was/felt ~ about what had happened** estaba/se sentía avergonzado por lo que había pasado; **she was in tears, saying how ~ she felt** estaba llorando y diciendo lo avergonzada *or* arrepentida que se sentía *or* estaba; **she was ~ that she had been so nasty** ◊ **she was ~ about having been so nasty** estaba avergonzada *or* se avergonzaba *or* se arrepentía de haber sido tan cruel; **to be ~ of o.s.** estar avergonzado de sí mismo; **you ought to be ~ of yourself!** ¡debería darte vergüenza *or* (*LAm*) pena!, ¡no te da vergüenza!
[2] (= *embarrassed*) **I was ~ to ask for money** me daba vergüenza *or* (*LAm*) pena pedir dinero; **I've done nothing, I'm ~ to say** me da vergüenza *or* (*LAm*) pena reconocerlo pero no he hecho nada; **I was too ~ to tell anyone** me sentía demasiado avergonzado como para decírselo a nadie; **it's nothing to be ~ of** no hay por qué avergonzarse *or* (*LAm*) apenarse; **I'm ~ of you** me avergüenzo de ti; **I felt ~ that the money spent on my education had been wasted** me daba vergüenza pensar que el dinero que se había gastado en mi educación no había servido para nada

ash blond(e) [æʃ'blɒnd] Ⓐ ADJ rubio ceniza
Ⓑ N rubio/a *m/f* ceniza

ash-coloured, **ash-colored** (*US*) ['æʃkʌləd] ADJ [1] (*lit*) color ceniza *inv*, ceniciento
[2] (= *pale*) pálido

ashen ['æʃn] ADJ [1] (= *greyish*) ceniciento
[2] (= *pale*) pálido
[3] (= *ashwood*) de fresno

Ashkenazi [,æʃkə'nɑːzɪ] Ⓐ ADJ askenazí
Ⓑ N (*pl* **Ashkenazim** [,æʃkə'nɑːzɪm]) askenazí *mf*

ashlar ['æʃlə'] N [1] sillar *m*
[2] (*also* **~ work**) sillería *f*

ashman ['æʃmæn] N (*pl* **ashmen**) (*US*) basurero *m*

ashore [ə'ʃɔː'] ADV en tierra; **to be ~** estar en tierra; **to go/come ~** desembarcar; **to put sb ~** desembarcar a algn, poner a algn en tierra; **to run ~** encallar

ashpan ['æʃpæn] N cenicero *m*, cajón *m* de la ceniza

ashram ['æʃrəm] N ashram *m*

ashtray ['æʃtreɪ] N cenicero *m*

ashy ['æʃɪ] ADJ lleno de ceniza

Asia ['eɪʃə] Ⓐ N Asia *f*
Ⓑ CPD ► **Asia Minor** N Asia *f* Menor

Asian ['eɪʃn] Ⓐ ADJ asiático; **~ flu** gripe *f* asiática
Ⓑ N asiático/a *m/f*

Asian-American ['eɪʃnə'merɪkən] Ⓐ ADJ

asiático-americano
Ⓑ N asiático-americano/a *m/f*

Asiatic [ˌeɪsɪˈætɪk] ADJ, N asiático/a *m/f*

aside [əˈsaɪd]

When **aside** *is an element in a phrasal verb, eg* **brush aside, cast aside, put aside, stand aside***, look up the verb.*

Ⓐ ADV [1] (*= to one side*) a un lado; **to set** *or* **put sth ~** apartar algo; **to cast ~** desechar, echar a un lado; **to step ~** hacerse a un lado; **joking ~** bromas aparte
[2] **~ from** (*= as well as*) aparte de, además de; (*= except for*) aparte de
Ⓑ N (*Theat*) aparte *m*; **to say sth in an ~** decir algo aparte

asinine [ˈæsɪnaɪn] ADJ [1] (*frm*) (*= ass-like*) asnal [2] (*= stupid*) estúpido

ask [ɑːsk]

Ⓐ TRANSITIVE VERB
Ⓑ INTRANSITIVE VERB
Ⓒ PHRASAL VERBS

Ⓐ TRANSITIVE VERB
[1] **= inquire** preguntar; **"how is Frank?" he ~ed** —¿cómo está Frank? —preguntó; **to ~ sb sth** preguntar algo a algn; **I ~ed him his name/the time** le pregunté su nombre/la hora; **to ~ o.s. sth** preguntarse algo; **did you ~ him about the job?** ¿le has preguntado por el trabajo?; (*in more detail*) ¿le has preguntado acerca del trabajo?; **I've been meaning to ~ you about that** llevo tiempo queriendo *or* hace tiempo que quiero preguntarte acerca de eso; **~ her about her plans for Christmas** pregúntale qué planes tiene para la Navidad; **~ me another!** ¡no tengo ni idea!; **don't ~ me!*** ¡yo qué sé!*, ¡qué sé yo! (*esp LAm**); **I ~ you!*** (*despairing*) ¿te lo puedes creer?; **~ him if he has seen her** pregúntale si la ha visto; **if you ~ me, I think she's crazy** para mí que está loca; **and where have you been, may I ~?** ¿y dónde has estado, si se puede saber?; **to ~ (sb) a question** hacer una pregunta (a algn); **I ~ed the teacher what to do next** le pregunté al profesor lo que tenía que hacer después; **~ them what time the party is** pregúntales a qué hora es la fiesta; **who ~ed you?*** ¿quién te ha preguntado a ti?; **~ her why she didn't come** pregúntale por qué no vino
[2] **= request** pedir; **to ~ sb a favour** ◊ **~ a favour of sb** pedir un favor a algn; **how much are they ~ing for the car?** ¿cuánto piden por el coche?; **they are ~ing £80,000 for the house** piden 80.000 libras por la casa; **that's ~ing the impossible** eso es pedir lo imposible; **it's not a lot to ~** no es mucho pedir; **that's ~ing a lot** eso es mucho pedir; **what more can you ~?** ¿qué más se puede pedir?; **to ~ sth of sb**: **he did everything ~ed of him** hizo todo lo que se le pidió; **all he ~ed of us was that we tell people about his plight** sólo nos pidió que habláramos a la gente de la difícil situación en que se encontraba; **to ~ that sth be done** pedir que se haga algo; **all I'm ~ing is that you keep an open mind** sólo te pido que *or* lo único que pido es que mantengas una actitud abierta; **to ~ to do sth**: **I ~ed to see the director** pedí ver al director; **he ~ed to go on the picnic** preguntó si podía ir (con ellos) de picnic; **to ~ sb to do sth** pedir a algn que haga algo; **we had to ~ him to leave** tuvimos que decirle *or* pedirle que se marchara; **that's ~ing too much** eso es pedir demasiado; **I think she's ~ing too much** creo que está exigiendo demasiado; *see also* **permission**
[3] **= invite** invitar; **have you been ~ed?** ¿te han invitado?; **to ~ sb to dinner** invitar a algn a cenar

Ⓑ INTRANSITIVE VERB
[1] **= inquire** preguntar; **he was too shy to ~** le dio vergüenza preguntar; **~ about our reduced rates for students** pregunta por *or* infórmate sobre nuestros descuentos para estudiantes; **he was ~ing about the Vikings** preguntaba acerca de *or* sobre los vikingos; **I ~ed about the possibility of staying on** pregunté acerca de *or* sobre la posibilidad de quedarme más tiempo, pregunté si era posible que me quedara más tiempo; **he was ~ing about you** estaba preguntando por ti; **"what's the matter?" — "don't ~"** —¿qué pasa? —más te vale no saberlo; **now you're ~ing!*** (*= what a difficult question*) ¡vaya con la preguntita!*; (*= who knows*) ¡quién sabe!; (*= wouldn't we all like to know*) ¡eso quisiera saber yo!*; **I was only ~ing** era sólo una pregunta; **"what has he gone and done now?" — "you may well ~!"** —¿qué es lo que ha hecho ahora? —¡buena pregunta!
[2] **= make request** pedir; **if you need anything, just ~** si quieres algo no tienes más que pedirlo; **the ~ing price** el precio que se pide/pedía *etc*; **I offered £5,000 below the ~ing price** les ofrecí 5.000 libras menos de lo que pedían; **it's yours for the ~ing** no tienes más que pedirlo y es tuyo

Ⓒ PHRASAL VERBS

►**ask after** VI + PREP [+ *person*] preguntar por; [+ *sb's health*] preguntar por, interesarse por; **Jane was ~ing after you** Jane (me) preguntaba por ti

►**ask along** VT + ADV invitar; **~ him along if you like** si quieres, dile que venga, invítale si quieres

►**ask around** VI + ADV preguntar por ahí; **~ around to find out which are the best schools** pregunta por ahí y entérate de cuáles son las mejores escuelas

►**ask back** VT + ADV (*for second visit*) volver a invitar; (*on reciprocal visit*) devolver la invitación a; **she ~ed me back to her house after the show** me invitó a su casa después del espectáculo

►**ask for** Ⓐ VI + PREP [1] (*= request*) pedir, solicitar (*frm*); **he wrote ~ing for help** escribió pidiendo *or* (*more frm*) solicitando ayuda; **to ~ for sth back** pedir que se devuelva algo
[2] (*= look for*) **to ~ for sb** preguntar por algn; **there's someone ~ing for you at reception** hay alguien en recepción que pregunta por ti
[3] (*in idiomatic phrases*) **he is all I could ~ for in a son** tiene todo lo que podría pedirle a un hijo; **he ~ed for it!** ¡él se lo ha buscado!; **you're ~ing for a good smack!** ¡si sigues así, te vas a ganar una buena bofetada!; **it's just ~ing for trouble** eso no es otra cosa que buscarse problemas
Ⓑ VT + PREP **to ~ sb for sth** pedir algo a algn

►**ask in** VT + ADV invitar a entrar, invitar a pasar; **to ~ sb in for a drink** invitar a algn a que pase a tomar algo

►**ask out** VT + ADV invitar a salir; **they never ~ her out** no la invitan nunca a salir (con ellos); **he ~ed her out to dinner** la invitó (a salir) a cenar

►**ask round** VT + ADV invitar (a casa); **they've ~ed us round for drinks** nos han invitado (a su casa) a tomar unas copas

ASK

• Translate **ask** by **preguntar** only in contexts where information is being sought:
I'll ask him
Voy a preguntárselo
Ask her what she thinks
Pregúntale qué le parece
We asked everywhere
Preguntamos en todas partes
• Use **pedir** when **ask** means "request" or "demand":
No one asked to see my passport
Nadie me pidió el pasaporte
We asked them to be here before five
Les pedimos que estuviesen *or* ***estuvieran aquí antes de las cinco***
He was asked to explain his behaviour
Le pidieron que explicara su comportamiento
! Pedir que is followed by the subjunctive.
For further uses and examples, see main entries at **ask**, **ask about** *and* **ask for** *etc.*

askance [əˈskɑːns] ADV **to look ~ at sb** mirar a algn con recelo *or* desconfianza; **to look ~ at sth** ver algo con recelo *or* desconfianza

askew [əˈskjuː] Ⓐ ADJ ladeado; **the picture is ~** el cuadro está torcido Ⓑ ADV de lado

aslant [əˈslɑːnt] Ⓐ ADV a través, oblicuamente Ⓑ PREP a través de

asleep [əˈsliːp] ADJ [1] (*= not awake*) dormido; **to be ~** estar dormido; **to be fast** *or* **sound ~** estar profundamente dormido; **to fall ~** dormirse, quedarse dormido
[2] (*= numb*) adormecido; **my foot's ~** se me ha (quedado) dormido el pie

ASLEF [ˈæzlef] N ABBR (*Brit*) = **Associated Society of Locomotive Engineers and Firemen**

AS level [eɪˈeslevl] N (*Brit*) (= **Advanced Subsidiary Level**) *certificado académico que se hace entre los* **GCSEs** *y los* **A Levels**;
→ GCSE, A LEVELS

ASM N ABBR [1] (*Mil*) = **air-to-surface missile** [2] (*Theat*) = **assistant stage manager**

asocial [eɪˈsəʊʃəl] ADJ [1] (*= solitary*) asocial, insociable [2] (*= antisocial*) antisocial

asp[1] [æsp] N áspid(e) *m*

asp[2] [æsp] = **aspen**

ASP ABBR = **American Selling Price**

asparagus [əsˈpærəgəs] Ⓐ N (*= plant*) espárrago *m*; (*= food*) espárragos *mpl* Ⓑ CPD ► **asparagus tips** NPL puntas *fpl* de espárrago

ASPCA N ABBR (*US*) = **American Society for the Prevention of Cruelty to Animals**

aspect [ˈæspekt] N [1] [*of situation*] aspecto *m*; **to study all ~s of a question** estudiar un asunto bajo todos sus aspectos; **seen from this ~** desde este punto de vista
[2] [*of building, room*] **a house with a northerly ~** una casa orientada hacia el norte
[3] (*Gram*) aspecto *m*

aspen [ˈæspən] N álamo *m* temblón

asperity [æsˈperɪtɪ] N aspereza *f*

aspersion [əsˈpɜːʃən] N calumnia *f*; **to cast ~s on sb** difamar *or* calumniar a algn

asphalt [ˈæsfælt] Ⓐ N [1] (*= material*) asfalto *m* [2] (*= surface, ground*) pista *f* asfaltada, recinto *m* asfaltado Ⓑ VT asfaltar Ⓒ CPD ► **asphalt jungle** N jungla *f* de asfalto

asphyxia [æsˈfɪksɪə] N asfixia *f*

asphyxiate [æsˈfɪksɪeɪt] Ⓐ VT asfixiar Ⓑ VI asfixiarse, morir asfixiado

asphyxiation [æsˌfɪksɪˈeɪʃən] N asfixia *f*

aspic [ˈæspɪk] N gelatina *f* (*de carne etc*)

➤ LANGUAGE IN USE: aspect 1 26.1, 26.3

aspidistra [ˌæspɪˈdɪstrə] N aspidistra *f*

aspirant [ˈæspɪrənt] N aspirante *mf*, candidato/a *m/f* (**to** a)

aspirate Ⓐ [ˈæspərɪt] ADJ aspirado
Ⓑ [ˈæspərɪt] N aspirada *f*
Ⓒ [ˈæspəreɪt] VT aspirar; **~d H** H *f* aspirada

aspiration [ˌæspəˈreɪʃən] N (*also Ling*) aspiración *f*

aspirational [ˌæspəˈreɪʃənl] ADJ [*person*] con aspiraciones; [*product*] que viste mucho, que queda muy bien

aspire [əsˈpaɪəʳ] VI **to ~ to sth** aspirar a algo; **we can't ~ to that** no aspiramos a tanto, nuestras pretensiones son más modestas; **he ~s to a new car** anhela tener un coche nuevo; **to ~ to do sth** aspirar a hacer algo, ambicionar hacer algo

aspirin [ˈæsprɪn] N (*pl* **aspirin, aspirins**) (*= substance, tablet*) aspirina *f*

aspiring [əsˈpaɪərɪŋ] ADJ (*= ambitious*) ambicioso; (*= budding*) en potencia, en ciernes; **this is good news for any ~ politician** eso es bueno para cualquier político en potencia *or* en ciernes

ass[1] [æs] N [1] (*Zool*) asno *m*, burro *m*
[2] (*) (*= fool*) imbécil *mf*; **the man's an ~** es un imbécil; **don't be an ~!** ¡no seas imbécil!; **what an ~ I am!** ¡soy un imbécil!, ¡qué burro soy!*; ✦*IDIOM* **to make an ~ of o.s.** quedar en ridículo

ass[2]** [æs] (*US*) N culo* *m*; **a piece of ~** (*= girl*) un bombón*; **to have a piece of ~** (*= sex*) echar un polvo**; *see also* **bust**[2], **chew**, **cover B3**, **save**[1] **A1**

assail [əˈseɪl] VT (*frm*) [1] (*= attack*) (*lit*) acometer, atacar; (*fig*) atacar; **he was ~ed by critics** le atacaron los críticos; **a sound ~ed my ear** un ruido penetró (en) mis oídos
[2] (*= bombard*) **to ~ sb with questions** asaltar *or* bombardear a algn a preguntas, freír a algn a preguntas*; **they ~ed her with questions** la asaltaron *or* bombardearon a preguntas, la frieron a preguntas*; **he was ~ed by doubts** ◊ **doubts ~ed him** le asaltaban las dudas

assailant [əˈseɪlənt] N asaltante *mf*, agresor(a) *m/f*; **she did not recognize her ~s** no reconoció a los que la agredieron; **there were four ~s** eran cuatro los agresores

Assam [æˈsæm] N Assam *m*

assassin [əˈsæsɪn] N asesino/a *m/f*

assassinate [əˈsæsɪneɪt] VT asesinar

assassination [əˌsæsɪˈneɪʃən] N asesinato *m*

assault [əˈsɔːlt] Ⓐ N [1] (*Mil, fig*) asalto *m*, ataque *m* (**on** a); **to make** *or* **mount an ~ on** asaltar
[2] (*Jur*) agresión *f*; **~ and battery** (*Jur*) lesiones *fpl*; *see also* **indecent**
Ⓑ VT [1] (*Mil*) asaltar, atacar
[2] (*Jur*) asaltar, agredir; (*sexually*) agredir sexualmente; (*= rape*) violar
Ⓒ CPD ► **assault course** N pista *f* americana ► **assault craft** N barcaza *f* de asalto ► **assault rifle** N fusil *m* de asalto, rifle *m* de asalto ► **assault troops** NPL tropas *fpl* de asalto

assay Ⓐ [əˈseɪ] N [*of metal, mineral, etc*] ensayo *m*; [*of gold*] ensayo *m*, aquilatamiento *m*
Ⓑ VT [1] [*+ metal, mineral, etc*] ensayar; [*+ gold*] ensayar, aquilatar; (*fig*) intentar, probar
[2] (††) (*= try*) **to ~ to** + INFIN intentar + *infin*
Ⓒ CPD ► **assay mark** N señal *f* de ensayo ► **assay office** N oficina *f* de ensayo

assemblage [əˈsemblɪdʒ] N [1] [*of people*] reunión *f*; [*of things*] colección *f*
[2] (*Mech*) montaje *m*

assemble [əˈsembl] Ⓐ VT [1] (*= bring together*) [*+ people, team, collection*] reunir; [*+ facts, evidence, ideas*] recopilar; (*Parl*) convocar; **the ~d dignitaries** los dignatarios reunidos, la reunión de dignatarios
[2] (*= put together*) [*+ device, machine, piece of furniture*] armar, montar
Ⓑ VI reunirse

assembler [əˈsembləʳ] N [1] (*= worker*) ensamblador(a) *m/f*, montador(a) *m/f*
[2] (*Comput*) ensamblador *m*

assembly [əˈsemblɪ] Ⓐ N [1] (*= meeting*) reunión *f*, asamblea *f*; (*= people present*) concurrencia *f*, asistentes *mpl*; **the right of ~** el derecho de reunión
[2] (*Pol*) asamblea *f*; **the Assembly** (*US*) la Asamblea
[3] (*Brit Scol*) reunión *f* general de todos los alumnos
[4] (*Tech*) montaje *m*, ensamblaje *m*
Ⓑ CPD ► **assembly language** N (*Comput*) lenguaje *m* ensamblador ► **assembly line** N cadena *f* de montaje ► **assembly line production** N producción *f* en cadena ► **assembly line worker** N trabajador(a) *m/f* en línea *or* cadena de montaje ► **assembly plant** N planta *f* de montaje, maquiladora *f* (*Mex*) ► **assembly room(s)** N(PL) salón *m* de celebraciones ► **assembly shop** N taller *m* de montaje

assemblyman [əˈsemblɪmən] N (*pl* **assemblymen**) (*US*) asambleísta *m*, miembro *m* de una asamblea

assemblywoman [əˈsemblɪwʊmən] N (*pl* **assemblywomen**) (*US*) asambleísta *f*, miembro *f* de una asamblea

assent [əˈsent] Ⓐ N (*= agreement*) asentimiento *m*, consentimiento *m*; (*= approval*) aprobación *f*; **royal ~** aprobación *f* real; **by common ~** de común acuerdo; **to nod one's ~** asentir con la cabeza
Ⓑ VI asentir (**to** a), consentir (**to** en)

assert [əˈsɜːt] VT [1] (*= declare*) afirmar, aseverar; [*+ innocence*] afirmar
[2] (*= insist on*) [*+ rights*] hacer valer
[3] (*= establish*) [*+ authority*] imponer
[4] **to ~ o.s.** imponerse

➤ **assertion** [əˈsɜːʃən] N afirmación *f*, aseveración *f*

assertive [əˈsɜːtɪv] ADJ [*manner, tone*] firme y enérgico; [*behaviour*] enérgico; **try to be a bit more ~** intenta ser un poco más firme y enérgico, intenta hacerte valer un poco más; **you were very ~ in that meeting** te mostraste muy firme y enérgico en esa reunión; **slowly she began to become more ~** poco a poco empezó a mostrarse más segura de sí misma *or* empezó a hacerse valer más

assertively [əˈsɜːtɪvlɪ] ADV [*speak, reply*] con firmeza, con convicción

assertiveness [əˈsɜːtɪvnɪs] Ⓐ N firmeza *f*
Ⓑ CPD ► **assertiveness course** N curso *m* de autoafirmación ► **assertiveness training** N ejercicios *mpl* de reafirmación personal

assess [əˈses] VT [1] (*= evaluate*) [*+ damage, property*] valorar, tasar; [*+ situation etc*] valorar; **how do you ~ your chances now?** ¿cómo valora sus posibilidades ahora?
[2] (*= calculate*) [*+ value, amount*] calcular (**at** en); [*+ income*] gravar
[3] (*Univ, Scol, Ind*) evaluar; **how did you ~ this candidate?** ¿cómo evaluó a este candidato?

assessable [əˈsesəbl] ADJ calculable, tasable; **~ income** ingresos *mpl* imponibles; **a theory not readily ~** una teoría difícil de enjuiciar

assessment [əˈsesmənt] N [1] (*= evaluation*) [*of damage, property*] valoración *f*, tasación *f*; (*= judgment*) juicio *m*, valoración *f*; **what is your ~ of the situation?** ¿qué juicio *or* valoración le merece la situación?
[2] (*Fin, Tax*) **tax ~** cálculo *m* de los ingresos, estimación *f* de la base impositiva
[3] (*Univ, Scol, Ind*) (*= appraisal*) evaluación *f*; *see also* **continuous**

assessor [əˈsesəʳ] N [1] (*Jur*) perito/a *m/f* asesor(a)
[2] (*Insurance*) perito/a *m/f* tasador(a)
[3] (*Educ*) examinador(a) *m/f*
[4] (*US*) [*of taxes etc*] tasador(a) *m/f*

asset [ˈæset] Ⓐ N [1] (*= advantage*) ventaja *f*; **she is a great ~ to the department** es una persona valiosísima en el departamento
[2] (*Fin etc*) bien *m*; (*= book-keeping item*) partida *f* del activo; **~s** (*on accounts*) haberes *mpl*, activo *msing*; **personal ~s** bienes *mpl* personales; **real ~s** bienes *mpl* muebles, bienes *mpl* raíces; **~s and liabilities** activo *msing* y pasivo *msing*; **~s in hand** activo *msing* disponible, bienes *mpl* disponibles
Ⓑ CPD ► **asset stripper** N (*Fin*) *especulador que compra empresas en crisis para vender sus bienes* ► **asset stripping** N (*Fin*) *acaparamiento de activos con vistas a su venta y a la liquidación de la empresa*

asseverate [əˈsevəreɪt] VT (*frm*) aseverar

asseveration [əˌsevəˈreɪʃən] N (*frm*) aseveración *f*

asshole** [ˈæshəʊl] (*esp US*) N [1] (*Anat*) culo* *m*
[2] (*= person*) gilipollas** *mf inv*

assiduity [ˌæsɪˈdjʊɪtɪ] N diligencia *f*

assiduous [əˈsɪdjʊəs] ADJ diligente

assiduously [əˈsɪdjʊəslɪ] ADV diligentemente

assign [əˈsaɪn] Ⓐ VT [1] (*= allot*) [*+ task*] asignar; [*+ room*] destinar; [*+ date*] señalar, fijar (**for** para); **which is the room ~ed to me?** ¿qué habitación se me ha destinado?
[2] [*+ person*] destinar; **to ~ sb to sth** destinar a algn a algo; **they ~ed him to the Paris embassy** lo destinaron a la embajada de París
[3] (*= attribute*) [*+ literary work, sculpture*] atribuir; [*+ reason*] señalar, indicar
[4] (*Jur*) [*+ property*] ceder
Ⓑ N (*Jur*) cesionario/a *m/f*

assignation [ˌæsɪgˈneɪʃən] N [1] (*= meeting*) [*of lovers*] cita *f* secreta
[2] (*= allocation*) [*of money, person, responsibility*] asignación *f*

assignee [ˌæsaɪˈniː] N (*Jur*) = **assign B**

assignment [əˈsaɪnmənt] N [1] (*= mission*) misión *f*; (*= task*) tarea *f*; **to be on (an) ~** estar cumpliendo una misión
[2] (*Scol, Univ*) trabajo *m*
[3] (*= allocation*) asignación *f*

assignor [ˌæsaɪˈnɔːʳ] N (*Jur*) cedente *mf*, cesionista *mf*

assimilate [əˈsɪmɪleɪt] Ⓐ VT asimilar
Ⓑ VI asimilarse

assimilation [əˌsɪmɪˈleɪʃən] N asimilación *f*

Assisi [əˈsiːzɪ] N Asís *m*

assist [əˈsɪst] Ⓐ VT (*= help*) [*+ person*] ayudar; [*+ development, growth etc*] fomentar, estimular; **to ~ sb to do sth** ayudar a algn a hacer algo; **we ~ed him to his car** le ayudamos a llegar a su coche
Ⓑ VI (*= help*) ayudar; **to ~ in sth** ayudar en algo; **to ~ in doing sth** ayudar a hacer algo
Ⓒ N (*Sport*) asistencia *f*

assistance [əˈsɪstəns] N ayuda *f*, auxilio *m*; **to be of ~ to** ◊ **give ~ to** ayudar a, prestar ayuda a; **can I be of any ~?** ¿puedo ayudarle?,

➤ LANGUAGE IN USE: assertion 26.1

¿le puedo servir en algo?; **to come to sb's ~** acudir en ayuda *or* auxilio de algn

assistant [ə'sɪstənt] Ⓐ N ayudante *mf*; (= *language assistant*) lector(a) *m/f*
Ⓑ CPD ► **assistant director** N (*Theat*) ayudante *mf* de dirección ► **assistant manager** N subdirector(a) *m/f* ► **assistant master** N (*Brit Scol†*) profesor *m* de instituto ► **assistant mistress** N (*Brit Scol†*) profesora *f* de instituto ► **assistant principal** N (*Scol*) subdirector(a) *m/f* ► **assistant professor** N (*US*) profesor(a) *m/f* agregado/a ► **assistant secretary** N subsecretario/a *m/f*

assistantship [ə'sɪstəntʃɪp] N [1] (*Brit*) (*at school*) lectorado *m*
[2] (*US*) (*at college*) agregaduría *f*, puesto *m* de profesor agregado

assisted [ə'sɪstɪd] ADJ **~ passage** pasaje *m* subvencionado; **~ place** (*Brit Scol*) *plaza de un colegio privado, subvencionada por el gobierno y destinada a alumnos seleccionados que no pueden sufragar las cuotas del mismo*; **~ suicide** suicidio *m* asistido

assizes [ə'saɪzɪz] NPL (*Brit Jur*) sesiones *fpl* jurídicas (regionales)

assn. ABBR = **association**

assoc. ABBR [1] = **association**
[2] = **associate(d)**

associate Ⓐ [ə'səʊʃɪɪt] ADJ [*company*] asociado
Ⓑ [ə'səʊʃɪɪt] N (= *colleague*) colega *mf*; (*in crime*) cómplice *mf*; (*also* **~ member**) [*of society*] miembro *mf* no numerario/a; [*of professional body*] colegiado/a *m/f*; [*of learned body*] miembro *mf* correspondiente; **Fred Bloggs and Associates** Fred Bloggs y Asociados
Ⓒ [ə'səʊʃɪeɪt] VT [1] (*mentally*) [+ *ideas, things, people*] asociar, relacionar; **to ~ one thing with another** asociar *or* relacionar una cosa con otra; **I always ~ you with Barcelona** siempre te asocio *or* relaciono con Barcelona
[2] (= *affiliate, connect*) vincular, asociar; **to be ~d with sth/sb: high blood pressure is ~d with heart disease** se vincula *or* asocia la tensión alta con las enfermedades coronarias; **he was ~d with the communist party** estaba vinculado *or* asociado con el partido comunista; **it is a privilege to be ~d with her** es un privilegio estar relacionado con ella; **I don't wish to be ~d** *or* **to ~ myself with it/him** no quiero tener nada que ver con ello/él
Ⓓ [ə'səʊʃɪeɪt] VI **to ~ with sb** relacionarse con algn, tratar con algn
Ⓔ [ə'səʊʃɪɪt] CPD ► **associate director** N subdirector(a) *m/f*, director(a) *m/f* adjunto/a ► **associate judge** N juez *mf* asesor(a) ► **Associate Justice** N (*US*) juez *mf* asociado/a ► **associate member** N [*of society*] miembro *mf* no numerario/a; [*of professional body*] colegiado/a *m/f*; [*of learned body*] miembro *mf* correspondiente ► **associate producer** N (*TV, Cine*) productor(a) *m/f* asociado/a ► **associate professor** N (*US*) profesor(a) *m/f* adjunto/a ► **associate's degree** N (*US*) licenciatura *f*

associated [ə'səʊʃɪeɪtɪd] Ⓐ ADJ [1] (= *connected*) asociado, relacionado; **engineering problems ~ with aircraft design** problemas de ingeniería asociados *or* relacionados con el diseño de aviones
[2] (*Comm*) asociado, afiliado
Ⓑ CPD ► **associated company** N compañía *f* asociada, compañía *f* afiliada

association [ə,səʊsɪ'eɪʃən] Ⓐ N [1] (= *act, partnership*) asociación *f*; **in ~ with** conjuntamente con; **to form an ~ with** asociarse con
[2] (= *organization*) sociedad *f*, asociación *f*
[3] (= *connection*) conexión *f*; **~ of ideas** asociación *f* de ideas
[4] **associations** (= *memories*) recuerdos *mpl*; **the name has unpleasant ~s** el nombre trae recuerdos desagradables; **the town has historic ~s** la ciudad posee connotaciones históricas
Ⓑ CPD ► **association football** N (*Brit*) fútbol *m*

associative [ə'səʊʃɪətɪv] ADJ [1] (*Math*) asociativo
[2] (*Comput*) **~ storage** almacenamiento *m* asociativo

assonance ['æsənəns] N asonancia *f*

assonant ['æsənənt] Ⓐ ADJ asonante
Ⓑ N asonante *f*

assonate ['æsəneɪt] VI asonar

assort [ə'sɔːt] VI concordar (**with** con), convenir (**with** a); **it ~s ill with his character** no cuadra con su carácter

assorted [ə'sɔːtɪd] ADJ surtido; **~ cakes** pasteles surtidos; **he dined with ~ ministers** cenó con diversos ministros

assortment [ə'sɔːtmənt] N [1] (*Comm*) surtido *m*
[2] (= *mixture*) mezcla *f*; (= *collection*) colección *f*; **there was a strange ~ of guests** había una extraña mezcla de invitados; **Peter was there with an ~ of girlfriends** allí estaba Peter con una colección de amigas; **quite an ~!** ¡aquí hay de todo!

asst. ABBR (= **assistant**) ayte.

assuage [ə'sweɪdʒ] VT (*liter*) [+ *feelings, anger*] aplacar; [+ *pain*] calmar, aliviar; [+ *passion*] mitigar, suavizar; [+ *desire*] satisfacer; [+ *appetite*] satisfacer, saciar; [+ *person*] apaciguar, sosegar; **he was not easily ~d** no resultaba fácil apaciguarlo *or* sosegarlo

▼ **assume** [ə'sjuːm] VT [1] (= *suppose*) suponer; **we may therefore ~ that …** así, es de suponer que …; **let us ~ that …** pongamos por caso *or* supongamos que …; **assuming that …** suponiendo que …, en el supuesto de que …; **you are assuming a lot** supones demasiado, eso es mucho suponer; **you resigned, I ~** dimitiste, me imagino
[2] (= *take on, take over*) [+ *power, control, responsibility*] asumir; [+ *authority*] (*unjustly*) apropiarse, arrogarse
[3] (= *adopt*) [+ *name, attitude, look of surprise*] adoptar; [+ *air*] darse

assumed [ə'sjuːmd] ADJ [*name*] falso, fingido; **under an ~ name** bajo *or* con (un) nombre falso

assumption [ə'sʌmpʃən] Ⓐ N [1] (= *supposition*) suposición *f*, supuesto *m*; **on the ~ that** suponiendo que, poniendo por caso que; **we cannot make that ~** no podemos dar eso por sentado; **to start from a false ~** partir de una base falsa
[2] (= *taking*) [*of power, responsibility*] asunción *f*
[3] **the Assumption** (*Rel*) la Asunción
Ⓑ CPD ► **Assumption Day** N Día *m* de la Asunción

assurance [ə'ʃʊərəns] Ⓐ N [1] (= *guarantee*) garantía *f*, promesa *f*; **you have my ~ that …** les aseguro que …; **I give you my ~ that …** le puedo asegurar que …; **I can give you no ~ about that** no les puedo garantizar nada
[2] (= *certainty*) certeza *f*, seguridad *f*; **with the ~ that …** con la seguridad de que …
[3] (= *confidence*) confianza *f*; (= *self-confidence*) seguridad *f*, aplomo *m*; **he spoke with ~** habló con seguridad *or* aplomo
[4] (*esp Brit*) (= *insurance*) seguro *m*; *see also* **life**
Ⓑ CPD ► **assurance company** N (*esp Brit*) compañía *f* de seguros

assure [ə'ʃʊəʳ] VT [1] (= *ensure*) asegurar, garantizar; **success was ~d** el éxito estaba asegurado; **to ~ o.s. of sth** asegurarse de algo
[2] (= *reassure*) asegurar; **I ~d him of my support** le aseguré mi apoyo; **you may rest ~d that …** ◊ **let me ~ you that …** tenga la (plena) seguridad de que …; **it is so, I ~ you** es así, se lo garantizo
[3] (*esp Brit Fin*) asegurar; **his life is ~d for £500,000** su vida está asegurada en 500.000 libras

assured [ə'ʃʊəd] Ⓐ ADJ [1] (= *self-assured*) confiado, sereno
[2] (= *certain*) seguro; **you have an ~ future** tienes un porvenir seguro
Ⓑ N **the ~** (*esp Brit Fin*) (*sing*) el asegurado/la asegurada; (*pl*) los asegurados/las aseguradas

assuredly [ə'ʃʊərɪdlɪ] ADV [1] (= *without doubt*) sin duda; **she is ~ the ideal person for the job** sin duda es la persona ideal para el puesto, no hay ninguna duda de que es la persona ideal para el puesto; **most ~** con toda seguridad
[2] (= *confidently*) con confianza, sin titubeos

ass-wipe** ['æswaɪp] N (*US*) [1] (= *toilet paper*) papel *m* del wáter*
[2] (= *person*) mamón/ona** *m/f*

Assyria [ə'sɪrɪə] N Asiria *f*

Assyrian [ə'sɪrɪən] Ⓐ ADJ asirio
Ⓑ N asirio/a *m/f*

AST N ABBR (*US, Canada*) = **Atlantic Standard Time**

aster ['æstəʳ] N áster *f*

asterisk ['æstərɪsk] Ⓐ N asterisco *m*
Ⓑ VT señalar con un asterisco, poner un asterisco a

astern [ə'stɜːn] ADV (*Naut*) a popa; **to fall ~** quedarse atrás; **to go ~** ciar, ir hacia atrás; **to make a boat fast ~** amarrar un barco por la popa; **~ of** detrás de

asteroid ['æstərɔɪd] N asteroide *m*

asthma ['æsmə] N asma *m or f*

asthmatic [æs'mætɪk] Ⓐ ADJ asmático
Ⓑ N asmático/a *m/f*

astigmatic [,æstɪg'mætɪk] ADJ astigmático

astigmatism [æs'tɪgmətɪzəm] N astigmatismo *m*

astir [ə'stɜːʳ] ADJ [1] **to be ~** (= *on the go*) estar activo, estar en movimiento
[2] (†) (= *out of bed*) estar levantado; **we were ~ early** nos levantamos temprano; **nobody was ~ at that hour** a tal hora todos estaban todavía en la cama

ASTM N ABBR (*US*) = **American Society for Testing Materials**

ASTMS N ABBR (*Brit*) = **Association of Scientific, Technical and Managerial Staff**

astonish [ə'stɒnɪʃ] VT asombrar, pasmar; **you ~ me!** (*iro*) ¡no me digas!, ¡vaya sorpresa!

astonished [ə'stɒnɪʃt] ADJ estupefacto, pasmado; **to be ~** asombrarse (**at** de); **I am ~ that …** me asombra que … + *subjun*

astonishing [ə'stɒnɪʃɪŋ] ADJ [*achievement, coincidence, news*] asombroso, pasmoso; **I find it ~ that …** me asombra *or* pasma que … + *subjun*, me parece increíble que … + *subjun*

astonishingly [ə'stɒnɪʃɪŋlɪ] ADV asombrosamente; **it was ~ easy** asombraba lo fácil que era, era asombrosamente fácil; **an ~ beautiful young woman** una joven de una belleza asombrosa; **she has ~ blue eyes** tiene unos ojos de un azul increíble; **he learned the language ~ quickly** aprendió la lengua con

➤ LANGUAGE IN USE: **assume 1** 26.1, 26.3

una rapidez asombrosa, fue asombroso lo rápido que aprendió la lengua; **~ (enough), he was right** por increíble que parezca, tenía razón

astonishment [əˈstɒnɪʃmənt] N asombro *m*; (*stronger*) estupefacción *f*; **a look of ~** una mirada de asombro; (*stronger*) una mirada de estupefacción; **her ~ at my good fortune** su asombro *or* sorpresa ante mi buena suerte; **to my ~** para mi asombro *or* sorpresa

astound [əˈstaʊnd] VT asombrar, pasmar

astounded [əˈstaʊndɪd] ADJ pasmado, estupefacto; **I am ~** estoy pasmado

astounding [əˈstaʊndɪŋ] ADJ asombroso, pasmoso; **~!** ¡esto es asombroso!; **I find it ~ that ...** me asombra *or* pasma que ... + *subjun*

astoundingly [əˈstaʊndɪŋlɪ] ADV asombrosamente; **he has done ~ well** le ha ido asombrosamente bien, es asombroso lo bien que le ha ido; **she has ~ blue eyes** tiene unos ojos de un azul increíble; **~, an American won the Tour de France** por asombroso que parezca, un americano ganó el Tour de France

astrakhan [ˌæstrəˈkæn] N astracán *m*

astral [ˈæstrəl] Ⓐ ADJ astral
Ⓑ CPD ► **astral projection** N viaje *m* astral

astray [əˈstreɪ] ADV [1] (*lit*) **to go ~** (= *get lost*) extraviarse
[2] (*fig*) **to go ~** (= *make a mistake*) equivocarse; (*morally*) ir por mal camino; **to lead sb ~** llevar a algn por mal camino; **I was led ~ by his voice** su voz me despistó

astride [əˈstraɪd] Ⓐ ADV a horcajadas
Ⓑ PREP [*horse, fence*] a horcajadas sobre

astringency [əsˈtrɪndʒənsɪ] N [1] (*Med*) astringencia *f*
[2] (*fig*) adustez *f*, austeridad *f*

astringent [əsˈtrɪndʒənt] Ⓐ ADJ [1] (*Med*) astringente
[2] (*fig*) adusto, austero
Ⓑ N (*Med*) astringente *m*

astro... [æstrəʊ] PREFIX astro...

astrolabe [ˈæstrəʊleɪb] N astrolabio *m*

astrologer [əsˈtrɒlədʒəʳ] N astrólogo/a *m/f*

astrological [ˌæstrəˈlɒdʒɪkəl] ADJ astrológico

astrologist [əsˈtrɒlədʒɪst] N astrólogo/a *m/f*

astrology [əsˈtrɒlədʒɪ] N astrología *f*

astronaut [ˈæstrənɔːt] N astronauta *mf*

astronautic [ˌæstrəʊˈnɔːtɪk] ADJ = **astronautical**

astronautical [ˌæstrəʊˈnɔːtɪkəl] ADJ astronáutico

astronautics [ˌæstrəʊˈnɔːtɪks] NSING astronáutica *f*

astronomer [əsˈtrɒnəməʳ] N astrónomo/a *m/f*

astronomic [ˌæstrəˈnɒmɪk] ADJ = **astronomical**

astronomical [ˌæstrəˈnɒmɪkəl] ADJ (*lit, fig*) astronómico

astronomically [ˌæstrəˈnɒmɪkəlɪ] ADV [*rise, grow, increase*] astronómicamente, exageradamente; **lobster is ~ expensive** la langosta está a precios astronómicos; **they set ~ high standards for their employees** exigen un nivel exageradamente alto a sus empleados

astronomy [əsˈtrɒnəmɪ] N astronomía *f*

astrophysicist [ˌæstrəʊˈfɪzɪsɪst] N astrofísico/a *m/f*

astrophysics [ˈæstrəʊˈfɪzɪks] NSING astrofísica *f*

Astroturf® [ˈæstrəʊtɜːf] N césped *m* artificial

Asturian [æˈstʊərɪən] Ⓐ ADJ asturiano
Ⓑ N [1] (= *person*) asturiano/a *m/f*
[2] (*Ling*) asturiano *m*

Asturias [æˈstʊərɪæs] N Asturias *f*

astute [əsˈtjuːt] ADJ [*person, decision*] astuto, sagaz; [*mind*] astuto; [*choice*] inteligente; **that was very ~ of you** en eso has sido muy listo

astutely [əsˈtjuːtlɪ] ADV [*decide*] astutamente, sagazmente; [*choose*] inteligentemente

astuteness [əsˈtjuːtnɪs] N astucia *f*, sagacidad *f*

asunder [əˈsʌndəʳ] ADV **to tear ~** (*liter*) hacer pedazos

ASV N ABBR (*US*) (= **American Standard Version**) *traducción americana de la Biblia*

Aswan [æsˈwɑːn] Ⓐ N Asuán *f*
Ⓑ CPD ► **Aswan High Dam** N Presa *f* de Asuán

asylum [əˈsaɪləm] Ⓐ N [1] (= *refuge*) asilo *m*; **to seek political ~** pedir asilo político; **to afford** *or* **give ~ to sb** [*place*] servir de asilo a algn; [*person*] dar asilo a algn
[2] (†) (= *mental hospital*) manicomio *m*
Ⓑ CPD ► **asylum seeker** N solicitante *mf* de asilo

asymmetric [ˌeɪsɪˈmetrɪk] ADJ = **asymmetrical**

asymmetrical [ˌeɪsɪˈmetrɪkəl] Ⓐ ADJ asimétrico
Ⓑ CPD ► **asymmetrical bars** NPL (*Sport*) barras *fpl* asimétricas

asymmetry [eɪˈsɪmɪtrɪ] N asimetría *f*

asymptomatic [æˌsɪmptəˈmætɪk] ADJ asintomático

asynchronous [æˈsɪŋkrənəs] ADJ asíncrono

AT N ABBR (= **automatic translation**) TA *f*

at [æt]

*When **at** is an element in a phrasal verb, eg **look at**, look up the verb.*

PREP [1] (*position*) [1·1] (*specifying rough location*) en; **there weren't many people at the party/lecture** no había mucha gente en la fiesta/conferencia; **at the hairdresser's/supermarket** en la peluquería/el supermercado; **at the office** en la oficina; **at school** en la escuela, en el colegio; **at sea** en el mar; **at table** en la mesa; BUT **at John's** en casa de Juan; ✦**IDIOMS where it's at: Glasgow's where it's at** en Glasgow es donde está la movida*, en Glasgow es donde está el rollo (*Sp**); **where we're at: I'll just run through where we're at** te voy a poner al tanto *or* al corriente de cuál es la situación
[1·2] (*specifying position*) **my room's at the back of the house** mi dormitorio está en la parte de atrás de la casa; **the dress fastens at the back** el vestido se abrocha por detrás; **at the bottom of the stairs** al pie de las escaleras; **to stand at the door** estar de pie *or* (*LAm*) parado en la puerta; **at the edge** en el borde; **my room's at the front of the house** mi dormitorio está en la parte delantera de la casa; **the dress fastens at the front** el vestido se abrocha por delante; **at the top** (*gen*) en lo alto; (*of mountain*) en la cumbre; **to be at the window** estar junto a la ventana; **he came in at the window** entró por la ventana
[1·3] (*esp Internet*) (= *name of @ symbol*) arroba *f*; **"my e-mail address is jones at collins dot uk"** (*jones@collins.uk*) —mi dirección electrónica Internet es jones arroba collins punto uk
[2] (*direction*) (= *towards*) hacia; **the car was coming straight at us** el coche venía directo hacia nosotros; **to look at sth** mirar algo
[3] (*time, age*) a; **at four o'clock** a las cuatro; **at midday** a mediodía; **at 16 he was already a household name** a los 16 años era ya un nombre muy conocido; **at lunchtime** a la hora de la comida, a la hora de almorzar; **at an early age** de pequeño/pequeña; **at Christmas** por *or* en Navidades; **at Easter** en Semana Santa; **at the moment** en este momento; **at that moment the bomb went off** en aquel momento estalló la bomba; **at night** de noche, por la noche; **at a time like this** en un momento como éste; **at my time of life** con los años que tengo
[4] (*rate*) a; **at 50p a kilo** a 50 peniques el kilo; **at 50p each** (a) 50 peniques cada uno; **at a high price** a un precio elevado; **at 4% interest** al 4% de interés; **two at a time** de dos en dos; **to go at 100 km an hour** ir a 100 km por hora
[5] (*activity*) **he's good at games** se le dan bien los deportes; **at it: while you're at it*** (= *doing it*) de paso; (= *by the way*) a propósito; **she's at it again*** otra vez con las mismas; **boys at play** muchachos que juegan, los muchachos cuando juegan; **I could tell she'd been at the whisky** se notaba que le había estado dando al whisky*; **at war** en guerra; **to be at work** (= *working*) estar trabajando; (= *in the office*) estar en la oficina
[6] (*manner*) **acting at its best** una actuación de antología; **at peace** en paz; **at a run** corriendo, a la carrera; **at full speed** a toda velocidad
[7] (*cause*) **to awaken at the least sound** despertarse al menor ruido; **at her cries** al escuchar sus gritos; **at my request** a petición mía; **at his suggestion** a sugerencia suya; **I was shocked/surprised at the news** me escandalizó/sorprendió la noticia

atavism [ˈætəvɪzəm] N atavismo *m*

atavistic [ˌætəˈvɪstɪk] ADJ atávico

ataxia [əˈtæksɪə] N ataxia *f*

ataxic [əˈtæksɪk] ADJ atáxico

ATB N = **all-terrain bike**

ATC N ABBR = **Air Training Corps**

ate [et, eɪt] PT *of* **eat**

A-test [ˈeɪtest] N prueba *f* de bomba atómica

atheism [ˈeɪθɪɪzəm] N ateísmo *m*

atheist [ˈeɪθɪɪst] N ateo/a *m/f*

atheistic [ˌeɪθɪˈɪstɪk] ADJ ateo, ateísta

Athenian [əˈθiːnɪən] Ⓐ ADJ ateniense
Ⓑ N ateniense *mf*

Athens [ˈæθɪnz] N Atenas *f*

athirst [əˈθɜːst] ADJ **to be ~ for** (*liter*) tener sed de

athlete [ˈæθliːt] Ⓐ N atleta *mf*
Ⓑ CPD ► **athlete's foot** N (*Med*) pie *m* de atleta

athletic [æθˈletɪk] Ⓐ ADJ [1] (*Sport*) [*club, association, event*] de atletismo
[2] (= *sporty*) [*person, body*] atlético; **he was tall, with an ~ build** era alto y atlético
Ⓑ CPD ► **athletic sports** NPL atletismo *msing*

athletically [æθˈletɪklɪ] ADV [1] (= *agilely*) [*jump, climb*] con agilidad, ágilmente
[2] (*Sport*) **~, she's outstanding** es una atleta excepcional; **~ talented youngsters** jóvenes con talento para el atletismo

athleticism [æθˈletsɪzəm] N atletismo *m*

athletics [æθˈletɪks] Ⓐ NSING (*Brit*) atletismo *m*; (*US*) deportes *mpl*
Ⓑ CPD ► **athletics coach** N entrenador(a) *m/f* de atletismo ► **athletics competition** N competición *f* atlética ► **athletics meeting** N competición *f* atlética, prueba *f* atlética ► **athletics track** N pista *f* de atletismo

at-home [ətˈhəʊm] N recepción *f* (*en casa particular*)

athwart [əˈθwɔːt] Ⓐ ADV de través, al través
Ⓑ PREP a través de

atishoo [əˈtɪʃuː] EXCL ¡(h)achís!

Atlantic [ətˈlæntɪk] Ⓐ ADJ atlántico
Ⓑ N **the ~ (Ocean)** el (Océano) Atlántico

Atlanticism [ət'læntɪsɪzəm] N atlantismo *m*

Atlanticist [ət'læntɪsɪst] ADJ, N atlantista *mf*

Atlantis [ət'læntɪs] N Atlántida *f*

atlas ['ætləs] Ⓐ N 1 (= *world atlas*) atlas *m inv*; (= *road atlas*) guía *f* de carreteras
2 **Atlas** (*Myth*) Atlas *m*, Atlante *m*
Ⓑ CPD ► **the Atlas Mountains** NPL los Atlas

ATM N ABBR (*US*) (= **Automated Teller Machine**) cajero *m* automático; **~ card** tarjeta *f* de cajero automático

atmosphere ['ætməsfɪəʳ] N 1 (= *air*) atmósfera *f*
2 (*fig*) ambiente *m*

atmospheric [,ætməs'ferɪk] Ⓐ ADJ 1 (*Met, Phys*) atmosférico
2 (*fig*) [*music, film, book*] evocador
Ⓑ CPD ► **atmospheric pollution** N contaminación *f* atmosférica ► **atmospheric pressure** N presión *f* atmosférica

atmospherics [,ætməs'ferɪks] NPL (*Rad*) interferencias *fpl*

atoll ['ætɒl] N atolón *m*

atom ['ætəm] Ⓐ N 1 (*Phys*) átomo *m*
2 (*fig*) pizca *f*; **there is not an ~ of truth in it** eso no tiene ni pizca de verdad; **if you had an ~ of sense** si tuvieras una gota de sentido común; **to smash sth to ~s** hacer algo añicos
Ⓑ CPD ► **atom bomb** N bomba *f* atómica ► **atom smasher** N acelerador *m* de partículas atómicas, rompeátomos *m inv*

atomic [ə'tɒmɪk] Ⓐ ADJ atómico
Ⓑ CPD ► **atomic age** N era *f* atómica *or* nuclear ► **atomic bomb** N bomba *f* atómica ► **atomic clock** N reloj *m* atómico ► **atomic energy** N energía *f* atómica *or* nuclear ► **Atomic Energy Authority** (*Brit*), **Atomic Energy Commission** (*US*) N Consejo *m* de Energía Nuclear ► **atomic nucleus** N núcleo *m* atómico ► **atomic number** N número *m* atómico ► **atomic particle** N partícula *f* atómica ► **atomic physics** NSING física *f* atómica ► **atomic pile** N pila *f* atómica ► **atomic power** N (= *nation*) potencia *f* nuclear ► **atomic power station**† N central *f* nuclear ► **atomic structure** N estructura *f* atómica ► **atomic theory** N teoría *f* de los átomos ► **atomic warfare** N guerra *f* atómica ► **atomic warhead** N cabeza *f* atómica ► **atomic weight** N peso *m* atómico

atomic-powered [ə'tɒmɪk'paʊəd] ADJ impulsado por energía atómica

atomize ['ætəmaɪz] VT atomizar, pulverizar

atomizer ['ætəmaɪzəʳ] N atomizador *m*, pulverizador *m*

atonal [æ'təʊnl] ADJ atonal

atone [ə'təʊn] VI **to ~ for** expiar

atonement [ə'təʊnmənt] N expiación *f*; **to make ~ for** enmendar, desagraviar; **Day of Atonement** Día *m* de la Expiación

atonic [æ'tɒnɪk] ADJ átono

atop [ə'tɒp] Ⓐ ADV encima
Ⓑ PREP (= *on*) encima de, sobre; [*mountain*] en la cumbre de, en la cima de; **he climbed ~ a tank** subió encima de un tanque

ATP N ABBR = **Association of Tennis Professionals**

at-risk [æt'rɪsk] Ⓐ ADJ [*group*] en peligro
Ⓑ CPD ► **at-risk register** N (*Brit Social Work*) ≈ registro *m* de delitos de violencia familiar *or* doméstica

atrium ['eɪtrɪəm] (*pl* **atria** *or* **atriums**) N atrio *m*

atrocious [ə'trəʊʃəs] ADJ 1 (= *shocking*) [*crime, treatment*] atroz
2 (*) (= *very bad*) [*film, food, spelling*] pésimo, espantoso; [*weather*] espantoso

atrociously [ə'trəʊʃəslɪ] ADV 1 (= *shockingly*) [*treat*] atrozmente; **he was ~ bad-tempered** tenía un genio atroz
2 (= *badly*) [*sing, spell, behave*] pésimamente, espantosamente

atrocity [ə'trɒsɪtɪ] N atrocidad *f*

atrophy ['ætrəfɪ] Ⓐ N (*Med*) atrofia *f*
Ⓑ VI atrofiarse
Ⓒ VT atrofiar

att. ABBR 1 (*Comm*) = **attached**
2 = **attorney**

attaboy* ['ætə,bɔɪ] EXCL (*esp US*) ¡bravo!, ¡dale!

attach [ə'tætʃ] Ⓐ VT 1 (= *fasten*) sujetar; (= *stick*) pegar; (= *tie*) atar, amarrar (*LAm*); (*with pin etc*) prender; (= *join up*) [+ *trailer etc*] acoplar; (= *put on*) [+ *seal*] poner; **you ~ it to the wall with rings** se sujeta a la pared con argollas; **to ~ o.s. to** [+ *group*] agregarse a, unirse a; **he ~ed himself to us** (*pej*) se pegó a nosotros
2 (*in letter*) adjuntar; **the document is ~ed** enviamos adjunto el documento; **the ~ed letter** la carta adjunta; **please find ~ed details of ...** les adjuntamos detalles de ...
3 (= *attribute*) [+ *importance, value*] dar, atribuir (**to** a)
4 (= *associate, connect*) **to ~ conditions (to sth)** imponer condiciones (a algo); *see also* **string A4**
5 (*Jur*) [+ *property*] incautar, embargar
Ⓑ VI 1 **to ~ to** (= *correspond to*) corresponder a, pertenecer a; **certain duties ~ to this post** ciertas responsabilidades corresponden a este puesto; **no blame ~es to you** no tienes culpa alguna
2 (*Chem*) [*compound, atom*] unirse (**to** a)

attaché [ə'tæʃeɪ] Ⓐ N agregado/a *m/f*; *see also* **cultural**
Ⓑ CPD ► **attaché case** N maletín *m*

attached [ə'tætʃt] ADJ 1 (= *close*) **they are very ~ (to each other)** se quieren mucho; **to be ~ to** (= *fond of*) [+ *person*] tener cariño a; [+ *theory*] estar apegado a; **to become ~ to sb** (*fig*) encariñarse con algn
2 **to be ~*** (= *married, spoken for*) no estar libre
3 (= *associated*) **the salary ~ to the post is ...** el sueldo que corresponde al puesto es ...; **to be ~ to an embassy** estar agregado a una embajada; **commission ~ to the Ministry of ...** comisión que depende del Ministerio de ...

attachment [ə'tætʃmənt] N 1 (= *accessory*) accesorio *m*, dispositivo *m*
2 (*Comput*) (= *document*) archivo *m* adjunto
3 (= *act of attaching*) unión *f*
4 (*to company, department etc*) adscripción *f* temporal; **to be on ~ (to)** estar adscrito temporalmente (a)
5 (= *affection*) cariño *m* (**to** por); (= *loyalty*) adhesión *f*
6 (*Jur*) incautación *f*, embargo *m*

attack [ə'tæk] Ⓐ N 1 (*Mil, Sport, fig*) ataque *m* (**on** a, contra, sobre); (= *assault*) atentado *m*, agresión *f*; **an ~ on sb's life** un atentado contra la vida de algn; **an ~ on the security of the state** un atentado contra la seguridad del estado; **to launch an ~** (*Mil, fig*) lanzar un ataque; **to leave o.s. open to ~** dejarse expuesto a un ataque; **to return to the ~** volver al ataque; **surprise ~** ataque por sorpresa; **to be/come under ~** ser atacado; ✦*PROV* **~ is the best form of defence** la mejor defensa es en el ataque
2 (*Med*) (*gen*) ataque *m*; (= *fit*) acceso *m*, crisis *f inv*; **an ~ of pneumonia** una pulmonía; **an ~ of nerves** un ataque de nervios, una crisis nerviosa; *see also* **heart**
Ⓑ VT 1 (*Mil, Sport, Med, fig*) atacar; (= *assault*) agredir; [*bull etc*] embestir; **it ~s the liver** ataca al hígado; **they mercilessly ~ed his Marxist approach** atacaron despiadadamente su enfoque marxista
2 (= *tackle*) [+ *job, problem*] enfrentarse con; (= *combat*) combatir; **we must ~ poverty** debemos combatir la pobreza
3 (*Chem*) atacar
Ⓒ VI atacar
Ⓓ CPD ► **attack dog** N perro *m* de presa

attackable [ə'tækəbl] ADJ atacable, expuesto al ataque

attacker [ə'tækəʳ] N agresor(a) *m/f*, atacante *mf*

attagirl* ['ætəgɜːl] EXCL (*esp US*) ¡bravo!, ¡dale!

attain [ə'teɪn] Ⓐ VT (= *achieve, reach*) [+ *knowledge*] lograr; [+ *happiness*] lograr, conquistar; [+ *goal, aim*] lograr, conseguir, alcanzar; [+ *age, rank*] llegar a, alcanzar; (= *get hold of*) conseguir
Ⓑ VI (*frm*) **to ~ to** llegar a

attainable [ə'teɪnəbl] ADJ alcanzable

attainder [ə'teɪndəʳ] N (*Jur*) extinción *f* de los derechos civiles de un individuo

attainment [ə'teɪnmənt] Ⓐ N 1 (= *achieving*) [*of knowledge*] logro *m*; [*of happiness*] logro *m*, conquista *f*; [*of independence, freedom*] conquista *f*, consecución *f*; [*of goal, aim*] logro *m*, consecución *f*; **difficult of ~** de difícil consecución, de difícil realización
2 (= *accomplishment*) logro *m*
3 **attainments** (= *skill*) talento *msing* (**in** para); (= *knowledge*) conocimientos *mpl* (**in** de)
Ⓑ CPD ► **attainment target** N (*Brit Scol*) nivel *m* básico estipulado

attempt [ə'tempt] Ⓐ N 1 (= *try*) intento *m*; **we'll do it or die in the ~** lo haremos o moriremos en el intento; **at the first ~** en el primer intento; **this is my first ~** es la primera vez que lo intento; **after several ~s they gave up** tras varios intentos *or* varias tentativas, se dieron por vencidos; **we had to give up the ~** tuvimos que renunciar a la empresa; **it was a good ~** fue un esfuerzo digno de alabanza; **to make an ~ to do sth** hacer una tentativa de hacer algo, intentar hacer algo; **he made no ~ to help** ni siquiera intentó ayudar; **he made two ~s at it** lo intentó dos veces; **to make an ~ on the record** tratar de batir el récord; **to make an ~ on the summit** tratar de llegar a la cumbre
2 (= *attack*) atentado *m*; **to make an ~ on sb's life** atentar contra la vida de algn
Ⓑ VT 1 [+ *task*] intentar realizar; [+ *exam question*] intentar responder a; **to ~ a reply** intentar responder, tratar de responder; **to ~ a smile** intentar sonreír; **to ~ suicide** intentar suicidarse
2 (= *try*) **to ~ to do sth** tratar de *or* intentar *or* (*esp LAm*) procurar hacer algo; **the pilot ~ed to land** el piloto trató de aterrizar

attempted [ə'temptɪd] ADJ **~ murder** tentativa *f* de asesinato, intento *m* de asesinato; **~ suicide** intento *m* de suicidio

attend [ə'tend] Ⓐ VT 1 (= *be present at*) [+ *meeting, school etc*] asistir a, acudir a; (*regularly*) [+ *school, church*] ir a
2 (= *wait upon*) [*waiter*] servir, atender; [*servant, helper*] ocuparse de; (*Med*) atender, asistir; (= *accompany*) acompañar; **~ed by six bridesmaids** acompañada por seis damas de honor
3 (*frm*) (*fig*) **a method ~ed by many risks**

un método que comporta muchos riesgos; **the policy was ~ed by many difficulties** la política tropezó con muchas dificultades
Ⓑ VI [1] (= *be present*) asistir, acudir
[2] (= *pay attention*) prestar atención, poner atención (*LAm*)

►**attend on**† VI + PREP = **attend upon**

►**attend to** VI + PREP [1] (= *pay attention to*) [+ *words, work, lesson, speech*] prestar atención a, poner atención en (*LAm*); [+ *advice*] seguir
[2] (= *deal with*) [+ *task, business*] ocuparse de, atender; (*Comm*) [+ *order*] tramitar; **to ~ to one's work** ocuparse de su trabajo
[3] (= *give help to*) servir a; **to ~ to a customer** atender a un(a) cliente; **are you being ~ed to?** (*in shop*) ¿le atienden?; **I'll ~ to you in a moment** un momentito y estoy con usted

►**attend upon**† VI + PREP [+ *person*] servir; [*servant, helper*] ocuparse de

attendance [əˈtendəns] Ⓐ N [1] (= *presence*) asistencia *f* (**at** a); **is my ~ necessary?** ¿debo asistir?, ¿es preciso que asista yo?; **to be in ~** asistir; **to be in ~ on the minister** acompañar al ministro, formar parte del séquito del ministro; *see also* **dance**
[2] (= *those present*) concurrencia *f*; **a large ~** una numerosa concurrencia; **what was the ~ at the meeting?** ¿cuántos asistieron a la reunión?; **we need an ~ of 1,000** hace falta atraer a un público de 1.000 personas
[3] (*Med*) asistencia *f*
Ⓑ CPD ► **attendance centre** N (*Brit Jur*) centro *m* de régimen abierto ► **attendance fee** N honorarios *mpl* por asistencia ► **attendance money** N pago *m* por asistencia ► **attendance officer** N (*Brit Scol*) encargado/a *m/f* del control de asistencia ► **attendance order** N (*Brit Scol*) *orden que exige a los padres la asistencia de sus hijos a la escuela* ► **attendance sheet** N hoja *f* de asistencia

attendant [əˈtendənt] Ⓐ N [1] (*in car park, museum*) guarda *mf*, celador(a) *m/f*; (*Theat*) acomodador(a) *m/f*; (*at wedding etc*) acompañante *mf*
[2] (= *servant*) sirviente/a *m/f*; **the prince and his ~s** el príncipe y su séquito
Ⓑ ADJ [1] (*frm*) (= *associated*) relacionado, concomitante; **the ~ circumstances** las circunstancias concomitantes; **the ~ difficulties** las dificultades intrínsecas; **old age and its ~ ills** la vejez y los achaques correspondientes; **the risks ~ on the exploration of the unknown** los riesgos que conlleva la exploración de lo desconocido
[2] (= *accompanying*) de compañía; **the ~ crowd** la gente que asistía; **to be ~ (up)on sb** atender a algn

attendee [əˌtenˈdiː] N (*esp US*) asistente *mf*

attention [əˈtenʃən] Ⓐ N [1] atención *f*; **(your) ~ please!** ¡atención por favor!; **to attract sb's ~** llamar la atención de algn; **to call** *or* **draw sb's ~ to sth** hacer notar algo a algn; **it has come to my ~ that ...** me he enterado de que ...; **it requires daily ~** hay que atenderlo a diario; **it will have my earliest ~** lo atenderé lo antes posible; **for the ~ of Mr. Jones** a la atención del Sr. Jones; **to pay ~ (to)** prestar atención (a); **he paid no ~** no hizo caso (**to that** de eso); **to pay special ~ to** fijarse de modo especial en, prestar especial atención a; **to turn one's ~ to** pasar a considerar, pasar a estudiar
[2] (*Mil*) **~!** ¡firme(s)!; **to come to ~** ponerse firme(s); **to stand at** *or* **to ~** estar firme(s)
[3] **attentions** [*of suitor, media*] atenciones *fpl*
Ⓑ CPD ► **attention deficit disorder** N trastorno *m* de déficit de atención ► **attention deficit hyperactivity disorder** N trastorno *m* hiperactivo de déficit de atención ► **attention span** N capacidad *f* de concentración

attention-seeking [əˈtenʃənˌsiːkɪŋ] ADJ que busca *or* intenta llamar la atención

attentive [əˈtentɪv] ADJ [1] (= *alert*) [*audience, pupil*] atento; **he isn't very ~ in class** no está muy atento en la clase; **to be ~ to sth/sb** prestar atención a algo/algn; **you have to be ~ to the customers' needs** tienes que estar pendiente de *or* prestar atención a las necesidades de los clientes
[2] (= *considerate, polite*) atento; **to be ~ to sb** ser atento con algn

attentively [əˈtentɪvlɪ] ADV (= *alertly, considerately*) atentamente

attentiveness [əˈtentɪvnɪs] N [1] (= *alertness*) atención *f*
[2] (= *consideration*) atención *f*

attenuate [əˈtenjʊeɪt] VT atenuar

attenuating [əˈtenjʊeɪtɪŋ] ADJ atenuante

attenuation [əˌtenjʊˈeɪʃən] N atenuación *f*, disminución *f*

attest [əˈtest] Ⓐ VT atestiguar; [+ *signature*] legalizar; **to ~ that ...** atestiguar que ...
Ⓑ VI **to ~ to** dar fe de, dar testimonio de

attestation [ætesˈteɪʃən] N (= *evidence*) testimonio *m*, atestación *f*; (= *authentication*) confirmación *f*, autenticación *f*

attested herd [əˌtestɪdˈhɜːd] N (*Brit Agr*) ganado *m* certificado

attic [ˈætɪk] Ⓐ N desván *m*, altillo *m* (*LAm*), entretecho *m* (*LAm*)
Ⓑ CPD ► **attic room** N desván *m*, altillo *m* (*LAm*), entretecho *m* (*LAm*)

Attila [ˈætɪlə] N Atila

attire [əˈtaɪəʳ] (*frm*) Ⓐ N traje *m*, vestido *m*; (*hum*) atavío *m*
Ⓑ VT vestir (**in** de); (*hum*) ataviar (**in** de)

attitude [ˈætɪtjuːd] Ⓐ N [1] (= *way of behaving*) actitud *f*; **you won't get anywhere with that ~** no vas a conseguir nada con esa actitud; **I don't like your ~** no me gusta tu actitud; **his ~ towards** *or* **to me has changed** su actitud con respecto a mí ha cambiado; **if that's your ~** si te pones en ese plan; **~ of mind** disposición *f* de ánimo
[2] (= *position, posture*) [2·1] (*mental*) postura *f*; **the government's ~ is negative** la postura del gobierno es negativa; **what's your ~ to this?** ¿cuál es tu postura a este respeto?
[2·2] (*physical*) (= *posture*) postura *f*, pose *f*; **to strike** *or* **adopt an ~** adoptar una pose
[3] (*esp US**) (= *spirit*) **women with ~** mujeres *fpl* con carácter, mujeres *f* con personalidad; **don't give me ~, girl!** ¡no te me pongas de morros, guapa!*
Ⓑ CPD ► **attitude problem** N **to have an ~ problem** tener un problema de actitud

attitudinal [ˌætɪˈtjuːdɪnəl] ADJ [*change, difference*] de actitud

attitudinize [ˌætɪˈtjuːdɪnaɪz] VI tomar posturas afectadas *or* teatrales

Attn, attn ABBR = **(for the) attention (of)**

attorney [əˈtɜːnɪ] Ⓐ N [1] (*US*) (*also* **~-at-law**) abogado/a *m/f*; *see also* **district**
[2] (= *representative*) apoderado/a *m/f*; **power of ~** procuración *f*, poderes *mpl*
Ⓑ CPD ► **Attorney General** (*pl* **Attorney Generals** *or* **Attorneys General**) N (*US*) ≈ ministro/a *m/f* de justicia, ≈ procurador(a) *m/f* general (*LAm*); (*Brit*) ≈ fiscal *mf* general del Estado

> **ATTORNEY**
>
> *En Estados Unidos un* **attorney** *puede defender a sus clientes tanto en las cortes federales como en las estatales. En ocasiones sólo cobran sus honorarios si ganan el caso (***no win, no fee***), lo cual les permite representar a clientes con pocos recursos sin cobrarles, si se trata de casos de gran repercusión social, con la esperanza de obtener beneficios considerables si lo ganan. Ésta es la razón por la que las compensaciones que se piden por daños y perjuicios suelen ser tan altas y llegan tantos casos a los tribunales. También existe la figura del abogado de oficio, que recibe el nombre de* **public defender**.
>
> ⇨ *Ver tb* LAWYERS

attract [əˈtrækt] VT [1] [+ *publicity, visitors*] atraer; [+ *interest*] atraer, suscitar; [+ *attention*] llamar
[2] (= *cause to like*) atraer; **to be ~ed to sb** sentirse atraído por algn
[3] (*Phys*) [*magnet*] atraer

attraction [əˈtrækʃən] N [1] (*between people, also Phys*) atracción *f*; **sexual ~** atracción *f* sexual; **I felt an instant ~ towards him** inmediatamente me sentí atraída por él
[2] (= *attractive feature*) encanto *m*, atractivo *m*; (= *inducement*) aliciente *m*; **city life has no ~ for me** para mí la vida en la ciudad no tiene ningún encanto *or* atractivo, no me atrae la vida en *or* de la ciudad; **one of the ~s of the quiet life** uno de los encantos *or* atractivos de la vida retirada; **one of the ~s was a free car** uno de los alicientes era un coche gratis; **the ~ of the plan is that ...** el atractivo del plan está en que ..., lo atractivo del plan es que ...; **spring ~s in Madrid** las diversiones de la primavera madrileña; **the main ~ at the party was Cindy** el interés de la fiesta se cifraba en Cindy; **the film has the special ~ of featuring Nicola Kidd** la película tiene la atracción especial de presentar a Nicola Kidd

attractive [əˈtræktɪv] ADJ [1] (= *appealing to senses*) [*woman, picture, house, features*] atractivo; [*voice, smile, personality*] atractivo, atrayente; [*name*] bonito; [*sound*] agradable; **to find sb ~** encontrar atractivo a algn; **he was immensely ~ to women** las mujeres lo encontraban muy atractivo, a las mujeres les parecía muy atractivo
[2] (= *interesting*) [*price, salary, offer*] atractivo; [*option, plan, prospect*] atrayente; **the idea was ~ to her** la idea la atraía
[3] (*Phys*) **~ power** fuerza *f* de atracción

attractively [əˈtræktɪvlɪ] ADV [1] (= *appealingly*) [*smile, laugh*] de manera atrayente; [*arranged, presented, packaged*] de manera atractiva; [*dressed, furnished*] con buen gusto; **an ~ illustrated guidebook** una guía con bonitas ilustraciones; **an ~ designed garden** un jardín de trazado atractivo
[2] (= *interestingly*) **the books are ~ priced** los libros tienen un precio que resulta atractivo; **it is an ~ simple solution** es una solución que resulta atractiva por su sencillez

attractiveness [əˈtræktɪvnɪs] N [*of person, place, voice, price, offer*] lo atractivo

attributable [əˈtrɪbjʊtəbl] ADJ **~ to** atribuible a

▼**attribute** Ⓐ [ˈætrɪbjuːt] N atributo *m*
Ⓑ [əˈtrɪbjuːt] VT (*gen, Literat, Art*) atribuir (**to** a); [+ *blame*] atribuir, achacar (**to** a); **to what would you ~ this?** ¿a qué atribuyes *or* achacas tú esto?

attribution [ˌætrɪˈbjuːʃən] N atribución *f*

➤ LANGUAGE IN USE: **attribute B** 17.1

attributive [əˈtrɪbjʊtɪv] ADJ (*Ling*) atributivo

attributively [əˈtrɪbjʊtɪvlɪ] ADV como atributo

attrit [əˈtrɪt] VT, **attrite** [əˈtraɪt] VT desgastar, agotar

attrition [əˈtrɪʃən] N 1 (= *wearing away*) desgaste *m*; **war of ~** guerra *f* de desgaste
2 (*Ind, Univ*) amortización *f* de puestos

attune [əˈtjuːn] VT **to be ~d to sth** (= *in touch with*) estar sensibilizado a algo; (= *in keeping with*) estar acorde con algo; **she is deeply ~d to the needs of the land** está profundamente sensibilizada a las necesidades del terreno; **a style of campaigning that is completely ~d to the electorate** un estilo de campaña que está totalmente en consonancia con el electorado; **he is so well ~d to her thoughts and moods that …** está tan compenetrado con sus pensamientos y cambios de humor que …; **to ~ o.s. to** ◊ **become ~d to** (= *start understanding*) sensibilizarse a; (= *get used to*) adaptarse a, acostumbrarse a

atty ABBR (*US*) = **attorney**

Atty Gen. ABBR = **Attorney General**

ATV N ABBR = **all-terrain vehicle**

atypical [ˌeɪˈtɪpɪkəl] ADJ atípico

atypically [ˌeɪˈtɪpɪklɪ] ADV atípicamente, de manera atípica

aubergine [ˈəʊbəʒiːn] Ⓐ N 1 (*esp Brit Bot*) berenjena *f*
2 (= *colour*) (color *m*) berenjena *f*
Ⓑ ADJ color berenjena *inv*

auburn [ˈɔːbən] ADJ [*hair*] color castaño rojizo *inv*

auction [ˈɔːkʃən] Ⓐ N 1 [*of goods etc*] subasta *f*, remate *m* (*LAm*); **to put up for ~** subastar, poner en pública subasta; **to sell at ~** vender en pública subasta
2 (*Bridge*) subasta *f*
Ⓑ VT (*also* **~ off**) subastar, rematar (*LAm*)
Ⓒ CPD ► **auction bridge** N bridge-remate *m* ► **auction house** N casa *f* de subastas ► **auction room** N sala *f* de subastas ► **auction sale** N subasta *f*, remate *m* (*LAm*)

auctioneer [ˌɔːkʃəˈnɪəʳ] N subastador(a) *m/f*, rematador(a) *m/f*

aud. ABBR = **audit, auditor**

audacious [ɔːˈdeɪʃəs] ADJ 1 (= *bold*) audaz, osado
2 (= *impudent*) atrevido, descarado

audaciously [ɔːˈdeɪʃəslɪ] ADV 1 (= *boldly*) audazmente, con audacia
2 (= *impudently*) con atrevimiento, descaradamente, con descaro

audacity [ɔːˈdæsɪtɪ] N 1 (= *boldness*) audacia *f*, osadía *f*
2 (= *impudence*) atrevimiento *m*, descaro *m*; **to have the ~ to do sth** tener el descaro de hacer algo

audibility [ˌɔːdɪˈbɪlɪtɪ] N audibilidad *f*

audible [ˈɔːdɪbl] ADJ audible; **his voice was scarcely ~** apenas se podía oír su voz, su voz era apenas perceptible; **there was an ~ gasp** se oyó un grito ahogado

audibly [ˈɔːdɪblɪ] ADV de forma audible

audience [ˈɔːdɪəns] Ⓐ N 1 (= *gathering*) público *m*; (*in theatre etc*) público *m*, auditorio *m*; **there was a big ~** asistió un gran público; **those in the ~** los que formaban/forman *etc* parte del público *or* de la audiencia; **TV ~s** telespectadores *mpl*
2 (= *interview*) audiencia *f* (**with** con); **to have an ~ with** tener audiencia con, ser recibido en audiencia por; **to grant sb an ~** dar audiencia *or* conceder (una) audiencia a algn; **to receive sb in ~** recibir a algn en audiencia
Ⓑ CPD ► **audience appeal** N **it's got ~ appeal** tiene gancho con el público ► **audience chamber** N sala *f* de audiencias ► **audience participation** N participación *f* del público ► **audience rating** N (*TV, Rad*) índice *m* de audiencia ► **audience research** N (*TV, Rad*) sondeo *m* de opiniones

audio [ˈɔːdɪəʊ] Ⓐ ADJ de audio
Ⓑ N audio *m*
Ⓒ CPD ► **audio book** N audiolibro *m* ► **audio cassette** N cassette *f*, cinta *f* de audio ► **audio equipment** N equipo *m* de audio ► **audio frequency** N audiofrecuencia *f* ► **audio recording** N grabación *f* en audio ► **audio system** N sistema *m* audio

audio… [ˈɔːdɪəʊ] PREFIX audio…

audiometer [ˌɔːdɪˈɒmɪtəʳ] N audiómetro *m*

audiotronic [ˌɔːdɪəʊˈtrɒnɪk] ADJ audioelectrónico

audiotyping [ˈɔːdɪəʊˌtaɪpɪŋ] N mecanografía *f* por dictáfono

audiotypist [ˈɔːdɪəʊˌtaɪpɪst] N mecanógrafo/a *m/f* de dictáfono

audiovisual [ˌɔːdɪəʊˈvɪzjʊəl] ADJ audiovisual; **~ aids** medios *mpl* audiovisuales; **~ equipment** equipo *m* audiovisual; **~ method** método *m* audiovisual

audit [ˈɔːdɪt] Ⓐ N auditoría *f*, revisión *f* de cuentas
Ⓑ VT 1 (*Fin*) auditar, realizar una auditoría de, revisar
2 (*US*) **to ~ a course** asistir a un curso como oyente

auditing [ˈɔːdɪtɪŋ] N **~ of accounts** auditoría *f*, revisión *f* de cuentas

audition [ɔːˈdɪʃən] Ⓐ N (*Theat, Cine, TV*) prueba *f*, audición *f*; **to give sb an ~** (*Theat*) hacer una prueba a algn, ofrecer una audición a algn
Ⓑ VI **he ~ed for the part** hizo una prueba *or* audición para el papel
Ⓒ VT hacer una prueba a, hacer una audición a; **he was ~ed for the part** le hicieron una prueba *or* audición para el papel

auditor [ˈɔːdɪtəʳ] N 1 (*Comm, Fin*) auditor(a) *m/f*; **~'s report** informe *m* de auditoría
2 (*US Univ*) oyente *mf*, estudiante *mf* libre

auditorium [ˌɔːdɪˈtɔːrɪəm] N (*pl* **auditoriums, auditoria** [ˌɔːdɪˈtɔːrɪə]) auditorio *m*, sala *f*

auditory [ˈɔːdɪtərɪ] ADJ auditivo

Audubon [ˈɔːdəbɒn] N **the ~ Society** (*US*) *sociedad para la conservación de la naturaleza*, ≈ ICONA *m*, ≈ ADENA *f*

AUEW N ABBR (*Brit*) = **Amalgamated Union of Engineering Workers**

au fait [əʊˈfeɪ] ADJ **to be ~ with sth** estar al corriente *or* al tanto de algo

Aug. ABBR (= **August**) ag.

Augean Stables [ɔːˈdʒiːənˈsteɪblz] NPL establos *mpl* de Augias

aught [ɔːt] N (†† *or liter*) algo, alguna cosa; (*with negation*) nada; **if there is ~ I can do** si puedo hacer algo, si puedo ayudarles de algún modo; **for ~ I care he can …** igual me da si él …; **for ~ I know** que yo sepa

augment [ɔːgˈment] Ⓐ VT aumentar
Ⓑ VI aumentar(se)

augmentation [ˌɔːgmenˈteɪʃən] N aumento *m*

augmentative [ɔːgˈmentətɪv] ADJ aumentativo

au gratin [əʊˈgrætɛ̃] ADJ (*Culin*) gratinado

augur [ˈɔːgəʳ] Ⓐ VT augurar, pronosticar; **it ~s no good** esto no promete nada bueno
Ⓑ VI **it ~s well/ill** es un buen/mal augurio (**for** para)

augury [ˈɔːgjʊrɪ] N augurio *m*, presagio *m*; **to take the auguries††** consultar los augurios

August [ˈɔːgəst] N agosto *m*; *see* **July** *for usage*

august [ɔːˈgʌst] ADJ (*frm*) augusto

Augustan [ɔːˈgʌstən] ADJ de Augusto; **the ~ age** (*Latin Literat*) el siglo de Augusto; (*English Literat*) la época neoclásica (del siglo XVIII)

Augustine [ɔːˈgʌstɪn] N Agustín

Augustinian [ˌɔːgəˈstɪnɪən] Ⓐ ADJ agustino
Ⓑ N agustino/a *m/f*

Augustus [ɔːˈgʌstəs] N Augusto

auk [ɔːk] N alca *f*; **little ~** mérgulo *m* marino

auld [ɔːld] ADJ (*Scot*) = **old**; **~ lang syne** tiempos *mpl* antiguos, los buenos tiempos de antaño; **Auld Reekie** Edimburgo *m*

> **AULD LANG SYNE**
>
> **Auld Lang Syne** *es el título de una canción tradicional escocesa que se canta en todo el Reino Unido y en EE.UU. al final de algunas fiestas y celebraciones sociales, y en especial para dar la bienvenida al Año Nuevo, a las doce de la noche de fin de año. Con la canción se intenta hacernos recordar los tiempos pasados para que se tengan presentes en esos momentos. Los primeros versos son:* **Should auld acquaintance be forgot, And never brought to mind, We'll tak' a cup o' kindness yet, For the sake of auld lang syne.**
>
> ⇨ *Ver tb* HOGMANAY

aunt [ɑːnt] Ⓐ N tía *f*; **my ~ and uncle** mis tíos *mpl*
Ⓑ CPD ► **Aunt Sally** N blanco *m* (*de insultos, críticas etc*)

auntie*, **aunty*** [ˈɑːntɪ] N 1 (= *relative*) tía *f*
2 **Auntie** (*Brit hum*) la BBC

au pair [ˈəʊˈpɛəʳ] Ⓐ ADJ **~ girl** au pair *f*
Ⓑ N (*pl* **au pairs**) au pair *mf*
Ⓒ VI **to ~ (for sb)** hacer de au pair (para algn)

aura [ˈɔːrə] N (*pl* **auras, aurae** [ˈɔːriː]) (= *atmosphere*) aura *f*, halo *m*; (*Rel*) aureola *f*; **a mystic ~** un halo místico; **an ~ of doom** un halo fatídico

aural [ˈɔːrəl] ADJ del oído; **~ exam** examen *m* de comprensión oral

aureole [ˈɔːrɪəʊl] N aureola *f*

au revoir [ˌəʊrəˈvwɑːʳ] ADV hasta la vista

auricle [ˈɔːrɪkl] N aurícula *f*

aurochs [ˈɔːrɒks] N uro *m*, aurochs *m*

aurora borealis [ɔːˈrɔːrəbɔːrɪˈeɪlɪs] N aurora *f* boreal

auspices [ˈɔːspɪsɪz] NPL **under the ~ of** bajo los auspicios de

auspicious [ɔːsˈpɪʃəs] ADJ (*frm*) [*day, time*] propicio; [*sign*] de buen augurio; [*occasion, moment*] feliz; **it was an ~ start to their election campaign** fue un comienzo lleno de buenos auspicios para su campaña electoral; **to make an ~ start** comenzar felizmente *or* con buenos auspicios

auspiciously [ɔːsˈpɪʃəslɪ] ADV con buenos auspicios, propiciamente; **to start ~** comenzar felizmente *or* con buenos auspicios

Aussie* [ˈɒzɪ] = **Australian**

austere [ɒsˈtɪəʳ] ADJ [*person, manner, life*] austero, severo

austerely [ɒsˈtɪəlɪ] ADV austeramente

austerity [ɒsˈterɪtɪ] N austeridad *f*

Australasia [ˌɔːstrəˈleɪzɪə] N Australasia *f*

Australasian [ˌɔːstrəˈleɪzɪən] Ⓐ ADJ australasia-

no
Ⓑ N australasiano/a *m/f*

Australia [ɒs'treɪlɪə] N Australia *f*

Australian [ɒs'treɪlɪən] Ⓐ ADJ australiano
Ⓑ N australiano/a *m/f*
Ⓒ CPD ► **Australian Rules Football** N fútbol *m* australiano

Austria ['ɒstrɪə] N Austria *f*

Austrian ['ɒstrɪən] Ⓐ ADJ austriaco, austríaco
Ⓑ N austriaco/a *m/f*, austríaco/a *m/f*

Austro- ['ɒstrəʊ] PREFIX austro-; **~Hungarian** austro-húngaro

AUT N ABBR (*Brit*) = **Association of University Teachers**

autarchy ['ɔːtɑːkɪ] N autarquía *f*

authentic [ɔː'θentɪk] ADJ 1 (= *genuine*) [*document, painting, data*] auténtico; **the ~ taste of Italy** el auténtico sabor de Italia
2 (= *realistic*) [*scene, atmosphere*] realista

authentically [ɔː'θentɪkəlɪ] ADV 1 (= *genuinely*) auténticamente; **~ Chinese dishes** auténticos *or* genuinos platos de China
2 (= *realistically*) [*furnished, restored*] fielmente

authenticate [ɔː'θentɪkeɪt] VT autentificar, autenticar

authentication [ɔːˌθentɪ'keɪʃn] N autentificación *f*, autenticación *f*

authenticity [ˌɔːθen'tɪsɪtɪ] N 1 (= *genuineness*) [*of text, painting*] autenticidad *f*
2 (= *realistic quality*) [*of decor, furniture*] realismo *m*

author ['ɔːθəʳ] Ⓐ N 1 (= *writer*) autor(a) *m/f*; **~! ~!** (*Theat*) ¡que salga el autor!; **~'s copy** (*signed by author*) ejemplar *m* autógrafo; (*belonging to author*) ejemplar *m* del autor
2 (*fig*) [*of plan, trouble etc*] autor(a) *m/f*, creador(a) *m/f*
Ⓑ VT (*esp Brit*) escribir, componer

authoress ['ɔːθərɪs] N autora *f*

authorial [ɔː'θɔːrɪəl] ADJ del autor

authoritarian [ˌɔːθɒrɪ'teərɪən] Ⓐ ADJ autoritario
Ⓑ N autoritario/a *m/f*

authoritarianism [ˌɔːθɒrɪ'teərɪənɪzəm] N autoritarismo *m*

authoritative [ɔː'θɒrɪtətɪv] ADJ 1 (= *reliable*) [*account, book, writer, professor*] de gran autoridad, acreditado; [*source, statement, information, study*] autorizado; [*newspaper*] serio
2 (= *commanding*) [*person, voice, manner*] autoritario

authoritatively [ɔː'θɒrɪtətɪvlɪ] ADV 1 (= *reliably*) [*speak, write*] con autoridad
2 (= *commandingly*) [*say, nod, behave*] de manera autoritaria, autoritariamente

authority [ɔː'θɒrɪtɪ] N 1 (= *power*) autoridad *f*; **those in ~** los que tienen la autoridad; **who is in ~ here?** ¿quién manda aquí?; **to be in ~ over** tener autoridad sobre
2 (= *authorization*) **to give sb the ~ to do sth** autorizar a algn a hacer algo, autorizar a algn para que haga algo; **to have ~ to do sth** tener autoridad *or* estar autorizado para hacer algo; **on one's own ~** por su propia autoridad; **to do sth without ~** hacer algo sin tener autorización
3 (= *official body*) autoridad *f*; **the authorities** las autoridades; **the customs authorities** las autoridades aduaneras; **to apply to the proper authorities** dirigirse a la autoridad competente; *see also* **health**, **local**, **regional**
4 (= *expert*) autoridad *f*; **he's an ~ (on)** es una autoridad (en)
5 (= *expert opinion*) autoridad *f*; **on the ~ of Plato** con la autoridad de Platón; **I have it on good ~ that ...** sé de buena fuente que ...
6 (= *authoritativeness*) autoridad *f*; **to speak with ~** hablar con autoridad *or* con conocimiento de causa

▼**authorization** [ˌɔːθəraɪ'zeɪʃən] N autorización *f*

▼**authorize** ['ɔːθəraɪz] VT (= *empower*) autorizar; (= *approve*) aprobar; **to ~ sb to do sth** autorizar a algn a hacer algo; **to be ~d to do sth** estar autorizado para hacer algo, tener autorización para hacer algo

authorized ['ɔːθəraɪzd] ADJ autorizado; **~ agent** agente *mf* oficial; **~ biography** biografía *f* oficial; **~ capital** (*Comm*) capital *m* autorizado, capital *m* escriturado; **~ distributor** distribuidor *m* autorizado; **Authorized Version** Versión *f* Autorizada (de la Biblia)

authorship ['ɔːθəʃɪp] N 1 [*of book etc*] autoría *f*; **of unknown ~** de autor desconocido
2 (= *profession*) profesión *f* de autor

autism ['ɔːtɪzəm] N autismo *m*

autistic [ɔː'tɪstɪk] ADJ autista

auto ['ɔːtəʊ] (*US*) Ⓐ N coche *m*, automóvil *m*, carro *m* (*LAm*)
Ⓑ CPD ► **auto repair** N reparación *f* de automóviles ► **auto worker** N trabajador(a) *m/f* de la industria automovilística *or* del automóvil

auto... ['ɔːtəʊ] PREFIX auto...

autobank ['ɔːtəʊbæŋk] N cajero *m* automático

autobiographic ['ɔːtəʊˌbaɪəʊ'græfɪk] ADJ = **autobiographical**

autobiographical ['ɔːtəʊˌbaɪəʊ'græfɪkəl] ADJ autobiográfico

autobiography [ˌɔːtəʊbaɪ'ɒgrəfɪ] N autobiografía *f*

autocade ['ɔːtəʊkeɪd] N caravana *f* de automóviles

autochthonous [ɔː'tɒkθənəs] ADJ autóctono

autocracy [ɔː'tɒkrəsɪ] N autocracia *f*

autocrat ['ɔːtəʊkræt] N autócrata *mf*

autocratic [ˌɔːtəʊ'krætɪk] ADJ autocrático

autocross ['ɔːtəʊkrɒs] N autocross *m*

autocue ['ɔːtəʊkjuː] N (*Brit TV*) autocue *m*, chuleta* *f*

autocycle ['ɔːtəʊsaɪkl] N ciclomotor *m*

auto-da-fe, auto-da-fé ['ɔːtəʊdɑː'feɪ] N (*pl* **autos-da-fe**) auto *m* de fe

autodidact ['ɔːtəʊˌdaɪdækt] N (*frm*) autodidacta *mf*

autodrome† ['ɔːtəʊdrəʊm] N autódromo *m*

autofocus ['ɔːtəʊfəʊkəs] N (*Phot*) autofoco *m*, autoenfoque *m*

autogiro ['ɔːtəʊ'dʒaɪərəʊ] N autogiro *m*

autograph ['ɔːtəgrɑːf] Ⓐ N 1 (= *signature*) autógrafo *m*
2 (= *manuscript*) autógrafo *m*
Ⓑ VT (= *sign*) firmar; [+ *book, photo*] dedicar
Ⓒ CPD ► **autograph album** N álbum *m* de autógrafos ► **autograph hunter** N cazador(a) *m/f* de autógrafos

autohypnosis ['ɔːtəʊhɪp'nəʊsɪs] N autohipnosis *f inv*

auto-immune [ˌɔːtəʊɪ'mjuːn] ADJ autoinmune

automat ['ɔːtəmæt] N 1 (*Brit*) máquina *f* expendedora
2 (*US*) restaurante *m* de autoservicio

automata [ɔː'tɒmətə] NPL *of* **automaton**

automate ['ɔːtəmeɪt] VT automatizar

automated ['ɔːtəˌmeɪtɪd] Ⓐ ADJ automatizado
Ⓑ CPD ► **automated teller, automated telling machine** N cajero *m* automático

automatic [ˌɔːtə'mætɪk] Ⓐ ADJ (*Tech, gen*) automático; **disqualification is ~** la descalificación es automática
Ⓑ N (= *pistol*) pistola *f* automática; (= *car*) coche *m* automático; (= *washing machine*) lavadora *f*
Ⓒ CPD ► **automatic data processing** N (*Comput*) proceso *m* automático de datos ► **automatic pilot** N (*Aer*) piloto *m* automático; **to be on ~ pilot** (*fig*) ir como un/una autómata ► **automatic transmission** N (*Aut*) transmisión *f* automática

automatically [ˌɔːtə'mætɪkəlɪ] ADV automáticamente

automation [ˌɔːtə'meɪʃən] N automatización *f*

automatism [ɔː'tɒmətɪzəm] N automatismo *m*

automaton [ɔː'tɒmətən] N (*pl* **automatons, automata**) autómata *m*

automobile ['ɔːtəməbiːl] (*US*) Ⓐ N coche *m*, automóvil *m*, carro *m* (*LAm*)
Ⓑ CPD ► **automobile industry** N industria *f* del automóvil

automotive [ɔːtə'məʊtɪv] ADJ automotor (*f*: automotora, automotriz)

autonomous [ɔː'tɒnəməs] ADJ autónomo

autonomy [ɔː'tɒnəmɪ] N autonomía *f*

autopilot ['ɔːtəʊpaɪlət] N (*Aer*) piloto *m* automático; **to be on ~** (*fig*) ir como un/una autómata

autopsy ['ɔːtɒpsɪ] N autopsia *f*

auto-reverse ['ɔːtəʊrɪ'vɜːs] N rebobinado *m* automático, autorreverse *m*

auto-suggestion ['ɔːtəʊsə'dʒestʃən] N (auto)sugestión *f*

auto-teller ['ɔːtəʊˌteləʳ] N cajero *m* automático

auto-timer ['ɔːtəʊˌtaɪməʳ] N programador *m* automático

autumn ['ɔːtəm] N (*esp Brit*) otoño *m*; **in ~** en otoño; **I like to go walking in (the) ~** me gusta salir a pasear en otoño; **in the ~ of 1998** en el otoño de 1998; **in early/late ~** a principios/a finales del otoño; **an ~ day** un día de otoño

autumnal [ɔː'tʌmnəl] ADJ otoñal, de(l) otoño

Auvergne [əʊ'veən] N Auvernia *f*

auxiliary [ɔːg'zɪlɪərɪ] Ⓐ ADJ auxiliar; **~ police** (*US*) cuerpo *m* de policía auxiliar; **~ staff** (*Brit Scol*) profesores *mpl* auxiliares
Ⓑ N 1 (*Med*) ayudante *mf*
2 (*Mil*) **auxiliaries** tropas *fpl* auxiliares
3 (*also* **~ verb**) verbo *m* auxiliar

AV Ⓐ N ABBR (= **Authorized Version**) *traducción inglesa de la Biblia*
Ⓑ ABBR = **audiovisual**

Av. ABBR (= **Avenue**) Av., Avda.

av. ABBR (= **average**) prom.

a.v., a/v ABBR = **ad valorem**

avail [ə'veɪl] (*liter*) Ⓐ N **it is of no ~** es inútil; **to be of little ~** ser de poco provecho; **of what ~ is it to ...?** ¿de qué sirve ... + *infin* ?; **to no ~** en vano
Ⓑ VT valer; **to ~ o.s. of** aprovechar(se de), valerse de
Ⓒ VI **it ~s nothing to** + INFIN de nada sirve + *infin*

availability [əˌveɪlə'bɪlɪtɪ] N 1 [*of goods, tickets*] disponibilidad *f*; **the high crime rate is due to the easy ~ of guns** el alto índice de criminalidad se debe a la fácil disponibilidad de armas *or* a lo fácil que es conseguir armas; **..., subject to ~** (*goods*) ..., siempre que haya existencias
2 [*of person*] **this depends on your ~ for work** esto depende de si estás disponible para trabajar

available [ə'veɪləbl] ADJ 1 [*object, service*] 1.1 (*with verb*) **to be ~**: **application forms are ~**

➤ LANGUAGE IN USE: **authorization** 9.2, 9.5 **authorize** 9.4, 9.5

here las solicitudes se pueden conseguir aquí; **it's ~ in other colours** también viene en otros colores; **this item is not ~ at the moment** no disponemos de *or* no tenemos este artículo en este momento; **television isn't yet ~ here** la televisión aún no ha llegado aquí; **to become ~**: **new treatments are becoming ~** están apareciendo nuevos tratamientos; **a place has become ~ on the course/flight** ha quedado una plaza libre en el curso/el vuelo; **~ for sth/sb**: **a car park is ~ for the use of customers** hay un aparcamiento a la disposición de los clientes; **there are three boats ~ for hire** hay tres botes que se pueden alquilar; **to be freely ~** ser fácil de conseguir; **the guide is ~ from all good bookshops** la guía se puede encontrar en todas las buenas librerías; **this service is ~ from all good travel agents** cualquier agencia de viaje de calidad le ofrecerá este servicio; **tickets are ~ from the box office** las entradas están a la venta en taquilla; **to make sth ~ to sb** [+ *resources*] poner algo a la disposición de algn

[1·2] (*with noun*) disponible; **according to the ~ information** según la información disponible *or* de que se dispone; **we did what we could in the time ~** hicimos lo que pudimos en el tiempo disponible *or* del que disponíamos; **I have very few days ~ at the moment** en este momento tengo muy pocos días libres; **he tried every ~ means to find her** hizo todo lo posible para encontrarla; **I'd like a seat on the first ~ flight** quiero una plaza en el primer vuelo que haya; **the money ~ for spending** el dinero disponible para gastos; **~ to sb**: **the information ~ to us** la información de la que disponemos

[2] [*person*] [2·1] (= *free, at hand*) libre; **are you ~ next Thursday?** ¿estás libre el jueves que viene?; **I'm ~ on this number** me puedes localizar en este número; **counsellors are ~ to talk to anyone who needs advice** los orientadores están a la disposición de *or* están disponibles para hablar con cualquiera que necesite consejo; **there's no-one ~ to take your call** no hay nadie que pueda atender a su llamada; **the Minister is not ~ for comment** el Ministro no se dispone a hacer comentarios; **to make o.s. ~**: **he made himself ~ in case anybody had any questions** se puso a disposición de cualquiera que tuviese preguntas

[2·2] (= *unattached*) [*man, woman*] soltero y sin compromiso

avalanche [ˈævəlɑːnʃ] N avalancha *f*; (*fig*) torrente *m*, avalancha *f*

avant-garde [ˈævɑːŋˈgɑːd] Ⓐ ADJ vanguardista, de vanguardia

Ⓑ N vanguardia *f*

avarice [ˈævərɪs] N avaricia *f*

avaricious [ˌævəˈrɪʃəs] ADJ avaro

avatar [ˈævətɑːʳ] N [*of deity*] avatar *m*

avdp ABBR = **avoirdupois**

Ave ABBR (= **avenue**) Av., Avda.

avenge [əˈvendʒ] VT vengar; **to ~ o.s.** vengarse (**on sb** en algn)

avenger [əˈvendʒəʳ] N vengador(a) *m/f*

avenging [əˈvendʒɪŋ] ADJ vengador

avenue [ˈævənjuː] N [1] (= *road*) avenida *f*, paseo *m*

[2] (*fig*) vía *f*, camino *m*; **to explore every ~** explorar todas las vías *or* todos los caminos

aver [əˈvɜːʳ] VT afirmar, asegurar

average [ˈævərɪdʒ] Ⓐ ADJ [1] (*Math, Statistics*) [*age, wage, price, speed*] medio, promedio *inv*

[2] (= *normal, typical*) medio; **the ~ American drives 10,000 miles per year** el americano medio hace unas 10.000 millas al año con su coche; **an ~ thirteen-year-old child could understand it** un niño de trece años de inteligencia media podría entenderlo; **that's ~ for a woman of your age** eso es lo normal para una mujer de tu edad; **of ~ ability** de capacidad media; **of ~ height** de estatura mediana *or* media; **the ~ man** el hombre medio; **he's not your ~ footballer*** no es el típico futbolista

[3] (= *mediocre*) mediocre; **a very ~ novel** una novela bastante mediocre; **an ~ piece of work** un trabajo de una calidad mediana; **"how was the film?" — "average"** —¿qué tal fue la película? —nada del otro mundo

Ⓑ N media *f*, promedio *m*; **to do an ~ of 150kph** hacer una media *or* un promedio de 150kph; **it takes an ~ of ten weeks for a house sale to be completed** como promedio la venta de una casa se lleva a término en unas diez semanas; **above ~** superior a la media *or* al promedio, por encima de la media *or* del promedio; **below ~** inferior a la media *or* al promedio, por debajo de la media *or* del promedio; **on ~** como promedio, por término medio; **a rough ~** una media aproximada; **to take an ~ of sth** calcular la media *or* el promedio de algo

Ⓒ VT [1] (*also* **~ out**) (= *calculate average of*) calcular la media de, calcular el promedio de

[2] (= *reach an average of*) **pay increases are averaging 9.75%** los aumentos de sueldo son, como media *or* promedio, del 9,75%; **we ~ eight hours' work a day** trabajamos por término medio unas ocho horas diarias, trabajamos una media *or* un promedio de unas ocho horas diarias; **the sales ~ 200 copies a week** el promedio de ventas es de unos 200 ejemplares a la semana; **the temperature ~d 13 degrees over the month** la temperatura media *or* promedio fue de unos 13 grados a lo largo del mes, la temperatura alcanzó una media *or* un promedio de unos 13 grados a lo largo del mes; **he ~d 140kph all the way** (*Aut*) hizo un promedio *or* una media de 140kph en todo el recorrido

Ⓓ ADV (*) regular; **she did ~ in the oral exam** el examen oral le fue regular

►**average down** VT + ADV **to ~ sth down** sacar el promedio *or* la media de algo tirando hacia abajo

►**average out** Ⓐ VT + ADV calcular la media de, calcular el promedio de

Ⓑ VI + ADV **it'll ~ out in the end** al final una cosa compensará por la otra; **to ~ out at** salir a un promedio *or* una media de; **it ~s out at 50p a glass** sale a un promedio *or* una media de 50 peniques el vaso; **our working hours ~ out at eight a day** trabajamos un promedio *or* una media de ocho horas al día

►**average up** VT + ADV **to ~ sth up** sacar el promedio *or* la media de algo tirando hacia arriba

AVERAGE, HALF

Position of "medio"

You should generally put **medio** after the noun when you mean "average" and before the noun when you mean "half":

...the average citizen...

...el ciudadano medio...

...the average salary...

...el salario medio...

...half a kilo of tomatoes...

...medio kilo de tomates...

For further uses and examples, see main entries at ***average*** *and* ***half****.*

averagely [ˈævərɪdʒlɪ] ADV regular; **she did ~ (well) in the oral exam** el examen oral le fue regular; **he performed very ~ at school** en los estudios le iba bastante regular; **we scored only ~** las puntuaciones que obtuvimos no pasaron de ser regulares

averse [əˈvɜːs] ADJ **to be ~ to sth** sentir repugnancia por algo; **to be ~ to doing sth** ser reacio a hacer algo; **he is ~ to getting up early** es reacio a levantarse temprano; **would you be ~ to having the meeting at your house?** ¿estarías dispuesto a celebrar la reunión en tu casa?; **I'm not ~ to an occasional drink** no me opongo a tomar una copa de vez en cuando

aversion [əˈvɜːʃən] Ⓐ N [1] (= *dislike*) aversión *f* (**to, for** hacia); **I have an ~ to garlic/cooking** el ajo/la cocina me repugna, tengo aversión por el ajo/la cocina; **I have an ~ to him** me repugna, le tengo aversión; **I took an ~ to it** empezó a repugnarme

[2] (= *hated thing*) cosa *f* aborrecida; **it is one of my ~s** es una de las cosas que me repugnan

Ⓑ CPD ► **aversion therapy** N terapia *f* por aversión, terapia *f* aversiva

avert [əˈvɜːt] VT [1] (= *turn away*) [+ *eyes, thoughts*] apartar (**from** de); [+ *suspicion*] desviar (**from** de); [+ *possibility*] evitar

[2] (= *prevent*) [+ *accident, danger etc*] prevenir

[3] (= *parry*) [+ *blows*] desviar

aviary [ˈeɪvɪərɪ] N pajarera *f*

aviation [ˌeɪvɪˈeɪʃən] Ⓐ N aviación *f*

Ⓑ CPD ► **aviation industry** N industria *f* de la aviación ► **aviation spirit** N gasolina *f* de aviación

aviator [ˈeɪvɪeɪtəʳ] N aviador(a) *m/f*

avid [ˈævɪd] ADJ [*collector, viewer*] ávido; [*supporter, fan*] ferviente; **an ~ reader** un ávido lector; **to be ~ for sth** estar ávido de algo

avidity [əˈvɪdɪtɪ] N avidez *f*

avidly [ˈævɪdlɪ] ADV ávidamente, con avidez; **to read ~** leer con avidez

Avignon [ˈævɪnjɔ̃] N Aviñón *m*

avionics [ˌeɪvɪˈɒnɪks] NSING aviónica *f*

avocado [ævəˈkɑːdəʊ] N (*pl* **avocados**) [1] (*also* **~ pear**) aguacate *m*, palta *f* (*Andes, S. Cone*)

[2] (= *tree*) aguacate *m*, palto *m* (*LAm*)

avocation [ˌævəʊˈkeɪʃən] N (*frm*) (= *minor occupation*) diversión *f*, distracción *f*; (= *employment*) vocación *f*

avoid [əˈvɔɪd] VT [+ *obstacle*] evitar, esquivar; [+ *argument, question, subject*] evitar, eludir; [+ *duty*] eludir; [+ *danger*] salvarse de; **are you trying to ~ me?** ¿me estás evitando *or* esquivando?; **I try to ~ him** procuro no tener nada que ver con él; **he ~s all his friends** huye de todos sus amigos; **this way we ~ London** por esta ruta evitamos pasar por Londres; **to ~ sb's eye** esquivar la mirada de algn; **to ~ tax** (*legally*) evitar pagar impuestos; (*illegally*) defraudar al fisco; **to ~ doing sth** evitar hacer algo; **he managed to ~ (hitting) the tree** logró esquivar el árbol; **I'm trying to ~ being seen by Jeremy** estoy intentando evitar que me vea Jeremy, estoy intentando que Jeremy no me vea; ✦***IDIOM*** **it's to be ~ed like the plague** de esto hay que huir como de la peste

avoidable [əˈvɔɪdəbl] ADJ evitable

avoidance [əˈvɔɪdəns] N **the ~ of fatty foods** el evitar los alimentos grasos; **you can improve your health by the ~ of stress** uno puede mejorar su salud evitando el estrés; *see also* **tax**

avoirdupois [ˌævədeˈpɔɪz] N *sistema de pesos usado, aunque cada vez menos, en países de* *habla inglesa (1 libra = 16 onzas = 453,50 gramos)*

avow [ə'vaʊ] VT (*frm*) 1 (= *recognize*) reconocer, admitir, confesar; **many men ~ they find blondes insipid and cold** muchos hombres admiten *or* reconocen *or* confiesan que las rubias les parecen frías e insípidas; **he ~ed himself beaten** reconoció *or* admitió que había perdido
2 (= *affirm*) afirmar, declarar

avowal [ə'vaʊəl] N (*frm*) 1 (= *recognition*) reconocimiento *m*, admisión *f*, confesión *f*
2 (= *affirmation*) afirmación *f*, declaración *f*

avowed [ə'vaʊd] ADJ (*frm*) [*purpose, opponent, supporter*] declarado; **their ~ aim is to disrupt society** su objetivo declarado es causar problemas en la sociedad

avowedly [ə'vaʊɪdlɪ] ADV (*frm*) declaradamente, abiertamente

AVP N ABBR (*US*) = **assistant vice-president**

avuncular [ə'vʌŋkjʊləʳ] ADJ como de tío; **~ advice** consejos *mpl* amistosos

aw [ɔː] EXCL ¡ay!

AWACS [eɪ'wæks] N ABBR (= **Airborne Warning and Control System**) AWACS *m*

▼**await** [ə'weɪt] VT 1 (= *wait for*) esperar, aguardar; **we ~ your instructions** esperamos *or* aguardamos sus instrucciones; **we ~ your reply with interest** aguardamos su respuesta con interés
2 (= *be in store for*) esperar, aguardar; **the fate that ~s him** la suerte que le espera; **a surprise ~s him** le espera *or* le aguarda una sorpresa

awake [ə'weɪk] (*pt* **awoke** *or* **awaked**; *pp* **awoken** *or* **awaked**) Ⓐ ADJ despierto; **to be ~** estar despierto; **fully ~** totalmente despierto; **I was still only half ~** aún estaba medio dormido; **coffee keeps me ~** (= *keeps me alert*) el café me mantiene despierto; (= *stops me sleeping*) el café me desvela; **the noise kept me ~** el ruido no me dejó dormir; **to lie ~**: **he lay ~ all night, thinking about his new job** no pudo dormir en toda la noche *or* estuvo desvelado toda la noche, pensando en su nuevo trabajo; **I'm not really ~ yet** aún no estoy despierto del todo; **to stay ~** mantenerse despierto, no dormirse; **I found it difficult to stay ~** me costaba mantenerme despierto, me costaba no dormirme; **I'm not going to stay ~ all night worrying about that** no voy a pasarme toda la noche en vela preocupándome por eso; **to be ~ to sth** (*fig*) ser consciente de algo; **wide ~** totalmente despierto
Ⓑ VT 1 (= *wake up*) despertar
2 (= *arouse*) [+ *suspicion, curiosity*] despertar; [+ *hope*] hacer nacer; [+ *memories*] reavivar, resucitar
Ⓒ VI 1 (*liter*) (= *wake up*) despertar; **I awoke from a deep sleep** desperté de un sueño profundo; **when are we going to ~ from this nightmare?** ¿cuándo vamos a despertar de esta pesadilla?; **she awoke to a lovely, sunny day** despertó y el día era precioso, soleado; **he awoke to find himself in hospital** al despertar(se) vio que se hallaba en el hospital
2 (= *become aware*) **to ~ to sth** darse cuenta de algo; **she awoke to the fact that ...** se dio cuenta de que ...; **he finally awoke to his responsibilities** finalmente tomó conciencia de sus responsabilidades

awaked† [ə'weɪkt] PT, PP *of* **awake**

awaken [ə'weɪkən] Ⓐ VT despertar; **to ~ sb to a danger** alertar a algn de un peligro
Ⓑ VI (*also* **to ~ from sleep**) despertar; **to ~ from one's illusions** desilusionarse, quitarse las ilusiones; **to ~ to a danger** darse cuenta de un peligro

awakening [ə'weɪknɪŋ] Ⓐ ADJ (*fig*) naciente
Ⓑ N despertar *m*; **he got a rude ~** tuvo una desagradable sorpresa

award [ə'wɔːd] Ⓐ N 1 (= *prize*) premio *m*; (*Mil*) (= *medal*) condecoración *f*
2 (*Jur*) (= *ruling*) fallo *m*, sentencia *f*; (= *sum of money*) (*punitive*) sanción *f*; (= *damages*) concesión *f*; **a record ~ for sexual harassment** una sanción récord por acoso sexual; **they are appealing against the ~ of £350,000 to Violet Bush** van a recurrir contra la concesión de £350.000 a Violet Bush
3 (= *act of awarding*) entrega *f*, concesión *f*; *see also* **pay**
Ⓑ VT 1 [+ *prize, medal*] conceder, otorgar; **the prize is not being ~ed this year** este año el premio se ha declarado desierto
2 (*Jur*) [+ *damages*] adjudicar
3 (*Sport*) **to ~ a penalty (against sb)** pitar *or* señalar (un) penalti (contra algn); **to ~ sb a penalty** conceder un penalti a algn
Ⓒ CPD ► **award(s) ceremony** N ceremonia *f* de entrega de premios ► **award winner** N premiado/a *m/f*, galardonado/a *m/f*

award-winning [ə'wɔːd,wɪnɪŋ] ADJ premiado, galardonado

aware [ə'wɛəʳ] ADJ 1 (= *cognizant*) **to be ~ that ...** saber que ..., ser consciente de que ...; **I am fully ~ that ...** tengo plena conciencia de que ...; **to be ~ (of)** ser consciente (de); **we are ~ of what is happening** somos conscientes de lo que ocurre; **our employees are ~ of this advertisement** los empleados de la empresa han sido informados de este anuncio; **not that I am ~ (of)** que yo sepa, no; **to become ~ of** enterarse de; **to make sb ~ of sth** hacer que algn se dé cuenta de algo
2 (= *knowledgeable*) **politically ~** con conciencia política; **sexually ~** enterado de lo sexual; **socially ~** sensibilizado con los temas sociales
3 (= *alert*) despierto

awareness [ə'wɛənɪs] N conciencia *f*, conocimiento *m*; **sexual ~ in the young** la conciencia sexual *or* los conocimientos sexuales de los jóvenes

awash [ə'wɒʃ] ADJ 1 (*with water*) inundado; **the house was ~** la casa estaba inundada; **the deck is ~** la cubierta está a flor de agua
2 (*fig*) **we are ~ with applicants** estamos inundados de solicitudes

away [ə'weɪ]

When ***away*** *is an element in a phrasal verb, eg* ***boil away, die away, get away****, look up the verb.*

Ⓐ ADV 1 (= *at or to a distance*) **far ~** ◊ **a long way ~** lejos; **~ in the distance** a lo lejos; **it's ten miles ~ (from here)** está a diez millas (de aquí); **~ from the noise** lejos del ruido; **keep the child ~ from the fire** no dejes que el niño se acerque al fuego; **White won with Peters only two strokes ~** ganó White con Peters a sólo dos golpes de distancia; **~ back in 1066** allá en 1066
2 (= *absent*) **to be ~** estar fuera, estar ausente; **to be ~ (from home)** estar fuera, estar ausente; **she's ~ today** hoy está fuera; **he's ~ for a week** está fuera una semana; **he's ~ in Bognor** está en Bognor; **she was ~ before I could shout** se fue antes de que yo pudiese gritar; **I must ~** (*liter or hum*) tengo que marcharme; **~ with you!*** (= *go away!*) ¡vete!, ¡fuera de aquí!; (*expressing disbelief*) ¡venga ya!, ¡anda ya!; (*joking*) ¡no digas bobadas; **~ with him!** ¡fuera!, ¡que se lo lleven de aquí!
3 (*Sport*) fuera (de casa); **they have won only two games ~** han ganado solamente dos partidos fuera (de casa); **to play ~** (*Sport*) jugar fuera; **Chelsea are ~ to Everton on Saturday** el Chelsea juega fuera, en campo del Everton, el sábado
4 (= *continuously*) sin parar; **to talk ~** no parar de hablar, seguir hablando; **I could hear her talking ~** la oía hablar sin parar; **to work ~** seguir trabajando, trabajar sin parar; **he was working ~ in the garden** estaba dale que te pego en el jardín, estaba trabajando sin parar en el jardín; **he was grumbling ~** no paraba de refunfuñar
Ⓑ ADJ **the ~ team** el equipo de fuera; **~ match** partido *m* fuera de casa; **~ win** victoria *f* fuera de casa

awe [ɔː] Ⓐ N (= *fear*) pavor *m*; (= *wonder*) asombro *m*; (= *reverence*) temor *m* reverencial; **to go** *or* **be in ~ of** ◊ **hold in ~** tener temor reverencial a
Ⓑ VT (= *impress*) impresionar; (= *frighten*) atemorizar; **in an ~d voice** con un tono de respeto y temor

awe-inspiring ['ɔːɪn,spaɪərɪŋ] ADJ = **awesome 1**

awesome ['ɔːsəm] ADJ 1 (= *impressive*) [*sight, beauty*] impresionante, imponente; [*achievement*] impresionante
2 (= *huge*) [*task, responsibility*] abrumador
3 (*esp US**) (= *excellent*) formidable

awe-struck ['ɔːstrʌk] ADJ pasmado, atemorizado

▼**awful** ['ɔːfəl] Ⓐ ADJ 1 (= *dreadful*) [*weather*] horrible, espantoso; [*clothes, crime*] horroroso, espantoso; [*smell, dilemma*] terrible; **what ~ weather!** ¡qué tiempo más horrible *or* espantoso!; **we met and I thought he was ~** le conocí y me cayó fatal; **you are ~!** (= *wicked*) ¡qué malo eres!, ¡qué mala idea tienes!; **to feel ~** (= *embarrassed, guilty*) sentirse fatal; (= *ill*) encontrarse *or* sentirse fatal; **I felt ~ about what had happened** me sentía fatal por lo que había ocurrido; **I have an ~ feeling something's going to happen** tengo la terrible sospecha de que va a pasar algo; **how ~!** ¡qué horror!; **how ~ for you!** ¡qué mal rato habrás pasado!; **to look ~** tener muy mal aspecto; **you look ~, are you feeling all right?** tienes muy mala cara *or* tienes muy mal aspecto, ¿te encuentras bien?; **for one ~ moment I thought I'd broken it** ¡fue horrible! por un momento pensé que se me había roto; **it smells ~** huele fatal; **prices have gone up something ~**‡ los precios han subido cosa mala*; **they beat him up something ~**‡ le dieron una tremenda paliza; **what an ~ thing to happen!** ¡qué cosa tan horrible *or* terrible!; **the ~ thing is that he thought we were joking** lo peor (del caso) es que él pensó que estábamos de broma; **you said some pretty ~ things** hiciste algunos comentarios muy hirientes; **I learned the ~ truth** supe la amarga verdad
2 (= *bad, poor*) **his English is ~** habla inglés fatal
3 (= *awesome*) imponente, tremendo
4 (*) (*as intensifier*) **there were an ~ lot of people** había un montón de gente*; **I've got an ~ lot of work to do** tengo un montón de trabajo*; **it's an ~ nuisance** es una molestia terrible; **he's an ~ bore** es terriblemente pesado; **she's got an ~ cheek!** ¡tiene una cara increíble!*; **it seems an ~ waste** parece un desperdicio terrible
Ⓑ ADV (*esp US**) **ten years is an ~ long time** diez años es un montón de tiempo*; **it's an ~**

➤ LANGUAGE IN USE: **await 1** 20.7 **awful A1** 14

long way to go está lejísimo; **it's ~ cold outside** fuera hace un frío horroroso*

awfully* ['ɔːflɪ] ADV [1] (*as intensifier*) **he's ~ nice** es majísimo; **it's ~ hard** *or* **difficult** es terriblemente difícil; **she works ~ hard** trabaja durísimo; **it was ~ hot** hacía un calor espantoso; **that's ~ good of you** es muy amable de su parte; **I'm ~ sorry** lo siento muchísimo; **would you mind ~ if we didn't go?** ¿te molestaría mucho que no fuéramos?; **thanks ~!**† ¡muchísimas gracias!
[2] (= *badly*) [*play, sing*] pésimamente, fatal

awfulness ['ɔːfʊlnɪs] N [1] (= *dreadfulness*) lo terrible; **the ~ of the situation kept coming back to him** lo terrible de la situación se le venía insistentemente a la cabeza; **he had to serve 18 years because of the ~ of his crimes** sus crímenes fueron tan horrorosos que tuvo que servir una condena de 18 años
[2] (= *poor quality*) **it gets mentioned, if only for its ~** se habla de eso, aunque sólo sea por lo malo que es

awhile [ə'waɪl] (*esp US*) ADV un rato, algún tiempo; **not yet ~** todavía no

awkward ['ɔːkwəd] ADJ [1] (= *inconvenient, difficult*) [*moment, time*] malo; [*shape*] incómodo, poco práctico; [*corner*] peligroso; **have I called at an ~ moment?** ¿he llamado en mal momento?; **this scandal comes at an ~ moment for the government** este escándalo llega en un momento difícil *or* en un mal momento para el gobierno; **to be at an ~ age** estar en una edad difícil; **he's being ~ about it** está poniendo inconvenientes; **he's an ~ customer*** es un tipo difícil*, es un sujeto de cuidado*; **Thursday is ~ for me** el jueves no me viene bien; **to make things ~ for sb** poner las cosas difíciles a algn, crear dificultades a algn; **it would be ~ to postpone my trip again** sería difícil volver a aplazar mi viaje; **it's not far, but it's ~ to get to by public transport** no está lejos, pero es complicado llegar en transporte público; **it's very ~ to carry** es muy difícil de llevar
[2] (= *embarrassing, uncomfortable*) [*silence*] embarazoso; [*problem, question*] delicado, difícil; [*situation*] delicado, violento; [*matter, subject*] delicado; **to feel ~** sentirse incómodo; **he had always felt ~ with Clara** siempre se había sentido incómodo con Clara, nunca se había sentido a gusto con Clara; **I felt ~ about asking her for a rise** me resultaba violento pedirle un aumento de sueldo; **there was an ~ moment when ...** hubo un momento violento *or* embarazoso cuando ...; **to put sb in an ~ position** poner a algn en una situación embarazosa *or* delicada, poner a algn en un compromiso
[3] (= *clumsy*) [*person, gesture, movement*] torpe; [*phrasing*] poco elegante, torpe; **to sleep in an ~ position** dormir en mala posición

awkwardly ['ɔːkwədlɪ] ADV [1] (= *uncomfortably*) [*say, shake hands*] con embarazo; **there was an ~ long silence** hubo un silencio largo y embarazoso; **Sonia patted her shoulder ~** Sonia, violenta *or* incómoda, le dio unas palmaditas en el hombro
[2] (= *clumsily*) [*move, walk, dance*] torpemente, con torpeza; [*translate*] con poca fluidez; **he expresses himself ~** se expresa mal, le cuesta expresarse; **he fell ~** cayó en mala postura; **the keyhole is ~ placed under the handle** el ojo de la cerradura está colocado bajo el picaporte, lo cual resulta incómodo

awkwardness ['ɔːkwədnɪs] N [1] (= *difficult nature*) [*of problem*] lo delicado; [*of situation*] lo delicado, lo violento; [*of person*] falta *f* de colaboración; [*of shape, design*] lo incómodo, lo poco práctico
[2] (= *embarrassment, discomfort*) embarazo *m*
[3] (= *clumsiness*) torpeza *f*

awl [ɔːl] N lezna *f*

awning ['ɔːnɪŋ] N toldo *m*

awoke [ə'wəʊk] PT *of* **awake**

awoken [ə'wəʊkən] PP *of* **awake**

AWOL ['eɪwɒl] ABBR (*Mil*) (= **absent without leave**) ausente sin permiso

awry [ə'raɪ] ADV **to be ~** estar de través, estar al sesgo, estar mal puesto; **to go ~** salir mal, fracasar; **with his hat on ~** con el sombrero torcido *or* ladeado

axe, ax (*US*) [æks] (A) N (= *tool*) hacha *f*; ✦*IDIOMS* **when the ~ fell** cuando se descargó el golpe; **to have an ~ to grind** tener un interés creado; **I have no ~ to grind** no tengo ningún interés personal; **to get** *or* **be given the ~** [*employee*] ser despedido; [*project*] ser cancelado
(B) VT [+ *budget*] recortar; [+ *project, service*] cancelar; [+ *jobs*] reducir; [+ *staff*] despedir

axes ['æksiːz] NPL *of* **axis**

axial ['æksɪəl] ADJ axial

axiom ['æksɪəm] N axioma *m*

axiomatic [,æksɪəʊ'mætɪk] ADJ axiomático

axis ['æksɪs] N (*pl* **axes** ['æksiːz]) [1] (*Geom etc*) eje *m*
[2] (*Anat*) axis *m inv*
[3] **the Axis** (*Hist*) el Eje

axle ['æksl] (A) N eje *m*, árbol *m*, flecha *f* (*Mex*)
(B) CPD ► **axle shaft** N palier *m*

ay ADV, N = **aye**[1]

ayatollah [aɪə'tɒlə] N ayatolá *m*, ayatollah *m*

aye[1] [aɪ] (A) ADV (*esp Scot, N. England*) sí; **~, ~ sir!** sí, mi capitán
(B) N sí *m*; **to vote ~** votar sí; **the ~s have it** se ha aprobado la moción; **there were 50 ~s and 3 noes** votaron 50 a favor y 3 en contra

aye[2]† [eɪ] ADV **for ever and ~** (*Scot*) por siempre jamás

AYH N ABBR (*US*) = **American Youth Hostels**

Aymara [,aɪmə'rɑː] (A) ADJ aimara, aimará
(B) N [1] (= *person*) aimara *mf*, aimará *mf*
[2] (*Ling*) aimara *m*, aimará *m*

AZ ABBR (*US*) = **Arizona**

azalea [ə'zeɪlɪə] N (*Bot*) azalea *f*

Azerbaijan [,æzəbaɪ'dʒɑːn] N Azerbaiyán *m*

Azerbaijani [,æzəbaɪ'dʒɑːnɪ] (A) ADJ azerbaiyano
(B) N azerbaiyano/a *m/f*

Azeri [ə'zɛərɪ] (A) ADJ azerí
(B) N [1] (= *person*) azerí *mf*
[2] (*Ling*) azerí *m*

Azores [ə'zɔːz] NPL Azores *fpl*

AZT N ABBR (= **azidothymidine**) AZT *m* (*medicina antisida*)

Aztec ['æztek] (A) ADJ azteca
(B) N azteca *mf*

azure ['eɪʒə'] (A) ADJ celeste, azul celeste *inv*
(B) N [1] (= *colour*) celeste *m*, azul *m* celeste
[2] (*Heraldry*) azur *m*

B b

B, b [biː] Ⓐ N 1 (= *letter*) B *f*, b *f*; **B for Bertie** B de Burgos; **number 7b** (*in house numbers*) número 7b
2 (*Mus*) **B** si *m*; **B major/minor** si mayor/menor; **B sharp/flat** si sostenido/bemol
3 (*Scol*) notable *m*
Ⓑ CPD ► **B road** N (*Brit*) ≈ carretera *f* comarcal *or* secundaria

b. ABBR (= **born**) n

BA 1 N ABBR (*Univ*) (= **Bachelor of Arts**) Lic. en Fil. y Let.; → DEGREE
2 N ABBR = **British Academy**
3 N ABBR = **British Association (for the Advancement of Science)**
4 ABBR (*Geog*) (= **Buenos Aires**) Bs.As.

BAA N ABBR = **British Airports Authority**

baa [bɑː] Ⓐ N balido *m*
Ⓑ EXCL ¡be!
Ⓒ VI balar

baa-lamb* [ˈbɑːlæm] N corderito *m*, borreguito *m*

babble [ˈbæbl] Ⓐ N [*of baby*] balbuceo *m*; [*of stream*] murmullo *m*; (*) (= *small talk*) cháchara *f*; **a ~ of voices arose** se oyó un murmullo de voces
Ⓑ VI 1 [*person*] (= *talk to excess*) parlotear*; (= *gossip*) chismorrear*, cotillear*
2 [*baby*] balbucear; [*stream*] murmurar
Ⓒ VT decir balbuceando

►**babble away, babble on** VI + ADV hablar sin parar

babbling [ˈbæblɪŋ] Ⓐ ADJ [*person*] hablador; [*baby*] balbuceante; [*stream*] que murmura, músico
Ⓑ N = **babble A**

babe [beɪb] Ⓐ N 1 (*liter*, †) criatura *f*
2 (*esp US**) chica *f*; (*in direct address*) nena* *f*
Ⓑ CPD ► **babe in arms** N niño/a *m/f* de pecho

babel [ˈbeɪbəl] N babel *m or f*; **Tower of Babel** Torre *f* de Babel

baboon [bəˈbuːn] N babuino *m*

Babs [bæbz] N (*familiar form*) *of* **Barbara**

baby [ˈbeɪbɪ] Ⓐ N 1 (= *infant*) bebé *mf*, bebe/a *m/f* (*Arg*), guagua *f* (*Andes*); (= *small child*) nene/a *m/f*, niño/a *m/f*; **she's having a ~ in May** va a tener un niño en mayo; **she's having the ~ in hospital** va a dar a luz en el hospital; **the ~ of the family** el benjamín/la benjamina; **don't be such a ~!** ¡no seas niño/niña!; ✦*IDIOMS* **I was left holding the ~*** me tocó cargar con el muerto; **to throw out the ~ with the bathwater** actuar con exceso de celo, pasarse*
2 (*US**) (= *girlfriend*) chica* *f*; (*in direct address*) nena* *f*, cariño *m*; (= *boyfriend*) chico* *m*; (*in direct address*) cariño
3 (*) (*fig*) 3·1 (= *special responsibility*) **the new system was his ~** el nuevo sistema fue obra suya; **that's not my ~** eso no es cosa mía
3·2 (*esp US*) (= *thing*) **that ~ cost me a fortune** ese chisme me costó una fortuna*
Ⓑ VT mimar, consentir
Ⓒ ADJ 1 (= *for a baby*) de niño; **~ clothes** ropita *f* de niño
2 (= *young*) **~ hedgehog** cría *f* de erizo; **~ rabbit** conejito *m*
3 (= *small*) pequeño; **~ car** coche *m* pequeño; **~ sweetcorn** mazorca *f* pequeña
Ⓓ CPD ► **baby batterer** N *persona que maltrata a los niños* ► **baby battering** N maltrato *m* de los niños ► **baby bed** N (*US*) cuna *f* ► **baby bonds** NPL (*US*) bonos *mpl* depreciados ► **baby boom** N boom *m* de natalidad ► **baby boomer** N niño/a *m/f* nacido/a en época de un boom de natalidad (*esp de los años 60*) ► **Baby bouncer**® N columpio *m* para bebés ► **baby boy** N nene *m* ► **baby break** N interrupción *f* de las actividades profesionales por maternidad ► **baby buggy** N cochecito *m* (de bebé) ► **baby carriage** N (*US*) cochecito *m* (de bebé) ► **baby face** N cara *f* de niño ► **baby food(s)** N(PL) comida *f* para bebés, potitos *mpl* (*Sp**) ► **baby girl** N nena *f* ► **baby grand** N (*Mus*) piano *m* de media cola ► **baby minder** N niñera *f* ► **baby seat** N (*Aut*) sillita *f or* asiento *m* de seguridad para bebés ► **baby shower** N (*US*) *fiesta con entrega de regalos a la madre y al recién nacido* ► **baby snatcher** N mujer *f* que roba un bebé ► **baby talk** N habla *f* infantil ► **baby tender** N (*US*) canguro *mf* ► **baby tooth*** N diente *m* de leche ► **baby walker** N andador *m*, tacatá *m* (*Sp**) ► **baby wipe** N toallita *f* húmeda

baby-doll pyjamas [ˌbeɪbɪdɒlpɪˈdʒɑːməz] NPL picardía *f* (*camisón corto con pantalones a juego*)

baby-faced [ˈbeɪbɪˌfeɪst] ADJ [*person*] con cara aniñada

Babygro® [ˈbeɪbɪˌgrəʊ] N (*pl* **Babygros**) pijama *m* de una pieza

babyhood [ˈbeɪbɪhʊd] N primera infancia *f*

babyish [ˈbeɪbɪɪʃ] ADJ infantil

Babylon [ˈbæbɪlən] N, **Babylonia** [ˌbæbɪˈləʊnɪə] N Babilonia *f*

Babylonian [ˌbæbɪˈləʊnɪən] Ⓐ ADJ babilónico; [*person*] babilonio
Ⓑ N babilonio/a *m/f*

baby-sit [ˈbeɪbɪsɪt] Ⓐ VI cuidar niños, hacer de canguro (*Sp*)
Ⓑ VT cuidar, hacer de canguro a (*Sp*)

baby-sitter [ˈbeɪbɪˌsɪtəʳ] N babysitter *mf*, canguro *mf* (*Sp*)

baby-sitting [ˈbeɪbɪˌsɪtɪŋ] N **I can't pay for ~** no puedo pagar un/una babysitter *or* un/una canguro; **I hate ~** no me gusta nada hacer de babysitter *or* canguro

baccalaureate [ˌbækəˈlɔːrɪɪt] N bachillerato *m*

baccarat [ˈbækərɑː] N bacará *m*, bacarrá *m*

bacchanalia [ˌbækəˈneɪlɪə] NPL bacanales *fpl*; (*fig*) bacanal *f*

bacchanalian [ˌbækəˈneɪlɪən] ADJ bacanal, báquico

Bacchic [ˈbækɪk] ADJ báquico

Bacchus [ˈbækəs] N Baco

baccy* [ˈbækɪ] N tabaco *m*

bachelor [ˈbætʃələʳ] Ⓐ N 1 (= *unmarried man*) soltero *m*; **confirmed ~** solterón *m*
2 (*Univ*) **Bachelor of Arts/Science** (= *degree*) licenciatura *f* en Filosofía y Letras/Ciencias; (= *person*) licenciado/a *m/f* en Filosofía y Letras/Ciencias; **~'s degree** licenciatura *f*; → DEGREE
Ⓑ CPD ► **bachelor flat** N piso *m or* (*LAm*) departamento *m* de soltero ► **bachelor girl** N (*US*) soltera *f* ► **bachelor party** N fiesta *f* para solteros

bachelorhood [ˈbætʃələhʊd] N soltería *f*

bacillary [bəˈsɪlərɪ] ADJ bacilar

bacillus [bəˈsɪləs] N (*pl* **bacilli** [bəˈsɪlaɪ]) bacilo *m*

▼**back** [bæk]

A NOUN	E ADJECTIVE
B ADVERB	F COMPOUNDS
C TRANSITIVE VERB	G PHRASAL VERBS
D INTRANSITIVE VERB	

When **back** *is an element in a phrasal verb, eg* ***come back, go back, put back****, look up the verb.*

Ⓐ NOUN
1 = ***part of body*** 1·1 [*of person*] espalda *f*; [*of animal*] lomo *m*; **I've got a bad ~** tengo la espalda mal, tengo un problema de espalda; **to shoot sb in the ~** disparar a algn por la espalda; **he was lying on his ~** estaba tumbado boca arriba; **to carry sth/sb on one's ~** llevar algo/a algn a la espalda; **to have one's ~ to sth/sb** estar de espaldas a algo/algn; **with his ~ to the light** de espaldas a la luz; **sitting ~ to ~** sentados espalda con espalda
1·2 ✦*IDIOMS* **behind sb's ~** a espaldas de algn; **they laughed at her behind her ~** se rieron de ella a sus espaldas; **she has been seeing David behind my ~** ha estado viendo a David a mis espaldas; **to break the ~ of sth*** (= *do the difficult part*) hacer la peor parte de algo; (= *do the main part*) hacer lo más gordo de algo*, hacer la mayor parte de algo; **to get off sb's ~*** dejar a algn en paz; **to get sb's ~ up*** poner negro a algn*, mosquear a algn*‡; **to live off the ~ of sb** vivir a costa de algn; **to be on sb's ~*** estar encima de algn; **my boss is always on my ~** mi jefe siempre está encima mío; **on the ~ of sth** a conse-

➤ LANGUAGE IN USE: back C2 11.2

cuencia de algo; **shares rose on the ~ of two major new deals** las acciones subieron a consecuencia de dos nuevos e importantes tratos; **to put one's ~ into sth** poner mucho esfuerzo *or* empeño en algo; **to put one's ~ into doing sth*** esforzarse a tope por hacer algo*, emplearse a fondo en hacer algo; **to put sb's ~ up*** poner negro a algn*, mosquear a algn‡; **to see the ~ of sb**: **I was glad to see the ~ of him** me alegró deshacerme de él; **the moment** *or* **as soon as your ~ is turned ...** en cuanto te descuidas ...; **to have one's ~ to the wall** estar entre la espada y la pared; *see also* **flat A1**, **stab A1**

2 (= ***reverse side***) [*of cheque, envelope*] dorso *m*, revés *m*; [*of hand*] dorso *m*; [*of head*] parte *f* de atrás, parte *f* posterior (*more frm*); [*of dress*] espalda *f*; [*of medal*] reverso *m*; **write your name on the ~** escriba su nombre en el reverso; **the ~ of the neck** la nuca; ✦***IDIOM*** **to know sth like the ~ of one's hand**: **I know Naples like the ~ of my hand** conozco Nápoles como la palma de la mano

3 (= ***rear***) [*of room, hall*] fondo *m*; [*of chair*] respaldo *m*; [*of car*] parte *f* trasera, parte *f* de atrás; [*of book*] (= *back cover*) tapa *f* posterior; (= *spine*) lomo *m*; **there was damage to the ~ of the car** la parte trasera *or* de atrás del coche resultó dañada; **at the ~ (of)** [+ *building*] en la parte de atrás (de); [+ *cupboard, hall, stage*] en el fondo (de); **there's a car park at the ~** hay un aparcamiento en la parte de atrás; **be quiet at the ~!** ¡los de atrás guarden silencio!; **they sat at the ~ of the bus** se sentaron en la parte de atrás del autobús, se sentaron al fondo del autobús; **he's at the ~ of all this trouble** él está detrás de todo este lío*; **ambition is at the ~ of it** la ambición es lo que ha causado todo esto*; **this idea had been at the ~ of his mind for several days** esta idea le había estado varios días rondándole la cabeza; **the ship broke its ~** el barco se partió por la mitad; **~ to front** al revés; **you've got your sweater on ~ to front** te has puesto el jersey al revés; **in ~ of the house** (*US*) detrás de la casa; **in the ~ of the car** en la parte trasera del coche; **I'll sit in the ~** yo me sentaré detrás; **the toilet's out the ~** el baño está fuera en la parte de atrás; **they keep the car round the ~** dejan el coche detrás de la casa; *see also* **beyond B**, **mind A1**

4 (***Sport***) (= *defender*) defensa *mf*; **the team is weak at the ~** la defensa del equipo es débil; **left ~** defensa *mf* izquierdo/a; **right ~** defensa *mf* derecho/a

Ⓑ ADVERB

1 (***in space***) atrás; **stand ~!** ¡atrás!; **keep (well) ~!** (= *out of danger*) ¡quédate ahí atrás!; **keep ~!** (= *don't come near me*) ¡no te acerques!; **meanwhile, ~ in London/~ at the airport** mientras, en Londres/en el aeropuerto; **he little suspected how worried they were ~ at home** qué poco sospechaba lo preocupados que estaban en casa; **~ and forth** de acá para allá; **to go ~ and forth** [*person*] ir de acá para allá; **there were phone calls ~ and forth** se hicieron un montón de llamadas el uno al otro; **~ from the road** apartado de la carretera

2 (***in time***) **some months ~** hace unos meses; **~ in the 12th century** allá en el siglo XII; **it all started ~ in 1980** todo empezó ya en 1980, todo empezó allá en 1980 (*liter*); **I saw her ~ in August** la vi el agosto pasado

3 (= ***returned***) **to be ~** volver; **when/what time will you be ~?** ¿cuándo/a qué hora vuelves?, ¿cuándo/a qué hora estarás de vuelta?; **he's not ~ yet** aún no ha vuelto, aún no está de vuelta; **the electricity is ~** ha vuelto la electricidad; **black is ~ (in fashion)** vuelve (a estar de moda) el negro, se vuelve a llevar el negro; **he went to Paris and ~** fue a París y volvió; **30 kilometres there and ~** 30 kilómetros ida y vuelta; **you can go there and ~ in a day** puedes ir y volver en un día; **she's now ~ at work** ya ha vuelto al trabajo; **the kids will be ~ at school tomorrow** los niños vuelven al colegio mañana; **I'll be ~ by 6** estaré de vuelta para las 6; **I'd like it ~** quiero que me lo devuelvan; **full satisfaction or your money ~** si no está totalmente satisfecho, le devolvemos el dinero; **everything is ~ to normal** todo ha vuelto a la normalidad; **I want it ~** quiero que me lo devuelvan; *see also* **hit back**

Ⓒ TRANSITIVE VERB

1 (= ***reverse***) [+ *vehicle*] dar marcha atrás a; **she ~ed the car into the garage** entró el coche en el garaje dando marcha atrás; **he ~ed the car into a wall** dio marcha atrás y chocó con un muro

2 (= ***support***) 2·1 (*also* **~ up**) [+ *plan, person*] apoyar; **they found a witness to ~ his claim** encontraron un testigo que apoyó lo que decía

2·2 (= *finance*) [+ *person, enterprise*] financiar

2·3 (*Mus*) [+ *singer*] acompañar

3 (= ***bet on***) [+ *horse*] apostar por; **I'm ~ing Manchester to win** yo apuesto por que va a ganar el Manchester; **to ~ the wrong horse** (*lit*) apostar por el caballo perdedor; **Russia ~ed the wrong horse in him** (*fig*) Rusia se ha equivocado al apoyar a él; **to ~ a winner** (*lit*) apostar por el ganador; **he is confident that he's ~ing a winner** (*fig*) (*person*) está seguro de que está dando su apoyo a un ganador; (*idea, project*) está seguro de que va a funcionar bien

4 (= ***attach backing to***) [+ *rug, quilt*] forrar

Ⓓ INTRANSITIVE VERB

1 (***person***) 1·1 (*in car*) dar marcha atrás; **she ~ed into me** dio marcha atrás y chocó conmigo

1·2 (= *step backwards*) echarse hacia atrás, retroceder; **he ~ed into a table** se echó hacia atrás y se dio con una mesa, retrocedió y se dio con una mesa

2 (= ***change direction***) [*wind*] cambiar de dirección (*en sentido contrario a las agujas del reloj*)

Ⓔ ADJECTIVE

1 (= ***rear***) [*leg, pocket, wheel*] de atrás, trasero; **the ~ row** la última fila

2 (= ***previous, overdue***) [*rent, tax, issue*] atrasado

Ⓕ COMPOUNDS ► **back alley** N callejuela *f* (*que recorre la parte de atrás de una hilera de casas*) ► **back boiler** N caldera *f* pequeña (*detrás de una chimenea*) ► **back burner** N quemador *m* de detrás; ✦***IDIOM*** **to put sth on the ~ burner** posponer algo, dejar algo para más tarde ► **back catalogue** N (*Mus*) catálogo *m* de grabaciones discográficas ► **back copy** N (*Press*) número *m* atrasado ► **the back country** N (*US*) zona *f* rural (*con muy baja densidad de población*); *see also* **backcountry** ► **back cover** N contraportada *f* ► **back door** N puerta *f* trasera; ✦***IDIOM*** **to do sth by** *or* **through the ~ door** hacer algo de forma encubierta ► **back formation** N (*Ling*) derivación *f* regresiva ► **back garden** N (*Brit*) jardín *m* trasero ► **back lot** N (*Cine*) exteriores *mpl* (del estudio); [*of house, hotel, company premises*] solar *m* trasero ► **back marker** N (*Brit Sport*) competidor(a) *m/f* rezagado/a ► **back matter** N [*of book*] apéndices *mpl* ► **back number** N [*of magazine, newspaper*] número *m* atrasado ► **back page** N contraportada *f* ► **back pain** N dolor *m* de espalda, dolor *m* lumbar ► **back passage** N (*Brit euph*) recto *m* ► **back pay** N atrasos *mpl* ► **back rest** N respaldo *m* ► **back road** N carretera *f* comarcal, carretera *f* secundaria ► **back room** N cuarto *m* interior; (*fig*) *lugar donde se hacen investigaciones secretas* ► **back seat** N asiento *m* trasero, asiento *m* de atrás; ✦***IDIOM*** **to take a ~ seat** mantenerse en un segundo plano ► **back somersault** N salto *m* mortal hacia atrás ► **back stop** N (*Sport*) *red que se coloca alrededor de una cancha para impedir que se escapen las pelotas* ► **back talk*** N (*US*) = **backchat** ► **back tooth** N muela *f* ► **back view** N **the ~ view of the hotel is very impressive** el hotel visto desde atrás es impresionante, la parte de atrás del hotel es impresionante ► **back vowel** N (*Ling*) vocal *f* posterior

Ⓖ PHRASAL VERBS

►**back away** VI + ADV 1 (*lit*) retroceder (**from** ante)

2 (*fig*) (*from promise, pledge, statement*) echarse atrás, dar marcha atrás (**from** en); **the government have been ~ing away from making such a commitment** el gobierno ha estado tratando de evitar comprometerse a tal cosa

►**back down** VI + ADV echarse atrás, dar marcha atrás; **to ~ down on sth** echarse atrás en algo, dar marcha atrás en algo

►**back off** VI + ADV (= *stop exerting pressure*) echarse atrás, dar marcha atrás (**from** en); (= *withdraw*) retirarse; **~ off!** ¡déjame en paz!, ¡déjame estar!; **she asked him to ~ off and give her some space** le pidió que no le estuviera encima y la dejara respirar; **the government has ~ed off from its decision** el gobierno se ha echado atrás *or* el gobierno ha dado marcha atrás en su decisión

►**back on to** VI + PREP **the house ~s on to the golf course** por atrás la casa da al campo de golf

►**back out** Ⓐ VI + ADV 1 (*lit*) [*vehicle, driver*] salir marcha atrás (**of** de); [*person*] salir hacia atrás (**of** de)

2 (*fig*) [*person*] (*of team*) retirarse (**of** de); (*of deal, duty*) echarse atrás (**of** en); **they are threatening to ~ out of the deal** amenazan con echarse atrás en el trato

Ⓑ VT + ADV [+ *vehicle*] sacar marcha atrás

►**back up** Ⓐ VT + ADV 1 (= *support*) [+ *person*] apoyar, respaldar

2 (= *confirm*) [+ *claim, theory*] respaldar

3 (= *reverse*) [+ *car*] dar marcha atrás a, hacer retroceder

4 (*Comput*) [+ *file*] hacer una copia de seguridad *or* de reserva de

5 (= *delay*) **the traffic was ~ed up for two miles** había una caravana (de tráfico) de dos millas, había retenciones (de tráfico) de dos millas

Ⓑ VI + ADV 1 (*in car*) (= *reverse*) dar marcha atrás

2 (= *queue*) **traffic is ~ing up for miles behind the accident** hay una caravana (de tráfico) de varias millas desde el lugar del accidente, hay retenciones (de tráfico) de varias millas desde el lugar del accidente

backache [ˈbækeɪk] N dolor *m* de espalda

backbench [ˈbækˈbentʃ] ADJ [*committee, revolt*] de los diputados sin cargo oficial; [*MP*] sin cargo oficial

backbencher [ˌbækˈbentʃəʳ] N (*Brit Parl*) *diputado sin cargo oficial en el gobierno o la oposición*

BACKBENCHER

Se conoce como **backbencher** *al parlamentario británico que no se sienta en los escaños (***benches***) de las primeras filas de la Cámara de los Comunes (***House of Commons***) junto al líder de su partido, por no pertenecer al Gobierno o a su equivalente en la oposición. Al no ser titulares de ningún cargo, les resulta más fácil hablar o votar en contra de la política oficial del partido. Se los conoce también colectivamente como los* **backbenches***.*

⇨ *Ver tb* FRONT BENCH

backbenches [ˌbæk'bentʃəz] NPL (*Brit Parl*) *escaños de los diputados sin cargo oficial en el gobierno o la oposición*; **the Tory ~** los diputados conservadores sin cargo oficial

backbite ['bækbaɪt] Ⓐ VI murmurar
Ⓑ VT [+ *absent person*] hablar mal de

backbiting ['bækbaɪtɪŋ] N murmuración *f*

backboard ['bækbɔːd] N (*US Sport*) tablero *m*

backbone ['bækbəʊn] N 1 (*Anat*) columna *f* vertebral, espina *f* dorsal; **a patriot to the ~** un patriota hasta la médula
2 (*fig*) (= *courage*) agallas *fpl*; (= *strength*) resistencia *f*; **the ~ of the organisation** el pilar de la organización

back-breaking ['bækbreɪkɪŋ] ADJ deslomador, matador

backchat ['bæktʃæt] N réplicas *fpl* (insolentes)

backcloth ['bækklɒθ] N (*Brit Theat, also fig*) telón *m* de fondo

backcomb ['bækkəʊm] VT (*Brit*) [+ *hair*] cardar

back-country ['bækˌkʌntrɪ] ADJ (= *rural*) rural; **~ jeep expeditions** expediciones *fpl* en jeep al campo

backdate ['bæk'deɪt] VT [+ *cheque*] poner fecha anterior a, antedatar; [+ *pay rise*] dar efecto retroactivo a; **a pay rise ~d to April** un aumento salarial con efecto retroactivo desde abril

backdrop ['bækdrɒp] N = **backcloth**

-backed [bækt] ADJ (*ending in compounds*) 1 **low-backed chair** silla *f* de respaldo bajo
2 **rubber-backed carpet** alfombra *f* con refuerzo de caucho

backer ['bækəʳ] N 1 (*Comm*) (= *guarantor*) fiador(a) *m/f*; (= *financier*) promotor(a) *m/f*, patrocinador(a) *m/f*
2 (*Pol*) (= *supporter*) partidario/a *m/f*
3 (= *one who bets*) apostante *mf*

backfire ['bæk'faɪəʳ] Ⓐ N (*Aut*) petardeo *m*
Ⓑ VI (*Aut*) petardear; **their plan ~d** (*fig*) les salió el tiro por la culata*

backgammon ['bækˌgæmən] N backgammon *m*

background ['bækgraʊnd] Ⓐ N 1 [*of picture etc*] fondo *m*; (*fig*) ambiente *m*; **on a red ~** sobre un fondo rojo; **in the ~** al *or* en el fondo; (*fig*) en segundo plano, en la sombra; **to stay in the ~** mantenerse en segundo plano, no buscar publicidad
2 [*of person*] formación *f*, educación *f*; **she comes from a wealthy ~** proviene de una familia acaudalada; **what is his ~?** ¿cuáles son sus antecedentes?
3 [*of situation, event*] antecedentes *mpl*; **the ~ to the crisis** los antecedentes de la crisis; **to fill in the ~ for sb** poner a algn en antecedentes
Ⓑ CPD ► **background music** N música *f* de fondo ► **background noise** N ruido *m* de fondo ► **background reading** N lecturas *fpl* de fondo, lecturas *fpl* preparatorias ► **background studies** NPL estudios *mpl* del ambiente histórico (*en que vivió un autor etc*) ► **background task** N (*Comput*) tarea *f* secundaria

backhand ['bækhænd] Ⓐ ADJ [*blow*] de revés; **~ drive/shot/stroke** (*Tennis*) revés *m*; **~ volley** (*Tennis*) volea *f* de revés
Ⓑ N (*Tennis*) revés *m*

backhanded ['bæk'hændɪd] ADJ 1 [*blow*] de revés
2 (*fig*) [*compliment*] ambiguo, equívoco

backhander* ['bæk'hændəʳ] N (*Brit*) 1 (= *blow*) revés *m*
2 (= *bribe*) soborno *m*, mordida *f* (*CAm, Mex*), coima *f* (*Andes, S. Cone*)

backing ['bækɪŋ] Ⓐ N 1 (= *support*) apoyo *m*; (*Comm*) respaldo *m* (financiero)
2 (*Mus*) acompañamiento *m*
3 (= *protective layer*) refuerzo *m*
Ⓑ CPD ► **backing group** N (*Mus*) grupo *m* de acompañamiento ► **backing singer** N (*Mus*) corista *mf* ► **backing store** N (*Comput*) memoria *f* auxiliar ► **backing vocals** NPL (*Mus*) coros *mpl*

backlash ['bæklæʃ] N (*fig*) reacción *f* en contra; (*Pol*) reacción *f* violenta; **the male ~** la violenta reacción masculina, el contraataque de los hombres

backless ['bæklɪs] ADJ [*dress*] sin espalda, muy escotado por detrás

back-line player ['bæklaɪnˌpleɪəʳ] N (*US*) defensa *mf*

backlist ['bæklɪst] N fondo *m* editorial

backlog ['bæklɒg] N **because of the ~ (of work/orders)** por el trabajo acumulado *or* atrasado/el volumen de pedidos pendientes; **a ~ of cases** un montón de casos atrasados

backpack ['bækpæk] Ⓐ N mochila *f*
Ⓑ VI hacer excursionismo de mochila

backpacker ['bækˌpækəʳ] N mochilero/a *m/f*

backpacking ['bækˌpækɪŋ] N **to go ~** hacer excursionismo de mochila

back-pedal ['bæk'pedl] VI (*on bicycle*) pedalear hacia atrás; (*fig*) echarse atrás, dar marcha atrás

back-pedalling ['bækˌpedəlɪŋ] N **~ is his speciality** (*fig*) echarse atrás *or* dar marcha atrás es su especialidad

backplate ['bækpleɪt] N (*US*) sesos *mpl* de cerdo

back-room boy ['bækrʊm,bɔɪ] N *persona que colabora en un proyecto de investigación sin obtener reconocimiento público*

backscratching* ['bækˌskrætʃɪŋ] N (*fig*) compadreo *m*

back-seat driver [ˌbæksiːt'draɪvəʳ] N *pasajero que siempre está dando consejos al conductor*

backshift ['bækʃɪft] N (*Brit Ind*) turno *m* de tarde

backside* ['bæk'saɪd] N trasero* *m*

backslapping ['bækˌslæpɪŋ] N espaldarazos *mpl*; **mutual ~** bombo *m* mutuo

backslash ['bækslæʃ] N (*Typ*) barra *f* inversa

backslide ['bæk'slaɪd] (*pt, pp* **backslid**) VI reincidir, recaer

backslider ['bæk'slaɪdəʳ] N reincidente *mf*

backsliding ['bæk'slaɪdɪŋ] N reincidencia *f*, recaída *f*

backspace ['bækspeɪs] (*Typ*) Ⓐ VI retroceder
Ⓑ N retroceso *m*, tecla *f* de retroceso

backspin ['bækspɪn] N (*Tennis, Cricket*) efecto *m* cortado; (*Billiards, Snooker*) efecto *m* bajo, efecto *m* de retroceso; **to give a ball ~** ◊ **put ~ on a ball** (*Tennis, Cricket*) cortar una pelota; (*Billiards, Snooker*) picar una bola

backstage ['bæk'steɪdʒ] Ⓐ N (= *off-stage*) bastidores *mpl*, espacio *m* entre bastidores; (= *dressing-rooms*) camarines *mpl*
Ⓑ ADJ entre bastidores
Ⓒ ADV entre bastidores; **to go ~** ir a los camarines

backstairs ['bæk'stɛəz] Ⓐ NPL escalera *f* de servicio
Ⓑ CPD [*staff*] de servicio; [*work*] doméstico; (*fig*) [*gossip, plot*] clandestino, subrepticio

backstitch ['bækstɪtʃ] Ⓐ N pespunte *m*
Ⓑ VT pespuntar

backstreet ['baekstriːt] Ⓐ N **the ~s** (*lit*) las callejuelas; (*quiet*) las calles tranquilas *or* apartadas del centro; (*poor*) las calles de los barrios bajos
Ⓑ CPD [*hotel, shop*] de barrio ► **backstreet abortion** N aborto *m* clandestino ► **backstreet abortionist** N abortista *mf* clandestino/a

backstroke ['bækstrəʊk] N espalda *f*; **the 100 metres ~** los 100 metros espalda

back-to-back ['bæktə'bæk] Ⓐ ADJ **~ credit** créditos *mpl* contiguos; **~ houses** (*Brit*) casas *fpl* adosadas (*por la parte trasera*)
Ⓑ ADV **to sit ~** sentarse *or* estar sentados espalda con espalda; **they showed two episodes ~** echaron dos capítulos seguidos

backtrack ['bæktræk] VI 1 (*on route, journey*) desandar el camino, dar marcha atrás
2 (*fig*) (*in account, explanation*) ir más atrás, retroceder; (= *renege*) (*on promise, decision*) echarse atrás, dar marcha atrás (**on** en)

backup ['bækʌp] Ⓐ N 1 (= *support*) apoyo *m*
2 (*US*) [*of traffic*] embotellamiento *m*
3 (*Comput*) (*also* **~ file**) copia *f* de seguridad
Ⓑ CPD [*train, plane*] suplementario; (*Comput*) [*disk, file*] de seguridad ► **backup copy** N (*Comput*) copia *f* de seguridad ► **backup lights** NPL (*US*) luces *fpl* de marcha atrás ► **backup operation** N operación *f* de apoyo ► **backup services** NPL servicios *mpl* auxiliares

backward ['bækwəd] Ⓐ ADJ 1 [*motion, glance*] hacia atrás; **~ and forward movement** movimiento *m* de vaivén
2 [*pupil, country*] atrasado
3 (= *reluctant*) tímido; **he wasn't ~ in claiming the money** no se mostró tímido a la hora de reclamar el dinero; **he's not ~ in coming forward** (*iro*) no peca de tímido
Ⓑ ADV 1 [*look*] atrás, hacia atrás; [*move*] hacia atrás; **to walk/fall ~** andar/caer hacia atrás; **to go ~ and forward** ir y venir, ir de acá para allá; **this is a step ~** (*fig*) esto supone un paso atrás; *see also* **bend over**
2 (= *in reverse*) al revés; **to read sth ~** leer algo para atrás; ✦**IDIOM to know sth ~*** saberse algo al dedillo *or* de pe a pa

backwardation [ˌbækwə'deɪʃən] N (*St Ex*) retraso *m* en la entrega de acciones; (= *fee*) prima *f* pagada por retraso en la entrega de acciones

backward-compatible ['bækwədkəm'pætɪbl] ADJ (*Comput, Tech*) *compatible con el modelo, sistema etc anterior*

backward-looking ['bækwədˌlʊkɪŋ] ADJ retrógrado

backwardness ['bækwədnɪs] N [*of country*] atraso *m*; [*of person*] (*socially*) timidez *f*; (*mentally*) retraso *m*

backwards ['bækwədz] ADV (*esp Brit*) = **backward B**

backwards-compatible ['bækwədzkəm'pætɪbl] ADJ = **backward-compatible**

backwash ['bækwɒʃ] N 1 (*Naut*) agua *f* de rechazo
2 (*fig*) reacción *f*, repercusiones *fpl*

backwater ['bækwɔːtəʳ] N 1 [*of river*] remanso *m*
2 (*fig*) lugar *m* atrasado

backwoods ['bækwʊdz] Ⓐ NPL región *f* apartada, ≈ Las Batuecas
Ⓑ CPD ► **backwoods community** N comunidad *f* rústica

backwoodsman ['bækwʊdzmən] N (*pl* **backwoodsmen**) 1 (*lit*) campesino/a *m/f*; (*pej*) patán *m*
2 (*fig*) (= *reactionary*) reaccionario/a *m/f*; (*Brit Pol*) *par que asiste con muy poca frecuencia a las sesiones de la Cámara de los Lores*

backyard ['bæk'jɑːd] N (*Brit*) patio *m* trasero; (*US*) jardín *m* trasero; **in one's own ~** en su misma puerta, delante de sus narices*; **"not in my ~"** (*slogan*) "no lo quiero en mi patio" (*residuos tóxicos etc*)

bacon ['beɪkən] N beicon *m* (*Sp*), tocino *m* (*LAm*), panceta *f* (*Arg*); **~ and eggs** huevos *mpl* con tocino; ✦***IDIOMS*** **to bring home the ~*** (= *earn one's living*) ganarse las habichuelas*; **to save sb's ~*** salvar el pellejo a algn*

bacteria [bæk'tɪərɪə] NPL bacterias *fpl*

bacterial [bæk'tɪərɪəl] ADJ bacteriano, bacterial

bacteriological [bæk,tɪərɪə'lɒdʒɪkəl] ADJ bacteriológico

bacteriologist [bæk,tɪərɪ'ɒlədʒɪst] N bacteriólogo/a *m/f*

bacteriology [bæk,tɪərɪ'ɒlədʒɪ] N bacteriología *f*

bacteriosis [,bæktɪərɪ'əʊsɪs] N bacteriosis *f*

bacterium [bæk'tɪərɪəm] N (*pl* **bacteria**) bacteria *f*

bad [bæd] Ⓐ ADJ (*compar* **worse**; *superl* **worst**)
1 (= *disagreeable*) malo; **I've had a ~ day at work** he tenido un mal día en el trabajo; **to taste ~** saber mal, no saber bueno; **she looked as if she had a ~ smell under her nose** parecía como si algo le oliera mal; **to go from ~ to worse** ir de mal en peor; *see also* **mood² A**, **temper A1**, **time A7**
2 (= *poor, inferior*) malo; **her English is ~** habla inglés mal; **his handwriting is ~** tiene mala letra; **business is ~** el negocio va mal; **to be ~ at sth** ser malo para algo; **I was ~ at sports** era muy malo para los deportes, los deportes se me daban mal; **he was a ~ driver** era un mal conductor; **that's not a ~ idea** ésa no es una mala idea; **I'm a ~ liar** no sé mentir; **~ light stopped play** se suspendió el partido debido a la falta de luz; **it would make me look ~ in the press** daría una mala imagen de mí en la prensa; **he wasn't ~-looking** no estaba mal; **~ management** mala administración; **this wine's not ~ at all** este vino no está nada mal; **too ~**: **it's too ~ you couldn't get tickets** es una pena *or* una lástima que no hayas podido conseguir entradas; **"that was my drink!"** — **"too ~!"** —¡ésa era mi bebida! —¡qué le vamos a hacer!; **if you don't like it, (that's) too ~!** si no te gusta, ¡peor para ti!; **the firm has had a ~ year** la empresa ha tenido un mal año
3 (= *serious, severe*) [*accident, mistake*] grave; [*headache*] fuerte; **she's got a ~ cold** está muy resfriada, tiene un resfriado fuerte; **the traffic was ~ today** hoy había mucho tráfico
4 (= *unfavourable*) malo; **the plane was diverted due to ~ weather** el avión fue desviado debido al mal tiempo; **you've come at a ~ time** vienes en un mal momento; **things are looking ~ for the government** las cosas se están poniendo feas para el gobierno; **it'll look ~ if we don't go** quedará mal que no vayamos; *see also* **book A1**
5 (= *harmful*) malo; **he was a ~ influence** era una mala influencia; **to be ~ for sth/sb**: **smoking is ~ for you** *or* **for your health** fumar es malo *or* perjudicial para la salud, fumar perjudica la salud; **soap is ~ for the skin** el jabón no es bueno para la piel
6 (= *wicked*) [*person, behaviour*] malo; **you ~ boy!** ¡qué niño más malo eres!; **they're a ~ lot*** no son buena gente; **he said a ~ word** ha dicho una palabrota; **it's too ~ of you!** ¿no te da vergüenza?; **it's really too ~ of him!** ¡realmente no tiene vergüenza!; *see also* **language A5**
7 **to feel ~ about sth** (= *sorry*): **I feel ~ about hurting his feelings** me sabe mal haber herido sus sentimientos; (= *guilty*) **are you trying to make me feel ~?** ¿estás intentando hacer que me sienta culpable?; **don't feel ~ (about it), it's not your fault** no te preocupes, no es culpa tuya
8 (= *ailing*) **I feel ~** me siento mal; **he has a ~ back** está mal de la espalda; **to be in a ~ way**: **the economy is in a ~ way** la economía va mal; **he looked in a ~ way** tenía mal aspecto
9 (= *rotten*) [*food*] podrido; [*milk*] cortado; [*tooth*] picado; **to go ~** pasarse, estropearse; *see also* **blood**
10 (*Fin*) [*cheque*] sin fondos; **a ~ debt** una deuda incobrable *or* de pago dudoso
Ⓑ N lo malo; **parents can have a powerful influence for good or ~** los padres pueden tener mucha influencia para lo bueno y para lo malo; **there's good and ~ in this news** esta noticia tiene su lado bueno y su lado malo; **there is both good and ~ in every human being** hay una parte buena y una parte mala en cada ser humano; **to take the ~ with the good** aceptar tanto lo bueno como lo malo
Ⓒ ADV (*) **he's hurt ~** está malherido; **she took it ~** se lo tomó a mal; **if you want it that ~ you can pay for it yourself** si tanto lo quieres, cómpratelo tú; **to need sth real ~** necesitar algo desesperadamente; **the way she looks at him, you can tell she's got it ~** por la forma en que lo mira, se nota que está colada por él*; **to be in ~ with sb**: **he's in ~ with the law** tiene problemas con la ley

baddie*, **baddy*** ['bædɪ] N (*Cine, often hum*) malo *m*

baddish ['bædɪʃ] ADJ bastante malo, más bien malo

bade [bæd] PT of **bid**

badge [bædʒ] N 1 (= *emblem*) insignia *f*; (*sewn on coat*) distintivo *m*; (*Brit*) (*metal*) chapa *f*; **~ of office** distintivo *m* or insignia *f* de su función
2 (*fig*) señal *f*

badger ['bædʒəʳ] Ⓐ N tejón *m*
Ⓑ VT acosar, atormentar (**for** para obtener); **to ~ sb into doing sth** acosar a algn hasta que haga algo; **stop ~ing me!** ¡deja ya de fastidiarme!

badinage ['bædɪnɑːʒ] N chanzas *fpl*, bromas *fpl*

badlands ['bædlændz] NPL (*US*) tierras *fpl* malas, *región yerma, esp en los estados de Nebraska y Dakota del Sur*

> **BAD**
>
> **"Malo" shortened to "mal"**
>
> • **Malo** must be shortened to **mal** before a masculine singular noun:
>
> He was in a bad mood
> ***Estaba de mal humor***
>
> **Position of "malo"**
>
> • **Mal**/**Mala** *etc* precedes the noun in general comments. Here, there is no comparison, implied or explicit, with something better:
>
> I'm afraid I have some bad news for you
> ***Me temo que traigo malas noticias para usted***
> I've had a bad day today
> ***Hoy he tenido un mal día***
>
> • **Malo**/**Mala** *etc* follows the noun when there is an implicit or explicit comparison with something good:
>
> ...his only bad day in the race...
> ***...su único día malo en la carrera...***
>
> **Ser/Estar malo**
>
> • Use **malo** with **ser** to describe inherent qualities and characteristics:
>
> Smoking is bad for your health
> ***Fumar es malo para la salud***
> This is a very bad film
> ***Esta película es malísima***
>
> • Use **malo** with **estar** to describe unpleasant food or else to mean "unwell":
>
> The food was really bad
> ***La comida estaba malísima***
> He's been unwell lately
> ***Ha estado malo últimamente***
>
> **Estar mal**
>
> • Use **estar** with the adverb **mal** to give a general comment on a situation that seems bad or wrong:
>
> Cheating in your exams is really bad
> ***Está muy mal que copies en los exámenes***
> In the space of an hour I've signed fifty books. Not bad
> ***En una hora he firmado cincuenta libros. No está mal***
> I managed to come second, which wasn't bad
> ***He conseguido acabar segundo, lo que no estuvo mal***
>
> *For further uses and examples, see main entry.*

badly ['bædlɪ] ADV 1 (= *poorly*) mal; **he did ~ in his exams** los exámenes le fueron mal; **things are going ~** las cosas van mal; **we came off ~ in the deal** salimos mal parados del negocio; **~ made/written/designed** mal hecho/escrito/diseñado; **to sleep ~** dormir mal; *see also* **pay B1**
2 (= *seriously, severely*) gravemente; **he was ~ injured** estaba gravemente herido; **they were ~ beaten** (*in contest*) sufrieron una seria derrota; (*physically*) les dieron una paliza tremenda; **to be ~ mistaken** estar muy equivocado; **it was a gamble that went ~ wrong** se corría un riesgo y salió muy mal; **the building was ~ damaged in the explosion** en la explosión el edificio resultó muy dañado
3 (= *unfavourably*) **to speak/think ~ of sb** hablar/pensar mal de algn; **to reflect ~ on sb** dejar mal a algn; **"how did he take it?"** — **"badly"** —¿qué tal se lo tomó? —fatal
4 (= *wrongly*) **to treat sb ~** tratar mal a algn; **to behave ~** portarse mal
5 (= *very much*) [*want, need*] **~-needed medical supplies** medicamentos *mpl* que se necesitan desesperadamente; **it ~ needs painting** hace mucha falta pintarlo; **he ~**

needs help necesita ayuda a toda costa; **they ~ wanted a child** estaban desesperados por tener un niño; **we ~ need another assistant** nos hace muchísima falta otro ayudante
[6] **to be ~ off** (= *poor*) andar *or* estar mal de dinero; **we are ~ off for coal** andamos mal de carbón; **you're not that ~ off, you only have to work 20 hours a week** no estás tan mal, sólo tienes que trabajar 20 horas por semana

badman ['bædmæn] (*pl* **badmen**) N (*esp US*) gángster *m*

bad-mannered ['bæd'mænəd] ADJ maleducado, grosero

badminton ['bædmɪntən] N bádminton *m*

badmouth* ['bæd,maʊθ] VT hablar pestes de*

badness ['bædnɪs] N [1] (= *wickedness*) maldad *f*
[2] (= *poor quality*) mala calidad *f*

bad-tempered ['bæd'tempəd] ADJ [*person*] (*temporarily*) de mal humor; (*permanently*) de mal genio, de mal carácter; [*argument*] fuerte; [*tone etc*] áspero, malhumorado

Bae N ABBR (= **British Aerospace**) ≈ CASA *f*

Baffin ['bæfɪn] N **~ Bay** Bahía *f* de Baffin; **~ Island** Tierra *f* de Baffin

baffle ['bæfl] Ⓐ VT [1] (= *perplex*) desconcertar; **at times you ~ me** a veces me desconciertas; **the problem ~s me** el problema me tiene perplejo, no le veo solución alguna al problema; **the police are ~d** la policía está desconcertada *or* perpleja
[2] (*frm*) (= *frustrate*) [+ *progress*] impedir; [+ *plan, attempt*] frustrar; **it ~s description** es imposible describirlo
Ⓑ N (*also* **~ board, ~ plate**) deflector *m*; (*Rad*) pantalla *f* acústica

bafflement ['bæflmənt] N desconcierto *m*, perplejidad *f*

baffling ['bæflɪŋ] ADJ [*action*] incomprensible, desconcertante; [*crime*] misterioso; [*problem*] dificilísimo

BAFTA ['bæftə] N ABBR = **British Academy of Film and Television Arts**

bag [bæg] Ⓐ N [1] [*of paper, plastic*] bolsa *f*; (= *large sack*) costal *m*; (= *handbag*) bolso *m*, cartera *f* (*LAm*); (= *suitcase*) maleta *f*, valija *f* (*LAm*), veliz *m* (*Mex*); (*carried over shoulder*) zurrón *m*, mochila *f*; **a ~ of sweets/chips** una bolsa de caramelos/patatas fritas; **to pack one's ~s** hacer las maletas; **they threw him out ~ and baggage** lo pusieron de patitas en la calle; **he was like a ~ of bones** estaba como un esqueleto; **it's a mixed ~*** hay un poco de todo; **the whole ~ of tricks*** todo el rollo*; **✦IDIOMS to be left holding the ~** (*US**) cargar con el muerto*; **to be in the ~*: it's in the ~** es cosa segura, está en el bote (*Sp**); **we had the game nearly in the ~** el partido estaba casi ganado, teníamos el partido casi en el bote (*Sp**); **not to be sb's ~** (*US**) **it's not his ~** no es lo suyo
[2] (*Hunting*) cacería *f*, piezas *fpl* cobradas; **a good day's ~** una buena cacería
[3] **bags** (= *baggage*) equipaje *m*; (*Brit**) (= *trousers*) pantalones *mpl*; **~s under the eyes** ojeras *fpl*
[4] **~s of** (*Brit**) (= *lots*) un montón de; **we've ~s of time** tenemos tiempo de sobra
[5] (= *woman*) **old ~*** bruja* *f*
Ⓑ VT [1] (*also* **~ up**) [+ *goods, groceries*] meter en una bolsa/en bolsas
[2] (*Hunting*) cazar; (= *shoot down*) derribar
[3] (*) (= *get possession of*) pillar*, hacerse con; (*Brit*) (= *claim in advance*) reservarse; **I ~s that** eso pa' mí
Ⓒ VI (*also* **~ out**) [*garment*] hacer bolsas
Ⓓ CPD ► **bag lady*** N indigente *f* vagabunda ► **bag snatcher** N ladrón/a *m/f* de bolsos

bagatelle [,bægə'tel] N [1] (= *trifle*) bagatela *f*
[2] (= *board game*) bagatelle *f*
[3] (*Billiards*) billar *m* romano
[4] (*Mus*) bagatela *f*

bagel ['beɪgl] N (*US*) *especie de bollo en forma de aro*

bagful ['bægfʊl] N bolsa *f* (lleno)

baggage ['bægɪdʒ] Ⓐ N [1] (= *luggage*) equipaje *m*; (*Mil*) bagaje *m*
[2] (*fig*) (*Psych*) bagaje *m*
[3] (†*) (= *woman*) bruja* *f*
Ⓑ CPD ► **baggage allowance** N límite *m* de equipaje ► **baggage car** N (*US*) furgón *m* de equipajes ► **baggage check** N talón *m* de equipaje ► **baggage (check)room** N (*US*) consigna *f* ► **baggage handler** N despachador(a) *m/f* de equipaje ► **baggage locker** N consigna *f* automática ► **baggage (re)claim** N recogida *f* de equipaje ► **baggage train** N tren *m* de equipajes

baggy ['bægɪ] ADJ (*compar* **baggier**; *superl* **baggiest**) ancho; [*trousers*] (*at the knees*) con bolsas en las rodillas; (= *wide*) abombachado

Baghdad [,bæg'dæd] N Bagdad *m*

bagpiper ['bægpaɪpər] N gaitero *m*

bagpipes ['bægpaɪps] NPL gaita *fsing*

bag-snatching ['bæg,snætʃɪŋ] N tirón *m* (de bolsos)

baguette [bæ'get] N baguette *f*, barrita *f* de pan

bah [bɑː] EXCL ¡bah!

Bahamas [bə'hɑːməz] NPL **the ~** las Bahamas

Bahrain [bɑː'reɪn] N Bahrein *m*

Bahraini [bɑː'reɪnɪ] Ⓐ ADJ bahreiní
Ⓑ N bahreiní *mf*

bail¹ [beɪl] (*Jur*) Ⓐ N (*Jur*) fianza *f*; **on ~** bajo fianza; **he's out on ~** está libre bajo fianza; **to be released on ~** ser puesto en libertad bajo fianza; **to jump ~*** fugarse estando bajo fianza; **to go** *or* **stand ~ for sb** pagar la fianza de algn
Ⓑ VT (*Jur*) (*also* **~ out**) pagar la fianza de
Ⓒ CPD ► **bail bandit*** N (*Brit*) *persona que comete un delito estando en libertad bajo fianza* ► **bail bond** N (*US*) fianza *f*

►**bail out** VT + ADV **to ~ sb out** (*Jur*) pagar la fianza de algn; (*fig*) echar un cable a algn

bail² [beɪl] N (*Cricket*) palito *m* corto

bail³ [beɪl] VT (*Naut*) achicar

►**bail out** Ⓐ VI + ADV (*Aer*) lanzarse *or* tirarse en paracaídas
Ⓑ VT + ADV (*US*) = **bale out**

bailiff ['beɪlɪf] N [1] (*Jur*) alguacil *m*
[2] (*on estate*) administrador(a) *m/f*

bailiwick ['beɪlɪwɪk] N [1] (*Jur*) alguacilazgo *m*
[2] (*esp US*) (*fig*) (= *speciality*) ámbito *m* de actuación

bain-marie [bẽmə'ri] N (*pl* **bains-marie**) baño *m* de María

bairn [beən] N (*Scot, N Eng*) niño/a *m/f*

bait [beɪt] Ⓐ N (*Fishing, Hunting*) cebo *m*; (*fig*) anzuelo *m*, cebo *m*; **✦IDIOMS to rise to the ~: he didn't rise to the ~** no picó; **to swallow the ~** (*lit*) picar; (*fig*) morder el anzuelo, caer en la trampa
Ⓑ VT [1] [+ *hook, trap*] cebar
[2] (= *torment*) [+ *person, animal*] atormentar

baize [beɪz] N paño *m*; **green ~** tapete *m* verde

bake [beɪk] Ⓐ VT [1] [+ *food*] cocer (al horno); [+ *bricks etc*] cocer; **to ~ one's own bread** hacer el pan en casa; **~d beans** judías *fpl* en salsa de tomate; **~d potato** patata *f* or (*LAm*) papa *f* al horno
[2] (= *harden*) endurecer
Ⓑ VI [1] [*person*] **I love to ~** me gusta hacer pasteles/pan *etc* al horno
[2] [*bread, cake*] hacerse en el horno
[3] (*fig*) (= *swelter*) **we were baking in the heat** nos asábamos de calor
Ⓒ N (*Brit Culin*) *pastel salado cocinado al horno esp con verduras o pescado*

bakehouse ['beɪkhaʊs] N (*pl* **bakehouses** ['beɪkhaʊzɪz]) tahona *f*, panadería *f*

Bakelite® ['beɪkəlaɪt] N baquelita *f*

baker ['beɪkər] N panadero/a *m/f*; [*of cakes*] pastelero/a *m/f*; **~'s (shop)** (*for bread*) panadería *f*; (*for cakes*) pastelería *f*; **~'s dozen** docena *f* de fraile

bakery ['beɪkərɪ] N (*for bread*) panadería *f*; (*for cakes*) pastelería *f*

bakeware ['beɪkweər] N fuentes *fpl* de horno

Bakewell tart [,beɪkwəl'tɑːt] N *tarta hecha a base de almendras, mermelada y azúcar en polvo*

baking ['beɪkɪŋ] Ⓐ N [1] (= *activity*) **she does the ~ on Monday** los lunes hace el pan/los pasteles *etc*
[2] (= *batch*) hornada *f*
Ⓑ ADJ (*) (= *hot*) **it's ~ (hot) in here** esto es un horno; **a ~ hot day** un día de calor asfixiante
Ⓒ CPD ► **baking chocolate** N (*US*) chocolate *m* fondant ► **baking dish** N fuente *f* para el horno ► **baking pan** N = **baking tin** ► **baking powder** N Royal® *m*, levadura *f* en polvo (*Sp*) ► **baking sheet** N = **baking tray** ► **baking soda** N bicarbonato *m* de soda ► **baking tin** N molde *m* (para el horno) ► **baking tray** N bandeja *f* de horno

baksheesh ['bækʃiːʃ] N propina *f*

bal. ABBR = **balance**

balaclava [,bælə'klɑːvə] N (*also* **~ helmet**) pasamontañas *m inv*

balalaika [,bælə'laɪkə] N balalaica *f*

balance ['bæləns] Ⓐ N [1] (= *equilibrium*) equilibrio *m*; **a nice ~ of humour and pathos** un sutil equilibrio entre el humor y el patetismo; **the ~ of his mind was disturbed** (*frm*) su mente estaba desequilibrada; **in ~** en equilibrio, equilibrado; **to keep one's ~** mantener el equilibrio; **to lose one's ~** perder el equilibrio; **the ~ of nature** el equilibrio de la naturaleza; **off ~: he's a bit off ~** (*mentally*) está un poco desequilibrado; **to catch sb off ~** pillar a algn desprevenido; **to throw sb off ~** (*lit*) hacer que algn pierda el equilibrio; (*fig*) desconcertar a algn; **on ~** (*fig*) teniendo *or* tomando en cuenta todos los factores, una vez considerados todos los factores (*frm*); **to be out of ~** [*mechanism, wheel*] estar desequilibrado; **~ of power** (*Mil, Comm*) equilibrio *m* de poder; (*Phys*) equilibrio *m* de fuerzas; **to redress the ~** restablecer el equilibrio; **he has no sense of ~** no tiene sentido del equilibrio; **to strike a ~** conseguir *or* establecer un equilibrio
[2] (= *scales*) balanza *f*; **to be** *or* **hang in the ~** (*fig*) estar pendiente de un hilo
[3] (*Comm*) saldo *m*; **what's my ~?** ¿qué saldo tengo?; **to pay off the ~ of an account** liquidar el saldo de una cuenta; **bank ~** saldo *m*; **~ carried forward** balance *m* a cuenta nueva; **closing ~** saldo *m* de cierre; **credit/debit ~** saldo *m* acreedor/deudor; **~ of payments/trade** balanza *f* de pagos/comercio
[4] (= *remainder*) [*of items*] resto *m*; [*of money*] saldo *m*; **~ due** saldo *m* deudor; **~ outstanding** saldo *m* pendiente
[5] (*Audio*) balance *m*
Ⓑ VT [1] (= *place in equilibrium*) [+ *weight*] equilibrar; [+ *object*] poner/mantener en equilibrio; (*Aut*) [+ *wheel*] nivelar; **he ~d the glass on top of the books** puso el vaso en equilibrio sobre los libros; **the seal ~d the ball on its nose** la foca mantenía la pelota

en equilibrio sobre su hocico; **he ~d himself on one foot** se mantuvo en equilibrio sobre un pie; **cats use their tails to ~ themselves** los gatos utilizan el rabo para equilibrarse

2 (= *compare*) comparar, sopesar; (= *make up for*) compensar; **this increase must be ~d against the rate of inflation** hay que sopesar este aumento y la tasa de inflación

3 (*Comm*) **to ~ an account** hacer el balance de una cuenta; **to ~ the books** hacer balance, hacer cuadrar las cuentas; **to ~ the budget** nivelar el presupuesto; **to ~ the cash** hacer caja

Ⓒ VI 1 (= *keep equilibrium*) mantener el equilibrio, mantenerse en equilibrio

2 (*Comm*) [*accounts*] cuadrar

Ⓓ CPD ► **balance sheet** N balance *m*, hoja *f* de balance ► **balance weight** N contrapeso *m*

►**balance out** Ⓐ VT + ADV (*fig*) compensar; **the two things ~ each other out** las dos cosas se compensan mutuamente

Ⓑ VI + ADV **the profits and losses ~ out** las ganancias y las pérdidas se compensan

►**balance up** VT + ADV finiquitar, saldar

balanced ['bælənst] ADJ [*meal, view, person, budget*] equilibrado; **evenly ~** ◊ **well ~** bien equilibrado; **a ~ diet** una dieta equilibrada

balancing ['bælənsɪŋ] Ⓐ N 1 (= *equilibrium*) **~ on a high wire is not easy** mantener el equilibrio en la cuerda floja no es fácil

2 (*Comm, Fin*) **~ of accounts** balance *m* de cuentas; **~ of the books** balance *m* de los libros

Ⓑ CPD ► **balancing act** N ✦*IDIOM* **to do a ~ act (between)** hacer malabarismos (con)

balcony ['bælkənɪ] N balcón *m*; (*interior, Theat*) galería *f*; (*large*) terraza *f*; **first/second ~** (*US Theat*) primer/segundo piso *m*

bald [bɔːld] Ⓐ ADJ (*compar* **balder**; *superl* **baldest**) 1 (= *hairless*) [*person, head*] calvo; (= *shaven*) pelado; **~ patch** (*on head*) calva *f*, claro *m*; (*on animal*) calva *f*; **he can't spend much on the barber's, with that ~ head of his** con lo calvo que está no puede gastar mucho en peluquería; **to go ~** quedarse calvo; ✦*IDIOM* **(as) ~ as an egg** *or* **a coot** más calvo que una bola de billar

2 (= *worn*) [*tyre*] desgastado, gastado; [*lawn*] pelado; **~ patches on the lawn/carpet** calvas *fpl* en el césped/la alfombra

3 (= *unadorned*) [*statement*] directo, sin rodeos; [*style*] escueto; **these are the ~ facts** estos son los hechos sin más

Ⓑ CPD ► **bald eagle** N águila *f* de cabeza blanca

balderdash ['bɔːldədæʃ] N tonterías *fpl*

bald-headed ['bɔːld'hedɪd] ADJ calvo; ✦*IDIOM* **to go ~ into*** lanzarse ciegamente a

balding ['bɔːldɪŋ] ADJ parcialmente calvo

baldly ['bɔːldlɪ] ADV (*fig*) [*state*] sin rodeos

baldness ['bɔːldnɪs] N 1 [*of person*] calvicie *f*

2 [*of tyre*] desgaste *m*

3 [*of statement*] lo directo; [*of style*] lo escueto

baldy* ['bɔːldɪ] N calvo *m*

bale¹ [beɪl] N [*of cloth*] bala *f*; [*of hay*] fardo *m*, bala *f*

bale² [beɪl] *see* **bale out**

►**bale out** VT + ADV (*Naut*) [+ *water*] achicar; [+ *ship*] achicar *or* sacar el agua de

Bâle [bɑːl] N Basilea *f*

Balearic [,bælɪ'ærɪk] ADJ **the ~ Islands** las Islas Baleares

Balearics [,bælɪ'ærɪks] NPL **the ~** las Baleares

baleful ['beɪlfʊl] ADJ [*influence, presence*] funesto, siniestro; [*look, stare*] torvo, hosco; **to give sb a ~ look** dirigir a algn una mirada torva *or* hosca, mirar a algn de forma torva *or* hosca

balefully ['beɪlfəlɪ] ADV [*stare, look, say*] siniestramente, con hostilidad

baler ['beɪlə^r] N (*Agr*) empacadora *f*, enfardadora *f*

balk [bɔːk] Ⓐ N 1 (*Agr*) caballón *m*

2 (*Billiards*) cabaña *f*

3 (= *building timber*) viga *f*

Ⓑ VT (= *thwart*) impedir; (= *miss*) perder, no aprovechar; **we were ~ed of the chance to see it** perdimos la oportunidad de verlo

Ⓒ VI **to ~ (at)** [*horse*] plantarse (ante); (*fig*) [*person*] **some students ~ at carrying out animal experiments** algunos estudiantes se muestran reacios *or* se resisten a llevar a cabo experimentos con animales

Balkan ['bɔːlkən] Ⓐ ADJ balcánico

Ⓑ N **the ~s** los Balcanes

balkanization ['bɔːlkənaɪ'zeɪʃən] N balcanización *f*

ball¹ [bɔːl] Ⓐ N 1 (*Tennis, Cricket, Golf etc*) pelota *f*; (*Ftbl*) balón *m*; (= *sphere*) bola *f*; **to play ~ (with sb)** (*lit*) jugar a la pelota (con algn); (*fig*) cooperar (con algn); **to roll (o.s.) up into a ~** hacerse un ovillo; **the ~ is with you** *or* **in your court** (*fig*) te corresponde a ti dar el siguiente paso; **that's the way the ~ bounces** (*US**) así es la vida, así son las cosas; **the whole ~ of wax** (*US**) (*fig*) toda la historia*; ✦*IDIOMS* **to be behind the eight ~** (*US*) estar en apuros; **to be on the ~** estar al tanto, ser muy despabilado; **you have to be on the ~ for this** para esto hay que estar al tanto; **to have a lot on the ~** (*US**) tener mucho talento; **to keep one's eye on the ~** no perder de vista lo principal; **to start/keep the ~ rolling** poner/mantener la cosa en marcha; **to be a ~ of fire**: **he's a real ~ of fire** es muy dinámico; **he's not exactly a ~ of fire** no es que sea muy dinámico que digamos; **to keep several ~s in the air** hacer varias cosas al mismo tiempo; **to pick up** *or* **take the ~ and run with it** tomar el testigo e intentarlo

2 (*Mil*) bala *f*; **~ and chain** (*lit*) grillete *m* con bola; (*fig*) atadura *f*

3 [*of wool*] ovillo *m*

4 (*Anat*) [*of foot*] pulpejo *m*; [*of thumb*] base *f*

5 (**) (= *testicle*) cojón** *m*, huevo** *m*

6 **balls** (*Brit***) (= *nonsense*) pavadas* *fpl*, huevadas *fpl* (*Andes, Chile***); (= *courage*) cojones** *mpl*, pelotas** *fpl*; ✦*IDIOM* **to break** *or* **bust sb's ~s** joder la existencia a algn**

Ⓑ VT 1 (*also* **~ up**) [+ *handkerchief etc*] hacer una bola con

2 (*esp US***) (= *have sex with*) echarse un polvo con**, tirarse**

Ⓒ VI 1 (*also* **~ up**) [*fist etc*] hacerse una bola

2 (*esp US***) (= *have sex*) echarse un polvo**, follar (*Sp***), chingar (*Mex***)

Ⓓ CPD ► **ball and socket joint** N junta *f* articulada ► **ball bearing** N cojinete *m* de bolas, balero *m* (*Mex*), rulemán *m* (*S. Cone*) ► **ball boy** N (*Tennis*) recogedor *m* de pelotas ► **ball control** N (*Ftbl*) dominio *m* del balón ► **ball game** N (*US*) partido *m* de béisbol; **this is a different ~ game*** (*fig*) esto es otro cantar*, esto es algo muy distinto; **it's a whole new ~ game*** (*fig*) las cosas han cambiado totalmente; → BASEBALL ► **ball girl** N (*Tennis*) recogedora *f* de pelotas ► **ball joint** N junta *f* articulada ► **ball lightning** N (*Met*) relámpago *m* en bola *or* en globo

►**ball up** Ⓐ VT + ADV 1 = **ball B**

2 (*US***) = **balls up**

Ⓑ VI + ADV = **ball C**

►**balls up**** VT + ADV estropear, joder**

ball² [bɔːl] N 1 (= *dance*) baile *m* de etiqueta

2 (*) (= *good time*) **we had a ~** lo pasamos en grande*

ballad ['bæləd] N balada *f*; (*Spanish*) romance *m*, corrido *m* (*Mex*)

ballade [bæ'lɑːd] N (*Mus*) balada *f*

ballast ['bæləst] Ⓐ N (*Naut*) (*fig*) lastre *m*; (*Rail*) balasto *m*; **in ~** en lastre

Ⓑ VT (*Naut*) lastrar; (*Rail*) balastar

ballcock ['bɔːlkɒk] N llave *f* de bola *or* de flotador

ballerina [,bælə'riːnə] N bailarina *f* (de ballet); **prima ~** primera bailarina *f*

ballet ['bæleɪ] Ⓐ N ballet *m*

Ⓑ CPD ► **ballet dancer** N bailarín/ina *m/f* (de ballet) ► **ballet school** N escuela *f* de ballet ► **ballet shoes** NPL zapatillas *fpl* de ballet ► **ballet skirt** N falda *f* de bailarina *or* de ballet

balletic [bæ'letɪk] ADJ [*grace, movements*] de bailarina, de ballet

ballgown ['bɔːlgaʊn] N traje *m* de fiesta, vestido *m* de gala

ballistic [bə'lɪstɪk] Ⓐ ADJ balístico; ✦*IDIOM* **to go ~*** subirse por las paredes*

Ⓑ CPD ► **ballistic missile** N misil *m* balístico

ballistics [bə'lɪstɪks] NSING balística *f*

balloon [bə'luːn] Ⓐ N globo *m*; (*in cartoons*) bocadillo *m*; **then the ~ went up*** luego se armó la gorda*; ✦*IDIOM* **to go down like a lead ~***: **that went down like a lead ~** eso cayó muy mal, eso cayo fatal*

Ⓑ VI 1 [*injury*] hincharse (como un tomate)

2 (*also* **to ~ out**) [*sail*] hincharse como un globo; [*skirt*] inflarse

ballooning [bə'luːnɪŋ] N **to go ~** montar en globo

balloonist [bə'luːnɪst] N ascensionista *mf*, aeronauta *mf*

ballot ['bælət] Ⓐ N (= *voting*) votación *f*; (= *paper*) papeleta *f* (de voto); **on the first ~** a la primera votación; **to take a ~ on sth** someter algo a votación; **there will be a ~ for the remaining places** se sortearán las plazas restantes; **to vote by secret ~** votar en secreto

Ⓑ VT **to ~ the members on a strike** someter la huelga a votación entre los miembros

Ⓒ VI 1 (= *vote*) votar

2 (= *draw lots*) **to ~ for** [+ *tickets*] rifar, sortear; **to ~ for a place** sortear un puesto

Ⓓ CPD ► **ballot box** N urna *f* ► **ballot box stuffing** N (*US*) fraude *m* electoral, pucherazo* *m* ► **ballot paper** N papeleta *f* (de voto)

balloting ['bælətɪŋ] N votación *f*

ballpark ['bɔːlpɑːk] Ⓐ N (*US*) estadio *m* de béisbol; ✦*IDIOM* **to be in the same ~**: **it's in the same ~** está en la misma categoría; → BASEBALL

Ⓑ CPD ► **ballpark estimate** N cálculo *m* aproximado ► **ballpark figure**, **ballpark number** N cifra *f* aproximada

ballplayer, **ball player** ['bɔːl,pleɪə^r] N (*US*) (*Baseball*) jugador(a) *m/f* de béisbol; (*Basketball*) baloncestista *mf*; (*Ftbl*) jugador(a) *m/f* de fútbol americano

ballpoint (pen) ['bɔːlpɔɪnt('pen)] N bolígrafo *m*, birome *m or f* (*S. Cone*)

ballroom ['bɔːlrʊm] Ⓐ N salón *m or* sala *f* de baile

Ⓑ CPD ► **ballroom dancing** N baile *m* de salón

balls-up** ['bɔːlzʌp], **ball-up**** ['bɔːlʌp] (*US*)

N cagada** *f*; **he made a ~ of the job** lo jodió todo**

ballsy* ['bɔ:lzɪ] ADJ de armas tomar*, con agallas*

bally* ['bælɪ] ADJ (*Brit*) puñetero*

ballyhoo* [,bælɪ'hu:] N (= *publicity*) bombo* *m*, propaganda *f* estrepitosa

balm [bɑ:m] N (*also fig*) bálsamo *m*

balmy ['bɑ:mɪ] ADJ (*compar* **balmier**; *superl* **balmiest**) [1] (*liter*) (= *soothing*) balsámico
[2] (= *mild*) [*breeze, air*] suave, cálido
[3] (*) = **barmy**

baloney* (*esp US*) [bə'ləʊnɪ] N tonterías *fpl*, chorradas *fpl* (*Sp**)

BALPA ['bælpə] N ABBR (= **British Airline Pilots' Association**) ≈ SEPLA *m*

balsa ['bɔ:lsə] N (*also* **~ wood**) (madera *f* de) balsa *f*

balsam ['bɔ:lsəm] N bálsamo *m*

balsamic [bɔ:l'sæmɪk] ADJ [*vinegar*] balsámico

balti ['bɔ:ltɪ] N (*Culin*) *especialidad de comida india con verduras o carne cocinadas en una cazuela de fondo cóncavo*

Baltic ['bɔ:ltɪk] Ⓐ ADJ báltico; **the ~ states** los estados bálticos; **one of the ~ ports** uno de los puertos del mar Báltico
Ⓑ N **the ~ (Sea)** el mar Báltico

balustrade [,bæləs'treɪd] N balaustrada *f*, barandilla *f*

bamboo [bæm'bu:] Ⓐ N (= *cane, plant*) bambú *m*
Ⓑ CPD ► **the Bamboo Curtain** N el Telón de Bambú ► **bamboo shoots** NPL brotes *mpl* de bambú

bamboozle* [bæm'bu:zl] VT enredar, engatusar; **she was ~d into buying it** la enredaron *or* engatusaron para que lo comprara

ban [bæn] Ⓐ N prohibición *f* (**on** de); **to be under a ~** estar prohibido; **to put a ~ on sth** prohibir algo; **to lift the ~ on sth** levantar la prohibición de algo
Ⓑ VT [+ *activity, book*] prohibir; [+ *person*] excluir (**from** de); **Ban the Bomb Campaign** Campaña *f* contra la Bomba Atómica; **he was ~ned from the club** le prohibieron la entrada en el club, lo excluyeron del club; **he was ~ned from driving** le retiraron el carnet de conducir; **the bullfighter was ~ned for three months** al torero le prohibieron torear durante tres meses

banal [bə'nɑ:l] ADJ banal

banality [bə'nælɪtɪ] N banalidad *f*

banana [bə'nɑ:nə] Ⓐ N (= *fruit*) plátano *m*, banana *f* (*LAm*); (= *tree*) platanero *m*, banano *m* (*LAm*)
Ⓑ CPD ► **banana boat** N barco *m* bananero ► **banana republic** N república *f* bananera ► **banana skin** N piel *f* de plátano; (*fig*) problema *m* no previsto ► **banana tree** N platanero *m*, banano *m* (*LAm*)

bananas* [bə'nɑ:nəz] ADJ chalado*; **to go ~** perder la chaveta* (**over** por)

band[1] [bænd] Ⓐ N [1] (= *strip of material*) faja *f*, tira *f*; (= *ribbon*) cinta *f*; (= *edging*) franja *f*; [*of cigar*] vitola *f*, faja *f*; [*of wheel*] fleje *m*; (= *ring*) anillo *m*, sortija *f* (*LAm*); (= *armband*) brazalete *m*; (= *hatband*) cintillo *m*; [*of harness*] correa *f*; (= *stripe*) raya *f*; [*of territory*] faja *f*; *see also* **rubber**[1] **B**
[2] (*Rad*) (= *waveband*) banda *f*
[3] [*of statistics, tax etc*] banda *f*
Ⓑ VT [+ *tax, property*] dividir en bandas
Ⓒ CPD ► **band saw** N sierra *f* de cinta

band[2] [bænd] N [1] (*Mus*) orquesta *f*, conjunto *m*; (*Mil*) (= *brass band*) banda *f*; (= *pop group*) grupo *m*; **then the ~ played** (*US**) (*fig*) y se armó la gorda*
[2] (= *group of people*) cuadrilla *f*, grupo *m*; (*pej*) (= *gang*) pandilla *f*

►**band together** VI + ADV juntarse, asociarse; (*pej*) apandillarse

bandage ['bændɪdʒ] Ⓐ N venda *f*
Ⓑ VT (*also* **to ~ up**) vendar; **with a ~d hand** con una mano vendada

Band-Aid® ['bændeɪd] N (*esp US*) tirita *f* (*Sp*), curita *f* (*LAm*)

bandan(n)a [bæn'dænə] N pañuelo *m*

B & B N ABBR (= **bed and breakfast**) *alojamiento y desayuno*; → BED AND BREAKFAST

bandbox ['bænd*b*ɒks] N sombrerera *f*

banding ['bændɪŋ] N (*Brit Scol*) calificaciones *fpl* por letras

bandit ['bændɪt] N bandido *m*; *see also* **one-armed**

banditry ['bændɪtrɪ] N bandolerismo *m*, bandidismo *m*

bandleader ['bænd*l*i:dəʳ] N líder *mf* de banda

bandmaster ['bænd*m*ɑ:stəʳ] N director *m* de banda

bandolier [,bændə'lɪəʳ] N bandolera *f*

bandsman ['bændzmən] N (*pl* **bandsmen**) músico *m* (de banda)

bandstand ['bænd*s*tænd] N quiosco *m* de música

bandwagon ['bænd,wægən] N ✦IDIOM **to jump** *or* **climb on the ~** subirse al carro *or* al tren

bandy[1] ['bændɪ] VT [+ *jokes, insults*] cambiar, intercambiar; **don't ~ words with me!** ¡no discuta conmigo!

►**bandy about** VT + ADV **the story was bandied about that ...** se rumoreaba que ...; **to ~ sb's name about** circular el nombre de algn

bandy[2] ['bændɪ], **bandy-legged** ['bændɪ-'legd] ADJ estevado

bane [beɪn] N (*liter*) (= *poison*) veneno *m*; (*fig*) plaga *f*, azote *m*; **it's the ~ of my life** me amarga la vida

baneful ['beɪnf*ʊ*l] ADJ (*liter*) (= *poisonous*) nocivo; (= *destructive*) funesto, fatal

banefully ['beɪnfəlɪ] ADV (*liter*) (= *poisonously*) nocivamente; (= *destructively*) funestamente, fatalmente

bang [bæŋ] Ⓐ N (= *noise*) [*of explosion*] estallido *m*; [*of door*] portazo *m*; [*of blow*] porrazo *m*, golpe *m*; **the door closed with a ~** la puerta se cerró de golpe; ✦IDIOMS **to go with a ~***: **it went with a ~** fue todo un éxito; **not with a ~ but a whimper** no con un estallido sino con un sollozo; **to get more ~ for the buck** *or* **more ~s for your bucks** (*esp US**) llevarse más por el mismo precio
Ⓑ ADV [1] **to go ~** hacer ¡pum!, estallar; **~ went £10*** adiós 10 libras
[2] (*) justo, exactamente; **~ in the middle** justo en (el) medio; **I ran ~ into a traffic jam** me encontré de repente en un embotellamiento; **it hit him ~ on the ear** le dio justo en la oreja, le dio en toda la oreja*; **~ on!** ¡acertado!; **the answer was ~ on** (*Brit*) la respuesta dio en el blanco; **~ on time** (*Brit*) a la hora justa; **it was ~ on target** (*Brit*) dio justo en el blanco; **~ up to date** totalmente al día; **to keep ~ up to date** mantenerse totalmente al día; **this production is ~ up to date** este montaje está de rabiosa actualidad
Ⓒ VT [1] (= *strike*) golpear; **to ~ the door** dar un portazo; **to ~ one's head (on sth)** dar con la cabeza (contra algo); **he ~ed himself against the wall** se dio contra la pared; **to ~ one's fist on the table** dar un puñetazo en la mesa
[2] (**) (= *have sex with*) echarse un polvo con**, tirarse**
Ⓓ VI (= *explode*) explotar, estallar; (= *slam*) [*door*] cerrarse de golpe; **downstairs a door ~ed** abajo se cerró de golpe una puerta; **to ~ at** *or* **on sth** dar golpes en algo
Ⓔ EXCL ¡pum!; (*of a blow*) ¡zas!

►**bang about, bang around** VI + ADV moverse ruidosamente

►**bang away** VI + ADV [*guns*] disparar estrepitosamente; [*workman*] martillear; **she was ~ing away on the piano** aporreaba el piano

►**bang down** VT + ADV [+ *receiver*] colgar de golpe; **he ~ed it down on the table** lo arrojó violentamente sobre la mesa

►**bang into** VI + PREP (= *collide with*) chocar con, darse contra

►**bang on*** VI + ADV (*Brit*) **to ~ on about sth** dar la tabarra con algo*

►**bang out** VT + ADV [+ *tune*] tocar ruidosamente

►**bang together** VT + ADV [+ *heads*] hacer chocar; **I'll ~ your heads together!** ¡voy a dar un coscorrón a los dos!; **the leaders should have their heads ~ed together** hay que obligar a los jefes a que lleguen a un acuerdo

►**bang up*** VT + ADV (*Brit*) [+ *prisoner*] encerrar (en su celda)

banger* ['bæŋəʳ] (*Brit*) N [1] (= *sausage*) salchicha *f*
[2] (= *firework*) petardo *m*
[3] (= *old car*) armatoste* *m*, cacharro* *m*

Bangkok [bæŋ'kɒk] N Bangkok *m*

Bangladesh [,bæŋglə'deʃ] N Bangladesh *m*

Bangladeshi [,bæŋglə'deʃɪ] Ⓐ ADJ bangladesí
Ⓑ N bangladesí *mf*

bangle ['bæŋgl] N brazalete *m*, pulsera *f*

bangs [bæŋz] NPL (*US*) (= *fringe*) flequillo *m*

bang-up* ['bæŋʌp] ADJ (*US*) tope, guay (*Sp**)

banish ['bænɪʃ] VT [+ *person*] expulsar, desterrar; (*fig*) [+ *thought, fear*] desterrar, apartar (**from** de); **to ~ a topic from one's conversation** desterrar un tema de la conversación

banishment ['bænɪʃmənt] N destierro *m*

banisters ['bænɪstəz] NPL barandilla *f*, pasamanos *m inv*

banjax* ['bændʒæks] VT dar una paliza a

banjo ['bændʒəʊ] N (*pl* **banjoes, banjos**) banjo *m*

bank[1] [bæŋk] Ⓐ N [1] [*of river etc*] orilla *f*; (= *small hill*) loma *f*; (= *embankment*) terraplén *m*; (= *sandbank*) banco *m*; (= *escarpment*) escarpa *f*; [*of clouds*] grupo *m*; [*of snow*] montículo *m*; [*of switches*] batería *f*, serie *f*; [*of phones*] equipo *m*, batería *f*; [*of oars*] hilera *f*
[2] (*Aer*) inclinación *f* lateral
Ⓑ VT [1] (*also* **~ up**) [+ *earth, sand*] amontonar, apilar; [+ *fire*] alimentar (*con mucha leña o carbón*)
[2] (*Aer*) ladear
Ⓒ VI [1] (*Aer*) ladearse
[2] **to ~ up** [*clouds etc*] acumularse

bank[2] [bæŋk] (*Comm, Fin*) Ⓐ N (*Fin*) banco *m*; (*in games*) banca *f*; (*also* **savings ~**) caja *f* de ahorros; **Bank of England** Banco *m* de Inglaterra; **Bank of International Settlements** (*US*) Banco *m* Internacional de Pagos; **Bank of Spain** Banco *m* de España; ✦IDIOM **to break the ~** hacer saltar *or* quebrar la banca
Ⓑ VT [+ *money*] depositar en un/el banco, ingresar
Ⓒ VI **we ~ with Smith** tenemos la cuenta en

el banco Smith
Ⓓ CPD ► **bank acceptance** N letra *f* de cambio ► **bank account** N cuenta *f* bancaria ► **bank balance** N saldo *m*; **this won't be good for my ~ balance** esto no será bueno para mi situación financiera ► **bank bill** N (*Brit*) letra *f* de cambio; (*US*) billete *m* de banco ► **bank book** N libreta *f* (de depósitos); (*in savings bank*) cartilla *f* ► **bank card** N tarjeta *f* bancaria ► **bank charges** NPL (*Brit*) comisión *f* ► **bank clerk** N (*Brit*) empleado/a *m/f* de banco ► **bank credit** N crédito *m* bancario ► **bank deposits** NPL depósitos *mpl* bancarios ► **bank draft** N letra *f* de cambio ► **bank giro** N giro *m* bancario ► **bank holiday** N (*Brit*) fiesta *f*, día *m* festivo, (día *m*) feriado *m* (*LAm*) ► **bank loan** N préstamo *m* bancario ► **bank manager** N director(a) *m/f* de banco ► **bank rate** N tipo *m* de interés bancario ► **bank robber** N ladrón *m* de banco ► **bank run** N (*US*) asedio *m* de un banco ► **bank statement** N estado *m* de cuenta ► **bank transfer** N transferencia *f* bancaria

►**bank on** VI + PREP contar con; **don't ~ on it** sería prudente no contar con eso, no puedes estar tan seguro de eso

> **BANK HOLIDAY**
>
> *El término* **bank holiday** *se aplica en el Reino Unido a todo día festivo oficial en el que cierran bancos y comercios, que siempre cae en lunes. Los más destacados coinciden con Navidad, Semana Santa, finales de mayo y finales de agosto. Al contrario que en los países de tradición católica, no se celebran las festividades dedicadas a los santos.*

bankable ['bæŋkəbl] ADJ [*idea*] válido, valedero; [*person*] taquillero

banker ['bæŋkə^r] Ⓐ N 1 (*Fin*) banquero/a *m/f*; **to be ~** (*in game*) tener la banca
2 (*Betting*) apuesta *f* fija
Ⓑ CPD ► **banker's card** N tarjeta *f* bancaria ► **banker's draft** N efecto *m* bancario ► **banker's order** N (*Brit*) orden *f* bancaria ► **banker's reference** N referencia *f* bancaria

banking[1] ['bæŋkɪŋ] N [*of earth*] terraplén *m*, rampas *fpl*

banking[2] ['bæŋkɪŋ] Ⓐ N (*Comm, Fin*) banca *f*
Ⓑ CPD bancario ► **banking account** N cuenta *f* bancaria ► **banking hours** NPL horas *fpl* bancarias ► **banking house** N casa *f* de banca

banknote ['bæŋknəʊt] N billete *m* de banco

bankroll ['bæŋkrəʊl] (*esp US*) Ⓐ N recursos *mpl* económicos
Ⓑ VT financiar

bankrupt ['bæŋkrʌpt] Ⓐ ADJ 1 (*Jur*) en quiebra; **to be ~** estar en quiebra; **to go ~** ir a la bancarrota, quebrar; **to be declared ~** declararse en quiebra
2 (*fig*) 2·1 (*) (= *penniless*) sin un duro (*Sp**), sin un peso (*LAm**)
2·2 (= *deficient*) **spiritually/morally ~** en franca decadencia espiritual/moral; **to be ~ of ideas** estar totalmente falto de ideas
Ⓑ N (*Jur*) quebrado/a *m/f*
Ⓒ VT 1 (*Jur*) llevar a la quiebra
2 (*) (*fig*) (= *impoverish*) arruinar; **to ~ o.s. buying pictures** arruinarse comprando cuadros
Ⓓ CPD ► **bankrupt's estate** N activo *m* or masa *f* de la quiebra

bankruptcy ['bæŋkrəptsɪ] Ⓐ N 1 (*Jur*) quiebra *f*
2 (*fig*) falta *f* (**of** de); **moral ~** decadencia *f* moral
Ⓑ CPD ► **bankruptcy court** N (*Brit*) tribunal *m* de quiebras ► **bankruptcy proceedings** NPL juicio *m* de insolvencia

banned substance [ˌbænd'sʌbstəns] N (*Sport*) sustancia *f* prohibida

banner ['bænə^r] Ⓐ N (= *flag*) bandera *f*; (= *placard*) pancarta *f*
Ⓑ CPD ► **banner ad*** N (*Internet*) banner *m* ► **banner headlines** NPL grandes titulares *mpl*

bannisters ['bænɪstəz] N = **banisters**

banns [bænz] NPL amonestaciones *fpl*; **to put up** *or* **call the ~** correr las amonestaciones

banquet ['bæŋkwɪt] Ⓐ N banquete *m*
Ⓑ VI banquetear
Ⓒ VT [+ *person*] dar un banquete en honor de

banqueting hall ['bæŋkwɪtɪŋˌhɔːl] N comedor *m* de gala, sala *f* de banquetes

banquette [bæŋ'ket] N banqueta *f* alargada

banshee ['bæn'ʃiː] N (*Irl*) *hada que anuncia una muerte en la familia*

bantam ['bæntəm] N gallina *f* bántam

bantamweight ['bæntəmweɪt] N (*Sport*) (= *boxer*) peso *m* gallo

banter ['bæntə^r] Ⓐ N bromas *fpl*, guasa *f*
Ⓑ VI bromear

bantering ['bæntərɪŋ] Ⓐ ADJ [*tone*] de chanza
Ⓑ N = **banter A**

Bantu [ˌbæn'tuː] Ⓐ ADJ bantú
Ⓑ N 1 (*pl* **Bantu** *or* **Bantus**) (= *person*) bantú *mf*; **the ~(s)** los bantú, los bantúes
2 (*Ling*) bantú *m*

bap [bæp] N (*Brit*) bollo *m* pequeño de pan

baptism ['bæptɪzəm] N (*in general*) bautismo *m*; (= *ceremony*) bautizo *m*; **~ of fire** bautismo *m* de fuego

baptismal [bæp'tɪzməl] ADJ bautismal

Baptist ['bæptɪst] Ⓐ N baptista *mf*, bautista *mf*; **St John the ~** San Juan Bautista
Ⓑ CPD ► **Baptist church** N Iglesia *f* Bautista

baptize [bæp'taɪz] VT bautizar; **he was ~d John** lo bautizaron con el nombre de Juan

bar[1] [bɑː^r] Ⓐ N 1 (= *piece*) [*of wood, metal*] barra *f*; [*of soap*] pastilla *f*; [*of chocolate*] tableta *f*
2 (= *lever*) palanca *f*; (*on electric fire*) resistencia *f*; [*of window, cage etc*] reja *f*; (*on door*) tranca *f*; **behind ~s** entre rejas; **to put sb behind ~s** encarcelar a algn; **to spend three years behind ~s** pasar tres años entre rejas
3 (= *hindrance*) obstáculo *m* (**to** para); **it is a ~ to progress** es un obstáculo para el progreso
4 (= *ban*) prohibición *f* (**on** de)
5 (= *pub*) bar *m*, cantina *f* (*esp LAm*); (= *counter*) barra *f*, mostrador *m*
6 (*Jur*) **the Bar** (= *persons*) el colegio de abogados; (= *profession*) la abogacía, la Barra (*Mex*); **the prisoner at the ~** el/la acusado/a; **to be called** *or* (*US*) **admitted to the Bar** recibirse de abogado, ingresar en la abogacía; *see also* **read B4**
7 (*Brit Mus*) (= *measure, rhythm*) compás *m*
Ⓑ VT 1 (= *obstruct*) [+ *way*] obstruir
2 (= *prevent*) [+ *progress*] impedir
3 (= *exclude*) excluir (**from** de); (= *ban*) prohibir; **to be ~red from a club** ser excluido de un club; **to ~ sb from doing sth** prohibir a algn hacer algo
4 (= *fasten*) [+ *door, window*] atrancar
Ⓒ CPD ► **bar billiards** N (*Brit*) billar *m* americano ► **bar chart** N cuadro *m* de barras ► **bar code** N código *m* de barras ► **bar girl*** N (*US*) camarera *f* de barra ► **bar graph** N (*esp US*) gráfico *m* de barras ► **bar stool** N taburete *m* (de bar)

bar[2] [bɑː^r] PREP salvo, con excepción de; **all ~ two** todos salvo *or* con excepción de dos; **~ none** sin excepción; **it was all over ~ the shouting** (*fig*) en realidad ya estaba concluido el asunto

barb [bɑːb] Ⓐ N 1 [*of arrow, hook*] lengüeta *f*; [*of feather*] barba *f*; (*Zool*) púa *f*
2 (*fig*) dardo *m*
Ⓑ CPD ► **barb wire** N = **barbed wire**

Barbadian [bɑː'beɪdɪən] Ⓐ ADJ de Barbados
Ⓑ N nativo/a *m/f* or habitante *mf* de Barbados

Barbados [bɑː'beɪdɒs] N Barbados *m*

barbarian [bɑː'bɛərɪən] Ⓐ ADJ bárbaro
Ⓑ N bárbaro/a *m/f*

barbaric [bɑː'bærɪk] ADJ bárbaro

barbarism ['bɑːbərɪzəm] N 1 (= *cruelty*) barbarie *f*
2 (*Gram*) barbarismo *m*

barbarity [bɑː'bærɪtɪ] N barbaridad *f*

barbarous ['bɑːbərəs] ADJ bárbaro

barbarously ['bɑːbərəslɪ] ADV bárbaramente

Barbary ['bɑːbərɪ] Ⓐ N Berbería *f*
Ⓑ CPD ► **Barbary ape** N macaco *m* ► **the Barbary Coast** N la costa berebere

barbecue ['bɑːbɪkjuː] Ⓐ N (= *grill*) barbacoa *f*; (= *party*) parrillada *f*, barbacoa *f*, asado *m* (*LAm*)
Ⓑ VT asar a la parrilla
Ⓒ CPD ► **barbecue sauce** N salsa *f* picante

barbed [bɑːbd] Ⓐ ADJ 1 [*arrow etc*] armado de lengüetas
2 (*fig*) [*criticism*] incisivo, mordaz
Ⓑ CPD ► **barbed wire** N alambre *m* de púas *or* de espino; **~-wire fence** cercado *m* de alambrada *or* de alambre de espino *or* (*LAm*) de alambrado

barbel ['bɑːbəl] N 1 (*Anat*) barbilla *f*, cococha *f*
2 (= *fish*) barbo *m*

barbell ['bɑːbel] N (*Sport*) haltera *f*, pesas *fpl*

barber ['bɑːbə^r] N peluquero *m*, barbero *m*; **at/to the ~'s (shop)** en/a la peluquería *or* barbería; **The Barber of Seville** El Barbero de Sevilla

barbershop ['bɑːbəʃɒp] (*US*) Ⓐ N barbería *f*
Ⓑ CPD ► **barbershop quartet** N *cuarteto vocal armónico de hombres que se especializa en canciones sentimentales de los años 20 y 30*

barbican ['bɑːbɪkən] N barbacana *f*

Barbie doll® ['bɑːbɪdɒl] N muñeca *f* Barbie®

barbitone ['bɑːbɪtəʊn] N barbitúrico *m*

barbiturate [bɑː'bɪtjʊrɪt] N barbitúrico *m*

barbs‡ [bɑːbz] NPL (*Drugs*) barbitúricos *mpl*

barcarol(l)e [ˌbɑːkə'rəʊl] N barcarola *f*

Barcelona [ˌbɑːsə'ləʊnə] N Barcelona *f*

bard [bɑːd] N (*liter*) bardo *m*, vate *m*; **the Bard** (= *Shakespeare*) el Vate; **the Bard of Avon** el Cisne del Avon

bare [bɛə^r] Ⓐ ADJ (*compar* **barer**; *superl* **barest**)
1 (= *uncovered*) [*body, skin, shoulders, person*] desnudo; [*head*] descubierto; [*feet*] descalzo; [*landscape*] pelado; [*tree*] sin hojas; [*ground*] árido, sin vegetación; [*floorboards*] sin alfombrar; (*Elec*) [*wire*] pelado, sin protección; **~ to the waist** desnudo hasta la cintura; **to sleep on ~ boards** dormir en una tabla; **in one's ~ feet** descalzo; **he put his ~ hand in the flame** puso la mano directamente en la llama; **he killed the lion with his ~ hands** mató al león sólo con las manos *or* sin armas; **to lay sth ~** [+ *flaw, mistake*] poner algo de manifiesto; [+ *intentions, plans*] poner algo al descubierto; **to lay ~ one's heart to sb** abrir el corazón a algn; **to lay ~ a secret** revelar un se-

creto; **~ of sth** desprovisto de algo; **~ patch** (*on lawn, carpet*) calva *f*
2 (= *empty, unadorned*) [*room*] sin muebles; [*wall*] desnudo; [*statement*] escueto; **the food cupboard was ~** la despensa estaba vacía; **they only told us the ~ facts** se limitaron a contarnos estrictamente los hechos
3 (= *meagre*) [*majority*] escaso; **the ~ bones** (*fig*) lo esencial; **to strip sth down to the ~ bones** reducir algo a lo esencial; **the ~ essentials** *or* **necessities** lo estrictamente indispensable; **to earn a ~ living** ganar lo justo para vivir; **the ~ minimum** lo justo, lo indispensable
4 (= *mere*) **the match lasted a ~ 18 minutes** el partido duró apenas 18 minutos; **sales grew at a ~ 2% a year** las ventas ascendieron apenas a un 2% al año
(B) VT [+ *body*] desnudar; [+ *wire*] pelar; [+ *sword*] desenvainar; **to ~ one's head** descubrirse; **to ~ one's soul to sb** abrir el corazón a algn; **the dog ~d its teeth** el perro enseñó *or* mostró los dientes

bareback ['bɛəbæk] ADV a pelo, sin silla; **to ride ~** montar a pelo

bare-bones ['bɛə'bəʊnz] ADJ (*esp US*) muy limitado

barefaced ['bɛəfeɪst] ADJ descarado; **a ~ lie** una mentira descarada; **it's ~ robbery** es un robo descarado

barefoot(ed) ['bɛə'fʊt(ɪd)] (A) ADJ descalzo
(B) ADV descalzo

bareheaded ['bɛə'hedɪd] ADJ con la cabeza descubierta

barelegged ['bɛə'legɪd] ADJ con las piernas descubiertas

barely ['bɛəlɪ] ADV 1 (= *scarcely*) apenas; **he can ~ read** apenas puede leer; **he looked around him with ~ concealed horror** miró a su alrededor disimulando apenas su horror; **there was ~ enough room for all of us** apenas había sitio para todos nosotros; **there was ~ anyone there** allí no había casi nadie; **I had ~ closed the door when the phone rang** apenas había cerrado la puerta cuando sonó el teléfono
2 (= *scantily*) **a ~ furnished room** una habitación escasamente amueblada

bareness ['bɛənɪs] N 1 (= *nakedness*) desnudez *f*
2 (= *emptiness*) [*of room*] lo vacío; [*of wall, tree*] desnudez *f*; [*of landscape*] desnudez *f*, lo pelado

Barents Sea ['bærənts'siː] N **the ~** el Mar de Barents

barf‡ [bɑːf] VI (*US*) vomitar, arrojar*

barfly* ['bɑːflaɪ] N (*US*) ≈ culo *m* de café*

bargain ['bɑːgɪn] (A) N 1 (= *agreement*) trato *m*; (= *transaction*) negocio *m*; (= *advantageous deal*) negocio *m* ventajoso; **it's a ~!** ¡trato hecho!, ¡de acuerdo!; **into the ~** (*fig*) para colmo; **you drive a hard ~** sabes regatear; **to make** *or* **strike a ~** cerrar un trato; **I'll make a ~ with you** hagamos un trato
2 (= *cheap thing*) ganga *f*; **~s** (*Comm*) artículos *mpl* de ocasión, oportunidades *fpl*; **it's a real ~** es una verdadera ganga
(B) VI 1 (= *negotiate*) negociar (**about** sobre; **for** para obtener; **with** con)
2 (= *haggle*) regatear
(C) CPD de ocasión ► **bargain basement**, **bargain counter** N sección *f* de ofertas *or* oportunidades ► **bargain hunter** N cazador(a) *m/f* de ofertas *or* oportunidades; **she's a real ~ hunter** siempre va a la caza de ofertas *or* oportunidades ► **bargain hunting** N caza *f* de ofertas *or* oportunidades; **to go ~ hunting** ir en busca de gangas; **I enjoy ~ hunting** me gusta ir de rebajas ► **bargain offer** N oferta *f* especial ► **bargain price** N precio *m* de ganga ► **bargain sale** N saldo *m*

►**bargain for** VI + PREP **I wasn't ~ing for that** yo no contaba con eso; **he got more than he ~ed for** resultó peor de lo que esperaba

►**bargain on** VI + PREP (= *count on*) contar con

bargaining ['bɑːgɪnɪŋ] (A) N (= *negotiation*) negociación *f*; (= *haggling*) regateo *m*
(B) CPD ► **bargaining chip**, **bargaining counter** N baza *f* a jugar, moneda *f* de cambio ► **bargaining power** N poder *m* de negociación ► **bargaining table** N mesa *f* de negociaciones

barge [bɑːdʒ] (A) N (*Naut*) barcaza *f*; (*towed*) lancha *f* a remolque, gabarra *f*; (*ceremonial*) falúa *f*
(B) VT (= *push*) empujar; (*Sport*) cargar contra
(C) VI **to ~ through a crowd** abrirse paso a empujones entre una multitud; **to ~ past sb** apartar a algn de un empujón
(D) CPD ► **barge pole** N bichero *m*; **I wouldn't touch it with a ~ pole** (*Brit**) (*fig*) yo no lo querría ni regalado

►**barge about, barge around** VI + ADV moverse pesadamente, dar tumbos

►**barge in** VI + ADV 1 (= *enter*) irrumpir
2 (*fig*) (= *interrupt*) meterse; **to ~ in on a conversation** entrometerse en una conversación

►**barge into** VI + PREP 1 [+ *person*] chocar contra; [+ *room*] irrumpir en
2 (*fig*) (= *interrupt*) interrumpir

bargee [bɑː'dʒiː] N (*Brit*) gabarrero *m*

bar-hopping ['bɑːˌhɒpɪŋ] N (*US*) **to go ~** ir de bar en bar, ir de copeo*

baritone ['bærɪtəʊn] (A) N barítono *m*
(B) CPD [*voice*] de barítono

barium ['bɛərɪəm] (A) N bario *m*
(B) CPD ► **barium meal** N sulfato *m* de bario

bark[1] [bɑːk] (A) N [*of tree*] corteza *f*
(B) VT [+ *tree*] descortezar; [+ *skin*] raer, raspar; **to ~ one's shins** desollarse las espinillas

bark[2] [bɑːk] (A) N [*of dog*] ladrido *m*; ✦**IDIOM his ~ is worse than his bite** perro ladrador, poco mordedor
(B) VI 1 [*dog*] ladrar (**at** a); [*fox*] aullir; ✦**IDIOM to be ~ing up the wrong tree** ir muy descaminado
2 (= *speak sharply*) vociferar (**at** a)
(C) VT (*also* **~ out**) [+ *order*] escupir, gritar

bark[3] [bɑːk] N (*liter, poet*) (= *boat*) barco *m*

barkeeper ['bɑːˌkiːpəʳ] N (*US*) tabernero/a *m/f*

barker ['bɑːkəʳ] N voceador(a) *m/f*, charlatán/ana *m/f* de feria

barking ['bɑːkɪŋ] (A) N [*of dog*] ladrido *m*; [*of fox*] aullido *m*
(B) ADJ (*Brit**) **~ (mad)** chiflado*, como una regadera*

barley ['bɑːlɪ] (A) N cebada *f*
(B) CPD ► **barley sugar** N azúcar *m* cande ► **barley water** N (*esp Brit*) hordiate *m*

barleyfield ['bɑːlɪfiːld] N cebadal *m*

barmaid ['bɑːmeɪd] N (*esp Brit*) camarera *f*, moza *f* (*LAm*)

barman ['bɑːmən] N (*pl* **barmen**) bárman *m*, camarero *m*

Bar Mitzvah, bar mitzvah [bɑː'mɪtsvə] N Bar Mitzvah *m*

barmy* ['bɑːmɪ] ADJ (*compar* **barmier**; *superl* **barmiest**) (*Brit*) chiflado*, chalado*; **you must be ~!** ¿estás loco?

barn [bɑːn] (A) N granero *m*; (= *raised barn*) troje *f*; (*US*) (*for horses*) cuadra *f*; (*for cattle*) establo *m*; (*for buses etc*) parque *m*, garaje *m*; **a great ~ of a house** una casa enorme, un caserón
(B) CPD ► **barn dance** N baile *m* campesino ► **barn door** N puerta *f* de granero ► **barn owl** N lechuza *f*

barnacle ['bɑːnəkl] N percebe *m*

barney* ['bɑːnɪ] N (*Brit*) (= *quarrel*) bronca *f*, agarrada* *f*

barnstorm ['bɑːnstɔːm] VI (*US*) *hacer una campaña electoral por las zonas rurales*

barnstorming ['bɑːnstɔːmɪŋ] ADJ (*Brit*) arrollador, arrasador

barnyard ['bɑːnjɑːd] (A) N corral *m*
(B) CPD ► **barnyard fowl(s)** NPL aves *fpl* de corral

barometer [bə'rɒmɪtəʳ] N barómetro *m*

barometric [ˌbærəʊ'metrɪk] (A) ADJ barométrico
(B) CPD ► **barometric pressure** N presión *f* barométrica

baron ['bærən] N 1 (= *member of nobility*) barón *m*; (*fig*) magnate *m*
2 **~ of beef** solomillo *m*

baroness ['bærənɪs] N baronesa *f*

baronet ['bærənɪt] N baronet *m*

baronetcy ['bærənɪtsɪ] N dignidad *f* del baronet

baronial [bə'rəʊnɪəl] ADJ baronial

barony ['bærənɪ] N baronía *f*

baroque [bə'rɒk] (A) ADJ (*Archit, Art, Mus*) barroco (*also fig*)
(B) N barroco *m*

barrack (*esp Brit*) ['bærək] VT abuchear

barracking ['bærəkɪŋ] (*esp Brit*) N abucheo *m*

barrack-room ['bærəkrʊm] (A) N dormitorio *m* de tropa
(B) CPD cuartelero ► **barrack-room ballad** N canción *f* cuartelera ► **barrack-room lawyer** N protestón/ona *m/f*

barracks ['bærəks] NPL 1 (*Mil*) cuartel *msing*; **confined to ~** arrestado en cuartel
2 (= *house*) caserón *m*; **a great ~ of a place** (*Brit*) una casa enorme, un caserón

barrack-square ['bærək'skwɛəʳ] N plaza *f* de armas

barracuda [ˌbærə'kjuːdə] N (*pl* **barracuda** *or* **barracudas**) barracuda *f*

barrage ['bærɑːʒ] (A) N 1 (= *dam*) presa *f*
2 (*Mil*) cortina *f* de fuego; [*of balloons etc*] aluvión *m*
3 (*fig*) **a ~ of noise** un estrépito; **a ~ of questions** una lluvia de preguntas; **there was a ~ of protests** se produjo un aluvión de protestas
(B) VT **to be ~d by sb** (*fig*) verse asediado por algn; **he was ~d by phone calls** se vio desbordado por un aluvión de llamadas
(C) CPD ► **barrage balloon** N globo *m* de barrera

barred [bɑːʳd] ADJ [*window etc*] enrejado, con reja

barrel ['bærəl] (A) N 1 (*gen*) barril *m*, tonel *m*; [*of oil*] barril *m*; (*for rain*) tina *f*; (*Tech*) tambor *m*; ✦**IDIOMS to have sb over a ~*** tener a algn con el agua al cuello*; **to scrape the (bottom of the) ~** rebañar las últimas migas
2 [*of gun, pen*] cañón *m*
(B) CPD ► **barrel organ** N organillo *m* ► **barrel vault** N bóveda *f* de cañón

barrel-chested ['bærəl'tʃestɪd] ADJ de pecho fuerte y grueso

barren ['bærən] ADJ [*soil*] árido; [*plant, woman*] estéril; **~ of** falto de, desprovisto de

barrenness ['bærənnɪs] N [*of soil*] aridez *f*; [*of woman*] esterilidad *f*

barrette [bəˈret] N (*US*) pasador *m* (para el pelo)

barricade [ˌbærɪˈkeɪd] Ⓐ N barricada *f*
Ⓑ VT cerrar con barricadas; **to ~ o.s. in a house** hacerse fuerte en una casa

barrier [ˈbærɪəʳ] Ⓐ N barrera *f*, valla *f*; (*Rail*) (*in station*) barrera *f*; (= *crash barrier*) valla *f* protectora; (*fig*) barrera *f*, obstáculo *m* (**to** para)
Ⓑ CPD ► **barrier cream** N crema *f* protectora ► **barrier method** N método *m* (de) barrera

barring [ˈbɑːrɪŋ] PREP excepto, salvo; **we shall be there ~ accidents** iremos a menos que suceda algo imprevisto

barrio [ˈbɑːrɪəʊ] N (*esp US*) barrio *m* hispano

barrister [ˈbærɪstəʳ] N (*Brit*) abogado/a *m/f*; → LAWYERS, QC/KC

bar-room [ˈbɑːˌrʊm] Ⓐ N (*US*) bar *m*, taberna *f*
Ⓑ CPD ► **bar-room brawl** N pelea *f* de taberna

barrow[1] [ˈbærəʊ] Ⓐ N (= *wheelbarrow*) carretilla *f*; (= *market stall*) carreta *f*
Ⓑ CPD ► **barrow boy** N (*Brit*) vendedor *m* callejero

barrow[2] [ˈbærəʊ] N (*Archeol*) túmulo *m*

Bart ABBR (*Brit*) = **Baronet**

bartender [ˈbɑːtendəʳ] N bárman *m*, camarero *m*

barter [ˈbɑːtəʳ] Ⓐ N trueque *m*
Ⓑ VT **to ~ sth (for sth)** trocar *or* cambiar algo (por algo)
Ⓒ VI **to ~ with sb (for sth)** negociar con algn (por algo)

►**barter away** VT + ADV [+ *rights, freedom*] malvender

Bartholomew [bɑːˈθɒləmjuː] N Bartolomé

barytone [ˈbærɪtəʊn] N viola *f* de bordón

basal [ˈbeɪsl] ADJ [1] (*lit, fig*) básico
[2] (*Physiol*) basal

basalt [ˈbæsɔːlt] N basalto *m*

base[1] [beɪs] Ⓐ N [1] (= *bottom, support*) [*of wall*] base *f*; [*of column*] base *f*, pie *m*; [*of vase, lamp*] pie *m*
[2] (= *basis, starting point*) base *f*
[3] (*Mil*) base *f*; [*of organization, company*] sede *f*; (= *residence*) lugar *m* de residencia; (= *workplace*) base *f*
[4] (*Baseball*) base *f*; ✦**IDIOMS to get to** *or* **reach first ~** (*esp US Baseball*) llegar a la primera base; (*fig*) alcanzar la primera meta; **to touch ~ with sb** (*esp US*) ponerse en contacto con algn; **to touch** *or* **cover all (the) ~s** (*esp US*) abarcarlo todo; **to be off ~** (*US**): **he's way off ~** está totalmente equivocado
[5] (*Math*) base *f*
[6] (*Drugs**) cocaína *f* (para fumar)
Ⓑ VT [1] (= *post, locate*) **to ~ sb at** [+ *troops*] estacionar a algn en; **we were ~d on Malta** nos estacionaron en Malta; **the job is ~d in London** el trabajo tiene su base en Londres; **where are you ~d now?** ¿dónde estás ahora?
[2] (= *found*) [+ *opinion, relationship*] **to ~ sth on** basar *or* fundar algo en; **to be ~d on** basarse *or* fundarse en; **a story ~d on fact** una historia basada en la realidad; **I ~ myself on the following facts** me apoyo en los hechos siguientes
Ⓒ CPD ► **base camp** N campo *m* base ► **base coat** N [*of paint*] primera capa *f* ► **base form** N (*Ling*) base *f* derivativa ► **base jumping** N *salto en paracaídas realizado ilegalmente desde rascacielos, puentes, etc.* ► **base lending rate** N tipo *m* de interés base ► **base period** N período *m* base ► **base rate** N tipo *m* de interés base

base[2] [beɪs] (*compar* **baser**, *superl* **basest**) ADJ
[1] [*action, motive*] vil, bajo
[2] [*metal*] bajo de ley
[3] (*US*) = **bass**[1]

baseball [ˈbeɪsbɔːl] Ⓐ N (= *sport*) béisbol *m*; (= *ball*) pelota *f* de béisbol
Ⓑ CPD ► **baseball cap** N gorra *f* de béisbol ► **baseball player** N jugador(a) *m/f* de béisbol

> **BASEBALL**
>
> *El* **baseball** *es el deporte nacional norteamericano. Dos equipos de nueve jugadores se enfrentan en un campo de cuatro bases que forman un rombo. El bateador (***batter***) intenta dar a la pelota que le ha tirado el lanzador (***pitcher***) y enviarla fuera del alcance de los fildeadores (***fielders***) para después correr alrededor del rombo de base en base y volver a su punto inicial. Existen dos ligas importantes en los Estados Unidos: la* **National League** *y la* **American League**. *Los equipos ganadores de estas dos ligas juegan después otra serie de partidos que se denominan* **World Series**.
>
> *Algunos aspectos de este deporte, tales como la camaradería y el espíritu de competición tanto entre equipos como entre miembros de un mismo equipo se usan a menudo en el cine como metáforas del modo de vida americano. Culturalmente el béisbol ha aportado, además de conocidas prendas de vestir como las botas o las gorras de béisbol, ciertas expresiones idiomáticas como* **a ballpark figure** *(una cifra aproximada) o* **a whole new ball game** *(una situación completamente distinta).*

baseboard [ˈbeɪsbɔːd] N (*US*) rodapié *m*

-based [beɪst] ADJ (*ending in compounds*) **coffee-based** basado en el café; **shore-based** con base en tierra; **sea-/land-based missile** misil *m* situado en una base marítima/terrestre; **to be London-based** [*person, job*] tener su base en Londres; [*organization, company*] tener su sede en Londres

Basel [ˈbɑːzəl] N Basilea *f*

baseless [ˈbeɪslɪs] ADJ infundado

baseline [ˈbeɪslaɪn] N [1] (*Tennis*) línea *f* de saque *or* de fondo
[2] (*Survey*) línea *f* de base
[3] (*fig*) (*on scale*) punto *m* de referencia

basely [ˈbeɪslɪ] ADV vilmente, de forma despreciable

baseman [ˈbeɪsmən] N (*pl* **basemen**) (*Baseball*) hombre *m* de base

basement [ˈbeɪsmənt] Ⓐ N sótano *m*
Ⓑ CPD ► **basement flat** (*Brit*), **basement apartment** (*US*) N (apartamento *m* *or* (*LAm*) departamento *m* de) sótano *m*

baseness [ˈbeɪsnɪs] N bajeza *f*, vileza *f*

bases[1] [ˈbeɪsiːz] NPL *of* **basis**

bases[2] [ˈbeɪsɪz] NPL *of* **base**[1]

bash* [bæʃ] Ⓐ N [1] (= *knock*) porrazo* *m*, golpe *m*
[2] (*Brit*) (= *attempt*) intento *m*; **I'll have a ~ (at it)** lo intentaré; **go on, have a ~!** ¡venga, inténtalo!
[3] (= *party*) fiesta *f*, juerga *f*
Ⓑ VT [+ *table, door*] golpear; [+ *person*] pegar; (*also* **~ about**) dar una paliza a
Ⓒ VI **to ~ away** = **bang away**

►**bash in*** VT + ADV [+ *door*] echar abajo; [+ *hat, car*] abollar; [+ *lid, cover*] forzar a golpes, cargarse a golpes*; **to ~ sb's head in** romper la crisma a algn*

►**bash on*** VI + ADV continuar (a pesar de todo); **~ on!** ¡adelante!

►**bash out*** VT + ADV (= *produce quickly*) sacar cantidad de*, sacar en cantidades industriales*

►**bash up*** VT + ADV [+ *car*] estrellar; (*Brit*) [+ *person*] pegar una paliza a

bashful [ˈbæʃfʊl] ADJ tímido, vergonzoso

bashfully [ˈbæʃfəlɪ] ADV tímidamente

bashfulness [ˈbæʃfʊlnɪs] N timidez *f*

bashing* [ˈbæʃɪŋ] N tunda *f*, paliza *f*; **to give sb a ~** dar una paliza a algn; **the team took a real ~** el equipo recibió una paliza*

BASIC [ˈbeɪsɪk] N ABBR (*Comput*) (= **Beginner's All-purpose Symbolic Instruction Code**) BASIC *m*

basic [ˈbeɪsɪk] Ⓐ ADJ [1] (= *fundamental*) [*reason, idea, problem*] básico, fundamental; [*knowledge*] básico, elemental; [*skills, vocabulary, needs*] básico; **~ French** francés *m* básico *or* elemental; **a ~ knowledge of Russian** unos conocimientos básicos *or* elementales de ruso; **a ~ right** un derecho fundamental; **~ to sth** básico *or* fundamental para algo
[2] (= *forming starting point*) [*salary, working hours*] base; **the ~ rate of income tax** el tipo impositivo *or* de gravamen básico
[3] (= *rudimentary*) [*equipment, furniture*] rudimentario; [*cooking*] muy sencillo, muy poco elaborado; **the hotel was extremely ~** el hotel era sumamente sencillo
[4] (*Chem*) básico; **~ salt** sal *f* básica; **~ slag** escoria *f* básica
Ⓑ NPL **~s such as bread and milk** alimentos básicos como el pan y la leche; **the ~s** los principios básicos; **to get back to ~s** volver a empezar por los principios básicos; **to get down to (the) ~s** ir a lo importante; **they had forgotten everything and we had to go back to ~s** lo habían olvidado todo y tuvimos que volver a empezar por los principios
Ⓒ CPD ► **basic airman** N (*US*) soldado *m* raso de la fuerzas aéreas ► **basic rate** N (*Fin*) tipo *m* de interés base ► **basic training** N (*Mil*) entrenamiento *m* básico ► **basic wage** N salario *m* base

basically [ˈbeɪsɪklɪ] ADV básicamente, fundamentalmente; **~ we agree** básicamente *or* fundamentalmente estamos de acuerdo; **it's ~ the same** es básicamente *or* fundamentalmente lo mismo; **he's ~ lazy** más que nada es perezoso, básicamente *or* fundamentalmente es perezoso; **it's ~ simple** en el fondo es sencillo; **well, ~, all I have to do is ...** bueno, básicamente *or* en pocas palabras, todo lo que tengo que hacer es ...

basil [ˈbæzl] N albahaca *f*

basilica [bəˈzɪlɪkə] N basílica *f*

basilisk [ˈbæzɪlɪsk] N basilisco *m*

basin [ˈbeɪsn] N [1] (*Culin*) bol *m*, cuenco *m*
[2] (= *washbasin*) palangana *f*; (*in bathroom*) lavabo *m*; [*of fountain*] taza *f*
[3] (*Geog*) cuenca *f*; [*of port*] dársena *f*

basis [ˈbeɪsɪs] Ⓐ N (*pl* **bases**) (= *foundation*) base *f*; **on a daily ~** diariamente, a base diaria; **on the ~ of what you've said** en base a lo que ha dicho
Ⓑ CPD ► **basis point** N (*Fin*) punto *m* base *or* básico

bask [bɑːsk] VI **to ~ in the sun** tomar el sol; **to ~ in the heat** disfrutar del calor; **to ~ in sb's favour** disfrutar del favor de algn; *see also* **reflect A2**

basket [ˈbɑːskɪt] Ⓐ N [1] (*big*) cesto *m*; (*two-handled*) canasta *f*; (*two-handled, for earth etc*) espuerta *f*; (= *hamper*) canasta *f*; (= *pannier*)

sera *f*, serón *m*; [*of balloon*] barquilla *f*
2 (*Basketball*) canasta *f*; **to score a ~** encestar, meter una canasta
3 **a ~ of currencies** (*Econ*) una cesta de monedas (nacionales), una canasta de divisas (*LAm*)
Ⓑ CPD ► **basket case*** N (= *person*) chalado/a* *m/f*, majareta *mf* (*Sp**); (= *country, organization*) caso *m* perdido ► **basket chair** N silla *f* de mimbre

basketball ['bɑːskɪtbɔːl] Ⓐ N (= *sport*) baloncesto *m*; (= *ball*) balón *m* de baloncesto
Ⓑ CPD ► **basketball player** N jugador(a) *m/f* de baloncesto

basketry ['bɑːskɪtrɪ] N = **basketwork**

basketwork ['bɑːskɪtwɜːk] N cestería *f*

Basle [bɑːl] N Basilea *f*

basmati rice [bəz'mætɪ'raɪs] N arroz *m* basmati (*arroz de grano largo con aromatizantes*)

Basque [bæsk] Ⓐ ADJ vasco
Ⓑ N 1 (= *person*) vasco/a *m/f*
2 (*Ling*) euskera *m*, vascuence *m*
Ⓒ CPD ► **the Basque Country** N el País Vasco, Euskadi *f* ► **the Basque Provinces** NPL las Vascongadas

bas-relief ['bæsrɪ,liːf] N bajorrelieve *m*

bass[1] [beɪs] (*Mus*) Ⓐ ADJ bajo
Ⓑ N (= *voice, singer, guitar*) bajo *m*; (= *double bass*) contrabajo *m*
Ⓒ CPD ► **bass baritone** N barítono *m* bajo ► **bass clef** N clave *f* de fa ► **bass drum** N bombo *m* ► **bass flute** N flauta *f* contralto ► **bass guitar** N bajo *m* ► **bass horn** N trompa *f* baja ► **bass strings** NPL instrumentos *mpl* de cuerda bajos ► **bass trombone** N trombón *m* bajo ► **bass tuba** N tuba *f* ► **bass viol** N viola *f* de gamba baja

bass[2] [bæs] N (= *fish*) róbalo *m*

basset ['bæsɪt] N (*also* **~ hound**) basset *m*

bassist ['beɪsɪst] N (*Mus*) bajista *mf*, bajo *m*

bassoon [bə'suːn] N bajón *m*, fagot *m*

bassoonist [bə'suːnɪst] N fagot *mf*, fagotista *mf*

basso profundo [,bæsəʊprə'fʊndəʊ] N bajo *m* profundo

bastard ['bɑːstəd] Ⓐ ADJ (= *illegitimate*) bastardo
Ⓑ N 1 (= *illegitimate child*) bastardo/a *m/f*
2 (** *pej*) cabrón/ona** *m/f*, hijo/a *m/f* de puta**, hijo/a *m/f* de la chingada (*Mex***); **you ~!** ¡cabrón!**; **you old ~!** ¡hijoputa!**; **that silly ~** ese idiota*; **this job is a real ~** este trabajo es muy jodido**

bastardized ['bɑːstədaɪzd] ADJ [*language*] corrupto

bastardy ['bɑːstədɪ] N (*Jur*) bastardía *f*

baste [beɪst] VT 1 (*Culin*) pringar
2 (*Sew*) hilvanar
3 (*) (= *beat*) dar una paliza a

basting ['beɪstɪŋ] N 1 (*Sew*) hilván *m*
2 (*) (= *beating*) paliza *f*, zurra *f*

bastion ['bæstɪən] N (*also fig*) baluarte *m*

Basutoland [bə'suːtəʊlænd] N (*formerly*) Basutolandia *f*

BASW N ABBR = **British Association of Social Workers**

bat[1] [bæt] N (*Zool*) murciélago *m*; **old ~*** (= *old woman*) bruja* *f*; ✦***IDIOMS*** **to be ~s** ◊ **have ~s in the belfry*** estar más loco que una cabra*; **to go like a ~ out of hell*** ir como alma que lleva el diablo, ir a toda hostia (*Sp**)

bat[2] [bæt] Ⓐ N 1 (*in ball games*) paleta *f*, pala *f*; (*in cricket, baseball*) bate *m*; ✦***IDIOMS*** **off one's own ~*** por cuenta propia; **right off the ~** (*US**) de repente
2 (*) (= *blow*) golpe *m*
Ⓑ VI (*Sport*) batear; ✦***IDIOM*** **to go (in) to ~ for sb** (= *support*) dar la cara por algn, salir en apoyo de algn
Ⓒ VT (*) (= *hit*) golpear, apalear; **to ~ sth around** (*US**) (= *discuss*) discutir acerca de algo

bat[3] [bæt] VT **he didn't ~ an eyelid** (*Brit*) ◊ **he didn't ~ an eye** (*US*) ni pestañeó; **without ~ting an eyelid** (*Brit*) ◊ **without ~ting an eye** (*US*) sin pestañear, sin inmutarse

batch [bætʃ] Ⓐ N 1 [*of goods etc*] lote *m*, remesa *f*; [*of papers*] pila *f*; [*of people*] grupo *m*; [*of bread*] hornada *f*
2 (*Comput*) lote *m*
Ⓑ CPD ► **batch file** N (*Comput*) fichero *m* BAT ► **batch mode** N (*Comput*) **in ~ mode** en tratamiento por lotes ► **batch processing** N (*Comput*) tratamiento *m* por lotes ► **batch production** N (*Ind*) producción *f* por lotes

bated ['beɪtɪd] ADJ **with ~ breath** sin respirar

bath [bɑːθ] Ⓐ N (*pl* **baths** [bɑːðz]) 1 (*esp Brit*) (*also* **~tub**) bañera *f*, tina *f* (*LAm*), bañadera *f* (*S. Cone*)
2 (= *act*) baño *m*; **to have** *or* **take a ~** darse un baño, bañarse; **to give sb a ~** dar un baño a algn, bañar a algn
3 (*Chem, Phot*) baño *m*
4 **baths** (*Brit*) (= *swimming pool*) piscina *f*, alberca *f* (*Mex*), pileta *f* (*S. Cone*)
Ⓑ VT (*Brit*) bañar, dar un baño a
Ⓒ VI (*Brit*) bañarse
Ⓓ CPD ► **bath chair** N silla *f* de ruedas ► **bath cube** N cubo *m* de sales para el baño ► **bath salts** NPL sales *fpl* de baño ► **bath sheet**, **bath towel** N toalla *f* de baño

bathe [beɪð] Ⓐ N (*Brit*) (= *swim*) baño *m*; **to go for a ~** ir a bañarse
Ⓑ VT 1 [+ *wound etc*] lavar
2 (*esp US*) bañar; **to ~ the baby** bañar al niño
3 (*fig*) **~d in light** bañado de luz; **~d in tears/sweat** bañado en lágrimas/sudor
Ⓒ VI 1 (*Brit*) (= *swim*) bañarse; **to go bathing** ir a bañarse
2 (*US*) (= *take bath*) bañarse

bather ['beɪðəʳ] N bañista *mf*

bathetic [bə'θetɪk] ADJ que pasa de lo sublime a lo trivial

bathhouse ['bɑːθhaʊs] N (*pl* **bathhouses** ['bɑːθhaʊzɪz]) baño *m*

bathing ['beɪðɪŋ] Ⓐ N el bañarse; **"no bathing"** "prohibido bañarse"
Ⓑ CPD ► **bathing beauty** N sirena *f* or belleza *f* de la playa ► **bathing cap** N (*US*) gorro *m* de baño ► **bathing costume** N (*Brit*) traje *m* de baño, bañador *m*, malla *f* (*S. Cone*) ► **bathing hut** N caseta *f* de playa ► **bathing machine** N (*Hist*) caseta *f* de playa movible ► **bathing suit** (*US*) N = **bathing costume** ► **bathing trunks** NPL bañador *m* (*de hombre*) ► **bathing wrap** N albornoz *m*

bathmat ['bɑːθmæt] N alfombra *f* de baño

bathos ['beɪθɒs] N paso *m* de lo sublime a lo trivial

bathrobe ['bɑːθrəʊb] N albornoz *m*

bathroom ['bɑːθrʊm] Ⓐ N cuarto *m* de baño; (*US*) (= *toilet*) servicio *m*, baño *m* (*esp LAm*); **to go to** *or* **use the ~** (*US*) ir al servicio
Ⓑ CPD ► **bathroom cabinet** N armario *m* de aseo ► **bathroom fittings** NPL aparatos *mpl* sanitarios ► **bathroom scales** NPL báscula *f* de baño

bathtub ['bɑːθtʌb] N (*esp US*) bañera *f*, tina *f* (*LAm*), bañadera *f* (*S. Cone*)

bathwater ['bɑːθwɔːtəʳ] N agua *f* del baño

bathysphere ['bæθɪsfɪəʳ] N batisfera *f*

batik [bə'tiːk] N (= *process, cloth*) batik *m*

batiste [bæ'tiːst] N batista *f*

batman ['bætmən] N (*pl* **batmen**) (*Brit Mil*) ordenanza *m*

baton ['bætən] Ⓐ N (*Mus*) batuta *f*; (*Mil*) bastón *m*; [*of policeman*] porra *f*; (*in race*) testigo *m*; ✦***IDIOMS*** **to hand on** *or* **pass the ~ to sb** entregar el testigo a algn; **to pick up the ~** recoger el testigo
Ⓑ CPD ► **baton charge** N carga *f* con bastones ► **baton round** N bala *f* de goma

batrachian [bə'treɪkɪən] N batracio *m*

batsman ['bætsmən] N (*pl* **batsmen**) (*Cricket*) bateador *m*

battalion [bə'tælɪən] N batallón *m*

batten ['bætn] Ⓐ N (*Brit Carpentry*) listón *m*; (*Naut*) junquillo *m*, sable *m*
Ⓑ VT [+ *roof, shutters*] sujetar con listones; **to ~ down the hatches** (*also fig*) atrancar las escotillas

►**batten on** VI + PREP explotar, aprovecharse de

batter[1] ['bætəʳ] N (*Culin*) mezcla *f* para rebozar; **in ~** rebozado

batter[2] ['bætəʳ] Ⓐ N (*Baseball, Cricket*) bateador(a) *m/f*; → BASEBALL, CRICKET
Ⓑ VT 1 [+ *person*] apalear; [+ *wife, baby*] maltratar; [*boxer*] magullar; [*wind, waves*] azotar; (*Mil*) cañonear, bombardear
2 (*verbally etc*) criticar ásperamente, poner como un trapo*

►**batter (away) at** VI + PREP dar grandes golpes en

►**batter down**, **batter in** VT + ADV [+ *door*] derribar a golpes

battered ['bætəd] Ⓐ ADJ (= *bruised*) magullado; [*hat*] estropeado; [*car*] abollado
Ⓑ CPD ► **battered baby** N niño/a *m/f* maltratado/a ► **battered wife** N mujer *f* maltratada

batterer ['bætərəʳ] N *persona que maltrata físicamente a su mujer o marido e hijos*; **wife-~** marido *m* violento

battering ['bætərɪŋ] Ⓐ N (= *blows*) paliza *f*; (*Mil*) bombardeo *m*; **the ~ of the waves** el golpear de las olas; **he got a ~ from the critics** los críticos fueron muy duros con él, los críticos lo pusieron como un trapo*
Ⓑ CPD ► **battering ram** N ariete *m*

battery ['bætərɪ] Ⓐ N 1 (*Elec*) (*dry*) pila *f*; (*wet*) batería *f*
2 (*Mil*) batería *f*
3 (= *series*) [*of tests*] serie *f*; [*of lights*] batería *f*, equipo *m*; [*of questions*] descarga *f*, sarta *f*
4 (*Agr*) batería *f*
5 (*Jur*) violencia *f*, agresión *f*
Ⓑ CPD ► **battery charger** N (*Elec*) cargador *m* de baterías ► **battery farm** N (*Brit*) granja *f* (avícola) de cría intensiva ► **battery farming** N (*Brit*) cría *f* (avícola) intensiva ► **battery fire** N (*Mil*) fuego *m* de batería ► **battery hen** N (*Brit*) gallina *f* de criadero ► **battery set** N (*Rad*) radio *f* de pilas, transistor *m*

battery-operated [,bætərɪ'ɒpəreɪtɪd] ADJ a pilas

battle ['bætl] Ⓐ N 1 (*Mil*) batalla *f*; **to do ~** librar batalla (**with** con); **to fight a ~** luchar; **the ~ was fought in 1346** la batalla se libró en 1346; **to join ~** (*frm*) trabar batalla
2 (*fig*) lucha *f* (**for control of** por el control de; **to control** por controlar); **to do ~ for** luchar por; **a ~ of wills** un duelo de voluntades; **a ~ of wits** un duelo de ingenio; **that's half the ~*** (con eso) ya hay medio camino andado*; **the ~ lines are drawn** (*fig*) todo está listo para la batalla; ✦***IDIOMS*** **to fight a losing ~** luchar por una causa perdida; **to win the ~**

but lose the war ganar la batalla pero perder la guerra
Ⓑ VI [1] (*Mil*) **the two armies ~d all day** los dos ejércitos se batieron durante todo el día
[2] (*fig*) luchar (**against** contra; **for** por; **to do** por hacer); **to ~ against the wind** luchar contra el viento; **to ~ for breath** esforzarse por respirar
Ⓒ VT (*esp US*) luchar contra, librar batalla contra
Ⓓ CPD ► **battle array** N **in ~ array** en formación *or* en orden de batalla ► **battle cruiser** N crucero *m* de batalla ► **battle cry** N (*Mil*) grito *m* de combate; (*fig*) lema *m*, consigna *f* ► **battle dress** N traje *m* de campaña ► **battle fatigue** N *trastorno mental postraumático provocado por el combate militar* ► **battle fleet** N flota *f* de guerra ► **battle order** N = **battle array** ► **battle royal** N batalla *f* campal ► **battle zone** N zona *f* de batalla
►**battle on** VI + ADV seguir luchando
►**battle out** VT + ADV **to ~ it out** enfrentarse
battle-axe, **battle-ax** (*US*) ['bætlæks] N [1] (= *weapon*) hacha *f* de guerra
[2] (* *pej*) (= *woman*) arpía *f*
battledore ['bætldɔːʳ] N raqueta *f* de bádminton; **~ and shuttlecock** *antiguo juego predecesor del bádminton*
battlefield ['bætlfiːld] N, **battleground** ['bætlgraʊnd] N campo *m* de batalla
battle-hardened ['bætl,hɑːdənd] ADJ endurecido por la lucha
battlements ['bætlmənts] NPL almenas *fpl*
battle-scarred ['bætl,skɑːd] ADJ (*gen*) marcado por la lucha; (*hum*) deteriorado
battleship ['bætlʃɪp] N [1] (*Mil*) acorazado *m*
[2] **~s** (= *game*) los barquitos (*juego*)
Battn ABBR (= **battalion**) Bón.
batty* ['bætɪ] ADJ (*compar* **battier**, *superl* **battiest**) (*esp Brit*) chiflado*, chalado*
bauble ['bɔːbl] N chuchería *f*
baud [bɔːd] (*Comput*) Ⓐ N baudio *m*
Ⓑ CPD ► **baud rate** N velocidad *f* (de transmisión) en baudios
baulk [bɔːlk] VI *see* **balk**
bauxite ['bɔːksaɪt] N bauxita *f*
Bavaria [bə'vɛərɪə] N Baviera *f*
Bavarian [bə'vɛərɪən] Ⓐ ADJ bávaro
Ⓑ N bávaro/a *m/f*
bawbee [bɔː'biː] N (*Scot hum*) medio penique *m*
bawd†† [bɔːd] N alcahueta *f*
bawdiness ['bɔːdɪnɪs] N lo verde
bawdy ['bɔːdɪ] ADJ (*compar* **bawdier**, *superl* **bawdiest**) subido de tono, verde*, colorado (*Mex**)
bawdyhouse†† ['bɔːdɪhaʊs] N (*pl* **bawdyhouses** ['bɔːdɪhaʊzɪz]) mancebía *f*
bawl [bɔːl] VI [1] (= *cry*) berrear
[2] (= *shout*) chillar; **to ~ at sb** gritar a algn
►**bawl out** VT + ADV [1] vocear, vociferar
[2] (*) (= *scold*) **to ~ sb out** echar una bronca a algn*
bay¹ [beɪ] N (*Geog*) bahía *f*; (*small*) abra *f*; (*very large*) golfo *m*; **the Bay of Biscay** el Golfo de Vizcaya
bay² [beɪ] Ⓐ N [1] (*Archit*) (*between two walls*) crujía *f*; (*also* **~ window**) ventana *f* salediza
[2] (*for parking*) parking *m*, área *f* de aparcamiento *or* (*LAm*) estacionamiento; (*for loading*) área *f* de carga
[3] (*Rail*) nave *f*
Ⓑ CPD ► **bay window** N ventana *f* salediza
bay³ [beɪ] Ⓐ VI [*dog*] aullar (**at** a); ✦*IDIOMS* **to ~ for blood** (*Brit*) clamar venganza; **to ~ for sb's blood** (*Brit*) pedir la cabeza de algn
Ⓑ N [1] (= *bark*) aullido *m*
[2] **at ~** (*Hunting*) acorralado (*also fig*); **to keep** *or* **hold sth/sb at ~** (*fig*) mantener algo/a algn a raya; **to bring to ~** (*Hunting*) acorralar (*also fig*)
bay⁴ [beɪ] Ⓐ ADJ [*horse*] bayo
Ⓑ N caballo *m* bayo
bay⁵ [beɪ] Ⓐ N (*Bot*) laurel *m*
Ⓑ CPD ► **bay leaf** N (hoja *f* de) laurel *m* ► **bay rum** N ron *m* de laurel *or* de malagueta
bayonet ['beɪənɪt] Ⓐ N bayoneta *f*; **with fixed ~s** con las bayonetas caladas; **at ~ point** a punta de bayoneta
Ⓑ VT herir/matar con la bayoneta
Ⓒ CPD ► **bayonet bulb** N (*Elec*) bombilla *f or* (*LAm*) foco *m* de bayoneta ► **bayonet charge** N carga *f* a la bayoneta ► **bayonet practice** N ejercicios *mpl* con bayoneta, prácticas *fpl* de bayoneta
Bayonne [baɪ'jɒn] N Bayona *f*
bayou ['baɪjuː] N (*US*) pantanos *mpl*
bazaar [bə'zɑːʳ] N bazar *m*
bazooka [bə'zuːkə] N bazuca *f*
BB Ⓐ N ABBR (= **Boys' Brigade**) *organización parecida a los Boy Scouts*
Ⓑ CPD ► **BB gun** N (*US*) *carabina de aire comprimido*
BBA N ABBR (*US Univ*) = **Bachelor of Business Administration**
BBB N ABBR (*US*) = **Better Business Bureau**
BBC N ABBR = **British Broadcasting Corporation**; **the ~** la BBC; → OPEN UNIVERSITY
BBFC N ABBR = **British Board of Film Classification**
bbl ABBR = **barrels**
BBQ N ABBR = **barbecue**
BBS N ABBR (*Comput*) = **bulletin board system**
BC Ⓐ ADV ABBR (= **Before Christ**) a. de C., a.C., A.C.
Ⓑ N ABBR (*Canada*) = **British Columbia**
BCD N ABBR (*Comput*) = **binary-coded decimal**
BCG N ABBR (= **Bacillus Calmette-Guérin**) BCG *m*
BCom [biː'kɒm] N ABBR = **Bachelor of Commerce**
BD Ⓐ N ABBR (*Univ*) = **Bachelor of Divinity**
Ⓑ ABBR = **bills discounted**
bd ABBR (*Fin*) = **bond**
B/D ABBR = **bank draft**
b/d ABBR (*Fin*) = **brought down**
BDS N ABBR (*Univ*) = **Bachelor of Dental Surgery**
BE N ABBR (*Fin*) (= **bill of exchange**) L/C

be [biː] (*present* **am, is, are**; *pt* **was, were**; *pp* **been**)

[A] INTRANSITIVE VERB	[C] MODAL VERB
[B] AUXILIARY VERB	

Ⓐ INTRANSITIVE VERB
[1] ***linking nouns, noun phrases, pronouns*** ser; **he's a pianist** es pianista; **he wants to be a doctor** quiere ser médico; **Monday's a holiday** el lunes es fiesta; **two and two are four** dos y dos son cuatro; **it's me!** ¡soy yo!; **it was me** fui yo; **who wants to be Hamlet?** ¿quién quiere hacer de *or* ser Hamlet?; **you be the patient and I'll be the doctor** tú eres el enfermo y yo seré el médico; **if I were you ...** yo en tu lugar ..., yo que tú ...*
[2] ***possession*** ser; **she's his sister** es su hermana; **it's mine** es mío
[3] ***characteristics seen as inherent*** ser; **the sky is blue** el cielo es azul; **it's (made of) plastic** es de plástico; **they're English** son ingleses; **he's tall** es alto; **it's round/enormous** es redondo/enorme; **she is boring** es aburrida; **I used to be poor but now I'm rich** antes era pobre pero ahora soy rico; **if I were rich** si fuera rico; **I'm from the south** soy del sur; **the book is in French** el libro es en francés

Use **estar** *with past participles used as adjectives describing the results of an action or process:*

it's broken está roto; **he's dead** está muerto
[4] ***changeable or temporary state*** estar; **it's dirty** está sucio; **she's bored/ill** está aburrida/enferma; **how are you?** ¿cómo estás?, ¿qué tal estás?; **how are you now?** ¿qué tal te encuentras ahora?; **I'm very well, thanks** estoy muy bien, gracias

In certain expressions where English uses **be** *+ adjective to describe feelings (***be cold/hot/hungry/thirsty***), Spanish uses* **tener** *with a noun:*

I'm cold/hot tengo frío/calor; **my feet are cold** tengo los pies fríos; **I'm hungry/thirsty** tengo hambre/sed; **be good!** ¡pórtate bien!; **you're late** llegas tarde; *see also* **afraid**, **sleepy**, **right**
[5] ***age*** **"how old is she?" — "she's nine"** —¿cuántos años tiene? —tiene nueve años; **she will be two tomorrow** mañana cumple dos años; **when I'm old** cuando sea viejo; **when I was young** cuando era joven
[6] ***= take place*** ser; **the meeting's today** la reunión es hoy; **the service will be at St Ninian's Church** el oficio será en la iglesia de San Ninian
[7] ***= be situated*** estar; **Edinburgh is in Scotland** Edimburgo está en Escocia; **it's on the table** está sobre *or* en la mesa; **where is the Town Hall?** ¿dónde está *or* queda el ayuntamiento?; **it's 5 km to the village** el pueblo está *or* queda a 5 kilómetros; **he won't be here tomorrow** mañana no estará aquí; **we've been here for ages** hace mucho tiempo que estamos aquí, llevamos aquí mucho tiempo, estamos aquí desde hace mucho tiempo; **here you are, (take it)** aquí tienes, (tómalo); **there's the church** ahí está la iglesia
[8] ***impersonal use*** [8·1] (*referring to weather*) hacer; **it's hot/cold** hace calor/frío; **it's too hot** hace demasiado calor; **it's fine** hace buen tiempo; *see also* **windy**, **sunny**, **foggy** *etc*
[8·2] (*referring to time, date etc*) ser; **it's eight o'clock** son las ocho; **it's morning in New York now** en Nueva York ahora es por la mañana; **wake up, it's morning** despierta, es de día; **what's the date (today)?** ¿qué fecha es hoy?; **it's the 3rd of May** es 3 de mayo; **it's Thursday today** hoy es jueves

BUT *note the following alternatives with* **estar**:

it's the 3rd of May estamos a 3 de mayo; **it's Thursday today** hoy estamos a jueves
[8·3] (*asking and giving opinion*) ser; **is it certain that ...?** ¿es verdad *or* cierto que ...?; **it is easy to make a mistake** es fácil cometer un fallo; **is it fair that she should be punished while ...?** ¿es justo que se la castigue mientras que ...?; **it is possible that he'll come** es posible que venga, puede (ser) que venga; **it is impossible to study all the time** es imposible estar siempre estudiando; **it is unbelievable that ...** es increíble que ...; [BUT] **it's not clear whether ...** no está claro si ...; **it would be wrong for us to do that** no estaría bien que nosotros hiciésemos eso
[8·4] (*emphatic*) ser; **it's me who does all the work** soy yo quien hace todo el trabajo; **it**

BE

"Ser" or "estar"?

You can use "ser":

• when defining or identifying by linking two nouns or noun phrases:

Paris is the capital of France
París es la capital de Francia
He was the most hated man in the village
Era el hombre más odiado del pueblo

• to describe essential or inherent characteristics (e.g. colour, material, nationality, race, shape, size *etc*):

His mother is German
Su madre es alemana
She was blonde
Era rubia

• with most impersonal expressions not involving past participles:

It is important to be on time
Es importante llegar a tiempo

NOTE: **Está claro que** is an exception:

It is obvious you don't understand
Está claro que no lo entiendes

• when telling the time or talking about time or age:

It is ten o'clock
Son las diez
It's very late. Let's go home
Es muy tarde. Vamos a casa
He lived in the country when he was young
Vivió en el campo cuando era joven

• to indicate possession or duty:

It's mine
Es mío
This is your responsibility
Este asunto es responsabilidad tuya

• with events in the sense of "take place":

The 1992 Olympic Games were in Barcelona
Los Juegos Olímpicos de 1992 fueron en Barcelona
"Where is the exam?" - "It's in Room 1"
"¿Dónde es el examen?" - "Es en el Aula Número 1"

! Compare this usage with that of **estar** *(see below)* to talk about location of places, objects and people.

You can use "estar":

• to talk about location of places, objects and people:

"Where is Zaragoza?" - "It's in Spain"
"¿Dónde está Zaragoza?" - "Está en España"
Your glasses are on the bedside table
Tus gafas están en la mesilla de noche

! But use **ser** with events in the sense of "take place" *(see above)*.

• to talk about changeable state, condition or mood:

The teacher is ill
La profesora está enferma
The coffee's cold
El café está frío
How happy I am!
¡Qué contento estoy!

! **Feliz**, however, which is seen as more permanent than **contento**, is used mainly with **ser**.

• to form progressive tenses:

We're having lunch. Is it ok if I call you later?
Estamos comiendo. Te llamaré luego, ¿vale?

Both "ser" and "estar" can be used with past participles

• Use **ser** in *passive* constructions:

This play was written by Lorca
Esta obra fue escrita por Lorca
He was shot dead (by a terrorist group)
Fue asesinado a tiros (por un grupo terrorista)

! The passive is not used as often in Spanish as it is in English.

• Use **estar** with past participles to describe the *results* of a previous action or event:

We threw them away because they were broken
Los tiramos a la basura porque estaban rotos
He's dead
Está muerto

• Compare the use of **ser** + PAST PARTICIPLE which describes *action* and **estar** + PAST PARTICIPLE which describes *result* in the following:

The window was broken by the firemen
La ventana fue rota por los bomberos
The window was broken
La ventana estaba rota
It was painted around 1925
Fue pintado hacia 1925
The floor is painted a dark colour
El suelo está pintado de color oscuro

• **Ser** and **estar** are both used in impersonal expressions with past participles. As above, the use of **ser** implies *action* while the use of **estar** implies *result*:

It is understood that the work was never finished
Es sabido que el trabajo nunca se llegó a terminar
It is a proven fact that vaccinations save many lives
Está demostrado que las vacunas salvan muchas vidas

Ser" and "estar" with adjectives

• Some adjectives can be used with both **ser** and **estar** but the meaning changes completely depending on the verb:

Es listo
He's clever
¿Estás listo?
Are you ready?
La química es aburrida
Chemistry is boring
Estoy aburrido
I'm bored

• Other adjectives can also be used with both verbs but the use of **ser** describes a *characteristic* while the use of **estar** implies a *change*:

Es muy guapo
He's very handsome
Estás muy guapa con ese vestido
You look great in that dress!
Es delgado
He's slim
¡Estás muy delgada!
You're (looking) very slim

For further uses and examples, see main entry.

was Peter who phoned fue Peter quien llamó; **why is it that she's so successful?** ¿cómo es que tiene tanto éxito?, ¿por qué tiene tanto éxito?; **it was then that ...** fue entonces cuando ...

9 *= exist* haber; **there is/are** hay; **what is (there) in that room?** ¿qué hay en esa habitación?; **there is nothing more beautiful** no hay nada más bello; **is there anyone at home?** ¿hay alguien en casa?; **there were six road accidents here last year** el año pasado hubo seis accidentes de tráfico aquí; **there must be an explanation** debe de haber una explicación; **there being no alternative solution ...** al no haber *or* no habiendo otra solución ...; **let there be light!** ¡hágase la luz!; *BUT* **there are three of us** somos tres; **there were three of them** eran tres; **after the shop there's the bus station** después de la tienda está la estación de autobuses; → *THERE*

10 *= cost* **how much was it?** ¿cuánto costó?; **the book is £20** el libro vale *or* cuesta 20 libras; **how much is it?** ¿cuánto es?; (*when paying*) ¿qué le debo? (*frm*)

11 *= visit* **has the postman been?** ¿ha venido el cartero?; **he has been and gone** vino y se fue; **I have been to see my aunt** he ido a ver a mi tía; **have you ever been to Glasgow?** ¿has estado en Glasgow alguna vez?; **I've been to China** he estado en China

12 *in noun compounds* futuro; **mother to be** futura madre *or* mamá *f*; **my wife to be** mi futura esposa

13 *in set expressions* **to be or not to be** ser o no ser; **been and***: **you've been and done it now!** ¡buena la has hecho!*; **that dog of yours has been and dug up my flowers!** ¡tu perro ha ido y me ha destrozado las flores!; **you're busy enough as it is** estás bastante ocupado ya con lo que tienes, ya tienes suficiente trabajo; **as things are** tal como están las cosas; **be that as it may** sea como fuere; **if it hadn't been for ...**: **if it hadn't been for you** *or* (*frm*) **had it not been for you, we would have lost** si no hubiera sido por ti *or* de no haber sido por ti, habríamos perdido; **let me be!** ¡déjame en paz!; **if that's what you want to do, then so be it** si eso es lo que quieres hacer, adelante; **what is it to you?*** ¿a ti qué te importa?; **what's it to be?** (*in bar etc*) ¿qué va a ser?, ¿qué vas a tomar?

Ⓑ AUXILIARY VERB

1 *forming passive* ser; **the house was destroyed by an earthquake** la casa fue destruida por un terremoto

The passive is not used as often in Spanish as in English, active and reflexive constructions often being preferred:

the box had been opened habían abierto la caja; **these cars are produced in Spain** estos coches se fabrican en España; **it is said that ...** dicen que ..., se dice que ...; **he was killed by a terrorist** lo mató un terrorista; **she was killed in a car crash** murió en un accidente de coche, resultó muerta en un accidente de coche (*frm*); **what's to be done?** ¿qué hay que hacer?; **it's a film not to be missed** es una película que no hay que perderse; **we searched everywhere for him, but he was nowhere to be seen** lo buscamos por todas partes pero no lo encontramos en ningún sitio

2 *forming continuous* estar; **it's raining** está lloviendo; **what are you doing?** ¿qué estás haciendo?, ¿qué haces?; **don't distract me when I'm driving** no me distraigas cuando estoy conduciendo; **he's always grumbling** siempre está quejándose; **he was studying until the early hours** estuvo estudiando hasta la madrugada

Use the present simple to talk about planned future events and the ***ir a*** *construction to talk about intention:*

they're coming tomorrow vienen mañana; **"it's a pity you aren't coming with us" — "but I am coming!"** —¡qué pena que no vengas con nosotros! —¡sí que voy!; **will you be seeing her tomorrow?** ¿la verás *or* la vas a ver mañana?; **will you be needing more?** ¿vas a necesitar más?; **I shall be seeing him** voy a verlo; **I'll be seeing you** hasta luego, nos vemos (*esp LAm*)

The imperfect tense can be used for continuous action in the past:

he was driving too fast conducía demasiado rápido; *see also* **for**, **since**

3 *verb substitute* 3·1 **he's older than you are** es mayor que tú; **he isn't as happy as he was** no está tan contento como antes; **"he's going to complain about you" — "oh, is he?"** —va a quejarse de ti —¿ah, sí?; **"I'm worried" — "so am I"** —estoy preocupado —yo también; **"I'm not ready" — "neither am I"** —no estoy listo —yo tampoco; **"you're tired" — "no, I'm not"** —estás cansado —no, ¡qué va!; **"you're not eating enough" — "yes I am"** —no comes lo suficiente —que sí; **"they're getting married" — "oh, are they?"** (*showing surprise*) —se casan —¿ah, sí? *or* —¡no me digas!; **"he isn't very happy" — "oh, isn't he?"** —no está muy contento —¿ah, no?; **"he's always late, isn't he?" — "yes, he is"** —siempre llega tarde, ¿verdad? —(pues) sí; **"is it what you expected?" — "no, it isn't"** —¿es esto lo que esperabas? —(pues) no; **"she's pretty" — "no, she isn't"** —es guapa —¡qué va!

3·2 (*in question tags*) **he's handsome, isn't he?** es guapo, ¿verdad?, es guapo, ¿no?, es guapo, ¿no es cierto?; **it was fun, wasn't it?** fue divertido, ¿verdad?, fue divertido, ¿no?; **she wasn't happy, was she?** no era feliz, ¿verdad?; **so he's back again, is he?** así que ha vuelto, ¿eh?; **you're not ill, are you?** ¿no estarás enfermo?

Ⓒ MODAL VERB *with infinitive construction*

1 *= must, have to* **you're to put on your shoes** tienes que ponerte los zapatos; **he's not to open it** no debe abrirlo, que no lo abra; **I am to do it** he de hacerlo yo, soy yo el que debe hacerlo; **I am not to speak to him** no tengo permiso para hablar con él; **I wasn't to tell you his name** no podía *or* debía decirte su nombre

2 *= should* deber; **he is to be congratulated on his work** debemos felicitarlo por su trabajo; **am I to understand that ...?** ¿debo entender que ...?; **she wrote "My Life", not to be confused with Bernstein's book of the same name** escribió "Mi Vida", que no debe confundirse con la obra de Bernstein que lleva el mismo título; **he was to have come yesterday** tenía que *or* debía haber venido ayer; **he is to be pitied** es digno de lástima

3 *= will* **the talks are to start tomorrow** las conversaciones darán comienzo mañana; **her house is to be sold** su casa se pondrá a la venta; **they are to be married in the summer** se casarán en el verano

4 *= can* **these birds are to be found all over the world** estos pájaros se encuentran por todo el mundo; **little traffic was to be seen** había poco tráfico; **you weren't to know** no tenías por qué saberlo

5 *expressing destiny* **this was to have serious repercussions** esto iba a tener serias repercusiones; **they were never to return** jamás regresaron; **it was not to be** no quiso el destino que así fuera

6 *in conditional sentences* **you must work harder if you are to succeed** debes esforzarte más si quieres triunfar; **if it was** *or* **were to snow ...** si nevase *or* nevara ...; **if I were to leave the job, would you replace me?** si yo dejara el puesto, ¿me sustituirías?

➤ LANGUAGE IN USE: bear² A3 7.3

B/E N ABBR 1 (*Fin*) (= **bill of exchange**) L/C
2 (*Fin*) = **Bank of England**

beach [bi:tʃ] Ⓐ N playa *f*
Ⓑ VT [+ *boat*] varar; [+ *whale*] embarrancar, encallar
Ⓒ CPD ► **beach ball** N balón *m* de playa ► **beach buggy** N buggy *m* ► **beach bum*** N playero/a *m/f* (de mucho cuidado)* ► **beach chair** N (*US*) tumbona *f* ► **beach hut** N caseta *f* de playa ► **beach pyjamas** NPL pijama *m* de verano ► **beach umbrella** N sombrilla *f* ► **beach volleyball** N voley-playa *m*, voleibol-playa *m* ► **beach wrap** N batín *m* (de playa)

beachcomber [ˈbi:tʃˌkəʊməʳ] N raquero/a *m/f*

beachhead [ˈbi:tʃhed] N cabeza *f* de playa

beachwear [ˈbi:tʃwɛəʳ] N ropa *f* de playa

beacon [ˈbi:kən] Ⓐ N 1 (*in port*) faro *m*; (*on aerodrome*) baliza *f*, aerofaro *m*; (*Rad*) radiofaro *m*; (= *fire*) almenara *f*
2 (= *hill*) hacho *m*
Ⓑ CPD ► **beacon light** N luz *f* de faro

bead [bi:d] N 1 (*gen*) cuenta *f*; [*of glass*] abalorio *m*; **beads** (= *necklace*) collar *m*; (*Rel*) rosario *m*; **to tell one's ~s** rezar el rosario
2 [*of dew, sweat*] gota *f*
3 [*of gun*] mira *f* globular; **to draw a ~ on** apuntar a

beaded [ˈbi:dɪd] ADJ [*dress, cushion*] bordado con cuentas; **his forehead was ~ with sweat** su frente estaba salpicada con gotas de sudor

beading [ˈbi:dɪŋ] N 1 (*Archit*) astrágalo *m*, contero *m*
2 (*Carpentry*) moldura *f*
3 (*on garment*) canutillo *m*, adorno *m* de cuentas

beadle [ˈbi:dl] N 1 (*Brit Univ*) bedel *m*
2 (*Rel*) pertiguero *m*

beady [ˈbi:dɪ] ADJ **~ eyes** ojos *mpl* pequeños y brillantes

beady-eyed [ˈbi:dɪˈaɪd] ADJ de ojos pequeños y brillantes

beagle [ˈbi:gl] N sabueso *m*, beagle *m*

beak [bi:k] N 1 [*of bird*] pico *m*; (*) (= *nose*) napia* *f*
2 (*Naut*) rostro *m*; **~ of land** promontorio *m*
3 (*Brit**) (= *judge*) magistrado/a *m/f*

beaked [bi:kt] ADJ picudo

beaker [ˈbi:kəʳ] N vaso *m*; (*Chem*) vaso *m* de precipitación

be-all [ˈbi:ˈɔ:l] N (*also* **~ and end-all**) único objeto *m*, única cosa *f* que importa; **he is the ~ of her life** él es el único objeto de su vida; **money is not the ~** el dinero no es lo único que importa

beam [bi:m] Ⓐ N 1 (*Archit*) viga *f*, travesaño *m*; [*of plough*] timón *m*; [*of balance*] astil *m*; (*Mech*) balancín *m*
2 (*Naut*) (= *timber*) bao *m*; (= *width*) manga *f*; *see also* **broad A1**
3 [*of light, laser*] rayo *m*; (*from beacon, lamp*) haz *m* de luz; (*from radio beacon*) haz *m* de radiofaro; **to drive on full** *or* **main ~** conducir con luz de carretera *or* con luces largas; ✦**IDIOMS to be on the ~*** seguir el buen camino; **to be (way) off ~** (*Brit**) andar (totalmente) descaminado
4 (= *smile*) sonrisa *f* radiante; **with a ~ of pleasure** con una sonrisa de placer
5 (*Sport*) barra *f* fija
Ⓑ VT 1 (= *transmit*) [+ *signal*] emitir
2 (= *smile*) **she ~ed her thanks at me** me lanzó una mirada de agradecimiento
Ⓒ VI 1 (= *shine*) brillar
2 (= *smile*) sonreír satisfecho; **~ing with pride** radiante de orgullo
Ⓓ CPD ► **beam lights** NPL (*Aut*) luces *fpl* largas

► **beam down** (*Sci Fi*) Ⓐ VT + ADV teletransportar
Ⓑ VI + ADV teletransportarse

► **beam up** (*Sci Fi*) Ⓐ VT + ADV teletransportar
Ⓑ VI + ADV teletransportarse

beam-ends [ˌbi:mˈendz] NPL (*Naut*) cabezas *fpl* de los baos (de un buque); **she was on her ~** (*Naut*) el buque escoraba peligrosamente; ✦**IDIOM they are on their ~** están en un grave aprieto, no tienen donde caerse muertos

beaming [ˈbi:mɪŋ] ADJ sonriente, radiante

bean [bi:n] Ⓐ N 1 (*gen*) frijol *m*, alubia *f* (*Sp*); (*kidney*) frijol *m*, judía *f* (*Sp*), poroto *m* (*S. Cone*); (*broad, haricot*) haba *f*; (*green*) habichuela *f*, judía *f* verde (*Sp*), ejote *m* (*Mex*), poroto *m* verde (*S. Cone*); (*coffee*) grano *m*; **not a ~!*** ¡nada en absoluto!; **I haven't a ~** (*Brit**) estoy pelado*, no tengo un duro (*Sp**), no tengo un peso (*LAm**); **I didn't make a ~ on the deal*** no saqué ni un céntimo del negocio; ✦**IDIOMS to be full of ~s** (*Brit**) estar lleno de vida; **to know how many ~s make five** (*Brit†**) saber cuántas son dos y dos; **he doesn't know ~s about it** (*US**) no sabe ni papa de eso*, no tiene ni zorra idea (*Sp**); **not to amount to a hill** *or* **row of ~s*** no valer nada; *see also* **spill¹ A1**
2 (*as form of address*) **hello, old ~!** (*Brit†**) ¡hola, macho! (*Sp**), ¡hola, viejo! (*LAm**)
3 (*US**) (= *head, brain*) coco* *m*
Ⓑ CPD ► **bean counter*** N (*pej*) *contable o gerente obsesionado por los números* ► **bean curd** N tofu *m*

beanbag [ˈbi:nbæg] N (*for throwing*) *saquito que se usa para realizar ejercicios gimnásticos*; (= *chair*) *asiento en forma de bolsa rellena de bolitas de poliestireno*

beanfeast* [ˈbi:nfi:st] N, **beano*** [ˈbi:nəʊ] N (*Brit*) (= *party*) fiesta *f*, juerga *f*; (= *meal*) comilona* *f*

beanpole [ˈbi:npəʊl] N emparrado *m*; **he's a real ~*** (*fig*) está como un espárrago*

beanshoots [ˈbi:nʃu:ts] NPL, **beansprouts** [ˈbi:nspraʊts] NPL (*Culin*) brotes *mpl* de soja

beanstalk [ˈbi:nstɔ:k] N judía *f*

bear¹ [bɛəʳ] Ⓐ N 1 (= *animal*) oso/a *m/f*; (*fig*) (= *man*) grandullón* *m*; **he was a huge ~ of a man** era un hombre grande como un oso; **the Great/Little Bear** la Osa Mayor/Menor; ✦**IDIOMS to be like a ~ with a sore head*** estar de un humor de perros*; **to be loaded for ~** (*US**) estar dispuesto para el ataque; *see also* **brown E**, **grizzly**, **polar**
2 (*also* **teddy ~**) osito *m* de peluche
3 (*Fin*) (= *pessimistic trader*) bajista *mf*
Ⓑ CPD ► **bear baiting** N *espectáculo en el que se azuzan a unos perros contra un oso* ► **bear cub** N osezno *m* ► **bear garden** N (*fig*) manicomio *m*, casa *f* de locos ► **bear hug** N fuerte abrazo *m* ► **bear market** N (*Fin*) mercado *m* bajista ► **bear pit** N (*fig*) manicomio *m*, casa *f* de locos

▼ **bear²** [bɛəʳ] (*pt* **bore**; *pp* **borne**) Ⓐ VT 1 (= *support*) [+ *weight*] aguantar, sostener; *see also* **-bearing**
2 (= *take on*) [+ *cost*] correr con, pagar; [+ *responsibility*] cargar con; (*fig*) [+ *burden*] soportar; **the government ~s some responsibility for this crisis** el gobierno tiene parte de responsabilidad en esta crisis; **he bore no responsibility for what had happened** no era responsable de lo que había pasado; **they**

~ most of the responsibility for elderly relatives cargan con la mayor parte de la responsabilidad de atender a familiares ancianos
[3] (= *endure*) [+ *pain, suspense*] soportar, aguantar; **I can't ~ the suspense** no puedo soportar *or* aguantar el suspense; **I can't ~ him** no lo puedo ver, no lo soporto *or* aguanto; **the dog can't ~ being shut in** el perro no soporta estar encerrado; **I can't ~ to look** no puedo mirar; **he can't ~ to talk about it** no puede hablar de ello; **he can't ~ to see her suffer** no soporta verla sufrir; *see also* **brunt**
[4] (= *bring*) [+ *news, gift*] traer; **a letter ~ing important news** una carta que trae/traía importantes noticias
[5] (= *carry*) llevar, portar (*liter*); **protesters ~ing placards** manifestantes *mfpl* llevando *or* portando pancartas; **to ~ arms** (*frm*) portar armas (*frm*); **he bore himself like a soldier** (*posture*) tenía un porte soldadesco; (*behaviour*) se comportó como un verdadero soldado; **there was dignity in the way he bore himself** había dignidad en su porte
[6] (= *have, display*) [+ *signature, date, message, title*] llevar; [+ *mark, scar*] conservar; **his ideas bore little relation to reality** sus ideas no tenían mucha relación con la realidad; **she bore no resemblance to the girl I knew 20 years ago** no se parecía en nada a la chica que había conocido 20 años atrás; **the room bore all the signs of a violent struggle** el cuarto conservaba todas las huellas de una riña violenta; **to ~ a grudge** guardar rencor; **she ~s him no ill-will** (*grudge*) no le guarda rencor; (*hostility*) no siente ninguna animadversión hacia él; *see also* **witness A2, mind A3**
[7] (= *stand up to*) [+ *examination*] resistir; **her story won't ~ scrutiny** su historia no resistirá un análisis; **it doesn't ~ thinking about*** da horror sólo pensarlo; **the film ~s comparison with far more expensive productions** la película puede compararse con producciones mucho más caras
[8] (*liter*) (= *produce*) [+ *fruit*] dar; (*frm*) [+ *child*] dar a luz a; (*Fin*) [+ *interest*] devengar; **her hard work bore fruit when she was promoted** sus esfuerzos dieron fruto cuando la ascendieron; **she bore him a daughter** le dio una hija
Ⓑ VI [1] (= *move*) **to ~ (to the) right/left** torcer *or* girar a la derecha/izquierda
[2] **to ~ on sth** (= *relate to*) guardar relación con algo, tener que ver con algo; (= *influence*) influir en algo; *see also* **bring 2**
[3] (= *afflict*) **his misdeeds bore heavily on his conscience** sus fechorías le pesaban en la conciencia

►**bear away** VT + ADV llevarse; **injured people were borne away in ambulances** se llevaron a los heridos en ambulancias; **the wreckage was borne away by** *or* **on the tide** los restos del naufragio fueron arrastrados por la corriente

►**bear down** VI + ADV [1] (= *come closer*) **to ~ down on sth/sb** echarse encima a algo/algn; **the ferry was ~ing down on us** el ferry se nos echaba encima
[2] (= *press down*) presionar; **you have to ~ down hard on the screw** hay que apretar fuerte el tornillo
[3] (= *push*) (*in childbirth*) empujar

►**bear in on, bear in upon** VI + ADV + PREP (*frm*) **after half an hour it was borne in (up)on him that no one was listening** después de media hora cayó en la cuenta de que *or* se percató de que nadie le estaba escuchando

►**bear off** VT + ADV = **bear away**

►**bear on** VI + PREP [+ *person*] interesar; [+ *subject*] tener que ver con

►**bear out** VT + ADV confirmar; **the facts seem to ~ out her story** los hechos parecen confirmar su historia; **their prediction was not borne out by events** sus predicciones no se vieron confirmadas por los sucesos; **perhaps you can ~ me out on this, Alan?** Alan, ¿me puedes confirmar que estoy en lo cierto?

►**bear up*** VI + ADV **how are you ~ing up?** ¿qué tal ese ánimo?; **she's ~ing up well under the circumstances** lo está llevando bien dadas las circunstancias; **"how are you?" — "~ing up!"** —¿qué tal? —¡voy aguantando!; **~ up! it's nearly over** ¡ánimo, que ya queda poco!; **the children bore up well during the visit to the museum** los niños aguantaron bien la vista al museo

►**bear with** VI + PREP tener paciencia con; **thank you for ~ing with us during this difficult time** gracias por tener paciencia con nosotros en estos tiempos difíciles; **if I repeat myself, please ~ with me** les ruego que tengan paciencia si me repito; **~ with it, it gets better** ten un poco de paciencia *or* aguanta un poco, ya verás como mejora; **if you'll ~ with me, I'll explain** si esperas un poco, te explico

bearable ['bɛərəbl] ADJ soportable

beard [bɪəd] Ⓐ N [1] barba *f*; **to have** *or* **wear a ~** llevar barba
[2] (*Bot*) arista *f*
Ⓑ VT desafiar

bearded ['bɪədɪd] ADJ (*gen*) con barba; (*heavily*) barbudo

beardless ['bɪədlɪs] ADJ barbilampiño, lampiño; [*youth*] imberbe

bearer ['bɛərəʳ] Ⓐ N [1] (= *bringer*) [*of tradition, culture, idea*] poseedor(a) *m/f*; [*of burden*] porteador(a) *m/f*, portador(a) *m/f*; [*of letter, news*] portador(a) *m/f*; **I hate to be the ~ of bad news** siento traer malas noticias, siento ser portador de malas noticias (*frm*)
[2] (= *possessor*) [*of cheque*] portador(a) *m/f*; [*of title*] poseedor(a) *m/f*; [*of credentials, office, passport*] titular *mf*
[3] (= *servant*) porteador *m*; (*also* **pall~**) portador(a) *m/f* del féretro; (*also* **stretcher-~**) camillero/a *m/f*; *see also* **flag C, standard C**
Ⓑ CPD ► **bearer bond** N título *m* al portador

bearing ['bɛərɪŋ] N [1] (= *relevance*) relación *f*; **this has no ~ on the matter** esto no tiene relación *or* no tiene nada que ver con el asunto; **this has a direct ~ on our future** esto influye directamente en nuestro futuro
[2] (*in navigation*) rumbo *m*; **to take a ~ (on sth)** tomar una demora (de algo); **to find** *or* **get one's ~s** (*fig*) orientarse; **to lose one's ~s** (*fig*) desorientarse
[3] (= *posture*) porte *m*; (= *behaviour*) comportamiento *m*, modales *mpl*
[4] (*Mech*) cojinete *m*; *see also* **ball D**
[5] (*Heraldry*) blasón *m*; *see also* **armorial**

-bearing ['bɛərɪŋ] ADJ (*ending in compounds*) **oil-bearing rock** roca *f* que contiene petróleo; **malaria-bearing mosquitos** mosquitos *mpl* portadores de malaria; **a large fruit-bearing tree** un gran árbol frutal; **non-weight-bearing exercise, such as swimming and cycling** un ejercicio que no implique cargar peso, como la natación o el ciclismo; *see also* **interest-bearing, load-bearing**

bearish ['bɛərɪʃ] ADJ [*person, attitude*] pesimista; [*market*] (de tendencia) bajista

bearskin ['bɛəskɪn] N [1] piel *f* de oso; **a ~ rug** una alfombra de piel de oso
[2] (*Mil*) *gorro militar de piel de oso*

beast [biːst] N [1] (= *animal*) bestia *f*; **~ of burden** bestia *f* de carga; **the king of the ~s** el rey de los animales; **the Beast** (*Rel*) la Bestia; **the mark of the Beast** (*Rel*) la marca de la Bestia; *see also* **wild D**
[2] (*) (= *person*) bestia* *mf*; **that ~ of a policeman** aquel bestia de policía*; **what a ~ he is!** ¡qué bruto *or* bestia es!*; **you ~!** ¡animal!*
[3] (*) (= *thing*) **it's a ~ of a day** es un día horrible*; **it's a ~ of a job** es un trabajo de chinos*; **a good thriller is a rare ~ indeed** escasean las buenas novelas/películas de suspense; **this is quite a different ~** esto ya es otra cosa

beastliness ['biːstlɪnɪs] N bestialidad *f*

beastly ['biːstlɪ] Ⓐ ADJ [1] (†*) (= *horrid*) espantoso; **that was a ~ thing to do** eso sí que fue cruel; **you were ~ to me** te portaste muy mal conmigo; **where's that ~ book?** ¿dónde está el maldito libro ese?
[2] (††) (= *animal*) bestial
Ⓑ ADV (*Brit*†*) **it's ~ awkward** es terriblemente difícil; **it's ~ cold** hace un frío de muerte

beat [biːt] (*vb: pt* **beat**; *pp* **beaten**) Ⓐ N [1] (= *stroke, blow*) [*of drum*] redoble *m*; [*of heart*] latido *m*; **her heart missed** *or* **skipped a ~** le dio un vuelco el corazón; **he replied without missing a ~** (*fig*) contestó sin alterarse
[2] (= *beating*) [*of drums*] redoble *m*; [*of waves, rain*] batir *m*; **the ~ of wings** el batir de alas; *see also* **drum**
[3] (*Mus*) (= *rhythm*) compás *m*, ritmo *m*; (= *rhythmic unit*) tiempo *m*; [*of conductor*] **his ~ is not very clear** no marca el compás con mucha claridad
[4] (= *route*) [*of policeman*] ronda *f*; **he had spent 20 years on the ~** había hecho la ronda durante 20 años; **we need more officers on the ~** deberíamos tener más agentes haciendo la ronda; **that's rather off my ~** (*fig*) no es lo mío; *see also* **pound A3**
[5] (*also* **beatnik**) beatnik *mf*
Ⓑ VT [1] (= *strike, thrash*) [+ *surface*] golpear, dar golpes en; [+ *drum*] tocar; [+ *carpet*] sacudir; [+ *metal*] batir; (*Culin*) [+ *eggs, cream*] batir; (*Hunting*) (*to raise game*) batir; **to ~ sth flat** aplanar algo a golpes; **I had Latin ~en into me at school** en el colegio me enseñaron latín a fuerza de golpes; **he ~ his fists on the table** aporreó la mesa con los puños, dio golpes con los puños en la mesa; **they had to ~ a path through the jungle** tuvieron que abrirse paso a través de la jungla; *see also* **breast, path A4.1, retreat, track A3**
[2] (= *beat up*) [+ *person*] pegar; **he was badly ~en** le habían dado una buena paliza; **to ~ sb's brains out*** partir la crisma a algn*, partir la cabeza a algn; **to ~ sb to death** matar a algn a golpes *or* de una paliza
[3] (= *flap*) [+ *wings*] batir
[4] (*Mus*) **to ~ time** marcar el compás
[5] (= *defeat*) [+ *team, adversary*] ganar a; [+ *problem*] superar; **he ~ Smith by five seconds** le ganó a Smith por cinco segundos; **Arsenal ~ Leeds 5-1** el Arsenal ganó 5-1 contra el Leeds, el Arsenal derrotó al Leeds 5-1; **she was easily ~en into third place** fue fácil ganarla haciéndola quedar en el tercer puesto; **she doesn't know when she's ~en** no sabe reconocer que ha perdido; **our prices cannot be ~en** nuestros precios son insuperables *or* imbatibles; **we've got to ~ inflation** tenemos

que superar la inflación; **"how did he escape?" — "(it) ~s me!"*** —¿cómo escapó? —¡no me lo explico! *or* —¡(no tengo) ni idea!; ***✦IDIOM*** **if you can't ~ them, join them** si no puedes con ellos, únete a ellos; *see also* **hollow C**

6 (= *better*) [+ *record*] batir; **he ~ his own previous best time** batió su propio récord; **it ~s sitting at home doing nothing*** es mejor que estar en casa sin hacer nada; **you can't ~ a nice cup of tea*** no hay nada mejor que una buena taza de té; **coffee ~s tea any day*** el café da cien vueltas al té; **that ~s everything!*** ¡eso es el colmo!; **can you ~ it** *or* **that?*** ¿has visto cosa igual?; **~ it!*** ¡lárgate!*

7 (= *pre-empt*) adelantarse; **if we leave early, we can ~ the rush hour** si salimos temprano, nos evitamos la hora punta; **I'll ~ you to that tree** ¿a que llego antes que tú a aquel árbol?, te echo una carrera hasta aquel árbol; **they determined to be the first to get there but the other team ~ them to it (by 36 hours)** estaban decididos a llegar los primeros pero el otro equipo les ganó *or* se les adelantó (en 36 horas); **I could see she was about to object but I ~ her to it** me di cuenta de que iba a poner objeciones pero me adelanté

Ⓒ VI 1 (= *hit*) **to ~ on** *or* **against** *or* **at sth** [*rain, waves*] azotar algo; [*person*] dar golpes en algo, golpear algo; **the waves ~ against the harbour wall** las olas azotaban el muro del puerto; **someone was ~ing on the door** alguien estaba dando golpes en *or* golpeando *or* aporreando la puerta; **she began ~ing at the flames with a pillow** empezó a apagar las llamas a golpes con una almohada

2 (= *sound rhythmically*) [*heart*] latir; [*drum*] redoblar; [*wings*] batir

3 (*Hunting*) (*to raise game*) batir; ***✦IDIOM*** **to ~ about the bush** andarse con rodeos; **let's not ~ about the bush** no nos andemos con rodeos; **stop ~ing about the bush!** ¡deja de andarte con rodeos!

Ⓓ ADJ (*) 1 (= *exhausted*) rendido, molido*; *see also* **dead A1**

2 (= *defeated*) **the problem has me ~** me doy por vencido con este problema; **Gerald had him ~ on the practical side of things** Gerald le daba mil vueltas en el aspecto práctico de las cosas

Ⓔ CPD ► **beat box** N caja *f* de ritmos ► **beat generation** N generación *f* beat ► **beat music** N *música rock de las décadas de los cincuenta y sesenta*

►**beat back** VT + ADV 1 (= *fight off*) [+ *attack*] rechazar; **England won 4-1, ~ing back challenges from the U.S. and France** Inglaterra ganó 4-1 frente al reto que suponían EEUU y Francia

2 (= *force back*) hacer retroceder; **they were ~en back by smoke and flames** el humo y las llamas les hicieron retroceder

►**beat down** Ⓐ VT + ADV 1 [+ *door*] derribar a golpes

2 [+ *seller*] **he tried to ~ me down on the price** intentó que le rebajase el precio, intentó que se lo dejase más barato; **I ~ him down to £20** conseguí que me lo rebajara a 20 libras

Ⓑ VI + ADV [*sun*] caer a plomo; [*rain*] caer con fuerza; **the rain was ~ing down outside** fuera la lluvia caía con fuerza

►**beat off** VT + ADV 1 [+ *competition*] **they ~ off competition from other companies to win the contract** derrotaron a otras compañías que competían por conseguir el contrato

2 [+ *attack, challenge*] = **beat back**

►**beat out** VT + ADV 1 [+ *flames*] apagar (a golpes)

2 (*Mus*) [+ *rhythm*] marcar; [+ *tune*] tocar (con mucho ritmo)

3 (*US*) (= *defeat*) [+ *person*] derrotar

4 [+ *dent*] quitar (a golpes)

►**beat up** VT + ADV 1 [+ *person*] dar una paliza a, pegar

2 (*Culin*) batir

►**beat up on** VI + ADV + PREP (*US**) (= *hit*) dar una paliza a, pegar; (= *bully*) intimidar; (= *criticize*) arremeter contra

beaten [ˈbiːtn] Ⓐ PP *of* **beat**

Ⓑ ADJ 1 (= *shaped, compacted*) [*metal, earth*] batido; ***✦IDIOM*** **off the ~ track** (= *isolated*) apartado, retirado; (= *unfrequented*) fuera de los lugares donde va todo el mundo; **to get off the ~ track** apartarse de los lugares donde va todo el mundo

2 (= *defeated*) [*person*] derrotado; **he was a ~ man** era un hombre derrotado

beaten-up* [ˈbiːtnˌʌp] ADJ [*car*] hecho un cacharro*; [*clothes*] hecho polvo*

beater [ˈbiːtəʳ] N 1 (*Culin*) batidora *f*; (*also* **carpet ~**) sacudidor *m*; *see also* **panel, wife, world B**

2 (*Hunting*) ojeador(a) *m/f*, batidor(a) *m/f*

beatific [ˌbiːəˈtɪfɪk] ADJ beatífico; **a ~ smile** una sonrisa beatífica

beatifically [ˌbiːəˈtɪfɪklɪ] ADV beatíficamente

beatification [biːˌætɪfɪˈkeɪʃən] N beatificación *f*

beatify [biːˈætɪfaɪ] VT beatificar

beating [ˈbiːtɪŋ] N 1 (= *striking*) [*of drum*] redoble *m*; [*of heart*] latido *m*, pulsación *f*; **the ~ of wings** el batir de alas; **the ~ of the rain/the waves** el batir *or* el azote de la lluvia/las olas

2 (= *punishment*) paliza *f*, golpiza *f* (*LAm*); **to get a ~** recibir una paliza; **to give sb a ~** dar una paliza a algn; **to take a ~: our team took a ~** a nuestro equipo le dieron una paliza*, nuestro equipo recibió una paliza*; **the dollar is taking a ~ on the currency markets** le están dando una paliza al dólar en los mercados de divisas*

3 (= *bettering*) **that score will take some ~** será difícil superar esa puntuación

4 (*Hunting*) batida *f*

beating-up [ˌbiːtɪŋˈʌp] N paliza *f*

beatitude [biːˈætɪtjuːd] N beatitud *f*; **the Beatitudes** las Bienaventuranzas

beatnik [ˈbiːtnɪk] N beatnik *mf*

Beatrice [ˈbɪətrɪs] N Beatriz

beat-up* [ˈbiːtʌp] ADJ hecho polvo*, de perras*

beau [bəʊ] Ⓐ N (*pl* **beaus** *or* **beaux** [bəʊz]) (= *fop*) petimetre *m*, dandy *m*; (= *ladies' man*) galán *m*; (= *suitor*) pretendiente *m*; (= *sweetheart*) novio *m*

Ⓑ ADJ **~ ideal** lo bello ideal; (= *person*) tipo *m* ideal

Beaufort scale [ˈbəʊfətˌskeɪl] N escala *f* Beaufort

beaut* [bjuːt] N **it's a ~** es sensacional, es pistonudo (*Sp**)

beauteous [ˈbjuːtɪəs] ADJ (*poet*) bello

beautician [bjuːˈtɪʃən] N esteticista *mf*

beautiful [ˈbjuːtɪfʊl] ADJ hermoso, bello, lindo (*esp LAm*); **what a ~ house!** ¡qué casa más preciosa!; **the ~ people** la gente guapa

beautifully [ˈbjuːtɪflɪ] ADV (= *wonderfully*) maravillosamente; (= *precisely*) perfectamente; **she plays ~** toca a la perfección; **that will do ~** así sirve perfectamente

beautify [ˈbjuːtɪfaɪ] VT embellecer

beauty [ˈbjuːtɪ] Ⓐ N 1 (= *quality*) belleza *f*, hermosura *f*; **the ~ of it is that ...** lo mejor de esto es que ...; **that's the ~ of it** eso es lo que tiene de bueno; ***✦PROVS*** **~ is in the eye of the beholder** todo es según el cristal con que se mira; **~ is only skin-deep** la belleza no lo es todo, la belleza es algo sólo superficial

2 (= *person, thing*) belleza *f*, preciosidad *f*; **isn't he a little ~?** (= *child*) ¡mira qué rico es el niño!; **she's no ~** no es ninguna belleza; **Beauty and the Beast** la Bella y la Bestia; **it's a ~** es una preciosidad; **that was a ~!** (= *stroke etc*) ¡qué golpe más fino!

3 **beauties** (= *attractions*) maravillas *fpl*; **the beauties of Majorca** las maravillas de Mallorca

Ⓑ CPD ► **beauty competition, beauty contest** N concurso *m* de belleza ► **beauty consultant** N esteticista *mf* ► **beauty cream** N crema *f* de belleza ► **beauty editor** N directora *f* de la sección de belleza ► **beauty parlour, beauty parlor** (*US*) N salón *m* de belleza ► **beauty product** N producto *m* de belleza ► **beauty queen** N reina *f* de la belleza ► **beauty salon** N salón *m* de belleza ► **beauty sleep** N (*hum*) primer sueño *m*; **I need my ~ sleep** necesito dormir mis horas (para luego estar bien) ► **beauty spot** N (*on face*) lunar *m* postizo; (*in country*) lugar *m* pintoresco

beaver [ˈbiːvəʳ] N 1 castor *m*

2 (*esp US***) coño** *m*

►**beaver away*** VI + ADV trabajar con empeño

bebop [ˈbiːbɒp] N bebop *m*

becalm [bɪˈkɑːm] VT **to be ~ed** estar encalmado

became [bɪˈkeɪm] PT *of* **become**

▼ **because** [bɪˈkɒz] Ⓐ CONJ porque; **I came ~ you asked me to** vine porque me lo pediste; **~ he was ill he couldn't go** no pudo ir por estar enfermo; **just ~ he has two cars he thinks he's somebody** sólo porque tiene dos coches se cree todo un personaje

Ⓑ **~ of** PREP por; **I did it ~ of you** lo hice por ti; **many families break up ~ of a lack of money** muchas familias se deshacen por *or* debido a la falta de dinero

bechamel [ˌbeɪʃəˈmel] N (*also* **~ sauce**) besamel *f*

beck[1] [bek] N ***✦IDIOM*** **to be at the ~ and call of** estar siempre a disposición de

beck[2] [bek] N (*N Eng*) arroyo *m*, riachuelo *m*

beckon [ˈbekən] Ⓐ VT 1 (= *signal*) llamar con señas, hacer señas a; **he ~ed me in/over** me hizo señas para que entrara/me acercara

2 (= *attract*) llamar, atraer

Ⓑ VI 1 (= *signal*) **to ~ to sb** llamar a algn con señas, hacer señas a algn

2 (= *be attractive*) [*bright lights, fame*] ejercer su atracción

3 (= *loom*) avecinarse, estar a la vuelta de la esquina

become [bɪˈkʌm] (*pt* **became**; *pp* **become**) Ⓐ VI 1 (= *grow to be*) **to ~ famous** hacerse famoso; **to ~ sad** ponerse triste; **to ~ ill** ponerse enfermo, enfermar; **to ~ old** hacerse *or* volverse viejo; **to ~ angry** enfadarse; **to ~ red** ponerse rojo, enrojecerse; **we became very worried** empezamos a inquietarnos muchísimo; **he became blind** (se) quedó ciego; **this is becoming difficult** esto se está poniendo difícil; **to ~ accustomed to sth** acostumbrarse a algo; **it became known that ...** se supo que ..., llegó a saberse que ...; **when he ~s 21** cuando cumpla los 21 años

2 (= *turn into*) convertirse en, transformarse

➤ LANGUAGE IN USE: **because A** 17.1, 26.3 **B** 17.1

BECOME, GO, GET

The translation of become/go/get/turn depends on the context and the type of change involved and how it is regarded. Very often there is more than one possible translation, or even a special verb to translate **get** + ADJECTIVE (e.g. **get angry** - **enfadarse**), but here are some general hints.

Become *etc* **+ adjective**

• Use **ponerse** to talk about temporary but normal changes:

I got quite ill
Me puse muy malo
He went pale
Se puso blanco
You've got very brown
Te has puesto muy moreno
He got very angry
Se puso furioso

• Use **volverse** to refer to sudden, longer-lasting and unpredictable changes, particularly those affecting the mind:

He has become very impatient in the last few years
Se ha vuelto muy impaciente estos últimos años
She went mad
Se volvió loca

• Use **quedar(se)** especially when talking about changes that are permanent, involve deterioration and are due to external circumstances. Their onset may or may not be sudden:

He went blind
(Se) quedó ciego
Goya went deaf
Goya (se) quedó sordo

NOTE: **Quedarse** is also used to talk about pregnancy:

She became pregnant
(Se) quedó embarazada

• Use **hacerse** for states resulting from effort or from a gradual, cumulative process:

They became very famous
Se hicieron muy famosos
The pain became unbearable
El dolor se hizo insoportable

• Use **llegar a ser** to suggest reaching a peak:

The heat became stifling
El calor llegó a ser agobiante

Become *etc* **+ noun**

• Use **hacerse** for career goals and religious or political persuasions:

He became a lawyer
Se hizo abogado
I became a Catholic in 1990
Me hice católico en 1990
He became a member of the Green Party
Se hizo miembro del Partido Verde

• Use **llegar a** + NOUN and **llegar a ser** + PHRASE for reaching a peak after a period of gradual change. This construction is often used to talk about professional accomplishments:

If you don't make more effort, you'll never get to be a teacher
Si no te esfuerzas más, no llegarás a profesor
Castelar became one of the most important politicians of his time
Castelar llegó a ser uno de los políticos más importantes de su época
Football became an obsession for him
El fútbol llegó a ser una obsesión para él

• Use **convertirse en** for long-lasting changes in character, substance and kind which take place gradually:

Those youngsters went on to become delinquents
Aquellos jóvenes se convirtieron después en delincuentes
Over the years I have become a more tolerant person
Con los años me he convertido en una persona más tolerante
Water turns into steam
El agua se convierte en vapor

• Use **quedar(se)** + ADJECTIVE to talk about changes, particularly when they are permanent, for the worse and due to external circumstances. Their onset may or may not be sudden:

She became a widow
(Se) quedó viuda

• To translate **have turned into** *or* **have become** *etc* + NOUN in emphatic phrases particularly about people, you can use **estar hecho un(a)** + NOUN:

Juan has become a really good pianist
Juan está hecho todo un pianista

For further uses and examples, see main entries at ***become***, ***go***, ***get*** *and* ***turn***.

en; **the building has ~ a cinema** el edificio se ha convertido *or* transformado en cine; **the gas ~s liquid** el gas se convierte en líquido
[3] (= *acquire position of*) (*through study*) hacerse; (*by promotion etc*) llegar a ser; **to ~ a doctor** hacerse médico; **to ~ professor** llegar a ser catedrático; **he became king in 1911** subió al trono en 1911; **later this lady became his wife** esta dama llegó a ser su esposa más tarde; **to ~ a father** convertirse en padre
Ⓑ IMPERS VB **what has ~ of him?** ¿qué ha sido de él?; **what will ~ of me?** ¿qué será de mí?; **whatever can have ~ of that book?** ¿dónde estará ese libro?
Ⓒ VT (= *look nice on*) favorecer, sentar bien; **that thought does not ~ you** ese pensamiento es indigno de ti

becoming† [bɪ'kʌmɪŋ] ADJ [1] (= *fetching*) [*clothes, hairstyle, hat*] favorecedor, sentador (*LAm*); **that dress is very ~** ese vestido es muy favorecedor, ese vestido te sienta muy bien
[2] (= *suitable*) [*conduct, language*] apropiado; **it is not ~ for young ladies to speak like that** no es apropiado que las señoritas hablen así, no es propio de señoritas hablar así

becomingly† [bɪ'kʌmɪŋlɪ] ADV [1] (= *fetchingly*) [*blush, smile*] de forma encantadora; [*dress*] de modo favorecedor
[2] (= *suitably*) apropiadamente

becquerel [ˌbekə'rel] N becquerelio *m*

BECTU ['bɛktu] N ABBR (*Brit*) = **Broadcasting, Entertainment, Cinematographic and Theatre Union**

BEd [biː'ed] N ABBR = **Bachelor of Education**

bed [bed] Ⓐ N [1] (= *furniture*) cama *f*; **I was in ~** estaba en la cama; **could you give me a ~ for the night?** ¿me puede hospedar *or* alojar esta noche?; **to get into ~** meterse en la cama; **to get sb into ~** (= *have sex*) llevarse a algn a la cama; **to get into ~ with sb** (*fig*) (= *agree to work together*) aliarse con algn; **to go to ~** acostarse; **to go to ~ with sb** acostarse con algn; **to make the ~** hacer la cama; **to put a child to ~** acostar a un niño; **to put a paper to ~** terminar la redacción de un número; **to stay in ~** (*because ill*) guardar cama; (*because lazy*) quedarse en la cama; **to take to one's ~** irse a la cama; ✦*IDIOMS* **to get out of ~ (on) the wrong side** (*Brit*) ◊ **get up (on) the wrong side of the ~** (*US*) levantarse con el pie izquierdo; **you've made your ~, now you must lie in** *or* **on it** quien mala cama hace en ella se yace
[2] [*of animal*] lecho *m*
[3] [*of river*] cauce *m*, lecho *m*; [*of sea*] fondo *m*
[4] (= *flower bed*) arriate *m*, parterre *m*; (= *vegetable bed*) arriate *m*; (= *oyster bed*) banco *m*, vivero *m*; ✦*IDIOM* **his life's no ~ of roses** su vida no es un lecho de rosas
[5] (= *layer*) [*of coal, ore*] estrato *m*, capa *f*; (*in road-building*) capa *f*; (*Archit, Tech*) base *f*; **served on a ~ of lettuce/rice** servido sobre una base de lechuga/arroz
Ⓑ VT [1] (*Archit etc*) fijar, engastar
[2] (†*) [+ *woman*] llevar a la cama, acostarse con
Ⓒ CPD ► **bed and board** N comida *f* y cama, pensión *f* completa ► **bed and breakfast** N pensión *f* (con desayuno) ► **bed bath** N (*Med*) **they gave her a ~ bath** la lavaron en la cama ► **bed jacket** N mañanita *f* ► **bed linen** N ropa *f* de cama ► **bed of nails** N cama *f* de clavos ► **bed rest** N reposo *m* en cama ► **bed settee** N sofá-cama *m*

►**bed down** Ⓐ VI + ADV (= *go to bed*) acostarse
Ⓑ VT + ADV [+ *children*] acostar; [+ *animals*] hacer un lecho para

►**bed out** VT + ADV [+ *plants*] plantar en un macizo

BED AND BREAKFAST

Se llama **Bed and Breakfast** *a una casa particular de hospedaje tanto en el campo como en la ciudad, que ofrece cama y desayuno a tarifas inferiores a las de un hotel. El servicio se suele anunciar con carteles colocados en las ventanas del establecimiento, en el jardín o en la carretera y en ellos aparece a menudo únicamente el símbolo* **B&B**.

bedaub [bɪ'dɔːb] VT embadurnar

bedbug ['bedbʌg] N chinche *m or f*

bedclothes ['bedkləʊðz] NPL ropa *fsing* de cama

bedcover ['bedkʌvəʳ] N = **bedspread**

bedcovers ['bedkʌvəz] NPL mantas *fpl*, frazadas *fpl* (*LAm*)

-bedded ['bedɪd] ADJ (*ending in compounds*) **twin-bedded room** habitación *f* doble

bedding ['bedɪŋ] Ⓐ N ropa *f* de cama; (*for animal*) cama *f*
Ⓑ CPD ► **bedding plant** N planta *f* de parterre

Bede [biːd] N Beda; **the Venerable ~** el venerable Beda

bedeck [bɪ'dek] VT adornar, engalanar

bedevil [bɪ'devəl] VT **to be ~led by problems** [*project*] estar plagado de problemas; **the team has been ~led by injuries** el equipo ha sufrido muchas lesiones; **an industry ~led by rising costs** una industria aquejada por el aumento de los costes

bedfellow ['bedfeləʊ] N compañero/a *m/f* de cama; **they are** *or* **make strange ~s** (*fig*) forman una extraña pareja

bedhead ['bedhed] N testero *m*, cabecera *f*

bedlam ['bedləm] N [1] (= *uproar*) alboroto *m*; **it was sheer ~** la confusión era total; **~**

broke out se armó la de San Quintín*
2 (*Hist*) (= *asylum*) manicomio *m*

bedmate [ˈbedmeɪt] N = **bedfellow**

Bedouin [ˈbedʊɪn] Ⓐ ADJ beduino
Ⓑ N (*pl* **Bedouin** *or* **Bedouins**) beduino/a *m/f*

bedpan [ˈbedpæn] N bacinilla *f* (de cama), cuña *f*

bedpost [ˈbedpəʊst] N columna *f or* pilar *m* de cama

bedraggled [bɪˈdrægld] ADJ [*person*] desaliñado; [*hair, feathers, fur*] enmarañado; [*flowers*] mustio

bedridden [ˈbedrɪdn] ADJ postrado en la cama

bedrock [ˈbedrɒk] N (*Geol*) lecho *m* de roca; (*fig*) lo fundamental, base *f*; ✦*IDIOM* **to get down to ~** ir a lo fundamental

bedroll [ˈbedrəʊl] N petate *m*

bedroom [ˈbedrʊm] Ⓐ N dormitorio *m*, habitación *f*, recámara *f* (*CAm, Mex*); **three-~ flat** piso *m or* (*LAm*) departamento *m* de tres dormitorios
Ⓑ CPD ► **bedroom eyes*** NPL ojos *mpl* seductores ► **bedroom farce** N (*Theat*) comedia *f* de alcoba ► **bedroom slippers** NPL pantuflas *fpl*, zapatillas *fpl* (*Sp*) ► **bedroom suburb** N (*US*) ciudad *f* dormitorio ► **bedroom suite** N juego *m* de muebles para dormitorio

-bedroomed [ˈbedrʊmd] ADJ (*ending in compounds*) **a five-bedroomed house** una casa con cinco dormitorios

Beds [beds] N ABBR (*Brit*) = **Bedfordshire**

bedside [ˈbedsaɪd] Ⓐ N cabecera *f*; **to wait at the ~ of** esperar a la cabecera de
Ⓑ CPD ► **bedside lamp** N lámpara *f* de noche ► **bedside manner** N **to have a good ~ manner** tener mucho tacto con los enfermos ► **bedside rug** N alfombrilla *f* de cama ► **bedside table** N mesilla *f* de noche

bedsit* [ˈbedsɪt] N, **bedsitter** [ˈbedˈsɪtəʳ] N, **bedsitting room** [ˈbedˈsɪtɪŋrʊm] N (*Brit*) *habitación amueblada, cuyo alquiler incluye cocina y baño comunes*

bedsocks [ˈbedsɒks] NPL calcetines *mpl* de cama

bedsore [ˈbedsɔːʳ] N úlcera *f* de decúbito

bedspread [ˈbedspred] N colcha *f*, cubrecama *m*

bedstead [ˈbedsted] N cuja *f*, armazón *m or f* de cama

bedstraw [ˈbedstrɔː] N (*Bot*) cuajaleche *m*, amor *m* de hortelano

bedtime [ˈbedtaɪm] Ⓐ N hora *f* de acostarse; **it's past your ~** ya deberías estar acostado; **ten o'clock is my usual ~** normalmente me voy a la cama a las diez; **bedtime!** ¡a la cama!
Ⓑ CPD ► **bedtime story** N cuento *m* (*para dormir a un niño*)

bed-wetting [ˈbedwetɪŋ] N incontinencia *f* nocturna, enuresis *f* (*frm*)

bedworthy* [ˈbed,wɜːðɪ] ADJ atractivo

bee [biː] Ⓐ N 1 (*Zool*) abeja *f*; ✦*IDIOMS* **to have a ~ in one's bonnet about sth** tener algo metido entre ceja y ceja; **he thinks he's the ~'s knees*** se cree la mar de listo *or* de elegante* *etc*
2 (*esp US*) círculo *m* social; *see also* **spelling**
Ⓑ CPD ► **bee eater** N (*Orn*) abejaruco *m*

Beeb* [biːb] N **the ~** (*Brit*) la BBC

beech [biːtʃ] Ⓐ N (= *tree*) haya *f*; (= *wood*) hayedo *m*
Ⓑ CPD ► **beech grove** N hayal *m* ► **beech tree** N haya *f*

beechmast [ˈbiːtʃmɑːst] N hayucos *mpl*

beechnut [ˈbiːtʃnʌt] N hayuco *m*

beechwood [ˈbiːtʃwʊd] N 1 (= *group of trees*) hayedo *m*, hayal *m*
2 (= *material*) (madera *f* de) haya *f*

beef [biːf] Ⓐ N 1 (*Culin*) carne *f* de vaca *or* (*LAm*) de res; **roast ~** rosbif *m*, carne *f* asada (*LAm*)
2 (*) (= *brawn*) músculos *mpl*
3 (*esp US**) (= *complaint*) queja *f*
Ⓑ VI (*) (= *complain*) quejarse (**about** de)
Ⓒ CPD ► **beef cattle** N ganado *m* vacuno ► **beef olive** N *picadillo envuelto en una lonja de carne y cocinado en salsa* ► **beef sausage** N salchicha *f* de carne de vaca ► **beef tea** N caldo *m* de carne (*para enfermos*)

►**beef up*** VT + ADV [+ *essay, speech*] reforzar, fortalecer

beefburger [ˈbiːf,bɜːgəʳ] N hamburguesa *f*

beefcake* [ˈbiːfkeɪk] N (*hum*) cachas* *m inv*

beefeater [ˈbiːf,iːtəʳ] N (*Brit*) alabardero *m* de la Torre de Londres

beefsteak [ˈbiːfsteɪk] N biftec *m*, bistec *m*, bife *m* (*S. Cone*)

beefy* [ˈbiːfɪ] ADJ (*compar* **beefier**; *superl* **beefiest**) (= *brawny*) fornido

beehive [ˈbiːhaɪv] N colmena *f*

beekeeper [ˈbiːkiːpəʳ] N apicultor(a) *m/f*, colmenero/a *m/f*

beekeeping [ˈbiː,kiːpɪŋ] N apicultura *f*

beeline [ˈbiːlaɪn] N ✦*IDIOM* **to make a ~ for sth/sb** ir directo *or* derecho a algo/algn

Beelzebub [biːˈelzɪbʌb] N Belcebú

been [biːn] PP *of* **be**

beep [biːp] Ⓐ N (*Brit*) pitido *m*; **please leave a message after the ~** deje un mensaje después de la señal
Ⓑ VI sonar
Ⓒ VT [+ *horn*] tocar

beeper [ˈbiːpəʳ] N localizador *m*, busca* *m*

beer [bɪəʳ] Ⓐ N cerveza *f*; **draught ~** cerveza *f* de barril; **light/dark ~** cerveza *f* rubia/negra; **we're only here for the ~** (*hum*) venimos en plan de diversión; ✦*IDIOM* **life isn't all ~ and skittles** (*Brit*) la vida no es un lecho de rosas, la vida no es todo Jauja*; *see also* **small A1**
Ⓑ CPD ► **beer barrel** N barril *m* de cerveza ► **beer belly*** N panza* *f* (*de beber cerveza*) ► **beer bottle** N botella *f* de cerveza ► **beer can** N bote *m or* lata *f* de cerveza ► **beer garden** N terraza *f* de verano, jardín *m* (de un bar) ► **beer glass** N jarra *f* de cerveza ► **beer gut*** N = **beer belly**

beerfest [ˈbɪəfest] N (*US*) festival *m* cervecero

beermat [ˈbɪəmæt] N posavasos *m inv*

beery [ˈbɪərɪ] ADJ [*smell*] a cerveza; [*person*] muy aficionado a la cerveza; [*party*] donde se bebe mucha cerveza; **it was a ~ affair** allí se bebió una barbaridad

beeswax [ˈbiːzwæks] N cera *f* de abejas

beet [biːt] Ⓐ N 1 (= *crop*) remolacha *f* forrajera
2 (*US*) = **beetroot**
Ⓑ CPD ► **beet sugar** N azúcar *m* de remolacha

beetle [ˈbiːtl] N escarabajo *m*

►**beetle off*** VI + ADV (*Brit*) marcharse

beetle-browed [ˈbiːtlˈbraʊd] ADJ cejialto, de cejas muy espesas

beetroot [ˈbiːtruːt] N (*Brit*) remolacha *f*, betabel *m* (*Mex*), betarraga *f* (*Chile, Bol*)

befall [bɪˈfɔːl] (*pt* **befell**; *pp* **befallen**) (*liter*) Ⓐ VT acontecer a, suceder a
Ⓑ VI acontecer, suceder; **whatever may ~** pase lo que pase

befallen [bɪˈfɔːlən] PP *of* **befall**

befell [bɪˈfel] PT *of* **befall**

befit [bɪˈfɪt] VT (*frm*) corresponder a; **he writes beautifully, as ~s a poet** escribe con gran belleza, como corresponde a un poeta; **it ill ~s him to speak thus** no es la persona más indicada para decir eso; **they offered him a post ~ting his experience** le ofrecieron un puesto acorde a su experiencia

befitting [bɪˈfɪtɪŋ] ADJ (*frm*) apropiado

befog [bɪˈfɒg] VT (*liter*) (= *confuse*) [+ *issue etc*] entenebrecer; [+ *person*] ofuscar, confundir

before [bɪˈfɔːʳ]

When ***before*** *is an element in a phrasal verb, eg* ***come before, go before****, look up the verb.*

Ⓐ PREP 1 (*in time, order, rank*) antes de; **~ Christ** antes de Cristo; **the week ~ last** hace dos semanas; **~ long** (*in future*) antes de poco; (*in past*) poco después; **~ going, would you ...** antes de marcharte, quieres ...; **income ~ tax** renta *f* bruta *or* antes de impuestos; **profits ~ tax** beneficios *mpl* preimpositivos
2 (*in place*) delante de; (= *in the presence of*) ante, delante de, en presencia de; **they were married ~ a judge** se casaron en presencia de un juez
3 (= *facing*) **the question ~ us** (*in meeting*) el asunto que tenemos que discutir; **the problem ~ us is ...** el problema que se nos plantea es ...; **the task ~ us** la tarea que tenemos por delante; **we still have two hours ~ us** tenemos todavía dos horas por delante; **a new life lay ~ him** una vida nueva se abría ante él
4 (= *rather than*) **I should choose this one ~ that** yo escogería éste antes que aquél; **death ~ dishonour!** ¡antes la muerte que el deshonor!
Ⓑ ADV 1 (*time*) antes; **a moment ~** un momento antes; **the day ~** el día anterior; **~, it used to be different** antes, todo era distinto; **on this occasion and the one ~** en esta ocasión y la anterior
2 (*place, order*) delante, adelante; **~ and behind** por delante y por detrás; **that chapter and the one ~** ese capítulo y el anterior
Ⓒ CONJ (*time*) antes de que; (*rather than*) antes que

beforehand [bɪˈfɔːhænd] ADV de antemano, con antelación

befoul [bɪˈfaʊl] VT (*liter*) ensuciar

befriend [bɪˈfrend] VT entablar amistad con, hacerse amigo de

befuddle [bɪˈfʌdl] VT (= *confuse*) atontar, confundir; (= *make tipsy*) atontar

befuddled [bɪˈfʌdld] ADJ (= *confused*) aturdido; **~ with drink** atontado por la bebida

beg [beg] Ⓐ VT 1 (= *implore*) rogar, suplicar; **I ~ you!** ¡te lo suplico!; **to ~ forgiveness** suplicar *or* implorar perdón; **he ~ged my help** suplicó mi ayuda; **to ~ sb for sth** suplicar algo a algn; **he ~ged me to help him** me suplicó que le ayudara; **I ~ to inform you** (*frm*) tengo el honor de informarle; **I ~ to differ** siento tener que disentir; ✦*IDIOM* **to ~ the question**: **some definitions of mental illness ~ the question of what constitutes normal behaviour** algunas definiciones de enfermedad mental dan por sentado lo que constituye un comportamiento normal
2 [*beggar*] [+ *food, money*] pedir; **he ~ged a pound** pidió una libra
Ⓑ VI 1 (= *implore*) **to ~ for** [+ *forgiveness, mercy*] implorar
2 [*beggar*] mendigar, pedir limosna; **there's some cake going ~ging*** queda un poco de tarta, ¿no la quiere nadie?

►**beg off*** VI + ADV (*US*) dar una excusa

BEFORE

Time

Adverb

• When **before** is an *adverb*, you can usually translate it using **antes**:

Why didn't you say so before?
¿Por qué no lo has dicho antes?
I had spoken to her before
Había hablado con ella antes

• But the **before** in **never before** and **ever before** is often not translated:

I've never been to Spain before
Nunca he estado en España
I had never been to a police station before
Nunca había estado (antes) en una comisaría
It's not true that the working class is earning more money than ever before
No es cierto que la clase obrera gane más dinero que nunca

• **The day/night/week** *etc* **before** should usually be translated using **el día/la noche/la semana anterior**:

The night before, he had gone to a rock concert
La noche anterior había ido a un concierto de rock

• In more formal contexts, where **before** could be substituted by **previously**, **anteriormente** is another option:

As I said before...
Como he dicho antes *or* ***anteriormente...***

• When **before** is equivalent to **already**, translate using **ya** (**antes**) or, in questions about whether someone has done what they are doing now before, using **¿es la primera vez que...?**:

"How about watching this film?" - "Actually, I've seen it before"
—¿Vemos esa película? —"Es que ya la he visto"
I had been to Glasgow a couple of times before
Ya había estado (antes) en Glasgow un par de veces
Have you been to Spain before?
¿Has estado ya en España? *or* ***¿Es la primera vez que vienes a España?***

• Translate **PERIOD OF TIME** + **before** using **hacía** + **PERIOD OF TIME**:

They had married nearly 40 years before
Se habían casado hacía casi 40 años

! Hacía is invariable in this sense.

Preposition

• When **before** is a *preposition*, you can usually translate it using **antes de**:

Please ring before seven
Por favor, llama antes de las siete
Shall we go for a walk before dinner?
¿Nos vamos a dar un paseo antes de cenar?

• But use **antes que** with names of people and personal pronouns when they stand in for a verb:

If you get there before me *or* before I do, wait for me in the bar
Si llegas antes que yo, espérame en el bar

• Translate **before** + **-ING** using **antes de** + **INFINITIVE**:

He said goodbye to the children before leaving
Se despidió de los niños antes de irse

Conjunction

• When **before** is a *conjunction*, you can usually translate it using **antes de que** + **SUBJUNCTIVE**:

I'll ask Peter about it before he goes away on holiday
Se lo preguntaré a Peter antes de que se vaya de vacaciones
We reached home before the storm broke
Llegamos a casa antes de que empezara la tormenta

• If the subject of both clauses is the same, **antes de** + **INFINITIVE** is usually used rather than **antes de que**:

Give me a ring before you leave the office
Llámame antes de salir de la oficina

NOTE: This construction is also sometimes used in colloquial Spanish when the subjects are different:

Before you arrived she was very depressed
Antes de llegar tú, estaba muy deprimida

For further uses and examples, see main entry.

began [bɪˈgæn] PT *of* **begin**

beget [bɪˈget] (*pt* **begot**, **begat** [bɪˈgæt]; *pp* **begotten**) VT (*frm*) engendrar (*also fig*)

begetter [bɪˈgetəʳ] N (*frm*) creador(a) *m/f*, instigador(a) *m/f*

beggar [ˈbegəʳ] Ⓐ N [1] mendigo/a *m/f*, pordiosero/a *m/f*; ✦*PROV* **~s can't be choosers** a buen hambre no hay pan duro
[2] (*) (= *fellow*) tío/a* *m/f*; **lucky ~!** ¡qué suerte tiene el tío/la tía!*; **poor little ~!** ¡pobrecito!
Ⓑ VT [1] (= *ruin*) arruinar
[2] (*fig*) (= *exceed*) excederse a; **it ~s description** es imposible describirlo; **it ~s belief** resulta totalmente inverosímil

beggarly [ˈbegəlɪ] ADJ miserable

beggary [ˈbegərɪ] N (*frm*) mendicidad *f*; **to reduce to ~** reducir a la miseria

begging [ˈbegɪŋ] Ⓐ N mendicidad *f*
Ⓑ CPD ► **begging bowl** N platillo *m* para limosnas; **to hold out a ~ bowl** (*fig*) pasar el platillo ► **begging letter** N *carta en la que se pide dinero*

▼**begin** [bɪˈgɪn] (*pt* **began**; *pp* **begun**) Ⓐ VT [1] (= *start*) empezar, comenzar; **to ~ doing sth** ◊ **~ to do sth** empezar a hacer algo; **it's ~ning to rain** está empezando a llover; **he ~s the day with a glass of orange juice** empieza el día con un zumo de naranja; **I can't ~ to thank you** no encuentro palabras para agradecerle; **it doesn't ~ to compare with ...** no puede ni compararse con ...; **this skirt began life as an evening dress** esta falda empezó siendo un traje de noche
[2] (= *undertake*) emprender; (= *set in motion*) iniciar; [+ *discussion*] entablar; **I was foolish ever to ~ it** hice mal en emprenderlo
Ⓑ VI [1] (= *start*) empezar, comenzar, iniciarse (*frm*); **the work will ~ tomorrow** el trabajo empezará *or* comenzará mañana; **the teacher began by writing on the board** el profesor empezó escribiendo en la pizarra; **let me ~ by saying ...** quiero comenzar diciendo ...; **~ning from Monday** a partir del lunes; **to ~ on sth** emprender algo; **to ~ with sth** comenzar por *or* con algo; **to ~ with, I'd like to know ...** en primer lugar, quisiera saber ...; **to ~ with there were only two of us** al principio sólo éramos dos
[2] (= *originate*) [*river*] nacer; [*rumour, custom*] originarse

beginner [bɪˈgɪnəʳ] N principiante *mf*; **it's just ~'s luck** es la suerte del principiante

beginning [bɪˈgɪnɪŋ] N [1] [*of speech, book, film etc*] principio *m*, comienzo *m*; **at the ~ of** al principio de; **at the ~ of the century** a principios de siglo; **the ~ of the end** el principio del fin; **right from the ~** desde el principio; **from ~ to end** de principio a fin, desde el principio hasta el final; **in the ~** al principio; **to make a ~** empezar
[2] (= *origin*) origen *m*; **from humble ~s** de orígenes modestos; **Buddhism had its ~s ...** el budismo tuvo sus orígenes ...; **he had the ~s of a beard** tenía un asomo de barba

begone†† [bɪˈgɒn] EXCL (*liter*) ¡fuera de aquí!

begonia [bɪˈgəʊnɪə] N begonia *f*

begot [bɪˈgɒt] PT *of* **beget**

begotten [bɪˈgɒtn] PP *of* **beget**; **God gave His only Begotten Son** Dios entregó a su Unigénito

begrime [bɪˈgraɪm] VT (*liter*) tiznar, ensuciar

begrudge [bɪˈgrʌdʒ] VT [1] (= *envy*) **to ~ sb sth** envidiar algo a algn; **I don't ~ him his success** no le envidio su éxito
[2] (= *give reluctantly*) dar de mala gana; **I don't ~ all the money I've spent** no me duele todo el dinero que he gastado

begrudgingly [bɪˈgrʌdʒɪŋlɪ] ADV de mala gana, a regañadientes

beguile [bɪˈgaɪl] VT [1] (= *deceive*) **to ~ sb into doing sth** engatusar a algn para que haga algo
[2] (= *enchant*) seducir, cautivar
[3] (*liter*) (= *pass*) [+ *time*] pasar (*de manera entretenida*)

beguiling [bɪˈgaɪlɪŋ] ADJ seductor, persuasivo

begun [bɪˈgʌn] PP *of* **begin**

behalf [bɪˈhɑːf] N **on** *or* (*US*) **in ~ of** en nombre de, de parte de; **a collection on ~ of orphans** una colecta en beneficio de los huérfanos, una colecta para los huérfanos; **I interceded on his ~** intercedí por él; **don't worry on my ~** no te preocupes por mí

behave [bɪˈheɪv] VI [1] [*person*] portarse (**to, towards** con), comportarse; **he ~d like an idiot** se comportó como un idiota; **to ~ (o.s.)** portarse bien; **did the children ~ themselves?** ¿se portaron bien los niños?; **~ (yourself)!** ¡compórtate!, ¡pórtate bien!; **if you ~ (yourself)** si te portas bien, si te comportas debidamente
[2] (*Mech etc*) funcionar

behaviour, **behavior** (*US*) [bɪˈheɪvjəʳ] Ⓐ N [1] [*of person*] conducta *f*, comportamiento *m*; **good ~** buena conducta *f*; **to be on one's best ~** comportarse lo mejor posible; **you must be on your best ~** tienes que portarte lo mejor posible
[2] (*Mech etc*) funcionamiento *m*
Ⓑ CPD ► **behaviour pattern** N patrón *m* de conducta

behavioural, **behavioral** (*US*) [bɪˈheɪvjərəl] ADJ [*problems, changes*] conductual; [*theory, science*] conductista

behaviourism, **behaviorism** (*US*) [bɪˈheɪvjərɪzəm] N conductismo *m*, behaviorismo *m*

behaviourist, **behaviorist** (*US*) [bɪˈheɪvjərɪst] Ⓐ ADJ conductista, behaviorista
Ⓑ N conductista *mf*, behaviorista *mf*

behead [bɪˈhed] VT decapitar

beheld [bɪˈheld] PT, PP *of* **behold**

behemoth [bɪˈhiːmɒθ] N (*liter*) (= *monster*) gigante *m*

behest [bɪˈhest] N (*frm*) **at his ~** a petición suya

behind [bɪˈhaɪnd]

*When **behind** is an element in a phrasal verb, eg **fall behind**, **stay behind**, look up the verb.*

Ⓐ PREP [1] (= *to the rear of*) detrás de; **~ the door** detrás de la puerta; **look ~ you!** ¡cuidado atrás!; **with his hands ~ his back** las ma-

➤ LANGUAGE IN USE: **begin B** 26.1

nos en la espalda
[2] (= *responsible for*) detrás de; **what's ~ all this?** ¿qué hay detrás de todo esto?
[3] (= *less advanced than*) **Hill is nine points ~ Schumacher** Hill tiene nueve puntos menos que Schumacher; **we're well ~ them in technology** nos dejan muy atrás *or* estamos muy a la zaga de ellos en tecnología
[4] (= *supporting*) **his family is ~ him** tiene el apoyo de su familia
[5] (= *in the past of*) **it's all ~ us now** todo eso ha quedado ya atrás
[6] (= *to one's credit*) **she has four novels ~ her** tiene cuatro novelas en el haber
Ⓑ ADV [1] (= *in or at the rear*) detrás, atrás; **to come from ~** venir desde atrás; **to follow close ~** seguir muy de cerca; **to attack sb from ~** atacar a algn por la espalda; **to leave sth ~** olvidar algo
[2] (= *behind schedule*) **to be a bit ~** estar algo atrasadillo; **to be ~ with the rent** tener atrasos de alquiler; **to be ~ with one's work** estar atrasado en el trabajo
[3] (= *less advanced*) **Pepe won with Paco only two strokes ~** ganó Pepe con Paco a sólo dos golpes de distancia
Ⓒ N (*) trasero *m*

behindhand [bɪ'haɪndhænd] ADV atrasado, con retraso

behold [bɪ'həʊld] (*pt, pp* **beheld**) VT (*liter*) contemplar; **behold!** ¡mire!; **~ the results!** ¡he aquí los resultados!; *see also* **lo**

beholden [bɪ'həʊldən] ADJ (*frm*) **to be ~ to sb** tener obligaciones con algn

beholder [bɪ'həʊldə'] N espectador(a) *m/f*, observador(a) *m/f*

behove, [bɪ'həʊv], **behoove** (*US*) [bɪ'huːv] IMPERS VT (*frm*) **it ~s him to** + INFIN le incumbe + *infin*

beige [beɪʒ] Ⓐ ADJ (color) beige *inv*
Ⓑ N beige *m*

Beijing ['beɪ'dʒɪŋ] N Pekín *m*

being ['biːɪŋ] N [1] (= *existence*) existencia *f*; **in ~** existente; **to come** *or* **be brought into ~** nacer
[2] (= *creature*) ser *m*; *see also* **human**

Beirut [beɪ'ruːt] N Beirut *m*

bejewelled, **bejeweled** (*US*) [bɪ'dʒuːəld] ADJ enjoyado

belabour, **belabor** (*US*) [bɪ'leɪbə'] VT (= *beat*) apalear; (*fig*) (*with insults*) atacar; (*with questions*) asediar (**with** con)

Belarus [belə'rʊs] N Bielorrusia *f*

Belarussian [ˌbelə'rʌʃən] Ⓐ ADJ bielorruso
Ⓑ N [1] (= *person*) bielorruso/a *m/f*
[2] (*Ling*) bielorruso *m*

belated [bɪ'leɪtɪd] ADJ tardío, atrasado

belatedly [bɪ'leɪtɪdlɪ] ADV con retraso

belay [bɪ'leɪ] VT amarrar (*dando vueltas en una cabilla*)

belch [beltʃ] Ⓐ N eructo *m*
Ⓑ VI eructar
Ⓒ VT (*also* **~ out**) [+ *smoke, flames*] arrojar, vomitar

beleaguered [bɪ'liːgəd] ADJ [1] [*city*] asediado
[2] (*fig*) (= *harassed*) atormentado, acosado

Belfast ['belfaːst] N Belfast *m*

belfry ['belfrɪ] N campanario *m*

Belgian ['beldʒən] Ⓐ ADJ belga
Ⓑ N belga *mf*

Belgium ['beldʒəm] N Bélgica *f*

Belgrade [bel'greɪd] N Belgrado *m*

belie [bɪ'laɪ] VT (= *fail to justify*) [+ *hopes etc*] defraudar; (= *prove false*) [+ *words*] contradecir, desmentir

▼**belief** [bɪ'liːf] N [1] (= *tenet, doctrine*) creencia *f*; (= *trust*) confianza *f*; (= *opinion*) opinión *f*; **contrary to popular ~ ...** al contrario de lo que muchos creen ...; **a man of strong ~s** un hombre de firmes convicciones; **to the best of my ~** según mi leal saber y entender; **it is my ~ that ...** estoy convencido de que ...; **I did it in the ~ that ...** lo hice creyendo que ...; **it's beyond ~** es increíble (**that** que); **wealthy beyond ~** de una fortuna increíble
[2] (*no pl*) (= *faith*) fe *f*; **his ~ in God** su fe en Dios

believable [bɪ'liːvəbl] ADJ creíble, verosímil

▼**believe** [bɪ'liːv] Ⓐ VT [1] (= *think*) creer; **I ~ so** creo que sí; **I ~ not** creo que no; **he is ~d to be abroad** se cree que está en el extranjero
[2] [+ *story, evidence, person*] creer; **don't you ~ it!** ¡no te lo creas!; **~ it or not, she bought it** aunque parezca mentira, lo compró; **it was hot, ~ (you) me** hacía calor, ¡y cómo!; **I couldn't ~ my eyes** no podía dar crédito a mis ojos; **do you really ~ the threat?** ¿crees de veras en la amenaza?; **I would never have ~d it of him** jamás le hubiera creído capaz de eso
Ⓑ VI creer; **to ~ in God** creer en Dios; **I don't ~ in corporal punishment** no soy partidario del castigo corporal; **we don't ~ in drugs** no aprobamos el uso de las drogas

believer [bɪ'liːvə'] N [1] (*Rel*) creyente *mf*, fiel *mf*
[2] (= *advocate*) partidario/a *m/f*; **to be a great ~ in ...** ser muy partidario de ...; **I am a ~ in letting things take their course** soy partidario de dejar que las cosas sigan su propio curso

Belisha beacon† [bɪˌlɪʃə'biːkən] N poste *m* luminoso (*de cruce de peatones*)

belittle [bɪ'lɪtl] VT (= *demean*) menospreciar; (= *minimize*) quitar importancia a, minimizar

Belize [be'liːz] N Belice *m*

Belizean [be'liːzɪən] Ⓐ ADJ beliceño
Ⓑ N beliceño/a *m/f*

bell [bel] Ⓐ N [1] (= *church bell*) campana *f*; (= *handbell*) campanilla *f*; (= *doorbell, electric bell*) timbre *m*; (*for cow*) cencerro *m*; (*for cat, on toy, dress etc*) cascabel *m*; **two/eight** *etc* **~s** (*Naut*) *las medias horas de cada guardia marítima*; ✦**IDIOMS** **to ring a ~**: **that rings a ~** eso me suena; **it doesn't ring a ~ with me** no me suena; **he was saved by the ~** (*lit*) (*Boxing*) le salvó la campana; (*fig*) se salvó por los pelos*
[2] [*of trumpet*] pabellón *m*; [*of flower*] campanilla *f*
[3] (*Brit**) (= *phone call*) **I'll give you a ~** te llamaré
Ⓑ CPD ► **bell glass**, **bell jar** N fanal *m*, campana *f* de cristal ► **bell pull** N campanilla *f* ► **bell push** N pulsador *m* de timbre ► **bell rope** N cuerda *f* de campana ► **bells and whistles*** NPL (*esp Comput*) elementos *mpl* accesorios; (*pej*) florituras *fpl* ► **bell tent** N pabellón *m* ► **bell tower** N campanario *m*

belladonna [ˌbelə'dɒnə] Ⓐ N (*Bot, Med*) belladona *f*
Ⓑ CPD ► **belladonna lily** N azucena *f* rosa

bell-bottomed ['bel'bɒtəmd] ADJ [*trousers*] acampanado

bell-bottoms ['bel'bɔtəmz] NPL pantalones *mpl* de campana

bellboy ['belbɔɪ] N botones *m inv*

bellbuoy ['belbɔɪ] N boya *f* de campana

belle [bel] N **the ~ of the ball** la reina del baile

belles-lettres ['bel'letr] NPL bellas letras *fpl*

bellhop ['belhɒp] N (*US*) botones *m inv*

bellicose ['belɪkəʊs] ADJ belicoso

bellicosity [ˌbelɪ'kɒsɪtɪ] N belicosidad *f*

belligerence [bɪ'lɪdʒərəns] N, **belligerency** [bɪ'lɪdʒərənsɪ] N agresividad *f*

belligerent [bɪ'lɪdʒərənt] Ⓐ ADJ beligerante
Ⓑ N parte *f* beligerante

belligerently [bɪ'lɪdʒərəntlɪ] ADV agresivamente

bellow ['beləʊ] Ⓐ N [*of bull etc*] bramido *m*; [*of person*] rugido *m*
Ⓑ VI [*animal*] bramar; [*person*] rugir
Ⓒ VT (*also* **~ out**) [+ *order, song*] gritar

bellows ['beləʊz] NPL fuelle *msing*; **a pair of ~** un fuelle

bell-ringer ['belˌrɪŋə'] N campanero/a *m/f*; (*as hobby*) campanólogo/a *m/f*

bell-ringing ['belˌrɪŋɪŋ] N campanología *f*

bell-shaped ['belʃeɪpt] ADJ acampanado

belly ['belɪ] Ⓐ N [1] (= *abdomen*) barriga* *f*, guata *f* (*Chile**)
[2] [*of vessel*] barriga *f*
Ⓑ VI (*also* **~ out**) [*sail*] hincharse
Ⓒ CPD ► **belly button*** N ombligo *m* ► **belly dance** N danza *f* del vientre ► **belly dancer** N danzarina *f* del vientre ► **belly flop** N panzazo* *m*; **to do a ~ flop** dar(se) un panzazo* ► **belly landing** N (*Aer*) aterrizaje *m* de panza; **to make a ~ landing** aterrizar de panza ► **belly laugh** N carcajada *f* (grosera)

bellyache* ['belɪeɪk] Ⓐ N dolor *m* de barriga*
Ⓑ VI (= *complain*) renegar, echar pestes* (**at** de)

bellyaching* ['belɪˌeɪkɪŋ] N quejas *fpl* constantes

bellyful* ['belɪfʊl] N (*fig*) **I've had a ~ (of)** estoy hasta la coronilla *or* las narices (de)*

belly-up* [ˌbelɪ'ʌp] ADV **to go ~** [*company, scheme*] irse al garete*, irse al traste

belong [bɪ'lɒŋ] VI [1] (= *be possession*) **to ~ to sb** pertenecer a algn; **who does this ~ to?** ¿a quién pertenece esto?, ¿de quién es esto?; **the house/the book doesn't ~ to you** la casa/el libro no te pertenece; **the land ~s to him** la tierra es de su propiedad, la tierra le pertenece
[2] (= *be product*) ser; **the handwriting ~s to a male** la letra es de hombre
[3] (= *be member*) **I used to ~ to the Labour Party** estuve afiliado a *or* fui miembro del partido laborista; **do you ~ to a church?** ¿perteneces a alguna iglesia?; **to ~ to a club** ser socio de un club
[4] (= *be appropriate*) **we truly ~ together** estamos verdaderamente hechos el uno para el otro; **those ideas ~ in the middle ages** esas ideas son de la edad media; **the future ~s to technology** el futuro está en manos de la tecnología
[5] (= *fit in*) **I feel I ~ here** aquí me siento en casa; **he feels the need to ~** siente la necesidad de ser parte de algún grupo; **I don't ~ here** éste no es mi sitio
[6] (= *have rightful place*) **it ~s on the shelf** va en el estante; **your toys don't ~ in the living room** el sitio de tus juguetes no es el salón, tus juguetes no deberían estar en el salón; **go back home where you ~** vuelve a casa, que es donde está tu sitio
[7] (= *be part*) ser; **that top ~s to this bottle** ese tapón es el de esta botella; **it ~s to the rodent family** pertenece a *or* es de la familia de los roedores; **Henry and I ~ to different generations** Henry y yo pertenecemos a distintas generaciones *or* somos de dos generaciones diferentes

➤ LANGUAGE IN USE: **belief 1** 6.2, 26.1 **believe A1** 26.3

belongings [bɪˈlɒŋɪŋz] NPL pertenencias *fpl*; *see also* **personal A2**

Belorussia [ˌbjeləʊˈrʌʃə] N = **Belarus**

Belorussian [ˌbeləʊˈrʌʃən] ADJ, N = **Belarussian**

beloved [bɪˈlʌvɪd] Ⓐ ADJ querido (**by, of** por); **my dearly ~ brethren ...** mis queridos hermanos ...
Ⓑ N querido/a *m/f*, amado/a *m/f*

below [bɪˈləʊ]

*When **below** is an element in a phrasal verb, eg **go below**, look up the verb.*

Ⓐ PREP [1] (= *under*) debajo de, bajo; **~ the bed** debajo de la cama, bajo la cama; **the room ~ this is my study** la habitación que está debajo de ésta es mi estudio; **her skirt reaches well ~ her knees** la falda le llega muy por debajo de las rodillas; **their readership has dropped to ~ 18,000** el número de lectores que tenían ha descendido por debajo de los 18.000; **to be ~ sb in rank** ser inferior a algn en rango; **~ average** inferior al promedio, inferior a *or* por debajo de la media; **~ freezing (point)** bajo cero; **five degrees ~ zero** cinco grados bajo cero; **~ (the) ground** bajo tierra; **temperatures ~ normal** temperaturas inferiores a las normales; **~ sea level** por debajo del nivel del mar; **~ the surface** por debajo de la superficie, bajo la superficie; **~ zero** = **below freezing (point)**
[2] (*Geog*) (= *downstream of*) más abajo de; **the Thames ~ Oxford** el Támesis más abajo de Oxford
Ⓑ ADV [1] (= *beneath*) abajo; **~, we could see the valley** abajo podíamos ver el valle; **the flat ~** el piso de abajo; **they live two floors ~** viven dos pisos más abajo; **decisions occur at departmental level or ~** las decisiones se toman a nivel de departamento o a un nivel inferior; **her name was written ~** su nombre estaba escrito debajo; **it was five (degrees) ~** hacía cinco grados bajo cero; **down ~** abajo; **far ~** mucho más abajo; **from ~** desde abajo; **here ~** (*lit*) aquí abajo; (= *not in sky*) aquí en la tierra; (= *in this life*) en este mundo; **immediately ~** justamente debajo
[2] (*in document*) **see ~** véase más abajo; **as stated ~** como se indica más abajo
[3] (*Naut*) (*also* **~ deck**) abajo; **to go ~** bajar

Belshazzar [belˈʃæzəʳ] N Baltasar; **~'s Feast** la Cena de Baltasar

belt [belt] Ⓐ N [1] (= *garment*) cinturón *m*, fajo *m* (*Mex*); (= *seat belt*) cinturón *m* de seguridad; ✦*IDIOMS* **to tighten one's ~** apretarse el cinturón; **that was below the ~** ese fue un golpe bajo; **he has three novels under his ~** tiene tres novelas en su haber; **it was a ~-and-braces job*** se tomaron todas las precauciones posibles
[2] (*Tech*) (= *conveyor belt etc*) correa *f*, cinta *f*
[3] (*Geog*) (= *zone*) zona *f*; **industrial ~** cinturón *m* industrial
Ⓑ VT (*) (= *thrash*) zurrar (con correa); **he ~ed me one** (= *slap*) me dio una torta*; (= *punch*) me dio un mamporro*
Ⓒ VI (*Brit**) (= *rush*) **he ~ed into the room** entró pitando en la habitación*; **he ~ed down the street** salió pitando por la calle abajo*; **to ~ past** pasar como una bala
Ⓓ CPD ► **belt bag** N riñonera *f*

►**belt along*** VI + ADV ir como una bala

►**belt down*** VT + ADV (*US*) [+ *drink*] cepillarse*

►**belt off*** VI + ADV salir pitando*

►**belt out*** Ⓐ VT + ADV [+ *song*] cantar a pleno pulmón
Ⓑ VI + ADV (*also* **to come ~ing out**) salir disparado

►**belt up** VI + ADV [1] (*Aut*) abrocharse el cinturón
[2] (*Brit**‡) (= *be quiet*) cerrar el pico*, callarse la boca‡; **~ up!** ¡cállate la boca!‡

belter* [ˈbeltəʳ] N [1] (= *singer*) **she's a ~** qué pulmones tiene; (= *song*) *canción cantada a pleno pulmón*
[2] (= *party*) bombazo* *m*

beltway [ˈbeltweɪ] N (*US*) carretera *f* de circunvalación

bemoan [bɪˈməʊn] VT lamentar

bemuse [bɪˈmjuːz] VT aturdir, confundir

bemused [bɪˈmjuːzd] ADJ aturdido, confuso

Ben [ben] N (*familiar form*) *of* **Benjamin**

ben [ben] N (*Scot*) (= *mountain*) montaña *f*; (= *room*) cuarto *m* interior

bench [bentʃ] N [1] (= *seat, workbench*) banco *m*; (*Sport*) banquillo *m*; (= *court*) tribunal *m*; **the Bench** (*Jur*) la magistratura; **to be on the ~** (*Jur*) ser juez, ser magistrado; (*Sport*) estar en el banquillo
[2] **benches** (*Brit Parl*) **on the Tory/Labour ~es** en los escaños conservadores/laboristas

benchmark [ˈbentʃmɑːk] Ⓐ N cota *f*
Ⓑ CPD ► **benchmark price** N precio *m* de referencia

benchwarmer* [ˈbentʃˌwɔːməʳ] N (*US Sport*) calientabanquillos *m*

bend [bend] (*vb: pt, pp* **bent**) Ⓐ N [1] (*gen*) curva *f*; (*in pipe etc*) ángulo *m*; (= *corner*) recodo *m*; (*Naut*) gaza *f*; **"dangerous bend"** "curva peligrosa"; ✦*IDIOM* **he's round the ~!** (*Brit**) ¡está chiflado!*; **to go round the ~** volverse loco; **to drive sb round the ~** volver loco a algn*
[2] **the ~s** (*Med*) la enfermedad de descompresión
[3] (*Heraldry*) banda *f*
Ⓑ VT [1] (= *make curved*) [+ *wire*] curvar, doblar; (= *cause to sag*) combar; [+ *arm, knee*] doblar; [+ *sail*] envergar; **on ~ed knee** de rodillas; **to ~ the rules for sb** adaptar las normas a beneficio de algn; **to ~ sb to one's will** doblar a algn a su voluntad; ✦*IDIOM* **to ~ sb's ear*** marear a algn*
[2] (= *incline*) [+ *body, head*] inclinar
[3] (= *direct*) [+ *efforts, steps etc*] dirigir (**to** a); **to ~ one's mind to a problem** aplicarse a un problema; *see also* **bent**
Ⓒ VI [1] [*branch*] doblarse; [*wire*] torcerse; [*arm, knee*] doblarse; [*road, river*] torcer (**to the left** a la izquierda)
[2] [*person*] (= *stoop*) inclinarse, doblarse

►**bend back** VT + ADV doblar hacia atrás

►**bend down** Ⓐ VT + ADV [+ *branch*] doblar; [+ *head*] inclinar
Ⓑ VI + ADV [*person*] agacharse

►**bend over** Ⓐ VT + ADV doblar
Ⓑ VI + ADV [*person*] inclinarse; ✦*IDIOM* **to ~ over backwards (to do sth)** hacer lo imposible (por hacer algo)

bender [ˈbendəʳ] N [1] **to go on a ~**‡ ir de juerga*, ir de borrachera*
[2] (*) (= *tent*) choza *f*

beneath [bɪˈniːθ] Ⓐ PREP [1] (= *below*) debajo de, bajo
[2] (*fig*) inferior a, por debajo de; **it would be ~ him to do such a thing** hacer tal cosa sería indigno de él; **she married ~ her** se casó con un hombre de clase inferior; **~ contempt** despreciable
Ⓑ ADV abajo, debajo

Benedict [ˈbenɪdɪkt] N Benito; (= *pope*) Benedicto

Benedictine [ˌbenɪˈdɪktɪn] Ⓐ ADJ benedictino
Ⓑ N benedictino *m*

benediction [ˌbenɪˈdɪkʃən] N bendición *f*

benefaction [ˌbenɪˈfækʃən] N (*frm*) (= *gift*) beneficio *m*

benefactor [ˈbenɪfæktəʳ] N bienhechor(a) *m/f*, benefactor(a) *m/f*

benefactress [ˈbenɪfæktrɪs] N bienhechora *f*, benefactora *f*

benefice [ˈbenɪfɪs] N beneficio *m*

beneficence [bɪˈnefɪsəns] N (*frm*) beneficencia *f*

beneficent [bɪˈnefɪsənt] ADJ (*frm*) benéfico

beneficial [ˌbenɪˈfɪʃəl] ADJ [1] (= *advantageous*) beneficioso; **~ to the health** beneficioso para la salud; **the change will be ~ to you** el cambio te resultará beneficioso
[2] (*Jur*) **~ owner** verdadero/a propietario/a *m/f*

beneficially [ˌbenɪˈfɪʃəlɪ] ADV beneficiosamente

beneficiary [ˌbenɪˈfɪʃərɪ] N (*Jur*) beneficiario/a *m/f*; (*Rel*) beneficiado *m*

benefit [ˈbenɪfɪt] Ⓐ N [1] (= *advantage*) beneficio *m*, provecho *m*; **to give sb the ~ of the doubt** dar a algn el beneficio de la duda; **for the ~ of one's health** en beneficio de la salud; **I'll try it on for your ~** lo probaré en tu honor; **to have the ~ of** tener la ventaja de; **to be of ~ to sb** beneficiar a algn; **to reap the ~ of** sacar el fruto de; **to be to the ~ of** ser provechoso a; **without ~ of** sin la ayuda de; **to marry without ~ of clergy** casarse por lo civil
[2] (*Admin*) (= *money*) ayuda *f*; (*also* **unemployment ~**) subsidio *m* de desempleo
[3] (*Theat, Sport*) (= *charity performance*) beneficio *m*
Ⓑ VI beneficiar(se), sacar provecho; **to ~ by/from** sacar provecho de
Ⓒ VT beneficiar
Ⓓ CPD ► **benefit association** N (*esp US*) sociedad *f* de beneficencia ► **benefit match** N partido *m* con fines benéficos ► **benefit performance** N función *f* benéfica ► **benefit society** N = **benefit association** ► **benefits package** N paquete *m* de beneficios

Benelux [ˈbenɪlʌks] N Benelux *m*; **the ~ countries** los países del Benelux

benevolence [bɪˈnevələns] N benevolencia *f*

benevolent [bɪˈnevələnt] Ⓐ ADJ [1] (= *kind*) benévolo, benevolente; **a ~ smile** una sonrisa benévola *or* benevolente
[2] (= *charitable*) [*organization, society*] benéfica, de beneficencia
Ⓑ CPD ► **benevolent fund** N fondos *mpl* benéficos

benevolently [bɪˈnevələntlɪ] ADV con benevolencia, benévolamente

BEng [ˌbiːˈeŋ] N ABBR (*Univ*) = **Bachelor of Engineering**

Bengal [beŋˈgɔːl] Ⓐ ADJ bengalí
Ⓑ N Bengala *f*
Ⓒ CPD ► **Bengal tiger** N tigre *m* de Bengala

Bengali [beŋˈgɔːlɪ] Ⓐ ADJ bengalí
Ⓑ N (= *person*) bengalí *mf*; (*Ling*) bengalí *m*

Benghazi [benˈgɑːzɪ] N Bengasi *m*

benighted [bɪˈnaɪtɪd] ADJ (*liter*) (*fig*) ignorante

benign [bɪˈnaɪn] ADJ [1] (= *kind*) [*person, view*] benevolente; [*smile, gesture*] benévolo, benevolente; **a policy of ~ neglect of the economy** una política en que, por su propio interés, se deja que la economía siga su curso sin interferir
[2] (= *favourable*) [*substance, influence*] benéfico; [*conditions*] favorable; [*climate*] benigno
[3] (*Med*) [*tumour, growth*] benigno

benignant [bɪˈnɪgnənt] ADJ benigno (*also Med*); (= *healthy*) saludable

benignly [bɪˈnaɪnlɪ] ADV [1] (= *kindly*) [*smile, say*] benévolamente, con benevolencia
[2] (= *favourably*) con benignidad, benignamente

Benjamin [ˈbendʒəmɪn] N Benjamín

benny†* [ˈbenɪ] N (*Drugs*) bencedrina® *f*

bent [bent] Ⓐ PT, PP *of* **bend**
Ⓑ ADJ [1] [*wire, pipe*] doblado; (= *twisted*) torcido
[2] (*esp Brit* pej*) (= *dishonest*) pringado (*Sp**), chueco (*LAm**), corrupto
[3] (*Brit* pej*) (= *homosexual*) del otro bando*, invertido
[4] **to be ~ on doing sth** (*fig*) (= *determined*) estar resuelto a *or* empeñado en hacer algo; **to be ~ on a quarrel** estar resuelto a *or* empeñado en provocar una riña; **to be ~ on pleasure** estar resuelto a *or* empeñado en divertirse
Ⓒ N (= *inclination*) inclinación *f*; (= *aptitude*) facilidad *f*; **of an artistic ~** con una inclinación artística, con inclinaciones artísticas; **to follow one's ~** seguir su inclinación; **he has a ~ for annoying people** tiene una facilidad para molestar a la gente

benumb [bɪˈnʌm] VT (*with cold*) entumecer; (= *frighten, shock*) paralizar

benumbed [bɪˈnʌmd] ADJ (= *cold*) [*person, fingers*] entumecido; (= *frightened, shocked*) paralizado

Benzedrine® [ˈbenzɪdriːn] N bencedrina® *f*

benzene [ˈbenziːn] N benceno *m*

benzine [ˈbenziːn] N bencina *f*

bequeath [bɪˈkwiːð] VT legar

bequest [bɪˈkwest] N legado *m*

berate [bɪˈreɪt] VT regañar

Berber [ˈbɜːbəʳ] Ⓐ ADJ bereber
Ⓑ N bereber *mf*

bereave [bɪˈriːv] (*pt, pp* **bereft**) VT privar (**of** de)

bereaved [bɪˈriːvd] ADJ afligido; **the ~** los familiares del difunto/de la difunta; **with the thanks of his ~ family** con el agradecimiento de su afligida familia

bereavement [bɪˈriːvmənt] N (= *loss*) pérdida *f*; (= *mourning*) duelo *m*; (= *sorrow*) pesar *m*

bereft [bɪˈreft] ADJ (*frm*) **to be ~ of** (= *not have to hand*) estar desprovisto de; (= *not possess*) estar falto de; (= *be robbed*) ser despojado de

beret [ˈbereɪ] N boina *f*; **the Red Berets** (*Mil*) los boinas rojas

bergamot [ˈbɜːgəmɒt] N bergamota *f*

beriberi [ˈberɪˌberɪ] N beriberi *m*

Bering Sea [ˈberɪŋˈsiː] N mar *m* de Bering

berk* [bɜːk] N (*Brit*) imbécil* *mf*, gilipollas *mf* (*Sp**), huevón/ona *m/f* (*LAm**)

berkelium [bɜːˈkiːlɪəm] N berkelio *m*

Berks [bɑːks] N ABBR (*Brit*) = **Berkshire**

Berlin [bɜːˈlɪn] Ⓐ N Berlín *m*; **East/West ~** Berlín Este/Oeste
Ⓑ CPD berlinés ► **the Berlin Wall** N el Muro de Berlín

Berliner [bɜːˈlɪnəʳ] N berlinés/esa *m/f*

berm [bɜːm] N (*US*) arcén *m*

Bermuda [bɜːˈmjuːdə] Ⓐ N las Bermudas
Ⓑ CPD ► **Bermuda shorts** NPL bermudas *fpl* ► **the Bermuda Triangle** N el triángulo de las Bermudas

Bern [bɜːn] N Berna *f*

Bernard [ˈbɜːnəd] N Bernardo

Bernese [bɜːˈniːz] Ⓐ ADJ bernés
Ⓑ CPD ► **Bernese Alps** NPL, **Bernese Oberland** N Alpes *mpl* Berneses

berry [ˈberɪ] N baya *f*; ♦**IDIOM brown as a ~** morenísimo

berserk [bəˈsɜːk] ADJ desquiciado; **to drive sb ~** desquiciar a algn; **to go ~** perder los estribos, ponerse hecho una furia*

Bert [bɜːt] N (*familiar form*) *of* **Albert, Herbert** *etc*

berth [bɜːθ] Ⓐ N [1] (*on ship, train*) (= *cabin*) camarote *m*; (= *bunk*) litera *f*
[2] (*Naut*) (*at wharf*) amarradero *m*; (*in marina etc*) punto *m* de atraque; ♦**IDIOM to give sb a wide ~** evitar el encuentro con algn
Ⓑ VI (*Naut*) atracar
Ⓒ VT (*Naut*) atracar

beryl [ˈberɪl] N berilo *m*

beryllium [beˈrɪljəm] N berilio *m*

beseech [bɪˈsiːtʃ] (*pt, pp* **besought**) VT **to ~ sb to do sth** suplicar a algn que haga algo

beseeching [bɪˈsiːtʃɪŋ] ADJ [*look*] suplicante; [*tone*] suplicante, de súplica

beseechingly [bɪˈsiːtʃɪŋlɪ] ADV en tono suplicante *or* de súplica; **to look at sb ~** mirar a algn suplicante

beset [bɪˈset] (*pt, pp* **beset**) VT [+ *person*] acosar; **he was ~ with** *or* **by fears** le acosaban los temores; **a policy ~ with dangers** una política plagada de peligros; **a path ~ with obstacles** (*fig*) un camino plagado de obstáculos

besetting [bɪˈsetɪŋ] ADJ [*vice, failing*] grande; **his ~ sin** su gran pecado

beside [bɪˈsaɪd] PREP [1] (= *at the side of*) al lado de, junto a; (= *near*) cerca de; **to be ~ o.s.** (*with anger*) estar fuera de sí; (*with joy*) estar loco de alegría; **that's ~ the point** eso no tiene nada que ver con el asunto, eso no viene al caso
[2] (= *compared with*) comparado con; **what is that ~ victory?** ¿y eso qué importa comparado con la victoria?
[3] (= *in addition to*) además de, aparte de; (= *apart from*) aparte de

besides [bɪˈsaɪdz] Ⓐ PREP [1] (= *in addition to*) además de, aparte de; **there were three of us ~ Mary** éramos tres además de *or* aparte de Mary; **there are others ~ ourselves who might be interested** además de nosotros *or* aparte de nosotros hay otros que pueden estar interesados; **~ which he was unwell** aparte de eso estaba malo, además estaba malo
[2] (= *apart from*) aparte de; **no one ~ you has the key** nadie, aparte de ti, tiene la llave; **Thomas was the only blond in the family, ~ the mother** Thomas era el único rubio de la familia, aparte de la madre
Ⓑ ADV [1] (= *in addition*) además; **he wrote a novel and several short stories ~** escribió una novela y además varias narraciones cortas; **and much more ~** y mucho más todavía
[2] (= *anyway*) además; **I didn't want to invite him, and ~, he said he was busy** no quería invitarlo, además dijo que estaba ocupado

besiege [bɪˈsiːdʒ] VT (*Mil*) (*fig*) asediar; **we were ~d with inquiries** nos inundaron con solicitudes de información; **we are ~d with calls** nos están llamando incesantemente

besieger [bɪˈsiːdʒəʳ] N sitiador(a) *m/f*

besmear [bɪˈsmɪəʳ] VT embarrar, embadurnar

besmirch [bɪˈsmɜːtʃ] VT manchar, mancillar

besom [ˈbiːzəm] N escoba *f*

besotted [bɪˈsɒtɪd] ADJ [1] (= *infatuated*) **he is ~ with her** anda loco por ella; **they are ~ with love** están enamoradísimos
[2] (= *foolish*) atontado, entontecido
[3] **~ with drink** embrutecido por la bebida

besought [bɪˈsɔːt] PT, PP *of* **beseech**

bespatter [bɪˈspætəʳ] VT salpicar (**with** de)

bespeak† [bɪˈspiːk] (*pt* **bespoke**; *pp* **bespoken** *or* **bespoke**) VT [1] (= *be evidence of*) indicar
[2] (= *order*) [+ *goods*] encargar, reservar

bespectacled [bɪˈspektɪkld] ADJ con gafas

bespoke [bɪˈspəʊk] Ⓐ PT, PP *of* **bespeak**
Ⓑ ADJ (*Brit*) [*garment*] hecho a la medida; [*tailor*] que confecciona a la medida

bespoken [bɪˈspəʊkən] PP *of* **bespeak**

besprinkle [bɪˈsprɪŋkl] VT (*with liquid*) salpicar, rociar (**with** de); (*with powder*) espolvorear (**with** de)

Bess [bes], **Bessie, Bessy** [ˈbesɪ] N (*familiar forms*) *of* **Elizabeth** Isabelita; **Good Queen ~** (*Brit Hist*) la buena reina Isabel

best [best] Ⓐ ADJ SUPERL *of* **good** el/la mejor; **to be ~** ser el/la mejor; **she wore her ~ dress** llevaba su mejor vestido; **the ~ pupil in the class** el/la mejor alumno/a de la clase; **the ~ one of all** el/la mejor de todos; **"~ before 20 June"** "consumir preferentemente antes del 20 de junio"; **to know what is ~ for sb** saber lo que más le conviene a algn; **my ~ friend** mi mejor amigo/a; **may the ~ man win!** ¡que gane el mejor!; **for the ~ part of the year** durante la mayor parte del año; **the ~ thing to do is …** lo mejor que se puede hacer es …
Ⓑ ADV SUPERL *of* **well** mejor; **John came off ~** Juan salió ganando; **as ~ I could** lo mejor que pude; **she did ~ of all in the test** hizo el test mejor que nadie; **you had ~ leave** lo mejor es que te vayas; **I had ~ go** más vale que vaya; **I had ~ see him at once** lo mejor sería verlo en seguida; **you know ~** tú sabes mejor; **when it comes to hotels I know ~** en cuestión de hoteles yo soy el que más sabe; **Mummy knows ~** estas cosas las decide mamá, mamá sabe lo que más conviene
Ⓒ N lo mejor; **he deserves the ~** se merece lo mejor; **all the ~!** (*as farewell*) ¡que tengas suerte!; **all the ~** ◊ **my ~** (*US*) (*ending letter*) un abrazo; **all the ~ to Jim!** ¡recuerdos para Jim!; **at ~** en el mejor de los casos; **he wasn't at his ~** no estaba en plena forma; **the garden is at its ~ in June** en junio es cuando el jardín luce más; **at the ~ of times** en las mejores circunstancias; **to do one's ~ (to do sth)** hacer todo lo posible (para *or* por hacer algo); **is that the ~ you can do?** ¿y eso es todo lo que puedes hacer?; **I acted for the ~** lo hice con la mejor intención; **it's all for the ~** todo conduce al bien a la larga; **to be the ~ of friends** ser muy amigos; **to get the ~ of it** salir ganando; **in order to get the ~ out of the car** para obtener el máximo rendimiento del coche; **we have had the ~ of the day** el buen tiempo se acabó por hoy; **let's hope for the ~** esperemos lo mejor; **to look one's ~** tener un aspecto inmejorable; **she's not looking her ~** está algo desmejorada; **to make the ~ of it** sacar el mayor partido posible; **the ~ of it is that …** lo mejor del caso es que …; **to play (the) ~ of three** jugar al mejor de tres; **I try to think the ~ of him** procuro conservar mi buena opinión de él; **to the ~ of my knowledge** que yo sepa; **I'll do it to the ~ of my ability** lo haré lo mejor que pueda; **she can dance with the ~ of them** sabe bailar como la que más; ♦**IDIOMS to get the ~ of the bargain** llevarse la mejor parte, salir ganando; **to have the ~ of both worlds** tenerlo todo; **to make the ~ of a bad job** sacar el mejor partido posible
Ⓓ VT (= *defeat, win over*) vencer
Ⓔ CPD ► **best boy** N (*Cine*) ayudante *mf* (*de*

rodaje) ► **best man** N (*at wedding*) padrino *m* de boda

BEST MAN

*En una boda tradicional el novio (***bridegroom***) va acompañado del* **best man***, un amigo íntimo o un pariente cercano que tiene la responsabilidad de asegurarse de que todo marche bien en el día de la boda (***wedding day***). No hay pues, madrina. El* **best man** *se encarga, entre otras cosas, de los anillos de boda, de llevar al novio a la iglesia a tiempo y de dar la bienvenida a los invitados. En el banquete de boda (***wedding reception***) lee los telegramas enviados por los que no han podido asistir, presenta los discursos que vayan a dar algunos invitados, da su propio discurso, casi siempre en clave de humor y sobre el novio, y propone un brindis por la pareja de recién casados (***newly-weds***).*

best-before date [bestbɪ'fɔːdeɪt] N (*Comm*) fecha *f* de consumo preferente

bestial ['bestɪəl] ADJ bestial

bestiality [ˌbestɪ'ælɪtɪ] N (= *behaviour*) bestialidad *f*; (*sexual*) bestialismo *m*

bestiary ['bestɪərɪ] N bestiario *m*

bestir [bɪ'stɜːʳ] VT (*liter*) **to ~ o.s.** menearse

bestow [bɪ'stəʊ] VT [+ *title, honour*] conferir (**on** a); [+ *affections*] ofrecer (**on** a); [+ *compliment*] hacer (**on** a)

bestowal [bɪ'stəʊəl] N [*of title, honour*] otorgamiento *m*; [*of money, gifts*] donación *f*; [*of affections*] ofrecimiento *m*

bestraddle [bɪ'strædl] VT [+ *horse*] montar a horcajadas, estar a horcajadas sobre

bestrew [bɪ'struː] (*pt* **bestrewed**; *pp* **bestrewed** *or* **bestrewn**) VT (*liter*) [+ *things*] desparramar, esparcir; [+ *surface*] sembrar, cubrir (**with** de)

bestridden [bɪ'strɪdn] PP *of* **bestride**

bestride [bɪ'straɪd] (*pt* **bestrode**; *pp* **bestridden**) VT [+ *horse*] montar a horcajadas; [+ *stream etc*] cruzar de un tranco; (*fig*) dominar

bestrode [bɪ'strəʊd] PT *of* **bestride**

bestseller ['best'seləʳ] N best-seller *m*, éxito *m* de ventas

best-selling ['best'selɪŋ] ADJ **our ~ line** nuestro producto de mayor venta; **for years it was our ~ car** durante años fue el coche que más se vendió

bet [bet] (*pt, pp* **bet**) Ⓐ VI 1 (= *place bet*) apostar; **I'm not a ~ting man** no me gusta apostar; **to ~ against sb** apostar que algn va a perder; **to ~ on sth/sb** apostar a *or* por algo/por algn; **I ~ on the wrong horse** aposté por el *or* al caballo que no debía; **they are forbidden to ~ on their own races** tienen prohibido apostar en sus propias carreras
2 (= *be certain*) **don't ~ on it!** ◊ **I wouldn't ~ on it!** ¡no estés tan seguro!; **(do you) want to ~** *or* **a ~?*** ¿qué te apuestas *or* juegas?; **"are you going?" — "you ~!"*** —¿vas a ir? —¡hombre, claro! *or* (*LAm*) —¡cómo no!; **"I'm so relieved it's all over" — "I'll ~"*** —es un alivio que todo haya pasado —ya me lo imagino
Ⓑ VT 1 (= *stake*) [+ *money*] apostar, jugar; **I ~ £10 on a horse called Premonition** aposté 10 libras a *or* por un caballo llamado Premonition, jugué 10 libras a un caballo llamado Premonition; **he ~ them (that) they would lose** hizo una apuesta con ellos a que perdían; **he ~ them £500 that they would lose** les apostó *or* jugó 500 libras a que perdían
2 (*) (= *predict*) apostar, jugarse; **I ~ you anything** *or* **any money he won't come** te apuesto *or* me juego lo que quieras a que no viene; **you can ~ she'll be there** puedes tener por seguro que estará allí; **"I ~ I can jump over that stream" — "I ~ you can't!"** —¡a que puedo saltar ese arroyo! —¡a que no!; **"it wasn't easy" — "I ~ it wasn't"** —no fue fácil —ya me imagino que no; **you can ~ your bottom dollar** *or* **your life that ...*** puedes apostarte lo que quieras a que ...; **"did you tell him off?" — "you ~ your life I did!"** —¿le reñiste? —¡ya lo creo!
Ⓒ N 1 (= *stake*) apuesta *f*; **a £5 ~** una apuesta de 5 libras; **I had a ~ on that horse** había apostado por ese caballo; **I've made a ~ with him that he can't do it** le he hecho una apuesta a que no puede hacerlo; **they placed ~s on who could get her to talk** apostaron a ver quién podía hacerla hablar; **place your ~s!** ¡hagan sus apuestas!; **to take ~s** aceptar apuestas; *see also* **hedge**
2 (= *prediction*) **it's my ~ he's up to no good** apuesto a que está tramando algo; **it's a fair** *or* **good ~ that interest rates will go up** es muy posible que los tipos de interés van a subir; **he's a good ~ for president** es el que más posibilidades tiene de conseguir la presidencia
3 (*) (= *option*) **it's our best ~** es la mejor opción que tenemos; **your best** *or* **safest ~ is to keep quiet about it** lo mejor que puedes hacer es no decir nada; **these companies are a safe ~ for investors** estas compañías no presentan ningún riesgo para los inversores

beta ['biːtə] Ⓐ N beta *f*
Ⓑ CPD ► **beta blocker** N (*Med*) betabloqueador *m*

betake [bɪ'teɪk] (*pt* **betook**; *pp* **betaken**) VT (*liter*) **to ~ o.s. to** dirigirse a, trasladarse a

betaken [bɪ'teɪkən] PP *of* **betake**

betel ['biːtəl] Ⓐ N betel *m*
Ⓑ CPD ► **betel nut** N betel *m*

bête noire ['beɪt'nwaːʳ] N bestia *f* negra, pesadilla *f*

bethink [bɪ'θɪŋk] (*pt, pp* **bethought**) VT (*liter*) **to ~ o.s. of** acordarse de

Bethlehem ['beθlɪhem] N Belén *m*

bethought [bɪ'θɔːt] PT, PP *of* **bethink**

betide [bɪ'taɪd] (*liter*) Ⓐ VT acontecer; *see also* **woe**
Ⓑ VI acontecer

betimes [bɪ'taɪmz] ADV (*liter*) (= *early*) temprano, al alba; (= *quickly*) rápidamente; (= *in good time*) a tiempo

betoken [bɪ'təʊkən] (*liter*) VT presagiar, anunciar

betook [bɪ'tʊk] PT *of* **betake**

betray [bɪ'treɪ] VT 1 (= *be disloyal to*) [+ *person, country, principles*] traicionar
2 (= *inform on*) delatar; **to ~ sb to the enemy** entregar a algn al enemigo
3 (= *reveal*) [+ *secret*] revelar; [+ *ignorance, fear*] delatar, revelar; **his accent ~s him** su acento lo delata; **his accent ~s him as a foreigner** su acento revela su origen extranjero; **his face ~ed a certain surprise** su cara delataba *or* revelaba cierto asombro

betrayal [bɪ'treɪəl] N 1 [*of person, country*] traición *f*; **a ~ of trust** un abuso de confianza
2 [*of secret, plot*] revelación *f*
3 [*of feelings, intentions*] descubrimiento *m*

betrayer [bɪ'treɪəʳ] N traidor(a) *m/f*; **she killed her ~** mató a quien la traicionó

betroth [bɪ'trəʊð] VT (*liter*) prometer en matrimonio (**to** a); **to be ~ed** (= *act*) desposarse; (= *state*) estar desposado

betrothal [bɪ'trəʊðəl] N (*liter*) desposorios *mpl*

betrothed [bɪ'trəʊðd] (*liter, hum*) Ⓐ ADJ prometido
Ⓑ N INV prometido/a *m/f*

▼ **better¹** ['betəʳ] Ⓐ ADJ COMPAR *of* **good** mejor; **he is ~ than you** es mejor que tú; **he's much ~** (*Med*) está mucho mejor; **that's ~!** ¡eso es!; **it is ~ to** + INFIN más vale + *infin*; **~ and ~** cada vez mejor; **she is ~ at dancing than her sister** se le da mejor bailar a ella que a su hermana; **it couldn't be ~** no podría ser mejor; **these products are ~ for the environment** estos productos son mejores para el medio ambiente; **to get ~** mejorar; (*Med*) mejorar(se), reponerse; **he's no ~ than a thief** no es más que un ladrón; **she's no ~ than she ought to be**† es una mujer que tiene historia; **to go one ~** hacer mejor todavía (**than** que); **it lasted the ~ part of a year** duró la mayor parte del año; **the sooner the ~** cuanto antes mejor; **it would be ~ to go now** sería mejor irse ya; *see also* **half A1, nature A2, day A3**
Ⓑ ADV COMPAR *of* **well** mejor; **all the ~** tanto mejor; **so you're both coming — all the ~!** así es que venís los dos, ¡tanto mejor!; **I feel all the ~ for having confided in someone** me siento mucho mejor después de haberme confiado a alguien; **he was all the ~ for it** le hizo mucho bien; **it would be all the ~ for a drop of paint** no le vendría mal una mano de pintura; **I had ~ go** más vale que me vaya, mejor me vaya (*esp LAm*); **he thinks he knows ~** cree que se lo sabe todo; **at his age he ought to know ~** a la edad que tiene debería tener más juicio; **but he knew ~ than to ...** pero sabía que no se debía ...; **he knows ~ than the experts** sabe más que los expertos; **they are ~ off than we are** están mejor de dinero que nosotros; **you'd be ~ off staying where you are** te convendría más quedarte; **so much the ~** tanto mejor; **write to her or, ~ still, go and see her** escríbele o, mejor aún, vete a verla; **they withdrew, the ~ to resist** se retiraron para poder resistir mejor; **to think ~ of it** cambiar de parecer; *see also* **late A3**
Ⓒ N 1 el/la mejor; **it's a change for the ~** es una mejora; **to get the ~ of** (= *beat*) vencer, quedar por encima de; **for ~ or worse** para bien o mal
2 **my ~s** mis superiores
Ⓓ VT mejorar; [+ *record, score*] superar; **to ~ o.s.** (*financially*) mejorar su posición; (*culturally, educationally*) superarse

better² ['betəʳ] N (= *gambler*) apostador(a) *m/f*

betterment ['betəmənt] N mejora *f*, mejoramiento *m*

betting ['betɪŋ] Ⓐ N **the ~ is that they'll divorce** se da casi por sentado que van a divorciarse; **what's the ~ he won't come back?** ¿qué te apuestas a que no vuelve?; **the latest ~ is ...** las últimas apuestas son ...
Ⓑ CPD ► **betting shop** N (*Brit*) casa *f* de apuestas ► **betting slip** N (*Brit*) boleto *m* de apuestas ► **betting tax** N impuesto *m* sobre las apuestas

bettor ['betəʳ] N (*US*) = **better²**

Betty ['betɪ] N (*familiar form*) *of* **Elizabeth** Isabelita

between [bɪ'twiːn] Ⓐ PREP 1 entre; **the shops are shut ~ two and four o'clock** las tiendas cierran de dos a cuatro; **~ now and May** de ahora a mayo; **I sat (in) ~ John and**

➤ LANGUAGE IN USE: **better¹ A** 5.4

Sue me senté entre John y Sue; **it's ~ five and six metres long** mide entre cinco y seis metros de largo
2 (= *amongst*) entre; **we shared it ~ us** nos lo repartimos entre los dos; **just ~ you and me** ◊ **just ~ ourselves** entre nosotros; **we only had £5 ~ us** teníamos sólo 5 libras entre todos; **we did it ~ the two of us** lo hicimos entre los dos
Ⓑ ADV (*also* **in ~**) (*time*) mientras tanto; (*place*) en medio, entre medio

betweentimes [bɪ'twiːntaɪmz] ADV, **betweenwhiles** [bɪ'twiːnwaɪlz] ADV mientras, entretanto

betwixt [bɪ'twɪkst] Ⓐ ADV **~ and between** entre lo uno y lo otro, entre las dos cosas
Ⓑ PREP (†† *liter*) = **between A**

bevel ['bevəl] Ⓐ ADJ biselado
Ⓑ N (= *tool*) (*also* **~ edge**) cartabón *m*, escuadra *f* falsa; (= *surface*) bisel *m*
Ⓒ VT biselar

bevel-edged [ˌbevl'edʒd] ADJ biselado

beverage ['bevərɪdʒ] N bebida *f*

bevvy* ['bevɪ] N (*Brit*) 1 (= *drink*) trago* *m*; **he's back on the ~** ha vuelto a la bebida
2 (= *drinking session*) **to go out on the ~** ir a emborracharse

bevy ['bevɪ] N [*of girls, women*] grupo *m*; [*of birds*] bandada *f*

bewail [bɪ'weɪl] VT lamentar

beware [bɪ'weəʳ] VI **to ~ of sth/sb** tener cuidado con algo/algn; **beware!** ¡cuidado!; **"beware of the dog!"** "¡cuidado con el perro!"; **"beware of pickpockets!"** "¡ojo con los carteristas!"; **"beware of imitations!"** (*Comm*) "desconfíe de las imitaciones"

bewhiskered [bɪ'wɪskəd] ADJ bigotudo

bewilder [bɪ'wɪldəʳ] VT desconcertar, dejar perplejo

bewildered [bɪ'wɪldəd] ADJ [*person*] desconcertado, perplejo; **he gave me a ~ look** me miró perplejo

bewildering [bɪ'wɪldərɪŋ] ADJ desconcertante

bewilderingly [bɪ'wɪldərɪŋlɪ] ADV de modo desconcertante; **a ~ complicated matter** un asunto de una complejidad increíble

bewilderment [bɪ'wɪldəmənt] N perplejidad *f*, desconcierto *m*; **to look around in ~** mirar alrededor perplejo *or* desconcertado

bewitch [bɪ'wɪtʃ] VT (= *cast a spell on*) hechizar; (= *seduce*) seducir, cautivar; (= *enchant*) encantar

bewitching [bɪ'wɪtʃɪŋ] ADJ cautivador

bewitchingly [bɪ'wɪtʃɪŋlɪ] ADV cautivadoramente; **~ beautiful** de una belleza cautivadora

beyond [bɪ'jɒnd] Ⓐ PREP 1 (*in space*) (= *further than*) más allá de; (= *on the other side of*) al otro lado de; **you can't go ~ the barrier** no se puede cruzar la barrera; **~ the convent walls** tras los muros del convento; **~ the seas** allende los mares
2 (*in time*) **she won't stay much ~ a month** no se quedará mucho más de un mes; **we can't see ~ 2010** no podemos ver más allá de 2010; **it was ~ the middle of June** era más de mediados de junio; **~ 12 o'clock** pasadas las 12; **it's ~ bedtime** ya se ha pasado la hora de irse a la cama
3 (= *surpassing, exceeding*) **the situation was ~ her control** la situación estaba fuera de su control; **what he has done is ~ my comprehension** lo que ha hecho me resulta incomprensible; **it's ~ me why ...*** no alcanzo a ver por qué ...; **this is getting ~ me** se me está haciendo imposible esto; **it's ~ belief** es increíble; **it's ~ doubt that ...** no cabe duda de que ...; **that's ~ a joke** eso es el colmo; **that job was ~ him** ese trabajo era demasiado para él *or* era superior a sus fuerzas; **his interests extend ~ the fine arts to philosophy** sus intereses se extienden más allá de las bellas artes a la filosofía; **~ repair** irreparable
4 (= *apart from*) aparte de; **I knew nothing ~ a few random facts** no sabía nada, aparte de algunos hechos aislados; **he has no personal staff, ~ a secretary** no tiene personal, aparte de una secretaria
Ⓑ ADV más allá; **next year and ~** el año que viene y después
Ⓒ N **the (great) ~** el más allá; **to live at the back of ~*** vivir en el quinto pino, vivir en el quinto infierno*

bezique [bɪ'ziːk] N *juego de cartas que se juega con dos barajas*

BF* N ABBR = **bloody fool**

b/f ABBR = **brought forward**

BFPO N ABBR (*Brit Mil*) = **British Forces Post Office**

b/fwd ABBR = **b/f**

bhp N ABBR = **brake horsepower**

Bhutan [buː'tɑːn] N Bután *m*

bi... [baɪ] PREFIX bi...

Biafra [bɪ'æfrə] N Biafra *f*

Biafran [bɪ'æfrən] Ⓐ ADJ de Biafra
Ⓑ N nativo/a *m/f or* habitante *mf* de Biafra

biannual [baɪ'ænjʊəl] ADJ semestral

biannually ['baɪ'ænjʊəlɪ] ADV semestralmente, dos veces al año

bias ['baɪəs] Ⓐ N 1 (= *inclination*) propensión *f*, predisposición *f* (**to, towards** a); **a course with a practical ~** un curso orientado a la práctica; **a right-wing ~** una tendencia derechista
2 (= *prejudice*) prejuicio *m* (**against** contra), parcialidad *f*
3 [*of material*] sesgo *m*, bies *m*; **to cut sth on the ~** cortar algo al sesgo *or* al bies
Ⓑ VT influir en; **to ~ sb for/against sth** predisponer a algn en pro/en contra de algo; **to be ~(s)ed in favour of** estar predispuesto a *or* en favor de; **to be ~(s)ed against** tener prejuicio contra
Ⓒ CPD ► **bias binding** N (*Sew*) bies *m*, ribete *m* al bies

bias(s)ed ['baɪəst] ADJ parcial

biathlon [baɪ'æθlən] N biatlón *m*

bib [bɪb] N (*for child*) babero *m*; (*on dungarees*) peto *m*; ✦**IDIOM in one's best ~ and tucker*** acicalado

Bible ['baɪbl] Ⓐ N Biblia *f*; **the Holy ~** la Santa Biblia
Ⓑ CPD ► **the Bible Belt** N (*US*) *los estados ultraprotestantes de EEUU* ► **Bible class** N (*for confirmation etc*) ≈ catequesis *f inv* ► **Bible college** N (*US*) colegio *m* evangelista ► **Bible school** N (*US*) escuela *f* de enseñanza de la Biblia ► **Bible story** N historia *f* de la Biblia ► **Bible study** N estudio *m* de la Biblia ► **Bible thumper*** N *creyente muy celoso de la Biblia*

biblical ['bɪblɪkəl] ADJ bíblico

biblio... ['bɪblɪəʊ] PREFIX biblio...

bibliographer [ˌbɪblɪ'ɒgrəfəʳ] N bibliógrafo/a *m/f*

bibliographic [ˌbɪblɪə'græfɪk] ADJ = **bibliographical**

bibliographical [ˌbɪblɪə'græfɪkəl] ADJ bibliográfico

bibliography [ˌbɪblɪ'ɒgrəfɪ] N bibliografía *f*

bibliomania [ˌbɪblɪəʊ'meɪnɪə] N bibliomanía *f*

bibliometric [ˌbɪblɪəʊ'metrɪk] ADJ bibliométrico

bibliometry [ˌbɪblɪ'ɒmɪtrɪ] N bibliometría *f*

bibliophile ['bɪblɪəʊfaɪl] N bibliófilo/a *m/f*

bibulous ['bɪbjʊləs] ADJ bebedor, borrachín

bicameral [baɪ'kæmərəl] ADJ bicameral

bicarb* ['baɪkɑːb] N = **bicarbonate of soda**

bicarbonate of soda [baɪ'kɑːbənɪtəv'səʊdə] N bicarbonato *m* de soda

bicentenary [ˌbaɪsen'tiːnərɪ] Ⓐ N bicentenario *m*
Ⓑ CPD (de) bicentenario ► **bicentenary celebrations** NPL celebraciones *fpl* de(l) bicentenario

bicentennial [baɪsen'tenɪəl] N, CPD (*US*) = **bicentenary**

biceps ['baɪseps] N bíceps *m inv*

bicker ['bɪkəʳ] VI discutir, reñir

bickering ['bɪkərɪŋ] N riñas *fpl*, discusiones *fpl*

bickie* ['bɪkɪ] N (*Brit*) (*esp baby talk*) galleta *f*

bicuspid [baɪ'kʌspɪd] Ⓐ ADJ bicúspide
Ⓑ N bicúspide *m*

bicycle ['baɪsɪkl] Ⓐ N bicicleta *f*; **to ride a ~** ir *or* montar en bicicleta
Ⓑ VI ir en bicicleta; **to ~ to Dover** ir en bicicleta a Dover
Ⓒ CPD ► **bicycle chain** N cadena *f* de bicicleta ► **bicycle clip** N pinza *f* para ir en bicicleta ► **bicycle kick** N (*Ftbl*) chilena *f* ► **bicycle lane** N carril *m* para ciclistas ► **bicycle pump** N bomba *f* de bicicleta ► **bicycle rack** N (*on floor, ground*) aparcamiento-bici *m*; (*on car roof*) portabicicletas *m inv* ► **bicycle shed** N cobertizo *m* para bicicletas ► **bicycle touring** N cicloturismo *m* ► **bicycle track** N pista *f* de ciclismo

bicyclist† ['baɪsɪklɪst] N ciclista *mf*

bid [bɪd] Ⓐ N 1 (*at auction*) oferta *f*, puja *f*; (*Fin*) oferta *f*; **the highest ~** la mejor oferta *or* puja; **to raise one's ~** subir su puja
2 (= *attempt*) tentativa *f*, intento *m*; **in a ~ to** en un intento de; **to make a ~ for freedom/power** hacer un intento para conseguir la libertad/el poder; **to make a ~ to do sth** hacer un intento para hacer algo
3 (*Cards*) marca *f*; **no ~** paso
Ⓑ VT 1 (*pt, pp* **bid**) (*at auction etc*) pujar; **to ~ £10 for** ofrecer 10 libras por
2 (*pt* **bad(e)**; *pp* **bidden**) (†, *also poet*) (= *order*) mandar; **to ~ sb to do sth** mandar a algn hacer algo
3 (*pt* **bad(e)**; *pp* **bidden**) **to ~ sb good morning** dar los buenos días a algn; *see also* **adieu**
Ⓒ VI (*pt, pp* **bid**) 1 (*at auction etc*) **to ~ (for)** pujar (por), hacer una oferta (por); **to ~ against sb** pujar contra algn
2 (= *try*) **to ~ for power/fame** intentar alcanzar el poder/la fama; **to ~ to do sth** intentar hacer algo
3 (*Cards*) marcar, declarar
4 (*liter*) **to ~ fair to** + INFIN prometer + *infin*, dar esperanzas de + *infin*
Ⓓ CPD ► **bid price** N precio *m* de oferta
►**bid up** VT + ADV [+ *item*] ofrecer más por; **to ~ up the price (of sth)** ofrecer un precio más alto (por algo)

biddable ['bɪdəbl] ADJ 1 [*person*] obediente, sumiso
2 (*Cards*) marcable

bidden ['bɪdn] PP *of* **bid**

bidder ['bɪdəʳ] N 1 (*at auction, Comm*) postor(a) *m/f*; **the highest ~** el/la mejor postor(a)
2 (*Cards*) declarante *mf*

bidding [ˈbɪdɪŋ] N 1 (*at auction*) ofertas *fpl*, puja *f*; **the ~ opened at £5** la primera puja fue de 5 libras; **there was keen ~ for the picture** hubo una rápida serie de ofertas por el cuadro; **to raise** *or* **up the ~** subir la puja
2 (*Cards*) declaración *f*; **to open the ~** abrir la declaración
3 (*frm*) (= *order*) orden *f*, mandato *m*; **they did it at her ~** lo hicieron cumpliendo sus órdenes; **to do sb's ~** cumplir las órdenes *or* el mandato de algn
4 (*Rel*) (*also* **~ prayers**) oraciones *fpl* de los fieles

biddy* [ˈbɪdɪ] N **old ~** viejecita *f*

bide [baɪd] VT **to ~ one's time** esperar la hora propicia

bidet [ˈbiːdeɪ] N bidet *m*, bidé *m*

bidirectional [baɪdɪˈrekʃənl] ADJ bidireccional

biennial [baɪˈenɪəl] Ⓐ ADJ 1 (= *every two years*) bienal
2 (*Bot*) bianual
Ⓑ N (= *plant*) planta *f* bienal

biennially [baɪˈenɪəlɪ] ADV bienalmente, cada dos años

bier [bɪəʳ] N andas *fpl* (*para el féretro*)

biff* [bɪf] Ⓐ N bofetada *f*
Ⓑ VT dar una bofetada a

bifocal [ˈbaɪˈfəʊkəl] Ⓐ ADJ bifocal
Ⓑ N **bifocals** gafas *fpl* bifocales

bifurcate [ˈbaɪfəkeɪt] VI bifurcarse

big [bɪg] Ⓐ ADJ (*compar* **bigger**, *superl* **biggest**)
1 (*in size*) [*house, book, city*] grande; **a ~ car** un coche grande; **a ~ stick** un palo grande; **this dress is too ~ for me** este vestido me queda demasiado grande; **how ~ is the wardrobe?** ¿cómo es de grande el armario?; **he was a ~ man** era un hombre corpulento; **a ~ woman** (= *heavily-built*) una mujer grande *or* grandota; (*euph*) (= *fat*) una mujer de grandes dimensiones; **there's a ~ backlog of applications** hay un montón de solicitudes atrasadas; **to take a ~ bite out of sth** dar un buen bocado a algo; **the ~ city** la gran ciudad; **I'm not a ~ eater*** no soy de mucho comer; **to get** *or* **grow ~(ger)** crecer; **he gave me a ~ kiss** me dio un besote *or* un beso fuerte; **he likes using ~ words** le gusta usar palabras difíciles; → GREAT, BIG, LARGE
2 (= *significant, serious*) [*change, problem*] grande; **the ~gest problem at the moment is unemployment** el mayor problema de hoy día es el desempleo; **the ~ question is, will he accept?** la cuestión es: ¿aceptará?; **it makes a ~ difference** eso cambia mucho las cosas; **you're making a ~ mistake** estás cometiendo un grave error; **a tragedy? that's rather a ~ word** ¿una tragedia? eso es llevar las cosas un poco lejos
3 (= *important*) [*company, bank*] importante, grande; **he's one of our ~gest customers** es uno de nuestros clientes más importantes, es uno de nuestros mayores clientes; **this is her ~ day** hoy es su gran día, hoy es un día muy importante para ella; **to be ~ in publishing/plastics** ser muy conocido en el mundo editorial/la industria del plástico; **the ~ match** el partido más importante
4 (*) (*in age*) [*girl, boy*] grande; **my ~ brother/sister** mi hermano/a mayor; **~ boys don't cry** los niños grandes no lloran; **you're a ~ girl now!** ¡ahora ya eres mayorcita!
5 (*) (*as intensifier*) **he's a ~ cheat/bully/liar** es un tramposo/un abusón/un mentiroso de marca mayor
6 (*in phrases*) **the ~ eight/ten** (*US Univ*) *las ocho/diez mayores universidades del centro oeste de EE.UU.*; **to have a ~ heart** tener un gran corazón; **what's the ~ hurry?*** ¿a qué viene tanta prisa?; **what's the ~ idea?*** ¿a qué viene eso?; **to have ~ ideas** hacerse ilusiones; **don't get any ~ ideas** no te hagas muchas ilusiones; **there's ~ money in tourism** se puede ganar mucho dinero con el turismo; **to make** *or* **earn ~ money** ganar mucho dinero; **to have a ~ mouth*** (*fig*) ser un bocazas*; **why don't you keep your ~ mouth shut!*** ¡no seas bocazas!*; **me and my ~ mouth!*** ¡quién me manda decir nada!; **Mr Big*** el número uno; **it was ~ of you to lend them the money** fue muy generoso de tu parte prestarles el dinero; **(that's) ~ of you!*** (*iro*) ¡qué generosidad la tuya! (*iro*); **to be ~ on sth/sb*** ser un fanático de algo/algn; **a ~ one** (*US**) un billete de mil dólares; **we're onto something ~!** ¡hemos dado con algo gordo!; **to do sth/things in a ~ way*** hacer algo/las cosas a lo grande; **I think boxing will take off in a ~ way here*** pienso que el boxeo va a tener una aceptación buenísima aquí; **the ~ wide world** el ancho mundo; ♦**IDIOM he's too ~ for his boots*** tiene muchos humos; **you're getting too ~ for your boots, young lady!*** se te están subiendo mucho los humos, señorita; *see also* **deal[1] A2**; → GREAT, BIG, LARGE
Ⓑ ADV (*) **to act ~** fanfarronear; **to go down ~** tener muchísimo éxito, ser un verdadero éxito; **to make it ~** triunfar; **she could have made it ~ as a singer** podría haber triunfado como cantante; **to talk ~** darse mucha importancia, fanfarronear; **to think ~** planear a lo grande, ser ambicioso
Ⓒ CPD ► **the Big Apple** N la Gran Manzana, Nueva York *f*; → CITY NICKNAMES ► **big band** N *orquesta grande que tocaba música de jazz o de baile y que fue muy popular entre los años 30 y 50* ► **the big bang** N (*Astron*) el big bang, la gran explosión; **the ~ bang theory** la teoría del big bang *or* de la gran explosión ► **Big Ben** N (*Brit*) Big Ben *m* ► **Big Brother** N (*Pol*) (*fig*) **Big Brother is watching you** el Gran Hermano te vigila ► **big business** N (*Ind, Comm*) las grandes empresas; **tourism is ~ business in Thailand** el turismo es un gran negocio en Tailandia ► **the big cats** N (*Zool*) los grandes felinos ► **big dipper** N (*at fair*) montaña *f* rusa; **the Big Dipper** (*US Astron*) la Osa Mayor ► **the Big Easy** N Nueva Orleans ► **big end** N (*Aut*) cabeza *f* de biela ► **big fish*** N (*fig*) (= *person*) pez *m* gordo* ► **big game** N caza *f* mayor; **~ game hunter** cazador(a) *m/f* de caza mayor; **~ game hunting** caza *f* mayor ► **the big hand** N (*used to or by children*) (*on clock*) la aguja grande ► **The Big Issue** N (*Brit*) *revista vendida por personas sin hogar*, ≈ La Farola (*Sp*) ► **big name*** N figura *f* importante ► **big noise***, **big shot*** N pez *m* gordo* ► **big talk** N fanfarronadas *fpl* ► **the big time*** N el estrellato, el éxito; **to make the ~ time** alcanzar el éxito, triunfar; *see also* **big-time** ► **big toe** N dedo *m* gordo (del pie) ► **big top** N (= *circus*) circo *m*; (= *main tent*) carpa *f* principal ► **big wheel** N (*at fair*) noria *f*; (*) (= *person*) personaje *m*, pez *m* gordo*

bigamist [ˈbɪgəmɪst] N bígamo/a *m/f*

bigamous [ˈbɪgəməs] ADJ bígamo

bigamy [ˈbɪgəmɪ] N bigamia *f*

big-boned [ˌbɪgˈbəʊnd] ADJ de huesos grandes, huesudo

biggie* [ˈbɪgɪ] N (= *song, film*) gran éxito *m*; (= *person, company*) uno/a *m/f* de los grandes; **some ~ in drugs** uno de los grandes en lo de las drogas; **the film is this summer's box-office ~** esta película es el gran éxito de taquilla de este verano

biggish [ˈbɪgɪʃ] ADJ bastante grande

bighead* [ˈbɪghed] N creído/a* *m/f*, engreído/a *m/f*

big-headed* [ˈbɪgˈhedɪd] ADJ creído*, engreído

big-hearted [ˈbɪgˈhɑːtɪd] ADJ generoso

bight [baɪt] N 1 (*Geog*) ensenada *f*, cala *f*; (= *bend*) recodo *m*
2 [*of rope*] gaza *f*, laza *f*

bigmouth* [ˈbɪgmaʊθ] N (*pl* **bigmouths** [ˈbɪgmaʊðz]) (= *loudmouth*) bocazas* *mf*; (= *gossipy person*) cotilla* *mf*

big-mouthed [ˈbɪgˈmaʊθt] ADJ 1 de boca grande
2 (*) (= *loudmouthed*) bocazas*; (= *gossipy*) cotilla*

bigot [ˈbɪgət] N intolerante *mf*

bigoted [ˈbɪgətɪd] ADJ intolerante

bigotry [ˈbɪgətrɪ] N intolerancia *f*

big-ticket [ˈbɪgˌtɪkɪt] ADJ (*US*) **~ item** compra *f* importante

big-time* [ˈbɪgˈtaɪm] Ⓐ ADJ **~ football/politics** fútbol *m*/política *f* de alto nivel; **a ~ politician/actor** un político/actor de primera línea; **a ~ banker** un banquero de categoría
Ⓑ ADV **he has tasted success ~** ha conocido el éxito con mayúsculas*; **they screwed (things) up ~** metieron la pata bien hondo*; **America lost ~** el equipo americano se llevó una soberana paliza*

bigwig* [ˈbɪgwɪg] N gerifalte *mf*, pez *m* gordo*

bijou [ˈbiːʒuː] ADJ **"bijou residence for sale"** (*Brit*) "se vende vivienda, verdadera monada"

bike* [baɪk] Ⓐ N (= *bicycle*) bici* *f*; (= *motorcycle*) moto *f*; **to ride a ~** (= *bicycle*) ir *or* montar en bici; (= *motorcycle*) ir en moto; **on your ~!** (*Brit**) ¡largo de aquí!*, ¡andando!*
Ⓑ VI ir en bici; **I ~d 10km** hice 10km en bici
Ⓒ CPD ► **bike lane** N carril *m* de bicicleta, carril *m* bici ► **bike rack** N (*on floor, ground*) aparcamiento-bici *m*; (*on car roof*) portabicicletas *m inv* ► **bike shed** N cobertizo *m* para bicicletas

biker* [ˈbaɪkəʳ] N motociclista *mf*

bikeway [ˈbaɪkweɪ] N (= *lane*) carril *m* de bicicletas; (= *track*) pista *f* de ciclismo

bikini [bɪˈkiːnɪ] Ⓐ N bikini *m* (*f in Arg*)
Ⓑ CPD ► **bikini bottom(s)** N(PL) parte *f* de abajo del bikini, braga *f* del bikini ► **bikini line** N entrepierna *f* ► **bikini top** N parte *f* de arriba del bikini

bilabial [baɪˈleɪbɪəl] Ⓐ ADJ bilabial
Ⓑ N bilabial *f*

bilateral [baɪˈlætərəl] ADJ bilateral

bilaterally [baɪˈlætərəlɪ] ADV bilateralmente

bilberry [ˈbɪlbərɪ] N arándano *m*

bile [baɪl] N 1 (*Med*) bilis *f*
2 (*fig*) (= *anger*) mal genio *m*, displicencia *f*

bilge [bɪldʒ] Ⓐ N 1 (*Naut*) pantoque *m*; (*also* **~ water**) aguas *fpl* de pantoque
2 (‡) (= *nonsense*) tonterías *fpl*
Ⓑ CPD ► **bilge pump** N (*Naut*) bomba *f* de achique ► **bilge water** N aguas *fpl* de pantoque

bilharzia [bɪlˈhɑːzɪə] N, **bilharziasis** [ˌbɪlhɑːˈzaɪəsɪs] N bilharzia *f*, bilharziosis *f*, bilharciosis *f*

bilingual [baɪˈlɪŋgwəl] ADJ bilingüe

bilingualism [baɪˈlɪŋgwəlɪzəm] N bilingüismo *m*

bilious [ˈbɪlɪəs] Ⓐ ADJ 1 (= *horrid*) [*colour*] bilioso
2 (= *sick*) [*person*] bilioso
3 (= *irritable*) bilioso

[4] (*Med*) **to be** *or* **feel ~** sentirse revuelto
Ⓑ CPD ► **bilious attack** N cólico *m* bilioso
biliousness [ˈbɪlɪəsnɪs] N (*Med*) trastornos *mpl* biliares
bilk* [bɪlk] VT (*US*) estafar, defraudar; **to ~ sb out of sth** estafar algo a algn
bill[1] [bɪl] Ⓐ N [1] (*esp Brit*) (*in restaurant, hotel etc*) cuenta *f*, adición *f* (*S. Cone*); **can we have the ~, please?** ¿nos trae la cuenta, por favor?; **to pay the ~** pagar la cuenta; **put it on my ~, please** póngalo en mi cuenta; **+IDIOM to foot the ~ (for sth)** correr con los gastos (de algo), pagar (algo)
[2] (*Comm, Fin*) (= *invoice*) factura *f*; **the gas ~** la factura del gas; **wage(s) ~** (*in industry*) gastos *mpl* de nómina *or* salariales; **~s discounted** efectos *mpl* descontados; **~s payable** efectos *mpl* a pagar; **~s receivable** efectos *mpl* a cobrar
[3] (*Parl*) proyecto *m* de ley; **the ~ passed the Commons** (*Brit*) el proyecto de ley fue aprobado en la Cámara de los Comunes
[4] (*US*) (= *banknote*) billete *m*; **a 5-dollar ~** un billete de 5 dólares
[5] (= *notice*) cartel *m*; **"stick no bills"** "prohibido fijar carteles"
[6] (*Theat*) programa *m*; **to head** *or* **top the ~** ser la atracción principal, encabezar el reparto; **+IDIOM that fills** *or* **fits the ~** eso cumple los requisitos
Ⓑ VT [1] (*Theat*) anunciar, presentar; **he is ~ed to appear next week** figura en el programa de la semana que viene; **it is ~ed as Britain's most interesting museum** lo presentan como el museo más interesante de Gran Bretaña
[2] (*Comm*) **to ~ sb for sth** extender *or* pasar a algn la factura de algo; **you've ~ed me for five instead of four** me ha puesto cinco en vez de cuatro en la factura
Ⓒ CPD ► **bill of exchange** N letra *f* de cambio ► **bill of fare** N carta *f*, menú *m* ► **bill of health** N **the doctor gave him a clean ~ of health** el médico le aseguró que estaba perfectamente ► **bill of lading** N conocimiento *m* de embarque ► **bill of rights** N declaración *f* de derechos ► **bill of sale** N escritura *f* de venta
bill[2] [bɪl] Ⓐ N [1] [*of bird*] pico *m*
[2] [*of anchor*] uña *f*
[3] (*Agr*) podadera *f*, podón *m*
[4] (*Geog*) promontorio *m*
Ⓑ VI **to ~ and coo** [*birds*] arrullarse; (*fig*) [*lovers*] arrullarse, hacerse arrumacos

> **BILL OF RIGHTS**
> *El conjunto de las diez enmiendas (***amendments***) originales a la Constitución de los Estados Unidos, en vigor desde 1791, recibe el nombre de* **Bill of Rights**. *Aquí se enumeran los derechos que tiene todo ciudadano norteamericano y se definen algunos de los poderes de los gobiernos estatales y federal. Se incluyen, por ejemplo, el derecho a la libertad de culto, de asociación y de prensa (***First Amendment***), el derecho a llevar armas (***Second Amendment***) y el derecho a un juicio justo (***Sixth Amendment***). Entre las enmiendas hechas a la Constitución después de 1791 están el derecho a la igualdad de protección legal para todos los ciudadanos (***Fourteenth Amendment***) y el derecho al voto (***Fifteenth Amendment***).*
> ⇨ AMENDMENT - FIFTH AMENDMENT

Bill [bɪl] N [1] (*familiar form*) *of* **William**
[2] (*Brit**) **the (Old) ~** la poli*, la pasma (*Sp**)
billboard [ˈbɪlbɔːd] N cartelera *f*
billet[1] [ˈbɪlɪt] Ⓐ N (*Mil*) alojamiento *m*
Ⓑ VT (*Mil*) **to ~ sb (on sb)** alojar a algn (en casa de algn)
billet[2] [ˈbɪlɪt] N (= *wood*) leño *m*
billet-doux [ˈbɪleɪˈduː] N (*pl* **billets-doux** [ˈbɪleɪˈduːz]) carta *f* amorosa
billeting [ˈbɪlətɪŋ] Ⓐ N acantonamiento *m*
Ⓑ CPD ► **billeting officer** N oficial *mf* de acantonamiento
billfold [ˈbɪlfəʊld] N (*US*) billetero *m*, cartera *f*
billhook [ˈbɪlhʊk] N podadera *f*, podón *m*
billiard [ˈbɪljəd] Ⓐ ADJ de billar
Ⓑ CPD ► **billiard ball** N bola *f* de billar ► **billiard cue** N taco *m* (de billar) ► **billiard hall** N sala *f* de billar, billares *mpl* ► **billiard table** N mesa *f* de billar
billiards [ˈbɪljədz] NSING billar *m*
billing[1] [ˈbɪlɪŋ] N (*Theat*) **to get top ~** ser la atracción principal, encabezar el reparto
billing[2] [ˈbɪlɪŋ] N **~ and cooing** (*fig*) besuqueo *m*, caricias *fpl*
billion [ˈbɪlɪən] N (*pl* **billion** *or* **billions**) (= *thousand million*) mil millones *mpl*; (*Brit*†) (= *million million*) billón *m*; **I've told you a ~ times** te lo he dicho infinidad de veces
billionaire [ˌbɪlɪəˈnɛəʳ] N billonario/a *m/f*
billow [ˈbɪləʊ] Ⓐ N oleada *f*; **the ~s** (*liter*) las olas, el mar
Ⓑ VI [*smoke*] salir en nubes; [*sail*] ondear
►**billow out** VI + ADV hincharse (*de viento etc*)
billowy [ˈbɪləʊɪ] ADJ [*sea, waves, smoke*] ondulante; [*sail*] ondeante
billposter [ˈbɪlˌpəʊstəʳ], **billsticker** [ˈbɪlˌstɪkəʳ] N pegador(a) *m/f* de carteles
Billy [ˈbɪlɪ] N (*familiar form*) *of* **William**
billy [ˈbɪlɪ] N (*US*) (*also* **~ club**) porra *f*
billycan [ˈbɪlɪkæn] N cazo *m*
billy goat [ˈbɪlɪgəʊt] N macho *m* cabrío
billy-o(h)* [ˈbɪlɪəʊ], **billy-ho*** [ˈbɪlɪhəʊ] ADV (*Brit*) **like ~** *or* **billy-ho** a todo tren*, a más no poder; **it's raining like ~** *or* **billy-ho** llueve a más no poder
BIM N ABBR = **British Institute of Management**
bimbo* [ˈbɪmbəʊ] N (*pl* **bimbos** *or* **bimboes**) (*pej*) *mujer guapa y tonta*, tía *f* buena sin coco (*Sp**)
bimonthly [ˈbaɪˈmʌnθlɪ] Ⓐ ADJ (= *every two months*) bimestral; (= *twice monthly*) bimensual, quincenal
Ⓑ ADV (= *every two months*) bimestralmente; (= *twice monthly*) bimensualmente, quincenalmente
Ⓒ N (= *two monthly publication*) revista *f* bimestral; (= *fortnightly publication*) revista *f* bimensual *or* quincenal
bin [bɪn] Ⓐ N (*for bread*) panera *f*; (*for coal*) carbonera *f*; (= *rubbish bin, dustbin*) cubo *m* de la basura, tarro *m* de la basura (*LAm*); (= *litter bin*) papelera *f*
Ⓑ VT (*) (= *throw away*) tirar
Ⓒ CPD ► **bin liner** N bolsa *f* de la basura
binary [ˈbaɪnərɪ] Ⓐ ADJ binario
Ⓑ CPD ► **binary code** N código *m* binario ► **binary notation** N notación *f* binaria ► **binary number** N número *m* binario ► **binary system** N sistema *m* binario
bind [baɪnd] (*pt, pp* **bound**) Ⓐ VT [1] (= *tie together*) atar; (= *tie down, make fast*) sujetar; (*fig*) unir (**to** a); **bound hand and foot** atado de pies y manos
[2] (= *encircle*) rodear (**with** de), ceñir (**with** con, de)
[3] [+ *wound, arm etc*] vendar; [+ *bandage*] enrollar
[4] (*Sew*) [+ *material, hem*] ribetear; (*Agr*) [+ *corn*] agavillar
[5] [+ *book*] encuadernar
[6] (= *oblige*) **to ~ sb to sth** obligar a algn a cumplir con algo; **to ~ sb to do sth** obligar a algn a hacer algo; **to ~ sb as an apprentice to** poner a algn de aprendiz con; *see also* **bound**[1]
[7] (*Culin*) unir, trabar
Ⓑ VI [*cement etc*] cuajarse; [*parts of machine*] trabarse
Ⓒ N (*Brit**) (= *nuisance*) lata* *f*; **it's a ~** es una lata*; **what a ~!** ¡qué lata!*; **to be in a ~** estar en apuros; **the ~ is that …** el problema es que …
►**bind on** VT + ADV prender
►**bind over** VT + ADV (*Brit Jur*) obligar a comparecer ante el magistrado; **to ~ sb over for six months** conceder a algn la libertad bajo fianza durante seis meses; **to ~ sb over to keep the peace** exigir a algn legalmente que no reincida
►**bind together** VT + ADV (*lit*) atar; (*fig*) unir
►**bind up** VT + ADV [1] [+ *wound*] vendar
[2] **to be bound up in** [+ *work, research etc*] estar absorto en; **to be bound up with** (= *connected to*) estar estrechamente ligado *or* vinculado a
binder [ˈbaɪndəʳ] N [1] (= *file*) carpeta *f*
[2] (*Agr*) agavilladora *f*
[3] [*of book*] encuadernador(a) *m/f*
bindery [ˈbaɪndərɪ] N taller *m* de encuadernación
binding [ˈbaɪndɪŋ] Ⓐ N [1] [*of book*] encuadernación *f*
[2] (*Sew*) ribete *m*
[3] (*on skis*) ataduras *fpl*
Ⓑ ADJ [1] [*agreement, contract, decision*] vinculante; [*promise*] que hay que cumplir; **to be ~ on sb** ser obligatorio para algn
[2] (*Med*) que estriñe
bindweed [ˈbaɪndwiːd] N convólvulo *m*, enredadera *f*
binge* [bɪndʒ] Ⓐ N [*of drinking*] borrachera *f*; [*of eating*] comilona* *f*, atracón* *m*; **to go on a ~** ir de juerga; **to go on a spending ~** salir de compras a despilfarrar el dinero
Ⓑ VI (*gen*) correrse un exceso; (*eating*) darse una comilona*, darse un atracón*; **to ~ on chocolate** darse un atracón *or* ponerse hasta arriba de chocolate*
bingo [ˈbɪŋgəʊ] Ⓐ N bingo *m*
Ⓑ EXCL ¡premio!
Ⓒ CPD ► **bingo hall** N bingo *m*
binnacle [ˈbɪnəkl] N bitácora *f*
binocular [bɪˈnɒkjʊləʳ] ADJ binocular
binoculars [bɪˈnɒkjʊləz] NPL gemelos *mpl*, prismáticos *mpl*; (*Mil*) anteojo *m* de campaña
binomial [baɪˈnəʊmɪəl] Ⓐ ADJ de dos términos
Ⓑ N binomio *m*
bint‡ [bɪnt] N (*Brit pej*) tía *f* (*Sp**), tronca‡ *f*, titi‡ *f*
binuclear [baɪˈnjuːklɪəʳ] ADJ binuclear
bio… [ˈbaɪəʊ] PREFIX bio…
bioactive [ˈbaɪəʊˈæktɪv] ADJ bioactivo
biochemical [ˈbaɪəʊˈkemɪkəl] ADJ bioquímico
biochemist [ˈbaɪəʊˈkemɪst] N bioquímico/a *m/f*
biochemistry [ˈbaɪəʊˈkemɪstrɪ] N bioquímica *f*
biodegradable [ˌbaɪədɪˈgreɪdəbl] ADJ biodegradable
biodegradation [ˌbaɪəʊˌdegrəˈdeɪʃən] N biodegradación *f*
biodegrade [ˌbaɪədɪˈgreɪd] Ⓐ VT biodegradar
Ⓑ VI biodegradarse
biodiversity [ˌbaɪədaɪˈvɜːsɪtɪ] N biodiversidad *f*

biodynamic [ˈbaɪəʊdaɪˈnæmɪk] ADJ biodinámico

bioengineering [ˈbaɪəʊendʒɪˈnɪərɪŋ] N bioingeniería *f*

biofeedback [ˌbaɪəʊˈfiːdbæk] N biofeedback *m*

biofuel [ˈbaɪəʊfjʊəl] N combustible *m* biológico

biogas [ˈbaɪəʊgæs] N biogás *m*

biogenesis [ˌbaɪəʊˈdʒenɪsɪs] N biogénesis *f*

biographee [baɪˌɒgrəˈfiː] N biografiado/a *m/f*

biographer [baɪˈɒgrəfəʳ] N biógrafo/a *m/f*

biographic [ˌbaɪəʊˈgræfɪk] ADJ = **biographical**

biographical [ˌbaɪəʊˈgræfɪkəl] ADJ biográfico

biography [baɪˈɒgrəfɪ] N biografía *f*

biological [ˌbaɪəˈlɒdʒɪkəl] Ⓐ ADJ biológico
Ⓑ CPD ► **biological clock** N reloj *m* biológico, reloj *m* interno ► **biological soap powder** N detergente *m* biológico ► **biological warfare** N guerra *f* biológica ► **biological weapons** NPL armas *fpl* biológicas

biologically [ˌbaɪəˈlɒdʒɪkəlɪ] ADV [*active, programmed, determined*] biológicamente; [*different*] desde el punto de vista biológico

biologist [baɪˈɒlədʒɪst] N biólogo/a *m/f*

biology [baɪˈɒlədʒɪ] N biología *f*

biomass [ˈbaɪəʊˌmæs] N biomasa *f*

biome [ˈbaɪəʊm] N biomedio *m*

biomedical [ˌbaɪəʊˈmedɪkl] ADJ biomédico

biometric [ˌbaɪəˈmetrɪk] ADJ [*data, technology, device*] biométrico

biometrics [ˌbaɪəˈmetrɪks] NSING, **biometry** [baɪˈɒmətrɪ] N biometría *f*

bionic [baɪˈɒnɪk] ADJ biónico

bionics [baɪˈɒnɪks] NSING electrónica *f* biológica

bio-organic [ˌbaɪəʊɔːˈgænɪk] ADJ bioorgánico

biophysical [ˌbaɪəʊˈfɪzɪkəl] ADJ biofísico

biophysicist [ˌbaɪəʊˈfɪzɪsɪst] N biofísico/a *m/f*

biophysics [ˌbaɪəʊˈfɪzɪks] NSING biofísica *f*

biopic* [ˈbaɪəʊˌpɪk] N biografía *f* cinematográfica

biopiracy [ˌbaɪəʊˈpaɪərəsɪ] N biopiratería *f*

bioprospecting [ˈbaɪəʊprɒsˌpektɪŋ] Ⓐ N bioprospección *f* Ⓑ ADJ [*company*] bioprospector

biopsy [ˈbaɪɒpsɪ] N biopsia *f*

biorhythm [ˈbaɪəʊrɪðəm] N biorritmo *m*

bioscopy [baɪˈɒskəpɪ] N bioscopia *f*

biosensor [ˈbaɪəʊˈsensəʳ] N biosensor *m*

biosphere [ˈbaɪəˌsfɪəʳ] N biosfera *f*

biostatistics [ˈbaɪəʊstəˈtɪstɪks] NPL bioestadística *fsing*

biosynthesis [ˌbaɪəʊˈsɪnθɪsɪs] N biosíntesis *f*

biosynthetic [ˌbaɪəʊˌsɪnˈθetɪk] ADJ biosintético

biotechnological [ˌbaɪəˌteknəˈlɒdʒɪkəl] ADJ biotecnológico

biotechnologist [ˌbaɪəʊtekˈnɒlədʒɪst] N biotecnólogo/a *m/f*

biotechnology [ˌbaɪəʊtekˈnɒlədʒɪ] N biotecnología *f*

bioterrorism [ˌbaɪəʊˈterərɪzəm] N bioterrorismo *m*

bioterrorist [ˌbaɪəʊˈterərɪst] Ⓐ ADJ bioterrorista Ⓑ N bioterrorista *m/f*

biotic [baɪˈɒtɪk] ADJ biótico

biotope [ˈbaɪəˌtəʊp] N biotopo *m*

biotype [ˈbaɪəˌtaɪp] N biotipo *m*

biowarfare [ˈbaɪəʊˈwɔːfɛəʳ] N guerra *f* bacteriológica

bioweapon [ˈbaɪəʊˌwepən] N arma *f* biológica

bipartisan [ˌbaɪˈpɑːtɪzæn] ADJ bipartidario

bipartite [baɪˈpɑːtaɪt] ADJ (= *consisting of two parts*) [*structure*] bipartido; [*treaty*] bipartito

biped [ˈbaɪped] N bípedo *m*

biplane [ˈbaɪpleɪn] N biplano *m*

bipolar [baɪˈpəʊləʳ] Ⓐ ADJ bipolar
Ⓑ CPD ► **bipolar disorder** trastorno *m* bipolar

bipolarize [baɪˈpəʊləraɪz] VT bipolarizar

birch [bɜːtʃ] Ⓐ N (= *tree, wood*) abedul *m*; (*for whipping*) vara *f*
Ⓑ VT (= *punish*) castigar con la vara
Ⓒ CPD ► **birch tree** N abedul *m*

birching [ˈbɜːtʃɪŋ] N azotamiento *m* (con la vara)

birchwood [ˈbɜːtʃwʊd] N (= *forest*) bosque *m* de abedules; (= *material*) abedul *m*

bird [bɜːd] Ⓐ N 1 (*gen small*) pájaro *m*; (*Zool, Culin*) ave *f*; **~ of ill omen** (*liter*) pájaro *m* de mal agüero; **a little ~ told me*** (*hum*) me lo dijo un pajarito; **the ~ has flown** (*fig*) el pájaro ha volado; ✦*IDIOMS* **they haven't yet told her about the ~s and the bees** todavía no le han explicado las cosas de la vida; **to kill two ~s with one stone** matar dos pájaros de un tiro; **to be strictly for the ~s*** ser cosa de poca monta *or* de tontos; **they're ~s of a feather** son lobos de una camada; ✦*PROVS* **~s of a feather flock together** Dios los cría y ellos se juntan; **a ~ in the hand is worth two in the bush** más vale pájaro en mano que ciento volando; *see also* **early C**
2 (*Brit Theat**) ✦*IDIOMS* **to get the ~** ganarse un abucheo, ser pateado; **to give sb the ~** abuchear a algn, patear a algn
3 (*Brit**) (= *girl*) chica *f*, pollita *f*, niña *f* (*LAm*); (= *girlfriend*) chica *f*, amiguita *f*
4 (*) (= *fellow*) tipo* *m*, tío* *m* (*Sp**); **he's a queer ~** es un bicho raro
5 (‡) (= *imprisonment*) **to do two years ~** pasar dos años a la sombra‡
Ⓑ CPD ► **bird bath** N pila *f* para pájaros ► **bird brain*** N casquivano/a *m/f* ► **bird call** N reclamo *m* ► **bird dog** N (*US*) perro *m* de caza ► **bird fancier** N criador(a) *m/f* de pájaros ► **bird flu** N gripe *f* aviar ► **bird nesting** N **to go ~ nesting** ir a buscar nidos ► **bird of paradise** N ave *f* del paraíso ► **bird of passage** N ave *f* de paso ► **bird of prey** N ave *f* de rapiña ► **bird sanctuary** N reserva *f* de pájaros ► **bird's nest** N nido *m* de pájaro ► **bird table** N *mesita de jardín para poner comida a los pájaros*

bird-brained* [ˈbɜːdbreɪnd] ADJ casquivano

birdcage [ˈbɜːdkeɪdʒ] N jaula *f* de pájaro; (*large, outdoor*) pajarera *f*

birdie [ˈbɜːdɪ] Ⓐ N 1 (*Golf*) birdie *m*, menos uno *m* 2 (*baby talk*) pajarito *m*; **watch the ~!** (*Phot**) ¡mira el pajarito!
Ⓑ VT (*Golf*) **to ~ a hole** hacer birdie *or* uno bajo par en un hoyo

bird-like [ˈbɜːdlaɪk] ADJ como un pájaro

birdlime [ˈbɜːdlaɪm] N liga *f*

birdseed [ˈbɜːdsiːd] N alpiste *m*

bird's-eye view [ˌbɜːdzaɪˈvjuː] N vista *f* de pájaro

birdshot [ˈbɜːdʃɒt] N perdigones *mpl*

bird-watcher [ˈbɜːdwɒtʃəʳ] N observador(a) *m/f* de aves

bird-watching [ˈbɜːdˌwɒtʃɪŋ] N observación *f* de aves; **to go ~** realizar observación de aves

biretta [bɪˈretə] N birrete *m*

Biro® [ˈbaɪrəʊ] N (*Brit*) bolígrafo *m*, birome *f* (*S. Cone*)

▼ **birth** [bɜːθ] Ⓐ N (*gen*) nacimiento *m*; (*Med*) parto *m*; (*fig*) nacimiento *m*, surgimiento *m*; **at ~** al nacer; **French by ~** francés de nacimiento; **of humble ~** de origen humilde; **place of ~** lugar *m* de nacimiento; **to give ~ to** (*lit*) dar a luz a; (*fig*) dar origen a; **to be in at the ~ of** (*fig*) asistir al nacimiento de; **the ~ of an idea** el origen de una idea
Ⓑ CPD ► **birth certificate** N partida *f* de nacimiento ► **birth control** N control *m* de la natalidad; **method of ~ control** método *m* anticonceptivo ► **birth control pill** N píldora *f* anticonceptiva ► **birth mother** N madre *f* biológica ► **birth pill** N = **birth control pill** ► **birth rate** N tasa *f* or índice *m* de natalidad

birthdate [ˈbɜːθdeɪt] N fecha *f* de nacimiento

▼ **birthday** [ˈbɜːθdeɪ] Ⓐ N [*of person*] cumpleaños *m inv*; [*of event etc*] aniversario *m*; **on my 21st ~** el día en que cumplo/cumplí 21 años; **happy ~!** ¡feliz cumpleaños!
Ⓑ CPD ► **birthday cake** N tarta *f* de cumpleaños ► **birthday card** N tarjeta *f* de cumpleaños ► **birthday party** N fiesta *f* de cumpleaños ► **birthday present** N regalo *m* de cumpleaños ► **birthday suit*** N **in one's ~ suit** (*hum*) en cueros*

birthing [ˈbɜːθɪŋ] ADJ [*pool, centre etc*] de partos, para el parto

birthmark [ˈbɜːθmɑːk] N antojo *m*, marca *f* de nacimiento

birthplace [ˈbɜːθpleɪs] N lugar *m* de nacimiento

birthright [ˈbɜːθraɪt] N derechos *mpl* de nacimiento; (*fig*) patrimonio *m*, herencia *f*; **it is the ~ of every Englishman** pertenece por derecho natural a todo inglés, es el patrimonio de todo inglés; ✦*IDIOM* **to sell one's ~ for a mess of pottage** vender su primogenitura por un plato de lentejas

birthstone [ˈbɜːθstəʊn] N piedra *f* natalicia

BIS N ABBR (*US*) (= **Bank of International Settlements**) BIP *m*

Biscay [ˈbɪskeɪ] N Vizcaya *f*

biscuit [ˈbɪskɪt] Ⓐ N (*Brit*) galleta *f*; (*US*) magdalena *f*; ✦*IDIOM* **that takes the ~!‡** ¡eso es el colmo!*
Ⓑ CPD ► **biscuit barrel** N galletero *m*

bisect [baɪˈsekt] VT bisecar

bisection [baɪˈsekʃən] N (*Math*) bisección *f*, división *f* en dos partes; (= *angle*) bisección *f*

bisector [baɪˈsektəʳ] N bisector *m*

bisexual [ˈbaɪˈseksjʊəl] Ⓐ ADJ bisexual
Ⓑ N bisexual *mf*

bisexuality [baɪˌseksjʊˈælɪtɪ] N bisexualidad *f*

bishop [ˈbɪʃəp] N 1 (*Rel*) obispo *m*; **yes, Bishop** sí, Ilustrísima 2 (*Chess*) alfil *m*

bishopric [ˈbɪʃəprɪk] N obispado *m*

bismuth [ˈbɪzməθ] N bismuto *m*

bison [ˈbaɪsən] N (*pl* **bison, bisons**) bisonte *m*

bisque [bɪsk] N (*Culin*) sopa *f* de mariscos; (*Sport*) ventaja *f*; (*Pottery*) bizcocho *m*, biscuit *m*

bistable [baɪˈsteɪbl] ADJ (*Comput*) biestable

bistro [ˈbiːstrəʊ] N bistro(t) *m*

bit¹ [bɪt] Ⓐ N 1 (= *piece*) trozo *m*, pedazo *m*; **~s of paper** trozos *mpl* or pedazos *mpl* de papel; **have you got a ~ of paper I can write on?** ¿tienes un trozo de papel para escribir?; **he washed off every ~ of dirt** se lavó hasta la última mancha de suciedad; **in ~s** (= *broken*) hecho pedazos; (= *dismantled*) desmontado, desarmado; **who owns this ~ of land?** ¿a quién pertenece este trozo *or* pedazo de tierra?; **~s and pieces** (= *items*) cosas *fpl*; (= *possessions*) cosas *fpl*, trastos* *mpl*; [*of fabric*] retales *mpl*, retazos *mpl*; **to ~s: to blow sth to ~s** hacer saltar algo en pedazos, volar algo en pedazos; **to come to ~s** (= *break*) hacerse pedazos; (= *be dismantled*) desmontarse, desarmarse; **to smash sth to ~s** hacer algo añicos *or* pedazos; **to tear sth to ~s** [+ *letter, document*] romper algo en pedazos; **the dogs tear the fox to ~s** los perros destrozan al zorro; **she tore the argument to ~s** hizo peda-

➤ LANGUAGE IN USE: birth A 24.1 birthday A 23.3

zos el argumento; ✦*IDIOMS* **to love sb to ~s*** querer un montón a algn*; **the professor pulled his essay to ~s** el profesor destrozó su trabajo; **he was thrilled to ~s with the present** estaba que no cabía en sí (de alegría) con el regalo, el regalo le hizo muchísima ilusión

2 **a ~ of** 2·1 (= *some*) un poco de; **with a ~ of luck** con un poco de suerte; **a ~ of advice** un consejo; **I need a ~ of peace and quiet** necesito un poco de paz y tranquilidad; **what you say won't make a ~ of difference** digas lo que digas no va a cambiar nada; **this is a ~ of all right!*** ¡esto está muy bien!, ¡esto no está nada mal!; **he's a ~ of all right*** ése está buenísimo *or* para comérselo*

2·2 (= *rather*) **he's a ~ of a liar** es bastante *or* un poco mentiroso; **it was a ~ of a shock** fue un golpe bastante duro; **I've got a ~ of a cold** estoy un poco resfriado; **I'm a ~ of a socialist** yo tengo algo de socialista; **quite a ~ of** bastante; **they have quite a ~ of money** tienen bastante dinero; **I've been seeing quite a ~ of her** la he estado viendo bastante

3 (*adverbial uses*) **a ~** un poco; **a ~ bigger/smaller** un poco más grande/pequeño; **a ~ later** poco después, un poco más tarde; **that sounds a ~ technical** eso suena un poco técnico; **it's a ~ awkward just now** ahora no es buen momento; **~ by ~** poco a poco; **our performance was every ~ as good as theirs** nuestra actuación fue tan buena como la suya en todos los aspectos; **she swept into the room, every ~ the actress** entró majestuosamente en la habitación, muy en su papel de actriz; **he looked every ~ the angelic child** tenía toda la pinta *or* todo el aspecto de un niño angelical; **a good ~** bastante; **it's a good ~ further than we thought** queda bastante más lejos de lo que creíamos; **a good ~ bigger/cheaper** bastante más grande/barato; **would you like a little ~ more?** ¿quieres un poquito más?; **that's a ~ much!** ¡eso pasa de castaño oscuro!; **it's a ~ much expecting you to take the blame** es demasiado esperar que tú asumas la culpa; **not a ~: I'm not a ~ surprised** no me sorprende lo más mínimo *or* en absoluto; **"wasn't he embarrassed?" — "not a ~ of it"** —¿y no le daba vergüenza? —qué va* *or* —en absoluto; **quite a ~** bastante; **they're worth quite a ~** valen bastante; **he's quite a ~ older than me** es bastante mayor que yo; **I've had a ~ too much to eat** me he pasado un poco comiendo, he comido un poco más de la cuenta

4 (= *part*) parte *f*; **he'd just got to the exciting ~** acababa de llegar a la parte emocionante; **to enjoy every ~ of sth** disfrutar algo totalmente

5 (*Brit**) (= *role*) **she's doing the prima donna ~** está haciendo su papel de diva; **it's important not to overdo the motherly ~** es importante no ser excesivamente maternal; **to do one's ~** aportar su granito de arena; **we must all do our ~ to put an end to starvation in the Third World** para erradicar el hambre en el Tercer Mundo todos debemos aportar nuestro granito de arena; **he did his ~ in the war** durante la guerra cumplió con su deber; **I've done my ~** yo he hecho mi parte *or* lo que me tocaba

6 (= *moment*) rato *m*, momento *m*; **I'll see you in a ~** te veo dentro de un momento *or* dentro de un ratito; **I waited quite a ~** esperé bastante tiempo *or* un buen rato

7 (= *coin*) (*Brit*) moneda *f*; (*US*) (= *12½ cents*) doce centavos y medio; **a tuppenny ~** una moneda de dos peniques; **two ~s** (*US*) 25 centavos; **for two ~s I'd throw it all in** por dos duros lo dejaría todo; **he was always throwing in his two ~s about how he'd put the economy to rights** siempre estaba dando su opinión *or* echando su cuarto a espadas sobre cómo arreglaría la economía

8 (*Comput*) bit *m*

9 (*Brit*‡ *pej*) (= *woman*) tía *f* (*Sp**); *see also* **side A6**

Ⓑ CPD ► **bit part** N (*Cine, Theat*) papel *m* de poca importancia, papel *m* pequeño

bit² [bɪt] N 1 [*of drill*] broca *f*

2 (*for horse*) freno *m*, bocado *m*; ✦*IDIOMS* **to be champing** *or* **chomping at the ~**: **I expect you're champing** *or* **chomping at the ~** supongo que te devora la impaciencia; **they were champing** *or* **chomping at the ~ to get started** no veían la hora de poner manos a la obra; **to get the ~ between one's teeth**: **once she gets the ~ between her teeth, there's no stopping her** una vez que se pone en marcha no hay quien la pare

bit³ [bɪt] PT *of* **bite**

bitch [bɪtʃ] Ⓐ N 1 [*of canines*] hembra *f*; [*of dog*] perra *f*

2 (‡) (= *woman*) bruja* *f*; **you ~!** ¡(tía) cerda!*, ¡lagarta! (*Sp**)

3 (‡) **this car is a ~** este coche es una lata*; **it's a ~ of a problem** es un problema que se las trae*; **life's a ~ (and then you die)** esta vida es un asco*, esta vida es una mierda‡

4 (*esp US*‡) (= *complaint*) queja *f*; **what's your ~?** ¿de qué coño te quejas tú?‡

Ⓑ VI (*) (= *complain*) quejarse (**about** de)

bitchiness* ['bɪtʃɪnɪs] N mala leche* *f*

bitchy* ['bɪtʃɪ] ADJ (*compar* **bitchier**; *superl* **bitchiest**) [*person*] malicioso; [*remark*] malintencionado, de mala leche (*Sp**); **to be ~ to sb** ser malicioso con algn; **that was a ~ thing to do** eso fue una puñalada trapera*, eso fue una guarrada (*Sp**)

bite [baɪt] (*vb: pt* **bit**; *pp* **bitten**) Ⓐ N 1 (= *act*) mordisco *m*; (= *wound*) [*of dog, snake etc*] mordedura *f*; [*of insect*] picadura *f*; (= *toothmark*) dentellada *f*; **to take a ~ at** morder; **the dog took a ~ at him** el perro intentó morderlo; **to take a ~ out of** [+ *apple etc*] dar un mordisco a; (*esp US*) (*fig*) [+ *savings, budget*] llevarse un pellizco de; ✦*IDIOMS* **he wants another** *or* **a second ~ at the cherry** quiere otra oportunidad, quiere probar otra vez; **to put the ~ on sb** (*US**) hacer cerrar el pico a algn*

2 (*) [*of food*] bocado *m*; **I've not had a ~ to eat** no he probado bocado; **do you fancy a ~ (to eat)?** ¿te apetece algo (de comer)?; **I'll get a ~ (to eat) on the train** tomaré algo en el tren

3 (*Fishing*) **are you getting any ~s?** ¿están picando?

4 (*fig*) (= *sharpness*) mordacidad *f*; [*of food, drink*] fuerza *f*; **a novel with ~** una novela mordaz; **a speech with ~** un discurso mordaz *or* incisivo; **without any ~** sin garra; **there's a ~ in the air** hace un frío cortante

Ⓑ VT 1 [*dog, person*] morder; [*bird, fish, insect*] picar; **it won't ~ (you)!*** ¡no te va a morder!, ¡no muerde!; **to ~ sth in two** partir algo en dos de un mordisco; **to ~ one's nails** comerse *or* morderse las uñas; **what's biting you?*** ¿qué mosca te ha picado?*; **to get bitten*** (= *be cheated*) dejarse timar; **to be bitten with the desire to do sth*** tener el gusanillo de hacer algo*; ✦*IDIOMS* **to ~ the bullet** enfrentarse al toro; **to ~ the dust** (= *die*) morder el polvo; (= *fail*) venirse abajo; **it's the old story of biting the hand that feeds you** ya sabes "cría cuervos (y te sacarán los ojos)"; **to ~ one's lip** *or* **tongue** morderse la lengua; ✦*PROV* **once bitten twice shy** el gato escaldado del agua fría huye

2 [*acid*] corroer; (*Mech*) asir, trabar

Ⓒ VI 1 [*dog, person*] morder; [*insect, fish*] picar; **to ~ at** tratar de morder

2 (*fig*) [*cuts, inflation etc*] hacerse sentir; **the strike is beginning to ~** la huelga empieza a hacer mella

►**bite back** Ⓐ VT + ADV [+ *words*] dejar sin decir, tragarse*

Ⓑ VI + ADV **the dog bit back** el perro mordió a su vez

►**bite into** VI + PREP [*person*] meter los dientes en; [*acid*] corroer

►**bite off** VT + ADV arrancar con los dientes; ✦*IDIOMS* **to ~ off more than one can chew** abarcar demasiado; **to ~ sb's head off** echar una bronca a algn*

►**bite on** VI + PREP morder

►**bite through** VI + PREP [+ *string, thread*] cortar con los dientes; [+ *tip, one's tongue*] morderse; **he fell and bit through his tongue** se cayó y se mordió la lengua

biter ['baɪtəʳ] N ✦*IDIOM* **the ~ bit** el cazador cazado

bite-size(d)* ['baɪt'saɪz(d)] ADJ 1 (*lit*) [*food*] cortado a taquitos *or* en dados; **bite-sized pieces of ham** taquitos *mpl* de jamón

2 (*fig*) [*information*] en cantidades digeribles, en pequeñas dosis

biting ['baɪtɪŋ] ADJ [*cold, wind*] cortante; [*criticism etc*] mordaz

bitten ['bɪtn] PP *of* **bite**

bitter ['bɪtəʳ] Ⓐ ADJ 1 (*in taste*) [*drink, medicine*] amargo; **it tasted ~** sabía amargo; ✦*IDIOM* **a ~ pill to swallow** un trago amargo

2 (= *icy*) [*weather, winter*] gélido, glacial; [*wind*] cortante, gélido; **it's ~ today!** hoy hace un frío gélido *or* glacial

3 (= *fierce*) [*enemy, hatred*] implacable; [*battle*] encarnizado; **a ~ struggle** una lucha enconada

4 (= *resentful*) [*person*] amargado, resentido; [*protest*] amargo; **to feel ~ about sth** estar amargo *or* resentido por algo

5 (= *painful*) [*disappointment*] amargo; **to carry on to the ~ end** continuar hasta el final (cueste lo que cueste); **to shed ~ tears** llorar lágrimas amargas

Ⓑ N 1 (*Brit*) (= *beer*) cerveza *f* amarga

2 **bitters** *licor amargo hecho con extractos de plantas*

Ⓒ CPD ► **bitter aloes** NPL áloes *mpl* amargos ► **bitter lemon** N (= *drink*) refresco *m* de limón ► **bitter orange** N (= *drink*) refresco *m* de naranja

bitterly ['bɪtəlɪ] ADV 1 (= *icily*) **it's ~ cold** hace un frío gélido *or* glacial; **a ~ cold day** un día gélido *or* glacial

2 (= *fiercely*) [*oppose*] implacablemente; [*hate*] implacablemente, a muerte; [*fight*] a muerte; [*criticize*] duramente; **a ~ contested match** un partido muy reñido

3 (= *deeply*) [*regret, resent*] amargamente; [*resentful, jealous, ashamed*] terriblemente; **I was ~ disappointed** sufrí una terrible *or* amarga decepción, quedé terriblemente decepcionado

4 (= *resentfully*) [*say, reply*] con rencor; [*speak, think*] amargamente, con rencor; [*complain*] amargamente; **she spoke ~ of her experiences** habló amargamente *or* con rencor de sus experiencias

5 (= *sorrowfully*) [*weep, cry*] amargamente

bittern ['bɪtɜːn] N avetoro *m* (común)

bitterness ['bɪtənɪs] N 1 (= *taste*) amargor *m*

2 (= *iciness*) crudeza *f*

[3] (= *fierceness*) [*of struggle, fight*] lo enconado; [*of hatred*] lo implacable
[4] (= *resentfulness*) amargura *f*, rencor *m*; **I accepted it without ~** lo acepté sin amargura *or* sin rencor; **I have no ~ towards you** no le guardo rencor; **a look of ~** una mirada de amargura
[5] (= *depth*) [*of disappointment*] amargura *f*

bittersweet ['bɪtəswiːt] ADJ (*lit, fig*) agridulce

bitty* ['bɪtɪ] ADJ [1] (*compar* **bittier**; *superl* **bittiest**) (= *disconnected*) deshilvanado
[2] (*US*) (= *small*) pequeñito

bitumen ['bɪtjʊmɪn] N betún *m*

bituminous [bɪ'tjuːmɪnəs] ADJ bituminoso

bivalent ['baɪ'veɪlənt] ADJ bivalente

bivalve ['baɪvælv] (A) ADJ bivalvo
(B) N (molusco *m*) bivalvo *m*

bivouac ['bɪvʊæk] (*vb: pt, pp* **bivouacked**) (A) N vivaque *m*
(B) VI vivaquear

bi-weekly ['baɪ'wiːklɪ] (A) ADJ [1] (= *fortnightly*) quincenal
[2] (= *twice weekly*) bisemanal
(B) ADV [1] (= *fortnightly*) quincenalmente
[2] (= *twice weekly*) bisemanalmente
(C) N [1] (= *fortnightly*) revista *f* quincenal
[2] (= *twice weekly*) revista *f* bisemanal

biz* [bɪz] N ABBR = **business**

bizarre [bɪ'zɑːʳ] ADJ (= *strange*) extraño, raro; [*dress, appearance etc*] estrafalario

bk ABBR [1] (= **book**) l., lib.
[2] (= **bank**) Bco., B.

bkcy ABBR = **bankruptcy**

bkg ABBR = **banking**

bkpt ABBR = **bankrupt**

BL N ABBR [1] = **British Library**
[2] = **Bachelor of Law**

B/L ABBR = **bill of lading**

blab* [blæb] (A) VT (*also* ~ **out**) [+ *secret*] soplar*
(B) VI (= *chatter*) chismorrear*, cotillear (*Sp**); (*to police etc*) cantar*

blabber* ['blæbəʳ] VI (*also* ~ **on**) charlotear, parlar

blabbermouth* ['blæbə,maʊθ] N (*pej*) bocazas* *mf*, cotilla *mf* (*Sp**)

black [blæk] (A) ADJ (*compar* **blacker**; *superl* **blackest**) [1] (*in colour*) negro; **(accident) ~ spot** (*Aut*) punto *m* negro; **~ and white photo** foto *f* en blanco y negro; **~ and white TV** TV *f* monocromo; **his face was ~ and blue** tenía la cara amoratada; **with a face as ~ as thunder** con cara de pocos amigos; ✦***IDIOM*** **to swear ~ and blue** jurar por todo lo más santo (**that** que)
[2] (*of race*) negro; **~ man** negro *m*; **~ woman** negra *f*
[3] (= *dark*) oscuro, tenebroso; **as ~ as pitch** ◊ **as ~ as your hat** oscuro como boca de lobo
[4] (= *dirty*) sucio; (*with smoke*) negro, ennegrecido
[5] (*Brit*) (*trade union parlance*) **to declare a product ~** boicotear un producto
[6] (*fig*) [*day, event*] negro, funesto, aciago; [*outlook*] negro; [*forecast*] pesimista; [*thought*] malévolo; [*rage*] negro; [*look*] ceñudo, de desaprobación; **a ~ day on the roads** una jornada negra en las carreteras; **he is not as ~ as he is painted** no es tan malo como lo pintan; **things look pretty ~** la situación es desconsoladora; **things were looking ~ for him** la situación se le presentaba muy difícil
(B) N [1] (= *colour*) negro *m*, color *m* negro; **a film in ~ and white** un film en blanco y negro; ✦***IDIOM*** **in ~ and white: I should like it in ~ and white** quisiera tenerlo por escrito; **there it is in ~ and white!** ¡ahí lo tiene en letras de molde!
[2] (= *person*) negro/a *m/f*
[3] (= *mourning*) luto *m*; **to be in ~** ◊ **wear ~** estar de luto
[4] (= *darkness*) oscuridad *f*, noche *f*
[5] **to stay in the ~** estar en números negros
(C) VT [1] ennegrecer; [+ *shoes*] limpiar, lustrar; **to ~ sb's eye** poner a algn el ojo amoratado, poner a algn el ojo a la funerala (*Sp**)
[2] (*Brit*) (*trade union parlance*) boicotear
(D) CPD ► **Black Africa** N el África negra ► **black arts** NPL magia *f* negra ► **black bass** N perca *f* negra, perca *f* truchada ► **black belt** N (*Sport*) cinturón *m* negro ► **black box** N (*Aer*) caja *f* negra ► **black coffee** N café *m* solo, tinto *m* (*Col*); (*large*) café *m* americano ► **black college** N (*US*) *universidad para gente de color* ► **black comedy** N comedia *f* negra ► **Black Country** N *región industrial al noroeste de Birmingham (Inglaterra)* ► **Black Death** N peste *f* negra ► **black economy** N economía *f* negra ► **Black English** N (*US*) *inglés hablado por los negros americanos* ► **black eye** N ojo *m* amoratado, ojo *m* a la funerala (*Sp**) ► **Black Forest** N Selva *f* Negra ► **Black Forest gâteau** N *pastel de chocolate, nata y guindas* ► **black goods** NPL géneros *mpl* sujetos a boicoteo ► **black grouse** N gallo *m* lira ► **black hole** N (*Astron*) agujero *m* negro ► **black humour** N humor *m* negro ► **black ice** N *hielo invisible en la carretera* ► **black line** N raya *f* en negro ► **black magic** N magia *f* negra ► **Black Maria** N (*Brit*) coche *m or* furgón *m* celular ► **black mark** N señal *f* roja; (*fig*) nota *f* adversa, punto *m* negativo ► **black market** N mercado *m* negro, estraperlo *m* (*Sp*) ► **black marketeer** N estraperlista *mf* (*Sp*) ► **Black Moslem** N musulmán *m* negro ► **Black Nationalism** N nacionalismo *m* negro ► **Black Panthers** NPL Panteras *fpl* negras ► **black pepper** N pimienta *f* negra ► **Black Power** N poder *m* negro ► **black pudding** N (*Brit*) morcilla *f*, moronga *f* (*Mex*) ► **Black Rod** N (*Brit Parl*) *dignatario de la Cámara de los Lores encargado de reunir a los Comunes en la apertura del Parlamento* ► **Black Sea** N Mar *m* Negro ► **black sheep (of the family)** N oveja *f* negra ► **Black Studies** N (*US*) *estudios de la cultura negra americana* ► **black tie** N corbata *f* de lazo, corbata *f* de smoking; **"~ tie"** (*on invitation*) "de etiqueta" ► **black tie dinner** N cena *f* de etiqueta ► **Black Watch** N (*Brit Mil*) *regimiento escocés* ► **black widow (spider)** N viuda *f* negra

►**black out** (A) VT + ADV (= *obliterate with ink etc*) suprimir; **to ~ out a house** apagar las luces de una casa, hacer que no sean visibles por fuera las luces de una casa; **the screen was ~ed out by the strike** (*TV*) debido a la huelga no había programas en la pantalla; **the storm ~ed out the city** la tormenta causó un apagón en la ciudad
(B) VI + ADV (= *faint*) desmayarse, perder el conocimiento

blackball ['blækbɔːl] (A) VT (= *vote against*) dar bola negra a, votar en contra de; (= *exclude*) dejar fuera
(B) N (= *ball*) bola *f* negra; (= *vote*) voto *m* en contra

blackberry ['blækbərɪ] N (= *fruit*) zarzamora *f*, mora *f*; (= *plant*) zarza *f*

blackberrying ['blæk,berɪɪŋ] N **to go ~** ir a coger zarzamoras

blackbird ['blækbɜːd] N mirlo *m*

blackboard ['blækbɔːd] N pizarra *f*

blackcap ['blækkæp] N (*Orn*) cucurra *f* capirotada

blackcock ['blækkɒk] N gallo *m* lira

blackcurrant [,blæk'kʌrənt] N (= *fruit*) grosella *f* negra; (= *bush*) grosellero *m* negro, casis *f inv*

blacken ['blækən] (A) VT [1] ennegrecer; (*by fire*) calcinar; [+ *face*] tiznar de negro
[2] (*fig*) [+ *reputation*] manchar
(B) VI ennegrecerse

blackguard† ['blægɑːd] (A) N canalla* *mf*
(B) VT vilipendiar

blackguardly† ['blægɑːdlɪ] ADJ vil, canallesco

blackhead ['blækhed] N espinilla *f*

black-headed gull [,blækhedɪd'gʌl] N gaviota *f* de cabeza negra

black-hearted [,blæk'hɑːtɪd] ADJ malvado, perverso

blacking ['blækɪŋ] N betún *m*

blackish ['blækɪʃ] ADJ negruzco; (*wine parlance*) aguindado

blackjack ['blækdʒæk] N (*esp US*) [1] (= *truncheon*) cachiporra *f* con puño flexible
[2] (= *flag*) bandera *f* pirata
[3] (*Cards*) veintiuna *f*

blackleg ['blækleg] (*Brit Ind*) (A) N esquirol *mf*
(B) VI ser esquirol, trabajar durante una huelga

blacklegging ['blæk,legɪŋ] N (*Brit Ind*) esquirolaje *m*

blacklist ['blæklɪst] (A) N lista *f* negra
(B) VT poner en la lista negra

blackmail ['blækmeɪl] (A) N chantaje *m*; **it's sheer ~!** ¡es un chantaje!
(B) VT chantajear; **to ~ sb into doing sth** chantajear a algn para que haga algo; **he was ~ed into it** lo hizo obligado por el chantaje

blackmailer ['blækmeɪləʳ] N chantajista *mf*

blackness ['blæknɪs] N negrura *f*; (= *darkness*) oscuridad *f*, tinieblas *fpl*

blackout ['blækaʊt] N [1] (*Elec*) apagón *m*
[2] (*Med*) desmayo *m*
[3] (*of news*) bloqueo *m* informativo, apagón *m* informativo; **there was a media ~ at the request of the police** hubo un bloqueo informativo en los medios de comunicación a petición de la policía

blackshirt ['blækʃɜːt] N (*Pol*) camisa negra *mf*

blacksmith ['blæksmɪθ] N herrero/a *m/f*; **~'s (forge)** herrería *f*

blackthorn ['blækθɔːn] N endrino *m*

blacktop ['blæktɒp] (*US*) (A) N (= *substance, road*) asfalto *m*
(B) VT asfaltar

bladder ['blædəʳ] N (*Anat*) vejiga *f*; [*of football etc*] cámara *f* de aire

blade [bleɪd] N [1] (= *cutting edge*) [*of knife, tool*] filo *m*; (= *flat part*) [*of weapon, razor etc*] hoja *f*; [*of skate*] cuchilla *f*
[2] [*of propeller*] paleta *f*; [*of oar*] pala *f*; (*Aut*) [*of wiper*] rasqueta *f*
[3] [*of grass etc*] brizna *f*
[4] (†) (= *gallant*) **(young) ~** galán *m*, joven *m* apuesto

blaeberry ['bleɪbərɪ] N arándano *m*

blag‡ [blæg] (A) N (= *robbery*) atraco *m*, robo *m* a mano armada
(B) VT (*Brit*) [+ *ticket*] sacar de gorra*; **to ~ one's way into a club** colarse de gorra en una discoteca*

blah* [blɑː] (A) ADJ (*US*) poco apetitoso
(B) N [1] (= *words*) paja *f*, palabrería *f*; **and there was a lot more ~, ~, ~** y hubo mucho más bla, bla, bla
[2] **the ~s** (*US*) la depre*

Blairite ['blɛəraɪt] N, ADJ (*Brit Pol*) blairista *mf*

blamable ['bleɪməbl] ADJ censurable, culpable

blame [bleɪm] Ⓐ N culpa *f*; **to bear** *or* **take the ~** asumir la culpa; **to lay** *or* **put the ~ (for sth) on sb** echar a algn la culpa (de algo)
Ⓑ VT 1 (= *hold responsible*) culpar, echar la culpa a; **to ~ sb (for sth)** echar a algn la culpa (de algo), culpar a algn (de algo); **to ~ sth on sb** culpar de algo a algn; **to be to ~ for** tener la culpa de; **I am not to ~** yo no tengo la culpa; **who's to ~?** ¿quién tiene la culpa?; **you have only yourself to ~** la culpa la tienes tú
2 (= *reproach*) censurar; **and I don't ~ him** y con toda la razón, y lo comprendo perfectamente

blameless ['bleɪmlɪs] ADJ (= *innocent*) inocente; (= *irreproachable*) intachable

blamelessly ['bleɪmlɪslɪ] ADV (= *innocently*) inocentemente; (= *irreproachably*) intachablemente

blameworthy ['bleɪmwɜːðɪ] ADJ [*action*] censurable, reprobable; [*person*] culpable

blanch [blɑːntʃ] Ⓐ VI [*person*] palidecer
Ⓑ VT (*Culin*) blanquear; (= *boil*) escaldar; **~ed almonds** almendras *fpl* peladas

blancmange [blə'mɒnʒ] N (*Brit*) crema *f* (de vainilla *etc*)

bland [blænd] ADJ (*compar* **blander**; *superl* **blandest**) 1 (*pej*) (= *dull*) [*food, taste*] soso, insípido; [*smile, expression*] insulso; [*music, book, film*] soso, anodino; [*statement*] anodino; **it tastes rather ~** tiene un sabor bastante soso
2 (= *mild*) [*person, action*] suave, afable; [*diet*] blando

blandish ['blændɪʃ] VT engatusar, halagar

blandishments ['blændɪʃmənts] NPL halagos *mpl*, lisonjas *fpl*

blandly ['blændlɪ] ADV (*pej*) [*say, reply*] débilmente; [*smile*] de manera insulsa

blank [blæŋk] Ⓐ ADJ 1 [*paper, space etc*] en blanco; [*tape*] virgen, sin grabar; [*wall*] liso, sin adorno; **the screen went ~** se fue la imagen de la pantalla
2 [*expression etc*] vacío, vago; **a ~ look** una mirada vacía *or* vaga; **a look of ~ amazement** una mirada de profundo asombro; **when I asked him he looked ~** cuando se lo pregunté se quedó mirando con una expresión vaga; **my mind went ~** se me quedó la mente en blanco
3 (= *unrelieved*) **in a state of ~ despair** en un estado de desesperación total
Ⓑ N 1 (= *void*) vacío *m*; (*in form*) espacio *m* en blanco; **my mind was a complete ~** no pude recordar nada; ✦**IDIOM to draw a ~** no llegar a ninguna parte
2 (*Mil*) cartucho *m* de fogueo; **to fire ~s** usar municiones de fogueo
Ⓒ VT (*Brit**) (= *snub*) dar de lado a
Ⓓ CPD ► **blank cartridge** N cartucho *m* de fogueo ► **blank cheque**, **blank check** (*US*) N cheque *m* en blanco; **to give sb a ~ cheque** dar a algn un cheque en blanco; (*fig*) dar carta blanca a algn (**to** para); ► **blank verse** N verso *m* blanco *or* suelto

►**blank out** VT + ADV [+ *feeling, thought*] desechar

blanket ['blæŋkɪt] Ⓐ N manta *f*, frazada *f* (*LAm*), cobija *f* (*LAm*); (*fig*) [*of snow*] manto *m*; [*of smoke, fog*] capa *f*; *see also* **security**, **wet D1**
Ⓑ ADJ [*statement, agreement*] general; [*ban*] global; [*coverage*] exhaustivo; **this insurance policy gives ~ cover** esta póliza de seguro es a todo riesgo
Ⓒ VT (*fig*) cubrir (**in, with** de, con), envolver (**by, in, with** en)
Ⓓ CPD ► **blanket bath** N = **bed bath** ► **blanket stitch** N punto *m* de festón

blankly ['blæŋklɪ] ADV **he looked at me ~** me miró sin comprender

blare [blɛəʳ] Ⓐ N [*of music, siren*] estruendo *m*; [*of trumpet*] trompetazo *m*
Ⓑ VT (*also* **~ out**) [+ *words, order*] vociferar; [+ *music*] tocar muy fuerte
Ⓒ VI (*also* **~ out**) [*music, siren*] sonar a todo volumen, resonar

blarney* ['blɑːnɪ] Ⓐ N labia* *f*
Ⓑ VT dar coba a*, engatusar
Ⓒ CPD ► **Blarney Stone** N *piedra del castillo de Blarney, al sudoeste de Irlanda, que se dice que transmite el don de la galantería al que la besa*; ✦**IDIOM to kiss the Blarney Stone** aprender a tener labia*

blasé ['blɑːzeɪ] ADJ [*attitude*] indiferente; **she's very ~ about the risks involved** le traen sin cuidado los riesgos que el asunto conlleva; **he's won so many Oscars he's become ~ about it** ha ganado tantos óscars que ya está de vuelta de ello *or* le da igual

blaspheme [blæs'fiːm] VI (= *swear*) blasfemar

blasphemer [blæs'fiːməʳ] N blasfemador(a) *m/f*, blasfemo/a *m/f*

blasphemous ['blæsfɪməs] ADJ blasfemo

blasphemously ['blæsfɪməslɪ] ADV [*act, argue*] blasfemamente; **to speak/curse ~** blasfemar

blasphemy ['blæsfɪmɪ] N blasfemia *f*

blast [blɑːst] Ⓐ N 1 [*of air, steam, wind*] ráfaga *f*; [*of sand, water*] chorro *m*; **(at) full ~** (*fig*) a toda marcha
2 (= *sound*) [*of whistle etc*] toque *m*; [*of bomb*] explosión *f*; **at each ~ of the trumpet** a cada trompetazo
3 (= *shock wave*) [*of explosion etc*] sacudida *f*, onda *f* expansiva
4 [*of criticism etc*] tempestad *f*, oleada *f*
5 (*) (= *fun*) **it was a ~** fue el desmadre*; **we got a real ~ out of the party** nos lo pasamos de miedo en la fiesta*
Ⓑ VT 1 (= *tear apart*) (*with explosives*) volar; (*by lightning*) derribar; (*Mil*) bombardear; **to ~ open** abrir con carga explosiva
2 (*Bot*) marchitar; (*with blight*) añublar; (*fig*) [+ *hopes, future*] malograr, echar por tierra
3 (= *shoot*) pegar un tiro a, abrir fuego contra
4 (= *criticize*) [+ *person*] emprenderla con; [+ *film, novel, report*] poner por los suelos
5 (*Sport*) [+ *ball*] estrellar
6 (= *send out*) [+ *air, water*] lanzar
Ⓒ VI (*also* **~ out**) [*music, siren*] sonar a todo volumen, resonar
Ⓓ EXCL (*Brit*‡) ¡maldita sea!*; **~ it!** ¡maldita sea!*
Ⓔ CPD ► **blast furnace** N alto horno *m*

►**blast away** Ⓐ VT + ADV [+ *rocks etc*] volar, quitar con explosivos
Ⓑ VI + ADV [*gun*] seguir disparando; **they were ~ing away at the town** seguían bombardeando el pueblo

►**blast off** VI + ADV [*spacecraft*] despegar

►**blast out** VT + ADV [*DJ*] [+ *music*] poner a todo volumen; [*group*] [+ *tune*] tocar a todo volumen

blasted ['blɑːstɪd] ADJ 1 (‡) (= *wretched*) condenado*, maldito*
2 (*liter*) [*landscape*] inhóspito

blasting ['blɑːstɪŋ] N 1 (*Tech*) voladura *f*; **"blasting in progress"** "explosión controlada en curso"
2 (*) (= *rebuke*) **to give sb a ~ for (having done) sth** echar una bronca *or* abroncar a algn por (haber hecho) algo*

blast-off ['blɑːstɒf] N [*of spacecraft*] despegue *m*

blatant ['bleɪtənt] ADJ [*injustice, lie*] flagrante; [*bully, coward, thief, liar*] descarado; **he's not only racist, but he's ~ about it** no sólo es un racista sino que además no lo disimula; **he was quite ~ about cheating in the exam** copió en el examen con todo descaro *or* sin ningún disimulo

blatantly ['bleɪtəntlɪ] ADV 1 (= *glaringly*) [*untrue, unfair*] descaradamente, obviamente; **its faults are ~ obvious** sus defectos saltan a la vista; **it's ~ obvious that ...** es a todas luces evidente que ...
2 (= *flagrantly*) [*ignore, encourage, disregard*] descaradamente, abiertamente; [*sexist, racist*] descaradamente

blather* ['blæðəʳ] Ⓐ N disparates *mpl*
Ⓑ VI charlatanear, decir tonterías; **to ~ (on) about sth** enrollarse con algo*, dar la tabarra con algo*

blaze¹ [bleɪz] Ⓐ N 1 (= *fire*) (*in hearth*) fuego *m*; (= *flare-up*) llamarada *f*; [*of buildings etc*] incendio *m*; (= *bonfire*) hoguera *f*; (= *glow*) [*of fire, sun etc*] resplandor *m*
2 (= *display*) derroche *m*; **a ~ of colour** un derroche de color
3 (= *outburst*) arranque *m*; **in a ~ of anger** en un arranque de cólera; **in a ~ of publicity** en medio de un gran despliegue publicitario
4 (†‡) **like ~s** hasta más no poder; **what the ~s ...?** ¿qué diablos ...?*; **go to ~s!** ¡vete a la porra!*
Ⓑ VI 1 [*fire*] arder; [*light*] resplandecer; **the sun was blazing** el sol brillaba implacablemente; **all the lights were blazing** brillaban todas las luces
2 [*eyes*] centellear; **to ~ with anger** estar muy indignado, echar chispas*
Ⓒ VT **the news was ~d across the front page** la noticia venía en grandes titulares en la primera plana

►**blaze abroad** VT + ADV (*liter*) [+ *news etc*] proclamar a voz en grito

►**blaze away** VI + ADV [*soldiers*] disparar continuamente

►**blaze down** VI + ADV **the sun was blazing down** el sol brillaba implacablemente

►**blaze forth** VI + ADV (*liter*) [*sun*] aparecer súbitamente; (*fig*) [*anger*] estallar

►**blaze out** VI + ADV [*fire*] llamear; [*sun*] resplandecer, relucir; [*light*] relucir; (*fig*) [*anger, hatred*] estallar

►**blaze up** VI + ADV [*fire*] llamear; (*fig*) [*feelings*] estallar

blaze² [bleɪz] Ⓐ N (*on animal*) mancha *f* blanca; (*on tree*) señal *f*
Ⓑ VT [+ *tree*] marcar; **to ~ a trail** (*also fig*) abrir camino

blazer ['bleɪzəʳ] N (= *jacket*) chaqueta *f* de sport, blazer *m*

blazing ['bleɪzɪŋ] ADJ 1 [*building etc*] en llamas; [*fire*] llameante; [*sun*] abrasador, ardiente; [*light*] brillante; [*eyes*] centelleante
2 (*) [*row, anger*] violento

blazon ['bleɪzn] Ⓐ N blasón *m*
Ⓑ VT (*fig*) proclamar

bldg ABBR = **building**

bleach [bliːtʃ] Ⓐ N lejía *f*
Ⓑ VT [+ *clothes*] blanquear; [+ *hair*] aclarar, decolorar
Ⓒ VI blanquearse

bleached [bliːtʃt] ADJ [*hair*] decolorado, (teñido de) rubio platino; [*clothes*] descolorido

bleachers ['bliːtʃəz] NPL (*US*) gradas *fpl*

bleaching ['bliːtʃɪŋ] Ⓐ N decoloración *f*
Ⓑ CPD ► **bleaching agent** N decolorante *m*

► **bleaching powder** N polvos *mpl* de blanqueo

bleak [bli:k] Ⓐ ADJ (*compar* **bleaker**, *superl* **bleakest**) [*landscape*] desolado, inhóspito; [*weather*] desapacible, crudo; [*smile, voice*] lúgubre, sombrío; [*future*] sombrío; [*welcome*] poco hospitalario; [*room*] lúgubre; **it was a ~, lonely existence out there** allá la vida era triste y desoladora; **it looks** *or* **things look rather ~ for him** las cosas no se le presentan muy alentadoras
Ⓑ N (= *fish*) breca *f*, albur *m*

bleakly ['bli:klı] ADV [*look*] desoladamente; [*smile*] lúgubremente, con aire sombrío; [*speak*] con desaliento, en tono sombrío

bleakness ['bli:knıs] N [*of landscape*] desolación *f*; [*of room, furnishings*] lo lúgubre; [*of weather*] crudeza *f*, desapacibilidad *f*; [*of prospects, future*] lo sombrío

bleary ['blıərı] ADJ (*compar* **blearier**, *superl* **bleariest**) (*with tears, sleep*) lloroso; (= *tired*) agotado

bleary-eyed ['blıərıaıd] ADJ con cara de sueño

bleat [bli:t] Ⓐ N **1** [*of sheep, goat*] balido *m*
2 (*) (= *complaint*) queja *f*
Ⓑ VI **1** [*sheep, goat*] balar
2 (*) (= *complain*) quejarse (**about** de), gimotear

bled [bled] PT, PP *of* **bleed**

bleed [bli:d] (*pt, pp* **bled**) Ⓐ VI **1** (*from cut, wound*) sangrar; [*tree*] exudar; **his nose is ~ing** le sangra la nariz; **to ~ to death** morir desangrado; **my heart ~s for him** (*iro*) ¡qué pena me da!
2 [*colours*] diluirse (**into** en), correrse (**into** en)
Ⓑ VT **1** (*Med*) sangrar
2 [+ *brakes, radiator*] desaguar, sangrar
3 (*) (= *exploit*) desangrar, sacar los cuartos a (*Sp**); ✦*IDIOMS* **to ~ sb dry** *or* **white** chupar la sangre a algn; **to ~ a country dry** *or* **white** explotar despiadadamente un país

bleeder ['bli:dəʳ] N **1** (*Med**) hemofílico/a *m/f*
2 (*Brit*‡) tipo/a* *m/f*, tío/a *m/f* (*Sp**); **poor ~!** ¡pobre desgraciado!; **he's a lucky ~!** ¡qué suerte tiene el tío! (*Sp**), ¡qué suertudo es! (*LAm**)

bleeding ['bli:dıŋ] Ⓐ ADJ **1** [*wound etc*] sangrante; (*fig*) [*heart*] dolorido
2 (*Brit*‡) condenado*, puñetero‡
Ⓑ ADV (*Brit*‡) **~ awkward** condenadamente difícil*
Ⓒ N (= *medical procedure*) sangría *f*; (= *blood loss*) desangramiento *m*, hemorragia *f*

bleeding-heart [,bli:dıŋ'hɑ:t] ADJ (*fig*) **~ liberal** liberal *mf* de gran corazón

bleep [bli:p] Ⓐ N (*Rad, TV*) pitido *m*
Ⓑ VI [*transmitter*] emitir pitidos
Ⓒ VT (*) (*in hospital etc*) llamar por el busca(personas)

bleeper ['bli:pəʳ] N (= *pager*) busca* *m inv*, buscapersonas *m inv*

blemish ['blemıʃ] Ⓐ N (*on fruit*) mancha *f*; (*on complexion*) imperfección *f*; (*fig*) (*on reputation*) tacha *f*
Ⓑ VT (= *spoil*) estropear

blench [blentʃ] VI (= *flinch*) acobardarse; (= *pale*) palidecer

blend [blend] Ⓐ N mezcla *f*
Ⓑ VT [+ *teas, food etc*] mezclar; [+ *colours*] mezclar, combinar
Ⓒ VI (= *harmonize*) armonizar (**with** con); **to ~ in with** armonizarse con; **to ~ into** [*colour*] fundirse con

blended ['blendıd] ADJ mezclado

blender ['blendəʳ] N **1** (*Culin*) licuadora *f*
2 (= *person*) catador(a) *m/f*; **tea ~** catador(a) *m/f* de té

bless [bles] VT **1** [*God, priest*] bendecir; **God ~ you!** ¡Dios te bendiga!; **God ~ the Pope!** ¡Dios guarde al Papa!; **~ you!** ¡qué cielo eres!; (*after sneezing*) ¡Jesús!; **and Paul, ~ him** *or* **~ his heart, had no idea that ...** y Paul, el pobre, no tenía ni idea de que ...; **to ~ o.s.** santiguarse
2 (*fig*) **they were never ~ed with children** Dios jamás les dio la bendición de los hijos; **she is ~ed with every virtue** la adornan mil virtudes; **I ~ the day I bought it** bendigo el día que lo compré; **well I'm ~ed!** ◊ **God ~ my soul!**†* ¡vaya por Dios!; **I'm ~ed if I know** (*Brit**) no tengo ni idea

blessed ['blesıd] Ⓐ ADJ **1** (*Rel*) (= *holy*) bendito, santo; (= *beatified*) beato; **the Blessed Virgin** la Santísima Virgen; **the Blessed Sacrament** el Santísimo Sacramento; **~ be Thy Name** bendito sea Tu Nombre; **of ~ memory** que Dios lo/la tenga en su gloria
2 (*liter*) (= *joyous*) feliz, maravilloso; **a day of ~ calm** un día de bendita tranquilidad
3 (*Brit*‡) (= *wretched*) santo*, dichoso*; **the whole ~ day** todo el santo día*; **where's that ~ book?** ¿dónde está ese dichoso libro?*; **we didn't find a ~ thing** no encontramos nada de nada*
Ⓑ NPL **the Blessed** los bienaventurados

blessedness ['blesıdnıs] N (*Rel*) bienaventuranza *f*, santidad *f*; (= *happiness*) dicha *f*, felicidad *f*

blessing ['blesıŋ] N **1** (*Rel*) bendición *f*
2 (= *advantage*) beneficio *m*; **the ~s of electricity** los beneficios de la electricidad; **the ~s of science** los adelantos de la ciencia; ✦*IDIOMS* **it's a ~ in disguise** no hay mal que por bien no venga; **it's a mixed ~** tiene sus pros y sus contras; **to count one's ~s** agradecer lo que se tiene; **you can count your ~s that ...** tienes que estar agradecido de que ...

blest [blest] ADJ, PP (*liter*) *of* **bless**

blether ['bleðəʳ] (*Scot*) = **blather**

blew [blu:] PT *of* **blow²**

blight [blaıt] Ⓐ N **1** (*Bot*) [*of plants, cereals, fruit, trees*] roya *f*
2 (*fig*) plaga *f*; **urban ~** desertización *f* urbana; **to cast a ~ on** *or* **over** arruinar
Ⓑ VT **1** (*Bot*) (= *wither*) marchitar
2 (*fig*) (= *spoil*) arruinar; (= *frustrate*) frustrar; [+ *urban scene*] desertizar

blighter†* ['blaıtəʳ] N (*Brit*) tipo/a* *m/f*, tío/a *m/f* (*Sp**); **you ~!** (*hum*) ¡menudo canalla estás hecho!*, ¡qué cabrito! (*Sp**); **what a lucky ~!** ¡qué suerte tiene el tío! (*Sp**), ¡qué suertudo es! (*LAm**)

Blighty†* ['blaıtı] N (*Brit Mil*) Inglaterra *f*

blimey‡ ['blaımı] EXCL (*Brit*) ¡caray!

blimp [blımp] N **1** (*esp US*) (= *airship*) zepelín *m*, dirigible *m*
2 (*Brit**) (= *person*) reaccionario/a *m/f*, militarista *mf*, patriotero/a *m/f*; **a (Colonel) Blimp** ≈ un carpetovetónico

blimpish ['blımpıʃ] ADJ (*Brit*) reaccionario

blind [blaınd] Ⓐ ADJ **1** (*lit*) (= *sightless*) ciego; **a ~ man** un ciego, un hombre ciego; **to go ~** quedar(se) ciego; **~ in one eye** tuerto; **the accident left him ~** el accidente lo dejó ciego; **to be ~ with tears** estar cegado por las lágrimas; ✦*IDIOMS* **(as) ~ as a bat*** más ciego que un topo; **to turn a ~ eye (to sth)** hacer la vista gorda (con algo); *see also* **colour-blind**
2 (*fig*) (= *unable to see*) ciego; **you've got to be ~ not to see that it's a trick** hay que estar ciego para no darse cuenta de que es un engaño; **I was so in love that I was ~** estaba tan enamorado que no podía ver claro; **to be ~ to sth** no poder ver algo; **he is ~ to her true character** no puede ver su verdadero carácter; **to be ~ to sb's faults** no ver los defectos de algn; **to be ~ to the consequences of one's actions** no ver las consecuencias de las acciones de uno; **I am not ~ to those considerations** no ignoro esas consideraciones; ✦*PROV* **love is ~** el amor es ciego
3 (= *irrational*) [*rage, panic, faith*] ciego; **a ~ guess** una respuesta al azar; **to be ~ with rage** estar cegado por la ira, estar ciego de ira
4 **a ~ bit of sth***: **it won't make a ~ bit of difference** va a dar exactamente lo mismo; **he didn't take a ~ bit of notice** no hizo ni caso; **it isn't a ~ bit of use** no sirve absolutamente para nada
5 (*Aer*) [*landing, flying*] guiándose sólo por los instrumentos
6 (= *without openings*) [*building, wall*] ciego; [*window*] condenado
Ⓑ N **1** **the ~** los ciegos; ✦*IDIOM* **it's a case of the ~ leading the ~** es como un ciego llevando a otro ciego
2 (= *shade*) persiana *f*; **Venetian ~** persiana *f* veneciana
3 (= *pretence*) pretexto *m*, subterfugio *m*; **it's all a ~** no es más que un pretexto *or* subterfugio
Ⓒ ADV (= *fly, land*) guiándose sólo por los instrumentos; **to bake pastry ~** cocer una masa en blanco *or* sin relleno; **to be ~ drunk*** estar más borracho que una cuba*; **he swore ~ that ...** juró y perjuró que ...
Ⓓ VT **1** (= *render sightless*) dejar ciego, cegar; **to be ~ed in an accident** quedar ciego después de un accidente
2 (= *dazzle*) [*sun, light*] deslumbrar, cegar; **to ~ sb with science** deslumbrar a algn con conocimientos
3 (*fig*) cegar; **to be ~ed by anger/hate** estar cegado por la ira/el odio, estar ciego de ira/odio; **her love ~ed her to his faults** su amor no le dejaba ver sus faltas
Ⓔ CPD ► **blind alley** N callejón *m* sin salida
► **blind corner** N curva *f* sin visibilidad
► **blind date** N (= *meeting*) cita *f* a ciegas; **to go on a ~ date with sb** tener una cita a ciegas con algn ► **blind man's buff** N gallina *f* ciega ► **blind spot** N (*Aut*) ángulo *m* muerto; (*Med*) punto *m* ciego; **I have a ~ spot about computers** ◊ **computers are a ~ spot with me** los ordenadores no son mi punto fuerte
► **blind test** N (*Marketing*) prueba *f* a ciegas

blinder ['blaındəʳ] N **1** **to play a ~ (of a match)** (*Brit**) jugar de maravilla
2 **blinders** (*US*) (= *blinkers*) anteojeras *fpl*

blindfold ['blaındfəʊld] Ⓐ ADJ con los ojos vendados; [*game of chess*] a la ciega; **I could do it ~** podría hacerlo con los ojos vendados
Ⓑ N venda *f*
Ⓒ VT vendar los ojos a

blinding ['blaındıŋ] ADJ [*light, glare*] cegador, deslumbrante; **I've got a ~ headache** tengo un dolor de cabeza que no veo

blindingly ['blaındıŋlı] ADV **a ~ obvious fact** un hecho de claridad meridiana; **it is ~ obvious that ...** es a todas luces evidente que ...

blindly ['blaındlı] ADV **1** (= *unseeingly*) [*grope, stumble*] a ciegas, a tientas; [*shoot*] a ciegas; **she stared ~ at the wall** se quedó mirando obnubilada a la pared

2 (= *unquestioningly*) [*follow, accept, obey*] ciegamente

blindness ['blaɪndnɪs] N ceguera *f*; **~ to the truth** ceguera frente a la verdad

blindworm ['blaɪndwɜːm] N lución *m*

blini ['blɪnɪ] N panqueque *m* ruso

blink [blɪŋk] Ⓐ N [*of eyes*] parpadeo *m*; (= *gleam*) destello *m*; ✦*IDIOMS* **in the ~ of an eye** en un abrir y cerrar de ojos; **to be on the ~*** (*TV etc*) estar averiado
Ⓑ VT [+ *eyes*] cerrar
Ⓒ VI [*eyes*] parpadear, pestañear; [*light*] parpadear

►**blink at** VI + PREP (= *ignore*) pasar por alto

blinkered ['blɪŋkəd] (*Brit*) ADJ [*horse*] con anteojeras; (*fig*) [*person*] estrecho de miras; [*view*] miope, estrecho

blinkers ['blɪŋkəz] NPL 1 (*Brit*) [*of horse*] anteojeras *fpl*
2 (*Aut*) intermitentes *mpl*, direccionales *mpl* (*Mex*)

blinking* ['blɪŋkɪŋ] ADJ (*Brit*) maldito; **you ~ idiot!** ¡imbécil!*

blip [blɪp] N 1 = **bleep** 2 (*fig*) (= *aberration*) irregularidad *f* momentánea; **this is just a ~** es un problema pasajero

bliss [blɪs] N 1 (*Rel*) (= *happy state*) dicha *f*; ✦*PROV* **ignorance is ~** ojos que no ven, corazón que no siente
2 (*) (*fig*) éxtasis *m*, arrobamiento *m*; **the concert was ~!** ¡el concierto fue una gloria!; **what ~!** ¡qué gustazo!*; **isn't he ~?** ¡qué encanto de hombre!

►**bliss out‡** VT + ADV (*esp US*) **to be ~ed out** flipar de gusto‡, estar en la gloria

blissful ['blɪsfʊl] ADJ 1 (= *happy*) dichoso; **in ~ ignorance** feliz en la ignorancia
2 (*) (= *wonderful*) maravilloso, estupendo

blissfully ['blɪsfəlɪ] ADV [*sigh, lounge*] con felicidad; **~ happy** sumamente feliz; **~ ignorant** feliz en la ignorancia

blister ['blɪstər] Ⓐ N (*on skin*) ampolla *f*; (*on paintwork*) burbuja *f*
Ⓑ VT ampollar
Ⓒ VI [*skin*] ampollarse; [*paintwork*] formar burbujas
Ⓓ CPD ► **blister pack** N envase *m* en lámina al vacío

blistering ['blɪstərɪŋ] ADJ 1 [*heat etc*] abrasador
2 [*criticism*] feroz, devastador
3 [*pace, speed*] frenético

blister-packed ['blɪstəˌpækt] ADJ envasado en lámina al vacío

blithe [blaɪð] ADJ (*liter*) alegre

blithely ['blaɪðlɪ] ADV (*liter*) [*continue, ignore*] alegremente

blithering* ['blɪðərɪŋ] ADJ **~ idiot** imbécil* *mf*

BLitt [ˌbiː'lɪt] N ABBR (*Univ*) = **Bachelor of Letters**

blitz [blɪts] Ⓐ N 1 (*Mil*) guerra *f* relámpago; (*Aer*) bombardeo *m* aéreo; **the Blitz** (*Brit Hist*) *el bombardeo alemán de Gran Bretaña en 1940 y 1941*
2 (*) (*fig*) campaña *f* (**on** contra); **I'm going to have a ~ on ironing tomorrow** mañana voy a atacar la plancha*
Ⓑ VT (*Mil*) bombardear

blitzed‡ [blɪtst] ADJ (= *drunk*) mamado‡, borracho como una cuba*

blitzkrieg ['blɪtskriːg] N 1 (*Mil*) guerra *f* relámpago
2 (*) (*fig*) (= *attack*) arremetida *f*

blizzard ['blɪzəd] N ventisca *f*; (*fig*) [*of letters, bills etc*] aluvión *m*, avalancha *f*

BLM N ABBR (*US*) = **Bureau of Land Management**

bloated ['bləʊtɪd] ADJ 1 (= *swollen*) [*stomach*] hinchado; [*face*] hinchado, abotargado; **to feel ~** sentirse hinchado
2 (*fig*) [*bureaucracy*] excesivo; [*budget, ego*] inflado; **~ with pride** henchido de orgullo

bloater ['bləʊtər] N arenque *m* ahumado

blob [blɒb] N (= *drop*) [*of ink etc*] gota *f*; (= *lump*) [*of mud etc*] grumo *m*; (= *stain*) mancha *f*

bloc [blɒk] N 1 (*Pol*) bloque *m*
2 **en ~** en bloque

block [blɒk] Ⓐ N 1 [*of stone*] bloque *m*; [*of wood*] zoquete *m*, tarugo *m*; (*for paving*) adoquín *m*; (*butcher's, executioner's*) tajo *m*; (= *toy*) (*also* **building ~**) cubo *m*; [*of brake*] zapata *f*; [*of cylinder*] bloque *m*; ✦*IDIOM* **on the ~** (*US**) con dinero contante y sonante*, a tocateja (*Sp**); *see also* **chip**
2 (= *building*) bloque *m*; (*esp US*) (= *group of buildings*) manzana *f*, cuadra *f* (*LAm*); **~ of flats** (*Brit*) bloque *m* de pisos (*Sp*), edificio *m* de departamentos (*LAm*); **to walk around the ~** dar la vuelta a la manzana; **three ~s from here** (*esp US*) a tres manzanas de aquí
3 (= *section*) [*of tickets, stamps*] serie *f*; **~ of seats** grupo *m* de asientos; **~ of shares** paquete *m* de acciones
4 (= *blockage*) (*in pipe*) (*gen*) atasco *m*; (*Med*) bloqueo *m*; **writer's ~** bloqueo *m* de escritor; **to have a mental ~** tener un bloqueo mental
5 (*Brit Typ*) molde *m*; (= *writing pad*) bloc *m*
6 (*Sport*) **blocks** (*also* **starting ~s**) tacos *mpl* de salida; **to be first/last off the ~s** ser el más rápido/lento en la salida; (*fig*) ser el más/menos madrugador
7 (*Comput*) bloque *m*
8 (*) (= *head*) ✦*IDIOM* **to knock sb's ~ off*** romper la crisma a algn*
Ⓑ VT 1 (= *obstruct*) [+ *road, gangway*] bloquear; [+ *traffic, progress*] estorbar, impedir; [+ *pipe*] obstruir; (*Parl*) [+ *bill*] bloquear; (*Comm*) [+ *account*] bloquear; (*Sport*) bloquear, parar; **to ~ sb's way** cerrar el paso a algn; **he stopped in the doorway, ~ing her view** se paró en la entrada, tapándole la vista; **am I ~ing your view?** ¿te estoy tapando?; **the road is ~ed in four places** el camino está cortado en cuatro lugares; **"road blocked"** "cerrado (por obras)"; **my nose is ~ed** tengo la nariz taponada
2 (*Comput*) agrupar
Ⓒ VI (*Sport*) bloquear, parar
Ⓓ CPD ► **block and tackle** N (*Tech*) aparejo *m* de poleas ► **block booking** N reserva *f* en bloque ► **block capitals** NPL (letras *fpl*) mayúsculas *fpl*; **in ~ capitals** en mayúsculas, en letra *or* caracteres de imprenta ► **block diagram** N diagrama *m* de bloques ► **block grant** N subvención *f* en bloque ► **block letters** NPL = **block capitals** ► **block release** N (*Brit Scol*) exención *f* por estudios ► **block vote** N voto *m* por representación

►**block in** VT + ADV (= *sketch roughly*) esbozar

►**block off** VT + ADV [+ *road etc*] cortar; (*accidentally*) bloquear

►**block out** VT + ADV 1 (= *suppress*) [+ *thought, idea*] desechar, apartar de la mente
2 (= *obscure*) [+ *light*] tapar; (= *erase*) borrar
3 (= *sketch roughly*) [+ *scheme, design*] esbozar

►**block up** VT + ADV 1 (= *obstruct*) [+ *passage*] obstruir; [+ *pipe*] atascar; **my nose is all ~ed up** tengo la nariz taponada
2 (= *fill in*) [+ *gap*] cerrar

blockade [blɒ'keɪd] Ⓐ N (*Mil, Ind*) bloqueo *m*; **to run a ~** burlar un bloqueo; **under ~** bloqueado
Ⓑ VT [+ *traffic*] bloquear

blockage ['blɒkɪdʒ] N (= *obstruction*) (*Med*) obstrucción *f*; (*in pipe*) atasco *m*

blockbuster* ['blɒkˌbʌstər] N 1 (= *film*) exitazo* *m*, gran éxito *m* de taquilla; (= *book*) exitazo* *m*, best-seller *m*
2 (*Mil*) bomba *f* revientamanzanas

blockhead* ['blɒkhed] N (*pej*) zopenco/a* *m/f*; **you ~!** ¡imbécil!*

blockhouse ['blɒkhaʊs] N (*pl* **blockhouses** ['blɒkhaʊzɪz]) blocao *m*

blog [blɒg] N (*Internet*) blog *m*

blogger [blɒgər] N (*Internet*) blogger *mf*

bloke* [bləʊk] N (*Brit*) (= *man*) tipo* *m*, tío *m* (*Sp**); (= *boyfriend*) amigo *m*

blokey* ['bləʊkɪ], **blok(e)ish*** ['bləʊkɪʃ] ADJ (*Brit*) [*man*] machote*, tío*; [*manners, gestures*] hombruno

blond(e) [blɒnd] Ⓐ ADJ rubio, güero (*CAm, Mex*), catire (*Carib*)
Ⓑ N rubio/a *m/f*, güero/a *m/f* (*CAm, Mex*), catire/a *m/f* (*Carib*)
Ⓒ CPD ► **blond(e) bombshell*** N rubia *f* explosiva*

blood [blʌd] Ⓐ N 1 (*lit*) sangre *f*; **to be after sb's ~** tenérsela jurada a algn*; **it makes my ~ boil** me saca de quicio*, hace que me hierva la sangre; **it makes my ~ boil to think how …** me hierve la sangre sólo de pensar que …; **in cold ~** a sangre fría; **to donate** *or* **give ~** donar *or* dar sangre; **to draw ~** (= *wound*) hacer sangre; (*Med*) sacar sangre; **to draw first ~** (*fig*) abrir el marcador, anotarse el primer tanto; **a ~ and guts film** una película sangrienta *or* violenta; **acting was in his ~** llevaba la profesión de actor en la sangre; **to sweat ~** (= *work hard*) sudar tinta *or* sangre*; (= *worry*) sudar la gota gorda*; **~ and thunder** (= *melodrama*) melodrama *m*; ✦*IDIOMS* **to have sb's ~ on one's hands** tener las manos manchadas con la sangre de algn; **to make one's ~ run cold**: **the look in his eyes made her ~ run cold** su mirada hizo que se le helara la sangre (en las venas); **to get ~ out of a stone** sacar agua de las piedras; **getting her to talk is like trying to get ~ out of a stone** hacer que hable es como sacar agua de las piedras; *see also* **bay**[3], **flesh**
2 (= *family, ancestry*) sangre *f*; **of noble/royal ~** de sangre noble/real; ✦*PROV* **~ is thicker than water** la sangre tira; *see also* **blue D**
3 (*fig*) 3·1 (= *people*) **fresh** *or* **new** *or* **young ~** savia *f* nueva
3·2 (= *feeling*) **bad ~** hostilidad *f*; **there had always been bad ~ between him and his in-laws** siempre había existido hostilidad entre él y la familia de su mujer
Ⓑ CPD ► **blood bank** N banco *m* de sangre ► **blood blister** N ampolla *f* de sangre ► **blood brother** N hermano *m* de sangre ► **blood cell** N glóbulo *m* ► **blood clot** N coágulo *m* de sangre ► **blood corpuscle** N glóbulo *m* sanguíneo ► **blood count** N hemograma *m*, recuento *m* sanguíneo *or* globular ► **blood donor** N donante *mf* de sangre ► **blood feud** N enemistad *f* mortal (*entre clanes, familias*) ► **blood group** N grupo *m* sanguíneo ► **blood heat** N temperatura *f* del cuerpo ► **blood money** N dinero *m* manchado de sangre, *(en pago por asesinato)*; *(as compensation) indemnización que se paga a la familia de alguien que ha sido asesinado* ► **blood orange** N naranja *f* sanguina ► **blood plasma** N plasma *m* sanguíneo ► **blood poisoning** N septicemia *f*, envenenamiento *m* de la

sangre ► **blood pressure** N tensión *f or* presión *f* arterial, presión *f* sanguínea; **to have high/low ~ pressure** tener la tensión alta/baja, tener hipertensión/hipotensión; **to take sb's ~ pressure** tomar la tensión a algn ► **blood pudding** N morcilla *f* ► **blood relation, blood relative** N **she is no ~ relation to him** ella y él no son de la misma sangre, ella y él no son (parientes) cosanguíneos (*frm*) ► **blood relationship** N consanguinidad *f*, lazo *m* de parentesco ► **blood sausage** N (*US*) = **blood pudding** ► **blood sport** N *deporte en el que se matan animales* ► **blood sugar (level)** N nivel *m* de azúcar en la sangre ► **blood supply** N riego *m* sanguíneo ► **blood test** N análisis *m inv* de sangre ► **blood transfusion** N transfusión *f* de sangre ► **blood type** N = **blood group** ► **blood vessel** N vaso *m* sanguíneo

blood-and-thunder ['blʌdən'θʌndəʳ] ADJ melodramático

bloodbath ['blʌdbɑːθ] N (*pl* **bloodbaths** ['blʌdbɑːðz]) carnicería *f*, baño *m* de sangre

bloodcurdling ['blʌd,kɜːdlɪŋ] ADJ espeluznante

bloodhound ['blʌdhaʊnd] N [1] (= *dog*) sabueso *m*
[2] (*) (= *detective*) detective *mf* privado/a

bloodily ['blʌdɪlɪ] ADV **the rebellion was ~ put down** reprimieron la rebelión de forma sangrienta; **a man was dying ~ on the floor** un hombre moría en el suelo en un baño de sangre *or* moría desangrado en el suelo

bloodiness ['blʌdɪnɪs] N (*lit*) lo sangriento; **the ~ of his deeds** el carácter sangriento de sus actos

bloodless ['blʌdlɪs] ADJ [1] (= *pale*) (*gen*) pálido; (*due to blood loss*) exangüe; **her face was ~** su rostro no tenía color, su rostro estaba pálido; (*due to blood loss*) su rostro estaba exangüe; **her lips were ~** sus labios apenas tenían color *or* eran casi blancos; (*due to accident, death*) sus labios estaban exangües
[2] (= *without bloodshed*) [*revolution, coup*] incruento, sin derramamiento de sangre
[3] (= *characterless*) [*film, novel, style*] soso, anodino; [*person*] sin sangre en las venas, con sangre de horchata

bloodlessly ['blʌdlɪslɪ] ADV sin derramamiento de sangre

bloodletting ['blʌd,letɪŋ] N (*Med*) sangría *f*; (*fig*) carnicería *f*, baño *m* de sangre

bloodline ['blʌdlaɪn] N línea *f* de sangre, línea *f* de parentesco por consanguinidad; **the Celtic royal ~ descended through the mother's side** la línea de sangre de la realeza celta venía por parte de la madre

blood-lust ['blʌdlʌst] N sed *f* de sangre

blood-red ['blʌd'red] ADJ [*fabric, paint, car*] de color rojo sangre, rojo sangre; [*sun, sky, sunset*] de un rojo encendido; [*flower*] encarnado

bloodshed ['blʌdʃed] N derramamiento *m* de sangre; **an act of mindless ~** un derramamiento de sangre sin sentido

bloodshot ['blʌdʃɒt] ADJ [*eye*] (*from crying, lack of sleep*) rojo, enrojecido; (*from anger*) inyectado en sangre

bloodstain ['blʌdsteɪn] N mancha *f* de sangre

bloodstained ['blʌdsteɪnd] ADJ manchado de sangre

bloodstock ['blʌdstɒk] N caballos *mpl* de pura sangre, purasangres *mpl*

bloodstone ['blʌdstəʊn] N restañasangre *m*, sanguinaria *f*

bloodstream ['blʌdstriːm] N **the ~** la corriente sanguínea, el flujo sanguíneo

bloodsucker ['blʌdsʌkəʳ] N (*Zool, fig*) sanguijuela *f*

bloodthirstiness ['blʌd,θɜːstɪnɪs] N [*of person, animal*] sed *f* de sangre, carácter *m* sanguinario; [*of film, book*] lo sangriento

bloodthirsty ['blʌdθɜːstɪ] ADJ (*compar* **bloodthirstier**; *superl* **bloodthirstiest**) (= *brutal*) sanguinario; (= *gory*) [*film, book*] sangriento

bloody ['blʌdɪ] Ⓐ ADJ (*compar* **bloodier**; *superl* **bloodiest**) [1] (*lit*) (= *bloodstained*) [*hands, dress*] ensangrentado, manchado de sangre; (= *cruel*) [*battle*] sangriento, cruento (*frm*); [*steak*] sanguinolento; **her fingers were cracked and ~** sus dedos estaban agrietados y sangraban; **to give sb a ~ nose** romper la nariz a algn
[2] (*Brit*‡) **shut the ~ door!** ¡cierra la puerta, coño!*‡, ¡me cago en diez, cierra esa puerta!‡; **that ~ dog!** ¡ese puñetero perro!‡; **you ~ idiot!** ¡maldito imbécil!*; **I'm a ~ genius!** ¡la leche, soy un genio!‡, ¡joder, qué genio soy!*‡; **~ hell!** ¡maldita sea!*, ¡joder!*‡
Ⓑ ADV (*Brit*‡) **not ~ likely!** ¡ni hablar!, ¡ni de coña!‡; **he can ~ well do it himself!** ¡que lo haga él, leche!‡ *or* coño!*‡; **that's no ~ good!** ¡me cago en la mar, eso no vale para nada!‡, ¡eso no vale para nada, joder!*‡; **it's a ~ awful place** es un sitio asqueroso, es un sitio de mierda*‡; **he runs ~ fast** corre que se las pela*, corre (de) la hostia*‡
Ⓒ VT **he had bloodied his knee when he fell** se había hecho sangre en la rodilla al caer; **she stared at her bloodied hands** se miró las manos manchadas de sangre; **he was bloodied but unbowed** (*fig*) había sufrido pero no se daba por vencido
Ⓓ CPD ► **Bloody Mary** N bloody mary *m*

bloody-minded* ['blʌdɪ'maɪndɪd] ADJ (*Brit*) [1] (= *stubborn*) terco, empecinado; **the ~ conservatism of some groups** el terco conservadurismo de algunos grupos
[2] (= *awkward*) atravesado, difícil; **you're just being ~** son ganas de ser atravesado *or* difícil, son ganas de fastidiar; **he didn't really want a replacement, he was just being ~ about it** no quería realmente un sustituto, lo hacía sólo para fastidiar

bloody-mindedness* ['blʌdɪ'maɪndɪdnɪs] (*Brit*) N [1] (= *stubbornness*) terquedad *f*, empecinamiento *m*
[2] (= *awkwardness*) **it's just ~ on his part** son ganas de fastidiar *or* de ser atravesado; **he did it out of sheer ~** lo hizo sólo para fastidiar

bloom [bluːm] Ⓐ N [1] (= *flower*) flor *f*; (*on fruit*) vello *m*, pelusa *f*; **in ~** en flor; **in full ~** en plena floración; **in the full ~ of youth** en la flor de la juventud; **to come into ~** florecer
[2] (*fig*) (*on complexion*) rubor *m*
Ⓑ VI [*flower*] abrirse; [*tree*] florecer; (*fig*) [*economy, industry*] prosperar

bloomer ['bluːməʳ] N [1] (*) (= *mistake*) planchazo* *m*, metedura *f* de pata*; **to make a ~** llevarse un planchazo*, meter la pata*
[2] **to be a late ~** (*fig*) ser una flor tardía, tardar en desarrollarse

bloomers ['bluːməz] NPL bombachos *mpl*, pantaletas *fpl* (*LAm*)

blooming ['bluːmɪŋ] Ⓐ ADJ [1] [*tree*] floreciente, en flor
[2] (*fig*) (= *flourishing*) radiante; **to be ~ with health** ◊ **be in ~ health** estar rebosante de *or* rebosar salud
[3] (*Brit**) **the ~ car wouldn't start** el maldito coche no arrancaba*; **get that ~ thing out of the way!** ¡quita eso de ahí, hombre!*
Ⓑ ADV (*Brit**) **I think it's ~ marvellous** a mí me parece genial*; **we had to lift this ~ great box** tuvimos que levantar un pedazo de caja enorme *or* una caja de agárrate y no te menees*

blooper* ['bluːpəʳ] N (*esp US*) = **bloomer 1**

blossom ['blɒsəm] Ⓐ N (= *collective*) flores *fpl*; (= *single*) flor *f*; **in ~** en flor
Ⓑ VI [*tree*] florecer; (*fig*) florecer, llegar a su apogeo; **it ~ed into love** se transformó en amor

►**blossom out** VI + ADV (*fig*) [*person*] alcanzar su plenitud, florecer

blot [blɒt] Ⓐ N [*of ink*] borrón *m*, mancha *f*; (*fig*) (*on reputation etc*) tacha *f*, mancha *f*; **the chimney is a ~ on the landscape** la chimenea afea el paisaje; ✦***IDIOM*** **a ~ on the family escutcheon** una mancha en el honor de la familia
Ⓑ VT [1] (= *spot*) (*with ink*) manchar; (*fig*) [+ *reputation*] desacreditar; ✦***IDIOM*** **to ~ one's copybook** (*Brit*) manchar su reputación
[2] (= *dry*) (*with blotter*) [+ *ink, writing*] secar
Ⓒ VI [*pen*] echar borrones; [*ink*] correrse

►**blot out** VT + ADV [1] (*lit*) [+ *words*] borrar
[2] (*fig*) [*mist, fog*] [+ *view*] tapar, ocultar; [+ *memories*] borrar

►**blot up** VT + ADV [+ *ink*] secar

blotch [blɒtʃ] N [*of ink, colour*] mancha *f*; (*on skin*) mancha *f*, erupción *f*

blotchy ['blɒtʃɪ] ADJ (*compar* **blotchier**; *superl* **blotchiest**) manchado, lleno de manchas

blotter ['blɒtəʳ] N [1] (= *blotting paper*) secante *m*
[2] (*US*) (= *notebook*) registro *m*

blotting-pad ['blɒtɪŋ,pæd] N secante *m*

blotting paper ['blɒtɪŋ,peɪpəʳ] N papel *m* secante

blotto‡ ['blɒtəʊ] ADJ **to be ~** (= *drunk*) estar mamado‡, estar como una cuba*

blouse [blaʊz] N [1] (= *woman's garment*) blusa *f*; **he's a big girl's ~*** es un mariquita*
[2] (*US Mil*) guerrera *f*

blouson ['bluːzɒn] N cazadora *f*

blow[1] [bləʊ] N [1] (= *hit*) golpe *m*; (= *slap*) bofetada *f*; **a ~ with a hammer/fist/elbow** un martillazo/un puñetazo/un codazo; **at one ~** de un solo golpe; **a ~-by-~ account** una narración pormenorizada; **to cushion** *or* **soften the ~** (*lit*) amortiguar el golpe; (*fig*) disminuir los efectos (*de un desastre etc*); **to deal** *or* **strike sb a ~** dar *or* asestar un golpe a algn; **to strike a ~ for freedom** (*fig*) dar un paso más hacia la libertad; **without striking a ~** sin violencia; **to come to ~s** (*lit, fig*) llegar a las manos
[2] (*fig*) (= *setback*) golpe *m*; **it is a cruel ~ for everybody** es un golpe cruel para todos; **the news came as a great ~** la noticia fue un duro golpe; **that's a ~!** ¡qué lástima!; **the affair was a ~ to his pride** la cosa le hirió en el amor propio; **it was the final ~ to our hopes** acabó de echar por tierra nuestras esperanzas

blow[2] [bləʊ] (*pt* **blew**; *pp* **blown**) Ⓐ VT [1] (= *move by blowing*) [*wind etc*] [+ *leaves papers*] hacer volar; **the wind blew the ship towards the coast** el viento llevó *or* empujó el barco hacia la costa; **the wind has ~n dust all over it** el viento lo ha cubierto de polvo; **the wind blew the door shut** el viento cerró la puerta de golpe; **to ~ sb a kiss** enviar *or* tirar un beso a algn
[2] [+ *trumpet, whistle*] tocar, sonar; [+ *glass*] soplar; [+ *egg*] vaciar (soplando); **to ~ bubbles** (*soap*) hacer pompas; (*gum*) hacer glo-

bos; **to ~ one's nose** sonarse (la nariz); **to ~ smoke in sb's face** *or* **eyes** (*lit*) echar el humo en la cara *or* los ojos a algn; (*US*) (*fig*) engañar a algn; **to ~ smoke rings** hacer anillos *or* aros de humo; ✦***IDIOMS*** **to ~ smoke up sb's ass** (*US***) lamer el culo a algn**, dar coba a algn*; **to ~ one's own trumpet** ◊ **~ one's own horn** (*US*) darse bombo*; **to ~ the whistle on sth/sb** dar la voz de alarma sobre algo/algn

3 (= *burn out, explode*) [+ *fuse*] fundir, quemar; [+ *tyre*] reventar; [+ *safe etc*] volar; **to ~ sth sky-high** volar algo en mil pedazos; **to ~ a theory sky-high** echar por tierra una teoría; **to ~ a matter wide open** destapar un asunto; ✦***IDIOMS*** **to ~ the lid off sth** sacar a la luz algo, dejar algo al descubierto; **to ~ sb's mind*** dejar alucinado a algn*; **to ~ one's top** ◊ **~ one's cork** *or* **stack** (*US*) reventar, estallar; **to ~ sth out of the water** echar por tierra algo, dar al traste con algo

4 (= *spoil, ruin*) **to ~ one's chance of doing sth*** echar a perder *or* desperdiciar la oportunidad de hacer algo; **to ~ sb's cover** desenmascarar a algn; **to ~ it*** pifiarla*; **now you've ~n it!*** ¡ahora sí que la has pifiado!*; **to ~ one's lines** (*US Theat**) perder el hilo, olvidar el papel; **to ~ a secret** revelar un secreto; *see also* **gaff[3]**

5 **to ~ money on sth*** malgastar dinero en algo

6 (*esp US***) (= *fellate*) mamársela a**, hacer una mamada a**

7 (*Drugs*) **to ~ grass‡** fumar hierba

8 (*) (*in exclamations*) **~ me!** ◊ **~ it!** ◊ **well I'm ~ed!** ¡caramba!; **~ this rain!** ¡dichosa lluvia!*; **I'll be ~ed if ...** que me cuelguen si ...*; **~ the expense!** ¡al cuerno el gasto!*

Ⓑ VI 1 [*wind, whale*] soplar; [*person*] (*from breathlessness*) jadear; **to ~ on one's fingers** soplarse los dedos; **to ~ on one's soup** enfriar la sopa soplando; **it's ~ing a gale** hace muchísimo viento; *see also* **hot B**, **wind[1] A1**

2 [*leaves etc*] (*with wind*) volar; **the door blew open/shut** se abrió/cerró la puerta con el viento

3 (= *make sound*) [*trumpet, siren*] sonar; **the referee blew for a foul** el árbitro pitó falta

4 [*fuse etc*] fundirse, quemarse; [*tyre*] reventar

5 (‡) (= *leave*) largarse*, pirarla (*Sp**); **I must ~** tengo que largarme*

Ⓒ N 1 [*of breath*] soplo *m*

2 (*Brit*‡) (= *marijuana*) maría‡ *f*; (*US*) (= *cocaine*) coca‡ *f*, perico‡ *m*

Ⓓ CPD ► **blow drier** N secador *m* de pelo ► **blow job**** N mamada** *f*; **to give sb a ~ job** mamársela *or* chupársela a algn**

►**blow about** Ⓐ VT + ADV [+ *leaves etc*] llevar de acá para allá

Ⓑ VI + ADV [*leaves etc*] moverse de acá para allá por el viento

►**blow away** Ⓐ VI + ADV [*hat*] salir volando, volarse

Ⓑ VT + ADV 1 [*wind*] [+ *leaves, rubbish*] hacer volar

2 (‡) (= *kill*) cargarse a*, liquidar*

3 (*) (= *defeat*) machacar*

4 (*) (= *impress*) dejar pasmado*

►**blow down** Ⓐ VT + ADV derribar

Ⓑ VI + ADV venirse abajo

►**blow in** VI + ADV 1 (= *collapse*) venirse abajo

2 (*) (= *enter*) entrar de sopetón*; **look who's ~n in!** ¡mira quién ha caído del cielo!*

►**blow off** Ⓐ VI + ADV 1 [*hat*] salir volando, volarse

2 (*Brit*‡) tirarse un pedo‡

Ⓑ VT + ADV [+ *gas*] dejar escapar; ✦***IDIOM*** **to ~ off steam** desfogarse

Ⓒ VT + PREP **to ~ the dust off a table** quitar el polvo de una mesa soplando

►**blow out** Ⓐ VT + ADV 1 (= *extinguish*) [+ *candle*] apagar (con un soplo); **the next day the storm had ~n itself out** al día siguiente la tormenta se había calmado

2 (= *swell out*) [+ *cheeks*] hinchar

3 **to ~ one's brains out*** pegarse un tiro, levantarse *or* volarse la tapa de los sesos*; **to ~ sb's brains out*** pegar un tiro a algn, levantar *or* volar la tapa de los sesos a algn*

Ⓑ VI + ADV 1 [*candle etc*] apagarse

2 [*tyre*] reventar; [*window*] romperse (*con la fuerza del viento etc*)

►**blow over** Ⓐ VT + ADV derribar, tumbar

Ⓑ VI + ADV 1 [*tree etc*] caer

2 [*storm*] pasar

3 (*fig*) [*dispute*] olvidarse

►**blow up** Ⓐ VT + ADV 1 (= *explode*) [+ *bridge etc*] volar

2 (= *inflate*) [+ *tyre etc*] inflar, hinchar (*Sp*)

3 (= *enlarge*) [+ *photo*] ampliar

4 (= *exaggerate*) [+ *event etc*] exagerar; **they blew it up out of all proportion** se exageró una barbaridad sobre eso, se sacó totalmente de quicio

5 (*) (= *reprimand*) **the boss blew the boy up** el jefe puso al chico como un trapo*

Ⓑ VI + ADV 1 [*explosive*] estallar, explotar; [*container*] estallar, reventar; **his allegations could ~ up in his face** con esas acusaciones le podría salir el tiro por la culata*

2 [*storm*] levantarse; **it's ~ing up for rain** con este viento tendremos lluvia

3 (*fig*) 3·1 [*row etc*] estallar; **now something else has ~n up** ahora ha surgido otra cosa

3·2 (*) (*in anger*) salirse de sus casillas*; **to ~ up at sb** perder los estribos con algn

blow-dry [ˈbləʊˌdraɪ] Ⓐ N (= *hairstyle*) **I'd like a cut and ~** quisiera un corte y secado a mano

Ⓑ VT [+ *style*] secar a mano

blower* [ˈbləʊəʳ] N (*Brit*) (= *telephone*) teléfono *m*; **who's on the ~?** ¿con quién hablas?; **get on the ~ to them** dales un toque (por teléfono)

blowfly [ˈbləʊflaɪ] N moscarda *f*, mosca *f* azul

blowgun [ˈbləʊɡʌn] N (*US*) cerbatana *f*

blowhard* [ˈbləʊhɑːd] N (*esp US*) fanfarrón/ona *m/f*

blowhole [ˈbləʊhəʊl] N 1 [*of whale*] orificio *m* nasal

2 (*in ice*) brecha *f*, orificio *m* (*para respirar*)

blowlamp [ˈbləʊlæmp] N soplete *m*

blown [bləʊn] Ⓐ PP *of* **blow[2]**

Ⓑ ADJ [*flower*] marchito

blow-out [ˈbləʊaʊt] N 1 (*Aut*) (= *burst tyre*) reventón *m*, pinchazo *m*, ponchada *f* (*Mex*)

2 (*Elec*) [*of fuse*] apagón *m*

3 [*of oil well*] explosión *f*

4 (‡) (= *big meal*) comilona* *f*, atracón* *m*

blowpipe [ˈbləʊpaɪp] N (= *weapon*) cerbatana *f*

blowsy [ˈblaʊzɪ] ADJ = **blowzy**

blowtorch [ˈbləʊtɔːtʃ] N soplete *m*

blow-up [ˈbləʊʌp] N 1 (*Phot*) ampliación *f*

2 (*) riña *f*, pelea *f* (**between** entre)

blowy* [ˈbləʊɪ] ADJ [*day*] de mucho viento; **on a ~ day in March** un día de marzo de mucho viento; **it's ~ here** aquí hay mucho viento

blowzy [ˈblaʊzɪ] ADJ (*compar* **blowzier**; *superl* **blowziest**) [*woman*] desaliñado; (= *red in face*) coloradote*

BLS N ABBR (*US*) = **Bureau of Labor Statistics**

BLT N ABBR = **bacon, lettuce and tomato**; **a ~ sandwich** *un sándwich de bacon, lechuga y tomate*

blub* [blʌb] VI (*Brit*) lloriquear

blubber[1] [ˈblʌbəʳ] N [*of whale, seal*] grasa *f*

blubber[2]* [ˈblʌbəʳ] Ⓐ N lloriqueo *m*; **she just wanted to have a good ~** tenía ganas de llorar

Ⓑ VI (= *weep*) lloriquear; **stop ~ing!** ¡deja ya de lloriquear!

Ⓒ VT decir lloriqueando

blubbery [ˈblʌbərɪ] ADJ (= *fat*) fláccido, fofo; **~ lips** labios *mpl* carnosos

bludgeon [ˈblʌdʒən] Ⓐ N cachiporra *f*

Ⓑ VT aporrear; **to ~ sb into doing sth** (*fig*) coaccionar *or* forzar a algn a hacer algo

blue [bluː] Ⓐ ADJ (*compar* **bluer**; *superl* **bluest**)

1 azul; [*body, bruise*] amoratado; **~ with cold** amoratado de frío; ✦***IDIOMS*** **once in a ~ moon** de Pascuas a Ramos; **you can shout till you're ~ in the face*** puedes gritar hasta hartarte; **to go like a ~ streak** (*US**) ir como un rayo; **to talk like a ~ streak** (*US**) hablar muy deprisa

2 (*) (= *obscene*) verde, colorado (*LAm*); **~ film** película *f* porno

3 (*) (= *sad*) triste, deprimido; **to feel ~** estar deprimido, estar tristón*; **to look ~** tener aspecto triste

4 (*Pol*) conservador

Ⓑ N 1 (= *colour*) azul *m*

2 (*Pol*) conservador(a) *m/f*; *see also* **true-blue**

3 (*Chem*) añil *m*

4 **the ~** (= *sky*) el cielo; (= *sea*) el mar; ✦***IDIOM*** **to come out of the ~** [*money, good news*] venir como cosa llovida del cielo, bajar del cielo; [*bad news*] caer como una bomba; **he said out of the ~** dijo de repente, dijo inesperadamente

5 **blues** (*Mus*) blues *m*; (= *feeling*) melancolía *f*, tristeza *f*; **he's got the ~s** está deprimido

6 **Dark/Light Blue** (*Brit Univ*) deportista *mf* representante de Oxford/Cambridge

Ⓒ VT 1 [+ *washing*] añilar, dar azulete a

2 (*Brit**) (= *squander*) despilfarrar

Ⓓ CPD ► **blue baby** N niño/a *m/f* azul, niño/a *m/f* cianótico/a ► **blue beret** N casco *m* azul ► **blue blood** N sangre *f* azul ► **blue book** N (*US Scol*) cuaderno *m* de exámenes ► **blue cheese** N queso *m* de pasta verde ► **blue chips** NPL = **blue-chip securities**; *see* **blue-chip** ► **blue jeans** NPL tejanos *mpl*, vaqueros *mpl* ► **blue pencil** N lápiz *m* negro (en la censura); *see also* **blue-pencil** ► **Blue Peter** N (*Naut*) bandera *f* de salida ► **blue shark** N tiburón *m* azul ► **blue whale** N ballena *f* azul ► **blue whiting** N bacaladilla *f*

Bluebeard [ˈbluːbɪəd] N Barba Azul

bluebell [ˈbluːbel] N campánula *f* azul; (*Scot*) (= *harebell*) campanilla *f*

blueberry [ˈbluːberɪ] N arándano *m*

bluebird [ˈbluːbɜːd] N pájaro *m* azul, azulejo *m* (de América)

blue-blooded [ˈbluːˈblʌdɪd] ADJ de sangre azul

bluebottle [ˈbluːˌbɒtl] N moscarda *f*

blue-chip [ˈbluːˈtʃɪp] Ⓐ ADJ [*company*] de primera (categoría); [*investment*] asegurado

Ⓑ CPD ► **blue-chip securities** NPL fianzas *fpl* fiables

blue-collar [ˈbluːˌkɒləʳ] Ⓐ ADJ [*job*] manual

Ⓑ CPD ► **blue-collar worker** N obrero/a *m/f*, trabajador(a) *m/f* manual

blue-eyed [ˈbluːˌaɪd] Ⓐ ADJ de ojos azules

Ⓑ CPD ► **blue-eyed boy** N (*fig*) consentido *m*, niño *m* mimado

bluegrass ['blu:grɑ:s] Ⓐ N (*US Bot*) *hierba norteamericana usada como forraje*
Ⓑ CPD ► **bluegrass music** N *música folk de Kentucky*
bluejacket ['blu:,dʒækɪt] N marinero *m* (de buque de guerra)
bluejay ['blu:dʒeɪ] N (*US*) arrendajo *m* azul
blueness ['blu:nɪs] N azul *m*, lo azul
blue-pencil ['blu:'pensl] VT tachar con lápiz negro (en la censura); *see also* **blue D**
blueprint ['blu:prɪnt] N (= *plan*) proyecto *m*, anteproyecto *m*; (= *drawing*) cianotipo *m*
blue-sky ['blu:skaɪ] ADJ [*project, research*] sin límites; **we need to do some ~ thinking** tenemos que ponernos a pensar sin ningún tipo de límite; **~ laws** (*US*) legislación *f* para regular la emisión y venta de valores
bluestocking† ['blu:,stɒkɪŋ] N (= *scholarly woman*) literata *f*, marisabidilla *f*
bluesy ['blu:zɪ] ADJ (*Mus*) de blues
bluetit ['blu:tɪt] N herrerillo *m* (común)
Bluetooth® ['blu:tu:θ] N, ADJ **~ technology** tecnología *f* Bluetooth®
blue-water ['blu:'wɔ:tər] ADJ (*Naut*) [*navy, ship*] de altura, pelágico
bluey* ['blu:ɪ] ADJ azulado
bluff[1] [blʌf] Ⓐ ADJ [1] [*cliff etc*] escarpado
[2] [*person*] franco, directo
Ⓑ N (*Geog*) risco *m*, peñasco *m*
bluff[2] [blʌf] Ⓐ N (= *act of bluffing*) farol *m*, bluff *m*; ✦*IDIOM* **to call sb's ~** poner a algn en evidencia
Ⓑ VT (= *deceive by pretending*) engañar, embaucar; **to ~ it out by ...** salvar la situación haciendo creer que …
Ⓒ VI farolear, tirarse un farol (*Sp**)
bluffer ['blʌfər] N farolero/a *m/f*
bluish ['blu:ɪʃ] ADJ azulado, azulino
blunder ['blʌndər] Ⓐ N metedura *f* de pata*, plancha *f* (*Sp**); **to make a ~** meter la pata*, tirarse una plancha (*Sp**)
Ⓑ VI [1] (= *err*) cometer un grave error, meter la pata*
[2] (= *move clumsily*) **to ~ about** andar dando tumbos; **to ~ into sth/sb** tropezar con algo/algn; **to ~ into sth** [+ *trap*] caer en algo; (*fig*) caer *or* meterse en algo
blunderbuss ['blʌndəbʌs] N trabuco *m*
blunderer ['blʌndərər] N metepatas* *mf*
blundering ['blʌndərɪŋ] Ⓐ ADJ [*person*] torpe, que mete la pata*; [*words, act*] torpe
Ⓑ N torpeza *f*
blunt [blʌnt] Ⓐ ADJ [1] (= *not sharp*) [*edge*] desafilado; [*point*] despuntado; **with a ~ instrument** con un instrumento contundente
[2] (= *outspoken*) [*manner, person*] directo, franco; [*statement*] terminante; **I will be ~ with you** voy a hablarte con franqueza; **he was very ~ with me** no se mordió la lengua conmigo
Ⓑ VT [+ *blade, knife*] desafilar; [+ *pencil*] despuntar; (*fig*) debilitar, mitigar
bluntly ['blʌntlɪ] ADV [*speak*] francamente, directamente
bluntness ['blʌntnɪs] N [1] [*of blade etc*] falta *f* de filo, lo poco afilado
[2] (= *outspokenness*) franqueza *f*
blur [blɜ:r] Ⓐ N (= *shape*) contorno *m* borroso; **everything is a ~ when I take off my glasses** todo se vuelve borroso cuando me quito los lentes; **the memory is just a ~** es un recuerdo muy vago; **my mind was a ~** todo se volvió borroso en mi mente
Ⓑ VT [1] (= *obscure*) [+ *writing*] borrar, hacer borroso; [+ *outline*] desdibujar; [+ *sight*] oscurecer, empañar; **my eyes were ~red with tears** las lágrimas me enturbiaban la vista
[2] (*fig*) [+ *memory*] enturbiar; [+ *judgment*] ofuscar
Ⓒ VI (= *be obscured*) desdibujarse, volverse borroso; **her eyes ~red with tears** las lágrimas le enturbiaban la vista
blurb [blɜ:b] N propaganda *f*
blurred [blɜ:d] ADJ [1] [*outline etc*] borroso, poco nítido; **a ~ photo** una foto movida *or* desenfocada
[2] (*fig*) [*memory*] borroso; **to be/become ~** estar/volverse borroso; **class distinctions are becoming ~** las diferencias de clase se están difuminando
blurt [blɜ:t] VT **to ~ out** [+ *secret*] dejar escapar; [+ *whole story*] contar de buenas a primeras
blush [blʌʃ] Ⓐ N [1] (*from embarrassment*) rubor *m*, sonrojo *m*; (= *glow*) tono *m* rosáceo; **the first ~ of dawn** la primera luz del alba; **in the first ~ of youth** en la inocencia de la juventud; **at first ~** a primera vista; **to bring a ~ to sb's face** hacer sonrojar a algn; **to spare** *or* **save his ~es** para que no se ruborice; **spare my ~es!** ¡qué cosas dices!
[2] (*US*) (= *make-up*) colorete *m*
Ⓑ VI ruborizarse, sonrojarse (**at** por; **with** de); **to make sb ~** hacer que algn se ruborice *or* se sonroje; **I ~ for you** siento vergüenza por ti; **I ~ to even think about it** me avergüenzo de sólo pensarlo; **she ~ed to the roots of her hair** se puso colorada como un tomate
blusher ['blʌʃər] N colorete *m*
blushing ['blʌʃɪŋ] ADJ ruboroso; [*bride*] candoroso
bluster ['blʌstər] Ⓐ N (= *empty threats*) fanfarronadas *fpl*, bravatas *fpl*
Ⓑ VI [*wind*] soplar con fuerza, bramar
Ⓒ VT **to ~ it out** defenderse echando bravatas, baladronear
blusterer ['blʌstərər] N fanfarrón/ona *m/f*
blustering ['blʌstərɪŋ] ADJ [*person*] jactancioso, fanfarrón
blustery ['blʌstərɪ] ADJ [*wind*] tempestuoso; [*day*] de mucho viento
Blu-Tack® ['blu:tæk] N Blu-Tack® *m*
Blvd ABBR (= **boulevard**) Blvr
BM N ABBR [1] = **British Museum**
[2] (*Univ*) = **Bachelor of Medicine**
BMA N ABBR = **British Medical Association**
BMC N ABBR = **British Medical Council**
BMJ N ABBR = **British Medical Journal**
B-movie ['bi:,mu:vɪ] N película *f* de la serie B
BMus N ABBR (*Univ*) = **Bachelor of Music**
BMX Ⓐ N ABBR (= **bicycle motocross**) ciclocross *m*
Ⓑ CPD ► **BMX bike** N bicicleta *f* de ciclocross
bn ABBR = **billion**
BNFL N ABBR = **British Nuclear Fuels Limited**
BNP N ABBR (= **British National Party**) *partido político de la extrema derecha*
BO N ABBR [1] (= **body odour**) olor *m* a sudor
[2] (*US*) = **box office**
b.o. ABBR (*Comm*) = **buyer's option**
B/O ABBR (*Fin*) = **brought over**
boa ['bəʊə] N [1] (*also* **~ constrictor**) boa *f*
[2] (= *garment*) boa *f* (de plumas)
Boadicea [,bəʊədɪ'sɪə] N Boadicea
boar [bɔ:r] N (= *male pig*) cerdo *m*, verraco *m*; **wild ~** jabalí *m*
board [bɔ:d] Ⓐ N [1] [*of wood*] tabla *f*, tablón *m*; (= *table*) mesa *f*; (*for chess etc*) tablero *m*; (= *ironing board*) tabla *f* de planchar; (= *notice board*) tablón *m*; (*in bookbinding*) cartón *m*; (*Comput*) placa *f*, tarjeta *f*; **above ~** (= *legitimate*) legítimo; (= *in order*) en regla, legal; **an increase across the ~** un aumento global *or* general; **to go by the ~** (= *go wrong*) ir al traste; (= *be abandoned*) abandonarse; **in ~s** (*book*) en cartoné; ✦*IDIOM* **to sweep the ~** ganar todas las bazas; (*in election*) copar todos los escaños
[2] (= *provision of meals*) comida *f*; **full ~** pensión *f* completa; **half ~** media pensión *f*; **~ and lodging** (*Brit*) casa *f* y comida
[3] (*Naut, Aer*) **on ~** a bordo; **on ~ (the) ship** a bordo del barco; **to go on ~** embarcarse, subir a bordo; ✦*IDIOM* **to take sth on ~** [+ *idea*] adoptar algo, asimilar algo
[4] (= *group of officials*) junta *f*, consejo *m*
[5] (*gas, water etc*) comisión *f*
[6] **the ~s** (*Theat*) las tablas; ✦*IDIOM* **to tread the ~s** (*as profession*) ser actor/actriz; (= *action*) salir a escena
Ⓑ VT [1] [+ *ship, plane*] subir a bordo de, embarcarse en; [+ *enemy ship*] abordar; [+ *bus, train*] subir a
[2] (*also* **~ up**) (= *cover with boards*) entablar
[3] (= *feed, lodge*) hospedar, dar pensión (completa) a
Ⓒ VI **to ~ with** hospedarse en casa de
Ⓓ CPD ► **board game** N juego *m* de tablero ► **board meeting** N reunión *f* de la junta directiva *or* del consejo de administración ► **board of directors** N junta *f* directiva, consejo *m* de administración ► **board of governors** N (*Brit Scol*) consejo *m* (*de un colegio, instituto etc*) ► **board of inquiry** N comisión *f* investigadora ► **Board of Trade** N (*Brit*) (*formerly*) Departamento *m* de Comercio y Exportación; (*US*) Cámara *f* de Comercio
►**board in** VT + ADV = **board up**
►**board out** VT + ADV [+ *person*] buscar alojamiento a; **he is ~ed out with relatives** vive con unos parientes (*pagando la pensión*)
►**board up** VT + ADV [+ *door, window*] entablar
boarder ['bɔ:dər] N (*in house*) huésped(a) *m/f*; (*Brit Scol*) interno/a *m/f*
boarding ['bɔ:dɪŋ] Ⓐ N entablado *m*
Ⓑ CPD ► **boarding card** N tarjeta *f* de embarque, pase *m* de embarque (*LAm*) ► **boarding house** N pensión *f*, casa *f* de huéspedes, residencial *f* (*S. Cone*) ► **boarding party** N pelotón *m* de abordaje ► **boarding pass** N = **boarding card** ► **boarding school** N internado *m*
boardroom ['bɔ:drʊm] N sala *f* de juntas
boardwalk ['bɔ:dwɔ:k] N (*US*) paseo *m* marítimo entablado
boast [bəʊst] Ⓐ N alarde *m*; **it is his ~ that ...** se jacta de que …; **to be the ~ of** ser el orgullo de
Ⓑ VT (*frm*) (= *pride o.s. on*) ostentar, jactarse de
Ⓒ VI presumir, alardear; **he ~s about** *or* **of his strength** presume de fuerte; **that's nothing to ~ about** eso no es motivo para vanagloriarse
boasted ['bəʊstɪd] ADJ alardeado, cacareado
boaster ['bəʊstər] N jactancioso/a *m/f*, fanfarrón/ona *m/f*
boastful ['bəʊstfʊl] ADJ jactancioso, fanfarrón
boastfully ['bəʊstfəlɪ] ADV jactanciosamente, con fanfarronería
boastfulness ['bəʊstfʊlnɪs] N jactancia *f*, fanfarronería *f*
boasting ['bəʊstɪŋ] N jactancia *f*, fanfarronadas *fpl*
boat [bəʊt] Ⓐ N (*gen*) barco *m*; (= *large ship*) buque *m*, navío *m*; (*small*) barca *f*; (= *rowing

boat) barca *f*, bote *m* (de remo); (= *racing eight, ship's boat*) bote *m*; **to go by ~** ir en barco; **to launch** *or* **lower the ~s** botar los botes al agua; ✦*IDIOMS* **to burn one's ~s** quemar las naves; **to miss the ~** perder el tren; **to push the ~ out*** tirar la casa por la ventana*; **to rock the ~** hacer olas; **we're all in the same ~*** estamos todos en la misma situación
Ⓑ CPD ► **boat deck** N cubierta *f* de botes ► **boat hook** N bichero *m* ► **boat people** NPL *refugiados que huyen en barco* ► **boat race** N regata *f*; **the Boat Race** (*Brit*) *carrera anual de remo entre Oxford y Cambridge* ► **boat train** N tren *m* que enlaza con el barco

boatbuilder ['bəʊt,bɪldəʳ] N constructor(a) *m/f* de barcos; **~'s (yard)** astillero *m*

boatbuilding ['bəʊt,bɪldɪŋ] N construcción *f* de barcos

boater ['bəʊtəʳ] N (= *hat*) canotié *m*

boatful ['bəʊtfʊl] N (*goods*) cargamento *m*; **the refugees arrived in ~s** llegaron barcos llenos de refugiados

boathouse ['bəʊthaʊs] N cobertizo *m* para botes

boating ['bəʊtɪŋ] Ⓐ N **to go ~** ir a dar un paseo en barca
Ⓑ CPD ► **boating holiday** N vacaciones *fpl* en barca ► **boating trip** N paseo *m* en barca

boatload ['bəʊtləʊd] N barcada *f*

boatman ['bəʊtmən] N (*pl* **boatmen**) barquero *m*

boatswain ['bəʊsn] N contramaestre *m*

boatyard ['bəʊtjɑːd] N astillero *m*

Bob [bɒb] N (*familiar form*) *of* **Robert**; ✦*IDIOM* **~'s your uncle!** (*Brit**) ¡y se acabó!, ¡y listo!

bob[1] [bɒb] Ⓐ N (= *jerk*) [*of head etc*] sacudida *f*, meneo *m*; (= *curtsy*) reverencia *f*
Ⓑ VI (= *jerk*) [*person*] menearse; [*animal*] moverse, menearse; **to ~ to sb** (= *curtsy*) hacer una reverencia a algn

►**bob about** VI + ADV (*in wind etc*) bailar; (*on water*) balancearse, mecerse

►**bob down** VI + ADV (= *duck*) agacharse

►**bob up** VI + ADV aparecer; (*fig*) (= *appear*) surgir, presentarse; **to ~ up and down** [*cork*] subir y bajar; [*boat*] cabecear; [*person*] levantarse y sentarse repetidas veces

bob[2] [bɒb] Ⓐ N (= *hairstyle*) pelo *m* a lo garçon
Ⓑ VT [+ *hair*] cortar a lo garçon

bob[3]* [bɒb] N (*pl inv*) (*Brit*) (*formerly*) (= *shilling*) chelín *m*; **that must be worth a few ~** eso tiene que valer un buen pico* *or* un dineral; **he's not short of a few ~** está forrado*

bob[4] [bɒb] N (= *bobsleigh*) bob *m*, bobsleigh *m*

bobbin ['bɒbɪn] N (*Tech*) carrete *m*, bobina *f*; (*Sew*) [*of cotton*] canilla *f*

bobble ['bɒbl] Ⓐ N [1] (*Brit*) (*on hat*) borla *f*
[2] (*US**) (= *mistake*) pifia* *f*
Ⓑ VI [*ball etc*] saltar, moverse de un lado para otro
Ⓒ VT (*US**) (= *handle ineptly*) pifiarla con*
Ⓓ CPD ► **bobble hat** N (*Brit*) gorro *m* con borla

Bobby ['bɒbɪ] N (*familiar form*) *of* **Robert**

bobby* ['bɒbɪ] N (*Brit*) (= *policeman*) poli* *m*

bobby pin ['bɒbɪ,pɪn] N (*US*) horquilla *f*, prendedor *m*

bobbysocks*, **bobbysox*** ['bɒbɪsɒks] NPL (*US*) escarpines *mpl*

bobbysoxer* ['bɒbɪsɒksəʳ] N (*US*) tobillera *f*

bobcat ['bɒbkæt] N (*US*) lince *m*

bobsled ['bɒbsled] N (*US*) bob *m*, bobsleigh *m*

bobsleigh ['bɒbsleɪ] N (*Brit*) bob *m*, bobsleigh *m*

bobtail ['bɒbteɪl] N (= *tail*) cola *f* corta; (= *animal*) animal *m* de cola corta, animal *m* rabón

bobtailed ['bɒbteɪld] ADJ rabicorto

Boccaccio [bɒ'kætʃɪəʊ] N Bocacio

Boche [bɒʃ] Ⓐ ADJ (*pej*) alemán, tudesco
Ⓑ N (*pej*) boche *m*, alemán *m*; **the ~** los alemanes

bock beer ['bɒk,bɪəʳ] N (*US*) cerveza *f* alemana

bod* [bɒd] N [1] (*Brit*) (= *person*) tipo/a* *m/f*, tío/a *m/f* (*Sp**)
[2] (= *body*) cuerpo *m*

bodacious‡ [bəʊ'deɪʃəs] ADJ (*US*) tremendo*, fabuloso*

bode [bəʊd] (*liter*) Ⓐ VT presagiar; **it ~s no good** no promete nada bueno
Ⓑ VI **it ~s well/ill** es de buen/mal agüero

bodega [bəʊ'deɪgə] N (= *grocery shop*) almacén *m*, tienda *f* de ultramarinos

bodge* [bɒdʒ] VT (*Brit*) = **botch**

bodice ['bɒdɪs] N [*of dress*] canesú *m*

bodice-ripping* ['bɒdɪsrɪpɪŋ] ADJ [*film, novel*] romanticón

-bodied ['bɒdɪd] ADJ (*ending in compounds*) de cuerpo ...; (*eg*) **small-bodied** de cuerpo pequeño; **full-bodied** [*cry*] fuerte; [*wine*] de mucho cuerpo

bodily ['bɒdɪlɪ] Ⓐ ADJ [*scar, injury*] en el cuerpo; [*comfort*] del cuerpo; [*pain*] corporal; [*fluid*] corporal, del cuerpo; **~ functions** funciones *fpl* fisiológicas; **~ needs** necesidades *fpl* corporales; **actual ~ harm** (*Jur*) daños *mpl* físicos, lesiones *fpl* corporales; **grievous ~ harm** (*Jur*) daños *mpl* físicos graves, lesiones *fpl* corporales graves
Ⓑ ADV **to lift sb ~** levantar a algn totalmente; **he hurled himself ~ at the Prince** se lanzó con todo su peso sobre el Príncipe; **the audience moved ~ to the front** el público se abalanzó en masa hacia la parte delantera

bodkin ['bɒdkɪn] N [1] (*Sew*) aguja *f* de jareta
[2] (*Typ*) punzón *m*
[3] (††) (= *for hair*) espadilla *f*

body ['bɒdɪ] Ⓐ N [1] [*of person, animal*] cuerpo *m*, tronco *m*; **~ and soul** (*as adv*) de todo corazón, con el alma; **to belong to sb ~ and soul** pertenecer a algn en cuerpo y alma; ✦*IDIOMS* **over my dead ~!*** ¡en sueños!, ¡ni pensarlo!; **to keep ~ and soul together** ir tirando; **her salary hardly keeps ~ and soul together** apenas se gana para vivir
[2] (= *corpse*) cadáver *m*
[3] (= *external structure*) armazón *m or f*, casco *m*; (*Aut*) (*also* **~work**) carrocería *f*
[4] (= *core*) [*of argument*] meollo *m*; **the main ~ of his speech** la parte principal *or* el meollo de su discurso
[5] (= *mass, collection*) [*of information, literature*] conjunto *m*, grueso *m*; [*of people*] grupo *m*; [*of water*] masa *f*; **a large ~ of people** un nutrido grupo de personas; **the student ~** [*of school*] el alumnado; [*of university*] el estudiantado; **the ~ politic** (*frm*) el estado; **a fine ~ of men** un buen grupo de hombres; **a large ~ of evidence** un buen conjunto de pruebas; **there is a ~ of opinion that ...** hay buen número de gente que opina que ...; **in a ~** todos juntos, en masa
[6] (= *organization*) organismo *m*, órgano *m*
[7] [*of wine*] cuerpo *m*; [*of hair*] volumen *m*, cuerpo *m*; **to give one's hair ~** dar volumen *or* cuerpo al cabello
[8] (*Astron, Chem*) cuerpo *m*; *see also* **foreign B**, **heavenly**
[9] (†*) (= *person*) tipo/a* *m/f*, tío/a *m/f* (*Sp**)
[10] = **body stocking**
Ⓑ CPD ► **body armour**, **body armor** (*US*) N *equipo de protección corporal* ► **body bag** N bolsa *f* para restos humanos ► **body blow** N (*fig*) golpe *m* duro, revés *m* ► **body clock** N reloj *m* biológico ► **body count** N (*US*) número *m or* balance *m* de las víctimas; **to do a ~ count** [*of those present*] hacer un recuento de la asistencia; [*of dead*] hacer un recuento de los muertos ► **body double** N (*Cine, TV*) doble *mf* ► **body fascism** N discriminación *f* por el (aspecto) físico ► **body fat** N grasa *f* corporal, grasa *f* (del cuerpo) ► **body language** N lenguaje *m* corporal, lenguaje *m* del cuerpo ► **body lotion** N loción *f* corporal ► **body mike*** N micro *m* de solapa* ► **body odour**, **body odor** (*US*) N olor *m* corporal ► **body repairs** NPL (*Aut*) reparación *f* de la carrocería ► **body repair shop** N = **body shop** ► **body scanner** N escáner *m* ► **body search** N registro *m* de la persona; *see also* **body-search** ► **body shop** N (*Aut*) taller *m* de reparaciones (*de carrocería*) ► **body snatcher** N (*Hist*) ladrón/a *m/f* de cadáveres ► **body stocking** N body *m*, bodi *m* ► **body suit** N = **body stocking** ► **body swerve** N (*Sport*) finta *f*, regate *m* ► **body temperature** N temperatura *f* corporal ► **body warmer** N chaleco *m* acolchado ► **body weight** N peso *m* (del cuerpo)

bodybuilder ['bɒdɪ,bɪldəʳ] N culturista *mf*

bodybuilding ['bɒdɪ,bɪldɪŋ] Ⓐ N culturismo *m*
Ⓑ CPD ► **bodybuilding exercises** NPL ejercicios *mpl* de musculación

bodyguard ['bɒdɪgɑːd] N (= *one person*) guardaespaldas *mf inv*, guarura *mf* (*Mex*); (= *group*) escolta *f*, guardia *f* personal; (*royal*) guardia *f* de corps

body-search ['bɒdɪsɜːtʃ] VT registrar (la persona de); *see also* **body**

bodywork ['bɒdɪwɜːk] N (*Aut*) carrocería *f*

Boer ['bəʊəʳ] Ⓐ ADJ bóer
Ⓑ N bóer *mf*
Ⓒ CPD ► **Boer War** N Guerra *f* Bóer, Guerra *f* del Transvaal

B. of E. N ABBR = **Bank of England**

boffin* ['bɒfɪn] N (*Brit*) cerebrito* *mf*

bog [bɒg] Ⓐ N [1] (= *swamp*) pantano *m*, ciénaga *f*
[2] (*Brit*‡) (= *toilet*) retrete *m*, meadero‡ *m*
Ⓑ CPD ► **bog paper**‡ N (*Brit*) papel *m* de wáter ► **bog roll**‡ N (*Brit*) rollo *m* de papel de wáter

►**bog down** VT + ADV **to get ~ged down (in)** quedar atascado (en), hundirse (en); (*fig*) empantanarse *or* atrancarse (en)

bogey ['bəʊgɪ] Ⓐ N [1] (= *goblin*) duende *m*, trasgo *m*; (= *bugbear*) pesadilla *f*; **that is our ~ team** ese es nuestro equipo pesadilla*
[2] (*Golf*) bogey *m*, más uno *m*
[3] (*Brit*‡) (*in nose*) moco *m*
[4] (*Brit**) (= *policeman*) poli* *m*
[5] (*Rail*) bogie *m*, boga *f*
Ⓑ VT (*Golf*) **to ~ a hole** hacer bogey *or* uno sobre par en un hoyo

bogeyman ['bəʊgɪ,mæn] N (*pl* **bogeymen**) coco* *m*

boggle* ['bɒgl] Ⓐ VI pasmarse, quedarse patidifuso*; **to ~ (at)** (= *hesitate*) quedarse patidifuso (ante)*; (= *be afraid*) quedarse helado (ante); **don't just stand and ~** no te quedes ahí parado con la boca abierta; **the imagination ~s** se queda uno alucinado*; **the mind ~s!** te quedas helado *or* patidifuso*
Ⓑ VT **it ~s the mind** te deja alucinado*

boggy ['bɒgɪ] ADJ (*compar* **boggier**; *superl* **boggiest**) pantanoso

bogie ['bəʊgɪ] N = **bogey**

Bogotá [ˌbɒgəʊ'tɑː] N Bogotá *m*

bog-standard* ['bɒg'stændəd] ADJ (*Brit*) normalito*, común y corriente

bogtrotter* ['bɒgˌtrɒtəʳ] N (*pej*) irlandés/esa *m/f*

bogus ['bəʊgəs] ADJ [*claim*] falso, fraudulento; [*interest*] fingido; [*doctor, policeman*] falso

bogy ['bəʊgɪ] N = **bogey**

Bohemia [bəʊ'hiːmɪə] N Bohemia *f*

Bohemian [bəʊ'hiːmɪən] Ⓐ ADJ (*Geog, fig*) bohemio
Ⓑ N (*Geog, fig*) bohemio/a *m/f*

Bohemianism [bəʊ'hiːmɪənɪzəm] N bohemia *f*, vida *f* bohemia

boho* ['bəʊhəʊ] Ⓐ ADJ bohemio
Ⓑ N bohemio/a *m/f*

boil[1] [bɔɪl] N (*Med*) divieso *m*, furúnculo *m*, chupón *m* (*Andes*), postema *f* (*Mex*)

boil[2] [bɔɪl] Ⓐ N **to be on the ~** estar hirviendo; (*fig*) [*situation*] estar a punto de estallar; [*person*] estar furioso; **to bring to the ~** ◊ **bring to a ~** (*US*) calentar hasta que hierva, llevar a ebullición; **to come to the ~** ◊ **come to a ~** (*US*) comenzar a hervir; (*fig*) entrar en ebullición; **to go off the ~** dejar de hervir
Ⓑ VT hervir, hacer hervir, calentar hasta que hierva; (*Culin*) [+ *liquid*] hervir; [+ *vegetables, meat*] herventar, cocer; [+ *egg*] pasar por agua
Ⓒ VI [1] hervir; **to ~ dry** quedarse sin caldo/agua
[2] (*fig*) **it makes me ~** me hace rabiar; **to ~ with rage** estar furioso; **to ~ with indignation** estar indignado; *see also* **blood**

►**boil away** VI + ADV (= *evaporate completely*) evaporarse, reducirse (por ebullición)

►**boil down** VT + ADV [+ *sauce etc*] reducir por cocción; (*fig*) reducir a forma más sencilla

►**boil down to** VI + ADV reducirse a; **it all ~s down to this** la cosa se reduce a lo siguiente

►**boil over** VI + ADV [1] [*liquid*] irse, rebosar
[2] (*fig*) desbordarse

►**boil up** VI + ADV (*lit*) [*milk*] hervir, subir; **anger was ~ing up in him** estaba a punto de estallar de ira; **they are ~ing up for a real row** se están enfureciendo de verdad

boiled [bɔɪld] Ⓐ ADJ hervido
Ⓑ CPD ► **boiled egg** N huevo *m* pasado por agua, huevo *m* a la copa (*Andes, S. Cone*) ► **boiled potatoes** NPL patatas *fpl* cocidas al agua ► **boiled shirt** N camisa *f* de pechera ► **boiled sweet** N (*Brit*) caramelo *m* con sabor a frutas

boiler ['bɔɪləʳ] Ⓐ N [1] (*for central heating*) caldera *f*; (*in ship, engine*) calderas *fpl*; (*Brit*) (*for washing clothes*) caldero *m*, calefón *m* (*S. Cone*)
[2] (*Culin*) gallina *f* vieja
Ⓑ CPD ► **boiler room** N sala *f* de calderas ► **boiler suit** N (*Brit*) mono *m*, overol *m* (*LAm*), mameluco *m* (*S. Cone*)

boilerhouse ['bɔɪləhaʊs] N (*pl* **boilerhouses** ['bɔɪləhaʊzɪz]) edificio *m* de la caldera

boilermaker ['bɔɪləˌmeɪkəʳ] N calderero/a *m/f*

boiling ['bɔɪlɪŋ] Ⓐ ADJ [1] (*gen*) hirviendo
[2] (*) (*fig*) [2·1] (= *very hot*) **I'm ~** estoy asado*; **it's ~ in here** aquí hace un calor terrible
[2·2] (= *angry*) echando chispas*
Ⓑ ADV (*) **it's ~ hot** (*weather*) hace un calor espantoso; **on a ~ hot day** un día de mucho calor; **I'm ~ hot** estoy asado*
Ⓒ CPD ► **boiling point** N punto *m* de ebullición

boil-in-the-bag meal [ˌbɔɪlɪnðəˌbæg'miːl] N *plato precocinado empaquetado en bolsas para cocción*

boisterous ['bɔɪstərəs] ADJ [1] (= *unrestrained*) [*person*] bullicioso, escandaloso; [*crowd*] bullicioso, alborotado; [*meeting*] bullicioso, tumultuoso
[2] (= *in high spirits*) [*child, game*] bullicioso, alborotado; [*party*] bullicioso, muy animado
[3] (= *rough*) [*sea, waves*] embravecido; [*wind*] tempestuoso

boisterously ['bɔɪstərəslɪ] ADV [*play*] bulliciosamente, alborotadamente; [*laugh*] escandalosamente

bold [bəʊld] Ⓐ ADJ (*compar* **bolder**, *superl* **boldest**) [1] (= *brave*) [*person, attempt, plan*] atrevido, audaz
[2] (= *forward*) [*child, remark*] atrevido, descarado; **if I may be** *or* **make so ~** (*frm*) si me permite el atrevimiento (*frm*); **to make ~ with sth** (*frm*) servirse de algo como si fuera suyo; ✦***IDIOM*** **(as) ~ as brass** más fresco que una lechuga*
[3] (= *striking*) [*colour, clothes, design*] llamativo; [*brush stroke, handwriting, move*] enérgico; [*shape, relief, contrast*] marcado
[4] (*Typ*) [*letters*] en negrita
Ⓑ N (*Typ*) negrita *f*
Ⓒ CPD ► **bold type** N negrita *f*

boldly ['bəʊldlɪ] ADV [1] (= *bravely*) [*speak, behave*] audazmente; **you must act ~ and confidently** debes actuar con audacia y seguridad en ti mismo; **to ~ go where no man has gone before** atreverse a ir donde ningún otro hombre ha estado antes
[2] (= *forwardly*) [*stare, announce, claim*] descaradamente, con atrevimiento
[3] (= *strikingly*) [*painted, drawn, written*] con energía; **he signed his name ~ at the bottom** firmó enérgicamente al pie; **a ~ designed airport** un aeropuerto con un diseño atrevido; **a ~ patterned fabric** una tela con un estampado llamativo; **a ~ coloured shirt** una camisa de color llamativo

boldness ['bəʊldnɪs] N [1] (= *daring*) audacia *f*
[2] (= *forwardness*) atrevimiento *m*, descaro *m*
[3] (= *striking quality*) [*of design, colours, clothes*] lo llamativo; [*of lines, strokes*] lo enérgico; [*of contrast*] lo marcado

bole [bəʊl] N tronco *m*

bolero [bə'lɛərəʊ] N bolero *m*

boletus [bəʊ'liːtəs] N (*pl* **boletuses** *or* **boleti** [bəʊ'liːˌtaɪ]) seta *f*

Bolivia [bə'lɪvɪə] N Bolivia *f*

Bolivian [bə'lɪvɪən] Ⓐ ADJ boliviano
Ⓑ N boliviano/a *m/f*

boll [bəʊl] N (*Bot*) cápsula *f*

bollard ['bɒləd] N (*Brit*) (*at roadside*) baliza *f*; (*Naut*) noray *m*, bolardo *m*

bollocking** ['bɒləkɪŋ] N (*Brit*) **to give sb a ~** echar una bronca a algn*, poner a algn como un trapo*

bollocks** ['bɒləks] (*Brit*) Ⓐ NPL cojones** *mpl*
Ⓑ N (= *nonsense*) pavadas* *fpl*, huevadas *fpl* (*Andes, Chile***)

Bollywood* ['bɒlɪwʊd] N (*hum*) *la industria cinematográfica de la India*

Bologna [bə'ləʊnjə] N Bolonia *f*

bolognese [bɒlə'njeɪz] ADJ **~ sauce** salsa *f* boloñesa

boloney [bə'ləʊnɪ] N [1] (*) = **baloney**
[2] (*US*) (= *sausage*) *tipo de salchicha*

Bolshevik ['bɒlʃəvɪk] Ⓐ ADJ bolchevique
Ⓑ N bolchevique *mf*

Bolshevism ['bɒlʃəvɪzəm] N bolchevismo *m*

Bolshevist ['bɒlʃəvɪst] Ⓐ ADJ bolchevista
Ⓑ N bolchevista *mf*

bolshie*, **bolshy*** ['bɒlʃɪ] (*Brit*) Ⓐ N (*Pol*) bolchevique *mf*
Ⓑ ADJ (*Pol*) bolchevique; (*fig*) rebelde, protestón

bolster ['bəʊlstəʳ] Ⓐ N (= *pillow*) cabezal *m*, almohadón *m* (*con forma cilíndrica*); (*Tech*) cojín *m*
Ⓑ VT (*fig*) (*also* **~ up**) reforzar; [+ *morale etc*] levantar

bolt [bəʊlt] Ⓐ N [1] (*on door, gun*) cerrojo *m*; [*of crossbow*] cuadrillo *m*; [*of lock*] pestillo *m*; (*Tech*) perno *m*, tornillo *m*; ✦***IDIOM*** **he's shot his ~** ha quemado su último cartucho
[2] [*of cloth*] rollo *m*
[3] (= *dash*) salida *f* repentina; (= *flight*) fuga *f*; **to make a ~ for it** echar a correr; **he made a ~ for the door** se lanzó hacia la puerta
[4] [*of lightning*] rayo *m*, relámpago *m*; ✦***IDIOM*** **it came like a ~ from the blue** cayó como una bomba
Ⓑ ADV **~ upright** rígido, muy erguido; **to sit ~ upright** incorporarse de golpe
Ⓒ VT [1] [+ *door etc*] echar el cerrojo a; (*Tech*) sujetar con tornillos, empernar; **to ~ two things together** unir dos cosas con pernos
[2] (*also* **~ down**) [+ *food*] engullir, tragar (*LAm*)
Ⓓ VI [1] (= *escape*) escaparse, huir; [*horse*] desbocarse
[2] (= *rush*) echar a correr; **to ~ past** pasar como un rayo
[3] (*US Pol*) separarse del partido
Ⓔ CPD ► **bolt hole** N (*Brit*) refugio *m*

►**bolt in** VI + ADV (= *rush in*) entrar precipitadamente

►**bolt on** VT + ADV (*Tech*) asegurar con perno

►**bolt out** Ⓐ VI + ADV (= *rush out*) salir de golpe
Ⓑ VT + ADV (= *lock out*) **to ~ sb out** dejar fuera a algn echando el cerrojo

bomb [bɒm] Ⓐ N bomba *f*; **the Bomb** la bomba atómica; ✦***IDIOMS*** **to go like a ~** (*Brit**): **it went like a ~** [*party, event*] resultó fenomenal*, fue un éxito; **this car goes like a ~** este coche va como un bólido*; **to cost a ~** (*Brit**) costar un ojo de la cara*; **to make a ~** (*Brit**) ganarse un fortunón*
Ⓑ VT [1] [+ *target*] bombardear
[2] (*US**) (= *fail*) suspender
Ⓒ VI (*US**) (= *fail*) fracasar; **the show ~ed** el espectáculo fracasó
Ⓓ CPD ► **bomb alert** N aviso *m* de bomba ► **bomb attack** N atentado *m* con bomba ► **bomb bay** N compartimento *m* de bombas ► **bomb crater** N cráter *m* de bomba ► **bomb disposal** N desactivación *f* or neutralización *f* de bombas ► **bomb disposal expert** N artificiero/a *m/f*, experto/a *m/f* en desactivar bombas ► **bomb disposal squad**, **bomb disposal unit** N brigada *f* de bombas ► **bomb factory** N *local clandestino de fabricación de bombas* ► **bomb scare** N amenaza *f* de bomba ► **bomb shelter** N refugio *m* antiaéreo ► **bomb site** N *lugar en el que ha estallado una bomba* ► **bomb warning** N = **bomb alert**

►**bomb along*** VI + ADV ir a toda marcha*, ir a toda hostia(*Sp**); **we were ~ing along at 150** íbamos a 150

►**bomb out** VT + ADV [+ *house*] volar; **the family was ~ed out** (*by terrorists*) a la familia les volaron la casa; (*by planes*) a la familia les bombardearon la casa

bombard [bɒm'bɑːd] VT (*Mil*) bombardear

(**with** con); **I was ~ed with questions** me acosaron *or* bombardearon a preguntas

bombardier [ˌbɒmbəˈdɪəʳ] N bombardero *m*

bombardment [bɒmˈbɑːdmənt] N (*Mil*) bombardeo *m*

bombast [ˈbɒmbæst] N (= *pomposity*) ampulosidad *f*, rimbombancia *f*; (= *words*) palabras *fpl* altisonantes, rimbombancia *f*; (= *boasts*) bravatas *fpl*

bombastic [bɒmˈbæstɪk] ADJ [*language, manner, style*] ampuloso, rimbombante; [*person*] pomposo

bombastically [bɒmˈbæstɪklɪ] ADV rimbombantemente

Bombay [bɒmˈbeɪ] Ⓐ N Bombay *m*
Ⓑ CPD ► **Bombay duck** N (*Culin*) *pescado seco utilizado en la elaboración del curry*

bomber [ˈbɒməʳ] Ⓐ N [1] (= *aircraft*) bombardero *m*
[2] (= *person*) terrorista *mf* que coloca bombas
Ⓑ CPD ► **bomber command** N jefatura *f* de bombardeo ► **bomber jacket** N chaqueta *f or* (*Sp*) cazadora *f* (*tipo aviador*) ► **bomber pilot** N piloto *m* de bombardero

bombing [ˈbɒmɪŋ] N bombardeo *m*

bombproof [ˈbɒmpruːf] ADJ a prueba de bombas

bombshell [ˈbɒmʃel] N [1] (*Mil*) (*formerly*) obús *m*, granada *f*
[2] (*fig*) [*of news etc*] bomba *f*; **it fell like a ~** cayó como una bomba
[3] (*) (= *attractive woman*) **she was a real ~** era todo un bombón*; *see also* **blond(e)**

bombsight [ˈbɒmsaɪt] N mira *f or* visor *m* de bombardeo

bona fide [ˈbəʊnəˈfaɪdɪ] ADJ (= *genuine*) auténtico; (= *legal*) legal

bona fides [ˈbəʊnəˈfaɪdɪz] N [*of person*] buena fe *f*

bonanza [bəˈnænzə] N (*fig*) (*in profits*) bonanza *f*

bonce* [bɒns] N (*Brit*) coco* *m*

bond [bɒnd] Ⓐ N [1] (= *link*) lazo *m*, vínculo *m*; **a ~ of friendship** un vínculo de amistad; **his word is as good as his ~** es un hombre de palabra, es de fiar; *see also* **marriage B**
[2] **bonds** (= *chains etc*) cadenas *fpl*
[3] (*Fin*) bono *m*; *see also* **premium C**
[4] (*Jur*) (= *bail*) fianza *f*
[5] (*Comm*) **in ~** en depósito bajo fianza; **to put goods into ~** depositar mercancías en el almacén aduanero; **to take goods out of ~** retirar mercancías del almacén aduanero
[6] (= *adhesion*) unión *f*
[7] (*Chem etc*) enlace *m*
Ⓑ VT [1] (*Tech*) [+ *materials*] (*also* **~ together**) unir, pegar
[2] (*Psych*) unir
Ⓒ VI [1] (*Tech*) adherirse (**with** a)
[2] (*Psych*) establecer lazos *or* vínculos afectivos; **she was having difficulty ~ing with the baby** no conseguía establecer vínculos afectivos con su bebé
Ⓓ CPD ► **bond washing** N (*Fin*) lavado *m* de bonos

bondage [ˈbɒndɪdʒ] N [1] (= *enslavement*) esclavitud *f*, cautiverio *m*; **to be in ~ to sth** ser esclavo de algo
[2] (= *sexual practice*) bondage *m*

bonded [ˈbɒndɪd] Ⓐ ADJ unido, vinculado; (*Comm*) en aduana
Ⓑ CPD ► **bonded goods** NPL mercancías *fpl* en almacén aduanero ► **bonded warehouse** N almacén *m* aduanero *or* de depósito

bondholder [ˈbɒndˌhəʊldəʳ] N obligacionista *mf*, titular *mf* de bonos

bonding [ˈbɒndɪŋ] N (*Psych*) vinculación *f* afectiva

bone [bəʊn] Ⓐ N [1] [*of human, animal etc*] hueso *m*; [*of fish*] espina *f*; **~s** [*of dead*] huesos *mpl*; (*more respectfully*) restos *mpl* mortales; **~ of contention** manzana *f* de la discordia; **chilled** *or* **frozen to the ~** congelado de frío; **to cut costs to the ~** reducir los gastos al mínimo; **I feel it in my ~s** tengo esa corazonada, me da en la nariz (*Sp**); **he won't make old ~s** no llegará a viejo; ✦**IDIOMS close to the ~** [*joke*] subido de tono; **I have a ~ to pick with you** tenemos una cuenta que ajustar; **to make no ~s about doing sth** no vacilar en hacer algo; **he made no ~s about it** no se anduvo con rodeos; **to work one's fingers to the ~** trabajar como un esclavo
[2] (= *substance*) hueso *m*
Ⓑ VT [+ *meat*] deshuesar; [+ *fish*] quitar las espinas a
Ⓒ CPD ► **bone china** N porcelana *f* fina ► **bone marrow** N médula *f* ósea
►**bone up*** VI + ADV quemarse las cejas (**on** estudiando), empollar (**on** sobre)

boned [bəʊnd] ADJ [1] [*meat*] deshuesado; [*fish*] sin espinas
[2] [*corset*] de ballenas

bone-dry [ˌbəʊnˈdraɪ] ADJ completamente seco

bonehead* [ˈbəʊnhed] N tonto/a *m/f*

boneheaded* [ˈbəʊnˈhedɪd] ADJ estúpido

bone-idle* [ˌbəʊnˈaɪdl] ADJ gandul, holgazán, flojo (*LAm*)

boneless [ˈbəʊnlɪs] ADJ [1] (*Anat*) sin hueso(s), deshuesado
[2] (*fig*) sin carácter, débil

bonemeal [ˈbəʊnmiːl] N harina *f* de huesos

boner [ˈbəʊnəʳ] N [1] (*US**) (= *blunder*) metedura *f* de pata*, plancha *f* (*Sp**); **to pull a ~** meter la pata*, tirarse una plancha (*Sp**)
[2] (‡) (= *erection*) erección *f*; **to have a ~** tenerla dura‡

boneshaker* [ˈbəʊnˌʃeɪkəʳ] N (*Aut etc*) armatoste* *m*, rácano* *m*; (= *bicycle*) *bicicleta antigua con ruedas sólidas y sin muelles*

bonfire [ˈbɒnfaɪəʳ] N (*for celebration*) hoguera *f*; (*for rubbish*) fogata *f*

bongo [ˈbɒŋgəʊ] N (*also* **~ drum**) bongó *m*

bonhomie [ˈbɒnɒmiː] N afabilidad *f*

bonk [bɒŋk] Ⓐ N [1] (*) (= *hit*) golpe *m*; **it went ~*** hizo ¡pum!, se oyó un ruido sordo
[2] (*Brit*‡) (= *sex*) **to have a ~** echarse un polvo**‡, follar (*Sp*‡*)
Ⓑ VI (*Brit*‡) (= *have sex*) echarse un polvo**‡, follar (*Sp*‡*)
Ⓒ VT [1] (*) (= *hit*) golpear, pegar
[2] (*Brit*‡) (= *have sex with*) tirarse a**‡, echarse un polvo con**‡

bonkers* [ˈbɒŋkəz] ADJ (*esp Brit*) **to be ~** estar chalado*, estar como una cabra*; **to go ~** perder la chaveta*

bonking‡ [ˈbɒŋkɪŋ] N (*Brit*) (= *sex*) joder**‡ *m*

bon mot [ˈbɒnˈməʊ] N agudeza *f*

Bonn [bɒn] N Bonn *m*

bonnet [ˈbɒnɪt] N [1] (*woman's*) gorra *f*; (*large, showy*) papalina *f*, toca *f*; (*esp Scot*) (*man's*) gorra *f* escocesa; (*baby's*) gorro *m*
[2] (*Brit Aut*) capó *m*, cofre *m* (*Mex*)

bonny [ˈbɒnɪ] ADJ (*compar* **bonnier**; *superl* **bonniest**) (*esp Scot*) (= *pretty*) [*child*] hermoso, lindo (*esp LAm*); [*dress*] bonito, lindo (*esp LAm*)

bonsai [ˈbɒnsaɪ] N bonsai *m*

bonus [ˈbəʊnəs] Ⓐ N [1] (*on wages*) prima *f*, bonificación *f*; (*insurance etc*) gratificación *f*; (*to shareholders*) dividendo *m* adicional
[2] (*fig*) ventaja *f*
Ⓑ CPD ► **bonus point** N (*in game, quiz*) punto *m* extra ► **bonus scheme** N plan *m* de incentivos ► **bonus shares** NPL acciones *fpl* gratuitas

bony [ˈbəʊnɪ] ADJ (*compar* **bonier**; *superl* **boniest**) [1] (= *having bones*) huesudo; [*fish*] espinoso, lleno de espinas
[2] (= *like bone*) óseo
[3] (= *thin*) [*person*] flaco, delgado

boo [buː] Ⓐ N rechifla *f*, abucheo *m*; ✦**IDIOM he wouldn't say ~ to a goose*** es incapaz de matar una mosca
Ⓑ EXCL ¡uh!
Ⓒ VT [+ *actor, referee*] abuchear, silbar; **he was ~ed off the stage** la rechifla le obligó a abandonar el escenario
Ⓓ VI silbar

boob [buːb] Ⓐ N [1] (*Brit**) (= *mistake*) metedura *f* de pata*; **to make a ~** meter la pata*
[2] (‡) (= *breast*) teta* *f*
Ⓑ VI (*) meter la pata*
Ⓒ CPD ► **boob tube** N (*US*) (= *TV set*) televisor *m*; (= *garment*) camiseta-tubo *f*

booboo* [ˈbuːbuː] N (*US*) metedura *f* de pata*

booby [ˈbuːbɪ] Ⓐ N [1] (= *fool*) bobo/a *m/f*
[2] **boobies**‡ tetas* *fpl*
Ⓑ CPD ► **booby hatch**‡ N (*US*) (= *mental hospital*) casa *f* de locos ► **booby prize** N premio *m* al último ► **booby trap** N trampa *f*; (*Mil etc*) trampa *f* explosiva, bomba *f* cazabobos

booby-trap [ˈbuːbɪtræp] VT poner trampa explosiva a; **the house had been ~ped** habían puesto una trampa explosiva en la casa; **~ped car** coche-bomba *m*; **~ped door** puerta *f* con sorpresa

boogie* [ˈbuːgɪ] Ⓐ N (= *dance*) bailoteo* *m*; **to go for a ~** irse de marcha*, darle marcha (al cuerpo)‡
Ⓑ VI bailotear*, dar marcha (al cuerpo)‡

boogie-woogie [ˈbuːgɪˌwuːgɪ] N bugui-bugui *m*

boo-hoo* [ˌbuːˈhuː] EXCL ¡bua!

booing [ˈbuːɪŋ] N abucheo *m*

book [bʊk] Ⓐ N [1] (= *publication*) libro *m*; **by the ~** según las reglas; **to play it** *or* **to go by the ~** seguir las reglas; **economics/her life is a closed ~ to me** la economía/su vida es un misterio para mí; **the ~ of Genesis** el libro del Génesis; **the Good Book** la Biblia; **in my ~** (*fig*) tal como yo lo veo, a mi modo de ver; **a ~ on politics** un libro de política; **that's one for the ~** eso es digno de mención; **his mind is an open ~** su mente es un libro abierto; ✦**IDIOMS to bring sb to ~** pedir cuentas a algn; **those who planned the murder were never brought to ~** nunca se les pidió cuentas a los que planearon el asesinato; **to be in sb's good/bad ~s**: **I'm in his bad ~s at the moment** en este momento estoy en su lista negra; **I was trying to get back in her good ~s** estaba intentando volver a congraciarme con ella; **to read sb like a ~**: **I know where he's off to - I can read him like a ~** sé dónde va, a mí no me engaña; **to suit sb's ~**: **it suits his ~ to play the easy-going liberal** le viene bien hacerse el liberal poco exigente, se hace el liberal poco exigente porque le conviene; **to throw the ~ at sb** castigar severamente a algn; *see also* **leaf**, **trick A2**, **turn-up**
[2] (*also* **notebook**) libreta *f*, librito *m*; (*also* **exercise ~**) cuaderno *m*
[3] (*also* **telephone ~**) guía *f*; **I'm in the ~** estoy en la guía
[4] (= *set*) [*of tickets, cheques*] talonario *m*; [*of matches*] estuche *m*; [*of stamps*] librito *m*; [*of*

samples] muestrario *m*
[5] **books** [5·1] (*Comm*) **the ~s** las cuentas, la contabilidad; **to keep the ~s** llevar las cuentas *or* los libros *or* la contabilidad; *see also* **cook**
[5·2] (= *register of members*) registro *msing*; **they had less than 30 members on their ~s** tenían menos de 30 miembros en el registro; **to take sb's name off the ~s** borrar a algn del registro; **he was the most expensive player on the ~s** era el jugador más caro que tenían fichado
[6] (*Jur*) (*also* **statute** ~) código *m*; *see also* **statute**
[7] (*Gambling*) **to make a ~ on sth** aceptar apuestas a algo; **to open** *or* **start a ~ on sth** empezar a aceptar apuestas a algo
[8] (*US Mus*) (= *libretto*) libreto *m*
(B) VT [1] (*Brit*) (= *reserve*) [+ *ticket, seat, room, table, flight*] reservar; **we ~ed the hotel rooms in advance** reservamos habitaciones en el hotel por adelantado; **all the restaurants are fully ~ed** todos los restaurantes están llenos; **have you ~ed your holiday yet?** ¿ya has reservado las vacaciones?
[2] (= *arrange*) [+ *appointment, time*] pedir; **I've ~ed an appointment with the dentist** he pedido hora con el dentista; **can we ~ a time to meet soon?** ¿podemos quedar un día de éstos?
[3] (= *engage*) [+ *performer, artiste*] contratar
[4] (*) (= *take name of*) [4·1] [*police*] **he was ~ed for speeding** lo multaron por exceso de velocidad; **they took him to the station and ~ed him for assault** lo llevaron a la comisaría y lo acusaron de agresión
[4·2] (*Sport*) [+ *player*] amonestar
[5] (= *note down*) [+ *order*] anotar
(C) VI (*Brit*) hacer una reserva, reservar; **to ~ into a hotel** hacer una reserva *or* reservar en un hotel
(D) CPD ► **book club** N club *m* del libro, club *m* de lectores ► **book fair** N feria *f* del libro ► **book jacket** N sobrecubierta *f* ► **book learning** N aprendizaje *m* (a través) de los libros, saber *m* libresco (*frm*); **~ learning is only part of school life** el aprendizaje de los libros es sólo una parte de la vida escolar ► **book post** N correo *m* de libros ► **book review** N crítica *f* *or* reseña *f* de un libro ► **book token** N vale *m* para libros, cheque *m* regalo para libros ► **book value** N valor *m* contable *or* en libros

►**book in** (*Brit*) (A) VI + ADV (= *record arrival*) registrarse; (= *reserve a room*) reservar habitación; **they ~ed in under false names** reservaron habitación bajo un nombre falso
(B) VT + ADV **they're ~ed in at the White Swan** tienen reservada una habitación en el White Swan; **I've ~ed you in with Dr Stuart for four o'clock** te he conseguido hora con el Dr. Stuart para las cuatro; **make sure you're ~ed in for antenatal care** asegúrate de que estás apuntada para la asistencia prevía al parto

►**book up** VT + ADV (*esp Brit*) [1] [+ *holiday*] hacer reserva de
[2] **to be ~ed up** [2·1] [*hotel, restaurant, flight*] **we are ~ed up all summer** no tenemos nada libre en todo el verano, lo tenemos todo reservado para todo el verano; **the hotel is ~ed up** el hotel está completo, todas las habitaciones del hotel están reservadas; **all the flights were ~ed up** todos los vuelos estaban completos, no quedaban plazas en ningún vuelo
[2·2] [*performer*] **the orchestra is ~ed up until 2002** la orquesta tiene un programa de actuaciones completo hasta 2002
[2·3] [*person*] **I'm ~ed up for tonight** tengo muchos compromisos para esta noche; **I'm ~ed up all next week** la semana que viene tengo un programa muy apretado

bookable ['bʊkəbl] ADJ (*Brit*) [1] (= *reservable*) [*seat*] que se puede reservar; **"seats bookable in advance"** "las entradas pueden reservarse con antelación"
[2] (*Sport*) [*offence*] sujeto a tarjeta amarilla

bookbinder ['bʊk,baɪndəʳ] N encuadernador(a) *m/f*

bookbinding ['bʊk,baɪndɪŋ] N encuadernación *f*

bookcase ['bʊkkeɪs] N librería *f*, estantería *f*, librero *m* (*Mex*)

bookend ['bʊkend] N sujetalibros *m inv*

bookie* ['bʊkɪ] N = **bookmaker**

booking ['bʊkɪŋ] (A) N [1] [*of hotel, holiday, restaurant*] reserva *f*; [*of performers*] contratación *f*; **to make a ~** hacer una reserva; **telephone ~** reserva *f* por teléfono; *see also* **block D**
[2] (= *engagement*) **the band has a ~ next week** han contratado al grupo para la semana que viene
[3] (*Sport*) [*of player*] **he had nine ~s last year** el año pasado recibió tarjeta amarilla nueve veces
(B) CPD ► **booking clerk** N taquillero/a *m/f* ► **booking conditions** NPL condiciones *fpl* de reserva ► **booking fee** N suplemento *m* por hacer la reserva ► **booking form** N formulario *m* de reserva ► **booking office** N (*Rail*) despacho *m* de billetes *or* (*LAm*) boletos; (*Theat*) taquilla *f*

BOOKER PRIZE

Booker Prize *es el nombre de un premio literario que se concede anualmente a una obra de ficción en inglés publicada en el Reino Unido, Irlanda o cualquier otro país de la* **Commonwealth**. *El premio, que viene otorgándose desde 1969 y es uno de los más conocidos en el Reino Unido, está financiado por la empresa* **Booker McConnell**. *La entrega de premios, en la que se anuncia el ganador, provoca un considerable interés en los medios de comunicación y se televisa en directo. La decisión de los jueces, normalmente escritores, catedráticos y críticos, suele generar bastante polémica.*

bookish ['bʊkɪʃ] ADJ [*learning*] basado en libros, libresco (*frm*); [*person*] estudioso; **her dowdy, ~ image** su imagen aburrida, de ratón de biblioteca*

bookkeeper ['bʊk,kiːpəʳ] N contable *mf*, tenedor(a) *m/f* de libros, contador(a) *m/f* (*LAm*)

bookkeeping ['bʊk,kiːpɪŋ] N contabilidad *f*, teneduría *f* de libros

booklet ['bʊklɪt] N folleto *m*

book-lover ['bʊk,lʌvəʳ] N bibliófilo/a *m/f*, amante *mf* de los libros

bookmaker ['bʊkmeɪkəʳ] N corredor *m* de apuestas; → GREYHOUND RACING

bookmaking ['bʊkmeɪkɪŋ] N apuestas *fpl*, correduría *f* de apuestas; **a ~ firm** una casa de apuestas

bookmark ['bʊkmɑːk] (A) N [1] (*for book*) marcador *m*, señalador *m*
[2] (*Internet*) marcador *m*, favorito *m*
(B) VT (*Internet*) marcar como sitio favorito, agregar a favoritos

bookmobile ['bʊkməʊ,biːl] N (*US*) biblioteca *f* ambulante, bibliobús *m* (*Sp*)

bookplate ['bʊkpleɪt] N ex libris *m*

bookrest ['bʊkrest] N atril *m*

bookseller ['bʊk,seləʳ] N librero/a *m/f*; **a ~'s** una librería

bookshelf ['bʊkʃelf] N (*pl* **bookshelves**) estante *m* (para libros); **bookshelves** estantería *fsing*

bookshop ['bʊkʃɒp] N (*esp Brit*) librería *f*

bookstall ['bʊkstɔːl] N (*at station*) quiosco *m* (de libros); (*at fair*) puesto *m* de libros

bookstore ['bʊkstɔːʳ] N (*esp US*) librería *f*

bookworm ['bʊkwɜːm] N (*fig*) ratón *m* de biblioteca*

Boolean ['buːlɪən] (A) ADJ booleano
(B) CPD ► **Boolean algebra** N álgebra *f* de Boole ► **Boolean logic** N lógica *f* booleana

boom[1] [buːm] N [1] (*Naut*) botalón *m*, botavara *f*
[2] (*across harbour*) barrera *f*
[3] [*of crane*] aguilón *m*; [*of microphone*] jirafa *f*

boom[2] [buːm] (A) N [*of guns*] estruendo *m*, estampido *m*; [*of thunder*] retumbo *m*, trueno *m*
(B) VI [*voice, radio*] (*also* ~ **out**) resonar, retumbar; [*sea*] bramar; [*gun*] tronar, retumbar
(C) VT (*also* ~ **out**) tronar

boom[3] [buːm] (A) N (*in an industry*) auge *m*, boom *m*; (= *period of growth*) expansión *f*; **in ~ conditions** en condiciones de prosperidad repentina
(B) VI [*prices*] estar en alza; [*commodity*] tener mucha demanda; [*industry, town*] gozar de un boom, estar en auge; **business is ~ing** el negocio está en auge
(C) CPD ► **boom economy** N economía *f* de alza ► **boom market** N mercado *m* de alza ► **boom town** N ciudad *f* beneficiaria del auge

boom-bust ['buːm'bʌst], **boom-and-bust** ['buːmənd'bʌst] ADJ (*Econ*) [*economy, market*] con grandes altibajos

boomerang ['buːməræŋ] (A) N bumerang *m*
(B) ADJ contraproducente, contrario a lo que se esperaba
(C) VI (*fig*) (= *backfire*) resultar contraproducente, tener el efecto contraproducente al buscado (**on** para); **it ~ed on him** le salió el tiro por la culata*

booming[1] ['buːmɪŋ] ADJ [*voice*] resonante, retumbante

booming[2] ['buːmɪŋ] ADJ (*Comm etc*) próspero, que goza de un boom, floreciente

boon [buːn] (A) N (= *blessing*) gran ayuda *f*; **it would be a ~ if he went** nos ayudaría muchísimo que él fuera; **it would be a ~ to humanity** sería un gran beneficio para la humanidad
(B) CPD ► **boon companion** N compañero/a *m/f* inseparable

boondocks* ['buːndɒks] NPL (*US*) **out in the ~** en el quinto pino

boondoggle* ['buːndɒgl] VI (*US*) enredar*

boons* [buːnz] NPL (*US*) = **boondocks**

boor [bʊəʳ] N palurdo/a *m/f*

boorish ['bʊərɪʃ] ADJ [*manners*] grosero

boorishly ['bʊərɪʃlɪ] ADV [*behave, speak*] groseramente

boorishness ['bʊərɪʃnɪs] N grosería *f*

boost [buːst] (A) N [1] (= *encouragement*) estímulo *m*, aliento *m*; **to give a ~ to** estimular, alentar
[2] (= *upward thrust*) (*to person*) empuje *m*, empujón *m*; (*to rocket*) impulso *m*, propulsión *f*
(B) VT [1] (= *increase*) [+ *sales, production*] fomentar, incrementar; [+ *confidence, hopes*] estimular; **to ~ sb's morale** levantar la moral a algn

➤ LANGUAGE IN USE: **booking A1** 21.4

2 (= *promote*) [+ *product*] promover, hacer publicidad de; [+ *person*] dar bombo a
3 (*Elec*) [+ *voltage*] elevar; [+ *radio signal*] potenciar
4 (*Space*) propulsar, lanzar

booster ['bu:stəʳ] Ⓐ N 1 (= *encouragement*) estímulo *m*
2 (*TV, Rad*) repetidor *m*
3 (*Elec*) elevador *m* de tensión
4 (*Space*) (*also* ~ **rocket**) cohete *m* secundario
5 (*Aer*) impulsor *m*, impulsador *m*
6 (*Mech*) aumentador *m* de presión
7 (*Med*) dosis *f inv* de refuerzo *or* recuerdo
Ⓑ CPD ► **booster injection** N dosis *f inv* de refuerzo *or* recuerdo, revacunación *f* ► **booster rocket** N cohete *m* secundario ► **booster shot** N = **booster injection** ► **booster station** N (*TV, Rad*) repetidor *m*

boot[1] [bu:t] Ⓐ N 1 bota *f*; (= *ankle boot*) borceguí *m*; ✦*IDIOMS* **to die with one's ~s on** morir con las botas puestas; **now the ~ is on the other foot** (*Brit*) ahora se ha dado vuelta a la tortilla; **to give sb the ~*** despedir a algn, poner a algn en la calle*; **to get** *or* **be given the ~*** ser despedido; **he was quaking** *or* **shaking** *or* **trembling in his ~s** le temblaban las piernas; **to lick sb's ~s** hacer la pelotilla a algn*; **to put the ~ in** (*Brit**) emplear la violencia; (*fig*) obrar decisivamente; *see also* **big A6**
2 (*Brit Aut*) maletero *m*, baúl *m* (*S. Cone*), maletera *f* (*Andes, Chile*), cajuela *f* (*Mex*)
3 (*US Aut*) (*also* **Denver** ~) cepo *m*
Ⓑ VT 1 (*) (= *kick*) dar un puntapié a; **to ~ sb out*** poner a algn de patitas en la calle*
2 (*Comput*) (*also* ~ **up**) cebar, inicializar
Ⓒ VI (*Comput*) (*also* ~ **up**) cebar, inicializar
Ⓓ CPD ► **boot boy*** N (*Brit*) camorrista *m* ► **boot camp** N (*in army*) campamento *m* militar; (= *prison*) *prisión civil con régimen militar* ► **boot polish** N betún *m* ► **boot sale** N (*Brit*) (*also* **car ~ sale**) mercadillo *m* (*en el que se exponen las mercancías en el maletero del coche*)

boot[2] [bu:t] **to ~** ADV (*liter*) además, por añadidura

bootblack ['bu:tblæk] N limpiabotas *mf inv*, bolero/a *m/f* (*Mex*), embolador(a) *m/f* (*Col*)

bootee [bu:'ti:] N (*baby's*) bota *f* de lana; (*woman's*) borceguí *m*

booth [bu:ð] N (*at fair*) puesto *m*; (*in restaurant*) reservado *m*; (*Telec, interpreter's, voting*) cabina *f*

booting-up [,bu:tɪŋ'ʌp] Ⓐ N (*Comput*) operación *f* de cargo, iniciación *f*
Ⓑ CPD ► **booting-up switch** N tecla *f* de iniciación

bootlace ['bu:tleɪs] N cordón *m*

bootleg ['bu:tleg] Ⓐ ADJ (= *illicit*) [*alcohol*] de contrabando; [*tape, edition*] pirata
Ⓑ N (*Mus*) grabación *f* pirata
Ⓒ VI contrabandear con licores
Ⓓ VT [+ *tape, recording*] grabar y vender ilegalmente

bootlegger ['bu:t,legəʳ] N [*of alcohol*] contrabandista *mf*; [*of tapes, recordings*] productor/a *m/f* de copias pirata

bootlicker* ['bu:tlɪkəʳ] N lameculos‡ *m*

bootlicking* ['bu:tlɪkɪŋ] Ⓐ ADJ pelotillero*
Ⓑ N pelotilleo* *m*

bootmaker ['bu:tmeɪkəʳ] N zapatero/a *m/f* que hace botas

boots [bu:ts] NSING (*Brit*) limpiabotas *mf inv* (de un hotel)

bootstrap ['bu:tstræp] N oreja *f*; ✦*IDIOM* **to pull oneself up by one's ~s** reponerse gracias a sus propios esfuerzos

booty ['bu:tɪ] N botín *m*

booze* [bu:z] Ⓐ N bebida *f*; **to go on the ~** darse a la bebida; **to be off the ~** haber dejado la bebida
Ⓑ VI (= *get drunk*) empinar el codo*; (= *go out drinking*) salir a beber
Ⓒ VT beber

boozer‡ ['bu:zəʳ] N 1 (= *person*) bebedor(a) *m/f*, tomador(a) *m/f* (*LAm*)
2 (*Brit*) (= *pub*) bar *m*

booze-up‡ ['bu:z,ʌp] N (*Brit*) *reunión social donde se bebe mucho alcohol*

boozy‡ ['bu:zɪ] ADJ [*person*] aficionado a la bebida, borracho; [*party*] donde se bebe bastante; [*song etc*] tabernario

bop[1]* [bɒp] (*Mus*) Ⓐ N bop *m*
Ⓑ VI menear el esqueleto*

bop[2]* [bɒp] VT (*esp US*) (= *hit*) cascar*

bo-peep [bəʊ'pi:p] N **to play ~** jugar tapándose la cara y descubriéndola de repente; **Little Bo-peep** *personaje de una poesía infantil, famoso por haber perdido sus ovejas*

boraces ['bɔ:rə,si:z] NPL *of* **borax**

boracic [bə'ræsɪk] ADJ bórico

borage ['bɒrɪdʒ] N borraja *f*

borax ['bɔ:ræks] N (*pl* **boraxes** *or* **boraces**) bórax *m*

Bordeaux [bɔ:'dəʊ] N 1 (*Geog*) Burdeos *m*
2 (= *wine*) burdeos *m*

bordello [bɔ:'deləʊ] N casa *f* de putas

border ['bɔ:dəʳ] Ⓐ N 1 (= *edge*) (*as decoration*) borde *m*, margen *m*; (*as boundary*) límite *m*
2 (= *frontier*) frontera *f*; **the Borders** (*Brit*) *la frontera entre Inglaterra y Escocia*
3 (*Sew*) orilla *f*, cenefa *f*
4 (*in garden*) arriate *m*, parterre *m*
Ⓑ VT 1 (= *adjoin*) bordear, lindar con; **it is ~ed on the north by ...** linda al norte con ...
2 (*Sew*) ribetear, orlar
Ⓒ CPD [*area, ballad*] fronterizo; [*guard*] de la frontera ► **border dispute** N disputa *f* fronteriza ► **border incident** N incidente *m* fronterizo ► **border patrol** N (*US*) patrulla *f* de fronteras ► **border post** N puesto *m* fronterizo ► **border town** N pueblo *m* fronterizo

►**border on, border upon** VI + PREP 1 [+ *area, country*] lindar con, limitar con
2 (*fig*) (= *come near to being*) rayar en; **with a self-confidence ~ing on arrogance** con una confianza en sí mismo que raya en la arrogancia

bordering ['bɔ:dərɪŋ] ADJ contiguo

borderland ['bɔ:dəlænd] N zona *f* fronteriza

borderline ['bɔ:dəlaɪn] Ⓐ N (*between districts*) límite *m*, línea *f* divisoria; **on the ~** (*between classes*) a medio camino; (*in exam etc*) en el límite
Ⓑ CPD ► **borderline case** N (= *situation, thing, person*) caso *m* dudoso

bore[1] [bɔ:ʳ] Ⓐ N 1 (= *tool*) taladro *m*, barrena *f*; (*Geol*) sonda *f*
2 (*also* ~ **hole**) perforación *f*
3 (= *diameter*) agujero *m*, barreno *m*; [*of gun*] calibre *m*; [*of cylinder*] alesaje *m*; **a 12-~ shotgun** una escopeta del calibre 12
Ⓑ VT [+ *hole, tunnel*] hacer, perforar; **to ~ a hole in** hacer *or* perforar un agujero en; **to ~ one's way through** abrirse camino por; **wood ~d by insects** madera *f* carcomida
Ⓒ VI **to ~ for oil** hacer perforaciones en busca de petróleo

bore[2] [bɔ:ʳ] Ⓐ N 1 (= *person*) pesado/a *m/f*, pelmazo/a* *m/f*; **what a ~ he is!** ¡qué hombre más pesado!, ¡es más pesado que el plomo!*
2 (= *event, task*) lata* *f*; **it's such a ~** es una lata*, es un rollo (*Sp**); **what a ~!** ¡qué lata!*, ¡qué rollo! (*Sp**)
Ⓑ VT aburrir; **to be ~d** ◊ **get ~d** aburrirse; **he's ~d to death** *or* **tears** ◊ **he's ~d stiff*** está aburrido como una ostra*, está muerto de aburrimiento; **to be ~d with** estar aburrido *or* harto de

bore[3] [bɔ:ʳ] PT *of* **bear**[2]

bore[4] [bɔ:ʳ] N (= *tidal wave*) marea *f*

boredom ['bɔ:dəm] N aburrimiento *m*

borehole ['bɔ:həʊl] N perforación *f*

Borgia ['bɔ:dʒjə] N Borja *m*

boric acid [,bɔ:rɪk'æsɪd] N ácido *m* bórico

boring ['bɔ:rɪŋ] ADJ (= *tedious*) aburrido, pesado; **she's so ~** es muy aburrida *or* pesada

born [bɔ:n] Ⓐ PP *of* **bear** nacido; **to be ~** (*lit*) nacer; (*fig*) [*idea*] surgir, nacer; **I was ~ in 1955** nací en 1955; **a daughter was ~ to them** les nació una hija; **to be ~ again** renacer, volver a nacer; **evil is ~ of idleness** la pereza es madre de todos los vicios; **he wasn't ~ yesterday!*** ¡no se chupa el dedo!*
Ⓑ ADJ [*actor, leader*] nato; **he is a ~ liar** es mentiroso por naturaleza; **a Londoner ~ and bred** londinense de casta y cuna; **in all my ~ days** en mi vida

-born [bɔ:n] ADJ (*ending in compounds*) **British-born** británico de nacimiento

born-again ['bɔ:nə,gen] ADJ renacido, vuelto a nacer

borne [bɔ:n] PP *of* **bear**[2]

-borne [-bɔ:n] ADJ (*ending in compounds*) llevado por, traído por

Borneo ['bɔ:nɪəʊ] N Borneo *m*

boron ['bɔ:rɒn] N boro *m*

borough ['bʌrə] N municipio *m*; (*in London, New York*) distrito *m*

borrow ['bɒrəʊ] VT pedir prestado (**from, of** a), tomar prestado; [+ *idea etc*] adoptar, apropiarse; [+ *word*] tomar (**from** de); **may I ~ your car?** ¿me prestas el coche?; **you can ~ it till I need it** te lo presto hasta que lo necesite

borrower ['bɒrəʊəʳ] N 1 [*of money*] prestatario/a *m/f*; ✦*PROV* **neither a ~ nor a lender be** ni prestes ni pidas prestado
2 (*in library*) usuario/a *m/f*

borrowing ['bɒrəʊɪŋ] Ⓐ N préstamo(s) *m(pl)* (**from** de)
Ⓑ CPD ► **borrowing power(s)** N(PL) capacidad *f* de endeudamiento

borstal ['bɔ:stl] Ⓐ N (*Brit*) correccional *m* de menores
Ⓑ CPD ► **borstal boy** N joven *m* delincuente (que ha pasado por el correccional)

borzoi ['bɔ:zɔɪ] N galgo *m* ruso

Bosch [bɒʃ] N El Bosco

bosh* [bɒʃ] N tonterías *fpl*

bo's'n ['bəʊsən] N = **boatswain**

Bosnia ['bɒznɪə] N Bosnia *f*

Bosnia Herzegovina ['bɒznɪə,hɜ:tsəgə'vi:nə] N Bosnia Herzegovina *f*

Bosnian ['bɒznɪən] Ⓐ ADJ bosnio
Ⓑ N bosnio/a *m/f*

bosom ['bʊzəm] Ⓐ N [*of woman*] seno *m*, pecho *m*; [*of garment*] pechera *f*; **in the ~ of the family** en el seno de la familia; ✦*IDIOM* **to take sb to one's ~** acoger amorosamente a algn
Ⓑ CPD ► **bosom friend** N amigo/a *m/f* íntimo/a *or* entrañable

bosomy ['bʊzəmɪ] ADJ tetuda*, de pecho abultado

Bosphorus ['bɒsfərəs] N Bósforo *m*

boss¹ [bɒs] Ⓐ N (*gen*) jefe/a *m/f*; (= *owner, employer*) patrón/ona *m/f*; (= *manager*) gerente *mf*; (= *foreman*) capataz *m*; [*of gang*] cerebro *m*; (*US Pol*) cacique *m*; **I like to be my own ~** quiero mandar en mis asuntos, quiero controlar mis propias cosas; **I'm the ~ here** aquí mando yo; **OK, you're the ~** vale, tú mandas
Ⓑ VT mangonear*, dar órdenes a
Ⓒ ADJ (*US**) chulo*

►**boss about, boss around** VT + ADV mangonear*, dar órdenes a

boss² [bɒs] N (= *bulge*) protuberancia *f*; (= *stud*) clavo *m*, tachón *m*; [*of shield*] ombligo *m*; (*Archit*) llave *f* de bóveda

BOSS N ABBR (*in South Africa*) = **Bureau of State Security**

boss-eyed [,bɒs'aɪd] ADJ bizco

bossiness ['bɒsɪnɪs] N carácter *m* mandón, tiranía *f*

bossy ['bɒsɪ] ADJ (*compar* **bossier**; *superl* **bossiest**) [*person*] mandón

Bostonian [bɒs'təʊnɪən] N bostoniano/a *m/f*

bosun ['bəʊsən] N = **boatswain**

botanic [bə'tænɪk] ADJ = **botanical**

botanical [bə'tænɪkəl] ADJ [*gardens*] botánico

botanist ['bɒtənɪst] N botánico/a *m/f*, botanista *mf*

botanize ['bɒtənaɪz] VI herborizar

botany ['bɒtənɪ] N botánica *f*

botch* [bɒtʃ] Ⓐ N (= *crude repair*) chapuza* *f*; **to make a ~ of** = B
Ⓑ VT (*also* **~ up**) hacer una chapuza de*; **to ~ it** estropearlo; **a ~ed job** una chapuza*

both [bəʊθ] Ⓐ ADJ ambos/as, los/las dos; **~ (the) boys** los dos *or* ambos chicos
Ⓑ PRON ambos/as *mpl/fpl*, los/las dos *mpl/fpl*; **~ of them** los dos; **~ of us** nosotros dos, los dos; **we ~ went** fuimos los dos; **they were ~ there** ◊ **~ of them were there** estaban allí los dos
Ⓒ ADV a la vez; **she was ~ laughing and crying** reía y lloraba a la vez; **I find it ~ impressive and vulgar** encuentro que es impresionante y vulgar a la vez; **he ~ plays and sings** canta y además toca; **~ you and I saw it** lo vimos tanto tú como yo, lo vimos los dos

bother ['bɒðəʳ] Ⓐ N [1] (= *nuisance*) molestia *f*, lata* *f*; **what a ~!** ¡qué lata!*; **it's such a ~ to clean** es una lata limpiarlo*, es muy incómodo limpiarlo
[2] (= *problems*) problemas *mpl*; **I found the street without any ~** encontré la calle sin problemas; **do you have much ~ with your car?** ¿tienes muchos problemas con el coche?; **he had a spot of ~ with the police** tuvo un pequeño problema con la policía
[3] (= *trouble*) molestia *f*; **it isn't any ~** ◊ **it's no ~** no es ninguna molestia; **I went to the ~ of finding one** me tomé la molestia de buscar uno
[4] (*Brit**) (= *violence*) **to go out looking for ~** salir a buscar camorra*
Ⓑ VT [1] (= *worry*) preocupar; (= *annoy*) molestar, fastidiar; **does the noise ~ you?** ¿le molesta el ruido?; **does it ~ you if I smoke?** ¿le molesta que fume?; **his leg ~s him** le duele la pierna; **to ~ o.s. about/with sth** molestarse *or* preocuparse por algo
[2] (= *inconvenience*) molestar; (= *pester*) dar la lata a*; **I'm sorry to ~ you** perdona la molestia; **don't ~ me!** ¡no me molestes!, ¡no fastidies!, ¡no me friegues! (*LAm**); **please don't ~ me about it now** le ruego que no me moleste con eso ahora
Ⓒ VI (= *take trouble*) tomarse la molestia (**to do** de hacer); **to ~ about/with** molestarse *or* preocuparse por; **don't ~** no te molestes, no te preocupes; **he didn't even ~ to write** ni siquiera se molestó en escribir
Ⓓ EXCL ¡porras!*

BOTH

Pronoun and adjective

- When **both** is a pronoun or adjective you can usually translate it using **los/las dos**:
  We're both climbers, Both of us are climbers
  Los dos somos alpinistas
  I know both of them *or* I know them both
  Los conozco a los dos
  Both (of the) sisters were blind
  Las dos hermanas eran ciegas
- Alternatively, in more formal speech, use **ambos/ambas**:
  We both liked it
  Nos gustó a ambos
  Both (of the) regions are autonomous
  Ambas regiones son autónomas

! Don't use the article with **ambos**.

"both ... and"

- **Both ... and** can be translated in a variety of ways, depending on what is referred to. If it relates to two individuals, you can usually use the invariable **tanto ... como**. Alternatively, you can often use **los/las dos**, though this may involve changing the syntax:
  Both Mary and Peter will be very happy here
  Tanto Mary como Peter van a ser muy felices aquí, Mary y Peter van a ser los dos muy felices aquí
  Both Mike and Clare could see something was wrong
  Tanto Mike como Clare veían que algo iba mal
- When talking about two groups or things use **tanto ... como** or, if **both ... and** is equivalent to "at one and the same time", use **a la vez**:
  The course is directed at both piano and violin teachers
  El curso está dirigido a profesores tanto de piano como de violín, El curso está dirigido a la vez a profesores de piano y de violín
- **Tanto ... como** can also be used with adverbs:
  He was a weak man both physically and mentally
  Era un hombre débil, tanto física como mentalmente

NOTE: When adverbs ending in **-mente** are linked together with a conjunction as here, only the last retains the **-mente**.

- When **both ... and** relates to verbs, you can usually use **y además**:
  He both paints and sculpts
  Pinta y además hace esculturas
- Use **a la vez** to comment on descriptions which are both true at the same time:
  The book is both interesting and depressing
  El libro es interesante y deprimente a la vez

For further uses and examples, see main entry.

botheration†* [,bɒðə'reɪʃən] EXCL ¡porras!*

bothered ['bɒðəd] ADJ [1] **I can't be ~** me da pereza, no tengo ganas, me da flojera (*LAm*); **I can't be ~ to go** me da pereza ir, no tengo ganas de ir, me da flojera ir (*LAm*)
[2] **"shall we stay in or go out?" — "I'm not ~"** —¿salimos o nos quedamos? —me da igual
[3] (= *disconcerted*) **to get ~** desconcertarse, ponerse nervioso; *see also* **hot A1**

bothersome ['bɒðəsəm] ADJ molesto

Bothnia ['bɒθnɪə] N **Gulf of ~** Golfo *m* de Botnia

Botswana [bɒ'tswɑːnə] N Botsuana *f*

bottle ['bɒtl] Ⓐ N [1] (*gen*) botella *f*; (*empty*) envase *m*; [*of ink, scent*] frasco *m*; (*baby's*) biberón *m*; ✦**IDIOM to hit** *or* **take to the ~*** darse a la bebida
[2] (*Brit**) (= *courage*) **it takes a lot of ~ to ...** hay que tener muchas agallas para ...*; **to lose one's ~** rajarse*
Ⓑ VT [1] [+ *wine*] embotellar; [+ *fruit*] envasar, enfrascar
[2] (*Brit**) **he ~d it** se rajó*
Ⓒ CPD ► **bottle bank** N contenedor *m* de vidrio ► **bottle brush** N escobilla *f*, limpiabotellas *m inv*; (*Bot*) callistemon *m* ► **bottle opener** N abrebotellas *m inv*, destapador *m* (*LAm*) ► **bottle party** N *fiesta a la que cada invitado contribuye con una botella*

►**bottle out*** VI + ADV (*Brit*) rajarse*; **they ~d out of doing it** se rajaron y no lo hicieron*

►**bottle up** VT + ADV [+ *emotion*] reprimir, contener

bottled ['bɒtld] ADJ **~ beer** cerveza *f* de botella; **~ gas** gas *m* de bombona; **~ water** agua *f* embotellada

bottle-fed ['bɒtlfed] ADJ alimentado con biberón

bottle-feed ['bɒtl,fiːd] VT criar con biberón

bottle-green ['bɒtl'griːn] Ⓐ ADJ verde botella *adj inv*
Ⓑ N verde *m* botella

bottleneck ['bɒtlnek] N (*on road*) embotellamiento *m*, atasco *m*; (*fig*) obstáculo *m*

bottler ['bɒtləʳ] N (= *person*) embotellador(a) *m/f*; (= *company*) embotelladora *f*

bottling ['bɒtlɪŋ] N embotellado *m*

bottom ['bɒtəm] Ⓐ N [1] [*of box, cup, sea, river, garden*] fondo *m*; [*of stairs, page, mountain, tree*] pie *m*; [*of list, class*] último/a *m/f*; [*of foot*] planta *f*; [*of shoe*] suela *f*; [*of chair*] asiento *m*; [*of ship*] quilla *f*, casco *m*; **at the ~ (of)** [+ *page, hill, ladder*] al pie (de); [+ *road*] al fondo (de); **the ~ has fallen out of the market** el mercado se ha venido abajo; **the ~ fell** *or* **dropped out of his world** se le vino el mundo abajo; **to knock the ~ out of** desfondar; **on the ~ (of)** (= *underside*) [+ *box, case etc*] en la parte inferior (de), en el fondo (de); [+ *shoe*] en la suela (de); [+ *sea, lake etc*] en el fondo (de); **to go to the ~** (*Naut*) irse a pique; **to send a ship to the ~** hundir un buque; **to touch ~** (*lit*) tocar fondo; (*fig*) tocar fondo, llegar al punto más bajo; **~s up!*** ¡salud!; *see also* **false A4**
[2] (= *buttocks*) trasero *m*
[3] (*fig*) (= *deepest part*) **at ~** en el fondo; **he's at the ~ of it** él está detrás de esto; ✦**IDIOMS to get to the ~ of sth** llegar al fondo de algo; **from the ~ of my heart** de todo corazón
[4] (*also* **~s**) [*of tracksuit, pyjamas*] pantalón *m*, parte *f* de abajo; [*of bikini*] braga *f*, parte *f* de abajo
Ⓑ ADJ (= *lowest*) más bajo; (= *last*) último; *see also* **dollar**
Ⓒ CPD ► **bottom drawer** N ajuar *m* ► **bottom floor** N planta *f* baja ► **bottom gear** N (*Aut*) primera *f* (marcha) ► **bottom half** N parte *f* de abajo, mitad *f* inferior ► **bottom line** N (= *minimum*) mínimo *m* aceptable; (= *essential point*) lo fundamental; **the ~ line is he has to go** a fin de cuentas

tenemos que despedirlo ► **bottom price** N precio *m* más bajo ► **bottom step** N primer peldaño *m* ► **bottom team** N colista *m*

►**bottom out** VI + ADV [*figures etc*] tocar fondo

bottomless ['bɒtəmlɪs] ADJ [*pit*] sin fondo, insondable; [*supply*] interminable

bottommost ['bɒtəmməʊst] ADJ más bajo, último

botulism ['bɒtjʊlɪzəm] N botulismo *m*

bouclé ['bu:kleɪ] Ⓐ N lana *f or* ropa *f* rizada
Ⓑ ADJ de lana rizada

boudoir ['bu:dwɑ:ʳ] N tocador *m*

bouffant ['bu:fɒŋ] ADJ [*hairdo*] crepado

bougainvillea [ˌbu:gən'vɪlɪə] N buganvilla *f*

bough [baʊ] N rama *f*

bought [bɔ:t] PT, PP *of* **buy**

bouillon ['bu:jɔ:ŋ] Ⓐ N caldo *m*
Ⓑ CPD ► **bouillon cube** N cubito *m* de caldo

boulder ['bəʊldəʳ] N canto *m* rodado

boulevard ['bu:ləvɑ:ʳ] N bulevar *m*, zócalo *m* (*Mex*)

bounce [baʊns] Ⓐ N 1 [*of ball*] (re)bote *m*; **to catch a ball on the ~** agarrar una pelota de rebote
2 (= *springiness*) [*of hair, mattress*] elasticidad *f*
3 (*fig*) (= *energy*) energía *f*, dinamismo *m*; **he's got plenty of ~** tiene mucha energía
Ⓑ VT 1 [+ *ball*] hacer (re)botar; **to ~ a baby on one's knee** hacer el caballito a un niño pequeño; **to ~ radio waves off the moon** hacer rebotar las ondas radiofónicas en la luna; **to ~ one's ideas off sb** exponer las ideas a algn para que dé su opinión
2 (*) [+ *cheque*] rechazar
3 (*) (= *eject*) plantar en la calle*, poner de patitas en la calle*
4 **I will not be ~d into it** no lo voy a hacer bajo presión, no voy a dejar que me presionen para hacerlo
Ⓒ VI 1 [*ball*] (re)botar
2 (*) [*cheque*] ser rechazado
3 (= *bound*) dar saltos; **he ~d up out of his chair** se levantó de la silla de un salto; **he ~d in** irrumpió alegremente
4 (= *be returned*) [*e-mail message*] ser devuelto

►**bounce back** VI + ADV (*fig*) [*person*] recuperarse

bouncer* ['baʊnsəʳ] N gorila* *m*

bouncing ['baʊnsɪŋ] ADJ **~ baby** niño/a *m/f* sanote

bouncy ['baʊnsɪ] Ⓐ ADJ (*compar* **bouncier**; *superl* **bounciest**) 1 [*ball*] con mucho rebote; [*hair*] con mucho cuerpo; [*mattress*] elástico
2 (*fig*) [*person*] enérgico, dinámico
Ⓑ CPD ► **bouncy castle** N castillo *m* inflable

bound¹ [baʊnd] Ⓐ N **bounds** (= *limits*) límite *m*; **out of ~s** zona *f* prohibida; **it's out of ~s to civilians** los civiles tienen la entrada prohibida; **to put a place out of ~s** prohibir la entrada a un lugar; **his ambition knows no ~s** su ambición no tiene límites; **to set ~s to one's ambitions** poner límites a sus ambiciones; **to keep sth within ~s** tener algo a raya; **it is within the ~s of possibility** cabe dentro de los límites de lo posible
Ⓑ VT (*gen passive*) limitar, rodear; **a field ~ed by woods** un campo rodeado de bosque; **on one side it is ~ed by the park** por un lado limita *or* linda con el parque

bound² [baʊnd] Ⓐ N (= *jump*) salto *m*; **at a ~** ◊ **in one ~** de un salto
Ⓑ VI [*person, animal*] saltar; [*ball*] (re)botar; **to ~ forward** avanzar a saltos; **he ~ed out of bed** se levantó de la cama de un salto; **his heart ~ed with joy** su corazón daba brincos de alegría
Ⓒ VT saltar por encima de

bound³ [baʊnd] Ⓐ PT, PP *of* **bind**
Ⓑ ADJ 1 (= *tied*) [*prisoner*] atado; **~ hand and foot** atado de pies y manos; **the problems are ~ together** existe una estrecha relación entre los problemas; **they are ~ up in each other** están absortos el uno en el otro; **he's ~ up in his work** está muy absorbido por su trabajo; **to be ~ up with sth** estar estrechamente ligado a algo
2 (= *sure*) **to be ~ to: we are ~ to win** seguro que ganamos, estamos seguros de ganar; **he's ~ to come** es seguro que vendrá, no puede dejar de venir; **it's ~ to happen** tiene forzosamente que ocurrir; **they'll regret it, I'll be ~** se arrepentirán de ello, estoy seguro
3 (= *obliged*) obligado; **he's ~ to do it** tiene que hacerlo; **you're not ~ to go** no estás obligado a ir; **I'm ~ to say that …** me siento obligado a decir que …, siento el deber de decir que …; **I feel ~ to tell you that …** me veo en la necesidad de decirte que …; **I feel ~ to him by gratitude** la gratitud hace que me sienta en deuda con él; **to be ~ by contract to sb** tener obligaciones contractuales con algn; *see also* **honour**

bound⁴ [baʊnd] ADJ **where are you ~ (for)?** ¿adónde se dirige usted?; **~ for** [*train, plane*] con destino a; [*ship, person*] con rumbo a; **he's ~ for London** se dirige a Londres; *see also* **homeward**

-bound [-baʊnd] ADJ (*ending in compounds*) **to be London-bound** [*person*] ir rumbo a Londres; **a Paris-bound flight/plane** un vuelo/avión con destino a París; **the south-bound carriageway** la calzada dirección sur

boundary ['baʊndərɪ] Ⓐ N 1 (= *border*) límite *m*; **to make ~ changes** (*Brit Pol*) hacer cambios en las circunscripciones
2 (*Cricket*) banda *f*
Ⓑ CPD ► **boundary line** N límite *m*, frontera *f* ► **boundary stone** N mojón *m*

bounden† ['baʊndən] ADJ **~ duty** obligación *f* ineludible

bounder†* ['baʊndəʳ] N (*Brit*) sinvergüenza *m*, granuja *m*

boundless ['baʊndlɪs] ADJ (*fig*) ilimitado, sin límite

bounteous ['baʊntɪəs], **bountiful** ['baʊntɪfʊl] ADJ [*crop etc*] abundante; [*person*] generoso, munífico

bounty ['baʊntɪ] Ⓐ N 1 (= *generosity*) generosidad *f*, munificencia *f*
2 (= *reward*) recompensa *f*; (*Mil*) premio *m* de enganche
Ⓑ CPD ► **bounty hunter** N cazarrecompensas *mf inv*

bouquet [bʊ'keɪ] N 1 [*of flowers*] ramo *m*, ramillete *m*
2 [*of wine*] buqué *m*

Bourbon ['bʊəbən] (*Hist*) Ⓐ N Borbón *m*
Ⓑ ADJ borbónico

bourbon ['bʊəbən] Ⓐ N Borbón *m*; (*US*) (*also* **~ whiskey**) whisky *m* americano, bourbon *m*
Ⓑ ADJ borbónico

bourgeois ['bʊəʒwɑ:] Ⓐ ADJ burgués
Ⓑ N burgués/esa *m/f*

bourgeoisie [ˌbʊəʒwɑ:'zi:] N burguesía *f*

bout [baʊt] N 1 [*of illness*] ataque *m*
2 (= *period*) [*of work*] tanda *f*; **drinking ~** juerga *f*, farra *f* (*LAm**)
3 (= *boxing match*) combate *m*, encuentro *m*; (*Fencing*) asalto *m*

boutique [bu:'ti:k] N boutique *f*, tienda *f* de ropa

bovine ['bəʊvaɪn] ADJ bovino; (*fig*) lerdo, estúpido

bovver* ['bɒvəʳ] Ⓐ N (*Brit*) camorra* *f*
Ⓑ CPD ► **bovver boots** NPL *botas de suela gruesa usadas por los punkis*

bow¹ [bəʊ] Ⓐ N 1 (= *weapon, Mus*) arco *m*; **~ and arrow** arco *m* y flechas
2 (= *knot*) lazo *m*; **to tie a ~** hacer un lazo
Ⓑ CPD ► **bow legs** NPL piernas *fpl* arqueadas ► **bow tie** N pajarita *f* ► **bow window** N mirador *m*, ventana *f* saledizа

bow² [baʊ] Ⓐ N (= *greeting*) reverencia *f*; **to make a ~** inclinarse (**to** delante de), hacer una reverencia (**to** a); **to make one's ~** presentarse, debutar; **to take a ~** salir a agradecer los aplausos, salir a saludar
Ⓑ VT 1 (= *lower*) [+ *head*] inclinar, bajar
2 (= *bend*) [+ *back*] encorvar, doblar; [+ *branches*] inclinar, doblar
3 **to ~ one's thanks** inclinarse en señal de agradecimiento
Ⓒ VI 1 (*in greeting*) inclinarse (**to** delante de), hacer una reverencia (**to** a); ✦***IDIOM*** **to ~ and scrape** mostrarse demasiado solícito
2 (= *bend*) [*branch etc*] arquearse, doblarse; **to ~ beneath** (*fig*) estar agobiado por
3 (*fig*) (= *yield*) inclinarse *or* ceder (**to** ante); **to ~ to the inevitable** resignarse a lo inevitable

►**bow down** Ⓐ VT + ADV (*lit, fig*) doblegar
Ⓑ VI + ADV (*lit, fig*) doblegarse

►**bow out** VI + ADV (*fig*) retirarse, despedirse

bow³ [baʊ] Ⓐ N (*Naut*) (*also* **~s**) proa *f*; **on the port/starboard ~** a babor/estribor; ✦***IDIOM*** **a shot across the ~s** un cañonazo de advertencia
Ⓑ CPD ► **bow doors** NPL portón *m* de proa ► **bow wave** N *ola causada por un barco al desplazarse por el agua*

Bow Bells [ˌbəʊ'belz] NPL *famoso campanario de Londres*; **born within the sound of ~** nacido en la zona alrededor de Bow Bells (*definición del puro Cockney londinense*)

bowdlerization [ˌbaʊdləraɪ'zeɪʃən] N expurgación *f*

bowdlerize ['baʊdləraɪz] VT [+ *book*] expurgar

bowel ['baʊəl] Ⓐ N 1 intestino *m*
2 **bowels** (*Anat*) intestinos *mpl*, vientre *msing*; (*fig*) entrañas *fpl*; **the ~s of the earth/ship** las entrañas de la tierra/del barco; **the ~s of compassion** (*liter*) la compasión
Ⓑ CPD ► **bowel movement** N evacuación *f* (del vientre)

bower ['baʊəʳ] N emparrado *m*, enramada *f*

bowing ['bəʊɪŋ] N (*Mus*) técnica *f* del arco; (*marked on score*) inicio *m* del golpe de arco; **his ~ was sensitive** su uso del arco era sensible; **to mark the ~** indicar *or* marcar los movimientos del arco

bowl¹ [bəʊl] N 1 (= *large cup*) tazón *m*, cuenco *m*; (= *dish*) (*for soup*) plato *m* sopero; (*for washing up*) palangana *f*, barreño *m*; (*for salad*) fuente *f*, ensaladera *f*; ✦***IDIOM*** **life isn't a ~ of cherries for her right now** actualmente su vida no es un camino de rosas *or* no es de color de rosa
2 (= *amount*) plato *m*
3 (= *hollow*) [*of lavatory*] taza *f*; [*of spoon*] cuenco *m*; [*of pipe*] cazoleta *f*; [*of fountain*] tazón *m*
4 (*US*) (= *stadium*) estadio *m*
5 (*Geog*) cuenca *f*

bowl² [bəʊl] Ⓐ N 1 (= *ball*) bola *f*, bocha *f*
2 **~s** (= *game*) (*Brit*) (*on green*) bochas *fpl*; (=

tenpin bowling) bolos *mpl*, boliche *m*
Ⓑ VT (*Cricket*) [+ *ball*] lanzar, arrojar; (*also* ~ **out**) [+ *batsman*] eliminar
Ⓒ VI 1 (*Cricket*) lanzar
2 **to go ~ing** (*Brit*) ir a jugar a las bochas; (*US*) ir a jugar al boliche
3 **we were ~ing down Knightsbridge** (*on foot*) caminábamos por Knightsbridge a toda prisa; (*in vehicle*) íbamos por Knightsbridge a toda velocidad

►**bowl along** VI + ADV (*on foot*) caminar a toda prisa; (*in vehicle*) ir a toda velocidad

►**bowl over** VT + ADV 1 (= *knock down*) tumbar, derribar
2 (*fig*) desconcertar, dejar atónito; **we were quite ~ed over by the news** la noticia nos desconcertó *or* sorprendió bastante; **she ~ed him over** ella lo dejó patidifuso*

bow-legged [ˈbəʊˈlegɪd] ADJ [*person*] estevado, que tiene las piernas en arco; [*stance*] con las piernas en arco

bowler[1] [ˈbəʊləʳ] N 1 (*Cricket, Rounders, etc*) lanzador(a) *m/f*; → CRICKET
2 (*US Sport*) jugador(a) *m/f* de bolos

bowler[2] [ˈbəʊləʳ] N (*Brit*) (*also* ~ **hat**) bombín *m*, sombrero hongo *m*

bowline [ˈbəʊlɪn] N bolina *f*

bowling [ˈbəʊlɪŋ] Ⓐ N 1 (*also* **tenpin** ~) bolos *mpl*, boliche *m*
2 (*on green*) bochas *fpl*
3 (*Cricket*) lanzamiento *m*
Ⓑ CPD ► **bowling alley** N bolera *f*, boliche *m* ► **bowling green** N campo *m* de bochas ► **bowling match** N (*Brit*) concurso *m* de bochas

bowman [ˈbəʊmən] N (*pl* **bowmen**) (= *archer*) arquero *m*; (*with crossbow*) ballestero *m*

bowsprit [ˈbəʊsprɪt] N bauprés *m*

bowstring [ˈbəʊstrɪŋ] N cuerda *f* de arco

bow-wow [ˈbaʊˈwaʊ] Ⓐ N (*baby talk*) (= *dog*) guau-guau *m*
Ⓑ EXCL ¡guau!

box[1] [bɒks] Ⓐ N 1 (*gen*) caja *f*; (= *large*) cajón *m*; (= *chest etc*) arca *f*, cofre *m*; (*for money etc*) hucha *f*; (*for jewels etc*) estuche *m*; **cardboard ~** caja *f* de cartón; **~ of matches** caja *f* de cerillas; **wine ~** *caja de cartón revestida de plástico por dentro y con una llave en el exterior por la que se vierte el vino*; ✦**IDIOM to be out of one's ~** (*Brit*‡) (*from drugs*) estar volado‡, estar colocado (*Sp**); (*from alcohol*) estar como una cuba*
2 (*in theatre, stadium*) palco *m*
3 **the ~** (*Brit**) (= *television*) la caja boba*, la tele*; **we saw it on the ~*** lo vimos en la tele*
4 (*Brit*) (= *road junction*) parrilla *f*
5 (*on form, to be filled in*) casilla *f*
6 (*Sport*) (= *protection*) protector *m*
7 (*also* **post-office ~**) apartado *m* de correos, casilla *f* de correo (*LAm*)
8 (*Typ*) (*surrounding table, diagram*) recuadro *m*
Ⓑ VT poner en una caja; **a ~ed set of six cups and saucers** un juego de seis tazas y platillos envasado en una caja de cartón; **to ~ the compass** cuartear la aguja
Ⓒ CPD ► **box camera** N cámara *f* de cajón ► **box file** N archivador *m*, archivo *m* ► **box girder** N viga *f* en forma de cajón, vigas *fpl* gemelas ► **box junction** N (*Brit Aut*) cruce *m* con parrilla ► **box kite** N *cometa en forma de cubo, abierto por dos lados* ► **box number** N apartado *m* de correos, casilla *f* de correo (*LAm*) ► **box office** N taquilla *f*, boletería *f* (*LAm*); **to be good ~ office** ser taquillero; *see also* **box-office** ► **box pleat** N (*Sew*) tablón *m* ► **box seat** N (*US Theat*) asiento *m* de palco ► **box spring** N muelle *m*

►**box in** VT + ADV 1 (= *fix wooden surround to*) [+ *bath*] tapar *or* cerrar con madera
2 (= *shut in*) [+ *car*] encajonar; **to get ~ed in** (*Sport*) encontrarse tapado
3 (*fig*) **to ~ sb in** acorralar a algn; **to feel ~ed in** sentirse acorralado

►**box off** VT + ADV compartimentar

►**box up** VT + ADV poner en una caja; (*fig*) constreñir

box[2] [bɒks] Ⓐ N (= *blow*) **a ~ on the ear** un cachete *m*
Ⓑ VT (*Sport*) boxear contra; **to ~ sb's ears**† guantear a algn, dar un mamporro a algn*
Ⓒ VI boxear; ✦**IDIOM to ~ clever** (*Brit**) andarse listo, montárselo bien*

box[3] [bɒks] N (*Bot*) boj *m*

boxcar [ˈbɒksˌkɑːʳ] N (*US*) furgón *m*

boxer [ˈbɒksəʳ] Ⓐ N 1 (*Sport*) boxeador(a) *m/f*
2 (= *dog*) bóxer *mf*
Ⓑ CPD ► **boxer shorts** NPL calzones *mpl*

boxing [ˈbɒksɪŋ] Ⓐ N boxeo *m*, box *m* (*LAm*)
Ⓑ CPD ► **Boxing Day** N (*Brit*) día *m* de San Esteban (*26 de diciembre*) ► **boxing gloves** NPL guantes *mpl* de boxeo ► **boxing match** N combate *m* de boxeo ► **boxing ring** N cuadrilátero *m*, ring *m*

> **BOXING DAY**
> *El día después de Navidad es* **Boxing Day**, *fiesta en todo el Reino Unido, aunque si el 26 de diciembre cae en domingo el día de descanso se traslada al lunes. El nombre proviene de una costumbre del siglo XIX, cuando en dicho día se daba un aguinaldo o pequeño regalo* (**Christmas box**) *a los comerciantes, carteros etc. En la actualidad es una fecha en la que se celebran importantes encuentros deportivos.*

box-office [ˈbɒksɒfɪs] Ⓐ ADJ taquillero
Ⓑ CPD ► **box-office receipts** NPL ingresos *mpl* de taquilla ► **box-office success** N éxito *m* de taquilla; *see also* **box**

boxroom [ˈbɒksrʊm] N (*Brit*) trastero *m*

boxwood [ˈbɒkswʊd] N boj *m*

boxy [ˈbɒksɪ] ADJ (*pej*) [*building*] amazacotado; [*car*] cuadrado

boy [bɔɪ] Ⓐ N 1 (= *small*) niño *m*; (= *young man*) muchacho *m*, chico *m*, joven *m* (*LAm*); (= *son*) hijo *m*; **oh ~!** ¡vaya!; **I have known him from a ~** lo conozco desde chico; ✦**IDIOMS to send a ~ to do a man's job** mandar a un muchacho a hacer un trabajo de hombre; **~s will be ~s** ¡los hombres, ya se sabe, son como niños!; *see also* **old C**
2 (*) (= *fellow*) chico *m*, hijo *m*; **that's the ~!** ◊ **that's my ~!** ¡bravo!; **but my dear ~!** ¡pero hijo!, ¡pero hombre!; **García and his ~s in the national team** García y sus muchachos del equipo nacional; **he's out with the ~s** ha salido con los amigos; **he's one of the ~s now** ahora es un personaje; **the ~s in blue** (*Brit**) la policía; *see also* **job A1**
3 (= *servant*) criado *m*
Ⓑ CPD ► **boy band** N (*Brit Mus*) *grupo de música pop masculino* ► **boy racer*** N (*Brit pej*) loco *m* del volante ► **boy scout** N (muchacho *m or* niño *m*) explorador *m* ► **boy wonder*** N niño *m* prodigio, joven promesa *m*

boycott [ˈbɔɪkɒt] Ⓐ N boicot *m*
Ⓑ VT [+ *firm, country*] boicotear

boyfriend [ˈbɔɪfrend] N amigo *m*; (= *fiancé etc*) novio *m*, pololo *m* (*Chile**)

boyhood [ˈbɔɪhʊd] N niñez *f*; (*as teenager*) adolescencia *f*

boyish [ˈbɔɪɪʃ] ADJ [*appearance, manner*] juvenil; (= *tomboyish*) (*of girl*) de muchacho, de chico; (*of small girl*) de niño

boy-meets-girl [ˈbɔɪmiːtsˈgɜːl] ADJ **a ~ story/film** una historia/película de amor entre un chico y una chica

boyo* [ˈbɔɪəʊ] N (*Brit*) (*often in direct address*) joven *m*, muchacho *m*

bozo‡ [ˈbəʊzəʊ] N (*esp US*) imbécil* *mf*

BP N ABBR 1 = **British Petroleum**
2 (= **blood pressure**) TA

Bp ABBR (= **Bishop**) ob., obpo.

B/P, b/p ABBR (*Comm*) = **bills payable**

bpi ABBR (*Comput*) = **bits per inch**

BPOE N ABBR (*US*) (= **Benevolent and Protective Order of Elks**) *organización benéfica*

bps ABBR (*Comput*) = **bits per second**

BR N ABBR = **British Rail** (*formerly*) *ferrocarriles británicos*, ≈ RENFE *f* (*Sp*)

Br ABBR 1 (= **Brother**) H., Hno.
2 = **British**

B/R ABBR = **bills receivable**

bra [brɑː] N sostén *m*, sujetador *m*, corpiño *m* (*Arg*)

brace [breɪs] Ⓐ N 1 (*Constr*) (= *strengthening piece*) abrazadera *f*, refuerzo *m*; (*Archit*) riostra *f*, tirante *m*; (*Naut*) braza *f*; (= *tool*) berbiquí *m*; **~ and bit** berbiquí *m* y barrena *f*
2 (*also* **~s**) (*for teeth*) corrector *msing*, aparato *msing*
3 **braces** (*Brit*) tirantes *mpl*, suspensores *mpl* (*LAm*)
4 (*Mus*) corchete *m*
5 (*Typ*) corchete *m*
6 (*pl inv*) (= *pair*) par *m*
Ⓑ VT (= *strengthen*) [+ *building*] asegurar, reforzar; **to ~ o.s.** prepararse (*para resistir una sacudida etc*); (*fig*) fortalecer su ánimo; **to ~ o.s. for** prepararse para; **to ~ o.s. against** agarrarse a

bracelet [ˈbreɪslɪt] N pulsera *f*, brazalete *m*

bracing [ˈbreɪsɪŋ] ADJ [*air, activity*] vigorizante

bracken [ˈbrækən] N helecho *m*

bracket [ˈbrækɪt] Ⓐ N 1 (*gen*) soporte *m*; (= *angle bracket*) escuadra *f*; (*Archit*) ménsula *f*, repisa *f*
2 (*Typ*) (*usu pl*) (*round*) paréntesis *m inv*; (*also* **square ~**) corchete *m*; (*angled*) corchete *m* (agudo); (*curly*) corchete *m*, llave *f*; **in ~s** entre paréntesis; *see also* **angle**[1] **D**, **square F**
3 (= *group*) clase *f*, categoría *f*; **he's in the £200,000 a year ~** pertenece a la categoría de los que ganan 200,000 libras al año; **income ~** nivel *m* de ingresos
Ⓑ VT 1 (*Constr*) (= *join by brackets*) asegurar con soportes/escuadras
2 (*Typ*) poner entre paréntesis/corchetes
3 (*fig*) (*also* **~ together**) agrupar, poner juntos; **to ~ sth with sth** agrupar algo con algo

►**bracket off** VT + ADV separar, poner aparte

brackish [ˈbrækɪʃ] ADJ [*water*] salobre

brad [bræd] N puntilla *f*, clavito *m*

brae [breɪ] N (*Scot*) ladera *f* de monte, pendiente *f*

brag [bræg] Ⓐ VI jactarse, fanfarronear (**about, of** de; **that** de que)
Ⓑ N (= *boast*) fanfarronada *f*, bravata *f*

braggart [ˈbrægət] N fanfarrón/ona *m/f*, jactancioso/a *m/f*

bragging [ˈbrægɪŋ] N fanfarronadas *fpl*

Brahman ['brɑːmən] N (*pl* **Brahmans**), **Brahmin** ['brɑːmɪn] N (*pl* **Brahmin** *or* **Brahmins**) brahmán/ana *m/f*

Brahmaputra ['brɑːmə'puːtrə] N Brahmaputra *m*

braid [breɪd] Ⓐ N [1] (*on dress, uniform*) galón *m*; **(gold) ~** galón *m* de oro
[2] (*esp US*) [*of hair*] trenza *f*
Ⓑ VT (*esp US*) [+ *hair*] trenzar, hacer trenzas en; [+ *material*] galonear

Braille [breɪl] Ⓐ N Braille *m*
Ⓑ CPD ► **Braille library** N biblioteca *f* Braille

brain [breɪn] Ⓐ N [1] (*Anat*) cerebro *m*; ✦*IDIOMS* **he's got politics on the ~** tiene la política metida en la cabeza; **to get one's ~ into gear*** poner la mente a carburar*
[2] **brains** [2·1] (*Anat, Culin*) sesos *mpl*; ✦*IDIOMS* **to beat sb's ~s out*** romper la crisma a algn*; **to blow one's ~s out*** volarse *or* levantarse la tapa de los sesos*
[2·2] (*) (= *intelligence*) inteligencia *f*, cabeza *f*; **he's got ~s** es muy listo, tiene mucha cabeza; **he's the ~s of the family** es el listo de la familia; *see also* **pick B5**, **rack[1] B1**
Ⓑ VT (*) romper la crisma a*
Ⓒ CPD ► **brain damage** N lesión *f* cerebral *or* medular ► **brain death** N muerte *f* clínica *or* cerebral ► **brain drain** N fuga *f* de cerebros ► **brain scan** N exploración *f* cerebral mediante escáner ► **brain scanner** N escáner *m* cerebral ► **brains trust**, **brain trust** (*US*) N grupo *m* de peritos; (*TV etc*) jurado *m* de expertos ► **brain teaser** N rompecabezas *m inv* ► **brain tumour**, **brain tumor** (*US*) N tumor *m* cerebral

brainchild ['breɪntʃaɪld] N parto *m* del ingenio, invento *m*

brain-damaged ['breɪn,dæmɪdʒd] ADJ **he was ~ by meningitis** sufrió lesiones cerebrales por la meningitis; **the child was ~ for life** el niño quedó con lesiones medulares de por vida

brain-dead ['breɪn,ded] ADJ [1] (*Med*) clínicamente muerto
[2] (*) (= *stupid*) subnormal*, tarado*

brainless ['breɪnlɪs] ADJ estúpido, tonto

brainpower ['breɪn,paʊə^r] N fuerza *f* intelectual

brainstorm ['breɪnstɔːm] Ⓐ N [1] (*Brit*) (*fig*) ataque *m* de locura, frenesí *m*
[2] (*US*) = **brainwave**
Ⓑ VI *hacer una puesta en común de ideas y sugerencias*
Ⓒ VT [+ *ideas*] poner en común

brainstorming ['breɪnstɔːmɪŋ] Ⓐ N puesta *f* en común, brainstorming *m*
Ⓑ CPD ► **brainstorming session** N reunión *f* para hacer una puesta en común

brainwash ['breɪnwɒʃ] VT lavar el cerebro a; **to ~ sb into doing sth** convencer a algn para que haga algo

brainwashing ['breɪn,wɒʃɪŋ] N lavado *m* de cerebro

brainwave ['breɪnweɪv] N [1] (*Brit**) idea *f* luminosa*, idea *f* genial*
[2] **brainwaves** (*Med*) ondas *fpl* cerebrales

brainwork ['breɪnwɜːk] N trabajo *m* intelectual

brainy* ['breɪnɪ] ADJ (*compar* **brainier**; *superl* **brainiest**) listo, inteligente

braise [breɪz] VT (*Culin*) cocer a fuego lento, estofar

brake[1] [breɪk] Ⓐ N (*Aut etc*) freno *m*; **to put the ~s on** (*Aut*) frenar; **to put the ~s on sth** (*fig*) poner freno a algo
Ⓑ VI frenar
Ⓒ VT frenar
Ⓓ CPD ► **brake block** N pastilla *f* de frenos ► **brake drum** N tambor *m* de freno ► **brake fluid** N líquido *m* de frenos ► **brake horsepower** N potencia *f* al freno ► **brake lever** N palanca *f* de freno ► **brake light** N luz *f* de freno ► **brake lining** N forro *m or* guarnición *f* del freno ► **brake pad** N pastilla *f* de frenos ► **brake pedal** N pedal *m* de freno ► **brake shoe** N zapata *f* del freno ► **brake van** N (*Brit Rail*) furgón *m* de cola

brake[2] [breɪk] N (= *vehicle*) break *m*; (= *estate car*) rubia *f*

brake[3] [breɪk] N (*Bot*) helecho *m*; (= *thicket*) soto *m*

brakesman ['breɪksmən] N (*pl* **brakesmen**) encargado *m* del montacargas de la mina

braking ['breɪkɪŋ] Ⓐ N (*Aut etc*) frenado *m*
Ⓑ CPD ► **braking distance** N distancia *f* de parada ► **braking power** N potencia *f* de freno

bramble ['bræmbl] N zarza *f*

bran [bræn] Ⓐ N salvado *m*
Ⓑ CPD ► **bran tub** N (*Brit*) sorteo *m* de regalos

branch [brɑːntʃ] Ⓐ N [1] [*of tree*] rama *f*; (*fig*) [*of science*] rama *f*; [*of government, police*] sección *f*; [*of industry*] ramo *m*
[2] (*Comm*) [*of company, bank*] sucursal *f*
[3] (*in road, railway, pipe*) ramal *m*
[4] [*of river*] brazo *m*; (*US*) [*of stream*] arroyo *m*
[5] [*of family*] rama *f*
Ⓑ VI [*road etc*] bifurcarse
Ⓒ CPD ► **branch line** N (*Rail*) ramal *m*, línea *f* secundaria ► **branch manager** N director(a) *m/f* de sucursal ► **branch office** N sucursal *f*

►**branch off** VI + ADV **after a few miles, a small road ~es off to the right** después de unas cuantas millas hay una carretera pequeña que sale hacia la derecha; **we ~ed off before reaching Madrid** tomamos un desvío antes de llegar a Madrid; **we ~ed off at Medina** tomamos el desvío de la carretera principal en Medina

►**branch out** VI + ADV (*fig*) extenderse

brand [brænd] Ⓐ N [1] (*Comm*) marca *f* (de fábrica)
[2] (*Agr*) (= *mark*) marca *f*; (= *iron*) hierro *m* de marcar
[3] (= *burning wood*) tizón *m*, tea *f*
Ⓑ VT [1] [+ *cattle*] marcar (con hierro candente)
[2] (*fig*) **to ~ sb as** tildar a algn de; **to ~ sth as** calificar algo de; **to be ~ed as a liar** ser tildado de mentiroso; **it is ~ed on my memory** lo tengo grabado en la memoria
[3] **~ed goods** (*Comm*) artículos *mpl* de marca
Ⓒ CPD ► **brand awareness** N conciencia *f* de marca ► **brand image** N imagen *f* de marca ► **brand loyalty** N fidelidad *f* a una marca ► **brand name** N nombre *m* de marca

branding iron ['brændɪŋ,aɪən] N hierro *m* (de marcar)

brandish ['brændɪʃ] VT [+ *weapon*] blandir

brand-new ['brænd'njuː] ADJ [*car, motorbike*] salido de fábrica, flamante; [*house, sofa*] completamente nuevo; [*boyfriend, TV series*] nuevo

brandy ['brændɪ] Ⓐ N coñac *m*, brandy *m*
Ⓑ CPD ► **brandy butter** N mantequilla *f* al coñac ► **brandy snap** N *barquillo con sabor a jengibre y generalmente relleno de nata*

brash [bræʃ] ADJ (*compar* **brasher**; *superl* **brashest**) [1] (= *over-confident*) presuntuoso; (= *rash*) impetuoso
[2] (= *crude*) [*colour*] chillón; [*taste*] vulgar

brashly ['bræʃlɪ] ADV [1] [*act*] (= *over-confidently*) presuntuosamente; (= *rashly*) impetuosamente
[2] (*with adj*) [*intrusive*] descaradamente

brashness ['bræʃnɪs] N (= *over-confidence*) presunción *f*; (= *rashness*) impetuosidad *f*

Brasilia [brə'zɪljə] N Brasilia *f*

brass [brɑːs] Ⓐ N [1] (= *metal*) latón *m*; *see also* **bold**
[2] (= *plate*) placa *f* conmemorativa; (*Rel*) plancha *f* sepulcral (de latón); **to clean the ~es** pulir los bronces
[3] **the ~** [3·1] (*Mus*) los metales
[3·2] (*Mil*) los jefazos; *see also* **top E**
[4] (*Brit**) (= *money*) pasta* *f*
[5] (*) (= *impudence*) cara* *f*; **he had the ~ to ask me for it** tuvo la cara de pedírmelo*
Ⓑ ADJ (= *made of brass*) (hecho) de latón; ✦*IDIOMS* **not to be worth a ~ farthing** no valer un ardite; **it's cold enough to freeze a ~ monkey** ◊ **it's ~ monkey weather** (*Brit**) ¡hace un frío que pela!*; **to get down to ~ tacks*** ir al grano*
Ⓒ CPD ► **brass band** N banda *f* de metal ► **brass hat*** N (*Mil*) jefazo/a* *m/f* ► **brass knuckles** NPL (*US*) nudilleras *fpl* ► **brass neck*** N cara(dura)* *f*, valor *m* ► **brass rubbing** N (= *art, object*) calco *m* de plancha sepulcral (de latón) ► **the brass section** N (*Mus*) los metales

►**brass off*** VT + ADV fastidiar

brassed off* ['brɑːst'ɒf] ADJ (*Brit*) **to be ~ with** estar hasta la coronilla *or* las narices de*

brasserie ['brɑːsərɪ] N brasserie *f*

brassica ['bræsɪkə] N brassica *f*, crucífera *f*

brassiere ['bræsɪə^r] N sostén *m*, sujetador *m*, corpiño *m* (*Arg*)

brassy ['brɑːsɪ] ADJ (*compar* **brassier**; *superl* **brassiest**) [1] (= *like brass*) (*in colour*) dorado, de color dorado; (= *cheap*) ordinario
[2] (= *harsh*) [*sound*] estridente; (= *metallic*) metálico
[3] [*person*] descarado

brat* [bræt] Ⓐ N (*pej*) mocoso/a* *m/f*
Ⓑ CPD ► **brat pack** N (*pej*) (= *actors etc*) *generación de jóvenes artistas con éxito*

bravado [brə'vɑːdəʊ] N (*pl* **bravados** *or* **bravadoes**) bravatas *fpl*, baladronadas *fpl*; **a piece of ~** una bravata; **out of sheer ~** de puro bravucón

brave [breɪv] Ⓐ ADJ (*compar* **braver**; *superl* **bravest**) [1] (= *courageous*) [*person, deed*] valiente, valeroso; **be ~!** ¡sé valiente!; **that was very ~ of you** has demostrado mucho valor al hacer eso; **she went in with a ~ smile** entró sonriendo valientemente; **try to put on a ~ smile** intenta sonreír aunque te cueste; **to make a ~ attempt to do sth** intentar valientemente hacer algo; ✦*IDIOM* **as ~ as a lion** más fiero que un león; *see also* **face**
[2] (*liter*) (= *splendid*) magnífico (*liter*); **a Brave New World** un mundo feliz
Ⓑ N [1] **the ~** los valientes; **the ~st of the ~** los más valientes entre los valientes
[2] (= *Indian*) guerrero *m*
Ⓒ VT [+ *weather*] afrontar, hacer frente a; [+ *death*] desafiar; **to ~ the storm** (*fig*) capear el temporal; **to ~ sb's anger** afrontar *or* hacer frente a la ira de algn

►**brave out** VT + ADV **to ~ it out** afrontar la situación

bravely ['breɪvlɪ] ADV valientemente, con valor; **she smiled ~** sonrió valiente *or* valientemente; **the flag was flying ~** la bandera ondeaba magnífica

bravery ['breɪvərɪ] N valentía *f*, valor *m*

bravo ['brɑː'vəʊ] EXCL (*pl* **bravoes** *or* **bravos**) ¡bravo!, ¡olé!

bravura [brəˈvʊərə] Ⓐ N [1] arrojo *m*, brío *m*
[2] (*Mus*) virtuosismo *m*
Ⓑ CPD [*display, performance*] brillante
brawl [brɔːl] Ⓐ N pelea *f*, reyerta *f*
Ⓑ VI pelear, pegarse
brawling [ˈbrɔːlɪŋ] Ⓐ ADJ pendenciero, alborotador
Ⓑ N peleas *fpl*, alboroto *m*
brawn [brɔːn] N [1] (*Brit Culin*) carne *f* en gelatina
[2] (= *strength*) fuerza *f* muscular
brawny [ˈbrɔːnɪ] ADJ fornido, musculoso
bray [breɪ] Ⓐ N [*of ass*] rebuzno *m*; (= *laugh*) carcajada *f*
Ⓑ VI [*ass*] rebuznar; [*trumpet*] sonar con estrépito
braze [breɪz] VT soldar
brazen [ˈbreɪzn] Ⓐ ADJ [1] (= *shameless*) descarado; **I couldn't do anything so ~ as that** yo nunca podría hacer algo con tanto descaro; **a ~ hussy** una desvergonzada, una descarada
[2] (= *made of brass*) de latón
Ⓑ VT **to ~ it out** echar cara (a la situación)
brazenly [ˈbreɪznlɪ] ADV descaradamente, con descaro
brazenness [ˈbreɪzənnɪs] N descaro *m*
brazier [ˈbreɪzɪəʳ] N brasero *m*
Brazil [brəˈzɪl] Ⓐ N Brasil *m*
Ⓑ CPD ► **Brazil nut** N nuez *f* del Brasil
Brazilian [brəˈzɪlɪən] Ⓐ ADJ brasileño
Ⓑ N brasileño/a *m/f*
BRCS N ABBR = **British Red Cross Society**
breach [briːtʃ] Ⓐ N [1] (= *violation*) [*of law etc*] violación *f*, infracción *f*; **~ of confidence** *or* **faith** abuso *m* de confianza; **~ of contract** incumplimiento *m* de contrato; **to be in ~ of a rule** incumplir una regla; **~ of the peace** (*Jur*) perturbación *f* del orden público; **~ of privilege** (*Parl*) abuso *m* del privilegio parlamentario; **~ of promise** incumplimiento *m* de la palabra de casamiento; **~ of security** fallo *m* de seguridad
[2] (= *gap*) (*in wall, Mil*) brecha *f*; ✦***IDIOMS*** **to fill the ~** ◊ **step into the ~** llenar el vacío
[3] (= *estrangement*) ruptura *f*; (*between friends*) (= *act*) rompimiento *m* de relaciones; (= *state*) desavenencia *f*; **to heal the ~** hacer las paces
Ⓑ VT [1] [+ *defences, wall*] abrir brecha en
[2] [+ *security*] poner en peligro
Ⓒ VI [*whale*] salir a la superficie
bread [bred] Ⓐ N [1] (= *food*) pan *m*; **white/brown/rye/wholemeal ~** pan *m* blanco/moreno/de centeno/integral; **~ and butter** pan *m* con mantequilla; (*) (*fig*) (= *living*) pan de cada día*; **to be on ~ and water** estar a pan y agua; **the ~ and wine** (*Rel*) el pan y el vino; ✦***IDIOMS*** **to break ~ with** sentarse a la mesa con; **to cast one's ~ on the waters** hacer el bien sin mirar a quién; **to earn one's daily ~** ganarse el pan; **to know which side one's ~ is buttered (on)** saber dónde aprieta el zapato; **to take the ~ out of sb's mouth** quitar el pan de la boca de algn; ✦***PROV*** **man cannot live by ~ alone** no sólo de pan vive el hombre; *see also* **bread-and-butter**
[2] (‡) (= *money*) pasta* *f*, lana *f* (*LAm**), plata *f* (*LAm**)
Ⓑ CPD ► **bread grains** NPL granos *mpl* panificables ► **bread pudding** N pudín *m* de leche y pan
bread-and-butter [ˈbredənˈbʌtəʳ] Ⓐ ADJ (*fig*) [*issues, needs*] básico, primario; [*product*] de más venta; [*customer*] más asiduo
Ⓑ CPD ► **bread-and-butter letter** N carta *f* de agradecimiento (*a una señora en cuya casa el invitado ha pasado varios días*) ► **bread-and-butter pudding** N pudín *m* de pan y mantequilla
breadbasket [ˈbred,bɑːskɪt] N [1] (= *container*) cesto *m* para el pan
[2] (*fig*) (= *country, area*) granero *m*
[3] (‡) (= *stomach*) panza* *f*, tripa *f* (*Sp**)
breadbin [ˈbredbɪn] N panera *f*
breadboard [ˈbredbɔːd] N (*in kitchen*) tabla *f* para cortar el pan; (*Comput*) circuito *m* experimental
breadbox [ˈbredbɒks] N (*US*) = **breadbin**
breadcrumb [ˈbredkrʌm] N [1] miga *f*, migaja *f*
[2] **breadcrumbs** (*Culin*) pan *m* rallado; **fish in ~s** pescado *m* empanado
breaded [ˈbredɪd] ADJ empanado
breadfruit [ˈbredfruːt] Ⓐ N (*pl* **breadfruit** *or* **breadfruits**) fruto *m* del árbol del pan
Ⓑ CPD ► **breadfruit tree** N árbol *m* del pan
breadknife [ˈbrednaɪf] N (*pl* **breadknives**) cuchillo *m* para cortar pan
breadline [ˈbredlaɪn] N (*US*) cola *f* del pan; ✦***IDIOM*** **on the ~** (*Brit*) en la miseria
breadstick [ˈbredstɪk] N piquito *m*, palito *m*
breadth [bretθ] N [1] (= *width*) anchura *f*, ancho *m*; **to be two metres in ~** tener dos metros de ancho
[2] (*fig*) [*of experience, knowledge*] amplitud *f*
breadthwise [ˈbretθwaɪz] ADV de lado a lado
breadwinner [ˈbred,wɪnəʳ] N sostén *m* de la familia
break [breɪk] (*vb: pt* **broke**; *pp* **broken**) Ⓐ N [1] (= *fracture*) rotura *f*; (*in bone*) fractura *f*; (*fig*) (*in relationship*) ruptura *f*; **to make a ~ with** romper con
[2] (= *gap*) (*in wall etc*) abertura *f*, brecha *f*; (= *crack*) grieta *f*; (*Typ*) (*on paper etc*) espacio *m*, blanco *m*; (*Elec*) (*in circuit*) corte *m*; **a ~ in the clouds** un claro entre las nubes
[3] (= *pause*) (*in conversation*) interrupción *f*, pausa *f*; (*in journey*) descanso *m*, pausa *f*; (= *stop*) parada *f*; (= *holiday*) vacaciones *fpl*; (= *rest*) descanso *m*; (= *tea break*) descanso *m* para tomar el té, once(s) *f(pl)* (*LAm*); (*Brit Scol*) recreo *m*; **a ~ in continuity** una solución de continuidad; **give me a ~!** ¡dame un respiro!; (*impatient*) ¡déjame, anda!; **to have** *or* **take a ~** descansar, tomarse un descanso; **to take a weekend ~** hacer una escapada de fin de semana; **with a ~ in her voice** con la voz entrecortada; **a ~ in the weather** un cambio del tiempo; **without a ~** sin descanso *or* descansar
[4] (*) (= *chance*) oportunidad *f*; **to give sb a ~** dar una oportunidad a algn; **lucky ~** golpe *m* de suerte, racha *f* de buena suerte
[5] (= *break-out*) fuga *f*; **to make a ~ for it*** tratar de fugarse
[6] **at ~ of day** (*liter*) al amanecer
[7] (*Tennis*) ruptura *f*; **two ~s of service** dos servicios rotos
[8] (*Billiards, Snooker*) tacada *f*, serie *f*
[9] (= *vehicle*) break *m*, volanta *f* (*LAm*)
Ⓑ VT [1] (= *smash*) [+ *glass etc*] romper; [+ *branch, stick*] romper, quebrar (*LAm*); [+ *ground*] roturar; [+ *code*] descifrar; [+ *conspiracy*] deshacer; [+ *drugs ring etc*] desarticular; **to ~ one's back** romperse la columna; **I'm not going to ~ my back to finish it today** no me voy a matar para terminarlo hoy; **to ~ sb's heart** romper *or* partir el corazón a algn; **to ~ one's leg** romperse la pierna; **~ a leg!*** (*Theat*) ¡buena suerte!; **to ~ surface** [*submarine, diver*] emerger, salir a la superficie; ✦***IDIOM*** **to ~ the ice** romper el hielo; *see also* **spirit A3**
[2] (= *surpass*) [+ *record*] batir, superar
[3] (= *fail to observe*) [+ *law, rule*] violar, quebrantar; [+ *appointment*] no acudir a; **he broke his word/promise** faltó a su palabra/promesa; **to ~ a date** faltar a una cita
[4] (= *weaken, destroy*) [+ *resistance, spirits*] quebrantar, quebrar (*LAm*); [+ *health*] quebrantar; [+ *strike*] romper, quebrar (*LAm*); [+ *habit*] perder; [+ *horse*] domar, amansar; [+ *bank*] (*in gambling*) quebrar, hacer quebrar; [+ *person*] (*financially*) arruinar; (*morally*) abatir, vencer; **to ~ sb of a habit** quitar una costumbre a algn
[5] (= *interrupt*) [+ *silence, spell*] romper; [+ *journey*] interrumpir; [+ *electrical circuit*] cortar, interrumpir
[6] (= *soften*) [+ *force*] mitigar, contener; [+ *impact, fall*] amortiguar
[7] (= *disclose*) [+ *news*] comunicar (**to** a)
[8] (= *leave*) **to ~ camp** levantar el campamento; **to ~ cover** salir al descubierto; **to ~ ranks** romper filas
[9] **to ~ sb's serve** *or* **service** (*Tennis*) romper el servicio de algn
[10] (*Naut*) [+ *flag*] desplegar
[11] (*US**) **can you ~ me a 100-dollar bill?** ¿me puede cambiar un billete de 100 dólares?
Ⓒ VI [1] (= *smash*) [*window, glass*] romperse; (*into pieces*) hacerse pedazos
[2] (= *be fractured*) [*chair*] romperse, partirse; [*branch, twig*] romperse, quebrarse (*LAm*); [*limb*] fracturarse; [*boil*] reventar; (*fig*) [*heart*] romperse, partirse
[3] (= *cease to function*) [*machine*] estropearse
[4] (= *arrive*) [*dawn, day*] apuntar, rayar; [*news*] darse a conocer; [*story*] revelarse; [*storm*] estallar; [*wave*] romper
[5] (= *give way*) [*health, spirits*] quebrantarse; [*weather*] cambiar; [*heat wave*] terminar; [*boy's voice*] mudarse; [*singing voice*] cascarse; [*bank*] quebrar
[6] (= *pause*) **let's ~ for lunch** vamos a hacer un descanso para comer
[7] **to ~ free** (*from chains, ropes etc*) soltarse; (*fig*) liberarse; **to ~ loose** desatarse, escaparse; (*fig*) desencadenarse
[8] **to ~ even** cubrir los gastos
[9] (*Boxing*) separarse
[10] (*Billiards, Snooker*) abrir el juego
[11] (*Sport*) [*ball*] torcerse, desviarse
Ⓓ CPD ► **break dancer** N bailarín/ina *m/f* de break ► **break dancing** N break *m* ► **break point** N (*Tennis*) punto *m* de break, punto *m* de ruptura; (*Comput*) punto *m* de interrupción
►**break away** VI + ADV [1] [*piece*] desprenderse, separarse
[2] (*Ftbl etc*) escapar, despegarse
[3] **to ~ away from** [+ *guard*] evadirse de; [+ *group*] (= *leave*) separarse de; (*from disagreement*) romper con
►**break down** Ⓐ VT + ADV [1] (= *destroy*) [+ *door etc*] echar abajo, derribar; [+ *resistance*] vencer, acabar con; [+ *suspicion*] disipar
[2] (= *analyse*) [+ *figures*] analizar, desglosar; [+ *substance*] descomponer
Ⓑ VI + ADV [*machine*] estropearse, malograrse (*Peru*), descomponerse (*LAm*); (*Aut*) averiarse, descomponerse (*LAm*); [*person*] (*under pressure*) derrumbarse; (*from emotion*) romper *or* echarse a llorar; [*health*] quebrantarse; [*talks etc*] fracasar; [*chemicals, waste*] descomponerse .
►**break forth** VI + ADV [*light, water*] surgir; [*storm*] estallar; **to ~ forth into song** ponerse a cantar
►**break in** Ⓐ VT + ADV [1] [+ *door*] forzar, echar abajo
[2] (= *train*) [+ *horse*] domar, amansar; [+ *re-*

cruit] formar
[3] [+ *shoes*] domar, acostumbrarse a
(B) VI + ADV [1] [*burglar*] forzar la entrada
[2] (= *interrupt*) (*on conversation*) interrumpir
►**break into** VI + PREP [1] [+ *house*] entrar a robar en, allanar; [+ *safe*] forzar
[2] (*Comm etc*) **to ~ into a new market** introducirse en un mercado nuevo; **to ~ into films** introducirse en el mundo cinematográfico
[3] (= *begin suddenly*) echar a, romper a; **to ~ into a run** echar *or* empezar a correr; **to ~ into song** ponerse a cantar
►**break off** (A) VT + ADV [1] [+ *piece etc*] partir
[2] (= *end*) [+ *engagement, talks*] romper; (*Mil*) [+ *action*] terminar
(B) VI + ADV [1] [*piece of rock, ice, handle*] desprenderse; [*twig, segment of orange*] desgajarse
[2] (= *stop*) interrumpirse, pararse
►**break out** (A) VI + ADV [1] [*prisoners*] fugarse, escaparse
[2] (= *begin*) [*fire, war, epidemic*] estallar; [*discussion, fighting, argument*] producirse
[3] **he broke out in spots** le salieron granos; **he broke out in a sweat** quedó cubierto de sudor
(B) VT + ADV [+ *champagne etc*] descorchar
►**break through** (A) VI + ADV [*sun*] salir; [*water etc*] abrirse paso, abrirse (un) camino; **to ~ through to** [+ *new seam*] [*miners*] llegar a, abrir un camino hasta
(B) VI + PREP [+ *defences, barrier*] atravesar; [+ *crowd*] abrirse paso entre
►**break up** (A) VT + ADV [1] [+ *rocks etc*] hacer pedazos, deshacer; [+ *ship*] desguazar
[2] (*fig*) [+ *crowd*] dispersar, disolver; [+ *meeting, organization*] disolver; [+ *gang*] desarticular; [+ *marriage*] deshacer; [+ *estate*] parcelar; [+ *industry*] desconcentrar; [+ *fight*] intervenir en; **~ it up!** ¡basta ya!
[3] (*US**) (= *cause to laugh*) hacer reír a carcajadas
(B) VI + ADV [1] [*ship*] hacerse pedazos; [*ice*] deshacerse
[2] (*fig*) [*partnership*] deshacerse, disolverse; [*marriage*] deshacerse; [*federation*] desmembrarse; [*group*] disgregarse; [*weather*] cambiar; [*crowd, clouds*] dispersarse; **they broke up after ten years of marriage** se separaron después de diez años de matrimonio
[3] (= *divide*) dividirse, desglosarse (**into** en)
[4] (*Brit*) [*pupils*] empezar las vacaciones; [*session*] levantarse, terminar; **the school ~s up tomorrow** las clases terminan mañana
[5] (*US**) (= *laugh*) reír a carcajadas
[6] (*Telec*) **the line's** *or* **you're ~ing up** no hay cobertura, no te oigo *or* no se te oye bien
►**break with** VI + PREP **to ~ with sth/sb** romper con algo/algn

breakable ['breɪkəbl] (A) ADJ (= *brittle*) quebradizo; (= *fragile*) frágil
(B) N **breakables** objetos *mpl* frágiles

breakage ['breɪkɪdʒ] N (= *act of breaking*) rotura *f*; (= *thing broken*) destrozo *m*

breakaway ['breɪkəweɪ] (A) ADJ [*group etc*] disidente
(B) N (*Sport*) escapada *f*
(C) CPD ► **breakaway state** N (*Pol*) estado *m* independizado

breakdown ['breɪkdaʊn] (A) N [1] (= *failure*) [*of system, electricity*] fallo *m*; [*of negotiations, marriage*] fracaso *m*; [*of vehicle, machine*] avería *f*, descompostura *f* (*LAm*)
[2] (*fig*) [*of talks*] ruptura *f*
[3] (*Med*) colapso *m*, crisis *f inv* nerviosa
[4] (= *analysis*) [*of numbers etc*] análisis *m inv*, desglose *m*; (*Chem*) descomposición *f*; (= *report*) informe *m* detallado
(B) CPD ► **breakdown service** N (*Brit Aut*) servicio *m* de asistencia en carretera ► **breakdown truck**, **breakdown van** N (*Brit Aut*) (camión *m*) grúa *f*

breaker ['breɪkəʳ] N (= *wave*) ola *f* grande

break-even [ˌbreɪk'iːvən] ADJ **~ chart** gráfica *f* del punto de equilibrio; **~ point** punto *m* de equilibrio

breakfast ['brekfəst] (A) N desayuno *m*; **to have ~** desayunar
(B) VI desayunar; **to ~ off** *or* **on eggs** desayunar huevos
(C) CPD ► **breakfast cereal** N cereales *mpl* para el desayuno ► **breakfast cup** N taza *f* de desayuno ► **breakfast room** N habitación *f* del desayuno ► **breakfast time** N hora *f* del desayuno ► **breakfast TV** N tele(visión) *f* matinal

break-in ['breɪkˌɪn] N robo *m* (con allanamiento de morada)

breaking ['breɪkɪŋ] (A) N [1] rotura *f*, rompimiento *m*
[2] **~ and entering** (*Jur*) violación *f* de domicilio, allanamiento *m* de morada
(B) CPD ► **breaking news** N noticia *fsing* de última hora ► **breaking point** N punto *m* de máxima tensión tolerable; (*fig*) [*of person*] límite *m*; **to reach ~ point** llegar al límite

breaking-up [ˌbreɪkɪŋ'ʌp] N [*of meeting etc*] disolución *f*, levantamiento *m* (de la sesión); [*of school*] fin *m* de las clases, fin *m* de curso

breakneck ['breɪknek] ADJ **at ~ speed** a una velocidad vertiginosa

break-out ['breɪkaʊt] N fuga *f*, evasión *f*

breakthrough ['breɪkθruː] N (*Mil*) avance *m*; (*in research etc*) adelanto *m* muy importante; **to achieve** *or* **make a ~** conseguir *or* hacer un adelanto muy importante

break-up ['breɪkʌp] (A) N [*of partnership*] disolución *f*; [*of couple*] separación *f*
(B) CPD ► **break-up value** N (*Comm*) valor *m* en liquidación

breakwater ['breɪkˌwɔːtəʳ] N rompeolas *m inv*

bream [briːm] N (= *sea bream*) besugo *m*

breast [brest] (A) N (= *chest*) pecho *m*; [*of woman*] seno *m*, pecho *m*; (*Culin*) [*of bird*] pechuga *f*; (*fig*) corazón *m*; **to beat one's ~** darse golpes de pecho; ✦*IDIOM* **to make a clean ~ of** confesar con franqueza; **to make a clean ~ of it** confesarlo todo, descargar la conciencia
(B) VT [1] [+ *waves*] hacer cara a, arrostrar
[2] (*Sport*) [+ *finishing tape*] romper
(C) CPD ► **breast cancer** N cáncer *m* de mama ► **breast milk** N leche *f* materna ► **breast pocket** N bolsillo *m* de pecho

breastbone ['brestbəʊn] N esternón *m*

breast-fed ['brestfed] ADJ criado a pecho

breast-feed ['brestfiːd] (*pt, pp* **breast-fed**) VT amamantar, criar a los pechos

breast-feeding ['brestˌfiːdɪŋ] N amamantamiento *m*, cría *f* a los pechos

breastplate ['brestpleɪt] N peto *m*

breaststroke ['breststrəʊk] N braza *f* de pecho; **to swim** *or* **do the ~** nadar a la braza

breastwork ['brestwɜːk] N parapeto *m*

breath [breθ] (A) N [1] (*lit*) (= *respiration*) aliento *m*; **you could smell the whisky on his ~** estaba claro que el aliento le olía a whisky; **without pausing for ~** sin detenerse ni un momento para recobrar el aliento *or* la respiración; **to have bad ~** tener mal aliento; **he stopped running to catch his ~** dejó de correr para recobrar el aliento *or* la respiración; **the pain made her catch her ~** el dolor hizo que se le cortara la respiración; **to draw ~** (*lit*) respirar; (*liter*) (= *exist*) **he was one of the meanest people who ever drew ~** era una de las personas más mezquinas que jamás ha visto este mundo; **to draw one's first ~** (*liter*) venir al mundo; **to draw one's last ~** (*liter*) exhalar el último suspiro (*liter*); **to get one's ~ back** recobrar el aliento *or* la respiración; **to hold one's ~** (*lit*) contener la respiración; (*fig*) **the whole world is holding its ~** el mundo entero está en vilo; **"he said he would be here" — "well, I wouldn't hold your ~"** —dijo que vendría —sí, pues yo le esperaría sentado*; **to lose one's ~** perder el aliento; **to be/get out of ~** estar/quedar sin aliento; **in the same** *or* **next ~** acto seguido; **she felt hot and short of ~** tenía calor y se ahogaba; **he was short of ~ after the climb** estaba sin aliento después de la escalada; **she has asthma and sometimes gets short of ~** tiene asma y a veces se ahoga *or* le falta el aliento; **she sucked in her ~** tomó aliento, aspiró; **to take a ~** respirar; **he took a deep ~** respiró hondo; **to take one's ~ away** dejar a uno sin habla; **he muttered something under his ~** dijo algo entre dientes *or* en voz baja; **to waste one's ~*** gastar saliva (en balde)*; *see also* **bated**, **save A4**
[2] (*fig*) (= *puff*) soplo *m*; **there wasn't a ~ of wind** no corría ni un soplo de viento; **we must avoid the slightest ~ of scandal** debemos evitar el más mínimo soplo de escándalo; **a ~ of fresh air**: **we went out for a ~ of fresh air** salimos a tomar el (aire) fresco; **she's like a ~ of fresh air** es como un soplo de aire fresco
(B) CPD ► **breath test** N (*Aut*) prueba *f* de alcoholemia; *see also* **breath-test**

breathable ['briːðəbl] ADJ [*air*] respirable, que se puede respirar; [*fabric, garment*] transpirable, que deja pasar el aire

breathalyse, **breathalyze** (*US*) ['breθəlaɪz] VT someter a la prueba de la alcoholemia *or* del alcohol

Breathalyser®, **Breathalyzer** (*US*) ['breθəlaɪzəʳ] (A) N alcoholímetro *m*
(B) CPD ► **Breathalyser test** N prueba *f* de la alcoholemia

breathe [briːð] (A) VT [1] [+ *air*] respirar; **to ~ air into a balloon** inflar un globo soplando; **he ~d alcohol all over me** el aliento le apestaba a alcohol; ✦*IDIOMS* **to ~ new life into sth** infundir nueva vida a algo; **to ~ one's last** (*liter*) (= *die*) exhalar el último suspiro
[2] (= *utter*) [+ *prayer*] decir en voz baja; **to ~ a sigh** suspirar, dar un suspiro; **I won't ~ a word** no diré nada *or* palabra
(B) VI [1] [*person, animal*] respirar; [*noisily*] resollar; **now we can ~ again** (*fig*) ahora podemos respirar tranquilos; *see also* **neck A1**
[2] [*wine*] respirar
[3] [*fabric*] transpirar, dejar pasar el aire
►**breathe in** VT + ADV, VI + ADV aspirar
►**breathe out** (A) VT + ADV exhalar
(B) VI + ADV espirar

breather* ['briːðəʳ] N (= *short rest*) respiro *m*, descanso *m*; **to take a ~** tomarse un respiro *or* descanso; **to give sb a ~** dejar que algn se tome un respiro *or* descanso

breathing ['briːðɪŋ] (A) N respiración *f*; **heavy ~** resuello *m*
(B) CPD ► **breathing apparatus** N respirador *m* ► **breathing space** N (*fig*) respiro *m* ► **breathing tube** N tubo *m* de respiración

breathless ['breθlɪs] ADJ [1] (*from exertion*) [*voice*] entrecortado; **he arrived ~** llegó sin alien-

to, llegó jadeando; **she was ~ from climbing the stairs** subir las escaleras la había dejado sin aliento; **it leaves you ~** corta la respiración; **at a ~ pace** a un ritmo acelerado
[2] (*with excitement*) **a ~ silence** un silencio intenso; **she was ~ with excitement** la emoción la había dejado sin aliento; **we were ~ with anticipation** esperábamos ansiosísimos

breathlessly [ˈbreθlɪslɪ] ADV [1] (*lit*) [*say, ask*] entrecortadamente, jadeante; [*walk, climb*] jadeando, con la respiración entrecortada
[2] (*fig*) [*watch, wait*] ansiosamente

breathlessness [ˈbreθlɪsnɪs] N falta *f* de aliento, dificultad *f* al respirar

breathtaking [ˈbreθ,teɪkɪŋ] ADJ [*sight*] imponente, impresionante; [*speed*] vertiginoso; [*effrontery*] pasmoso; **the view is ~** la vista corta la respiración, la vista es imponente *or* impresionante

breathtakingly [ˈbreθ,teɪkɪŋlɪ] ADV **~ beautiful** de una belleza impresionante, tan hermoso que corta la respiración; **~ simple** de una sencillez impresionante *or* pasmosa; **to go ~ fast** ir a una velocidad vertiginosa

breath-test [ˈbreθtest] VT someter a la prueba de la alcoholemia *or* del alcohol; *see also* **breath**

breathy [ˈbreθɪ] ADJ [*voice*] entrecortado

bred [bred] PT, PP *of* **breed**

-bred [bred] ADJ (*ending in compounds*) criado, educado; **well-bred** bien educado, formal

breech [briːtʃ] Ⓐ N [*of gun*] recámara *f*
Ⓑ CPD ► **breech birth, breech delivery** N (*Med*) parto *m* de nalgas; **he was a ~ birth** nació de nalgas

breeches [ˈbriːtʃɪz] Ⓐ NPL calzones *mpl*; **riding ~** pantalones *mpl* de montar; ✦**IDIOM to wear the ~** llevar los pantalones *or* calzones
Ⓑ CPD ► **breeches buoy** N (*Naut*) boya *f* pantalón

breechloader [ˈbriːtʃ,ləʊdəʳ] N arma *f* de retrocarga

breed [briːd] (*vb: pt, pp* **bred**) Ⓐ N (*lit*) [*of animal*] raza *f*; [*of plant*] variedad *f*; (*fig*) estirpe *f*
Ⓑ VT [1] [+ *animals*] criar; **town bred** criado en la ciudad; **they are bred for show** se crían para las exposiciones; **we ~ them for hunting** los criamos para la caza
[2] (*fig*) [+ *hate, suspicion*] crear, engendrar
Ⓒ VI [*animals*] reproducirse, procrear; **they ~ like flies** *or* **rabbits** se multiplican como conejos

breeder [ˈbriːdəʳ] N [1] (= *person*) criador(a) *m/f*
[2] (= *animal*) reproductor(a) *m/f*
[3] (*Phys*) (*also* **~ reactor**) reactor *m*

breeding [ˈbriːdɪŋ] Ⓐ N [1] (*Bio*) reproducción *f*
[2] [*of stock*] cría *f*
[3] [*of person*] (*also* **good ~**) educación *f*, crianza *f*; **bad ~** ◊ **ill ~** mala crianza *f*, falta *f* de educación; **he has (good) ~** es una persona educada; **it shows bad ~** muestra una falta de educación
Ⓑ CPD ► **breeding ground** N (*Bio*) lugar *m* de cría; (*fig*) caldo *m* de cultivo (**of, for** de, para); ► **breeding season** N época *f* de reproducción

breeks [briːks] NPL (*Scot*) pantalones *mpl*

breeze [briːz] Ⓐ N [1] (= *wind*) brisa *f*
[2] **it's a ~*** es coser y cantar*; **to do sth in a ~** (*US**) hacer algo con los ojos cerrados; *see also* **shoot B4**
Ⓑ VI **to ~ in** entrar como si nada; **to ~ through sth*** hacer algo con los ojos cerrados

breeze-block [ˈbriːzblɒk] N (*Brit*) bovedilla *f*

breezily [ˈbriːzɪlɪ] ADV (= *cheerfully*) alegremente; (= *nonchalantly*) despreocupadamente

breezy [ˈbriːzɪ] ADJ (*compar* **breezier**, *superl* **breeziest**) [1] [*day, weather*] de viento; [*spot*] desprotegido del viento; **it's ~** hace viento
[2] [*person's manner*] (= *cheerful*) animado, alegre; (= *nonchalant*) despreocupado

Bren carrier [ˈbren,kærɪəʳ] N = **Bren gun carrier**, *see* **Bren gun**

Bren gun [ˈbren,gʌn] Ⓐ N fusil *m* ametrallador
Ⓑ CPD ► **Bren gun carrier** N vehículo *m* de transporte ligero (con fusil ametrallador)

brethren [ˈbreðrɪn] NPL (*irr pl* (*esp Rel*) *of* **brother**) hermanos *mpl*

Breton [ˈbretən] Ⓐ ADJ bretón
Ⓑ N [1] (= *person*) bretón/ona *m/f*
[2] (*Ling*) bretón *m*

breve [briːv] N (*Mus, Typ*) breve *f*

breviary [ˈbriːvɪərɪ] N (*Rel*) breviario *m*

brevity [ˈbrevɪtɪ] N (= *shortness*) brevedad *f*; (= *conciseness*) concisión *f*; ✦**PROV ~ is the soul of wit** lo bueno si breve dos veces bueno

brew [bruː] Ⓐ N [*of beer*] variedad *f* (de cerveza); [*of tea, herbs*] infusión *f*
Ⓑ VT [1] [+ *beer*] elaborar; [+ *tea*] hacer, preparar
[2] (*fig*) [+ *scheme, mischief*] tramar
Ⓒ VI [1] [*beer*] elaborarse; [*tea*] hacerse
[2] (*fig*) [*storm*] avecinarse; [*plot*] tramarse; **there's trouble ~ing** algo se está tramando

►**brew up*** VI + ADV (*Brit*) preparar el té

brewer [ˈbruːəʳ] N cervecero/a *m/f*

brewery [ˈbruːərɪ] N cervecería *f*, fábrica *f* de cerveza

brew-up [ˈbruːʌp] N **let's have a ~** (*Brit**) vamos a tomar un té

briar [ˈbraɪəʳ] N [1] (= *thorny bush*) zarza *f*; (= *wild rose*) escaramujo *m*, rosa *f* silvestre; (= *hawthorn*) espino *m*; (= *heather*) brezo *m*
[2] (= *pipe*) pipa *f* de brezo

bribable [ˈbraɪbəbl] ADJ sobornable

bribe [braɪb] Ⓐ N soborno *m*, mordida *f* (*CAm, Mex**), coima *f* (*Andes, S. Cone**); **to take a ~** dejarse sobornar (**from** por)
Ⓑ VT sobornar, comprar*; **to ~ sb to do sth** sobornar a algn para que haga algo

bribery [ˈbraɪbərɪ] N soborno *m*, mordida *f* (*CAm, Mex**), coima *f* (*Andes, S. Cone**)

bric-à-brac [ˈbrɪkəbræk] N (*no pl*) chucherías *fpl*, curiosidades *fpl*

brick [brɪk] Ⓐ N [1] (*Constr*) ladrillo *m*, tabique *m* (*Mex*); **~s and mortar** construcción *f*, edificios *mpl*; ✦**IDIOMS to come down on sb like a ton of ~s*** echar una bronca de miedo a algn*; **to drop a ~** (*Brit**) meter la pata*, tirarse una plancha (*Sp**); ✦**PROV you can't make ~s without straw** sin paja ho hay ladrillos
[2] (*Brit*) (= *toy*) cubo *m*
[3] [*of ice cream*] bloque *m*
[4] (†*) (= *person*) **he's a ~** es buen chico; **be a ~ and lend it to me** préstamelo como buen amigo
Ⓑ CPD de ladrillo(s) ► **brick kiln** N horno *m* de ladrillos ► **brick wall** N pared *f* de ladrillos; ✦**IDIOM to beat one's head against a ~ wall** esforzarse en balde

►**brick in** VT + ADV [+ *window etc*] tapar con ladrillos *or* (*Mex*) tabiques

►**brick up** VT + ADV [+ *window etc*] tapar con ladrillos *or* (*Mex*) tabiques

brickbat [ˈbrɪkbæt] N trozo *m* de ladrillo; (*fig*) crítica *f*

brick-built [ˈbrɪk,bɪlt] ADJ construido de ladrillos

brickie* [ˈbrɪkɪ] N (*Brit*) albañil *mf*, paleta *mf* (*Sp**)

bricklayer [ˈbrɪk,leɪəʳ] N albañil *mf*

bricklaying [ˈbrɪk,leɪɪŋ] N albañilería *f*

brick-red [ˈbrɪkred] Ⓐ ADJ rojo ladrillo
Ⓑ N rojo *m* ladrillo

brickwork [ˈbrɪkwɜːk] N enladrillado *m*, ladrillos *mpl*

brickworks [ˈbrɪkwɜːks] N, **brickyard** [ˈbrɪk,jɑːd] N ladrillar *m*

bridal [ˈbraɪdl] Ⓐ ADJ nupcial
Ⓑ CPD ► **bridal suite** N suite *f* nupcial

bride [braɪd] N novia *f*; **the ~ and groom** los novios; **~ of Christ** (*Rel*) esposa *f* de Cristo

bridegroom [ˈbraɪdgrʊm] N novio *m*; → BEST MAN

bridesmaid [ˈbraɪdzmeɪd] N dama *f* de honor

bridge[1] [brɪdʒ] Ⓐ N [1] (*gen*) puente *m* (*also Mus*); **to build a ~ between two communities** (*fig*) crear un vínculo (de unión) entre dos comunidades; **we must rebuild our ~s** (*fig*) tenemos que restablecer las relaciones; ✦**IDIOMS to burn one's ~s** quemar las naves; **we'll cross that ~ when we come to it** trataremos ese problema en su momento; **don't cross your ~s before you come to them** no adelantes los acontecimientos; **much water has flowed under the ~ since then** mucho ha llovido desde entonces
[2] (*Naut*) puente *m* de mando
[3] [*of nose*] caballete *m*; [*of spectacles*] puente *m*
[4] (*Dentistry*) puente *m*
Ⓑ VT tender un puente sobre; **to ~ a gap** (*fig*) llenar un vacío
Ⓒ CPD ► **bridge building** N construcción *f* de puentes; (*fig*) restablecimiento *m* de relaciones

bridge[2] [brɪdʒ] Ⓐ N (*Cards*) bridge *m*
Ⓑ CPD ► **bridge party** N reunión *f* de bridge
► **bridge player** N jugador(a) *m/f* de bridge
► **bridge roll** N *tipo de bollo pequeño y alargado*

bridgehead [ˈbrɪdʒhed] N (*Mil*) cabeza *f* de puente

Bridget [ˈbrɪdʒɪt] N Brígida

bridging loan [ˈbrɪdʒɪŋ,ləʊn] N (*Brit Fin*) crédito *m* puente

bridle [ˈbraɪdl] Ⓐ N [*of horse*] brida *f*, freno *m*
Ⓑ VT [+ *horse*] frenar, detener
Ⓒ VI picarse, ofenderse (**at** por)
Ⓓ CPD ► **bridle path** N camino *m* de herradura

brief [briːf] Ⓐ ADJ (*compar* **briefer**, *superl* **briefest**) [1] (= *short*) [*visit, period, career*] breve, corto; [*glimpse, moment, interval*] breve
[2] (= *concise*) [*speech, description, statement*] breve; **please be ~** sea breve, por favor; **he was ~ and to the point** fue breve y yendo al grano; **in ~** en resumen, en suma
[3] (= *skimpy*) [*panties, bathing costume, shorts*] diminuto, breve
Ⓑ N [1] (*Jur*) escrito *m*; **to hold a ~ for sb** (*fig*) ser partidario de algn, abogar por algn; **I hold no ~ for those who ...** no soy partidario de los que ..., no abogo por los que ...; **I hold no ~ for him** no lo defiendo
[2] (= *instructions, remit*) instrucciones *fpl*; **his ~ is to negotiate a solution to the conflict** sus instrucciones son solucionar el conflicto mediante negociaciones; **it's not part of my ~ to sort out disputes** no entra dentro de mi competencia solventar disputas
[3] **briefs** (*man's*) calzoncillos *mpl*, slip *m*, calzones *mpl* (*LAm*); (*woman's*) bragas *fpl* (*Sp*), calzones *mpl* (*LAm*)

Ⓒ VT [1] (*Jur, Mil*) (= *instruct*) dar instrucciones a; **the pilots were ~ed** dieron instrucciones a los pilotos
[2] (= *inform, prepare*) informar; **we were ~ed on recent developments** nos informaron sobre los acontecimientos recientes

briefcase [ˈbriːfkeɪs] N cartera *f*, maletín *m*

briefer [ˈbriːfəʳ] N (*esp Mil*) informador(a) *m/f*

briefing [ˈbriːfɪŋ] N (= *meeting*) sesión *f* informativa; (*written*) informe *m*

briefly [ˈbriːflɪ] ADV [1] (= *for short time*) [*speak, reply, smile, pause*] brevemente; **she visited us ~** nos hizo una breve *or* corta visita; **"good morning," he said, looking up ~** "buenos días," dijo, levantando la vista fugazmente; **I wondered ~ if he were lying** por un momento me pregunté si no estaría mintiendo; **he was ~ detained by the police** la policía lo tuvo detenido durante un corto espacio de tiempo
[2] (= *in brief*) [*tell, reply, describe*] en pocas palabras, en resumen; **the facts, ~, are these** los hechos, en pocas palabras *or* en resumen, son éstos; **~, we still don't know** en resumen *or* en suma, aún no lo sabemos

briefness [ˈbriːfnɪs] N brevedad *f*

brier [ˈbraɪəʳ] N = **briar**

brig [brɪg] N (*Naut*) bergantín *m*

Brig. ABBR = **Brigadier**

brigade [brɪˈgeɪd] N (*Mil*) brigada *f*; (*fire etc*) cuerpo *m*; **one of the old ~** un veterano

brigadier [ˌbrɪgəˈdɪəʳ] Ⓐ N general *mf* de brigada
Ⓑ CPD ► **brigadier general** N general *mf* de brigada

brigand [ˈbrɪgənd] N bandido *m*, bandolero *m*

brigandage [ˈbrɪgəndɪdʒ] N bandidaje *m*, bandolerismo *m*

bright [braɪt] Ⓐ ADJ (*compar* **brighter**; *superl* **brightest**) [1] (= *vivid, shining*) [*light, sun, reflection*] brillante, luminoso; [*star, metal*] brillante; [*surface*] resplandeciente; [*fire*] luminoso; [*uniform, bird, flower*] lleno de colorido; [*eyes*] brillante; [*colour*] fuerte, vivo; **~ red** rojo fuerte; **her eyes were ~ with excitement** sus ojos brillaban de excitación
[2] (= *sunny*) [*day, weather*] radiante, soleado; [*room, house*] luminoso, con mucha luz; **a ~ October day** un radiante *or* soleado día de octubre; **a ~, sunny day** un día de sol radiante; **the outlook is ~er for tomorrow** (*Met*) la previsión meteorológica para mañana es que hará mejor tiempo
[3] (= *cheerful*) [*person*] alegre, animado; [*face, expression, smile*] radiante; [*voice*] lleno de animación; **~ and breezy** radiante y lleno de vida; ✦*IDIOM* **to look on the ~ side** ver el lado positivo de las cosas
[4] (= *clever*) [*person*] listo, inteligente; [*idea*] brillante, genial; **was it your ~ idea to let the children do the washing-up?** (*iro*) ¿ha sido tuya la brillante *or* genial idea de dejar que los niños laven los platos?; **whose ~ idea was that?** (*iro*) ¿quién tuvo *or* de quién fue esa brillante idea?; ✦*IDIOM* **as ~ as a button** más listo que el hambre
[5] (= *promising*) [*future*] brillante, prometedor; [*outlook, prospects, start*] prometedor; **the future looks ~ (for him)** el futuro se le presenta brillante *or* prometedor; **I can see a ~ future ahead of you** te auguro un futuro brillante; **the outlook is ~er** las perspectivas son más prometedoras
Ⓑ ADV **to get up ~ and early** levantarse tempranito
Ⓒ CPD ► **bright lights** NPL (*US Aut*) luces *fpl* largas; **he was attracted by the ~ lights of the big city** (*fig*) se sentía atraído por las luces de neón de la gran ciudad (*fig*) ► **bright spark*** N (*iro*) listillo/a *m/f*; **you're a ~ spark, aren't you!** ¡te has pasado de listo!

brighten [ˈbraɪtn] (*also* **~ up**) Ⓐ VT [1] (= *make lighter*) [+ *room*] dar más luz a, iluminar más; (*TV*) [+ *picture*] dar brillo a
[2] (= *make more cheerful*) [+ *room*] alegrar; [+ *situation*] mejorar
Ⓑ VI [1] [*person*] animarse, alegrarse; [*eyes*] iluminarse, brillar
[2] [*weather*] despejarse; [*prospects*] mejorar

bright-eyed [ˈbraɪtˈaɪd] ADJ de ojos vivos

brightly [ˈbraɪtlɪ] ADV [1] (= *brilliantly*) [*shine*] intensamente, con intensidad; [*burn*] con intensidad; **~ lit** radiantemente iluminado
[2] (= *vividly*) **~ coloured flowers** flores *fpl* de colores vivos; **~ painted pictures** cuadros *mpl* pintados con llamativos colores; **~ patterned shawls** mantones *mpl* con unos diseños llamativos
[3] (= *cheerily*) [*smile, say, answer*] alegremente

brightness [ˈbraɪtnɪs] Ⓐ N [1] [*of light, sun, fire, eyes, metal*] brillo *m*, resplandor *m*; [*of morning, day*] claridad *f*, luminosidad *f*; [*of colour*] viveza *f*
[2] (= *cheerfulness*) alegría *f*, animación *f*
[3] (= *cleverness*) inteligencia *f*
[4] (= *promise*) [*of future, prospects*] lo prometedor
Ⓑ CPD ► **brightness control** N (*TV*) botón *m* de ajuste del brillo

brill[1] [brɪl] N (*pl* **brill** *or* **brills**) rodaballo *m* menor

brill[2]* [brɪl] Ⓐ ADJ (*Brit*) (= *brilliant*) genial*, fenómeno*
Ⓑ EXCL ¡fantástico!*

brilliance [ˈbrɪljəns] N, **brilliancy** [ˈbrɪljənsɪ] N [1] (= *brightness*) [*of light*] resplandor *m*, brillo *m*; [*of colour*] luminosidad *f*; [*of gemstone*] resplandor *m*, fulgor *m*, brillo *m*
[2] (= *cleverness*) [*of student, scientist*] brillantez *f*, genialidad *f*

brilliant [ˈbrɪljənt] Ⓐ ADJ [1] (= *bright*) [*sunshine*] resplandeciente, radiante; [*light*] brillante; [*colour*] brillante, luminoso; [*smile*] radiante; **his teeth were (a) ~ white** tenía los dientes de un blanco reluciente
[2] (= *clever*) [*person, idea, mind*] brillante, genial; [*thesis*] brillante
[3] (= *outstanding*) [*career, future*] brillante; [*success, victory*] rotundo; **the party was a ~ success** la fiesta fue un éxito rotundo *or* total
[4] (*) (= *wonderful*) [*book, film, restaurant*] genial*, buenísimo; **we had a ~ time in Spain** lo pasamos fenomenal *or* genial en España*; **she's ~ with children** se le dan fenomenal los niños*; **she's ~ at making cakes** se le da fenomenal hacer pasteles*; **brilliant!** ¡fantástico!, ¡genial!*
Ⓑ N (= *diamond*) brillante *m*

brilliantine [ˈbrɪljəntiːn] N brillantina *f*

brilliantly [ˈbrɪljəntlɪ] ADV [1] (= *brightly*) [*shine*] intensamente, con intensidad; **~ lit** *or* **illuminated** radiantemente iluminado; **a ~ sunny morning** una mañana de sol radiante; **~ coloured** de colores vivos *or* brillantes
[2] (= *superbly*) [*play, perform, act*] brillantemente; [*written, executed*] con brillantez; **she played ~** tocó brillantemente, tocó genial*; **the strategy worked ~** la estrategia funcionó a la perfección; **he succeeded ~ in politics** tuvo una brillante carrera política; **a ~ simple idea** una idea brillante y sencilla; **he was ~ successful** tuvo un éxito rotundo *or* total

Brillo pad® [ˈbrɪləʊˌpæd] N estropajo *m* de aluminio

brim [brɪm] Ⓐ N [*of cup*] borde *m*; [*of hat*] ala *f*
Ⓑ VI (*also* **~ over**) rebosar, desbordarse; **to ~ with** rebosar de

brimful [ˈbrɪmˈfʊl] ADJ lleno hasta el borde; **~ of** *or* **with confidence** lleno *or* rebosante de confianza

brimstone [ˈbrɪmstəʊn] N azufre *m*

brindled [ˈbrɪndld] ADJ manchado, mosqueado

brine [braɪn] N (*for preserving*) salmuera *f*; (*liter*) (= *sea*) piélago *m* (*liter*), mar *m or f*

bring [brɪŋ] (*pt, pp* **brought**) VT [1] [*person, object*] [+ *news, luck etc*] traer; [+ *person*] llevar, conducir; **~ it over here** tráelo para acá; **~ it closer** acércalo; **to ~ sth to an end** terminar con algo; **to ~ a matter to a conclusion** concluir un asunto, llevar un asunto a su desenlace; **it brought us to the verge of disaster** nos llevó al borde del desastre; **I was not brought into the matter at any stage** no me dieron voz en este asunto en ningún momento; *see also* **book A1**
[2] (= *cause*) traer; **the hot weather ~s storms** el calor trae tormenta; **to ~ influence/pressure to bear (on)** ejercer influencia/presión (sobre); **you ~ nothing but trouble** no haces más que causarme problemas; **it brought tears to her eyes** hizo que se le llenaran los ojos de lágrimas; **this brought him to his feet** esto hizo que se levantara; **he brought it upon himself** se lo buscó él mismo
[3] (*Jur*) [+ *charge*] hacer, formular; [+ *suit*] entablar; **no charges will be brought** no se hará ninguna acusación; **the case was brought before the judge** la causa fue vista por el juez
[4] (= *yield*) [+ *profit etc*] dar, producir; **to ~ a good price** alcanzar un buen precio
[5] (= *induce*) **to ~ sb to do sth** hacer que algn haga algo; **he was brought to see his error** le hicieron ver su error; **it brought me to realize that ...** me hizo comprender que ...; **he couldn't ~ himself to tell her/touch it** no se sentía con el valor suficiente para decírselo/tocarlo

►**bring about** VT + ADV [1] [+ *change*] provocar; [+ *crisis, death, war*] ocasionar, provocar
[2] [+ *boat*] virar, dar la vuelta a

►**bring along** VT + ADV traer consigo, llevar consigo

►**bring away** VT + ADV llevarse

►**bring back** VT + ADV (*lit*) [+ *person, object*] traer de vuelta; [+ *thing borrowed*] devolver; [+ *monarchy etc*] restaurar; (*to life*) devolver la vida a; **she brought a friend back for coffee** trajo una amiga a casa a tomar café; **it ~s back memories** trae recuerdos

►**bring down** VT + ADV [1] (= *lower*) [+ *prices*] bajar
[2] (*Mil, Hunting*) abatir, derribar
[3] (= *topple*) [+ *opponent*] derribar; [+ *government*] derrocar

►**bring forth** VT + ADV [+ *child*] dar a luz a; (*fig*) [+ *protests, criticism*] dar lugar a, suscitar (*frm*)

►**bring forward** VT + ADV [1] [+ *evidence, idea*] presentar; [+ *argument*] exponer; [+ *suggestion*] proponer; [+ *offer*] hacer
[2] (= *advance time of*) [+ *date, meeting*] adelantar
[3] (*Book-keeping*) pasar a otra cuenta; **brought forward** saldo *m* anterior

►**bring in** VT + ADV [1] [+ *person*] hacer entrar, hacer pasar; [+ *object*] traer; [+ *heavy object*] entrar; [+ *meal*] servir; [+ *harvest*] recoger; [+

suspect] detener, llevar a la comisaría; **to ~ in the police** pedir la intervención de la policía; **~ him in!** ¡que entre!, ¡que pase!
[2] (= *yield*) [+ *income*] producir, proporcionar; [+ *wages*] sacar
[3] (= *introduce*) [+ *fashion, custom*] introducir; (*Pol*) [+ *bill*] presentar, introducir; **to ~ in a verdict** (*Jur*) pronunciar un veredicto
[4] (= *attract*) atraer; **this should ~ in the masses** esto debería atraer a las masas

► **bring off** VT + ADV [1] [+ *plan*] lograr, conseguir; [+ *success*] obtener; **he didn't ~ it off*** no le salió*
[2] [+ *people from wreck*] rescatar

► **bring on** VT + ADV [1] (= *cause*) [+ *illness, quarrel*] producir, causar
[2] (= *stimulate*) [+ *crops*] hacer crecer *or* madurar; [+ *flowers*] hacer florecer; [+ *growth*] estimular, favorecer
[3] (*Theat, Sport*) [+ *performer*] presentar; [+ *player*] sacar (de la reserva), hacer salir

► **bring out** VT + ADV [1] (= *take out*) sacar; [+ *argument*] sacar a relucir
[2] (= *introduce*) [+ *product, model*] sacar, lanzar al mercado; [+ *book*] publicar, sacar
[3] (= *reveal*) [+ *colour, meaning*] realzar; **to ~ out the best in sb** sacar a la luz lo mejor que hay en algn
[4] (= *develop*) [+ *quality*] sacar a la luz, despertar
[5] (= *give confidence to*) [+ *person*] ayudar a adquirir confianza

► **bring over** VT + ADV [1] [+ *person, object*] ir a buscar
[2] (= *convert*) [+ *person*] convertir, convencer

► **bring round** VT + ADV [1] (= *persuade*) convencer
[2] (= *steer*) [+ *conversation*] llevar, dirigir
[3] [+ *unconscious person*] hacer volver en sí, reanimar

► **bring to** VT + ADV [1] [+ *unconscious person*] hacer volver en sí, reanimar
[2] (*Naut*) pairear, poner al pairo

► **bring together** VT + ADV reunir; [+ *enemies*] reconciliar

► **bring under** VT + ADV (= *subjugate*) someter

► **bring up** VT + ADV [1] (= *carry*) subir; [*person*] hacer subir
[2] (= *rear*) [+ *child*] criar, educar; **a well brought up child** un niño bien educado; **she was badly brought up** la criaron de manera poco satisfactoria; **he was brought up to believe that ...** lo educaron en la creencia de que ...; **where were you brought up?** (*iro*) ¡cómo se ve que no has ido a colegios de pago!
[3] [+ *subject*] sacar a colación, sacar a relucir; (*in meeting*) plantar
[4] (= *vomit*) devolver, vomitar
[5] **to ~ sb up short** parar a algn en seco
[6] **to ~ up the rear** (*Mil*) cerrar la marcha
[7] **to ~ sb up in court** (*Jur*) hacer comparecer a algn ante el magistrado

bring-and-buy sale [ˌbrɪŋəndˈbaɪseɪl] N (*Brit*) *venta de objetos usados con fines benéficos*

brink [brɪŋk] N (*lit, fig*) borde *m*; **on the ~ of sth** al borde de algo; **to be on the ~ of doing sth** estar a punto de hacer algo

brinkmanship [ˈbrɪŋkmənʃɪp] N política *f* arriesgada

briny [ˈbraɪnɪ] Ⓐ ADJ salado, salobre
Ⓑ N **the ~**† (*also hum*) el mar

briquette [brɪˈket] N briqueta *f*

brisk [brɪsk] ADJ (*compar* **brisker**; *superl* **briskest**) [*walk*] enérgico; [*person, voice, movement*] enérgico, dinámico; [*manner*] brusco; [*wind, day*] fresco; [*trade*] activo; **at a ~ pace** con paso brioso *or* enérgico; **business is ~** (*in shop etc*) el negocio lleva un buen ritmo; **trading was ~ today** (*St Ex*) hoy hubo mucho movimiento en la bolsa, hoy el mercado estuvo muy dinámico

brisket [ˈbrɪskɪt] N carne *f* de pecho (para asar)

briskly [ˈbrɪsklɪ] ADV [*speak, say*] enérgicamente; [*walk, trot, march*] con brío, con paso enérgico; **these goods are selling ~** estos artículos se están vendiendo mucho

briskness [ˈbrɪsknɪs] N [*of walk, movement*] brío *m*; [*of manner*] brusquedad *f*; [*of trade*] dinamismo *m*

brisling [ˈbrɪzlɪŋ] N espadín *m* (noruego)

bristle [ˈbrɪsl] Ⓐ N [*of brush, on animal*] cerda *f*; [*of beard*] **~(s)** barba *f* (incipiente)
Ⓑ VI [1] [*hair etc*] erizarse, ponerse de punta; **to ~ with** (*fig*) estar erizado de; **he ~d with anger** se enfureció
[2] (*fig*) [*person*] resentirse (**at** de)
Ⓒ CPD ► **bristle brush** N cepillo *m* de púas

bristly [ˈbrɪslɪ] ADJ (*compar* **bristlier**; *superl* **bristliest**) [*beard, hair*] erizado; **to have a ~ chin** tener la barba crecida

Bristol [ˈbrɪstəl] N **~ board** cartulina *f*; *see also* **shipshape**

bristols‡ [ˈbrɪstəlz] NPL (*Brit*) (= *breasts*) tetas* *fpl*

Brit* [brɪt] N británico/a *m/f*; (*loosely*) inglés/esa *m/f*

Britain [ˈbrɪtən] N (*also* **Great ~**) Gran Bretaña *f*; (*loosely*) Inglaterra *f*

> **BRITAIN**
>
> *A veces se usa el término* **England** *para referirse a la totalidad del país, aunque no es un término usado con precisión; sin embargo, mucha gente confunde a menudo los nombres* **Britain, Great Britain, United Kingdom** *y* **British Isles.**
> *Se denomina* **Great Britain** *a la isla que comprende Inglaterra, Escocia y Gales. Desde el punto de vista administrativo, el término también incluye las islas menores cercanas, a excepción de la Isla de Man (***Isle of Man***) y las Islas Anglonormandas o Islas del Canal de la Mancha (***Channel Islands***).*
> **United Kingdom (of Great Britain and Northern Ireland)**, *o* **UK**, *es la unidad política que comprende Gran Bretaña e Irlanda del Norte.*
> **British Isles** *es el término geográfico que abarca Gran Bretaña, Irlanda, la Isla de Man y las Islas Anglonormandas. En lo político, el término comprende dos estados soberanos: el Reino Unido y la República de Irlanda.*
> *El término* **Britain** *se utiliza fundamentalmente para referirse al Reino Unido, y en algunas ocasiones también a la isla, a Gran Bretaña.*

Britannia [brɪˈtænɪə] N Britania *f* (*figura que representa simbólicamente a Gran Bretaña*); → RULE BRITANNIA

Britannic [brɪˈtænɪk] ADJ **His/Her ~ Majesty** su Majestad Británica

britches [ˈbrɪtʃəz] NPL = **breeches**

Briticism [ˈbrɪtɪsɪzəm] N (*US*) modismo *m or* vocablo *m etc* del inglés británico

British [ˈbrɪtɪʃ] Ⓐ ADJ (*gen*) británico; (*loosely*) inglés; **the best of ~ (luck)!*** ¡y un cuerno!*
Ⓑ NPL **the ~** los británicos; (*loosely*) los ingleses
Ⓒ CPD ► **British Asian** N britanico/a *m/f* de origen asiático ► **British Council** N (*in other countries*) Consejo *m* Británico ► **the British disease** N (*Ind hum*) *la falta de motivación laboral de los años 60-70 en el Reino Unido* ► **British English** N inglés *m* británico ► **the British Isles** NPL las Islas Británicas ► **British Legion** N *organización de veteranos de las dos guerras mundiales*; → LEGION ► **British Museum** N Museo *m* Británico ► **British Summer Time** N *hora de verano en Gran Bretaña* ► **British Thermal Unit** N unidad *f* térmica británica

> **BRITISH COUNCIL**
>
> *El* **British Council** *se creó en 1935 para fomentar la cultura británica en el extranjero y actualmente tiene delegaciones en más de 100 países. Sus principales cometidos son la organización de actividades culturales, tales como exposiciones y conferencias, con el fin de dar a conocer el arte, la ciencia y la literatura del país, así como la enseñanza del inglés, además de ayudar a aquellos que desean estudiar en el Reino Unido.*

Britisher [ˈbrɪtɪʃəʳ] N (*US*) británico/a *m/f*, natural *mf* de Gran Bretaña

Briton [ˈbrɪtən] N británico/a *m/f*; (*loosely*) inglés/esa *m/f*

Brittany [ˈbrɪtənɪ] N Bretaña *f*

brittle [ˈbrɪtl] ADJ (*compar* **brittler**; *superl* **brittlest**) quebradizo

brittleness [ˈbrɪtlnɪs] N lo quebradizo

Bro. ABBR (= **Brother**) H., Hno.

broach [brəʊtʃ] VT [1] [+ *cask*] espitar; [+ *bottle etc*] abrir
[2] [+ *subject*] abordar, sacar a colación; **he didn't ~ the subject** no sacó el tema a colación, no abordó ese tema

broad [brɔːd] Ⓐ ADJ (*compar* **broader**; *superl* **broadest**) [1] (= *wide*) [*road*] ancho, amplio; [*shoulders*] ancho; [*forehead*] despejado, amplio; [*smile*] de oreja a oreja, abierto (*liter*); **it is three metres ~** tiene tres metros de ancho; **a ~ expanse of lawn** una amplia extensión de césped; **to be ~ in the shoulder** [*person*] ser ancho de hombros *or* de espaldas; [*garment*] ser ancho de hombros; ✦**IDIOMS** **to be ~ in the beam*** (*pej*) [*person*] tener un buen trasero*, tener buenas posaderas*; **it's as ~ as it's long*** lo mismo da
[2] (= *general, extensive*) [*outline, objectives, view*] general; **in ~ terms** en términos generales; **the ~ outlines of sth** las líneas generales de algo; **to be in ~ agreement** estar de acuerdo en líneas generales
[3] (= *wide-ranging*) [*education, syllabus*] amplio; [*range, spectrum*] amplio, extenso; [*mind*] abierto; **a ~ spectrum of opinion** un amplio espectro de opiniones; **a film with ~ appeal** una película que atrae a una amplia gama de público; **it has ~er implications** tiene repercusiones en más aspectos; **in its ~est sense** en su sentido más amplio
[4] (= *unsubtle*) [*hint*] claro
[5] (= *strong*) [*accent*] cerrado; **(in) ~ Scots/Yorkshire** (con) un acento escocés/de Yorkshire cerrado
[6] (= *coarse*) **~ humour** humor *m* ordinario *or* basto; **a ~ joke** una broma ordinaria *or* grosera
[7] **in ~ daylight** en plena luz del día
Ⓑ N [1] (*US**) tipa* *f*, tía *f* (*Sp**)
[2] (= *widest part*) **the ~ of the back** la parte más ancha de la espalda; **the (Norfolk) Broads** (*Geog*) *área de estuarios en Norfolk*
Ⓒ CPD ► **broad bean** N (*esp Brit*) haba *f*

gruesa ► **broad jump** N (*US*) salto *m* de longitud

broadband ['brɔːdbænd] Ⓐ N banda *f* ancha Ⓑ CPD ► **broadband access** N acceso *m* de banda ancha

broad-based ['brɔːd'beɪst] ADJ = **broadly-based**

broad-brimmed ['brɔːd'brɪmd] ADJ [*hat*] de ala ancha

broadcast ['brɔːdkɑːst] (*vb: pt, pp* **broadcast**)
Ⓐ N (*Rad, TV*) emisión *f*, programa *m*
Ⓑ VT 1 (*TV*) [+ *match, event*] transmitir; (*Rad*) emitir, radiar
2 (*Agr*) sembrar a voleo
3 (*fig*) [+ *news, rumour*] divulgar, difundir
Ⓒ VI (*TV, Rad*) [*station*] transmitir, emitir; [*person*] hablar por la radio/televisión
Ⓓ ADV [*sow*] a voleo
Ⓔ CPD (*Agr*) [*seed*] sembrado a voleo ► **broadcast journalism** N periodismo *m* de radio y televisión ► **broadcast journalist** N periodista *mf* de radio y televisión ► **broadcast media** NPL medios *mpl* de radiodifusión y teledifusión ► **broadcast news** N noticias *fpl* de radio y televisión ► **broadcast satellite** N satélite *m* de retransmisiones

broadcaster ['brɔːdkɑːstəʳ] N (*Rad, TV*) locutor(a) *m/f*

broadcasting ['brɔːdkɑːstɪŋ] Ⓐ N (*TV*) teledifusión *f*, transmisión *f*; (*Rad*) radiodifusión *f*
Ⓑ CPD ► **broadcasting station** N emisora *f*

broadcloth ['brɔːdklɒθ] N velarte *m*

broaden ['brɔːdn] Ⓐ VT [+ *road*] ensanchar; [+ *horizons, outlook*] ampliar; **travel ~s the mind** los viajes son muy educativos
Ⓑ VI (*also* **~ out**) ensancharse

broadleaved ['brɔːd'liːvd] ADJ de hoja ancha

broadloom ['brɔːdluːm] ADJ **~ carpet** alfombra *f* sin costuras

broadly ['brɔːdlɪ] ADV 1 (= *by and large*) [*agree, accept*] en líneas generales; **~ similar** parecido en líneas generales; **~ speaking** en general, hablando en términos generales; **it is ~ true that ...** en líneas generales es verdad que ...
2 (= *widely*) [*smile, grin*] abiertamente, de oreja a oreja
3 (= *unsubtly*) [*hint*] claramente

broadly-based ['brɔːdlɪ,beɪst] ADJ que cuenta con una base amplia; **a ~ coalition** una coalición que representa gran diversidad de intereses

broad-minded ['brɔːd'maɪndɪd] ADJ tolerante, de miras amplias

broad-mindedness ['brɔːd'maɪndɪdnɪs] N amplitud *f* de criterio, tolerancia *f*

broadness ['brɔːdnɪs] N 1 (*in dimension*) anchura *f*, extensión *f*
2 [*of accent*] lo cerrado

broadsheet ['brɔːdʃiːt] N periódico *m* de gran formato; → TABLOIDS AND BROADSHEETS

broad-shouldered ['brɔːd'ʃəʊldəd] ADJ ancho de espaldas

broadside ['brɔːdsaɪd] Ⓐ N (*Naut*) (= *side*) costado *m*; (= *shots*) (*also fig*) andanada *f*; **to fire a ~** (*lit, fig*) soltar *or* disparar una andanada; **~ on** (*as adv*) de costado
Ⓑ ADV **to be moored ~ to sth** estar amarrado de costado a algo

broadsword ['brɔːd,sɔːd] N sable *m*

Broadway ['brɔːd,weɪ] Ⓐ N Broadway *m* (*calle de Nueva York famosa por sus teatros*); → OFF-BROADWAY
Ⓑ CPD [*musical, theatre*] de Broadway

broadways ['brɔːdweɪz] ADV, **broadwise** ['brɔːdwaɪz] ADV a lo ancho, por lo ancho; **~ on to the waves** de costado a las olas

brocade [brəʊ'keɪd] N brocado *m*

broccoli ['brɒkəlɪ] N brécol *m*, brócoli *m*

brochure ['brəʊʃjʊəʳ] N folleto *m*

brogue[1] [brəʊg] N (= *shoe*) zapato *m* grueso de cuero

brogue[2] [brəʊg] N (= *accent*) acento *m* regional (*sobre todo irlandés*)

broil [brɔɪl] VT (*US Culin*) asar a la parrilla

broiler ['brɔɪləʳ] Ⓐ N 1 (= *chicken*) pollo *m* para asar
2 (*US*) (= *grill*) parrilla *f*, grill *m*
Ⓑ CPD ► **broiler house** N batería *f* de engorde

broiling ['brɔɪlɪŋ] ADJ [*sun*] achicharrante; **it's ~ hot** hace un calor achicharrante

broke [brəʊk] Ⓐ PT *of* **break**
Ⓑ ADJ 1 (*) (*incorrect usage*) (= *broken*) estropeado; ✦*IDIOM* **if it ain't ~, don't fix it*** no hay que complicar las cosas *or* complicarse la vida sin necesidad
2 (*) (= *penniless*) pelado*; **I'm ~** estoy pelado*, estoy sin un duro (*Sp**), estoy sin un peso (*LAm**); **to go ~** arruinarse; ✦*IDIOM* **to go for ~** jugarse el todo por el todo; *see also* **flat B1**

broken ['brəʊkən] Ⓐ PP *of* **break**
Ⓑ ADJ 1 [*object*] roto, quebrado (*LAm*); [*bone*] roto, fracturado; [*skin*] cortado; **"do not use on ~ skin"** "no aplicar si hay cortes o heridas en la piel"; **he sounds like a ~ record** parece un disco rallado
2 (= *not working*) [*machine*] estropeado, averiado
3 (= *uneven*) [*road surface*] accidentado
4 (= *ruined*) [*health, spirit*] quebrantado; [*heart*] roto, destrozado; **to die of a ~ heart** morir de pena; **~ in health** deshecho, muy decaído; **a ~ man** un hombre deshecho; **a ~ reed** (*fig*) una persona quemada
5 (= *interrupted*) [*line*] quebrado; [*voice*] entrecortado; [*sleep*] interrumpido; [*cloud*] fragmentario; **he speaks ~ English** chapurrea el inglés; **she had a ~ night** durmió mal, despertándose a cada momento
6 (= *failed*) [*marriage*] deshecho; **a ~ home** una familia dividida
7 [*promise*] roto, quebrantado

broken-down ['brəʊkən'daʊn] ADJ [*machine, car*] averiado, estropeado, descompuesto (*Mex*); [*house*] destartalado, desvencijado

broken-hearted ['brəʊkən'hɑːtɪd] ADJ con el corazón destrozado *or* partido

brokenly ['brəʊkənlɪ] ADV [*say etc*] en tono angustiado, con palabras entrecortadas

broker ['brəʊkəʳ] Ⓐ N (*Comm*) agente *mf*; (= *stockbroker*) corredor(a) *m/f* de bolsa, bolsista *mf*
Ⓑ VT [+ *deal, agreement*] negociar

brokerage ['brəʊkərɪdʒ] N corretaje *m*

broking ['brəʊkɪŋ] N = **brokerage**

brolly* ['brɒlɪ] N (*Brit*) paraguas *m inv*

bromide ['brəʊmaɪd] N 1 (*Chem, Typ*) bromuro *m*
2 (*fig*) (= *platitude*) perogrullada *f*

bromine ['brəʊmiːn] N bromo *m*

bronchial ['brɒŋkɪəl] Ⓐ ADJ bronquial
Ⓑ CPD ► **bronchial asthma** N asma *f* bronquial ► **bronchial tubes** NPL bronquios *mpl*

bronchitic [brɒŋ'kɪtɪk] ADJ bronquítico

bronchitis [brɒŋ'kaɪtɪs] N bronquitis *f*

bronchopneumonia [,brɒŋkəʊnjuː'məʊnɪə] N bronconeumonía *f*

broncho-pulmonary ['brɒŋkəʊ'pʌlmənərɪ] ADJ broncopulmonar

bronchus ['brɒŋkəs] N (*pl* **bronchi** ['brɒŋkaɪ]) bronquio *m*

bronco ['brɒŋkəʊ] N (*US*) potro *m* cerril

broncobuster* ['brɒŋkəʊ,bʌstəʳ] N (*US*) domador *m* de potros cerriles

brontosaurus [,brɒntə'sɔːrəs] N (*pl* **brontosauruses** *or* **brontosauri** [,brɒntə'sɔːraɪ]) brontosaurio *m*

Bronx cheer* [,brɒŋks'tʃɪəʳ] N (*US*) pedorreta‡ *f*

bronze [brɒnz] Ⓐ N 1 (= *metal, sculpture*) bronce *m*
2 [*of skin*] bronceado *m*
Ⓑ VI [*person*] broncearse
Ⓒ VT [+ *skin*] broncear
Ⓓ ADJ (= *made of bronze*) de bronce; [*colour*] color de bronce
Ⓔ CPD ► **the Bronze Age** N la Edad de Bronce ► **bronze medal** N medalla *f* de bronce ► **bronze medallist** N medallero/a *m/f* de bronce

bronzed [brɒnzd] ADJ [*person*] bronceado

bronzing ['brɒnzɪŋ] ADJ [*powder, gel*] bronceador

brooch [brəʊtʃ] N prendedor *m*, broche *m*; (*ancient*) fíbula *f*

brood [bruːd] Ⓐ N (*gen*) cría *f*, camada *f*; [*of chicks*] nidada *f*; [*of insects etc*] generación *f*; (*hum*) [*of children*] prole *f*
Ⓑ VI 1 [*bird*] empollar
2 (*fig*) [*person*] ponerse melancólico; **to ~ on** *or* **over** dar vueltas a; **you mustn't ~ over it** no debes darle tantas vueltas; **disaster ~ed over the town** se cernía el desastre sobre la ciudad
Ⓒ CPD ► **brood mare** N yegua *f* de cría

brooding ['bruːdɪŋ] ADJ [*evil, presence etc*] siniestro, amenazador

broodings ['bruːdɪŋs] NPL meditaciones *fpl*

broody ['bruːdɪ] ADJ 1 [*hen*] clueca; (*) [*woman*] con ganas de tener hijos
2 (= *pensive*) triste, melancólico

brook[1] [brʊk] N (= *stream*) arroyo *m*

brook[2] [brʊk] VT (*frm*) (= *tolerate*) tolerar, admitir; **he ~s no opposition** no admite oposición

brooklet ['brʊklɪt] N arroyuelo *m*

broom [bruːm, brʊm] Ⓐ N 1 (= *brush*) escoba *f*; **new ~** (*fig*) escoba *f* nueva; ✦*PROV* **a new ~ sweeps clean** escoba nueva barre bien
2 (*Bot*) retama *f*, hiniesta *f*
Ⓑ CPD ► **broom closet** (*US*), **broom cupboard** (*Brit*) N armario *m* de los artículos de limpieza

broomstick ['brʊmstɪk] N palo *m* de escoba

Bros. ABBR (= **Brothers**) Hnos

broth [brɒθ] N caldo *m*

brothel ['brɒθl] N burdel *m*, prostíbulo *m*

brother ['brʌðəʳ] Ⓐ N (*gen, Rel*) hermano *m*; (*Trade Union etc*) compañero *m*; **hey, ~!*** ¡oye, colega!*, ¡oye, tío! (*Sp**); **oh, ~!*** ¡vaya hombre!
Ⓑ CPD ► **brother workers** NPL colegas *mpl*

brotherhood ['brʌðəhʊd] N 1 fraternidad *f*; **the ~ of man** la fraternidad humana
2 (= *group*) hermandad *f*

brother-in-arms ['brʌðəɪn'ɑːmz] N (*pl* **brothers-in-arms**) compañero *m* de armas

brother-in-law ['brʌðərɪnlɔː] N (*pl* **brothers-in-law**) cuñado *m*, hermano *m* político

brotherly ['brʌðəlɪ] ADJ fraterno, fraternal

brougham [bruːm] N break *m*

brought [brɔːt] PT, PP *of* **bring**

brouhaha* ['bruːhɑːhɑː] N barullo *m*

brow [braʊ] N 1 (= *forehead*) frente *f*; (*also* **eyebrow**) ceja *f*; *see also* **knit**
2 [*of hill*] cumbre *f*, cima *f*; [*of cliff*] borde *m*

browbeat ['braʊbi:t] (*pt* **browbeat**; *pp* **browbeaten**) VT intimidar, convencer con amenazas; **to ~ sb into doing sth** intimidar a algn para que haga algo

brown [braʊn] Ⓐ ADJ (*compar* **browner**; *superl* **brownest**) 1 (*gen*) marrón, color café (*LAm*); [*hair*] castaño; [*leather*] marrón
2 (= *tanned*) moreno, bronceado; [*skin*] moreno; **to go ~** ponerse moreno, broncearse; ✦*IDIOM* **as ~ as a berry** muy moreno, bronceadísimo
Ⓑ N marrón *m*, color *m* café (*LAm*); [*of eyes, hair*] castaño *m*
Ⓒ VT 1 [*sun*] [+ *person*] broncear, poner moreno
2 (*Culin*) dorar
Ⓓ VI 1 [*leaves etc*] volverse de color marrón
2 [*skin*] ponerse moreno, broncearse
3 (*Culin*) dorarse
Ⓔ CPD ► **brown ale** N cerveza *f* oscura *or* negra ► **brown bear** N oso *m* pardo ► **brown belt** N (*in judo, karate*) cinturón *m* marrón ► **brown bread** N pan *m* negro, pan *m* moreno (*Sp*) ► **brown egg** N huevo *m* moreno ► **brown goods** NPL (productos *mpl* de) línea *f* marrón, (productos *mpl* de) gama *f* marrón ► **brown owl** N (*Orn*) autillo *m* ► **brown paper** N papel *m* de estraza ► **brown rice** N arroz *m* integral ► **brown sauce** N (*Brit*) *salsa de condimento, con sabor agridulce* ► **brown study** N ✦*IDIOM* **to be in a ~ study**† estar absorto en sus pensamientos, estar en Babia* ► **brown sugar** N azúcar *m* moreno

►**brown off*** VT + ADV (*Brit*) fastidiar

browned-off* [,braʊnd'ɒf] ADJ (*Brit*) **I'm ~** estoy harto *or* hasta las narices* (**with** de)

brownfield ['braʊnfi:ld] [*site, land*] previamente urbanizado

brownie ['braʊnɪ] N 1 (= *fairy*) duende *m*
2 (*also* **Brownie Guide**) niña *f* exploradora; ✦*IDIOM* **to earn** *or* **win Brownie points** (*hum*) apuntarse tantos a favor, hacer méritos
3 (*US*) (= *cookie*) pastelillo *m* de chocolate y nueces

browning ['braʊnɪŋ] N (*Brit Culin*) aditamento *m* colorante

brownish ['braʊnɪʃ] ADJ pardusco, que tira a moreno

brown-nose‡ ['braʊn,nəʊz] (*US*) Ⓐ N lameculos** *mf inv*
Ⓑ VT lamer el culo a**

Brownshirt ['braʊnʃɜ:t] N (*Hist*) *soldado de las SA en la Alemania nazi*

brownstone ['braʊnstəʊn] N (*US*) (casa *f* construida con) piedra *f* caliza de color rojizo

browse [braʊz] Ⓐ VI 1 (*in shop*) echar una ojeada, curiosear; **to spend an hour browsing in a bookshop** pasar una hora hojeando los libros en una librería
2 [*animal*] pacer
3 (*Internet*) curiosear
Ⓑ VT 1 (*also* **~ through**) [+ *book*] hojear; [+ *clothes*] mirar, echar un vistazo a
2 [*animal*] [+ *grass*] pacer; [+ *trees*] ramonear
Ⓒ N **to have a ~ (around)** echar una ojeada *or* un vistazo

►**browse on** VI + PREP [*animal*] pacer

browser ['braʊzəʳ] N 1 (*in shop*) *persona que entra a una tienda a curiosear*
2 (*Internet*) navegador *m*

brucellosis [,bru:sə'ləʊsɪs] N brucelosis *f*

Bruges [bru:ʒ] N Brujas *f*

bruise [bru:z] Ⓐ N (*on person*) cardenal *m*, moretón *m* (*esp LAm*); (*on fruit*) maca *f*, magulladura *f*
Ⓑ VT 1 [+ *leg etc*] magullar, amoratar (*esp LAm*); [+ *fruit*] magullar, dañar
2 (*fig*) [+ *feelings*] herir
Ⓒ VI **I ~ easily** me salen cardenales *or* moretones con facilidad

bruiser* ['bru:zəʳ] N gorila* *m*

bruising ['bru:zɪŋ] ADJ [*experience*] doloroso, penoso; [*match*] durísimo, violento

Brum* [brʌm] N (*Brit*) = **Birmingham**

Brummie* ['brʌmɪ] N (*Brit*) nativo/a *m/f or* habitante *mf* de Birmingham

brunch [brʌntʃ] N desayuno-almuerzo *m*

brunette [bru:'net] Ⓐ N morena *f*, morocha *f* (*LAm*), prieta *f* (*Mex*)
Ⓑ ADJ moreno

brunt [brʌnt] N **the ~ of the attack** lo más fuerte del ataque; **the ~ of the work** la mayor parte del trabajo; **to bear the ~ of sth** aguantar lo más recio *or* duro de algo

brush [brʌʃ] Ⓐ N 1 (*gen*) cepillo *m*; (= *sweeping brush*) cepillo *m*, escobilla *f*; (= *scrubbing brush*) cepillo *m* de cerda; (= *shaving brush, decorator's*) brocha *f*; (= *paint brush*) (*artist's*) pincel *m*; (*Elec*) (= *contact*) escobilla *f*; **shoe ~** cepillo *m* para zapatos
2 (= *act of brushing*) cepillado *m*; **give your coat a ~** cepíllate el abrigo; **let's give it a ~** vamos a pasar el cepillo
3 (= *tail*) [*of fox*] rabo *m*, hopo *m*
4 (= *skirmish*) roce *m*
5 (= *light touch*) toque *m*
6 (= *undergrowth*) maleza *f*, broza *f*
Ⓑ VT 1 (= *clean*) [+ *floor*] cepillar; [+ *clothes, hair*] cepillar; **to ~ one's shoes** limpiarse los zapatos; **to ~ one's teeth** lavarse los dientes, cepillarse los dientes
2 (= *touch lightly*) rozar

►**brush against** VI + PREP rozar (al pasar)

►**brush aside** VT + ADV (*fig*) no hacer caso de, dejar a un lado

►**brush away** VT + ADV (*gen*) quitar (con cepillo *or* la mano *etc*)

►**brush down** VT + ADV cepillar, limpiar; [+ *horse*] almohazar

►**brush off** Ⓐ VT + ADV 1 [+ *mud*] quitar (con cepillo *or* la mano etc)
2 (*fig*) (= *dismiss*) no hacer caso de
Ⓑ VI + ADV **the mud ~es off easily** el barro sale *or* se quita fácilmente

►**brush past** Ⓐ VIT + ADV rozar al pasar
Ⓑ VI + ADV pasar muy cerca

►**brush up** VT + ADV 1 [+ *crumbs*] recoger
2 (= *improve, revise*) (*also* **~ up on**) repasar, refrescar

brushed [brʌʃt] ADJ [*nylon, denim etc*] afelpado

brush-off* ['brʌʃɒf] N **to give sb the ~** mandar a algn a paseo*, zafarse de algn

brushstroke ['brʌʃstrəʊk] N pincelada *f*; **in broad ~s** (*fig*) a grandes rasgos

brush-up ['brʌʃʌp] N **to have a wash and ~** lavarse y arreglarse

brushwood ['brʌʃwʊd] N maleza *f*, monte *m* bajo; (= *faggots*) broza *f*, leña *f* menuda

brushwork ['brʌʃwɜ:k] N pincelada *f*, técnica *f* del pincel; **Turner's ~** la pincelada de Turner, la técnica del pincel de Turner

brusque [bru:sk] ADJ [*comment, manner etc*] brusco, áspero; [*person*] brusco; **he was very ~ with me** me trató con poca cortesía *or* con aspereza

brusquely ['bru:sklɪ] ADV bruscamente, con brusquedad, abruptamente

brusqueness ['bru:sknɪs] N brusquedad *f*, aspereza *f*

Brussels ['brʌslz] Ⓐ N Bruselas *f*
Ⓑ CPD ► **Brussels sprout** N col *f* de Bruselas

brutal ['bru:tl] ADJ 1 (= *savage*) [*person, murder, attack*] brutal; [*tone, remark*] cruel; **the government's ~ treatment of political prisoners** la brutalidad *or* la crueldad con la que el gobierno trata a los prisioneros políticos
2 (= *stark*) [*honesty, frankness*] descarnada; [*reality*] crudo; [*change*] brutal
3 (= *harsh*) [*weather, climate*] crudo, riguroso

brutality [bru:'tælɪtɪ] N [*of person*] brutalidad *f*; [*of murder*] salvajismo *m*, crueldad *f*; *see also* **police B**

brutalize ['bru:təlaɪz] VT brutalizar

brutally ['bru:təlɪ] ADV 1 (= *savagely*) [*attack, murder, suppress*] de manera brutal, brutalmente
2 (= *starkly*) [*say, reply, expose*] crudamente, descarnadamente; **let me be ~ honest with you** voy a serte tremendamente sincero; **the talks had been ~ frank** las conversaciones habían sido francas y crudas; **a ~ competitive world** un mundo despiadadamente competitivo; **the choice is ~ clear** la elección es de una claridad cruel *or* despiadada

brute [bru:t] Ⓐ N (= *animal*) bestia *f*; (= *person*) bruto/a *m/f*, bestia *mf*; **you ~!** ¡bestia!, ¡animal!*; **it's a ~ of a problem*** es un problema de los más feos
Ⓑ ADJ [*force, strength*] bruto; [*fact*] crudo; [*emotion*] tosco

brutish ['bru:tɪʃ] ADJ bruto

Brutus ['bru:təs] N Bruto

Brylcreem® ['brɪlkri:m] Ⓐ N gomina *f*, fijador *m* (*de pelo*)
Ⓑ VT engominar, echarse gomina en

BS N ABBR 1 (= **British Standard**) *norma de calidad*
2 (*US Univ*) = **Bachelor of Science**; → DEGREE
3 (*esp US*‡) = **bullshit**

bs N ABBR 1 (*Comm*) = **bill of sale**
2 (*Comm, Fin*) = **balance sheet**

BSA N ABBR (*US*) = **Boy Scouts of America**

BSB N ABBR (= **British Sky Broadcasting**) *emisora de televisión por satélite*

BSC N ABBR = **Broadcasting Standards Council**

BSc N ABBR (*Univ*) = **Bachelor of Science**; → DEGREE

BSE N ABBR = **bovine spongiform encephalopathy**

BSI N ABBR (*Brit*) (= **British Standards Institution**) *organismo que fija niveles de calidad de los productos*

BST N ABBR (*Brit*) = **British Summer Time**

BT N ABBR (= **British Telecom**) ≈ Telefónica *f* (*Sp*)

Bt ABBR = **Baronet**

BTA N ABBR = **British Tourist Authority**

BTEC ['bi:tek] N ABBR (*Brit*) = **Business and Technology Education Council** 1 (= *organization*) *institución responsable de los estudios de ciencia y tecnología empresarial*
2 (= *diploma*) *estudios de ciencia y tecnología empresarial*

bt fwd ABBR = **brought forward**

BTU, **btu** N ABBR = **British Thermal Unit**

BTW* ABBR (= **by the way**) por cierto

bubble ['bʌbl] Ⓐ N (*in liquid*) burbuja *f*; (*in paint*) ampolla *f*; (= *soap bubble*) pompa *f*; (*in cartoon*) bocadillo *m*, globo *m*; **to blow ~s** (*with soap*) hacer pompas; (*with bubble gum*) hacer globos; **the ~ burst** (*fig*) se deshizo la burbuja
Ⓑ VI [*champagne, bath water*] burbujear; (= *bubble forth*) borbotar

Ⓒ CPD ► **bubble and squeak** N (*Brit Culin*) *carne picada frita con patatas y col* ► **bubble bath** N gel *m* de baño ► **bubble car** N coche-cabina *m*, huevo *m* ► **bubble gum** N chicle *m* (de globo) ► **bubble memory** N memoria *f* de burbuja ► **bubble pack** N envasado *m* en lámina ► **bubble wrap** N envoltorio *m* de plástico con burbujas

►**bubble over** VI + ADV [*boiling liquid*] derramarse; (*fig*) (*with happiness etc*) rebosar (**with** de)

►**bubble up** VI + ADV [*liquid*] burbujear, borbotear

bubblejet printer [ˈbʌbldʒetˈprɪntəʳ] N impresora *f* de inyección de burbujas

bubbly [ˈbʌblɪ] Ⓐ ADJ (*compar* **bubblier**; *superl* **bubbliest**) (*lit*) burbujeante, con burbujas; (*) (*fig*) [*person*] lleno de vida, dicharrachero
Ⓑ N (*) (= *champagne*) champaña *f*

bubonic plague [bjuːˌbɒnɪkˈpleɪg] N peste *f* bubónica

buccaneer [ˌbʌkəˈnɪəʳ] Ⓐ N (*Hist*) bucanero *m*; (*fig*) emprendedor(a) *m/f*
Ⓑ VI piratear

buccaneering [ˌbʌkəˈnɪərɪŋ] ADJ (*fig*) aventurero

Bucharest [ˌbuːkəˈrest] N Bucarest *m*

buck [bʌk] Ⓐ N [1] (= *male*) [*of deer*] ciervo *m* (macho); [*of rabbit*] conejo *m* (macho); (= *antelope*) antílope *m*
[2] (*US**) (= *dollar*) dólar *m*; **to make a ~** hacer dinero; **to make a fast** *or* **quick ~** hacer dinero fácil
[3] ✦***IDIOMS* to pass the ~*** escurrir el bulto*, pasar la pelota*; **to pass the ~ to sb** cargar el muerto a algn*, pasar la pelota a algn*; **the ~ stops here** yo soy el responsable/nosotros somos los responsables
[4] (*in gym*) potro *m*
[5] (*US**) **young ~** joven *m*
[6] (†) (= *dandy*) galán *m*, dandy *m*
Ⓑ ADJ (= *male*) macho
Ⓒ ADV **~ naked** (*US**) en cueros*
Ⓓ VI [1] [*horse*] corcovear
[2] (*US*) (= *move violently*) **she ~ed against her captor** se volvió con fuerza contra su captor; **the revolver ~ed violently upwards** el revólver dio una sacudida hacia arriba; **to ~ against** (*fig*) [+ *rules, authority*] rebelarse contra
[3] **to ~ for sth** (*US**) buscar algo
Ⓔ VT [1] (*esp US*) [+ *rider*] derribar, desarzonar
[2] **to ~ the market** (*Fin*) ir en contra del mercado; **to ~ the system** rebelarse contra el sistema; **to ~ the trend** ir en contra de la tendencia
Ⓕ CPD ► **buck nigger** N (*Hist*) negrazo *m* ► **buck private** N (*US Mil*) soldado *mf* raso ► **buck rabbit** N conejo *m* (macho) ► **buck sergeant** N (*US Mil*) sargento *mf* chusquero ► **buck's fizz** N *sangría hecha con champán u otro vino espumoso y zumo de naranja* ► **buck teeth** NPL dientes *mpl* salientes

►**buck up*** Ⓐ VI + ADV [1] (= *cheer up*) animarse, levantar el ánimo; **~ up!** ¡ánimo!
[2] (= *hurry up*) espabilarse, apurarse (*LAm*); **~ up!** ¡espabílate!, ¡date prisa!
Ⓑ VT + ADV [1] (= *cheer up*) animar, dar ánimos a; **we were very ~ed up by what he said** lo que dijo nos levantó mucho el ánimo
[2] (= *hurry up*) dar prisa a
[3] **you'll have to ~ your ideas up** tendrás que moverte, tendrás que ponerte a trabajar en serio

bucket [ˈbʌkɪt] Ⓐ N cubo *m*, balde *m* (*LAm*); (*child's*) cubito *m*; [*of waterwheel etc*] cangilón *m*; **a ~ of water** un cubo *or* (*LAm*) un balde de agua; ✦***IDIOMS* to rain ~s*** llover a cántaros; **to weep ~s*** llorar a mares; *see also* **kick B1**
Ⓑ VI [1] (*) (= *hurtle*) ir a toda velocidad, ir a toda pastilla (*Sp**)
[2] **the rain is ~ing down*** ◊ **it's ~ing (down)*** está lloviendo a cántaros
Ⓒ CPD ► **bucket seat** N asiento *m* envolvente ► **bucket shop** N (*Fin*) agencia *f* de bolsa fraudulenta; (*Brit*) (*for air tickets*) agencia *f* de viajes que vende barato

bucketful [ˈbʌkɪtfʊl] N cubo *m* (lleno), balde *m* (lleno) (*LAm*); **by the ~** a cubos; (*fig*) a montones, en grandes cantidades

buckle [ˈbʌkl] Ⓐ N [*of shoe, belt*] hebilla *f*
Ⓑ VT [1] [+ *shoe, belt*] abrochar
[2] (= *warp*) [+ *wheel, girder*] combar, torcer
[3] [+ *knees*] doblar
Ⓒ VI [*wheel, girder*] combarse, torcerse; [*knees*] doblarse

►**buckle down** VI + ADV ponerse a trabajar; **to ~ down to a job** dedicarse en serio a una tarea

►**buckle in** VT + ADV **to ~ a baby in** abrochar el cinturón de un niño

►**buckle on** VT + ADV [+ *armour, sword*] ceñirse

►**buckle to** VI + ADV ponerse a trabajar

►**buckle up** VI + ADV (*US*) ponerse el cinturón de seguridad

buckra [ˈbʌkrə] N (*US pej*) blanco *m*

buckram [ˈbʌkrəm] N bucarán *m*

Bucks [bʌks] N ABBR (*Brit*) = **Buckinghamshire**

bucksaw [ˈbʌksɔː] N sierra *f* de arco

buckshee‡ [bʌkˈʃiː] (*Brit*) Ⓐ ADJ gratuito
Ⓑ ADV gratis

buckshot [ˈbʌkʃɒt] N perdigón *m*, posta *f*

buckskin [ˈbʌkskɪn] N (cuero *m* de) ante *m*

buckthorn [ˈbʌkθɔːn] N espino *m* cerval

buck-toothed [ˈbʌkˈtuːθt] ADJ de dientes salientes, dientudo (*LAm**)

buckwheat [ˈbʌkwiːt] N alforfón *m*, trigo *m* sarraceno

bucolic [bjuːˈkɒlɪk] Ⓐ ADJ bucólico
Ⓑ N **the Bucolics** las Bucólicas

bud¹ [bʌd] Ⓐ N [*of flower*] capullo *m*; (*on tree, plant*) brote *m*, yema *f*; **in ~** [*tree*] en brote; *see also* **nip¹ B**
Ⓑ VI [*flower, tree*] brotar, echar brotes
Ⓒ VT (*Hort*) injertar de escudete

bud²* [bʌd] N (*US*) = **buddy**

Budapest [ˌbjuːdəˈpest] N Budapest *m*

Buddha [ˈbʊdə] N Buda *m*

Buddhism [ˈbʊdɪzəm] N budismo *m*

Buddhist [ˈbʊdɪst] Ⓐ ADJ budista
Ⓑ N budista *mf*

budding [ˈbʌdɪŋ] ADJ (*fig*) [*talent*] en ciernes

buddleia [ˈbʌdlɪə] N budleia *f*

buddy [ˈbʌdɪ] Ⓐ N (*esp US*) amigo *m*, amigote* *m*, compadre *m* (*LAm*), cuate *m* (*Mex**), pata *m* (*Peru**); (*in direct address*) hermano* *m*, macho *m* (*Sp**)
Ⓑ CPD ► **buddy movie** N *película en la que los personajes centrales son un par de amigotes* ► **buddy system*** N **they use the ~ system** emplean el amiguismo, se ayudan mutuamente

budge [bʌdʒ] Ⓐ VT (= *move*) mover, hacer que se mueva; **I couldn't ~ him an inch** (*fig*) no lo pude convencer
Ⓑ VI (= *move*) moverse; (*fig*) ceder, rendirse; **he didn't dare to ~** no se atrevía a moverse; **he won't ~ an inch** (*fig*) no cede lo más mínimo

►**budge up** VI + ADV moverse un poco, correrse a un lado

budgerigar [ˈbʌdʒərɪgɑːʳ] N periquito *m*

budget [ˈbʌdʒɪt] Ⓐ N presupuesto *m*; **the Budget** (*Brit Pol*) los Presupuestos Generales del Estado; **my ~ won't stretch** *or* **run to steak** mi presupuesto no me permite comprar bistec
Ⓑ VI planear el presupuesto
Ⓒ VT [+ *sum*] asignar; **the movie is only ~ed at $10m** a la película se le ha asignado un presupuesto de sólo 10 millones de dólares; **~ed costs** costos *mpl* presupuestados
Ⓓ CPD (*Econ*) presupuestario; (= *cut-price*) [*holiday, prices*] económico ► **budget account** N cuenta *f* presupuestaria ► **budget day** N día *m* de la presentación de los Presupuestos Generales del Estado ► **budget deficit** N déficit *m* presupuestario ► **budget plan** N plan *m* presupuestario ► **budget speech** N discurso *m* en el que se presentan los Presupuestos Generales del Estado

►**budget for** VI + PREP hacer un presupuesto para; **we hadn't ~ed for the price increase** no habíamos contado con el aumento de precios

BUDGET

*Cuando el Ministro de Economía y Hacienda británico (***Chancellor of the Exchequer***) presenta los presupuestos generales del Estado al Parlamento cada noviembre, en el país se refieren a ellos simplemente como* **the Budget**, *el cual suele incluir cambios en los impuestos y en las prestaciones sociales. Su discurso se televisa en su totalidad, para que los ciudadanos se enteren por sí mismos de cómo afectarán los cambios a su declaración de la renta, así como al precio de artículos tales como la gasolina, el alcohol o el tabaco.*

budgetary [ˈbʌdʒɪtrɪ] ADJ [*control, deficit, policy, year*] presupuestario

budgeting [ˈbʌdʒɪtɪŋ] N elaboración *f* de un presupuesto, presupuesto *m*; **with careful ~** con buena administración

budgie* [ˈbʌdʒɪ] N = **budgerigar**

Buenos Aires [ˌbwenəsˈaɪərɪz] Ⓐ N Buenos Aires *msing*
Ⓑ ADJ bonaerense, porteño (*Arg**)

buff¹ [bʌf] Ⓐ ADJ [*colour*] de color de ante
Ⓑ N piel *f* de ante; **in the ~*** en cueros*
Ⓒ VT (*also* **~ up**) lustrar, pulir

buff²* [bʌf] N aficionado/a *m/f*, entusiasta *mf*; **film ~** cinéfilo/a *m/f*

buffalo [ˈbʌfələʊ] N (*pl* **buffalo** *or* **buffaloes**) [1] búfalo *m*
[2] (*esp US*) (= *bison*) bisonte *m*

buffer¹ [ˈbʌfəʳ] Ⓐ N (*Brit Rail*) (*on carriage*) tope *m*; (*in station*) parachoques *m inv*, amortiguador *m* (de choques); (*US Aut*) parachoques *m inv*; (*Comput*) memoria *f* intermedia; ✦***IDIOM* the plan suddenly hit the ~s** el plan frenó de golpe
Ⓑ VT (*fig*) (= *protect*) proteger
Ⓒ CPD ► **buffer state** N estado *m* tapón ► **buffer zone** N zona *f* parachoques

buffer²* [ˈbʌfəʳ] N **old ~** (*Brit*) mastuerzo *m*, carca* *m*

buffering [ˈbʌfərɪŋ] N (*Comput*) almacenamiento *m* en memoria intermedia

buffet¹ [ˈbʌfɪt] Ⓐ N (= *blow*) golpe *m*
Ⓑ VT (= *hit*) abofetear; [*sea, wind*] zarandear

buffet² [ˈbʊfeɪ] Ⓐ N (*for refreshments*) cantina *f*, cafetería *f*; (= *meal*) buffet *m* (libre), comida *f*

buffet
Ⓑ CPD ► **buffet car** N (*Brit Rail*) coche-restaurante *m* ► **buffet lunch** N almuerzo *m* buffet ► **buffet meal** N buffet *m* (libre), comida *f* buffet ► **buffet supper** N cena *f* buffet

buffeting [ˈbʌfɪtɪŋ] N [*of sea etc*] el golpear; **to get a ~ from** sufrir los golpes de

buffoon [bəˈfuːn] N bufón *m*, payaso *m*

buffoonery [bəˈfuːnərɪ] N bufonadas *fpl*

bug [bʌg] Ⓐ N [1] (*Zool*) chinche *mf*; (*esp US**) (= *any insect*) bicho *m*
[2] (*) (= *germ*) microbio *m*; (*fig*) (= *obsession*) gusanillo *m*; **flu ~** virus *m inv* de la gripe; **there's a ~ going around** hay un virus que corre por ahí; **I've got the travel ~** me ha picado el gusanillo de los viajes
[3] (*) (= *hidden microphone*) micrófono *m* oculto
[4] (*esp US**) (= *defect, snag*) traba *f*, pega *f*
[5] (*Comput*) virus *m inv*
[6] (*US**) (= *small car*) coche *m* compacto
[7] (*US**) (= *enthusiast*) aficionado/a *m/f*, entusiasta *mf*
Ⓑ VT [1] (*) [+ *telephone*] intervenir, pinchar*; [+ *room*] poner un micrófono oculto en; [+ *person*] escuchar clandestinamente a, pinchar el teléfono de*; **my phone is ~ged** mi teléfono está pinchado*; **do you think this room is ~ged?** ¿crees que en esta habitación hay un micro oculto?
[2] (*) (= *annoy*) fastidiar, molestar; **don't ~ me!** ¡deja de molestar(me) *or* fastidiar!; **what's ~ging you?** ¿qué mosca te ha picado?*
Ⓒ CPD ► **bug hunter*** N entomólogo/a *m/f*

►**bug out‡** VI + ADV (*US*) largarse*

bugaboo [ˈbʌgəbuː] N (*US*) espantajo *m*, coco *m*

bugbear [ˈbʌgbeəʳ] N pesadilla *f*

bug-eyed* [ˌbʌgˈaɪd] ADJ **to be ~** mirar con los ojos saltones

bug-free* [ˈbʌgˈfriː] ADJ (*Comput*) libre de virus, sin virus

bugger [ˈbʌgəʳ] Ⓐ N [1] (*Jur*) sodomita *mf*
[2] (*Brit***) (= *person*) hijo/a *m/f* de puta‡, gilipollas *mf* (*Sp*‡); **he's a lucky ~!** ¡qué suerte tiene el cabrón!‡; **that silly ~** ese cabrón‡, ese gilipollas (*Sp*‡); **some poor ~** algún desgraciado*; **I don't give a ~!** ¡me importa un carajo!‡; **don't play silly ~s!** ¡deja de hacer pendejadas!‡, ¡no des el coñazo! (*Sp*‡)
[3] (*Brit***) (= *nuisance, annoyance*) **it's a ~** es jodidísimo**
Ⓑ EXCL (*Brit*) **~ (it** *or* **me)!**** ¡mierda!**
Ⓒ VT [1] (*Jur*) cometer sodomía con
[2] (*Brit***) **(well) I'll be ~ed!** ¡no me jodas!**; **lawyers be ~ed!** ¡que se jodan los abogados!**; **I'll be ~ed if I will** paso de hacerlo ¡qué coño!**

►**bugger about****, **bugger around**** (*Brit*)
Ⓐ VT + ADV **to ~ sb about** joder a algn**
Ⓑ VI + ADV hacer pendejadas‡, hacer el gilipollas (*Sp*‡)

►**bugger off**** (*Brit*) VI + ADV largarse*; **~ off!** ¡vete a la mierda!**, ¡vete a tomar por culo! (*Sp***), ¡chinga tu madre! (*Mex***)

►**bugger up**** (*Brit*) VT + ADV **to ~ sth up** joder algo**

bugger-all** [ˈbʌgəˌɔːl] N (*Brit*) nada

buggery [ˈbʌgərɪ] N sodomía *f*

bugging [ˈbʌgɪŋ] Ⓐ N (*Telec*) intervención *f*
Ⓑ CPD ► **bugging device** N micrófono *m* oculto

buggy [ˈbʌgɪ] N [1] (*also* **baby ~**) (*Brit*) (= *push-chair*) sillita *f* de paseo; (*US*) (= *pram*) cochecito *m* (de niño)
[2] (*horse-drawn*) calesa *f*
[3] (*Golf*) cochecito *m*; *see also* **beach, moon**

bughouse‡ [ˈbʌghaʊs] N (*pl* **bughouses** [ˈbʌghaʊzɪz]) (*US*) (= *asylum*) casa *f* de locos, manicomio *m*

bugle [ˈbjuːgl] N corneta *f*, clarín *m*

bugler [ˈbjuːgləʳ] N corneta *mf*

bug-ridden [ˈbʌgˌrɪdn] ADJ **this house is ~** esta casa está llena de bichos

build [bɪld] (*vb: pt, pp* **built**) Ⓐ N (= *physique*) figura *f*, tipo *m*; **of powerful ~** fornido
Ⓑ VT [1] [+ *house*] construir, hacer; [+ *ship*] construir; [+ *nest*] hacer; [+ *fire*] preparar; **to ~ a mirror into a wall** empotrar un espejo en la pared; **a house built into the hillside** una casa construida en la ladera; **this car wasn't built for speed** este coche no está hecho para correr; **built to last** hecho para durar; *see also* **castle**
[2] (*fig*) [+ *empire, organization*] levantar; [+ *relationship*] establecer; [+ *trust, confidence*] cimentar; [+ *self-confidence*] desarrollar; [+ *words, sequence*] formar
Ⓒ VI [1] (*Constr*) edificar, construir
[2] (= *increase*) [*pressure, sound, speed*] aumentar; [*excitement*] crecer

►**build in** VT + ADV [1] [+ *cupboard*] empotrar; (*Mech*) incorporar
[2] [+ *safeguards*] incluir, incorporar

►**build on** Ⓐ VT + ADV (= *add*) añadir; **to ~ a garage on to a house** añadir un garaje a una casa; **the garage is built on to the house** la casa tiene un garaje anexo
Ⓑ VI + PREP (*fig*) **now we have a base to ~ on** ahora tenemos una base sobre la que podemos construir

►**build up** Ⓐ VT + ADV [1] [+ *area, town etc*] urbanizar; **the area was built up years ago** la zona fue urbanizada hace años
[2] (= *establish*) [+ *business, firm*] levantar; [+ *reputation*] labrarse; [+ *impression*] crear; **to ~ up a lead** tomar la delantera; **he had built up a picture in his mind of what she was like** se había formado una imagen mental de cómo era ella
[3] (= *increase*) [+ *stocks etc*] acumular; [+ *sales, numbers*] incrementar; **to ~ up one's strength** fortalecerse; **to ~ up one's hopes** hacerse ilusiones; **to ~ up sb's confidence** dar más confianza en sí mismo a algn; **to ~ up one's (self-)confidence** desarrollar la confianza en sí mismo
Ⓑ VI + ADV (= *increase*) [*pressure, sound, speed*] aumentar; (*Fin*) [*interest*] acumularse; [*excitement*] crecer

builder [ˈbɪldəʳ] N (= *company*) constructor(a) *m/f*; (= *worker*) albañil *mf*; (= *contractor*) contratista *mf*; (*fig*) fundador(a) *m/f*

building [ˈbɪldɪŋ] Ⓐ N [1] (= *house, office etc*) edificio *m*; (*at exhibition*) pabellón *m*
[2] (= *activity*) construcción *f*
Ⓑ CPD ► **building block** N (= *toy*) bloque *m* de construcción; (*fig*) elemento *m* esencial, componente *m* básico ► **building contractor** N contratista *mf* de construcciones ► **the building industry** N la industria de la construcción ► **building land** N tierra *f* para construcción, terrenos *mpl* edificables ► **building lot** N solar *m* (para construcción) ► **building materials** NPL material *msing* de construcción ► **building permit** N permiso *m* de obras ► **building plot** N = **building lot** ► **building site** N obra *f* ► **building society** N (*Brit*) sociedad *f* de crédito hipotecario ► **the building trade** N la industria de la construcción ► **building worker** N obrero/a *m/f or* trabajador(a) *m/f* de la construcción ► **building works** NPL obras *fpl* de construcción

build-up [ˈbɪldʌp] N [1] [*of pressure, tension, traffic*] aumento *m*; [*of gas*] acumulación *f*, concentración *f*; [*of forces*] concentración *f*
[2] (= *publicity*) propaganda *f*; **to give sth/sb a good ~** hacer mucha propaganda a favor de algo/algn

built [bɪlt] Ⓐ PT, PP *of* **build**
Ⓑ ADJ **heavily/slightly ~** [*person*] fornido/menudo

-built [bɪlt] ADJ (*ending in compounds*) **American-built** de construcción americana; **brick-built** construido de ladrillos

built-in [ˈbɪltˈɪn] Ⓐ ADJ [*wardrobe, mirror*] empotrado; (*as integral part of*) incorporado
Ⓑ CPD ► **built-in obsolescence** N caducidad *f* programada *or* controlada

built-up [ˈbɪltˈʌp] N **~ area** zona *f* urbanizada

bulb [bʌlb] N [1] (*Bot*) bulbo *m*, camote *m* (*Mex*); [*of garlic*] cabeza *f*
[2] (*Elec*) bombilla *f*, bombillo *m* (*LAm*), foco *m* (*LAm*)
[3] [*of thermometer*] cubeta *f*, ampolleta *f*

bulbous [ˈbʌlbəs] ADJ [*shape*] bulboso

Bulgar [ˈbʌlgəʳ] N (*Hist*) búlgaro/a *m/f*

Bulgaria [bʌlˈgeərɪə] N Bulgaria *f*

Bulgarian [bʌlˈgeərɪən] Ⓐ ADJ búlgaro
Ⓑ N [1] (= *person*) búlgaro/a *m/f*
[2] (*Ling*) búlgaro *m*

bulge [bʌldʒ] Ⓐ N [1] (*in surface, of curve*) abombamiento *m*, protuberancia *f*; (*in pocket*) bulto *m*
[2] (*in birth rate, sales*) alza *f*, aumento *m*; **the postwar ~ in the birth rate** la explosión demográfica de la posguerra
Ⓑ VI [*pocket etc*] estar abultado; [*eyes*] saltarse; **his pockets ~d with apples** iba con los bolsillos repletos de manzanas; **their eyes ~d at the sight** se les saltaron los ojos al verlo

bulging [ˈbʌldʒɪŋ] ADJ [*pocket*] muy lleno; [*suitcase*] que está para reventar; [*eyes*] saltón

bulimia [bjuːˈlɪmɪə] N bulimia *f*

bulimic [bjuːˈlɪmɪk] Ⓐ ADJ bulímico
Ⓑ N bulímico/a *m/f*

bulk [bʌlk] Ⓐ N [1] (= *size*) [*of thing*] bulto *m*; [*of person*] corpulencia *f*, masa *f*; **the enormous ~ of the ship** la enorme mole del buque; **he set his full ~ down in a chair** dejó caer todo el peso de su cuerpo en un sillón
[2] (= *main part*) **the ~ of** la mayoría de; **the ~ of the work** la mayor parte del trabajo; **the ~ of the army** el grueso del ejército
[3] (*Comm*) **to buy in ~** (= *in large quantities*) comprar al por mayor; **in ~** (= *not pre-packed*) suelto, a granel
Ⓑ VI **to ~ large** tener un puesto importante, ocupar un lugar importante
Ⓒ CPD ► **bulk buying** N compra *f* al por mayor ► **bulk carrier** N (buque *m*) granelero *m* ► **bulk goods** NPL mercancías *fpl* a granel ► **bulk purchase** N compra *f* al por mayor

bulkhead [ˈbʌlkhed] N (*Naut*) mamparo *m*

bulkiness [ˈbʌlkɪnɪs] N volumen *m*, lo abultado

bulky [ˈbʌlkɪ] ADJ (*compar* **bulkier**; *superl* **bulkiest**) [*parcel*] abultado; [*person*] corpulento

bull[1] [bʊl] Ⓐ N [1] (*Zool*) toro *m*; (= *male*) [*of elephant, seal*] macho *m*; ✦*IDIOMS* **like a ~ in a china shop** como un elefante en una cristalería; **to take the ~ by the horns** coger *or* (*LAm*) agarrar el toro por los cuernos; *see also* **red A1**
[2] (*Fin*) alcista *mf*
[3] (‡) (= *nonsense*) sandeces* *fpl*, chorradas *fpl* (*Sp**); **to talk a lot of ~** decir sandeces*, decir chorradas (*Sp**)

[4] (*Mil**) trabajos *mpl* rutinarios
(B) ADJ (*Zool*) macho
(C) VT (*Fin*) **to ~ the market** hacer subir el mercado comprando acciones especulativamente
(D) CPD ► **bull bars** NPL (*Aut*) defensa *fsing* (delantera *or* frontal) ► **bull calf** N (*Zool*) becerro *m* ► **bull dyke*** N (*pej*) camionera* *f* ► **bull market** N (*Fin*) mercado *m* en alza *or* alcista ► **bull neck** N cuello *m* de toro ► **bull terrier** N bulterrier *m*

bull² [bʊl] N (*Rel*) bula *f*

bulldog ['bʊldɒg] (A) N dogo *m*, buldog *m*
(B) CPD ► **the bulldog breed** N los ingleses (*con su aspecto heroico y porfiado*) ► **Bulldog® clip** N pinza *f*

bulldoze ['bʊldəʊz] VT [1] (*Constr*) [+ *site*] nivelar (con motoniveladora); [+ *building*] arrasar (con motoniveladora)
[2] (*fig*) [+ *opposition*] arrollar; **I was ~d into doing it** me forzaron a hacerlo; **the government ~d the bill through parliament** el gobierno hizo presiones para que se aprobara el proyecto de ley en el parlamento

bulldozer ['bʊldəʊzəʳ] N motoniveladora *f*, bulldozer *m*

bullet ['bʊlɪt] (A) N bala *f*; **to go by like a ~** pasar como (una) bala *or* un rayo; ✦**IDIOM to bite the ~** enfrentarse al toro
(B) CPD ► **bullet hole** N agujero *m* de bala ► **bullet train** N tren *m* de gran velocidad (*japonés*) ► **bullet wound** N balazo *m*

bulletin ['bʊlɪtɪn] (A) N (= *statement*) comunicado *m*, parte *m*; (= *journal*) boletín *m*
(B) CPD ► **bulletin board** N (*US*) tablón *m* de anuncios; (*Comput*) tablero *m* de noticias

bulletproof ['bʊlɪtpruːf] (A) ADJ antibalas, a prueba de balas
(B) CPD ► **bulletproof glass** N vidrio *m* antibalas *or* a prueba de balas ► **bulletproof vest** N chaleco *m* antibalas *or* a prueba de balas

bullfight ['bʊlfaɪt] N corrida *f* (de toros)

bullfighter ['bʊlfaɪtəʳ] N torero/a *m/f*

bullfighting ['bʊlfaɪtɪŋ] N toreo *m*, tauromaquia *f*; **I hate ~** odio los toros

bullfinch ['bʊlfɪntʃ] N camachuelo *m*

bullfrog ['bʊlfrɒg] N rana *f* toro

bullhorn ['bʊlhɔːn] N (*US*) megáfono *m*

bullion ['bʊljən] N oro *m*/plata *f* en barras *or* en lingotes

bullish ['bʊlɪʃ] ADJ optimista; (*Fin*) (de tendencia) alcista

bull-necked ['bʊl'nekt] ADJ de cuello de toro

bullock ['bʊlək] N buey *m*

bullring ['bʊlrɪŋ] N plaza *f* de toros

bull's-eye ['bʊlzaɪ] N [1] [*of target*] blanco *m*; **to hit the ~** ◊ **score a ~** (*lit, fig*) dar en el blanco
[2] (= *sweet*) caramelo *m* de menta
[3] (= *lantern*) linterna *f* sorda
[4] (*Naut*) ojo *m* de buey

bullshit** ['bʊlʃɪt] (A) N (= *nonsense*) sandeces* *fpl*, chorradas *fpl* (*Sp**)
(B) VI decir sandeces*, decir chorradas (*Sp**)
(C) VT **don't ~ me now** no me vengas ahora con sandeces *or* chorradas*

bullshitter** ['bʊl'ʃɪtəʳ] N fanfarrón/ona *m/f*

bully¹ ['bʊlɪ] (A) N [1] (= *person*) matón/ona *m/f*, peleón/ona *m/f*
[2] (*Brit Hockey*) (*also* **~-off**) saque *m*
(B) VT (*also* **~ around**) intimidar; **to ~ sb into doing sth** intimidar a algn para que haga algo

►**bully off** VI + ADV (*Brit Hockey*) sacar

bully²* ['bʊlɪ] (A) ADJ (†) (= *first-rate*) de primera
(B) EXCL **~ for you!** ¡bravo!

bully³* ['bʊlɪ] N (*Mil*) (*also* **~ beef**) carne *f* de vaca conservada en lata

bully-boy* ['bʊlɪ,bɔɪ] (A) N matón *m*, esbirro *m*
(B) CPD ► **bully-boy tactics** NPL táctica *fsing* de matón

bullying ['bʊlɪɪŋ] (A) ADJ [*person*] matón, valentón; [*attitude*] amedrentador, propio de matón
(B) N intimidación *f*, abuso *m*

bulrush ['bʊlrʌʃ] N espadaña *f*

bulwark ['bʊlwək] N (*Mil, fig*) baluarte *m*; (*Naut*) borda *f*

bum¹* [bʌm] (A) N (*Brit Anat*) culo* *m*; ✦**IDIOM to put ~s on seats** (*Theat etc*) llenar el teatro *or* cine etc
(B) CPD ► **bum bag** N riñonera *f* ► **bum boy**** N (*Brit pej*) maricón* *m*

bum²* [bʌm] (A) N (*esp US*) (= *idler*) holgazán/ana *m/f*, vago/a *m/f*; (= *tramp*) vagabundo/a *m/f*; (= *scrounger*) gorrón/ona* *m/f*; (*as term of general disapproval*) vago/a *m/f*; ✦**IDIOMS to go** *or* **live on the ~** [*scrounger*] vivir de gorra; [*tramp*] vagabundear; **to give sb the ~'s rush** echar a algn a patadas*
(B) ADJ [1] (= *worthless*) sin ningún valor
[2] (*esp US*) (= *false*) falso
(C) VT [+ *money, food*] gorrear*; **he ~med a cigarette off me** me gorreó un pitillo*
(D) CPD ► **bum deal** N **I knew I was getting a ~ deal** sabía que se estaban aprovechando de mí ► **bum rap** N acusación *f* falsa ► **bum steer** N bulo *m*

►**bum around*** VI + ADV holgazanear

bumble ['bʌmbl] VI (= *walk unsteadily*) andar de forma vacilante, andar a tropezones; (*fig*) trastabillar

bumblebee ['bʌmblbiː] N abejorro *m*

bumbling ['bʌmblɪŋ] (A) ADJ (= *inept*) inepto, inútil; (= *muttering*) que habla a tropezones
(B) N divagación *f*

bumf* [bʌmf] N [1] (*Brit pej*) (= *papers, information*) papeleo* *m*, papeles *mpl*
[2] (= *lavatory paper*) papel *m* higiénico

bummer* ['bʌməʳ] N (= *nuisance*) latazo* *m*; (= *disaster*) desastre *m*; **what a ~!** ¡vaya desastre!

bump [bʌmp] (A) N [1] (= *blow, noise*) choque *m*, topetazo *m*; (= *jolt of vehicle*) sacudida *f*; (*Aer*) rebote *m*; (*in falling*) batacazo *m*; **things that go ~ in the night** cosas que hacen ruidos misteriosos en la noche; ✦**IDIOM to come down to earth with a ~** volver a la realidad de un golpe
[2] (= *swelling*) bollo *m*, abolladura *f*; (*on skin*) chichón *m*, hinchazón *f*; (*on road etc*) bache *m*
(B) VT [+ *car*] chocar contra; **to ~ one's head** darse un golpe en la cabeza; **to ~ one's head on a door** dar con la cabeza contra una puerta
(C) VI **to ~ along** (= *move joltingly*) avanzar dando sacudidas; **the economy continues to ~ along the bottom** (*Brit*) la economía continúa arrastrándose por los suelos

►**bump against** VI + PREP chocar contra, topetar, dar contra

►**bump into** VI + PREP [1] [+ *person, vehicle*] chocar contra, dar con *or* contra
[2] (*) (= *meet*) tropezar con, toparse con; **fancy ~ing into you!** ¡qué casualidad encontrarte aquí!

►**bump off*** VT + ADV (= *kill*) cargarse a*

►**bump up*** VT + ADV [1] (= *increase*) [+ *price*] subir, aumentar
[2] **he was ~ed up to first-class on his flight home** en el viaje de vuelta lo pusieron en primera clase

►**bump up against** VI + PREP = **bump into 1**

bumper¹ ['bʌmpəʳ] (A) N (*Brit Aut*) parachoques *m inv*; **traffic is ~ to ~ as far as the airport** hay una caravana que llega hasta el aeropuerto
(B) CPD ► **bumper car** N auto *m* de choque ► **bumper sticker** N pegatina *f* de parachoques

bumper² ['bʌmpəʳ] (A) N (= *glass*) copa *f* llena
(B) ADJ [*crop, harvest*] abundante
(C) CPD ► **bumper issue** N edición *f* especial

bumph* [bʌmf] N (*Brit*) = **bumf**

bumpkin ['bʌmpkɪn] N (*also* **country ~**) (*pej*) pueblerino/a *m/f*, paleto/a *m/f* (*Sp**)

bump-start ['bʌmpstɑːt] (A) N **to give a car a ~** empujar un coche para que arranque
(B) VT [+ *car*] empujar para que arranque

bumptious ['bʌmpʃəs] ADJ engreído, presuntuoso

bumpy ['bʌmpɪ] ADJ (*compar* **bumpier**, *superl* **bumpiest**) [*surface*] desigual; [*road*] lleno de baches; [*journey, flight*] agitado, con mucho traqueteo

bun [bʌn] (A) N [1] (*Culin*) bollo *m*, magdalena *f*; (*Brit*) (= *cake*) pastel *m*; ✦**IDIOM to have a ~ in the oven*** estar en estado
[2] (= *hairstyle*) moño *m*; **to wear one's hair in a ~** recogerse el pelo en un moño
[3] **buns** (*US**) trasero* *msing*
(B) CPD ► **bun fight*** N *merienda servida para mucha gente*

bunch [bʌntʃ] (A) N [1] [*of flowers*] ramo *m*; (*small*) ramillete *m*; [*of bananas, grapes*] racimo *m*; [*of keys*] manojo *m*; **to wear one's hair in ~es** (*Brit*) llevar coletas; **the best** *or* **pick of the ~*** (*fig*) el/la mejor de todos
[2] (*) (= *set of people*) grupo *m*, pandilla *f*; **they're an odd ~** son gente rara; **they're a ~ of traitors** son una panda de traidores; ✦**IDIOM the best of a bad ~** entre malos, los mejores; *see also* **mixed A1**
[3] (*US**) **a ~ of** (= *several, many*) un montón de; **a ~ of times** un montón de veces
[4] **thanks a ~!*** (*iro*) ¡hombre, pues te lo agradezco!, ¡gracias mil!
(B) VT [+ *objects*] agrupar, juntar

►**bunch together** (A) VT + ADV agrupar, juntar
(B) VI + ADV [*people*] agruparse, apiñarse

►**bunch up** (A) VT + ADV [1] [+ *dress, skirt*] arremangar
[2] **they sat ~ed up on the bench** se apretujaban en el banco
(B) VI + ADV apretujarse

bundle ['bʌndl] (A) N [1] [*of clothes, rags*] bulto *m*, fardo *m*, lío *m*; [*of sticks*] haz *m*; [*of papers*] legajo *m*; **~ of joy** (= *baby*) bebé *mf*; **he's a ~ of nerves** es un manojo de nervios; **he's not exactly a ~ of laughs** no es muy divertido que digamos
[2] (*) (= *money*) **to make a ~** ganarse un dineral*, ganarse un pastón (*Sp**); **it cost a ~** costó un dineral *or* una millonada*
[3] (= *large number*) montón *m*; **to go a ~ on*** volverse loco por*
[4] (*Comput*) paquete *m*
(B) VT [1] (*also* **~ up**) [+ *clothes*] atar en un bulto
[2] (= *put hastily*) guardar sin orden; **the body was ~d into the car** metieron el cadáver en el coche a la carrera
(C) CPD ► **bundled software** N (*Comput*) paquete *m* de software

►**bundle off** VT + ADV [+ *person*] despachar;

they ~d him off to Australia lo despacharon a Australia

►**bundle out** VT + ADV **to ~ sb out** echar a algn; **they ~d him out into the street** lo pusieron de patitas en la calle*

►**bundle up** VT + ADV [+ *clothes, belongings*] liar, atar

bung [bʌŋ] Ⓐ N [1] [*of cask*] tapón *m*
[2] (*Brit**) (= *bribe*) soborno *m*
Ⓑ VT (*Brit*) [1] (*also* **~ up**) [+ *pipe, hole*] tapar, taponar; **to be ~ed up** [*sink, pipe*] estar atascado, estar obstruido; **my nose is ~ed up*** tengo la nariz tapada
[2] (*) (= *throw*) echar; (= *put*) poner, meter; **~ it over** échalo para acá

►**bung in*** VT + ADV (= *include*) añadir

►**bung out*** VT + ADV tirar, botar

bungalow [ˈbʌŋɡələʊ] N chalé *m*, bungalow *m*

bungee jumping [ˈbʌndʒiːˈdʒʌmpɪŋ] N bungee *m*, banyi *m*; (*from bridge*) puenting *m*, puentismo *m*; **to go ~** hacer bungee *or* banyi; (*from bridge*) hacer puenting *or* puentismo

bunghole [ˈbʌŋhəʊl] N piquera *f*, boca *f* (de tonel)

bungle [ˈbʌŋɡl] Ⓐ N chapuza* *f*
Ⓑ VT [+ *work*] hacer chapuceramente; **to ~ it** hacer una chapuza*, amolarlo (*Mex**); **to ~ an opportunity** desperdiciar una oportunidad

bungled [ˈbʌŋɡld] ADJ **a ~ job** una chapuza*; **a ~ operation** una operación mal ejecutada

bungler [ˈbʌŋɡləʳ] N chapucero/a *m/f*

bungling [ˈbʌŋɡlɪŋ] ADJ torpe, desmañado

bungy jumping [ˈbʌndʒiːˈdʒʌmpɪŋ] N = **bungee jumping**

bunion [ˈbʌnjən] N (*Med*) juanete *m*

bunk¹ [bʌŋk] Ⓐ N (*Naut*) litera *f*, camastro *m*; (*Rail, child's*) litera *f*; (*) (= *bed*) cama *f*
Ⓑ CPD ► **bunk bed** N litera *f*

bunk²* [bʌŋk] (*Brit*) Ⓐ N **to do a ~** = **B**
Ⓑ VI largarse*, escaquearse (*Sp**)

►**bunk off*** (*Brit*) Ⓐ VI + ADV (*from school, work*) escaquearse (*Sp**)
Ⓑ VI + PREP **to ~ off school** hacer novillos *or* rabona

bunk³* [bʌŋk] N (= *nonsense*) bobadas* *fpl*; **~!** ¡bobadas!*; **history is ~** la historia son bobadas*

bunker [ˈbʌŋkəʳ] Ⓐ N [1] (= *coal bunker*) carbonera *f*; (*Naut*) pañol *m* del carbón
[2] (*Mil*) refugio *m* antiaéreo/antinuclear, búnker *m*
[3] (*Golf*) búnker *m*
Ⓑ VT [1] (*Naut*) proveer de carbón
[2] **to be ~ed** (*Golf*) tener la pelota en un búnker; (*fig*) (*) estar en un atolladero

bunkhouse [ˈbʌŋkhaʊs] N (*pl* **bunkhouses** [ˈbʌŋkhaʊzɪz]) (*US*) casa *f* de dormitorios (para trabajadores de hacienda)

bunkum* [ˈbʌŋkəm] N bobadas* *fpl*

bunk-up* [ˌbʌŋkˈʌp] N **to give sb a ~** ayudar a algn a subir

bunny [ˈbʌnɪ] Ⓐ N [1] (*baby talk*) (= *rabbit*) conejito *m*
[2] (*US**) (= *pretty girl*) bombón* *m*, tía *f* buena (*Sp**)
Ⓑ CPD ► **bunny girl** N conejita *f* ► **bunny rabbit** N (*baby talk*) conejito *m*

Bunsen burner [ˌbʌnsnˈbɜːnəʳ] N mechero *m* Bunsen

bunting¹ [ˈbʌntɪŋ] N (*Orn*) escribano *m*

bunting² [ˈbʌntɪŋ] N (= *decoration*) banderitas *fpl*, empavesado *m*; (= *cloth*) lanilla *f*

buoy [bɔɪ] (*US*) [ˈbuːɪ] Ⓐ N boya *f*
Ⓑ VT [+ *channel*] aboyar, señalar con boyas

►**buoy up** VT + ADV (*lit*) [+ *person, boat*] mantener a flote; (*fig*) [+ *spirits etc*] levantar; [+ *person*] animar, alentar

buoyancy [ˈbɔɪənsɪ] N [1] (*Phys*) [*of ship, object*] capacidad *f* para flotar, flotabilidad *f*; [*of liquid*] sustentación *f* hidraúlica; (*Aer*) fuerza *f* ascensional
[2] (*fig*) optimismo *m*
[3] (*Fin*) [*of market, prices*] tendencia *f* al alza

buoyant [ˈbɔɪənt] ADJ [1] (*Phys*) [*ship, object*] flotante, boyante (*Tech*); **fresh water is not so ~ as salt water** en el agua dulce no se flota tanto como en la salada
[2] (= *bouncy*) [*mood, person*] optimista; [*step*] ligero
[3] (*Fin*) [*market, prices*] con tendencia al alza

buoyantly [ˈbɔɪəntlɪ] ADV [*walk*] con paso ligero; [*recover, return*] con optimismo

BUPA [ˈbuːpə] N ABBR (= **British United Provident Association**) *seguro médico privado*

buppie*, **buppy*** [ˈbʌpɪ] N ABBR (= **black upwardly mobile professional**) *yuppie negro*

bur [bɜːʳ] N = **burr**

burble [ˈbɜːbl] VI [1] [*baby*] hacer gorgoritos; [*stream*] burbujear
[2] (*pej*) [*person*] (= *talk*) farfullar

burbot [ˈbɜːbət] N lota *f*

burbs*, **'burbs*** [bɜːbz] NPL (*US*) = **suburbs**

burden [ˈbɜːdn] Ⓐ N [1] (= *load*) carga *f*; (= *weight*) peso *m*
[2] (*fig*) [*of taxes, years*] peso *m*, carga *f*; **the ~ of proof lies with him** él lleva la carga de la prueba; **to be a ~ to sb** ser una carga para algn; **he carries a heavy ~** tiene que cargar con una gran responsabilidad; **to make sb's life a ~** amargar la vida a algn
[3] (*Naut*) arqueo *m*
[4] (= *chief theme*) [*of speech etc*] tema *m* principal
[5] (= *chorus*) [*of song*] estribillo *m*
Ⓑ VT cargar (**with** con); **to be ~ed with** tener que cargar con; **don't ~ me with your troubles** no me vengas con tus problemas

burdensome [ˈbɜːdnsəm] ADJ gravoso, oneroso

burdock [ˈbɜːdɒk] N (*Bot*) bardana *f*

bureau [ˈbjʊərəʊ] Ⓐ N (*pl* **bureaus** *or* **bureaux** [ˈbjʊərəʊz]) [1] (= *organization*) [1·1] (= *travel/employment agency*) agencia *f*, oficina *f*
[1·2] (*US*) (= *government department*) departamento *m*; *see also* **federal**
[2] (= *piece of furniture*) [2·1] (*Brit*) (= *desk*) buró *m*, escritorio *m*
[2·2] (*US*) (= *chest of drawers*) cómoda *f*
Ⓑ CPD ► **bureau de change** [ˌbjʊərəʊdəˈʃɒndʒ] N caja *f* de cambio ► **Bureau of Indian affairs** N (*US*) Departamento *m* de Asuntos Indios ► **bureau of standards** N (*US*) oficina *f* de pesos y medidas

BUREAU OF INDIAN AFFAIRS

La agencia del gobierno estadounidense denominada **Bureau of Indian Affairs** *(***Departamento de Asuntos Indios***) se encarga de todos los asuntos relacionados con los indios nativos norteamericanos. Este organismo, fundado en 1824 como parte del Ministerio de Guerra, llevaba en un principio la gestión de las reservas indias. Hoy en día trabaja conjuntamente con los indios para tratar de mejorar su situación, elaborando programas de salud y bienestar social y dando facilidades para la educación y el empleo. Desde la década de los sesenta viene proporcionando también asistencia técnica y formación para que puedan gestionar sus tierras y recursos.*

bureaucracy [bjʊəˈrɒkrəsɪ] N burocracia *f*; (*pej*) papeleo* *m*, trámites *mpl*

bureaucrat [ˈbjʊərəʊkræt] N burócrata *mf*

bureaucratic [ˌbjʊərəʊˈkrætɪk] ADJ burocrático

burg* [bɜːɡ] N (*US often hum, pej*) (= *town*) burgo *m*

burgeon [ˈbɜːdʒən] VI (*Bot*) retoñar; (*fig*) empezar a prosperar (rápidamente); [*trade etc*] florecer

burgeoning [ˈbɜːdʒənɪŋ] ADJ [*industry, market*] en vías de expansión, que empieza a prosperar *or* florecer; [*career*] que empieza a prosperar *or* florecer; [*population*] en aumento

burger [ˈbɜːɡəʳ] N hamburguesa *f*

burgess [ˈbɜːdʒɪs] N (*Brit*) ciudadano/a *m/f*; (††) (*Parl*) diputado/a *m/f*

burgh [ˈbʌrə] N (*Scot*) villa *f*

burgher [ˈbɜːɡəʳ] N (†† *or liter*) (= *bourgeois*) burgués/esa *m/f*; (= *citizen*) ciudadano/a *m/f*

burglar [ˈbɜːɡləʳ] Ⓐ N ladrón/ona *m/f*
Ⓑ CPD ► **burglar alarm** N alarma *f* antirrobo

burglarize [ˈbɜːɡləraɪz] VT (*US*) robar (de una casa *etc*)

burglar-proof [ˈbɜːɡləpruːf] ADJ a prueba de ladrones

burglary [ˈbɜːɡlərɪ] N robo *m* (*en una casa*); (*Jur*) allanamiento *m* de morada

burgle [ˈbɜːɡl] VT (*Brit*) robar (*de una casa etc*)

Burgundian [bɜːˈɡʌndɪən] Ⓐ ADJ borgoñón
Ⓑ N borgoñón/ona *m/f*

Burgundy [ˈbɜːɡəndɪ] N [1] (*Geog*) Borgoña *f*
[2] (= *wine*) vino *m* de Borgoña

burial [ˈberɪəl] Ⓐ N entierro *m*; **I like the idea of ~ at sea** me gusta la idea de que mi cadáver sea arrojado al mar
Ⓑ CPD ► **burial ground** N cementerio *m*, camposanto *m*, panteón *m* (*LAm*) ► **burial mound** N túmulo *m* ► **burial place** N lugar *m* de sepultura ► **burial service** N funerales *mpl* ► **burial vault** N panteón *m* familiar, cripta *f*

Burkina-Faso [bɜːˈkiːnəˈfæsəʊ] N Burkina Faso *f*

burlap [ˈbɜːlæp] N (*esp US*) arpillera *f*

burlesque [bɜːˈlesk] Ⓐ ADJ burlesco
Ⓑ N [1] (= *parody*) parodia *f*
[2] (*US Theat*) revista *f* de estriptise
Ⓒ VT parodiar
Ⓓ CPD ► **burlesque show** N (*US*) revista *f* de estriptise

burly [ˈbɜːlɪ] ADJ (*compar* **burlier**; *superl* **burliest**) fornido, fuerte

Burma [ˈbɜːmə] N Birmania *f*

Burmese [bɜːˈmiːz] Ⓐ ADJ birmano
Ⓑ N birmano/a *m/f*

burn¹ [bɜːn] (*vb: pt, pp* **burned**, **burnt**) Ⓐ N [1] (*Med*) quemadura *f*
[2] (*Space*) [*of rocket*] fuego *m*
Ⓑ VT [1] (*gen*) quemar; [+ *house, building*] incendiar; [+ *corpse*] incinerar; [+ *mouth, tongue*] quemar, escaldar; **to ~ a house to the ground** incendiar y arrasar una casa; **to ~ a hole in sth** hacer un agujero en algo quemándolo; **to ~ sth to ashes** reducir algo a cenizas; **to be ~ed alive** ser quemado vivo; **to be ~t to death** morir abrasado; **to ~ one's finger/hand** quemarse el dedo/la mano; **I've ~t myself!** ¡me he quemado!, ¡me quemé! (*LAm*); **I ~t the toast** se me ha quemado la tostada; ✦***IDIOMS*** **to ~ one's boats** *or* **bridges** quemar las naves; **to ~ the candle at both ends** hacer de la noche día; **to ~ one's fingers** ◊ **get one's fingers ~ed** pi-

llarse los dedos; **money ~s a hole in his pocket** el dinero le quema las manos
[2] [*sun*] [+ *person, skin*] tostar; [+ *plants*] abrasar; **with a face ~ed by the sun** con la cara tostada al sol
[3] [+ *fuel*] consumir, usar
Ⓒ VI [1] [*fire, building etc*] arder, quemarse; (= *catch fire*) incendiarse; **to ~ to death** morir abrasado
[2] [*skin*] (*in sun*) quemarse, tostarse
[3] [*meat, pastry etc*] quemarse
[4] [*light, gas*] estar encendido
[5] (*fig*) **to ~ with anger/passion** *etc* arder de rabia/pasión *etc*; **to ~ with desire for** desear ardientemente; **to ~ with impatience** consumirse de impaciencia; **to ~ to do sth** desear ardientemente hacer algo

►**burn away** Ⓐ VT + ADV quemar
Ⓑ VI + ADV [1] (= *be consumed*) consumirse
[2] (= *go on burning*) seguir ardiendo, arder bien

►**burn down** Ⓐ VT + ADV [+ *building*] incendiar
Ⓑ VI + ADV [1] [*house*] incendiarse
[2] [*candle, fire*] apagarse

►**burn off** VT + ADV [+ *paint etc*] quitar con soplete; [+ *weeds*] quemar

►**burn out** Ⓐ VT + ADV [1] (= *destroy*) [+ *building*] reducir a cenizas; (*criminally*) incendiar
[2] [+ *person*] incendiar la casa de
[3] (*Elec*) fundir, quemar
[4] **the fire had ~t itself out** (*in hearth*) el fuego se había apagado; [*forest fire*] el incendio se había extinguido; **he's ~t himself out** (*fig*) está quemado
Ⓑ VI + ADV [1] [*fuse*] fundirse
[2] [*candle, fire*] apagarse

►**burn up** Ⓐ VI + ADV [1] [*fire*] echar llamas, arder más
[2] [*rocket etc*] desintegrarse
Ⓑ VT + ADV [1] [+ *rubbish etc*] quemar; [+ *crop*] abrasar
[2] (= *consume*) [+ *calories, energy*] quemar
[3] (*US**) (= *make angry*) sacar de quicio*

burn² [bɜːn] N (*Scot*) arroyo *m*, riachuelo *m*

burner [ˈbɜːnəʳ] N (*on cooker etc*) quemador *m*; *see also* **back**

burning [ˈbɜːnɪŋ] Ⓐ N [1] (= *singeing*) **there's a smell of ~** huele a quemado; **I can smell ~** huelo a quemado
[2] (= *setting on fire*) quema *f*; **the ~ (down) of the Embassy during the riots** la quema de la embajada durante los disturbios
Ⓑ ADJ [1] (= *on fire*) [*building, forest*] en llamas; [*coals, flame*] ardiente; [*candle*] encendido; **the ~ bush** (*Bible*) la zarza ardiente, la zarza que ardía sin consumirse
[2] (= *hot*) [*sun*] abrasador, ardiente; [*sand*] ardiente; [*desert*] infernal; [*face, skin*] ardiendo; [*thirst, fever*] abrasador; [*sensation*] de ardor, de escozor; **they drank some water to cool their ~ throats** bebieron agua para refrescar sus ardientes gargantas; **with a ~ face** (*through embarrassment, shame*) con la cara ardiendo de vergüenza
[3] (= *intense*) [*desire, passion, eyes*] ardiente; [*ambition*] que quema; [*hatred*] violento; [*question, topic*] candente
Ⓒ ADV **~ hot**: **his forehead was ~ hot** su frente estaba ardiendo; **don't touch that, it's ~ hot!** ¡no toques eso! ¡está ardiendo!; **it's ~ hot today!** ¡hoy hace un calor abrasador!

burnish [ˈbɜːnɪʃ] VT [1] [+ *metal*] bruñir
[2] (*fig*) [+ *image*] mejorar

burnoose, burnous(e) [bɜːˈnuːz] N albornoz *m*

> **BURNS NIGHT**
>
> *En la noche del 25 de enero,* **Burns Night**, *se celebra el aniversario del nacimiento del poeta escocés Robert Burns (1759-1796). Los escoceses de todo el mundo se reúnen para celebrar su vida y obra haciendo una cena en su honor (***Burns Supper***), en la que, al son de la gaita, se sirve* **haggis** *(asaduras de cordero, avena y especias cocidas en las tripas del animal) con patatas y puré de nabos. Después de la cena se cantan canciones de Burns, se leen sus poemas y se hacen discursos de carácter festivo relacionados con ellos.*

burnt [bɜːnt] Ⓐ PT, PP *of* **burn**
Ⓑ ADJ quemado; ✦*PROV* **a ~ child dreads the fire** el gato escaldado del agua fría huye; **it has a ~ taste** sabe a quemado
Ⓒ CPD ► **burnt almonds** NPL almendras *fpl* tostadas ► **burnt offering** N (*Rel*) holocausto *m*; **I forgot to turn off the oven and we had a ~ offering for dinner** (*hum*) se me olvidó apagar el horno y tuvimos carbón para cenar ► **burnt orange** N (= *colour*) naranja *m* oscuro ► **burnt sienna** N (= *colour*) siena *f* tostada ► **burnt sugar** N azúcar *m* quemado ► **burnt umber** N (= *colour*) siena *m* tostado

burnt-out [ˌbɜːntˈaʊt] ADJ [*person*] quemado

burp* [bɜːp] Ⓐ N eructo *m*
Ⓑ VI eructar
Ⓒ VT [+ *baby*] hacer eructar

burqa [ˈbɜːkə] N burqa *m*, burka *m*

burr [bɜːʳ] N (*Bot*) erizo *m*

burrow [ˈbʌrəʊ] Ⓐ N [*of animal*] madriguera *f*; [*of rabbit*] conejera *f*
Ⓑ VT [+ *hole*] cavar; **to ~ one's way** abrirse camino cavando (**into** en)
Ⓒ VI [*animal*] hacer una madriguera; **to ~ into** hacer madrigueras en, horadar; (*fig*) investigar minuciosamente; **he ~ed under the bedclothes** se metió debajo de la ropa de cama

bursar [ˈbɜːsəʳ] N (*Univ etc*) tesorero/a *m/f*; [*of school*] administrador(a) *m/f*

bursary [ˈbɜːsərɪ] N (*Brit Univ*) beca *f*

burst [bɜːst] (*vb: pt, pp* **burst**) Ⓐ N [1] (*in pipe*) reventón *m*
[2] [*of shell etc*] estallido *m*, explosión *f*; [*of shots*] ráfaga *f*; **a ~ of activity** un arranque repentino de actividad; **in a ~ of anger** en un arranque de cólera; **a ~ of applause** una salva de aplausos; **a ~ of laughter** una carcajada; **he put on a ~ of speed** aceleró bruscamente
Ⓑ ADJ **a ~ blood vessel** un derrame; **a ~ pipe** una tubería reventada; **a ~ tyre** un neumático reventado, una llanta pinchada (*LAm*)
Ⓒ VT [+ *pipe, balloon, bag, tyre, bubble*] reventar; [+ *banks, dam*] romper; **the river has ~ its banks** el río se ha desbordado; **to ~ open a door** abrir una puerta de golpe
Ⓓ VI [*balloon, tyre, boil, boiler, bubble, pipe*] reventar(se); [*dam*] romperse; [*shell, firework*] explotar, estallar; [*storm*] desatarse, desencadenarse; (*fig*) [*heart*] partirse; **~ing at the seams** lleno a reventar; **I'm ~ing for the loo** (*Brit**) estoy que reviento*, tengo que ir al wáter; **the door ~ open** la puerta se abrió de golpe; **I was ~ing to tell you*** reventaba de ganas de decírtelo; **to be ~ing with pride** no caber dentro de sí de orgullo; **he was ~ing with impatience** reventaba de impaciencia; **London is ~ing with young people** Londres está que bulle de juventud

►**burst forth** VI + ADV [*plants, buds*] brotar; [*water*] salir a chorro; [*sun*] aparecer de repente; [*anger, violence*] estallar

►**burst in** VI + ADV entrar violentamente; **he ~ in on the meeting** irrumpió en la reunión

►**burst into** VI + PREP [1] **to ~ into a room** irrumpir en un cuarto
[2] **to ~ into flames** estallar en llamas; **to ~ into song** romper *or* ponerse a cantar; **to ~ into tears** echarse a llorar

►**burst out** VI + ADV [1] **to ~ out of a room** salir repentinamente de un cuarto; **to be ~ing out of a dress*** no caber en un vestido
[2] **to ~ out laughing** echarse a reír; **to ~ out singing** romper *or* ponerse a cantar; **"no!" he ~ out** —¡no!, —gritó con pasión

►**burst through** VI + PREP [+ *barrier*] romper (violentamente); **the sun ~ through the clouds** el sol apareció de repente entre las nubes

bursting [ˈbɜːstɪŋ] Ⓐ N (*Comput*) separación *f* de hojas
Ⓑ CPD ► **bursting point** N **filled to ~ point** lleno a reventar

burthen†† [ˈbɜːðən] = **burden**

burton* [ˈbɜːtn] (*Brit*) N **it's gone for a ~** (= *broken etc*) se ha ido al traste*; (= *lost*) se ha perdido; **he's gone for a ~** (*Brit**) [*pilot, driver*] estiró la pata*, la palmó (*Sp*‡)

Burundi [bəˈrʊndɪ] N Burundi *m*

bury [ˈberɪ] VT [1] [+ *body, treasure*] enterrar; (*fig*) [+ *memory, matter*] echar tierra sobre; **buried by an avalanche** sepultado por una avalancha; **he wanted to be buried at sea** quería que su cadáver fuera arrojado al mar; **to be buried alive** ser enterrado vivo; ✦*IDIOMS* **to ~ the hatchet** ◊ **~ the tomahawk** (*US*) enterrar el hacha de guerra
[2] (= *conceal*) **he buried his face in his hands** escondió la cara entre las manos; **it's buried away in the library** está en algún rincón de la biblioteca; **to ~ o.s. in the country** perderse en la campiña; **the bullet buried itself in a tree** la bala se empotró en un árbol
[3] (= *engross*) **buried in thought** ensimismado, absorto en sus pensamientos; **she buried herself in her book** se ensimismó en la lectura, se enfrascó en el libro
[4] (= *plunge*) [+ *claws, knife*] clavar (**in** en); **to ~ a dagger in sb's heart** clavar un puñal en el corazón de algn
[5] (*Sport**) (= *defeat*) aplastar*

bus [bʌs] (*pl* **buses,** (*US*) **buses** *or* **busses**) Ⓐ N [1] (= *city bus*) autobús *m*, colectivo *m* (*Ven, Arg*), micro *m* (*Chile, Bol*), camión *m* (*Mex*); (= *coach*) autocar *m*, flota *f* (*Bol, Col*); **to come/go by ~** venir/ir en autobús *etc*; ✦*IDIOM* **to miss the ~** perder el tren
[2] (‡) (= *car*) cacharro* *m*; (= *plane*) avión *m* viejo
[3] (*Comput*) bus *m*
Ⓑ VT llevar en autobús; **the children are ~sed to school** los niños van al colegio en autobús
Ⓒ VI [1] (= *go by bus*) ir en autobús *etc*
[2] (*US**) (*in cafe*) quitar los platos de la mesa
Ⓓ CPD ► **bus conductor** N cobrador(a) *m/f* ► **bus conductress** N cobradora *f* ► **bus depot** N cochera *f* de autobuses *etc* ► **bus driver** N conductor(a) *m/f* de autobús *etc* ► **bus lane** N (*Brit*) carril *m* de autobuses *etc*, carril-bus *m* ► **bus route** N recorrido *m* del autobús *etc*; **the house is on a ~ route** pasa un autobús por delante de la casa ► **bus service** N servicio *m* de autobuses *etc* ► **bus shelter** N marquesina *f* de autobús ► **bus station** N estación *f* de autobuses *etc* ► **bus stop** N parada *f*, paradero *m* (*LAm*) ► **bus ticket** N billete *m* de autobús; *see also* **bus A1**

busbar ['bʌzbɑːʳ] N [1] (*Comput*) bus *m*
[2] (*Tech*) barra *f* ómnibus

busboy ['bʌsbɔɪ] N (*US*) ayudante *m* de camarero

busby ['bʌzbɪ] N (*Brit*) gorro *m* alto de piel negra

bush[1] [bʊʃ] Ⓐ N [1] (= *shrub*) arbusto *m*, mata *f*; (= *thicket*) (*also* **~es**) matorral *m*; ✦***IDIOM*** **to beat about the ~** andarse con rodeos *or* por las ramas
[2] (*in Africa, Australia*) **the ~** el monte
Ⓑ CPD ► **bush baby** N (*Zool*) lemúrido *m* ► **bush fire** N incendio *m* de monte ► **bush telegraph*** N (*fig*) teléfono *m* árabe*

bush[2] [bʊʃ] N (*Tech*) cojinete *m*

bushed [bʊʃt] ADJ [1] (*) (= *exhausted*) agotado, hecho polvo*; (= *puzzled*) perplejo, pasmado
[2] (*Australia*) perdido en el monte

bushel ['bʊʃl] N *medida de áridos (Brit = 36,37 litros; US = 35,24 litros)*

bush-league* ['bʊʃˌliːg] ADJ (*US Baseball*) de calidad mediocre

bushman ['bʊʃmən] N (*pl* **bushmen**) bosquimano *m*, bosquimán *m*

bushmeat ['bʊʃmiːt] N *carne de animales silvestres o salvajes*

bushranger ['bʊʃˌreɪndʒəʳ] N (*Australia*) bandido *m*

bushwhack ['bʊʃˌwæk] (*US*) Ⓐ VI abrirse camino por el bosque
Ⓑ VT (= *ambush*) tender una emboscada a

bushwhacker ['bʊʃˌwækəʳ] N (*US*) pionero/a *m/f*, explorador(a) *m/f*

bushy ['bʊʃɪ] ADJ (*compar* **bushier**; *superl* **bushiest**) [*plant*] parecido a un arbusto; [*ground*] lleno de arbustos; [*hair*] espeso, tupido; [*beard, eyebrows*] poblado

bushy-tailed [ˌbʊʃɪ'teɪld] ADJ **bright-eyed and ~** rebosante de energía y entusiasmo

busily ['bɪzɪlɪ] ADV afanosamente; **he was ~ engaged in painting it** lo estaba pintando afanosamente; **everyone was ~ writing** todos escribían con ahínco

business ['bɪznɪs] Ⓐ N [1] (= *commerce*) negocios *mpl*, comercio *m*; **~ is good at the moment** el negocio va bien por el momento; **~ is ~** los negocios son los negocios; **~ as usual** (= *general slogan*) aquí no ha pasado nada; (= *notice outside shop*) "seguimos atendiendo al público durante las reformas"; **~ before pleasure** primero es la obligación que la devoción; **to carry on ~ as** tener un negocio de; **to do ~ with** negociar con; **he's in ~** se dedica al comercio; **he's in ~ in London** trabaja en una empresa comercial de Londres; **he's in the selling ~** se dedica al comercio; **now we're in ~*** ya caminamos; **if we can find a car we're in ~*** si encontramos un coche empezamos a rodar; **to go into ~** dedicarse al comercio; **the shop is losing ~** la tienda está perdiendo clientela; **he means ~** habla en serio; **I'm here on ~** estoy (en viaje) de negocios; **to go abroad on ~** ir al extranjero en viaje de negocios; **to go out of ~** quebrar; **to put sb out of ~** hacer que algn quiebre; **to set up in ~ as** montar un negocio de; **to set sb up in ~** montar un negocio a algn; **to get down to ~** ir al grano
[2] (= *firm*) negocio *m*, empresa *f*
[3] (= *trade, profession*) oficio *m*, ocupación *f*; **what ~ are you in?** ¿a qué se dedica usted?; **he's got the biggest laugh in the ~** tiene la risa más fuerte que hay por aquí
[4] (= *task, duty, concern*) asunto *m*, responsabilidad *f*; **to send sb about his ~** echar a algn con cajas destempladas; **the ~ before the meeting** (*frm*) los asuntos a tratar; **I have ~ with the minister** tengo asuntos que tratar con el ministro; **what ~ have you to intervene?** ¿con qué derecho interviene usted?; **we're not in ~ to** + *INFIN* no tenemos por costumbre + *infin*; **we are not in the ~ of subsidizing scroungers** no tenemos por costumbre costearles la vida a los gorrones; **mind your own ~!** ◊ **none of your ~!*** ¡y a ti qué te importa!, ¡no te metas!*; **that's my ~** eso es cosa mía; **it is my ~ to** + *INFIN* me corresponde + *infin*; **I will make it my ~ to tell him** yo me encargaré de decírselo; **it's no ~ of mine** yo no tengo nada que ver con eso, no es cosa mía; **you had no ~ doing that** no tenías derecho a hacerlo; **they're working away like nobody's ~** están trabajando como locos; **it's none of his ~** no es asunto suyo; **any other ~** (*on agenda*) ruegos *mpl* y preguntas
[5] (*) (= *affair, matter*) asunto *m*, cuestión *f*; **the Suez ~** el asunto de Suez, la cuestión Suez; **it's a nasty ~** es un asunto feo; **finding a flat can be quite a ~** encontrar piso *or* (*LAm*) un departamento puede ser muy difícil; **did you hear about that ~ yesterday?** ¿te contaron algo de lo que pasó ayer?; **I can't stand this ~ of doing nothing** no puedo con este plan de no hacer nada; **what a ~ this is!** ¡vaya lío!
[6] (*Theat*) acción *f*, gag *m*
[7] **the dog did its ~*** el perro hizo sus necesidades
[8] **he's/it's the ~*** es fantástico
Ⓑ CPD ► **business address** N dirección *f* comercial *or* profesional ► **business administration** N (*as course*) administración *f* de empresas ► **business agent** N agente *mf* de negocios ► **business associate** N socio/a *m/f*, asociado/a *m/f* ► **business card** N tarjeta *f* de visita ► **business centre**, **business center** (*US*) N centro *m* financiero ► **business class** N (*Aer*) clase *f* preferente ► **business college** N escuela *f* de administración de empresas ► **business consultancy** N asesoría *f* empresarial ► **business consultant** N asesor(a) *m/f* de empresas ► **business deal** N trato *m* comercial ► **business district** N zona *f* comercial ► **business end*** N (*fig*) [*of tool, weapon*] punta *f* ► **business expenses** NPL gastos *mpl* (comerciales) ► **business hours** NPL horas *fpl* de oficina ► **business language** N lenguaje *m* comercial ► **business lunch** N comida *f* de negocios ► **business machines** NPL máquinas *fpl* para la empresa ► **business management** N dirección *f* empresarial ► **business manager** N (*Comm, Ind*) director(a) *m/f* comercial, gerente *mf* comercial; (*Theat*) secretario/a *m/f* ► **business park** N parque *m* industrial ► **business people** NPL empresarios *mpl*, gente *f* de negocios ► **business plan** N plan *m* de empresa ► **business practice** N práctica *f* empresarial ► **business premises** NPL local *msing* comercial ► **business school** N = **business college** ► **business sense** N cabeza *f* para los negocios ► **business Spanish** N español *m* comercial ► **(Faculty of) Business Studies** N (Facultad *f* de) Ciencias *fpl* Empresariales ► **business suit** N traje *m* de oficina *or* de calle ► **business trip** N viaje *m* de negocios

businesslike ['bɪznɪslaɪk] ADJ [*approach, transaction, firm, person, manner*] formal, serio

businessman ['bɪznɪsmæn] N (*pl* **businessmen**) (*gen*) hombre *m* de negocios; (= *trader*) empresario *m*; *see also* **small D**

businesswoman ['bɪznɪsˌwʊmən] N (*pl* **businesswomen**) mujer *f* de negocios; (= *trader*) empresaria *f*

busing ['bʌsɪŋ] N = **bussing**

busk [bʌsk] VI (*Brit*) tocar música (en la calle)

busker ['bʌskəʳ] N (*Brit*) músico/a *m/f* callejero/a

busload ['bʌsləʊd] N autobús *m* lleno; **they came by the ~** (*fig*) vinieron en masa, vinieron en tropel

busman ['bʌsmən] N (*pl* **busmen**) conductor *m*/cobrador *m* de autobús; **~'s holiday** (*fig*) *ocupación del ocio parecida a la del trabajo diario*

bussing ['bʌsɪŋ] N (*US*) transporte *m* escolar

bust[1] [bʌst] Ⓐ N [1] (*Art*) busto *m*
[2] (= *bosom*) pecho *m*
Ⓑ CPD ► **bust measurement** N talla *f* de pecho

bust[2] [bʌst] Ⓐ ADJ [1] (*) (= *broken*) estropeado, escacharrado (*Sp**)
[2] (*) (= *bankrupt*) **to go ~** [*business*] quebrar, irse a pique*; [*person*] arruinarse
Ⓑ N [1] (*Police‡*) (= *raid*) redada *f*
[2] (*US**) (= *failure*) pifia* *f*
Ⓒ VT [1] (*) (= *break*) destrozar, escacharrar (*Sp**); ✦***IDIOMS*** **to ~ a gut‡** echar los bofes*; **to ~ one's ass** (*US*‡*) ir de culo‡
[2] (*Police‡*) (= *arrest*) agarrar, trincar (*Sp**); (= *raid*) hacer una redada en; **the police ~ed him for drugs** la policía lo agarró por cuestión de drogas, la policía lo trincó por cuestión de drogas (*Sp**); **the police ~ed the place** la policía hizo una redada en el local
[3] (*esp US**) (= *demote*) [+ *officer*] degradar
Ⓓ VI (*) romperse, estropearse; **New York or ~!** ¡o Nueva York o nada!

►**bust up*** Ⓐ VT + ADV [+ *marriage, friendship*] romper
Ⓑ VI + ADV [*friends*] reñir, pelearse; **to ~ up with sb** (= *quarrel*) reñir *or* pelearse con algn; (= *break up*) romper con algn

bustard ['bʌstəd] N avutarda *f*

buster* ['bʌstəʳ] N (*in direct address*) macho *m* (*Sp**), tío *m* (*Sp**)

-buster ['bʌstəʳ] N (*ending in compounds*) **sanctions-buster** infractor(a) *m/f* de sanciones; **crime-buster** *persona que esclarece crímenes*

bustier ['buːstɪeɪ] N bustier *m*

bustle[1] ['bʌsl] Ⓐ N (= *activity*) ajetreo *m*, bullicio *m*; (= *haste*) prisa *f*
Ⓑ VI (*also* **~ about**) ir y venir; **to ~ in/out** entrar/salir afanosamente; **bustling with activity** rebosante de actividad

bustle[2] ['bʌsl] N (*Hist*) [*of dress*] polisón *m*

bustling ['bʌslɪŋ] ADJ [*streets*] animado, lleno de movimiento; [*crowd*] animado, afanoso

bust-up* ['bʌstʌp] N (= *quarrel*) riña *f*, bronca* *f*; (= *break-up*) ruptura *f*

busty* ['bʌstɪ] ADJ tetuda*

busway ['bʌsweɪ] N (*US*) carril *m* de autobuses, carril-bus *m*

busy ['bɪzɪ] Ⓐ ADJ (*compar* **busier**; *superl* **busiest**) [1] [*person*] ocupado; **are you ~?** ¿está ocupado?; **he's a ~ man** es un hombre muy ocupado; **to be ~ doing sth** estar ocupado haciendo algo; **she's ~ studying/cooking** está ocupada estudiando/cocinando; **to be ~ at** *or* **on** *or* **with** estar ocupado en *or* con; **he's ~ at his work** está ocupado en su trabajo; **to get ~** empezar a trabajar; (= *hurry*) menearse, darse prisa; **let's get ~** ¡a trabajar!; **to keep ~** mantenerse ocupado; **to keep sb ~** ocupar a algn; ✦***IDIOM*** **as ~ as a bee** ocupadísimo, atareadísimo
[2] [*day, time*] activo, ajetreado; **the busiest**

season is the autumn la época de mayor actividad es el otoño
3 [*place, town*] concurrido; [*scene*] animado, lleno de movimiento
4 [*telephone, line*] comunicando, ocupado
Ⓑ VT **to ~ o.s. with/doing sth** ocuparse con/en hacer algo
Ⓒ CPD ► **Busy Lizzie** N (*Bot*) alegría *f* de la casa ► **busy signal** N (*esp US Telec*) señal *f* de comunicando, tono *m* (de) ocupado

busybody ['bɪzɪbɒdɪ] N entrometido/a *m/f*

but [bʌt] Ⓐ CONJ 1 (*contrasting*) pero; **she was poor ~ she was honest** era pobre pero honrada; **I want to go ~ I can't afford it** quiero ir, pero no tengo el dinero; **~ it does move!** ¡pero sí se mueve!
2 (*in direct contradiction*) sino; **he's not Spanish ~ Italian** no es español sino italiano; **he didn't sing ~ he shouted** no cantó sino que gritó
3 (*subordinating*) **we never go out ~ it rains** nunca salimos sin que llueva; **I never go there ~ I think of you** nunca voy allá sin pensar en ti; ✦*PROV* **it never rains ~ it pours** llueve sobre mojado
4 (*as linker*) **~ then he couldn't have known** por otro lado, no podía saber *or* haberlo sabido; **~ then you must be my cousin!** ¡entonces tú debes ser mi primo!
Ⓑ ADV sólo, solamente, no más que; **she's ~ a child** no es más que una niña; **all ~ naked** casi desnudo; **you can ~ try** con intentar no se pierde nada; **if I could ~ speak to him** si solamente pudiese hablar con él; **one cannot ~ admire him** no se puede sino admirarle; **had I ~ known** de haberlo sabido (yo), si lo hubiera sabido
Ⓒ PREP (= *except*) menos, excepto, salvo; **anything ~ that** cualquier cosa menos eso; **everyone ~ him** todos menos él; **~ for you** si no fuera por ti; **the last ~ one** el/la penúltimo/a; **the last ~ three** el tercero antes del último; **there is nothing for it ~ to pay up** no hay más remedio que pagar; **who ~ she could have said something like that?** ¿quién sino ella podría haber dicho semejante cosa?
Ⓓ N pero *m*, objeción *f*; **no ~s about it!** ¡no hay pero que valga!; **come on, no ~s, off to bed with you!** ¡vale ya! no hay pero que valga, ¡a la cama!

butane ['bju:teɪn] Ⓐ N butano *m*; (*US*) (*for camping*) camping gas *m*
Ⓑ CPD ► **butane gas** N gas *m* butano

butch* [bʊtʃ] Ⓐ ADJ [*woman*] marimacho; [*man*] macho
Ⓑ N (= *woman*) marimacho *m or f*; (= *man*) macho *m*

butcher ['bʊtʃəʳ] Ⓐ N 1 (*gen, also fig*) carnicero/a *m/f*; **~'s (shop)** carnicería *f*; **at the ~'s** en la carnicería
2 (*US*) vendedor(a) *m/f* de dulces
3 ✦*IDIOM* **let's have a ~'s** (*Brit**) déjame verlo; → RHYMING SLANG
Ⓑ VT [+ *animal*] matar; (*fig*) hacer una carnicería con, masacrar

butchery ['bʊtʃərɪ] N (*lit*) carnicería *f*; (*fig*) matanza *f*, carnicería *f*

butler ['bʌtləʳ] N mayordomo *m*

butt¹ [bʌt] N (= *barrel*) tonel *m*; (*for rainwater*) tina *f*, aljibe *m*

butt² [bʌt] Ⓐ N 1 (*also* **~-end**) cabo *m*, extremo *m*; [*of gun*] culata *f*; [*of cigar*] colilla *f*
2 (*US**) (= *cigarette*) colilla *f*
3 (*esp US**) (= *bottom*) trasero* *m*, culo* *m*; ✦*IDIOM* **to work one's ~ off** romperse los cuernos*
Ⓑ CPD ► **butt cheeks*** NPL (*US*) nalgas *fpl*

butt³ [bʌt] N 1 (*Archery, Shooting*) (= *target*) blanco *m*; **the ~s** el campo de tiro al blanco
2 (*fig*) blanco *m*; **she's the ~ of his jokes** ella es el blanco de sus bromas

BUT

There are three main ways of translating the conjunction **but**: **pero**, **sino** and **sino que**.

Contrasting

• To introduce a contrast or a new idea, use **pero**:

Strange but interesting
Extraño pero interesante
I thought he would help me but he refused
Creí que me ayudaría, pero se negó

• In informal language, **pero** can be used at the start of a comment:

But where are you going to put it?
Pero ¿dónde lo vas a poner?

! In formal language, **sin embargo** or **no obstante** may be preferred:

But, in spite of the likely benefits, he still opposed the idea
Sin embargo *or* ***No obstante, a pesar de las probables ventajas, todavía se oponía a la idea***

Correcting a previous negative

• When **but** or **but rather** introduces a noun phrase, prepositional phrase or verb in the infinitive which corrects a previous negative, translate **but** using **sino**:

Not wine, but vinegar
No vino, sino vinagre
They aren't from Seville, but from Bilbao
No son de Sevilla, sino de Bilbao
His trip to London was not to investigate the case but to hush it up
Su viaje a Londres no fue para investigar el caso sino para taparlo

• When **but** or **but rather** introduces a verb clause (or requires a verb clause in Spanish) which corrects a previous negative, translate using **sino que**:

He's not asking you to do what he says but (rather) to listen to him
No te pide que hagas lo que él dice, sino que le escuches

Not only ... but also

• When the **but also** part of this construction contains SUBJECT + VERB, translate using **no sólo** or **no solamente ... sino que también** or **sino que además**:

It will not only cause tension, but it will also damage the economy
No sólo *or* ***No solamente provocará tensiones, sino que además*** *or* ***sino que también dañará la economía***

• When the **but also** part does not contain SUBJECT + VERB, translate using **no sólo** or **no solamente ... sino también** or **sino además**:

Not only rich but also powerful
No sólo *or* ***No solamente rico sino también*** *or* ***sino además poderoso***
We don't only want to negotiate but also to take decisions
No queremos sólo *or* ***solamente negociar, sino también tomar decisiones***

For further uses and examples, see main entry.

butt⁴ [bʌt] Ⓐ N (= *push with head*) cabezazo *m*; [*of goat*] topetazo *m*
Ⓑ VT [*goat*] topetar; [*person*] dar un cabezazo a; **to ~ one's head against** dar un cabezazo contra; **to ~ one's way through** abrirse paso a cabezazos

► **butt in** VI + ADV (= *interrupt*) interrumpir; (= *meddle*) meterse

► **butt into** VI + PREP [+ *conversation*] meterse en; [+ *meeting*] interrumpir

► **butt out*** VI + ADV (*US*) no entrometerse; **~ out!** ¡no te metas donde no te importa!

butter ['bʌtəʳ] Ⓐ N mantequilla *f*, manteca *f* (*Arg*); ✦*IDIOM* **~ wouldn't melt in his mouth** es una mosquita muerta*
Ⓑ VT [+ *bread*] untar con mantequilla
Ⓒ CPD ► **butter bean** N *tipo de frijol blanco o judía blanca* ► **butter dish** N mantequera *f* ► **butter icing** N glaseado *m* de mantequilla ► **butter knife** N cuchillo *m* de mantequilla

► **butter up*** VT + ADV (*Brit*) dar jabón a*

butterball* ['bʌtəbɔ:l] N (*US*) gordo/a *m/f*

buttercup ['bʌtəkʌp] N ranúnculo *m*

butter-fingered* ['bʌtə,fɪŋgəd] ADJ torpe

butterfingers* ['bʌtə,fɪŋgəz] N manazas* *mf*; **~!** ¡premio!

butterfly ['bʌtəflaɪ] Ⓐ N 1 (*Zool*) mariposa *f*; ✦*IDIOM* **I've got butterflies (in my stomach)** tengo los nervios en el estómago, estoy nerviosísimo
2 (*Swimming*) mariposa *f*
Ⓑ CPD ► **butterfly effect** N efecto *m* mariposa ► **butterfly knot** N nudo *m* de lazo ► **butterfly mind** N mentalidad *f* frívola ► **butterfly net** N manga *f* de mariposas ► **butterfly nut** N tuerca *f* de mariposa ► **butterfly stroke** N braza *f* de mariposa

buttermilk ['bʌtəmɪlk] N suero *m* de leche, suero *m* de manteca

butterscotch ['bʌtəskɒtʃ] N *dulce de azúcar terciado con mantequilla*

buttery ['bʌtərɪ] N despensa *f*

buttocks ['bʌtəks] NPL nalgas *fpl*

button ['bʌtn] Ⓐ N 1 (*on garment, machine*) botón *m*; **on the ~*** [*arrive*] en punto; (= *absolutely exact*) exacto; ✦*IDIOM* **to press** *or* **push the right ~** dar en la tecla
2 (*US*) (= *badge*) insignia *f*
3 **Buttons** (*esp Brit*) (*in hotel*) botones *m inv*
Ⓑ VT (*also* **~ up**) abrochar, abotonar; ✦*IDIOM* **to ~ one's lip*** no decir ni mu*
Ⓒ VI abrocharse; **it ~s in front** se abrocha por delante
Ⓓ CPD ► **button mushroom** N champiñón *m* pequeño

button-down ['bʌtndaʊn] ADJ [*shirt*] con cuello de botones; [*collar*] de botones

buttoned-up* ['bʌtnd,ʌp] ADJ [*person*] reservado

buttonhole ['bʌtnhəʊl] Ⓐ N 1 [*of garment*] ojal *m*
2 (*Brit*) (= *flower*) *flor que se lleva en el ojal*
Ⓑ VT (*fig*) enganchar; **I was ~d by Brian** Brian me enganchó y no me dejaba irme

buttonhook ['bʌtnhʊk] N abotonador *m*

button-through dress [,bʌtnθru:'dres] N vestido *m* abrochado por delante

buttress ['bʌtrɪs] Ⓐ N 1 (*Archit*) contrafuerte *m*
2 (*fig*) apoyo *m*, sostén *m*
Ⓑ VT 1 (*Archit*) apuntalar
2 (*fig*) reforzar, apoyar

butty* ['bʌtɪ] N (*Brit*) bocadillo *m*

buxom ['bʌksəm] ADJ con mucho pecho

buy [baɪ] (*vb: pt, pp* **bought**) Ⓐ N compra *f*; **a bad ~** una mala compra; **a good ~** una buena compra; **this month's best ~** la mejor oferta del mes

Ⓑ VT [1] (= *purchase*) comprar; **to ~ sth for sb** ◊ **~ sb sth** comprar algo a algn; **he bought me a bracelet** me compró una pulsera; **let me ~ it for you** deja que te lo compre; **to ~ sth from sb** comprar algo a algn; **I bought it from my brother/the shop on the corner** se lo compré a mi hermano/lo compré en la tienda de la esquina; **I can't get anyone to ~ it off me*** no consigo que me lo compre nadie; **you can ~ them cheaper in the supermarket** en el supermercado los venden más baratos; **money couldn't ~ it** no se puede comprar con dinero; **their victory was dearly bought** la victoria les costó cara
[2] (= *bribe*) sobornar, comprar*
[3] (*) (= *believe*) creer, tragar; **he won't ~ that explanation** no se va a tragar esa explicación*; **all right, I'll ~ it** bueno, te creo
[4] **he bought it**‡ (= *died*) estiró la pata*, la palmó (*Sp*‡)

►**buy back** VT + ADV volver a comprar

►**buy in** VT + ADV (*Brit*) [+ *food*] proveerse *or* abastecerse de; (*St Ex*) comprar; (*Fin*) comprar (por cuenta del dueño)

►**buy into** VI + PREP [1] [+ *company*] comprar acciones de
[2] (*fig*) (*) [+ *idea*] apoyar

►**buy off*** VT + ADV (= *bribe*) sobornar, comprar*

►**buy out** VT + ADV (*Comm*) [+ *business, partner*] comprar su parte de; **to ~ o.s. out of the army** *pagar una suma de dinero para dejar el ejército antes del periodo acordado*

►**buy up** VT + ADV [+ *property*] acaparar; [+ *stock*] comprar todas las existencias de

buy-back option ['baɪbæk,ɒpʃən] N opción *f* de recompra

buyer ['baɪəʳ] Ⓐ N comprador(a) *m/f*
Ⓑ CPD ► **buyer's market** N mercado *m* favorable al comprador

buying ['baɪɪŋ] Ⓐ N compra *f*
Ⓑ CPD ► **buying power** N poder *m* adquisitivo

buy-out ['baɪaʊt] Ⓐ N compra *f* de la totalidad de las acciones; **management ~** compra *f* de acciones por los gerentes; **workers' ~** compra *f* de una empresa por los trabajadores
Ⓑ CPD ► **buy-out clause** N cláusula *f* de rescisión

buzz [bʌz] Ⓐ N [1] [*of insect, device*] zumbido *m*; [*of conversation*] rumor *m*
[2] (*) (= *telephone call*) llamada *f* (telefónica), telefonazo* *m*; **to give sb a ~** dar un telefonazo a algn*, dar un toque a algn (*Sp**)
[3] (*) (= *thrill*) **to get a ~ from sth** gozar con algo; **driving fast gives me a ~** conducir a toda velocidad me entusiasma
[4] (*) (= *rumour*) rumor *m*
Ⓑ VT [1] (*) (= *call by buzzer*) llamar por el interfono; (*US Telec*) dar un telefonazo *or* (*Sp*) un toque a*
[2] (*Aer*) [+ *plane, building, ship*] pasar rozando
Ⓒ VI [1] [*insect*] zumbar
[2] [*ears, crowd*] zumbar; **my head is ~ing** me zumba la cabeza
[3] (*fig*) **the school ~ed with the news** todo el colegio comentaba la noticia
Ⓓ CPD (= *trendy*) [*phrase, topic*] de moda ► **buzz bomb** N bomba *f* volante ► **buzz saw** N sierra *f* circular

►**buzz about, buzz around*** VI + ADV [*person*] trajinar

►**buzz off**‡ VI + ADV (*esp Brit*) largarse*; **~ off!** ¡largo de aquí!*

buzzard ['bʌzəd] N (*Brit*) águila *f* ratonera; (*US*) buitre *m*, gallinazo *m* (*LAm*), zopilote *m* (*CAm, Mex*)

buzzer ['bʌzəʳ] N [1] (= *intercom*) portero *m* automático, interfono *m*
[2] (= *factory hooter*) sirena *f*
[3] (*electronic*) (*on cooker, timer etc*) timbre *m*

buzzing ['bʌzɪŋ] N zumbido *m*

buzzword* ['bʌzwɜːd] N palabra *f* que está de moda, cliché *m*

b.v. ABBR = **book value**

BVM N ABBR = **Blessed Virgin Mary**

b/w ABBR (= **black and white**) b/n

---

by [baɪ]

> Ⓐ PREPOSITION Ⓑ ADVERB
> *When* **by** *is the second element in a phrasal verb, eg* **go by**, **stand by**, *look up the verb. When it is part of a set combination, eg* **by chance**, **by degrees**, **by half**, *look up the other word.*

Ⓐ PREPOSITION

[1] [*= close to*] al lado de, junto a; **the house by the church** la casa que está al lado de *or* junto a la iglesia; **come and sit by me** ven y siéntate a mi lado *or* junto a mí; **I've got it by me** lo tengo a mi lado; **"where's the bank?" — "it's by the post office"** —¿dónde está el banco? —está al lado de *or* junto a la oficina de correos; **the house by the river** la casa que hay junto al río; [BUT] **a holiday by the sea** unas vacaciones en la costa

[2] [*= via*] por; **he came in by the back door/by the window** entró por la puerta de atrás/por la ventana; **which route did you come by?** ¿por dónde *or* por qué camino *or* por qué ruta viniste?; **I went by Dover** fui por Dover

[3] [*= past*] por delante de; **she walked by me** pasó por delante de mí; **he rushed by me without seeing me** pasó deprisa por delante de mí sin verme; **we drove by the cathedral** pasamos con el coche por delante de la catedral

[4] [*= during*] **by day** de día; **by night** de noche; **by day he's a bank clerk and by night he's a security guard** de día es un empleado de banco y de noche es guarda de seguridad; [BUT] **a postcard of London by night** una postal nocturna de Londres

[5] [*in expressions of time*] [5·1] (= *not later than*) para; **we must be there by four o'clock** tenemos que estar allí para las cuatro; **can you finish it by tomorrow?** ¿puedes terminarlo para mañana?; **I'll be back by midnight** estaré de vuelta antes de *or* para la medianoche; **applications must be submitted by 21 April** las solicitudes deben presentarse antes del 21 de abril; **by the time I got there it was too late** cuando llegué ya era demasiado tarde; **it'll be ready by the time you get back** estará listo para cuando regreses; **by that time** *or* **by then I knew** para entonces ya lo sabía
[5·2] (*in year, on date, on day*) **by tomorrow/Tuesday, I'll be in France** mañana/el martes ya estaré en Francia; **by yesterday it was clear that …** ayer ya se veía claro que …; **by 30 September we had spent £500** a 30 de septiembre habíamos gastado 500 libras; **by 1998 the figure had reached …** en 1998 la cifra había llegado a …; **by 2010 the figure will have reached …** hacia el año 2010 la cifra habrá llegado a …

[6] [*indicating amount or rate*] **to reduce sth by a third** reducir algo en una tercera parte; **to rent a house by the month** alquilar una casa por meses; **letters were arriving by the sackload** las cartas llegaban a montones; **it seems to be getting bigger by the minute/day** parece que va creciendo minuto a minuto/día a día; **to sell sth by the dozen** vender algo por docenas; **we get paid by the hour** nos pagan por horas; **we sell by the kilo** vendemos por kilos; **we charge by the kilometre** cobramos por kilómetro; **little by little** poco a poco; **one by one** uno tras otro, uno a uno; **two by two** de dos en dos

[7] [*indicating agent, cause*] por; **the thieves were caught by the police** los ladrones fueron capturados por la policía, la policía capturó a los ladrones; [BUT] **surrounded by enemies** rodeado de enemigos; **a painting by Picasso** un cuadro de Picasso; **who's that song by?** ¿de quién es esa canción?; **he had a daughter by his first wife** tuvo una hija con su primera mujer

[8] [*indicating transport, method, etc*] **by air** [*travel*] en avión; [*send*] por avión, por vía aérea; **by bus/car** en autobús/coche; **to pay by cheque** pagar con cheque; **made by hand** hecho a mano; **by land** por tierra; **by the light of the moon/a candle** a la luz de la luna/de una vela; **by rail** *or* **train** en tren; **by sea** por mar

[9] [*with gerund*] **by working hard** a fuerza de mucho trabajar, trabajando mucho; **he ended by saying that …** terminó diciendo que …

[10] [*= according to*] según; **by my watch it's five o'clock** según mi reloj son las cinco; **by my calculations** según mis cálculos; [BUT] **to call sth by its proper name** llamar algo por su nombre; **it's all right by me** por mí no hay problema *or* está bien; **if that's okay by you** si no tienes inconveniente

[11] [*measuring difference*] **she missed the plane by a few minutes** perdió el avión por unos minutos; **we beat them to Joe's house by five minutes** llegamos a casa de Joe cinco minutos antes que ellos; **broader by a metre** un metro más ancho; **she's lighter than her brother by only a couple of pounds** pesa sólo un par de libras menos que su hermano; **it's too short by a metre** es un metro más corto de lo que tendría que ser; **it missed me by inches** no me dio por un pelo, me pasó rozando

[12] [*in measurements, sums*] **a room 3 metres by 4** una habitación de 3 metros por 4; **to divide by** dividir por *or* entre; **to multiply by** multiplicar por

[13] **by oneself** solo; **he was all by himself** estaba solo; **I did it all by myself** lo hice yo solo; **don't leave the two of them alone by themselves** no los dejes solos

[14] [*with compass point*] **north by northeast** nornordeste; **south by southwest** sudsudoeste, sursuroeste

[15] [*in oaths*] por; **I swear by Almighty God** juro por Dios Todopoderoso; **by heaven*** por Dios

Ⓑ ADVERB

[1] [*= past*] **a train hurtled by** pasó un tren a toda velocidad; **they wouldn't let me by** no me dejaban pasar; **she rushed by without stopping** pasó a toda prisa, sin pararse

[2] [*in set expressions*] **by and by**: **I'll be with you by and by** enseguida estoy contigo; **you'll be sorry by and by** no tardarás en arrepentirte; **by and by we heard voices** al poco rato oímos unas voces; **close** *or* **hard by** muy cerca; **by and large** en general, por lo general; **to put sth by** poner algo a un lado

bye¹* [baɪ] EXCL (= *goodbye*) adiós, hasta luego, chao *or* chau (*esp LAm*); **~ for now!** ¡hasta luego!

bye² [baɪ] N [1] (*Sport*) bye *m*; **to have a ~** pasar a la segunda eliminatoria por sorteo
[2] **by the ~** por cierto, a propósito

bye-bye* [ˌbaɪˈbaɪ] EXCL ¡adiós!, ¡hasta luego!, chao *or* chau (*esp LAm*)

bye-byes [ˈbaɪˌbaɪz] NPL (*baby talk*) **to go ~** dormirse, quedar dormido; **it's time to go ~** es hora de acostarte

bye-election [ˈbaɪɪˌlekʃən] N = **by-election**

bye-law [ˈbaɪlɔː] N = **by-law**

by-election [ˈbaɪɪˌlekʃən] N elección *f* parcial; → MARGINAL SEAT

BY-ELECTION

Se denomina **by-election** *en el Reino Unido y otros países de la* **Commonwealth** *a las elecciones convocadas con carácter excepcional cuando un escaño queda desierto por fallecimiento o dimisión de un parlamentario* (**Member of Parliament**)*. Dichas elecciones tienen lugar únicamente en el área electoral representada por el citado parlamentario, su* **constituency***.*

Byelorussia [ˌbjeləʊˈrʌʃə] N Bielorrusia *f*

Byelorussian [ˌbjeləʊˈrʌʃən] (A) ADJ bielorruso
(B) N [1] (= *person*) bielorruso/a *m/f*
[2] (*Ling*) bielorruso *m*

bygone [ˈbaɪgɒn] (A) ADJ [*days, times*] pasado
(B) N **✦IDIOM to let ~s be ~s** olvidar el pasado; **let ~s be ~s** lo pasado, pasado está

by-law [ˈbaɪlɔː] N ordenanza *f* municipal

by-line [ˈbaɪlaɪn] N (*Press*) pie *m* de autor

by-name [ˈbaɪneɪm] N sobrenombre *m*; (= *nickname*) apodo *m*, mote *m*

BYOB* ABBR (= **bring your own bottle**) trae botella

bypass [ˈbaɪpɑːs] (A) N [1] (= *road*) circunvalación *f*, carretera *f* de circunvalación
[2] (*Elec*) desviación *f*
[3] (*Med*) (operación *f* de) by-pass *m*; **a heart ~** un by-pass de corazón; **to have a humour/charisma ~** (*hum*) no tener ni gota de sentido del humor/carisma
(B) VT [1] [+ *town*] evitar entrar en
[2] (*fig*) [+ *person, difficulty*] evitar
(C) CPD ► **bypass operation** N (operación *f* de) by-pass *m* ► **bypass surgery** N cirugía *f* de by-pass

by-play [ˈbaɪpleɪ] N (*Theat*) acción *f* aparte, escena *f* muda

by-product [ˈbaɪˌprɒdəkt] N (*Chem etc*) subproducto *m*, derivado *m*; (*fig*) consecuencia *f*, resultado *m*

byre [ˈbaɪəʳ] N establo *m*

by-road [ˈbaɪrəʊd] N camino *m* vecinal, carretera *f* secundaria

bystander [ˈbaɪˌstændəʳ] N (= *spectator*) espectador(a) *m/f*; (= *witness*) testigo *mf*; **an innocent ~** un transeúnte que pasaba/pasa *etc* por allí

byte [baɪt] N (*Comput*) byte *m*, octeto *m*

byway [ˈbaɪweɪ] N camino *m* poco frecuentado; **the ~s of history** los aspectos poco conocidos de la historia

byword [ˈbaɪwɜːd] N [1] sinónimo *m*; **his name is a ~ for success** su nombre es sinónimo de éxito
[2] (= *slogan*) palabra *f* de moda

by-your-leave [ˌbaɪˌjɔːˈliːv] N **without so much as a ~** sin siquiera pedir permiso, sin más ni más

Byzantine [baɪˈzæntaɪn] (A) ADJ bizantino
(B) N bizantino/a *m/f*

Byzantium [baɪˈzæntɪəm] N Bizancio *m*

C c

C[1], **c**[1] [siː] N [1] (= *letter*) C, c *f*; **C for Charlie** C de Carmen
[2] (*Mus*) **C** do *m*; **C major/minor** do mayor/menor; **C sharp/flat** do sostenido/bemol

C[2] ABBR [1] (*Literat*) (= **chapter**) cap., c., c/
[2] (*Geog*) = **Cape**
[3] (= **Celsius, Centigrade**) C
[4] (*Pol*) = **Conservative**

c[2] ABBR [1] (*US Fin*) (= **cent**) c
[2] (= **century**) S.
[3] = **circa** (= *about*) h.
[4] (*Math*) = **cubic**
[5] (= **carat**) qts., quil.

c. ABBR (= **chapter**) cap., c., c/

C.14 (A) N ABBR (= **carbon 14**) C-14
(B) CPD ► **C.14 dating** N datación *f* por C-14

CA N ABBR [1] = **Central America**
[2] = **chartered accountant**
[3] (*US*) = **California**
[4] (*Brit*) (= **Consumers' Association**) ≈ OCU *f* (*Sp*)

ca. ABBR (= **circa**) h.

C/A ABBR [1] (= **current account**) cta., cte., c/c
[2] = **credit account**
[3] = **capital account**

CAA N ABBR [1] (*Brit*) (= **Civil Aviation Authority**) ≈ Aviación *f* Civil
[2] (*US*) = **Civil Aeronautics Authority**

CAB N ABBR (*Brit*) (= **Citizens' Advice Bureau**) *oficina que facilita información gratuita sobre materias legales*; → CITIZENS' ADVICE BUREAU

cab [kæb] (A) N [1] (= *taxi*) taxi *m*, colectivo *m* (*LAm*)
[2] [*of lorry etc*] cabina *f*
[3] (††) (*horse-drawn*) cabriolé *m*, coche *m* de caballos
(B) CPD ► **cab driver** N taxista *mf* ► **cab rank**, **cab stand** N parada *f* de taxis

cabal [kəˈbæl] N (= *clique*) contubernio *m*, camarilla *f*; (= *conspiracy*) conspiración *f*

cabala [kəˈbɑːlə] N = **cabbala**

cabaret [ˈkæbəreɪ] N cabaret *m*

cabbage [ˈkæbɪdʒ] (A) N [1] (*Bot*) col *f*, repollo *m*
[2] (*fig*) (= *person*) vegetal *m*
(B) CPD ► **cabbage white (butterfly)** N mariposa *f* de la col

cabbala [kəˈbɑːlə] N cábala *f*

cabbalistic [ˌkæbəˈlɪstɪk] ADJ cabalístico

cabbie*, **cabby*** [ˈkæbɪ] N [*of taxi*] taxista *mf*; (††) [*of horse-drawn cab*] cochero *m*

caber [keɪbəʳ] N (*Scot*) tronco *m*; *see* **toss B2**; → HIGHLAND GAMES

cabin [ˈkæbɪn] (A) N [1] (= *hut*) cabaña *f*
[2] (*Naut*) camarote *m*; [*of lorry, plane*] cabina *f*
(B) CPD ► **cabin boy** N grumete *m* ► **cabin class** N (*Naut*) segunda clase *f* ► **cabin crew** N (*Aer*) tripulación *f* de pilotaje ► **cabin cruiser** N yate *m* de crucero (a motor) ► **cabin trunk** N baúl *m*

cabinet [ˈkæbɪnɪt] (A) N [1] (= *cupboard*) armario *m*; (*for display*) vitrina *f*; (*for medicine*) botiquín *m*; (*Rad, TV*) caja *f*
[2] (*Pol*) (*also* **Cabinet**) consejo *m* de ministros, gabinete *m* ministerial
(B) CPD ► **cabinet crisis** N crisis *f inv* del gobierno ► **cabinet meeting** N consejo *m* de ministros ► **Cabinet Minister** N ministro/a *m/f* (del Gabinete)

> **CABINET**
>
> *El Consejo de Ministros británico (***Cabinet***) se compone de unos veinte ministros, escogidos por el Primer Ministro (***Prime Minister***). Su función es la de planificar la legislación importante y defender la política del Gobierno en los debates.*
>
> *En Estados Unidos el* **Cabinet** *tiene meramente carácter consultivo, su función es aconsejar al Presidente. Sus miembros, escogidos por él y nombrados con el consentimiento del Senado (***Senate***), son jefes de departamentos ejecutivos o altos cargos del gobierno, pero no pueden ser miembros del Congreso (***Congress***). Existe otro grupo de asesores del Presidente, que actúan a un nivel menos oficial, que se conoce como* **kitchen cabinet**.

cabinetmaker [ˈkæbɪnɪtˌmeɪkəʳ] N ebanista *mf*

cabinetmaking [ˈkæbɪnɪtˌmeɪkɪŋ] N ebanistería *f*

cable [ˈkeɪbl] (A) N [1] (= *rope, Elec, cablegram*) cable *m*
[2] = **cable television**
(B) VT [1] [+ *news, money*] mandar por cable, cablegrafiar; [+ *person*] mandar un cable a
[2] (*TV*) [+ *city, homes*] instalar la televisión por cable en
(C) CPD ► **cable address** N dirección *f* cablegráfica ► **cable car** N teleférico *m*, funicular *m* ► **cable railway** N (*aerial*) teleférico *m*; (*funicular*) funicular *m* aéreo ► **cable stitch** N punto *m* de trenza ► **cable television** N televisión *f* por cable ► **cable transfer** N (*Fin*) transferencia *f* por cable

cablecast [ˈkeɪblˌkɑːst] (A) N emisión *f* de televisión por cable
(B) VT emitir por cable

cablegram [ˈkeɪblgræm] N cablegrama *m*

cableway [ˈkeɪblweɪ] N teleférico *m*, funicular *m* aéreo

cabling [ˈkeɪblɪŋ] N (*Elec*) (= *cables*) red *f* de cables, cableado *m*; (= *process*) cableado *m*

cabman [ˈkæbmən] N (*pl* **cabmen**) [1] (= *taxi driver*) taxista *m*
[2] (††) [*of horse-drawn cab*] cochero *m*

caboodle [kəˈbuːdl] N **the whole (kit and) ~*** todo el rollo*, toda la pesca*

caboose [kəˈbuːs] N (*US*) furgón *m* de cola

cacao [kəˈkɑːəʊ] N cacao *m*

cache [kæʃ] (A) N [1] (= *stores*) víveres *mpl* escondidos; [*of contraband, arms, explosives*] alijo *m*
[2] (*Comput*) = **cache memory**
(B) VT (= *hide*) esconder, ocultar; (= *hoard*) acumular
(C) CPD ► **cache memory** N (*Comput*) (memoria *f*) cache *m or f*

cachet [ˈkæʃeɪ] N caché *m*, cachet *m*

cack‡ [kæk] N (*Brit*) (*lit, fig*) mierda‡ *f*

cack-handed* [ˌkækˈhændɪd] ADJ (*esp Brit*) (= *clumsy*) [*person*] patoso*, desmañado; [*attempt, version*] chapucero*, torpe

cackle [ˈkækl] (A) N [*of hen*] cacareo *m*; (= *laugh*) risa *f* aguda; (= *chatter*) parloteo *m*; **cut the ~!*** ¡corta el rollo!*
(B) VI [*hen*] cacarear; [*person*] reírse a carcajada limpia, carcajearse

CACM N ABBR (= **Central American Common Market**) MCCA *m*

cacophonous [kəˈkɒfənəs] ADJ cacofónico

cacophony [kæˈkɒfənɪ] N cacofonía *f*

cactus [ˈkæktəs] (*pl* **cactuses, cacti** [ˈkæktaɪ]) N cacto *m*, cactus *m inv*

CAD [kæd] N ABBR (= **computer-aided design**) DAO *m*, DAC *m* (*LAm*)

cad†* [kæd] N canalla *m*, sinvergüenza *m*; **you ~!** ¡canalla!*

cadaster, cadastre [kəˈdæstəʳ] N catastro *m*

cadaver [kəˈdeɪvəʳ] N (*esp US*) cadáver *m*

cadaverous [kəˈdævərəs] ADJ cadavérico

CADCAM [ˈkædˌkæm] N ABBR = **computer-aided design and manufacture**

caddie, caddy[1] [ˈkædɪ] (*Golf*) (A) N caddie *mf*
(B) VI **to ~ for sb** hacer de caddie a algn

caddis fly [ˈkædɪsflaɪ] N frígano *m*

caddish†* [ˈkædɪʃ] ADJ desvergonzado, canallesco; **~ trick** canallada *f*

caddy[1] [ˈkædɪ] N = **caddie**

caddy[2] [ˈkædɪ] N [1] (*also* **tea ~**) cajita *f* para té
[2] (*US*) (= *shopping trolley*) carrito *m* de la compra

cadence [ˈkeɪdəns] N (*Mus*) [*of voice*] cadencia *f*; (= *rhythm*) ritmo *m*, cadencia *f*; **the ~s of prose** el ritmo de la prosa

cadenza [kəˈdenzə] N cadencia *f*

cadet [kəˈdet] (A) N [1] (*Mil etc*) cadete *m*
[2] (= *younger son*) hijo *m* menor
(B) CPD ► **cadet corps** N (*Brit*) (*in school*) cuerpo *m* de alumnos que reciben entrenamiento militar; (*Police*) cuerpo *m* de cadetes

► **cadet school** N escuela *f* en la que se ofrece instrucción militar

cadge* [kædʒ] (*Brit*) Ⓐ VT [+ *money, cigarette etc*] gorronear*, sablear*; **could I ~ a lift from you?** ¿me puedes llevar?, ¿me das un aventón? (*Mex*)
Ⓑ VI gorronear*, vivir de gorra*; **you can't ~ off me** no te molestes en pedirme nada

cadger* ['kædʒəʳ] N (*Brit*) gorrón/ona* *m/f*, sablista* *mf*

Cadiz [kə'dɪz] N Cádiz *m*

cadmium ['kædmɪəm] N cadmio *m*

cadre ['kædrɪ] N (*Mil etc*) cuadro *m*; (*Pol*) (= *worker, official*) delegado/a *m/f*

CAE N ABBR (= **computer-aided engineering**) IAO *f*, IAC *f* (*LAm*)

caecum, **cecum** (*US*) ['si:kəm] N (*pl* **caeca** ['si:kə]) (intestino *m*) ciego *m*

Caesar ['si:zəʳ] N César

Caesarean, **Cesarean** (*US*) [si:'zɛərɪən] N (*also* **~ operation** *or* **section**) (operación *f* de) cesárea *f*

caesium, **cesium** (*US*) ['si:zɪəm] N cesio *m*

caesura [sɪ'zjʊərə] N (*pl* **caesuras** *or* **caesurae** [sɪ'zjʊəri:]) cesura *f*

CAF, **c.a.f.** N ABBR (= **cost and freight**) C y F

café ['kæfeɪ] Ⓐ N café *m*
Ⓑ CPD ► **café society** N la gente de moda

cafeteria [ˌkæfɪ'tɪərɪə] N (restaurante *m* de) autoservicio *m*; (*in factory, office*) cafetería *f*, comedor *m*

caff* [kæf] N (*Brit*) = **café**

caffein(e) ['kæfi:n] N cafeína *f*

caffeine-free [ˌkæfi:n'fri:] ADJ [*beverage*] sin cafeína

caftan ['kæftæn] N caftán *m*

cage [keɪdʒ] Ⓐ N jaula *f*; (*in mine*) jaula *f* de ascensor
Ⓑ VT enjaular; **like a ~d tiger** como una fiera enjaulada
Ⓒ CPD ► **cage(d) bird** N pájaro *m* de jaula

cagey ['keɪdʒɪ] (*compar* **cagier**; *superl* **cagiest**) ADJ (= *reserved*) reservado; (= *cautious*) cauteloso; **he was very ~ about it** en eso se anduvo con mucha reserva; **Michael was ~ about his plans after resigning** Michael mantenía celosamente en secreto sus planes tras dimitir

cagily ['keɪdʒɪlɪ] ADV [*say*] cautelosamente, con cautela

caginess ['keɪdʒɪnɪs] N [*of person, reply*] cautela *f*

cagoule [kə'gu:l] N chubasquero *m*; (*without zip*) canguro *m*

cahoots* [kə'hu:ts] NPL ✦*IDIOM* **to be in ~ with sb** estar conchabado con algn*

CAI N ABBR (= **computer-aided instruction**) IAO *f*

caiman ['keɪmən] N caimán *m*

Cain [keɪn] N Caín; ✦*IDIOM* **to raise ~*** armar la gorda, protestar enérgicamente

cairn [kɛən] N montón *m* de piedras colocadas como señal

Cairo ['kaɪərəʊ] N El Cairo

caisson ['keɪsən] N (*Mech*) cajón *m* hidráulico; (*Naut*) cajón *m* de suspensión; [*of dry-dock*] puerta *f* de dique; (*Mil*) cajón *m* de municiones

cajole [kə'dʒəʊl] VT engatusar, camelar; **to ~ sb into doing sth** engatusar a algn para que haga algo

cajolery [kə'dʒəʊlərɪ] N zalamerías *fpl*

Cajun ['keɪdʒən] Ⓐ ADJ cajún; **~ cookery** cocina *f* tipo cajún
Ⓑ N [1] (= *person*) cajún *mf*
[2] (*Ling*) cajún *m*

CAJUN

A los habitantes del sur de Luisiana que hablan un dialecto francés se les llama **Cajuns**. *Son los descendientes de los canadienses franceses expulsados de Nueva Escocia por los británicos en 1755, llamada entonces Acadia (***Cajun** *es la forma acortada de* **Acadian**). *El dialecto combina francés arcaico con inglés y español, junto con algunas palabras y frases hechas indias. Tanto su comida picante como su música se conocen hoy en el mundo entero.*

cake [keɪk] Ⓐ N [1] (*large*) tarta *f*, pastel *m*, torta *f* (*LAm*); (*small*) pastel *m*, queque *m* (*LAm*); (*sponge, plain*) bizcocho *m*, pan *m* dulce; **the way the national ~ is divided** (*fig*) la forma en que está repartida la tarta *or* está repartido el pastel nacional; ✦*IDIOMS* **it's a piece of ~*** es pan comido, está tirado*; **to go** *or* **sell like hot ~s*** venderse como rosquillas; **to have one's ~ and eat it**: **he wants to have his ~ and eat it** quiere nadar y guardar la ropa; **that takes the ~!*** ¡es el colmo!
[2] (= *bar*) [*of chocolate*] barra *f*; [*of soap*] pastilla *f*
Ⓑ VT **~d with mud** embarrado, cubierto de barro seco
Ⓒ VI [*blood*] coagularse; [*mud*] endurecerse
Ⓓ CPD ► **cake mix** N polvos *mpl* para hacer pasteles ► **cake shop** N pastelería *f* ► **cake tin** N (*for baking*) molde *m* para pastel; (*for storing*) caja *f* de pastel

caked [keɪkt] Ⓐ PT, PP *of* **cake**
Ⓑ ADJ *see* **cake B**

Cal. ABBR = **California**

cal. N ABBR = **calorie**

calabash ['kæləbæʃ] N calabaza *f*

calaboose* ['kæləbu:s] N (*US*) jaula *f*; (= *prison*) cárcel *f*

calamine ['kæləmaɪn] N (*also* **~ lotion**) (loción *f* de) calamina *f*

calamitous [kə'læmɪtəs] ADJ calamitoso, desastroso

calamity [kə'læmɪtɪ] N calamidad *f*, desastre *m*

calcareous [kæl'kɛərɪəs] ADJ calcáreo

calcicole ['kælsɪˌkəʊl] N calcícola *f*

calcicolous [kæl'sɪkələs] ADJ calcícola

calcification [ˌkælsɪfɪ'keɪʃən] N calcificación *f*

calcifugous [kæl'sɪfjəgəs] ADJ calcífugo

calcify ['kælsɪfaɪ] Ⓐ VT calcificar
Ⓑ VI calcificarse

calcium ['kælsɪəm] Ⓐ N calcio *m*
Ⓑ CPD ► **calcium carbonate** N carbonato *m* de calcio ► **calcium chloride** N cloruro *m* de calcio

calculable ['kælkjʊləbl] ADJ calculable

calculate ['kælkjʊleɪt] Ⓐ VT [1] (= *measure*) [+ *weight, speed, number, distance*] calcular
[2] (= *judge*) [+ *effects, consequences, risk*] calcular
[3] (= *intend*) **his words were ~d to cause pain** había planeado expresamente sus palabras para hacer daño; **this is ~d to give him a jolt** el propósito de esto es darle una sacudida; **a move ~d to improve his popularity** una operación diseñada *or* pensada para darle mayor popularidad
Ⓑ VI (*Math*) calcular, hacer cálculos

►**calculate on** VI + PREP (= *count on*) contar con

calculated ['kælkjʊleɪtɪd] ADJ (= *deliberate*) [*insult, action*] deliberado, intencionado; **(to take) a ~ risk** (correr) un riesgo calculado

calculating ['kælkjʊleɪtɪŋ] Ⓐ ADJ (= *scheming*) [*person*] calculador
Ⓑ CPD ► **calculating machine** N calculadora *f*, máquina *f* de calcular

calculation [ˌkælkjʊ'leɪʃən] N (*Math*) (= *estimation*) cálculo *m*; **to make** *or* **do a ~** realizar un cálculo

calculator ['kælkjʊleɪtəʳ] N (= *machine*) calculadora *f*

calculus ['kælkjʊləs] N (*pl* **calculuses** *or* **calculi** ['kælkjʊlaɪ]) (*Math*) cálculo *m*; **integral/differential ~** cálculo *m* integral/diferencial

Calcutta [kæl'kʌtə] N Calcuta *f*

Caledonia [ˌkælə'dəʊnɪə] N Caledonia *f*

Caledonian [ˌkælɪ'dəʊnɪən] Ⓐ ADJ caledoniano
Ⓑ N caledoniano/a *m/f*

calendar ['kæləndəʳ] Ⓐ N [1] (= *chart*) calendario *m*
[2] (= *year*) calendario *m*; **the Church ~** el calendario eclesiástico; **the university ~** (*Brit*) el calendario universitario; **the most important event in the sporting ~** el acontecimiento más importante del año *or* calendario deportivo
[3] (*Jur*) lista *f* (de pleitos)
Ⓑ CPD ► **calendar month** N mes *m* civil ► **calendar year** N año *m* civil

calf[1] [kɑ:f] Ⓐ N (*pl* **calves**) [1] (= *young cow*) becerro/a *m/f*, ternero/a *m/f*; (= *young seal, elephant etc*) cría *f*; (= *young whale*) ballenato *m*; **the cow is in** *or* **with ~** la vaca está preñada; ✦*IDIOM* **to kill the fatted ~** celebrar una fiesta de bienvenida
[2] = **calfskin**
Ⓑ CPD ► **calf love** N amor *m* juvenil

calf[2] [kɑ:f] N (*pl* **calves**) (*Anat*) pantorrilla *f*, canilla *f* (*esp LAm*)

calfskin ['kɑ:fskɪn] N piel *f* de becerro

caliber ['kælɪbəʳ] N (*US*) = **calibre**

calibrate ['kælɪbreɪt] VT [+ *gun*] calibrar; [+ *scale of measuring instrument*] graduar

calibrated ['kælɪbreɪtɪd] ADJ calibrado

calibration [ˌkælɪ'breɪʃən] N [*of gun etc*] calibración *f*; [*of measuring instrument*] graduación *f*

calibre, **caliber** (*US*) ['kælɪbəʳ] N [1] [*of rifle*] calibre *m*
[2] [*of person*] calibre *m*, talla *f*; **a man of his ~** un hombre de su calibre *or* talla; **then he showed his real ~** luego demostró su verdadero valor *or* su verdadera talla; **the high ~ of the research staff** el alto nivel de los investigadores

calico ['kælɪkəʊ] Ⓐ N (*pl* **calicoes** *or* **calicos**) calicó *m*, percal *m*
Ⓑ ADJ [*jacket, shirt etc*] de percal

Calif. ABBR = **California**

California [ˌkælɪ'fɔ:nɪə] N California *f*

Californian [ˌkælɪ'fɔ:nɪən] Ⓐ ADJ californiano
Ⓑ N californiano/a *m/f*

californium [ˌkælɪ'fɔ:nɪəm] N californio *m*

calipers ['kælɪpəz] NPL (*US*) = **callipers**

caliph ['keɪlɪf] N califa *m*

caliphate ['keɪlɪfeɪt] N califato *m*

calisthenics [ˌkælɪs'θenɪks] NSING (*US*) = **calisthenics**

CALL [kɔ:l] N ABBR = **computer-assisted language learning**

▼ **call** [kɔ:l] Ⓐ N [1] (= *cry*) llamada *f*, llamado *m* (*LAm*); (= *shout*) grito *m*; [*of bird*] canto *m*, reclamo *m*; (*imitating bird's cry*) reclamo *m*; (*imitating animal's cry*) chilla *f*; **they came at my ~** acudieron a mi llamada; **please give me a ~ at seven** (*in hotel*) despiérteme a las siete,

➤ LANGUAGE IN USE: call A2, B3, C2 27

por favor; (*at friend's*) llámame a las siete; **within ~** al alcance de la voz
2 (*Telec*) llamada *f*; **long-distance ~** conferencia *f*; **to make a ~** llamar (por teléfono), hacer una llamada, telefonear (*esp LAm*)
3 (= *appeal, summons, invitation*) llamamiento *m*, llamado (*LAm*); (*Aer*) (*for flight*) anuncio *m*; (*Theat*) (*to actor*) llamamiento *m*; **a ~ went to the fire brigade** se llamó a los bomberos; **he's had a ~ to the Palace** le han llamado a palacio; **to answer the ~** (*Rel*) acudir al llamamiento; **the boat sent out a ~ for help** el barco emitió una llamada de socorro; **there were ~s for the Minister's resignation** hubo quienes pidieron la dimisión del ministro; **a ~ for a strike** una convocatoria de huelga; **a ~ for congress papers** una convocatoria de ponencias para un congreso; **to be on ~** (= *on duty*) estar de guardia; (= *available*) estar disponible; **money on ~** dinero *m* a la vista; **the minister sent out a ~ to the country to remain calm** el ministro hizo un llamamiento al país para que conservara la calma
4 (= *lure*) llamada *f*; **the ~ of duty** la llamada del deber; **to answer the ~ of nature** (*euph*) hacer sus necesidades fisiológicas; **the ~ of the sea** la llamada del mar; **the ~ of the unknown** la llamada de lo desconocido
5 (= *visit*) (*also Med*) visita *f*; **the boat makes a ~ at Vigo** el barco hace escala en Vigo; **to pay a ~ on sb** ir a ver a algn, hacer una visita a algn; **port of ~** puerto *m* de escala
6 (= *need*) motivo *m*; **you had no ~ to say that** no tenías motivo alguno para decir eso; **there is no ~ for alarm** no tienen por qué asustarse
7 (= *demand*) demanda *f* (**for** de); **there isn't much ~ for these now** hay poca demanda de éstos ahora
8 (= *claim*) **to have first ~ on sth** (*resources etc*) tener prioridad en algo; (*when buying it*) tener opción de compra sobre algo; **there are many ~s on my time** hay muchos asuntos que requieren mi atención; **the UN has many ~s on its resources** la ONU reparte sus recursos en muchos frentes
9 (*Bridge*) marca *f*, voz *f*; **whose ~ is it?** ¿a quién le toca declarar?
10 ✦*IDIOM* **to have a close ~** escapar por un pelo, salvarse de milagro; **that was a close ~** eso fue cosa de milagro
Ⓑ VT 1 (= *shout out*) [+ *name, person*] llamar, gritar; **did you ~ me?** ¿me llamaste?; **they ~ed me to see it** me llamaron para que lo viese; *see also* **attention A1**, **halt A1**, **name A2**, **shot B4**, **tune A1**
2 (= *summon*) [+ *doctor, taxi*] llamar; [+ *meeting, election*] convocar; **to be ~ed to the Bar** (*Brit Jur*) licenciarse como abogado, recibirse de abogado (*LAm*); **he felt ~ed to serve God** se sentía llamado a servir al Señor; **to ~ a strike** convocar una huelga; **to ~ sb as a witness** citar a algn como testigo
3 (*Telec*) llamar (por teléfono); **I'll ~ you tomorrow** te llamo mañana; **London ~ed you this morning** esta mañana le llamaron desde Londres; **don't ~ us, we'll ~ you** no se moleste en llamar, nosotros le llamaremos
4 (= *announce*) [+ *flight*] anunciar
5 (= *waken*) despertar, llamar; **please ~ me at eight** me llama *or* despierta a las ocho, por favor
6 (= *name, describe*) llamar; **to be ~ed** llamarse; **I'm ~ed Peter** me llamo Peter; **what are you ~ed?** ¿cómo te llamas?; **they ~ each other by their surnames** se llaman por los apellidos; **what are they ~ing him?** ¿qué nombre le van a poner?; **they're ~ing the boy John** al niño le van a llamar John; **I ~ed him a liar** lo llamé mentiroso; **are you ~ing me a liar?** ¿me está diciendo que soy un mentiroso?, ¿me está llamando mentiroso?
7 (= *consider*) **I ~ it an insult** para mí eso es un insulto; **let's ~ it £50** quedamos en 50 libras; **I had nothing I could ~ my own** no tenía más que lo puesto; **what time do you ~ this?** (*iro*) ¿qué hora crees que es?; **~ yourself a friend?** (*iro*) ¿y tú dices que eres un amigo?; ✦*IDIOM* **let's ~ it a day*** ya basta por hoy
8 [+ *result*] (*of election, race*) hacer público, anunciar; **it's too close to ~** la cosa está muy igualada *or* reñida
9 (*Bridge*) declarar; **to ~ three spades** declarar tres picas
10 (*US Sport*) [+ *game*] suspender
Ⓒ VI 1 (= *shout*) [*person*] llamar; (= *cry, sing*) [*bird*] cantar; **did you ~?** ¿me llamaste?; **to ~ to sb** llamar a algn
2 (*Telec*) **who's ~ing?** ¿de parte de quién?, ¿quién (le) llama?; **London ~ing** (*Rad*) aquí Londres
3 (= *visit*) pasar (a ver); **please ~ again** (*Comm*) gracias por su visita
Ⓓ CPD ► **call centre** N (*Brit Telec*) centro *m* de atención al cliente, call centre *m* ► **call girl** N prostituta *f* (*que concierta citas por teléfono*) ► **call letters** NPL (*US Telec*) letras *fpl* de identificación, indicativo *m* ► **call loan** N (*Fin*) préstamo *m* cobrable a la vista ► **call money** N (*Fin*) dinero *m* a la vista ► **call number** N (*US*) [*of library book*] número *m* de catalogación ► **call option** N (*St Ex*) opción *f* de compra a precio fijado ► **call sign** N (*Rad*) (señal *f* de) llamada *f* ► **call signal** N (*Telec*) código *m* de llamada

►**call aside** VT + ADV [+ *person*] llamar aparte

►**call at** VI + PREP [+ *house*] visitar, pasar por; [+ *port*] hacer escala en

►**call away** VT + ADV **he was ~ed away** tuvo que salir *or* marcharse, se vio obligado a ausentarse (*frm*) (**from** de); **to be ~ed away on business** tener que ausentarse por razones de trabajo *or* asuntos de negocios

►**call back** Ⓐ VT + ADV 1 (*Telec*) (= *call again*) volver a llamar a; (= *return call*) devolver la llamada a
2 (= *recall*) hacer volver
Ⓑ VI + ADV 1 (*Telec*) (= *call again*) volver a llamar; (= *return call*) devolver la llamada; **can you ~ back later? I'm busy just now** ¿puede volver a llamar dentro de un rato? ahora no puedo atenderlo
2 (= *return*) volver, regresar (*LAm*); **I'll ~ back later** volveré más tarde

►**call down** VT + ADV 1 (*liter*) [+ *blessings*] pedir (**on** para); **to ~ curses down on sb** maldecir a algn, lanzar maldiciones contra algn
2 (*US**) (= *scold*) echar la bronca a*, poner verde a*

►**call for** VI + PREP 1 (= *summon*) [+ *wine, bill*] pedir; **to ~ for help** pedir auxilio
2 (= *demand*) [+ *courage, action*] exigir, requerir; **this ~s for firm measures** esto exige *or* requiere unas medidas contundentes; **this ~s for a celebration!** ¡esto hay que celebrarlo!
3 (= *collect*) [+ *person*] pasar a buscar; [+ *goods*] recoger
4 (*US*) (= *predict*) pronosticar, prever

►**call forth** VT + ADV sacar; [+ *remark*] inspirar; [+ *protest*] motivar, provocar

►**call in** Ⓐ VT + ADV 1 (= *summon*) hacer entrar; [+ *doctor, expert, police*] llamar a
2 (*Comm etc*) (= *withdraw*) [+ *faulty goods, currency*] retirar; [+ *book, loan*] pedir la devolución de
Ⓑ VI + ADV venir, pasar; **to ~ in on sb** pasar a ver a algn; **we can ~ in on James on the way home** podemos pasar a ver a James de camino a casa; **~ in any time** ven cuando quieras, pasa por aquí cuando quieras

►**call off** VT + ADV 1 (= *cancel*) [+ *meeting, race*] cancelar, suspender; [+ *deal*] anular; [+ *search*] abandonar, dar por terminado; **the strike was ~ed off** se desconvocó la huelga
2 [+ *dog*] llamar (*para que no ataque*)

►**call on** VI + PREP 1 (= *visit*) pasar a ver
2 (*also* **~ upon**) (= *appeal*) **to ~ (up)on sb for help** pedir ayuda a algn, acudir a algn pidiendo ayuda; **to ~ (up)on sb to do sth** (= *appeal*) apelar a algn para que haga algo; (= *demand*) exigir a algn que haga algo; **he ~ed (up)on the nation to be strong** hizo un llamamiento a la nación para que se mostrara fuerte
3 (*also* **~ upon**) (= *invite to speak*) ceder *or* pasar la palabra a; **I now ~ (up)on Mr Brown to speak** cedo la palabra al Sr. Brown

►**call out** Ⓐ VT + ADV 1 (= *shout out*) [+ *name*] gritar
2 (= *summon*) [+ *doctor, rescue services*] llamar; [+ *troops*] hacer intervenir; **to ~ workers out on strike** llamar a los obreros a la huelga
Ⓑ VI + ADV (*in pain, for help etc*) gritar

►**call out for** VI + PREP (= *require*) pedir; (= *summon, ask for*) llamar; **to ~ out for help** pedir ayuda; **the situation ~s out for an urgent solution** la situación exige una solución urgente; **to ~ out for sb to do sth** pedir a algn que haga algo

►**call over** VT + ADV llamar

►**call round** VI + ADV pasar por casa; **I'll ~ round in the morning** pasaré por ahí por la mañana; **to ~ round to see sb** ir de visita a casa de algn

►**call together** VT + ADV convocar, reunir

►**call up** VT + ADV 1 (*Mil*) llamar para el servicio militar
2 (*Telec*) llamar (por teléfono)
3 [+ *memories*] traer a la memoria

►**call upon** VI + PREP (*frm*) *see* **call on**

callable [ˈkɔːləbəl] ADJ (*Fin*) redimible, amortizable

callback [ˈkɔːlbæk] N (*Comm*) retirada *f* (*de productos con defecto de origen*)

callbox [ˈkɔːlbɒks] N (*Brit*) cabina *f* (telefónica)

callboy [ˈkɔːlbɔɪ] N (*Theat*) traspunte *m*; (*in hotel*) botones *m inv*

called-up capital [ˌkɔːldʌpˈkæpɪtl] N capital *m* desembolsado

caller [ˈkɔːləʳ] N 1 (= *visitor*) visita *f*; **the first ~ at the shop** el primer cliente de la tienda
2 (*Brit Telec*) persona *f* que llama; **~, please wait** espere por favor

calligrapher [kəˈlɪgrəfəʳ] N calígrafo/a *m/f*

calligraphic [ˌkælɪˈgræfɪk] ADJ caligráfico

calligraphy [kəˈlɪgrəfɪ] N caligrafía *f*

call-in [ˈkɔːlɪn] N (*also* **~ program**) (*US*) (programa *m*) coloquio *m* (por teléfono)

calling [ˈkɔːlɪŋ] Ⓐ N (= *vocation*) vocación *f*, profesión *f*
Ⓑ CPD ► **calling card** N (*esp US*) tarjeta *f* de visita comercial

callipers, **calipers** (*US*) [ˈkælɪpəz] NPL (*Med*) soporte *msing* ortopédico; (*Math*) calibrador *msing*

callisthenics, **calisthenics** (*US*) [ˌkælɪsˈθenɪks] NSING calistenia *f*

➤ LANGUAGE IN USE: call back A1, B1 27

callosity [kæ'lɒsɪtɪ] N callo *m*, callosidad *f*
callous ['kæləs] Ⓐ ADJ [1] [*person, remark*] insensible, cruel; [*treatment, murder, crime, attack*] despiadado, cruel; **his ~ disregard for their safety** su cruel indiferencia ante su seguridad
[2] (*Med*) calloso
Ⓑ N (*Med*) callo *m*
calloused ['kæləsd] ADJ [*fingers, hands*] encallecido, calloso
callously ['kæləslɪ] ADV despiadadamente, cruelmente
callousness ['kæləsnɪs] N insensibilidad *f*, crueldad *f*
callow ['kæləʊ] ADJ (= *immature*) [*youth*] imberbe, bisoño
call-up ['kɔːlʌp] Ⓐ N [1] (*Mil*) llamada *f* al servicio militar; [*of reserves*] movilización *f*; (= *conscription*) servicio *m* militar obligatorio
[2] (*Sport*) convocatoria *f*; **to get a ~ into a squad** ser convocado para jugar con un equipo
Ⓑ CPD ► **call-up papers** NPL (*Mil*) notificación *fsing* de llamada a filas
callus ['kæləs] N (*pl* **calluses**) = **callous**
callused ['kæləst] ADJ = **calloused**
calm [kɑːm] Ⓐ ADJ (*compar* **calmer**; *superl* **calmest**) [1] (= *unruffled*) [*person, voice, place*] tranquilo; **to grow ~** tranquilizarse, calmarse; **to keep** *or* **remain ~** mantener la calma; **keep ~!** ¡tranquilo(s)!, ¡calma!; **on ~er reflection, she decided that it would be a mistake** tras un periodo de calma y reflexión, decidió que sería un error; **(cool,) ~ and collected** tranquilo y con dominio de sí mismo; **I feel ~er now** ahora estoy más tranquilo *or* calmado
[2] (= *still*) [*sea, lake, water, weather*] en calma; [*day, evening*] sin viento; **the sea was dead ~** el mar estaba en calma chicha
[3] (*Fin*) [*market, trading*] sin incidencias
Ⓑ N calma *f*, tranquilidad *f*; **the ~ before the storm** (*lit, fig*) la calma antes de la tormenta; (*Naut*) **a dead ~** una calma chicha
Ⓒ VT (*also* **~ down**) [+ *person*] calmar, tranquilizar; **to ~ o.s.** calmarse, tranquilizarse; **~ yourself!** ¡cálmate!, ¡tranquilízate!; **to ~ sb's fears** tranquilizar a algn
Ⓓ VI [*sea, wind*] calmarse
► **calm down** Ⓐ VT + ADV = **calm C**
Ⓑ VI + ADV [*person*] tranquilizarse, calmarse; [*wind*] amainar, calmarse; **~ down!** ¡cálmate!, ¡tranquilízate!; (*to excited child*) ¡tranquilízate!
calming ['kɑːmɪŋ] ADJ tranquilizante, calmante
calmly ['kɑːmlɪ] ADV [*walk*] tranquilamente; [*speak, discuss, reply*] con calma, tranquilamente; [*react, think*] con calma
calmness ['kɑːmnɪs] N [*of person, voice*] calma *f*, tranquilidad *f*; [*of weather, sea*] calma *f*
Calor gas® ['kælə,gæs] N (*Brit*) butano *m*
caloric [,kə'lɒrɪk] Ⓐ ADJ calórico, térmico
Ⓑ CPD ► **caloric energy** N energía *f* calórica *or* térmica
calorie ['kælərɪ] N caloría *f*; **she's very ~-conscious** es muy cuidadosa con la línea; **a ~-controlled diet** un régimen de bajo contenido calórico
calorific [,kælə'rɪfɪk] Ⓐ ADJ calorífico
Ⓑ CPD ► **calorific value** N (*Phys*) valor *m* calorífico
calque [kælk] N calco *m* (**on** de)
calumniate [kə'lʌmnɪeɪt] VT (*frm*) calumniar
calumny ['kæləmnɪ] N (*frm*) calumnia *f*
Calvados ['kælvə,dɒs] N Calvados *m*
Calvary ['kælvərɪ] N Calvario *m*
calve [kɑːv] VI parir
calves [kɑːvz] NPL *of* **calf**[1,2]
Calvin ['kælvɪn] N Calvino
Calvinism ['kælvɪnɪzəm] N calvinismo *m*
Calvinist ['kælvɪnɪst] Ⓐ ADJ calvinista
Ⓑ N calvinista *mf*
Calvinistic [,kælvɪ'nɪstɪk] ADJ calvinista
calypso [kə'lɪpsəʊ] N calipso *m*
calyx ['keɪlɪks] N (*pl* **calyxes** *or* **calyces** ['keɪlɪsiːz]) cáliz *m*
cam[1] [kæm] N leva *f*
cam[2]* [kæm] N ABBR = **camera**
CAM [kæm] N ABBR (= **computer-aided manufacture**) FAO *f*
camaraderie [,kæmə'rɑːdərɪ] N compañerismo *m*
camber ['kæmbəʳ] Ⓐ N (*in road*) combadura *f*
Ⓑ VT combar, arquear
Ⓒ VI combarse, arquearse
Cambodia [kæm'bəʊdɪə] N Camboya *f*
Cambodian [kæm'bəʊdɪən] Ⓐ ADJ camboyano
Ⓑ N camboyano/a *m/f*
cambric ['keɪmbrɪk] N batista *f*
Cambs ABBR (*Brit*) = **Cambridgeshire**
camcorder ['kæmkɔːdəʳ] N videocámara *f*, filmadora *f* (*LAm*)
came [keɪm] PT *of* **come**
camel ['kæməl] Ⓐ N [1] (= *animal*) camello *m*
[2] (= *colour*) color *m* camello
Ⓑ CPD ► **camel coat** N (*also* **~hair coat**) abrigo *m* de pelo de camello ► **camel hair** N pelo *m* de camello
camellia [kə'miːlɪə] N camelia *f*
cameo ['kæmɪəʊ] Ⓐ N [1] (= *jewellery*) camafeo *m*
[2] (*Cine*) (*also* **~ role**) papel *m* de estrella invitada
Ⓑ CPD ► **cameo brooch** N camafeo *m*
camera ['kæmərə] Ⓐ N [1] (*Phot*) cámara *f*, máquina *f* fotográfica; (*Cine, TV*) cámara *f*; **on ~** delante de la cámara, en cámara; **to be on ~** estar enfocado
[2] (*Jur*) **in ~** a puerta cerrada
Ⓑ CPD ► **camera angle** N ángulo *m* de la cámara ► **camera crew** N equipo *m* de cámara ► **camera phone** N teléfono *m* con cámara ► **camera-ready copy** N material *m* preparado para la cámara
cameraman ['kæmərəmæn] N (*pl* **cameramen**) cámara *mf*, operador(a) *m/f*
camera-shy ['kæmərə,ʃaɪ] ADJ **to be ~** cohibirse en presencia de la cámara
camerawork ['kæmərə,wɜːk] N (*Cine*) manejo *m* de la cámara
Cameroon, **Cameroun** [,kæmə'ruːn] N Camerún *m*
Cameroonian [,kæmə'ruːnɪən] Ⓐ ADJ camerunés, camerunense
Ⓑ N camerunés/esa *m/f*, camerunense *mf*
camiknickers ['kæmɪ,nɪkəz] NPL *especie de body holgado o camisón y braga de una sola pieza*
camisole ['kæmɪsəʊl] N camisola *f*
camomile ['kæməʊmaɪl] Ⓐ N camomila *f*
Ⓑ CPD ► **camomile tea** N manzanilla *f*
camouflage ['kæməflɑːʒ] Ⓐ N camuflaje *m*
Ⓑ VT camuflar
camp[1] [kæmp] Ⓐ N [1] (= *collection of tents*) campamento *m*; (= *organized site*) camping *m*; **to make** *or* **pitch ~** poner *or* montar el campamento, acampar; **to break** *or* **strike ~** levantar el campamento
[2] (*Pol etc*) bando *m*, facción *f*; ✦*IDIOM* **to have a foot in both ~s** tener intereses en ambos bandos
Ⓑ VI [1] (*in tent*) acampar; **to go ~ing** ir de camping
[2] (*) (= *stay*) alojarse temporalmente
Ⓒ CPD ► **camp bed** N cama *f* de campaña, cama *f* plegable, catre *m* (*LAm*) ► **camp chair** N silla *f* plegable ► **camp follower** N (= *sympathizer*) simpatizante *mf*; (*Mil*) (= *prostitute*) prostituta *f*; (= *civilian worker*) trabajador(a) *m/f* civil ► **camp site** N camping *m* ► **camp stool** N taburete *m* plegable ► **camp stove** N hornillo *m* de camping
► **camp out** VI + ADV pasar la noche al aire libre; **to ~ out on the beach** pasar la noche en la playa
camp[2] [kæmp] Ⓐ ADJ [1] (= *affected, theatrical*) amanerado, afectado
[2] (= *effeminate*) afeminado; ✦*IDIOM* **to be as ~ as a row of tents*** tener mucha pluma*, ser mariquita perdido*
Ⓑ N [1] (*Theat*) (*also* **high ~**) amaneramiento *m*
[2] (= *effeminacy*) lo afeminado
Ⓒ VT **to ~ it up*** parodiarse a sí mismo
campaign [kæm'peɪn] Ⓐ N (*Mil*) (*fig*) campaña *f*; **election ~** campaña *f* electoral
Ⓑ VI (*Mil*) (*fig*) hacer campaña; **to ~ for/against** hacer campaña a favor de/en contra de
Ⓒ CPD ► **campaign trail** N recorrido *m* electoral ► **campaign worker** N colaborador(a) *m/f* en una campaña política
campaigner [kæm'peɪnəʳ] N [1] (*Mil*) **old ~** veterano/a *m/f*
[2] (= *supporter*) defensor(a) *m/f*, partidario/a *m/f*; **a ~ for sth** un partidario *or* defensor de algo; **environmental ~s** defensores del medio ambiente; **a ~ against sth** un luchador contra algo
campanile [,kæmpə'niːlɪ] N campanario *m*
campanologist [,kæmpə'nɒlədʒɪst] N campanólogo/a *m/f*
campanology [,kæmpə'nɒlədʒɪ] N campanología *f*
camper ['kæmpəʳ] N [1] (= *person*) campista *mf*; (*in holiday camp*) veraneante *mf*
[2] (*also* **~ van**) caravana *f*, autocaravana *f*
campfire ['kæmp'faɪə] N hoguera *f* de campamento; [*of scouts*] reunión *f* alrededor de la hoguera
campground ['kæmpgraʊnd] N (*US*) cámping *m*
camphor ['kæmfəʳ] N alcanfor *m*
camphorated ['kæmfəreɪtɪd] ADJ alcanforado
camping ['kæmpɪŋ] Ⓐ N cámping *m*
Ⓑ CPD ► **Camping gas**® N (*Brit*) (= *gas*) gas *m* butano; (*US*) (= *stove*) cámping gas® *m* ► **camping ground** N (terreno *m* de) cámping *m* ► **camping site** N = **camping ground** ► **camping van** N caravana *f*, autocaravana *f*
campion ['kæmpɪən] N colleja *f*
campus ['kæmpəs] N (*pl* **campuses**) (*Univ*) (= *district*) ciudad *f* universitaria; (= *internal area*) recinto *m* universitario, campus *m inv*
CAMRA ['kæmrə] N ABBR (*Brit*) (= **Campaign for Real Ale**) *organización para la defensa y promoción de la cerveza tradicional*
camshaft ['kæmʃɑːft] N (*Aut*) árbol *m* de levas
▼ **can**[1] [kæn] MODAL AUX VB (*neg* **cannot**, **can't**; *condit, pt* **could**) [1] (= *be able to*) poder; **he ~ do it if he tries hard** puede hacerlo si se esfuerza; **I ~'t** *or* **cannot go any further** no puedo seguir; **I'll tell you all I ~** te diré todo lo que pueda; **he will do all he ~ to help you** hará lo posible por ayudarte; **you ~ but ask** con preguntar no se pierde nada; **they couldn't help it** ellos no tienen la culpa;

► LANGUAGE IN USE: **can**[1] **1** 1.1, 4, 9.1, 9.2, 9.3, 9.4, 10.4, 12.3, 15.3, 15.4, 16.3, 16.4 **can**[1] **2** 15.4 **4** 4, 9.1 **5** 16.3

"have another helping" — "I really couldn't" —¿otra ración? —no puedo
[2] (= *know how to*) saber; **he ~'t swim** no sabe nadar; **~ you speak Italian?** ¿sabes (hablar) italiano?
[3] (= *may*) poder; **~ I use your telephone?** ¿puedo usar su teléfono?; **~ I have your name?** ¿me dice su nombre?; **could I have a word with you?** ¿podría hablar contigo un momento?; **~'t I come too?** ¿puedo ir también?
[4] (*with verbs of perception: not translated*) **I ~ hear it** lo oigo; **I couldn't see it anywhere** no lo veía en ninguna parte; **I ~'t understand why** no comprendo por qué
[5] (*expressing disbelief, puzzlement*) **that cannot be!** ¡eso no puede ser!, ¡es imposible!; **he ~'t have said that** no puede haber dicho eso; **they ~'t have left already!** ¡no es posible que ya se han ido!; **how could you lie to me!** ¿cómo pudiste mentirme?; **how ~ you say that?** ¿cómo te atreves a decir eso?; **you ~'t be serious!** ¿lo dices en serio?; **it ~'t be true!** ¡no puede ser!; **what ~ he want?** ¿qué querrá?; **where on earth ~ she be?** ¿dónde demonios puede estar?
[6] (*expressing possibility, suggestion etc*) **he could be in the library** puede que esté en la biblioteca; **you could try telephoning his office** ¿por qué no le llamas a su despacho?; **they could have forgotten** puede (ser) que se hayan olvidado; **you could have told me!** ¡podías habérmelo dicho!; **it could have been a wolf** podía ser un lobo; **I reckon you could have got a job last year** creo que podías obtener un trabajo el año pasado
[7] (= *want to*) **I'm so happy I could cry** soy tan feliz que me dan ganas de llorar *or* que me voy a echar a llorar; **I could have cried** me daban ganas de llorar; **I could scream!** ¡es para volverse loco!
[8] (= *be occasionally capable of*) **she ~ be very annoying** a veces te pone negro; **it ~ get very cold here** aquí puede llegar a hacer mucho frío
[9] (*in comparisons*) **I'm doing it as well as I ~** lo hago lo mejor que puedo; **as cheap as ~ be** lo más barato posible; **as big as big ~ be** lo más grande posible; **she was as happy as could be** estaba de lo más feliz
[10] **could do with: I could do with a drink** ¡qué bien me vendría una copa!; **we could do with a bigger house** nos convendría una casa más grande; → ABLE, CAN

can² [kæn] Ⓐ N [1] (= *container*) (*for foodstuffs*) bote *m*, lata *f*; (*for oil, water etc*) bidón *m*; **a ~ of beer** una lata de cerveza; ✦*IDIOMS* **a ~ of worms*** un asunto peliagudo; **to open a ~ of worms*** abrir la caja de Pandora; **(to be left) to carry the ~** (*Brit**) pagar el pato
[2] (*esp US*) (= *garbage can*) cubo *m or* (*LAm*) bote *m or* tarro *m* de la basura
[3] (*Cine*) [*of film*] lata *f*; ✦*IDIOM* **it's in the ~*** está en el bote*
[4] (*US‡*) (= *prison*) chirona* *f*
[5] (*US‡*) (= *toilet*) wáter *m*
[6] (*US‡*) (= *buttocks*) culo‡ *m*
Ⓑ VT [1] [+ *food*] enlatar, envasar; ✦*IDIOM* **~ it!** (*US‡*) ¡cállate!
[2] (*US**) (= *dismiss*) [+ *employee*] despedir
Ⓒ CPD ► **can opener** N abrelatas *m inv*

Canaan ['keɪnən] N Canaán *m*

Canaanite ['keɪnənaɪt] N canaanita *mf*

Canada ['kænədə] N Canadá *m*

Canadian [kə'neɪdɪən] Ⓐ ADJ canadiense
Ⓑ N canadiense *mf*

canal [kə'næl] Ⓐ N [1] (*for barge*) canal *m*
[2] (*Anat*) tubo *m*
Ⓑ CPD ► **canal boat** N barcaza *f* ► **the Canal Zone** N (*US*) (= *Panama*) (*formerly*) la zona del Canal de Panamá

canalization [,kænəlaɪ'zeɪʃən] N canalización *f*

canalize ['kænəlaɪz] VT canalizar

canapé ['kænəpeɪ] N (*Culin*) canapé *m*

canard [kæ'nɑːd] N bulo *m*, chisme *m*

Canaries [kə'nɛərɪz] NPL **the ~** las Canarias

canary [kə'nɛərɪ] Ⓐ N canario *m*
Ⓑ CPD ► **the Canary Islands** NPL las Islas Canarias ► **canary seed** N alpiste *m* ► **canary yellow** N amarillo *m* canario

canary-yellow [kə,nɛərɪ'jeləʊ] ADJ (de color) amarillo canario *inv*

canasta [kə'næstə] N canasta *f*

Canberra ['kænbərə] N Canberra *f*

cancan ['kænkæn] N cancán *m*

▼ **cancel** ['kænsəl] (*pt, pp* **cancelled, canceled** (*US*)) Ⓐ VT [1] [+ *reservation, taxi*] anular, cancelar; [+ *room*] anular la reserva de; [+ *holiday, party, plans*] suspender; [+ *flight, train, performance*] suspender, cancelar; [+ *order, contract*] anular; [+ *permission etc*] retirar; (*Aut*) [+ *indicator*] quitar
[2] (= *mark, frank*) [+ *stamp*] matar; [+ *cheque*] anular
[3] (= *delete*) [+ *name, word*] borrar, suprimir
[4] (*Math*) anular
Ⓑ VI [*tourist etc*] cancelar la reserva/el vuelo *etc*
Ⓒ CPD ► **cancel key** N tecla *f* de anulación

► **cancel out** Ⓐ VT + ADV (*Math*) anular; (*fig*) contrarrestar, compensar; **they ~ each other out** (*Math*) se anulan mutuamente; (*fig*) se contrarrestan, una cosa compensa la otra; **the disadvantages ~ out the benefits** las desventajas anulan los beneficios; **the reduction in noise would be ~led out by the extra traffic** la reducción del ruido se vería neutralizada *or* contrarrestada por el tráfico adicional
Ⓑ VI + ADV (*Math*) anularse

cancellation [,kænsə'leɪʃən] Ⓐ N [1] [*of reservation, taxi*] anulación *f*, cancelación *f*; [*of room*] anulación *f* de reserva; [*of holiday, party, plans*] cancelación *f*; [*of flight, train, performance*] suspensión *f*, cancelación *f*; [*of order, contract*] anulación *f*; **"cancellations will not be accepted after …"** (*for travel, hotel*) "no se admiten cancelaciones de reserva después del …"; (*for theatre etc*) "no se admite la devolución de localidades después del …"
[2] (*Post*) (= *mark*) matasellos *m inv*; (= *act*) inutilización *f*
Ⓑ CPD ► **cancellation fee** N tarifa *f* por cancelación

Cancer ['kænsəʳ] N [1] (= *sign, constellation, also Geog*) Cáncer *m*; *see also* **tropic**
[2] (= *person*) cáncer *mf*; **I'm (a) ~** soy cáncer

cancer ['kænsəʳ] Ⓐ N (*Med*) cáncer *m*
Ⓑ CPD ► **cancer patient** N enfermo/a *m/f* de cáncer ► **cancer research** N investigación *f* del cáncer ► **cancer specialist** N cancerólogo/a *m/f*, oncólogo/a *m/f* ► **cancer stick‡** N (*Brit*) pito* *m*, fumata‡ *m*

cancer-causing ['kænsə,kɔːzɪŋ] ADJ cancerígeno

Cancerian [kæn'sɪərɪən] N **to be a ~** ser Cáncer

cancerous ['kænsərəs] ADJ canceroso; **to become ~** cancerarse

candelabra [,kændɪ'lɑːbrə] N (*pl* **candelabra** *or* **candelabras**) candelabro *m*

C and F [,siːənd'ef] (*Comm*) ABBR = **Cost and Freight** (*Comm*) C y F

candid ['kændɪd] Ⓐ ADJ [*person, interview, remark, statement*] franco, sincero; **to be quite ~ …** hablando con franqueza …; **he is delightfully ~ about his business affairs** es increíblemente franco *or* sincero acerca de sus negocios
Ⓑ CPD ► **candid camera** N cámara *f* indiscreta

candida ['kændɪdə] N (*Med*) afta *f*

candidacy ['kændɪdəsɪ] N (*esp US*) candidatura *f*

candidate ['kændɪdeɪt] N (*for job*) aspirante *mf* (**for** a), solicitante *mf* (**for** de); (*for election, examination*) candidato/a *m/f* (**for** a); (*in competitive examination*) opositor(a) *m/f* (**for a post** a un puesto); **the overweight are prime ~s for heart disease** los obesos son los que presentan más riesgo de padecer enfermedades cardiacas

candidature ['kændɪdətʃəʳ] N (*Brit*) candidatura *f*

candidly ['kændɪdlɪ] ADV francamente, con franqueza

candidness ['kændɪdnɪs] N franqueza *f*

candied ['kændɪd] Ⓐ ADJ azucarado
Ⓑ CPD ► **candied fruit** N fruta *f* escarchada ► **candied peel** N piel *f* almibarada

candle ['kændl] Ⓐ N vela *f*, candela *f*; (*in church*) cirio *m*; ✦*IDIOMS* **to hold a ~ to sb**: **you can't hold a ~ to him** no le llegas ni a la suela de los zapatos; **it's not worth the ~** no merece *or* vale la pena; *see also* **burn¹ B1**
Ⓑ CPD ► **candle end** N cabo *m* de vela ► **candle grease** N cera *f* derretida ► **candle holder** N = **candlestick**

candlelight ['kændllaɪt] N luz *f* de una vela; **by ~** a la luz de las velas

candlelit ['kændllɪt] ADJ alumbrado por velas; **a ~ supper for two** una cena para dos con velas

Candlemas ['kændlmæs] N Candelaria *f* (*2 febrero*)

candlepower ['kændl,paʊəʳ] N bujía *f*

candlestick ['kændlstɪk] N (*single*) candelero *m*; (*low, with handle*) palmatoria *f*; (*large, ornamental*) candelabro *m*; (*in church*) cirial *m*

candlewick ['kændlwɪk] N [1] (= *cloth*) tela *f* de algodón afelpada, chenille *f*
[2] (= *wick of candle*) pabilo *m*, mecha *f* (de vela)

can-do* [,kæn'duː] ADJ (*US*) [*person, organization*] dinámico

candour, candor (*US*) ['kændəʳ] N franqueza *f*, sinceridad *f*

C & W [,siːən'dʌbljuː] N ABBR = **Country and Western**; *see* **country B**

candy ['kændɪ] Ⓐ N [1] (= *sugar candy*) azúcar *m* cande
[2] (*US*) (= *sweets*) golosinas *fpl*, caramelos *mpl*, dulces *mpl*; ✦*IDIOM* **it's like taking ~ from a baby** es coser y cantar
Ⓑ VT [+ *fruit*] escarchar
Ⓒ CPD ► **candy bar** N (*US*) barrita *f* de caramelo; (*chocolate*) chocolatina *f* ► **candy store** N (*US*) confitería *f*, bombonería *f*; ✦*IDIOM* **like a kid in a ~ store** (*esp US*) como el rey/la reina del mambo, como si fuera el amo/ama del mundo

candyfloss ['kændɪflɒs] (*Brit*) N algodón *m* de azúcar; (*pej*) (*fig*) morralla *f*

candy-striped ['kændɪ,straɪpt] ADJ a rayas de colores

cane [keɪn] Ⓐ N [1] (*Bot*) caña *f*; (*for baskets, chairs etc*) mimbre *m*
[2] (= *stick*) (*for walking*) bastón *m*; (*for punish-*

➤ LANGUAGE IN USE: cancel A1 21.4

ment) vara *f*, palmeta *f*; **to get the ~** (*Scol*) ser castigado con la vara *or* palmeta
Ⓑ VT [+ *pupil*] castigar con la vara *or* palmeta
Ⓒ CPD ► **cane chair** N silla *f* de mimbre ► **cane liquor** N caña *f* ► **cane sugar** N azúcar *m* de caña

canine [ˈkænaɪn] Ⓐ ADJ canino
Ⓑ N [1] (= *dog*) canino *m*
[2] (*also* **~ tooth**) colmillo *m*, diente *m* canino

caning [ˈkeɪnɪŋ] N **to give sb a ~** castigar a algn con la vara *or* palmeta; (*fig*) (*) dar una paliza a algn*

canister [ˈkænɪstəʳ] N (*for tea, coffee*) lata *f*, bote *m*; [*of gas*] bombona *f*; (*for film*) lata *f*

canker [ˈkæŋkəʳ] Ⓐ N (*Med*) úlcera *f* en la boca; (*Bot*) cancro *m*; (= *scourge*) cáncer *m*
Ⓑ VT (*Med*) ulcerar
Ⓒ VI (*Med*) ulcerarse

cankerous [ˈkæŋkərəs] ADJ ulceroso

cannabis [ˈkænəbɪs] Ⓐ N (*Bot*) cáñamo *m* (índico); (= *drug*) cannabis *m*
Ⓑ CPD ► **cannabis resin** N resina *f* de hachís

canned [kænd] Ⓐ PT, PP *of* **can**[2]
Ⓑ ADJ [1] [*food*] enlatado, en lata; **~ foods** conservas *fpl* alimenticias
[2] (*) (= *recorded*) [*music*] grabado, enlatado; **~ laughter** (*TV, Rad*) risas *fpl* grabadas
[3] (‡) (= *drunk*) mamado, tomado (*LAm*)

cannelloni [ˌkænɪˈləʊnɪ] NPL canelones *mpl*

cannery [ˈkænərɪ] N fábrica *f* de conservas

cannibal [ˈkænɪbəl] Ⓐ ADJ antropófago
Ⓑ N caníbal *mf*, antropófago/a *m/f*

cannibalism [ˈkænɪbəlɪzəm] N canibalismo *m*

cannibalistic [ˌkænɪbəˈlɪstɪk] ADJ canibalesco

cannibalization [ˌkænɪbəlaɪˈzeɪʃən] N [*of machine, product*] canibalización *f*

cannibalize [ˈkænɪbəlaɪz] VT [+ *car etc*] desguazar, desmontar

canning [ˈkænɪŋ] Ⓐ N enlatado *m*
Ⓑ CPD ► **canning factory** N fábrica *f* de conservas ► **canning industry** N industria *f* conservera

cannon [ˈkænən] Ⓐ N (*pl* **cannon** *or* **cannons**)
[1] (*Mil*) cañón *m*; (*collectively*) artillería *f*
[2] (*Brit Billiards*) carambola *f*
Ⓑ VI (*Brit Billiards*) hacer carambola
Ⓒ CPD ► **cannon fodder** N carne *f* de cañón ► **cannon shot** N cañonazo *m*, disparo *m* de cañón; (= *ammunition*) bala *f* de cañón; **within ~-shot** a tiro de cañón

► **cannon into** VI + PREP chocar con *or* contra

► **cannon off** VI + PREP rebotar contra

cannonade [ˌkænəˈneɪd] N cañoneo *m*

cannonball [ˈkænənbɔːl] N bala *f* de cañón

cannot [ˈkænɒt] NEG *of* **can**[1]

canny [ˈkænɪ] ADJ (*compar* **cannier**; *superl* **canniest**) (*esp Scot*) astuto

canoe [kəˈnuː] Ⓐ N canoa *f*; (*Sport*) piragua *f*
Ⓑ VI ir en canoa

canoeing [kəˈnuːɪŋ] N piragüismo *m*

canoeist [kəˈnuːɪst] N piragüista *mf*

canon [ˈkænən] Ⓐ N [1] (*Rel etc*) (= *decree*) canon *m*; (= *rule, norm*) canon *m*, norma *f*
[2] (= *priest*) canónigo *m*
[3] (*Mus*) canon *m*
[4] (*Literat*) [*of single author*] bibliografía *f* autorizada, catálogo *m* autorizado de obras; (*more broadly*) corpus *m inv*
Ⓑ CPD ► **canon law** N (*Rel*) derecho *m* canónico

canonical [kəˈnɒnɪkəl] ADJ canónico

canonization [ˌkænənaɪˈzeɪʃən] N canonización *f*

canonize [ˈkænənaɪz] VT canonizar

canonry [ˈkænənrɪ] N canonjía *f*

canoodle* [kəˈnuːdl] VI (*esp Brit*) besuquearse*

canopy [ˈkænəpɪ] N [1] (= *outside shop*) toldo *m*
[2] (*of cockpit*) cubierta *f* exterior de la cabina
[3] (*above bed, throne*) dosel *m*; (*over king, pope, bishop*) palio *m*; (*over altar*) baldaquín *m*; (*over tomb*) doselete *m*; **a ~ of stars** un manto *or* un firmamento de estrellas; **a ~ of leaves** un manto de hojas

cant[1] [kænt] Ⓐ N (= *slope*) inclinación *f*, sesgo *m*; [*of crystal etc*] bisel *m*
Ⓑ VT inclinar, sesgar
Ⓒ VI inclinarse, ladearse

► **cant over** VI + ADV volcar

cant[2] [kænt] Ⓐ N [1] (= *hypocrisy*) hipocresía(s) *f(pl)*
[2] (= *jargon*) jerga *f*
Ⓑ VI camandulear

can't [kɑːnt] NEG *of* **can**[1]

Cantab [kænˈtæb] ADJ ABBR (*Brit*) = **Cantabrigiensis, of Cambridge**

Cantabrian [kænˈtæbrɪən] ADJ cantábrico

cantaloup [ˈkæntəluːp] N cantalupo *m*

cantankerous [kænˈtæŋkərəs] ADJ cascarrabias *inv*, gruñón

cantata [kænˈtɑːtə] N cantata *f*

canteen [kænˈtiːn] N [1] (= *restaurant*) cantina *f*, comedor *m*
[2] (= *bottle*) cantimplora *f*
[3] **a ~ of cutlery** un juego de cubiertos

canter [ˈkæntəʳ] Ⓐ N medio galope *m*; **to go for a ~** ir a dar un paseo a caballo; **at a ~** a medio galope; ✦*IDIOM* **to win in** *or* **at a ~** (*Brit*) (*fig*) ganar fácilmente
Ⓑ VI ir a medio galope

Canterbury [ˈkæntəbərɪ] Ⓐ N Cantórbery *m*
Ⓑ CPD ► **Canterbury Tales** NPL Cuentos *mpl* de Cantórbery

cantharides [kænˈθærɪdiːz] NPL polvo *m* de cantárida

canticle [ˈkæntɪkl] N cántico *m*; **the Canticles** el Cantar de los Cantares

cantilever [ˈkæntɪliːvəʳ] Ⓐ N viga *f* voladiza
Ⓑ CPD ► **cantilever bridge** N puente *m* voladizo

canting [ˈkæntɪŋ] ADJ hipócrita

canto [ˈkæntəʊ] N canto *m*

canton [ˈkæntɒn] N (*Admin, Pol*) cantón *m*

cantonal [ˈkæntənl] ADJ cantonal

Cantonese [ˌkæntəˈniːz] Ⓐ ADJ cantonés
Ⓑ N [1] (= *person*) cantonés/esa *m/f*
[2] (*Ling*) cantonés *m*

cantonment [kənˈtuːnmənt] N acantonamiento *m*

Canuck‡ [kəˈnʊk] N (*pej*) (= *Canadian, French Canadian*) canuck *mf*

Canute [kəˈnjuːt] N Canuto

canvas [ˈkænvəs] Ⓐ N [1] (= *cloth*) lona *f*; (*Naut*) velas *fpl*, velamen *m*; **under ~** en tienda de campaña, en carpa (*LAm*); (*Naut*) con el velamen desplegado
[2] (*Art*) lienzo *m*
Ⓑ CPD ► **canvas chair** N silla *f* de lona ► **canvas shoes** NPL zapatos *mpl* de lona; (*rope-soled*) alpargatas *fpl*

canvass [ˈkænvəs] Ⓐ VT [1] (*Pol*) [+ *district*] hacer campaña en; [+ *voters*] solicitar el voto de; [+ *votes*] solicitar
[2] (*US*) [+ *votes*] escudriñar
[3] (*Comm*) [+ *district, opinions*] sondear; [+ *orders*] solicitar; [+ *purchaser*] solicitar pedidos de
[4] (= *discuss*) [+ *possibility, question*] discutir, someter a debate
Ⓑ VI [1] (*Pol*) solicitar votos, hacer campaña (**for** a favor de)
[2] (*Comm*) buscar clientes
Ⓒ N [1] (*Pol*) (*for votes*) solicitación *f*; **to make a door-to-door ~** ir solicitando votos de puerta en puerta
[2] (*Comm*) (= *inquiry*) sondeo *m*

canvasser [ˈkænvəsəʳ] N [1] (*Pol*) persona *f* que hace campaña electoral para un partido en una zona concreta
[2] (*Comm*) promotor(a) *m/f*

canvassing [ˈkænvəsɪŋ] N solicitación *f* (de votos); **to go out ~** salir a solicitar votos

canyon [ˈkænjən] N cañón *m*

CAP N ABBR (*Pol*) (= **Common Agricultural Policy**) PAC *f*

cap [kæp] Ⓐ N [1] (= *hat*) gorra *f*; (*soldier's*) gorra *f* militar; (*for swimming*) gorro *m* de baño; (*servant's etc*) cofia *f*; (*Univ*) bonete *m*; **~ and gown** (*Univ*) toga *f* y bonete; ✦*IDIOMS* **to go ~ in hand** ir con el sombrero en la mano; **if the ~ fits, wear it** el que se pica, ajos come; **to set one's ~ at sb**† proponerse conquistar a algn; **to put on one's thinking ~** ponerse a pensar detenidamente; **I must put on my thinking ~** tengo que meditarlo
[2] (*Brit Sport*) **he's got his ~ for England** ◊ **he's an England ~** forma parte de la selección nacional inglesa, juega con la selección nacional inglesa
[3] (= *lid, cover*) [*of bottle*] tapón *m*; (*made of metal*) chapa *f*, tapón *m*; [*of pen*] capuchón *m*
[4] [*of gun*] cápsula *f* (fulminante)
[5] [*of mushroom*] sombrerete *m*, sombrerillo *m*
[6] [*of tooth*] (*artificial*) funda *f*
[7] (*Mech*) casquete *m*; (*Aut*) (= *radiator/petrol cap*) tapón *m*
[8] (= *contraceptive*) diafragma *m*
[9] (= *percussion cap*) cápsula *f* (fulminante)
Ⓑ VT [1] [+ *bottle etc*] tapar; [+ *tooth*] enfundar; [+ *oil-well*] encapuchar, tapar
[2] (= *surpass*) [+ *story, joke*] **see if you can ~ that story** a ver si cuentas un chiste mejor que ése; **I can ~ that** yo sé algo mejor sobre el mismo asunto; **and to ~ it all, he …** y para colmo, él …
[3] (= *complete*) coronar, completar
[4] (= *limit*) [+ *expenditure*] restringir; [+ *council etc*] imponer un límite presupuestario a
[5] (*Brit Sport*) [+ *player*] seleccionar (para el equipo nacional), incluir en la selección nacional

cap. ABBR (*Typ*) (= **capital (letter)**) may

capability [ˌkeɪpəˈbɪlɪtɪ] N (= *competence*) competencia *f*; (= *potential ability*) capacidad *f*; **to have the ~ to do sth** ser capaz de hacer algo, tener capacidad para hacer algo; **the ~ for rational thought** la capacidad de raciocinio; **within/beyond one's capabilities** dentro de/más allá de sus posibilidades; **military/nuclear ~** potencial *m* militar/nuclear

capable [ˈkeɪpəbl] ADJ [1] (= *competent*) competente, capaz; **she's a very ~ speaker** es una oradora muy competente *or* capaz; **she's very ~** es muy competente *or* capaz; **I can leave the matter in your very ~ hands** si te confío a ti el asunto, estará en buenas manos
[2] (= *able to*) capaz; (= *predisposed towards*) susceptible; **sports cars ~ of reaching 150mph** coches deportivos que pueden alcanzar *or* que son capaces de alcanzar las 150 millas por hora; **it's ~ of some improvement** (*frm*) se puede mejorar algo; **such men are ~ of anything** hombres así son capaces de cualquier cosa

capably [ˈkeɪpəblɪ] ADV competentemente

capacious [kə'peɪʃəs] ADJ [*room*] amplio, espacioso; [*container*] de mucha cabida, grande; [*dress*] ancho, holgado

capacitance [kə'pæsɪtəns] N (*Elec*) capacitancia *f*

capacitor [kə'pæsɪtəʳ] N (*Elec*) capacitor *m*

capacity [kə'pæsɪtɪ] Ⓐ N [1] [*of container etc*] capacidad *f*; (= *seating capacity*) cabida *f*, aforo *m*; (*Aut*) cilindrada *f*; (= *carrying capacity*) capacidad *f* de carga; **what is the ~ of this hall?** ¿cuántos caben en esta sala?; **filled to ~** al completo
[2] (= *position*) calidad *f*; **in my ~ as Chairman** en mi calidad de presidente; **in what ~ were you there?** ¿en calidad de qué estabas allí?; **I've worked for them in various capacities** he trabajado para ellos desempeñando distintas funciones
[3] (= *ability*) capacidad *f*; **her capacities** su capacidad *or* aptitud; **her ~ for research** su capacidad *or* aptitud para la investigación; **to work at full ~** [*machine, factory*] funcionar a pleno rendimiento
Ⓑ CPD ► **capacity audience** N lleno *m*; **there was a ~ audience in the theatre** hubo un lleno en el teatro ► **capacity booking** N reserva *f* total ► **capacity crowd** N = **capacity audience**

caparison [kə'pærɪsn] Ⓐ N caparazón *m*, gualdrapa *f*; [*of person*] vestido *m* rico, galas *fpl*; (= *harness etc*) equipo *m*
Ⓑ VT engualdrapar; **gaily ~ed** brillantemente enjaezado; (*fig*) brillantemente vestido

cape[1] [keɪp] Ⓐ N (*Geog*) cabo *m*; **the Cape** (= *Cape Province*) la provincia del Cabo; (= *Cape of Good Hope*) el Cabo de Buena Esperanza
Ⓑ CPD ► **Cape Canaveral** N Cabo *m* Cañaveral ► **Cape Cod** N Cape Cod ► **Cape Coloureds** NPL *personas de padres racialmente mixtos (que habitan en la provincia del Cabo)* ► **cape honeysuckle** N madreselva *f* siempreviva, bignonia *f* del Cabo ► **Cape Horn** N Cabo *m* de Hornos ► **Cape of Good Hope** N Cabo *m* de Buena Esperanza ► **Cape Province** N Provincia *f* del Cabo ► **Cape Town** N El Cabo, Ciudad *f* del Cabo ► **Cape Verde Islands** NPL Islas *fpl* de Cabo Verde

cape[2] [keɪp] N (= *garment*) capa *f*; (*short*) capotillo *m*, esclavina *f*; [*of policeman, cyclist*] chubasquero *m*; (*Bullfighting*) capote *m*

caper[1] ['keɪpəʳ] N (*Culin*) alcaparra *f*

caper[2] ['keɪpəʳ] Ⓐ N [1] [*of horse*] cabriola *f*; **to cut ~s** hacer cabriolas
[2] (= *escapade*) travesura *f*; (*) (= *business*) lío *m*, embrollo *m*; **that was quite a ~** eso sí que fue un número*; **I don't bother with taxes and all that ~** no me molesto con impuestos y cosas así; **how did your Spanish ~ go?** ¿qué tal el viajecito por España?
Ⓑ VI [1] [*horse*] hacer cabriolas; [*other animal*] brincar, corcovear; [*child*] juguetear, brincar; **to ~ about** brincar, juguetear
[2] (*) (= *go*) ir, correr; **he went ~ing off to Paris** se marchó a París como si tal cosa

capercaillie [,kæpə'keɪlɪ] N urogallo *m*

capful ['kæpfʊl] N **one ~ to four litres of water** un tapón por cada cuatro litros de agua

capillarity [,kæpɪ'lærɪtɪ] N capilaridad *f*

capillary [kə'pɪlərɪ] Ⓐ ADJ capilar
Ⓑ N capilar *m*

capital ['kæpɪtl] Ⓐ ADJ [1] (*Jur*) capital
[2] (= *chief*) capital
[3] (= *essential*) capital, primordial; **of ~ importance** de capital importancia
[4] [*letter*] mayúsculo; **~ Q** Q *f* mayúscula; **he's Conservative with a ~ C** es conservador con mayúscula
[5] (†*) (= *splendid*) magnífico, estupendo; **~!** ¡magnífico!, ¡estupendo!
Ⓑ N [1] (*also* **~ letter**) mayúscula *f*; **~s** (*large*) mayúsculas *fpl*, versales *fpl*; (*small*) versalitas *fpl*; **please write in ~s** escribir en letras de imprenta
[2] (*also* **~ city**) capital *f*
[3] (*Fin*) capital *m*; **to make ~ out of sth** (*fig*) sacar provecho de algo
[4] (*Archit*) capitel *m*
Ⓒ CPD ► **capital account** N cuenta *f* de capital ► **capital allowance** N desgravación *f* sobre bienes de capital ► **capital assets** NPL activo *msing* fijo ► **capital expenditure** N inversión *f* de capital ► **capital gain(s)** N(PL) plusvalía *f* ► **capital gains tax** N impuesto *m* sobre las plusvalías ► **capital goods** NPL bienes *mpl* de equipo ► **capital growth** N aumento *m* del capital ► **capital investment** N inversión *f* de capital ► **capital levy** N impuesto *m* sobre el capital ► **capital offence**, **capital offense** (*US*) N delito *m* capital ► **capital outlay** N desembolso *m* de capital ► **capital punishment** N pena *f* de muerte ► **capital reserves** NPL reservas *fpl* de capital ► **capital sentence** N condena *f* a la pena de muerte ► **capital ship** N acorazado *m* ► **capital spending** N capital *m* adquisitivo ► **capital stock** N (= *capital*) capital *m* social *or* comercial; (= *shares*) acciones *fpl* de capital ► **capital sum** N capital *m* ► **capital transfer tax** N (*Brit*) impuesto *m* sobre plusvalía de cesión

capital-intensive [,kæpɪtlɪn'tensɪv] ADJ de utilización intensiva de capital

capitalism ['kæpɪtəlɪzəm] N capitalismo *m*

capitalist ['kæpɪtəlɪst] Ⓐ ADJ capitalista
Ⓑ N capitalista *mf*

capitalistic [,kæpɪtə'lɪstɪk] ADJ capitalista

capitalization [kə,pɪtəlaɪ'zeɪʃən] N capitalización *f*

capitalize [kə'pɪtəlaɪz] Ⓐ VT [1] (*Fin*) (= *provide with capital*) capitalizar
[2] [+ *letter, word*] escribir con mayúscula
Ⓑ VI **to ~ on** sacar provecho de, aprovechar

capitation [,kæpɪ'teɪʃən] Ⓐ N (= *act*) capitación *f*; (= *tax*) impuesto *m* por cabeza
Ⓑ CPD ► **capitation grant** N subvención *f* por capitación

Capitol ['kæpɪtol] N (*US*) Capitolio *m*

> **CAPITOL**
>
> *El Capitolio (**Capitol**) es el edificio en el que se reúne el Congreso de los Estados Unidos (**Congress**), situado en la ciudad de Washington. Al estar situado en la colina llamada **Capitol Hill**, también se suele hacer referencia a él con ese nombre en los medios de comunicación.*
> *Por otra parte a menudo se llama **Capitol**, por extensión, al edificio en el que tienen lugar las sesiones parlamentarias de la cámara de representantes de muchos estados.*

capitulate [kə'pɪtjʊleɪt] VI (*Mil*) (= *surrender*) rendirse, capitular (**to** ante); (*fig*) claudicar, capitular (**to** ante)

capitulation [kə,pɪtjʊ'leɪʃən] N (*Mil, fig*) capitulación *f*, rendición *f*

capon ['keɪpən] N capón *m*

cappuccino [,kæpə'tʃiːnəʊ] N capuchino *m*

caprice [kə'priːs] N capricho *m*, antojo *m*

capricious [kə'prɪʃəs] ADJ caprichoso, antojadizo

capriciously [kə'prɪʃəslɪ] ADV caprichosamente

Capricorn ['kæprɪkɔːn] N [1] (= *sign, constellation, also Geog*) Capricornio *m*; *see also* **tropic**
[2] (= *person*) capricornio *mf*; **she's (a) ~** es capricornio

caps [kæps] NPL ABBR (*Typ*) (= **capitals, capital letters**) may

capsicum ['kæpsɪkəm] N pimiento *m*

capsize [kæp'saɪz] Ⓐ VT volcar; (*Naut*) hacer zozobrar, tumbar
Ⓑ VI volcarse, dar una vuelta de campana; (*Naut*) zozobrar

capstan ['kæpstən] N cabrestante *m*

capsule ['kæpsjuːl] Ⓐ N (*all senses*) cápsula *f*
Ⓑ ADJ [*version, summary*] conciso, sucinto

Capt. ABBR (*Mil*) = **Captain**

captain ['kæptɪn] Ⓐ N (*Mil, Naut, Sport*) capitán/ana *m/f*; (*Aer*) comandante *mf*; (*US Police*) comisario/a *m/f* de distrito; **~ of industry** magnate *mf* de la industria, gran industrial *mf*
Ⓑ VT [+ *team*] capitanear; **a team ~ed by Grace** un equipo capitaneado por Grace

captaincy ['kæptənsɪ] N capitanía *f*

caption ['kæpʃən] Ⓐ N (= *heading*) título *m*, titular *m*; (*on photo, cartoon*) leyenda *f*, pie *m*; (*in film*) subtítulo *m*
Ⓑ VT [+ *essay, article*] titular; [+ *photo, cartoon*] poner una leyenda a

captious ['kæpʃəs] ADJ (*liter*) criticón, reparón

captivate ['kæptɪveɪt] VT encantar, cautivar

captivating ['kæptɪveɪtɪŋ] ADJ cautivador, fascinante

captive ['kæptɪv] Ⓐ ADJ [*animal, bird, person*] cautivo; **to take sb ~** hacer prisionero a algn; **to hold sb ~** tener *or* mantener prisionero *or* cautivo a algn; **he had a ~ audience** la gente no tenía más remedio que escucharle; **~ market** mercado *m* cautivo
Ⓑ N cautivo/a *m/f*, preso/a *m/f*

captivity [kæp'tɪvɪtɪ] N cautiverio *m*, cautividad *f*; **bred in ~** criado en cautividad; **to hold** *or* **keep sb in ~** tener a algn en cautividad *or* en cautiverio

captor ['kæptəʳ] N captor(a) *m/f*, apresador(a) *m/f*

capture ['kæptʃəʳ] Ⓐ N [1] [*of animal, soldier, escapee*] captura *f*, apresamiento *m*; [*of city etc*] toma *f*, conquista *f*
[2] (*Comput*) captura *f*, recogida *f*
[3] (= *thing caught*) presa *f*
Ⓑ VT [1] [+ *animal*] apresar; [+ *soldier, escapee*] capturar, apresar; [+ *city etc*] tomar, conquistar; (*Comm*) [+ *market*] conquistar, acaparar; [+ *leadership*] apoderarse de
[2] (= *attract*) [+ *attention, interest*] captar; **a film that has ~d the imagination of teenagers** una película que ha cautivado la imaginación de los adolescentes; **this phenomenon has ~d the attention of many scientists** este fenómeno ha llamado la atención de muchos científicos; **the woman who has ~d his heart** la mujer que le ha arrebatado el corazón
[3] (= *convey, evoke*) captar, reflejar; **to ~ sth on film** captar algo con la cámara
[4] [+ *data*] capturar, recoger

capuchin ['kæpjʊʃɪn] N [1] (= *cowl*) capucho *m*
[2] (*Zool*) mono *m* capuchino
[3] **Capuchin** (*Rel*) capuchino *m*

car [kɑːʳ] Ⓐ N [1] (*Aut*) coche *m*, automóvil *m* (*frm*), carro *m* (*LAm*), auto *m* (*S. Cone*); **by ~** en coche
[2] (*esp US*) [*of train*] vagón *m*, coche *m*
[3] (= *tramcar*) tranvía *m*
[4] [*of cable railway*] coche *m*; [*of lift*] caja *f*; [*of balloon etc*] barquilla *f*

➤ LANGUAGE IN USE: **capacity** A3 15.4

Ⓑ CPD ► **car accident** N accidente *m* de coche, accidente *m* de tráfico ► **car allowance** N extra *m* por uso de coche propio ► **car bomb** N coche-bomba *m* ► **car boot sale** N (*Brit*) mercadillo *m* (*en el que se exponen las mercancías en el maletero del coche*) ► **car chase** N persecución *f* de coches; **there followed a ~ chase along the motorway** se persiguió luego al coche por la autopista ► **car ferry** N transbordador *m* para coches ► **car hire** N alquiler *m* de coches; **~-hire firm** empresa *f* de alquiler de coches ► **car industry** N industria *f* del automóvil ► **car insurance** N seguro *m* de automóvil ► **car journey** N viaje *m* en coche ► **car licence** N permiso *m* de conducir ► **car number** N (*Brit*) matrícula *f* ► **car park** N aparcamiento *m*, parking *m*, (playa *f* de) estacionamiento *m* (*LAm*) ► **car phone** N teléfono *m* móvil (de coche) ► **car pool** N [*of company*] parque *m* móvil; (= *sharing*) uso *m* compartido de coches ► **car radio** N radio *f* de coche, autorradio *f* ► **car rental** N = **car hire** ► **car sickness** N mareo *m* al ir en coche; **to suffer ~ sickness** marearse (en coche) ► **car wash** N tren *m* or túnel *m* de lavado (de coches) ► **car worker** N trabajador(a) *m/f* de la industria del automóvil

CAR BOOT SALE

En los mercadillos británicos llamados **car boot sales** *la gente vende todo tipo de objetos usados de los que quiere deshacerse, como ropa, muebles, libros, etc, que exhiben en los maleteros de sus coches. Normalmente tienen lugar en aparcamientos u otros espacios abiertos y los propietarios de los vehículos han de pagar una pequeña tarifa por aparcar. Los mercadillos más importantes atraen también a comerciantes y en ellos se venden tanto artículos usados como nuevos. En otras ocasiones se organizan para recaudar dinero con fines benéficos.*

Caracas [kəˈrækəs] N Caracas *m*

carafe [kəˈræf] N garrafa *f*

caramel [ˈkærəməl] Ⓐ N (= *substance, flavour, sweet*) caramelo *m*
Ⓑ CPD ► **caramel cream**, **caramel custard** N flan *m*

caramelize [ˈkærəməlaɪz] Ⓐ VT caramelizar, acaramelar
Ⓑ VI caramelizarse, acaramelarse

carapace [ˈkærəpeɪs] N carapacho *m*

carat [ˈkærət] N quilate *m*; **24-~ gold** oro *m* de 24 quilates

caravan [ˈkærəvæn] Ⓐ N [1] (*Brit Aut*) remolque *m*, caravana *f*, tráiler *m* (*LAm*); (*gipsies'*) carromato *m*
[2] (*in desert*) caravana *f*
Ⓑ VI **to go ~ning** ir de vacaciones en una caravana
Ⓒ CPD ► **caravan site** N camping *m* para caravanas

caravanette [ˌkærəvəˈnet] N (*Brit*) caravana *f* pequeña

caravanserai, **caravansary** [ˌkærəˈvænsəraɪ, ˌkærəˈvænsərɪ] N caravasar *m*

caravel [kærəˈvel] N carabela *f*

caraway [ˈkærəweɪ] Ⓐ N alcaravea *f*
Ⓑ CPD ► **caraway seeds** NPL carvis *mpl*

carbide [ˈkɑːbaɪd] N carburo *m*

carbine [ˈkɑːbaɪn] N carabina *f*

carbohydrate [ˈkɑːbəʊˈhaɪdreɪt] N (*Chem*) hidrato *m* de carbono; (= *starch in food*) fécula *f*

carbolic [kɑːˈbɒlɪk] N (*also* **~ acid**) ácido *m* carbólico *or* fénico; (*also* **~ soap**) jabón *m* con fenol

carbon [ˈkɑːbən] Ⓐ N [1] (*Chem*) carbono *m*
[2] (*Elec*) carbón *m*
[3] (= *carbon paper*) papel *m* de calco, papel *m* carbón, papel *m* carbónico (*S. Cone*)
Ⓑ CPD ► **carbon copy** N (*typing*) copia *f* hecha con papel de carbón; (*fig*) vivo retrato *m*; **he's a ~ copy of my uncle** es el vivo retrato de mi tío, es calcado a mi tío ► **carbon credit** N crédito *m* de carbono ► **carbon dating** N datación *f* utilizando carbono 14 ► **carbon dioxide** N bióxido *m* de carbono ► **carbon fibre** N fibra *f* de carbono ► **carbon monoxide** N monóxido *m* de carbono ► **carbon paper** N papel *m* de calco, papel *m* carbón, papel *m* carbónico (*S. Cone*) ► **carbon ribbon** N cinta *f* mecanográfica de carbón ► **carbon tetrachloride** N tetracloruro *m* de carbono

carbonaceous [ˌkɑːbəˈneɪʃəs] ADJ carbonoso

carbonate [ˈkɑːbənɪt] N carbonato *m*

carbonated [ˈkɑːbəneɪtɪd] ADJ [*water*] con gas; **~ drink** bebida *f* gaseosa

carbon-date [ˌkɑːbənˈdeɪt] VT datar mediante la prueba del carbono 14

carbonic acid [kɑːˌbɒnɪkˈæsɪd] N ácido *m* carbónico

carboniferous [ˌkɑːbəˈnɪfərəs] ADJ carbonífero

carbonization [ˌkɑːbənaɪˈzeɪʃən] N carbonización *f*

carbonize [ˈkɑːbənaɪz] Ⓐ VT carbonizar
Ⓑ VI carbonizarse

carbonless paper [ˈkɑːbənlɪsˈpeɪpəʳ] N papel *m* autocopiativo

carborundum [ˌkɑːbəˈrʌndəm] N carborundo *m*

carboy [ˈkɑːbɔɪ] N garrafón *m*

carbuncle [ˈkɑːbʌŋkl] N [1] (*Med*) carbunc(l)o *m*
[2] (= *ruby*) carbúnculo *m*, carbunco *m*

carburation [ˌkɑːbjʊˈreɪʃən] N carburación *f*

carburettor, **carburetor** (*US*) [ˌkɑːbjʊˈretəʳ] N carburador *m*

carcass, **carcase** [ˈkɑːkəs] N [1] [*of animal*] res *f* muerta; (= *body*) cuerpo *m*; (= *dead body*) cadáver *m*; ✦**IDIOM** **to save one's ~** salvar el pellejo
[2] [*of building, vehicle*] carcasa *f*, armazón *m* or *f*

carcinogen [kɑːˈsɪnədʒen] N carcinógeno *m*

carcinogenic [ˌkɑːsɪnəˈdʒenɪk] ADJ cancerígeno, carcinógeno

carcinoma [ˌkɑːsɪˈnəʊmə] N (*pl* **carcinomas** *or* **carcinomata** [ˌkɑːsɪˈnəʊmətə]) carcinoma *m*

card[1] [kɑːd] Ⓐ N [1] (= *greetings card, visiting card etc*) tarjeta *f*; (= *membership card, press card*) carnet *m*, carné *m*
[2] (= *index card*) ficha *f*
[3] (= *playing card*) carta *f*, naipe *m*; **a pack of ~s** una baraja; **to play ~s** jugar a las cartas *or* los naipes; **to lose money at ~s** perder el dinero jugando a las cartas
[4] (*at dance, race*) programa *m*
[5] (= *thin cardboard*) cartulina *f*
[6] (†*) (= *person*) **isn't he a ~?** ¡qué gracia tiene el tío!, ¡qué tipo más salado!
[7] ✦**IDIOMS** **to ask for one's ~s** (*Brit**) dejar su puesto, renunciar; **to get one's ~s** (*Brit**) ser despedido; **to have a ~ up one's sleeve** guardarse una carta bajo la manga; **to hold all the ~s** tener los triunfos en la mano; **to lay one's ~s on the table** poner las cartas sobre la mesa *or* boca arriba; **it's on** *or* (*US*) **in the ~s** es probable; **it's quite on** *or* (*US*) **in the ~s that ...** es perfectamente posible que ... + *subjun*; **to play** *or* **keep one's ~s close to one's chest** *or* (*US*) **close to the vest** no soltar prenda; **to play one's ~s right** jugar bien sus cartas; *see also* **Christmas**, **house A1**
Ⓑ VT (*US**) **to ~ sb** verificar los papeles de identidad de algn
Ⓒ CPD ► **card catalogue** N fichero *m*, catálogo *m* de fichas ► **card game** N juego *m* de naipes *or* cartas ► **card index** N fichero *m*; *see also* **card-index** ► **card reader** N lector *m* de fichas ► **card stacker** N depósito *m* de descarga de fichas ► **card table** N mesa *f* de juego ► **card trick** N truco *m* de cartas ► **card vote** N voto *m* por delegación

card[2] [kɑːd] (*Tech*) Ⓐ N carda *f*
Ⓑ VT cardar

cardamom [ˈkɑːdəməm] N cardamomo *m*

cardboard [ˈkɑːdbɔːd] Ⓐ N cartón *m*; (*thin*) cartulina *f*
Ⓑ CPD ► **cardboard box** N caja *f* de cartón ► **cardboard city*** N *área en la que los vagabundos duermen a la intemperie*, ≈ zona *f* de chabolas ► **cardboard cut-out** N figura *f* de cartón

card-carrying member [ˌkɑːdˌkærɪɪŋˈmembəʳ] N miembro *mf* con carnet

cardholder [ˈkɑːdˌhəʊldəʳ] N [*of political party, organization*] miembro *mf* con carnet; [*of credit card*] titular *mf* (de tarjeta de crédito); [*of library*] socio *mf* (de una biblioteca); [*of restaurant etc*] asiduo/a *m/f*

cardiac [ˈkɑːdɪæk] Ⓐ ADJ cardíaco
Ⓑ CPD ► **cardiac arrest** N paro *m* cardíaco

cardie* [ˈkɑːdɪ] N ABBR (*Brit*) = **cardigan**

cardigan [ˈkɑːdɪgən] N chaqueta *f* de punto, rebeca *f*

cardinal [ˈkɑːdɪnl] Ⓐ ADJ cardinal; **a ~ rule** una regla primordial *or* fundamental; **of ~ importance** de capital importancia
Ⓑ N (*Rel*) cardenal *m*
Ⓒ CPD ► **cardinal number** N (*Math*) número *m* cardinal ► **cardinal point** N punto *m* cardinal ► **cardinal sin** N (*Rel*) pecado *m* capital ► **cardinal virtue** N virtud *f* cardinal

card-index [ˌkɑːdˈɪndeks] VT fichar, catalogar

cardio... [ˈkɑːdɪəʊ] PREFIX cardio...

cardiogram [ˈkɑːdɪəʊˌgræm] N cardiograma *m*

cardiograph [ˈkɑːdɪəʊˌgræf] N cardiógrafo *m*

cardiological [ˌkɑːdɪəˈlɒdʒɪkəl] ADJ cardiológico

cardiologist [ˌkɑːdɪˈɒlɪdʒɪst] N cardiólogo/a *m/f*

cardiology [ˌkɑːdɪˈɒlədʒɪ] N cardiología *f*

cardiopulmonary [ˈkɑːdɪəʊˈpʌlmənərɪ] ADJ cardiopulmonar

cardiorespiratory [ˈkɑːdɪəʊˈrespərətɔːrɪ] ADJ cardiorrespiratorio

cardiovascular [ˌkɑːdɪəʊˈvæskjʊləʳ] ADJ cardiovascular

cardphone [ˈkɑːdˌfəʊn] N (*Brit*) teléfono *m* de tarjeta

Cards ABBR (*Brit*) = **Cardiganshire**

cardsharp [ˈkɑːdˌʃɑːp] N, **cardsharper** [ˈkɑːdˌʃɑːpəʳ] N fullero/a *m/f*, tahur *m*

CARE [keəʳ] N ABBR (*US*) (= **Cooperative for American Relief Everywhere**) *sociedad benéfica*

care [keəʳ] Ⓐ N [1] (= *anxiety*) preocupación *f*, inquietud *f*; **he has many ~s** hay muchas cosas que le preocupan; **full of ~s** lleno de inquietudes; **he hasn't a ~ in the world** no le preocupa nada
[2] (= *carefulness*) cuidado *m*, atención *f*; **have a ~, sir!**† ¡mire usted lo que está diciendo!; **to take ~** tener cuidado; **take ~!** (*as warning*)

¡cuidado!, ¡ten cuidado!; (*as good wishes*) ¡cuídate!; **to take ~ to** + INFIN cuidar de que + *subjun*, asegurarse de que + *subjun*; **to take ~ not to** + INFIN guardarse de + *infin*; **take ~ not to drop it!** ¡cuidado no lo vayas a dejar caer!, ¡procura no soltarlo!; **"with care"** "¡atención!", "¡con cuidado!"; (*on box*) "frágil"; **convicted of driving without due ~ and attention** declarado culpable de conducir sin la debida precaución

3 (= *charge*) cargo *m*, cuidado *m*; (*Med*) asistencia *f*, atención *f* médica; **to be in the ~ of** estar bajo la custodia de; **he is in the ~ of Dr Wood** le asiste *or* atiende el doctor Wood; **the parcel was left in my ~** dejaron el paquete a mi cargo *or* cuidado; **the child has been taken into ~** pusieron al niño en un centro de protección de menores; **Mr López ~ of** (*abbr* **c/o**) **Mr. Jones** (*on letter*) Sr. Jones, para (entregar al) Sr. López; **to take ~ of** (= *take charge of*) encargarse de, ocuparse de; (= *look after*) cuidar a; **that takes ~ of that** con eso todo queda arreglado; **that can take ~ of itself** eso se resolverá por sí mismo; **I'll take ~ of him!*** ¡yo me encargo de él!; **she can take ~ of herself** sabe cuidar de sí misma; **I'll take ~ of this** (*bill etc*) esto corre de mi cuenta; **to take good ~ of o.s.** cuidarse mucho

Ⓑ VI (= *be concerned*) preocuparse (**about** por), interesarse (**about** por); **we need more people who ~** necesitamos más gente que se preocupe por los demás, necesitamos más personas que se interesen por el prójimo; **I don't ~** no me importa, me da igual *or* lo mismo; **I don't ~ either way** me da lo mismo; **for all I ~, you can go** por mí, te puedes ir; **that's all he ~s about** es lo único que le interesa; **as if I ~d!** ¿y a mí qué?; **to ~ deeply about** [+ *person*] querer mucho a; [+ *thing*] interesarse mucho por; **who ~s?** ¿qué me importa?, ¿y qué?

Ⓒ VT 1 (= *be concerned*) **I don't ~ what you think** no me importa tu opinión; **what do I ~?** ¿a mí qué me importa?; **I don't ~ twopence** *or* **a fig** *or* **a hoot!** ¡me importa un comino!; **I couldn't ~ less what people say** (*Brit*) me importa un bledo lo que diga la gente; **I couldn't ~ less** ◊ **I could ~ less** (*US*) eso me trae sin cuidado

2 (*frm*) (= *like*) **to ~ to**: **I shouldn't ~ to meet him** no me gustaría conocerle; **if you ~ to** si quieres; **would you ~ to tell me?** ¿quieres decírmelo?; **would you ~ to take a walk?** ¿te apetece dar un paseo?; **would you ~ to come this way?** si no tiene inconveniente en pasar por aquí, por aquí si es tan amable *or* (*LAm*) si gusta

Ⓓ CPD ► **care giver** N (*professional*) cuidador(a) *m/f* (*de atención domiciliaria*); (= *relative, friend*) *persona que cuida de un incapacitado* ► **care label** N (*on garment*) etiqueta *f* de instrucciones de lavado ► **care order** N (*Brit Jur, Social Work*) *orden judicial para la puesta de un niño bajo tutela estatal* ► **care worker** N asistente *mf* social, cuidador(a) *m/f*

►**care for** VI + PREP 1 (= *look after*) [+ *people*] cuidar a; [+ *things*] cuidar de; **well ~d for** (bien) cuidado, bien atendido

2 (= *like*) tener afecto a, sentir cariño por; (*amorously*) sentirse atraído por; **I don't much ~ for him** no me resulta simpático; **she no longer ~s for him** ya no le quiere; **I know he ~s for you a lot** sé que te tiene mucho cariño; **I don't ~ for coffee** no me gusta el café; **I don't ~ for the idea** no me hace gracia la idea; **would you ~ for a drink?** ¿te apetece una copa?

careen [kəˈriːn] Ⓐ VT carenar
Ⓑ VI inclinarse, escorar

career [kəˈrɪəʳ] Ⓐ N (= *occupation*) profesión *f*; (= *working life*) carrera *f* profesional; **he made a ~ (for himself) in advertising** se dedicó a la publicidad, desarrolló su carrera profesional en el campo de la publicidad

Ⓑ VI correr a toda velocidad; **to ~ down the street** correr calle abajo; **to ~ into a wall** estrellarse contra un muro

Ⓒ CPD [*diplomat, soldier*] de carrera; [*criminal*] profesional ► **career girl** N mujer *f* de carrera ► **career move** N cambio *m* (en la trayectoria) profesional; **a good/bad ~ move** una buena/mala decisión para la trayectoria profesional ► **career prospects** NPL perspectivas *fpl* profesionales ► **careers advisor** (*Brit*), **careers counselor** (*US*) N (*Scol*) *persona encargada de la guía vocacional de los alumnos* ► **careers guidance** N (*Brit*) guía *f* vocacional ► **careers office** N oficina *f* de guía vocacional ► **careers officer** N consejero/a *m/f* de orientación profesional ► **careers service** N servicio *m* de orientación profesional ► **careers teacher** N (*Brit Scol*) = **careers advisor** ► **career woman** N mujer *f* de carrera

careerist [kəˈrɪərɪst] N ambicioso/a *m/f*, arribista *mf*

carefree [ˈkɛəfriː] ADJ despreocupado, alegre

careful [ˈkɛəfʊl] ADJ 1 (= *taking care, cautious*)
1·1 cuidadoso, cauteloso; **he's a ~ driver** es un conductor prudente, conduce con prudencia *or* cuidado

1·2 **to be ~** tener cuidado; **(be) ~!** ¡(ten) cuidado!; **she's very ~ about what she eats** pone mucho cuidado en *or* es muy prudente con lo que come; **be ~ of the dog** ten cuidado con el perro; **be ~ that he doesn't hear you** procura que no te oiga, ten cuidado de que no te oiga; **be ~ to shut the door** no te olvides de cerrar la puerta; **he was ~ to point out that ...** se cuidó de señalar que ...; **he was ~ not to offend her** tuvo cuidado de no ofenderle; **be ~ not to drop it** ◊ **be ~ (that) you don't drop it** procura que no se te caiga, ten cuidado de que no se te caiga; **we have to be very ~ not to be seen** tenemos que tener mucho cuidado de que no nos vean; **you can't be too ~** todos las precauciones son pocas; **be ~ what you say to him** (ten) cuidado con lo que le dices; **to be ~ with sth** tener cuidado con algo; **be ~ with the glasses** cuidado con los vasos; **he's very ~ with his money** es muy ahorrador; (*pej*) es muy tacaño

2 (= *painstaking*) [*work*] cuidadoso, esmerado; [*writer*] cuidadoso, meticuloso; [*planning, examination*] meticuloso, cuidadoso; **after ~ consideration of all the relevant facts** después de considerar todos los datos cuidadosamente; **after weeks of ~ preparation** después de semanas de cuidadosos *or* intensos preparativos; **we have made a ~ study of the report** hemos estudiado el informe cuidadosamente *or* detenidamente; **after giving this problem ~ thought, I believe that ...** después de pensar detenidamente sobre este problema, creo que ...

carefully [ˈkɛəfəlɪ] ADV 1 (= *cautiously*) [*drive, step*] con cuidado; [*choose*] con cuidado, cuidadosamente; [*reply*] con cautela; **he chose his words ~** escogió con cuidado *or* cuidadosamente sus palabras; **I have to spend ~** tengo que tener cuidado a la hora de gastar dinero; **she ~ avoided looking at him** tuvo cuidado de no mirarlo; **think ~ before you answer** piénsalo bien antes de contestar; **to go** *or* **tread ~** (*lit, fig*) andar con cuidado

2 (= *painstakingly*) (*gen*) cuidadosamente; [*listen*] atentamente

carefulness [ˈkɛəfəlnɪs] N cuidado *m*

careless [ˈkɛəlɪs] ADJ 1 (= *negligent*) [*person*] descuidado; [*appearance*] descuidado, desaliñado; [*handwriting*] poco cuidado; **~ driving** conducción *f* negligente; **~ driver** conductor(a) *m/f* negligente; **a ~ mistake** una falta de atención, un descuido; **she was producing work that was ~** no ponía cuidado en el trabajo que hacía; **it was ~ of her to do that** no fue muy prudente de *or* por su parte hacer eso; **how ~ of me!** ¡qué descuido!; **his spelling is ~** no pone cuidado en la ortografía; **you shouldn't be so ~ with money** deberías tener más cuidado con el dinero, deberías mirar más el dinero

2 (= *thoughtless*) [*remark, comment*] desconsiderado; **she is ~ of others** no le importan los demás, es desconsiderada con los demás

3 (= *carefree*) [*existence, days*] despreocupado

carelessly [ˈkɛəlɪslɪ] ADV 1 (= *negligently*) [*write, leave, handle*] sin cuidado, sin la debida atención; [*drive*] imprudentemente, con negligencia

2 (= *casually*) [*say, reply*] a la ligera; [*drop, toss*] despreocupadamente

carelessness [ˈkɛəlɪsnɪs] N 1 (= *negligence*) falta *f* de atención, falta *f* de cuidado; **through sheer ~** por simple falta de atención *or* cuidado; **the ~ of his work** la falta de atención *or* cuidado con la que hace su trabajo

2 (= *casualness*) despreocupación *f*

carer [ˈkɛərəʳ] N (*professional*) cuidador(a) *m/f* (*de atención domiciliaria*); (*relative, friend*) *persona que cuida de un incapacitado*

caress [kəˈres] Ⓐ N caricia *f*
Ⓑ VT acariciar

caret [ˈkærət] N signo *m* de intercalación

caretaker [ˈkɛəˌteɪkəʳ] Ⓐ N 1 (*Brit*) [*of school, flats etc*] portero/a *m/f*, conserje *mf*; (= *watchman*) vigilante *m*

2 (*US*) (= *care giver*) cuidador(a) *m/f* (*de atención domiciliaria*)

Ⓑ CPD ► **caretaker government** N gobierno *m* de transición ► **caretaker manager** N (*Sport*) entrenador(a) *m/f* provisional *or* suplente

careworn [ˈkɛəwɔːn] ADJ [*person*] agobiado; [*face, frown*] preocupado, lleno de ansiedad

carfare [ˈkɑːfɛəʳ] N (*US*) pasaje *m*, precio *m* (del billete)

cargo [ˈkɑːgəʊ] Ⓐ N (*pl* **cargoes** *or* (*esp US*) **cargos**) cargamento *m*, carga *f*
Ⓑ CPD ► **cargo boat** N buque *m* de carga, carguero *m* ► **cargo plane** N avión *m* de carga

carhop [ˈkɑːhɒp] N (*US*) camarero/a *m/f* de un restaurante "drive-in"

Caribbean [ˌkærɪˈbiːən] ADJ caribe; **the ~ (Sea)** el (Mar) Caribe

caribou [ˈkærɪbuː] N (*pl* **caribous** *or* **caribou**) caribú *m*

caricature [ˈkærɪkətjʊəʳ] Ⓐ N caricatura *f*; (*in newspaper*) dibujo *m* cómico; **it was a ~ of a ceremony** (*fig*) fue una parodia de ceremonia
Ⓑ VT caricaturizar

caricaturist [ˌkærɪkəˈtjʊərɪst] N caricaturista *mf*

CARICOM [ˈkærɪˌkɒm] N ABBR (= **Caribbean Community and Common Market**) CMCC *f*

caries [ˈkɛəriːz] NSING caries *f inv*

carillon [kəˈrɪljən] N carillón *m*

caring [ˈkɛərɪŋ] Ⓐ ADJ afectuoso, bondadoso; **the ~ professions** las profesiones humanitarias; **the ~ society** la sociedad humanitaria

Ⓑ N (= *care*) cuidado *m*; (= *affection*) afecto *m*, cariño *m*; (= *help*) ayuda *f*, auxilio *m*

carious [ˈkɛərɪəs] ADJ cariado

car-jacker [ˈkɑːˌdʒækəʳ] N *ladrón que asalta a sus víctimas en sus propios automóviles*

carjacking [ˈkɑːˌdʒækɪŋ] N *asalto generalmente acompañado de robo e intimidación a una persona en su propio automóvil*

Carlism [ˈkɑːlɪzəm] N carlismo *m*

Carlist [ˈkɑːlɪst] Ⓐ ADJ carlista
Ⓑ N carlista *mf*

Carmelite [ˈkɑːməlaɪt] Ⓐ ADJ carmelita
Ⓑ N carmelita *mf*

carmine [ˈkɑːmaɪn] Ⓐ ADJ carmín, de carmín
Ⓑ N carmín *m*

carnage [ˈkɑːnɪdʒ] N matanza *f*, carnicería *f*

carnal [ˈkɑːnl] ADJ (*frm*) carnal; **to have ~ knowledge of** tener conocimiento carnal de

carnation [kɑːˈneɪʃən] N clavel *m*

carnival [ˈkɑːnɪvəl] Ⓐ N carnaval *m*; (*US*) parque *m* de atracciones
Ⓑ CPD ► **carnival queen** N reina *f* del carnaval *or* de la fiesta

carnivore [ˈkɑːnɪvɔːʳ] N [1] (*Zool*) carnívoro/a *m/f*
[2] (*hum*) (= *non-vegetarian*) carnívoro/a *m/f*, no vegetariano/a *m/f*

carnivorous [kɑːˈnɪvərəs] ADJ [1] [*animal*] carnívoro
[2] (*hum*) (= *non-vegetarian*) carnívoro, no vegetariano

carob [ˈkærəb] N (= *bean*) algarroba *f*; (= *tree*) algarrobo *m*

carol [ˈkærəl] Ⓐ N (*also* **Christmas ~**) villancico *m*
Ⓑ VI (*liter*) cantar alegremente
Ⓒ CPD ► **carol singer** N *persona que canta villancicos en Navidad*

Carolingian [kærəˈlɪnʒɪən] ADJ carolingio

carotene [ˈkærətiːn] N caroteno *m*

carotid [kəˈrɒtɪd] N (*also* **~ artery**) carótida *f*

carousal [kəˈraʊzəl] N (*liter*) jarana *f*, parranda *f*

carouse [kəˈraʊz] VI (*liter*) ir de juerga *or* jarana

carousel [ˌkæruːˈsel] N [1] (*US*) (= *merry-go-round*) tiovivo *m*, carrusel *m*
[2] (*Phot*) bombo *m* de diapositivas
[3] (*at airport*) cinta *f* de equipajes

carp¹ [kɑːp] N (*pl* **carp** *or* **carps**) (= *fish*) carpa *f*

carp² [kɑːp] VI (= *complain*) quejarse, poner pegas; **to ~ at** criticar

carpal [ˈkɑːpl] Ⓐ ADJ carpiano
Ⓑ N (*also* **~ bone**) carpo *m*
Ⓒ CPD ► **carpal tunnel syndrome** N síndrome *m* del túnel carpiano

Carpathians [kɑːˈpeɪθɪənz] NPL **the ~** los montes Cárpatos

carpenter [ˈkɑːpɪntəʳ] N carpintero/a *m/f*

carpentry [ˈkɑːpɪntrɪ] N carpintería *f*

carpet [ˈkɑːpɪt] Ⓐ N alfombra *f*; (*small*) tapete *m*; (*fitted*) moqueta *f*; **a ~ of leaves** (*fig*) una alfombra de hojas; ✦*IDIOMS* **to be on the ~*** tener que aguantar un rapapolvo*; **to roll out the red ~ for sb** recibir a algn con todos los honores, ponerle a algn la alfombra roja; **they tried to sweep it under the ~** quisieron echar tierra sobre el asunto, trataron de esconder los trapos sucios
Ⓑ VT [1] [+ *floor*] (*wall to wall*) enmoquetar; (*with individual rugs*) alfombrar (**with** de)
[2] (*) (= *scold*) **to ~ sb** echar un rapapolvo a algn*
Ⓒ CPD ► **carpet bag** N (*US*) maletín *m*, morral *m* ► **carpet bombing** N bombardeo *m* de arrasamiento ► **carpet slippers** NPL zapatillas *fpl* ► **carpet square**, **carpet tile** N loseta *f* ► **carpet sweeper** N escoba *f* mecánica

carpetbagger [ˈkɑːpɪtˌbægəʳ] N [1] (*US Pol*) aventurero/a *m/f* político/a
[2] (*Fin pej*) *oportunista que trata de sacar beneficio de una operación de conversión de una sociedad de crédito hipotecario en entidad bancaria*

carpet-bomb [ˈkɑːpɪtˌbɒm] VT arrasar con bombas

carpeted [ˈkɑːpɪtɪd] ADJ [*floor*] alfombrado; **~ with** (*fig*) cubierto de

carpeting [ˈkɑːpɪtɪŋ] N alfombrado *m*, tapizado *m*; (*wall to wall*) moqueta *f*

carping [ˈkɑːpɪŋ] Ⓐ ADJ criticón, reparón
Ⓑ N quejas *fpl* constantes

carport [ˈkɑːpɔːt] N cochera *f*

carrel, **carrell** [ˈkærəl] N (*in library*) (= *desk*) mesa *f* de estudio; (= *room*) sala *f* de estudio

carriage [ˈkærɪdʒ] Ⓐ N [1] (*Brit Rail*) vagón *m*, coche *m*
[2] (*horse-drawn*) coche *m*, carruaje *m*
[3] [*of typewriter*] carro *m*; (= *gun carriage*) cureña *f*
[4] (= *bearing*) [*of person*] porte *m*
[5] (*Comm*) (= *transportation*) transporte *m*, flete *m*; (= *cost*) porte *m*, flete *m*; **~ forward** porte debido; **~ free** franco de porte; **~ inwards/outwards** gastos *mpl* de transporte a cargo del comprador/vendedor; **~ paid** portes pagados
Ⓑ CPD ► **carriage clock** N reloj *m* de mesa ► **carriage drive** N calzada *f* ► **carriage return** N (*on typewriter etc*) tecla *f* de retorno ► **carriage trade** N (*US*) sector *m* de transporte de mercancías

carriageway [ˈkærɪdʒweɪ] N (*Brit Aut*) calzada *f*; *see also* **dual**

carrier [ˈkærɪəʳ] Ⓐ N [1] (*Comm*) (= *person*) transportista *mf*; (= *company*) empresa *f* de transportes
[2] (= *airline*) aerotransportista *m*, aerolínea *f*
[3] (*Med*) [*of disease*] portador(a) *m/f*
[4] (*also* **aircraft ~**) portaaviones *m inv*; (*also* **troop ~**) (*Aer*) avión *m* de transporte de tropas; (*Naut*) (= *troopship*) barco *m* de transporte de tropas
[5] (= *basket etc*) portaequipajes *m inv*; (*on cycle*) cesta *f*
[6] (*Brit*) (*also* **~ bag**) bolsa *f* (de papel *or* plástico)
Ⓑ CPD ► **carrier bag** N bolsa *f* (de papel *or* plástico) ► **carrier pigeon** N paloma *f* mensajera

carrion [ˈkærɪən] Ⓐ N carroña *f*
Ⓑ CPD ► **carrion crow** N corneja *f* negra

carrot [ˈkærət] Ⓐ N zanahoria *f*; ✦*IDIOM* **to dangle a ~ in front of sb** *or* **offer sb a ~** ofrecer un incentivo a algn
Ⓑ CPD ► **carrot cake** N pastel *m* de zanahoria

carrot-and-stick [ˈkærətənd'stɪk] ADJ **a ~ policy** la política del palo y la zanahoria

carroty [ˈkærətɪ] ADJ [*hair*] pelirrojo

carrousel [ˌkæruːˈsel] N (*US*) = **carousel**

carry [ˈkærɪ] Ⓐ VT [1] (= *take*) llevar; **I carried the tray into the kitchen** llevé la bandeja a la cocina; **he carries our lives in his hands** nuestras vidas están en sus manos; **to ~ sth around with one** llevar algo consigo; **I've been ~ing your umbrella around since last week** llevo cargando con tu paraguas desde la semana pasada; **as fast as his legs could ~ him** tan rápido como le permitían sus piernas, a todo correr; **to ~ one's audience with one** (*fig*) ganarse al público; **to ~ sth in one's head** tener algo en mente; **he carries his drink well** aguanta mucho bebiendo
[2] (= *support*) [+ *burden*] sostener; **it's too heavy to ~** pesa mucho para llevarlo encima *or* para cargar con ello
[3] (= *have on one's person*) [+ *money, documents*] llevar (encima); **he always carries a gun** siempre lleva pistola (encima); **are you ~ing any money?** ¿llevas dinero (encima)?
[4] (= *transport*) [+ *goods*] transportar; [+ *passengers, message*] llevar; **the train does not ~ passengers** el tren no lleva pasajeros; **this bus carries 60 passengers** este autobús tiene asientos para 60 personas; **the wind carried the sound to him** el viento llevó el sonido hasta él
[5] (*Comm*) (= *stock*) [+ *goods*] tener, tratar en
[6] (*Med*) [+ *disease*] transmitir, ser portador de
[7] (= *involve*) [+ *consequence*] acarrear; [+ *responsibility*] conllevar; [+ *interpretation*] encerrar, llevar implícito; [+ *meaning*] tener; [+ *authority etc*] revestir; **the offence carries a £50 fine** la infracción será penalizada con una multa de 50 libras; **a crime which carries the death penalty** un delito que lleva aparejada la pena de muerte
[8] (= *have, be provided with*) [+ *guarantee*] tener, llevar; [+ *warning*] llevar
[9] [*newspaper etc*] [+ *story*] traer, imprimir; **both papers carried the story** ambos periódicos traían la noticia; **this journal does not ~ reviews** esta revista no tiene reseñas
[10] (= *extend*) extender, prolongar; **to ~ sth too far** (*fig*) llevar algo demasiado lejos
[11] (*Math*) [+ *figure*] llevarse; (*Fin*) [+ *interest*] llevar
[12] (= *approve*) [+ *motion*] aprobar; [+ *proposition*] hacer aceptar; **the motion was carried** la moción fue aprobada
[13] (= *win*) [+ *election, point*] ganar; (*Parl*) [+ *seat*] ganar; ✦*IDIOMS* **to ~ the day** triunfar; **to ~ all** *or* **everything before one** arrasar con todo
[14] **to ~ o.s.** portarse; **he carries himself like a soldier** se comporta como un soldado; **she carries herself well** se mueve con garbo
[15] [*pregnant woman*] [+ *child*] estar encinta de
Ⓑ VI [1] [*sound*] oírse; **she has a voice which carries** tiene una voz que se oye bastante lejos
[2] [*pregnant woman*] **she's ~ing†** está embarazada
Ⓒ N [*of ball, shot*] alcance *m*

►**carry along** VT + ADV llevar; [*flood, water*] arrastrar

►**carry away** VT + ADV [1] (*lit*) llevarse
[2] (*fig*) entusiasmar; **to get carried away by sth** entusiasmarse con algo

►**carry back** VT + ADV [1] (*lit*) [+ *object*] traer
[2] (*fig*) **that music carries me back to the 60s** esa música me hace recordar los 60
[3] (*Fin*) cargar (sobre cuentas anteriores)

►**carry down** VT + ADV bajar

►**carry forward** VT + ADV (*Math, Fin*) pasar a la página/columna siguiente; **carried forward** suma y sigue

►**carry off** VT + ADV [1] (*lit*) llevarse
[2] (*fig*) (= *seize, win*) llevarse; [+ *prize*] alzarse con, arramblar con; [+ *election*] ganar; **he carried it off very well** salió muy airoso de la situación
[3] (= *kill*) matar, llevar a la tumba

►**carry on** Ⓐ VT + ADV [1] (= *continue*) [+ *tradition etc*] seguir, continuar
[2] (= *conduct*) [+ *conversation*] mantener; [+ *business, trade*] llevar (adelante)
Ⓑ VI + ADV [1] (= *continue*) continuar, seguir; **if**

you ~ on like that si sigues así; **we ~ on somehow** de algún modo vamos tirando; **~ on!** ¡siga!; (*in talking*) ¡prosigue!; **to ~ on doing sth** seguir haciendo algo
2 (*) (= *make a fuss*) montar un número*, armarla*; **to ~ on about sth** machacar sobre algo; **how he carries on!** ¡no para nunca!, ¡está dale que dale!; **don't ~ on so!** ¡no hagas tanto escándalo!
3 (*) (= *have an affair*) tener un lío* (**with sb** con algn)

►**carry out** VT + ADV 1 (= *accomplish etc*) [+ *plan*] llevar a cabo; [+ *threat, promise, order*] cumplir; **he never carried out his intention to write to her** tenía intención de escribirla, pero nunca lo hizo
2 (= *perform, implement*) [+ *idea, search etc*] realizar; [+ *test, experiment*] verificar; [+ *work*] realizar, llevar a cabo; **to ~ out repairs** hacer reparaciones

►**carry over** VT + ADV 1 (= *postpone*) posponer
2 (= *pass on*) transmitir; **a tradition carried over from one generation to the next** una tradición transmitida de generación en generación
3 (*Comm*) pasar a cuenta nueva

►**carry through** Ⓐ VT + ADV 1 (= *accomplish*) [+ *task*] llevar a término
2 (= *sustain*) [+ *person*] sostener
Ⓑ VT + PREP **to ~ sb through a crisis** ayudar a algn a superar una crisis; **we have enough food to ~ us through the winter** tenemos comida suficiente para pasar todo el invierno

►**carry up** VT + ADV subir

carryall ['kærɪɔːl] N (*US*) = **holdall**

carry-back ['kærɪbæk] N (*Fin*) traspaso *m* al período anterior

carrycot ['kærɪkɒt] N (*Brit*) cuna *f* portátil, capazo *m*

carrying charge ['kærɪɪŋˌtʃɑːdʒ] N (*Comm*) costo *m* de géneros no en venta (*almacenados etc*)

carrying-on ['kærɪɪŋ'ɒn] N 1 [*of work, business etc*] continuación *f*
2 **carryings-on*** (= *romantic intrigues*) plan *m*, relaciones *fpl* amorosas (ilícitas)

carry-on* [ˌkærɪ'ɒn] N (= *fuss*) jaleo* *m*, lío* *m*, follón* *m*; **what a ~!** ¡qué jaleo *or* follón!*; **there was a great ~ about the tickets** se armó un tremendo lío a causa de los billetes*; **did you ever see such a ~?** ¿se ha visto un jaleo igual?*

carry-out ['kærɪˌaʊt] Ⓐ ADJ [*meal etc*] para llevar
Ⓑ N (= *food*) comida *f* para llevar; (*esp Scot*) (= *drink*) bebida *f* para llevar

carry-over ['kærɪ'əʊvəʳ] N (= *surplus*) remanente *m*, sobrante *m*; (*Comm*) suma *f* anterior (para traspasar), suma *f* que pasa de una página (de cuenta) a la siguiente; (*St Ex*) aplazamiento *m* de pago hasta el próximo día de ajuste de cuentas

car-sick ['kɑːˌsɪk] ADJ **to be/get ~** marearse (en el coche)

cart [kɑːt] Ⓐ N (*horse-drawn*) carro *m*; (*heavy*) carretón *m*; (= *hand cart*) carretilla *f*, carro *m* de mano; (*US*) (*for shopping*) carrito *m*; (*US*) (*motorized*) cochecito *m*; ✦***IDIOM*** **to put the ~ before the horse** empezar la casa por el tejado
Ⓑ VT (*) llevar, acarrear; **I had to ~ his books about all day** tuve que cargar con sus libros todo el día
Ⓒ CPD ► **cart track** N (= *rut*) carril *m*, rodada *f*; (= *road*) camino *m* (para carros)

►**cart away***, **cart off*** VT + ADV llevarse

cartage ['kɑːtɪdʒ] N acarreo *m*, porte *m*

carte blanche [kɑːt'blɑ̃ːnʃ] N carta *f* blanca; **to give sb ~** dar carta blanca a algn

cartel [kɑː'tel] N (*Comm*) cartel *m*

carter ['kɑːtəʳ] N carretero *m*

Cartesian [kɑː'tiːzɪən] Ⓐ ADJ cartesiano
Ⓑ N cartesiano/a *m/f*

Carthage ['kɑːθɪdʒ] N Cartago *f*

Carthaginian [ˌkɑːθə'dʒɪnɪən] Ⓐ ADJ cartaginés
Ⓑ N cartaginés/esa *m/f*

carthorse ['kɑːthɔːs] N caballo *m* de tiro

Carthusian [kɑː'θjuːzɪən] Ⓐ ADJ cartujo
Ⓑ N cartujo/a *m/f*

cartilage ['kɑːtɪlɪdʒ] N cartílago *m*

cartilaginous [ˌkɑːtɪ'lædʒɪnəs] ADJ cartilaginoso

cartload ['kɑːtləʊd] N carretada *f* (*also fig*); **by the ~** a carretadas, a montones

cartographer [kɑː'tɒgrəfəʳ] N cartógrafo/a *m/f*

cartographic [ˌkɑːtəʊ'græfɪk] ADJ cartográfico

cartographical [ˌkɑːtəʊ'græfɪkəl] ADJ = **cartographic**

cartography [kɑː'tɒgrəfɪ] N cartografía *f*

cartomancy ['kɑːtəmænsɪ] N cartomancia *f*

carton ['kɑːtən] N [*of milk*] envase *m* de cartón, caja *f*; [*of ice-cream, yogurt*] vasito *m*; [*of cigarettes*] cartón *m*

cartoon [kɑː'tuːn] N 1 (*in newspaper etc*) viñeta *f*, chiste *m*; (= *comic strip*) historieta *f*
2 (*Art*) (= *sketch for fresco etc*) cartón *m*
3 (*Cine, TV*) dibujos *mpl* animados

cartoonist [ˌkɑː'tuːnɪst] N dibujante *mf*

cartridge ['kɑːtrɪdʒ] Ⓐ N (*gen, also Comput*) cartucho *m*; (*for pen*) recambio *m*
Ⓑ CPD ► **cartridge belt** N cartuchera *f*, canana *f* ► **cartridge case** N cartucho *m* ► **cartridge paper** N papel *m* de dibujo ► **cartridge player** N lector *m* de cartucho

cartwheel ['kɑːtwiːl] N 1 (= *wheel*) rueda *f* de carro
2 (*Gymnastics*) voltereta *f* lateral, rueda *f*; **to do** *or* **turn a ~** dar una voltereta lateral, hacer la rueda

cartwright ['kɑːtraɪt] N carretero/a *m/f*

carve [kɑːv] Ⓐ VT (*Culin*) [+ *meat*] trinchar; [+ *stone, wood*] tallar, esculpir; [+ *name on tree etc*] grabar; **to ~ one's way through the crowd** (*fig*) abrirse camino a la fuerza por entre la multitud
Ⓑ VI (*Culin*) trinchar la carne

►**carve out** VT + ADV [+ *piece of wood*] tallar; [+ *piece of land*] limpiar; [+ *statue, figure*] esculpir; [+ *tool*] tallar; **to ~ out a career for o.s.** abrirse camino

►**carve up** VT + ADV 1 [+ *meat*] trinchar
2 (*fig*) [+ *country*] repartirse; (*) [+ *person*] coser a puñaladas

carver ['kɑːvəʳ] N 1 (= *knife*) cuchillo *m* de trinchar, trinchante *m*; **carvers** cubierto *m* de trinchar
2 (*Culin*) (= *person*) trinchador(a) *m/f*

carvery ['kɑːvərɪ] N restaurante *m* que se especializa en asados

carve-up ['kɑːvˌʌp] N (= *division*) división *f*, repartimiento *m*; (*Pol etc*) arreglo *m*

carving ['kɑːvɪŋ] Ⓐ N (= *act*) tallado *m*; (= *ornament*) talla *f*, escultura *f*
Ⓑ CPD ► **carving knife** N cuchillo *m* de trinchar, trinchante *m*

caryatid [ˌkærɪ'ætɪd] N (*pl* **caryatids** *or* **caryatides** [ˌkærɪ'ætɪdiːz]) cariátide *f*

Casablanca [ˌkæsə'blæŋkə] N Casablanca *f*

Casanova [ˌkæsə'nəʊvə] N (*fig*) casanova *m*, conquistador *m*

cascade [kæs'keɪd] Ⓐ N cascada *f*, salto *m* de agua; (*fig*) [*of sparks*] cascada *f*; [*of letters*] aluvión *m*; [*of stones*] lluvia *f*
Ⓑ VI caer en cascada

cascara [kæs'kɑːrə] N (*Pharm*) cáscara *f* sagrada

case¹ [keɪs] Ⓐ N 1 (*Brit*) (= *suitcase*) maleta *f*, valija *f* (*S. Cone*), veliz *m* (*Mex*); (= *briefcase*) cartera *f*, maletín *m*, portafolio(s) *m* (*LAm*); (= *packing case*) cajón *m*; [*of drink*] caja *f*; (*for jewellery*) joyero *m*, estuche *m*; (*for camera, guitar, gun etc*) funda *f*; (*for spectacles*) (*soft*) funda *f*; (*hard*) estuche *m*; (*for watch*) caja *f*; (= *display case*) vitrina *f*; [*of window*] marco *m*, bastidor *m*; [*of cartridge*] funda *f*, cápsula *f*
2 (*Typ*) caja *f*; **lower ~** minúscula *f*; **upper ~** mayúscula *f*
Ⓑ VT 1 (= *encase*) **her leg was ~d in plaster** tenía la pierna escayolada *or* enyesada; **~d in concrete** revestido de hormigón
2 **to ~ the joint‡** estudiar el terreno para un robo

case² [keɪs] Ⓐ N 1 (*gen, Med, instance*) caso *m*; **it's a sad ~** es un caso triste; **it's a hopeless ~** (*Med*) es un caso de desahucio; **a fever ~** un caso de fiebre; **he's working on the train-robbery ~** está investigando el caso del robo del tren; **as the ~ may be** según el caso; **it's a ~ for the police** éste es asunto para la policía, esto es cosa de la policía; **it's a ~ of ...** se trata de ...; **it's a clear ~ of murder** es un claro caso de homicidio; **a ~ in point** un ejemplo al respecto *or* que hace al caso; **if that is the ~** en ese caso
2 (*Jur*) (*gen*) caso *m*, proceso *m*; (= *particular dispute*) causa *f*, pleito *m*; (= *argument*) argumento *m*, razón *f*; **the Dreyfus ~** el proceso de Dreyfus; (*more loosely*) el asunto Dreyfus; **there is no ~ to answer** no hay acusación para contestar; **there's a strong ~ for reform** hay buenos fundamentos para exigir una reforma; **there's a ~ for saying that ...** puede decirse razonablemente que ...; **there is a ~ for that attitude** hay argumentos en favor de esa actitud; **the ~ for the defence** la defensa; **the ~ for the prosecution** la acusación; **to have a good** *or* **strong ~** tener buenos argumentos *or* buenas razones; **to make (out) a ~ for sth** dar razones para algo, presentar argumentos en favor de algo; **to make the ~ for doing nothing** exponer las razones para no hacer nada; **to put** *or* **state one's ~** presentar sus argumentos, exponer su caso; **to rest one's ~** terminar la presentación de su alegato
3 (*with "in"*) **(just) in ~** por si acaso, por si las moscas*; **in ~ he comes** por si viene, (en) caso de que venga; **in your ~** en tu caso; **in any ~** de todas formas, en cualquier caso, en todo caso; **in most ~s** en la mayoría de los casos; **in no ~** en ningún caso, de ninguna manera; **in ~ of emergency** en caso de emergencia; **as in the ~ of** como en el caso de; **in such a ~** en tal caso; **in that ~** en ese caso
4 (*Ling*) caso *m*
5 (*) (= *eccentric person*) **he's a ~** es un tipo raro*, es un caso
6 (‡) **get off my ~!** ¡déjame ya en paz!; **to be on sb's ~** estar siempre encima de algn; **to get on sb's ~** meterse en la vida de algn
Ⓑ CPD ► **case file** N historial *m* ► **case grammar** N gramática *f* de caso ► **case history** N (*Med*) historial *m* médico *or* clínico; **what is the patient's ~ history?** ¿cuál es el historial del enfermo?; **I'll give you the full ~ history** le contaré la historia con todos los detalles ► **case law** N jurisprudencia *f* ► **case**

study N estudio *m* de casos ► **case system** N (*Ling*) sistema *m* de casos

casebook ['keɪsbʊk] N diario *m*, registro *m*

case-hardened ['keɪs,hɑːdnd] ADJ (*Tech*) cementado; (*fig*) [*person*] insensible, poco compasivo

caseload ['keɪsləʊd] N *número de encargos asignados a un(a) profesional*

casement ['keɪsmənt] N (*also* ~ **window**) ventana *f* de bisagras; (= *frame*) marco *m* de ventana

case-sensitive ['keɪs,sensɪtɪv] ADJ (*Comput*) capaz de distinguir mayúsculas de minúsculas

casework ['keɪswɜːk] N (*Sociol*) asistencia *f or* trabajo *m* social individualizado

caseworker ['keɪs,wɜːkəʳ] N asistente *mf* social

cash [kæʃ] Ⓐ N 1 (= *coins, notes*) (dinero *m* en) efectivo *m*, metálico *m*; **to pay (in) ~** pagar al contado *or* en efectivo; **~ on delivery** envío *m or* entrega *f* contra reembolso; **~ down** al contado; **to pay ~ (down) for sth** pagar algo al contado; **~ in hand** efectivo en caja; *see also* **hard C**
2 (*) (= *money*) dinero *m*, pasta *f* (*Sp**), plata *f* (*LAm**); **to be short of ~** andar mal de dinero; **I haven't any ~ on me** no llevo dinero encima
Ⓑ VT [+ *cheque*] cobrar, hacer efectivo; **to ~ sb a cheque** cambiarle a algn un cheque
Ⓒ CPD ► **cash account** N cuenta *f* de caja ► **cash advance** N adelanto *m* ► **cash bar** N bar *m* privado (*sin barra libre*) ► **cash box** N caja *f* para el dinero, alcancía *f* ► **cash card** N tarjeta *f* de cajero automático ► **cash cow** N producto *m* muy rentable ► **cash crop** N cultivo *m* comercial ► **cash deficit** N déficit *m* de caja ► **cash desk** N caja *f* ► **cash discount** N descuento *m* por pago al contado ► **cash dispenser** N (*Brit*) cajero *m* automático ► **cash flow** N flujo *m* de caja, movimiento *m* de efectivo; **~-flow problems** problemas *mpl* de cash-flow ► **cash income** N ingresos *mpl* al contado ► **cash offer** N oferta *f* de pago al contado ► **cash order** N orden *f* de pago al contado ► **cash payment** N pago *m* al contado ► **cash price** N precio *m* al contado ► **cash prize** N premio *m* en metálico ► **cash ratio** N coeficiente *m* de caja ► **cash receipts** NPL total *m* cobrado ► **cash reduction** N = **cash discount** ► **cash register** N caja *f* registradora ► **cash reserves** NPL reserva *fsing* en efectivo ► **cash sale** N venta *f* al contado ► **cash squeeze** N restricciones *fpl* económicas ► **cash terms** NPL = **cash payment** ► **cash value** N valor *m* en dinero

►**cash in** VT + ADV [+ *investment, policy*] cobrar

►**cash in on*** VI + PREP **to ~ in on sth** sacar partido *or* provecho de algo

►**cash up** VI + ADV (*Brit*) contar el dinero recaudado

cash-and-carry ['kæʃən'kærɪ] Ⓐ N (= *shop*) autoservicio *m* mayorista
Ⓑ ADJ [*goods, business*] de venta al por mayor

cashback ['kæʃbæk] N 1 (= *discount*) devolución *f*
2 (*at supermarket etc*) *retirada de dinero en efectivo de un establecimiento donde se ha pagado con tarjeta; también dinero retirado*

cashbook ['kæʃbʊk] N libro *m* de caja

cashew [kæ'ʃuː] N (*also* ~ **nut**) anacardo *m*

cashier [kæ'ʃɪəʳ] Ⓐ N cajero/a *m/f*
Ⓑ VT (*Mil*) separar del servicio, destituir
Ⓒ CPD ► **cashier's check** N (*US*) cheque *m* bancario

cashless ['kæʃlɪs] ADJ **the ~ society** la sociedad sin dinero

cashmere [kæʃ'mɪəʳ] Ⓐ N cachemir *m*, cachemira *f*
Ⓑ CPD de cachemir, de cachemira

cashpoint ['kæʃ,pɔɪnt] N (*Brit*) cajero *m* automático

casing ['keɪsɪŋ] N (*Tech*) (*gen*) cubierta *f*; [*of boiler*] revestimiento *m*; [*of cylinder*] camisa *f*; [*of tyre*] llanta *f*; [*of window*] marco *m*

casino [kə'siːnəʊ] N casino *m*

cask [kɑːsk] N (*for wine*) cuba *f*; (*large*) tonel *m*

casket ['kɑːskɪt] N (*for jewels*) estuche *m*, cofre *m*; (*esp US*) (= *coffin*) ataúd *m*

Caspian Sea ['kæspɪən,siː] N Mar *m* Caspio

Cassandra [kə'sændrə] N Casandra

cassava [kə'sɑːvə] N mandioca *f*

casserole ['kæsərəʊl] Ⓐ N (= *utensil*) cacerola *f*, cazuela *f*; (= *food*) guiso *m*, cazuela *f*
Ⓑ VT hacer un guiso de

cassette [kæ'set] Ⓐ N casette *m*, cassette *m*
Ⓑ CPD ► **cassette deck** N platina *f*, pletina *f* ► **cassette player** N casette *m*, cassette *m* ► **cassette recorder** N casette *m*, cassette *m* ► **cassette tape** N = **cassette**

cassis [kæ'siːs] N cassis *m*

Cassius ['kæsɪəs] N Casio

cassock ['kæsək] N sotana *f*

cassowary ['kæsəweərɪ] N casuario *m*

cast [kɑːst] (*vb: pt, pp* **cast**) Ⓐ N 1 (= *throw*) [*of net, line*] lanzamiento *m*
2 (= *mould*) molde *m*; (*Med*) (= *plaster cast*) escayola *f*; [*of worm*] forma *f*; **leg in ~** pierna *f* enyesada *or* escayolada; **~ of features** facciones *fpl*, fisonomía *f*; **~ of mind** temperamento *m*
3 (*Tech*) (= *metal casting*) pieza *f* fundida
4 [*of play etc*] reparto *m*; **~ (and credits)** (*Cine, TV*) reparto *m*
5 (*Med*) (= *squint*) estrabismo *m*; **to have a ~ in one's eye** tener estrabismo en un ojo
Ⓑ VT 1 (= *throw*) echar, lanzar; [+ *net, anchor etc*] echar
2 (*fig*) [+ *shadow*] proyectar; [+ *light*] arrojar (**on** sobre); [+ *blame, glance, spell*] echar; [+ *horoscope*] hacer; **to ~ doubt upon sth** poner algo en duda; **to ~ one's eyes over sth** echar una mirada a algo; **to ~ lots** echar a suertes; **to ~ one's vote** votar, dar su voto
3 (= *shed*) [+ *horseshoe, skin*] mudar
4 [+ *metal*] fundir; [+ *statue, clay*] moldear, vaciar
5 (*Theat*) [+ *part, play*] hacer el reparto de; **to ~ an actor in the part of** dar a un actor el papel de; **he was ~ as Macbeth** le dieron el papel de Macbeth; **we shall ~ the play on Tuesday** haremos el reparto de los papeles de la obra el martes
Ⓒ VI (*Fishing*) lanzar, arrojar
Ⓓ CPD ► **cast iron** N hierro *m* fundido *or* colado; *see also* **cast-iron**

►**cast about for, cast around for** VI + PREP [+ *job, answer*] buscar, andar buscando

►**cast aside** VT + ADV (= *reject*) descartar, desechar

►**cast away** VT + ADV 1 (= *throw away*) desechar, tirar
2 (*Naut*) **to be ~ away** naufragar; **to be ~ away on an island** naufragar y llegar a una isla

►**cast back** VT + ADV **to ~ one's thoughts back to** rememorar

►**cast down** VT + ADV 1 (= *lower*) [+ *eyes*] bajar
2 (*fig*) desanimar; **to be ~ down** estar deprimido

►**cast in** VT + ADV, VI + ADV **to ~ in (one's lot) with sb** compartir el destino de algn

►**cast off** Ⓐ VT + ADV 1 (*lit*) desechar, abandonar; [+ *burden*] deshacerse de, quitarse de encima; [+ *clothing*] quitarse; [+ *wife*] repudiar; [+ *mistress*] dejar; **the slaves ~ off their chains** los esclavos se deshicieron de sus cadenas
2 (*Naut*) soltar las amarras de, desamarrar
3 (*Knitting*) [+ *stitch*] cerrar
Ⓑ VI + ADV 1 (*Naut*) soltar amarras
2 (*Knitting*) cerrar

►**cast on** VT + ADV, VI + ADV (*Knitting*) montar

►**cast out** VT + ADV (*liter*) expulsar

►**cast up** VT + ADV 1 (*lit*) echar
2 (*Math, Fin*) [+ *account*] sumar
3 (*fig*) (= *reproach*) **to ~ sth up to** *or* **at sb** echar en cara algo a algn

castanets [,kæstə'nets] NPL castañuelas *fpl*

castaway ['kɑːstəweɪ] N náufrago/a *m/f*

caste [kɑːst] Ⓐ N casta *f*; **to lose ~** desprestigiarse
Ⓑ ADJ de casta

castellated ['kæstəleɪtɪd] ADJ almenado

caster ['kɑːstəʳ] Ⓐ N = **castor**
Ⓑ CPD ► **caster sugar** N (*Brit*) azúcar *m* extrafino, azúcar *m* lustre

castigate ['kæstɪgeɪt] VT (*frm*) reprobar, censurar

castigation [,kæstɪ'geɪʃən] N (*frm*) reprobación *f*, censura *f*

Castile [kæs'tiːl] N Castilla *f*

Castilian [kæs'tɪlɪən] Ⓐ ADJ castellano
Ⓑ N 1 (= *person*) castellano/a *m/f*
2 (*Ling*) castellano *m*

casting ['kɑːstɪŋ] Ⓐ N 1 (*Tech*) pieza *f* fundida, pieza *f* de fundición
2 (*Cine, Theat*) reparto *m*
Ⓑ CPD ► **casting couch** N (*Cine hum*) diván *m* del director (del reparto) ► **casting vote** N voto *m* decisivo, voto *m* de calidad

cast-iron ['kɑːst,aɪən] ADJ 1 (*lit*) (hecho) de hierro fundido
2 (*fig*) [*will*] inquebrantable, férreo; [*case*] irrebatible; [*excuse*] frente a la que no se puede decir nada

castle ['kɑːsl] Ⓐ N 1 (= *building*) castillo *m*; **✦IDIOM to build ~s in the air** *or* (*Brit*) **in Spain** construir castillos en el aire
2 (*Chess*) torre *f*
Ⓑ VI (*Chess*) enrocar

castling ['kɑːslɪŋ] N (*Chess*) enroque *m*

cast-off ['kɑːstɒf] Ⓐ ADJ [*clothing etc*] de desecho, en desuso
Ⓑ N (= *garment*) ropa *f* de desecho; **our players are mostly ~s from the first team** la mayoría de nuestros jugadores vienen descartados del primer equipo; **society's ~s** los marginados de la sociedad

castor ['kɑːstəʳ] Ⓐ N 1 (*on furniture*) ruedecilla *f*
2 (= *sifter*) (*for sugar*) azucarero *m*
Ⓑ CPD ► **castor oil** N aceite *m* de ricino ► **castor oil plant** N ricino *m* ► **castor sugar** N = **caster sugar**

castrate [kæs'treɪt] VT castrar

castration [kæs'treɪʃən] N castración *f*

castrato [kæs'trɑːtəʊ] N (*pl* **castrato** *or* **castrati** [kæs'trɑːtɪ]) castrato *m*

Castroism ['kæstrəʊɪzəm] N castrismo *m*

Castroist ['kæstrəʊɪst] Ⓐ ADJ castrista
Ⓑ N castrista *mf*

casual ['kæʒjʊəl] Ⓐ ADJ 1 (= *not planned*) [*walk, stroll*] sin rumbo fijo, al azar; [*meeting, encounter*] fortuito; [*caller*] ocasional; **it was**

just a ~ **conversation between strangers** no era más que una conversación para pasar el rato entre extraños; **to the ~ eye** a simple vista; **he ran a ~ eye down the page** le echó un vistazo a la página; **a ~ glance** una ojeada; **to the ~ observer** para el observador ocasional; **a ~ remark** un comentario hecho a la ligera; **she gave him a ~ wave** lo saludó informalmente con la mano
2 (= *offhand*) [*attitude*] despreocupado, poco serio; [*manner*] informal; [*tone*] informal, poco serio; **he tried to appear/sound ~** intentó parecer/sonar relajado; **he was very ~ about it** no le dio mucha importancia; **to assume a ~ air** hacer como si nada
3 (= *informal*) [*discussion*] informal; [*clothing*] de sport, informal; **~ wear** ropa de sport, ropa informal
4 (= *occasional*) [*drinker, drug user, relationship*] esporádico; **he's just a ~ acquaintance** es un conocido nada más; **~ sex** relaciones *fpl* sexuales promiscuas
5 (= *temporary*) [*labour, work, employment*] eventual; **on a ~ basis** temporalmente, eventualmente; **~ worker** (*in office, factory*) trabajador(a) *m/f* eventual; (*on farm*) trabajador(a) *m/f* temporero/a, jornalero/a *m/f*
(B) N **casuals** (= *shoes*) zapatos *mpl* de sport; (= *clothes*) ropa *f* de sport, ropa *f* informal

casually [ˈkæʒjʊəlɪ] ADV 1 (= *offhandedly*) [*walk, lean*] con aire despreocupado, despreocupadamente; [*look, wave*] despreocupadamente; [*mention, say, ask*] de pasada; **I said it quite ~** lo dije sin darle importancia
2 (= *informally*) [*dress*] de manera informal; [*talk*] informalmente; **they were smartly but ~ dressed** iban vestidos de manera informal pero elegante

casualness [ˈkæʒjuəlnɪs] N 1 (= *offhandedness*) despreocupación *f*
2 (= *informality*) informalidad *f*, naturalidad *f*

casualty [ˈkæʒjʊəltɪ] (A) N 1 (*Mil*) (*dead*) baja *f*; (*wounded*) herido/a *m/f*; **there were heavy casualties** hubo muchas bajas
2 (*in accident*) (*dead*) víctima *f*; (*wounded*) herido/a *m/f*; **Casualty** (= *hospital department*) Urgencias; **fortunately there were no casualties** por fortuna no hubo víctimas *or* heridos
3 (*fig*) **a ~ of modern society** una víctima de la sociedad moderna
(B) CPD ► **casualty department** N (servicio *m* de) urgencias *fpl* ► **casualty list** N (*Mil*) lista *f* de bajas; (*in accident*) lista *f* de víctimas ► **casualty ward** N sala *f* de urgencias

casuist [ˈkæzjʊɪst] N (*frm*) casuista *mf*; (*pej*) sofista *mf*

casuistry [ˈkæzjʊɪstrɪ] N (*frm*) casuística *f*; (*pej*) sofismas *mpl*, razonamiento *m* falaz

CAT [ˈkæt] (A) N ABBR 1 = **computer-aided teaching**
2 (= **computerized axial tomography**) TAC *m or f*
3 (= **computer-assisted translation**) TAO *f*
4 = **College of Advanced Technology**
(B) CPD ► **CAT scan** N escáner *m* TAC; **to have a ~ scan: I'm going to have a ~ scan** me van a hacer un (escáner) TAC

cat [kæt] (A) N 1 (*domestic*) gato/a *m/f*; (= *lion etc*) felino/a *m/f*; ✦*IDIOMS* **to put** *or* **set the ~ among the pigeons: that's put** *or* **set the ~ among the pigeons!** ¡eso ha puesto a los perros en danza!, ¡ya se armó la gorda!*; **something the ~ has brought** *or* **dragged in: he looked like something the ~ had brought** *or* **dragged in*** estaba hecho un desastre; **look what the ~ brought** *or* **dragged in!*** (*iro*) (*expressing dislike*) ¡vaya facha *or* pinta que traes!; (*as greeting*) ¡anda, mira quién viene por aquí!; **to let the ~ out of the bag** irse de la lengua; **the ~'s out of the bag** se ha descubierto todo el pastel; **to be like a ~ on hot bricks** *or* **on a hot tin roof** estar sobre ascuas; **to look like the ~ that ate the canary** *or* (*Brit*) **that got the cream** estar más ancho que largo, no caber en sí de satisfacción; **to fight like ~ and dog** llevarse como el perro y el gato; **to play a game of ~ and mouse** *or* **a ~-and-mouse game with sb** jugar al gato y ratón con algn; **not to have a ~ in hell's chance*** no tener la más mínima posibilidad; **to see which way the ~ jumps** esperar a ver de qué lado caen las peras; **the ~'s pyjamas** *or* **whiskers***: **he thinks he's the ~'s pyjamas** *or* **whiskers*** se cree la mar de listo*; **there isn't room to swing a ~** aquí no cabe un alfiler; **(has the) ~ got your tongue?*** ¿te ha comido la lengua el gato?; ✦*PROVS* **when the ~'s away, the mice will play** cuando el gato no está, bailan los ratones; **~s have nine lives** los gatos tienen siete vidas; *see also* **curiosity**, **fat C**, **rain C**, **skin B1**, **scald**, **swing C1**
2 (*US‡*) (= *person*) tío/a* *m/f*, tipo/a* *m/f*; **he's a real cool ~** es un tío la mar de chulo*
3 (††) (= *cat-o'-nine-tails*) azote *m*
4 (*) (= *catalytic converter*) catalizador *m*
(B) CPD ► **cat basket** N (*for carrying*) cesto *m* para llevar al gato; (*for sleeping*) cesto *m* del gato ► **cat burglar** N (ladrón/ona *m/f*) balconero/a *m/f* ► **cat's cradle** N (juego *m* de la) cuna *f* ► **cat flap** N gatera *f* ► **cat food** N comida *f* para gatos ► **cat litter** N arena *f* higiénica (para gatos) ► **cat's whisker** N (*Rad*) cable *m* antena

cataclysm [ˈkætəklɪzəm] N cataclismo *m*

cataclysmic [ˌkætəˈklɪzmɪk] ADJ de cataclismo

catacombs [ˈkætəkuːmz] NPL catacumbas *fpl*

catafalque [ˈkætəfælk] N catafalco *m*

Catalan [ˈkætəlæn] (A) ADJ catalán
(B) N 1 (= *person*) catalán/ana *m/f*
2 (*Ling*) catalán *m*

catalepsy [ˈkætlepsɪ] N catalepsia *f*

cataleptic [ˌkætəˈleptɪk] (A) ADJ cataléptico
(B) N cataléptico/a *m/f*

catalogue, **catalog** (*US*) [ˈkætəlɒg] (A) N catálogo *m*; (*also* **card ~**) fichero *m*; (*US*) (= *pamphlet, prospectus*) folleto *m*; **a whole ~ of complaints** (*fig*) toda una serie de quejas
(B) VT catalogar, poner en un catálogo; **it is not catalog(u)ed** no consta en el catálogo

Catalonia [ˌkætəˈləʊnɪə] N Cataluña *f*

Catalonian [ˌkætəˈləʊnɪən] = **Catalan**

catalyse, **catalyze** (*US*) [ˈkætəlaɪz] VT catalizar

catalysis [kəˈtælɪsɪs] N (*pl* **catalyses** [kəˈtæləˌsiːz]) catálisis *f*

catalyst [ˈkætəlɪst] N (*Chem, fig*) catalizador *m*

catalytic [ˌkætəˈlɪtɪk] (A) ADJ catalítico
(B) CPD ► **catalytic converter** N (*Aut*) catalizador *m*

catamaran [ˌkætəməˈræn] N catamarán *m*

catapult [ˈkætəpʌlt] (A) N 1 (*Brit*) (= *slingshot*) tirador *m*, tirachinas *m inv*
2 (*Aer, Mil*) catapulta *f*
(B) VT 1 (*Aer*) catapultar
2 (*fig*) **he was ~ed to fame** fue catapultado a la fama
(C) VI (*fig*) **his record ~ed to number one** su disco subió catapultado al número uno

cataract [ˈkætərækt] N 1 (= *waterfall*) catarata *f*
2 (*Med*) catarata *f*

catarrh [kəˈtɑːʳ] N catarro *m*

catastrophe [kəˈtæstrəfɪ] N catástrofe *f*

catastrophic [ˌkætəˈstrɒfɪk] ADJ catastrófico

catastrophically [ˌkætəˈstrɒfɪklɪ] ADV catastróficamente

catatonic [ˌkætəˈtɒnɪk] (A) ADJ catatónico
(B) N catatónico/a *m/f*

catbird [ˈkætbɜːd] N ✦*IDIOM* **to be (sitting) in the ~ seat** (*US**) sentirse seguro

catcall [ˈkætkɔːl] (*Theat etc*) (A) N **catcalls** silbido *msing*
(B) VI silbar

catch [kætʃ] (*vb: pt, pp* **caught**) (A) N 1 [*of ball etc*] cogida *f*, parada *f*; [*of trawler*] pesca *f*; [*of single fish*] presa *f*, pesca *f*, captura *f*; **good ~!** (*Sport*) ¡la cogiste! ¡bien hecho!, ¡bien agarrada! (*LAm*); **he's a good ~*** (*as husband etc*) es un buen partido
2 (= *fastener*) cierre *m*; (*Brit*) (*on door*) pestillo *m*; (*Brit*) (*on box, window*) cerradura *f*; (= *small flange*) fiador *m*
3 (= *trick*) trampa *f*; (= *snag*) pega *f*; **where's the ~?** ¿cuál es la trampa?; **there must be a ~ here somewhere** aquí debe de haber trampa; **a question with a ~ to it** una pregunta capciosa *or* de pega; **the ~ is that ...** la dificultad es que ...
4 **with a ~ in one's voice** con la voz entrecortada
5 (= *game*) catch-can *m*, lucha *f*
(B) VT 1 (= *grasp*) asir; [+ *ball*] coger, agarrar (*LAm*); [+ *fish*] pescar; [+ *thief*] coger, atrapar; **~!** ¡cógelo!, ¡toma!; **to be caught between two alternatives** estar entre la espada y la pared, no saber a qué carta quedarse; **a toaster with a tray to ~ the breadcrumbs** un tostador con una bandeja para recoger las migas; **to ~ sb's attention** *or* **eye** llamar la atención de algn; ✦*IDIOM* **to be caught like a rat in a trap** estar atrapado como un ratón
2 (= *take by surprise*) pillar *or* coger *or* (*LAm*) tomar de sorpresa; **to ~ sb doing sth** sorprender *or* pillar a algn haciendo algo; **to ~ o.s. doing sth** sorprenderse a sí mismo haciendo algo; **you won't ~ me doing that** yo sería incapaz de hacer eso, nunca me verás haciendo eso; **they caught him in the act** le cogieron *or* pillaron con las manos en la masa; **we never caught them at it** no los sorprendimos nunca in fraganti; **we won't get caught like that again** no volveremos a caer en esta trampa; **he got caught in the rain** la lluvia lo pilló desprevenido; **you've caught me at a bad moment** me has pillado en un mal momento; ✦*IDIOM* **he was caught off stride** *or* **off balance*** lo cogieron con la guardia baja
3 (= *contact, get hold of*) **I tried to ~ you on the phone** traté de hablar contigo por teléfono; **when can I ~ you next?** ¿cuándo podemos quedar otra vez para esto?; **(I'll) ~ you later!*** ¡nos vemos!
4 [+ *bus, train etc*] coger, tomar (*LAm*); **we only just caught the train** por poco perdimos el tren; **hurry if you want to ~ it** date prisa si quieres llegar a tiempo
5 (= *hear*) oír; (= *understand*) comprender, entender; **I didn't quite ~ what you said** no oí bien lo que dijiste
6 (= *see, hear, visit*) [+ *TV programme, film*] ver; [+ *radio programme*] oír, escuchar; [+ *exhibition, concert*] ir a; **to ~ the post** (= *be in time for*) llegar antes de la recogida del correo
7 (*Med*) [+ *disease*] coger, pillar, contagiarse de; **to ~ (a) cold** resfriarse; **you'll ~ your**

death (of cold)!* ¡(te) vas a agarrar un buen resfriado!; ✦**IDIOM to ~ a cold*** (*in business deal etc*) tener un tropiezo económico
8 (= *capture*) [+ *atmosphere, likeness*] saber captar, plasmar; **the painter has caught her expression** el pintor ha sabido captar su expresión; **to ~ the mood of the times** definir el espíritu de la época
9 (= *trap*) **I caught my fingers in the door** me pillé los dedos en la puerta; **I caught my coat on that nail** mi chaqueta se enganchó en ese clavo
10 (= *hit*) **to ~ sb a blow** pegar un golpe a algn; **the punch caught him on the arm** recibió el puñetazo en el brazo; **I caught my head on that beam** me di con la cabeza en esa viga; **she caught me one on the nose*** me pegó en la nariz
11 (= *receive, come into contact with*) **this room ~es the morning sun** este cuarto recibe el sol de la mañana; **her brooch caught the light** su broche reflejaba la luz; **the light was ~ing her hair** la luz brillaba en su pelo
12 **to ~ one's breath** contener la respiración
13 **to ~ it*** merecerse una regañina (**from** de); **you'll ~ it!*** ¡las vas a pagar!, ¡te va a costar caro!; **he caught it good and proper*** le cayó una buena
Ⓒ VI 1 (= *hook*) engancharse (**on** en); (= *tangle*) enredarse; **her dress caught in the door** se pilló el vestido con la puerta; **her dress caught on a nail** se le enganchó el vestido en un clavo
2 [*fire, wood*] prender, encenderse; (*Culin*) [*rice, vegetables etc*] quemarse
Ⓓ CPD ► **catch cry** N slogan *m*, eslogan *m* ► **catch phrase** N muletilla *f*, frase *f* de moda ► **catch question** N pregunta *f* capciosa, pregunta *f* de pega

►**catch at** VI + PREP [+ *object*] tratar de coger *or* (*LAm*) agarrar; [+ *opportunity*] aprovechar

►**catch on** VI + ADV 1 (= *become popular*) cuajar, tener éxito; **it never really caught on** no logró establecerse de verdad
2 (= *understand*) caer en la cuenta; (= *get the knack*) coger el truco; **to ~ on to** comprender

►**catch out** VT + ADV (*esp Brit*) (*with trick question*) hundir; **to ~ sb out** sorprender *or* pillar a algn; **you won't ~ me out again like that** no me vas a pillar así otra vez; **we were caught out by the rise in the dollar** la subida del dólar nos cogió desprevenidos

►**catch up** Ⓐ VT + ADV 1 **to ~ sb up** (*walking, working etc*) alcanzar a algn
2 (= *enmesh*) **we were caught up in the traffic** nos vimos bloqueados por el tráfico; **a society caught up in change** una sociedad afectada por cambios; **to be caught up in the excitement** participar de la emoción
3 (= *grab*) [+ *weapon, pen etc*] recoger, agarrar
Ⓑ VI + ADV **to ~ up (on *or* with one's work)** ponerse al día (en el trabajo); **to ~ up on one's sleep** recuperar el sueño atrasado; **to ~ up with** [+ *person*] alcanzar; [+ *news etc*] ponerse al corriente de; **the police finally caught up with him in Vienna** al final la policía dio con él *or* lo localizó en Viena; **the truth has finally caught up with him** ya no le queda más remedio que enfrentarse a la verdad

catch-22 [ˌkætʃˌtwentɪˈtuː] N **a ~22 situation** un callejón sin salida, un círculo vicioso

catch-all [ˈkætʃˌɔːl] Ⓐ ADJ [*regulation, clause etc*] general; [*phrase*] para todo
Ⓑ N *algo que sirve para todo*

catcher [ˈkætʃəʳ] N (*Baseball*) apañador(a) *m/f*, receptor(a) *m/f*

catching [ˈkætʃɪŋ] ADJ 1 (*Med*) contagioso
2 (*fig*) [*enthusiasm, laughter*] contagioso

catchment [ˈkætʃmənt] Ⓐ N [*of river*] cuenca *f* hidrográfica
Ⓑ CPD ► **catchment area** N (*Brit*) zona *f* de captación ► **catchment basin** N cuenca *f*

catchpenny [ˈkætʃˌpenɪ] ADJ llamativo (y barato), hecho para venderse al instante; **~ solution** solución *f* atractiva (pero poco recomendable)

catchword [ˈkætʃwɜːd] N (= *catch phrase*) [*of person*] muletilla *f*; (*Pol*) eslogan *m*; (*Typ*) reclamo *m*

catchy [ˈkætʃɪ] ADJ (*compar* **catchier**; *superl* **catchiest**) [*tune, slogan*] pegadizo; [*name, title*] fácil de recordar, con gancho

catechism [ˈkætɪkɪzəm] N (= *instruction*) catequesis *f inv*, catequismo *m*; (= *book*) catecismo *m*

catechist [ˈkætɪkɪst] N catequista *mf*

catechize [ˈkætɪkaɪz] VT catequizar

categoric [ˌkætɪˈgɒrɪk] ADJ = **categorical**

categorical [ˌkætɪˈgɒrɪkəl] ADJ categórico, terminante; [*refusal*] rotundo

categorically [ˌkætɪˈgɒrɪkəlɪ] ADV [*state etc*] de modo terminante; [*refuse*] rotundamente

categorization [ˌkætɪgəraɪˈzeɪʃən] N categorización *f*

categorize [ˈkætɪgəraɪz] VT clasificar; **to ~ sth as** calificar algo de, clasificar algo como

category [ˈkætɪgərɪ] Ⓐ N categoría *f*
Ⓑ CPD ► **Category A prisoner** N (*Brit*) preso/a *m/f* peligroso/a

cater [ˈkeɪtəʳ] VI 1 (= *provide food*) proveer de comida (**for** a)
2 (*fig*) **to ~ for** *or* (*US*) **to** atender a, ofrecer (sus) servicios a; **we ~ for group bookings** (*Brit*) nos ocupamos de las reservas de grupos; **to ~ for** *or* (*US*) **to sb's needs** atender las necesidades de algn; **to ~ for** *or* (*US*) **to all tastes** atender a todos los gustos; **this magazine ~s for** *or* (*US*) **to the under-21's** esta revista está dirigida a gente por debajo de los 21 años

cater-cornered [ˈkeɪtəˈkɔːnəd] (*US*) Ⓐ ADJ diagonal
Ⓑ ADV diagonalmente

caterer [ˈkeɪtərəʳ] N proveedor(a) *m/f* de catering

catering [ˈkeɪtərɪŋ] Ⓐ N servicio *m* de comidas; **a career in ~** una carrera en la hostelería; **who did the ~?** ¿quién se encargó del servicio de comidas?
Ⓑ CPD ► **catering company** N empresa *f* de hostelería ► **catering industry**, **catering trade** N hostelería *f*, restauración *f*

caterpillar [ˈkætəpɪləʳ] Ⓐ N 1 (*Zool*) oruga *f*
2 (*also* **Caterpillar tractor**®) tractor *m* de oruga
Ⓑ CPD ► **Caterpillar track**® N rodado *m* de oruga

caterwaul [ˈkætəwɔːl] VI [*person*] aullar; [*cat*] maullar

caterwauling [ˈkætəˌwɔːlɪŋ] N [*of person*] chillidos *mpl*, aullidos *mpl*; [*of cat*] maullidos *mpl*

catfish [ˈkætfɪʃ] N (*pl* **catfish** *or* **catfishes**) siluro *m*, bagre *m*

catgut [ˈkætgʌt] N cuerda *f* de tripa; (*Med*) catgut *m*

Cath. ABBR 1 = **Cathedral**
2 = **Catholic**

Catharine [ˈkæθərɪn] N Catalina

catharsis [kəˈθɑːsɪs] N (*pl* **catharses**) catarsis *f*

cathartic [kəˈθɑːtɪk] Ⓐ ADJ 1 (*Med*) catártico, purgante
2 (*fig*) catártico
Ⓑ N (*Med*) purgante *m*

cathedral [kəˈθiːdrəl] Ⓐ N catedral *f*
Ⓑ CPD ► **cathedral church** N iglesia *f* catedral ► **cathedral city** N ciudad *f* episcopal

Catherine [ˈkæθərɪn] Ⓐ N Catalina
Ⓑ CPD ► **Catherine wheel** N (= *firework*) girándula *f*

catheter [ˈkæθɪtəʳ] N catéter *m*

catheterize [ˈkæθɪtəˌraɪz] VT [+ *bladder, person*] entubar

cathode [ˈkæθəʊd] Ⓐ N cátodo *m*
Ⓑ CPD ► **cathode ray** N rayo *m* catódico ► **cathode ray tube** N tubo *m* de rayos catódicos

catholic [ˈkæθəlɪk] Ⓐ ADJ 1 **(Roman) Catholic** católico; **the Catholic Church** la Iglesia Católica
2 (= *wide-ranging*) [*tastes, interests*] católico
Ⓑ N **Catholic** católico/a *m/f*

Catholicism [kəˈθɒlɪsɪzəm] N catolicismo *m*

cathouse‡ [ˈkæthaʊs] N (*pl* **cathouses** [ˈkæthaʊzɪz]) (*US*) casa *f* de putas

Cathy [ˈkæθɪ] N (*familiar form*) *of* **Catharine, Catherine**

catkin [ˈkætkɪn] N amento *m*, candelilla *f*

cat-lick* [ˈkætlɪk] N mano *f* de gato; **to give o.s. a ~** lavarse a lo gato

catlike [ˈkætlaɪk] ADJ felino, gatuno

catmint [ˈkætmɪnt] N hierba *f* gatera, nébeda *f*

catnap* [ˈkætnæp] Ⓐ N siestecita *f*, sueñecito *m*; **to take a ~** echarse una siestecita *or* un sueñecito
Ⓑ VI echarse una siestecita, echarse un sueñecito

catnip [ˈkætnɪp] N (*US*) = **catmint**

Cato [ˈkeɪtəʊ] N Catón

cat-o'-nine-tails [ˈkætəˈnaɪnteɪlz] N azote *m* (con nueve ramales)

Cat's-eye® [ˈkætsˌaɪ] N (*Brit Aut*) catafaro *m*

cat's-paw [ˈkætspɔː] N (*fig*) instrumento *m*

catsuit [ˈkætsuːt] N traje *m* de gato

catsup [ˈkætsəp] N (*US*) catsup *m*, salsa *f* de tomate

cattery [ˈkætərɪ] N residencia *f* para gatos

cattiness [ˈkætɪnɪs] N malicia *f*, rencor *m*

cattle [ˈkætl] Ⓐ NPL ganado *msing*
Ⓑ CPD ► **cattle breeder** N criador(a) *m/f* de ganado ► **cattle breeding** N crianza *f* de ganado ► **cattle crossing** N paso *m* de ganado ► **cattle drive** N (*US*) recogida *f* de ganado ► **cattle egret** N garcilla *f* bueyera ► **cattle grid** N (*Brit*) rejilla *f* de retención (de ganado) ► **cattle market** N mercado *m* ganadero *or* de ganado; (*also fig*) feria *f* de ganado ► **cattle prod** N picana *f* ► **cattle raising** N ganadería *f* ► **cattle ranch** N finca *f* ganadera, estancia *f* (*LAm*) ► **cattle rustler** N (*US*) ladrón *m* de ganado, cuatrero *m* ► **cattle shed** N establo *m* ► **cattle show** N feria *f* de ganado ► **cattle truck** N (*Aut*) camión *m* de ganado; (*Brit Rail*) vagón *m* para ganado

cattleman [ˈkætlmæn] N (*pl* **cattlemen**) ganadero *m*

catty* [ˈkætɪ] ADJ (*compar* **cattier**; *superl* **cattiest**) [*person, remark*] malicioso

Catullus [kəˈtʌləs] N Catulo

CATV N ABBR = **community antenna television**

catwalk [ˈkætwɔːk] N pasarela *f*

Caucasian [kɔːˈkeɪzɪən] Ⓐ ADJ (*by race*) caucásico; (*Geog*) caucasiano

Ⓑ N (*by race*) caucásico/a *m/f*; (*Geog*) caucasiano/a *m/f*

Caucasus ['kɔːkəsəs] N Cáucaso *m*

caucus ['kɔːkəs] Ⓐ N (*pl* **caucuses**) (*Brit*) camarilla *f* (política), junta *f* secreta; (*US*) (= *meeting*) junta *f* ejecutiva; (= *committee*) comité *m* ejecutivo, comisión *f* ejecutiva
Ⓑ VI reunirse (para tomar decisiones)

caudal ['kɔːdl] ADJ caudal

caught [kɔːt] PT, PP *of* **catch**

cauldron ['kɔːldrən] N caldera *f*, calderón *m*; **a ~ of unrest** (*fig*) una caldera *or* olla a presión

cauliflower ['kɒlɪflaʊə^r] Ⓐ N coliflor *f*
Ⓑ CPD ► **cauliflower cheese** N coliflor *f* con queso ► **cauliflower ear** N oreja *f* deformada por los golpes

caulk [kɔːk] VT calafatear

causal ['kɔːzəl] ADJ causal

causality [kɔː'zælɪtɪ] N causalidad *f*

causally ['kɔːzəlɪ] ADV causalmente; **they are ~ related** guardan una relación de causa y efecto

causation [kɔː'zeɪʃən] N causalidad *f*

causative ['kɔːzətɪv] ADJ causativo

▼ **cause** [kɔːz] Ⓐ N [1] (= *origin*) causa *f*; (= *reason*) motivo *m*, razón *f*; **~ and effect** (relación de) causa y efecto; **with good ~** con razón; **to be the ~ of** ser causa de; **there's no ~ for alarm** no hay por qué inquietarse; **to give ~ for complaint** dar motivo de queja; **you have ~ to be worried** usted tiene motivo para estar preocupado; **to show ~** (*frm*) aducir argumentos convincentes
[2] (= *purpose*) causa *f*; **in the ~ of justice** por la justicia; **to make common ~ with** hacer causa común con; **it's all in a good ~** se está haciendo por una buena causa; **to die in a good ~** morir por una causa noble; **to take up sb's ~** apoyar la campaña de algn; *see also* **lost C**
[3] (*Jur*) causa *f*, pleito *m*
Ⓑ VT causar, provocar; [+ *accident, trouble*] causar; **I don't want to ~ you any inconvenience** no quisiera causarle ninguna molestia; **to ~ sb to do sth** hacer que algn haga algo
Ⓒ CPD ► **cause célèbre** [,kɔːzseɪ'lebr] N pleito *m or* caso *m* célebre

causeway ['kɔːzweɪ] N calzada *f or* carretera *f* elevada; (*in sea*) arrecife *m*

caustic ['kɔːstɪk] Ⓐ ADJ [1] (*Chem*) cáustico
[2] (*fig*) [*remark etc*] mordaz, sarcástico
Ⓑ CPD ► **caustic soda** N sosa *f* cáustica

cauterize ['kɔːtəraɪz] VT cauterizar

caution ['kɔːʃən] Ⓐ N [1] (= *care*) cautela *f*, prudencia *f*; **"caution!"** (*Aut*) "¡cuidado!", "¡precaución!"; **proceed with ~** actúe con precaución; ✦*IDIOM* **to throw ~ to the winds** abandonar la prudencia
[2] (= *warning*) advertencia *f*, aviso *m*; (*Brit Police*) amonestación *f*
[3] **he's a ~**†* (= *amusing*) es un tío divertidísimo; (= *odd*) es un tío muy raro
Ⓑ VT **to ~ sb** (*Brit Police*) amonestar a algn; **to ~ sb against doing sth** advertir a algn que no haga algo

cautionary ['kɔːʃənərɪ] ADJ [*tale*] de escarmiento, aleccionador; **to sound a ~ note** recomendar precaución

cautious ['kɔːʃəs] ADJ (= *careful*) cuidadoso; (= *wary*) cauteloso, prudente; **to make a ~ statement** hacer una declaración prudente; **to play a ~ game** jugar con mucha prudencia

cautiously ['kɔːʃəslɪ] ADV cautelosamente, con cautela; **~ optimistic** moderadamente *or* prudentemente optimista

cautiousness ['kɔːʃəsnɪs] N cautela *f*, prudencia *f*

cavalcade [,kævəl'keɪd] N cabalgata *f*; (*fig*) desfile *m*

cavalier [,kævə'lɪə^r] Ⓐ N caballero *m*; (††) galán *m*; (*Brit Hist*) *partidario del Rey en la Guerra Civil inglesa (1641-49)*
Ⓑ ADJ (*pej*) (= *offhand*) desdeñoso

cavalierly [,kævə'lɪəlɪ] ADV (*pej*) desdeñosamente

cavalry ['kævəlrɪ] Ⓐ N caballería *f*
Ⓑ CPD ► **cavalry charge** N carga *f* de caballería ► **cavalry officer** N oficial *m* de caballería ► **cavalry twill** N *tela asargada utilizada para confeccionar pantalones*

cavalryman ['kævəlrɪmən] N (*pl* **cavalrymen**) soldado *m* de caballería

cave[1] [keɪv] Ⓐ N cueva *f*, caverna *f*
Ⓑ CPD ► **cave dweller** N cavernícola *mf*, troglodita *mf* ► **cave painting** N pintura *f* rupestre

►**cave in** VI + ADV [1] [*ceiling*] derrumbarse, desplomarse; [*ground*] hundirse
[2] (*) (*fig*) (= *submit*) ceder, rendirse

cave[2]†* ['keɪvɪ] EXCL (*Brit Scol*) **~!** ¡ojo!, ¡ahí viene!; **to keep ~** estar a la mira

caveat ['kævɪæt] N advertencia *f*; (*Jur*) advertencia *f* de suspensión; **to enter a ~** hacer una advertencia

cave-in ['keɪvɪn] N [*of roof etc*] derrumbe *m*, derrumbamiento *m*; [*of pavement etc*] socavón *m*

caveman ['keɪvmæn] N (*pl* **cavemen**) [1] (*Anthropology*) hombre *m* de las cavernas, cavernícola *m*, troglodita *m*; (*more loosely*) hombre *m* prehistórico
[2] (* *hum*) (*aggressively masculine*) machote* *m*

caver ['keɪvə^r] N espeleólogo/a *m/f*

cavern ['kævən] N caverna *f*

cavernous ['kævənəs] ADJ [*eyes, cheeks*] hundido; [*pit, darkness*] cavernoso

cavewoman ['keɪvwʊmən] N (*pl* **cavewomen**) mujer *f* de las cavernas, cavernícola *f*, troglodita *f*; (*more loosely*) mujer *f* prehistórica

caviar(e) ['kævɪɑː^r] N caviar *m*

cavil ['kævɪl] (*pt, pp* **cavilled, caviled** (*US*)) Ⓐ N reparo *m* Ⓑ VI poner peros *or* reparos (**at** a)

caving ['keɪvɪŋ] N espeleología *f*; **to go ~** (*gen*) hacer espeleología; (*on specific occasion*) ir en una expedición espeleológica

cavity ['kævɪtɪ] Ⓐ N cavidad *f*; (*in tooth*) caries *f inv*; **nasal cavities** fosas *fpl* nasales
Ⓑ CPD ► **cavity wall** N pared *f* con cámara de aire, doble pared *f* ► **cavity wall insulation** N aislamiento *m* con cámara de aire

cavort [kə'vɔːt] VI dar *or* hacer cabriolas, dar brincos; (*fig*) divertirse ruidosamente

cavy ['keɪvɪ] N conejillo *m* de Indias, cobaya *m*

caw [kɔː] Ⓐ N graznido *m* Ⓑ VI graznar

cawing ['kɔːɪŋ] N graznidos *mpl*, el graznar

cayenne ['keɪen] N (*also* **~ pepper**) pimentón *m* picante

cayman ['keɪmən] Ⓐ N caimán *m*
Ⓑ CPD ► **the Cayman Islands** NPL las Islas Caimán

CB Ⓐ N ABBR [1] (= **Citizens' Band Radio**) BC *f*
[2] (= **Companion (of the Order) of the Bath**) *título honorífico británico*
Ⓑ ABBR (*Mil*) = **confined to barracks**
Ⓒ CPD ► **CB Radio** N radio *f* de BC, BC *f*

CBC N ABBR = **Canadian Broadcasting Corporation**

CBE N ABBR (= **Commander (of the Order) of the British Empire**) *título honorífico británico*

CBI N ABBR (= **Confederation of British Industry**) ≈ CEOE *f*

CBS N ABBR (*US*) (= **Columbia Broadcasting System**) *cadena de televisión*

CC N ABBR (*Brit*) (*formerly*) (= **County Council**) gobierno *m* de un condado

cc ABBR [1] (= **cubic centimetre(s)**) cc, cm^3
[2] = **carbon copy, carbon copies**

CCA N ABBR (*US*) = **Circuit Court of Appeals**

CCC N ABBR (*US*) = **Commodity Credit Corporation**

CCTV N ABBR = **closed-circuit television**

CCU N ABBR (*US Med*) = **coronary care unit**

CD Ⓐ N ABBR [1] (= **compact disc**) CD *m*
[2] (= **Corps Diplomatique**) C.D.
[3] = **Civil Defence (Corps)**
[4] (*US Pol*) = **Congressional District**
[5] (*Pol*) = **Conference on Disarmament**
Ⓑ CPD ► **CD burner, CD writer** N grabadora *f* de CDs

CDC N ABBR (*US*) = **Centers for Disease Control and Prevention**

CD-I® ADJ ABBR (= **compact disc interactive**) CD-I *m*

Cdr. ABBR (*Brit Naut, Mil*) (= **commander**) Cdte.; **~ R. Thomas** (*on envelope*) Cdte. R. Thomas

CD-ROM [,siːdiː'rɒm] Ⓐ N ABBR (= **compact disc read-only memory**) CD-ROM *m*
Ⓑ CPD ► **CD-ROM drive** N unidad *f* de CD-ROM

CDT N ABBR [1] (*US*) = **Central Daylight Time**
[2] (*Brit Scol*) = **Craft, Design and Technology**

CDV, CD-video N ABBR = **compact disc video**

CE N ABBR = **Church of England**

cease [siːs] Ⓐ VT (= *stop*) cesar, parar; (= *suspend*) suspender; (= *end*) terminar; **to ~ work** suspender el trabajo, terminar de trabajar; **~ fire!** ¡alto el fuego!
Ⓑ VI cesar (**to do, doing** de hacer); **to ~ from doing sth** dejar de hacer algo, cesar de hacer algo

ceasefire [,siːs'faɪə^r] Ⓐ N alto *m* el fuego, cese *m* de hostilidades
Ⓑ CPD ► **ceasefire line** N línea *f* del alto el fuego

ceaseless ['siːslɪs] ADJ incesante, continuo

ceaselessly ['siːslɪslɪ] ADV incesantemente, sin cesar

Cecil ['sesl] N Cecilio

Cecily ['sɪsɪlɪ] N Cecilia

cecum ['siːkəm] N (*pl* **ceca**) (*US*) = **caecum**

CED N ABBR (*US*) = **Committee for Economic Development**

cedar ['siːdə^r] Ⓐ N cedro *m*
Ⓑ ADJ [*wood, table etc*] de cedro

cede [siːd] VT [+ *territory*] ceder (**to** a); [+ *argument*] reconocer, admitir

cedilla [sɪ'dɪlə] N cedilla *f*

CEEB N ABBR (*US*) = **College Entry Examination Board**

ceilidh ['keɪlɪ] N *baile con música y danzas tradicionales escocesas o irlandesas*

ceiling ['siːlɪŋ] Ⓐ N [1] [*of room*] techo *m*; (*Archit*) cielo *m* raso; *see also* **hit B3**
[2] (*Aer*) techo *m*
[3] (*fig*) (= *upper limit*) límite *m*, tope *m*; **to fix a ~ for** ◊ **put a ~ on** fijar el límite de
Ⓑ CPD ► **ceiling price** N precio *m* tope

celandine ['seləndaɪn] N celidonia *f*

celeb* [sɪ'leb] N famoso/a *m/f*

celebrant ['selɪbrənt] N celebrante *m*

▼ **celebrate** ['selɪbreɪt] Ⓐ VT [1] [+ *birthday, special occasion*] celebrar; (*with a party*) festejar; [+ *anniversary etc*] conmemorar; **what are you celebrating?** ¿qué festejáis?, ¿cuál es el mo-

➤ LANGUAGE IN USE: **cause B** 17.1, 26.3 **celebrate A** 25.2

tivo de esta fiesta?; **we're celebrating his arrival** estamos celebrando su llegada; **he ~d his birthday by scoring two goals** celebró su cumpleaños marcando dos goles

2 [+ *mass*] celebrar, decir; [+ *marriage*] celebrar

(B) VI divertirse, festejar

celebrated ['selıbreıtıd] ADJ célebre, famoso

celebration [,selı'breıʃən] N 1 (= *act*) celebración *f*, festejo *m*; **in ~ of** para celebrar

2 (= *party*) fiesta *f*, guateque *m*; (= *festivity*) festividad *f*; **we must have a ~** hay que celebrarlo *or* festejarlo, hay que hacer una fiesta; **the jubilee ~s** las conmemoraciones *or* los festejos del aniversario

celebratory [,selı'breıtərı] ADJ [*event etc*] de celebración; **let's have a ~ dinner** vamos a ofrecer una cena para celebrarlo

celebrity [sı'lebrıtı] N (= *fame, person*) celebridad *f*

celeriac [sə'lerıæk] N apio-nabo *m*

celerity [sı'lerıtı] N (*frm*) celeridad *f*

celery ['selərı] N apio *m*; **head/stick of ~** cabeza *f*/tallo *m* de apio

celestial [sı'lestıəl] ADJ (*lit, fig*) celestial

celibacy ['selıbəsı] N celibato *m*

celibate ['selıbıt] (A) ADJ célibe

(B) N célibe *mf*

cell [sel] (A) N 1 (*in prison, monastery etc*) celda *f*

2 (*Bio, Pol*) célula *f*

3 (*Elec*) pila *f*

(B) CPD ► **cell biology** N biología *f* celular

cellar ['seləʳ] N sótano *m*; (*for wine*) bodega *f*; **to keep a good ~** tener buena bodega

cellist ['tʃelıst] N violoncelista *mf*, violonchelista *mf*

cellmate ['selmeıt] N compañero/a *m/f* de celda

cello ['tʃeləʊ] N violoncelo *m*, violonchelo *m*

Cellophane® ['seləfeın] N celofán *m*

cellphone ['sel,fəʊn] N = **cellular telephone**

cellular ['seljʊləʳ] (A) ADJ (*Bio*) celular

(B) CPD ► **cellular blanket** N manta *f* con tejido muy suelto ► **cellular telephone** N teléfono *m* celular

cellulite ['seljʊlaıt] N celulitis *f*

cellulitis [,selju'laıtıs] N celulitis *f*

celluloid ['seljʊlɔıd] (A) N celuloide *m*; **on ~** (*Cine*) en el celuloide, en el cine

(B) ADJ (*Cine*) del celuloide, cinematográfico

cellulose ['seljʊləʊs] N celulosa *f*

Celsius ['selsıəs] ADJ celsius, centígrado; **20 degrees ~** 20 grados centígrados

Celt [kelt, selt] N celta *mf*

Celtiberia [,keltaı'bıərı] N Celtiberia *f*

Celtiberian [,keltaı'bıərıən] (A) ADJ celtibérico

(B) N celtíbero/a *m/f*

Celtic ['keltık, 'seltık] (A) ADJ celta, céltico

(B) N (*Ling*) celta *m*

cembalo ['tʃembələʊ] N (*pl* **cembalos** *or* **cembali** ['tʃembəlı]) clavicordio *m*, clave *m*

cement [sə'ment] (A) N cemento *m*; (= *glue*) cola *f*

(B) VT 1 (*Constr*) cementar, cubrir de cemento

2 (*fig*) cimentar

(C) CPD ► **cement mixer** N hormigonera *f*

cementation [,si:men'teıʃən] N cementación *f*

cemetery ['semıtrı] N cementerio *m*

cenotaph ['senətɑ:f] N cenotafio *m*

censer ['sensəʳ] N incensario *m*

censor ['sensəʳ] (A) N censor(a) *m/f*

(B) VT censurar

censorious [sen'sɔ:rıəs] ADJ (*frm*) hipercrítico

censorship ['sensəʃıp] N censura *f*

censurable ['senʃərəbl] ADJ censurable

censure ['senʃəʳ] (A) N censura *f*; **vote of ~** voto de censura

(B) VT censurar

census ['sensəs] (A) N (*pl* **censuses**) censo *m*; **to take a ~ of** levantar el censo de

(B) CPD ► **census taker** N (*US*) encuestador(a) *m/f* del censo

cent [sent] N (= *division of dollar*) centavo *m*; (= *division of euro*) céntimo; **I haven't a ~** (*US**) no tengo ni un céntimo *or* (*LAm*) ni un peso

cent. ABBR 1 (= **centigrade**) C

2 = **central**

3 (= **century**) s

centaur ['sentɔ:ʳ] N centauro *m*

centenarian [,sentı'nεərıən] (A) ADJ centenario

(B) N centenario/a *m/f*

centenary [sen'ti:nərı] (*esp Brit*) N centenario *m*; **the ~ celebrations for …** las festividades para celebrar el centenario de …

centennial [sen'tenıəl] (A) ADJ centenario

(B) N (*US*) = **centenary**

center *etc* ['sentəʳ] (*US*) = **centre** *etc*

centesimal [sen'tesıməl] ADJ centesimal

centigrade ['sentıgreıd] ADJ centígrado; **30 degrees ~** 30 grados centígrados

centigram(me) ['sentıgræm] N centigramo *m*

centilitre, **centiliter** (*US*) ['sentı,li:təʳ] N centilitro *m*

centime ['sɑ̃:nti:m] N céntimo *m*

centimetre, **centimeter** (*US*) ['sentı,mi:təʳ] N centímetro *m*

centipede ['sentıpi:d] N ciempiés *m inv*

central ['sentrəl] (A) ADJ 1 (= *in the middle*) central; **the houses are arranged around a ~ courtyard** las casas están distribuidas alrededor de un patio central

2 (= *near the centre of town*) [*house, office, location*] céntrico; **I'm looking for somewhere more ~** busco algo más céntrico; **his flat is very ~** su piso está muy céntrico; **it's in ~ Paris** está en el centro de París

3 (= *principal*) [*figure, problem, idea, fact*] central, fundamental; [*role*] fundamental; [*aim*] principal; **of ~ importance** de la mayor importancia, primordial; **the issue of Aids is ~ to the plot of the film** el tema del SIDA es fundamental en el argumento de la película; **it is ~ to our policy** es un punto clave de nuestra política

4 (*Admin, Pol*) [*committee, planning, control etc*] central

(B) N (*US*) (= *exchange*) central *f* telefónica

(C) CPD ► **Central African Republic** N República *f* Centroafricana ► **Central America** N Centroamérica *f*, América *f* Central ► **Central Asia** N Asia *f* Central ► **central bank** N banco *m* central ► **central casting** N (*Cine*) departamento *m* de reparto *or* casting; **a Texan farmer straight from** *or* **out of ~ casting** (*fig hum*) un granjero tejano de pura cepa *or* con toda la barba ► **Central Daylight Time** N (*US*) horario *m* de verano de la zona central (de Estados Unidos) ► **Central Europe** N Europa *f* Central ► **central government** N gobierno *m* central ► **central heating** N calefacción *f* central ► **central locking** N (*Aut*) cierre *m* centralizado ► **central nervous system** N sistema *m* nervioso central ► **central processing unit** N (*Comput*) unidad *f* central de proceso ► **central reservation** N (*Brit Aut*) mediana *f* ► **Central Standard Time** N (*US*) horario *m* de la zona central (de Estados Unidos); *see also* **Central American**, **Central Asian**, **Central European**

Central American [,sentrələ'merıkən] (A) N centroamericano/a *m/f*

(B) ADJ centroamericano, de América Central

Central Asian [,sentrəl'eıʃn] ADJ centroasiático, de Asia Central

Central European [,sentrəljʊərə'pi:ən] (A) N centroeuropeo/a *m/f*

(B) ADJ centroeuropeo, de Europa Central

(C) CPD ► **Central European Time** N horario *m* de la zona central europea

centralism ['sentrəlızəm] N (*Pol*) centralismo *m*

centralist ['sentrəlıst] ADJ centralista

centrality [sen'trælıtı] N (*frm*) centralidad *f*

centralization [,sentrəlaı'zeıʃən] N centralización *f*

centralize ['sentrəlaız] VT centralizar

centralized ['sentrəlaızd] ADJ centralizado

centrally ['sentrəlı] ADV [*positioned, located*] en el centro, en un sitio céntrico; **~ heated** con calefacción central; **~ planned economy** economía *f* de planificación central; **he lives ~** vive en el centro

centre, **center** (*US*) ['sentəʳ] (A) N 1 (= *middle*) centro *m*; [*of chocolate*] relleno *m*; **in the ~** en el centro; **the man at the ~ of the controversy** el hombre sobre el que gira la polémica

2 (= *focus*) centro *m*; **the ~ of attention** el centro de atención; **the ~ of attraction** el centro de atracción; **a ~ of intrigue** un centro de intrigas

3 (= *place for specific activity*) centro *m*; **health ~** centro *m* de salud, centro *m* médico

4 (*Pol*) centro *m*

5 (*Sport*) (= *player, kick*) centro *m*

(B) VT 1 (= *place in centre*) centrar; **to feel ~d** (*mentally*) estar centrado

2 (*Sport*) [+ *ball*] pasar al centro, centrar

3 (= *concentrate*) concentrar (**on** en)

(C) VI **to ~ (a)round/in/on** concentrarse en; [*hopes etc*] cifrarse en

(D) CPD ► **centre court** N (*Tennis*) pista *f* central ► **centre forward** N (*Sport*) (delantero/a *m/f*) centro *mf* ► **centre of gravity** N centro *m* de gravedad ► **centre party** N (*Pol*) partido *m* centrista ► **centre spread** N (*Brit Press*) páginas *fpl* centrales ► **centre stage** N (*Theat*) centro *m* del escenario; **to take ~ stage** adquirir protagonismo, pasar a un primer plano

centre-back ['sentə'bæk] N (*Sport*) defensa *mf* centro, escoba *m*

centreboard, **centerboard** (*US*) ['sentəbɔ:d] N orza *f* de deriva

-centred, **-centered** (*US*) ['sentəd] ADJ (*ending in compounds*) centrado en, basado en; **home-centred** centrado en el hogar

centrefold, **centerfold** (*US*) ['sentə,fəʊld] N póster *m* central, encarte *m* central

centre-half [,sentə'hɑ:f] N (*pl* **centre-halves** [,sentə'hɑ:vz]) (*Sport*) medio *mf* centro

centrepiece, **centerpiece** (*US*) ['sentəpi:s] N centro *m* de mesa; (*fig*) atracción *f* principal

centrifugal [sen'trıfjʊgəl] ADJ centrífugo

centrifuge ['sentrıfju:ʒ] (A) N centrifugadora *f*

(B) VT centrifugar

centripetal [sen'trıpıtl] ADJ centrípeto

centrism ['sentrızəm] N centrismo *m*

centrist ['sentrıst] (A) ADJ centrista

(B) N centrista *mf*

centuries-old ['sentjʊrız,əʊld] ADJ secular

centurion [sen'tjʊərıən] N centurión *m*

century ['sentjʊrɪ] N 1 (= *100 years*) siglo *m*; **in the 20th ~** en el siglo veinte
2 (*Cricket*) cien puntos *mpl*, cien carreras *fpl*

CEO N ABBR (*US*) = **Chief Executive Officer**

ceramic [sɪ'ræmɪk] ADJ de cerámica

ceramics [sɪ'ræmɪks] N (= *art*) cerámica *fsing*; (= *objects*) cerámicas *fpl*

cereal ['sɪərɪəl] Ⓐ ADJ cereal
Ⓑ N (= *crop*) cereal *m*; (= *breakfast cereal*) cereales *mpl*

cerebellum [,serɪ'beləm] N (*pl* **cerebellums** *or* **cerebella** [,serɪ'belə]) cerebelo *m*

cerebral ['serɪbrəl] (*US*) [sə'ri:brəl] Ⓐ ADJ 1 (*Med*) cerebral
2 (= *intellectual*) cerebral, intelectual
Ⓑ CPD ► **cerebral palsy** N parálisis *f* cerebral

cerebration [,serɪ'breɪʃən] N (*frm*) meditación *f*, actividad *f* mental

cerebrum ['serəbrəm] N (*pl* **cerebrums** *or* **cerebra** ['serəbrə]) cerebro *m*

ceremonial [,serɪ'məʊnɪəl] Ⓐ ADJ [*rite*] ceremonial; [*dress*] de ceremonia, de gala
Ⓑ N ceremonial *m*

ceremonially [,serɪ'məʊnɪəlɪ] ADV con ceremonia

ceremonious [,serɪ'məʊnɪəs] ADJ ceremonioso

ceremoniously [,serɪ'məʊnɪəslɪ] ADV ceremoniosamente

➤**ceremony** ['serɪmənɪ] N ceremonia *f*; ✦**IDIOM to stand on ~** andarse con ceremonias *or* cumplidos; **let's not stand on ~** dejémonos de ceremonias *or* cumplidos

cerise [sə'ri:z] Ⓐ ADJ (de) color de cereza
Ⓑ N cereza *f*

CERN [sɜ:n] N ABBR = **Conseil Européen pour la Recherche Nucléaire**

cert* [sɜ:t] N ABBR (*Brit*) (= **certainty**) **it's a (dead) ~** es cosa segura; **he's a (dead) ~ for the job** sin duda le darán el puesto

cert. ABBR 1 = **certificate**
2 = **certified**

➤**certain** ['sɜ:tən] Ⓐ ADJ 1 (= *convinced*) **to be ~** [*person*] estar seguro; **I'm ~ he's hiding something** estoy seguro de que está ocultando algo; **to be ~ about sth** estar seguro de algo; **to feel ~** estar seguro; **to be ~ of sth** estar seguro de algo; **I am ~ of it** estoy seguro de ello; **you don't sound very ~** no pareces estar muy seguro
2 (= *sure*) **for ~**: **I can't say for ~** no puedo decirlo con seguridad *or* a ciencia cierta; **we don't know for ~ what caused the accident** no sabemos con seguridad *or* a ciencia cierta lo que causó el accidente; **he's up to something, that's for ~** trama algo, de eso no hay duda *or* eso es seguro; **to make ~ of sth** asegurarse de algo; **you should make ~ of your facts** debes asegurarte de que los datos son ciertos; **to make ~ that** asegurarse de que; **I wanted to make absolutely ~ that this was the right number** quería asegurarme del todo de que este número era el correcto; **I made ~ that he kept his promise** me aseguré de que cumpliese su promesa
3 (= *definite, guaranteed*) [*defeat, death, winner*] seguro; [*cure*] definitivo; [*fact*] cierto, seguro; **one thing is ~ ...** una cosa es segura ...; **it is ~ that ...** es seguro que ...; **it's almost ~ that her husband is dead** es casi seguro que *or* se tiene la casi completa seguridad de que su marido está muerto; **the hospital is facing almost ~ closure** el hospital se enfrenta al cierre casi inevitable; **it is far from ~ that they can win this election** no es ni mucho menos seguro *or* no está nada claro que puedan ganar estas elecciones; **he has been there four times to my ~ knowledge** me consta que *or* sé con certeza que ha estado allí cuatro veces; **in the ~ knowledge that ...** con la seguridad *or* certeza de que ...; **nothing's ~ in this world** no hay nada seguro en este mundo
4 + INFIN **be ~ to tell her** no dejes *or* olvides de decírselo; **he is ~ to be there** (es) seguro que estará allí; **there's ~ to be an argument** con seguridad se producirá una discusión; (*less formal*) seguro que habrá una discusión; **there's ~ to be strong opposition to these proposals** está garantizado que estas propuestas se enfrentarán a una fuerte oposición; **the plans are almost ~ to go ahead** los planes se llevarán a cabo casi con toda seguridad
5 (= *particular*) cierto; **on a ~ day in May** cierto día de mayo; **a ~ Mr/Mrs Smith** un tal Señor/una tal Señora Smith; **of a ~ age** de cierta edad; **in ~ circumstances** en ciertas *or* determinadas circunstancias; **a ~ number of people/years** un cierto número de personas/años; **a ~ person told me that ...** cierta persona me dijo que ...; **she has a ~ something** tiene algo *or* un no sé qué; **at ~ times of the day/month/year** en ciertos momentos del día/ciertos días del mes/ciertas épocas del año
6 (= *slight*) [*impatience, bitterness, courage*] cierto; **there's a ~ amount of confusion about the arrangements** existe una cierta confusión *or* un cierto grado de confusión sobre los preparativos; **to a ~ degree** *or* **extent** hasta cierto punto
Ⓑ PRON (*frm*) ciertos/as *mpl/fpl*, algunos/as *mpl/fpl*; **~ of our leaders** ciertos líderes nuestros, algunos de nuestros líderes

➤**certainly** ['sɜ:tənlɪ] ADV 1 (= *undoubtedly*) con toda certeza, sin duda alguna; **if nothing is done there will ~ be an economic crisis** si no se hace nada, con toda certeza *or* sin duda alguna se producirá una crisis económica; **your answer is almost ~ right** casi seguro que *or* casi con seguridad tu respuesta está bien; **it is ~ true that ...** desde luego es verdad *or* cierto que ...
2 (= *definitely*) **something should ~ be done about that** decididamente, deberían hacer algo al respecto; **I will ~ get it finished by tomorrow** definitivamente lo termino para mañana; **it's ~ better** desde luego es mucho mejor; **this computer is ~ an improvement on the old one** este ordenador es sin ninguna duda mejor que el antiguo; **it ~ impressed me** ya lo creo que me impresionó; **I shall ~ be there** no faltaré, seguro que estaré; **you ~ did that well** desde luego eso lo hiciste bien; **I would ~ like to try** desde luego (que) me gustaría probar; **such groups most ~ exist** esos grupos existen con toda seguridad
3 (*in answer to questions, requests*) **"could you give me a lift?" — "certainly!"** —¿me podrías llevar? —¡claro (que sí)! *or* ¡por supuesto! *or* ¡faltaría más!; **~ madam!** ¡con mucho gusto, señora!, ¡por supuesto, señora!; **"wouldn't you agree?" — "oh, ~"** —¿estás de acuerdo? —sí, desde luego; **"had you forgotten?" — "~ not"** —¿se le había olvidado? —por supuesto que no *or* claro que no; **"would you ever eat snake?" — "~ not!"** —¿comerías serpiente? —¡qué va!; **"will you accept his offer?" — "~ not!"** —¿vas a aceptar su oferta? —¡qué va! *or* ¡de ninguna manera!; **"can I go on my own?" — "~ not!"** —¿puedo ir sola? —¡de eso nada! *or* ¡ni hablar!
4 (= *granted*) **~, she has potential, but ...** desde luego tiene posibilidades, pero ..., no hay duda de que tiene posibilidades, pero ...

certainty ['sɜ:təntɪ] N 1 (*no pl*) (= *conviction*) certeza *f*, seguridad *f*; **I can't say with any ~ that this will happen** no puedo decir con ninguna certeza *or* seguridad que esto vaya a suceder
2 (= *sure fact*) **faced with the ~ of disaster** ante la seguridad *or* lo inevitable del desastre; **we know for a ~ that ...** sabemos a ciencia cierta que ...; **it's a ~** es cosa segura; **there are no certainties in modern Europe** en la Europa moderna no hay nada seguro, pocas cosas son seguras en la Europa moderna; **there is no ~ that they will be alive** no existe la seguridad *or* la certeza de que vayan a estar vivos

Cert. Ed. N ABBR = **Certificate of Education**

certifiable [,sɜ:tɪ'faɪəbl] ADJ 1 [*fact, claim*] certificable
2 (*Med*) declarado demente; (*) (= *mad*) loco, demente

certificate [sə'tɪfɪkɪt] N certificado *m*; (*Univ etc*) diploma *m*, título *m*; **birth/death/marriage ~** partida *f* de nacimiento/defunción/matrimonio; **~ of airworthiness** certificado de aeronavegabilidad; **~ of deposit** certificado de depósito; **~ of incorporation** escritura *f* de constitución (*de una sociedad anónima*); **~ of origin** certificado de origen; **Certificate of Secondary Education** (*Brit Scol*) (*formerly*) ≈ Título *m* de BUP; **X ~** (*Cine*) (para) mayores de 18 años

certificated [sə'tɪfɪkeɪtɪd] ADJ titulado, diplomado

certification [,sɜ:tɪfɪ'keɪʃən] N certificación *f*

certified ['sɜ:tɪfaɪd] Ⓐ ADJ 1 [*cheque*] certificado; [*translation*] confirmado, jurado
2 [*person*] (*in profession*) titulado, diplomado; (= *declared insane*) demente
Ⓑ CPD ► **certified copy** N copia *f* certificada
► **certified mail** N (*US*) correo *m* certificado
► **certified public accountant** N (*US*) contable *mf* diplomado/a

certify ['sɜ:tɪfaɪ] VT 1 (= *confirm*) certificar; **certified as a true copy** confirmada como copia auténtica; **to ~ that...** declarar que...
2 (*Med*) **to ~ sb (insane)** certificar que algn no está en posesión de sus facultades mentales; **you ought to be certified!*** (*esp hum*) ¡estás como una cabra!, ¡estás para que te encierren!

certitude ['sɜ:tɪtju:d] N certidumbre *f*

cerumen [sɪ'ru:men] N cerumen *m*

cervical ['sɜ:vɪkəl] Ⓐ ADJ cervical
Ⓑ CPD ► **cervical cancer** N cáncer *m* cervical *or* del cuello del útero ► **cervical smear** N frotis *m* cervical, citología *f*

cervix ['sɜ:vɪks] N (*pl* **cervixes** *or* **cervices** [sə'vaɪsi:z]) cuello *m* del útero

Cesarean [si:'zɛərɪən] N (*US*) = **Caesarean**

cesium ['si:zɪəm] N (*US*) = **caesium**

cessation [se'seɪʃən] N (*frm*) cese *m*, suspensión *f*; **~ of hostilities** cese *m* de hostilidades

cession ['seʃən] N cesión *f*

cesspit ['sespɪt], **cesspool** ['sespu:l] N pozo *m* negro; (*fig*) sentina *f*

CET N ABBR = **Central European Time**

cetacean [sɪ'teɪʃɪən] Ⓐ ADJ cetáceo
Ⓑ N cetáceo *m*

Cetnik ['tʃetnɪk] ADJ, N chetnik *mf*

Ceylon [sɪ'lɒn] N (*Hist*) Ceilán *m*

Ceylonese [sɪlɒ'ni:z] (*Hist*) Ⓐ ADJ ceilanés
Ⓑ N ceilanés/esa *m/f*

➤ LANGUAGE IN USE: **ceremony** 25.1 **certain A1** 16.1 **A2** 15.1, 16.1 **A3** 16.1, 26.3 **certainly 1** 15.1

CF, cf[1] N ABBR (= **cost and freight**) C y F

cf[2] ABBR (= **confer, compare**) cfr., cf.

C/F, c/f, c/fwd ABBR = **carried forward**

CFC N ABBR (= **chlorofluorocarbon**) CFC *m*

CFE Ⓐ N ABBR (*Brit*) = **college of further education**
Ⓑ NPL ABBR = **Conventional Forces in Europe**

CFO N ABBR = **chief financial officer**

CG N ABBR = **coastguard**

cg ABBR (= **centigram(s), centigramme(s)**) cg

CGA N ABBR (*Comput*) = **colour graphics adaptor**

CH N ABBR (*Brit*) (= **Companion of Honour**) *título honorífico*

ch ABBR 1 (*Literat*) (= **chapter**) cap., c., c/
2 (*Fin*) (= **cheque**) ch.
3 (*Rel*) = **church**

Ch. ABBR (= **chapter**) cap., c., c/

c.h. ABBR (= **central heating**) cal.cen.

cha-cha(-cha) ['tʃɑːtʃɑː('tʃɑː)] N cha-cha-chá *m*

Chad [tʃæd] Ⓐ N Chad *m*; **Lake ~** Lago *m* Chad
Ⓑ ADJ chadiano

chador ['tʃʌdəʳ] N chador *m*

chafe [tʃeɪf] Ⓐ VT 1 (= *rub against*) [+ *skin etc*] rozar, raspar
2 (= *warm*) calentar frotando
Ⓑ VI 1 (= *become sore*) irritar; **to ~ against sth** rozar *or* raspar algo
2 (*fig*) impacientarse *or* irritarse (**at** por)

chaff [tʃɑːf] Ⓐ N 1 (= *husks*) cascarilla *f*, ahechaduras *fpl*; (= *animal food*) pienso *m*, forraje *m*; *see also* **wheat**
2 (*fig*) paja *f*
Ⓑ VT zumbarse de, tomar el pelo a

chaffinch ['tʃæfɪntʃ] N pinzón *m* (vulgar)

chafing dish ['tʃeɪfɪŋdɪʃ] N calientaplatos *m inv*

chagrin ['ʃægrɪn] Ⓐ N (= *anger*) disgusto *m*; (= *disappointment*) desilusión *f*, desazón *f*; **to my ~** con gran disgusto mío
Ⓑ VT mortificar, disgustar

chain [tʃeɪn] Ⓐ N 1 (*lit*) cadena *f*; **to pull the ~** [*of lavatory*] tirar de la cadena
2 **chains** (= *fetters*) cadenas *fpl*, grillos *mpl*; (*Aut*) cadenas *fpl*; **in ~s** encadenado
3 (*fig*) **~ of mountains** cordillera *f*; **~ of shops** cadena *f* de tiendas; **~ of command** cadena *f* de mando; **~ of events** serie *f* de acontecimientos; **to form a human ~** formar una cadena humana
4 (= *measure*) *medida de longitud equivalente a 22 yardas o 20,12 metros*
Ⓑ VT encadenar; **he was ~ed to the wall** estaba encadenado a la pared
Ⓒ CPD ► **chain gang** N (*US*) cadena *f* de presidiarios ► **chain letter** N carta *f* que circula en cadena (*con promesa de una ganancia cuantiosa para los que siguen las indicaciones que da*) ► **chain lightning** N relámpagos *mpl* en zigzag ► **chain mail** N cota *f* de malla ► **chain pump** N bomba *f* de cangilones ► **chain reaction** N reacción *f* en cadena ► **chain smoker** N fumador(a) *m/f* empedernido/a ► **chain stitch** N (*Sew*) punto *m* de cadeneta, cadeneta *f* ► **chain store** N tienda *f* que pertenece a una cadena

►**chain up** VT + ADV encadenar

chain-link fence [ˌtʃeɪnlɪŋk'fens] N valla *f* de tela metálica

chainsaw ['tʃeɪnˌsɔː] N sierra *f* de cadena

chain-smoke ['tʃeɪnˌsməʊk] VI fumar un pitillo tras otro

chair [tʃɛəʳ] Ⓐ N 1 (*gen*) silla *f*; (= *armchair*) sillón *m*, butaca *f*; (= *wheelchair*) silla *f* (de ruedas); (= *seat*) lugar *m*, asiento *m*; **please take a ~** siéntese *or* tome asiento por favor
2 (*Univ*) cátedra *f*
3 [*of meeting*] presidencia *f*; (= *chairman*) presidente *m*; **to be in the ~** ◊ **take the ~** presidir; **to address the ~** dirigirse al presidente
4 **the ~** (*US*) (= *electric chair*) la silla eléctrica
Ⓑ VT 1 [+ *person*] llevar a hombros; **they ~ed him off the ground** le sacaron del campo a hombros
2 [+ *meeting*] presidir

chairback ['tʃɛəbæk] N respaldo *m*

chairbound ['tʃɛəbaʊnd] ADJ en silla de ruedas

chairlift ['tʃɛəlɪft] N telesilla *m or f*, teleférico *m*

chairman ['tʃɛəmən] N (*pl* **chairmen**) presidente/a *m/f*; **~'s report** informe *m* del presidente

chairmanship ['tʃɛəmənʃɪp] N (= *post*) presidencia *f*; (= *art*) arte *m* de presidir reuniones

chairoplane ['tʃɛərəʊˌpleɪn] N silla *f* colgante

chairperson ['tʃɛəˌpɜːsn] N presidente/a *m/f*

chairwarmer* ['tʃɛəˌwɔːməʳ] N (*US*) calientasillas *mf inv*

chairwoman ['tʃɛəˌwʊmən] N (*pl* **chairwomen**) presidenta *f*

chaise longue ['ʃeɪz'lɔ̃ːŋ] N (*pl* **chaise-longues**) tumbona *f*

chakra ['tʃækrə] N chakra *m*

chalet ['ʃæleɪ] N chalet *m*, chalé *m*

chalice ['tʃælɪs] N (*Rel*) cáliz *m*; *see also* **poison B2**

chalk [tʃɔːk] Ⓐ N (*Geol*) creta *f*; (*for writing*) tiza *f*, gis *m* (*Mex*); **a (piece of) ~** una tiza *f*, un gis *m* (*Mex*); ✦*IDIOMS* **by a long ~** (*Brit**) de lejos; **not by a long ~** (*Brit**) ni con mucho, ni mucho menos; **to be as different as ~ and cheese** ser como el día y la noche
Ⓑ VT [+ *message*] escribir con tiza; [+ *luggage*] marcar con tiza

►**chalk up** VT + ADV (*lit*) apuntar; (*fig*) [+ *success, victory*] apuntarse

chalkboard ['tʃɔːkbɔːd] N (*US*) pizarra *f*

chalkface ['tʃɔːkfeɪs] N **the teacher at the ~** el maestro en su clase, el profesor delante de la pizarra; **those at the ~** los que enseñan

chalkpit ['tʃɔːkpɪt] N cantera *f* de creta

chalktalk* ['tʃɔːktɔːk] N (*US*) charla *f* ilustrada en la pizarra

chalky ['tʃɔːkɪ] ADJ (*compar* **chalkier**; *superl* **chalkiest**) (*Geol*) cretáceo

challenge ['tʃælɪndʒ] Ⓐ N 1 (*to game, fight etc*) desafío *m*, reto *m*; [*of sentry*] alto *m*; **to issue a ~ to sb** desafiar a algn; **to rise to the ~** ponerse a la altura de las circunstancias; **to take up a ~** aceptar un desafío
2 (= *bid*) (*for leadership etc*) intento *m* (**for** por); **Vigo's ~ for the league leadership** la tentativa que hace el Vigo para hacerse con el liderato de la liga
3 (*fig*) desafío *m*, reto *m*; **this task is a great ~** esta tarea representa un gran desafío; **the ~ of the 21st century** el reto del siglo XXI; **the ~ of new ideas** el reto de las nuevas ideas
4 (*Jur*) recusación *f*
Ⓑ VT 1 (*to duel*) desafiar, retar; [*sentry*] dar el alto a
2 [+ *speaker*] hablar en contra de; **to ~ sb to do sth** desafiar *or* retar a algn a que haga algo
3 (= *dispute*) [+ *fact, point*] poner en duda; **I ~ that conclusion** dudo que esa conclusión sea acertada
4 (*Jur*) recusar

challenger ['tʃælɪndʒəʳ] N desafiador(a) *m/f*; (= *competitor*) aspirante *mf*; (= *opponent*) contrincante *mf*

challenging ['tʃælɪndʒɪŋ] ADJ 1 (= *provocative*) [*remark, look, tone*] desafiante
2 (= *stimulating*) [*book*] estimulante, provocador; (= *demanding*) [*job, task*] que supone un desafío *or* un reto

challengingly ['tʃælɪndʒɪŋlɪ] ADV 1 (= *defiantly*) [*say*] en tono desafiante; [*act*] con una actitud desafiante, provocadoramente
2 (= *demandingly*) [*difficult*] de forma que supone un desafío *or* un reto

chamber ['tʃeɪmbəʳ] Ⓐ N 1 [*of parliament*] cámara *f*; (†) (= *esp bedroom*) aposento† *m*; **chambers** [*of judge*] despacho *m*; [*of barrister*] bufete *m*; **the Upper/Lower Chamber** (*Pol*) la Cámara Alta/Baja; **~ of commerce** cámara de comercio
2 [*of gun*] recámara *f*
Ⓑ CPD ► **chamber concert** N concierto *m* de cámara ► **chamber music** N música *f* de cámara ► **chamber orchestra** N orquesta *f* de cámara ► **chamber pot** N orinal *m*

chamberlain ['tʃeɪmbəlɪn] N chambelán *m*, gentilhombre *m* de cámara

chambermaid ['tʃeɪmbəmeɪd] N (*in hotel*) camarera *f*

chambray ['tʃæmbreɪ] N (*US*) = **cambric**

chameleon [kə'miːlɪən] N camaleón *m*

chamfer ['tʃæmfəʳ] Ⓐ N chaflán *m*, bisel *m*
Ⓑ VT chaflanar, biselar

chammy ['ʃæmɪ] N gamuza *f*

chamois N 1 ['ʃæmwɑː] (*Zool*) gamuza *f*
2 ['ʃæmɪ] (*also* **~ leather**) gamuza *f*

chamomile ['kæməʊmaɪl] N = **camomile**

champ[1] [tʃæmp] VI **to ~ at** morder, mordiscar; [+ *bit*] tascar, morder; ✦*IDIOM* **to be ~ing at the bit (to do sth)** estar impaciente (por hacer algo)

champ[2]* [tʃæmp] N = **champion**

Champagne [ʃæm'peɪn] N Champaña *f*

champagne [ʃæm'peɪn] Ⓐ N champán *m*, champaña *m or f*
Ⓑ CPD ► **champagne breakfast** N desayuno *m* con champán ► **champagne glass** N copa *f* de champán

champers* ['ʃæmpəz] N (*hum*) champán *m*

champion ['tʃæmpɪən] Ⓐ N campeón/ona *m/f*; [*of cause*] defensor(a) *m/f*, paladín *m*; **boxing ~** campeón de boxeo; **world ~** campeón mundial
Ⓑ ADJ 1 (= *award-winning*) campeón; **a ~ athlete** un campeón de atletismo
2 (*) magnífico, estupendo; **~!** ¡magnífico!, ¡estupendo!
Ⓒ VT defender, abogar por

championship ['tʃæmpɪənʃɪp] N 1 (= *contest*) campeonato *m*
2 [*of cause*] defensa *f*

▼**chance** [tʃɑːns] Ⓐ N 1 (= *fate*) azar *m*; (= *coincidence*) casualidad *f*; **by ~** por casualidad; **we met by ~ in Paris** nos encontramos por casualidad en París; **do you have a room available, by any ~?** ¿no tendrá por casualidad una habitación libre?, ¿por casualidad tiene una habitación libre?; **to leave nothing to ~** no dejar nada al azar *or* a la casualidad, no dejar ningún cabo suelto *or* por atar; **to trust sth to ~** dejar algo al azar; *see also* **game**[1] **A1.1**
2 (= *opportunity*) oportunidad *f*, ocasión *f*; **~ would be a fine thing!*** ¡ojalá!, ¡ya quisiera yo!; **you'll never get another ~ like this** nunca se te presentará otra oportunidad *or* ocasión como ésta; **all those eligible will**

➤ LANGUAGE IN USE: **chance A3** 15.2, 16.2

get a ~ to vote todas las personas que cumplan los requisitos podrán votar; **to give sb a ~**: **he didn't give me a ~ to say anything** no me dio (la) oportunidad de decir nada; **give me a ~, I've only just got here!** ¡espera un ratito, acabo de llegar!; **he never had a ~ in life** nunca tuvo suerte en la vida; **given half a ~ he'd eat the lot*** si se le dejara, se lo comería todo; **you always wanted to ride a horse, and here's your ~** siempre quisiste montar a caballo, ahora tienes la oportunidad; **to jump** *or* **leap at the ~** aprovechar la oportunidad *or* ocasión, no dejar escapar la oportunidad *or* ocasión; **it's the ~ of a lifetime** es la oportunidad de mi/tu/su *etc* vida; **to have an eye on** *or* **to the main ~*** (*pej*) estar a la que salta*; **to miss one's ~** perder la *or* su oportunidad; **she's gone out, now's your ~!** ha salido, ¡ésta es tu oportunidad!; **they decided to give me a second ~** decidieron darme una segunda oportunidad

[3] (= *possibility*) posibilidad *f*; **his ~s of survival are slim** tiene escasas posibilidades de sobrevivir, sus posibilidades de sobrevivir son escasas; **the ~s are that ...** lo más probable es que ...; **it has a one in 11,000 ~ (of winning)** tiene una posibilidad entre 11.000 (de ganar); **to have a good ~ of success** tener bastantes posibilidades de éxito; **to be in with a ~** (*Brit**) tener muchas posibilidades; **I had very little ~ of winning** tenía muy pocas posibilidades de ganar; **he has no ~ of winning** no tiene ninguna posibilidad de ganar, no tiene posibilidad alguna de ganar; **no ~!*** (*refusing*) ¡ni hablar!*; (*dismissing a possibility*) ¡qué va!*; **there is a slight ~ she may still be there** puede que exista una pequeña posibilidad de que todavía esté allí; **they don't stand a ~ (of winning)** no tienen ninguna posibilidad *or* posibilidad alguna (de ganar); **he never stood a ~, the truck went straight into him** no pudo hacer nada, el camión se fue derecho a él; *see also* **fat A5**

[4] (= *risk*) riesgo *m*; **I'll take that ~** correré ese riesgo, me arriesgaré; **I'm not taking any ~s** no quiero arriesgarme; **you shouldn't take any ~s where your health is concerned** no deberías correr riesgos *or* arriesgarte cuando se trata de tu salud; **we decided to take a ~ on the weather** decidimos arriesgarnos con el tiempo

Ⓑ VT [1] (= *run the risk of*) [+ *rejection, fine*] arriesgarse a; **to ~ doing sth** arriesgarse a hacer algo; **to ~ it*** jugársela, arriesgarse; ✦*IDIOM* **to ~ one's arm** *or* **one's luck** probar suerte

[2] (*frm*) (= *happen*) **to ~ to do sth** hacer algo por casualidad; **she ~d to look up at that moment** en ese momento dio la casualidad de que levantó la vista *or* levantó la vista por casualidad; **I ~d to catch sight of her as she passed** la vi por casualidad cuando pasaba

Ⓒ CPD ► **chance meeting** N encuentro *m* fortuito *or* casual ► **chance remark** N comentario *m* casual

►**chance on, chance upon** VI + PREP [+ *object*] tropezar(se) con, encontrar por casualidad; [+ *person*] tropezar(se) con, encontrarse por casualidad con

chancel [ˈtʃɑːnsəl] N coro *m* y presbiterio

chancellery [ˈtʃɑːnsərɪ] N cancillería *f*

chancellor [ˈtʃɑːnsələʳ] N (*Pol*) canciller *mf*; (*Univ*) rector(a) *m/f* honorario/a; **Chancellor of the Exchequer** Ministro/a *m/f* (*LAm*) Secretario/a *m/f* de Economía y Hacienda; **Lord Chancellor** *jefe de la administración de la justicia en Inglaterra y Gales, y presidente de la Cámara de los Lores*

chancer* [ˈtʃænsəʳ] N (*Brit*) trepa* *mf*

chancery [ˈtʃɑːnsərɪ] N [1] (*Brit Jur*) (*also* **Chancery Division**) *sala del High Court que se ocupa de causas de derecho privado*; **ward in ~** *pupilo/a bajo la protección del tribunal*

[2] (*US*) = **chancellery**

[3] (*US Jur*) (*also* **Court of Chancery**) tribunal *m* de equidad

chancre [ˈʃæŋkəʳ] N chancro *m*

chancy* [ˈtʃɑːnsɪ] ADJ (*compar* **chancier**; *superl* **chanciest**) arriesgado

chandelier [ˌʃændəˈlɪəʳ] N araña *f* (de luces)

chandler [ˈtʃɑːndləʳ] N velero *m*

change [tʃeɪndʒ] Ⓐ N [1] (*gen*) cambio *m*; (= *transformation*) transformación *f*; (= *alteration*) modificación *f*; (= *variation*) variación *f*; [*of skin*] muda *f*; **the day out made a refreshing ~** el día fuera de casa nos dio un buen cambio de aire; **to resist ~** resistirse a las innovaciones; **~ of address** cambio de domicilio; **to have a ~ of air** cambiar de aires; **the ~ of air has done me good** el cambio de aires me ha sentado bien; **a ~ for the better** un cambio para bien; **a ~ of clothes** ropa para cambiarse; (= *underclothes*) una muda; **just for a ~** para variar; **~ of heart** cambio de idea; **he's had a ~ of heart** ha cambiado de idea; **~ of horses** relevo *m* de los tiros; **a ~ in policy** un cambio de política; **the ~ of life** (*Med*) la menopausia; **~ of ownership** cambio de dueño; **~ of scene** cambio de aires; **a ~ for the worse** un cambio para mal; ✦*IDIOM* **to get no ~ out of sb** no conseguir sacar nada a algn; ✦*PROV* **a ~ is as good as a rest** un cambio de aires da fuerzas para seguir; *see also* **ring² B1**

[2] (= *small coins*) cambio *m*, suelto *m*, sencillo *m*, feria *f* (*Mex**); (*for a larger coin*) cambio *m*; (= *money returned*) vuelta *f*, vuelto *m* (*LAm*); **can you give me ~ for one pound?** ¿tiene cambio de una libra?, ¿puede cambiarme una moneda de una libra?; **keep the ~** quédese con la vuelta; **you won't get much ~ out of a pound if you buy sugar** con una libra no te va a sobrar mucho si compras azúcar

Ⓑ VT [1] (*by substitution*) [+ *address, name etc*] cambiar; [+ *clothes, colour*] cambiar de; **to ~ trains/buses/planes (at)** hacer transbordo (en), cambiar de tren/autobús/avión (en); **to ~ gear** (*Aut*) cambiar de marcha; **to get ~d** cambiarse; **to ~ hands** cambiar de mano *or* de dueño; **he wants to ~ his job** quiere cambiar de trabajo; **to ~ one's mind** cambiar de opinión *or* idea; **to ~ places** cambiar de sitio; **I'm going to ~ my shoes** voy a cambiarme de zapatos; **let's ~ the subject** cambiemos de tema

[2] (= *exchange*) (*in shop*) cambiar (**for** por); **can I ~ this dress for a larger size?** ¿puedo cambiar este vestido por otro de una talla mayor?

[3] (= *alter*) [+ *person*] cambiar; (*fig*) evolucionar; (= *transform*) transformar (**into** en); **I find him much ~d** le veo muy cambiado; **the prince was ~d into a frog** el príncipe se transformó en rana

[4] [+ *money*] cambiar; **to ~ pounds into dollars** cambiar libras en dólares; **can you ~ this note for me?** ¿me hace el favor de cambiar este billete?

[5] (= *put fresh nappy on*) [+ *baby*] cambiar (el pañal de)

Ⓒ VI [1] (= *alter*) cambiar; **you've ~d!** ¡cómo has cambiado!, ¡pareces otro!; **you haven't ~d a bit!** ¡no has cambiado en lo más mínimo!

[2] (= *be transformed*) transformarse (**into** en)

[3] (= *change clothes*) cambiarse, mudarse; **she ~d into an old skirt** se cambió y se puso una falda vieja

[4] (= *change trains*) hacer transbordo, cambiar de tren; (= *change buses*) hacer transbordo, cambiar de autobús; **all ~!** ¡fin de trayecto!

Ⓓ CPD ► **change machine** N máquina *f* de cambio ► **change purse** N (*US*) monedero *m*

►**change around** Ⓐ VT + ADV (= *rearrange*) cambiar de posición

Ⓑ VI + ADV cambiar

►**change down** VI + ADV (*Brit Aut*) cambiar a una velocidad inferior

►**change over** Ⓐ VI + ADV (*from sth to sth*) cambiar (**to** a); [*players etc*] cambiar(se)

Ⓑ VT + ADV cambiar

►**change round** *see* **change around**

►**change up** VI + ADV (*Brit Aut*) cambiar a una velocidad superior

changeability [ˌtʃeɪndʒəˈbɪlɪtɪ] N [*of situation, weather*] variabilidad *f*, lo cambiante; [*of person*] volubilidad *f*, lo cambiante

changeable [ˈtʃeɪndʒəbl] ADJ [*situation, weather*] variable; [*person*] voluble, inconstante

changeless [ˈtʃeɪndʒlɪs] ADJ inmutable

changeling [ˈtʃeɪndʒlɪŋ] N *niño sustituido por otro*

changeover [ˈtʃeɪndʒˌəʊvəʳ] N cambio *m*

changing [ˈtʃeɪndʒɪŋ] Ⓐ ADJ cambiante; **a ~ world** un mundo en perpetua evolución

Ⓑ N **the ~ of the Guard** el cambio *or* relevo de la Guardia

Ⓒ CPD ► **changing room** N (*Brit*) vestuario *m*

channel [ˈtʃænl] Ⓐ N (= *watercourse, TV channel*) canal *m*; (= *strait*) estrecho *m*; (= *deepest part of river*) cauce *m*; (*fig*) [*of communication*] vía *f*; **irrigation ~** acequia *f*, canal *m* de riego; **green/red ~** (*Customs*) pasillo *m* verde/rojo; **to go through the usual ~s** seguir las vías normales; **the (English) Channel** el Canal (de la Mancha); **~ of distribution** vía *f* *or* canal *m* de distribución

Ⓑ VT (= *hollow out*) [+ *course*] acanalar; (= *direct*) [+ *river*] encauzar; (*fig*) [+ *interest, energies*] encauzar, dirigir (**into** a)

Ⓒ CPD ► **the Channel Islands** NPL las Islas Anglonormandas *or* del Canal de la Mancha ► **the Channel Tunnel** N el túnel del Canal de la Mancha

►**channel off** VT + ADV (*lit, fig*) [+ *water, energy, resources*] canalizar

channel-hop [ˈtʃænlhɒp] VI (*Brit TV*) hacer zapping

channel-hopping [ˈtʃænlˈhɒpɪŋ] N (*Brit TV*) zapping *m*

channel-surf [ˈtʃænlˌsɜːf] (*US*) = **channel-hop**

channel-surfing [ˈtʃænlˌsɜːfɪŋ] (*US*) = **channel-hopping**

chant [tʃɑːnt] Ⓐ N (*Mus, Rel*) canto *m*; [*of crowd*] grito *m*, consigna *f*; (*fig*) (*monotonous*) sonsonete *m*; **plain ~** (*Rel*) canto llano

Ⓑ VT (*Mus, Rel*) cantar; [+ *slogan*] gritar (rítmicamente), corear; (*fig*) salmodiar, recitar en tono monótono

Ⓒ VI (*Mus, Rel*) cantar; (*at demonstration etc*) gritar (rítmicamente)

chantey [ˈʃæntɪ] N (*US*) saloma *f*

chaos [ˈkeɪɒs] Ⓐ N caos *m*; **to be in ~** [*house*] estar en completo desorden; [*country*] estar en el caos; *see* **organized**

Ⓑ CPD ► **chaos theory** N teoría *f* del caos

chaotic [keɪˈɒtɪk] ADJ caótico

chap[1] [tʃæp] Ⓐ N (*on lip*) grieta *f*
Ⓑ VT agrietar
Ⓒ VI agrietarse

chap[2]* [tʃæp] N (= *man*) tío* *m*, tipo* *m*; **a ~ I know** un tío que conozco; **he's a nice ~** es buen chico, es buena persona; **he's very deaf, poor ~** es muy sordo, el pobre; **how are you, old ~?** ¿qué tal, amigo *or* (*S. Cone*) viejo?; **be a good ~ and say nothing** sé buen chico y no digas nada; **poor little ~** pobrecito *m*

chap[3] [tʃæp] N (*Anat*) mandíbula *f*; (= *cheek*) mejilla *f*

chap. ABBR (= **chapter**) cap., c., c/

chapat(t)i [tʃə'pætɪ, tʃə'pɑːtɪ] N (*pl* **chapat(t)i** *or* **chapat(t)is** *or* **chapat(t)ies**) chapatti *m* (*en la cocina india, pan de forma achatada, sin levadura*)

chapel ['tʃæpəl] N 1 (= *part of church*) capilla *f*; (= *nonconformist church*) templo *m*
2 (*as adj*) **it doesn't matter whether they're church or ~** no importa si son protestantes de la Iglesia Anglicana o de fuera de ella
3 [*of union*] división *f* sindical

chaperon(e) ['ʃæpərəʊn] Ⓐ N acompañante *f* (de señoritas), carabina *mf* (*Sp**)
Ⓑ VT acompañar a, hacer de carabina a (*Sp**)

chaplain ['tʃæplɪn] N capellán *m*; **~ general** (*Mil*) vicario *m* general castrense

chaplaincy ['tʃæplənsɪ] N capellanía *f*

chaplet ['tʃæplɪt] N guirnalda *f*, corona *f* de flores; (= *necklace*) collar *m*; (*Rel*) rosario *m*

chapped [tʃæpt] ADJ [*skin*] agrietado

chappy* ['tʃæpɪ] N = **chap**[2]

chaps [tʃæps] NPL (*US*) zahones *mpl*, chaparreras *fpl*

chapter ['tʃæptəʳ] Ⓐ N 1 [*of book*] capítulo *m*; ✦*IDIOM* **~ and verse** con pelos y señales, con todo lujo de detalles; **he can quote you ~ and verse** él te lo puede citar textualmente
2 (*Rel*) cabildo *m*
3 (= *branch of society, organization*) sección *f*
4 (*fig*) (= *period*) **a ~ of accidents** una serie de desgracias
Ⓑ CPD ► **chapter house** N sala *f* capitular

char[1] [tʃɑːʳ] Ⓐ VT (= *burn black*) carbonizar
Ⓑ VI carbonizarse

char[2] [tʃɑːʳ] Ⓐ N (= *charwoman*) = **charlady**
Ⓑ VI limpiar, trabajar como asistenta

char[3]‡ [tʃɑːʳ] N (*Brit*) té *m*

charabanc† ['ʃærəbæŋ] N (*Brit*) autobús *m*, autocar *m* (*Sp*)

character ['kærɪktəʳ] Ⓐ N 1 (= *nature*) [*of thing*] carácter *m*, naturaleza *f*; [*of person*] carácter *m*, personalidad *f*; **a man of good ~** un hombre de buena reputación; **to bear a good ~** tener buena reputación; **that is more in ~ for him** eso es más típico de él; **his sudden concern for me was completely out of ~ (for him)** su inesperado interés por mí no era nada típico de él
2 (*in novel, play*) (= *person*) personaje *m*; (= *role*) papel *m*; **chief ~** protagonista *mf*
3 (= *energy, determination*) carácter *m*; **a man of ~** un hombre de carácter; **he lacks ~** le falta carácter
4 (*) (= *person*) tipo/a* *m/f*, individuo/a *m/f*; **he's a very odd ~** es un tipo muy raro*; **he's quite a ~** es todo un personaje
5 (*Comput, Typ, Bio*) carácter *m*
Ⓑ CPD ► **character actor** N actor *m* de carácter ► **character actress** N actriz *f* de carácter ► **character assassination** N difamación *f* ► **character code** N (*Comput*) código *m* de caracteres ► **character part** N (*Theat*) papel *m* de carácter ► **character reference** N informe *m*, referencia *f* ► **character set** N (*Typ*) juego *m* de caracteres ► **character sketch** N esbozo *m* de carácter ► **character space** N (*Typ*) espacio *m* (de carácter)

characterful ['kærɪktəfʊl] ADJ [*wine, singer*] con (mucho) carácter

characteristic [ˌkærɪktə'rɪstɪk] Ⓐ ADJ característico (**of** de)
Ⓑ N característica *f*

characteristically [ˌkærɪktə'rɪstɪkəlɪ] ADV característicamente, de modo característico; **he was in ~ jovial mood** como es típico de él, estaba de muy buen talante

characterization [ˌkærɪktəraɪ'zeɪʃən] N (*in novel*) caracterización *f*

characterize ['kærɪktəraɪz] VT (= *be characteristic of*) caracterizar; (= *describe*) calificar (**as** de)

characterless ['kærɪktəlɪs] ADJ sin carácter

charade [ʃə'rɑːd] N (*frm, pej*) payasada *f*, farsa *f*; **charades** (= *game*) charada *f*

charcoal ['tʃɑːkəʊl] Ⓐ N carbón *m* vegetal; (*Art*) carboncillo *m*
Ⓑ CPD ► **charcoal drawing** N dibujo *m* al carbón *or* al carboncillo

charcoal-burner ['tʃɑːkəʊlˌbɜːnəʳ] N carbonero *m*

charcoal-grey [ˌtʃɑːkəʊl'greɪ] ADJ gris marengo *inv*

charge [tʃɑːdʒ]

A NOUN	C INTRANSITIVE VERB
B TRANSITIVE VERB	D COMPOUNDS

Ⓐ NOUN
1 *= accusation* (*Jur*) cargo *m*, acusación *f*; (*fig*) acusación *f*; **the ~s were dropped** retiraron los cargos *or* la acusación; **what is the ~?** ¿de qué se me acusa?; **the ~ was murder** lo acusaron de asesinato; **to lay o.s. open to the ~ of …** exponerse a que le acusen de …; **to bring a ~ against sb** formular *or* presentar cargos contra algn; **he will appear in court on a ~ of murder** *or* **murder ~** comparecerá ante el tribunal acusado de asesinato; **he was arrested on a ~ of murder** *or* **murder ~** lo detuvieron bajo acusación de asesinato; *see also* **press B9**
2 *Mil* **to put sb on a ~** arrestar a algn
3 *= fee* precio *m*; (*professional*) honorarios *mpl*; (*Telec*) **charges** tarifa *fsing*; **~ for admission** precio *m* de entrada; **is there a ~?** ¿hay que pagar (algo)?; **is there a ~ for delivery?** ¿se paga el envío?; **there's no ~** es gratis; **"no charge for admission"** "entrada gratis", "entrada gratuita"; **extra ~** recargo *m*, suplemento *m*; **free of ~** gratis; **interest ~s** cargos *mpl* en concepto de interés; **to make a ~ for (doing) sth** cobrar por (hacer) algo; **for a small ~, we can supply …** por una pequeña cantidad, podemos proporcionarle …; *see also* **prescription B**, **reverse C3**, **service C**
4 *US = charge account* **cash or ~?** ¿al contado o a crédito?
5 *= responsibility* **I've been given ~ of this class** han puesto a esta clase a mi cargo; **to have ~ of sb/sth** hacerse cargo de algn/algo; **the patients under her ~** los pacientes a su cargo
◆ **in charge**: **the person in ~** el/la encargado/a; **who is in ~ here?** ¿quién es el encargado aquí?; **look, I'm in ~ here!** ¡oye, aquí mando yo!
◆ **in charge of**: **to be in ~ of** [+ *department, operation*] estar al frente *or* al cargo de; **he's in ~ of the shop when I'm out** se encarga de la tienda cuando yo no estoy; **it is illegal for anyone under 16 to be left in ~ of young children** es ilegal dejar a niños pequeños a cargo *or* al cuidado de alguien menor de 16 años
◆ **to put sb in charge of** [+ *department, operation*] poner a algn al frente *or* al cargo de; [+ *ship, plane*] poner a algn al mando de; **to put sb in ~ of doing sth** encargar a algn que haga algo
◆ **to take charge** (*of firm, project*) hacerse cargo (**of** de); **he took ~ of the situation at once** se hizo cargo de la situación inmediatamente; **will you take ~ of the situation while I'm away?** ¿te puedes hacer cargo de la situación mientras no esté yo?
6 *= person* **the teacher and her ~s** la maestra y los alumnos a su cargo; **the nurse and her ~s** la enfermera y los enfermos a su cargo
7 *electrical* carga *f*; **there is no ~ left in the battery** la batería está descargada; ✦*IDIOM* **to get a ~ out of sth**: **I got a big ~ out of working with the Philharmonic Orchestra** disfruté muchísimo trabajando con la Orquesta Filarmónica
8 *= explosive* carga *f*
9 *= attack* (*by people, army*) carga *f*, ataque *m*; (*by bull*) embestida *f*; *see also* **sound B1**
10 *= financial burden* carga *f*; **to be a ~ on …** ser una carga para …
11 *Heraldry* blasón *m*

Ⓑ TRANSITIVE VERB
1 *Jur, fig* (= *accuse*) acusar (**with** de); **he was ~d with stealing a car** lo acusaron del robo de un coche; **to find sb guilty/not guilty as ~d** declarar a algn culpable/inocente de los delitos que se le imputan; **he ~d the minister with lying about the economy** acusó al ministro de mentir acerca de la economía; **to ~ that** (*US*) alegar que
2 *= ask for* [+ *price*] cobrar; **what did they ~ you for it?** ¿cuánto te cobraron?; **what are they charging for the work?** ¿cuánto cobran *or* piden por el trabajo?; **to ~ 3% commission** cobrar un 3% de comisión
3 *= record as debt* **to ~ sth (up) to sb** ◊ **~ sth (up) to sb's account** cargar algo en la cuenta de algn; **~ it (up) to my card** cárguelo a mi tarjeta
4 *= attack* [*person, army*] cargar contra, atacar; [*bull etc*] embestir
5 *Elec* (*also* **~ up**) [+ *battery*] cargar
6 *= order* **to ~ sb to do sth** ordenar a algn hacer *or* que haga algo; **to ~ sb with a mission** confiar una misión a algn; **I am ~d with the task of modernizing the company** me han encargado la tarea de modernizar la empresa
7 (*US: in library*) **to ~ a book** [*reader*] rellenar la ficha del préstamo; [*librarian*] registrar un libro como prestado

Ⓒ INTRANSITIVE VERB
1 *= ask for a fee* cobrar; **they'll mend it but they'll ~!** lo arreglarán, pero ¡te va a salir caro!
2 *= attack* [*person, army*] atacar; [*bull*] embestir; **~!** ¡a la carga!; **he ~d into the room** irrumpió en la habitación
3 *Elec* (*also* **~ up**) [*battery*] cargarse; **leave the battery to ~ (up) for a couple of hours** deja que la batería se cargue durante un par de horas

Ⓓ COMPOUNDS ► **charge account** N (*US*) cuenta *f* de crédito ► **charge card** N (*Brit Comm*) tarjeta *f* (de) cliente; (*US*) (= *credit card*) tarjeta *f* de crédito

chargeable ['tʃɑːdʒəbl] ADJ [1] (*Jur*) [*offence*] imputable; **to be ~ with** [*person*] ser susceptible de ser acusado de
[2] **to be ~ to** [+ *person*] correr a cargo de; [+ *account*] cargarse a
charge-cap ['tʃɑːdʒkæp] VT (*Brit*) [+ *local authority*] fijar un tope a los impuestos de
charged [tʃɑːdʒd] ADJ (*Elec*) cargado, con carga
chargé d'affaires ['ʃɑːʒeɪdæ'fɛəʳ] (*pl* **chargés d'affaires**) N encargado *m* de negocios
chargehand ['tʃɑːdʒhænd] N (*Brit*) capataz *m*
charger ['tʃɑːdʒəʳ] N (*Elec*) cargador *m*; (= *war-horse*) corcel *m*, caballo *m* de guerra
char-grilled [,tʃɑːʳ'grɪld] ADJ a la brasa
charily ['tʃɛərɪlɪ] ADV (= *warily*) cautelosamente; (= *sparingly*) parcamente, con parquedad
chariot ['tʃærɪət] N carro *m* (*romano, de guerra etc*)
charioteer [,tʃærɪə'tɪəʳ] N auriga *m*
charisma [kæ'rɪzmə] N carisma *m*
charismatic [,kærɪz'mætɪk] ADJ carismático
charitable ['tʃærɪtəbl] ADJ [1] (= *helping needy*) [*organization, society, institution, donation*] benéfico; **~ trust** fundación *f* benéfica; **to have ~ status** tener categoría de organización benéfica; **~ work** obras *fpl* benéficas, obras *fpl* de beneficiencia
[2] (= *kindly*) [*person, deed, gesture*] benévolo, caritativo; [*remark, view*] comprensivo; **to be ~ to sb** mostrarse benévolo con algn; **to take a ~ view of sth** tener una visión comprensiva de algo, adoptar un punto de vista comprensivo sobre algo
charitably ['tʃærɪtəblɪ] ADV [*say, act*] caritativamente, con benevolencia
charity ['tʃærɪtɪ] Ⓐ N [1] (= *goodwill*) caridad *f*; **out of ~** por caridad; ✦*PROV* **~ begins at home** la caridad bien entendida empieza por uno mismo
[2] (= *financial relief*) obras *fpl* benéficas; (= *alms*) limosnas *fpl*; **all proceeds go to ~** todo lo recaudado se destinará a obras benéficas; **he gave the money to ~** donó el dinero a una organización benéfica; **to live on ~** vivir de la caridad; **to raffle sth for ~** rifar algo para fines benéficos
[3] (= *organization*) organización *f* benéfica
[4] (= *act*) **it would be a ~ if ...** sería una obra de caridad si ...
Ⓑ CPD ► **charity appeal** N cuestación *f* para obras benéficas ► **charity shop** N (*Brit*) *tienda de artículos de segunda mano que dedica su recaudación a causas benéficas*
charlady ['tʃɑːleɪdɪ] N (*Brit*) mujer *f* de la limpieza, asistenta *f*
charlatan ['ʃɑːlətən] N charlatán/tana *m/f*
Charlemagne ['ʃɑːləmeɪn] N Carlomagno
Charles [tʃɑːlz] N Carlos
charleston ['tʃɑːlstən] N charlestón *m*
charley horse* ['tʃɑːlɪhɔːs] N (*US*) calambre *m*
Charlie* ['tʃɑːlɪ] N [1] (*Brit†*) (= *fool*) imbécil *m*; **I felt a right ~!** ¡me sentí como un idiota!; **he must have looked a right ~!** ¡debía parecer un verdadero imbécil!* [2] (*familiar form*) of **Charles** Carlitos; **~ Chaplin** Charlot
Charlotte ['ʃɑːlət] N Carlota
charm [tʃɑːm] Ⓐ N [1] (= *attractiveness*) encanto *m*, atractivo *m*; (= *pleasantness*) simpatía *f*; **he has great ~** es verdaderamente encantador, tiene un fuerte atractivo; **to turn on the ~** ponerse fino; **to fall victim to sb's ~s** sucumbir a los encantos de algn
[2] (= *magic spell*) hechizo *m*; (*recited*) ensalmo *m*; **it worked like a ~** funcionó a las mil maravillas
[3] (= *object*) dije *m*, amuleto *m*
Ⓑ VT [1] (= *delight*) encantar; **we were ~ed by Granada** nos encantó Granada
[2] (= *entice with charm*) **to ~ one's way out of a situation** utilizar su encanto para salir de un apuro; ✦*IDIOM* **he could ~ the birds out of the trees** con su encanto es capaz de conseguir todo lo que se propone
[3] (= *bewitch*) encantar, hechizar; **~ed circle** círculo *m* privilegiado; ✦*IDIOM* **to lead a ~ed life** tener suerte en todo
Ⓒ CPD ► **charm bracelet** N pulsera *f* amuleto *or* de dijes ► **charm offensive** N ofensiva *f* amistosa; **to launch a ~ offensive** lanzar una ofensiva amistosa ► **charm school*** N = **finishing school**
►**charm away** VT + ADV hacer desaparecer como por magia, llevarse misteriosamente
charmer ['tʃɑːməʳ] N persona *f* encantadora
charming ['tʃɑːmɪŋ] ADJ [*place*] encantador; [*person*] encantador, simpático; **how ~ of you!** ¡qué detalle!; **~!** (*iro*) ¡qué simpático! (*iro*)
charmingly ['tʃɑːmɪŋlɪ] ADV de modo encantador; **a ~ simple dress** un vestido sencillo pero muy mono; **as you so ~ put it** (*iro*) como tú tan finamente has indicado (*iro*)
charmless ['tʃɑːmlɪs] ADJ [*place*] sin encanto, poco atractivo; [*person*] sin atractivo, sin chispa*
charnel-house ['tʃɑːnlhaʊs] N (*pl* **charnel-houses** ['tʃɑːnlhaʊzɪz]) osario *m*
charred [tʃɑːd] ADJ carbonizado
chart [tʃɑːt] Ⓐ N [1] (= *table*) tabla *f*, cuadro *m*; (= *graph*) gráfica *f*, gráfico *m*; (*Met*) mapa *m*; (*Naut*) (= *map*) carta *f* (de navegación); **weather ~** mapa meteorológico
[2] (*Mus*) **the ~s*** la lista de éxitos; **to be in the ~s** [*record, pop group*] estar en la lista de éxitos
Ⓑ VT (= *plot*) [+ *course*] trazar; (= *record on graph*) [+ *sales, growth, etc*] hacer una gráfica de, representar gráficamente; (= *follow*) [+ *progress*] reflejar; **the book ~s the rise and fall of the empire** el libro describe la grandeza y decadencia del imperio; **the diagram ~s the company's progress** el diagrama muestra *or* refleja el progreso de la compañía
Ⓒ CPD ► **chart topper*** N éxito *m* discográfico
charter ['tʃɑːtəʳ] Ⓐ N [1] (= *authorization*) carta *f*; [*of city*] fuero *m*; [*of organization*] estatutos *mpl*; [*of company*] escritura *f* de constitución; **royal ~** cédula *f* real
[2] (= *hire*) (*Naut*) alquiler *m*; (*Aer*) fletamento *m*; **this boat is available for ~** este barco se alquila
Ⓑ VT [1] [+ *organization*] aprobar los estatutos de; [+ *company*] aprobar la escritura de constitución de
[2] [+ *bus*] alquilar; [+ *ship, plane*] fletar
Ⓒ CPD ► **charter flight** N vuelo *m* chárter ► **charter plane** N avión *m* chárter
chartered ['tʃɑːtəd] ADJ [*surveyor*] colegiado; [*librarian*] diplomado (*con un mínimo de dos años de experiencia*); [*company*] legalmente constituido; **~ accountant** (*Brit, Canada*) censor(a) *m/f* jurado/a de cuentas, contador(a) *m/f* público/a (*LAm*)
charterer ['tʃɑːtərəʳ] N fletador(a) *m/f*
Chartism ['tʃɑːtɪzəm] N (*Hist*) cartismo *m*
Chartist ['tʃɑːtɪst] N **the ~s** (*Hist*) los cartistas
charwoman ['tʃɑː,wʊmən] N (*pl* **charwomen**) mujer *f* de la limpieza, asistenta *f*
chary ['tʃɛərɪ] ADJ (*compar* **charier**, *superl* **chariest**) [1] (= *wary*) cauteloso; **he's ~ of getting involved** evita inmiscuirse
[2] (= *sparing*) **she's ~ in her praise** no se prodiga en alabanzas
chase[1] [tʃeɪs] Ⓐ N persecución *f*; **the ~** (= *hunting*) la caza; **a car ~** una persecución de coches; **to give ~ to** dar caza a, perseguir; **to join in the ~ for sth** unirse a los que buscan algo
Ⓑ VT (= *pursue*) perseguir; **he's started chasing girls*** ya anda detrás de las chicas; **to ~ sb for money** reclamar dinero a algn
Ⓒ VI correr; **I've been chasing all over the place looking for you** te he estado buscando por todas partes; **to ~ after sb** (= *pursue*) correr tras algn; (= *seek out*) ir *or* andar a la caza de algn
►**chase away, chase off** VT + ADV ahuyentar
►**chase down** VT + ADV [1] (= *track down*) localizar
[2] (*US*) (= *catch*) recabar, tratar de localizar
►**chase out** VT + ADV echar fuera
►**chase up** VT + ADV [+ *information*] recabar, tratar de localizar; [+ *person*] buscar; [+ *matter*] investigar; **I'll ~ him up about it** se lo voy a recordar; **I'll ~ it up for you** investigaré lo que está pasando con lo tuyo; **to ~ up debts** reclamar el cobro de las deudas
chase[2] [tʃeɪs] VT [+ *metal*] grabar, adornar grabando, cincelar
chaser ['tʃeɪsəʳ] N *bebida tomada inmediatamente después de otra distinta, p.ej., una copita de licor después de una cerveza*
chasm ['kæzəm] N (*Geol*) sima *f*; (*fig*) abismo *m*
chassis ['ʃæsɪ] N (*pl* **chassis**) [1] (*Aut*) chasis *m inv*
[2] (*Aer*) tren *m* de aterrizaje
chaste [tʃeɪst] ADJ casto
chastely ['tʃeɪstlɪ] ADV castamente
chasten ['tʃeɪsn] VT castigar, escarmentar
chastened ['tʃeɪsnd] Ⓐ PT, PP *of* **chasten**
Ⓑ ADJ (*by experience*) escarmentado; [*tone*] sumiso; **they seemed much ~** parecían haberse arrepentido
chasteness ['tʃeɪstnɪs] N castidad *f*
chastening ['tʃeɪsnɪŋ] ADJ [*experience*] aleccionador
chastise [tʃæs'taɪz] VT (= *scold*) regañar; (= *punish*) castigar
chastisement ['tʃæstɪzmənt] N castigo *m*
chastity ['tʃæstɪtɪ] N castidad *f*
chasuble ['tʃæzjʊbl] N casulla *f*
chat [tʃæt] Ⓐ N charla *f*, plática *f* (*CAm*); **to have a ~ with** (*gen*) charlar con, platicar con (*CAm*); (= *discuss*) hablar con; **I'll have a ~ with him about it** hablaré con él de *or* sobre ello
Ⓑ VI [1] (= *talk*) charlar, platicar (*CAm*) (**with, to** con)
[2] (*Internet*) chatear
Ⓒ CPD ► **chat room** N (*Internet*) canal *m* de charla, grupo *m* de discusión, chat *m* ► **chat show** N programa *m* de entrevistas ► **chat show host** N presentador *m* de programa de entrevistas ► **chat show hostess** N presentadora *f* de programa de entrevistas
►**chat up*** VT + ADV (*Brit*) (= *try to pick up*) tratar de ligar*; [+ *influential person*] dar jabón a*
chatline ['tʃætlaɪn] N *servicio telefónico que permite a los que llaman conversar unos con otros sobre distintos temas*
chattels ['tʃætlz] NPL bienes *mpl* muebles; (*loosely*) cosas *fpl*, enseres *mpl*; *see also* **goods**
chatter ['tʃætəʳ] Ⓐ N (*gen*) charla *f*; (*excessive*) cháchara *f*, cotorreo *m*; [*of birds, monkeys*] parloteo *m*

Ⓑ VI [*person*] (*gen*) charlar; (*excessively*) estar de cháchara, cotorrear; [*birds, monkeys*] parlotear; **her teeth were ~ing** le castañeteaban los dientes; **she does ~ so** es muy habladora; **stop ~ing!** ¡silencio!

chatterbox* ['tʃætəbɒks], **chatterer** ['tʃætərəʳ] N charlatán/ana* *m/f*, parlanchín/ina* *m/f*, platicón/ona *m/f* (*Mex**)

chattering ['tʃætərɪŋ] Ⓐ N [*of person*] parloteo *m*; (*excessive*) charloteo *m*; [*of birds, monkeys*] parloteo *m*; [*of teeth*] castañeteo *m*
Ⓑ CPD ► **the chattering classes*** NPL (*Brit pej*) los intelectualoides*

chatty ['tʃætɪ] ADJ (*compar* **chattier**; *superl* **chattiest**) [*person*] hablador; [*letter*] afectuoso y lleno de noticias; [*style*] informal

chat-up line ['tʃætʌp,laɪn] N **a good ~** una buena frase para entrarle a algn*

chauffeur ['ʃəʊfəʳ] Ⓐ N chófer *mf*, chofer *mf* (*LAm*)
Ⓑ VT llevar en coche (**to the station** a la estación); **I had to ~ him all over town** (*iro*) tuve que hacer de chófer y llevarle de una punta a otra de la ciudad
Ⓒ VI hacer de chófer (**for** para)

chauffeur-driven ['ʃəʊfə,drɪvən] ADJ **~ car** coche *m* con chófer *or* (*LAm*) chofer

chauvinism ['ʃəʊvɪnɪzəm] N (= *male chauvinism*) machismo *m*; (= *nationalism*) chovinismo *m*, patriotería *f*

chauvinist ['ʃəʊvɪnɪst] Ⓐ N (= *male chauvinist*) machista *m*; (= *nationalist*) chovinista *mf*, patriotero/a *m/f*
Ⓑ ADJ (= *male chauvinist*) machista; (= *nationalist*) chovinista, patriotero; **(male) ~ pig*** (*pej*) machista asqueroso (*pej*)

chauvinistic [,ʃəʊvɪ'nɪstɪk] ADJ = **chauvinist B**

CHE ABBR = **Campaign for Homosexual Equality**

ChE ABBR (*esp US*) [1] = **Chemical Engineer**
[2] = **Chief Engineer**

cheap [tʃiːp] Ⓐ ADJ (*compar* **cheaper**; *superl* **cheapest**) [1] (= *inexpensive*) [*goods, labour, shop, ticket*] barato; [*imports*] a bajo precio; [*loan, credit*] a bajo interés; **it's ten pence ~er** es diez peniques más barato; **it's ~er to buy than to rent** sale más económico *or* barato comprar que alquilar; **gas cookers are ~er to run** las cocinas de gas salen *or* resultan más económicas; **these cars are very ~ to produce** la fabricación de estos coches sale muy barata; **~ labour** mano *f* de obra barata; **~ money** dinero *m* barato; **dresses at ridiculously ~ prices** vestidos a unos precios regalados; **it's ~ at the price*** está bien de precio, es barato para lo que es; **that's ~ at half the price!*** ¡es más que regalado!; **~ rate** tarifa *f* reducida; ✦*IDIOM* **~ and cheerful** bueno, bonito y barato; *see also* **dirt-cheap**
[2] (= *poor-quality*) [*product*] barato, corriente; **beware of ~ imitations!** ¡esté al tanto de imitaciones baratas!; **~ and nasty** ordinario, chabacano
[3] (= *vulgar, mean*) [*joke*] ordinario, chabacano; [*behaviour, tactics*] rastrero; [*remark, question*] de mal gusto; [*opportunism, sensationalism*] barato; [*promises*] fácil; **a ~ laugh** la risa fácil; **~ thrills** placeres *mpl* baratos; **a ~ trick** una mala pasada
[4] (= *not deserving respect*) bajo, indigno; **to feel ~** sentirse humillado; **they hold life ~ there** allí la vida no vale nada; **to look ~** parecer ordinario, tener un aspecto ordinario; **to make o.s. ~** rebajarse, humillarse
Ⓑ ADV [*buy, sell*] barato; **it's going ~** se vende barato; **quality doesn't come ~** la calidad hay que pagarla
Ⓒ N **on the ~*** (*pej*) [*decorate, travel*] en plan barato*; **to do sth on the ~** hacer algo en plan barato*; **to buy** *or* **get sth on the ~** comprar algo por poco dinero *or* a bajo precio
Ⓓ CPD ► **cheap shot** N golpe *m* bajo

cheapen ['tʃiːpən] Ⓐ VT (= *make cheaper*) [+ *cost*] abaratar; (*fig*) (= *debase*) [+ *sb's name, work*] degradar; **to ~ o.s.** hacer cosas indignas, rebajarse
Ⓑ VI abaratarse

cheapie* ['tʃiːpɪ] Ⓐ ADJ de barato*
Ⓑ N (= *ticket, meal etc*) ganga *f*

cheap-jack ['tʃiːpdʒæk] Ⓐ ADJ [*product*] de bajísima calidad, malísimo; [*furniture*] muy mal hecho; [*person*] chapucero
Ⓑ N (= *person*) chapucero/a *m/f*, baratillero *m*

cheaply ['tʃiːplɪ] ADV [*buy, sell*] barato, a bajo precio; [*produce goods*] a bajo precio; [*live, eat, decorate, furnish*] con poco dinero; **two can live as ~ as one** dos pueden vivir por el mismo dinero que uno

cheapness ['tʃiːpnɪs] N [1] (= *low cost*) lo barato, baratura *f*
[2] (= *poor quality*) lo corriente, ordinariez *f*

cheapo* ['tʃiːpəʊ] ADJ baratejo

cheapshot* ['tʃiːpʃɒt] VT **to ~ sb** (*US*) hablar mal de algn

cheapskate* ['tʃiːpskeɪt] N tacaño/a *m/f*, roñoso/a* *m/f*

cheat [tʃiːt] Ⓐ N [1] (= *person*) tramposo/a *m/f*; (*at cards*) tramposo/a *m/f*, fullero/a *m/f*
[2] (= *fraud*) estafa *f*, fraude *m*; (= *trick*) trampa *f*; **it was a ~** fue una estafa *or* un timo, hubo trampa
Ⓑ VT (= *swindle*) estafar, timar; (= *trick*) engañar; **to ~ sb out of sth** estafar algo a algn; **to feel ~ed** sentirse defraudado
Ⓒ VI hacer trampa(s); (*in exam*) copiar

►**cheat on** VI + PREP (*esp US*) [+ *person*] engañar

cheater ['tʃiːtəʳ] N (*esp US*) (= *person*) = **cheat A1**

cheating ['tʃiːtɪŋ] N trampa *f*; (*at cards*) trampas *fpl*, fullerías *fpl*; **that's ~** eso es trampa; **no ~!** ¡sin hacer trampas!

Chechen ['tʃetʃən] Ⓐ ADJ checheno
Ⓑ N (*pl* **Chechen** *or* **Chechens**) checheno/a *m/f*

Chechnya [tʃɪtʃ'njɑː] N Chechenia *f*

check [tʃek] Ⓐ N [1] (= *inspection*) control *m*, inspección *f*, chequeo *m*; (*Mech*) revisión *f*; (*Med*) chequeo *m*; **he has regular ~s on his blood pressure** le controlan la tensión con regularidad; **security ~** control *m* de seguridad; **to keep a ~ on sth/sb** controlar algo/a algn, vigilar algo/a algn; **to run** *or* **make a ~ on sth** comprobar *or* revisar algo; **to run** *or* **make a ~ on sb** hacer averiguaciones *or* indagaciones sobre algn
[2] (= *restraint*) **~s and balances** (*US Pol*) *mecanismo de equilibrio de poderes*; **to act as a ~ on sth** poner freno a algo, servir de freno a algo; **to hold** *or* **keep sth in ~** tener algo controlado *or* bajo control; **population growth must be held in ~** hay que tener *or* mantener el crecimiento demográfico bajo control; **she kept her temper in ~** controlaba *or* contenía su genio; **to hold** *or* **keep sb in ~** controlar a algn, mantener a algn a raya
[3] (*Chess*) jaque *m*; **~!** ¡jaque!; **to be in ~** estar (en) jaque; **to put sb in ~** dar *or* hacer jaque a algn
[4] (= *square*) cuadro *m*; (= *fabric*) tela *f* a cuadros, tela *f* de cuadros; **a red and white ~ dress** un vestido rojo y blanco a *or* de cuadros
[5] (*US*) (= *bill*) cuenta *f*
[6] (*US*) = **cheque**
[7] (*US*) (= *tick*) marca *f*, señal *f*; **~!** ¡vale!*
[8] (*US*) (= *tag, ticket*) resguardo *m*
Ⓑ VT [1] (= *examine*) [+ *ticket, passport*] controlar, revisar; [+ *merchandise, premises*] inspeccionar, controlar; [+ *tyres, oil*] revisar, comprobar; [+ *temperature, pressure*] controlar; **he ~ed his watch every hour** miraba el reloj cada hora; **he stopped to ~ his map** se detuvo para leer *or* mirar el mapa; **~ each item for flaws** compruebe todos los artículos para ver que no tengan defectos; **~ the phone book for local suppliers** mire en la guía telefónica para encontrar proveedores en su zona
[2] (= *confirm, verify*) [+ *facts, figures*] comprobar; **please ~ the number and dial again** por favor, compruebe que el número es el correcto y vuelva a marcar; **~ the seasoning** pruébelo para ver que esté sazonado a su gusto; **~ that he's gone before you do it** asegúrate de que *or* comprueba que se ha ido antes de hacerlo; **to ~ sth against sth** comparar *or* cotejar algo con algo
[3] (*) (= *look at*) (*also* **~ out**) mirar; **wow, ~ that car!** ¡hala! ¡mira *or* fíjate qué coche!
[4] (= *hold back*) [+ *attack, advance, progress*] detener, frenar; **to ~ the spread of AIDS** detener *or* frenar la propagación del SIDA; **to ~ o.s.** contenerse, refrenarse
[5] (*US*) (= *tick*) marcar, señalar
[6] (*US*) [+ *luggage*] (*at airport*) facturar, chequear (*LAm*); (*at station*) dejar en consigna; [+ *clothes, property*] (*in cloakroom*) dejar (en el guardarropa)
[7] (*Chess*) [+ *king*] dar jaque a
Ⓒ VI [1] (= *confirm*) comprobar, chequear (*esp LAm*); **I'm not sure he's here, I'll just ~** no estoy seguro de que esté aquí, iré a comprobar(lo) *or* iré a mirar; **I'll need to ~ with the manager** lo tendré que consultar con el encargado
[2] (= *examine*) **to ~ for sth**: **they ~ed for broken bones** lo examinaron para ver si tenía algún hueso roto; **~ periodically for wear and tear** compruebe periódicamente el deterioro; **he ~ed on her several times during the night** fue a verla varias veces durante la noche para asegurarse de que estaba bien
[3] (= *hesitate*) pararse en seco, pararse de repente
[4] (*US*) (= *agree*) concordar (**with** con)

►**check in** Ⓐ VI + ADV [1] (= *register*) (*at airport*) facturar *or* (*LAm*) chequear (el equipaje); (*at hotel*) registrarse; (*at clinic, hospital*) ingresar
[2] (*US*) (= *communicate*) **he ~s in with us by phone every week** se pone en contacto con nosotros *or* nos llama por teléfono todas las semanas
Ⓑ VT + ADV [+ *luggage*] facturar, chequear (*LAm*); [+ *person*] (*at hotel*) registrar; (*at airport*) facturar el equipaje de; **go to that desk and someone will ~ you in** vaya a ese mostrador y allí le facturarán el equipaje

►**check off** VT + ADV **to ~ items off on a list** comprobar puntos en una lista

►**check on** VI + ADV [+ *information, time etc*] verificar; **to ~ on sb** investigar a algn

►**check out** Ⓐ VI + ADV [1] (*of hotel*) (pagar y) marcharse (**of** de)
[2] (*US*) (= *agree*) cuadrar; **their credentials ~ out** sus credenciales cuadran; **his alibi ~s out** su coartada concuerda (con los hechos)
Ⓑ VT + ADV [1] (= *investigate*) **the police had to ~ out the call** la policía tuvo que investigar la llamada
[2] (= *confirm*) [+ *facts, statement*] comprobar, verificar

[3] (*) (= *look at*) mirar; **~ out the girl in the pink shirt!** ¡mira a esa chica con la camisa rosa!
[4] [+ *purchases*] [*customer*] pagar; [*cashier*] pasar por la caja

►**check over** VT + ADV revisar, escudriñar

►**check up** VT + ADV **can you ~ up what time the film starts?** ¿puedes confirmar *or* mirar a qué hora empieza la película?; **they never ~ up to see how much it costs** nunca comprueban *or* miran cuánto cuesta

►**check up on** VI + PREP [1] (= *confirm*) [+ *story*] comprobar, verificar; **he phoned me to ~ up on some facts** me llamó para comprobar *or* verificar cierta información
[2] (= *investigate*) **we've ~ed up on you and it seems you are telling the truth** hemos hecho indagaciones *or* averiguaciones sobre usted y parece que nos está diciendo la verdad; **I'm sure he knew I was ~ing up on him** estoy seguro de que sabía que lo estaba espiando *or* vigilando

CHECKS AND BALANCES

El sistema de **checks and balances** *es uno de los principios de gobierno de Estados Unidos, cuyo objetivo es prevenir abusos de poder por parte de uno de los tres poderes del Estado. Para garantizar la libertad dentro del marco constitucional, los padres de la Constitución estadounidense crearon un sistema por el que tanto el poder del Presidente, como el del Congreso, el de los Tribunales o el de los gobiernos de cada estado puede ser sometido a debate o, si fuera necesario, controlado por el resto de los poderes.*

checkbook ['tʃekbʊk] N (*US*) = **chequebook**

checked [tʃekt] ADJ = **chequered 1**

checker ['tʃekəʳ] N [1] (= *examiner*) verificador(a) *m/f*
[2] (*US*) (*in supermarket*) cajero/a *m/f*; (*in cloakroom*) encargado/a *m/f* de guardarropa

checkerboard ['tʃekəbɔːd] N (*US*) tablero *m* de damas

checkered ['tʃekəd] ADJ (*US*) = **chequered**

checkers ['tʃekəz] NPL (*US*) damas *fpl*

check-in ['tʃekɪn] N (*also* **~ desk**) (*at airport*) mostrador *m* de facturación; **your ~ time is an hour before departure** la facturación es una hora antes de la salida

checking ['tʃekɪŋ] Ⓐ N control *m*, comprobación *f*
Ⓑ CPD ► **checking account** N (*US*) cuenta *f* corriente

checking-in [ˌtʃekɪŋ'ɪn] N (*Aer*) facturación *f*

checklist ['tʃeklɪst] N lista *f* de control (*con la que se coteja algo*)

checkmate ['tʃek'meɪt] Ⓐ N (*in chess*) mate *m*, jaque *m* mate; (*fig*) callejón *m* sin salida; **~!** ¡jaque mate!
Ⓑ VT [1] (*in chess*) dar mate a
[2] (*fig*) poner en un callejón sin salida a; **to be ~d** estar en un callejón sin salida

checkout ['tʃekaʊt] Ⓐ N (*in supermarket*) (*also* **~ counter**) caja *f*; (*in hotel*) = **checkout time**
Ⓑ CPD ► **checkout girl** N cajera *f* (de supermercado) ► **checkout time** N hora *f* a la que hay que dejar libre la habitación

checkpoint ['tʃekpɔɪnt] N (punto *m* de) control *m*, retén *m* (*LAm*)

checkroom ['tʃekrʊm] N (*US*) guardarropa *m*; (*Rail*) consigna *f*; (*euph*) lavabo *m*

checkup ['tʃekʌp] N (*Med*) (*at doctor's*) reconocimiento *m* general, chequeo *m*; (*at dentist's*) revisión *f*; (*Aut*) [*of vehicle*] revisión *f*

cheddar ['tʃedəʳ] N (*also* **~ cheese**) queso *m* cheddar

cheek [tʃiːk] Ⓐ N [1] (*Anat*) mejilla *f*, carrillo *m*; (= *buttock*) nalga *f*; **they were dancing ~ to ~** bailaban muy apretados; ✦**IDIOMS ~ by jowl (with)** codo a *or* con codo (con); **to turn the other ~** poner la otra mejilla
[2] (*) (= *impudence*) descaro *m*, cara* *f*, frescura *f*; **what a ~!** ◊ **of all the ~!** ¡qué cara!*, ¡qué caradura!*, ¡qué frescura!; **to have the ~ to do sth** tener la cara de hacer algo
Ⓑ VT (*) portarse como un fresco con*

cheekbone ['tʃiːkbəʊn] N pómulo *m*

cheekily* ['tʃiːkɪlɪ] ADV descaradamente, con frescura

cheekiness* ['tʃiːkɪnɪs] N descaro *m*, frescura *f*

cheeky ['tʃiːkɪ] ADJ (*compar* **cheekier**; *superl* **cheekiest**) [*person*] descarado, fresco; [*question*] indiscreto, descarado; [*grin*] malicioso; **don't be ~!** ¡no seas descarado!

cheep [tʃiːp] Ⓐ N [*of bird*] pío *m*
Ⓑ VI piar

cheer [tʃɪəʳ] Ⓐ N [1] (= *applause*) ovación *f*, aclamación *f*; (= *hurrah*) vítor *m*, viva *m*; **a ~ went up from the crowd** la multitud prorrumpió en ovaciones *or* vítores; **there were loud ~s at this** esto fue muy aplaudido; **three ~s for the president!** ¡viva el presidente!, ¡tres hurras por el presidente!
[2] (= *comfort*) consuelo *m*; **the inflation figures offer little ~ to the government** el nivel de inflación brinda poco consuelo al gobierno
[3] (= *state of mind*) **be of good ~** (*liter*) ¡ánimo!
Ⓑ EXCL **~s!** (= *toast*) ¡salud!; (*Brit**) (= *thank you*) ¡gracias!; (= *goodbye*) ¡hasta luego!
Ⓒ VT [1] (= *applaud*) [+ *winner etc*] aclamar, vitorear
[2] (*also* **~ up**) (= *gladden*) alegrar, animar; **I was much ~ed by the news** me alegró mucho la noticia
Ⓓ VI (= *shout*) dar vivas, dar vítores

►**cheer on** VT + ADV animar (*con aplausos or gritos*)

►**cheer up** Ⓐ VI + ADV animarse, alegrarse; **~ up!** ¡anímate!, ¡ánimo!
Ⓑ VT + ADV alegrar, animar; [+ *person*] levantar el ánimo a

cheerful ['tʃɪəfʊl] ADJ [*person, expression, voice, atmosphere*] alegre, jovial; [*occasion*] feliz; [*place*] alegre, animado; [*colour*] alegre, vivo; [*fire*] acogedor; [*news, prospect, outlook*] alentador; **to be ~ about sth** alegrarse de *or* por algo; **she felt she had nothing to be ~ about** sintió que no tenía nada por lo que alegrarse; **she was very ~ about moving into her new flat** la idea de mudarse al nuevo piso la alegraba mucho; **to feel ~** ◊ **be in a ~ mood** estar de buen humor

cheerfully ['tʃɪəfəlɪ] ADV [1] (= *cheerily*) [*smile, say, greet*] alegremente, jovialmente; **the nursery is ~ painted** la guardería está pintada con colores alegres
[2] (= *blithely*) alegremente, tranquilamente; **he ~ ignored the doctor's advice** ignoró alegremente *or* tranquilamente los consejos del médico
[3] (= *gladly*) **I could ~ strangle him** con mucho gusto lo estrangularía; **she ~ agreed to try using his method** aceptó de buena gana probar su método

cheerfulness ['tʃɪəfʊlnɪs] N [*of person, smile*] alegría *f*, jovialidad *f*; [*of place*] alegría *f*, animación *f*

cheerily ['tʃɪərɪlɪ] ADV alegremente, jovialmente

cheering ['tʃɪərɪŋ] Ⓐ ADJ [*news*] bueno, esperanzador; [*prospect*] alentador
Ⓑ N ovaciones *fpl*, vítores *mpl*

cheerio* ['tʃɪərɪ'əʊ] EXCL (*Brit*) ¡hasta luego!, ¡chau! (*LAm*)

cheerleader ['tʃɪəˌliːdəʳ] N (*esp US*) animador(a) *m/f*

cheerless ['tʃɪəlɪs] ADJ triste, sombrío

cheery ['tʃɪərɪ] ADJ (*compar* **cheerier**; *superl* **cheeriest**) [*person*] alegre, jovial; [*room, atmosphere*] acogedor; [*voice*] risueño, alegre; [*letter*] alegre

cheese [tʃiːz] Ⓐ N [1] (= *dairy product*) queso *m*; **say ~!** (*Phot*) ¡a ver, una sonrisa!; **hard ~!*** ¡mala pata!
[2] (*) (= *person*) **big ~** pez *m* gordo
Ⓑ VT (*Brit**) **I'm ~d off with this** estoy hasta las narices de esto*
Ⓒ CPD ► **cheese dish** N tabla *f* de quesos ► **cheese sauce** N salsa *f* de queso, ≈ salsa *f* Mornay

cheeseboard ['tʃiːzbɔːd] N tabla *f* de quesos

cheeseburger ['tʃiːzˌbɜːgəʳ] N hamburguesa *f* con queso

cheesecake ['tʃiːzkeɪk] N tarta *f or* (*LAm*) pay *m* de queso; (*) (*fig*) *fotos, dibujos etc de chicas atractivas en traje o actitud incitante*

cheesecloth ['tʃiːzklɒθ] N estopilla *f*

cheeseparing ['tʃiːzˌpɛərɪŋ] Ⓐ ADJ tacaño
Ⓑ N economías *fpl* pequeñas

cheesy ['tʃiːzɪ] ADJ [1] [*taste, smell*] a queso; [*socks, feet*] maloliente
[2] (*) horrible, sin valor
[3] [*grin*] de hiena

cheetah ['tʃiːtə] N guepardo *m*

chef [ʃef] N cocinero/a *m/f* jefe/a, chef *m*

chef-d'oeuvre [ʃe'dɜːvrə] N (*pl* **chefs-d'oeuvre** [ʃe'dɜːvrə]) obra *f* maestra

Chekhov ['tʃekɒf] N Chejov

chemical ['kemɪkəl] Ⓐ ADJ químico
Ⓑ N sustancia *f* química, producto *m* químico
Ⓒ CPD ► **chemical engineer** N ingeniero/a *m/f* químico/a ► **chemical engineering** N ingeniería *f* química ► **chemical warfare** N guerra *f* química ► **chemical weapon** N arma *f* química

chemically ['kemɪkəlɪ] ADV químicamente; [*do, carry out*] por medios químicos

chemise [ʃə'miːz] N blusa *f* camisera

chemist ['kemɪst] N (= *scientist*) químico/a *m/f*; (*Brit*) (= *pharmacist*) farmacéutico/a *m/f*; **~'s (shop)** farmacia *f*; **all-night ~'s** farmacia de turno *or* de guardia

chemistry ['kemɪstrɪ] Ⓐ N química *f*; **the ~ between them is right** (*fig*) están muy compenetrados
Ⓑ CPD ► **chemistry laboratory** N laboratorio *m* de química ► **chemistry set** N juego *m* de química

chemo* ['kiːməʊ] N (= *chemotherapy*) quimio* *f*

chemotherapy ['kiːməʊ'θerəpɪ] N quimioterapia *f*

chenille [ʃə'niːl] N felpilla *f*

▼**cheque**, **check** (*US*) [tʃek] Ⓐ N (*Brit*) cheque *m*, talón *m* (bancario) (*Sp*); **a ~ for £20** un cheque por *or* de 20 libras; **to make out** *or* **write a ~ (for £100/to Rodríguez)** extender un cheque (de 100 libras/a favor de Rodríguez); **to pay by ~** pagar con cheque; **bad ~** cheque *m* sin fondos *or* sin provisión
Ⓑ CPD ► **cheque card** N (*also* **~ guarantee card**) tarjeta *f* de identificación bancaria

➤ LANGUAGE IN USE: **cheque** A 20.6

chequebook, **checkbook** (*US*) ['tʃekbʊk] N talonario *m* de cheques, chequera *f* (*LAm*); **~ journalism** periodismo *m* a golpe de talonario

chequered, **checkered** (*US*) ['tʃekəd] ADJ [1] (= *checked*) [*tablecloth, shirt, pattern*] a cuadros, de cuadros
[2] (= *varied*) **a ~ career** una carrera accidentada *or* llena de altibajos

chequers ['tʃekəz] N damas *fpl*

cherish ['tʃerɪʃ] VT [+ *person*] querer, apreciar; [+ *hope*] abrigar, acariciar; [+ *memory*] conservar

cherished ['tʃerɪʃt] ADJ [*memory*] precioso, entrañable; [*possession*] preciado; [*privilege*] apreciado; **it's a long-~ dream of mine to go to Florence** ir a Florencia es un sueño que llevo albergando desde hace tiempo

cheroot [ʃə'ru:t] N puro *m* (cortado en los dos extremos)

cherry ['tʃerɪ] Ⓐ N (= *fruit*) cereza *f*; (= *tree, wood*) cerezo *m*
Ⓑ CPD [*pie, jam*] de cereza ► **cherry brandy** N aguardiente *m* de cerezas ► **cherry orchard** N cerezal *m* ► **cherry red** N rojo *m* cereza ► **cherry tree** N cerezo *m*

cherry-pick ['tʃerɪpɪk] VT (*fig*) escoger cuidadosamente, seleccionar cuidadosamente

cherry-red [,tʃerɪ'red] ADJ (de) color rojo cereza

cherub ['tʃerəb] N (*pl* **cherubs**) [1] querubín *m*, angelito *m*
[2] (*Rel*) (*pl* **cherubim** ['tʃerəbɪm]) querubín *m*

cherubic [tʃe'ru:bɪk] ADJ querúbico

chervil ['tʃɜ:vɪl] N perifollo *m*

Ches ABBR (*Brit*) = **Cheshire**

Cheshire cat ['tʃeʃə'kæt] N ✦**IDIOM** **to grin like a ~** sonreír de oreja a oreja

chess [tʃes] Ⓐ N ajedrez *m*
Ⓑ CPD ► **chess player** N jugador(a) *m/f* de ajedrez, ajedrecista *mf* ► **chess set** N (juego *m* de) ajedrez *m* ► **chess tournament** N torneo *m* de ajedrez

chessboard ['tʃesbɔ:d] N tablero *m* de ajedrez

chessman ['tʃesmæn] N (*pl* **chessmen**) pieza *f* de ajedrez

chest [tʃest] Ⓐ N [1] (*Anat*) pecho *m*; **to have ~ trouble** tener problemas respiratorios, padecer de los bronquios; **to have a cold on the ~** tener el pecho resfriado; ✦**IDIOM** **to get sth off one's ~*** desahogarse
[2] (= *box*) cofre *m*, arca *f*; **~ of drawers** cómoda *f*
Ⓑ CPD [*pain*] de pecho ► **chest cold** N resfriado *m* de pecho ► **chest expander** N tensor *m*, extensor *m* ► **chest freezer** N congelador *m* de arcón ► **chest infection** N infección *f* de las vías respiratorias ► **chest measurement**, **chest size** N anchura *f* de pecho; [*of clothes*] talla *f* (*de chaqueta etc*) ► **chest specialist** N especialista *mf* de las vías respiratorias ► **chest X-ray** N radiografía *f* torácica

chesterfield ['tʃestəfi:ld] N (*esp US*) sofá *m*

chestnut ['tʃesnʌt] Ⓐ N [1] (= *fruit*) castaña *f*; (= *tree, colour*) castaño *m*
[2] (= *horse*) caballo *m* castaño
[3] (*) (= *story*) historia *f*; **not that old ~!** ¡ya estamos con la misma historia de siempre!
Ⓑ ADJ (*also* **~ brown**) [*hair*] (de color) castaño *inv*
Ⓒ CPD ► **chestnut tree** N castaño *m*

chesty* ['tʃestɪ] ADJ (*compar* **chestier**; *superl* **chestiest**) (*Brit*) [*cough*] de pecho; [*person*] que tiene el pecho cargado *or* congestionado; **you sound a bit ~** por la voz parece que tienes el pecho cargado *or* congestionado

Chetnik ['tʃetnɪk] Ⓐ ADJ chetnik
Ⓑ N chetnik *mf*

cheval glass [ʃə'vælglɑ:s] N psique *f*

chevron ['ʃevrən] N (*Mil*) galón *m*; (*Heraldry*) cheurón *m*

chew [tʃu:] Ⓐ N [1] (= *action*) **to give sth a ~** masticar algo
[2] (*Brit*) (= *sweet*) caramelo *m* masticable; (= *dog treat*) golosina *f* para perros
Ⓑ VT [+ *food etc*] mascar, masticar; **the goats had ~ed off all the flower heads** las cabras se habían comido todas las flores; ✦**IDIOMS** **to ~ sb's ass** (*US***) poner verde a algn*; **to ~ the fat‡** *or* **rag‡** estar de palique*, dar a la lengua*, charlar
Ⓒ VI **to ~ on** [+ *problem*] rumiar, dar vueltas a

►**chew out** VT + ADV (*US*) = **chew up 1**

►**chew over** VT + ADV (= *consider*) rumiar, considerar; (= *reflect on*) dar vueltas a

►**chew up** VT + ADV [1] [+ *food*] masticar bien
[2] (= *damage*) estropear; **this cassette player is ~ing up all my tapes** este casete está estropeando todas mis cintas
[3] (*) (= *scold*) echar una bronca a

chewing gum ['tʃu:ɪŋgʌm] N chicle *m*, goma *f* de mascar

chewy ['tʃu:ɪ] ADJ (*compar* **chewier**; *superl* **chewiest**) difícil de masticar; [*meat*] fibroso, correoso; [*sweet*] masticable

chiaroscuro [kɪ,ɑ:rəs'kʊərəʊ] N claroscuro *m*

chic [ʃi:k] Ⓐ ADJ elegante
Ⓑ N chic *m*, elegancia *f*

chicanery [ʃɪ'keɪnərɪ] N embustes *mpl*, sofismas *mpl*; **a piece of ~** una triquiñuela

Chicano [tʃɪ'kɑ:nəʊ] Ⓐ ADJ chicano
Ⓑ N chicano/a *m/f*

chichi ['ʃi:ʃi:] ADJ afectado, cursi*

chick [tʃɪk] N [1] (= *baby bird*) pajarito *m*; (= *baby hen*) pollito *m*, polluelo *m*
[2] (‡) (= *woman*) chica *f*, chavala *f* (*Sp*)

chickadee ['tʃɪkədi:] N carbonero *m*

chicken ['tʃɪkɪn] Ⓐ N (= *hen*) gallina *f*; (= *cock*) pollo *m*; (*as food*) pollo; (*) (= *coward*) gallina *mf*; **roast ~** pollo asado; ✦**IDIOMS** **to be ~*** dejarse intimidar, acobardarse; **to play ~*** jugar a quién es más valiente; **it's a ~ and egg situation** es aquello de la gallina y el huevo; **the ~s are coming home to roost** ahora se ven las consecuencias; ✦**PROV** **don't count your ~s before they're hatched** no hagas las cuentas de la lechera; *see also* **spring D**
Ⓑ CPD ► **chicken farmer** N avicultor(a) *m/f* ► **chicken farming** N avicultura *f* ► **chicken feed** N (*lit*) pienso *m* para gallinas; **it's ~ feed to him** para él es una bagatela ► **chicken liver** N hígado *m* de pollo ► **chicken run** N corral *m* ► **chicken wire** N tela *f* metálica, alambrada *f*

►**chicken out*** VI + ADV rajarse; **to ~ out of sth/doing sth: he ~ed out of the audition** se rajó y no se presentó a la prueba; **he ~ed out of asking her to dinner** se rajó y no la invitó a cenar, no se atrevió a invitarla a cenar

chicken-hearted ['tʃɪkɪn,hɑ:tɪd] ADJ cobarde, gallina

chickenpox ['tʃɪkɪnpɒks] N varicela *f*

chickpea ['tʃɪkpi:] N garbanzo *m*

chickweed ['tʃɪkwi:d] N pamplina *f*

chicory ['tʃɪkərɪ] N (*in coffee*) achicoria *f*; (*as salad*) escarola *f*

chide [tʃaɪd] (*pt* **chid**; *pp* **chidden**, **chid**) VT (*liter*) reprender

chief [tʃi:f] Ⓐ ADJ (= *principal*) [*reason etc*] principal, mayor; (*in rank*) jefe, de más categoría
Ⓑ N [*of organization*] jefe/a *m/f*; [*of tribe*] jefe/a *m/f*, cacique *m*; (*) (= *boss*) jefe/a *m/f*, patrón(ona) *m/f*; **yes, ~!** ¡sí, jefe!; **Chief of Staff** (*Mil*) Jefe del Estado Mayor; **... in ~** ... en jefe
Ⓒ CPD ► **chief constable** N (*Brit*) jefe/a *m/f* de policía ► **chief executive** N (*Brit*) (*local government*) director(a) *m/f*; [*of company*] (*also* **~ executive officer**) director(a) *m/f* general ► **chief inspector** N (*Brit Police*) inspector(a) *m/f* jefe ► **chief justice** N (*US*) presidente/a *m/f* del Tribunal Supremo ► **chief superintendent** N (*Brit Police*) comisario/a *m/f* jefe/a

chiefly ['tʃi:flɪ] ADV principalmente, sobre todo

chieftain ['tʃi:ftən] N jefe/a *m/f*, cacique *m* (*LAm*)

chiffchaff ['tʃɪftʃæf] N mosquitero *m* común

chiffon ['ʃɪfɒn] Ⓐ N gasa *f*
Ⓑ CPD de gasa

chignon ['ʃi:njɔ̃n] N moño *m*

chihuahua [tʃɪ'wɑ:wɑ:] N chihuahua *m*

chilblain ['tʃɪlbleɪn] N sabañón *m*

child [tʃaɪld] Ⓐ N (*pl* **children**) niño/a *m/f*; (= *son/daughter*) hijo/a *m/f*; (*Jur*) (= *non-adult*) menor *mf*; **I have known him since he was a ~** lo conozco desde niño; **to be with ~**† estar encinta; **to get sb with ~**† dejar a algn encinta; **it's ~'s play** es un juego de niños
Ⓑ CPD ► **child abuse** N (*with violence*) malos tratos *mpl* a niños; (*sexual*) abuso *m* sexual de niños ► **child abuser** N (*with violence*) *persona que maltrata a un niño*; (*sexual*) *persona que abusa sexualmente de un niño* ► **child benefit** N subsidio *m* familiar (por hijos) ► **child guidance** N psicopedagogía *f* ► **child guidance centre** N centro *m* psicopedagógico ► **child labour**, **child labor** (*US*) N trabajo *m* de menores ► **child lock** N (*on door*) cerradura *f* de seguridad para niños ► **child prodigy** N niño/a *m/f* prodigio ► **children's home** N centro *m* de acogida de menores ► **children's literature** N literatura *f* infantil ► **child welfare** N protección *f* a *or* de la infancia

CHILDREN IN NEED

La organización benéfica **Children in Need** *(Niños Necesitados), fundada por la* **BBC** *en 1972, recauda dinero en beneficio de los niños necesitados en el Reino Unido y en el extranjero. Se la conoce sobre todo por los* **telethons** *(telemaratones) que organiza anualmente: los programas de TV en los que se invita a los televidentes a llamar para hacer donativos y a organizar sus propias campañas de ayuda para niños enfermos, minusválidos, pobres, etc.*

childbearing ['tʃaɪld,beərɪŋ] Ⓐ N (= *act*) parto *m*; (*as statistic*) natalidad *f*
Ⓑ ADJ **~ women** las mujeres fecundas, las mujeres que producen hijos; **women of ~ age** las mujeres en edad de tener hijos

childbed ['tʃaɪldbed] N parturición *f*

childbirth ['tʃaɪldbɜ:θ] N parto *m*, alumbramiento *m* (*frm*); **to die in ~** morir de parto

childcare ['tʃaɪldkeə'] Ⓐ N cuidado *m* de los niños
Ⓑ CPD ► **childcare facilities** NPL guarderías *fpl*

childhood ['tʃaɪldhʊd] N niñez *f*, infancia *f*; **from ~** desde niño; ✦**IDIOM** **to be in one's second ~** estar en su segunda infancia; *see also* **sweetheart**

childish ['tʃaɪldɪʃ] ADJ [1] (*slightly pej*) infantil, pueril; **don't be ~!** ¡no seas niño!
[2] [*disease*] infantil, de la infancia; **~ ailment** enfermedad *f* infantil *or* de la infancia

childishly [ˈtʃaɪldɪʃlɪ] ADV de modo infantil *or* pueril, como un niño; **she behaved ~** se portó como una niña

childishness [ˈtʃaɪldɪʃnɪs] N infantilismo *m*, puerilidad *f*

childless [ˈtʃaɪldlɪs] ADJ sin hijos

childlike [ˈtʃaɪldlaɪk] ADJ de niño; **with a ~ faith** con una confianza ingenua

childminder [ˈtʃaɪldˌmaɪndəʳ] N (*Brit*) niñera *f*

childminding [ˈtʃaɪldˌmaɪndɪŋ] N (*Brit*) cuidado *m* de niños

childproof [ˈtʃaɪldˌpruːf] ADJ a prueba de niños; **child-proof (door) lock** cerradura *f* de seguridad para niños

children [ˈtʃɪldrən] NPL *of* **child**

child-resistant [ˈtʃaɪldˌrɪzɪstənt] ADJ = **childproof**

Chile [ˈtʃɪlɪ] N Chile *m*

Chilean [ˈtʃɪlɪən] Ⓐ ADJ chileno
Ⓑ N chileno/a *m/f*

chili [ˈtʃɪlɪ] N (*pl* **chilies**) (*also* **chilli pepper**) chile *m*, ají *m* (*S. Cone*), guindilla *f* (*Sp*); **~ con carne** chile con carne; **~ powder** chile en polvo; **~ sauce** salsa *f* de ají

chill [tʃɪl] Ⓐ N (= *coldness*) frío *m*; (*Med*) resfriado *m*; (= *mild fever*) escalofrío *m*; **there's a ~ in the air** hace fresco; **to catch a ~** (*Med*) resfriarse; **to cast a ~ over** enfriar el ambiente de; **to take the ~ off** [+ *room*] calentar un poco, templar; [+ *wine*] templar
Ⓑ ADJ [*wind*] frío
Ⓒ VT [+ *wine*] enfriar; [+ *food*] refrigerar; **serve ~ed** sírvase bien frío; **to ~ sb's blood** (*fig*) helarle la sangre en las venas a algn; **to be ~ed to the bone** estar helado hasta los huesos

►**chill out*** VI + ADV (*esp US*) tranquilizarse, relajarse; **~ out, man!** ¡tranqui tronco!*

chiller [ˈtʃɪləʳ] N (= *film*) película *f* de terror

chilliness [ˈtʃɪlɪnɪs] N frío *m*; (*fig*) frialdad *f*

chilling [ˈtʃɪlɪŋ] ADJ (*fig*) escalofriante

chillness [ˈtʃɪlnɪs] N = **chilliness**

chill-out* [ˈtʃɪlaʊt] ADJ [*music*] relajante

chilly [ˈtʃɪlɪ] ADJ (*compar* **chillier**, *superl* **chilliest**) 1 (= *cold*) [*weather, water, day, room*] frío; **to be** *or* **feel ~** [*person*] tener frío; **I feel a bit ~** tengo un poco de frío; **it's ~ today** hace fresquito hoy 2 (= *unfriendly*) frío

chime [tʃaɪm] Ⓐ N (= *sound*) [*of church bells*] repique *m*; [*of clock*] campanada *f*; (= *set*) juego *m* de campanas, carillón *m*; **a ~ of bells** un carillón
Ⓑ VT [+ *bell*] tocar
Ⓒ VI repicar, sonar; **the clock ~d six** el reloj dio las seis

►**chime in*** VI + ADV (= *butt in*) meter baza; (= *say*) decir; **to ~ in with** (*in conversation*) meter baza hablando de; (= *harmonize*) estar en armonía con

chimera [kaɪˈmɪərə] N quimera *f*

chimerical [kaɪˈmerɪkəl] ADJ quimérico

chiming [ˈtʃaɪmɪŋ] Ⓐ ADJ **~ clock** reloj *m* de carillón
Ⓑ N [*of church bells*] repiqueteo *m*; [*of clock*] campanadas *fpl*

chimney [ˈtʃɪmnɪ] Ⓐ N 1 [*of building*] chimenea *f*
2 [*of lamp*] tubo *m*
3 (*Mountaineering*) olla *f*, chimenea *f*
Ⓑ CPD ► **chimney breast** N (*Brit*) campana *f* de chimenea ► **chimney corner** N rincón *m* de la chimenea ► **chimney pot** N cañón *m* de chimenea ► **chimney stack** N fuste *m* de chimenea ► **chimney sweep** N deshollinador(a) *m/f*

chimneypiece [ˈtʃɪmnɪˌpiːs] N (*Brit*) repisa *f* de chimenea

chimp* [tʃɪmp] N = **chimpanzee**

chimpanzee [ˌtʃɪmpænˈziː] N chimpancé *m*

chin [tʃɪn] Ⓐ N barbilla *f*, mentón *m*; **double ~** papada *f*; ✦***IDIOMS*** **to keep one's ~ up*** no desanimarse; **(keep your) ~ up!** ¡no te desanimes!, ¡ánimo!; **to take it on the ~*** encajar el golpe; (*fig*) (= *put up with*) soportarlo
Ⓑ VT (*Brit**) (= *punch*) dar una hostia a*; (= *reprimand*) echar un rapapolvo a*
Ⓒ VI (*US**) charlar; *see also* **chuck[1]**

china[1] [ˈtʃaɪnə] Ⓐ N (= *crockery*) loza *f*, vajilla *f*; (= *fine china*) porcelana *f*
Ⓑ CPD [*cup, plate etc*] de porcelana ► **china cabinet** N vitrina *f* de la porcelana ► **china clay** N caolín *m* ► **china doll** N muñeca *f* de porcelana

china[2]†* [ˈtʃaɪnə] N amigo *m*, compinche *m*; **here you are, my old ~** toma, macho*

China [ˈtʃaɪnə] Ⓐ N China *f*
Ⓑ CPD ► **China Sea** N Mar *m* de China ► **China tea** N té *m* de China

Chinaman† [ˈtʃaɪnəmən] N (*pl* **Chinamen**) (*pej in US*) chino *m*

Chinatown [ˈtʃaɪnətaʊn] N barrio *m* chino

chinaware [ˈtʃaɪnəweəʳ] N porcelana *f*

chinch (bug) [ˈtʃɪntʃ(bʌg)] N (*US*) chinche *m or f* de los cereales

chinchilla [tʃɪnˈtʃɪlə] N chinchilla *f*

chin-chin†* [ˌtʃɪnˈtʃɪn] EXCL ¡chin-chin!

Chinese [ˌtʃaɪˈniːz] Ⓐ ADJ chino; **a ~ man** un chino; **a ~ woman** una china
Ⓑ N 1 (= *person*) chino/a *m/f*; **the ~** (= *people*) los chinos
2 (*Ling*) chino *m*
Ⓒ CPD ► **Chinese chequers** NPL damas *fpl* chinas ► **Chinese lantern** N farolillo *m* chino ► **Chinese leaves** NPL col *fsing* china

chink[1] [tʃɪŋk] N (= *slit*) (*in wall*) grieta *f*, hendidura *f*; (*in door*) resquicio *m*; **a ~ of light** un hilo de luz; ✦***IDIOM*** **it's the ~ in his armour** es su punto débil *or* su talón de Aquiles

chink[2] [tʃɪŋk] Ⓐ N (= *sound*) sonido *m* metálico, tintineo *m*
Ⓑ VT [+ *metal*] hacer sonar; [+ *glass*] hacer tintinear
Ⓒ VI [*metal*] sonar; [*glass*] tintinear

Chink‡ [tʃɪŋk] N (*offensive*) chino/a *m/f*

chinless [ˈtʃɪnlɪs] ADJ (*fig*) (= *spineless*) apocado

chinos [ˈtʃiːnəʊz] NPL chinos *mpl* (*pantalones de algodón a veces con pinzas*)

chintz [tʃɪnts] N cretona *f*

chintzy [ˈtʃɪntsɪ] ADJ 1 [*style*] coqueto
2 (*US*) (= *poor-quality*) basto, ordinario

chin-ups [ˈtʃɪnʌps] NPL **to do ~** hacer flexiones (de brazos) (*en barra o espalderas*)

chinwag* [ˈtʃɪnwæg] N **to have a ~** charlar, darle al palique

chip [tʃɪp] Ⓐ N 1 (= *piece*) pedacito *m*; (= *splinter*) [*of glass, wood*] astilla *f*; (= *stone*) lasca *f*; ✦***IDIOMS*** **he's a ~ off the old block** de tal palo tal astilla; **to have a ~ on one's shoulder** ser un resentido
2 (*Culin*) **chips** (*Brit*) (= *French fries*) patatas *fpl* fritas, papas *fpl* fritas (*esp LAm*); (*US*) (= *crisps*) patatas *fpl* (fritas) de bolsa, chips *mpl*
3 (= *break, mark*) mella *f*; (*on rim of vessel*) desportilladura *f*
4 (*Gambling*) ficha *f*; ✦***IDIOMS*** **he's had his ~s*** se le acabó la suerte; **to hand** *or* **cash in one's ~s*** palmarla*; **when the ~s are down** cuando llega el momento de la verdad
5 (*Comput*) chip *m*
6 (*Golf*) (= *chip shot*) chip *m*
Ⓑ VT [+ *cup, plate*] desconchar, desportillar; [+ *furniture*] desportillar; [+ *surface*] picar; [+ *paint, varnish*] desconchar, desprender
Ⓒ VI [*pottery*] desconcharse, desportillarse; [*paint, varnish*] desconcharse
Ⓓ CPD ► **chip and PIN** N *tecnología de identificación del usuario mediante una tarjeta chip que debe ir acompañada por un número PIN* ► **chip and PIN card** N tarjeta *f* chip con número PIN ► **chip shop*** N pescadería *f* (*donde se vende principalmente pescado rebozado y patatas fritas*)

►**chip away** Ⓐ VT + ADV [+ *paint*] desconchar
Ⓑ VI + ADV [*paint, varnish*] desconcharse; **to ~ away at** [+ *lands*] ir usurpando; [+ *authority*] ir minando *or* debilitando; **they ~ped away at her resistance** fueron debilitando su resistencia

►**chip in*** VI + ADV 1 (= *contribute*) contribuir (**with** con); (= *share costs*) compartir los gastos
2 (= *interrupt*) interrumpir (**with** diciendo)

►**chip off** Ⓐ VI + ADV [*paint etc*] desconcharse, desprenderse (en escamas)
Ⓑ VT + ADV [+ *paint etc*] desconchar, desprender

chip-based [ˈtʃɪpˌbeɪst] ADJ **~ technology** tecnología *f* a base de microchips

chipboard [ˈtʃɪpbɔːd] N madera *f* aglomerada, aglomerado *m*

chipmunk [ˈtʃɪpmʌŋk] N ardilla *f* listada

chipolata [ˌtʃɪpəˈlɑːtə] N (*Brit*) salchicha *f* fina

chipper* [ˈtʃɪpəʳ] ADJ alegre, contento

chippings [ˈtʃɪpɪŋz] NPL gravilla *fsing*; **"loose chippings"** "gravilla suelta"

chippy* [ˈtʃɪpɪ] N 1 (*US*) tía* *f*, fulana* *f*
2 (*Brit*) *tienda que vende pescado frito con patatas fritas*

chiromancer [ˈkaɪərəmænsəʳ] N quiromántico/a *m/f*, quiromante *mf*

chiropodist [kɪˈrɒpədɪst] N (*Brit*) podólogo/a *m/f*, pedicuro/a *m/f*

chiropody [kɪˈrɒpədɪ] N (*Brit*) podología *f*, pedicura *f*

chiropractic [ˌkaɪərəʊˈpræktɪk] Ⓐ ADJ quiropráctico Ⓑ N quiropráctica *f*

chiropractor [ˈkaɪrəʊˌpræktəʳ] N quiropráctico *m*

chirp [tʃɜːp] Ⓐ N [*of birds*] pío *m*, gorjeo *m*; [*of crickets*] chirrido *m*, canto *m*
Ⓑ VI [*birds*] piar, gorjear; [*crickets*] chirriar, cantar

chirpy* [ˈtʃɜːpɪ] ADJ (*compar* **chirpier**, *superl* **chirpiest**) alegre, animado

chirrup [ˈtʃɪrəp] N, VI *see* **chirp**

chisel [ˈtʃɪzl] (*vb: pt, pp* **chiselled** (*Brit*) *or* **chiseled** (*US*)) Ⓐ N (*for wood*) formón *m*, escoplo *m*; (*for stone*) cincel *m*
Ⓑ VT 1 (*also* **~ out**) [+ *wood*] tallar; [+ *stone*] cincelar; (= *carve*) tallar, labrar; **~led features** (*fig*) facciones *fpl* marcadas
2 (*) (= *swindle*) timar, estafar

chiseller, **chiseler** (*US*) [ˈtʃɪzləʳ] N gorrón *m*

chit[1] [tʃɪt] N (= *note*) vale *m*

chit[2] [tʃɪt] N **a ~ of a girl** una muchachita no muy crecida

chitchat [ˈtʃɪttʃæt] N (= *gossip*) chismes *mpl*, habladurías *fpl*; (= *chatter*) **"what did you talk about?" - "oh, nothing in particular, just ~"** —¿de qué hablasteis? —de nada en particular, sólo estuvimos dándole al palique

chitlings [ˈtʃɪtlɪŋz] NPL, **chitlins** [ˈtʃɪtlɪnz] NPL, **chitterlings** [ˈtʃɪtəlɪŋz] NPL menudos *mpl* de cerdo (comestibles)

chitty [ˈtʃɪtɪ] N = **chit[1]**

chiv* [tʃɪv] N chori* *m*, navaja *f*

chivalresque [ʃɪvəl'resk] ADJ, **chivalric** [ʃɪ'vælrɪk] ADJ caballeresco

chivalrous ['ʃɪvəlrəs] ADJ caballeroso

chivalrously ['ʃɪvəlrəslɪ] ADV caballerosamente

chivalry ['ʃɪvəlrɪ] N (= *courteousness*) caballerosidad *f*; (*in medieval times*) caballería *f*

chives [tʃaɪvz] NPL cebollinos *mpl*

chivvy* ['tʃɪvɪ] VT (*Brit*) perseguir, acosar; **to ~ sb into doing sth** no dejar en paz a algn hasta que hace algo

►**chivvy up*** VT + ADV [+ *person*] espabilar

chlamydia [clə'mɪdɪə] N (*Med*) clamidia *f*

chloral ['klɔːrəl] N cloral *m*

chlorate ['klɔːreɪt] N clorato *m*

chloric ['klɔːrɪk] Ⓐ ADJ clórico
Ⓑ CPD ► **chloric acid** N ácido *m* clórico

chloride ['klɔːraɪd] Ⓐ N cloruro *m*
Ⓑ CPD ► **chloride of lime** N cloruro *m* de cal

chlorinate ['klɒrɪneɪt] VT clorar, tratar con cloro

chlorinated ['klɒrɪneɪtɪd] ADJ **~ water** agua *f* clorinada

chlorination [,klɔːrɪ'neɪʃən] N cloración *f*, tratamiento *m* con cloro

chlorine ['klɔːriːn] Ⓐ N cloro *m*
Ⓑ CPD ► **chlorine monoxide** N monóxido *m* de cloro ► **chlorine nitrate** N nitrato *m* de cloro

chlorofluorocarbon [,klɔːrə,flʊərə'kɑːbən] N clorofluorocarbono *m*

chloroform ['klɒrəfɔːm] Ⓐ N cloroformo *m*
Ⓑ VT cloroformizar, cloroformar (*LAm*)

chlorophyll ['klɒrəfɪl] N clorofila *f*

choc* [tʃɒk] N = **chocolate**

chocaholic* [,tʃɒkə'hɒlɪk] N adicto/a *m/f* al chocolate

choc-ice ['tʃɒkaɪs] N (*Brit*) helado *m* cubierto de chocolate

chock [tʃɒk] Ⓐ N (= *wedge*) calzo *m*, cuña *f*
Ⓑ VT calzar, poner un calzo *or* una cuña a

chock-a-block* ['tʃɒkə'blɒk] ADJ de bote en bote, hasta los topes; **~ of** *or* **with** atestado de, totalmente lleno de

chocker* ['tʃɒkə^r] ADJ **to be ~** estar harto (**with** de)

chock-full* ['tʃɒk'fʊl] ADJ atestado, lleno a rebosar

chocolate ['tʃɒklɪt] Ⓐ N chocolate *m*; (= *individual sweet*) bombón *m*; **hot** *or* **drinking ~** chocolate caliente; **a box of ~s** una caja de bombones *or* chocolatinas
Ⓑ CPD [*biscuit, cake, egg*] de chocolate; [*colour*] (*also* **~ brown**) (de color) chocolate ► **chocolate biscuit** N galleta *f* de chocolate ► **chocolate éclair** N relámpago *m* de chocolate

chocolate-box ['tʃɒklɪt,bɒks] ADJ [*look, picture*] de postal de Navidad

choice [tʃɔɪs] Ⓐ ADJ [1] (= *selected*) selecto, escogido; (= *high quality*) de primera calidad
[2] (*hum*) [*example, remark*] apropiado, oportuno; [*language*] fino
Ⓑ N [1] (= *act of choosing*) elección *f*, selección *f*; (= *right to choose*) opción *f*; **it's your ~** ◊ **the ~ is yours** usted elige; **for ~** preferentemente; **it was not a free ~** no pude elegir libremente; **I did it from ~** lo hice de buena gana; **he did it but not from ~** lo hizo pero de mala gana; **to make one's ~** elegir; **the house of my ~** mi casa predilecta; **the prince married the girl of his ~** el príncipe se casó con la joven que había elegido; **the drug/weapon of ~** la droga/el arma preferida; **to take one's ~** elegir; **take your ~!** ¡elija usted!, ¡escoja usted!
[2] (= *thing chosen*) preferencia *f*, elección *f*; **this book would be my ~** este libro es el que yo escogería
[3] (= *variety*) surtido *m*; **we have a wide ~** (*Comm*) tenemos un gran surtido; **you have a wide ~** tienes muchas posibilidades
[4] (= *option*) opción *f*, alternativa *f*; **he gave me two ~s** me dio a elegir entre dos opciones; **to have no ~** no tener alternativa, no tener opción; **he had no ~ but to go** no tuvo más remedio que ir

choir ['kwaɪə^r] Ⓐ N [1] (*Mus*) coro *m*, coral *f*
[2] (*Archit*) coro *m*
Ⓑ CPD ► **choir school** N *escuela primaria para niños cantores* ► **choir stall** N silla *f* de coro; *see also* **practice A4**

choirboy ['kwaɪəbɔɪ] N niño *m* de coro

choirmaster ['kwaɪə,mɑːstə^r] N director *m* de coro, maestro *m* de coros

choke [tʃəʊk] Ⓐ N (*Aut*) (e)stárter *m*, chok(e) *m* (*LAm*); (*Mech*) obturador *m*, cierre *m*
Ⓑ VT [1] [+ *person*] ahogar, asfixiar; (*with hands*) estrangular; **in a voice ~d with emotion** con una voz ahogada *or* sofocada por la emoción
[2] [+ *pipe etc*] atascar, obstruir; **a canal ~d with weeds** un canal atascado por las hierbas; **a street ~d with traffic** una calle congestionada por el tráfico
Ⓒ VI [*person*] ahogarse, asfixiarse; **to ~ to death** morir asfixiado; **to ~ on a fishbone** atragantarse con una espina; **to ~ with laughter** morirse de risa

►**choke back** VT + ADV [+ *tears*] tragarse; [+ *feelings*] ahogar

►**choke down** VT + ADV [+ *rage, sobs*] ahogar

►**choke off** VT + ADV (*fig*) [+ *supply, suggestions etc*] cortar; [+ *discussion*] cortar por lo sano; [+ *person*] cortar

►**choke up** Ⓐ VT + ADV [+ *pipe, drain*] obstruir
Ⓑ VI + ADV [1] [*pipe, drain*] atascarse
[2] [*person*] quedarse sin habla

choked [tʃəʊkt] ADJ [1] (= *strangled*) **a ~ cry** un grito ahogado *or* entrecortado; **in a ~ voice** con voz entrecortada; **~ with emotion** ahogado por la emoción
[2] (*Brit**) (= *angry, upset*) disgustado; **I still feel ~ about him leaving** aún me dura el disgusto de que se fuera

choker ['tʃəʊkə^r] N [1] (= *necklace*) gargantilla *f*; (*hum*) cuello *m* alto
[2] (*Mech*) obturador *m*
[3] (*) (= *disappointment*) fastidio *m*
[4] (*esp US**) (= *person*) agobiado/a* *m/f*

choking ['tʃəʊkɪŋ] Ⓐ ADJ asfixiador, asfixiante
Ⓑ N ahogo *m*, asfixia *f*

choky* ['tʃəʊkɪ] N (= *prison*) trena* *f*; (= *cell*) unidad *f* de aislamiento

cholera ['kɒlərə] N cólera *m*

choleric ['kɒlərɪk] ADJ colérico

cholesterol [kə'lestərɒl] N colesterol *m*

chomp* [tʃɒmp] Ⓐ VT mascar
Ⓑ VI mascar; *see also* **bit²**

Chomskyan ['tʃɒmskɪən] ADJ de Chomsky, chomskiano

choo-choo* ['tʃuːtʃuː] N (*Brit child language*) chu-chu *m*, tren *m*

choose [tʃuːz] (*pt* **chose**; *pp* **chosen**) Ⓐ VT [1] (*gen*) elegir, escoger; (= *select*) [+ *team*] seleccionar; [+ *candidate*] elegir; **he was chosen (as) leader** fue elegido líder; **there is nothing to ~ between them** vale tanto el uno como el otro, no veo la diferencia entre ellos
[2] (= *opt*) **to ~ to do sth** optar por hacer algo; **if I don't ~ to** si no quiero
Ⓑ VI elegir, escoger; **to ~ between** elegir entre; **there are several to ~ from** hay varios entre los que elegir; **as/when I ~** como/cuando me parezca*, como/cuando me dé la gana (*Sp**)

choosey, choosy ['tʃuːzɪ] ADJ (*gen*) exigente; (*about food*) delicado; (= *touchy*) quisquilloso; **he's a bit ~ about it** en esto es algo difícil de contentar; **I'm ~ about who I go out with** yo no salgo con un cualquiera; **in his position he can't be ~** su posición no le permite darse el lujo de escoger

chop¹ [tʃɒp] Ⓐ N [1] (= *blow*) golpe *m* cortante; (= *cut*) tajo *m*
[2] (*Culin*) chuleta *f*
[3] (*Brit**) (*fig*) **to get the ~** [*project*] ser rechazado *or* desechado; [*person*] (= *be sacked*) ser despedido; **to give sb the ~** despedir a algn; **he's for the ~** le van a despedir; **this programme is for the ~** este programa se va a suprimir
Ⓑ VT [1] [+ *wood*] cortar, talar; [+ *meat, vegetables*] picar; **to ~ one's way through** abrirse camino a con un machete
[2] (*Brit**) [+ *person*] despedir
[3] (*Sport*) [+ *ball*] cortar

►**chop at** VI + PREP tratar de tajar

►**chop down** VT + ADV [+ *tree*] talar

►**chop off** VT + ADV [1] (*lit*) cortar de un tajo; **they ~ped off his head** le cortaron la cabeza
[2] (*fig*) recortar, reducir

►**chop up** VT + ADV desmenuzar; [+ *meat*] picar

chop² [tʃɒp] VI (*Brit**) **to ~ and change** cambiar constantemente de opinión

chopper ['tʃɒpə^r] N [1] (= *axe*) hacha *f*; [*of butcher*] tajadera *f*, cuchilla *f*
[2] (*) (= *helicopter*) helicóptero *m*; (*Brit*) (= *bicycle*) *bicicleta de manillar alto y asiento alargado*; (*US*) (= *motorbike*) *motocicleta de manillar alto y asiento alargado*

chopping ['tʃɒpɪŋ] CPD ► **chopping block, chopping board** N tajo *m*, tabla *f* de cortar ► **chopping knife** N tajadera *f*, cuchilla *f*

choppy ['tʃɒpɪ] ADJ (*compar* **choppier**; *superl* **choppiest**) [*sea, weather*] picado, agitado

chops* [tʃɒps] NPL (*Anat*) boca *fsing*, labios *mpl*; **to lick one's ~** relamerse, chuparse los dedos

chopsticks ['tʃɒpstɪks] NPL palillos *mpl*

chop suey [,tʃɒp'suːɪ] N chop suey *m*

choral ['kɔːrəl] Ⓐ ADJ coral
Ⓑ CPD ► **choral society** N orfeón *m*

chorale [kɒ'rɑːl] N coral *m*

chord [kɔːd] N [1] (*Mus*) acorde *m*; ✦**IDIOMS to strike a ~** sonarle (algo a uno); **we must strike a common ~** tenemos que encontrar un punto en común; **this struck a responsive ~ with everyone** esto produjo una reacción positiva en todos; **to touch the right ~** despertar emociones
[2] (*Math, Anat*) cuerda *f*

chore [tʃɔː^r] N faena *f*, tarea *f*; (*pej*) tarea *f* rutinaria; **to do the (household) ~s** hacer los quehaceres domésticos

choreograph ['kɒrɪə,græf] VT coreografiar

choreographer [,kɒrɪ'ɒgrəfə^r] N coreógrafo/a *m/f*

choreographic [,kɒrɪəʊ'græfɪk] ADJ coreográfico

choreography [,kɒrɪ'ɒgrəfɪ] N coreografía *f*

chorister ['kɒrɪstə^r] N corista *mf*; (*US*) director(a) *m/f* de un coro

chortle ['tʃɔːtl] Ⓐ N risa *f* alegre

Ⓑ VI reírse alegremente; **to ~ over sth** reírse satisfecho por algo

chorus ['kɔːrəs] Ⓐ N (*pl* **choruses**) [1] [*of singers, play*] coro *m*; (*in musical*) conjunto *m*; **in ~** a coro; **to sing in ~** cantar a coro
[2] (= *refrain*) estribillo *m*; **to join in the ~** unirse en el estribillo
[3] (*fig*) **a ~ of praise greeted the book** el libro fue recibido por un coro de aprobación *or* alabanzas; **a ~ of shouts greeted this** esto fue recibido por un coro de exclamaciones
Ⓑ VT (= *speak in unison*) decir a coro; (= *answer*) contestar a coro
Ⓒ CPD ► **chorus girl** N corista *f* ► **chorus line** N línea *f* de coro

chose [tʃəʊz] PT *of* **choose**

chosen ['tʃəʊzn] Ⓐ PP *of* **choose**
Ⓑ ADJ preferido, predilecto; **the ~ few** la minoría privilegiada; **the Chosen (People)** el pueblo elegido; **their ~ representative** el representante que han elegido
Ⓒ N **one of the ~** uno de los elegidos

chough [tʃʌf] N chova *f* (piquirroja)

choux pastry ['ʃuː'peɪstrɪ] N masa *f* de profiteroles

chow¹ [tʃaʊ] N (= *dog*) chow-chow *m*, perro *m* chino

chow²* [tʃaʊ] N (*esp US*) (= *food*) comida *f*

chowder ['tʃaʊdəʳ] N (*esp US*) sopa *f* de pescado

chow mein [tʃaʊ'meɪn] N *plato de la cocina china de tallarines rehogados con carne o verduras*

Chris [krɪs] N (*familiar form*) *of* **Christopher**

Christ [kraɪst] Ⓐ N Cristo *m*
Ⓑ EXCL **~!*** ¡hostia(s)!*, ¡carajo! (*LAm*)

christen ['krɪsn] VT [1] (*Rel*) bautizar
[2] (= *name*) bautizar con el nombre de; **they ~ed him Jack after his uncle** le pusieron Jack como su tío
[3] (*) (= *use for first time*) estrenar

Christendom ['krɪsndəm] N cristiandad *f*

▼ **christening** ['krɪsnɪŋ] Ⓐ N bautizo *m*, bautismo *m*
Ⓑ CPD ► **christening gown, christening robe** N faldón *m* de bautizo

Christian ['krɪstɪən] Ⓐ ADJ cristiano
Ⓑ N cristiano/a *m/f*
Ⓒ CPD ► **Christian Democrat** N (*Pol*) democratacristiano/a *m/f*, democristiano/a *m/f* ► **Christian Democrat(ic) Party** N (*Pol*) partido *m* democratacristiano, partido *m* democristiano ► **Christian name** N nombre *m* de pila ► **Christian Science** N Ciencia *f* Cristiana ► **Christian Scientist** N Científico/a *m/f* Cristiano/a

Christianity [,krɪstɪ'ænɪtɪ] N cristianismo *m*

Christianize ['krɪstɪənaɪz] VT cristianizar

Christlike ['kraɪstlaɪk] ADJ como Cristo

▼ **Christmas** ['krɪsməs] Ⓐ N Navidad *f*; (= *season*) Navidades *fpl*; **at ~** en Navidad, por Navidades; **happy** *or* **merry ~!** ¡Feliz Navidad!, ¡Felices Pascuas!; *see also* **father C**
Ⓑ CPD [*decorations, festivities*] de Navidad, navideño/a ► **Christmas box** N (*Brit*) aguinaldo *m* ► **Christmas cake** N pastel *m* de Navidad, tarta *f* de Navidad ► **Christmas card** N crismas *m inv*, tarjeta *f* de Navidad ► **Christmas carol** N villancico *m* ► **Christmas club** N club *m* de ahorros (*que los reparte por Navidades*) ► **Christmas Day** N día *m* de Navidad ► **Christmas dinner** N comida *f* de Navidad ► **Christmas Eve** N Nochebuena *f* ► **Christmas Island** N Isla *f* Christmas ► **Christmas party** N fiesta *f* de Navidad ► **Christmas present** N regalo *m* de Navidad ► **Christmas pudding** N (*esp Brit*) pudin *m* de Navidad ► **Christmas rose** N eléboro *m* negro ► **Christmas stocking** N ≈ zapatos *mpl* de Reyes ► **Christmas time** N Navidades *fpl*, Pascua *f* de Navidad ► **Christmas tree** N árbol *m* de Navidad

> **CHRISTMAS DINNER**
> *La comida de Navidad (***Christmas dinner***) que se celebra en familia el día 25, es un momento central de las celebraciones navideñas. En ella se suele comer pavo relleno asado (***roast turkey with stuffing***) acompañado de coles de Bruselas y patatas asadas. En el Reino Unido el postre tradicional es* **Christmas pudding***, un pastel hecho a base de frutas secas, especias y brandy al que se le añade* **brandy butter***, una mezcla de mantequilla, azúcar y brandy.*

Christmassy* ['krɪsməsɪ] ADJ navideño, propio de Navidad

Christopher ['krɪstəfəʳ] N Cristóbal

chromatic [krə'mætɪk] ADJ (*Mus, Tech*) cromático

chromatogram [krəʊ'mætə,græm] N cromatograma *m*

chromatography [,krəʊmə'tɒgrəfɪ] N cromatografía *f*

chrome [krəʊm] Ⓐ N cromo *m*
Ⓑ CPD ► **chrome steel** N acero *m* al cromo, acerocromo *m* ► **chrome yellow** N amarillo *m* de cromo

chromium ['krəʊmɪəm] Ⓐ N cromo *m*
Ⓑ CPD ► **chromium plating** N cromado *m*

chromium-plated ['krəʊmɪəm,pleɪtɪd] ADJ cromado

chromosomal [,krəʊmə'səʊməl] ADJ cromosomático, cromosómico

chromosome ['krəʊməsəʊm] N cromosoma *m*

chronic ['krɒnɪk] ADJ [1] [*invalid, disease*] crónico
[2] (= *inveterate*) [*smoker*] empedernido; [*liar*] incorregible
[3] (*Brit**) [*weather, person*] horrible, malísimo; **I had toothache something ~** me dolían las muelas horriblemente

chronically ['krɒnɪkəlɪ] ADV **to be ~ sick** sufrir una enfermedad crónica; **beer is ~ scarce** hay una escasez permanente de cerveza

chronicle ['krɒnɪkl] Ⓐ N crónica *f*; **Chronicles** (*Bible*) Crónicas *fpl*
Ⓑ VT (= *recount*) hacer una crónica de

chronicler ['krɒnɪkləʳ] N cronista *mf*

chronological [,krɒnə'lɒdʒɪkəl] ADJ cronológico; **in ~ order** en orden cronológico

chronologically [,krɒnə'lɒdʒɪkəlɪ] ADV por orden cronológico

chronology [krə'nɒlədʒɪ] N cronología *f*

chronometer [krə'nɒmɪtəʳ] N cronómetro *m*

chrysalis ['krɪsəlɪs] N (*pl* **chrysalises** ['krɪsəlɪsɪz]) (*Bio*) crisálida *f*

chrysanth* [krɪ'sænθ] N (*Brit*) = **chrysanthemum**

chrysanthemum [krɪ'sænθəməm] N crisantemo *m*

chub [tʃʌb] N (*pl* **chub** *or* **chubs**) cacho *m*

chubby ['tʃʌbɪ] ADJ (*compar* **chubbier**, *superl* **chubbiest**) [*baby, hands*] rechoncho, regordete; [*face, cheeks*] mofletudo

chuck¹ [tʃʌk] Ⓐ N [1] (*) (= *throw*) tiro *m*, echada *f*
[2] (*) **to get the ~** (*from job*) ser despedido; **to give sb the ~** (*from relationship*) dar la patada a algn*, plantar a algn*
[3] **a ~ under the chin** una palmada cariñosa en la barbilla
Ⓑ VT [1] (*) (= *throw*) tirar, echar
[2] (*) (= *throw away*) (*also* **~ away**) tirar, botar (*LAm*); [+ *money*] tirar; [+ *chance*] desperdiciar
[3] (*) (= *give up*) (*also* **~ up, ~ in**) [+ *job*] dejar, plantar*; [+ *boyfriend, girlfriend*] dar la patada a*, plantar*; **so I had to ~ it** así que tuve que dejarlo; **~ it!** ¡basta ya!, ¡déjalo!
[4] **to ~ sb under the chin** dar una palmada cariñosa bajo la barbilla a algn

►**chuck away*** VT + ADV [+ *old clothes, books*] tirar, botar (*LAm*); [+ *money*] despilfarrar; [+ *chance*] desperdiciar

►**chuck in*** VT + ADV abandonar, renunciar a; **I'm thinking of ~ing it in** estoy pensando en mandarlo a paseo

►**chuck out*** VT + ADV [+ *rubbish*] tirar, botar (*LAm*); [+ *person*] echar (fuera); [+ *employee*] despedir, dar el pasaporte a*

►**chuck up** Ⓐ VT + ADV (*) abandonar, renunciar a
Ⓑ VI + ADV (*US**) (= *vomit*) arrojar*

chuck² [tʃʌk] Ⓐ N [1] (*also* **~ steak**) bistec *m* de pobre
[2] (*US**) (= *food*) manduca* *f*; → DUDE RANCH
Ⓑ CPD ► **chuck wagon** N carromato *m* de provisiones

chuck³ [tʃʌk] = **chock**

chuck⁴ [tʃʌk] N (*Tech*) portabrocas *m inv*

chucker-out* ['tʃʌkər'aʊt] N (*Brit*) gorila *m* (*en la entrada de un local*)

chuckle ['tʃʌkl] Ⓐ N risita *f*, risa *f* sofocada; **we had a good ~ over that** nos reímos bastante con eso
Ⓑ VI reírse entre dientes, soltar una risita; **to ~ at** *or* **over** reírse con

chuddar ['tʃʌdəʳ] N chador *m*

chuffed* [tʃʌft] ADJ (*Brit*) (= *pleased*) satisfecho, contento; **he was pretty ~ about it** estaba la mar de contento por eso

chug [tʃʌg] VI [*steam engine*] resoplar; [*motor*] traquetear; **the train ~ged past** pasó el tren resoplando

►**chug along** VI + ADV [*car, train*] ir despacio resoplando; (*fig*) ir tirando

chukka, chukker ['tʃʌkəʳ] N (*Polo*) tiempo *m* de un partido de polo

chum* [tʃʌm] N amiguete* *m*, colega *mf*, cuate *mf* (*Mex**), pata *mf* (*Peru**); (= *child*) amiguito/a *m/f*; (*in direct address*) amigo; **to be great ~s** ser íntimos amigos; **to be ~s with sb** ser amigo de algn

►**chum up*** VI + ADV hacerse amigos; **to ~ up with sb** hacerse amigo de algn

chummy* ['tʃʌmɪ] ADJ muy amigo; **they're very ~** son muy amigos; **he's very ~ with the boss** es muy amigo del jefe; **he got ~ with the boss** se hizo amigo del jefe

chump [tʃʌmp] Ⓐ N [1] (*) (= *idiot*) tonto/a *m/f*; **you ~!** ¡imbécil!
[2] (*) (= *head*) cabeza *f*; ✦IDIOM **to be off one's ~** estar chiflado
Ⓑ CPD ► **chump chop** N (*Brit*) *chuleta gruesa con hueso*

chunk [tʃʌŋk] N [*of bread, cheese etc*] pedazo *m*, trozo *m*; (*) [*of land, time, money*] cantidad *f* considerable

chunky ['tʃʌŋkɪ] ADJ (*compar* **chunkier**, *superl* **chunkiest**) [*person*] fornido; [*furniture, mug*] achaparrado; [*knitwear*] grueso, de lana gorda

Chunnel ['tʃʌnl] N (*hum*) túnel *m* bajo el Canal de la Mancha

chunter* ['tʃʌntəʳ] VI (*Brit*) (*also* **~ on**) (= *mutter*) murmurar; (= *complain*) gruñir, refunfuñar*

➤ LANGUAGE IN USE: christening A 25.2 Christmas A 23.2

church [tʃɜːtʃ] Ⓐ N 1 (= *building*) (*gen*) iglesia *f*; (*Protestant*) templo *m*
2 (= *service*) (*Catholic*) misa *f*; (*Protestant*) oficio *m*; **to go to ~** (*Catholic*) ir a misa; (*Protestant*) ir al oficio; **after ~** después de la misa *or* del oficio
3 (= *institution*) **the Church** la Iglesia; **Church and State** Iglesia y Estado; **to enter the Church** hacerse cura *or (Protestant)* pastor
Ⓑ CPD [*doctrine*] de la Iglesia ► **Church Fathers** NPL Padres *mpl* de la Iglesia ► **church hall** N sacristía *f* ► **church music** N música *f* sacra *or* religiosa ► **Church of England** N Iglesia *f* Anglicana ► **Church of Scotland** N Iglesia *f* Presbiteriana Escocesa ► **church school** N colegio *m* religioso ► **church service** N oficio *m*, servicio *m* religioso ► **church wedding** N boda *f* eclesiástica, boda *f* por la iglesia; **they want a ~ wedding** quieren casarse por la iglesia

CHURCHES OF ENGLAND/SCOTLAND

*La Iglesia Anglicana (***Church of England***) es la iglesia oficial de Inglaterra. Tiene su origen en la ruptura de Enrique VIII con la Iglesia católica en el siglo XVI. En ella se unen aspectos de la tradición católica y de la protestante. Su dirigente oficial es el monarca y su jefe espiritual el Arzobispo de Canterbury. Al clero se le permite contraer matrimonio y, desde 1992, las mujeres pueden ejercer el sacerdocio, cambio al que se opuso radicalmente la corriente conservadora.*
*La Iglesia Presbiteriana Escocesa (***Church of Scotland***) es la iglesia nacional de Escocia, pero no depende de ninguna autoridad civil. Sigue la doctrina calvinista y se rige según las normas presbiterianas, lo que significa que está gobernada a nivel local, por* **ministers** *y dirigentes laicos (***elders***). Tanto hombres como mujeres pueden ejercer el sacerdocio. Hay una reunión anual (***General Assembly***) en la que se discuten asuntos nacionales, presidida por un* **Moderator***, que es elegido anualmente.*
⇨ *Ver tb* ARCHBISHOP

churchgoer [ˈtʃɜːtʃˌɡəʊəʳ] N fiel *mf*
churchman [ˈtʃɜːtʃmən] N (*pl* **churchmen**) 1 (= *priest*) sacerdote *m*, eclesiástico *m*
2 (= *member*) fiel *m* practicante
churchwarden [ˈtʃɜːtʃˈwɔːdn] N capillero *m*
churchwoman [ˈtʃɜːtʃˌwʊmən] N (*pl* **churchwomen**) fiel *f* practicante
churchy* [ˈtʃɜːtʃɪ] ADJ (*pej*) (= *pious*) beato; (= *churchgoing*) que va mucho a la iglesia, que toma muy en serio las cosas de la iglesia
churchyard [ˈtʃɜːtʃjɑːd] N cementerio *m*, campo *m* santo
churl [tʃɜːl] N (= *person*) patán *m*
churlish [ˈtʃɜːlɪʃ] ADJ (= *rude*) grosero, maleducado; (= *unfriendly*) poco amistoso, arisco; (= *mean*) mezquino; **it would be ~ not to thank him** sería muy grosero *or* maleducado no darle las gracias
churlishly [ˈtʃɜːlɪʃlɪ] ADV (= *rudely*) groseramente, sin educación
churlishness [ˈtʃɜːlɪʃnɪs] N (= *rudeness*) grosería *f*, mala educación *f*; (= *unfriendliness*) conducta *f* poco amistosa; (= *meanness*) mezquindad *f*
churn [tʃɜːn] Ⓐ N (*for butter*) mantequera *f*; (*Brit*) (*for milk*) lechera *f*
Ⓑ VT 1 [+ *butter*] batir *or* hacer en una mantequera
2 (*fig*) (*also* **~ up**) [+ *sea, mud*] revolver, agitar
Ⓒ VI [*sea*] revolverse, agitarse; **her stomach was ~ing** se le revolvía el estómago
►**churn out** VT + ADV (*pej*) [+ *books, goods*] producir en serie, producir en masa
chute [ʃuːt] N 1 (*for rubbish*) vertedero *m*
2 (*Brit*) (*in playground, swimming pool*) tobogán *m*
3 (*) (= *parachute*) paracaídas *m inv*
chutney [ˈtʃʌtnɪ] N salsa *f* picante (de frutas y especias)
chutzpa(h)* [ˈxʊtspə] N (*esp US*) cara *f* dura
CI ABBR = **Channel Islands**
C.I. N ABBR = **Consular Invoice**
CIA N ABBR (*US*) (= **Central Intelligence Agency**) CIA *f*
ciao* [tʃaʊ] EXCL ¡chao!
cicada [sɪˈkɑːdə] N (*pl* **cicadas** *or* **cicadae** [sɪˈkɑːdiː]) cigarra *f*
Cicero [ˈsɪsərəʊ] N Cicerón
Ciceronian [ˌsɪsəˈrəʊnɪən] ADJ ciceroniano
CID N ABBR (*Brit*) = **Criminal Investigation Department**; **~ man/woman** ◊ **~ officer** policía *mf or* oficial *mf* del Departamento de Investigación Criminal
cider [ˈsaɪdəʳ] Ⓐ N sidra *f*
Ⓑ CPD ► **cider apple** N manzana *f* de sidra ► **cider press** N lagar *m* para hacer sidra ► **cider vinegar** N vinagre *m* de sidra
CIF, c.i.f. N ABBR (= **cost, insurance, freight**) c.s.f.
cig* [sɪɡ] N (*Brit*) = **cigarette**
cigar [sɪˈɡɑːʳ] Ⓐ N puro *m*, cigarro *m*
Ⓑ CPD ► **cigar case** N cigarrera *f* ► **cigar holder** N boquilla *f* de puro ► **cigar lighter** N (*Aut*) encendedor *m* de puro
cigarette [ˌsɪɡəˈret] Ⓐ N cigarrillo *m*, cigarro *m*; **he had a ~** (se) fumó un cigarrillo *or* cigarro
Ⓑ CPD ► **cigarette ash** N ceniza *f* de cigarrillo ► **cigarette card** N cromo *m* (coleccionable) ► **cigarette case** N pitillera *f*, cigarrera *f* (*LAm*) ► **cigarette end** N colilla *f* ► **cigarette holder** N boquilla *f* ► **cigarette lighter** N encendedor *m*, mechero *m* ► **cigarette machine** N máquina *f* de tabaco ► **cigarette paper** N papel *m* de fumar
cigar-shaped [sɪˈɡɑːʃeɪpt] ADJ en forma de puro
ciggy* [ˈsɪɡɪ] N (*Brit*) = **cigarette**
CIM N ABBR (*Comput*) = **computer-integrated manufacturing**
C.-in-C. N ABBR = **Commander-in-Chief**
cinch* [sɪntʃ] N **it's a ~** (= *easy thing*) está tirado, es pan comido; (= *sure thing*) es cosa segura
cinchona [sɪŋˈkəʊnə] Ⓐ N quino *m*
Ⓑ CPD ► **cinchona bark** N quina *f*
cinder [ˈsɪndəʳ] Ⓐ N 1 (= *ember*) carbonilla *f*; ✦***IDIOM*** **to be burned to a ~** [*food etc*] quedar carbonizado
2 **cinders** (= *ashes*) cenizas *fpl*
Ⓑ CPD ► **cinder block** N (*US*) ladrillo *m* de cenizas ► **cinder track** N (*Sport*) pista *f* de ceniza
Cinderella [ˌsɪndəˈrelə] N Cenicienta *f*; **it's the ~ of the arts** es la hermana pobre de las artes
cine [ˈsɪnɪ] CPD (*Brit*) ► **cine camera** N cámara *f* cinematográfica ► **cine film** N película *f* de cine ► **cine projector** N proyector *m* de películas
cinéaste [ˈsɪnɪæst] N cinéfilo/a *m/f*
cinema [ˈsɪnəmə] (*esp Brit*) Ⓐ N cine *m*; **the silent/talking ~** el cine mudo/sonoro
Ⓑ CPD ► **cinema complex** N cine *m* multisalas
cinema-going [ˈsɪnəməˌɡəʊɪŋ] (*esp Brit*) Ⓐ N **~ is very popular among the young** el ir al cine es muy popular entre los jóvenes
Ⓑ ADJ **the ~ public** el público aficionado al cine
Cinemascope® [ˈsɪnəməskəʊp] N Cinemascope® *m*
cinematic [ˌsɪnɪˈmætɪk] ADJ cinemático
cinematograph [ˌsɪnɪˈmætəɡrɑːf] N (*Brit*) cinematógrafo *m*
cinematographer [ˌsɪnəməˈtɒɡrəfəʳ] N cinematógrafo/a *m/f*
cinematography [ˌsɪnəməˈtɒɡrəfɪ] N cinematografía *f*
cinerary [ˈsɪnərərɪ] ADJ cinerario
cinnabar [ˈsɪnəbɑːʳ] N cinabrio *m*
cinnamon [ˈsɪnəmən] N canela *f*
cipher [ˈsaɪfəʳ] Ⓐ N 1 (= *0, zero*) cero *m*; (= *any number, initials*) cifra *f*; (= *Arabic numeral*) cifra *f*, número *m*
2 (= *secret writing*) cifra *f*, código *m*; **in ~** cifrado, en clave
3 (= *monogram*) monograma *m*
4 (*fig*) (= *person*) **he's a mere ~** es un cero a la izquierda
Ⓑ VT 1 [+ *code, calculations, communications*] cifrar
2 (*Math*) calcular
circa [ˈsɜːkə] PREP hacia; **~ 1500** hacia (el año) 1500
circadian [səˈkeɪdɪən] ADJ circadiano; **~ cycle** ciclo *m* circadiano
circle [ˈsɜːkl] Ⓐ N 1 (*gen*) círculo *m*; **to stand in a ~** formar un corro; ✦***IDIOMS*** **to come full ~** volver al punto de partida; **to go round in ~s*** dar vueltas sobre lo mismo, no avanzar; **it had us running round in ~s*** nos tuvo dando vueltas sin orden ni concierto; *see also* **vicious**
2 (= *set of people*) círculo *m*, grupo *m*; **John and his ~** Juan y sus amigos, Juan y su peña; **in certain ~s** en ciertos medios; **in business ~s** en el mundo de los negocios; **the family ~** el círculo familiar; **to move in fashionable ~s** frecuentar los ambientes que están de moda; **an inner ~ of ministers** un grupo de ministros que ostentan mayor poder; **she moves in wealthy ~s** frecuenta la buena sociedad
3 (*Brit Theat*) anfiteatro *m*
Ⓑ VT 1 (= *surround*) cercar, rodear; (= *move round*) girar alrededor de, dar vueltas alrededor de; **the lion ~d its prey** el león se movió alrededor de la presa; **the cosmonaut ~d the earth** el cosmonauta dio la vuelta a la tierra; **the aircraft ~d the town twice** el avión dio dos vueltas sobre la ciudad
2 (= *draw round*) poner un círculo alrededor de, rodear con un círculo
Ⓒ VI dar vueltas
circlet [ˈsɜːklɪt] N (*worn on head*) diadema *f*; (*worn on finger*) anillo *m*; (*worn on arm*) aro *m*, brazalete *m*
circuit [ˈsɜːkɪt] Ⓐ N 1 (= *route*) circuito *m*; (= *course*) recorrido *m*; (= *long way round*) rodeo *m*; (= *lap by runner*) vuelta *f*
2 (*Brit Jur*) distrito *m*
3 (*Cine*) cadena *f*
4 (*esp Brit*) (= *sports track*) pista *f*
5 (*Aut, Elec*) circuito *m*; *see also* **short-circuit**
Ⓑ CPD ► **circuit board** N (*Elec*) tarjeta *f* de

circuitos ► **circuit breaker** N (*Elec*) cortacircuitos *m inv* ► **circuit court** N (*US Jur*) tribunal *m* superior ► **circuit switching network** N (*Elec*) red *f* de conmutación de circuito ► **circuit training** N (*Sport*) circuito *m* de entrenamiento

circuitous [sɜːˈkjʊɪtəs] ADJ [*route*] tortuoso, sinuoso; [*method*] tortuoso, solapado

circuitry [ˈsɜːkɪtrɪ] N circuitería *f*, sistema *m* de circuitos

circular [ˈsɜːkjʊləʳ] Ⓐ ADJ circular, redondo; **~ motion** movimiento *m* circular; **~ tour** circuito *m*
Ⓑ N (*in firm*) circular *f*; (= *advertisement*) panfleto *m*
Ⓒ CPD ► **circular saw** N sierra *f* circular

circularity [ˌsɜːkjʊˈlærɪtɪ] N circularidad *f*

circularize [ˈsɜːkjʊləraɪz] VT enviar circulares a

circulate [ˈsɜːkjʊleɪt] Ⓐ VI (*gen*) circular
Ⓑ VT (*gen*) poner en circulación; [+ *letter, papers etc*] hacer circular; [+ *news*] hacer circular

circulating [ˈsɜːkjʊleɪtɪŋ] Ⓐ ADJ circulante
Ⓑ CPD ► **circulating assets** NPL activo *msing* circulante ► **circulating capital** N capital *m* circulante ► **circulating library** N (*US*) biblioteca *f* circulante ► **circulating medium** N (*Fin*) medios *mpl* monetarios

circulation [ˌsɜːkjʊˈleɪʃən] N 1 (*gen*) circulación *f*; **to withdraw sth from ~** retirar algo de la circulación; **to put into ~** poner en circulación; **he's back in ~*** se está dejando ver otra vez
2 (= *number of papers printed*) tirada *f*
3 (*Med*) **she has poor ~** tiene mala circulación

circulatory [ˌsɜːkjʊˈleɪtərɪ] ADJ circulatorio

circum... [ˈsɜːkəm] PREFIX circun..., circum...

circumcise [ˈsɜːkəmsaɪz] VT circuncidar

circumcision [ˌsɜːkəmˈsɪʒən] N circuncisión *f*

circumference [səˈkʌmfərəns] N circunferencia *f*

circumflex [ˈsɜːkəmfleks] Ⓐ N circunflejo *m*
Ⓑ CPD ► **circumflex accent** N acento *m* circunflejo

circumlocution [ˌsɜːkəmləˈkjuːʃən] N circunloquio *m*, rodeo *m*

circumnavigate [ˌsɜːkəmˈnævɪgeɪt] VT circunnavegar

circumnavigation [ˈsɜːkəmˌnævɪˈgeɪʃən] N circunnavegación *f*

circumscribe [ˈsɜːkəmskraɪb] VT (*lit*) circunscribir; (*fig*) (= *limit*) limitar, restringir

circumspect [ˈsɜːkəmspekt] ADJ circunspecto, prudente

circumspection [ˌsɜːkəmˈspekʃən] N circunspección *f*, prudencia *f*

circumspectly [ˈsɜːkəmspektlɪ] ADV prudentemente

▼ **circumstance** [ˈsɜːkəmstəns] (*usu pl*) N 1 circunstancia *f*; **in** *or* **under the ~s** en *or* dadas las circunstancias; **under no ~s** de ninguna manera, bajo ningún concepto; **owing to ~s beyond our control** debido a circunstancias ajenas a nuestra voluntad; **~s alter cases** las circunstancias cambian los casos; **were it not for the ~ that ...** si no se diera la circunstancia de que ...; **a victim of ~** una víctima de las circunstancias; *see also* **pomp**
2 (= *economic situation*) **to be in easy/poor ~s** estar en buena/mala situación económica; **what are your ~s?** ¿cuál es su situación económica?; **if the family ~s allow it** si lo permite la situación económica de la familia

circumstantial [ˌsɜːkəmˈstænʃəl] ADJ [*report, statement*] detallado; **~ evidence** (*Jur*) pruebas *fpl* circunstanciales

circumstantiate [ˌsɜːkəmˈstænʃɪeɪt] VT probar refiriendo más detalles, corroborar, confirmar

circumvent [ˌsɜːkəmˈvent] VT [+ *law, rule*] burlar; [+ *difficulty, obstacle*] salvar, evitar

circumvention [ˌsɜːkəmˈvenʃən] N acción *f* de burlar *or* salvar; **the ~ of this obstacle will not be easy** no va a ser fácil salvar este obstáculo

circus [ˈsɜːkəs] N (*pl* **circuses**) 1 (= *entertainment*) circo *m*
2 (*in place names*) plaza *f*, glorieta *f*

cirrhosis [sɪˈrəʊsɪs] N cirrosis *f*

cirrocumulus [ˌsɪrəʊˈkjuːmjʊləs] N (*pl* **cirrocumuli** [ˌsɪrəʊˈkjuːmjʊlaɪ]) cirrocúmulo *m*

cirrostratus [ˌsɪrəʊˈstrɑːtəs] N (*pl* **cirrostrati** [ˌsɪrəʊˈstrɑːtaɪ]) cirrostrato *m*

cirrus [ˈsɪrəs] N (*pl* **cirri** [ˈsɪraɪ]) cirro *m*

CIS N ABBR (= **Commonwealth of Independent States**) CEI *f*

cissy* [ˈsɪsɪ] N mariquita* *m*

Cistercian [sɪsˈtɜːʃən] Ⓐ ADJ cisterciense; **~ Order** Orden *f* del Císter
Ⓑ N cisterciense *m*

cistern [ˈsɪstən] N [*of WC*] cisterna *f*; (= *tank*) depósito *m*; (*for hot water*) termo *m*; (*for rainwater*) aljibe *m*, cisterna *f*

citadel [ˈsɪtədl] N ciudadela *f*; (*in Spain, freq*) alcázar *m*; (*fig*) reducto *m*

citation [saɪˈteɪʃən] Ⓐ N cita *f*; (*US Jur*) citación *f*; (*Mil*) mención *f*, citación *f*
Ⓑ CPD ► **citation index** N índice *m* de citación

cite [saɪt] VT 1 (= *quote*) citar
2 (*Jur*) **he was ~d to appear in court** lo citaron para que se compareciera ante el tribunal
3 (*Mil*) mencionar, citar

citizen [ˈsɪtɪzn] Ⓐ N [*of state*] ciudadano/a *m/f*, súbdito/a *m/f*; [*of city*] habitante *mf*, vecino/a *m/f*
Ⓑ CPD ► **Citizens' Advice Bureau** N (*Brit*) *organización voluntaria británica que asesora legal o financieramente* ► **citizen's arrest** N *arresto realizado por un ciudadano ordinario* ► **Citizens' Band** N (*Rad*) banda *f* ciudadana

CITIZENS' ADVICE BUREAU

Las oficinas de información al ciudadano, ***Citizens' Advice Bureaux*** *o* ***CABs****, se crearon en 1939 para asesorar al pueblo británico sobre las normas que había que cumplir en tiempos de guerra. Después pasaron a ser un servicio de asesoramiento general al público, ofreciendo información gratuita y ayuda en problemas de carácter diverso. Actualmente se encargan de aconsejar en lo concerniente a la vivienda, problemas económicos, prestaciones y servicios sociales y derechos del consumidor. Existen unas 900 oficinas por todo el país, financiadas con dinero público y en las que trabajan normalmente voluntarios dirigidos por una persona que cobra por su trabajo.*

citizenry [ˈsɪtɪznrɪ] N ciudadanos *mpl*, ciudadanía *f*

citizenship [ˈsɪtɪznʃɪp] N ciudadanía *f*

citrate [ˈsɪtreɪt] N citrato *m*

citric [ˈsɪtrɪk] ADJ **~ acid** ácido *m* cítrico

citron [ˈsɪtrən] N (= *fruit*) cidra *f*; (= *tree*) cidro *m*

citrus [ˈsɪtrəs] Ⓐ N (*pl* **citruses**) cidro *m*
Ⓑ CPD ► **citrus fruits** NPL cítricos *mpl*, agrios *mpl*

city [ˈsɪtɪ] Ⓐ N ciudad *f*; **the City** (*Brit Fin*) *el centro financiero de Londres*
Ⓑ CPD municipal, de la ciudad ► **city centre, city center** (*US*) N centro *m* de la ciudad ► **city council** N concejo *m* municipal, ayuntamiento *m* ► **city desk** N (*Brit Press*) sección *f* de noticias financieras (de un periódico); (*US Press*) sección *f* de noticias de la ciudad (de un periódico) ► **city dweller** N habitante *mf* de una ciudad ► **city editor** N redactor(a) *m/f* encargado/a de las noticias financieras ► **city fathers** NPL concejales *mpl* ► **city hall** N palacio *m* municipal; (*US*) ayuntamiento *m* ► **city limits** NPL perímetro *msing* urbano ► **city manager** N administrador(a) *m/f* municipal ► **city news** N (*Brit*) noticias *fpl* financieras; (*US*) noticias *fpl* de la ciudad ► **city page** N (*Fin*) sección *f* de información financiera ► **city plan** N (*US*) plano *m* de la ciudad ► **city planner** N (*US*) urbanista *mf* ► **city planning** N (*US*) urbanismo *m* ► **city slicker*** N (*pej*) capitalino/a* *m/f* ► **City Technology College** N (*Brit*) ≈ Centro *m* de formación profesional

CITY NICKNAMES

Las ciudades estadounidenses a menudo tienen apodos por los que se las conoce informalmente. Por ejemplo, a Nueva York se la llama ***Big Apple****, ya que* ***apple*** *en argot significa gran ciudad. Chicago es* ***Windy City*** *debido a los fuertes vientos que vienen del lago Michigan. A Nueva Orleans la llaman* ***Big Easy****, por la tranquilidad con la que se lo toman todo sus habitantes. Detroit tiene el apelativo de* ***Motown****, que es un compuesto de* ***Motor*** *y* ***Town****, por las fábricas de coches que hay en ella.*
A otras ciudades estadounidenses se las conoce por sus iniciales, como por ejemplo, Los Angeles, ***LA*** *y Dallas,* ***Big D*** *o por una parte de su nombre como* ***Vegas****, en lugar de* ***Las Vegas*** *o* ***Corpus*** *por* ***Corpus Christi****, en Texas.*
También hay veces en las que se usa una versión acortada del nombre, como ocurre en el caso de San Francisco y Philadelphia, a las que se llama ***Frisco*** *y* ***Philly*** *respectivamente.*

cityscape [ˈsɪtɪskeɪp] N paisaje *m* urbano

city-state [ˈsɪtɪˌsteɪt] N ciudad-estado *f*

civet [ˈsɪvɪt] N algalia *f*

civic [ˈsɪvɪk] Ⓐ ADJ [*rights, duty*] cívico; [*authorities*] municipal
Ⓑ CPD ► **civic centre** N (*Brit*) conjunto *m* de edificios municipales; *see also* **pride A1**

civics [ˈsɪvɪks] NPL cívica *fsing*; (*as course*) educación *fsing* cívica

civies* [ˈsɪvɪz] NPL (*US*) = **civvies**

civil [ˈsɪvl] Ⓐ ADJ 1 (= *societal*) [*strife, conflict*] civil; [*unrest*] social
2 (= *not military*) [*aviation, ship*] civil
3 (= *not religious*) [*ceremony, service, marriage*] civil
4 (*Jur*) (= *not criminal*) [*case, action, proceedings, charge*] civil; [*penalty*] por infracción de la ley; [*court*] de lo Civil
5 (= *polite*) [*person*] cortés, atento; [*behaviour*] cortés; **to be ~ to sb** ser cortés *or* atento con algn; **that's very ~ of you** es usted muy amable; *see also* **tongue**
Ⓑ CPD ► **Civil Aviation Authority** N Aviación *f* Civil ► **civil defence, civil defense** (*US*) N defensa *f* civil ► **civil disobedience** N

➤ LANGUAGE IN USE: circumstance 1 14

desobediencia *f* civil ► **civil engineer** N ingeniero/a *m/f* civil, ingeniero/a *m/f* de caminos (canales y puertos) (*Sp*) ► **civil engineering** N ingeniería *f* civil, ingeniería *f* de caminos (canales y puertos) (*Sp*) ► **civil law** N derecho *m* civil ► **civil liberties** N libertades *fpl* civiles ► **civil list** N (*Brit*) *presupuesto de la casa real aprobado por el parlamento* ► **civil marriage** N matrimonio *m* civil ► **civil rights** N derechos *mpl* civiles; **~ rights leader** defensor(a) *m/f* de los derechos civiles ► **civil rights movement** N movimiento *m* pro derechos civiles ► **civil servant** N funcionario/a *m/f* (del Estado) ► **Civil Service** N administración *f* pública ► **civil status** N estado *m* civil ► **civil war** N guerra *f* civil; **the American Civil War** la guerra de Secesión ► **civil wedding** N boda *f* civil

civilian [sɪ'vɪlɪən] Ⓐ ADJ (= *non-military*) civil; **in ~ clothes** vestido/a de paisano *or* civil; **there were no ~ casualties** no hubo bajas entre la población civil
Ⓑ N civil *mf*

civility [sɪ'vɪlɪtɪ] N 1 (= *politeness*) cortesía *f*, amabilidad *f*
2 (*usu pl*) (= *polite remark*) cortesía *f*, cumplido *m*

civilization [,sɪvɪlaɪ'zeɪʃən] N civilización *f*

civilize ['sɪvɪlaɪz] VT civilizar

civilized ['sɪvɪlaɪzd] ADJ 1 (= *socially advanced*) [*society, country, world, people*] civilizado; **to become ~** civilizarse
2 (= *refined, decent*) [*person, manner*] educado; [*behaviour, conversation, company*] civilizado; [*meal, place, tastes*] refinado; [*time of day*] decente; **he never phones at a ~ hour** nunca llama a una hora decente; **how ~! real champagne!** ¡qué refinado *or* cuánto refinamiento! ¡champán de verdad!; **I know we disagree, but we could at least be ~ about it** sé que no estamos de acuerdo, pero vamos a ser civilizados por lo menos

civilizing ['sɪvɪlaɪzɪŋ] ADJ **she has had a ~ influence on him** bajo su influencia se ha vuelto más civilizado *or* refinado

civilly ['sɪvɪlɪ] ADV cortésmente, atentamente

civism ['sɪvɪzəm] N civismo *m*

civvies* ['sɪvɪz] NPL traje *msing* civil; **in ~** vestido/a de paisano *or* civil

civvy* ['sɪvɪ] ADJ **~ street** (*Brit*) la vida civil

CJD N ABBR (= **Creutzfeldt-Jakob disease**) *enfermedad de Creutzfeldt-Jakob*

CKD ADJ ABBR = **completely knocked down**; *see* **knock down**

cl ABBR (= **centilitre(s)**) cl

clack [klæk] VI (= *chatter*) charlar, chismear; **this will make the tongues ~** esto será tema para los chismosos

clad [klæd] ADJ vestido (**in** de)

cladding [klædɪŋ] N (*Tech*) revestimiento *m*

claim [kleɪm] Ⓐ N 1 (= *demand*) (*for rights, wages*) reivindicación *f*, demanda *f*; (*for damages, on insurance*) reclamación *f*; (*for expenses, benefit*) solicitud *f*; (*Jur*) demanda *f*; **pay** *or* **wage ~** reivindicación *f* salarial; **to file a ~** (*Jur*) presentar *or* interponer una demanda; **she lost her ~ for damages** el tribunal rechazó su demanda de daños y perjuicios; **to make a ~** (*on insurance*) reclamar; **we made a ~ on our insurance** reclamamos al seguro; **have you made a ~ since last year?** (*for benefit*) ¿ha solicitado alguna ayuda estatal desde el año pasado?; **there are many ~s on my time** tengo una agenda muy apretada; **to put in a ~ (for sth)** (*for expenses*) presentar una solicitud (de algo); (*on insurance*) reclamar (algo)
2 (= *right*) (*to property, title*) derecho *m*; **he renounced his ~ to the throne** renunció a su derecho al trono; **they will not give up their ~ to the territory** no renunciarán a su reivindicación del territorio; **the town's main ~ to fame is its pub** este pueblo se destaca más que nada por el bar; **to lay ~ to sth** (*lit*) reclamar algo; (*fig*) atribuirse algo; **he cannot lay ~ to much originality** no puede atribuirse mucha originalidad, no puede presumir de original; *see also* **stake B2.1**, **prior A1**
3 (= *assertion*) afirmación *f*; **he rejected ~s that he had had affairs with six women** desmintió las afirmaciones de que había tenido seis amantes; **I make no ~ to be infallible** no pretendo ser infalible
Ⓑ VT 1 (= *demand as due*) [+ *rights*] reivindicar; [+ *lost property*] reclamar; [+ *allowance, benefit*] (= *apply for*) solicitar; (= *receive*) cobrar; **if you wish to ~ expenses you must provide receipts** si desea que se le reembolsen los gastos debe presentar los recibos; **25% of people who are entitled to ~ State benefits do not do so** el 25% de las personas que tienen derecho a cobrar ayuda del Estado no lo hace; **to ~ damages from sb** demandar a algn por daños y perjuicios; **he ~ed damages for negligence on the part of the hospital** exigió que el hospital le compensara por haber cometido negligencia, demandó al hospital por negligencia
2 (= *state title to*) [+ *territory*] reivindicar; [+ *victory*] atribuirse; [+ *prize*] llevarse; [+ *throne*] reclamar; **neither side can ~ victory in this war** ninguno de los dos bandos puede atribuirse la victoria en esta guerra; **Graf ~ed a fourth Wimbledon title** Graf se llevó su cuarto título de Wimbledon; **~ your prize by ringing the competition hotline** llévese el premio llamando a la línea directa del concurso; **he was too modest to ~ the credit** era demasiado modesto como para atribuirse el mérito; **so far no one has ~ed responsibility for the bomb** hasta ahora nadie ha reivindicado la colocación de de la bomba
3 (= *assert*) **he ~s a 70% success rate** afirma *or* alega que resuelve satisfactoriamente un 70% de los casos; **to ~ that** afirmar que; **they ~ the police opened fire without warning** afirman que la policía abrió fuego sin previo aviso; **I do not ~ that everyone can do this** no estoy diciendo que todo el mundo pueda hacer esto; **he ~s to have seen her** afirma haberla visto; **these products ~ to be environmentally safe** se afirma que estos productos no dañan el medio ambiente
4 (= *require*) [+ *attention*] requerir, exigir; **something else ~ed her attention** otra cosa requirió *or* exigió su atención
5 (= *take*) [+ *life*] cobrarse; **the accident ~ed four lives** el accidente se cobró cuatro vidas
Ⓒ VI (= *make demand*) presentar reclamación; **make sure you ~ within a month of the accident** asegúrese de presentar reclamación antes de un mes desde la fecha del accidente; **to ~ for sth** reclamar (los gastos de) algo; **I ~ed for damage to the carpet after the flood** reclamé los gastos del deterioro de la alfombra tras la inundación
Ⓓ CPD ► **claim form** N (*for benefit*) (impreso *m* de) solicitud *f*; (*for expenses*) impreso *m* de reembolso

claimant ['kleɪmənt] N (*in court*) demandante *mf*; (*Brit*) [*of benefit*] solicitante *mf*; (*to throne*) pretendiente *mf*

clairvoyance [klɛə'vɔɪəns] N clarividencia *f*

clairvoyant(e) [klɛə'vɔɪənt] Ⓐ ADJ clarividente, vidente
Ⓑ N clarividente *mf*, vidente *mf*

clam [klæm] Ⓐ N 1 (*Zool*) almeja *f*
2 (*US**) (= *dollar*) dólar *m*
Ⓑ CPD ► **clam chowder** N (*US*) sopa *f* de almejas

►**clam up*** VI + ADV cerrar el pico*, no decir ni pío

clambake ['klæmbeɪk] N (*US Culin*) merienda *f* en la playa *or* en el campo (*en la que se cocinan y comen almejas*); (*) (= *party*) fiesta *f*

clamber ['klæmbəʳ] Ⓐ N subida *f*
Ⓑ VI trepar, subir gateando (**over** sobre; **up** a)

clammy ['klæmɪ] ADJ (*compar* **clammier**; *superl* **clammiest**) (= *damp*) frío y húmedo; (= *sticky*) pegajoso

clamor ['klæməʳ] N (*US*) = **clamour**

clamorous ['klæmərəs] ADJ clamoroso, vociferante, ruidoso

clamour, **clamor** (*US*) ['klæməʳ] Ⓐ N clamor *m*
Ⓑ VI clamorear, vociferar; **to ~ for sth** clamar algo, pedir algo a voces

clamp [klæmp] Ⓐ N 1 (= *brace*) abrazadera *f*; (*Aut*) (*on parked car*) cepo *m*; (= *laboratory clamp*) grapa *f*; (*on bench*) cárcel *f*
2 (*Agr*) ensilado *m*, montón *m*
Ⓑ VT 1 (= *secure*) (*with brace*) afianzar *or* sujetar con abrazadera; (*in laboratory*) afianzar *or* sujetar con grapa; (*on bench*) afianzar *or* sujetar con cárcel; **he ~ed it in his hand** lo agarró con la mano; **he ~ed his hand down on it** lo sujetó firmemente con la mano
2 [+ *car*] poner un cepo en

►**clamp down** VI + ADV **to ~ down (on)** [+ *tax evasion, crime etc*] poner frenos (a), tomar fuertes medidas (contra)

clampdown ['klæmpdaʊn] N restricción *f* (**on** de), prohibición *f* (**on** en)

clan [klæn] N (*also fig*) clan *m*

clandestine [klæn'destɪn] ADJ clandestino

clandestinely [klæn'destɪnlɪ] ADV clandestinamente

clang [klæŋ] Ⓐ N ruido *m* metálico fuerte
Ⓑ VI sonar mucho, hacer estruendo; **the gate ~ed shut** la puerta se cerró ruidosamente
Ⓒ VT hacer sonar

clanger* ['klæŋəʳ] N (*Brit*) plancha *f* (*Sp**), metedura *f or* (*LAm*) metida *f* de pata*; ♦***IDIOM*** **to drop a ~** meter la pata*, tirarse una plancha (*Sp**)

clangor ['klæŋgəʳ] N (*US*) = **clangour**

clangorous ['klæŋgərəs] ADJ estrepitoso, estruendoso

clangour, **clangor** (*US*) ['klæŋgəʳ] N estruendo *m*

clank [klæŋk] Ⓐ N sonido *m* metálico seco
Ⓑ VI sonar; **the train went ~ing past** el tren pasó con gran estruendo
Ⓒ VT hacer sonar

clannish ['klænɪʃ] ADJ exclusivista, con fuerte sentimiento de tribu

clansman ['klænzmən] N (*pl* **clansmen**) miembro *m* del clan

clanswoman ['klænz,wʊmən] N (*pl* **clanswomen**) miembro *f* del clan

clap¹ [klæp] Ⓐ N 1 (*on shoulder, of the hands*) palmada *f*; **a ~ of thunder** un trueno
2 (= *applause*) aplauso *m*; **to get a ~** recibir un aplauso; **to give sb a ~** dar un aplauso a algn
Ⓑ VT 1 (= *applaud*) [+ *person, play, announce-*

ment] aplaudir; **to ~ one's hands** dar palmadas, batir las palmas; **to ~ sb on the back** dar a algn una palmada en la espalda
2 (= *place*) poner; **he ~ped his hat on** se encasquetó el sombrero; **to ~ a hand over sb's mouth** tapar la boca a algn con la mano; **to ~ eyes on** clavar la vista en; **to ~ sth shut** cerrar algo de golpe; **they ~ped him in prison*** lo metieron en la cárcel
Ⓒ VI aplaudir

clap²*‡ [klæp] N **the ~** (= *disease*) gonorrea *f*

clapboard ['klæpbɔːd] N (*US*) chilla *f*, tablilla *f*

clapped-out* [ˌklæpt'aʊt] ADJ (*Brit*) [*car, bus etc*] desvencijado; [*person*] para el arrastre

clapper ['klæpəʳ] N [*of bell*] badajo *m*; (*Cine*) claqueta *f*; ✦**IDIOM to run like the ~s** (*Brit**) correr como loco

clapperboard ['klæpəˌbɔːd] N (*Cine*) claqueta *f*

clapping ['klæpɪŋ] N (= *applause*) aplausos *mpl*; (= *sound of hands*) palmoteo *m*

claptrap* ['klæptræp] N (*pej*) burradas *fpl*, disparates *mpl*

claque [klæk] N claque *f*

claret ['klærət] N 1 (= *wine*) vino *m* de Burdeos
2 (= *colour*) burdeos *m*

clarification [ˌklærɪfɪ'keɪʃən] N aclaración *f*

clarify ['klærɪfaɪ] VT 1 [+ *statement etc*] aclarar, clarificar
2 [+ *liquid, butter*] clarificar

clarinet [ˌklærɪ'net] N clarinete *m*

clarinettist [ˌklærɪ'netɪst] N clarinetista *mf*

clarion ['klærɪən] Ⓐ N (toque *m* de) trompeta *f*
Ⓑ CPD ► **clarion call** N llamada *f* fuerte y sonora

clarity ['klærɪtɪ] N 1 [*of statement etc*] claridad *f*
2 [*of image, sound*] claridad *f*, nitidez *f*
3 [*of water, glass*] claridad *f*, transparencia *f*; [*of air*] pureza *f*

clash [klæʃ] Ⓐ N 1 (= *noise*) estruendo *m*, fragor *m*; [*of cymbals*] ruido *m* metálico
2 [*of armies, personalities*] choque *m*; (= *conflict*) choque *m*, conflicto *m*; (= *confrontation*) enfrentamiento *m*; [*of interests, opinions*] conflicto *m*; [*of dates, programmes*] coincidencia *f*; [*of colours*] desentono *m*; **a ~ with the police** un choque *or* un enfrentamiento con la policía; **a ~ of wills** un conflicto de voluntades
Ⓑ VT [+ *cymbals, swords*] golpear
Ⓒ VI 1 [*personalities, interests*] oponerse, chocar; [*colours*] desentonar; [*dates, events*] coincidir
2 (= *disagree*) estar en desacuerdo; (= *argue*) pelear; (*Mil*) encontrarse, enfrentarse (**with** con)

clasp [klɑːsp] Ⓐ N 1 [*of brooch, necklace*] cierre *m*; [*of belt etc*] broche *m*; [*of book*] broche *m*, manecilla *f*
2 **with a ~ of the hand** con un apretón de manos
Ⓑ VT 1 (= *fasten*) abrochar
2 (= *take hold of*) agarrar; (= *hold hands*) apretar; **to ~ one's hands (together)** juntar las manos; **to ~ sb's hands** apretar las manos a algn, estrechar las manos de algn
3 (= *embrace*) abrazar; **to ~ sb to one's bosom** estrechar a algn contra el pecho
Ⓒ CPD ► **clasp knife** N navaja *f*

class [klɑːs] Ⓐ N 1 (*gen, Scol, Bio, Sociol*) clase *f*; **the ~ of 82** la promoción del 82; **ruling/middle/working ~** clase *f* dirigente/media/obrera; **first ~** primera clase *f*; **lower ~es** clase *fsing* baja; **upper ~** clase *f* alta
2 (= *category*) categoría *f*; **~ of degree** (*Brit Univ*) *tipo de título universitario según la nota con que se ha obtenido*; **a good ~ (of) novel** una novela de buena calidad; **it's just not in the same ~** no se puede comparar; **in a ~ of one's own** sin par *or* igual; **it's in a ~ by itself** no tiene par *or* igual, es único en su género
3 (= *style*) **to have ~** tener clase
Ⓑ VT clasificar; **to ~ sb as sth** clasificar a algn de algo
Ⓒ ADJ (= *classy*) [*player, actor*] de primera clase
Ⓓ CPD ► **class distinction** N (*Sociol*) diferencia *f* de clase ► **class list** N (*Scol*) lista *f* de clase; (*Univ*) lista *f* de estudiantes aprobados para la licenciatura ► **class society** N (*Pol*) sociedad *f* formada por clases ► **class struggle** N (*Sociol*) lucha *f* de clases ► **class system** N sistema *m* de clases sociales ► **class teacher** N (*Brit*) tutor(a) *m/f* ► **class war(fare)** N = **class struggle**

class-conscious ['klɑːs'kɒnʃəs] ADJ con conciencia de clase

class-consciousness ['klɑːs'kɒnʃəsnɪs] N conciencia *f* de clase

classic ['klæsɪk] Ⓐ ADJ 1 (= *timeless, traditional*) clásico; **she was dressed in a ~ black suit** vestía un clásico traje de chaqueta negro
2 (*) (= *wonderful, memorable*) memorable; (= *hilarious*) genial*; **it was ~** fue genial*; **the film "Casablanca" produced some ~ lines** la película "Casablanca" nos dejó varias frases memorables; **the president came out with a ~ line** el presidente salió con una frase de las que hacen época
Ⓑ N 1 (= *book, play*) clásico *m*; **it is a ~ of its kind** es un clásico en su género
2 **classics** (*Univ*) clásicas *fpl*
3 (*) (= *hilarious remark or event*) **that was a ~!** ¡fue genial!*
Ⓒ CPD ► **classic car** N coche *m* antiguo (*de coleccionista*)

classical ['klæsɪkəl] ADJ [*ballet, style, Greece, Latin*] clásico; [*musician, recording*] de música clásica; **~ music** música *f* clásica; **~ scholar** académico/a *m/f* especializado/a en lenguas clásicas; **~ times** la época clásica

classically ['klæsɪkəlɪ] ADV [*educated, trained*] en la tradición clásica; **a ~ trained pianist** un pianista formado en la tradición clásica *or* con una formación clásica; **she is ~ beautiful** es de una belleza clásica; **the ~ undesirable son-in-law** el típico yerno indeseable

classicism ['klæsɪsɪzəm] N clasicismo *m*

classicist ['klæsɪsɪst] N clasicista *mf*

classifiable ['klæsɪfaɪəbl] ADJ clasificable

classification [ˌklæsɪfɪ'keɪʃən] N clasificación *f*

classified ['klæsɪfaɪd] Ⓐ ADJ (= *secret*) [*document etc*] confidencial, secreto; **~ information** información *f* confidencial, información *f* secreta
Ⓑ N 1 (*Press*) **late night ~** últimas noticias con los resultados del fútbol
2 **classifieds** (*also* **~ advertisements**) anuncios *mpl* por palabras
Ⓒ CPD ► **classified advertisement** N anuncio *m* por palabras ► **classified results** NPL (*Brit Sport*) clasificación *fsing* ► **classified section** N (*Press*) sección *f* de anuncios por palabras

classify ['klæsɪfaɪ] VT 1 (= *sort*) clasificar (**in, into** en); **to ~ sth under the letter B** clasificar algo bajo la letra B
2 (= *restrict access to*) [+ *information*] clasificar como secreto

classism ['klɑːsɪzəm] N clasismo *m*

classist ['klɑːsɪst] ADJ clasista

classless ['klɑːslɪs] ADJ [*society*] sin clases

classmate ['klɑːsmeɪt] N (*Brit*) compañero/a *m/f* de clase, condiscípulo/a *m/f*

classroom ['klɑːsrʊm] N aula *f*, clase *f*

classy* ['klɑːsɪ] ADJ (*compar* **classier**, *superl* **classiest**) elegante, de buen tono

clatter ['klætəʳ] Ⓐ N (= *loud noise*) estruendo *m*; [*of plates*] estrépito *m*; [*of hooves*] trápala *f*; [*of train*] triquitraque *m*; (= *hammering*) martilleo *m*
Ⓑ VI [*metal object etc*] hacer estrépito, hacer estruendo; [*hooves*] trapalear; **to ~ in/out** entrar/salir estrepitosamente; **to come ~ing down** caer ruidosamente; **to ~ down the stairs** bajar ruidosamente la escalera

Claudius ['klɔːdɪəs] N Claudio

clause [klɔːz] N (*Ling*) oración *f*; (*in contract, law*) cláusula *f*; (*in will*) disposición *f*

claustrophobia [ˌklɔːstrə'fəʊbɪə] N claustrofobia *f*

claustrophobic [ˌklɔːstrə'fəʊbɪk] Ⓐ ADJ claustrofóbico
Ⓑ N *persona que padece de claustrofobia*

clavichord ['klævɪkɔːd] N clavicordio *m*

clavicle ['klævɪkl] N clavícula *f*

claw [klɔː] Ⓐ N 1 (*Zool*) [*of cat, bird etc*] garra *f*; [*of lobster*] pinza *f*
2 (*Tech*) garfio *m*, gancho *m*
3 **claws*** (= *fingers*) dedos *mpl*, mano *fsing*; **to get one's ~s into sb** (= *attack*) atacar con rencor a algn; (= *dominate*) dominar a algn; **to get one's ~s on** agarrarse de *or* a; **get your ~s off that!** ¡fuera las manos!; **to show one's ~s** sacar las uñas
Ⓑ VT 1 (= *scratch*) arañar; (= *tear*) desgarrar; **to ~ sth to shreds** desgarrar algo completamente, hacer algo trizas
2 **to ~ one's way somewhere** abrirse camino a toda costa; **to ~ one's way to the top** (*fig*) abrirse paso hasta la cima a toda costa
Ⓒ CPD ► **claw hammer** N martillo *m* de orejas

►**claw at** VI + PREP (= *scratch*) arañar; (= *tear*) desgarrar

►**claw back** VT + ADV (*fig*) volver a tomar, tomar otra vez para sí

clawback ['klɔːbæk] N (*Econ*) *desgravación fiscal obtenida por devolución de impuestos*

clay [kleɪ] Ⓐ N arcilla *f*, barro *m*
Ⓑ CPD ► **clay court** N (*Tennis*) pista *f* de tierra batida ► **clay pigeon** N plato *m* de barro; (*US*) (*fig*) (= *victim*) víctima *f* ► **clay pigeon shooting** N tiro *m* al plato, tiro *m* al pichón ► **clay pipe** N pipa *f* de cerámica ► **clay pit** N pozo *m* de arcilla

clayey ['kleɪɪ] ADJ arcilloso

clean [kliːn] Ⓐ ADJ (*compar* **cleaner**, *superl* **cleanest**) 1 (= *not dirty*) [*clothes, sheets, floor, face*] limpio; [*air, water*] limpio, puro; **he washed the floor ~** fregó el suelo; **the rain washed the streets ~** la lluvia limpió las calles; **to come ~** (*lit*) quedar limpio; (*fig*) (*) confesarlo todo; **to come ~ about sth*** confesar algo; **to have ~ hands** (*lit, fig*) tener las manos limpias; **to wipe sth ~** limpiar algo; ✦**IDIOMS to make a ~ breast of it** confesarlo todo; **to make a ~ sweep** (= *complete change*) hacer tabla rasa; (= *win everything*) arrasar; **to make a ~ sweep of sth** (*of prizes, awards*) arrasar con algo; **to make a ~ sweep of the votes** acaparar todos los votos, barrer; **as ~ as a whistle** *or* **new pin*** limpio como los chorros del oro, limpio como la patena
2 (= *fresh*) [*smell*] a limpio; [*taste*] refrescante
3 (= *new, unused*) [*sheet of paper, page*] en blanco, en limpio; **to make a ~ copy** hacer una copia en limpio

[4] (= *not indecent*) [*joke*] inocente; [*film, life*] decente; **keep it ~!** ¡no seas indecente!; **~ living** vida *f* sana
[5] (= *smooth, even*) [*movement*] fluido; [*shot*] certero; [*cut*] limpio; [*sound*] nítido, claro; [*features, outline*] nítido, bien definido; **a ~ break** (*Med*) una fractura limpia; **a ~ break with the totalitarian past** una ruptura radical con el pasado totalitario; **to make a ~ break** cortar por lo sano; **I need (to make) a ~ break with the past** necesito romper con el pasado totalmente
[6] (= *fair*) [*fight, game, match*] limpio; [*player*] que juega limpio
[7] (= *untarnished*) [*image, reputation*] bueno, impecable; **they gave him a ~ bill of health** le declararon en perfecto estado de salud; **a ~ driving licence** un carnet de conducir sin infracciones; **to have a ~ record** (*gen*) tener un historial limpio; (*no criminal record*) no tener antecedentes penales; **we have a ~ safety record** nuestro historial de seguridad está limpio *or* no registra incidentes
[8] (= *environmentally friendly*) [*machine, substance, energy*] no contaminante
[9] (*Nuclear Physics*) (= *uncontaminated*) [*area, person, object*] no contaminado
[10] (= *ritually pure*) [*animal*] puro
[11] (= *trouble-free*) [*operation, job, getaway*] sin problemas
[12] (‡) (= *innocent*) **they can't touch me, I'm ~** no me pueden hacer nada, tengo las manos limpias*
[13] (‡) (= *not in possession of drugs, weapon, stolen property*) **he's ~** no lleva nada encima; **his room was ~** no encontraron nada en su habitación
Ⓑ ADV [1] (*) (= *completely*) **he ~ forgot** lo olvidó por completo; **he got ~ away** se escapó sin dejar rastro; **it went ~ through the window** pasó limpiamente por la ventana; **I'm ~ out of them** no me queda ni uno; **he jumped ~ over the fence** saltó la valla limpiamente
[2] (= *fairly*) **to fight/play ~** luchar/jugar limpio
Ⓒ N limpieza *f*, aseo *m* (*LAm*); (= *wash*) lavado *m*; **the windows could do with a ~** no estaría de más limpiar las ventanas; **to give sth a ~** limpiar algo; **to give sth a quick ~** dar una pasada (rápida) a algo; **to give sth a good ~** limpiar algo bien
Ⓓ VT [+ *room, carpet, windows, shoes*] limpiar; [+ *vegetables, clothes*] lavar; [+ *car*] lavar, limpiar; [+ *blackboard*] borrar; [+ *wound, cut*] desinfectar; **to ~ one's teeth** lavarse los dientes
Ⓔ VI [1] (*around the house*) limpiar; **her mother cooked and ~ed all day** su madre se pasaba el día cocinando y limpiando
[2] (= *be cleaned*) **that floor ~s easily** este suelo es muy fácil de limpiar
Ⓕ CPD ► **clean sweep** N **to make a ~ sweep of sth** (*esp Sport*) arrasar con algo, barrer con algo

►**clean down** VT + ADV limpiar

►**clean off** VT + ADV [+ *dirt, rust*] limpiar

►**clean out** VT + ADV [1] [+ *room, cupboard*] vaciar; **to ~ out a box** limpiar (el interior de) una caja
[2] (*) (*fig*) (= *leave penniless*) dejar limpio/a*, dejar pelado/a*; (*in robbery*) limpiar*; **the burglars came back to ~ me out again** los ladrones volvieron para limpiarme (la casa) de nuevo; **we were ~ed out** nos dejaron sin blanca

►**clean up** Ⓐ VT + ADV [1] [+ *room, mess*] limpiar, asear; **to ~ o.s. up** lavarse, ponerse decente
[2] (*fig*) [+ *city, television etc*] limpiar, quitar lo indecente de; [+ *act, play*] suprimir los pasajes indecentes de
Ⓑ VI + ADV [1] (= *tidy*) limpiar; **to ~ up after a party** limpiar después de una fiesta; **to ~ up after sb** limpiar lo que ha dejado *or* ensuciado otro
[2] (*) (= *make profit*) hacer mucho dinero (**on** con); **he ~ed up on that deal** hizo mucho dinero con ese negocio

clean-break divorce [ˌkliːnˌbreɪkdɪˈvɔːs] N *divorcio en el que se renuncia a la pensión alimenticia por un bien que se puede capitalizar*

clean-cut [ˈkliːnˈkʌt] ADJ [1] (= *clearly outlined*) claro, bien definido; [*outline*] nítido
[2] [*person*] de buen parecer; (= *smart*) de aspecto elegante

cleaner [ˈkliːnəʳ] N [1] (= *man*) encargado *m* de la limpieza; (= *woman*) encargada *f* de la limpieza, asistenta *f*; **~'s (shop)** tintorería *f*, lavandería *f*; ✦**IDIOM to take sb to the ~'s**: **we'll take them to the ~'s*** les dejaremos sin blanca*, les dejaremos limpios*; *see also* **vacuum**
[2] (= *substance*) producto *m* de limpieza

cleaning [ˈkliːnɪŋ] Ⓐ N limpieza *f*, limpia *f* (*LAm*); **to do the ~** hacer la limpieza
Ⓑ CPD ► **cleaning fluid** N líquido *m* de limpieza ► **cleaning lady, cleaning woman** N señora *f* de la limpieza

clean-limbed [ˌkliːnˈlɪmd] ADJ bien proporcionado

cleanliness [ˈklenlɪnɪs] N limpieza *f*; **the importance of personal ~** la importancia del aseo *or* de la higiene personal; ✦**PROV ~ is next to godliness** la limpieza lo es todo

clean-living [ˌkliːnˈlɪvɪŋ] ADJ de vida sana

cleanly[1] [ˈkliːnlɪ] ADV [1] (= *without polluting*) [*burn, operate*] de forma limpia, sin contaminar
[2] (= *neatly*) [*cut, break*] limpiamente; [*hit, catch*] con habilidad, con destreza
[3] (= *fairly*) [*play, fight*] limpiamente

cleanly[2] [ˈklenlɪ] ADJ [*person, animal*] limpio, aseado

cleanness [ˈkliːnnɪs] N [1] [*of clothes, sheets etc*] limpieza *f*; [*of air, water*] pureza *f*
[2] (= *smoothness*) [*of cut, fracture*] limpieza *f*; [*of outline, features*] nitidez *f*; [*of movement*] fluidez *f*
[3] (= *fairness*) [*of fight, game*] limpieza *f*

clean-out [ˈkliːnaʊt] N limpieza *f*

cleanse [klenz] VT [+ *skin*] limpiar (**of** de); (*fig*) [+ *soul etc*] purificar

cleanser [ˈklenzəʳ] N (= *detergent*) detergente *m*; (= *disinfectant*) desinfectante *m*; (= *cosmetic*) leche *f or* crema *f* limpiadora

clean-shaven [ˈkliːnˈʃeɪvn] ADJ (= *beardless*) sin barba ni bigote, totalmente afeitado; (= *smooth-faced*) lampiño

cleansing [ˈklenzɪŋ] Ⓐ ADJ (*for complexion*) limpiador; (*fig*) purificador
Ⓑ N limpieza *f*
Ⓒ CPD ► **cleansing cream** N crema *f* desmaquilladora ► **cleansing department** N departamento *m* de limpieza ► **cleansing lotion** N loción *f* limpiadora

clean-up [ˈkliːnʌp] N limpia *f*, limpieza *f*

▼**clear** [klɪəʳ] Ⓐ ADJ (*compar* **clearer**; *superl* **clearest**) [1] (= *unambiguous*) [*meaning, explanation*] claro; **a ~ case of murder** un caso claro de homicidio; **now let's get this ~ ...** vamos a dejar esto claro ...; **to make it ~ that ...** dejar claro *or* bien sentado que ...; **to make o.s. ~** explicarse claramente; **do I make myself ~?** ¿me explico bien?; **he's a ~ thinker** tiene la mente lúcida *or* despejada
[2] (= *obvious*) [*motive, consequence*] claro, evidente; **it is (absolutely) ~ to me that ...** no me cabe (la menor) duda de que ...; **it became ~ that ...** empezó a verse claro que ...; **it's not ~ whether ...** no está claro si ...; ✦**IDIOMS as ~ as crystal** más claro que el agua; **as ~ as day** más claro que el sol; **as ~ as mud*** nada claro
[3] (= *certain*) [*understanding, proof*] seguro, cierto; **he was perfectly ~ that he did not intend to go** dijo claramente *or* tajantemente que no pensaba ir; **are we ~ that we want this?** ¿estamos seguros de que queremos esto?; **I'm not very ~ about this** no tengo una idea muy clara de esto; **I'm not ~ whether ...** no tengo claro si ...
[4] (= *transparent*) [*water, glass*] claro, transparente; **a ~ soup** una sopa clara
[5] [*sky, weather*] despejado; [*air*] puro; **on a ~ day** en un día despejado
[6] (= *bright*) [*light, colour*] claro; **~ blue eyes** ojos azul claro; *see also* **light**[1] **A1**
[7] [*photograph, outline*] claro, preciso; [*complexion*] terso; **to have a ~ head** tener la cabeza despejada
[8] (= *distinct*) [*sound, impression, voice*] claro; ✦**IDIOM as ~ as a bell**: **I could hear his voice as ~ as a bell** oía su voz como si estuviera a mi lado, oía su voz con toda claridad
[9] (= *unobstructed*) [*road, space*] libre, despejado; **all ~!** ¡vía libre!, ¡adelante!; **to get a ~ look at sb/sth** poder ver algn/algo bien; **to be ~ of sth** (= *free of*) estar libre de algo; (= *away from*) estar lejos de algo; **we had a ~ view** teníamos una buena vista, se veía bien
[10] (= *untroubled*) [*conscience*] limpio, tranquilo
[11] (*after deductions*) **a ~ profit** una ganancia neta; **£3 ~ profit** una ganancia neta de 3 libras
[12] **a ~ majority** una mayoría absoluta; **to win by a ~ margin** ganar por un amplio margen; **a ~ winner** un ganador absoluto
[13] (= *complete*) **three ~ days** tres días enteros
[14] (= *without commitments*) [*day, afternoon*] libre; [*diary*] despejado
Ⓑ ADV [1] *see* **loud 2**
[2] (= *completely*) **he jumped ~ across the river** atravesó el río limpiamente de un salto; **you could hear it ~ across the valley** se oía claramente desde el otro lado del valle
[3] (= *free*) **to get ~ away** escaparse sin dejar rastro alguno; **to get ~ of** (= *get rid of*) deshacerse de; **when we get ~ of London** (= *away from*) cuando estemos fuera de Londres; **to keep ~ of sb/sth**: **keep ~ of the wall** no te acerques a la pared; **I decided to keep ~ of him** decidí evitarle; **keep ~ of my daughter!** ¡no te acerques a mi hija!, ¡mantente alejado de mi hija!; **to stand ~ of sth** mantenerse apartado de algo; **stand ~ of the doors!** ¡apártense de las puertas!
[4] (*Brit Sport*) (= *ahead*) **to be seven metres/seconds/points ~ of sb** estar siete metros/segundos/puntos por delante de algn; *see also* **steer**[1]
[5] (= *net*) **he'll get £250 ~** sacará 250 libras netas
[6] (*esp US*) **~ to sth** (= *as far as*) hasta algo; **they went ~ to Mexico** llegaron hasta México
Ⓒ N [1] **to be in the ~** (= *out of debt*) estar libre de deudas; (= *free of suspicion*) quedar fuera de toda sospecha; (= *free of danger*) estar fuera de peligro
[2] **message in ~** mensaje *m* no cifrado
Ⓓ VT [1] (= *remove obstacles etc from*) [+ *place,*

➤ LANGUAGE IN USE: **clear A2** 15.1, 16.1, 26.3

surface] despejar; [+ *road, railway track*] dejar libre, despejar; [+ *site*] desmontar; [+ *woodland*] despejar, desbrozar; [+ *court, hall*] desocupar, desalojar (de público *etc*); [+ *pipe*] desatascar; [+ *postbox*] recoger las cartas de; **to ~ one's conscience** descargar la conciencia; **to ~ one's head** despejar la cabeza; **to ~ sth of sth** despejar algo de algo; **to ~ a space for sth/sb** hacer sitio para algo/algn; **to ~ the table** recoger *or* quitar la mesa; **to ~ one's throat** carraspear, aclararse la voz; **to ~ the way for sth** (*fig*) dejar el camino libre para algo; **✦IDIOM to ~ the air** (= *clarify things*) aclarar las cosas; (= *ease tensions*) relajar el ambiente

2 [+ *liquid*] aclarar, clarificar; (*Med*) [+ *blood*] purificar

3 (*Sport*) [+ *ball*] despejar

4 (= *get over*) [+ *fence etc*] salvar, saltar por encima de; (= *get past*) [+ *rocks etc*] pasar sin tocar; **the plane just ~ed the roof** el avión no tocó el tejado por poco, el avión pasó casi rozando el tejado; **to ~ two metres** [*jumper*] saltar dos metros; **this part has to ~ that by at least one centimetre** entre esta pieza y aquélla tiene que haber un espacio de un centímetro al menos

5 (= *declare innocent etc*) [+ *person*] absolver, probar la inocencia de; **he was ~ed of murder** fue absuelto de asesinato; **to ~ o.s. of a charge** probar su inocencia de una acusación

6 (= *authorize*) **you will have to be ~ed by Security** será preciso que le acredite la Seguridad; **the plan will have to be ~ed with the director** el plan tendrá que ser aprobado por el director

7 **to ~ a cheque** (= *accept*) aceptar *or* dar el visto bueno a un cheque; (= *double check*) compensar un cheque

8 (*Comm etc*) [+ *debt*] liquidar, saldar; [+ *profit*] sacar (una ganancia de); [+ *goods etc*] liquidar; **he ~ed £50 on the deal** sacó 50 libras del negocio; **he ~s £250 a week** se saca 250 libras a la semana; **we have just about ~ed our costs** nos ha llegado justo para cubrir los gastos; **"half-price to clear"** "liquidación a mitad de precio"

9 (*Comput*) despejar

Ⓔ VI 1 (= *improve*) [*weather*] (*also* **~ up**) despejarse; [*sky*] despejarse; [*fog*] disiparse

2 [*liquid*] aclararse, clarificarse

3 [*cheque*] ser compensado

4 (*Sport*) despejar

Ⓕ CPD ► **clear round** N (*Showjumping*) ronda *f* sin penalizaciones

►**clear away** Ⓐ VT + ADV [+ *things, clothes etc*] quitar (de en medio); [+ *dishes*] retirar

Ⓑ VI + ADV 1 (= *clear the table*) quitar los platos, quitar la mesa

2 [*mist*] disiparse

►**clear off** Ⓐ VT + ADV [+ *debt*] liquidar, saldar

Ⓑ VI + ADV (*) (= *leave*) largarse*, mandarse mudar (*LAm*); **~ off!** ¡lárgate!*, ¡fuera de aquí!

►**clear out** Ⓐ VT + ADV [+ *room*] ordenar y tirar los trastos de; [+ *cupboard*] vaciar; [+ *objects*] quitar; **he ~ed everyone out of the room** hizo salir a todo el mundo de la habitación; **he ~ed everything out of the room** despejó la habitación de cosas

Ⓑ VI + ADV = **clear off B**

►**clear up** Ⓐ VT + ADV 1 (= *resolve*) [+ *matter, difficulty*] aclarar; [+ *mystery, crime*] resolver, esclarecer; [+ *doubt*] resolver, aclarar, disipar

2 (= *tidy*) [+ *room, books, toys*] ordenar

Ⓑ VI + ADV 1 [*weather*] despejarse

2 [*illness*] curarse

3 (= *tidy up*) ponerlo todo en orden, ordenar

clearance ['klɪərəns] Ⓐ N 1 (= *act of clearing*) [*of road etc*] despeje *m*; [*of land*] desmonte *m*, roza *f*

2 (= *height, width etc*) margen *m* (*de altura, anchura etc*)

3 (= *authorization*) (*by customs*) despacho *m* de aduana; (*by security*) acreditación *f*; (*Fin*) compensación *f*; **~ for take-off** (*Aer*) pista libre para despegar

4 (*Ftbl*) despeje *m*

Ⓑ CPD ► **clearance sale** N liquidación *f*, realización *f* (*LAm*)

clear-cut ['klɪə'kʌt] ADJ [*decision, victory*] claro; [*statement*] sin ambages

clear-eyed [,klɪər'aɪd] ADJ de ojos claros; (*fig*) clarividente

clear-headed ['klɪə'hedɪd] ADJ lúcido, de mente despejada

clear-headedness ['klɪə'hedɪdnɪs] N lucidez *f*

clearing ['klɪərɪŋ] Ⓐ N 1 (*in wood*) claro *m*

2 (*Fin*) liquidación *f*

Ⓑ CPD ► **clearing account** N (*Fin*) cuenta *f* de compensación ► **clearing bank** N (*Brit Fin*) banco *m* central ► **clearing house** N (*Fin*) cámara *f* de compensación

clearly ['klɪəlɪ] ADV 1 (= *unambiguously*) [*define, state, forbid*] claramente

2 (= *rationally*) [*think*] con claridad

3 (= *distinctly*) [*see, speak, hear*] claramente, con claridad; **~ visible** claramente visible; **~ marked** marcado claramente

4 (= *obviously*) evidentemente, obviamente; **~, the police cannot break the law in order to enforce it** evidentemente *or* obviamente la policía no puede ir contra la ley para aplicarla; **a very pleasant man, educated and ~ intelligent** un hombre muy agradable, educado y obviamente inteligente; **he was ~ not convinced** estaba claro *or* era evidente que no estaba convencido; **the owner of the house was ~ not expecting us** estaba claro *or* era evidente que el dueño de la casa no nos esperaba

clearness ['klɪənɪs] N claridad *f*

clear-out ['klɪəraʊt] N **to have a good ~** limpiarlo todo, despejarlo todo

clear-sighted ['klɪə'saɪtɪd] ADJ clarividente, perspicaz

clear-sightedness ['klɪə'saɪtɪdnɪs] N clarividencia *f*, perspicacia *f*

clear-up rate ['klɪə'rʌpreɪt] N (*Police*) *ratio de casos resueltos por número de denuncias*

clearway ['klɪəweɪ] N (*Brit*) carretera *f* en la que está prohibido parar

cleat [kli:t] N abrazadera *f*, listón *m*, fiador *m*

cleavage ['kli:vɪdʒ] N 1 (= *division, split*) escisión *f*, división *f*

2 [*of woman*] escote *m*

cleave[1] [kli:v] (*pt* **clove, cleft**; *pp* **cloven, cleft**) VT (= *split*) partir; [+ *water*] surcar

cleave[2] [kli:v] VI **to ~ to** adherirse a, no separarse de; **to ~ together** ser inseparables

cleaver ['kli:vər] N cuchilla *f* de carnicero

clef [klef] N (*Mus*) clave *f*

cleft [kleft] Ⓐ PT, PP *of* **cleave**[1]

Ⓑ ADJ **~ chin** barbilla *f* partida; **✦IDIOM to be in a ~ stick** estar entre la espada y la pared

Ⓒ N (*in rock*) grieta *f*, hendidura *f*; (*in chin*) partición *f*

Ⓓ CPD ► **cleft palate** N (*Med*) fisura *f* del paladar

cleg [kleg] N tábano *m*

clematis ['klemətɪs] N clemátide *f*

clemency ['klemənsɪ] N clemencia *f*

Clement ['klemənt] N Clemente

clement ['klemənt] ADJ clemente, benigno

clementine ['kleməntaɪn] N clementina *f*

clench [klentʃ] VT [+ *teeth*] apretar; [+ *fist*] cerrar; **to ~ sth in one's hands** apretar algo en las manos; **the ~ed fist** el puño cerrado

Cleopatra [,kli:ə'pætrə] N Cleopatra

clerestory ['klɪə,stɔ:rɪ] N triforio *m*

clergy ['klɜ:dʒɪ] NPL clero *m*

clergyman ['klɜ:dʒɪmən] N (*pl* **clergymen**) clérigo *m*; (*Anglican*) pastor *m* anglicano; (*Protestant*) pastor *m* protestante

clergywoman ['klɜ:dʒɪ,wʊmən] N (*pl* **clergywomen**) (*Anglican*) pastora *f* anglicana; (*Protestant*) pastora *f* protestante

cleric ['klerɪk] N eclesiástico *m*, clérigo *m*

clerical ['klerɪkəl] ADJ 1 (*Comm*) [*job*] de oficina; **~ error** error *m* de copia; **~ grades** (*Civil Service etc*) oficinistas *mpl*; **~ staff** personal *m* de oficina; **~ work** trabajo *m* de oficina; **~ worker** oficinista *mf*

2 (*Rel*) clerical; **~ collar** alzacuello(s) *m*

clericalism ['klerɪkə,lɪzəm] N clericalismo *m*

clerihew ['klerɪhju:] N *estrofa inglesa de cuatro versos, de carácter festivo*

clerk [klɑ:k, (*US*) klɜ:k] Ⓐ N 1 (*Comm*) oficinista *mf*, empleado/a *m/f*; (*in civil service*) funcionario/a *m/f*; (*in bank*) empleado/a *m/f*; (*in hotel*) recepcionista *mf*; (*Jur*) escribano *m*; *see also* **town B**

2 (*US*) (= *shop assistant*) dependiente/a *m/f*, vendedor(a) *m/f*

3 (*Rel*††) clérigo *m*

Ⓑ VI (*US*) trabajar como dependiente

Ⓒ CPD ► **clerk of works** N (*Brit Constr*) maestro/a *m/f* de obras

clerkship ['klɑ:kʃɪp, (*US*) 'klɜ:kʃɪp] N empleo *m* de oficinista; (*Jur*) escribanía *f*

clever ['klevər] ADJ (*compar* **cleverer**; *superl* **cleverest**) 1 (= *intelligent*) [*person*] inteligente, listo; **~ girl!** ¡qué chica más lista!; **that was ~ of you** ¡qué listo eres!; **that wasn't very ~, was it?*** eso ha sido una metedura de pata ¿no te parece?*

2 (= *skilful*) [*craftsman, sportsman*] hábil, habilidoso; [*piece of work, action*] hábil, ingenioso; **he is very ~ with his hands** es muy mañoso, es muy hábil *or* habilidoso con las manos; **she is very ~ with cars** entiende de coches, tiene mano para los coches; **to be ~ at sth** tener aptitud para algo

3 (= *ingenious*) [*book, idea, design*] ingenioso

4 (*often pej*) (= *smart, astute*) [*politician, lawyer, criminal*] astuto, listo; [*move, approach, plan*] astuto, ingenioso; [*trick, hoax, technique, advertising*] ingenioso; **he was too ~ for us** fue más listo que nosotros; **he did some ~ book-keeping** hizo la contabilidad con bastante maña; **don't get ~ (with me)!*** ¡no te hagas el listo (conmigo)!; **to be too ~ by half*** pasarse de listo; **✦IDIOMS ~ Dick** (*Brit**) ◊ **~ clogs** (*Brit**) sabelotodo *mf inv*, listorro/a* *m/f*; *see also* **half 1**

clever-clever* ['klevə,klevər] ADJ sabihondo; **he's very ~** es un siete ciencias

cleverly ['klevəlɪ] ADV 1 (= *intelligently*) [*deduce, work out*] de forma inteligente, con inteligencia; **she ~ worked out the answer** supo averiguar la respuesta de forma inteligente *or* con inteligencia

2 (= *skilfully*) hábilmente, ingeniosamente; **the photographer ~ framed the shot with trees** el fotógrafo encuadró hábilmente *or* ingeniosamente la fotografía entre árboles; **~ constructed** ingeniosamente construido; **it is ~ designed** tiene un diseño ingenioso

3 (*often pej*) (= *astutely*) [*avoid, plan, disguise*] astutamente, con maña

cleverness ['klevənɪs] N 1 (= *intelligence*) inteligencia *f*
2 (= *skill*) habilidad *f*
3 (= *ingenuity*) ingenio *m*
4 (= *astuteness*) [*of person*] astucia *f*, maña *f*; [*of trick, technique, plan*] lo ingenioso

clew [klu:] N (*US*) = **clue**

cliché ['kli:ʃeɪ] N cliché *m*, tópico *m*

cliched, clichéd ['kli:ʃeɪd] ADJ [*image, view, argument*] manido, muy visto; [*song*] de siempre

click [klɪk] Ⓐ N [*of camera etc*] golpecito *m* seco, clic *m*; [*of heels*] taconeo *m*; [*of tongue*] chasquido *m*; [*of gun*] piñoneo *m*; [*of typewriter etc*] tecleo *m*
Ⓑ VT [+ *tongue*] chasquear; (*Comput*) hacer click en; **to ~ one's heels** dar un taconazo
Ⓒ VI 1 [*camera etc*] hacer clic; [*gun*] piñonear; [*typewriter etc*] teclear; **the door ~ed shut** la puerta se cerró con un golpecito seco
2 (*) (= *be understood*) quedar claro/a; **it didn't ~ with me until …** no caí en la cuenta hasta (que) …; **suddenly it all ~ed (into place)** de pronto, todo encajaba (en su sitio)
3 (*) (= *be a success*) [*product, invention*] ser un éxito; [*two people*] congeniar, gustarse inmediatamente; **to ~ with sb** congeniar *or* conectar con algn
4 (*Comput*) hacer click; **to ~ on an icon** hacer click en un icono

clickable ['klɪkəbl] (*Comput*) cliqueable

clicking ['klɪkɪŋ] N chasquido *m*

client ['klaɪənt] Ⓐ N cliente/a *m/f*; **my ~** (*in court*) mi defendido
Ⓑ CPD ► **client state** N (*Pol*) estado *m* satélite, estado *m* cliente

clientele [,kli:ɑ̃:n'tel] N clientela *f*

cliff [klɪf] Ⓐ N (= *sea cliff*) acantilado *m*; [*of mountain etc*] risco *m*, precipicio *m*
Ⓑ CPD ► **cliff dweller*** N (*US*) (*fig*) *persona que habita en un bloque*

cliffhanger ['klɪf,hæŋəʳ] N (= *film*) película *f* melodramática, película *f* de suspense; **the match was a real ~** el partido fue un suspense hasta el último momento

cliff-hanging ['klɪf,hæŋɪŋ] ADJ muy emocionante (por su final dudoso y apasionante), que tiene a todos pendientes de su resultado; [*drama*] de suspense

clifftop ['klɪftɒp] Ⓐ N lo alto de un acantilado; **I have a beautiful house on a ~** tengo una casa hermosa encima de un acantilado
Ⓑ ADJ en *or* por lo alto de un acantilado; **a ~ walk** un paseo por el acantilado

climacteric [klaɪ'mæktərɪk] Ⓐ ADJ climactérico
Ⓑ N período *m* climactérico

climactic [klaɪ'mæktɪk] ADJ culminante

climate ['klaɪmɪt] Ⓐ N clima *m*; (*fig*) ambiente *m*; **the ~ of opinion** (*fig*) la opinión general
Ⓑ CPD ► **climate change** N cambio *m* climático

climatic [klaɪ'mætɪk] ADJ climático

climatological [,klaɪmətə'lɒdʒɪkəl] ADJ climatológico

climatologist [,klaɪmə'tɒlədʒɪst] N climatólogo/a *m/f*

climatology [,klaɪmə'tɒlədʒɪ] N climatología *f*

climax ['klaɪmæks] Ⓐ N 1 (= *high point*) punto *m* culminante, apogeo *m*; [*of play etc*] clímax *m inv*; **to reach a ~** llegar a su punto álgido, alcanzar una cima de intensidad
2 (= *sexual climax*) orgasmo *m*
Ⓑ VI 1 (= *reach high point*) llegar a un *or* su clímax
2 (= *achieve orgasm*) tener un orgasmo

climb [klaɪm] Ⓐ N (*gen*) subida *f*, ascenso *m*; [*of mountain*] escalada *f*; (*fig*) ascenso *m*; **it was a stiff ~** la subida fue penosa
Ⓑ VT (*also* **~ up**) [+ *tree, ladder etc*] trepar, subir a; [+ *staircase*] subir (por); [+ *mountain*] escalar; [+ *cliff*] trepar por; [+ *wall*] trepar (a); **to ~ a rope** trepar por una cuerda
Ⓒ VI 1 [*person, plant*] trepar, subir; **to ~ along a ledge** subir por un saliente; **to ~ over a wall** franquear *or* saltar una tapia; **to ~ to power** (*fig*) subir al poder
2 [*road*] ascender; [*plane*] elevarse, remontar el vuelo; [*price, sun*] subir; **the path ~s higher yet** la senda llega aún más arriba

► **climb down** Ⓐ VI + PREP [+ *tree etc*] bajar; **to ~ down a cliff** bajar por un precipicio Ⓑ VI + ADV 1 [*person*] (*from tree etc*) bajar
2 (*fig*) rendirse; (= *retract statement etc*) desdecirse, retractarse

► **climb into** VI + PREP **to ~ into an aircraft** subir a un avión; **to ~ into a tree** trepar a un árbol

► **climb out** VI + ADV salir trepando

► **climb out of** VI + PREP salir trepando de

► **climb up** Ⓐ VI + PREP **to ~ up a rope** trepar por una cuerda; **to ~ up a cliff** trepar por un precipicio
Ⓑ VI + ADV subir, trepar

climbdown ['klaɪmdaʊn] N vuelta *f* atrás, retroceso *m*

climber ['klaɪməʳ] N 1 (= *mountaineer*) montañista *mf*, alpinista *mf*, andinista *mf* (*LAm*)
2 (*Bot*) trepadora *f*, enredadera *f*
3 (*fig*) (*also* **social ~**) arribista *mf*, trepador(a) *m/f*

climbing ['klaɪmɪŋ] Ⓐ N (= *rock climbing*) montañismo *m*, alpinismo *m*, andinismo *m* (*LAm*); **to go ~** hacer montañismo *or* alpinismo, ir de escalada Ⓑ CPD ► **climbing frame** N *estructura metálica en la cual los niños juegan trepando* ► **climbing irons** NPL garfios *mpl*

clime [klaɪm] N (*liter*) (= *climate*) clima *m*; (= *country*) región *f*; **in warmer/sunnier ~s** en tierras *or* regiones más cálidas/soleadas; **he went off to foreign ~s** se marchó a tierras extranjeras

clinch [klɪntʃ] Ⓐ N 1 (*Boxing*) clinch *m*
2 (‡) (= *embrace*) abrazo *m*; **in a ~** abrazados, agarrados (*LAm*); **to go into a ~** abrazarse, agarrarse (*LAm*)
Ⓑ VT 1 (= *secure*) afianzar; [+ *nail*] remachar, roblar
2 (= *settle decisively*) [+ *deal*] cerrar, firmar; [+ *argument*] remachar, terminar; [+ *agreement*] cerrar; **to ~ matters** para acabar de remacharlo; **that ~es it** está decidido, ni una palabra más

clincher* ['klɪntʃəʳ] N **that was the ~** eso fue el punto clave, eso fue el argumento irrebatible

clinching ['klɪntʃɪŋ] ADJ [*argument*] decisivo, irrebatible

cling [klɪŋ] (*pt, pp* **clung**) VI 1 (= *hold on*) (*to person*) pegarse (**to** a); (*affectionately*) agarrarse, aferrarse (**to** a); (*to rope*) agarrarse (**to** a, de); (*to belief, opinion*) aferrarse, seguir fiel (**to** a); **they clung to one another** no se desprendían de su abrazo
2 (= *stick*) [*clothes*] (*to skin*) pegarse (**to** a); **a dress that ~s to the figure** un vestido que se pega al cuerpo; **the smell clung to her clothes** la ropa se quedó impregnada del olor
3 (= *stay close*) (*to friend, mother etc*) no separarse (**to** de); **to ~ together** (*fig*) no separarse (ni un momento)

Clingfilm® ['klɪŋfɪlm] N film *m* adherente (para envolver alimentos)

clinging ['klɪŋɪŋ] ADJ 1 (*pej*) (= *overdependent*) [*person*] pegajoso; **~ vine** (*US*) (*fig*) lapa* *mf*
2 [*dress*] ceñido
3 [*odour*] tenaz

clingwrap ['klɪŋræp] N = **Clingfilm**

clingy* ['klɪŋɪ] ADJ 1 [*person*] pegajoso
2 [*clothes*] ceñido

clinic ['klɪnɪk] N (*in NHS hospital*) consultorio *m*; (= *private hospital*) clínica *f*; (*for guidance*) consultorio *m*

clinical ['klɪnɪkəl] Ⓐ ADJ 1 (*Med*) clínico
2 (= *unemotional, cool*) frío
Ⓑ CPD ► **clinical depression** N depresión *f* clínica ► **clinical psychologist** N psicólogo/a *m/f* clínico/a ► **clinical psychology** N psicología *f* clínica ► **clinical thermometer** N termómetro *m* clínico ► **clinical trials** NPL ensayos *mpl* clínicos

clinically ['klɪnɪkəlɪ] ADV 1 (*Med*) clínicamente; **~ dead** clínicamente muerto
2 (= *coldly*) fríamente

clinician [klɪ'nɪʃən] N médico/a *m/f* de clínica

clink¹ [klɪŋk] Ⓐ N [*of coins*] tintín *m*, tintineo *m*; [*of glasses*] choque *m*
Ⓑ VT hacer sonar, hacer tintinear; **to ~ glasses with sb** entrechocar la copa con algn
Ⓒ VI [*coins*] tintinear

clink²‡ [klɪŋk] N (= *jail*) trena‡ *f*

clinker ['klɪŋkəʳ] N 1 (= *burnt out coal*) escoria *f* de hulla
2 (= *paving material*) ladrillo *m* duro
3 (*US‡*) (= *gaffe*) metedura *f* de pata; (= *failed film, play*) birria* *f*

clinker-built ['klɪŋkə,bɪlt] ADJ (*Naut*) de tingladillo

clip¹ [klɪp] Ⓐ N 1 (= *cut*) tijeretazo *m*, tijeretada *f*; (= *shearing*) esquila *f*, esquileo *m*; (= *wool*) cantidad *f* de lana esquilada
2 (*Cine*) secuencia *f*; **some ~s from Kevin Costner's latest film** unas secuencias de la última película de Kevin Costner
3 (= *blow*) golpe *m*, cachete *m*; **at a (fast) ~** (*US*) a toda pastilla
Ⓑ VT 1 (= *cut*) cortar; (= *cut to shorten*) acortar; [+ *hedge*] podar; [+ *ticket*] picar; (*also* **~ off**) [+ *wool*] trasquilar, esquilar; [+ *hair*] recortar; (*also* **~ out**) [+ *article from newspaper*] recortar; [+ *words*] comerse, abreviar; ✦***IDIOM*** **to ~ sb's wings** cortar las alas a algn
2 (= *hit*) golpear, dar un cachete a
Ⓒ CPD ► **clip joint*** N (*US*) bar *m* (muy caro)

► **clip off** VT + ADV cortar, quitar cortando

► **clip out** VT + ADV recortar

clip² [klɪp] Ⓐ N (= *clamp*) grapa *f*; (= *paper clip*) sujetapapeles *m inv*, clip *m*, grampa *f* (*S. Cone*); [*of pen*] sujetador *m*; (= *hair clip*) horquilla *f*, clip *m*; (= *brooch*) alfiler *m*, clip *m*, abrochador *m* (*LAm*); [*of cyclist*] pinza *f*
Ⓑ VT sujetar

► **clip on** Ⓐ VT + ADV [+ *brooch*] prender, sujetar; [+ *document*] sujetar con un clip
Ⓑ VI + ADV **it ~s on here** se fija aquí (con clip)

► **clip together** VT + ADV unir

clipboard ['klɪp,bɔ:d] N tablilla *f* con sujetapapeles, carpeta *f* sujetapapeles

clip-clop ['klɪp'klɒp] N *ruido de los cascos del caballo*

clip-on ['klɪpɒn] ADJ [*badge*] para prender, con prendedor; [*earrings*] de pinza

clipped [klɪpt] ADJ [*accent*] entrecortado; [*style*] sucinto; [*hair*] corto

clipper ['klɪpəʳ] N (*Naut*) clíper *m*

clippers ['klɪpəz] NPL (*for hair*) maquinilla *fsing* (para el pelo); (*for nails*) cortaúñas *msing inv*; (*for hedge*) tijeras *fpl* de podar

clippie†* ['klɪpɪ] N (*Brit*) cobradora *f* (de autobús)

clipping ['klɪpɪŋ] N (*from newspaper*) recorte *m*

clique [kli:k] N camarilla *f*

cliquey ['kli:kɪ] ADJ exclusivista

cliquish ['kli:kɪʃ] ADJ = **cliquey**

cliquishness ['kli:kɪʃnɪs] N exclusivismo *m*

cliquy ['kli:kɪ] ADJ = **cliquey**

clitoral ['klɪtərəl] ADJ del clítoris

clitoridectomy [,klɪtərɪ'dektəmɪ] N clitoridectomía *f*

clitoris ['klɪtərɪs] N clítoris *m*

Cllr ABBR = **Councillor**

cloak [kləʊk] Ⓐ N capa *f*, manto *m*; **under the ~ of darkness** (*fig*) al amparo de la oscuridad
Ⓑ VT (= *cover*) cubrir (**in, with** de); (*fig*) encubrir, disimular; **a ~ed figure** una silueta envuelta *or* embozada en una capa

cloak-and-dagger ['kləʊkən'dægəʳ] ADJ [*activity*] clandestino; [*play*] de capa y espada; [*story*] de agentes secretos

cloakroom ['kləʊkrʊm] N 1 (*for coats*) guardarropa *m*, ropero *m*
2 (*Brit euph*) (= *toilet*) lavabo *m*, servicios *mpl*, baño *m* (*LAm*)

clobber‡ ['klɒbəʳ] Ⓐ N 1 (= *clothes*) ropa *f*, traje *m*
2 (*Brit*) (= *gear*) bártulos* *mpl*, trastos *mpl* (*Sp**)
Ⓑ VT 1 (= *defeat*) cascar*
2 (= *beat up*) dar una paliza a

cloche [klɒʃ] N campana *f* de cristal

clock [klɒk] Ⓐ N 1 (= *timepiece*) (*gen*) reloj *m*; [*of taxi*] taxímetro *m*; (= *speedometer*) velocímetro *m*; (= *milometer*) cuentakilómetros *m inv*; **you can't put the ~ back** (= *return to past*) no puedes volver al pasado; (= *stop progress*) no se puede detener el progreso; **to keep one's eyes on** *or* **watch the ~** mirar mucho el reloj (ansiando abandonar el trabajo); **to work against the ~** trabajar contra reloj; **alarm ~** despertador *m*; **around the ~** *see* **round the clock**; **grandfather ~** reloj *m* de pie, reloj *m* de caja; **30,000 miles on the ~** (*Aut*) 30.000 millas en el cuentakilómetros; **it's only got 60 miles on the ~** este coche ha hecho solamente 60 millas; **round the ~** las veinticuatro horas del día; **the garage is open round the ~** el garaje está abierto las veinticuatro horas del día; **we have surveillance round the ~** tenemos vigilancia de veinticuatro horas, tenemos vigilancia permanente; **to sleep round the ~** dormir un día entero
2 (‡) (= *face*) jeta *f*
Ⓑ VT 1 (= *time, measure*) [+ *runner, time*] cronometrar; **we ~ed 80mph** alcanzamos una velocidad de 80 millas por hora
2 (*Brit**) (= *hit*) **he ~ed him one** le dio un bofetón*
Ⓒ CPD ► **clock radio** N radio-despertador *m* ► **clock repairer** N relojero/a *m/f* ► **clock tower** N torre *f* de reloj ► **clock watcher** N *persona que mira mucho el reloj ansiando abandonar el trabajo*

►**clock in** VI + ADV (= *mark card*) fichar, picar; (= *start work*) entrar a trabajar

►**clock off** VI + ADV (= *mark card*) fichar *or* picar la salida; (= *leave work*) salir del trabajo

►**clock on** VI + ADV = **clock in**

►**clock out** VI + ADV = **clock off**

►**clock up** VT + ADV (*Aut*) hacer; **he ~ed up 250 miles** (*Aut*) hizo 250 millas

clockface ['klɒkfeɪs] N esfera *f* de reloj

clockmaker ['klɒk,meɪkəʳ] N relojero/a *m/f*

clockwise ['klɒkwaɪz] ADJ, ADV en el sentido de las agujas del reloj

clockwork ['klɒkwɜːk] Ⓐ N **to go like ~** funcionar como un reloj
Ⓑ CPD [*toy*] de cuerda ► **clockwork train** N tren *m* de cuerda

clod [klɒd] N 1 [*of earth*] terrón *m*
2 (= *person*) patán *m*, zoquete *mf*; **you ~!** ¡bestia!

clodhopper ['klɒd,hɒpəʳ] N patán *m*

clodhopping ['klɒdhɒpɪŋ] ADJ [*person*] torpón, desgarbado; [*boots*] basto, pesado

clog [klɒg] Ⓐ N zueco *m*, chanclo *m*
Ⓑ VT (*also* **~ up**) [+ *pipe, drain, machine, mechanism*] atascar
Ⓒ VI (*also* **~ up**) atascarse

cloister ['klɔɪstəʳ] N claustro *m*; **cloisters** soportales *mpl*

cloistered ['klɔɪstəd] ADJ **to lead a ~ life** llevar una vida de ermitaño

clonal ['kləʊnəl] ADJ clónico

clone [kləʊn] Ⓐ N clon *m*; (*Comput*) clónico *m*
Ⓑ VT clonar

cloning ['kləʊnɪŋ] N clonación *f*, clonaje *m*

clonk [klɒŋk] Ⓐ N (= *sound*) ruido *m* hueco
Ⓑ VI (= *make sound*) hacer un ruido hueco

close[1] [kləʊs] Ⓐ ADV (*compar* **closer**, *superl* **closest**) cerca; **the shops are very ~** las tiendas están muy cerca; **the hotel is ~ to the station** el hotel está cerca de la estación; **she was ~ to tears** estaba a punto de llorar; **according to sources ~ to the police** según fuentes allegadas a la policía; **~ by** muy cerca; **come ~r** acércate más; **to come ~ to** acercarse a; **we came very ~ to losing the match** estuvimos a punto de perder el partido, faltó poco para que perdiéramos el partido; **that comes ~ to an insult** eso es casi un insulto; **the runners finished very ~** los corredores llegaron casi al mismo tiempo; **to fit ~** ajustarse al cuerpo; **to follow ~ behind** seguir muy de cerca; **to hold sb ~** abrazar fuertemente a algn; **to keep ~ to the wall** ir arrimado a la pared; **he must be ~ on 50** debe andar cerca de los 50; **it's ~ on six o'clock** son casi las seis; **stay ~ to me** no te alejes *or* separes de mí; **~ together** juntos, cerca uno del otro; **to look at sth ~ up** mirar algo de cerca
Ⓑ ADJ 1 (= *near*) [*place*] cercano, próximo; [*contact*] directo; [*connection*] estrecho, íntimo; **~ combat** lucha *f* cuerpo a cuerpo; **at ~ quarters** de cerca; **to come a ~ second to sb/sth** disputarle la primera posición a algn/algo; **he was the ~st thing to a real worker among us** entre nosotros él tenía más visos de ser un obrero auténtico, de nosotros él era el que tenía más visos de ser un obrero; ✦**IDIOM it was a ~ shave*** se salvaron por un pelo *or* de milagro
2 (= *intimate*) [*relative*] cercano; [*friend*] íntimo; **we have only invited ~ relations** sólo hemos invitado a parientes cercanos; **she's a ~ friend of mine** es una amiga íntima mía; **I'm very ~ to my sister** estoy muy unida a mi hermana; **they're very ~ (to each other)** están muy unidos; **a ~ circle of friends** un estrecho círculo de amigos
3 (= *almost equal*) [*result, election, fight*] muy reñido; [*scores*] casi iguales; **it was a very ~ contest** fue una competición muy reñida; **to bear a ~ resemblance to** tener mucho parecido con
4 (= *exact, detailed*) [*examination, study*] detallado; [*investigation, questioning*] minucioso; [*surveillance, control*] estricto; [*translation*] fiel, exacto; **to pay ~ attention to sb/sth** prestar mucha atención a algn/algo; **to keep a ~ watch on sb** mantener a algn bajo estricta vigilancia
5 (= *not spread out*) [*handwriting, print*] compacto; [*texture, weave*] compacto, tupido; [*formation*] cerrado
6 (= *stuffy*) [*atmosphere, room*] sofocante, cargado; [*weather*] pesado, bochornoso; **it's ~ this afternoon** hace bochorno esta tarde
7 (= *secretive*) reservado; (= *mean*) tacaño
8 (*Ling*) [*vowel*] cerrado
Ⓒ N recinto *m*
Ⓓ CPD ► **close company** N (*Brit Fin*) sociedad *f* exclusiva, compañía *f* propietaria ► **close corporation** N (*US*) = **close company** ► **close season** N (*Hunting, Fishing*) veda *f*; (*Ftbl*) temporada *f* de descanso (*de la liga de fútbol*)

close[2] [kləʊz] Ⓐ N (= *end*) final *m*, conclusión *f*; **at the ~** al final; **at the ~ of day** a la caída de la tarde; **at the ~ of the year** al final del año; **to bring sth to a ~** terminar algo, concluir algo; **to draw to a ~** tocar a su fin, estar terminando
Ⓑ VI 1 (= *shut*) [*shop*] cerrar; [*door, window*] cerrarse; **the doors ~ automatically** las puertas se cierran automáticamente; **the shops ~ at five thirty** las tiendas cierran a las cinco y media; **this window does not ~ properly** esta ventana no cierra bien; **his eyes ~d** se le cerraron los ojos
2 (= *end*) terminar, terminarse, concluir; (*Fin*) **shares ~d at 120p** al cierre las acciones estaban a 120 peniques
Ⓒ VT 1 (= *shut*) cerrar; [+ *hole*] tapar; **please ~ the door** cierra la puerta, por favor; **"road closed"** "cerrado el paso"; **to ~ one's eyes** cerrar los ojos; **to ~ one's eyes to sth** (= *ignore*) hacer la vista gorda a algo; **to ~ the gap between two things** llenar el hueco entre dos cosas; **~ your mouth when you're eating!** ¡no abras la boca comiendo!; **to ~ ranks** cerrar filas
2 (= *end*) [+ *discussion, meeting*] cerrar, poner fin a; [+ *ceremony*] clausurar, dar término a; [+ *bank account*] liquidar; [+ *account*] (*Comm*) saldar; [+ *bargain, deal*] cerrar

►**close down** Ⓐ VI + ADV [*business*] (*gen*) cerrarse definitivamente; (*by order*) clausurarse; (*TV, Rad*) cerrar (la emisión)
Ⓑ VT + ADV (*gen*) cerrar definitivamente; (*by legal order*) clausurar

►**close in** Ⓐ VI + ADV [*hunters*] acercarse rodeando, rodear; [*night*] caer; [*darkness, fog*] cerrarse; **the days are closing in** los días son cada vez más cortos; **night was closing in** caía ya la noche
Ⓑ VT + ADV [+ *area*] cercar, rodear

►**close in on** VI + ADV + PREP **to ~ in on sb** rodear a algn, cercar a algn

►**close off** VT + ADV [+ *road*] cerrar al tráfico, cerrar al público; [+ *supply*] cortar; [+ *access*] bloquear

►**close on** VI + PREP 1 (= *get nearer to*) acercarse a
2 (*US*) = **close in on**

►**close out** VT + ADV (*US Fin*) liquidar

►**close round** VI + PREP **the crowd ~d round him** la multitud se agolpó en torno suyo; **the clouds ~d round the peak** las nubes envolvieron la cumbre; **the waters ~d round it** lo envolvieron las aguas

►**close up** Ⓐ VI + ADV [*flower*] cerrarse del todo; [*people in queue*] arrimarse; [*ranks*] apretarse; [*wound*] cicatrizarse; **~ up, please** arrímense, por favor
Ⓑ VT + ADV [+ *building*] cerrar (del todo); [+ *pipe, opening*] tapar, obstruir; [+ *wound*] cerrar

►**close with** VI + PREP (= *begin to fight*) enzarzarse con

close-cropped ['kləʊs'krɒpt] ADJ (cortado) al rape, rapado

closed [kləʊzd] Ⓐ ADJ (*gen*) cerrado; [*hearing, meeting*] a puerta cerrada; **her eyes were ~** tenía los ojos cerrados; **sociology is a ~ book to me** la sociología es un misterio para mí; **the case is ~** (*Jur*) el caso está cerrado; **behind ~ doors** (*fig*) a puerta cerrada; **to have a ~ mind** ser de miras estrechas, ser de mente cerrada; **it's ~ on Sundays** los domingos está cerrado, cierra los domingos; **the road is ~ to traffic** la carretera está cerrada al tráfico; **the door was ~ to us** (*fig*) para nosotros las puertas estaban cerradas
Ⓑ CPD ► **closed primary** N (*US Pol*) *elección primaria reservada a los miembros de un partido* ► **closed season** N (*Hunting, Fishing*) veda *f*; (*Ftbl, Rugby*) temporada *f* de descanso (*de la liga de fútbol*) ► **closed session** N (*Jur*) sesión *f* a puerta cerrada; **in ~ session** en sesión a puerta cerrada ► **closed shop** N (*Ind*) *empresa con todo el personal afiliado obligatoriamente a un solo sindicato*

closed-circuit ['kləʊzd,sɜːkɪt] CPD ► **closed-circuit television** N televisión *f* circuito cerrado

closed-door ['kləʊzd,dɔːʳ] ADJ (*US*) [*meeting, session*] a puerta cerrada

close-down ['kləʊzdaʊn] N cierre *m*

close-fisted ['kləʊs'fɪstɪd] ADJ tacaño

close-fitting ['kləʊs'fɪtɪŋ] ADJ ceñido, ajustado

close-grained [,kləʊs'greɪnd] ADJ [*wood*] tupido

close-harmony [,kləʊs,hɑːmənɪ] CPD ► **close-harmony singing** N canto *m* en estrecha armonía

close-knit ['kləʊsnɪt] ADJ [*family*] muy unido

closely ['kləʊslɪ] ADV [1] (= *carefully*) [*look, examine*] atentamente, de cerca; **to watch ~** fijarse, prestar mucha atención; **to listen ~** escuchar con atención, escuchar atentamente; **a ~ guarded secret** un secreto celosamente guardado
[2] (= *nearly*) **to resemble sth/sb ~** parecerse mucho a algo/algn; **~ related/connected** estrechamente relacionado/unido; **~ contested** muy reñido; **~ packed** [*case*] repleto; **this will be a ~ fought race** será una carrera muy reñida

closeness ['kləʊsnɪs] N [1] (= *nearness*) proximidad *f*; [*of resemblance*] parecido *m*; [*of translation*] fidelidad *f*
[2] [*of friendship*] intimidad *f*
[3] [*of weather, atmosphere*] pesadez *f*, bochorno *m*; [*of room*] mala ventilación *f*
[4] [*of election*] lo muy reñido
[5] (= *secretiveness*) reserva *f*; (= *meanness*) tacañería *f*

close-run [,kləʊs'rʌn] ADJ **~ race** carrera *f* muy reñida

close-set ['kləʊs,set] ADJ [*eyes*] muy juntos

closet ['klɒzɪt] Ⓐ N [1] (= *toilet*) wáter *m*, lavabo *m*
[2] (*US*) (= *cupboard*) armario *m*, placar(d) *m* (*LAm*); (*for clothes*) ropero *m*; **to come out of the ~** (*fig*) anunciarse públicamente
Ⓑ VT **to be ~ed with sb** estar encerrado con algn
Ⓒ CPD [*fascist, racist*] secreto/a, no declarado/a ► **closet gay** N gay *m* no declarado

close-up ['kləʊsʌp] Ⓐ N primer plano *m*; **in ~** en primer plano
Ⓑ CPD ► **close-up lens** N teleobjetivo *m*

closing ['kləʊzɪŋ] Ⓐ ADJ último, final; **~ speech** discurso *m* de clausura; **in the ~ stages** en las últimas etapas; **when is ~ time?** ¿a qué hora cierran?; **his ~ words were …** sus palabras finales fueron …
Ⓑ CPD ► **closing date** N fecha *f* tope, fecha *f* límite ► **closing down** N cierre *m* ► **closing down sale** N liquidación *f* por cierre ► **closing entry** N (*in account*) asiento *m* de cierre ► **closing price** N (*St Ex*) cotización *f* de cierre ► **closing time** N (*Brit*) hora *f* de cerrar

closure ['kləʊʒəʳ] N [1] (= *close-down*) cierre *m*
[2] (= *end*) fin *m*, conclusión *f*
[3] (*Parl*) clausura *f*

clot [klɒt] Ⓐ N [1] (*Med*) embolia *f*; [*of blood*] coágulo *m*; **~ on the brain** embolia *f* cerebral
[2] (*) (= *fool*) papanatas *mf inv*, tonto/a *m/f* del bote; **you ~!** ¡bobo!
Ⓑ VI (*Med*) coagularse

cloth [klɒθ] Ⓐ N [1] (= *material*) paño *m*, tela *f*; **bound in ~** encuadernado en tela
[2] (*for cleaning*) trapo *m*
[3] (= *tablecloth*) mantel *m*; **to lay the ~** poner la mesa
[4] (*Rel*) **the ~** el clero; **a man of the ~** un clérigo
Ⓑ CPD ► **cloth cap** N (*Brit*) gorra *f* de paño

clothbound ['klɒθ,baʊnd] ADJ **~ book** libro *m* encuadernado en tela

clothe [kləʊð] VT [1] [+ *family*] vestir (**in, with** de)
[2] (*fig*) cubrir, revestir (**in, with** de)

cloth-eared ['klɒθɪəd] ADJ sordo como una tapia

clothed [kləʊðd] ADJ vestido

clothes [kləʊðz] Ⓐ NPL ropa *fsing*, vestidos *mpl*; **to put one's ~ on** vestirse, ponerse la ropa; **to take one's ~ off** quitarse la ropa, desvestirse
Ⓑ CPD ► **clothes basket** N canasta *f* de la ropa sucia ► **clothes brush** N cepillo *m* de la ropa ► **clothes drier, clothes dryer** N secadora *f* ► **clothes hanger** N percha *f*, gancho *m* (*LAm*) ► **clothes horse** N tendedero *m* plegable; (*US**) (= *model*) modelo *mf*; **she's a ~ horse** (*US**) está obsesionada con los trapos* ► **clothes line** N cuerda *f* para (tender) la ropa ► **clothes moth** N polilla *f* ► **clothes peg, clothes pin** (*US*) N pinza *f* de la ropa ► **clothes rack** N tendedero *m* ► **clothes rope** N = **clothes line** ► **clothes shop** N tienda *f* (de ropa)

clothespole ['kləʊðzpəʊl], **clothesprop** ['kləʊðzprɒp] N palo *m* de tendedero

clothier ['kləʊðɪəʳ] N ropero *m*; (= *tailor*) sastre *m*; **~'s (shop)** pañería *f*, ropería *f*; (= *tailor's*) sastrería *f*

clothing ['kləʊðɪŋ] Ⓐ N ropa *f*, vestimenta *f*; **article of ~** prenda *f* de vestir
Ⓑ CPD ► **clothing allowance** N extra *m* para ropa de trabajo ► **clothing industry** N industria *f* textil ► **the clothing trade** N la industria de la confección

clotted cream [,klɒtɪd'kriːm] N (*Culin*) nata *f* cuajada

clotting agent ['klɒtɪŋ,eɪdʒənt] N agente *m* coagulante

cloture ['kləʊtʃəʳ] Ⓐ N (*US Pol*) clausura *f*
Ⓑ CPD ► **cloture rule** N control del tiempo de intervención (*en un debate*)

cloud [klaʊd] Ⓐ N nube *f* (*also fig*); **a ~ of dust/smoke/gas/insects** una nube de polvo/humo/gases/insectos; ✦*IDIOMS* **to be under a ~** (= *under suspicion*) estar bajo sospecha; (= *resented*) estar desacreditado; **to have one's head in the ~s** estar en las nubes; **to be on ~ nine** estar en el séptimo cielo; **every ~ has a silver lining** no hay mal que por bien no venga
Ⓑ VT [1] (= *make cloudy*) [+ *vision*] nublar; [+ *liquid*] enturbiar; [+ *mirror*] empañar
[2] (*fig*) (= *confuse*) aturdir; **to ~ the issue** complicar el asunto
Ⓒ VI (*also* **to ~ over**) nublarse (*also fig*)

►**cloud over** VI + ADV nublarse

cloudberry ['klaʊdbərɪ] N (*US*) camemoro *m*

cloudburst ['klaʊdbɜːst] N chaparrón *m*

cloud-cuckoo-land [,klaʊd'kʊkuː,lænd], **cloudland** ['klaʊdlænd] (*US*) N **to be in ~** estar en babia, estar con la cabeza en el aire (*LAm*)

cloudiness ['klaʊdɪnɪs] N [1] (*Met*) lo nublado, lo nuboso
[2] (= *murkiness*) lo turbio

cloudless ['klaʊdlɪs] ADJ sin nubes, despejado

cloudy ['klaʊdɪ] ADJ (*compar* **cloudier**; *superl* **cloudiest**) [1] (*Met*) [*sky*] nublado, cubierto de nubes; [*day, weather*] nublado; **it's ~ today** hoy está nublado
[2] (= *murky*) [*liquid*] turbio
[3] (= *unclear*) [*policy, ideas, memory*] confuso
[4] (= *misty*) [*eyes, glass*] empañado

clout¹ [klaʊt] Ⓐ N [1] (= *blow*) tortazo *m*
[2] (= *influence, power*) influencia *f*, peso *m*, palanca *f* (*LAm*)
Ⓑ VT dar un tortazo a

clout² [klaʊt] N ✦*PROV* **ne'er cast a ~ till May be out** hasta el cuarenta de mayo no te quites el sayo

clove¹ [kləʊv] N [1] (= *spice*) clavo *m*
[2] **~ of garlic** diente *m* de ajo

clove² [kləʊv] Ⓐ PT *of* **cleave¹**
Ⓑ CPD ► **clove hitch** N ballestrinque *m*

cloven ['kləʊvn] PP *of* **cleave¹**

cloven-footed [,kləʊvn'fʊtɪd] ADJ [*animal*] de pezuña hendida; [*devil*] con pezuña

cloven hoof [,kləʊvn'huːf] N pata *f* hendida

clover ['kləʊvəʳ] N trébol *m*; ✦*IDIOM* **to be in ~*** vivir a cuerpo de rey

cloverleaf ['kləʊvəliːf] N (*pl* **cloverleaves**) [1] (*Bot*) hoja *f* de trébol
[2] (*Aut*) cruce *m* en trébol

clown [klaʊn] Ⓐ N [1] (*in circus*) payaso/a *m/f*, clown *mf*; **to make a ~ of o.s.** hacer el ridículo
[2] (*) patán *m*, zoquete *mf*
Ⓑ VI (*also* **~ about** *or* **around**) hacer el payaso; **stop ~ing!** ¡déjate de tonterías!

clowning ['klaʊnɪŋ] N payasadas *fpl*

clownish ['klaʊnɪʃ] ADJ [*person*] cómico; [*behaviour*] de payaso; [*sense of humour*] de payaso, tonto

cloy [klɔɪ] VI empalagar

cloying ['klɔɪɪŋ] ADJ empalagoso

cloyingly ['klɔɪɪŋlɪ] ADV empalagosamente; **~ sweet** tan dulce que empalaga, empalagosamente dulce

cloze test ['kləʊz,test] N *test consistente en rellenar los espacios en blanco de un texto*

CLU N ABBR (*US*) = **Chartered Life Underwriter**

club [klʌb] Ⓐ N [1] (= *stick*) porra *f*, cachiporra *f*
[2] (= *golf club*) palo *m*

3 **clubs** (*Cards*) (*in Spanish pack*) bastos *mpl*; (*in conventional pack*) tréboles *mpl*
4 (= *association*) club *m*; (= *gaming club*) casino *m*; (= *building*) centro *m*, club *m*; **a golf ~** un club de golf; **the youth ~** el club juvenil; **join the ~!** (*fig*) ¡ya somos dos!; **to be in the ~** (*hum*) estar en estado; **he put her in the ~** él la dejó en estado
5 (= *disco*) discoteca *f*
Ⓑ VT [+ *person*] aporrear, dar porrazos a; **to ~ sb to death** matar a algn a porrazos
Ⓒ VI **to ~ together** (*esp Brit*) (= *join forces*) unir fuerzas; **we all ~bed together to buy him a present** le compramos un regalo entre todos
Ⓓ CPD ► **club car** N (*US Rail*) coche *m* club ► **club class** N clase *f* club ► **club foot** N pie *m* zopo ► **club member** N socio/a *m/f* del club ► **club sandwich** N *bocadillo vegetal con pollo y beicon* ► **club steak** N (*US*) bistec *m* culer

clubbable* [ˈklʌbəbl] ADJ sociable

clubber [ˈklʌbəʳ] N discotequero/a *m/f*

clubbing* [ˈklʌbɪŋ] N (*Brit*) ir de discotecas; **to go ~** ir de discotecas

club-footed [ˈklʌb,fʊtɪd] ADJ con el pie zopo

clubhouse [ˈklʌbhaʊs] N (*pl* **clubhouses**) sede *f* de un club

clubland [ˈklʌblænd] N (*esp Brit*) *zona de las discotecas de moda*

clubroom [ˈklʌbrʊm] N salón *m*, sala *f* de reuniones

cluck [klʌk] Ⓐ N 1 [*of hen*] cloqueo *m*
2 (*with tongue*) chasquido *m* (de la lengua)
Ⓑ VI 1 [*hen*] cloquear
2 [*person*] chasquear con la lengua

►**cluck over** VI + PREP **she ~ed over the children** con los niños estaba como la gallina con sus polluelos

clue, clew (*US*) [kluː] Ⓐ N (*in guessing game*) pista *f*; (*in a crime*) pista *f*, indicio *m*; [*of crossword*] indicación *f*; **an important ~** una pista importante; **I haven't a ~*** no tengo ni idea; **can you give me a ~?** ¿me das una pista?
Ⓑ VT **to ~ sb up*** informar a algn

clued up* [,kluːdˈʌp] ADJ **~ (on)** al tanto (de), al corriente (de)

clueless* [ˈkluːlɪs] ADJ despistado, que no tiene ni idea

clump¹ [klʌmp] N [*of trees, shrubs*] grupo *m*; [*of flowers, grass*] mata *f*; [*of earth*] terrón *m*

clump² [klʌmp] Ⓐ N [*of feet*] pisada *f* fuerte
Ⓑ VI **to ~ about** caminar dando pisadas fuertes

clumpy [ˈklʌmpɪ] ADJ (*compar* **clumpier**, *superl* **clumpiest**) [*shoes*] grandón, grandote

clumsily [ˈklʌmzɪlɪ] ADV 1 (= *awkwardly*) [*walk, express, apologize*] con torpeza, torpemente
2 (= *roughly*) [*produced*] toscamente, chapuceramente

clumsiness [ˈklʌmzɪnɪs] N (= *awkwardness*) torpeza *f*; (= *tactlessness*) falta *f* de tacto

clumsy [ˈklʌmzɪ] ADJ (*compar* **clumsier**, *superl* **clumsiest**) 1 (= *awkward*) [*person, action*] torpe, patoso; [*movement*] torpe, desgarbado; [*remark, apology*] torpe, poco delicado; [*tool*] pesado, difícil de manejar
2 (= *crudely made*) [*painting, forgery*] tosco, chapucero

clung [klʌŋ] PT, PP *of* **cling**

Cluniac [ˈkluːnɪæk] Ⓐ ADJ cluniacense
Ⓑ N cluniacense *m*

clunk [klʌŋk] Ⓐ N 1 (= *sound*) sonido *m* metálico sordo
2 (*US**) cabeza *mf* hueca
Ⓑ VI (= *make sound*) sonar a hueco

clunker‡ [ˈklʌŋkəʳ] N (*US*) cacharro* *m*

clunky [ˈklʌŋkɪ] ADJ (*compar* **clunkier**, *superl* **clunkiest**) macizo

cluster [ˈklʌstəʳ] Ⓐ N [*of trees, houses, people, stars*] grupo *m*; [*of flowers*] macizo *m*; [*of plants*] mata *f*; [*of fruit*] racimo *m*
Ⓑ VI [*people, things*] agruparse, apiñarse; [*plants*] arracimarse; **to ~ round sb/sth** apiñarse en torno a algn/algo
Ⓒ CPD ► **cluster bomb** N bomba *f* de dispersión, bomba *f* de racimo

clutch¹ [klʌtʃ] Ⓐ N 1 (*Aut*) embrague *m*, cloche *m* (*LAm*); (= *pedal*) (pedal *m* del) embrague *m or* cloche *m*; **to let the ~ in** embragar; **to let the ~ out** desembragar
2 (= *grasp*) **to make a ~ at sth** tratar de agarrar algo; **to fall into sb's ~es** caer en las garras de algn; **to get sth out of sb's ~es** hacer que algn ceda la posesión *or* se desprenda de algo
3 (*US**) (= *crisis*) crisis *f inv*
Ⓑ VT (= *catch hold of*) asir, agarrar (*esp LAm*); (= *hold tightly*) apretar, agarrar; **she ~ed my arm and begged me not to go** se me agarró al brazo y me suplicó que no me marchara
Ⓒ VI **to ~ at** tratar de agarrar; (*fig*) aferrarse a; **he ~ed at my hand** trató de agarrarme la mano; **to ~ at a hope** aferrarse a una esperanza; ✦***IDIOM*** **to ~ at straws** aferrarse a cualquier esperanza

clutch² [klʌtʃ] N [*of eggs*] nidada *f*

clutter [ˈklʌtəʳ] Ⓐ N desorden *m*, confusión *f*; **in a ~** en desorden, en un montón
Ⓑ VT atestar; **to ~ up a room** amontonar cosas en un cuarto; **to be ~ed up with sth** estar atestado de algo

CM ABBR (*US*) = **North Mariana Islands**

cm ABBR (= **centimetre(s)**) cm

Cmdr ABBR (*Mil*) (= **Commander**) Cdte

CNAA N ABBR (*Brit*) (= **Council for National Academic Awards**) *organismo no universitario que otorga diplomas*

CND N ABBR = **Campaign for Nuclear Disarmament**

CNN N ABBR (*US*) (= **Cable News Network**) *agencia de noticias*

CO N ABBR 1 (*Mil*) = **Commanding Officer**
2 (*Brit Admin*) (= **Commonwealth Office**) *Ministerio de Relaciones con la Commonwealth*
3 = **conscientious objector**
4 (*US*) = **Colorado**

co- [kəʊ] PREFIX co-

Co. ABBR 1 [keʊ] (*Comm*) (= **company**) Cía., S.A.; **Joe and ~*** Joe y compañía
2 = **county**

c/o ABBR 1 (= **care of**) c/d, a/c
2 (*Comm*) = **cash order**

coach [kəʊtʃ] Ⓐ N 1 (*esp Brit*) (= *bus*) autobús *m*, autocar *m* (*Sp*), coche *m* de línea, pullman *m* (*LAm*), camión *m* (*Mex*), micro *m* (*Arg*); (*Brit Rail*) coche *m*, vagón *m*, pullman *m* (*Mex*); (*horse-drawn*) diligencia *f*; (*ceremonial*) carroza *f*
2 (*Sport*) (= *trainer*) entrenador(a) *m/f*; **the Spanish ~** el entrenador del equipo español
3 (= *tutor*) profesor(a) *m/f* particular
Ⓑ VT [+ *team*] entrenar, preparar; [+ *student*] enseñar, preparar; **to ~ sb in French** enseñar francés a algn; **to ~ sb in a part** preparar a algn para un papel
Ⓒ CPD ► **coach building** N (*Brit*) construcción *f* de carrocerías ► **coach driver** N (*Brit*) conductor(a) *m/f* de autobús, conductor(a) *m/f* de autocar (*Sp*) ► **coach operator** N compañía *f* de autobuses, compañía *f* de autocares (*Sp*) ► **coach station** N estación *f* de autobuses ► **coach tour** N (*Brit*) gira *f* en autocar, viaje *m* en autocar ► **coach trip** N (*Brit*) excursión *f* en autobús, excursión *f* en autocar (*Sp*)

coachbuilder [ˈkəʊtʃ,bɪldəʳ] N (*Brit Aut*) carrocero *m*

coaching [ˈkəʊtʃɪŋ] N 1 (*Sport*) (= *training*) entrenamiento *m*
2 (*esp US*) (= *tuition*) enseñanza *f* particular

coachload [ˈkəʊtʃləʊd] N (*Brit*) autobús *m* (lleno), autocar *m* (lleno) (*Sp*); **they came by the ~** vinieron en masa

coachman [ˈkəʊtʃmən] N (*pl* **coachmen**) cochero *m*

coachwork [ˈkəʊtʃwɜːk] N (*Brit*) carrocería *f*

coagulant [kəʊˈægjʊlənt] N coagulante *m*

coagulate [kəʊˈægjʊleɪt] Ⓐ VT coagular
Ⓑ VI coagularse

coagulation [kəʊ,ægjʊˈleɪʃən] N coagulación *f*

coal [kəʊl] Ⓐ N carbón *m*; (*soft*) hulla *f*; ✦***IDIOMS*** **to carry ~s to Newcastle** llevar leña al monte *or* agua al mar; **to haul sb over the ~s** echarle una bronca a algn; **to heap ~s of fire on sb's head** avergonzar a algn devolviéndole bien por mal
Ⓑ VI (*Naut*) tomar carbón
Ⓒ CPD ► **coal bunker** N carbonera *f* ► **coal cellar** N carbonera *f* ► **coal dust** N polvillo *m* de carbón, carbonilla *f* ► **coal fire** N chimenea *f* de carbón ► **coal gas** N gas *m* de hulla ► **coal hod** N cubo *m* de carbón ► **coal industry** N industria *f* del carbón ► **coal measures** NPL depósitos *mpl* de carbón ► **coal merchant** N carbonero *m* ► **coal mine** N mina *f* de carbón ► **coal miner** N minero/a *m/f* del carbón ► **coal mining** N minería *f* del carbón ► **coal oil** N (*US*) parafina *f* ► **coal pit** N mina *f* de carbón, pozo *m* de carbón ► **coal scuttle** N cubo *m* para carbón ► **coal shed** N carbonera *f* ► **coal strike** N huelga *f* de mineros ► **coal tar** N alquitrán *m* mineral ► **coal tit** N carbonero *m* garrapinos ► **coal yard** N patio *m* del carbón

coal-black [ˈkəʊlˈblæk] ADJ negro como el carbón

coal-burning [ˈkəʊl,bɜːnɪŋ] ADJ que quema carbón

coalesce [,kəʊəˈles] VI (= *merge, blend*) fundirse; (= *join together*) unirse, incorporarse

coalescence [,kəʊəˈlesəns] N (= *merging*) fusión *f*; (= *joining together*) unión *f*, incorporación *f*

coalface [ˈkəʊlfeɪs] N frente *m* donde empieza la veta de carbón

coalfield [ˈkəʊlfiːld] N yacimiento *m* de carbón, cuenca *f* minera

coal-fired [,kəʊlˈfaɪəd] ADJ que quema carbón

coalition [,kəʊəˈlɪʃən] Ⓐ N (*Pol*) coalición *f*
Ⓑ CPD ► **coalition government** N gobierno *m* de coalición

coalman [ˈkəʊlmən] N (*pl* **coalmen**) carbonero *m*

coarse [kɔːs] Ⓐ ADJ (*compar* **coarser**, *superl* **coarsest**) 1 (= *rough*) [*texture*] basto, áspero; [*sand*] grueso; [*skin*] áspero
2 (= *badly made*) burdo, tosco
3 (= *vulgar*) [*character, laugh, remark*] ordinario, tosco; [*joke*] verde
Ⓑ CPD ► **coarse fishing** N pesca *f* de agua dulce (*excluyendo salmón y trucha*)

coarse-grained [ˈkɔːsgreɪnd] ADJ de grano grueso; (*fig*) tosco, basto

coarsely ['kɔːslɪ] ADV 1 (= *crudely*) [*made*] toscamente
2 (= *vulgarly*) [*laugh, say*] groseramente

coarsen ['kɔːsn] Ⓐ VT [+ *person*] embrutecer; [+ *skin*] curtir
Ⓑ VI [*person*] embrutecerse; [*skin*] curtirse

coarseness ['kɔːsnɪs] N 1 (= *roughness*) [*of texture*] aspereza *f*; [*of fabrication*] tosquedad *f*
2 (= *lack of refinement*) falta *f* de finura, falta *f* de elegancia
3 (= *vulgarity*) [*of person, remark*] ordinariez *f*, tosquedad *f*; [*of joke*] lo verde

coast [kəʊst] Ⓐ N (= *shore*) costa *f*; (= *coastline*) litoral *m*; **it's on the west ~ of Scotland** está en la costa oeste de Escocia; ✦*IDIOM* **the ~ is clear** (= *there is no one about*) no hay moros en la costa; (= *the danger is over*) pasó el peligro
Ⓑ VI (*also* **~ along**) (*Aut*) ir en punto muerto; (*on sledge, cycle*) deslizarse cuesta abajo; (*fig*) avanzar sin esfuerzo

coastal ['kəʊstəl] ADJ costero; **~ defences** defensas *fpl* costeras; **~ traffic** (*Naut*) cabotaje *m*

coaster ['kəʊstəʳ] N 1 (*Naut*) buque *m* costero, barco *m* de cabotaje; (*US*) trineo *m*
2 (= *small mat for drinks*) posavasos *m inv*

coastguard ['kəʊstgɑːd] Ⓐ N (= *person*) guardacostas *mf inv*; (= *organization*) servicio *m* de guardacostas
Ⓑ CPD ► **coastguard station** N puesto *m* de guardacostas ► **coastguard vessel** N guardacostas *m*

coastline ['kəʊstlaɪn] N litoral *m*

coast-to-coast ['kəʊstə'kəʊst] (*US*) Ⓐ ADJ de costa a costa
Ⓑ ADV de costa a costa

coat [kəʊt] Ⓐ N 1 (= *winter/long coat*) abrigo *m*; (= *jacket*) chaqueta *f* (*Sp*), americana *f*, saco *m* (*LAm*); (*chemist's*) bata *f*; ✦*IDIOM* **to cut one's ~ according to one's cloth** adaptarse a las circunstancias
2 (*animal's*) (= *hide*) pelo *m*, pelaje *m*; (= *wool*) lana *f*
3 (= *layer*) capa *f*; **a ~ of paint** una mano de pintura
4 **~ of arms** escudo *m* (de armas)
Ⓑ VT cubrir, revestir (**with** de); (*with a liquid*) bañar (**with** en); **to ~ sth with paint** dar una mano de pintura a algo
Ⓒ CPD ► **coat hanger** N percha *f*, gancho *m* (*LAm*)

coated ['kəʊtɪd] ADJ [*tongue*] saburral

coating ['kəʊtɪŋ] N capa *f*, baño *m*; [*of paint*] mano *f*

coatstand ['kəʊtstænd] N perchero *m*

coattails ['kəʊtteɪlz] NPL faldón *msing*; ✦*IDIOM* **to ride on sb's ~** salir adelante gracias al favor de algn, lograr el éxito a la sombra de algn

co-author ['kəʊ,ɔːθəʳ] Ⓐ N coautor(a) *m/f*
Ⓑ VT (*US*) escribir conjuntamente

coax [kəʊks] VT **to ~ sth out of sb** sonsacar algo a algn (engatusándolo); **to ~ sb into/out of doing sth** engatusar a algn para que haga/no haga algo; **to ~ sb along** mimar a algn

coaxial [,kəʊ'æksɪəl] ADJ coaxial; **~ cable** (*Comput*) cable *m* coaxial

coaxing ['kəʊksɪŋ] Ⓐ ADJ mimoso
Ⓑ N mimos *mpl*, halagos *mpl*

coaxingly ['kəʊksɪŋlɪ] ADV mimosamente

cob [kɒb] N 1 (= *swan*) cisne *m* macho
2 (= *horse*) jaca *f* fuerte
3 (= *loaf*) pan *m* redondo
4 (= *nut*) avellana *f*
5 (= *maize*) mazorca *f*

cobalt ['kəʊbɒlt] Ⓐ N cobalto *m*
Ⓑ CPD ► **cobalt blue** N azul *m* cobalto ► **cobalt bomb** N bomba *f* de cobalto

cobber* ['kɒbəʳ] N (*Australia*) amigo *m*, compañero *m*; (*in direct address*) amigo

cobble ['kɒbl] Ⓐ N = **cobblestone**
Ⓑ VT 1 (*also* **~ up**) [+ *shoes*] remendar
2 [+ *street*] empedrar, adoquinar

►**cobble together** VT + ADV (*pej*) hacer apresuradamente

cobbled ['kɒbld] ADJ **~ street** calle *f* empedrada, calle *f* adoquinada

cobbler ['kɒbləʳ] N zapatero/a *m/f* (remendón/ona)

cobblers ['kɒbləz] NPL (*Brit*) 1 (*Anat***) cojones** *mpl*
2 (*) (*fig*) chorradas* *fpl*

cobblestone ['kɒblstəʊn] N adoquín *m*

COBOL [ʊʃθkəʊbɒl] N (*Comput*) COBOL *m*

cobra ['kəʊbrə] N cobra *f*

cobweb ['kɒbweb] N telaraña *f*; **to blow away the ~s** (*fig*) despejar la mente

cobwebbed ['kɒbwebd] ADJ cubierto de telarañas, lleno de telarañas

coca ['kəʊkə] N coca *f*

cocaine [kə'keɪn] Ⓐ N cocaína *f*
Ⓑ CPD ► **cocaine addict** N cocainómano/a *m/f* ► **cocaine addiction** N adicción *f* a la cocaína

coccyx ['kɒksɪks] N (*pl* **coccyges** [kɒk'saɪdʒiːz]) cóccix *m inv*

cochineal ['kɒtʃɪniːl] N cochinilla *f*

cochlea ['kɒklɪə] N (*pl* **cochleae** ['kɒklɪiː]) cóclea *f*, caracol *m* óseo

cock [kɒk] Ⓐ N 1 (*esp Brit*) (= *rooster*) gallo *m*; (= *other male bird*) macho *m*; **old ~!*** ¡amigo!, ¡viejo!; ✦*IDIOM* **~ of the walk** gallito *m* del lugar
2 (= *tap*) (*also* **stopcock**) llave *f* de paso
3 (**) (= *penis*) polla** *f*
4 [*of gun*] martillo *m*; **to go off at half ~** (*fig*) [*plan*] ponerse en práctica sin la debida preparación
Ⓑ VT 1 [+ *gun*] amartillar; [+ *head*] ladear; **to ~ one's eye at** mirar con intención a, guiñar el ojo a; ✦*IDIOM* **to ~ a snook at sb/sth** (*Brit*) (*fig*) burlarse de algn/algo
2 (*also* **~ up**) [+ *ears*] aguzar; **to keep one's ears ~ed** mantenerse alerta, aguzar el oído *or* la oreja
Ⓒ CPD ► **cock sparrow** N gorrión *m* macho ► **cock teaser**** N calientapollas** *f inv*

►**cock up**** VT + ADV **to ~ sth up** (*Brit*) joder algo**

cockade [kɒ'keɪd] N escarapela *f*

cock-a-doodle-doo ['kɒkəduːdl'duː] EXCL ¡quiquiriquí!

cock-a-hoop ['kɒkə'huːp] ADJ contentísimo

cockamamie*, **cockamamy*** [,kɒkə'meɪmɪ] ADJ (*US*) que no tiene ni pies ni cabeza*

cock-and-bull ['kɒkən'bʊl] ADJ **~ story** cuento *m* chino

cockatoo [,kɒkə'tuː] N cacatúa *f*

cockchafer ['kɒk,tʃeɪfəʳ] N abejorro *m*

cockcrow ['kɒkkrəʊ] N **at ~** al amanecer

cocked [kɒkt] ADJ **~ hat** sombrero *m* de tres picos; ✦*IDIOM* **to knock sth into a ~ hat** ser muy superior a algo

cocker ['kɒkəʳ] N (*also* **~ spaniel**) cocker *m*

cockerel ['kɒkrəl] N gallito *m*, gallo *m* joven

cockeyed ['kɒkaɪd] ADJ 1 (= *crooked*) torcido, chueco (*LAm*)
2 (= *absurd*) disparatado

cockfight ['kɒkfaɪt] N pelea *f* de gallos

cockfighting ['kɒk,faɪtɪŋ] N la pelea de gallos, peleas *fpl* de gallos

cockiness* ['kɒkɪnɪs] N engreimiento *m*

cockle ['kɒkl] N (*Zool*) berberecho *m*; ✦*IDIOM* **to warm the ~s of sb's heart** llenar a algn de ternura

cockleshell ['kɒklʃel] N 1 (= *shell*) concha *f* de berberecho
2 (= *boat*) cascarón *m* de nuez

cockney ['kɒknɪ] Ⓐ N 1 (= *person*) *persona nacida en el este de Londres y especialmente de clase obrera*
2 (= *dialect*) dialecto *m* de esa zona
Ⓑ ADJ *del este de Londres y especialmente de clase obrera*; → RHYMING SLANG

> **COCKNEY**
>
> *Se llama* **cockneys** *a las personas de la zona este de Londres conocida como* **East End**, *un barrio tradicionalmente obrero, aunque según la tradición un* **cockney** *auténtico ha de haber nacido dentro del área en la que se oye el repique de las campanas de la iglesia de* **Mary-Le-Bow**, *en la* **City** *londinense. Este término también hace referencia al dialecto que se habla en esta parte de Londres, aunque a veces también se aplica a cualquier acento de la clase trabajadora londinense. El actor Michael Caine es un* **cockney** *famoso.*
>
> ⇨ *Ver tb* RHYMING SLANG

cockpit ['kɒkpɪt] N 1 (*Aer*) cabina *f*
2 (*for cockfight*) reñidero *m*

cockroach ['kɒkrəʊtʃ] N cucaracha *f*

cockscomb ['kɒkskəʊm] N cresta *f* de gallo

cocksucker** ['kɒk,sʌkəʳ] N cabrón‡ *m*, mamón‡ *m*

cocksure ['kɒk'ʃʊəʳ] ADJ creído, engreído

cocktail ['kɒkteɪl] Ⓐ N (= *drink*) combinado *m*, cóctel *m*; **fruit ~** macedonia *f* de frutas; **prawn ~** cóctel *m* de gambas
Ⓑ CPD ► **cocktail bar** N (*in hotel*) bar *m* (*de cócteles*), coctelería *f* ► **cocktail cabinet** N mueble-bar *m* ► **cocktail dress** N vestido *m* de fiesta ► **cocktail lounge** N salón *m* de fiestas ► **cocktail onion** N cebolla *f* perla ► **cocktail party** N cóctel *m* ► **cocktail sausage** N salchichita *f* de aperitivo ► **cocktail shaker** N coctelera *f*

cockup‡ ['kɒkʌp] N (*Brit*) **what a ~!** ¡qué lío!, ¡qué desmadre!; **to make a ~ of sth** fastidiar algo, joder algo**; **there's been a ~ over my passport** me han armado un follón con el pasaporte*

cocky* ['kɒkɪ] ADJ (*compar* **cockier**; *superl* **cockiest**) (*pej*) creído

cocoa ['kəʊkəʊ] Ⓐ N cacao *m*; (= *drink*) chocolate *m*; **a cup of ~** una taza de chocolate
Ⓑ CPD ► **cocoa bean** N grano *m* de cacao ► **cocoa butter** N mantequilla *f* de cacao ► **cocoa powder** N cacao *m* en polvo

coconut ['kəʊkənʌt] Ⓐ N 1 (= *nut*) coco *m*
2 (= *tree*) cocotero *m*
Ⓑ CPD ► **coconut matting** N estera *f* de fibra de coco ► **coconut oil** N aceite *m* de coco ► **coconut palm** N cocotero *m* ► **coconut shy** N tiro *m* al coco ► **coconut tree** N cocotero *m*

cocoon [kə'kuːn] Ⓐ N capullo *m*
Ⓑ VT envolver

COD ABBR 1 (*Brit*) (= **cash on delivery**) C.A.E.
2 (*US*) (= **collect on delivery**) C.A.E.

cod [kɒd] N (*pl* **cod** *or* **cods**) bacalao *m*

coda ['kəʊdə] N coda *f*

coddle ['kɒdl] VT [1] (*also* **mollycoddle**) consentir, mimar
[2] (*Culin*) **~d eggs** *huevos cocidos a fuego lento*

code [kəʊd] Ⓐ N [1] (= *cipher*) clave *f*, cifra *f*; **in ~** en clave, cifrado; **it's written in ~** está cifrado *or* escrito en clave
[2] (*Telec*) prefijo *m*, código *m*; (*Comput*) código *m*; **what is the ~ for London?** ¿cuál es el prefijo *or* código de Londres?; **postal ~** código *m* postal, distrito *m* postal
[3] [*of laws*] código *m*; **~ of behaviour** código *m* de conducta; **~ of practice** código *m* profesional; *see also* **highway B**
Ⓑ VT [+ *message*] poner en clave, cifrar
Ⓒ CPD ► **code book** N libro *m* de códigos ► **code dating** N fechación *f* en código ► **code letter** N letra *f* de código ► **code name** N alias *m inv*, nombre *m* en clave; (*Pol*) nombre *m* de guerra; *see also* **code-name** ► **code number** N (*Tax*) ≈ número *m* de identificación fiscal ► **code word** N palabra *f* en clave

coded ['kəʊdɪd] ADJ en cifra, en clave (*also fig*)

codeine ['kəʊdiːn] N (*Pharm*) codeína *f*

code-name ['kəʊdneɪm] VT dar nombre en clave a; **the operation was ~d Albert** la operación tuvo el nombre en clave de Albert

codex ['kəʊdeks] N (*pl* **codices**) códice *m*

codfish ['kɒdfɪʃ] N (*pl* **codfish** *or* **codfishes**) bacalao *m*

codger* ['kɒdʒəʳ] N (*also* **old ~**) sujeto *m*, vejete *m*

codices ['kɒdɪˌsiːz] NPL *of* **codex**

codicil ['kɒdɪsɪl] N codicilo *m*

codify ['kəʊdɪfaɪ] VT codificar

coding ['kəʊdɪŋ] Ⓐ N codificación *f*
Ⓑ CPD ► **coding sheet** N hoja *f* de programación

cod-liver oil ['kɒdlɪvəʳ'ɔɪl] N aceite *m* de hígado de bacalao

codpiece ['kɒdpiːs] N (*Hist*) bragueta *f*

co-driver ['kəʊdraɪvəʳ] N (*Aut*) copiloto *mf*

codswallop‡ ['kɒdzwɒləp] N (*Brit*) chorradas* *fpl*

coed* ['kəʊ'ed] Ⓐ ADJ mixto
Ⓑ N [1] (*US*) (= *female student*) alumna *f* de un colegio mixto
[2] (*Brit*) (= *school*) colegio *m* mixto
Ⓒ ADJ, ABBR = **coeducational**

co-edition ['kəʊɪˌdɪʃən] N edición *f* conjunta

coeducation ['kəʊˌedjʊ'keɪʃən] N enseñanza *f* mixta

coeducational ['kəʊˌedjʊ'keɪʃənl] ADJ mixto

coefficient [ˌkəʊɪ'fɪʃənt] N coeficiente *m*

coelacanth ['siːləkænθ] N celacanto *m*

coerce [kəʊ'ɜːs] VT obligar, coaccionar; **to ~ sb into doing sth** obligar a algn a hacer algo, coaccionar a algn para que haga algo

coercion [kəʊ'ɜːʃən] N coacción *f*; **under ~** obligado a ello, a la fuerza

coercive [kəʊ'ɜːsɪv] ADJ coactivo, coercitivo

coeval [kəʊ'iːvəl] Ⓐ ADJ coetáneo (**with** de), contemporáneo (**with** de)
Ⓑ N coetáneo/a *m/f*, contemporáneo/a *m/f*

coexist ['kəʊɪg'zɪst] VI coexistir (**with** con)

coexistence ['kəʊɪg'zɪstəns] N coexistencia *f*

coexistent ['kəʊɪg'zɪstənt] ADJ coexistente

co-extensive [ˌkəʊɪk'stensɪv] ADJ de la misma extensión (**with** que)

C of C N ABBR = **Chamber of Commerce**

C of E [ˌsiːəv'iː] N ABBR (= **Church of England**) Iglesia *f* anglicana; **to be ~*** ser anglicano

coffee ['kɒfɪ] Ⓐ N café *m*; **a cup of ~** una taza de café, un café; **white ~** (*milky*) café *m* con leche; (*with dash of milk*) café *m* cortado; **black ~** café *m* solo, tinto *m* (*Col*); (*large*) café *m* americano; **two white ~s, please** dos cafés con leche, por favor
Ⓑ CPD ► **coffee bar** N café *m*, cafetería *f* ► **coffee bean** N grano *m* de café ► **coffee break** N descanso *m* (para tomar café) ► **coffee cake** N (*Brit*) pastel *m* de café ► **coffee cup** N taza *f* para café, tacita *f*, pocillo *m* (*LAm*) ► **coffee filter** N filtro *m* de café ► **coffee grounds** NPL poso *msing* de café ► **coffee house** N café *m* ► **coffee machine** N (*small*) máquina *f* de café, cafetera *f*; (= *vending machine*) máquina *f* expendedora de café ► **coffee maker** N máquina *f* de hacer café, cafetera *f* ► **coffee mill** N molinillo *m* de café ► **coffee morning** N tertulia *f* formada para tomar el café por la mañana ► **coffee percolator** N = **coffee maker** ► **coffee plantation** N cafetal *m* ► **coffee service**, **coffee set** N servicio *m* de café ► **coffee shop** N café *m* ► **coffee spoon** N cucharilla *f* de café ► **coffee table** N mesita *f* para servir el café ► **coffee whitener** N leche *f* en polvo

coffee-coloured, **coffee-colored** (*US*) ['kɒfɪˌkʌləd] ADJ (de) color café

coffeepot ['kɒfɪpɒt] N cafetera *f*

coffee-table book ['kɒfɪteɪblˌbʊk] N libro *m* de gran formato (*bello e impresionante*)

coffer ['kɒfəʳ] N [1] (= *chest*) cofre *m*, arca *f*; **coffers** (*fig*) tesoro *msing*, fondos *mpl*
[2] (*Archit*) (= *sunken panel*) artesón *m*
[3] = **cofferdam**

cofferdam ['kɒfədæm] N ataguía *f*

coffin ['kɒfɪn] N ataúd *m*

C of I [ˌsiːəv'aɪ] N ABBR = **Church of Ireland**

co-founder [ˌkəʊ'faʊndəʳ] N cofundador(a) *m/f*

C of S [ˌsiːəv'es] N ABBR [1] (*Rel*) = **Church of Scotland**
[2] (*Mil*) = **Chief of Staff**

cog [kɒg] N diente *m* (de rueda dentada); **✦IDIOM just a ~ in the wheel** una pieza del mecanismo, nada más

cogency ['kəʊdʒənsɪ] N convicción *f*, contundencia *f*

cogent ['kəʊdʒənt] ADJ convincente, contundente

cogently ['kəʊdʒəntlɪ] ADV de modo convincente, de forma contundente

cogitate ['kɒdʒɪteɪt] VI meditar, reflexionar

cogitation [ˌkɒdʒɪ'teɪʃən] N meditación *f*, reflexión *f*

cognac ['kɒnjæk] N coñac *m*

cognate ['kɒgneɪt] Ⓐ ADJ cognado (**with** con), afín
Ⓑ N cognado *m*

cognition [kɒg'nɪʃən] N cognición *f*

cognitive ['kɒgnɪtɪv] ADJ cognitivo, cognoscitivo; **~ modelling** modelización *f* cognoscitiva

cognizance ['kɒgnɪzəns] N conocimiento *m*; **to be within one's ~** ser de la competencia de uno; **to take ~ of** tener en cuenta

cognizant ['kɒgnɪzənt] ADJ **to be ~ of** saber, estar enterado de

cognomen [kɒg'nəʊmen] N (*frm*) (*pl* **cognomens** *or* **cognomina**) (= *surname*) apellido *m*; (= *nickname*) apodo *m*

cognoscenti [ˌkɒnəʊ'ʃentɪ] NPL expertos *mpl*, peritos *mpl*

cogwheel ['kɒgwiːl] N rueda *f* dentada

cohabit [kəʊ'hæbɪt] VI cohabitar (**with sb** con algn)

cohabitation [ˌkəʊhæbɪ'teɪʃən] N cohabitación *f*

cohere [kəʊ'hɪəʳ] VI adherirse, pegarse; [*ideas*] formar un conjunto sólido, ser consecuentes

coherence [kəʊ'hɪərəns] N coherencia *f*

coherent [kəʊ'hɪərənt] ADJ [*person, theory, argument, behaviour*] coherente, congruente; [*account, speech*] coherente; **incapable of ~ speech** incapaz de hablar coherentemente

coherently [kəʊ'hɪərəntlɪ] ADV [*think, speak, argue, act*] coherentemente, de manera coherente, con coherencia; [*behave*] coherentemente, de manera coherente

cohesion [kəʊ'hiːʒən] N cohesión *f*

cohesive [kəʊ'hiːsɪv] ADJ (*fig*) cohesivo, unido

cohesiveness [kəʊ'hiːsɪvnɪs] N cohesión *f*

cohort ['kəʊhɔːt] N cohorte *f*

COHSE ['kəʊzɪ] N ABBR (*Brit*) (*formerly*) = **Confederation of Health Service Employees**

COI N ABBR (*Brit*) = **Central Office of Information**

coif [kɔɪf] N cofia *f*

coiffed ['kwɑːft] ADJ (*frm*) peinado

coiffeur [kwɒ'fɜːʳ] N peluquero *m*

coiffure [kwɒ'fjʊəʳ] N peinado *m*

coiffured [kwɒ'fjʊəd] ADJ (*frm*) peinado

coil [kɔɪl] Ⓐ N [1] (= *roll*) rollo *m*; (= *single loop*) vuelta *f*; [*of hair*] rizo *m*; [*of snake*] anillo *m*; [*of smoke*] espiral *f*
[2] (*Aut, Elec*) bobina *f*, carrete *m*
[3] (= *contraceptive*) espiral *f*, DIU *m*
Ⓑ VT arrollar, enrollar; **to ~ sth up** enrollar algo; **to ~ sth round sth** enrollar algo alrededor de algo
Ⓒ VI [1] [*snake*] enroscarse; **to ~ up (into a ball)** hacerse un ovillo; **to ~ round sth** enroscarse alrededor de algo
[2] [*smoke*] subir en espiral

coiled [kɔɪld] ADJ arrollado, enrollado

coin [kɔɪn] Ⓐ N moneda *f*; **a 20p ~** una moneda de 20 peniques; **to toss a ~** echar una moneda al aire, jugárselo a cara o cruz; **to pay sb back in his own ~** pagar a algn en *or* con la misma moneda
Ⓑ VT [+ *money*] acuñar; (*fig*) [+ *word*] inventar, acuñar; **he must be ~ing money*** debe de estar haciéndose de oro; **to ~ a phrase** (*hum*) para decirlo así, si me permite la frase

coinage ['kɔɪnɪdʒ] N (= *system*) moneda *f*, sistema *m* monetario; (= *act*) acuñación *f*; (*fig*) [*of word*] invención *f*

coinbox ['kɔɪnbɒks] N (*Telec*) depósito *m* de monedas

coincide [ˌkəʊɪn'saɪd] VI [1] (= *happen at same time*) coincidir; **to ~ with** coincidir con
[2] (= *agree*) estar de acuerdo; **to ~ with** estar de acuerdo con

coincidence [kəʊ'ɪnsɪdəns] N coincidencia *f*, casualidad *f*; **what a ~!** ¡qué coincidencia!, ¡qué casualidad!

coincident [kəʊ'ɪnsɪdənt] ADJ [1] (= *simultaneous*) [*events*] coincidente; **~ with her marriage ...** al mismo tiempo que su boda ...
[2] (= *identical*) [*ideas, opinions*] coincidente; **to be ~ with** coincidir con

coincidental [kəʊˌɪnsɪ'dentl] ADJ [1] (= *by chance*) fortuito, casual
[2] (= *simultaneous*) coincidente

coincidentally [ˌkəʊɪnsɪ'dentəlɪ] ADV por casualidad, casualmente; **not ~, we arrived at the same time** no es una casualidad que llegáramos al mismo tiempo

coin-op* ['kɔɪnˌɒp] N ABBR (= **coin-operated laundry**) *lavandería que funciona con monedas*

coin-operated ['kɔɪn'ɒpəreɪtɪd] ADJ [*machine, laundry*] que funciona con monedas

coinsurance [ˌkəʊɪnˈʃʊərəns] N coaseguro *m*, seguro *m* copartícipe

coinsurer [ˌkəʊɪnˈʃʊərəʳ] N coasegurador(a) *m/f*

coital [ˈkɔɪtəl] ADJ (*frm*) coital; *see also* **post-coital**

coitus [ˈkɔɪtəs] N coito *m*; **~ interruptus** coitus *m* interruptus

Coke® [kəʊk] N Coca-Cola® *f*

coke [kəʊk] N 1 (= *fuel*) coque *m*
2 (*) (= *cocaine*) coca *f*

Col ABBR 1 (*Mil*) (= **Colonel**) Cnel., Cor.; **~. T. Richard** (*on envelope*) Cnel. T. Richard, Cor. T. Richard
2 (*US*) = **Colorado**

col. ABBR 1 (= **column**) col, col.[a]
2 = **colour**

COLA [ˈkəʊlə] N ABBR (*US Fin*) = **cost-of-living adjustment**

colander [ˈkʌləndəʳ] N colador *m*, escurridor *m*

cold [kəʊld] Ⓐ ADJ (*compar* **colder**; *superl* **coldest**) 1 (= *lacking heat*) frío; **a ~ buffet** un buffet frío; **to be ~** [*person*] tener frío; [*thing*] estar frío; **I'm ~** tengo frío; **my hands are ~** tengo las manos frías; **it was ~** ◊ **the weather was ~** hacía frío; **the house was ~** la casa estaba fría, en la casa hacía frío; **to get ~** [*food, coffee*] enfriarse; **your dinner's getting ~** se te está enfriando la cena; **the nights are getting ~er** está haciendo más frío por las noches; **I'm getting ~** me está entrando frío; **no, no, you're getting ~er** (*in game*) no, no, cada vez más frío; **to go ~: your coffee's going ~** se te está enfriando el café; **I went ~ at the very thought** sólo de pensarlo me entraron escalofríos; **the trail went ~ in Athens** las huellas desaparecieron en Atenas; ✦*IDIOM* **to pour** *or* **throw ~ water on** *or* **over sth** poner pegas *or* trabas a algo; *see also* **comfort A1**, **foot A1**
2 (= *hostile*) [*look, voice, person*] frío; **to get** *or* **receive a ~ reception** [*person*] tener un recibimiento frío; [*proposal*] tener una acogida fría; **to give sb a ~ reception** recibir a algn con frialdad; **to give sth a ~ reception** acoger algo con frialdad; **the proposal was given a ~ reception by the banks** los bancos acogieron la propuesta con frialdad; **to be ~ to** *or* **with sb** mostrarse frío con algn
3 (*) (= *indifferent*) ✦*IDIOM* **to leave sb ~** dejar frío a algn; **his music leaves me ~** su música me deja frío
4 (= *dispassionate*) **he approached everything with ~ logic** lo enfocaba todo con fría lógica; **the ~ facts** la cruda realidad; *see also* **blood A1**, **light[1] A1**
5 [*colour, light*] frío
6 **from ~** en frío; **I can't sing it from ~** no puedo cantarlo en frío
7 (= *unconscious*) *see also* **out A15**
Ⓑ N 1 (= *cold weather*) frío *m*; **her hands were blue with ~** tenía las manos moradas del frío; **come in out of the ~!** ¡entra, que hace frío!; **to feel the ~** ser friolento *or* (*Sp*) friolero; ✦*IDIOM* **to leave sb out in the ~** (*fig*) dejar a algn al margen, dar a algn a un lado; **she felt left out in the ~** sintió que la habían dejado al margen *or* dado de lado
2 (*Med*) resfriado *m*, catarro *m*, constipado *m*, resfrío *m* (*LAm*); **I've got a ~** estoy resfriado *or* acatarrado *or* constipado; **to catch a ~** resfriarse, constiparse; **to have a chest ~** tener el pecho congestionado *or* cargado; **you'll catch your death of ~*** vas a pillar un resfriado de muerte; **to get a ~** resfriarse, constiparse; **to give sb a/one's ~** contagiar *or* pegar un/el resfriado a algn; **to have a head ~** estar resfriado *or* constipado
Ⓒ ADV 1 (= *abruptly*) **she turned him down ~** lo rechazó rotundamente; **he stopped ~ in his tracks** se paró en seco
2 (= *without preparation*) **he played his part ~** representó su papel en frío *or* sin haberse preparado de antemano; **to come to sth ~** llegar a algo frío *or* sin preparación
Ⓓ CPD ► **cold calling** N venta *f* en frío ► **cold cream** N crema *f* hidratante ► **cold cuts** NPL (*US*) = **cold meats** ► **cold fish** N (*fig*) persona *f* seca ► **cold frame** N vivero *m* para plantas ► **cold front** N (*Met*) frente *m* frío ► **cold meats** NPL fiambres *fpl*, embutidos *mpl* ► **cold snap** N ola *f* de frío ► **cold sore** N herpes *m inv* labial, pupa* *f* ► **cold start** N (*Aut*) arranque *m* en frío ► **cold storage** N conservación *f* en cámaras frigoríficas; **to put sth into ~ storage** [+ *food*] refrigerar algo; (*) (*fig*) [+ *project*] aparcar algo* ► **cold store** N cámara *f* frigorífica ► **cold sweat** N sudor *m* frío; **he broke into a ~ sweat** le entró un sudor frío ► **cold turkey*** N mono* *m*, síndrome *m* de abstinencia; **to go ~ turkey** dejar la droga en seco; **he quit smoking ~ turkey** dejó de fumar a base de aguantarse el mono* ► **cold war** N guerra *f* fría

cold-blooded [ˈkəʊldˈblʌdɪd] ADJ (*Zool*) de sangre fría; (*fig*) desalmado, despiadado

cold-bloodedly [ˈkəʊldˈblʌdɪdlɪ] ADV a sangre fría

cold-hearted [ˈkəʊldˈhɑːtɪd] ADJ insensible, cruel

coldly [ˈkəʊldlɪ] ADV (*fig*) fríamente, con frialdad

coldness [ˈkəʊldnɪs] N 1 (*lit*) (= *lack of heat*) frío *m*
2 (*fig*) (= *hostility*) frialdad *f*

cold-shoulder [ˈkəʊldˈʃəʊldəʳ] VT (*rebuff*) volver la espalda a

coleslaw [ˈkəʊlslɔː] N *ensalada de col, zanahoria, cebolla y mayonesa*

coley [ˈkəʊlɪ] N abadejo *m*

colic [ˈkɒlɪk] N (*esp of horses, children*) cólico *m*

colicky [ˈkɒlɪkɪ] ADJ [*baby*] que padece de cólicos; [*pain*] de cólico; **to be ~** tener un cólico

Coliseum [ˌkɒlɪˈsiːəm] N Coliseo *m*

colitis [kɒˈlaɪtɪs] N colitis *f*

collaborate [kəˈlæbəreɪt] VI (*also Pol*) colaborar; **to ~ on sth/in doing sth** colaborar en algo; **to ~ with sb** colaborar con algn

collaboration [kəˌlæbəˈreɪʃən] N colaboración *f*; (*Pol*) colaboracionismo *m*; **in ~** en colaboración (**with** con)

collaborationist [kəˈlæbəˈreɪʃənɪst] ADJ colaboracionista

collaborative [kəˈlæbərətɪv] ADJ **by a ~ effort** por un esfuerzo común, ayudándose unos a otros; **it's a ~ work** es un trabajo de colaboración

collaboratively [kəˈlæbərətɪvlɪ] ADV en colaboración

collaborator [kəˈlæbəreɪtəʳ] N colaborador(a) *m/f*; (*Pol*) colaboracionista *mf*

collage [kɒˈlɑːʒ] N collage *m*

collagen [ˈkɒlədʒən] N colágeno *m*

collapse [kəˈlæps] Ⓐ N (*Med*) colapso *m*; [*of building, roof, floor*] hundimiento *m*, desplome *m*; [*of government*] caída *f*; [*of plans, scheme*] fracaso *m*; (*financial*) ruina *f*; [*of civilization, society*] ocaso *m*; (*Comm*) [*of business*] quiebra *f*; [*of prices*] hundimiento *m*, caída *f*
Ⓑ VI 1 [*person*] (*Med*) sufrir un colapso; (*with laughter*) morirse (de risa); [*building, roof, floor*] hundirse, desplomarse; [*civilization, society*] desaparecer, extinguirse; [*government*] caer; [*scheme*] fracasar; [*business*] quebrar; [*prices*] hundirse, bajar repentinamente; **the bridge ~d during the storm** el puente se vino abajo durante la tormenta; **the deal ~d** el negocio fracasó; **the company ~d** la compañía quebró *or* se hundió
2 (= *fold down*) plegarse, doblarse

collapsible [kəˈlæpsəbl] ADJ plegable

collar [ˈkɒləʳ] Ⓐ N 1 [*of coat, shirt*] cuello *m*; ✦*IDIOM* **to get hot under the ~** sulfurarse
2 (= *necklace*) collar *m*
3 (*for dog*) collar *m*
4 (*Med*) collarín *m*
5 (*Tech*) (*on pipe etc*) collar *m*
Ⓑ VT (*) [+ *person*] abordar, acorralar; [+ *object*] (= *get for o.s.*) apropiarse
Ⓒ N ► **collar button** N (*US*) = **collarstud** ► **collar size** N medida *f* del cuello

collarbone [ˈkɒləbəʊn] N clavícula *f*

collarstud [ˈkɒləstʌd] N (*Brit*) botón *m* de camisa

collate [kɒˈleɪt] VT cotejar

collateral [kɒˈlætərəl] Ⓐ N 1 (*Fin*) garantía *f* subsidiaria
2 (= *person*) colateral *mf*
Ⓑ CPD ► **collateral loan** N préstamo *m* colateral ► **collateral security** N garantía *f* colateral

collation [kəˈleɪʃən] N 1 [*of texts*] cotejo *m*
2 (= *meal*) colación *f*

colleague [ˈkɒliːg] N colega *mf*

collect [kəˈlekt] Ⓐ VT 1 (= *assemble*) reunir, juntar; [+ *facts, documents*] recopilar, reunir; (= *collect in*) recoger; **the teacher ~ed the exercise books** el maestro recogió los cuadernos; **to ~ o.s.** *or* **one's thoughts** (*fig*) reponerse, recobrar el dominio de uno mismo
2 (*as hobby*) [+ *stamps, valuables*] coleccionar
3 (= *call for, pick up*) [+ *person*] recoger, pasar por (*LAm*); [+ *post, rubbish*] recoger; [+ *books*] coger, recoger; [+ *subscriptions, rent*] cobrar; [+ *taxes*] recaudar; [+ *ticket*] recoger; **I'll ~ you at eight** vengo a recogerte a las ocho; **their mother ~s them from school** su madre los recoge del colegio, su madre los pasa a buscar por el colegio; **I'll go and ~ the mail** voy por el correo
4 (= *gather*) [+ *dust, water*] acumular, retener
Ⓑ VI 1 (= *gather*) [*people*] reunirse, congregarse; [*water*] estancarse; [*dust*] acumularse
2 (= *collect money*) hacer una colecta; **I'm ~ing for UNICEF** estoy haciendo una colecta para la UNICEF; **to ~ for charity** recaudar *or* recolectar fondos con fines benéficos
3 (= *pick up*) **~ on delivery** (*US*) contra reembolso
Ⓒ ADV **to call ~** (*US Telec*) llamar a cobro revertido
Ⓓ CPD ► **collect call** N (*US*) llamada *f* a cobro revertido

collectable [kəˈlektəbl] N coleccionable *m*

collected [kəˈlektɪd] ADJ 1 (= *cool*) sosegado, tranquilo
2 (= *compiled*) **the ~ works of Shakespeare** las obras completas de Shakespeare

collectible [kəˈlektəbl] N coleccionable *m*

collecting [kəˈlektɪŋ] Ⓐ N coleccionismo *m*, el coleccionar
Ⓑ CPD ► **collecting box**, **collecting tin** N bote *m* de cuestación, lata *f* petitoria

collection [kəˈlekʃən] Ⓐ N 1 (= *act of collecting*) [*of post, rubbish*] recogida *f*; [*of taxes*] recaudación *f*; **to await ~** estar listo para ser recogido
2 (= *things collected*) [*of pictures, stamps*] co-

lección *f*; (*pej*) montón *m*; **my CD ~** mi colección de CDs
[3] (= *money*) colecta *f*; **a ~ for charity** una colecta para obras benéficas; **to make a ~ for** hacer una colecta a beneficio de
[4] (= *group of people*) grupo *m*
(B) CPD ► **collection charges** NPL (*Fin, Comm*) gastos *mpl* de recogida ► **collection plate** N cepillo *m*, platillo *m*

collective [kəˈlektɪv] (A) N [1] (= *co-operative*) colectivo *m*
[2] (*also* **~ noun**) (*Ling*) colectivo *m*
(B) ADJ colectivo
(C) CPD ► **collective bargaining** N negociación *f* del convenio colectivo ► **collective farm** N granja *f* colectiva ► **collective noun** N sustantivo *m* colectivo, nombre *m* colectivo ► **collective ownership** N propiedad *f* colectiva ► **collective security** N seguridad *f* colectiva ► **collective unconscious** N subconsciente *m* colectivo

collectively [kəˈlektɪvlɪ] ADV colectivamente

collectivism [kəˈlektɪvɪzəm] N colectivismo *m*

collectivist [kəˈlektɪvɪst] ADJ colectivista

collectivization [kəˌlektɪvaɪˈzeɪʃən] N colectivización *f*

collectivize [kəˈlektɪvaɪz] VT colectivizar

collector [kəˈlektəʳ] N [*of taxes*] recaudador(a) *m/f*; [*of stamps*] coleccionista *mf*; **~'s item** *or* **piece** pieza *f* de coleccionista; *see also* **ticket C**

colleen [ˈkɒliːn] N (*Irl*) muchacha *f*

college [ˈkɒlɪdʒ] N (= *part of university*) colegio *m* universitario, escuela *f* universitaria; (*US*) [*of university*] ≈ facultad *f*; [*of agriculture, technology*] escuela *f*; [*of music*] conservatorio *m*; (= *body*) colegio *m*; **College of Advanced Technology** (*Brit*) politécnico *m*; **College of Further Education** Escuela de Formación Profesional; **to go to ~** seguir estudios superiores

> **COLLEGE**
>
> *En el Reino Unido* **college** *es un término que designa a cualquier institución de estudios no primarios. Puede hacer referencia a centros que otorgan un título de licenciado en materias específicas, como arte o música, o a centros de formación profesional. Además algunas universidades como Oxford y Cambridge se componen de* **colleges** *en los que los estudiantes tienen también alojamiento.*
>
> *En la universidad estadounidense, un* **college** *es normalmente una división administrativa, semejante a una facultad, como por ejemplo* **College of Arts and Science** *o* **College of Medicine**. *En ellos se pueden estudiar carreras de cuatro años tras las que se obtiene el título de* **bachelor's degree**. *Los cursos de postgrado se imparten en* **graduate schools**. *Por otra parte, en los centros denominados* **junior colleges** *o* **community colleges** *se otorga un diploma llamado* **associate degree** *después de dos años de estudio y también se imparten clases de formación profesional a gente que está ya trabajando.*
>
> ⇨ *Ver tb* DEGREE

collegiate [kəˈliːdʒɪɪt] ADJ [1] (*Rel*) colegial, colegiado; **~ church** iglesia *f* colegial
[2] (*Univ*) que tiene colegios, organizado a base de colegios

collide [kəˈlaɪd] VI **to ~ (with)** (*lit, fig*) chocar (con), colisionar (con)

collie [ˈkɒlɪ] N perro *m* pastor escocés, collie *m*

collier [ˈkɒlɪəʳ] N [1] (= *miner*) minero *m* (de carbón)
[2] (= *ship*) barco *m* carbonero

colliery [ˈkɒlɪərɪ] N (*Brit*) mina *f* de carbón

collision [kəˈlɪʒən] (A) N choque *m*, colisión *f*; **to come into ~ with** chocar con, colisionar con
(B) CPD ► **collision course** N **to be on a ~ course** (*fig*) ir camino del enfrentamiento

collocate [ˈkɒləkət] (*Ling*) (A) N colocador *m*
(B) VI [ˈkɒləkeɪt] **to ~ with** colocarse con

collocation [ˌkɒləˈkeɪʃən] N colocación *f*

colloquia [kəˈləʊkwɪə] NPL *of* **colloquium**

colloquial [kəˈləʊkwɪəl] ADJ coloquial, familiar

colloquialism [kəˈləʊkwɪəlɪzəm] N (= *word*) palabra *f* familiar; (= *expression*) expresión *f* familiar; (= *style*) estilo *m* familiar

colloquially [kəˈləʊkwɪəlɪ] ADV coloquialmente

colloquium [kəˈləʊkwɪəm] N (*pl* **colloquiums** *or* **colloquia**) coloquio *m*

colloquy [ˈkɒləkwɪ] N coloquio *m*

collude [kəˈluːd] VI confabularse (**with** con)

collusion [kəˈluːʒən] N confabulación *f*, connivencia *f*; **to be in ~ with** confabular *or* conspirar con

collusive [kəˈluːsɪv] ADJ (*frm*) [*behaviour*] colusivo, connivente

collywobbles* [ˈkɒlɪˌwɒblz] N (*fig*) nerviosismo *m*, ataque *m* de nervios

Colo. ABBR (*US*) = **Colorado**

Cologne [kəˈləʊn] N Colonia *f*

cologne [kəˈləʊn] N (*also* **eau de ~**) agua *f* de colonia, colonia *f*

Colombia [kəˈlɒmbɪə] N Colombia *f*

Colombian [kəˈlɒmbɪən] (A) ADJ colombiano
(B) N colombiano/a *m/f*

colon[1] [ˈkəʊlən] N (*pl* **colons** *or* **cola**) (*Anat*) colon *m*

colon[2] [ˈkəʊlən] N (*pl* **colons**) (*Typ*) dos puntos *mpl*

colonel [ˈkɜːnl] N coronel *m*

colonial [kəˈləʊnɪəl] (A) ADJ colonial; **the ~ power** el poder colonizador
(B) N colono *m*

colonialism [kəˈləʊnɪəlɪzəm] N colonialismo *m*

colonialist [kəˈləʊnɪəlɪst] N colonialista *mf*

colonic [kəʊˈlɒnɪk] (A) ADJ de colon
(B) CPD ► **colonic irrigation** N lavado *m* de colon

colonist [ˈkɒlənɪst] N (= *pioneer*) colonizador(a) *m/f*; (= *inhabitant*) colono *m*

colonization [ˌkɒlənaɪˈzeɪʃən] N colonización *f*

colonize [ˈkɒlənaɪz] VT colonizar

colonnade [ˌkɒləˈneɪd] N columnata *f*, galería *f*

colony [ˈkɒlənɪ] N (*pl* **colonies**) colonia *f*

colophon [ˈkɒləfən] N colofón *m*, pie *m* de imprenta

color *etc* [ˈkʌləʳ] N, VT, VI (*US*) = **colour** *etc*

Colorado beetle [ˌkɒləˌrɑːdəʊˈbiːtl] N escarabajo *m* de la patata, dorífora *f*

colorant [ˈkʌlərənt] N (*US*) = **colourant**

coloration [ˌkʌləˈreɪʃən] N colorido *m*, colores *mpl*, coloración *f*

coloratura [ˌkɒlərəˈtʊərə] N [1] (= *passage*) coloratura *f*
[2] (= *singer*) soprano *f* de coloratura

colorcast [ˈkʌləkɑːst] (*US*) (A) N programa *m* de TV en color
(B) VT transmitir en color

colossal [kəˈlɒsl] ADJ colosal, descomunal

colossally [kəˈlɒsəlɪ] ADV colosalmente, descomunalmente

colossus [kəˈlɒsəs] N (*pl* **colossi** *or* **colossuses**) coloso *m*

colostomy [kəˈlɒstəmɪ] N colostomía *f*

colostrum [kəˈlɒstrəm] N colostro *m*, calostro *m*

colour, color (*US*) [ˈkʌləʳ] (A) N [1] (= *shade*) color *m*; **what ~ is it?** ¿de qué color es?; **they come in different ~s** los hay de varios colores; **to change ~** cambiar *or* mudar de color; **it was green in ~** era de color verde; **as time goes by my memories take on a different ~** (*fig*) con el paso de los años mis recuerdos van tomando otro color; ✦*IDIOM* **let's see the ~ of your money!** (*hum*) ¡a ver la pasta!*
[2] (= *colourfulness*) color *m*; **splashes of ~** salpicones *fpl or* notas *fpl* de color; **what this room needs is a touch of ~** lo que este cuarto necesita es un toque de color; **in ~** (*TV, Cine*) en color
[3] (= *dye, paint, pigment*) color *m*; **the latest lip and eye ~s** los últimos colores para labios y ojos
[4] (= *complexion*) color *m*; **the ~ drained from his face** palideció, se le fue el color de la cara; **the ~ rose to her face** se le subieron los colores; **to put the ~ back in sb's cheeks** devolverle el color *or* los colores a algn; ✦*IDIOM* **to be off ~** estar indispuesto
[5] (= *race*) color *m*; **people of ~** (*US*) personas *fpl* de color
[6] **colours** [*of country, team*] colores *mpl*; (= *flag*) bandera *f*; (*Mil*) estandarte *m*; **the Hungarian national ~s** los colores húngaros; (= *flag*) la bandera húngara; **to salute the ~s** saludar a la bandera; **the battalion's ~s** el estandarte del batallón; **he was wearing the team's ~s** vestía los colores del equipo; ✦*IDIOMS* **with flying ~s**: **she passed her exams with flying ~s** aprobó los exámenes con unas notas excelentes; **he has come out of all the tests with flying ~s** ha salido airoso de todas las pruebas; **to nail one's ~s to the mast**: **he nailed his ~s to the mast** hizo constar sus opiniones; **to show one's true ~s** ◊ **show o.s. in one's true ~s** demostrar cómo se es de verdad; *see also* **flying A**
[7] (= *authenticity, vividness*) color *m*, colorido *m*; **an article full of local ~** un artículo lleno de colorido local
[8] (= *pretext*) **under the ~ of ...** bajo la apariencia de ...
[9] (*Mus*) (*also* **tone ~**) timbre *m*
(B) VT [1] (= *apply colour to*) [+ *picture*] (*with paint*) pintar; (*with crayons*) colorear
[2] (= *dye, tint*) teñir; **to ~ one's hair** teñirse *or* tintarse el pelo
[3] (= *influence*) influir en; **his politics are ~ed by his upbringing** sus opiniones políticas están influenciadas por su educación; **you must not allow it to ~ your judgement** no debes permitir que influya en tu juicio
(C) VI [1] (= *blush*) ponerse colorado, sonrojarse
[2] (= *change colour*) tomar color; **fry the onion until it begins to ~** fría la cebolla hasta que empiece a coger color
[3] (*with crayons*) [*child*] colorear
(D) CPD [*film, photograph, slide*] en *or* (*LAm*) a color ► **colour bar** N barrera *f* racial ► **colour blindness** N daltonismo *m* ► **colour filter** N (*Phot*) filtro *m* de color ► **colour guard** N (*Mil*) portaestandarte *mf* ► **colour line** N barrera *f* de color ► **colour match** N coordinación *f* de colores ► **colour prejudice** N prejuicio *m* racial ► **colour scheme** N combinación *f* de colores ► **colour sergeant** N (*Mil*) sargento *mf* por-

taestandarte ► **colour supplement** N (*Journalism*) suplemento *m* a color ► **colour television** N televisión *f* en color, televisión *f* a color (*LAm*)

►**colour in** VT + ADV (*with crayons*) colorear; (*with paint*) pintar

colourant, colorant (*US*) ['kʌlərənt] N colorante *m*

colour-blind, color-blind (*US*) ['kʌləblaɪnd] ADJ daltónico

colour-coded, color-coded (*US*) ['kʌlə'kəʊdɪd] ADJ con código de colores

coloured, colored (*US*) ['kʌləd] Ⓐ ADJ [1] [*pencils, glass, chalk, beads*] de colores; **brightly ~ silks** sedas *fpl* de colores vivos
[2] (= *biased*) parcial; **a highly ~ tale** una historia de lo más parcial
[3] (†) (= *black*) [*person*] de color
Ⓑ N [1] (†) (= *black*) persona *f* de color
[2] (*in South Africa*) *persona de padres racialmente mixtos*
[3] **coloureds** (= *clothes*) ropa *fsing* de color

-coloured, -colored (*US*) [ˌkʌləd] ADJ (*ending in compounds*) **rust-coloured** de color de herrumbre, color herrumbre; **gold-coloured** (de color) dorado; **straw-coloured** (de) color paja; **coffee-coloured** (de) color café

colourfast, colorfast (*US*) ['kʌləfɑːst] ADJ no desteñible

colourful, colorful (*US*) ['kʌləfəl] ADJ [1] (= *bright*) [*display, image*] lleno de color, lleno de colorido; [*procession*] lleno de colorido; [*clothes, design, pattern*] de colores vivos; **a bunch of ~ flowers** un ramo de flores de vistosos colores
[2] (= *picturesque*) [*figure, character, story, history*] pintoresco; [*description, account, style*] colorista; [*scene*] vivo, animado; **her ~ past** (*euph*) su movidito pasado*
[3] (*euph*) (= *vulgar*) [*language*] subido de tono

colourfully, colorfully (*US*) ['kʌləfʊlɪ] ADV [1] (= *brightly*) [*decorated, painted*] con colores muy vivos; [*dressed*] de forma muy vistosa
[2] (= *in picturesque terms*) [*describe*] con mucho colorido; **he swore ~** utilizó expresiones muy subidas de tono

colouring, coloring (*US*) ['kʌlərɪŋ] Ⓐ N (*gen*) colorido *m*; (= *substance*) colorante *m*; (= *complexion*) tez *f*; **"no artificial colouring"** "sin colores artificiales"; **food ~** colorante *m*; **high ~** sonrojamiento *m*
Ⓑ CPD ► **colouring book** N libro *m* (con dibujos) para colorear

colourist, colorist (*US*) ['kʌlərɪst] N [1] (= *artist*) colorista *mf*
[2] (= *hairdresser*) *peluquero especializado en tintes*

colourless, colorless (*US*) ['kʌləlɪs] ADJ sin color, incoloro; (*fig*) (= *dull*) [*person*] soso; **a ~ liquid** un líquido transparente

colourway ['kʌləweɪ] N (*Brit*) combinación *f* de colores

colt [kəʊlt] N potro *m*

coltish ['kəʊltɪʃ] ADJ juguetón, retozón

coltsfoot ['kəʊltsfʊt] N (*pl* **coltsfoots**) uña *f* de caballo, fárfara *f*

Columbia [kə'lʌmbɪə] N **(District of) ~** (*US*) Distrito *m* de Columbia

Columbine ['kɒləmbaɪn] N Columbina

columbine ['kɒləmbaɪn] N aguileña *f*

Columbus [kə'lʌmbəs] Ⓐ N Colón
Ⓑ CPD ► **Columbus Day** N Día *m* de la Raza

column ['kɒləm] Ⓐ N (*gen*) columna *f*; (*in newspaper*) columna *f*, sección *f*; **fifth ~** quinta columna *f*; **spinal ~** (*Anat*) columna *f* vertebral
Ⓑ CPD ► **column inch** N **they gave the news only two ~ inches** dieron sólo dos pulgadas de columna a la noticia

columnist ['kɒləmnɪst] N columnista *mf*, articulista *mf*

colza ['kɒlzə] N colza *f*

coma ['kəʊmə] N coma *m*; **to be in a ~** estar en (estado de) coma

comatose ['kəʊmətəʊs] ADJ comatoso

comb [kəʊm] Ⓐ N [1] (*for hair*) peine *m*; (*ornamental*) peineta *f*; (*for horse*) almohaza *f*; **to run a ~ through one's hair** peinarse, pasarse un peine
[2] [*of fowl*] cresta *f*
[3] (= *honeycomb*) panal *m*
[4] (*Tech*) carda *f*
Ⓑ VT [1] [+ *hair*] peinar; **to ~ one's hair** peinarse
[2] (= *search*) [+ *countryside*] registrar a fondo, peinar; **we've been ~ing the town for you** te hemos buscado por toda la ciudad
[3] (*Tech*) [+ *wool*] cardar

►**comb out** VT + ADV [+ *hair*] desenmarañar; **they ~ed out the useless members of the staff** se deshicieron de los miembros del personal inútiles

combat ['kɒmbæt] Ⓐ N combate *m*
Ⓑ VT (*fig*) combatir, luchar contra
Ⓒ CPD ► **combat duty** N servicio *m* de frente ► **combat jacket** N guerrera *f* ► **combat troops** NPL tropas *fpl* de combate ► **combat zone** N zona *f* de combate

combatant ['kɒmbətənt] N combatiente *mf*

combative ['kɒmbətɪv] ADJ combativo

combe [kuːm] N = **coomb**

combination [ˌkɒmbɪ'neɪʃən] Ⓐ N [1] (*gen*) combinación *f*; (= *mixture*) mezcla *f*; **a ~ of circumstances** un conjunto *or* una combinación de circunstancias
[2] [*of safe*] combinación *f*
[3] **combinations** (= *undergarment*) combinación *f*
Ⓑ CPD ► **combination lock** N cerradura *f* de combinación

combinatory [ˌkɒmbɪ'neɪtərɪ] ADJ combinacional

combine [kəm'baɪn] Ⓐ VT **to ~ (with)** combinar (con); **the film ~s humour with suspense** la película combina el humor con el suspense; **to ~ business with pleasure** combinar los negocios con el placer; **expertise ~d with charm** la pericia combinada con la simpatía; **he ~s all the qualities of a leader** reúne todas las cualidades de un líder; **it's difficult to ~ a career with a family** es difícil compaginar la profesión con la vida familiar; **a ~d effort** un esfuerzo conjunto; **a ~d operation** (*Mil*) una operación conjunta
Ⓑ [kəm'baɪn] VI [1] (= *join together*) combinarse, unirse; **to ~ with** aunarse con; **to ~ against sth/sb** unirse en contra de algo/algn
[2] (*Chem*) **to ~ (with)** combinarse (con), mezclarse (con)
Ⓒ ['kɒmbaɪn] N [1] (*Comm*) asociación *f*
[2] (*also* **~ harvester**) cosechadora *f*
Ⓓ ['kɒmbaɪn] CPD ► **combine harvester** N cosechadora *f*

combings ['kəʊmɪŋz] NPL peinaduras *fpl*

combo* ['kɒmbəʊ] N (*pl* **combos**) [1] (*Mus*) grupo *m*, conjunto *m*
[2] (= *clothes*) conjunto *m*

combs* [kɒmz] NPL combinación *f*

combustible [kəm'bʌstɪbl] Ⓐ ADJ combustible
Ⓑ N combustible *m*

combustion [kəm'bʌstʃən] Ⓐ N combustión *f*; *see also* **internal**
Ⓑ CPD ► **combustion chamber** N cámara *f* de combustión

come [kʌm] (*pt* **came**; *pp* **come**) Ⓐ VI [1] (*gen*) venir; (= *arrive*) llegar; **we have ~ to help you** hemos venido a ayudarte; **when did he ~?** ¿cuándo llegó?; **they came late** llegaron tarde; **the letter came this morning** la carta llegó esta mañana; **(I'm) coming!** ¡voy!, ¡ya voy!; **he came running/dashing** *etc* **in** entró corriendo/volando *etc*; **the day/time will ~ when …** ya llegará el día/la hora (en) que …; **it will be two years ~ March** en marzo hará dos años; **a week ~ Monday** ocho días a partir del lunes; **we'll ~ after you** te seguiremos; **~ and see us soon** ven a vernos pronto; **it may ~ as a surprise to you …** puede que te asombre *or* (*LAm*) extrañe …; **it came as a shock to her** le afectó mucho; **to ~ for sth/sb** venir por *or* (*LAm*) pasar por algo/algn; **to ~ from** (= *stem from*) [*word, custom*] venir de, proceder de, provenir de; (= *originate from*) [*person*] ser de; **she has just ~ from London** acaba de venir *or* (*LAm*) regresar de Londres; **I ~ from Wigan** soy de Wigan; **where do you ~ from?** ¿de dónde eres?; **this necklace ~s from Spain** este collar es de España; **I don't know where you're coming from** (*US**) no alcanzo a comprender la base de tu argumento; **to ~ and go** ir y venir; **people were coming and going all day** la gente iba y venía todo el día; **the pain ~s and goes** el dolor va y viene; **the picture ~s and goes** (*TV*) un momento tenemos imagen y al siguiente no; **~ home** ven a casa; **it never came into my mind** no pasó siquiera por mi mente; **we came to a village** llegamos a un pueblo; **to ~ to a decision** llegar a una decisión; **the water only came to her waist** el agua le llegaba sólo hasta la cintura; **it came to me that there was a better way to do it** se me ocurrió que había otra forma mejor de hacerlo; **when it ~s to choosing, I prefer wine** si tengo que elegir, prefiero vino; **when it ~s to mathematics …** en cuanto a *or* en lo que se refiere a las matemáticas …; **when your turn ~s** cuando llegue tu turno; **they have ~ a long way** (*lit*) han venido desde muy lejos; (*fig*) han llegado muy lejos; **~ with me** ven conmigo
[2] (= *have its place*) venir; **May ~s before June** mayo viene antes de junio; **it ~s on the next page** viene en la pagina siguiente; **work ~s before pleasure** primero el trabajo, luego la diversión; **the adjective ~s before the noun** el adjetivo precede al sustantivo; **he came third** llego en tercer lugar
[3] (= *happen*) pasar, ocurrir; **recovery came slowly** la recuperación fue lenta; **how does this chair ~ to be broken?** ¿cómo es que esta silla está rota?; **how ~?*** ¿cómo es eso?, ¿cómo así?, ¿por qué?; **how ~ you don't know?*** ¿cómo es que no lo sabes?; **no good will ~ of it** de eso no saldrá nada bueno; **nothing came of it** todo quedó en nada; **that's what ~s of being careless** eso es lo que pasa *or* ocurre por la falta de cuidado; **no harm will ~ to him** no le pasará nada; **~ what may** pase lo que pase
[4] (= *be, become*) **I have ~ to like her** ha llegado a caerme bien; **I came to think it was all my fault** llegué a la conclusión de que era culpa mía; **now I ~ to think of it** ahora que lo pienso, pensándolo bien; **it came to pass that …** (*liter*) aconteció que …; **those shoes ~ in two colours** esos zapatos vienen en dos colores; **the button has ~ loose** el botón se

ha soltado; **it ~s naturally to him** lo hace sin esfuerzo, no le cuesta nada hacerlo; **it'll all ~ right in the end** al final, todo se arreglará; **my dreams came true** mis sueños se hicieron realidad

5 (*) (= *have orgasm*) correrse (*Sp***), acabar (*LAm***)

6 (*in phrases*) **~ again?*** ¿cómo (dice)?; **he's as good as they ~** es bueno como él solo; **he's as stupid as they ~** es tonto de remate; **I like my tea just as it ~s** me gusta el té hecho de cualquier modo; **they don't ~ any better than that** mejores no los hay; **to ~ between two people** (= *interfere*) meterse *or* entrometerse entre dos personas; (= *separate*) separar a dos personas; **nothing can ~ between us** no hay nada que sea capaz de separarnos; **cars like that don't ~ cheap** los coches así no son baratos; **come, come!** ¡vamos!; **the new ruling ~s into force next year** la nueva ley entra en vigor el año que viene; **I don't know whether I'm coming or going** no sé lo que me hago; **he had it coming to him*** se lo tenía bien merecido; **if it ~s to it** llegado el caso; **oh, ~ now!** ¡vamos!; **I could see it coming** lo veía venir; **~ to that ...** si vamos a eso ...; **in (the) years to ~** en los años venideros

Ⓑ VT **don't ~ that game with me!*** ¡no me vengas con esos cuentos!; **that's coming it a bit strong** eso me parece algo exagerado, no es para tanto

►**come about** VI + ADV suceder, ocurrir; **how did this ~ about?** ¿cómo ha sido esto?

►**come across** Ⓐ VI + ADV 1 (= *make an impression*) **to ~ across well/badly** causar buena/mala impresión; **she ~s across as a nice girl** da la impresión de ser una chica simpática; **it didn't ~ across like that** no lo entendimos en ese sentido, no es ésa la impresión que nos produjo

2 (*US*) (= *keep one's word*) cumplir la palabra

Ⓑ VI + PREP (= *find*) dar con, topar con, encontrarse con; **I came across a dress that I hadn't worn for years** di con *or* me encontré un vestido que hacía años que no me ponía

►**come across with** VI + PREP [+ *money*] apoquinar*; **to ~ across with the information** soltar prenda

►**come along** VI + ADV 1 **~ along!** (*in friendly tone*) ¡vamos!, ¡venga!, ¡ándale! (*esp Mex*), ¡ándele! (*Mex*); (*impatiently*) ¡date prisa!, ¡apúrate! (*LAm*)

2 (= *accompany*) acompañar; **are you coming along?** ¿vienes?, ¿nos acompañas?; **you'll have to ~ along with me to the station** usted tendrá que acompañarme a la comisaría

3 (= *progress*) ir; **how is the book coming along?** ¿qué tal va el libro?; **it's coming along nicely** va bien

4 (= *arrive*) [*chance*] presentarse; **then who should ~ along but Alex** entonces se presentó nada más ni nada menos que Alex

►**come apart** VI + ADV deshacerse, caer en pedazos

►**come around** VI + ADV = **come round**

►**come at** VI + PREP 1 [+ *solution*] llegar a

2 (= *attack*) atacar, precipitarse sobre

►**come away** VI + ADV 1 (= *leave*) marcharse, salir; **~ away from there!** ¡sal *or* quítate de ahí!

2 (= *become detached*) separarse, desprenderse

►**come back** VI + ADV 1 (= *return*) volver, regresar (*LAm*); **my brother is coming back tomorrow** mi hermano vuelve mañana; **would you like to ~ back for a cup of tea?** ¿quieres volver a casa a tomar un té?; **to ~ back to what we were discussing ...** volviendo a lo anterior ...; **it all ~s back to money** todo viene a ser cuestión de dinero

2 (*) (= *reply*) **can I ~ back to you on that one?** ¿te importa si dejamos ese punto para mas tarde?; **when accused, he came back with a counter-accusation** cuando le acusaron, respondió con una contraacusación

3 (= *return to mind*) **it's all coming back to me** ahora sí me acuerdo

►**come before** VI + PREP (*Jur*) [*person*] comparecer ante; **his case came before the courts** su caso llegó a los tribunales

►**come by** Ⓐ VI + PREP (= *obtain*) conseguir, adquirir; **how did she ~ by that name?** ¿cómo adquirió ese nombre?

Ⓑ VI + ADV 1 (= *pass*) pasar; **could I ~ by please?** ¿me permite?, ¿se puede?

2 (= *visit*) visitar, entrar a ver; **next time you ~ by** la próxima vez que vengas por aquí

►**come down** Ⓐ VI + PREP bajar; **to ~ down the stairs** bajar las escaleras

Ⓑ VI + ADV 1 (= *descend*) [*person, prices, temperature*] bajar (**from** de; **to** a); [*rain*] caer; [*plane*] (= *land*) aterrizar; (= *crash*) estrellarse; **to ~ down in the world** venir a menos; **to ~ down hard on sb** ser duro con algn; **she came down on them like a ton of bricks** se les echó encima; **to ~ down against a policy** declararse en contra de una política; **so it ~s down to this** así que se reduce a esto; **if it ~s down to it, we'll have to move** si es necesario habrá que mudarse; **to ~ down on sb's side** tomar partido por algn; **if it ~s down heads** [*coin*] si sale cara

2 (= *be transmitted*) [*heirloom*] pasar; [*tradition*] ser transmitido

3 [*building*] (= *be demolished*) ser derribado/a; (= *fall down*) derrumbarse

►**come down with** VI + PREP 1 (= *become ill from*) caer enfermo de, enfermar de; **to ~ down with flu** caer enfermo *or* enfermar de gripe

2 (*) (= *pay out*) apoquinar

►**come forward** VI + ADV 1 (= *advance*) avanzar

2 (= *volunteer*) ofrecerse, presentarse; **to ~ forward with a suggestion** ofrecer una sugerencia

3 (= *respond*) responder

►**come in** VI + ADV [*person*] entrar; [*train, person in race*] llegar; [*tide*] crecer; **~ in!** ¡pase!, ¡entre!, ¡siga! (*LAm*); **the Tories came in at the last election** en las últimas elecciones, ganaron los conservadores; **where do I ~ in?** y yo ¿qué hago?, y yo ¿qué pinto?; **they have no money coming in** no tienen ingresos *or* (*LAm*) entradas; **he has £500 coming in each week** tiene ingresos *or* (*LAm*) entradas de 500 libras por semana; **he came in last** (*in race*) llegó el último; **it will ~ in handy** vendrá bien; **to ~ in for criticism/praise** ser objeto de críticas/elogios; **to ~ in on a deal** tomar parte en un negocio

►**come into** VI + PREP 1 (= *inherit*) [+ *legacy*] heredar; **he came into a fortune** heredó una fortuna, le correspondió una fortuna

2 (= *be involved in*) tener que ver con, ser parte de; **melons don't ~ into it** los melones no tienen que ver, los melones no hacen al caso

►**come of** VI + PREP **to ~ of a good family** ser de buena familia; *see also* **age A2**

►**come off** Ⓐ VI + ADV 1 [*button*] caerse; [*stain*] quitarse; **does this lid ~ off?** ¿se puede quitar esta tapa?

2 (= *take place, come to pass*) tener lugar, realizarse

3 (= *succeed*) tener éxito, dar resultados; **to ~ off well/badly** (= *turn out*) salir bien/mal

4 (= *acquit o.s.*) portarse; **to ~ off best** salir mejor parado, salir ganando

5 (*Theat*) **the play came off in January** la obra dejó de figurar en la cartelera en enero

Ⓑ VI + PREP 1 (= *separate from*) **she came off her bike** se cayó de la bicicleta; **the car came off the road** el coche se salió de la carretera; **the label came off the bottle** la etiqueta se desprendió de la botella; **~ off it!*** ¡vamos, anda!, ¡venga ya!; **I told him to ~ off it** le dije que dejase de hacer el tonto

2 (= *give up*) dejar; **it's time you came off the pill** es hora de dejar la píldora

►**come on** Ⓐ VI + ADV 1 **~ on!** (*expressing encouragement*) ¡vamos!, ¡venga!, ¡ándale! (*esp Mex*), ¡ándele! (*Mex*); (*urging haste*) ¡date prisa!, ¡apúrate! (*LAm*); (*expressing disbelief*) ¡venga ya!

2 (= *progress*) ir; [*plant*] crecer, desarrollarse; **how is the book coming on?** ¿qué tal va el libro?; **it's coming on nicely** va bien

3 (= *start*) empezar; **winter is coming on now** ya está empezando el invierno; **I feel a cold coming on** me está entrando un catarro; *see also* **come on to**

4 (*Theat*) salir a escena

5 [*light*] encenderse

6 (*US*) (*fig*) **he came on sincere** fingía ser sincero

Ⓑ VI + PREP = **come upon**

►**come on to** VI + PREP 1 (= *start discussing*) [+ *question, topic, issue*] pasar a; **I'll ~ on to that in a moment** ◊ **I'm coming on to that next** de eso hablaré en seguida

2 (*esp US**) (*sexually*) tirar los tejos a*, insinuarse a

►**come out** VI + ADV 1 (= *emerge*) [*person, object, sun, magazine*] salir (**of** de); [*qualities*] mostrarse; [*news*] divulgarse, difundirse; [*scandal*] descubrirse, salir a la luz; [*film*] estrenarse; **we came out of the cinema at ten** salimos del cine a las diez; **her book ~s out in May** su libro sale en mayo; **the idea came out of an experiment** la idea surgió a raíz de un experimento; **he came out of it with credit** salió con honor; *see also* **closet**

2 (= *open*) [*flower*] abrirse, florecer

3 (*into the open*) [*debutante*] ser presentada en sociedad, ponerse de largo; [*homosexual*] declararse; **to ~ out on strike** declararse en huelga; (*fig*) **to ~ out for/against sth** declararse en pro/en contra de algo

4 [*stain*] (= *be removed*) quitarse; [*dye*] (= *run*) desteñirse; **I don't think this stain will ~ out** no creo que esta mancha se vaya a quitar

5 (= *become covered with*) **he came out in a rash** le salió un sarpullido; **he came out in spots** le salieron granos; **I came out in a sweat** empecé a sudar, me cubrí de sudor

6 (*in conversation*) **to ~ out with a remark** salir con un comentario; **you never know what he's going to ~ out with next!*** ¡nunca se sabe por dónde va a salir!

7 (= *turn out*) salir; **it all came out right** todo salió bien; **none of my photos came out** no salió ninguna de mis fotos; **you always ~ out well in photos** siempre sales bien en las fotos; **it ~s out at £5 a head** sale a 5 libras por cabeza

►**come over** Ⓐ VI + ADV 1 (*lit*) venir, venirse; **they came over to England for a holiday** se vinieron a Inglaterra de vacaciones; **you'll soon ~ over to my way of thinking** (*fig*) ya me darás la razón

2 (*) (= *feel suddenly*) ponerse; **she came over quite ill** se puso bastante mala; **he came over all shy** de repente le dió vergüenza; **I came over all dizzy** me mareé
3 (= *give impression*) **how did he ~ over?** ¿qué impresión produjo?; **to ~ over well/badly** causar buena/mala impresión; **her speech came over very well** su discurso causó buena impresión; **to ~ over as** dar la impresión de ser, dar una imagen de
Ⓑ VI + PREP **I don't know what's ~ over him!** ¡no sé lo que le pasa!; **a feeling of weariness came over her** le invadió una sensación de cansancio; **a change came over him** se operó en él un cambio

►**come round** VI + ADV 1 (= *visit*) **~ round whenever you like** pasa por la casa cuando quieras; **he is coming round to see us tonight** viene a vernos *or* pasará a vernos esta noche
2 (= *occur regularly*) llegar; **I shall be glad when payday ~s round** ya estoy esperando el día de pago
3 (= *make detour*) dar un rodeo, desviarse; **I had to ~ round by the Post Office to post a letter** tuve que desviarme hasta Correos para echar una carta
4 (= *change one's mind*) dejarse convencer; **she'll soon ~ round to my way of thinking** no tardará en darme la razón; **he came round to our view** adoptó nuestra opinión
5 (= *throw off bad mood*) tranquilizarse, calmarse; (= *cheer up*) animarse; **leave him alone, he'll soon ~ round** déjalo en paz, ya se calmará
6 (= *regain consciousness, esp after anaesthetic*) volver en sí; **he came round after about ten minutes** volvió en sí después de unos diez minutos

►**come through** Ⓐ VI + ADV 1 (= *survive*) sobrevivir; (= *recover*) recuperarse; **he's badly injured, but he'll ~ through all right** está malherido, pero se recuperará *or* se pondrá bien
2 [*telephone call*] llegar; **the call came through from France at 10p.m.** a las 10 de la noche lograron comunicar desde Francia
Ⓑ VI + PREP 1 (= *survive*) [+ *war, danger*] sobrevivir; (*uninjured*) salir ileso/a de; [+ *illness*] recuperarse de
2 (= *pass*) [+ *test*] superar

►**come through with** VI + PREP (*US*) = **come up with**

►**come to** Ⓐ VI + PREP [*amount*] ascender a, sumar; **how much does it ~ to?** ¿cuánto es en total?, ¿a cuánto asciende?; **it ~s to £15 altogether** en total son 15 libras; **so it ~s to this** así que viene a ser esto; **what are we coming to?** ¿adónde va a parar todo esto?
Ⓑ VI + ADV (= *regain consciousness, esp after accidental knock-out*) recobrar el conocimiento; **he came to in hospital** recobró el conocimiento en el hospital

►**come together** VI + ADV (= *assemble*) reunirse, juntarse; **great qualities ~ together in his work** en su obra se dan cita grandes cualidades; **it's all coming together now** [*project, plan*] parece que ya empieza a tomar forma

►**come under** VI + PREP **it ~s under the heading of vandalism** se puede clasificar de vandalismo; **he came under the teacher's influence** cayó bajo la influencia del profesor; **to ~ under attack** sufrir un ataque, verse atacado

►**come up** Ⓐ VI + ADV 1 (= *ascend*) [*person*] subir; [*sun*] salir; [*plant*] aparecer; **~ up here!** ¡sube aquí!; **he has ~ up in the world** ha subido mucho en la escala social
2 (= *crop up*) [*difficulty*] surgir; [*matters for discussion*] plantearse, mencionarse; **something's ~ up so I'll be late home** ha surgido algo, así es que llegaré tarde a casa; **to ~ up for sale** ponerse a la venta
3 (*Jur*) [*accused*] (= *appear in court*) comparecer; [*lawsuit*] (= *be heard*) oírse, presentarse; **to ~ up before the judge** comparecer ante el juez; **his case ~s up tomorrow** su proceso se verá mañana
4 (*Univ*) matricularse; **he came up to Oxford last year** (*Brit*) se matriculó en la universidad de Oxford el año pasado
Ⓑ VI + PREP subir; **to ~ up the stairs** subir las escaleras

►**come up against** VI + PREP [+ *problem*] tropezar con; [+ *enemy*] tener que habérselas con; **she came up against complete opposition to her proposals** tropezó con una oposición total ante sus propuestas

►**come upon** VI + PREP (= *find*) [+ *object, person*] topar(se) con, encontrar

►**come up to** VI + PREP 1 (= *reach*) llegar hasta; **the water came up to my waist** el agua me llegaba hasta la cintura
2 (= *approach*) acercarse a; **she came up to me and kissed me** se me acercó y me besó
3 (*fig*) estar a la altura de, satisfacer; **it didn't ~ up to our expectations** no estuvo a la altura de lo que esperábamos; **the goods didn't ~ up to the required standard** la mercancía no satisfacía el nivel de calidad requerido; *see also* **scratch A3**

►**come up with** VI + PREP 1 (= *suggest, propose*) [+ *idea, plan*] proponer, sugerir; [+ *suggestion*] hacer; [+ *solution*] ofrecer, sugerir
2 (= *find*) [+ *money*] encontrar; **eventually he came up with the money** por fin encontró el dinero

COME, GO

Although **come** and **venir** usually imply motion towards the speaker while **go** and **ir** imply motion away from them, there are some differences between the two languages. In English we sometimes describe movement as if from the other person's perspective. In Spanish, this is not the case.

- For example when someone calls you:
  I'm coming
  Ya voy
- Making arrangements over the phone or in a letter:
  I'll come and pick you up at four
  Iré a recogerte a las cuatro
  Can I come too?
  ¿Puedo ir yo también?
  Shall I come with you?
  ¿Voy contigo?
- So, use **ir** rather than **venir** when going towards someone else or when joining them to go on somewhere else.
- Compare:
  Are you coming with us? (*viewed from the speaker's perspective*)
  ¿(Te) vienes con nosotros?

For further uses and examples, see main entries at ***come*** *and* ***go****.*

comeback ['kʌmbæk] N 1 (= *reaction*) (*usually adverse*) reacción *f*
2 (*US*) (= *response*) réplica *f*; (*witty*) respuesta *f* aguda
3 (= *return*) **to make a ~** (*Theat*) volver a las tablas; (*Cine*) volver a los platós; **he is making a ~ to professional football** está listo para volver al fútbol profesional; **butter has made a ~ in the British diet** la mantequilla ha recobrado su importancia en la dieta británica
4 (= *redress*) **to have no ~** no poder pedir cuentas, no poder reclamar

Comecon ['kɒmɪkɒn] N ABBR (*formerly*) (= **Council for Mutual Economic Aid**) COMECON *m*

comedian [kə'mi:dɪən] N humorista *mf*, cómico/a *m/f*

comedic [kə'mi:dɪk] ADJ (*frm*) [*moment, performance*] cómico

comedienne [kə,mi:dɪ'en] N humorista *f*, cómica *f*

comedown ['kʌmdaʊn] N (= *humiliation*) humillación *f*; **the house is a bit of a ~ from the mansion she is used to** la casa representa un cierto bajón de nivel en comparación con la mansión a la que ha estado acostumbrada

comedy ['kɒmɪdɪ] Ⓐ N (*gen*) comedia *f*; (= *humour of situation*) comicidad *f*; **~ of manners** comedia *f* de costumbres
Ⓑ CPD ► **comedy show** N (*TV*) programa *m* de humor

come-hither ['kʌm'hɪðə^r] ADJ [*look*] insinuante, provocativo

comeliness ['kʌmlɪnɪs] N (*liter*) gracia *f*, encanto *m*, donaire† *m*

comely ['kʌmlɪ] ADJ (*compar* **comelier**; *superl* **comeliest**) (*liter*) lindo

come-on* ['kʌm,ɒn] N 1 (= *enticement*) insinuación *f*, invitación *f*; **to give sb the ~** insinuársele a algn
2 (*Comm*) truco *m*, señuelo *m*

comer ['kʌmə^r] N **the first ~** el primero/la primera en llegar; **he has defended his title against all ~s** ha defendido su título contra todos los contendientes

comestible [kə'mestɪbl] ADJ (*frm*) comestible

comestibles [kə'mestɪblz] NPL (*frm*) comestibles *mpl*

comet ['kɒmɪt] N cometa *m*

comeuppance [ˌkʌm'ʌpəns] N ✦*IDIOM* **to get one's ~** llevarse su merecido

COMEX ['kɒmeks] N ABBR (*US*) = **Commodities Exchange**

comfort ['kʌmfət] Ⓐ N 1 (= *solace*) consuelo *m*; **you're a great ~ to me** eres un gran consuelo para mí; **if it's any ~ to you** si te sirve de consuelo; **that's cold** *or* **small ~** eso no me consuela nada; **the exam is too close for ~** el examen está demasiado cerca para que me sienta tranquilo; **to give ~ to the enemy** dar aliento al enemigo; **to take ~ from sth** consolarse con algo; **I take ~ in** *or* **from the fact/knowledge that …** me consuelo sabiendo que …
2 (= *well-being*) confort *m*, comodidad *f*; (= *facility*) comodidad *f*; **to live in ~** vivir cómodamente; **with every modern ~** con todo confort, con toda comodidad; **he likes his home ~s** le gusta rodearse de las comodidades del hogar
Ⓑ VT (= *give solace*) consolar, confortar
Ⓒ CPD ► **comfort food** N *comida como terapia contra la depresión* ► **comfort station** N (*US*) servicios *mpl*, aseos *mpl*, baño *m* (*LAm*) ► **comfort zone** N [*of activity, job*] terreno *m* conocido

comfortable ['kʌmfətəbl] ADJ 1 (*physically*) [*chair, shoes, position*] cómodo; [*room, house, hotel*] confortable, cómodo; [*temperature*] agradable; **are you ~, sitting there?** ¿estás cómodo sentado ahí?; **you don't look very ~** no pareces estar muy cómodo; **I'm not ~ in**

these shoes no estoy *or* voy cómodo con estos zapatos; **to make o.s. ~** ponerse cómodo
[2] (*mentally, emotionally*) cómodo, a gusto; **I'm not ~** *or* **I don't feel ~ at formal dinners** no me siento cómodo *or* a gusto en las cenas formales; **she wasn't ~ about giving him the keys** no se sentía a gusto dejándole las llaves; **to feel ~ with sb/sth** sentirse cómodo *or* a gusto con algn/algo; **he came closer to the truth than was ~** se acercó de manera inquietante a la verdad
[3] (*financially*) [*income*] bueno, suficiente; [*life, lifestyle*] holgado; **he's ~** está en buena posición económica
[4] (= *easy*) [*lead, majority, margin*] amplio, holgado; **a ~ job** un buen empleo, un empleo cómodo y bien pagado; **he was elected with a ~ majority** fue elegido por una amplia mayoría, fue elegido por una mayoría holgada; **to have a ~ win over sb** vencer a algn fácilmente
[5] (*Med*) estable; **he was described as ~ in hospital last night** anoche el hospital describió su condición como estable

comfortably [ˈkʌmfətəblɪ] ADV [1] (*physically*) [*sit, rest, lie*] cómodamente; [*sleep*] confortablemente; **sitting ~** cómodamente sentado; **~ furnished** amueblado confortablemente; **these shoes fit ~** voy muy cómodo con estos zapatos; **we are settled ~ in our new home** ya nos hemos acomodado en la casa nueva
[2] (*financially*) [*live*] holgadamente, con desahogo; **to be ~ off** vivir holgadamente *or* con desahogo, disfrutar de una posición acomodada *or* desahogada (*frm*)
[3] (= *easily*) [*manage*] sin problemas; [*win, defeat*] fácilmente, sin problemas; [*afford*] sin problemas, cómodamente; **the desk fits ~ into this corner** el escritorio cabe holgadamente *or* de sobra en esta esquina

comforter [ˈkʌmfətəʳ] N [1] (*baby's*) chupete *m*, chupón *m* (*LAm*)
[2] (*US*) (= *blanket*) edredón *m*
[3] (= *scarf*) bufanda *f*

comforting [ˈkʌmfətɪŋ] ADJ consolador, (re)confortante; [*words*] de consuelo

comfortless [ˈkʌmfətlɪs] ADJ incómodo, sin comodidad

comfrey [ˈkʌmfrɪ] N consuelda *f*

comfy* [ˈkʌmfɪ] ADJ (*compar* **comfier**; *superl* **comfiest**) [*chair, room*] cómodo; [*bed*] cómodo y calentito; **I'm nice and ~ here** estoy súper a gusto *or* súper cómoda aquí*

comic [ˈkɒmɪk] Ⓐ ADJ cómico; (= *amusing*) gracioso, divertido
Ⓑ N [1] (= *person*) cómico/a *m/f*
[2] (*esp Brit*) (= *paper*) cómic *m*; (*children's*) revista *f* de historietas, tebeo *m* (*Sp*)
[3] **comics** (*US*) = **comic strip**
Ⓒ CPD ► **comic book** N (*esp US*) libro *m* de cómics ► **comic opera** N ópera *f* bufa *or* cómica ► **comic relief** N toque *m* humorístico *or* cómico (*en una obra dramática*) ► **comic strip** N historieta *f*, tira *f* cómica ► **comic verse** N poesía *f* humorística *or* cómica

comical [ˈkɒmɪkəl] ADJ cómico, gracioso

comically [ˈkɒmɪkəlɪ] ADV de manera cómica, graciosamente

coming [ˈkʌmɪŋ] Ⓐ ADJ [1] (= *approaching*) [*weeks, months, years*] próximo, venidero (*frm*); **in the ~ weeks** en las próximas semanas, en las semanas venideras (*frm*); **the ~ year** el año que viene, el próximo año; **this ~ Friday** el viernes que viene, el próximo viernes; **the ~ election** las próximas elecciones; **~ generations** las generaciones venideras (*frm*)
[2] (= *promising*) [*politician, actor*] prometedor; **it's the ~ thing*** es lo que se va a poner de moda, es lo que se va a llevar
Ⓑ N llegada *f*; **the ~ of spring** la llegada de la primavera; **the ~ of Christ** el advenimiento de Cristo; **~ of age** (llegada *f* a la) mayoría *f* de edad; **the ~s and goings of the guests** las idas y venidas de los invitados; **there was too much ~ and going** había demasiado ir y venir de gente; *see also* **second[1] E**

> **COMIC RELIEF**
>
> **Comic Relief** *es una campaña con fines benéficos organizada por actores y humoristas para recaudar dinero y paliar así la pobreza, especialmente en África. La cadena de televisión* **BBC** *le dedica cada dos años una noche entera y en el programa actores, humoristas y famosos hacen números cómicos, informando a la vez sobre proyectos para luchar contra la pobreza e invitando al público a que llame y haga donativos. Como muestra de apoyo mucha gente lleva narices rojas de plástico (***red noses***) o las ponen en la parte frontal del coche.*

coming-out [ˈkʌmɪŋˈaʊt] N presentación *f* en sociedad

Comintern [ˈkɒmɪntɜːn] N ABBR (*Pol*) (= **Communist International**) Comintern *f*

comm. ABBR [1] = **commerce**
[2] = **commercial**
[3] = **committee**

comma [ˈkɒmə] N coma *f*; *see also* **inverted**

command [kəˈmɑːnd] Ⓐ N [1] (= *order*) (*esp Mil*) orden *f*; (*Comput*) orden *f*, comando *m*; **he gave the ~ (to attack/retreat)** dio la orden (de atacar/retirarse); **his ~s were obeyed at once** sus órdenes se cumplieron de inmediato; **at** *or* **by the ~ of sb** por orden de algn; **by royal ~** por real orden
[2] (= *control*) [*of army, ship*] mando *m*; **to be at sb's ~** [*resources, money, troops*] estar a la disposición de algn; [*men*] estar a las órdenes de algn, estar bajo el mando de algn; **to have at one's ~** [+ *resources, money, troops*] disponer de, tener a su disposición; [+ *men*] tener a sus órdenes, estar al mando de; **to have ~ of sth** estar al mando de algo; **to be in ~ (of sth)** estar al mando (de algo); **who is in ~ here?** ¿quién manda aquí?; **to be in ~ of one's faculties** estar en posesión de sus facultades; **to be in ~ of the situation** ser dueño de la situación; **to take ~ of sth** asumir el mando de algo; **under the ~ of** bajo el mando de
[3] (= *mastery*) dominio *m*; **his ~ of English** su dominio del inglés; **to have a good ~ of English** dominar el inglés; **~ of the seas** dominio de los mares
[4] (= *authority*) (*Mil, Naut*) mando *m*, jefatura *f*; **second in ~** segundo *m*; (*Naut*) segundo *m* de a bordo; *see also* **high D**
Ⓑ VT [1] (= *order*) **to ~ sb to do sth** mandar *or* ordenar a algn que haga algo; **to ~ sth to be done** mandar *or* ordenar que se haga algo
[2] (= *be in control of*) [+ *soldiers, army*] mandar, estar al mando de; [+ *ship*] comandar
[3] (= *have at one's disposal*) [+ *resources, money, services*] disponer de, contar con
[4] (= *deserve and get*) [+ *attention*] ganarse; [+ *respect*] imponer; [+ *sympathy*] merecerse, hacerse acreedor de; [+ *price*] venderse a, venderse por; [+ *fee*] exigir
[5] (= *overlook*) [+ *area*] dominar; [+ *view*] tener, disfrutar de
Ⓒ CPD ► **command key** N (*Comput*) tecla *f* de comando ► **command language** N (*Comput*) lenguaje *m* de comandos ► **command line** N (*Comput*) orden *f*, comando *m* ► **command module** N (*on a space rocket*) módulo *m* de mando ► **command performance** N gala *f* (a petición) real ► **command post** N puesto *m* de mando

commandant [ˌkɒmənˈdænt] N comandante *mf*

commandeer [ˌkɒmənˈdɪəʳ] VT [1] (= *requisition*) [+ *building, stores, ship etc*] requisar, expropiar; [+ *men*] reclutar a la fuerza
[2] (*) tomar, apropiarse (de)

commander [kəˈmɑːndəʳ] N (*Mil*) comandante *mf*; (*Hist*) [*of chivalric order*] comendador *m*; (*Naut*) capitán *m* de fragata

commander-in-chief [kəˈmɑːndərɪnˈtʃiːf] N (*pl* **commanders in chief**) jefe/a *m/f* supremo/a, comandante/a *m/f* en jefe

commanding [kəˈmɑːndɪŋ] Ⓐ ADJ [*appearance*] imponente; [*tone of voice*] autoritario, imperioso; [*lead*] abrumador; [*position*] dominante
Ⓑ CPD ► **commanding officer** N (*Mil*) comandante *mf*

commandingly [kəˈmɑːndɪŋlɪ] ADV [*speak*] de forma autoritaria, imperiosamente

commandment [kəˈmɑːndmənt] N (*Bible*) mandamiento *m*; **the Ten Commandments** los diez mandamientos

commando [kəˈmɑːndəʊ] N (*pl* **commandos** *or* **commandoes**) (= *man, group*) comando *m*

commemorate [kəˈmeməreɪt] VT conmemorar

commemoration [kəˌmeməˈreɪʃən] Ⓐ N conmemoración *f*; **in ~ of** en conmemoración de
Ⓑ CPD [*service, ceremony*] de conmemoración

commemorative [kəˈmemərətɪv] Ⓐ ADJ conmemorativo
Ⓑ N (*US*) (= *stamp*) sello *m* conmemorativo; (= *coin*) moneda *f* conmemorativa

commence [kəˈmens] (*frm*) Ⓐ VT comenzar; **to ~ doing** *or* **to do sth** comenzar a hacer algo; **to ~ proceedings (against sb)** (*Jur*) entablar demanda (a algn)
Ⓑ VI comenzar

commencement [kəˈmensmənt] N [1] (*frm*) (= *start*) comienzo *m*, principio *m*
[2] (*US Univ*) (ceremonia *f* de) graduación *f*, (ceremonia *f* de) entrega *f* de diplomas

commend [kəˈmend] VT [1] (= *praise*) elogiar; **to ~ sb for** *or* **on sth** elogiar a algn por algo; **to ~ sb for his action** elogiar la acción de algn; **her entry was highly ~ed** (*in competition*) su participación recibió una mención elogiosa *or* especial
[2] (= *recommend*) recomendar; **I ~ him to you** se lo recomiendo; **it has little to ~ it** poco se puede decir en su favor; **the plan does not ~ itself to me** el proyecto no me resulta aceptable
[3] (= *entrust*) encomendar (**to** a); **to ~ sb's/one's soul to God** encomendar el alma de algn/su alma a Dios
[4] († *frm*) **~ me to Mr White** (= *give respects*) presente mis respetos al Sr. White (*frm*)

commendable [kəˈmendəbl] ADJ encomiable, loable

commendably [kəˈmendəblɪ] ADV **it was ~ short** tuvo el mérito de ser breve; **you have been ~ prompt** le felicito por la prontitud

commendation [ˌkɒmenˈdeɪʃən] N [1] (= *praise*) elogio *m*, encomio *m*; (*Mil*) distinción *f*
[2] (= *recommendation*) recomendación *f*

commensurable [kəˈmenʃərəbl] ADJ conmensurable, comparable (**with** con)

commensurate [kəˈmenʃərɪt] ADJ **~ with** en proporción a, que corresponde a; **"salary**

commensurate with experience" "sueldo según experiencia"

▼**comment** [ˈkɒment] Ⓐ N (= *remark*) (*written or spoken*) comentario *m*, observación *f*; (= *gossip*) comentarios *mpl*; **no ~** sin comentarios; **to make a ~** hacer un comentario *or* una observación; **she made the ~ that ...** observó que ...; **he made no ~** no hizo ningún comentario; **to cause ~** (= *cause gossip*) provocar comentarios
Ⓑ VI hacer observaciones *or* comentarios, comentar; **to ~ on** [+ *text*] comentar, hacer un comentario de; [+ *subject*] hacer observaciones *or* comentarios acerca de; (*to the press*) hacer declaraciones sobre
Ⓒ VT (*in conversation*) observar; **to ~ that ...** observar que ...

commentary [ˈkɒməntərɪ] Ⓐ N (*gen*) comentario *m*; (*Rad, TV*) (*on sporting event*) crónica *f*; (*on text*) comentario *m* (de texto)
Ⓑ CPD ► **commentary box** N cabina *f* de prensa

commentate [ˈkɒmənteɪt] (*Rad, TV*) Ⓐ VT hacer la crónica de
Ⓑ VI hacer la crónica, comentar

commentator [ˈkɒmənteɪtəʳ] N (*Rad, TV*) comentarista *mf*

commerce [ˈkɒmɜːs] N comercio *m*; **Chamber of Commerce** Cámara *f* de Comercio

commercial [kəˈmɜːʃəl] Ⓐ ADJ comercial
Ⓑ N (*TV*) (= *advert*) anuncio *m*, spot *m* publicitario
Ⓒ CPD ► **commercial art** N arte *m* publicitario ► **commercial artist** N dibujante *mf* publicitario/a ► **commercial bank** N banco *m* comercial, banco *m* mercantil ► **commercial break** N (*TV*) espacio *m* publicitario, pausa *f* publicitaria ► **commercial centre** N centro *m* comercial ► **commercial college** N escuela *f* de secretariado ► **commercial law** N derecho *m* mercantil ► **commercial paper** N (*esp US*) efectos *mpl* negociables, papel *m* comercial ► **commercial property** N propiedad *f* comercial ► **commercial radio** N radio *f* comercial ► **commercial television** N televisión *f* privada ► **commercial traveller, commercial traveler** (*US*) N viajante *mf* (de comercio) ► **commercial value** N valor *m* comercial; **"no commercial value"** "sin valor comercial" ► **commercial vehicle** N vehículo *m* comercial

commercialism [kəˈmɜːʃəlɪzəm] N (*often pej*) comercialismo *m* (*pej*), mercantilismo *m* (*pej*)

commercialization [kəˌmɜːʃəlaɪˈzeɪʃən] N comercialización *f*

commercialize [kəˈmɜːʃəlaɪz] VT comercializar

commercially [kəˈmɜːʃəlɪ] ADV [*viable, competitive, produced*] comercialmente; **it is not ~ available** no puede adquirirse en el mercado

commie* [ˈkɒmɪ] Ⓐ ADJ rojo
Ⓑ N rojo/a *m/f*

commiserate [kəˈmɪzəreɪt] VI **friends called to ~ when they found out I hadn't got the job** cuando me rechazaron para el trabajo mis amigos me llamaron para decirme lo mucho que lo sentían; **"I know how you feel," he ~d** —sé cómo te sientes —le dijo a modo de consuelo

commiseration [kəˌmɪzəˈreɪʃən] N conmiseración *f*; **my ~s to the runner-up** lo siento mucho por el que ha llegado segundo

commissar [ˈkɒmɪsɑːʳ] N comisario/a *m/f*

commissariat [ˌkɒmɪˈseərɪət] N comisaría *f*

commissary [ˈkɒmɪsərɪ] N [1] comisario/a *m/f* político/a
[2] (*US*) (= *shop*) economato *m*

➤ LANGUAGE IN USE: **comment A** 26.1, 26.2

commission [kəˈmɪʃən] Ⓐ N [1] (= *committee*) comisión *f*; **~ of inquiry** comisión *f* investigadora
[2] (= *order for work, esp of artist*) comisión *f*
[3] (*for salesman*) comisión *f*; **to sell things on ~** *or* **on a ~ basis** vender cosas a comisión; **I get 10% ~** me dan el 10 por ciento de comisión
[4] (*Mil*) (= *position*) graduación *f* de oficial; (= *warrant*) nombramiento *m*
[5] (= *use, service*) servicio *m*; **to put into ~** poner en servicio; **to be out of ~** estar fuera de servicio; **to put out of ~** inutilizar; **to take out of ~** retirar del servicio
[6] [*of crime*] perpetración *f*
Ⓑ VT [1] [+ *artist etc*] hacer un encargo a; [+ *picture*] encargar, comisionar (*esp LAm*); [+ *article*] encargar; **to ~ sb to do sth** encargar a algn que haga algo
[2] (*Mil*) [+ *officer*] nombrar; [+ *ship*] poner en servicio; **~ed officer** oficial *mf*
Ⓒ CPD ► **commission agent** N comisionista *mf*

commissionaire [kəˌmɪʃəˈneəʳ] N (*Brit, Canada*) portero *m*, conserje *m*

commissioner [kəˈmɪʃənəʳ] N (= *official*) comisario/a *m/f*; (= *member of commission*) comisionado/a *m/f*; **~ for oaths** (*Brit*) notario/a *m/f* público/a; **~ of police** inspector(a) *m/f* jefe de policía

commissioning editor [kəˈmɪʃənɪŋˈedɪtəʳ] N jefe(a) *m/f* de sección, responsable *mf* de departamento

commit [kəˈmɪt] Ⓐ VT [1] [+ *crime, sin, error*] cometer; **to ~ suicide** suicidarse; *see also* **perjury**
[2] (= *consign*) [+ *resources*] asignar, destinar; [+ *troops*] enviar; (*Parl*) [+ *bill*] remitir a una comisión; **to ~ sb** (*to mental hospital*) internar a algn; **to ~ sth to sb's charge** confiar algo a algn; **to ~ sth to the flames** arrojar algo al fuego; **to ~ sth to memory** aprender algo de memoria; **to ~ sth to paper** poner algo por escrito; **to ~ sb to prison** encarcelar a algn; **to ~ sb for trial** remitir a algn al tribunal; **to ~ sth to writing** poner algo por escrito
[3] (= *pledge*) comprometer; **accepting this offer does not ~ you to anything** aceptar esta oferta no le compromete a nada; **I am ~ted to help him** me he comprometido a ayudarle; **he is ~ted to change** está dedicado a buscar una forma de cambiar; **we are deeply ~ted to this policy** creemos firmemente en esta política
[4] **to ~ o.s. (to)** comprometerse (a); **I can't ~ myself** no puedo comprometerme; **without ~ting myself** sin compromiso por mi parte
Ⓑ VI **to ~ to sb/sth** comprometerse con algn/a algo

commitment [kəˈmɪtmənt] N [1] (= *obligation*) obligación *f*; **he has heavy teaching ~s** tiene muchas obligaciones como profesor; **family ~s** obligaciones familiares
[2] (= *pledge*) **to give a ~ to do sth** comprometerse a hacer algo; **she would give no ~** no quiso comprometerse
[3] (= *devotion*) entrega *f*, devoción *f*

committal [kəˈmɪtl] N [1] (*Jur*) **~ for trial** (auto *m* de) procesamiento *m*; **~ to prison** encarcelamiento *m*, (auto *m* de) prisión *f*
[2] (*to mental asylum*) reclusión *f*
[3] (= *burial*) entierro *m*

committed [kəˈmɪtɪd] ADJ comprometido; **a ~ writer** un escritor comprometido

committee [kəˈmɪtɪ] Ⓐ N comité *m*, comisión *f*; **to be** *or* **sit on a ~** ser miembro de un comité; **~ of inquiry** (*Parl*) comisión *f* investigadora; *see also* **executive C, management B**
Ⓑ CPD ► **committee meeting** N reunión *f* del comité ► **committee member** N miembro *mf* del comité ► **committee stage** N (*Parl*) *fase en la que un proyecto de ley está siendo estudiado por un comité*

commode [kəˈməʊd] N (*with chamber pot*) silla *f* con orinal; (= *chest of drawers*) cómoda *f*

commodious [kəˈməʊdɪəs] ADJ grande, espacioso

commodity [kəˈmɒdɪtɪ] Ⓐ N artículo *m* (de consumo *or* de comercio), producto *m*, mercancía *f*, mercadería *f* (*LAm*); (*Fin, St Ex*) materia *f* prima
Ⓑ CPD ► **commodity exchange** N bolsa *f* de artículos de consumo ► **commodity markets** NPL mercados *mpl* de materias primas ► **commodity trade** N comercio *m* de materias primas

commodore [ˈkɒmədɔːʳ] N comodoro *m*

common [ˈkɒmən] Ⓐ ADJ [1] (= *usual, ordinary*) [*event, experience, name, species*] común, corriente; [*misconception, mistake*] común, frecuente; **this butterfly is ~ in Spain** esta mariposa es común *or* corriente en España; **it is ~ for these animals to die young** es corriente *or* frecuente que estos animales mueran jóvenes; **it is a ~ belief that ...** es una creencia extendida *or* generalizada que ...; **~ belief has it that ...** según la opinión generalizada ...; **it's (just) ~ courtesy** es una cortesía elemental; **the ~ man** el hombre de la calle, el hombre medio; **it's a ~ occurrence** es corriente que suceda; **in ~ parlance** en lenguaje corriente; **the ~ people** la gente corriente; **it is ~ practice in the USA** es una práctica común en EE.UU.; **pigeons are a ~ sight in London** es corriente *or* frecuente ver palomas en Londres; **the ~ soldier** el soldado raso; **to have the ~ touch** saber tratar con la gente corriente; **in ~ use** de uso corriente; ✦*IDIOM* **~ or garden** (*esp Brit**) común y corriente, normal y corriente
[2] (= *shared*) [*cause, aim, language*] común; **to work for a ~ aim** cooperar para un mismo fin *or* para un objetivo común; **by ~ agreement** *or* **consent** de común acuerdo; **for the ~ good** para el bien común, para el bien de todos; **~ ground** (*fig*) puntos *mpl* en común, puntos *mpl* de confluencia *or* acuerdo; **they discussed several issues of ~ interest** hablaron de varios asuntos de interés común *or* de interés mutuo; **it is ~ knowledge that ...** es del dominio público que ...; **the desire for freedom is ~ to all people** todo el mundo comparte el deseo de la libertad
[3] (*pej*) (= *vulgar*) [*person, behaviour, speech*] ordinario, basto; ✦*IDIOM* **as ~ as muck*** de lo más ordinario, más basto que la lija (del cuatro)
[4] (*Zool, Bot*) común; **the ~ house fly** la mosca común
Ⓑ N [1] (= *land*) campo *m* comunal, ejido *m*
[2] (*Brit Pol*) **the Commons** (la Cámera de) los Comunes; *see also* **House A3**
[3] **in ~: we have a lot in ~ (with other people)** tenemos mucho en común (con otra gente); **we have nothing in ~** no tenemos nada en común; **in ~ with many other companies, we advertise in the local press** al igual que otras muchas empresas, nos anunciamos en la prensa local
Ⓒ CPD ► **the Common Agricultural Policy** N la Política Agrícola Común ► **common cold** N resfriado *m* común ► **common core**

N (*Scol*) (*also* **~-core syllabus**) asignaturas *fpl* comunes ► **common currency** N **to become/be ~ currency** [*idea, belief*] convertirse en/ser moneda corriente ► **common denominator** N (*Math*) común denominador *m*; **lowest ~ denominator** mínimo común denominador *m* ► **Common Entrance** N (*Brit Scol*) *examen de acceso a un colegio de enseñanza privada* ► **common factor** N (*Math*) factor *m* común ► **common land** N propiedad *f* comunal ► **common law** N (*Jur*) (*established by custom*) derecho *m* consuetudinario; (*based on precedent*) jurisprudencia *f*; *see also* **common-law** ► **the Common Market** N el Mercado Común ► **common noun** N nombre *m* común ► **common ownership** N (= *joint ownership*) copropiedad *f*; (*Pol*) (= *collective ownership*) propiedad *f* colectiva ► **the Book of Common Prayer** N la liturgia de la Iglesia Anglicana ► **common room** N (*esp Brit*) (*for students*) sala *f* de estudiantes; (*for teachers*) sala *f* de profesores ► **common salt** N sal *f* común ► **common sense** N sentido *m* común; *see also* **commonsense** ► **common stock** N (*US St Ex*) acciones *fpl* ordinarias ► **common time** N (*Mus*) cuatro *m* por cuatro ► **common wall** N pared *f* medianera

COMMON LAW

Se llama **common law** *o* **case law** *(derecho consuetudinario o jurisprudencia), al conjunto de leyes basadas en el fallo de los tribunales, a diferencia de las leyes establecidas por escrito en el Parlamento. El derecho consuetudinario inglés se desarrolló después de la conquista normanda, cuando los jueces basaban sus decisiones en la tradición o en el precedente judicial. La jurisprudencia sigue usándose como base del sistema legal anglosajón, aunque va perdiendo vigencia por el desarrollo del derecho escrito.*

⇨ *Ver tb* ACT OF PARLIAMENT, CONSTITUTION

commonality [ˌkɒmə'nælɪtɪ], **commonalty** ['kɒmənəltɪ] N 1 (*frm*) (= *things in common*) cosas *fpl* en común; **there is a ~ of interests between them** tienen muchos intereses en común
2 **the ~** (= *ordinary people*) el común de la gente, la plebe

commoner ['kɒmənəʳ] N 1 (= *not noble*) plebeyo/a *m/f*
2 (*at Oxford Univ etc*) estudiante *mf* que no tiene beca del colegio

common-law ['kɒmən,lɔː] ADJ [*marriage*] consensual; [*spouse*] en unión consensual

commonly ['kɒmənlɪ] ADV 1 (= *usually, frequently*) [*called*] comúnmente; [*prescribed*] frecuentemente; **more ~ known as …** más comúnmente conocido como …; **anorexia is more ~ found among women** la anorexia es más común *or* corriente entre las mujeres; **an orchid which is not ~ found in this country** una orquídea que no es corriente encontrar *or* que no se encuentra frecuentemente en este país; **it is ~ the case that …** es corriente que …, frecuentemente se da el caso de que …; **acupuncture is ~ used in China** la acupuntura es una práctica muy común en China
2 (= *generally*) **the ~ held view** la opinión extendida *or* generalizada; **it is ~ accepted as the best in the world** es aceptado por todos como el mejor del mundo; **it is ~ believed that …** es una creencia extendida *or* generalizada que …; **the disease is ~ thought to be caused by a virus** es una creencia extendida *or* generalizada que esta enfermedad está causada por un virus
3 (= *vulgarly*) [*behave, speak, dress*] ordinariamente, vulgarmente

commonness ['kɒmənnɪs] N 1 (= *frequency*) frecuencia *f*
2 (= *vulgarity*) ordinariez *f*

commonplace ['kɒmənpleɪs] Ⓐ ADJ (= *normal*) común, normal, corriente; (*pej*) vulgar, ordinario; **it is ~ to see this sort of thing** es frecuente *or* corriente ver este tipo de cosas
Ⓑ N (= *event*) cosa *f* común y corriente; (= *statement*) tópico *m*, lugar *m* común

Commons ['kɒmənz] NPL (*Pol*) = **common B2**

commonsense ['kɒmən,sens] ADJ racional, lógico; **the ~ thing to do is …** lo lógico es …

Commonwealth ['kɒmənwelθ] N **the ~** la Comunidad Británica de Naciones; (*Brit Hist*) la república de Cromwell; **the ~ of Independent States** la Comunidad de Estados Independientes; **the ~ of Kentucky** el estado de Kentucky; **the ~ of Puerto Rico** el estado de Puerto Rico

COMMONWEALTH

La **Commonwealth** *(Comunidad Británica de Naciones) es una asociación de estados soberanos, la mayoría de los cuales eran colonias británicas en el pasado, establecida para fomentar el comercio y los lazos de amistad entre ellos. Actualmente se compone de más de cincuenta estados miembros, entre los cuales se encuentran el Reino Unido, Australia, Canadá, la India, Jamaica, Kenia, Nueva Zelanda, Nigeria, Pakistán y Sudáfrica. Los países miembros reconocen al soberano británico como* **Head of the Commonwealth** *y se reúnen anualmente para debatir asuntos políticos y económicos. Además, cada cuatro años uno de los países miembros es el anfitrión de la competición deportiva conocida como* **Commonwealth Games**.

commotion [kə'məʊʃən] N (= *noise*) alboroto *m*; (= *activity*) jaleo *m*, tumulto *m*, confusión *f*; (*civil*) disturbio *m*; **to cause a ~** provocar *or* causar un alboroto; **to make a ~** (= *noise*) armar un alboroto; (= *fuss*) armar un lío*; **there was a ~ in the crowd** se armó un lío entre los espectadores; **what a ~!** ¡qué alboroto!

communal ['kɒmjuːnl] ADJ [*property, ownership*] comunal; [*living room, dining room, facilities*] común; [*activities*] comunitario

communally ['kɒmjuːnəlɪ] ADV [*live, eat*] en comunidad; **to act ~** obrar como comunidad; **the property is held ~** la propiedad pertenece a la comunidad

commune ['kɒmjuːn] Ⓐ N (= *group*) comuna *f*
Ⓑ [kə'mjuːn] VI 1 (*Rel*) (*esp US*) comulgar
2 **to ~ with** estar en contacto con; **to ~ with nature/one's soul** estar en contacto con la naturaleza/su alma

communicable [kə'mjuːnɪkəbl] ADJ (*gen*) comunicable; [*disease*] transmisible

communicant [kə'mjuːnɪkənt] N (*Rel*) comulgante *mf*

communicate [kə'mjuːnɪkeɪt] Ⓐ VT **to ~ sth (to sb)** [+ *thoughts, information*] comunicar algo (a algn); (*frm*) [+ *disease*] transmitir algo (a algn)
Ⓑ VI (= *speak*) comunicarse (**with** con); **we ~ by letter/telephone** mantenemos correspondencia/estamos en contacto telefónico; **they just can't ~** no se entienden en absoluto

communicating [kə'mjuːnɪkeɪtɪŋ] ADJ **~ rooms** habitaciones *fpl* que se comunican

communication [kə,mjuːnɪ'keɪʃən] Ⓐ N 1 (= *verbal or written contact*) contacto *m*; (= *exchange of information*) comunicación *f*; **to be in/get into ~ with** (*frm*) estar/ponerse en contacto con; **there has been a breakdown of** *or* **in ~ between the police and the community** el diálogo entre la policía y la comunidad ha sufrido un deterioro
2 (= *message*) mensaje *m*, comunicación *f*
3 **communications** comunicaciones *fpl*; **good/poor ~s** buenas/malas comunicaciones
Ⓑ CPD ► **communication cord** N (*Rail*) timbre *m* *or* palanca *f* de alarma ► **communication problem** N (*personal*) problema *m* de expresión; (*within organization*) problema *m* de comunicación ► **communication skills** NPL habilidad *f* *or* aptitud *f* para comunicarse ► **communications network** N red *f* de comunicaciones ► **communications satellite** N satélite *m* de comunicaciones ► **communications software** N paquete *m* de comunicaciones

communicative [kə'mjuːnɪkətɪv] ADJ comunicativo

communicator [kə'mjuːnɪkeɪtəʳ] N (= *person*) comunicador(a) *m/f*; **to be a good/bad ~** saber/no saber comunicarse

communion [kə'mjuːnɪən] Ⓐ N (*Rel*) comunión *f*; **to take** *or* **receive ~** comulgar
Ⓑ CPD ► **communion rail** N comulgatorio *m* ► **communion service** N comunión *f* ► **communion table** N mesa *f* de comunión

communiqué [kə'mjuːnɪkeɪ] N comunicado *m*

communism ['kɒmjʊnɪzəm] N comunismo *m*

communist ['kɒmjʊnɪst] Ⓐ ADJ comunista
Ⓑ N comunista *mf*
Ⓒ CPD ► **Communist party** N partido *m* comunista

community [kə'mjuːnɪtɪ] Ⓐ N 1 (= *people at large*) comunidad *f*, sociedad *f*; (= *people locally*) comunidad *f*; **the local ~** el vecindario
2 (*cultural etc*) comunidad *f*, colectividad *f*; **the black ~** la población negra; **the artistic ~** el mundillo artístico; **the English ~ in Rome** la colectividad *or* colonia inglesa de Roma
3 **the Community** (= *EEC*) la Comunidad
Ⓑ CPD ► **community care** N (*Brit*) política *f* de integración social de enfermos y ancianos ► **community centre** N centro *m* social ► **community charge** N (*Brit Admin*) (*formerly*) (contribución *f* de) capitación *f* ► **community chest** N (*US*) fondo *m* para beneficencia social ► **community college** N (*US*) *establecimiento docente de educación terciaria donde se realizan cursos de dos años* ► **community health centre** N centro *m* médico comunitario ► **Community law** N derecho *m* comunitario ► **community life** N vida *f* comunitaria ► **community policing** N *política policial de acercamiento a la comunidad* ► **Community policy** N (*EC*) política *f* comunitaria ► **community politics** N política *f* local ► **Community regulations** NPL normas *fpl* comunitarias ► **community service** N trabajo *m* comunitario (*prestado en lugar de cumplir una pena de prisión*) ► **community singing** N canto *m* colectivo ► **community spirit** N sentimiento *m* de comunidad, civismo *m* ► **community worker** N asistente *mf* social

communize ['kɒmjuːnaɪz] VT comunizar

commutable [kə'mjuːtəbl] ADJ (*gen, Jur*) conmutable

commutation [ˌkɒmjʊˈteɪʃən] Ⓐ N (*gen, Fin*) conmutación *f*; (*US Rail etc*) uso *m* de un billete de abono
Ⓑ CPD ► **commutation ticket** N (*US*) billete *m* de abono

commute [kəˈmjuːt] Ⓐ VI viajar diariamente (de la casa al trabajo); **I live in Brighton but I ~ to London** vivo en Brighton pero voy todos los días a trabajar a Londres; **she ~s between Oxford and London** para ir al trabajo viaja *or* se desplaza diariamente de Oxford a Londres
Ⓑ VT [+ *payment*] conmutar (**for/into** por/en); [+ *sentence*] conmutar (**to** por)
Ⓒ N viaje *m* diario al trabajo

commuter [kəˈmjuːtəʳ] Ⓐ N *persona que viaja cada día de su casa a su trabajo*
Ⓑ CPD ► **the commuter belt** N zona *f* de los barrios exteriores ► **commuter services** NPL servicios *mpl* de cercanías ► **commuter train** N tren *m* de cercanías

commuting [kəˈmjuːtɪŋ] N ~ **is very stressful** el viajar para ir al trabajo provoca mucho estrés

compact¹ Ⓐ [kəmˈpækt] ADJ (= *small*) compacto; (= *dense*) apretado, sólido; [*style*] breve, conciso
Ⓑ [kəmˈpækt] VT [+ *snow, earth*] comprimir (**into** en); (= *condense*) [+ *text, activities*] condensar
Ⓒ [kəmˈpækt] VI [*snow*] comprimirse
Ⓓ [ˈkɒmpækt] N 1 (*also* **powder** ~) polvera *f*
2 (*US Aut*) (*also* ~ **car**) utilitario *m*
Ⓔ [ˈkɒmpækt] CPD ► **compact car** N (*US*) utilitario *m* ► **compact disc** N disco *m* compacto, compact *m* ► **compact disc player** N lector *m* de discos compactos

compact² [ˈkɒmpækt] N (= *agreement*) pacto *m*, convenio *m*

compactly [kəmˈpæktlɪ] ADV (= *in a neat way*) de modo compacto; (= *tightly*) apretadamente, sólidamente; (= *concisely*) brevemente, concisamente

compactness [kəmˈpæktnɪs] N [*of house, room*] compacidad *f*; [*of style*] concisión *f*

companion [kəmˈpænjən] Ⓐ N 1 (= *accompanying person*) compañero/a *m/f*; (*lady's*) señora *f* de compañía; **travelling ~** compañero/a *m/f* de viaje
2 (= *book*) guía *f*, manual *m*
3 (= *one of pair of objects*) compañero *m*, pareja *f*
4 (*Naut*) lumbrera *f*; (= *companionway*) escalerilla *f* (que conduce a los camarotes)
Ⓑ CPD ► **companion volume** N tomo *m* complementario

companionable [kəmˈpænjənəbl] ADJ [*person*] sociable, amigable; **they sat in ~ silence** estaban sentados en amigable silencio

companionably [kəmˈpænjənəblɪ] ADV amigablemente

companionship [kəmˈpænjənʃɪp] N (= *company*) compañía *f*; (= *friendship, friendliness*) compañerismo *m*

companionway [kəmˈpænjənweɪ] N (*Naut*) escalerilla *f* (que conduce a los camarotes)

company [ˈkʌmpənɪ] Ⓐ N 1 (= *companionship*) compañía *f*; **it's ~ for her** le hace compañía; **he's good/poor ~** es/no es muy agradable estar con él; **to keep sb ~** hacer compañía a algn, acompañar a algn; ✦*PROV* **two's ~(, three's a crowd)** dos es compañía, tres es multitud
2 (= *group, friends*) **to keep bad ~** andar en malas compañías; **to get into bad ~** tener malas compañías; **to be in good ~** (*fig*) estar bien acompañado; **to join ~ with** reunirse con; **to part ~** separarse (**with** de); (*fig*) (= *come apart, unstuck*) desprenderse, soltarse (**with** de); **present ~ excepted** mejorando lo presente, salvando a los presentes; ✦*PROV* **a man is known by the ~ he keeps** dime con quién andas y te diré quién eres
3 (*no pl*) (= *guests*) visita *f*, invitados *mpl*; **we have ~** tenemos visita *or* invitados; **are you expecting ~?** ¿esperas visita?
4 (*Comm*) (= *firm*) compañía *f*, empresa *f*; (= *association*) sociedad *f*; **Smith and Company** Smith y Compañía; **he's a ~ man** se desvive por la empresa; **in ~ time** en horas de trabajo; *see also* **limited**
5 (*Mil*) compañía *f*, unidad *f*; **ship's ~** tripulación *f*
6 (*Theat*) compañía *f* (de teatro)
Ⓑ CPD ► **company car** N coche *m* de la empresa ► **company commander** N capitán *m* de compañía ► **company director** N director(a) *m/f* de empresa ► **company law** N derecho *m* de compañías ► **company lawyer** N (*Brit Jur*) abogado *mf* empresarial; (*working within company*) abogado *mf* de la compañía ► **company policy** N política *f* de la empresa ► **company secretary** N administrador(a) *m/f* de empresa ► **company union** N (*US*) sindicato *m* de empresa

comparability [kɒmpərəˈbɪlɪtɪ] N comparabilidad *f*

comparable [ˈkɒmpərəbl] ADJ comparable; ~ **to** *or* **with** comparable a *or* con; **a ~ case** un caso análogo; **they are not ~** no se los puede comparar

comparably [ˈkɒmpərəblɪ] ADV **salaries in line with ~ qualified professions** sueldos a la par con los de las profesiones similares

comparative [kəmˈpærətɪv] Ⓐ ADJ 1 (= *relative*) relativo; **before becoming famous she had lived in ~ obscurity** había vivido en relativa oscuridad antes de hacerse famosa
2 [*study*] comparativo, comparado
3 (*Gram*) comparativo
Ⓑ N (*Gram*) comparativo *m*
Ⓒ CPD ► **comparative literature** N literatura *f* comparada

▼**comparatively** [kəmˈpærətɪvlɪ] ADV (= *relatively*) relativamente; [*consider, view*] desde un punto de vista relativo; **the books can be studied ~** se puede hacer un estudio comparado de los libros

▼**compare** [kəmˈpɛəʳ] Ⓐ VT 1 (*gen*) comparar; (= *put side by side*) [+ *texts*] cotejar; **to ~ sth/sb with** *or* **to sth/sb** comparar algo/a algn con *or* a algo/algn; **Oxford is small ~d with London** Oxford es pequeño en comparación a *or* comparado con Londres; **as ~d with** comparado con; ✦*IDIOM* **to ~ notes with sb** cambiar impresiones con algn
2 (*Gram*) formar los grados de comparación de
Ⓑ VI **she can't ~ with you** no se la puede comparar contigo; **it doesn't ~ with yours** no se lo puede comparar al tuyo, no tiene comparación con el tuyo; **how do they ~?** ¿cuáles son sus cualidades respectivas?; **how do they ~ for speed?** ¿cuál tiene mayor velocidad?; **how do the prices ~?** ¿qué tal son los precios en comparación?; **it ~s favourably with the other** no pierde por comparación con el otro, supera al otro; **it ~s poorly with the other** es inferior al otro
Ⓒ N **beyond ~** (*poet*) incomparable, sin comparación, sin par

▼**comparison** [kəmˈpærɪsn] N 1 (*between things, people*) comparación *f*; **there's no ~ (between them)** no hay comparación (entre ellos), no se puede comparar (el uno con el otro); **in** *or* **by ~ (with)** en comparación (con); **this one is large in ~** éste es grande en comparación; **to draw a ~** establecer una comparación; **it will bear** *or* **stand ~ with the best** se puede comparar con los mejores
2 (*Gram*) comparación *f*

compartment [kəmˈpɑːtmənt] N compartimiento *m*; (*Brit Rail*) compartimiento *m*

compartmentalization [ˌkɒmpɑːtˌmentəlaɪˈzeɪʃən] N compartimentación *f*

compartmentalize [ˌkɒmpɑːtˈmentəlaɪz] VT dividir en categorías; (*pej*) aislar en compartimientos estancos, compartimentar

compass [ˈkʌmpəs] Ⓐ N 1 (*Naut etc*) brújula *f*
2 (*Math*) (*usu pl*) compás *m*; **a pair of ~es** un compás
3 (*frm*) (= *range*) alcance *m*; (= *area*) ámbito *m*; **beyond my ~** fuera de mi alcance; **within the ~ of the plan** dentro de lo abarcado por el plan
Ⓑ VT (*frm*) (= *cover, take in*) abarcar; (*liter*) (= *surround*) rodear
Ⓒ CPD ► **compass card** N (*Naut*) rosa *f* de los vientos ► **compass course** N ruta *f* magnética ► **compass rose** N = **compass card**

compassion [kəmˈpæʃən] N compasión *f*; **to have ~ for sth/for** *or* **on sb** tener compasión por *or* de algo/algn, compadecerse de algo/algn; **to feel ~ for sb** sentir compasión por *or* de algn; **to move sb to ~** mover a algn a la compasión

compassionate [kəmˈpæʃənɪt] Ⓐ ADJ [*person*] compasivo; **on ~ grounds** por compasión
Ⓑ CPD ► **compassionate leave** N permiso *m* por motivos familiares

compassionately [kəmˈpæʃənɪtlɪ] ADV compasivamente, con compasión

compatibility [kəmˌpætəˈbɪlɪtɪ] N compatibilidad *f*

compatible [kəmˈpætɪbl] Ⓐ ADJ compatible; **we weren't really ~** la verdad es que no éramos compatibles; **to be ~ with sth/sb** ser compatible con algo/algn; **an IBM-~ computer** un ordenador compatible con IBM
Ⓑ N (*Comput*) compatible *m*; **an IBM-~** un compatible con IBM

compatriot [kəmˈpætrɪət] N compatriota *mf*

compel [kəmˈpel] VT 1 (= *oblige*) obligar; **to ~ sb to do sth** obligar a algn a hacer algo, compeler a algn a hacer algo (*frm*); **I feel ~led to say that ...** me veo obligado a decir que ...
2 (= *command*) [+ *respect, obedience*] imponer; [+ *admiration*] ganarse

compelling [kəmˈpelɪŋ] ADJ 1 (= *convincing*) [*argument, evidence*] convincente; [*curiosity*] irresistible; **I went there for ~ reasons** fui porque tenía razones de peso; **to make a ~ case for sth** exponer unos argumentos convincentes a favor de algo
2 (= *riveting*) [*account, film, book*] fascinante, apasionante; **his new novel makes ~ reading** su nueva novela es fascinante *or* apasionante

compellingly [kəmˈpelɪŋlɪ] ADV [*write, tell*] de manera convincente, de modo convincente; [*attractive*] irresistiblemente; [*persuasive*] terriblemente

compendious [kəmˈpendɪəs] ADJ compendioso

compendium [kəmˈpendɪəm] N (*pl* **compendiums** *or* **compendia** [kəmˈpendɪə]) compendio *m*; ~ **of games** juegos *mpl* reunidos

compensate [ˈkɒmpənseɪt] Ⓐ VT 1 compensar; (*for loss, damage*) indemnizar, resarcir; **to**

➤ LANGUAGE IN USE: **comparatively** 5.1 **compare A1** 5.1 **comparison 1** 5.1, 5.5, 26.3

~ sb for sth compensar a algn por algo; (*for loss, damage*) indemnizar a algn por algo, resarcir a algn de algo
[2] (= *reward*) recompensar
Ⓑ VI **to ~ for sth** compensar algo

compensation [ˌkɒmpən'seɪʃən] Ⓐ N (= *award etc*) compensación *f*; (*for loss, damage*) indemnización *f*, resarcimiento *m*; (= *reward*) recompensa *f*; **they got £2,000 ~** recibieron 2.000 libras de indemnización; **in ~ (for)** en compensación (por)
Ⓑ CPD ► **compensation fund** N fondo *m* de compensación

compensatory [ˌkɒmpən'seɪtərɪ] Ⓐ ADJ compensatorio
Ⓑ CPD ► **compensatory damages** NPL indemnización *fsing* por daños y perjuicios ► **compensatory finance** N financiación *f* compensatoria

compere, compère ['kɒmpɛəʳ] Ⓐ N presentador(a) *m/f*, animador(a) *m/f*
Ⓑ VT [+ *show*] presentar
Ⓒ VI actuar de presentador

compete [kəm'piːt] VI (*as rivals*) competir (**against, with** con; **for** por); (= *take part*) tomar parte (**in** en), presentarse (**in** a); (*Comm*) competir, hacer la competencia; **there are 50 students competing for six places** hay 50 estudiantes compitiendo por seis puestos; **there are many firms competing for a share in the market** hay muchas empresas compitiendo por una participación en el mercado; **his poetry can't ~ with Eliot's** no se puede comparar su poesía con la de Eliot; **I can't ~ with that racket*** no puedo hablar por encima de esa bulla*

competence ['kɒmpɪtəns], **competency** ['kɒmpɪtənsɪ] N [1] (= *ability*) competencia *f*, capacidad *f*; **her ~ as a nurse** su competencia *or* capacidad como enfermera; **he has achieved a certain level of ~ in reading** ha conseguido un cierto nivel de competencia en la lectura
[2] (= *jurisdiction*) competencia *f*; **that is not within my ~** eso está fuera de mi competencia, eso no me compete

competent ['kɒmpɪtənt] ADJ [1] (= *proficient*) [*person, pilot, nurse*] competente, capaz; **to be ~ at sth** ser competente en algo; **students must be ~ in five basic subjects** los estudiantes tienen que ser competentes en *or* dominar cinco asignaturas fundamentales; **to feel ~ to do sth** sentirse capacitado para hacer algo
[2] (= *satisfactory*) [*work, performance*] aceptable; **his work is ~, but not very original** su trabajo es aceptable pero no muy original; **a ~ knowledge of the language** un conocimiento *or* dominio suficiente del idioma; **he did a very ~ job** hizo su trabajo muy bien; **a highly ~ piece of work** un trabajo muy bien hecho
[3] (*Jur*) [*court*] competente; [*witness*] hábil

competently ['kɒmpɪtəntlɪ] ADV [*handle, perform, play*] competentemente, de forma muy competente

competing [kəm'piːtɪŋ] ADJ [*product, bid, offer*] rival; [*interests*] conflictivo; **there are ~ claims on my time** hay muchas cosas que requieren mi tiempo

competition [ˌkɒmpɪ'tɪʃən] N [1] (= *competing*) competencia *f*, rivalidad *f*; **in ~ with** en competencia con; **there was keen ~ for the prize** se disputó reñidamente el premio
[2] (*Comm*) competencia *f*; **unfair ~** competencia desleal
[3] (= *contest*) concurso *m*; (*eg for Civil Service posts*) oposición *f*; (*Sport*) competición *f*; **to go in for a ~** ◊ **enter a ~** inscribirse en *or* presentarse a un concurso; **60 places to be filled by ~** 60 vacantes a cubrir por oposición

competitive [kəm'petɪtɪv] ADJ [*person*] competitivo; [*spirit*] competitivo, de competencia; [*exam, selection*] por concurso *or* oposiciones; (*Comm*) competitivo; **we must make ourselves more ~** tenemos que hacernos más competitivos; **we must improve our ~ position** tenemos que mejorar nuestras posibilidades de competir; **the technology has given them a ~ advantage** la tecnología les ha dado una ventaja competitiva; **~ sports** deportes *mpl* competitivos; *see also* **edge A5**

competitively [kəm'petɪtɪvlɪ] ADV [*think, behave*] con espíritu competidor; [*swim, run, play etc*] a nivel de competición; **~ priced** a precio competitivo; **their products are ~ priced** sus productos tienen precios competitivos

competitiveness [kəm'petɪtɪvnɪs] N [*of person*] espíritu *m* competitivo, espíritu *m* de competencia; [*of prices*] competitividad *f*

competitor [kəm'petɪtəʳ] N (= *rival*) competidor(a) *m/f*, rival *mf*; (*in contest*) concursante *mf*; (*Sport*) competidor(a) *m/f*, participante *mf*; (*eg for Civil Service post*) opositor(a) *m/f*; (*Comm*) competidor(a) *m/f*; **our ~s beat us to it** se nos adelantó la competencia

compilation [ˌkɒmpɪ'leɪʃən] Ⓐ N (= *act*) [*of list, catalogue*] compilación *f*; [*of information*] recopilación *f*; (= *document*) compilación *f*
Ⓑ CPD ► **compilation album** N (*Mus*) álbum *m* recopilatorio

compile [kəm'paɪl] VT [+ *list, catalogue*] compilar (*also Comput*); [+ *information*] recopilar

compiler [kəm'paɪləʳ] N [*of catalogue, list, dictionary*] compilador(a) *m/f* (*also Comput*); [*of information*] recopilador(a) *m/f*

complacency [kəm'pleɪsənsɪ] N, **complacence** [kəm'pleɪsns] N autosuficiencia *f*, satisfacción *f* de sí mismo *or* consigo

complacent [kəm'pleɪsənt] ADJ [*person*] (demasiado) pagado de sí mismo; **a ~ look** una expresión de autosatisfacción; **we can't afford to be ~** no podemos permitirnos el lujo de confiarnos, no podemos dormirnos en los laureles

complacently [kəm'pleɪsəntlɪ] ADV de modo satisfecho; **he looked at me ~** me miró con expresión de autosatisfacción

complain [kəm'pleɪn] VI [1] (= *grumble*) quejarse (**about, of** de; **to** a); **to ~ that** quejarse de que; **they ~ed to the neighbours** se quejaron a los vecinos; **I can't ~** yo no me quejo
[2] (= *make a formal complaint*) reclamar (**about** por; **to** ante); **we're going to ~ to the manager** vamos a reclamar al director; **you should ~ to the police** tendrías que denunciarlo a la policía
[3] (*Med*) **to ~ of** quejarse de

complainant [kəm'pleɪnənt] N (*Jur*) demandante *mf*, querellante *mf*

complaint [kəm'pleɪnt] Ⓐ N [1] (= *statement of dissatisfaction*) queja *f*; (*to manager of shop etc*) reclamación *f*; (*to police*) denuncia *f*; **I had no ~s about the service** no tenía ninguna queja del servicio; **to have cause for ~** tener motivo de queja; **to make** *or* **lodge a ~** reclamar, formular una queja
[2] (= *cause of dissatisfaction*) motivo *m* de queja
[3] (*Med*) (= *illness*) mal *m*, dolencia *f*
Ⓑ CPD ► **complaints book** N libro *m* de reclamaciones ► **complaints department** N sección *f* de reclamaciones ► **complaints procedure** N procedimiento *m* para presentar reclamaciones

complaisance [kəm'pleɪzəns] N (*liter*) complacencia *f*, sumisión *f*

complaisant [kəm'pleɪzənt] ADJ (*gen*) servicial, cortés; [*wife, husband*] consentido, sumiso

-complected [kəm'plektɪd] ADJ (*ending in compounds*) (*US*) = **-complexioned**

complement Ⓐ ['kɒmplɪmənt] N [1] (*gen*) complemento *m*; **to be a ~ to** complementar a; **this wine is the perfect ~ to smoked salmon** este vino complementa perfectamente al salmón ahumado
[2] [*of staff*] (*esp on ship*) dotación *f*, personal *m*; **the orchestra did not have its full ~ of brass** la orquesta no contaba con su sección de metales completa
Ⓑ ['kɒmplɪment] VT complementar

complementary [ˌkɒmplɪ'mentərɪ] ADJ complementario; **the skirt and jacket are ~** la falda y la chaqueta son del mismo traje

complete [kəm'pliːt] Ⓐ ADJ [1] (= *whole*) entero; **a ~ office block was burnt to the ground** un bloque de oficinas entero quedó reducido a cenizas
[2] (= *finished*) terminado; **the work of restoring the farmhouse is ~** la restauración de la granja está terminada
[3] (= *total*) [*control, lack*] total, absoluto; [*change*] total; [*surprise*] auténtico; **in ~ agreement** totalmente de acuerdo, en completo acuerdo; **in ~ contrast to sth/sb** todo lo contrario que algo/algn; **it's a ~ disaster** es un completo desastre, es un desastre total; **the man's a ~ idiot** es un auténtico idiota; **it is a ~ mistake to think that ...** es totalmente erróneo pensar que ...; **he is the ~ opposite of me** no nos parecemos en nada; **to my ~ satisfaction** para mi completa *or* total satisfacción
[4] (= *full*) [*list, set, group*] completo; **the Complete Works of Shakespeare** las Obras Completas de Shakespeare; **at last her happiness was ~** por fin, su dicha era completa; **no garden is ~ without a bed of rose bushes** ningún jardín puede considerarse completo si no tiene un arriate de rosales
[5] (= *all-round*) [*novelist, footballer*] completo, perfecto; **he is the ~ film-maker** es el director de cine completo *or* perfecto
[6] **~ with: a mansion ~ with swimming pool** una mansión con piscina y todo; **he arrived ~ with equipment** llegó con todo su equipo; **the diary comes ~ with a ballpoint pen** la agenda viene con bolígrafo incluido; **it comes ~ with instructions** viene con sus correspondientes instrucciones
Ⓑ VT [1] (= *make up*) [+ *set, collection, team*] completar; [+ *misfortune, happiness*] colmar; **a grey silk tie ~d the outfit** una corbata de seda gris completaba el conjunto
[2] (= *finish*) [+ *work*] terminar, acabar; [+ *contract*] cumplir, llevar a cabo; **the course takes three years to ~** se tarda tres años en hacer el curso; **to ~ a prison sentence** cumplir una pena de cárcel
[3] (= *fill in*) [+ *form, questionnaire*] rellenar; **~ the application form** rellene la solicitud

completely [kəm'pliːtlɪ] ADV completamente, totalmente; **something ~ different** algo completamente *or* totalmente diferente; **~ and utterly ridiculous** total y absolutamente ridículo; **almost ~** casi completamente, casi por completo; **I'm sorry, I ~ forgot** lo siento, me olvidé completamente *or* totalmente *or* por completo; **she's not ~ recovered yet** aún no está completamente *or* totalmente *or* del todo recuperada

completeness [kəmˈpliːtnɪs] N [*of report, study, information*] lo completo; **at varying stages of ~** en diferentes fases de finalización

completion [kəmˈpliːʃən] Ⓐ N finalización *f*, terminación *f*, conclusión *f*; **to be nearing ~** estar a punto de finalizarse *or* terminarse *or* concluirse, estar llegando a su finalización *or* conclusión; **on ~ of contract** cuando se cumpla el contrato
Ⓑ CPD ► **completion date** N (*Jur*) (*for work*) fecha *f* de cumplimiento; (*in house-buying*) fecha de entrega (de llaves)

complex [ˈkɒmpleks] Ⓐ ADJ (= *difficult*) complejo, complicado; (= *consisting of different parts*) complejo; (*Ling*) compuesto
Ⓑ N [1] (*Psych*) complejo *m*; **inferiority/ Oedipus ~** complejo *m* de inferioridad/ Edipo; **he's got a ~ about his nose** está acomplejado por su nariz, su nariz lo acompleja
[2] [*of buildings*] complejo *m*; **sports ~** complejo *m* deportivo; **housing ~** colonia *f* de viviendas, urbanización *f*; **shopping ~** complejo *m* comercial

complexion [kəmˈplekʃən] N tez *f*, cutis *m*; (*in terms of colour*) tez *f*, piel *f*; (*fig*) cariz *m*, aspecto *m*; **that puts a different ~ on it** eso le da otro cariz *or* aspecto

-complexioned [kəmˈplekʃnd] ADJ (*ending in compounds*) de piel …; **dark-complexioned** de piel morena; **light-complexioned** de piel blanca

complexity [kəmˈpleksɪtɪ] N complejidad *f*, lo complejo

compliance [kəmˈplaɪəns] N (*with rules etc*) conformidad *f*; (= *submissiveness*) sumisión *f* (**with** a); **in ~ with** conforme a, en conformidad con

compliant [kəmˈplaɪənt] ADJ sumiso

complicate [ˈkɒmplɪkeɪt] VT complicar

complicated [ˈkɒmplɪkeɪtɪd] ADJ complicado; **to become ~** ◊ **get ~** complicarse

complication [ˌkɒmplɪˈkeɪʃən] N complicación *f*; **it seems there are ~s** parece que han surgido complicaciones *or* dificultades

complicity [kəmˈplɪsɪtɪ] N complicidad *f* (**in** en)

compliment Ⓐ [ˈkɒmplɪmənt] N [1] (= *respect*) cumplido *m*; (= *flirtation*) piropo *m*; (= *flattery*) halago *m*; **what a nice ~!** ¡qué detalle!; **that was meant as a ~** lo dije con buena intención; **to pay sb a ~** (*respectful*) hacer cumplidos a algn; (*amorous*) echar piropos a algn; (= *flatter*) halagar a algn; **to return the ~** devolver el cumplido; **I take it as a ~ that …** me halaga (el) que …
[2] **compliments** (= *greetings*) saludos *mpl*; **my ~s to the chef** mi enhorabuena al cocinero; **the ~s of the season** felicidades *fpl*; **to send one's ~s to sb** enviar saludos a algn; **"with ~s"** "con un atento saludo"; **with the ~s of the management** obsequio de la casa; **with the ~s of Mr Pearce** con un atento saludo del Sr. Pearce, de parte del Sr. Pearce; **with the author's ~s** homenaje *m or* obsequio *m* del autor
Ⓑ [ˈkɒmplɪment] VT **to ~ sb on sth/on doing sth** felicitar a algn por algo/por conseguir algo; **they ~ed me on my Spanish** me felicitaron por mi español
Ⓒ [ˈkɒmplɪmənt] CPD ► **compliment(s) slip** N nota *f* de saludo, saluda *m* (*Admin*)

complimentary [ˌkɒmplɪˈmentərɪ] ADJ [1] [*remark etc*] elogioso; **he was very ~ about the play** habló de la obra en términos muy favorables
[2] (= *free*) [*copy of book etc*] de obsequio; **~ ticket** invitación *f*

complin, compline [ˈkɒmplɪn] N completas *fpl*

comply [kəmˈplaɪ] VI **to ~ with** [+ *rules*] cumplir; [+ *laws*] acatar; [+ *orders*] obedecer; [+ *wishes, request*] acceder a

component [kəmˈpəʊnənt] Ⓐ ADJ componente; **its ~ parts** (*of structure, device*) las piezas que lo integran; (*of organization, concept*) las partes que lo integran
Ⓑ N (= *part*) componente *m*; (*Tech*) pieza *f*
Ⓒ CPD ► **components factory** N fábrica *f* de componentes, maquiladora *f* (*LAm*)

comport [kəmˈpɔːt] (*frm*) Ⓐ VI **to ~ with** concordar con
Ⓑ VT **to ~ o.s.** comportarse

comportment [kəmˈpɔːtmənt] N (*frm*) comportamiento *m*

compose [kəmˈpəʊz] VT [1] [+ *music*] componer; [+ *poetry, letter*] escribir; **to be ~d of** constar de, componerse de
[2] **to ~ o.s.** calmarse, serenarse

composed [kəmˈpəʊzd] ADJ tranquilo, sereno

composedly [kəmˈpəʊzɪdlɪ] ADV tranquilamente, serenamente

composer [kəmˈpəʊzəʳ] N compositor(a) *m/f*

composite [ˈkɒmpəzɪt] Ⓐ ADJ compuesto
Ⓑ CPD ► **composite motion** N moción *f* compuesta

composition [ˌkɒmpəˈzɪʃən] N [1] (*Mus*) (= *act of composing, thing composed*) composición *f*; (*Literat*) redacción *f*
[2] (*Art*) (= *make-up*) composición *f*

compositional [ˌkɒmpəˈzɪʃənl] ADJ [*skill, style*] de composición

compositor [kəmˈpɒzɪtəʳ] N cajista *mf*

compos mentis [ˈkɒmpɒsˈmentɪs] ADJ **to be ~** estar en su sano *or* entero juicio; (*Jur*) estar en pleno uso de sus facultades mentales; **he normally takes a good hour to become ~** generalmente no es persona *or* no se espabila hasta que no pasa más de una hora

compost [ˈkɒmpɒst] Ⓐ N compost *m*, fertilizante *m* orgánico
Ⓑ CPD ► **compost heap** N montón *m* de desechos para formar el compost

composting [ˈkɒmpɒstɪŋ] N compostación *f*

composure [kəmˈpəʊʒəʳ] N calma *f*, serenidad *f*; **to recover** *or* **regain one's ~** recobrar la calma

compote [ˈkɒmpəʊt] N compota *f*

compound [ˈkɒmpaʊnd] Ⓐ N [1] (*Chem*) compuesto *m*
[2] (= *word*) palabra *f* compuesta
[3] (= *enclosed area*) recinto *m* (cercado)
Ⓑ [ˈkɒmpaʊnd] ADJ [1] (*Chem*) compuesto
[2] [*number, sentence, tense*] compuesto
[3] [*fracture*] múltiple
Ⓒ [kəmˈpaʊnd] VT (*fig*) [+ *problem, difficulty*] agravar; **to ~ a felony** aceptar dinero para no entablar juicio
Ⓓ [kəmˈpaʊnd] VI (*Jur etc*) **to ~ with** capitular con
Ⓔ [ˈkɒmpaʊnd] CPD ► **compound interest** N interés *m* compuesto

compounding [ˈkɒmpaʊndɪŋ] N composición *f*

comprehend [ˌkɒmprɪˈhend] Ⓐ VT [1] (= *understand*) comprender, entender
[2] (= *include*) comprender, abarcar
Ⓑ VI comprender

comprehensible [ˌkɒmprɪˈhensəbl] ADJ comprensible

comprehensibly [ˌkɒmprɪˈhensəblɪ] ADV comprensiblemente, de modo comprensible

comprehension [ˌkɒmprɪˈhenʃən] Ⓐ N [1] (= *understanding*) comprensión *f*; **it is beyond ~** es incomprensible
[2] (*Scol*) (= *exercise*) prueba *f* de comprensión
Ⓑ CPD ► **comprehension test** N test *m* de comprensión

comprehensive [ˌkɒmprɪˈhensɪv] Ⓐ ADJ [1] (= *complete*) [*list, guide, range*] completo; [*report, description, study*] exhaustivo; [*account, view*] de conjunto, integral; [*knowledge*] extenso; [*training*] completo, exhaustivo; [*victory, defeat*] aplastante
[2] (*Brit Scol*) **~ education** *sistema de enseñanza secundaria que abarca a alumnos de todos los niveles de aptitud*; **~ school** instituto *m* (de segunda enseñanza)
[3] (*Insurance*) (*also* **fully ~**) [*insurance, policy, cover*] a todo riesgo
Ⓑ N (*also* **~ school**) instituto *m* (de segunda enseñanza)

COMPREHENSIVE SCHOOLS

La mayoría de las escuelas de educación secundaria en el Reino Unido se conocen como **comprehensive schools** *y ofrecen una gran variedad de asignaturas para cubrir las necesidades educativas de alumnos con diferentes aptitudes. Fueron creadas en los años sesenta en un intento de fomentar la igualdad de oportunidades y acabar con la división tradicional entre los centros selectivos de enseñanzas teóricas (***grammar schools***) y otros de enseñanza básicamente profesional (***secondary modern schools***).*

⇨ *Ver tb* GRAMMAR SCHOOL, EDUCATION

comprehensively [ˌkɒmprɪˈhensɪvlɪ] ADV (= *thoroughly*) de forma exhaustiva; **the book is ~ illustrated** el libro está ampliamente ilustrado; **they were ~ beaten by the Italian champions** sufrieron una derrota aplastante frente a *or* ante los campeones italianos

compress Ⓐ [kəmˈpres] VT (*gen*) comprimir; [+ *text etc*] condensar
Ⓑ [ˈkɒmpres] N (*Med*) compresa *f*

compressed [kəmˈprest] Ⓐ ADJ comprimido
Ⓑ CPD ► **compressed air** N aire *m* comprimido ► **compressed charge** N (*US*) precio *m* inclusivo

compression [kəmˈpreʃən] N compresión *f*

compressor [kəmˈpresəʳ] Ⓐ N compresor *m*
Ⓑ CPD ► **compressor unit** N unidad *f* de compresión

comprise [kəmˈpraɪz] VT (= *include*) comprender; (= *be made up of*) constar de, consistir en

compromise [ˈkɒmprəmaɪz] Ⓐ N [1] (= *agreement*) arreglo *m*, solución *f* intermedia; **to reach a ~ (over sth)** llegar a un arreglo (sobre algo)
[2] (= *giving in*) transigencia *f*; **there can be no ~ with treason** no transigimos con la traición
Ⓑ VI [1] (= *reach an agreement*) llegar a un arreglo; **so we ~d on seven** así que, ni para uno ni para otro, convinimos en siete
[2] (= *give in*) transigir, transar (*LAm*); **to ~ with sb over sth** transigir con algn sobre algo; **to agree to ~ (with sb)** avenirse a transigir (con algn); **in the end I agreed to ~** terminé dando mi brazo a torcer

ⓒ VT [1] (= *endangering safety of*) poner en peligro
[2] (= *bring under suspicion*) [+ *reputation, person*] comprometer; **to ~ o.s.** comprometerse
ⓓ CPD [*decision, solution*] intermedio

compromising ['kɒmprəmaɪzɪŋ] ADJ [*situation*] comprometedor; [*mind, spirit*] acomodaticio

comptometer [kɒmp'tɒmɪtəʳ] N máquina *f* de calcular

comptroller [kən'trəʊləʳ] N interventor(a) *m/f*

compulsion [kəm'pʌlʃən] N [1] (= *urge*) compulsión *f*
[2] (= *force*) **under ~** a la fuerza, bajo coacción; **you are under no ~** no tienes ninguna obligación

compulsive [kəm'pʌlsɪv] ADJ compulsivo; *see also* **viewing**

compulsively [kəm'pʌlsɪvlɪ] ADV compulsivamente

compulsorily [kəm'pʌlsərɪlɪ] ADV por fuerza, forzosamente

➤**compulsory** [kəm'pʌlsərɪ] ⓐ ADJ obligatorio
ⓑ CPD ► **compulsory liquidation** N liquidación *f* obligatoria ► **compulsory purchase** N expropiación *f* ► **compulsory purchase order** N orden *f* de expropiación ► **compulsory redundancy** N despido *m* forzoso

compunction [kəm'pʌŋkʃən] N escrúpulo *m*; **without ~** sin escrúpulo

computation [,kɒmpjʊ'teɪʃən] N [1] (*gen*) (*often pl*) cómputo *m*, cálculo *m*
[2] (*Comput*) computación *f*

computational [,kɑmpjʊ'teɪʃənl] ⓐ ADJ computacional
ⓑ CPD ► **computational linguistics** N lingüística *f* computacional

compute [kəm'pjuːt] VT computar, calcular

computer [kəm'pjuːtəʳ] ⓐ N ordenador *m* (*Sp*), computador *m* (*LAm*), computadora *f* (*LAm*); **we do it by ~ now** ahora lo hacemos con el ordenador; **the records have all been put on ~** todos los registros han entrado en (el) ordenador; **she's in ~s** se dedica a la informática, trabaja en algo de informática
ⓑ CPD ► **computer animation** N animación *f* por ordenador ► **computer crime** N delitos *mpl* informáticos ► **computer dating service** N agencia *f* matrimonial por ordenador ► **computer expert** N experto/a *m/f* en ordenadores ► **computer game** N videojuego *m* ► **computer graphics** NPL gráficas *fpl* por ordenador ► **computer language** N lenguaje *m* de ordenador ► **computer literacy** N competencia *f* en la informática ► **computer model** N modelo *m* informático ► **computer operator** N operador(a) *m/f* de ordenador ► **computer peripheral** N periférico *m* ► **computer printout** N impresión *f* (de ordenador) ► **computer program** N programa *m* de ordenador ► **computer programmer** N programador(a) *m/f* de ordenadores ► **computer programming** N programación *f* de ordenadores ► **computer science** N informática *f* ► **computer scientist** N informático/a *m/f* ► **computer simulation** N simulación *f* por ordenador ► **computer skills** NPL conocimientos *mpl* de informática ► **computer studies** NPL = **computer science** ► **computer typesetting** N composición *f* por ordenador ► **computer user** N usuario/a *m/f* de ordenador

computer-aided [kəm'pjuːtər'eɪdɪd], **computer-assisted** [kəm'pjuːtərə'sɪstɪd] ADJ asistido por ordenador *or* (*LAm*) computador *or* computadora

computer-controlled [kəm'pjuːtəkən'trəʊld] ADJ controlado por ordenador *or* (*LAm*) computador *or* computadora

computerese [kəm,pjuːtə'riːz] N jerga *f* informática

computer-generated [kəm,pjuːtə'dʒenəreɪtɪd] ADJ [*graphics, images*] realizado *or* creado por ordenador *or* (*LAm*) computador *or* computadora

computerization [kəm,pjuːtəraɪ'zeɪʃən] N computerización *f*, computarización *f*

computerize [kəm'pjuːtəraɪz] VT [+ *company, hospital, system, accounts*] informatizar; [+ *data, information, records*] computerizar, computarizar, informatizar; **we're ~d now** ya nos hemos informatizado

computer-literate [kəm,pjuːtə'lɪtərɪt] ADJ **to be computer literate** saber cómo utilizar un ordenador

computer-operated [kəm,pjuːtər'ɒpəreɪtɪd] ADJ operado por ordenador *or* (*LAm*) computador *or* computadora, computerizado

computing [kəm'pjuːtɪŋ] ⓐ N informática *f*
ⓑ CPD ► **computing problem** N problema *m* de cómputo ► **computing task** N tarea *f* de computar

comrade ['kɒmrɪd] N compañero/a *m/f*, camarada *mf*; (*Pol*) camarada *mf*

comrade-in-arms ['kɒmrɪdɪn'ɑːmz] N compañero *m* de armas

comradely ['kɒmreɪdlɪ] ADJ de camarada; **I gave him some ~ advice** le di unos consejos de camarada; **we did it in a ~ spirit** lo hicimos como camaradas

comradeship ['kɒmrɪdʃɪp] N compañerismo *m*, camaradería *f*

Comsat® ['kɒmsæt] N ABBR (*US*) (= **communications satellite**) COMSAT® *m*

con[1]* [kɒn] ⓐ VT estafar, timar; **I've been ~ned!** ¡me han estafado!; **to ~ sb into doing sth** engañar a algn para que haga algo
ⓑ N estafa *f*, timo *m*; **it was all a big ~** no fue más que una estafa
ⓒ CPD ► **con artist**, **con man** N estafador(a) *m/f*, timador(a) *m/f* ► **con trick** N = **confidence trick**

con[2] [kɒn] N (= *disadvantage*) contra *m*; **the pros and ~s** los pros y los contras

con[3]†† [kɒn] VT (*also* **to ~ over**) estudiar, repasar

con[4]‡ [kɒn] N (= *prisoner*) preso/a *m/f*

Con. ABBR (*Brit*) [1] = **Conservative**
[2] = **constable**

conc. ABBR = **concessions**; **admission £5 (~ £4)** entrada: 5 libras (tarifa reducida: 4 libras) (*para jubilados, parados, estudiantes, etc*)

concatenate [kɒn'kætɪ,neɪt] VT (*frm*) concatenar

concatenation [kɒn,kætɪ'neɪʃən] N (*frm*) concatenación *f*

concave ['kɒn'keɪv] ADJ cóncavo

concavity [kɒn'kævɪtɪ] N concavidad *f*

conceal [kən'siːl] VT [+ *object, news*] ocultar; [+ *emotions, thoughts*] disimular; (*Jur*) encubrir; **~ed lighting** luces *fpl* indirectas; **~ed turning** (*Aut*) cruce *m* poco visible

concealment [kən'siːlmənt] N [*of object*] ocultación *f*; [*of emotion*] disimulación *f*; (*Jur*) encubrimiento *m*; **place of ~** escondrijo *m*

concede [kən'siːd] ⓐ VT [+ *point, argument*] reconocer, conceder; [+ *game, territory*] ceder; **to ~ that** admitir que; **to ~ defeat** darse por vencido
ⓑ VI ceder, darse por vencido

conceit [kən'siːt] N [1] (= *pride*) vanidad *f*, presunción *f*, engreimiento *m*
[2] (*Literat*) concepto *m*

conceited [kən'siːtɪd] ADJ vanidoso, engreído; **to be ~ about** envanecerse con *or* de *or* por

conceitedly [kən'siːtɪdlɪ] ADV con vanidad *or* engreimiento

conceivable [kən'siːvəbl] ADJ imaginable, concebible

conceivably [kən'siːvəblɪ] ADV **you may ~ be right** es posible que tenga razón; **it cannot ~ be true** no es posible que sea verdad; **more than one could ~ need** más de lo que se podría imaginar como necesidad

conceive [kən'siːv] ⓐ VT [1] [+ *child*] concebir
[2] (= *imagine*) concebir; **to ~ a dislike for sth/sb** cobrar antipatía a algo/algn
ⓑ VI [1] (= *become pregnant*) concebir
[2] (= *think*) **to ~ of sth** imaginar algo; **to ~ of doing sth** imaginarse haciendo algo; **I cannot ~ of anything worse** no me puedo imaginar nada peor; **I cannot ~ why** no entiendo porqué

concelebrant [kən'selɪ,brənt] N (*frm*) concelebrante *m*

concelebrate [kən'selɪbreɪt] VT (*frm*) [+ *mass*] concelebrar

concentrate ['kɒnsəntreɪt] ⓐ VT [1] [+ *efforts, thoughts*] concentrar; **to ~ one's efforts on sth/on doing sth** centrar *or* concentrar los esfuerzos en algo/en hacer algo; **he ~d his mind on the task ahead** se concentró *or* se centró en la tarea que tenía por delante
[2] (= *group together*) [+ *troops etc*] concentrar, reunir; **heavy industry is ~d in the north of the country** la industria pesada se concentra en el norte del país
ⓑ VI [1] (= *pay attention*) concentrarse; **I couldn't ~** no me podía concentrar; **~!** ¡concéntrate!; **to ~ on sth** concentrarse en algo; **I was concentrating on my homework** me estaba concentrando en los deberes
[2] (= *focus on*) **to ~ on sth** centrarse en algo; **the talks are expected to ~ on practical issues** se espera que las conversaciones se centren en *or* giren en torno a cuestiones prácticas; **to ~ on doing sth** concentrarse *or* centrarse en hacer algo
[3] (= *come together*) [*troops, crowd*] concentrarse, reunirse
ⓒ N (*Chem*) concentrado *m*

concentrated ['kɒnsən,treɪtɪd] ADJ concentrado

concentration [,kɒnsən'treɪʃən] ⓐ N concentración *f*
ⓑ CPD ► **concentration camp** N campo *m* de concentración

concentric [kən'sentrɪk] ADJ concéntrico

concept ['kɒnsept] ⓐ N concepto *m*; **have you any ~ of how hard it is?** ¿tienes idea de lo difícil que es?
ⓑ CPD ► **concept album** N (*Mus*) volumen *m* monográfico

conception [kən'sepʃən] N [1] [*of child, idea*] concepción *f*; *see also* **immaculate**
[2] (= *idea*) concepto *m*; **a bold ~** un concepto grandioso; **he has not the remotest ~ of …** no tiene ni la menor idea de …

conceptual [kən'septjʊəl] ⓐ ADJ conceptual
ⓑ CPD ► **conceptual art** N arte *m* conceptual

conceptualization [kən,septjʊəlaɪ'zeɪʃən] N conceptualización *f*

conceptualize [kən'septjʊəlaɪz] VT conceptualizar

➤ LANGUAGE IN USE: **compulsory A** 10.1, 10.3

conceptually [kən'septjʊəlɪ] ADV conceptualmente, como concepto; **~, the idea made sense** como concepto, la idea podía funcionar

concern [kən'sɜːn] Ⓐ N [1] (= *business*) asunto *m*; **it's no ~ of yours** no es asunto tuyo; **technical aspects were the ~ of the army** de los aspectos técnicos se encargaba el ejército, los aspectos técnicos eran asunto del ejército; **if they want to go ahead, that's their ~** si quieren seguir adelante, es asunto suyo; **what ~ is it of yours?** ¿qué tiene que ver contigo?
[2] (= *anxiety*) preocupación *f*; **his health is giving cause for ~** su salud está dando motivo de preocupación; **to express ~ about sth** expresar preocupación por algo; **it is a matter for ~ that …** es motivo de preocupación el (hecho de) que …; **with an expression** *or* **a look of ~** con cara preocupada *or* de preocupación; **there is ~ that …** preocupa que …
[3] (= *interest, regard*) interés *m*; **my main ~ is the welfare of my children** mi interés principal *or* lo que más me preocupa es el bienestar de mis hijos; **it's of no ~ to me** me tiene sin cuidado, a mí no me importa; **out of ~ for her feelings, I didn't say anything** no dije nada por no herir sus sentimientos; **out of ~ for the public's safety** por la seguridad pública
[4] (= *firm*) negocio *m*, empresa *f*; **a family ~** un negocio familiar; **a going ~** un negocio próspero, una empresa próspera; **the farm is not a going ~** la granja no es un buen negocio
Ⓑ VT [1] (= *affect*) afectar, concernir; **it ~s me directly** me afecta *or* concierne directamente; **it doesn't ~ you at all** no te afecta *or* concierne para nada
[2] (= *interest, involve*) **please contact the department ~ed** póngase en contacto con la sección correspondiente; **it is best for all ~ed** es lo mejor para todas las partes interesadas; **as far as I am ~ed** por *or* en lo que a mí se refiere, por *or* en lo que a mí respecta; **she can go to hell as far as I'm ~ed** por mí se puede ir a la porra*, por *or* en lo que a mí respecta se puede ir a la porra*; **I was just another student as far as he was ~ed** para él yo no era más que otra estudiante; **to ~ o.s. with sth**: **I didn't ~ myself with politics** no me metí en política; **don't ~ yourself with things you can do nothing about** no te preocupes por cosas que están fuera de tu alcance; **those ~ed** los interesados; **to whom it may ~** (*frm*) a quien corresponda; **to be ~ed with sth**: **essential reading for anyone ~ed with children** lecturas fundamentales para cualquiera al que le interesen los niños; **they are mainly ~ed with maximizing profits** su interés principal es maximizar los beneficios
[3] (= *be about*) **my question ~s money** mi pregunta hace referencia al dinero; **chapter two is ~ed with the civil war** el capítulo dos trata de la guerra civil
[4] (= *worry*) preocupar; **it ~s me that …** me preocupa el hecho de que …

concerned [kən'sɜːnd] ADJ [1] (= *worried*) preocupado; **to be ~ about sth/sb** estar preocupado por algo/algn; **I'm not nagging, I'm ~ about you** no es que quiera darte la lata, estoy preocupado por ti *or* me preocupas; **to be ~ at** *or* **by sth** estar preocupado por algo; **doctors are ~ at his slow recovery** los médicos están preocupados por *or* a los médicos les preocupa la lentitud con la que se está recuperando; **to be ~ for sth/sb** estar preocupado por algo/algn; **he was ~ for his son's happiness** le preocupaba la felicidad de su hijo; **he sounded very ~** parecía estar muy preocupado; **he was ~ that he might have hurt her** le preocupaba que pudiera haberle hecho daño
[2] **to be ~ to do sth** poner mucho interés en hacer algo; **Britain was ~ to avoid war** Gran Bretaña puso mucho interés en evitar la guerra; *see also* **concern B2**

concerning [kən'sɜːnɪŋ] PREP [1] (= *with regard to*) con respecto a, con relación a, en lo que se refiere a (*frm*); **~ your last remark, …** con respecto *or* relación a su último comentario, …, en lo que se refiere a su último comentario, …
[2] (= *about*) sobre, acerca de; **theories ~ evolution** teorías sobre *or* acerca de la evolución; **something ~ his mother** algo que tenía que ver con su madre, algo relacionado con su madre

concert Ⓐ ['kɒnsət] N concierto *m*; **to give a ~** dar un concierto; **in ~** (*Mus*) en concierto; **in ~ with** (*Mus*) en concierto con; (*fig*) (= *in agreement with*) de común acuerdo con
Ⓑ [kən'sɜːt] VT concertar
Ⓒ ['kɒnsət] CPD ► **concert grand** N piano *m* de cola ► **concert hall** N sala *f* de conciertos ► **concert party** N (*Theat*) grupo *m* de artistas de revista; (*Fin*) *conjunto de inversores que se pone de acuerdo en secreto para adquirir la mayoría de las acciones de una empresa* ► **concert performer** N concertista *mf* ► **concert pianist** N pianista *mf* de concierto ► **concert pitch** N diapasón *m* normal; **at ~ pitch** (*fig*) en plena forma, en un momento excelente ► **concert ticket** N entrada *f* de concierto ► **concert tour** N gira *f* de conciertos

concerted [kən'sɜːtɪd] ADJ [*campaign, attack*] coordinado, organizado; [*attempt*] coordinado, concertado; **to make a ~ effort (to do sth)** aunar *or* coordinar los esfuerzos (por hacer algo)

concertgoer ['kɒnsət,gəʊəʳ] N aficionado/a *m/f* a los conciertos; **we are regular ~s** vamos con regularidad a los conciertos

concertina [,kɒnsə'tiːnə] Ⓐ N concertina *f*
Ⓑ VI **the vehicles ~ed into each other** los vehículos quedaron hechos un acordeón
Ⓒ CPD ► **concertina crash** N (*Aut*) choque *m* *or* colisión *f* en cadena

concertmaster ['kɒnsət,mɑːstəʳ] N (*US*) primer violín *m*

concerto [kən'tʃeətəʊ] N (*pl* **concertos, concerti** [kən'tʃeətiː]) concierto *m*

concession [kən'seʃən] N [1] (= *reduction*) concesión *f*; (*on tax*) desgravación *f*, exención *f*; **price ~** reducción *f*
[2] (= *franchise*) concesión *f*; (= *exploration rights*) (*for oil*) derechos *mpl* de exploración

concessionaire [kən,seʃə'neəʳ] N (*esp US*) concesionario/a *m/f*

concessionary [kən'seʃənərɪ] Ⓐ ADJ [*ticket, fare*] reducido
Ⓑ N concesionario/a *m/f*

conch [kɒntʃ] N (*pl* **conchs** *or* **conches**) [1] (= *shell*) caracola *f*
[2] (*Archit*) cóclea *f*

concierge [,kɔ̃ːnsɪ'eəʒ] N conserje *m*

conciliate [kən'sɪlɪeɪt] VT conciliar

conciliation [kən,sɪlɪ'eɪʃən] Ⓐ N conciliación *f*
Ⓑ CPD ► **conciliation service** N servicio *m* de conciliación

conciliator [kən'sɪlɪeɪtəʳ] N conciliador(a) *m/f*; (*Ind*) árbitro *mf*

conciliatory [kən'sɪlɪətərɪ] ADJ conciliador

concise [kən'saɪs] ADJ conciso

concisely [kən'saɪslɪ] ADV concisamente, con concisión

conciseness [kən'saɪsnɪs] N, **concision** [kən'sɪʒən] N concisión *f*

conclave ['kɒnkleɪv] N cónclave *m*

conclude [kən'kluːd] Ⓐ VT [1] (= *end*) acabar, concluir; **"to be ~d"** [*serial*] "terminará en el próximo episodio"
[2] (= *finalize*) [+ *treaty*] concertar, pactar; [+ *agreement*] llegar a, concertar; [+ *deal*] cerrar
[3] (= *infer*) concluir; **it was ~d that …** se concluyó que …; **what are we to ~ from that?** ¿que conclusión se saca de eso?; **from your expression I ~ that you are angry** por tu expresión deduzco que estás enfadado
[4] (*US*) (= *decide*) decidir (**to do sth** hacer algo)
Ⓑ VI (= *end*) terminar, concluir; **he ~d by saying** terminó diciendo; **the judge ~d in his favour** el juez decidió a su favor; **to ~ I must say …** para concluir *or* terminar, debo decir …

concluding [kən'kluːdɪŋ] ADJ final

conclusion [kən'kluːʒən] N [1] (= *end*) conclusión *f*, término *m*; **to reach a happy ~** llegar a feliz término; **in ~** para concluir *or* terminar, en conclusión; **to bring sth to a ~** concluir algo
[2] (= *signing*) [*of treaty, agreement, deal*] firmar *m*
[3] (= *inference*) conclusión *f*; **to come to the ~ that** llegar a la conclusión de que; **draw your own ~s** extraiga usted las conclusiones oportunas; **to jump to ~s** sacar conclusiones precipitadas; *see also* **foregone**

conclusive [kən'kluːsɪv] ADJ [*answer, victory*] concluyente, decisivo; [*proof*] concluyente

conclusively [kən'kluːsɪvlɪ] ADV concluyentemente

concoct [kən'kɒkt] VT [+ *food, drink*] confeccionar; [+ *lie, story*] inventar; [+ *plot*] tramar, fraguar

concoction [kən'kɒkʃən] N [1] (= *food*) mezcla *f*, mejunje *m*; (= *drink*) brebaje *m*
[2] (= *act*) [*of food, drink*] confección *f*; [*of story*] invención *f*

concomitant [kən'kɒmɪtənt] (*frm*) Ⓐ ADJ concomitante
Ⓑ N hecho *m* concomitante

concord ['kɒŋkɔːd] N [1] (= *harmony*) concordia *f*
[2] (= *treaty*) acuerdo *m*
[3] (*Mus, Gram*) concordancia *f*

concordance [kən'kɔːdəns] N [1] (= *agreement*) concordancia *f*
[2] (= *index, book*) concordancias *fpl*

concordant [kən'kɔːdənt] ADJ concordante

concordat [kɒn'kɔːdæt] N concordato *m*

Concorde ['kɒŋkɔːd] N Concorde *m*; **to fly by ~** volar en Concorde

concourse ['kɒŋkɔːs] N [1] [*of people*] concurrencia *f*; [*of rivers*] confluencia *f*
[2] (*in building, station*) explanada *f*

concrete ['kɒnkriːt] Ⓐ ADJ [1] (= *not abstract*) concreto
[2] (*Constr*) de hormigón *or* (*LAm*) concreto
Ⓑ N hormigón *m*
Ⓒ VT **to ~ a path** cubrir un sendero de hormigón
Ⓓ CPD ► **concrete jungle** N jungla *f* de asfalto ► **concrete mixer** N hormigonera *f* ► **concrete noun** N nombre *m* concreto

concretion [kən'kriːʃən] N concreción *f*

➤ LANGUAGE IN USE: concern B2 26.2 concerned 1 26.1 conclude B 26.1, 26.2 conclusion 1, 3 26.1

concretize [ˈkɒnkrɪtaɪz] VT concretar

concubine [ˈkɒŋkjʊbaɪn] N concubina *f*

concupiscence [kənˈkjuːpɪsəns] N (*frm*) concupiscencia *f*

concupiscent [kənˈkjuːpɪsənt] ADJ (*frm*) concupiscente

concur [kənˈkɜːʳ] VI 1 (= *agree*) estar de acuerdo (**with** con)
2 (= *happen at the same time*) concurrir

concurrence [kənˈkʌrəns] N 1 (*frm*) (= *consent*) conformidad *f*
2 (= *coincidence*) concurrencia *f*

concurrent [kənˈkʌrənt] Ⓐ ADJ concurrente; **~ with** concurrente con
Ⓑ CPD ► **concurrent processing** N procesamiento *m* concurrente

concurrently [kənˈkʌrəntlɪ] ADV al mismo tiempo, simultáneamente

concuss [kənˈkʌs] VT (*Med*) producir una conmoción cerebral a

concussed [kənˈkʌst] ADJ **to be ~** sufrir una conmoción cerebral

concussion [kənˈkʌʃən] N (*Med*) conmoción *f* cerebral

▼**condemn** [kənˈdem] VT (= *sentence, censure*) condenar; [+ *building*] declarar en ruina; [+ *food*] declarar insalubre; **to ~ sb to death** condenar a algn a muerte; **the ~ed cell** la celda de los condenados a muerte; **the ~ed man** el reo de muerte; **such conduct is to be ~ed** tal conducta es censurable

▼**condemnation** [ˌkɒndemˈneɪʃən] N (= *sentencing*) condena *f*; (= *censure*) censura *f*

condemnatory [ˌkɒndemˈneɪtərɪ] ADJ condenatorio

condensation [ˌkɒndenˈseɪʃən] N 1 (= *vapour*) vaho *m*
2 (= *summary*) resumen *m*

condense [kənˈdens] Ⓐ VT 1 [+ *vapour*] condensar; **~d milk** leche *f* condensada
2 [+ *text*] abreviar, resumir
Ⓑ VI condensarse

condenser [kənˈdensəʳ] N condensador *m*

condescend [ˌkɒndɪˈsend] VI **to ~ to sb** tratar a algn con condescendencia; **to ~ to do sth** dignarse (a) hacer algo, condescender a hacer algo

condescending [ˌkɒndɪˈsendɪŋ] ADJ [*attitude, tone, smile*] condescendiente; **in a ~ way** de manera condescendiente; **he's very ~** tiene una actitud muy condescendiente, se cree muy superior; **they were so ~** su actitud fue tan condescendiente; **to be ~ to** *or* **towards sb** tratar a algn con condescendencia

condescendingly [ˌkɒndɪˈsendɪŋlɪ] ADV con condescendencia; **to treat people ~** tratar a la gente con condescendencia; **he ~ agreed to do it** accedió hacerlo como si de un favor se tratara

condescension [ˌkɒndɪˈsenʃən] N condescendencia *f*

condiment [ˈkɒndɪmənt] N condimento *m*

condition [kənˈdɪʃən] Ⓐ N 1 (= *state*) condición *f*, estado *m*; **in good ~** en buenas condiciones, en buen estado; **to keep o.s. in ~** mantenerse en forma; **living ~s** condiciones de vida; **to be in no ~ to do sth** no estar en condiciones de hacer algo; **to be out of ~** no estar en forma; **physical ~** estado físico; **physical ~s** condiciones físicas; **in poor ~** en malas condiciones; **weather ~s** estado del tiempo; **working ~s** condiciones de trabajo
2 (= *stipulation*) condición *f*; **on ~ that** a condición de que; **on no ~** bajo ningún concepto; **I'll do it on one ~** lo haré, con una condición; **on this ~** con esta condición; **~s of sale** condiciones de venta
3 (= *circumstance*) circunstancia *f*; **under existing ~s** en las circunstancias actuales
4 (= *disease*) enfermedad *f*, padecimiento *m*; **he has a heart ~** tiene una afección cardíaca
5 (*social*) clase *f*; **of humble ~** de clase humilde
Ⓑ VT 1 (= *make healthy*) [+ *hair*] condicionar
2 (= *determine*) determinar; **to be ~ed by** depender de
3 (*Psych*) (= *train*) condicionar

conditional [kənˈdɪʃənl] Ⓐ ADJ condicional; **~ offer** oferta *f* condicional; **~ tense/clause** tiempo *m*/oración *f* condicional; **to be ~ upon** depender de
Ⓑ N condicional *m*

conditionally [kənˈdɪʃnəlɪ] ADV condicionalmente, con reservas

conditioned [kənˈdɪʃənd] Ⓐ ADJ condicionado
Ⓑ CPD ► **conditioned reflex** N reflejo *m* condicionado

conditioner [kənˈdɪʃənəʳ] N (*for hair*) suavizante *m*, acondicionador *m* (*LAm*), enjuague *m* (*LAm*); (*for skin*) crema *f* suavizante; (= *fabric conditioner*) suavizante *m*

conditioning [kənˈdɪʃənɪŋ] Ⓐ ADJ **~ shampoo** champú *m* acondicionador
Ⓑ N (*social*) condicionamiento *m*; *see also* **air B**

condo* [ˈkɒndəʊ] N (*US*) = **condominium**

condole [kənˈdəʊl] VI (*frm*) **to ~ with sb** condolerse de algn

condolence [kənˈdəʊləns] N (*usu pl*) pésame *m*; **to send one's ~s** dar el pésame; **please accept my ~s** le acompaño en el sentimiento

condom [ˈkɒndəm] N condón *m*, preservativo *m*

condominium [ˌkɒndəˈmɪnɪəm] N (*pl* **condominiums**) 1 (*US*) (= *building*) bloque *m* de pisos, condominio *m* (*LAm*) (*en copropiedad de los que lo habitan*); (= *apartment*) piso *m* or apartamento *m* (en propiedad), condominio *m* (*LAm*)
2 (*Pol*) condominio *m*

condone [kənˈdəʊn] VT consentir, tolerar

condor [ˈkɒndɔːʳ] N cóndor *m*

conduce [kənˈdjuːs] VI **to ~ to** conducir a

conducive [kənˈdjuːsɪv] ADJ **~ to** conducente a

conduct Ⓐ [ˈkɒndʌkt] N (= *behaviour*) comportamiento *m*, conducta *f*; [*of business etc*] dirección *f*, manejo *m*
Ⓑ [kənˈdʌkt] VT 1 (= *guide*) llevar, conducir; **~ed tour** visita *f* con guía; **we were ~ed to the interview room** nos llevaron *or* condujeron a la sala de entrevistas; **we were ~ed round by Lord Rice** Lord Rice actuó de guía
2 [+ *heat, electricity*] conducir
3 [+ *campaign*] dirigir, llevar; [+ *legal case*] presentar; (*Mus*) dirigir; **I don't like the way they ~ business** no me gusta la forma en que llevan los negocios, no me gusta la forma de hacer negocios que tienen; **to ~ a correspondence with sb** estar en correspondencia con algn, cartearse con algn
4 (= *behave*) **to ~ o.s.** comportarse
Ⓒ [kənˈdʌkt] VI (*Mus*) dirigir
Ⓓ [ˈkɒndʌkt] CPD ► **conduct report** N (*Scol*) informe *m* de conducta

conduction [kənˈdʌkʃən] N (*Elec*) conducción *f*

conductive [kənˈdʌktɪv] ADJ conductivo

conductivity [ˌkɒndʌkˈtɪvɪtɪ] N conductividad *f*

conductor [kənˈdʌktəʳ] N 1 (*Mus*) director(a) *m/f*; (*on bus*) cobrador(a) *m/f*; (*US Rail*) revisor(a) *m/f*
2 (*Phys*) [*of heat, electricity*] conductor *m*; (*also* **lightning ~**) pararrayos *m inv*

conductress [kənˈdʌktrɪs] N cobradora *f*

conduit [ˈkɒndɪt] N conducto *m*

cone [kəʊn] N 1 (*Math*) cono *m*; **traffic ~** cono *m* señalizador
2 (*Bot*) piña *f*
3 (*also* **ice cream ~**) cucurucho *m*
►**cone off** VT + ADV [+ *road*] cerrar *or* cortar con conos

coney [ˈkəʊnɪ] N (*US*) conejo *m*

confab* [ˈkɒnfæb] N = **confabulation**

confabulate [kənˈfæbjʊleɪt] VI conferenciar

confabulation [kənˌfæbjʊˈleɪʃən] N conferencia *f*

confection [kənˈfekʃən] N 1 (*Culin*) dulce *m*, confite *m*
2 (= *thing produced*) creación *f*
3 (= *manufacture*) confección *f*, hechura *f*

confectioner [kənˈfekʃənəʳ] N confitero/a *m/f*; **~'s (shop)** confitería *f*, dulcería *f* (*LAm*); **~'s sugar** (*US*) azúcar *m* glas(eado)

confectionery [kənˈfekʃənərɪ] N (= *sweets*) dulces *mpl*, golosinas *fpl*; (*Brit*) (= *cakes*) pasteles *mpl*

confederacy [kənˈfedərəsɪ] N (= *alliance*) confederación *f*; (= *plot*) complot *m*; **the Confederacy** (*US*) los Estados Confederados

confederate Ⓐ [kənˈfedərɪt] ADJ confederado
Ⓑ [kənˈfedərɪt] N 1 (*pej*) (= *accomplice*) cómplice *mf*
2 (*US Hist*) confederado/a *m/f*
Ⓒ [kənˈfedəreɪt] VT confederar
Ⓓ [kənˈfedəreɪt] VI confederarse

confederation [kənˌfedəˈreɪʃən] N confederación *f*

confer [kənˈfɜːʳ] Ⓐ VT **to ~ sth on sb** [+ *honour*] conceder *or* otorgar algo a algn; [+ *title*] conferir *or* conceder algo a algn
Ⓑ VI conferenciar, estar en consultas; **to ~ with sb** consultar con algn

conferee [ˌkɒnfɜːˈriː] N (*US*) congresista *mf*

conference [ˈkɒnfərəns] Ⓐ N (= *discussion, meeting*) reunión *f*, conferencia *f*; (= *assembly*) asamblea *f*, congreso *m*; (*party political, academic*) congreso *m*; **to be in ~** estar en una reunión; *see also* **press D**, **video**
Ⓑ CPD ► **conference call** N conferencia *f* ► **conference centre** N (= *town*) ciudad *f* de congresos; (= *building*) palacio *m* de congresos; (*in institution*) centro *m* de conferencias ► **conference hall** N sala *f* de conferencias *or* congresos ► **conference member** N congresista *mf* ► **conference room** N sala *f* de conferencias ► **conference system** N sistema *m* de conferencias ► **conference table** N mesa *f* negociadora

conferencing [ˈkɒnfərənsɪŋ] Ⓐ N (*Comput*) conferencia *f*; *see also* **video**
Ⓑ CPD ► **conferencing system** N sistema *m* de conferencias

conferment [kənˈfɜːmənt], **conferral** [kənˈfɜːrəl] N [*of honour*] otorgamiento *m*, concesión *f* (**on** a); [*of title*] concesión *f* (**on** a)

▼**confess** [kənˈfes] Ⓐ VT 1 [+ *crime, sin*] confesar; [+ *guilt, error*] confesar, reconocer; **to ~ that ...** confesar que ...; **to ~ one's guilt** confesar *or* reconocer ser culpable; **to ~ o.s. guilty of** [+ *sin, crime*] confesarse culpable de; **I ~ myself totally ignorant** me confieso totalmente ignorante en eso
2 (*Rel*) **to ~ sb** confesar a algn
Ⓑ VI 1 (= *admit*) confesar; **he ~ed to the murder** se confesó culpable del asesinato, confesó haber cometido el asesinato; **to ~ to**

doing sth confesarse culpable de haber hecho algo; **I must ~, I like your car** debo reconocer que me gusta tu coche; **to ~ to a liking for sth** reconocerse aficionado a algo
[2] (*Rel*) confesarse

confessed [kən'fest] ADJ declarado

confession [kən'feʃən] N [1] (= *act, document*) confesión *f*; **to make a ~** confesar, hacer una confesión; **to make a full ~** confesarlo todo, confesar de plano
[2] (*Rel*) **to go to ~** confesarse; **to hear sb's ~** confesar a algn; **~ of faith** profesión *f* de fe

confessional [kən'feʃənl] N confesionario *m*

confessor [kən'fesəʳ] N (*Rel*) (= *priest*) confesor *m*; (= *adviser*) director *m* espiritual

confetti [kən'feti:] N confeti *m*

confidant [,kɒnfɪ'dænt] N confidente *m*

confidante [,kɒnfɪ'dænt] N confidenta *f*

confide [kən'faɪd] (A) VT (= *tell*) [+ *secret*] confiar; **he ~d to me that …** me confió que …, me dijo en confianza que …; **to ~ sth to sb** confiar algo a algn, contar algo en confianza a algn
(B) VI [1] (= *trust*) **to ~ in sb** confiarse a algn, hacer confidencias a algn; **please ~ in me** puedes fiarte de mí
[2] (= *tell secrets*) **to ~ in sb** confiarse a algn; **to ~ in** *or* **to sb that …** confiar a algn que …, confesar a algn en secreto que …

confidence ['kɒnfɪdəns] (A) N [1] (= *trust*) confianza *f*; **to gain sb's ~** ganarse la confianza de algn; **to have (every) ~ in sb** tener (entera) confianza en algn; **to have (every) ~ that** estar seguro de que; **to inspire ~** inspirar confianza; **a motion of no ~** moción *f* de censura; **to put one's ~ in sth/sb** confiar en algo/algn
[2] (*also* **self-~**) confianza *f* (en sí mismo), seguridad *f* (en sí mismo); **to gain ~** ganar confianza *or* seguridad (en sí mismo); **he lacks ~** le falta confianza *or* seguridad (en sí mismo)
[3] (= *secrecy*) confianza *f*; **in ~** en confianza; **to tell sb (about) sth in strict ~** decir algo a algn en la más estricta confianza; **"write in ~ to Michelle Davis"** "escriba a Michelle Davis: discreción garantizada"; **to take sb into one's ~** confiarse a algn
[4] (= *revelation*) confidencia *f*; **they exchanged ~s** se hicieron confidencias
(B) CPD ► **confidence man** N timador *m*, estafador *m* ► **confidence trick**, **confidence game** (*esp US*) N timo *m*, estafa *f* ► **confidence trickster** N timador/a *m/f*, estafador/a *m/f*

confident ['kɒnfɪdənt] ADJ [*person*] seguro, seguro de sí mismo; [*prediction*] hecho con seguridad, hecho con confianza; [*performance, smile, reply, manner*] lleno de seguridad, lleno de confianza; **to be ~ that** estar seguro de que; **to be ~ of doing sth** confiar en hacer algo; **he is ~ of success** confía en obtener el éxito; **to feel** *or* **be ~ about sth** tener confianza en algo; **the prime minister is in ~ mood** el primer ministro está lleno de confianza

confidential [,kɒnfɪ'denʃəl] ADJ [*information, remark*] confidencial, secreto; [*secretary, tone of voice*] de confianza; **"confidential"** (*on letter etc*) "confidencial"

confidentiality [,kɒnfɪ,denʃɪ'ælɪtɪ] N confidencialidad *f*

confidentially [,kɒnfɪ'dənʃəlɪ] ADV confidencialmente, en confianza

confidently ['kɒnfɪdəntlɪ] ADV [*predict, promise*] con seguridad, con confianza; [*smile, stride, enter*] con seguridad; [*speak, reply*] con un tono de seguridad *or* confianza; **"sure," he said ~** —claro —dijo lleno de confianza; **we ~ expect that …** creemos con toda confianza que …

confiding [kən'faɪdɪŋ] ADJ **in a ~ tone** en tono de confianza; **he is too ~** es demasiado confiado

confidingly [kən'faɪdɪŋlɪ] ADV como disponiéndose a hacer una confidencia

configuration [kən,fɪgjʊ'reɪʃən] N (*gen, Comput*) configuración *f*

configure [kən'fɪgəʳ] VT (*Comput*) configurar

confine [kən'faɪn] VT [1] (= *imprison*) encerrar (**in, to** en); **to be ~d to bed** tener que guardar cama; **to be ~d to one's room** no poder dejar su cuarto
[2] (= *limit*) limitar; **to ~ o.s. to doing sth** limitarse a hacer algo; **please ~ yourself to the facts** por favor, limítese a los hechos; **the damage is ~d to this part** el daño afecta sólo a esta parte; **this bird is ~d to Spain** esta ave existe únicamente en España
[3] (*Med*†) **to be ~d** [*woman*] estar de parto

confined [kən'faɪnd] ADJ reducido; **a ~ space** un espacio reducido

confinement [kən'faɪnmənt] N [1] (= *imprisonment*) prisión *f*, reclusión *f*; **to be in solitary ~** estar incomunicado, estar en pelota‡; **~ to barracks** arresto *m* en cuartel
[2] (*Med*†) parto *m*

confines ['kɒnfaɪnz] NPL confines *mpl*, límites *mpl*

confirm [kən'fɜ:m] VT [1] (= *prove*) confirmar
[2] (*Rel*) confirmar

confirmation [,kɒnfə'meɪʃən] N [1] (= *proof*) confirmación *f*
[2] (*Rel*) confirmación *f*

confirmed [kən'fɜ:md] ADJ [*bachelor, alcoholic*] empedernido; [*atheist*] inveterado, redomado

confiscate ['kɒnfɪskeɪt] VT confiscar, incautarse de

confiscation [,kɒnfɪs'keɪʃən] N confiscación *f*, incautación *f*

conflagration [,kɒnflə'greɪʃən] N conflagración *f*, incendio *m*

conflate [kən'fleɪt] VT combinar

conflation [kən'fleɪʃən] N combinación *f*

conflict (A) ['kɒnflɪkt] N conflicto *m*; **to be in ~ with sth/sb** estar en conflicto con algo/algn; **the theories are in ~** las teorías están en conflicto *or* se contradicen; **to come into ~ with** entrar en conflicto con; **~ of interests** conflicto *m* de intereses, incompatibilidad *f* (de intereses); **~ of evidence** contradicción *f* de testimonios
(B) [kən'flɪkt] VI [*ideas, evidence, statements etc*] estar reñido (**with** con); [*interests*] estar en conflicto (**with** con); **that ~s with what he told me** eso contradice lo que me dijo

conflicting [kən'flɪktɪŋ] ADJ [*reports, evidence*] contradictorio; [*interests*] opuesto

confluence ['kɒnflʊəns] N confluencia *f*

conform [kən'fɔ:m] VI (= *comply*) (*to laws*) someterse (**to** a); (*to standards*) ajustarse (**to** a); [*people*] (*socially*) adaptarse, amoldarse; **he will ~ to the agreement** se ajustará al acuerdo

conformation [,kɒnfə'meɪʃən] N conformación *f*, estructura *f*

conformism [kən'fɔ:mɪzəm] N conformismo *m*

conformist [kən'fɔ:mɪst] (A) ADJ conformista
(B) N conformista *mf*

conformity [kən'fɔ:mɪtɪ] N conformidad *f*; **in ~ with** conforme a *or* con

confound [kən'faʊnd] VT (= *confuse*) confundir; (= *amaze*) pasmar, desconcertar; **~ it!**† ¡demonio!; **~ him!**† ¡maldito sea!*

confounded [kən'faʊndɪd] ADJ condenado*, maldito*††

confront [kən'frʌnt] VT (= *face squarely*) hacer frente a; (= *face defiantly*) enfrentarse con; **to ~ sb with sth** confrontar a algn con algo; **to ~ sb with the facts** exponer delante de algn los hechos; **the problems which ~ us** los problemas con los que nos enfrentamos; **we were ~ed by the river** estábamos delante el río

confrontation [,kɒnfrən'teɪʃən] N enfrentamiento *m*, confrontación *f*

confrontational [,kɒnfrən'teɪʃənəl] ADJ [*approach, attitude, style*] confrontacional, agresivo

Confucian [kən'fju:ʃən] (A) ADJ de Confucio
(B) N confuciano/a *m/f*

Confucianism [kən'fju:ʃənɪzəm] N confucianismo *m*, confucionismo *m*

Confucius [kən'fju:ʃəs] N Confucio

confuse [kən'fju:z] VT [1] (= *perplex*) confundir, desconcertar; **you're just confusing me** no haces más que confundirme, lo único que haces es confundirme más
[2] (= *mix up*) confundir; **to ~ the issue** complicar el asunto; **to ~ A and B** confundir A con B

confused [kən'fju:zd] ADJ [1] [*situation etc*] confuso
[2] (= *perplexed*) confuso, confundido, desconcertado; **to be ~** estar confuso *or* confundido; **to get ~** (= *muddled up*) hacerse un lío; (= *perplexed*) confundirse, desconcertarse; **his mind is ~** tiene la cabeza trastornada

confusedly [kən'fju:zɪdlɪ] ADV confusamente

confusing [kən'fju:zɪŋ] ADJ [*instructions, message*] confuso; **it's a very ~ situation** la situación es muy confusa; **the traffic signs are ~** las señales de tráfico están poco claras; **it's all very ~** es muy difícil de entender

confusingly [kən'fju:zɪŋlɪ] ADV [*written, explained*] de manera confusa; **~, two of them had the same name** para mayor confusión, dos de ellos tenían el mismo nombre

confusion [kən'fju:ʒən] N [1] (= *disorder*) desorden *m*; **to be in ~** estar en desorden; **to retire in ~** retirarse en desorden
[2] (= *perplexity*) confusión *f*, desorientación *f*; **people were in a state of ~** la gente estaba desorientada
[3] (= *commotion*) confusión *f*; **in all the ~ I forgot it** lo olvidé en medio de tanta confusión; **I heard a ~ of voices** oí unas voces confusas
[4] (= *embarrassment*) **to be covered in ~** estar avergonzado

confute [kən'fju:t] VT refutar

conga ['kɒŋgə] N [1] (= *dance*) conga *f*
[2] (*also* **~ drum**) congas *fpl*

congeal [kən'dʒi:l] (A) VT coagular, cuajar
(B) VI coagularse, cuajarse

congenial [kən'dʒi:nɪəl] ADJ (*frm*) [*atmosphere, environment, place*] agradable; [*person, company*] simpático, agradable; **to find sb ~** tener simpatía a algn; **the land proved ~ to farming** la tierra resultó ser buena para la agricultura; **he found few people ~ to him** conoció a pocas personas con las que congeniara

congenital [kən'dʒenɪtl] ADJ congénito

congenitally [kən'dʒenɪtlɪ] ADV congénitamente

conger ['kɒŋgər] N (*also* **~ eel**) congrio *m*

➤ LANGUAGE IN USE: **confidence A3** 19.4 **confirm 1** 19.5, 20.3, 20.5, 21.4

congested [kən'dʒestɪd] ADJ [1] [*street, building etc*] atestado de gente; **to get ~ with** llenarse de, atestarse de; **it's getting very ~ in here** esto se está llenando demasiado
[2] (*Med*) congestionado

congestion [kən'dʒestʃən] Ⓐ N [1] [*of traffic*] congestión *f*; [*of people*] aglomeración *f*
[2] (*Med*) congestión *f*
Ⓑ CPD ► **congestion charge(s)** N(PL) tasa *fsing* por congestión

congestive [kən'dʒestɪv] ADJ (*Med*) congestivo; **~ heart failure** insuficiencia *f* cardíaca congestiva

conglomerate Ⓐ [kən'glɒmərɪt] N (*Comm*) conglomerado *m*
Ⓑ [kən'glɒməreɪt] VT conglomerar, aglomerar
Ⓒ [kən'glɒməreɪt] VI conglomerarse, aglomerarse

conglomeration [kən,glɒmə'reɪʃən] N conglomeración *f*

Congo ['kɒŋgəʊ] N **the ~** el Congo; **Republic of the ~** República *f* del Congo

Congolese [,kɒŋgəʊ'li:z] Ⓐ ADJ congoleño
Ⓑ N congoleño/a *m/f*

congrats* [kən'græts] EXCL (*esp Brit*) ¡enhorabuena!, ¡felicidades!

congratulate [kən'grætjuleɪt] VT felicitar; **to ~ sb (on sth/on doing sth)** felicitar a algn (por algo/por hacer algo); **my friends ~d me on passing my test** mis amigos me felicitaron por aprobar el examen

▼ **congratulations** [kən,grætjʊ'leɪʃənz] NPL felicitaciones *fpl* (**on** por); **~!** ¡enhorabuena!, ¡felicidades!; **~ on your new job!** ¡enhorabuena *or* felicidades por tu nuevo trabajo!

congratulatory [kən'grætjʊlətərɪ] ADJ de felicitación

congregate ['kɒŋgrɪgeɪt] VI reunirse, congregarse

congregation [,kɒŋgrɪ'geɪʃən] N [1] (*Rel*) fieles *mpl*, feligreses *mpl*
[2] (= *assembly*) reunión *f*

congregational [,kɒŋgrɪ'geɪʃənl] ADJ congregacionalista

congregationalist [,kɒŋgrɪ'geɪʃənəlɪst] N congregacionalista *mf*

congress ['kɒŋgres] Ⓐ N (= *meeting*) congreso *m*; **Congress** (*Pol*) el Congreso
Ⓑ CPD ► **congress member** N miembro *mf* del congreso, congresista *mf*; → CABINET, CAPITOL

> **CONGRESS**
>
> *En el Congreso de Estados Unidos (**Congress**) se elaboran y aprueban las leyes federales. Consta de dos cámaras: la Cámara de Representantes (**House of Representatives**), cuyos 435 miembros son elegidos cada dos años por voto popular directo y en número proporcional a los habitantes de cada estado, y el Senado (**Senate**), con 100 senadores (**senators**), 2 por estado, de los que un tercio se elige cada dos años y el resto cada seis.*

congressional [kɒŋ'greʃənl] ADJ del congreso

congressman ['kɒŋgresmən] N (*pl* **congressmen**) (*US*) diputado *m*, miembro *m* del Congreso

congresswoman ['kɒŋgres,wʊmən] N (*pl* **congresswomen**) (*US*) diputada *f*, miembro *f* del Congreso

congruence ['kɒŋgrʊəns] N, **congruency** ['kɒŋgrʊənsɪ] N congruencia *f*

congruent ['kɒŋgrʊənt] ADJ congruente

congruity [kɒŋ'gru:ɪtɪ] N congruencia *f* (**with** con)

congruous ['kɒŋgrʊəs] ADJ congruo (**with** con)

conic ['kɒnɪk] Ⓐ ADJ cónico
Ⓑ CPD ► **conic section** N sección *f* cónica

conical ['kɒnɪkəl] ADJ cónico

conifer ['kɒnɪfə^r] N conífera *f*

coniferous [kə'nɪfərəs] ADJ conífero

conjectural [kən'dʒektʃərəl] ADJ conjetural

conjecture [kən'dʒektʃə^r] Ⓐ N **it's only ~** son conjeturas, nada más Ⓑ VT conjeturar Ⓒ VI conjeturar

conjoin [kən'dʒɔɪn] (*frm*) Ⓐ VT aunar, unir
Ⓑ VI aunarse, unirse

conjoint [kɒn'dʒɔɪnt] ADJ (*frm*) conjunto

conjointly ['kɒn'dʒɔɪntlɪ] ADV (*frm*) conjuntamente

conjugal ['kɒndʒʊgəl] ADJ [*rights, bliss*] conyugal; **~ duties** deberes *mpl* conyugales, débito *msing* conyugal (*Jur*); **~ visit** vis a vis* *m*, visita *f* del cónyuge

conjugate ['kɒndʒʊgeɪt] (*Ling*) Ⓐ VT conjugar
Ⓑ VI conjugarse

conjugation [,kɒndʒʊ'geɪʃən] N (*Ling*) conjugación *f*

conjunct [kən'dʒʌŋkt] ADJ (*Astron*) en conjunción

conjunction [kən'dʒʌŋkʃən] N [1] (*Ling*) conjunción *f*
[2] **in ~ with** junto con, juntamente con

conjunctive [kən'dʒʌŋktɪv] ADJ conjuntivo

conjunctivitis [kən,dʒʌŋktɪ'vaɪtɪs] N conjuntivitis *f*

conjuncture [kən'dʒʌŋktʃə^r] N coyuntura *f*

conjure[1] ['kʌndʒə^r] VI hacer juegos de manos; **he ~s with handkerchiefs** hace trucos con pañuelos; **a name to ~ with** un personaje importante, una figura destacada

► **conjure away** VT + ADV conjurar, hacer desaparecer

► **conjure up** VT + ADV [1] [*conjurer*] [+ *rabbit etc*] hacer aparecer
[2] (*fig*) [+ *memories, visions*] evocar; [+ *meal*] preparar en un abrir y cerrar de ojos

conjure[2] [kən'dʒʊə^r] VT (*liter*) suplicar; **to ~ sb to do sth** suplicar a algn que haga algo

conjurer, **conjuror** ['kʌndʒərə^r] N ilusionista *mf*, prestidigitador(a) *m/f*

conjuring ['kʌndʒərɪŋ] Ⓐ N ilusionismo *m*, prestidigitación *f*
Ⓑ CPD ► **conjuring trick** N juego *m* de manos

conjuror ['kʌndʒərə^r] N = **conjurer**

conk* [kɒŋk] N [1] (*Brit*) (= *nose*) narigón* *m*
[2] (= *blow*) golpe *m*
[3] (*US*) (= *head*) coco* *m*, cholla *f* (*Mex**)

► **conk out*** VI + ADV [1] (= *break down*) averiarse, fastidiarse*, descomponerse (*LAm*)
[2] (= *die*) estirar la pata*; (= *fall asleep*) dormir como un tronco*

conker* ['kɒŋkə^r] N (*Brit*) castaña *f* de Indias; **conkers** (= *game*) juego *m* de las castañas

Conn ABBR (*US*) = **Connecticut**

connect [kə'nekt] Ⓐ VT [1] (= *join*) conectar; [+ *road, railway, airline*] unir; [+ *pipes, drains*] empalmar (**to** a); **to ~ sth (up) to the mains** (*Elec*) conectar algo a la red eléctrica
[2] (= *install*) [+ *cooker, telephone*] conectar
[3] (*Telec*) [+ *caller*] poner, comunicar (*LAm*) (**with** con); **please ~ me with Mr Lyons** póngame con el Sr. Lyons, por favor; **"I am trying to ~ you"** "estoy intentando ponerle al habla"
[4] (= *associate*) vincular, asociar; **to ~ sth/sb (with)** vincular *or* asociar algo/a algn (con); **I never ~ed you with that** nunca te vinculé *or* asocié con eso, nunca creí que tuvieras nada que ver con eso
Ⓑ VI [*trains, planes*] enlazar (**with** con); [*road, pipes, electricity*] empalmar (**with** con)

connected [kə'nektɪd] Ⓐ ADJ [1] (= *related*) [*concepts, events*] relacionado; **to be ~ (to** *or* **with)** estar relacionado (con); **what firm are you ~ with?** ¿con qué empresa estás conectado *or* relacionado?; **are these matters ~?** ¿tienen alguna relación entre sí estas cuestiones?; **to be well ~** estar bien relacionado
[2] (*Bot, Jur*) conexo
[3] (*fig*) [*argument etc*] conexo
Ⓑ CPD ► **connected speech** N discurso *m* conexo

connecting [kə'nektɪŋ] Ⓐ ADJ [*rooms etc*] comunicado; **bedroom with ~ bathroom** habitación comunicada con el baño
Ⓑ CPD ► **connecting flight** N vuelo *m* de enlace ► **connecting rod** N biela *f*

connection [kə'nekʃən] N [1] (*Rail etc*) enlace *m*; (*Elec, Tech*) conexión *f*, empalme *m*; (*Telec*) línea *f*, comunicación *f*; **we missed our ~** perdimos el enlace; **to make a ~** hacer enlace, empalmar; **our ~s with the town are poor** son malas nuestras comunicaciones con la ciudad; **there's a loose ~** (*Elec*) hay un hilo suelto; **we've got a bad ~** (*Telec*) no se oye bien
[2] (= *relationship*) relación *f* (**between** entre; **with** con); **in ~ with** en relación a, con respecto a; **there's no ~ between the two events** no hay ninguna relación *or* conexión entre los dos sucesos; **in this ~** a este respecto; **"no ~ with any other firm"** "ésta es una firma independiente"
[3] **connections** (= *relatives*) parientes *mpl*; (= *business connections*) relaciones *fpl*, contactos *mpl*; **we have ~s everywhere** tenemos relaciones con todas partes; **you have to have ~s** hay que tener buenas relaciones

connective [kə'nektɪv] Ⓐ ADJ conjuntivo
Ⓑ N conjunción *f* Ⓒ CPD ► **connective tissue** N tejido *m* conjuntivo

connectivity [,kɒnek'tɪvɪtɪ] N conectividad *f*

connector [kə'nektə^r] N (*Elec*) conector *m*

connexion [kə'nekʃən] N = **connection**

conning tower ['kɒnɪŋ,taʊə^r] N [*of submarine*] torre *f* de mando

connivance [kə'naɪvəns] N [1] (= *tacit consent*) consentimiento *m* (**at** en), connivencia *f* (*frm*) (**at** en); **with the ~ of** con el consentimiento *or* (*frm*) la connivencia de
[2] (= *conspiracy*) connivencia *f* (*frm*), complicidad *f*

connive [kə'naɪv] VI [1] (= *condone*) hacer la vista gorda (**at** a)
[2] (= *conspire*) confabularse; **to ~ with sb to do sth** confabularse con algn para hacer algo

conniving [kə'naɪvɪŋ] ADJ intrigante, mañoso

connoisseur [,kɒnə'sɜ:^r] N conocedor(a) *m/f*, entendido/a *m/f*; **an art ~** un entendido en arte; **a wine ~** un entendido en vinos, un enólogo

connotation [,kɒnəʊ'teɪʃən] N connotación *f*

connotative ['kɒnə,teɪtɪv] ADJ connotativo

connote [kɒ'nəʊt] VT connotar

connubial [kə'nju:bɪəl] ADJ conyugal, connubial

conquer ['kɒŋkə^r] Ⓐ VT [+ *territory, nation etc*] conquistar; [+ *fear, enemy*] vencer
Ⓑ VI triunfar

conquering ['kɒŋkərɪŋ] ADJ vencedor, victorioso

➤ LANGUAGE IN USE: **congratulations** 23.6, 24.1, 24.2

conqueror [ˈkɒŋkərəʳ] N conquistador(a) *m/f*

conquest [ˈkɒŋkwest] N conquista *f*

conquistador [kɒnˈkwɪstədɔːʳ] N conquistador *m*

Cons. ABBR (*Brit*) = **Conservative**

consanguinity [ˌkɒnsæŋˈgwɪnɪtɪ] N consanguinidad *f*

conscience [ˈkɒnʃəns] Ⓐ N conciencia *f*; **in all ~** en conciencia; **bad ~** mala conciencia; **to have a clear ~** tener la conciencia tranquila *or* limpia; **I have a clear ~ about it** tengo la conciencia tranquila *or* limpia al respecto; **with a clear ~** con la conciencia tranquila *or* limpia; **I have a guilty ~ (about it)** me remuerde la conciencia (por ello); **I could not in ~ say that** en conciencia no podría decir eso; **the ~ of the nation** la voz de la conciencia del país; **to have sth on one's ~** tener algo pesando sobre la conciencia, tener cargo *or* remordimiento de conciencia por algo; **I have it on my ~** me está remordiendo la conciencia por ello; **social ~** conciencia *f* social; **a doctor with a social ~** un médico socialmente concienciado *or* con conciencia social
Ⓑ CPD ► **conscience money** N *dinero que se paga para descargar la conciencia* ► **conscience raising** N = **consciousness raising**

conscience-stricken [ˈkɒnʃənsˌstrɪkən] ADJ lleno de remordimientos

conscientious [ˌkɒnʃɪˈenʃəs] Ⓐ ADJ concienzudo
Ⓑ CPD ► **conscientious objector** N objetor(a) *m/f* de conciencia

conscientiously [ˌkɒnʃɪˈenʃəslɪ] ADV concienzudamente

conscientiousness [ˌkɒnʃɪˈenʃəsnɪs] N diligencia *f*, escrupulosidad *f*

conscious [ˈkɒnʃəs] Ⓐ ADJ [1] (= *aware*) **to be ~ of sth/of doing sth** ser consciente de algo/de hacer algo; **to be ~ that** tener (plena) conciencia de que; **to become ~ of sth** darse cuenta de algo; **to become ~ that** darse cuenta de que; **she became ~ of him looking at her** se dio cuenta de que él la miraba; **environmentally ~** consciente de los problemas medioambientales; **politically ~** con conciencia política
[2] (= *deliberate*) [*decision*] deliberado; [*prejudice*] consciente; [*error, irony, insult*] intencional, deliberado; **they made a ~ choice** *or* **decision not to have children** decidieron deliberadamente no tener hijos; **he made a ~ effort to look as though he was enjoying himself** se esforzó deliberadamente por aparentar que se estaba divirtiendo
[3] (*Med*) consciente; **to be ~** estar consciente, tener conocimiento; **to be fully ~** estar totalmente consciente; **to become ~** recobrar el reconocimiento, volver en sí
[4] (*Psych*) [*memory, thought*] consciente; **the ~ mind** la conciencia; **to remain below the level of ~ awareness** quedarse en el subconsciente; **on a ~ level** conscientemente
Ⓑ N (*Psych*) **the ~** la conciencia; **at a level below the ~** por debajo de los niveles de conciencia

-conscious [-ˌkɒnʃəs] ADJ (*ending in compounds*) **security-conscious** consciente de los problemas relativos a la seguridad

consciously [ˈkɒnʃəslɪ] ADV [1] (= *deliberately*) conscientemente, deliberadamente
[2] (= *with full awareness*) [*remember, think*] conscientemente; **to be ~ aware of sth** ser plenamente consciente de algo

consciousness [ˈkɒnʃəsnɪs] Ⓐ N [1] (= *awareness*) conciencia *f*, consciencia *f* (**of** de); **to raise sb's ~ of sth** concienciar a algn sobre algo (*Sp*), concientizar a algn sobre algo (*LAm*)
[2] (*Med*) conocimiento *m*; **to lose ~** perder el conocimiento; **to regain ~** recobrar el conocimiento, volver en sí
Ⓑ CPD ► **consciousness raising** N concienciación *f* (*Sp*), concientización *f* (*LAm*)

conscript Ⓐ [ˈkɒnskrɪpt] N recluta *mf*, conscripto/a *m/f* (*LAm*)
Ⓑ [kənˈskrɪpt] VT (*Mil*) reclutar, llamar a filas

conscripted [kənˈskrɪptɪd] ADJ [*labourer etc*] reclutado a la fuerza, forzado; **~ troops** reclutas *mpl*, conscriptos *mpl* (*LAm*)

conscription [kənˈskrɪpʃən] N servicio *m* militar obligatorio, conscripción *f* (*LAm*)

consecrate [ˈkɒnsɪkreɪt] VT consagrar

consecration [ˌkɒnsɪˈkreɪʃən] N consagración *f*

consecutive [kənˈsekjʊtɪv] ADJ [1] (= *successive*) consecutivo; **on three ~ days** tres días consecutivos *or* seguidos
[2] (*Ling*) consecutivo

consecutively [kənˈsekjʊtɪvlɪ] ADV consecutivamente

consensual [kənˈsensjʊəl] ADJ [*approach, decision etc*] consensuado; [*sex*] consentido

consensus [kənˈsensəs] N consenso *m*; **the ~ of opinion** el consenso general

consent [kənˈsent] Ⓐ N consentimiento *m*; **with the ~ of** con el consentimiento de; **without his ~** sin su consentimiento; **by common ~** de *or* por común acuerdo; **by mutual ~** de *or* por mutuo acuerdo; **the age of ~** la edad en la que es válido el consentimiento en las relaciones sexuales
Ⓑ VI **to ~ (to sth/to do sth)** consentir (en algo/en hacer algo)

consenting [kənˈsentɪŋ] ADJ **~ party** parte *f* que da su consentimiento; **between ~ adults** entre personas de edad para consentir

▼ **consequence** [ˈkɒnsɪkwəns] N [1] (= *result*) consecuencia *f*; **to take the ~s** aceptar las consecuencias; **in ~** por consiguiente, por lo tanto; **in ~ of (which)** como consecuencia de (lo cual)
[2] (= *importance*) importancia *f*, trascendencia *f*; **it is of no ~** no tiene importancia, es de poca trascendencia

consequent [ˈkɒnsɪkwənt] ADJ consiguiente

consequential [ˌkɒnsɪˈkwenʃəl] ADJ [1] (= *resulting*) consiguiente, resultante; **the moves ~ upon this decision** las medidas consiguientes a *or* resultantes de esta decisión
[2] (= *important*) importante

consequently [ˈkɒnsɪkwəntlɪ] ADV por consiguiente, por lo tanto

conservancy [kənˈsɜːvənsɪ] N conservación *f*

conservation [ˌkɒnsəˈveɪʃən] Ⓐ N conservación *f*, protección *f*; **energy ~** la conservación de la energía
Ⓑ CPD ► **conservation area** N zona *f* declarada de patrimonio histórico-artístico; (= *nature reserve*) zona *f* protegida; *see also* **nature B**

conservationism [ˌkɒnsəˈveɪʃənɪzəm] N conservacionismo *m*

conservationist [ˌkɒnsəˈveɪʃənɪst] N conservacionista *mf*, ecologista *mf*

conservatism [kənˈsɜːvətɪzəm] N conservadurismo *m*

Conservative [kənˈsɜːvətɪv] (*Brit*) Ⓐ ADJ (*Pol*) conservador; **~ Party** Partido *m* Conservador
Ⓑ N (*Pol*) conservador(a) *m/f*; **to vote ~** votar a favor del partido Conservador

conservative [kənˈsɜːvətɪv] ADJ [1] (= *conventional*) [*person, suit, colour, ideas*] conservador
[2] (= *cautious*) [*attitude, approach, guess*] prudente, cauteloso; **a ~ estimate** un cálculo prudente *or* cauteloso

conservatively [kənˈsɜːvətɪvlɪ] ADV (= *conventionally*) **he dresses very ~** es muy conservador en su forma de vestir, viste de forma muy conservadora; **~ minded people** gente con ideas muy conservadoras

conservatoire [kənˈsɜːvətwɑːʳ] N conservatorio *m*

conservatory [kənˈsɜːvətrɪ] N invernadero *m*

conserve [kənˈsɜːv] Ⓐ VT [+ *natural resources, environment, historic buildings*] conservar, preservar; [+ *moisture*] conservar; [+ *energy, water*] ahorrar, conservar; **to ~ one's energies** ahorrar (las) energías
Ⓑ N conserva *f*

▼ **consider** [kənˈsɪdəʳ] VT [1] (= *think about*) [+ *problem, possibility*] considerar, pensar en; **~ how much you owe him** piensa en *or* considera lo que le debes; **to ~ doing sth: have you ever ~ed going by train?** ¿has pensado alguna vez (en) ir en tren?, ¿has considerado alguna vez ir en tren?; **we ~ed cancelling our holiday** pensamos en cancelar nuestras vacaciones; **would you ~ buying it?** ¿te interesa comprarlo?; **I'm ~ing resigning** estoy pensando en dimitir, estoy considerando la posibilidad de dimitir; **he is being ~ed for the post** lo están considerando para el puesto; **we are ~ing the matter** estamos estudiando el asunto; **it is my ~ed opinion that …** después de haberlo pensado *or* considerado detenidamente, creo que …; **to ~ one's position** (*euph*) (= *consider resigning*) pensar en dimitir, estudiar la conveniencia de dimitir; **he refused even to ~ it** se negó a pensarlo *or* considerarlo siquiera; **I wouldn't ~ it for a moment** yo ni me lo plantearía siquiera
[2] (= *take into account*) tomar *or* tener en cuenta; **when one ~s that …** cuando uno toma o tiene en cuenta que …; **you must ~ other people's feelings** hay que tomar *or* tener en cuenta los sentimientos de los demás; **all things ~ed** pensándolo bien
[3] (= *be of the opinion*) considerar; **I ~ that …** considero que …
[4] (= *regard as*) considerar; **I ~ it an honour** lo considero un honor; **I ~ the matter closed** para mí el tema está cerrado; **to ~ o.s.: I ~ myself happy** me considero feliz; **to ~ sb to be intelligent** considerar a algn inteligente; **he is ~ed to be the best** se le considera el mejor; **he ~s it a waste of time** lo considera una pérdida de tiempo; **~ yourself lucky!** ¡date por satisfecho!; **~ yourself dismissed** considérese despedido

considerable [kənˈsɪdərəbl] ADJ considerable; **a ~ number of applicants** un número considerable de solicitudes; **a ~ sum of money** una suma considerable de dinero; **they achieved a ~ degree of success** tuvieron un éxito considerable; **we had ~ difficulty** tuvimos bastante dificultad; **I'd been living in England for a** *or* **some ~ time** llevaba bastante tiempo viviendo en Inglaterra; **to a** *or* **some ~ extent** en gran parte; **the building suffered ~ damage** el edificio sufrió daños de consideración

considerably [kənˈsɪdərəblɪ] ADV bastante, considerablemente

considerate [kənˈsɪdərɪt] ADJ [*person, action*] atento, considerado; **to be ~ towards** ser atento con; **it's most ~ of you** es muy amable de su parte

➤ LANGUAGE IN USE: **consequence 1** 2.3 **consider 1** 8.4, 26.1

considerately [kənˈsɪdərɪtlɪ] ADV con consideración

consideration [kən,sɪdəˈreɪʃən] N 1 (= *thought, reflection*) consideración *f*; **after due ~** tras (darle) la debida consideración; **without due ~** sin (darle) la debida consideración; **we are giving the matter our ~** estamos estudiando *or* considerando la cuestión; **in ~ of** en consideración a; **to take sth into ~** tener *or* tomar algo en cuenta *or* consideración; **taking everything into ~** teniendo en cuenta todo; **after some ~, he decided to ...** tras considerarlo, decidió ...; **the issue is under ~** la cuestión se está estudiando
2 (= *thoughtfulness*) consideración *f*; **as a mark of my ~** en señal de respeto; **out of ~ for sb/sb's feelings** por consideración a algn/los sentimientos de algn; **to show ~ for sb/sb's feelings** respetar a algn/los sentimientos de algn
3 (= *factor*) **his age is an important ~** su edad es un factor importante; **that is a ~** eso debe tomarse en cuenta; **money is the main ~** el dinero es la consideración principal; **it's of no ~** no tiene importancia
4 (= *payment*) retribución *f*; **for a ~** por una gratificación

considering [kənˈsɪdərɪŋ] Ⓐ PREP teniendo en cuenta, en vista de; **~ the circumstances** teniendo en cuenta las circunstancias
Ⓑ CONJ (*also* **~ that**) en vista de que, teniendo en cuenta que; **~ (that) it was my fault** teniendo en cuenta que la culpa fue mía
Ⓒ ADV después de todo, a fin de cuentas; **I got a good mark, ~** después de todo *or* a fin de cuentas, saqué buena nota

consign [kənˈsaɪn] VT 1 (*Comm*) (= *send*) enviar, consignar
2 (*frm*) (= *commit, entrust*) confiar; **to ~ to oblivion** sepultar en el olvido

consignee [,kɒnsaɪˈniː] N consignatario/a *m/f*

consigner [kənˈsaɪnəʳ] N = **consignor**

consignment [kənˈsaɪnmənt] Ⓐ N envío *m*, remesa *f*; **goods on ~** mercancías *fpl* en consignación
Ⓑ CPD ► **consignment note** N talón *m* de expedición

consignor [kənˈsaɪnəʳ] N remitente *mf*

consist [kənˈsɪst] VI **to ~ of** constar de, consistir en; **to ~ in sth/in doing sth** consistir en algo/en hacer algo

consistency [kənˈsɪstənsɪ] N 1 (= *constancy*) [*of person, action, behaviour*] coherencia *f*, uniformidad *f*; [*of results*] lo regular; **the manager was impressed by the ~ of her work** el jefe quedó impresionado por la calidad que caracterizaba todo su trabajo
2 (= *cohesion*) [*of argument*] coherencia *f*, lógica *f*; **their statements lack ~** sus declaraciones no concuerdan
3 (= *density*) [*of paste, mixture*] consistencia *f*

consistent [kənˈsɪstənt] ADJ 1 (= *constant*) [*person, action, behaviour*] consecuente, coherente; [*results*] uniforme; [*work, performance*] de calidad constante
2 (= *cohesive*) [*argument*] coherente, lógico; **he made various statements which were not ~** realizó varias declaraciones que no concordaban; **his actions are not ~ with his beliefs** sus actos no son consecuentes con sus ideas; **that is not ~ with what you told me** eso no encaja *or* no concuerda con lo que me dijiste

consistently [kənˈsɪstəntlɪ] ADV 1 (= *regularly*) [*refuse, deny, oppose, support*] sistemáticamente; [*work, perform*] con un nivel de calidad constante; **the quality of this product has been ~ high over the last few years** el nivel de calidad de este producto se ha mantenido durante los últimos años; **the rate of inflation has been ~ low** el nivel de inflación se ha mantenido bajo; **she has had ~ good marks** en general sus notas han sido buenas; **he ~ achieved marks of over 90%** sus notas estaban habitualmente por encima del 90%
2 (= *logically*) [*argue, behave*] consecuentemente; **to act ~** obrar con consecuencia

consolation [,kɒnsəˈleɪʃən] Ⓐ N consuelo *m*; **that's one ~** esto es un consuelo, por lo menos; **if it's any ~ to you** si te consuela de algún modo; **it is some ~ to know that ...** me reconforta saber que ...
Ⓑ CPD ► **consolation prize** N premio *m* de consolación

consolatory [kənˈsɒlətərɪ] ADJ consolador

console[1] [kənˈsəʊl] VT consolar; **to ~ sb for sth** consolar a algn por algo

console[2] [ˈkɒnsəʊl] N (= *control panel*) consola *f*

consolidate [kənˈsɒlɪdeɪt] Ⓐ VT 1 (= *strengthen*) [+ *position, influence*] consolidar
2 (= *combine*) concentrar, fusionar
Ⓑ VI 1 (= *strengthen*) consolidarse
2 (= *combine*) concentrarse, fusionarse

consolidated [kənˈsɒlɪdeɪtɪd] ADJ consolidado; **~ accounts** cuentas *fpl* consolidadas; **~ balance sheet** hoja *f* de balance consolidado; **~ fund** fondo *m* consolidado

consolidation [kən,sɒlɪˈdeɪʃən] N 1 (= *strengthening*) consolidación *f*
2 (= *combining*) concentración *f*, fusión *f*

consoling [kənˈsəʊlɪŋ] ADJ consolador, reconfortante

consols [ˈkɒnsɒlz] NPL (*Brit Fin*) fondos *mpl* consolidados

consommé [ˈkɑn,sɒmeɪ] N consomé *m*, caldo *m*

consonance [ˈkɒnsənəns] N consonancia *f*

consonant [ˈkɒnsənənt] Ⓐ N consonante *f*
Ⓑ ADJ **~ with** de acuerdo *or* en consonancia con

consonantal [,kɒnsəˈnæntl] ADJ consonántico

consort [ˈkɒnsɔːt] Ⓐ N consorte *mf*; **prince ~** príncipe *m* consorte
Ⓑ [kənˈsɔːt] VI **to ~ with sb** (*often pej*) asociarse con algn

consortium [kənˈsɔːtɪəm] N (*pl* **consortia** [kənˈsɔːtɪə]) consorcio *m*

conspectus [kənˈspektəs] N vista *f* general

conspicuous [kənˈspɪkjʊəs] Ⓐ ADJ 1 (= *attracting attention*) [*clothes*] llamativo; [*person, behaviour*] que llama la atención; [*notice, attempt*] visible; **to be ~ by one's/its absence** brillar por su ausencia; **I felt ~ in that ridiculous outfit** vestido de aquella manera tan ridícula tenía la impresión de que todo el mundo me miraba *or* tenía la impresión de ser el objeto de atención; **I left the keys in a ~ place** dejé las llaves en un lugar bien visible; **to make o.s. ~** llamar la atención
2 (= *noticeable*) [*bravery*] destacado, manifiesto; [*difference*] manifiesto, notorio; **he was ~ for his courage** destacaba por su valor; **a ~ lack of sth** una carencia manifiesta de algo; **the film was a ~ failure/success** la película fue un fracaso/éxito rotundo
Ⓑ CPD ► **conspicuous consumption** N (*Econ*) consumo *m* ostentoso

conspicuously [kənˈspɪkjʊəslɪ] ADV 1 (= *so as to attract attention*) [*behave, act*] de modo que llama la atención; [*dressed*] de forma muy llamativa
2 (= *noticeably*) [*worried, uncomfortable, embarrassed*] visiblemente; **to be ~ absent** brillar por su ausencia; **he has remained ~ silent on the issue** de forma ostensible, ha guardado silencio respecto al asunto; **she had been ~ successful** obtuvo un éxito rotundo; **they have ~ failed to solve the problem** es muy evidente que no han conseguido resolver el problema

conspiracy [kənˈspɪrəsɪ] Ⓐ N (= *plotting*) conspiración *f*, conjuración *f*; (= *plot*) complot *m*, conjura *f*
Ⓑ CPD ► **conspiracy theory** N teoría *f* de la conspiración

conspirator [kənˈspɪrətəʳ] N conspirador(a) *m/f*

conspiratorial [kən,spɪrəˈtɔːrɪəl] ADJ de conspirador

conspiratorially [kən,spɪrəˈtɔːrɪəlɪ] ADV [*behave*] con complicidad

conspire [kənˈspaɪəʳ] VI 1 [*people*] conspirar; **to ~ with sb against sth/sb** conspirar con algn contra algo/algn; **to ~ to do sth** conspirar para hacer algo
2 [*events*] **to ~ against/to do sth** conjurarse *or* conspirar contra/para hacer algo

constable [ˈkʌnstəbl] N (*Brit*) (*also* **police ~**) agente *mf* de policía, policía *mf*; (*as form of address*) señor(a) policía

constabulary [kənˈstæbjʊlərɪ] N policía *f*

Constance [ˈkɒnstəns] N Constanza

constancy [ˈkɒnstənsɪ] N 1 (= *regularity*) [*of temperature etc*] constancia *f*
2 (= *faithfulness*) fidelidad *f*

constant [ˈkɒnstənt] Ⓐ ADJ 1 (= *unchanging*) [*temperature, velocity*] constante; **to remain ~** permanecer constante
2 (= *continual*) [*quarrels, interruptions, complaints*] constante, continuo; **to be in ~ use** usarse continuamente; **to be in ~ pain** sufrir dolor continuamente
3 (= *faithful*) [*friend, companion*] leal, fiel
Ⓑ N (*Math, Phys*) constante *f*

Constantine [ˈkɒnstəntaɪn] N Constantine

Constantinople [,kɒnstæntɪˈnəʊpl] N Constantinopla *f*

constantly [ˈkɒnstəntlɪ] ADV (= *continuously*) constantemente, continuamente; **to be ~ changing** estar cambiando constantemente *or* continuamente; **she's ~ complaining** se está quejando constantemente *or* continuamente; **"gates constantly in use"** "vado permanente"

constellation [,kɒnstəˈleɪʃən] N constelación *f*

consternation [,kɒnstəˈneɪʃən] N consternación *f*; **in ~** consternado; **there was general ~** hubo una consternación general

constipate [ˈkɒnstɪpeɪt] VT estreñir

constipated [ˈkɒnstɪpeɪtɪd] ADJ estreñido; **to be ~** estar estreñido

constipation [,kɒnstɪˈpeɪʃən] N estreñimiento *m*

constituency [kənˈstɪtjʊənsɪ] Ⓐ N (= *district*) distrito *m* electoral, circunscripción *f* electoral; (= *people*) electorado *m*
Ⓑ CPD ► **constituency party** N partido *m* local

constituent [kənˈstɪtjʊənt] Ⓐ N 1 (= *component*) constitutivo *m*, componente *m*
2 (*Pol*) (= *voter*) elector(a) *m/f*
Ⓑ ADJ [*part*] constitutivo, integrante
Ⓒ CPD ► **constituent assembly** N cortes *fpl* constituyentes

constitute [ˈkɒnstɪtjuːt] VT 1 (= *amount to*) significar, constituir; (= *make up*) constituir, componer

[2] (*frm*) (= *appoint, set up*) constituir; **to ~ o.s. a judge** constituirse en juez

constitution [ˌkɒnstɪ'tjuːʃən] N [1] (*Pol*) constitución *f* [2] (= *health*) constitución *f*

> **CONSTITUTION**
>
> *El Reino Unido no tiene una constitución escrita. La Constitución británica está compuesta por el derecho legislado en el Parlamento (**statute law**) y por el derecho consuetudinario (**common law**), además de aquellas normas y prácticas necesarias para el funcionamiento del gobierno. Las leyes constitucionales pueden ser modificadas o derogadas por el Parlamento como cualquier otra ley.*
>
> ⇨ *Ver tb* ACT OF PARLIAMENT, COMMON LAW

constitutional [ˌkɒnstɪ'tjuːʃənl] Ⓐ ADJ constitucional
Ⓑ N paseo *m*
Ⓒ CPD ► **constitutional monarchy** N monarquía *f* constitucional ► **constitutional reform** N reforma *f* constitucional ► **constitutional law** N derecho *m* político

constitutionality [ˌkɒnstɪtjuːʃə'nælɪtɪ] (*frm*) N constitucionalidad *f*

constitutionally [ˌkɒnstɪ'tjuːʃənəlɪ] ADV según la constitución

constrain [kən'streɪn] VT (= *oblige*) obligar; **to ~ sb to do sth** obligar a algn a hacer algo; **to feel/be ~ed to do sth** sentirse/verse obligado a hacer algo

constrained [kən'streɪnd] ADJ [*atmosphere*] constrictivo; [*voice, manner, smile*] constreñido

constraint [kən'streɪnt] N [1] (= *compulsion*) coacción *f*, fuerza *f*; **under ~** obligado (a ello)
[2] (= *limit*) restricción *f*; **budgetary ~s** restricciones presupuestarias
[3] (= *restraint*) reserva *f*, cohibición *f*; **to feel a certain ~** sentirse algo cohibido

constrict [kən'strɪkt] VT [+ *muscle*] oprimir; [+ *vein*] estrangular; [+ *movements*] restringir

constricted [kən'strɪktɪd] ADJ [*space*] limitado, reducido; [*freedom, movement*] restringido; (*Phon*) constrictivo; **to feel ~** (*by clothes etc*) sentirse constreñido; **I feel ~ by these regulations** me siento constreñido por estas reglas

constricting [kən'strɪktɪŋ] ADJ [*dress, ideology*] estrecho

constriction [kən'strɪkʃən] N [*of vein*] estrangulamiento *m*

constrictive [kən'strɪktɪv] ADJ = **constricting**

constrictor [kən'strɪktəʳ] N constrictor *f*

construct Ⓐ [kən'strʌkt] VT construir
Ⓑ ['kɒnstrʌkt] N construcción *f*

construction [kən'strʌkʃən] Ⓐ N [1] (= *act, structure, building*) construcción *f*; **under ~** ◊ **in course of ~** en construcción
[2] (*fig*) (= *interpretation*) interpretación *f*; **to put a wrong ~ on sth** interpretar algo mal; **it depends what ~ one places on his words** depende de cómo se interpreten sus palabras
[3] (*Ling*) construcción *f*
Ⓑ CPD ► **construction company** N compañía *f* constructora ► **construction engineer** N ingeniero/a *m/f* de la construcción ► **construction industry** N industria *f* de la construcción

constructional [kən'strʌkʃənl] ADJ estructural; **~ toy** juguete *m* con que se construyen modelos

constructive [kən'strʌktɪv] ADJ constructivo

constructively [kən'strʌktɪvlɪ] ADV constructivamente

➤ LANGUAGE IN USE: contact B 21.2

constructivism [kən'strʌktɪvɪzəm] N constructivismo *m*

constructivist [kən'strʌktɪvɪst] Ⓐ ADJ constructivista
Ⓑ N constructivista *mf*

constructor [kən'strʌktəʳ] N constructor *m*

construe [kən'struː] VT interpretar

consul ['kɒnsəl] N (= *diplomatic official*) cónsul *mf*; **~ general** cónsul *mf* general

consular ['kɒnsjʊləʳ] ADJ consular

consulate ['kɒnsjʊlɪt] N consulado *m*

consulship ['kɒnsəlʃɪp] N consulado *m*

consult [kən'sʌlt] Ⓐ VT [1] [+ *book, person, doctor*] consultar
[2] (*frm*) (= *show consideration for*) [+ *one's interests*] tener en cuenta
Ⓑ VI consultar; **to ~ together** reunirse para hacer consultas; **people should ~ more** la gente debería consultar más entre sí; **to ~ with** (*US*) consultar con, aconsejarse con

consultancy [kən'sʌltənsɪ] Ⓐ N (*Comm*) consultoría *f*; (*Med*) puesto *m* de especialista
Ⓑ CPD ► **consultancy fees** NPL (*Comm*) derechos *mpl* de asesoría; (*Med*) derechos *mpl* de consulta

consultant [kən'sʌltənt] Ⓐ N [1] (*gen*) consultor(a) *m/f*, asesor(a) *m/f*; **to act as ~ to** asesorar
[2] (*Brit Med*) especialista *mf*
Ⓑ CPD ► **consultant engineer** N ingeniero *mf* consejero ► **consultant paediatrician** N especialista *mf* en pediatría ► **consultant physician** N médico *mf* especialista ► **consultant psychiatrist** N psiquiatra *mf* especialista

consultation [ˌkɒnsəl'teɪʃən] N (= *act*) consulta *f*; (= *meeting*) negociaciones *fpl*; **in ~ with** tras consultar a

consultative [kən'sʌltətɪv] ADJ consultivo; **~ document** documento *m* consultivo; **I was there in a ~ capacity** yo estuve en calidad de asesor

consulting [kən'sʌltɪŋ] ADJ **~ hours** (*Brit Med*) horas *fpl* de consulta; **~ room** (*Brit Med*) consultorio *m*, consulta *f*

consumable [kən'sjuːməbl] ADJ (*Econ etc*) consumible; **~ goods** bienes *mpl* consumibles, artículos *mpl* de consumo

consumables [kən'sjuːməblz] NPL bienes *mpl* consumibles, artículos *mpl* de consumo

consume [kən'sjuːm] VT [1] (= *eat*) consumir, comerse; (= *drink*) consumir, beber
[2] (= *use*) [+ *resources, fuel*] consumir; [+ *space, time etc*] ocupar
[3] (= *destroy*) (*by fire*) consumir; **the house was ~d by fire** la casa fue consumida *or* arrasada por las llamas; **to be ~d with envy/grief** estar muerto de envidia/pena

consumer [kən'sjuːməʳ] Ⓐ N consumidor(a) *m/f*; **the ~** el consumidor
Ⓑ CPD ► **consumer behaviour, consumer behavior** (*US*) N comportamiento *m* del consumidor ► **consumer choice** N libertad *f* del consumidor para elegir ► **consumer credit** N crédito *m* al consumidor ► **consumer demand** N demanda *f* de consumo ► **consumer durables** NPL bienes *mpl* (de consumo) duraderos ► **consumer goods** NPL bienes *mpl* de consumo ► **consumer price index** N índice *m* de precios al consumo ► **consumer product** N producto *m* al consumidor ► **consumer protection** N protección *f* del consumidor ► **consumer research** N estudios *mpl* de mercado ► **consumer resistance** N resistencia *f* por parte del consumidor ► **consumer rights** NPL derechos *mpl* del consumidor ► **the consumer society** N la sociedad de consumo ► **consumer survey** N encuesta *f* sobre consumo; *see also* **product A1**

consumerism [kən'sjuːmərɪzəm] N consumismo *m*

consuming [kən'sjuːmɪŋ] ADJ arrollador, apasionado; [*passion*] dominante, avasallador

consummate Ⓐ [kən'sʌmɪt] ADJ consumado; [*skill*] sumo
Ⓑ ['kɒnsʌmeɪt] VT consumar

consummation [ˌkɒnsʌ'meɪʃən] N consumación *f*

consumption [kən'sʌmpʃən] N [1] [*of food, fuel etc*] (= *act, amount*) consumo *m*; **not fit for human ~** [*food*] no apto para el consumo humano
[2] (†) (= *tuberculosis*) tisis *f*

consumptive [kən'sʌmptɪv] (*Med*) Ⓐ ADJ tísico Ⓑ N tísico/a *m/f*

cont. ABBR (= **continued**) sigue

▼**contact** ['kɒntækt] Ⓐ N [1] (= *connection*) contacto *m*; **to come into ~ with** tocar; (*violently*) chocar con
[2] (= *communication*) comunicación *f*; **to be in ~ with sth/sb** estar en contacto con algo/algn; **to get into ~ with** ponerse en contacto con; **to lose ~ (with sb)** perder el contacto (con algn); **to make ~ (with sb)** ponerse en contacto (con algn); **I seem to make no ~ with him** me resulta imposible comunicar con él; *see also* **radio D**
[3] (*Elec*) contacto *m*; **to make/break a ~** (*in circuit*) hacer/interrumpir el contacto
[4] (= *personal connection*) relación *f*; (*pej*) enchufe *m*, cuña *f* (*LAm*), hueso *m* (*Mex**), muñeca *f* (*S. Cone**); (= *intermediary*) contacto *m*; **he has a lot of ~s** tiene muchas relaciones; **business ~s** relaciones *fpl* comerciales; **he rang up one of his business ~s** llamó a uno de sus colegas comerciales; **you have to have a ~ in the business** hay que tener un buen enchufe en el negocio; **he's got good ~s** tiene buenas relaciones
[5] = **contact lens**
Ⓑ VT (*gen*) contactar con, ponerse en contacto con; (*by telephone etc*) comunicar con; **where can we ~ you?** ¿cómo podemos ponernos en contacto contigo?, ¿dónde podemos encontrarte?
Ⓒ CPD ► **contact adhesive** N adhesivo *m* de contacto ► **contact breaker** N (*Elec*) interruptor *m* ► **contact details** NPL información *f* de contacto ► **contact lens** N lente *f* de contacto, lentilla *f* ► **contact man** N intermediario *m* ► **contact number** N número *m* de contacto ► **contact print** N contact *m*

contagion [kən'teɪdʒən] N contagio *m*

contagious [kən'teɪdʒəs] ADJ contagioso

contain [kən'teɪn] VT (*all senses*) contener; **to ~ o.s.** contenerse

container [kən'teɪnəʳ] Ⓐ N [1] (= *box, jug etc*) recipiente *m*; (= *package, bottle*) envase *m*
[2] (*Comm*) (*for transport*) contenedor *m*, contáiner *m*
Ⓑ CPD ► **container depot** N terminal *f* para portacontenedores ► **container lorry** N portacontenedores *m inv* ► **container port** N puerto *m* para contenedores ► **container ship** N portacontenedores *m inv*, buque *m* contenedor ► **container terminal** N terminal *f* para portacontenedores ► **container train** N portacontenedores *m inv* ► **container transport** N transporte *m* en contenedores

containerization [kənˌteɪnəraɪ'zeɪʃən] N transporte *m* en contenedores

containerize [kənˈteɪnəraɪz] VT (*Comm*) [+ *goods*] transportar en contenedores, contenerizar

containment [kənˈteɪnmənt] N (*Pol*) contención *f*

contaminant [kənˈtæmɪnənt] N contaminante *m*

contaminate [kənˈtæmɪneɪt] VT [1] (*lit*) contaminar; **to be ~d by** contaminarse con *or* de
[2] (*fig*) corromper, contaminar

contamination [kənˌtæmɪˈneɪʃən] N contaminación *f*

contango [kənˈtæŋgəʊ] N (*St Ex*) *aplazamiento de pago hasta el próximo día de ajuste de cuentas*

contd., cont'd ABBR (= **continued**) sigue

contemplate [ˈkɒntempleɪt] VT [1] (= *gaze at*) contemplar; **I ~ the future with misgiving** el futuro lo veo dudoso
[2] (= *consider*) contemplar; (= *reflect upon*) considerar; **we ~d a holiday in Spain** nos planteamos unas vacaciones en España; **he ~d suicide** pensó en suicidarse; **to ~ doing sth** pensar en hacer algo; **when do you ~ doing it?** ¿cuándo se propone hacerlo?
[3] (= *expect*) contar con

contemplation [ˌkɒntemˈpleɪʃən] N contemplación *f*, meditación *f*

contemplative [kənˈtemplətɪv] ADJ contemplativo

contemplatively [kənˈtemplətɪvlɪ] ADV pensativamente

contemporaneous [kənˌtempəˈreɪnɪəs] ADJ contemporáneo

contemporaneously [kənˌtempəˈreɪnɪəslɪ] ADV contemporáneamente

contemporary [kənˈtempərərɪ] Ⓐ ADJ contemporáneo; **~ with** contemporáneo de
Ⓑ N contemporáneo/a *m/f*

contempt [kənˈtempt] N desprecio *m*, desdén *m*; **to hold sth/sb in ~** despreciar algo/a algn; **it's beneath ~** es más que despreciable; **to bring into ~** desprestigiar, envilecer; **to hold in ~** despreciar; (*Jur*) declarar en rebeldía; **~ of court** (*Jur*) desacato *m* (a los tribunales)

contemptible [kənˈtemptəbl] ADJ despreciable, desdeñable

contemptuous [kənˈtemptjʊəs] ADJ [*person*] desdeñoso (**of** con); [*manner*] despreciativo, desdeñoso; [*gesture*] despectivo; **to be ~ of** desdeñar, menospreciar

contemptuously [kənˈtemptjʊəslɪ] ADV desdeñosamente, con desprecio

contend [kənˈtend] Ⓐ VT **to ~ that** afirmar que, sostener que
Ⓑ VI **to ~ (with sb) for sth** competir (con algn) por algo; **we have many problems to ~ with** se nos plantean muchos problemas; **you'll have me to ~ with** tendrás que vértelas conmigo; **he has a lot to ~ with** tiene que enfrentarse a muchos problemas

contender [kənˈtendəʳ] N (= *rival*) competidor(a) *m/f*; (*Sport etc*) contendiente *mf*

contending [kənˈtendɪŋ] ADJ rival, opuesto

content¹ [kənˈtent] Ⓐ ADJ [1] (= *happy*) contento (**with** con); **to be ~** estar contento; **he is ~ to watch** se conforma *or* se contenta con mirar
[2] (= *satisfied*) satisfecho (**with** con)
Ⓑ N (= *happiness*) contento *m*; (= *satisfaction*) satisfacción *f*; **to one's heart's ~** hasta hartarse, a más no poder; **you can complain to your heart's ~** protesta cuanto quieras
Ⓒ VT (= *make happy*) contentar; (= *satisfy*) satisfacer; **to ~ o.s. with sth/with doing sth** contentarse *or* darse por contento con algo/con hacer algo

content² [ˈkɒntent] N [1] **contents** [*of box, packet etc*] contenido *msing*; [*of book*] índice *msing* (de materias)
[2] (= *subject matter, amount*) contenido *m*

contented [kənˈtentɪd] ADJ satisfecho, contento

contentedly [kənˈtentɪdlɪ] ADV con satisfacción, contentamente

contentedness [kənˈtentɪdnɪs] N contento *m*, satisfacción *f*

contention [kənˈtenʃən] N [1] (= *strife*) discusión *f*; (= *dissent*) disensión *f*; **teams in ~** equipos rivales
[2] (= *point*) opinión *f*, argumento *m*; **it is our ~ that …** pretendemos que …, sostenemos que …

contentious [kənˈtenʃəs] ADJ [1] (= *controversial*) [*issue, view, proposal*] conflictivo, muy discutido
[2] (= *argumentative*) [*person*] que le gusta discutir

contentment [kənˈtentmənt] N contento *m*, satisfacción *f*

contest Ⓐ [ˈkɒntest] N (= *struggle*) contienda *f*, lucha *f*; (*Boxing, Wrestling*) combate *m*; (= *competition, quiz*) concurso *m*; (*Sport*) competición *f*; **beauty ~** concurso *m* de belleza; **a fishing ~** una competición de pesca
Ⓑ [kənˈtest] VT [+ *argument, will etc*] impugnar, rebatir; [+ *election, seat*] presentarse como candidato/a a; [+ *legal suit*] defender; **I ~ your right to do that** pongo en tela de juicio que usted tenga el derecho de hacer eso; **the seat was not ~ed** no hubo disputa por el escaño, en las elecciones se presentó un solo candidato
Ⓒ [kənˈtest] VI **to ~ against** contender con; **they are ~ing for a big prize** se disputan un premio importante

contestant [kənˈtestənt] N (*in competition*) concursante *mf*; (*Sport etc*) contrincante *mf*, contendiente *mf*

context [ˈkɒntekst] N contexto *m*; **in/out of ~** en/fuera de contexto; **we must see this in ~** tenemos que ver esto en su contexto; **to put sth in ~** poner algo en su contexto; **it was taken out of ~** fue sacado de su contexto

contextual [kənˈtekstjʊəl] ADJ contextual

contextualize [kənˈtekstjʊəlaɪz] VT contextualizar

contiguity [ˈkɒntɪgjuːɪtɪ] N contigüidad *f*

contiguous [kənˈtɪgjʊəs] ADJ contiguo (**to** a)

continence [ˈkɒntɪnəns] N continencia *f*

continent¹ [ˈkɒntɪnənt] ADJ continente

continent² [ˈkɒntɪnənt] N [1] (*Geog*) continente *m*
[2] (*Brit*) **the Continent** el continente europeo, Europa *f* (continental); **on the Continent** en Europa (continental)

continental [ˌkɒntɪˈnentl] Ⓐ ADJ [1] (*Geog*) continental
[2] (*Brit*) (= *European*) continental, europeo
Ⓑ N (*Brit*) europeo/a *m/f* (continental)
Ⓒ CPD ► **continental breakfast** N desayuno *m* estilo europeo ► **continental drift** N deriva *f* continental ► **continental quilt** N edredón *m* ► **continental shelf** N plataforma *f* continental

contingency [kənˈtɪndʒənsɪ] Ⓐ N eventualidad *f*, contingencia *f*; **to provide for every ~** tener en cuenta cualquier eventualidad *or* contingencia; **should the ~ arise** en caso de presentarse la eventualidad; **£50 for contingencies** 50 libras en caso de que surja una eventualidad *or* para gastos imprevistos
Ⓑ CPD ► **contingency funds** NPL fondos *mpl* para imprevistos ► **contingency planning** N planificación *f* para una eventual emergencia ► **contingency plans** NPL medidas *fpl* para casos de emergencia

contingent [kənˈtɪndʒənt] Ⓐ ADJ **to be ~ upon** depender de
Ⓑ N [1] (*Mil*) contingente *m*
[2] (= *group*) representación *f*

continual [kənˈtɪnjʊəl] ADJ (= *continuous*) continuo; (= *persistent*) constante

continually [kənˈtɪnjʊəlɪ] ADV continuamente, constantemente

continuance [kənˈtɪnjʊəns] N continuación *f*

continuation [kənˌtɪnjʊˈeɪʃən] N [1] (= *maintenance*) prosecución *f*; (= *resumption*) reanudación *f*
[2] (= *sth continued*) prolongación *f*; (= *story, episode*) continuación *f*

continue [kənˈtɪnjuː] Ⓐ VT [1] (= *carry on*) [+ *policy, tradition*] seguir
[2] (= *resume*) [+ *story etc*] reanudar, continuar; **~d on page ten** sigue en la página diez; **to be ~d** continuará
Ⓑ VI [1] (= *carry on*) continuar; **"and so," he ~d** —y de este modo —continuó; **to ~ doing** *or* **to do sth** continuar *or* seguir haciendo algo; **she ~d talking to her friend** continuó *or* siguió hablando con su amiga; **to ~ on one's way** seguir su camino; **to ~ with sth** seguir con algo
[2] (= *remain*) seguir; **to ~ in office** seguir en su puesto; **to ~ in a place** seguir en un sitio
[3] (= *extend*) prolongarse, seguir; **the road ~s for two miles** la carretera se prolonga *or* sigue dos millas más; **the forest ~s to the sea** el bosque se prolonga *or* sigue hasta el mar

continuing [kənˈtɪnjʊɪŋ] Ⓐ ADJ [*argument*] irresoluto; [*correspondence*] continuado
Ⓑ CPD ► **continuing education** N *cursos de enseñanza para adultos*

continuity [ˌkɒntɪˈnjuːɪtɪ] Ⓐ N continuidad *f*
Ⓑ CPD ► **continuity man/girl** N (*Cine*) secretario/a *m/f* de rodaje

continuo [kənˈtɪnjʊəʊ] N continuo *m*

continuous [kənˈtɪnjʊəs] Ⓐ ADJ continuo
Ⓑ CPD ► **continuous assessment** N evaluación *f* continua ► **continuous (feed) paper** N papel *m* continuo ► **continuous inventory** N inventario *m* continuo ► **continuous performance** N (*in cinema*) sesión *f* continua ► **continuous stationery** N papel *m* continuo

continuously [kənˈtɪnjʊəslɪ] ADV continuamente

continuum [kənˈtɪnjʊəm] N (*pl* **continuums** *or* **continua**) continuo *m*

contort [kənˈtɔːt] VT retorcer

contortion [kənˈtɔːʃən] N (= *act*) retorcimiento *m*; (= *movement*) contorsión *f*

contortionist [kənˈtɔːʃənɪst] N contorsionista *mf*

contour [ˈkɒntʊəʳ] Ⓐ N contorno *m*
Ⓑ CPD ► **contour flying** N vuelo *m* rasante ► **contour line** N curva *f* de nivel ► **contour map** N plano *m* acotado

contoured [ˈkɒntʊəd] ADJ [*surface, seat*] contorneado

contra… [ˈkɒntrə] PREFIX contra…

contraband [ˈkɒntrəbænd] Ⓐ N contrabando *m*
Ⓑ CPD de contrabando

contrabass [ˌkɒntrəˈbeɪs] N contrabajo *m*

contrabassoon [ˌkɒntrəbəˈsuːn] N contrafagot *m*

contraception [ˌkɒntrəˈsepʃən] N contracepción *f*, anticoncepción *f*

contraceptive [ˌkɒntrəˈseptɪv] Ⓐ ADJ anticonceptivo
Ⓑ N anticonceptivo *m*, contraceptivo *m*
Ⓒ CPD ► **contraceptive pill** N píldora *f* anticonceptiva

contract Ⓐ [ˈkɒntrækt] N 1 (= *document*) contrato *m*; **~ of employment** *or* **service** contrato *m* de trabajo; **breach of ~** incumplimiento *m* de contrato; **by ~** por contrato; **to enter into a ~ (with sb) (to do sth/for sth)** firmar un contrato (con algn) (para hacer algo/de algo); **to place a ~ with** dar un contrato a; **to sign a ~** firmar un contrato; **to put work out to ~** sacar una obra a contrato; **to be under ~ to do sth** hacer algo bajo contrato; **they are under ~ to X** tienen contrato con X, tienen obligaciones contractuales con X
2 (*fig*) **there's a ~ out for him** le han puesto precio
Ⓑ [kənˈtrækt] VT 1 (= *acquire*) [+ *disease, debt*] contraer; [+ *habit*] tomar, adquirir
2 (= *enter into*) [+ *alliance*] entablar, establecer; [+ *marriage*] contraer
3 (*Ling*) (= *shorten*) contraer
Ⓒ [kənˈtrækt] VI 1 (= *become smaller*) [*metal*] contraerse, encogerse
2 [*muscles, face*] contraerse
3 (*Ling*) [*word, phrase*] contraerse
4 (*Comm*) **to ~ (with sb) to do sth** comprometerse por contrato (con algn) a hacer algo; **to ~ for** contratar
Ⓓ [ˈkɒntrækt] CPD ► **contract bridge** N bridge *m* de contrato ► **contract date** N fecha *f* contratada, fecha *f* de contrato ► **contract killer** N asesino *m* a sueldo ► **contract killing** N asesinato *m* pagado ► **contract price** N precio *m* contractual, precio *m* contratado ► **contract work** N trabajo *m* bajo contrato

► **contract in** VI + ADV tomar parte (**to** en)

► **contract out** Ⓐ VT + ADV **this work is ~ed out** este trabajo se hace fuera de la empresa con un contrato aparte
Ⓑ VI + ADV (*Brit*) optar por no tomar parte (**of** en)

contracting [kənˈtræktɪŋ] ADJ **~ party** contratante *mf*

contraction [kənˈtrækʃən] N contracción *f*

contractor [kənˈtræktəʳ] N contratista *mf*

contractual [kənˈtræktʃʊəl] Ⓐ ADJ [*duty, obligation*] contractual
Ⓑ CPD ► **contractual liability** N responsabilidad *f* contractual

contractually [kənˈtræktʃʊəlɪ] ADV contractualmente; **a ~ binding agreement** un acuerdo vinculante por contrato; **we are ~ bound to finish it** estamos obligados a terminarlo por contrato

▼ **contradict** [ˌkɒntrəˈdɪkt] VT (= *be contrary to*) contradecir; (= *declare to be wrong*) desmentir; (= *argue*) replicar, discutir; **don't ~ me!** ¡no me repliques!

contradiction [ˌkɒntrəˈdɪkʃən] N contradicción *f*; **to be a ~ in terms** ser contradictorio

contradictory [ˌkɒntrəˈdɪktərɪ] ADJ contradictorio

contradistinction [ˌkɒntrədɪsˈtɪŋkʃən] N **in ~ to** a diferencia de

contraflow [ˈkɒntrəfləʊ] N (*Brit Aut*) (*also* **~ system**) sistema *m* de contracorriente

contraindication [ˌkɒntrəˌɪndɪˈkeɪʃən] N contraindicación *f*

contralto [kənˈtræltəʊ] Ⓐ N (*pl* **contraltos** *or* **contralti** [kənˈtræltɪ]) (= *person*) contralto *f*
Ⓑ CPD [*voice*] de contralto

contraption* [kənˈtræpʃən] N (= *gadget*) artilugio *m*, aparato *m*; (= *vehicle*) armatoste *m*

contrapuntal [ˌkɒntrəˈpʌntl] ADJ de contrapunto

contrarian [kənˈtreərɪən] (*frm*) Ⓐ ADJ inconformista
Ⓑ N *persona que deliberadamente lleva la contraria*; **he is by nature a ~** por naturaleza le gusta llevar la contraria

contrarily [kənˈtreərɪlɪ] ADV (= *perversely*) tercamente

contrariness [kənˈtreərɪnɪs] N (= *perverseness*) terquedad *f*

contrariwise [kənˈtreərɪwaɪz] ADV (= *on the contrary*) al contrario; (= *on the other hand*) por otra parte; (= *in opposite direction*) en sentido contrario; (= *the other way round*) a la inversa

contrary [ˈkɒntrərɪ] Ⓐ ADJ 1 [*direction*] contrario; [*opinions*] opuesto; **~ to** en contra de, contrario a; **~ to what we thought** en contra de lo que pensábamos
2 [kənˈtreərɪ] (= *perverse*) terco
Ⓑ N contrario *m*; **on the ~** al contrario, todo lo contrario; **quite the ~** muy al contrario; **he holds the ~** él sostiene lo contrario; **the ~ seems to be true** parece que es al revés; **I know nothing to the ~** yo no sé nada en sentido contrario; **unless we hear to the ~** a no ser que nos digan lo contrario

▼ **contrast** Ⓐ [ˈkɒntrɑːst] N (*gen*) contraste *m*; **in ~ to** *or* **with** a diferencia de, en contraste con; **to form a ~ to** *or* **with** contrastar con
Ⓑ [kənˈtrɑːst] VT **to ~ with** comparar con, contrastar con
Ⓒ [kənˈtrɑːst] VI **to ~ with** contrastar con, hacer contraste con

contrasting [kənˈtrɑːstɪŋ] ADJ [*opinion*] opuesto; [*colour*] que hace contraste

contrastive [kənˈtrɑːstɪv] ADJ (*Ling*) contrastivo

contravene [ˌkɒntrəˈviːn] VT (= *infringe*) [+ *law*] contravenir; (= *go against*) ir en contra de; (= *dispute*) oponerse a

contravention [ˌkɒntrəˈvenʃən] N contravención *f*

contretemps [ˈkɔ̃ntrətɑ̃ːŋ] N (*pl* **contretemps**) contratiempo *m*, revés *m*

contribute [kənˈtrɪbjuːt] Ⓐ VT [+ *money, ideas*] contribuir, aportar (*esp LAm*); [+ *facts, information etc*] aportar; [+ *help*] prestar; [+ *article to a newspaper*] escribir; **she ~d £10 to the collection** contribuyó con 10 libras a la colecta
Ⓑ VI (*to charity, collection*) contribuir (**to** a); (*to newspaper*) colaborar (**to** en); (*to discussion*) intervenir (**to** en); (= *help in bringing sth about*) contribuir; **everyone ~d to the success of the play** todos contribuyeron al éxito de la obra; **it all ~d to the muddle** todo sirvió para aumentar la confusión

contribution [ˌkɒntrɪˈbjuːʃən] N (= *money*) contribución *f*, aporte *m* (*esp LAm*); (*to journal*) artículo *m*, colaboración *f*; (*to discussion*) intervención *f*, aportación *f*; [*of information etc*] aportación *f*; (*to pension fund*) cuota *f*, cotización *f*

contributor [kənˈtrɪbjʊtəʳ] N [*of money*] persona *f* que contribuye; [*of taxes*] contribuyente *mf*; (*to journal*) colaborador(a) *m/f*

contributory [kənˈtrɪbjʊtərɪ] ADJ [*cause, factor*] que contribuye, contribuyente; **~ pension scheme** plan *m* cotizable de jubilación

contrite [ˈkɒntraɪt] ADJ arrepentido; (*Rel*) contrito

contritely [ˈkɒntraɪtlɪ] ADV [*say etc*] en tono arrepentido

contrition [kənˈtrɪʃən] N arrepentimiento *m*; (*Rel*) contrición *f*

contrivance [kənˈtraɪvəns] N (= *machine, device*) artilugio *m*, aparato *m*; (= *invention*) invención *f*, invento *m*; (= *stratagem*) estratagema *f*

contrive [kənˈtraɪv] Ⓐ VT [+ *plan, scheme*] inventar, idear; **to ~ a means of doing sth** inventar una manera de hacer algo
Ⓑ VI **to ~ to do** (= *manage, arrange*) lograr hacer; (= *try*) procurar hacer

contrived [kənˈtraɪvd] ADJ artificial

control [kənˈtrəʊl] Ⓐ N 1 (= *command*) control *m* (**over** sobre); **troops regained ~ of the capital** las tropas recuperaron el control de la capital; **he is giving up ~ of the company** va a ceder el control de la empresa; **to gain ~ of** [+ *company, territory*] hacerse con el control de; **they have no ~ over their pupils** no pueden controlar a sus alumnos; **to be in ~ (of sth)**: **who is in ~?** ¿quién manda?; **they are in complete ~ of the situation** tienen la situación totalmente controlada *or* dominada; **people feel more in ~ of their lives** la gente se siente más dueña de su vida, la gente siente que tiene mayor control de su vida; **his party has lost ~ of the Senate** su partido perdió el control del Senado; **to take ~ of a company** hacerse con el control de una empresa; **it was time to take ~ of her life again** era hora de volver a tomar las riendas de su vida; **under British ~** bajo dominio *or* control británico; **to be under private ~** estar en manos de particulares
2 (= *power to restrain*) control *m*; **due to circumstances beyond our ~** debido a circunstancias ajenas a nuestra voluntad; **to lose ~ (of o.s.)** perder el control *or* dominio de uno mismo; **he lost ~ of the car** perdió el control del coche; **to be out of ~** estar fuera de control; **the children were getting out of ~** los niños se estaban descontrolando; **the car went out of ~** el coche quedó fuera de control; **everything is under ~** todo está bajo control; **I brought my temper under ~** dominé *or* controlé el genio; **to bring** *or* **get a fire under ~** conseguir dominar *or* controlar un incendio; **to keep sth/sb under ~** mantener algo/a algn bajo control
3 (= *restraint*) restricción *f*; **they want greater ~s on arms sales** quieren mayores restricciones en la venta de armamento; **arms ~** control *m* de armamentos; **birth ~** control *m* de la natalidad; **price/wage ~** reglamentación *f or* control *m* de precios/salarios
4 (*Tech*) 4·1 **controls** mandos *mpl*; **to be at the ~s** estar a (cargo de) los mandos; **to take over the ~s** hacerse cargo de los mandos
4·2 (= *knob, switch*) botón *m*; **volume ~** botón *m* del volumen
5 (*in experiment*) testigo *m*
6 (= *checkpoint*) control *m*; **an agreement to abolish border ~s** un acuerdo para eliminar los controles en las fronteras; **passport ~** control *m* de pasaportes
7 (*Sport*) (= *mastery*) dominio *m*; **his ball ~ is very good** su dominio del balón es muy bueno, domina bien el balón
Ⓑ VT 1 (= *command*) [+ *country, territory, business, organization*] controlar
2 (= *restrain*) [+ *crowd, child, animal, disease*] controlar; [+ *fire, emotions, temper*] controlar, dominar; **to ~ the spread of malaria** conte-

➤ LANGUAGE IN USE: contradict 12.1 contrast A 26.3

ner la propagación de la malaria; **to ~ o.s.** controlarse, dominarse; **~ yourself!** ¡contrólese!, ¡domínese!
[3] (= *regulate*) [+ *activity, prices, wages, expenditure*] controlar, regular; [+ *traffic*] dirigir; **legislation to ~ immigration** legislación para controlar *or* regular la inmigración; **he was trying to ~ the conversation** estaba intentando llevar las riendas de la conversación
[4] (= *operate*) [+ *machine, vehicle*] manejar, controlar; [+ *horse*] controlar, dominar
Ⓒ CPD ► **control column** N palanca *f* de mando ► **control freak*** N **he's a total ~ freak** tiene la manía de controlarlo todo ► **control group** N (*in experiment*) grupo *m* testigo ► **control key** N (*Comput*) tecla *f* de control ► **control knob** N (*Rad, TV*) botón *m* de mando ► **control panel** N tablero *m* de control ► **control room** N (*Mil, Naut*) sala *f* de mandos; (*Rad, TV*) sala *f* de control ► **control tower** N (*Aer*) torre *f* de control

controllable [kən'trəʊləbl] ADJ controlable

controlled [kən'trəʊld] ADJ [1] (= *restrained*) [*emotion*] contenido; **she was very ~** tenía gran dominio de sí misma; **she spoke in a ~ voice** al hablar, su voz no reveló lo que sentía
[2] (= *regulated*) controlado; **~ economy** economía *f* dirigida; **~ explosion** explosión *f* controlada
[3] (= *restricted*) [*drug, substance*] *que se dispensa únicamente con receta médica*

-controlled [kən'trəʊld] ADJ (*ending in compounds*) **a Labour-controlled council** un ayuntamiento laborista *or* gobernado por los laboristas; **a government-controlled organization** una organización bajo control gubernamental; **computer-controlled equipment** equipamiento computerizado

controller [kən'trəʊlə^r] N (*Comm*) interventor(a) *m/f*; (*Aer*) controlador(a) *m/f*; **air-traffic ~** controlador(a) *m/f* aéreo/a

controlling [kən'trəʊlɪŋ] ADJ [1] [*factor*] determinante
[2] (*Fin*) **a ~ interest** una participación mayoritaria

▼**controversial** [,kɒntrə'vɜːʃəl] ADJ controvertido, polémico; **euthanasia is a ~ subject** la eutanasia es un tema controvertido *or* polémico

controversially [,kɒntrə'vɜːʃəlɪ] ADV de forma controvertida, de forma polémica

controversy [kɒn'trɒvəsɪ] N controversia *f*, polémica *f*; (= *debate*) polémica *f*; **there was a lot of ~ about it** hubo mucha controversia *or* polémica en torno a eso; **to cause ~** ocasionar controversia *or* polémica

controvert ['kɒntrəvɜːt] VT contradecir

contumacious [,kɒntjʊ'meɪʃəs] ADJ (*frm*) contumaz

contumaciously [,kɒntjʊ'meɪʃəslɪ] ADV (*frm*) contumazmente

contumacy ['kɒntjʊməsɪ] N (*frm*) contumacia *f*

contumely ['kɒntjʊmɪlɪ] N (*frm*) contumelia *f*

contusion [kən'tjuːʒən] N (*Med*) contusión *f*

conundrum [kə'nʌndrəm] N (= *riddle*) acertijo *m*, adivinanza *f*; (= *problem*) enigma *m*

conurbation [,kɒnɜː'beɪʃən] N (*Brit*) conurbación *f*

convalesce [,kɒnvə'les] VI convalecer

convalescence [,kɒnvə'lesəns] N convalecencia *f*

convalescent [,kɒnvə'lesənt] Ⓐ ADJ convaleciente
Ⓑ N convaleciente *mf*
Ⓒ CPD ► **convalescent home** N clínica *f* de reposo

convection [kən'vekʃən] N convección *f*

convector [kən'vektə^r] N (*also* **~ heater, convection heater**) calentador *m* de convección

convene [kən'viːn] Ⓐ VT convocar
Ⓑ VI reunirse

convener [kən'viːnə^r] N (*esp Brit*) coordinador(a) *m/f* sindical

convenience [kən'viːnɪəns] Ⓐ N [1] (= *comfort*) comodidad *f*; (= *advantage*) ventaja *f*, provecho *m*; **at your earliest ~** tan pronto como le sea posible; **you can do it at your own ~** puede hacerlo cuando le venga mejor *or* (*LAm*) le convenga; **for your ~ an envelope is enclosed** para facilitar su contestación adjuntamos un sobre; **it is a great ~ to be so close** resulta muy práctico estar tan cerca
[2] (= *amenity*) comodidad *f*, confort *m*; *see* **public C, modern**
Ⓑ CPD ► **convenience foods** NPL comidas *fpl* fáciles de preparar; (= *ready-cooked meals*) platos *mpl* preparados

convenient [kən'viːnɪənt] ADJ [1] (= *suitable*) conveniente; [*tool, device*] práctico, útil; [*size*] idóneo, cómodo; **if it is ~ to you** si le viene bien; **when it is ~ for you** cuando le venga bien; **would tomorrow be ~?** ¿le viene bien mañana?; **is it ~ to call tomorrow?** ¿le viene bien llamar mañana?; **it is ~ to live here** resulta práctico vivir aquí; **her death was certainly ~ for him** (*iro*) es cierto que su muerte fue oportuna para él; **at a ~ moment** en un momento oportuno; **we looked for a ~ place to stop** buscamos un sitio apropiado para parar; **it's not a ~ time for me** a esa hora no me viene bien
[2] (= *near*) [*place*] bien situado, accesible; **the house is ~ for the shops** la casa está muy cerca de las tiendas; **the hotel is ~ for the airport** el hotel está bien situado con respecto al aeropuerto; **he put it on a ~ chair** lo puso en una silla que estaba a mano

conveniently [kən'viːnɪəntlɪ] ADV (= *handily*) convenientemente; (= *suitably*) [*time*] oportunamente; **the house is ~ situated** la casa está en un sitio muy práctico; **it fell ~ close** cayó muy cerca; **when you ~ can do so** cuando puedas hacerlo sin que te cause molestia; **he very ~ forgot to write it down** (*iro*) muy oportunamente *or* mira por donde, se olvidó de apuntarlo (*iro*)

convenor [kən'viːnə^r] N = **convener**

convent ['kɒnvənt] Ⓐ N convento *m*
Ⓑ CPD ► **convent school** N colegio *m* de monjas

convention [kən'venʃən] N [1] (= *custom*) convención *f*; **you must follow ~** hay que seguir los convencionalismos
[2] (= *meeting*) asamblea *f*, congreso *m*
[3] (= *agreement*) convenio *m*, convención *f*

conventional [kən'venʃənl] ADJ [*behaviour, tastes, weapons, method*] convencional; [*person*] tradicional, convencional; [*belief, values*] tradicional; [*style, clothes*] clásico, tradicional; **~ medicine** la medicina tradicional *or* convencional; **she was not beautiful in the ~ sense of the word** no era una belleza en el sentido generalmente aceptado de la palabra; **~ wisdom** (*frm*) la opinión convencional

conventionalism [kən'venʃənəlɪzəm] N convencionalismo *m*

conventionally [kən'venʃənəlɪ] ADV [*dress, behave*] de manera convencional; [*produced, grown*] de manera tradicional; **~ educated students** estudiantes educados de manera convencional *or* tradicional; **~ beautiful women** mujeres con una belleza convencional *or* clásica

conventioneer [kən,venʃə'nɪə^r] N (*esp US*) asistente *mf* a un congreso, congresista *mf*

converge [kən'vɜːdʒ] VI converger, convergir; **the crowd ~d on the square** la muchedumbre se dirigió a la plaza

convergence [kən'vɜːdʒəns] N convergencia *f*

convergent [kən'vɜːdʒənt], **converging** [kən'vɜːdʒɪŋ] ADJ convergente

conversant [kən'vɜːsənt] ADJ **~ with** versado en, familiarizado con; **to become ~ with** familiarizarse con

conversation [,kɒnvə'seɪʃən] Ⓐ N conversación *f*, plática *f* (*LAm*); **we had a long ~** tuvimos una larga conversación; **to have a ~ with sb** conversar *or* (*LAm*) platicar con algn; **what was your ~ about?** ¿de qué hablabas?; **I said it just to make ~** lo dije sólo por decir algo
Ⓑ CPD ► **conversation mode** N (*Comput*) modo *m* de conversación ► **conversation piece** N **it was a ~ piece** fue tema de conversación ► **conversation stopper*** N **that was a ~ stopper*** eso nos *etc* dejó a todos sin saber qué decir

conversational [,kɒnvə'seɪʃənl] Ⓐ ADJ [*style, tone*] familiar; **her ~ skills were somewhat lacking** no era muy buena conversadora; **he has the ~ skills of a two-year-old** habla como un niño de dos anos
Ⓑ CPD ► **conversational mode** N (*Comput*) modo *m* de conversación

conversationalist [,kɒnvə'seɪʃnəlɪst] N conversador(a) *m/f*; **to be a good ~** brillar en la conversación; **he's not much of a ~** no es muy buen conversador

conversationally [,kɒnvə'seɪʃnəlɪ] ADV en tono familiar

converse[1] [kən'vɜːs] VI **to ~ (with sb) (about sth)** conversar *or* (*LAm*) platicar (con algn) (sobre algo); **to ~ by signs** hablar por señas

converse[2] ['kɒnvɜːs] Ⓐ N (*Math, Logic*) proposición *f* recíproca; (*gen*) inversa *f*; **but the ~ is true** pero la verdad es al revés
Ⓑ ADJ contrario, opuesto; (*Logic*) recíproco

conversely [kɒn'vɜːslɪ] ADV a la inversa

conversion [kən'vɜːʃən] Ⓐ N [1] (*gen, Rel*) conversión *f* (**into** en; **to** a)
[2] (= *house conversion*) reforma *f*, remodelación *f*
[3] (*Rugby, US Football*) transformación *f*
[4] (*Jur*) apropiación *f* ilícita
Ⓑ CPD ► **conversion kit** N equipo *m* de conversión ► **conversion (loan) stock** N obligaciones *fpl* convertibles ► **conversion table** N tabla *f* de equivalencias

convert ['kɒnvɜːt] Ⓐ N converso/a *m/f*; **to become a ~** convertirse, hacerse converso
Ⓑ [kən'vɜːt] VT [1] [+ *appliance*] adaptar; [+ *house*] reformar, convertir (**into** en); (*Fin*) [+ *currency*] convertir (**to, into** en); (*Rel*) convertir (**to** a); (*fig*) convencer (**to** a); **to ~ sth into** convertir algo en, transformar algo en
[2] (*Rugby, US Football*) transformar
[3] (*Jur*) apropiarse ilícitamente (**to one's own use** para uso propio)
Ⓒ [kən'vɜːt] VI convertirse (**to** a)

converter [kən'vɜːtə^r] N (*Elec*) convertidor *m*

convertibility [kən,vɜːtə'bɪlɪtɪ] N convertibilidad *f*

convertible [kən'vɜːtəbl] Ⓐ ADJ [*currency*] convertible; [*car*] descapotable; [*settee*] transformable
Ⓑ N (= *car*) descapotable *m*
Ⓒ CPD ► **convertible debenture** N obliga-

➤ LANGUAGE IN USE: **controversial** 26.3

ción *f* convertible ► **convertible loan stock** N obligaciones *fpl* convertibles

convertor [kən'vɜːtəʳ] = **converter**

convex ['kɒn'veks] ADJ convexo

convexity [kɒn'veksɪtɪ] N convexidad *f*

convey [kən'veɪ] VT [1] [+ *goods, oil*] transportar, llevar; [+ *sound, smell*] llevar; [+ *current*] transmitir; (*slightly frm*) [+ *person*] conducir, acompañar (*LAm*)
[2] [+ *thanks, congratulations*] comunicar; [+ *meaning, ideas*] expresar; **to ~ to sb that ...** comunicar a algn que ...; **the name ~s nothing to me** el nombre no me dice nada; **what does this music ~ to you?** ¿qué es lo que te evoca esta música?
[3] (*Jur*) traspasar, transferir

conveyance [kən'veəns] N [1] (= *act*) (*no pl*) transporte *m*, transmisión *f*; (*Jur*) [*of property*] traspaso *m*
[2] (*frm*) (= *vehicle*) vehículo *m*, medio *m* de transporte; **public ~** vehículo *m* de servicio público
[3] (*Jur*) (= *deed*) escritura *f* de traspaso

conveyancer [kən'veənsəʳ] N (*Brit Jur*) *persona que formaliza el traspaso de la propiedad de inmuebles*, ≈ notario/a *m/f*

conveyancing [kən'veənsɪŋ] N (*Brit Jur*) preparación *f* de escrituras de traspaso

conveyor [kən'veɪəʳ] Ⓐ N portador *m*, transportador *m*; (= *belt*) = **conveyor belt**
Ⓑ CPD ► **conveyor belt** N cinta *f* transportadora

convict ['kɒnvɪkt] Ⓐ N (= *prisoner*) presidiario/a *m/f*
Ⓑ [kən'vɪkt] VT declarar culpable (**of** de), condenar; **a ~ed murderer** un asesino convicto y confeso; **he was ~ed of drunken driving** fue condenado por conducir en estado de embriaguez
Ⓒ [kən'vɪkt] VI [*jury*] condenar
Ⓓ ['kɒnvɪkt] CPD ► **convict settlement** N colonia *f* de presidiarios

conviction [kən'vɪkʃən] N [1] (*Jur*) condena *f*; **there were 12 ~s for theft** hubo 12 condenas por robo; **to have no previous ~s** no tener antecedentes penales
[2] (= *belief*) convicción *f*, creencia *f*; **it is my ~ that ...** creo firmemente que ...
[3] (= *persuasion, persuasiveness*) **he said with ~** dijo con convicción; **without much ~** no muy convencido; **to carry ~** ser convincente; **open to ~** dispuesto a dejarse convencer

▼ **convince** [kən'vɪns] VT convencer; **to ~ sb (of sth/that)** convencer a algn (de algo/de que); **I am not ~d** no estoy convencido, no me convence

convinced [kən'vɪnst] ADJ [*Christian etc*] convencido

convincing [kən'vɪnsɪŋ] ADJ convincente

convincingly [kən'vɪnsɪŋlɪ] ADV de forma convincente

convivial [kən'vɪvɪəl] ADJ [*person, company*] sociable, agradable; [*evening, atmosphere*] alegre, agradable

conviviality [kən,vɪvɪ'ælɪtɪ] N alegría *f* y buen humor; **there was an atmosphere of ~** había un ambiente de alegría y buen humor

convocation [,kɒnvə'keɪʃən] N (*frm*) (= *act*) convocación *f*; (= *meeting*) asamblea *f*

convoke [kən'vəʊk] VT convocar

convoluted ['kɒnvə,luːtɪd] ADJ [*shape*] enrollado, enroscado; [*argument*] enrevesado

convolution [,kɒnvə'luːʃən] N circunvolución *f*

convolvulus [kən'vɒlvjʊləs] N (*pl* **convolvuluses** *or* **convolvuli** [kən'vɒlvjʊlaɪ]) enredadera *f*

convoy ['kɒnvɔɪ] Ⓐ N (= *procession*) convoy *m*; (= *escort*) escolta *f*; **in/under ~** en convoy
Ⓑ VT convoyar, escoltar

convulse [kən'vʌls] VT [1] (*often pass*) [*earthquake etc*] sacudir; (*fig*) [*war, riot*] convulsionar, conmocionar
[2] (*fig*) **to be ~d with laughter** desternillarse de risa; **to be ~d with anger** estar ciego de ira; **to be ~d with pain** retorcerse de dolor

convulsion [kən'vʌlʃən] N [1] (= *fit, seizure*) convulsión *f*; **to have ~s** tener convulsiones
[2] (*fig*) conmoción *f*; **they were in ~s*** [*of laughter*] se desternillaban de risa

convulsive [kən'vʌlsɪv] ADJ [*movement*] convulsivo; [*laughter*] incontenible

convulsively [kən'vʌlsɪvlɪ] ADV [*shake, jerk*] convulsivamente

cony ['kəʊnɪ] N (*US*) conejo *m*

coo[1] [kuː] VI [*dove*] arrullar; [*baby*] hacer gorgoritos

coo[2]* [kuː] EXCL (*Brit*) ¡toma!, ¡vaya!

co-occur [,kəʊə'kɜːʳ] VI coocurrir

co-occurrence [,kəʊə'kʌrəns] N coocurrencia *f*

cooing ['kuːɪŋ] N arrullos *mpl*

cook [kʊk] Ⓐ N cocinero/a *m/f*; ✦***PROV*** **too many ~s spoil the broth** demasiadas cocineras estropean el caldo
Ⓑ VT [1] (*Culin*) [+ *rice, vegetables*] cocinar, guisar; (= *boil*) cocer; (= *grill*) asar (a la parrilla); (= *fry*) freír; **to ~ a meal** preparar *or* hacer una comida; ✦***IDIOM*** **to ~ sb's goose*** hacer la pascua a algn
[2] (*) (= *falsify*) [+ *accounts*] falsificar; ✦***IDIOM*** **to ~ the books** amañar las cuentas
Ⓒ VI [1] [*food*] cocinarse, cocer; **what's ~ing?*** (*fig*) ¿qué se guisa?, ¿qué pasa?
[2] [*person*] cocinar, guisar (*esp LAm*); **can you ~?** ¿sabes cocinar?

►**cook up** VT + ADV [1] (*Culin*) preparar
[2] (*) [+ *excuse, story*] inventar; [+ *plan*] tramar

cookbook ['kʊkbʊk] N = **cookery book**

cooked [kʊkt] Ⓐ ADJ [*breakfast*] caliente
Ⓑ CPD ► **cooked meats** NPL fiambres *fpl*

cooker ['kʊkəʳ] N [1] (*Brit*) (= *stove*) cocina *f*, horno *m* (*esp LAm*); (*US*) olla *f* para cocinar; **gas/electric ~** cocina *f* de gas/eléctrica
[2] (= *cooking apple*) manzana *f* para cocer

cookery ['kʊkərɪ] Ⓐ N cocina *f*; **French ~** la cocina francesa; **I'm no good at ~** yo no sé nada de cocina
Ⓑ CPD ► **cookery book** N (*Brit*) libro *m* de cocina ► **cookery course** N curso *m* de cocina

cookhouse ['kʊkhaʊs] N cocina *f*; (*Mil*) cocina *f* móvil de campaña

cookie ['kʊkɪ] N [1] (*esp US*) (= *biscuit*) galleta *f*; **that's the way the ~ crumbles*** así es la vida
[2] (*) (= *person*) tipo/a* *m/f*, tío/a* *m/f*; **she's a smart ~** es una chica lista; **a tough ~** un tío duro*
[3] (*Internet*) cookie *f*

cooking ['kʊkɪŋ] Ⓐ N [1] (= *art*) cocina *f*; **typical Galician ~** la típica cocina gallega; **her ~ is a delight** sus platos son una delicia
[2] (= *process*) cocción *f*
Ⓑ CPD [*utensils, salt*] de cocina; [*chocolate*] de hacer ► **cooking apple** N manzana *f* para cocer ► **cooking foil** N papel *m* de aluminio ► **cooking salt** N sal *f* de cocina ► **cooking time** N tiempo *m* de cocción

cookout ['kʊkaʊt] N (*US*) barbacoa *f*, comida *f* hecha al aire libre

cookware ['kʊkweəʳ] N batería *f* de cocina

cool [kuːl] Ⓐ ADJ (*compar* **cooler**; *superl* **coolest**) [1] (= *not hot*) [*air, room, skin, drink*] fresco; **it was a ~ day** el día estaba fresco; **it's getting** *or* **turning ~er** está empezando a refrescar; **it's nice and ~ in here** aquí dentro hace fresquito *or* se está fresquito; **"keep in a cool place"** "guardar en un lugar fresco"; **it helps you to keep ~** [*food, drink*] refresca; [*clothing, fan*] ayuda a mantenerse fresco
[2] (= *light, comfortable*) [*dress, fabric*] fresco
[3] (= *pale*) [*colour, shade, blue*] fresco
[4] (= *calm*) [*person, manner, action, tone*] sereno; **his ~ handling of the situation** el aplomo con el que *or* la sangre fría con la que manejó la situación; **~, calm and collected** tranquilo y con dominio de sí mismo; **to keep** *or* **stay ~** no perder la calma; **keep ~!** ¡tranquilo!; **to keep a ~ head** no perder la calma; **to play it ~*** tomárselo con calma, hacer como si nada
[5] (*pej*) (= *audacious*) [*behaviour*] fresco, descarado; **did you see the ~ way he asked me to do it?** ¿viste la frescura con la que me pidió que lo hiciese?; **as ~ as you please** más fresco que una lechuga*; **he's a ~ customer*** es un fresco, es un caradura; **we paid a ~ £200,000 for that house*** pagamos la friolera de 200.000 libras por esa casa; ✦***IDIOM*** **to be as ~ as a cucumber*** estar más fresco que una lechuga*
[6] (= *distant, unenthusiastic*) [*person, response*] frío; **a ~ welcome** *or* **reception** un recibimiento frío; **relations were ~ but polite** la relación era fría *or* distante pero correcta; **to be ~ towards** *or* **with sb** mostrarse frío con algn, tratar a algn con frialdad
[7] (‡) (= *trendy, stylish*) [*object, person*] guay (*Sp*‡); **hey, (that's really) ~!** ¡ala, qué guay!‡, ¡ala, cómo mola! (*Sp*‡); **it's ~ to say you like computers** queda muy bien decir que te gustan los ordenadores
[8] (‡) (= *acceptable*) **don't worry, it's ~** tranqui, no pasa nada*; **he's ~** es un tipo legal (*Sp**)
Ⓑ N [1] (= *low temperature*) frescor *m*; **in the ~ of the evening** en el frescor de la tarde; **to keep sth in the ~** guardar algo en un lugar fresco
[2] (= *calm*) **to keep/lose one's ~*** no perder/perder la calma
Ⓒ VT [1] [+ *brow, room*] refrescar; [+ *engine*] refrigerar; [+ *hot food or drink*] dejar enfriar; [+ *wine, soft drink*] poner a enfriar; ✦***IDIOM*** **to ~ one's heels** esperar impaciente
[2] (= *dampen*) [+ *emotions, feelings*] enfriar; **~ it!*** ¡tranquilo!
Ⓓ VI [1] (*also* **to ~ down**) [*air, liquid*] enfriarse; [*weather*] refrescar; **the air ~s in the evenings here** aquí refresca al atardecer; **the room had ~ed considerably** la habitación estaba mucho más fresca, ahora hacía bastante más fresco en la habitación
[2] (= *abate*) [*feeling, emotion*] enfriarse; **her passion for Richard had begun to ~** su pasión por Richard había empezado a enfriarse; **by Monday tempers had ~ed** el lunes los ánimos se habían calmado
Ⓔ CPD ► **cool box** N nevera *f* portátil

►**cool down** Ⓐ VT + ADV [1] (= *make colder*) enfriar
[2] (= *make calmer*) **to ~ sb down** calmar a algn
Ⓑ VI + ADV [1] (= *become colder*) [*object*] enfriarse; [*person*] refrescarse, tener menos calor

➤ LANGUAGE IN USE: **convince** 6.2, 15.1, 16.1, 26.2

2 (= *become calmer*) [*person, situation*] calmarse; **~ down!** ¡cálmese!

►**cool off** VI + ADV (= *become less angry*) calmarse; (= *lose enthusiasm*) perder (el) interés, enfriarse; (= *become less affectionate*) distanciarse, enfriarse

coolant ['kuːlənt] N (*Tech*) (líquido *m*) refrigerante *m*

cooler ['kuːlə^r] N 1 (= *cool box*) nevera *f* portátil

2 (*) (= *prison*) chirona* *f*, trena* *f*

cool-headed ['kuːl,hedɪd] ADJ sereno, imperturbable

coolie ['kuːlɪ] N cooli *m*, culi *m*

cooling ['kuːlɪŋ] Ⓐ ADJ refrescante

Ⓑ CPD ► **cooling tower** N (*at power station*) torre *f* de refrigeración ► **cooling fan** N ventilador *m*

cooling-off period [,kuːlɪŋ'ɒf,pɪərɪəd] N (*Ind*) plazo *m* de negociación; (*Comm*) plazo *m* de prueba

coolly ['kuːlɪ] ADV 1 (= *calmly*) [*react, behave*] con serenidad, con sangre fría; **he reacted ~ in the midst of the crisis** mostró mucha sangre fría en medio de la crisis; **he very ~ put out his hand and picked up the snake** con una serenidad *or* con una sangre fría increíble alargó la mano y cogió la serpiente

2 (= *unemotionally*) [*say, reply*] con tranquilidad, con sangre fría; **she ~ denied everything** negó todo con una sangre fría increíble

3 (*pej*) (= *audaciously*) descaradamente, con mucha frescura

4 (= *unenthusiastically*) fríamente, con frialdad

coolness ['kuːlnɪs] N 1 (= *coldness*) [*of water, air, weather*] frescor *m*

2 (= *calmness*) tranquilidad *f*, serenidad *f*; (*in battle, crisis*) sangre *f* fría

3 (*pej*) (= *audacity*) frescura *f*, descaro *m*

4 (= *lack of enthusiasm*) [*of welcome, person*] frialdad *f*; **her ~ towards him** su frialdad con él

coomb [kuːm] N garganta *f*, desfiladero *m*

coon [kuːn] N 1 (*Zool*) = **raccoon**

2 (** *offensive*) (= *Negro*) negro/a *m/f* (*pej*)

coop [kuːp] N gallinero *m*

►**coop up** VT + ADV encerrar

co-op* ['kəʊ,ɒp] N 1 (= *shop*) = **cooperative**

2 (*US*) = **cooperative apartment**

3 (*US Univ*) = **cooperative**

cooper ['kuːpə^r] N tonelero/a *m/f*

cooperage ['kuːpərɪdʒ] N tonelería *f*

cooperate [kəʊ'ɒpəreɪt] VI cooperar, colaborar; **to ~ with sb (in sth/to do sth)** cooperar con algn (en algo/para hacer algo)

cooperation [kəʊ,ɒpə'reɪʃən] N cooperación *f*, colaboración *f*

cooperative [kəʊ'ɒpərətɪv] Ⓐ ADJ 1 [*attitude*] colaborador, cooperador; [*person*] servicial, dispuesto a ayudar

2 [*farm etc*] cooperativo

Ⓑ N cooperativa *f*

Ⓒ CPD ► **cooperative society** N (*Brit*) cooperativa *f*

cooperatively [kəʊ'ɒpərətɪvlɪ] ADV (= *jointly*) en cooperación, en colaboración, conjuntamente; (= *obligingly*) servicialmente

co-opt [kəʊ'ɒpt] VT **to ~ sb (onto sth)** nombrar (como miembro) a algn (para algo)

co-option [kəʊ'ɒpʃən] N cooptación *f*

coordinate Ⓐ [kəʊ'ɔːdnɪt] N 1 (*usu pl*) (*on map*) coordenada *f*

2 **coordinates** (= *clothes*) coordinados *mpl*

Ⓑ [kəʊ'ɔːdɪneɪt] VT [+ *movements, work*] coordinar; [+ *efforts*] aunar

coordinating [kəʊ'ɔːdɪneɪtɪŋ] ADJ [*committee, body, centre*] coordinador; [*fabric, wallpaper, skirt, shoes*] haciendo juego, a juego (*Sp*)

coordination [kəʊ,ɔːdɪ'neɪʃən] N coordinación *f*

coordinator [kəʊ'ɔːdɪneɪtə^r] N coordinador(a) *m/f*

coot [kuːt] N 1 (*Orn*) focha *f* (común), fúlica *f*

2 (*) (= *fool*) bobo/a *m/f*

co-owner [,kəʊ'əʊnə^r] N copropietario/a *m/f*

co-ownership [,kəʊ'əʊnəʃɪp] N copropiedad *f*

cop* [kɒp] Ⓐ N 1 (= *policeman*) poli *m* (*Sp**), cana *m* (*S. Cone**); **the ~s** la pasma (*Sp**), la cana (*S. Cone**); **~s and robbers** (= *game*) policías y ladrones

2 (*Brit*) **it's not much ~** no es gran cosa; **it's a fair ~!** ¡está bien!

Ⓑ VT 1 (*Brit*) (= *catch*) [+ *person*] pescar, pillar; [+ *beating, fine*] ganarse; **he ~ped six months** se cargó seis meses; **you'll ~ it!** ¡te la vas a ganar!; **I ~ped it from the headmaster** el director me puso como un trapo; **~ this!** ¡hay que ver esto!; **~ hold of this** coge (*Sp*) *or* toma esto

2 (*US Jur*) **to ~ a plea** *declararse culpable de un delito menor para obtener una sentencia más leve*

3 (*US*) [+ *drugs*] comprar

Ⓒ CPD ► **cop shop*** N (*Brit*) comisaría *f*

►**cop off with*** VI + PREP (*Brit*) liarse con*, ligar con*, enrollarse con (*Sp**)

►**cop out*** VI + ADV escabullirse, rajarse

co-partner ['kəʊ'pɑːtnə^r] N consocio *mf*, copartícipe *mf*

co-partnership ['kəʊ'pɑːtnəʃɪp] N asociación *f*, cogestión *f*, coparticipación *f*

cope[1] [kəʊp] VI 1 arreglárselas; **he's coping pretty well** se las está arreglando bastante bien; **we shall be able to ~ better next year** podremos arreglarnos mejor el año que viene; **can you ~?** ¿tú puedes con esto?; **how are you coping?** ¿cómo lo llevas?*; **he can't ~ any more** ya no puede más

2 **to ~ with** [+ *task, person*] poder con; [+ *situation*] enfrentarse con; [+ *difficulties, problems*] (= *tackle*) hacer frente a, abordar; (= *solve*) solucionar

cope[2] [kəʊp] N (*Rel*) capa *f* pluvial

Copenhagen [,kəʊpn'heɪgən] N Copenhague *m*

Copernicus [kə'pɜːnɪkəs] N Copérnico

copestone ['kəʊpstəʊn] N (piedra *f* de) albardilla *f*

copier ['kɒpɪə^r] N (= *photocopier*) fotocopiadora *f*

co-pilot ['kəʊ'paɪlət] N copiloto *mf*

coping ['kəʊpɪŋ] Ⓐ N (*Constr*) albardilla *f*, mojinete *m*

Ⓑ CPD ► **coping stone** N = **copestone**

copious ['kəʊpɪəs] ADJ copioso, abundante

copiously ['kəʊpɪəslɪ] ADV copiosamente, en abundancia

cop-out* ['kɒpaʊt] N evasión *f* de responsabilidad

copper ['kɒpə^r] Ⓐ N 1 (= *material*) cobre *m*

2 (= *utensil*) caldera *f* de lavar

3 (*Brit**) (= *coin*) perra *f* (chica), centavo *m* (*LAm*); (= *penny*) penique *m*; **it costs a few ~s** vale unos peniques

4 (*Brit*) *see* **cop A1**

Ⓑ ADJ 1 (= *made of copper*) de cobre

2 (= *colour*) cobrizo

Ⓒ CPD ► **copper beech** N haya *f* roja *or* de sangre ► **copper sulphate** N sulfato *m* de cobre

copper-bottomed [,kɒpə'bɒtəmd] ADJ con fondo de cobre; (*fig*) totalmente fiable, de máxima seguridad

copper-coloured, **copper-colored** (*US*) ['kɒpə,kʌləd] ADJ cobrizo

copperhead ['kɒpəhed] N víbora *f* cobriza

copperplate ['kɒpəpleɪt] N (*also* **~ writing**) letra *f* caligrafiada, caligrafía *f*

coppersmith ['kɒpəsmɪθ] N cobrero/a *m/f*

coppery ['kɒpərɪ] ADJ cobreño; [*colour*] cobrizo

coppice ['kɒpɪs] N soto *m*, bosquecillo *m*

copra ['kɒprə] N copra *f*

co-presidency [kəʊ'prezɪdənsɪ] N copresidencia *f*

co-president [kəʊ'prezɪdənt] N copresidente/a *m/f*

co-processor [,kəʊ'prəʊsesə^r] N coprocesador *m*; **graphics ~** coprocesador *m* de gráficos

co-produce [,kəʊprə'djuːs] VT coproducir

co-production [,kəʊprə'dʌkʃən] N coproducción *f*

copse [kɒps] N soto *m*, bosquecillo *m*

Copt [kɒpt] N copto/a *m/f*

'copter*, **copter*** ['kɒptə^r] N ABBR (= **helicopter**) helicóptero *m*

Coptic ['kɒptɪk] Ⓐ ADJ copto

Ⓑ CPD ► **the Coptic Church** N la Iglesia Copta

copula ['kɒpjʊlə] N (*pl* **copulas** *or* **copulae** ['kɒpjʊliː]) cópula *f*

copulate ['kɒpjʊleɪt] VI copular

copulation [,kɒpjʊ'leɪʃən] N cópula *f*

copulative ['kɒpjʊlətɪv] ADJ copulativo

copy ['kɒpɪ] Ⓐ N 1 (*gen*) (= *duplicate*) copia *f*; [*of photograph*] copia *f*; [*of painting*] copia *f*, imitación *f*; (= *carbon copy*) copia *f* (en papel carbón); **rough ~** borrador *m*; **fair ~** copia en limpio; **to make a ~ of** hacer *or* sacar una copia de

2 [*of book, newspaper*] ejemplar *m*; [*of magazine*] número *m*

3 (= *no pl*) (*Press*) (= *written material*) original *m*, manuscrito *m*; **there's plenty of ~ here** tenemos aquí un material abundante; **a murder is always good ~** un asesinato es siempre un buen tema; **to make good ~** ser una noticia de interés

Ⓑ VT 1 (= *imitate*) copiar, imitar; (*Scol*) (= *cheat*) copiar

2 (= *make copy of*) (*gen*) sacar una copia de; (*in writing, Comput*) copiar; (*with carbon*) sacar una copia/copias al carbón; (= *photocopy*) fotocopiar; **to ~ from** copiar de

3 (= *send a copy to*) enviar una copia (**to** a)

4 (*Rad, Telec*) recibir

Ⓒ CPD ► **copy boy** N (*Press*) chico *m* de los recados de la redacción ► **copy editor** N editor(a) *m/f*, corrector(a) *m/f* de manuscritos ► **copy machine** N fotocopiadora *f* ► **copy typist** N mecanógrafo/a *m/f*

►**copy down** VT + ADV anotar, tomar nota de

►**copy out** VT + ADV copiar

copybook ['kɒpɪbʊk] Ⓐ N cuaderno *m* de escritura; ✦*IDIOM* **to blot one's ~** manchar su reputación

Ⓑ CPD perfecto; **the pilot made a ~ landing** el piloto hizo un aterrizaje de libro

copycat* ['kɒpɪkæt] Ⓐ N imitador(a) *m/f*

Ⓑ CPD ► **copycat crime** N crimen *m* que trata de emular a otros

copy-edit ['kɒpɪ'edɪt] VT editar y corregir

copying ['kɒpɪɪŋ] Ⓐ N [1] (= *imitation*) **children learn by ~** los niños aprenden por imitación
[2] (*Scol*) (= *cheating*) **~ will be severely punished** el que sea descubierto copiando recibirá un severo castigo
Ⓑ CPD ► **copying ink** N (*for machine use*) tinta *f* de copiar ► **copying machine** N copiadora *f*

copyist ['kɒpɪɪst] N copista *mf*

copyreader ['kɒpɪˌriːdəʳ] N corrector(a) *m/f*

copyright ['kɒpɪraɪt] Ⓐ ADJ protegido por los derechos de(l) autor
Ⓑ N derechos *mpl* de autor, propriedad *f* literaria; **the book is still in ~** siguen vigentes los derechos del autor de este libro; **it will be out of ~ in 2020** los derechos de(l) autor terminarán en 2020; **"~ reserved"** "es propiedad", "copyright"
Ⓒ VT registrar como propiedad literaria

copywriter ['kɒpɪˌraɪtəʳ] N escritor(a) *m/f* de material publicitario

coquetry ['kɒkɪtrɪ] N coquetería *f*

coquette [kə'ket] N coqueta *f*

coquettish [kə'ketɪʃ] ADJ coqueta

coquettishly [kə'ketɪʃlɪ] ADV coquetamente, con coquetería

cor‡ [kɔːʳ] EXCL (*Brit*) ¡caramba!; **~ blimey!** ¡Dios mío!*

coracle ['kɒrəkl] N barquilla *f* de cuero

coral ['kɒrəl] Ⓐ N coral *m*
Ⓑ CPD de coral, coralino ► **coral island** N isla *f* coralina ► **coral necklace** N collar *m* de coral ► **coral reef** N arrecife *m* de coral ► **Coral Sea** N Mar *m* del Coral

cor anglais ['kɔːr'ɔ̃ŋgleɪ] N (*pl* **cors anglais**) corno *m* inglés

corbel ['kɔːbəl] N ménsula *f*, repisa *f*

cord [kɔːd] Ⓐ N [1] (= *thick string*) cuerda *f*; (*for pyjamas, curtains, of window*) cordón *m*; (*Elec*) cable *m*
[2] (*also* **umbilical ~**) cordón *m* umbilical; **✦IDIOM to cut** *or* **sever the ~** soltar amarras; *see also* **spinal, vocal**
[3] (= *material*) pana *f*; **cords** (= *trousers*) pantalones *mpl* de pana
Ⓑ VT atar con cuerdas

cordage ['kɔːdɪdʒ] N cordaje *m*, cordería *f*

cordial ['kɔːdɪəl] Ⓐ ADJ cordial, afectuoso
Ⓑ N (*Brit*) (= *drink*) cordial *m*; (= *liqueur*) licor *m*

cordiality [ˌkɔːdɪ'ælɪtɪ] N cordialidad *f*

cordially ['kɔːdɪəlɪ] ADV cordialmente, afectuosamente; **I ~ detest him** le odio cordialmente

cordite ['kɔːdaɪt] N cordita *f*

cordless ['kɔːdlɪs] Ⓐ ADJ [*iron, kettle, tool*] sin cable
Ⓑ CPD ► **cordless telephone** N teléfono *m* inalámbrico *or* sin hilos

cordon ['kɔːdn] Ⓐ N cordón *m*
Ⓑ VT (*also* **to ~ off**) acordonar
Ⓒ CPD ► **cordon sanitaire** N (*Pol*) cordón *m* sanitario

cordon bleu [ˌkɔːdɔ̃n'blɜː] Ⓐ N cordón *m* azul; (*Culin*) cocinero/a *m/f* de primera clase
Ⓑ CPD de primera clase

Cordova ['kɔːdəvə] N Córdoba *f*

Cordovan ['kɔːdəvən] Ⓐ ADJ cordobés
Ⓑ N cordobés/esa *m/f*; (= *leather*) cordobán *m*

corduroy ['kɔːdərɔɪ] Ⓐ N pana *f*; **corduroys** pantalones *mpl* de pana
Ⓑ CPD ► **corduroy road** N (*US*) camino *m* de troncos

CORE [kɔːʳ] N ABBR (*US*) = **Congress of Racial Equality**

core [kɔːʳ] Ⓐ N [1] [*of fruit*] corazón *m*; [*of earth*] centro *m*, núcleo *m*; [*of cable, nuclear reactor*] núcleo *m*
[2] (*fig*) [*of problem etc*] esencia *f*, meollo *m*; [*of group etc*] centro *m*; **English to the ~** inglés hasta los tuétanos; **rotten to the ~** corrompido hasta la médula; **shocked to the ~** profundamente afectado; **a hard ~ of resistance** un núcleo *or* foco arraigado de resistencia; **the hard ~ of unemployment** los parados que tienen pocas posibilidades de salir de esa situación
Ⓑ VT [+ *fruit*] deshuesar
Ⓒ CPD ► **core business** N actividad *f* principal ► **core curriculum** N (*Scol*) asignaturas *fpl* comunes ► **core memory** N (*Comput*) memoria *f* de núcleos ► **core subject** N (*Scol, Univ*) asignatura *f* común ► **core time** N período *m* nuclear

co-religionist ['kəʊrɪ'lɪdʒənɪst] N correligionario/a *m/f*

corer ['kɔːrəʳ] N (*Culin*) despepitadora *f*

co-respondent ['kəʊrɪs'pɒndənt] N (*Jur*) codemandado/a *m/f*

Corfu [kɔː'fuː] N Corfú *m*

corgi ['kɔːgɪ] N perro/a *m/f* galés/esa

coriander [ˌkɒrɪ'ændəʳ] N culantro *m*, cilantro *m*

Corinth ['kɒrɪnθ] N Corinto *m*

Corinthian [kə'rɪnθɪən] ADJ corintio

cork [kɔːk] Ⓐ N [1] (= *substance*) corcho *m*
[2] (= *stopper*) corcho *m*, tapón *m*
Ⓑ VT [+ *bottle*] (*also* **~ up**) tapar con corcho, taponar
Ⓒ CPD de corcho ► **cork oak, cork tree** N alcornoque *m*

corkage ['kɔːkɪdʒ] N *precio que se cobra en un restaurante por abrir una botella traida de fuera*

corked [kɔːkt] ADJ [*wine*] con sabor a corcho

corker*† ['kɔːkəʳ] N [1] (= *lie*) bola* *f*; (= *story*) historia *f* absurda
[2] (*Sport*) (= *shot, stroke*) golpe *m* de primera; (= *good player*) crac* *m*; (= *attractive girl*) tía *f* buena*; **that's a ~!** ¡es cutre!*

corkscrew ['kɔːkskruː] Ⓐ N sacacorchos *m inv*
Ⓑ ADJ en espiral
Ⓒ VI subir en espiral

corm [kɔːm] N (*Bot*) bulbo *m*

cormorant ['kɔːmərənt] N cormorán *m* (grande)

corn¹ [kɔːn] Ⓐ N [1] (*Brit*) (= *wheat*) trigo *m*; (*gen term*) cereales *mpl*; (*US*) (= *maize*) maíz *m*; (= *individual grains*) granos *mpl*
[2] (*) (= *sentimentality*) sentimentalismo *m*, sensiblería *f*
Ⓑ CPD ► **corn bread** N (*US*) pan *m* de maíz ► **corn on the cob** N mazorca *f* de maíz, choclo *m* (*Andes, S. Cone*), elote *m* (*Mex*) ► **corn exchange** N bolsa *f* de granos ► **corn meal** N (*US*) harina *f* de maíz ► **corn oil** N aceite *m* de maíz ► **corn poppy** N amapola *f*

corn² [kɔːn] Ⓐ N (*Med*) callo *m*; **✦IDIOM to tread on sb's ~s** (*Brit*) herir las sensibilidades de algn
Ⓑ CPD ► **corn plaster** N emplasto *m or* parche *m* para callos

Corn ABBR (*Brit*) = **Cornwall**

cornball* ['kɔːnbɔːl] N (*US*) paleto/a‡ *m/f*

corncob ['kɔːnkɒb] N (*esp US*) mazorca *f* de maíz

corncrake ['kɔːnkreɪk] N guión *m* de codornices

cornea ['kɔːnɪə] N (*pl* **corneas** *or* **corneae** ['kɔːnɪiː]) córnea *f*

corneal ['kɔːnɪəl] ADJ corneal

corned beef [ˌkɔːnd'biːf] N carne *f* de vaca en conserva

cornelian [kɔː'niːlɪən] N cornalina *f*

corner ['kɔːnəʳ] Ⓐ N [1] (= *angle*) [*of object*] (*outer*) ángulo *m*, esquina *f*; (*inner*) rincón *m*; [*of mouth*] comisura *f*; [*of eye*] rabillo *m*; (= *bend in road*) curva *f*, recodo *m*; (*where two roads meet*) esquina *f*; **in the ~ of the room** en un rincón de la habitación; **the ~ of a table/page** la esquina de una mesa/página; **it's just around the ~** está a la vuelta de la esquina; **prosperity is just around the ~** la prosperidad está a la vuelta de la esquina; **to cut a ~** (*Aut*) tomar una curva muy cerrada; **out of the ~ of one's eye** con el rabillo del ojo; **to go round the ~** doblar la esquina; **to turn the ~** doblar la esquina; (*fig*) salir del apuro; **a two-~ed fight** una pelea entre dos; **✦IDIOMS to be in a (tight) ~** estar en un aprieto; **to cut ~s** atajar; (= *save money, effort etc*) ahorrar dinero/trabajo *etc*; **to drive sb into a ~** poner a algn entre la espada y la pared, acorralar a algn; **to paint o.s. into a ~** verse acorralado
[2] (*fig*) (= *cranny, place*) **a picturesque ~ of Soria** un rincón pintoresco de Soria; **in every ~** por todos los rincones; **every ~ of Europe** todos los rincones de Europa; **the four ~s of the world** las cinco partes del mundo; **in odd ~s** en cualquier rincón
[3] (*Ftbl*) (*also* **~ kick**) córner *m*, saque *m* de esquina
[4] (*Comm*) monopolio *m*; **he made a ~ in peanuts** se hizo con el monopolio de los cacahuetes, acaparó el mercado de los cacahuetes
Ⓑ VT [1] [+ *animal, fugitive*] acorralar, arrinconar; (*fig*) [+ *person*] (= *catch to speak to*) abordar, detener
[2] (*Comm*) [+ *market*] acaparar
Ⓒ VI (*Aut*) tomar las curvas
Ⓓ CPD ► **corner cupboard** N rinconera *f*, esquinera *f* ► **corner flag** N (*Ftbl*) banderola *f* de esquina ► **corner house** N casa *f* que hace esquina ► **corner kick** N (*Ftbl*) córner *m*, saque *m* de esquina ► **corner seat** N asiento *m* del rincón, rinconera *f* ► **corner shop, corner store** (*US*) N tienda *f* de la esquina, tienda *f* pequeña del barrio ► **corner table** N mesa *f* rinconera

cornering ['kɔːnərɪŋ] N **the new suspension allows much safer ~** (*Aut*) la nueva suspensión proporciona un mayor agarre en las curvas

cornerstone ['kɔːnəstəʊn] N (*lit, fig*) piedra *f* angular

cornet ['kɔːnɪt] N [1] (*Mus*) corneta *f*
[2] (*Brit*) (= *ice cream*) cucurucho *m*

cornfield ['kɔːnfiːld] N [*of wheat*] trigal *m*, campo *m* de trigo; (*US*) [*of maize*] maizal *m*, milpa *f*

cornflakes ['kɔːnfleɪks] NPL copos *mpl* de maíz, cornflakes *mpl*; (*loosely*) cereales *mpl*

cornflour ['kɔːnflaʊəʳ] N (*Brit*) harina *f* de maíz, maicena *f*

cornflower ['kɔːnflaʊəʳ] Ⓐ N aciano *m*
Ⓑ ADJ (*also* **~ blue**) azul aciano *inv*

cornice ['kɔːnɪs] N (*Archit*) cornisa *f*

corniche ['kɔːniːʃ, kɔː'niːʃ] N (*also* **~ road**) corniche *f*

Cornish ['kɔːnɪʃ] Ⓐ ADJ de Cornualles
Ⓑ N (*Ling*) córnico *m*

Ⓒ CPD ► **Cornish pasty** N empanada *f* de Cornualles (*con cebolla, patata y carne*)

cornstarch ['kɔːnstɑːtʃ] N (*US*) = **cornflour**

cornucopia [ˌkɔːnjʊ'kəʊpɪə] N cuerno *m* de la abundancia

Cornwall ['kɔːnwəl] N Cornualles *m*

corny* ['kɔːnɪ] ADJ (*compar* **cornier**, *superl* **corniest**) [*joke, story*] trillado, muy visto; [*film, play*] sensiblero, sentimental

corolla [kə'rɒlə] N corola *f*

corollary [kə'rɒlərɪ] N corolario *m*

corona [kə'rəʊnə] N (*pl* **coronas** *or* **coronae** [kə'rəʊniː]) (*Anat, Astron*) corona *f*; (*Elec*) descarga *f* de corona; (*Archit*) corona *f*, alero *m*

coronary ['kɒrənərɪ] Ⓐ ADJ coronario
Ⓑ N (*also* ~ **thrombosis**) infarto *m*, trombosis *f* coronaria

coronation [ˌkɒrə'neɪʃən] N coronación *f*

coroner ['kɒrənəʳ] N juez *mf* de instrucción

coronet ['kɒrənɪt] N corona *f* (de marqués *etc*); (= *diadem*) diadema *f*

Corp ABBR [1] (*Comm, Fin*) (= **Corporation**) S.A.
[2] (*Pol*) = **Corporation**
[3] (*Mil*) = **Corporal**

corpora ['kɔːpərə] NPL *of* **corpus**

corporal ['kɔːpərəl] Ⓐ ADJ corporal
Ⓑ N (*Mil*) cabo *m*
Ⓒ CPD ► **corporal punishment** N castigo *m* corporal

corporate ['kɔːpərɪt] Ⓐ ADJ (= *joint*) [*ownership, responsibility*] corporativo, colectivo; [*action, effort*] combinado; (= *of company, firm*) [*image, planning, identity, growth*] corporativo
Ⓑ CPD ► **corporate body** N corporación *f* ► **corporate car** N (*US*) coche *m* de la empresa ► **corporate name** N nombre *m* social ► **corporate strategy** N estrategia *f* de la empresa

corporately ['kɔːpərɪtlɪ] ADV corporativamente, como corporación

corporation [ˌkɔːpə'reɪʃən] Ⓐ N [1] (*Comm*) corporación *f*; (*US*) (= *limited company*) sociedad *f* anónima
[2] [*of city*] ayuntamiento *m*
[3] (*Brit**) (= *paunch*) panza* *f*
Ⓑ CPD corporativo ► **corporation tax** N (*Brit*) impuesto *m* sobre sociedades

corporatism ['kɔːpərətɪzəm] N corporacionismo *m*

corporatist ['kɔːpərətɪst] ADJ [*theory, tendencies*] corporativista

corporeal [kɔː'pɔːrɪəl] ADJ corpóreo

corps [kɔːʳ] Ⓐ N (*pl* **corps** [kɔːz]) (*Mil*) cuerpo *m* (de ejército); *see also* **diplomatic**, **press D**
Ⓑ CPD ► **corps de ballet** N cuerpo *m* de baile

corpse [kɔːps] N cadáver *m*

corpulence ['kɔːpjʊləns] N corpulencia *f*

corpulent ['kɔːpjʊlənt] ADJ corpulento

corpus ['kɔːpəs] Ⓐ N (*pl* **corpuses** *or* **corpora**) cuerpo *m*
Ⓑ CPD ► **corpus delicti** N cuerpo *m* del delito ► **Corpus Christi** N Corpus *m*

corpuscle ['kɔːpʌsl] N [*of blood*] glóbulo *m*, corpúsculo *m*

corral [kə'rɑːl] (*US*) Ⓐ N corral *m*
Ⓑ VT acorralar

correct [kə'rekt] Ⓐ ADJ [1] (= *accurate*) correcto; **(that's) ~!** ¡correcto!, ¡exacto!; **is this spelling ~?** ¿está bien escrito esto?; **your suspicions are ~** está en lo cierto con sus sospechas; **"correct fare only"** (*in buses etc*) "importe exacto"; **to be ~** [*person*] tener razón, estar en lo cierto; **am I ~ in saying that ...?** ¿me equivoco al decir que ...?, ¿estoy en lo cierto al decir que ...?; **he was normally ~ in his calculations** normalmente sus cálculos eran exactos; **he was ~ to blame the government** estuvo en lo cierto cuando culpó al gobierno; **the president was ~ to reject the offer** el presidente hizo bien al rechazar la oferta; **it is ~ to say that ...** es acertado decir que ...; **have you got the ~ time?** ¿tiene la hora exacta?
[2] (= *appropriate*) adecuado; **the ~ weight for your height and build** el peso adecuado dadas su altura y constitución; **in the ~ place** en su sitio
[3] (= *proper*) [*person, behaviour, manners*] correcto; [*dress*] apropiado; **it's the ~ thing to do** es lo correcto
Ⓑ VT [1] (= *put right*) [+ *mistake, habit, exam, eyesight*] corregir; [+ *person*] corregir, rectificar; [+ *imbalance*] eliminar; [+ *clock*] poner en hora; **"I don't mean tomorrow," she ~ed herself** —no, no mañana —se corrigió; **~ me if I'm wrong** dime si tengo razón o no; **~ me if I'm wrong, but ...** a lo mejor me equivoco, pero ...; **I stand ~ed** reconozco mi error
[2] (*frm*) (= *punish*) castigar; (= *admonish*) reprender

correcting fluid [kəˌrektɪŋ'fluːɪd] N corrector *m*

correction [kə'rekʃən] N [1] (*gen*) corrección *f*, rectificación *f*; (*on page*) tachadura *f*; **I am open to ~ but ...** corregidme si me equivoco, pero ...
[2] (*esp US*) (= *punishment*) corrección *f*; **a house of ~**† un correccional, un reformatorio

correctional [kə'rekʃənəl] (*US*) Ⓐ ADJ penitenciario
Ⓑ CPD ► **correctional facility** N centro *m* penitenciario ► **correctional officer** N funcionario/a *m/f* de prisiones

corrective [kə'rektɪv] Ⓐ ADJ correctivo
Ⓑ N correctivo *m*
Ⓒ CPD ► **corrective glasses** NPL gafas *fpl* correctoras ► **corrective surgery** N cirugía *f* correctiva

correctly [kə'rektlɪ] ADV [1] (= *accurately, in right way*) [*answer, pronounce, predict*] correctamente; **if I remember ~** si mal no recuerdo; **if I understand you ~** si le he entendido bien
[2] (= *respectably, decently*) [*behave, proceed*] correctamente
[3] (= *appropriately*) **she refused, quite ~, to give in to his demands** se negó, con toda la razón, a ceder a sus exigencias; **when an accident happens, quite ~, questions are asked** como debe ser, cuando ocurre un accidente se hacen indagaciones

correctness [kə'rektnɪs] N [1] (= *accuracy*) [*of answer, amount, term, calculation*] exactitud *f*
[2] (= *appropriateness*) [*of method, approach*] lo apropiado, lo adecuado
[3] (= *decency*) [*of person, behaviour, dress*] corrección *f*

correlate ['kɒrɪleɪt] Ⓐ VT establecer una correlación entre, correlacionar; **to ~ sth with sth** poner algo en correlación con algo
Ⓑ VI tener correlación; **to ~ with** estar en correlación con

correlation [ˌkɒrɪ'leɪʃən] N correlación *f*

correlative [kɒ'relətɪv] Ⓐ ADJ correlativo
Ⓑ N correlativo *m*

correspond [ˌkɒrɪs'pɒnd] VI [1] (= *be in accordance*) corresponder (**with** con); (= *be equivalent*) equivaler (**to** a)
[2] (*by letter*) escribirse, mantener correspondencia (**with** con)

correspondence [ˌkɒrɪs'pɒndəns] Ⓐ N [1] (= *agreement*) correspondencia *f*, conexión *f* (**between** entre)
[2] (= *letter-writing*) correspondencia *f*; **to be in ~ with sb** mantener correspondencia con algn
[3] (= *letters*) correspondencia *f*
Ⓑ CPD ► **correspondence college** N centro *m* de enseñanza por correspondencia ► **correspondence column** N (*Press*) (sección *f* de) cartas *fpl* al director ► **correspondence course** N curso *m* por correspondencia

correspondent [ˌkɒrɪs'pɒndənt] N (*Press*) corresponsal *mf*; (= *letter-writer*) corresponsal *mf*; **I'm a hopeless ~** soy muy mala para escribir cartas

corresponding [ˌkɒrɪs'pɒndɪŋ] ADJ correspondiente

correspondingly [ˌkɒrɪs'pɒndɪŋlɪ] ADV (= *as a result*) por consecuencia; (= *proportionately*) proporcionalmente, en la misma medida

corridor ['kɒrɪdɔːʳ] N pasillo *m*, corredor *m*; **the ~s of power** los pasillos del poder

corroborate [kə'rɒbəreɪt] VT corroborar, confirmar

corroboration [kəˌrɒbə'reɪʃən] N corroboración *f*, confirmación *f*

corroborative [kə'rɒbərətɪv] ADJ corroborativo, confirmatorio

corrode [kə'rəʊd] Ⓐ VT (*lit, fig*) corroer
Ⓑ VI corroerse

corroded [kə'rəʊdɪd] ADJ corroído

corrosion [kə'rəʊʒən] N corrosión *f*

corrosive [kə'rəʊzɪv] ADJ corrosivo; (*fig*) destructivo

corrugated ['kɒrəgeɪtɪd] Ⓐ ADJ ondulado
Ⓑ CPD ► **corrugated cardboard** N cartón *m* ondulado ► **corrugated iron** N hierro *m* ondulado, calamina *f* (*LAm*) ► **corrugated paper** N papel *m* ondulado

corrupt [kə'rʌpt] Ⓐ ADJ [1] (= *depraved*) pervertido, depravado
[2] (= *dishonest*) corrompido, venal
[3] (*Comput*) [*text, file*] corrompido
Ⓑ VT [1] (= *deprave*) pervertir, corromper
[2] (= *bribe*) sobornar
[3] [+ *language*] corromper; (*Comput*) [+ *text, file*] corromper
Ⓒ CPD ► **corrupt practices** NPL (= *dishonesty, bribery*) corrupción *fsing*

corruptible [kə'rʌptəbl] ADJ corruptible

corruption [kə'rʌpʃən] N [1] (= *depravity*) perversión *f*, corrupción *f*
[2] (= *dishonesty*) corrupción *f*, venalidad *f*
[3] [*of language*] corrupción *f*; (*Comput*) [*of text, file*] corrupción *f*

corsage [kɔː'sɑːʒ] N (= *flowers*) ramillete *m*; (= *bodice*) cuerpo *m*

corsair ['kɔːseəʳ] N corsario *m*

cors anglais ['kɔːz'ɔ̃ŋgleɪ] NPL *of* **cor anglais**

corset ['kɔːsɪt] N faja *f*; (*old style*) corsé *m*

corseted ['kɔːsɪtɪd] ADJ encorsetado

Corsica ['kɔːsɪkə] N Córcega *f*

Corsican ['kɔːsɪkən] Ⓐ ADJ corso
Ⓑ N corso/a *m/f*

cortège [kɔː'teɪʒ] N (= *procession*) cortejo *m*, comitiva *f*; (= *retinue*) séquito *m*; (= *funeral cortège*) cortejo *m* fúnebre

cortex ['kɔːteks] N (*pl* **cortices** ['kɔːtɪsiːz]) (*Anat, Bot*) córtex *m*, corteza *f*

corticoids ['kɔːtɪkɔɪdz] NPL, **corticosteroids**

['kɔːtɪkəʊ'stɪərɔɪdz] NPL corticoides *mpl*, corticoesteroides *mpl*

cortisone ['kɔːtɪzəʊn] N cortisona *f*

Corunna [kə'rʌnə] N La Coruña

coruscating ['kɒrəskeɪtɪŋ] ADJ [*humour*] chispeante

corvette [kɔː'vet] N corbeta *f*

cos[1] [kɒs] N (*Brit*) (*also* ~ **lettuce**) lechuga *f* romana

cos[2] [kɒs] ABBR = **cosine**

cos[3]‡, **'cos**‡ [kɒz] CONJ = **because**

COS, **c.o.s.** ABBR (*Comm*) = **cash on shipment**

cosh [kɒʃ] (*Brit*) Ⓐ N porra *f*, cachiporra *f*
Ⓑ VT aporrear

cosignatory ['kəʊ'sɪgnətərɪ] N cosignatario/a *m/f*

cosily ['kəʊzɪlɪ] ADV (= *warmly, comfortably*) cómodamente, agradablemente; [*chat*] íntimamente

cosine ['kəʊsaɪn] N coseno *m*

cosiness ['kəʊzɪnɪs] N [*of room*] lo acogedor; (= *intimacy*) intimidad *f*

COSLA ['kɒzlə] N ABBR (*Scot*) = **Convention of Scottish Local Authorities**

cosmetic [kɒz'metɪk] Ⓐ ADJ cosmético; **the changes are merely ~** (*fig*) los cambios son puramente cosméticos
Ⓑ N (*often pl*) cosmético *m*
Ⓒ CPD ► **cosmetic preparation** N cosmético *m* ► **cosmetic surgery** N cirugía *f* estética

cosmetician [kɒzmɪ'tɪʃən] N cosmetólogo/a *m/f*

cosmic ['kɒzmɪk] Ⓐ ADJ cósmico
Ⓑ CPD ► **cosmic rays** NPL rayos *mpl* cósmicos

cosmogony [kɒz'mɒgənɪ] N cosmogonía *f*

cosmographer [kɒz'mɒgrəfəʳ] N cosmógrafo/a *m/f*

cosmography [kɒz'mɒgrəfɪ] N cosmografía *f*

cosmology [kɒz'mɒlədʒɪ] N cosmología *f*

cosmonaut ['kɒzmənɔːt] N cosmonauta *mf*

cosmopolitan [ˌkɒzmə'pɒlɪtən] Ⓐ ADJ cosmopolita
Ⓑ N cosmopolita *mf*

cosmos ['kɒzmɒs] N cosmos *m*

co-sponsor ['kəʊ'spɒnsəʳ] N (*esp Advertising*) copatrocinador(a) *m/f*

Cossack ['kɒsæk] Ⓐ ADJ cosaco *m*
Ⓑ N cosaco/a *m/f*

cosset ['kɒsɪt] VT mimar, consentir

cossie* ['kɒzɪ] N (*Brit*) bañador *m*

cost [kɒst] Ⓐ N [1] (= *expense*) (*often pl*) coste *m*, costo *m* (*esp LAm*); (= *amount paid, price*) precio *m*; **at ~** (*Comm*) a (precio de) coste; **at all ~s, at any ~, whatever the ~** (*fig*) cueste lo que cueste, a toda costa; **she cared for her elderly mother at great ~ to her own freedom** cuidó de su madre anciana pagando un precio muy alto a costa de su propia libertad; **these are solutions that can be implemented at little ~** estas son soluciones que pueden ponerse en práctica y que son poco costosas; **at the ~ of his life/health** a costa de su vida/salud; **to bear the ~ of** (*lit*) pagar *or* correr con los gastos de; (*fig*) sufrir las consecuencias de; **to count the ~ of sth/of doing sth** pensar en los riesgos de algo/de hacer algo; **without counting the ~** sin pensar en los riesgos; **to my ~** a mis expensas
[2] **costs** [2·1] (*Jur*) costas *fpl*; **he was ordered to pay ~s** se le condenó a pagar las costas
[2·2] (= *expenses*) gastos *mpl*
Ⓑ VT [1] (*pt, pp* **cost**) costar, valer; **it ~ £2** costó 2 libras; **how much does it ~?** ¿cuánto cuesta?, ¿cuánto vale?, ¿a cuánto está?; **what will it ~ to have it repaired?** ¿cuánto va a costar repararlo?; **it ~ him a lot of money** le costó mucho dinero; **it'll ~ you*** te va a salir caro; **it ~ him his life/job** le costó la vida/el trabajo; **it ~ me a great deal of time/effort** me robó mucho tiempo/me costó mucho esfuerzo; **it ~s nothing to be polite** no cuesta nada ser educado; **whatever it ~s, ~ what it may** (*also fig*) cueste lo que cueste; ✦**IDIOM to ~ the earth**: **it ~s the earth*** cuesta un riñón, cuesta un ojo de la cara
[2] (*pt, pp* **costed**) (*Comm*) [+ *articles for sale*] calcular el coste de; [+ *job*] calcular el presupuesto de; **the job was ~ed at £5000** se calculó que el coste del trabajo ascendería a 5.000 libras; **it has not been properly ~ed** no se ha calculado detalladamente el coste
Ⓒ CPD ► **cost accountant** N contable *mf* de costes *or* (*esp LAm*) costos ► **cost accounting** N contabilidad *f* de costes *or* (*esp LAm*) costos ► **cost analysis** N análisis *m inv* de costes *or* (*esp LAm*) costos ► **cost centre** N centro *m* (de determinación) de costes *or* (*esp LAm*) costos ► **cost control** N control *m* de costes *or* (*esp LAm*) costos ► **cost of living** N coste *m* *or* (*esp LAm*) costo *m* de la vida; **~-of-living allowance** subsidio *m* por coste; **~-of-living bonus** plus *m* de carestía de vida, prima *f* por coste de la vida; **~-of-living increase** incremento *m* según el coste de la vida; **~-of-living index** índice *m* del coste *or* (*LAm*) de (la) vida ► **cost price** N (*Brit*) precio *m* de coste *or* (*LAm*) costo; **at ~ price** a precio de coste

►**cost out** VT + ADV presupuestar

co-star ['kəʊstɑːʳ] Ⓐ N coprotagonista *mf*, coestrella *mf*
Ⓑ VI **to ~ with sb** figurar con algn como protagonista
Ⓒ VT **the film ~s A and B** la película presenta como protagonistas a A y B *or* está coprotagonizada por A y B

Costa Rica ['kɒstə'riːkə] N Costa Rica *f*

Costa Rican ['kɒstə'riːkən] Ⓐ ADJ costarricense
Ⓑ N costarricense *mf*

cost-benefit analysis [ˌkɒst,benəfɪtə'næləsɪs] N análisis *m* coste-beneficio *or* (*LAm*) costo-beneficio

cost-conscious ['kɒst,kɒnʃəs] ADJ consciente de (los) costes *or* (*LAm*) costos

cost-cutting ['kɒst,kʌtɪŋ] N recorte *m* de costes *or* (*LAm*) costos

cost-effective [ˌkɒstɪ'fektɪv] ADJ rentable

cost-effectiveness [ˌkɒstɪ'fektɪvnɪs] N rentabilidad *f*, relación *f* coste-rendimiento *or* (*LAm*) costo-rendimiento

coster ['kɒstəʳ], **costermonger** ['kɒstə,mʌŋgəʳ] N (*Brit*) vendedor *m* ambulante

costing ['kɒstɪŋ] N cálculo *m* del coste

costive ['kɒstɪv] ADJ estreñido

costliness ['kɒstlɪnɪs] N (= *expensiveness*) alto precio *m*, lo caro; (= *great value*) suntuosidad *f*

costly ['kɒstlɪ] ADJ (*compar* **costlier**; *superl* **costliest**) (= *expensive*) (*lit, fig*) costoso; (= *valuable*) suntuoso

cost-plus [ˌkɒst'plʌs] N (*Comm*) precio *m* de coste más beneficio; **on a ~ basis** a base de precio de coste más beneficio

costume ['kɒstjuːm] Ⓐ N [1] [*of country*] traje *m*; (= *fancy dress*) disfraz *m*; (= *lady's suit*) traje *m* sastre; (= *bathing costume*) bañador *m*, traje *m* de baño
[2] **costumes** (*Theat*) vestuario *msing*
Ⓑ CPD ► **costume ball** N baile *m* de disfraces ► **costume designer** N (*Cine, TV*) diseñador(a) *m/f* de vestuario ► **costume drama** N obra *f* dramática de época ► **costume jewellery** (*Brit*), **costume jewelry** (*US*) N bisutería *f*, joyas *fpl* de fantasía ► **costume party** N (*US*) = **costume ball** ► **costume piece**, **costume play** N = **costume drama**

costumier [kɒs'tjuːmɪəʳ], **costumer** (*esp US*) [kɒs'tjuːməʳ] N sastre *m* de teatro

cosy, **cozy** (*US*) ['kəʊzɪ] Ⓐ ADJ (*compar* **cosier**, *superl* **cosiest**) [1] (= *warm*) [*room, atmosphere*] acogedor; [*clothes*] de abrigo, caliente
[2] (= *friendly*) [*chat*] íntimo, personal
[3] (*pej*) (= *convenient*) [*arrangement, relationship*] de lo más cómodo; (= *easy, comfortable*) [*life*] holgado
Ⓑ N (*for teapot, egg*) *cubierta que se utiliza para mantener el té de una tetera, los huevos etc calientes*

►**cosy up***, **cozy up*** (*US*) VI + ADV **to ~ up to sb** (*US*) (*fig*) tratar de quedar bien con algn

cot [kɒt] Ⓐ N (*Brit*) (*for baby*) cuna *f*; (*US*) (= *folding bed*) cama *f* plegable, catre *m*
Ⓑ CPD ► **cot death** N (*Brit*) muerte *f* en la cuna

coterie ['kəʊtərɪ] N grupo *m*; (= *clique*) peña *f*, camarilla *f*

coterminous [kəʊ'tɜːmɪnəs] (*frm*) ADJ (*Geog*) colindante (**with** con); [*concepts, ideas*] coincidente (**with** con); **to be ~ with** (*Geog*) colindar con; [*concepts, ideas*] coincidir con

Cotswolds ['kɒtswəʊldz] NPL *región montañosa de relieve suave del suroeste de Inglaterra*

cottage ['kɒtɪdʒ] Ⓐ N (= *country house*) casita *f* de campo, quinta *f* (*LAm*); (= *humble dwelling*) choza *f*, barraca *f*; (*US*) vivienda *f* campestre, quinta *f*
Ⓑ CPD ► **cottage cheese** N requesón *m* ► **cottage hospital** N (*Brit*) hospital *m* rural ► **cottage industry** N industria *f* artesanal *or* casera ► **cottage loaf** N (*Brit*) pan *m* casero ► **cottage pie** N (*Brit*) *pastel de carne cubierta de puré de patatas*

cottager ['kɒtɪdʒəʳ] N (*Brit*) aldeano/a *m/f*; (*US*) veraneante *mf* (en una casita de campo)

cotter ['kɒtəʳ] N chaveta *f*

cotton ['kɒtn] Ⓐ N (= *cloth*) algodón *m*; (= *plant, industry etc*) algodonero *m*; (*Brit*) (= *thread*) hilo *m* (de algodón); (*US*) = **cotton wool**
Ⓑ CPD [*shirt, dress*] de algodón ► **cotton belt** N (*US Geog*) zona *f* algodonera ► **cotton bud** N bastoncillo *m* de algodón ► **cotton candy** N (*US*) algodón *m* (azucarado) ► **the cotton industry** N la industria algodonera ► **cotton mill** N fábrica *f* de algodón ► **cotton reel** N carrete *m* de hilo, bobina *f* de hilo ► **cotton swab** N (*US*) = **cotton bud** ► **cotton waste** N borra *f* de algodón ► **cotton wool** N (*Brit*) algodón *m* hidrófilo

►**cotton on*** VI + ADV (*Brit*) **to ~ on (to sth)** caer en la cuenta (de algo)

cottongrass ['kɒtngrɑːs] N algodonosa *f*, algodoncillo *m* (silvestre)

cotton-picking* ['kɒtn,pɪkɪŋ] ADJ (*US*) condenado*

cottonseed oil ['kɒtnsiːd,ɔɪl] N aceite *m* de algodón

cottontail ['kɒtnteɪl] N (*US*) conejo *m* (de cola blanca)

cottonwood ['kɒtnwʊd] N (*US*) álamo *m* de Virginia

cotyledon [ˌkɒtɪ'liːdən] N cotiledón *m*

couch [kaʊtʃ] Ⓐ N sofá *m*; (*Med*) (*in doctor's surgery*) camilla *f*; (*psychiatrist's*) diván *m*; ✦**IDIOM to be on the ~** (*esp US*) ir al psicoa-

nalista
Ⓑ VT expresar; **~ed in jargon** redactado en jerigonza
Ⓒ CPD ► **couch grass** N hierba *f* rastrera ► **couch potato*** N teleadicto/a *m/f*, *persona que se apalanca en el sofá*

couchette [kuːˈʃet] N (*on train, ferry*) litera *f*

cougar [ˈkuːgəʳ] N puma *m*

cough [kɒf] Ⓐ N tos *f*; **to have a bad ~** tener mucha tos
Ⓑ VI [1] toser
[2] (‡) (= *confess*) cantar*
Ⓒ CPD ► **cough drop** N pastilla *f* para la tos ► **cough mixture** N jarabe *m* para la tos ► **cough sweet** NPL caramelo *m* para la tos ► **cough syrup** N = **cough mixture**

►**cough up** Ⓐ VT + ADV [1] [+ *blood, phlegm*] escupir, arrojar; (*Med*) expectorar
[2] (*fig*) (*) [+ *money*] soltar
Ⓑ VI + ADV (*fig*) (*) soltar la pasta*

coughing [ˈkɒfɪŋ] N toser *m*, toses *fpl*; **fit of ~** acceso *m* de tos; **you couldn't hear the symphony for ~** el público tosía tanto que apenas se oía la sinfonía

could [kʊd] PT, COND *of* **can**[1]; → ABLE, CAN

couldn't [ˈkʊdnt] = **could not**; *see* **can**[1]

could've [ˈkʊdəv] = **could have**; *see* **can**[1]

coulomb [ˈkuːlɒm] N culombio *m*

council [ˈkaʊnsl] Ⓐ N [1] (= *committee*) consejo *m*, junta *f*; (*Rel*) concilio *m*; *see also* **security B**
[2] (*in local government*) concejo *m* municipal; **city/town ~** ayuntamiento *m*; **you should write to the ~ about it** deberías escribir al ayuntamiento acerca de eso; **the ~ should move the rubbish** les corresponde a los servicios municipales recoger la basura
[3] (= *meeting*) reunión *f*, sesión *f*; **~ of war** consejo *m* de guerra
Ⓑ CPD ► **Council of Europe** N Consejo *m* de Europa ► **council flat** N (*Brit*) piso *m* *or* (*LAm*) departamento *m* de protección oficial ► **council house** N (*Brit*) casa *f* de protección oficial ► **council housing** N (*Brit*) viviendas *fpl* de protección oficial ► **council (housing) estate** N (*Brit*) urbanización *f* *or* barrio *m* de viviendas de protección oficial ► **council meeting** N pleno *m* municipal ► **Council of Ministers** N Consejo *m* de Ministros (*de la Unión Europea*) ► **council tax** N (*Brit*) *impuesto municipal* ► **council tenant** N (*Brit*) inquilino/a *m/f* (de una vivienda de protección oficial)

councillor, **councilor** (*US*) [ˈkaʊnsɪləʳ] N concejal(a) *m/f*

councilman [ˈkaʊnsɪlmən] N (*pl* **councilmen**) (*US*) concejal *m*

councilwoman [ˈkaʊnsl,wʊmən] N (*pl* **councilwomen**) (*US*) concejala *f*

counsel [ˈkaʊnsəl] Ⓐ N [1] (*frm, liter*) (= *advice*) consejo *m*; **to hold/take ~ (with sb) about sth** consultar *or* pedir consejo (a algn) sobre algo; **to keep one's own ~** guardar silencio; **a ~ of perfection** un ideal imposible
[2] (*Jur*) (*pl inv*) abogado/a *m/f*; **~ for the defence** (*Brit*) abogado/a *m/f* defensor(a); **~ for the prosecution** (*Brit*) fiscal *mf*; **Queen's** *or* **King's Counsel** (*Brit*) abogado/a *m/f* del Estado
Ⓑ VT [+ *person*] (*frm*) aconsejar; (*Med etc*) orientar; [+ *prudence etc*] recomendar; **to ~ sb to do sth** aconsejar a algn que haga algo

counselling, **counseling** (*US*) [ˈkaʊnsəlɪŋ] Ⓐ N (*gen*) (= *advice*) asesoramiento *m*; (*Psych*) asistencia *f* sociopsicológica; (*Brit Scol*) ayuda *f* psicopedagógica
Ⓑ CPD ► **counselling service** N servicio *m* de orientación; (*Univ*) servicio *m* de orientación universitaria

counsellor, **counselor** (*US*) [ˈkaʊnsələʳ] N [1] (*Psych*) consejero/a *m/f*; (= *adviser*) asesor(a) *m/f*
[2] (*US Scol*) consejero/a *m/f*, asesor(a) *m/f*
[3] (*Irl, US Jur*) (*also* **~-at-law**) abogado/a *m/f*

count[1] [kaʊnt] Ⓐ N [1] (= *act of counting*) recuento *m*; [*of votes*] escrutinio *m*, recuento *m*; (*Boxing*) cuenta *f*; **to keep/lose ~ (of sth)** llevar/perder la cuenta (de algo); **at the last ~** en el último recuento; **to make** *or* **do a ~ of sth** hacer un recuento de algo; **to be out for the ~** estar fuera de combate
[2] (= *total*) recuento *m*; **the final ~** (*in election*) el último recuento; **hold the stretch for a ~ of ten, then relax** estírese y cuente hasta diez, luego relájese; *see also* **pollen**, **sperm**
[3] (*Jur*) cargo *m*; **he was found guilty on all ~s** fue declarado culpable de todos los cargos; **he was indicted on two ~s of murder** le fueron imputados dos cargos por asesinato
[4] (= *point*) **you're wrong on both ~s** estás equivocado en los dos aspectos; **I think she deserves recognition on two ~s** creo que merece reconocimiento por dos motivos
Ⓑ VT [1] (= *add up, check*) contar; **she was ~ing the days until he came home** contaba los días que faltaban para su vuelta; **to ~ the cost of (doing) sth** (*lit*) reparar en el coste de (hacer) algo; (*fig*) reparar en las consecuencias de (hacer) algo; *see also* **chicken**, **blessing**, **cost A1**
[2] (= *include*) contar; **not ~ing the children** sin contar a los niños; **ten ~ing him** diez con él, diez contándolo a él
[3] (= *consider*) considerar; **I ~ you among my friends** te cuento entre mis amigos, te considero amigo mío; **I ~ myself lucky** me considero feliz; **~ yourself lucky!** ¡date por satisfecho!
Ⓒ VI [1] (= *add up, recite numbers*) contar; **can you ~?** ¿sabes contar?; **~ing from the left** contando de izquierda a derecha; **~ing from today/last Sunday** a partir de hoy/contando desde el domingo pasado; **to ~ (up) to ten** contar hasta diez
[2] (= *be considered, be valid*) valer, contar; **that doesn't ~** eso no vale, eso no cuenta; **every second ~s** cada segundo cuenta *or* es importante; **it will ~ <u>against</u> him** irá en su contra; **to ~ <u>as</u>: two children ~ as one adult** dos niños cuentan como un adulto; **a conservatory ~s as an extension** un jardín de invierno cuenta como una ampliación de la casa; **ability ~s <u>for</u> little here** aquí la capacidad que se tenga sirve de muy poco
Ⓓ CPD ► **count noun** N (*Gram*) sustantivo *m* contable

►**count down** VI + ADV **~ down from ten to one** cuenta hacia atrás del diez al uno; **children tend to ~ down to Christmas** los niños suelen contar los días que quedan para Navidad

►**count in*** VT + ADV incluir; **~ me in!** ¡yo me apunto!, ¡cuenta conmigo!; **to ~ sb in on sth** contar con algn para algo

▼►**count on** VI + PREP [1] (= *rely on*) contar con; **we're ~ing on him** contamos con él; **I wouldn't ~ on it!** ¡no contaría con ello!; **he's ~ing on winning** cuenta con ganar; **he can be ~ed on to ruin everything** puedes contar con que él estropeará todo; **I can always ~ on you to cheer me up** siempre puedo contar contigo para que me levantes el ánimo
[2] (= *expect*) contar con; **I hadn't ~ed on this** no había contado con esto

►**count out** VT + ADV [1] (= *count*) [+ *money*] ir contando; [+ *small objects*] contar (uno por uno)
[2] (= *exclude*) [+ *possibility*] descartar; **we can't ~ out the possibility that they'll attack** no podemos descartar la posibilidad de que ataquen
[3] (*) **if that's what I have to do, you can ~ me out** si eso es lo que tengo que hacer, no cuentes conmigo; **(you can) ~ me out of this!** ¡no cuentes conmigo para esto!, ¡dejame fuera de esto!
[4] (*Boxing*) **the referee ~ed him out** el árbitro terminó la cuenta antes de que se levantara; **to be ~ed out** ser declarado fuera de combate

►**count toward(s)** VI + PREP contar para; **this work ~s towards your final degree** este trabajo cuenta para la nota final de la licenciatura; **the time he has already spent in prison will ~ towards his sentence** el tiempo que ya ha pasado en la cárcel se descontará de su condena

►**count up** VT + ADV contar

►**count upon** VI + PREP = **count on**

count[2] [kaʊnt] N (= *nobleman*) conde *m*

countable [ˈkaʊntəbl] ADJ contable; **~ noun** (*Ling*) nombre *m* contable

countdown [ˈkaʊntdaʊn] N cuenta *f* atrás, cuenta *f* regresiva (*LAm*)

countenance [ˈkaʊntɪnəns] (*frm*) Ⓐ N [1] (*liter*) (= *face*) semblante *m*, rostro *m*; **to keep one's ~** contener la risa, no perder la serenidad; **to lose ~** desconcertarse; **to be out of ~** estar desconcertado; **to put sb out of ~** desconcertar a algn
[2] (*frm*) (*no pl*) (= *approval*) consentimiento *m*; **to give** *or* **lend ~ to** [+ *news*] acreditar
Ⓑ VT (*frm*) (= *permit*) **to ~ sth** consentir *or* permitir algo; **to ~ sb doing sth** permitir a algn que haga algo

counter[1] [ˈkaʊntəʳ] Ⓐ N [1] [*of shop*] mostrador *m*; [*of canteen*] barra *f*; (= *position in post office, bank*) ventanilla *f*; **you can buy it over the ~** (*Med*) esto se compra sin receta médica; ✦***IDIOM*** **to buy under the ~** comprar de estraperlo *or* bajo mano; *see also* **over-the-counter**
[2] (*in game*) ficha *f*
[3] (*Tech*) contador *m*
Ⓑ CPD ► **counter staff** N personal *m* de ventas

counter[2] [ˈkaʊntəʳ] Ⓐ ADV **~ to** contrario a, en contra de; **to run ~ to** ir en sentido contrario a, ser contrario a
Ⓑ VT [+ *blow*] responder a, parar; [+ *attack*] contestar a, hacer frente a; **to ~ sth with sth/by doing sth** contestar a algo con algo/haciendo algo
Ⓒ VI **to ~ with** contestar *or* responder con

counter... [ˈkaʊntəʳ] PREFIX contra...

counteract [,kaʊntəˈrækt] VT contrarrestar

counter-argument [ˈkaʊntər,ɑːgjʊmənt] N contraargumento *m*, argumento *m* en contrario

counter-attack [ˈkaʊntərə,tæk] Ⓐ N contraataque *m*
Ⓑ VT, VI contraatacar

counter-attraction [ˈkaʊntərə,trækʃən] N atracción *f* rival

counterbalance [ˈkaʊntə,bæləns] Ⓐ N contrapeso *m*; (*fig*) compensación *f*
Ⓑ VT contrapesar; (*fig*) compensar

counterbid [ˈkaʊntəbɪd] Ⓐ N contraoferta *f*; **to make/launch a ~** hacer/presentar una

➤ LANGUAGE IN USE: **count on 1** 11.3

contraoferta
Ⓑ VT, VI contraofertar

counterblast ['kaʊntəblɑːst] N respuesta *f* vigorosa (**to** a)

counterblow ['kaʊntəbləʊ] N contragolpe *m*

countercharge ['kaʊntətʃɑːdʒ] N contraacusación *f*

countercheck ['kaʊntətʃek] Ⓐ N segunda comprobación *f*
Ⓑ VT comprobar por segunda vez

counterclaim ['kaʊntəkleɪm] N (*Jur*) contrademanda *f*

counterclockwise ['kaʊntə'klɒkwaɪz] ADV (*US*) en sentido contrario al de las agujas del reloj

counter-culture ['kaʊntə,kʌltʃəʳ] N contracultura *f*

counter-espionage ['kaʊntər'espɪənɑːʒ] N contraespionaje *m*

counterexample ['kaʊntərɪg,zɑːmpl] N contraejemplo *m*

counterfeit ['kaʊntəfiːt] Ⓐ ADJ (= *false*) falsificado
Ⓑ N falsificación *f*; (= *coin*) moneda *f* falsa; (= *note*) billete *m* falso
Ⓒ VT falsificar

counterfoil ['kaʊntəfɔɪl] N (*Brit*) matriz *f* (*Sp*), talón *m* (*LAm*)

counter-gambit ['kaʊntəgæmbɪt] N táctica *f* contraataque

counter-indication ['kaʊntər,ɪndɪ'keɪʃən] N contraindicación *f*

counter-insurgency ['kaʊntərɪn'sɜːdʒənsɪ] N medidas *fpl* antiinsurrectivas

counter-insurgent ['kaʊntərɪn'sɜːdʒənt] N contrainsurgente *mf*

counterintelligence ['kaʊntərɪn,telɪdʒəns] N = **counter-espionage**

countermand ['kaʊntəmɑːnd] VT revocar, cancelar

counter-measure ['kaʊntəmeʒəʳ] N contramedida *f*

counter-move ['kaʊntəmuːv] N contrajugada *f*; (*fig*) contraataque *m*; (= *manoeuvre*) contramaniobra *f*

counter-offensive ['kaʊntərə'fensɪv] N contraofensiva *f*

counter-order ['kaʊntər,ɔːdəʳ] N contraorden *f*

counterpane ['kaʊntəpeɪn] N colcha *f*, cubrecama *m*

counterpart ['kaʊntəpɑːt] N (= *equivalent*) equivalente *m*; (= *person*) homólogo/a *m/f*

counterpoint ['kaʊntəpɔɪnt] Ⓐ N (*Mus, fig*) contrapunto *m*
Ⓑ VT (*fig*) poner el contrapunto a

counterpoise ['kaʊntəpɔɪz] Ⓐ N contrapeso *m*
Ⓑ VT contrapesar

counter-productive [,kaʊntəprə'dʌktɪv] ADJ contraproducente

counter-proposal ['kaʊntəprə,pəʊzəl] N contrapropuesta *f*

counterpunch ['kaʊntəpʌntʃ] N contragolpe *m*

Counter-Reformation ['kaʊntə,refə'meɪʃən] N Contrarreforma *f*

counter-revolution ['kaʊntərevə'luːʃən] N contrarrevolución *f*

counter-revolutionary ['kaʊntərevə'luːʃənrɪ]
Ⓐ ADJ contrarrevolucionario
Ⓑ N contrarrevolucionario/a *m/f*

countersign ['kaʊntəsaɪn] Ⓐ N (*Mil*) contraseña *f*
Ⓑ VT refrendar

countersink ['kaʊntəsɪŋk] (*pt* **countersank** ['kaʊntəsæŋk], *pp* **countersunk** ['kaʊntəsʌŋk]) VT [+ *hole*] avellanar; [+ *screw*] encastrar

counter-stroke ['kaʊntəstrəʊk] N contragolpe *m*

countersunk ['kaʊntəsʌŋk] ADJ [*screw*] encastrado

countertenor ['kaʊntə,tenəʳ] Ⓐ N contratenor *m*
Ⓑ CPD [*voice*] de contratenor

countervailing ['kaʊntə,veɪlɪŋ] Ⓐ ADJ compensatorio
Ⓑ CPD ► **countervailing duties** NPL aranceles *mpl* compensatorios

counterweigh [,kaʊntə'weɪ] VT contrapesar

counterweight ['kaʊntəweɪt] Ⓐ N (*lit, fig*) contrapeso *m*
Ⓑ VT (*lit*) contrabalancear; (*fig*) contrarrestar, contrabalancear

countess ['kaʊntɪs] N condesa *f*

counting ['kaʊntɪŋ] N cálculo *m*

countless ['kaʊntlɪs] ADJ incontable, innumerable; **on ~ occasions** infinidad *f* de veces

countrified ['kʌntrɪfaɪd] ADJ rústico

country ['kʌntrɪ] Ⓐ N [1] (= *nation*) país *m*; (= *people*) pueblo *m*; **to go to the ~** (*Brit Pol*) convocar a elecciones generales
[2] (= *fatherland*) patria *f*; **to die for one's ~** morir por la patria; **love of ~** amor a la patria
[3] (*no pl*) (= *countryside*) campo *m*; **we had to leave the road and go across ~** tuvimos que dejar la carretera e ir a través del campo; **in the ~** en el campo; **to live off the ~** vivir de lo que produce la tierra
[4] (*no pl*) (= *terrain, land*) terreno *m*, tierra *f*; **this is good fishing ~** ésta es buena tierra para la pesca; **unknown ~** (*also fig*) terreno desconocido; **mountainous ~** región *f* montañosa; **there is some lovely ~ further south** más al sur el paisaje es muy bonito
Ⓑ CPD ► **country and western (music)** N música *f* country, música *f* ranchera (*Mex*) ► **country bumpkin** N (*pej*) patán *m*, paleto/a *m/f* ► **country club** N club *m* campestre ► **country cottage** N casita *f* (en el campo) ► **country cousin** N (*fig*) pueblerino/a *m/f* ► **country dance** N baile *m* regional ► **country dancing** N danza *f* folklórica ► **country dweller** N persona *f* que vive en el campo ► **country folk** NPL gente *f* del campo ► **country gentleman** N hacendado *m* ► **country house** N casa *f* de campo, quinta *f*; (= *farm*) finca *f* (*esp LAm*), rancho *m* (*Mex*) ► **country life** N vida *f* campestre *or* del campo ► **country mile*** N ✦*IDIOM* **to miss sth by a ~ mile** (*US*) quedarse a una legua de algo ► **country music** N = **country and western (music)** ► **country park** N parque *m* ► **country people** NPL = **country folk** ► **country road** N camino *m* vecinal ► **country seat** N casa *f* solariega, hacienda *f* (*LAm*)

country-born [,kʌntrɪ'bɔːn] ADJ nacido en el campo

country-bred [,kʌntrɪ'bred] ADJ criado en el campo

countryman ['kʌntrɪmən] N (*pl* **countrymen**)
[1] (= *rural dweller*) hombre *m* del campo, campesino *m*
[2] (= *fellow-countryman*) compatriota *mf*

countryside ['kʌntrɪsaɪd] N campo *m*

countrywide [,kʌntrɪ'waɪd] ADJ nacional

countrywoman ['kʌntrɪ,wʊmən] N (*pl* **countrywomen**) [1] (= *rural dweller*) campesina *f*
[2] (= *fellow-countrywoman*) compatriota *f*

county ['kaʊntɪ] Ⓐ N (*Brit*) condado *m*; (*US*) (= *subdivision of state*) comarca *f*, provincia *f*
Ⓑ CPD ► **county boundary** N límite *m* comarcal *or* provincial ► **county clerk's office** N (*US*) registro *m* civil ► **county council**, **county commission** (*US*) N ≈ diputación *f* provincial ► **county court** N (*Brit*) juzgado *m* de primera instancia ► **county cricket** N (*Brit*) *partidos de cricket entre los condados* ► **county family** N (*Brit*) familia *f* aristocrática rural ► **county recorder's office** N (*US*) ≈ registro *m* de la propiedad ► **county road** N (*US*) ≈ carretera *f* secundaria ► **county seat** N (*US*) = **county town** ► **county town** N (*Brit*) capital *f* de condado

coup [kuː] Ⓐ N [1] (*Pol*) (*also* **~ d'état**) golpe *m* (de estado)
[2] (= *triumph*) éxito *m*; **to bring off a ~** obtener un éxito inesperado
Ⓑ CPD ► **coup de grace** N golpe *m* de gracia ► **coup de théâtre** N golpe *m* de efecto

coupé ['kuːpeɪ] N (*Aut*) cupé *m*

couple ['kʌpl] Ⓐ N [1] (= *pair*) par *m*; **a ~ of** un par de
[2] (= *partners*) pareja *f*; (= *married couple*) matrimonio *m*; **young ~** matrimonio *m* joven
[3] (= *two or three*) **just a ~ of minutes** dos minutos nada más; **I know a ~ of lads who can do the job** conozco a un par de chicos que pueden hacer el trabajo; **we had a ~ in a bar*** tomamos un par de copas en un bar
Ⓑ VT [1] [+ *names etc*] unir, juntar; [+ *ideas*] asociar; **to ~ sth with sth** unir algo a algo, juntar algo con algo
[2] (*Tech*) **to ~ (on *or* up)** acoplar (a), enganchar (a)
Ⓒ VI (*Zool*) copularse

coupledom ['kʌpldəm] N convivencia *f* en pareja

coupler ['kʌpləʳ] N (*Comput*) acoplador *m*; (*US Rail*) enganche *m*; *see also* **acoustic**

couplet ['kʌplɪt] N pareado *m*

coupling ['kʌplɪŋ] N [1] (*Tech*) acoplamiento *m*; (*Aut, Rail*) enganche *m*
[2] (*sexual*) cópula *f*

coupon ['kuːpɒn] N (= *voucher in newspaper, advertisement*) cupón *m*; (*for price reduction or gifts*) vale *m*; (= *football pools coupon*) boleto *m* (de quiniela)

courage ['kʌrɪdʒ] N valor *m*, valentía *f*; **~!** ¡ánimo!; **I haven't the ~ to refuse** no tengo valor para negarme; **to have the ~ of one's convictions** obrar de acuerdo con su conciencia; **to pluck up one's ~** ◊ **take one's ~ in both hands** armarse de valor; **to take ~ from** cobrar ánimos *or* sacar fuerzas de

courageous [kə'reɪdʒəs] ADJ valiente, valeroso

courageously [kə'reɪdʒəslɪ] ADV valientemente

courgette [kʊə'ʒet] N (*Brit*) calabacín *m*, calabacita *f*

courier ['kʊrɪəʳ] N (= *messenger*) mensajero/a *m/f*; (= *tourist guide*) guía *mf* de turismo

▼**course** [kɔːs] Ⓐ N [1] (= *route, direction*) [*of ship, plane*] rumbo *m*; [*of river*] curso *m*; [*of planet*] órbita *f*; **on a southerly ~** con rumbo sur; **to change ~** (*lit*) cambiar de rumbo; **the government has changed ~ on Europe** el gobierno ha dado un nuevo rumbo *or* giro a su política con respecto a Europa; **to be/go off ~** (*lit, fig*) haberse desviado/desviarse de su rumbo; **the plane was 300 miles off ~** el avión se había desviado 300 millas de su rumbo; **the boat was blown off ~** el viento desvió al barco de su rumbo; **we are on ~ for victory** vamos bien encaminados para la victoria; **to plot a ~ (for Jamaica)** trazar el

➤ LANGUAGE IN USE: **course A4** 9.2, 11.1, 11.2, 11.3, 15.1

rumbo (para ir a Jamaica); **to set (a) ~ for** (*Naut*) poner rumbo a; *see also* **collision**
2 (= *line of action*) **I'd advise you not to follow that ~** te aconsejaría que no escogieras ese camino; **the best ~ would be to ...** lo mejor sería ...; **we have to decide on the best ~ of action** tenemos que decidir cuáles son las mejores medidas a tomar; **it's the only ~ left open to him** es la única opción que le queda
3 (= *process*) curso *m*; **it changed the ~ of history/of her life** cambió el curso de la historia/de su vida; **in the normal** *or* **ordinary ~ of events** normalmente; **in the ~ of:** **in the ~ of my work** en el cumplimiento de mi trabajo; **in the ~ of conversation** en el curso *or* transcurso de la conversación; **in** *or* **during the ~ of the next few days** en el curso de los próximos días; **in** *or* **during the ~ of the journey** durante el viaje; **to let things take** *or* **run their ~** dejar que las cosas sigan su curso; *see also* **due A3**, **event 1**, **matter A5**
4 **of ~** claro, desde luego, por supuesto, cómo no (*esp LAm*), sí pues (*S. Cone*); **of ~! I should have known** ¡pero si está claro! me lo tenía que haber imaginado; **"can I have a drink?" — "of ~ you can"** —¿puedo tomar algo de beber? —claro *or* desde luego *or* por supuesto que sí; **I've read about her in the papers, of ~** por supuesto, la conozco de los periódicos; **of ~, I may be wrong** claro que puedo estar confundido; **of ~ not!** (*answering*) ¡claro que no!, ¡por supuesto que no!; **"can I go?" — "of ~ not** *or* **of ~ you can't"** —¿puedo ir? —claro que no *or* ni hablar *or* por supuesto que no
5 (*Scol, Univ*) curso *m*; **to go on a ~** ir a hacer un curso; **a ~ in business administration** un curso de administración de empresas; **short ~** cursillo *m*; **~ of study** (*gen*) estudios *mpl*; (*Univ*) carrera *f*, estudios *mpl*; **to take** *or* **do a ~ in** *or* **on sth** hacer un curso de algo
6 (*Med*) (= *regimen*) **she was put on a ~ of steroids** le recetaron esteroides, le pusieron un tratamiento a base de esteroides; **a ~ of treatment** un tratamiento
7 (*Sport*) (= *distance*) recorrido *m*; (= *surface*) pista *f*; (= *racecourse*) hipódromo *m*; **golf ~** campo *m* *or* (*S. Cone*) cancha *f* (de golf); ✦*IDIOM* **to stay the ~** no cejar, aguantar hasta el final; *see also* **obstacle**
8 (*Culin*) plato *m*; **main ~** plato *m* principal; **a three-~ meal** una comida de tres platos
9 (*Naut*) (= *sail*) vela *f* mayor
10 (*Constr*) (= *layer*) [*of bricks*] hilada *f*
Ⓑ VI [*water, air*] correr; [*tears*] rodar; [*sweat*] caer; (*fig*) [*emotion*] invadir; **it sent the blood coursing through his veins** hacía que la sangre corriera por sus venas; **rage/relief ~d through him** le invadió la ira/una sensación de alivio
Ⓒ VT (*Hunting*†) cazar
Ⓓ CPD ► **course work** N trabajos *mpl* (para clase)

coursing ['kɔːsɪŋ] N caza *f* con perros

court [kɔːt] Ⓐ N 1 (*Jur*) tribunal *m*, juzgado *m*, corte *f* (*esp LAm*); (= *officers and/or public*) tribunal *m*; **he was brought before the ~ on a charge of theft** fue procesado por robo; **in open ~** en pleno tribunal; **to rule sth out of ~** no admitir algo; **to settle (a case) out of ~** llegar a un acuerdo las partes (sin ir a juicio); **to take sb to ~ (over sth)** llevar a algn a los tribunales *or* ante el tribunal (por algo); *see also* **crown C**, **high D**, **magistrate**, **out-of-court**, **supreme**
2 (*Tennis*) pista *f*, cancha *f*; **hard/grass ~** pista *f* *or* cancha *f* dura/de hierba
3 (*royal*) (= *palace*) palacio *m*; (= *people*) corte *f*; **at ~** en la corte; **to hold ~** (*fig*) dar audiencia, recibir en audiencia
4 (*Archit*) patio *m*
5 **to pay ~ to**† hacer la corte a
Ⓑ VT 1 [+ *woman*] pretender *or* cortejar a
2 (*fig*) (= *seek*) [+ *favour*] intentar conseguir; [+ *death, disaster*] buscar, exponerse a; **to ~ favour with sb** intentar congraciarse con algn
Ⓒ VI (†) ser novios; **are you ~ing?** ¿tienes novio?; **they've been ~ing for three years** llevan tres años de relaciones; **a ~ing couple** una pareja de novios
Ⓓ CPD ► **court action** N **she was threatened with ~ action** la amenazaron con llevarla a juicio, la amenazaron con presentar una demanda judicial contra ella ► **court of appeal** N tribunal *m* de apelación ► **court card** N (*esp Brit*) figura *f* ► **court circular** N noticiario *m* de la corte ► **court of inquiry** N comisión *f* de investigación ► **court of justice**, **court of law** N tribunal *m* de justicia ► **court order** N mandato *m* judicial ► **Court of Session** N (*Scot*) Tribunal *m* Supremo de Escocia ► **court shoe** N (*Brit*) escarpín *m*

Courtelle® [kɔː'tel] N Courtelle® *f*

courteous ['kɜːtɪəs] ADJ cortés, atento

courteously ['kɜːtɪəslɪ] ADV cortésmente

courtesan [ˌkɔːtɪ'zæn] N cortesana *f*

courtesy ['kɜːtɪsɪ] Ⓐ N (= *politeness*) cortesía *f*; (= *polite act*) atención *f*, gentileza *f*; **by ~ of** (por) cortesía de; **to exchange courtesies** intercambiar cumplidos de etiqueta; **will you do me the ~ of ...?** si fuera tan amable de ..., haga el favor de ...; **you might have had the ~ to tell me** podrías haber tenido la gentileza de decírmelo; **I'll do it out of ~** lo haré por cortesía
Ⓑ CPD ► **courtesy bus** N autobús *m* de cortesía ► **courtesy call** N visita *f* de cumplido ► **courtesy car** N coche *m* de cortesía ► **courtesy card** N (*US*) tarjeta *f* (de visita) ► **courtesy coach** N (*Brit*) autocar *m* *or* autobús *m* de cortesía ► **courtesy light** N (*Aut*) luz *f* interna ► **courtesy title** N título *m* de cortesía ► **courtesy visit** N = **courtesy call**

courthouse ['kɔːthaʊs] N (*pl* **courthouses** ['kɔːthaʊzɪz]) (*esp US Jur*) palacio *m* de justicia

courtier ['kɔːtɪəʳ] N cortesano/a *m/f*

courtly ['kɔːtlɪ] Ⓐ ADJ cortés, elegante, fino
Ⓑ CPD ► **courtly love** N amor *m* cortés

court-martial ['kɔːt'mɑːʃəl] Ⓐ N (*pl* **courts-martial, court-martials**) consejo *m* de guerra, tribunal *m* militar
Ⓑ VT juzgar en consejo de guerra

courtroom ['kɔːtrʊm] N sala *f* de justicia, sala *f* de tribunal

courtship ['kɔːtʃɪp] N (= *act*) cortejo *m*; (= *period*) noviazgo *m*

courtyard ['kɔːtjɑːd] N patio *m*

cousin ['kʌzn] N primo/a *m/f*; **first ~** primo/a *m/f* carnal; **second ~** primo/a *m/f* segundo/a

couth [kuːθ] N (*US*) buenos modales *mpl*

couture [kuː'tjʊəʳ] N alta costura *f*

couturier [kuː'tʊərɪˌeɪ] N modisto *m*

cove[1] [kəʊv] N (*Geog*) cala *f*, ensenada *f*; (*US*) (= *valley*) valle *m*

cove[2]* [kəʊv] N (*Brit*†) (= *fellow*) tío* *m*

coven ['kʌvən] N aquelarre *m*

covenant ['kʌvɪnənt] Ⓐ N 1 (*legal*) pacto *m*, convenio *m*; (*also* **tax ~**) (*Brit*) *sistema de contribuciones caritativas con beneficios fiscales para el beneficiario*; *see also* **deed**
2 **Covenant** (*Bible*) Alianza *f*
Ⓑ VT pactar, concertar; **to ~ £20 a year to a charity** concertar el pago de 20 libras anuales a una sociedad benéfica
Ⓒ VI **to ~ with sb for sth** pactar algo con algn

covenanter ['kʌvɪnəntəʳ] N (*Scot Hist*) firmante *mf* de un pacto

Coventry ['kɒvəntrɪ] N ✦*IDIOM* **to send sb to ~** (*Brit*) hacer el vacío a algn

cover ['kʌvəʳ] Ⓐ N 1 (*gen*) [*of dish, saucepan*] tapa *f*, tapadera *f*; [*of furniture, typewriter*] funda *f*; [*of lens*] tapa *f*; (*for book*) forro *m*; (*for merchandise, on vehicle*) cubierta *f*
2 (= *bedspread*) cubrecama *m*, colcha *f*; (*often pl*) (= *blanket*) manta *f*, frazada *f* (*LAm*), cobija *f* (*LAm*)
3 [*of magazine*] portada *f*; [*of book*] cubierta *f*, tapa *f*; **to read a book from ~ to ~** leer un libro de cabo a rabo
4 (*Comm*) (= *envelope*) sobre *m*; **under separate ~** por separado; *see also* **first-day cover**
5 (*no pl*) (= *shelter*) cobijo *m*, refugio *m*; (*for hiding*) escondite *m*; (= *covering fire*) cobertura *f*; **to break ~** salir al descubierto; **to run for ~** correr a cobijarse; (*fig*) ponerse a buen recaudo; **to take ~ (from)** (*Mil*) ponerse a cubierto (de); (= *shelter*) protegerse *or* resguardarse (de); **under ~** a cubierto; (= *indoors*) bajo techo; **under ~ of darkness** al amparo de la oscuridad
6 (*no pl*) (*Fin, Insurance*) cobertura *f*; **without ~** (*Fin*) sin cobertura; **full/fire ~** (*Insurance*) cobertura total/contra incendios
7 (*in espionage etc*) tapadera *f*; **to blow sb's ~*** (*accidentally*) poner a algn al descubierto; (*intentionally*) desenmascarar a algn
8 (*frm*) (*at table*) cubierto *m*
9 (*Mus*) = **cover version**
Ⓑ VT 1 **to ~ sth (with)** [+ *surface, wall*] cubrir algo (con *or* de); [+ *saucepan, hole, eyes, face*] tapar algo (con); [+ *book*] forrar algo (con); [+ *chair*] tapizar algo (con); **to ~ one's face with one's hands** taparse la cara con las manos; **to be ~ed in** *or* **with snow/dust/chocolate** estar cubierto de nieve/polvo/chocolate; **~ed with confusion/shame** lleno de confusión/muerto de vergüenza; ✦*IDIOM* **to ~ o.s. with glory/disgrace** cubrirse de gloria/hundirse en la miseria
2 (= *hide*) [+ *feelings, facts, mistakes*] ocultar; [+ *noise*] ahogar; **to ~ (up) one's tracks** (*lit, fig*) borrar las huellas
3 (= *protect*) (*Mil, Sport*) cubrir; **to keep sb ~ed** cubrir a algn; **I've got you ~ed!** ¡te tengo a tiro!, ¡te estoy apuntando!; **the soldiers ~ed our retreat** los soldados nos cubrieron la retirada; **he only said that to ~ himself** lo dijo sólo para cubrirse; ✦*IDIOMS* **to ~ one's back*** ◊ **~ one's ass**** cubrirse las espaldas
4 (*Insurance*) cubrir; **what does your travel insurance ~ you for?** ¿qué (cosas) cubre tu seguro de viaje?; **the house is ~ed against fire** la casa está asegurada contra incendios
5 (= *be sufficient for*) [+ *cost, expenses*] cubrir, sufragar; **to ~ a loss** cubrir una pérdida; **£10 will ~ everything** con 10 libras será suficiente
6 (= *take in, include*) incluir; **goods ~ed by this invoice** los artículos incluídos en esta factura; **such factories will not be ~ed by this report** tales fábricas no se verán incluídas en este informe; **we must ~ all possibilities** debemos tener en cuenta todas las posibilidades
7 (= *deal with*) [+ *problem, area*] abarcar; [+ *points in discussion*] tratar, discutir; **his speech ~ed most of the points raised** su discurso

abarcó la mayoría de los puntos planteados; **his work ~s many different fields** su trabajo abarca muchas especialidades distintas; **no law ~s a situation like this** ninguna ley contempla una situación semejante

8 [+ *distance*] recorrer, cubrir; **we ~ed eight miles in one hour** recorrimos ocho millas en una hora; **to ~ a lot of ground** (*in travel, work*) recorrer mucho trecho; (= *deal with many subjects*) abarcar muchos temas

9 (*Press*) (= *report on*) cubrir; **all the newspapers ~ed the story** todos los periódicos cubrieron el caso; **he was sent to ~ the riots** lo enviaron para que hiciera un reportaje de los disturbios

10 (*Mus*) **to ~ a song** hacer una versión de una canción

11 (= *inseminate*) [+ *animal*] cubrir

C VI **to ~ for sb** (*at work etc*) suplir a algn; (= *protect*) encubrir a algn

D CPD ► **cover charge** N (*in restaurant*) (precio *m* del) cubierto *m* ► **cover girl** N modelo *f* de portada ► **cover letter** N (*US*) carta *f* de explicación ► **cover note** N (*Brit Insurance*) ≈ seguro *m* provisional ► **cover price** N precio *m* de venta al público ► **cover story** N (*Press*) tema *m* de portada; (*in espionage etc*) tapadera *f* ► **cover version** N (*Mus*) versión *f*

►**cover in** VT + ADV cubrir; (= *put roof on*) poner un techo a, techar

►**cover over** VT + ADV [+ *surface, object, hole*] cubrir, tapar; [+ *problem*] tapar, esconder

►**cover up** A VT + ADV 1 [+ *child, object*] cubrir completamente, tapar

2 (*fig*) (= *hide*) [+ *facts*] ocultar; [+ *emotions*] disimular

B VI + ADV 1 (*with clothes*) abrigarse, taparse

2 (*fig*) **to ~ up for sb** encubrir a algn

coverage ['kʌvərɪdʒ] N 1 (*Press*) reportaje *m*; **to give full ~ to an event** (= *report widely*) dar amplia difusión a un suceso; (= *report in depth*) informar a fondo sobre un suceso

2 (*Insurance*) cobertura *f*

coveralls ['kʌvərɔːlz] NPL (*US*) (= *overalls*) mono *msing*

covered wagon [ˌkʌvəd'wægən] N carreta *f* entoldada

covering ['kʌvərɪŋ] A N 1 (= *wrapping*) cubierta *f*, envoltura *f*; (= *dress etc*) abrigo *m*

2 (= *layer*) **a ~ of snow/dust/icing** una capa de nieve/polvo/azúcar glaseado

B CPD ► **covering letter** N (*Brit*) carta *f* de explicación

coverlet ['kʌvəlɪt] N sobrecama *m*, colcha *f*, cobertor *m*

covert ['kʌvət] A ADJ (*gen*) secreto, encubierto; [*glance*] furtivo, disimulado

B N soto *m*, matorral *m*

C CPD ► **covert attack** N ataque *m* por sorpresa

covertly ['kʌvətlɪ] ADV [*observe*] encubiertamente

cover-up ['kʌvərʌp] N encubrimiento *m*; **there's been a ~** están tratando de encubrir el asunto

covet ['kʌvɪt] VT codiciar

covetous ['kʌvɪtəs] ADJ [*person*] codicioso; [*glance*] ávido

covetousness ['kʌvɪtəsnɪs] N codicia *f*

covey ['kʌvɪ] N 1 (*Orn*) nidada *f* (*de perdices*)

2 (*fig*) grupo *m*

cow¹ [kaʊ] A N 1 (*Zool*) vaca *f*; (= *female of other species*) hembra *f*; ✦**IDIOM till the ~s come home** hasta que las ranas críen pelo

2 (‡ *pej*) (= *woman*) estúpida *f*, bruja *f*

B CPD ► **cow house** N establo *m* ► **cow parsley** N perejil *m* de monte ► **cow town*** N (*US*) pueblucho *m* de mala muerte

cow² [kaʊ] VT [+ *person*] intimidar, acobardar; **a ~ed look** una mirada temerosa

coward ['kaʊəd] N cobarde *mf*

cowardice ['kaʊədɪs], **cowardliness** ['kaʊədlɪnɪs] N cobardía *f*

cowardly ['kaʊədlɪ] ADJ cobarde

cowbell ['kaʊbel] N cencerro *m*

cowboy ['kaʊbɔɪ] A N 1 vaquero *m*, gaucho *m* (*Arg*); (*Cine etc*) cowboy *m*; **~s and Indians** (= *game*) indios *mpl* y americanos

2 (*Brit** *pej*) chorizo/a *m/f* (*Sp*); **he's a real ~** es un auténtico chorizo; **the ~s of the building trade** los piratas de la construcción

B CPD ► **cowboy boots** NPL botas *fpl* camperas ► **cowboy hat** N sombrero *m* de cowboy

cowcatcher ['kaʊˌkætʃəʳ] N rastrillo *m* delantero, quitapiedras *m inv*

cower ['kaʊəʳ] VI encogerse (de miedo); **the servants were ~ing in a corner** los criados se habían refugiado medrosos en un rincón

cowgirl ['kaʊgɜːl] N vaquera *f*

cowherd ['kaʊhɜːd] N pastor(a) *m/f* de ganado, vaquero/a *m/f*

cowhide ['kaʊhaɪd] N cuero *m*

cowl [kaʊl] N (= *hood*) capucha *f*; (= *garment*) cogulla *f*; [*of chimney*] sombrerete *m*

cowlick ['kaʊlɪk] N (*US*) chavito *m*, mechón *m*

cowling ['kaʊlɪŋ] N cubierta *f*

cowman ['kaʊmən] N (*pl* **cowmen**) vaquero *m*; (= *owner*) ganadero *m*

co-worker ['kəʊ'wɜːkəʳ] N colaborador(a) *m/f*

cowpat ['kaʊpæt] N mierda *f* de vaca, boñiga *f*

cowpoke* ['kaʊpəʊk] N (*US*) vaquero *m*

cowpox ['kaʊpɒks] N vacuna *f*

cowrie ['kaʊrɪ] N cauri *m*

cowshed ['kaʊʃed] N establo *m*

cowslip ['kaʊslɪp] N (*Bot*) primavera *f*, prímula *f*

cox [kɒks] A N timonel *mf*

B VT gobernar

C VI hacer *or* actuar de timonel

coxcomb ['kɒkskəʊm] N cresta *f* de gallo

coxless pairs [ˌkɒkslɪs'peəz] N dos *m* sin timonel

coxswain ['kɒksn] N timonel *mf*

Coy ABBR (*Mil*) = **company**

coy [kɔɪ] ADJ (*compar* **coyer**, *superl* **coyest**) 1 (= *demure*) [*person, smile*] tímido; (*pej*) (= *coquettish*) coqueta, coquetón

2 (= *evasive*) esquivo, reticente

coyly ['kɔɪlɪ] ADV 1 (= *demurely*) tímidamente; (*pej*) (= *coquettishly*) con coquetería

2 (= *evasively*) con evasivas

coyness ['kɔɪnɪs] N 1 (= *demureness*) timidez *f*; (*pej*) (= *coquettishness*) coquetería *f*

2 (= *evasiveness*) evasivas *fpl*, reticencias *fpl*

coyote [kɔɪ'əʊtɪ] N coyote *m*

coypu ['kɔɪpuː] N (*pl* **coypus** *or* **coypu**) coipo *m*

coz* [kɒz] = **cousin**

'coz‡ [kɒz] = **because**

coziness ['kəʊzɪnɪs] N (*US*) = **cosiness**

cozy ['kəʊzɪ] ADJ (*US*) = **cosy**

cozzie* ['kɒzɪ] N (*Brit, Australia*) = **cossie**

CP N ABBR 1 (*Pol*) (= **Communist Party**) PC *m*

2 (*Comm*) (= **carriage paid**) pp

3 = **Cape Province**

cp ABBR (= **compare**) comp

C/P, c/p ABBR (= **carriage paid**) pp

CPA N ABBR 1 (*US Fin*) = **Certified Public Accountant**

2 = **critical path analysis**

CPI N ABBR (*US*) (= **Consumer Price Index**) IPC *m*

cpi ABBR (*Comput*) = **characters per inch**

Cpl N ABBR (*Mil*) = **Corporal**

CP/M N ABBR (= **Control Program for Microprocessors**) CP/M *m*

CPO N ABBR 1 (*Naut*) = **Chief Petty Officer**

2 = **Crime Prevention Officer**

CPR N ABBR = **cardiopulmonary resuscitation**

cps ABBR (*Comput*) 1 (= **characters per second**) cps

2 = **cycles per second**

CPSA N ABBR (*Brit*) (= **Civil and Public Services Association**) *sindicato de funcionarios*

CPU N ABBR (*Comput*) (= **central processing unit**) UPC *f*, UCP *f*

CPVE N ABBR (*Brit*) = **Certificate of Prevocational Education**

Cr ABBR 1 (*Comm*) (= **credit**) H.

2 (*Comm*) (= **creditor**) acr.

3 (*Pol*) = **councillor**

crab [kræb] A N 1 (*Zool*) cangrejo *m*, jaiba *f* (*LAm*); **the Crab** (*Astron*) (la constelación de) Cáncer; ✦**IDIOM to catch a ~** (*Rowing*) fallar con el remo, dar una calada

2 **crabs** (*Med*) ladillas *fpl*

B VI **to ~ (about)** (*US**) quejarse (acerca de)

C CPD ► **crab apple** N (= *fruit*) manzana *f* silvestre; (= *tree*) manzano *m* silvestre ► **crab grass** N garranchuelo *m* ► **crab louse** N ladilla *f*

crabbed ['kræbd] ADJ 1 [*writing*] apretado, indescifrable

2 [*mood*] malhumorado, hosco

crabby* ['kræbɪ] ADJ malhumorado, hosco

crabmeat ['kræbmiːt] N carne *f* de cangrejo

crabwise ['kræbˌwaɪz] A ADJ [*movement*] como de cangrejo, lateral

B ADV [*move*] como cangrejo, lateralmente

crack [kræk] A N 1 (= *fracture*) (*in plate, glass*) raja *f*; (*in wall, ceiling, ice*) grieta *f*; (*in skin*) grieta *f*; (*fig*) (*in system, relationship*) grieta *f*; ✦**IDIOM to paper over the ~s** (*fig*) disimular las grietas

2 (= *slight opening*) rendija *f*; **I opened the door a ~** abrí un poquito la puerta

3 (= *noise*) [*of twigs*] crujido *m*; [*of whip*] chasquido *m*; [*of rifle*] estampido *m*, estallido *m*; [*of thunder*] estampido *m*, estruendo *m*; ✦**IDIOMS to get a fair ~ of the whip** tener la oportunidad de demostrar lo que vale; **to give sb a fair ~ of the whip** dar la oportunidad a algn de demostrar lo que vale

4 (= *blow*) golpe *m*; **he got a nasty ~ on the head** se llevó un buen golpe en la cabeza

5 (*) (= *attempt*) intento *m*; **to have** *or* **take a ~ at sth** intentar algo; **he was anxious to have the first ~ at it** estaba deseoso de ser el primero en intentarlo

6 (*) (= *joke, insult*) comentario *m* burlón; **he made a silly ~ about our new car** hizo un chiste tonto sobre nuestro coche nuevo

7 (= *drug*) crack *m*

8 **at the ~ of dawn** al romper el alba; **I'm not getting up at the ~ of dawn!*** ¡no me voy a levantar con el canto del gallo!*

9 (*) (= *fun*) **it's good ~** es muy divertido

B ADJ [*team, sportsperson, troops*] de primera; **he's a ~ shot** es un tirador de primera

C VT 1 (= *break*) [+ *glass, pottery*] rajar; [+ *wood, ground, wall*] agrietar, resquebrajar; [+ *ice*] resquebrajar; [+ *skin*] agrietar; (*fig*) (*) [+ *person*] derrotar; **to ~ sb's resolve** hacerle perder la determinación a algn

2 (= *break open*) [+ *nut*] cascar; [+ *egg*] cascar, romper; [+ *safe*] forzar; (*fig*) (*) [+ *market*]

entrar en, introducirse en; [+ *drugs/spy ring*] desarticular; **to ~ (open) a bottle*** abrir una botella; *see also* **nut A2**
3 (= *hit*) golpear; **he fell and ~ed his head on the pavement** se cayó y se golpeó la cabeza con la acera
4 (= *cause to sound*) [+ *whip*] chasquear, restallar; [+ *finger joints*] hacer crujir; ✦**IDIOM to ~ the whip** apretarle a algn las clavijas
5 (*) (= *tell*) [+ *joke*] contar; **to ~ jokes** bromear, contar chistes
6 (= *solve*) [+ *problem, case*] resolver; [+ *code*] descifrar; **the police think they've ~ed it** la policía cree haberlo resuelto
7 **to ~ a smile** sonreír
Ⓓ VI 1 (= *break*) [*glass, pottery*] rajarse; [*wall, wood, ground*] agrietarse, resquebrajarse; [*ice*] resquebrajarse; [*skin*] agrietarse
2 [*voice*] (*with emotion*) quebrarse
3 (= *yield, break down*) [*person*] desmoronarse; **I thought his nerve would ~** creía que iba a perder el valor; **to ~ under the strain** [*person*] desmoronarse bajo la presión, sufrir una crisis nerviosa a cause de la presión; [*relationship*] desmoronarse; [*alliance*] desmoronarse *or* quebrantarse bajo la presión
4 (= *make noise*) [*thunder*] retumbar; [*whip*] chasquear; [*dry wood, joints*] crujir
5 **to get ~ing*** poner manos a la obra; **you'd better get ~ing** más te vale poner manos a la obra; **I promised to get ~ing on** *or* **with the decorating** le prometí que empezaría a pintar inmediatamente
Ⓔ CPD ► **crack cocaine** N crack *m* ► **crack house** N (*Drugs*) *lugar donde se vende crack or cocaína dura*
►**crack down** VI + ADV **to ~ down (on sth/sb)** tomar medidas enérgicas *or* duras (contra algo/algn)
►**crack up*** Ⓐ VI + ADV 1 (= *break down*) [*person*] desmoronarse, sufrir una crisis nerviosa; [*relationship*] desmoronarse; [*alliance*] desmoronarse, quebrantarse
2 (= *laugh*) troncharse de risa*
Ⓑ VT + ADV **the film's not all it's ~ed up to be** la película no es tan buena como se dice; **he's not all he's ~ed up to be** no es tan maravilloso como lo pintan*
crackajack* [ˈkrækədʒæk] N, ADJ (*US*) = **crackerjack**
crack-brained* [ˈkrækbreɪnd] ADJ loco
crackdown [ˈkrækdaʊn] N campaña *f* (**on** contra), medidas *fpl* enérgicas (**on** contra)
cracked [krækt] ADJ 1 [*cup, plate*] rajado; [*wall*] agrietado; [*lips*] cortado, agrietado; [*skin*] agrietado; **the bone's not really broken, only ~** el hueso no está rota en realidad, sólo tiene una fisura pequeña
2 [*voice*] cascado
3 (*) (= *mad*) chiflado*, tarado*
cracker [ˈkrækəʳ] N 1 (= *firework*) buscapiés *m inv*
2 (*also* **Christmas ~**) sorpresa *f* (navideña)
3 (= *biscuit*) galleta *f* salada, cráker *m*
4 (*Brit**) **a ~ of a game** un partido fenomenal*
crackerjack* [ˈkrækədʒæk] Ⓐ N (= *person*) as* *m*; (= *thing*) bomba* *f*
Ⓑ ADJ bomba*, súper*
crackers* [ˈkrækəz] ADJ (*Brit*) lelo, chiflado*
crackhead* [ˈkræk,hed] N adicto/a *m/f* al crack
cracking [ˈkrækɪŋ] Ⓐ N 1 (*Chem*) [*of petroleum*] craqueo *m*
2 (= *cracks*) grietas *fpl*, agrietamiento *m*
Ⓑ ADJ (*Brit**) 1 (= *very fast*) **at a ~ speed** *or* **pace** a toda pastilla*
2 (= *excellent*) de órdago*
Ⓒ ADV (*Brit**) **this book is a ~ good read** este libro es superameno
crackle [ˈkrækl] Ⓐ N (*usu no pl*) (= *noise*) [*of twigs burning*] crepitación *f*, chisporroteo *m*; [*of frying*] chisporroteo *m*; [*of dry leaves*] crujido *m*; [*of shots*] traqueteo *m*; (*on telephone*) interferencia *f*
Ⓑ VI [*burning twigs*] crepitar, chisporrotear; [*bacon*] chisporrotear; [*dry leaves*] crujir; [*shots*] traquetear; [*phone line*] tener interferencias
crackling [ˈkræklɪŋ] N 1 (= *no pl*) (*Culin*) chicharrones *mpl*
2 (= *sound*) chisporroteo *m*; (*on radio, telephone*) interferencias *fpl*
crackly [ˈkrækəlɪ] ADJ [*phone line, noise*] chirriante, chisporroteante
crackpot* [ˈkrækpɒt] Ⓐ ADJ tonto
Ⓑ N chiflado/a* *m/f*, excéntrico/a *m/f*
crack-up [ˈkrækʌp] N (*Med*) crisis *f inv* nerviosa, colapso *m* nervioso; (*Fin etc*) quiebra *f*
cradle [ˈkreɪdl] Ⓐ N 1 (= *cot, birthplace etc*) cuna *f*; ✦**IDIOMS from the ~ to the grave** desde que nació, nacen *etc* hasta que murió, mueren *etc*; **to rob the ~*** casarse con una persona mucho más joven
2 [*of telephone*] soporte *m*, horquilla *f*
3 (*Constr*) andamio *m* volante
Ⓑ VT [+ *child*] mecer, acunar; [+ *object*] abrazar; **to ~ a child in one's arms** mecer un niño en los brazos
Ⓒ CPD ► **cradle snatcher*** N **she's a ~ snatcher** siempre va detrás de los jovencitos
cradlesong [ˈkreɪdlsɒŋ] N canción *f* de cuna
craft [krɑːft] Ⓐ N 1 (= *trade*) oficio *m*
2 (= *no pl*) (= *skill*) destreza *f*, habilidad *f*
3 (= *handicraft*) artesanía *f*; **arts and ~s** artesanías *fpl*
4 (*pej*) (= *cunning*) astucia *f*, maña *f*
5 (= *boat*) (*pl inv*) barco *m*, embarcación *f*
Ⓑ VT hacer (a mano); **~ed products** productos *mpl* de artesanía
Ⓒ CPD ► **craft fair** N feria *f* de artesanía ► **craft union** N sindicato *m* de obreros especializados ► **craft work** N artesanía *f*
craftily [ˈkrɑːftɪlɪ] ADV astutamente
craftiness [ˈkrɑːftɪnɪs] N astucia *f*
craftsman [ˈkrɑːftsmən] N (*pl* **craftsmen**) artesano *m*
craftsmanship [ˈkrɑːftsmənʃɪp] N (*no pl*) (= *skill*) destreza *f*, habilidad *f*; (= *workmanship*) trabajo *m*
craftsperson [ˈkrɑːfts,pɜːsn] N (*pl* **craftspeople**) artesano/a *m/f*
craftswoman [ˈkrɑːfts,wʊmən] N (*pl* **craftswomen**) artesana *f*
crafty [ˈkrɑːftɪ] ADJ (*compar* **craftier**; *superl* **craftiest**) 1 [*person*] astuto, vivo; [*action*] hábil
2 [*gadget etc*] ingenioso
crag [kræg] N peñasco *m*, risco *m*
craggy [ˈkrægɪ] ADJ (*compar* **craggier**; *superl* **craggiest**) [*rock*] rocoso, escarpado; [*features*] hosco, arrugado
cram [kræm] Ⓐ VT 1 (= *stuff*) meter (**into** en); **we can't ~ any more in** es imposible meter más; **to ~ food into one's mouth** llenarse la boca de comida; **to ~ things into a case** ir metiendo cosas en una maleta hasta que ya no cabe más nada; **she ~med her hat down over her eyes** se enfundó el sombrero hasta los ojos
2 (= *fill*) llenar a reventar (**with** de); **the hall is ~med** la sala está de bote en bote; **the room was ~med with furniture** la habitación estaba atestada de muebles; **his head is ~med with strange ideas** tiene la cabeza llena de ideas raras; **to ~ o.s. with food** atiborrarse de comida, darse un atracón*
3 (*Scol*) [+ *subject*] empollar, aprender apresuradamente; [+ *pupil*] preparar apresuradamente para un examen
Ⓑ VI 1 [*people*] apelotonarse (**into** en); **can I ~ in here?** ¿hay un hueco para mí aquí?; **seven of us ~med into the Mini** los siete logramos encajarnos en el Mini
2 [*pupil*] (*for exam*) empollar
cram-full [ˈkræmˈfʊl] ADJ atestado (**of** de), de bote en bote
crammer [ˈkræməʳ] N (*Scol*) (= *pupil*) empollón/ona *m/f*; (= *teacher*) profesor(a) *m/f* (*que prepara rapidísimamente a sus alumnos para los exámenes*)
cramp[1] [kræmp] Ⓐ N (*Med*) calambre *m*; **writer's ~** calambre *m* en las manos (por escribir mucho)
Ⓑ VT (= *restrict*) [+ *development*] poner obstáculos a, poner trabas a; ✦**IDIOM to ~ sb's style** cortar las alas a algn
cramp[2] [kræmp] N (*Tech*) grapa *f*; (*Archit*) pieza *f* de unión, abrazadera *f*
cramped [kræmpt] ADJ [*position*] encogido, incómodo; [*room etc*] estrecho; [*writing*] menudo, apretado; **to live in ~ conditions** vivir en la estrechez; **they were all ~ together** estaban apiñados; **we are very ~ for space** apenas hay espacio para moverse
crampon [ˈkræmpən] N garfio *m*; (*Mountaineering*) crampón *m*
cramponning [ˈkræmpənɪŋ] N (*Mountaineering*) uso *m* de crampones
cranberry [ˈkrænbərɪ] Ⓐ N arándano *m*
Ⓑ CPD ► **cranberry sauce** N salsa *f* de arándanos
crane [kreɪn] Ⓐ N 1 (*Orn*) grulla *f*
2 (*Tech*) grúa *f*
Ⓑ VT 1 **to ~ one's neck** estirar el cuello
2 (*also* **to ~ up**) levantar con grúa
Ⓒ VI (*also* **~ forward**) inclinarse estirando el cuello; **to ~ to see sth** estirar el cuello para ver algo
Ⓓ CPD ► **crane driver, crane operator** N operador(a) *m/f* de grúa
cranefly [ˈkreɪnflaɪ] N típula *f*
cranial [ˈkreɪnɪəl] ADJ craneal
cranium [ˈkreɪnɪəm] N (*pl* **craniums** *or* **crania** [ˈkreɪnɪə]) cráneo *m*
crank[1] [kræŋk] Ⓐ N (*Tech*) manivela *f*, manubrio *m*
Ⓑ VT (*also* **~ up**) [+ *engine*] hacer arrancar con la manivela
►**crank out*** VT + ADV producir penosamente
►**crank up*** VT + ADV 1 [+ *hearing aid*] subir; [+ *music*] poner más fuerte; **to ~ up the volume** subir el volumen
2 (= *intensify*) [+ *campaign, bombing*] intensificar
crank[2]* [kræŋk] N (= *eccentric person*) excéntrico/a *m/f*; (*US*) (= *bad-tempered person*) ogro* *m*, cascarrabias* *mf inv*
crankcase [ˈkræŋkkeɪs] N cárter *m*
crankshaft [ˈkræŋkʃɑːft] N cigüeñal *m*
cranky* [ˈkræŋkɪ] ADJ (*compar* **crankier**; *superl* **crankiest**) (= *strange*) [*idea, person*] excéntrico; (*US*) (= *bad-tempered*) malhumorado, enojón (*LAm*)
cranny [ˈkrænɪ] N grieta *f*
crap** [kræp] Ⓐ N 1 (= *faeces*) mierda** *f*
2 (= *nonsense*) estupideces *fpl*, macanas* *fpl*, gilipolleces *fpl* (*Sp**), huevadas *fpl* (*Chile, Andes***), boludeces *fpl* (*S. Cone***); **that's ~** eso

son gilipolleces*, eso es una chorrada*; **to talk ~** decir gilipolleces*, decir chorradas*
3 (= *unwanted items*) porquería *f*
Ⓑ ADJ [*joke, job*] pésimo; **the film was ~** la película era una mierda**; **to be ~** ser una mierda**; **I'm ~ at football** yo jugando al fútbol soy una mierda** *or* soy malísimo
Ⓒ VI cagar**
► **crap out**** VI + ADV (*US*) 1 (= *back down*) rajarse*
2 (= *fail*) fracasar
crape [kreɪp] N = **crepe**
crappy** ['kræpɪ] ADJ chungo*
craps [kræps] NSING (*US*) (= *game*) dados *mpl*; **to shoot ~** jugar a los dados
crapulous ['kræpjʊləs] ADJ (*frm*) crapuloso, ebrio
crash [kræʃ] Ⓐ N 1 (= *noise*) estrépito *m*; (= *thunder*) estruendo *m*; (= *explosion*) estallido *m*
2 (= *accident*) (*Aut*) choque *m*; (*Aer*) accidente *m*; **to have a ~** (*Aut*) tener un accidente de coche, chocar con el coche; **to be in a car/plane ~** tener un accidente de coche/aviación
3 (*Fin*) [*of stock exchange*] crac *m*; [*of business*] (= *failure*) quiebra *f*; **the 1929 ~** la crisis económica de 1929
Ⓑ VT 1 (= *smash*) [+ *car, aircraft etc*] estrellar (**into** contra); **he ~ed his head against the wall** se estrelló la cabeza contra la pared
2 (*) (= *gatecrash*) **to ~ a party** colarse en una fiesta*
Ⓒ VI 1 (= *fall noisily*) caer con estrépito; (= *move noisily*) moverse de manera ruidosa; **to come ~ing down** caer con gran estrépito
2 (= *have accident*) tener un accidente; (*Aer*) estrellarse, caer a tierra; (= *collide*) [*two vehicles*] chocar; **to ~ into/through** chocar *or* estrellarse contra
3 (*Fin*) [*business*] quebrar; [*stock exchange*] sufrir una crisis; **when the stock market ~ed** cuando la bolsa se derrumbó
4 (*Comput*) bloquearse, colgarse (*Sp*)
5 (*) (= *sleep*) dormir, pasar la noche
Ⓓ ADV **he went ~ into a tree** dio de lleno contra un árbol
Ⓔ EXCL ¡zas!, ¡pum!
Ⓕ CPD [*diet etc*] intensivo, acelerado ► **crash barrier** N (*Brit Aut*) quitamiedos *m inv*; (*at stadium etc*) valla *f* protectora ► **crash course** N curso *m* intensivo *or* acelerado ► **crash dive** N [*of submarine*] inmersión *f* de emergencia ► **crash helmet** N casco *m* protector ► **crash landing** N aterrizaje *m* forzoso *or* de emergencia ► **crash pad*** N guarida *f*, lugar *m* donde dormir ► **crash programme** (*Brit*), **crash program** (*US*) N programa *m* de urgencia
► **crash out*** Ⓐ VT + ADV **to be ~ed out** estar hecho polvo*
Ⓑ VI + ADV (= *collapse*) caer redondo; (= *sleep*) dormirse
crashing ['kræʃɪŋ] ADJ (†) **a ~ bore** una paliza*, un muermo*
crashingly ['kræʃɪŋlɪ] ADV (†) [*dull, boring*] tremendamente
crash-land ['kræʃlænd] Ⓐ VT [+ *aircraft*] poner forzosamente en tierra
Ⓑ VI aterrizar forzosamente
crass [kræs] ADJ (*pej*) (= *extreme*) [*stupidity*] extremo; [*mistake*] craso; (= *coarse*) [*person, behaviour*] grosero, maleducado; [*performance*] malo, desastroso
crassly ['kræslɪ] ADV estúpidamente, tontamente
crassness ['kræsnɪs] N estupidez *f*
crate [kreɪt] Ⓐ N 1 cajón *m* de embalaje, jaula *f*
2 (*) (= *car etc*) armatoste *m*, cacharro* *m*
Ⓑ VT (*also* **~ up**) embalar (en cajones)
crater ['kreɪtəʳ] N cráter *m*
cravat(e) [krə'væt] N pañuelo *m*
crave [kreɪv] VT 1 (*also* **~ for**) [+ *food*] tener antojo de; [+ *affection, attention*] reclamar
2 (= *beg*) [+ *pardon*] suplicar; [+ *permission*] implorar, rogar
craven ['kreɪvən] ADJ (*liter*) cobarde
cravenly ['kreɪvənlɪ] ADV (*liter*) cobardemente
cravenness ['kreɪvənnɪs] N (*liter*) cobardía *f*
craving ['kreɪvɪŋ] N (*for food etc*) antojo *m*; (*for affection, attention*) anhelo *m*, ansias *fpl*; **to get a ~ for sth** encapricharse por algo
craw [krɔː] N ✦*IDIOM* **to stick in one's ~***: **it really sticks in my ~ that she thinks ...** no trago con que ella piense que ...
crawfish ['krɔːfɪʃ] N (*pl* **crawfish** *or* **crawfishes**) (*US*) = **crayfish**
crawl [krɔːl] Ⓐ N 1 (= *slow pace*) [*of traffic*] **the traffic went at a ~** la circulación avanzaba a paso de tortuga; **the ~ to the coast** la cola de coches hasta la costa
2 (*Swimming*) crol *m*; **to do the ~** nadar a crol
Ⓑ VI 1 (= *drag o.s.*) arrastrarse; [*child*] andar a gatas, gatear; **to ~ in/out** meterse/salirse a gatas; **the fly ~ed up the window** la mosca subió despacito por el cristal
2 (= *move slowly*) [*traffic*] avanzar lentamente, formar caravana; [*time*] alargarse interminablemente; **the cars were ~ing along** los coches avanzaban a paso de tortuga
3 (*) (= *suck up*) **to ~ to sb** dar coba a algn*, hacer la pelota a algn*
4 **to be ~ing with vermin** estar plagado *or* cuajado de bichos; *see also* **flesh**
Ⓒ CPD ► **crawl space** N (*US*) (*between floors*) *espacio entre plantas para tuberías o cables*
crawler ['krɔːləʳ] Ⓐ N (*Mech*) tractor *m* de oruga
Ⓑ CPD ► **crawler lane** N (*Brit Aut*) carril *m* (de autopista) para vehículos lentos
crayfish ['kreɪfɪʃ] N (*pl* **crayfish** *or* **crayfishes**) (*freshwater*) cangrejo *m or* (*LAm*) jaiba *f* de río; (*saltwater*) cigala *f*
crayon ['kreɪən] Ⓐ N (*Art*) pastel *m*, lápiz *m* de tiza; (*child's*) lápiz *m* de color
Ⓑ VT dibujar al pastel
craze [kreɪz] N (= *fashion*) moda *f* (**for** de); (= *fad*) manía *f* (**for** por); **it's the latest ~** es la última moda, es el último grito
crazed [kreɪzd] ADJ 1 [*look, person*] loco, demente
2 [*pottery, glaze*] agrietado, cuarteado
crazily ['kreɪzɪlɪ] ADV 1 (= *madly*) [*shout, argue, laugh*] como (un) loco
2 (= *crookedly*) [*tilt, lean*] de modo peligroso, peligrosamente
craziness ['kreɪzɪnɪs] N (= *madness*) [*of person*] locura *f*; [*of behaviour, idea*] insensatez *f*
crazy ['kreɪzɪ] Ⓐ ADJ (*compar* **crazier**, *superl* **craziest**) 1 (= *mad*) loco, chiflado*; **you were ~ to do it** fue una locura hacerlo; **you would be ~ to do that** tendrías que estar loco para hacer eso; **it would be ~ for him to give up his job** sería una locura que dejase el trabajo; **to drive sb ~** (= *drive mad*) volver loco a algn; (= *infuriate*) sacar de quicio a algn; **it's enough to drive you ~** es para volverse loco; **to go ~** (= *mad*) volverse loco; (= *excited*) ponerse como loco; (= *angry*) ponerse como un energúmeno; **it was a ~ idea** fue una locura *or* un disparate, era una idea descabellada *or* disparatada; **everyone shouted like ~** todos gritaban como locos; **they were selling like ~** se estaban vendiendo como rosquillas *or* como pan caliente*; **it sounds ~** parece una locura; **~ talk** disparates *mpl*, tonterías *fpl*; **I've done some ~ things in my time** he hecho algunas locuras en mi vida; **~ with grief/anxiety** loco de pena/preocupación; **it's a ~ world** el mundo está loco, es un mundo de locos
2 (*) (= *keen*) **he's football ~** es un fanático del fútbol; **to be ~ about sb** estar loco por algn; **they're ~ about football** el fútbol les vuelve locos; **I'm not ~ about it** no es que me vuelva loco, no me entusiasma
3 **to lean at a ~ angle** inclinarse de modo peligroso
Ⓑ N (*US**) loco/a *m/f*
Ⓒ CPD ► **crazy bone** N (*US*) hueso *m* del codo ► **crazy house*** N (*US*) casa *f* de locos*, manicomio *m* ► **crazy paving** N pavimento *m* de baldosas irregulares ► **crazy quilt** N (*US*) edredón *m* de retazos
CRC N ABBR 1 (*US*) = **Civil Rights Commission**
2 = **Camera-Ready Copy**
CRE N ABBR (*Brit*) = **Commission for Racial Equality**
creak [kriːk] Ⓐ N [*of wood, shoe etc*] crujido *m*; [*of hinge etc*] chirrido *m*, rechinamiento *m*
Ⓑ VI crujir; (= *squeak*) chirriar, rechinar
creaky ['kriːkɪ] ADJ rechinador; (*fig*) poco sólido
cream [kriːm] Ⓐ N 1 (*on milk*) nata *f*, crema *f* (*LAm*); **~ of tartar** crémor *m* tártaro; **~ of tomato soup** sopa *f* de crema de tomate; **~ of wheat** (*US*) sémola *f*; *see also* **double F**, **single C**, **whipped**
2 (*fig*) flor *f* y nata, crema *f*; **the ~ of society** la flor y nata de la sociedad; **the ~ of the crop** lo mejor de lo mejor
3 (= *lotion*) (*for face, shoes etc*) crema *f*, pomada *f*; **shoe ~** betún *m*; **face ~** crema *f* para la cara
Ⓑ ADJ 1 (= *cream-coloured*) color crema *inv*
2 (= *made with cream*) de nata *or* (*LAm*) crema
Ⓒ VT 1 [+ *milk*] desnatar, descremar (*LAm*); [+ *butter*] batir
2 (*also* **~ together**) (= *mix*) batir; **~ed potatoes** puré *msing* de patatas *or* (*LAm*) papas
3 (*US**) [+ *enemy, opposing team*] arrollar, aplastar
4 **to ~ one's pants**** correrse sin querer**
Ⓓ CPD ► **cream cake** N pastel *m* de nata *or* (*LAm*) crema ► **cream cheese** N queso *m* crema ► **cream cracker** N galleta *f* de soda ► **cream puff** N petisú *m*, pastel *m* de nata *or* (*LAm*) crema ► **cream soda** N gaseosa *f* de vainilla ► **cream tea** N (*Brit*) *merienda en cafetería que suele constar de té, bollos, mermelada y nata*
► **cream off*** VT + ADV [+ *best talents, part of profits*] separar lo mejor de
creamery ['kriːmərɪ] N 1 (*on farm*) lechería *f*; (= *butter factory*) fábrica *f* de productos lácteos
2 (= *small shop*) lechería *f*
creaminess ['kriːmɪnɪs] N cremosidad *f*
creamy ['kriːmɪ] ADJ (*compar* **creamier**, *superl* **creamiest**) [*taste, texture*] cremoso; [*colour*] color crema *inv*
crease [kriːs] Ⓐ N 1 (= *fold*) raya *f*; (= *wrinkle*) arruga *f*
2 (*Cricket*) línea *f* de bateo
Ⓑ VT [+ *paper*] doblar; (*esp several times*) plegar; [+ *clothes*] arrugar; **to ~ one's trousers** (= *press crease in*) hacer la raya a los pantalones
Ⓒ VI arrugarse
► **crease up*** (*Brit*) Ⓐ VT + ADV **he was ~d up (with laughter)** se tronchaba (de risa)

Ⓑ VI + ADV **he ~d up (with laughter)** se tronchaba (de risa)

creaseless ['kri:slɪs], **crease-resistant** ['kri:srɪ,zɪstənt] ADJ inarrugable

create [kri:'eɪt] Ⓐ VT [1] (*gen, Comput*) crear; [+ *character*] inventar; [+ *rôle*] encarnar; [+ *fashion*] desarrollar; [+ *fuss, noise*] armar; [+ *problem*] causar, crear; **to ~ an impression** impresionar, causar buena impresión
[2] (= *appoint*) nombrar; **he was ~d a peer by the Queen** fue nombrado par por la reina
Ⓑ VI (*Brit**) (= *make a fuss*) montar un número*, armar un lío*

creation [kri:'eɪʃən] N [1] creación *f*; **the Creation** (*Rel*) la Creación
[2] (= *dress etc*) modelo *m*

creationism [kri:'eɪʃənɪzəm] N creacionismo *m*

creationist [kri:'eɪʃənɪst] N creacionista *mf*

creative [kri:'eɪtɪv] Ⓐ ADJ [*person, talent, energy, solution*] creativo; **the ~ use of language** el uso creativo del lenguaje; **~ thinking** creatividad *f*
Ⓑ CPD ► **creative accounting** N contabilidad *f* embellecida ► **creative writing** N escritura *f* creativa

creatively [kri:'eɪtɪvlɪ] ADV con creatividad

creativity [,kri:eɪ'tɪvɪtɪ] N creatividad *f*

creator [krɪ'eɪtəʳ] N creador(a) *m/f*; **the Creator** (*Rel*) el Creador

creature ['kri:tʃəʳ] Ⓐ N [1] (*gen*) criatura *f*; (= *animal*) animal *m*; (= *insect etc*) bicho *m*
[2] (= *person*) **pay no attention to that ~** no hagas caso de esa individua; **poor ~!** ¡pobrecito!; **wretched ~!** ¡desgraciado!; **~ of habit** esclavo/a *m/f* de la costumbre
[3] (*pej*) (= *dependent person*) títere *m*
Ⓑ CPD ► **creature comforts** NPL comodidades *fpl* (materiales)

crèche [kreɪʃ] N (*Brit*) guardería *f*

cred* [kred] N = **street cred**

credence ['kri:dəns] N **to give ~ to** dar crédito a

credentials [krɪ'denʃəlz] NPL (= *identifying papers*) credenciales *fpl*; (= *letters of reference*) referencias *fpl*; [*of diplomat*] cartas *fpl* credenciales; **what are his ~ for the post?** ¿qué méritos alega para el puesto?

credibility [,kredə'bɪlɪtɪ] Ⓐ N (*no pl*) credibilidad *f*
Ⓑ CPD ► **credibility gap** N falta *f* de credibilidad ► **credibility rating** N índice *m* de credibilidad

credible ['kredɪbl] ADJ (*gen*) creíble, digno de crédito; [*person*] plausible; [*witness*] de integridad

credibly ['kredɪblɪ] ADV creíblemente, verosímilmente

credit ['kredɪt] Ⓐ N [1] (*Fin*) [1·1] (*in account*) (= *positive balance*) **his account is in ~** su cuenta tiene saldo positivo *or* está en números negros; **as long as you stay in ~** *or* **keep your account in ~** mientras pueda mantener un saldo positivo; **you have £10 to your ~** tiene 10 libras en el haber, tiene un saldo a favor de 10 libras; *see also* **letter A2**
[1·2] (*for purchases*) crédito *m*; **they were refused ~** se les denegó un crédito; **is his ~ good?** ¿se le puede dar crédito sin riesgo?; **to give sb ~** conceder un crédito a algn; **interest-free ~** crédito *m* sin intereses; **to buy sth on ~** comprar algo a crédito *or* a plazos; **"no credit given"** "no se fía"; **"credit terms available"** "se vende a plazos", "facilidades de pago"
[1·3] (*Accounting*) saldo *m* acreedor, saldo *m* positivo; **on the ~ side** (*lit*) en el haber; (*fig*) entre los aspectos positivos
[2] (= *honour*) honor *m*; **he's a ~ to his family** es un orgullo para su familia, honra a su familia; **it does you ~** dice mucho a tu favor, te honra; **with a skill that would have done ~ to an expert** con una habilidad que hubiera sido el orgullo de un experto; **to his ~, I must point out that ...** debo decir en su favor que ...
[3] (= *recognition*) mérito *m*; **they deserve ~ for not giving up** merecen que se les reconozca el mérito de no haberse rendido; **~ where it's** *or* **~'s due** a cada uno según sus méritos; **to get the ~ (for sth)** llevarse el mérito (de algo); **I did the work and he got all the ~** yo hice el trabajo y él se llevó todo el mérito; **to give sb ~ for (doing) sth** reconocer a algn el mérito de (haber hecho) algo; **to take the ~ for (doing) sth** llevarse el mérito de (haber hecho) algo; **it would be wrong for us to take all the ~** no estaría bien que nos llevásemos todo el mérito
[4] (= *credence*) **he's a lot better than people give him ~ for** es bastante mejor que lo que la gente cree; **I gave you ~ for more sense** te creía más sensato; **I have to give some ~ to his story** tengo que reconocer que su historia tiene algo de verdad
[5] **credits** (*Cine, TV*) (= *titles*) títulos *mpl* de crédito, créditos *mpl*; (= *achievements*) logros *mpl*; **she has a long list of stage ~s** cuenta con una larga lista de éxitos *or* logros en escena
[6] (*esp US Univ*) (= *award*) crédito *m*, unidad *f* de valor académico
Ⓑ VT [1] (= *believe*) creer; **it's hard to ~ that such things went on** es difícil de creer que pasaran cosas semejantes; **would you ~ it!** ¡parece mentira!
[2] (= *attribute*) **I ~ed him with more sense** le creía más sensato; **~ me with SOME sense!** ¡no me tomes por idiota!; **he is ~ed with the discovery** se le atribuye a él el descubrimiento; **you don't ~ her with a mind of her own** no te das cuenta de que ella sabe lo que quiere
[3] (*Comm*) [+ *money, interest*] abonar, ingresar; **the money was ~ed to his account** el dinero se abonó *or* se ingresó en su cuenta; **we ~ you with the interest monthly** le abonamos *or* ingresamos el interés mensualmente
Ⓒ CPD ► **credit account** N cuenta *f* de crédito ► **credit agency** N agencia *f* de créditos ► **credit balance** N saldo *m* acreedor, saldo *m* positivo ► **credit card** N tarjeta *f* de crédito ► **credit entry** N anotación *f* en el haber ► **credit facilities** NPL facilidades *fpl* de crédito ► **credit limit** N límite *m* de crédito ► **credit line** N línea *f* de crédito ► **credit note** N nota *f* de crédito ► **credit rating** N clasificación *f* crediticia; (*fig*) credibilidad *f*; **the government's ~ rating has plummeted** la credibilidad del gobierno ha caído en picado ► **credit reference** N informe *m* de crédito ► **credit squeeze** N restricciones *fpl* de crédito ► **credit union** N cooperativa *f* de crédito

creditable ['kredɪtəbl] ADJ loable, encomiable

creditably ['kredɪtəblɪ] ADV de modo loable

creditor ['kredɪtəʳ] N acreedor(a) *m/f*

creditworthiness ['kredɪt,wɜ:ðɪnɪs] N solvencia *f*

creditworthy ['kredɪt,wɜ:ðɪ] ADJ solvente

credo ['kreɪdəʊ] N credo *m*

credulity [krɪ'dju:lɪtɪ] N credulidad *f*

credulous ['kredjʊləs] ADJ crédulo

credulously ['kredjʊləslɪ] ADV con credulidad

creed [kri:d] N (= *religion*) credo *m*, religión *f*; (= *system of beliefs*) credo *m*; **the Creed** (*Rel*) el Credo

creek [kri:k] N (*Brit*) (= *inlet*) cala *f*, ensenada *f*; (*US*) (= *stream*) riachuelo *m*; ✦**IDIOM up the ~ (without a paddle)*** (= *in difficulties*) en un lío *or* (*LAm*) aprieto

creel [kri:l] N nasa *f*, cesta *f* (de pescador)

creep [kri:p] (*pt, pp* **crept**) Ⓐ VI [1] [*animal*] deslizarse, arrastrarse; [*plant*] trepar
[2] [*person*] (*stealthily*) ir cautelosamente; (*slowly*) ir muy despacio; **to ~ in/out/up/down** entrar/salir/subir/bajar sigilosamente; **to ~ about on tiptoe** andar a *or* de puntillas; **to ~ along** [*traffic*] avanzar a paso de tortuga; **to ~ up on sb** acercarse sigilosamente a algn
[3] (*fig*) **it made my flesh ~** me puso la carne de gallina; **doubts began to ~ in** las dudas empezaron a aparecer; **an error crept in** se deslizó un error; **he felt old age ~ing up on him** sintió como la vida le ganaba años; **fear crept over him** le invadió el terror
Ⓑ N [1] (*) (= *person*) **what a ~!** ¡qué lameculos es!*; **he's a ~** (= *weird*) ¡qué tipo más raro!, ¡qué bicho!
[2] **it gives me the ~s*** me da miedo, me da escalofríos

creeper ['kri:pəʳ] N [1] (*Bot*) enredadera *f*
[2] **creepers** (*US*) (= *rompers*) (*for baby*) pelele *m*

creeping ['kri:pɪŋ] Ⓐ ADJ (*Med etc*) progresivo; [*barrage*] móvil
Ⓑ CPD ► **creeping inflation** N inflación *f* progresiva

creepy* ['kri:pɪ] ADJ (*compar* **creepier**; *superl* **creepiest**) horripilante, escalofriante

creepy-crawly* ['kri:pɪ'krɔ:lɪ] N (*Brit*) bicho *m*

cremate [krɪ'meɪt] VT incinerar

cremation [krɪ'meɪʃən] N cremación *f*, incineración *f*

crematorium [,kremə'tɔ:rɪəm] N (*pl* **crematoriums** *or* **crematoria** [,kremə'tɔ:rɪə]), **crematory** (*US*) ['kremə,tɔ:rɪ] crematorio *m*

crème caramel [,kremkærə'mel] N flan *m*

crème de la crème ['kremdəlɑ:'krem] N **the ~** la crème de la crème, la flor y nata

crème de menthe ['kremdəmɒ:nθ] N licor *m* de crema de menta

crenellated ['krenɪleɪtɪd] ADJ almenado

crenellations [,krenɪ'leɪʃənz] NPL almenas *fpl*

Creole ['kri:əʊl] Ⓐ ADJ criollo
Ⓑ N [1] (= *person*) criollo/a *m/f*
[2] (*Ling*) lengua *f* criolla

creosote ['krɪəsəʊt] Ⓐ N creosota *f*, chapote *m* (*Mex*)
Ⓑ VT echar creosota a

crepe, crêpe [kreɪp] Ⓐ N [1] (= *fabric*) crespón *m*
[2] (*also* **~ rubber**) crepé *m*; **~-soled shoes** zapatos *mpl* de suela de crepé
[3] (= *pancake*) crepa *f*
Ⓑ CPD ► **crepe bandage** N venda *f* de crespón ► **crepe de Chine** N crep(é) *m* de China ► **crepe paper** N papel *m* crepé ► **crepe sole** N (*on shoes*) suela *f* de crepé

crept [krept] PT, PP *of* **creep**

crepuscular [krɪ'pʌskjʊləʳ] ADJ (*liter*) crepuscular

crescendo [krɪ'ʃendəʊ] N (*pl* **crescendos** *or* **crescendi** [krɪ'ʃendɪ]) (*Mus*) (*fig*) crescendo *m*

crescent ['kresnt] Ⓐ ADJ creciente
Ⓑ N (= *shape*) medialuna *f*; (= *street*) calle en

forma de semicírculo
Ⓒ CPD ► **crescent moon** N luna *f* creciente

cress [kres] N berro *m*

crest [krest] Ⓐ N [*of bird, wave*] cresta *f*; [*of turkey*] moco *m*; [*of hill*] cima *f*, cumbre *f*; (*on helmet*) penacho *m*; (*Heraldry*) blasón *m*; ✦*IDIOM* **to be on the ~ of a wave** estar en la cresta de la ola
Ⓑ VT [+ *hill*] coronar, alcanzar la cima de
Ⓒ VI (*US*) llegar al máximo, alcanzar su punto más alto; **the flood ~ed at two metres** las aguas llegaron a dos metros sobre su nivel normal

crested ['krestɪd] ADJ [*bird etc*] crestado, con cresta; [*notepaper*] con escudo

crestfallen ['krest,fɔːlən] ADJ cariacontecido

cretaceous [krɪ'teɪʃəs] ADJ cretáceo

Cretan ['kriːtən] Ⓐ ADJ cretense
Ⓑ N cretense *mf*

Crete [kriːt] N Creta *f*

cretin* ['kretɪn] N (*Med*) cretino/a *m/f*; (*pej*) cretino/a *m/f*, imbécil *mf*

cretinous ['kretɪnəs] ADJ cretino; (* *pej*) imbécil

cretonne [kre'tɒn] N cretona *f*

crevasse [krɪ'væs] N grieta *f*

crevice ['krevɪs] N grieta *f*, hendedura *f*

crew[1] [kruː] Ⓐ N 1 (*Aer, Naut*) tripulación *f*; (*Navy*) dotación *f*; (*excluding officers*) marineros *mpl* rasos; **three ~ were drowned** perecieron ahogados tres tripulantes
2 (*Cine, Rowing, gen*) (= *team*) equipo *m*
3 (= *gang*) pandilla *f*, banda *f*; **they looked a sorry ~** daba lástima verlos
Ⓑ VI **to ~ for sb** hacer de tripulación para algn
Ⓒ VT tripular
Ⓓ CPD ► **crew cut** N pelado *m* al rape

crew[2] [kruː] PT *of* **crow**

crewman ['kruːmən] N (*pl* **crewmen**) 1 (*Naut*) tripulante *mf*
2 (*TV etc*) miembro *mf* del equipo (*de cámara etc*)

crew-neck ['kruːnek] N cuello *m* de barco; (*also* **~ sweater**) suéter *m* con cuello de barco

crib [krɪb] Ⓐ N 1 (*Brit*) (*for infant*) pesebre *m*; (*US*) (*for toddler*) cuna *f*; (*Rel*) Belén *m*; (= *manger*) cuadra *f*; **portable ~** (*US*) cuna *f* portátil
2 (*Scol**) (= *illicit copy*) plagio *m*; (*in exam*) chuleta* *f*; (= *translation*) traducción *f*
Ⓑ VT (*Scol**) plagiar, tomar (**from** de)
Ⓒ VI (*Scol**) usar una chuleta*
Ⓓ CPD ► **crib death** N (*US*) muerte *f* en la cuna

cribbage ['krɪbɪdʒ] N *juego de cartas que se juega utilizando un tablero de puntuación*

crick [krɪk] Ⓐ N **to have a ~ in one's neck/back** tener tortícolis/lumbago
Ⓑ VT **to ~ one's neck** tener tortícolis; **to ~ one's back** tener un ataque de lumbago

cricket[1] ['krɪkɪt] N (*Zool*) grillo *m*

cricket[2] ['krɪkɪt] Ⓐ N (= *sport*) críquet *m*, crícket *m*; **that's not ~** (*fig*) es una jugada sucia
Ⓑ CPD ► **cricket ball** N pelota *f* de críquet ► **cricket bat** N bate *m* de críquet ► **cricket match** N partido *m* de críquet ► **cricket pavilion** N caseta *f* de críquet ► **cricket pitch** N terreno *m* de juego de críquet

cricketer ['krɪkɪtə'] N criquetero/a *m/f*, jugador(a) *m/f* de críquet

cricketing ['krɪkɪtɪŋ] ADJ de cricket; **his brief ~ career** su corta trayectoria como jugador de cricket

crier ['kraɪə'] N *see* **town B**

crikey‡ ['kraɪkɪ] EXCL (*Brit*) ¡caramba!

> **CRICKET**
>
> *El críquet se practica en todo el Reino Unido y los países de la* **Commonwealth**, *aunque se considera un juego típicamente inglés. Se juega sobre todo en verano al aire libre, sobre hierba y se puede reconocer inmediatamente porque todos los jugadores van vestidos de blanco. Tiene unas reglas un tanto complejas: hay dos equipos de 11 jugadores. En el primer equipo todos los jugadores batean por turnos, mientras que en el otro equipo hay un boleador (***bowler***) y diez fildeadores (***fielders***) en puntos estratégicos del campo. El boleador lanza la pelota al bateador (***batsman***). Éste intenta a su vez lanzarla lo más lejos posible y así tener tiempo para correr de un poste (***wicket***) a otro y conseguir puntos, llamados por ello (***runs***). Los fildeadores del equipo contrario intentan atrapar la pelota lanzada por el bateador para evitar que consiga más puntos. Si atrapan la pelota en el aire o si dan en el* **wicket** *con ella, el bateador es eliminado. Cuando todos los bateadores del primer equipo han sido eliminados, se cambian los papeles. Un partido puede durar varios días seguidos.*
>
> *Como ocurre con el béisbol en Estados Unidos, algunas expresiones de críquet han pasado a la lengua cotidiana, entre otras,* **a sticky wicket** *(una situación difícil).*

crime [kraɪm] Ⓐ N 1 (= *offence*) delito *m*; (*very serious*) crimen *m*; **to commit a ~** cometer un delito; **the scene of the ~** el lugar del delito; **a ~ against humanity** un crimen contra la humanidad; **it's not a ~!** (*fig*) ¡no es para tanto!; **it's a ~ to let that food go to waste** es un crimen echar a perder esa comida
2 (= *activity*) delincuencia *f*; **~ is rising** la delincuencia va en aumento; ✦*PROV* **~ doesn't pay** el crimen no compensa
Ⓑ CPD ► **crime of passion** N crimen *m* pasional ► **crime prevention** N prevención *f* del crimen ► **crime rate** N índice *m* de criminalidad ► **Crime Squad** N ≈ Brigada *f* de Investigación Criminal (*Sp*) ► **crime statistics** NPL estadísticas *fpl* del crimen ► **crime wave** N ola *f* de crímenes *or* delitos ► **crime writer** N autor(a) *m/f* de novelas policíacas

Crimea [kraɪ'mɪə] N Crimea *f*

Crimean War [kraɪ'mɪən'wɔː'] N Guerra *f* de Crimea

criminal ['krɪmɪnl] Ⓐ N criminal *mf*
Ⓑ ADJ 1 (*Jur*) [*act, activity, behaviour*] delictivo; [*investigation, organization*] criminal; [*trial, case*] penal; **he had done nothing ~** no había cometido ningún delito; **to bring ~ charges against sb** formular *or* presentar cargos en contra de algn, entablar un proceso penal contra algn
2 (= *shameful*) **it would be ~ to throw them away** sería un crimen tirarlos; **it was a ~ waste of resources** era un crimen desperdiciar recursos así
Ⓒ CPD ► **criminal assault** N intento *m* de violación ► **criminal code** N código *m* penal ► **criminal court** N juzgado *m* de lo penal ► **criminal damage** N delito *m* de daños ► **criminal intent** N intención *f* dolosa ► **Criminal Investigation Department** N (*Brit*) ≈ Brigada *f* de Investigación Criminal (*Sp*) ► **the criminal justice system** N el sistema penal ► **criminal law** N derecho *m* penal ► **criminal lawyer** N penalista *mf*, abogado/a *m/f* criminalista ► **criminal negligence** N negligencia *f* criminal ► **criminal record** N antecedentes *mpl* penales; **to have a ~ record** tener antecedentes penales

criminality [,krɪmɪ'nælɪtɪ] N criminalidad *f*

criminalization [,krɪmɪnəlaɪ'zeɪʃən] N criminalización *f*

criminalize ['krɪmɪnəlaɪz] VT criminalizar

criminally ['krɪmɪnəlɪ] ADV 1 (*Jur*) **they are ~ liable** se les puede imputar delito; **the hospital staff had been ~ negligent** el personal del hospital había cometido delito por negligencia; **they are ~ responsible from the age of 16** son responsables desde el punto de vista penal a partir de los 16 años; **the ~ insane** los delincuentes psicóticos
2 (= *shamefully*) vergonzosamente; **the pay was ~ poor** el sueldo era tan bajo que daba vergüenza, el sueldo era vergonzosamente bajo

criminologist [,krɪmɪ'nɒlədʒɪst] N criminalista *mf*

criminology [,krɪmɪ'nɒlədʒɪ] N criminología *f*

crimp [krɪmp] VT [+ *hair*] rizar, encrespar

crimped [krɪmpt] ADJ rizado, con rizos, encrespado

Crimplene® ['krɪmpliːn] N ≈ crepé *m* de poliéster

crimson ['krɪmzn] Ⓐ ADJ carmesí
Ⓑ N carmesí *m*

cringe [krɪndʒ] VI 1 (= *shrink back*) encogerse (**at** ante); **to ~ with fear** encogerse de miedo; **to ~ with embarrassment** morirse de vergüenza; **it makes me ~** me da horror
2 (= *fawn*) acobardarse, agacharse (**before** ante)

cringing ['krɪndʒɪŋ] ADJ servil, rastrero

crinkle ['krɪŋkl] Ⓐ N arruga *f*
Ⓑ VT arrugar
Ⓒ VI arrugarse

crinkle-cut ['krɪnkl,cʌt] ADJ [*chips, crisps*] ondulado

crinkly ['krɪŋklɪ] ADJ (*compar* **crinklier**; *superl* **crinkliest**) [*hair*] (= *very curly*) rizado, crespo; [*paper etc*] (= *having wrinkles, creases*) arrugado; [*leaves etc*] crespado

crinoline ['krɪnəliːn] N miriñaque *m*, crinolina *f*

cripes‡ [kraɪps] EXCL ¡caramba!*

cripple ['krɪpl] Ⓐ N (*lame*) cojo/a *m/f*, lisiado/a *m/f*; (*disabled*) minusválido/a *m/f*; (*maimed*) mutilado/a *m/f*; **he's an emotional ~** tiene serios traumas
Ⓑ VT 1 (*physically*) lisiar, mutilar
2 (*fig*) [+ *ship, plane*] inutilizar; [+ *production, exports*] paralizar

crippled ['krɪpld] Ⓐ ADJ 1 (= *maimed*) tullido, lisiado; (= *disabled*) minusválido; **he is ~ with arthritis** está paralizado por la artritis
2 (*fig*) [*plane, vehicle*] averiado; [*factory*] (*after bomb etc*) paralizado
Ⓑ NPL **the ~** (= *maimed*) los tullidos; (= *disabled*) los minusválidos

crippling ['krɪplɪŋ] ADJ [*disease*] que conduce a la parálisis; [*blow, defect*] muy grave, muy severo; [*taxes, debts*] abrumador, agobiante

crisis ['kraɪsɪs] Ⓐ N (*pl* **crises** ['kraɪsiːz]) crisis *f inv*; (*Med*) punto *m* crítico; **to come to a ~** entrar en crisis; **we've got a ~ on our hands** estamos enfrentándonos a una crisis
Ⓑ CPD ► **crisis centre** (*Brit*), **crisis center** (*US*) N (*for disaster*) ≈ centro *m* coordinador de rescate; (*for personal help*) ≈ teléfono *m* de la esperanza; (*for battered women*) centro *m* de ayuda (*a las mujeres maltratadas*) ► **crisis management** N gestión *f* de crisis

crisp [krɪsp] Ⓐ ADJ (*compar* **crisper**; *superl* **crispest**) [1] (= *fresh, crunchy*) [*lettuce, salad*] fresco; [*apple, snow, bacon, leaves*] crujiente; [*paper*] limpio; [*banknote*] nuevecito; [*linen*] almidonado
[2] (= *cold, clear*) [*air*] vivificante, vigorizante; [*day, morning*] frío y despejado; **the weather was clear and ~** el día estaba frío y despejado
[3] (= *sharp*) [*voice, sound*] bien definido, nítido; [*image*] nítido
[4] (= *tight*) [*curl*] apretado
[5] (= *brisk, curt*) [*tone, reply*] seco, tajante; [*statement, phrase*] escueto; **a ~ prose style** una prosa escueta
Ⓑ N (*Brit*) (*also* **potato ~**) patata *f* frita (*de bolsa*), papa *f* (frita) (*de bolsa*) (*LAm*); ✦**IDIOM burnt to a ~** [*toast etc*] chamuscado; [*person*] (= *sunburnt*) achicharrado

crispbread ['krɪspbred] N pan *m* tostado (escandinavo)

crisper ['krɪspəʳ] N (*in fridge*) cajón *m* de las verduras (*del frigorífico*)

crisply ['krɪsplɪ] ADV [*pressed, ironed*] cuidadosamente; [*say, reply*] secamente; [*speak, write*] de manera concisa, de manera sucinta; **~ fried onion rings** crujientes aros de cebolla fritos

crispness ['krɪspnɪs] N [1] (= *crunchiness*) [*of lettuce, salad*] frescura *f*; [*of apple, snow, bacon*] lo crujiente; [*of linen*] lo almidonado
[2] (= *coldness, clarity*) [*of air*] lo vivificante, lo vigorizante; [*of weather*] lo frío y despejado
[3] (= *sharpness*) [*of voice, sound, image*] nitidez *f*
[4] (= *briskness*) [*of tone, reply*] sequedad *f*

crispy ['krɪspɪ] ADJ [*food*] crujiente

criss-cross ['krɪskrɒs] Ⓐ ADJ entrecruzado
Ⓑ N **a ~ of paths** veredas *fpl* entrecruzadas
Ⓒ VI entrecruzarse

criss-crossed ['krɪskrɒst] ADJ entrelazado; **~ by** surcado de

crit* [krɪt] N [*of play, book etc*] crítica *f*

criterion [kraɪ'tɪərɪən] N (*pl* **criterions** *or* **criteria** [kraɪ'tɪərɪə]) criterio *m*

critic ['krɪtɪk] N (= *reviewer*) crítico/a *m/f*; (= *faultfinder*) criticón/ona *m/f*

critical ['krɪtɪkəl] Ⓐ ADJ [1] (= *important*) [*factor, element*] crítico; [*issue*] apremiante; [*problem*] muy serio; **it is ~ to understand what is happening** es de vital importancia entender lo que está ocurriendo; **of ~ importance** de vital importancia; **how you finance a business is ~ to its success** el éxito de un negocio depende de forma crucial de cómo se financie
[2] (= *decisive*) [*moment, stage*] crítico; **it was a ~ time for the nation** fue un período crítico para la nación; **at a ~ juncture** en una coyuntura crítica
[3] (= *perilous, serious*) [*situation, state*] crítico
[4] (*Med*) [*patient, condition, illness*] grave; **to be on the ~ list** estar en la lista de enfermos graves; **to be off the ~ list** estar fuera de peligro
[5] (= *fault-finding*) [*attitude, remark, report*] crítico; **he's too ~** siempre está criticando, critica demasiado; **to watch sb with a ~ eye** observar a algn con ojo crítico; **to be ~ of sth/sb** criticar algo/a algn
[6] (= *analytical*) [*person, reader, analysis*] crítico
[7] (*Cine, Literat, Mus, Theat*) crítico; **the film met with ~ acclaim** la película fue aplaudida por la crítica; **to be a ~ success** [*book, play etc*] ser un éxito de crítica
[8] (*Phys, Nuclear Physics*) [*temperature, pressure*] crítico; **to go ~** empezar una reacción en cadena
Ⓑ CPD ► **critical angle** N (*Aer, Opt*) ángulo *m* crítico ► **critical edition** N edición *f* crítica ► **critical essays** NPL ensayos *mpl* de crítica ► **critical mass** N masa *f* crítica ► **critical path analysis** N análisis *m inv* del camino crítico

critically ['krɪtɪkəlɪ] ADV [1] (= *crucially*) **~ important** crucial
[2] (*Med*) [*ill, injured*] gravemente, de gravedad
[3] (= *seriously*) **we are running ~ low on food supplies** nuestras provisiones de alimentos están quedando reducidas a unos niveles críticos
[4] (= *disparagingly*) [*speak, say*] con desaprobación, en tono de crítica
[5] (= *analytically*) [*study, examine, watch*] con ojo crítico, críticamente
[6] (*Cine, Lit, Mus, Theat*) **the band's ~ acclaimed new album** el nuevo disco del grupo, aclamado por la crítica; **his first two books were ~ acclaimed** sus dos primeros libros tuvieron muy buena acogida por parte de la crítica

criticism ['krɪtɪsɪzəm] N crítica *f* (*also Literat, Cine etc*)

criticize ['krɪtɪsaɪz] VT, VI (= *review, find fault*) criticar; **I don't wish to ~, but ...** no quisiera criticar, pero ...

critique [krɪ'tiːk] Ⓐ N crítica *f*
Ⓑ VT evaluar; **to ~ sb's work/performance** evaluar el trabajo/la actuación de algn

croak [krəʊk] Ⓐ N [*of raven*] graznido *m*; [*of frog*] croar *m*, canto *m*; [*of person*] gruñido *m*
Ⓑ VI [1] [*raven*] graznar; [*frog*] croar, cantar; [*person*] carraspear
[2] (*) (= *die*) estirar la pata*, espicharla*
Ⓒ VT (= *say*) decir con voz ronca

croaky ['krəʊkɪ] ADJ [*voice*] ronco

Croat ['krəʊæt] N croata *mf*

Croatia [krəʊ'eɪʃə] N Croacia *f*

Croatian [krəʊ'eɪʃən] Ⓐ ADJ croata
Ⓑ N croata *mf*

crochet ['krəʊʃeɪ] Ⓐ N ganchillo *m*, croché *m*
Ⓑ VT hacer en croché, hacer de ganchillo
Ⓒ VI hacer ganchillo *or* croché
Ⓓ CPD ► **crochet hook** N aguja *f* de ganchillo

crock [krɒk] Ⓐ N [1] (= *earthenware pot*) vasija *f* de barro; ✦**IDIOM it's a ~ of shit** (*esp US***) es una sandez*, es una gilipollez (*Sp***), es una pendejada (*Andes, Mex**), es una huevada (*Andes, S. Cone**)
[2] (*) (= *person*) (*also* **old ~**) carcamal* *m*, vejete/a* *m/f*; (= *car etc*) cacharro* *m*
Ⓑ VT lisiar, incapacitar

crockery ['krɒkərɪ] N (*Brit*) loza *f*, vajilla *f*

crocodile ['krɒkədaɪl] Ⓐ N cocodrilo *m*; **to walk in a ~** andar en doble fila
Ⓑ CPD ► **crocodile tears** NPL (*fig*) lágrimas *fpl* de cocodrilo

crocus ['krəʊkəs] N (*pl* **crocuses**) azafrán *m*

Croesus ['kriːsəs] N Creso

croft [krɒft] N (*Scot*) (= *small farm*) granja *f* pequeña

crofter ['krɒftəʳ] N (*Scot*) arrendatario/a *m/f* de una granja pequeña

crofting ['krɒftɪŋ] (*Scot*) Ⓐ N minifundismo *m*, agricultura *f* en pequeña escala
Ⓑ CPD [*community*] de granjas pequeñas

croissant [krwɑːsɑ̃ːŋ] N croissant *m*, cruasán *m*, medialuna *f* (*esp LAm*)

crone [krəʊn] N bruja *f*, vieja *f*

crony* ['krəʊnɪ] N (*pej*) (= *friend*) compinche* *mf*, amigote/a* *mf*

cronyism ['krəʊnɪɪzəm] N amiguismo *m*

crook [krʊk] Ⓐ N [1] (*shepherd's*) cayado *m*; (*bishop's*) báculo *m*; (= *hook*) gancho *m*; *see also* **hook A1**
[2] **the ~ of one's arm** el pliegue del codo
[3] (*) (= *thief*) ladrón/ona *m/f*; (= *villain*) maleante *mf*
[4] (= *curve*) codo *m*, recodo *m*
Ⓑ VT (*fig*) [+ *finger*] doblar; **to ~ one's arm** empinar el codo
Ⓒ ADJ (*Australia**) (= *ill*) mal

crooked ['krʊkɪd] ADJ [1] (= *not straight*) torcido, chueco (*LAm*); (= *bent over*) encorvado, doblado; [*path*] sinuoso, tortuoso; [*smile*] torcido
[2] (*) (= *dishonest*) [*deal*] sucio; [*means*] nada honrado; [*person*] nada honrado, criminal

crookedly ['krʊkɪdlɪ] ADV [*smile*] con un rictus, torciendo la boca

crookedness ['krʊkɪdnɪs] N [1] (*lit*) sinuosidad *f*
[2] (*fig*) criminalidad *f*

croon [kruːn] VT, VI canturrear, cantar en voz baja

crooner ['kruːnəʳ] N cantante *mf* melódico/a

crooning ['kruːnɪŋ] N canturreo *m*, tarareo *m*

crop [krɒp] Ⓐ N [1] (= *species grown*) cultivo *m*; (= *produce*) [*of fruit, vegetables*] cosecha *f*; [*of cereals*] cereal *m*; (*fig*) montón *m*
[2] (*Orn*) buche *m*
[3] [*of whip*] mango *m*; (= *riding crop*) fusta *f*, látigo *m* de montar
Ⓑ VT (= *cut*) [+ *hair*] cortar al rape; [*animal*] [+ *grass*] pacer
Ⓒ CPD ► **crop circle** N *círculo misterioso en los sembrados* ► **crop dusting** N = **crop spraying** ► **crop rotation** N rotación *f* de cultivos ► **crop sprayer** N (= *device*) fumigadora *f* (de cultivos), sulfatadora *f*; (= *plane*) avión *m* fumigador ► **crop spraying** N fumigación *f* aérea, aerofumigación *f* (de cultivos)

►**crop out** VI + ADV (*Geol*) aflorar

►**crop up** VI + ADV [1] (*Geol*) aflorar
[2] (*fig*) (= *arise*) surgir, presentarse; **something must have ~ped up** habrán tenido algún problema, habrá pasado *or* surgido algo; **the subject ~ped up during the conversation** el tema surgió durante la conversación

cropper* ['krɒpəʳ] N [1] ✦**IDIOM to come a ~** (= *fall*) darse un batacazo*, cazar la liebre*; (= *fail*) [*person*] llevarse una buena plancha *or* un buen planchazo*; [*project*] irse al garete*
[2] (*Agr*) agricultor(a) *m/f*; *see also* **sharecropper**

croquet ['krəʊkeɪ] N (= *game*) croquet *m*

croquette [krəʊ'ket] N (*Culin*) croqueta *f*

crosier ['krəʊʒəʳ] N báculo *m* (pastoral)

cross [krɒs] Ⓐ N [1] (= *sign, decoration*) cruz *f*; **to sign with a ~** marcar con una cruz; **to make the sign of the ~** hacer la señal de la cruz (**over** sobre), santiguarse; **the Cross** (*Rel*) la Cruz; ✦**IDIOM to bear a/one's ~**: **we each have our ~ to bear** cada quien carga su cruz; **it's one of the ~es we women have to bear** es una de las cruces que tenemos las mujeres
[2] (*Bio, Zool*) cruce *m*, cruzamiento *m*; (*fig*) mezcla *f*; **it's a ~ between a horse and a donkey** es un cruce *or* cruzamiento de caballo y burro; **the game is a ~ between squash and tennis** el juego es una mezcla de squash y tenis, el juego está a medio camino entre el squash y el tenis
[3] (= *bias*) **cut on the ~** cortado al bies *or* al sesgo
[4] (*Ftbl*) centro *m*, pase *m* cruzado
Ⓑ ADJ [1] (= *angry*) enfadado, enojado (*LAm*);

(= *vexed*) molesto; **to be/get ~ with sb (about sth)** enfadarse *or* (*LAm*) enojarse con algn (por algo); **it makes me ~ when that happens** me da mucha rabia que pase eso; **don't be/get ~ with me** no te enfades *or* (*LAm*) enojes conmigo; **they haven't had a ~ word in ten years** no han cruzado palabra en diez años, llevan diez años sin cruzar palabra

2 (= *diagonal etc*) transversal, oblicuo

Ⓒ VT 1 (= *go across*) [*person*] [+ *road, room*] cruzar; [+ *bridge*] cruzar, pasar; [+ *ditch*] cruzar, salvar; [+ *river, sea, desert*] cruzar, atravesar; [+ *threshold*] cruzar, traspasar; **this road ~es the motorway** esta carretera atraviesa la autopista; **the bridge ~es the river here** el puente atraviesa el río por aquí; **it ~ed my mind that ...** se me ocurrió que ...; **they have clearly ~ed the boundary into terrorism** está claro que han traspasado la frontera que separa del terrorismo; **the word never ~ed his lips** jamás pronunció esa palabra; **a smile ~ed her lips** una sonrisa se dibujó en sus labios, esbozó una sonrisa; **we'll ~ that bridge when we come to it** (*fig*) no anticipemos problemas

2 (= *draw line across*) [+ *cheque*] cruzar; **~ed cheque** (*Brit*) cheque *m* cruzado; **to ~ o.s.** santiguarse; **~ my heart!** (*in promise*) ¡te lo juro!; **to ~ a "t"** poner el rabito a la "t"

3 (= *place crosswise*) [+ *arms, legs*] cruzar; **keep your fingers ~ed for me** ¡deséame suerte!; **I got a ~ed line** (*Telec*) había (un) cruce de líneas; **they got their lines ~ed** (*fig*) hubo un malentendido entre ellos; ✦***IDIOMS*** **to ~ sb's palm with silver** dar una moneda de plata a algn; **to ~ swords with sb** cruzar la espada con algn; *see also* **wire A1**

4 (= *thwart*) [+ *person*] contrariar, ir contra; [+ *plan*] desbaratar; **to be ~ed in love** sufrir un fracaso sentimental

5 [+ *animals, plants*] cruzar

Ⓓ VI 1 (= *go to other side*) cruzar, ir al otro lado; **he ~ed from one side of the room to the other to speak to me** cruzó *or* atravesó la sala para hablar conmigo, fue hasta el otro lado de la sala para hablar conmigo; **to ~ from Newhaven to Dieppe** pasar *or* cruzar de Newhaven a Dieppe

2 (= *intersect*) [*roads etc*] cruzarse; *see also* **path A4.1**

3 (= *meet and pass*) [*letters, people*] cruzarse

► **cross off** VT + ADV tachar

► **cross out** VT + ADV borrar; **"~ out what does not apply"** "táchese lo que no proceda"

► **cross over** Ⓐ VI + ADV (= *cross the road*) cruzar; (*fig*) (= *change sides*) cambiar de chaqueta, ser un/una tránsfuga

Ⓑ VI + PREP [+ *road*] cruzar; [+ *bridge*] cruzar, pasar

crossbar ['krɒsbɑːʳ] N [*of bicycle*] barra *f*; [*of goalpost*] travesaño *m*, larguero *m*

crossbeam ['krɒsbiːm] N viga *f* transversal

cross-bencher ['krɒs'bentʃəʳ] N diputado/a *m/f* independiente

crossbill ['krɒsbɪl] N piquituerto *m* común

crossbones ['krɒsbəʊnz] NPL tibias *fpl* cruzadas; *see* **skull**

cross-border ['krɒs'bɔːdəʳ] Ⓐ ADJ [*conflict*] fronterizo; [*trade*] internacional, transfronterizo; [*raid*] a través de la frontera, fronterizo

Ⓑ CPD ► **cross-border security** N seguridad *f* en la frontera

crossbow ['krɒsbəʊ] N ballesta *f*

crossbred ['krɒsbred] ADJ cruzado, híbrido

crossbreed ['krɒsbriːd] Ⓐ N cruce *m*, híbrido *m*

Ⓑ VT (*pt* **crossbred**) cruzar

cross-Channel ['krɒs,tʃænl] ADJ **~ services** servicios *mpl* a través del Canal de la Mancha; **~ ferry** transbordador *m* que cruza el Canal de la Mancha

cross-check ['krɒstʃek] Ⓐ N comprobación *f* adicional, verificación *f*

Ⓑ VT comprobar una vez más *or* por otro sistema, verificar

cross-compiler ['krɒskəm'paɪləʳ] N compilador *m* cruzado

cross-country ['krɒs'kʌntrɪ] Ⓐ ADJ [*route, walk*] a campo traviesa

Ⓑ CPD ► **cross-country race** N cross *m inv*, campo *m* a través ► **cross-country running** N cross *m* ► **cross-country skiing** N esquí *m* de fondo

cross-cultural ['krɒs'kʌltʃərəl] ADJ transcultural

cross-current ['krɒs'kʌrənt] N contracorriente *f*

cross-disciplinary [,krɒs'dɪsɪplɪnərɪ] ADJ multidisciplinario

cross-dress ['krɒsdres] VI travestirse

cross-dresser ['krɒsdresəʳ] N travesti *mf*, travestido/a *m/f*

cross-dressing [,krɒs'dresɪŋ] N travestismo *m*

cross-examination ['krɒsɪg,zæmɪ'neɪʃən] N (*Jur*) repreguntas *fpl*; (*fig*) interrogatorio *m*

cross-examine ['krɒsɪg'zæmɪn] VT (*Jur*) repreguntar; (*fig*) interrogar (severamente)

cross-eyed ['krɒsaɪd] ADJ bizco

cross-fertilize ['krɒs'fɜːtɪlaɪz] VT fecundar por fertilización cruzada

crossfire ['krɒsfaɪəʳ] N fuego *m* cruzado; **we were caught in the ~** quedamos atrapados en medio del tiroteo *or* en el fuego cruzado; (*fig*) nos veíamos atacados por ambos lados

cross-grained ['krɒsgreɪnd] ADJ de fibras cruzadas

cross-hatching ['krɔːs,hætʃɪŋ] N sombreado *m* con rayas

crossing ['krɒsɪŋ] Ⓐ N 1 (*esp by sea*) travesía *f*

2 (= *road junction*) cruce *m*; (= *pedestrian crossing*) paso *m* de peatones; (= *level crossing*) paso *m* a nivel; **cross at the ~** crucen en el paso de peatones

Ⓑ CPD ► **crossing guard** N (*US*) *persona encargada de ayudar a los niños a cruzar la calle* ► **crossing point** N paso *m*; (*at border*) paso *m* fronterizo

cross-legged ['krɒs'legd] ADV **to sit ~ on the floor** sentarse en el suelo con las piernas cruzadas

crossly ['krɒslɪ] ADV con enfado *or* (*LAm*) enojo; **"what do you mean!" he said ~** —¿qué quieres decir con eso? —dijo enfadado *or* (*LAm*) enojado

crossover ['krɒsəʊvəʳ] N 1 (*Aut etc*) paso *m*

2 (*Mus*) fusión *f*

cross-party ['krɒs'pɑːtɪ] ADJ **~ support** apoyo *m* multilateral

crosspatch* ['krɒspætʃ] N gruñón/ona *m/f*, cascarrabias *mf*

crosspiece ['krɒspiːs] N travesaño *m*

cross-ply ['krɒsplaɪ] ADJ (*Aut*) [*tyre*] a carcasa diagonal

cross-pollination ['krɒs,pɒlɪ'neɪʃən] N polinización *f* cruzada

cross-purposes ['krɒs'pɜːpəsɪz] NPL **I think we're at ~** me temo que hemos tenido un malentendido; **we were talking at ~** hablábamos de cosas distintas

cross-question ['krɒs'kwestʃən] VT (*Jur*) repreguntar; (*fig*) interrogar

cross-questioning ['krɒs'kwestʃənɪŋ] N (*Jur*) repreguntas *fpl*; (*fig*) interrogación *f*

cross-refer [,krɒsrɪ'fɜːʳ] VT remitir (**to** a)

cross-reference ['krɒs'refərəns] Ⓐ N remisión *f*

Ⓑ VT poner referencia cruzada a; **to ~ A to Q** hacer una remisión de A a Q, poner en A una nota que remite al usuario a Q

crossroads ['krɒsrəʊdz] NSING cruce *m*, encrucijada *f*; **to be at a ~** (*fig*) estar en una encrucijada

cross-section ['krɒs'sekʃən] N (*Bio etc*) corte *m or* sección *f* transversal; [*of population*] muestra *f* (representativa)

cross-stitch ['krɒsstɪtʃ] Ⓐ N punto *m* de cruz

Ⓑ VT coser en punto de cruz

crosstalk ['krɒstɔːk] Ⓐ N (*Brit*) réplicas *fpl* agudas

Ⓑ CPD ► **crosstalk act** N (*Theat*) diálogo *m* ágil salpicado de humor

cross-tie ['krɒs,taɪ] N (*US*) durmiente *m*, traviesa *f*

cross-vote [,krɒs'vəʊt] VI votar en contra del partido

crosswalk ['krɒs,wɔːk] N (*US*) paso *m* de peatones

crosswind ['krɒswɪnd] N viento *m* de costado

crosswise ['krɒswaɪz] ADV transversalmente

crossword ['krɒswɜːd] N **~ (puzzle)** crucigrama *m*

crotch [krɒtʃ] N 1 (*also* **crutch**) (*Anat*) [*of garment*] entrepierna *f*

2 [*of tree*] horquilla *f*

crotchet ['krɒtʃɪt] N (*Brit Mus*) negra *f*

crotchety ['krɒtʃɪtɪ] ADJ arisco, malhumorado

crouch [kraʊtʃ] VI (*also* **~ down**) [*person*] agacharse, ponerse en cuclillas; [*animal*] agazaparse

croup¹ [kruːp] N (*Med*) crup *m*

croup² [kruːp] N [*of horse*] grupa *f*

croupier ['kruːpɪeɪ] N crupier *mf*

crouton, croûton ['kruːtɒn] N cuscurro *m*, picatoste *m*

crow [krəʊ] Ⓐ N 1 (= *bird*) cuervo *m*; **as the ~ flies** en línea recta, a vuelo de pájaro; **stone the ~s!*** ¡caray!*

2 (= *noise*) [*of cock*] cacareo *m*; [*of baby, person*] grito *m*; **a ~ of delight** un gorjeo de placer

Ⓑ VI 1 (*pt* **crowed, crew**) [*cock*] cacarear, cantar

2 (*pt* **crowed**) [*child*] gorjear; (*fig*) jactarse, pavonearse; **to ~ over** *or* **about sth** jactarse de algo, felicitarse por algo; **it's nothing to ~ about** no hay motivo para sentirse satisfecho

crowbar ['krəʊbɑːʳ] N palanca *f*

crowd [kraʊd] Ⓐ N 1 (= *mass of people*) multitud *f*, muchedumbre *f*; **he disappeared into the ~** desapareció entre la multitud *or* la muchedumbre *or* el gentío; **she lost him in the ~** lo perdió de vista entre la multitud *or* la muchedumbre *or* el gentío; **~s of people** una multitud de gente; **there was quite a ~** había bastante gente; **they always go round in a ~** siempre salen en grupo; **accidents always draw a ~** los accidentes siempre atraen a un gentío; **she's the sort of person who stands out in a ~** es la típica persona que (se) destaca en un grupo de gente

2 (= *spectators*) público *m*, espectadores *mpl*; **a ~ of 10,000 watched the parade** 10.000 espectadores presenciaron el desfile; **the away/home ~** (*Ftbl*) los seguidores del equipo

visitante/de casa; **the match drew a big ~** el partido atrajo mucho público; **he certainly draws the ~s** [*performer*] no cabe duda de que atrae mucho público
3 (*) (= *social group*) gente *f*; **I don't like that ~ at all** esa gente no me gusta nada; **she got in with a nice ~ at work** se juntó con (una) gente maja en el trabajo; **all the old ~ have come out for the occasion** la antigua pandilla ha salido para celebrar la ocasión
4 (= *common people*) **the ~: she's just one of the ~** es del montón; **to follow the ~** (*fig*) dejarse llevar por los demás *or* por la corriente; **he likes to stand out from the ~** le gusta distinguirse de los demás
Ⓑ VT 1 (= *fill*) [+ *place*] atestar, llenar; **demonstrators ~ed the streets** los manifestantes atestaron *or* llenaron las calles; **new buildings ~ the narrow lanes of the old town** los nuevos edificios se apiñan en los estrechos callejones del casco viejo; **the thoughts that ~ed her mind** los pensamientos que le inundaban la mente
2 (= *squeeze, force*) apiñar; **they ~ed the prisoners into trucks** apiñaron a los prisioneros en unos camiones
3 (= *press against*) empujar; **they ~ed me against the wall** me empujaron contra la pared
4 (*fig*) (= *harass*) agobiar; **I do things at my own pace, so don't ~ me** deja de agobiarme, me gusta trabajar a mi ritmo
Ⓒ VI (= *gather together*) apiñarse; **they ~ed at the window to see him** se apiñaron en la ventana para verlo; **to ~ in** entrar en tropel; **memories ~ed in on me** me inundó una ola de recuerdos; **dense vegetation ~ed in on both sides of the road** la vegetación crecía espesa a ambos lados de la carretera; **I feel as if everything's ~ing in on me** me siento desbordado por todo; **we all ~ed into her little flat** todos nos metimos en su pisito, abarrotándolo de gente; **thousands of people have ~ed into the capital** miles de personas han llegado en tropel a la capital; **to ~ around** *or* **round sth/sb** apiñarse alrededor de algo/algn
Ⓓ CPD ► **crowd control** N control *m* de masas ► **crowd scene** N (*Cine, Theat*) escena *f* masiva *or* multitudinaria

► **crowd out** VT + ADV 1 (= *not let in*) desplazar; **exotic plants move in, ~ing native species out** las plantas exóticas se trasladan, desplazando a las especies autóctonas
2 (= *fill*) [*people*] atestar; **the bar was ~ed out** el bar estaba atestado (de gente)

crowded ['kraʊdɪd] ADJ [*room*] (*with people*) atestado (de gente), abarrotado (de gente); [*meeting, event*] muy concurrido; [*day*] lleno de actividad; **it's very ~ here** esto está atestado *or* abarrotado (de gente); **she has a very ~ schedule** tiene una agenda muy apretada; **~ urban areas** zonas *fpl* urbanas muy pobladas; **they live in ~ conditions** viven hacinados; **every room is ~ with furniture** todas las habitaciones están abarrotadas de muebles; **the bar gets very ~ after nine o'clock** el bar se llena de gente a partir de las nueve; **the houses are ~ together** las casas están apiñadas

crowd-puller ['kraud,pʊləʳ] N gran atracción *f*; **the show is bound to be a ~** no cabe duda de que este espectáculo atraerá a mucho público

crowfoot ['krəʊfʊt] N (*pl* **crowfoots**) ranúnculo *m*

crowing ['krəʊɪŋ] N [*of cock*] canto *m*, cacareo *m*; [*of child*] gorjeo *m*; (*fig*) cacareo *m*

crown [kraʊn] Ⓐ N 1 (= *headdress, monarchy*) corona *f*
2 (*Jur*) **the Crown** el Estado
3 (*Sport*) (= *championship title*) campeonato *m*, título *m*
4 (= *top*) [*of hat*] copa *f*; [*of head*] coronilla *f*; [*of hill*] cumbre *f*, cima *f*; [*of tooth*] corona *f*; **the ~ of the road** el centro de la calzada
Ⓑ VT 1 [+ *king etc*] coronar; **he was ~ed king** fue coronado rey; **all the ~ed heads of Europe** todos los monarcas europeos
2 (*usu pass*) (= *cap, round off*) coronar, rematar; **and to ~ it all it began to snow** y para colmo (de desgracias) *or* para remate empezó a nevar; **I wouldn't exactly say our efforts were ~ed with success** (*iro*) yo no me atrevería a decir que nuestros esfuerzos se vieron coronados por el éxito
3 [+ *tooth*] poner una corona en
4 (*Draughts*) [+ *piece*] coronar
5 (*) (= *hit*) golpear en la cabeza; **I'll ~ you if you do that again!** ¡como lo vuelves a hacer te rompo la crisma!*
Ⓒ CPD ► **crown colony** N (*Brit*) colonia *f* ► **crown court** N (*Brit Jur*) ≈ Audiencia *f* provincial ► **crown jewels** NPL joyas *fpl* de la corona ► **crown lands** NPL propiedad *f* de la corona ► **crown prince** N príncipe *m* heredero ► **crown princess** N princesa *f* heredera

crowning ['kraʊnɪŋ] Ⓐ ADJ [*achievement*] supremo, máximo; **the house's ~ glory is its garden** el máximo *or* mayor atractivo de la casa es el jardín
Ⓑ N (= *ceremony*) coronación *f*

crow's-feet ['krəʊz'fiːt] NPL (= *wrinkles*) patas *fpl* de gallo

crow's-nest ['krəʊznest] N (*Naut*) cofa *f* de vigía

CRT N ABBR (= **cathode ray tube**) TRC *m*

crucial ['kruːʃəl] ADJ decisivo, crucial; **the next few weeks will be ~ for this government** las próximas semanas van a ser decisivas *or* cruciales para este gobierno; **their cooperation is ~ to the success of the project** su colaboración resulta crucial para el éxito del proyecto; **to play a ~ role in sth** desempeñar un papel decisivo *or* crucial en algo

crucially ['kruːʃəlɪ] ADV **to be ~ important** ser de crucial importancia; **their future is ~ dependent** *or* **depends ~ on this decision** su futuro depende de forma crucial de esta decisión; **~, he failed to secure the backing of the banks** lo verdaderamente crucial fue que no logró asegurarse el respaldo de los bancos

crucible ['kruːsɪbl] N crisol *m* (*also fig*)

crucifix ['kruːsɪfɪks] N crucifijo *m*

crucifixion [,kruːsɪ'fɪkʃən] N crucifixión *f*

cruciform ['kruːsɪfɔːm] ADJ cruciforme

crucify ['kruːsɪfaɪ] VT 1 (*lit*) crucificar
2 (*fig*) **he'll ~ me when he finds out!** ¡cuando se entere me mata!; **the newspapers are ~ing him** los periódicos se están ensañando con él

crud* [krʌd] N (*esp US*) porquería *f*

cruddy* ['krʌdɪ] ADJ asqueroso

crude [kruːd] Ⓐ ADJ (*compar* **cruder**; *superl* **crudest**) 1 (= *unprocessed*) [*oil*] crudo; [*steel, materials*] bruto; [*sugar*] sin refinar
2 (= *primitive*) [*device, bomb, method, hut*] rudimentario; [*table, door*] tosco, basto; [*drawing, piece of work*] tosco, burdo; **to make a ~ attempt at doing sth** hacer un burdo intento de hacer algo
3 (= *coarse*) [*person, behaviour, language, joke*] grosero, ordinario
Ⓑ N (*also* **~ oil**) crudo *m*

crudely ['kruːdlɪ] ADV 1 (= *primitively*) [*carved, constructed, drawn*] toscamente, burdamente
2 (= *coarsely*) [*speak, behave, joke, gesture*] groseramente, ordinariamente; **to put it ~** hablando en plata*

crudeness ['kruːdnɪs], **crudity** ['kruːdɪtɪ] N 1 (= *primitiveness*) [*of device, bomb, weapon, method, hut*] lo rudimentario; [*of table, drawing, piece of work*] tosquedad *f*
2 (= *coarseness*) [*of language, person, behaviour, joke*] grosería *f*, ordinariez *f*

crudités ['kruːdɪ'teɪ] NPL crudités *mpl*

cruel ['krʊəl] ADJ (*compar* **crueller**; *superl* **cruellest**) cruel; **they were very ~ to her** fueron muy crueles con ella; **it's a ~ fact** es un hecho brutal; ✦***PROV*** **you have to be ~ to be kind** quien bien te quiere te hará llorar

cruelly ['krʊəlɪ] ADV cruelmente

cruelty ['krʊəltɪ] N crueldad *f* (**to** con, hacia); **society for the prevention of ~ to animals** sociedad *f* protectora de los animales

cruet ['kruːɪt] N (= *oil and vinegar*) vinagrera *f*, alcuza *f* (*Bol, Chile*); (= *stand*) vinagreras *fpl*, alcuzas *fpl* (*Bol, Chile*)

cruise [kruːz] Ⓐ N crucero *m*; **to go on a ~** hacer un crucero
Ⓑ VI 1 [*ship, fleet*] navegar; [*holidaymaker*] hacer un crucero; [*plane*] volar; **the car was cruising (along) at 80km/h** el coche marchaba plácidamente a una velocidad de 80km/h; **we are cruising at an altitude of 33,000 ft** estamos volando a una altura (de crucero) de 33.000 pies; **cruising speed** velocidad *f* de crucero; **cruising altitude** altura *f* *or* altitud *f* de crucero
2 (*fig*) **to ~ to victory** vencer fácilmente
3 (*) (= *pick up men/women*) ir de ligue*, ir a ligar*
Ⓒ VT [*ship*] [+ *waters, seas*] surcar; [*vehicle*] [+ *streets*] circular por; **there were plenty of taxis cruising the streets** había muchos taxis circulando por la calle
Ⓓ CPD ► **cruise control** N control *m* de crucero ► **cruise missile** N misil *m* de crucero

► **cruise around** VI + ADV (*US*) pasear en coche

cruiser ['kruːzəʳ] N (*Naut*) crucero *m*

cruiserweight ['kruːzəweɪt] N (*Boxing*) peso *m* semipesado

cruller ['krʌləʳ] N (*US*) buñuelo *m*

crumb [krʌm] N 1 [*of bread, cake etc*] miga *f*
2 (*fig*) (= *small piece*) migaja *f*; **a ~ of comfort** algo de consuelo; **~s of knowledge/information** fragmentos *mpl* de conocimiento/información; ✦***IDIOM*** **to live off** *or* **on the ~s from sb's table** vivir de las migajas de algn

crumble ['krʌmbl] Ⓐ VT [+ *bread*] desmigar, desmigajar; [+ *earth, cheese etc*] desmenuzar
Ⓑ VI 1 [*bread*] desmigarse, desmigajarse; [*earth, cheese etc*] desmenuzarse; [*building, plaster etc*] desmoronarse
2 (*fig*) [*hopes, power, self-confidence*] desmoronarse, venirse abajo; [*coalition*] venirse abajo, derrumbarse

crumbly ['krʌmblɪ] ADJ [*earth*] quebradizo; [*cheese*] que se desmenuza con facilidad; (*Culin*) [*mixture*] quebradizo; (*US*) [*pastry*] sobado

crummy* ['krʌmɪ] ADJ 1 (= *bad*) miserable; [*hotel*] de mala muerte*; **you can keep your ~ job** puede usted quedarse su empleo de pacotilla
2 (= *unwell*) fatal*; **I'm feeling ~** me siento fatal*

crumpet ['krʌmpɪt] N 1 (*esp Brit Culin*) ≈ bollo *m* blando para tostar

[2] (*Brit*‡) (= *girl*) jai‡ *f*, tía* *f*; (= *girls*) las jais‡, las tías*; **a bit of ~** (*Brit*‡) una jai‡, una tía*

crumple ['krʌmpl] Ⓐ VT (*also* **~ up**) [+ *paper*] estrujar; [+ *clothes*] arrugar
Ⓑ VI [*material*] arrugarse; [*person*] (= *fall*) desplomarse; (= *lose one's nerve*) desmoronarse, venirse abajo; **she ~d to the floor** se desplomó; **he just ~d and lost all his confidence** se desmoronó *or* se vino abajo y perdió toda la confianza; **his face ~d and he started to cry** se le descompuso el rostro y se echó a llorar
Ⓒ CPD ► **crumple zone** N (*Aut*) zona *f* de deformación absorbente

crunch [krʌntʃ] Ⓐ N crujido *m*; (*fig*) crisis *f*, punto *m* decisivo; ✦*IDIOMS* **when it comes to the ~** cuando llega el momento de la verdad; **if it comes to the ~** si llega el momento
Ⓑ VT (*with teeth*) mascar, ronzar; [+ *ground etc*] hacer crujir; (*fig*) [+ *numbers*] devorar; **to ~ an apple/a biscuit** mascar *or* ronzar una manzana/una galleta
Ⓒ VI [*gravel, snow, glass*] crujir; **the tyres ~ed on the gravel** la grava crujía bajo el peso de los neumáticos, los neumáticos hacían crujir la grava
Ⓓ CPD [*meeting, match*] decisivo, crucial

crunchy ['krʌntʃɪ] ADJ (*compar* **crunchier**; *superl* **crunchiest**) crujiente

crupper ['krʌpəʳ] N [*of horse*] anca *f*, grupa *f*; (= *part of harness*) baticola *f*

crusade [kruː'seɪd] Ⓐ N cruzada *f*; (*fig*) campaña *f*, cruzada *f*
Ⓑ VI (*fig*) **to ~ for/against sth** hacer una campaña en pro de/en contra de algo

crusader [kruː'seɪdəʳ] N cruzado *m*; (*fig*) paladín *m*, campeón/ona *m/f*

crush [krʌʃ] Ⓐ N [1] (= *crowd*) aglomeración *f*, multitud *f*; [*of cars*] masa *f*; **there was an awful ~** hubo la mar de gente; **there's always a ~ in the tube** el metro va siempre atestado de gente; **I lost my handbag in the ~** perdí el bolso en la aglomeración; **they died in the ~** murieron aplastados
[2] (*) (= *infatuation*) enamoramiento *m*; **to have a ~ on sb** estar enamorado de algn, perder la chaveta por algn*
[3] (*Brit*) **orange ~** naranjada *f*
Ⓑ VT [1] (= *squash*) aplastar, apachurrar (*Andes, CAm*); (= *crumple*) [+ *paper*] estrujar; [+ *clothes*] arrugar; (= *grind, break up*) [+ *stones*] triturar, moler; [+ *grapes*] exprimir, prensar; [+ *garlic*] machacar; [+ *ice*] picar; [+ *scrap metal*] comprimir; **to ~ sth into a case** meter algo a la fuerza en una maleta; **to ~ sth to a pulp** hacer papilla algo
[2] (*fig*) [+ *enemy, opposition, resistance*] doblegar, aplastar; [+ *argument*] aplastar, abrumar; [+ *hopes*] defraudar
Ⓒ VI [*clothes*] arrugarse; **can we all ~ in?** ¿habrá sitio para todos?
Ⓓ CPD ► **crush barrier** N barrera *f* de seguridad

crusher ['krʌʃəʳ] N (*for paper, stone, food*) trituradora *f*; **garlic ~** triturador *m* de ajos

crushing ['krʌʃɪŋ] ADJ [*defeat, blow, reply*] aplastante; [*grief, etc*] abrumador; [*argument*] decisivo; [*burden*] agobiador

crushingly ['krʌʃɪŋlɪ] ADV [*dull, familiar*] terriblemente

crush-resistant [,krʌʃrɪ'zɪstənt] ADJ inarrugable

crust [krʌst] Ⓐ N [*of bread etc*] corteza *f*; (= *dry bread*) mendrugo *m*; [*of pie*] pasta *f*; (*Med*) (*on wound, sore*) costra *f*; [*of wine*] depósito *m*, poso *m*; (= *layer*) capa *f*; (*Geol*) corteza *f*; **there were only a few ~s to eat** para comer sólo había unos pocos mendrugos; **a thin ~ of ice** una fina capa de hielo; **the earth's ~** la corteza terrestre; *see also* **earn A**, **upper C**
Ⓑ VT **frost ~ed the windscreen** el parabrisas tenía una capa de hielo; **boots ~ed with mud** botas con barro incrustado

crustacean [krʌs'teɪʃən] N crustáceo *m*

crusty ['krʌstɪ] ADJ (*compar* **crustier**; *superl* **crustiest**) [1] [*bread*] crujiente; [*loaf*] de corteza dura
[2] (*) [*person*] arisco, malhumorado

crutch [krʌtʃ] N [1] (*Med*) muleta *f*; (*fig*) (= *support*) apoyo *m*
[2] = **crotch 1**

crux [krʌks] N (*pl* **cruxes** *or* **cruces** ['kruːsiːz]) **the ~ of the matter** lo esencial *or* el meollo *or* el quid del asunto

cry [kraɪ] Ⓐ N [1] (= *call, shout*) grito *m*; (= *howl*) [*of animal*] aullido *m*; [*of street vendor*] pregón *m*; **to give a ~ of surprise** dar un grito de sorpresa; **"jobs, not bombs" was their ~** su grito de guerra fue —trabajo sí, bombas no; **a ~ for help** (*lit*) un grito de socorro *or* auxilio; (*fig*) una llamada de socorro *or* auxilio; **the hounds were in full ~** los perros seguían de cerca la presa; **the crowd was in full ~ after him** la multitud lo perseguía con gritos; **the newspapers are in full ~ over the scandal** la prensa ha puesto el grito en el cielo por el escándalo; *see also* **far B**
[2] (= *watchword*) lema *m*, slogan *m*
[3] (= *weep*) llanto *m*; **to have a ~** llorar; **she had a good ~** lloró largamente
Ⓑ VI [1] (= *call out, shout*) gritar, llamar (en voz alta); **they are ~ing for his resignation** piden a gritos que dimita; **he cried (out) with pain** dio un grito de dolor; **to ~ for help/mercy** pedir socorro/clemencia a voces
[2] (= *weep*) llorar; **he was ~ing for his mother** lloraba por su madre; **I cried for joy** lloraba de alegría; **she was ~ing with rage** lloraba de rabia; **I laughed till I cried** terminé llorando de la risa; **I'll give him something to ~ about!*** le voy a dar de qué llorar; **to ~ over sth** llorar por algo; ✦*PROV* **it's no good ~ing over spilt milk** a lo hecho, pecho; *see also* **shoulder A1**
Ⓒ VT [1] (*also* **to ~ out**) (= *call*) gritar; [+ *warning*] lanzar a gritos; [+ *wares*] pregonar
[2] **to ~ o.s. to sleep** llorar hasta dormirse

►**cry down** VT + ADV despreciar, desacreditar

►**cry off** VI + ADV (= *withdraw*) retirarse; (*) (= *back out*) rajarse

►**cry out** Ⓐ VI + ADV (= *call out, shout*) lanzar un grito, echar un grito; **to ~ out against** protestar contra, poner el grito en el cielo por; **the system is ~ing out for reform** (*fig*) el sistema pide la reforma a gritos *or* necesita urgentemente reformarse; **this car is ~ing out to be resprayed** este coche está pidiendo a gritos una mano de pintura; **for ~ing out loud!*** ¡por Dios!
Ⓑ VT + ADV [1] (= *call*) gritar; [+ *warning*] lanzar a gritos
[2] **to ~ one's eyes** *or* **heart out** llorar a lágrima viva *or* a moco tendido

crybaby ['kraɪ,beɪbɪ] N llorón/ona *m/f*

crying ['kraɪɪŋ] Ⓐ ADJ [*child*] que llora; (= *whining*) llorón; (*) [*need*] urgente; **it's a ~ shame*** (= *pity*) es una verdadera lástima; (= *outrage*) es una auténtica vergüenza
Ⓑ N (= *weeping*) llanto *m*; (= *sobbing*) lloriqueo *m*

cryogenics [,kraɪə'dʒenɪks] N criogenia *f*

cryonics [kraɪ'ɒnɪks] N criogenética *f*

cryosurgery [,kraɪəʊ'sɜːdʒərɪ] N criocirugía *f*

crypt [krɪpt] N cripta *f*

cryptic ['krɪptɪk] ADJ [*message, clue*] críptico; [*comment*] enigmático, críptico; (= *coded*) en clave

cryptically ['krɪptɪkəlɪ] ADV enigmáticamente, de forma críptica

crypto- ['krɪptəʊ] PREFIX cripto-

crypto-communist ['krɪptəʊ'kɒmjʊnɪst] N criptocomunista *mf*

cryptogram ['krɪptəʊgræm] N criptograma *m*

cryptographer [krɪp'tɒgrəfəʳ] N criptógrafo/a *m/f*

cryptographic(al) [,krɪptə'græfɪk(əl)] ADJ criptográfico

cryptography [krɪp'tɒgrəfɪ] N criptografía *f*

crystal ['krɪstl] Ⓐ N cristal *m*; **quartz/rock ~** cristal de roca
Ⓑ ADJ (= *clear*) [*water, lake*] cristalino
Ⓒ CPD [*glass, vase*] de cristal ► **crystal ball** N bola *f* de cristal ► **crystal set** N (*Rad*) receptor *m* de cristal

crystal-clear ['krɪstl'klɪəʳ] ADJ (*lit*) [*water*] cristalino; (= *obvious*) evidente, más claro que el agua

crystal-gazing ['krɪstl,geɪzɪŋ] N (*fig*) adivinación *f* (*del futuro en la bola de cristal*)

crystalline ['krɪstəlaɪn] ADJ cristalino

crystallize ['krɪstəlaɪz] Ⓐ VT (*Chem*) cristalizar; [+ *fruit*] escarchar; (*fig*) cristalizar, resolver; **~d fruits** frutas *fpl* escarchadas
Ⓑ VI (*Chem*) cristalizarse; (*fig*) concretarse, cristalizarse

crystallographer [,krɪstə'lɒgrəfəʳ] N cristalógrafo/a *m/f*

crystallography [,krɪstə'lɒgrəfɪ] N cristalografía *f*

CSA N ABBR [1] (*Brit*) = **Child Support Agency**
[2] (*US*) = **Confederate States of America**

CSC N ABBR (*Brit*) (= **Civil Service Commission**) *comisión de reclutamiento de funcionarios*

CSE N ABBR (*Brit Scol*) (= **Certificate of Secondary Education**) ≈ BUP *m* (*Sp*)

CSEU N ABBR (*Brit*) = **Confederation of Shipbuilding and Engineering Unions**

CS gas [,siː,es'gæs] N (*Brit*) gas *m* lacrimógeno

CST N ABBR (*US*) = **Central Standard Time**

CSU N ABBR (*Brit*) = **Civil Service Union**

CT ABBR [1] (*Fin*) = **cable transfer**
[2] (*US*) = **Connecticut**

ct ABBR [1] (= **carat**) qts., quil.
[2] = **cent**

Ct. ABBR (*US*) = **Connecticut**

CTC N ABBR = **City Technology College**

CTT N ABBR (*Brit*) = **Capital Transfer Tax**

cu. ABBR = **cubic**

cub [kʌb] Ⓐ N [1] (= *animal*) cachorro *m*; **wolf/lion ~** cachorro *m* de lobo/león
[2] (*also* **~ scout**) lobato *m*, niño *m* explorador
[3] (*Brit*†) (= *youngster*) jovenzuelo *m*
Ⓑ CPD ► **cub reporter** N periodista *mf* novato/a

Cuba ['kjuːbə] N Cuba *f*

Cuban ['kjuːbən] Ⓐ ADJ cubano
Ⓑ N cubano/a *m/f*

cubbyhole ['kʌbɪhəʊl] N (= *small room*) cuchitril *m*; (= *cupboard*) armario *m* pequeño; (= *pigeonhole*) casilla *f*

cube [kjuːb] Ⓐ N [1] (= *solid*) cubo *m*; [*of sugar*] terrón *m*; [*of ice*] cubito *m*; [*of cheese*] dado *m*, cubito *m*
[2] (= *number*) **the ~ of four** cuatro (elevado) al cubo

Ⓑ VT (*Math*) cubicar, elevar al cubo
Ⓒ CPD ► **cube root** N (*Math*) raíz *f* cúbica

cubic ['kju:bɪk] Ⓐ ADJ cúbico
Ⓑ CPD ► **cubic capacity** N capacidad *f* cúbica ► **cubic foot** N pie *m* cúbico ► **cubic measure** N medida *f* cúbica ► **cubic metre** N metro *m* cúbico

cubicle ['kju:bɪkəl] N (*in hospital, dormitory*) cubículo *m*; (*in swimming baths*) caseta *f*

cubism ['kju:bɪzəm] N cubismo *m*

cubist ['kju:bɪst] Ⓐ ADJ cubista
Ⓑ N cubista *mf*

cubit ['kju:bɪt] N codo *m*

cuckold ['kʌkəld] Ⓐ N cornudo *m*
Ⓑ VT poner los cuernos a

cuckoo ['kʊku:] Ⓐ N cuco *m*, cuclillo *m*
Ⓑ ADJ (*) loco, lelo*
Ⓒ CPD ► **cuckoo clock** N reloj *m* de cuco, cucú *m*

cuckoopint [ˌkʊku:'paɪnt] N aro *m*

cucumber ['kju:kʌmbəʳ] N pepino *m*; *see also* **cool A5**

cud [kʌd] N **to chew the ~** [*animal*] rumiar; (= *think over*) reflexionar, dar vueltas a las cosas

cuddle ['kʌdl] Ⓐ N abrazo *m*
Ⓑ VT abrazar, apapachar (*Mex**)
Ⓒ VI [*two persons*] abrazarse, estar abrazados; **to ~ down** [*child in bed*] acurrucarse (en la cama); **to ~ up to sb** arrimarse a algn

cuddly ['kʌdlɪ] ADJ (*compar* **cuddlier**; *superl* **cuddliest**) [*person*] rico, tierno; [*animal*] cariñoso; [*toy*] de peluche

cudgel ['kʌdʒəl] Ⓐ N porra *f*; ✦***IDIOM*** **to take up the ~s for sth/sb** salir a la defensa de algo/algn
Ⓑ VT aporrear

cue [kju:] Ⓐ N 1 (*Billiards*) taco *m*
2 (*Theat*) (*verbal, by signal*) pie *m*, entrada *f*; (*Mus*) (*by signal*) entrada *f*; **to give sb his ~** (*Theat*) dar el pie *or* la entrada a algn; (*Mus*) dar a algn su entrada; **that gave me my ~** (*fig*) eso me sirvió de indicación; **to come in on ~** entrar en el momento justo; **then, right on ~ for the photographers, she threw him a kiss** entonces, en el momento justo para los fotógrafos, ella le lanzó un beso; ✦***IDIOM*** **to take one's ~ from sb** seguir el ejemplo de algn
Ⓑ CPD ► **cue ball** N (*Billiards*) bola *f* jugadora; (*Snooker*) bola *f* blanca ► **cue card** N letrero *m* (*apuntando lo que se ha de decir*) ► **cue word** N palabra *f* clave

►**cue in** VT + ADV (*Rad, TV, Mus*) dar la entrada a; (*Theat*) dar el pie a, dar la entrada a; **to ~ sb in on sth** (*US**) poner a algn al tanto *or* al corriente de algo

cuff¹ [kʌf] Ⓐ N bofetada *f*
Ⓑ VT abofetear

cuff² [kʌf] N [*of sleeve*] puño *m*; (*US*) [*of trousers*] vuelta *f*; **cuffs*** (= *handcuffs*) esposas *fpl*; ✦***IDIOM*** **off the ~** (*as adv*) de improviso; (*as adj*) improvisado; *see also* **off-the-cuff**

cufflinks ['kʌflɪŋks] NPL gemelos *mpl*, mancuernas *fpl* (*CAm, Mex*)

cu.ft. ABBR = **cubic foot, cubic feet**

cu.in. ABBR = **cubic inch(es)**

cuisine [kwɪ'zi:n] N cocina *f*

cul-de-sac ['kʌldə'sæk] (*pl* **culs-de-sac, cul-de-sacs**) N (*lit*) calle *f* sin salida, calle *f* cortada; (*fig*) callejón *m* sin salida

culinary ['kʌlɪnərɪ] ADJ culinario

cull [kʌl] Ⓐ VT (= *select*) [+ *fruit*] entresacar; [+ *flowers*] coger; (= *kill selectively*) [+ *deer, seals*] matar selectivamente
Ⓑ N [*of deer, seals*] matanza *f* selectiva; **seal ~** matanza *f* selectiva de focas

culminate ['kʌlmɪneɪt] VI **to ~ in** culminar en

culminating ['kʌlmɪneɪtɪŋ] ADJ culminante

culmination [ˌkʌlmɪ'neɪʃən] N culminación *f*, punto *m* culminante; **it is the ~ of a great deal of effort** es la culminación de grandes esfuerzos

culottes [kjʊ:'lɒts] NPL falda *fsing* pantalón

culpability [ˌkʌlpə'bɪlɪtɪ] N (*frm*) culpabilidad *f*

culpable ['kʌlpəbl] Ⓐ ADJ (*frm*) culpable
Ⓑ CPD ► **culpable homicide** N homicidio *m* sin premeditación

culprit ['kʌlprɪt] N culpable *mf*; (*Jur*) acusado/a *m/f*

cult [kʌlt] Ⓐ N culto *m* (**of** a); **to make a ~ of sth** rendir culto a algo
Ⓑ CPD ► **cult figure** N ídolo *m*

cultivable ['kʌltɪvəbl] ADJ cultivable

cultivar ['kʌltɪvɑ:ʳ] N (*Bot*) variedad *f* cultivada

cultivate ['kʌltɪveɪt] VT 1 [+ *crop, land, friendships*] cultivar
2 (*fig*) [+ *habit*] cultivar

cultivated ['kʌltɪveɪtɪd] Ⓐ ADJ (*fig*) [*person*] cultivado, culto; [*tastes, voice*] refinado
Ⓑ CPD ► **cultivated land** N tierras *fpl* cultivadas

cultivation [ˌkʌltɪ'veɪʃən] N 1 (*Agr*) cultivo *m*
2 (*fig*) [*of habit, qualities*] cultivo *m*

cultivator ['kʌltɪveɪtəʳ] N 1 (= *person*) cultivador(a) *m/f*
2 (= *machine*) cultivadora *f*

cultural ['kʌltʃərəl] Ⓐ ADJ cultural
Ⓑ CPD ► **cultural attaché** N agregado/a *m/f* cultural

culturally ['kʌltʃərəlɪ] ADV [*diverse*] culturalmente, desde el punto de vista cultural; **to be ~ aware/sensitive** estar pendiente de/sensibilizado con la cultura; **~, they have much in common with their neighbours** culturalmente hablando, tienen mucho en común con sus vecinos

culture ['kʌltʃəʳ] Ⓐ N 1 (= *the arts*) cultura *f*; (= *civilization*) civilización *f*, cultura *f*
2 (= *education, refinement*) cultura *f*; **she has no ~** carece de cultura, es una inculta
3 (*Agr*) (= *breeding*) cría *f*; [*of plants, etc*] cultivo *m*
Ⓑ VT [+ *tissue etc*] cultivar
Ⓒ CPD ► **culture clash** N choque *m* de culturas, choque *m* cultural ► **culture fluid** N caldo *m* de cultivo ► **culture gap** N vacío *m* cultural ► **culture medium** N caldo *m* de cultivo ► **culture shock** N choque *m* cultural ► **culture vulture*** N (*hum*) cultureta* *mf*

cultured ['kʌltʃəd] Ⓐ ADJ [*person*] culto, cultivado; [*tastes, voice*] refinado
Ⓑ CPD ► **cultured pearl** N perla *f* cultivada

culvert ['kʌlvət] N alcantarilla *f* (debajo de una carretera)

cum [kʌm] PREP con; **it's a sort of kitchen-~-library** es algo así como cocina y biblioteca combinadas; **I was butler-~-gardener to Lady Jane** yo fui mayordomo y jardinero a la vez en el servicio de Lady Jane

cu. m. ABBR (= **cubic metre(s), cubic meter(s)**) m^3

Cumb ABBR (= **Cumberland**) *antigua provincia del noroeste de Inglaterra*

cumbersome ['kʌmbəsəm], **cumbrous** ['kʌmbrəs] ADJ (= *bulky*) voluminoso, de mucho bulto; (= *awkward*) incómodo; **he was muffled in thick and ~ clothing** las abultadas ropas de abrigo casi le tapaban la cara; **the machine was slow and ~ to use** la máquina resultaba lenta y aparatosa *or* lenta e incómoda (de manejar); **~ administrative procedures** procedimientos *mpl* administrativos engorrosos

cumin ['kʌmɪn] N comino *m*

cum laude [kʊm'laʊdeɪ] ADJ (*Univ*) cum laude

cummerbund ['kʌməbʌnd] N faja *f*

cumulative ['kju:mjʊlətɪv] ADJ cumulativo

cumulonimbus [ˌkju:mjʊləʊ'nɪmbəs] N (*pl* **cumulonimbi** [ˌkju:mjʊləʊ'nɪmbaɪ]) cumulonimbo *m*

cumulus ['kju:mələs] N (*pl* **cumuli** ['kju:mjʊlaɪ]) cúmulo *m*

cuneiform ['kju:nɪfɔ:m] ADJ cuneiforme

cunnilingus [ˌkʌnɪ'lɪŋgəs] N cunnilingus *m*

cunning ['kʌnɪŋ] Ⓐ ADJ 1 (*pej*) (= *sly*) taimado, vivo (*LAm*)
2 (= *clever*) [*person*] astuto, ingenioso; [*plan, scheme, device*] ingenioso
3 (*US**) (= *cute*) mono, precioso
Ⓑ N (= *slyness*) astucia *f*; (= *cleverness*) ingenio *m*

cunningly ['kʌnɪŋlɪ] ADV 1 (= *slyly*) astutamente
2 (= *cleverly*) [*contrived, designed*] astutamente, sutilmente; [*disguised*] astutamente

cunt** [kʌnt] N 1 (= *genitals*) coño** *m*, concha *f* (*Andes, S. Cone***)
2 (= *person*) hijo/a *m/f* de puta**

CUP N ABBR = **Cambridge University Press**

cup [kʌp] Ⓐ N (*for tea, etc*) taza *f*; (= *amount*) (*also* **~ful**) taza *f*; (*Sport etc*) (= *prize*) copa *f*; (*Rel*) (= *chalice*) cáliz *m*; [*of brassiere*] copa *f*; **a ~ of tea** una taza de té, un té; **coffee ~** tacita *f*, pocillo *m* (*LAm*); **how's your ~?** ¿quieres más té/café *etc*?; **his ~ of sorrow was full** le agobiaba el dolor; ✦***IDIOMS*** **to be in one's ~s** estar borracho; **to be sb's ~ of tea***: **it's not everyone's ~ of tea*** no es del gusto de todos; **he's not my ~ of tea*** no es de mi agrado, no es santo de mi devoción; **football isn't my ~ of tea*** a mí el fútbol no me va; *see also* **paper C**
Ⓑ VT **to ~ one's hands** (*for shouting*) formar bocina con las manos; (*for drinking*) ahuecar las manos; **to ~ one's hands round sth** rodear algo con las manos
Ⓒ CPD ► **cup final** N (*Ftbl*) final *m* de copa ► **cup tie** N (*Ftbl*) partido *m* de copa

cup-bearer ['kʌpˌbeərəʳ] N copero *m*

cupboard ['kʌbəd] Ⓐ N (*free-standing*) armario *m*; (*built-in*) armario *m*, closet/clóset *m* (*LAm*), placar(d) *m* (*S. Cone*)
Ⓑ CPD ► **cupboard love** N (*Brit*) amor *m* interesado

cupcake ['kʌpkeɪk] N pastelito *m*

cupful ['kʌpfʊl] N taza *f*; **two ~s of milk** dos tazas de leche

Cupid ['kju:pɪd] N Cupido *m*

cupidity [kju:'pɪdɪtɪ] N (*frm*) codicia *f*

cupola ['kju:pələ] N cúpula *f*

cuppa* ['kʌpə] N (*Brit*) taza *f* de té

cur [kɜ:ʳ] N perro *m* de mala raza; (= *person*) canalla *m*

curable ['kjʊərəbl] ADJ curable

curaçao ['kjʊərəsəʊ] N curaçao *m*

curacy ['kjʊərəsɪ] N (*as parish priest*) curato *m*; (*as assistant*) coadjutoría *f*

curare [kjʊə'rɑ:rɪ] N curare *m*

curate ['kjʊərɪt] N (= *parish priest*) cura *m*; (= *assistant*) coadjutor *m*; ✦***IDIOM*** **to be like the ~'s egg**: **it's like the ~'s egg** (*Brit*) tiene su lado bueno y su lado malo

curative ['kjʊərətɪv] ADJ curativo

curator [kjʊəˈreɪtəʳ] N [*of museum*] director(a) *m/f*; [*of museum department*] conservador(a) *m/f*

curatorial [ˌkjʊərəˈtɔːrɪəl] ADJ **the museum's ~ staff** el equipo de conservadores del museo; **~ expertise** conocimientos *mpl* de conservación

curb [kɜːb] Ⓐ N [1] (*fig*) freno *m*; **to put a ~ on sth** poner freno a algo, refrenar algo
[2] (*US*) = **kerb**
Ⓑ VT (*fig*) [+ *temper, impatience etc*] dominar, refrenar; [+ *spending*] restringir; [+ *inflation*] poner freno a, frenar

curbstone [ˈkɜːbstəʊn] N (*US*) = **kerbstone**

curd [kɜːd] Ⓐ N (*usu pl*) cuajada *f*
Ⓑ CPD ► **curd cheese** N requesón *m*; *see also* **bean B**, **lemon C**

curdle [ˈkɜːdl] Ⓐ VT (= *form curds in*) cuajar; (= *separate*) [+ *milk, sauce*] cortar; **it was enough to ~ the blood** fue para helar la sangre a uno
Ⓑ VI (= *form curds*) cuajarse; (= *separate*) [*milk, sauce*] cortarse

cure [kjʊəʳ] Ⓐ N (= *remedy*) remedio *m*; (= *course of treatment*) cura *f*; (= *process of recovery*) curación *f*; **there is no known ~** no existe curación; **to be beyond ~** [*person*] padecer una enfermedad incurable; [*situation, injustice*] ser irremediable; **to take a ~** (*for illness*) tomar un remedio
Ⓑ VT [1] (*Med*) [+ *disease, patient*] curar; (*fig*) [+ *poverty, injustice, evil*] remediar; **to ~ sb of a habit** quitar a algn un vicio; ✦*PROV* **what can't be ~d must be endured** hay cosas que no queda más remedio que aguantar
[2] (= *preserve*) (*in salt*) salar; (*by smoking*) curar; (*by drying*) secar; [+ *animal hide*] curtir

cure-all [ˈkjʊərɔːl] N panacea *f*, curalotodo *m*

curettage [ˌkjʊəˈretɪdʒ] N legrado *m*, raspado *m*

curfew [ˈkɜːfjuː] N toque *m* de queda

curie [ˈkjʊərɪ] N curie *m*

curing [ˈkjʊərɪŋ] N curación *f*; *see also* **cure**

curio [ˈkjʊərɪəʊ] N curiosidad *f*

curiosity [ˌkjʊərɪˈɒsɪtɪ] Ⓐ N [1] (= *inquisitiveness*) curiosidad *f* (**about** por, acerca de); **out of ~** por curiosidad; ✦*PROV* **~ killed the cat** la curiosidad mata al hombre
[2] (= *rare thing*) curiosidad *f*
Ⓑ CPD ► **curiosity shop** N tienda *f* de curiosidades ► **curiosity value** N **its only attraction is its ~ value** su único interés es el valor que tiene como rareza

curious [ˈkjʊərɪəs] ADJ [1] (= *inquisitive*) curioso; **I'd be ~ to know** tengo curiosidad por saberlo; **she was ~ about her sister's new boyfriend** sentía curiosidad por conocer al nuevo novio de su hermana; **"do you want to know for any special reason?" — "no, I'm just ~"** —¿quieres saberlo por alguna razón especial? —no, sólo por curiosidad
[2] (= *strange*) curioso; **it's ~ that she didn't say why** es curioso que no dijese por qué; **it's ~ how we keep meeting each other** es curioso que siempre nos estemos encontrando

curiously [ˈkjʊərɪəslɪ] ADV [1] (= *inquisitively*) [*ask, look*] con curiosidad
[2] (= *oddly*) [*silent, reticent*] curiosamente; **~, he didn't object** curiosamente, no puso objeciones; **~ shaped** con una forma curiosa; **~ enough, it's true** curiosamente *or* aunque parezca extraño, es cierto

curl [kɜːl] Ⓐ N [*of hair*] rizo *m*; (= *ringlet*) bucle *m*, sortija *f*; [*of smoke etc*] espiral *m*, voluta *f*
Ⓑ VT [+ *hair*] rizar; [+ *paper*] arrollar; **she ~ed her lip in scorn** hizo una mueca de desprecio
Ⓒ VI [*hair*] rizarse; [*paper*] arrollarse; [*leaf*] abarquillarse; [*waves*] encresparse
► **curl up** VI + ADV [*paper, stale bread*] arrollarse; [*leaf*] abarquillarse; [*cat, dog*] hacerse una pelota; [*person*] hacerse un ovillo, acurrucarse; **she lay ~ed up on the bed** estaba acurrucada encima de la cama; **to ~ up into a ball** hacerse un ovillo; **to ~ up with a book** acurrucarse con un libro; **to ~ up with embarrassment/laughter*** morirse de vergüenza/risa

curler [ˈkɜːləʳ] N (*for hair*) rulo *m*, bigudí *m*, rulero *m* (*S. Cone*)

curlew [ˈkɜːluː] N zarapito *m*

curlicue [ˈkɜːlɪkjuː] N floritura *f*, floreo *m*

curling [ˈkɜːlɪŋ] Ⓐ N (*Sport*) curling *m*
Ⓑ CPD ► **curling iron(s)** N(PL), **curling tongs** NPL (*for hair*) tenacillas *fpl* de rizar

curl-paper [ˈkɜːlˌpeɪpəʳ] N papillote *m*

curly [ˈkɜːlɪ] ADJ (*compar* **curlier**; *superl* **curliest**) [*hair, eyelashes, lettuce*] rizado; [*writing*] de trazo ondulado, lleno de florituras

curly-haired [ˌkɜːlɪˈhɛəd], **curly-headed** [kɜːlɪˈhedɪd] ADJ de pelo rizado

curmudgeon† [kɜːˈmʌdʒən] N cascarrabias *mf inv*

curmudgeonly† [kɜːˈmʌdʒənlɪ] ADJ [*person*] arisco, cascarrabias; [*attitude*] de viejo cascarrabias

currant [ˈkʌrənt] Ⓐ N (= *dried grape*) pasa *f* de Corinto; (= *bush*) grosellero *m*; (= *fruit*) grosella *f*
Ⓑ CPD ► **currant bun** N bollo *m* con pasas, pan *m* de pasas (*LAm*)

currency [ˈkʌrənsɪ] Ⓐ N [1] (= *monetary system, money*) moneda *f*; **foreign ~** moneda *f* extranjera, divisas *fpl*; *see also* **paper C**
[2] (*fig*) aceptación *f*; **his theory had wide ~ in America** su teoría tuvo amplia aceptación en América; **these things are the ~ of everyday life** estas cosas son el pan nuestro de cada día; **to gain ~** [*views, ideas*] darse a conocer, difundirse; **it was his writing that gave the term ~** el término se dio a conocer gracias a sus escritos
Ⓑ CPD ► **currency market** N mercado *m* monetario, mercado *m* de divisas ► **currency note** N pagaré *m* fiscal, pagaré *m* de tesorería ► **currency restrictions** NPL restricciones *fpl* monetarias ► **currency snake** N serpiente *f* monetaria ► **currency unit** N unidad *f* monetaria

current [ˈkʌrənt] Ⓐ ADJ [*fashion, tendency*] actual; [*price, word*] corriente; [*year, month, week*] presente, en curso; **the ~ month/year** el presente mes/año, el mes/año en curso; **the ~ issue of the magazine** el último número de la revista; **her ~ boyfriend** su novio de ahora; **to be in ~ use** estar en uso corriente; **a word in ~ use** una palabra de uso corriente; **the ~ opinion is that …** actualmente se cree que …; **this idea/method is still quite ~** esta idea/este método se usa bastante todavía
Ⓑ N (*all senses*) corriente *f*; **direct/alternating ~** corriente *f* directa/alterna; ✦*IDIOMS* **to go against the ~** ir contra la corriente; **to go with the ~** dejarse llevar por la corriente
Ⓒ CPD ► **current account** N (*Brit*) cuenta *f* corriente ► **current affairs** NPL temas *mpl* de actualidad ► **current assets** NPL activo *msing* corriente ► **current events** N = **current affairs** ► **current liabilities** NPL pasivo *msing* corriente

currently [ˈkʌrəntlɪ] ADV actualmente, en la actualidad

curriculum [kəˈrɪkjʊləm] Ⓐ N (*pl* **curriculums** *or* **curricula** [kəˈrɪkjʊlə]) [*of school*] plan *m* de estudios; [*of college/university course*] programa *m* de estudios
Ⓑ CPD ► **curriculum vitae** N (*esp Brit*) curriculum *m* (vitae), historial *m* (profesional)

curried [ˈkʌrɪd] ADJ al curry

curry[1] [ˈkʌrɪ] Ⓐ N curry *m*
Ⓑ VT preparar con curry
Ⓒ CPD ► **curry powder** N curry *m* en polvo

curry[2] [ˈkʌrɪ] VT [+ *horse*] almohazar

currycomb [ˈkʌrɪkəʊm] N almohaza *f*

curse [kɜːs] Ⓐ N [1] (= *malediction, spell*) maldición *f*; **to put a ~ on sb** maldecir a algn; **a ~ on it!** ¡maldito sea!
[2] (= *bane*) maldición *f*, azote *m*; **drought is the ~ of Spain** la sequía es el azote de España; **it's been the ~ of my life** me ha amargado la vida, ha sido mi cruz; **the ~ of it is that …** lo peor (del caso) es que …
[3] (= *oath*) palabrota *f*; **to utter a ~** blasfemar; **~s!*** ¡maldito sea!, ¡maldición!
[4] (*) (= *menstruation*) **the ~** la regla, el período
Ⓑ VT [+ *luck, stupidity*] maldecir; [+ *person*] echar pestes de; **~ it!** ¡maldito sea!; **I ~ the day I met him** maldita sea la hora en que lo conocí; **to be ~d with** padecer, tener que soportar; **he seemed to be ~d with bad luck** parecía que la mala suerte le perseguía; **to ~ o.s.** maldecirse (**for being a fool** por tonto)
Ⓒ VI blasfemar, echar pestes, soltar palabrotas; **to ~ and swear** echar sapos y culebras

cursed [ˈkɜːsɪd] ADJ maldito

cursive [ˈkɜːsɪv] ADJ cursivo

cursor [ˈkɜːsəʳ] Ⓐ N (*Comput*) cursor *m*
Ⓑ CPD ► **cursor key** N tecla *f* del cursor

cursorily [ˈkɜːsərɪlɪ] ADV [*glance*] brevemente, de forma somera; [*read*] por encima, de forma somera

cursory [ˈkɜːsərɪ] ADJ [*examination, inspection*] somero, superficial; [*nod*] brusco; **at a ~ glance** a primera vista; **to give sth a ~ glance** mirar algo brevemente *or* de forma somera

curt [kɜːt] ADJ [*person, tone*] seco, corto; [*nod*] brusco

curtail [kɜːˈteɪl] VT (= *restrict*) restringir; (= *cut short*) acortar, abreviar; (= *reduce*) [+ *expenditure*] reducir

curtailment [kɜːˈteɪlmənt] N (= *restriction*) restricción *f*; (= *shortening*) acortamiento *m*; [*of expenditure*] reducción *f*

curtain [ˈkɜːtn] Ⓐ N [1] (*gen, Mil*) cortina *f*; (= *lace, small etc*) visillo *m*; (*Theat*) telón *m*; **to draw the ~s** (*together*) correr las cortinas; (*apart*) abrir las cortinas; **a ~ of fire** (*Mil*) una cortina de fuego; **when the final ~ came down** cuando el telón bajó por última vez; **it'll be ~s for you!*** será el acabóse para ti; ✦*IDIOMS* **to raise the ~ on sth** dar el pistoletazo de salida a algo; **to bring the ~ down on sth** poner punto final a algo; *see also* **safety B**
[2] (*fig*) [*of secrecy*] halo *m*; [*of mist*] manto *m*
Ⓑ VT proveer de cortinas
Ⓒ CPD ► **curtain call** N (*Theat*) llamada *f* a escena ► **curtain hook** N colgadero *m* de cortina ► **curtain pole** N = **curtain rod** ► **curtain rail** N riel *m* (de las cortinas) ► **curtain ring** N anilla *f* (de las cortinas) ► **curtain rod** N barra *f* (de las cortinas) ► **curtain wall** N [*of house, building*] muro *mpl* de cerramiento; [*of castle*] (= *low wall outside*)

contramuralla *f*, falsabraga *f*; (*between bastions or towers*) lienzo *m*, muralla *f*

► **curtain off** VT + ADV [+ *separate room*] separar con cortina; [+ *bed, area*] encerrar con cortina

curtained ['kɜ:tənd] ADJ [*door etc*] con cortina(s)

curtain-raiser ['kɜ:tn,reɪzəʳ] N pieza *f* preliminar

curtly ['kɜ:tlɪ] ADV [*say, reply*] bruscamente, secamente; [*nod*] bruscamente

curtness ['kɜ:tnɪs] N brusquedad *f*

curtsey, curtsy ['kɜ:tsɪ] Ⓐ N reverencia *f*; **to drop** *or* **make a curts(e)y** hacer una reverencia

Ⓑ VI hacer una reverencia (**to** a)

curvaceous* [kɜ:'veɪʃəs] ADJ [*woman*] de buen cuerpo, curvilíneo

curvature ['kɜ:vətʃəʳ] N [1] (*Math*) curvatura *f*
[2] **~ of the spine** (*Med*) escoliosis *f inv*, desviación *f* de columna

curve [kɜ:v] Ⓐ N (*gen*) curva *f*

Ⓑ VT [+ *spine, back*] encorvar, doblar

Ⓒ VI [*road, line, etc*] torcerse, hacer curva; [*surface*] combarse; **the walls ~ inward/outward** las paredes están combadas hacia dentro/fuera; **the road ~s round the mountain** la carretera va haciendo curvas *or* dando vueltas alrededor de la montaña; **the boomerang ~d through the air** el bumerán describió *or* hizo una curva en el aire; **a wide, curving staircase** una amplia escalera en curva

curved [kɜ:vd] ADJ curvo, encorvado

curvy ['kɜ:vɪ] ADJ [*line*] curvo; [*road etc*] serpentino, con muchas curvas; [*figure, woman*] curvilíneo

cushion ['kʊʃən] Ⓐ N (*gen*) cojín *m*; [*of chair, for knees etc*] almohadilla *f*; [*of air, moss*] colchón *m*; (= *edge of billiard table*) banda *f*

Ⓑ VT [+ *blow, fall*] amortiguar; **to ~ sb against sth** proteger a algn de algo

Ⓒ CPD ► **cushion cover** N funda *f* de cojín

cushy* ['kʊʃɪ] ADJ **a ~ job** un chollo*, un hueso (*Mex**); **to have a ~ life** *or* **time** tener la vida arreglada

cusp [kʌsp] N (*Bot, Astron*) cúspide *f*; [*of tooth*] corona *f*; [*of moon*] cuerno *m*

cuspidor ['kʌspɪdɔ:ʳ] N (*US*) escupidera *f*, salivadera *f* (*S. Cone*)

cuss* [kʌs] Ⓐ N (*US*) tipo* *m*, tío* *m*

Ⓑ VT, VI = **curse C**

cussed* ['kʌsɪd] ADJ [1] terco, cabezón
[2] = **cursed**

cussedness* ['kʌsɪdnɪs] N terquedad *f*; **out of sheer ~*** de puro terco

custard ['kʌstəd] Ⓐ N ≈ natillas *fpl* (*utilizada como acompañante en algunos postres*); (*also* **egg ~**) flan *m*

Ⓑ CPD ► **custard apple** N (*Bot*) chirimoya *f* ► **custard cream** N (= *biscuit*) galleta *f* de crema ► **custard pie** N pastel *m* de natillas; (= *missile*) torta *f* de crema ► **custard powder** N polvos *mpl* para (hacer) natillas ► **custard tart** N pastel *m* de crema

custodial [kʌs'təʊdɪəl] ADJ [1] **~ sentence** condena *f* de prisión
[2] **~ staff** (*in museum etc*) personal *m* de vigilancia

custodian [kʌs'təʊdɪən] N (*gen*) custodio/a *m/f*, guardián/ana *m/f*; [*of museum etc*] conservador(a) *m/f*

custody ['kʌstədɪ] N (*Jur*) [*of children*] custodia *f*; (= *police custody*) detención *f*; **the mother has ~ of the children** la madre tiene la custodia de los hijos; **to be in ~** estar detenido; **to take sb into ~** detener a algn; **in safe ~** bajo custodia, en buenas manos, bajo segura custodia; **in the ~ of** al cargo *or* cuidado de, bajo la custodia de

custom ['kʌstəm] Ⓐ N [1] (= *habit, usual behaviour*) costumbre *f*; **social ~s** costumbres *fpl* sociales; **it is her ~ to go for a walk each evening** tiene la costumbre de *or* tiene por costumbre dar un paseo cada tarde, acostumbra *or* suele dar un paseo cada tarde
[2] (*Comm*) clientela *f*; (= *total sales*) caja *f*, ventas *fpl*; **to attract ~** atraer clientela; **to get sb's ~** ganar la clientela de algn; **we've not had much ~ today** hoy hemos tenido pocos clientes; **the shop has lost a lot of ~** la tienda ha perdido muchos clientes; *see also* **customs**

Ⓑ CPD (*esp US*) *see* **custom-built, custom-made**

customarily ['kʌstəmərɪlɪ] ADV por regla general, normalmente

customary ['kʌstəmərɪ] ADJ [*place, time*] acostumbrado, de costumbre, habitual; [*wit, good humour etc*] acostumbrado, habitual; [*practice*] normal, habitual; **it's ~ to** + INFIN es la costumbre + *infin*

custom-built ['kʌstəm,bɪlt] ADJ hecho de encargo

customer ['kʌstəməʳ] Ⓐ N [1] cliente *mf*
[2] (*Brit**) tipo/a* *m/f*, tío/a* *m/f*; **he's an awkward ~** es un tipo *or* un tío difícil*; **ugly ~** antipático/a

Ⓑ CPD ► **customer profile** N perfil *m* del cliente ► **customer service** N servicio *m* de atención al cliente ► **customer service department** N departamento *m* de atención al cliente ► **customer services** NPL (= *counter*) mostrador *m* de información y atención al cliente

customize ['kʌstəmaɪz] VT [+ *car*] adaptar al gusto del cliente, adaptar por encargo del cliente; [+ *product*] personalizar; **~d software** software *m* a medida del usuario

custom-made ['kʌstəm'meɪd] ADJ [*furniture, clothing*] a medida, hecho a medida; [*car*] hecho de encargo

customs ['kʌstəmz] Ⓐ NPL aduana *fsing*; (*also* **~ duty**) derechos *mpl* de aduana; **to go through (the) ~** pasar por la aduana; **Customs and Excise** (*Brit*) Aduanas *fpl* y Arbitrios

Ⓑ CPD ► **customs clearance** N despacho *m* aduanero ► **customs declaration** N declaración *f* aduanera ► **customs house** N aduana *f* ► **customs inspection** N inspección *f* de aduanas ► **customs inspector** N inspector(a) *m/f* de aduanas, aduanero/a *m/f* ► **customs invoice** N factura *f* de aduana ► **customs officer** N oficial *mf* de aduanas, vista *mf* (de aduanas), aduanero/a *m/f* ► **customs post** N puesto *m* aduanero ► **Customs Service** N (*US*) aduana *f*, servicio *m* aduanero

cut [kʌt] (*vb: pt, pp* **cut**) Ⓐ N [1] (*in skin*) corte *m*, cortadura *f*; (= *wound*) herida *f*; (*Med*) (= *incision*) corte *m*, incisión *f*; (= *slash*) tajo *m*; (*with knife*) cuchillada *f*; (*with whip*) latigazo *m*; (*Cards*) corte *m*; **he's got a ~ on his forehead** tiene un corte en la frente; **he had a ~ on his chin from shaving** se había hecho un corte *or* se había cortado en la barbilla al afeitarse; **he was treated for minor ~s and bruises** recibió asistencia médica por heridas y hematomas; **there's a ~ in his jacket** lleva una raja en la chaqueta; ✦***IDIOMS*** **to be a ~ above sb**: **he's a ~ above the others** está por encima de los demás; **the ~ and thrust of politics** la esgrima política; **the unkindest ~ of all** el golpe más duro
[2] (= *reduction*) (*in wages, prices, production*) rebaja *f*, reducción *f*; (*in expenditure, budget*) corte *m*, recorte *m*; (*in tax, interest rates*) bajada *f*, rebaja *f*; (*in staff, workforce*) reducción *f*, recorte *f*; (= *deletion*) corte *m*; (= *deleted part*) trozo *m* suprimido; (*Elec*) apagón *m*, corte *m*; **public spending ~s** cortes *mpl* presupuestarios; **wage ~s** rebajas *fpl* de sueldo; **to take a ~ in salary** aceptar una reducción de sueldo; **they made some ~s in the text** hicieron algunos cortes en el texto, suprimieron algunas cosas del texto
[3] [*of clothes etc*] corte *m*; [*of hair*] corte *m*, peinado *m*
[4] [*of meat*] (= *part of animal*) corte *m* (de carne); (= *piece*) trozo *m*; (= *slice*) tajada *f*
[5] (*) (= *share*) parte *f*, tajada *f*; **the salesman gets a ~ of 5%** el vendedor recibe su parte de 5%
[6] (= *woodcut*) grabado *m*; (*US*) foto *f*, diagrama *m*, dibujo *m*
[7] **~ and paste** (*Comput*) cortar y pegar
[8] *see* **short E**

Ⓑ VT [1] [+ *meat, bread, cards*] cortar; **to ~ one's finger** cortarse el dedo; **to ~ sb free** (*from wreckage*) liberar a algn; (*when tied up*) desatar *or* soltar a algn; **to ~ sth in half** cortar algo por la mitad; **to ~ sth open** [+ *fruit, vegetable, body, package*] abrir algo; **I ~ my hand open on a tin** me corté la mano en una lata; **he ~ his head open** se abrió la cabeza; **to ~ sth (in)to pieces** cortar algo en pedazos; **to ~ an army to pieces** aniquilar un ejército; **to ~ sth to size** cortar algo a la medida; **to ~ sb's throat** degollar a algn; **he is ~ting his own throat** (*fig*) labra su propia ruina; **to ~ sth in two** cortar *or* partir algo en dos; ✦***IDIOM*** **you could ~ the atmosphere with a knife** se mascaba *or* respiraba la tensión en el ambiente; *see also* **fine[1] B2, ice A1, loss A2, tooth A1**
[2] (= *shape*) [+ *stone, glass, jewel*] tallar; [+ *key, hole*] hacer; [+ *channel*] abrir, excavar; [+ *engraving, record*] grabar; **to ~ one's way through** abrirse camino por; *see also* **coat A1**
[3] (= *clip, trim*) [+ *hedge, grass*] cortar; [+ *corn, hay*] segar; **to get one's hair ~** cortarse el pelo
[4] (= *reduce*) [+ *wages, prices, production*] reducir, rebajar (**by 5%** en un 5 por cien); [+ *expenditure*] reducir, recortar; [+ *taxes, interest rates*] bajar, rebajar; [+ *staff, workforce*] reducir, recortar; [+ *speech, text*] acortar, hacer cortes en; [+ *film*] cortar, hacer cortes en; (= *delete*) [+ *passage*] suprimir, cortar; (= *interrupt*) interrumpir, cortar; **she ~ two seconds off the record** mejoró *or* rebajó la plusmarca en dos segundos; **we ~ the journey time by half** reducimos el tiempo de viaje a la mitad; **to ~ sth/sb short** interrumpir algo/a algn; *see also* **corner A1**
[5] (*fig*) (= *hurt*) herir; ✦***IDIOM*** **to ~ sb to the quick**: **it ~ me to the quick** me tocó en lo vivo
[6] (= *intersect with*) [*road*] cruzar, atravesar; (*Math*) [*line*] cortar
[7] (*esp US**) **to ~ classes** hacer novillos*, ausentarse de clase; **to ~ sb dead** negar el saludo *or* (*LAm*) cortar a algn
[8] (= *turn off*) [+ *engine*] parar; (= *stop*) [+ *electricity supply*] cortar, interrumpir; **~ all this soft-soaping and tell me what you want*** deja ya de darme coba y dime qué quieres*
[9] (= *adulterate*) [+ *cocaine etc*] cortar
[10] (= *succeed*) **he couldn't ~ it as a singer** como cantante no daba la talla

Ⓒ VI [1] [*person, knife*] cortar; [*material*] cortarse; **paper ~s easily** el papel se corta fácilmente; **she ~ into the melon** cortó el melón; **will that cake ~ into six?** ¿se puede dividir el pastel en seis?; ✦***IDIOMS*** **to ~ loose (from sth)** deshacerse (de algo); **it ~s both ways** tiene doble filo

[2] (*Math etc*) [*lines*] cortarse

[3] (= *hurry*) **I must ~ along now** tengo que marcharme ya; ✦***IDIOMS*** **to ~ and run*** largarse*, escaparse; **to ~ to the chase** (*esp US**) ir al grano, dejar de marear la perdiz*

[4] (*Cine, TV*) (= *change scene*) cortar y pasar; **they ~ from the palace to the castle scene** cortan y pasan del palacio a la escena del castillo; **cut!** ¡corten!

[5] (*Cards*) cortar

Ⓓ ADJ [*flowers*] cortado; [*glass*] tallado; **~ price** a precio reducido, rebajado, de rebaja

►**cut across** VT + PREP [1] atajar por; **to ~ across a field** atajar por un campo; **to ~ across country** atajar por el campo

[2] (*fig*) **this ~s across the usual categories** esto rebasa las categorías establecidas

►**cut along** VI + ADV irse de prisa

►**cut away** VT + ADV cortar, eliminar

►**cut back** Ⓐ VT + ADV [1] (= *prune*) [+ *plant*] podar

[2] (= *reduce*) [+ *production, expenditure, staff*] reducir, recortar; **to ~ sth back by 50%** reducir algo en un 50 por ciento

Ⓑ VI + ADV [1] (= *make savings*) economizar; **to ~ back on sth** = **cut down B**

[2] (*Cine*) (= *flash back*) volver (**to** a)

►**cut down** Ⓐ VT + ADV [1] [+ *tree*] cortar, talar; [+ *enemy*] matar; [+ *clothes*] acortar

[2] (= *reduce*) [+ *consumption*] reducir; [+ *expenditure*] reducir, recortar; [+ *text*] acortar, abreviar; ✦***IDIOM*** **to ~ sb down to size** bajar los humos a algn

Ⓑ VI + ADV **you're drinking too much, you really should ~ down** bebes demasiado, deberías moderarte; **to ~ down on** [+ *fat*] reducir el consumo de; [+ *expenditure*] moderar, reducir; [+ *public services*] recortar, reducir; **I'm ~ting down on coffee and cigarettes** estoy intentando tomar menos café y fumar menos

►**cut in** Ⓐ VI + ADV (*in conversation*) interrumpir; (*Aut*) meterse delante; **to ~ in on a conversation** interrumpir una conversación

Ⓑ VT + ADV (*) **to ~ sb in (on sth)** incluir a algn (en algo)

►**cut into** VI + PREP **to ~ into one's holidays** interrumpir sus vacaciones; **we shall have to ~ into our savings** tendremos que usar una parte de los ahorros

►**cut off** VT + ADV [1] (*with scissors, knife*) cortar; (= *amputate*) amputar, quitar; **they ~ off his head** le cortaron la cabeza; ✦***IDIOM*** **to ~ off one's nose to spite one's face*** tirar piedras contra su propio tejado

[2] (= *disconnect*) [+ *telephone, gas*] cortar, desconectar; **we've been ~ off** (*Telec*) nos han cortado la comunicación

[3] (= *interrupt*) **to ~ sb off in the middle of a sentence** cortar *or* interrumpir a algn en mitad de una frase, no dejar terminar a algn; **to ~ off sb's supplies** cortar *or* interrumpir el suministro a algn

[4] (= *isolate*) aislar; **I feel very ~ off, living out here in the country** me siento muy aislado, viviendo aquí en el campo; **~ off by floods** aislado por las inundaciones; **we were ~ off by the snow** quedamos bloqueados por la nieve; **the village was ~ off for several days by the snow** la aldea quedó aislada *or* incomunicada por la nieve durante varios días; **to ~ o.s. off from sth/sb** aislarse de algo/algn; **to ~ off the enemy's retreat** cortar la retirada al enemigo; ✦***IDIOM*** **to ~ sb off without a penny** desheredar completamente a algn

►**cut out** Ⓐ VT + ADV [1] [+ *article, picture*] recortar; [+ *dress, skirt etc*] cortar; [+ *diseased part*] extirpar; ✦***IDIOMS*** **to be ~ out for sth/to do sth** estar hecho para ser algo/hacer algo; **he's not ~ out to be a poet** no tiene madera de poeta; **you'll have your work ~ out for you** te va a costar trabajo; **he had his work ~ out to finish it** tuvo que trabajar duro para terminarlo

[2] (= *exclude*) [+ *unnecessary details*] eliminar, suprimir; [+ *light*] tapar; [+ *intermediary, middleman*] saltarse a, eliminar; **he ~ his nephew out of his will** borró de su testamento la mención del sobrino; **you can ~ that out for a start!*** ¡para empezar deja de hacer eso!; **~ out the singing!*** ¡basta ya de cantar!; **~ it out!*** ¡basta ya!

[3] (= *give up*) [+ *fatty food*] dejar de comer; **to ~ out alcohol** dejar de beber

[4] (= *delete*) suprimir

Ⓑ VI + ADV [*car engine*] pararse; (*Elec*) cortarse, interrumpirse

►**cut through** VI + PREP [1] (*lit*) [+ *bone, cable*] atravesar, traspasar; [+ *jungle, undergrowth*] abrirse camino a través de

[2] (= *take short cut via*) atajar por, cortar por; **to ~ through the lane** atajar *or* cortar por el callejón

[3] (= *circumvent*) saltarse, sortear; **we have to find a way to ~ through all this red tape** hay que encontrar la manera de saltarse *or* sortear todo este papeleo

►**cut up** Ⓐ VT + ADV [1] [+ *food, paper, wood*] cortar en pedazos; [+ *meat*] picar; (= *wound*) herir, acuchillar

[2] (*) **to be ~ up about sth** (= *hurt*) estar muy afectado por algo; (= *annoyed*) estar muy molesto por algo; **he was very ~ up by the death of his son** estaba muy afectado por la muerte de su hijo

Ⓑ VI + ADV ✦***IDIOM*** **to ~ up rough*** ponerse agresivo

cut-and-dried [ˌkʌtən'draɪd], **cut-and-dry** [ˌkʌtən'draɪ] ADJ [*answer*] concreto; [*situation, issue*] definido, claro; **this situation is not as ~ as it may seem** la situación no está tan definida *or* clara como podría parecer

cutaneous [kjuː'teɪnɪəs] ADJ cutáneo

cutback ['kʌtbæk] N [1] (*in expenditure, staff, production*) recorte *m*, reducción *f*; **to make ~s (in sth)** hacer *or* realizar recortes (en algo)

[2] (*Cine*) (= *flashback*) flashback *m*

cute [kjuːt] ADJ [1] (= *sweet*) [*face, animal, baby*] lindo, precioso, mono*, rico*; [*person*] guapo; **isn't he ~!** (= *baby, pet*) ¡qué lindo es!, ¡qué mono *or* rico es!* (= *man*) ¡es guapísimo!

[2] (*esp US*) (= *clever*) listo, vivo (*LAm*); (= *affecting prettiness etc*) presumido

cutesy* ['kjuːtsɪ] ADJ (*pej*) [*person, painting, clothes*] cursi

cut-glass ['kʌt'glɑːs] ADJ de vidrio tallado

cuticle ['kjuːtɪkl] N cutícula *f*

cutie* ['kjuːtɪ] N (*US*) monada* *f*, ricura* *f*

cutie pie* ['kjuːtɪpaɪ] N (*US*) = **cutie**

cutlass ['kʌtləs] N alfanje *m*

cutler ['kʌtlə^r] N cuchillero *m*

cutlery ['kʌtlərɪ] N (*Brit*) cubiertos *mpl*, cubertería *f*; *see also* **canteen**

cutlet ['kʌtlɪt] N chuleta *f*; **a veal ~** una chuleta de ternera

cutoff ['kʌtɒf] Ⓐ N [1] (*also* **~ point**) (= *limit*) límite *m*

[2] (*Mech*) (*in pipe or duct*) cierre *m*, corte *m*; (*Elec*) valor *m* límite, corte *m*

[3] (*US*) atajo *m*

[4] **cutoffs*** tejanos *mpl* cortados, vaqueros *mpl* cortados

Ⓑ ADJ [*jeans*] cortado

Ⓔ CPD ► **cutoff date** N fecha *f* tope, fecha *f* límite ► **cutoff voltage** N tensión *f* de corte ► **cutoff switch** N conmutador *m* de corte, limitador *m* de potencia

cut-out ['kʌtaʊt] N [1] (= *paper, cardboard figure*) recorte *m*, figura *f* recortada; (*child's*) (*for cutting out*) recortable *m*, diseño *m* para recortar [2] (*Elec*) (= *switch*) cortacircuitos *m inv*, automático *m*; (*Mech*) válvula *f* de escape

cut-price ['kʌtpraɪs] ADJ [*goods*] a precio reducido, rebajado, de ocasión; [*shop*] de saldos

cut-rate [ˌkʌt'reɪt] ADJ = **cut-price**

cutter ['kʌtə^r] N [1] (= *tool*) cortadora *f*; (*for paper, cardboard*) cutter *m*; **wire ~s** cizalla *fsing*, cortaalambres *m*

[2] (= *person*) cortador(a) *m/f*

[3] (= *boat*) cúter *m*; (*US*) (= *coastguard*) patrullero *m*, guardacostas *m*

cut-throat ['kʌtθrəʊt] Ⓐ N (= *murderer*) asesino/a *m/f*

Ⓑ ADJ (= *fierce*) [*competition*] feroz, encarnizado

Ⓒ CPD ► **cut-throat razor** N navaja *f* (de afeitar)

cutting ['kʌtɪŋ] Ⓐ N [1] [*of plant*] esqueje *m*

[2] (*from newspaper*) recorte *m*; (*Cine*) montaje *m*

[3] (*for road, railway*) desmonte *m*, zanja *f*

Ⓑ ADJ (= *sharp*) [*edge, wind etc*] cortante; (*fig*) [*remark*] mordaz

Ⓒ CPD ► **cutting board** N plancha *f* para cortar ► **cutting edge** N filo *m*; (*fig*) vanguardia *f* ► **cutting room** N (*Cine*) sala *f* de montaje

cutting-edge ['kʌtɪŋˌedʒ] ADJ [*research, design*] más vanguardista; **~ technology** la tecnología más vanguardista

cuttlefish ['kʌtlfɪʃ] N (*pl* **cuttlefish** *or* **cuttlefishes**) jibia *f*, sepia *f*

cut-up* [ˌkʌt'ʌp] ADJ (*US*) gracioso

CV N ABBR (= **curriculum vitae**) C.V. *m*

CW N ABBR [1] = **chemical weapons**

[2] = **chemical warfare**

CWO, **cwo** ABBR [1] (*Comm*) = **cash with order**

[2] = **chief warrant officer**

CWS N ABBR = **Cooperative Wholesale Society**

cwt ABBR = **hundredweight(s)**

cyanide ['saɪənaɪd] N cianuro *m*; **~ of potassium** cianuro *m* potásico

cyanose ['saɪənəʊz] N cianosis *f*

cybercafé ['saɪbəˌkæfeɪ] N cibercafé *m*

cybernetic [ˌsaɪbə'netɪk] ADJ cibernético

cybernetics [ˌsaɪbə'netɪks] NSING cibernética *f*

cyberpunk ['saɪbəpʌŋk] N (*Literat*) ciberpunk *m*

cybersex ['saɪbəseks] N cibersexo *m*

cyberspace ['saɪbəspeɪs] N ciberespacio *m*

cyberterrorism ['saɪbəˌterərɪsm] N ciberterrorismo *m*

cyberterrorist ['saɪbəˌterərɪst] Ⓐ ADJ ciberterrorista Ⓑ N ciberterrorista *mf*

cyborg ['saɪbɔːg] N ciborg *m*, organismo *m* cibernético

cyclamate ['sɪkləmeɪt] N ciclamato *m*

cyclamen ['sɪkləmən] N ciclamen *m*

cycle ['saɪkl] Ⓐ N [1] (= *bicycle*) bicicleta *f*; **racing ~** bicicleta *f* de carreras

[2] [*of seasons, poems etc*] ciclo *m*; **life ~** ciclo *m* vital; **menstrual ~** ciclo *m* menstrual; **a 10-second ~** un ciclo de 10 segundos

Ⓑ VI (= *travel*) ir en bicicleta; **we ~d to the coast** fuimos en bicicleta a la costa; **I ~ to school** voy al colegio en bicicleta; **can you ~?** ¿sabes montar en bicicleta?
Ⓒ CPD ► **cycle clip** N pinza *f* para ir en bicicleta ► **cycle lane** N (*Brit*) carril *m* de bicicleta, carril *m* bici ► **cycle path** N carril *m* de bicicleta ► **cycle race** N carrera *f* ciclista ► **cycle rack** N soporte *m* para bicicletas; (*on car roof*) baca *f* para transportar bicicletas ► **cycle ride** N paseo *m* en bicicleta; **to go for a ~ ride** ir a dar un paseo en bicicleta ► **cycle shed** N cobertizo *m* para bicicletas ► **cycle track** N (*in countryside*) ruta *f* para ciclistas, senda *f* para ciclistas; (*Sport*) pista *f* de ciclismo, velódromo *m*

cycler ['saɪkləʳ] N (*US*) ciclista *mf*

cycleway ['saɪklweɪ] N ruta *f* para ciclistas

cyclic(al) ['saɪklɪk(əl)] ADJ cíclico

cycling ['saɪklɪŋ] Ⓐ N ciclismo *m*; **to go ~** ir *or* montar en bicicleta, hacer ciclismo; **the roads round here are ideal for ~** las carreteras de por aquí son ideales para ir *or* montar en bicicleta
Ⓑ CPD ► **cycling holiday** N vacaciones *fpl* en bicicleta ► **cycling shorts** NPL culotes *mpl*, culotte(s) *m(pl)*

cyclist ['saɪklɪst] N ciclista *mf*

cyclone ['saɪkləʊn] N ciclón *m*

Cyclops ['saɪklɒps] N (*pl* **Cyclopses** *or* **Cyclopes** [saɪ'kləʊpiːz]) cíclope *m*

cyclostyle ['saɪkləʊstaɪl] Ⓐ N ciclostil(o) *m*
Ⓑ VT reproducir en ciclostil(o)

cyclostyled ['saɪkləʊstaɪld] ADJ en ciclostil(o)

cyclotron ['saɪklətrɒn] N ciclotrón *m*

cygnet ['sɪgnɪt] N pollo *m* de cisne

cylinder ['sɪlɪndəʳ] Ⓐ N [1] (= *shape*) cilindro *m*
[2] (*Tech*) cilindro *m*; **a 6-~ engine** un motor de 6 cilindros; ✦***IDIOM*** **to fire on all ~s** emplearse a fondo, dar el do de pecho
Ⓑ CPD ► **cylinder block** N bloque *m* de cilindros ► **cylinder capacity** N cilindrada *f* ► **cylinder head** N culata *f* de cilindro ► **cylinder head gasket** N junta *f* de culata

cylindrical [sɪ'lɪndrɪkəl] ADJ cilíndrico

cymbal ['sɪmbəl] N (*freq pl*) címbalo *m*, platillo *m*

cynic ['sɪnɪk] N cínico/a *m/f*

cynical ['sɪnɪkəl] ADJ cínico

cynically ['sɪnɪklɪ] ADV cínicamente, con cinismo

cynicism ['sɪnɪsɪzəm] N cinismo *m*

cynosure ['saɪnəʃʊəʳ] N **~ of every eye** blanco *m* de todas las miradas

CYO N ABBR (*US*) = **Catholic Youth Organization**

cypher ['saɪfəʳ] = **cipher**

cypress ['saɪprɪs] N ciprés *m*

Cypriot ['sɪprɪət] Ⓐ ADJ chipriota
Ⓑ N chipriota *mf*

Cyprus ['saɪprəs] N Chipre *f*

Cyrillic [sɪ'rɪlɪk] Ⓐ ADJ cirílico
Ⓑ N cirílico *m*

cyst [sɪst] N quiste *m*

cystic ['sɪstɪk] Ⓐ ADJ cístico
Ⓑ CPD ► **cystic fibrosis** N fibrosis *f* cística

cystitis [sɪs'taɪtɪs] N cistitis *f*

cytological [,saɪtə'lɒdʒɪkəl] ADJ citológico

cytology [saɪ'tɒlədʒɪ] N citología *f*

cytoplasm ['saɪtəʊplæzm] N citoplasma *m*

cytotoxic [,saɪtəʊ'tɒksɪk] ADJ citotóxico

CZ ABBR (*US Geog*) = **Canal Zone**

czar [zɑːʳ] N zar *m*

czarina [zɑː'riːnə] N zarina *f*

czarism ['zɑːrɪzəm] N zarismo *m*

czarist ['zɑːrɪst] ADJ, N zarista *mf*

Czech [tʃek] Ⓐ ADJ checo; **the ~ Republic** la República Checa
Ⓑ N [1] (= *person*) checo/a *m/f*
[2] (*Ling*) checo *m*

Czechoslovak ['tʃekəʊ'sləʊvæk] (*Hist*) Ⓐ ADJ checoslovaco
Ⓑ N checoslovaco/a *m/f*

Czechoslovakia ['tʃekəʊslə'vækɪə] N (*Hist*) Checoslovaquia *f*

Czechoslovakian ['tʃekəʊslə'vækɪən] (*Hist*) Ⓐ ADJ checoslovaco
Ⓑ N checoslovaco/a *m/f*

Dd

D¹, d¹ [diː] N [1] (= *letter*) D, d *f*; **D for David** D de Dolores
[2] (*Mus*) **D** re *m*; **D major/minor** re mayor/menor; **D sharp/flat** re sostenido/bemol

D² (A) N (*Scol*) (= *mark around 50%*) aprobado *m*, suficiente *m*
(B) ABBR (*US Pol*) = **Democrat(ic)**

d² ABBR [1] (= **date**) fha.
[2] (= **daughter**) hija *f*
[3] (= **died**) m.
[4] (*Rail etc*) = **depart(s)**
[5] (*Brit*†) = **penny**

DA N ABBR (*US Jur*) = **District Attorney**

D/A ABBR = **deposit account**

dab¹ [dæb] (A) N [1] (= *light stroke*) toque *m*; (= *blow*) golpecito *m*
[2] (= *small amount*) pizca *f*; [*of paint*] ligero brochazo *m*; [*of liquid*] gota *f*
[3] **dabs** (*esp Brit*‡) huellas *fpl* digitales
(B) VT (= *touch lightly*) tocar ligeramente; (*with cream, butter*) untar ligeramente; (*with paint, water*) dar unos toques a; **to ~ a stain off** quitar una mancha humedeciéndola; **to ~ on** untar ligeramente

►**dab at** VI + PREP **to ~ at one's mouth/eyes** limpiarse la boca/los ojos (*dándose toquecitos*)

dab² [dæb] N (= *fish*) lenguado *m*

dab³* [dæb] (A) ADJ ✦***IDIOM*** **to be a ~ hand at (doing) sth** (*Brit*) ser un hacha para (hacer) algo
(B) ADV **~ in the middle** (*US*) en el mismo centro

dabble [ˈdæbl] (A) VT salpicar, mojar; **to ~ one's hands/feet in water** chapotear con las manos/los pies en el agua
(B) VI (*fig*) **to ~ in sth** hacer algo/interesarse por algo superficialmente; **to ~ in politics** ser politiquero, politiquear; **to ~ in shares** jugar a la bolsa; **I only ~ in it** para mí es un pasatiempo nada más

dabbler [ˈdæbləʳ] N (*pej*) aficionado/a *m/f* (**in** a), diletante *mf*; **he's just a ~** es un simple aficionado, para él es un pasatiempo nada más

dabchick [ˈdæbtʃɪk] N somorgujo *m* menor

Dacca [ˈdækə] N Dacca *f*

dace [deɪs] N (*pl* **dace** *or* **daces**) albur *m*

dacha [ˈdætʃə] N dacha *f*

dachshund [ˈdækshʊnd] N perro *m* salchicha

Dacron® [ˈdækrɒn] N (*US*) Dacrón® *m*

dactyl [ˈdæktɪl] N dáctilo *m*

dactylic [dækˈtɪlɪk] ADJ dactílico

dad* [dæd] N papá *m*

Dada [ˈdɑːdɑː] (A) N dada *m*, dadaísmo *m*
(B) ADJ dadaísta

dadaism [ˈdɑːdɑːɪzəm] N dadaísmo *m*

dadaist [ˈdɑːdɑːɪst] (A) ADJ dadaísta
(B) N dadaísta *mf*

daddy* [ˈdædɪ] N = **dad**

daddy-long-legs [ˈdædɪˈlɒŋlegz] N (*Brit*) típula *f*

dado [ˈdeɪdəʊ] N (*pl* **dadoes** *or* **dados**) [*of wall*] friso *m*; (*Archit*) [*of pedestal*] dado *m*

daemon [ˈdiːmən] N demonio *m*

daff* [dæf] N ABBR (*Brit*) = **daffodil**

daffodil [ˈdæfədɪl] N narciso *m*

daffy* [ˈdæfɪ] ADJ chiflado*

daft* [dɑːft] ADJ (*compar* **dafter**; *superl* **daftest**)
[1] (= *silly*) [*person*] tonto, bobo, tarado (*S. Cone**); [*idea, action, question*] tonto; **don't be ~** no seas tonto *or* bobo; **he's not as ~ as he looks** no es tan tonto como parece; **if you're ~ enough to pay £600** si eres tan bobo como para pagar 600 libras; **the ~ things some people do!** ¡hay que ver las estupideces que hace la gente!; ✦***IDIOMS*** **to be ~ in the head*** estar mal de la cabeza*, estar tocado del ala*; **to be as ~ as a brush*** ser más tonto que Abundio*
[2] (= *crazy*) **to be ~ about sb** estar loco por algn; **he's ~ about football** le apasiona el fútbol, el fútbol le vuelve loco

dagger [ˈdægəʳ] N [1] (= *knife*) daga *f*, puñal *m*; ✦***IDIOMS*** **to be at ~s drawn (with sb)** estar a matar (con algn); **to look ~s at sb** fulminar a algn con la mirada
[2] (*Typ*) cruz *f*, obelisco *m*

dago‡ [ˈdeɪgəʊ] N (*pl* **dagos** *or* **dagoes**) (*pej*) *término ofensivo aplicado a españoles, portugueses e italianos*

daguerrotype [dəˈgɛrəʊˌtaɪp] N daguerrotipo *m*

dahlia [ˈdeɪlɪə] N dalia *f*

Dáil [dɔɪl] N (*also* **~ Éireann**) *Cámara baja del Parlamento de la República de Irlanda*

daily [ˈdeɪlɪ] (A) ADJ [1] (= *occurring each day*) diario; **there are ~ flights from Manchester to Munich** hay vuelos diarios de Manchester a Munich, hay vuelos de Manchester a Munich diariamente; **on a ~ basis** (= *every day*) diariamente; **they are paid on a ~ basis** (= *by the day*) les pagan por días *or* por día trabajado; (= *every day*) les pagan cada día; **our ~ bread** el pan nuestro de cada día; **~ newspaper** diario *m*, periódico *m*; **incidents of this kind are a ~ occurrence** este tipo de incidentes ocurre diariamente *or* a diario
[2] (= *normal, everyday*) cotidiano; **the ~ grind** la rutina diaria; **the ~ life of a primary school teacher** la vida cotidiana de un profesor de primaria; **we went about our ~ lives as if nothing had happened** continuamos con nuestra vida normal como si nada hubiera pasado; **the ~ round** la rutina diaria
(B) ADV diariamente, a diario; **incidents of this kind happen ~** este tipo de incidentes ocurre diariamente *or* a diario; **the ticket office is open ~** la taquilla abre diariamente *or* todos los días; **twice ~** dos veces al día
(C) N [1] (= *newspaper*) diario *m*, periódico *m*
[2] (*esp Brit**) **~ (help** *or* **woman)** asistenta *f*, chacha* *f*

daintily [ˈdeɪntɪlɪ] ADV [*walk*] elegantemente, con pasos delicados; [*eat*] (= *delicately*) con delicadeza, delicadamente; (= *affectedly*) remilgadamente, melindrosamente; **the fish was ~ served** se sirvió el pescado exquisitamente presentado; **a plate of ~ cut sandwiches** un plato de sandwiches delicadamente cortados

daintiness [ˈdeɪntɪnɪs] N [*of person, hands, vase*] finura *f*, delicadeza *f*; [*of steps*] elegancia *f*, delicadeza *f*; [*of figure*] gracia *f*, delicadeza *f*

dainty [ˈdeɪntɪ] (A) ADJ (*compar* **daintier**; *superl* **daintiest**) [1] (= *delicate*) [*person, hands, vase*] fino, delicado; [*steps*] elegante, delicado; [*figure*] delicado; [*food, clothes*] exquisito, refinado; **a ~ morsel** un bocado exquisito
[2] (= *fastidious*) delicado, melindroso
(B) N bocado *m* exquisito; **dainties** exquisiteces *fpl*

daiquiri [ˈdaɪkɪrɪ] N daiquiri *m*, daiquirí *m*

dairy [ˈdɛərɪ] (A) N (= *shop*) lechería *f*; (*on farm*) vaquería *f*
(B) CPD [*products*] lácteo ► **dairy butter** N mantequilla *f* casera ► **dairy cattle**, **dairy cows** NPL vacas *fpl* lecheras ► **dairy farm** N granja *f* de productos lácteos ► **dairy farmer** N ganadero/a *m/f* de vacuno de leche ► **dairy farming** N industria *f* láctera, industria *f* lactaria ► **dairy herd** N ganado *m* lechero ► **dairy ice cream** N helado *m* de nata ► **dairy produce** N productos *mpl* lácteos

dairymaid [ˈdɛərɪmeɪd] N lechera *f*

dairyman [ˈdɛərɪmən] N (*pl* **dairymen**) lechero *m*

dais [ˈdeɪɪs] N estrado *m*

daisy [ˈdeɪzɪ] (A) N margarita *f*; ✦***IDIOM*** **to be pushing up the daisies*** criar malvas*
(B) CPD ► **daisy chain** N (*lit*) guirnalda *f* de margaritas; (*fig*) serie *f*

daisywheel [ˈdeɪzɪˌwiːl] (A) N margarita *f*
(B) CPD ► **daisywheel printer** N impresora *f* de margarita

Dakar [ˈdækəʳ] N Dakar *m*

Dalai Lama [ˈdælaɪˈlɑːmə] N Dalai Lama *m*

dale [deɪl] N valle *m*; **the (Yorkshire) Dales** los valles de Yorkshire

dalliance [ˈdælɪəns] N [1] (*liter*) (*amorous*) coqueteo *m*, flirteo *m*
[2] (*esp hum*) (*with hobby, politics etc*) escarceos *mpl*

dally ['dælɪ] VI [1] (= *dawdle*) tardar; **to ~ over sth** perder el tiempo con algo; *see also* **dilly-dally**
[2] (= *amuse o.s.*) divertirse; **to ~ with** [+ *lover*] coquetear con, tener escarceos amorosos con; [+ *idea*] entretenerse con
Dalmatia [dæl'meɪʃə] N Dalmacia *f*
Dalmatian [dæl'meɪʃən] Ⓐ N (= *person*) dálmata *mf*
Ⓑ ADJ dálmata
dalmatian [dæl'meɪʃən] N (= *dog*) perro *m* dálmata
daltonism ['dɔːltənɪzəm] N daltonismo *m*
dam¹ [dæm] Ⓐ N (= *wall*) dique *m*, presa *f*; (= *reservoir*) presa *f*, embalse *m*
Ⓑ VT (*also* **~ up**) poner un dique a, represar; (*fig*) reprimir, contener
► **dam up** VT + ADV = **dam B**
dam²‡ [dæm] ADJ = **damn D, damned A2**
dam³ [dæm] N (*Zool*) madre *f*
damage ['dæmɪdʒ] Ⓐ N [1] (*gen*) daño *m*; (*visible, eg on car*) desperfectos *mpl*; (*to building, area*) daños *pl*; **to do** *or* **cause ~ to** [+ *building*] causar daños a; [+ *machine*] causar desperfectos en; **the bomb did a lot of ~** la bomba causó muchos daños; **not much ~ was caused to the car** el coche no sufrió grandes desperfectos
[2] (*fig*) (*to chances, reputation etc*) perjuicio *m*, daño *m*; **to do** *or* **cause ~ to sth/sb** causar perjuicio a algo/algn, perjudicar algo/a algn; **the ~ is done** el daño ya está hecho; ✦*IDIOM* **what's the ~?*** (= *cost*) ¿cuánto va a ser?, ¿qué se debe?
[3] **damages** (*Jur*) daños *mpl* y perjuicios; *see also* **recover A2**
Ⓑ VT (= *harm*) dañar; [+ *machine*] averiar, causar desperfectos en; [+ *health, chances, reputation*] perjudicar; **to be ~d in a collision** sufrir daños en un choque
Ⓒ CPD ► **damage limitation exercise** N campaña *f* para minimizar los daños
damaging ['dæmɪdʒɪŋ] ADJ (*gen*) dañino; (*fig*) perjudicial (**to** para)
damascene ['dæməsiːn] Ⓐ ADJ damasquinado, damasquino
Ⓑ VT damasquinar
Damascus [də'mɑːskəs] N Damasco *m*
damask ['dæməsk] Ⓐ ADJ [*cloth*] adamascado; [*steel*] damasquinado
Ⓑ N (= *cloth*) damasco *m*; (= *steel*) acero *m* damasquinado
Ⓒ VT [+ *cloth*] adamascar; [+ *steel*] damasquinar
Ⓓ CPD ► **damask rose** N rosa *f* de Damasco
dame [deɪm] N [1] **Dame** (*Brit*) (= *title*) *título aristocrático para mujeres equivalente a "sir"*
[2] (*esp Brit*†) dama *f*, señora *f*; (*Brit Theat*) *personaje de mujer anciana en las pantomimas británicas interpretado por un actor*; → PANTOMIME
[3] (*US*†*) (= *woman*) tía* *f*, gachí *f* (*Sp*‡)
damfool‡ ['dæm'fuːl] ADJ = **damn-fool**
dammit‡ ['dæmɪt] EXCL ¡maldita sea!*; ✦*IDIOM* **as near as ~** (*Brit*) casi, por un pelo
damn [dæm] Ⓐ VT [1] (*Rel*) (= *condemn*) condenar; **the effort was ~ed from the start** desde el principio el intento estaba condenado a fracasar; **the critics ~ed the book** los críticos pusieron *or* tiraron el libro por los suelos; **I'll see him ~ed first** antes lo veré colgado; ✦*IDIOM* **to ~ sth/sb with faint praise** despachar algo/a algn con tímidos elogios
[2] (= *swear at*) maldecir
[3] (‡) (*in exclamations*) **~ it!** ¡maldita sea!*; **~ him/you!** ¡maldito sea/seas!*; **~ this car!** ¡al diablo con este coche!; **well I'll be ~ed!** ¡caramba!*, ¡vaya!*; **I'll be ~ed if I will!** ¡ni en broma!, ¡ni pensarlo!, ¡ni de coña! (*Sp*‡)
Ⓑ EXCL (‡) ¡maldita sea!*, ¡caray!*, ¡me cago en la leche! (*Sp*‡), ¡carajo! (*LAm*‡‡)
Ⓒ N (‡) **I don't give a ~** me importa un pito *or* bledo*, me importa un carajo‡‡; **it's not worth a ~** no vale un pimiento*, no vale un carajo‡‡
Ⓓ ADJ (‡) maldito*, condenado*, fregado (*LAm**); **~ Yankee** (*US*) sucio/a yanqui *mf*
Ⓔ ADV (‡) **it's ~ hot/cold!** ¡vaya calor/frío que hace!, ¡hace un calor/frío del demonio!*; **he's ~ clever!** ¡mira que es listo!, ¡es más listo que el hambre!*; **he ~ near killed me** por poco me mata, casi me mata; **"did you tell him so?" — "~ right, I did!"** —¿eso le dijiste? —¡pues claro! *or* ¡ya lo creo!; **I should ~ well think so!** ¡hombre, eso espero!
damnable†* ['dæmnəbl] ADJ detestable
damnably†* ['dæmnəblɪ] ADV terriblemente
damn-all‡ ['dæm'ɔːl] Ⓐ ADJ **it's ~ use** no sirve para nada en absoluto
Ⓑ N **he does ~** no da (ni) golpe*; **I know ~ about it** (*Brit*) no tengo ni pajolera idea del tema*
damnation [dæm'neɪʃən] Ⓐ N (*Rel*) perdición *f*
Ⓑ EXCL (*) ¡maldición!
damned [dæmd] Ⓐ ADJ [1] [*soul*] condenado, maldito
[2] (‡) maldito*, condenado*, fregado (*LAm**); **that ~ book** ese maldito libro; **it's a ~ shame** es una verdadera lástima *or* pena
Ⓑ ADV (‡) muy, extraordinariamente; **it's ~ awkward** es terriblemente difícil; **it's ~ hot!** ¡vaya calor/frío que hace!, ¡hace un calor del demonio!*
Ⓒ N **the ~** las almas en pena
damnedest* ['dæmdɪst] N **to do one's ~ to succeed** hacer lo imposible para tener éxito
damn-fool‡ ['dæmfuːl] ADJ estúpido, tonto; **some ~ driver** algún imbécil de conductor; **that's a ~ thing to say!** ¡qué estupidez *or* tontería!
damning ['dæmɪŋ] ADJ [*evidence*] irrefutable
Damocles ['dæməkliːz] N Damocles
damp [dæmp] Ⓐ ADJ (*compar* **damper**, *superl* **dampest**) [*house, air, skin, grass*] húmedo; **wipe with a ~ cloth** límpielo con un trapo húmedo; **~ conditions are the worst enemy of old manuscripts** la humedad es el peor enemigo de los manuscritos; **it smells ~ in here** aquí huele a humedad *or* a húmedo; **a ~ patch** una mancha de humedad; ✦*IDIOM* **to be a ~ squib**: **the concert was a bit of a ~ squib** el concierto fue decepcionante, nos llevamos un chasco con el concierto
Ⓑ N (*also* **~ness**) humedad *f*; *see also* **rising D**
Ⓒ VT [1] (= *moisten*) humedecer
[2] = **dampen 2**
[3] (= *deaden*) [+ *sounds*] amortiguar; [+ *vibration*] mitigar
Ⓓ CPD ► **damp course** N aislante *m* hidrófugo
► **damp down** VT + ADV [+ *fire*] sofocar
dampen ['dæmpən] VT [1] (= *moisten*) humedecer
[2] (*fig*) [+ *hopes*] frustrar; [+ *enthusiasm, zeal*] enfriar; **his words ~ed her hopes** sus palabras frustraron sus esperanzas, sus palabras le hicieron perder las esperanzas; **I don't want to ~ your enthusiasm, but ...** no quiero enfriar tu entusiasmo, pero ..., no quiero hacer que pierdas tu entusiasmo, pero ...; **to ~ sb's spirits** desanimar *or* desalentar a algn; **to ~ sb's ardour** apagar el ardor de algn
dampener ['dæmpənəʳ] N ✦*IDIOM* **to put a ~ on** = **to put a damper on**
damper ['dæmpəʳ] N (*Mus*) sordina *f*, apagador *m*; [*of fire*] regulador *m* de tiro; (*Tech*) amortiguador *m*; ✦*IDIOM* **to put a ~ on** [*sad news*] [+ *celebration, party*] poner una nota de tristeza a; **to put a ~ on things*** aguar la fiesta
dampish ['dæmpɪʃ] ADJ algo húmedo
damply ['dæmplɪ] ADV [1] (= *wetly*) **his T-shirt clung ~ to him** la camiseta mojada se le ceñía al cuerpo; **her hair clung ~ to her cheeks** el pelo mojado se le pegaba a las mejillas
[2] (*fig*) (= *unenthusiastically*) sin ganas, sin (mucho) entusiasmo
dampness ['dæmpnɪs] N humedad *f*
damp-proof ['dæmppruːf] Ⓐ ADJ hidrófugo, a prueba de humedad
Ⓑ VT aislar contra la humedad
Ⓒ CPD ► **damp-proof course** N = **damp course**
damsel† ['dæmzəl] N damisela *f*, doncella *f*; **a ~ in distress** (*hum*) una dama en apuros
damson ['dæmzən] N (= *fruit*) ciruela *f* damascena; (= *tree*) ciruelo *m* damasceno
Dan [dæn] N (*familiar form*) *of* **Daniel**
dan [dæn] N (*Sport*) dan *m*
dance [dɑːns] Ⓐ N [1] (= *act*) baile *m*; (= *art of dancing*) danza *f*, baile *m*; **~ of death** danza *f* de la muerte; ✦*IDIOM* **to lead sb a (merry) ~** (*Brit*) traer loco a algn
[2] (= *event*) baile *m*
Ⓑ VT bailar; ✦*IDIOM* **to ~ attendance on sb** desvivirse por algn
Ⓒ VI bailar; (*artistically*) bailar, danzar; (*fig*) (= *skip*) saltar, brincar; **shall we ~?** ¿quieres bailar?; **to ~ about** (*with pain, joy etc*) saltar; **to ~ for joy** saltar *or* brincar de alegría; ✦*IDIOM* **to ~ to sb's tune** bailar al son que algn toca
Ⓓ CPD ► **dance band** N orquesta *f* de baile ► **dance class** N clase *f* de baile ► **dance floor** N pista *f* de baile ► **dance hall** N salón *m* de baile, sala *f* de fiestas ► **dance music** N música *f* de baile
dancer ['dɑːnsəʳ] N (*gen*) bailarín/ina *m/f*; (*flamenco*) bailaor(a) *m/f*
dancing ['dɑːnsɪŋ] Ⓐ N baile *m*
Ⓑ CPD ► **dancing girl** N bailarina *f* ► **dancing partner** N pareja *f* de baile ► **dancing shoes** NPL (*gen*) zapatos *mpl* de baile; (*for ballet*) zapatillas *fpl* de ballet
D and C N ABBR = **dilation and curettage**
dandelion ['dændɪlaɪən] N diente *m* de león
dander ['dændəʳ] N ✦*IDIOM* **to get sb's ~ up**† sacar a algn de sus casillas
dandified ['dændɪfaɪd] ADJ guapo, acicalado
dandle ['dændl] VT hacer saltar sobre las rodillas
dandruff ['dændrəf] Ⓐ N caspa *f*
Ⓑ CPD ► **dandruff shampoo** N champú *m* anticaspa
dandy ['dændɪ] Ⓐ N (*pej*) (= *man*) dandi *m*, petimetre *m*
Ⓑ ADJ (*esp US**) excelente, chachi (*Sp**), macanudo (*LAm**); **fine and ~** perfecto
Dane [deɪn] N danés/esa *m/f*
dang* [dæŋ] EXCL (*euph*) = **damn B**
danger ['deɪndʒəʳ] Ⓐ N peligro *m*; **to be in ~** estar en peligro, correr peligro; **to be in ~ of falling** correr el peligro *or* riesgo de caer; **there is a ~ of** hay peligro *or* riesgo de; **there was no ~ that he would be discovered** no había peligro de que lo descubrieran; **(to be) out of ~** (*gen, Med*) (estar) fuera de peligro; **to be a ~ to sth/sb/o.s.** ser un peligro para

algo/para algn/para sí mismo; **"danger men at work"** "¡atención *or* ¡peligro obras!"; **"danger keep out"** "¡peligro de muerte! prohibido el acceso"
Ⓑ CPD ► **danger area** N = **danger zone** ► **danger list** N (*Med*) **to be on the ~ list** estar grave ► **danger money** N plus *m* de peligrosidad ► **danger point** N punto *m* crítico ► **danger signal** N señal *f* de peligro ► **danger zone** N área *f or* zona *f* de peligro

dangerous ['deɪndʒrəs] ADJ [*animal, disease, person, place*] peligroso; [*strategy, decision, operation*] peligroso, arriesgado; [*driver*] peligroso, temerario; [*substance, drug*] peligroso, nocivo; **he was jailed for ~ driving** lo metieron en la cárcel por conducir con imprudencia temeraria; **it is ~ to play on railway lines** es peligroso jugar en las vías del tren

dangerously ['deɪndʒrəslɪ] ADV peligrosamente, de forma peligrosa; **he was driving ~ close to the car in front** conducía tan pegado al coche de delante que era peligroso; **I came ~ close to hitting him** faltó muy poco para que le pegara; **he didn't die, but he came ~ close to it** no murió, pero estuvo a punto *or* le faltó poco; **to drive ~** conducir de forma temeraria; (*Jur*) conducir con imprudencia temeraria; **~ high** peligrosamente alto; **to be ~ ill** estar gravemente enfermo; **to live ~** (= *take risks*) llevar una vida arriesgada, vivir al límite; **go on, live ~, have another glass of wine!** (*hum*) venga, un día es un día, ¡tómate otra copa de vino!; **~ low** peligrosamente bajo

dangle ['dæŋgl] Ⓐ VT [1] [+ *arm, leg*] colgar; [+ *object on string etc*] dejar colgado
[2] (*fig*) [+ *tempting offer*] **to ~ sth in front of** *or* **before sb** tentar a algn con algo
Ⓑ VI colgar, pender; **to keep sb dangling** (*fig*) tener a algn pendiente

Daniel ['dænjəl] N Daniel

Danish ['deɪnɪʃ] Ⓐ N [1] (*Ling*) danés *m*
[2] **the ~** los daneses
[3] (*esp US*) = **Danish pastry**
Ⓑ ADJ danés, dinamarqués
Ⓒ CPD ► **Danish blue (cheese)** N queso *m* azul danés ► **Danish pastry** N *bollo de masa de hojaldre con pasas, manzana o crema*

dank [dæŋk] ADJ (*compar* **danker**; *superl* **dankest**) húmedo y oscuro

Dante ['dæntɪ] N Dante

Danube ['dænju:b] N Danubio *m*

Daphne ['dæfnɪ] N Dafne

dapper ['dæpəʳ] ADJ (= *smart*) [*man, appearance*] pulcro

dapple ['dæpl] VT motear a colores

dappled ['dæpld] ADJ moteado; [*horse*] rodado

DAR N ABBR (*US*) (= **Daughters of the American Revolution**) *una organización de mujeres descendientes de combatientes de la Guerra de la Independencia americana*

> **DAR**
>
> *La organización* **Daughters of the American Revolution** *o* **DAR***, fundada en 1890, está formada por mujeres que descienden de familias que lucharon para defender las colonias contra los británicos durante la Guerra de la Independencia americana (1775-1783). Sus miembros han trabajado mucho para fomentar el patriotismo y preservar los lugares históricos.*
> *Políticamente, es una organización muy conservadora que incluso se ha opuesto a la existencia de las Naciones Unidas.*

Darby and Joan ['dɑ:bɪən'dʒəʊn] Ⓐ NPL *el matrimonio ideal, de ancianos que siguen viviendo en la mayor felicidad*
Ⓑ CPD ► **Darby and Joan club** N (*Brit*) club *m* para personas de la tercera edad

Dardanelles [,dɑ:də'nelz] NPL Dardanelos *mpl*

dare [dɛəʳ] Ⓐ N (= *challenge*) reto *m*, desafío *m*; **I did it for a ~** me retaron, por eso lo hice
Ⓑ VT [1] (= *challenge*) desafiar, retar; **to ~ sb to do sth** desafiar *or* retar a algn a hacer algo; **I ~ you!** ¡a que no te atreves!
[2] (= *be so bold*) atreverse; **to ~ (to) do sth** atreverse a hacer algo; **I ~n't** no me atrevo; **I ~n't tell him** no me atrevo a decírselo; **how ~ you!** ¡cómo te atreves!, ¡qué cara!; **don't** *or* **just you ~!*** ¡ni se te ocurra!
[3] **I ~ say** (= *in my opinion*) en mi opinión; (= *possibly*) puede ser, tal vez; **I ~ say that ...** no me sorprendería que + *subjun*; **I ~ say you're tired** supongo que estás cansado; **~ I say it** me atrevería a decir
[4] (*liter*) [+ *sb's anger*] hacer frente a

daredevil ['dɛə,devl] Ⓐ ADJ temerario
Ⓑ N temerario/a *m/f*, atrevido/a *m/f*

daren't [dɛənt] = **dare not**

Dar-es-Salaam [,dɑ:ressə'lɑ:m] N Dar-es-Salaam *m*

daring ['dɛərɪŋ] Ⓐ ADJ [1] (= *bold*) [*plan, escape*] arriesgado; [*person*] atrevido, audaz
[2] (= *provocative*) [*film, clothes*] atrevido
Ⓑ N audacia *f*, atrevimiento *m*

daringly ['dɛərɪŋlɪ] ADV atrevidamente, osadamente

Darius [də'raɪəs] N Darío

dark [dɑ:k] Ⓐ ADJ (*compar* **darker**; *superl* **darkest**) [1] (= *not illuminated*) oscuro; **a ~ night** una noche cerrada; **the room/house was ~** (= *poky*) era una habitación/casa oscura; (= *badly-lit*) la habitación/casa estaba oscura; (= *lights not on*) la habitación/casa estaba a oscuras; **it was already ~ outside** ya había oscurecido, ya era de noche; **to get ~** oscurecerse, ponerse oscuro; (*at night-time*) oscurecer, hacerse de noche; **it gets ~ early in winter** en invierno oscurece pronto, en invierno se hace de noche pronto; **the ~ side of the moon** la cara oculta de la luna
[2] (*in colour*) [*colour, clothes*] oscuro; [*complexion, hair*] moreno, prieto (*Mex*); [*cloud*] gris; **~ blue/red** *etc* azul/rojo *etc* oscuro; **he is tall and ~** es alto y moreno, es alto y prieto (*Mex*)
[3] (= *sad, gloomy*) [*day, period*] aciago; [*mood, thoughts*] sombrío; **these are ~ days for the steel industry** son días aciagos para la industria del acero
[4] (= *obscure, mysterious*) oscuro; **the ~ recesses of the human mind** los oscuros recovecos de la mente humana; **~est Africa** lo más recóndito de África; **a ~ corner of the world** un rincón recóndito del mundo; **to keep sth ~*** no decir ni pío de algo*; **keep it ~!*** ¡de esto ni una palabra a nadie!; ✦**IDIOM he's a ~ horse** es una incógnita, es un enigma
[5] (= *sinister*) [*secret, plan, threat*] siniestro; **who performed the ~ deed?** ¿quién llevó a cabo el vil acto?; **I got some ~ looks from Janet** Janet me lanzaba miradas asesinas
Ⓑ N **after ~** después del anochecer; **until ~** hasta el anochecer; **I want to leave before ~** quiero salir antes de que anochezca, quiero salir antes del anochecer; **the ~** la oscuridad; **he is afraid of the ~** le tiene miedo a la oscuridad; **why are you sitting in the ~?** ¿por qué estás sentado en lo oscuro?; ✦**IDIOMS to be in the ~ about sth*** no saber nada sobre algo; **I'm still in the ~ (about it)*** aún no sé nada (de eso); **to keep/leave sb in the ~ about sth*** mantener/dejar a algn desinformado de algo, ocultar algo a algn; *see* **shot B5**
Ⓒ CPD ► **the Dark Ages** NPL la Alta Edad Media; **we're still living in the ~ ages** (*fig*) todavía vivimos en la Edad Media ► **dark chocolate** N chocolate *m* amargo, chocolate *m* negro ► **dark glasses** NPL gafas *fpl* oscuras ► **dark matter** N (*Astron*) materia *f* oscura

darken ['dɑ:kən] Ⓐ VT [+ *sky*] oscurecer; [+ *colour*] hacer más oscuro; **a ~ed room** un cuarto oscuro; ✦**IDIOM to ~ sb's door**: **never ~ my door again!** ¡no vuelvas nunca por aquí!
Ⓑ VI [*room, landscape*] oscurecerse; [*sky*] (*at nightfall*) oscurecerse; (= *cloud over*) nublarse; [*colour*] ponerse más oscuro; (*fig*) [*face, future*] ensombrecerse

darkey‡ ['dɑ:kɪ] N = **darkie**

dark-eyed [,dɑ:k'aɪd] ADJ de ojos oscuros

darkie†‡ ['dɑ:kɪ] N (*Brit pej*) negro/a *m/f*

darkish ['dɑ:kɪʃ] ADJ [*colour*] algo oscuro, tirando a oscuro; [*hair, complexion*] algo moreno, tirando a moreno

darkly ['dɑ:klɪ] ADV (= *mysteriously*) enigmáticamente; (= *threateningly*) de manera amenazante; **the newspapers hinted ~ at conspiracies** los periódicos hacían enigmáticas referencias a conspiraciones; **"we'll see," he said ~** —ya veremos —dijo en tono amenazante; **~ comic** lleno de humor negro; **the freckles stood out ~ against her pale skin** las pecas resaltaban oscuras en su blanca piel; **a ~ handsome man** un atractivo hombre moreno

darkness ['dɑ:knɪs] N [1] (= *blackness*) [*of complexion, hair, sky*] oscuridad *f*; **in the ~ of the night** en la oscuridad *or* lo oscuro de la noche; **the house was in ~** la casa estaba a oscuras; **~ fell, and we returned home** cayó la noche y volvimos a casa
[2] (= *evil*) el mal; **the forces of ~** las fuerzas del mal; **the powers of ~** los poderes del mal

darkroom ['dɑ:krʊm] N (*Phot*) cuarto *m* oscuro

dark-skinned [,dɑ:k'skɪnd] ADJ moreno, morocho (*LAm*)

darky‡ ['dɑ:kɪ] N = **darkie**

darling ['dɑ:lɪŋ] Ⓐ N [1] (*gen*) cariño *m*, querido/a *m/f*; **yes, ~** sí, cariño *or* querida; **come here, ~** (*to child*) ven aquí, cielo; **be a ~ and ...*** sé bueno y ...; **she's a little ~** (*child*) es un encanto
[2] (= *favourite*) preferido/a *m/f*; **the ~ of the muses** el preferido de las musas
Ⓑ ADJ [1] (= *beloved*) querido
[2] (*) (= *lovely*) [*house, dress*] mono; **what a ~ dress/house!** ¡qué vestido más mono/casa más mona!, ¡qué monada de vestido/casa!

darn[1] [dɑ:n] Ⓐ N (*Sew*) zurcido *m*, zurcidura *f*
Ⓑ VT [+ *socks, cloth*] zurcir

darn[2]* [dɑ:n] (*esp US*) Ⓐ EXCL **~ (it)!** ¡caray!*
Ⓑ ADJ = **darned A**
Ⓒ ADV = **darned B**

darned* [dɑ:nd] (*esp US*) Ⓐ ADJ condenado, maldito; **I'll be ~!** ¡mecachis!*
Ⓑ ADV **free to do as you ~ well please** libre de hacer lo que te dé la real gana*; **we start working pretty ~ early** empezamos a trabajar tela de pronto*

darning ['dɑ:nɪŋ] Ⓐ N (= *action*) zurcido *m*; (= *items to be darned*) cosas *f* por zurcir
Ⓑ CPD ► **darning needle** N aguja *f* de zurcir ► **darning wool** N hilo *m* de zurcir

dart [dɑ:t] Ⓐ N [1] (= *movement*) movimiento *m* rápido; **to make a ~ for** precipitarse hacia
[2] (*Sport*) dardo *m*, rehilete *m*; **~s** (= *game*) dardos *mpl*; **to play ~s** jugar a los dardos

3 (= *weapon*) dardo *m*, flecha *f*
4 (*Sew*) pinza *f*
Ⓑ VT [+ *look*] lanzar
Ⓒ VI **to ~ in/out** entrar/salir como una flecha; **to ~ at** *or* **for sth** lanzarse *or* precipitarse hacia algo

►**dart away, dart off** VI + ADV salir como una flecha

dartboard ['dɑːtbɔːd] N diana *f*

Darwinian [dɑː'wɪnɪən] Ⓐ ADJ darwiniano
Ⓑ N darwinista *mf*

Darwinism ['dɑːwɪnɪzəm] N darwinismo *m*

Darwinist ['dɑːwɪnɪst] Ⓐ ADJ darwinista
Ⓑ N darwinista *mf*

dash [dæʃ] Ⓐ N 1 (= *small quantity*) [*of liquid*] gota *f*, chorrito *m*; [*of salt, pepper*] pizca *f*; [*of colour*] toque *m*; **with a ~ of soda** con una gota *or* un chorrito de sifón
2 (= *punctuation mark*) (*also Morse*) raya *f*
3 (= *rush*) carrera *f*; **there was a mad ~ for the exit** todos se precipitaron hacia la salida; **to make a ~ at** *or* **towards** precipitarse hacia; **we had to make a ~ for it** tuvimos que salir corriendo
4 (*US Sport*) **the 100-meter ~** los 100 metros lisos
5 (= *flair, style*) brío *m*; ✦***IDIOM* to cut a ~** destacar
6 (*Aut*) = **dashboard**
Ⓑ VT 1 (= *throw*) **to ~ sth to the ground** tirar *or* arrojar algo al suelo; **to ~ sth to pieces** hacer añicos algo, estrellar algo; **to ~ one's head against sth** dar con la cabeza contra algo
2 (*fig*) [+ *hopes*] frustrar, defraudar; **to ~ sb's spirits** desanimar a algn
Ⓒ VI 1 (= *smash*) estrellarse; **the waves are ~ing against the rock** las olas rompen contra la roca
2 (= *rush*) ir de prisa, precipitarse; **to ~ away/back** salir/volver corriendo; **to ~ in/out** entrar/salir disparado; **to ~ past** pasar como un rayo; **to ~ up** [*person*] llegar corriendo; [*car*] llegar a toda velocidad; **I must ~*** me voy corriendo
Ⓓ EXCL **~ it (all)!**†* ¡demontre!*, ¡porras!*

►**dash off** Ⓐ VT + ADV [+ *letter, drawing*] hacer a la carrera
Ⓑ VI + ADV salir corriendo, marcharse apresuradamente

dashboard ['dæʃbɔːd] N (*Aut*) salpicadero *m*

dashed†* [dæʃt] ADJ (*euph*) = **damned A2**

dashing ['dæʃɪŋ] ADJ [*man*] gallardo, apuesto

dashingly ['dæʃɪŋlɪ] ADV [*behave*] gallardamente, arrojadamente; [*dress*] garbosamente

dastardly ['dæstədlɪ] ADJ ruin, vil

DAT N ABBR = **digital audio tape**

data ['deɪtə] Ⓐ NPL (*with sing or pl vb*) datos *mpl*
Ⓑ CPD ► **data bank** N banco *m* de datos ► **data capture** N grabación *f* de datos ► **data collection** N recogida *f* de datos, recopilación *f* de datos ► **data dictionary**, **data directory** N guía *f* de datos ► **data entry** N entrada *f* de datos ► **data file** N archivo *m* de datos ► **data link** N medio *m* de transmisión de datos ► **data management** N gestión *f* de datos ► **data preparation** N preparación *f* de datos ► **data processing** N (= *action*) procesamiento *m* de datos, proceso *m* de datos; (= *science*) informática *f* ► **data processor** N procesador *m* de datos ► **data protection** N protección *f* de datos ► **data transmission** N transmisión *f* de datos, telemática *f*

database ['deɪtəbeɪs] Ⓐ N base *f* de datos
Ⓑ CPD ► **database manager** N (= *software*) gestor *m* de base de datos

datable ['deɪtəbl] ADJ datable, fechable (**to** en)

Datapost® ['deɪtəpəʊst] N (*Brit*) **by ~** por correo urgente

date[1] [deɪt] Ⓐ N 1 (= *year, day of month*) fecha *f*; **what's the ~ today?** ◊ **what ~ is it today?** ¿qué fecha es hoy?; **~ of birth** fecha *f* de nacimiento; **closing ~** fecha *f* tope; **at an early ~** (*in the future*) en fecha próxima, dentro de poco; **at some future ~** en alguna fecha futura; **~ of issue** fecha *f* de emisión; **at a later ~** en una fecha posterior; **opening ~** fecha *f* de apertura; **to ~** hasta la fecha; *see also* **out-of-date**, **up-to-date**
2 (= *appointment*) cita *f*, compromiso *m*; (*with girlfriend, boyfriend*) cita *f*; **to have a ~ with sb** tener una cita con algn; **have you got a ~ tonight?** ¿tienes algún compromiso para esta noche?; **to make a ~ with sb** citarse *or* quedar con algn; **they made a ~ for eight o'clock** se citaron para las ocho, quedaron a las ocho
3 (= *person one is dating*) pareja *f*, acompañante *mf*; **who's your ~ for tonight?** ¿con quién sales esta noche?
4 (= *concert etc*) actuación *f*
Ⓑ VT 1 (= *put date on*) [+ *letter*] fechar, poner fecha a
2 (= *establish age of*) [+ *object*] fechar, datar
3 (= *show age of*) [+ *person*] **you remember the Tremeloes? that really ~s you!** ¿recuerdas a los Tremeloes? ¡eso demuestra lo viejo que eres!
4 (= *go out with*) [+ *girl etc*] salir con, pololear con (*Chile*)
Ⓒ VI 1 (= *show age*) pasar de moda
2 **to ~ back to** [+ *time*] remontarse a; **to ~ from** datar de
3 (= *go out with sb*) **is she dating?** ¿sale con chicos?; **they've been dating for three months** llevan saliendo juntos tres meses
Ⓓ CPD ► **date rape** N violación *f* durante una cita amorosa ► **date stamp** N (*on library book, fresh food*) sello *m* de fecha; (= *postmark*) matasellos *m inv*; *see also* **date-stamp**

date[2] [deɪt] N (*Bot*) (= *fruit*) dátil *m*; (*also* **~ palm**) palmera *f* datilera

dated ['deɪtɪd] ADJ [*clothes, ideas*] pasado de moda, anticuado

dateline ['deɪtlaɪn] N 1 (*Geog*) línea *f* de cambio de fecha
2 (*in newspaper*) **~ Beirut** fechado en Beirut

date-stamp ['deɪtstæmp] VT estampar la fecha en; *see also* **date**

dating ['deɪtɪŋ] Ⓐ N (*Archeol*) datación *f*
Ⓑ CPD ► **dating agency** N agencia *f* de contactos ► **dating service** N servicio *m* de contactos

dative ['deɪtɪv] Ⓐ ADJ dativo
Ⓑ N (*also* **~ case**) dativo *m*

datum ['deɪtəm] N (*pl* **data**) dato *m*; *see also* **data**

daub [dɔːb] Ⓐ N (= *smear*) mancha *f*; (= *bad painting*) pintarrajo *m*
Ⓑ VT (= *smear*) embadurnar; **to ~ a wall with paint** ◊ **~ paint onto a wall** embadurnar una pared de pintura
Ⓒ VI pintarrajear

dauber ['dɔːbəʳ], **daubster** ['dɔːbstəʳ] N pintor(a) *m/f* de brocha gorda, mal(a) pintor(a) *m/f*

daughter ['dɔːtəʳ] N hija *f*; → DAR

daughterboard ['dɔːtə,bɔːd] N (*Comput*) placa *f* hija

daughter-in-law ['dɔːtərɪnlɔː] N (*pl* **daughters-in-law**) nuera *f*, hija *f* política

daunt [dɔːnt] VT (= *inhibit*) amedrentar; (= *dishearten*) desmoralizar, desalentar; **nothing ~ed** sin dejarse amedrentar, sin inmutarse

daunting ['dɔːntɪŋ] ADJ (= *inhibiting*) abrumador, amedrentador; (= *disheartening*) desalentador, desmoralizante; **a ~ task** una tarea abrumadora, una gigantesca tarea

dauntless ['dɔːntlɪs] ADJ [*person*] intrépido; [*courage*] tenaz

dauntlessly ['dɔːntlɪslɪ] ADV **to carry on ~** continuar sin amilanarse, continuar impávido

dauphin ['dɔːfɪn] N (*Hist*) delfín *m*

Dave [deɪv] N (*familiar form*) *of* **David**

davenport ['dævnpɔːt] N (*US*) sofá *m* cama; (*Brit*) (= *desk*) escritorio *m* pequeño

David ['deɪvɪd] N David

davit ['dævɪt] N pescante *m*

Davy Jones ['deɪvɪ'dʒəʊnz] N **~' locker** (*Naut*) el fondo del mar (*tumba de los marineros ahogados*)

dawdle ['dɔːdl] Ⓐ VI (*in walking*) andar muy despacio; (*over food, work*) entretenerse, demorarse
Ⓑ VT **to ~ away** malgastar

dawdler ['dɔːdləʳ] N (= *idler*) holgazán/ana *m/f*, ocioso/a *m/f*; (= *slowcoach*) rezagado/a *m/f*

dawdling ['dɔːdlɪŋ] Ⓐ ADJ (= *lagging behind*) rezagado
Ⓑ N pérdida *f* de tiempo

dawn [dɔːn] Ⓐ N 1 (= *daybreak*) amanecer *m*; **at ~** al amanecer; **to get up with the ~** levantarse al amanecer; **from ~ to dusk** de sol a sol
2 (*liter*) (= *beginning*) albores *mpl*; **the ~ of the radio age** los albores de la era de la radio
Ⓑ VI [*day*] amanecer; **a new epoch has ~ed** ha nacido una época nueva
Ⓒ CPD ► **dawn chorus** N (*Brit*) canto *m* de los pájaros al amanecer ► **dawn raid** N (*Police*) *redada efectuada en la madrugada*; (*Fin*) *compra inesperada de acciones de una empresa como paso previo a una OPA*

►**dawn (up)on** VI + PREP **it suddenly ~ed on him that …** se dio cuenta *or* cayó en la cuenta de repente de que …

dawning ['dɔːnɪŋ] Ⓐ ADJ [*hope etc*] naciente
Ⓑ N (= *beginning*) albores *mpl*; **the ~ of the space age** los albores de la era espacial; **the first ~ of hope** el primer atisbo *or* rayo de esperanza

day [deɪ] Ⓐ N 1 (= *24 hours*) día *m*; **what ~ is it today?** ¿qué día es hoy?; **he works eight hours a ~** trabaja ocho horas al día; **twice a ~** dos veces al día; **the ~ after** el día siguiente; **the ~ after tomorrow** pasado mañana; **~ after ~** día tras día; **two ~s ago** hace dos días; **any ~** un día cualquiera; **any ~ now** cualquier día de éstos; **any old ~*** el mejor día; **the ~ before** el día anterior; **the ~ before yesterday** anteayer; **the ~ before his birthday** la víspera de su cumpleaños; **two ~s before Christmas** dos días antes de Navidad; **~ by ~** de un día para otro, de día a día (*LAm*); **every ~** cada día, todos los días; **one fine ~** el día menos pensado; **on the following ~** al día siguiente; **for ~s on end** durante días; **from ~ to ~** de día en día; **from one ~ to the next** de un día a otro; **to live from ~ to ~** *or* **from one ~ to the next** vivir al día; **~ in ~ out** un día sí y otro también; **you don't look a ~ older** no pasan por ti los días, no pareces un día más viejo; **on the ~ everything will be all right** para el día en cuestión todo estará en orden; **one ~** un día; **the other ~** el otro día; **every other ~** un día sí y otro no; **some ~** un día; **(on) that ~** aquel día; **that ~ when we ...** aquel día en que nosotros ...; **one of these ~s** un día de éstos; **this ~ next week** ◊ **this ~ week** (*Brit*) (de) hoy en ocho días; **50 years ago to the ~** (hoy) hace exactamente 50 años; ✦*IDIOMS* **he's fifty if he's a ~*** debe tener cincuenta años mínimo; **to carry** *or* **win the ~** ganar la victoria; **to give sb his ~ in court** dar a algn la oportunidad de explicarse; **to make sb's ~**: **it made my ~ to see him smile** me hizo feliz verlo sonreír; **that'll be the ~, when he offers to pay!*** ¡él nos invitará cuando las ranas críen pelo!; *see also* **black A6**

2 (= *daylight hours, working hours*) jornada *f*; **to work an eight-hour ~** trabajar una jornada de ocho horas; **it's a fine ~** hace buen tiempo hoy; **to work all ~** trabajar todo el día; **a ~ at the seaside** un día de playa; **to travel by ~** ◊ **travel during the ~** viajar de día; **paid by the ~** pagado por día; **good ~!** ¡buenos días!; **to work ~ and night** trabajar día y noche; **a ~ off** un día libre; **to take a ~ off** darse un día libre, no presentarse en el trabajo; **on a fine/wet ~** un día bonito/lluvioso; **one summer's ~** un día de verano; **~ of reckoning** (*fig*) día *m* de ajustar cuentas; **to work ~s** trabajar de día; ✦*IDIOMS* **it's all in a ~'s work** son gajes del oficio; **to call it a ~*** (*for good*) darse por vencido, abandonar; (*for today*) dejarlo por hoy; **let's call it a ~** terminemos ya

3 (= *period*) **during the early/final ~s of the strike** durante los primeros/últimos días de la huelga; **it has seen better ~s** ya no vale lo que antes; **until my dying ~** hasta la muerte; **it's early ~s yet** todavía es pronto; **the happiest ~s of your life** los mejores días de su vida; **in those ~s** en aquellos tiempos; **in ~s to come** en días venideros; **in this ~ and age** ◊ **in the present ~** hoy en día; **in my ~** en mis tiempos; **in Queen Victoria's ~** en la época de la reina Victoria; **he was famous in his ~** fue famoso en sus tiempos; **in the good old ~s** en los viejos tiempos; **these ~s** hoy en día; **those were the ~s, when ...** esa fue la buena época, cuando ...; **to this ~** hasta el día de hoy; **in his younger ~s** en su juventud; ✦*IDIOM* **to have had one's ~**: **he's had his ~** pasó de moda, está acabado; *see also* **dog A1, time A1, A5**

Ⓑ CPD ► **day bed** N (*US*) meridiana *f* ► **day boarder** N (*Brit Scol*) alumno/a *m/f* de media pensión ► **day boy** N (*Brit Scol*) externo *m* ► **day centre** N (*Brit*) centro *m* de día ► **day girl** N (*Brit Scol*) externa *f* ► **day job** N trabajo *m* habitual, ocupación *f* habitual; ✦*IDIOM* **don't give up the ~ job!** (*hum*) ¡sigue en lo tuyo! ► **Day of Judgement** N día *m* del Juicio Final ► **day labourer**, **day laborer** (*US*) N jornalero *m* ► **day nurse** N enfermero/a *m/f* de día ► **day nursery** N guardería *f* ► **day release course** N (*Brit Comm, Ind*) curso *m* de un día a la semana (para trabajadores) ► **day return (ticket)** N (*Brit*) billete *m* de ida y vuelta en el día ► **day school** N colegio *m* sin internado ► **day shift** N (*in factory etc*) turno *m* de día ► **day trip** N excursión *f* (de un día); **to go on a ~ trip to London** ir un día de excursión *or* (*LAm*) de paseo a Londres ► **day tripper** N excursionista *mf*

daybook ['deɪbʊk] N (*Brit*) diario *m* de entradas y salidas, libro *m* de entradas y salidas; (*US*) agenda *f*

daybreak ['deɪbreɪk] N amanecer *m*; **at ~** al amanecer

daycare ['deɪkɛəʳ] Ⓐ N servicio *m* de guardería
Ⓑ CPD ► **daycare centre**, **daycare center** (*US*) N guardería *f* ► **daycare services** NPL (*Brit*) servicios *mpl* de guardería

daydream ['deɪdriːm] Ⓐ N ensueño *m*, ilusión *f*
Ⓑ VI soñar despierto

Day-glo® ['deɪgləʊ] ADJ [*colours etc*] fosforescente, fosforito*

daylight ['deɪlaɪt] Ⓐ N luz *f* (del día); **at ~** (= *dawn*) al amanecer; **in the ~** ◊ **by ~** de día; **in broad ~** a plena luz del día, en pleno día; ✦*IDIOMS* **to see ~**: **I am beginning to see ~** (= *understand*) empiezo a ver las cosas claras; (= *approach the end of a job*) ya vislumbro el final; **to beat** *or* **knock the (living) ~s out of sb*** dar una tremenda paliza a algn; **to scare the (living) ~s out of sb*** dar un susto de muerte a algn; **it's ~ robbery!** (*Brit*) ¡es un robo *or* una estafa!
Ⓑ CPD ► **daylight attack** N ataque *m* diurno ► **daylight hours** NPL horas *fpl* de luz

daylight-saving time [ˌdeɪlaɪt'seɪvɪŋˌtaɪm] N (*US*) horario *m* de verano

daylong ['deɪˌlɒŋ] Ⓐ ADJ que dura todo el día
Ⓑ ADV todo el día

day-old ['deɪ'əʊld] ADJ [*chick*] de un día

dayroom ['deɪrʊm] N (*in hospital etc*) *sala de estar para los internos*

daytime ['deɪtaɪm] Ⓐ N día *m*; **in the ~** de día
Ⓑ ADJ de día; **please give a ~ telephone number** por favor dé un teléfono de contacto durante el día
Ⓒ CPD ► **daytime TV** N programación *f* de televisión matinal *or* matutina, televisión *f* matinal *or* matutina

day-to-day ['deɪtə'deɪ] ADJ cotidiano, diario; **the ~ running of the centre** la gestión cotidiana *or* diaria del centro; **on a ~ basis** día por día, de día a día (*LAm*)

daze [deɪz] Ⓐ N aturdimiento *m*; **to be in a ~** estar aturdido
Ⓑ VT 1 [*drug, blow*] atontar, aturdir; (= *confuse*) aturdir
2 (*fig*) [*news*] aturdir, atolondrar

dazed [deɪzd] ADJ (= *confused*) aturdido

dazzle ['dæzl] Ⓐ N deslumbramiento *m*
Ⓑ VT deslumbrar; **he was ~d by the bright light** lo deslumbró el resplandor de la luz; **she was ~d by his knowledge of the world** (se) quedó deslumbrada por su conocimiento del mundo

dazzling ['dæzlɪŋ] ADJ (*lit, fig*) deslumbrante

dazzlingly ['dæzlɪŋlɪ] ADV [*shine*] deslumbradoramente; **~ beautiful** de una belleza deslumbrante

DB ABBR = **database**

dB ABBR (= **decibel**) dB

DBMS N ABBR = **database management system**

DBS N ABBR 1 = **direct broadcasting by satellite**
2 = **direct broadcasting satellite**

DC N ABBR 1 (*Elec*) (= **direct current**) C.C.
2 (*US*) = **District of Columbia**

DCC® N ABBR = **digital compact cassette**

DCF N ABBR = **discounted cash-flow**

DCI N ABBR (*Brit*) = **Detective Chief Inspector**

DD N ABBR 1 (*Univ*) = **Doctor of Divinity**
2 (*Comm, Fin*) = **direct debit**
3 (*US Mil*) = **dishonorable discharge**

dd ABBR (*Comm*) 1 = **delivered**
2 = **dated**
3 = **demand draft**

D/D ABBR = **direct debit**

DC - DISTRICT OF COLUMBIA

District of Columbia *es el distrito donde se encuentra el gobierno de Estados Unidos. No forma parte de ningún estado, sino que es un distrito autónomo que comprende únicamente la capital del país, Washington. Se halla en el este de los Estados Unidos y tiene un área de unos 180 kilómetros cuadrados, donados por los estados de Maryland y Virginia. Normalmente se hace referencia a este distrito mediante sus siglas,* **DC**, *y se usa después del nombre de la capital:* **Washington DC**.

D-day ['diːdeɪ] N (*Hist*) el día D, el día de la invasión aliada de Normandía (*6 junio 1944*); (*fig*) día *m* D

DDS N ABBR (*US*) 1 (*Univ*) = **Doctor of Dental Science**
2 (*Univ*) = **Doctor of Dental Surgery**

DDT N ABBR (= **dichlorodiphenyltrichloroethane**) DDT *m*

DE Ⓐ ABBR (*US*) = **Delaware**
Ⓑ N ABBR (*Brit*) = **Department of Employment**

de... [diː] PREFIX de...

DEA N ABBR (*US*) (= **Drug Enforcement Administration**) *departamento para la lucha contra la droga*

deacon ['diːkən] N diácono *m*

deaconess ['diːkənes] N diaconisa *f*

deactivate [diː'æktɪveɪt] VT desactivar

dead [ded] Ⓐ ADJ 1 [*person, animal, plant*] muerto, difunto (*frm*); [*leaf*] marchito, seco; **~ man** muerto *m*; **the ~ king** el difunto rey; **to be ~** estar muerto; **he's been ~ for two years** hace dos años que murió; **~ or alive** vivo o muerto; **to be ~ on arrival** (*in hospital*) ingresar cadáver; **~ and buried** (*lit, fig*) muerto y bien muerto; **to drop (down) ~** caer muerto; **drop ~!*** ¡vete al cuerno!*; **to fall down ~** caer muerto; ✦*IDIOMS* **over my ~ body!*** ¡ni muerto!, ¡ni de chiste!; **as ~ as a dodo** *or* **a doornail** *or* **mutton** más muerto que mi abuela; **~ duck**: **he's a ~ duck** está quemado; **that issue is a ~ duck** esa cuestión ya no tiene interés; **to be ~ on one's feet** estar hecho migas *or* polvo*; **~ from the neck up*** bruto, imbécil, zoquete*; **to flog a ~ horse** ◊ **beat a ~ horse** (*US*) machacar en hierro frío; **you're ~ meat!*** ¡te vas a enterar!, ¡vas a ver lo que es bueno!; **I wouldn't be seen ~ there** ni muerto ni vivo me verán allí; **to be ~ in the water** [*economy, talks etc*] haberse ido al garete; [*politician, sportsperson etc*] estar acabado; **he/she was ~ to the world** (= *asleep*) estaba dormido/a como un tronco; ✦*PROV* **~ men tell no tales** los muertos no hablan

2 (*) (= *finished with*) **is that glass/drink ~?** ¿ha terminado su vaso?, ¿puedo levantar su vaso?

3 (= *inactive*) [*volcano, fire*] apagado; [*cigarette, match*] gastado; [*battery*] agotado; [*telephone line*] cortado, desconectado; [*wire*] sin corriente; [*language, love, town, party*] muerto; [*custom*] anticuado; (*Sport*) [*ball*] parado, fuera de juego; **the line has gone ~** (*Telec*) la línea está cortada *or* muerta

4 (= *numb*) **my fingers have gone ~** (*gen*) se me han dormido los dedos; (*with cold*) se me han entumecido los dedos; **he is ~ to all pity** es incapaz de sentir compasión

5 (= *complete*) [*silence, calm*] total, completo; (= *exact*) [*centre*] justo; **a ~ cert*** una cosa segura; **to fall into a ~ faint** desmayarse totalmente; **a ~ loss*** (= *person*) un inútil; (= *thing*)

una birria; **a ~ ringer for*** el doble de, la viva imagen de; **to come to a ~ stop** pararse en seco

Ⓑ ADV 1 (= *completely, exactly*) **he stopped ~** se paró en seco; **"dead slow"** (*Aut*) "reducir la marcha"; (*Naut*) "muy despacio"; **to be ~ against sth** estar totalmente opuesto a algo; **~ ahead** todo seguido, todo derecho; **~ between the eyes** justo entre los ojos; **~ level** completamente plano; **to be ~ set on doing sth** estar decidido a hacer algo; **to be ~ set against sth** estar totalmente opuesto a algo; **~ straight** todo seguido, todo derecho; **~ on target** justo en el blanco; **~ on time** a la hora exacta

2 (*Brit**) (= *very*) **to be ~ beat** estar hecho polvo*; **~ broke** sin un duro; **~ certain** completamente seguro; **~ drunk** borracho perdido; **~ easy** facilón, chupado‡; **~ tired** muerto (de cansancio)

3 ✦*IDIOM* **to cut sb ~*** hacer el vacío a algn

Ⓒ N 1 **the ~** los muertos *mpl*; **to come back** *or* **rise from the ~** resucitar

2 **at ~ of night** ◊ **in the ~ of night** a altas horas de la noche; **in the ~ of winter** en pleno invierno

Ⓓ CPD ► **dead end** N (*lit, fig*) callejón *m* sin salida; **to come to a ~ end** (*fig*) llegar a un punto muerto; *see also* **dead-end** ► **dead hand** N (*fig*) [*of state, bureaucracy*] peso *m* muerto ► **dead heat** N (*Sport*) empate *m*; *see also* **dead-heat** ► **dead letter** N letra *f* muerta ► **dead march** N marcha *f* fúnebre ► **dead matter** N materia *f* inanimada ► **dead reckoning** N estima *f* ► **Dead Sea** N Mar *m* Muerto; **the Dead Sea Scrolls** los manuscritos del Mar Muerto ► **the dead season** N (*Tourism*) la temporada baja ► **dead weight** N peso *m* muerto; [*of vehicle*] tara *f*; (*fig*) lastre *m*, carga *f* inútil

dead-and-alive ['dedənə'laɪv] ADJ aburrido, monótono

deadbeat* ['dedbiːt] N (*US*) haragán/ana *m/f*

deadbolt ['dedbəʊlt] N cerrojo *m* de seguridad

deaden ['dedn] VT [+ *noise, shock*] amortiguar; [+ *feeling*] embotar; [+ *pain*] aliviar, calmar

dead-end ['ded'end] ADJ [*street*] sin salida; [*job*] sin porvenir; **~ kids** (*US*) chicos *mpl* de la calle; *see also* **dead D**

deadening ['dednɪŋ] ADJ [*boredom*] de mala muerte

dead-heat ['ded'hiːt] VI (*Sport*) empatar (**with** con); *see also* **dead D**

deadline ['dedlaɪn] N (*Press, Comm*) fecha *f* tope; **to meet a ~** respetar un plazo; **we cannot meet the government's ~** no podemos terminarlo *etc* en el plazo señalado por el gobierno

deadliness ['dedlɪnɪs] N 1 [*of poison*] letalidad *f*; [*of aim*] certeza *f*

2 (= *boredom*) tedio *m*

deadlock ['dedlɒk] Ⓐ N punto *m* muerto; **to reach ~** llegar a un punto muerto, quedar estancado; **the ~ is complete** no se ve salida alguna

Ⓑ VT **to be ~ed** estar en un punto muerto

deadly ['dedlɪ] Ⓐ ADJ (*compar* **deadlier**; *superl* **deadliest**) 1 (= *lethal*) [*poison, disease, combination*] mortal; [*weapon, attack*] mortífero; **he has a ~ aim with a rifle** tiene una puntería infalible con el rifle; **to use ~ force (against sb)** (*Police, Mil*) abrir fuego (contra algn)

2 (= *devastating*) **with ~ accuracy** (*Sport etc*) con precisión mortífera; (*Mil etc*) con precisión letal *or* mortal; **he was in ~ earnest** iba muy en serio; **to be ~ enemies** ser enemigos mortales, ser enemigos a muerte; **she argued with ~ logic** argumentaba con una lógica aplastante; **she levelled a ~ look at Nick** le lanzó una mirada asesina a Nick; **there was ~ silence** se hizo un silencio sepulcral; *see also* **seven A**

3 (*) (= *very boring*) aburridísimo

Ⓑ ADV **it was ~ cold** hacía un frío de muerte; **the trip was ~ dull** el viaje fue un aburrimiento de muerte, el viaje fue aburridísimo; **she was ~ pale** estaba pálida como un cadáver, tenía una palidez cadavérica (*liter*); **she thought he was joking but he was ~ serious** ella pensaba que bromeaba, pero lo decía completamente en serio

Ⓒ CPD ► **deadly nightshade** N belladona *f*

deadness ['dednɪs] N inercia *f*, falta *f* de vida

dead-nettle ['ded,netl] N ortiga *f* muerta

deadpan ['ded,pæn] ADJ [*face, humour*] inexpresivo

deadstock [,ded'stɒk] N aperos *mpl*

deadwood ['ded,wʊd] N (= *person*) persona *f* inútil; (= *people*) gente *f* inútil; (= *things*) cosas *fpl* inútiles; **to get rid of the ~** (*in organization*) eliminar al personal inútil

deaf [def] Ⓐ ADJ (*compar* **deafer**; *superl* **deafest**) 1 (= *unable to hear*) sordo; **~ in one ear** sordo de un oído; ✦*IDIOM* **to be as ~ as a (door)post** estar más sordo que una tapia

2 (= *unwilling to hear*) **~ to all appeals** sordo a todos los ruegos; ✦*IDIOMS* **to turn a ~ ear to sth** hacer oídos sordos *or* no prestar oídos a algo; **the plea fell on ~ ears** el ruego cayó en saco roto

Ⓑ NPL **the deaf** los sordos *mpl*

Ⓒ CPD ► **deaf aid** N audífono *m*, sonotone® *m*

deaf-and-dumb ['defən'dʌm] ADJ [*person, alphabet*] sordomudo

deafen ['defn] VT ensordecer

deafening ['defnɪŋ] ADJ ensordecedor

deaf-mute ['def'mjuːt] N sordomudo/a *m/f*

deafness ['defnɪs] N sordera *f*

▼**deal**[1] [diːl] (*vb: pt, pp* **dealt**) Ⓐ N 1 (= *agreement*) acuerdo *m*, trato *m*; **a new ~ for the miners** un nuevo acuerdo salarial para los mineros; **we're looking for a better ~** buscamos un arreglo más equitativo; **it's a ~!*** ¡trato hecho!; **to do** *or* **make a ~ with sb** hacer un trato con algn, llegar a un acuerdo con algn; **the New Deal** (*US Pol*) *la nueva política económica de los EE.UU. aplicada por Roosevelt entre 1933 y 1940*; **pay ~** acuerdo *m* salarial; ✦*IDIOM* **it's a done ~** (*esp US*) es cosa hecha *or* segura, está atado y bien atado

2 (= *transaction*) trato *m*, transacción *f*; **the company lost thousands of pounds on the ~** la empresa perdió miles de libras con ese trato *or* en esa transacción; **arms ~** venta *f* de armas; **big ~!** (*iro*) ¡vaya cosa!; **he only asked me out for a drink, what's the big ~?** sólo me invitó a tomar algo por ahí, ¿qué tiene eso de raro?; **this sort of thing happens every day, it's no big ~** estas cosas pasan todos los días, no es nada del otro mundo; **business ~** (*between companies, countries*) acuerdo *m or* trato *m* comercial; (*by individual*) negocio *m*; **to make a big ~ (out) of sth*** dar mucha *or* demasiada importancia a algo; **I tried not to make a big ~ out of it but I was really annoyed** intenté no darle mucha *or* demasiada importancia pero estaba muy enfadado; **don't make such a big ~ out of it!** ¡no hagas una montaña de un grano de arena!

3 (= *treatment*) trato *m*; **a bad/fair/good ~** un trato malo/justo/bueno; **homeowners are getting a bad ~ from this government** los propietarios de viviendas están saliendo malparados con este gobierno; **working women are not getting a fair ~** las mujeres que trabajan no están recibiendo un trato justo; *see also* **raw A7**, **square B6**

4 (= *bargain*) ganga *f*; **they are offering good ~s on flights to Australia** tienen viajes a Australia a muy buen precio

5 (= *amount*) **he had a ~ of work to do†** tenía mucho trabajo que hacer; **a good ~** ◊ **a great ~** mucho; **a good** *or* **great ~ of money** una gran cantidad de dinero, mucho dinero; **it can save you a good ~ of time** te puede ahorrar mucho tiempo; **there's a good ~ of truth in what you say** hay mucho de verdad en lo que dices; **she's a good ~ cleverer than her brother** es mucho *or* bastante más inteligente que su hermano; **she knew a great ~ about him** sabía muchas cosas sobre él; **"does he get out much?" — "not a great ~"** —¿sale mucho? —no mucho *or* demasiado; **it means a great ~ to me** significa mucho para mí; **he thinks a great ~ of his father** admira mucho a su padre; **the new law will not make a great ~ of difference to the homeless** la nueva ley apenas va a afectar a la gente sin hogar

6 (*Cards*) (= *distribution*) reparto *m*; **whose ~ is it?** ¿a quién le toca dar *or* repartir?

Ⓑ VT 1 [+ *blow*] asestar, dar; **to ~ a blow to sth/sb** (*fig*) ser un golpe para algo/algn; **the news dealt a severe blow to their hopes/the economy** la noticia fue un duro golpe para sus esperanzas/la economía

2 (*Cards*) dar, repartir; **I was dealt a very bad hand** (*at cards*) me dieron una mano malísima; (*fig*) (= *had bad luck*) tuve muy mala suerte

Ⓒ VI (*Cards*) dar, repartir

►**deal in** VI + PREP 1 (*Comm*) [+ *goods*] comerciar con, negociar con; [+ *antiques, used cars*] dedicarse a la compraventa de; [+ *drugs*] traficar con; (*Fin, St Ex*) [+ *stocks, shares, currency*] operar con; **he was suspected of ~ing in smuggled tobacco** se sospechaba que se dedicaba al contrabando de tabaco; **we're ~ing in facts here, not theories** aquí estamos tratando con hechos, nada de teoría

2 (*Cards*) [+ *person*] **~ me in on the next hand** a mí me das (cartas) en la siguiente ronda

►**deal out** VT + ADV [+ *playing cards, plates*] repartir; [+ *punishment*] imponer; **you have to make the best of what life ~s out to you** tienes que sacar el máximo provecho de lo que te toca en la vida; **the injustice dealt out to her family** la injusticia que se había cometido con su familia

►**deal with** VI + PREP 1 (= *have dealings with*) tratar con; **you're ~ing with professionals here** ahora estás tratando con profesionales; **they ~ a lot with the Far East** hacen mucho negocio *or* comercian mucho con el Extremo Oriente; **we don't ~ with hostage takers** no negociamos con secuestradores

2 (= *handle, cope with*) [+ *problem, task*] ocuparse de, encargarse de; [+ *difficult person*] manejar, tratar; (= *attend to*) [+ *customer, order, application, complaint*] atender; [+ *person*] manejar, tratar; **he ~s with all the paperwork** él se ocupa *or* se encarga de todo el papeleo; **don't worry, I'm ~ing with it** no te preocupes, ya me ocupo *or* encargo de ello; **my boss will ~ with you from now on** a partir de ahora mi jefe será quien le atienda; **she knows how to ~ with difficult customers** sabe (cómo) manejar *or* tratar a los clientes difíci-

➤ LANGUAGE IN USE: **deal**[1] **A1** 13

les; **she's not easy to ~ with** tiene un carácter difícil; **the way that banks ~ with complaints** la forma en que los bancos atienden las quejas; **I'll ~ with your questions afterwards** contestaré (a) sus preguntas después; **we teach people how to ~ with stress** enseñamos a la gente a lidiar con el estrés

3 (= *sort out, solve*) [+ *problem*] solucionar, resolver; [+ *emotion*] superar; **have you dealt with that paperwork yet?** ¿has resuelto todo el papeleo ya?, ¿has terminado ya todo el papeleo?; **don't worry, I've dealt with it** no te preocupes, ya lo he *or* tengo solucionado; **I'll see that the problem is dealt with** yo me ocuparé de que se solucione *or* se resuelva el problema; **he couldn't ~ with his jealousy** no podía superar los celos que sentía; **I'll ~ with you later!** (= *rebuke, punish*) ¡luego me encargaré de ti!; **anyone who disobeys will be severely dealt with** cualquiera que desobedezca será tratado con mucha severidad

4 (= *be about*) [*book, film*] tratar de

deal[2] [diːl] Ⓐ N 1 (= *wood*) (*pine*) madera *f* de pino; (*fir*) madera *f* de abeto

2 (= *plank*) tablón *m*; (= *beam*) viga *f*

Ⓑ ADJ **a ~ table** una mesa de pino

dealer [ˈdiːləʳ] N 1 (*Comm*) comerciante *mf* (**in** de); (*in cattle, horses*) tratante *mf* (**in** de); (= *retailer*) (*gen*) distribuidor(a) *m/f*, proveedor(a) *m/f*; (*in cars*) concesionario/a *m/f*; **your local Honda ~** su concesionario Honda más próximo; **he's a ~ in stolen goods** es comerciante de mercancías robadas; **a major London currency ~** un importante agente de cambio londinense; **he's a property/second-hand car ~** se dedica a la compraventa de propiedades/coches de segunda mano; *see also* **antique C, arm**[2] **D, drug C, scrap C**

2 (*Cards*) repartidor(a) *m/f* de cartas; **the ~ gave him a nine** el que repartía le dio un nueve

dealership [ˈdiːləʃɪp] N (*US*) representación *f*, concesión *f*

dealing [ˈdiːlɪŋ] N 1 (*Comm*) **we have a reputation for honest ~** tenemos fama de ser honrados en nuestros negocios

2 (*St Ex*) transacciones *fpl* (bursátiles); **a computerized ~ system** un sistema informatizado de transacciones (bursátiles); **~ was sluggish today** hoy ha habido muy poco movimiento *or* muy poca actividad (bursátil); **when ~ started the price soared** cuando se abrió el mercado (bursátil) la cotización se disparó

3 (*in drugs, arms*) tráfico *m* (**in** de); *see also* **insider B, wheeling**

4 (*also* **~ out**) (*gen, Cards*) reparto *m*

dealings [ˈdiːlɪŋz] NPL 1 (= *relationship*) trato *msing*, relaciones *fpl*; **our aim is to be honest in our ~ with our customers** nuestro objetivo es la honradez en nuestro trato con los clientes; **he was not very successful in his ~ with women** no le iba muy bien en sus relaciones con las mujeres; **have you had any ~ with them?** ¿ha tratado con ellos alguna vez?

2 (*Comm, Fin*) negocios *mpl*; **we have a lot of ~ with her company** hacemos mucho(s) negocio(s) con su empresa; **his business ~ suffered as a result of the restrictions** sus negocios se vieron afectados por las restricciones; **he was accused of illegal share ~** lo acusaron de operar ilegalmente en la Bolsa

dealt [delt] PT, PP of **deal**[1]

dean [diːn] N (*Rel*) deán *m*; (*Univ*) decano *m*; **Dean's list** (*US Univ*) lista de honor académica *f*

➤ LANGUAGE IN USE: **death A1** 24.5

DEAN'S LIST

Se llama **Dean's List** *a la relación honorífica de alumnos que se hace en muchas universidades estadounidenses al final de cada año académico o al final de la carrera. En algunas universidades para figurar en ella se ha de haber obtenido A o B en todas las asignaturas, aunque normalmente la lista se basa en la nota media, conocida como* **grade-point average**. *Los estudiantes que han recibido la máxima puntuación, A, en todo, aparecen a veces en otra lista, llamada* **scholars' list** *o* **president's list**. *En algunas escuelas también publican listas similares, conocidas como* **honor roll**.

dear [dɪəʳ] Ⓐ ADJ (*compar* **dearer**; *superl* **dearest**) 1 (= *loved*) querido; **she's a very ~ friend of mine** es una amiga mía muy querida; **my ~est friend** mi amigo más querido, mi amigo del alma

2 (= *lovable*) **he's a ~ boy, but rather impetuous** es un chico muy majo, pero un poco impulsivo; **what a ~ little boy!** ¡este niño es un encanto!; **what a ~ little necklace that is!*** ¡qué bonita que es esa gargantilla!

3 (= *precious*) **it's my ~est wish** es mi mayor deseo; **to hold sth ~** apreciar algo; **the values and beliefs which our society holds ~** los valores y las creencias que nuestra sociedad aprecia; **I had to leave everything I held most ~** tuve que dejar atrás todas las cosas que más quería; **his family life was very ~ to him** su familia era muy importante para él; **your country is very ~ to me** tengo su país en mucha estima; **it is a subject ~ to her heart** es uno de sus temas preferidos; *see also* **life A2**

4 (*in letter writing*) **Dear Daddy** Querido papá; **Dear Peter** Estimado Peter; (*to closer friend*) Querido Peter; **Dear Mr/Mrs Smith** Estimado Sr./Estimada Sra. Smith; (*more formally*) Distinguido Sr./Distinguida Sra. Smith; **Dear Mr and Mrs Smith** Estimados señores (de) Smith; **Dear Madam** Estimada Señora, Muy señora mía, De mi/nuestra consideración (*esp LAm*); **Dear Sir(s)** Estimado(s) Señor(es), Muy señor(es) mío(s), De mi/nuestra consideración (*esp LAm*); **Dear Sir or Madam** Estimado Señor(a)

5 (*form of address*) querido; **my ~ fellow, I won't hear of it†** amigo mío *or* mi querido amigo, ni se le ocurra; **my ~ girl, nothing could be further from the truth** querida, estás muy equivocada

6 (= *expensive*) [*product, shop, price*] caro; **~ money** (*Fin*) dinero *m* caro

Ⓑ EXCL **~, ~, have you hurt your knee?** ¡ay, mi niño! ¿te has hecho daño en la rodilla?; **~ me, it's nearly one o'clock!** ¡madre mía, es casi la una!; **oh ~, we're going to be late** vaya hombre *or* vaya por Dios, vamos a llegar tarde; **~, oh ~, look at the mess you're in!** ay, Dios mío *or* qué horror, ¡mira qué desastre vienes hecho!

Ⓒ N (*) (*as form of address*) cariño *m*; **come along, ~** ven, cariño; **would you be a ~ and pass me my book?** anda, sé bueno y pásame el libro; **(you) poor ~!** ¡pobrecito!; **he's such a ~** es un cielo, es un encanto

Ⓓ ADV [*sell, buy, pay*] caro; **it cost me ~** (*fig*) me costó caro

dearie* [ˈdɪərɪ] N (*esp Brit*) (= *form of address*) cariño *m*; (*as excl*) **~ me!** ¡madre mía!

dearly [ˈdɪəlɪ] ADV 1 (= *very much*) mucho, de verdad; **I loved him ~** lo quería mucho *or* de verdad; **I should ~ love to go** me encantaría ir; **his ~ beloved wife** su amada esposa; **~ beloved, we are gathered here today ...** queridos *or* amados hermanos, estamos aquí reunidos hoy ...; **the ~ departed** (*frm*) el queridísimo difunto/la queridísima difunta

2 (= *at great cost*) caro; **victory for the Russians was ~ bought** los rusos pagaron un precio muy alto por la victoria; **to cost sb ~** costar caro a algn; **it cost him ~** le costó caro; **to pay ~ for sth** pagar algo caro; **he paid ~ for his mistake** pagó caro su error

dearness [ˈdɪənɪs] N (= *expensiveness*) alto precio *m*, lo caro

dearth [dɜːθ] N [*of food, resources, money*] escasez *f*; [*of ideas*] carencia *f*

▼**death** [deθ] Ⓐ N 1 muerte *f*, fallecimiento *m*; **to be in at the ~** (*Hunting*) ver el final de la caza; **it will be the ~ of him** (*lit*) será su perdición; **you'll be the ~ of me** (*fig*) vas a acabar conmigo; **till ~ us do part** hasta que la muerte nos separe; **this is ~ to our hopes** esto acaba con nuestras esperanzas; **it was ~ to the company** arruinó la empresa; **~ to traitors!** ¡muerte a los traidores!; **a fight to the ~** una lucha a muerte; **to fight to the ~** luchar a muerte; ✦**IDIOMS to catch one's ~ (of cold)** coger un catarro de muerte; **to be at ~'s door** estar a las puertas de la muerte; **to hold on like grim ~** estar firmemente agarrado; (*fig*) resistir con la mayor firmeza; **to look like ~ warmed up** *or* (*US*) **warmed over*** estar muy demacrado, estar hecho una pena

2 **to ~: to be bored to ~*** estar muerto de aburrimiento; **it frightens me to ~** me da un miedo espantoso; **to put sb to ~** dar muerte a algn; **to sentence sb to ~** condenar a algn a muerte; **I'm sick to ~ of it*** estoy hasta la coronilla de ello; **he's working himself to ~** trabaja tanto que va a acabar con su vida; **he works his men to ~** a sus hombres los mata a trabajar; **it worries me to ~** me preocupa muchísimo

Ⓑ CPD ► **death benefit** N (*Insurance*) indemnización *f* por fallecimiento ► **death blow** N golpe *m* mortal ► **death camp** N campo *m* de exterminio ► **death cell** N celda *f* de los condenados a muerte ► **death certificate** N partida *f* de defunción ► **death duties** NPL (*Brit*) impuesto *m* de sucesiones ► **death house** N (*US*) pabellón *m* de los condenados a muerte ► **death knell** N toque *m* de difuntos, doble *m*; **it sounded the ~ knell of the empire** (*fig*) anunció el fin del imperio, presagió la caída del imperio ► **death march** N marcha *f* fúnebre ► **death mask** N mascarilla *f* ► **death penalty** N pena *f* de muerte ► **death rate** N tasa *f* de mortalidad, mortalidad *f* ► **death rattle** N estertor *m* ► **death ray** N rayo *m* mortal ► **death roll** N número *m* de víctimas, lista *f* de víctimas ► **death row** N (*US*) celdas *fpl* de los condenados a muerte, corredor *m* de la muerte ► **death sentence** N pena *f* de muerte ► **death squad** N escuadrón *m* de la muerte ► **death threat** N amenaza *f* de muerte ► **death throes** NPL agonía *fsing* ► **death toll** N número *m* de víctimas ► **death warrant** N orden *f* de ejecución; ✦**IDIOM to sign one's own ~ warrant** firmar su sentencia de muerte ► **death wish** N ganas *fpl* de morir

deathbed [ˈdeθbed] Ⓐ N lecho *m* de muerte; **on one's ~** en su lecho de muerte

Ⓑ CPD ► **deathbed confession** N confesión *f* en el lecho de muerte ► **deathbed conversion** N conversión *f* in artículo mortis ► **deathbed repentance** N arrepentimiento *m* de última hora

death-dealing ['deθdi:lıŋ] ADJ (*liter*) [*blow, missile*] mortífero, letal

deathless ['deθlıs] ADJ inmortal

deathlike ['deθlaık] ADJ como de muerto, cadavérico

deathly ['deθlı] Ⓐ ADJ (*compar* **deathlier**, *superl* **deathliest**) [*appearance, pallor*] cadavérico; [*silence*] sepulcral
Ⓑ ADV **~ pale** pálido como un muerto

death's-head ['deθshed] Ⓐ N calavera *f*
Ⓑ CPD ► **death's-head moth** N mariposa *f* de la muerte

deathtrap ['deθtræp] N (= *place*) lugar *m* peligroso; (= *vehicle*) vehículo *m* peligroso; **this car's a ~** este coche es un peligro *or* una trampa mortal

deathwatch beetle [,deθwɒtʃ'bi:tl] N reloj *m* de la muerte (*tipo de carcoma*)

deb* [deb] N = **debutante**

debacle, **débâcle** [deı'bɑ:kl] N debacle *f*, desastre *m*; (*Mil*) derrota *f*

debag ['di:'bæg] VT (*Brit hum*) quitar (violentamente) los pantalones a

debar [dı'bɑ:ʳ] VT excluir; **to ~ sb from sth** excluir a algn de algo; **to ~ sb from doing sth** prohibir a algn hacer algo

debark [dı'bɑ:k] VI (*US*) desembarcar

debarkation [di:bɑ:'keıʃən] N (*US*) desembarco *m*

debase [dı'beıs] VT 1 (= *degrade*) [+ *language*] corromper; [+ *person, culture, tradition*] degradar; **to ~ o.s. (by doing sth)** degradarse (haciendo algo)
2 (= *devalue*) [+ *currency*] devaluar

debasement [dı'beısmənt] N 1 [*of language*] corrupción *f*; [*of person, culture, tradition*] degradación *f*
2 [*of currency*] devaluación *f*

▼ **debatable** [dı'beıtəbl] ADJ discutible

debate [dı'beıt] Ⓐ VT [+ *topic, question, idea*] debatir, discutir
Ⓑ VI discutir, debatir; **to ~ with sb (about** *or* **on** *or* **upon sth)** discutir con algn (sobre algo); **to ~ with o.s. (about** *or* **on** *or* **upon sth)** vacilar (sobre algo); **we ~d whether to go or not** dudamos *or* nos planteamos si ir o no
Ⓒ N debate *m*, discusión *f*; **after much ~** después de mucho discutir; **that is open to ~** ése es un tema discutido

debater [dı'beıtəʳ] N polemista *mf*; **he was a brilliant ~** brillaba en los debates

debating [dı'beıtıŋ] Ⓐ N **~ is a difficult skill to learn** el saber debatir es una habilidad difícil de adquirir
Ⓑ CPD ► **debating society** N círculo *m* de debates

debauch [dı'bɔ:tʃ] VT [+ *person, morals, taste*] depravar, corromper; [+ *woman*] seducir

debauched [dı'bɔ:tʃt] ADJ depravado, libertino

debaucher [dı'bɔ:tʃəʳ] N [*of person, taste, morals*] corruptor *m*; [*of woman*] seductor *m*

debauchery [dı'bɔ:tʃərı] N libertinaje *m*, depravación *f*

debenture [dı'bentʃəʳ] Ⓐ N (*Fin*) bono *m*, obligación *f*
Ⓑ CPD ► **debenture bond** N obligación *f* ► **debenture capital** N capital *m* en obligaciones ► **debenture holder** N obligacionista *mf* ► **debenture stock** N obligaciones *fpl*

debilitate [dı'bılıteıt] VT debilitar

debilitating [dı'bılıteıtıŋ] ADJ debilitante, que debilita

debility [dı'bılıtı] N debilidad *f*

debit ['debıt] Ⓐ N (*in the books of a business*) pasivo *m*; (*in a bank account*) debe *m*, débito *m*; (= *individual sum taken*) cargo *m*
Ⓑ VT **to ~ an account with a sum** cargar una suma en cuenta; **to ~ sb with a sum** cargar una suma en la cuenta de algn; **to ~ an account directly** domiciliar una cuenta; *see also* **direct D**
Ⓒ CPD ► **debit balance** N saldo *m* deudor ► **debit card** N tarjeta *f* de débito ► **debit entry** N débito *m* ► **debit note** N nota *f* de cargo ► **debit side** N debe *m*; (*fig*) desventaja *f*; **on the ~ side** (*lit*) en el debe; (*fig*) entre las desventajas

debonair [,debə'nɛəʳ] ADJ (= *elegant*) gallardo; (= *courteous*) cortés; (= *cheerful*) alegre

debone [di:'bəʊn] VT [+ *meat*] deshuesar; [+ *fish*] quitar las espinas a

Deborah ['debərə] N Débora

debouch [dı'baʊtʃ] VI (*frm*) **to ~ into** [*river*] desembocar en

Debrett [də'bret] N *libro de referencia de la aristocracia del Reino Unido*; (*loosely*) anuario *m* de la nobleza

debrief [,di:'bri:f] VT hacer dar parte

debriefing [,di:'bri:fıŋ] N informe *m* sobre una operación *etc*

debris ['debri:] N [*of building, construction*] escombros *mpl*; [*of aeroplane*] restos *mpl*; (*Geol*) rocalla *f*

debt [det] Ⓐ N 1 (= *money owed*) deuda *f*; **bad ~** deuda incobrable; **foreign ~** (*Pol*) deuda *f* externa *or* exterior; **a ~ of honour** una deuda de honor; **to be in ~ (to sb)** tener deudas *or* estar endeudado (con algn); **I am five pounds in ~** debo cinco libras (**to** a); **to get into ~** ◊ **run into ~** ◊ **run up ~s** contraer deudas; **to be out of ~** tener las deudas saldadas
2 (*fig*) **a ~ of gratitude** una deuda de agradecimiento; **to be in sb's ~** estar en deuda con algn
Ⓑ CPD ► **debt collection** N cobro *m* de morosos ► **debt collector** N cobrador(a) *m/f* de morosos ► **debt ratio** N tasa *f* de endeudamiento ► **debt relief** N alivio *m* de deuda ► **debt service**, **debt servicing** N (*US*) amortización *f* de la deuda

debtor ['detəʳ] Ⓐ N deudor(a) *m/f*
Ⓑ CPD ► **debtor nation** N nación *f* deudora

debt-ridden ['det,rıdn] ADJ agobiado por las deudas

debug [,di:'bʌg] VT 1 (*Tech*) resolver los problemas de, suprimir las pegas de; (*Comput*) depurar, quitar los fallos a
2 (= *remove mikes from*) quitar los micrófonos ocultos de

debugger [,di:'bʌgəʳ] N (*Comput*) programa *m* de depuración

debugging [,di:'bʌgıŋ] N (*Comput*) depuración *f*

debunk ['di:'bʌŋk] VT [+ *theory, claim, person, institution*] desacreditar

debut, **début** ['deıbu:] Ⓐ N (*Theat*) (= *first appearance*) debut *m*, presentación *f*; (*fig*) primer acto *m*; **to make one's ~** (*Theat*) debutar, hacer su presentación; (*in society*) presentarse en sociedad, ponerse de largo
Ⓑ VI [*artist, actor*] debutar; [*film, play*] estrenarse
Ⓒ CPD ► **debut album** N (*Mus*) álbum *m* de debut, álbum *m* de presentación

debutante, **débutante** ['debju:tɑ̃:nt] N joven *f* que se presenta en sociedad, debutante *f*

Dec. ABBR (= **December**) dic., dic.ᵉ, D.

dec. ABBR = **deceased**

decade ['dekeıd] N década *f*, decenio *m*

decadence ['dekədəns] N decadencia *f*

decadent ['dekədənt] ADJ [*habits, person*] decadente

de-caff* ['di:kæf] N ABBR = **decaffeinated coffee**

decaffeinated [,di:'kæfıneıtıd] Ⓐ ADJ [*beverage, tea*] sin cafeína
Ⓑ CPD ► **decaffeinated coffee** N café *m* descafeinado, descafeinado *m*

decagram(me) ['dekəgræm] N decagramo *m*

decal [dı'kæl] N (*US*) calcomanía *f*

decalcification ['di:,kælsıfı'keıʃən] N descalcificación *f*

decalcify [,di:'kælsıfaı] VT descalcificar

decalitre, **decaliter** (*US*) ['dekə,li:təʳ] N decalitro *m*

Decalogue ['dekəlɒg] N **the ~** el Decálogo

decametre, **decameter** (*US*) ['dekə,mi:təʳ] N decámetro *m*

decamp [dı'kæmp] VI 1 (*Mil*) levantar el campamento
2 (*) (= *make off*) escaparse; (= *move*) irse (**to** a)

decant [dı'kænt] VT [+ *wine etc*] decantar

decanter [dı'kæntəʳ] N licorera *f*

decapitate [dı'kæpıteıt] VT decapitar

decapitation [dı,kæpı'teıʃən] N decapitación *f*, degollación *f*

decarbonization ['di:,kɑ:bənaı'zeıʃən] N (*Aut*) descarburación *f*; [*of steel*] descarbonación *f*

decarbonize [di:'kɑ:bənaız] VT (*Aut*) descarburar

decasyllable ['dekəsıləbl] N decasílabo *m*

decathlete [dı'kæθli:t] N decatlonista *mf*, decatleta *mf*

decathlon [dı'kæθlən] N decatlón *m*

decay [dı'keı] Ⓐ N 1 [*of vegetation, food*] putrefacción *f*, descomposición *f*; [*of teeth*] caries *f*; [*of building*] desmoronamiento *m*, ruina *f*
2 (*fig*) [*of civilization*] decadencia *f*; [*of faculties*] deterioro *m*
Ⓑ VI 1 (= *rot*) [*leaves, food*] pudrirse, descomponerse; [*teeth*] cariarse; [*building*] desmoronarse
2 (*fig*) [*civilization*] decaer, estar en decadencia; [*faculties*] deteriorarse
Ⓒ VT [+ *vegetation, food*] pudrir, descomponer; [+ *teeth*] cariar

decayed [dı'keıd] ADJ 1 [*wood, food*] podrido; [*tooth*] cariado
2 (*fig*) [*family*] venido a menos

decaying [dı'keııŋ] ADJ 1 [*food*] podrido, en estado de descomposición; [*vegetation*] podrido; [*flesh*] en estado de descomposición, en descomposición; [*tooth*] cariado; [*building*] muy deteriorado, ruinoso; [*stone*] que se descompone
2 (*fig*) [*civilization*] decadente, en decadencia

decease [dı'si:s] (*frm*) Ⓐ N fallecimiento *m*, defunción *f*
Ⓑ VI fallecer

deceased [dı'si:st] Ⓐ ADJ (*Jur, Police*) difunto
Ⓑ N **the ~** el/la difunto/a

deceit [dı'si:t] N (= *misleading*) engaño *m*; (= *fraud*) fraude *m*; (= *deceitfulness*) falsedad *f*; **he was involved in a web of lies and ~** estaba metido en una maraña de mentiras y engaños; **they won the voters over by ~** con-

➤ LANGUAGE IN USE: **debatable** 12.2

quistaron a los votantes engañándolos *or* mediante engaños

deceitful [dɪ'si:tfʊl] ADJ [*person*] falso; [*child*] mentiroso; [*statement, behaviour*] engañoso

deceitfully [dɪ'si:tfəlɪ] ADV engañosamente

deceitfulness [dɪ'si:tfʊlnɪs] N falsedad *f*

deceive [dɪ'si:v] VT engañar; **she ~d me into thinking that ...** me engañó, haciéndome pensar que ...; **don't be ~d by appearances** no te dejes engañar por las apariencias; **let nobody be ~d by this** que nadie se llame a engaño por esto; **he thought his eyes were deceiving him** no creía lo que veían sus ojos; **if my memory does not ~ me** si mal no recuerdo; **to ~ o.s.** engañarse

deceiver [dɪ'si:vəʳ] N impostor(a) *m/f*, embustero/a *m/f*; [*of women*] seductor *m*

decelerate [di:'seləreɪt] VI (*Aut*) desacelerar, decelerar; (*fig*) frenarse, ralentizarse

deceleration ['di:ˌselə'reɪʃən] N desaceleración *f*, deceleración *f*, disminución *f* de velocidad

December [dɪ'sembəʳ] N diciembre *m*; *see* **July** *for usage*

decency ['di:sənsɪ] N [1] (= *propriety*) decencia *f*, decoro *m*; **to have a sense of ~** tener sentido del decoro; **offence against ~** atentado *m* contra el pudor
[2] (= *politeness*) educación *f*; **it is no more than common ~ to let him know** hay que avisarle, aunque sólo sea por una cuestión de educación
[3] (= *kindness*) bondad *f*, amabilidad *f*; **he had the ~ to phone me** tuvo la amabilidad de llamarme
[4] **decencies** buenas costumbres *fpl*

decent ['di:sənt] ADJ [1] (= *respectable*) [*person, house*] decente; (= *proper*) [*clothes, behaviour, language*] decoroso, decente; **are you ~?** (*hum*) ¿estás visible?
[2] (= *kind*) amable; **he was very ~ to me** fue muy amable conmigo, se portó muy bien conmigo; **he's a ~ sort** es buena persona
[3] (= *passable*) [*salary, meal*] adecuado, decente; **a ~ sum** una cantidad considerable

decenter [di:'sentəʳ] VT (*US*) = **decentre**

decently ['di:səntlɪ] ADV [1] (= *respectably*) decentemente, decorosamente
[2] (= *kindly*) amablemente, con amabilidad; **he very ~ offered it to me** muy amablemente me lo ofreció

decentralization [di:ˌsentrəlaɪ'zeɪʃən] N descentralización *f*

decentralize [di:'sentrəlaɪz] VT descentralizar

decentre, **decenter** (*US*) [di:'sentəʳ] VT descentrar

deception [dɪ'sepʃən] N engaño *m*

deceptive [dɪ'septɪv] ADJ engañoso

deceptively [dɪ'septɪvlɪ] ADV **the village looks ~ near** el pueblo parece engañosamente cerca; **he was ~ obedient** no era tan sumiso como parecía

deceptiveness [dɪ'septɪvnɪs] N carácter *m* engañoso

decibel ['desɪbel] N decibelio *m*

decide [dɪ'saɪd] Ⓐ VT (*gen*) decidir; **to ~ where to go/what to do** decidir adónde ir/qué hacer; **to ~ to do sth** decidir hacer algo; **it was ~d that** se decidió que; **that ~d me** eso me convenció
Ⓑ VI decidir, decidirse; **to ~ against sth** decidirse en contra de algo; **to ~ against doing sth** decidirse en contra de hacer algo, decidir no hacer algo; **to ~ for** *or* **in favour of sb** decidirse por algn, decidir a favor de algn; **to ~ in favour of sth** decidirse por algo; **to ~ in favour of doing sth** determinar *or* resolver hacer algo; **the judge ~d in his favour** el juez decidió *or* resolvió a su favor

► **decide on** VI + PREP **to ~ on sth** decidirse por algo; **to ~ on doing sth** decidir hacer algo

decided [dɪ'saɪdɪd] ADJ [1] (= *distinct*) [*difference, improvement*] indudable, marcado
[2] (= *categorical*) [*person, tone, manner*] resuelto, decidido; [*opinion*] firme, categórico

decidedly [dɪ'saɪdɪdlɪ] ADV [1] (= *without doubt*) indudablemente, sin duda; (= *very, markedly*) decididamente; **it is ~ difficult** indudablemente es difícil
[2] (= *resolutely*) con resolución, con decisión

decider [dɪ'saɪdəʳ] N (*Brit Sport*) (= *game*) partido *m* decisivo; (= *replay*) partido *m* de desempate, desempate *m*; (= *point, goal*) gol *m etc* decisivo

deciding [dɪ'saɪdɪŋ] ADJ decisivo, determinante; **the ~ factor** el factor decisivo *or* determinante; **the ~ goal/point** el gol/punto decisivo; **the ~ vote** el voto decisivo

deciduous [dɪ'sɪdjʊəs] ADJ [*tree*] de hoja caduca

decile ['desɪl] N decil *m*

decilitre, **deciliter** (*US*) ['desɪˌli:təʳ] N decilitro *m*

decimal ['desɪməl] Ⓐ ADJ decimal; **to three ~ places** con tres decimales
Ⓑ N decimal *m*
Ⓒ CPD ► **decimal currency** N moneda *f* decimal ► **decimal fraction** N fracción *f* decimal ► **decimal point** N coma *f* decimal, coma *f* de decimales ► **decimal system** N sistema *m* métrico decimal

decimalization [ˌdesɪməlaɪ'zeɪʃən] N conversión *f* al sistema decimal, decimalización *f*

decimalize ['desɪməlaɪz] VT convertir al sistema decimal

decimate ['desɪmeɪt] VT (*lit, fig*) diezmar

decimation [ˌdesɪ'meɪʃən] N (*lit, fig*) aniquilación *f*

decimetre, **decimeter** (*US*) ['desɪˌmi:təʳ] N decímetro *m*

decipher [dɪ'saɪfəʳ] VT (*lit, fig*) descifrar

decipherable [dɪ'saɪfərəbl] ADJ descifrable

decision [dɪ'sɪʒən] Ⓐ N [1] (*after consideration*) decisión *f*, determinación *f*; (*Jur*) fallo *m*; **to come to** *or* **reach a ~** llegar a una decisión; **to make** *or* **take a ~** tomar *or* adoptar una decisión
[2] (= *resoluteness*) resolución *f*, decisión *f*
Ⓑ CPD ► **decision table** N (*Comput*) tabla *f* de decisiones

decision-maker [dɪ'sɪʒən,meɪkəʳ] N persona *f* que toma decisiones

decision-making [dɪ'sɪʒən,meɪkɪŋ] Ⓐ N toma *f* de decisiones; **he's good at ~** es bueno tomando decisiones
Ⓑ CPD ► **decision-making process** N proceso *m* decisorio ► **decision-making unit** N unidad *f* de adopción de decisiones

decisive [dɪ'saɪsɪv] ADJ [1] (= *conclusive*) [*victory, factor, influence*] decisivo, determinante
[2] (= *resolute*) [*manner, reply*] decidido, tajante; [*person*] decidido, resuelto

decisively [dɪ'saɪsɪvlɪ] ADV [1] (= *conclusively*) **to be ~ beaten** ser derrotado de modo decisivo
[2] (= *resolutely*) con decisión, con resolución

decisiveness [dɪ'saɪsɪvnɪs] N [*of manner, reply*] carácter *m* tajante; [*of person*] firmeza *f*, decisión *f*

deck [dek] Ⓐ N [1] (*Naut*) cubierta *f*; **to go up on ~** subir a la cubierta; **below ~** bajo cubierta; ✦*IDIOMS* **to clear the ~s** despejar el terreno; **to hit the ~*** caer al suelo
[2] [*of bus*] piso *m*; **top** *or* **upper ~** piso *m* de arriba; **bottom** *or* **lower ~** piso *m* de abajo
[3] (*esp US*) [*of cards*] baraja *f*
[4] (*also* **record ~**) tocadiscos *m inv*; (*also* **cassette ~**) pletina *f*
[5] (*US Drugs**) saquito *m* de heroína
Ⓑ VT [1] (*also* **~ out**) [+ *room*] adornar, engalanar (**with** con); [+ *person*] ataviar, engalanar (**with** con); **all ~ed out** [*room*] adornado, todo engalanado; [*person*] de punta en blanco
[2] (‡) (= *knock down*) derribar de un golpe
Ⓒ CPD ► **deck cabin** N cabina *f* de cubierta ► **deck cargo** N carga *f* de cubierta

deckchair ['dek,tʃɛəʳ] N tumbona *f*, perezosa *f* (*LAm*)

-decker ['dekəʳ] N (*ending in compounds*) **single-decker** (= *bus*) autobús *m* de un piso; **three-decker** (*Naut*) barco *m* de tres cubiertas; *see also* **double-decker**

deckhand ['dekhænd] N marinero *m* de cubierta

deckhouse ['dekhaʊs] N (*pl* **deckhouses** ['dek,haʊzɪz]) camareta *f* alta

declaim [dɪ'kleɪm] Ⓐ VI declamar
Ⓑ VT declamar

declamation [ˌdeklə'meɪʃən] N declamación *f*

declamatory [dɪ'klæmətərɪ] ADJ declamatorio

declaration [ˌdeklə'reɪʃən] Ⓐ N (*written*) declaración *f*; **~ of war/love** declaración de guerra/amor
Ⓑ CPD ► **the Declaration of Independence** N (*US Hist*) la Declaración de Independencia (*de Estados Unidos*)

declare [dɪ'klɛəʳ] Ⓐ VT [1] [+ *intentions, love*] declarar; [+ *dividend, result*] anunciar; **she ~d that she knew nothing about it** declaró *or* manifestó que no sabía nada al respecto; **to ~ war (on** *or* **against sb)** declarar la guerra (a algn); **to ~ o.s.** declararse; **to ~ o.s. against/in favour of sth** pronunciarse *or* declararse en contra de/a favor de algo; **he ~d himself beaten** se dio por vencido; **to ~ o.s. surprised** confesar su sorpresa
[2] (*Fin*) [+ *income*] declarar; **to ~ sth to the customs** declarar algo en la aduana; **have you anything to ~?** ¿tiene usted algo que declarar?
[3] (*Bridge*) declarar
Ⓑ VI [1] (= *pronounce*) **to ~ for** ◊ **~ in favour of** pronunciarse a favor de
[2] (*in exclamation*) **well, I ~!**† ¡vaya por Dios!
[3] (*Bridge*) declarar

declared [dɪ'klɛəd] ADJ declarado, abierto

declarer [dɪ'klɛərəʳ] N (*Bridge*) declarante *mf*

déclassé [deɪ'klæseɪ] ADJ desprestigiado, empobrecido

declassify [di:'klæsɪfaɪ] VT [+ *information*] levantar el secreto oficial que pesa sobre

declension [dɪ'klenʃən] N (*Ling*) declinación *f*

declinable [dɪ'klaɪnəbl] ADJ declinable

▼ **decline** [dɪ'klaɪn] Ⓐ N [1] (= *decrease*) (*in numbers, sales*) descenso *m*, disminución *f* (**in** de); (*in support, interest*) disminución *f*; **to be on the ~** ir disminuyendo
[2] (= *deterioration*) decadencia *f*, declive *m*, deterioro *m*; (*in standards*) descenso *m*, declive *m*; (*Med*) debilitamiento *m*; **the ~ of the Roman Empire** la decadencia del Imperio Romano; **to fall into ~** [*industry, town*] entrar en decadencia, entrar en declive; **to go into a ~** (*Med*) ir debilitándose
Ⓑ VT [1] (= *refuse*) rehusar, rechazar, declinar (*frm*); **to ~ to do sth** rehusar hacer algo, declinar hacer algo (*frm*)

➤ LANGUAGE IN USE: **decline C2** 19.5

2 (*Ling*) declinar
C VI 1 (= *decrease*) [*power, influence*] disminuir; (= *deteriorate*) decaer; (*in health*) debilitarse, decaer; **to ~ in importance** ir perdiendo importancia
2 (= *refuse*) negarse, rehusar
3 (*Ling*) declinarse

declining [dɪˈklaɪnɪŋ] ADJ [*industry*] en decadencia; **~ interest** pérdida *f* de interés; **in my ~ years** en mis últimos años

declivity [dɪˈklɪvɪtɪ] N declive *m*

declutch [ˈdiːˈklʌtʃ] VI desembragar; **to double ~** hacer un doble desembrague (*hacer una reducción de marcha soltando antes el embrague al pasar por punto muerto*)

decoction [dɪˈkɒkʃən] N decocción *f*

decode [ˈdiːˈkəʊd] VT descifrar; (*Ling, TV*) descodificar

decoder [diːˈkəʊdəʳ] N (*Comput, TV*) descodificador *m*

decoding [diːˈkəʊdɪŋ] N (*Comput*) descodificación *f*

decoke (*Brit Aut*) A [ˈdiːkəʊk] N descarburación *f*
B [diːˈkəʊk] VT descarburar

decollate [ˌdiːkəˈleɪt] VT separar, alzar

décolletage [deɪˈkɒlətɑːʒ] N escote *m*

décolleté(e) [deɪˈkɒlteɪ] ADJ [*dress*] escotado; [*woman*] en traje escotado

decolonization [diːˌkɒlənaɪˈzeɪʃən] N descolonización *f*

decolonize [diːˈkɒlənaɪz] VT descolonizar

decommission [ˌdiːkəˈmɪʃən] VT [+ *nuclear power station*] desmantelar; [+ *warship, aircraft, weapon*] desguazar, desmantelar

decommissioning [ˌdiːkəˈmɪʃənɪŋ] N [*of nuclear power station*] desmantelamiento *m*; [*of warship, aircraft, weapon*] desguace *m*, desmantelamiento *m*

decompartmentalization [ˌdiːkɒmpɑːtˌmentəlaɪˈzeɪʃən] N descompartimentación *f*

decompartmentalize [ˌdiːkɒmpɑːtˈmentəlaɪz] VT descompartimentar

decompose [ˌdiːkəmˈpəʊz] A VT (= *rot*) descomponer, pudrir
B VI descomponerse, pudrirse

decomposition [ˌdiːkɒmpəˈzɪʃən] N descomposición *f*, putrefacción *f*

decompress [ˌdiːkəmˈpres] VT descomprimir

decompression [ˌdiːkəmˈpreʃən] A N descompresión *f*
B CPD ► **decompression chamber** N cámara *f* de descompresión ► **decompression sickness** N aeroembolismo *m*, embolia *f* gaseosa

decongestant [ˌdiːkənˈdʒestənt] N anticongestivo *m*, descongestionante *m*

decongestion [ˌdiːkənˈdʒestʃən] N descongestión *f*

deconstruct [ˌdiːkənˈstrʌkt] VT deconstruir

deconstruction [ˌdiːkənˈstrʌkʃən] N deconstrucción *f*

decontaminate [ˌdiːkənˈtæmɪneɪt] VT descontaminar

decontamination [ˈdiːkənˌtæmɪˈneɪʃən] N descontaminación *f*

decontextualize [diːkənˈtekstjʊəlaɪz] VT descontextualizar

decontrol [ˌdiːkənˈtrəʊl] A N liberalización *f*
B VT (*esp US*) [+ *prices, trade*] liberalizar

décor [ˈdeɪkɔːʳ] N (*of house, room etc*) decoración *f*; (*Theat*) decorado *m*

decorate [ˈdekəreɪt] VT 1 (= *adorn*) decorar, adornar (**with** de)
2 (= *paint*) [+ *room, house*] pintar; (= *paper*) empapelar
3 (= *honour*) condecorar

decorating [ˈdekəreɪtɪŋ] N **I got someone in to do the ~** traje a una persona para que pintara/empapelara la casa; **interior ~** decoración *f* de interiores, interiorismo *m*

decoration [ˌdekəˈreɪʃən] N 1 (= *act*) decoración *f*
2 (= *ornament*) adorno *m*
3 (= *medal*) condecoración *f*

decorative [ˈdekərətɪv] A ADJ (*in function*) de adorno, decorativo; (= *pleasant*) hermoso, elegante
B CPD ► **decorative arts** NPL artes *fpl* decorativas

decorator [ˈdekəreɪtəʳ] N (= *painter and decorator*) pintor *m* empapelador; (= *interior decorator*) interiorista *mf*, decorador(a) *m/f*

decorous [ˈdekərəs] ADJ [*behaviour, appearance*] decoroso

decorously [ˈdekərəslɪ] ADV decorosamente

decorum [dɪˈkɔːrəm] N decoro *m*

decouple [diːˈkʌpl] VT (*frm*) escindir (*frm*), desconectar

decoy A [ˈdiːkɔɪ] N (= *bird*) (*artificial*) señuelo *m*, reclamo *m*; (*live*) cimbel *m*, señuelo *m*, reclamo *m*; (*fig*) (= *bait*) cebo *m*, señuelo *m*
B [dɪˈkɔɪ] VT atraer (con señuelo)
C [ˈdiːkɔɪ] CPD ► **decoy duck** N pato *m* de reclamo

decrease A [ˈdiːkriːs] N (*gen*) disminución *f*, reducción *f*; (*in wages*) descenso *m*, bajada *f*; (*in prices*) bajada *f*, disminución *f*; **a ~ in speed/strength** una reducción de velocidad/fuerza; **a ~ of 50%** una reducción del 50%; **to be on the ~** ir disminuyendo
B [diːˈkriːs] VT [+ *quantity, pressure, dose, speed*] disminuir, reducir; [+ *wages*] bajar, reducir
C [diːˈkriːs] VI 1 [*power, strength, popularity, temperature, pressure*] disminuir; [*enthusiasm, interest*] disminuir, decaer; **to ~ by 10%** bajar *or* disminuir un 10%
2 (*Knitting*) menguar

decreasing [diːˈkriːsɪŋ] ADJ decreciente

decreasingly [diːˈkriːsɪŋlɪ] ADV decrecientemente

decree [dɪˈkriː] A N decreto *m*; **to issue a ~** promulgar un decreto; **~ absolute/nisi** (= *divorce*) sentencia *f* definitiva/condicional de divorcio
B VT (*gen*) decretar

decrepit [dɪˈkrepɪt] ADJ [*person*] decrépito; [*building*] deteriorado, en mal estado

decrepitude [dɪˈkrepɪtjuːd] N [*of person*] decrepitud *f*; [*of building*] deterioro *m*, mal estado *m*

decriminalization [ˌdiːˈkrɪmɪnəlaɪˈzeɪʃən] N despenalización *f*

decriminalize [diːˈkrɪmɪnəlaɪz] VT despenalizar

decry [dɪˈkraɪ] VT (= *strongly criticize*) criticar, censurar; (= *belittle*) menospreciar

dedicate [ˈdedɪkeɪt] VT 1 [+ *book*] dedicar (**to** a); [+ *church, monument*] dedicar, consagrar (**to** a); **to ~ one's life to sth/to doing sth** dedicar *or* consagrar su vida a algo/a hacer algo; **to ~ o.s. to sth/to doing sth** dedicarse *or* consagrarse a algo/a hacer algo
2 (*US*) (= *inaugurate*) [+ *official building*] inaugurar oficialmente

dedicated [ˈdedɪkeɪtɪd] ADJ 1 [*person*] totalmente entregado; **a very ~ teacher** un maestro totalmente entregado a su trabajo; **~ followers of classical music** devotos seguidores de la música clásica
2 (*Comput*) especializado, dedicado; **~ word processor** procesador *m* de textos especializado *or* dedicado

dedication [ˌdedɪˈkeɪʃən] N 1 (= *act*) dedicación *f*, consagración *f*
2 (= *quality*) dedicación *f*, entrega *f*, devoción *f*
3 (*in book*) dedicatoria *f*

deduce [dɪˈdjuːs] VT deducir; **to ~ sth from sth** deducir algo de algo; **what do you ~ from that?** ¿qué conclusión sacas de eso?; **to ~ (from sth) that ...** deducir (de algo) que ...; **as can be ~d from** según se deduce *or* se desprende de

deducible [dɪˈdjuːsɪbl] ADJ deducible (**from** de)

deduct [dɪˈdʌkt] VT restar, descontar (**from** de); [+ *tax*] deducir (**from** de)

deductible [dɪˈdʌktəbl] ADJ deducible, descontable; (*for tax purposes*) desgravable, deducible

deduction [dɪˈdʌkʃən] N 1 (= *inference*) deducción *f*, conclusión *f*; **what are your ~s?** ¿cuáles son sus conclusiones?
2 (= *act of deducting*) deducción *f*; (= *amount deducted*) descuento *m*; **tax ~s** desgravaciones *fpl* fiscales, deducciones *fpl* fiscales

deductive [dɪˈdʌktɪv] ADJ deductivo

deed [diːd] A N 1 (= *act*) acto *m*, acción *f*; (= *result*) hecho *m*; **brave ~** hazaña *f*; **good ~** buena acción *f*
2 (*Jur*) escritura *f*; **~ of covenant** *documento contractual mediante el que una persona se compromete a donar cantidades regulares de dinero a una entidad benéfica*; **~ of partnership** contrato *m* de sociedad; **~ of transfer** escritura *f* de traspaso
B VT (*US Jur*) [+ *property*] transferir por acto notarial
C CPD ► **deed poll** N *escritura mediante la cual una persona se cambia el apellido oficialmente*; **to change one's name by ~ poll** cambiarse el apellido oficialmente

deejay* [ˈdiːdʒeɪ] N pinchadiscos* *mf inv*

deem [diːm] VT (*frm*) juzgar, considerar; **she ~s it wise to ...** considera prudente ...; **he was ~ed to have consented** se juzgó que había dado su consentimiento

deep [diːp] A ADJ (*compar* **deeper**; *superl* **deepest**) 1 (= *extending far down*) [*hole*] profundo, hondo; [*cut, wound, water*] profundo; [*pan, bowl, container*] hondo; **the water is two metres ~** el agua tiene una profundidad de dos metros; **they tramped through ~ snow** avanzaban con dificultad por una espesa capa de nieve; **the ~ end** (*of swimming pool*) lo hondo, la parte honda; **to be ~ in snow/water** estar hundido en la nieve/el agua; **he was waist-~/thigh-~ in water** el agua le llegaba a la cintura/al muslo; **the van was axle-~ in mud** la furgoneta estaba metida en barro hasta el eje; **the snow lay ~** había una espesa capa de nieve; **a ~ *or* ~-pile carpet** una alfombra de pelo largo; ◆***IDIOMS*** **to go off (at) the ~ end*** enfadarse, ponerse de morros*; **I was thrown in (at) the ~ end*** me echaron *or* arrojaron a los leones*; **to be in ~ water** estar hasta el cuello (de problemas)
2 (= *extending far back*) [*shelf, cupboard*] hondo; [*border, hem*] ancho; **a cupboard a metre ~** un armario de un metro de fondo; **a plot 30 metres ~** un terreno de 30 metros de fondo; **the spectators were standing six ~** los espectadores estaban de pie de seis en fondo
3 (= *immersed*) **to be ~ in debt** estar cargado de deudas; **to be ~ in thought/in a book** estar sumido *or* absorto en sus pensamientos/en la lectura
4 (= *low-pitched*) [*voice*] grave, profundo; [*note, sound*] grave

[5] (= *intense*) [*emotion, relaxation, concern*] profundo; [*recession*] grave; [*sigh*] profundo, hondo; **to take a ~ breath** respirar profundamente *or* hondo *or* a pleno pulmón; **the play made a ~ impression on me** la obra me impresionó profundamente; **to be in ~ mourning** estar de luto riguroso; **she fell into a ~ sleep** se quedó profundamente dormida; **they expressed their ~ sorrow at her loss** le expresaron su profundo pesar por la pérdida que había sufrido; **to be in ~ trouble** estar en grandes apuros
[6] [*colour*] intenso, subido; [*tan*] intenso
[7] (= *profound*) **it's too ~ for me** no lo entiendo, no alcanzo a entenderlo; **they're adventure stories, they're not intended to be ~** son historias de aventuras, sin intención de ir más allá
[8] (= *unfathomable*) [*secret, mystery*] bien guardado; **he's a ~ one*** es un misterio
Ⓑ ADV [1] (= *far down*) **don't go in too ~ if you can't swim** no te metas muy hondo si no sabes nadar; **he thrust his hand ~ into his pocket** metió la mano hasta el fondo del bolsillo; **the company is sliding even ~er into the red** la empresa está cada vez más cargada de deudas; **~ down he's a bit of a softie** en el fondo es un poco blandengue; **to go ~: his anger clearly went ~** la ira le había calado muy hondo; **I was in too ~ to pull out** estaba demasiado metido para echarme atrás; **to run ~: the roots of racial prejudice run ~** los prejuicios raciales están profundamente arraigados; *see also* **dig C2, still A1**
[2] (= *a long way inside*) **~ in the forest** en lo hondo *or* profundo del bosque; **he gazed ~ into her eyes** la miró profundamente a los ojos; **~ in one's heart** en lo más profundo del corazón; **~ in the heart of the countryside** en medio del campo; **they worked ~ into the night** trabajaron hasta muy entrada la noche
Ⓒ N (*liter*) [1] (= *sea*) **the ~** el piélago *m*; **creatures of the ~** criaturas *fpl* de las profundidades
[2] (= *depths*) **in the ~ of winter** en pleno invierno
Ⓓ CPD ► **deep breathing** N gimnasia *f* respiratoria, ejercicios *mpl* respiratorios ► **deep freeze** N (*domestic*) congelador *m*; *see also* **deep-freeze** ► **deep fryer** N freidora *f* ► **the Deep South** N (*US*) los estados del sureste de EE.UU. ► **deep space** N espacio *m* interplanetario ► **deep structure** N (*Ling*) estructura *f* profunda ► **deep vein thrombosis** N trombosis *f* venosa profunda

deep-chested [ˈdiːpˈtʃestɪd] ADJ ancho de pecho

deepen [ˈdiːpən] Ⓐ VT [+ *hole*] hacer más profundo; [+ *voice*] hacer más grave, ahuecar; [+ *colour*] intensificar; [+ *understanding*] aumentar; [+ *love, friendship*] hacer más profundo *or* intenso, ahondar; [+ *crisis*] agudizar, acentuar
Ⓑ VI [*water*] hacerse más profundo *or* hondo; [*voice*] hacerse más grave *or* profundo; [*frown*] acentuarse; [*colour, emotion*] intensificarse; [*night*] avanzar, cerrarse; [*darkness*] hacerse más profundo; [*mystery, suspicion*] aumentar; [*understanding, love, friendship*] hacerse más profundo *or* intenso; [*crisis*] agudizarse, acentuarse; **the colour in her face ~ed** se puso aún más colorada

deepening [ˈdiːpənɪŋ] ADJ [*darkness, gloom, conflict, division*] cada vez más profundo; [*unease*] cada vez mayor; [*friendship*] cada vez más profundo *or* intenso; [*crisis*] que se agudiza, que se acentúa

deep-felt [ˈdiːpˈfelt] ADJ profundo; **a ~ need** una profunda necesidad

deep-freeze [ˈdiːpˈfriːz] VT (*at home*) congelar; (*in factory*) ultracongelar; *see also* **deep**

deep-freezing [ˌdiːpˈfriːzɪŋ] N (*at home*) congelación *f*; (*in factory*) ultracongelación *f*

deep-frozen [ˌdiːpˈfrəʊzn] ADJ ultracongelado

deep-fry [ˈdiːpˈfraɪ] VT freír en aceite abundante

deep-laid [ˈdiːpˈleɪd] ADJ [*plan*] bien preparado

deeply [ˈdiːplɪ] ADV [1] [*dig*] en profundidad; [*drink*] a grandes tragos; [*breathe, sigh*] profundamente, hondo; [*sleep, regret*] profundamente; [*think*] a fondo; **to blush ~** enrojecer violentamente; **to go ~ into sth** entrar de lleno en algo; **a ~ held conviction** una convicción profunda; **they looked ~ into each other's eyes** se miraron profundamente a los ojos; **to love sb ~** querer profundamente a algn; **to regret sth ~** lamentar algo profundamente
[2] (= *profoundly, intensely*) [*worrying, sceptical, disappointed, shocked*] sumamente; [*concerned, troubled, grateful, religious*] profundamente; [*offensive, unhappy, depressed*] terriblemente; **to be ~ in debt** estar lleno de deudas, estar cargado de deudas; **it remains a ~ divided nation** sigue siendo una nación muy dividida; **I was ~ embarrassed by his question** su pregunta me hizo sentirme muy violenta; **~ embedded dirt** suciedad profundamente incrustado; **I was ~ hurt by her remarks** sus comentarios me hirieron en lo más hondo *or* profundo, sus comentarios me dolieron mucho; **we are ~ indebted to you** le debemos muchísimo; **to be ~ in love** estar profundamente enamorado; **she appeared to be ~ moved** parecía estar muy *or* profundamente conmovida; **we were ~ saddened by his death** su muerte nos entristeció profundamente; **~ tanned** con un bronceado intenso

deep-rooted [ˈdiːpˈruːtɪd] ADJ (*Bot, fig*) profundamente arraigado

deep-sea [ˈdiːpˈsiː] Ⓐ ADJ [*creature, plant*] abisal, de alta mar; [*fisherman*] de altura
Ⓑ CPD ► **deep-sea diver** N buzo *m* ► **deep-sea diving** N buceo *m* de altura ► **deep-sea fishing** N pesca *f* de gran altura

deep-seated [ˈdiːpˈsiːtɪd] ADJ profundamente arraigado

deep-set [ˈdiːpˈset] ADJ [*eyes*] hundido

deep-six* [ˌdiːpˈsɪks] VT (*US*) (= *throw out*) tirar; (= *kill*) cargarse*

deer [dɪəʳ] N (*pl* **deer** *or* **deers**) ciervo *m*, venado *m* (*esp LAm*); (= *red deer*) ciervo *m* común; (= *roe deer*) corzo *m*; (= *fallow deer*) gamo *m*

deerhound [ˈdɪəhaʊnd] N galgo *m* (para cazar venados), galgo *m* escocés (de pelo lanoso)

deerskin [ˈdɪəskɪn] N piel *f* de ciervo, gamuza *f*

deerstalker [ˈdɪəˌstɔːkəʳ] N [1] (= *person*) cazador *m* de ciervos al acecho
[2] (= *hat*) gorro *m* de cazador

deerstalking [ˈdɪəˌstɔːkɪŋ] N caza *f* de venado

de-escalate [ˌdiːˈeskəleɪt] VT [+ *tension*] reducir; [+ *crisis, conflict*] desacelerar, frenar la escalada de; [+ *war*] frenar la escalada de

de-escalation [diːˌeskəˈleɪʃən] N (*Mil, Pol*) freno *m* a la escalada

deface [dɪˈfeɪs] VT [+ *wall, monument*] llenar de pintadas; [+ *work of art, poster, book*] pintarrajear

de facto [deɪˈfæktəʊ] ADJ, ADV de facto, de hecho

defalcation [ˌdiːfælˈkeɪʃən] N desfalco *m*

defamation [ˌdefəˈmeɪʃən] N difamación *f*

defamatory [dɪˈfæmətərɪ] ADJ [*article, statement*] difamatorio

defame [dɪˈfeɪm] VT difamar, calumniar

default [dɪˈfɔːlt] Ⓐ N [1] (*on contract*) incumplimiento *m* (**on** de); (*on payment*) impago *m* (**on** de); **to be in ~** estar en mora; **judgment by ~** juicio *m* en rebeldía; **he won by ~** ganó por incomparecencia de su adversario; **we must not let it go by ~** no debemos dejarlo escapar por descuido *or* sin hacer nada; **in ~ of** a falta de
[2] (*Comput*) valor *m* por defecto
Ⓑ VI [1] (= *not pay*) no pagar, faltar al pago; **to ~ on one's payments** no pagar los plazos
[2] (*Sport*) (= *not appear*) no presentarse, no comparecer
[3] (*Comput*) **it always ~s to the C drive** siempre va a la unidad de disco C por defecto
Ⓒ CPD ► **default option** N (*Comput*) opción *f* por defecto

defaulter [dɪˈfɔːltəʳ] N [1] (*Comm, Fin*) (*on payments*) moroso/a *m/f*
[2] (*Mil*) rebelde *mf*

defaulting [dɪˈfɔːltɪŋ] ADJ [1] (*St Ex*) moroso
[2] (*Jur*) en rebeldía

defeat [dɪˈfiːt] Ⓐ N [*of army, team*] derrota *f*; [*of ambition, plan*] fracaso *m*; [*of bill, amendment*] rechazo *m*; **eventually he admitted ~** al final se dio por vencido
Ⓑ VT [+ *army, team, opponent*] vencer, derrotar; [+ *plan, ambition*] hacer fracasar, frustrar; [+ *hopes*] frustrar, defraudar; (*Pol*) [+ *party*] derrotar; [+ *bill, amendment*] rechazar; (*fig*) vencer; **this will ~ its own ends** esto será contraproducente; **the problem ~s me** el problema me supera; **it ~ed all our efforts** burló todos nuestros esfuerzos

defeated [dɪˈfiːtɪd] ADJ [*army, team, player*] derrotado; **he left the room a ~ man** cuando abandonó la sala era un hombre derrotado

defeatism [dɪˈfiːtɪzəm] N derrotismo *m*

defeatist [dɪˈfiːtɪst] Ⓐ ADJ derrotista
Ⓑ N derrotista *mf*

defecate [ˈdefəkeɪt] VI defecar

defecation [ˌdefəˈkeɪʃən] N defecación *f*

defect Ⓐ [ˈdiːfekt] N (*gen*) defecto *m*; (*mental*) deficiencia *f*; **moral ~** defecto *m* moral; *see also* **speech B**
Ⓑ [dɪˈfekt] VI (*Pol*) desertar (**from** de; **to** a); **he ~ed to the USA** desertó de su país para irse a los EE.UU.

defection [dɪˈfekʃən] N (*Pol*) (*to different country*) deserción *f*; (*to different party*) cambio *m* de filas, defección *f* (*frm*)

defective [dɪˈfektɪv] Ⓐ ADJ defectuoso; **~ verb** (*Ling*) verbo *m* defectivo; **to be ~ in sth** [*person*] ser deficiente en algo
Ⓑ N [1] (= *person*) persona *f* anormal; **mental ~** deficiente *mf* mental
[2] (*Gram*) defectivo *m*

defector [dɪˈfektəʳ] N (*to different country*) desertor(a) *m/f*; (*to different party*) tránsfuga *mf*

defence, defense (*US*) [dɪˈfens] Ⓐ N (*all senses*) defensa *f*; **as a ~ against** como defensa contra; **the body's ~s against disease** las defensas del organismo contra la enfermedad; **the case for the ~** el argumento de la defensa; **counsel for the ~** abogado/a *m/f* defensor(a); **Department of Defense** (*US*) = **Ministry of Defence**; **in his ~** en su defensa; **what have you to say in your own ~?** ¿qué tiene usted que decir *or* alegar en defensa propia?; **in ~ of sth** en defensa de algo; **to come out in ~ of** salir en defensa de; **Minister of Defence** (*Brit*) Ministro *m* de Defensa; **Ministry of Defence** (*Brit*) Ministerio *m* de

Defensa; **Secretary (of State) for Defence** (*Brit*) ◊ **Secretary of Defense** (*US*) Ministro *m* de Defensa; **witness for the ~** testigo *mf* de cargo, testigo *mf* de la defensa
Ⓑ CPD [*policy, strategy, costs*] de defensa ► **defence counsel** N abogado/a *m/f* defensor(a) ► **defence forces** NPL fuerzas *fpl* defensivas ► **defence mechanism** N mecanismo *m* de defensa ► **defence spending** N gastos *mpl* de defensa

defenceless, **defenseless** (*US*) [dɪ'fenslɪs] ADJ indefenso

defencelessness, **defenselessness** (*US*) [dɪ'fenslɪsnɪs] N indefensión *f*

defend [dɪ'fend] Ⓐ VT (*all senses*) defender (**against** contra; **from** de); **to ~ o.s.** defenderse
Ⓑ VI (*Sport*) jugar de defensa

defendant [dɪ'fendənt] N (*Jur*) (*civil*) demandado/a *m/f*; (*criminal*) acusado/a *m/f*

defender [dɪ'fendəʳ] N (*gen*) defensor(a) *m/f*; (*Sport*) defensa *mf*

defending [dɪ'fendɪŋ] ADJ **~ champion** (*Sport*) campeón *m* vigente; **~ counsel** (*Jur*) abogado/a *m/f* defensor(a)

defense [dɪ'fens] N (*US*) = **defence**

defenseless [dɪ'fenslɪs] ADJ (*US*) = **defenceless**

defenselessness [dɪ'fenslɪsnɪs] N (*US*) = **defencelessness**

defensible [dɪ'fensɪbl] ADJ defendible; [*action*] justificable

defensive [dɪ'fensɪv] Ⓐ ADJ [*attitude, measures, play*] defensivo
Ⓑ N defensiva *f*; **to be/go on the ~** estar/ponerse a la defensiva
Ⓒ CPD ► **defensive works** NPL fortificaciones *fpl*

defensively [dɪ'fensɪvlɪ] ADV [*say*] en tono defensivo; (*Sport*) [*play*] de defensa

defensiveness [dɪ'fensɪvnɪs] N (= *tone*) tono *m* defensivo; (= *attitude*) actitud *f* defensiva

defer¹ [dɪ'fɜːʳ] VT [1] (= *postpone*) [+ *meeting, business*] posponer, diferir; [+ *payment*] aplazar, diferir, postergar (*LAm*)
[2] (*Mil*) [+ *conscript*] dar una prórroga a; **his military service was ~red** le concedieron una prórroga militar

defer² [dɪ'fɜːʳ] VI (= *submit*) **to ~ to sth** deferir a algo (*frm*); **in this I ~ to you** a este respecto defiero a su opinión (*frm*), a este respecto me adhiero a su opinión; **to ~ to sb's (greater) knowledge** deferir a los (mayores) conocimientos de algn (*frm*)

deference ['defərəns] N deferencia *f*, respeto *m*; **out of** *or* **in ~ to sb/sb's age** por deferencia *or* respeto a algn/la edad de algn

deferential [ˌdefə'renʃəl] ADJ deferente, respetuoso

deferentially [ˌdefə'renʃəlɪ] ADV deferentemente, respetuosamente

deferment [dɪ'fɜːmənt], **deferral** [dɪ'fɜːrəl] N (= *postponement*) aplazamiento *m*; (*Mil*) prórroga *f*

deferred [dɪ'fɜːd] CPD ► **deferred annuity** N anualidad *f* diferida ► **deferred credit** N crédito *m* diferido ► **deferred liabilities** NPL pasivo *msing* diferido ► **deferred payment** N pago *m* a plazos

defiance [dɪ'faɪəns] N (= *attitude*) desafío *m*; (= *resistance*) resistencia *f* terca; **a gesture/an act of ~** un gesto/acto desafiante; **in ~ of the law** desafiando a la ley

defiant [dɪ'faɪənt] ADJ (= *insolent*) [*person*] atrevido, insolente; (= *challenging*) [*tone, stare*] desafiante, retador

defiantly [dɪ'faɪəntlɪ] ADV [*act*] atrevidamente, insolentemente; [*say, answer*] en tono desafiante *or* retador, en son de reto

defibrillator [dɪ'faɪbrɪˌleɪtəʳ] N desfibrilador *m*

deficiency [dɪ'fɪʃənsɪ] Ⓐ N [1] (*gen*) deficiencia *f*; (= *lack*) falta *f*; (*Med*) (= *weakness*) debilidad *f*; **vitamin ~** avitaminosis *f*, déficit *m* vitamínico
[2] (*in system, plan, character etc*) defecto *m*
[3] (*Fin*) déficit *m*
Ⓑ CPD ► **deficiency disease** N mal *m* carencial

deficient [dɪ'fɪʃənt] ADJ (*gen*) deficiente; (*in quantity*) insuficiente; (= *incomplete*) incompleto; (= *defective*) defectuoso; **to be ~ in sth** estar falto de algo; **his diet is ~ in vitamin C** su dieta está falta de vitamina C; **mentally ~** deficiente mental

deficit ['defɪsɪt] Ⓐ N (*esp Fin*) déficit *m*; **the balance of payments is in ~** la balanza de pagos es deficitaria
Ⓑ CPD ► **deficit financing** N financiación *f* mediante déficit ► **deficit spending** N gasto *m* deficitario

defile¹ ['diːfaɪl] N desfiladero *m*

defile² [dɪ'faɪl] VT [+ *honour*] manchar; [+ *flag*] ultrajar; [+ *sacred thing, memory*] profanar; [+ *language*] corromper; [+ *woman*] deshonrar

defilement [dɪ'faɪlmənt] N [*of person, community*] corrupción *f*; [*of sacred thing, memory*] profanación *f*; [*of language*] corrupción *f*; [*of woman*] deshonra *f*

definable [dɪ'faɪnəbl] ADJ definible

define [dɪ'faɪn] VT [1] (= *give definition for*) definir; (= *characterize*) caracterizar; (= *delimit*) determinar, delimitar; (= *outline*) destacar; **she doesn't ~ herself as a feminist** no se define como feminista; **how would you ~ yourself politically?** ¿cómo se definiría políticamente?
[2] (*Comput*) definir

definite ['defɪnɪt] ADJ [1] (= *fixed*) [*time, offer, plan*] definitivo; [*decision, agreement*] final; **I don't have any ~ plans** no tengo ningún plan definitivo; **are you ready to make a ~ order?** ¿puede mandarnos ya un pedido en firme?; **it is ~ that he will retire** ya es seguro *or* definitivo que se jubilará; **14 September is ~ for the trip** el 14 de septiembre es la fecha definitiva para el viaje; **nothing ~** nada definitivo; **I don't intend to go, and that's ~** no pienso ir, y no voy a cambiar de idea; **is that ~?** ¿es seguro?
[2] (= *clear*) [*improvement, advantage*] indudable; [*feeling, impression*] inequívoco; [*increase*] claro; **he had a ~ advantage** tuvo una ventaja indudable; **it's a ~ possibility** es una posibilidad clara; **there is a ~ possibility that we will get the contract** está claro que existe la posibilidad de que consigamos el contrato, es muy posible que consigamos el contrato
[3] (= *sure*) **are you ~ about that?** ¿estás seguro de eso?; **to know sth for ~** saber algo con seguridad; **I don't know** *or* **can't say for ~ yet** no lo sé seguro todavía, no puedo asegurarlo todavía
[4] (= *emphatic*) [*manner, tone*] firme, terminante; [*views, opinions*] firme; **he was very ~ about it** lo dijo de forma categórica; **he was very ~ about wanting to resign** dijo categóricamente que quería dimitir
[5] (*Ling*) **~ article** artículo *m* definido; **past ~ (tense)** (tiempo *m*) pretérito *m*

definitely ['defɪnɪtlɪ] ADV [1] (= *definitively*) [*agree, arrange, decide*] definitivamente; **I haven't ~ decided on law school** todavía no he decidido hacer derecho definitivamente; **the date has not yet been ~ decided** aún no se ha decidido una fecha definitiva; **they have not said ~ whether they will attend** no han dicho de forma definitiva que vayan a asistir
[2] (= *certainly*) **something should ~ be done about that** decididamente, deberían hacer algo al respecto; **yes, we ~ do need a car** sí, está clarísimo que necesitamos un coche, sí, decididamente necesitamos un coche; **he is ~ leaving** es seguro que se va, definitivamente se va; **they are ~ not for sale** definitivamente no están a la venta; **I'll ~ go** seguro que iré; **she ~ said two o'clock** estoy seguro de que dijo a las dos en punto; **she said ~ two o'clock** dijo que seguro que a los dos en punto; **I will ~ get it finished by tomorrow** definitivamente lo termino para mañana, seguro que lo termino para mañana; **it's ~ better** es sin duda mejor; **"are you going to Greece this summer?" — "yes, ~"** —¿te vas a Grecia este verano? —sí, seguro; **"do you think she'll pass?" — "definitely"** — ¿crees que aprobará? —seguro *or* sin duda; **"will you accept his offer?" — "~ not!"** —¿vas a aceptar su oferta? —¡de ninguna manera!; **"can I go on my own?" — "~ not!"** —¿puedo ir solo? —¡ni hablar!
[3] (= *emphatically*) [*say, deny*] terminantemente, categóricamente; [*state*] firmemente

definition [ˌdefɪ'nɪʃən] N [1] [*of word, concept*] definición *f*; [*of powers, boundaries, duties*] delimitación *f*; **by ~** por definición
[2] (*Phot*) nitidez *f*, definición *f*

definitive [dɪ'fɪnɪtɪv] ADJ definitivo; **it is the ~ work on Mahler** es la obra más autorizada sobre Mahler

definitively [dɪ'fɪnɪtɪvlɪ] ADV de manera definitiva, definitivamente

deflate [diː'fleɪt] Ⓐ VT [1] [+ *tyre*] desinflar, deshinchar; [+ *economy*] reducir la inflación de, deflactar
[2] (= *humble*) [+ *pompous person*] bajar los humos a
[3] (= *depress*) desanimar, desalentar; **at this news he felt very ~d** con esta noticia se desanimó por completo
Ⓑ VI [*tyre*] desinflarse, deshincharse; [*economy*] sufrir deflación

deflation [diː'fleɪʃən] N [*of tyre etc*] desinflamiento *m*; (*Econ*) deflación *f*

deflationary [diː'fleɪʃənərɪ] ADJ (*Econ*) deflacionario

deflationist [diː'fleɪʃənɪst] ADJ deflacionista

deflator [diː'fleɪtəʳ] N medida *f* deflacionista

deflect [dɪ'flekt] Ⓐ VT [+ *ball, bullet*] desviar; (*fig*) [+ *person*] desviar (**from** de)
Ⓑ VI [*ball, bullet*] desviarse

deflection [dɪ'flekʃən] N desvío *m*, desviación *f*

deflector [dɪ'flektəʳ] N deflector *m*

defloration [ˌdiːflɔː'reɪʃən] N desfloración *f*

deflower [diː'flaʊəʳ] VT desflorar

defog [diː'fɒg] VT desempañar

defogger [diː'fɒgəʳ] N (*US*) luneta *f* térmica, dispositivo *m* antivaho

defoliant [diː'fəʊlɪənt] N defoliante *m*

defoliate [diː'fəʊlɪeɪt] VT defoliar

defoliation [ˌdiːfəʊlɪ'eɪʃən] N defoliación *f*

deforest [diː'fɒrɪst] VT deforestar, despoblar de árboles

deforestation [diːˌfɒrə'steɪʃən] N deforestación *f*, despoblación *f* forestal

deform [dɪ'fɔːm] VT deformar

deformation [ˌdiːfɔːˈmeɪʃən] N deformación *f*
deformed [dɪˈfɔːmd] ADJ [*person, limb, body*] deforme; [*structure*] deformado
deformity [dɪˈfɔːmɪtɪ] N deformidad *f*
defraud [dɪˈfrɔːd] VT (*frm*) [+ *person, authorities*] estafar, defraudar; **to ~ sb of sth** estafar algo a algn; **he ~ed the firm of £1,000** le estafó 1.000 libras a la compañía
defrauder [dɪˈfrɔːdəʳ] N defraudador(a) *m/f*
defray [dɪˈfreɪ] VT (*frm*) sufragar, costear; **to ~ sb's expenses** sufragar *or* costear los gastos de algn
defrayal [dɪˈfreɪəl], **defrayment** [dɪˈfreɪmənt] N pago *m*
defreeze [diːˈfriːz] VT descongelar
defrock [diːˈfrɒk] VT apartar del sacerdocio
defrost [diːˈfrɒst] VT [+ *refrigerator*] descongelar, deshelar; [+ *frozen food*] descongelar
defroster [diːˈfrɒstəʳ] N (*US*) descongelador *m*; (*Aut*) spray *m* antihielo
deft [deft] ADJ (*compar* **defter**; *superl* **deftest**) diestro, hábil
deftly [ˈdeftlɪ] ADV diestramente, con destreza, hábilmente
deftness [ˈdeftnɪs] N destreza *f*, habilidad *f*
defunct [dɪˈfʌŋkt] ADJ (*frm*) 1 [*company, organization*] desaparecido, extinto; [*idea*] caduco; [*scheme*] paralizado, suspendido
2 (= *deceased*) difunto
defuse [diːˈfjuːz] VT [+ *bomb*] desactivar; (*fig*) [+ *tension*] calmar, apaciguar; [+ *situation*] reducir la tensión de
defy [dɪˈfaɪ] VT 1 (= *challenge*) [+ *person*] desafiar, retar; **I ~ you to do it** te desafío a hacerlo
2 (= *refuse to obey*) [+ *person*] desobedecer, enfrentarse a; [+ *order*] contravenir
3 (= *fly in the face of*) **it defies definition** se escapa a toda definición; **it defies description** resulta imposible describirlo, es indescriptible; **to ~ gravity** desafiar la ley de la gravedad; **people defied the bad weather to get away for Easter** a pesar del mal tiempo, la gente salió de vacaciones durante la Semana Santa; **to ~ death** (= *face without fear*) desafiar a la muerte; (= *narrowly escape*) escapar de una muerte segura
degeneracy [dɪˈdʒenərəsɪ] N degeneración *f*, depravación *f*
degenerate Ⓐ [dɪˈdʒenərɪt] ADJ degenerado
Ⓑ [dɪˈdʒenərɪt] N degenerado/a *m/f*
Ⓒ [dɪˈdʒenəreɪt] VI degenerar (**into** en); **the debate ~d into a shouting match** el debate degeneró en una discusión a voz en grito
degeneration [dɪˌdʒenəˈreɪʃən] N degeneración *f*
degenerative [dɪˈdʒenərətɪv] ADJ [*disease*] degenerativo
deglamourize [diːˈglæməˌraɪz] VT quitar el atractivo de
degradable [dɪˈgreɪdəbl] ADJ degradable
degradation [ˌdegrəˈdeɪʃən] N degradación *f*
degrade [dɪˈgreɪd] Ⓐ VT 1 (*gen*) degradar; **to ~ o.s.** degradarse
2 (*Chem, Phys*) (= *break down*) degradar
3 (*Mil*) [+ *weaponry etc*] mermar, diezmar
Ⓑ VI 1 (*gen*) degradarse
2 (*Chem, Phys*) (= *break down*) degradarse
degrading [dɪˈgreɪdɪŋ] ADJ degradante
degree [dɪˈgriː] Ⓐ N 1 (*gen, Geog, Math*) grado *m*; **ten ~s below freezing** diez grados bajo cero
2 (= *extent*) punto *m*, grado *m*; **to such a ~ that ...** hasta tal punto que ...; **a high ~ of uncertainty** un alto grado de incertidumbre; **with varying ~s of success** con mayor o menor éxito; **they have some** *or* **a certain ~ of freedom** tienen cierto grado de libertad; **to some** *or* **a certain ~** hasta cierto punto; **to the highest ~** en sumo grado; **he is superstitious to a ~** (*esp Brit*) es sumamente supersticioso
3 (= *stage in scale*) grado *m*; **by ~s** poco a poco, gradualmente, por etapas; **first/second/third ~ burns** quemaduras *fpl* de primer/segundo/tercer grado; **first ~ murder** ◊ **murder in the first ~** homicidio *m* en primer grado; **second ~ murder** ◊ **murder in the second ~** homicidio *m* en segundo grado; ✦**IDIOM to give sb the third ~** interrogar a algn brutalmente, sacudir a algn*
4 (*Univ*) título *m*; **first ~** licenciatura *f*; **higher ~** doctorado *m*; **honorary ~** doctorado *m* "honoris causa"; **she's got a ~ in English** es licenciada en filología inglesa; **to get a ~** sacar un título; **to take a ~ in** (= *study*) hacer la carrera de; (= *graduate*) licenciarse en
5 (= *social standing*) rango *m*, condición *f* social
Ⓑ CPD ► **degree course** N (*Brit Univ*) licenciatura *f*; **to do a ~ course** hacer una licenciatura

➤ LANGUAGE IN USE: degree A4 19.2

DEGREE

Al título universitario equivalente a la licenciatura se le conoce como **Bachelor's degree**, *que se obtiene generalmente tras tres años de estudios. Las titulaciones más frecuentes son las de Letras:* **Bachelor of Arts** *o* **BA** *y Ciencias:* **Bachelor of Science** *o* **BSc** *en el Reino Unido,* **BS** *en Estados Unidos.*
En el Reino Unido, la mayoría de los estudiantes reciben un **honours degree**, *cuyas calificaciones, en orden descendente son:* **first** *(1) la nota más alta, seguida de* **upper second** *(2-1),* **lower second** *(2-2) y* **third** *(3). En algunas ocasiones se puede obtener un* **ordinary degree**, *por ejemplo en el caso de que no se aprueben los exámenes para obtener el título pero los examinadores consideren que a lo largo de la carrera se han tenido unos resultados mínimos satisfactorios.*
En Estados Unidos los estudiantes no reciben calificaciones en sus titulaciones de fin de carrera, pero sí existe la matrícula de honor (**honours**), *que puede ser, de menor a mayor importancia:* **cum laude**, **magna cum laude** *y* **summa cum laude**.
Master's degree *es normalmente un título que se recibe tras estudios de postgrado, en los que se combinan horas lectivas o investigación con una tesina final, conocida como* **dissertation**. *Las titulaciones más frecuentes son las de* **Master of Arts** *o* **MA**, **Master of Science** *o* **MSc** *y* **Master of Business Administration** *o* **MBA**. *El título se concede con la única calificación de apto. En algunas universidades, como las escocesas, el título de* **master's degree** *no es de postgrado, sino que corresponde a la licenciatura.*
El título universitario más alto es el de doctorado, **doctorate** *o* **doctor's degree**, *abreviado normalmente como* **PhD** *o* **DPhil**.

dehumanization [diːˌhjuːmənaɪˈzeɪʃən] N deshumanización *f*
dehumanize [diːˈhjuːmənaɪz] VT deshumanizar
dehumanizing [diːˈhjuːmənaɪzɪŋ] ADJ deshumanizante
dehumidifier [ˌdiːhjuːˈmɪdɪfaɪəʳ] N deshumidificador *m*
dehumidify [ˌdiːhjuːˈmɪdɪfaɪ] VT (*US*) deshumedecer
dehydrate [diːˈhaɪdreɪt] VT deshidratar
dehydrated [ˌdiːhaɪˈdreɪtɪd] ADJ (*Med, Tech*) deshidratado; [*vegetables*] seco; [*milk, eggs*] en polvo
dehydration [ˌdiːhaɪˈdreɪʃən] N deshidratación *f*
de-ice [diːˈaɪs] VT descongelar
de-icer [ˈdiːˈaɪsəʳ] N (*Aer*) descongelador *m*; (*Aut*) descongelante *m*
de-icing [diːˈaɪsɪŋ] N descongelación *f*
deictic [ˈdaɪktɪk] N deíctico *m*
deification [ˌdiːɪfɪˈkeɪʃən] N deificación *f*
deify [ˈdiːɪfaɪ] VT deificar
deign [deɪn] VT **to ~ to do sth** dignarse hacer algo
deism [ˈdiːɪzəm] N deísmo *m*
deist [ˈdiːɪst] N deísta *mf*
deity [ˈdiːɪtɪ] N deidad *f*; **the Deity** Dios *m*
deixis [ˈdaɪksɪs] N deixis *f*
déjà vu [deɪʒɑːˈvuː] N déjà vu *m*
dejected [dɪˈdʒektɪd] ADJ [*person, look*] desanimado, abatido
dejectedly [dɪˈdʒektɪdlɪ] ADV [*sit, gaze*] con desánimo, desalentado; [*say*] con tono de abatimiento
dejection [dɪˈdʒekʃən] N (= *emotion*) desánimo *m*, abatimiento *m*
de jure [ˌdeɪˈdʒʊərɪ] ADJ, ADV de iure
dekko* [ˈdekəʊ] N (*Brit*) vistazo *m*; **let's have a ~*** déjame verlo
Del. ABBR (*US*) = **Delaware**
del. ABBR = **delete**
delay [dɪˈleɪ] Ⓐ N (= *hold-up*) retraso *m*, demora *f* (*esp LAm*); (= *act of delaying*) retraso *m*, dilación *f*; (*to traffic*) retención *f*, atasco *m*; (*to train*) retraso *m*; **the tests have caused some ~** las pruebas han ocasionado algún retraso; **there will be ~s to traffic** habrá retenciones *or* atascos en las carreteras; **"delays possible until Dec 2000"** "posibles retenciones hasta Diciembre de 2000"; **without ~** sin demora; **these measures should be implemented without further ~** estas medidas deben ponerse en práctica sin más demora
Ⓑ VT (= *hold up*) [+ *person*] retrasar, entretener; [+ *train*] retrasar; [+ *start, opening*] retrasar, demorar (*LAm*); (= *postpone*) aplazar, demorar (*LAm*); (= *obstruct*) impedir; **the train was ~ed for two hours** el tren se retrasó dos horas; **we decided to ~ our departure** decidimos retrasar la salida; **what ~ed you?** ¿por qué has tardado tanto?; **to ~ doing sth: we ~ed going out until Jane arrived** retrasamos la salida hasta que llegara Jane; **the illness could have been treated if you hadn't ~ed going to the doctor** se hubiera podido tratar la enfermedad si no hubieras tardado tanto en ir al médico; **~ed broadcast** (*US*) transmisión *f* en diferido; **~ed effect** efecto *m* retardado
Ⓒ VI tardar, demorarse (*LAm*); **don't ~!** (*in doing sth*) ¡no pierdas tiempo!; (*on the way*) ¡no te entretengas!, ¡no tardes!, ¡no te demores! (*LAm*)
delayed-action [dɪˈleɪdˈækʃən] ADJ de acción retardada; **~ bomb** bomba *f* de acción retardada
delayering [diːˈleɪərɪŋ] N (*Admin*) reducción *f* de niveles jerárquicos
delaying [dɪˈleɪɪŋ] Ⓐ ADJ [*action*] dilatorio
Ⓑ CPD ► **delaying tactics** NPL tácticas *fpl* dilatorias
delectable [dɪˈlektəbl] ADJ delicioso

delectation [ˌdiːlekˈteɪʃən] N deleite *m*, delectación *f* (*frm*)

delegate Ⓐ [ˈdelɪgɪt] N delegado/a *m/f* (**to** en)
Ⓑ [ˈdelɪgeɪt] VT [+ *task, power*] delegar (**to** en); [+ *person*] delegar (**to do sth** para hacer algo); **I was ~d to do it** me delegaron para hacerlo; **that task cannot be ~d** ese cometido no se puede delegar en otro

delegation [ˌdelɪˈgeɪʃən] N (= *act, group*) delegación *f*

delete [dɪˈliːt] Ⓐ VT tachar, suprimir (**from** de); (*Comput*) borrar, suprimir; **"delete where inapplicable"** "táchese lo que no proceda"
Ⓑ CPD ► **delete key** N tecla *f* de borrado, tecla *f* de supresión

deleterious [ˌdelɪˈtɪərɪəs] ADJ (*frm*) nocivo, perjudicial (**to** para)

deletion [dɪˈliːʃən] N supresión *f*, tachadura *f*; (*Comput*) borrado *m*, supresión *f*

delft [delft] N porcelana *f* de Delft

Delhi [ˈdelɪ] N Delhi *m*

deli* [ˈdelɪ] N = **delicatessen**

deliberate Ⓐ [dɪˈlɪbərɪt] ADJ [1] (= *intentional*) deliberado, premeditado
[2] (= *cautious*) prudente
[3] (= *unhurried*) pausado, lento
Ⓑ [dɪˈlɪbəreɪt] VT (= *think about*) [+ *issue, question*] reflexionar sobre, deliberar sobre; (= *discuss*) deliberar sobre, discutir; **I ~d what to do** estuve pensando qué debería hacer; **I ~d whether to do it** estuve pensando *or* deliberando si hacerlo o no
Ⓒ [dɪˈlɪbəreɪt] VI (= *think*) reflexionar, meditar (**on** sobre); (= *discuss*) deliberar (**on** sobre)

deliberately [dɪˈlɪbərɪtlɪ] ADV [1] (= *intentionally*) a propósito, deliberadamente; (*with adj*) [*rude, misleading*] deliberadamente
[2] (= *cautiously*) prudentemente; (= *slowly*) lentamente, pausadamente

deliberation [dɪˌlɪbəˈreɪʃən] N [1] (= *consideration*) deliberación *f*, reflexión *f*; (= *discussion*) (*usu pl*) deliberación *f*, discusión *f*; **after due ~** después de pensarlo bien
[2] (= *slowness*) pausa *f*, lentitud *f*; (= *caution*) prudencia *f*

deliberative [dɪˈɪbərətɪv] ADJ deliberativo

delicacy [ˈdelɪkəsɪ] N [1] (= *fineness, subtlety*) [*of flavour, workmanship, instrument*] delicadeza *f*
[2] (= *fragility*) [*of china, person, balance*] fragilidad *f*
[3] (= *sensitivity, awkwardness*) [*of situation, problem*] lo delicado; **a matter of some ~** un asunto algo delicado
[4] (= *tact*) [*of person, inquiry*] delicadeza *f*
[5] (= *special food*) exquisitez *f*, manjar *m* exquisito

delicate [ˈdelɪkɪt] ADJ [1] (= *fine, subtle*) [*features, fabric, workmanship, instrument*] delicado; [*flavour, fragrance, food*] exquisito; [*touch*] suave
[2] (= *fragile*) [*china, balance, ecosystem*] frágil; [*person, health, skin, liver*] delicado; **I'm feeling rather ~ this morning** (*hum*) estoy un tanto delicado esta mañana (*hum*)
[3] (= *sensitive, awkward*) [*situation, problem, task, negotiations*] delicado, difícil

delicately [ˈdelɪkɪtlɪ] ADV [1] [*say, act*] con delicadeza, delicadamente; **~ worded** expresado con delicadeza; **... as you so ~ put it** (*iro*) ... como tú tan delicadamente *or* con tanta delicadeza has expresado
[2] [*flavoured, scented, carved*] exquisitamente; **this may upset the ~ balanced ecosystem** esto puede alterar el frágil equilibrio del ecosistema

delicatessen [ˌdelɪkəˈtesn] N (= *shop*) charcutería *f*, rotisería *f* (*S. Cone*)

delicious [dɪˈlɪʃəs] ADJ [*food, taste, smell*] delicioso, exquisito, riquísimo; [*sensation*] delicioso

deliciously [dɪˈlɪʃəslɪ] ADV deliciosamente, exquisitamente

delight [dɪˈlaɪt] Ⓐ N [1] (= *feeling of joy*) deleite *m*, placer *m*; (= *jubilation*) regocijo *m*; **much to her ~, they lost** perdieron, con gran regocijo de su parte; **to take ~ in sth** disfrutar con algo, deleitarse con algo; **to take ~ in doing sth** disfrutar haciendo algo, deleitarse en hacer algo
[2] (= *pleasurable thing*) encanto *m*; **one of the ~s of Majorca** uno de los encantos de Mallorca; **the book is sheer ~** el libro es una verdadera delicia *or* maravilla; **she is a ~ to teach** (*said of schoolgirl*) es un placer ser su maestra; **a ~ to the eye** un placer para la vista
Ⓑ VT [+ *person*] encantar, deleitar
Ⓒ VI **to ~ in sth** disfrutar con algo, deleitarse con algo; **to ~ in doing sth** disfrutar haciendo algo, deleitarse en hacer algo

▼ **delighted** [dɪˈlaɪtɪd] ADJ **delighted!** ¡encantado!; **I'd be ~** con (mucho) gusto; **to be ~ at** *or* **with sth** estar encantado con algo; **we are ~ with it** estamos encantados con ello; **(I'm) ~ to meet you** (estoy) encantado de conocerlo, mucho gusto de conocerlo; **I was ~ to hear the news** me alegró mucho recibir la noticia; **we shall be ~ to come** estaremos encantados de ir

delightedly [dɪˈlaɪtɪdlɪ] ADV con alegría; **she smiled ~** sonrió encantada, sonrió contentísima

delightful [dɪˈlaɪtfʊl] ADJ [*person*] encantador; [*outfit*] precioso; [*food, breeze*] delicioso

delightfully [dɪˈlaɪtfəlɪ] ADV (*after vb*) [*play, dance, etc*] maravillosamente; **the water was ~ cool** el agua estaba tan fresquita que daba gusto

Delilah [dɪˈlaɪlə] N Dalila

delimit [diːˈlɪmɪt] VT delimitar

delimitation [ˌdiːlɪmɪˈteɪʃən] N delimitación *f*

delineate [dɪˈlɪnɪeɪt] VT [1] (= *draw*) [+ *outline*] delinear, trazar
[2] (= *describe*) [+ *character*] describir, pintar; [+ *plans*] trazar
[3] (= *delimit*) definir

delineation [dɪˌlɪnɪˈeɪʃən] N delineación *f*

delinquency [dɪˈlɪŋkwənsɪ] N delincuencia *f*; *see also* **juvenile A**

delinquent [dɪˈlɪŋkwənt] Ⓐ ADJ delincuente
Ⓑ N delincuente *mf*; *see also* **juvenile A**

delirious [dɪˈlɪrɪəs] ADJ [1] (*Med*) delirante; **to be ~** delirar, desvariar
[2] (*fig*) (*with happiness etc*) loco; **to be ~ with joy** estar loco de alegría

deliriously [dɪˈlɪrɪəslɪ] ADV [*rant, rave*] con desvarío, como un loco; **to be ~ happy** estar loco de alegría; **to be ~ in love** estar locamente enamorado

delirium [dɪˈlɪrɪəm] Ⓐ N (*pl* **delirium** *or* **deliria** [dɪˈlɪrɪə]) (*Med, fig*) delirio *m*
Ⓑ CPD ► **delirium tremens** N delírium *m* tremens

delist [diːˈlɪst] (*St Ex*) Ⓐ VT *quitar de la lista de compañías o títulos admitidos a cotización oficial*
Ⓑ VI *dejar de formar parte de la lista de compañías que cotizan en Bolsa*

deliver [dɪˈlɪvəʳ] Ⓐ VT [1] (= *hand over*) [+ *goods*] entregar (**to** a); [+ *mail*] repartir; [+ *message*] llevar, comunicar; **he ~ed me home safely** me acompañó hasta casa, me dejó en casa; **he ~ed the goods*** (*fig*) cumplió *or* hizo lo que se esperaba de él
[2] (†) (= *save*) librar (**from** de); **~ us from evil** líbranos del mal
[3] (= *give*) [+ *speech, verdict*] pronunciar; [+ *lecture*] dar; **to ~ an ultimatum** dar un ultimátum
[4] (= *throw*) [+ *blow, punch*] asestar, dar; [+ *ball, missile*] lanzar
[5] (= *surrender, hand over*) (*also* **~ up, ~ over**) entregar (**to** a); **to ~ a town (up** *or* **over) into the hands of the enemy** entregar una ciudad al enemigo; **to ~ o.s. up** entregarse (**to** a)
[6] (*Med*) [+ *baby*] asistir en el parto de; **Doctor Hamilton ~ed the twins** el Doctor Hamilton asistió en el parto de los gemelos; **she was ~ed of a child†** (*frm*) dio a luz (a) un niño
[7] **to ~ o.s. of** (*frm*) [+ *speech*] pronunciar; [+ *opinion*] expresar; [+ *remark*] hacer (con solemnidad)
Ⓑ VI [1] (*Comm*) **"we deliver"** "(servicio de) entrega a domicilio"
[2] (*) cumplir lo prometido; **the match promised great things but didn't ~** el partido prometía mucho, pero no estuvo a la altura de lo que se esperaba

deliverance [dɪˈlɪvərəns] N (*poet*) liberación *f* (**from** de)

deliverer [dɪˈlɪvərəʳ] N (= *saviour*) libertador(a) *m/f*, salvador(a) *m/f*

▼ **delivery** [dɪˈlɪvərɪ] Ⓐ N [1] [*of goods*] entrega *f*; [*of mail*] reparto *m*; **allow 28 days for ~** la entrega se realizará en un plazo de 28 días; **the balance is payable on ~** el saldo pendiente se hará efectivo a la entrega; **to take ~ of** recibir; **General Delivery** (*US*) Lista *f* de Correos
[2] [*of speaker*] presentación *f* oral, forma *f* de hablar en público
[3] (*Med*) parto *m*, alumbramiento *m* (*frm*)
[4] (= *saving*) liberación *f* (**from** de)
Ⓑ CPD [*date, order, time*] de entrega ► **delivery boy** N recadero *m*, mensajero *m* ► **delivery charge** N gastos *mpl* de envío ► **delivery man** N repartidor *m* ► **delivery note** N nota *f* de entrega, albarán *m* (de entrega) ► **delivery room** N (*Med*) sala *f* de partos ► **delivery service** N servicio *m* de entrega a domicilio ► **delivery truck** (*US*), **delivery van** (*Brit*) N furgoneta *f* de reparto, camioneta *f* de reparto

dell [del] N vallecito *m*

delouse [diːˈlaʊs] VT despiojar, espulgar

Delphi [ˈdelfaɪ] N Delfos *m*

Delphic [ˈdelfɪk] ADJ délfico

delphinium [delˈfɪnɪəm] N (*pl* **delphiniums** *or* **delphinia** [delˈfɪnɪə]) espuela *f* de caballero

delta [ˈdeltə] N [1] (*Geog*) delta *m*
[2] (= *letter*) delta *f*

delta-winged [ˈdeltəˈwɪŋgd] ADJ con alas en delta

deltoid [ˈdeltɔɪd] Ⓐ ADJ deltoideo
Ⓑ N deltoides *m*

delude [dɪˈluːd] VT engañar; **to ~ sb into thinking (that) ...** hacer creer a algn (que) ...; **to ~ o.s.** engañarse; **to ~ o.s. into thinking (that) ...** engañarse pensando (que) ...

deluded [dɪˈluːdɪd] ADJ iluso, engañado

deluge [ˈdeljuːdʒ] Ⓐ N [*of rain*] diluvio *m*; [*of floodwater*] inundación *f*; **the Deluge** (*Rel*) el Diluvio; **a ~ of protests** una avalancha de protestas

➤ LANGUAGE IN USE: **delighted** 7.2, 11.3, 13, 24.1, 24.2 **delivery A1** 20.1, 20.3, 20.4

Ⓑ VT (*fig*) inundar (**with** de); **he was ~d with gifts** se vio inundado de regalos, le llovieron los regalos; **he was ~d with questions** lo acribillaron a preguntas, le llovieron las preguntas; **we are ~d with work** tenemos trabajo hasta encima de las cabezas, estamos hasta las cejas de trabajo

delusion [dɪ'lu:ʒən] N (= *false impression*) engaño *m*, error *m*; (= *hope*) ilusión *f*; (*Psych*) delirio *m*; **~s of grandeur** delirios *mpl* de grandeza; **to labour under a ~** abrigar una falsa ilusión; **she's labouring under the ~ that she's going to get the job** abriga la falsa ilusión de que va a conseguir el puesto, se engaña pensando que va a conseguir el puesto

delusive [dɪ'lu:sɪv], **delusory** [dɪ'lu:sərɪ] ADJ engañoso, ilusorio

de luxe [dɪ'lʌks] ADJ de lujo

delve [delv] VI **to ~ into** [+ *pocket, cupboard*] hurgar en, rebuscar en; [+ *subject*] profundizar en, ahondar en; [+ *past*] hurgar en; **we must ~ deeper** tenemos que profundizar *or* ahondar todavía más

Dem. (*US Pol*) Ⓐ N ABBR = **Democrat**
Ⓑ ADJ ABBR = **Democratic**

demagnetize [di:'mægnɪtaɪz] VT desimantar

demagogic [,demə'gɒgɪk] ADJ demagógico

demagogue, **demagog** (*US sometimes*) ['deməgɒg] N demagogo/a *m/f*

demagoguery [demə'gɒgərɪ] N demagogia *f*

demagogy ['deməgɒgɪ] N demagogia *f*

de-man [,di:'mæn] VT (*Brit*) (= *reduce manpower in*) reducir el personal en

demand [dɪ'mɑ:nd] Ⓐ N [1] (= *request*) petición *f*, solicitud *f* (**for** de); **his ~ for compensation was rejected** rechazaron su petición *or* solicitud de indemnización; **on ~** a libre disposición de todos, a petición; **abortion on ~** aborto *m* libre; **by popular ~** a petición del público
[2] (= *urgent claim*) exigencia *f*; (*for payment*) aviso *m*, reclamación *f*; (*Pol, Ind*) reivindicación *f*; **the ~s of duty** las exigencias del deber; **final ~** (*for payment of bill*) último aviso *m*; **there are many ~s on my time** tengo muchas ocupaciones; **it makes great ~s on our resources** pone a prueba nuestros recursos; **her children make great ~s on her time** sus hijos absorben gran parte de su tiempo
[3] (*Comm*) demanda *f* (**for** de); **~ for coal is down** ha bajado la demanda de carbón; **there is a ~ for** existe demanda de; **to be in great ~** ◊ **be much in ~** tener mucha demanda; (*fig*) [*person*] estar muy solicitado, ser muy popular
Ⓑ VT [1] (= *insist on*) exigir; (= *claim*) reclamar; **I ~ed to know why** insistí en que me explicaran por qué; **he ~ed to see my passport** insistió en *or* exigió ver mi pasaporte; **to ~ that** insistir en que; **"who are you?" he ~ed** —¿quién es usted? —preguntó; **to ~ sth (from *or* of sb)** exigir algo (a algn); **I ~ an explanation** exijo una explicación; **I ~ my rights** reclamo mis derechos
[2] (= *require*) exigir, requerir; **the job ~s care** el trabajo exige *or* requiere cuidado
Ⓒ CPD ► **demand bill** N letra *f* a la vista ► **demand curve** N curva *f* de la demanda ► **demand draft** N letra *f* a la vista ► **demand management** N control *m* de la demanda ► **demand note** N pagaré *m* a la vista

demanding [dɪ'mɑ:ndɪŋ] ADJ [*person*] exigente; [*work*] (= *tiring*) agotador; [*part, role*] difícil; **it's a very ~ job** es un trabajo que exige mucho; **a ~ child** un niño que requiere mucha atención

de-manning [,di:'mænɪŋ] N (*Brit Ind*) reducción *f* de personal, despidos *mpl*

demarcate ['di:mɑ:keɪt] VT demarcar

demarcation [,di:mɑ:'keɪʃən] Ⓐ N demarcación *f*
Ⓑ CPD ► **demarcation dispute** N conflicto *m* de competencias laborales ► **demarcation line** N línea *f* de demarcación

démarche ['deɪmɑ:ʃ] N gestión *f*, diligencia *f*

dematerialize [,dɪmə'ti:ərɪəlaɪz] VI desmaterializarse

demean [dɪ'mi:n] VT degradar; **to ~ o.s.** rebajarse, degradarse

demeaning [dɪ'mi:nɪŋ] ADJ degradante

demeanour, **demeanor** (*US*) [dɪ'mi:nə^r] N conducta *f*, comportamiento *m*; (= *bearing*) porte *m*

demented [dɪ'mentɪd] ADJ demente; (*fig*) loco

dementedly [dɪ'mentɪdlɪ] ADV (*fig*) como un loco

dementia [dɪ'menʃɪə] N demencia *f*; **senile ~** demencia *f* senil

demerara [,demə'reərə] N (*also* **~ sugar**) azúcar *m* moreno

demerge [,di:'mɜ:dʒ] VT (*Brit*) [+ *company*] dividir, fragmentar, separar

demerger [,di:'mɜ:dʒə^r] N (*Brit*) división *f*, fragmentación *f*, separación *f*

demerit [di:'merɪt] N (*usu pl*) demérito *m*, desmerecimiento *m*

demesne [dɪ'meɪn] N (*Jur*) heredad *f*; [*of manor, country house*] tierras *fpl* solariegas

demi... ['demɪ] PREFIX semi…, medio…

demigod ['demɪgɒd] N semidiós *m*

demijohn ['demɪdʒɒn] N damajuana *f*

demilitarization ['di:,mɪlɪtəraɪ'zeɪʃən] N desmilitarización *f*

demilitarize ['di:'mɪlɪtəraɪz] VT desmilitarizar; **~d zone** zona *f* desmilitarizada

demimonde [,demɪ'mɒnd] N mujeres *fpl* mundanas

demise [dɪ'maɪz] N (*frm*) (= *death*) fallecimiento *m*; (*fig*) [*of institution etc*] desaparición *f*

demisemiquaver ['demɪsemɪ,kweɪvə^r] N (*Brit*) fusa *f*

demist [di:'mɪst] VT (*Aut*) desempañar

demister [di:'mɪstə^r] N (*Aut*) luneta *f* térmica, dispositivo *m* antivaho

demisting [di:'mɪstɪŋ] N eliminación *f* del vaho

demitasse ['demɪtæs] N [*of coffee*] taza *f* pequeña, tacita *f* (de café)

demi-vegetarian [,demɪvedʒɪ'teərɪən] N semi-vegetariano/a *m/f*

demo* ['deməʊ] = **demonstration** Ⓐ N [1] (*Brit Pol*) manifestación *f*, mani* *f*
[2] (*Comm*) [*of machine, product*] demostración *f*
[3] = **demo tape**
Ⓑ CPD ► **demo disk** N (*Mus*) disco *m* de demostración; (*Comput*) disquete *m* de demostración ► **demo tape** N (*Mus*) cinta *f* de demostración

demob* [di:'mɒb] (*Brit*) Ⓐ N = **demobilization**
Ⓑ VT = **demobilize**

demobilization ['di:,məʊbɪlaɪ'zeɪʃən] N desmovilización *f*

demobilize [di:'məʊbɪlaɪz] VT desmovilizar

democracy [dɪ'mɒkrəsɪ] N democracia *f*

democrat ['deməkræt] N demócrata *mf*; **Christian Democrat** democratacristiano/a *m/f*, democristiano/a *m/f*; **Social Democrat** socialdemócrata *mf*

democratic [,demə'krætɪk] ADJ [1] [*country, society, government, election*] democrático
[2] (*US Pol*) **Democratic** [*candidate, nomination, convention*] demócrata; **the Democratic Party** el Partido Demócrata; **the Democratic Congress** el congreso demócrata; **the Democratic Republic of ...** la República Democrática de …; *see also* **liberal C**, **social C**
[3] (= *egalitarian*) [*style, ethos, boss, atmosphere*] democrático

democratically [,demə'krætɪklɪ] ADV democráticamente

democratization [dɪ,mɒkrətaɪ'zeɪʃən] N democratización *f*

democratize [dɪ'mɒkrətaɪz] VT democratizar

démodé [deɪ'mɒdeɪ] ADJ pasado de moda

demographer [dɪ'mɒgrəfə^r] N demógrafo/a *m/f*

demographic [,demə'græfɪk] ADJ demográfico

demographics [,demə'græfɪks] NPL estadísticas *fpl* demográficas, perfil *msing* demográfico

demography [dɪ'mɒgrəfɪ] N demografía *f*

demolish [dɪ'mɒlɪʃ] VT [+ *building*] demoler, derribar, echar abajo; (*fig*) [+ *argument*] echar por tierra; [+ *opposition*] arrasar; (*hum*) [+ *cake*] zamparse*

demolisher [dɪ'mɒlɪʃə^r] N (*lit, fig*) demoledor(a) *m/f*

demolition [,demə'lɪʃən] Ⓐ N demolición *f*, derribo *m*
Ⓑ CPD ► **demolition squad** N equipo *m* de demolición ► **demolition zone** N zona *f* de demolición

demon ['di:mən] Ⓐ N demonio *m*; **he's a ~ for work*** es una fiera para el trabajo
Ⓑ ADJ [1] **the ~ drink** el demonio de la bebida
[2] (*) **he's a ~ squash-player** es un as del squash*, jugando al squash es fabuloso*

demonetization [di:,mʌnɪtaɪ'zeɪʃən] N desmonetización *f*

demonetize [di:'mʌnɪtaɪz] VT desmonetizar

demoniac [dɪ'məʊnɪæk] Ⓐ ADJ = **demoniacal**
Ⓑ N demoníaco/a *m/f*, demoniaco/a *m/f*

demoniacal [,di:mə'naɪəkəl] ADJ demoníaco, demoniaco, diabólico

demonic [dɪ'mɒnɪk] ADJ [1] (*lit*) [*forces, possession, influence*] demoníaco
[2] (*fig*) = **demoniacal**

demonize ['di:mənaɪz] VT demonizar

demonology [,di:mə'nɒlədʒɪ] N demonología *f*

demonstrable ['demənstrəbl] ADJ demostrable

demonstrably ['demənstrəblɪ] ADV manifiestamente; **a ~ false statement** una afirmación manifiestamente falsa

demonstrate ['demənstreɪt] Ⓐ VT [1] (= *prove*) [+ *theory*] demostrar, probar; **you have to ~ that you are reliable** tienes que demostrar que se puede confiar en ti
[2] (= *explain*) [+ *method, product*] hacer una demostración de
[3] (= *display*) [+ *emotions*] manifestar, expresar; [+ *talent, ability*] demostrar
Ⓑ VI (*Pol*) manifestarse (**against** en contra de; **in support of** en apoyo de; **in favour of** a favor de)

demonstration [,demən'streɪʃən] Ⓐ N [1] (= *illustration*) demostración *f*
[2] (= *manifestation*) muestra *f*, demostración *f*
[3] (*Pol*) manifestación *f*; **to hold a ~** hacer una manifestación
Ⓑ CPD ► **demonstration model** N modelo *m* de muestra

demonstrative [dɪˈmɒnstrətɪv] Ⓐ ADJ 1 [*person*] expresivo; **not very ~** más bien reservado
2 **to be ~ of sth** (= *illustrative*) demostrar algo
3 (*Gram*) demostrativo
Ⓑ N demostrativo *m*

demonstratively [dɪˈmɒnstrətɪvlɪ] ADV efusivamente, calurosamente

demonstrator [ˈdemənstreɪtəʳ] N (*Pol*) manifestante *mf*; (*Univ etc*) ayudante *mf*, auxiliar *mf*; (*in shop*) demostrador(a) *m/f*

demoralization [dɪˌmɒrəlaɪˈzeɪʃən] N desmoralización *f*

demoralize [dɪˈmɒrəlaɪz] VT desmoralizar

demoralizing [dɪˈmɒrəlaɪzɪŋ] ADJ desmoralizador

Demosthenes [dɪˈmɒsθəniːz] N Demóstenes

demote [dɪˈməʊt] VT (*gen*) rebajar de categoría; (*Mil*) degradar

demotic [dɪˈmɒtɪk] ADJ demótico

demotion [dɪˈməʊʃən] N (*gen*) descenso *m* de categoría; (*Mil*) degradación *f*

demur [dɪˈmɜːʳ] Ⓐ VI (*frm*) objetar, poner reparos (**at** a)
Ⓑ N **without ~** sin poner reparos, sin objeción

demure [dɪˈmjʊəʳ] ADJ [*person*] (= *modest*) recatado; (= *coy*) tímido y algo coqueto; [*clothing, appearance*] recatado; **in a ~ little voice** en tono dulce y algo coqueta

demurely [dɪˈmjʊəlɪ] ADV (= *modestly*) recatadamente; (= *coyly*) con coqueta timidez

demureness [dɪˈmjʊənɪs] N recato *m*

demurrage [dɪˈmʌrɪdʒ] N (*Naut*) estadía *f*; (*Comm*) sobrestadía *f*

demurrer [dɪˈmʌrəʳ] N (*Jur*) ≈ excepción *f* perentoria

demutualize [diːˈmjuːtjʊəlaɪz] VI (*Fin*) dejar de ser una mutualidad

demystification [diːˌmɪstɪfɪˈkeɪʃən] N desmitificación *f*

demystify [diːˈmɪstɪfaɪ] VT desmitificar

demythification [diːˌmɪθɪfɪˈkeɪʃən] N desmitificación *f*

demythify [diːˈmɪθɪˌfaɪ] VT desmitificar

demythologize [ˌdiːmɪˈθɒlədʒaɪz] VT desmitificar

den [den] N 1 (*wild animal's*) guarida *f*; [*of fox*] madriguera *f*; **a ~ of iniquity** *or* **vice** un antro de vicio y perversión; **a ~ of thieves** una guarida de ladrones
2 (*US*) (= *private room*) estudio *m*, gabinete *m*

denationalization [ˈdiːˌnæʃnəlaɪˈzeɪʃən] N desnacionalización *f*

denationalize [diːˈnæʃnəlaɪz] VT desnacionalizar

denatured [diːˈneɪtʃəd] Ⓐ ADJ [*food*] desnaturalizado
Ⓑ CPD ► **denatured alcohol** N (*US*) alcohol *m* desnaturalizado

dendrochronology [ˌdendrəʊkrəˈnɒlədʒɪ] N dendrocronología *f*

dengue [ˈdeŋgɪ] N dengue *m*

denial [dɪˈnaɪəl] N 1 [*of accusation, guilt*] negación *f*; **he shook his head in ~** negó con la cabeza; **he met the accusation with a flat ~** negó *or* desmintió rotundamente la acusación; **the government issued an official ~** el gobierno lo desmintió oficialmente, el gobierno emitió un desmentido oficial
2 (= *refusal*) [*of request*] denegación *f*; (= *rejection*) rechazo *m*; [*of report, statement*] desmentido *m*, mentís *m inv*; **a ~ of justice** una denegación de justicia
3 (= *self-denial*) abnegación *f*; **to be in ~ about sth** no querer reconocer algo

denier [ˈdenɪəʳ] N 1 (= *weight*) denier *m*; **25 ~ stockings** medias *fpl* de 25 denier
2 (= *coin*) denario *m*

denigrate [ˈdenɪgreɪt] VT denigrar

denigration [ˌdenɪˈgreɪʃən] N denigración *f*

denigratory [ˌdenɪˈgreɪtərɪ] ADJ denigratorio

denim [ˈdenɪm] Ⓐ N tela *f* vaquera; **denims** vaqueros *mpl*, bluyín *msing* (*esp LAm*)
Ⓑ CPD ► **denim jacket** N chaqueta *f* vaquera, cazadora *f* vaquera, saco *m* de vaquero (*LAm*)

denizen [ˈdenɪzn] N (*liter*) morador(a) *m/f*, habitante *mf*; **the ~s of the deep** los moradores de las profundidades del mar (*liter*)

Denmark [ˈdenmɑːk] N Dinamarca *f*

denominate [dɪˈnɒmɪneɪt] VT denominar

denomination [dɪˌnɒmɪˈneɪʃən] N 1 (= *class*) clase *f*, categoría *f*
2 (*Rel*) confesión *f*
3 [*of coin*] valor *m*; [*of measure, weight*] unidad *f*
4 (= *name*) denominación *f*

denominational [dɪˌnɒmɪˈneɪʃənl] ADJ (*Rel*) confesional; (*US*) [*school*] confesional, religioso

denominator [dɪˈnɒmɪneɪtəʳ] N (*Math*) denominador *m*; *see also* **common C**

denotation [ˌdiːnəʊˈteɪʃən] N 1 (*gen*) denotación *f* (*also Ling, Philos*); (= *meaning*) sentido *m*
2 (= *symbol*) símbolo *m*, señal *f*

denotative [dɪˈnəʊtətɪv] ADJ (*Ling*) denotativo

denote [dɪˈnəʊt] VT denotar, indicar; [*word*] significar; (*Ling, Philos*) denotar

denouement, dénouement [deɪˈnuːmɒn] N desenlace *m*

denounce [dɪˈnaʊns] VT (= *accuse publicly*) censurar, denunciar; (*to police etc*) denunciar; [+ *treaty*] denunciar, abrogar

denouncement [dɪˈnaʊnsmənt] N = **denunciation**

denouncer [dɪˈnaʊnsəʳ] N denunciante *mf*

dense [dens] ADJ (*compar* **denser**; *superl* **densest**) 1 (= *thick*) [*forest, vegetation, fog*] denso, espeso; [*crowd*] nutrido; [*population*] denso
2 [*Phys*] [*liquid, substance*] denso
3 (*) [*person*] corto de entendederas*, duro de mollera*

densely [ˈdenslɪ] ADV densamente; **~ packed pages** páginas repletas de información; **~ populated** densamente poblado

denseness [ˈdensnɪs] N 1 (= *stupidity*) estupidez *f*
2 = **density**

density [ˈdensɪtɪ] N 1 (= *thickness*) [*of forest, vegetation, fog*] densidad *f*, lo espeso; [*of population*] densidad *f*
2 (*Phys*) [*of material, substance*] densidad *f*; **single/double ~ disk** disco *m* de densidad sencilla/de doble densidad

dent [dent] Ⓐ N (*in metal*) abolladura *f*; (*in wood*) muesca *f*, marca *f*; **to make a ~ in sth** [+ *metal*] abollar algo; [+ *wood*] hacer una muesca *or* marca en algo; **it's made a ~ in my savings*** se ha comido una buena parte de mis ahorros*
Ⓑ VT 1 [+ *car, hat etc*] abollar
2 (*fig*) [+ *enthusiasm, confidence*] hacer mella en; **his reputation was somewhat ~ed** su reputación quedó un tanto en entredicho; **his pride was somewhat ~ed** su orgullo resultó un tanto herido

dental [ˈdentl] Ⓐ ADJ dental
Ⓑ N (*Ling*) dental *f*
Ⓒ CPD ► **dental appointment** N cita *f* con el dentista ► **dental floss** N seda *f* dental, hilo *m* dental ► **dental hygienist** N higienista *mf* dental ► **dental nurse** N auxiliar *mf* en odontología, enfermero/a *m/f* dental ► **dental science** N odontología *f* ► **dental surgeon** N odontólogo/a *m/f*, dentista *mf* ► **dental technician** N protésico/a *m/f* dental

dented [ˈdentɪd] ADJ abollado, con abolladuras

dentifrice [ˈdentɪfrɪs] N (*frm*) dentífrico *m*

dentine [ˈdentiːn] N dentina *f*, esmalte *m* dental

dentist [ˈdentɪst] N dentista *mf*, odontólogo/a *m/f*; **at the ~'s** en el dentista; **~'s chair** silla *f* del dentista; **~'s surgery** ◊ **~'s office** (*US*) clínica *f* dental, consultorio *m* dental

dentistry [ˈdentɪstrɪ] N odontología *f*, dentistería *f* (*CAm*)

dentition [denˈtɪʃən] N dentición *f*

denture [ˈdentʃəʳ] N dentadura *f*; **dentures** dentadura *f* postiza

denuclearize [diːˈnjuːklɪəraɪz] VT desnuclearizar; **a ~d zone** una zona desnuclearizada

denude [dɪˈnjuːd] VT 1 (*Geol, Geog*) denudar
2 (= *strip*) despojar (**of** de)

denuded [dɪˈnjuːdɪd] ADJ [*terrain*] denudado; **~ of** despojado de

denunciation [dɪˌnʌnsɪˈeɪʃən] N (*gen*) denuncia *f*

denunciator [dɪˈnʌnsɪeɪtəʳ] N denunciante *mf*

Denver boot [ˌdenvəˈbuːt], **Denver clamp** [ˌdenvəˈklæmp] N (*US*) cepo *m*

▼**deny** [dɪˈnaɪ] VT 1 [+ *charge*] negar, rechazar; [+ *report*] desmentir; [+ *possibility, truth of statement*] negar; **to ~ having done sth** negar haber hecho algo; **to ~ that ...** negar que ...; **he denies that he said it** ◊ **he denies having said it** niega haberlo dicho; **I don't ~ it** no lo niego; **she denied everything** lo negó todo; **there's no ~ing it** no se puede negar, es innegable
2 (= *refuse*) [+ *request*] denegar; **to ~ sb sth** negar algo a algn, privar a algn de algo; **to ~ o.s. sth** privarse de algo; **he was not going to be denied his revenge** nada iba a impedir su venganza
3 (= *renounce*) [+ *faith*] renegar de

deodorant [diːˈəʊdərənt] N desodorante *m*

deodorize [diːˈəʊdəraɪz] VT desodorizar

deontology [ˌdiːɒnˈtɒlədʒɪ] N deontología *f*

deoxidize [diːˈɒksɪdaɪz] VT desoxidar

deoxygenate [ˌdiːˈɒksɪdʒəneɪt] VT deoxigenar

deoxyribonucleic acid [diːˌɒksɪˌraɪbəʊnjuːˌkleɪɪkˈæsɪd] N ácido *m* desoxirribonucleico

dep. ABBR = **departs, departure** (*on timetables*) salida

depart [dɪˈpɑːt] Ⓐ VI [*person*] partir, irse, marcharse (**from** de); [*train etc*] salir (**at** a; **for** para; **from** de); **to ~ from** [+ *custom, truth etc*] apartarse de, desviarse de; **the train is about to ~** el tren está a punto de salir
Ⓑ VT **to ~ this life** *or* **this world** (*liter or hum*) dejar este mundo

departed [dɪˈpɑːtɪd] Ⓐ ADJ 1 (= *bygone*) [*days etc*] pasado
2 (*liter, euph*) (= *dead*) difunto
Ⓑ NPL **the ~** (*sing*) el difunto, la difunta; (*pl*) los difuntos, las difuntas

department [dɪˈpɑːtmənt] Ⓐ N 1 (*gen*) departamento *m*; (*in shop*) sección *f*; (*Admin*) sección *f*, oficina *f*; **the toy ~** la sección de juguetes; **the English ~** el departamento de inglés
2 [*of government*] ministerio *m*, secretaría *f*

➤ LANGUAGE IN USE: **deny 1** 26.3

(*Mex*); **Department of Employment** (*Brit*) Ministerio *m or* (*Mex*) Secretaría *f* de Trabajo; **Department of State** (*US*) Ministerio *m or* (*Mex*) Secretaría *f* de Asuntos Exteriores
[3] (*) [*of activity*] **gardening is my wife's ~** del jardín se encarga mi mujer; **men? I don't have any problems in that ~** ¿los hombres? no tengo ningún problema en ese campo
(B) CPD ► **department store** N (grandes) almacenes *mpl*, tienda *f* por departamento (*Carib*)

departmental [ˌdiːpɑːtˈmentl] (A) ADJ departamental
(B) CPD ► **departmental head** N jefe *m* de departamento/sección ► **departmental policy** N política *f* del departamento

departmentalization [ˌdiːpɑːtˌmentəlaɪˈzeɪʃən] N división *f* en departamentos, compartimentación *f*

departmentalize [ˌdiːpɑːtˈmentəˌlaɪz] VT dividir en departamentos, compartimentar

departure [dɪˈpɑːtʃəʳ] (A) N [1] [*of person*] partida *f*, marcha *f* (**from** de); [*of train, plane*] salida *f* (**from** de); **the ~ of this flight has been delayed** se ha retrasado la salida de este vuelo; **his sudden ~ worried us** su marcha repentina nos dejó preocupados; **"Departures"** (*Aer, Rail*) "Salidas"; **point of ~** punto *m* de partida; **to take one's ~** (*frm*) marcharse
[2] (*fig*) (*from custom, principle*) desviación *f* (**from** de); **this is a ~ from the norm** esto se aparta de la norma; **this is a ~ from the truth** esto no representa la verdad
[3] (= *trend, course*) **a new ~** un rumbo nuevo, una novedad
(B) CPD ► **departure board** N (*Aer, Rail*) tablón *m* de salidas, panel *m* de salidas ► **departure gate** N (*Aer*) puerta *f* de embarque ► **departure language** N (*Ling*) lengua *f* de origen ► **departure lounge** N (*Aer*) sala *f* de embarque ► **departure time** N hora *f* de salida

depend [dɪˈpend] VI [1] (= *rely*) **to ~ (up)on** contar con; **you can ~ on me!** ¡cuenta conmigo!; **can we ~ on you to do it?** ¿podemos contar contigo para hacerlo?, ¿podemos confiar en que tú lo hagas?; **you can ~ on it!** ¡tenlo por seguro!; **you can ~ on him to be late** ten por seguro que llegará tarde
[2] (= *be dependent*) **to ~ (up)on** depender de; **he ~s on her for everything** depende de ella para todo; **he has to ~ on his pen** tiene que vivir de su pluma
[3] (= *be influenced by*) **to ~ on** depender de; **your success ~s on how hard you work** tu éxito depende del trabajo que hagas; **it (all) ~s on the weather** (todo) depende del tiempo; **it (all) ~s what you mean** depende de lo que quieras decir; **that ~s** eso depende; **~ing on the weather, we can go tomorrow** según el tiempo que haga, podemos ir mañana

dependability [dɪˌpendəˈbɪlɪtɪ] N [*of person*] seriedad *f*, formalidad *f*; [*of machine*] fiabilidad *f*

dependable [dɪˈpendəbl] ADJ [*person*] serio, formal, cumplidor; [*machine*] fiable

dependance [dɪˈpendəns] N = **dependence**

dependant [dɪˈpendənt] N *persona a cargo de algn*; **I have no ~s** no tengo cargas familiares; **how many ~s does he have?** ¿cuántas personas tiene a su cargo?

dependence [dɪˈpendəns] N dependencia *f* (**on** de); **she wants to be cured of her ~ on tranquillizers** quiere curarse de su dependencia de los tranquilizantes; **his ~ on her for financial support** su dependencia económica de ella; **~ on drugs** ◊ **drug ~** drogodependencia *f* (*frm*)

dependency [dɪˈpendənsɪ] N [1] (*Pol*) (= *territory*) posesión *f*, dominio *m*
[2] (= *dependence*) dependencia *f*; **~ culture** cultura *f* de dependencia

dependent [dɪˈpendənt] (A) ADJ [1] (= *reliant*) **he has no ~ relatives** no tiene cargas familiares, no tiene familiares a su cargo; **to be ~ on** *or* **upon sth/sb** depender de algo/algn; **to be financially ~ on sb** depender económicamente de algn; **to be ~ on drugs** ser drogodependiente (*frm*); **to become ~ on** *or* **upon sth/sb** llegar a depender de algo/algn; **he had become ~ on her for affection** había llegado a depender de ella afectivamente
[2] (*Ling*) [*clause*] subordinado
[3] (= *conditional*) **to be ~ on** *or* **upon sth** depender de algo; **tourism is ~ on (the) climate** el turismo depende del clima
(B) N (*esp US*) = **dependant**

depersonalize [diːˈpɜːsənəlaɪz] VT despersonalizar

depict [dɪˈpɪkt] VT (*in picture*) representar, pintar; (*in words*) describir

depiction [dɪˈpɪkʃən] N (*in picture*) representación *f*; (*in writing*) descripción *f*

depilatory [dɪˈpɪlətərɪ] (A) ADJ depilatorio
(B) N (*also* **~ cream**) depilatorio *m*, crema *f* depilatoria

deplane [diːˈpleɪn] VI (*US*) bajar del avión, desembarcar

deplete [dɪˈpliːt] VT (= *reduce*) mermar; (= *exhaust totally*) agotar; **stocks have been ~d by overfishing** la fauna marina se ha visto mermada debido a una actividad pesquera desmesurada; **substances that ~ the ozone layer** sustancias que destruyen la capa de ozono; **Lee's exhausted and ~d army** el ejército cansado y diezmado de Lee; **that holiday rather ~d our savings** esas vacaciones mermaron *or* redujeron bastante nuestros ahorros

depleted uranium [dɪˈpliːtɪdjʊəˈreɪnɪəm] N uranio *m* empobrecido

depletion [dɪˈpliːʃən] N (= *reduction*) reducción *f*, merma *f*; (= *exhaustion*) agotamiento *m*; **the ~ of the ozone layer** la rarefacción *or* destrucción de la capa de ozono

▼**deplorable** [dɪˈplɔːrəbl] ADJ [1] (= *sad*) lamentable; **it would be ~ if** sería lamentable que + *subjun*
[2] (= *disgraceful*) deplorable; **it is ~ that** es deplorable que + *subjun*

deplorably [dɪˈplɔːrəblɪ] ADV (= *sadly*) lamentablemente; (= *disgracefully*) deplorablemente; **in ~ bad taste** de un mal gusto lamentable

deplore [dɪˈplɔːʳ] VT (= *regret*) lamentar; (= *censure*) deplorar; **it is to be ~d** (= *unfortunate*) es lamentable; (= *disgraceful*) es deplorable

deploy [dɪˈplɔɪ] (A) VT [1] (*Mil*) desplegar
[2] (*fig*) [+ *resources*] utilizar
(B) VI (*Mil*) desplegarse

deployment [dɪˈplɔɪmənt] N [1] (*Mil*) despliegue *m*
[2] (*fig*) [*of resources*] utilización *f*

depolarization [diːˌpəʊləraɪˈzeɪʃən] N despolarización *f*

depolarize [diːˈpəʊləˌraɪz] VT despolarizar

depoliticize [ˌdiːpəˈlɪtɪsaɪz] VT despolitizar

depopulate [diːˈpɒpjʊleɪt] VT despoblar

depopulation [ˈdiːˌpɒpjʊˈleɪʃən] N [*of region*] despoblación *f*

deport [dɪˈpɔːt] VT [1] (= *expel*) deportar
[2] (= *behave*) **to ~ o.s.**† comportarse

deportation [ˌdiːpɔːˈteɪʃən] (A) N deportación *f*
(B) CPD ► **deportation order** N orden *f* de deportación

deportee [ˌdiːpɔːˈtiː] N deportado/a *m/f*

deportment [dɪˈpɔːtmənt] N (= *behaviour*) conducta *f*, comportamiento *m*; (= *carriage*) porte *m*

depose [dɪˈpəʊz] (A) VT [+ *ruler*] deponer, destituir
(B) VI (*Jur*) declarar, deponer

deposit [dɪˈpɒzɪt] (A) N [1] (*in bank*) depósito *m*; **to have £50 on ~** tener 50 libras en cuenta de ahorros
[2] (*Comm*) (= *part payment*) (*on hire purchase, car*) depósito *m*, enganche *m* (*Mex*); (*on house*) desembolso *m* inicial, entrada *f* (*Sp*); (= *returnable security*) señal *f*, fianza *f*; **to put down a ~ of £50** dejar un depósito de 50 libras; **he paid a £2,000 ~ on the house** hizo un desembolso inicial de 2.000 libras para la casa, dio una entrada de 2.000 libras para la casa (*Sp*); **to lose one's ~** (*Brit Pol*) perder el depósito
[3] (*Chem*) poso *m*, sedimento *m*
[4] (*Geol*) [*of gas*] depósito *m*; [*of mineral*] yacimiento *m*
(B) VT [1] (= *put down*) depositar; (= *leave*) [+ *luggage*] consignar, dejar (en consigna); [+ *eggs*] poner; [+ *object*] depositar (**with** en), dejar (**with** con)
[2] (*in bank*) [+ *money*] depositar, ingresar (**in** en); **I want to ~ £10 in my account** quiero ingresar 10 libras en mi cuenta; **to ~ £2,000 on a house** hacer un desembolso inicial *or* (*Sp*) dar una entrada de 2.000 libras para una casa
[3] (*Geol, Chem*) depositar
(C) CPD ► **deposit account** N cuenta *f* de ahorros ► **deposit slip** N hoja *f* de ingreso

depositary [dɪˈpɒzɪtərɪ] N [1] (= *person*) depositario/a *m/f*
[2] = **depository**

deposition [ˌdiːpəˈzɪʃən] N [1] [*of ruler*] deposición *f*, destitución *f*
[2] (*Jur*) declaración *f*, deposición *f*

depositor [dɪˈpɒzɪtəʳ] N (*Fin*) depositante *mf*, impositor(a) *m/f*

depository [dɪˈpɒzɪtərɪ] (A) N (= *storage place*) almacén *m*; (*fig*) (= *person*) depositario/a *m/f*
(B) CPD ► **depository library** N (*US*) biblioteca *f* de depósito

depot [ˈdepəʊ] (A) N (= *storehouse*) almacén *m*, depósito *m*; (*for vehicles*) parque *m*, cochera *f*; (= *bus station*) terminal *f*; (*US Rail*) estación *f*; (*Mil*) depósito *m*
(B) CPD ► **depot ship** N buque *m* nodriza

depravation [ˌdeprəˈveɪʃən] N = **depravity**

deprave [dɪˈpreɪv] VT depravar

depraved [dɪˈpreɪvd] ADJ depravado

depravity [dɪˈprævɪtɪ] N depravación *f*

deprecate [ˈdeprɪkeɪt] VT (*frm*) (= *censure*) desaprobar, lamentar; (= *disparage*) menospreciar

deprecating [ˈdeprɪkeɪtɪŋ] ADJ [*tone*] de desaprobación; [*smile*] de desprecio

deprecatingly [ˈdeprɪkeɪtɪŋlɪ] ADV (= *disapprovingly*) con desaprobación; (= *disparagingly*) con desprecio

deprecatory [ˈdeprɪkətərɪ] ADJ [*attitude, gesture*] de desaprobación; [*smile*] de disculpa

depreciate [dɪˈpriːʃɪeɪt] (A) VI [*currency, shares*] depreciarse
(B) VT [1] (*Fin*) [+ *value*] depreciar; [+ *assets*] depreciar, amortizar
[2] (= *belittle*) menospreciar, desdeñar

depreciation [dɪˌpriːʃɪˈeɪʃən] (A) N [*of value*] depreciación *f*; [*of assets*] depreciación *f*, amortización *f*

➤ LANGUAGE IN USE: **deplorable 2** 14

Ⓑ CPD ► **depreciation account** N cuenta *f* de amortización ► **depreciation allowance** N reservas *fpl* para depreciaciones

depredations [ˌdeprɪˈdeɪʃənz] NPL estragos *mpl*, expolios *mpl*; **the ~ of time** los estragos del tiempo

depress [dɪˈpres] VT 1 [+ *person*] (= *make miserable*) deprimir, abatir; (= *discourage*) desalentar; (*Psych*) tener un efecto depresivo sobre; (*Med*) [+ *immune system*] deprimir
2 (*Fin*) [+ *trade, price*] reducir
3 (*frm*) (= *press down*) [+ *button, accelerator*] apretar; [+ *lever*] bajar

depressant [dɪˈpresnt] Ⓐ ADJ (*Med*) depresivo
Ⓑ N (*Med*) depresivo *m*

depressed [dɪˈprest] ADJ 1 [*person*] deprimido, abatido; **to feel ~ (about sth)** estar deprimido *or* abatido (por algo); **to get ~ (about sth)** deprimirse (por algo)
2 (*Fin*) [*market, economy, industry*] deprimido; **the government has tried to reduce unemployment in ~ areas** el gobierno ha intentado reducir el desempleo de las zonas deprimidas; **share prices were ~ following the announcement** los precios de las acciones habían caído tras el anuncio
3 (*Med frm*) [*bone*] hundido; [*immune system*] disminuido; **a ~ fracture** una fractura por aplastamiento

depressing [dɪˈpresɪŋ] ADJ deprimente; **what a ~ thought!** ¡qué idea tan deprimente!

depressingly [dɪˈpresɪŋlɪ] ADV [*say, reply*] tristemente; **Dad had become ~ weak** era deprimente ver lo débil que se había quedado papá; **it all sounded ~ familiar** me sonaba todo tanto que era deprimente; **it was a ~ familiar story** era una historia tan sabida *or* oída que resultaba deprimente

depression [dɪˈpreʃən] N 1 (= *dejection*) depresión *f*, abatimiento *m*
2 (*Met*) depresión *f*
3 (*Econ*) depresión *f*, crisis *f inv* (económica); **the Depression** la Depresión
4 (= *hollow*) (*in surface*) depresión *f*; (*in ground, road*) bache *m*, hoyo *m*

depressive [dɪˈpresɪv] Ⓐ ADJ depresivo
Ⓑ N depresivo/a *m/f*

depressurization [dɪˌpreʃəraɪˈzeɪʃən] N despresurización *f*

depressurize [diːˈpreʃəˌraɪz] VT despresurizar

deprivation [ˌdeprɪˈveɪʃən] N (*Psych*) (= *act*) privación *f*; (= *state*) necesidad *f*; **he lived a life of ~** vivía en la necesidad, vivió una vida llena de privaciones; **the ~s of the past thirty years** las privaciones de los últimos treinta años; **sleep ~** falta *f* de sueño; **social ~** marginación *f* social

deprive [dɪˈpraɪv] VT **to ~ sb of sth** privar a algn de algo; **to ~ o.s. of sth** privarse de algo; **they had been ~d of their freedom** les habían privado de su libertad; **they were ~d of affection as children** de niños no recibieron el suficiente afecto; **he was ~d of sleep/food for seven days** no le dejaron dormir/no le dieron de comer durante siete días; **the brain was ~d of oxygen** el cerebro no recibía su aporte de oxígeno; **"would you like some chocolate?" — "no thanks, I don't want to ~ you"** (*hum*) —¿quieres chocolate? —no, gracias, para ti

deprived [dɪˈpraɪvd] ADJ [*child, family*] necesitado, desventajado; [*area, district*] marginado; **she had a ~ childhood** tuvo una niñez llena de privaciones; **emotionally ~ children** niños con carencias afectivas; **to feel ~** sentirse en desventaja

deprogramme, deprogram (*US*) [diːˈprəʊɡræm] VT desprogramar

Dept, dept. ABBR (= **department**) Dep., Dpto.

depth [depθ] Ⓐ N 1 [*of water, hole, shelf*] profundidad *f*; [*of room, building*] fondo *m*; [*of hem*] ancho *m*; [*of colour, feelings*] intensidad *f*; [*of voice*] gravedad *f*, profundidad *f*; **at a ~ of three metres** a tres metros de profundidad; **~ of field** (*Phot*) profundidad *f* de campo; **the trench was two metres in ~** la zanja tenía dos metros de profundidad; **to study a subject in ~** estudiar un tema a fondo *or* en profundidad; **it shows a great ~ of knowledge of the subject** muestra un conocimiento muy profundo de la materia; **to get out of one's ~** (*lit*) perder pie; (*fig*) meterse en honduras, salirse de su terreno; **to be out of one's ~** (*lit*) no tocar fondo, no hacer pie; (*fig*) **I'm out of my ~ with physics** no entiendo nada de física; **he felt out of his ~ with these people** se sentía perdido entre esta gente; **it is deplorable that anyone should sink to such ~s** es deplorable que uno pueda caer tan bajo
2 **the ~s: in the ~s of the sea** en las profundidades del mar, en el fondo del mar; **to be in the ~s of despair** estar hundido en la desesperación; **in the ~s of winter** en lo más crudo del invierno; *see also* **plumb D2**
Ⓑ CPD ► **depth charge** N carga *f* de profundidad

deputation [ˌdepjʊˈteɪʃən] N (= *group*) delegación *f*

depute [dɪˈpjuːt] VT [+ *job, authority*] delegar; **to ~ sth to sb** delegar algo en algn; **to ~ sb to do sth** delegar a algn para que haga algo

deputize [ˈdepjʊtaɪz] VI **to ~ for sb** desempeñar las funciones de algn, sustituir a algn

deputy [ˈdepjʊtɪ] Ⓐ N suplente *mf*, sustituto/a *m/f*; (*Pol*) diputado/a *m/f*; (= *agent*) representante *mf*
Ⓑ CPD ► **deputy chairman** N vicepresidente/a *m/f* ► **deputy director** N director(a) *m/f* adjunto/a, subdirector(a) *m/f* ► **deputy head** N (= *deputy manager*) subdirector(a) *m/f*; (= *deputy head teacher*) subdirector(a) *m/f*, ≈ jefe/a *m/f* de estudios ► **deputy manager** N subdirector(a) *m/f* ► **deputy minister** N viceministro/a *m/f*

derail [dɪˈreɪl] Ⓐ VT hacer descarrilar
Ⓑ VI descarrilar

derailment [dɪˈreɪlmənt] N descarrilamiento *m*

derange [dɪˈreɪndʒ] VT 1 (= *upset*) [+ *plans*] desarreglar, descomponer
2 (*mentally*) [+ *person*] volver loco, desquiciar

deranged [dɪˈreɪndʒd] ADJ [*person*] loco, desquiciado; [*mind*] perturbado; **to be (mentally) ~** estar desquiciado, ser un perturbado mental

derangement [dɪˈreɪndʒmənt] N 1 (= *disturbance*) desarreglo *m*
2 (*Med*) trastorno *m* mental

derby[1] [ˈdɑːbɪ, (*US*) ˈdɜːbɪ] N 1 (*Sport*) **local ~** derbi *m*
2 **the Derby** (*Brit Horse racing*) el Derby (*importante carrera de caballos en Inglaterra*)

derby[2] [ˈdɜːbɪ] N (*US*) (*also* **~ hat**) sombrero *m* hongo, bombín *m*

Derbys ABBR (*Brit*) = **Derbyshire**

deregulate [diːˈreɡjʊleɪt] VT desregular

deregulation [diːˌreɡjʊˈleɪʃən] N desregulación *f*

derelict [ˈderɪlɪkt] Ⓐ ADJ (= *abandoned*) abandonado; (= *ruined*) en ruinas
Ⓑ N (= *person*) indigente *mf*; (= *ship*) derrelicto *m*; (= *building*) edificio *m* abandonado

dereliction [ˌderɪˈlɪkʃən] N [*of property*] abandono *m*; **~ of duty** negligencia *f*

deride [dɪˈraɪd] VT ridiculizar, mofarse de

de rigueur [dərɪˈɡɜːʳ] ADV de rigor

derision [dɪˈrɪʒən] N mofa *f*, burla *f*, irrisión *f*; **this was greeted with hoots of ~** esto fue recibido con gran mofa *or* sonoras burlas, esto provocó gran irrisión

derisive [dɪˈraɪsɪv] ADJ [*laughter*] burlón

derisively [dɪˈraɪsɪvlɪ] ADV burlonamente

derisory [dɪˈraɪsərɪ] ADJ 1 [*amount*] irrisorio
2 = **derisive**

derivation [ˌderɪˈveɪʃən] N [*of word*] derivación *f*

derivative [dɪˈrɪvətɪv] Ⓐ ADJ (*Chem, Ling*) derivado; (= *unoriginal*) [*literary work, style*] poco original
Ⓑ N (*Chem, Ling, Fin*) derivado *m*

derive [dɪˈraɪv] Ⓐ VT [+ *comfort, pleasure*] encontrar (**from** en); [+ *profit*] sacar, obtener (**from** de); **it ~s its name** *or* **its name is ~d from the Latin word "linum"** su nombre viene *or* procede del latín "linum"; **~d demand** demanda *f* indirecta
Ⓑ VI **to ~ from** [*word, name*] proceder de, venir de; [*view, notion*] basarse en; [*problem, power, fortune*] provenir de

dermatitis [ˌdɜːməˈtaɪtɪs] N dermatitis *f inv*

dermatologist [ˌdɜːməˈtɒlədʒɪst] N dermatólogo/a *m/f*

dermatology [ˌdɜːməˈtɒlədʒɪ] N dermatología *f*

dermis [ˈdɜːmɪs] N dermis *f*

derogate [ˈderəɡeɪt] VI **to ~ from** (= *detract from*) quitar mérito *or* valor a; (= *reduce*) [+ *authority*] menoscabar; (= *deviate from*) desviarse de

derogation [ˌderəˈɡeɪʃən] N [*of authority*] menoscabo *m* (**from** de); (= *deviation*) desviación *f*, descarrío *m* (*liter*) (**from** de)

derogatory [dɪˈrɒɡətərɪ] ADJ despectivo; **he was very ~ about her singing** hizo comentarios muy despectivos de su forma de cantar

derrick [ˈderɪk] N (*in port*) grúa *f*; (*above oil well*) torre *f* de perforación, derrick *m*

derring-do [ˈderɪŋˈduː] N (*liter*) **tales of ~** relatos *mpl* épicos; **deeds of ~** gestas *fpl*, hazañas *fpl*

derringer [ˈderɪndʒəʳ] N *pistola de cañón corto y calibre ancho*

derv [dɜːv] N (*Brit*) gasoil *m*

dervish [ˈdɜːvɪʃ] N derviche *mf*; (*fig*) salvaje *mf*

DES N ABBR (*Brit*) (*formerly*) = **Department of Education and Science**

desalinate [diːˈsælɪneɪt] VT desalinizar

desalination [diːˌsælɪˈneɪʃən] Ⓐ N desalinización *f*
Ⓑ CPD ► **desalination plant** N planta *f* desalinizadora

descale [diːˈskeɪl] VT desincrustar; **descaling agent/product** agente *m*/producto *m* desincrustante

descant [ˈdeskænt] N (*Mus*) contrapunto *m*

descend [dɪˈsend] Ⓐ VT 1 (*frm*) (= *go down*) [+ *stairs*] descender, bajar
2 (= *originate*) **to be ~ed from sb** descender de algn
Ⓑ VI 1 (*frm*) (= *go down*) descender, bajar (**from** de); *see also* **descending**
2 (= *invade, take over*) **to ~ (up)on** [*fog, silence*] caer sobre; [*army, reporters*] invadir; (*hum*) [*visitors*] invadir; **we've got the whole family ~ing on us this weekend** nos va a invadir toda la familia este fin de semana
3 (= *sink*) **I'd never ~ to that level** nunca me rebajaría a ese nivel; **to ~ to doing sth**

rebajarse a hacer algo

4 (= *be inherited*) [*property, custom*] pasar (**to** a)

5 (= *originate*) **to ~ from** [+ *ancestors*] descender de; **his family ~s from William the Conqueror** su familia desciende de Guillermo el Conquistador

descendant [dɪˈsendənt] N descendiente *mf*; **to leave no ~s** no dejar descendencia

descending [dɪˈsendɪŋ] ADJ descendente; **in ~ order of importance** por orden decreciente *or* descendente de importancia

descent [dɪˈsent] N 1 (= *going down*) descenso *m*, bajada *f*; (= *slope*) cuesta *f*, pendiente *f*; (= *fall*) descenso *m* (**in** de)

2 (= *raid*) ataque *m* (**on** sobre), incursión *f* (**on** en)

3 (= *ancestry*) ascendencia *f* (**from** de); **of Italian ~** de ascendencia italiana; **line of ~** linaje *m*; **he claimed ~ from Peter the Great** afirmaba descender de Pedro el Grande

descramble [ˈdiːˈskræmbl] VT (*TV*) descodificar

descrambler [ˈdiːˈskræmbləʳ] N (*TV*) descodificador *m*

describe [dɪsˈkraɪb] VT 1 [+ *scene, person*] describir; **~ him for us** descríbenoslo; **the feeling is impossible to ~** la sensación es indescriptible; **she ~s herself as an executive** se define como una ejecutiva; **I wouldn't ~ her as a feminist** no la calificaría de *or* describiría como feminista

2 (*Geom*) [+ *circle*] describir

description [dɪsˈkrɪpʃən] N 1 [*of person, scene, object*] descripción *f*; **do you know anyone of this ~?** ¿sabe de alguien que responda a esta descripción?; **beyond ~** indescriptible; *see also* **answer B2**

2 (= *sort*) **he carried a gun of some ~** llevaba un arma de algún tipo; **of every ~** de toda clase

descriptive [dɪsˈkrɪptɪv] ADJ descriptivo

descriptivism [dɪsˈkrɪptɪvɪzəm] N descriptivismo *m*

descriptivist [dɪsˈkrɪptɪvɪst] N descriptivista *mf*

descry [dɪsˈkraɪ] VT (*liter*) divisar

Desdemona [ˌdezdɪˈməʊnə] N Desdémona

desecrate [ˈdesɪkreɪt] VT profanar

desecration [ˌdesɪˈkreɪʃən] N profanación *f*

deseed [ˌdiːˈsiːd] VT [+ *fruit*] despepitar

desegregate [diːˈsegrəgeɪt] VT abolir la segregación de

desegregation [ˈdiːˌsegrəˈgeɪʃən] N abolición *f* de la segregación

deselect [ˌdiːsɪˈlekt] VT no renovar la candidatura de, no reelegir

deselection [diːsɪˈlekʃən] N no renovación *f* de la candidatura, rechazo *m* de la reelección

desensitize [diːˈsensɪtaɪz] VT insensibilizar; (*Phot*) hacer insensible a la luz

desert¹ [ˈdezət] (A) N desierto *m*

(B) CPD [*climate, region*] desértico; [*tribe, people*] del desierto ► **desert boots** NPL botines *mpl* de ante ► **desert island** N isla *f* desierta ► **desert rat** N (*Mil*) rata *f* del desierto

desert² [dɪˈzɜːt] (A) VT (*Mil, Jur etc*) desertar de; [+ *person*] abandonar; **his courage ~ed him** su valor le abandonó *or* se esfumó

(B) VI (*Mil*) desertar (**from** de; **to** a)

deserted [dɪˈzɜːtɪd] ADJ [*place, street*] desierto; [*husband, wife*] abandonado

deserter [dɪˈzɜːtəʳ] N (*Mil*) desertor(a) *m/f*; (*Pol*) tránsfuga *mf*

desertification [ˌdezɜːtɪfɪˈkeɪʃən] N desertización *f*

desertify [deˈzɜːtɪfaɪ] VT desertizar

desertion [dɪˈzɜːʃən] N (*Mil*) deserción *f*; [*of spouse*] abandono *m*

deserts [dɪˈzɜːts] NPL ✦***IDIOMS*** **to get one's just ~** llevarse su merecido; **to give sb his/her just ~** dar a algn su merecido

deserve [dɪˈzɜːv] (A) VT merecer; **to ~ to do sth** merecer hacer algo; **he ~s to win** merece ganar; **he got what he ~d** se llevó su merecido; **it's an area of France that ~s further exploration** es una región de Francia digna de ser explorada más a fondo

(B) VI **to ~ well of** merecer ser bien tratado por; **I thought I ~d better than that** opinaba que me tenían que haber tratado mejor

deservedly [dɪˈzɜːvɪdlɪ] ADV con razón, merecidamente; **and ~ so** y con razón

deserving [dɪˈzɜːvɪŋ] ADJ [*cause*] meritorio; **to be ~ of** merecer, ser digno de

deshabille [ˌdezəˈbiːl] N desabillé *m*

desiccant [ˈdesɪkənt] N secante *m*

desiccate [ˈdesɪkeɪt] VT desecar

desiccated [ˈdesɪkeɪtɪd] (A) ADJ 1 (= *dried*) seco

2 (*fig*) [*person*] marchito, mustio

(B) CPD ► **desiccated coconut** N coco rallado y seco

desiccation [ˌdesɪˈkeɪʃən] N desecación *f*

desideratum [dɪˌzɪdəˈrɑːtəm] N (*pl* **desiderata** [dɪˌzɪdəˈrɑːtə]) desiderátum *m*

design [dɪˈzaɪn] (A) N 1 [*of building*] (= *plan, drawing*) proyecto *m*, diseño *m*; (= *ground plan*) distribución *f*; (= *preliminary sketch*) boceto *m*; (= *pattern*) motivo *m*; [*of cloth, wallpaper etc*] dibujo *m*; (= *style*) estilo *m*, líneas *fpl*; (= *art of design*) diseño *m*; **industrial ~** diseño *m* industrial

2 (= *intention*) intención *f*, propósito *m*; (= *plan*) plan *m*, proyecto *m*; **by ~** a propósito, adrede; **whether by accident or ~, he managed it** lo consiguió, ya sea por casualidad o a propósito; **grand ~** plan *m* general; (*Mil*) estrategia *f* general; **to have ~s on sth/sb** tener las miras puestas en algo/algn

(B) VT 1 [+ *building etc*] diseñar, proyectar; [+ *dress, hat*] diseñar; [+ *course*] estructurar; **a well ~ed house** una casa bien diseñada; **a well ~ed programme** un programa bien concebido; **we will ~ an exercise plan specially for you** elaboraremos un programa de ejercicios especial para usted

2 (= *intend*) **to be ~ed for sth/sb: a course ~ed for foreign students** un curso concebido *or* pensado para los estudiantes extranjeros; **a product ~ed for sensitive skin** un producto creado para pieles delicadas; **it was not ~ed for that** [*tool*] no fue diseñado para eso; **to be ~ed to do sth: clothes that are ~ed to appeal to young people** ropa que está diseñada para atraer a la juventud; **the strike was ~ed to cause maximum disruption** la huelga se planeó para causar el mayor trastorno posible

(C) CPD ► **design department** N departamento *m* de diseño, departamento *m* de proyectos ► **design engineer** N ingeniero/a *m/f* diseñador(a) ► **design fault** N fallo *m* de diseño ► **design studio** N estudio *m* de diseño

designate (A) [ˈdezɪgneɪt] VT (= *name*) denominar; (= *appoint*) nombrar, designar; (= *indicate*) señalar, indicar; **to ~ sb to do sth** nombrar *or* designar a algn para hacer algo; **I was ~d as their representative** me nombraron *or* designaron representante de su grupo; **some of the rooms were ~d as offices** destinaron algunas de las habitaciones a oficinas; **the woodland has been ~d (as) a bird sanctuary** el bosque ha sido declarado reserva ornitológica

(B) [ˈdezɪgnɪt] ADJ designado, nombrado

designation [ˌdezɪgˈneɪʃən] N (= *title*) denominación *f*; (= *appointment*) nombramiento *m*, designación *f*

designedly [dɪˈzaɪnɪdlɪ] ADV de propósito

designer [dɪˈzaɪnəʳ] (A) N [*of machines etc*] diseñador(a) *m/f*; (= *fashion designer*) diseñador(a) *m/f* de moda, modisto/a *m/f*; (*in theatre*) escenógrafo/a *m/f*; (*TV*) diseñador(a) *m/f*

(B) CPD ► **designer baby** N bebé *m* de diseño ► **designer clothes** NPL ropa *fsing* de diseño ► **designer drug** N droga *f* de diseño, droga *f* de laboratorio ► **designer jeans** NPL vaqueros *mpl* de marca ► **designer label** N marca *f* de moda ► **designer stubble** N barba *f* de tres días (*según la moda*)

designing [dɪˈzaɪnɪŋ] (A) ADJ intrigante

(B) N diseño *m*, el diseñar

desirability [dɪˌzaɪərəˈbɪlɪtɪ] N [*of plan*] conveniencia *f*; [*of person*] atractivo *m*; **the ~ of the plan is not in question** nadie pone en duda la conveniencia del proyecto

desirable [dɪˈzaɪərəbl] ADJ [*woman*] deseable, atractiva; [*offer*] atrayente; [*property*] deseable; [*action*] conveniente, deseable; **"experience desirable but not essential"** "la experiencia se valorará pero no es imprescindible"; **I don't think it ~ to tell him** *or* **that we tell him** no creo que sea conveniente decírselo

desirably [dɪˈzaɪərəblɪ] ADV **~ located** con una situación ideal

desire [dɪˈzaɪəʳ] (A) N deseo *m* (**for** de; **to do sth** de hacer algo); **I have no ~ to see him** no tengo el más mínimo deseo de verlo

(B) VT 1 (= *want*) [+ *wealth, success*] desear; **to ~ to do sth** desear hacer algo; **it leaves much to be ~d** deja mucho que desear

2 (*sexually*) [+ *person*] desear

3 (= *request*) **to ~ that ...** rogar que ...; **to ~ sb to do sth** rogar a algn que haga algo

desirous [dɪˈzaɪərəs] ADJ (*frm*) deseoso (**of** de); **to be ~ of** desear; **to be ~ that** desear que + *subjun*; **to be ~ to do sth** desear hacer algo

desist [dɪˈzɪst] VI **to ~ from sth** desistir de algo; **to ~ from doing sth** dejar *or* desistir de hacer algo; **we begged him to ~** le rogamos que desistiera *or* que lo dejara

desk [desk] (A) N 1 (*in office, study etc*) escritorio *m*, mesa *f* de trabajo; (*Scol*) pupitre *m*; (= *bureau*) escritorio *m*

2 (= *section*) [*of ministry, newspaper*] sección *f*

3 (*Brit*) (*in airport, hospital*) mostrador *m*; (*in shop, restaurant*) (*for payment*) caja *f*; (*in hotel*) recepción *f*

(B) CPD ► **desk clerk** N (*US*) recepcionista *mf* ► **desk diary** N agenda *f* de escritorio ► **desk job** N trabajo *m* de oficina ► **desk lamp** N lámpara *f* de escritorio ► **desk pad** N bloc *m* de notas ► **desk study** N estudio *m* sobre el papel

desk-bound [ˈdeskbaʊnd] ADJ sedentario

desktop [ˈdesktɒp] (A) ADJ [*computer*] de sobremesa, de escritorio

(B) CPD ► **desktop publishing** N autoedición *f*

desolate (A) [ˈdesəlɪt] ADJ [*place*] desolado, desierto; [*outlook, future*] desolador; [*person*] (= *griefstricken*) desolado, afligido; (= *friendless*) solitario

(B) [ˈdesəleɪt] VT [+ *place*] asolar, arrasar; [+ *person*] desolar, afligir; **we were utterly ~d** quedamos profundamente desolados *or* afligidos

desolately [ˈdesəlɪtlɪ] ADV [*say*] tristemente

desolation [ˌdesəˈleɪʃən] N 1 (= *deserted state*) [*of landscape*] desolación *f*

2 (= *grief*) [*of person*] desolación *f*, desconsuelo *m*

3 (= *act*) asolamiento *m*, arrasamiento *m*

despair [dɪsˈpɛəʳ] Ⓐ N 1 (= *emotion*) desesperación *f*; **to be in ~** estar desesperado

2 (= *person*) **he is the ~ of his parents** trae locos a sus padres

Ⓑ VI perder la esperanza, desesperarse; **to ~ of sth** perder la esperanza de algo; **we ~ed of ever seeing her again** perdimos la esperanza de volver a verla; **don't ~!** ¡ánimo!, ¡anímate!

despairing [dɪsˈpɛərɪŋ] ADJ [*look, sigh*] de desesperación; [*parent, sufferer*] desesperado

despairingly [dɪsˈpɛərɪŋlɪ] ADV desesperadamente

despatch [dɪsˈpætʃ] = **dispatch**

desperado [ˌdespəˈrɑːdəʊ] N (*pl* **desperado(e)s**) bandido *m*

desperate [ˈdespərɪt] ADJ 1 [*person, act, attempt, situation*] desesperado; **to feel ~** estar desesperado; **to be ~ for sth** necesitar algo urgentemente; **I'm ~ (for the lavatory)!*** me muero de ganas de ir al lavabo; **to get** *or* **grow ~** desesperarse; **to resort to ~ measures** recurrir a medidas desesperadas, recurrir a fruto de la de desesperación; **you're going out with her? you must be ~!** (*hum*) ¿sales con ésa? ¡muy desesperado debes estar!; **to be in ~ need of sth** necesitar algo urgentemente; **the company's ~ financial position** la crítica posición económica de la empresa; **to do something ~** cometer un acto desesperado, cometer una locura, hacer algo a la desesperada; **to be ~ to do sth: I was ~ to see her** estaba desesperada por verla, quería verla a toda costa, me moría por verla; **she was ~ to find a new job** estaba desesperada por encontrar otro trabajo; **both countries are ~ to avoid war** ambos países quieren evitar la guerra a toda costa

2 (*) (= *very bad*) [*book, film, meal*] atroz, pésimo; **the play was pretty ~** la obra era atroz *or* pésima

desperately [ˈdespərɪtlɪ] ADV 1 (= *urgently, frantically*) [*say, look*] desesperadamente, con desesperación; [*try, struggle, look for*] desesperadamente; [*fight*] encarnizadamente; [*need, require*] urgentemente, desesperadamente; **to hope ~ for sth** desear algo con todas sus fuerzas; **to be ~ in love** estar locamente *or* perdidamente enamorado; **to be ~ in need of sth** necesitar algo urgentemente; **I ~ wanted to become a film director** quería ser director de cine más que nada en el mundo *or* con todo el alma

2 (= *horribly*) [*lonely, thin, shy, poor*] terriblemente; **we're not ~ busy at the moment** no estamos lo que se dice terriblemente ocupados en este momento; **it's ~ cold** hace un frío terrible; **to try ~ hard to do sth** esforzarse mucho por hacer algo; **I'm ~ hungry** me muero de hambre; **~ ill** muy grave, gravemente enfermo; **I'm not ~ keen on the idea*** la idea no me vuelve loco; **to be ~ short of sth** andar escasísimo de algo; **he's ~ unhappy** es terriblemente desdichado; **my parents were ~ worried** mis padres estaban preocupadísimos

3 (*) (= *very much, very*) **"do you want to have children?" — "not ~"*** —¿quieres tener hijos? —no estoy desesperado por tenerlos; **it's not ~ important/urgent** no es terriblemente importante/urgente; **I'm not ~ keen** no es que me entusiasme; **"hungry?" — "not ~"** —¿tienes hambre? —puedo aguantar

desperation [ˌdespəˈreɪʃən] N desesperación *f*; **she drove him to ~** le llevó al borde de la desesperación, le hizo caer en la desesperación; **in (sheer) ~** ◊ **out of (sheer) ~** a la desesperada, de pura desesperación

despicable [dɪsˈpɪkəbl] ADJ vil, despreciable

despicably [dɪsˈpɪkəblɪ] ADV despreciablemente; [*behave*] de manera despreciable

despise [dɪsˈpaɪz] VT despreciar

despite [dɪsˈpaɪt] PREP a pesar de, pese a

despoil [dɪsˈpɔɪl] VT despojar (**of** de)

despondency [dɪsˈpɒndənsɪ] N, **despondence** [dɪsˈpɒndəns] N abatimiento *m*, desaliento *m*, pesimismo *m*

despondent [dɪsˈpɒndənt] ADJ (= *dejected*) abatido, desanimado; (= *disheartened*) descorazonado; [*letter etc*] de tono triste, pesimista; **he was very ~ about our chances** habló en términos pesimistas de nuestras posibilidades; **he was too ~ to smile** le faltaron ánimos para sonreír

despondently [dɪsˈpɒndəntlɪ] ADV **he sighed ~** suspiró desanimado

despot [ˈdespɒt] N déspota *mf*

despotic [desˈpɒtɪk] ADJ déspota

despotically [desˈpɒtɪkəlɪ] ADV despóticamente

despotism [ˈdespətɪzəm] N despotismo *m*

des. res.* [ˈdezˈrez] N = **desirable residence**

dessert [dɪˈzɜːt] Ⓐ N postre *m*; **what's for ~?** ¿qué hay de postre?

Ⓑ CPD ► **dessert apple** N manzana *f* para repostería ► **dessert plate** N plato *m* de postre ► **dessert wine** N vino *m* dulce (*para el postre*)

dessertspoon [dɪˈzɜːtspuːn] N cuchara *f* de postre

destabilization [diːˌsteɪbɪlaɪˈzeɪʃən] N desestabilización *f*

destabilize [diːˈsteɪbɪlaɪz] VT desestabilizar

destination [ˌdestɪˈneɪʃən] N destino *m*

destine [ˈdestɪn] VT destinar (**for, to** para)

destined [ˈdestɪnd] ADJ 1 (= *intended*) **~ for** destinado a

2 (= *fated*) **to be ~ to do sth** estar destinado a hacer algo; **it was ~ to fail** estaba destinado *or* condenado a fracasar; **she was ~ for greater things** estaba destinada *or* predestinada a llegar lejos; **it was ~ to happen this way** tenía que ocurrir así; **we were ~ never to meet again** el destino no quiso que nos volviéramos a encontrar

3 (= *travelling*) **~ for London** con destino a Londres

destiny [ˈdestɪnɪ] N (= *fate*) destino *m*

destitute [ˈdestɪtjuːt] ADJ 1 (= *poverty-stricken*) indigente; **to be (utterly) ~** estar en la (más absoluta) miseria

2 (= *lacking*) **~ of** desprovisto de

destitution [ˌdestɪˈtjuːʃən] N indigencia *f*, miseria *f*

destroy [dɪsˈtrɔɪ] VT (*gen*) destruir, destrozar; (= *kill*) matar; [+ *pet*] sacrificar; [+ *vermin*] exterminar; (*fig*) [+ *relationship, hopes etc*] destrozar, acabar con; **the factory was ~ed by a fire** la fábrica quedó destrozada *or* fue arrasada por un incendio

destroyer [dɪsˈtrɔɪəʳ] N (*Naut*) destructor *m*

destruct [dɪˈstrʌkt] Ⓐ VT destruir

Ⓑ VI destruirse; *see also* **self-destruct**

Ⓒ CPD ► **destruct button** N botón *m* de destrucción ► **destruct mechanism** N mecanismo *m* de destrucción

destructible [dɪsˈtrʌktəbl] ADJ destructible

destruction [dɪsˈtrʌkʃən] N 1 (*gen*) destrucción *f*; (*fig*) [*of reputation*] destrucción *f*; [*of person*] ruina *f*, perdición *f*; **to test a machine to ~** someter una máquina a pruebas límite; *see also* **scene A2**

2 (= *ruins, damage*) destrozos *mpl*

destructive [dɪsˈtrʌktɪv] ADJ [*weapon, person, behaviour, influence, emotion*] destructivo; [*effect*] destructor; [*child*] destrozón; [*criticism, comment*] destructivo, negativo; [*relationship*] destructivo, dañino; **the ~ power of nuclear weapons** el poder destructivo *or* destructor de las armas nucleares; **to be ~ of** *or* **to sth: products that are ~ of** *or* **to the environment** productos que destruyen el medio ambiente

destructively [dɪsˈtrʌktɪvlɪ] ADV destructivamente, de modo destructivo; **the storm struck violently and ~** la tormenta se abatió violenta y destructiva

destructiveness [dɪˈstrʌktɪvnɪs] N [*of fire, war, weapon*] capacidad *f* destructora; [*of child*] tendencia *f* destructiva; [*of criticism, attitude, behaviour*] carácter *m* destructivo

destructor [dɪsˈtrʌktəʳ] N (*Brit*) (*also* **refuse ~**) incinerador *m* de basuras, quemador *m* de basuras

desuetude [dɪˈsjʊɪtjuːd] N (*frm*) desuso *m*; **to fall into ~** caer en desuso

desulphurization [ˌdiːsʌlfəraɪˈzeɪʃən] N desulfurización *f*

desultory [ˈdesəltərɪ] (*frm*) ADJ [*way of working etc*] poco metódico; [*applause*] poco entusiasta; [*gunfire*] intermitente, esporádico; **they made ~ conversation** entablaron sin ganas una conversación

det. ABBR 1 = **detached**

2 = **detective**

detach [dɪˈtætʃ] VT (= *separate*) separar (**from** de); (= *unstick*) despegar; (*Mil*) destacar; **to ~ o.s. from a group** separarse de un grupo; **to ~ o.s. from a situation** distanciarse de una situación

detachable [dɪˈtætʃəbl] ADJ [*collar, lining*] postizo, separable; [*parts*] desmontable, extraíble

detached [dɪˈtætʃt] Ⓐ ADJ 1 (= *separate*) separado, suelto; (*from friends, family*) distanciado; **to become ~ (from)** [*part, fragment*] desprenderse (de); **she had become ~ from reality** había perdido contacto con la realidad; **they live ~ from everything** viven desligados de todo

2 (= *impartial*) [*opinion*] objetivo, imparcial; (= *unemotional*) [*manner*] indiferente; **to take a ~ view of** considerar objetivamente

Ⓑ CPD ► **detached house** N casa *f* independiente, chalet *m* individual ► **detached retina** N desprendimiento *m* de la retina

detachment [dɪˈtætʃmənt] N 1 (= *separation*) separación *f*, desprendimiento *m*

2 (= *impartiality*) objetividad *f*, imparcialidad *f*; (= *indifference*) indiferencia *f*; **an air of ~** un aire de indiferencia

3 (*Mil*) destacamento *m*

▼ **detail** [ˈdiːteɪl] Ⓐ N 1 (*gen*) detalle *m*; **there are still one or two ~s to sort out** hay todavía un par de detalles *or* cosas que concretar; **to go into ~(s)** entrar en detalles, pormenorizar; **down to the last ~** hasta el más mínimo detalle; **for further ~s contact J. Sims** para más información póngase en contacto con J. Sims

2 (*taken collectively*) detalles *mpl*; **the wonderful ~ of the painting** la maravillosa minuciosidad del cuadro; **attention to ~** minuciosidad *f*; **in ~** en detalle, detalladamente

3 (*Mil*) destacamento *m*

➤ LANGUAGE IN USE: **detail A1** 19.1, 20.1 **A2** 26.1, 26.2

Ⓑ VT [1] [+ *facts, story*] detallar
[2] (*Mil*) destacar (**to do sth** para hacer algo)

detailed ['di:teɪld] ADJ [*information, report, description*] detallado, pormenorizado; [*plan, map, instructions, knowledge, picture*] detallado; [*examination, investigation*] minucioso, detenido; [*history*] pormenorizado

detain [dɪ'teɪn] VT [1] (= *arrest*) detener, arrestar
[2] (= *keep waiting*) retener; **I was ~ed at the office** me entretuve *or* demoré en la oficina; **I was ~ed by fog** me retrasé por la niebla; **don't let me ~ you** no quiero entretenerla

detainee [,di:teɪ'ni:] N detenido/a *m/f*

detect [dɪ'tekt] VT (= *discover*) descubrir; (= *notice*) percibir, detectar; [+ *crime*] descubrir; [+ *criminal*] identificar; (*Tech*) (*by radar etc*) detectar

detectable [dɪ'tektəbl] ADJ perceptible, detectable

detection [dɪ'tekʃən] N (= *discovery*) descubrimiento *m*; (= *perception*) percepción *f*; (*by detective*) investigación *f*; (*Tech*) detección *f*; **to escape ~** [*criminal*] no ser descubierto; [*mistake*] pasar desapercibido

detective [dɪ'tektɪv] Ⓐ N detective *mf*; **private ~** detective *mf* privado/a
Ⓑ CPD ► **detective chief inspector** N (*Brit*) ≈ comisario *m* ► **detective chief superintendent** N (*Brit*) ≈ comisario/a *m/f* jefe ► **detective constable** N (*Brit*) ≈ agente *mf* (de policía) ► **detective inspector** N (*Brit*) ≈ inspector(a) *m/f* (de policía) ► **detective sergeant** N (*Brit*) ≈ oficial *mf* de policía ► **detective story** N novela *f* policíaca ► **detective superintendent** N (*Brit*) ≈ comisario/a *m/f* (de policía) ► **detective work** N (*fig*) trabajo *m* detectivesco, trabajo *m* de investigación

detector [dɪ'tektəʳ] Ⓐ N (= *gadget*) detector *m*
Ⓑ CPD ► **detector van** N (*Brit*) camioneta *f* de detección (*de televisores sin licencia*)

détente ['deɪtɑ̃:nt] N distensión *f*

detention [dɪ'tenʃən] Ⓐ N [*of criminal, spy*] detención *f*, arresto *m*; [*of schoolchild*] castigo *m*; **to get a ~** quedarse castigado después de clase
Ⓑ CPD ► **detention centre, detention center** (*US*) N centro *m* de detención ► **detention home** N (*US*) centro *m* de rehabilitación

deter [dɪ'tɜ:ʳ] VT (= *discourage*) desalentar; (= *dissuade*) disuadir; (= *prevent*) impedir; **to ~ sb from doing sth** (= *dissuade*) disuadir a algn de hacer algo; (= *prevent*) impedir a algn hacer algo, impedir a algn que haga algo; **I was ~red by the cost** el precio me hizo abandonar la idea; **a weapon which ~s nobody** un arma que no asusta a nadie, un arma sin poder disuasorio; **don't let the weather ~ you** no desistas por el mal tiempo

detergent [dɪ'tɜ:dʒənt] Ⓐ ADJ detergente
Ⓑ N detergente *m*

deteriorate [dɪ'tɪərɪəreɪt] VI [*work, situation, weather, condition*] empeorar; [*health*] empeorar, deteriorarse; [*materials, building, relationship*] deteriorarse; **he was worried about her deteriorating health** le preocupaba que cada vez estuviera peor de salud; **the meeting ~d into a free-for-all** la reunión degeneró en una pelea

deterioration [dɪ,tɪərɪə'reɪʃən] N [*of work, situation, condition*] empeoramiento *m* (**in, of** de); [*of health*] deterioro *m*, empeoramiento *m* (**in, of** de); [*of materials, building, relationship*] deterioro *m* (**in, of** de)

determinable [dɪ'tɜ:mɪnəbl] ADJ determinable

> ➤ LANGUAGE IN USE: **determined** 8.2

determinant [dɪ'tɜ:mɪnənt] Ⓐ ADJ determinante
Ⓑ N determinante *m*

determinate [dɪ'tɜ:mɪnɪt] ADJ (*frm*) (= *fixed*) determinado; (*Jur*) [*sentence*] definitivo

determination [dɪ,tɜ:mɪ'neɪʃən] N [1] (= *resolve*) determinación *f*, resolución *f*, decisión *f*; **he set off with great ~** partió muy resuelto; **in his ~ to do it** por su determinación *or* decisión a hacerlo
[2] (= *ascertaining*) [*of cause, position*] determinación *f*

determinative [dɪ'tɜ:mɪnətɪv] Ⓐ ADJ determinativo
Ⓑ N determinativo *m*

determine [dɪ'tɜ:mɪn] VT [1] (= *ascertain, define*) [+ *cause, meaning*] determinar; [+ *price, date*] fijar, determinar; [+ *scope, limits, boundary*] definir, determinar; **to ~ what is to be done** determinar *or* decidir lo que hay que hacer; **to ~ whether sth is true** determinar si algo es verdad
[2] (= *be the deciding factor in*) [+ *fate, character*] determinar; **demand ~s supply** la demanda determina la oferta; **to be ~d by** depender de
[3] (= *make determined*) **to ~ sb to do sth** hacer que algn se decida a hacer algo; **this ~d him to go** esto hizo que se decidiera a ir
[4] (= *resolve*) **to ~ to do sth** decidir hacer algo, determinar hacer algo

►**determine on** VI + PREP [+ *course of action*] optar por, decidirse por

determined [dɪ'tɜ:mɪnd] ADJ [*person*] decidido, resuelto; [*effort*] resuelto, enérgico; **he walked in with a ~ look on his face** entró con aire resuelto; **her refusal made me even more ~** su negativa sólo sirvió para que me decidiese aún más; **to be ~ that ...** estar decidido a que + *subjun*; **she is ~ that her children should go to college** está decidida a que sus hijos vayan a la universidad; **to be ~ to do sth** estar decidido *or* resuelto a hacer algo; **she's ~ to pass the exam** está decidida *or* resuelta a aprobar el examen; **his enemies are ~ to ruin him** sus enemigos se han empeñado en arruinarle, sus enemigos quieren arruinarle a toda costa; **to make a ~ attempt** *or* **effort to do sth** poner todo su empeño en hacer algo

determinedly [dɪ'tɜ:mɪndlɪ] ADV [*say*] resueltamente; [*persevere*] con determinación; **he walked in ~** entró con aire resuelto *or* decidido; **he was ~ optimistic** estaba resuelto a ver el lado bueno

determiner [dɪ'tɜ:mɪnəʳ] N determinante *m*

determining [dɪ'tɜ:mɪnɪŋ] ADJ **~ factor** factor *m* determinante

determinism [dɪ'tɜ:mɪnɪzəm] N determinismo *m*

determinist [dɪ'tɜ:mɪnɪst] Ⓐ ADJ determinista
Ⓑ N determinista *mf*

deterministic [dɪ,tɜ:mɪ'nɪstɪk] ADJ determinista

deterrence [dɪ'terəns] N disuasión *f*

deterrent [dɪ'terənt] Ⓐ N (*also Mil*) elemento *m* disuasivo, elemento *m* disuasorio; **to act as a ~** servir de elemento disuasivo; **nuclear ~** fuerza *f* nuclear disuasiva; **these penalties are no ~ to criminals** estos castigos no disuaden a los criminales
Ⓑ ADJ disuasivo, disuasorio

detest [dɪ'test] VT detestar, aborrecer; **to ~ doing sth** detestar *or* odiar hacer algo

detestable [dɪ'testəbl] ADJ detestable, aborrecible

detestation [,di:tes'teɪʃən] (*frm*) N detestación *f*, odio *m*, aborrecimiento *m*; **to hold in ~** detestar, odiar, aborrecer

dethrone [di:'θrəʊn] VT destronar

dethronement [di:'θrəʊnmənt] N destronamiento *m*

detonate ['detəneɪt] Ⓐ VT hacer detonar
Ⓑ VI detonar, estallar

detonation [,detə'neɪʃən] N detonación *f*

detonator ['detəneɪtəʳ] N detonador *m*

detour ['di:tʊəʳ] Ⓐ N rodeo *m*, vuelta *f*; (*Aut*) desvío *m*; **to make a ~** desviarse, dar un rodeo
Ⓑ VT (*US*) desviar
Ⓒ VI (*US*) desviarse, dar un rodeo

detox* ['di:'tɒks] Ⓐ N = **detoxication, detoxification**
Ⓑ VT = **detoxicate, detoxify**

detoxicate [di:'tɒksɪkeɪt] VT = **detoxify**

detoxication [di:,tɒksɪ'keɪʃən], **detoxification** [di:,tɒksɪfɪ'keɪʃən] Ⓐ N desintoxicación *f*
Ⓑ CPD ► **detoxification centre, detoxification center** (*US*) N centro *m* de desintoxicación ► **detoxification programme, detoxification program** (*US*) N programa *f* de desintoxicación

detoxify [di:'tɒksɪfaɪ] VT [+ *alcoholic*] desintoxicar; [+ *chemical*] eliminar la toxicidad de

detract [dɪ'trækt] VI **to ~ from** [+ *value*] quitar mérito *or* valor a; [+ *reputation*] empañar

detraction [dɪ'trækʃən] N detracción *f*

detractor [dɪ'træktəʳ] N detractor(a) *m/f*

detrain [di:'treɪn] VI bajarse del tren

detriment ['detrɪmənt] N detrimento *m*, perjuicio *m*; **to the ~ of** en detrimento *or* perjuicio de; **without ~ to** sin (causar) detrimento *or* perjuicio a

detrimental [,detrɪ'mentl] ADJ perjudicial (**to** para)

detritus [dɪ'traɪtəs] N (*frm*) detrito(s) *m(pl)*, detritus *m*

de trop [də'trəʊ] (*frm*) ADV **to be ~** estar de más, sobrar

deuce[1] [dju:s] N (*Tennis*) cuarenta iguales *mpl*, deuce *m*

deuce[2]† [dju:s] N **a ~ of a row** un tremendo jaleo; **a ~ of a mess** una terrible confusión; **the ~ it is!** ¡qué demonio!; **what/where the ~ ...?** ¿qué/dónde demonios ...?; **to play the ~ with** estropear, echar a perder

deuced [dju:st] Ⓐ ADJ maldito
Ⓑ ADV diabólicamente, terriblemente

deuterium [dju:'tɪərɪəm] Ⓐ N deuterio *m*
Ⓑ CPD ► **deuterium oxide** N óxido *m* deutérico

Deuteronomy [,dju:tə'rɒnəmɪ] N Deuteronomio *m*

deutschmark ['dɔɪtʃmɑ:k] N marco *m* alemán

devaluate [di:'væljʊeɪt] VT = **devalue**

devaluation [,dɪvæljʊ'eɪʃən] N (*Fin*) devaluación *f*; [*of person*] subvaloración *f*

devalue ['di:'vælju:] VT (*Fin*) devaluar; [+ *person*] subvalorar, subestimar

devastate ['devəsteɪt] VT (= *destroy*) [+ *place*] devastar, asolar; (*fig*) [+ *opponent, opposition*] aplastar, arrollar; (= *overwhelm*) [+ *person*] dejar desolado, dejar destrozado; **we were simply ~d** estábamos verdaderamente desolados *or* destrozados

devastating ['devəsteɪtɪŋ] ADJ [1] (= *destructive*) [*flood, storm, consequence*] devastador; [*attack*] demoledor; **nuclear war would be ~ for Europe** una guerra nuclear tendría un efecto devastador sobre Europa
[2] (= *crushing*) [*blow, loss*] tremendo; [*argu-*

ment, opposition, logic, defeat] aplastante; [*news*] terrible; [*criticism, report*] demoledor; [*wit*] apabullante; **the ~ news that she had cancer** la terrible noticia de que tenía cáncer; **the news is ~** la noticia es un golpe tremendo *or* durísimo; **a strike would be ~ to the economy** una huelga sería un golpe tremendo para la economía
3 (= *stunning*) [*beauty, woman, charm*] irresistible

devastatingly [ˈdevəsteɪtɪŋlɪ] ADV [*beautiful*] irresistiblemente; [*effective, successful, funny*] tremendamente; **a ~ attractive woman** una mujer de un atractivo irresistible; **a ~ simple solution** una solución terriblemente simple; **these missiles are ~ accurate** estos misiles tienen una precisión devastadora; **she demolished his arguments briefly and ~** destruyó sus argumentos de forma lacónica y aplastante

devastation [ˌdevəˈsteɪʃən] N 1 (= *act*) devastación *f*
2 (= *state*) devastación *f*, destrozos *mpl*

develop [dɪˈveləp] Ⓐ VT 1 (= *make bigger, stronger etc*) [+ *mind, body*] desarrollar; (*fig*) [+ *argument, idea*] desarrollar; **I ~ed his original idea** yo desarrollé su idea original
2 (= *generate*) [+ *plan*] elaborar; [+ *process*] perfeccionar
3 (= *acquire*) [+ *interest, taste, habit*] adquirir; [+ *disease*] contraer; [+ *tendency*] coger, desarrollar; [+ *engine trouble*] empezar a tener; **she ~ed a liking for whisky** le cogió el gusto al whisky
4 (= *build on*) [+ *region*] desarrollar, fomentar; [+ *land*] urbanizar; [+ *site*] ampliar; **this land is to be ~ed** se va a construir en *or* urbanizar este terreno
5 (= *exploit*) [+ *resources, mine etc*] explotar
6 (*Phot*) revelar; **to get a film ~ed** revelar un carrete
Ⓑ VI 1 (= *change, mature*) desarrollarse; **girls ~ faster than boys** las chicas se desarrollan más rápido que los chicos; **to ~ into** convertirse *or* transformarse en; **the argument ~ed into a fight** la discusión se convirtió en una pelea
2 (= *progress*) [*country*] desarrollarse; **how is the book ~ing?** ¿qué tal va el libro?
3 (= *come into being*) aparecer; [*symptoms*] aparecer, mostrarse; **a crack was ~ing in the wall** se estaba abriendo una grieta en la pared
4 (= *come about*) [*idea, plan, problem*] surgir; **it later ~ed that ...** más tarde quedó claro que ...

developed [dɪˈveləpt] ADJ [*country, world*] desarrollado; [*sense of humour, justice etc*] profundo

developer [dɪˈveləpəʳ] N 1 (*also* **property ~**) promotor(a) *m/f* inmobiliario/a
2 (*Physiol*) **I was a late ~** maduré tarde
3 (*Phot*) revelador *m*

developing [dɪˈveləpɪŋ] Ⓐ ADJ [*country*] en (vías de) desarrollo; [*crisis, storm*] que se avecina
Ⓑ N (*Phot*) revelado *m*
Ⓒ CPD ► **developing bath** N baño *m* de revelado

development [dɪˈveləpmənt] Ⓐ N 1 (*gen*) desarrollo *m*; (= *unfolding*) evolución *f*
2 (= *change in situation*) novedad *f*, cambio *m*; (= *event*) acontecimiento *m*; **there are no new ~s to report** no se registra ninguna novedad *or* ningún cambio; **what is the latest ~?** ¿hay alguna novedad?; **awaiting ~s** en espera de novedades
3 [*of resources*] explotación *f*; [*of land*] urbanización *f*
4 (= *area of new housing*) urbanización *f*
Ⓑ CPD ► **development agency** N agencia *f* de desarrollo ► **development area** N ≈ zona *f* de urgente reindustrialización, ≈ polo *m* de desarrollo ► **development bank** N banco *m* de desarrollo ► **development company** N [*of property*] promotora *f* inmobiliaria; [*of resources*] compañía *f* de explotación ► **development corporation** N [*of new town*] corporación *f* de desarrollo, corporación *f* de promoción ► **development officer** N director(a) *m/f* de promoción ► **development plan** N plan *m* de desarrollo

developmental [dɪˌveləpˈmentl] Ⓐ ADJ [*process*] de desarrollo; [*abnormality*] del desarrollo
Ⓑ CPD ► **developmental psychologist** N psicólogo/a *m/f* del desarrollo ► **developmental psychology** N psicología *f* del desarrollo

deviance [ˈdiːvɪəns], **deviancy** [ˈdiːvɪənsɪ] N (*gen*) (*also Psych*) desviación *f*

deviant [ˈdiːvɪənt] Ⓐ ADJ (*gen*) (*also Psych, Ling*) desviado
Ⓑ N *persona de conducta desviada*

deviate [ˈdiːvɪeɪt] VI desviarse (**from** de)

deviation [ˌdiːvɪˈeɪʃən] N desviación *f* (**from** de)

deviationism [ˌdiːvɪˈeɪʃənɪzəm] N desviacionismo *m*

deviationist [ˌdiːvɪˈeɪʃənɪst] Ⓐ ADJ desviacionista
Ⓑ N desviacionista *mf*

device [dɪˈvaɪs] N 1 (= *gadget*) aparato *m*; (= *mechanism*) mecanismo *m*, dispositivo *m*; (= *explosive*) artefacto *m*; **nuclear ~** ingenio *m* nuclear
2 (= *scheme*) estratagema *f*, recurso *m*; **to leave sb to his own ~s** dejar a algn hacer lo que le dé la gana; (*to solve problem*) dejar que algn se las arregle solo
3 (= *emblem*) emblema *m*; (= *motto*) lema *m*

devil [ˈdevl] Ⓐ N 1 (= *evil spirit*) demonio *m*, diablo *m*; **the Devil** el Diablo; **go to the ~!**‡ ¡vete al diablo!‡, ¡vete a la porra! (*Sp**); **the ~ take it!**† ¡que se lo lleve el diablo!; **~s on horseback** *ciruelas pasas envueltas en beicon servidas sobre pan tostado*; ✦***IDIOMS*** **to be between the ~ and the deep blue sea** estar entre la espada y la pared; **(to) give the ~ his due** ser justo hasta con el diablo; **to play the ~ with** arruinar, estropear; **to play (the) ~'s advocate** hacer de abogado del diablo; **to raise the ~** armar la gorda; **speak** *or* **talk of the ~!*** hablando del rey de Roma (por la puerta asoma); ✦***PROVS*** **better the ~ you know** vale más lo malo conocido que lo bueno por conocer; **the ~ finds work for idle hands** cuando el diablo no tiene que hacer con el rabo mata moscas; *see also* **luck**
2 (*) (= *person*) demonio *m*; **poor ~** pobre diablo, pobrecito/a *m/f*; **go on, be a ~!** ¡anda, atrévete *or* lánzate!; **you little ~!** ¡qué diablillo *or* malo eres!
3 (*) (*as intensifier*) **the ~ it is!** ¡qué demonio!; **a ~ of a noise** un ruido de todos los demonios; **it was the ~ of a job to do!** ¡menudo trabajo que (me) costó!; **we had the ~ of a job** *or* **the ~'s own job to find it** nos costó horrores encontrarlo; **I'm in the ~ of a mess** estoy en un lío tremendo; **to work/run like the ~** trabajar/correr como un descosido; **how/what/why/who the ~ ...?** ¿cómo/qué/por qué/quién demonios ...?; **there will be the ~ to pay** esto va a costar caro
4 (*Jur*) aprendiz *m* (de abogado); (*Typ*) aprendiz *m* de imprenta
Ⓑ VT 1 [+ *meat*] asar con mucho picante
2 (*US**) fastidiar
Ⓒ VI **to ~ for** (*Jur*) trabajar de aprendiz para

devilfish [ˈdevlfɪʃ] N (*pl* **devilfish** *or* **devilfishes**) raya *f*, manta *f*

devilish [ˈdevlɪʃ] Ⓐ ADJ (= *wicked*) diabólico; (= *mischievous*) travieso
Ⓑ ADV (†) (= *devilishly*) la mar de, sumamente; **~ cunning** la mar de ingenioso

devilishly [ˈdevlɪʃlɪ] ADV [*behave*] endemoniadamente; **~ clever** la mar de listo, sumamente listo

devil-may-care [ˈdevlmeɪˈkɛəʳ] ADJ despreocupado; (= *rash*) temerario, arriesgado

devilment [ˈdevlmənt] N = **devilry**

devilry [ˈdevlrɪ] N (= *wickedness*) maldad *f*, crueldad *f*; (= *mischief*) diablura *f*, travesura *f*, pillería *f*

devious [ˈdiːvɪəs] ADJ 1 (= *twisting, winding*) [*path*] tortuoso, sinuoso; [*argument*] intrincado, enrevesado
2 (= *crafty*) [*means*] dudoso, artero; [*person*] taimado

deviously [ˈdiːvɪəslɪ] ADV [*act, behave*] taimadamente

deviousness [ˈdiːvɪəsnɪs] N 1 (= *twistiness*) tortuosidad *f*
2 (= *craftiness*) [*of person*] artería *f*

devise [dɪˈvaɪz] VT (= *conceive*) [+ *strategy*] concebir, idear; [+ *gadget*] inventar; [+ *plan*] elaborar; [+ *solution*] encontrar; **to ~ a way to kill sb** tramar la muerte de algn

deviser [dɪˈvaɪzəʳ] N [*of scheme, plan*] inventor(a) *m/f*

devitalize [diːˈvaɪtəlaɪz] VT privar de vitalidad

devoid [dɪˈvɔɪd] ADJ **~ of** desprovisto de

devolution [ˌdiːvəˈluːʃən] N delegación *f* (de poderes); (*Pol*) traspaso *m* de competencias; (*Brit Pol*) descentralización *f*; **most Welsh people want ~** la mayoría de los galeses quieren la autonomía

devolve [dɪˈvɒlv] Ⓐ VT [+ *power*] delegar; [+ *government*] descentralizar
Ⓑ VI recaer (**on, upon** sobre); **it ~d on me to tell him** me tocó a mí decírselo

Devonian [deˈvəʊnɪən] ADJ (*Geol*) devónico

devote [dɪˈvəʊt] VT **to ~ sth to sth** dedicar algo a algo; **he ~d three chapters to Japanese politics** dedicó tres capítulos a la política japonesa; **she ~d four years to studying history** dedicó cuatro años a estudiar historia; **she ~d her life to finding a cure for the disease** dedicó *or* consagró su vida a encontrar una cura para la enfermedad; **they do not ~ enough attention to their children** no dedican la suficiente atención a sus hijos; **we will ~ 30% of the money to research** asignaremos *or* destinaremos el 30% del dinero a la investigación; **to ~ o.s. to sth** dedicarse a algo

devoted [dɪˈvəʊtɪd] ADJ [*wife, husband, mother, son, etc*] abnegado; [*couple, family*] unido; [*friend*] leal, fiel; [*follower, admirer*] ferviente; **a ~ Manchester United fan** una forofa del Manchester United; **a ~ Beatles fan** una devota fan de los Beatles; **years of ~ service** años de dedicación y servicio; **to be ~ to sb** adorar a algn, sentir devoción por algn; **they are ~ to one another** se adoran, sienten devoción el uno por el otro; **to be ~ to sth** estar dedicado a algo; **this chapter is ~ to politics** este capítulo está dedicado a la política; **organizations ~ to helping children** organizaciones de ayuda a la infancia; **the institute is ~ to discovering young artists** el instituto se dedica al descubrimiento de jóvenes artistas

devotedly [dɪˈvəʊtɪdlɪ] ADV [*care for, love, follow*] con devoción; [*loyal*] fervientemente

devotee [ˌdevəʊˈtiː] N 1 (*Rel*) devoto/a *m/f*
2 (= *enthusiast*) partidario/a *m/f* (**of** de)

devotion [dɪˈvəʊʃən] N 1 (*to spouse, relative, football team, pop star*) (*also Rel*) devoción *f* (**to** por); (*to friend*) lealtad *f* (**to** a); (*to studies, duty, work, cause*) dedicación *f* (**to** a)
2 **devotions** (*Rel*) oraciones *fpl*; **to be at one's ~s** estar rezando

devotional [dɪˈvəʊʃənl] ADJ piadoso, devoto

devour [dɪˈvaʊəʳ] VT [+ *food*] devorar; **to be ~ed with jealousy** morirse de envidia; **to be ~ed with curiosity** verse devorado *or* corroído por la curiosidad

devouring [dɪˈvaʊərɪŋ] ADJ (*fig*) [*passion*] devorador; [*curiosity*] acuciante

devout [dɪˈvaʊt] ADJ 1 (*Rel*) [*Christian, Muslim, Methodist, etc*] devoto; **they're very ~** son muy devotos *or* piadosos; **she's a ~ Catholic** es muy católica
2 (= *fervent*) [*Communist*] convencido; [*supporter*] ferviente; [*thanks, prayer*] sincero; **it was his ~ wish that his son should become a lawyer** deseaba de todo corazón que su hijo se hiciese abogado

devoutly [dɪˈvaʊtlɪ] ADV [*pray*] con devoción; [*hope, wish*] de todo corazón; [*believe*] fervientemente; **~ religious** muy religioso

dew [djuː] N rocío *m*

dewdrop [ˈdjuːdrɒp] N gota *f* de rocío

dewlap [ˈdjuːlæp] N papada *f*

dewpond [ˈdjuːpɒnd] N charca *f* formada por el rocío

dewy [ˈdjuːɪ] ADJ (*compar* **dewier**; *superl* **dewiest**) [*grass*] cubierto de rocío; [*eyes*] húmedo

dewy-eyed [ˈdjuːɪˈaɪd] ADJ (= *innocent*) ingenuo

dexterity [deksˈterɪtɪ] N (*physical, mental*) destreza *f*, habilidad *f*

dexterous ADJ, **dextrous** [ˈdekstrəs] ADJ diestro, hábil; **by the ~ use of** por el diestro uso de

dexterously, **dextrously** [ˈdekstrəslɪ] ADV [*pass, snatch etc*] con destreza; [*avoid*] diestramente, hábilmente

dextrose [ˈdekstrəʊs] N dextrosa *f*

DfEE N ABBR (*Brit*) = **Department for Education and Employment**

DG Ⓐ N ABBR (= **Director General**) D.G. *mf*
Ⓑ ABBR (= **Deo gratias**) a.D.g.

dg ABBR (= **decigram, decigrams**) dg

DH N ABBR (*Brit*) = **Department of Health**

DHSS N ABBR (*Brit*) (*formerly*) = **Department of Health and Social Security**

DI N ABBR 1 = **Donor Insemination**
2 (*Brit Police*) = **Detective Inspector**

Di [daɪ] N (*familiar form*) *of* **Diana**

di... [daɪ] PREFIX di...

diabetes [ˌdaɪəˈbiːtiːz] NSING diabetes *f inv*

diabetic [ˌdaɪəˈbetɪk] Ⓐ ADJ [*patient*] diabético; [*chocolate*] para diabéticos
Ⓑ N diabético/a *m/f*

diabolic [ˌdaɪəˈbɒlɪk] ADJ 1 [*forces, powers*] diabólico
2 = **diabolical 1**

diabolical [ˌdaɪəˈbɒlɪkəl] ADJ 1 (= *devilish*) [*laughter, plan, plot*] diabólico
2 (*) (= *very bad*) horrendo; **it's a ~ liberty!** ¡es un descaro intolerable!

diabolically [ˌdaɪəˈbɒlɪkəlɪ] ADV 1 (= *devilishly*) [*behave, laugh*] diabólicamente; **~ difficult** endemoniadamente difícil; **it was ~ hot** hacía un calor de infierno
2 (*) (= *very badly*) [*play, sing etc*] pésimamente, fatal*

diachronic [ˌdaɪəˈkrɒnɪk] ADJ diacrónico

diacritic [ˌdaɪəˈkrɪtɪk] Ⓐ ADJ diacrítico
Ⓑ N signo *m* diacrítico

diacritical [ˌdaɪəˈkrɪtɪkəl] ADJ diacrítico

diadem [ˈdaɪədem] N diadema *f*

diaeresis, **dieresis** (*US*) [daɪˈerɪsɪs] N (*pl* **diaereses** [daɪˈerɪsiːz]) diéresis *f inv*

diagnose [ˈdaɪəgnəʊz] VT (*Med, fig*) diagnosticar; **she was ~d with cancer** le diagnosticaron (un) cáncer

diagnosis [ˌdaɪəgˈnəʊsɪs] N (*pl* **diagnoses** [ˌdaɪəgˈnəʊsiːz]) (= *opinion, conclusion*) diagnóstico *m* (*also Med*)

diagnostic [ˌdaɪəgˈnɒstɪk] ADJ diagnóstico

diagnostics [ˌdaɪəgˈnɒstɪks] NSING diagnóstica *f*, diagnosis *f*

diagonal [daɪˈægənl] Ⓐ ADJ diagonal
Ⓑ N diagonal *f*

diagonally [daɪˈægənəlɪ] ADV [*cut, fold*] diagonalmente, en diagonal; **to go ~ across** cruzar diagonalmente; **~ opposite** diagonalmente opuesto

diagram [ˈdaɪəgræm] N (= *plan*) esquema *m*; (= *chart*) gráfica *f*; (*Math*) diagrama *m*

diagrammatic [ˌdaɪəgrəˈmætɪk] ADJ esquemático

▼**dial** [ˈdaɪəl] Ⓐ N 1 [*of clock*] esfera *f*, carátula *f* (*Mex*); [*of instrument*] esfera *f*, cuadrante *m*; [*of radio*] dial *m*; (*Aut*) (*on dashboard*) cuadrante *m*; (= *tuner*) selector *m*; [*of telephone*] disco *m*
2 (*) (= *face*) jeta* *f*, cara *f*
Ⓑ VT (*Telec*) marcar, discar (*LAm*); **to ~ a wrong number** equivocarse de número (al marcar); **can I ~ Bombay direct?** ¿puedo llamar a Bombay directamente?, ¿hay discado directo a Bombay? (*LAm*); **to ~ 999** ◊ **~ 911** (*US*) llamar al teléfono de emergencia
Ⓒ VI (*Telec*) marcar, discar (*LAm*)
Ⓓ CPD ► **dial code** N (*US*) prefijo *m* ► **dial tone** N (*US*) señal *f* de marcar, tono *m* de marcar

dial. ABBR = **dialect**

dialect [ˈdaɪəlekt] Ⓐ N dialecto *m*
Ⓑ CPD ► **dialect atlas** N atlas *m inv* lingüístico ► **dialect survey** N estudio *m* dialectológico ► **dialect word** N dialectalismo *m*

dialectal [ˌdaɪəˈlektl] ADJ dialectal

dialectic [ˌdaɪəˈlektɪk] Ⓐ N dialéctica *f*
Ⓑ ADJ dialéctico

dialectical [ˌdaɪəˈlektɪkəl] Ⓐ ADJ dialéctico
Ⓑ CPD ► **dialectical materialism** N materialismo *m* dialéctico

dialectics [ˌdaɪəˈlektɪks] N dialéctica *f*

dialectology [ˌdaɪəlekˈtɒlədʒɪ] N dialectología *f*

dialling, **dialing** (*US*) [ˈdaɪəlɪŋ] Ⓐ N marcación *f*, discado *m* (*LAm*)
Ⓑ CPD ► **dialling code** N (*Brit*) prefijo *m* ► **dialling tone** N (*Brit*) señal *f* de marcar, tono *m* de marcar

dialogue, **dialog** (*US*) [ˈdaɪəlɒg] Ⓐ N diálogo *m*
Ⓑ VI dialogar

dial-up service [ˈdaɪəl,ʌpˈsɜːvɪs] N servicio *m* de enlace entre cuadrantes

dialysis [daɪˈælɪsɪs] N (*pl* **dialyses** [daɪˈælɪˌsiːz]) (*Med*) diálisis *f inv*

diamanté [diːəˈmɑːnteɪ] Ⓐ N strass *m*
Ⓑ CPD de strass

diameter [daɪˈæmɪtəʳ] N diámetro *m*; **it is one metre in ~** tiene un diámetro de un metro, tiene un metro de diámetro

diametric [ˌdaɪəˈmetrɪk] ADJ = **diametrical**

diametrical [ˌdaɪəˈmetrɪkəl] ADJ diametral

diametrically [ˌdaɪəˈmetrɪkəlɪ] ADV **~ opposed** diametralmente opuesto (**to** a)

diamond [ˈdaɪəmənd] Ⓐ N 1 (= *mineral*) diamante *m*; (= *jewel*) brillante *m*, diamante *m*; ✦*IDIOM* **~ cut ~** tal para cual
2 (= *shape*) rombo *m*
3 (*Cards*) (= *standard pack*) diamante *m*; (*Spanish cards*) oro *m*; **diamonds** (= *suit*) diamantes *mpl*; (*in Spanish pack*) oros *mpl*; **the Queen of ~s** la dama *or* reina de diamantes
4 (*Baseball*) campo *m* de béisbol
Ⓑ CPD ► **diamond jubilee** N sexagésimo aniversario *m* ► **diamond merchant** N comerciante *mf* en diamantes ► **diamond mine** N mina *f* de diamantes ► **diamond necklace** N collar *m* de diamantes ► **diamond ring** N anillo *m* de diamantes, sortija *f* de diamantes ► **diamond wedding (anniversary)** N bodas *fpl* de diamante

diamond-cutter [ˈdaɪəmənd,kʌtəʳ] N diamantista *mf*

diamond-shaped [ˈdaɪəmənd,ʃeɪpt] ADJ de forma de rombo, en forma de rombo

diamorphine [ˌdaɪəˈmɔːfiːn] N diamorfina *f*

Diana [daɪˈænə] N Diana

diapason [ˌdaɪəˈpeɪzən] N diapasón *m*

diaper [ˈdaɪəpəʳ] (*US*) Ⓐ N pañal *m*
Ⓑ CPD ► **diaper pin** N imperdible *m*, seguro *m* (*LAm*)

diaphanous [daɪˈæfənəs] ADJ diáfano

diaphragm [ˈdaɪəfræm] N 1 (*Anat*) diafragma *m*
2 (= *contraceptive*) diafragma *m*

diarist [ˈdaɪərɪst] N diarista *mf*

diarrhoea, **diarrhea** (*US*) [ˌdaɪəˈriːə] N diarrea *f*; *see also* **verbal**

diary [ˈdaɪərɪ] N (= *journal*) diario *m*; (*for engagements*) agenda *f*; **I keep a ~** estoy escribiendo un diario; *see* **desk B**

diaspora [daɪˈæspərə] N diáspora *f*

diastole [daɪˈæstəlɪ] N diástole *f*

diastolic [ˌdaɪəˈstɒlɪk] ADJ **~ pressure** presión *f* diastólica

diatonic [ˌdaɪəˈtɒnɪk] Ⓐ ADJ diatónico
Ⓑ CPD ► **diatonic scale** N escala *f* diatónica

diatribe [ˈdaɪətraɪb] N diatriba *f* (**against** contra)

dibber [ˈdɪbəʳ] N (*Brit*) plantador *m*

dibble [ˈdɪbl] Ⓐ N plantador *m*
Ⓑ VT (*also* **to ~ in**) plantar con plantador

dibs [dɪbz] N 1 (*Brit*†*) (= *money*) parné** *m*; (= *game of jacks*) taba(s) *f(pl)*
2 (*US**) **~ on the cookies!** ¡las galletas pa' mí!; **I want ~ on this one if we get him alive** si sigue vivo cuando lo cojamos pido ser el primero en darle una buena paliza

dice [daɪs] Ⓐ N dado *m*; (*as pl*) dados *mpl*; (= *shapes*) cubitos *mpl*; **no ~!** (*US**) ¡ni hablar!, ¡nada de eso!; *see also* **load B3**
Ⓑ VT [+ *vegetables*] cortar en cubitos; **~d vegetables** menestra *f* de verduras
Ⓒ VI jugar a los dados; **to ~ with death** jugar con la muerte

dicey* [ˈdaɪsɪ] ADJ (*compar* **dicier**; *superl* **diciest**) (*Brit*) (= *uncertain*) incierto, dudoso; (= *hazardous*) peligroso, arriesgado

dichotomy [dɪˈkɒtəmɪ] N dicotomía *f*

Dick [dɪk] N (*familiar form*) *of* **Richard**

dick [dɪk] N 1 (*US**) sabueso *mf*
2 (**) polla *f* (*Sp***), verga** *f*

➤ LANGUAGE IN USE: **dial** B 27

dickens ['dɪkɪnz] (*euph*) = **devil A 3**

Dickensian [dɪ'kenzɪən] ADJ dickensiano

dicker ['dɪkəʳ] VI [1] vacilar, titubear
[2] (*US Comm*) regatear, cambalachear

dickey* ['dɪkɪ] Ⓐ N [1] (= *shirt front*) pechera *f* postiza
[2] (*Brit*) (*also* ~ **bow**) pajarita *f* (*Sp*), corbata *f* de moño (*LAm*)
[3] (*Brit*) (*also* ~ **seat**) spider *m*
Ⓑ CPD ► **dickey bird** N (*baby talk*) pajarito *m*; ✦*IDIOM* **I won't say a ~ bird*** no diré ni pío*

dickhead** ['dɪkhed] N imbécil* *mf*, gilipollas** *mf inv*

dicky* ['dɪkɪ] ADJ (*compar* **dickier**, *superl* **dickiest**) [1] = **dickey**
[2] **to have a ~ heart** (*Brit*) tener el corazón fastidiado

dicta ['dɪktə] NPL *of* **dictum**

Dictaphone® ['dɪktəfəʊn] N dictáfono® *m*

dictate Ⓐ [dɪk'teɪt] VT [1] (*to secretary*) [+ *letter*] dictar
[2] (= *order*) mandar; [+ *terms, conditions*] imponer; **he decided to act as circumstances ~d** decidió actuar según (mandasen) las circunstancias
Ⓑ [dɪk'teɪt] VI dictar; **to ~ to one's secretary** dictar a su secretaria
Ⓒ ['dɪkteɪt] N mandato *m*; **dictates** dictados *mpl*; **the ~s of conscience/reason** los dictados de la conciencia/razón

► **dictate to** VI + PREP [+ *person*] dar órdenes a; **I won't be ~d to** a mi nadie me da órdenes

dictation [dɪk'teɪʃən] N (*to secretary, schoolchild etc*) dictado *m*; **to take (a) ~** escribir al dictado; **at ~ speed** a velocidad de dictado

dictator [dɪk'teɪtəʳ] N dictador(a) *m/f*

dictatorial [,dɪktə'tɔːrɪəl] ADJ [*manner etc*] dictatorial

dictatorially [dɪktə'tɔːrɪəlɪ] ADV dictatorialmente

dictatorship [dɪk'teɪtəʃɪp] N dictadura *f*

diction ['dɪkʃən] N (= *pronunciation*) dicción *f*; (*Literat*) lengua *f*, lenguaje *m*

dictionary ['dɪkʃənrɪ] N diccionario *m*

dictum ['dɪktəm] N (*pl* **dictums** *or* **dicta** ['dɪktə]) sentencia *f*, aforismo *m*; (*Jur*) dictamen *m*

did [dɪd] PT *of* **do**

didactic [daɪ'dæktɪk] ADJ (= *educational*) didáctico; (= *moralistic*) [*tone*] moralizador

didactically [dɪ'dæktɪkəlɪ] ADV didácticamente

diddle* ['dɪdl] VT estafar, timar; **to ~ sb out of sth** estafar algo a algn

didn't ['dɪdənt] = **did not**

Dido [daɪdəʊ] N Dido

die¹ [daɪ] (*pres part* **dying**) VI [1] [*person, animal, plant*] morir (**of, from** de); **her father was dying** su padre se moría *or* se estaba muriendo *or* estaba moribundo; **to ~ a natural death** morir de muerte natural; **to ~ a violent death** tener una muerte violenta; **he ~d a hero** murió convertido en un héroe; **to ~ for one's country** morir por la patria; **the secret ~d with her** se llevó el secreto a la tumba; **I nearly ~d!*** (*laughing*) ¡me moría de la risa!; (*with embarrassment*) ¡me moría de vergüenza!; (*with fear*) ¡casi me muero del susto!; ✦*IDIOMS* **to ~ like flies** morir como chinches, caer como moscas; **a dress/house to ~ for*** un vestido/una casa para caerse de espaldas*, un vestido/una casa de ensueño; ✦*PROVS* **never say ~*** no hay que darse por vencido; **old habits ~ hard** genio y figura hasta la sepultura
[2] (*fig*) [*friendship, interest*] morir, desaparecer; [*light*] extinguirse; [*engine*] pararse, apagarse; **the day was dying fast** (*liter*) la luz del día iba apagándose rápidamente
[3] **to be dying to do sth** morirse de ganas de hacer algo; **I'm dying for a cigarette** me muero de ganas de fumar un cigarrillo

► **die away** VI + ADV [*voice, sound*] irse apagando

► **die back** VI + ADV (*Bot*) secarse

► **die down** VI + ADV [*fire*] apagarse; [*wind, storm*] remitir, amainar; [*battle*] hacerse menos violento; [*shelling*] disminuir; [*discontent, excitement, protests*] calmarse, apaciguarse

► **die off** VI + ADV [*plants, animals*] morirse, desaparecer

► **die out** VI + ADV [*custom*] desaparecer, caer en desuso; [*family, race, species*] extinguirse; [*fire*] apagarse, extinguirse; [*showers*] desaparecer

die² [daɪ] N [1] (*pl* **dice** [daɪs]) dado *m*; ✦*IDIOM* **the ~ is cast** la suerte está echada
[2] (*pl* **dies**) (= *stamp*) troquel *m*, cuño *m*; (= *mould*) matriz *f*, molde *m*; *see also* **straight A3**

die-casting ['daɪ'kɑːstɪŋ] N fundición *f* a troquel

diectic [daɪ'ektɪk] N diéctico *m*

diehard ['daɪhɑːd] Ⓐ ADJ acérrimo
Ⓑ N intransigente *mf*

dieldrin ['diːldrɪn] N dieldrina *f*

dielectric [,daɪə'lektrɪk] Ⓐ ADJ dieléctrico
Ⓑ N dieléctrico *m*

dieresis [daɪ'erɪsɪs] N (*pl* **diereses** [daɪ'erɪsiːz]) (*US*) = **diaeresis**

diesel ['diːzəl] Ⓐ N [1] (= *car, train*) vehículo *m* diesel
[2] (= *fuel*) gasóleo *m*, gasoil *m*
Ⓑ CPD ► **diesel engine** N motor *m* diesel ► **diesel fuel, diesel oil** N gasóleo *m*, gasoil *m* ► **diesel train** N tren *m* diesel

diesel-electric ['diːzəlɪ'lektrɪk] ADJ dieseleléctrico

die-sinker ['daɪ,sɪŋkəʳ] N grabador *m* de troqueles

die-stamp ['daɪ,stæmp] VT grabar

diet¹ ['daɪət] Ⓐ N [1] (= *customary food*) dieta *f*, alimentación *f*
[2] (= *slimming diet*) régimen *m*, dieta *f*; **to be/go on a ~** estar/ponerse a régimen *or* dieta; **to put sb on a ~** poner a algn a régimen *or* dieta
Ⓑ VI estar a régimen
Ⓒ CPD [*soft drink*] light *inv*

diet² ['daɪət] N (*Pol*) dieta *f*

dietary ['daɪətərɪ] Ⓐ ADJ [*supplement*] dietético; [*needs, habits*] alimenticio
Ⓑ CPD ► **dietary fibre** N fibra *f* dietética

dieter ['daɪətəʳ] N persona *f* que está a régimen *or* dieta

dietetic [,daɪɪ'tetɪk] ADJ [*research*] dietético; (*US*) [*meal, food, drink*] de régimen

dietetics [,daɪə'tetɪks] N dietética *f*

dietician [,daɪɪ'tɪʃən] N médico/a *m/f* especialista en dietética, dietista *mf*

differ ['dɪfəʳ] VI [1] (= *be unlike*) ser distinto, diferenciarse, diferir (*frm*) (**from** de)
[2] (= *disagree*) [*people*] no estar de acuerdo, discrepar; [*texts, versions*] discrepar; **to ~ with sb (on** *or* **over** *or* **about sth)** no estar de acuerdo con algn (en algo), discrepar de algn (en algo); **I beg to ~** siento tener que disentir *or* discrepar, lamento estar en desacuerdo *or* no estar de acuerdo; *see also* **agree B2**

difference ['dɪfrəns] N [1] (= *dissimilarity*) diferencia *f* (**between** entre); **I see no ~ between them** no veo diferencia alguna entre ellos; **a car with a ~** un coche diferente *or* especial; **that makes all the ~** eso cambia totalmente la cosa; **it makes no ~** da igual, da lo mismo; **it makes no ~ to me** me da igual *or* lo mismo; **it will make no ~ to us** nos dará igual *or* lo mismo, no nos afectará en lo más mínimo; **what ~ does it make?** ¿qué más da?; **it makes a lot of ~** importa mucho; *see also* **split C2**
[2] (*between numbers, amounts*) diferencia *f*; **I'll pay the ~** yo pagaré la diferencia
[3] (= *change*) **the ~ in her is amazing!** ¡cuánto ha cambiado!
[4] (*euph*) (= *quarrel*) riña *f*; **a ~ of opinion** un desacuerdo; *see also* **put aside, settle**

different ['dɪfrənt] ADJ [1] (= *not alike*) diferente, distinto; **the two brothers couldn't be more ~ from each other** los dos hermanos no podían ser más diferentes *or* distintos el uno del otro; **that's ~ to** *or* **from what I was told** eso es diferente de *or* a lo que me contaron, eso es distinto de *or* a lo que me contaron; **that's quite a ~ matter** eso es harina de otro costal; *see also* **chalk**
[2] (= *changed*) **I feel a ~ person** me siento otro
[3] (= *various*) varios, distintos; **~ people noticed it** varias *or* distintas personas lo vieron
[4] (*iro*) (= *distinctive*) distinto, original; **"what do you think of my new hairstyle?" — "well ... it's certainly ~"** —¿qué te parece mi nuevo peinado? —pues ... desde luego es algo distinto *or* original

differential [,dɪfə'renʃəl] Ⓐ ADJ [*rate*] diferencial
Ⓑ N [1] (*esp Brit Econ*) diferencial *m*; *see also* **wage**
[2] (*Math*) diferencial *f*
Ⓒ CPD ► **differential calculus** N cálculo *m* diferencial ► **differential equation** N ecuación *f* diferencial

differentiate [,dɪfə'renʃɪeɪt] Ⓐ VT [1] (*gen*) diferenciar, distinguir (**from** de); **to ~ A from B** (= *tell the difference*) distinguir A de B; (= *make the difference*) diferenciar A de B
[2] (*Math*) diferenciar
Ⓑ VI [1] (*gen*) distinguir (**between** entre)
[2] (*Bio*) diferenciarse

differentiation [,dɪfərenʃɪ'eɪʃən] N diferenciación *f*

differently ['dɪfrəntlɪ] ADV de modo distinto; **she wanted to do things ~** quería hacer las cosas de otro modo *or* de modo distinto

difficult ['dɪfɪkəlt] ADJ [1] (= *hard*) [*task, book, question*] difícil; [*writer*] complicado, complejo; **there's nothing ~ about it** no es nada difícil; **it is ~ to describe the feeling** es difícil describir la sensación; **these dogs are ~ to control** estos perros son difíciles de controlar; **many youngsters find it ~ to get work** a muchos jóvenes les resulta difícil encontrar trabajo; **it was ~ for him to leave her** le resultó difícil dejarla; **she is determined to make life ~ for him** está decidida a hacerle la vida imposible; **to put sb in a ~ position** poner a algn en una posición comprometida; **she is determined to make things ~ for him** está decidida a hacerle la vida imposible; **this is a ~ time for us** son tiempos difíciles para nosotros; → EASY, DIFFICULT, IMPOSSIBLE
[2] (= *awkward*) [*person, child, character*] difícil; **why are you always trying to be ~?** ¿por qué siempre estás intentando crear problemas?

difficulty ['dɪfɪkəltɪ] N [1] (= *hardness*) dificultad *f*; **to have ~ (in) doing sth** tener dificultades para hacer algo, resultarle difícil a algn

➤ LANGUAGE IN USE: **difference 1** 5.3, 26.3 **different 1** 5.3

hacer algo; **he has ~ (in) walking** tiene dificultades para andar, le resulta difícil andar; **I had no ~ finding the house** no tuve problemas para encontrar la casa, no me resultó difícil encontrar la casa; **with ~** con dificultad; **with great ~** con gran dificultad; **with the greatest ~** a duras penas

[2] (= *problem*) problema *m*, dificultad *f*; **to get into ~** *or* **difficulties** [*person*] (*gen*) meterse en problemas *or* apuros; (*while swimming*) empezar a tener problemas; [*ship*] empezar a peligrar; **to have difficulties with sth** tener problemas con algo; **to be in difficulties** *or* **~** estar teniendo problemas; **they are in financial difficulties** tienen problemas económicos, están pasando dificultades económicas; **to make difficulties for sb** crear problemas a algn; *see also* **learning, run into**

diffidence [ˈdɪfɪdəns] N inseguridad *f*, falta *f* de confianza en sí mismo

diffident [ˈdɪfɪdənt] ADJ inseguro, cohibido

diffidently [ˈdɪfɪdəntlɪ] ADV tímidamente, de forma insegura

diffract [dɪˈfrækt] Ⓐ VT difractar
Ⓑ VI difractarse

diffraction [dɪˈfrækʃən] N difracción *f*

diffuse Ⓐ [dɪˈfjuːs] ADJ (= *spread out*) [*light*] difuso; (= *long-winded*) [*style, writer*] difuso, prolijo
Ⓑ [dɪˈfjuːz] VT [+ *light*] difundir; [+ *heat*] difundir, esparcir; [+ *information, ideas*] difundir
Ⓒ [dɪˈfjuːz] VI [*heat, gas*] difundirse, esparcirse

diffused [dɪˈfjuːzd] ADJ difuso

diffuseness [dɪˈfjuːsnɪs] N [*of style, writer*] prolijidad *f*

diffusion [dɪˈfjuːʒən] N [*of light, heat, information, ideas*] difusión *f*

dig [dɪg] (*vb: pt, pp* **dug**) Ⓐ N [1] (*Archeol*) excavación *f*
[2] (= *prod*) (*gen*) empujón *m*; (*with elbow*) codazo *m*
[3] (*) (= *taunt*) indirecta *f*, pulla *f*; **to have a ~ at sb** lanzar una indirecta *or* una pulla a algn
Ⓑ VT [1] [+ *hole*] [*person*] cavar, excavar; [*machine*] excavar; [*animal*] cavar, escarbar; **✦IDIOM to ~ one's own grave** cavar su propia tumba
[2] (= *break up*) [+ *ground*] remover
[3] (= *cultivate*) [+ *garden*] cultivar, cavar en
[4] (= *add*) [+ *fertilizer, compost*] meter (**into** en), añadir (**into** a)
[5] (= *extract*) [+ *coal*] extraer, sacar
[6] (= *thrust*) **to ~ sth into sth** clavar algo en algo, hundir algo en algo
[7] (= *prod*) empujar; (*with elbow*) dar un codazo a; **to ~ sb in the ribs** dar a algn un codazo en las costillas
[8] (*esp US*†*) (= *enjoy*) **I don't ~ jazz** no me gusta el jazz, el jazz no me dice nada; **I really ~ that** eso me chifla*; **~ this!** ¡mira esto!
Ⓒ VI [1] [*person*] (*gen*) cavar; (*Archeol, Tech*) excavar; [*dog, pig*] escarbar; **to ~ for gold** excavar en busca de oro
[2] (= *search*) ahondar; **to ~ deeper into a subject** ahondar *or* profundizar en un tema; **he dug into his pockets for a coin** hurgó en los bolsillos para buscar una moneda; **✦IDIOM to ~ deep into one's pocket** rascarse el bolsillo

►**dig in** Ⓐ VI + ADV [1] (*) (= *eat*) meter mano a la comida; **~ in!** ¡a comer!
[2] (*also* **~ o.s. in**) (*Mil*) atrincherarse; (*fig*) (*in negotiations, argument*) atrincherarse en su postura
Ⓑ VT + ADV [1] (= *add*) [+ *fertilizer, compost*] añadir al suelo
[2] (= *thrust*) [+ *nails, claws, knife*] clavar, hundir; **✦IDIOM to ~ in one's heels** mantenerse en sus trece, empecinarse
[3] (*Mil*) **his troops are now well dug in** sus tropas se hallan ahora bien atrincheradas

►**dig into** VI + PREP [1] (= *use up*) [*reserves*] consumir, usar; **I had to ~ into my savings to pay for it** tuve que recurrir a *or* echar mano de mis ahorros para pagarlo
[2] (= *investigate*) [+ *sb's past*] remover, hurgar en
[3] (*) (= *start*) [+ *food*] hincar el diente a, atacar; **to ~ into a meal** hincar el diente a una comida

►**dig out** VT + ADV [1] [+ *buried object*] (*gen*) desenterrar, sacar; (*from rubble*) sacar (de entre los escombros)
[2] (= *extract*) [+ *thorn in flesh*] extraer, quitar
[3] (= *search out*) buscar

►**dig over** VT + ADV [+ *earth*] remover; [+ *garden*] remover la tierra de

►**dig up** VT + ADV [1] [+ *potatoes*] sacar; [+ *weeds*] arrancar; [+ *plant*] desarraigar; [+ *flowerbed*] cavar en, remover la tierra de; [+ *roadway*] levantar; [+ *grave*] abrir; [+ *treasure, body, artifacts*] desenterrar
[2] [+ *information*] desenterrar, sacar a la luz; *see also* **dirt, past**

digest Ⓐ [daɪˈdʒest] VT [1] [+ *food*] digerir; **easy to ~** fácil de digerir
[2] (= *assimilate*) [+ *information, news*] asimilar, digerir
[3] (= *summarize*) resumir
Ⓑ [daɪˈdʒest] VI digerir
Ⓒ [ˈdaɪdʒest] N [1] (= *summary*) resumen *m*
[2] (= *journal*) boletín *m*
[3] (*Jur*) digesto *m*, recopilación *f* de leyes

digestible [dɪˈdʒestəbl] ADJ [1] [*food*] digerible; **easily ~** fácil de digerir
[2] (= *understandable*) [*information*] asimilable, fácil de digerir; **he presents the information in an easily ~ form** presenta la información de un modo fácil de digerir *or* fácilmente asimilable

digestion [dɪˈdʒestʃən] N digestión *f*

digestive [dɪˈdʒestɪv] Ⓐ ADJ digestivo
Ⓑ N (*also* **~ biscuit**) galleta *f* dulce integral, bizcocho *m* (*LAm*)
Ⓒ CPD ► **digestive juices** NPL jugos *mpl* digestivos, jugos *mpl* gástricos ► **digestive system** N aparato *m* digestivo ► **digestive tract** N tubo *m* digestivo

digger [ˈdɪgəʳ] N [1] (= *machine*) excavadora *f*; (= *person*) (*Archeol*) excavador(a) *m/f*
[2] (*) (= *Australian*) australiano/a *m/f*; *see also* **ditch**

digging [ˈdɪgɪŋ] N [1] (*with spade, of hole*) **Helen always did the ~** Helen era la que siempre cavaba
[2] (*Min*) excavación *f*
[3] **diggings** (*Min, Archeol*) excavaciones *fpl*

digit [ˈdɪdʒɪt] N [1] (*Math*) dígito *m*, cifra *f*
[2] (= *finger, toe*) dedo *m*

digital [ˈdɪdʒɪtəl] Ⓐ ADJ [*watch, display, recording*] digital
Ⓑ CPD ► **digital camera** N cámara *f* digital ► **digital radio** N radio *f* digital ► **digital television** N televisión *f* digital

digitalis [ˌdɪdʒɪˈteɪlɪs] N digital *f*

digitally [ˈdɪdʒɪtlɪ] ADV [*scan, record, store*] digitalmente; **~ remastered** [*sound recording*] reprocesado digitalmente

digitize [ˈdɪdʒɪtaɪz] VT digitalizar

digitizer [ˈdɪdʒɪtaɪzəʳ] N digitalizador *m*

diglossia [daɪˈglɒsɪə] N diglosia *f*

dignified [ˈdɪgnɪfaɪd] ADJ [*person*] de aspecto solemne, de aspecto digno; [*manner, air*] solemne, digno; [*bearing*] solemne, majestuoso; [*silence*] decoroso; **it's not ~ to do that** no es elegante hacer eso

dignify [ˈdɪgnɪfaɪ] VT [1] (= *exalt*) dignificar
[2] (= *lend credence to*) (*gen*) honrar, otorgar reconocimiento a; (*with title*) dar un título altisonante a; **I see no point in ~ing this speculation with a comment** me parece que estas especulaciones no son siquiera dignas de comentario

dignitary [ˈdɪgnɪtərɪ] N dignatario/a *m/f*

dignity [ˈdɪgnɪtɪ] N [1] (= *self-esteem*) dignidad *f*; **that would be beneath my ~** no me rebajaría a eso; **✦IDIOM to stand on one's ~** ponerse en su lugar
[2] (= *solemnity*) [*of occasion*] solemnidad *f*
[3] (= *respectability*) [*of work, labour*] dignidad *f*, honorabilidad *f*

digress [daɪˈgres] VI hacer una digresión; (*pej*) divagar; **to ~ from the subject** apartarse del tema; **but I ~** (*often hum*) pero me estoy apartando del tema

digression [daɪˈgreʃən] N digresión *f*

digressive [daɪˈgresɪv] ADJ que se aparta del tema principal

digs* [dɪgz] NPL (*Brit*) alojamiento *msing*; **to be in ~** estar alojado, vivir en una pensión, estar de patrona*†

dike [daɪk] N = **dyke**

diktat [dɪkˈtɑːt] N dictado *m*, imposición *f*

dilapidated [dɪˈlæpɪdeɪtɪd] ADJ [*building*] desmoronado, ruinoso; [*vehicle*] desvencijado

dilapidation [dɪˌlæpɪˈdeɪʃən] N [*of building*] estado *m* ruinoso

dilate [daɪˈleɪt] Ⓐ VI [1] [*veins, pupils, cervix*] dilatarse
[2] (*frm*) (= *expatiate*) **to ~ (up)on sth** explayarse sobre algo
Ⓑ VT dilatar; **her pupils were ~d** tenía las pupilas dilatadas

dilation [daɪˈleɪʃən] N dilatación *f*; **~ and curettage** (*Med*) raspado *m*, legrado *m*

dilatoriness [ˈdɪlətərɪnɪs] N (*frm*) tardanza *f*, demora *f*

dilatory [ˈdɪlətərɪ] ADJ (*frm*) [*person*] lento, tardo; [*tactics*] dilatorio; **to be ~ in replying** tardar mucho en contestar

dildo [ˈdɪldəʊ] N consolador *m*

dilemma [daɪˈlemə] N dilema *m*; **to be in a ~** estar en *or* tener un dilema; *see also* **horn**

dilettante [ˌdɪlɪˈtæntɪ] N (*pl* **dilettantes** *or* **dilettanti** [ˌdɪlɪˈtæntɪ]) diletante *mf*

dilettantism [ˌdɪləˈtæntɪzəm] N diletantismo *m*

diligence [ˈdɪlɪdʒəns] N diligencia *f*

diligent [ˈdɪlɪdʒənt] ADJ [*person*] diligente; [*work, search*] concienzudo

diligently [ˈdɪlɪdʒəntlɪ] ADV diligentemente

dill [dɪl] Ⓐ N eneldo *m*
Ⓑ CPD ► **dill pickle** N (*US*) pepinillos *mpl* en vinagre al eneldo

dilly* [ˈdɪlɪ] N (*US*) **she's a ~** (= *girl*) está muy bien*; **it's a ~** (= *problem*) es un rompecabezas

dilly-dally* [ˈdɪlɪdælɪ] VI [1] (= *loiter*) entretenerse, demorarse
[2] (= *hesitate*) andarse con titubeos

dilly-dallying [ˈdɪlɪdælɪɪŋ] N [1] (= *loitering*) pérdida *f* de tiempo
[2] (= *hesitation*) vacilación *f*, titubeo *m*

dilute [daɪˈluːt] Ⓐ VT [1] [+ *fruit juice, flavour*] diluir; **"~ to taste"** (*in instructions*) "diluya a su gusto"
[2] (*fig*) [+ *power*] debilitar; [+ *effect*] reducir
Ⓑ ADJ diluido

dilution [daɪˈluːʃən] N 1 [*of substance, flavour*] disolución *f*, dilución *f* (*frm*)
2 (*fig*) [*of power*] debilitamiento *m*; [*of effectiveness*] reducción *f*

dim [dɪm] Ⓐ ADJ (*compar* **dimmer**; *superl* **dimmest**) 1 (= *not bright*) [*light*] débil, tenue; [*room*] oscuro, poco iluminado; **she read the letter by the ~ light of a torch** leyó la carta con la ayuda de la débil *or* tenue luz de una linterna; **even in the ~ light the furniture looked dirty** incluso con la poca luz que había los muebles parecían sucios; **her eyes were ~ with tears** sus ojos estaban nublados por las lágrimas; **to grow ~** [*light*] atenuarse, ir atenuándose; [*room*] oscurecer, ir oscureciendo; **his eyes had grown ~ with age** (*liter*) su vista se había ido debilitando con la edad
2 (= *indistinct*) [*figure, shape, outline*] borroso; [*memory*] borroso, vago; **in the ~ and distant past** en un pasado muy remoto
3 (= *gloomy*) [*prospects*] poco prometedor; **to take a ~ view of sth*** ver algo con malos ojos
4 (*) (= *unintelligent*) corto, lerdo*; **he's a bit ~** es un poco corto, no tiene muchas luces
Ⓑ VT 1 (= *make less bright*) [+ *light*] bajar, atenuar; [+ *room*] oscurecer; [+ *colours*] apagar; [+ *metals*] deslucir, deslustrar; [+ *eyesight*] debilitar; **to ~ the lights** (*in room, theatre*) bajar *or* atenuar la luz; **to ~ one's (head)lights** poner las luces cortas *or* de cruce, poner las luces bajas (*LAm*); **she looked at him through eyes ~med by tears** lo miró con los ojos nublados por las lágrimas
2 (= *dampen, diminish*) [+ *hopes*] hacer perder, empañar (*liter*); [+ *senses*] debilitar; **the passing years had not ~med her beauty** el paso de los años no había marchitado su belleza; **to ~ sb's spirits** desanimar a algn, desalentar a algn
3 (= *fade*) [+ *outline, memory*] borrar
Ⓒ VI 1 (= *become less bright*) [*light*] atenuarse, ir atenuándose; [*metal*] deslucirse, ir desluciéndose; [*colour*] apagarse, ir apagándose; [*eyesight*] debilitarse, ir debilitándose
2 (= *diminish*) [*hopes*] ir perdiéndose, ir empañándose (*liter*); [*beauty*] marchitarse, ir marchitándose
3 (= *fade*) [*outline, memory*] hacerse borroso

dime [daɪm] (*US*) Ⓐ N (*Canada, US*) *moneda de diez centavos*; **they're a ~ a dozen** son muy baratos; (*fig*) los hay a montones*
Ⓑ CPD ► **dime novel** N novelucha *f* ► **dime store** N ≈ todo a cien *m* (*Sp*) (*tienda que vende mercadería barata*)

dimension [dɪˈmenʃən] N 1 (*Phys, Math*) dimensión *f*
2 **dimensions** (= *size, scope*) dimensiones *fpl*; **they did not realize the ~s of the problem** no se daban cuenta de las dimensiones *or* de la envergadura *or* del alcance del problema
3 (= *aspect*) dimensión *f*; **the human ~ of the tragedy** la dimensión humana de la tragedia

-dimensional [daɪˈmenʃənl] ADJ (*ending in compounds*) *see* **three-dimensional**, **two-dimensional**

diminish [dɪˈmɪnɪʃ] Ⓐ VT (*gen*) disminuir; [+ *numbers, speed, strength*] disminuir, reducir
Ⓑ VI (*gen*) disminuir

diminished [dɪˈmɪnɪʃt] Ⓐ ADJ [*value*] reducido; [*ability*] limitado; (*Mus*) [*interval*] disminuido; **a ~ staff** una plantilla reducida
Ⓑ CPD ► **diminished responsibility** N (*Jur*) responsabilidad *f* disminuida

diminishing [dɪˈmɪnɪʃɪŋ] ADJ [*number*] decreciente, cada vez menor; [*value, resources, funds*] cada vez menor, cada vez más reducido; [*strength*] cada vez menor; **the law of ~ returns** la ley de rendimiento decreciente

diminuendo [dɪˌmɪnjʊˈendəʊ] Ⓐ N (*Mus*) diminuendo *m*
Ⓑ VI hacer un diminuendo

diminution [ˌdɪmɪˈnjuːʃən] N (*frm*) disminución *f*

diminutive [dɪˈmɪnjʊtɪv] Ⓐ ADJ 1 (= *very small*) diminuto
2 (*Ling*) diminutivo
Ⓑ N (*Ling*) diminutivo *m*

dimly [ˈdɪmlɪ] ADV 1 [*shine, glow*] débilmente, tenuemente; **~ lit** poco iluminado, iluminado con una luz tenue
2 (= *vaguely*) [*remember, recollect*] vagamente; **I ~ remember ...** recuerdo vagamente ...; **I was ~ aware that ...** era vagamente consciente de que ...; **you could ~ make out the shape** apenas se entreveía la forma

dimmer [ˈdɪmər] Ⓐ N 1 (*on light switch*) regulador *m* de intensidad de luz
2 (*US Aut*) interruptor *m* de las luces cortas *or* de cruce, interruptor *m* de las luces bajas (*LAm*)
Ⓑ CPD ► **dimmer switch** N regulador *m* de intensidad de luz

dimming [ˈdɪmɪŋ] N [*of light*] oscurecimiento *m*; [*of reputation*] empañamiento *m*

dimness [ˈdɪmnɪs] N 1 [*of light*] lo tenue; [*of room*] penumbra *f*, la poca luz; [*of eyesight*] debilidad *f*
2 [*of figure, shape, outline*] lo borroso; [*of memory*] vaguedad *f*
3 [*of prospects*] lo poco prometedor
4 (*) (= *stupidity*) cortedad *f*, torpeza *f*

dimple [ˈdɪmpl] Ⓐ N 1 (*in chin, cheek*) hoyuelo *m*
2 (= *small depression*) hoyito *m*
Ⓑ VT [+ *hand, arm, thigh*] hacer hoyitos en; [+ *water*] rizar
Ⓒ VI [*water*] rizarse; **her cheeks ~d, she had a lovely smile** le salían hoyuelos en las mejillas, tenía una sonrisa preciosa

dimpled [ˈdɪmpld] ADJ [*cheek, chin*] con hoyuelo; [*hand, arm, thigh*] con hoyitos

dimwit* [ˈdɪmwɪt] N lerdo/a* *m/f*

dim-witted* [ˈdɪmˈwɪtɪd] ADJ lerdo*, corto de alcances

DIN [dɪn] N ABBR = **Deutsche Industrie Normen**

din [dɪn] Ⓐ N [*of traffic, roadworks*] estruendo *m*, estrépito *m*; [*of voices, music*] alboroto *m*, bulla* *f*
Ⓑ VT **to ~ sth into sb** inculcar algo a algn; **I had it ~ned into me as a child** me lo inculcaron desde niño
Ⓒ VI **his words still ~ned in my head** el eco de sus palabras aún resonaba en mi cabeza

dinar [ˈdiːnɑː] N dinar *m*

din-dins* [ˈdɪndɪns] NPL (*baby talk*) (= *mid-day meal*) comidita *f*; (= *evening meal*) cenita *f*

dine [daɪn] Ⓐ VI (*frm*) cenar; **to ~ on** *or* **off sth** cenar algo
Ⓑ VT *see* **wine**

►**dine in** VI + ADV cenar en casa

►**dine out** VI + ADV cenar fuera; **this was a story he could ~ out for months on** (*fig*) a esta historia le podía sacar muchísimo partido

diner [ˈdaɪnər] N 1 (= *person*) comensal *mf*
2 (*Rail*) coche *m* comedor, vagón *m* restaurante, buffet *m* (*Peru*)
3 (*US*) (= *eating place*) casa *f* de comidas, lonchería *f* (*LAm*); (= *transport café*) cafetería *f* de carretera

dinero* [dɪˈnɛərəʊ] N (*US*) guita* *f*, pasta *f* (*Sp**), plata *f* (*LAm**), lana *f* (*LAm**)

dinette [dɪˈnet] Ⓐ N pequeño comedorcito *m*; **kitchen-~** cocina-comedor *f*
Ⓑ CPD ► **dinette set** N (*US*) vajilla *f* de diario

ding-a-ling [ˌdɪŋəˈlɪŋ] N 1 [*of bell, telephone*] tilín *m*
2 (*US‡*) bobo/a* *m/f*

dingbat‡ [ˈdɪŋbæt] N gilipollas‡ *m*

ding-dong* [ˈdɪŋˈdɒŋ] Ⓐ N 1 (= *sound*) **~!** ¡din dan!, ¡din don!
2 (= *argument*) agarrada* *f*, bronca *f*
Ⓑ ADJ **a ~ battle** una batalla campal

dinghy [ˈdɪŋgɪ] N (= *rubber dinghy*) lancha *f* neumática; (= *sailing dinghy*) bote *m*

dinginess [ˈdɪndʒɪnɪs] N (= *shabbiness*) [*of furniture, decor*] lo deslucido, falta *f* de lustre; (= *gloominess*) [*of town, house, room*] lo sombrío, lobreguez *f*; (= *dirtiness*) suciedad *f*

dingo [ˈdɪŋgəʊ] N (*pl* **dingoes**) dingo *m*

dingy [ˈdɪndʒɪ] ADJ (*compar* **dingier**; *superl* **dingiest**) (= *shabby*) [*furniture, decor*] deslustrado, deslucido; (= *gloomy*) [*town, house, room*] sombrío, lóbrego; (= *dirty*) sucio

dining [ˈdaɪnɪŋ] CPD ► **dining car** N coche *m* comedor, vagón *m* restaurante ► **dining hall** N comedor *m*, refectorio *m* ► **dining room** N comedor *m* ► **dining table** N mesa *f* de comedor

dink‡ [dɪŋk] N (*US*) tontorrón(ona)‡ *m/f*

dinkie* [ˈdɪŋkɪ] N ABBR (= **double** *or* **dual income no kids**) *pareja sin hijos con dos sueldos*

dinky* [ˈdɪŋkɪ] ADJ (*Brit*) (*compar* **dinky**; *superl* **dinkiest**) (= *small*) pequeñito; (= *nice*) mono, precioso

▼**dinner** [ˈdɪnər] Ⓐ N (= *evening meal*) cena *f*; (= *lunch*) almuerzo *m*, comida *f*, lonche *m* (*Mex*); (= *banquet*) cena *f* de gala; **to have ~** (*in the evening*) cenar; (*at midday*) almorzar, comer; **can you come to ~?** ¿puedes venir a cenar?; **we're having people to ~** tenemos invitados para *or* a cenar; **to go out to ~** salir a cenar (fuera); **we sat down to ~ at 10.30** nos sentamos a cenar a las 10.30
Ⓑ CPD ► **dinner bell** N campana *f* de la cena ► **dinner dance** N cena *f* seguida de baile ► **dinner duty** N (*Scol*) supervisión *f* de comedor ► **dinner jacket** N esmoquin *m*, smoking *m* ► **dinner knife** N cuchillo *m* grande ► **dinner lady** N *empleada que da el servicio de comidas en las escuelas* ► **dinner party** N cena *f* (*con invitados*) ► **dinner plate** N plato *m* llano ► **dinner roll** N panecillo *m* ► **dinner service** N vajilla *f* ► **dinner table** N mesa *f* de comedor ► **dinner time** N hora *f* de cenar/comer ► **dinner trolley, dinner wagon** N carrito *m* de la comida; *see also* **school C**

dinosaur [ˈdaɪnəsɔːr] N 1 (= *reptile*) dinosaurio *m*
2 (= *old-fashioned person*) carcamal* *mf*; (= *old-fashioned organization*) reliquia *f* del pasado

dint[1] [dɪnt] N **by ~ of** a fuerza de

dint[2] [dɪnt] = **dent**

diocesan [daɪˈɒsɪsən] ADJ diocesano

diocese [ˈdaɪəsɪs] N diócesis *f inv*

diode [ˈdaɪəʊd] N diodo *m*

Dionysian [ˌdaɪəˈnɪzɪən] ADJ dionisiaco

Dionysius [ˌdaɪəˈnɪsɪəs] N Dionisio

diorama [daɪəˈrɑːmə] N diorama *m*

dioxide [daɪˈɒksaɪd] N dióxido *m*; *see also* **carbon B**, **sulphur B**

dioxin [daɪˈɒksɪn] N dioxina *f*

➤ LANGUAGE IN USE: **dinner A** 25.2, 25.3

DIP [dɪp] N ABBR (*Comput*) = **Dual-In-Line Package**

dip [dɪp] Ⓐ N 1 (= *swim*) baño *m*, chapuzón *m*, zambullida *f* (*LAm*); **to go for a ~** ir a darse un baño *or* un chapuzón
2 (= *slope*) declive *m*, pendiente *f*; (= *hollow*) hondonada *f*, depresión *f*
3 (*Geol*) [*of rock strata, fault*] inclinación *f*; **angle of ~** buzamiento *m*, angulo *m* de inclinación; **magnetic ~** inclinación *f* (magnética)
4 (*Culin*) salsa *f* (*para mojar*)
5 (*Agr*) (*for sheep, poultry*) baño *m* de desinfección; *see* **lucky B**
Ⓑ VT 1 (= *thrust*) (*into liquid*) sumergir, bañar (**in, into** en); [+ *pen*] mojar (**in, into** en); [+ *hand*] (*into bag*) meter (**in, into** en); [+ *ladle, scoop*] meter (**in, into** en); [+ *sheep*] bañar con desinfectante
2 (= *lower*) [+ *flag*] bajar, saludar con; (*Aer*) [+ *wings*] saludar con; **to ~ one's (head)lights** (*Brit*) poner las luces cortas *or* de cruce, poner las luces bajas (*LAm*); **~ped headlights** luces *fpl* cortas *or* de cruce, luces *fpl* bajas (*LAm*)
Ⓒ VI 1 (= *slope down*) [*road*] bajar en pendiente; [*land*] formar una hondonada
2 (= *move down*) [*bird, plane*] bajar en picado; [*temperature*] bajar; [*sun*] esconderse; **the sun ~ped below the hill** el sol se escondió tras la colina
3 (= *draw on*) **to ~ into one's savings** (*fig*) echar mano de los ahorros
4 (= *read superficially*) **to ~ into a book** hojear un libro
Ⓓ CPD ► **dip switch** N (*Aut*) interruptor *m* de las luces cortas *or* de cruce, interruptor *m* de las luces bajas (*LAm*)

Dip. ABBR = **Diploma**

Dip Ed [dɪp'ɛd] N ABBR (*Brit Univ*) (= **Diploma in Education**) *título de magisterio*

diphtheria [dɪf'θɪərɪə] N difteria *f*

diphthong ['dɪfθɒŋ] N diptongo *m*

diphthongize ['dɪfθɒŋaɪz] Ⓐ VT diptongar
Ⓑ VI diptongarse

diploma [dɪ'pləʊmə] N diploma *m*

diplomacy [dɪ'pləʊməsɪ] N 1 (*Pol*) diplomacia *f*
2 (= *tact*) diplomacia *f*

diplomat ['dɪpləmæt] N diplomático/a *m/f*

diplomatic [ˌdɪplə'mætɪk] Ⓐ ADJ 1 (*Pol*) diplomático
2 (= *tactful*) diplomático
Ⓑ CPD ► **diplomatic bag** N valija *f* diplomática ► **diplomatic corps** N cuerpo *m* diplomático ► **diplomatic immunity** N inmunidad *f* diplomática ► **diplomatic pouch** N (*US*) = **diplomatic bag** ► **diplomatic relations** NPL **to break off ~ relations** romper las relaciones diplomáticas ► **diplomatic service** N servicio *m* diplomático

diplomatically [ˌdɪplə'mætɪkəlɪ] ADV [*say, act*] diplomáticamente; [*isolated*] desde el punto de vista diplomático

diplomatist [dɪ'pləʊmətɪst] N diplomático/a *m/f*

dipole ['daɪˌpəʊl] N 1 (*Elec*) dipolo *m*
2 (*TV, Rad*) (*also* **~ aerial**) antena *f* dipolar, dipolar *f*

dipper[1] ['dɪpə^r] N (*Orn*) mirlo *m* acuático

dipper[2] ['dɪpə^r] N **big ~** (*at fair*) montaña *f* rusa; **the Big Dipper** (*US Astron*) la Osa Mayor

dipper[3] ['dɪpə^r] N (*Culin*) cazo *m*, cucharón *m*

dipping ['dɪpɪŋ] N (*Agr*) baño *m* de desinfección

dippy* ['dɪpɪ] ADJ chiflado*

dipso* ['dɪpsəʊ] N = **dipsomaniac**

➤ LANGUAGE IN USE: **directory** 27

dipsomania [ˌdɪpsəʊ'meɪnɪə] N dipsomanía *f*

dipsomaniac [ˌdɪpsəʊ'meɪnɪæk] N dipsomaníaco/a *m/f*, dipsómano/a *m/f*

dipstick ['dɪpstɪk] N 1 (*Aut*) varilla *f* del aceite, cala *f*
2 (**) (= *fool*) capullo *m* (*Sp***), gilipollas *mf inv* (*Sp***)

diptych ['dɪptɪk] N díptico *m*

dir. ABBR (= **director**) Dir., Dtor(a).

dire [daɪə^r] ADJ (*superl* **direst**) 1 (= *terrible*) [*event, consequences, results*] nefasto, funesto; [*situation*] desesperado; [*warning, prediction*] alarmante; [*poverty*] extremo; **to be in ~ need of sth** necesitar algo desesperadamente; **to be in ~ straits** estar en un serio aprieto *or* apuro
2 (*) (= *awful*) [*film, book*] pésimo, malísimo

direct [daɪ'rekt] Ⓐ ADJ 1 (= *without detour*) [*route, train, flight*] directo
2 (= *immediate*) [*cause, result*] directo; [*contact, control, responsibility, descendant*] directo; **"keep away from ~ heat"** "no exponer directamente al calor"; **to make a ~ hit** dar en el blanco; **he's the ~ opposite** es exactamente el contrario
3 (= *straightforward, not evasive*) [*answer, refusal*] claro, inequívoco; [*manner, character*] abierto, franco
Ⓑ ADV 1 (= *straight*) [*go, fly, pay*] directamente; **we fly ~ to Santiago** volamos directo *or* directamente a Santiago
2 (= *frankly*) con franqueza, sin rodeos
Ⓒ VT 1 (= *aim*) [+ *remark, gaze, attention*] dirigir (**at, to** a)
2 (= *give directions to*) **can you ~ me to the station?** ¿me puede indicar cómo llegar a la estación?
3 (= *control*) [+ *traffic, play, film*] dirigir
4 (= *instruct*) **to ~ sb to do sth** mandar a algn hacer algo; **to ~ that …** mandar que …
Ⓓ CPD ► **direct access** N (*Comput*) acceso *m* directo ► **direct action** N acción *f* directa ► **direct advertising** N publicidad *f* directa ► **direct cost** N costo *m* directo ► **direct current** N (*Elec*) corriente *f* continua ► **direct debit** N pago *m* a la orden ► **direct debiting** N domiciliación *f* (de pagos) ► **direct dialling** N servicio *m* (telefónico) automático, discado *m* directo (*LAm*) ► **direct free kick** N golpe *m* libre directo ► **direct grant school** N (*Brit*†) escuela *f* subvencionada ► **direct mail** N publicidad *f* por correo, correspondencia *f* directa ► **direct mail shot** N (*Brit*) campaña *f* publicitaria por correo, mailing *m* ► **direct marketing** N márketing *m* directo ► **direct object** N (*Gram*) complemento *m* directo ► **direct rule** N gobierno *m* directo ► **direct selling** N ventas *fpl* directas ► **direct speech** N (*Ling*) estilo *m* directo ► **direct tax** N impuesto *m* directo ► **direct taxation** N tributación *f* directa

direction [dɪ'rekʃən] Ⓐ N 1 (= *course*) dirección *f*; **in the ~ of** hacia, en dirección a; **sense of ~** sentido *m* de la orientación; **in the opposite ~** en sentido contrario; **in all ~s** por todos lados; **they ran off in different ~s** salieron corriendo cada uno por su lado
2 (*fig*) (= *purpose*) orientación *f*; (= *control*) mando *m*; [*of play, film*] dirección *f*
3 **directions** (= *instructions*) (*for use*) instrucciones *fpl*; (*to a place*) señas *fpl*; **~s for use** modo *m* de empleo, instrucciones *fpl* de uso
Ⓑ CPD ► **direction finder** N radiogoniómetro *m* ► **direction indicator** N (*Aut*) intermitente *m*

directional [dɪ'rekʃənl] ADJ direccional; **~ aerial** antena *f* dirigida; **~ light** (*Aut*) intermitente *m*

directionless [dɪ'rekʃənlɪs] ADJ [*activity*] sin dirección, que no conduce a ninguna parte; **to be/feel ~** andar/sentirse sin rumbo ni dirección

directive [dɪ'rektɪv] N directiva *f*

directly [dɪ'rektlɪ] Ⓐ ADV 1 (= *exactly*) justo; **~ above/below sth/sb** justo encima de/debajo de algo/algn; **~ opposite sth/sb** justo enfrente de algo/algn; **the sun was ~ overhead** el sol caía de pleno
2 (= *straight*) [*go, fly, look, pay*] directamente; **my salary is paid ~ into my account** me ingresan el sueldo directamente en mi cuenta; **he was looking ~ at me when he said it** me estaba mirando directamente a la cara cuando lo dijo
3 (= *personally*) [*affect*] directamente; **this decision doesn't affect us ~** esta decisión no nos afecta directamente; **I hold you ~ responsible for this!** ¡te considero el responsable directo de esto!
4 (= *immediately*) inmediatamente; **~ after/before sth** inmediatamente después de/antes de algo; **the two murders are not ~ related** *or* **linked** los dos asesinatos no están directamente relacionados; **to be ~ descended from sb** descender directamente de algn, descender de algn por línea directa
5 (= *shortly*) enseguida, de inmediato; **she will be here ~** vendrá enseguida *or* de inmediato
6 (= *frankly*) [*speak, explain*] con franqueza
Ⓑ CONJ (*esp Brit*) (= *as soon as*) en cuanto; **~ he heard the door close he picked up the telephone** en cuanto oyó cerrarse la puerta cogió el teléfono; **~ you hear it, …** en cuanto lo oigas, …

directness [daɪ'rektnɪs] N [*of person, speech, reply*] franqueza *f*

director [dɪ'rektə^r] N [*of company*] directivo/a *m/f*; (*on board of directors*) miembro *mf* del consejo de administración, consejero/a *m/f*; [*of institution, department*] (*also Theat, Cine, Rad, TV*) director(a) *m/f*; **~'s cut** (*Cine*) versión *f* íntegra; **~ general** director(a) *m/f* general; **Director of Public Prosecutions** (*Brit*) ≈ Fiscal *mf* General del Estado; *see also* **board D, executive C, funeral B, managing, music B**

directorate [daɪ'rektərɪt] N 1 (= *post*) dirección *f*, cargo *m* de director
2 (= *body*) junta *f* directiva, consejo *m* de administración

directorial [daɪrek'tɔːrɪəl] ADJ [*talent, experience*] como director; [*career, work*] de director; **to make one's ~ debut** debutar como director

directorship [dɪ'rektəʃɪp] N (= *post*) dirección *f*, cargo *m* de director; (= *term as director*) gerencia *f*, periodo *m* de gestión

➤ **directory** [dɪ'rektərɪ] Ⓐ N (*also* **telephone ~**) guía *f* (telefónica); (= *street directory*) callejero *m*, guía *f* de calles; (= *trade directory*) directorio *m* de comercio; (*Comput*) directorio *m*
Ⓑ CPD ► **directory assistance** N (*US*) información *f* (telefónica) ► **directory enquiries** N (*Brit*) = **directory assistance**

dirge [dɜːdʒ] N canto *m* fúnebre, endecha *f*

dirigible ['dɪrɪdʒəbl] Ⓐ ADJ dirigible
Ⓑ N dirigible *m*

dirk [dɜːk] N (*Scot*) puñal *m*

dirndl ['dɜːndl] N falda *f* acampanada

dirt [dɜːt] Ⓐ N 1 (= *unclean matter*) suciedad *f*; (= *piece of dirt*) suciedad *f*, mugre *f*; **to treat**

sb like ~* tratar a algn como si fuese basura, tratar a patadas a algn; **✦IDIOM to dig up ~ on sb** sacar los trapos sucios de algn
2 (= *earth*) tierra *f*; (= *mud*) barro *m*, lodo *m*
3 (*) (= *obscenity*) porquerías *fpl*, cochinadas* *fpl*; **this book is nothing but ~** este libro está lleno de porquerías *or* cochinadas*
Ⓑ CPD ► **dirt farmer*** N (*US*) pequeño granjero *m* (sin obreros) ► **dirt road** N (*US*) camino *m* de tierra ► **dirt track** N (*Sport*) pista *f* de ceniza; (= *road*) camino *m* de tierra

dirt-cheap* [ˈdɜːtˈtʃiːp] ADJ tirado de precio*, baratísimo, regalado

dirtily [ˈdɜːtɪlɪ] ADV 1 (= *not cleanly*) [*eat, drink*] sin modales; **they live ~** viven rodeados de suciedad
2 (= *indecently*) [*laugh, smile*] lascivamente
3 (= *unfairly*) [*act, behave*] de una forma traicionera; **to play ~** [*footballer*] jugar sucio; **to fight ~** [*boxer*] no luchar limpiamente

dirtiness [ˈdɜːtɪnɪs] N suciedad *f*

dirty [ˈdɜːtɪ] Ⓐ ADJ (*compar* **dirtier**; *superl* **dirtiest**) 1 (= *unclean*) [*hands, clothes, dishes*] sucio; **your hands are ~** tienes las manos sucias; **to get (o.s.) ~** ensuciarse; **to get sth ~** ensuciar algo; **to get one's hands ~** ensuciarse *or* mancharse las manos; **his ~ habits get on my nerves** tiene unas costumbres asquerosas que me sacan de quicio; **cleaning the cooker is a ~ job** limpiar la cocina es un trabajo muy sucio; **there was a ~ mark on his shirt** tenía una mancha en la camisa; **✦IDIOM to wash one's ~ linen in public** sacar los trapos sucios a relucir; *see also* **nappy A**
2 (= *dull*) [*grey, white*] sucio; **the sky was a ~ grey** el cielo tenía un color gris sucio
3 (= *nasty*) [*weather*] horrible, feo; [*night*] horrible
4 (= *indecent*) [*story, joke*] verde, colorado (*Mex*); [*book*] cochino*, de guarrerías (*Sp**); [*magazine, film*] porno*; [*laugh*] lascivo; **to have a ~ mind** tener una mente pervertida, tener una mente guarra (*Sp**); **~ old man** viejo *m* verde; **~ weekend** (*Brit* hum*) fin *m* de semana de lujuria (*hum*); **to go on a ~ weekend (with sb)** ir a pasar un fin de semana de lujuria (con algn); **~ word** palabrota *f*, lisura *f* (*Andes, S. Cone*); **communism has become almost a ~ word** "comunismo" se ha convertido casi en una palabrota
5 (*) (= *underhand*) sucio; **~ business** negocio *m* sucio; **~ money** dinero *m* sucio; **~ play** (*Sport*) juego *m* sucio; **there are some ~ players in the team** algunos de los miembros del equipo juegan sucio; **~ pool** (*US**) juego *m* sucio; **a ~ trick** una mala pasada, una jugarreta*; **to play a ~ trick on sb** jugar una mala pasada a algn, hacer una jugarreta a algn*; **~ tricks** chanchullos *mpl*; **~ tricks department** *sección de actividades secretas para desacreditar al contrario*; **~ war** guerra *f* sucia; **to do sb's ~ work: he always gets other people to do his ~ work** siempre consigue que los demás le hagan el trabajo sucio
6 (*) (= *despicable*) asqueroso*, de mierda**; **you're a ~ liar‡** eres un cerdo mentiroso‡, eres un mentiroso de mierda**; **you ~ rat!‡** ¡canalla!‡, ¡cerdo!‡
7 (*) (= *angry*) **to give sb a ~ look** echar una mirada asesina a algn*
Ⓑ ADV 1 (*Sport*) (= *unfairly*) **to fight ~** [*boxer*] no luchar limpiamente; **to play ~** [*footballer*] jugar sucio
2 (= *indecently*) **to talk ~** decir cochinadas*, decir guarrerías (*Sp**)
3 (‡) **~ great: a ~ great dog/lorry/hole** un perrazo/camionazo/agujerazo*; **his ~ great hands** sus manazas*, sus manotas*
Ⓒ VT ensuciar; **don't ~ your clothes** no te ensucies la ropa
Ⓓ N **to do the ~ on sb** (*Brit**) jugar una mala pasada a algn, hacer una jugarreta a algn*
Ⓔ CPD ► **dirty bomb** N bomba *f* sucia

dirty-minded [ˌdɜːtɪˈmaɪndɪd] ADJ con la mente sucia

disability [ˌdɪsəˈbɪlɪtɪ] Ⓐ N 1 (= *state*) invalidez *f*, discapacidad *f*, minusvalía *f*; (= *injury, illness, condition*) discapacidad *f*, minusvalía *f*; **people with a ~** los discapacitados, los minusválidos
2 (*fig*) desventaja *f*
Ⓑ CPD ► **disability allowance** N (*permanent*) subsidio *m* por incapacidad laboral permanente; (*temporary*) subsidio *m* por incapacidad laboral transitoria ► **disability pension** N pensión *f* de invalidez

disable [dɪsˈeɪbl] VT 1 (= *cripple*) [+ *person*] dejar inválido
2 (= *make unfit for use*) [+ *tank, gun, device*] inutilizar
3 (= *disqualify*) incapacitar, inhabilitar (**for** para)

disabled [dɪsˈeɪbld] Ⓐ ADJ [*person*] minusválido, discapacitado
Ⓑ NPL **the ~** los discapacitados, los minusválidos

disablement [dɪsˈeɪblmənt] N 1 (= *state*) invalidez *f*, discapacidad *f*, minusvalía *f*
2 [*of tank, gun, device*] inutilización *f*

disabuse [ˌdɪsəˈbjuːz] VT desengañar (**of** de); **I was rapidly ~d of this notion** pronto me desengañé de esta idea, pronto salí del error

disadvantage [ˌdɪsədˈvɑːntɪdʒ] Ⓐ N desventaja *f*, inconveniente *m*; **to sb's ~** perjudicial para algn; **to the ~ of** en perjuicio *or* detrimento de; **to be at a ~** estar en desventaja, estar en una situación desventajosa; **this put him at a ~** esto lo dejó en situación desventajosa
Ⓑ VT perjudicar

disadvantaged [ˌdɪsədˈvɑːntɪdʒd] Ⓐ ADJ [*person*] perjudicado; **she comes from a ~ background** proviene de un entorno desfavorecido Ⓑ NPL **the ~** los desfavorecidos, los marginados

disadvantageous [ˌdɪsædvɑːnˈteɪdʒəs] ADJ (= *unfavourable*) [*circumstances*] desventajoso

disaffected [ˌdɪsəˈfektɪd] ADJ desafecto (**towards** hacia)

disaffection [ˌdɪsəˈfekʃən] N descontento *m*, desafección *f*

disaffiliate [ˌdɪsəˈfɪlɪeɪt] VI desafiliarse (**from** de)

▼**disagree** [ˌdɪsəˈgriː] VI 1 (= *have different opinion*) no estar de acuerdo, estar en desacuerdo; **to ~ with sb (on** *or* **about sth)** no estar de acuerdo *or* estar en desacuerdo con algn (sobre algo); **I ~ with you** no estoy de acuerdo contigo, no comparto tu opinión
2 (= *not approve*) **I ~ with bullfighting** yo no apruebo los toros, no me gustan los toros
3 (= *quarrel*) reñir, discutir (**with** con)
4 (= *not coincide*) [*accounts, versions*] diferir, no cuadrar (**with** con); **their findings ~** sus conclusiones difieren
5 (= *make unwell*) **to ~ with sb** [*climate, food*] sentar mal a algn; **onions ~ with me** las cebollas me sientan mal

disagreeable [ˌdɪsəˈgriːəbl] ADJ 1 (= *unpleasant*) [*experience, task*] desagradable; **she was very ~ to us** nos trató con bastante aspereza
2 (= *bad-tempered*) [*person*] desagradable, antipático; [*tone of voice*] malhumorado, áspero; **he's rather ~ in the mornings** por la mañana suele estar de bastante mal humor

disagreeableness [ˌdɪsəˈgriːəblnɪs] N [*of task, experience*] desagrado *m*; [*of person*] antipatía *f*

disagreeably [ˌdɪsəˈgriːəblɪ] ADV [*say*] con aspereza, de mala manera; **a ~ pungent taste** un sabor agrio de lo más desagradable

▼**disagreement** [ˌdɪsəˈgriːmənt] N 1 (*with opinion*) desacuerdo *m*, disconformidad *f*; **the talks ended in ~** no se alcanzó un acuerdo *or* no hubo acuerdo en las conversaciones
2 (= *quarrel*) riña *f*, discusión *f*
3 (*between accounts, versions*) discrepancia *f* (**with** con)

disallow [ˈdɪsəˈlaʊ] VT 1 [+ *claim*] rechazar
2 (*Ftbl*) [+ *goal*] anular
3 (*Jur*) [+ *evidence*] desestimar, rechazar; [+ *conviction*] anular, invalidar

disambiguate [ˌdɪsæmˈbɪgjʊeɪt] VT [+ *term, phrase*] desambiguar

disambiguation [ˌdɪsæmbɪgjʊˈeɪʃən] N desambiguación *f*

disappear [ˌdɪsəˈpɪəʳ] Ⓐ VI desaparecer; **he ~ed from sight** *or* **view** desapareció de la vista; **to make sth ~** hacer desaparecer algo
Ⓑ VT (*) hacer desaparecer

disappearance [ˌdɪsəˈpɪərəns] N desaparición *f*

disappeared [ˌdɪsəˈpɪəd] NPL (*Pol*) **the ~** los desaparecidos

disappoint [ˌdɪsəˈpɔɪnt] Ⓐ VT [+ *person*] defraudar, decepcionar, desilusionar; [+ *hopes, ambitions*] defraudar; **her daughter ~ed her** su hija la defraudó *or* decepcionó; **the course ~ed her** el curso la defraudó *or* decepcionó *or* desilusionó; **she has been ~ed in love** el amor la ha defraudado *or* decepcionado
Ⓑ VI decepcionar

▼**disappointed** [ˌdɪsəˈpɔɪntɪd] ADJ [*person*] decepcionado, desilusionado; [*hopes*] frustrado; **she'll be terribly ~ when she hears the news** se llevará una gran decepción *or* una desilusión muy grande cuando se entere de la noticia; **she's ~ about** *or* **at having to give up her career** siente mucho tener que dejar su carrera; **to be ~ by sth** estar decepcionado por algo; **I'm ~ in you** me has defraudado, me has decepcionado; **she gave me a ~ look** me miró decepcionada, me dirigió una mirada de decepción; **I was ~ that my mother was not there** me sentí defraudada porque mi madre no estaba allí, me decepcionó (el) que mi madre no estuviera allí; **to be ~ to see/learn sth** quedar decepcionado *or* defraudado al ver/enterarse de algo; **we were ~ not to see her** sentimos mucho no verla; **to be ~ with sth** estar decepcionado con algo; **they are ~ with the result** están decepcionados con el resultado, el resultado los ha decepcionado; **if you see him on stage you won't be ~** si lo ves actuar no te defraudará *or* decepcionará

disappointing [ˌdɪsəˈpɔɪntɪŋ] ADJ decepcionante; **it's ~ that nobody wants to help** es decepcionante que nadie quiera ayudar; **the film/hotel was very ~** la película/el hotel fue una decepción; **how ~!** ¡qué decepción!, ¡qué desilusión!

disappointingly [ˌdɪsəˈpɔɪntɪŋlɪ] ADV [*react, lose*] de manera decepcionante; **the boat performed ~ in the race** el barco tuvo una actuación decepcionante en la regata; **progress is ~ slow** el progreso es tan lento que resulta decepcionante; **~, nothing happened** lamentablemente, no pasó nada, lo decepcionante fue que no pasó nada

➤ LANGUAGE IN USE: **disagree 1** 12.1 **disagreement 1** 12.1 **disappointed** 14

disappointment [ˌdɪsəˈpɔɪntmənt] N 1 (= *feeling*) decepción *f*, desilusión *f*; **to our ~** para nuestra decepción, para nuestra gran desilusión; **reserve your place now to avoid ~** haga ahora su reserva para no llevarse una desilusión
2 (= *cause of regret*) **he is a big ~ to us** nos ha decepcionado muchísimo; **the holiday was such a ~!** ¡las vacaciones fueron una decepción tan grande!, ¡las vacaciones fueron tan decepcionantes!; **~s in love** desengaños *mpl* amorosos

disapproval [ˌdɪsəˈpruːvəl] N desaprobación *f*; **she pursed her lips in ~** frunció los labios en un gesto de desaprobación

disapprove [ˌdɪsəˈpruːv] VI **to ~ of sth** estar en contra de algo, desaprobar algo; **to ~ of sb** mirar mal a algn, no mirar con buenos ojos a algn; **her father ~d of me** su padre me miraba mal *or* no me miraba con buenos ojos; **I think he ~s of me** creo que no me mira con buenos ojos, creo que me tiene poca simpatía; **he ~s of gambling** está en contra del juego, desaprueba la práctica del juego; **I strongly ~** yo estoy firmemente en contra; **I wanted to go but father ~d** yo quería ir pero papá no quiso permitirlo; **your mother would ~** tu madre estaría en contra *or* lo desaprobaría

disapproving [ˌdɪsəˈpruːvɪŋ] ADJ [*look, glance*] de desaprobación

disapprovingly [ˌdɪsəˈpruːvɪŋlɪ] ADV [*look, frown*] con desaprobación; **he shook his head ~** hizo un gesto de desaprobación con la cabeza

disarm [dɪsˈɑːm] Ⓐ VT 1 (*Mil*) [+ *troops, attacker*] desarmar
2 (= *deactivate*) [+ *bomb*] desactivar
3 (= *conciliate*) [+ *opponent*] desarmar
4 (= *render ineffective*) [+ *criticism*] echar por tierra, desbaratar; [+ *opposition*] desbaratar
Ⓑ VI (*Mil*) desarmarse

disarmament [dɪsˈɑːməmənt] N desarme *m*; **nuclear ~** desarme *m* nuclear

disarmer [dɪsˈɑːməʳ] N partidario/a *m/f* del desarme

disarming [dɪsˈɑːmɪŋ] ADJ [*smile*] que desarma, encantador; [*modesty*] que desarma; [*frankness*] apabullante

disarmingly [dɪsˈɑːmɪŋlɪ] ADV [*smile*] encantadoramente; [*frank*] apabullantemente; **he was ~ modest** era tan modesto que (te) desarmaba

disarrange [ˌdɪsəˈreɪndʒ] VT desarreglar, descomponer

disarranged [ˌdɪsəˈreɪndʒd] ADJ [*bed*] deshecho; [*hair*] despeinado; [*clothes*] desarreglado

disarray [ˌdɪsəˈreɪ] N (*frm*) [*of house, flat*] desorden *m*; [*of clothes*] desaliño *m*; [*of institution, economy, government*] desorganización *f*; **to be in ~** [*house, flat*] estar totalmente desordenado; [*clothes*] estar muy desarreglado *or* desaliñado; [*thoughts*] estar en desorden; [*institution, economy, government*] estar sumido en el caos, estar totalmente desorganizado; **the troops fled in ~** las tropas huyeron a la desbandada; **this threw our plans into ~** esto dio al traste con nuestros planes

disassemble [ˌdɪsəˈsembl] Ⓐ VT desmontar, desarmar
Ⓑ VI desmontarse, desarmarse

disassociate [ˌdɪsəˈsəʊʃɪˌeɪt] = **dissociate**

disaster [dɪˈzɑːstəʳ] Ⓐ N 1 (= *catastrophe*) desastre *m*; *see also* **court B2**, **strike B2**
2 (= *inept person*) desastre *m*
Ⓑ CPD ► **disaster area** N zona *f* catastrófica, zona *f* de desastre; **he's a walking ~ area** (*hum*) es un puro desastre ► **disaster fund** N fondo *m* de ayuda para casos de desastre

disastrous [dɪˈzɑːstrəs] ADJ 1 (= *catastrophic*) [*decision, reforms*] desastroso, catastrófico; [*earthquake, flood*] catastrófico; **that would be ~!** ¡eso sería una catástrofe!; **with ~ consequences** con consecuencias desastrosas *or* nefastas
2 (*) (= *unsuccessful*) [*marriage, cake, novel*] desastroso; **his first movie was ~** su primera película fue desastrosa *or* un desastre

disastrously [dɪˈzɑːstrəslɪ] ADV 1 (= *catastrophically*) desastrosamente; **the race started ~ for Smith** la carrera tuvo un comienzo desastroso para Smith; **to go ~ wrong** salir terriblemente mal
2 (*) (= *atrociously*) pésimamente; **we performed ~** actuamos pésimamente, tuvimos una actuación horrorosa

disavow [ˌdɪsəˈvaʊ] VT 1 (= *reject*) [+ *one's principles, religion*] abdicar de, abjurar de; [+ *one's past*] renegar de
2 (= *deny*) **they ~ed any knowledge of his activities** negaban tener conocimiento de sus actividades

disavowal [ˌdɪsəˈvaʊəl] N 1 (= *rejection*) abdicación *f*
2 (= *denial*) desmentido *m*

disband [dɪsˈbænd] Ⓐ VT [+ *army*] licenciar; [+ *organization*] disolver
Ⓑ VI disolverse

disbar [dɪsˈbɑːʳ] VT [+ *barrister*] inhabilitar para el ejercicio de la abogacía, prohibir ejercer; **he was ~red** le prohibieron ejercer la abogacía

disbarment [dɪsˈbɑːmənt] N inhabilitación *f* (*para el ejercicio de la abogacía*)

disbelief [ˌdɪsbəˈliːf] N incredulidad *f*; **in ~** con incredulidad

disbelieve [ˌdɪsbəˈliːv] Ⓐ VT [+ *person*] no creer a; [+ *story*] no creer
Ⓑ VI (*esp Rel*) no creer (**in** en)

disbeliever [ˌdɪsbəˈliːvəʳ] N incrédulo/a *m/f*; (*Rel*) descreído/a *m/f*

disbelieving [ˌdɪsbɪˈliːvɪŋ] ADJ incrédulo

disburden [dɪsˈbɜːdn] (*frm*) VT descargar; **to ~ o.s. of** descargarse de

disburse [dɪsˈbɜːs] VT (*frm*) desembolsar

disbursement [dɪsˈbɜːsmənt] N (*frm*) desembolso *m*

disc, disk (*US*) [dɪsk] Ⓐ N (*gen, Anat*) disco *m*; (= *identity disc*) chapa *f*; (*Comput*) = **disk**; *see also* **slip C4**
Ⓑ CPD ► **disc brakes** NPL (*Aut*) frenos *mpl* de disco ► **disc jockey** N discjockey *mf*, pinchadiscos* *mf inv*

disc. ABBR (*Comm*) = **discount**

discard Ⓐ [dɪsˈkɑːd] VT [+ *unwanted thing*] deshacerse de; [+ *idea, plan*] desechar, descartar; [+ *clothing*] desembarazarse de; [+ *habit*] renunciar a; (*Cards*) descartarse de; [+ *person*] desembarazarse de
Ⓑ [dɪsˈkɑːd] VI (*Cards*) descartarse
Ⓒ [ˈdɪskɑːd] N (*Cards*) descarte *m*; (= *unwanted thing*) desecho *m*

discern [dɪˈsɜːn] VT 1 (= *see*) distinguir
2 (= *taste, smell*) distinguir, apreciar
3 (= *detect*) [+ *problem, mistake*] localizar; [+ *sb's intentions*] discernir; **two major trends may be ~ed** se pueden distinguir dos tendencias fundamentales

discernible [dɪˈsɜːnəbl] ADJ 1 (= *perceptible*) [*difference*] perceptible, apreciable; [*effect*] apreciable; **for no ~ reason** sin un motivo aparente
2 (= *visible*) distinguible

discernibly [dɪˈsɜːnəblɪ] ADV [*affected*] visiblemente; [*different*] sensiblemente, notablemente

discerning [dɪˈsɜːnɪŋ] ADJ [*person*] entendido; [*eye*] experto; **~ taste** muy buen gusto *m*

discernment [dɪˈsɜːnmənt] N (= *good judgment*) discernimiento *m*; (= *good taste*) buen gusto *m*

discharge Ⓐ [ˈdɪstʃɑːdʒ] N 1 [*of cargo*] descarga *f*; [*of gun*] descarga *f*, disparo *m*
2 (= *release*) [*of patient*] alta *f*; [*of prisoner*] liberación *f*, puesta *f* en libertad; [*of bankrupt*] rehabilitación *f*; **he got his ~** (*Mil*) lo licenciaron
3 (= *dismissal*) [*of worker*] despido *m*; (*Mil*) baja *f*
4 (= *emission*) (*Elec*) descarga *f*; [*of liquid, waste*] vertido *m*; [*of gas, chemicals*] emisión *f*; (*Med*) (*from wound*) secreción *f*, supuración *f*; (*from vagina*) flujo *m* vaginal
5 (= *completion*) [*of duty*] ejercicio *m*, cumplimiento *m*
Ⓑ [dɪsˈtʃɑːdʒ] VT 1 (= *unload*) [+ *ship, cargo*] descargar
2 (= *fire*) [+ *gun*] descargar, disparar; [+ *shot*] hacer; [+ *arrow*] disparar
3 (= *release*) [+ *patient*] dar de alta, dar el alta a; [+ *prisoner*] liberar, poner en libertad; [+ *bankrupt*] rehabilitar; **they ~d him from hospital on Monday** le dieron de *or* el alta el lunes
4 (= *dismiss*) [+ *employee*] despedir; [+ *soldier*] dar de baja del ejército
5 (= *emit*) [+ *liquid, waste*] verter; [+ *gas, chemicals*] emitir; (*Med*) [+ *pus*] segregar, supurar
6 (= *settle*) [+ *debt*] saldar
7 (= *complete*) [+ *task, duty*] cumplir
Ⓒ [dɪsˈtʃɑːdʒ] VI [*river*] desembocar (**into** en); [*battery*] decargarse; [*wound, sore*] supurar

disci [ˈdɪskaɪ] NPL *of* **discus**

disciple [dɪˈsaɪpl] N (*Rel*) discípulo/a *m/f*; (*fig*) discípulo/a *m/f*, seguidor(a) *m/f*

disciplinarian [ˌdɪsɪplɪˈnɛərɪən] N **he was a strict ~** imponía una férrea disciplina (en el cumplimiento de las normas)

disciplinary [ˈdɪsɪplɪnərɪ] ADJ [*committee, hearing*] disciplinario; **~ action** *or* **measure** medida *f* disciplinaria; **~ procedures** procedimiento *m* disciplinario

discipline [ˈdɪsɪplɪn] Ⓐ N 1 (= *obedience*) disciplina *f*; (= *punishment*) castigo *m*; (= *self-control*) autodisciplina *f*; **to keep** *or* **maintain ~** mantener la disciplina
2 (= *field of study*) disciplina *f*
Ⓑ VT 1 (= *punish*) [+ *pupil, soldier*] castigar; [+ *employee*] sancionar
2 (= *control*) [+ *child*] disciplinar; [+ *one's mind*] adiestrar; **to ~ o.s. (to do sth)** disciplinarse (para hacer algo)

disciplined [ˈdɪsɪplɪnd] ADJ [*person, approach*] disciplinado

disclaim [dɪsˈkleɪm] VT [+ *statement*] desmentir, negar; [+ *responsibility*] negar; (*Jur*) renunciar a; **he ~ed all knowledge of it** dijo que no sabía nada en absoluto de ello

disclaimer [dɪsˈkleɪməʳ] N (*Jur*) [*of a right*] renuncia *f*; (= *denial*) (*to newspaper etc*) desmentido *m*; **to issue a ~** declarar descargo *or* limitación de responsabilidad

disclose [dɪsˈkləʊz] VT revelar

disclosure [dɪsˈkləʊʒəʳ] N revelación *f*

disco [ˈdɪskəʊ] Ⓐ ABBR (= **discotheque**) disco *f*, discoteca *f*
Ⓑ CPD ► **disco dancing** N baile *m* de música disco ► **disco music** N música *f* disco

discography [dɪsˈkɒgrəfɪ] N discografía *f*

discolour, **discolor** (*US*) [dɪsˈkʌləʳ] Ⓐ VT (= *fade*) de(s)colorar; (= *stain*) manchar
Ⓑ VI (= *lose colour*) de(s)colorarse; (= *run*) desteñir

discolouration, **discoloration** (*US*) [dɪs,kʌləˈreɪʃən] N (= *fading*) de(s)coloramiento *m*; (= *staining*) mancha *f*

discoloured, **discolored** (*US*) [dɪsˈkʌləd] ADJ (= *faded*) de(s)colorado; (= *stained*) manchado

discombobulate [ˌdɪskəmˈbɒbjʊˌleɪt] VT (*esp US*) [+ *person, plans*] dislocar

discomfit [dɪsˈkʌmfɪt] VT desconcertar

discomfiture [dɪsˈkʌmfɪtʃəʳ] N (*frm*) desconcierto *m*, turbación *f*

discomfort [dɪsˈkʌmfət] N (= *lack of comfort*) incomodidad *f*; (= *uneasiness*) incomodidad *f*, turbación *f*; (*physical*) molestia *f*, malestar *m*; **the injury gave him some ~** la herida le causaba molestia

discomposure [ˌdɪskəmˈpəʊʒəʳ] N (*frm*) desconcierto *m*, confusión *f*

disconcert [ˌdɪskənˈsɜːt] VT desconcertar

disconcerting [ˌdɪskənˈsɜːtɪŋ] ADJ desconcertante

disconcertingly [ˌdɪskənˈsɜːtɪŋlɪ] ADV de modo desconcertante; **he spoke in a ~ frank way** desconcertó a todos hablando con tanta franqueza

disconnect [ˌdɪskəˈnekt] VT 1 (*gen*) desconectar
2 (*Telec*) **I've been ~ed** (*for non-payment*) me han cortado el teléfono *or* la línea (por no pagar); (*in mid-conversation*) se ha cortado

disconnected [ˌdɪskəˈnektɪd] ADJ (*fig*) inconexo

disconnection [ˌdɪskəˈnekʃən] N desconexión *f*, corte *m* (*de línea/suministro*)

disconsolate [dɪsˈkɒnsəlɪt] ADJ desconsolado

disconsolately [dɪsˈkɒnsəlɪtlɪ] ADV desconsoladamente

discontent [ˌdɪskənˈtent] N descontento *m*, malestar *m*

discontented [ˌdɪskənˈtentɪd] ADJ descontento (**with, about** con)

discontentment [ˌdɪskənˈtentmənt] N descontento *m*

discontinuance [ˌdɪskɒnˈtɪnjʊəns] N = **discontinuation**

discontinuation [ˌdɪskənˌtɪnjʊˈeɪʃən] N (*frm*) [*of practice*] abandono *m*; [*of production*] suspensión *f*, interrupción *f*

discontinue [ˌdɪskənˈtɪnjuː] VT [+ *production, payment*] suspender; [+ *practice*] abandonar; (*Comm*) [+ *product*] dejar de fabricar; (*Med*) [+ *treatment*] interrumpir, suspender; **"discontinued"** (*Comm*) "fin de serie"

discontinuity [ˌdɪskɒntɪˈnjuːɪtɪ] N (= *lack of continuity*) discontinuidad *f*; (= *interruption*) interrupción *f*

discontinuous [ˌdɪskənˈtɪnjʊəs] ADJ (= *interrupted*) interrumpido; (*Math*) [*curve*] discontinuo

discord [ˈdɪskɔːd] N 1 (= *quarrelling*) discordia *f*; **to sow ~ among** sembrar la discordia entre, sembrar cizaña entre
2 (*Mus*) disonancia *f*

discordant [dɪsˈkɔːdənt] ADJ [*ideas, opinions*] discorde, opuesto; [*sound*] disonante

discotheque [ˈdɪskəʊtek] N discoteca *f*

▼**discount** Ⓐ [ˈdɪskaʊnt] N (*gen*) descuento *m*, rebaja *f*; **to give a 10% ~** dar un descuento del 10%; **to sell (sth) at a ~** vender (algo) con descuento *or* a precio reducido
Ⓑ [dɪsˈkaʊnt] VT 1 (= *lower price of*) [+ *merchandise*] descontar, rebajar; **~ed cash flow** cashflow *m* actualizado
2 (= *disregard*) [+ *report, rumour*] descartar
Ⓒ [ˈdɪskaʊnt] CPD ► **discount house** N (*US*) tienda *f* de rebajas ► **discount price** N **they are available at ~ prices** se venden con descuento ► **discount rate** N tasa *f* de descuento ► **discount store** N (*US*) economato *m*

discourage [dɪsˈkʌrɪdʒ] VT 1 (= *dishearten*) desanimar, desalentar; **to get** *or* **become ~d** desanimarse, desalentarse
2 (= *deter*) [+ *offer, advances*] rechazar; [+ *tendency, relationship*] oponerse a; **smoking is ~d** se recomienda no fumar
3 (= *dissuade*) **to ~ sb from doing sth** disuadir a algn de hacer algo; **I don't want to ~ you, but …** no pretendo disuadirte *or* desanimarte, pero …

discouragement [dɪsˈkʌrɪdʒmənt] N 1 (= *depression*) desánimo *m*, desaliento *m*
2 (= *dissuasion*) disuasión *f*
3 (= *deterrent*) impedimento *m*; **it's a real ~ to progress** es un verdadero impedimento para el progreso

discouraging [dɪsˈkʌrɪdʒɪŋ] ADJ desalentador; **he was ~ about it** habló de ello en tono pesimista

discourse Ⓐ [ˈdɪskɔːs] N 1 (= *talk*) conversación *f*, plática *f* (*LAm*)
2 (= *essay*) tratado *m*
3 (*Ling*) discurso *m*
Ⓑ [dɪsˈkɔːs] VI **to ~ (up)on sth** disertar sobre algo
Ⓒ [ˈdɪskɔːs] CPD ► **discourse analysis** N análisis *m inv* del discurso

discourteous [dɪsˈkɜːtɪəs] ADJ descortés

discourteously [dɪsˈkɜːtɪəslɪ] ADV descortésmente

discourtesy [dɪsˈkɜːtɪsɪ] N descortesía *f*

discover [dɪsˈkʌvəʳ] VT 1 [+ *new country, species, talent*] descubrir; [+ *object*] (*after search*) encontrar, hallar
2 (= *notice*) [+ *loss, mistake*] darse cuenta de; **I ~ed that I'd left it at home** me di cuenta de que lo había dejado en casa

discoverer [dɪsˈkʌvərəʳ] N descubridor(a) *m/f*

discovery [dɪsˈkʌvərɪ] N 1 (= *finding*) [*of new country, drug, talent*] descubrimiento *m*
2 (= *thing or person found*) descubrimiento *m*

discredit [dɪsˈkredɪt] Ⓐ N (= *dishonour*) descrédito *m*, deshonor *m*; **it was to the general's ~ that …** fue un descrédito para el general que …; **to bring ~ (up)on sth/sb** desacreditar algo/a algn, suponer un descrédito para algo/algn
Ⓑ VT 1 (= *prove untrue*) [+ *theory*] rebatir, refutar; **that theory is now ~ed** esa teoría ya ha sido rebatida *or* refutada
2 (= *cast doubt upon*) poner en duda; **all his evidence is thus ~ed** por lo tanto se pone en duda todo su testimonio
3 (= *sully reputation of*) [+ *family*] deshonrar, desacreditar; [+ *organization, profession*] desacreditar

discreditable [dɪsˈkredɪtəbl] ADJ deshonroso, vergonzoso

discreet [dɪsˈkriːt] ADJ [*person, inquiry, decor, uniform*] discreto; **at a ~ distance** a una distancia prudencial

discreetly [dɪsˈkriːtlɪ] ADV [*speak, behave, leave, dress*] discretamente, con discreción

discrepancy [dɪsˈkrepənsɪ] N discrepancia *f* (**between** entre)

discrete [dɪsˈkriːt] ADJ [*stages, phases, events*] específico, separado

discretion [dɪsˈkreʃən] N 1 (= *tact*) discreción *f*; ✦**PROV ~ is the better part of valour** una retirada a tiempo es una victoria
2 (= *judgment*) criterio *m*, juicio *m*; **use your own ~** usa tu propio criterio *or* juicio; **I will leave it to your ~** te lo dejaré a tu criterio *or* juicio; **at the ~ of the judge** a discreción *or* a criterio del juez; **the age of ~** (la edad de) la madurez

discretionary [dɪsˈkreʃənərɪ] ADJ discrecional

discriminate [dɪsˈkrɪmɪneɪt] Ⓐ VI 1 (= *distinguish*) distinguir (**between** entre)
2 (= *show prejudice*) **to ~ against sb** discriminar a algn; **to ~ in favour of sb** hacer discriminaciones en favor de algn
3 (= *show good judgment*) tener buen criterio
Ⓑ VT distinguir (**from** de)

discriminating [dɪsˈkrɪmɪneɪtɪŋ] ADJ [*person*] entendido; [*taste*] refinado

discrimination [dɪsˌkrɪmɪˈneɪʃən] N 1 (= *prejudice*) discriminación *f* (**against** de, contra; **in favour of** a favor de); **racial/sexual ~** discriminación *f* racial/sexual
2 (= *good judgment*) buen criterio *m*, discernimiento *m*

discriminatory [dɪsˈkrɪmɪnətərɪ] ADJ [*duty etc*] discriminatorio

discursive [dɪsˈkɜːsɪv] ADJ divagador, prolijo; (*Ling, Philos*) discursivo

discus [ˈdɪskəs] N (*pl* **discuses** *or* **disci**) (*Sport*) 1 (= *object*) disco *m*; **to throw the ~** lanzar el disco
2 (= *event*) **she won a gold medal in the ~** ganó la medalla de oro en la prueba de disco

▼**discuss** [dɪsˈkʌs] VT 1 (= *talk about*) [+ *topic*] hablar de, discutir; [+ *person*] hablar de; [+ *problem, essay*] cambiar opiniones sobre, discutir
2 (*in exam question*) [+ *statement*] tratar, analizar

discussant [dɪsˈkʌsənt] N (*US*) miembro *mf* de la mesa (de la sección de un congreso)

discussion [dɪsˈkʌʃən] Ⓐ N discusión *f*; **we had a long ~ about it** hablamos largo y tendido de ello, tuvimos una larga discusión sobre ello; **to come up for ~** someterse a discusión; **it is under ~** se está discutiendo
Ⓑ CPD ► **discussion document** N proposición *f* (para el debate) ► **discussion group** N coloquio *m* ► **discussion paper** N = **discussion document**

disdain [dɪsˈdeɪn] Ⓐ N desdén *m*, desprecio *m*
Ⓑ VT **to ~ sth** desdeñar *or* despreciar algo; **to ~ to do sth** no dignarse (a) hacer algo

disdainful [dɪsˈdeɪnfʊl] ADJ [*look, expression, attitude*] desdeñoso, de desdén; **to be ~ of sth** desdeñar *or* despreciar algo, mostrar desdén *or* desprecio hacia algo; **to be ~ towards** *or* **of sb** desdeñar *or* despreciar a algn, mostrar desdén *or* desprecio hacia algn

disdainfully [dɪsˈdeɪnfəlɪ] ADV desdeñosamente, con desdén

disease [dɪˈziːz] N enfermedad *f*; (*fig*) mal *m*, enfermedad *f*

diseased [dɪˈziːzd] ADJ [*person, animal, plant*] enfermo; [*tissue*] dañado, afectado; [*mind*] enfermo, morboso

disembark [ˌdɪsɪmˈbɑːk] VT, VI desembarcar

disembarkation [ˌdɪsembɑːˈkeɪʃən] N [*of goods*] desembarque *m*; [*of persons*] desembarco *m*

disembodied [ˌdɪsɪmˈbɒdɪd] ADJ incorpóreo

disembowel [ˌdɪsɪmˈbaʊəl] VT desentrañar, destripar

disempower [ˌdɪsɪmˈpaʊəʳ] VT restar autoridad a, despojar de sus derechos a

➤ LANGUAGE IN USE: discount A 20.1 discuss 1 26.1

disenchanted [ˌdɪsɪnˈtʃɑːntɪd] ADJ desencantado, desilusionado; **to be ~ with sth/sb** estar desencantado *or* desilusionado con algo/algn; **to become ~ with sth/sb** quedar desencantado *or* desilusionado con algo/algn

disenchantment [ˌdɪsɪnˈtʃɑːntmənt] N desencanto *m*, desilusión *f*

disenfranchise [ˌdɪsɪnˈfræntʃaɪz] VT privar del derecho de voto

disengage [ˌdɪsɪnˈɡeɪdʒ] Ⓐ VT [1] (= *free*) soltar; **she gently ~d her hand (from his)** soltó su mano (de la de él) con suavidad
[2] (*Mil*) [+ *troops*] retirar
[3] (*Mech*) desacoplar, desconectar; **to ~ the clutch** desembragar, soltar el embrague
Ⓑ VI [1] (*Mil*) retirarse
[2] (*Fencing*) separarse

disengaged [ˌdɪsɪnˈɡeɪdʒd] ADJ libre, desocupado

disengagement [ˌdɪsɪnˈɡeɪdʒmənt] N [1] (*Mil*) retirada *f*
[2] (*Mech*) desacoplamiento *m*, desconexión *f*

disentangle [ˌdɪsɪnˈtæŋɡl] VT [1] [+ *string, hair*] desenredar, desenmarañar (**from** de); **to ~ o.s. from** (*fig*) desenredarse de
[2] (*fig*) [+ *problem, mystery*] desentrañar, esclarecer

disequilibrium [ˌdɪsiːkwɪˈlɪbrɪəm] N desequilibrio *m*

disestablish [ˌdɪsɪsˈtæblɪʃ] VT [*church*] separar del Estado

disestablishment [ˌdɪsɪsˈtæblɪʃmənt] N [*of church*] separación *f* del Estado

disfavour, **disfavor** (*US*) [dɪsˈfeɪvəʳ] N [1] (= *disapproval*) desaprobación *f*; **to fall into ~** [*custom, practice*] caer en desuso; [*person*] caer en desgracia; **to look with ~ on sth** ver algo con malos ojos, desaprobar algo
[2] (= *disservice*) **to do sb a ~** ◊ **do a ~ to sb** hacer un flaco favor a algn, no hacer ningún favor a algn

disfigure [dɪsˈfɪɡəʳ] VT [+ *face, body*] desfigurar; [+ *area*] afear

disfigured [dɪsˈfɪɡəd] ADJ desfigurado

disfigurement [dɪsˈfɪɡəmənt] N [*of face, body*] desfiguración *f*; [*of area*] afeamiento *m*

disfranchise [ˈdɪsˈfræntʃaɪz] VT = **disenfranchise**

disgorge [dɪsˈɡɔːdʒ] VT [1] [+ *food*] [*person, animal*] vomitar, arrojar; [*bird*] desembuchar
[2] [+ *contents, passengers*] **the coaches were disgorging hordes of tourists** de los autocares manaban hordas de turistas; **the ship ~d its cargo of oil into the sea** el barco derramó su cargamento de petróleo en el mar

disgrace [dɪsˈɡreɪs] Ⓐ N [1] (= *state of shame*) deshonra *f*, ignominia *f*; **there is no ~ in being poor** no es ninguna deshonra ser pobre; **to be in ~** [*adult*] estar totalmente desacreditado, haber caído en desgracia; [*pet, child*] estar castigado; **she was sent home in ~** la mandaron a casa castigada; **to bring ~ on** deshonrar
[2] (= *shameful thing*) vergüenza *f*; **it's a ~** es una vergüenza; **you're a ~!** ¡lo tuyo es una vergüenza!; **to be a ~ to the school/family** ser una deshonra para la escuela/la familia
[3] (= *downfall*) caída *f*
Ⓑ VT [+ *family, country*] deshonrar; **he ~d himself** se deshonró; **he was ~d and banished** lo destituyeron de su cargo y lo desterraron

disgraceful [dɪsˈɡreɪsfʊl] ADJ vergonzoso; [*behaviour*] escandaloso; **disgraceful!** ¡qué vergüenza!

disgracefully [dɪsˈɡreɪsfəlɪ] ADV vergonzosamente; [*behave*] escandalosamente

disgruntled [dɪsˈɡrʌntld] ADJ (= *unhappy*) [*employee, staff, customer*] descontento; (= *bad-tempered*) contrariado, malhumorado

disguise [dɪsˈɡaɪz] Ⓐ N disfraz *m*; **to be in ~** estar disfrazado
Ⓑ VT [+ *person*] disfrazar (**as** de); [+ *voice*] simular, cambiar; [+ *feelings*] ocultar, disimular; [+ *bad points, error*] ocultar; **to ~ o.s. as** disfrazarse de; **she ~d herself as a man** se disfrazó de hombre

disgust [dɪsˈɡʌst] Ⓐ N [1] (= *revulsion*) repugnancia *f*, asco *m*; **it fills me with ~** me da asco
[2] (= *anger*) indignación *f*; **she left in ~** se marchó indignada
Ⓑ VT dar asco a, repugnar; **the thought ~s me** la idea me repugna; **you ~ me** me das asco

disgusted [dɪsˈɡʌstɪd] ADJ [*viewer, reader, customer*] indignado; [*tone, voice*] de indignación; **I am ~ at the way we were treated** estoy indignado por la manera en que nos trataron; **he was ~ by his failure** estaba muy enojado consigo mismo por su fracaso; **I am ~ with you** estoy indignado contigo

disgustedly [dɪsˈɡʌstɪdlɪ] ADV (= *with revulsion*) con asco; (= *angrily*) con indignación; **... he said ~** ... dijo indignado

disgusting [dɪsˈɡʌstɪŋ] ADJ [1] (= *revolting*) [*habit, taste, smell, food, place*] asqueroso, repugnante; [*person*] repugnante; **you're ~** me das asco, eres repugnante; **the kitchen is in a ~ mess** la cocina está que da asco, la cocina está asquerosa; **how ~!** ¡qué asco!; **it looks ~** tiene una pinta asquerosa; **it smells ~** tiene un olor asqueroso *or* repugnante, huele que da asco; **it tastes ~** tiene un sabor asqueroso *or* repugnante
[2] (= *obscene*) [*book, film, photo*] repugnante, asqueroso; [*language*] indecente, cochino*
[3] (= *disgraceful*) [*attitude, behaviour, manners*] vergonzoso; **she returned the book in a ~ condition** devolvió el libro en un estado vergonzoso
[4] (*) (= *terrible*) [*weather*] asqueroso, de perros*

disgustingly [dɪsˈɡʌstɪŋlɪ] ADV asquerosamente; **it was ~ dirty** estaba asquerosamente sucio, estaba tan sucio que daba asco; **they are ~ rich** son tan ricos que da asco

dish [dɪʃ] Ⓐ N [1] (= *plate*) plato *m*; (= *serving dish*) fuente *f*; (= *food*) plato *m*, platillo *m* (*Mex*); **to wash** *or* **do the ~es** fregar los platos; **a typical Spanish ~** un plato típico español
[2] (*TV*) antena *f* parabólica; (*Astron*) reflector *m*
[3] (*) (= *girl, boy*) bombón* *m*
Ⓑ VT [+ *hopes, chances*] desbaratar
Ⓒ CPD ► **dish aerial** (*Brit*), **dish antenna** (*US*) N antena *f* parabólica ► **dish soap** N (*US*) lavavajillas *m inv*

►**dish out** VT + ADV [+ *food*] servir; [+ *money*] repartir; [+ *advice*] dar, impartir; [+ *punishment*] infligir, impartir; [+ *criticism*] hacer

►**dish up** Ⓐ VT + ADV [1] (= *serve*) [+ *food*] servir
[2] (= *present*) ofrecer; **he ~ed up the same old arguments** repitió los argumentos de siempre
Ⓑ VI + ADV servir

dishabille [ˌdɪsæˈbiːl] N desnudez *f*

disharmony [ˈdɪsˈhɑːmənɪ] N discordia *f*; (*Mus*) disonancia *f*

dishcloth [ˈdɪʃklɒθ] N (*pl* **dishcloths** [ˈdɪʃklɒðz]) (*for washing*) bayeta *f*; (*for drying*) paño *m* (de cocina), trapo *m*

dishearten [dɪsˈhɑːtn] VT desalentar, desanimar; **don't be ~ed!** ¡ánimo!, ¡no te desanimes!

disheartening [dɪsˈhɑːtnɪŋ] ADJ desalentador

dishevelled, **disheveled** (*US*) [dɪˈʃevəld] ADJ [*hair*] despeinado; [*clothes*] desarreglado, desaliñado

dishmop [ˈdɪʃmɒp] N fregona *f* para lavar los platos

dishonest [dɪsˈɒnɪst] ADJ [*person*] poco honrado, deshonesto; [*means, plan*] fraudulento, deshonesto

dishonestly [dɪsˈɒnɪstlɪ] ADV fraudulentamente, deshonestamente; **to act ~** obrar con poca honradez *or* de forma poco honrada

dishonesty [dɪsˈɒnɪstɪ] N [*of person*] falta *f* de honradez, deshonestidad *f*; [*of declaration*] falsedad *f*; [*of means*] carácter *m* fraudulento, fraudulencia *f*

dishonour, **dishonor** (*US*) [dɪsˈɒnəʳ] Ⓐ N deshonra *f*, deshonor *m*; **to bring** *or* **cast ~ on sth/sb** traer la deshonra a algo/a algn, deshonrar algo/a algn
Ⓑ VT [+ *country, family*] deshonrar; [+ *cheque*] devolver, rechazar; [+ *debt*] dejar sin pagar, incumplir el pago de; [+ *promise*] faltar a, no cumplir

dishonourable, **dishonorable** (*US*) [dɪsˈɒnərəbl] ADJ deshonroso; **~ discharge** (*US Mil*) baja *f* por conducta deshonrosa

dishonourably, **dishonorably** (*US*) [dɪsˈɒnərəblɪ] ADV deshonrosamente; **to be ~ discharged** ser dado de baja con deshonor *or* por conducta deshonrosa

dishrack [ˈdɪʃræk] N escurreplatos *m inv*, escurridor *m*

dishrag [ˈdɪʃræɡ] N trapo *m* para fregar los platos, bayeta *f*

dishtowel [ˈdɪʃtaʊəl] N (*US*) paño *m* de cocina, trapo *m*

dishware [ˈdɪʃweəʳ] N (*US*) loza *f*, vajilla *f*

dishwasher [ˈdɪʃˌwɒʃəʳ] N (= *machine*) lavaplatos *m inv*, lavavajillas *m inv*; (= *person*) (*in restaurant*) friegaplatos *mf inv*, lavaplatos *mf inv*

dishwater [ˈdɪʃwɔːtəʳ] N agua *f* de lavar platos; (*fig*) agua *f* sucia

dishy* [ˈdɪʃɪ] ADJ (*Brit*) guapísimo; **he's/she's really ~** está buenísimo/buenísima

disillusion [ˌdɪsɪˈluːʒən] Ⓐ N desilusión *f*; (*more intense*) desencanto *m*
Ⓑ VT desilusionar; (*more intensely*) desencantar

disillusioned [ˌdɪsɪˈluːʒənd] ADJ desilusionado; (*more intense*) desencantado; **to be/become ~ with sth/sb** estar/quedar desilusionado con algo/algn; (*more intensely*) estar/quedar desencantado con algo/algn

disillusionment [ˌdɪsɪˈluːʒənmənt] N desilusión *f*; (*more intense*) desencanto *m*

disincentive [ˌdɪsɪnˈsentɪv] N factor *m* desmotivador (**to** para)

disinclination [ˌdɪsɪnklɪˈneɪʃən] N (*frm*) poca disposición *f* (**for** a; **to do sth** a hacer algo); **one of his characteristics was an extreme ~ to part with money** una de sus características era su extremado apego al dinero; **they showed a marked ~ to compromise** se mostraron manifiestamente reacios a comprometerse

disinclined [ˈdɪsɪnˈklaɪnd] ADJ (*frm*) **to be ~ to do sth** estar poco dispuesto a hacer algo, ser reacio a hacer algo; **I feel very ~ to go** no tengo ningunas ganas de ir

disinfect [ˌdɪsɪnˈfekt] VT desinfectar

disinfectant [ˌdɪsɪnˈfektənt] N desinfectante *m*

disinfection [ˌdɪsɪnˈfekʃən] N desinfección *f*

disinflation [ˌdɪsɪnˈfleɪʃən] N reducción *f* de la inflación

disinflationary [ˌdɪsɪnˈfleɪʃənərɪ] ADJ desinflacionista

disinformation [ˌdɪsɪnfəˈmeɪʃən] N desinformación *f*

disingenuous [ˌdɪsɪnˈdʒenjʊəs] ADJ falso, poco sincero

disingenuousness [ˌdɪsɪnˈdʒenjʊəsnɪs] N falsedad *f*, falta *f* de sinceridad

disinherit [ˈdɪsɪnˈherɪt] VT desheredar

disintegrate [dɪsˈɪntɪgreɪt] Ⓐ VI [1] (*lit*) [*rock*] desintegrarse; [*piece of machinery, furniture, toy*] destrozarse
[2] (*fig*) [*country, family, organization, rock*] desintegrarse
Ⓑ VT [+ *rock*] desintegrar

disintegration [dɪsˌɪntɪˈgreɪʃən] N desintegración *f*

disinter [ˈdɪsɪnˈtɜːʳ] VT [+ *corpse*] desenterrar, exhumar; [+ *idea, law*] desenterrar

disinterest [dɪsˈɪntrəst] N [1] (= *indifference*) desinterés *m*, apatía *f*
[2] (= *impartiality*) imparcialidad *f*

disinterested [dɪsˈɪntrɪstɪd] ADJ [1] (= *impartial*) desinteresado, imparcial
[2] (= *uninterested*) indiferente

disinterestedly [dɪsˈɪntrɪstɪdlɪ] ADV [1] (= *impartially*) de manera desinteresada, desinteresadamente
[2] (= *uninterestedly*) con indiferencia

disinterestedness [dɪsˈɪntrɪstɪdnɪs] N [1] (= *impartiality*) imparcialidad *f*
[2] (= *indifference*) desinterés *m*

disinterment [ˌdɪsɪnˈtɜːmənt] N exhumación *f*, desenterramiento *m*

disinvest [ˌdɪsɪnˈvest] VI desinvertir (**from** de)

disinvestment [ˌdɪsɪnˈvestmənt] N desinversión *f*

disjointed [dɪsˈdʒɔɪntɪd] ADJ [*words, sentences, arguments*] inconexo, deslavazado

disjointedly [dɪsˈdʒɔɪntɪdlɪ] ADV de forma incoherente, de forma inconexa

disjunctive [dɪsˈdʒʌŋktɪv] ADJ disyuntivo

disk [dɪsk] Ⓐ N [1] (*esp US*) = **disc**
[2] (*Comput*) disco *m*; **single-/double-sided ~** disco *m* de una cara/dos caras
Ⓑ CPD ► **disk drive** N unidad *f* de disco
► **disk operating system** N sistema *m* operativo de disco

diskette [dɪsˈket] N disquete *m*, diskette *m*

diskless [ˈdɪsklɪs] ADJ sin disco(s)

▼**dislike** [dɪsˈlaɪk] Ⓐ N [1] (= *antipathy*) aversión *f*, antipatía *f* (**of** a, hacia); **to take a ~ to sb** coger *or* (*LAm*) tomar antipatía a algn
[2] (= *thing disliked*) **likes and ~s** aficiones *fpl* y fobias *or* manías, cosas *fpl* que gustan y cosas que no
Ⓑ VT [+ *person*] tener antipatía a; (*more intensely*) tener aversión a; **I ~ her intensely** le tengo mucha antipatía *or* auténtica aversión; **it's not that I ~ him** no es que me caiga mal, no es que yo le tenga antipatía; **I ~ pop music/flying** no me gusta la música pop/ir en avión

dislocate [ˈdɪsləʊkeɪt] VT [1] (= *put out of joint*) [+ *bone*] dislocarse; **he ~d his shoulder** se dislocó el hombro
[2] (= *disrupt*) [+ *traffic*] trastornar; [+ *plans*] trastocar
[3] (= *displace*) [+ *person*] desplazar

dislocation [ˌdɪsləʊˈkeɪʃən] N [1] (*Med*) dislocación *f*
[2] (= *disruption*) [*of traffic*] trastorno *m*; [*of plans*] trastocamiento *m*
[3] (= *displacement*) desplazamiento *m*

dislodge [dɪsˈlɒdʒ] VT [1] (= *remove*) [+ *stone, obstruction*] sacar; [+ *enemy*] desalojar (**from** de); [+ *party, ruler*] desbancar
[2] (= *cause to fall*) hacer caer

disloyal [ˈdɪsˈlɔɪəl] ADJ desleal (**to** con)

disloyalty [ˈdɪsˈlɔɪəltɪ] N deslealtad *f* (**to** con)

dismal [ˈdɪzməl] ADJ [1] (= *gloomy, depressing*) [*weather*] deprimente; [*place*] sombrío, deprimente; [*day, tone, thought*] sombrío; [*person*] taciturno, de carácter sombrío; **to be in a ~ mood** estar *or* sentirse abatido
[2] (= *poor*) [*performance, condition*] pésimo; [*future*] desalentador, poco prometedor; **my prospects of getting a job are ~/pretty ~** mis posibilidades de conseguir un trabajo son ínfimas/bastante escasas; **a ~ failure** un rotundo fracaso

dismally [ˈdɪzməlɪ] ADV [1] (= *sadly*) [*say, reply*] en tono sombrío
[2] (= *poorly*) **to perform ~** [*actor*] actuar pésimamente; [*athlete*] tener una actuación pésima; **to fail ~** fracasar estrepitosamente
[3] (*as intensifier*) **the play was ~ bad** la obra fue pésima

dismantle [dɪsˈmæntl] VT [+ *machine*] desmontar, desarmar; [+ *fort, ship*] desmantelar; [+ *system, organization*] desmantelar

dismast [dɪsˈmɑːst] VT desarbolar

dismay [dɪsˈmeɪ] Ⓐ N consternación *f*; **there was general ~** todos estaban consternados; **in ~** consternado; **(much) to my ~** para (gran) consternación mía; **to fill sb with ~** consternar a algn
Ⓑ VT consternar; **I am ~ed to hear that ...** me da pena *or* me produce consternación enterarme de que ...; **don't look so ~ed!** ¡no te aflijas!

dismember [dɪsˈmembəʳ] VT desmembrar

dismemberment [dɪsˈmembəmənt] N desmembramiento *m*, desmembración *f*

dismiss [dɪsˈmɪs] Ⓐ VT [1] (*from job*) [+ *worker*] despedir; [+ *official*] destituir; **to be ~ed from the service** (*Mil*) ser dado de baja, ser separado del servicio
[2] (= *send away*) (*gen*) despachar; [+ *troops*] dar permiso (para irse); **class ~ed!** (*Scol*) eso es todo por hoy
[3] (= *reject, disregard*) [+ *thought*] rechazar, apartar de sí; [+ *request*] rechazar; [+ *possibility*] descartar, desechar; [+ *problem*] hacer caso omiso de; **with that he ~ed the matter** con eso dio por concluido el asunto
[4] (*Jur*) [+ *court case*] anular; [+ *appeal*] desestimar, rechazar; **the case was ~ed** el tribunal absolvió al acusado
[5] (= *beat*) [+ *opponent*] vencer
Ⓑ VI (*Mil*) romper filas; **dismiss!** ¡rompan filas!

dismissal [dɪsˈmɪsəl] N [1] (*from job*) [*of worker*] despido *m*; [*of official*] destitución *f*
[2] [*of suggestion, idea*] rechazo *m*
[3] (*Jur*) desestimación *f*

dismissive [dɪsˈmɪsɪv] ADJ (= *disdainful*) [*gesture, wave, attitude*] despectivo, desdeñoso; **he said in a ~ tone** dijo como quien no quería tomar la cosa en serio; **he was very ~ about it** parecía no tomar la cosa en serio; **he is very ~ of her capabilities** siempre está infravalorando *or* subestimando sus capacidades

dismissively [dɪsˈmɪsɪvlɪ] ADV [1] (= *disdainfully*) [*speak, wave*] despectivamente, con desdén
[2] (*sending sb away*) **"that's all," he said ~** —eso es todo —se limitó a decir él

dismount [dɪsˈmaʊnt] Ⓐ VI desmontar; **she ~ed from her horse** desmontó (del caballo), se apeó *or* se bajó del caballo
Ⓑ VT [+ *rider*] desmontar

Disneyland [ˈdɪznɪˌlænd] N Disneylandia *f*

disobedience [ˌdɪsəˈbiːdɪəns] N desobediencia *f*

disobedient [ˌdɪsəˈbiːdɪənt] ADJ desobediente

disobey [ˈdɪsəˈbeɪ] Ⓐ VT [+ *person, rule*] desobedecer
Ⓑ VI desobedecer

disobliging [ˈdɪsəˈblaɪdʒɪŋ] ADJ poco servicial

disorder [dɪsˈɔːdəʳ] Ⓐ N [1] (= *confusion, untidiness*) desorden *m*; **to be in ~** estar en desorden; **to retreat in ~** retirarse a la desbandada
[2] (*Pol*) (= *rioting*) disturbios *mpl*
[3] (*Med*) dolencia *f*, trastorno *m*; **mental ~** trastorno *m* mental
Ⓑ VT [1] (= *make untidy*) desordenar
[2] (*Med*) [+ *mind*] trastornar

disordered [dɪsˈɔːdəd] ADJ [1] [*room, thoughts*] desordenado
[2] (*Med*) [*mind*] trastornado

disorderly [dɪsˈɔːdəlɪ] ADJ [1] (= *untidy, disorganized*) [*room, queue*] desordenado; [*person, mind*] poco metódico; **the ~ flight of the refugees** la caótica huída de los refugiados
[2] (= *unruly*) [*behaviour*] indisciplinado, turbulento; [*crowd*] indisciplinado, alborotado; [*hooligan*] desmandado; [*meeting*] turbulento; **to become ~** [*meeting, person*] alborotarse; **~ conduct** (*Jur*) alteración *f* del orden público; **~ house** (*euph*) (= *brothel*) burdel *m*, prostíbulo *m*; (= *gambling den*) casa *f* de juego; **to keep a ~ house** (= *brothel*) regentar un burdel *or* prostíbulo; (= *gambling den*) regentar una casa de juego; *see also* **drunk B**

disorganization [dɪsˌɔːgənaɪˈzeɪʃən] N desorganización *f*

disorganize [dɪsˈɔːgənaɪz] VT (*gen*) desorganizar; [+ *communications*] interrumpir

disorganized [dɪsˈɔːgənaɪzd] ADJ desorganizado

disorient [dɪsˈɔːrɪənt] VT = **disorientate**

disorientate [dɪsˈɔːrɪənteɪt] VT desorientar

disown [dɪsˈəʊn] VT [1] (= *repudiate*) [+ *son, daughter, husband, wife*] desconocer, repudiar
[2] (= *deny*) [+ *responsibility*] negar; [+ *belief*] renegar de

disparage [dɪsˈpærɪdʒ] VT [+ *person, achievements*] menospreciar, despreciar

disparagement [dɪsˈpærɪdʒmənt] N menosprecio *m*

disparaging [dɪsˈpærɪdʒɪŋ] ADJ [*remark*] despectivo; **to be ~ about sth/sb** menospreciar algo/a algn

disparagingly [dɪsˈpærɪdʒɪŋlɪ] ADV **to speak ~ of** hablar en términos despreciativos de

disparate [ˈdɪspərɪt] ADJ dispar

disparity [dɪsˈpærɪtɪ] N (= *inequality, dissimilarity*) disparidad *f*

dispassionate [dɪsˈpæʃnɪt] ADJ (= *unbiased*) [*appraisal, observer*] imparcial; (= *unemotional*) [*voice, tone*] desapasionado

dispassionately [dɪsˈpæʃnɪtlɪ] ADV de modo desapasionado, sin apasionamientos

▼**dispatch** [dɪsˈpætʃ] Ⓐ N [1] (= *sending*) [*of person*] envío *m*; [*of goods*] envío *m*, expedición *f*
[2] (= *report*) (*in press*) reportaje *m*, informe *m*; (= *message*) despacho *m*; (*Mil*) parte *m*, comunicado *m*; **to be mentioned in ~es** (*Mil*)

➤ LANGUAGE IN USE: **dislike A1** 7.3 **dispatch B1** 20.4, 20.5

recibir menciones de elogio (*por su valor en combate*)
[3] (= *promptness*) (*frm*) celeridad *f*, prontitud *f*
(B) VT [1] (= *send*) [+ *letter, goods*] enviar, expedir; [+ *messenger, troops*] enviar
[2] (= *deal with*) [+ *business*] despachar
[3] (= *carry out*) [+ *duty*] ejercer, realizar
[4] (*hum*) (= *eat*) [+ *food*] despachar
[5] (= *kill*) despachar
(C) CPD ► **dispatch box** N (*Brit*) cartera *f* ► **dispatch case** N portafolios *m inv* ► **dispatch department** N departamento *m* de envíos ► **dispatch documents** NPL documentos *mpl* de envío ► **dispatch note** N nota *f* de envío, nota *f* de expedición ► **dispatch rider** N (= *motorcyclist*) mensajero/a *m/f* (*con moto*); (= *horseman*) correo *m*; (*Mil*) correo *m*

dispatcher [dɪs'pætʃəʳ] N transportista *m*

dispel [dɪs'pel] VT [+ *fog, smell, doubts, fear, worry*] disipar

dispensable [dɪs'pensəbl] ADJ prescindible

dispensary [dɪs'pensərɪ] N (*gen*) dispensario *m*; (*in hospital*) farmacia *f*

dispensation [ˌdɪspen'seɪʃən] N [1] (= *exemption*) exención *f*
[2] (= *distribution*) [*of drugs*] dispensación *f*
[3] (= *implementation*) [*of justice*] administración *f*
[4] (*Rel*) dispensa *f*; **~ of Providence** designio *m* divino
[5] (= *ruling*) decreto *m*

dispense [dɪs'pens] VT [1] (= *distribute*) [+ *food, money*] repartir; [+ *advice*] ofrecer; [+ *drug, prescription*] despachar; **this machine ~s coffee** esta máquina expende café
[2] (= *implement*) [+ *justice*] administrar
[3] (= *exempt*) **to ~ sb from sth** dispensar *or* eximir a algn de algo

►**dispense with** VI + PREP [1] (= *do without*) prescindir de
[2] (= *get rid of*) deshacerse de

dispenser [dɪs'pensəʳ] N [1] (= *person*) farmacéutico/a *m/f*
[2] (= *container*) (*for soap*) dosificador *m*; (= *machine*) distribuidor *m* automático, máquina *f* expendedora; **cash ~** (*Brit*) cajero *m* automático

dispensing chemist [dɪs'pensɪŋ'kemɪst] N (= *shop*) farmacia *f*; (= *person*) farmacéutico/a *m/f*

dispersal [dɪs'pɜːsəl] N (= *scattering*) [*of army, crowd*] dispersión *f*; [*of light*] descomposición *f*

dispersant [dɪs'pɜːsənt] N (*Chem*) dispersante *m*

disperse [dɪs'pɜːs] (A) VT (= *scatter*) [+ *crowd*] dispersar; [+ *news*] propagar; [+ *light*] descomponer
(B) VI [*crowd, army, troops*] dispersarse; [*mist*] disiparse

dispersion [dɪs'pɜːʃən] N = **dispersal**

dispirit [dɪs'pɪrɪt] VT desanimar, desalentar

dispirited [dɪs'pɪrɪtɪd] ADJ desanimado, desalentado

dispiritedly [dɪs'pɪrɪtɪdlɪ] ADV con desánimo, con desaliento

dispiriting [dɪs'pɪrɪtɪŋ] ADJ desalentador

displace [dɪs'pleɪs] VT [1] (*Phys*) [+ *liquid, mass*] desplazar
[2] (= *replace*) reemplazar
[3] (= *remove from office*) destituir
[4] (= *force to leave home*) desplazar

displaced [dɪs'pleɪst] ADJ **~ person** desplazado/a *m/f*

➤ LANGUAGE IN USE: **disposal 4** 3

displacement [dɪs'pleɪsmənt] N [1] (*Phys*) [*of liquid, mass*] desplazamiento *m*
[2] (= *replacement*) reemplazo *m*
[3] (= *removal*) eliminación *f*; (= *dismissal*) destitución *f*
[4] (= *forced relocation*) desplazamiento *m*
[5] (*Psych*) [*of energy*] sublimación *f*

display [dɪs'pleɪ] (A) N [1] (= *act of displaying*) [*of merchandise*] exposición *f*; (*in gallery, museum*) exposición *f*, exhibición *f*; [*of emotion, interest*] manifestación *f*, demostración *f*; [*of force*] despliegue *m*; **to be on ~** estar expuesto
[2] (= *array*) [*of merchandise*] muestrario *m*, surtido *m*; (*in gallery, museum*) exposición *f*; **window ~** (*in shop*) escaparate *m*
[3] (= *show*) (*Mil*) exhibición *f*, demostración *f*; **a firework(s) ~** fuegos *mpl* artificiales
[4] (= *ostentation*) **the party made a ~ of unity** el partido se esforzó en dar una imagen de unidad
[5] (*Comput*) (= *act*) visualización *f*
(B) VT [1] (= *put on view*) [+ *goods, painting, exhibit*] exponer, exhibir; [+ *notice, results*] exponer, hacer público
[2] (= *show*) [+ *emotion, ignorance*] mostrar, manifestar; [+ *courage*] demostrar, hacer gala de
[3] (= *show ostentatiously*) [+ *one's knowledge*] alardear de, hacer alarde de
[4] (*Comput*) desplegar, visualizar
(C) CPD ► **display advertising** N (*Press*) pancartas *fpl* publicitarias, publicidad *f* gráfica ► **display case** N vitrina *f* ► **display screen**, **display unit** N (*Comput*) monitor *m* ► **display window** N escaparate *m*

displease [dɪs'pliːz] VT (= *be disagreeable to*) desagradar; (= *annoy*) disgustar

displeased [dɪs'pliːzd] ADJ **to be ~ at sth/sb** estar disgustado con algo/algn

displeasing [dɪs'pliːzɪŋ] ADJ desagradable

displeasure [dɪs'pleʒəʳ] N desagrado *m*, disgusto *m*

disport [dɪs'pɔːt] VT **to ~ o.s.** divertirse

disposable [dɪs'pəʊzəbl] (A) ADJ [1] (= *not reusable*) [*nappy*] desechable, de usar y tirar; **~ goods** productos *mpl* desechables *or* no reutilizables
[2] (= *available*) disponible; **~ assets** activos *mpl* disponibles; **~ income** renta *f* disponible
(B) N (= *nappy*) pañal *m* desechable, pañal *m* de usar y tirar

▼**disposal** [dɪs'pəʊzəl] N [1] (= *sale, transfer*) [*of goods*] venta *f*; [*of property*] traspaso *m*; [*of rights*] enajenación *f*
[2] [*of waste*] **refuse ~** eliminación *f* de basuras; *see also* **bomb D**
[3] (= *distribution*) [*of ornaments, furniture*] disposición *f*, colocación *f*; [*of troops*] despliegue *m*
[4] (= *availability for use*) disposición *f*; **to put sth at sb's ~** poner algo a disposición de algn; **to have sth at one's ~** tener algo a su disposición, disponer de algo; **it's/I'm at your ~** está/estoy a tu disposición

dispose [dɪs'pəʊz] VT [1] (= *arrange*) [+ *furniture, ornaments*] disponer, colocar; [+ *troops*] desplegar
[2] (*frm*) (= *incline*) predisponer; **her behaviour did not ~ me to help her** su comportamiento no me predisponía a ayudarla, su comportamiento no hacía que me sintiese inclinado a ayudarla
[3] (= *decide*) disponer, decidir

►**dispose of** VI + PREP [1] (= *get rid of*) [+ *evidence, body*] deshacerse de; [+ *rubbish*] tirar, botar (*LAm*)
[2] (= *sell, transfer*) [+ *goods*] vender; [+ *property*] traspasar; [+ *rights*] enajenar, ceder
[3] (= *deal with*) [+ *matter, problem*] resolver; [+ *business*] despachar
[4] (= *disprove*) [+ *argument*] echar por tierra
[5] (= *have at one's command*) disponer de
[6] (*hum*) (= *eat*) [+ *food*] comerse, despachar
[7] (= *kill*) matar, despachar

disposed [dɪs'pəʊzd] ADJ (*frm*) **to be ~ to do sth** estar dispuesto a hacer algo; **to be favourably ~ towards sth/sb** tener una disposición favorable hacia algo/algn; *see also* **ill-disposed**, **well-disposed**

disposition [ˌdɪspə'zɪʃən] N [1] (= *temperament*) carácter *m*, temperamento *m*
[2] (= *placing*) [*of ornaments, furniture*] disposición *f*, colocación *f*; [*of troops*] despliegue *m*
[3] (= *inclination*) predisposición *f* (**to** a); **I have no ~ to help him** no estoy dispuesto a ayudarle
[4] **dispositions** preparativos *mpl*; **to make one's ~s** hacer preparativos

dispossess ['dɪspə'zes] VT [+ *tenant*] desahuciar; **to ~ sb of** desposeer *or* despojar a algn de

disproportion [ˌdɪsprə'pɔːʃən] N desproporción *f*

disproportionate [ˌdɪsprə'pɔːʃnɪt] ADJ desproporcionado (**to** en relación con)

disproportionately [ˌdɪsprə'pɔːʃnɪtlɪ] ADV desproporcionadamente

disprove [dɪs'pruːv] VT [+ *theory, argument*] refutar, rebatir; [+ *claim, allegation*] desmentir

disputable [dɪs'pjuːtəbl] ADJ discutible

disputation [ˌdɪspjuː'teɪʃən] N debate *m*

disputatious [ˌdɪspjuː'teɪʃəs] ADJ discutidor, disputador

dispute [dɪs'pjuːt] (A) N (= *quarrel*) disputa *f*, discusión *f*; (= *debate*) discusión *f*; (= *controversy*) polémica *f*, controversia *f*; (= *industrial dispute*) conflicto *m*; (*Jur*) contencioso *m*; **it is beyond ~ that ...** es indudable que ...; **in** *or* **under ~** [*territory*] en litigio
(B) VT [1] (= *gainsay*) [+ *statement, claim*] poner en duda; **I ~ that** lo dudo; **I do not ~ the fact that ...** no niego *or* no discuto que ...
[2] (= *fight for*) **to ~ possession of a house with sb** tener un contencioso con algn sobre la posesión de una casa; **the final will be ~d between Agassi and Sampras** Agassi y Sampras se disputarán la final
(C) VI (= *argue*) discutir (**about, over** sobre)

disputed [dɪs'pjuːtɪd] ADJ [*decision*] discutido; [*territory*] en litigio; **a ~ matter** un asunto contencioso, un asunto en litigio

disqualification [dɪsˌkwɒlɪfɪ'keɪʃən] N [1] (= *act, effect*) inhabilitación *f*; (*Sport*) descalificación *f*
[2] (= *thing that disqualifies*) impedimento *m*

disqualify [dɪs'kwɒlɪfaɪ] VT **to ~ sb (from)** (= *disable*) inhabilitar *or* incapacitar a algn (para); (*Sport*) descalificar a algn (para); **to ~ sb from driving** retirar el permiso de conducir a algn

disquiet [dɪs'kwaɪət] (A) N preocupación *f*, inquietud *f*
(B) VT inquietar

disquieting [dɪs'kwaɪətɪŋ] ADJ inquietante

disquietude [dɪs'kwaɪɪtjuːd] N (*frm*) inquietud *f*, intranquilidad *f*

disquisition [ˌdɪskwɪ'zɪʃən] N disquisición *f*

disregard ['dɪsrɪ'gɑːd] (A) N (= *indifference*) (*for feelings, money, danger*) indiferencia *f* (**for** por, hacia); (= *non-observance*) [*of law, rules*] desacato *m* (**of** a, de); **with complete ~ for** sin atender en lo más mínimo a; **with complete**

~ for his own safety haciendo caso omiso de su propia seguridad
Ⓑ VT [+ *remark, feelings*] hacer caso omiso de; [+ *authority, duty*] desatender

disrepair [ˈdɪsrɪˈpɛəʳ] N **in a state of ~** en mal estado; **to fall into ~** [*house*] desmoronarse; [*machinery etc*] deteriorarse

disreputable [dɪsˈrepjʊtəbl] ADJ [*person, place*] de mala fama; [*clothing*] desaliñado

disreputably [dɪsˈrepjʊtəblɪ] ADV vergonzosamente

disrepute [ˈdɪsrɪˈpjuːt] N **to bring into ~** desprestigiar; **to fall into ~** desprestigiarse

disrespect [ˈdɪsrɪsˈpekt] N falta *f* de respeto; **I meant no ~** no quería ofenderle

disrespectful [ˌdɪsrɪsˈpektfʊl] ADJ irrespetuoso; **to be ~ to** *or* **towards sb** faltar al respeto a algn

disrespectfully [ˌdɪsrɪsˈpektfəlɪ] ADV irrespetuosamente; **... he said ~** ... dijo de forma irrespetuosa

disrobe [ˈdɪsˈrəʊb] (*frm*) Ⓐ VT desnudar, desvestir
Ⓑ VI desnudarse

disrupt [dɪsˈrʌpt] VT [+ *meeting, communications etc*] interrumpir; [+ *plans*] alterar, trastocar

disruption [dɪsˈrʌpʃən] N [*of meeting, communications*] interrupción *f*; [*of plans*] alteración *f*

disruptive [dɪsˈrʌptɪv] ADJ perjudicial

dissatisfaction [ˈdɪsˌsætɪsˈfækʃən] N insatisfacción *f* (**with** con)

dissatisfied [ˈdɪsˈsætɪsfaɪd] ADJ descontento, insatisfecho (**with** con); **everyone was ~ with the result** el resultado dejó descontento *or* insatisfecho a todo el mundo

dissect [dɪˈsekt] VT [+ *animal*] disecar; (*fig*) analizar minuciosamente

dissection [dɪˈsekʃən] N [*of animal*] disección *f*; (*fig*) análisis *m inv* minucioso

dissemble [dɪˈsembl] Ⓐ VT ocultar, disimular
Ⓑ VI disimular

disseminate [dɪˈsemɪneɪt] VT [+ *information*] divulgar, difundir

dissemination [dɪˌsemɪˈneɪʃən] N diseminación *f*, difusión *f*

dissension [dɪˈsenʃən] N disensión *f*, desacuerdo *m*

dissent [dɪˈsent] Ⓐ N disentimiento *m*, disconformidad *f*; (*Rel, Pol*) disidencia *f*
Ⓑ VI disentir (**from** de), estar disconforme (**from** con); (*Rel*) disidir

dissenter [dɪˈsentəʳ] N (*Pol, Rel*) disidente *mf*

dissentient [dɪˈsenʃɪənt] (*frm*) Ⓐ ADJ = **dissenting**
Ⓑ N disidente *mf*

dissenting [dɪˈsentɪŋ] ADJ [*voice*] discrepante; **there was one ~ voice** hubo una voz discrepante *or* en contra; **a long ~ tradition** una larga tradición de disidencia

dissertation [ˌdɪsəˈteɪʃən] N disertación *f*; (*US Univ*) tesis *f inv*; (*Brit Univ*) tesina *f*

disservice [ˈdɪsˈsɜːvɪs] N perjuicio *m*; **to do sb a ~** perjudicar a algn

dissidence [ˈdɪsɪdəns] N disidencia *f*

dissident [ˈdɪsɪdənt] Ⓐ ADJ disidente
Ⓑ N disidente *mf*

dissimilar [ˈdɪˈsɪmɪləʳ] ADJ distinto, diferente (**to** de)

dissimilarity [ˌdɪsɪmɪˈlærɪtɪ] N desemejanza *f* (**between** entre)

dissimulate [dɪˈsɪmjʊleɪt] VT disimular

dissimulation [dɪˌsɪmjʊˈleɪʃən] N disimulación *f*

dissipate [ˈdɪsɪpeɪt] Ⓐ VT [1] (= *dispel*) [+ *fear, doubt etc*] disipar
[2] (= *waste*) [+ *efforts, fortune*] derrochar
Ⓑ VI disiparse

dissipated [ˈdɪsɪpeɪtɪd] ADJ [*person*] disipado, licencioso; [*behaviour, life*] disoluto

dissipation [ˌdɪsɪˈpeɪʃən] N [1] (= *act of dispelling*) disipación *f*; (= *waste*) derroche *m*, desperdicio *m*
[2] (= *debauchery*) disipación *f*, libertinaje *m*

dissociate [dɪˈsəʊʃɪeɪt] VT disociar (**from** de); **to ~ o.s. from sth/sb** disociarse *or* desligarse de algo/algn

dissociation [dɪˌsəʊsɪˈeɪʃən] N disociación *f*

dissoluble [dɪˈsɒljʊbl] ADJ disoluble

dissolute [ˈdɪsəluːt] ADJ disoluto

dissolution [ˌdɪsəˈluːʃən] N (*gen, Pol*) disolución *f*

dissolvable [dɪˈzɒlvəbl] ADJ soluble

dissolve [dɪˈzɒlv] Ⓐ VT (*gen, Comm*) disolver
Ⓑ VI (*gen*) disolverse; **it ~s in water** se disuelve en agua; **the crowd ~d** la muchedumbre se dispersó; **she ~d into tears** se deshizo en lágrimas

dissonance [ˈdɪsənəns] N disonancia *f*

dissonant [ˈdɪsənənt] ADJ disonante

dissuade [dɪˈsweɪd] VT disuadir (**from** de); **to ~ sb from doing sth** disuadir a algn de hacer algo

dissuasion [dɪˈsweɪʒən] N disuasión *f*

dissuasive [dɪˈsweɪsɪv] ADJ (*gen*) [*voice, person*] disuasivo; [*powers*] disuasorio

dist. ABBR [1] (= **distance**) dist
[2] (= **district**) dist

distaff [ˈdɪstɑːf] Ⓐ N rueca *f*
Ⓑ CPD ► **the distaff side** N la rama femenina; **on the ~ side** por parte de madre

distance [ˈdɪstəns] Ⓐ N [1] (*in space*) distancia *f*; **what ~ is it from here to London?** ¿qué distancia hay de aquí a Londres?; **we followed them at a ~** les seguimos a distancia; **at a ~ of two metres** a dos metros de distancia; **I can't see her face at this ~** a esta distancia no puedo ver su cara; **within easy ~ (of sth)** a poca distancia (de algo), no muy lejos (de algo); **the hotel is a fair ~ from the airport** el hotel está bastante lejos del aeropuerto; **from a ~** desde lejos; **from a ~ you look like your mother** desde lejos te pareces a tu madre; **he had no choice but to admire her from a ~** no podía hacer otra cosa más que admirarla desde lejos; **to go the ~** (*Sport*) llegar hasta el final; **a lot of people start the course with enthusiasm but are unable to go the ~** muchos empiezan el curso con entusiasmo pero son incapaces de completarlo; **it's a good ~ (from here)** está muy *or* bastante lejos (de aquí); **to be within hearing ~** estar al alcance de la voz; **in the ~** a lo lejos; **in the near ~** a poca distancia; **in the middle ~** en segundo término; **in the far ~** muy a lo lejos, en la lejanía; **to keep one's ~** (*lit*) mantenerse a distancia; (*fig*) guardar las distancias; **keep your ~!** ¡mantén la distancia!; **to keep sb at a ~** (*fig*) guardar las distancias con algn; **he can't walk long ~s yet** aún no puede andar largas distancias; **it's no ~** está cerquísima, está a nada de aquí; **it's only a short ~ away** está a poca distancia, está bastante cerca; **stopping ~** (*Aut*) distancia *f* de parada; **to be within striking ~ of sth** estar muy cerca de algo, estar a un paso *or* dos pasos de algo; **it is within walking ~** se puede ir andando; *see also* **long-distance**
[2] (*in time*) **at a ~ of 400 years** después de 400 años; **at this ~ in time** después de tanto tiempo
Ⓑ VT **to ~ o.s.** (*from problems, situations etc*) distanciarse (**from sth** de algo)
Ⓒ CPD ► **distance learning** N enseñanza *f* a distancia, enseñanza *f* por correspondencia ► **distance race** N carrera *f* de larga distancia ► **distance runner** N corredor(a) *m/f* de fondo

distant [ˈdɪstənt] ADJ [1] (*in space*) [*country, land*] distante, lejano; [*star, galaxy*] lejano, remoto; [*sound*] lejano; **the nearest hospital was 200km ~** el hospital más cercano se hallaba a 200km (de distancia); **the school is 2km ~ from the church** la escuela está a 2km (de distancia) de la iglesia; **as Neptune is so ~ from the sun** como Neptuno está tan lejos del sol; **in a ~ part of the country** en una remota región del país; **we could hear ~ thunder** se oían truenos lejanos *or* en la distancia; **we had a ~ view of the sea** veíamos el mar a lo lejos
[2] (*in time*) [*future, past, ancestor*] lejano; **in the ~ future** en un lejano futuro; **in the not too** *or* **very ~ future** en un futuro no demasiado *or* no muy lejano; **last summer's drought is a ~ memory** la sequía del verano pasado es ya un recuerdo lejano; **in the ~ past** en un lejano pasado, en un pasado remoto; **at some ~ point in the future** en algún momento del futuro lejano; **a ~ prospect** una remota posibilidad
[3] (= *not closely related*) [*relative, cousin*] lejano; [*connection*] remoto
[4] (= *aloof*) [*person, manner, voice*] distante; **he is courteous but ~** es cortés pero distante; **to become ~** volverse distante; **she became increasingly ~ towards him** se distanció cada vez más de él
[5] (= *removed*) **all this seems so ~ from the Spain of today** todo esto parece muy alejado de la realidad española de hoy, todo esto parece no tener nada que ver con la España de hoy; **Steve gradually became more ~ from reality** poco a poco, Steve se iba alejando cada vez más de la realidad; **he has become somewhat ~ from the day-to-day operations of the department** se ha distanciado un tanto de las operaciones diarias del departamento
[6] (= *distracted*) [*person, look*] ausente; **there was a ~ look in her eyes** tenía la mirada ausente *or* ida

distantly [ˈdɪstəntlɪ] ADV [1] (= *not closely*) [*resemble*] ligeramente; **to be ~ related to sb** ser pariente lejano de algn; **we are ~ related** somos parientes lejanos
[2] (= *far away*) **Rose heard a buzzer sound ~** Rose oyó el sonido de un timbre a lo lejos *or* en la distancia; **he looked down at the pigeons flying ~ below** miró hacia abajo a las palomas que volaban muy por debajo de él
[3] (= *in a detached manner*) [*greet, say*] con frialdad, fríamente
[4] (= *distractedly*) [*smile, nod*] distraídamente

distaste [ˈdɪsˈteɪst] N aversión *f* (**for** por, a); **she looked at his grubby clothes with ~** miró su ropa mugrienta con expresión de repugnancia

distasteful [dɪsˈteɪstfʊl] ADJ desagradable; [*task*] ingrato; **it is ~ to me to have to do this** no me resulta nada grato tener que hacer esto

Dist. Atty. ABBR (*US*) = **District Attorney**

distemper[1] [dɪsˈtempəʳ] Ⓐ N (= *paint*) temple *m*
Ⓑ VT pintar al temple

distemper² [dɪsˈtempəʳ] N (*Vet*) moquillo *m*; (*fig*) mal *m*

distend [dɪsˈtend] Ⓐ VT dilatar, hinchar
Ⓑ VI dilatarse, hincharse

distension [dɪsˈtenʃən] N distensión *f*, dilatación *f*, hinchazón *f*

distich [ˈdɪstɪk] N dístico *m*

distil, **distill** (*US*) [dɪsˈtɪl] VT destilar; **~led water** agua *f* destilada

distillation [ˌdɪstɪˈleɪʃən] N destilación *f*

distiller [dɪsˈtɪləʳ] N destilador *m*

distillery [dɪsˈtɪlərɪ] N destilería *f*

distinct [dɪsˈtɪŋkt] ADJ 1 (= *different*) [*types, species, groups*] diferente, distinto; **the book is divided into two ~ parts** el libro está dividido en dos partes bien diferenciadas; **~ from** diferente a, distinto a; **engineering and technology are disciplines quite ~ from one another** la ingeniería y la tecnología son disciplinas muy diferentes *or* distintas; **as ~ from** a diferencia de
2 (= *clear, definite*) [*shape, memory*] claro, definido; [*image, sound*] claro, nítido; [*increase, rise, fall*] marcado; [*advantage, disadvantage*] claro, obvio; [*possibility, improvement*] claro; [*lack*] evidente; [*flavour*] inconfundible; **we noticed a ~ change in her attitude** notamos un claro cambio en su actitud; **he had the ~ feeling that they were laughing at him** tuvo la clara sensación de que se estaban riendo de él; **I got the ~ impression that …** tuve la clara impresión de que …; **there is a ~ possibility that …** existe una clara posibilidad de que … + *subjun*; **there are ~ signs of progress** existen señales evidentes *or* inconfundibles de progreso

distinction [dɪsˈtɪŋkʃən] N 1 (= *difference*) distinción *f*; **to draw a ~ between** hacer una distinción entre
2 (= *eminence*) distinción *f*; **a man of ~** un hombre distinguido; **a writer of ~** un escritor destacado; **to gain** *or* **win ~** distinguirse (**as** como); **you have the ~ of being the first** a usted le corresponde el honor de ser el primero
3 (*Univ, Scol*) sobresaliente *m*; **he got a ~ in English** le dieron un sobresaliente en inglés

distinctive [dɪsˈtɪŋktɪv] ADJ [*sound, colour*] característico; [*flavour, smell, voice*] inconfundible, característico; [*plumage, fur*] distintivo, característico; [*style*] característico, particular; [*clothing, decor*] peculiar, particular; **one of the ~ features of Elizabethan architecture** uno de los rasgos característicos de la arquitectura isabelina; **stone walls are a ~ feature of the countryside** los muros de piedra son característicos del campo; **what was most ~ about him was his extreme nervousness** lo que más le caracterizaba era su extremo nerviosismo

distinctively [dɪsˈtɪŋktɪvlɪ] ADV [*dressed*] de forma muy peculiar, de forma muy particular; [*furnished*] de una forma muy particular, de una forma muy personal; **the decor has a ~ masculine feel to it** la decoración tiene un aire claramente *or* ostensiblemente masculino; **~ patterned** con un diseño muy particular

distinctiveness [dɪsˈtɪŋktɪvnɪs] N peculiaridad *f*

distinctly [dɪsˈtɪŋktlɪ] ADV 1 (= *clearly*) [*see, hear, remember*] claramente, perfectamente; [*promise*] definitivamente; [*prefer*] claramente; **I ~ remember locking the door** recuerdo claramente *or* perfectamente haber cerrado la puerta; **he speaks very ~** habla con mucha claridad
2 (= *very*) [*odd*] verdaderamente; [*uncomfortable, nervous*] realmente; [*better*] marcadamente; **his was a ~ unhappy childhood** su infancia fue verdaderamente desdichada; **she was ~ unhappy about the new arrangements** estaba realmente *or* muy descontenta con los nuevos planes; **it was ~ cold outside** fuera hacía verdadero *or* mucho frío; **it is ~ awkward** es realmente difícil; **he is ~ lacking in imagination** carece totalmente de imaginación; **his work has a ~ modern flavour** su trabajo tiene un inconfundible sabor a moderno; **it is ~ possible that …** bien podría ser que … + *subjun*

distinguish [dɪsˈtɪŋgwɪʃ] Ⓐ VT 1 (= *differentiate*) distinguir; **they are so alike, it's hard to ~ them** son tan parecidos que es difícil distinguirlos; **he is unable to ~ brown from green** *or* **brown and green** no es capaz de distinguir el marrón del verde *or* el marrón y el verde
2 (= *make different*) distinguir (**from** de); **it is his professionalism that ~es him from his rivals** su profesionalismo es lo que le distingue de sus rivales; **to ~ o.s.** destacarse (**as** como); **he ~ed himself during his career in the army** se destacó durante su carrera en el ejército; **you've really ~ed yourself!** (*iro*) ¡te has lucido! (*iro*)
3 (= *characterize*) caracterizar; **her work is ~ed by its excellent presentation** su trabajo se caracteriza por una excelente presentación
4 (= *discern*) [+ *landmark*] distinguir, vislumbrar; [+ *voice*] distinguir; [+ *change*] distinguir, reconocer
Ⓑ VI distinguir (**between** entre); **I can't ~ between the two of them** no puedo distinguir entre los dos

distinguishable [dɪsˈtɪŋgwɪʃəbl] ADJ 1 (= *possible to differentiate*) distinguible; **the two types are easily ~** los dos tipos son fácilmente distinguibles, los dos tipos se distinguen fácilmente; **~ groups such as the disabled** grupos que se pueden diferenciar, como los minusválidos; **this vintage port is ~ by its deep red colour** este oporto añejo se caracteriza por su color rojo oscuro; **the copy is barely ~ from the original** la copia apenas puede distinguirse del original; **she is barely ~ from her younger sister** casi no se la puede distinguir de su hermana menor
2 (= *discernible*) **to be clearly ~** [*landmark, shape*] distinguirse claramente *or* fácilmente; **no words were ~** no se distinguía ninguna palabra con claridad

distinguished [dɪsˈtɪŋgwɪʃt] Ⓐ ADJ [*guest, appearance, career*] distinguido; [*professor, scholar, writer*] distinguido, eminente; **he retired after 25 years of ~ service** se retiró tras 25 años de distinguido servicio; **to look ~** tener un aspecto distinguido
Ⓑ CPD ► **distinguished service professor** N (*US Univ*) *profesor de universidad Americana que ocupa una cátedra de prestigio*

distinguishing [dɪsˈtɪŋgwɪʃɪŋ] ADJ distintivo; **~ features** (*of landscape, sb's work*) rasgos *mpl* característicos, características *fpl*; (*of animal*) rasgos *mpl* distintivos; **~ mark** marca *f* distintiva

distort [dɪsˈtɔːt] VT [+ *shape etc*] deformar; [+ *sound, image*] distorsionar; (*fig*) [+ *judgment*] distorsionar; [+ *truth*] tergiversar; **a ~ed impression** una impresión distorsionada

distorted [dɪsˈtɔːtɪd] ADJ (*lit, fig*) distorsionado; **he gave us a ~ version of the events** nos dio una versión distorsionada de los hechos

distortion [dɪsˈtɔːʃən] N [*of shape*] deformación *f*; [*of sound, image*] distorsión *f*; (*fig*) distorsión *f*; [*of truth*] tergiversación *f*

distr. ABBR 1 = **distribution**
2 = **distributor**

distract [dɪsˈtrækt] VT [+ *person*] **to ~ sb (from sth)** distraer a algn (de algo); **to ~ sb's attention (from sth)** desviar la atención de algn (de algo); **she is easily ~ed** se distrae fácilmente

distracted [dɪsˈtræktɪd] ADJ 1 (= *preoccupied*) distraído
2 (†) (= *mad*) loco; **like one ~** como un loco; **to be ~ with anxiety** estar loco de inquietud

distractedly [dɪsˈtræktɪdlɪ] ADV 1 (= *absently*) [*speak, behave*] distraídamente
2 (= *madly*) locamente, como un loco

distracting [dɪsˈtræktɪŋ] ADJ que distrae la atención, molesto

distraction [dɪsˈtrækʃən] N 1 (= *interruption*) distracción *f*
2 (= *entertainment*) diversión *f*
3 (= *distress, anxiety*) aturdimiento *m*; **to drive sb to ~** volver loco a algn

distrain [dɪsˈtreɪn] VI (*Jur*) **to ~ upon** secuestrar, embargar

distraint [dɪsˈtreɪnt] N (*Jur*) secuestro *m*, embargo *m*

distrait [dɪsˈtreɪ] ADJ (*liter*) distraído

distraught [dɪsˈtrɔːt] ADJ afligido, alterado (*LAm*); **in a ~ voice** con una voz embargada por la emoción

distress [dɪsˈtres] Ⓐ N 1 (= *pain*) dolor *m*; (= *mental anguish*) angustia *f*, aflicción *f*; (*Med*) (*after exertion*) agotamiento *m*, fatiga *f*; **to be in great ~** estar sufriendo mucho
2 (= *danger*) peligro *m*; **to be in ~** [*ship etc*] estar en peligro
3 (= *poverty*) miseria *f*; **to be in financial ~** pasar apuros económicos
Ⓑ VT (*physically*) doler; (*mentally*) angustiar, afligir; (*Med*) agotar, fatigar; **I am very ~ed at the news** estoy muy afligido por la noticia; **I am ~ed to hear that …** lamento profundamente enterarme de que …
Ⓒ CPD ► **distress rocket** N cohete *m* de señales ► **distress signal** N señal *f* de socorro

distressed [dɪsˈtrest] ADJ 1 (= *upset*) afligido, angustiado
2 (†) (= *poverty-stricken*) **in ~ circumstances** en penuria económica, en dificultades económicas

distressful [dɪsˈtresfʊl] ADJ = **distressing**

distressing [dɪsˈtresɪŋ] ADJ [*situation, experience*] angustioso, doloroso; [*poverty, inadequacy*] acuciante

distressingly [dɪsˈtresɪŋlɪ] ADV dolorosamente, penosamente; **a ~ bad picture** un cuadro tan malo que daba pena

distribute [dɪsˈtrɪbjuːt] VT (= *deal out, spread out*) repartir; (*Comm*) [+ *goods*] distribuir

distribution [ˌdɪstrɪˈbjuːʃən] Ⓐ N [*of wealth, population etc*] distribución *f*; (= *handing out*) reparto *m*; (*Comm*) [*of goods*] distribución *f*; (*Ling*) distribución *f*
Ⓑ CPD ► **distribution cost** N gastos *mpl* de distribución ► **distribution network** N red *f* de distribución ► **distribution rights** NPL derechos *mpl* de distribución

distributional [ˌdɪstrɪˈbjuːʃənəl] ADJ distribucional

distributive [dɪsˈtrɪbjʊtɪv] Ⓐ ADJ distributivo
Ⓑ N (*Ling*) adjetivo *m* distributivo
Ⓒ CPD ► **distributive trade** N comercio *m* de distribución

distributor [dɪsˈtrɪbjʊtəʳ] N 1 (= *person handing out*) repartidor(a) *m/f*, distribuidor(a) *m/f*
2 (*Comm*) (= *firm*) compañía *f* distribuidora, distribuidora *f*; (*Cine*) distribuidora *f*
3 (*Elec, Mech*) distribuidor *m*; (*Aut*) distribuidor *m* (del encendido), delco® *m* (*Sp*)

distributorship [dɪsˈtrɪbjʊtəʃɪp] N (*Comm*) (= *company*) compañía *f* distribuidora, distribuidora *f*; (= *right to supply*) distribución *f*

district [ˈdɪstrɪkt] Ⓐ N [*of country*] región *f*, zona *f*; [*of town*] distrito *m*, barrio *m*; (= *administrative area*) (*gen*) (*Pol*) distrito *m*; **postal ~** distrito *m* postal
Ⓑ CPD ► **district attorney** N (*US*) fiscal *mf* (de distrito) ► **district commissioner** N (*Brit*) jefe/a *m/f* de policía de distrito ► **district council** N (*Brit*) municipio *m* ► **district court** N (*US*) tribunal *m* de distrito ► **district manager** N representante *mf* regional ► **district nurse** N (*Brit*) *enfermero/a de la Seguridad Social encargado/a de una zona determinada*

distrust [dɪsˈtrʌst] Ⓐ N desconfianza *f* (**of** en), recelo *m* (**of** de)
Ⓑ VT desconfiar de, recelar de

distrustful [dɪsˈtrʌstfʊl] ADJ desconfiado, receloso

disturb [dɪsˈtɜːb] VT 1 (= *bother*) [+ *person, animal*] molestar; **"please do not disturb"** "se ruega no molestar"; **sorry to ~ you** perdona la molestia; **try not to ~ Joseph, he's asleep** intenta no despertar a Joseph, está durmiendo
2 (= *interrupt*) [+ *order, balance*] alterar; [+ *meeting, sleep*] interrumpir; [+ *silence*] romper; **a car alarm ~ed her sleep** una alarma de coche interrumpió su sueño *or* la despertó; **to ~ the peace** (*Jur*) alterar el orden público; **they ~ed a burglar breaking into their house** sorprendieron a un ladrón que estaba intentando entrar en su casa; **her constant questions ~ed his concentration** sus constantes preguntas le impedían concentrarse
3 (= *worry*) preocupar; (= *upset*) afectar; **the news ~ed him greatly** la noticia le preocupó enormemente; **the photos of the war victims ~ed her** las fotos de las víctimas de guerra la afectaron
4 (= *disarrange*) [+ *papers*] desordenar; [+ *water, sediment*] agitar; **somebody had been in her room and ~ed her things** alguien había estado en su cuarto y había revuelto sus cosas; **the police asked if anything had been ~ed** la policía preguntó si había algo fuera de su sitio

disturbance [dɪsˈtɜːbəns] N 1 (= *act, state*) perturbación *f*; **~ of the peace** (*Jur*) alteración *f* del orden público
2 (*social, political*) disturbio *m*; (*in house, street*) alboroto *m*; [*of mind*] trastorno *m*; (= *fight*) altercado *m*, bronca *f* (*LAm*); **to cause a ~** armar alboroto; **there was a ~ in the crowd** hubo un altercado entre algunos de los espectadores; **the ~s in the north** los disturbios en el norte
3 (= *nuisance*) molestia *f*
4 (= *interruption*) interrupción *f* (**to** de)

disturbed [dɪsˈtɜːbd] ADJ 1 (= *worried*) preocupado, angustiado; (= *upset*) afectado; **I was ~ to hear that …** me afectó mucho el enterarme de que …; **he was ~ that …** le preocupaba que ... + *subjun*, le inquietaba que ... + *subjun*
2 (*Psych*) 2·1 (= *unhappy*) [*childhood, adolescence*] problemático; **children from ~ backgrounds** niños que proceden de hogares con problemas
2·2 (= *unbalanced*) [*person, mind*] trastornado; [*behaviour*] desequilibrado; **she is very ~** está muy trastornada, tiene muchos problemas mentales; **to be emotionally/mentally ~** tener trastornos afectivos/mentales
3 (= *interrupted*) [*sleep*] interrumpido; **to have a ~ night** dormir mal

disturbing [dɪsˈtɜːbɪŋ] ADJ [*influence, thought*] perturbador; [*event*] inquietante, preocupante; **it is ~ that …** es inquietante que …

disturbingly [dɪsˈtɜːbɪŋlɪ] ADV de manera inquietante; **a ~ large number** un número tan grande que resulta inquietante; **the bomb fell ~ close** la bomba cayó tan cerca que causó inquietud

disunited [ˈdɪsjʊˈnaɪtɪd] ADJ desunido

disunity [ˌdɪsˈjuːnɪtɪ] N desunión *f*

disuse [ˈdɪsˈjuːs] N desuso *m*; **to fall into ~** caer en desuso

disused [ˈdɪsˈjuːzd] ADJ abandonado

disyllabic [ˌdɪsɪˈlæbɪk] ADJ disílabo

ditch [dɪtʃ] Ⓐ N (*gen*) zanja *f*; (*at roadside*) cuneta *f*; (= *irrigation channel*) acequia *f*; (*as defence*) foso *m*
Ⓑ VT (*) (= *get rid of*) [+ *car*] deshacerse de; [+ *person*] dejar plantado*; **to ~ a plane** hacer un amaraje forzoso

ditching [ˈdɪtʃɪŋ] N 1 (= *digging ditches*) abertura *f* de zanjas; **hedging and ~** mantenimiento *m* de setos y zanjas
2 (*Aer*) amaraje *m*

ditchwater [ˈdɪtʃˌwɔːtəʳ] N ✦**IDIOM to be as dull as ~*** ser muy soso, no tener gracia ninguna

dither [ˈdɪðəʳ] Ⓐ N **to be in a ~** ◊ **be all of a ~** (= *be nervous*) estar muy nervioso; (= *hesitate*) no saber qué hacer, vacilar
Ⓑ VI (= *be nervous*) estar nervioso; (= *hesitate*) no saber qué hacer, vacilar; **to ~ over a decision** vacilar al tomar una decisión

ditherer [ˈdɪðərəʳ] N (*esp Brit*) indeciso/a *m/f*; **don't be such a ~!** ¡no seas tan indeciso!

dithery [ˈdɪðərɪ] ADJ (= *nervous*) nervioso; (= *hesitant*) indeciso, vacilante; (*from old age*) chocho

ditto [ˈdɪtəʊ] Ⓐ N ídem, lo mismo; **"I'd like coffee" — "~ (for me)"** —yo quiero café —yo lo mismo *or* y yo; **"~," said Graham** —yo también —dijo Graham
Ⓑ CPD ► **ditto marks**, NPL **ditto sign** N comillas *fpl*

ditty [ˈdɪtɪ] N cancioncilla *f*

diuretic [ˌdaɪjʊəˈretɪk] Ⓐ ADJ diurético
Ⓑ N diurético *m*

diurnal [daɪˈɜːnl] ADJ diurno

diva [ˈdiːvə] N (*pl* **divas** *or* **dive** [ˈdiːvɪ]) diva *f*

divan [dɪˈvæn] N diván *m*; (*Brit*) (*also* **~ bed**) cama *f* turca

dive [daɪv] Ⓐ N 1 (*into water*) salto *m* de cabeza (al agua), zambullida *f*, clavado *m* (*CAm, Mex*); (*by professional diver, of submarine*) inmersión *f*
2 (*Aer*) picado *m*, picada *f* (*LAm*)
3 (= *leap*) **to make a ~ for sth** lanzarse *or* abalanzarse sobre algo
4 (*Ftbl*) estirada *f*; **to take a ~** (*Ftbl*) tirarse a la piscina (*dejarse caer deliberadamente con la intención de conseguir un tiro libre o un penalty*)
5 (*fig*) (= *fall*) **his reputation has taken a ~*** su reputación ha caído en picado
6 (*pej*, *) (= *club etc*) garito *m*
Ⓑ VI 1 [*swimmer*] tirarse, zambullirse, dar un clavado (*CAm, Mex*), clavarse (*CAm, Mex*); (*artistically*) saltar; (*underwater*) bucear; [*submarine*] sumergirse; **the kids were diving for coins** los niños se tiraban al agua para recoger monedas; **to ~ for pearls** buscar perlas; **to ~ into the water** tirarse al agua, zambullirse
2 (*Aer*) bajar en picado
3 (= *leap*) **the goalkeeper ~d for the ball** el portero se lanzó a parar el balón; **to ~ for cover** precipitarse en busca de cobijo; **he ~d for the exit** se precipitó hacia la salida; **he ~d into the crowd** se metió entre la muchedumbre; **to ~ into one's pocket** meter la mano en el bolsillo; **to ~ into a bar** entrar a toda prisa en un bar; **I ~d into the shop for a paper** pasé corriendo por la tienda a por un periódico, me metí corriendo a la tienda a por un periódico
4 (= *fall*) [*prices etc*] bajar de golpe, caer en picado *or* (*LAm*) picada

dive-bomb [ˈdaɪvbɒm] VT [+ *town etc*] bombardear en picado

dive-bomber [ˈdaɪvˌbɒməʳ] N bombardero *m* en picado

dive-bombing [ˈdaɪvˌbɒmɪŋ] N bombardeo *m* en picado

diver [ˈdaɪvəʳ] N 1 (= *swimmer*) saltador(a) *m/f*, clavadista *mf* (*LAm*); (= *deep-sea diver*) submarinista *mf*, buzo *m*; (*sub-aqua*) escafandrista *mf*
2 (*Orn*) colimbo *m*

diverge [daɪˈvɜːdʒ] VI [*roads*] bifurcarse; (*fig*) [*opinions*] divergir (**from** de)

divergence [daɪˈvɜːdʒəns] N divergencia *f*

divergent [daɪˈvɜːdʒənt] ADJ divergente

divers [ˈdaɪvɜːz] ADJ (*liter*) diversos, varios

diverse [daɪˈvɜːs] ADJ (= *varied*) diverso, variado

diversification [daɪˌvɜːsɪfɪˈkeɪʃən] N diversificación *f*

diversify [daɪˈvɜːsɪfaɪ] Ⓐ VT (*gen*) (*also Comm*) diversificar
Ⓑ VI (*Comm*) diversificarse, ampliar el campo de acción

diversion [daɪˈvɜːʃən] N 1 (*Brit*) [*of traffic*] desviación *f*, desvío *m*; **"Diversion"** (*road sign*) "Desvío"
2 (= *distraction*) **to create a ~** (*gen*) distraer; (*Mil*) producir una diversión
3 (= *pastime*) diversión *f*

diversionary [daɪˈvɜːʃnərɪ] ADJ de diversión

diversity [daɪˈvɜːsɪtɪ] N [*of opinions etc*] diversidad *f*

divert [daɪˈvɜːt] VT 1 [+ *traffic, train etc*] desviar; [+ *conversation*] cambiar
2 (= *amuse*) divertir, entretener

diverting [daɪˈvɜːtɪŋ] ADJ divertido

divest[1] [daɪˈvest] VT **to ~ sb of sth** despojar a algn de algo; **to ~ o.s. of one's rights** renunciar a sus derechos; **he ~ed himself of his coat** (*frm*) se despojó de su abrigo (*frm*)

divest[2] [daɪˈvest] VT, VI (*US Fin*) desinvertir

divestment [daɪˈvestmənt] N (*US Fin*) desinversión *f*

divide [dɪˈvaɪd] Ⓐ VT 1 (= *separate*) separar; **the Pyrenees ~ France from Spain** los Pirineos separan Francia de España
2 (*also* **~ up**) (= *split*) [+ *money, work, kingdom*] dividir, repartir (**among, between** entre); [+ *sweets*] repartir (**among, between** entre); [+ *apple, orange, cake*] partir, dividir (**among, between** entre; **into** en); **they ~d it among themselves** se lo repartieron entre sí; **when he died his property was ~d between his daughters** cuando murió su propiedad se repartió *or* se dividió entre sus hijas; **she tried to ~ her time fairly between the children** intentaba repartir su tiempo de forma equitativa entre los niños; **the house has been ~d into flats** la casa se ha dividido en

apartamentos; **~ the dough into four pieces** dividir la masa en cuatro trozos

3 (*Math*) dividir; **48 ~d by 8 is 6** 48 dividido entre *or* por 8 es 6; **~ 6 into 36** divide 36 entre *or* por 6; **you can't ~ 7 into 50** 50 no es divisible entre *or* por 7

4 (= *cause disagreement among*) [+ *friends, political parties*] dividir

5 (*Pol*) (*Brit*) **to ~ the House** hacer que la Cámara proceda a la votación

Ⓑ VI 1 (= *separate*) [*road, river*] bifurcarse

2 (*also* **~ up**) (= *split*) [*cells, people*] dividirse; **we ~d into groups for the first activity** nos dividimos en grupos para la primera actividad; **~ and rule** divide y vencerás

3 (*Math*) dividir

4 (*Brit Pol*) votar; **the House ~d** la Cámara procedió a la votación

Ⓒ N 1 (*US Geog*) línea *f* divisoria de aguas, divisoria *f* de aguas

2 (*fig*) (= *gap*) división *f*; **there is a clear ~ between the upper and lower classes** hay una clara división entre las clases superiores y las inferiores

► **divide off** Ⓐ VT + ADV dividir, separar

Ⓑ VI + ADV dividirse

► **divide out** VT + ADV [+ *sweets, biscuits*] repartir (**between, among** entre)

► **divide up** Ⓐ VT + ADV [+ *money, work, kingdom*] dividir, repartir (**between, among** entre); [+ *sweets*] repartir (**between, among** entre); [+ *apple, orange, cake*] partir, dividir (**between, among** entre; **into** en)

Ⓑ VI + ADV [*people*] dividirse; **we ~d up to look for the missing child** nos dividimos para buscar al niño que se había perdido; **~ up into pairs** dividíos en parejas

divided [dɪˈvaɪdɪd] Ⓐ ADJ 1 (= *disunited*) [*nation, government, society*] dividido; **public opinion was ~** la opinión pública estaba dividida; **to have ~ loyalties** sufrir un conflicto de lealtades; **to be ~ on** *or* **over sth** [*people*] tener opiniones divididas sobre algo; **opinions are ~ on** *or* **over that** las opiniones respecto a eso están muy divididas

2 (*Bot*) seccionado

Ⓑ CPD ► **divided highway** N (*US*) autovía *f* ► **divided skirt** N (*US*) falda *f* pantalón

dividend [ˈdɪvɪdend] Ⓐ N 1 (*Fin*) dividendo *m*

2 (*fig*) beneficio *m*; **this should pay handsome ~s** esto ha de proporcionar grandes beneficios

Ⓑ CPD ► **dividend cover** N cobertura *f* de dividendo ► **dividend warrant** N cédula *f* de dividendo

dividers [dɪˈvaɪdəz] NPL compás *msing* de puntas

dividing [dɪˈvaɪdɪŋ] Ⓐ ADJ [*wall, fence*] divisorio

Ⓑ CPD ► **dividing line** N línea *f* divisoria

divination [ˌdɪvɪˈneɪʃən] N adivinación *f*

divine[1] [dɪˈvaɪn] Ⓐ ADJ (*Rel*) divino; (*fig*) sublime; (*) divino, maravilloso

Ⓑ N teólogo *m*

Ⓒ CPD ► **divine right** N derecho *m* divino ► **divine service** N culto *m*, oficio *m* divino

divine[2] [dɪˈvaɪn] VT adivinar

divinely [dɪˈvaɪnlɪ] ADV (*Rel*) divinamente; (*fig*) sublimemente; (*) divinamente, maravillosamente

diviner [dɪˈvaɪnəʳ] N adivinador(a) *m/f*; (= *water diviner*) zahorí *mf*

diving [ˈdaɪvɪŋ] Ⓐ N (*professional*) submarinismo *m*, buceo *m*; (*sporting*) salto *m* de trampolín, clavado *m* (*CAm, Mex*); (*from side of pool*) salto *m*, zambullida *f*

Ⓑ CPD ► **diving bell** N campana *f* de buzo ► **diving board** N trampolín *m* ► **diving suit** N escafandra *f*, traje *m* de buceo

divining rod [dɪˈvaɪnɪŋrɒd] N varilla *f* de zahorí

divinity [dɪˈvɪnɪtɪ] N 1 (= *deity, quality*) divinidad *f*

2 (*as study*) teología *f*

divisible [dɪˈvɪzəbl] ADJ divisible

division [dɪˈvɪʒən] Ⓐ N 1 (*gen, Math*) división *f*; (= *sharing*) reparto *m*, distribución *f*; **~ of labour** división *f* del trabajo

2 (*Comm*) (= *department*) sección *f*

3 (*Mil, Brit Police*) división *f*

4 (= *partition*) separación *f*, división *f*; (= *line*) línea *f* divisoria; (*Ftbl etc*) división *f*

5 (= *conflict, discord*) discordia *f*; **there is a ~ of opinion about this** las opiniones respecto a esto están divididas

6 (*Brit Parl*) votación *f*; **to call a ~** exigir una votación; **approved without a ~** aprobado por unanimidad

Ⓑ CPD ► **division sign** N (*Math*) signo *m* de división

divisional [dɪˈvɪʒənl] ADJ de división

divisive [dɪˈvaɪsɪv] ADJ divisivo, causante de divisiones

divisiveness [dɪˈvaɪsɪvnɪs] N **the ~ of this decision** las disensiones causadas/que serán causadas por esta decisión

divisor [dɪˈvaɪzəʳ] N divisor *m*

divorce [dɪˈvɔːs] Ⓐ N 1 (*Jur*) divorcio *m*; **to get a ~** divorciarse (**from** de)

2 (*fig*) separación *f* (**from** de)

Ⓑ VT 1 (*Jur*) divorciarse de; **to get ~d** divorciarse

2 (*fig*) separar; **to ~ sth from sth** separar algo de algo

Ⓒ VI divorciarse

Ⓓ CPD ► **divorce court** N tribunal *m* de pleitos matrimoniales ► **divorce proceedings** NPL pleito *msing* de divorcio ► **divorce rate** N tasa *f* de divorcio

divorcé [dəˈvɔːseɪ] N divorciado *m*

divorced [dɪˈvɔːst] ADJ divorciado

divorcee [dɪˌvɔːˈsiː] N divorciado/a *m/f*

divot [ˈdɪvɪt] N (= *piece of turf*) (*gen*) terrón *m*; (*Golf*) chuleta *f*

divulge [daɪˈvʌldʒ] VT divulgar, revelar

divvy[1]* [ˈdɪvɪ] Ⓐ N, ABBR (*Brit*) = **dividend**

Ⓑ VT (*also* **to ~ up**) repartir

divvy[2]‡ [ˈdɪvɪ] N (*Brit*) (= *fool*) tontaina* *mf*

Dixie [ˈdɪksɪ] N *el sur de los Estados Unidos*

dixie [ˈdɪksɪ] N (*Brit Mil*) (*also* **~ can**) olla *f*, marmita *f*

> **DIXIE**
>
> **Dixie** *o* **Dixieland** *es el sobrenombre con el que se conoce de forma global a los estados sureños de EE.UU., en especial a los once estados que formaron los Estados Confederados de América durante la Guerra Civil: Alabama, Arkansas, Georgia, Florida, Louisiana, Mississippi, Carolina del Norte, Carolina del Sur, Tennessee, Texas y Virginia. También se usa como un adjetivo para describir características de los estados sureños y de sus habitantes, así como el jazz que surgió en ellos. Se supone que el nombre* **Dixie** *proviene de Louisiana, donde los billetes de diez dólares llevaban impreso en el anverso la palabra francesa* **dix**. *Para otros la palabra proviene de la línea simbólica Mason-Dixon, que separa el norte del sur.*
>
> ⇨ *Ver tb* MASON-DIXON LINE

DIY ABBR (= **do-it-yourself**) bricolaje *m*

dizzily [ˈdɪzɪlɪ] ADV 1 (= *giddily*) [*walk, sway*] con una sensación de mareo; **her head began to spin ~** la cabeza empezó a darle vueltas y vueltas

2 (*fig*) [*rise, fall*] vertiginosamente

3 (*) (= *in a scatterbrained way*) de manera atolondrada; **she has been behaving rather ~ lately** ha estado bastante atolondrada últimamente

4 (*in a silly way*) con aire alelado; **she smiled ~** sonrió alelada

dizziness [ˈdɪzɪnɪs] N (*gen*) mareo *m*; (*caused by height*) vértigo *m*; **to have an attack of ~** tener *or* sufrir un mareo

dizzy Ⓐ [ˈdɪzɪ] ADJ 1 (= *giddy*) [*person*] mareado; **to feel ~** (*because ill, drunk etc*) estar mareado, marearse; **if I look down I feel ~** si miro hacia abajo me da vértigo; **changes in altitude make you ~** los cambios de altitud causan mareo *or* hacen que te mareas; **you're making me ~** me estás mareando; **this drug may make you ~** este medicamento puede provocarle mareos; **it makes one ~ to think of it** marea sólo de pensarlo; **she had a ~ spell** tuvo *or* le dio un mareo; **to be ~ with success** estar borracho de éxito

2 (*fig*) [*pace, speed*] vertiginoso; **she rose to the ~ heights of director's secretary** ascendió ni más ni menos que al puesto de secretaria del director

3 (*) (= *scatterbrained*) atolondrado

Ⓑ VT (= *confuse*) aturdir; **they had been dizzied by the pace of technological change** el ritmo del cambio tecnológico les había aturdido

DJ Ⓐ N ABBR (= **disc-jockey**) pinchadiscos *mf*

Ⓑ ABBR (= **dinner-jacket**) smoking *m*

Djakarta [dʒəˈkɑːtə] N Yakarta *f*

djellabah [ˈdʒeləbə] N chilaba *f*

DJIA N ABBR (*US St Ex*) = **Dow Jones Industrial Average**

Djibouti [dʒɪˈbuːtɪ] N Yibuti *m*

dl ABBR (= **decilitre(s)**) dl

DLit(t) [ˌdiːˈlɪt] N ABBR 1 = **Doctor of Letters**

2 = **Doctor of Literature**

DLO N ABBR (= **dead-letter office**) *oficina de Correos que se encarga de las cartas que no llegan a su destino*

DM ABBR (= **Deutschmark**) DM

dm ABBR (= **decimetre(s)**) dm

D-mark [ˈdiːmɑːk] N ABBR (= **Deutschmark**) DM *m*

DMU N ABBR = **decision-making unit**

DMus ABBR = **Doctor of Music**

DMZ N ABBR = **demilitarized zone**

DNA Ⓐ N ABBR (= **deoxyribonucleic acid**) ADN *m*

Ⓑ CPD ► **DNA fingerprinting, DNA profiling** N identificación *f* mediante el análisis del ADN ► **DNA testing** N pruebas *fpl* del ADN

DNB N ABBR = **Dictionary of National Biography**

DNF ABBR (*Athletics*) = **did not finish**

DNS ABBR (*Athletics*) = **did not start**

do[1] [duː] (*3rd pers sing present* **does**; *pt* **did**; *pp* **done**)

A TRANSITIVE VERB	D NOUN
B INTRANSITIVE VERB	E PHRASAL VERBS
C AUXILIARY VERB	

Ⓐ TRANSITIVE VERB

1 hacer; **what are you doing tonight?** ¿qué haces esta noche?; **I would never do a thing like that** yo nunca haría una cosa así;

what's this doing on my chair? ¿qué hace esto en mi silla?; **I've got nothing to do** no tengo nada que hacer; **he does nothing but complain** no hace más que quejarse; **what's to be done?** ¿qué se puede hacer?; **what's the weather doing?** ¿qué tal tiempo hace?; **to do sth again** volver a hacer algo, hacer algo de nuevo; **it will have to be done again** habrá que volver a hacerlo, habrá que hacerlo de nuevo; **what's he ever done for me?** ¿qué ha hecho él por mí?; **what can I do for you?** ¿en qué puedo servirle?, ¿qué se le ofrece? (*LAm*); **could you do something for me?** ¿me podrías hacer un favor?; **what are we going to do for money?** ¿de dónde vamos a sacar dinero?; **that dress doesn't do a lot for you*** este vestido no te queda muy bien; **the new measures will do a lot for small businesses** las nuevas medidas serán de gran ayuda para las pequeñas empresas; **after the accident she couldn't do much for herself** después del accidente casi no podía valerse por sí misma; **if you do anything to him I'll kill you** si le haces algo te mato; **what's he done to his hair?** ¿qué se ha hecho en el pelo?; **I could see what the stress was doing to him** era evidente cómo le estaba afectando el estrés; **what have you done with my slippers?** ¿dónde has puesto mis zapatillas?; **what am I going to do with you?** ¿qué voy a hacer contigo?; **what are you doing with yourself these days?** ¿qué haces ahora?; **what am I going to do with myself for the rest of the day?** ¿qué puedo hacer el resto del día?; **she didn't know what to do with herself once the children had left home** se encontró un poco perdida cuando sus hijos se fueron de casa; *see also* **living B1**

2 *= carry out* [+ *work, essay*] hacer; **the work is being done by a local builder** un albañil de la zona está haciendo el trabajo; **I've got a few jobs that need doing around the house** tengo algunas cosas que hacer en la casa; **she was doing the crossword** estaba haciendo el crucigrama; **to do the washing** hacer la colada

Some **do** *+ noun combinations require a more specific Spanish verb:*

Edmund does all the accounts Edmund se encarga de *or* lleva la contabilidad; **to do the cooking** cocinar; **he did a drawing/portrait of her** la dibujó/retrató, hizo un dibujo/retrato de ella; **to do one's duty (by sb)** cumplir con su deber (con algn); **to do the ironing** planchar; **we did a lot of talking** hablamos mucho

3 *= clean* **to do the dishes** lavar los platos; **to do the silver** limpiar la plata; **to do one's teeth** lavarse los dientes

4 *= arrange, prepare* [+ *vegetables*] preparar; [+ *room*] hacer, arreglar; **this room needs doing** hay que hacer *or* arreglar esta habitación; **to do the flowers** arreglar las flores; **to do one's nails** hacerse *or* arreglarse las uñas; *see also* **hair A1**

5 *= spend* pasar; **he did six years (in jail)** pasó seis años en la cárcel; **he did two years as ambassador in Lagos** estuvo dos años como embajador en Lagos; **I did five years as a policeman** fui policía durante cinco años; **they have to do two years military service** tienen que hacer dos años de servicio militar

6 *= finish* **I've only done three pages** sólo he hecho tres páginas; **now you've (gone and) done it!*** ¡ahora sí que la has hecho buena!*; **that's done it!*** **we're stuck now** ¡la hemos fastidiado!* ahora no podemos salir de aquí; **that does it!*** **that's the last time I lend him my car** ¡es el colmo! *or* ¡hasta aquí hemos llegado!, es la última vez que le dejo el coche; **have you done moaning?*** ¿has acabado de quejarte?; *see also* **good B2, C2**

7 *= offer, make available* **they do a summer course in painting** dan un curso de verano de pintura; **we only do one make of gloves** sólo tenemos una marca de guantes; **they do an estate version of this car** fabrican un modelo familiar de este coche; **we do evening meals if ordered in advance** servimos cenas si se encargan con antelación; **I can do you a discount on this model** le puedo hacer un descuento en este modelo

8 *= study* [+ *university course, option*] hacer, estudiar; **I want to do Physics at university** quiero hacer *or* estudiar física en la universidad; **to do Italian** hacer *or* estudiar italiano; **we're doing Orwell this term** estamos estudiando a Orwell este trimestre

9 *Theat* [+ *play*] representar, poner; [+ *part*] hacer; **he did King Lear in a BBC production** hizo (el papel) de King Lear en una producción de la BBC

10 *= mimic* [+ *person*] imitar; **he does his maths master to perfection** imita a su profesor de matemáticas a la perfección; **she was doing the worried mother bit‡** hacía el numerito de la típica madre preocupada*

11 *Aut, Rail etc* (= *travel at*) [+ *speed*] ir a; (= *cover*) [+ *distance*] cubrir; **the car can do 100 miles per hour** el coche puede ir a 100 millas por hora; **the car was doing 100 miles per hour** el coche iba a 100 millas por hora; **we've done 200km already** ya hemos hecho 200km; **we did London to Edinburgh in 8 hours** fuimos de Londres a Edimburgo en 8 horas

12 *= attend to* **the barber said he'd do me next** el barbero dijo que después me tocaría a mí; **they do you very well in this hotel** en este hotel te dan muy buen servicio; *see also* **proud 1**

13 ** = visit* [+ *city, museum*] visitar, recorrer; [+ *country*] visitar, viajar por; **we did six countries in an 8-week tour** visitamos seis países durante un viaje de 8 semanas

14 ** = be suitable, sufficient for* **will a kilo do you?** ¿le va bien un kilo?; **that'll do me nicely** (= *be suitable*) eso me vendrá muy bien; (= *suffice*) con eso me basta

15 ** = cheat* estafar, timar; (= *rob*) robar; **I've been done!** ¡me han estafado *or* timado!

16 ** = prosecute* procesar; (= *fine*) multar; **she was done for shoplifting** la procesaron por robar en una tienda; **he was done for speeding** le multaron por exceso de velocidad

17 ** = beat up* dar una paliza a; **I'll do you if I get hold of you!** ¡te voy a dar una paliza como te pille!

Ⓑ INTRANSITIVE VERB

1 *= act* hacer; **do as I do** haz como yo; **you would do better to accept** sería aconsejable que aceptaras; **he did right** hizo lo correcto; **do as you think best** haga lo que mejor le parezca; **do as you are told!** ¡haz lo que te digo!; **she was up and doing at 6 o'clock** a las 6 de la mañana ya estaba levantada y trajinando; **you would do well to take his advice** harías bien en seguir su consejo; **you could do a lot worse than marry her** casarte con ella no es lo peor que podrías hacer; *see also* **well A1**

2 *= get on* **he did badly in the exam** le fue mal en el examen; **the team hasn't done badly this season** al equipo no le ha ido mal esta temporada; **you didn't do so badly** no lo has hecho del todo mal; **you can do better than that** (*essay, drawing*) puedes hacerlo mejor; (*iro*) (= *find better excuse*) ¡y qué más!; **how is your father doing?** ¿cómo está tu padre?, ¿cómo le va a tu padre?; **how are you doing?*** ¿qué tal?, ¿cómo te va?; **how did you do in the audition?** ¿qué tal *or* cómo te fue en la audición?; **he's doing well at school** le va bien en el colegio; **her son's doing well for himself** a su hijo le van muy bien las cosas; **his business is doing well** los negocios le van bien; **the patient is doing well** el paciente está respondiendo bien; **the roses are doing well this year** las rosas han florecido muy bien este año

◆ **how do you do?** (*greeting*) ¿cómo está usted?, gusto en conocerlo (*LAm*); (*as answer*) ¡mucho gusto!, ¡encantado!

3 *= be suitable* **it doesn't do to upset her** cuidado con ofenderla; **will this one do?** ¿te parece bien éste?; **this room will do** esta habitación ya me va bien; **will it do if I come back at eight?** ¿va bien si vuelvo a las ocho?; **will tomorrow do?** ¿iría bien mañana?; **it's not exactly what I wanted, but it will** *or* **it'll do** no es exactamente lo que quería pero servirá; **this coat will do as a blanket** este abrigo servirá de manta; **that will have to do** tendremos que conformarnos con eso; **that won't do, you'll have to do it again** así no está bien, tendrás que volver a hacerlo; **you can't go on your own, that would never do!** no podemos consentir que vayas sola, ¡eso no puede ser!; *see also* **make A4**

4 *= be sufficient* bastar; **three bottles of wine should do** bastará con tres botellas de vino; **will £20 do?** ¿bastarán 20 libras?, ¿tendrás bastante con 20 libras?; **that'll do** con eso basta; **that will do!** ¡basta ya!; **that will do for the moment** de momento ya está bien

5 *= happen* **there's not much doing in this town** no hay mucha animación en esta ciudad; **"could you lend me £50?" — "nothing doing!"** —¿me podrías prestar 50 libras? —¡de ninguna manera! *or* —¡ni hablar!

6 ** = finish* (*in past tenses only*) terminar, acabar; **have you done?** ¿ya has terminado *or* acabado?; **don't take it away, I've not done yet** no te lo lleves, ¡aún no he terminado *or* acabado!; **I haven't done telling you** ¡no he terminado de contarte!; **I've done with travelling** ya no voy a viajar más, he renunciado a los viajes; **I've done with all that nonsense** ya no tengo nada que ver *or* ya he terminado con todas esas tonterías; **have you done with that book?** ¿has terminado con este libro?

7 ** = clean* hacer la limpieza (en casa); **I've got a lady who does for me** tengo una señora que me viene a hacer la limpieza en la casa

Ⓒ AUXILIARY VERB

There is no equivalent in Spanish to the use of **do** *in questions, negative statements and negative commands.*

1 *in questions* **do you understand?** ¿comprendes?, ¿entiendes?; **where does he live?** ¿dónde vive?; **didn't you like it?** ¿no te gustó?; **why didn't you come?** ¿por qué no viniste?

2 *negation* **I don't understand** no entiendo *or* comprendo; **don't let's argue** no discutamos; **don't worry!** ¡no te preocupes!; **don't you tell me what to do!** ¡no me digas lo que tengo que hacer!; **she did not go** no fue

3 *for emphasis* **DO tell me!** ¡dímelo, por favor!; **DO sit down** siéntese, por favor, tome asiento, por favor (*frm*); **she DOES look lovely in that dress** está preciosa con este vestido; **I DO hope so** así lo espero; **I DO wish I could come with you** ¡ojalá pudiera ir contigo!; **but I DO like it!** ¡sí que me gusta!, ¡por supuesto que me gusta!; **so you DO know him!** ¡así que sí lo conoces!; **but I DID do it** pero sí que lo hice

4 *with inversion* **rarely does it happen that …** rara vez ocurre que …; **not once did they offer to pay** no se ofrecieron a pagar ni una sola vez

5 *verb substitute* 5·1 **you speak better than I do** tú hablas mejor que yo; **"did you fix the car?" — "I did"** —¿arreglaste el coche? —sí; **"I love it" — "so do I"** —me encanta —a mí también; **I don't like sport and neither does he** no me gusta el deporte ni a él tampoco; **you didn't see him but I did** tú no lo viste pero yo sí; **I told him he'd fail and he did** le dije que iba a suspender y suspendió; **he went for a walk as he often did** fue a dar un paseo como solía hacer; **she always says she'll come but she never does** siempre dice que vendrá pero nunca viene; **"he borrowed the car" — "oh he did, did he?"** —pidió el coche prestado —¿ah sí? ¡no me digas!; **I like this colour, don't you?** me gusta este color, ¿a ti no?; **"do you speak English?" — "yes, I do/no I don't"** —¿habla usted inglés? —sí, hablo inglés/no, no hablo inglés; **"may I come in?" — "(please) do!"** —¿se puede pasar? —¡pasa (por favor)!; **"who made this mess?" — "I did"** —¿quién lo ha desordenado todo? —fui yo; **"shall I ring her again?" — "no, don't!"** —¿la llamo otra vez? —¡no, no la llames!

5·2 (*in question tags*) **he lives here, doesn't he?** vive aquí, ¿verdad? *or* ¿no es cierto? *or* ¿no?; **I don't know him, do I?** no lo conozco, ¿verdad?; **it doesn't matter, does it?** no importa, ¿no?; **she said that, did she?** ¿eso es lo que dijo?

Ⓓ NOUN

1 *Brit* = party* fiesta *f*; (= *formal gathering*) reunión *f*; **they had a big do for their twenty-fifth anniversary** dieron una gran fiesta por su vigésimo quinto aniversario

2 *in phrases* **the do's and don'ts of buying a house** lo que debe y lo que no debe hacerse al comprar una casa; **he gave us a series of dos and don'ts** nos explicó lo que podíamos y lo que no podíamos hacer; **fair dos!*** (= *be fair*) ¡hay que ser justo!, ¡seamos justos!; (= *fair shares*) ¡a partes iguales!; **it's a poor do when …** es una vergüenza cuando …

Ⓔ PHRASAL VERBS

►**do away with** VI + PREP 1 (= *get rid of*) [+ *controls*] suprimir, eliminar; [+ *nuclear weapons*] eliminar, acabar con; [+ *injustice, exploitation, system*] acabar con; [+ *capital punishment*] abolir; **it does away with the need for a middleman** con esto ya no hace falta el intermediario, con esto uno se ahorra el intermediario

2 (*) (= *kill*) matar, liquidar*; **to do away with o.s.** matarse, suicidarse

►**do by** VI + PREP **to do well/badly by sb** portarse bien/mal con algn, tratar bien/mal a algn; **he did well by his mother** se portó bien con su madre; **employees felt hard done by** los empleados se sintieron injustamente tratados; ✦*PROV* **do as you would be done by** trata como quieres ser tratado; *see also* **hard B2**

►**do down** VT + ADV (*Brit*) 1 (= *denigrate*) menospreciar; **to do o.s. down** subestimarse

2 (= *cheat*) timar, estafar; (= *play false*) hacer una mala pasada a

►**do for*** VI + PREP 1 (= *kill*) acabar con, matar; **smoking will do for him in the end** el tabaco acabará con él, el tabaco lo acabará matando; **I thought we were done for** pensaba que nos íbamos a matar; **one false move and he was done for** un movimiento en falso y era hombre muerto

2 (= *finish off*) **as a politician he's done for** como político está acabado; **they've seen him, he's done for!** lo han visto, ¡está perdido!; **if I can't talk to my own wife about these things, I'm done for** si ni siquiera puedo hablar con mi mujer de estas cosas, estoy acabado*; **I'm done for** (= *exhausted*) estoy rendido *or* molido*

►**do in*** VT + ADV 1 (= *kill*) liquidar*, cargarse*

2 (= *exhaust*) reventar*, hacer polvo*; **he's absolutely done in** está totalmente reventado*, está hecho polvo*

3 (= *ruin*) [+ *back*] hacerse daño en, fastidiar (*Sp**); [+ *engine*] cargarse (*Sp**), arruinar (*LAm*); **he'll do the engine in, driving the way he does** se cargará el motor conduciendo de esa manera (*Sp**)

►**do out** VT + ADV 1 (*Brit*) [+ *room*] (= *clean*) limpiar a fondo

2 [+ *room*] (= *paint*) pintar; (= *wallpaper*) empapelar; (= *furnish*) decorar; **a room done out in Mexican style** una habitación decorada al estilo mejicano

3 **to do sb out of sth***: **he has done me out of thousands of pounds** me quedé sin miles de libras por su culpa; **he did her out of a job** le quitó el trabajo, se quedó sin el trabajo por su culpa; **they did me out of my big chance** me pisaron mi gran oportunidad*

►**do over** VT + ADV 1 (*US**) (= *repeat*) volver a hacer, hacer de nuevo

2 (= *redecorate*) volver a pintar/empapelar; (= *refurnish*) volver a decorar

3 (*Brit**) (= *beat up*) dar una paliza a*

►**do up** VT + ADV 1 (= *fasten*) [+ *shoes, shoelaces*] atar; [+ *dress*] (*gen*) abrochar; (*with zip*) cerrar *or* subir la cremallera de; [+ *buttons, coat, necklace*] abrochar; [+ *tie*] hacer el nudo de; [+ *zip*] cerrar, subir

2 (= *wrap up*) [+ *parcel*] envolver; **have you done up that parcel yet?** ¿has envuelto ya ese paquete?

3 (= *renovate*) [+ *house*] reformar, hacer reformas en

4 (= *dress up*) **she was all done up in her best clothes** iba de punta en blanco*; **Mark was done up in a beret and cravat*** Mark iba luciendo una boina y un fular

►**do with** VI + PREP 1 (= *need*) **I could do with some help/a beer** no me vendría mal un poco de ayuda/una cerveza; **we could have done with you there** nos hiciste mucha falta; **you could do with a bath** te vendría bien un baño

2 (= *have connection with*) **it is to do with**: **"what did you want to see her about?" — "it's to do with her application"** —¿de qué querías hablarle? —es respecto a su solicitud; **it's nothing to do with me** no tiene nada que ver conmigo; **to have to do with** tener que ver con; **that has nothing to do with you!** ¡eso no tiene nada que ver contigo!; **what has that got to do with it?** ¿eso qué tiene que ver?; **that has nothing to do with it!** ¡eso no tiene nada que ver!; **I won't have anything to do with it/him** no quiero tener nada que ver con este asunto/con él, no quiero saber nada de este asunto/de él

3 (*) **I can't be doing with pop music** tengo mejores cosas que hacer que escuchar música pop; **I can't be doing with his finicky eating habits** no soporto sus manías a la hora de comer

►**do without** VI + PREP **I can't do without my computer** yo no puedo pasar sin el ordenador; **"I haven't brought my gym kit" — "you'll have to do without then!"** —no he traído mi equipo de gimnasia —pues vas a tener que apañártelas sin él; **you can't do without money** no se puede vivir sin dinero; **I can do without your advice** no necesito tus consejos; **I could do without them poking their noses in*** no necesito que vengan ellos metiendo las narices en lo que no les importa*; **this bus strike is something I could do without*** esta huelga de autobuses es lo último que me faltaba

do² [dəʊ] N (*Mus*) do *m*

do. ABBR (= **ditto**) lo mismo, ídem, íd.

DOA ADJ ABBR (= **dead on arrival**) ingresó cadáver

d.o.b. N ABBR = **date of birth**

Doberman ['dəʊbəmən] N (*also* ~ **pinscher**) dóberman *m*

doc [dɒk] Ⓐ N (*esp US**) = **doctor**
Ⓑ ABBR (= **document**) doc.

docile ['dəʊsaɪl] ADJ dócil, sumiso

docility [dəʊ'sɪlɪtɪ] N docilidad *f*

dock¹ [dɒk] N (*Bot*) acedera *f*, ramaza *f*

dock² [dɒk] VT 1 [+ *animal's tail*] cortar, cercenar (*frm*)

2 (*Brit*) **to ~ sb's pay** descontar dinero del sueldo a algn; **I've been ~ed £1** me han descontado una libra

dock³ [dɒk] Ⓐ N 1 (*Naut*) dársena *f*, muelle *m*; (*with gates*) dique *m*; **to be in ~** (*Brit**) [*ship*] estar en puerto; [*car*] estar en el taller

2 **docks** muelles *mpl*, puerto *m*

Ⓑ VT [+ *ship*] atracar; [+ *spacecraft*] acoplar

Ⓒ VI 1 (*Naut*) atracar; (*loosely*) llegar; **the ship has ~ed** el barco ha atracado; **we ~ed at five** llegamos a las cinco, entramos en el puerto a las cinco; **when we ~ed at Vigo** cuando llegamos a Vigo

2 [*spacecraft*] acoplarse (**with** a)

Ⓓ CPD ► **dock dues** NPL derechos *mpl* de atraque *or* de dársena ► **dock labourer**, **dock laborer** (*US*) N = **dock worker** ► **dock walloper*** N (*US*) = **dock worker** ► **dock warrant** N resguardo *m* de muelle, conocimiento *m* de almacén ► **dock worker** N trabajador *m* portuario

dock⁴ [dɒk] N (*Brit*) (*in court*) banquillo *m* de los acusados

docker ['dɒkəʳ] N (*Brit*) estibador *m*

docket ['dɒkɪt] N 1 (= *label*) etiqueta *f*, marbete *m*; (*esp Brit*) (= *certificate*) resguardo *m*, certificado *m*; (= *bill*) factura *f*

2 (*US Jur*) lista *f* de casos pendientes

docking ['dɒkɪŋ] Ⓐ N [*of spacecraft*] atraque *m*, acoplamiento *m*

Ⓑ CPD ► **docking manoeuvre**, **docking maneuver** (*US*) N maniobra *f* de atraque

dockland(s) ['dɒklænd(z)] N(PL) (*Brit*) zona *f* del puerto, zona *f* portuaria

dockyard ['dɒkjɑːd] N astillero *m*

doctor ['dɒktəʳ] Ⓐ N 1 (*Med*) médico/a *m/f*; **to go to the ~'s** ir al médico; **Doctor Brown** el doctor Brown; **to be under the ~*** estar bajo tratamiento médico; ✦*IDIOM* **it was just what the ~ ordered*** fue mano de santo

[2] (*Univ*) doctor(a) *m/f* (**of** en); → [DEGREE]
Ⓑ VT [1] (= *tamper with*) [+ *food, drink*] adulterar; [+ *document*] manipular
[2] (= *treat*) [+ *cold*] tratar, curar; **to ~ o.s.** automedicarse
[3] (*) (= *castrate*) [+ *cat, dog etc*] castrar
Ⓒ CPD ► **doctor's degree** N doctorado *m* ► **doctor's excuse** (*US*), **doctor's line** (*Brit*), **doctor's note** (*Brit*) N baja *f* (médica)

► **doctor up** VT + ADV [+ *machine etc*] remendar, arreglar de cualquier modo

doctoral ['dɒktərəl] Ⓐ ADJ doctoral
Ⓑ CPD ► **doctoral dissertation** N (*US*) = **doctoral thesis** ► **doctoral thesis** N (*Brit*) tesis *f inv* doctoral

doctorate ['dɒktərɪt] N doctorado *m*; → [DEGREE]

doctrinaire [ˌdɒktrɪ'neəʳ] Ⓐ ADJ doctrinario
Ⓑ N doctrinario/a *m/f*

doctrinal [dɒk'traɪnl] ADJ doctrinal

doctrine ['dɒktrɪn] N doctrina *f*

docudrama ['dɒkjʊˌdrɑːmə] N docudrama *m*

document Ⓐ ['dɒkjʊmənt] N documento *m*
Ⓑ ['dɒkjʊment] VT documentar
Ⓒ ['dɒkjʊmənt] CPD ► **document case**, **document holder** N portadocumentos *m inv* ► **document reader** N (*Comput*) lector *m* de documentos

documentary [ˌdɒkjʊ'mentərɪ] Ⓐ ADJ documental; (*Comm, Fin*) documentario
Ⓑ N (*Cine, TV*) documental *m*
Ⓒ CPD ► **documentary bill of exchange** N letra *f* de cambio documentaria ► **documentary evidence** N pruebas *fpl* documentales ► **documentary (letter of) credit** N crédito *m* documentario

documentation [ˌdɒkjʊmen'teɪʃən] N documentación *f*

docu-soap ['dɒkjʊsəʊp] N (*TV*) *documental sobre la vida cotidiana de un grupo de personas*

DOD N ABBR (*US*) = **Department of Defense**

dodder ['dɒdəʳ] VI (*walking*) renquear; [*hand*] temblequear

dodderer ['dɒdərəʳ] N chocho *m*

doddering ['dɒdərɪŋ], **doddery** ['dɒdərɪ] ADJ renqueante, chocho (*pej*)

doddle* ['dɒdl] N **it's a ~** (*Brit*) es pan comido*, está chupado

Dodecanese [ˌdəʊdɪkə'niːz] NPL **the ~** el Dodecaneso

dodecaphonic [ˌdəʊdekə'fɒnɪk] ADJ dodecafónico

dodge [dɒdʒ] Ⓐ N [1] (= *movement*) regate *m*; (*Boxing etc*) finta *f*
[2] (*Brit**) (= *trick*) truco *m*
Ⓑ VT (= *elude*) [+ *blow, ball*] esquivar; [+ *pursuer*] dar esquinazo a; [+ *acquaintance, problem*] evitar; [+ *tax*] evadir; [+ *responsibility, duty, job*] eludir; **to ~ the issue** eludir el tema
Ⓒ VI escabullirse; (*Boxing*) hacer una finta; **to ~ out of the way** echarse a un lado; **to ~ behind a tree** ocultarse tras un árbol; **to ~ round a corner** escabullirse detrás de una esquina

► **dodge about** VI + ADV ir de aquí para allá

dodgem ['dɒdʒəm] N (*Brit*) (*also* **~ car**) coche *m* de choque; **the ~s** los coches de choque

dodger ['dɒdʒəʳ] N (= *trickster*) tunante/a *m/f*, gandul *mf*

dodgy* ['dɒdʒɪ] ADJ (*Brit*) (*compar* **dodgier**; *superl* **dodgiest**) [1] (= *dishonest*) [*person*] de poco fiar, poco fiable; [*business, deal, district*] oscuro, chungo (*Sp**); [*practice*] dudoso; **there's something ~ about him** hay algo en él que me da mala espina*; **the whole business seemed a bit ~** todo el asunto parecía un poco oscuro
[2] (= *unreliable, uncertain*) [*plan*] arriesgado; [*weather*] inestable; **the clutch is a bit ~** el embrague no anda muy bien, el embrague está un poco chungo (*Sp**); **he's in a ~ situation financially** su situación económica es un poco peliaguda; **the sausages looked ~** las salchichas tenían una pinta sospechosa; **to have a ~ back** tener la espalda fastidiada, estar fastidiado de la espalda; **to have a ~ heart** estar fastidiado del corazón

dodo ['dəʊdəʊ] N (*pl* **dodos** *or* **dodoes**) [1] (*Zool*) dodó *m*; *see also* **dead A1**
[2] (*US**) (= *fool*) bobo/a *m/f*

DOE N ABBR [1] (*Brit*) = **Department of the Environment**
[2] (*US*) = **Department of Energy**

doe [dəʊ] N (*pl* **does** *or* **doe**) (= *deer*) cierva *f*, gama *f*; (= *rabbit*) coneja *f*; (= *hare*) liebre *f*

doer ['dʊːəʳ] N [1] (= *author of deed*) hacedor(a) *m/f*
[2] (= *active person*) persona *f* enérgica, persona *f* dinámica

does [dʌz] 3RD PERS SING *of* **do**

doeskin ['dəʊskɪn] N ante *m*, piel *f* de ante

doesn't ['dʌznt] = **does not**

doff [dɒf] VT (*frm*) quitarse; **to ~ one's hat** quitarse el sombrero

dog [dɒg] Ⓐ N [1] (*Zool*) perro/a *m/f*; ✦**IDIOMS ~ eat ~**: **it's ~ eat ~ in this place** aquí se despedazan unos a otros; **to go to the ~s*** [*person*] echarse a perder; [*nation, country*] ir a la ruina; **~'s breakfast*** revoltijo *m*; **to have a ~'s chance**: **he hasn't a ~'s chance** no tiene la más remota posibilidad; **it's a ~'s life** es una vida de perros; **to be dressed up like a ~'s dinner*** ir hecho un adefesio; **to be a ~ in the manger** [*person*] ser como el perro del hortelano; **to put on the ~** (*US**) vestirse de punta en blanco; **to be top ~** ser el gallo del lugar, triunfar; **the ~'s bollocks** (*Brit***) la hostia**; ✦**PROVS every ~ has its day** a cada cerdo le llega su San Martín; **let sleeping ~s lie** más vale no meneallo
[2] (= *male*) (*fox*) macho *m*
[3] (*) (*term of abuse*) canalla *m*, bribón *m*; **you ~!** ¡canalla!; (*hum*) ¡tunante!
[4] (*) (= *unattractive girl*) callo *m* (malayo)*
[5] (*) (= *person*) **dirty ~** tío *m* guarro*, tipo *m* asqueroso*; **you lucky ~!** ¡qué suerte tienes!; **he's a lucky ~** es un tío suertudo; ✦**IDIOM there's life in the old ~ yet** (al abuelo) aún le queda cuerda para rato
[6] **the ~s** (*Brit**) (= *greyhounds*) las carreras de galgos; → [GREYHOUND RACING]
[7] (*Brit**) (= *telephone*) teléfono *m*
Ⓑ VT (= *follow closely*) seguir (de cerca); **he ~s my footsteps** me sigue los pasos; **he was ~ged by ill luck** le perseguía la mala suerte
Ⓒ CPD ► **dog basket** N cesto *m* del perro ► **dog biscuit** N galleta *f* de perro ► **dog breeder** N criador(a) *m/f* de perros ► **dog collar** N collar *m* de perro; (*Rel hum*) gola *f*, alzacuello(s) *m inv* ► **dog days** NPL canícula *f* ► **dog fancier** N (= *connoisseur*) entendido/a *m/f* en perros; (= *breeder*) criador(a) *m/f* de perros ► **dog food** N comida *f* para perros ► **dog fox** N zorro *m* macho ► **dog guard** N (*Aut*) reja *f* separadora ► **dog handler** N (*Police*) adiestrador(a) *m/f* de perros ► **dog Latin** N latín *m* macarrónico ► **dog licence** N permiso *m* para perros ► **dog paddle** N braza *f* de perro (*forma de nadar*); *see also* **dog-paddle** ► **dog rose** N escaramujo *m*, rosal *m* silvestre ► **dog show** N exposición *f* canina ► **Dog Star** N Sirio *m* ► **dog tag** N (*US Mil*) placa *f* de identificación ► **dog track** N (*Sport*) canódromo *m*

dogcart ['dɒgkɑːt] N dócar *m*

doge [dəʊdʒ] N dux *m*

dog-eared ['dɒgɪəd] ADJ sobado, muy manoseado

dog-end* ['dɒgend] N colilla *f*, toba* *f*

dogfight ['dɒgfaɪt] N (*Aer*) combate *m* aéreo (reñido y confuso); (*) (= *squabble*) trifulca *f*, refriega *f*

dogfish ['dɒgfɪʃ] N (*pl* **dogfish** *or* **dogfishes**) perro *m* marino, cazón *m*

dogged ['dɒgɪd] ADJ (= *obstinate*) porfiado, terco; (= *tenacious*) tenaz

doggedly ['dɒgɪdlɪ] ADV tenazmente

doggedness ['dɒgɪdnɪs] N tenacidad *f*

doggerel ['dɒgərəl] N coplas *fpl* de ciego, malos versos *mpl*

doggie ['dɒgɪ] N = **doggy**

doggo* ['dɒgəʊ] ADV (*Brit*) **to lie ~** quedarse escondido

doggone* [ˌdɒg'gɒn] (*US*) Ⓐ EXCL ¡maldita sea!
Ⓑ ADJ condenado, maldito

doggy* ['dɒgɪ] Ⓐ N (*baby talk*) perrito *m*; **to have sex ~ fashion** hacer el amor al estilo perrito
Ⓑ CPD ► **doggy bag** N bolsita *f* con los restos de la comida (*en restaurante*) ► **doggy paddle** N braza *f* de perro; *see also* **doggy-paddle**

doggy-paddle ['dɒgˌɪpædl] VI nadar como los perros; *see also* **doggy**

doghouse ['dɒghaʊs] N (*pl* **doghouses** ['dɒghaʊzɪz]) (*US*) caseta *f* del perro; ✦**IDIOM to be in the ~*** [*person*] estar castigado

dogleg ['dɒgleg] N (*in road etc*) codo *m*, ángulo *m* abrupto

doglike ['dɒglaɪk] ADJ de perro

dogma ['dɒgmə] N (*pl* **dogmas** *or* **dogmata** ['dɒgmətə]) dogma *m*

dogmatic [dɒg'mætɪk] ADJ dogmático

dogmatically [dɒg'mætɪkəlɪ] ADV dogmáticamente

dogmatism ['dɒgmətɪzəm] N dogmatismo *m*

dogmatist ['dɒgmətɪst] N dogmático/a *m/f*

dogmatize ['dɒgmətaɪz] VI dogmatizar

do-gooder* ['duː'gʊdəʳ] N (*pej*) hacedor(a) *m/f* de buenas obras

dog-paddle ['dɒgˌpædl] VI nadar como los perros; *see also* **dog C**

dogsbody* ['dɒgzbɒdɪ] N (*Brit*) burro *m* de carga; **to be the general ~** ser el burro de carga de todo el mundo

dog-tired* ['dɒg'taɪəd] ADJ rendido*, hecho polvo*

dogtrot ['dɒgtrɒt] N trote *m* lento

dogwatch ['dɒgwɒtʃ] N (*Naut*) guardia *f* de cuartillo

doily ['dɔɪlɪ] N (*under cake*) blonda *f*; (*under ornament*) pañito *m* de adorno

doing ['duːɪŋ] N [1] **this is your ~** esto es cosa tuya; **it was none of my ~** yo no he tenido nada que ver; **it will take a lot of** *or* **some ~** va a ser muy difícil hacerlo, costará mucho hacerlo; **that takes some ~!** ¡eso no es nada fácil!; *see also* **nothing A**
[2] **doings** (= *activities*) actividades *fpl*; (= *actions*) acciones *fpl*; (= *happenings*) sucesos *mpl*; **he recounted the day's ~s** hizo recuento de las actividades del día

doings* ['duːɪŋz] NSING (*Brit*) (= *thing*) chisme

m; **that ~ with two knobs** aquel chisme con dos botones

do-it-yourself ['du:ɪtjə'self] Ⓐ N bricolaje *m*
Ⓑ CPD ► **do-it-yourself enthusiast, do-it-yourself expert** N aficionado/a *m/f* al bricolaje ► **do-it-yourself kit** N modelo *m* para armar ► **do-it-yourself shop** N tienda *f* de bricolaje

do-it-yourselfer* [,du:ɪtjə'selfəʳ] N aficionado/a *m/f* al bricolaje, bricolero/a *m/f*

Dolby® ['dɒlbɪ] N Dolby® *m*

doldrums ['dɒldrəmz] NPL (*Naut*) zona *f* de las calmas ecuatoriales; ✦*IDIOM* **to be in the ~** [*person*] estar abatido; [*business*] estar estancado; (*St Ex*) estar en calma

dole* [dəʊl] (*Brit*) Ⓐ N subsidio *m* de paro, paro *m*; **to be on the ~** estar parado, cobrar el paro
Ⓑ CPD ► **dole queue** N cola *f* del paro

►**dole out** VT + ADV repartir, distribuir

doleful ['dəʊlfʊl] ADJ triste

dolefully ['dəʊlfəlɪ] ADV tristemente

doll [dɒl] Ⓐ N [1] (= *toy*) muñeca *f*
[2] (*esp US**) (= *girl*) muñeca *f*, preciosidad *f*; **you're a ~ to help me** eres un ángel, gracias por ayudarme
Ⓑ CPD ► **doll's house** N casa *f* de muñecas

►**doll up*** VT + ADV emperifollar, emperejilar; **to ~ o.s. up** emperifollarse, emperejilarse

dollar ['dɒləʳ] Ⓐ N dólar *m*; ✦*IDIOMS* **you can bet your bottom ~ that ...** puedes apostarte lo que quieras a que ...; **it's ~s to doughnuts that ...** (*US**) es tan cierto como hay Dios que ...*
Ⓑ CPD ► **dollar area** N zona *f* del dólar ► **dollar bill** N billete *m* de un dólar ► **dollar diplomacy** N (*US Pol*) diplomacia *f* a golpe de dólar ► **dollar rate** N cambio *m* del dólar ► **dollar sign** N signo *m* del dólar

dollop ['dɒləp] N [*of jam, ketchup etc*] pegote *m*

dolly ['dɒlɪ] Ⓐ N [1] (* *baby talk*) (= *doll*) muñequita *f*
[2] (*) (= *girl*) chica *f*, jovencita *f*
[3] (*Cine, TV*) travelín *m*, plataforma *f* rodante
[4] (*US*) carretilla *f*
Ⓑ CPD ► **dolly bird**‡ N (*Brit*) niña *f* mona*

dolomite ['dɒləmaɪt] N dolomía *f*, dolomita *f*

Dolomites ['dɒləmaɪts] NPL **the ~** las Dolomitas, los Alpes Dolomíticos

dolphin ['dɒlfɪn] N delfín *m*

dolphinarium [,dɒlfɪ'nɛərɪəm] N delfinario *m*

dolt* [dəʊlt] N imbécil *mf*; **you ~!** ¡imbécil!

domain [dəʊ'meɪn] Ⓐ N [1] (= *lands etc*) dominio *m*, propiedad *f*
[2] (*fig*) campo *m*, competencia *f*; **the matter is now in the public ~** el asunto es ya del dominio público
Ⓑ CPD ► **domain name** N (*Internet*) nombre *m* de dominio

dome [dəʊm] N (*on building etc*) cúpula *f*; (*Geog*) colina *f* redonda

domed [dəʊmd] ADJ [*roof*] abovedado; [*forehead*] en forma de huevo

Domesday Book ['du:mzdeɪ,bʊk] N **the ~** el Domesday Book (*libro del registro catastral realizado en Inglaterra en 1086*)

domestic [də'mestɪk] Ⓐ ADJ [1] (= *household*) [*activities, duty, life, animal*] doméstico; [*fuel*] de uso doméstico; [*harmony, quarrel*] familiar; [*violence*] en el hogar; **for ~ use** para uso doméstico; **she does ~ work for a living** trabaja como empleada del hogar *or* empleada doméstica; **a scene of ~ bliss** una escena de felicidad familiar *or* doméstica
[2] (= *home-loving*) casero, hogareño
[3] (*Econ, Pol*) (= *internal*) [*flight, industry, news, economy, politics*] nacional; [*market, consumption, policy*] nacional, interior; [*affairs, problems*] nacional, interno
Ⓑ N doméstico/a *m/f*, empleado/a *m/f* doméstico/a
Ⓒ CPD ► **domestic appliance** N aparato *m* doméstico, aparato *m* de uso doméstico ► **domestic help** N empleado/a *m/f* del hogar, empleado/a *m/f* doméstico/a ► **domestic science** N (*esp Brit Scol*) economía *f* doméstica, hogar *m* (*Sp*) ► **domestic science teacher** N (*esp Brit Scol*) profesor(a) *m/f* de economía doméstica, profesor(a) *m/f* de hogar (*Sp*) ► **domestic servant** N sirviente/a *m/f*, doméstico/a *m/f* ► **domestic service** N servicio *m* doméstico; **to be in ~ service** trabajar en el servicio doméstico ► **domestic staff** N (*in hospital, institution*) personal *m* de servicio; (*in private household*) servicio *m* doméstico ► **domestic worker** N empleado/a *m/f* doméstico/a

domestically [də'mestɪkəlɪ] ADV [1] (= *nationally*) nacionalmente; **~ and internationally** nacional e internacionalmente; **a ~ produced article** un artículo producido en el país; **~ produced goods** productos *mpl* nacionales
[2] (= *in the home*) **he's not very ~ inclined** (= *not homely*) no es lo que se dice una persona muy casera; (= *not keen on housework*) no le van mucho las tareas de la casa

domesticate [də'mestɪkeɪt] VT [+ *wild animal*] domesticar

domesticated [də'mestɪkeɪtɪd] ADJ [*animal*] domesticado; [*person*] casero, hogareño

domestication [dəʊ,mestɪ'keɪʃən] N domesticación *f*

domesticity [,dəʊmes'tɪsɪtɪ] N domesticidad *f*

domicile ['dɒmɪsaɪl] (*frm*) Ⓐ N (*also* **place of ~**) domicilio *m*
Ⓑ VT **to be ~d in** tener domicilio en

domiciliary [,dɒmɪ'sɪlɪərɪ] ADJ domiciliario

dominance ['dɒmɪnəns] N [1] (= *supremacy*) [*of person*] dominio *m* (**over** sobre); [*of class, nation*] dominio *m*, dominación *f* (**over** sobre)
[2] (= *predominance*) predominio *m*
[3] (*Bio, Ecol*) [*of gene, species, male*] dominancia *f*

dominant ['dɒmɪnənt] Ⓐ ADJ [1] (= *supremely powerful*) [*person, factor, role*] dominante; **Britain was once ~ in the world market** Gran Bretaña fue en su día una nación dominante en el mercado mundial
[2] (= *predominant*) [*feature, theme*] predominante
[3] (*Bio, Ecol*) [*gene, species, male*] dominante
[4] (*Mus*) dominante; **~ seventh** séptima *f* dominante
Ⓑ N (*Mus*) dominante *f*

dominate ['dɒmɪneɪt] VT, VI dominar

dominating ['dɒmɪneɪtɪŋ] ADJ dominante, dominador

domination [,dɒmɪ'neɪʃən] N (= *act of dominating*) dominación *f*; (= *control*) dominio *m*

dominatrix [,dɒmɪ'neɪtrɪks] N (*pl* **dominatrices** [,dɒmɪnə'traɪsi:z]) ama *f* (*prostituta especializada en servicios sadomasoquistas*)

domineer [,dɒmɪ'nɪəʳ] VI dominar, tiranizar (**over** a)

domineering [,dɒmɪ'nɪərɪŋ] ADJ dominante, autoritario

Dominic ['dɒmɪnɪk] N Domingo

Dominica [,dɒmɪ'ni:kə] N Dominica *f*

Dominican [də'mɪnɪkən] Ⓐ ADJ dominicano
Ⓑ N [1] (*Pol*) dominicano/a *m/f*
[2] (*Rel*) dominico *m*, dominicano *m*
Ⓒ CPD ► **Dominican Republic** N República *f* Dominicana

dominion [də'mɪnɪən] N [1] (= *control*) dominio *m*; **to hold** *or* **have ~ over sb** ejercer dominio sobre algn
[2] (*Brit Pol*) dominio *m*

domino ['dɒmɪnəʊ] Ⓐ N (*pl* **dominoes**) [1] (= *piece in game*) ficha *f* de dominó; **~es** (= *game*) dominó *msing*; **to play ~es** jugar al dominó, jugar dominó (*LAm*)
[2] (= *dress*) dominó *m*
Ⓑ CPD ► **domino effect** N (*Pol*) reacción *f* en cadena ► **domino theory** N (*Pol*) teoría *f* de la reacción en cadena

Domitian [də'mɪʃɪən] N Domiciano

don[1] [dɒn] N [1] (*Brit Univ*) catedrático/a *m/f*
[2] (*US*) **a Mafia ~** un capo de la Mafia

don[2] [dɒn] VT (*liter*) [+ *garment*] ponerse, ataviarse con

donate [dəʊ'neɪt] VT donar; **to ~ blood** donar sangre

donation [dəʊ'neɪʃən] N [1] (= *act*) donación *f*
[2] (= *gift*) donativo *m*, donación *f*; **to make a ~ to a fund** hacer un donativo *or* una donación a un fondo

done [dʌn] Ⓐ PP of **do**[1]
Ⓑ ADJ [1] (= *finished*) terminado, acabado; **the job's ~** el trabajo está terminado *or* acabado; **it's as good as ~** eso está hecho; **to get ~ with sth** terminar *or* acabar de hacer algo; **why don't you tell him and have ~ with it?** ¿por qué no se lo dices y acabas de una vez?; ✦*PROV* **what's ~ cannot be undone** a lo hecho, pecho; *see also* **over C**, **say A3**
[2] (= *accepted*) **it's just not ~!** ¡eso no se hace!; **it's not ~ to voice your opinions here** aquí está mal visto que uno exprese sus opiniones; **it's not ~ to put your elbows on the table** poner los codos en la mesa es de mala educación
[3] (*in exclamations*) **done!** (= *agreed*) ¡trato hecho!; **well ~!** ¡muy bien!, ¡bravo!
[4] (*Culin*) **the vegetables are ~** la verdura está cocida *or* hecha; **how do you like your steak ~?** ¿cómo te gusta el filete?; **I like my steak well ~** me gusta el filete muy hecho
[5] (= *exhausted*) agotado, hecho polvo*; *see also* **do for 2**, **do in 2**

dong** [dɒŋ] N verga** *f*, polla *f* (*Sp***)

Don Juan [dɒn'hwa:n] N (*fig*) Don Juan *m*

donkey ['dɒŋkɪ] Ⓐ N burro *m*; **female ~** burra *f*; ✦*IDIOM* **for ~'s years** (*Brit**) durante un porrón de *or* muchísimos años; **I haven't seen him for ~'s years** (*Brit**) hace siglos que no lo veo; *see also* **hind**[1]
Ⓑ CPD ► **donkey derby** N (*Brit*) carrera *f* de burros ► **donkey jacket** N (*Brit*) chaqueta *f* de lanilla de trabajo ► **donkey engine** N pequeña máquina *f* de vapor, motor *m* auxiliar ► **donkey work*** N (*Brit*) trabajo *m* pesado

donnish ['dɒnɪʃ] ADJ [*life, discussion etc*] de erudito, de profesor; (*in appearance*) de aspecto erudito; (*pej*) profesoril, pedantesco

donor ['dəʊnəʳ] Ⓐ N donante *mf*
Ⓑ CPD ► **donor card** N carnet *m* de donante ► **donor organ** N órgano *m* donado

Don Quixote [dɒn'kwɪksət] N Don Quijote

don't [dəʊnt] Ⓐ = **do not**
Ⓑ N *see* **do**[1] **D2**
Ⓒ CPD ► **the don't knows** NPL los que no saben

donut ['dəʊnʌt] N (*esp US*) = **doughnut**

doodah* ['du:dɑ:], **doodad*** (*US*) ['du:dæd] N (*Brit*) (= *thing*) chisme *m*

doodle ['du:dl] Ⓐ N dibujito *m*, garabato *m*
Ⓑ VI hacer dibujitos, hacer garabatos

doodlebug ['du:dlbʌg] N (*Brit*) bomba *f* volante

doohickey* [ˌdu:'hɪkɪ] N (*US*) trasto *m*

doolally‡ [ˌdu:'lælɪ] ADJ tarumba*

doom [du:m] Ⓐ N (= *terrible fate*) destino *m* funesto; (= *death*) muerte *f*; (*Rel*) juicio *m* final; **a sense of ~** una sensación de desastre; **it's all ~ and gloom here** aquí reina el catastrofismo
Ⓑ VT (= *destine*) condenar (**to** a); **~ed to failure** condenado al fracaso; **to be ~ed to die** estar condenado a morir; **the ~ed ship** el buque siniestrado

doom-laden ['du:mˌleɪdn] ADJ [*warning, prophecy*] aciago

doomsday ['du:mzdeɪ] Ⓐ N día *m* del juicio final; **till ~** (*fig*) hasta el día del juicio final
Ⓑ CPD ► **the doomsday scenario** N la peor de las perspectivas, la perspectiva más catastrófica

doomwatcher ['du:mˌwɒtʃə^r] N cataclismista *mf*, catastrofista *mf*

doomwatching ['du:mˌwɒtʃɪŋ] N cataclismismo *m*, catastrofismo *m*

Doona® ['du:nə] N (*Australia*) edredón *m*

door [dɔ:^r] Ⓐ N 1 (= *hinged object*) [*of room, vehicle*] puerta *f*; **to answer the ~** (ir a) abrir la puerta; **she answered the ~ as soon as I knocked** llamé a la puerta y vino a abrir al momento; **"performance starts at 8pm, doors open at 7"** "la actuación empieza a las 8, pero las puertas se abrirán a las 7"; **to shut** *or* **slam the ~ in sb's face** cerrar la puerta a algn en las narices*, dar a algn con la puerta en las narices*; ✦***IDIOMS*** **to lay the blame for sth at sb's ~** echar la culpa de algo a algn; **the blame is always laid at the ~ of the government** siempre se le echa la culpa al gobierno; **I'm not sure his death can be laid at the doctor's ~** no estoy seguro de que se le pueda achacar su muerte al médico, no estoy seguro de que se pueda echar la culpa *or* culpar al médico de su muerte; **to close the ~ on sth** (= *make impossible*) cerrar la puerta a algo; (= *bring to an end*) poner punto final a algo; **behind closed ~s** a puerta cerrada; **to open the ~ to sth** abrir la(s) puerta(s) a algo; **meeting him opened the ~ to success for me** el encuentro con él me abrió la(s) puerta(s) al éxito; **this could open the ~ to a flood of claims for compensation** esto podría dar pie a una avalancha de reclamaciones de indemnización; ✦***PROV*** **as one ~ shuts, another opens** cuando una puerta se cierra, otra se abre; *see also* **darken A, knock C1, sliding, slam B1**
2 (= *entrance*) puerta *f*; **he stopped at the ~ of his office** se detuvo a *or* en la puerta de su oficina; **to pay at the ~** (*Cine, Theat*) pagar a la entrada *or* al entrar; **to be on the ~** [*of nightclub*] hacer de portero, estar en la puerta; (*Theat*) hacer de acomodador(a) *m/f*; **"tickets £5 in advance, £6 on the door"** "la entrada cuesta 5 libras por adelantado, 6 en la puerta"; **to see** *or* **show sb to the ~** acompañar a algn a la puerta; **to show sb the ~** (*euph*) decir a algn dónde está la puerta
3 (= *building*) puerta *f*; **she lived a few ~s down from me** ella vivía unas cuantas puertas más abajo (de mí); **three ~s down the street** tres puertas más abajo; **(from) ~ to ~** de puerta en puerta; **it took seven hours to get there, ~ to ~** de puerta a puerta tardamos siete horas; **next ~** (= *in the next house*) en la casa de al lado; (= *in the next room*) en la habitación de al lado; **out of ~s** al aire libre; *see also* **foot A1**
Ⓑ CPD ► **door chain** N cadena *f* (de seguridad) de la puerta ► **door handle** N (*gen*) picaporte *m*; [*of car*] manija *f* ► **door jamb** N jamba *f* de la puerta ► **door key** N llave *f* (de la puerta) ► **door knocker** N aldaba *f*, llamador *m*

doorbell ['dɔ:bel] N timbre *m*

do-or-die ['du:ə'daɪ] ADJ [*effort*] extraordinario; **it's ~** es todo o nada

doorframe ['dɔ:freɪm] N marco *m* de la puerta

doorkeeper ['dɔ:ˌki:pə^r] N portero/a *m/f*, conserje *mf*

doorknob ['dɔ:nɒb] N pomo *m* de la puerta, manilla *f* (*LAm*)

doorman ['dɔ:mən] N (*pl* **doormen**) [*of hotel, block of flats*] portero/a *m/f*, conserje *mf*

doormat ['dɔ:mæt] N felpudo *m*, estera *f*; ✦***IDIOM*** **to treat sb like a ~**: **he treats her like a ~** le trata como a un esclava, la pisotea

doornail ['dɔ:neɪl] N *see* **dead A1**

doorpost ['dɔ:pəʊst] N jamba *f* de puerta

doorstep ['dɔ:step] Ⓐ N (= *threshold*) umbral *m*; (= *step*) peldaño *m* de la puerta; **on our ~** en la puerta de casa; **we don't want an airport on our ~** no queremos un aeropuerto aquí tan cerca
Ⓑ VT (*Brit**) *ir los periodistas a la casa de una persona para hacerle fotos o una entrevista, a menudo en contra de su voluntad*

doorstop ['dɔ:stɒp] N tope *m*

door-to-door ['dɔ:tədɔ:^r] Ⓐ ADJ [*selling*] a domicilio
Ⓑ CPD ► **door-to-door salesman** N vendedor *m* a domicilio

doorway ['dɔ:weɪ] N [*of house*] entrada *f*, puerta *f*; [*of block of flats, building*] portal *m*; (*fig*) puertas *fpl*, sendero *m*

dope [dəʊp] Ⓐ N 1 (*) (= *drugs*) drogas *fpl*; (= *cannabis*) chocolate* *m*, mota *f* (*LAm*); (*Sport*) estimulante *m*; **to do ~** (*esp US*) drogarse
2 (*) (= *information*) información *f*, informes *mpl*; **to give sb the ~** informar a algn; **what's the ~ on him?** ¿qué es lo que se sabe de él?
3 (*) (= *stupid person*) idiota *mf*, imbécil *mf*; **you ~!** ¡bobo!
4 (= *varnish*) barniz *m*
Ⓑ VT [+ *horse, person*] drogar; [+ *food, drink*] adulterar con drogas
Ⓒ CPD ► **dope fiend*** N drogata* *mf* ► **dope peddler***, **dope pusher*** N camello* *m* ► **dope sheet*** N (*US Horse racing*) periódico *m* de carreras de caballos ► **dope test** N prueba *f* antidoping, control *m* antidoping
►**dope up*** VT + ADV **to be ~d up on** *or* **with Valium** ir ciego a Valium*

dopehead* ['dəʊphed] N porrero/a* *m/f*

dopey* ['dəʊpɪ] ADJ (*compar* **dopier**, *superl* **dopiest**) (= *drugged*) drogado, colocado*; (= *fuddled*) atontado; (= *stupid*) corto*

doping ['dəʊpɪŋ] N (*Sport*) dopaje *m*, doping *m*

Doppler effect ['dɒplərɪˌfekt] N (*Astron*) efecto *m* Doppler

dopy ['dəʊpɪ] = **dopey**

Dordogne [dɔr'dɔɲ] N (= *region*) Dordoña *f*; (= *river*) Dordoña *m*

Doric ['dɒrɪk] ADJ (*Archit*) dórico

dork‡ [dɔ:k] N (*esp US*) zumbado/a *m/f*

dorm* [dɔ:m] N = **dormitory**

dormancy ['dɔ:mənsɪ] N [*of volcano*] inactividad *f*; [*of virus*] estado *m* latente; [*of plant*] reposo *m* (vegetativo)

dormant ['dɔ:mənt] ADJ [*volcano*] inactivo; (*Bio, Bot*) durmiente; [*energy*] latente; **to lie ~** (*lit*) estar inactivo; (*fig*) quedar por realizarse

dormer ['dɔ:mə^r] N (*also* **~ window**) buhardilla *f*, lucerna *f*

dormice ['dɔ:maɪs] NPL *of* **dormouse**

dormitory ['dɔ:mɪtrɪ] Ⓐ N 1 (= *bedroom*) dormitorio *m*
2 (*US*) (= *hall of residence*) residencia *f*
Ⓑ CPD ► **dormitory suburb** N (*Brit*) barrio *m* dormitorio ► **dormitory town** N (*Brit*) ciudad *f* dormitorio

Dormobile® ['dɔ:məbi:l] N (*Brit*) combi *f*

dormouse ['dɔ:maʊs] N (*pl* **dormice**) lirón *m*

Dorothy ['dɒrəθɪ] N Dorotea

Dors ABBR (*Brit*) = **Dorset**

dorsal ['dɔ:sl] Ⓐ ADJ dorsal
Ⓑ CPD ► **dorsal fin** N aleta *f* dorsal

dory[1] ['dɔ:rɪ] N (= *fish*) gallo *m*, pez *m* de San Pedro

dory[2] ['dɔ:rɪ] N (= *boat*) arenera *f*

DOS [dɒs] N ABBR = **disk operating system**

dosage ['dəʊsɪdʒ] N [*of medicine*] dosificación *f*; (*in instructions for use of medication*) posología *f*; (= *amount*) dosis *f inv*

dose [dəʊs] Ⓐ N 1 [*of medicine*] dosis *f inv*; ✦***IDIOM*** **like a ~ of salts***: **it went through her like a ~ of salts*** le hizo hacer de vientre en menos que canta un gallo*
2 (*fig*) (= *amount*) dosis *f inv*; **in small ~s** en pequeñas dosis *or* cantidades
3 (*) [*of flu*] ataque *m*
Ⓑ VT 1 (*also* **~ up**) medicar (**with** con); **to ~ o.s. (up)** medicarse (**with** con)
2 [+ *wine*] adulterar

dosh‡ [dɒʃ] N (*Brit*) guita* *f*, pasta *f* (*Sp**), plata *f* (*LAm**), lana *f* (*LAm**)

doss* [dɒs] (*Brit*) Ⓐ N 1 (= *bed*) camastro *m*; (= *sleep*) sueño *m*
2 (= *easy task*) **he thought the course would be a ~** pensó que el curso sería pan comido*
Ⓑ VI 1 (*also* **~ down**) (= *sleep*) echarse a dormir
2 (= *laze*) **to ~ around** gandulear, no hacer nada

dosser* ['dɒsə^r] N (*Brit*) vagabundo/a *m/f*, pobre *mf*

dosshouse* ['dɒshaʊs] N (*pl* **dosshouses** ['dɒshaʊzɪz]) (*Brit*) pensión *f* de mala muerte

dossier ['dɒsɪeɪ] N (*gen*) informe *m*, dossier *m*; (*Admin*) expediente *m* (**on** sobre)

DOT N ABBR (*US*) = **Department of Transportation**

Dot [dɒt] N (*familiar form*) *of* **Dorothy**

dot [dɒt] Ⓐ N punto *m*; **~s and dashes** (*Morse*) puntos y rayas; **~, ~, ~** (*Typ*) puntos suspensivos; **at seven o'clock on the ~** a las siete en punto; **to pay on the ~** pagar puntualmente; ✦***IDIOM*** **since the year ~** (*Brit*) desde los tiempos de Maricastaña
Ⓑ VT 1 [+ *letter*] poner el punto sobre; ✦***IDIOM*** **to ~ the i's and cross the t's** poner los puntos sobre las íes; *see also* **dotted line**
2 (= *scatter*) esparcir, desparramar; **they are ~ted about the country** están esparcidos por todo el país; **~ted with flowers** salpicado de flores
3 (= *speckle*) puntear, motear, salpicar de puntos
4 (*) (= *hit*) **to ~ sb a blow** pegar *or* arrear* un golpe a algn; **he ~ted him one** le pegó *or* arreó* (un porrazo)
Ⓒ CPD ► **dot command** N (*Comput*) instruc-

ción *f* (precedida) de punto ► **dot prompt** N (*Comput*) indicación *f* de punto

dotage [ˈdəʊtɪdʒ] N chochez *f*; **to be in one's ~** chochear, estar chocho

dotcom, dot.com [ˈdɒtˈkɒm] N puntocom *f*

dote [dəʊt] VI **to ~ on** adorar, chochear por

doting [ˈdəʊtɪŋ] ADJ 1 (= *loving*) **her ~ parents** sus padres, que la adoran
2 (= *senile*) chocho

dot-matrix printer [ˌdɒtˌmeɪtrɪksˈprɪntəʳ] N impresora *f* matricial de agujas

dotted line [ˌdɒtɪdˈlaɪn] N línea *f* de puntos; **"tear along the ~"** "cortar por la línea de puntos"; ✦**IDIOM to sign on the ~** firmar

dotty* [ˈdɒtɪ] ADJ (*compar* **dottier**, *superl* **dottiest**) (*Brit*) [*person*] chiflado*; [*idea, scheme*] estrafalario, disparatado; **you must be ~!** ¿estás loco o qué?; **it's driving me ~** esto me trae loco

double [ˈdʌbl] Ⓐ ADJ 1 (= *twice*) doble; **it is ~ what it was** es el doble de lo que era; **my income is ~ that of my neighbour** gano dos veces más que mi vecino, gano el doble que mi vecino; **he's ~ your age** te dobla la edad; **he's ~ the age of his sister** le dobla en edad a su hermana; **~ the size** el doble de grande; **~ the amount of money** el doble de dinero; **twins: ~ the trouble, and ~ the fun!** mellizos: el doble de problemas ¡y el doble de diversión!
2 (= *extra-big*) doble; **a ~ dose of cough mixture** una dosis doble de jarabe para la tos; **a ~ helping of ice cream** una porción doble de helado; **a ~ whisky** un whisky doble
3 (= *two, dual*) **it is spelt with a ~ "m"** se escribe con dos emes; **~ five two six (5526)** (*Telec*) cinco, cinco, dos, seis, cincuenta y cinco, veintiséis; **a box with a ~ bottom** una caja con doble fondo; **to lead a ~ life** llevar una doble vida; **it serves a ~ purpose** sirve un doble propósito; **throw a ~ six to commence play** para empezar el juego tiene que sacar un seis doble al tirar los dados; **the egg had a ~ yolk** el huevo tenía dos yemas; *see also* **figure A4**
Ⓑ ADV 1 (= *twice as much*) [*cost, pay*] el doble; **he earns ~ what I earn** gana el doble que yo; **you should have bought ~ that amount** deberías haber comprado el doble; **if you land on a pink square it counts ~** si caes en una casilla rosa vale el doble *or* vale por dos; **to see ~** ver doble
2 (= *in half*) por la mitad; **the blanket had been folded ~** habían doblado la manta por la mitad; **to be bent ~** (*with age*) estar encorvado; **to be bent ~ with pain** retorcerse de dolor
Ⓒ N 1 (= *drink*) doble *m*
2 (= *double room*) habitación *f* doble
3 (*Cine*) (= *stand-in*) doble *mf*
4 (= *lookalike*) doble *mf*
5 (*in games*) doble *m*; **throw a ~ to start** para empezar tienes que sacar un doble; **~ or quits** ◊ **~ or nothing** doble o nada
6 **doubles** (*Tennis, Badminton*) dobles *mpl*; **to play ~s** jugar dobles; **a game of mixed/ladies' ~s** un partido de dobles mixtos/femeninos
7 (*Sport*) (= *double victory*) **the ~** el doblete
8 **at the ~*** (= *very quickly*) a la carrera, corriendo; **they ate their food at the ~** comieron a la carrera, comieron corriendo; **get into bed, at the ~!** ¡a la cama corriendo!
9 **on the ~*** (= *immediately*) ya mismo; **we'd better go on the ~** mejor vamos ya mismo
Ⓓ VT 1 (= *increase twofold*) [+ *money, quantity, profits*] doblar, duplicar; [+ *price, salary*] doblar; [+ *efforts*] redoblar; **think of a number and ~ it** piensa en un número y multiplícalo por dos *or* duplícalo; **he ~d my offer** ofreció el doble que yo; **he has already ~d his birth weight** ya pesa el doble de lo que pesaba al nacer
2 (*also* **~ over**) (= *fold*) [+ *paper, blanket*] doblar
3 (*Theat*) **he ~s the parts of courtier and hangman** hace dos papeles, el de cortesano y el de verdugo; **he's doubling the part of Kennedy for Steve Newman** es el doble de Steve Newman en el papel de Kennedy
4 (*in card games*) doblar; **to ~ one's stake** doblar la apuesta; **I'll ~ you!** ¡te doblo la apuesta!
5 (= *circumnavigate*) [+ *headland*] doblar
Ⓔ VI 1 (= *become twice as great*) [*quantity*] doblarse, duplicarse; **these figures have ~d since last year** estas cifras se han duplicado desde el año pasado
2 (= *have two functions*) **to ~ as sth** hacer las veces de algo; **the sofa ~s as a spare bed** el sofá hace las veces de cama para los invitados
3 (*Theat*) **to ~ for sb** doblar a algn; **he ~d as Hamlet's father** también hizo el papel del padre de Hamlet
4 (= *change direction suddenly*) girar sobre sí mismo
5 (*Bridge*) doblar
Ⓕ CPD ► **double agent** N doble agente *mf* ► **double bar** N (*Mus*) barra *f* doble ► **double bass** N contrabajo *m* ► **double bassoon** N contrafagot *m* ► **double bed** N cama *f* de matrimonio ► **double bend** N (*Aut*) curva *f* en S ► **double bill** N (*Cine*) programa *m* doble ► **double bind** N dilema *m* sin solución, callejón *m* sin salida* ► **double bluff** N **perhaps, he thought, it's a kind of ~ bluff** quizás, pensó, intenta hacerme creer que está mintiendo pero en realidad dice la verdad ► **double boiler** N (*US*) cazos *mpl* para hervir al baño María ► **double booking** N (= *booking for two*) reserva *f* para dos; (= *over-booking*) doble reserva *f* ► **double chin** N papada *f* ► **double cream** N (*Brit*) crema *f* doble, nata *f* (para montar) (*Sp*), doble crema *f* (*Mex*) ► **double dealer** N traidor(a) *m/f* ► **double density disk** N (*Comput*) disco *m* de doble densidad ► **double doors** NPL puerta *fsing* de dos hojas ► **double Dutch*** N (*Brit*) chino* *m*; **it's ~ Dutch to me** para mí es chino*; **to talk ~ Dutch*** hablar en chino* ► **double eagle** N doble eagle *m* ► **double entry** N partida *f* doble ► **double entry book-keeping** N contabilidad *f* por partida doble ► **double exposure** N (*Phot*) doble exposición *f* ► **double fault** N (*Tennis*) falta *f* doble; *see also* **double-fault** ► **double feature** N (*Cine*) sesión *f* doble, programa *m* doble ► **double first** N (*Univ*) *título universitario británico con nota de sobresaliente en dos especialidades* ► **double flat** N (*Mus*) doble bemol *m* ► **double glazing** N doble acristalamiento *m*, doble ventana *f* ► **double helix** N (*Chem*) hélice *f* doble ► **double indemnity** N (*US Insurance*) doble indemnización *f* ► **double indemnity coverage** N (*US*) seguro *m* de doble indemnización ► **double jeopardy** N (*US Jur*) procesamiento *m* por segunda vez ► **double knitting** N lana *f* de doble hebra ► **double knot** N nudo *m* doble ► **double lock** N cerradura *f* doble; *see also* **double-lock** ► **double marking** N doble corrección *f* ► **double meaning** N doble sentido *m* ► **double negative** N (*Gram*) doble negación *f* (*construcción gramatical, incorrecta en inglés, en la que se utilizan dos formas negativas*) ► **double pay** N paga *f* doble; **everybody gets ~ pay on Sundays** todo el mundo recibe paga doble los domingos ► **double pneumonia** N pulmonía *f* doble ► **double room** N habitación *f* doble ► **double saucepan** N (*Brit*) cazos *mpl* para hervir al baño María ► **double sharp** N (*Mus*) doble sostenido *m* ► **double spacing** N **in ~ spacing** a doble espacio ► **double standard** N **to have ~ standards** ◊ **have a ~ standard** aplicar una regla para unos y otra para otros ► **double star** N estrella *f* binaria ► **double stopping** N doble cuerda *f* ► **double take** N **to do a ~ take** (= *look twice*) tener que mirar dos veces; **when I told him the news, he did a ~ take** cuando le di la noticia no daba crédito a sus oídos *or* no se lo creía ► **double talk** N lenguaje *m* con doble sentido ► **double time** N (*Ind, Comm*) tarifa *f* doble; **we earn ~ time on Sundays** los domingos nos pagan el doble; (*Mil*) **in ~ time** a paso ligero ► **double track** N vía *f* doble ► **double vision** N doble visión *f*, diplopía *f* ► **double whammy*** N palo *m* doble* ► **double windows** NPL ventanas *fpl* dobles ► **double yellow lines** NPL (*Aut*) *línea doble amarilla de prohibido aparcar*, ≈ línea *fsing* amarilla continua

►**double back** Ⓐ VI + ADV [*person*] volver sobre sus pasos; **to ~ back on itself** [*road*] volver sobre sí mismo
Ⓑ VT + ADV [+ *blanket*] doblar

►**double over** VT + ADV doblar

►**double up** Ⓐ VT + ADV **to be ~d up with laughter** troncharse de risa; **to be ~d up with pain** doblarse de dolor
Ⓑ VI + ADV 1 (= *bend over*) doblarse; **he ~d up with laughter** se partió de la risa
2 (= *share bedroom*) compartir (una habitación)

double-acting [ˌdʌblˈæktɪŋ] ADJ de doble acción

double-barrelled [ˈdʌblˌbærəld] ADJ 1 [*gun*] de dos cañones
2 (*Brit*) [*surname*] compuesto

double-blind [ˈdʌblˌblaɪnd] ADJ **~ experiment** *experimento en el que ni el analizador ni el sujeto conoce las características*; **~ method** *método según el cual ni el analizador ni el sujeto conoce las características del producto*

double-book [ˌdʌblˈbʊk] VT **I was ~ed** (*in diary of engagements*) tenía dos compromisos para la misma hora; **we found the room had been ~ed** encontramos que habían reservado la habitación para dos parejas distintas

double-breasted [ˈdʌblˈbrestɪd] ADJ cruzado, con botonadura doble

double-check [ˈdʌblˈtʃek] Ⓐ VT volver a comprobar, comprobar de nuevo; **to ~ that ...** volver a comprobar que ..., asegurarse bien de que ...
Ⓑ VI volver a comprobar, asegurarse bien; **to ~ with sb** confirmarlo con algn
Ⓒ N doble comprobación *f*, revisión *f*

double-click [ˈdʌblˌklɪk] (*Comput*) Ⓐ VI hacer doble click (**on** en)
Ⓑ VT hacer doble click en

double-cross* [ˈdʌblˈkrɒs] Ⓐ N engaño *m*, trampa *f*, traición *f*
Ⓑ VT traicionar, engañar

double-date [ˌdʌblˈdeɪt] Ⓐ VT engañar con otro/otra
Ⓑ VI salir dos parejas

double-dealing [ˈdʌblˈdiːlɪŋ] N trato *m* doble, juego *m* doble, duplicidad *f*

double-decker [ˈdʌblˈdekəʳ] Ⓐ N (*also* **~ bus**) autobús *m* de dos pisos

Ⓑ CPD ► **double-decker sandwich** N sandwich *m* club

double-declutch [ˌdʌbldiːˈklʌtʃ] VI (*Aut*) hacer un doble desembragaje

double-digit [ˌdʌblˈdɪdʒɪt] ADJ de dos dígitos

double-edged [ˈdʌblˈedʒd] ADJ [*remark*] con segundas; ✦*IDIOM* **it's a ~ sword** es un arma de doble filo

double entendre [ˈduːblɑ̃ːnˈtɑ̃ːndr] N equívoco *m*, frase *f* ambigua

double-faced [ˌdʌblˈfeɪst] ADJ [*material*] reversible; (*pej*) [*person*] de dos caras

double-fault [ˌdʌblˈfɔːlt] VI (*Tennis*) cometer doble falta; *see also* **double fault**

double-figure [ˌdʌblˈfɪgəʳ] ADJ = **double-digit**

double-glaze [ˌdʌblˈgleɪz] VT **to ~ a window** termoaislar una ventana

double-glazed [ˌdʌblˈgleɪzd] ADJ con doble acristalamiento

double-header [ˈdʌblˌhedəʳ] N (*esp US Sport*) *dos encuentros consecutivos entre los mismos o diferentes equipos*

double-jointed [ˈdʌblˈdʒɔɪntɪd] ADJ con articulaciones muy flexibles

double-lock [ˌdʌblˈlɒk] VT cerrar con dos vueltas; *see also* **double lock**

double-page spread [ˌdʌblpeɪdʒˈspred] N doble página *f*

double-park [ˌdʌblˈpɑːk] VI (*Aut*) aparcar en doble fila, estacionar en doble fila

double-parking [ˌdʌblˈpɑːkɪŋ] N (*Aut*) aparcamiento *m* en doble fila, estacionamiento *m* en doble fila

double-quick [ˌdʌblˈkwɪk] Ⓐ ADV rapidísimamente, en un santiamén; (*Mil*) a paso ligero
Ⓑ ADJ **in ~ time** rapidísimamente, en un santiamén

double-sided disk [ˌdʌblˌsaɪdɪdˈdɪsk] N disco *m* de dos caras

double-space [ˌdʌblˈspeɪs] VT escribir a doble espacio

double-spaced [ˈdʌblˈspeɪst] ADV a doble espacio

doublespeak [ˈdʌblˈspiːk] N (*pej*) doble lenguaje *m*

doublet [ˈdʌblɪt] N 1 (††) (= *garment*) jubón *m*
2 (*Ling*) doblete *m*

doublethink [ˈdʌblθɪŋk] N razonamiento *m* contradictorio; **a piece of ~** una contradicción en sí misma

doubleton [ˈdʌbltən] N dubletón *m*

doubling [ˈdʌblɪŋ] N [*of number*] multiplicación *f* por dos; [*of letter*] duplicación *f*

doubly [ˈdʌblɪ] ADV 1 (= *twice as*) [*important, difficult, dangerous*] doblemente; **we are ~ determined to win this time** esta vez estamos doblemente *or* mucho más empeñados en ganar; **you'll have to be ~ careful from now on** a partir de ahora tienes que tener el doble de cuidado; **since then she has been ~ careful to lock the door** desde entonces se cuida todavía más de cerrar la puerta con llave; **he has to work ~ hard to make up for lost time** tiene que trabajar el doble para recuperar el tiempo perdido; **to make ~ sure** asegurarse muy bien
2 (= *in two ways*) por partida doble; **Fran was ~ mistaken** Fran estaba equivocada por partida doble; **it's a delicious dessert, ~ so when you use cream instead of milk** es un postre riquísimo, y el doble de rico si usas nata en vez de leche

▼**doubt** [daʊt] Ⓐ N (= *uncertainty, qualm*) duda *f*; **there is some ~ about it** sobre esto existen dudas; **beyond ~** fuera de duda; **beyond all reasonable ~** más allá de toda duda; **to cast ~ on** poner en duda; **to clear up sb's ~s** sacar a algn de dudas; **to have one's ~s about sth** tener sus dudas acerca de algo; **to be in ~** [*person*] tener dudas, dudar; [*sb's honesty etc*] ser dudoso; **she was in ~ whether to …** dudaba si …; **the matter is still in some ~** el caso sigue siendo dudoso; **if** *or* **when in ~** en caso de duda; **no ~!** ¡sin duda!; **no ~ he will come** seguro que viene; **there is no ~ of that** de eso no cabe duda; **there is no ~ that** es indudable que, no cabe duda de que; **I have no ~ that it is true** no me cabe duda de que es verdad; **let there be no ~ about it** que nadie dude de esto; **the marks left no ~ about how he died** las señales no dejaban lugar a dudas sobre cómo murió; **to throw ~ on** poner en duda; **without (a) ~** sin duda (alguna); *see also* **plant B2**
Ⓑ VT 1 [+ *truth of statement etc*] dudar; **I ~ it very much** lo dudo mucho; **I never ~ed you** nunca tuve dudas acerca de ti; **to ~ sb's loyalty** dudar de la lealtad de algn
2 (= *be uncertain*) **to ~ whether** *or* **if** dudar si; **I don't ~ that he will come** no dudo que vaya a venir
Ⓒ VI dudar; **~ing Thomas** (*fig*) incrédulo/a *m/f*, escéptico/a *m/f*

doubter [ˈdaʊtəʳ] N escéptico/a *m/f*

▼**doubtful** [ˈdaʊtfʊl] ADJ 1 (= *uncertain*) [*result, success, future*] incierto, dudoso
2 (= *unconvinced*) [*expression*] de duda; **"all right then," he said in a ~ tone** —bueno, vale —dijo con un tono de duda en la voz; **Jeremy nodded his head, but he still looked ~** Jeremy asintió pero no parecía aún convencido; **I'm a bit ~** no estoy convencido del todo; **to be ~ that** dudar que + *subjun*; **he was ~ that he would be able to lift it** dudaba que pudiera levantarlo; **I am ~ whether we should accept the offer** dudo si deberíamos aceptar la oferta o no; **to be ~ about sth** tener dudas sobre algo
3 (= *unlikely*) dudoso; **a reconciliation between the two sides seems ~** una reconciliación entre las dos partes parece dudosa; **it is ~ that they will reach an agreement** es dudoso *or* poco probable que lleguen a un acuerdo; **it is ~ that there will be any survivors** se duda *or* es poco probable que haya sobrevivientes; **for a moment it seemed ~ that he would move at all** por un momento pareció que no se iba a mover en absoluto; **it is ~ whether** es poco probable que + *subjun*; **~ starter** (*Sport*) participante *mf* dudoso
4 (= *questionable*) [*taste, reputation, quality, value*] dudoso; **in ~ taste** de dudoso gusto; **the weather looks a bit ~** el tiempo no parece muy estable

doubtfully [ˈdaʊtfəlɪ] ADV 1 (= *unconvincedly*) sin estar convencido; **Ralph looked at him ~** Ralph lo miró muy poco convencido; **"I suppose not," he said ~** —supongo que no —dijo él poco convencido *or* sin demasiado convencimiento
2 (= *questionably*) dudosamente; **the painting is ~ ascribed to Picasso** el cuadro se ha atribuído dudosamente a Picasso

doubtfulness [ˈdaʊtfʊlnɪs] N 1 (= *uncertainty*) incertidumbre *f*, dudas *fpl*; (= *hesitation*) vacilación *f*, duda *f*; **there is some ~ as to whether he did indeed live there** existe cierta incertidumbre *or* existen algunas dudas sobre si realmente vivió ahí
2 (= *questionable quality*) carácter *m* dudoso

▼**doubtless** [ˈdaʊtlɪs] ADV sin duda, seguramente

douceur [duːˈsɜːʳ] N (*frm*) (= *gift, tip etc*) gratificación *f*

douche [duːʃ] Ⓐ N ducha *f*; (*Med*) jeringa *f*
Ⓑ VT duchar
Ⓒ VI ducharse

dough [dəʊ] N 1 (*Culin*) masa *f*, pasta *f*
2 (‡) (= *money*) guita* *f*, pasta *f* (*Sp**), plata *f* (*LAm**), lana *f* (*LAm**)

doughboy* [ˈdəʊbɔɪ] N (*US*) soldado *m* de infantería; (*Hist*) *soldado de la Primera Guerra Mundial*

doughnut [ˈdəʊnʌt] N donut® *m*, dona *f* (*LAm*)

doughty [ˈdaʊtɪ] ADJ (*compar* **doughtier**; *superl* **doughtiest**) [*person*] valiente, esforzado; [*deed*] hazañoso

doughy [ˈdəʊɪ] ADJ pastoso

dour [ˈdʊəʳ] ADJ (= *grim*) adusto, arisco; **a ~ Scot** un escocés adusto *or* arisco; **a ~ struggle** una batalla muy reñida

Douro [ˈdʊərəʊ] N Duero *m*

douse [daʊs] VT (*with water*) mojar (**with** con); [+ *flames, light*] apagar

dove[1] [dʌv] N (*Orn*) paloma *f*; (*Pol*) (= *person opposed to war*) pacifista *mf*

dove[2] [dəʊv] (*US*) PT *of* **dive**

dovecote [ˈdʌvkɒt] N palomar *m*

dove-grey [ˌdʌvˈgreɪ] ADJ gris paloma

Dover [ˈdəʊvəʳ] Ⓐ N Dover *m*
Ⓑ CPD ► **Dover sole** N lenguado *m*

dovetail [ˈdʌvteɪl] Ⓐ N (*also* **~ joint**) cola *f* de milano
Ⓑ VT 1 (*Carpentry*) ensamblar a cola de milano
2 (*fig*) (= *fit*) encajar; (= *link*) enlazar
Ⓒ VI (*fig*) encajar, enlazar; **to ~ with** encajar perfectamente con

dovish [ˈdʌvɪʃ] ADJ (*Pol*) blando

dowager [ˈdaʊədʒəʳ] Ⓐ N viuda *f* de un noble
Ⓑ CPD ► **dowager duchess** N duquesa *f* viuda

dowdiness [ˈdaʊdɪnɪs] N falta *f* de elegancia

dowdy [ˈdaʊdɪ] ADJ (*compar* **dowdier**; *superl* **dowdiest**) [*person*] anticuado, trasnochado; [*clothes*] trasnochado, pasado de moda

dowel [ˈdaʊəl] N clavija *f*

Dow Jones average [ˌdaʊdʒəʊnzˈævərɪdʒ], **Dow Jones index** [ˌdaʊdʒəʊnzˈɪndeks] N (*US Fin*) índice *m* Dow-Jones

down[1] [daʊn]

When ***down*** *is an element in a phrasal verb, eg* ***back down, glance down, play down,*** *look up the verb.*

Ⓐ ADV 1 (*physical movement*) abajo, hacia abajo; (= *to the ground*) a tierra; **there was snow all the way ~ to London** estuvo nevando todo el camino hasta Londres; **to fall ~** caerse; **I ran all the way ~** bajé toda la distancia corriendo
2 (*static position*) abajo; (= *on the ground*) por tierra, en tierra; **to be ~** (*Aer*) haber aterrizado, estar en tierra; [*person*] haber caído, estar en tierra; **I'll be ~ in a minute** ahora bajo; **he isn't ~ yet** (*eg for breakfast*) todavía no ha bajado; **the blinds are ~** estan bajadas las persianas; **the sun is ~** el sol se ha puesto; **~ below** allá abajo; **~ by the river** abajo en la ribera; **~ here** aquí (abajo); **~ on the shore** abajo en la playa; **~ there** allí (abajo)
3 (*Geog*) **he came ~ from Glasgow to London** ha bajado *or* venido de Glasgow a Londres; **to be ~ from college** haber terminado el curso universitario; **he lives ~ South** vive en el sur; **~ under** (*Brit**) en Australia o en Nueva Zelanda; **to go ~ under** (*Brit**) (= *to Australia*) ir a Australia; (= *to New Zealand*) ir a

➤ LANGUAGE IN USE: doubt A 15.1, 16.1, 26.3 B2 16.1, 16.2 doubtful 1 16.2 doubtless 26.3

Nueva Zelanda

4 (*in writing*) **write this ~** apunta esto; **you're ~ for the next race** estás inscrito para la próxima carrera; **you're ~ for Tuesday** te hemos apuntado para el martes

5 (*in volume, degree, status*) **the tyres are ~** los neumáticos están desinflados; **his temperature is ~** le ha bajado la temperatura; **the price of meat is ~** ha bajado el precio de la carne; **England are two goals ~** Inglaterra está perdiendo por dos tantos; **I'm £20 ~** he perdido 20 libras; **I'm ~ to my last cigarette** me queda un cigarrillo nada más

6 (*indicating a series or succession*) **from the year 1600 ~ to the present day** desde el año 1600 hasta el presente; **from the biggest ~ to the smallest** desde el más grande hasta el más pequeño

7 (= *ill*) **I've been ~ with flu** he estado con gripe

8 **~ to: it's ~ to him** (= *due to, up to*) le toca a él, le incumbe a él; **it's all ~ to us now** ahora nosotros somos los únicos responsables

9 (*as deposit*) **to pay £50 ~** pagar un depósito de 50 libras, hacer un desembolso inicial de 50 libras

10 (*in exclamations*) **down!** ¡abajo!; (*to dog*) ¡quieto!; **~ with traitors!** ¡abajo los traidores!

11 (= *completed etc*) **one ~, five to go** uno en el bote y quedan cinco

12 (*esp US*) **to be ~ on sb** tener manía *or* inquina a algn*

Ⓑ PREP 1 (*indicating movement*) **he went ~ the hill** fue cuesta abajo; **to go ~ the road** ir calle abajo; **he's gone ~ the pub*** se ha ido al bar; **looking ~ this road, you can see …** mirando carretera abajo, se ve …; **he ran his finger ~ the list** pasó el dedo por la lista; **the rain was running ~ the trunk** la lluvia corría por el tronco

2 (= *at a lower point on*) **he lives ~ the street (from us)** vive en esta calle, más abajo de nosotros; **~ the ages** a través de los siglos; **face ~** boca abajo; **~ river** río abajo (**from** de)

Ⓒ ADJ 1 (= *depressed*) deprimido

2 (= *not functioning*) **the computer is ~** el ordenador no funciona; **the power lines are ~** los cables de alta tensión están cortados; **the telephone lines are ~** las líneas de teléfono están cortadas

3 (*Brit*) [*train, line*] de bajada

Ⓓ VT (*) 1 [+ *food*] devorar; [+ *drink*] beberse (de un trago), tragarse; **he ~ed a pint of beer** tragó una pinta de cerveza

2 [+ *opponent*] tirar al suelo, echar al suelo; [+ *plane*] derribar, abatir; ♦***IDIOM*** **to ~ tools** (*Brit*) declararse en huelga

Ⓔ N **to have a ~ on sb** (*Brit**) tenerle manía *or* inquina a algn*

Ⓕ CPD ► **down bow** N (*Mus*) descenso *m* de arco ► **down cycle** N (*Econ*) ciclo *m* de caída ► **down payment** N (*Fin*) (= *initial payment*) entrada *f*; (= *deposit*) desembolso *m* inicial

down² [daʊn] N (*on bird*) plumón *m*, flojel *m*; (*on face*) bozo *m*; (*on body*) vello *m*; (*on fruit*) pelusa *f*; (*Bot*) vilano *m*

down³ [daʊn] N (*Geog*) colina *f*; **the Downs** (*Brit*) las Downs (*colinas del sur de Inglaterra*)

down-and-out ['daʊnən,aʊt] Ⓐ N (= *tramp*) indigente *mf*, vagabundo/a *m/f*

Ⓑ ADJ **to be ~** no tener donde caerse muerto, estar sin un cuarto

down-at-heel ['daʊnət'hiːl] ADJ [*person, appearance*] desastrado; [*bar, café*] de mala muerte; [*shoes*] gastado

downbeat ['daʊn,biːt] Ⓐ ADJ (= *gloomy*) pesimista, deprimido; (= *unemphatic*) [*tone, statement*] moderado

Ⓑ N (*Mus*) compás *m* acentuado

downcast ['daʊnkɑːst] ADJ (= *sad*) abatido; [*eyes*] bajo, alicaído

downer* ['daʊnəʳ] N 1 (= *tranquilizer*) tranquilizante *m*

2 (= *depressing experience*) experiencia *f* deprimente

downfall ['daʊnfɔːl] N 1 (= *collapse*) caída *f*

2 (= *ruin*) perdición *f*, ruina *f*; **it will be his ~** será su perdición

downgrade ['daʊngreɪd] Ⓐ N **to be on the ~** ir cuesta abajo, estar en plena decadencia

Ⓑ [daʊn'greɪd] VT [+ *job, hotel*] bajar de categoría; **he's been ~d to assistant manager** le han bajado a ayudante de dirección

downhearted ['daʊn'hɑːtɪd] ADJ descorazonado; **don't be ~** no te dejes desanimar

downhill ['daʊn'hɪl] Ⓐ ADV cuesta abajo; **to go ~** [*road*] bajar; [*car*] ir cuesta abajo; (*fig*) [*person*] ir cuesta abajo; [*industry*] estar en declive, estar de capa caída; [*company*] ir de mal en peor

Ⓑ ADJ en pendiente; [*skiing*] de descenso; **it was ~ all the way after that** (*fig*) (= *got easier*) a partir de entonces la cosa fue más fácil; (= *got worse*) a partir de entonces la cosa fue de mal en peor

down-home* [,daʊn'həʊm] ADJ (*US*) (= *from the South*) del sur; (= *narrow-minded*) cerrado de miras

Downing Street ['daʊnɪŋ,striːt] N Downing Street (*calle de Londres en que están las residencias oficiales del ministro de Hacienda y del primer ministro británicos*)

> **DOWNING STREET**
>
> **Downing Street** *es la calle de Londres, cerrada al público, donde se encuentran las residencias oficiales del Primer Ministro* (**Prime Minister**) *y del Ministro de Economía y Hacienda* (**Chancellor of the Exchequer**), *normalmente en los Nºs 10 y 11 respectivamente. Los términos* **Downing Street**, **Number Ten**, *o* **Ten Downing Street** *se usan a menudo en los medios de comunicación para referirse al Primer Ministro o al Gobierno.*

down-in-the-mouth ['daʊnɪnðə'maʊθ] ADJ decaído, deprimido

download [,daʊn'ləʊd] VT (*Comput*) descargar

downloadable [,daʊn,ləʊdəbl] ADJ (*Comput*) descargable

downloading [,daʊn'ləʊdɪŋ] N (*Comput*) descarga *f*

downmarket [,daʊn'mɑːkɪt] Ⓐ ADJ [*product*] para el sector popular del mercado

Ⓑ ADV **to go ~** buscar clientela en el sector popular

downpipe ['daʊn,paɪp] N (*Brit*) canal *f* bajante, bajante *f or m*

downplay ['daʊn'pleɪ] VT quitar importancia a, restar importancia a

downpour ['daʊnpɔːʳ] N aguacero *m*, chaparrón *m*, chubasco *m* (*LAm*)

downright ['daʊnraɪt] Ⓐ ADJ [*nonsense, lie*] patente, manifiesto; [*refusal*] categórico

Ⓑ ADV [*rude, angry*] realmente

downside ['daʊnsaɪd] N (*fig*) pega *f*, desventaja *f*, lo malo (**of** de)

downsize [,daʊn'saɪz] Ⓐ VT hacer recortes de personal en, hacer recortes de plantilla en (*Sp*)

Ⓑ VI reducir (el) personal, reducir (la) plantilla (*Sp*)

Down's Syndrome ['daʊnz,sɪndrəʊm] N síndrome *m* de Down; **a ~ child** un niño con síndrome de Down

downstairs ['daʊn'steəz] Ⓐ ADJ (= *on the ground floor*) de la planta baja; (= *on the floor underneath*) del piso de abajo; **a ~ window** una ventana de la planta baja

Ⓑ ADV en la planta baja, abajo; **to fall ~** caer por las escaleras; **to come/go ~** bajar la escalera

Ⓒ N **the ~** [*of building*] la planta baja

downstate ['daʊn,steɪt] (*US*) Ⓐ N campo *m*, sur *m* del estado

Ⓑ ADJ del campo, del sur del estado

Ⓒ ADV [*be*] en el campo, en el sur; [*go*] al campo, hacia el sur

downstream ['daʊn'striːm] ADV río abajo (**from** de); **to go ~** ir río abajo; **to swim ~** nadar con la corriente; **a town ~ from Soria** una ciudad pasando Soria río abajo; **about 5km ~ from Zamora** a unos 5km de Zamora río abajo

downstroke ['daʊnstrəʊk] N 1 (*with pen*) pierna *f*; (*by child when learning*) palote *m*

2 (*Mech*) carrera *f* descendente

downswept ['daʊnswept] ADJ [*wings*] con caída posterior

downswing ['daʊnswɪŋ] N (*fig*) recesión *f*, caída *f*

downtime ['daʊn,taɪm] N tiempo *m* de inactividad, tiempo *m* muerto

down-to-earth ['daʊntʊ'ɜːθ] ADJ (= *natural*) [*person*] natural, llano; (= *practical*) [*person, policy, outlook*] práctico, realista

downtown ['daʊn'taʊn] (*US*) Ⓐ ADV al centro

Ⓑ ADJ **~ San Francisco** el centro de San Francisco

downtrend ['daʊn,trend] N (*Econ*) tendencia *f* a la baja; **in** *or* **on a ~** en baja

downtrodden ['daʊn,trɒdn] ADJ [*person*] oprimido, pisoteado

downturn ['daʊntɜːn] N (*in economy*) deterioro *m*; (*in sales, production*) disminución *f*

downward ['daʊnwəd] Ⓐ ADJ [*curve, movement*] descendente; [*slope*] hacia abajo; [*tendency*] a la baja

Ⓑ ADV [*go, look*] hacia abajo; **from the President ~** todos, incluso el Presidente

downwards ['daʊnwədz] ADV (*esp Brit*) = **downward**

downwind ['daʊn,wɪnd] ADV a favor del viento

downy ['daʊnɪ] ADJ velloso; (= *and soft*) blando, suave

dowry ['daʊrɪ] N dote *f*

dowse [daʊz] VT = **douse**

dowser ['daʊzəʳ] N zahorí *mf*

doyen ['dɔɪən] N decano *m*

doyenne ['dɔɪen] N decana *f*

doz. ABBR (= **dozen**) doc.

doze [dəʊz] Ⓐ N sueñecito *m*, siestecita *f*; **to have a ~** (*after meal*) echar una siestecita

Ⓑ VI dormitar

►**doze off** VI + ADV dormirse

dozen ['dʌzn] N docena *f*; **80p a ~** 80 peniques la docena; **a ~ eggs** una docena de huevos; **they arrived in their ~s** *or* **by the ~** llegaban docenas de ellos; **~s of times/people** cantidad *f* de veces/gente

dozy ['dəʊzɪ] ADJ (*compar* **dozier**; *superl* **doziest**) 1 (= *sleepy*) amodorrado, soñoliento

2 (*Brit**) (= *stupid*) corto*, lerdo*

DP N ABBR = **data processing**

DPh, DPhil [,diː'fɪl] N ABBR = **Doctor of Philosophy**; → DEGREE

d.p.i. ABBR (= **dots per inch**) p.p.p.

DPM N ABBR = **Diploma in Psychological Medicine**

DPP N ABBR (*Brit Jur*) = **Director of Public Prosecutions**

DPT N ABBR (= **diphtheria, pertussis, tetanus**) vacuna *f* trivalente

dpt ABBR (= **department**) dto

DPW N ABBR (*US*) = **Department of Public Works**

DQ ABBR (*Athletics*) = **Disqualified**

Dr ABBR 1 (*Med*) (= **Doctor**) Dr(a)
2 (*Fin*) = **debtor**
3 (= *street*) = **Drive**

dr ABBR 1 = **debtor**
2 = **dram**
3 = **drachma**

drab [dræb] Ⓐ ADJ (*compar* **drabber**; *superl* **drabbest**) [*colour*] apagado; [*life*] monótono, gris
Ⓑ N 1 (= *fabric*) *tela de color marrón o gris apagado*
2 *see* **dribs**

drabness ['dræbnɪs] N [*of life*] monotonía *f*; [*of clothes, colours*] lo soso

drachm [dræm] N 1 (*Pharm*) (= *measure*) dracma *f*
2 = **drachma**

drachma ['drækmə] N (*pl* **drachmas** *or* **drachmae** ['drækmi:]) dracma *m* (*sometimes f*)

draconian [drə'kəʊnɪən] ADJ draconiano, severo, riguroso

Dracula ['drækjʊlə] N Drácula *m*

draft [drɑ:ft] Ⓐ N 1 (= *outline*) (*in writing*) borrador *m*; (= *drawing*) boceto *m*
2 (*Mil*) (= *detachment*) destacamento *m*; (= *reinforcements*) refuerzos *mpl*; **the ~** (*US Mil*) (= *conscription*) la llamada a filas, el servicio militar
3 (*Comm*) (*also* **banker's ~**) letra *f* de cambio, giro *m*
4 (*Comput*) borrador *m*
5 (*US*) = **draught**
Ⓑ VT 1 (*also* **~ out**) [+ *document*] (= *write*) redactar; [+ *first attempt*] hacer un borrador de; [+ *scheme*] elaborar, trazar
2 (*Mil*) (*for specific duty*) destacar; (= *send*) mandar (**to** a); (*US Mil*) (= *conscript*) reclutar, llamar al servicio militar; (*fig*) forzar, obligar
Ⓒ CPD ► **draft agreement** N proyecto *m* de (un) acuerdo ► **draft bill** N anteproyecto *m* de ley ► **draft board** N (*US Mil*) junta *f* de reclutamiento ► **draft card** N (*US Mil*) cartilla *f* militar ► **draft dodger** N (*US Mil*) prófugo *m* ► **draft excluder** N (*US*) burlete *m* ► **draft law** N = **draft bill** ► **draft horse** (*US*) N caballo *m* de tiro ► **draft letter** N borrador *m* de carta; (*more formal*) proyecto *m* de carta ► **draft version** N versión *f* preliminar

draftee [drɑ:f'ti:] N (*US Mil*) recluta *mf*

draftiness ['drɑ:ftɪnɪs] N (*US*) = **draughtiness**

draft-proof ['drɑ:ftpru:f] ADJ (*US*) = **draught-proof**

draft-proofing ['drɑ:ft,pru:fɪŋ] N (*US*) = **draught-proofing**

draftsman ['drɑ:ftsmən] N (*US*) = **draughtsman**

draftsmanship ['drɑ:ftsmənʃɪp] N (*US*) = **draughtsmanship**

draftswoman ['drɑ:fts,wʊmən] N (*US*) = **draughtswoman**

drafty ['drɑ:ftɪ] ADJ (*US*) = **draughty**

drag [dræg] Ⓐ N 1 (= *restraint*) **the satellite acts like a ~ on the shuttle** el satélite hace más lento el avance del transbordador espacial; **the region is a ~ on the country's financial resources** (*fig*) la región supone una sangría *or* un desaguadero para los recursos económicos del país; **these conservative institutions were seen as a ~ on progress** (*fig*) estas instituciones conservadoras eran consideradas un obstáculo *or* estorbo para el progreso
2 (*Aer*) (= *resistance*) resistencia *f* aerodinámica
3 (*) (= *boring thing*) lata* *f*, rollo *m* (*Sp**); **what a ~!** ¡qué lata!*, ¡qué rollo! (*Sp**); **she's a real ~!** ¡qué tía más pesada!*
4 (*) (*on cigarette*) chupada *f*, calada *f* (*Sp*); **he took a long ~ on his cigarette** le dio una chupada *or* (*Sp*) calada larga al cigarro
5 (= *women's clothes*) **he was wearing ~** iba vestido de mujer, iba travestido; **a man in ~** un hombre vestido de mujer, un hombre travestido
6 **the main ~** (*US**) la avenida principal
7 (= *dragnet*) red *f* barredera; (= *dredge*) draga *f*
8 (*US**) (= *influence*) enchufe* *m*
Ⓑ VT 1 (= *pull*) arrastrar; **he ~ged his chair towards the table** arrastró su silla hacia la mesa; **they ~ged the man out of the car** sacaron al hombre del coche a rastras; **she managed to ~ herself clear of the wreckage** consiguió salir a duras penas del coche siniestrado; ✦**IDIOM** **to ~ sb's (good) name through the mud** *or* **dirt** arrastrar el buen nombre de algn por el lodo
2 (= *trail*) [+ *injured limb, coat*] arrastrar; **I don't want to ~ the children round the supermarket** no quiero ir tirando de los niños por el supermercado; **to ~ one's feet** (*lit*) arrastrar los pies; **to ~ one's feet** *or* **heels** (*fig*) dar largas (al asunto); **the government has been ~ging its feet** *or* **heels on this issue** el gobierno ha estado dando largas a este asunto
3 (= *force*) **the government didn't want to ~ the nation into a war** el gobierno no quería arrastrar al país a una guerra; **I have to ~ myself into the office in the mornings** por las mañanas me cuesta muchísimo (trabajo) ir a la oficina; **I don't want to get ~ged into your argument** no quiero que me mezcléis en vuestra discusión; **we had to ~ the truth out of him** tuvimos que sacarle la verdad a la fuerza
4 (= *dredge, search*) [+ *sea bed, river*] dragar
Ⓒ VI 1 (= *go very slowly*) [*time*] pasar muy lentamente; [*film, play*] hacerse pesado; **the minutes ~ged by** los minutos pasaban muy lentamente *or* se alargaban sin fin
2 (= *trail*) [*skirt, coat*] arrastrar; **her skirt was ~ging on the floor** la falda le iba arrastrando por el suelo, iba arrastrando la falda por el suelo
3 (= *not keep pace*) rezagarse
4 (= *dredge, search*) **to ~ for sth** dragar en busca de algo
Ⓓ CPD ► **drag artist** N transformista *m*, travesti *m* ► **drag car** N coche *m* trucado ► **drag hunt** N *deporte en el que los perros salen a la caza de un objeto perfumado en lugar de un animal* ► **drag (para)chute** N paracaídas *m inv* de frenado ► **drag queen*** N drag-queen* *f*, reinona* *f*, travesti *m* ► **drag race** N (*US Aut*) *carrera de coches trucados de salida parada* ► **drag show** N espectáculo *m* de drag-queens*, espectáculo *m* de reinonas*, espectáculo *m* de travestismo

►**drag about** VT + ADV arrastrar de un lado a otro

►**drag along** VT + ADV [+ *person*] arrastrar

►**drag away** VT + ADV 1 (*lit*) [+ *person*] llevar a la fuerza
2 (*fig*) **I'm sorry to ~ you away from your meal** siento interrumpirte la comida, siento hacerte levantar de la mesa; **you can never ~ him away from the television** no hay forma de apartarlo del televisor, no hay forma de despegarlo del televisor*; **if you can ~ yourself away from the luxury of the hotel** si puedes desprenderte del lujo del hotel

►**drag down** VT + ADV **you may have made a terrible mistake but you're not going to ~ me down with you** habrás cometido un grave error pero no voy a cargar con las consecuencias yo también; **he could ~ down the entire party in this election** podría hacer fracasar a todo el partido en estas elecciones; **I'm not going to be ~ged down to your level** no me vas a arrastrar a tu mismo nivel

►**drag in** VT + ADV [+ *subject*] sacar a relucir; *see also* **cat A1**

►**drag on** VI + ADV [*meeting, conversation*] alargarse; [*film, play*] hacerse pesadísimo; [*speech*] hacerse interminable; **the case could ~ on for months** el caso podría alargarse durante meses

►**drag out** VT + ADV [+ *process*] alargar

►**drag up** VT + ADV 1 [+ *subject*] **do you have to ~ that up again?** ¿otra vez tienes que sacar a relucir eso?; **this ~ged up painful memories for her** esto despertó en ella recuerdos dolorosos
2 (*Brit**) (= *bring up*) [+ *person*] **where were you ~ged up?** ¿dónde te han enseñado eso?, ¿dónde has aprendido esos modales?

draglift ['dræglɪft] N (*Ski*) arrastre *m*, remonte *m*

dragnet ['drægnet] N 1 (= *net*) red *f* de arrastre, red *f* barredera
2 (*fig*) (*by police*) operación *f* policial de captura, emboscada *f*
3 (*US Pol*) dragadora *f*

dragon ['drægən] N 1 (*Myth*) dragón *m*
2 (*) (= *woman*) bruja *f*

dragonfly ['drægənflaɪ] N libélula *f*, caballito *m* del diablo

dragoon [drə'gu:n] Ⓐ N (*Mil*) dragón *m*
Ⓑ VT **to ~ sb into (doing) sth** obligar *or* forzar a algn a (hacer) algo

dragster ['drægstəʳ] N coche *m* trucado

drain [dreɪn] Ⓐ N 1 (= *outlet*) (*in house*) desagüe *m*; (*in street*) boca *f* de alcantarilla, sumidero *m*; (*Agr*) zanja *f* de drenaje; **the ~s** (= *sewage system*) el alcantarillado *msing*; ✦**IDIOMS** **to throw one's money down the ~*** tirar el dinero (por la ventana); **to go down the ~*** perderse, echarse a perder; *see also* **laugh B**
2 (*fig*) (= *source of loss*) **to be a ~ on** [+ *energies, resources*] consumir, agotar; **they are a great ~ on our reserves** ellos se llevan gran parte de nuestras reservas; **it has been a great ~ on her** la ha agotado
Ⓑ VT 1 (*Agr*) [+ *land, marshes, lake*] drenar, desecar; [+ *vegetables, last drops*] escurrir; [+ *glass, radiator etc*] vaciar; (*Med*) [+ *wound etc*] drenar
2 (*fig*) agotar, consumir; **to feel ~ed (of energy)** sentirse agotado *or* sin fuerzas; **the country is being ~ed of wealth** al país lo están empobreciendo
Ⓒ VI [*washed dishes, vegetables*] escurrir; [*liquid*] desaguar; [*stream*] desembocar (**into** en)

►**drain away** Ⓐ VT + ADV [+ *liquid*] (*from vegetables etc*) escurrir; (*Med, Mech*) drenar
Ⓑ VI + ADV [*liquid*] irse; [*strength*] agotarse

►**drain off** Ⓐ VT + ADV [+ *liquid*] (*from vegetables etc*) escurrir; (*Med, Mech*) drenar
Ⓑ VI + ADV [*liquid*] irse

drainage ['dreɪnɪdʒ] Ⓐ N 1 [*of land*] (*naturally*) desagüe *m*; (*artificially*) drenaje *m*; [*of lake*] desecación *f*
2 (= *sewage system*) alcantarillado *m*
Ⓑ CPD ► **drainage area, drainage basin** N (*Geol*) cuenca *f* hidrográfica ► **drainage channel** N zanja *f* de drenaje ► **drainage tube** N (*Med*) tubo *m* de drenaje

drainboard ['dreɪnbɔːd] N (*US*) = **draining board**

drainer ['dreɪnəʳ] N escurridor *m*

draining board ['dreɪnɪŋˌbɔːd] N escurridero *m*

drainpipe ['dreɪnpaɪp] Ⓐ N tubo *m* de desagüe, cañería *f*
Ⓑ CPD ► **drainpipe trousers** NPL (*Brit*) pantalones *mpl* de pitillo

Drake [dreɪk] N Draque

drake [dreɪk] N pato *m* (macho)

Dralon® ['dreɪlɒn] N Dralón® *m*

DRAM, D-RAM ['diːræm] ABBR (*Comput*) = **dynamic random access memory**

dram [dræm] N (*Brit*) [*of drink*] trago *m*; (*Pharm*) dracma *f*

drama ['drɑːmə] Ⓐ N 1 (= *dramatic art*) teatro *m*; (= *play*) obra *f* dramática, drama *m*
2 (*fig*) (= *event*) drama *m*; (= *excitement*) dramatismo *m*
Ⓑ CPD ► **drama critic** N crítico/a *m/f* de teatro ► **drama queen*** N (*pej*) peliculero/a *m/f*; **you're such a ~ queen** eres demasiado peliculero ► **drama school** N escuela *f* de arte dramático ► **drama student** N estudiante *mf* de arte dramático

dramatic [drə'mætɪk] ADJ 1 (= *marked*) [*increase, rise, decline*] espectacular; [*change*] radical, drástico; [*improvement*] espectacular, impresionante; [*effect*] espectacular, dramático
2 (= *exciting*) [*entrance*] espectacular, teatral; [*escape*] espectacular; [*decor*] de gran efecto, efectista; **she lifted the lid with a ~ gesture** levantó la tapa con gesto teatral
3 (*Theat*) [*works, film*] dramático, teatral; **~ art** arte *m* dramático; **the ~ arts** las artes dramáticas

dramatically [drə'mætɪkəlɪ] ADV 1 (= *markedly*) [*change*] radicalmente; [*increase, improve, rise, fall*] espectacularmente; **this plan is ~ different** este plan es radicalmente diferente; **the results were ~ better** los resultados fueron notablemente mejores
2 (= *theatrically*) [*pause, sigh*] de forma teatral, con mucho teatro
3 (*Theat*) desde el punto de vista dramático; **~, it was very effective** desde el punto de vista dramático funcionó muy bien

dramatics [drə'mætɪks] Ⓐ NSING (*Theat*) arte *m* dramático, teatro *m*; **amateur ~** teatro *m* amateur, teatro *m* de aficionados
Ⓑ NPL (= *histrionics*) dramatismo *msing*; **George's ~ were beginning to irritate me** el dramatismo de George me estaba empezando a irritar

dramatis personae ['dræmətɪspɜː'səʊnaɪ] N personajes *mpl* (*del drama etc*)

dramatist ['dræmətɪst] N dramaturgo/a *m/f*

dramatization [ˌdræmətaɪ'zeɪʃən] N dramatización *f*

dramatize ['dræmətaɪz] VT 1 [+ *events etc*] dramatizar; (*Cine, TV*) (= *adapt*) [+ *novel*] adaptar a la televisión/al cine
2 (= *exaggerate*) dramatizar, exagerar

Drambuie® [dræm'bjuːɪ] N Drambuie® *m*

drank [dræŋk] PT *of* **drink**

drape [dreɪp] Ⓐ VT [+ *object*] cubrir (**with** con, de); **~ this round your shoulders** ponte esto sobre los hombros; **he ~d a towel about himself** se cubrió con una toalla; **he ~d an arm about my shoulders** me rodeó los hombros con el brazo
Ⓑ **drapes** NPL (*US*) cortinas *fpl*

draper ['dreɪpəʳ] N pañero/a *m/f*

drapery ['dreɪpərɪ] N 1 (= *draper's shop*) pañería *f*, mercería *f* (*LAm*)
2 (= *cloth for hanging*) colgaduras *fpl*; (*as merchandise*) pañería *f*, mercería *f* (*LAm*)

drastic ['dræstɪk] ADJ [*measures, change, reduction*] drástico; [*effect*] notorio; **to take ~ action** tomar medidas drásticas

drastically ['dræstɪkəlɪ] ADV drásticamente; **to be ~ reduced** sufrir una reducción drástica; **he ~ revised his ideas** cambió radicalmente *or* drásticamente de ideas; **it/things went ~ wrong** salió/las cosas salieron muy mal

drat* [dræt] EXCL **~!** ◊ **~ it!** ¡maldita sea!*, ¡mecachis!*

dratted* ['drætɪd] ADJ maldito*

draught, draft (*US*) [drɑːft] Ⓐ N 1 [*of air*] corriente *f* de aire; (*for fire*) tiro *m*; **there's a ~ from the window** entra corriente por la ventana; ✦**IDIOM to feel the ~** pasar apuros (económicos)
2 (= *drink*) trago *m*; **he took a long ~ of cider** se echó un buen trago de sidra; **at one ~** de un trago; **on ~** de barril
3 (*Med*) dosis *f inv*
4 (*Naut*) calado *m*
Ⓑ CPD ► **draught beer** N cerveza *f* de barril ► **draught excluder** N burlete *m* ► **draught horse** N caballo *m* de tiro

draughtboard ['drɑːftbɔːd] N (*Brit*) tablero *m* de damas

draughtiness, draftiness (*US*) ['drɑːftɪnɪs] N corriente *f* de aire

draught-proof, draft-proof (*US*) ['drɑːftpruːf] ADJ a prueba de corrientes de aire

draught-proofing, draft-proofing (*US*) ['drɑːftˌpruːfɪŋ] N burlete *m*

draughts [drɑːfts] N (*Brit*) juego *m* de damas; **to play ~** jugar a las damas

draughtsman, draftsman (*US*) ['drɑːftsmən] N (*pl* **draughtsmen**) 1 (*in drawing office*) delineante *mf*, dibujante *mf*
2 (*Brit*) (*in game*) dama *f*, pieza *f*

draughtsmanship, draftsmanship (*US*) ['drɑːftsmənʃɪp] N (= *skill*) arte *m* del delineante; (= *quality*) habilidad *f* para el dibujo

draughtswoman, draftswoman (*US*) ['drɑːftsˌwʊmən] N (*pl* **draughtswomen**) dibujante *f*

draughty, drafty (*US*) ['drɑːftɪ] ADJ (*compar* **draughtier**, *superl* **draughtiest**) [*room*] con mucha corriente; [*street corner*] de mucho viento

draw [drɔː] (*vb: pt* **drew**, *pp* **drawn**) Ⓐ N 1 (= *lottery*) lotería *f*; (= *picking of ticket*) sorteo *m*; **the ~ takes place on Saturday** el sorteo es el sábado; **it's the luck of the ~** es la suerte
2 (= *equal score*) empate *m*; (*Chess*) tablas *fpl*; **the match ended in a ~** el partido terminó en empate
3 (= *attraction*) atracción *f*
4 **to beat sb to the ~** (*lit*) desenfundar más rápido que algn; (*fig*) adelantarse a algn; **to be quick on the ~** (*lit*) ser rápido en sacar la pistola; (*fig*) ser muy avispado
5 [*of chimney*] tiro *m*
Ⓑ VT 1 (= *pull*) [+ *bolt, curtains*] (*to close*) correr; (*to open*) descorrer; [+ *caravan, trailer*] tirar, jalar (*LAm*); **she drew him to one side** lo llevó a un lado; **she drew him towards her** lo atrajo hacia sí; **we drew him into the plan** le persuadimos para que participara en el proyecto; **to ~ a bow** tensar un arco; **he drew his finger along the table** pasó el dedo por la superficie de la mesa; **to ~ one's hand over one's eyes** pasarse la mano por los ojos; **he drew his hat over his eyes** se caló el sombrero hasta los ojos
2 (= *extract*) [+ *gun, sword, confession, tooth*] sacar; [+ *cheque*] girar; [+ *salary*] cobrar; [+ *number, prize*] sacarse; [+ *trumps*] arrastrar; (*Culin*) [+ *fowl*] destripar; (*Med*) [+ *boil*] hacer reventar; **to ~ a bath** preparar el baño; **to ~ blood** sacar sangre; **to ~ (a) breath** respirar; **to ~ a card** robar una carta; **to ~ comfort from sth** hallar consuelo en algo; **to ~ inspiration from sth** encontrar inspiración en algo; **to ~ lots** echar suertes; **to ~ a smile from sb** arrancar una sonrisa a algn; *see also* **breath A1**
3 (= *attract*) [+ *attention, crowd, customer*] atraer; **their shouts drew him to the place** llegó al lugar atraído por sus gritos; **to feel ~n to sb** simpatizar con algn; **he refuses to be ~n** se niega a hablar de ello, se guarda de hacer comentario alguno
4 (= *cause*) [+ *laughter*] causar, provocar; [+ *applause*] despertar, motivar; [+ *criticism*] provocar; **it drew no reply** no hubo contestación a esto
5 (= *sketch*) [+ *scene, person*] dibujar; [+ *plan, line, circle, map*] trazar; (*fig*) [+ *situation*] explicar; [+ *character*] trazar; **to ~ a picture** hacer un dibujo; **to ~ a picture of sb** hacer un retrato de algn; ✦**IDIOM to ~ the line at sth**: **I ~ the line at (doing) that** a (hacer) eso no llego
6 (= *formulate*) [+ *conclusion*] sacar (**from** de); **to ~ a comparison between A and B** comparar A con B; **to ~ a distinction** distinguir (**between** entre)
7 (*Sport, Games*) **to ~ a match/game** (*gen*) empatar un partido; (*Chess*) entablar
8 (*Naut*) **the boat ~s two metres** el barco tiene un calado de dos metros
9 (*Tech*) [+ *wire*] estirar
Ⓒ VI 1 (= *move*) **he drew ahead of the other runners** se adelantó a los demás corredores; **to ~ to an end** llegar a su fin; **the train drew into the station** el tren entró en la estación; **the two horses drew level** los dos caballos se igualaron; **to ~ near** acercarse; **the car drew over to the kerb** el coche se acercó a la acera; **he drew to one side** se apartó; **to ~ towards** acercarse a
2 (*Cards*) **to ~ for trumps** echar triunfos
3 [*chimney etc*] tirar
4 (= *infuse*) [*tea*] reposar
5 (= *be equal*) [*two teams, players*] empatar; (*Chess*) entablar; **we drew two all** empatamos a dos; **the teams drew for second place** los equipos empataron en segundo lugar
6 (= *sketch*) dibujar

►**draw ahead** VI + ADV adelantarse (**of** a)

►**draw aside** Ⓐ VT + ADV [+ *covering*] apartar; [+ *curtain*] descorrer; [+ *person*] apartar, llevar a un lado
Ⓑ VI + ADV ir aparte, apartarse

►**draw away** Ⓐ VT + ADV apartar, llevar aparte
Ⓑ VI + ADV alejarse, apartarse; (*in race*) dejar atrás a los otros; **to ~ away from the kerb** apartarse *or* alejarse de la acera; **he drew away from her** se alejó *or* apartó de ella

►**draw back** Ⓐ VT + ADV [+ *object, hand*] retirar; [+ *curtains*] descorrer
Ⓑ VI + ADV (= *move back*) echarse atrás (**from**

de); **to ~ back from doing sth** no atreverse a hacer algo

►**draw down** VT + ADV [1] (= *pull down*) [+ *blind*] bajar
[2] (*fig*) [+ *blame, ridicule*] atraer

►**draw forth** VT + ADV [+ *comment etc*] motivar, provocar, dar lugar a

►**draw in** (A) VI + ADV [1] [*car*] (= *stop*) detenerse, pararse (*LAm*); [*train*] (= *enter station*) entrar en la estación
[2] (*Brit*) **the days are ~ing in** los días se van acortando, los días se van haciendo más cortos
(B) VT + ADV [1] [+ *breath, air*] aspirar
[2] (= *pull back in*) [+ *claws*] retraer
[3] (= *attract*) [+ *crowds*] atraer

►**draw off** VT + ADV [1] [+ *gloves*] quitarse
[2] [+ *liquid*] vaciar, trasegar
[3] [+ *pursuers*] apartar, desviar

►**draw on** (A) VI + ADV [*night*] acercarse
(B) VI + PREP [+ *source*] inspirarse en; [+ *text*] poner a contribución; [+ *resources*] usar, hacer uso de, explotar; [+ *experience*] recurrir a, servirse de; [+ *bank account*] retirar dinero de; **he drew on his own experience to write the book** recurrió a *or* se sirvió de su propia experiencia para escribir el libro
(C) VT + ADV [1] [+ *gloves*] ponerse
[2] **to ~ sb on** engatusar a algn

►**draw out** (A) VT + ADV [1] (= *take out*) [+ *handkerchief, money from bank*] sacar; **to ~ sb out (of his shell)** (*fig*) hacer que algn salga de sí mismo
[2] (= *prolong*) [+ *meeting etc*] alargar
[3] (= *lengthen*) [+ *wire*] estirar
(B) VI + ADV [1] [*train etc*] arrancar
[2] [*days*] hacerse más largos

►**draw together** (A) VT + ADV reunir, juntar
(B) VI + ADV reunirse, juntarse; (*fig*) hacerse más unidos

►**draw up** (A) VT + ADV [1] (= *formulate*) [+ *will, contract*] redactar; [+ *report etc*] redactar, preparar; [+ *plan*] elaborar, trazar
[2] (= *move*) [+ *chair*] acercar; [+ *troops*] ordenar, disponer; **to ~ o.s. up (to one's full height)** enderezarse, erguirse
[3] (= *raise*) levantar, alzar; (*from well*) [+ *water*] sacar
(B) VI + ADV [*car etc*] detenerse, parar

►**draw upon** VI + PREP *see* **draw on B**

drawback ['drɔːbæk] N inconveniente *m*, desventaja *f*

drawbridge ['drɔːbrɪdʒ] N puente *m* levadizo

drawee [drɔː'iː] N girado/a *m/f*, librado/a *m/f*

drawer[1] [drɔːr] N (*in desk etc*) cajón *m*; *see also* **top E**

drawer[2] ['drɔːər] N (*Comm*) girador(a) *m/f*, librador(a) *m/f*

drawers† [drɔːz] NPL (*man's*) calzoncillos *mpl*; (*woman's*) bragas *fpl*

drawing ['drɔːɪŋ] (A) N [1] (= *picture*) dibujo *m*
[2] (= *activity*) **I'm no good at ~** no sirvo para el dibujo, no se me da bien el dibujo
(B) CPD ► **drawing account** N cuenta *f* de anticipos, fondo *m* para gastos ► **drawing board** N mesa *f* de dibujo; ♦*IDIOM* **back to the ~ board!** ¡a comenzar de nuevo! ► **drawing office** N oficina *f* de delineación ► **drawing paper** N papel *m* de dibujo ► **drawing pen** N tiralíneas *m inv* ► **drawing pin** N chincheta *f* (*Sp*), chinche *m or f* (*LAm*) ► **drawing power** N [*of speaker, entertainer*] poder *m* de convocatoria, tirón* *m* ► **drawing rights** N derechos *mpl* de giro ► **drawing room** N salón *m*, sala *f*

drawl [drɔːl] (A) N voz *f* cansina; **a Southern ~** un acento del sur
(B) VT decir alargando las palabras
(C) VI hablar alargando las palabras

drawn [drɔːn] (A) PP *of* **draw**
(B) ADJ [1] (= *haggard*) (*with tiredness*) demacrado, ojeroso; (*with pain*) macilento
[2] (= *with no winner*) [*game*] empatado
[3] (= *prolonged*) **long ~ out** larguísimo, prolongado
[4] (= *unsheathed*) **with ~ sword** con la espada en la mano
(C) CPD ► **drawn butter** N (*US*) mantequilla *f* derretida

drawstring ['drɔːstrɪŋ] N cordón *m*

dray [dreɪ] N carro *m* pesado

dread [dred] (A) N terror *m*, pavor *m*; **to fill sb with ~** infundir terror a algn; **he lives in ~ of being caught** vive aterrorizado por la idea de que lo cojan *or* (*LAm*) agarren
(B) VT tener pavor a; **I ~ going to the dentist** me da pavor ir al dentista; **I ~ what may happen when he comes** me horroriza lo que pueda pasar cuando venga; **I ~ to think of it*** ¡sólo pensarlo me da horror!
(C) ADJ espantoso

dreadful ['dredfʊl] ADJ [*crime, sight, suffering*] espantoso; [*news, accident, experience*] espantoso, terrible; [*disease, person, noise*] terrible; [*night, moment, place*] horrible; [*book, film*] pésimo; [*weather, conditions*] pésimo, fatal (*Sp**); [*situation, mistake*] horroroso, terrible; **how ~!** ¡qué horror!; **he is a ~ coward** es un cobarde asqueroso; **a ~ business** un asunto horroroso; **I feel ~!** (= *ill*) ¡me encuentro muy mal!, ¡me encuentro fatal! (*Sp**); (= *ashamed*) ¡qué vergüenza me da!, ¡qué pena me da! (*LAm*), me da muchísima vergüenza *or* (*LAm*) pena; **I feel ~ about forgetting his birthday** me siento fatal por haber olvidado su cumpleaños*; **to look ~** (= *ill*) tener mala cara*; (= *unattractive*) [*person*] estar horrible, tener una pinta horrorosa*; [*thing*] quedar horroroso; **I look ~ in this hat** estoy horrible con este sombrero, tengo una pinta horrorosa con este sombrero*; **that brown wallpaper looks ~** ese papel pintado marrón queda horroroso

dreadfully* ['dredfəlɪ] ADV [1] (= *very*) [*boring*] mortalmente; [*late, difficult*] increíblemente, muy; **I'm ~ sorry** lo siento muchísimo; **I felt something was ~ wrong** sentía que había pasado algo horrible
[2] (= *very much*) [*suffer*] muchísimo, lo indecible; [*hurt*] a rabiar; **I miss Janet ~** echo muchísimo de menos a Janet
[3] (= *badly*) [*behave, treat, sing*] muy mal, espantosamente, fatal (*Sp**)

dreadlocks ['dredlɒks] NPL *rizos de estilo rastafari*

dreadnought ['drednɔːt] N (*Hist*) acorazado *m*

▼**dream** [driːm] (*vb: pt, pp* **dreamed, dreamt**) (A) N [1] (*while asleep*) sueño *m*; **a bad ~** una pesadilla; **I had a ~ that my father had died** soñé que mi padre se había muerto; **to have a ~ about sth/sb** soñar con algo/algn; **to see sth in a ~** ver algo en sueños; **sweet ~s!** ¡que sueñes con los angelitos!; *see also* **wet D**
[2] (= *daydream*) sueño *m*, ensueño *m*; **she goes about in a ~** siempre está en las nubes
[3] (= *fantasy, ideal*) sueño *m*; **my (fondest) ~ is to ...** el sueño de mi vida es ..., mi mayor ilusión es ...; **the house/man/woman of my ~s** mi casa/hombre/mujer ideal, la casa/el hombre/la mujer de mis sueños; **the museum was an archaeologist's ~** para un arqueólogo, el museo era un sueño; **he thinks he's every girl's ~** se cree que es el tipo ideal para cualquier chica; **the American Dream** el sueño americano; **it was like a ~ come true** fue como un sueño hecho realidad; **a ~ holiday in Jamaica** unas vacaciones de ensueño en Jamaica; **in your ~s!*** ¡ni en sueños!*; **she succeeded beyond her wildest ~s** consiguió más éxito del que jamás había soñado; **never in my wildest ~s did I expect to win** ni en mis sueños más dorados hubiera podido imaginar que ganaría; **he lives in a ~ world** vive en un mundo de fantasía *or* de ensueño; **in a ~ world no one would be poor** en un mundo ideal, nadie sería pobre; *see also* **pipe D**
[4] (*) (= *marvel*) **"how was the holiday?" — "it was a ~!"** —¿qué tal las vacaciones? —¡de ensueño!; **it worked like a ~** funcionó de maravilla *or* a las mil maravillas; **that car goes like a ~** ese coche funciona de maravilla
(B) VT [1] (*while asleep*) soñar; **I ~ed that I was being chased** soñé que me perseguían; **I ~ed a strange ~** tuve un sueño extraño
[2] (= *imagine*) soñar, imaginarse; **you must have ~ed it** lo habrás soñado, te lo habrás imaginado; **I never ~ed that she would accept** jamás soñé con que aceptaría, jamás me imaginé que aceptaría
[3] (*as ambition*) **I ~ that my son will find a good job** mi sueño es que mi hijo encuentre un buen trabajo
(C) VI [1] (*while asleep*) soñar (**of, about** con)
[2] (= *daydream*) estar en las nubes; **I'm sorry, I was ~ing** disculpa, estaba en las nubes *or* pensando en las musarañas
[3] (= *fantasize*) soñar; **she ~ed of having her own business** soñaba con llegar a tener su propio negocio; **they have a lifestyle most of us only ~ of** *or* **about** llevan un tren de vida que para la mayoría de nosotros no pasa de ser un sueño; **~ on!*** ¡ni en sueños!*
[4] (= *imagine*) soñar, imaginarse; (*in neg context*) imaginarse; **there were more than I'd ever ~ed of** había más de lo que jamás hubiera podido soñar *or* imaginar; **who would ever ~ of a disaster like this?** ¿quién hubiera podido imaginarse una catástrofe así?
[5] (= *consider*) **"will you ask them?" — "I wouldn't ~ of it!"** —¿les preguntarás? —¡ni pensarlo! *or* ¡ni en sueños!*; **I wouldn't ~ of going!** ¿ir? ¡ni pensarlo! *or* ¡ni en sueños!*; **I wouldn't ~ of doing such a thing** jamás se me ocurriría hacer tal cosa
(D) CPD ► **dream house** N casa *f* de ensueño; **my ~ house** la casa de mis sueños ► **dream ticket** N (*Pol*) candidatos *mpl* ideales

►**dream away** VT + ADV **to ~ away the day** pasar el día soñando

►**dream up** VT + ADV [+ *plan*] trazar, idear; **only you could ~ up such a stupid idea** sólo a ti se te podría ocurrir una idea tan tonta

dreamboat* ['driːmbəʊt] N bombón* *m*

dreamer ['driːmər] N (= *impractical person*) soñador(a) *m/f*; **he's a bit of a ~** (= *idealistic*) es un soñador; (= *absent-minded*) es un despistado

dreamily ['driːmɪlɪ] ADV como si estuviera soñando

dreamland ['driːmlænd] N reino *m* del ensueño, país *m* de los sueños; (= *utopia*) utopía *f*

dreamless ['driːmlɪs] ADJ sin sueños

dreamlike ['driːmlaɪk] ADJ de ensueño, como de sueño

dreamt [dremt] PT, PP *of* **dream**

dreamy ['driːmɪ] ADJ (*compar* **dreamier**; *superl* **dreamiest**) [*character, person*] soñador; [*smile, tone*] distraído; [*music*] de ensueño, suave

➤ LANGUAGE IN USE: **dream** A3 8.3

dreariness [ˈdrɪərɪnɪs] N [*of landscape, weather*] lo inhóspito; [*of routine, job*] monotonía *f*, lo aburrido

dreary [ˈdrɪərɪ] ADJ (*compar* **drearier**; *superl* **dreariest**) [*landscape, weather*] gris, inhóspito; [*life, work*] monótono, aburrido; [*book, speech*] pesado

dredge[1] [dredʒ] Ⓐ N (*Mech*) draga *f*
Ⓑ VT [+ *river, canal*] dragar
► **dredge up** VT + ADV sacar con draga; (*fig*) [+ *unpleasant facts*] sacar a la luz

dredge[2] [dredʒ] N (*Culin*) espolvoreador *m*

dredger[1] [ˈdredʒəʳ] N (= *ship*) draga *f*

dredger[2] [ˈdredʒəʳ] N (*Culin*) espolvoreador *m*

dredging[1] [ˈdredʒɪŋ] N dragado *m*, obras *fpl* de dragado

dredging[2] [ˈdredʒɪŋ] N (*Culin*) espolvoreado *m*

dregs [dregz] NPL 1 [*of tea, coffee etc*] posos *mpl*, heces *fpl*; **to drain a glass to the ~** apurar un vaso (hasta las heces)
2 (*fig*) **the ~ of society** la escoria de la sociedad

drench [drentʃ] Ⓐ VT empapar (**with** de); **to get ~ed** empaparse; **he was ~ed to the skin** estaba empapado *or* calado hasta los huesos
Ⓑ N (*Vet*) poción *f*

drenching [ˈdrentʃɪŋ] Ⓐ ADJ [*rain*] torrencial
Ⓑ N **to get a ~** empaparse

Dresden [ˈdrezdən] Ⓐ N Dresde *m*
Ⓑ CPD ► **Dresden china** N loza *f* de Dresde

dress [dres] Ⓐ N 1 (= *frock*) vestido *m*
2 (= *clothing*) ropa *f*; **he's usually smart in his ~** suele vestir con elegancia; **a Maori in Western ~** un maorí vestido a la forma occidental; **they were wearing traditional Nepalese ~** vestían el traje tradicional *or* típico de Nepal; **formal ~ will be required** el traje de etiqueta es de rigor; *see also* **evening B**
Ⓑ VT 1 (= *put clothes on*) vestir; **she ~ed the baby in clean clothes** le puso ropita limpia al niño; **he hasn't learned how to ~ himself yet** todavía no ha aprendido a vestirse; *see also* **dressed**
2 (*Culin*) [+ *salad*] aliñar, aderezar; [+ *meat, fish*] preparar y condimentar
3 (= *decorate, arrange*) [+ *hair*] peinar, arreglar; [+ *shop window*] decorar; [+ *Christmas tree*] adornar, decorar
4 (*Med*) [+ *wound*] vendar
5 (*Agr*) [+ *land*] abonar
6 (*Mil*) [+ *troops*] alinear
7 [+ *stone, metal*] dar el acabado a; [+ *skins*] curtir
Ⓒ VI 1 (= *put on clothes*) vestirse; **he ~ed quickly and left** se vistió deprisa y se marchó
2 (= *wear specified clothes*) vestir; **she ~es very well** viste muy bien, va muy bien vestida; **she always used to ~ in jeans/black** solía ir siempre vestida con vaqueros/de negro; **to ~ to the left/right** colgar hacia la izquierda/derecha
3 (= *wear formal clothes*) **to ~ for dinner** [*man*] ponerse smoking para cenar; [*woman*] ponerse traje de noche para cenar; **they always ~ for dinner** siempre (se) ponen elegantes para cenar
4 (*Mil*) alinearse; **right ~!** ¡vista a la derecha!
Ⓓ CPD ► **dress circle** N anfiteatro *m*, (piso *m*) principal *m* ► **dress coat** N frac *m* ► **dress code** N *regulaciones en materia de indumentaria o uniforme* ► **dress designer** N modisto/a *m/f* ► **dress length** N (= *material*) corte *m* de vestido ► **dress parade** N (*US Mil*) desfile *m* de gala ► **dress rehearsal** N ensayo *m* general ► **dress sense** N gusto *m* para vestir; **he has no ~ sense** no tiene gusto para vestir; **he has immaculate ~ sense** tiene un gusto impecable para vestir ► **dress shirt** N camisa *f* de frac, camisa *f* de etiqueta ► **dress suit** N traje *m* de etiqueta ► **dress uniform** N (*Mil*) uniforme *m* de gala
► **dress down** Ⓐ VI + ADV vestirse informalmente
Ⓑ VT + ADV (*) (= *rebuke*) reprender
► **dress up** Ⓐ VI + ADV (*in smart clothes*) ponerse elegante; (*formally*) vestirse de etiqueta; (*in fancy dress*) disfrazarse
Ⓑ VT + ADV 1 (*in smart clothes*) poner elegante; (*in fancy dress*) disfrazar; **you're all ~ed up, are you going somewhere?** vas muy elegante, ¿es que vas a algún sitio?; **to ~ sb up as sth** disfrazar *or* vestir a algn de algo; *see also* **nine B**
2 (= *improve appearance of*) [+ *facts, events*] disfrazar; **it was a pile of scrap metal ~ed up as art** era un montón de chatarra disfrazado de arte; **they ~ed the setback up as a triumph** hicieron creer que el revés había sido en realidad un triunfo

dressage [ˈdresɑːʒ] N *método de adiestramiento de caballos para que realicen movimientos controlados*

dressed [drest] Ⓐ ADJ vestido; **to be casually ~** ir (vestido) informal *or* de sport; **to be smartly ~** ir (vestido) elegante; **~ as a man/woman** vestido de hombre/mujer; **to be ~ for tennis/the country** ir vestido para jugar al tenis/para ir al campo; **fully ~** completamente vestido; **to get ~** vestirse; **~ in black** vestido de negro; **to be ~ in a skirt/trousers** llevar falda/pantalones; ✦**IDIOM to be ~ to kill*** ir despampanante*; *see also* **dress, dress up, well-dressed**
Ⓑ CPD ► **dressed crab** N cangrejo *m* preparado

dresser [ˈdresəʳ] N 1 (= *furniture*) (*in kitchen*) aparador *m*; (= *dressing table*) tocador *m*
2 (*Theat*) ayudante *mf* de camerino
3 (= *person*) **he's an elegant ~** se viste elegantemente

dressing [ˈdresɪŋ] Ⓐ N 1 (= *act*) **allow time for ~** déjese tiempo suficiente para vestirse
2 (*Med*) (= *bandage*) vendaje *m*
3 (*Culin*) (= *salad dressing*) aliño *m*
4 (*Agr*) (= *fertilizer*) abono *m*, fertilizante *m*
Ⓑ CPD ► **dressing case** N neceser *m* ► **dressing gown** N bata *f* ► **dressing room** N (*Theat*) camerino *m*; (*Sport*) vestuario *m* ► **dressing station** N (*Mil*) puesto *m* de socorro ► **dressing table** N tocador *m*

dressing-down [ˈdresɪŋˈdaʊn] N **to give sb a ~*** echar un rapapolvo a algn*

dressmaker [ˈdresmeɪkəʳ] N modista *f*, costurera *f*

dressmaking [ˈdresmeɪkɪŋ] N costura *f*, corte *m* y confección

dressy* [ˈdresɪ] ADJ (*compar* **dressier**; *superl* **dressiest**) [*person*] de mucho vestir; [*clothing*] elegante

drew [druː] PT *of* **draw**

dribble [ˈdrɪbl] Ⓐ N 1 [*of saliva*] babeo *m*; [*of water*] gotitas *fpl*; **the water came out in a ~** (*thin stream*) salía un hilillo de agua; (*dripping*) el agua goteaba; **a ~ of water** (= *thin stream*) un hilillo de agua; (= *drops*) gotas de agua
2 (*Ftbl*) control *m* del balón; (*past opponents*) regate *m*, dribling *m*
Ⓑ VT 1 [+ *liquid*] **he ~d his milk all down his chin** le chorreaba la leche por la barbilla
2 (*Ftbl*) regatear, driblar
Ⓒ VI 1 [*baby*] babear; [*liquid*] gotear
2 (*Ftbl*) controlar el balón; **to ~ past sb** regatear *or* driblar a algn

dribbler [ˈdrɪbləʳ] N (*Sport*) driblador *m*

driblet [ˈdrɪblɪt] N adarme *m*; **in ~s** por adarmes

dribs [drɪbz] NPL ✦**IDIOM in ~ and drabs** poco a poco, con cuentagotas; **the money came in in ~ and drabs** el dinero fue llegando poco a poco *or* con cuentagotas; **the guests arrived in ~ and drabs** los invitados fueron llegando poco a poco

dried [draɪd] Ⓐ PT, PP *of* **dry**
Ⓑ ADJ [*flowers, mushrooms, lentils*] seco; [*milk*] en polvo
Ⓒ CPD ► **dried fruit(s)** N frutas *fpl* pasas

dried-out [ˌdraɪdˈaʊt] ADJ [*alcoholic*] seco

dried-up [ˌdraɪdˈʌp] ADJ [*river-bed, stream, oasis*] seco

drier [ˈdraɪəʳ] N = **dryer**

drift [drɪft] Ⓐ N 1 (= *deviation from course*) deriva *f*; (= *movement*) movimiento *m*; (= *change of direction*) cambio *m* (de dirección); **the ~ to the city** el movimiento migratorio hacia la ciudad; **the ~ from the land** el éxodo rural, la despoblación del campo; **the ~ of events** la marcha de los acontecimientos
2 (= *meaning*) [*of questions*] significado *m*; **to catch sb's ~** seguir *or* entender a algn; **I don't get your ~** no te entiendo
3 (= *mass*) [*of snow*] ventisquero *m*; [*of sand*] montón *m*; [*of clouds, leaves*] banco *m*; (*Geol*) morrena *f*; **continental ~** deriva *f* continental
Ⓑ VI 1 (*in wind, current*) dejarse llevar, ir a la deriva; (= *be off course*) [*boat*] ir a la deriva; [*person*] vagar, ir a la deriva; **to ~ downstream** dejarse llevar río abajo; **he ~ed into marriage** se casó sin pensárselo; **to let things ~** dejar las cosas como están; **to ~ from job to job** cambiar a menudo de trabajo sin propósito fijo
2 [*snow, sand*] amontonarse
Ⓒ VT (= *carry*) impeler, llevar; (= *pile up*) amontonar
Ⓓ CPD ► **drift ice** N hielo *m* flotante ► **drift net** N traína *f*
► **drift apart** VI + ADV irse separando poco a poco
► **drift away** VI + ADV dejarse llevar por la corriente
► **drift off** VI + ADV (= *doze off*) dormirse, quedarse dormido

drifter [ˈdrɪftəʳ] N 1 (*Naut*) trainera *f*
2 (= *person*) vago/a *m/f*, vagabundo/a *m/f*

drifting [ˈdrɪftɪŋ] N nieve *f* acumulada (*después de una tormenta*)

driftwood [ˈdrɪftwʊd] N madera *f* de deriva

drill[1] [drɪl] Ⓐ N 1 (*for wood, metal*) taladradora *f*, taladro *m*; (= *bit*) broca *f*; (*Min*) (*for oil etc*) barrena *f*, perforadora *f*; (= *dentist's drill*) fresa *f*; (= *pneumatic drill*) martillo *m* neumático
2 (*Agr*) (= *furrow*) surco *m*; (= *machine*) sembradora *f*
Ⓑ VT [+ *wood, road*] taladrar, perforar; [+ *tooth*] agujerear; [+ *oil well*] perforar; (*Agr*) sembrar con sembradora; **he ~ed a hole in the wall** hizo *or* taladró un agujero en la pared
Ⓒ VI perforar (**for** en busca de)

drill[2] [drɪl] Ⓐ N (= *exercises*) (*Mil*) instrucción *f*; (*Scol*) ejercicios *mpl*; **fire ~** simulacro *m* de incendio; **you all know the ~*** todos sabéis lo que hay que hacer; **what's the ~?*** ¿qué es lo que tenemos que hacer?
Ⓑ VT [+ *soldiers*] ejercitar; **to ~ pupils in grammar** hacer ejercicios de gramática con

los alumnos; **to ~ good manners into a child** enseñar buenos modales a un niño; **I had it ~ed into me as a boy** me lo inculcaron de niño
Ⓒ VI (*Mil*) hacer instrucción

drill[3] [drɪl] N (= *fabric*) dril *m*

drilling[1] ['drɪlɪŋ] Ⓐ N (*for oil etc*) perforación *f*
Ⓑ CPD ► **drilling platform** N plataforma *f* de perforación ► **drilling rig** N torre *f* de perforación

drilling[2] ['drɪlɪŋ] N (*Mil*) instrucción *f*

drily ['draɪlɪ] ADV 1 (= *with dry humour*) **... he said ~** ... dijo con un humor cargado de ironía
2 (= *unemotionally*) secamente, con sequedad
3 **he coughed ~** emitió una tos seca

drink [drɪŋk] (*vb: pt* **drank**; *pp* **drunk**) Ⓐ N 1 (= *liquid to drink*) bebida *f*; **there's food and ~ in the kitchen** hay comida y bebidas en la cocina, hay cosas de comer y de beber en la cocina; **have you got ~s for the children?** ¿habéis traído algo para que beban los niños?; **I need a ~ of water** necesito un poco de agua; **cold ~s** (*non-alcoholic*) refrescos *mpl*; **to give sb a ~** darle algo de beber a algn; **can I have a ~?** ¿me podrías dar algo de beber *or* (*LAm*) tomar?; **hot ~s will be available** se servirá café y té; **I felt better after a hot ~** me sentía mejor después de beber algo caliente; *see also* **meat A1**, **soft B**
2 (= *glass of alcohol*) copa *f*, trago *m*; **to go (out) for a ~** salir a tomar algo, salir a tomar una copa; **they've asked us round for ~s** nos han invitado a su casa a tomar algo *or* a tomar unas copas; **to have a ~** tomar algo; **we had a ~ or two** tomamos unas copas *or* unos tragos; *see also* **drive B7**
3 (= *alcoholic liquor*) alcohol *m*, bebida *f*; **he's given up ~** ha dejado de beber, ha dejado el alcohol *or* la bebida; **he has a ~ problem** tiene problemas con el alcohol *or* la bebida; **to take to ~** darse a la bebida; *see also* **worse A**
4 **the ~*** (= *the water*) (*gen*) el agua; (= *sea*) el mar
Ⓑ VT beber, tomar (*esp LAm*); **would you like something to ~?** ¿quieres tomar algo?; **in the end he drank himself to death** al final la bebida lo llevó a la tumba; **this coffee isn't fit to ~** este café no se puede beber; **to ~ sb's health** brindar por la salud de algn; **we drank ourselves into a stupor** bebimos hasta perder el sentido; **to ~ sb under the table*** darle cien vueltas a algn bebiendo; **to ~ a toast to sth/sb** brindar por algo/algn
Ⓒ VI 1 (= *imbibe liquid*) beber; **to ~ from the bottle** beber de la botella; **to ~ out of paper cups** beber en vasos de plástico
2 (= *imbibe alcohol*) beber, tomar (*LAm*); **he doesn't ~** no bebe (alcohol), no toma (alcohol) (*esp LAm*); **don't ~ and drive** si bebes, no conduzcas; **he ~s like a fish** bebe como una esponja; **to ~ to sth/sb** brindar por algo/algn

► **drink down** VT + ADV beber de un trago

► **drink in** VT + ADV 1 (*fig*) [+ *fresh air*] respirar; [+ *story, sight, atmosphere*] empaparse de; [+ *words*] estar pendiente de; **he stood, ~ing in the view** se quedó parado, empapándose de la vista; **she sat there ~ing in his words** estaba ahí sentada, pendiente de sus palabras; **the children were ~ing it all in** a los niños no les escapaba nada
2 [*plant, soil*] absorber

► **drink up** Ⓐ VT + ADV [+ *one's drink*] terminar de beber, terminar de tomar (*LAm*); [+ *all drink available*] beberse, tomarse (*LAm*)
Ⓑ VI + ADV **~ up now, please!** ¡terminen sus bebidas!

drinkable ['drɪŋkəbl] ADJ (= *not poisonous*) potable; (= *palatable*) aceptable, que se deja beber; **quite ~** nada malo

drink-driving ['drɪŋk'draɪvɪŋ] Ⓐ N el conducir en estado de embriaguez, el manejar en estado de embriaguez (*LAm*); **he was arrested for ~** lo arrestaron por conducir en estado de embriaguez (*frm*), lo arrestaron por conducir borracho; **there are strict laws on ~** hay leyes muy estrictas en lo que respecta a conducir en estado de embriaguez
Ⓑ CPD ► **drink-driving campaign** N campaña *f* contra el alcohol en carretera ► **drink-driving offence** N delito *m* de conducir en estado de embriaguez; **~ offences must be severely dealt with** conducir en estado de embriaguez debe ser severamente castigado; **he was guilty of several ~ offences** le habían detenido varias veces por conducir en estado de embriaguez

drinker ['drɪŋkə^r] N bebedor(a) *m/f*; **he was a heavy ~** era un bebedor empedernido

drinking ['drɪŋkɪŋ] Ⓐ N 1 [*of any liquid*] **my sore throat made ~ painful** al tener la garganta irritada me dolía mucho al beber
2 [*of alcohol*] **his ~ caused his marriage to break up** la bebida fue la causa de la ruptura de su matrimonio; **she had to put up with his ~** tuvo que aguantar sus borracheras; **heavy ~ can cause weight problems** beber mucho puede ocasionar problemas de peso; **I'm not a ~ person** no soy bebedor, no bebo mucho
Ⓑ CPD ► **drinking bout** N juerga *f*, farra *f* (*LAm**) ► **drinking chocolate** N chocolate *m* (*bebida*) ► **drinking companion** N compañero/a *m/f* de copas ► **drinking fountain** N fuente *f* (de agua potable) ► **drinking session** N juerga *f*, farra *f* (*LAm**) ► **drinking song** N canción *f* de taberna ► **drinking trough** N abrevadero *m*, camellón *m* ► **drinking water** N agua *f* potable

drinking-up time ['drɪŋkɪŋʌp] N *tiempo permitido para terminar las bebidas en el pub antes de cerrar*

drip [drɪp] Ⓐ N 1 (= *droplet*) gota *f*
2 (= *dripping sound*) goteo *m*; **the ~, ~, ~ of the tap was beginning to irritate her** el constante goteo del grifo estaba empezando a irritarla; **she could hear the constant ~ of the rain outside** oía el constante gotear de la lluvia fuera
3 (*) (= *spineless person*) soso/a *m/f*
4 (*Med*) gotero *m*, gota a gota *m inv*; **she is on a ~** tiene puesto un gotero *or* gota a gota
Ⓑ VT **the children came in ~ping water all over the floor** los niños entraron chorreando agua por todo el suelo; **try not to ~ sauce onto the table cloth** procura que la salsa no gotee en el mantel; **you're ~ping paint all over the place** estás chorreando pintura por todas partes, lo estás poniendo todo perdido de pintura; **her knee was ~ping blood** su rodilla estaba chorreando sangre
Ⓒ VI [*tap, faucet*] gotear; **oil was ~ping from under the car** el coche perdía aceite; **the rain was ~ping down the wall** las gotas de lluvia se deslizaban por la pared; **sweat was ~ping from his brow** le caían gotas de sudor de la frente; **blood ~ped from her finger** le caían gotas de sangre del dedo; **I washed my jumper and left it to ~** lavé el jersey y lo dejé escurrir; *see also* **dripping**

drip-dry ['drɪp'draɪ] ADJ inarrugable

drip-feed ['drɪp,fiːd] Ⓐ N alimentación *f* gota a gota, gota a gota *m inv*; **to be on a ~** recibir alimentación gota a gota
Ⓑ VT (*pt, pp* **drip-fed**) alimentar gota a gota

dripmat ['drɪpmæt] N posavasos *m inv*

dripping ['drɪpɪŋ] Ⓐ N (*Culin*) pringue *m or f*
Ⓑ ADJ 1 (= *soaking*) [*washing, coat*] que chorrea, que gotea; [*person, hair*] empapado; **to be ~ wet*** estar empapado *or* chorreando; **~ with blood** chorreando sangre; **to be ~ with sweat** estar sudando a chorros, estar chorreando de sudor; **his voice was ~ with sarcasm** su voz rezumaba sarcasmo; **women ~ with diamonds and furs** mujeres cargadas de diamantes y pieles
2 [*tap, gutter*] que gotea

drippy* ['drɪpɪ] ADJ [*person, idea, book*] ñoño

drivability [,draɪvə'bɪlɪtɪ] N manejabilidad *f*, capacidad *f* de maniobras

drive [draɪv] (*vb: pt* **drove**; *pp* **driven**) Ⓐ N 1 (= *journey, outing*) **it's a long ~** se tarda mucho en coche; **it's only a short ~ from here** desde aquí se tarda poco en coche; **one hour's ~ from London** a una hora en coche de Londres; **it's a 50 mile ~** está a una distancia de 50 millas; **to go for a ~** ir a dar una vuelta *or* un paseo en coche; *see also* **test D**
2 (= *private road*) (*in front of garage*) entrada *f*; (*to large house*) camino *m* (de acceso), avenida *f*; **his car was parked in the ~** su coche estaba aparcado en la entrada
3 (*Tennis*) golpe *m* directo, drive *m*; (*Golf*) drive *m*
4 (= *energy, motivation*) empuje *m*, dinamismo *m*; **to have ~** tener empuje *or* dinamismo; **to lack ~** no tener empuje *or* dinamismo
5 (*Psych*) (= *impulse*) impulso *m*, instinto *m*; **sex ~** libido *f*, líbido *f*, apetito *m* sexual; **to have a high/low sex ~** tener la libido *or* líbido alta/baja, tener mucho/poco apetito sexual
6 (= *campaign, effort*) campaña *f*; **a recruitment ~** una campaña de reclutamiento; **a sales ~** una promoción de ventas; **the ~ towards industrialization** el camino hacia la industrialización
7 (*Tech*) (= *power transmission system*) transmisión *f*, propulsión *f*; (*Aut*) **four-wheel ~** tracción *f* en las cuatro ruedas; **a four-wheel ~ jeep** un jeep con tracción en las cuatro ruedas; **front-wheel/rear-wheel ~** tracción *f* delantera/trasera; **a left-hand/right-hand ~ car** un coche con el volante a la izquierda/derecha
8 (= *gear position in automatic car*) marcha *f*; **to put the car in ~** poner el coche en marcha
9 (*Comput*) (*also* **disk ~**) unidad *f* de disco; **CD-ROM ~** unidad *f* de CD-ROM
10 (= *tournament*) **whist ~** certamen *m* de whist
11 (*Mil*) (= *attack*) ofensiva *f*
Ⓑ VT 1 (= *operate*) [+ *car, bus, train*] conducir, manejar (*LAm*); [+ *racing car, speedboat*] pilotar; **he ~s a taxi** es taxista; **she ~s a Mercedes** tiene un Mercedes
2 (= *carry*) [+ *passenger*] llevar (en coche); **I'll ~ you home** te llevo a tu casa; **he drove me to the station** me llevó a la estación
3 (= *power*) [+ *machine, vehicle*] hacer funcionar
4 (= *cause to move*) **they ~ the cattle to new pastures** conducen el ganado a otros pastos; **the wind drove the rain into our eyes** el viento hacía que la lluvia nos azotaba en los ojos; **a strong wind was driving the clouds across the sky** un viento fuerte arrastraba las nubes por el cielo; **the gale drove the ship off course** el temporal hizo que el barco perdiera su rumbo; **troops drove the demonstrators off the streets**

las tropas obligaron a los manifestantes a abandonar las calles

5 (= *push, hammer*) [+ *nail, stake*] clavar (**into** en); **to ~ a post into the ground** clavar *or* hincar un poste en el suelo; **she drove her fist straight into his face** le dio con el puño justo en la cara; *see also* **home B2**

6 (= *excavate*) [+ *tunnel*] abrir, construir; [+ *hole*] perforar; [+ *furrow*] hacer

7 (= *force*) **I was ~n to it** me vi forzado a ello; **competition has ~n prices down** la competencia ha hecho que bajen los precios; **hunger eventually drove him out of the house** finalmente el hambre lo empujó a salir de la casa; **high prices are driving local people out of the area** el que los precios sean tan altos está haciendo que la gente se vaya a vivir a otras zonas; **the recession drove them into bankruptcy** la recesión los llevó a la bancarrota; **to ~ sb to despair** llevar a algn a la desesperación; **to ~ sb to drink: his worries drove him to drink** sus problemas le llevaron a la bebida; **it's enough to ~ you to drink** (*hum*) te crispa los nervios; **to ~ sb mad** volver loco a algn; *see also* **bargain A1**, **home B2**

8 (= *impel, motivate*) empujar, mover; **he was ~n by greed/ambition** lo empujaba *or* movía la avaricia/ambición; **to ~ sb to do sth** ◊ **~ sb into doing sth** empujar *or* llevar a algn a hacer algo; **depression drove him to attempt suicide** la depresión le empujó *or* llevó a intentar suicidarse; **what drove you to write this book?** ¿qué le empujó *or* llevó a escribir este libro?

9 (= *overwork*) **to ~ sb hard** hacer trabajar mucho a algn; **she is driving herself too hard** se está exigiendo demasiado

10 (*Sport*) [+ *ball*] mandar

Ⓒ VI 1 (= *operate vehicle*) conducir, manejar (*LAm*); **can you ~?** ¿sabes conducir *or* (*LAm*) manejar?; **to ~ on the left** circular por la izquierda

2 (= *go*) **he drove alone** hizo el viaje en coche solo; **we've ~n 50 miles in the last hour** hemos recorrido 80km (con el coche) en la última hora; **next time we'll ~ there** la próxima vez iremos en coche; **he ~s around in an expensive car** va por ahí en un coche de esos caros; **to ~ at 50km an hour** ir (en un coche) a 50km por hora; **we'll ~ down in the car this weekend** este fin de semana bajaremos en coche; **he drove into a wall** chocó con un muro; **to ~ to London** ir a Londres en coche

3 (= *handle*) conducirse, manejarse (*LAm*); **the new Ford ~s really well** el nuevo Ford se conduce *or* (*LAm*) se maneja muy bien

4 (= *beat*) **heavy rain drove against the window** la fuerte lluvia azotaba el cristal

Ⓓ CPD ► **drive shaft** N (*Aut*) árbol *m* motor

►**drive along** Ⓐ VT + ADV [*wind, current*] empujar

Ⓑ VI + ADV [*vehicle*] circular; [*person*] conducir

►**drive at*** VI + PREP (*fig*) (= *intend, mean*) insinuar, dar a entender; **what are you driving at?** ¿qué (es lo que) estás insinuando *or* dando a entender?

►**drive away** Ⓐ VT + ADV 1 (= *chase away*) [+ *person*] ahuyentar; [+ *cares*] alejar, quitarse de encima; **the smoke drove the mosquitos away** el humo ahuyentó a los mosquitos; **in the end his jealousy drove her away** al final sus celos la ahuyentaron

2 (*in vehicle*) llevarse (en coche)

Ⓑ VI + ADV = **drive off B**

►**drive back** Ⓐ VT + ADV 1 (= *force to retreat*) [+ *person, army*] hacer retroceder

2 (*in vehicle*) llevar de vuelta (en coche)

Ⓑ VI + ADV volver (en coche)

►**drive off** Ⓐ VT + ADV (= *force to retreat*) [+ *enemy*] ahuyentar; (= *force to leave*) expulsar, echar

Ⓑ VI + ADV irse, marcharse (en coche); [*vehicle*] partir

►**drive on** Ⓐ VI + ADV [*person, vehicle*] (*after accident*) no parar; (*after stopping*) seguir adelante; **~ on!** ¡siga!

Ⓑ VT + ADV (= *incite, encourage*) empujar, mover; **it was the desire to win that drove her on** era su deseo de ganar lo que la empujaba *or* movía (a seguir)

►**drive on to** VI + PREP [+ *ferry*] embarcar en

►**drive out** VT + ADV (= *force to leave*) **invading tribes drove them out** las tribus invasoras los expulsaron de sus tierras; **the smell drove me out** el olor me obligó a salir; **it is said to ~ out evil spirits** se dice que ahuyenta a los espíritus malignos

►**drive over** Ⓐ VT + ADV (= *convey*) llevar en coche

Ⓑ VI + PREP (= *crush*) aplastar

Ⓒ VI + ADV (= *come*) venir en coche; (= *go*) ir en coche; **we drove over in two hours** vinimos en dos horas; **we drove over to see them** fuimos a verlos (en coche)

►**drive up** Ⓐ VT + ADV [+ *price*] hacer subir

Ⓑ VI + ADV [*person*] acercarse (en coche); [*vehicle*] pararse; **the car drove up in front of the police station** el coche se paró delante de la comisaría; **he drove up in a limousine** se acercó en una limusina

driveability [ˌdraɪvəˈbɪlɪtɪ] N = **drivability**

drive-by [ˈdraɪvbaɪ] N (*also* **~ shooting**) tiroteo *m* desde el coche

drive-in [ˈdraɪvɪn] (*esp US*) Ⓐ N (= *restaurant*) *restaurante donde se sirve al cliente en su automóvil*; (= *cinema*) autocine *m*

Ⓑ ADJ [*bank etc*] *dispuesto para el uso del automovilista en su coche*; **~ cinema** autocine *m*; **a ~ movie** una película de autocine

DRIVE-IN

En Estados Unidos el término **drive-in** *hace referencia a todos aquellos establecimientos, como cines, restaurantes o bancos, especialmente construidos para que el cliente pueda hacer uso de sus servicios sin tener que abandonar el vehículo que conduce. El primero de estos establecimientos se abrió en 1933. El término también se usa como adjetivo, como por ejemplo en* **a drive-in movie**. *A veces se usa la forma* **drive-through** *o* **drive-thru**, *que se aplica especialmente a las hamburgueserías, bancos y otros establecimientos en los que las transacciones son muy breves y no hay necesidad de aparcar el vehículo.*

drivel* [ˈdrɪvl] Ⓐ N (= *nonsense*) tonterías *fpl*, chorradas* *fpl*, babosadas *fpl* (*LAm**)

Ⓑ VI decir tonterías, decir chorradas*, decir babosadas (*LAm**)

driven [ˈdrɪvn] PP *of* **drive**

-driven [ˈdrɪvn] ADJ (*ending in compounds*) que funciona con, accionado por; **electricity-driven** que funciona con electricidad, accionado por electricidad; **steam-driven** impulsado por vapor, a vapor

driver [ˈdraɪvəʳ] Ⓐ N 1 [*of car, bus*] conductor(a) *m/f*, chofer *mf* (*LAm*); [*of taxi*] taxista *mf*; [*of lorry*] camionero/a *m/f*; [*of carriage*] cochero *m*; (*Brit*) [*of train*] maquinista *mf*; **he's a bus ~** es conductor de autobús; **she's an excellent ~** conduce muy bien

2 (*Golf*) driver *m*

Ⓑ CPD ► **driver's license** N (*US*) permiso *m* de conducir *or* (*LAm*) manejar, carnet *m* de conducir *or* (*LAm*) manejar ► **driver's seat** N = **driving seat**

drive-through, **drive-thru** [ˈdraɪvθruː] N (*US*) = **drive-in**

drive-up window [draɪvʌpˈwɪndəʊ] N (*US*) taquilla *f* para automovilistas

driveway [ˈdraɪvweɪ] N entrada *f*

drive-yourself service [ˌdraɪvjɔːˈselfˌsɜːvɪs] N servicio *m* de alquiler sin chófer

driving [ˈdraɪvɪŋ] Ⓐ N (*Aut*) **his ~ was a bit erratic** su forma de conducir *or* (*LAm*) manejar era bastante imprevisible; **we share the ~** nos turnamos al volante; **why don't you let me do the ~?** ¿por qué no me dejas conducir *or* (*LAm*) manejar a mí?; *see also* **drunken 1**, **reckless**

Ⓑ ADJ [*force*] impulsor; [*rain*] torrencial; [*wind*] azotador; **she is the ~ force behind the organization** ella es la (fuerza) impulsora de la organización

Ⓒ CPD ► **driving belt** N correa *f* de transmisión ► **driving instructor** N profesor(a) *m/f* de autoescuela ► **driving lesson** N clase *f* de conducir *or* (*LAm*) manejar ► **driving licence** N (*Brit*) permiso *m* de conducir *or* (*LAm*) manejar, carnet *m* de conducir *or* (*LAm*) manejar; **provisional/full ~ license** permiso *m* de conducir provisional/definitivo, carnet *m* de conducir provisional/definitivo ► **driving mirror** N retrovisor *m*, espejo *m* retrovisor ► **driving range** N *zona de un campo de golf para practicar tiros de salida* ► **driving school** N autoescuela *f* ► **driving seat** N asiento *m* del conductor; ✦***IDIOM*** **to be in the ~ seat** estar al mando; **he's in the ~ seat now** ahora él es quien manda ► **driving test** N examen *m* de conducir *or* (*LAm*) manejar ► **driving wheel** N (*Tech*) rueda *f* motriz

DRIVING LICENCE/DRIVER'S LICENSE

*En el Reino Unido se puede obtener el permiso de conducir desde los 17 años. Aunque la mayoría de la gente aprende a conducir en una autoescuela, también se puede solicitar un permiso provisional (***provisional (driving) licence***) mientras se está aprendiendo, el cual permite llevar un coche siempre y cuando el conductor novato vaya acompañado por otra persona con al menos tres años de carnet. Este carnet provisional no lleva la fotografía del conductor y no es obligatorio llevarlo encima cuando se conduce, aunque la policía puede pedir que se presente el documento en comisaría. Una vez obtenido el carnet definitivo (***full driving licence***), no hace falta renovarlo hasta los setenta años.*

La edad para obtener el permiso de conducir en Estados Unidos varía, según el estado, entre 15 y 21 años. Sin embargo, los jóvenes pueden obtener un permiso **junior**, *para conducir en determinadas circunstancias, por ejemplo, para ir a clase. Este carnet se ha de llevar siempre encima y es un documento válido para acreditar la identidad o la edad, que tiene que renovarse a los 4 ó 6 años. Sólo tiene validez estatal, por lo que si alguien se traslada a otro estado debe sacar otro carnet, para lo cual debe hacer otro examen escrito.*

En ambos países son los conductores que no han aprobado aún el examen de conducir quienes llevan la L, llamada **L-plate** *(de* **learner***).*

drizzle ['drɪzl] Ⓐ N llovizna *f*, garúa *f* (*LAm*)
Ⓑ VI lloviznar

drizzly ['drɪzlɪ] ADJ lloviznoso

droll [drəʊl] ADJ gracioso, divertido

dromedary ['drɒmɪdərɪ] N dromedario *m*

drone [drəʊn] Ⓐ N [1] (= *male bee*) zángano *m*
[2] (= *noise*) [*of bees, engine*] zumbido *m*; [*of voice*] tono *m* monótono
[3] (= *sponger*) parásito/a *m/f*
Ⓑ VI [*bee, engine, aircraft*] zumbar; [*voice, person*] (*also* ~ **on**) hablar monótonamente; **he ~d on and on** hablaba y hablaba en tono monótono

drool [dru:l] VI (= *slobber*) babear; **she ~ed over the kittens/her grandchildren** (*fig*) se le caía la baba con los gatitos/sus nietos

droop [dru:p] Ⓐ VI [*head*] inclinarse; [*shoulders*] encorvarse; [*flower*] marchitarse; **his spirits ~ed** quedó abatido *or* desanimado
Ⓑ VT inclinar, dejar caer (**over** por)

drooping ['dru:pɪŋ] ADJ [*flower*] marchito; [*ears, head*] gacho; [*movement*] lánguido, desmayado

droopy ['dru:pɪ] ADJ [1] [*moustache, tail, breasts*] colgón
[2] (*hum*) (= *tired*) mustio

drop [drɒp] Ⓐ N [1] [*of liquid*] gota *f*; **"would you like some milk?" — "just a ~"** — ¿quieres leche? —una gota nada más; **in three weeks we didn't have a ~ of rain** no cayó ni una gota en tres semanas; **would you like a ~ of soup?** ¿quieres un poco de sopa?; **there's just a ~ left** queda sólo una gota; **he's had a ~ too much*** ha bebido más de la cuenta; **I haven't touched a ~** no he probado una sola gota; ✦*IDIOM* **a ~ in the ocean** una gota de agua en el mar
[2] **drops** (*Med*) gotas *fpl*
[3] (= *sweet*) pastilla *f*
[4] (= *fall*) (*in price*) bajada *f*, caída *f*; (*in demand*) disminución *f*, reducción *f*; **a ~ of 10%** una bajada del 10 por ciento; **to take a ~ in salary** aceptar un salario más bajo; **a ~ in temperature** una bajada de las temperaturas; ✦*IDIOM* **at the ~ of a hat** con cualquier pretexto
[5] (= *steep incline*) pendiente *f*; (= *fall*) caída *f*; **a ~ of ten metres** una caída de diez metros
[6] (*by parachute*) [*of supplies, arms etc*] lanzamiento *m*
[7] (*for secret mail*) escondrijo *m* (*para correo secreto*)
[8] ✦*IDIOM* **to have the ~ on sb** (*US**) llevar la delantera a algn, tener ventaja sobre algn
[9] (*Theat*) telón *m* de boca
Ⓑ VT [1] (= *let fall*) [1·1] (*deliberately*) [+ *object*] dejar caer; (= *release, let go of*) soltar; [+ *bomb, parachutist*] lanzar; [+ *anchor*] echar; [+ *liquid*] echar gota a gota; **the cat ~ped the mouse at my feet** el gato soltó al ratón junto a mis pies; **don't ~ your coat onto the floor, hang it up** no sueltes el abrigo en el suelo, cuélgalo; **to ~ a letter in the postbox** echar una carta al buzón; **~ it!*** (*gun*) ¡suéltalo!
[1·2] (*accidentally*) **I ~ped the glass** se me cayó el vaso; **I've ~ped a stitch** (*Knitting*) se me escapó un punto
[2] (= *lower*) [+ *eyes, voice, price, hem*] bajar
[3] (= *set down*) (*from car*) [+ *object, person*] dejar; (*from boat*) [+ *cargo, passengers*] descargar; **could you ~ me at the station?** ¿me puedes dejar en la estación?
[4] (= *utter casually*) [+ *remark, name, clue*] soltar; **to ~ (sb) a hint about sth** echar (a algn) una indirecta sobre algo; **to ~ a word in sb's ear** decir algo a algn en confianza
[5] (= *send casually*) [+ *postcard, note*] echar; **to ~ sb a line** mandar unas líneas a algn
[6] (= *omit*) (*from text*) suprimir; **to ~ one's h's** *or* **aitches** no pronunciar las haches; **I've been ~ped from the team** me han sacado del equipo
[7] (= *abandon*) [+ *conversation, correspondence*] dejar; [+ *candidate*] rechazar; [+ *boyfriend*] dejar, plantar; [+ *friend*] romper con; [+ *charges*] retirar; [+ *claim, plan*] renunciar a, abandonar; **we had to ~ what we were doing** tuvimos que dejar lo que estábamos haciendo; **they ~ped him like a hot brick** lo abandonaron como a perro sarnoso; **I'm going to ~ chemistry** no voy a dar más química; **to ~ everything** soltarlo todo; **~ it!*** (*subject*) ¡ya está bien!; **let's ~ the subject** cambiemos de tema
[8] (= *lose*) [+ *game*] perder
[9] (*Drugs*) **to ~ acid‡** tomar ácido
Ⓒ VI [1] (= *fall*) [*object, person*] caer(se); **to ~ with exhaustion** caer rendido; **~ dead!*** ¡vete al cuerno!*; **I'm fit to ~*** estoy que no me tengo; **he let it ~ that …** reveló que …; **so we let the matter ~** así que dejamos el asunto
[2] (= *decrease*) [*wind*] calmarse, amainar; [*temperature, price, voice*] bajar; [*numbers, crowd, demand*] disminuir; **the temperature will ~ tonight** la temperatura bajará esta noche
Ⓓ CPD ► **drop goal** N (*Rugby*) drop *m* ► **drop handlebars** NPL manillar *msing* de (bicicleta de) carreras ► **drop kick** N puntapié *m* de botepronto ► **drop shot** N dejada *f* ► **drop zone** N (*Aer*) zona *f* de salto

►**drop across*** VI + ADV **we ~ped across to see him** nos dejamos caer por su casa*; **he ~ped across to see us** se dejó caer por casa*

►**drop away** VI + ADV [*attendance etc*] disminuir

►**drop back** VI + ADV quedarse atrás

►**drop behind** VI + ADV (*in race, competition*) quedarse atrás; (*in work etc*) rezagarse

►**drop by** VI + ADV = **drop in**

►**drop down** VI + ADV caerse; (= *crouch*) agacharse; **we ~ped down to the coast** bajamos hacia la costa

►**drop in*** VI + ADV (= *visit*) pasar por casa *etc*, dejarse caer por casa *etc*; **do ~ in any time** ven a vernos cuando quieras; **to ~ in on** pasar por casa de; **they ~ped in on us yesterday** pasaron por casa ayer, nos visitaron de improviso ayer

►**drop off** Ⓐ VI + ADV [1] (= *fall asleep*) dormirse
[2] (= *decline*) [*sales, interest*] disminuir
[3] [*part*] desprenderse, soltarse
Ⓑ VT + ADV (*from car*) [+ *person, thing*] dejar; **could you ~ me off at the station?** ¿me puedes dejar en la estación?

►**drop out** VI + ADV [*contents etc*] derramarse, salirse; (*fig*) (*from competition*) retirarse; **to ~ out of society/university** abandonar la sociedad/la universidad; **to ~ out of a team** salirse de un equipo; **to ~ out of a race** abandonar una carrera; **he ~ped out of my life** desapareció de mi vida

►**drop round** Ⓐ VT + ADV **I'll ~ it round to you** pasaré por casa para dártelo
Ⓑ VI + ADV = **drop in**

drop-dead‡ ['drɒpded] ADJ **a ~ cute boy** un chico que te mueres* *or* te cagas‡; **a ~ gorgeous girl** una chica guapa hasta no poder más; **a ~ gorgeous song** una canción chulísima *or* que te mueres*

drop-leaf table [drɒpli:f'teɪbl] N mesa *f* de ala(s) abatible(s)

droplet ['drɒplɪt] N gotita *f*

drop-off ['drɒpɒf] N disminución *f*

dropout ['drɒpaʊt] N [1] (*from society*) marginado/a *m/f*; (*from university*) *estudiante que abandona la universidad antes de graduarse*
[2] (*Rugby*) puntapié *m* de saque

dropper ['drɒpəʳ] N (*Med etc*) cuentagotas *m inv*

dropping-out [ˌdrɒpɪŋ'aʊt] N automarginación *f*; (*Univ*) abandono *m* de los estudios

droppings ['drɒpɪŋz] NPL [*of bird, animal*] excrementos *mpl*, cacas* *fpl*

dropsical ['drɒpsɪkəl] ADJ hidrópico

dropsy ['drɒpsɪ] N hidropesía *f*

dross [drɒs] N (*fig*) escoria *f*

drought [draʊt] N sequía *f*

drove [drəʊv] Ⓐ PT *of* **drive**
Ⓑ N [*of cattle*] manada *f*; **~s of people** una multitud de gente; **they came in ~s** acudieron en tropel

drover ['drəʊvəʳ] N boyero *m*, pastor *m*

drown [draʊn] Ⓐ VT [1] [+ *people, animals*] ahogar; [+ *land*] inundar; **to ~ o.s.** ahogarse; **a boy was ~ed here yesterday** un chico se ahogó ayer aquí; ✦*IDIOM* **like a ~ed rat** calado hasta los huesos
[2] (*also* ~ **out**) [+ *sound*] ahogar; **his cries were ~ed by the noise of the waves** sus gritos se perdieron en el estruendo de las olas; *see also* **sorrow A**
Ⓑ VI ahogarse, perecer ahogado; **a boy ~ed here yesterday** un chico se ahogó *or* pereció ahogado ayer aquí

drowning ['draʊnɪŋ] N ahogo *m*

►**drown out** VT + ADV [+ *voice, sound, words*] ahogar

drowse [draʊz] VI dormitar; **to ~ off** adormilarse

drowsily ['draʊzɪlɪ] ADV **"what?" she asked ~** —¿qué? —preguntó soñolienta *or* medio dormida

drowsiness ['draʊzɪnɪs] N (= *sleepiness*) somnolencia *f*; (= *sluggishness*) modorra *f*, sopor *m*; **these tablets may cause ~** estas pastillas pueden producir somnolencia

drowsy ['draʊzɪ] ADJ (*compar* **drowsier**; *superl* **drowsiest**) [1] (= *sleepy*) [*person*] adormilado, soñoliento, somnoliento (*frm*); [*smile, look, voice*] soñoliento, somnoliento (*frm*); **"who?" he asked in a ~ voice** —¿quién? —preguntó con voz soñoliento *or* con voz de sueño; **to be** *or* **feel ~** [*person*] tener sueño *or* modorra, estar soñoliento *or* adormilado; (*because of medication*) tener somnolencia; **to become** *or* **grow ~** quedarse adormilado; **she grew ~ and was put to bed** se quedaba adormilada y la acostaron, se estaba quedando dormida y la acostaron; **I became pleasantly ~** me empezó a entrar un sueñecito agradable; **these tablets will make you ~** estas pastillas le producirán somnolencia
[2] (= *soporific*) [*afternoon, atmosphere*] soporífero; [*countryside*] apacible

drub [drʌb] VT (= *thrash*) apalear, vapulear; (*fig*) (= *defeat*) dar una paliza a*, cascar*

drubbing ['drʌbɪŋ] N (= *thrashing*) paliza *f*; (*fig*) (= *defeat*) paliza* *f*

drudge [drʌdʒ] Ⓐ N (= *person*) esclavo/a *m/f*; (= *job*) trabajo *m* pesado
Ⓑ VI trabajar como un esclavo

drudgery ['drʌdʒərɪ] N trabajo *m* pesado; **to take the ~ out of work** hacer el trabajo menos pesado

drug [drʌg] Ⓐ N (*Med*) medicamento *m*, fármaco *m*; (= *addictive substance*) droga *f*; (= *illegal substance*) droga *f*, narcótico *m*; **to take ~s** drogarse; **he's on ~s** se droga; **hard/soft ~s** drogas *fpl* duras/blandas; ✦***IDIOM* to be a ~ on the market** ser invendible
Ⓑ VT [+ *person*] drogar; [+ *wine etc*] echar una droga en; **to be in a ~ged sleep** dormir bajo los efectos de una droga; **to ~ o.s.** drogarse
Ⓒ CPD ► **drug abuse** N toxicomanía *f* ► **drug abuser** N toxicómano/a *m/f* ► **drug addict** N drogadicto/a *m/f* ► **drug addiction** N drogadicción *f*, toxicomanía *f* ► **drug baron** N capo *m* ► **drug check** N prueba *f* de la droga, control *m* antidoping ► **drug dealer** N traficante *mf* de drogas ► **drug dependency** N drogodependencia *f* ► **drug habit** N adicción *f* (a las drogas) ► **drug peddler**, **drug pusher** N traficante *mf* de drogas, camello* *mf* ► **drug raid** (*US*) N redada *f* antidroga ► **drug ring** (*US*) N red *f* de narcotráfico ► **drug runner**, **drug smuggler** N narcotraficante *mf* ► **drug squad** N brigada *f* antidrogas, brigada *f* de estupefacientes ► **drugs raid** N redada *f* antidroga ► **drugs ring** N red *f* de narcotráfico ► **drug taker** N = **drug user** ► **drug traffic** N narcotráfico *m*, tráfico *m* de drogas ► **drug trafficker** N traficante *mf* de drogas, narcotraficante *mf* ► **drug trafficking** N narcotráfico *m*, tráfico *m* de drogas ► **drug user** N consumidor(a) *m/f* de drogas, drogadicto/a *m/f*

druggist ['drʌgɪst] N (*US*) farmacéutico/a *m/f*

druggy⁑ ['drʌgɪ], **drugster⁑** ['drʌgstəʳ] N drogata⁑ *mf*, drogota⁑ *mf*

drug-related ['drʌgrɪ,leɪtɪd] ADJ relacionado con la droga; **~ crime** drogodelincuencia *f*

drugstore ['drʌgstɔːʳ] N (*US*) *tienda de comestibles, periódicos y medicamentos*

drug-taking ['drʌg,teɪkɪŋ] N consumo *m* de drogas

druid ['druːɪd] N druida *m*

drum [drʌm] Ⓐ N [1] (*Mus*) tambor *m*; **to play (the) ~s** tocar la batería; ✦***IDIOM* to beat** *or* **bang the ~ for sth/sb** dar bombo a algo/algn, anunciar algo/a algn a bombo y platillo
[2] (= *container*) (*for oil*) bidón *m*; (*Tech*) (= *cylinder, machine part*) tambor *m*
[3] (*Anat*) (*also* **eardrum**) tímpano *m*
Ⓑ VT **to ~ one's fingers on the table** tamborilear con los dedos sobre la mesa; **to ~ sth into sb** (*fig*) meter algo a algn en la cabeza por la fuerza; **I had it ~med into me as a child** de niño me hicieron comprender eso a la fuerza *or* a fuerza de repetírmelo
Ⓒ VI (*Mus*) tocar el tambor *etc*; (= *tap*) (*with fingers*) tamborilear; **the noise was ~ming in my ears** el ruido me estaba taladrando los oídos; **his words ~med in my mind** el eco de sus palabras resonaba en mi cabeza
Ⓓ CPD ► **drum brake** N (*Aut*) freno *m* de tambor ► **drum machine** N caja *f* de ritmos ► **drum major** N (*Brit*) tambor *m* mayor ► **drum majorette** N (*esp US*) bastonera *f*

►**drum out** VT + ADV **to ~ sb out** expulsar a algn

►**drum up** VT + ADV [+ *enthusiasm*] despertar; [+ *support*] movilizar; [+ *trade*] fomentar

drumbeat ['drʌm,biːt] N redoble *m*

drumhead ['drʌmhed] Ⓐ N parche *m* de tambor
Ⓑ CPD ► **drumhead court-martial** N consejo *m* de guerra sumarísimo

drumkit ['drʌmkɪt] N batería *f*

drummer ['drʌməʳ] N (*in military band etc*) tambor *m*; (*in jazz/pop group*) batería *mf*

drumming ['drʌmɪŋ] N tamborileo *m*

drumroll ['drʌm,rəʊl] N redoble *m*

drumstick ['drʌmstɪk] N [1] (*Mus*) baqueta *f*, palillo *m* de tambor
[2] (= *chicken leg*) muslo *m*

drunk [drʌŋk] Ⓐ PP *of* **drink**
Ⓑ ADJ [1] (*compar* **drunker**; *superl* **drunkest**) borracho, tomado (*LAm*); **~ and disorderly behaviour** (*Jur*) embriaguez *f* y alteración *f* del orden público; **he was arrested for being ~ and disorderly** lo detuvieron por embriaguez y alteración del orden público; **to get ~** emborracharse; **to get sb ~** emborrachar a algn; **to be ~ on whisky** estar borracho de whisky; **to get ~ on wine** emborracharse de vino; ✦***IDIOM* to be as ~ as a lord** *or* **a skunk*** estar borracho como una cuba*
[2] (*fig*) ebrio; **to be ~ on** *or* **with success** estar ebrio de éxito
Ⓒ N borracho/a *m/f*
Ⓓ CPD ► **drunk driver** N conductor(a) *m/f* en estado de embriaguez ► **drunk driving** N (*esp US*) = **drink-driving**

drunkard ['drʌŋkəd] N borracho/a *m/f*

drunken ['drʌŋkən] ADJ [1] (= *intoxicated*) [*person*] borracho; [*brawl, orgy*] de borrachos; [*night, evening*] de borrachera; [*violence*] provocado por el alcohol; [*voice*] de borracho, de cazallero; **a ~ old man** un viejo borracho; **her ~ husband** el borracho de su marido; **~ driving** conducir *or* (*LAm*) manejar en estado de embriaguez; **a ~ party** una juerga; **in a ~ rage** en un ataque de furia provocado por el alcohol; **in a ~ state** borracho; **in a ~ stupor** flotando en los vapores del alcohol
[2] (*fig*) (= *crooked*) **at a ~ angle** torcido

drunkenly ['drʌŋkənlɪ] ADV [*walk*] tambaleándose (borracho), haciendo eses*; [*speak, say, sing*] con voz de borracho; **the two men were arguing ~** los dos hombres discutían borrachos; **he staggered ~ out of the pub** salió del bar tambaleándose borracho *or* haciendo eses*

drunkenness ['drʌŋkənnɪs] N (= *state*) borrachera *f*, embriaguez *f* (*more frm*); (= *habit, problem*) alcoholismo *m*

drupe [druːp] N drupa *f*

druthers* ['drʌðəz] N (*US*) **if I had my ~*** si por mí fuera

dry [draɪ] Ⓐ ADJ (*compar* **drier**, *superl* **driest**) [1] (= *not moist*) [*clothes, paint, leaves, weather*] seco; [*climate*] árido, seco; **it was warm and ~ yesterday afternoon** ayer hizo una tarde cálida y seca; **wait till the glue is ~** espere a que la cola se seque; **he rubbed himself ~ with a towel** se secó frotándose con una toalla; **her throat/mouth was ~** ◊ **she had a ~ throat/mouth** tenía la garganta/boca seca; **his mouth was ~ with fear** tenía la boca seca de miedo; **her eyes were ~** (= *without tears*) no había lágrimas en sus ojos; **there wasn't a ~ eye in the house** no había nadie que no estuviera llorando; **for ~ skin/hair** para piel seca/pelo seco; **"keep in a dry place"** "mantener en un lugar seco"; **~ bread** (*without butter*) pan *m* sin mantequilla; (*stale*) pan *m* seco; **a ~ cough** una tos seca; **to get ~** secarse; **on ~ land** en tierra firme; **to run ~** [*river, well*] secarse; [*inspiration*] agotarse; **to wipe sth ~** secar algo (con un trapo); ✦***IDIOM* as ~ as a bone** más seco que una pasa
[2] (*) (= *thirsty*) **to be** *or* **feel ~** tener sed, estar seco*
[3] (*) (= *prohibiting alcohol*) [*country, state*] seco; **due to a storm, the island was ~ for a week** a causa de una tormenta, durante una semana no hubo ni una gota de alcohol en la isla
[4] (= *wry*) [*humour, wit*] mordaz; [*laugh*] sardónico; **he has a very ~ sense of humour** tiene un sentido del humor muy mordaz *or* cargado de ironía
[5] (= *harsh*) **it broke with a ~ snapping sound** se rompió con un ruido seco
[6] (= *uninteresting*) [*lecture, subject, book*] árido; [*voice*] seco; ✦***IDIOM* as ~ as dust** terriblemente árido
[7] (= *not sweet*) [*wine, sherry, cider*] seco; [*champagne*] brut, seco; **a ~ white wine** un vino blanco seco
[8] (= *not producing milk*) **the old cow went ~** la vaca vieja se quedó sin leche
Ⓑ N **the ~** (*Brit*) lo seco; **such cars grip the road well, even in the ~** estos coches se agarran bien al firme, incluso en seco; **come on into the ~** métete aquí que no llueve
Ⓒ VT secar; **to ~ one's hands/eyes** secarse las manos/las lágrimas; **to ~ the dishes** secar los platos; **to ~ o.s.** secarse
Ⓓ VI [1] (= *become dry*) secarse; **leave it to ~** déjalo que se seque; **would you rather wash or ~?** ¿prefieres lavar o secar?
[2] (*esp Brit Theat*) quedarse en blanco
Ⓔ CPD ► **dry cell** N pila *f* seca ► **dry cleaner's** N tintorería *f*, tinte *m* (*Sp*) ► **dry cleaning** N limpieza *f* en seco ► **dry dock** N dique *m* seco ► **dry fly** N (*Fishing*) mosca *f* seca ► **dry ginger** N ginebra *f* seca ► **dry goods** NPL (*US*) artículos *mpl* de confección ► **dry goods store** N (*US*) mercería *f* ► **dry ice** N nieve *f* carbónica ► **dry measure** N medida *f* para áridos ► **dry rot** N *putrefacción seca de la madera causada por un hongo* ► **dry run** N (*fig*) ensayo *m* ► **the dry season** N la estación seca ► **dry shampoo** N champú *m* seco ► **dry shave** N **to have a ~ shave** afeitarse en seco ► **dry ski slope** N pista *f* artificial de esquí ► **dry stone wall** N muro *m* seco

►**dry off** Ⓐ VI + ADV [*clothes etc*] secarse
Ⓑ VT + ADV secar

►**dry out** Ⓐ VI + ADV [1] (*lit*) (= *dry*) secarse
[2] (*) (*fig*) [*alcoholic*] seguir una cura de desintoxicación de alcohol
Ⓑ VT + ADV [1] (*lit*) (= *dry*) [+ *clothes, ground, food, skin*] secar
[2] (*) (*fig*) [+ *alcoholic*] curar del alcoholismo

►**dry up** VI + ADV [1] [*river, well*] secarse; [*moisture*] evaporarse, desaparecer; [*source of supply*] agotarse
[2] (= *dry the dishes*) secar los platos
[3] (*) (= *fall silent*) [*speaker*] callarse; **~ up!** ¡cierra el pico!*

dry-as-dust ['draɪəz'dʌst] ADJ terriblemente árido

dry-clean ['draɪ'kliːn] VT limpiar en seco, lavar en seco; **"~ only"** (*on label*) "limpiar *or* lavar en seco"

dryer ['draɪəʳ] N (*for hair*) secador *m*; (*for clothes*) (= *machine*) secadora *f*; (= *rack*) tendedero *m*

dry-eyed ['draɪ'aɪd] ADJ sin lágrimas

drying ['draɪɪŋ] Ⓐ ADJ [*wind*] seco
Ⓑ CPD ► **drying cupboard** N armario *m* de tender ► **drying room** N habitación *f* de tender

drying-up ['draɪɪŋ'ʌp] N [*of river, well*] desecación *f*; [*of skin*] deshidratación *f*; **to do the ~** secar los platos

dryly ['draɪlɪ] ADV = **drily**

dryness ['draɪnɪs] N [1] [*of hair, skin, climate*] sequedad *f*
[2] [*of wit, humour*] mordacidad *f*
[3] [*of wine, sherry, cider, champagne*] lo seco
[4] [*of lecture, subject, book*] aridez *f*

dry-shod ['draɪ'ʃɒd] ADV a pie enjuto

DS N ABBR (*Brit Police*) = **Detective Sergeant**
D/s ABBR (= **days after sight**) a ... días vista
DSC (*Brit*) N ABBR (= **Distinguished Service Cross**) ≈ cruz *f* al mérito militar
DSc N ABBR (*Univ*) = **Doctor of Science**
DSM (*Brit*) N ABBR (= **Distinguished Service Medal**) ≈ medalla *f* al mérito militar
DSO (*Brit*) N ABBR = **Distinguished Service Order**
DSS N ABBR (*Brit*) = **Department of Social Security**
DST N ABBR (*US*) = **Daylight Saving Time**
DT N ABBR (*Comput*) = **data transmission**
DTD N ABBR (= **Document Type Definition**) DTD *f*
DTI N ABBR (*Brit Admin*) = **Department of Trade and Industry**
DTP N ABBR = **desktop publishing**
DTs* NPL ABBR = **delirium tremens**
DU N ABBR = **depleted uranium**
dual ['djʊəl] Ⓐ ADJ doble
Ⓑ CPD ► **dual carriageway** N (*Brit*) autovía *f*, carretera *f* de doble calzada ► **dual control** N doble mando *m* ► **dual nationality** N doble nacionalidad *f* ► **dual ownership** N condominio *m* ► **dual personality** N doble personalidad *f*
dualism ['djʊəlɪzəm] N dualismo *m*
dualist ['djʊəlɪst] Ⓐ ADJ dualista
Ⓑ N dualista *mf*
duality [djʊ'ælɪtɪ] N dualidad *f*
dual-purpose ['djʊəl'pɜːpəs] ADJ de doble uso
dub [dʌb] VT [1] (*Cine*) doblar; **the film was ~bed into Spanish** la película estaba doblada al español
[2] (= *nickname*) apodar; **they ~bed him "Shorty"** lo apodaron "Shorty"
[3] [+ *knight*] armar caballero a
Dubai [duː'baɪ] N Dubai *m*
dubbin ['dʌbɪn] N adobo *m* impermeable, cera *f*
dubbing ['dʌbɪŋ] Ⓐ N (*Cine*) doblaje *m*
Ⓑ CPD ► **dubbing mixer** N mezclador(a) *m/f* de sonido
dubiety [djuː'baɪətɪ] N incertidumbre *f*
dubious ['djuːbɪəs] ADJ [1] (= *questionable*) [*reputation, claim, privilege, taste*] dudoso; [*person, character, motives*] sospechoso; [*company, offer*] poco fiable; [*business deal, practice*] sospechoso, turbio; [*idea, measure*] discutible; [*compliment*] equívoco; **to have the ~ honour/pleasure of doing sth** tener el dudoso honor/placer de hacer algo; **that paté looks a bit ~*** ese paté tiene una pinta un poco sospechosa; **of ~ benefit** de beneficios dudosos; **of ~ origin** de origen dudoso; **of ~ quality** de dudosa calidad
[2] (= *unsure*) [*look, smile*] indeciso; **to be ~** tener dudas *or* reservas; **I was ~ at first, but he convinced me** al principio tenía mis dudas *or* reservas, pero él me convenció; **I'm very ~ about it** tengo grandes dudas *or* reservas sobre ello; **I am ~ that** *or* **whether the new law will achieve anything** tengo mis dudas *or* reservas sobre si la nueva ley va a lograr algo; **he looked ~** parecía tener dudas *or* reservas, parecía dudar; **he sounded ~** parecía tener dudas *or* reservas, parecía dudar
dubiously ['djuːbɪəslɪ] ADV [*look at, smile*] con recelo, con desconfianza; [*say*] con desconfianza; **a concerto ~ attributed to Albinoni** un concierto atribuido sin verdadera fundamento a Albinoni
Dublin ['dʌblɪn] Ⓐ N Dublín *m*
Ⓑ CPD ► **Dublin Bay prawn** N cigala *f*
Dubliner ['dʌblɪnəʳ] N dublinés/esa *m/f*

ducal ['djuːkəl] ADJ ducal
ducat ['dʌkɪt] N ducado *m* (*moneda*)
duchess ['dʌtʃɪs] N duquesa *f*
duchy ['dʌtʃɪ] N ducado *m* (*territorio*)
duck[1] [dʌk] Ⓐ N (*pl* **ducks** *or* **duck**) [1] (*Orn*) pato *m*; (*female*) pata *f*; **wild ~** pato *m* salvaje; ✦*IDIOMS* **to be a dead ~**: **he's a dead ~** está quemado; **that issue is a dead ~** esa cuestión ya no tiene interés; **to play ~s and drakes** hacer saltar una piedra plana sobre el agua; **to play ~s and drakes with** despilfarrar; **to take to sth like a ~ to water** sentirse como pez en el agua en *or* con algo, encontrarse en seguida en su elemento con algo; *see also* **lame D**, **water A1**
[2] (*Cricket*) cero *m*; **to make a ~** ◊ **be out for a ~** (*Brit*) ser eliminado a cero
[3] (= *movement*) (*under water*) zambullida *f*; (*to escape, avoid*) agachada *f*; (*Boxing*) finta *f*, esquiva *f*
[4] (*) (*as form of address*) **yes, ~(s)** (*Brit*) sí, cariño
Ⓑ VT [1] (= *plunge in water*) [+ *person, head*] zambullir
[2] (= *lower*) **to ~ one's head** agachar la cabeza
[3] (= *avoid*) [+ *problem, question*] eludir, esquivar
Ⓒ VI (*also* **~ down**) agacharse, agachar la cabeza; (*in fight*) esquivar el golpe; (*under water*) sumergirse
Ⓓ CPD ► **duck soup*** N (*US*) (*fig*) **it's just ~ soup** es pan comido, es coser y cantar
►**duck out of*** VI + PREP escabullirse de
duck[2] [dʌk] N (*US*) dril *m*
duckbill ['dʌkbɪl], **duck-billed platypus** ['dʌkbɪld'plætɪpəs] N ornitorrinco *m*
duckboard ['dʌkbɔːd] N pasadera *f*
duckie* ['dʌkɪ] N (*Brit*) = **ducky**
ducking ['dʌkɪŋ] N zambullida *f*; **to give sb a ~** meter la cabeza en el agua a algn
ducking-and-diving* [ˌdʌkɪŋən'daɪvɪŋ] N **he did a lot of ~ in London's drug-world** estuvo metido en muchos trapicheos en el mundo de la droga de Londres*; **~ is all part of political life** los políticos saben siempre cómo escaquearse*
duckling ['dʌklɪŋ] N patito *m*
duckpond ['dʌkpɒnd] N estanque *m* de patos
duckweed ['dʌkwiːd] N lenteja *f* de agua
ducky* ['dʌkɪ] Ⓐ N **~!** ¡cariño!
Ⓑ ADJ (*US*) muy mono
duct [dʌkt] N [1] (*for ventilation, liquid*) conducto *m*
[2] (*Anat*) conducto *m*, canal *m*
ductile ['dʌktaɪl] ADJ (*Tech*) [*metal*] dúctil
ductless ['dʌktlɪs] Ⓐ ADJ endocrino
Ⓑ CPD ► **ductless gland** N glándula *f* endocrina
dud* [dʌd] Ⓐ ADJ [1] (= *useless*) [*cheque*] sin fondos; [*merchandise*] invendible; (= *not working*) [*machine etc*] estropeado; [*shell, bomb*] que no estalla
[2] (= *false*) [*coin, note*] falso
Ⓑ N (= *thing*) filfa *f*; (= *person*) desastre *m*, inútil *mf*; (= *coin*) moneda *f* falsa; (= *shell*) obús *m* que no estalla
dude* [djuːd] (*US*) Ⓐ N (= *guy*) tío* *m*, tipo* *m*; (= *dandy*) petimetre *m*
Ⓑ CPD ► **dude ranch** N rancho *m* para turistas

> **DUDE RANCH**
>
> *Se llama* **dude ranch** *a un rancho del oeste de Estados Unidos que se abre a los turistas para ofrecerles el sabor de la vida del oeste al aire libre. Puede ser un rancho que funciona como tal en la realidad o uno que recrea la atmósfera tradicional de los vaqueros. Los turistas pueden montar a caballo, ayudar en las tareas del rancho o probar la comida hecha en el carromato* (**chuck-wagon**) *alrededor de la hoguera.* **Dude** *es una palabra que pertenece al argot americano, usada para referirse a una persona de ciudad muy bien vestida o a alguien del este.*

dudgeon ['dʌdʒən] N **in high ~** muy enojado, enfurecido
duds* [dʌdz] NPL (= *clothes*) prendas *fpl* de vestir, trapos* *mpl*
▼**due** [djuː] Ⓐ ADJ [1] (= *expected*) **when is the plane ~ (in)?** ¿a qué hora llega el avión?; **the train is ~ (in)** *or* **~ to arrive at eight** el tren llega a las ocho, el tren tiene su hora de llegada a las ocho; **the train was ~ (in) ten minutes ago** el tren tenía que haber llegado hace diez minutos; **the results are ~ (in) today** está previsto que los resultados salgan hoy; **the magazine/film/record is ~ out in December** la revista/la película/el disco sale en diciembre; **I'm ~ in Chicago tomorrow** mañana me esperan en Chicago; **he is ~ back tomorrow** estará de vuelta mañana, está previsto que vuelva mañana; **when is it ~ to happen?** ¿para cuándo se prevé?; **it is ~ to be demolished** tienen que demolerlo; **when is the baby ~?** ¿cuándo se espera que nazca el niño?
[2] (= *owing*) [*sum, money*] pagadero, pendiente; **it's ~ on the 30th** el plazo vence el día 30; **he's ~ a salary raise** (*US*) le corresponde un aumento de sueldo; **I am ~ six days' leave** se me deben seis días de vacaciones; **when is the rent ~?** ¿cuándo se paga el alquiler?, ¿cuándo hay que pagar el alquiler?; **I feel I'm about ~ a holiday!** ¡me parece que necesito unas vacaciones!; **to fall ~** (*Fin*) vencer; **he is ~ for a rise** le corresponde un aumento de sueldo; **I have £50 ~ to me** me deben 50 libras; **our thanks are ~ to him** le estamos muy agradecidos; **they must be treated with the respect ~ to their rank** deben ser tratados con el respeto que su rango merece
[3] (= *appropriate*) [*care, attention*] debido; **to drive without ~ care and attention** (*Jur*) conducir *or* (*LAm*) manejar sin el cuidado y la atención debidos; **after ~ consideration** después de la debida consideración; **we'll let you know in ~ course** le avisaremos a su debido tiempo; **he has never received ~ credit for his achievements** nunca ha recibido el crédito que merece por sus logros; **~ process (of law)** (*Jur*) (el buen hacer de) la justicia; **with (all) ~ respect (to Mrs Harrison)** con el debido respeto (hacia la señora Harrison)
[4] **~ to** (= *caused by*) debido a; **~ to repairs, the garage will be closed next Saturday** esta gasolinera estará cerrada por obras el próximo sábado; **his death was ~ to natural causes** su muerte se debió a causas naturales; **what's it ~ to?** ¿a qué se debe?; **it is ~ to you that he is alive today** gracias a ti está todavía vivo
Ⓑ ADV **~ west of** justo hacia el oeste de; **to face ~ north** [*person*] mirar justo hacia el norte; [*building*] estar orientado completamente hacia el norte; **to go ~ north** ir derecho hacia el norte
Ⓒ N [1] (= *due credit*) **to give him his ~, he did try hard** para ser justo, se esforzó mucho
[2] **dues** (= *club, union fees*) cuota *fsing*; (= *taxes*) derechos *mpl*; **harbour/port ~s** dere-

➤ LANGUAGE IN USE: due A2 20.6, 20.7 A4 17.1

chos *mpl* de puerto; ✦*IDIOM* **to pay one's ~s** cumplir con su deber
Ⓓ CPD ► **due date** N (*Fin*) [*of loan, debt*] fecha *f* de vencimiento; **when is your ~ date?** (*for birth*) ¿cuándo cumples?; **she is five days past her ~ date** cumplió hace cinco días, salió de cuentas hace cinco días (*Sp*)

duel ['djʊəl] Ⓐ N duelo *m*; **to fight a ~** batirse en duelo
Ⓑ VI batirse en duelo

duellist, **duelist** (*US*) ['djʊəlɪst] N duelista *m*

duet [djuː'et] N (= *players, composition*) dúo *m*; **to sing/play a ~** cantar/tocar a dúo

duff[1]* [dʌf] (*Brit*) ADJ (= *useless*) inútil; (= *poor quality*) de tres al cuarto

duff[2]* [dʌf] VT **to ~ sb up** dar una paliza a algn

duff[3] [dʌf] N (*Culin*) budín *m*, pudín *m*

duff[4]‡ [dʌf] N culo‡ *m*; **he just sits on his ~ all day** pasa el día sin hacer nada; **get off your ~!** ¡no te quedes ahí sentado y haz algo!

duffel-bag ['dʌfəlbæg] N bolsa *f* de lona; (*Mil*) talego *m* (*para efectos de uso personal*)

duffel-coat ['dʌfəlkəʊt] N trenca *f*

duffer* ['dʌfəʳ] N zoquete* *m*

duffle-bag ['dʌfəlbæg] N = **duffel-bag**

duffle-coat ['dʌfəlkəʊt] N = **duffel-coat**

dug[1] [dʌg] PT, PP *of* **dig**

dug[2] [dʌg] N (*Zool*) teta *f*, ubre *f*

dugout ['dʌgaʊt] N [1] (*Ftbl*) caseta *f*
[2] (*Mil*) refugio *m* subterráneo

DUI N ABBR (*US*) (= **driving under (the) influence (of alcohol)**) conducción *f or* (*LAm*) manejo *m* bajo los efectos del alcohol

duke [djuːk] N duque *m*

dukedom ['djuːkdəm] N ducado *m* (*título*)

dukes‡ [djuːks] NPL puños *mpl*

dulcet ['dʌlsɪt] ADJ dulce, suave

dulcimer ['dʌlsɪməʳ] N dulcémele *m*

dull [dʌl] Ⓐ ADJ (*compar* **duller**; *superl* **dullest**)
[1] (= *boring*) [*person, speech, book, evening, job*] aburrido, pesado; [*place*] aburrido, soso; [*style, food*] soso; **deadly ~** terriblemente aburrido, aburridísimo; **there's never a ~ moment here in the office** aquí en la oficina no nos aburrimos nunca; ✦*IDIOM* **as ~ as ditchwater** terriblemente aburrido
[2] (= *not bright*) [*colour, metal, glow*] apagado; [*eyes*] apagado, sin brillo; [*hair, skin, complexion*] sin brillo; [*weather*] nublado; [*sky, day*] gris; **his eyes were ~ and lifeless** sus ojos estaban apagados y sin vida; **~, lifeless hair** pelo sin brillo, sin vida; **it will be ~ at first** (*Met*) al principio estará nublado
[3] (= *not sharp*) [*pain, feeling, sound*] sordo; **it fell with a ~ thud** *or* **thump** cayó con un golpe sordo
[4] (= *lethargic, withdrawn*) [*person, mood*] deprimido, desanimado
[5] (= *slow-witted*) [*person, mind*] torpe; [*pupil*] lento; **his senses** *or* **faculties are growing ~** está perdiendo facultades; **to be ~ of hearing** ser duro de oído
[6] (= *blunt*) [*blade, knife*] romo
[7] (*Comm*) [*trade, business, market*] flojo
Ⓑ VT [+ *senses, blade*] embotar; [+ *emotions*] enfriar; [+ *pain*] aliviar; [+ *sound*] amortiguar; [+ *mind, memory*] entorpecer; [+ *colour*] apagar; [+ *mirror, metal*] deslustrar, quitar el brillo de; [+ *sensitivity*] embrutecer; [+ *grief*] atenuar; **the explosion ~ed her hearing** la explosión la dejó dura de oído
Ⓒ VI [*light*] amortiguarse; [*colour*] apagarse, perder intensidad; [*metal*] deslustrarse, perder brillo; [*memory*] entorpecerse; [*senses*] embotarse; **his eyes ~ed** sus ojos perdieron brillo

dullard ['dʌləd] N zoquete* *m*

dullness ['dʌlnɪs] N [1] (= *lack of interest*) [*of book, lecture, person*] lo aburrido, pesadez *f*
[2] (= *lack of brightness*) [*of colour, metal*] falta *f* de brillo, lo opaco; [*of landscape*] monotonía *f*; [*of room*] lo lúgubre; [*of sound, pain*] lo sordo
[3] (= *slow-wittedness*) [*of person*] torpeza *f*; **~ of hearing** dureza *f* de oído

dullsville* ['dʌlzvɪl] N (*US*) **it's ~ here*** esto es un muermo*

dully ['dʌllɪ] ADV [1] (= *boringly*) [*speak, write*] de manera aburrida
[2] (= *dimly*) [*glow, gleam, shine*] pálidamente, débilmente
[3] (= *without enthusiasm*) [*say, reply*] sin entusiasmo; [*think*] de forma confusa; **he looked ~ about the room** sus ojos recorrieron la habitación sin entusiasmo
[4] (= *with a muffled sound*) sordamente, con ruido sordo
[5] (= *with a dull pain*) **his arm throbbed ~** tenía un dolor sordo en el brazo

duly ['djuːlɪ] ADV [1] (= *as expected*) [*arrive, land*] como estaba previsto; **he ~ arrived at three** llegó a las tres, como estaba previsto; **I was ~ grateful for his assistance** como cabe esperar, le agradecí su asistencia; **the visitors were ~ impressed** los visitantes quedaron muy impresionados, como era de esperar
[2] (= *properly*) [*elect, sign*] debidamente; **the point was ~ noted in the minutes** se tomó debida nota de ese punto

dumb [dʌm] ADJ (*compar* **dumber**; *superl* **dumbest**) [1] (*Med*) mudo; (*with surprise etc*) sin habla; **a ~ person** un mudo; **to become ~** quedar mudo; **she's deaf and ~** es sordomuda; **~ animals** animales *mpl* indefensos; **the ~ millions** los millones que no tienen voz; **to be struck ~** (*fig*) quedarse sin habla
[2] (*) (= *stupid*) tonto, bobo; **to act ~** hacerse el tonto; **don't be so ~!** ¡no seas tonto *or* bobo!; **that was a really ~ thing I did!** ¡lo que hice fue una verdadera tontería *or* bobada!; **he says some ~ things** ¡dice cada tontería *or* bobada!; **~ blonde** rubia *f* descerebrada *or* sin seso; ✦*IDIOM* **as ~ as an ox** más bruto que un arado
► **dumb down** VT + ADV embrutecer, empobrecer intelectualmente

dumb-ass‡ ['dʌmæs] (*US*) ADJ, N burro/a *m/f*

dumbbell ['dʌmbel] N [1] (*in gymnastics*) pesa *f*
[2] (*) (= *fool*) bobo/a *m/f*

dumbcluck* ['dʌmklʌk] N borde* *mf*

dumbfound [dʌm'faʊnd] VT dejar mudo; **we were ~ed** nos quedamos mudos de asombro

dumbness ['dʌmnɪs] N [1] (*Med*) mudez *f*
[2] (*) (= *stupidity*) estupidez *f*

dumbo* ['dʌmbəʊ] N tonto/a *m/f*

dumbstruck ['dʌmstrʌk] ADJ **we were ~** nos quedamos mudos de asombro

dumbwaiter ['dʌm'weɪtəʳ] N (= *lift*) montaplatos *m inv*; (*Brit*) (*at table*) bandeja *f* giratoria

dum-dum bullet [ˌdʌmdʌm'bʊlɪt] N bala *f* dum-dum

dummy ['dʌmɪ] Ⓐ ADJ (= *not real*) [*gun*] de juguete; [*ammunition*] de fogueo; [*container*] vacío
Ⓑ N [1] (*for clothes*) maniquí *m*
[2] (*for baby*) chupete *m*
[3] (*Comm*) (= *sham object*) envase *m* vacío
[4] (*Ftbl*) finta *f*
[5] (*Bridge*) muerto *m*
[6] (*) (= *idiot*) tonto/a *m/f*
Ⓒ CPD ► **dummy assault**, **dummy attack** N simulacro *m* de ataque ► **dummy company** N empresa *f* fantasma ► **dummy number** N (*Press*) número *m* cero ► **dummy run** N (*Brit*) ensayo *m*, prueba *f*

dump [dʌmp] Ⓐ N [1] (= *place for refuse*) vertedero *m*, basurero *m*, basural *m* (*LAm*), tiradero(s) *m(pl)* (*Mex*); (= *pile of rubbish*) montón *m* de basura; **a rubbish ~** un vertedero, un basurero
[2] (*Mil*) depósito *m*
[3] (* *pej*) (= *town*) poblacho *m*; (= *hotel etc*) cuchitril *m*; **it's a real ~!** ¡es una auténtica pocilga!
[4] (*Comput*) vuelco *m* de memoria, volcado *m* de memoria
[5] ✦*IDIOM* **to be (down) in the ~s*** tener murria, estar deprimido
[6] **to have a ~** (*Brit*‡) (= *defecate*) jiñar‡, cagar‡
Ⓑ VT [1] [+ *rubbish etc*] verter, descargar
[2] (*) (= *put down*) [+ *parcel*] dejar, soltar; [+ *passenger*] dejar, plantar*; [+ *sand, load*] descargar, verter; **to ~ sth down*** poner algo (con mucho ruido); **can I ~ this here?*** ¿puedo dejar esto aquí?
[3] (*) (= *get rid of*) [+ *person*] deshacerse de, librarse de; [+ *girlfriend, boyfriend*] plantar*
[4] (= *reject*) rechazar
[5] (= *throw away*) [+ *thing*] tirar
[6] (*Comm*) [+ *goods*] inundar el mercado de
[7] (*Comput*) volcar
Ⓒ VI (*Brit*‡) (= *defecate*) jiñar‡, cagar‡

dumper ['dʌmpəʳ] N (*also* **~ truck**) volquete *m*

dumping ['dʌmpɪŋ] Ⓐ N [1] [*of rubbish, waste*] vertido *m*; **"no dumping"** "prohibido verter basuras"
[2] (*Comm*) dúmping *m*
Ⓑ CPD ► **dumping ground** N vertedero *m*

dumpling ['dʌmplɪŋ] N *bola de masa hervida para servir con guiso*

Dumpster® ['dʌmpstəʳ] N (*US*) contenedor *m* de escombros *or* deshechos

dumptruck ['dʌmptrʌk] N (*US*) volquete *m*

dumpy ['dʌmpɪ] ADJ regordete

dun[1] [dʌn] ADJ pardo

dun[2] [dʌn] VT **to ~ sb** apremiar a algn para que pague lo que debe; (*fig*) dar la lata a algn*

dunce [dʌns] N (*Scol*) zopenco/a *m/f*

dunderhead ['dʌndəhed] N zoquete* *m*

Dundonian [dʌn'dəʊnɪən] Ⓐ N habitante *mf* de Dundee, nativo/a *m/f* de Dundee
Ⓑ ADJ de Dundee

dune [djuːn] Ⓐ N duna *f*
Ⓑ CPD ► **dune buggy** N buggy *m* (*vehículo para terrenos arenosos*)

dung [dʌŋ] Ⓐ N [*of horse, camel etc*] excrementos *mpl*; (*as manure*) estiércol *m*
Ⓑ CPD ► **dung beetle** N escarabajo *m* pelotero

dungarees [ˌdʌŋgə'riːz] NPL (*for work*) mono *msing*, overol *m* (*LAm*); (*casual wear*) pantalón *msing* de peto

dungeon ['dʌndʒən] N calabozo *m*, mazmorra *f*

dunghill ['dʌŋhɪl] N estercolero *m*

dunk [dʌŋk] VT [1] [+ *biscuit, cake etc*] mojar
[2] (*Basketball*) machacar

Dunkirk [dʌn'kɜːk] N Dunquerque *m*

dunno‡ [də'nəʊ] = **(I) don't know** no sé, ni flores*

dunnock ['dʌnək] N acentor *m* (común)

dunny* ['dʌnɪ] N (*Australia*) retrete *m*, wáter *m*

duo ['djuːəʊ] N (*pl* **duos** *or* **dui** ['djuːiː]) (*Mus, Theat*) dúo *m*

duodecimal [ˌdjuːəʊ'desɪməl] ADJ duodecimal

duodenal [ˌdjuːəʊˈdiːnl] Ⓐ ADJ duodenal
Ⓑ CPD ► **duodenal ulcer** N úlcera *f* de duodeno

duodenum [ˌdjuːəʊˈdiːnəm] N (*pl* **duodenums** *or* **duodena** [ˌdjuːəʊˈdiːnə]) duodeno *m*

duopoly [djʊˈɒpəlɪ] N duopolio *m*

dupe [djuːp] Ⓐ N inocentón/ona *m/f*; **to be the ~ of** ser víctima de
Ⓑ VT (= *trick*) engañar, embaucar; (= *swindle*) timar; **to ~ sb (into doing sth)** engañar *or* embaucar a algn (para que haga algo)

duple [ˈdjuːpl] Ⓐ ADJ (= *double*) (*gen*) doble
Ⓑ CPD ► **duple time** N (*Mus*) tiempo *m* doble

duplex [ˈdjuːpleks] (*US*) N (*also* **~ house**) *casa para dos familias formada por dos viviendas adosadas*; (*also* **~ apartment**) dúplex *m inv*

duplicate Ⓐ [ˈdjuːplɪkeɪt] VT 1 (= *copy*) [+ *document, letter*] duplicar; (*on machine*) copiar
2 (= *repeat*) [+ *action*] repetir
Ⓑ [ˈdjuːplɪkɪt] N (= *copy of letter etc*) duplicado *m*, copia *f*; **in ~** por duplicado
Ⓒ [ˈdjuːplɪkɪt] ADJ [*copy*] duplicado
Ⓓ [ˈdjuːplɪkɪt] CPD ► **duplicate key** N duplicado *m* de una llave

duplicating machine [ˈdjuːplɪkeɪtɪŋməˈʃiːn] N multicopista *f*

duplication [ˌdjuːplɪˈkeɪʃən] N (= *copying*) duplicación *f*; (= *repetition*) repetición *f* innecesaria

duplicator [ˈdjuːplɪkeɪtə^r] N multicopista *f*

duplicitous [djuːˈplɪsɪtəs] ADJ (*frm*) tramposo

duplicity [djuːˈplɪsɪtɪ] N (*frm*) doblez *f*, duplicidad *f*

Dur ABBR (*Brit*) = **Durham**

durability [ˌdjʊərəˈbɪlɪtɪ] N durabilidad *f*, lo duradero

durable [ˈdjʊərəbl] Ⓐ ADJ duradero; **~ goods** (*US*) bienes *mpl* (de consumo) duraderos *or* no perecederos
Ⓑ **durables** NPL bienes *mpl* (de consumo) duraderos *or* no perecederos; *see also* **consumer B**

duration [djʊəˈreɪʃən] N duración *f*; **courses are of two years' ~** los cursos tienen una duración de dos años; **for the ~ of the war** mientras dure la guerra

Dürer [ˈdjʊərə^r] N Durero

duress [djʊəˈres] N **under ~** bajo presión

Durex® [ˈdjʊəreks] N preservativo *m*

during [ˈdjʊərɪŋ] PREP 1 (= *throughout*) durante
2 (= *in the course of*) durante

durst†† [dɜːst] PT *of* **dare**

dusk [dʌsk] N 1 (= *nightfall*) anochecer *m*, atardecer *m*; **at ~** al anochecer *or* atardecer
2 (= *gloom*) oscuridad *f*; **in the gathering ~** en la creciente oscuridad

dusky [ˈdʌskɪ] ADJ [*pink, blue*] oscuro; [*complexion*] moreno

dust [dʌst] Ⓐ N 1 (*in house, on ground*) polvo *m*; **there was thick ~** ◊ **the ~ lay thick** había una gruesa capa de polvo; **to raise a cloud of ~** levantar una nube de polvo; **to raise a lot of ~** (*lit*) levantar mucho polvo; (*fig*) (= *cause a scandal*) levantar una polvareda; ✦***IDIOMS*** **to kick up** *or* **raise a ~*** armar un escándalo; **if you ask for a volunteer, you won't see her for ~!*** ¡en cuanto pides un voluntario pone los pies en polvorosa!; **when the ~ has settled** cuando haya pasado la tempestad; **to throw ~ in sb's eyes** engañar a algn; *see also* **ash² A**; *see* **bite B1**; *see also* **dry A6**, **gather A1**
2 (*) (= *act of dusting*) **to give sth a ~** quitar el polvo a algo; **she gave the ornaments a quick ~** le quitó un poco el polvo a los adornos
Ⓑ VT 1 [+ *furniture*] quitar el polvo a *or* de; [+ *room*] limpiar el polvo a *or* de; ✦***IDIOM*** **it's done and ~ed** (*Brit*) todo ha terminado; **the deal is done and ~ed** el trato está cerrado
2 (*with flour, icing sugar*) espolvorear; **to ~ o.s. with talc** ponerse talco; *see also* **dust down, dust off**
Ⓒ VI (= *clean up*) limpiar el polvo
Ⓓ CPD ► **dust bowl** N (*Geog*) *terreno erosionado por el viento* ► **dust cloth** N (*US*) trapo *m* del polvo ► **dust cover** N [*of book*] sobrecubierta *f*; (*for furniture*) guardapolvo *m* ► **dust devil** N remolino *m* de polvo ► **dust jacket** N sobrecubierta *f* ► **dust sheet** N (*Brit*) guardapolvo *m*, funda *f* ► **dust storm** N vendaval *m* de polvo, tormenta *f* de polvo

►**dust down** VT + ADV 1 (*lit*) [+ *furniture, shelf*] quitar el polvo a *or* de, desempolvar; **he stood and ~ed down his suit** se levantó y se sacudió el polvo del traje
2 (*fig*) desempolvar; **they ~ed down a project that had been shelved years ago** desempolvaron un proyecto que había sido aparcado hacía años; **to ~ o.s. down** sobreponerse; **he ~ed himself down and started again** se sobrepuso y volvió a empezar

►**dust off** VT + ADV = **dust down**

►**dust out** VT + ADV [+ *box, cupboard*] quitar el polvo a *or* de

dustbag [ˈdʌstbæg] N bolsa *f* de aspiradora

dustbin [ˈdʌstbɪn] (*Brit*) Ⓐ N cubo *m* de la basura
Ⓑ CPD ► **dustbin liner** N bolsa *f* de basura

dustcart [ˈdʌstkɑːt] N camión *m* de la basura

dustcloud [ˈdʌstklaʊd] N polvareda *f*

duster [ˈdʌstə^r] N 1 (= *cloth for dusting*) trapo *m*; (*for blackboard*) borrador *m*; **feather ~** plumero *m*
2 (*US*) (= *housecoat*) guardapolvo *m*

dustheap [ˈdʌsthiːp] N basurero *m*

dusting [ˈdʌstɪŋ] Ⓐ N 1 (= *cleaning*) limpieza *f*
2 (*) (= *beating*) paliza *f*
3 (*Culin*) (= *sprinkling*) espolvoreado *m*
Ⓑ CPD ► **dusting powder** N polvos *mpl* secantes

dustman [ˈdʌstmən] N (*pl* **dustmen**) (*Brit*) basurero *m*

dustpan [ˈdʌstpæn] N cogedor *m*

dust-proof [ˈdʌstpruːf] ADJ a prueba de polvo

dust-up* [ˈdʌstʌp] N (*Brit*) pelea *f*, bronca *f*; **to have a ~ with** pelearse con, tener una bronca con

dusty [ˈdʌstɪ] ADJ (*compar* **dustier**; *superl* **dustiest**) 1 (= *covered in dust*) [*town, ground, track, atmosphere*] polvoriento; [*furniture, book, car*] cubierto de polvo; **to get ~** [*table, book*] cubrirse de polvo; [*room, house*] llenarse de polvo
2 (= *greyish*) grisáceo; **~ blue** azul *m* grisáceo; **~ pink** rosa *m* grisáceo, rosa *m* viejo
3 (*Brit**) **a ~ answer** *or* **reply** una respuesta evasiva; **"how are you?" — "not so ~** *or* **not too ~, thanks"** —¿cómo estás? —no mal del todo, gracias

Dutch [dʌtʃ] Ⓐ ADJ holandés; **she's ~** es holandesa; ✦***IDIOMS*** **to be in ~ with sb** (*US**) estar en la lista negra de algn; **to talk to sb like a ~ uncle** decirle cuatro verdades a algn
Ⓑ N 1 (*Ling*) neerlandés *m*, holandés *m*
2 **the ~** (= *people*) los holandeses
Ⓒ ADV ✦***IDIOM*** **to go ~*** [*two people*] pagar a medias; [*more than two*] pagar a escote
Ⓓ CPD ► **Dutch auction** N subasta *f* a la baja ► **Dutch barn** N *granero abierto a los lados con el tejado curvo* ► **Dutch cap** N diafragma *m* ► **Dutch courage** N *envalentonamiento del que ha bebido* ► **Dutch elm disease** N enfermedad *f* del olmo, grafiosis *f* ► **Dutch oven** N olla *f* ► **Dutch school** N (*Art*) escuela *f* holandesa ► **Dutch treat** N *comida etc en la que cada uno paga lo suyo*

Dutchman [ˈdʌtʃmən] N (*pl* **Dutchmen**) holandés *m*; **it's him or I'm a ~*** que me maten si no es él

Dutchwoman [ˈdʌtʃˌwʊmən] N (*pl* **Dutchwomen**) holandesa *f*

dutiable [ˈdjuːtɪəbl] ADJ sujeto a derechos de aduana

dutiful [ˈdjuːtɪfʊl] ADJ [*child*] obediente; [*husband*] sumiso; [*employee*] cumplido

dutifully [ˈdjuːtɪfəlɪ] ADV obedientemente, sumisamente

▼**duty** [ˈdjuːtɪ] Ⓐ N 1 (*moral, legal*) deber *m*, obligación *f*; **it is my ~ to inform you that …** es mi deber *or* obligación informarles de que …; **I feel it to be my ~** creo que es mi deber; **it was his ~ to tell the police** su deber era decírselo a la policía; **I am ~ bound to say that …** es mi deber decir que …; **to do one's ~ (by sb)** cumplir con su deber (hacia algn, para con algn); **to fail in one's ~** faltar a su deber; **to make it one's ~ to do sth** encargarse de hacer algo; **it is no part of my ~ to do this** no me corresponde a mí hacer esto; **out of a sense of ~** por sentido del deber
2 (= *task, responsibility*) función *f*, responsabilidad *f*; **my duties consist of …** mis funciones *or* responsabilidades son …; **to do ~ as** servir de; **to do ~ for** servir en lugar de; **to neglect one's duties** faltar a sus responsabilidades; **to be off ~** (*gen*) estar libre; **an off ~ policeman** un policía fuera de servicio; **to be on ~** (*Med*) [*doctor, nurse, sentry*] estar de guardia; [*policeman*] estar de servicio; (*Admin, Scol*) estar de turno; **to go on ~** entrar de servicio; **to take up one's duties** entrar en funciones
3 (*Fin*) (= *tax*) derechos *mpl*; **to pay ~ on sth** pagar derechos por algo
Ⓑ CPD ► **duty call** N visita *f* de cumplido ► **duty officer** N (*Mil*) oficial *mf* de servicio ► **duty roster, duty rota** N lista *f* de turnos

duty-free [ˈdjuːtɪˈfriː] Ⓐ ADJ [*goods, perfume*] libre de impuestos, exento de derechos de aduana
Ⓑ CPD ► **duty-free shop** N tienda *f* "duty free"

duty-paid [ˌdjuːtɪˈpeɪd] ADJ con aranceles pagados

duvet [ˈduːveɪ] (*Brit*) Ⓐ N edredón *m* (nórdico)
Ⓑ CPD ► **duvet cover** N funda *f* de edredón (nórdico)

DV ADV ABBR = **Deo volente** (= *God willing*) D. m.

DVD Ⓐ N ABBR (= **digital versatile** *or* **video disc**) DVD *m*, disco *m* de vídeo digital, disco digital polivalente
Ⓑ CPD ► **DVD burner** N grabadora *f* de DVDs ► **DVD player** lector *m* de DVDs ► **DVD-Rom** DVD-Rom *m* ► **DVD writer** N grabadora *f* de DVDs

DVLA N ABBR (*Brit*) (= **Driver and Vehicle Licensing Agency**) *organismo encargado de la expedición de permisos de conducir y matriculación de vehículos*, ≈ DGT *f* (*Sp*)

DVLC N ABBR (*Brit*) (= **Driver and Vehicle Licensing Centre**) *centro de donde se expiden los permisos de conducir y matriculación de vehículos*, ≈ DGT *f* (*Sp*)

DVM N ABBR (*US Univ*) = **Doctor of Veterinary Medicine**

➤ LANGUAGE IN USE: **duty A1** 10.1

dwarf [dwɔːf] Ⓐ ADJ (*gen*) enano
Ⓑ N (*pl* **dwarfs** *or* **dwarves** [dwɔːvz]) enano/a *m/f*
Ⓒ VT (= *dominate*) [+ *building, person*] empequeñecer, hacer que parezca pequeño; [+ *achievement*] eclipsar
Ⓓ CPD ► **dwarf bean** N judía *f* enana, fríjol *m*

dweeb* [dwiːb] N (*esp US*) memo/a* *m/f*

dwell [dwel] (*pt, pp* **dwelt**) VI (*poet*) morar, vivir
►**dwell on, dwell upon** VI + PREP 1 (= *think about*) dar vueltas a, pensar obsesivamente en; (= *talk about*) insistir en (hablar de); **don't let's ~ upon it** no hay que insistir
2 (= *emphasize*) hacer hincapié en; (= *lengthen*) [+ *note, syllable*] alargar, poner énfasis en

dweller ['dweləʳ] N morador(a) *m/f*, habitante *mf*

dwelling ['dwelɪŋ] Ⓐ N (*frm, poet*) morada *f*, vivienda *f*
Ⓑ CPD ► **dwelling house** N (*frm*) casa *f* particular

dwelt [dwelt] PT, PP *of* **dwell**

dwindle ['dwɪndl] VI reducirse, menguar; **to ~ to** quedar reducido a; **to ~ away** [*money, sound*] disminuir, menguar; **his life was dwindling away** se consumía poco a poco

dwindling ['dwɪndlɪŋ] Ⓐ ADJ (*gen*) menguante
Ⓑ N disminución *f*

dye [daɪ] Ⓐ N tinte *m*; **hair ~** tinte *m* para el pelo
Ⓑ VT [+ *fabric, hair*] teñir; **to ~ sth red** teñir algo de rojo; **to ~ one's hair blond** teñirse el pelo de rubio

dyed-in-the-wool ['daɪdɪnðə'wʊl] ADJ (*fig*) testarudo

dyeing ['daɪɪŋ] N tinte *m*, tintura *f*

dyer ['daɪəʳ] N tintorero/a *m/f*; **~'s** tintorería *f*

dyestuff ['daɪstʌf] N tinte *m*, colorante *m*

dyeworks ['daɪwɜːks] NPL tintorería *fsing*

dying ['daɪɪŋ] Ⓐ PRESENT PARTICIPLE *of* **die**
Ⓑ ADJ [*man*] moribundo, agonizante; [*moments*] final; [*custom, race*] en vías de extinción; **his ~ words were …** sus últimas palabras fueron …
Ⓒ NPL **the ~** los moribundos

dyke [daɪk] N 1 (= *barrier*) dique *m*; (= *channel*) canal *m*, acequia *f*; (= *causeway*) calzada *f*; (= *embankment*) terraplén *m*
2 (** *offensive*) (= *lesbian*) tortillera** *f*

dynamic [daɪ'næmɪk] Ⓐ ADJ (*Phys, fig*) dinámico
Ⓑ N dinámica *f*

dynamically [daɪ'næmɪkəlɪ] ADV dinámicamente

dynamics [daɪ'næmɪks] NSING dinámica *f*

dynamism ['daɪnəmɪzəm] N dinamismo *m*

dynamite ['daɪnəmaɪt] Ⓐ N 1 (= *explosive*) dinamita *f*
2 (*fig*) (*) **he's ~!** ¡es estupendo!; **the story is ~** (*Press*) la noticia es una bomba *or* pura dinamita
Ⓑ VT [+ *bridge etc*] dinamitar, volar con dinamita

dynamo ['daɪnəməʊ] N dínamo *f*, dinamo *f*, dínamo *m* (*LAm*), dinamo *m* (*LAm*)

dynastic [daɪ'næstɪk] ADJ dinástico

dynasty ['dɪnəstɪ] N dinastía *f*

d'you [djuː] ABBR = **do you**

dysentery ['dɪsntrɪ] N disentería *f*

dysfunction [dɪs'fʌŋkʃən] N disfunción *f*

dysfunctional [dɪs'fʌŋkʃənəl] ADJ disfuncional

dyslexia [dɪs'leksɪə] N dislexia *f*

dyslexic [dɪs'leksɪk] Ⓐ ADJ disléxico
Ⓑ N disléxico/a *m/f*

dysmenorrhoea, dysmenorrhea (*US*) [ˌdɪsmenə'rɪə] N dismenorrea *f*

dyspepsia [dɪs'pepsɪə] N dispepsia *f*

dyspeptic [dɪs'peptɪk] ADJ dispéptico

dysphasia [dɪs'feɪzɪə] N disfasia *f*

dystrophy ['dɪstrəfɪ] N distrofia *f*; **muscular ~** distrofia *f* muscular

Ee

E¹, **e** [iː] Ⓐ N [1] (= *letter*) E, e *f*; **E for Edward** E de Enrique
[2] (*Mus*) **E** mi *m*; **E major/minor** mi mayor/menor; **E sharp/flat** mi sostenido/bemol
[3] (*Brit*) = **elbow**; **to give sb the big E*** [+ *lover*] dejar plantado *or* plantar a algn*; [+ *employee*] echar a algn a la calle*, despedir a algn
Ⓑ CPD ► **E number** N número *m* E

E² ABBR [1] (= **east**) E
[2] (*Drugs**) (= **ecstasy**) éxtasis *m*

e- [iː] PREFIX electrónico

EA ABBR (*US*) = **educational age**

ea ABBR (= **each**) c/u

each [iːtʃ] Ⓐ ADJ cada; **~ day** cada día; **~ house has its own garden** todas las casas tienen jardín; **~ one of them** cada uno (de ellos); **~ and every one of them** todos y cada uno de ellos
Ⓑ PRON [1] cada uno; **~ of us** cada uno de nosotros, cada quien (*LAm*); **he gave ~ of us £10** nos dio 10 libras a cada uno; **a little of ~** un poco de cada
[2] **~ other: they looked at ~ other** se miraron (uno a otro); **they help ~ other** se ayudan mutuamente *or* entre ellos; **people must help ~ other** hay que ayudarse (uno a otro); **they love ~ other** se quieren; **we write to ~ other** nos escribimos; **they don't know ~ other** no se conocen; **they were sorry for ~ other** se compadecían entre ellos; **their houses are next to ~ other** sus casas están una al lado de la otra *or* (*LAm*) juntas
Ⓒ ADV **we gave them one apple ~** les dimos una manzana por persona; **they cost £5 ~** costaron 5 libras cada uno

eager [ˈiːgəʳ] ADJ [1] [*person*] (= *enthusiastic*) entusiasta, entusiasmado; (= *impatient*) impaciente, ansioso; (= *hopeful*) ilusionado; **don't be so ~!** ¡ten paciencia!; **to be ~ to do sth: we were ~ to leave** estábamos impacientes *or* ansiosos por marcharnos; **he is ~ to find a new job** está impaciente *or* ansioso por encontrar otro trabajo; **the children are ~ to go camping** los niños están deseando ir de acampada; **to be ~ to help** estar deseoso de ayudar; **to be ~ to learn** tener muchas ganas *or* muchos deseos de aprender; **to be ~ to please** desear complacer; **to be ~ to succeed** estar ansioso por triunfar; **to be ~ for** [+ *affection, knowledge, power*] tener ansias de; [+ *vengeance*] tener sed de; **to be ~ for change** ansiar *or* desear mucho un cambio; **to be ~ for sb to do sth** estar ansioso porque algn haga algo, estar deseando que algn haga algo; **he was ~ for me to meet his family** estaba ansioso porque conociera a su familia, estaba deseando que conociera a su familia; **to be ~ for sth to happen** ansiar que algo pase, desear ardientemente que algo pase; ✦***IDIOM* to be an ~ beaver*** ser muy diligente
[2] [*desire*] vivo, ardiente

eagerly [ˈiːgəlɪ] ADV (= *enthusiastically*) [*say, accept*] con entusiasmo; (= *impatiently*) [*await, anticipate*] con impaciencia, ansiosamente; (= *hopefully*) con ilusión; (= *avidly*) [*read, listen*] con avidez

eagerness [ˈiːgənɪs] N (= *enthusiasm*) entusiasmo *m*; (= *impatience*) impaciencia *f*; (= *hopefulness*) ilusión *f*; **~ to do sth: ~ to succeed** ansias *fpl* de éxito; **~ to learn/leave** ganas *fpl* de aprender/marcharse, ansias *fpl* de aprender/marcharse; **~ to help/please** deseo *m* de ayudar/agradar; **in his ~ to get there first** en su ansia por llegar el primero

EAGGF N ABBR (= **European Agricultural Guidance and Guarantee Fund**) FEOGA *m*

eagle [ˈiːgl] N águila *f*; **with (an) ~ eye** con ojos de lince

eagle-eyed [ˈiːglˈaɪd] ADJ [*person*] **to be ~** tener ojos de lince

eaglet [ˈiːglɪt] N aguilucho *m*

E & OE [ˌiːəndˈəʊiː] ABBR (= **errors and omissions excepted**) s.e.u.o.

ear¹ [ɪəʳ] Ⓐ N [1] (*Anat*) (= *outer part*) oreja *f*; (= *rest of organ*) oído *m*; **she has small ~s** tiene las orejas pequeñas; **he could not believe his ~s** no daba crédito a sus oídos; **he was grinning from ~ to ~** la mueca le llegaba de oreja a oreja; **he whispered in her ~** le susurró al oído; **inner/middle/outer ~** oído *m* interno/medio/externo; **to prick up one's ~s** [*person*] aguzar el oído; [*animal*] empinar las orejas; **he was looking for a sympathetic ~** buscaba a alguien que le escuchara; **a word in your ~** una palabra en confianza; ✦***IDIOMS* to be all ~s** ser todo oídos; **to bend sb's ~*** machacar la cabeza a algn*; **I bet his ~s were burning** apuesto a que le zumbaban *or* pitaban los oídos; **to close one's ~s to sth** hacer caso omiso de algo; **they closed their ~s to everything that was being said** hicieron caso omiso de todo lo que se dijo; **to fall** *or* **crash down around** *or* **about one's ~s** venirse abajo; **the house is falling down around my ~s** la casa se está viniendo abajo; **it brought their world crashing down around their ~s** hizo que el mundo se les viniera abajo; **to fall on deaf ~s** caer en oídos sordos; **it goes in one ~ and out the other** por un oído le/me entra y por otro le/me sale; **to have/keep one's ~(s) to the ground** estar con la oreja pegada*, estar al tanto; **to have sb's ~** tener enchufe con algn*; **to lend an ~ (to sth)** prestar atención (a algo); **they're always willing to lend an ~ and offer advice** siempre están dispuestos a escuchar y dar consejos; **to listen with half an ~** escuchar a medias; **to be out on one's ~*** verse en la calle (sin trabajo)*; **if you don't work harder, you'll be out on your ~** como no arrimes más el hombro te verás en la calle*; **to pin back one's ~s*** escuchar bien; **to shut one's ~s to sth** = **to close one's ears to sth**; **to give sb a thick ~*** dar una torta *or* un tortazo a algn*; **to be up to one's ~s (in sth)*** (*in work, papers*) estar hasta arriba (de algo); (*in difficulties, debt, scandal*) estar hasta el cuello (de algo); **to have money/houses coming out of one's ~s** tener dinero/casas para dar y tomar; **I had football/pizza coming out of my ~s** el fútbol/la pizza me salía por las orejas, estaba harto de fútbol/pizza; **to be wet behind the ~s*** estar verde*; *see also* **cauliflower**, **deaf**, **flea**, **pig**, **box²**
[2] (= *sense of hearing*) oído *m*; **her voice was very pleasing to the ~** tenía una voz muy agradable al oído; **to play sth by ~** (*lit*) tocar algo de oído; **we don't know what to expect, we'll just have to play it by ~** (*fig*) no sabemos a qué atenernos, tendremos que improvisar sobre la marcha; **she has an ~ for languages** tiene oído para los idiomas; **she has a good ~ (for music)** tiene buen oído (para la música)
Ⓑ CPD ► **ear lobe** N lóbulo *m* de la oreja ► **ear, nose and throat department** N sección *f* de otorrinolaringología ► **ear, nose and throat specialist** N otorrinolaringólogo/a *m/f* ► **ear trumpet** N trompetilla *f* acústica ► **ear wax** N cerumen *m*, cera *f* de los oídos

ear² [ɪəʳ] N [*of cereal*] espiga *f*

earache [ˈɪəreɪk] N dolor *m* de oídos; **to have ~** tener dolor de oídos

eardrops [ˈɪədrɒps] NPL (*Med*) gotas *fpl* para el oído

eardrum [ˈɪədrʌm] N tímpano *m*

earflap [ˈɪəflæp] N orejera *f*

earful* [ˈɪəfʊl] N [1] **I got an ~ of Wagner** me llenaron los oídos de Wagner; **she gave me an ~ of her complaints** me soltó el rollo de sus quejas*; **get an ~ of this** (*Brit*) escucha esto
[2] (= *telling-off*) **to give sb an ~** echar la *or* una bronca a algn*, regañar a algn

earhole* [ˈɪəhəʊl] N agujero *m* de la oreja

earl [ɜːl] N conde *m*

earldom [ˈɜːldəm] N condado *m*

early [ˈɜːlɪ] (*compar* **earlier**, *superl* **earliest**) Ⓐ ADJ [1] (= *before appointed time*) **to be ~** llegar temprano *or* pronto; **you're ~!** ¡llegas temprano *or* pronto!; **you're five minutes ~** llegas con cinco minutos de adelanto; **I was half an hour ~ for the meeting** llegué a la reunión con media hora de adelanto, llegué a la reunión media hora antes de que empezase
[2] (= *before usual time*) [*death, menopause*] pre-

maturo, temprano; **Easter is ~ this year** la Semana Santa cae pronto este año; **~ frosts** heladas *fpl* prematuras *or* tempranas; **to have an ~ lunch** almorzar temprano, comer temprano; **she was pressurized into an ~ marriage** la presionaron para que se casase muy joven; **to have an ~ night** acostarse temprano; **~ retirement** jubilación *f* anticipada; **it was an ~ summer** el verano se había adelantado, el verano había llegado pronto

3 (= *soon*) pronto; **it's too ~ to say** es demasiado pronto para saber; **it will happen in March at the earliest** ocurrirá en marzo como muy pronto; **at your earliest convenience** (*Comm*) con la mayor brevedad posible

4 (= *towards beginning*) 4·1 (*of morning*) **we need two seats on an ~ flight** necesitamos dos plazas en un vuelo que salga por la mañana temprano *or* un vuelo a primera hora de la mañana; **to get up at an ~ hour** levantarse temprano, levantarse de madrugada; **to keep ~ hours** acostarse y levantarse temprano; **we arrived home in the ~ hours (of the morning)** llegamos a casa de madrugada; **we worked until the ~ hours of the morning** trabajamos hasta altas horas de la madrugada; **it was ~ in the morning** era muy de mañana, era muy temprano; **in the ~ morning** a primeras horas de la mañana; **we went for an ~ morning drive** nos fuimos a dar un paseo en coche por la mañana temprano; **to be an ~ riser** ser madrugador; **to get off to** *or* **make an ~ start** salir temprano

4·2 [*period, process*] **the ~ days/months/years of sth** los primeros días/meses/años de algo; **in the ~ 60s/70s** a principios de los 60/70; **she's in her ~ forties/seventies** tiene poco más de cuarenta/setenta años, tiene cuarenta/setenta y pocos (años); **she became famous in her ~ thirties** se hizo famosa a los treinta y pocos; **there were two ~ goals** se marcaron dos goles al inicio del partido; **in ~ January/March** a principios de enero/marzo; **it's still ~** (*in process*) es pronto todavía; **the ~ afternoon** a primera hora de la tarde; **at an ~ age** a una edad temprana; **from an ~ age** desde pequeño, desde una edad temprana (*frm*); **his ~ career/childhood** los primeros años de su carrera/infancia; **an ~ diagnosis** un diagnóstico precoz; **it was ~ evening** era media tarde; **we'll arrive there in the ~ evening** llegaremos a media tarde; **her ~ life** los primeros años de su vida; **in the ~ spring** a principios de la primavera; **it flowers from ~ spring to ~ autumn** florece desde principios de la primavera a principios del otoño; **the disease is hard to detect in its ~ stages** es difícil detectar la enfermedad en sus fases iniciales; **at an earlier stage of the project** en una etapa anterior del proyecto; **he's in his ~ teens** tendrá unos trece o catorce años; **he began painting in his ~ teens** empezó a pintar a los trece o catorce años; **his ~ youth** su primera juventud; ✦*IDIOM* **it's ~ days yet: we may have to modify the plans, but it's ~ days yet** (*esp Brit*) quizás tengamos que modificar los planes, pero aún es pronto para saberlo

5 (= *first*) [*man, Church*] primitivo; [*settlers, pioneers, Christians*] primer; **the ~ Victorians** los primeros victorianos; **an ~ Victorian table** una mesa de principios de la era victoriana; **Shakespeare's ~ work** las primeras obras de Shakespeare

6 (*Hort*) [*fruit, vegetable, crop*] temprano

Ⓑ ADV 1 (= *ahead of time*) [*arrive, leave, get up, go to bed*] temprano, pronto; **he arrived ten minutes ~** llegó diez minutos antes de la hora, llegó con diez minutos de anticipación; **he took his summer holiday ~** se tomó las vacaciones de verano pronto; **to book ~** reservar con anticipación; **I don't want to get there too ~** no quiero llegar demasiado pronto; ✦*PROV* **~ to bed, ~ to rise (makes a man healthy, wealthy and wise)** a quien madruga, Dios le ayuda; *see also* **bright B**

2 (= *soon*) pronto; **the earliest I can do it is Tuesday** lo más pronto que lo podré hacer será el martes; **a month earlier** un mes antes; **as ~ as possible** lo más pronto posible, cuanto antes; **as ~ as 1978** ya en 1978

3 (= *towards beginning of sth*) 3·1 (*in morning*) temprano; **you get up too ~** te levantas demasiado temprano, madrugas demasiado

3·2 (*in period, process*) **~ in sth**: **~ in the afternoon** a primera hora de la tarde; **~ in the book** en las primeras páginas del libro; **~ in the war** a principios de la guerra; **~ in the week** a principios de semana; **~ in the year** a principios de año; **~ in 1915** a principios de 1915; **~ in his life** en su juventud; **Red Ribbon fell ~ in the race** Red Ribbon tuvo una caída al principio de la carrera; **~ last century** a principios del siglo pasado; **~ next year** a principios del año que viene; **~ on in his career** en los primeros años de su carrera; **earlier on** anteriormente, antes; **~ this month** a principios de (este) mes; **~ today** a primera hora de hoy

Ⓒ CPD ► **early bird*** N madrugador(a) *m/f*; ✦*PROV* **it's the ~ bird that catches the worm** al que madruga Dios le ayuda ► **early closing** N (*also* **~-closing day**) (*Brit*) *día en que muchas tiendas sólo abren por la mañana*; **~ closing is on Mondays** el lunes muchas tiendas sólo abren por la mañana ► **the Early Middle Ages** NPL la Alta Edad Media ► **early warning system** N sistema *m* de alarma *or* alerta precoz; **pain acts as the body's ~ warning system** el dolor actúa como un sistema de alarma precoz

earmark ['ɪəmɑːk] VT destinar (**for** a)

earmuff ['ɪəmʌf] N orejera *f*

earn [ɜːn] Ⓐ VT [+ *money, wages etc*] ganar; (*Comm*) [+ *interest*] devengar; [+ *praise*] ganarse; **she ~s £5 an hour** gana 5 libras a la hora; **to ~ one's living** ganarse la vida; **~ed income** ingresos *mpl* devengados, renta *f* salarial *or* del trabajo; **it ~ed him the nickname of Crazy Harry** le valió el apodo de Crazy Harry; ✦*IDIOM* **to ~ a** *or* **one's crust*** ganarse el pan, ganarse los garbanzos

Ⓑ VI **to be ~ing** estar trabajando

earner ['ɜːnəʳ] N asalariado/a *m/f*; **there are three ~s in the family** en la familia hay tres personas asalariadas *or* que ganan un sueldo; **the shop is a nice little ~** (*Brit**) la tienda es rentable *or* una buena fuente de ingresos

earnest¹ ['ɜːnɪst] Ⓐ ADJ (= *serious*) [*person, character etc*] serio, formal; (= *sincere*) sincero; (= *eager*) [*wish, request*] vivo, ferviente; **it is my ~ wish that** deseo fervientemente que + *subjun*

Ⓑ N **in ~** en serio; **are you in ~?** ¿lo dices en serio?

earnest² ['ɜːnɪst] N prenda *f*, señal *f*; **~ money** fianza *f*

earnestly ['ɜːnɪstlɪ] ADV [*speak*] en serio; [*work*] afanosamente, con empeño; [*pray*] fervorosamente, fervientemente; **I ~ entreat you** (*frm or liter*) se lo suplico de todo corazón

earnestness ['ɜːnɪstnɪs] N (= *seriousness*) seriedad *f*, formalidad *f*; (= *sincerity*) sinceridad *f*

earning ['ɜːnɪŋ] Ⓐ N **earnings** (= *wages*) sueldo *msing*, salario *msing*; (= *income*) ingresos *mpl*; (= *profits*) ganancias *fpl*, beneficios *mpl*; **average ~s rose two percent last year** los ingresos medios aumentaron un dos por ciento el año pasado

Ⓑ CPD ► **earning potential** N potencial *m* de rentabilidad ► **earning power** N poder *m* adquisitivo ► **earnings related benefit** N prestación *f* calculada según los ingresos

earphones ['ɪəfəʊnz] NPL (*Telec etc*) auriculares *mpl*

earpiece ['ɪəpiːs] N (*Telec*) auricular *m*

ear-piercing ['ɪə,pɪəsɪŋ] ADJ penetrante, que taladra el oído

earplugs ['ɪəplʌgz] NPL tapones *mpl* para los oídos

earring ['ɪərɪŋ] N (= *long*) pendiente *m*, arete *m* (*LAm*); (= *round*) arete *m*, zarcillo *m*; (= *stud*) pendiente *m* (en forma de bolita)

earshot ['ɪəʃɒt] N **to be within ~** estar al alcance del oído; **to be out of ~** estar fuera del alcance del oído

ear-splitting ['ɪə,splɪtɪŋ] ADJ que rompe el tímpano, que taladra el oído, ensordecedor

earth [ɜːθ] Ⓐ N 1 (= *the world*) **(the) Earth** la Tierra; **here on ~** en este mundo; **she looks like nothing on ~*** está hecha un desastre; **it tasted like nothing on ~*** (= *good*) sabía de maravilla*; (= *bad*) sabía a rayos*; **nothing on ~ would make me do it** no lo haría por nada del mundo; **nothing on ~ will stop me now** no lo dejo ahora por nada del mundo; **what/where/who on ~ ...?*** ¿qué/dónde/quién demonios *or* diablos ...?; **what on ~ are you doing here?** ¿qué demonios *or* diablos haces aquí?; **why on ~ do it now?** ¿por qué demonios *or* diablos vamos a hacerlo ahora?; ✦*IDIOMS* **to come down to ~** volver a la realidad; **it must have cost the ~!*** ¡te habrá costado un ojo de la cara!; **to promise the ~** prometer el oro y el moro; *see also* **planet**

2 (= *ground*) tierra *f*, suelo *m*; (= *soil*) tierra *f*; **to fall to ~** caer al suelo

3 [*of fox*] madriguera *f*, guarida *f*; **to go to ~** [*fox*] meterse en su madriguera; [*person*] esconderse, refugiarse; **to run to ~** [+ *animal*] cazar *or* atrapar en su guarida; [+ *person*] perseguir y encontrar

4 (*Elec*) toma *f* de tierra, tierra *f*

Ⓑ VT (*Elec*) [+ *apparatus*] conectar a tierra

Ⓒ CPD ► **earth cable, earth lead** N cable *m* de toma de tierra ► **earth mother** N (*Myth*) la madre tierra; (*) (= *woman*) venus *f* ► **earth sciences** NPL *ciencias concernientes a la Tierra*; (= *geology*) geología *f*

► **earth up** VT + ADV (*Agr*) [+ *plant*] acollar

earthbound ['ɜːθbaʊnd] ADJ (= *moving towards earth*) en dirección a la Tierra; (= *stuck on earth*) terrestre; (= *unimaginative*) prosaico

earthen ['ɜːθən] ADJ de tierra; [*pot*] de barro

earthenware ['ɜːθənwɛəʳ] Ⓐ N loza *f* (de barro)

Ⓑ CPD de barro

earthling ['ɜːθlɪŋ] N terrícola *mf*

earthly ['ɜːθlɪ] Ⓐ ADJ 1 (= *terrestrial*) terrenal; (= *worldly*) mundano; **~ paradise** paraíso *m* terrenal

2 (*) (= *possible*) **there is no ~ reason to think ...** no existe razón alguna para pensar ...; **it's of no ~ use** no sirve para nada

Ⓑ N (*Brit**) **he hasn't an ~** no tiene posibilidad alguna, no tiene ninguna esperanza

earthquake ['ɜːθkweɪk] N terremoto *m*

earthscape ['ɜːθskeɪp] N *vista de la tierra desde una nave espacial*

earth-shaking ['ɜːθ,ʃeɪkɪŋ] ADJ, **earth-shattering** ['ɜːθ,ʃætərɪŋ] ADJ trascendental

earthward ['ɜːθwəd] ADV hacia la tierra

earthwards ['ɜːθwədz] ADV (*esp Brit*) = **earthward**

earthwork ['ɜːθwɜːk] N terraplén *m*

earthworm ['ɜːθwɜːm] N lombriz *f*

earthy ['ɜːθɪ] ADJ [1] (= *like earth*) [*colour*] terroso; **an ~ taste** un sabor a tierra
[2] (= *uncomplicated*) [*character*] sencillo
[3] (= *vulgar*) [*humour*] grosero

earwig ['ɪəwɪɡ] N tijereta *f*

ease [iːz] Ⓐ N [1] (= *effortlessness*) facilidad *f*; **the ~ with which he found work** la facilidad con la que encontró trabajo; **for ~ of reference** para facilitar la referencia; **the camera's ~ of use** la facilidad de uso de la cámara; **with ~** con facilidad
[2] (= *relaxed state*) **his ~ with money** su soltura *or* ligereza con el dinero; **people immediately feel at ~ with her** la gente inmediatamente se siente a gusto *or* cómoda con ella; **he was completely at ~ with himself** se encontraba completamente a gusto consigo mismo; **I would feel more at ~ if I knew where she was** me sentiría más tranquilo si supiera dónde está; **to put sb at his/her ~** hacer que algn se relaje, tranquilizar a algn; **to put** *or* **set sb's mind at ~** tranquilizar a algn; **if it will put your mind at ~ I'll tell you** si te tranquiliza te lo digo; **his ~ of manner** su naturalidad; **to take one's ~** descansar; *see also* **ill A2**
[3] (= *comfort*) comodidad *f*; **a life of ~** una vida cómoda *or* desahogada; **to live a life of ~** vivir cómodamente
[4] (*Mil*) **stand at ~!** ◊ **stand easy!** (*Mil*) ¡descansen!; **at ~, Sergeant** descanse, Sargento
Ⓑ VT [1] (= *relieve, lessen*) [+ *pain, suffering*] aliviar; [+ *pressure, tension*] aliviar, relajar; [+ *burden*] aligerar; [+ *impact, effect*] mitigar, paliar; [+ *sanctions, restrictions*] relajar; **these measures will ~ the burden on small businesses** estas medidas aligerarán la carga de las pequeñas empresas; **she gave them money to ~ her conscience** les dio dinero para quedarse con la conciencia tranquila; **it will ~ her mind to know the baby's all right** le tranquilizará saber que el bebé está bien; **aid to help ~ the plight of refugees** ayuda para paliar la difícil situación de los refugiados; **attempts to ~ traffic congestion** intentos de descongestionar el tráfico; **this will help to ~ the workload** esto ayudará para hacer menos pesado el trabajo
[2] (= *facilitate*) [+ *transition, task*] facilitar
[3] (= *loosen*) aflojar
[4] (= *move carefully*) **he ~d the car into the parking space** aparcó el coche en el aparcamiento con cuidado; **she ~d her foot off the clutch** soltó el pie del embrague con cuidado; **he ~d himself into the chair** se sentó con cuidado en la silla
Ⓒ VI [1] (= *diminish*) [*pain*] ceder, disminuir; [*tension*] disminuir; [*wind, rain*] amainar; [*interest rates*] bajar
[2] (= *improve*) [*situation*] calmarse

►**ease off** Ⓐ VI + ADV [1] (= *diminish*) [*pain*] ceder, disminuir; [*rain*] amainar; [*pressure*] disminuir; **the snow had ~d off** había dejado de nevar con tanta fuerza
[2] (= *take things more easily*) tomarse las cosas con más tranquilidad
[3] (= *work less hard*) aflojar el ritmo (de trabajo)
Ⓑ VT + ADV [1] (= *remove*) [+ *lid*] quitar; [+ *shoes, boots*] quitarse
[2] (= *stop pressing on*) [+ *accelerator, clutch*] soltar

►**ease up** VI + ADV [1] (= *take things more easily*) tomarse las cosas con más tranquilidad; **if you don't ~ up, you'll make yourself ill** como no te tomes las cosas con más tranquilidad te vas a poner malo
[2] (= *work less intensively*) bajar el ritmo (de trabajo); **we can't afford to ~ up yet** no podemos relajarnos *or* bajar el ritmo todavía
[3] (= *relax*) relajarse; **~ up a bit!** ¡relájate un poco!
[4] (= *slow down*) [*runner*] aflojar el paso, aminorar la marcha; [*driver, car*] reducir *or* disminuir la velocidad, aminorar la marcha
[5] **to ~ up on** [+ *restrictions, sanctions*] relajar, aflojar; **you'd better ~ up on the chocolate** más vale que dejes de comer tanto chocolate; **~ up on him, he's only a child** no seas tan estricto con él, es sólo un niño

easel ['iːzl] N caballete *m*

easily ['iːzɪlɪ] ADV [1] (= *without difficulty*) [*win, climb, break, tire, cry*] fácilmente, con facilidad; **he makes friends ~** hace amigos fácilmente *or* con facilidad; **he talked ~ about himself** habló sobre sí mismo de forma relajada; **don't give up so ~** no te rindas tan fácilmente; **she's ~ pleased/upset** es fácil complacerla/disgustarla, se contenta/disgusta fácilmente; **the park is ~ accessible by car** el parque tiene fácil acceso con coche; **don't worry, it's ~ done** (*replying to apology*) no te preocupes, le puede pasar a cualquiera; **there were ~ 500 at the meeting** había fácilmente 500 en la reunión; **it holds four litres ~** caben cuatro litros largos, caben cuatro litros fácilmente; **that will cost you £50 ~** eso te costará fácilmente *or* por lo menos 50 libras; **as ~ as (if)** con la misma facilidad que (si)
[2] (= *very possibly*) perfectamente, fácilmente; **he may ~ change his mind** puede perfectamente *or* fácilmente cambiar de opinión, fácilmente cambia de opinión (*LAm*); **it could very ~ happen again** podría perfectamente *or* fácilmente ocurrir de nuevo; **this could ~ be his last race** bien podría ser ésta su última carrera
[3] (= *by far*) con mucho; **he was ~ the best candidate** era con mucho el mejor candidato; **there was ~ enough to go round** había más que suficiente para todos

easiness ['iːzɪnɪs] N [*of task, exam question*] lo fácil; [*of laughter, voice, tone*] naturalidad *f*; [*of manner*] soltura *f*, naturalidad *f*

east [iːst] Ⓐ N este *m*, oriente *m*; **the East** (= *Orient*) el Oriente; (*Pol*) el Este; **in the ~ of the country** al este *or* en el este del país; **the wind is in the** *or* **from the ~** el viento viene del este; **to the ~ of** al este de
Ⓑ ADJ [*side*] este, del este, oriental; **an ~ wind** un viento del este; **the ~ coast** la costa este, la costa oriental
Ⓒ ADV (= *eastward*) hacia el este; (= *in the east*) al este, en el este; **we were travelling ~** viajábamos hacia el este; **~ of the border** al este de la frontera; **it's ~ of London** está al este de Londres
Ⓓ CPD ► **East Africa** N África *f* Oriental ► **East Berlin** N Berlín *m* Este ► **the East End** N [*of London*] *zona del Este de Londres* ► **East Germany** N Alemania *f* Oriental ► **the East Indies** NPL las Indias Orientales ► **the East Side** N [*of New York*] *zona del Este de Nueva York*

eastbound ['iːstbaʊnd] ADJ [*traffic*] en dirección este; [*carriageway*] de dirección este, en dirección este

Eastender [ˌiːst'endəʳ] N nativo/a *m/f or* habitante *mf* del este de Londres

Easter ['iːstəʳ] Ⓐ N Pascua *f* (de Resurrección), Semana *f* Santa; **at ~** por Pascua, en Semana Santa; **the ~ holidays** las vacaciones de Semana Santa
Ⓑ CPD ► **Easter bonnet** N sombrero *m* de primavera ► **Easter Day** N Domingo *m* de Resurrección ► **Easter egg** N huevo *m* de Pascua ► **Easter Island** N Isla *f* de Pascua ► **Easter Monday** N lunes *m inv* de Pascua de Resurrección ► **Easter parade** N procesión *f* de Semana Santa ► **Easter Sunday** N Domingo *m* de Resurrección ► **Easter week** N Semana *f* Santa

easterly ['iːstəlɪ] Ⓐ ADJ [*wind*] del este; **we were headed in an ~ direction** íbamos hacia el este *or* rumbo al este *or* en dirección este; **the most ~ point in Wales** el punto más oriental *or* más al este de Gales
Ⓑ N viento *m* del este

eastern ['iːstən] Ⓐ ADJ del este, oriental; **the ~ part of the island** la parte oriental *or* la parte este de la isla; **the ~ coast** la costa este *or* oriental; **in ~ Spain** en el este *or* al este de España; **~ religions** religiones orientales
Ⓑ CPD ► **the Eastern bloc** N (*Pol Hist*) el bloque del Este ► **Eastern Europe** N Europa *f* del Este, Europa *f* Oriental

easterner ['iːstənəʳ] N (*esp US*) habitante *mf* del este

easternmost ['iːstənməʊst] ADJ más oriental, más al este; **the ~ point of Spain** el punto más oriental *or* más al este de España

Eastertide ['iːstətaɪd] N (*liter*) = **Easter**

east-facing ['iːst,feɪsɪŋ] ADJ con cara al este, orientado hacia el este; **~ slope** vertiente *f* este

East German [ˌiːst'dʒɜːmən] Ⓐ N (= *person*) alemán/ana *m/f* oriental
Ⓑ ADJ germanooriental

east-northeast [ˌiːstnɔːθ'iːst] Ⓐ N estenor(d)este *m*
Ⓑ ADJ estenor(d)este
Ⓒ ADV (= *toward east-northeast*) hacia el estenor(d)este; [*situated*] al estenor(d)este

east-southeast [ˌiːstsaʊθ'iːst] Ⓐ N estesudeste *m*, estesureste *m*
Ⓑ ADJ estesudeste, estesureste
Ⓒ ADV (= *toward east-southeast*) hacia el estesudeste *or* estesureste; (*situated*) al estesudeste *or* estesureste, en el estesudeste *or* estesureste

eastward ['iːstwəd] Ⓐ ADJ [*movement, migration*] hacia el este, en dirección este
Ⓑ ADV hacia el este, en dirección este

eastwards ['iːstwədz] ADV (*esp Brit*) = **eastward B**

easy ['iːzɪ] Ⓐ ADJ (*compar* **easier**, *superl* **easiest**) [1] (= *not difficult*) [*task, job, decision, victory*] fácil; **it is ~ to see that ...** es fácil ver que ...; **he's ~ to work with** es fácil trabajar con él; **he's ~ to get on with** es muy fácil llevarse bien con él; **fluorescent jackets are ~ to see at night** las chaquetas fluorescentes son fáciles de ver por la noche; **there are no ~ answers** no hay respuestas fáciles; **to be far from ~** no ser nada fácil; **he came in an ~ first** llegó el primero sin problemas; **that's ~ for you to say** para ti es fácil decirlo; **to have it ~** tenerlo fácil; **the ~ life** la vida fácil; **~ listening** (= *music*) música *f* fácil de escuchar; **they made it very ~ for us** nos lo pusieron muy fácil; **"Russian made ~"** "ruso sin esfuerzo"; **to be no ~ matter** no ser cosa fácil; **it's an ~ mistake to make** es un error que se comete fácilmente; **~ money** dinero *m* fácil; **to be none too ~** no ser nada fácil; **to be ~ on the eye/ear** ser *or* resultar agradable a la vista/al oído; **eat something that's ~ on**

the stomach come algo que sea fácil de digerir; **to go for** *or* **take the ~ option** optar por lo más fácil; **that's the ~ part** eso es lo fácil; **~ pickings** botín *m* fácil; **~ prey** presa *f* fácil; **to be within ~ reach of sth** estar muy cerca de algo; **to make ~ reading** ser fácil de leer; **to have an ~ ride** *(fig)* tener las cosas fáciles; **that's easier said than done!** ¡eso se dice pronto!, es fácil decirlo, pero hacerlo ...; **I'd love to tell her to get lost but that's easier said than done** me encantaría mandarla al cuerno pero no es tan fácil de hacer; **in** *or* **by ~ stages** por etapas fáciles de superar; **to be no ~ task** no ser cosa fácil; **to buy sth on ~ terms** *(Comm)* comprar algo con facilidades de pago; **to have an ~ time** no tener problemas; **to take the ~ way out** *(fig)* optar por el camino más fácil; ✦***IDIOMS*** **it's as ~ as ABC** *or* **falling off a log** *or* **pie** es facilísimo; **to be on ~ street** estar forrado
[2] (= *relaxed*) [*life*] cómodo, relajado; [*manners*] relajado, natural; [*disposition, conversation, conscience*] tranquilo; [*smile*] fácil; [*voice, tone, style*] natural; [*pace*] lento, pausado; [*movement*] suelto, relajado; **I'm ~*** (= *not particular*) me es igual *or* me da igual; **to feel ~ (in one's mind)** sentirse tranquilo; **I don't feel ~ about leaving the children with that woman** no me siento tranquilo dejando a los niños con esa mujer; **we relaxed into ~ laughter** nos relajamos y empezamos a reírnos con naturalidad; **he has** *or* **enjoys an ~ relationship with his stepchildren** tiene una relación muy buena *or* se lleva muy bien con los hijos de su mujer; **you can rest ~** puedes estar tranquilo; **to be on ~ terms with sb** estar en confianza con algn
[3] (= *promiscuous*) [*woman*] fácil; **a woman of ~ virtue**† una mujer ligera de cascos
Ⓑ ADV **we can all breathe ~ now** ahora todos podemos respirar tranquilos; **taking orders doesn't come ~ to him** no le resulta fácil obedecer órdenes; **~ come, ~ go** tal y como viene se va; **~ does it!** ¡despacio!, ¡cuidado!, ¡con calma!; **go ~ with the sugar** no te pases con el azúcar; **go ~ on him** no seas muy duro con él; **to take things ~** ◊ **take it ~** (= *rest*) descansar; (= *go slowly*) tomárselo con calma; **take it ~!*** (= *don't worry*) ¡cálmete!, ¡no te pongas nervioso!; (= *don't rush*) ¡despacio!, ¡no corras!; *see also* **stand C1**
Ⓒ CPD ► **easy chair** N butaca *f*, sillón *m* *(Sp)*

easy-care [ˈiːzɪkɛəʳ] ADJ *(Brit) que no necesita cuidados especiales*

easy-going [ˈiːzɪˈgəʊɪŋ] ADJ [*person*] acomodadizo; [*attitude*] de trato fácil, relajado; **she's very ~ and gets on well with everybody** es una persona de trato fácil y se lleva bien con todos

easy-peasy* [ˌiːzɪˈpiːzɪ] ADJ *(Brit child language)* tirado*, chupado‡

eat [iːt] *(pt* **ate**; *pp* **eaten)** Ⓐ VT comer; **there's nothing to ~** no hay nada de *or* que comer; **would you like something to ~?** ¿quieres comer algo?; **he won't ~ you*** no te va a morder; **what's ~ing you?*** ¿qué mosca te ha picado?; **to ~ one's fill** hartarse; **to ~ one's lunch** comer, almorzar; **to ~ one's way through the menu** pedir todos los platos de la carta; ✦***IDIOMS*** **he's ~ing us out of house and home*** come por ocho; **to ~ one's words** tragarse las palabras
Ⓑ VI comer; **he ~s like a horse** come más que una lima nueva; **he always ~s well** siempre tiene buen apetito; ✦***IDIOM*** **I've got him ~ing out of my hand** lo tengo dominado

►**eat away** VT + ADV (= *wear away*) desgastar; (= *corrode*) corroer; [*mice etc*] roer

►**eat away at** VI + PREP [1] [*waves, sea*] desgastar; [*acid, rust*] corroer; [*rot, damp*] comerse; [*mice etc*] roer; [*insect pest*] comerse, devorar
[2] *(fig)* devorar

►**eat in** VI + ADV comer en casa

►**eat into** VI + PREP (= *wear away*) desgastar; [+ *metal*] [*acid*] corroer; [+ *savings*] mermar; [+ *leisure time*] reducir

►**eat out** Ⓐ VI + ADV comer fuera
Ⓑ VT + ADV **to ~ one's heart out** consumirse; **... Marcel Proust, ~ your heart out!*** ... ¡chúpate esa, Marcel Proust!*

►**eat up** Ⓐ VT + ADV [+ *food*] comerse; **it ~s up electricity** consume mucha electricidad; **to ~ up the miles** tragar los kilómetros; **to be ~en up with envy** consumirse de envidia
Ⓑ VI + ADV **~ up!** ¡venga, come!, ¡apúrate! *(LAm)*

> **EASY, DIFFICULT, IMPOSSIBLE**
>
> • **Fácil**, **difícil** and **imposible** are followed directly by the infinitive when they qualify the action itself:
> Solving the problem is easy *or* It's easy to solve the problem
> ***Es fácil resolver el problema***
> It is sometimes difficult/impossible to control oneself
> ***En ocasiones es difícil/imposible controlarse***
>
> • When the adjective qualifies a noun or pronoun rather than the verb, **de** is inserted before the infinitive:
> The problem is easy to solve
> ***El problema es fácil de resolver***
> That's difficult *or* hard to believe
> ***Eso es difícil de creer***
> Semtex is impossible to detect
> ***El Semtex es imposible de detectar***
>
> **!** Remember in this case to make the adjective agree with the noun or pronoun it describes:
> Some of his works are difficult to classify
> ***Algunas de sus obras son difíciles de encasillar***
>
> *For further uses and examples, see main entry.*

eatable [ˈiːtəbl] ADJ (= *fit to eat*) comible, pasable; (= *edible*) comestible

eatables* [ˈiːtəblz] NPL comestibles *mpl*

eaten [ˈiːtn] PP *of* **eat**

eater [ˈiːtəʳ] N [1] (= *person*) **to be a big ~** tener siempre buen apetito, ser comilón; **I'm not a big ~** yo como bastante poco
[2] (= *apple*) manzana *f* de mesa

eatery* [ˈiːtərɪ] N *(US)* restaurante *m*

eating [ˈiːtɪŋ] Ⓐ N [1] (= *act*) el comer
[2] **to be good ~** ser sabroso
Ⓑ CPD ► **eating apple** N manzana *f* de mesa ► **eating disorder** N desorden *m* alimenticio ► **eating olives** NPL aceitunas *fpl* de boca

eating-house [ˈiːtɪŋhaʊs] N *(pl* **eating-houses** [ˈiːtɪŋhaʊzɪz]) restaurante *m*

eats* [iːts] NPL comida *fsing*, comestibles *mpl*; **let's get some ~** vamos a comer algo

eau de Cologne [ˈəʊdəkəˈləʊn] N (agua *f* de) colonia *f*

eaves [iːvz] NPL alero *msing*

eavesdrop [ˈiːvzdrɒp] VI escuchar a escondidas; **to ~ on a conversation** escuchar una conversación a escondidas

eavesdropper [ˈiːvzˌdrɒpəʳ] N fisgón(ona) *m/f* *(que escucha conversaciones a escondidas)*

ebb [eb] Ⓐ N [*of tide*] reflujo *m*; **the ~ and flow** [*of tide*] el flujo y reflujo; *(fig)* los altibajos; ✦***IDIOM*** **to be at a low ~** [*person, spirits*] estar decaído; [*business*] estar de capa caída; **at a low ~ in his fortunes** en un bache de su vida
Ⓑ VI bajar, menguar; *(fig)* decaer; **to ~ and flow** [*tide*] fluir y refluir; **life is ~ing from him** le están abandonando sus últimas fuerzas
Ⓒ CPD ► **ebb tide** N marea *f* baja, bajamar *f*

►**ebb away** VI + ADV *(fig)* menguar, disminuir

Ebola [iːˈbəʊlə] N ébola *m*; **the ~ virus** el virus ébola

ebonite [ˈebənaɪt] N ebonita *f*

ebony [ˈebənɪ] Ⓐ N ébano *m*
Ⓑ CPD de ébano

e-book [ˈiːbʊk] N libro *m* electrónico

e-business [ˈiːˌbɪznɪs] N [1] (= *company*) negocio *m* electrónico
[2] (= *commerce*) comercio *m* electrónico, comercio *m* E

EBRD N ABBR (= **European Bank for Reconstruction and Development**) BERD *m*

EBU N ABBR (= **European Broadcasting Union**) UER *f*

ebullience [ɪˈbʌlɪəns] N entusiasmo *m*, animación *f*

ebullient [ɪˈbʌlɪənt] ADJ entusiasta, animado

EC Ⓐ N ABBR (= **European Community**) CE *f*
Ⓑ CPD [*directive, membership, states etc*] de la CE

eccentric [ɪkˈsentrɪk] Ⓐ ADJ excéntrico
Ⓑ N excéntrico/a *m/f*; **she was a bit of an ~** era un poco excéntrica

eccentrically [ɪkˈsentrɪkəlɪ] ADV [*behave, dress*] de manera excéntrica

eccentricity [ˌeksənˈtrɪsɪtɪ] N excentricidad *f*

Ecclesiastes [ɪˌkliːzɪˈæstiːz] N *(Bible)* **the Book of ~** el Libro de Eclesiastés

ecclesiastic [ɪˌkliːzɪˈæstɪk] N eclesiástico *m*

ecclesiastical [ɪˌkliːzɪˈæstɪkəl] ADJ eclesiástico

ECG N ABBR (= **electrocardiogram, electrocardiograph**) ECG *m*

ECGD N ABBR (= **Export Credits Guarantee Department**) *servicio de garantía financiera a la exportación*

echelon [ˈeʃəlɒn] N (= *level*) nivel *m*; (= *degree*) grado *m*; *(Mil)* escalón *m*; **the upper ~s of the corporation** los cuadros directivos de la compañía

echo [ˈekəʊ] Ⓐ N *(pl* **echoes**) *(gen, fig)* eco *m*
Ⓑ VT [+ *sound*] repetir; [+ *opinion etc*] hacerse eco de
Ⓒ VI [*sound*] resonar, hacer eco; [*place*] resonar; **his footsteps ~ed in the street** se oía el eco de sus pasos *or* sus pasos resonaban en la calle; **the valley ~ed with shouts** resonaban los gritos por el valle
Ⓓ CPD ► **echo chamber** N cámara *f* de resonancia ► **echo sounder** N sonda *f* acústica

echolocation [ˌekəʊləʊˈkeɪʃən] N ecolocación *f*

ECJ N ABBR = **European Court of Justice**

ECLA N ABBR (= **Economic Commission for Latin America**) CEPAL *f*

éclair [ˈeɪklɛəʳ] N *pastelito relleno de nata y cubierto de chocolate*

eclampsia [ɪˈklæmpsɪə] N eclampsia *f*

éclat [ˈeɪklɑː] N brillo *m*; (= *success*) éxito *m* brillante; **with great ~** brillantemente

eclectic [ɪˈklektɪk] ADJ, N ecléctico/a *m/f*

eclecticism [ɪˈklektɪsɪzəm] N eclecticismo *m*

eclipse [ɪˈklɪps] Ⓐ N eclipse *m*; **partial/total ~** eclipse *m* parcial/total
Ⓑ VT *(lit, fig)* eclipsar

eclogue [ˈeklɒg] N égloga *f*

eclosion [ɪˈkləʊʒən] N eclosión *f*

ECM N ABBR [1] = **electronic counter-measure**
[2] (*US*) (= **European Common Market**) MCE *m*

ecobalance ['i:kəʊ,bæləns] N equilibrio *m* ecológico

ecoclimatic [,i:kəʊklaɪ'mætɪk] ADJ ecoclimático

eco-friendly ['i:kəʊ'frendlɪ] ADJ amigo de la ecología, ecológicamente puro

eco-labelling, **eco-labeling** (*US*) [,i:kəʊ'leɪbəlɪŋ] N ecoetiquetado *m*

E-coli [,i:'kəʊlaɪ] N (*Med*) E. coli *m*

ecological [,i:kəʊ'lɒdʒɪkəl] ADJ ecológico

ecologically [,i:kəʊ'lɒdʒɪkəlɪ] ADV ecológicamente; **an ~ sound scheme** un plan ecológicamente razonable, un plan razonable desde el punto de vista ecológico; **~, the new fishing regulations are a good move** desde el punto de vista ecológico, la nueva normativa sobre la pesca es una buena medida

ecologist [ɪ'kɒlədʒɪst] N (= *scientist*) ecólogo/a *m/f*; (= *conservationist*) ecologista *mf*

ecology [ɪ'kɒlədʒɪ] Ⓐ N ecología *f*
Ⓑ CPD ► **ecology movement** N movimiento *m* ecologista

e-commerce ['ɪ:,kɒmɜ:s] N comercio *m* electrónico, comercio *m* E

econometric [ɪ,kɒnə'metrɪk] ADJ econométrico

econometrician [ɪ,kɒnəmə'trɪʃən] N econometrista *mf*

econometrics [ɪ,kɒnə'metrɪks] NSING econometría *f*

econometrist [ɪ,kɒnə'metrɪst] N econometrista *mf*

economic [,i:kə'nɒmɪk] Ⓐ ADJ [1] (= *financial*) [*problems, development, geography*] económico
[2] (= *profitable*) [*business, price*] rentable
Ⓑ CPD ► **economic aid** N ayuda *f* económica ► **economic forecast** N previsiones *fpl* económicas ► **economic growth** N crecimiento *m* económico ► **economic sanctions** NPL sanciones *fpl* económicas

economical [,i:kə'nɒmɪkəl] ADJ [*person, method, car*] económico; **it's more ~ to have a diesel-engined car** resulta más económico tener un coche de gasoil; **my car is very ~ to run** mi coche me sale muy económico; **to be ~ with the truth** no decir toda la verdad, no ser muy pródigo con la verdad

economically [,i:kə'nɒmɪkəlɪ] ADV [1] (= *financially*) económicamente; **~ depressed areas** áreas *fpl* económicamente deprimidas; **an ~ powerful country** un país de gran poder económico; **~ speaking** respecto a la economía, económicamente hablando; **~, the plan makes good sense** desde el punto de vista económico, el plan tiene sentido
[2] (= *cheaply*) [*use, live*] de manera económica; **this machine could be more ~ operated** esta máquina se podría operar a un costo más bajo; **to be ~ priced** tener un precio módico *or* muy económico
[3] (= *concisely*) [*write, describe*] con economía de palabras

economics [,i:kə'nɒmɪks] Ⓐ NSING (= *science*) economía *f*; **he's doing ~ at university** estudia económicas en la universidad; *see also* **home D**
Ⓑ NPL (= *financial aspects*) aspectos *mpl* económicos; **the ~ of the situation** los aspectos económicos de la situación; **the ~ of the third world countries** la economía de los países tercermundistas

economist [ɪ'kɒnəmɪst] N economista *mf*

economize [ɪ'kɒnəmaɪz] Ⓐ VI economizar; **to ~ on sth** economizar en algo
Ⓑ VT economizar, ahorrar

economy [ɪ'kɒnəmɪ] Ⓐ N [1] (= *thrift*) economía *f*; (= *a saving*) ahorro *m*; **~ of scale** economía *f* de escala; **to make economies** economizar, ahorrar
[2] (= *system*) economía *f*
Ⓑ CPD ► **economy class** N clase *f* económica *or* turista ► **economy class syndrome** N síndrome *m* de la clase turista ► **economy drive** N **to have an ~ drive** economizar, ahorrar ► **economy pack** N (*Comm*) envase *m* familiar ► **economy size** N tamaño *m* familiar

ecosensitive ['i:kəʊ'sensɪtɪv] ADJ ecosensible

ecosphere ['i:kəʊ,sfɪəʳ] N ecosfera *f*

ecosystem ['i:kəʊ,sɪstɪm] N ecosistema *m*

eco-tourism [,i:kəʊ'tʊərɪzəm] N ecoturismo *m*, turismo *m* verde *or* ecológico

ecotype ['i:kə,taɪp] N ecotipo *m*

eco-warrior* ['i:kəʊ,wɒrɪəʳ] N activista *mf* del ecologismo, ecologista *mf* militante

ECS N ABBR (*Comput*) = **extended character set**

ECSC N ABBR (*formerly*) (= **European Coal and Steel Community**) CECA *f*

ecstasy ['ekstəsɪ] N [1] (*Rel, fig*) éxtasis *m inv*; **to go into ecstasies over sth** extasiarse ante algo; **to be in ~** estar en éxtasis; **to be in ecstasies** estar en éxtasis
[2] (*Drugs**) éxtasis *m inv*

ecstatic [eks'tætɪk] ADJ (*Rel*) extático; (*fig*) contentísimo, eufórico

ecstatically [eks'tætɪkəlɪ] ADV (*Rel*) en estado de éxtasis; (*fig*) con gran euforia

ECT N ABBR = **electroconvulsive therapy**; *see* **electroconvulsive therapy**

ectomorph ['ektəʊ,mɔ:f] N ectomorfo *m*

ectopic pregnancy [ek,tɒpɪk'pregnənsɪ] N embarazo *m* ectópico

ectoplasm ['ektəʊplæzəm] N ectoplasma *m*

ECU ['eɪkju:] N ABBR (= **European Currency Unit**) ECU *m*, UCE *f*

Ecuador [,ekwə'dɔ:ʳ] N Ecuador *m*

Ecuadoran [,ekwə'dɔ:rən], **Ecuadorian** [,ekwə'dɔ:rɪən] Ⓐ ADJ ecuatoriano
Ⓑ N ecuatoriano/a *m/f*

ecumenical [,i:kjʊ'menɪkəl] Ⓐ ADJ ecuménico
Ⓑ CPD ► **ecumenical council** N consejo *m* ecuménico ► **ecumenical movement** N movimiento *m* ecuménico

ecumenicism [,i:kjʊ'menɪsɪzəm], **ecumenism** [i:'kju:mənɪzəm] N ecumenismo *m*

eczema ['eksɪmə] N eczema *m*, eccema *m*; **she's got ~** tiene eczema

Ed [ed] N (*familiar form*) *of* **Edward**

ed ABBR [1] (= **edition**) ed
[2] (= **editor**) ed
[3] (= **edited by**) en edición de

Edam ['i:dæm] N (*also* **~ cheese**) queso *m* de Edam, queso *m* de bola

EDC N ABBR = **European Defence Community**

eddy ['edɪ] Ⓐ N remolino *m*
Ⓑ VI [*water*] hacer remolinos, arremolinarse

edelweiss ['eɪdlvaɪs] N edelweiss *m*

edema [ɪ'di:mə] N (*esp US*) = **oedema**

Eden ['i:dn] N Edén *m*

edentate [ɪ'denteɪt] Ⓐ ADJ desdentado
Ⓑ N desdentado/a *m/f*

EDF N ABBR (= **European Development Fund**) FED *m*

edge [edʒ] Ⓐ N [1] (= *border, rim*) [*of cliff, wood, chair, bed*] borde *m*; [*of town*] afueras *fpl*; [*of lake, river*] orilla *f*; [*of cube, brick*] arista *f*; [*of paper*] borde *m*, margen *m*; [*of coin*] canto *m*; **the fabric was fraying at the ~s** la tela se estaba deshilachando por los bordes; **she was standing at the water's ~** estaba de pie en la orilla del agua; **the trees at the ~ of the road** los árboles que bordean la carretera; **he sat down on the ~ of the bed** se sentó al borde la cama; **a house on the ~ of town** una casa a las afueras de la ciudad; **someone pushed him over the ~ of the cliff** alguien lo empujó por el borde del precipicio; ✦*IDIOMS* **to live close to the ~** vivir al límite; **to be on ~** tener los nervios de punta; **my nerves are on ~ today** hoy tengo los nervios de punta, hoy estoy de los nervios; **to set sb's teeth on ~** [*sound, voice*] dar dentera a algn; [*person*] poner los pelos de punta a algn; **to drive/push sb over the ~** llevar a algn al límite; **to be on the ~ of one's seat** estar en suspense *or* vilo *or* ascuas
[2] (= *brink*) borde *m*; **he was on the ~ of a breakthrough** estaba al borde de un gran adelanto
[3] (= *sharp side*) [*of blade*] filo *m*; **to put an ~ on sth** afilar algo; **army life will smooth the rough ~s off him** la vida militar le calmará; *see also* **cutting B**, **leading B**
[4] (= *sharpness*) **there was an ~ to her voice** había un tono de crispación en su voz; **his performance lacked ~** a su interpretación le faltaba mordacidad; **the wind had a sharp ~** hacía un viento cortante; **to take the ~ off sth**: **talking to her took the ~ off my grief** hablar con ella mitigó mi dolor; **that took the ~ off my appetite** con eso maté el hambre *or* engañé el estómago
[5] (= *advantage*) ventaja *f*; **their technology gave them the competitive ~** su tecnología les dio una posición de ventaja con respecto a la competencia; **to have the** *or* **an ~ on** *or* **over sb** llevar la delantera a algn, llevar ventaja a algn
Ⓑ VT [1] (= *provide border for*) [+ *garment*] ribetear; [+ *path*] bordear; **a top ~d with lace** un top ribeteado con encaje; **a teak tray ~d with brass** una bandeja de teca con el borde de bronce; **narrow green leaves ~d with red** hojas verdes delgadas con los bordes rojos
[2] (= *move carefully*) **he ~d the car into the traffic** sacó el coche con cuidado y se unió al resto del tráfico; **she ~d her way through the crowd** se abrió paso poco a poco entre la multitud; **the song ~d its way up the charts** la canción fue poco a poco subiendo puestos en las listas de éxitos
[3] (= *sharpen*) **her voice was ~d with panic** había un tono de pánico en su voz
Ⓒ VI (= *move slowly*) **she ~d away from him** poco a poco se alejó de él; **he ~d closer to the telephone** se acercó lentamente al teléfono; **to ~ forward** avanzar poco a poco; **Labour have ~d into the lead** el partido laborista ha conseguido tomar la delantera por muy poco; **to ~ past** pasar con dificultad

► **edge out** Ⓐ VT + ADV (= *defeat*) [+ *rival, opposing team*] derrotar por muy poco; **Germany and France have ~d out the British team** Alemania y Francia han derrotado a Gran Bretaña por muy poco; **they were ~d out of the number one slot** les arrebataron el primer puesto por muy poco
Ⓑ VI + ADV **the car ~d out into the traffic** el coche salió con cuidado y se unió al resto del tráfico

► **edge up** VI + ADV [1] [*shares, currency, price*] subir poco a poco
[2] **to ~ up to sb** acercarse con cautela a algn

edgeways ['edʒweɪz], **edgewise** ['edʒwaɪz]

ADV de lado, de canto; **I couldn't get a word in ~*** no pude meter baza*

edgily ['edʒılı] ADV [*say*] con tono crispado

edginess ['edʒınıs] N crispación *f*

edging ['edʒıŋ] N borde *m*; [*of ribbon, silk*] ribete *m*

edgy ['edʒı] ADJ crispado

edibility [ˌedı'bılətı] N comestibilidad *f*

edible ['edıbl] ADJ comestible

edict ['i:dıkt] N (*Hist*) edicto *m*; (*Jur*) decreto *m*, auto *m*; (*Pol*) decreto *m*; (*by mayor*) bando *m*, edicto *m*

edification [ˌedıfı'keıʃən] N enseñanza *f*

edifice ['edıfıs] N (*frm*) edificio *m* (imponente)

edify ['edıfaı] VT edificar

edifying ['edıfaııŋ] ADJ edificante

Edinburgh ['edınbərə] N Edimburgo *m*

EDINBURGH FESTIVAL

El Festival de Edimburgo, el mayor festival de este tipo del mundo, se celebra cada año en agosto durante tres semanas, en las que el festival está presente en toda la ciudad. Además del programa oficial del festival, que ofrece actuaciones de artistas de categoría internacional, también hay una enorme cantidad de actividades artísticas de todo tipo, desde lo más tradicional hasta lo más extravagante, teatro, danza, música, artistas callejeros etc., a lo que se llama **Fringe Festival**, *pues comenzó siendo un festival alternativo al oficial. Al mismo tiempo, se celebra un festival de jazz, otro de cine y una exhibición militar llamada* **Military Tattoo**, *que tiene lugar en el Castillo de Edimburgo.*

edit ['edıt] Ⓐ VT (= *be in charge of*) [+ *newspaper, magazine, etc*] dirigir; (= *prepare for printing*) corregir, revisar; (= *cut*) cortar, reducir; (*Cine, TV*) montar; (*Rad*) editar; (*Comput*) editar; **~ed by** [*newspaper*] bajo la dirección de; [*text, book*] edición de, editado por
Ⓑ N corrección *f*
Ⓒ CPD ► **edit key** N tecla *f* de edición

►**edit out** VT + ADV eliminar, suprimir

editing ['edıtıŋ] N (= *management*) [*of magazine*] redacción *f*; [*of newspaper, dictionary*] dirección *f*; (= *preparation for printing*) [*of article, series of texts, tape*] edición *f*; [*of film*] montaje *m*, edición *f*; [*of video*] edición *f*; (*Comput*) edición *f*

edition [ı'dıʃən] N (*gen*) edición *f*; (= *number printed*) tirada *f*, impresión *f*

editor ['edıtəʳ] N [*of newspaper, magazine*] director(a) *m/f*; (= *publisher's editor*) redactor(a) *m/f*; (*Cine, TV*) montador(a) *m/f*, editor(a) *m/f*; (*Rad*) editor(a) *m/f*; **~'s note** nota *f* de la redacción; **the sports ~** el/la redactor(a) de la sección de deportes

editorial [ˌedı'tɔ:rıəl] Ⓐ ADJ [*decision, control, page, policy*] editorial; [*board, meeting, assistant*] de redacción; **~ experience** experiencia *f* en edición de textos; **~ staff** redacción *f*
Ⓑ N (= *article*) editorial *m*, artículo *m* de fondo

editorialist [ˌedı'tɔ:rıəlıst] N (*US*) editorialista *mf*

editorialize [ˌedı'tɔ:rıəlaız] VI editorializar

editorially [ˌedı'tɔ:rıəlı] ADV desde el punto de vista editorial

editor-in-chief ['edıtərın'tʃi:f] N jefe/a *m/f* de redacción

editorship ['edıtəʃıp] N dirección *f*

Edmund ['edmənd] N Edmundo

EDP N ABBR (= **electronic data processing**) PED *m*

EDT N ABBR (*US*) = **Eastern Daylight Time**

educability [ˌedjʊkə'bılıtı] N educabilidad *f*

educable ['edjʊkəbl] ADJ educable

educate ['edjʊkeıt] VT (= *teach*) enseñar; (= *train*) educar, formar; (= *provide instruction in*) instruir; **where were you ~d?** ¿dónde cursó sus estudios?; **he is being privately ~d** cursa estudios en un colegio privado

educated ['edjʊkeıtıd] ADJ [*person, voice*] culto; **an ~ guess** una suposición bien fundamentada

education [ˌedjʊ'keıʃən] Ⓐ N educación *f*, formación *f*; (= *teaching*) enseñanza *f*; (= *knowledge, culture*) cultura *f*; (= *studies*) estudios *mpl*; (= *training*) formación *f*; (*Univ*) (= *subject*) pedagogía *f*; **Ministry of Education** Ministerio *m or* (*LAm*) Secretaría *f* de Educación; **primary/secondary ~** enseñanza *f* primaria/secundaria, primera/segunda enseñanza *f*; **higher ~** educación *f* superior, enseñanza *f* superior; **physical/political ~** educación *f* física/política; **literary/professional ~** formación *f* literaria/profesional; **there should be more investment in ~** debería invertirse más dinero en educación; **she works in ~** trabaja en la enseñanza; **I never had much ~** pasé poco tiempo en la escuela; **they paid for his ~** le pagaron los estudios
Ⓑ CPD ► **education authority** N (*Brit*) ≈ delegación *f* de educación, ≈ consejería *f* de educación (*Sp*) ► **education department** N (*Brit*) [*of local authority*] ≈ departamento *m* de educación; (= *ministry*) Ministerio *m* de Educación

educational [ˌedjʊ'keıʃənl] Ⓐ ADJ [1] (= *instructive*) [*film, book, toy, visit*] educativo, instructivo; [*role*] docente; [*function*] docente, educativo; [*event, experience*] educativo
[2] (= *relating to education*) [*system*] educativo, de enseñanza; [*needs, opportunities, supplies, material*] educativo; [*establishment, institution*] docente, de enseñanza; [*achievement, qualification*] académico; [*standards*] de educación; [*policy*] educacional, relativo a la educación; [*methods*] educativo, de educación; [*theory*] pedagógico; **falling ~ standards** estándares *mpl* de educación cada vez más bajos
Ⓑ CPD ► **educational adviser** N (*Brit Scol, Admin*) consejero/a *m/f* de enseñanza ► **educational psychologist** N psicopedagogo/a *m/f* ► **educational psychology** N psicopedagogía *f* ► **educational technology** N tecnología *f* educativa ► **educational television** N televisión *f* educativa

educationalist [ˌedjʊ'keıʃnəlıst] N (*esp Brit*) pedagogo/a *m/f*

educationally [ˌedjʊ'keıʃnəlı] ADV [*stimulate, encourage*] desde el punto de vista educativo; **~, the school is very good** desde el punto de vista educativo, el colegio es muy bueno; **~ backward adults** adultos *mpl* con carencias educativas; **~ deprived children** niños *mpl* privados de educación; **~ sound principles** principios *mpl* con una base pedagógica sólida; **~ subnormal** con dificultades de aprendizaje

educationist [ˌedjʊ'keıʃnıst] N (*esp Brit*) = **educationalist**

educative ['edjʊkətıv] ADJ educativo

educator ['edjʊkeıtəʳ] N educador(a) *m/f*

educe [ı'dju:s] VT educir, sacar

edutainment [ˌedjʊ'teınmənt] N (*esp US*) *juego de ordenador ameno y educativo al mismo tiempo*

Edward ['edwəd] N Eduardo; **~ the Confessor** Eduardo el Confesor

Edwardian [ed'wɔ:dıən] Ⓐ ADJ eduardiano
Ⓑ N eduardiano/a *m/f*

EE ABBR = **electrical engineer**

EEC N ABBR (= **European Economic Community**) CEE *f*

EEG N ABBR = **electroencephalogram**

eel [i:l] N anguila *f*

e'en [i:n] (*poet*) = **even**

EENT ABBR (*US Med*) = **eye, ear, nose and throat**

EEOC N ABBR (*US*) (= **Equal Employment Opportunity Commission**) *comisión que investiga la discriminación racial o sexual en el empleo*

e'er [ɛəʳ] (*poet*) = **ever**

eerie ['ıərı] ADJ [*sound, experience*] sobrecogedor, espeluznante; [*silence*] estremecedor, inquietante, sobrecogedor

eerily ['ıərılı] ADV [*deserted*] misteriosamente; [*similar, familiar*] sorprendentemente; **the whole town was ~ quiet** el pueblo entero estaba sumido en un silencio inquietante; **his footsteps echoed ~ along the High Street** sus pasos resonaron de manera sobrecogedora por la calle Mayor

EET N ABBR = **Eastern European Time**

eff‡ [ef] VI **he was ~ing all over the place** soltaba palabrotas por todas partes; **he told her to ~ off** la mandó a la mierda‡; ✦*IDIOM* **to ~ and blind** soltar palabrotas*

efface [ı'feıs] VT borrar; **to ~ o.s.** no hacerse notar, lograr pasar inadvertido

effect [ı'fekt] Ⓐ N [1] (*gen*) efecto *m*; (= *result*) resultado *m*, consecuencia *f*; **to feel the ~(s) of** sentir los efectos de; **to such good ~ that …** con tan buenos resultados que …; **to have an ~ on sb** hacer efecto a algn; **to have an ~ on sth** afectar (a) algo; **it will have the ~ of preventing …** tendrá como consecuencia impedir …; **to have the desired ~** producir el efecto deseado; **to have no ~** ◊ **be of no ~** no surtir efecto; **in ~** (= *in fact*) en realidad; (= *practically*) de hecho; **to be in ~** (*Jur*) estar vigente, tener vigencia; **to come into ~** (*Jur*) entrar en vigor; **to put into ~** [+ *rule*] poner en vigor; [+ *plan*] poner en práctica; **to take ~** [*drug*] surtir efecto; **to no ~** inútilmente, sin resultado; **with ~ from April** (*esp Brit*) a partir de abril; **an increase with immediate ~** un aumento efectivo a partir de hoy
[2] (= *sense*) [*of words etc*] sentido *m*; **a circular to this ~ will be issued next week** la próxima semana se hará pública una circular en este sentido; **an announcement to the ~ that …** un aviso informando de que …; **his letter is to the ~ that …** en su carta manifiesta que …; **to the same ~** en el mismo sentido; **or words to that ~** o algo por el estilo
[3] (= *impression*) efecto *m*, impresión *f*; **a pleasing ~** una impresión agradable; **to create an ~** impresionar; **he said it for ~** lo dijo sólo para impresionar; **special ~s** (*Cine, TV*) efectos *mpl* especiales
[4] **effects** (= *property*) efectos *mpl*; **personal ~s** efectos *mpl* personales
Ⓑ VT (*frm*) (= *bring about*) [+ *sale, purchase, payment, reform, reduction*] efectuar; [+ *cure, improvement, transformation*] lograr; **to ~ change** lograr *or* efectuar un cambio; **to ~ a saving** hacer un ahorro

effective [ı'fektıv] Ⓐ ADJ [1] (= *efficient, useful*) [*treatment, method, deterrent, system*] efectivo, eficaz; [*remark, argument*] eficaz; **the method is simple, but ~** el método es simple pero

efectivo *or* eficaz; **to be ~ against sth** [*drug*] ser eficaz contra algo; **~ capacity** (*Tech*) capacidad *f* útil; **to be ~ in doing sth** ser eficaz para hacer algo; **~ life** (*Pharm*) vida *f* útil; **~ power** (*Tech*) potencia *f* real; **~ ways of reducing pollution** formas *fpl* efectivas *or* eficaces de reducir la polución
2 (= *striking*) [*display, outfit, decoration*] impresionante, logrado; [*combination*] logrado; **to look ~** causar efecto; **blinds can look very ~** las persianas pueden causar muy buen efecto *or* mucho efecto
3 (= *operative*) **to become ~** entrar en vigor, hacerse efectivo (**from, on** a partir de); **~ date** fecha *f* de vigencia, fecha *f* efectiva; **it will be ~ from April 1** entrará en vigor *or* será efectivo a partir del 1 de abril
4 (= *actual*) [*aid, contribution, leader*] real; [*control, increase*] efectivo; [*income*] en efectivo
5 (*Econ, Fin*) [*demand, interest rate*] efectivo
Ⓑ **effectives** NPL (*Mil*) efectivos *mpl*

effectively [ɪ'fektɪvlɪ] ADV 1 (= *efficiently*) [*treat, teach, work*] eficazmente, de manera eficaz; [*function*] de manera eficaz; **it's very difficult to treat this disease ~** es muy difícil tratar esta enfermedad eficazmente *or* de manera eficaz
2 (= *strikingly*) [*displayed, decorated, combined*] de manera impresionante, con mucho efecto
3 (= *in effect*) realmente, de hecho; **the contest was ~ won in the first five minutes** realmente *or* de hecho, el concurso estaba ganado en los primeros cinco minutos

effectiveness [ɪ'fektɪvnɪs] N 1 (= *efficiency*) [*of method, system*] eficacia *f*, eficiencia *f*; [*of treatment, deterrent, argument*] eficacia *f*
2 (= *striking quality*) efecto *m*

effectual [ɪ'fektjʊəl] ADJ eficaz

effectually [ɪ'fektjʊəlɪ] ADV (*frm*) eficazmente, con eficacia

effectuate [ɪ'fektjʊeɪt] VT (*frm*) efectuar, lograr

effeminacy [ɪ'femɪnəsɪ] N afeminación *f*, afeminamiento *m*

effeminate [ɪ'femɪnɪt] ADJ afeminado

effervesce [,efə'ves] VI 1 (*lit*) [*liquid*] estar en efervescencia; **to begin to ~** entrar en efervescencia
2 (*fig*) [*person*] rebosar vitalidad

effervescence [,efə'vesns] N efervescencia *f*

effervescent [,efə'vesnt] ADJ 1 (*lit*) efervescente
2 (*fig*) [*person*] rebosante de vitalidad

effete [ɪ'fi:t] ADJ agotado, cansado

effeteness [ɪ'fi:tnɪs] N cansancio *m*

efficacious [,efɪ'keɪʃəs] ADJ (*frm*) [*remedy, method*] eficaz, efectivo (**against** contra); **to be ~ in the treatment of sth** ser eficaz para *or* efectivo en el tratamiento de algo

efficacy ['efɪkəsɪ] N (*frm*) eficacia *f*

efficiency [ɪ'fɪʃənsɪ] N 1 [*of person, manager*] eficiencia *f*; [*of method, remedy, product, army*] eficacia *f*
2 (*Mech, Phys*) [*of machine*] rendimiento *m*

efficient [ɪ'fɪʃənt] ADJ 1 [*person, manager*] eficaz, eficiente; [*method, remedy, product, system*] eficaz; [*service, company, organization, army*] eficiente; **to be ~ at doing sth** ser eficiente a la hora de hacer algo
2 (*esp Mech, Phys*) [*machine*] de buen rendimiento

efficiently [ɪ'fɪʃəntlɪ] ADV 1 (= *competently, well*) eficientemente, de manera eficiente; **she works ~** trabaja eficientemente *or* de manera eficiente; **she dealt with my application very ~** tramitó mi solicitud de manera muy eficiente; **our muscles need oxygen to work ~** los músculos necesitan oxígeno para trabajar con eficacia; **the new machine works ~** la máquina nueva da un buen rendimiento
2 (= *effectively*) de manera eficaz; **use "Cleano" to banish stains ~** utilice "Cleano" para acabar con las manchas de manera eficaz

effigy ['efɪdʒɪ] N efigie *f*

effing‡ ['efɪŋ] ADJ (*Brit euph*) = **fucking**

effloresce [,eflə'res] VI (*Chem*) eflorescer

efflorescence [,eflə'resns] N 1 (*Chem, Med*) eflorescencia *f*; (*Bot*) floración *f*
2 (*fig*) (*liter*) florecimiento *m*, prosperidad *f*

efflorescent [,eflɔ:'resnt] ADJ eflorescente

effluent ['eflʊənt] N aguas *fpl* residuales

effluvium [e'flu:vɪəm] N (*pl* **effluviums** *or* **effluvia** [e'flu:vɪə]) efluvio *m*, emanación *f*, tufo *m*

effort ['efət] N 1 (= *hard work*) esfuerzo *m*; **all his ~ was directed to ...** todos sus esfuerzos iban dirigidos a ...; **it was an ~ to get up** ◊ **getting up was an ~** levantarse resultaba un esfuerzo; **put a bit of ~ into it!** ¡esfuérzate un poco!, ¡pon un poco más de esfuerzo!; **to spare no ~ to do sth** no regatear esfuerzos para hacer algo; **without ~** sin ningún esfuerzo; **it's not worth the ~** no merece la pena; **it's well worth the ~** merece la pena
2 (= *attempt*) intento *m*, tentativa *f*; **it's not bad for a first ~** no está mal para ser su primer intento *or* la primera vez que lo intenta; **a good ~** un feliz intento; **in an ~ to solve the problem/be polite** en un esfuerzo por resolver el problema/ser amable; **his latest ~** (*hum*) su último intento; **what did you think of his latest ~?** ¿qué te pareció su última obra?; **to make an ~ to do sth** esforzarse en hacer algo, hacer un esfuerzo por hacer algo; **he made no ~ to be polite** no hizo ningún esfuerzo por ser amable; **please make every ~ to come** haz un esfuerzo por venir; **thank you for making the ~ to be here** gracias por tomarse la molestia de venir; **it was a pretty poor ~** fue un intento bastante flojo; **the war ~** *los esfuerzos realizados por la población civil durante una guerra*

effortless ['efətlɪs] ADJ [*success, victory*] fácil; [*charm, superiority, grace*] natural; **she danced across the room with light, ~ movements** cruzó la habitación bailando con movimientos ligeros, hechos sin esfuerzo; **with ~ ease** sin ningún esfuerzo; **to make sth seem ~** hacer que algo parezca muy fácil; **an author renowned for his ~ style** un autor famoso por su estilo fluido

effortlessly ['efətlɪslɪ] ADV [*win, succeed*] fácilmente; [*move, lift*] sin ningún esfuerzo

effrontery [ɪ'frʌntərɪ] N descaro *m*; **he had the ~ to say that ...** tuvo el descaro de decir que ...

effusion [ɪ'fju:ʒən] N efusión *f*

effusive [ɪ'fju:sɪv] ADJ [*person, welcome, letter*] efusivo; **we were embarrassed by his ~ apologies** la efusividad con la que se disculpó nos hizo sentirnos violentos

effusively [ɪ'fju:sɪvlɪ] ADV efusivamente, con efusión

effusiveness [ɪ'fju:sɪvnɪs] N efusividad *f*

E-fit ['i:fɪt] N fotorrobot *f* digital, retrato *m* robot digital

EFL N ABBR = **English as a Foreign Language**; → TEFL/EFL, TESL/ESL, ELT, TESOL/ESOL

EFT N ABBR = **electronic funds transfer**

eft [eft] N tritón *m*

EFTA ['eftə] N ABBR (= **European Free Trade Association**) AELC *f*

EFTPOS N ABBR = **electronic funds transfer at point of sale**

EFTS N ABBR = **electronic funds transfer system**

e.g. ADV, ABBR = **exempli gratia** (= *for example*) p.ej.

EGA N ABBR = **enhanced graphics adaptor**

egalitarian [ɪ,gælɪ'tɛərɪən] ADJ igualitario

egalitarianism [ɪ,gælɪ'tɛərɪənɪzəm] N igualitarismo *m*

egg [eg] Ⓐ N 1 huevo *m*, blanquillo *m* (*Mex*); (= *cell*) óvulo *m*; **fried/scrambled/soft-boiled/hard-boiled ~** huevo *m* frito/revuelto/pasado por agua/duro; **boiled ~** huevo *m* pasado por agua, huevo *m* a la copa (*Andes, S. Cone*); ✦**IDIOMS** **to have ~ on one's face*** quedar en ridículo; **as sure as ~s are** *or* **is ~s** como que dos y dos son cuatro, sin ningún género de dudas; ✦**PROV** **don't put all your ~s in one basket** no te lo juegues todo a una carta
2 (*) (= *person*) **bad ~** sinvergüenza *mf*; **she's a good ~** es una buena persona
Ⓑ CPD ► **egg beater** N batidor *m* de huevos; (*US**) helicóptero *m* ► **egg cup** N huevera *f* ► **egg custard** N natillas *fpl* ► **egg flip** N ponche *m* (de huevo) ► **egg roll** N (= *sandwich*) panecito *m* de huevo duro; (= *paté*) *paté a base de huevo con carne de cerdo y legumbres* ► **egg timer** N reloj *m* de arena (*para cocer huevos*) ► **egg whisk** N batidor *m* de huevos ► **egg white** N clara *f* de huevo ► **egg yolk** N yema *f* de huevo

►**egg on** VT + ADV (= *urge*) incitar; **to ~ sb on to do sth** incitar a algn a hacer algo

egg-and-spoon race ['egən,spu:n,reɪs] N juego *m* del huevo con la cuchara

egghead* ['eghed] N (*pej*) (= *intellectual*) lumbrera *f*, intelectual *mf*

eggnog ['eg'nɒg] N yema *f* mejida, ponche *m* de huevo

eggplant ['egplɑ:nt] N (*esp US*) berenjena *f*

egg-shaped ['egʃeɪpt] ADJ en forma de huevo

eggshell ['egʃel] N cáscara *f* de huevo

egis ['i:dʒəs] (*US*) = **aegis**

eglantine ['egləntaɪn] N eglantina *f*

EGM N ABBR = **extraordinary general meeting**

ego ['i:gəʊ] Ⓐ N 1 (*Psych*) **the ~** el ego, el yo
2 (= *pride*) orgullo *m*; **to boost one's ~** alimentar el ego
Ⓑ CPD ► **ego trip*** N **to be on an ~ trip** creerse el centro del universo *or* el ombligo del mundo

egocentric [,egəʊ'sentrɪk] ADJ egocéntrico

egocentrical [,egəʊ'sentrɪkəl] ADJ = **egocentric**

egoism ['egəʊɪzəm] N egoísmo *m*

egoist ['egəʊɪst] N egoísta *mf*

egoistical [,egəʊ'ɪstɪkəl] ADJ egoísta

egomania [,i:gəʊ'meɪnɪə] N egocentrismo *m* exagerado

egomaniac [,egəʊ'meɪnɪæk] N ególatra *mf*

egosurf ['i:gəʊ,sɜ:f] VI buscarse en la Red

egotism ['egəʊtɪzəm] N egolatría *f*, egocentrismo *m*

egotist ['egəʊtɪst] N ególatra *mf*, egocéntrico(a) *m/f*

egotistic [,egəʊ'tɪstɪk] ADJ egotista

egotistical [,egəʊ'tɪstɪkəl] ADJ = **egotistic**

egregious [ɪ'gri:dʒəs] ADJ atroz, enorme; [*liar etc*] notorio

egress ['i:gres] N (*frm*) salida *f*

egret ['i:gret] N garceta *f*

Egypt ['i:dʒɪpt] N Egipto *m*

Egyptian [ɪˈdʒɪpʃən] Ⓐ ADJ egipcio
Ⓑ N egipcio/a *m/f*

Egyptologist [ˌiːdʒɪpˈtɒlədʒɪst] N egiptólogo/a *m/f*

Egyptology [ˌiːdʒɪpˈtɒlədʒɪ] N egiptología *f*

eh [eɪ] EXCL (= *please repeat*) ¿cómo?, ¿qué?; (*inviting assent*) ¿no?, ¿verdad?, ¿no es así?

EIB N ABBR (= **European Investment Bank**) BEI *m*

eider [ˈaɪdəʳ] N = **eider duck**

eiderdown [ˈaɪdədaʊn] N edredón *m*

eider duck [ˈaɪdəˈdʌk] N eider *m*, pato *m* de flojel

eidetic [aɪˈdetɪk] ADJ [*memory, vision*] eidético

Eiffel Tower [ˌaɪfəlˈtaʊəʳ] N torre *f* Eiffel

eight [eɪt] Ⓐ ADJ ocho; **she's ~** tiene ocho años
Ⓑ N ocho *m*; ✦*IDIOM* **he's had one over the ~*** lleva una copa de más; *see* **five** *for usage*

eighteen [ˈeɪˈtiːn] Ⓐ ADJ dieciocho; **she's ~** tiene dieciocho años
Ⓑ N dieciocho; *see* **five** *for usage*

eighteenth [ˈeɪˈtiːnθ] Ⓐ ADJ decimoctavo; **on her ~ birthday** cuando cumple/cumplió los dieciocho años
Ⓑ N decimoctavo/a *m/f*; (= *fraction*) decimoctava parte *f*, dieciochoavo *m*; *see* **fifth** *for usage*

eighth [eɪtθ] Ⓐ ADJ octavo; **the ~ floor** el octavo piso; **the ~ of August** el ocho de agosto; **~ note** (*US Mus*) corchea *f*
Ⓑ N octavo/a *m/f*; (= *fraction*) octava parte *f*, octavo *m*; *see* **fifth** *for usage*

eightieth [ˈeɪtɪɪθ] Ⓐ ADJ octogésimo; **the ~ anniversary** el ochenta aniversario
Ⓑ N octogésimo/a *m/f*; (= *fraction*) octogésima parte *f*, octogésimo *m*; *see* **fifth** *for usage*

eighty [ˈeɪtɪ] Ⓐ ADJ ochenta; **she's ~** tiene ochenta años
Ⓑ N ochenta *m*; **the eighties** los años ochenta; **to be in one's eighties** tener más de ochenta años; *see* **five** *for usage*

Eire [ˈɛərə] N Eire *m*, República *f* de Irlanda

EIS N ABBR (= **Educational Institute of Scotland**) *sindicato de profesores*

Eisteddfod [aɪsˈteðvɒd] N *festival galés en el que se celebran concursos de música y poesía*

EISTEDDFOD

En Gales un **eisteddfod** *es un concurso de poesía, canto, música y danza, en el que las canciones, los poemas y los relatos son mayormente en galés. Cada año tienen lugar muchos de estos* **eisteddfodau** *por todo Gales y el nivel de competición suele ser muy alto en los concursos más importantes. En Llangollen, al noreste de Gales, se celebra anualmente un concurso internacional en el que hay participantes de todo el mundo, pero el concurso principal, el* **National Eisteddfod** *se celebra en un lugar diferente cada año.*

▼**either** [ˈaɪðəʳ] Ⓐ ADJ 1 (= *one or other*) (*positive*) cualquiera de los dos; (*negative*) ninguno de los dos; **~ day would suit me** cualquiera de los dos días me viene bien; **I don't like ~ book** no me gusta ninguno de los dos libros; **you can do it ~ way** puedes hacerlo de este modo o del otro
2 (= *each*) cada; **in ~ hand** en cada mano; **on ~ side of the road** a ambos lados de la carretera
Ⓑ PRON (*positive*) cualquiera de los dos; (*negative*) ninguno de los dos; **"which bus will you take?" — "either"** —¿qué autobús vas a coger? —cualquiera de los dos; **give it to ~ of them** dáselo a cualquiera de los dos; **~ of us** cualquiera de nosotros; **I don't want ~ of them** no quiero ninguno de los dos; **I don't like ~ of them** no me gusta ninguno de los dos
Ⓒ CONJ **either ... or** o ... o; **~ come in or stay out** o entra o quédate fuera; **I have never been to ~ Paris or Rome** no he estado nunca ni en París ni en Roma; **you can have ~ ice cream or yoghurt** puedes tomar o helado o yogur
Ⓓ ADV tampoco; **he can't sing ~** tampoco sabe cantar; **no, I haven't ~** no, yo tampoco; **I don't like milk and I don't like eggs ~** no me gusta la leche y tampoco me gustan los huevos

➤ LANGUAGE IN USE: **either** C 26.2

ejaculate [ɪˈdʒækjʊleɪt] Ⓐ VT 1 (= *cry out*) exclamar
2 [+ *semen*] eyacular
Ⓑ VI (*Physiol*) eyacular

ejaculation [ɪˌdʒækjʊˈleɪʃən] N 1 (= *cry*) exclamación *f*
2 (*Physiol*) eyaculación *f*

ejaculatory [ɪˈdʒækjʊlətərɪ] ADJ (*Physiol*) eyaculador

eject [ɪˈdʒekt] Ⓐ VT (*Aer, Tech*) [+ *bomb, flames*] expulsar; [+ *cartridge*] expulsar, eyectar; [+ *troublemaker*] echar; [+ *tenant*] desahuciar
Ⓑ VI [*pilot*] eyectarse

ejection [ɪˈdʒekʃən] N expulsión *f*; [*of tenant*] desahucio *m*; [*of pilot*] eyección *f*

ejector [ɪˈdʒektəʳ] Ⓐ N (*Tech*) expulsor *m*
Ⓑ CPD ► **ejector seat** N (*Aer*) asiento *m* eyectable

eke [iːk] VT **to ~ out** [+ *food, supplies*] escatimar; [+ *money, income*] hacer que alcance; **to ~ out a living** ganarse la vida a duras penas

EKG N ABBR (*US*) = **ECG**

el* [el] N ABBR (*US*) = **elevated railroad**

elaborate [ɪˈlæbərɪt] Ⓐ ADJ [*design, hairstyle, costume, ceremony*] muy elaborado; [*plan*] detallado, muy elaborado; [*architecture*] con mucha ornamentación; [*furniture*] con muchos adornos, muy recargado; [*equipment, network, preparations*] complicado; [*meal*] muy complicado de hacer; [*excuse*] rebuscado; **an ~ hoax** un elaborado engaño
Ⓑ [ɪˈlæbəreɪt] VT 1 (= *develop*) [+ *plan, theory*] elaborar, desarrollar
2 (= *explain*) [+ *idea, point*] explicar en detalle, desarrollar
Ⓒ [ɪˈlæbəreɪt] VI **he refused to ~** se negó a dar más detalles; **would you care to ~?** ¿le importaría explicarlo de forma más detallada?; **he ~d on it** lo explicó con más detalles

elaborately [ɪˈlæbərɪtlɪ] ADV 1 (= *ornately*) [*decorated, carved, dressed*] de forma muy elaborada; [*describe*] de forma muy detallada, de forma muy minuciosa; [*bow*] con mucha afectación
2 (= *carefully*) [*planned*] cuidadosamente, minuciosamente

elaboration [ɪˌlæbəˈreɪʃən] N elaboración *f*

élan [eɪˈlɑːn, eɪˈlæn] N (*liter*) elán *m*

elapse [ɪˈlæps] VI pasar, transcurrir

elastic [ɪˈlæstɪk] Ⓐ ADJ elástico; (*fig*) flexible
Ⓑ N (*in garment*) elástico *m*, jebe *m* (*S. Cone*)
Ⓒ CPD ► **elastic band** N (*esp Brit*) gomita *f*, goma *f* elástica

elasticated [ɪˈlæstɪkeɪtɪd] ADJ (*Brit*) [*waist, waistband*] con elástico

elasticity [ˌiːlæsˈtɪsɪtɪ] N elasticidad *f*; (*fig*) flexibilidad *f*

Elastoplast® [ɪˈlæstəˌplɑːst] N esparadrapo *m*

elate [ɪˈleɪt] VT regocijar

elated [ɪˈleɪtɪd] ADJ (= *excited*) entusiasmado; (= *happy*) eufórico, alborozado

elation [ɪˈleɪʃən] N (= *excitement*) entusiasmo *m*; (= *happiness*) euforia *f*, alborozo *m*, júbilo *m*

Elba [ˈelbə] N Elba *f*

elbow [ˈelbəʊ] Ⓐ N (*Anat*) codo *m*; (*in road*) recodo *m*; **at one's ~** al alcance de la mano; **out at the ~(s)** raído, descosido; ✦*IDIOM* **he doesn't know his arse** *or* **ass from his ~**** confunde el culo con las témporas*
Ⓑ VT **to ~ sb aside** apartar a algn a codazos; **to ~ one's way through the crowd** abrirse paso a codazos por la muchedumbre
Ⓒ CPD ► **elbow grease*** N **it's a matter of ~ grease** es una cuestión de esfuerzo; **use a bit of ~ grease!** ¡dale con más fuerza!; **it will take a bit of ~ grease to shift this** va a costar trabajo mover esto ► **elbow joint** N articulación *f* del codo ► **elbow room** N (= *space*) espacio *m* para moverse; (= *leeway*) margen *m* de maniobra

elbow-rest [ˈelbəʊˌrest] N [*of chair*] brazo *m*

elder[1] [ˈeldəʳ] Ⓐ ADJ [*brother etc*] mayor; **my ~ sister** mi hermana mayor; **~ statesman** viejo estadista *m*; (*fig*) persona *f* respetada; **Pliny the Elder** Plinio el Viejo
Ⓑ N (= *senior*) mayor *m*; [*of tribe*] anciano *m*; (*in certain Protestant churches*) *persona laica que ejerce funciones educativas, pastorales y/o administrativas*; **my ~s** mis mayores; **don't criticize your ~s and betters** no critiques a tus mayores; → CHURCHES OF ENGLAND/SCOTLAND

elder[2] [ˈeldəʳ] N (*Bot*) saúco *m*

elderberry [ˈeldəˌberɪ] Ⓐ N baya *f* del saúco
Ⓑ CPD ► **elderberry wine** N vino *m* de saúco

elderly [ˈeldəlɪ] Ⓐ ADJ mayor, de edad; **an ~ gentleman** un señor mayor, un caballero de edad avanzada; **an ~ man** un anciano; **to be getting ~** ir para viejo
Ⓑ NPL **the ~** las personas mayores, los ancianos

eldest [ˈeldɪst] ADJ [*child*] mayor; **my ~ sister** mi hermana mayor; **he's the ~** él es el mayor; **the ~ of the four** el mayor de los cuatro

Eleanor [ˈelɪnəʳ] N Leonor

elec ABBR 1 = **electric**
2 = **electricity**

elect [ɪˈlekt] Ⓐ VT 1 (*Pol etc*) elegir (**to** para); **he was ~ed chairman** fue elegido presidente
2 (= *choose*) elegir; **he ~ed to remain** eligió quedarse
Ⓑ ADJ (*after noun*) electo; **the president ~** el/la presidente/a electo/a
Ⓒ N **the ~** los elegidos, los predestinados

elected [ɪˈlektɪd] ADJ elegido; **~ government** gobierno *m* elegido

election [ɪˈlekʃən] Ⓐ N (*gen*) elección *f*; **general ~** elecciones *fpl or* comicios *mpl* generales; **to call/hold an ~** convocar elecciones
Ⓑ CPD ► **election agent** N secretario/a *m/f* electoral ► **election campaign** N campaña *f* electoral ► **election day** N día *m* de las elecciones ► **election expenses** NPL gastos *mpl* de la campaña electoral ► **the election machine** N el aparato electoral

electioneer [ɪˌlekʃəˈnɪəʳ] VI hacer campaña (electoral); (*pej*) hacer electoralismo

electioneering [ɪˌlekʃəˈnɪərɪŋ] N campaña *f* electoral; (*pej*) electoralismo *m*

elective [ɪˈlektɪv] Ⓐ ADJ 1 (*Univ*) [*course*] optativo, opcional; [*assembly*] electivo
2 [*surgery*] optativo
Ⓑ N (*US Scol*) asignatura *f* optativa, optativa *f*

elector [ɪˈlektəʳ] N elector(a) *m/f*

electoral [ɪ'lektərəl] Ⓐ ADJ electoral
Ⓑ CPD ► **electoral college** N colegio *m* electoral ► **electoral register, electoral roll** N registro *m* electoral, censo *m* electoral (*Sp*) ► **electoral vote** N (*US Pol*) voto *m* electoral

ELECTORAL COLLEGE

*Los norteamericanos no votan directamente a su Presidente o a su vicepresidente, sino que votan a unos compromisarios (***electors***) que a su vez se comprometen a votar a determinados candidatos. Estos compromisarios conforman el* **electoral college***, tal y como se contempla en la Constitución. El número de votos que tiene un estado para elegir al Presidente es igual al de senadores y diputados. Cada partido político elige a un grupo de compromisarios y en el día de las elecciones presidenciales el pueblo vota al grupo que apoya al candidato de su elección. Como el grupo que gana usa todos los votos del estado para votar a su candidato, podría ocurrir, en teoría, que un candidato ganara el voto popular pero no las elecciones, si le han apoyado colegios electorales con un número pequeño de votos.*

electorally [ɪ'lektərəlɪ] ADV [*popular, damaging, disastrous*] desde el punto de vista electoral; [*compete, succeed*] (*gen*) electoralmente; (*in specific election*) en las elecciones

electorate [ɪ'lektərɪt] N electorado *m*

electric [ɪ'lektrɪk] Ⓐ ADJ [*appliance, current, motor*] eléctrico; **the atmosphere was ~** (*fig*) el ambiente era electrizante, el ambiente estaba cargado de electricidad
Ⓑ CPD [*blanket, cooker, fire, guitar, mixer, organ*] eléctrico ► **electric bill** N (*US*) factura *f* or (*Sp*) recibo *m* de la electricidad ► **electric blue** N azul *m* eléctrico ► **electric chair** N silla *f* eléctrica; **to go to the ~ chair** acabar en la silla eléctrica ► **electric charge** N carga *f* eléctrica ► **electric eel** N anguila *f* eléctrica ► **electric eye** N célula *f* fotoeléctrica ► **electric fence** N valla *f* electrificada, cercado *m* electrificado ► **electric field** N campo *m* eléctrico ► **electric kettle** N hervidora *f* de agua eléctrica ► **electric light** N luz *f* eléctrica ► **electric ray** N (*Zool*) torpedo *m* ► **electric shock** N (*from wire, socket*) descarga *f* eléctrica; (*from static electricity*) calambre *m*; **I got an ~ shock from the tap** el grifo me dio calambre ► **electric shock treatment** N tratamiento *m* por electrochoque ► **electric storm** N tormenta *f* eléctrica ► **electric window(s)** N(PL) (*Aut*) elevalunas *m inv* eléctrico

electrical [ɪ'lektrɪkəl] Ⓐ ADJ [*equipment, appliance, component, system*] eléctrico; **an ~ fault** un fallo (en el sistema) eléctrico; **household ~ goods** electrodomésticos *mpl*
Ⓑ CPD ► **electrical engineer** N (= *electrician*) técnico/a *m/f* electricista; (*with university degree*) ingeniero/a *m/f* electrotécnico/a ► **electrical engineering** N electrotecnia *f*; (*at university*) ingeniería *f* eléctrica ► **electrical failure** N fallo *m* eléctrico ► **electrical fitter** N técnico/a *m/f* electricista ► **electrical fittings** NPL accesorios *mpl* eléctricos ► **electrical storm** N tormenta *f* eléctrica ► **electrical tape** N cinta *f* aislante ► **electrical wiring** N instalación *f* eléctrica

electrically [ɪ'lektrɪkəlɪ] ADV **~ charged** cargado de electricidad; **to be ~ controlled** controlarse eléctricamente; **to be ~ driven/powered** funcionar eléctricamente; **to be ~ operated** manejarse eléctricamente *or* por medio de la electricidad, funcionar eléctricamente

electric-blue [ɪ,lektrɪk'bluː] ADJ (de color) azul eléctrico

electrician [ɪlek'trɪʃən] N electricista *mf*

electricity [ɪlek'trɪsɪtɪ] Ⓐ N electricidad *f*; **to switch on/off the ~** encender/apagar la electricidad *or* la luz
Ⓑ CPD ► **electricity bill** N (*Brit*) factura *f or* (*Sp*) recibo *m* de la electricidad ► **electricity board** N (*Brit*) compañía *f* eléctrica, compañía *f* de luz (*LAm*) ► **electricity dispute** N conflicto *m* del sector eléctrico

electrics* [ɪ'lektrɪks] NPL **the ~** (*Brit*) [*of car, appliance*] el sistema eléctrico; [*of building*] la instalación eléctrica

electrification [ɪ'lektrɪfɪ'keɪʃən] N electrificación *f*

electrify [ɪ'lektrɪfaɪ] VT [1] (= *charge with electricity*) [+ *railway system*] electrificar; **electrified fence** valla *f* electrificada, cercado *m* eléctrico
[2] (*fig*) electrizar

electrifying [ɪ'lektrɪfaɪɪŋ] ADJ [*performance*] electrizante

electro... [ɪ,lektrəʊ] PREFIX electro...

electrocardiogram [ɪ,lektrəʊ'kɑːdɪəgræm] N electrocardiograma *m*

electrocardiograph [ɪ,lektrəʊ'kɑːdɪəgræf] N electrocardiógrafo *m*

electrochemical [ɪ,lektrəʊ'kemɪkəl] ADJ electroquímico

electrochemistry [ɪ,lektrəʊ'kemɪstrɪ] N electroquímica *f*

electroconvulsive therapy [ɪ,lektrəʊkən-vʌlsɪv''θerəpɪ] N electroterapia *f*; *see* **ECT**

electrocute [ɪ'lektrəʊkjuːt] VT electrocutar

electrocution [ɪ,lektrəʊ'kjuːʃən] N electrocución *f*

electrode [ɪ'lektrəʊd] N electrodo *m*

electrodialysis [ɪ,lektrəʊdaɪ'æləsɪs] N electrodiálisis *f*

electrodynamic [ɪ,lektrəʊdaɪ'næmɪk] ADJ electrodinámico

electrodynamics [ɪ'lektrəʊdaɪ'næmɪks] NSING electrodinámica *f*

electroencephalogram [ɪ,lektrəʊen-'sefələ,græm] N electroencefalograma *m*

electroencephalograph [ɪ'lektrəʊɪn-'sefələgrɑːf] N electroencefalógrafo *m*

electrolyse [ɪ'lektrəʊ,laɪz] VT electrolizar

electrolysis [ɪlek'trɒlɪsɪs] N electrólisis *f inv*

electrolyte [ɪ'lektrəʊ,laɪt] N electrolito *m*

electromagnet [ɪ'lektrəʊ'mægnɪt] N electroimán *m*

electromagnetic [ɪ'lektrəʊmæg'netɪk] ADJ electromagnético

electromagnetism [ɪ,lektrəʊ'mægnɪtɪzəm] N electromagnetismo *m*

electromechanical [ɪ,lektrəʊmɪ'kænɪkəl] ADJ electromecánico

electromechanics [ɪ,lektrəʊmɪ'kænɪks] NSING electromecánica *f*

electrometallurgy [ɪ,lektrəʊmɪ'tælədʒɪ] N electrometalurgia *f*

electrometer [ɪlek'trɒmɪtə^r] N electrómetro *m*

electromotive [ɪ,lektrəʊ'məʊtɪv] ADJ electromotor

electron [ɪ'lektrɒn] Ⓐ N electrón *m*
Ⓑ CPD ► **electron camera** N cámara *f* electrónica ► **electron gun** N cañón *m* de electrones ► **electron microscope** N microscopio *m* electrónico

electronic [ɪlek'trɒnɪk] Ⓐ ADJ [*equipment, circuit, information, signal*] electrónico; **the ~ age** la edad de la electrónica
Ⓑ CPD ► **electronic banking** N banca *f* informatizada ► **electronic data processing** N procesamiento *m* electrónico de datos ► **electronic engineer** N ingeniero/a *m/f* electrónico/a ► **electronic engineering** N ingeniería *f* electrónica ► **electronic funds transfer** N transferencia *f* electrónica de fondos ► **electronic mail** N correo *m* electrónico ► **electronic mailbox** N buzón *m* electrónico ► **electronic music** N música *f* electrónica ► **electronic news gathering** N recogida *f* electrónica de noticias ► **electronic point of sale** N punto *m* de venta electrónico ► **electronic publishing** N edición *f* electrónica ► **electronic shopping** N compra *f* computerizada ► **electronic surveillance** N vigilancia *f* electrónica ► **electronic tagging** N etiquetado *m* electrónico

electronically [ɪlek'trɒnɪklɪ] ADV electrónicamente

electronics [ɪlek'trɒnɪks] Ⓐ NSING (= *science*) electrónica *f*
Ⓑ NPL [*of machine*] componentes *mpl* electrónicos
Ⓒ CPD ► **electronics engineer** N ingeniero/a *m/f* electrónico/a ► **electronics industry** N industria *f* electrónica ► **electronics manufacturer** N fabricante *mf* de productos electrónicos

electrophysiological [ɪ,lektrəʊ,fɪzɪə'lɒdʒɪkəl] ADJ electrofisiológico

electrophysiology [ɪ,lektrəʊ,fɪzɪ'ɒlədʒɪ] N electrofisiología *f*

electroplate [ɪ'lektrəʊpleɪt] VT galvanizar, electrochapar

electroplated [ɪ'lektrəʊpleɪtɪd] ADJ galvanizado, electrochapado

electroplating [ɪ'lektrəʊpleɪtɪŋ] N (= *process*) galvanoplastia *f*

electroshock therapy [ɪ,lektrəʊʃɒk'θerəpɪ] N electroterapia *f*

electroshock treatment [ɪ,lektrəʊʃɒk'triːt-mənt] N electrochoque *m*

electrostatic [ɪ,lektrəʊ'stætɪk] ADJ electrostático

electrostatics [ɪ,lektrəʊ'stætɪks] NSING electrostática *f*

electrosurgery [ɪ,lektrəʊ'sɜːdʒərɪ] N electrocirugía *f*

electrosurgical [ɪ,lektrəʊ'sɜːdʒɪkəl] ADJ electroquirúrgico

electrotechnological [ɪ,lektrəʊ,teknə'lɒdʒɪkəl] ADJ electrotecnológico

electrotechnology [ɪ,lektrəʊtek'nɒlədʒɪ] N electrotecnología *f*

electrotherapeutic [ɪ,lektrəʊ,θerə'pjuːtɪk] ADJ electroterapéutico

electrotherapeutics [ɪ,lektrəʊ,θerə'pjuːtɪks] N electroterapia *f*

electrotherapist [ɪ,lektrəʊ'θerəpɪst] N electroterapeuta *mf*

electrotherapy [ɪ,lektrəʊ'θerəpɪ] N electroterapia *f*

electrotype [ɪ'lektrəʊ,taɪp] Ⓐ N electrotipo *m*
Ⓑ VT electrotipar

elegance ['elɪgəns] N elegancia *f*

elegant ['elɪgənt] ADJ [1] (= *stylish*) [*person, clothes, movement*] elegante; **she looked very ~** estaba muy elegante
[2] (= *polished*) [*writer, style, writing*] elegante

elegantly ['elɪgəntlɪ] ADV [1] [*move, dance, dress, furnish*] con elegancia, elegantemente;

an ~ simple room una habitación de una elegancia sencilla; **an ~ simple idea** una idea simple e inteligente
2 *[written, described]* con elegancia

elegiac [ˌelɪˈdʒaɪək] ADJ elegíaco

elegy [ˈelɪdʒɪ] N elegía *f*

element [ˈelɪmənt] N 1 *(gen, Chem)* elemento *m*; *(Elec)* resistencia *f*; (= *factor*) factor *m*; **an ~ of surprise** un elemento de sorpresa; **an ~ of truth** una parte de verdad; **it's the personal ~ that counts** es el factor personal el que cuenta; ✦**IDIOMS to be in one's ~** estar en su elemento, estar como pez en el agua; **to be out of one's ~** estar fuera de su elemento
2 **elements** 2·1 (= *rudiments*) elementos *mpl*, nociones *fpl* básicas; **the ~s of mathematics** las nociones básicas de las matemáticas
2·2 (= *weather*) **open to the ~s** a la intemperie; **to brave the ~s** arrostrar la tempestad; (= *go out*) salir a la intemperie

elemental [ˌelɪˈmentl] ADJ elemental

elementary [ˌelɪˈmentərɪ] Ⓐ ADJ 1 (= *basic*) *[idea, precautions, rules]* elemental, básico; **~ politeness requires that ...** la cortesía más elemental requiere que ...; **~, my dear Watson!** ¡elemental, querido Watson!
2 (= *introductory*) *[maths, level, exercises]* elemental, básico; **~ reading and writing skills** habilidades *fpl* de lectura y escritura básicas
Ⓑ CPD ► **elementary education** N *(US)* enseñanza *f* primaria ► **elementary particle** N partícula *f* elemental ► **elementary school** N *(US)* escuela *f* de enseñanza primaria ► **elementary student** N *(US)* alumno/a *m/f* de (la escuela) primaria ► **elementary teacher** N *(US)* maestro/a *m/f* de (enseñanza) primaria

elephant [ˈelɪfənt] N *(pl* **elephants** *or* **elephant***)* elefante *m*; *see also* **white C**

elephantiasis [ˌelɪfənˈtaɪəsɪs] N elefantiasis *f inv*

elephantine [ˌelɪˈfæntaɪn] ADJ *(fig)* elefantino

elevate [ˈelɪveɪt] VT 1 *(lit)* (= *raise*) elevar
2 *(in rank)* ascender (**to** a); *(Rel)* alzar; *(fig)* elevar

elevated [ˈelɪveɪtɪd] Ⓐ ADJ *(lit)* elevado; *(fig)* elevado, sublime
Ⓑ CPD ► **elevated railway** *(US)*, **elevated railroad** *(US)* N ferrocarril *m* urbano elevado

elevating [ˈelɪveɪtɪŋ] ADJ *[reading]* enriquecedor

elevation [ˌelɪˈveɪʃən] N 1 *(lit)* (= *act*) elevación *f*
2 *(in rank)* ascenso *m*; *(fig)* elevación *f*
3 *[of style]* sublimidad *f*
4 (= *hill*) elevación *f*; (= *height*) *(esp above sea level)* altitud *f*
5 *(Archit)* alzado *m*

elevator [ˈelɪveɪtəʳ] Ⓐ N 1 *(US)* (= *lift*) ascensor *m*, elevador *m (Mex)*
2 (= *hoist for goods*) montacargas *m inv*
3 *(Aer)* timón *m* de profundidad
4 *(Agr)* elevador *m* de granos
5 *(US)* *(also* **~ shoe***)* zapato *m* de tacón alto
Ⓑ CPD ► **elevator car** N *(US)* caja *f or* cabina *f* de ascensor ► **elevator shaft** N *(US)* hueco *m* del ascensor

eleven [ɪˈlevn] Ⓐ ADJ once
Ⓑ N once *m*; *(Sport)* once *m*, alineación *f*; **the ~ plus** *(Brit Scol)* *(formerly)* *examen selectivo realizado por niños mayores de 11 años*; *see* **five** *for usage*

elevenses* [ɪˈlevnzɪz] NPL *(Brit)* tentempié *m* de las once, onces *fpl (LAm)*; **to have ~** tomar un tentempié a las once, tomar las onces *(LAm)*

eleventh [ɪˈlevnθ] Ⓐ ADJ undécimo; ✦**IDIOM at the ~ hour** a última hora
Ⓑ N undécimo/a *m/f*; (= *fraction*) undécima parte *f*, onceavo *m*; *see* **fifth** *for usage*

elf [elf] N *(pl* **elves***)* duende *m*, elfo *m*; *(Nordic Myth)* elfo *m*

elfin [ˈelfɪn] ADJ de duende(s), mágico; *(Nordic Myth)* de elfo(s)

Elgin Marbles [ˈelgɪnˈmɑːblz] NPL **the ~** los mármoles del Partenón

elicit [ɪˈlɪsɪt] VT [+ *interest*] suscitar; [+ *reaction*] provocar; **to ~ sth (from sb)** [+ *reply, support, information*] obtener algo (de algn); **my comment ~ed no response from him** no respondió a mi comentario

elide [ɪˈlaɪd] Ⓐ VT *[vowel, syllable]* elidir
Ⓑ VI *[vowel, syllable]* elidirse

eligibility [ˌelɪdʒəˈbɪlɪtɪ] N elegibilidad *f*

eligible [ˈelɪdʒəbl] ADJ elegible; (= *desirable*) deseable, atractivo; **to be ~ for** (= *suitable*) cumplir los requisitos para; (= *entitled*) tener derecho a; **an ~ young man** un buen partido; **he's the most ~ bachelor in town** es el soltero más cotizado de la ciudad

Elijah [ɪˈlaɪdʒə] N Elías

eliminate [ɪˈlɪmɪneɪt] VT *(gen)* eliminar; [+ *suspect, possibility*] descartar; [+ *bad language, mistakes, details*] suprimir, eliminar

elimination [ɪˌlɪmɪˈneɪʃən] Ⓐ N (= *suppression*) supresión *f*, eliminación *f*; (= *being eliminated*) eliminación *f*; **by process of ~** por eliminación
Ⓑ CPD ► **elimination round** N eliminatoria *f*

eliminator [ɪˈlɪmɪneɪtəʳ] N *(Boxing)* combate *m* eliminatorio

Elishah [ɪˈlaɪʃə] N Elíseo

elision [ɪˈlɪʒən] N elisión *f*

elite, élite [eɪˈliːt] Ⓐ N élite *f*
Ⓑ CPD *[group, unit, force]* de élite; *[school, university]* de élite, exclusivo

elitism [ɪˈliːtɪzəm] N elitismo *m*

elitist [ɪˈliːtɪst] Ⓐ ADJ elitista
Ⓑ N elitista *mf*

elixir [ɪˈlɪksəʳ] N elixir *m*

Elizabeth [ɪˈlɪzəbəθ] N Isabel

Elizabethan [ɪˌlɪzəˈbiːθən] Ⓐ ADJ isabelino
Ⓑ N isabelino/a *m/f*

elk [elk] N *(pl* **elk** *or* **elks***)* *(Zool)* alce *m*

ellipse [ɪˈlɪps] N elipse *f*

ellipsis [ɪˈlɪpsɪs] N *(pl* **ellipses** [ɪˈlɪpsiːz]*)* (= *omission*) elipsis *f inv*; (= *dots*) puntos *mpl* suspensivos

elliptic [ɪˈlɪptɪk] ADJ = **elliptical**

elliptical [ɪˈlɪptɪkəl] ADJ elíptico

elliptically [ɪˈlɪptɪkəlɪ] ADV de manera elíptica

elm [elm] N *(also* **~ tree***)* olmo *m*

elocution [ˌeləˈkjuːʃən] N elocución *f*

elocutionist [ˌeləˈkjuːʃənɪst] N profesor(a) *m/f* de elocución, recitador(a) *m/f*

elongate [ˈiːlɒŋgeɪt] VT [+ *material, object*] alargar, extender

elongated [ˈiːlɒŋgeɪtɪd] ADJ alargado

elongation [ˌiːlɒŋˈgeɪʃən] N (= *act*) alargamiento *m*; (= *part elongated*) extensión *f*

elope [ɪˈləʊp] VI *[two persons]* fugarse para casarse; **to ~ with sb** *[one person]* fugarse con algn

elopement [ɪˈləʊpmənt] N fuga *f*

eloquence [ˈeləkwəns] N elocuencia *f*

eloquent [ˈeləkwənt] ADJ *[person, speech]* elocuente; *[gesture, look, silence]* revelador, elocuente; **his lawyer made an ~ plea for leniency** su abogado solicitó con elocuencia que el juez fuese indulgente; **to be ~ proof of sth** ser una prueba fehaciente de algo; *see also* **wax²**

eloquently [ˈeləkwəntlɪ] ADV *[speak, express]* con elocuencia, elocuentemente; *[write, demonstrate]* elocuentemente; *[nod, smile]* de manera elocuente

El Salvador [elˈsælvədɔːʳ] N El Salvador

else [els] ADV 1 *(after pron)* **all ~** todo lo demás; **anybody ~** cualquier otro; **anybody ~ would do it** cualquier otro lo haría; **I don't know anyone ~ here** aquí no conozco a nadie más; **anything ~: anything ~ is impossible** cualquier otra cosa es imposible; **have you anything ~ to tell me?** ¿tienes algo más que decirme?; **anything ~, sir?** *(in shop)* ¿algo más, señor?; **anywhere ~** en cualquier otro sitio; **everyone ~** todos los demás; **everything ~** todo lo demás; **nobody ~** nadie más; **nobody ~ knows** no lo sabe nadie más; **nothing ~** nada más; **there was nothing ~ I could do** no había otro remedio; **nothing ~, thank you** *(in shop)* nada más, gracias, es todo, gracias; **nowhere ~** en ningún otro sitio; **somebody ~** otra persona; **somebody ~'s coat** el abrigo de otro; **there's somebody ~, isn't there?** hay alguien más, ¿verdad?; **something ~** otra cosa; (*) (= *wonderful*) estupendo; **somewhere ~** en otro sitio, en otra parte
2 *(after interrog)* **how ~?** ¿de qué otra manera?; **what ~ ...?** ¿qué más ...?; **where ~ ...?** ¿en qué otro sitio ...?, ¿dónde más ...? *(LAm)*; **where ~ can he have gone?** ¿a qué otro sitio habrá podido ir?; **who ~ ...?** ¿quién si no ...?, ¿quién más ...?; **who ~ could do it as well as you?** ¿quién si no *or* quién más podría hacerlo tan bien como usted?
3 *(adv of quantity)* **there is little ~ to be done** poco se puede hacer aparte de eso; **he said that, and much ~** dijo eso y mucho más
4 (= *otherwise*) **or ~** si no; **red or ~ black** rojo o bien negro; **or ~ I'll do it** si no, lo hago yo; **keep quiet or ~ go away** cállate o vete; **do as I say, or ~!*** *(expressing threat)* ¡haz lo que te digo o si no verás!
5 *(standing alone)* **how could I have done it ~?** ¿de qué otro modo hubiera podido hacerlo?

elsewhere [ˈelsˈwɛəʳ] ADV *[be]* en otra parte, en otro sitio; *[go, send]* a otra parte, a otro sitio; **the document must be ~** el documento debe estar en otra parte *or* en otro sitio; **her thoughts were ~** tenía la cabeza en otra parte; **conditions are worse ~ in the country** las condiciones son peores en otros lugares *or* en otras partes del país; **we had to look ~ for entertainment** tuvimos que buscar diversión en otra parte

ELT N ABBR = **English Language Teaching**; *see* **English C** → TEFL/EFL, TESL/ESL, ELT, TESOL/ESOL

elucidate [ɪˈluːsɪdeɪt] VT aclarar, elucidar

elucidation [ɪˌluːsɪˈdeɪʃən] N aclaración *f*, elucidación *f*

elude [ɪˈluːd] VT [+ *pursuer*] burlar; [+ *capture, arrest*] eludir, escapar a; [+ *grasp, blow*] esquivar, zafarse de; [+ *question*] eludir; [+ *obligation*] eludir, zafarse de; **the answer has so far ~d us** hasta ahora no hemos dado con la respuesta; **his name ~s me** ahora no recuerdo su nombre; **success has ~d him** el éxito le ha eludido *or* le ha sido esquivo

elusive [ɪˈluːsɪv] ADJ *[prey, enemy]* esquivo, escurridizo; *[thoughts, word]* inaprensible; *[success]* esquivo, difícil de conseguir; **he is very ~** no es fácil encontrarlo

elusively [ɪ'lu:sɪvlɪ] ADV **to behave ~** comportarse de manera esquiva; **... he said ~** ... dijo, esquivo, ... dijo, mostrándose esquivo

elusiveness [ɪ'lu:sɪvnɪs] N carácter *m* esquivo

elusory [ɪ'lu:sərɪ] = **elusive**

elver ['elvəʳ] N angula *f*

elves [elvz] NPL *of* **elf**

Elysium [ɪ'lɪzɪəm] N Elíseo *m*

EM N ABBR (*US*) 1 = **Engineer of Mines**
2 = **enlisted man**

emaciated [ɪ'meɪsɪeɪtɪd] ADJ demacrado; **to become ~** demacrarse

emaciation [ɪ,meɪsɪ'eɪʃən] N demacración *f*

e-mail, **email** ['i:meɪl] Ⓐ N email *m*, correo *m* electrónico
Ⓑ VT **to ~ sb** mandar un email *or* un correo electrónico a algn; **to ~ sth to sb** ◊ **~ sb sth** mandar algo a algn por Internet, mandar algo a algn en un email *or* en un correo electrónico
Ⓒ CPD ► **e-mail account** N cuenta *f* de correo ► **e-mail address** N email *m*, dirección *f* electrónica; **"my ~ address is jones at collins dot uk"** (*jones@collins.uk*) —mi email *or* dirección electrónica es jones arroba collins punto uk

emanate ['eməneɪt] VI **to ~ from** [*idea, proposal*] surgir de; [*light, smell*] emanar de, proceder de

emanation [,emə'neɪʃən] N emanación *f*

emancipate [ɪ'mænsɪpeɪt] VT [+ *women, slaves*] emancipar; (*fig*) liberar

emancipated [ɪ'mænsɪpeɪtɪd] ADJ [*women, slaves*] emancipado; (*fig*) libre

emancipation [ɪ,mænsɪ'peɪʃən] N [*of women, slaves*] emancipación *f*; (*fig*) liberación *f*

emasculate [ɪ'mæskjʊleɪt] VT castrar, emascular (*frm*); (*fig*) mutilar, estropear

emasculated [ɪ'mæskjʊleɪtɪd] ADJ castrado, emasculado; (*fig*) [*text, film*] mutilado; [*style*] empobrecido

embalm [ɪm'bɑ:m] VT embalsamar

embalmer [ɪm'bɑ:məʳ] N embalsamador(a) *m/f*

embalming [ɪm'bɑ:mɪŋ] Ⓐ N embalsamamiento *m* Ⓑ CPD ► **embalming fluid** N líquido *m* embalsamador

embankment [ɪm'bæŋkmənt] N [*of path, railway*] terraplén *m*; [*of canal, river*] dique *m*

embargo [ɪm'bɑ:gəʊ] Ⓐ N (*pl* **embargoes**) (*Comm, Naut*) embargo *m*; (= *prohibition*) prohibición *f* (**on** de); **there is an ~ on arms** está prohibido comerciar con armas, hay un embargo del comercio de armas; **there is an ~ on that subject** está prohibido discutir ese asunto; **to lift an ~** levantar un embargo *or* una prohibición; **to put an ~ on sth** establecer un embargo sobre algo, embargar algo; (*fig*) (= *prohibit*) prohibir algo; **to be under (an) ~** estar embargado
Ⓑ VT prohibir; (*Jur*) embargar

embark [ɪm'bɑ:k] Ⓐ VT embarcar
Ⓑ VI (*Naut, Aer*) embarcarse (**for** con rumbo a; **on** en); **to ~ on** [+ *journey*] emprender; [+ *business venture, explanation, discussion*] lanzarse a, embarcarse en

embarkation [,embɑ:'keɪʃən] Ⓐ N [*of goods*] embarque *m*; [*of people*] embarco *m*
Ⓑ CPD ► **embarkation card** N tarjeta *f* de embarque

embarrass [ɪm'bærəs] VT hacer pasar vergüenza a, avergonzar, apenar (*LAm*); **you seem to enjoy ~ing me** parece que disfrutas haciéndome pasar vergüenza *or* avergonzándome; **I was ~ed by the question** la pregunta me avergonzó, la pregunta hizo sentirme violenta; **his decision could ~ the government** su decisión podría poner al gobierno en una situación embarazosa *or* comprometida

embarrassed [ɪm'bærəst] ADJ [*silence*] violento, incómodo; [*laugh*] nervioso; **to be ~: I was so ~!** ¡me dio tanta vergüenza!, ¡me sentí tan violento!; **many people are ~ about discussing their age** a mucha gente le da vergüenza hablar de su edad; **it's nothing to be ~ about** no hay por qué avergonzarse; **I feel ~ when I have to speak in public** me da vergüenza cuando tengo que hablar en público, me da corte cuando tengo que hablar en público (*Sp**); **to be financially ~** estar *or* andar mal de dinero, tener dificultades económicas; **he sang so badly I was** *or* **felt ~ for him** cantó tan mal que sentí vergüenza ajena; **she was ~ to be seen with him** le daba vergüenza que la vieran con él, le daba corte que la vieran con él (*Sp**)

embarrassing [ɪm'bærəsɪŋ] ADJ [*experience, situation*] embarazoso, violento; [*question, mistake*] embarazoso; [*performance*] penoso; **that was an ~ moment for me** pasé muchísima vergüenza, fue un momento muy embarazoso; **he finds it ~ to talk about himself** le da vergüenza hablar de sí mismo, le resulta violento hablar de sí mismo, le da corte hablar de sí mismo (*Sp**); **he has put the government in an ~ position** (= *awkward*) ha puesto al gobierno en una situación embarazosa *or* comprometida; **he tries to dance like a teenager - it's ~ to watch** intenta bailar como un quinceañero - da vergüenza ajena verlo

embarrassingly [ɪm'bærəsɪŋlɪ] ADV [*fail, flop*] de manera vergonzosa, bochornosamente; **there were ~ few people** era vergonzoso la poca gente que había; **her acting was ~ bad** actuó de pena*

embarrassment [ɪm'bærəsmənt] N 1 (= *state*) vergüenza *f*, pena *f* (*LAm*); **I am in a state of some ~** mi situación es algo delicada; **financial ~** dificultades *fpl* económicas; **to have an ~ of riches** tener mucho donde elegir
2 (= *cause*) molestia *f*, vergüenza *f*; **you are an ~ to us** eres un estorbo para nosotros

embassy ['embəsɪ] N embajada *f*; **the British Embassy in Rome** la embajada británica en Roma; **the Spanish Embassy** la embajada de España

embattled [ɪm'bætld] ADJ [*army*] en orden de batalla; [*city*] sitiado

embed [ɪm'bed] VT [+ *weapon, teeth*] clavar, hincar (**in** en); [+ *jewel*] engastar, incrustar; (*Ling*) incrustar; **it is ~ded in my memory** lo tengo clavado en la memoria; **to ~ itself in** empotrarse en

embedding [ɪm'bedɪŋ] N (*gen, Ling*) incrustación *f*

embellish [ɪm'belɪʃ] VT (= *decorate*) embellecer (**with** con); (*fig*) [+ *story, truth*] adornar (**with** con)

embellishment [ɪm'belɪʃmənt] N embellecimiento *m*; (*fig*) adorno *m*

ember ['embəʳ] N brasa *f*, ascua *f*; **the dying ~s** el rescoldo

embezzle [ɪm'bezl] VT [+ *funds, money*] malversar, desfalcar

embezzlement [ɪm'bezlmənt] N malversación *f* (de fondos), desfalco *m*

embezzler [ɪm'bezləʳ] N malversador(a) *m/f*, desfalcador(a) *m/f*

embitter [ɪm'bɪtəʳ] VT [+ *person*] amargar; [+ *relationship, dispute*] envenenar

embittered [ɪm'bɪtəd] ADJ resentido, amargado; **to be very ~** estar muy amargado, estar muy resentido (**about** por; **against** contra)

embittering [ɪm'bɪtərɪŋ] ADJ [*experience*] amargo

embitterment [ɪm'bɪtəmənt] N amargura *f*

emblazon [ɪm'bleɪzən] VT engalanar *or* esmaltar con colores brillantes; (*fig*) escribir *or* adornar de modo llamativo

emblem ['embləm] N emblema *m*

emblematic [,emblɪ'mætɪk] ADJ emblemático

embodiment [ɪm'bɒdɪmənt] N encarnación *f*; **to be the very ~ of virtue** ser la encarnación de la virtud, ser la virtud en persona

embody [ɪm'bɒdɪ] VT 1 [+ *spirit, quality*] encarnar; [+ *idea, thought, theory*] expresar, plasmar (**in** en)
2 (= *include*) incorporar (**in** en)

embolden [ɪm'bəʊldən] VT **to ~ sb to do sth** animar a algn a hacer algo, envalentonar a algn para que haga algo

embolism ['embəlɪzəm] N (*Med*) embolia *f*

emboss [ɪm'bɒs] VT [+ *metal, leather*] repujar; [+ *paper*] gofrar, estampar (en relieve); **~ed with the royal arms** con el escudo real en relieve

embossed [ɪm'bɒst] ADJ [*writing paper*] con membretes en relieve; [*metal, velvet, leather*] repujado, labrado; [*wallpaper*] labrado

embouchure [,ɒmbʊ'ʃʊəʳ] N (*Mus*) boquilla *f*

embrace [ɪm'breɪs] Ⓐ N abrazo *m*
Ⓑ VT 1 [+ *person*] abrazar
2 [+ *offer*] aceptar; [+ *opportunity*] aprovechar; [+ *course of action*] adoptar; [+ *doctrine, party*] adherirse a; [+ *religion*] abrazar; [+ *cause, profession*] dedicarse a
3 (= *include*) abarcar
Ⓒ VI abrazarse

embrasure [ɪm'breɪʒəʳ] N (*Archit*) alféizar *m*; (*Mil*) tronera *f*, aspillera *f*

embrocation [,embrəʊ'keɪʃən] N embrocación *f*, linimento *m*

embroider [ɪm'brɔɪdəʳ] Ⓐ VT 1 (= *sew*) bordar
2 (*fig*) (= *embellish*) [+ *truth, facts, story*] adornar
Ⓑ VI bordar

embroidered [ɪm'brɔɪdəd] ADJ 1 [*silk, linen, tablecloth*] bordado; **~ in silk** bordado en seda
2 (*fig*) [*story, version*] adornado

embroidery [ɪm'brɔɪdərɪ] Ⓐ N bordado *m*; **I do ~ in the afternoon** bordo por las tardes
Ⓑ CPD ► **embroidery frame** N bastidor *m*, tambor *m* de bordar ► **embroidery silk** N hilo *m* de bordar ► **embroidery thread** N = **embroidery silk**

embroil [ɪm'brɔɪl] VT enredar; **to ~ sb in sth** enredar a algn en algo; **to ~ o.s. in sth** ◊ **get ~ed in sth** enredarse en algo; **to ~ sb with** indisponer a algn con; **to ~ A with B** mezclar a A con B

embroilment [ɪm'brɔɪlmənt] N embrollo *m*

embryo ['embrɪəʊ] Ⓐ N embrión *m*; (*fig*) germen *m*, embrión *m*; **in ~** en embrión
Ⓑ CPD [*research*] embrionario

embryologist [,embrɪ'ɒlədʒɪst] N embriólogo/a *m/f*

embryology [,embrɪ'ɒlədʒɪ] N embriología *f*

embryonic [,embrɪ'ɒnɪk] ADJ embrionario

emcee ['em'si:] (*US*) Ⓐ N presentador(a) *m/f*
Ⓑ VT presentar; **to ~ a show** presentar un espectáculo

EMCF N ABBR (= **European Monetary Cooperation Fund**) FECOM *m*

em dash ['emdæʃ] N (*Typ*) raya *f*

emend [ɪ'mend] VT enmendar

emendation [ˌiːmen'deɪʃən] N enmienda *f*

emerald ['emərəld] (A) N (= *stone*) esmeralda *f*; (= *colour*) verde *m* esmeralda
(B) ADJ (*also* ~ **green**) verde esmeralda
(C) CPD [*necklace, bracelet, ring*] de esmeraldas
► **the Emerald Isle** N la verde Irlanda

emerge [ɪ'mɜːdʒ] VI salir (**from** de); [*truth*] saberse, resplandecer; [*facts, problems*] surgir, presentarse; [*theory, new nation*] surgir; **it ~s that** resulta que; **what has ~d from this inquiry?** ¿qué se saca de esta investigación?

emergence [ɪ'mɜːdʒəns] N aparición *f*

emergency [ɪ'mɜːdʒənsɪ] (A) N [1] (*gen*) emergencia *f*; **quick! this is an ~!** ¡rápido! ¡es una emergencia!; **prepared for any ~** preparado para cualquier emergencia, prevenido contra toda eventualidad (*frm*); **she is good in an ~** es buena en casos de emergencia; **in case of ~, please call ...** en caso de emergencia, por favor llamen al ...; **there is a national ~** existe una crisis nacional; **to declare a state of ~** declarar el estado de excepción
[2] (*Med*) urgencia *f*; **she was admitted for ~ surgery** fue admitida para ser sometida a una operación de urgencia; *see also* **accident B**
(B) CPD [*meeting, measures, talks, airstrip*] de emergencia ► **emergency brake** N (*esp US*) freno *m* de mano ► **emergency call** N llamada *f* de urgencia ► **emergency case** N caso *m* de emergencia ► **emergency centre** N centro *m* de emergencia ► **emergency exit** N salida *f* de emergencia ► **emergency fund** N fondos *mpl* de reserva ► **emergency landing** N aterrizaje *m* forzoso ► **emergency lane** N (*US*) arcén *m* ► **emergency operation** N operación *f* de urgencia ► **emergency powers** NPL poderes *mpl* extraordinarios ► **emergency ration** N ración *f* de reserva ► **emergency room** N (*US Med*) sala *f* de urgencias ► **emergency services** NPL (= *police, fire brigade, ambulance*) servicios *mpl* de urgencia, servicios *mpl* de emergencia ► **emergency stop** N (*Aut*) parada *f* de emergencia ► **emergency supply** N provisión *f* de reserva ► **emergency ward** N sala *f* de urgencias

emergent [ɪ'mɜːdʒənt] ADJ [*countries*] emergente

emerging [ɪ'mɜːdʒɪŋ] ADJ = **emergent**

emeritus [iː'merɪtəs] ADJ emérito

emery ['emərɪ] (A) N esmeril *m*
(B) CPD ► **emery board** N lima *f* de uñas ► **emery cloth** N tela *f* de esmeril ► **emery paper** N papel *m* de esmeril

emetic [ɪ'metɪk] (A) ADJ emético, vomitivo
(B) N emético *m*, vomitivo *m*

emigrant ['emɪgrənt] (A) ADJ emigrante
(B) N emigrante *mf*

emigrate ['emɪgreɪt] VI emigrar

emigration [ˌemɪ'greɪʃən] N emigración *f*

émigré(e) ['emɪgreɪ] N emigrado/a *m/f*

Emily ['emɪlɪ] N Emilia

eminence ['emɪnəns] N [1] (= *fame*) prestigio *m*, renombre *m*; **to gain** *or* **win ~** alcanzar prestigio (**as** como)
[2] (*frm*) (= *hill*) promontorio *m*, prominencia *f*
[3] (*Rel*) (= *title of cardinal*) eminencia *f*; **His/Your Eminence** Su/Vuestra Eminencia

eminent ['emɪnənt] ADJ [1] (= *distinguished*) [*doctor, scientist*] eminente, ilustre; **she is ~ in the field of avionics** es una eminencia en el campo de la aviónica
[2] (*frm*) (= *great*) [*charm, fairness, good sense*] extraordinario; **she was chosen for her ~ suitability for the job** la eligieron por ser sumamente idónea para el puesto

➤ LANGUAGE IN USE: **emphasize 1** 26.1

eminently ['emɪnəntlɪ] ADV [*suitable, qualified, respectable*] sumamente; **his earliest work is ~ forgettable** sus primeras obras no tienen nada de memorables

emir [e'mɪəʳ] N emir *m*

emirate [e'mɪərɪt] N emirato *m*

emissary ['emɪsərɪ] N emisario/a *m/f*

emission [ɪ'mɪʃən] (A) N [1] [*of light, smell*] emisión *f*; (*Anat*) [*of semen*] expulsión *f*
[2] **emissions** (= *fumes*) emisiones *fpl*
(B) CPD ► **emission controls** NPL controles *mpl* de emisiones

emit [ɪ'mɪt] VT [+ *sparks*] echar; [+ *light, signals*] emitir; [+ *smoke, heat, smell*] despedir; [+ *cry*] dar; [+ *sound*] producir

emitter [ɪ'mɪtəʳ] N (*Electronics*) emisor *m*

Emmanuel [ɪ'mænjʊəl] N Manuel

Emmy ['emɪ] N (*pl* **Emmys** *or* **Emmies**) (*US TV*) Emmy *m*

emollient [ɪ'mɒlɪənt] (A) ADJ emoliente
(B) N emoliente *m*

emolument [ɪ'mɒljʊmənt] N (*often pl*) (*frm*) (= *salary*) emolumentos *mpl*; (= *fees*) honorarios *mpl*

e-money ['iːmʌnɪ] N dinero *m* electrónico

emote* [ɪ'məʊt] VI actuar de una manera muy emocionada

emoticon [ɪ'məʊtɪkɒn] N emoticón *m*, emoticono *m*

emotion [ɪ'məʊʃən] N [1] (= *passion*) emoción *f*; **her voice trembled with ~** su voz temblaba de emoción; **he never shows any ~** nunca deja ver ninguna emoción; **the split between reason and ~** la división entre la razón y los sentimientos, el conflicto entre los dictados de la mente y del corazón
[2] (= *sensation*) (*eg happiness, love, fear, anger*) sentimiento *m*; **he struggled to control his ~s** luchaba para controlar sus sentimientos

emotional [ɪ'məʊʃənl] (A) ADJ [1] (= *concerning the emotions*) [*well-being, problem, tension, development*] emocional; [*abuse, need, relationship*] afectivo; [*support, disorder*] emocional, afectivo; **on an ~ level** a nivel emocional; **to be on an ~ roller coaster** sufrir altibajos emocionales; **to be an ~ wreck** estar destrozado emocionalmente
[2] (= *emotive, moving*) [*scene, farewell, welcome, subject*] emotivo; [*experience, situation, appeal, speech*] emotivo, conmovedor
[3] (= *excitable*) [*outburst*] impulsivo; [*response*] emotivo; **Latins are very ~ people** los latinos son muy expresivos con sus sentimientos; **to become** *or* **get ~** reaccionar de una forma emocional; **there's no need to get all ~!** ¡no te pongas así!
[4] (= *sentimental*) [*person, behaviour*] sentimental, emotivo; [*decision*] impulsivo; **I got very ~ when the time came to say goodbye** a la hora de despedirnos me puse muy sentimental; **to become** *or* **get ~** emocionarse; **he became** *or* **got very ~ at the farewell party** se emocionó mucho en la fiesta de despedida
(B) CPD ► **emotional baggage** N (*fig*) bagaje *m* emocional ► **emotional blackmail** N chantaje *m* emocional

emotionalism [ɪ'məʊʃnəlɪzəm] N emoción *f*, emotividad *f*; (*pej*) sentimentalismo *m*

emotionally [ɪ'məʊʃnəlɪ] ADV [1] (= *mentally*) [*mature, unstable*] emocionalmente; **~ I was a wreck** emocionalmente *or* desde el punto de vista emocional estaba destrozado; **to remain ~ detached** no involucrarse emocionalmente; **to be ~ drained** estar agotado emocionalmente; *see also* **deprived**
[2] (= *with emotion*) [*speak, appeal*] emotivamente, de forma conmovedora; [*respond*] emotivamente; **an ~ charged atmosphere** una atmósfera cargada de emotividad; **an ~ worded article** un artículo redactado con mucha emotividad
[3] (= *sentimentally*) **they became ~ involved** entablaron una relación sentimental

emotionless [ɪ'məʊʃənlɪs] ADJ sin emoción

emotive [ɪ'məʊtɪv] ADJ emotivo

empanel [ɪm'pænl] VT [+ *jury*] seleccionar; **to ~ sb for a jury** inscribir a algn para jurado

empathetic [ˌempə'θetɪk] ADJ = **empathic**

empathetically [ˌempə'θetɪkəlɪ] ADV = **empathically**

empathic [ˌempə'θetɪk] ADJ comprensivo, empático

empathically [ˌempə'θetɪkəlɪ] ADV con comprensión, con empatía

empathize ['empəθaɪz] VI identificarse (**with** con)

empathy ['empəθɪ] N identificación *f*, empatía *f*; **to feel ~ with sb** identificarse con algn

emperor ['empərəʳ] (A) N emperador *m*
(B) CPD ► **emperor penguin** N pingüino *m* emperador *or* real

emphasis ['emfəsɪs] N (*pl* **emphases** ['emfəsiːz]) [1] (*in word*) acento *m*; (*in sentence*) énfasis *m inv*; **the ~ is on the first syllable** el acento (re)cae en la primera sílaba; **to put ~ on a word** enfatizar una palabra
[2] (*fig*) énfasis *m inv*; **there has been a change of ~** ya no se hace hincapié en lo mismo; **he said it twice, for ~** lo dijo dos veces, para enfatizar *or* para recalcar; **the ~ is on sport** se da más énfasis al deporte; **this year the ~ is on femininity** este año se resalta la feminidad; **to place** *or* **put** *or* **lay ~ on sth** hacer hincapié en algo, poner énfasis en algo; **too much ~ is placed on research** se pone demasiado énfasis en la investigación, se hace demasiado hincapié en la investigación; **to put special ~ on sth** poner especial énfasis en algo; **to speak with ~** hablar con énfasis

➤ **emphasize** ['emfəsaɪz] VT [1] [+ *word, syllable*] enfatizar; [+ *fact, point*] hacer hincapié en, enfatizar, subrayar, recalcar; **I must ~ that ...** debo insistir en que ...
[2] (*Ling*) acentuar
[3] [*garment*] (= *accentuate*) hacer resaltar

emphatic [ɪm'fætɪk] ADJ [1] (= *forceful*) [*statement, declaration, response*] categórico, contundente; [*denial, refusal*] categórico, rotundo; [*tone, gesture*] enérgico, enfático; [*condemnation*] categórico, enérgico; **Wendy was ~, "you must do it," she said** Wendy fue categórica, -debes hacerlo, dijo; **she's ~ that business is improving** mantiene firmemente que el negocio está mejorando; **they were quite ~ that they were not going** dijeron categóricamente que no iban; **Pat was ~ about how valuable the course was** Pat hizo hincapié en lo valioso que era el curso; **they were ~ in denying their involvement** negaron categóricamente su participación; **an ~ no** un no rotundo; **an ~ yes** un sí contundente
[2] (= *decisive*) [*victory, win*] rotundo; [*success*] arrollador; [*defeat*] aplastante; [*winner, result*] contundente

emphatically [ɪm'fætɪkəlɪ] ADV [1] (= *forcefully*) [*say, reply, reject*] categóricamente, enérgicamente; [*deny, refuse*] rotundamente, categóricamente; **he shook his head ~** dijo que no con la cabeza de manera rotunda; **most ~** [*say, reply*] de la forma más contundente;

[*deny, refuse*] de la forma más rotunda
[2] (= *definitely*) decididamente, sin lugar a dudas

emphysema [emfɪˈsiːmə] N enfisema *m*

Empire [ˈempaɪəʳ] ADJ [*costume, furniture*] estilo Imperio

empire [ˈempaɪəʳ] Ⓐ N imperio *m*
Ⓑ CPD ► **the Empire State** N (*US*) el estado de Nueva York

empire-builder [ˈempaɪəˌbɪldəʳ] N (*fig*) constructor(a) *m/f* de imperios

empire-building [ˈempaɪəˌbɪldɪŋ] N (*fig*) construcción *f* de imperios

empiric [emˈpɪrɪk] ADJ = **empirical**

empirical [emˈpɪrɪkəl] ADJ [*method*] empírico

empirically [emˈpɪrɪkəlɪ] ADV empíricamente

empiricism [emˈpɪrɪsɪzəm] N empirismo *m*

empiricist [emˈpɪrɪsɪst] N empírico/a *m/f*

emplacement [ɪmˈpleɪsmənt] N (*Mil*) emplazamiento *m*

emplane [ɪmˈpleɪn] VI (*US*) subir al avión, embarcar (en avión)

employ [ɪmˈplɔɪ] Ⓐ VT [+ *person*] emplear, dar empleo a; [+ *object, method*] emplear, usar; [+ *time*] ocupar; **the factory ~s 600 people** la fábrica da empleo a 600 trabajadores; **thousands of people are ~ed in tourism** miles de personas trabajan en el sector del turismo
Ⓑ N **to be in the ~ of sb** (*frm*) (*as company employee*) ser empleado de algn; (*as servant*) estar al servicio de algn

employable [ɪmˈplɔɪəbl] ADJ [*person*] con capacidad para trabajar; [*skill*] útil, utilizable

employee [ˌemplɔɪˈiː] Ⓐ N empleado/a *m/f*
Ⓑ CPD ► **employee rights** NPL derechos *mpl* de los trabajadores

employer [ɪmˈplɔɪəʳ] N (= *business person*) empresario/a *m/f*; (= *boss*) patrón/ona *m/f*; **the ~s' federation** ◊ **the ~s' organization** la patronal; **the ~'s interests** los intereses empresariales; **my ~** mi jefe

employment [ɪmˈplɔɪmənt] Ⓐ N empleo *m*, trabajo *m*; **to be in ~** tener empleo *or* trabajo; **to find ~** encontrar empleo *or* trabajo; **to give ~ to** emplear a, dar trabajo a; **to look for ~** buscar empleo *or* trabajo; **conditions of ~** condiciones *fpl* de empleo; **full ~** pleno empleo *m*; **a high level of ~** un alto nivel de empleo; **her ~ prospects are poor** tiene pocas posibilidades de colocarse; **Secretary (of State) for** *or* **Minister of Employment** (*Brit*) ◊ **Secretary for Employment** (*US*) Ministro *m* de Trabajo; **Department of Employment** (*Brit*) Ministerio *m* de Trabajo
Ⓑ CPD ► **employment agency** N agencia *f* de colocación ► **employment exchange** N (*Brit*) oficina *f* de empleo ► **employment office** N (*US*) = **employment exchange** ► **employment statistics** NPL estadística *f* del empleo, cifras *fpl* del paro

emporium [emˈpɔːrɪəm] N (*pl* **emporiums** *or* **emporia** [emˈpɔːrɪə]) almacenes *mpl*, emporio *m* (*LAm*)

empower [ɪmˈpaʊəʳ] VT [1] (= *authorize*) **to ~ sb to do sth** autorizar a algn para hacer algo
[2] [+ *women, workers, minorities*] atribuir poderes a

empowerment [ɪmˈpaʊəmənt] N [*of women, workers, minorities*] atribución *f* de poder

empress [ˈemprɪs] N emperatriz *f*

emptiness [ˈemptɪnɪs] N [1] (= *bareness, barrenness*) desolación *f*, vacío *m*; **the ~ of the desert** la desolación *or* el vacío del desierto
[2] (= *void*) vacío *m*; **the ~ he felt inside** el vacío que sentía en su interior; **the ~ of his life** el vacío *or* (*frm*) la vacuidad de su vida

empty [ˈemptɪ] Ⓐ ADJ (*compar* **emptier**; *superl* **emptiest**) [1] (= *containing nothing, nobody*) [*box, bottle, glass, street, room, hands*] vacío; [*seat, chair*] (*in bus, restaurant*) libre, desocupado; (*in living room*) vacío; [*place*] desierto; [*landscape*] desierto, desolado; [*gun*] descargado; [*post, job*] vacante; **the flat next door is ~** (= *unoccupied*) el piso de al lado está desocupado; **to be ~ of sth**: **the parks are ~ of children** en los parques no hay niños; **his face was ~ of all expression** su rostro no expresaba ninguna emoción; **she was staring into ~ space** miraba al infinito; **there was an ~ space at the table** había un sitio vacío *or* sin ocupar en la mesa; **on an ~ stomach** en ayunas, con el estómago vacío; ✦**PROV ~ vessels make the most noise** mucho ruido y pocas nueces
[2] (= *meaningless*) [*threat, promise, dream*] vano; [*words, rhetoric*] hueco, vacío; [*exercise*] inútil; [*life*] sin sentido, vacío; **it's an ~ gesture** es un gesto vacío; **she felt trapped in an ~ marriage** se sentía atrapada en una relación matrimonial vacía; **his promises were just so much ~ talk** sus promesas no eran más que palabras huecas *or* vanas; **my life is ~ without you** mi vida no tiene sentido sin ti
[3] (= *numb*) [*person*] vacío; [*feeling*] de vacío; **when I heard the news I felt ~** cuando me enteré de la noticia me sentí vacío
Ⓑ N [1] (*usu pl*) (= *empty bottle*) envase *m* (vacío), casco *m* (vacío); (= *empty glass*) vaso *m* (vacío)
[2] (*Aut*) **the car was running on ~** el coche estaba con el depósito vacío; **I was running on ~** (*fig*) no me quedaba energía
Ⓒ VT [+ *container, tank, glass, plate*] vaciar; **television has emptied the cinemas** la televisión ha dejado los cines vacíos; **I emptied the dirty water down the drain** tiré el agua sucia por el sumidero; **she emptied the ashtray into the bin** vació el cenicero en el cubo de la basura; **we emptied the cupboards of junk** vaciamos los armarios de trastos; **he emptied the gun of bullets** descargó la pistola; **I tried to ~ my mind of distractions** intenté vaciar la mente de distracciones; **I emptied the contents of the bag onto the bed** vacié la bolsa en la cama; **to ~ out one's pockets** vaciarse los bolsillos; **he emptied the water out of his boots** se sacó el agua de las botas
Ⓓ VI [1] (= *become empty*) [*room, building, theatre, bath*] vaciarse; [*street*] quedarse desierto, vaciarse; [*train, coach, plane*] quedarse vacío, vaciarse; **the auditorium quickly emptied of students** los estudiantes desalojaron el auditorio rápidamente
[2] (= *flow*) **to ~ into sth** [*river*] desembocar en algo

empty-handed [ˈemptɪˈhændɪd] ADJ **to arrive/leave/return ~** llegar/marcharse/volver con las manos vacías

empty-headed [ˈemptɪˈhedɪd] ADJ casquivano

Empyrean [ɛmpɪˈriːən] N **the ~** (*liter*) el empíreo

em rule [ˈemruːl] N (*Typ*) raya *f*

EMS N ABBR (= **European Monetary System**) SME *m*

EMT N ABBR = **emergency medical technician**

EMU N ABBR (= **economic and monetary union**) UME *f*, UEM *f*

emu [ˈiːmjuː] N emú *m*

emulate [ˈemjʊleɪt] VT emular (*also Comput*)

emulation [ˌemjʊˈleɪʃən] N emulación *f* (*also Comput*)

emulator [ˈemjʊˌleɪtəʳ] N (*Comput*) emulador *m*

emulsifier [ɪˈmʌlsɪˌfaɪəʳ] N agente *m* emulsionador, emulsionante *m*

emulsify [ɪˈmʌlsɪfaɪ] VT emulsionar

emulsion [ɪˈmʌlʃən] N (= *liquid*) emulsión *f*; (*also* **~ paint**) pintura *f* emulsión

EN N ABBR (*Brit*) (= **Enrolled Nurse**) ≈ ATS *mf*

enable [ɪˈneɪbl] VT [1] (= *make able*) **to ~ sb to do sth** permitir a algn hacer algo
[2] (= *make possible*) posibilitar; **the new system will ~ better communication between doctor and patient** el nuevo sistema posibilitará *or* hará posible una mejor comunicación entre el médico y el paciente

enact [ɪˈnækt] VT [1] (*Jur*) decretar (**that** que); [+ *law*] promulgar
[2] (= *perform*) [+ *play, scene, part*] representar

enactment [ɪˈnæktmənt] N [1] [*of law*] promulgación *f*
[2] [*of play, scene, part*] representación *f*

enamel [ɪˈnæməl] Ⓐ N (*gen, of teeth*) esmalte *m*
Ⓑ VT esmaltar
Ⓒ CPD ► **enamel jewellery** N alhajas *fpl* de esmalte ► **enamel paint** N (pintura *f* al) esmalte *m* ► **enamel saucepan** N cacerola *f* esmaltada

enamelled, **enameled** (*US*) [ɪˈnæməld] ADJ esmaltado

enamelling, **enameling** (*US*) [ɪˈnæməlɪŋ] N esmaltado *m*

enamelware [ɪˈnæməlweəʳ] N utensilios *mpl* de hierro esmaltado

enamour, **enamor** (*US*) [ɪˈnæməʳ] VT **to be ~ed of** (*liter, hum*) [+ *person*] estar enamorado de; [+ *thing*] estar entusiasmado con

encamp [ɪnˈkæmp] VI acamparse

encampment [ɪnˈkæmpmənt] N campamento *m*

encapsulate [ɪnˈkæpsjʊleɪt] VT [1] (= *enclose*) encerrar
[2] (*fig*) (= *summarize*) resumir
[3] (*Pharm*) encapsular

encase [ɪnˈkeɪs] VT encerrar; (*Tech*) revestir; **to be ~d in** estar revestido de

encash [ɪnˈkæʃ] VT cobrar, hacer efectivo

encashment [ɪnˈkæʃmənt] N cobro *m*

encephalic [ensɪˈfælɪk] ADJ encefálico

encephalitis [ˌensefəˈlaɪtɪs] N encefalitis *f*

encephalogram [ɪnˈsefələgræm] N encefalograma *m*

enchain [ɪnˈtʃeɪn] VT (*frm*) encadenar

enchant [ɪnˈtʃɑːnt] VT (*often passive*) encantar; (= *use magic on*) encantar, hechizar; **we were ~ed with the place** el sitio nos encantó

enchanter [ɪnˈtʃɑːntəʳ] N hechicero/a *m/f*

enchanting [ɪnˈtʃɑːntɪŋ] ADJ encantador

enchantingly [ɪnˈtʃɑːntɪŋlɪ] ADV de manera encantadora, deliciosamente

enchantment [ɪnˈtʃɑːntmənt] N (= *act*) encantamiento *m*; (= *delight*) encanto *m*; (= *charm, spell*) encantamiento *m*, hechizo *m*; **it lent ~ to the scene** le daba encanto a la escena

enchantress [ɪnˈtʃɑːntrɪs] N hechicera *f*

enchilada [ˌentʃɪˈlædə] N enchilada *f*; **big ~** (*US**) peso *m* pesado

encircle [ɪnˈsɜːkl] VT rodear (**with** de); (*Mil*) sitiar; [+ *waist, shoulders*] ceñir; **it is ~d by a wall** está rodeado de una tapia

encirclement [ɪnˈsɜːklmənt] N (*Mil*) envolvimiento *m*

encircling [ɪnˈsɜːklɪŋ] ADJ [*movement*] envolvente

enc(l). ABBR (= **enclosure(s), enclosed**) adj.

enclave ['enkleɪv] N enclave *m*

enclitic [ɪn'klɪtɪk] ADJ enclítico

▼**enclose** [ɪn'kləʊz] VT 1 [+ *land, garden*] cercar, vallar; **to ~ with** cercar *or* vallar con
2 (= *put in a receptacle*) meter, encerrar
3 (= *include*) encerrar
4 (*with letter*) remitir adjunto, adjuntar; **I ~ a cheque** (remito) adjunto un cheque

enclosed [ɪn'kləʊzd] ADJ 1 (*with letter*) adjunto; **please find ~** le enviamos adjunto *or* anexo; **the ~ letter** la carta adjunta
2 [*garden, land*] cercado, vallado

enclosure [ɪn'kləʊʒəʳ] N 1 (= *act*) cercamiento *m*
2 (= *place*) recinto *m*; (*at racecourse*) reservado *m*
3 (*in letter*) anexo *m*

encode [ɪn'kəʊd] VT 1 (= *encrypt*) codificar, cifrar
2 (*Ling*) cifrar

encoder [ɪn'kəʊdəʳ] N (*Comput*) codificador *m*

encoding [ɪn'kəʊdɪŋ] N (*Comput, Ling*) codificación *f*

encomium [ɪn'kəʊmɪəm] N (*pl* **encomiums** *or* **encomia** [ɪn'kəʊmɪə]) elogio *m*, encomio *m*

encompass [ɪn'kʌmpəs] VT 1 (= *surround*) cercar, rodear (**with** de)
2 (= *include*) abarcar
3 (= *bring about*) lograr, efectuar

encore [ɒŋ'kɔːʳ] Ⓐ EXCL ¡otra!
Ⓑ N bis *m*; **to call for an ~** pedir un bis; **to give an ~** hacer un bis, repetir a petición del público; **to sing a song as an ~** cantar como bis una canción
Ⓒ VT [+ *song*] pedir un bis de; [+ *person*] pedir un bis *or* otra a

encounter [ɪn'kaʊntəʳ] Ⓐ N (= *meeting, fight*) encuentro *m*
Ⓑ VT [+ *person*] encontrar, encontrarse con; [+ *difficulty, danger, enemy*] tropezar con
Ⓒ CPD ► **encounter group** N grupo *m* de encuentro

encourage [ɪn'kʌrɪdʒ] VT [+ *person*] animar, alentar; [+ *industry, growth*] estimular, fomentar; **to ~ sb to do sth** animar a algn a hacer algo; **the discovery ~d him in his belief that she was still alive** el hallazgo reafirmó su creencia de que aún seguía viva

encouragement [ɪn'kʌrɪdʒmənt] N (= *act*) estímulo *m*; [*of industry*] fomento *m*; (= *support*) aliento *m*, ánimo(s) *m(pl)*; **to give ~ to** dar ánimos a, animar; **to give ~ to the enemy** dar aliento al enemigo

encouraging [ɪn'kʌrɪdʒɪŋ] ADJ [*smile*] alentador; [*news, prospect*] alentador, halagüeño; [*words*] de aliento; **it is not an ~ prospect** es una perspectiva poco halagüeña; **he was always very ~** siempre me daba ánimos

encouragingly [ɪn'kʌrɪdʒɪŋlɪ] ADV [*speak, say*] en tono alentador; [*smile, nod*] de modo alentador; **the theatre was ~ full** el teatro estaba lleno, lo cual resultaba alentador; **~, inflation is slowing down** resulta alentador que la inflación se vaya ralentizando

encroach [ɪn'krəʊtʃ] VI avanzar; **to ~ (up)on** [+ *time*] quitar; [+ *rights*] usurpar; [+ *land*] (*of neighbour*) invadir, traspasar los límites de; [+ *land*] (*by sea*) hurtar, invadir; [+ *someone's subject*] invadir

encroachment [ɪn'krəʊtʃmənt] N usurpación *f* (**on** de); **this new ~ on our liberty** esta nueva usurpación de nuestra libertad

encrust [ɪn'krʌst] VT incrustar (**with** de)

encrustation [ˌɪnkrʌs'teɪʃn] N incrustación *f*

encrusted [ɪn'krʌstɪd] ADJ **~ with** incrustado de

encrypt [ɪn'krɪpt] VT codificar

encryption [ɪn'krɪpʃən] N codificación *f*

encumber [ɪn'kʌmbəʳ] VT [+ *person, movement*] estorbar; (*with debts*) cargar; [+ *place*] llenar (**with** de); **to be ~ed with** tener que cargar con; [+ *debts*] estar cargado de

encumbrance [ɪn'kʌmbrəns] N estorbo *m*; (*Fin, Jur*) carga *f*, gravamen *m*; **without ~** (*frm*) sin familia

encyclical [en'sɪklɪkəl] N encíclica *f*

encyclopaedia, **encyclopedia** [enˌsaɪkləʊ'piːdɪə] N enciclopedia *f*

encyclopaedic, **encyclopedic** [enˌsaɪkləʊ'piːdɪk] ADJ enciclopédico

encyclopaedist, **encyclopedist** [enˌsaɪkləʊ'piːdɪst] N enciclopedista *mf*

end [end] Ⓐ N 1 [*of street*] final *m*; [*of line, table*] extremo *m*; [*of rope, stick*] punta *f*; [*of estate*] límite *m*; (*Sport*) lado *m*; [*of town*] parte *f*, zona *f*; **at the ~ of** [+ *street, corridor*] al final de; [+ *rope, cable*] en la punta de; **to change ~s** (*Sport*) cambiar de lado; **the ~s of the earth** (*fig*) el ultimo rincón del mundo; **to go to the ~s of the earth** ir hasta el fin del mundo; **from one ~ to the other** de un extremo a otro; **the ~ of the line** (*fig*) el término, el acabóse; **to stand sth on ~** poner algo de punta; **his hair stood on ~** se le puso el pelo de punta; **the ~ of the road** (*fig*) el término, el acabóse; **from ~ to ~** de punta a punta; **to place ~ to ~** poner uno tras otro; **to read a book to the very ~** leer un libro hasta el mismo final; **to start at the wrong ~** empezar por el fin; ✦**IDIOMS to keep one's ~ up*** (*in undertaking*) hacer su parte; (*) (*in argument*) defenderse bien; **to tie up the loose ~s** atar cabos; **to make ~s meet** hacer llegar *or* alcanzar el dinero; **to get hold of the wrong ~ of the stick** tomar el rábano por las hojas; **to be at the ~ of one's tether** no poder más, no aguantar más; *see also* **deep A1**, **shallow A1**
2 [*of time, process, journey, resources*] fin *m*, final *m*; [*of story*] fin *m*, conclusión *f*; **the ~ of the empire** el fin del imperio; **at the ~ of three months** al cabo de tres meses; **at the ~ of the century** a fines del siglo; **towards the ~ of** [+ *book, film*] hacia el final de; [+ *century*] hacia fines de; [+ *month*] hacia fin de; **that was the ~ of him** así terminó él; **that's the ~ of the matter** asunto concluido; **that was the ~ of that!** ¡y se acabo!; **that was the ~ of our car*** así se acabó el coche; **we'll never hear the ~ of it*** esto va a ser cuento de nunca acabar; **there's no ~ to it*** esto no se acaba nunca; **we see no ~ to it** no entrevemos posibilidad alguna de que termine; **to be at an ~** [*meeting, interview*] haber concluido; **to be at the ~ of** [+ *strength, patience*] estar al límite de; **we're at the ~ of our supplies** se nos están agotando las provisiones; **we are almost at the ~ of our holidays** se nos están acabando las vacaciones; **to be at the ~ of one's resources** haber agotado los recursos; **to come to a bad ~** acabar mal; **to the bitter ~** hasta el último suspiro; **to bring to an ~** [+ *work, speech, relationship*] dar por terminado; **to come to an ~** llegar a su fin, terminarse; **to draw to an ~** llegar a su fin, terminarse; **I am getting to the ~ of my patience** estoy llegando al límite de mi paciencia; **in the ~** al fin; **to make an ~ of** acabar con, poner fin a; **I enjoyed it no ~*** me gustó muchísimo; **to think no ~ of sb** tener un muy alto concepto de algn; **no ~ of*** la mar de*; **it caused no ~ of trouble** causó la mar de problemas; **no ~ of an expert** sumamente experto, más experto que nadie; **three days on ~** tres días seguidos; **for days on ~** día tras día, durante una infinidad de días; **for hours on ~** hora tras hora; **to put an ~ to** [+ *argument, relationship, sb's tricks*] poner fin a, acabar con; **that's the ~!*** ¡eso es el colmo!; **he's the ~!*** ¡es el colmo!; **that movie is the ~!** (*US**) esa película es el no va más; **without ~** interminable; **the ~ of the world** el fin del mundo; **it's not the ~ of the world*** el mundo no se va a acabar por eso; ✦**IDIOM at the ~ of the day** al fin y al cabo, a fin de cuentas
3 (= *death*) (*liter or hum*) muerte *f*; **to meet one's ~** encontrar la muerte
4 (= *remnant*) [*of loaf, candle, meat*] resto *m*, cabo *m*; **the ~ of a roll** [*of cloth, carpet*] el retal de un rollo; *see also* **cigarette B**
5 (= *aim*) fin *m*, propósito *m*; **an ~ in itself** un fin en sí; **the ~ justifies the means** el fin justifica los medios; **to achieve one's ~** alcanzar su objetivo; **to no ~** en vano; **to the ~ that ...** a fin de que + *subjun*; **to this ~** ◊ **with this ~ in view** con este propósito; **with what ~?** ¿para qué?
Ⓑ VT [+ *argument*] terminar, poner fin a; [+ *book*] concluir; [+ *speech*] concluir, terminar; [+ *relationship*] terminar; [+ *abuse, speculation*] acabar con; **that was the meal to ~ all meals!*** ¡eso fue el no va más en comidas!; **to ~ one's days** vivir sus últimos días; **to ~ it all*** suicidarse; **to ~ one's life** suicidarse
Ⓒ VI [*lesson, work, war, meeting*] terminar, acabar; (*more frm*) concluir; [*road*] terminar(se); [*period of time, programme, film, story*] terminar; **to ~ by saying** terminar diciendo; **to ~ in** terminar en; **to ~ with** terminar con
Ⓓ CPD ► **end game** N (*Chess*) fase *f* final ► **the end house** N la última casa ► **end line** N (*Basketball*) línea *f* de fondo ► **end note** N nota *f* final ► **end product** N (*Ind*) producto *m* final; (*fig*) consecuencia *f* ► **end result** N resultado *m* ► **end user** N usuario/a *m/f* final

►**end off** VT + ADV poner fin a

►**end up** VI + ADV terminar (**in** en); [*road, path*] llevar, conducir (**in** a)

end-all ['endɔːl] N *see* **be-all**

endanger [ɪn'deɪndʒəʳ] VT [+ *life, health, position*] poner en peligro; **an ~ed species** (*of animal*) una especie en peligro de extinción

endear [ɪn'dɪəʳ] VT **to ~ sb to** [+ *others*] ganar para algn la simpatía de; **this did not ~ him to the public** esto no le granjeó las simpatías de la gente; **to ~ o.s. to sb** ganarse la simpatía de algn

endearing [ɪn'dɪərɪŋ] ADJ [*person, smile*] entrañable, simpático; [*characteristic, quality*] atractivo, atrayente; [*personality, habit*] encantador; **she has a very ~ manner** tiene una manera de ser encantadora

endearingly [ɪn'dɪərɪŋlɪ] ADV [*say, smile*] de manera encantadora; **he is ~ shy/eccentric** es encantadoramente tímido/excéntrico

endearment [ɪn'dɪəmənt] N cariño *m*; **term of ~** palabra *f* de cariño

endeavour, **endeavor** (*US*) [ɪn'devəʳ] Ⓐ N (= *attempt*) intento *m*, tentativa *f*; (= *effort*) esfuerzo *m*; **in spite of my best ~s** a pesar de todos mis esfuerzos; **to make/use every ~ to do sth** procurar por todos los medios hacer algo
Ⓑ VI **to ~ to do sth** procurar hacer algo, esforzarse por hacer algo

endemic [en'demɪk] ADJ endémico

➤ LANGUAGE IN USE: **enclose 4** 20.2, 20.3, 20.6

ending ['endɪŋ] N 1 (= *end*) fin *m*, final *m*; [*of book, story, play*] final *m*, desenlace *m*; **the tale has a happy ~** el cuento tiene un final *or* desenlace feliz 2 (*Ling*) terminación *f*

endive ['endaɪv] N endibia *f*

endless ['endlɪs] ADJ 1 (= *interminable*) [*road, queue, summer, speech*] interminable; [*variety, patience, desert*] infinito; [*supply*] inacabable, inagotable; **the list is ~** la lista es interminable; **this job is ~** este trabajo no se acaba nunca; **an ~ round of meetings** una ronda interminable de reuniones
2 (= *countless*) continuo; **I'm tired of his ~ questions/complaining** estoy cansada de sus continuas preguntas/quejas; **he asked me ~ questions** me hizo un sinfín de preguntas; **the possibilities are ~** las posibilidades son infinitas
3 (*Tech*) [*screw, belt*] sin fin *adj inv*

endlessly ['endlɪslɪ] ADV [*repeat*] una y otra vez, hasta la saciedad; [*discuss*] hasta la saciedad; [*argue*] continuamente; [*talk*] sin parar; [*recycle*] una y otra vez; **she talks ~ about her job** no para de hablar de su trabajo; **the desert stretched ~ before her** el desierto se extendía interminable ante ella; **he could see his life stretching out ~ before him** veía su vida extendiéndose interminablemente ante sus ojos; **she is ~ patient** tiene una paciencia infinita

endocardium [endəʊ'kɑːdɪəm] N (*pl* **endocardia** [endəʊ'kɑːdɪə]) endocardio *m*

endocarp ['endəkɑːp] N endocarpio *m*

endocrine ['endəʊkraɪn] Ⓐ ADJ endocrino
Ⓑ N glándula *f* endocrina
Ⓒ CPD ► **endocrine gland** N glándula *f* endocrina ► **endocrine system** N sistema *m* endocrino

endocrinologist [ˌendəʊkraɪ'nɒlədʒɪst] N endocrinólogo/a *m/f*

endodontics [ˌendəʊ'dɒntɪks] NSING endodoncia *f*

endogenous [ˌen'dɒdʒɪnəs] ADJ endógeno

endomorph ['endəʊmɔːf] N endomorfo/a *m/f*

endorphin [ˌen'dɔːfɪn] N endorfina *f*

endorse [ɪn'dɔːs] VT 1 (= *sign*) [+ *cheque, document*] endosar
2 (= *approve*) [+ *opinion, claim, plan*] aprobar; (= *support*) [+ *decision*] respaldar
3 (*Brit Aut*) **to ~ a licence** anotar los detalles de una sanción en el permiso de conducir

endorsee [ɪnˌdɔː'siː] N endosatario/a *m/f*

endorsement [ɪn'dɔːsmənt] N 1 (= *signature*) endoso *m*
2 (= *approval*) aprobación *f*; (= *support*) respaldo *m*
3 (*Brit Aut*) (*on licence*) nota *f* de sanción

endorser [ɪn'dɔːsəʳ] N endosante *mf*

endoscope ['endəʊˌskəʊp] N endoscopio *m*

endoscopy [ˌen'dɒskəpɪ] N endoscopia *f*

endow [ɪn'daʊ] VT 1 (= *found*) [+ *prize, professorship*] fundar, crear; (= *donate*) dotar, hacer una donación a
2 (*fig*) **to be ~ed with** estar dotado de

endowment [ɪn'daʊmənt] Ⓐ N 1 (= *act*) dotación *f*; (= *creation*) fundación *f*, creación *f*; (= *amount*) donación *f* 2 (*fig*) dote *f*
Ⓑ CPD ► **endowment assurance** N seguro *m* mixto, seguro *m* de vida-ahorro ► **endowment insurance** N = **endowment assurance** ► **endowment mortgage** N (*Brit*) hipoteca *f* avalada por una dote ► **endowment policy** N (*Brit*) póliza *f* dotal

endpaper ['endpeɪpəʳ] N guarda *f*

endue [ɪn'djuː] VT dotar (**with** de)

endurable [ɪn'djʊərəbl] ADJ aguantable, soportable

endurance [ɪn'djʊərəns] Ⓐ N resistencia *f*; **to come to the end of one's ~** no poder más, llegar a sus límites; **past** *or* **beyond ~** inaguantable, insoportable; **to be tried beyond ~** ser puesto a prueba; **it tested his powers of ~** puso a prueba su resistencia
Ⓑ CPD ► **endurance race** N carrera *f* de resistencia ► **endurance test** N prueba *f* de resistencia

endure [ɪn'djʊəʳ] Ⓐ VT (= *suffer*) [+ *pain, heat*] resistir, aguantar; (= *tolerate*) aguantar, soportar; **she can't ~ being laughed at** no soporta que se rían de ella; **I can't ~ being corrected** no aguanto que me corrijan; **to ~ doing sth** aguantar hacer algo; **I can't ~ him** no lo puedo ver, no lo aguanto *or* soporto; **I can't ~ it a moment longer** no lo aguanto un momento más
Ⓑ VI (= *last*) durar; (= *not give in*) aguantar, resistir

enduring [ɪn'djʊərɪŋ] ADJ duradero, perdurable; **an ~ friendship** una amistad duradera; **an ~ affection/memory** un cariño/un recuerdo duradero

endways ['endweɪz] ADV (= *end to end*) de punta; (= *with end facing*) de lado, de canto

ENE ABBR (= **east-northeast**) ENE

ENEA N ABBR = **European Nuclear Energy Authority**

enema ['enɪmə] N (*pl* **enemas** *or* **enemata** ['enɪmətə]) enema *m*

enemy ['enəmɪ] Ⓐ N (= *person*) enemigo/a *m/f*; (*Mil*) enemigo *m*; **the ~ within** el enemigo en casa; **to go over to the ~** pasarse al enemigo; **to make an ~ of sb** enemistarse con algn; **✦IDIOM he is his own worst ~** su peor enemigo es él mismo
Ⓑ CPD [*territory, forces, aircraft*] enemigo ► **enemy alien** N extranjero/a *m/f* enemigo/a

enemy-occupied [ˌenəmɪ'ɒkjʊpaɪd] ADJ [*territory*] ocupado por el enemigo

energetic [ˌenə'dʒetɪk] ADJ [*person*] activo, lleno de energía; [*activity, sport*] que requiere mucha energía, duro; [*walk*] duro; [*campaign*] activo; [*performance*] lleno de energía; [*protest, efforts*] vigoroso; [*denial, refusal*] enérgico; **I've had a very ~ day** he tenido un día muy activo; **to feel ~** sentirse lleno de energía; **I'm not feeling very ~ today** hoy no me siento con muchas energías

energetically [ˌenə'dʒetɪkəlɪ] ADV [*play, run*] con energía; [*work, deny*] enérgicamente; [*campaign*] activamente, vigorosamente

energize ['enədʒaɪz] VT activar, dar energía a

energizing ['enədʒaɪzɪŋ] ADJ [*food*] energético, que da energías

energy ['enədʒɪ] Ⓐ N (*gen*) energía *f*; (= *strength*) vigor *m*; **electrical/atomic/solar ~** energía *f* eléctrica/atómica/solar; **Secretary (of State) for Energy** Secretario/a *m/f* (de Estado) de Energía; **Minister of Energy** Ministro/a *m/f* de Energía
Ⓑ CPD ► **energy conservation** N conservación *f* de la energía ► **energy crisis** N crisis *f inv* energética ► **energy food** N comida *f* energética *or* que da energías ► **energy level** N nivel *m* energético ► **energy needs** NPL necesidades *fpl* energéticas ► **energy policy** N política *f* de energía ► **energy resources** NPL recursos *mpl* energéticos ► **energy saving** N ahorro *m* de energía

energy-efficient ['enədʒɪɪˌfɪʃənt] ADJ [*light bulb, refrigerator*] de bajo consumo; [*building, system, industry*] energéticamente eficiente

energy-giving ['enədʒɪˌgɪvɪŋ] ADJ [*food etc*] energético, que da energías

energy-intensive [ˌenədʒɪɪn'tensɪv] ADJ [*industry*] consumidor de gran cantidad de energía

energy-saving ['enədʒɪˌseɪvɪŋ] ADJ [*device, system*] que ahorra energía; [*policy*] para ahorrar energía

enervate ['enɜːveɪt] VT enervar, debilitar

enervating ['enɜːveɪtɪŋ] ADJ enervador

enfeeble [ɪn'fiːbl] VT debilitar

enfeeblement [ɪn'fiːblmənt] N debilitación *f*

enfilade [ˌenfɪ'leɪd] VT enfilar

enfold [ɪn'fəʊld] VT envolver; **to ~ sb in one's arms** abrazar a algn, estrechar a algn entre los brazos

enforce [ɪn'fɔːs] VT 1 (= *make effective*) [+ *law*] hacer cumplir; [+ *argument*] imponer; [+ *claim*] hacer valer; [+ *rights*] hacer respetar; [+ *demand*] insistir en; [+ *sentence*] ejecutar
2 (= *compel*) [+ *obedience, attendance*] imponer (**on** a)

enforceable [ɪn'fɔːsəbl] ADJ [*law, rule*] ejecutable, que se puede hacer cumplir

enforced [ɪn'fɔːst] ADJ [*idleness, exile, silence*] forzoso, forzado

enforcement [ɪn'fɔːsmənt] N [*of law*] aplicación *f*; [*of sentence*] ejecución *f*; **law ~ agency** organismo *m* de seguridad del Estado

enfranchise [ɪn'fræntʃaɪz] VT (*Pol*) conceder el derecho de voto a; (= *free*) emancipar; [+ *slave*] liberar

enfranchisement [ɪn'fræntʃɪzmənt] N emancipación *f* (**of** de); (*Pol*) concesión *f* del derecho de votar (**of** a)

ENG N ABBR = **electronic news gathering**

Eng ABBR 1 = **England** 2 = **English**

engage [ɪn'geɪdʒ] Ⓐ VT 1 (= *hire*) [+ *servant, lawyer, worker*] contratar
2 (= *attract*) [+ *attention*] llamar, captar
3 (= *occupy*) [+ *attention, interest*] ocupar; **to ~ sb in conversation** entablar conversación con algn; **to ~ the enemy in battle** entablar batalla *or* combate con el enemigo
4 (*Mech*) [+ *cog*] engranar con; [+ *coupling*] acoplar; [+ *gear*] meter; **to ~ the clutch** embragar
Ⓑ VI 1 **to ~ in** [+ *discussion*] entablar; [+ *politics*] meterse en; [+ *sport*] tomar parte en
2 (= *initiate battle*) entablar batalla, entablar combate
3 (*Mech*) engranar (**with** con)

engagé [ɑ̃ːŋgæ'ʒeɪ] ADJ [*writer, artist*] comprometido

▼ **engaged** [ɪn'geɪdʒd] Ⓐ ADJ 1 **to be ~** (= *busy*) [*seat, person*] estar ocupado; (*Brit*) [*toilet*] estar ocupado; **to be ~ in** estar ocupado en, dedicarse a; **what are you ~ in?** ¿a qué se dedica Vd?
2 (*Brit Telec*) **to be ~** estar comunicando *or* (*LAm*) ocupado
3 **to be ~ (to be married)** estar prometido; [*2 persons*] estar prometidos, ser novios; **they've been ~ for two years** llevan dos años de relaciones formales; **to get ~** prometerse (**to** con); **the ~ couple** los novios
Ⓑ CPD ► **engaged signal, engaged tone** N señal *f* de comunicando *or* (*LAm*) ocupado

▼ **engagement** [ɪn'geɪdʒmənt] Ⓐ N 1 (*to marry*) compromiso *m*; (= *period of engagement*) noviazgo *m*; **they announced their ~ yesterday** anunciaron su compromiso ayer; **the ~ lasted ten months** el noviazgo duró diez meses; **the ~ is announced of Miss A to Mr B** la Srta. A y el Sr. B han anunciado su compromiso (matrimonial)

➤ LANGUAGE IN USE: engaged A3 24.2 engagement A1 24.2 A2 25.2

2 (= *appointment*) compromiso *m*, cita *f*; **I have a previous ~** ya tengo un compromiso
3 (= *undertaking*) compromiso *m*; **to enter into an ~ to do sth** comprometerse a hacer algo
4 (*Mil*) (= *battle*) batalla *f*, combate *m*
5 (= *contract*) contrato *m*; **a long ~ at a theatre** un contrato largo con un teatro
Ⓑ CPD ► **engagement book** N dietario *m*; (*at work*) agenda *f* de trabajo ► **engagement diary** N = **engagement book** ► **engagement party** N fiesta *f* de compromiso ► **engagement ring** N anillo *m* de compromiso *or* de pedida

engaging [ɪn'geɪdʒɪŋ] ADJ atractivo; [*enthusiasm etc*] contagioso

engagingly [ɪn'geɪdʒɪŋlɪ] ADV [*smile, write*] de manera atractiva, con encanto; **he was ~ honest about the reasons for his action** se ganó nuestra simpatía con su honestidad al explicar los motivos de su acto

engender [ɪn'dʒendəʳ] VT engendrar; (*fig*) engendrar, suscitar

engine ['endʒɪn] Ⓐ N 1 (= *motor*) (*in car, ship, plane*) motor *m*
2 (*Rail*) locomotora *f*, máquina *f*; **facing the ~** de frente a la máquina; **with your back to the ~** de espaldas a la máquina
Ⓑ CPD ► **engine block** N (*Aut*) bloque *m* del motor ► **engine driver** N (*Brit*) [*of train*] maquinista *mf* ► **engine failure** N avería *f* del motor ► **engine room** N (*Naut*) sala *f* de máquinas ► **engine shed** N (*Brit Rail*) cochera *f* de tren ► **engine trouble** N = **engine failure**

-engined ['endʒɪnd] ADJ (*ending in compounds*) **four-engined** de cuatro motores, cuatrimotor; **petrol-engined** con motor de gasolina

engineer [ˌendʒɪ'nɪəʳ] Ⓐ N ingeniero/a *m/f*; (*for repairs*) técnico/a *m/f*; (*US Rail*) maquinista *mf*; **ship's ~** ingeniero/a *m/f* naval; **electrical/TV ~** técnico/a *m/f* electricista/de televisión; **the Royal Engineers** (*Mil*) el Cuerpo de Ingenieros
Ⓑ VT (= *contrive*) [+ *plan*] maquinar; [+ *meeting*] organizar

engineering [ˌendʒɪ'nɪərɪŋ] Ⓐ N ingeniería *f*
Ⓑ CPD ► **engineering factory** N fábrica *f* de maquinaria ► **engineering industry** N industria *f* de ingeniería ► **engineering works** N taller *m* de ingeniería

England ['ɪŋglənd] N Inglaterra *f*

English ['ɪŋglɪʃ] Ⓐ ADJ inglés
Ⓑ N (*Ling*) inglés *m*; **Old ~** inglés *m* antiguo; **King's/Queen's ~** inglés *m* correcto; **in plain ~** en el habla corriente, ≈ en cristiano*; **~ as a Foreign Language** inglés para extranjeros; **~ as a Second Language** inglés como segunda lengua; **the ~** (= *people*) los ingleses
Ⓒ CPD ► **English breakfast** N desayuno *m* inglés *or* a la inglesa ► **the English Channel** N el Canal de la Mancha ► **English Heritage** N ≈ Patrimonio *m* Histórico-Artístico ► **English Language Teaching** N enseñanza *f* del inglés ► **English speaker** N anglohablante *mf*

ENGLISH

En el Reino Unido, se llama **Received Pronunciation** *o* **RP** *a un tipo de acento no asociado a ninguna región en concreto (si bien tuvo su origen en el inglés hablado en el sur de Inglaterra) que hoy en día usan especialmente las personas educadas en colegios privados, las clases dirigentes y los locutores en los informativos nacionales de la BBC. En los medios de comunicación se acepta ya el uso de acentos regionales siempre y cuando se use la norma lingüística, es decir, utilicen un inglés gramaticalmente correcto, el llamado* **Standard English**. *La pronunciación* **RP** *suele también tomarse como norma en la enseñanza del inglés británico como lengua extranjera. Todavía goza de cierto prestigio, aunque la gran mayoría de la población habla con el acento de su región, que puede ser más o menos marcado según su educación o clase social.*
El inglés americano difiere del inglés británico principalmente en la pronunciación, aunque también hay diferencias ortográficas y léxicas. Tiene también una pronunciación estándar, conocida por el nombre de **Network Standard**, *que es la que se usa en los medios de comunicación, así como diversas variedades regionales. A diferencia del Reino Unido, la asociación de acento y clase social no es muy evidente.*

Englishman ['ɪŋglɪʃmən] N (*pl* **Englishmen**) inglés *m*

English-speaking ['ɪŋglɪʃˌspiːkɪŋ] ADJ de habla inglesa, anglohablante

Englishwoman ['ɪŋglɪʃˌwʊmən] N (*pl* **Englishwomen**) inglesa *f*

Eng Lit ['ɪŋ'lɪt] N ABBR = **English Literature**

engorged [ɪn'gɔːdʒd] ADJ dilatado, hinchado; **to become ~** dilatarse, hincharse

engrave [ɪn'greɪv] VT (*Art, Typ*) grabar; (*fig*) grabar, imprimir

engraver [ɪn'greɪvəʳ] N (= *person*) grabador(a) *m/f*

engraving [ɪn'greɪvɪŋ] N (= *picture*) grabado *m*

engross [ɪn'grəʊs] VT 1 [+ *attention, person*] absorber
2 (*Jur*) copiar

engrossed [ɪn'grəʊst] ADJ absorto; **to be ~ in work/reading/one's thoughts** estar absorto en el trabajo/la lectura/los pensamientos; **to become ~ in** [+ *activity*] dedicarse por completo a

engrossing [ɪn'grəʊsɪŋ] ADJ absorbente

engulf [ɪn'gʌlf] VT (= *swallow up*) tragar; (= *immerse*) sumergir, hundir; **to be ~ed by** (*lit*) quedar sumergido bajo; **she felt ~ed by her grief** se sentía abrumada *or* hundida por el desconsuelo

enhance [ɪn'hɑːns] VT [+ *beauty, attraction*] realzar, dar realce a; [+ *position, reputation, chances*] mejorar; [+ *value, powers*] aumentar

enhancement [ɪn'hɑːnsmənt] N [*of beauty, attraction*] realce *m*, intensificación *f*; [*of reputation*] mejora *f*; [*of value, powers*] aumento *m*, incremento *m*

enigma [ɪ'nɪgmə] N enigma *m*

enigmatic [ˌenɪg'mætɪk] ADJ enigmático

enigmatically [ˌenɪg'mætɪkəlɪ] ADV enigmáticamente

enjambement [ɪn'dʒæmmənt] N encabalgamiento *m*

enjoin [ɪn'dʒɔɪn] VT (*frm*) [+ *obedience, silence, discretion*] imponer, exigir; **to ~ sth on sb** imponer algo a algn; **to ~ sb to sth/to do sth** exigir a algn algo/hacer algo; **to ~ sb from doing sth** (*US*) prohibir a algn hacer algo

▼ **enjoy** [ɪn'dʒɔɪ] VT 1 (= *take pleasure in*) [+ *meal, wine, occasion*] disfrutar de, disfrutar; **to ~ sth/doing sth: I ~ reading** me gusta leer; **did you ~ the game?** ¿te gustó el partido?; **I hope you ~ your holiday** que lo pases muy bien en las vacaciones; **to ~ life** disfrutar de la vida; **~ your meal!** ¡que aproveche!; **to ~ o.s.** pasarlo bien, divertirse; **we really ~ed ourselves** lo pasamos en grande, nos divertimos mucho; **he ~ed himself in London/on holiday** (se) lo pasó bien en Londres/las vacaciones; **~ yourself!** ¡que lo pases bien!, ¡que te diviertas!
2 (= *have benefit of*) [+ *good health, income, respect*] disfrutar de, gozar de; [+ *advantage*] poseer

enjoyable [ɪn'dʒɔɪəbl] ADJ (= *pleasant*) agradable; (= *amusing*) divertido

enjoyment [ɪn'dʒɔɪmənt] N 1 (= *pleasure*) placer *m*; **he listened with real ~** escuchó con verdadero placer; **to find ~ in sth/in doing sth** disfrutar *or* gozar de algo/haciendo algo
2 (= *possession*) [*of good health etc*] posesión *f*, disfrute *m*

enlarge [ɪn'lɑːdʒ] Ⓐ VT (*Phot*) ampliar; (*Med*) dilatar; [+ *house, business, circle of friends*] ampliar, extender
Ⓑ VI 1 extenderse, aumentarse
2 **to ~ (up)on** (= *explain*) entrar en detalles sobre

enlarged [ɪn'lɑːdʒd] ADJ [*edition*] aumentado; (*Med*) [*organ, gland*] hipertrofiado

enlargement [ɪn'lɑːdʒmənt] N (= *act*) aumento *m*; (*Phot*) ampliación *f*

enlarger [ɪn'lɑːdʒəʳ] N (*Phot*) ampliadora *f*

enlighten [ɪn'laɪtn] VT (= *inform*) informar, instruir; (*Rel frm*) iluminar; **can you ~ me?** ¿puedes explicármelo *or* aclarármelo?; **to ~ sb about** *or* **on sth** (= *inform*) poner a algn al corriente de algo; (= *clarify*) aclarar algo a algn

enlightened [ɪn'laɪtnd] ADJ [*person, society, policy, attitude*] progresista; **an ~ despot** un déspota ilustrado; **in this ~ age** *or* **in these ~ times** (*esp iro*) en esta época de tantos adelantos *or* progresos

enlightening [ɪn'laɪtnɪŋ] ADJ informativo; [*experience etc*] instructivo

enlightenment [ɪn'laɪtnmənt] N 1 (= *clarification*) **we need some ~ on this point** necesitamos una aclaración sobre este punto
2 (= *tolerance*) progresismo *m*; **sexual ~** progresismo *m* sexual; **the (Age of) Enlightenment** el Siglo de las Luces
3 (*Rel*) iluminación *f*; **spiritual ~** iluminación *f* espiritual

enlist [ɪn'lɪst] Ⓐ VT 1 (*Mil*) reclutar, alistar; **~ed man** (*US Mil*) soldado *m* raso
2 [+ *support etc*] conseguir
Ⓑ VI (*Mil*) alistarse (**in** en)

enlistment [ɪn'lɪstmənt] N alistamiento *m*

enliven [ɪn'laɪvn] VT (= *stimulate*) animar; (= *make lively*) avivar, animar

en masse [ɑ̃ːŋ'mæs] ADV en masa, masivamente

enmesh [ɪn'meʃ] VT (*lit*) coger en una red; **to get ~ed in** enredarse en

enmity ['enmɪtɪ] N (= *hatred*) enemistad *f*

ennoble [ɪ'nəʊbl] VT ennoblecer

ennui [ɑ̃ː'nwiː] N tedio *m*, hastío *m*

enology *etc* [iː'nɒlədʒɪ] N (*US*) = **oenology** *etc*

enormity [ɪ'nɔːmɪtɪ] N [*of task*] enormidad *f*; [*of crime, action*] gravedad *f*

enormous [ɪ'nɔːməs] ADJ 1 (*in physical size*) [*building, object*] enorme, inmenso; [*person, animal*] enorme; **an ~ great thing*** una cosa grandísima
2 (*fig*) [*patience, relief*] enorme; [*effort, variety*] enorme, inmenso; [*problems, difficulties*] enorme, muy grande; [*profits, losses*] enorme, cuantioso; [*appetite*] voraz; **he was on our side, and that made an ~ difference** él estaba de nuestra parte y eso supuso una enorme diferencia; **an ~ amount/number of sth** una

➤ LANGUAGE IN USE: **enjoy 1** 7.2

cantidad enorme de algo; **the country's industrial success has been bought at an ~ cost to the environment** el medio ambiente ha pagado un precio muy alto por el éxito industrial del país; **it gives me ~ pleasure to welcome Ed Lilly** es para mí un inmenso placer dar la bienvenida a Ed Lilly; **I get ~ pleasure from reading** la lectura es una enorme fuente de placer para mí

enormously [ɪˈnɔːməslɪ] ADV *[improve, vary, help]* enormemente; *[enjoy]* muchísimo, enormemente; *[like]* muchísimo; *[important, difficult, popular]* tremendamente; *[relieved]* inmensamente, enormemente; **it's ~ expensive** es tremendamente *or* enormemente caro, es carísimo; **he runs an ~ successful business** dirige un negocio muy próspero; **he launched an ~ successful stage career** inició una carrera teatral de enorme éxito

enough [ɪˈnʌf] Ⓐ ADJ suficiente, bastante; **we have ~ apples** tenemos suficientes *or* bastantes manzanas; **I've got ~ problems of my own** ya tengo suficientes *or* bastantes problemas con los míos; **I haven't ~ room** no tengo suficiente *or* bastante espacio, no tengo espacio suficiente; **did you get ~ sleep?** ¿has dormido bastante *or* lo suficiente?; **they didn't have ~ money to pay the rent** no tenían suficiente dinero (como) para pagar el alquiler; **more than ~ money/time** dinero/tiempo más que suficiente, dinero/tiempo de sobra; **to be proof ~ that ...** *(frm)* ser prueba suficiente de que ..., probar a las claras que ...

Ⓑ ADV [1] *(WITH VB)* *[suffer, help, talk]* bastante, lo suficiente; **I can't thank you ~** no puedo agradecértelo bastante *or* lo suficiente; **he opened the door just ~ to see out** abrió la puerta lo suficiente *or* lo bastante *or* lo justo (como) para poder mirar fuera

[2] *(WITH ADJ)* (lo) suficientemente, lo bastante; **it's not big ~** no es (lo) suficientemente grande, no es lo bastante grande; **he's old ~ to go alone** es (lo) suficientemente mayor *or* es lo bastante mayor (como) para ir solo; **that's a good ~ excuse** ésa es una buena excusa; **I'm sorry, that's not good ~** lo siento, pero eso no basta; **she seems happy ~** parece bien contenta; **she was fool ~** *or* **stupid ~ to listen to him** fue tan estúpida que le hizo caso; **he was kind ~ to lend me the money** tuvo la bondad *or* amabilidad de prestarme el dinero; **it's hard ~ to cope with two children, let alone with five** ya es difícil defenderse con dos niños, cuanto peor con cinco; *see also* **fair A1**, **sure B4**

[3] *(WITH ADV)* **he can't do it fast ~** no lo puede hacer lo bastante *or* lo suficientemente rápido, no lo puede hacer con la suficiente rapidez; **when he saw her coming he couldn't get away fast ~** cuando la vio venir desapareció todo lo rápido que pudo; **he hadn't prepared the report carefully ~** no había preparado el informe con la debida atención; **curiously** *or* **oddly** *or* **strangely ~** por extraño *or* raro que parezca; **you know well ~ that ...** sabes muy bien *or* de sobra que ...; **they seem to be settling down well ~** parece que se están adaptando bastante bien; **he writes well ~, I suppose** no escribe mal, supongo; *see also* **funnily**

Ⓒ PRON bastante, suficiente; **there are ~ for everyone** hay bastantes *or* suficientes para todos; **will £15 be ~?** ¿habrá bastante *or* suficiente con 15 libras?, ¿bastarán 15 libras?, ¿serán suficientes 15 libras?; **that's ~, thanks** con eso basta *or* ya es suficiente, gracias; **that's ~!** ¡basta ya!, ¡ya está bien!; **as if that weren't ~** por si eso fuera poco; **have you had ~ to eat?** ¿has comido bastante *or* lo suficiente?; **you don't eat ~** no comes bastante *or* lo suficiente; **we don't get paid ~** no nos pagan bastante *or* lo suficiente; **I have ~ to do without taking on more work** tengo ya bastante que hacer (como) para aceptar más trabajo; **we earn ~ to live on** ganamos lo bastante *or* lo suficiente (como) para vivir; **it's ~ to drive you mad*** es (como) para volverse loco; **enough's enough!** ¡basta ya!, ¡ya está bien!; **it is ~ for us to know that ...** nos basta con saber que ...; **we've got more than ~** tenemos más que suficiente(s) *or* más que de sobra; **he has had more than ~ to drink** ha bebido más de la cuenta; **I've had ~ of his silly behaviour** ya estoy harto de sus tonterías; **you can never have ~ of this scenery** nunca se cansa uno de este paisaje; **I think you have said ~** creo que ya has dicho bastante *or* suficiente; ✦***PROV*** **enough is as good as a feast** rogar a Dios por santos mas no por tantos

enquire *etc* [ɪnˈkwaɪəʳ] *see* **inquire** *etc*

enrage [ɪnˈreɪdʒ] VT enfurecer, hacer rabiar

enrapture [ɪnˈræptʃəʳ] VT embelesar, extasiar

enrich [ɪnˈrɪtʃ] VT [1] (= *improve*) [1·1] [+ *sb's life, society, language*] enriquecer; **it was an ~ing experience** fue una experiencia enriquecedora

[1·2] [+ *food*] enriquecer; [+ *soil*] fertilizar, abonar

[1·3] *(Phys)* [+ *uranium*] enriquecer

[2] (= *make wealthy*) enriquecer

enriched [ɪnˈrɪtʃt] ADJ *[food, uranium]* enriquecido; **bread ~ with folic acid** pan *m* enriquecido con ácido fólico

enrichment [ɪnˈrɪtʃmənt] N [1] (= *improvement*) [1·1] *[of sb's life, society, of language]* enriquecimiento *m*

[1·2] *[of soil]* fertilización *f*

[1·3] *(Phys)* *[of uranium]* enriquecimiento *m*

[2] *(financial)* enriquecimiento *m*

enrol, **enroll** *(US)* [ɪnˈrəʊl] Ⓐ VT [+ *member*] inscribir; [+ *student*] matricular; *(Mil)* alistar

Ⓑ VI *(on a course)* matricularse, inscribirse; *(in a club)* inscribirse, hacerse socio

enrolment, **enrollment** *(US)* [ɪnˈrəʊlmənt] N [1] *[of member]* inscripción *f*; *[of student]* matrícula *f*, inscripción *f*

[2] (= *numbers*) matrícula *f*

en route [ɑ̃ːnˈruːt] ADV **to be ~ for** *or* **to** ir camino de *or* a; **to be ~ from** venir de camino de; **it was stolen ~** se lo robaron durante el viaje

ensconce [ɪnˈskɒns] VT **to ~ o.s.** instalarse cómodamente, acomodarse; **to be ~d in** estar cómodamente instalado en

ensemble [ɑ̃ːnsɑ̃ːmbl] N [1] (= *whole*) conjunto *m*; (= *general effect*) impresión *f* de conjunto

[2] (= *dress*) conjunto *m*

[3] *(Mus)* conjunto *m* (musical)

enshrine [ɪnˈʃraɪn] VT *(fig)* encerrar, englobar; **to be ~d in law** ser consagrado por la ley

enshroud [ɪnˈʃraʊd] VT *(liter)* *(lit)* envolver, cubrir; **the case remains ~ed in mystery** el caso permanece envuelto en misterio

ensign [ˈensaɪn] N [1] (= *flag*) enseña *f*, pabellón *m*; *see also* **red C**, **white C**

[2] *(US Naut)* (= *rank*) alférez *mf*

enslave [ɪnˈsleɪv] VT esclavizar

enslavement [ɪnˈsleɪvmənt] N esclavitud *f*; (= *action*) esclavización *f*

ensnare [ɪnˈsneəʳ] VT *(lit, fig)* atrapar, coger en una trampa

ensue [ɪnˈsjuː] VI (= *follow*) seguir(se); (= *result*) resultar (**from** de)

> **ENOUGH**
>
> **Agreement**
>
> • When used as an *adjective* or *pronoun*, **bastante**, like **suficiente**, agrees with the noun it describes or refers to:
>
> Are there enough potatoes?
> ***¿Hay bastantes patatas?***
> Eggs? Yes, there are enough
> ***¿Huevos? Sí, hay bastantes***
>
> • Don't add an "s" to the *adverb* **bastante** (*i.e.* when it modifies an adjective or verb other than **ser**, **parecer** *etc*):
>
> They're not poor enough to get money from the State
> ***No son lo bastante pobres (como) para recibir dinero del Estado***
> We've studied these photographs enough
> ***Ya hemos estudiado bastante estas fotografías***
>
> **After verbs - adverbial Use**
>
> • When a purpose is implied or stated, translate using **lo suficiente** or, especially in affirmative phrases, **lo bastante**:
>
> We know enough to be able to say that these techniques are safe
> ***Sabemos lo suficiente*** *or* ***lo bastante (como) para afirmar que estas técnicas son seguras***
>
> • When no purpose is implied or stated, translate using either **bastante** or **lo suficiente**:
>
> He says he hasn't had enough to eat
> ***Dice que no ha comido bastante*** *or* ***no ha comido lo suficiente***
> We shall never be able to thank you enough
> ***Nunca se lo podremos agradecer bastante*** *or* ***lo suficiente***
>
> **After adjectives and adverbs**
>
> • Translate using **lo + bastante** + ADJECTIVE/ADVERB or **(lo) suficientemente** + ADJECTIVE/ADVERB:
>
> He isn't good enough to take part in the Olympics
> ***No es lo bastante*** *or* ***(lo) suficientemente bueno (como) para participar en las Olimpiadas***
> She couldn't run fast enough to catch him
> ***No pudo correr lo bastante*** *or* ***(lo) suficientemente rápido (como) para atraparlo*** ◇ ***No pudo correr lo bastante*** *or* ***lo suficiente (como) para atraparlo***
>
> **To be enough**
>
> • **To be enough** can often be translated using **bastar**:
>
> That's enough!
> ***¡Basta ya!***
> That's enough to feed an army!
> ***Con eso basta para dar de comer a un regimiento***
>
> **NOTE:** As **bastar** is an impersonal verb, it often takes an indirect object:
>
> Promises are no longer enough for him
> ***Ya no le bastan las promesas***
> That's enough for him
> ***Con eso le basta***
>
> *For further uses and examples, see main entry.*

ensuing [ɪnˈsjuːɪŋ] ADJ (= *subsequent*) subsiguiente; (= *resulting*) consiguiente

en suite [ɑ̃ˈswiːt] ADJ **with bathroom ~** ◊ **with an ~ bathroom** con baño adjunto

ensure [ɪnˈʃʊəʳ] VT asegurar (**that** que)

ENT ABBR *(Med)* = **ear, nose and throat**

➤ LANGUAGE IN USE: ensure 20.3

entail [ɪn'teɪl] Ⓐ VT 1 (= *necessitate*) suponer, implicar; [+ *hardship, suffering*] acarrear, traer consigo; **it ~s a lot of work** supone *or* implica mucho trabajo; **it ~ed buying a new car** supuso comprar un coche nuevo; **what does the job ~?** ¿en qué consiste el trabajo?
2 (*Jur*) vincular
Ⓑ N (*Jur*) vínculo *m*

entangle [ɪn'tæŋgl] VT 1 [+ *thread etc*] enredar, enmarañar
2 (*fig*) **to become ~d in sth** verse envuelto en algo, enredarse en algo; **to get ~d with sb** liarse con algn*

entanglement [ɪn'tæŋglmənt] N 1 (= *being entangled*) enredo *m*; (*fig*) lío* *m*
2 (= *love affair*) lío *m* amoroso*
3 (*Mil*) alambrada *f*

entente [ɑ̃:n'tɑ̃:nt] N (*Pol*) entente *f*

enter ['entəʳ] Ⓐ VT 1 (= *go into, come into*) [+ *room, country, tunnel*] entrar en; [+ *bus, train*] subir a; **the phrase has already ~ed the language** la frase ya ha entrado en el idioma; **where the River Wyre ~s the Thames** donde el río Wyre confluye con el Támesis; **the ship ~ed harbour** el barco entró en el puerto; **the thought never ~ed my head** jamás se me ocurrió, jamás se me pasó por la cabeza; **to ~ hospital** (*frm*) ingresar en el hospital
2 (= *penetrate*) [+ *market*] introducirse en; (*sexually*) penetrar
3 (= *join*) [+ *army, navy*] alistarse en, enrolarse en; [+ *college, school*] entrar en; [+ *company, organization*] incorporarse a, entrar a formar parte de; [+ *profession*] ingresar en, entrar en; [+ *discussion, conversation*] unirse a, intervenir en; [+ *war*] entrar en; **he ~ed the church** se hizo sacerdote; **he decided to ~ a monastery** decidió hacerse monje; **he ~ed politics at a young age** se metió en la política cuando era joven
4 (= *go in for*) [+ *live competition, exam*] presentarse a; [+ *race, postal competition*] participar en, tomar parte en
5 (= *enrol*) [+ *pupil*] (*for school*) matricular, inscribir; (*for examination*) presentar; **how many students are you ~ing this year?** ¿a cuántos alumnos presentas este año?; **to ~ sth/sb for sth: he ~ed his son for Eton** matriculó *or* inscribió a su hijo en Eton; **to ~ a horse for a race** inscribir a un caballo para una carrera; **she had intended to ~ the piece of work for a competition** su intención había sido presentar el trabajo a un concurso
6 (= *write down*) [+ *name*] escribir, apuntar; [+ *claim, request*] presentar, formular; (*Fin*) [+ *amount, transaction*] registrar, anotar; (*Comm*) [+ *order*] registrar, anotar; **~ your answers in the boxes provided** escriba las respuestas en las casillas
7 (= *begin*) entrar en; **as the war ~s its second month** al entrar la guerra en su segundo mes; **the crisis is ~ing a new phase** la crisis está entrando en una nueva fase
8 (*Comput*) [+ *data*] introducir
9 (*Jur*) **to ~ an appeal** presentar un recurso de apelación; **to ~ a plea of guilty/not guilty** declararse culpable/no culpable
Ⓑ VI 1 (= *come in, go in*) entrar; **~!** (*frm*) ¡adelante!, ¡pase!
2 (*Theat*) entrar en escena; **~, stage left** entra en escena por la izquierda del escenario; **~ Macbeth** entra en escena Macbeth
3 **to ~ for** [+ *live competition*] (= *put name down for*) inscribirse en; (= *take part in*) presentarse a; [+ *race, postal competition*] (= *put name down for*) inscribirse en; (= *take part in*) participar en; **are you going to ~ for the exam?** ¿te vas a presentar al examen?

►**enter into** VI + PREP 1 (= *engage in*) [+ *agreement*] llegar a; [+ *contract*] firmar; [+ *relationship, argument*] iniciar; [+ *explanation, details*] entrar en; [+ *conversation, correspondence, negotiations*] entablar; **to ~ into the spirit of things** ambientarse; *see also* **partnership A2**
2 (= *affect*) [+ *plans, calculations*] influir en; **do their wishes ~ into your plans at all?** ¿sus deseos influyen para algo en tus planes?; **money doesn't ~ into it** el dinero no tiene nada que ver

►**enter on, enter upon** VI + PREP [+ *career*] emprender; [+ *period, term of office*] empezar; (*Comm, Fin*) [+ *transaction, investment*] realizar

►**enter up** VT + ADV [+ *facts, information*] escribir, anotar; [+ *diary, ledger*] poner al día

enteric [en'terɪk] Ⓐ ADJ entérico
Ⓑ CPD ► **enteric fever** N fiebre *f* entérica

enteritis [ˌentə'raɪtɪs] N enteritis *f inv*

enterprise ['entəpraɪz] Ⓐ N 1 (= *firm, undertaking*) empresa *f*
2 (= *initiative*) iniciativa *f*; **free ~** la libre empresa; **private ~** la empresa privada
Ⓑ CPD ► **the enterprise culture** N la cultura empresarial ► **enterprise zone** N *zona declarada de especial interés para el fomento de actividades empresariales*

enterprising ['entəpraɪzɪŋ] ADJ [*person, spirit*] emprendedor; [*company, idea, scheme*] innovador; **that was ~ of her!** ¡qué emprendedora!

enterprisingly ['entəpraɪzɪŋlɪ] ADV con mucha iniciativa

entertain [ˌentə'teɪn] Ⓐ VT 1 (= *amuse*) [+ *audience*] divertir, entretener
2 (= *offer hospitality to*) [+ *guest*] recibir; **to ~ sb to dinner** (*frm*) invitar a algn a cenar
3 (= *consider*) [+ *idea, hope*] abrigar; [+ *proposal*] tomar en consideración; [+ *doubts*] albergar; **I wouldn't ~ it for a moment** jamás se me ocurriría tal cosa
Ⓑ VI 1 (= *amuse*) [*book, film, performer*] entretener
2 (= *have visitors*) recibir visitas; **they ~ a good deal** reciben muchos invitados

entertainer [ˌentə'teɪnəʳ] N artista *mf*

entertaining [ˌentə'teɪnɪŋ] Ⓐ ADJ [*person*] divertido; [*film, book, account, evening*] entretenido, ameno
Ⓑ N **I like ~** me gusta tener invitados; **she does a lot of ~** invita a gente a menudo, recibe a menudo (*frm*)

entertainingly [ˌentə'teɪnɪŋlɪ] ADV [*say, talk*] de manera divertida, de modo ameno; **an ~ irreverent book** un libro irreverente y divertido

entertainment [ˌentə'teɪnmənt] Ⓐ N 1 (= *amusement*) [*of guests*] entretenimiento *m*; [*of audience*] diversión *f*; **for your ~** para divertiros
2 (= *show*) espectáculo *m*; (= *musical entertainment*) concierto *m*; **to put on an ~** organizar un espectáculo; **the world of ~** el mundo del espectáculo
Ⓑ CPD ► **entertainment allowance** N gastos *mpl* de representación ► **entertainment expenses** NPL = **entertainment allowance** ► **entertainment guide** N guía *f* del ocio ► **entertainment tax** N impuesto *m* de espectáculos ► **the entertainment world** N el mundo del espectáculo

enthral, enthrall (*US*) [ɪn'θrɔ:l] VT (*gen passive*) cautivar, embelesar; **we listened ~led** escuchamos embelesados

enthralling [ɪn'θrɔ:lɪŋ] ADJ cautivador, embelesador

enthrone [ɪn'θrəʊn] VT (*lit*) entronizar; (*fig*) [+ *idea*] consagrar

enthronement [ɪn'θrəʊnmənt] N (*lit*) entronización *f*; (*fig*) consagración *f*

enthuse [ɪn'θu:z] VI **to ~ over** *or* **about sth/sb** entusiasmarse con algo/algn

enthusiasm [ɪn'θu:zɪæzəm] N 1 (= *excitement*) entusiasmo *m* (**for** por); **without ~** sin entusiasmo; **the news aroused little ~ in the White House** la noticia despertó poco entusiasmo en la Casa Blanca; **the idea filled her with ~** la idea la entusiasmó; **to show ~ for sth** mostrarse entusiasmado por algo; *see also* **work up A1**
2 (= *interest, hobby*) interés *m*; **photography is one of her many ~s** la fotografía es uno de sus muchos intereses

enthusiast [ɪn'θu:zɪæst] N entusiasta *mf*; **he is a jazz/bridge ~** es un entusiasta del jazz/bridge; **a Vivaldi ~** un enamorado *or* entusiasta de Vivaldi

enthusiastic [ɪnˌθu:zɪ'æstɪk] ADJ [*skier, supporter, crowd, applause*] entusiasta; **to be ~ about** [+ *photography, chess, art*] ser un entusiasta de; [+ *idea, suggestion*] estar entusiasmado con; **to be ~ about doing sth** estar entusiasmado por hacer algo; **to become ~ about sth** entusiasmarse con algo; **she was less than ~ about the idea** no le entusiasmaba nada la idea; **I tried to sound ~** intenté parecer entusiasmado

enthusiastically [ɪnˌθu:zɪ'æstɪkəlɪ] ADV [*greet, support, speak*] con entusiasmo; **he shouted ~** gritó entusiasmado

entice [ɪn'taɪs] VT (= *tempt*) atraer, tentar; (= *seduce*) seducir; **to ~ sb away from sb** convencer a algn de que deje a algn; **to ~ sb into a room** engatusar a algn para que entre en una habitación; **to ~ sb into doing sth** *or* **to do sth** tentar a algn a hacer algo; **to ~ sb with food/an offer** tentar a algn con comida/una oferta

enticement [ɪn'taɪsmənt] N 1 (= *attraction*) tentación *f*, atracción *f*
2 (= *seduction*) seducción *f*
3 (= *bait*) atractivo *m*

enticing [ɪn'taɪsɪŋ] ADJ tentador, atractivo

enticingly [ɪn'taɪsɪŋlɪ] ADV atractivamente, de manera atractiva

entire [ɪn'taɪəʳ] ADJ 1 (= *whole*) entero; **the ~ world** el mundo entero, todo el mundo; **she cleaned the ~ house** limpió toda la casa, limpió la casa entera; **he didn't speak throughout the ~ evening** no habló en toda la tarde; **his ~ earnings for a year** la totalidad de sus ingresos anuales; **he has my ~ confidence** tiene toda mi confianza
2 (= *complete*) completo; **an ~ dinner service** una vajilla completa

entirely [ɪn'taɪəlɪ] ADV 1 (= *completely*) [*satisfied, convinced*] completamente, enteramente; [*different*] totalmente, completamente; [*possible*] totalmente; **that's another matter ~** eso es otra cosa, eso es una cosa completamente distinta; **I don't ~ agree** no estoy totalmente de acuerdo; **that is not ~ true** eso no es del todo *or* no es enteramente cierto
2 (= *exclusively*) enteramente, exclusivamente; **it's ~ up to you** depende de ti exclusivamente, depende enteramente de ti; **it was his fault ~** fue totalmente *or* enteramente culpa suya; **the concert was devoted ~ to Mozart** el concierto estuvo enteramente *or* exclusivamente dedicado a Mozart, el concierto estuvo dedicado a Mozart en su totalidad; **to**

be made ~ of wood estar hecho totalmente de madera

entirety [ɪn'taɪərətɪ] N **in its ~** en su totalidad, íntegramente

entitle [ɪn'taɪtl] VT **1** [+ *book etc*] titular; **the book is ~d ...** el libro se titula ...
2 (= *give right*) dar derecho a; **to ~ sb to sth/to do sth** dar derecho a algn a algo/a hacer algo; **to be ~d to sth/to do sth** tener derecho a algo/a hacer algo; **you are quite ~d to do as you wish** tienes todo el derecho a hacer lo que quieras; **I think I am ~d to some respect** creo que se me debe cierto respeto

entitlement [ɪn'taɪtlmənt] N derecho *m*; **holiday ~** derecho *m* a vacaciones

entity ['entɪtɪ] N entidad *f*; **legal ~** persona *f* jurídica

entomb [ɪn'tu:m] VT (*liter*) sepultar

entombment [ɪn'tu:mmənt] N (*liter*) sepultura *f*

entomological [,entəmə'lɒdʒɪkəl] ADJ entomológico

entomologist [,entə'mɒlədʒɪst] N entomólogo/a *m/f*

entomology [,entə'mɒlədʒɪ] N entomología *f*

entourage [,ɒntʊ'rɑ:ʒ] N séquito *m*

entr'acte ['ɒntrækt] N intermedio *m*, entreacto *m*

entrails ['entreɪlz] NPL entrañas *fpl*; (*US*) asadura *f*, menudos *mpl*

entrain [ɪn'treɪn] VI (*esp Mil*) tomar el tren (**for** a)

entrance[1] ['entrəns] Ⓐ N **1** (= *way in*) entrada *f*; **front/back ~** entrada *f* principal/trasera
2 (= *act*) entrada *f* (**into** en); (*into profession etc*) ingreso *m*; (*Theat*) entrada *f* en escena; **to make one's ~** hacer su entrada; (*Theat*) entrar en escena
3 (= *right to enter*) (derecho *m* de) entrada *f*; **to gain ~ to** [+ *a place*] conseguir entrar en *or* acceder a; [+ *a profession etc*] conseguir ingresar en
Ⓑ CPD ► **entrance card** N pase *m* ► **entrance exam(ination)** N (*to school*) examen *m* de ingreso ► **entrance fee** N (*to a show*) (precio *m* de) entrada *f*; (*to a club, society etc*) cuota *f* de ingreso ► **entrance hall** N vestíbulo *m*, antesala *f* ► **entrance qualifications** NPL = **entrance requirements** ► **entrance ramp** N (*US Aut*) rampa *f* de acceso ► **entrance requirements** NPL requisitos *mpl* de ingreso

entrance[2] [ɪn'trɑ:ns] VT **1** (= *bewitch*) encantar, hechizar
2 (*gen passive*) (= *captivate*) **we listened ~d** escuchamos extasiados *or* embelesados

entrancing [ɪn'trɑ:nsɪŋ] ADJ [*film, music*] fascinante; **she looked ~** estaba cautivadora

entrancingly [ɪn'trɑ:nsɪŋlɪ] ADV [*play, dance, sing*] maravillosamente; **she is ~ beautiful** tiene una belleza cautivadora; **it's ~ simple** es tan sencillo que resulta fascinante

entrant ['entrənt] N (*in race, competition*) participante *mf*, concurrente *mf*; (*in exam*) candidato/a *m/f*; (*to profession*) principiante *mf*

entrap [ɪn'træp] VT coger en una trampa; (*fig*) entrampar

entrapment [ɪn'træpmənt] N (*Jur*) *acción por la que agentes de la ley incitan a algn a cometer un delito para poder arrestarlo*; **he complained of ~** se quejó de que le habían hecho caer en una trampa

entreat [ɪn'tri:t] VT rogar, suplicar; **to ~ sb to do sth** suplicar a algn que haga algo

entreating [ɪn'tri:tɪŋ] Ⓐ ADJ suplicante
Ⓑ N súplicas *fpl*, imploraciones *fpl*

entreatingly [ɪn'tri:tɪŋlɪ] ADV [*look, ask*] de modo suplicante

entreaty [ɪn'tri:tɪ] N súplica *f*, ruego *m*; **they ignored our entreaties** hicieron caso omiso de nuestras súplicas *or* nuestros ruegos; **a look of ~** una mirada suplicante

entrée ['ɒntreɪ] N **1** (= *entrance*) entrada *f*
2 (*Culin*) plato *m* fuerte *or* principal

entrench [ɪn'trentʃ] VT **1** (= *consolidate*) consolidar, afianzar; **to ~ o.s.** consolidarse, afianzarse; **to ~ o.s. in a position/an idea** atrincherarse en una posición/idea
2 (*Mil*) atrincherar; **to ~ o.s.** atrincherarse

entrenched [ɪn'trentʃt] ADJ **1** (*pej*) (= *established*) [*idea, belief, attitude*] arraigado; [*position, power*] afianzado; **deeply ~** [*idea, belief, attitude*] profundamente arraigado; [*position, power*] firmemente afianzado; **to be ~ in the belief/view that ...** mantener obcecadamente la creencia/opinión de que ...; **he's too ~ in the past** está demasiado anclado en el pasado
2 (*Mil*) atrincherado

entrenchment [ɪn'trentʃmənt] N **1** (*Mil*) trinchera *f*
2 (= *establishment*) [*of rights, standards*] afianzamiento *m*

entrepôt ['ɒntrəpəʊ] N (= *town*) centro *m* comercial, centro *m* de distribución; (= *warehouse*) almacén *m*, depósito *m*

entrepreneur [,ɒntrəprə'nɜ:ʳ] N (*Comm*) empresario/a *m/f*; (*Fin*) capitalista *mf*

entrepreneurial [,ɒntrəprə'nɜ:rɪəl] ADJ empresarial

entrepreneurship [,ɒntrəprə'nɜ:ʃɪp] N espíritu *m* empresarial *or* emprendedor; **to promote ~** promover la iniciativa empresarial

entropy ['entrəpɪ] N entropía *f*

entrust [ɪn'trʌst] VT **to ~ sth to sb** ◊ **~ sb with sth** confiar algo a algn

entry ['entrɪ] Ⓐ N **1** (= *entrance*) **1·1** (= *act of entering*) (*into organization*) entrada *f* (**into** en); (*into profession*) ingreso *m* (**into** en); (= *access*) acceso *m* (**into** a); **Britain's ~ into the EC** la entrada de Gran Bretaña en la CE; **she was denied ~ into the country** le negaron acceso al país; **~ into the hall had been forbidden** se había prohibido el acceso a la sala; **"no entry"** "prohibida la entrada"; (*Aut*) "prohibido el paso"; **he gained ~ to the house by breaking a window** consiguió entrar en la casa rompiendo una ventana; **they opposed France's ~ into the war** se opusieron a que Francia entrara en la guerra; **to make one's ~** hacer su entrada; **point of ~** (*into country*) punto *m* de entrada; **port of ~** puerto *m* de entrada
1·2 (= *doorway, hall*) entrada *f*
2 (= *sth recorded*) (*in diary*) anotación *f*, apunte *m*; (*in account*) entrada *f*, partida *f*, rubro *m* (*LAm*); (*in record, ship's log*) entrada *f*, apunte *m*; (*in reference book*) entrada *f*
3 (*in competition*) (= *total of competitors*) participantes *mpl*; (= *person*) participante *mf*; **the first correct ~ pulled from our postbag on January 24** la primera carta con la respuesta correcta que se saque de nuestra saca de correo el día 24 de enero; **entries must be submitted by March 29** las cartas/los cuentos/los diseños *etc* deben llegar antes del 29 de marzo; **the winning ~ in a writing competition** la obra ganadora de un concurso de redacción
Ⓑ CPD ► **entry fee** N cuota *f* de inscripción ► **entry form** N formulario *m* de inscripción, impreso *m* de inscripción ► **entry permit** N permiso *m* de entrada ► **entry phone** N portero *m* automático ► **entry qualifications**, **entry requirements** NPL requisitos *mpl* de entrada ► **entry word** N (*US*) (*in reference book*) entrada *f*

entry-level ['entrɪlevl] ADJ **1** (= *starting*) [*salary, position*] inicial
2 (*Comput*) básico

entwine [ɪn'twaɪn] VT (= *plait*) entrelazar; (= *twist around*) enroscar

enumerate [ɪ'nju:məreɪt] VT (= *list*) enumerar

enumeration [ɪ,nju:mə'reɪʃən] N enumeración *f*

enunciate [ɪ'nʌnsɪeɪt] VT [+ *word, sound*] pronunciar, articular; [+ *theory, idea*] enunciar

enunciation [ɪ,nʌnsɪ'eɪʃən] N [*of word, sound*] pronunciación *f*, articulación *f*; [*of theory, idea*] enunciación *f*

enuresis [,enjʊə'ri:sɪs] N enuresis *f*

enuretic [,enjʊ'retɪk] ADJ enurético

envelop [ɪn'veləp] VT (*lit, fig*) envolver (**in** en)

envelope ['envələʊp] N [*of letter*] sobre *m*; (*fig*) (= *wrapping*) funda *f*

enveloping [ɪn'veləpɪŋ] ADJ [*movement*] envolvente

envelopment [ɪn'veləpmənt] N envolvimiento *m*

envenom [ɪn'venəm] VT envenenar

enviable ['envɪəbl] ADJ envidiable

envious ['envɪəs] ADJ [*person*] envidioso; [*glance, look, tone*] de envidia; **to be ~ that** tener envidia de que + *subjun*, tener envidia porque; **she's ~ that you have what she doesn't** tiene envidia de que tú tengas *or* porque tú tienes lo que ella no tiene; **it makes me ~** me da envidia; **to be ~ of sth/sb** tener envidia de algo/algn, envidiar algo/a algn; **I am ~ of your good luck** envidio tu suerte

enviously ['envɪəslɪ] ADV con envidia

environment [ɪn'vaɪərənmənt] N **1** (= *surroundings*) (*gen*) entorno *m*, ambiente *m*; (*Zool, Bot*) entorno *m*, medio *m*; **a safe working ~** un entorno *or* un ambiente de trabajo seguro; **a working-class ~** un entorno *or* ambiente de clase trabajadora; **to observe animals in their natural ~** observar a los animales en su entorno *or* medio natural; **the ~** (*Ecol*) el medio ambiente; **measures to protect the ~** medidas *fpl* para proteger el medio ambiente; **Department of the Environment** (*Brit*) Ministerio *m* del Medio Ambiente
2 (*Comput*) entorno *m*

environmental [ɪn,vaɪərən'mentl] Ⓐ ADJ **1** (= *ecological*) [*pollution, policy, issues*] medioambiental; [*problems, disaster, damage*] ecológico, medioambiental; [*group, movement*] ecologista; [*impact*] ambiental; **it will have disastrous ~ effects** tendrá efectos desastrosos en el medio ambiente
2 (= *situational*) **the ~ factors in mental illness** la influencia de los factores del medio ambiente en las enfermedades mentales
Ⓑ CPD ► **environmental health** N salud *f* ambiental ► **Environmental Health Department** N (*Brit*) Departamento *m* de Sanidad y Medio Ambiente ► **environmental health officer** N (*Brit*) funcionario/a *m/f* del Departamento de Sanidad y Medio Ambiente ► **environmental health regulation** N normativa *f* de sanidad y medio ambiente ► **Environmental Health Service** N Servicio *m* de Sanidad y Medio Ambiente ► **En-**

vironmental Protection Agency N (*US*) Organización *f* de Protección del Medio Ambiente ► **environmental studies** NPL (= *subject*) ecología *fsing*; (= *research*) estudios *mpl* medioambientales

environmentalism [ɪn,vaɪrən'mentəlɪzəm] N ambientalismo *m*

environmentalist [ɪn,vaɪrən'mentəlɪst] Ⓐ ADJ ambiental, ecologista
Ⓑ N ecologista *mf*

environmentally [ɪn,vaɪərən'mentlɪ] ADV [1] (= *ecologically*) **we're more ~ aware now** ahora somos más conscientes del medio ambiente; **their policies are ~ sound** las medidas que adoptan son correctos desde el punto de vista medioambiental; **their products are ~ friendly** sus productos son ecológicos, sus productos no dañan el medio ambiente; **~ sensitive areas** zonas *fpl* de riesgo medioambiental
[2] (= *in the environment*) **an ~ acquired** *or* **induced disease** una enfermedad que se adquiere a través del medio ambiente

environment-friendly [ɪn'vaɪrənment'frendlɪ] ADJ ecológico, que no daña el medio ambiente

environs [ɪn'vaɪərənz] N alrededores *mpl*, inmediaciones *fpl*

envisage [ɪn'vɪzɪdʒ] VT [1] (= *expect*) prever; **it is ~d that ...** se prevé que ...; **an increase is ~d next year** está previsto un aumento para el año que viene
[2] (= *imagine*) imaginarse; **it is hard to ~ such a situation** es difícil imaginarse tal situación

envision [ɪn'vɪʒən] VT (*US*) = **envisage**

envoy ['envɔɪ] N (= *messenger*) mensajero/a *m/f*; (= *diplomat*) enviado/a *m/f*; **special ~** enviado/a *m/f* especial

envy ['envɪ] Ⓐ N envidia *f*; **a look of ~** una mirada de envidia; **filled with ~** lleno de envidia; **to do sth out of ~** hacer algo por envidia; **it was the ~ of everyone** era la envidia de todos; ✦***IDIOM*** **to be green with ~** morirse de envidia
Ⓑ VT envidiar, tener envidia de; **she envies her sister** envidia a su hermana, tiene envidia de su hermana, le tiene envidia a su hermana; **I don't ~ you!** ¡no te envidio!, ¡no te tengo ninguna envidia!; **to ~ sb sth** envidiar algo a algn; **she envied him his confidence** le envidiaba la seguridad que tenía en sí mismo

enzyme ['enzaɪm] N enzima *f*

EOC N ABBR (*Brit*) (= **Equal Opportunities Commission**) ≈ PIO *m* (*Sp*)

Eocene ['iːəʊsiːn] ADJ (*Geol*) eoceno

eolithic [,iːəʊ'lɪθɪk] ADJ eolítico

eon ['iːən, 'iːɒn] N (*US*) = **aeon**

EP N ABBR (= **extended play**) maxi-single *m*

EPA N ABBR (*US*) = **Environmental Protection Agency**

epaulette ['epɔːlet] N charretera *f*

epee, epée ['epeɪ] N espada *f* de esgrima

ephedrine ['efɪdrɪn] N efedrina *f*

ephemera [ɪ'femərə] NPL (*pl* **ephemeras** *or* **ephemerae** [ɪ'femə,riː]) (= *transitory items*) cosas *fpl* efímeras; (= *collectables*) objetos *mpl* coleccionables (*sin valor*)

ephemeral [ɪ'femərəl] ADJ efímero

Ephesians [ɪ'fiːʒənz] NPL efesios *mpl*

epic ['epɪk] Ⓐ ADJ épico; (*fig*) (*) excepcional, épico
Ⓑ N epopeya *f*; (= *film*) película *f* épica

epicene ['epɪsiːn] ADJ epiceno

epicentre, epicenter (*US*) ['epɪsentəʳ] N epicentro *m*

epicure ['epɪkjʊəʳ] N gastrónomo/a *m/f*

epicurean [,epɪkjʊ'riːən] Ⓐ ADJ epicúreo
Ⓑ N epicúreo *m*

epicureanism [,epɪkjʊə'rɪənɪzəm] N epicureísmo *m*

epidemic [,epɪ'demɪk] Ⓐ ADJ epidémico
Ⓑ N epidemia *f*; (*fig*) ola *f*

epidermis [,epɪ'dɜːmɪs] N epidermis *f*

epidural [,epɪ'djʊərəl] Ⓐ ADJ epidural
Ⓑ N (*also* **~ anaesthetic**) (anestesia *f*) epidural *f*

epiglottis [,epɪ'glɒtɪs] N (*pl* **epiglottises** *or* **epiglottides** [,epɪ'glɒtɪ,diːz]) epiglotis *f inv*

epigram ['epɪgræm] N epigrama *m*

epigrammatic [,epɪgrə'mætɪk] ADJ epigramático

epigrammatical [,epɪgrə'mætɪkəl] ADJ = **epigrammatic**

epigraph ['epɪgrɑːf] N epígrafe *m*

epigraphy [ɪ'pɪgrəfɪ] N epigrafía *f*

epilepsy ['epɪlepsɪ] N epilepsia *f*

epileptic [,epɪ'leptɪk] Ⓐ ADJ epiléptico
Ⓑ N epiléptico/a *m/f*
Ⓒ CPD ► **epileptic fit** N ataque *m* de epilepsia, acceso *m* epiléptico

epilogue ['epɪlɒg] N epílogo *m*

Epiphany [ɪ'pɪfənɪ] N Epifanía *f*

episcopacy [ɪ'pɪskəpəsɪ] N episcopado *m*

episcopal [ɪ'pɪskəpəl] ADJ episcopal

episcopalian [ɪ,pɪskə'peɪlɪən] Ⓐ ADJ episcopalista
Ⓑ N **Episcopalian** episcopalista *mf*

episcopate [ɪ'pɪskəʊpət] N episcopado *m*

episode ['epɪsəʊd] N (= *event*) acontecimiento *m*; (*TV, Rad*) capítulo *m*, episodio *m*; (*Press*) entrega *f*; (*Med*) ataque *m*

episodic [,epɪ'sɒdɪk] ADJ episódico

epistemological [ɪ,pɪstɪmə'lɒdʒɪkəl] ADJ epistemológico

epistemology [ɪ,pɪstə'mɒlədʒɪ] N epistemología *f*

epistle [ɪ'pɪsl] N (*hum*) (= *letter*) epístola *f*; **Epistle** (*Rel*) Epístola *f*

epistolary [ɪ'pɪstələrɪ] ADJ epistolar

epitaph ['epɪtɑːf] N epitafio *m*

epithet ['epɪθet] N epíteto *m*

epitome [ɪ'pɪtəmɪ] N representación *f*, paradigma *m*; **to be the ~ of virtue** ser la virtud en persona *or* personificada

epitomize [ɪ'pɪtəmaɪz] VT personificar, resumir; **he ~d resistance to the enemy** él era el paradigma de la resistencia al enemigo; **she ~s today's career woman** es el prototipo de la mujer de carrera moderna

EPNS N ABBR = **electroplated nickel silver**

epoch ['iːpɒk] N época *f*; **to mark an ~** hacer época, marcar un hito

epochal ['epəkəl] ADJ (*frm*) = **epoch-making**

epoch-making ['iːpɒk,meɪkɪŋ] ADJ que hace época

eponymous [ɪ'pɒnɪməs] ADJ epónimo

EPOS ['iːpɒs] N ABBR (= **electronic point of sale**) *sistema computerizado en tiendas para registrar el precio de las compras*

epoxy resin [ɪ'pɒksɪ'rezɪn] N resina *f* epoxídica

EPROM ['iːprɒm] N ABBR (*Comput*) = **erasable programmable read only memory**

Epsom salts ['epsɒm,sɔːlts] NPL epsomita *fsing*

EPU N ABBR (= **European Payments Union**) UEP *f*

EPW N ABBR (*US*) = **enemy prisoner of war**

equable ['ekwəbl] ADJ [*climate etc*] estable; [*person*] ecuánime; [*tone*] tranquilo, afable

equably ['ekwəblɪ] ADV sosegadamente, con ecuanimidad

equal ['iːkwəl] Ⓐ ADJ [1] (= *identical in size, value*) [*number, amount*] igual; **the cake was divided into twelve ~ parts** el pastel estaba dividida en doce partes iguales; **to be of ~ importance/value** tener igual importancia/el mismo valor; **with ~ ease/indifference** con igual *or* la misma facilidad/indiferencia; **to come ~ first/second** (*in competition*) compartir el primer/segundo puesto; (*in race*) llegar ambos en primer/segundo lugar; **to be ~ in sth: they are ~ in strength** son igual de fuertes, tienen la misma fuerza; **they are ~ in size** son del mismo tamaño, son iguales de tamaño; **they are ~ in value** tienen el mismo valor, tienen igual valor; **on ~ terms** de igual a igual; **all** *or* **other things being ~** si no intervienen otros factores; **an amount ~ to half your salary** una cantidad equivalente a la mitad de tu sueldo; **to be ~ to sth** (= *equivalent*) equivaler a algo; **his silence was ~ to an admission of guilt** su silencio equivalía a una admisión de culpabilidad; **a metre is ~ to 39 inches** un metro equivale a 39 pulgadas; **she is ~ to her mother in intelligence** es tan inteligente como su madre, es igual de inteligente que su madre; ✦***PROV*** **we are all ~ before** *or* **in the eyes of God** todos somos iguales a los ojos de Dios; *see also* **footing**
[2] (= *capable*) **to be/feel ~ to sth: I'm confident that he is ~ to the task** tengo la seguridad de que está capacitado para desempeñar la tarea; **she did not feel ~ to going out** no se sentía con fuerzas *or* ánimo para salir; **she was ~ to the situation** estaba a la altura de la situación
Ⓑ N [1] (= *person*) igual *mf*; **she is his ~** ella es su igual; **she has no ~** no hay nadie que se la iguale; **they are intellectual ~s** intelectualmente están a la par; **to treat sb as an ~** tratar a algn de igual a igual
[2] (= *thing*) **to have no ~** ◊ **be without ~** no tener igual; **the film has no ~ in cinema history** la película no tiene igual en la historia del cine; **a talent without ~** un talento sin igual *or* sin par
Ⓒ VT [1] (*Math*) ser igual a; **let x ~ y** si x es igual a y, suponiendo que x sea igual a y; **two plus two ~s four** dos y dos son cuatro
[2] [+ *record, rival, quality*] igualar; **there is nothing to ~ it** no hay nada que se le iguale, no hay nada que lo iguale; **prices not to be ~led** precios sin competencia
Ⓓ CPD ► **equal opportunities** NPL igualdad *fsing* de oportunidades ► **Equal Opportunities Commission** N (*Brit*) Comisión *f* para la Igualdad de Oportunidades ► **equal opportunities** *or* **opportunity employer** N empresa *f* no discriminatoria ► **equal pay** N igual salario *m*; **~ pay for ~ work** igual salario *or* el mismo salario para el mismo trabajo ► **equal rights** NPL igualdad *fsing* de derechos ► **equals sign, equal sign** N (*Math*) signo *m* de igual ► **equal time** N (*US Rad, TV*) derecho *m* de respuesta

equality [ɪ'kwɒlɪtɪ] N igualdad *f*; **~ of opportunity** igualdad *f* de oportunidades

equalization [,iːkwəlaɪ'zeɪʃən] Ⓐ N igualización *f*; (*Fin*) compensación *f*
Ⓑ CPD ► **equalization account** N cuenta *f* de compensación ► **equalization fund** N fondo *m* de compensación

equalize ['iːkwəlaɪz] Ⓐ VT igualar
Ⓑ VI (*Brit Sport*) empatar

equalizer ['iːkwəlaɪzəʳ] N [1] (*Brit Sport*) tanto *m* del empate
[2] (*US**) (= *pistol*) pipa* *f*, pistola *f*

▼**equally** [ˈiːkwəlɪ] ADV **1** (= *evenly*) [*divide, share*] equitativamente, por igual; **the fence posts should be ~ spaced** el espacio entre los postes de la valla debería ser igual
2 (= *in the same way*) por igual; **all foreigners should be treated ~** todos los extranjeros deberían ser tratados por igual *or* con igualdad; **this rule applies ~ to everyone** esta regla se aplica a todos por igual; **this applies ~ to men and to women** esto se aplica tanto a los hombres como a las mujeres
3 (= *just as*) [*important, difficult, responsible*] igualmente, igual de; [*well*] igual de; **her mother was ~ disappointed** su madre estaba igualmente decepcionada *or* igual de decepcionada; **she gave the task to her ~ capable assistant** le encargó la tarea a su asistente, que estaba igualmente capacitado *or* que estaba igual de capacitado; **his second novel was ~ successful** su segunda novela tuvo el mismo éxito; **she is ~ as intelligent as her sister** es igual de inteligente que su hermana, es tan inteligente como su hermana
4 (= *by the same token*) al mismo tiempo; **she cannot marry him, but ~ she cannot live alone** no se puede casar con él, pero, al mismo tiempo, no puede vivir sola; **~, you must remember ...** asimismo *or* al mismo tiempo, hay que recordar ...

equanimity [ˌekwəˈnɪmɪtɪ] N ecuanimidad *f*

equate [ɪˈkweɪt] Ⓐ VT **1** (= *compare*) equiparar (**to, with** con); (= *link*) identificar (**to, with** con)
2 (*Math*) poner en ecuación
Ⓑ VI **to ~ to** equivaler a

equation [ɪˈkweɪʒən] N **1** (*Math*) ecuación *f*; **to enter (into) the ~** (*fig*) entrar en juego; **fairness did not seem to enter into the ~** la justicia no parecía entrar en juego
2 (= *linking*) **the ~ of sth with sth** la identificación de algo con algo

equator [ɪˈkweɪtəʳ] N ecuador *m*

equatorial [ˌekwəˈtɔːrɪəl] Ⓐ ADJ ecuatorial
Ⓑ CPD ► **Equatorial Guinea** N Guinea *f* Ecuatorial

equerry [ˈekwərɪ] N caballerizo *m* del rey

equestrian [ɪˈkwestrɪən] Ⓐ ADJ ecuestre
Ⓑ N caballista *mf*, jinete *mf*

equestrianism [ɪˈkwestrɪənɪsm] N equitación *f*

equi... [ˈiːkwɪ] PREFIX equi...

equidistant [ˈiːkwɪˈdɪstənt] ADJ equidistante

equilateral [ˈiːkwɪˈlætərəl] ADJ equilátero

equilibrium [ˌiːkwɪˈlɪbrɪəm] N (*pl* **equilibriums** *or* **equilibria** [ˌiːkwɪˈlɪbrɪə]) equilibrio *m*; **to maintain/lose one's ~** (*also fig*) mantener/perder el equilibrio

equine [ˈekwaɪn] ADJ equino

equinoctial [ˌiːkwɪˈnɒkʃəl] ADJ equinoccial

equinox [ˈiːkwɪnɒks] N equinoccio *m*

equip [ɪˈkwɪp] VT [+ *office, workshop*] equipar (**with** con); [+ *person*] proveer (**with** de); **to be ~ped with** [*person*] estar provisto de; [*machine etc*] estar equipado con, estar dotado de; **he is well ~ped for the job** está bien preparado para el trabajo; **to be well ~ped to** (+ *INFIN*) estar bien preparado para + *infin*

equipment [ɪˈkwɪpmənt] N (*gen*) equipo *m*; (= *tools, utensils etc*) herramientas *fpl*; (*mental*) aptitud *f*, dotes *fpl*

equipoise [ˈiːkwɪpɔɪz] N (*frm*) estabilidad *f*

equitable [ˈekwɪtəbl] ADJ (*frm*) equitativo

equitably [ˈekwɪtəblɪ] ADV (*frm*) equitativamente, de forma equitativa

equity [ˈekwɪtɪ] N **1** (= *fairness*) equidad *f*; (*Jur*) derecho *m* de equidad, derecho *m* natural
2 (*Fin*) [*of debtor*] valor *m* líquido; (*also* **~ capital**) neto *m* patrimonial, patrimonio *m* neto
3 **equities** (*St Ex*) acciones *fpl* ordinarias
4 **Equity** (*Brit Theat*) *sindicato de actores*

equivalence [ɪˈkwɪvələns] N equivalencia *f*

▼**equivalent** [ɪˈkwɪvələnt] Ⓐ ADJ equivalente (**to** a; **in** en); **to be ~ to** equivaler a
Ⓑ N equivalente *m*

equivocal [ɪˈkwɪvəkəl] ADJ [*statement, behaviour*] equívoco

equivocally [ɪˈkwɪvəklɪ] ADV de manera equívoca *or* ambigua

equivocate [ɪˈkwɪvəkeɪt] VI ser evasivo

equivocation [ɪˌkwɪvəˈkeɪʃən] N evasivas *fpl*

ER ABBR **1** (= **Elizabeth Regina**) *la reina Isabel*
2 (*US Med*) = **emergency room**

er* [ɜː] EXCL (*in hesitation*) esto (*Sp*), este (*LAm*)

ERA N ABBR **1** (*US Pol*) = **Equal Rights Amendment**
2 (*Brit*) = **Education Reform Act**

era [ˈɪərə] N era *f*; **to mark an ~** hacer época

eradicate [ɪˈrædɪkeɪt] VT [+ *disease, crime, superstition, injustice*] erradicar; [+ *poverty, discrimination*] acabar con, erradicar; [+ *weeds*] desarraigar, arrancar

eradication [ɪˌrædɪˈkeɪʃən] N erradicación *f*

erase [ɪˈreɪz] Ⓐ VT **1** (*gen, Comput*) borrar
2 (*US‡*) (= *kill*) liquidar*
Ⓑ CPD ► **erase head** N cabezal *m* borrador

eraser [ɪˈreɪzəʳ] N (*esp US*) (= *rubber*) goma *f* de borrar

Erasmism [ɪˈræzmɪzəm] N erasmismo *m*

Erasmist [ɪˈræzmɪst] Ⓐ ADJ erasmista
Ⓑ N erasmista *mf*

Erasmus [ɪˈræzməs] N Erasmo

erasure [ɪˈreɪʒəʳ] N borradura *f*, raspadura *f*; (*Comput*) borrado *m*

ERDF N ABBR (= **European Regional Development Fund**) FEDER *m*

ere [eəʳ] (*poet*) Ⓐ PREP antes de; **~ long** dentro de poco
Ⓑ CONJ antes de que

erect [ɪˈrekt] Ⓐ ADJ [*person, head, posture*] erguido, derecho; [*plant, stem*] vertical, recto; [*tail, ears*] tieso, parado (*LAm*); (*Physiol*) [*penis*] erecto
Ⓑ ADV **to walk ~** caminar derecho *or* erguido; **to hold o.s.** *or* **stand ~** mantenerse derecho *or* erguido
Ⓒ VT [+ *monument, statue, temple*] erigir (*frm*); [+ *mast, wall, building, barricade*] levantar; [+ *tent, scaffolding*] montar

erectile [ɪˈrektaɪl] ADJ eréctil

erection [ɪˈrekʃən] N **1** (= *act*) erección *f*, construcción *f*; (= *assembly*) montaje *m*
2 (= *building*) construcción *f*
3 (*Anat*) [*of penis*] erección *f*

erectly [ɪˈrektlɪ] ADV erguidamente

erector set [ɪˈrektəset] N (*US*) juego *m* de construcciones

erg [ɜːg] N ergio *m*, erg *m*

ergative [ˈɜːgətɪv] ADJ (*Ling*) ergativo

ergo [ˈɜːgəʊ] CONJ (*frm or hum*) ergo

ergonomic [ˌɜːgəʊˈnɒmɪk] ADJ ergonómico

ergonomically [ˌɜːgəʊˈnɒmɪklɪ] ADV atendiendo a principios ergonómicos

ergonomics [ˌɜːgəʊˈnɒmɪks] NSING ergonomía *f*

ergonomist [ɜːˈgɒnəmɪst] N ergonomista *mf*, ergónomo/a *m/f*

ergot [ˈɜːgət] N cornezuelo *m* (del centeno)

ergotism [ˈɜːgətɪzəm] N ergotismo *m*

Eric [ˈerɪk] N Erico

Erie [ˈɪərɪ] N **Lake ~** el Lago Erie

Erin [ˈɪərɪn] N Erín *m* (*nombre antiguo y sentimental de Irlanda*)

ERISA [əˈrɪsə] N ABBR (*US*) (= **Employee Retirement Income Security Act**) *ley que regula pensiones de jubilados*

Eritrea [ˌerəˈtreɪə] N Eritrea *f*

Eritrean [erɪˈtreɪən] Ⓐ ADJ eritreo
Ⓑ N (= *person*) eritreo/a *m/f*

ERM N ABBR (= **Exchange Rate Mechanism**) mecanismo *m* de cambios

ermine [ˈɜːmɪn] N (*pl* **ermines** *or* **ermine**) armiño *m*

Ernest [ˈɜːnɪst] N Ernesto

ERNIE [ˈɜːnɪ] N ABBR (*Brit*) (= **Electronic Random Number Indicator Equipment**) *ordenador utilizado para sortear los bonos del Estado premiados*

erode [ɪˈrəʊd] Ⓐ VT **1** (*lit*) (*Geol*) erosionar; [*acid*] corroer
2 (*fig*) [+ *confidence, power, authority*] mermar; [+ *support, rights*] reducir; **inflation has ~d the value of their savings** la inflación ha mermado el valor de sus ahorros
Ⓑ VI **1** (*Geol*) erosionarse
2 (*fig*) [*confidence*] mermarse; [*support*] disminuir; **support for his party is eroding** el apoyo a su partido está disminuyendo

erogenous [ɪˈrɒdʒənəs] Ⓐ ADJ erógeno
Ⓑ CPD ► **erogenous zone** N zona *f* erógena

Eros [ˈɪərɒs] N Eros

erosion [ɪˈrəʊʒən] N **1** (*Geol*) erosión *f*; [*of metal*] corrosión *f*
2 (*fig*) desgaste *m*

erosive [ɪˈrəʊzɪv] ADJ erosivo, erosionante

erotic [ɪˈrɒtɪk] ADJ erótico

erotica [ɪˈrɒtɪkə] NPL literatura *f* erótica

eroticism [ɪˈrɒtɪsɪzəm] N erotismo *m*

eroticize [ɪˈrɒtɪsaɪz] VT erotizar

erotomania [ɪˌrɒtəʊˈmeɪnɪə] N erotomanía *f*

err [ɜːʳ] VI (= *be mistaken*) equivocarse; (= *sin*) pecar; **to ~ on the side of mercy/caution** *etc* pecar de piadoso/cauteloso *etc*; ✦*PROV* **to ~ is human** errar es de humanos, quien tiene boca se equivoca

errand [ˈerənd] Ⓐ N recado *m*, mandado *m* (*esp LAm*); **to run ~s** hacer recados; **~ of mercy** tentativa *f* de salvamento
Ⓑ CPD ► **errand boy** N recadero *m*, mandadero *m* (*esp LAm*)

errant [ˈerənt] ADJ (*frm*) errante; *see also* **knight C**

errata [eˈrɑːtə] NPL *of* **erratum**

erratic [ɪˈrætɪk] ADJ [*person*] (*by temperament*) imprevisible, voluble; (*in performance*) irregular; [*behaviour, mood*] imprevisible, variable; [*movement, pattern, pulse, breathing*] irregular; [*results, progress, performance*] desigual, poco uniforme; **police officers noticed his ~ driving** los policías notaron que conducía de modo irregular; **I work ~ hours** tengo un horario de trabajo irregular

erratically [ɪˈrætɪkəlɪ] ADV [*behave*] de forma imprevisible; [*work, drive, play*] de modo irregular; [*breathe*] de forma irregular, irregularmente; **his heart was beating ~** su corazón latía irregularmente *or* de forma irregular

erratum [eˈrɑːtəm] N (*pl* **errata**) errata *f*

erroneous [ɪˈrəʊnɪəs] ADJ erróneo

erroneously [ɪˈrəʊnɪəslɪ] ADV erróneamente

▼**error** [ˈerəʳ] Ⓐ N error *m*, equivocación *f*; **~s and omissions excepted** salvo error u omisión; **by ~** por error, por equivocación; **to be in ~** estar equivocado; **human ~** error *m* hu-

► LANGUAGE IN USE: **equally 2** 26.1 **equivalent A** 5.2 **error A** 20.7

mano; **spelling ~** falta *f* de ortografía; **typing ~** error *m* de mecanografía; **✦IDIOM to see the ~ of one's ways** reconocer su error
Ⓑ CPD ► **error message** N (*Comput*) mensaje *m* de error

ersatz ['ɛəzæts] Ⓐ ADJ sucedáneo
Ⓑ N sucedáneo *m*

erstwhile ['ɜːstwaɪl] ADJ (*liter*) antiguo

erudite ['erʊdaɪt] ADJ erudito

eruditely ['erʊdaɪtlɪ] ADV eruditamente

erudition [ˌerʊ'dɪʃən] N erudición *f*

erupt [ɪ'rʌpt] VI [1] [*volcano*] (= *begin to erupt*) entrar en erupción; (= *go on erupting*) estar en erupción
[2] (*fig*) [*spots*] hacer erupción; [*war, fighting, anger*] estallar; **he ~ed into the room** irrumpió en el cuarto

eruption [ɪ'rʌpʃən] N [1] [*of volcano, spots*] erupción *f*
[2] (*fig*) [*of war, fighting, anger*] estallido *m*

erysipelas [ˌerɪ'sɪpɪləs] N erisipela *f*

erythrocyte [ɪ'rɪθrəʊˌsaɪt] N eritrocito *m*

ES N ABBR = **expert system**

ESA N ABBR (= **European Space Agency**) AEE *f*

Esau ['iːsɔː] N Esaú

escalate ['eskəleɪt] Ⓐ VI [1] [*costs, prices*] subir vertiginosamente; **production costs have ~d** los costes de producción han subido vertiginosamente; **escalating costs** costes *mpl* que van en continuo aumento; **the cost of the project has ~d to £8.7 million** el coste del proyecto ha subido vertiginosamente a 8,7 millones de libras
[2] [*violence, tension, conflict*] intensificarse; **the violence could ~ into a war** la violencia podría intensificarse hasta llegar a una guerra
Ⓑ VT [+ *conflict*] intensificar; [+ *demands*] aumentar

escalation [ˌeskə'leɪʃən] N [*of costs, prices*] aumento *m* (vertiginoso), escalada *f*; [*of tension, conflict*] intensificación *f*; [*of violence*] intensificación *f*, escalada *f*; **the threat of nuclear ~ remains** sigue en pie la amenaza de una intensificación del conflicto nuclear

escalator ['eskəleɪtə'] Ⓐ N escalera *f* mecánica
Ⓑ CPD ► **escalator clause** N (*Comm*) cláusula *f* de revisión *or* actualización

escalope ['eskə'lɒp] N (*Brit*) escalope *m*, filete *m*

escapade [ˌeskə'peɪd] N (= *adventure*) aventura *f*; (= *misdeed*) travesura *f*

escape [ɪs'keɪp] Ⓐ N [1] (*from detention*) fuga *f*; (*from country*) huida *f*; **there is no ~ from this prison** no hay forma de escapar *or* fugarse de esta cárcel; **to make one's ~** escapar(se)
[2] (*from injury, harm*) **there was no ~ from the noise** no había forma de escapar al ruido; **she saw prostitution as her only means of ~ from poverty** vió la prostitución como el único medio de escapar a la pobreza; **to have a lucky** *or* **narrow ~** (*lit, fig*) salvarse por los pelos; **he had a lucky** *or* **narrow ~** (*from death*) tuvo suerte de escapar *or* salir con vida, se salvó por los pelos
[3] (*from real world*) evasión *f*; **for me television is an ~** a mí la televisión me sirve de evasión
[4] [*of water, gas*] fuga *f*, escape *m*
Ⓑ VT [1] (= *avoid*) [+ *pursuer*] escapar de, librarse de; [+ *punishment, death*] librarse de; [+ *consequences*] evitar; **they managed to ~ capture/detection** consiguieron evitar que les capturaran/detectaran; **they jumped out of the window to ~ the fire** saltaron por la ventana para escapar del fuego; **they were lucky to ~ injury** tuvieron mucha suerte de salir ilesos; **there was no way I could ~ meeting him** no había manera de poder evitar verme con él; **they left the country to ~ the press** se fueron del país para escapar de la prensa; **he just ~d being run over** por poco lo atropellan
[2] (= *elude*) **his name ~s me** no logro acordarme de su nombre; **nothing ~s her** no se le escapa nada; **it had ~d his notice** *or* **attention that ...** se le había escapado que ...
[3] (*esp liter*) (= *issue from*) **a cry ~d his lips** dejó escapar un grito
Ⓒ VI [1] (= *get away*) (*gen*) escaparse; [*prisoner*] fugarse, escapar(se); **to ~ from** [+ *prison*] escapar(se) de, fugarse de; [+ *cage*] escaparse de; [+ *danger, harm*] huir de; [+ *reality*] evadirse de; **he kept me talking and I couldn't ~ from him** hacía que siguiera hablando y no podía escaparme de él; **he wanted to ~ from the world for a while** quería evadirse del mundo durante un tiempo; **in winter I think of escaping to the sun** en invierno pienso en escaparme a un sitio con sol; **he ~d to a neutral country** huyó a un país neutral; **she ~d unhurt** salió ilesa; **he ~d with a few bruises** sólo sufrió algunas magulladuras; **he was lucky to ~ with his life** tuvo suerte de salir con vida
[2] (= *leak*) [*liquid, gas*] salirse
[3] (= *issue*) **a moan ~d from her lips** dejó escapar un gemido; **tendrils of hair were escaping from under her hat** algunos mechones de pelo le salían por debajo del sombrero
Ⓓ CPD ► **escape artist** N escapista *mf* ► **escape attempt** N intento *m* de fuga ► **escape clause** N (*in agreement*) cláusula *f* de excepción ► **escape hatch** N (*in plane, space rocket*) escotilla *f* de salvamento ► **escape key** N (*Comput*) tecla *f* de escape ► **escape pipe** N tubo *m* de desagüe ► **escape plan** N plan *m* de fuga ► **escape route** N ruta *f* de escape ► **escape valve** N válvula *f* de escape ► **escape velocity** N (*Aer*) velocidad *f* de escape

escaped [ɪs'keɪpt] ADJ [*prisoner*] fugado; [*animal*] escapado

escapee [ɪskeɪ'piː] N (*from prison*) fugitivo/a *m/f*, prófugo/a *m/f*

escapement [ɪs'keɪpmənt] N [*of watch*] escape *m*

escapism [ɪs'keɪpɪzəm] N escapismo *m*, evasión *f*

escapist [ɪs'keɪpɪst] Ⓐ ADJ escapista; **~ literature** literatura *f* de evasión
Ⓑ N escapista *mf*

escapologist [ˌeskəɪ'pɒlədʒɪst] N escapista *mf*

escarpment [ɪs'kɑːpmənt] N escarpa *f*

eschatological [ˌeskətə'lɒdʒɪkəl] ADJ (*Rel*) escatológico

eschatology [ˌeskə'tɒlədʒɪ] N (*Rel*) escatología *f*

eschew [ɪs'tʃuː] VT evitar, renunciar a

escort ['eskɔːt] Ⓐ N [1] (= *group*) séquito *m*, acompañamiento *m*; (*lady's*) acompañante *m*
[2] (= *girl from agency*) señorita *f* de compañía
[3] (*Mil, Naut*) escolta *f*; **to travel under ~** viajar con escolta; **a police ~** una escolta policial
Ⓑ [ɪs'kɔːt] VT [1] acompañar; **to ~ sb home** acompañar a algn a su casa; **to ~ sb in** acompañar a algn al entrar
[2] (*Mil, Naut*) escoltar
Ⓒ ['eskɔːt] CPD ► **escort agency** N agencia *m* de servicios de compañía ► **escort duty** N servicio *m* de escolta ► **escort vessel** N buque *m* escolta

escrow ['eskrəʊ] Ⓐ N depósito *m* en fideicomiso; **in ~** en depósito
Ⓑ CPD ► **escrow account** N (*Fin*) cuenta *f* de plica

escudo [ɛs'kuːdəʊ] N (*pl* **escudos**) escudo *m*

escutcheon [ɪs'kʌtʃən] N escudo *m* de armas, blasón *m*; (*fig*) honor *m*

ESE ABBR (= **east-southeast**) ESE

ESF N ABBR (= **European Social Fund**) FSE *m*

Eskimo ['eskɪməʊ] Ⓐ ADJ esquimal
Ⓑ N (*pl* **Eskimos, Eskimo**) [1] (= *person*) esquimal *mf*
[2] (*Ling*) esquimal *m*

ESL N ABBR = **English as a Second Language**; → TEFL/EFL, TESL/ESL, ELT, TESOL/ESOL

ESN ADJ ABBR = **educationally subnormal**

ESOL N ABBR = **English for Speakers of Other Languages**; → TEFL/EFL, TESL/ESL, ELT, TESOL/ESOL

esophagus [ɪ'sɒfəgəs] N (*pl* **esophaguses** *or* **esophagi** [ɪ'sɒfəˌdʒaɪ]) (*US*) = **oesophagus**

esoteric [ˌesəʊ'terɪk] ADJ esotérico

ESP N ABBR [1] (= **extrasensory perception**) percepción *f* extrasensorial
[2] = **English for Special Purposes**

esp. ABBR = **especially**

espadrille [ˌespə'drɪl] N alpargata *f*

espalier [ɪ'spæljə'] N espaldar *m*

esparto [e'spɑːtəʊ] N esparto *m*

especial [ɪs'peʃəl] ADJ (*frm*) especial, particular

especially [ɪs'peʃəlɪ] ADV [1] (= *particularly*) especialmente; **~ in summer/when it rains** especialmente *or* sobre todo en verano/cuando llueve; **why me, ~?** ¿por qué yo precisamente?
[2] (= *expressly*) especialmente; **I came ~ to see you** vine especialmente para verte; **to do sth ~ for sb/sth** hacer algo especialmente para algn/algo
[3] (= *more than usually*) [*important, difficult, sensitive*] especialmente, particularmente; **she did ~ well in her French exam** el examen de francés le fue especialmente *or* particularmente bien; **"is she pretty?" — "not ~"** —¿es guapa? —no especialmente

Esperantist [ˌespə'ræntɪst] N esperantista *mf*

Esperanto [ˌespə'ræntəʊ] N esperanto *m*

espionage [ˌespɪə'nɑːʒ] N espionaje *m*; **industrial ~** espionaje *m* industrial

esplanade [ˌesplə'neɪd] N paseo *m* marítimo; (*Mil*) explanada *f*

espousal [ɪ'spaʊzl] N (*frm*) adherencia *f* (**of** a), adopción *f* (**of** de)

espouse [ɪs'paʊz] VT (*frm*) [+ *cause*] adherirse a; [+ *plan*] adoptar

espresso [es'presəʊ] Ⓐ N café *m* exprés
Ⓑ CPD ► **espresso bar** N café *m*, cafetería *f* (*donde se sirve café exprés*)

esprit de corps ['espriːdə'kɔː'] N espíritu *m* de cuerpo

espy [ɪs'paɪ] VT (*liter*) divisar

Esq. ABBR (*Brit frm*) (= **esquire**) Don, D.

esquire [ɪs'kwaɪə'] N (*Brit*) (*on envelope*) Señor don; **Colin Smith Esquire** Sr. D. Colin Smith

▼**essay** Ⓐ ['eseɪ] N (*Literat*) ensayo *m*; (*Scol, Univ*) trabajo *m*
Ⓑ [e'seɪ] VT (*frm*) probar, ensayar; [+ *task*] intentar; **to ~ to** (+ *INFIN*) intentar + *infin*

essayist ['eseɪɪst] N (*Literat*) ensayista *mf*

essence ['esəns] N [1] esencia *f*; **the ~ of the matter is ...** lo esencial del asunto es ...; **in ~** en lo esencial; **time is of the ~** el tiempo

➤ LANGUAGE IN USE: essay A 26.1

es primordial
2 (= *extract*) esencia *f*, extracto *m*

▼**essential** [ɪ'senʃəl] Ⓐ ADJ 1 (= *necessary*) esencial, imprescindible; **it is ~ that** es esencial que, es imprescindible que; **it is ~ to** (+ *INFIN*) es esencial *or* imprescindible + *infin*; **it is absolutely ~ to remain calm** es absolutamente esencial *or* es imprescindible mantener la calma; **in this job accuracy is ~** para este trabajo la exactitud es esencial *or* imprescindible *or* es un imperativo; **a list of ~ reading** una lista de lecturas esenciales; **~ services** servicios *mpl* básicos
2 (= *fundamental*) [*quality, fact, difference, element*] fundamental, esencial; **play is an ~ part of a child's development** el juego es una parte fundamental *or* esencial en el desarrollo del niño; **man's ~ goodness** la bondad esencial *or* fundamental del ser humano
Ⓑ N 1 (= *necessary thing*) **in my job a car is an ~** en mi trabajo, un coche es una necesidad; **the ~s of everyday life** las necesidades básicas de la vida diaria; **we have all the ~s** tenemos todo lo necesario; **we picked up a few ~s for the trip** tomamos algunas cosas esenciales para el viaje; **accuracy is one of the ~s** la exactitud es uno de los elementos esenciales *or* fundamentales; **we can only take the bare ~s with us** sólo podemos llevarnos lo imprescindible
2 **essentials** (= *fundamentals*) **the ~s of German grammar** los rudimentos de la gramática alemana; **in all ~s** fundamentalmente
Ⓒ CPD ► **essential oil** N aceite *m* esencial

essentially [ɪ'senʃəlɪ] ADV 1 (= *at bottom*) básicamente; **~, it is a story of ordinary people** básicamente, es una historia de gente normal; **she was ~ a generous person** era básicamente *or* en esencia una persona generosa
2 (= *on the whole*) en lo esencial, en lo fundamental; **~, we agree** estamos de acuerdo en lo esencial *or* fundamental; **his theory is ~ correct** su teoría es correcta en lo esencial, fundamentalmente *or* en lo fundamental su teoría es correcta

EST N ABBR 1 (*US*) = **Eastern Standard Time**
2 = **electric shock treatment**

est. ABBR 1 = **estimate(d)**
2 = **established**; **~ 1888** se fundó en 1888

▼**establish** [ɪs'tæblɪʃ] VT 1 (= *set up*) [+ *business, state, committee*] establecer, fundar; [+ *custom, rule, peace, order*] establecer; [+ *precedent*] establecer, sentar; [+ *relations*] establecer, entablar; [+ *power, authority*] afirmar; [+ *reputation*] ganarse; **to ~ sb in a business** poner un negocio a algn; **the book ~ed him as a writer** el libro lo consagró como escritor; **to ~ o.s.** establecerse, consolidarse
2 (= *prove*) [+ *fact, rights*] comprobar, demostrar; [+ *identity*] verificar; [+ *sb's innocence*] probar, demostrar; **we have ~ed that …** hemos comprobado que …
3 (= *find out, discover*) averiguar; [+ *date*] determinar

established [ɪs'tæblɪʃt] ADJ [*person, business*] establecido, consolidado; [*custom*] establecido, arraigado; [*fact*] probado; [*church*] oficial, del Estado; [*staff*] fijo, en plantilla; **a well-~ business** un negocio establecido *or* consolidado

establishment [ɪs'tæblɪʃmənt] N 1 (= *setting-up*) establecimiento *m*; (= *creation*) creación *f*
2 (= *proof*) [*of innocence, guilt*] determinación *f*
3 (= *business, house*) establecimiento *m*; **a teaching/nursing ~** un centro de enseñanza/de reposo; **they have a smaller ~ nowadays** ahora mantienen una casa más modesta, tienen menos servicio ahora
4 (*Admin, Mil, Naut*) (= *personnel*) personal *m*; **to be on the ~** estar en plantilla
5 **the Establishment** la clase dirigente; **the literary/musical Establishment** las altas esferas del mundo literario/musical; *see also* **anti-Establishment**

ESTABLISHMENT

En el Reino Unido el término **Establishment** *hace referencia a la clase dirigente, es decir, al Gobierno, los altos cargos de la Administración pública, la Iglesia, las Fuerzas Armadas y a otras personas en puestos de influencia. Por lo general, se piensa que esta clase dirigente apoya el status quo tanto a nivel político como cultural o social.*
En Estados Unidos, el **Establishment** *se asocia sobre todo con Washington, donde se encuentra el gobierno federal, y en concreto con aquellos que estudiaron en universidades del noreste, especialmente* **Yale** *y* **Harvard**.
⇨ *Ver tb* IVY LEAGUE

estate [ɪs'teɪt] Ⓐ N 1 (= *land*) finca *f*, hacienda *f*; (= *country estate*) finca *f*, hacienda *f* (*LAm*), estancia *f* (*S. Cone*); (= *housing estate*) urbanización *f*; (= *industrial estate*) polígono *m* industrial
2 (= *property*) propiedad *f*; (= *assets*) patrimonio *m*; [*of deceased*] herencia *f*; **she left a large ~** dejó una gran herencia; **personal ~** patrimonio *m* personal; *see also* **real D**
3 (*Pol*) estado *m*; *see also* **fourth C, third D**
4 (*Brit*) = **estate car**
Ⓑ CPD ► **estate agency** N (*esp Brit*) agencia *f* inmobiliaria ► **estate agent** N (*esp Brit*) agente *mf* inmobiliario/a ► **estate car** N (*Brit*) ranchera *f*, coche *m* familiar, rural *f* (*S. Cone*), camioneta *f* (*LAm*) ► **estate duty** N (*Brit*) impuesto *m* de sucesiones

esteem [ɪs'tiːm] Ⓐ VT (*frm*) 1 [+ *person*] estimar, apreciar; **my ~ed colleague** mi estimado colega
2 (= *consider*) considerar, estimar; **I would ~ it an honour** lo consideraría un honor
Ⓑ N estima *f*, aprecio *m*; **to hold sb in high ~** tener a algn en gran estima; **he lowered himself in my ~** bajó en mi estima; **he went up in my ~** ganó valor a mis ojos

ester ['estəʳ] N (*Chem*) éster *m*

Esther ['estəʳ] N Ester

esthete ['iːsθiːt] N (*US*) *etc* = **aesthete** *etc*

esthetics [iːs'θetɪks] N (*US*) = **aesthetics**

Esthonia [es'təʊnɪə] N = **Estonia**

Esthonian [es'təʊnɪən] ADJ, N = **Estonian**

estimable ['estɪməbl] ADJ estimable

estimate ['estɪmɪt] Ⓐ N 1 (= *judgment*) estimación *f*, cálculo *m*; (= *approximate assessment*) (*for work etc*) presupuesto *m*; **to form an ~ of sth/sb** formarse una opinión de algo/algn; **to give sb an ~ of** [+ *cost etc*] presentar a algn un presupuesto de; **rough ~** cálculo *m* aproximativo; **at a rough ~** aproximadamente
2 **Estimates** (*Parl*) presupuestos *mpl* generales del Estado
Ⓑ ['estɪmeɪt] VT (= *judge*) calcular aproximadamente; (= *assess*) juzgar, estimar; **to ~ that** calcular que; **to ~ the cost at …** calcular el precio en …
Ⓒ ['estɪmeɪt] VI **to ~ for** [+ *building work etc*] hacer un presupuesto de

estimation [ˌestɪ'meɪʃən] N 1 (= *judgment*) juicio *m*, opinión *f*; **according to** *or* **in my ~** a mi juicio, en mi opinión; **what is your ~ of him?** ¿qué concepto tienes de él?
2 (= *esteem*) estima *f*, aprecio *m*

estimator ['estɪmeɪtəʳ] N tasador(a) *m/f*

Estonia [e'stəʊnɪə] N Estonia *f*

Estonian [e'stəʊnɪən] Ⓐ ADJ estonio
Ⓑ N 1 (= *person*) estonio/a *m/f*
2 (*Ling*) estonio *m*

estrange [ɪs'treɪndʒ] VT enajenar, distanciar (**from** de)

estranged ['ɪstreɪndʒd] ADJ separado; **his ~ wife** su mujer que vive separada de él; **to become ~** separarse

estrangement [ɪs'treɪndʒmənt] N distanciamiento *m*

estrogen ['iːstrəʊdʒən] N (*US*) = **oestrogen**

estrous ['estrəs] N (*US*) = **oestrous**

estrus ['estrəs] N (*US*) = **oestrus**

estuary ['estjʊərɪ] Ⓐ N estuario *m*, ría *f*
Ⓑ CPD ► **Estuary English** N (*Brit*) *variedad de inglés que se ha puesto de moda entre los jóvenes de zonas adyacentes al estuario del Támesis, en el SE de Inglaterra*

ET N ABBR (*US*) = **Eastern Time**

ETA N ABBR = **estimated time of arrival**

e-tail ['iːteɪl] Ⓐ N venta *f* via *or* por Internet
Ⓑ CPD ► **e-tail site** sitio *m* de venta via *or* por Internet

e-tailer ['iːteɪləʳ] N vendedor *m* en línea, vendedor *m* via *or* por Internet

e-tailing ['iːteɪlɪŋ] N venta *f* en línea, venta *f* via *or* por Internet

et al [et'æl] ABBR (= **et alii, and others**) y col., y otros

etc ABBR (= **et cetera**) etc.

etcetera [ɪt'setrə] Ⓐ ADV etcétera
Ⓑ **etceteras** NPL extras *mpl*, adornos *mpl*

etch [etʃ] VT grabar al aguafuerte; (*fig*) grabar; **it is ~ed on my memory forever** lo tengo grabado para siempre en mi memoria

etching ['etʃɪŋ] N (= *process*) grabado *m* al aguafuerte; (= *print made from plate*) aguafuerte *m or f*; **he invited her in to see his ~s** (*hum*) la invitó a entrar a ver su colección de sellos

ETD N ABBR = **estimated time of departure**

eternal [ɪ'tɜːnl] Ⓐ ADJ 1 (= *everlasting*) [*life, bliss*] eterno
2 (*pej*) (= *incessant*) constante; **in the background was that ~ hum** se oía aquel constante zumbido de fondo; **can't you stop this ~ quarrelling?** ¿no podéis dejar de pelearos constantemente?
Ⓑ CPD ► **the eternal triangle** N el triángulo amoroso

eternally [ɪ'tɜːnəlɪ] ADV 1 (= *everlastingly*) [*exist, live*] eternamente; [*damned, joined*] para siempre, eternamente
2 (*fig*) (= *perpetually*) [*grateful, optimistic, young*] eternamente; [*quarrel, criticize*] constantemente; **why do you have to be ~ quarrelling?** ¿por qué os tenéis que estar constantemente *or* siempre peleando?; **he's ~ complaining** se pasa la vida quejándose

eternity [ɪ'tɜːnɪtɪ] Ⓐ N eternidad *f*; **it seemed like an ~** pareció una eternidad *or* un siglo
Ⓑ CPD ► **eternity ring** N anillo *m* de brillantes

ETF N ABBR = **electronic transfer of funds**

ethane ['iːθeɪn] N etano *m*

ethanol ['eθənɒl] N etanol *m*

ether ['iːθəʳ] N (*Chem*) éter *m*

ethereal [ɪ'θɪərɪəl] ADJ (*fig*) etéreo

ethic ['eθɪk] N ética *f*; *see also* **work D**

➤ LANGUAGE IN USE: **essential A1** 10.1 **establish 2** 26.1

ethical ['eθɪkəl] ADJ ético; (= *honourable*) honrado

ethically ['eθɪklɪ] ADV [*behave*] éticamente, con ética; [*sound, unacceptable*] desde el punto de vista ético

ethics ['eθɪks] Ⓐ NSING (= *subject*) ética *fsing* Ⓑ NPL (= *honourableness*) moralidad *f*

Ethiopia [,i:θɪ'əʊpɪə] N Etiopía *f*

Ethiopian [,i:θɪ'əʊpɪən] Ⓐ ADJ etíope Ⓑ N etíope *mf*

ethnic ['eθnɪk] Ⓐ ADJ 1 (= *racial*) [*origin, community*] étnico; [*conflict, tension*] racial 2 (= *non-Western*) [*music*] étnico; [*food, jewellery*] exótico Ⓑ N (*esp US*) (= *person*) *miembro de una minoría étnica*; **white ~** *miembro de una minoría étnica de raza blanca* Ⓒ CPD ► **ethnic cleansing** N limpieza *f* étnica ► **ethnic group** N etnia *f*, grupo *m* étnico ► **ethnic minority** N minoría *f* étnica

ethnically ['eθnɪklɪ] ADV [*pure, homogeneous, distinct*] étnicamente; **it is one of the most ~ diverse areas of the world** es una de las zonas de más diversidad étnica del mundo; **an ~ mixed region** una región con una gran mezcla de razas *or* de etnias; **~ related violence** violencia *f* de origen racial; **~ cleansed areas** zonas *fpl* en las que ha tenido lugar una limpieza étnica; **~, it's not a stable country** desde el punto de vista étnico, no es un país estable

ethnicity [eθ'nɪsɪtɪ] N etnicidad *f*

ethnocentric [,eθnəʊ'sentrɪk] ADJ etnocéntrico

ethnocentrism [,eθnəʊ'sentrɪzəm] N etnocentrismo *m*

ethnographer [eθ'nɒgrəfəʳ] N etnógrafo/a *m/f*

ethnographic [,eθnəʊ'græfɪk] ADJ etnográfico

ethnography [eθ'nɒgrəfɪ] N etnografía *f*

ethnolinguistics [,eθnəʊlɪŋ'gwɪstɪks] N etnolingüística *f*

ethnological [,eθnəʊ'lɒdʒɪkl] ADJ etnológico

ethnologist [eθ'nɒlədʒɪst] N etnólogo/a *m/f*

ethnology [eθ'nɒlədʒɪ] N etnología *f*

ethnomusicology [,eθnəʊmju:zɪ'kɒlədʒɪ] N etnomusicología *f*

ethos ['i:θɒs] N [*of culture, group*] espíritu *m*, escala *f* de valores

ethyl ['i:θaɪl] N etilo *m*

ethylene ['eθɪli:n] N etileno *m*

e-ticket ['i:tɪkɪt] N billete *m* electrónico (*Sp*) boleto *m* electrónico (*LAm*)

etiolated ['i:tɪəleɪtɪd] ADJ 1 (*Bot*) decolorado, reblanquecido 2 (*fig*) (*frm*) desmayado, lánguido

etiology [,i:tɪ'ɒlədʒɪ] N etiología *f*

etiquette ['etɪket] N etiqueta *f*, protocolo *m*; **court ~** (*royal*) ceremonial *m* de la corte; (*Jur*) protocolo *m* de la corte; **legal ~** ética *f* legal; **professional ~** ética *f* profesional; **~ demands that ...** la etiqueta *or* el protocolo exige que ...; **it is not good ~** no está bien visto

Eton crop ['i:tn'krɒp] N corte *m* a lo garçon

Etruscan [ɪ'trʌskən] Ⓐ ADJ etrusco Ⓑ N 1 (= *person*) etrusco/a *m/f* 2 (*Ling*) etrusco *m*

et seq. ABBR (= **et sequentia**) y sigs

ETU N ABBR (*Brit*) (= **Electrical Trades Union**) *sindicato de electricistas*

ETV N ABBR (*US*) = **Educational Television**

etymological [,etɪmə'lɒdʒɪkəl] ADJ etimológico

etymologically [,etɪmə'lɒdʒɪkəlɪ] ADV etimológicamente

etymologist [,etɪ'mɒlədʒɪst] N etimólogo/a *m/f*, etimologista *mf*

etymology [,etɪ'mɒlədʒɪ] N etimología *f*

etymon ['etɪmɒn] N (*pl* **etymons, etyma** ['etɪmə]) étimo *m*

EU N ABBR (= **European Union**) UE *f*

eucalyptus [,ju:kə'lɪptəs] N (*pl* **eucalyptuses** *or* **eucalypti** [,ju:kə'lɪptaɪ]) (= *tree*) eucalipto *m*; (= *oil*) esencia *f* de eucalipto

Eucharist ['ju:kərɪst] N Eucaristía *f*

Eucharistic [ju:kə'rɪstɪk] ADJ de la Eucaristía, eucarístico

Euclid ['ju:klɪd] N Euclides

Euclidean [ju:'klɪdɪən] ADJ euclidiano

Eugene [ju:'ʒeɪn] N Eugenio

eugenic [ju:'dʒenɪk] ADJ eugenésico

eugenics [ju:'dʒenɪks] NSING eugenesia *f*

eulogistic [,ju:lə'dʒɪstɪk] ADJ elogioso, ensalzador

eulogize ['ju:lədʒaɪz] VT elogiar, encomiar

eulogy ['ju:lədʒɪ] N elogio *m*, encomio *m*

eunuch ['ju:nək] N eunuco *m*

euphemism ['ju:fɪmɪzəm] N eufemismo *m*; **a ~ for ...** un eufemismo de ...

euphemistic [,ju:fɪ'mɪstɪk] ADJ eufemístico

euphonic [ju:'fɒnɪk] ADJ eufónico

euphonious [ju:'fəʊnɪəs] ADJ = **euphonic**

euphonium [ju:'fəʊnɪəm] N bombardino *m*

euphony ['ju:fənɪ] N eufonía *f*

euphoria [ju:'fɔ:rɪə] N euforia *f*

euphoric [ju:'fɒrɪk] ADJ [*person, atmosphere, laughter*] eufórico

Euphrates [ju:'freɪti:z] N Eufrates *m*

Eurasia [jʊə'reɪʃə] N Eurasia *f*

Eurasian [jʊə'reɪʃn] Ⓐ ADJ eurasiático Ⓑ N eurasiático/a *m/f*

Euratom [jʊər'ætəm] N ABBR = **European Atomic Energy Commission**

eureka [jʊə'ri:kə] EXCL ¡eureka!

eurhythmics [ju:'rɪðmɪks] NSING euritmia *f*

Euripides [jʊ'rɪpɪdi:z] N Eurípides

euro ['jʊərəʊ] N euro *m*

Euro..., euro... ['jʊərəʊ] PREFIX euro...

Eurobonds ['jʊərəʊbɒndz] NPL eurobonos *mpl*

Eurocentric ['jʊərəʊsentrɪk] ADJ eurocentrista, centrado en Europa

Eurocentrism ['jʊərəʊ,sentrɪzəm] N eurocentrismo *m*

Eurocheque ['jʊərəʊtʃek] Ⓐ N eurocheque *m* Ⓑ CPD ► **Eurocheque card** N tarjeta *f* de eurocheque

Eurocommunism ['jʊərəʊ,kɒmjʊnɪzəm] N eurocomunismo *m*

Eurocommunist ['jʊərəʊ,kɒmjʊnɪst] Ⓐ ADJ eurocomunista Ⓑ N eurocomunista *mf*

Eurocrat ['jʊərəʊkræt] N (*hum, pej*) eurócrata *mf* (*burócrata de la UE*)

Eurocredit ['jʊərəʊ,kredɪt] N Eurocrédito *m*

Eurocurrency ['jʊərəʊ,kʌrənsɪ] N eurodivisa *f*

Eurodollar ['jʊərəʊ,dɒləʳ] N eurodólar *m*

Euroland ['jʊərəʊlænd] N zona *f* (del) euro, territorio *m* (del) euro

Euromarket Euromart ['jʊərəʊ,mɑ:t] N euromercado *m*, Mercado *m* Común

Euro-MP ['jʊərəʊ,em,pi:] N ABBR (= **Member of the European Parliament**) eurodiputado/a *m/f*

Europe ['jʊərəp] N Europa *f*; **to go into** *or* **join ~** (*Brit Pol*) entrar en la Unión Europea

European [,jʊərə'pi:ən] Ⓐ ADJ europeo Ⓑ N europeo/a *m/f* Ⓒ CPD ► **European Commission** N Comisión *f* Europea ► **European Court of Justice** N Tribunal *m* de Justicia Europeo ► **European Currency Unit** N Unidad *f* de Cuenta Europea, ECU *m* ► **European Economic Community** N Comunidad *f* Económica Europea ► **European Monetary System** N Sistema *m* Monetario Europeo ► **European Parliament** N Parlamento *m* Europeo ► **European plan** N (*US*) habitación *f* (de hotel) con servicios (pero sin comidas) ► **European Union** N Unión *f* Europea

europeanization [,jʊərə,pɪənaɪ'zeɪʃən] N europeización *f*

europeanize [,jʊərə'pɪənaɪz] VT europeizar

Europhile ['jʊərəʊfaɪl] Ⓐ N europeísta *mf* Ⓑ ADJ europeísta

Europhobe ['jʊərəʊfəʊb] N eurófobo/a *m/f*

Europol ['jʊərəʊpɒl] N Europol *f*

Euro-sceptic ['jʊərəʊskeptɪk], **Eurosceptic** N euroescéptico/a *m/f*

Euro-size ['jʊərəʊ,saɪz] N **~ 1** (*Comm*) talla *f* europea 1

Eurospeak ['jʊərəʊspi:k] N (*hum*) jerga *f* burocrática de la UE

Eurostar® ['jʊərəʊ,stɑ:ʳ] N Eurostar® *m*

Eurotunnel ['jʊərəʊ,tʌnl] N Eurotúnel *m*

Eurovision ['jʊərəvɪʒən] Ⓐ N Eurovisión *f* Ⓑ CPD ► **Eurovision Song Contest** N Festival *m* de Eurovisión

Eurozone ['jʊərəʊzəʊn] N eurozona *f*, zona *f* euro

Eurydice [jʊ'rɪdɪsi:] N Eurídice

Eustachian tube [ju:,steɪʃən'tju:b] N trompa *f* de Eustaquio

euthanasia [,ju:θə'neɪzɪə] N eutanasia *f*

evacuate [ɪ'vækjʊeɪt] Ⓐ VT 1 [+ *people*] evacuar; **he was ~d to a hospital in Haifa** lo evacuaron a un hospital de Haifa 2 [+ *building, area*] evacuar 3 (*frm*) [+ *bowels*] evacuar Ⓑ VI 1 [*people, troops*] **civilians were given the order to ~** les dieron órdenes a los civiles de que evacuaran la zona; **the British decided to ~** los británicos decidieron abandonar el lugar 2 (*frm*) [*bowels*] evacuar

evacuation [ɪ,vækjʊ'eɪʃən] N 1 [*of people*] evacuación *f* 2 [*of building, area*] evacuación *f* 3 (*frm*) [*of bowels*] evacuación *f*

evacuee [ɪ,vækjʊ'i:] N evacuado/a *m/f*

evade [ɪ'veɪd] VT [+ *capture, pursuers*] eludir; [+ *punishment, blow*] evitar; [+ *question, issue, responsibility*] eludir, evadir; [+ *military service*] eludir, zafarse de; [+ *taxation, customs duty*] evadir, sustraerse a; [+ *sb's gaze*] esquivar

evaluate [ɪ'væljʊeɪt] VT 1 (= *assess value of*) valorar, calcular el valor de 2 (= *judge*) evaluar; **to ~ evidence** evaluar las pruebas

evaluation [ɪ,væljʊ'eɪʃən] N 1 [*of value*] valoración *f*, cálculo *m* 2 [*of evidence etc*] evaluación *f*

evaluative [ɪ'væljʊətɪv] ADJ evaluativo

evanescent [,i:və'nesnt] ADJ (*liter*) evanescente, fugaz, efímero

evangelical [,i:væn'dʒelɪkəl] Ⓐ ADJ (*Rel*) evangélico Ⓑ N evangélico/a *m/f*

evangelism [ɪ'vændʒə,lɪzəm] N evangelismo *m*

evangelist [ɪ'vændʒəlɪst] N 1 (= *writer*) (*also* **Evangelist**) Evangelista *m*; **St John the Evangelist** San Juan Evangelista 2 (= *preacher*) evangelizador(a) *m/f*

evangelize [ɪ'vændʒɪlaɪz] Ⓐ VT evangelizar Ⓑ VI predicar el Evangelio

evaporate [ɪˈvæpəreɪt] Ⓐ VT evaporar
Ⓑ VI [*liquid*] evaporarse; (*fig*) [*hopes, fears, anger*] desvanecerse

evaporated milk [ɪˌvæpəreɪtɪdˈmɪlk] N leche *f* evaporada

evaporation [ɪˌvæpəˈreɪʃən] N evaporación *f*

evasion [ɪˈveɪʒən] N evasión *f*; (= *evasive answer etc*) evasiva *f*; *see also* **tax C**

evasive [ɪˈveɪzɪv] ADJ [*answer, person*] evasivo; **to be ~ (about sth)** mostrarse evasivo (acerca de algo); **to take ~ action** (*Mil*) adoptar tácticas evasivas

evasively [ɪˈveɪzɪvlɪ] ADV evasivamente; **"it was no problem," I said ~** —no hubo problema —dije evasivamente; **he answered ~** contestó con evasivas; **"I can't remember the exact details," she answered ~** —no recuerdo los detalles exactos —contestó evasivamente *or* de forma evasiva

evasiveness [ɪˈveɪzɪvnɪs] N esquivez *f*; **voters are fed up with the party's ~ on economic matters** los votantes están hartos de la esquivez del partido en cuestiones económicas

eve[1] [iːv] N víspera *f*; **on the ~ of** (*lit*) en la víspera de; (*fig*) en vísperas de

eve[2] [iːv] N (*liter*) (= *evening*) tarde *f*

Eve [iːv] N Eva

▼ **even** [ˈiːvən] Ⓐ ADJ [1] (= *smooth, flat*) [*surface, ground*] plano; **the floorboards are not very ~** las tablas del suelo no están muy niveladas; **to make sth ~** nivelar algo, allanar algo
[2] (= *uniform*) [*speed, temperature, progress*] constante; [*breathing*] regular; [*distribution, colour, work*] uniforme; **he has ~ features** tiene facciones regulares; *see also* **keel**
[3] (= *equal*) [*quantities, distances*] igual; [*distribution*] equitativo; **divide the dough into 12 ~ pieces** divida la masa en 12 piezas iguales; **a more ~ distribution of wealth** una distribución más equitativa de la riqueza; **to break ~** llegar a cubrir los gastos; **he has an ~ chance of winning the election** (*Brit*) tiene las mismas posibilidades de ganar las elecciones que de perderlas, tiene un cincuenta por ciento de posibilidades de ganar las elecciones; **to get ~ with sb** ajustar cuentas con algn; **I'll get ~ with you for that!** ¡me las pagarás por eso!*; **that makes us ~** (*in game*) así quedamos empatados; (*regarding money*) así quedamos en paz *or* (*LAm*) a mano; **they are an ~ match** (*in sports, games*) los dos son igual de buenos; (*fig*) no le tiene nada que envidiar el uno al otro; **I'll give you ~ money that Arsenal will win** (*Brit*) para mí que Arsenal tiene las mismas posibilidades de ganar que de perder; **the odds are about ~** (*Brit*) las posibilidades son más o menos iguales; **our score is ~** estamos igualados *or* empatados; **to be ~ with sb** (*in game*) estar igualado con algn; (*regarding money*) estar en paz *or* (*LAm*) a mano con algn; ♦**IDIOM to give sb an ~ break** (*esp US*) dar a algn su *or* una oportunidad; *see also* **even-handed, even-stevens**
[4] (= *calm*) **he has an ~ temper** no se altera fácilmente; **to say sth with an ~ voice** decir algo sin alterar la voz; **to keep one's voice ~** no alterar la voz; *see also* **even-tempered**
[5] (= *not odd*) [*number*] par
Ⓑ ADV [1] hasta, incluso; **I have ~ forgotten his name** hasta *or* incluso he olvidado su nombre; **~ on Sundays** hasta *or* incluso los domingos; **~ the priest was there** hasta *or* incluso el cura estaba allí; **pick them all, ~ the little ones** recógelos todos incluso los pequeños; **~ I know that!** ¡eso lo sé hasta yo!; **and he ~ sings** e incluso canta; **if you ~ tried a bit harder** si tan sólo te esforzaras un poco más
[2] (*with compar adj or adv*) aún, todavía; **~ faster** aún *or* todavía más rápido; **~ better** aún *or* todavía mejor; **~ more easily** aún *or* todavía más fácilmente; **~ less money** aún *or* todavía menos dinero
[3] (*with negative*) **not ~ ...** ni siquiera ...; **he can't ~ read** ni siquiera sabe leer; **he didn't ~ kiss me** ni me besó siquiera; **don't ~ think about it!** ¡ni lo pienses!; **without ~ reading it** sin leerlo siquiera
[4] (*in phrases*) **~ as**: **~ as he spoke the door opened** en ese mismo momento se abrió la puerta; **~ as a child I used to drink cider** incluso de niño solía beber sidra; **~ as he had wished it** (*frm*) exactamente como él lo había deseado; **~ if** aunque + *subjun*, incluso si + *subjun*; **~ if you tried** aunque lo intentaras, incluso si lo intentaras, así lo procuraras (*LAm*); **not ... ~ if** ◊ **not ~ if**: **he won't talk to you ~ if you do go there** no hablará contigo aunque vayas allí; **I wouldn't do it ~ if you paid me a fortune** no lo haría aunque me pagaras una fortuna; **I couldn't be prouder, not ~ if you were my own son** no me sentiría más orgulloso, aunque fuera mi propio hijo; **~ now** todavía; **~ now, you could still change your mind** todavía estás a tiempo de cambiar de idea; **~ so** aun así; **~ so he was disappointed** aun así, quedó decepcionado; **yes but ~ so ...** sí, pero aun así ...; **~ then** aun así; **and ~ then she wasn't happy** y aún así no estaba contenta; **~ though** aunque; **he didn't listen, ~ though he knew I was right** no me hizo caso, aunque sabía que tenía razón; **~ when** incluso cuando; **~ when I was young I never had any ambition** incluso cuando era joven no tenía ninguna ambición; **he never gets depressed, ~ when things go badly** nunca se deprime, incluso *or* ni siquiera cuando las cosas andan mal; **not ~ when** ni siquiera cuando; **we were never in love, not ~ when we got married** nunca estuvimos enamorados, ni siquiera cuando nos casamos
Ⓒ VT [1] (= *smooth, flatten*) [+ *surface, ground*] nivelar, allanar
[2] (= *equalize*) igualar; **to ~ the score** (*lit*) igualar el marcador; **he was determined to ~ the score** (= *get revenge*) estaba decidido *or* empeñado a desquitarse
Ⓓ **evens** NPL (*esp Brit*) **the bookmakers are offering ~s** los corredores de apuestas ofrecen el doble de la cantidad aportada

►**even out** Ⓐ VT + ADV [1] (= *smooth*) [+ *surface*] allanar, nivelar
[2] (= *equalize*) [+ *number, score*] igualar; **to ~ things out** (= *bring greater equality*) nivelar la situación *or* las cosas
[3] (= *regularize*) [+ *expenses, work, exports*] nivelar; **to ~ out the peaks and troughs** nivelar los altibajos
Ⓑ VI + ADV [1] (= *become equal*) nivelarse, quedar compensado
[2] (= *become more regular*) **the work will ~ out** el trabajo irá siendo más regular

►**even up** Ⓐ VT + ADV (*lit, fig*) igualar, poner parejos; **to ~ things up** nivelar la situación *or* las cosas
Ⓑ VI + ADV **to ~ up with sb** ajustar cuentas con algn

even-handed [ˈiːvənˈhændɪd] ADJ [*person*] imparcial; [*distribution*] equitativo

even-handedly [ˈiːvənˈhændɪdlɪ] ADV [*behave*] imparcialmente; [*distribute*] equitativamente

evening [ˈiːvnɪŋ] Ⓐ N (*before dark*) tarde *f*; (*after dark*) noche *f*; **in the ~** por la tarde/noche; **this ~** esta tarde/noche; **tomorrow/yesterday ~** mañana/ayer por la tarde/noche; **on Sunday ~** el domingo por la tarde/noche; **~ was coming on** estaba atardeciendo/anocheciendo; **she spends her ~s knitting** pasa las tardes haciendo punto; **good ~!** (*early*) ¡buenas tardes!; (*after sunset*) ¡buenas noches!
Ⓑ CPD ► **evening class** N clase *f* nocturna ► **evening dress** N (*woman's*) traje *m* de noche; (*man's*) traje *m* de etiqueta; **in ~ dress** (*man, woman*) vestido/a de etiqueta ► **evening fixture** N (*Sport*) partido *m* por la noche ► **evening institute** N escuela *f* nocturna ► **evening match** N = **evening fixture** ► **evening paper** N periódico *m* de la tarde, vespertino *m* ► **evening performance** N (*Theat*) función *f* de noche ► **evening prayers** NPL = **evening service** ► **evening service** N (*Rel*) vísperas *fpl*, misa *f* vespertina ► **evening star** N estrella *f* de Venus

evenly [ˈiːvənlɪ] ADV [1] (= *uniformly*) [*breathe, flow*] con regularidad, regularmente; [*mix*] uniformemente; **the cake should rise ~** el pastel debe subir de manera uniforme *or* todo por igual; **distribute the sugar ~ over the fruit** distribuye el azúcar por igual sobre la fruta; **the rise in unemployment was ~ spread across the country** el aumento del desempleo afectaba de forma regular a todo el país; **space the curtain rings ~** coloque los aros de las cortinas a la misma distancia unos de otros
[2] (= *equally*) [*distribute, share*] por igual; (*more frm*) equitativamente, parejo (*LAm*); **the wealth is ~ distributed** la riqueza está dividida equitativamente *or* por igual; **to divide/split sth ~** dividir algo a partes iguales; **public opinion is fairly ~ divided** la opinión pública está dividida en partes bastante iguales; **they are ~ matched** están muy igualados
[3] (= *calmly*) [*say, reply, ask*] sin alterarse, serenamente; [*look at*] serenamente

evenness [ˈiːvənnɪs] N [1] (= *smoothness*) [*of ground, surface*] lo liso, lo nivelado
[2] (= *uniformity*) [*of speed, temperature, progress*] lo constante; [*of breathing, features*] regularidad *f*; [*of distribution, colours*] uniformidad *f*
[3] (= *calmness*) **~ of temper** serenidad *f*, ecuanimidad *f*; **the ~ of his voice did not betray the anger he felt inside** el tono sosegado de su voz no revelaba la ira que sentía dentro

evensong [ˈiːvənsɒŋ] N vísperas *fpl*, misa *f* vespertina

even-stevens* [ˌiːvənˈstiːvənz] ADV **to be ~ with sb** estar en paz con algn; (*in competition*) ir parejo con algn; **they're pretty well ~** están más o menos igualados

event [ɪˈvent] N [1] (= *happening*) acontecimiento *m*; **this is quite an ~!** ¡esto es todo un acontecimiento!; **in** *or* **during the course of ~s** en el curso de los acontecimientos; **in the normal course of ~s** normalmente, por lo común; **current ~s** temas *mpl* de actualidad; **to be expecting a happy ~** estar en estado de buena esperanza; ♦**IDIOM to be wise after the ~** mostrar sabiduría cuando ya no hay remedio
[2] (= *case*) **at all ~s** ◊ **in any ~** pase lo que pase, en todo caso; **in either ~** en cualquiera de los dos casos; **in the ~ ...** (*Brit*) resultó que ...; **in the ~ of ...** en caso de ...; **in the ~ of his dying** en caso de que muriese; **in the ~ that ...** en caso de que + *subjun*; **in that ~** en ese caso
[3] (*in a programme*) número *m*; (= *ceremony*) acto *m*; **coming ~s** atracciones *fpl* venideras;

➤ LANGUAGE IN USE: **even** B4 26.3

programme of ~s (*civic*) programa *m* de actos; (= *shows*) programa *m* de atracciones
4 (*Sport*) prueba *f*; *see also* **field D**, **track A4, D**

even-tempered ['iːvən'tempəd] ADJ ecuánime, apacible

eventer [ɪ'ventəʳ] N (*Horse riding*) *jinete participante en el concurso completo*

eventful [ɪ'ventfʊl] ADJ [*journey, match*] lleno de incidentes; [*life*] azaroso

eventide home ['iːvəntaɪd,həʊm] N hogar *m* de ancianos

eventing [ɪ'ventɪŋ] N concursos *mpl* hípicos (de tres días)

eventual [ɪ'ventʃʊəl] ADJ final

eventuality [ɪ,ventʃʊ'ælɪtɪ] N eventualidad *f*; **in that ~** ante esa eventualidad; **in the ~ of** ante la eventualidad de; **to be ready for any ~** estar preparado para cualquier eventualidad

eventually [ɪ'ventʃʊəlɪ] ADV 1 (= *finally*) finalmente, al final; **he ~ agreed that she was right** finalmente *or* al final admitió que ella tenía razón; **he ~ became Prime Minister** finalmente *or* con el tiempo llegó a ser primer ministro
2 (= *at some future time*) con el tiempo; **I'll get round to it ~** lo haré con el tiempo

eventuate [ɪ'ventjʊeɪt] VI **to ~ in** (*US*) resultar en

ever ['evəʳ] ADV 1 (= *always*) siempre; **~ after** desde entonces; **they lived happily ~ after** vivieron felices; **as ~** como siempre; (*ending letter*) un abrazo …; **for ~** (= *always*) siempre; **for ~ and ~** ◊ **for ~ and a day** por siempre jamás; (= *until end of time*) para siempre; **~ ready** siempre dispuesto; **~ since** (*as adv*) desde entonces; (*as conj*) desde que; **yours ~** (*ending letter*) un abrazo …
2 (= *at any time*) **all she ~ does is make jam** se pasa la vida haciendo mermelada; **if you ~ go there** si vas allí alguna vez; **nothing ~ happens** nunca pasa nada; **we haven't ~ tried it** nunca lo hemos probado; **did you ~ find it?** ¿lo encontraste por fin?; **did you ~ meet him?** ¿llegaste a conocerlo?; **have you ~ been there?** ¿has estado allí alguna vez?; **better than ~** mejor que nunca; **hardly ~** casi nunca; **seldom, if ~** rara vez o nunca; **now, if ~, is the time** *or* **moment to …** ahora o nunca es el momento de …; **he's a liar if ~ there was one** él sí que es un mentiroso; **a nice man, if ~ I saw one** hombre simpático donde los haya *or* si los hay; **more than ~** más que nunca; **more beautiful than ~** más hermoso que nunca; ✦***IDIOM*** **did you ~?*** ¡habráse visto!
3 (*used as intensifier*) **is it ~ big!** (*US**) ¡qué grande es!, ¡si vieras lo grande que es!; **as if I ~ would!** ¿me crees capaz de hacer algo semejante?; **as soon as ~ you can** lo antes *or* lo más pronto posible; **before ~ you were born** antes de que nacieras; **never ~** (nunca) jamás; **~ so** (*esp Brit**) muy; **it's ~ so cold** hace un frío terrible; **we're ~ so grateful** estamos muy agradecidos; **~ so many things** tantísimas cosas, la mar de cosas; **~ so much** mucho, muchísimo; **he's ~ so nice** es simpatiquísimo; **why ~ did you do it?** ¿por qué demonios lo hiciste?; **why ~ not?** ¿y por qué no?
4 (*after superl*) **it's the best ~** jamás ha habido mejor; **the coldest night ~** la noche más fría que nunca hemos tenido

ever-changing [evə'tʃeɪndʒɪŋ] ADJ siempre variable, infinitamente mudable

Everest ['evərɪst] N (*also* **Mount ~**) (monte *m*) Everest *m*

Everglades ['evəgleɪdz] NPL **the ~** (*US*) los Everglades, *región pantanosa subtropical de Florida, al sur del Lago Okeechobee*

evergreen ['evəgriːn] Ⓐ ADJ 1 [*tree, shrub*] de hoja perenne
2 [*memory*] imperecedero; [*song*] clásico, de toda la vida
Ⓑ N (= *tree*) árbol *m* de hoja perenne; (= *plant*) planta *f* de hoja perenne
Ⓒ CPD ► **evergreen oak** N encina *f*

ever-growing ['evə'grəʊɪŋ] ADJ = **ever-increasing**

ever-increasing [,evərɪn'kriːsɪŋ] ADJ [*number, size*] cada vez mayor, creciente; [*population, threat, need*] creciente

everlasting [,evə'lɑːstɪŋ] ADJ (= *eternal*) [*gratitude, shame, regret*] eterno; [*fame*] imperecedero; **~ life** la vida eterna; **to her ~ regret, she refused the offer** para su eterno arrepentimiento, rechazó la oferta

everlastingly [,evə'lɑːstɪŋlɪ] ADV [*grateful*] eternamente; [*patient*] infinitamente

evermore ['evə'mɔːʳ] ADV eternamente; **for ~** por siempre jamás, para siempre jamás

every ['evrɪ] ADJ 1 (= *each*) cada *inv*; **~ day** cada día; **~ three days** ◊ **~ third day** cada tres días; **~ few days** cada dos o tres días; **~ bit of the cake** la torta entera; **~ bit as clever as …** tan *or* (*LAm*) igual de listo como …; **I have to account for ~ last penny** tengo que dar cuentas de cada penique que gasto; **I enjoyed ~ minute of the party** disfruté cada minuto de la fiesta; **~ now and then** ◊ **~ now and again** de vez en cuando; **~ other** *or* **second month** un mes sí y otro no, cada dos meses; **~ other person has a car** de cada dos personas una tiene coche; **he'd eaten ~ single chocolate** se había comido todos los bombones, se había comido hasta el último bombón; **~ single time** cada vez sin excepción; **~ so often** cada cierto tiempo, de vez en cuando; **he brings me a present ~ time he comes** cada vez que viene me trae un regalo; **this recipe gives you perfect results ~ time** esta receta siempre le dará resultados perfectos; ✦***IDIOMS*** **(it's) ~ man for himself** ¡sálvese quien pueda!; **~ man Jack of them voted against** todos y cada uno de ellos votaron en contra; ✦***PROV*** **~ little helps** un grano no hace granero pero ayuda al compañero, todo es ayuda
2 (= *all*) **he was following my ~ move** me vigilaba constantemente; **not ~ child is as fortunate as you** no todos los niños son tan afortunados como tú; **~ one of them passed the exam** todos ellos aprobaron el examen; **he criticized her at ~ opportunity** no dejaba escapar oportunidad alguna para criticarla; **he spends ~ penny he earns** gasta hasta el último centavo que gana; **in ~ way** en todos los aspectos; **his ~ wish** todos sus deseos; **I mean ~ word I say** lo digo muy en serio
3 (= *any*) todo; **~ parent will have experienced this at one time or another** todo padre se habrá encontrado con esto en algún momento
4 (= *all possible*) **I gave you ~ assistance** te ayudé en todo lo que podía; **she had ~ chance** se le dieron todas las posibilidades; **I have ~ confidence in him** tengo entera *or* plena confianza en él; **~ effort is being made to trace him** se está haciendo todo lo posible para localizarlo; **I have ~ reason to think that …** tengo razones sobradas para pensar que …; **we wish you ~ success** te deseamos todo el éxito posible

everybody ['evrɪbɒdɪ] PRON todos/as, todo el mundo; **~ else** todos los demás

everyday ['evrɪdeɪ] ADJ [*occurrence, experience*] cotidiano; [*expression*] corriente; [*use*] diario, cotidiano; [*shoes, clothes*] de uso diario; **for ~ (use)** de diario; **in ~ use** de uso corriente; **~ clothes** ropa *f* de diario

everyman ['evrɪmæn] N hombre *m* cualquiera, hombre *m* de la calle

everyone ['evrɪwʌn] PRON = **everybody**

everyplace ['evrɪpleɪs] ADV (*US*) = **everywhere**

everything ['evrɪθɪŋ] PRON todo; **~ is ready** todo está dispuesto; **~ nice had been sold** se había vendido todo lo bonito; **he sold ~** lo vendió todo; **~ you say is true** es verdad todo lo que dices; **time is ~** el tiempo lo es todo; **money isn't ~** el dinero no lo es todo; **he did ~ possible** hizo todo lo posible; **I've argued with him and ~, but he won't listen** he razonado y todo eso con él, pero no quiere escuchar

everywhere ['evrɪwɛəʳ] ADV [*go*] a todas partes; [*be*] en todas partes; **I looked ~** busqué en todas partes; **~ in Spain** en todas partes de España; **~ you go you'll find the same** en todas partes encontrarás lo mismo

everywoman ['evrɪ,wʊmən] N mujer *f* cualquiera

evict [ɪ'vɪkt] VT [+ *tenant*] desahuciar, desalojar

eviction [ɪ'vɪkʃən] Ⓐ N desahucio *m*, desalojo *m*
Ⓑ CPD ► **eviction notice** N aviso *m* de desalojo ► **eviction order** N orden *f* de desalojo

evidence ['evɪdəns] Ⓐ N 1 (= *proof*) pruebas *fpl*; **~ of/that …** pruebas de/de que …; **circumstantial ~** pruebas *fpl* circunstanciales; **there is no ~ against him** no hay pruebas contra él; **to hold sth in ~** esgrimir algo como prueba; **what ~ is there for this belief?** ¿qué pruebas corroboran esta creencia?
2 (= *sign*) indicio *m*, señal *f*; **to show ~ of** dar muestras de
3 (= *testimony*) testimonio *m*; **to call sb in ~** llamar a algn como testigo; **to give ~** prestar declaración, deponer (*more frm*); **to turn King's** *or* **Queen's** *or* (*US*) **State's ~** delatar a un cómplice
4 **to be in ~** (= *noticeable*) estar bien visible
Ⓑ VT 1 (= *make evident*) manifestar; [+ *emotion*] dar muestras de
2 (= *prove*) probar, demostrar; **as is ~d by the fact that …** según lo demuestra el hecho de que …

evident ['evɪdənt] ADJ evidente, manifiesto; **his distress was ~** era evidente *or* manifiesta su aflicción; **it is ~ from the way he talks …** resulta evidente por su forma de hablar …; **it is ~ from his speech that …** su discurso deja patente que …; **as is ~ from her novel** como queda bien claro en su novela; **to be ~ in** manifestarse en; **it is ~ that …** queda patente *or* manifiesto que …; **as is all too ~** como queda bien patente

evidently ['evɪdəntlɪ] ADV 1 (= *clearly*) evidentemente; **the two men ~ knew each other** evidentemente, los dos hombres se conocían, era evidente que los dos hombres se conocían; **he was ~ very angry** era evidente que estaba muy enfadado
2 (= *apparently*) aparentemente, por lo visto; **"was it suicide?" — "~ not"** —¿fue un suicidio? —por lo visto, no *or* —parece que no

evil ['iːvl] Ⓐ ADJ 1 (= *wicked*) [*person, deed, thought*] malvado; [*reputation*] de malvado; [*spirit*] maligno, maléfico; [*influence*] maléfico, funesto; [*place, plan*] diabólico; [*hour, times*] funesto; [*effect*] nocivo; **to put the ~ eye on**

sb ◊ **give sb the ~ eye** echar el mal de ojo a algn; **an ~ spell** un maleficio; **~ tongues may say that …** las malas lenguas dirán que …; **he had his ~ way with her** se aprovechó de ella, se la llevó al huerto (*hum*); **the ~ weed** (= *tobacco*) el vicio (*hum*)
[2] (= *nasty*) [*smell, taste*] horrible; **to put off the ~ day** posponer el día funesto; **to have an ~ temper** tener un genio endiablado
Ⓑ N [1] (= *wickedness*) mal *m*; **the conflict between good and ~** el conflicto entre el bien y el mal; **there wasn't a trace of ~ in her** no había ni un rastro del maldad en ella; **the forces of ~** las fuerzas del mal; **to speak ~ of sb** hablar mal de algn
[2] (= *harmful thing*) mal *m*; **the lesser of two ~s** el menor de dos males; **a necessary ~** un mal necesario; **social ~s** males *mpl* sociales

evildoer [ˈiːvlduːəʳ] N malhechor(a) *m/f*

evilly [ˈiːvɪlɪ] ADV [*behave, plot*] malvadamente; [*laugh, smile*] diabólicamente, malvadamente

evil-minded [ˈiːvlˈmaɪndɪd] ADJ (= *suspicious*) malpensado; (= *nasty*) malintencionado

evil-smelling [ˈiːvlˈsmelɪŋ] ADJ fétido, maloliente, hediondo

evil-tempered [ˈiːvlˈtempəd] ADJ de muy mal genio *or* carácter

evince [ɪˈvɪns] VT mostrar, dar señales de

eviscerate [ɪˈvɪsəreɪt] VT destripar

evocation [ˌevəˈkeɪʃən] N evocación *f*

evocative [ɪˈvɒkətɪv] ADJ evocador (**of** de)

evocatively [ɪˈvɒkətɪvlɪ] ADV de manera evocadora

evoke [ɪˈvəʊk] VT [+ *memories*] evocar; [+ *admiration*] suscitar, provocar

evolution [ˌiːvəˈluːʃən] N [1] (= *development*) desarrollo *m*
[2] (*Bio*) evolución *f*

evolutionary [ˌiːvəˈluːʃnərɪ] ADJ evolutivo

evolve [ɪˈvɒlv] Ⓐ VT [1] [+ *system, theory, plan*] desarrollar
[2] [+ *gas, heat*] desprender
Ⓑ VI [1] [*species*] evolucionar
[2] [*system, plan, science*] desarrollarse

ewe [juː] N oveja *f*

ewer [ˈjuːəʳ] N aguamanil *m*

ex [eks] Ⓐ PREP (= *out of*) **ex dividend** sin dividendo; **the price ex works** el precio de *or* en fábrica, el precio franco fábrica; *see also* **ex officio**
Ⓑ N (*) **my ex** (= *husband*) mi ex (marido); (= *wife*) mi ex (mujer); (= *boyfriend, girlfriend*) mi ex (novio/a)

ex- [eks] PREFIX (= *former*) ex; **the ~ambassador to Moscow** el ex embajador en Moscú; **the ~leader of** el antiguo jefe de; **~minister** ex-ministro/a *m/f*; **~president** ex-presidente/a *m/f*; *see also* **ex-husband**, **ex-serviceman** *etc*

exacerbate [eksˈæsəbeɪt] VT [+ *pain, disease*] exacerbar; [+ *relations, situation*] empeorar

exact [ɪgˈzækt] Ⓐ ADJ [1] (= *precise*) [*number, copy, translation*] exacto; [*meaning, instructions, time, amount, date, location*] exacto, preciso; [*cause, nature*] preciso; **his ~ words were …** lo que dijo, textualmente, era …; **to be ~, there were three of us** para ser exactos, éramos tres, en concreto, éramos tres; **can you be more ~?** precise, por favor; **to be an ~ likeness of sth/sb** ser exactamente igual a algo/algn; **until this ~ moment** hasta este preciso momento; **to be the ~ opposite (of)** ser exactamente *or* justo lo contrario (de); **the ~ same place/house** (*US*) exactamente el mismo sitio/la misma casa
[2] (= *meticulous*) [*description, analysis, scientist, work, study*] preciso, meticuloso; [*instrument*] preciso
Ⓑ VT [+ *money, payment, obedience, allegiance*] (= *demand*) exigir; (= *obtain*) obtener (**from** de); [+ *promise*] conseguir, arrancar; [+ *taxes*] recaudar; **to ~ revenge** vengarse
Ⓒ CPD ► **exact science** N ciencia *f* exacta; **history is not an ~ science** la historia no es una ciencia exacta ► **the exact sciences** NPL las ciencias exactas

exacting [ɪgˈzæktɪŋ] ADJ [*task, activity, profession*] duro; [*boss, person*] exigente; [*conditions*] severo, riguroso

exaction [ɪgˈzækʃən] N exacción *f*

exactitude [ɪgˈzæktɪtjuːd] N exactitud *f*

▼ **exactly** [ɪgˈzæktlɪ] ADV [*know, resemble*] exactamente; [*calculate, measure, describe*] exactamente, con precisión; **at ~ five o'clock** a las cinco en punto; **what did you tell him ~?** ◊ **what ~ did you tell him?** ¿qué le dijiste exactamente?; **that's ~ what I was thinking** eso es exactamente lo que yo estaba pensando; **he's ~ like his father** es exactamente igual que su padre, es clavado a su padre*; **nobody knows who ~ will be in charge** nadie sabe con exactitud quién será el encargado; **I wanted to get everything ~ right** quería hacerlo todo a la perfección; **"do you mean that we are stuck here?" — "exactly!"** —¿quieres decir que no nos podemos mover de aquí? —¡exacto! *or* —¡efectivamente!; **he wasn't ~ pleased** (*iro*) no estaba precisamente contento, no estaba muy contento, que digamos; **it's not ~ interesting** (*iro*) no es lo que se dice interesante; **"is she sick?" — "not ~"** —¿está enferma? —no exactamente

exactness [ɪgˈzæktnɪs] N [*of words, translation, copy*] exactitud *f*; [*of measurement, description, instructions*] precisión *f*

exaggerate [ɪgˈzædʒəreɪt] Ⓐ VT exagerar
Ⓑ VI exagerar

exaggerated [ɪgˈzædʒəreɪtɪd] ADJ exagerado

exaggeratedly [ɪgˈzædʒəreɪtɪdlɪ] ADV exageradamente

exaggeration [ɪgˈzædʒəreɪʃən] N exageración *f*

exalt [ɪgˈzɔːlt] VT (= *elevate*) exaltar, elevar; (= *praise*) ensalzar

exaltation [ˌegzɔːlˈteɪʃən] N exaltación *f*, elevación *f*; (= *praise*) ensalzamiento *m*

exalted [ɪgˈzɔːltɪd] ADJ (= *high*) [*position*] elevado; [*person*] eminente; (= *elated*) excitado

exam* [ɪgˈzæm] N = **examination**

examination [ɪgˌzæmɪˈneɪʃən] N [1] (*Scol, Univ*) (= *test*) examen *m*; **our chemistry ~** nuestro examen de química; **to take** *or* **sit an ~** presentarse a un examen; **to take an ~ in** examinarse de; **oral ~** examen *m* oral
[2] (= *inspection*) [*of premises*] inspección *f*; [*of luggage*] registro *m*; [*of account*] revisión *f*, inspección *f*; [*of witness, suspect*] interrogatorio *m*; **on ~** al examinarlo/examinarlos *etc*
[3] (= *inquiry*) investigación *f*, estudio *m* (**into** de); **the matter is under ~** el asunto está siendo investigado *or* estudiado
[4] (*Med*) reconocimiento *m*

▼ **examine** [ɪgˈzæmɪn] VT [1] [+ *student, candidate*] examinar; **I was ~d in maths** me examinaron de matemáticas
[2] (= *inspect*) [+ *premises*] inspeccionar; [+ *luggage*] registrar; [+ *witness, suspect, accused*] interrogar
[3] (= *investigate*) estudiar, investigar; **we are examining the question** estamos estudiando *or* investigando la cuestión
[4] (*Med*) [+ *patient*] examinar, hacer un reconocimiento médico a; [+ *part of body*] examinar

examinee [ɪgˌzæmɪˈniː] N examinando/a *m/f*

examiner [ɪgˈzæmɪnəʳ] N examinador(a) *m/f*

▼ **example** [ɪgˈzɑːmpl] N (*gen*) ejemplo *m*; (= *copy, specimen*) ejemplar *m*; **for ~** por ejemplo; **to quote sth/sb as an ~** citar algo/a algn como ejemplo; **to follow sb's ~** seguir el ejemplo de algn; **to set a good/bad ~** dar buen/mal ejemplo; **to make an ~ of sb/punish sb as an ~** dar a algn un castigo ejemplar

exasperate [ɪgˈzɑːspəreɪt] VT exasperar, sacar de quicio

exasperated [ɪgˈzɑːspəreɪtɪd] ADJ exasperado; **to be ~ at** *or* **with sth/sb** estar exasperado con algo/algn; **we were ~ with Joe/the situation** Joe/la situación nos tenía exasperados, estábamos exasperados con Joe/la situación; **to become** *or* **get** *or* **grow ~** exasperarse

exasperating [ɪgˈzɑːspəreɪtɪŋ] ADJ [*person, situation, problem*] exasperante; **you're so ~!** ¡sacas de quicio a cualquiera!; **it's so ~!** ¡es exasperante!, es para volverse loco*

exasperatingly [ɪgˈzɑːspəreɪtɪŋlɪ] ADV **the train was ~ slow** el tren era tan lento que me (*or* lo, etc) exasperaba; **she's ~ stupid** es tan estúpida que le saca a uno de quicio, es de una estupidez exasperante

exasperation [ɪgˌzɑːspəˈreɪʃən] N exasperación *f*; **"hurry!" he cried in ~** —¡date prisa! —gritó exasperado *or* con exasperación

ex cathedra [ekskəˈθiːdrə] ADJ, ADV ex cátedra

excavate [ˈekskəveɪt] VT excavar

excavation [ˌekskəˈveɪʃən] N excavación *f*

excavator [ˈekskəveɪtəʳ] N (= *machine*) excavadora *f*; (= *person*) excavador(a) *m/f*

exceed [ɪkˈsiːd] VT [+ *estimate*] exceder (**by** en); [+ *number*] pasar de, exceder de; [+ *limit, bounds, speed limit*] sobrepasar, rebasar; [+ *rights*] ir más allá de, abusar de; [+ *powers, instructions*] excederse en; [+ *expectations, fears*] superar; **a fine not ~ing £50** una multa que no pase de 50 libras

exceedingly [ɪkˈsiːdɪŋlɪ] ADV sumamente, extremadamente

excel [ɪkˈsel] Ⓐ VT superar; **to ~ o.s.** (*often iro*) lucirse, pasarse (*LAm*)
Ⓑ VI **to ~ at** *or* **in** sobresalir en, destacar en; **to ~ as** destacarse como

excellence [ˈeksələns] N excelencia *f*

Excellency [ˈeksələnsɪ] N Excelencia *f*; **His ~** su Excelencia *f*; **yes, Your ~** sí, Excelencia

▼ **excellent** [ˈeksələnt] ADJ excelente

excellently [ˈeksələntlɪ] ADV excelentemente, muy bien; **to do sth ~** hacer algo muy bien

excelsior [ekˈselsɪɔːʳ] N (*US*) virutas *fpl* de embalaje

except [ɪkˈsept] Ⓐ PREP **~ (for)** excepto, salvo, menos; **~ that/if/when/where** *etc* salvo que/si/cuando/donde *etc*; **there is nothing we can do ~ wait** no nos queda otra (cosa) que esperar
Ⓑ VT excluir, exceptuar (**from** de); **present company ~ed** con excepción de los presentes

excepting [ɪkˈseptɪŋ] PREP excepto, salvo; **always ~ the possibility that …** excluyendo la posibilidad de que …; **not ~ …** incluso …, inclusive …

exception [ɪkˈsepʃən] N excepción *f*; **to make an ~** hacer una excepción; **to take ~ to sth** ofenderse por algo; **with the ~ of** a excepción de; **without ~** sin excepción; **the ~**

➤ LANGUAGE IN USE: **exactly** 11.1 **examine 3** 26.1, 26.2 **example** 26.2 **excellent** 13

proves the rule la excepción confirma la regla

exceptionable [ɪk'sepʃənəbl] ADJ [*conduct*] censurable, objetable; [*proposal*] impugnable, refutable

exceptional [ɪk'sepʃənl] Ⓐ ADJ [*courage, ability, circumstances*] excepcional; [*achievement, performance*] extraordinario, excepcional; **your wife was a most ~ woman** su esposa era una mujer de lo más excepcional
Ⓑ CPD ► **exceptional child** N (*US Scol*) (= *gifted*) niño/a *m/f* superdotado/a; (= *handicapped*) niño/a *m/f* que requiere una atención diferenciada

exceptionally [ɪk'sepʃənəlɪ] ADV [*difficult, valuable, intelligent, high*] excepcionalmente, extraordinariamente; [*good, large, easy, rare*] extraordinariamente; **an ~ talented player** un jugador de un talento excepcional *or* extraordinario; **~, in times of emergency we can ...** de forma excepcional, en casos de urgencia podemos ...

excerpt ['eksɜːpt] N extracto *m*

excess [ɪk'ses] Ⓐ N [1] (= *surplus*) exceso *m*; **an ~ of** [+ *precautions, enthusiasm, details*] un exceso de; **a sum in ~ of £100,000** una cifra superior a las 100.000 libras; **the painting is expected to fetch in ~ of £100,000** se espera que el cuadro se venda por una cifra superior a las 100.000 libras; **I don't smoke or drink to ~** no fumo ni bebo en exceso; **to carry sth to ~** llevar algo al extremo
[2] (= *overindulgence*) excesos *mpl*; **she was sick of her life of ~** estaba harta de su vida de excesos; **the ~es of the regime** los excesos del régimen; (*more serious*) las atrocidades del régimen
[3] (*Brit Insurance*) franquicia *f*
Ⓑ ADJ [1] (= *surplus*) **always remove ~ fat from pork** quítele siempre el exceso de grasa a la carne de cerdo; **she lost the ~ weight she had gained on holiday** perdió los kilos de más que había engordado durante las vacaciones; **she burns off ~ energy by cycling** quema el exceso de energía montando en bicicleta
[2] (= *additional*) [*profit, charge*] extraordinario
Ⓒ CPD ► **excess baggage** N exceso *m* de equipaje ► **excess demand** N exceso *m* de demanda ► **excess fare** N suplemento *m* ► **excess luggage** N = **excess baggage** ► **excess profits tax** N impuesto *m* sobre los beneficios extraordinarios ► **excess supply** N exceso *m* de oferta ► **excess weight** N exceso *m* de peso

excessive [ɪk'sesɪv] ADJ [*amount, use, consumption, heat*] excesivo; [*demands, interest, ambition*] excesivo, desmesurado; [*price*] excesivo, abusivo; **the use of ~ force by the police** el uso excesivo de la fuerza por parte de la policía; **the accident was caused by the driver's ~ speed** el exceso de velocidad con que iba el conductor causó el accidente; **the dangers of ~ drinking** los peligros de beber en exceso; **£10? that's a bit ~** ¿10 libras? eso es un poco exagerado, ¿10 libras? eso es pasarse*

excessively [ɪk'sesɪvlɪ] ADV [*eat, smoke, worry, spend*] demasiado, en exceso; [*ambitious, optimistic, proud, cautious*] excesivamente; **prices are ~ high** los precios son excesivamente *or* demasiado altos

exchange [ɪks'tʃeɪndʒ] Ⓐ N [1] (= *act*) [*of prisoners, publications, stamps*] intercambio *m*, canje *m*; [*of ideas, information, contracts*] intercambio *m*; **in ~ for** a cambio de; **~ of gunfire** tiroteo *m*; **~ of views** cambio *m* de impresiones; **~ of words** diálogo *m*
[2] (= *barter*) trueque *m*
[3] (*Fin*) [*of currency*] cambio *m*; **foreign ~** (= *money*) divisas *fpl*, moneda *f* extranjera
[4] (= *building*) (*for trade in corn, cotton*) lonja *f*; (= *stock exchange*) bolsa *f*; **(telephone) ~** (*public*) central *f* telefónica; (*private*) centralita *f*, conmutador *m* (*LAm*)
Ⓑ VT [1] (*gen*) cambiar (**for** por); [+ *prisoners, publications, stamps*] canjear (**for** por; **with** con); [+ *greetings, shots*] cambiar; [+ *courtesies*] hacerse; [+ *blows*] darse; **we ~d glances** nos miramos el uno al otro, cruzamos una mirada
[2] (= *barter*) trocar
Ⓒ CPD ► **exchange control** N control *m* de cambios ► **exchange rate** N tipo *m* de cambio ► **Exchange Rate Mechanism** N mecanismo *m* de paridades *or* de cambio del Sistema Monetario Europeo ► **exchange restrictions** NPL restricciones *fpl* monetarias ► **exchange value** N contravalor *m* ► **exchange visit** N visita *f* de intercambio

exchangeable [ɪks'tʃeɪndʒəbl] ADJ cambiable; [*prisoners, publications, stamps*] canjeable

exchequer [ɪks'tʃekəʳ] N (= *government department*) hacienda *f*, tesoro *m*; (= *treasury funds*) fisco *m*, fondos *mpl*; **the Exchequer** (*Brit Pol*) la Hacienda, el Fisco

excisable [ek'saɪzəbl] ADJ tasable

excise[1] ['eksaɪz] N (*also* **~ duty**) impuestos *mpl* indirectos; (*Brit*) (= *department*) **the Customs and Excise** la Aduana

excise[2] [ek'saɪz] VT [1] (*Med*) (= *remove*) extirpar
[2] (= *delete*) suprimir, eliminar

excision [ek'sɪʒən] N (*Med*) extirpación *f*; (= *deletion*) supresión *f*, eliminación *f*

excitability [ɪk'saɪtə'bɪlɪtɪ] N [*of person*] excitabilidad *f*; [*of mood, temperament*] nerviosismo *m*

excitable [ɪk'saɪtəbl] ADJ [*person, creature*] excitable; [*mood, temperament*] nervioso

excite [ɪk'saɪt] VT [1] (= *make excited*) entusiasmar; **what ~s me about the idea is ...** lo que me entusiasma *or* me parece excitante de la idea es ...; **don't ~ yourself, Grandpa** no te excites *or* agites, abuelo
[2] (= *arouse*) [+ *curiosity, admiration, envy*] provocar, suscitar; [+ *enthusiasm, interest*] despertar, suscitar; [+ *anger, passion*] provocar; [+ *imagination*] estimular; [+ *desire*] incitar, despertar
[3] (*sexually*) excitar
[4] (*Phys*) [+ *atom, particle*] excitar
[5] (*Med*) [+ *nerve, heart*] excitar

excited [ɪk'saɪtɪd] ADJ [1] (= *exhilarated*) [*adult*] entusiasmado; [*child*] excitado, alborotado; [*voice, chatter*] excitado; [*cry, shout*] de excitación; **I'm very ~ about the new house** la nueva casa me hace mucha ilusión, estoy muy ilusionado *or* entusiasmado con la nueva casa; **to get ~ (about sth)** entusiasmarse (con algo); **the children are getting ~ about the trip** los niños están cada vez más ilusionados *or* más entusiasmados con la idea del viaje; **don't get ~, I only said she MIGHT come** ¡tranquilízate!, solo dije que *puede* que venga; **it's nothing to get ~ about** no es para tanto
[2] (= *agitated*) [*person, animal*] agitado, nervioso; [*crowd*] alborotado; [*state*] de agitación, de nerviosismo; [*voice*] nervioso, excitado; **to get ~** [*person*] excitarse, ponerse nervioso; [*crowd*] alborotarse; [*discussion*] acalorarse; **don't get ~! I'm not suggesting that ...** ¡no te excites! *or* ¡no te pongas nervioso! *or* ¡no te acalores! no estoy sugiriendo que ...
[3] (*sexually*) excitado; **to get ~** excitarse
[4] (*Phys*) [*atom, molecule*] excitado

excitedly [ɪk'saɪtɪdlɪ] ADV [*wave, shout*] con excitación; **they were talking ~** hablaban muy excitados

excitement [ɪk'saɪtmənt] N [1] (= *exhilaration*) emoción *f*, excitación *f*; **why all the ~?** ◊ **what's all the ~ about?** ¿a qué se debe tanta excitación?; **she's looking for a bit of ~ in her life** está buscando algo de emoción en su vida; **in her ~, she forgot to close the door** con la emoción, se olvidó de cerrar la puerta; **the book has caused great ~ in literary circles** el libro ha causado mucha conmoción en círculos literarios
[2] (= *agitation*) agitación *f*, alboroto *m*
[3] (*sexual*) excitación *f*

exciting [ɪk'saɪtɪŋ] ADJ [1] (= *exhilarating*) [*experience, day, game*] emocionante; [*idea, possibility, discovery*] apasionante; [*person*] fascinante; [*book, play, film*] emocionante, apasionante; **it was not an ~ prospect** no era una perspectiva muy fascinante; **how ~!** ¡qué ilusión!
[2] (*sexually*) excitante

excitingly [ɪk'saɪtɪŋlɪ] ADV [*describe, write*] de manera emocionante; **it was an ~ close finish** la llegada fue muy reñida y emocionante

exclaim [ɪks'kleɪm] Ⓐ VT exclamar
Ⓑ VI **to ~ at sth** exclamar ante algo

exclamation [,eksklə'meɪʃən] Ⓐ N exclamación *f*
Ⓑ CPD ► **exclamation mark**, **exclamation point** (*US*) N (*Ling*) signo *m* de admiración

exclamatory [eks'klæmətərɪ] ADJ exclamativo

exclude [ɪks'kluːd] VT [1] (= *keep out*) excluir
[2] (= *discount*) [+ *mistakes*] exceptuar; [+ *possibility of error*] evitar
[3] (*Scol*) [+ *pupil*] expulsar

excluding [ɪks'kluːdɪŋ] PREP excepto, menos; **everything ~ the piano** todo excepto *or* menos el piano

exclusion [ɪks'kluːʒən] Ⓐ N exclusión *f*; **to the ~ of** con exclusión de
Ⓑ CPD ► **exclusion clause** N claúsula *f* de exclusión ► **(total) exclusion zone** N zona *f* de exclusión (total)

exclusionary [ɪks'kluːʒənrɪ] ADJ (*frm*) exclusivista; **the club had ~ policies** el club practicaba una política exclusivista

exclusive [ɪks'kluːsɪv] Ⓐ ADJ [1] (= *for nobody else*) [*information, use, interview, pictures*] exclusivo; **an ~ report/story** (*Press*) un reportaje en exclusiva; **to have (the) ~ rights to sth** tener la exclusiva *or* los derechos exclusivos para algo; **many of their designs are ~ to our store** muchos de sus diseños son exclusivos nuestros
[2] (= *select*) [*area, club, resort, restaurant*] selecto, exclusivo; **we attended an ~ gathering of theatre people** asistimos a una selecta reunión de gente del teatro
[3] (= *undivided*) [*interest, attention*] exclusivo
[4] (= *not inclusive*) **from 1st to 15th ~** del 1 al 15 exclusive; **~ of sth** sin incluir algo, excluyendo algo; **~ of postage and packing** gastos *mpl* de envío y empaquetado exclusivos, sin incluir gastos de envío y empaquetado; **~ of taxes** impuestos *mpl* excluidos, excluyendo los impuestos; *see also* **mutually**
Ⓑ N (*Press*) (= *story*) exclusiva *f*, reportaje *m* en exclusiva

exclusively [ɪks'kluːsɪvlɪ] ADV exclusivamente; **this is not ~ the fault of the government** esto no es culpa del gobierno exclusivamente; **available ~ from ...** de venta exclusiva en ...

exclusiveness [ɪks'kluːsɪvnɪs] N exclusividad *f*
exclusivity [ɪksklu:'sɪvətɪ] N exclusividad *f*
excommunicate [,ekskə'mjuːnɪkeɪt] VT excomulgar
excommunication ['ekskə,mjuːnɪ'keɪʃən] N excomunión *f*
ex-con* [,eks'kɒn] N ex presidiario/a *m/f*
excoriate [ɪks'kɔːrɪeɪt] VT (*frm*) [*+ person, organization, idea*] vilipendiar
excrement ['ekskrɪmənt] N excremento *m*
excrescence [ɪks'kresns] N excrecencia *f*
excreta [eks'kriːtə] NPL excremento *msing*
excrete [eks'kriːt] VT (*frm*) excretar
excretion [eks'kriːʃən] N (= *act*) excreción *f*; (= *substance*) excremento *m*
excretory [eks'kriːtərɪ] ADJ excretorio
excruciating [ɪks'kruːʃɪeɪtɪŋ] ADJ 1 [*pain, suffering, noise*] atroz, insoportable
2 (*) (= *very bad*) [*film, speech, party*] horroroso
excruciatingly [ɪks'kruːʃɪeɪtɪŋlɪ] ADV [*hurt, suffer*] terriblemente; **it was ~ funny** era para morirse de risa; **it was ~ painful** dolía terriblemente
exculpate ['ekskʌlpeɪt] VT exculpar
excursion [ɪks'kɜːʃən] Ⓐ N (= *journey*) excursión *f*; (*fig*) digresión *f*
Ⓑ CPD ► **excursion ticket** N billete *m* de excursión ► **excursion train** N tren *m* de recreo
excursionist [ɪk'skɜːʃənɪst] N excursionista *mf*
excursus [ek'skɜːsɪz] N excursus *m inv*
excusable [ɪks'kjuːzəbl] ADJ perdonable, disculpable
▼**excuse** Ⓐ [ɪks'kjuːs] N (= *justification*) excusa *f*, disculpa *f*; (= *pretext*) pretexto *m*; **there's no ~ for this** esto no admite disculpa; **it's only an ~** es un pretexto nada más; **on the ~ that ...** con el pretexto de que ...; **to make ~s for sb** presentar disculpas por algn; **he's only making ~s** está buscando pretextos; **he made his ~s and left** presentó sus excusas y se marchó; **he gives poverty as his ~** alega su pobreza; **what's your ~ this time?** ¿qué excusa *or* disculpa me das esta vez?
Ⓑ [ɪks'kjuːz] VT 1 (= *forgive*) disculpar, perdonar; **to ~ sb sth** perdonar algo a algn; **~ me!** (*asking a favour*) por favor, perdón; (*interrupting sb*) perdóneme; (*when passing*) perdón, con permiso; (= *sorry*) ¡perdón!; (*on leaving table*) ¡con permiso!; **~ me?** (*US*) ¿perdone?, ¿mande? (*Mex*); **now, if you will ~ me ...** con permiso ...; **if you will ~ me I must go** con permiso de ustedes tengo que marcharme; **may I be ~d for a moment?** ¿puedo salir un momento?
2 (= *justify*) justificar; **that does not ~ his conduct** eso no justifica su conducta; **to ~ o.s. (for sth/for doing sth)** pedir disculpas (por algo/por haber hecho algo)
3 (= *exempt*) **to ~ sb (from sth/from doing sth)** dispensar *or* eximir a algn (de algo/de hacer algo); **to ~ o.s. (from sth/from doing sth)** dispensarse (de algo/de hacer algo); **after ten minutes he ~d himself** después de diez minutos pidió permiso y se fue; **to ask to be ~d** pedir permiso; **I must ask to be ~d this time** esta vez les ruego que me dispensen *or* disculpen
ex-directory [,eksdɪ'rektərɪ] (*Brit*) ADJ **the number is ~** el número no figura en la guía; **they are ~** su número no figura en la guía; **he had to go ~** tuvo que pedir que su número no figurara en la guía
execrable ['eksɪkrəbl] ADJ (*frm*) execrable (*frm*), abominable (*frm*)
execrably ['eksɪkrəblɪ] ADV (*frm*) execrablemente (*frm*)
execrate ['eksɪkreɪt] VT (*frm*) execrar (*frm*), abominar (de) (*frm*)
execration [,eksɪ'kreɪʃən] N (*frm*) execración *f* (*frm*), abominación *f* (*frm*)
executable ['eksɪkjuːtəbl] Ⓐ ADJ ejecutable
Ⓑ CPD ► **executable file** N (*Comput*) fichero *m* ejecutable
executant [ɪg'zekjʊtənt] N ejecutante *mf*
▼**execute** ['eksɪkjuːt] VT 1 (= *put to death*) (*gen*) ejecutar; (*by firing squad*) fusilar
2 (= *carry out, perform*) [*+ plan*] llevar a cabo, ejecutar; [*+ work of art*] realizar; [*+ order*] ejecutar, cumplir; [*+ scheme, task, duty*] desempeñar; [*+ will*] ejecutar; [*+ document*] otorgar; (*Comput*) ejecutar
execution [,eksɪ'kjuːʃən] N 1 (= *putting to death*) (*gen*) ejecución *f*; (*by firing squad*) fusilamiento *m*
2 (= *carrying out*) [*of plan*] ejecución *f*; [*of act, crime*] comisión *f*; **in the ~ of one's duty** en el cumplimiento de sus deberes
executioner [,eksɪ'kjuːʃnəʳ] N verdugo *m*
executive [ɪg'zekjʊtɪv] Ⓐ ADJ 1 (= *managerial*) [*powers, role*] ejecutivo; [*position, duties, decision*] directivo, de nivel ejecutivo; [*pay, salaries*] de los ejecutivos; [*offices, suite*] (= *for executives*) para ejecutivos; (= *used by executives*) de los ejecutivos; [*car*] de ejecutivo
2 (*esp Brit**) (= *up-market*) [*briefcase, chair, toy*] de ejecutivo
Ⓑ N 1 (= *person*) ejecutivo/a *m/f*; **a sales ~** un(a) ejecutivo/a de ventas; *see also* **chief C**
2 (= *group*) [*of company*] comité *m* ejecutivo; [*of trade union, party*] ejecutiva *f*; **to be on the ~** [*of company*] pertenecer al comité ejecutivo; [*of trade union, party*] pertenecer a la ejecutiva
3 (= *part of government*) poder *m* ejecutivo, ejecutivo *m*
Ⓒ CPD ► **executive board** N (*Admin, Ind*) junta *f* directiva ► **executive chairman** N presidente/a *m/f* ejecutivo/a ► **executive committee** N (*Admin, Ind*) comité *m* ejecutivo ► **executive director** N (*Brit*) director(a) *m/f* ejecutivo/a ► **executive officer** N (*US Mil, Naut*) segundo/a comandante *m/f* ► **executive president** N presidente/a *m/f* ejecutivo/a ► **executive privilege** N (*US Pol*) inmunidad *f* del poder ejecutivo ► **executive producer** N (*Cine, Theat, TV*) productor(a) *m/f* ejecutivo/a ► **executive secretary** N secretario/a *m/f* de dirección

> **EXECUTIVE PRIVILEGE**
>
> *Se conoce como* **executive privilege** *el derecho que tiene el Presidente de Estados Unidos a no revelar cierta información al Congreso o a la judicatura en lo que se refiere a las actividades de su oficina. Suelen alegarse normalmente motivos de seguridad nacional o la necesidad de no desvelar ciertas conversaciones privadas del gobierno, pero no puede pedirse por razones personales. Varios presidentes han pedido durante su mandato que se les concediera este derecho de forma absoluta, pero los tribunales se lo han denegado. Durante el escándalo Watergate, el presidente Richard Nixon intentó acogerse a este derecho para no revelar ciertas grabaciones de conversaciones telefónicas de la Comisión de Investigación del Senado, pero le fue denegado por el Tribunal Supremo.*

executor [ɪg'zekjʊtəʳ] N [*of will*] albacea *mf*, testamentario/a *m/f*
executrix [ɪg'zekjʊtrɪks] N (*pl* **executrixes** *or* **executrices** [ɪg,zekjʊ'traɪsiːz]) albacea *f*, testamentaria *f*
exegesis [,eksɪ'dʒiːsɪs] N (*pl* **exegeses** [,eksɪ'dʒiːsiːz]) exégesis *f*
exemplar ['ɪgzemplɑː] (*frm*) N 1 (= *example*) ejemplar *m*
2 (= *model*) ejemplo *m*
exemplary [ɪg'zemplərɪ] ADJ ejemplar
exemplification [ɪg,zemplɪfɪ'keɪʃən] N ejemplificación *f*
exemplify [ɪg'zemplɪfaɪ] VT (= *illustrate*) ejemplificar, ilustrar; (= *be an example of*) demostrar; **as exemplified by his refusal to cooperate** según lo demuestra su negativa de cooperar
exempt [ɪg'zempt] Ⓐ ADJ exento (**from** de); **to be ~ from paying** estar exento de pagar; **~ from tax** libre de impuestos
Ⓑ VT **to ~ sth/sb (from sth/from doing sth)** eximir algo/a algn (de algo/de hacer algo), dispensar algo/a algn (de algo/de hacer algo)
exemption [ɪg'zempʃən] Ⓐ N exención *f* (**from** de); **tax ~** exención *f* de impuestos, exención *f* tributaria
Ⓑ CPD ► **exemption certificate** N certificado *m* de exención
exercise ['eksəsaɪz] Ⓐ N 1 (*physical, also Scol*) ejercicio *m*; **to do (physical) ~s** hacer gimnasia; **to take ~** hacer ejercicio
2 (= *carrying out*) ejercicio *m*; **in the ~ of my duties** en el ejercicio de mi cargo
3 (*Mil*) (= *manoeuvres*) maniobras *fpl*
4 **exercises** (*Sport*) ejercicios *mpl*; (*US*) (= *ceremony*) ceremonia *fsing*
Ⓑ VT 1 (= *use*) [*+ authority, right, influence*] ejercer; [*+ patience, tact*] emplear, hacer uso de; **to ~ care** tener cuidado, proceder con cautela; **to ~ restraint** contenerse, mostrarse comedido
2 (= *preoccupy*) [*+ mind*] preocupar
3 (*physically*) [*+ muscle, limb*] ejercitar; [*+ horse, team*] entrenar; [*+ dog*] sacar a pasear
Ⓒ VI hacer ejercicio
Ⓓ CPD ► **exercise bicycle** N bicicleta *f* estática ► **exercise bike** N = **exercise bicycle** ► **exercise book** N cuaderno *m* de ejercicios
exercycle ['eksəsaɪkl] = **exercise bicycle**
exert [ɪg'zɜːt] VT [*+ strength, force*] emplear; [*+ influence, authority*] ejercer; **to ~ o.s.** (*physically*) esforzarse (**to do sth** por hacer algo); (= *overdo things*) esforzarse *or* trabajar demasiado; **don't ~ yourself!** (*iro*) ¡no te vayas a quebrar *or* herniar! (*iro*); **he doesn't ~ himself at all** no hace el más mínimo esfuerzo
exertion [ɪg'zɜːʃən] N esfuerzo *m*; (= *overdoing things*) esfuerzo *m* excesivo, trabajo *m* excesivo
exeunt ['eksɪʌnt] VI (*Theat*) salen, se van
exfoliant [eks'fəʊlɪənt] N exfoliante *m*
exfoliate [eks'fəʊlɪeɪt] Ⓐ VT exfoliar
Ⓑ VI exfoliarse
exfoliation [eks,fəʊlɪ'eɪʃən] N exfoliación *f*
ex gratia [,eks'greɪʃə] ADJ [*payment*] ex-gratia, graciable
exhalation [,ekshə'leɪʃən] N exhalación *f*
exhale [eks'heɪl] Ⓐ VT [*+ air, fumes*] despedir
Ⓑ VI espirar
exhaust [ɪg'zɔːst] Ⓐ N (= *fumes*) gases *mpl* de escape; (*Aut*) escape *m*; (*also* **~ pipe**) tubo *m* de escape *m*
Ⓑ VT (*all senses*) agotar; **to be ~ed** estar agotado; **to ~ o.s.** agotarse
Ⓒ CPD ► **exhaust fumes**, **exhaust gases**

➤ LANGUAGE IN USE: **excuse B1** 18.1 **execute 2** 20.3

NPL gases *mpl* de escape ► **exhaust system** N sistema *m* de escape

exhaustible [ɪg'zɔːstəbl] ADJ [*resource*] que se puede agotar, limitado

exhausting [ɪg'zɔːstɪŋ] ADJ agotador

exhaustion [ɪg'zɔːstʃən] N (= *fatigue*) agotamiento *m*; (= *nervous exhaustion*) postración *f* nerviosa

exhaustive [ɪg'zɔːstɪv] ADJ exhaustivo

exhaustively [ɪg'zɔːstɪvlɪ] ADV de modo exhaustivo, exhaustivamente

exhaustiveness [ɪg'zɔːstɪvnɪs] N exhaustividad *f*

exhibit [ɪg'zɪbɪt] Ⓐ N (= *painting, object*) (*in museum, art gallery*) objeto *m* expuesto; (*Jur*) prueba *f* instrumental, documento *m*; **to be on ~** estar expuesto
Ⓑ VT [+ *painting, object*] exponer; [+ *film*] exhibir, presentar; [+ *signs of emotion*] mostrar, manifestar; [+ *courage, skill, ingenuity*] demostrar
Ⓒ VI [*painter, sculptor*] exponer (sus obras)

exhibition [,eksɪ'bɪʃən] Ⓐ N [1] (= *act, instance*) manifestación *f*; (= *public show*) exposición *f*; **to be on ~** estar expuesto; **to make an ~ of o.s.** quedar en ridículo; **an ~ of bad temper** una demostración de mal genio
[2] (*Brit Univ*) beca *f*
Ⓑ CPD ► **exhibition game** N partido *m* de exhibición ► **exhibition match** N = **exhibition game**

exhibitionism [,eksɪ'bɪʃənɪzəm] N exhibicionismo *m*

exhibitionist [,eksɪ'bɪʃənɪst] Ⓐ ADJ exhibicionista
Ⓑ N exhibicionista *mf*

exhibitor [ɪg'zɪbɪtə^r] N expositor(a) *m/f*

exhilarate [ɪg'zɪləreɪt] VT alegrar, entusiasmar; **to feel ~d** sentirse muy entusiasmado *or* alegre

exhilarating [ɪg'zɪləreɪtɪŋ] ADJ estimulante, vigorizador

exhilaration [ɪg,zɪlə'reɪʃən] N (= *elation*) alegría *f*, regocijo *m*; (= *excitement*) excitación *f*; **the ~ of speed** lo emocionante de la velocidad

exhort [ɪg'zɔːt] VT **to ~ sb (to sth/to do sth)** exhortar a algn (a algo/a hacer algo)

exhortation [,egzɔː'teɪʃən] N exhortación *f*

exhumation [,eks*h*juː'meɪʃən] N exhumación *f*

exhume [eks'hjuːm] VT exhumar, desenterrar

ex-husband [,eks'hʌzbənd] N ex marido *m*

exigence ['eksɪdʒəns] N = **exigency**

exigency [ɪg'zɪdʒənsɪ] N (= *need*) exigencia *f*; (= *emergency*) caso *m* de urgencia

exigent ['eksɪdʒənt] ADJ exigente; (= *urgent*) urgente

exiguous [eg'zɪgjʊəs] ADJ exiguo

exile ['eksaɪl] Ⓐ N [1] (= *state*) exilio *m*, destierro *m*; **he spent many years in ~** vivió muchos años en el exilio, vivió muchos años exiliado; **government in ~** gobierno *m* en el exilio; **to send sb into ~** desterrar a algn, mandar a algn al exilio
[2] (= *person*) exiliado/a *m/f*, desterrado/a *m/f*
Ⓑ VT desterrar, exiliar

exiled ['eksaɪld] ADJ exiliado

exist [ɪg'zɪst] VI [1] (= *live*) vivir; (= *survive*) subsistir; **I just ~ed from one visit to the next** de una visita a la otra me limitaba a sobrevivir; **to ~ on very little money** vivir *or* subsistir con muy poco dinero; **you can't ~ on packet soup!** no puedes vivir sólo a base de sopa de sobre
[2] (= *occur, be in existence*) existir; **it only ~s in her imagination** sólo existe en su imaginación; **there ~s a possibility that** *or* **the possibility ~s that she is still alive** existe la posibilidad de que siga con vida; **I want to live, not just ~** quiero vivir, no simplemente existir; **to cease to ~** dejar de existir; **to continue to ~** [*situation, conditions, doubt*] persistir; [*institution, person*] (*after death*) seguir existiendo

existence [ɪg'zɪstəns] N existencia *f*; (= *way of life*) vida *f*; **to be in ~** existir; **to come into ~** nacer; **the only one in ~** el único existente

existent [ɪg'zɪstənt] ADJ existente, actual

existential [,egzɪs'tenʃəl] ADJ existencial

existentialism [,egzɪs'tenʃəlɪzəm] N existencialismo *m*

existentialist [,egzɪs'tenʃəlɪst] Ⓐ ADJ existencialista
Ⓑ N existencialista *mf*

existing [ɪg'zɪstɪŋ] ADJ [*customers, products, facilities*] existente; [*law, arrangements, system*] actual, existente; **under ~ circumstances** en las circunstancias actuales *or* existentes

exit ['eksɪt] Ⓐ N (= *place, act*) salida *f*; (*esp Theat*) mutis *m inv*; **"no exit"** "prohibida la salida"; **to make one's ~** salir, marcharse
Ⓑ VI (*Theat*) hacer mutis; (*Comput*) salir; **~ Hamlet** vase Hamlet
Ⓒ VT (*Comput*) salir de; **if we have to ~ the plane** (*US*) si tenemos que abandonar el avión, si tenemos que salir del avión
Ⓓ CPD ► **exit permit** N permiso *m* de salida ► **exit poll** N (*Pol*) *encuesta de votantes a la salida del colegio electoral* ► **exit ramp** N (*US*) vía *f* de acceso ► **exit visa** N visa *f or* visado *m* de salida

ex nihilo [,eks'nɪhɪləʊ] ADV ex nihilo

exodus ['eksədəs] N (*gen, Rel*) éxodo *m*; **there was a general ~** hubo un éxodo general

ex officio [,eksə'fɪʃɪəʊ] Ⓐ ADV [*act*] ex officio, oficialmente
Ⓑ ADJ [*member*] nato, ex officio

exonerate [ɪg'zɒnəreɪt] VT **to ~ sb (from)** [+ *obligations, blame*] exonerar a algn (de)

exoneration [ɪg,zɒnə'reɪʃən] N exculpación *f*

exorbitance [ɪg'zɔːbɪtəns] N exorbitancia *f*

exorbitant [ɪg'zɔːbɪtənt] ADJ [*rent, price, fee*] exorbitante, abusivo; [*demands*] desorbitado, desmesurado

exorbitantly [ɪg'zɔːbɪtəntlɪ] ADV exorbitantemente; **it was ~ expensive** era exorbitantemente caro; **to pay sb/charge sb ~** pagar/cobrar a algn una cantidad exorbitante *or* abusiva; **some bosses are paid ~** a algunos jefes se les paga unos salarios exorbitantes; **~ priced shoes** zapatos *mpl* a precios exorbitantes *or* abusivos

exorcise ['eksɔːsaɪz] VT [+ *person, evil spirit*] exorcizar

exorcism ['eksɔːsɪzəm] N exorcismo *m*

exorcist ['eksɔːsɪst] N exorcista *mf*

exotic [ɪg'zɒtɪk] Ⓐ ADJ [*flower, bird, fruit, food, place*] exótico; [*holiday*] en un lugar exótico
Ⓑ N (*Bot*) planta *f* exótica

exotica [ɪg'zɒtɪkə] NPL objetos *mpl* exóticos

exotically [ɪg'zɒtɪklɪ] ADV [*named, dressed, designed*] exóticamente, de forma exótica

exoticism [ɪg'zɒtɪsɪzəm] N exotismo *m*

expand [ɪks'pænd] Ⓐ VT [1] [+ *market, operations, business*] ampliar; [+ *metal*] dilatar; [+ *number*] aumentar; [+ *chest*] expandir; [+ *wings*] abrir, desplegar; [+ *influence, knowledge*] aumentar, ampliar
[2] (= *develop*) [+ *statement, notes*] ampliar
[3] (= *broaden*) [+ *experience, mind*] ampliar, extender; [+ *horizons*] ampliar, ensanchar
Ⓑ VI [1] [*gas, metal, lungs*] dilatarse; [*market, operations, business*] ampliarse; **to ~ (up)on** [+ *notes, story*] ampliar, desarrollar
[2] [*person*] (= *relax*) distenderse

expanded [ɪks'pændɪd] Ⓐ ADJ (*Metal, Tech*) dilatado
Ⓑ CPD ► **expanded polystyrene** N poliestireno *m* dilatado

expander [ɪks'pændə^r] N = **chest expander**

expanding [ɪks'pændɪŋ] ADJ [*metal*] dilatable; [*bracelet*] expandible; [*market, industry, profession*] en expansión; **the ~ universe** el universo en expansión; **~ file** carpeta *f* de acordeón; **a job with ~ opportunities** un empleo con perspectivas de futuro; **a rapidly ~ industry** una industria en rápida expansión

expanse [ɪks'pæns] N extensión *f*; [*of wings*] envergadura *f*

expansion [ɪks'pænʃən] Ⓐ N [*of metal*] dilatación *f*; [*of town, economy, territory*] desarrollo *m*; [*of subject, idea, trade, market*] ampliación *f*, desarrollo *m*; [*of production, knowledge*] aumento *m*, extensión *f*; [*of number*] aumento *m*; (*Math*) desarrollo *m*
Ⓑ CPD ► **expansion board** N (*Comput*) placa *f* de expansión ► **expansion bottle** N (*Aut*) depósito *m* del agua ► **expansion bus** N (*Comput*) bus *m* de expansión ► **expansion card** N (*Comput*) tarjeta *f* de expansión ► **expansion slot** N (*Comput*) ranura *f* para tarjetas de expansión ► **expansion tank** N (*Aut*) depósito *m* del agua

expansionism [ɪks'pænʃənɪzəm] N expansionismo *m*

expansionist [ɪks'pænʃənɪst] ADJ expansionista

expansive [ɪks'pænsɪv] ADJ [1] (= *affable*) comunicativo, sociable, expansivo (*liter*); **he was becoming more ~ as he relaxed** se volvía más comunicativo *or* sociable a medida que se relajaba; **he was in an ~ mood** estaba muy comunicativo *or* sociable
[2] (= *broad*) [*area, room*] extenso; [*view*] extenso, amplio; **with an ~ gesture he indicated the wonderful view** abrió los brazos señalando la fantástica vista
[3] (= *expanding*) [*economy, phase*] expansivo
[4] (*Phys*) expansivo

expansively [ɪks'pænsɪvlɪ] ADV [1] (= *affably*) [*welcome, say, smile*] calurosamente
[2] (= *in detail*) [*relate, write*] extensamente; **he talked ~ of his travels** habló extensamente sobre sus viajes, se explayó sobre sus viajes

expansiveness [ɪk'spænsɪvnɪs] N [*of person*] carácter *m* sociable

expat [eks'pæt] (*) N = **expatriate**

expatiate [eks'peɪʃɪeɪt] VI **to ~ on sth** hablar extensamente sobre algo

expatriate [eks'pætrɪɪt] Ⓐ N expatriado/a *m/f*
Ⓑ ADJ expatriado
Ⓒ VT desterrar; **to ~ o.s.** expatriarse

expect [ɪks'pekt] Ⓐ VT [1] (= *anticipate, hope for, wait for*) esperar; **I did not know what to ~** yo no sabía qué esperar; **it's not what I ~ed** no es lo que yo esperaba; **you know what to ~** ya sabes a qué atenerte; **we'll ~ you for supper** te esperamos a cenar; **is he ~ing you?** ¿tiene usted cita con él?; **it's easier than I ~ed** es más fácil de lo que esperaba; **to ~ to do sth** esperar hacer algo; **they ~ to arrive tomorrow** esperan llegar mañana; **I ~ him to arrive soon** creo que llegará pronto; **it is ~ed that ...** se espera que + *subjun*, se prevé que; **we ~ great things of him** tenemos depositadas grandes esperanzas en él; **I ~ed as much** ◊ **just what I ~ed** ya me lo imaginaba *or* figuraba; **that was (only) to be**

~ed eso era de esperar; **as was to be ~ed** ◊ **as might have been ~ed** ◊ **as one might ~** como era de esperar; **when least ~ed** el día menos pensado; **~ me when you see me*** no cuentes conmigo

2 (= *suppose*) imaginarse, suponer; **I ~ so** supongo que sí, a lo mejor; **yes, I ~ it is** así tenía que ser; **I ~ it was John** me imagino que fue John; **I ~ she's there by now** me imagino que ya habrá llegado; **I ~ he'll be late** seguro que llega tarde

3 (= *require*) **to ~ sth (of/from sb)** esperar algo (de algn); **I think you're ~ing too much of me** creo que esperas demasiado de mí; **to ~ sb to do sth** esperar que algn haga algo; **I ~ you to be punctual** cuento con que serás puntual; **how can you ~ me to sympathize?** ¿y me pides compasión?; **you can't ~ too much from him** no debes esperar demasiado de él; **she can't be ~ed to know that** no se puede esperar *or* pretender que sepa eso; **what do you ~ me to do about it?** ¿qué pretendes que haga yo?; **it is hardly to be ~ed that ...** apenas cabe esperar que + *subjun*

Ⓑ VI **she's ~ing** está encinta, está en estado

expectancy [ɪks'pektənsɪ] N (= *state*) expectación *f*; (= *hope, chance*) expectativa *f* (**of** de); **there was a buzz of ~ in the air** había un clima de expectación en el ambiente; **life ~** esperanza *f* de vida

expectant [ɪks'pektənt] ADJ [*person, crowd*] expectante; [*look*] de esperanza; **~ mother** mujer *f* encinta, futura madre *f*

expectantly [ɪks'pektəntlɪ] ADV con expectación

expectation [ˌekspek'teɪʃən] N 1 (= *state*) expectación *f*; **in ~ of** en espera de, previendo

2 (= *hope*) expectativa *f*, esperanza *f*; **against** *or* **contrary to all ~(s)** en contra de todos los pronósticos *or* todas las expectativas; **it didn't live up to our ~s** no estuvo a la altura de lo que esperábamos; **the holiday didn't come up to my ~s** las vacaciones no resultaron tan buenas como me esperaba; **the response exceeded all our ~s** la respuesta sobrepasó todas nuestras expectativas; **to fall below one's ~s** no llegar a lo que se esperaba

expectorant [eks'pektərənt] Ⓐ N expectorante *m*

Ⓑ ADJ expectorante

expectorate [eks'pektəreɪt] VT expectorar

expedience [ɪks'piːdɪəns], **expediency** [ɪks'piːdɪənsɪ] N conveniencia *f*, oportunidad *f*; (*pej*) oportunismo *m*

expedient [ɪks'piːdɪənt] Ⓐ ADJ (= *convenient, politic*) oportuno, conveniente

Ⓑ N recurso *m*

expedite ['ekspɪdaɪt] VT (= *speed up*) [+ *business, deal*] acelerar; [+ *official matter, legal matter*] dar curso a; [+ *process, preparations*] facilitar; [+ *task*] despachar (con prontitud); **to ~ matters** acelerar las cosas

expedition [ˌekspɪ'dɪʃən] N expedición *f*; **to go on a fishing/hunting ~** ir de pesca/caza, hacer una expedición de pesca/caza; **to go on a shopping ~** ir de compras *or* de tiendas

expeditionary [ˌekspɪ'dɪʃənrɪ] ADJ expedicionario; **~ force** cuerpo *m* expedicionario

expeditious [ˌekspɪ'dɪʃəs] ADJ rápido, pronto

expeditiously [ˌekspɪ'dɪʃəslɪ] ADV con toda prontitud

expel [ɪks'pel] VT [+ *air*] (*from container*) arrojar, expeler; [+ *person*] expulsar; **to get ~led** (*from school*) ser expulsado

expend [ɪks'pend] VT [+ *money*] gastar; [+ *time, effort, energy*] dedicar (**on** a); [+ *resources*] consumir, agotar; [+ *ammunition*] usar

expendability [ɪksˌpendə'bɪlətɪ] N prescindibilidad *f*

expendable [ɪks'pendəbl] Ⓐ ADJ [*equipment*] fungible; [*person, luxury*] prescindible

Ⓑ NPL **expendables** equipo *m* or material *m* fungible

expenditure [ɪks'pendɪtʃə^r] N [*of money*] gasto *m*, desembolso *m*; [*of time, effort*] gasto *m*, empleo *m*; (= *money spent*) gastos *mpl*; **I resent the ~ of time and effort on trivialities** me molesta el empleo de *or* me molesta emplear tiempo y esfuerzo en cosas triviales; *see also* **capital C**, **public C**

expense [ɪks'pens] Ⓐ N (= *cost*) gasto *m*, costo *m*; **expenses** gastos *mpl*; **travelling/repair ~s** gastos *mpl* de viaje/reparación; **with all ~s paid** con todos los gastos pagados; **at great ~** gastándose muchísimo dinero; **at my ~** a cuenta mía; **they thought they would have a joke at my ~** querían reírse a costa mía; **at the ~ of** (*fig*) a costa de; **you needn't go to the ~ of buying a new one** no es preciso que te gastes dinero en comprar uno nuevo; **they went to great ~ to send her to a private school** se metieron en muchos gastos para mandarla a un colegio privado; **to meet the ~ of** hacer frente a *or* correr con los gastos de; **he apologized for putting us to so much ~** se disculpó por habernos ocasionado tantos gastos; **regardless of ~** sin escatimar gastos; **to be a great ~ to sb** suponer a algn un gasto importante; *see also* **business B**

Ⓑ CPD ► **expense account** N cuenta *f* de gastos de representación

expensive [ɪks'pensɪv] ADJ [*goods, shop, hobby*] caro; **it is very ~ to live in London** resulta muy caro vivir en Londres; **learning to drive is an ~ business** aprender a conducir sale caro *or* resulta muy costoso; **he has ~ tastes** tiene gustos caros; **she has an ~ lifestyle** lleva un tren de vida caro; **it was an ~ mistake** el error nos ha salido caro

expensively [ɪks'pensɪvlɪ] ADV **he loves to eat ~** le gusta la comida cara; **she was ~ dressed** vestía con ropa cara; **they had been ~ educated** habían recibido una educación cara; **we can do that fairly easily and not too ~** podemos hacer eso fácilmente y sin gastar mucho *or* y sin que nos cueste mucho; **the room was ~ furnished** la habitación estaba amueblada por todo lo alto

expensiveness [ɪks'pensɪvnɪs] N lo caro

▼**experience** [ɪks'pɪərɪəns] Ⓐ N 1 (= *knowledge*) experiencia *f*; **to learn by ~** aprender por la experiencia; **I know from bitter/personal ~** lo sé por mi amarga experiencia/por experiencia propia; **he has no ~ of grief/being out of work** no conoce la tristeza/el desempleo

2 (= *skill, practice*) práctica *f*, experiencia *f*; **he has plenty of ~** tiene mucha práctica; **have you any previous ~?** ¿tiene usted experiencia previa?; **practical ~** experiencia *f* práctica; **teaching ~** experiencia *f* docente; **a driver with ten years' ~** un conductor con diez años de experiencia; *see also* **work D**

3 (= *event*) experiencia *f*, aventura *f*; **to have a pleasant/frightening ~** tener una experiencia agradable/aterradora; **it was quite an ~** fue toda una experiencia

Ⓑ VT (= *feel*) [+ *emotion, sensation*] experimentar; (= *suffer*) [+ *defeat, loss, hardship*] sufrir; [+ *difficulty*] tener, tropezar con; **he ~s some difficulty/pain in walking** tiene dificultades/dolor al andar; **he ~d a loss of hearing after the accident** después del accidente, sufrió una pérdida del oído

experienced [ɪks'pɪərɪənst] ADJ [*teacher, nurse*] con experiencia; **"experienced drivers required"** "se necesitan conductores con experiencia"; **we need someone more ~** necesitamos a alguien con más experiencia; **she is not ~ enough** no tiene la suficiente experiencia; **to be ~ (in sth/in doing sth)** tener experiencia (en algo/en hacer algo); **to the ~ eye/ear** para el ojo/oído experto; **with an ~ eye** con ojo experto; **to be sexually ~** tener experiencia sexual

experiential [ɪksˌpɪərɪ'enʃəl] ADJ (*Philos*) experiencial

experiment [ɪks'perɪmənt] Ⓐ N (*gen*) experimento *m*; **to perform** *or* **carry out an ~** realizar un experimento; **as an ~** ◊ **by way of ~** como experimento

Ⓑ VI (*gen*) experimentar; (*scientifically*) experimentar, hacer experimentos; **he ~ed on fellow students** experimentó *or* hizo experimentos con sus compañeros; **youngsters who ~ with drugs** jóvenes *mpl* que experimentan con drogas; **~ with different methods to find the best one for you** experimenta *or* prueba con distintos métodos para encontrar el que te va mejor

experimental [eksˌperɪ'mentl] ADJ [*science, method, music*] experimental; [*theatre, novel*] vanguardista; [*cinema*] de arte y ensayo; **to be at** *or* **in the ~ stage** estar en la fase experimental; **he gave an ~ tug at the door handle** hizo el experimento de tirar del picaporte

experimentally [eksˌperɪ'mentəlɪ] ADV [*study, test, introduce*] experimentalmente, de forma experimental; [*try out*] como experimento; **he lifted the cases ~ to see how heavy they were** hizo el experimento de levantar las maletas para ver lo que pesaban

experimentation [eksˌperɪmen'teɪʃən] N experimentación *f*

experimenter [ɪks'perɪmentə^r] N investigador(a) *m/f*

expert ['ekspɜːt] Ⓐ ADJ [*craftsman, surgeon*] experto, especialista; (*Jur*) [*evidence, witness*] pericial; **we'll need an ~ opinion** necesitaremos la opinión de un experto *or* especialista; **he ran an ~ eye over the photographs** echó un vistazo a las fotografías con ojo experto; **to be ~ at (doing) sth** ser experto en (hacer) algo; **~ system** (*Comput*) sistema *m* experto; **~ valuation** tasación *f* pericial

Ⓑ N experto/a *m/f*; **to be an ~ at (doing) sth** ser un experto en (hacer) algo; **he's an ~ on computers** es un experto en ordenadores; **I'm no ~ on the subject** no soy un experto en la materia; **he's a computer ~** es especialista en ordenadores; **to examine sth with the eye of an ~** examinar algo con ojo experto

expertise [ˌekspə'tiːz] N (= *experience*) experiencia *f*; (= *knowledge*) conocimientos *mpl*; (= *skills*) pericia *f*

expertly ['ekspɜːtlɪ] ADV con habilidad, con pericia (*more frm*); **she drove ~ through the traffic** condujo con habilidad *or* con pericia entre el tráfico; **he handled the controls ~** manejaba expertamente los mandos, manejaba los mandos con la habilidad de un experto

expertness ['ekspɜːtnɪs] N pericia *f*

expiate ['ekspɪeɪt] VT expiar

expiation [ˌekspɪ'eɪʃən] N expiación *f*

expiatory ['ekspɪətərɪ] ADJ expiatorio

➤ LANGUAGE IN USE: **experience A2** 19.2

expiration [ˌekspaɪə'reɪʃən] N 1 = **expiry**
2 [*of breath*] espiración *f*

expire [ɪks'paɪəʳ] VI 1 (= *end*) [*time, period*] terminar, finalizar; [*ticket, passport*] caducar, vencer; [*lease, contract*] vencer, expirar; **my passport has ~d** mi pasaporte ha caducado *or* vencido
2 (*frm*) (= *die*) expirar
3 (= *breathe out*) espirar

expiry [ɪks'paɪərɪ] Ⓐ N [*of time, period*] terminación *f*, finalización *f*; [*of visa, passport*] vencimiento *m*, caducidad *f*; [*of lease, contract*] vencimiento *m*, expiración *f*
Ⓑ CPD ► **expiry date** N [*of visa, contract*] fecha *f* de vencimiento; [*of medicine, food item*] fecha *f* de caducidad

explain Ⓐ [ɪks'pleɪn] VT (= *make clear*) [+ *meaning, problem*] explicar; [+ *plan*] explicar, exponer; [+ *mystery*] explicar, aclarar; (= *account for*) [+ *conduct*] explicar, justificar; **I ~ed it to him** se lo expliqué; **that ~s it** eso lo explica, con eso queda todo aclarado; **to ~ o.s.** (*clearly*) explicarse; (*morally*) justificarse, defenderse; **kindly ~ yourself!** ¡explíquese Vd!
Ⓑ VI **will you call him and ~?** ¿le llamas tú y se lo explicas?; **I tried to ~, but …** intenté explicárselo, pero …
► **explain away** VT + ADV dar explicaciones (convincentes) de, justificar; (= *excuse*) disculpar; **try and ~ that away!** ¡a ver cómo justificas eso!

explainable [ɪks'pleɪnəbl] ADJ explicable

explanation [ˌeksplə'neɪʃən] N (= *act, statement*) explicación *f*; [*of plan*] explicación *f*, exposición *f*; [*of problem, mystery*] aclaración *f*; (= *excuse*) disculpa *f*; **what is the ~ of this?** ¿cómo se explica esto?; **there must be some ~** tiene que haber alguna explicación; **to offer** *or* **give an ~** dar explicaciones; **they gave no ~ for the delay** no dieron ninguna explicación por el retraso

explanatory [ɪks'plænətərɪ] ADJ explicativo; [*note*] aclaratorio

expletive [eks'pliːtɪv] Ⓐ N (*Gram*) palabra *f* expletiva; (= *oath*) palabrota *f*, improperio *m*
Ⓑ ADJ (*Gram*) expletivo

explicable [eks'plɪkəbl] ADJ explicable

explicate ['eksplɪkeɪt] VT (*frm*) explicar; [+ *poem, painting*] comentar

explicit [ɪks'plɪsɪt] ADJ [*instructions, reference, intention*] explícito, claro; [*description, picture*] gráfico; [*statement, denial*] categórico; **the ~ nature of the photographs** el carácter gráfico de las fotos; **to describe sth in ~ detail** describir algo gráficamente; **he was ~ about his intentions** fue explícito *or* claro acerca de sus intenciones; **he was ~ on this point** fue muy claro sobre esto; **sexually ~** con claro contenido sexual

explicitly [ɪks'plɪsɪtlɪ] ADV [*state, mention, acknowledge*] explícitamente, de forma explícita; [*forbid, reject, deny*] categóricamente; [*racist, political*] explícitamente, claramente; **~ sexual photographs** fotografías *fpl* con claro contenido sexual

explicitness [ɪk'splɪsɪtnɪs] N [*of instructions, reference*] carácter *m* explícito, lo explícito; [*of description, picture*] lo gráfico; [*of statement*] lo categórico

explode [ɪks'pləʊd] Ⓐ VI estallar, explotar, hacer explosión; (*fig*) reventar, estallar; **to ~ with laughter** estallar en carcajadas; **to ~ with anger** tener un arrebato de ira; **to ~ with jealousy** tener un ataque de celos
Ⓑ VT 1 hacer estallar, hacer explotar, explosionar
2 (= *refute*) [+ *rumour*] desmentir; [+ *myth, theory*] echar por tierra

exploit ['eksplɔɪt] Ⓐ N hazaña *f*, proeza *f*
Ⓑ [ɪks'plɔɪt] VT [+ *resources*] explotar, aprovechar; (*pej*) [+ *person, situation*] explotar

exploitable [eks'plɔɪtəbl] ADJ explotable

exploitation [ˌeksplɔɪ'teɪʃən] N explotación *f*

exploitative [eks'plɔɪtətɪv] ADJ explotador

exploiter [eks'plɔɪtəʳ] N explotador(a) *m/f*

exploration [ˌeksplɔː'reɪʃən] N (*gen, Med*) exploración *f*; [*of subject*] análisis *m inv*, estudio *m*

exploratory [eks'plɒrətərɪ] ADJ [*surgery, research, study*] exploratorio; [*discussions*] preliminares, de tanteo; [*drilling*] de sondeo

explore [ɪks'plɔːʳ] Ⓐ VT 1 [+ *country*] explorar; (*Med*) examinar
2 (*fig*) [+ *problems, subject*] investigar; [+ *opinion*] sondear; **to ~ every possibility** considerar todas las posibilidades; **to ~ every avenue** estudiar todas las vías posibles
Ⓑ VI explorar

explorer [ɪks'plɔːrəʳ] N explorador(a) *m/f*

explosion [ɪks'pləʊʒən] N 1 (*gen*) explosión *f*; (= *noise*) explosión *f*, estallido *m*
2 (*fig*) (= *outburst*) [*of anger*] arranque *m*, arrebato *m*; [*of laughter*] estallido *m*; [*of feeling, emotion*] arrebato *m*; **there has been an ~ of interest in her books** el interés por sus libros ha experimentado un auge repentino; **population ~** explosión *f* demográfica; **price ~** aumento *m* general de precios

explosive [ɪks'pləʊzɪv] Ⓐ ADJ 1 (*lit*) [*gas, mixture, force*] explosivo; **an ~ device** un artefacto explosivo
2 (*fig*) [*combination, growth*] explosivo; [*situation, issue*] explosivo, candente; **he has an ~ temper** tiene un temperamento explosivo
Ⓑ N explosivo *m*
Ⓒ CPD ► **explosives expert** N artificiero/a *m/f*

explosively [ɪks'pləʊsɪvlɪ] ADV 1 (*lit*) **sodium reacts ~ with water** el sodio reacciona con el agua produciendo una explosión, el sodio explota en contacto con el agua
2 (*fig*) 2·1 (= *angrily*) **"shut up!" — she said ~** —¡cállate! —explotó
2·2 (= *by leaps and bounds*) **the number of customers has grown ~** el número de clientes ha crecido vertiginosamente

explosiveness [ɪk'spləʊzɪvnɪs] N carácter *m* explosivo

expo ['ekspəʊ] N ABBR (= **exposition**) expo *f*

exponent [eks'pəʊnənt] N [*of idea*] exponente *mf*; [*of cause*] partidario/a *m/f*; (= *interpreter*) intérprete *mf*; (*Gram, Math*) exponente *m*

exponential [ˌekspəʊ'nenʃəl] ADJ exponencial

exponentially [ˌekspəʊ'nenʃlɪ] ADV de manera exponencial

export ['ekspɔːt] Ⓐ N (= *act*) exportación *f*; (= *commodity*) artículo *m* de exportación; *see also* **invisible**
Ⓑ [eks'pɔːt] VT exportar
Ⓒ ['ekspɔːt] CPD [*market, goods, permit, licence*] de exportación ► **export credit** N crédito *m* a la exportación ► **export drive** N campaña *f* de exportación ► **export duty** N derechos *mpl* de exportación ► **export earnings** N ganancias *fpl* por exportación ► **export sales** NPL ventas *fpl* de exportación ► **export trade** N comercio *m* de exportación

exportable [eks'pɔːtəbl] ADJ exportable

exportation [ˌekspɔː'teɪʃən] N exportación *f*

exporter [eks'pɔːtəʳ] N exportador(a) *m/f*

exporting [ek'spɔːtɪŋ] Ⓐ ADJ exportador
Ⓑ CPD ► **exporting company** N empresa *f* exportadora ► **exporting country** N país *m* exportador

expose [ɪks'pəʊz] VT (= *uncover*) dejar al descubierto; (= *leave unprotected*) exponer; (= *display*) exponer, presentar; (*Phot*) exponer; (*fig*) (= *reveal*) [+ *plot, crime*] poner al descubierto; [+ *criminal, imposter*] desenmascarar; [+ *weakness, one's ignorance*] revelar, poner en evidencia; **to be ~d to view** estar a la vista de todos; **to ~ one's head to the sun** exponer la cabeza al sol; **to ~ sb/o.s. to ridicule** poner a algn/ponerse en ridículo; **to ~ o.s. to** [+ *risk, danger*] exponerse a; **to ~ o.s.** (*sexually*) hacer exhibicionismo

exposé [ek'spəʊzeɪ] N exposición *f*, revelación *f*

exposed [ɪks'pəʊzd] ADJ 1 (= *unsheltered*) [*hillside, site, garden*] desprotegido, expuesto; **the house is in an ~ position** la casa está en un lugar desprotegido *or* expuesto; **~ to the wind** desprotegido del viento, expuesto al viento
2 (= *vulnerable*) desprotegido, expuesto; **this leaves the party in an ~ position** esto deja al partido en una posición desprotegida *or* expuesta; **~ to enemy fire** expuesto al fuego enemigo
3 (= *uncovered*) [*pipe, brickwork, skin*] al descubierto; [*nerve*] al descubierto, expuesto; [*wire*] al aire; **use on all ~ parts of the body** aplíquese en las zonas del cuerpo que estén al descubierto
4 (*Phot*) [*film*] (*in normal process*) expuesto; (= *ruined*) velado

exposition [ˌekspə'zɪʃən] N 1 [*of facts, theories*] exposición *f*; **to give an ~ of sth** hacer una exposición de algo
2 (= *exhibition*) exposición *f*

expostulate [ɪks'pɒstjʊleɪt] Ⓐ VI protestar, reconvenir; **to ~ with sb about sth** discutir con algn por algo
Ⓑ VT protestar

expostulation [ɪksˌpɒstjʊ'leɪʃən] N protesta *f*

exposure [ɪks'pəʊʒəʳ] Ⓐ N 1 (= *contact, laying open*) (*to weather, heat, cold, light*) exposición *f*; **this strategy reduces your ~ to risk** (*Fin*) esta estrategia reduce el riesgo al que está expuesto; **to die of ~** morir de frío, morir por estar a la intemperie
2 (= *disclosure*) [*of plot*] denuncia *f*; [*of imposter, criminal*] desenmascaramiento *m*; **to threaten sb with ~** amenazar con desenmascarar *or* descubrir a algn
3 (= *public exposure*) publicidad *f*; **he's getting a lot of ~** está recibiendo mucha publicidad; *see also* **indecent**
4 (= *outlook*) orientación *f*; **a house with a southerly ~** una casa orientada hacia el sur
5 (*Phot*) (*gen*) exposición; (= *aperture*) abertura *f* de diafragma; (= *speed*) velocidad *f* de obturación; (= *photo*) foto *f*, fotografía *f*
Ⓑ CPD ► **exposure meter** N (*Phot*) fotómetro *m*, exposímetro *m*

expound [ɪks'paʊnd] Ⓐ VT [+ *theory, one's views*] exponer, explicar
Ⓑ VI **to ~ on sth** exponer algo en profundidad

ex-president [ˌeks'prezɪdənt] N ex presidente/a *m/f*

express [ɪks'pres] Ⓐ VT 1 (*verbally, nonverbally*) expresar; **her eyes ~ed annoyance** sus ojos expresaban irritación; **they ~ed interest in …** expresaron su interés en …; **he ~ed his surprise at the result** expresó su sorpresa ante el resultado; **I'd like to ~ my thanks to everyone for …** quiero expresar

► LANGUAGE IN USE: explain 26.3

mi agradecimiento a todos por …; **she had ~ed a wish to meet them** había manifestado su deseo de conocerlos; **to ~ o.s.** expresarse; **to ~ o.s. in** *or* **through** [+ *art, music etc*] expresarse a través de
[2] (= *send*) [+ *letter, parcel*] enviar por correo urgente *or* exprés
[3] (*Math*) (= *represent*) expresar; **here it is ~ed as a percentage** aquí está expresado en forma de porcentaje
[4] (*frm*) (= *squeeze out*) [+ *juice*] exprimir (**from** de); [+ *milk*] sacarse
Ⓑ ADJ [1] (*frm*) (= *specific*) [*purpose, intention*] expreso; **to give sb ~ instructions to do sth** dar instrucciones expresas a algn para que se haga algo; **~ warranty** garantía *f* escrita
[2] (= *fast*) [*letter, delivery, mail*] urgente, exprés; [*laundry, photography service*] rápido; **to send sth by ~ delivery** *or* **mail** enviar algo por correo urgente *or* exprés, enviar algo exprés
Ⓒ ADV **to send** *or* **post sth ~** enviar algo por correo urgente *or* exprés; **to travel ~** viajar en un tren rápido *or* expreso
Ⓓ N (= *train*) expreso *m*, rápido *m*
Ⓔ CPD ► **express train** N expreso *m*, rápido *m*

expression [ɪks'preʃən] N (*gen, facial*) expresión *f*; (= *feeling*) expresión *f*; (= *token*) señal *f*; (*Ling*) frase *f*, expresión *f*; **she had a puzzled ~ on her face** había una expresión de perplejidad en su rostro; **as an ~ of gratitude** en señal de agradecimiento *or* gratitud; **if you'll pardon the ~** con perdón de la expresión

expressionism [eks'preʃənɪzəm] N expresionismo *m*

expressionist [eks'preʃənɪst] Ⓐ ADJ expresionista
Ⓑ N expresionista *mf*

expressionless [ɪks'preʃənlɪs] ADJ sin expresión, inexpresivo

expressive [ɪks'presɪv] ADJ [*person, face, language*] expresivo; [*ability*] de expresión; **to be ~ of sth** (*frm*) expresar algo; **his gesture was ~ of anger** su gesto expresaba rabia

expressively [ɪks'presɪvlɪ] ADV de forma expresiva, expresivamente

expressiveness [ɪks'presɪvnɪs] N expresividad *f*

expressly [ɪks'preslɪ] ADV [1] (= *explicitly*) [*state, inform, deny, forbid*] explícitamente, claramente; [*instruct*] expresamente
[2] (= *specially*) expresamente, especialmente

expresso [ɪk'spresəʊ] N = **espresso**

expressway [ɪks'preswei] N (*US*) autopista *f*

expropriate [eks'prəʊprɪeɪt] VT expropiar

expropriation [eks,prəʊprɪ'eɪʃən] N expropiación *f*

expulsion [ɪks'pʌlʃən] Ⓐ N expulsión *f*; **in doing this she was risking ~** (*from school*) haciendo esto se arriesgaba a que la expulsaran
Ⓑ CPD ► **expulsion order** N orden *f* de expulsión

expunge [ɪks'pʌndʒ] VT suprimir

expurgate ['ekspɜːgeɪt] VT expurgar

exquisite [eks'kwɪzɪt] ADJ [1] [*craftmanship, food, manners*] exquisito; [*object, ornament*] (= *beautiful*) de una belleza exquisita; (= *tasteful*) de un gusto exquisito; **a woman of ~ beauty** una mujer de una belleza exquisita; **he has ~ taste** tiene un gusto exquisito; **in ~ detail** con una atención exquisita a los detalles
[2] (= *keen*) [*pleasure, irony*] exquisito; [*joy, pain*] muy intenso

exquisitely [eks'kwɪzɪtlɪ] ADV [1] (= *tastefully*) [*embroidered, decorated, dressed*] con un gusto exquisito; (= *skilfully*) [*made, carved*] de forma exquisita; **an ~ carved figure of an angel** una figura de un ángel tallada de forma exquisita; **her dress was ~ detailed** su vestido tenía unos detalles exquisitos
[2] (*as intensifier*) **~ beautiful/delicate** de una belleza/delicadeza exquisita; **~ painful** sumamente doloroso

ex-service [,eks'sɜːvɪs] ADJ (*Brit Mil*) retirado del servicio activo

ex-serviceman ['eks'sɜːvɪsmən] N (*pl* **ex-servicemen**) militar *m* retirado, ex militar *m*

ex-servicewoman [,eks'sɜːvɪs,wʊmən] N (*pl* **ex-servicewomen**) militar *f* retirada, ex militar *f*

ex-smoker ['eks'sməʊkəʳ] N (*US*) persona *f* que ha dejado de fumar

ext ABBR [1] (*Telec*) (= **extension**) Ext
[2] (= **exterior**) Ext

extant [eks'tænt] ADJ existente

extemporaneous [ɪks,tempə'reɪnɪəs], **extemporary** [ɪks'tempərərɪ] ADJ improvisado

extempore [eks'tempərɪ] Ⓐ ADV de improviso
Ⓑ ADJ improvisado

extemporize [ɪks'tempəraɪz] VI improvisar

extend [ɪks'tend] Ⓐ VT [1] (= *stretch out*) [+ *hand, arm*] extender; (*to sb*) tender, alargar
[2] (= *offer*) [+ *one's friendship, help, hospitality*] ofrecer; [+ *one's thanks, congratulations, condolences, welcome*] dar; [+ *invitation*] enviar; [+ *credit*] extender, otorgar
[3] (= *prolong*) [+ *road, line, visit*] prolongar
[4] (= *enlarge*) [+ *building*] ampliar; [+ *knowledge, research*] ampliar, profundizar en; [+ *powers, business*] ampliar, aumentar; [+ *frontiers*] extender; [+ *vocabulary*] enriquecer, aumentar
[5] (= *push to the limit*) [+ *athlete*] pedir el máximo esfuerzo a; **that child is not sufficiently ~ed** a ese niño no se le exige el rendimiento que es capaz de dar; **the staff is fully ~ed** el personal trabaja a pleno rendimiento; **to ~ o.s.** trabajar al máximum, esforzarse
Ⓑ VI [1] [*land, wall*] **to ~ to** *or* **as far as** extenderse a *or* hasta, llegar hasta; **the farm ~s over 40,000 hectares** la finca abarca unas 40.000 hectáreas
[2] (*fig*) **to ~ to** abarcar, incluir; **does that ~ to me?** ¿eso me incluye a mí?
[3] [*meeting*] **to ~ to** *or* **into** prolongarse hasta; **to ~ for** prolongarse por espacio de, prolongarse durante

extendable [ɪk'stendɪbl] ADJ extensible

extended [ɪk'stendɪd] Ⓐ ADJ (= *stretched out*) extendido; (= *prolonged*) [*stay*] prolongado; **to grant sb ~ credit** conceder a algn un crédito ilimitado; **he has been granted ~ leave** se le ha concedido una prórroga del permiso
Ⓑ CPD ► **extended family** N familia *f* extendida ► **extended forecast** N (*US*) pronóstico *m* a largo plazo ► **extended memory** N (*Comput*) memoria *f* extendida ► **extended play** N EP *m*, maxi-single *m*

extended-play [ɪk,stendɪd'pleɪ] ADJ [*record*] EP *inv*, de duración ampliada; **~ single** maxi-single *m*

extensible [ɪks'tensɪbl] ADJ extensible

extension [ɪks'tenʃən] Ⓐ N (= *act, part added*) extensión *f*; [*of powers*] ampliación *f*; [*of building*] ampliación *f*; [*of road, stay, visit*] prolongación *f*; [*of term, contract, credit*] prórroga *f*; (*Telec*) extensión, interno *m* (*S. Cone*), anexo *m* (*S. Cone*); **~ three one three seven, please** con la extensión tres uno tres siete, por favor; **by ~** por extensión
Ⓑ CPD ► **extension cable** N = **extension lead** ► **extension courses** NPL *cursos externos organizados por una universidad* ► **extension ladder** N escalera *f* extensible ► **extension lead** N (*Elec*) alargador *m*, alargadera *f*

extensive [ɪks'tensɪv] ADJ [1] (= *covering large area*) [*grounds, estate, area*] extenso; [*network, tour*] extenso, amplio; [*surgery*] de envergadura; [*burns*] de consideración
[2] (= *comprehensive*) [*collection, list*] extenso; [*range, reforms, interests*] amplio; [*enquiry, tests, research*] exhaustivo; [*knowledge*] vasto, amplio; **it got ~ coverage in the British papers** obtuvo una amplia cobertura en la prensa británica
[3] (= *considerable*) [*damage, investments*] considerable, importante; [*experience*] amplio, vasto; [*repairs*] de consideración; [*powers*] amplio; **many buildings suffered ~ damage in the blast** la explosión causó daños considerables *or* importantes en muchos edificios; **to make ~ use of sth** usar *or* utilizar algo mucho; **the machine developed a fault after ~ use** la máquina falló después de usarse mucho

extensively [ɪks'tensɪvlɪ] ADV [1] (= *on a large scale*) [*work, travel*] mucho; [*write, speak*] ampliamente, mucho; [*damage*] considerablemente; [*restore, modify*] considerablemente, en gran parte; **he travelled ~ in Mexico** viajó mucho por México; **the story was covered ~ in the papers** la historia tuvo una amplia cobertura en la prensa; **these grapes are grown ~ in Bordeaux** estas uvas se cultivan extensamente en Burdeos
[2] (= *in detail*) [*discuss, write*] mucho; [*study, research, revise*] exhaustivamente, a fondo; **I have quoted ~ from the article** he utilizado muchas citas del artículo

extent [ɪks'tent] N [1] (*in space*) [*of land, road*] extensión *f*
[2] (= *scope*) [*of knowledge, damage, activities*] alcance *m*; [*of power*] límite *m*; **the ~ of the problem** el alcance *or* la envergadura del problema; **we did not know the ~ of his injuries until later** no tuvimos conocimiento del alcance de sus lesiones hasta más tarde
[3] (= *degree*) [*of commitment, loss*] grado *m*; **to what ~?** ¿hasta qué punto?; **to a certain** *or* **to some ~** hasta cierto punto; **to a large ~** en gran parte *or* medida; **to a small ~** en menor grado; **to such an ~ that** hasta tal punto que; **to the ~ of** (= *as far as*) hasta el punto de; (*in money*) por la cantidad de; **to that ~, she is right** en ese sentido, ella tiene razón

extenuate [eks'tenjʊeɪt] VT atenuar, mitigar, disminuir (la gravedad de)

extenuating [eks'tenjʊeɪtɪŋ] ADJ **~ circumstances** circunstancias *fpl* atenuantes

exterior [eks'tɪərɪəʳ] Ⓐ ADJ [*wall, door, surface*] exterior
Ⓑ N exterior *m*; (= *outward appearance*) apariencia *f*, aspecto *m* exterior; **on the ~** (*lit, fig*) por fuera

exteriorize [eks'tɪərɪəraɪz] VT exteriorizar

exterminate [eks'tɜːmɪneɪt] VT exterminar

extermination [eks,tɜːmɪ'neɪʃən] N [*of people*] exterminio *m*; [*of pests*] exterminación *f*

exterminator [eks'tɜːmɪneɪtəʳ] N (*US*) exterminador *m* de plagas

extern ['ekstɜːn] N (*US Med*) externo/a *m/f*

external [eks'tɜːnl] Ⓐ ADJ [1] (= *outer*) [*wall, surface*] externo, exterior; [*appearance, injury, gills, skeleton*] externo; **"for external use only"** (*Med*) "de uso tópico *or* externo"
[2] (= *outside*) [*world, influences, factor*] externo

➤ LANGUAGE IN USE: **extend A2** 24.5

[3] (= *foreign*) [*affairs, relations*] exterior
Ⓑ N **externals** las apariencias *fpl*; **to judge by ~s** juzgar por las apariencias
Ⓒ CPD ► **external account** N cuenta *f* con el exterior ► **external audit** N auditoría *f* externa ► **external debt** N deuda *f* externa, deuda *f* exterior ► **external degree** N (*Brit Univ*) licenciatura *f* por libre ► **external examination** N examen *m* externo ► **external examiner** N examinador(a) *m/f* externo/a ► **external student** N (*Brit Univ*) alumno/a *m/f* externo/a, alumno/a *m/f* libre ► **external trade** N comercio *m* exterior

externalize [ɪks'tɜːnəlaɪz] VT [+ *ideas, feelings*] exteriorizar

externally [eks'tɜːnəlɪ] ADV [1] (= *on the outside, outwardly*) por fuera, exteriormente; **~, it looks like a car** por fuera *or* exteriormente parece un coche; **~, he seemed calm** por fuera *or* exteriormente parecía tranquilo
[2] (*Med*) [*apply, use*] tópicamente, externamente; **"to be used externally"** "de uso tópico *or* externo"; **to examine a patient ~** hacer un reconocimiento externo de un paciente
[3] (*by outsiders*) **the proofreading is done ~** la corrección de pruebas se hace con personal de fuera; **~ imposed conditions** condiciones impuestas desde el exterior

extinct [ɪks'tɪŋkt] ADJ [*volcano*] extinto, apagado; [*animal, race*] extinto, desaparecido; **to become ~** extinguirse, desaparecer; **dinosaurs are ~** los dinosaurios se extinguieron

extinction [ɪks'tɪŋkʃən] N extinción *f*

extinguish [ɪks'tɪŋgwɪʃ] VT [+ *fire*] extinguir, apagar; [+ *light, cigarette*] apagar; (*fig*) [+ *hope, faith*] destruir; (= *suppress*) [+ *title*] suprimir

extinguisher [ɪks'tɪŋgwɪʃəʳ] N [1] (*for fire*) extintor *m*, extinguidor *m* (*LAm*)
[2] (*for candle*) apagador *m*, apagavelas *m inv*

extirpate ['ekstɜːpeɪt] VT extirpar

extirpation [ˌekstə'peɪʃən] N extirpación *f*

extn ABBR (*Telec*) (= **extension**) Ext.

extol, **extoll** (*US*) [ɪks'təʊl] VT [+ *merits, virtues*] ensalzar, alabar; [+ *person*] alabar, elogiar

extort [ɪks'tɔːt] VT [+ *promise, confession*] obtener por la fuerza, arrancar; **to ~ money from sb** extorsionar a algn; (*less frm*) arrancar dinero a algn con amenazas

extortion [ɪks'tɔːʃən] N extorsión *f*, exacción *f*; (*by public figure*) concusión *f*

extortionate [ɪks'tɔːʃənɪt] ADJ [*price*] abusivo, exorbitante; [*demand*] excesivo, desmesurado

extortioner [ɪks'tɔːʃənəʳ], **extortionist** [ɪks'tɔːʃənɪst] N extorsionador(a) *m/f*; (= *official*) concusionario *m*

extra ['ekstrə] Ⓐ ADJ [1] (= *reserve*) de más, de sobra; **take an ~ pair of shoes** lleva un par de zapatos de más *or* de sobra; **take some ~ money just to be on the safe side** coge dinero de más *or* de sobra para más seguridad
[2] (= *additional*) más *inv*, adicional (*more frm*); **he gave me an ~ blanket** me dio una manta más; **we need two ~ chairs** necesitamos dos sillas más; **they laid on some ~ trains** pusieron algunos trenes adicionales *or* más; **I've set an ~ place at the table** he puesto otro cubierto en la mesa, he puesto un cubierto más en la mesa; **to earn an ~ £20 a week** ganar 20 libras más a la semana; **to go to ~ expense** gastar de más; **to work ~ hours** trabajar horas extra; **the ~ money will come in handy** el dinero extra vendrá bien; **~ pay** sobresueldo *m*; **five tons ~ to requirements** un excedente de cinco toneladas
[3] (= *special, added*) excepcional; **you must make an ~ effort** tienes que hacer un esfuerzo excepcional *or* extra; **for ~ whiteness** para una mayor blancura, para conseguir una blancura excepcional; **for ~ safety** para mayor seguridad; **take ~ care!** ¡ten muchísimo cuidado!
[4] (= *over, spare*) de más, de sobra; **an ~ chromosome** un cromosoma de más *or* de sobra; **these copies are ~** estas copias sobran
[5] (= *not included in price*) **wine is ~** el vino es aparte *or* no está incluido; **postage and packing ~** los gastos de envío son aparte, gastos de envío no incluidos; **~ charge** recargo *m*, suplemento *m*; **they delivered it at no ~ charge** lo enviaron sin recargo
Ⓑ ADV [1] (= *more*) más; **it is better to pay a little ~ for better quality** es mejor pagar un poco más y ganar en calidad; **you have to pay ~ for a single room** hay que pagar más por una habitación individual, hay un recargo por habitación individual; **wine costs ~** el vino es aparte *or* no está incluido; **send 95p ~ for postage and packing** manda 95 peniques de más para los gastos de envío
[2] (= *especially*) extraordinariamente, super*; **to sing ~ loud** cantar extraordinariamente fuerte, cantar super fuerte*; **he did ~ well in the written exam** el examen escrito le salió extraordinariamente bien, el examen escrito le salió super bien*; **he was ~ polite/nice to her** fue super educado/amable con ella*, fue re(te) educado/amable con ella (*esp LAm**); **to be ~ careful** tener un cuidado excepcional; **~ fine** [*nib*] extrafino; **to work ~ hard** trabajar super duro*; **~ large** [*size*] muy grande; **~ special** muy especial, super especial*; **to take ~ special care over sth** tomar extremadas precauciones en algo; **~ strong** [*bag, glue, mint*] extra fuerte; [*coffee*] super cargado; [*nylon*] reforzado
Ⓒ N [1] (= *luxury, addition*) extra *m*; **(optional) ~s** (*Aut*) extras *mpl*
[2] (= *charge*) extra *m*; **there are no hidden ~s** no hay extras escondidos
[3] (*Cine*) extra *mf*
[4] (*Press*) número *m* extraordinario; **"~, ~! read all about it!"** "¡extra, extra! ¡últimas noticias!"
[5] (*US*) (= *gasoline*) súper *f*
[6] (*US*) (= *spare part*) repuesto *m*
Ⓓ CPD ► **extra time** N (*Ftbl*) prórroga *f*

extra... ['ekstrə] PREFIX extra…

extract ['ekstrækt] Ⓐ N (*from book, film*) extracto *m*, fragmento *m*; (*Pharm*) extracto *m*; (*Culin*) [*of beef, yeast*] extracto *m*, concentrado *m*; **~s from "Don Quijote"** (*as book*) selecciones *fpl* del "Quijote"
Ⓑ [ɪks'trækt] VT [1] (= *take out*) [+ *cork, tooth*] sacar; [+ *bullet*] (*from wound*) extraer; [+ *mineral*] extraer, obtener; [+ *juice*] exprimir
[2] (= *obtain*) [+ *information, money*] obtener, sacar; [+ *confession*] sacar, arrancar
[3] (= *select*) (*from book etc*) seleccionar
[4] (*Math*) extraer

extraction [ɪks'trækʃən] N (*gen*) extracción *f*; **of Spanish ~** de extracción española

extractor [ɪks'træktəʳ] Ⓐ N extractor *m*
Ⓑ CPD ► **extractor fan** N (*Brit*) extractor *m* de humos

extracurricular [ˌekstrəkə'rɪkjʊləʳ] ADJ (*Scol*) [*activities*] extraescolar

extraditable ['ekstrədaɪtəbl] ADJ sujeto a extradición

extradite ['ekstrədaɪt] VT extraditar; **to ~ sb (from/to)** extraditar a algn (de/a)

extradition [ˌekstrə'dɪʃən] Ⓐ N extradición *f*
Ⓑ CPD ► **extradition agreement** N acuerdo *m* de extradición ► **extradition warrant** N orden *f* de extradición

extramarital [ˌekstrə'mærɪtəl] ADJ [*affair, sex*] extramarital, fuera del matrimonio

extramural ['ekstrə'mjʊərəl] ADJ [*course*] externo, de extensión; (*Univ*) [*activities*] extracurricular; **Department of Extramural Studies** (*Brit Univ*) Departamento *m* de Cursos de Extensión

extraneous [eks'treɪnɪəs] ADJ [*influence*] extraño, externo; [*issue*] irrelevante, superfluo; **~ to** ajeno a

extraordinaire [eksˌtrɔːdɪ'neəʳ] ADJ (*after n*) sin igual; **he's a film-maker ~** es un cineasta como no hay otro igual

extraordinarily [ɪks'trɔːdnrɪlɪ] ADV [1] (= *exceptionally*) [*difficult, beautiful, kind*] extraordinariamente
[2] (= *strangely*) **~, nobody was killed in the explosion** lo increíble es que nadie muriese en la explosión

extraordinary [ɪks'trɔːdnrɪ] ADJ [1] (= *exceptional*) [*courage, career, skill, person*] extraordinario; **there's nothing ~ about that** eso no tiene nada de extraordinario *or* increíble
[2] (= *strange*) [*tale, adventure, action*] increíble, insólito; **it's an ~ building** es un edificio increíble; **I find it ~ that he hasn't replied** me parece increíble que no haya contestado; **how ~!** (= *strange*) ¡qué raro!, ¡qué extraño!; (= *incredible*) ¡es increíble!
[3] (*frm*) (= *additional, special*) [*meeting, measure, powers*] extraordinario; **~ general meeting** junta *f* general extraordinaria; **~ meeting of shareholders** junta *f* extraordinaria de accionistas; **~ reserve** (*Fin*) reserva *f* extraordinaria

extrapolate [ɪks'træpəleɪt] Ⓐ VT extrapolar; **to ~ sth from sth** extrapolar algo a partir de algo
Ⓑ VI hacer una extrapolación; **to ~ (from sth)** hacer una extrapolación (a partir de algo)

extrapolation [ɪksˌtræpə'leɪʃən] N extrapolación *f*

extrasensory ['ekstrə'sensərɪ] Ⓐ ADJ extrasensorial
Ⓑ CPD ► **extrasensory perception** N percepción *f* extrasensorial

extraterrestrial [ˌekstrətə'restrɪəl] ADJ extraterrestre

extraterritorial ['ekstrəˌterɪ'tɔːrɪəl] ADJ extraterritorial

extravagance [ɪks'trævəgəns] N [1] (= *wastefulness*) derroche *m*, despilfarro *m*
[2] (= *indulgence*) extravagancia *f*; **buying a yacht is just an ~** comprar un yate es una extravagancia; **I know it's an ~, but I love lobster** ya sé que es una extravagancia, pero me encanta la langosta; **caviare! I'm not used to such ~** ¡caviar! no estoy acostumbrada a estos lujos
[3] (*fig*) [*of praise*] lo excesivo; [*of claim, opinion*] lo extraordinario; [*of behaviour, gesture*] lo extravagante

extravagant [ɪks'trævəgənt] ADJ [1] (= *wasteful, lavish*) [*person*] derrochador, despilfarrador; [*taste*] caro; [*lifestyle*] de muchos lujos; [*gift*] caro; [*price*] exorbitante, desorbitado; **I'd love to go but isn't it a bit ~?** me encantaría ir pero ¿no te parece un poco caro?, me encantaría ir pero ¿no te parece una extravagancia?; **it was very ~ of him to buy this ring** se ha pasado comprando este anillo; **to be ~ with electricity/one's money** derrochar electricidad/el dinero
[2] (= *exaggerated*) [*praise*] excesivo; [*claim,*

opinion] extraordinario; [*behaviour, person, design*] extravagante; [*gesture*] exagerado; **to be ~ in one's praise of sth/sb** excederse elogiando a algo/algn
[3] (= *odd*) raro, extravagante; **you have the most ~ ideas** se te ocurren unas ideas de lo más extravagantes *or* raras

extravagantly [ɪks'trævəgəntlɪ] ADV [1] (= *wastefully, lavishly*) [*spend*] profusamente, con gran despilfarro; [*live, decorate*] por todo lo alto, con todo lujo; **to use sth ~** derrochar algo; **the room was ~ furnished** la habitación estaba amueblada por todo lo alto *or* con mucho lujo
[2] (= *exaggeratedly*) [*praise, thank*] excesivamente, exageradamente; [*dress, behave*] de forma extravagante

extravaganza [eks,trævə'gænzə] N (= *show*) gran espectáculo *m*; (= *film*) película *f* espectacular; (= *building*) espectáculo *m* arquitectónico

extravehicular [,ekstrəvɪ'hɪkjʊləʳ] ADJ fuera de la nave

extreme [ɪks'tri:m] Ⓐ ADJ [1] (= *very great*) [*heat, danger, poverty, discomfort*] extremo; [*care, caution*] sumo, extremo; [*sorrow, anger*] profundo, enorme; **a matter of ~ importance** una cuestión de suma importancia; **in ~ old age** en *or* a una edad muy avanzada
[2] (= *exceptional*) [*case, circumstances*] extremo
[3] (= *radical*) [*views, opinion*] extremista; [*behaviour*] extremado; [*method, action, measure*] extremo; **the ~ left/right** (*Pol*) la extrema izquierda/derecha; **to be ~ in one's opinions** tener opiniones extremistas; **there's no need to be so ~** no es necesario llegar a esos extremos
[4] (= *furthest*) [*point,*] extremo; **the ~ opposite** el extremo opuesto; **winds from the ~ north** vientos de la región más septentrional; **the room at the ~ end of the corridor** la habitación al final del todo del pasillo
Ⓑ N extremo *m*; **she's a woman of ~s** es una mujer de extremos; **to be driven to ~s** verse obligado a tomar medidas extremas; **to go to ~s** tomar medidas extremas; **to go to any ~** llegar a cualquier extremo; **to go from one ~ to the other** pasar de un extremo al otro; **to take** *or* **carry sth to ~s** llevar algo al extremo; **~s of temperature** las temperaturas extremas; **in the ~** (*frm*) en extremo, en sumo grado
Ⓒ CPD ► **extreme sports** NPL deportes *mpl* de aventura, deportes *mpl* extremos
► **extreme unction** N (*Rel*) extremaunción *f*

extremely [ɪks'tri:mlɪ] ADV sumamente, extremadamente; **it is ~ difficult** es dificilísimo, es sumamente difícil, es extremadamente difícil; **he did ~ well in the exam** el examen le salió sumamente bien; **we are ~ glad** nos alegramos muchísimo; **it's ~ unlikely that you'll win** es muy poco probable que ganes

extremism [ɪks'tri:mɪzəm] N extremismo *m*

extremist [ɪks'tri:mɪst] Ⓐ ADJ extremista
Ⓑ N extremista *mf*

extremity [ɪks'tremɪtɪ] N [1] (= *end*) (*usu pl*) extremo *m*, punta *f*
[2] (*fig*) [*of despair etc*] extremo *m*; **in his ~, he went to her for help** ante la necesidad, acudió a ella en busca de ayuda
[3] **extremities** (*Anat*) extremidades *fpl*

extricate ['ekstrɪkeɪt] VT (= *disentangle*) desenredar; (= *free*) [+ *victim*] rescatar, sacar; **to ~ o.s. from** [+ *difficulty, situation*] lograr salir de; **he ~d himself from her grip** logró soltarse de la mano de ella

extrication [,ekstrɪ'keɪʃən] N (*frm*) (*lit*) [*of trapped person, object*] extracción *f*; (*fig*) (*from situation*) salida *f*

extrinsic [eks'trɪnsɪk] ADJ extrínseco

extrovert ['ekstrəʊvɜ:rt] Ⓐ ADJ extrovertido
Ⓑ N extrovertido/a *m/f*

extroverted ['ekstrəvɜ:tɪd] ADJ (*esp US*) = **extrovert A**

extrude [eks'tru:d] VT extrudir

extrusion [eks'tru:ʒən] N extrusión *f*

exuberance [ɪg'zu:bərəns] N [1] [*of person*] (= *euphoria*) euforia *f*; (= *enthusiasm*) entusiasmo *m*; **youthful ~** el entusiasmo (excesivo) de la juventud
[2] [*of style, painting*] exuberancia *f*; [*of film, music*] vitalidad *f*
[3] (*Bot*) (= *vigour*) [*of growth, foliage*] exuberancia *f*

exuberant [ɪg'zu:bərənt] ADJ [1] [*person*] (= *euphoric*) eufórico; (= *enthusiastic*) entusiasta; **he felt ~** estaba eufórico
[2] [*style, colour, painting*] exuberante; [*film, music, show*] lleno de vitalidad
[3] (*Bot*) (= *vigorous*) [*growth, foliage*] exuberante

exuberantly [ɪg'zu:bərəntlɪ] ADV [1] (= *euphorically*) [*laugh, shout*] eufóricamente
[2] (*Bot*) (= *vigorously*) [*grow*] de forma exuberante

exude [ɪg'zju:d] Ⓐ VT [1] [+ *liquid*] rezumar, exudar; [+ *odour*] desprender
[2] (*fig*) [+ *optimism, confidence, enthusiasm*] rebosar; [+ *sympathy, hostility*] rezumar
Ⓑ VI rezumar, exudar

exult [ɪg'zʌlt] VI **to ~ in** *or* **at** *or* **over** regocijarse por

exultant [ɪg'zʌltənt] ADJ [*person, shout, expression*] exultante, jubiloso

exultantly [ɪg'zʌltəntlɪ] ADV jubilosamente

exultation [,egzʌl'teɪʃən] N exultación *f*, júbilo *m*

ex-wife [,eks'waɪf] N (*pl* **ex-wives**) ex mujer *f*

ex-works [,eks'wɜ:ks] ADJ (*Brit*) [*price*] franco fábrica, de fábrica, en fábrica

eye [aɪ] Ⓐ N [1] (*gen*) ojo *m*; **to have good ~s** tener buena vista; **to rub one's ~s** restregarse los ojos; **I couldn't believe my (own) ~s** no daba crédito a lo que veían mis ojos; **black ~** ojo *m* morado *or* amoratado; **I gave him a black ~** le puse un ojo morado; **she had a black ~** tenía *or* llevaba un ojo morado; **to catch sb's ~** llamar la atención de algn; **he accidentally caught her ~ and looked away** su mirada se cruzó por casualidad con la de ella y apartó la vista; **it was the biggest one I'd ever clapped ~s on** era el más grande que jamás me había echado a la cara; **to cry one's ~s out** llorar a moco tendido *or* a lágrima viva; **there wasn't a dry ~ in the house** no había ojos sin lágrimas en todo el teatro; **to have an ~** *or* **a keen ~ for a bargain** tener mucha vista *or* buen ojo para las gangas; **we need someone with an ~ for detail** nos hace falta alguien que sea meticuloso; **he's got his ~ on you** (= *monitoring*) no te quita ojo, no te pierde de vista; (= *attracted to*) te tiene echado el ojo; **I've got my ~ on that sofa in the sale** le tengo echado el ojo a ese sofá que vimos en las rebajas; **she had ~s only for me** sólo tenía ojos para mí, no tenía ojos más que para mí; **it hits you in the ~** salta a la vista; **in the ~s of** a los ojos de; **in the ~s of the law** a los ojos de la ley; **to keep an ~ on sth/sb** (= *watch*) vigilar algo/a algn, echar una mirada a algo/algn; (= *look after*) cuidar algo/a algn; **keep your ~s on the road!** ¡no quites los ojos de la carretera!; **I'm keeping an ~ on things while the boss is away** yo estoy al cargo del negocio mientras el jefe está fuera; **at ~ level** a la altura de los ojos; **to look sb (straight) in the ~** mirar a algn (directamente) a los ojos; **with the naked ~** a simple vista; **he couldn't keep his ~s off the girl** se le fueron los ojos tras la chica; **to keep an ~ out** *or* **one's ~s open for sth/sb** estar pendiente de algo/algn; **keep an ~ out for the postman** estáte atento *or* pendiente a ver si ves al cartero; **keep an ~ out for snakes** cuidado por si hay culebras; **keep your ~s open for bag-snatchers!** ¡mucho ojo, no te vayan a dar el tirón!; **I haven't seen any recently but I'll keep my ~s open** últimamente no he visto ninguno pero estaré al tanto; **I could hardly keep my ~s open** se me cerraban los ojos; **I saw it with my own ~s** lo vi con mis propios ojos; **to be in the public ~** estar a la luz pública; **~s right/left/front!** ¡vista a la derecha/izquierda/al frente!; **to run one's ~ over sth** (*from curiosity*) recorrer algo con la vista; (*checking*) echar un vistazo a algo; **as far as the ~ can see** hasta donde alcanza la vista; **it's five years since I last set** *or* **laid ~s on him** hace cinco años que no lo veo; **the sun is in my ~s** me da el sol en los ojos; **he didn't take his ~s off her for one second** no le quitó los ojos de encima ni por un segundo; **with an ~ to sth/to doing sth** con vistas *or* miras a algo/a hacer algo; **with an ~ to the future** cara al futuro; **use your ~s!*** ¡abre los ojos!; **it happened before my very ~s** ocurrió delante de mis propios ojos; **the grass grows before your very ~s** crece la hierba a ojos vistas; **under the watchful ~ of** bajo la atenta mirada de; **to look at sth with** *or* **through the ~s of an expert** ver algo con ojos de experto; ✦***IDIOMS*** **he was all ~s** era todo *or* (*LAm*) puros ojos; **to have ~s in the back of one's head** tener ojos en la nuca; **he must have ~s in the back of his head!** ¡no se le escapa una!; **I haven't got ~s in the back of my head** (*iro*) ¿te crees que tengo ojos en la nuca o qué?; **to give sb the (glad) ~*** tirar los tejos a algn con miraditas*; **there's more to this than meets the ~** esto tiene más enjundia de lo que parece, esto tiene su miga; **the decision was one in the ~ for the president*** la decisión supuso un auténtico varapalo para el presidente; **to open sb's ~s to sth** abrir los ojos de algn a algo; **to keep one's ~s peeled** estar alerta; **to do sth with one's ~s (wide) open** hacer algo con los ojos abiertos; **to make (sheep's) ~s at sb*** lanzar miraditas insinuantes a algn, hacer ojitos a algn*; **to shut one's ~s to** [+ *truth, evidence, dangers*] cerrar los ojos a; [+ *sb's shortcomings*] hacer la vista gorda a; **I don't see ~ to ~ with him** no estoy de acuerdo con él; **in the twinkling of an ~** en un abrir y cerrar de ojos; **to be up to one's ~s** (*in work etc*) estar hasta aquí *or* agobiado de trabajo; ✦***PROV*** **an ~ for an ~ (and a tooth for a tooth)** ojo por ojo (y diente por diente); *see also* **blind A, feast B, mind A1, sight**
[2] [*of potato*] yema *f*
[3] [*of storm*] ojo *m*
[4] (*Sew*) [*of needle*] ojo *m*; [*of hook and eye*] hembra *f* de corchete
Ⓑ VT mirar detenidamente, observar; **she ~d him sullenly/with suspicion** lo miró detenidamente con gesto hosco/con recelo; **she ~d the package curiously** observó (detenidamente) el paquete con curiosidad; **I didn't like the way they ~d me up and down** no me gustaba la forma que tenían de mirarme de

arriba abajo; **an expensive leather jacket I had ~d for some time** una cazadora de cuero muy cara a la que hacía tiempo (que) le había echado el ojo

Ⓒ CPD ► **eye contact** N contacto *m* ocular ► **eye doctor** N (*US*) oculista *mf* ► **eye dropper** N cuentagotas *m inv* ► **eye drops** NPL gotas *fpl* para los ojos ► **eye patch** N parche *m* ► **eye pencil** N lápiz *m* de ojos ► **eye shadow** N sombra *f* de ojos ► **eye socket** N cuenca *f* del ojo ► **eye test** N test *m* visual *or* de visión

►**eye up** VT + ADV **he ~d up his fellow passengers** estudió detenidamente *or* pasó revista a sus compañeros de viaje; **he was ~ing the girl up** se comía a la joven con los ojos; *see also* **talent A3**

eyeball [ˈaɪbɔːl] Ⓐ N globo *m* ocular; **to be ~ to ~** (= *in confrontation*) enfrentarse cara a cara; ✦*IDIOM* **to be up to one's ~s in debt** estar hasta arriba de deudas; **to be drugged up to the ~s: they've got him drugged up to the ~s*** lo tienen medicado a tope

Ⓑ VT (*US*) clavar la mirada en

eyebath [ˈaɪbɑːθ] N [1] (= *small bowl*) lavaojos *m inv*

[2] (= *action*) baño *m* ocular *or* de ojos

eyebrow [ˈaɪbraʊ] Ⓐ N ceja *f*; **to raise one's ~s** arquear las cejas; **he looked at her with raised ~s** la miró asombrado *or* sorprendido; **he never raised an ~ at it** no se sorprendió en lo más mínimo, ni se inmutó; **there were a lot of raised ~s when she was appointed** mucha gente se sorprendió cuando la nombraron a ella

Ⓑ CPD ► **eyebrow pencil** N lápiz *m* de cejas ► **eyebrow tweezers** NPL pinzas *fpl* para las cejas

eye-catcher [ˈaɪˌkætʃəʳ] N *cosa que llama la atención*

eye-catching [ˈaɪˌkætʃɪŋ] ADJ llamativo, vistoso

eyecup [ˈaɪˌkʌp] N = **eyebath 1**

-eyed [aɪd] ADJ (*ending in compounds*) de ojos; **green-eyed** de ojos verdes; **one-eyed** tuerto

eyeful [ˈaɪfʊl] N **he got an ~ of mud** el lodo le dio de lleno en el ojo; **get an ~ of this!*** ¡echa un vistazo a esto!, ¡mira esto!; **she's quite an ~!*** ¡está buenísima!*

eyeglass [ˈaɪglɑːs] N lente *m or f*; (*worn in the eye*) monóculo *m*; **eyeglasses** (*esp US*) gafas *fpl* (*Sp*), lentes *mpl or fpl* (*LAm*)

eyelash [ˈaɪlæʃ] N pestaña *f*; *see also* **false A4**

eyelet [ˈaɪlɪt] N ojete *m*

eyelid [ˈaɪlɪd] N párpado *m*; *see also* **bat**[3]

eyeliner [ˈaɪˌlaɪnəʳ] N lápiz *m* de ojos, delineador *m* de ojos

eye-opener* [ˈaɪˌəʊpnəʳ] N [1] revelación *f*, sorpresa *f* grande; **it was a real ~ to** *or* **for me** fue una verdadera revelación para mí

[2] (*US*) copa *f* para despertarse

eyepiece [ˈaɪpiːs] N ocular *m*

eyeshade [ˈaɪʃeɪd] N visera *f*

eyesight [ˈaɪsaɪt] N vista *f*; **to have good/poor ~** tener buena/mala vista

eyesore [ˈaɪsɔːʳ] N monstruosidad *f*

eyestrain [ˈaɪstreɪn] N vista *f* cansada, fatiga *f* visual; **inadequate lighting can cause ~** una iluminación insuficiente puede cansar la vista *or* producir fatiga visual

eyetooth [ˈaɪtuːθ] N (*pl* **eyeteeth**) colmillo *m*; ✦*IDIOM* **I'd give my eyeteeth for a car like that/to see it*** daría cualquier cosa por un coche como ese/por verlo

eyewash [ˈaɪwɒʃ] N (*Med*) colirio *m*; **it's a lot of ~!** ¡es puro cuento!

eyewitness [ˈaɪˌwɪtnɪs] N testigo *mf* presencial *or* ocular

eyrie [ˈaɪərɪ] N aguilera *f*

Ezekiel [ɪˈziːkɪəl] N Ezequiel

e-zine [ˈiːziːn] N (*Internet*) revista *f* electrónica, revista *f* digital

F f

F[1], **f**[1] [ef] N 1 (= *letter*) F, f *f*; **F for Frederick** F de Francia
2 (*Mus*) **F** fa *m*; **F major/minor** fa mayor/menor; **F sharp/flat** fa sostenido/bemol

F[2] ABBR 1 = **Fahrenheit**
2 (*Rel*) (= **Father**) P., P.ᵉ

f[2] ABBR 1 (*Math*) = **foot, feet**
2 (= **following**) sig., sgte.
3 (*Bio*) (= **female**) hembra *f*

FA N ABBR 1 (*Brit Sport*) (= **Football Association**) ≈ AFE *f*; **FA Cup** Copa *f* de la FA
2 (‡) = **Fanny Adams**

fa [fɑː] N (*Mus*) fa *m*

FAA N ABBR (*US*) = **Federal Aviation Administration**

fab* [fæb] ADJ (*Brit*) fabuloso, bárbaro*, macanudo (*S. Cone**), chévere (*Col, Ven**)

Fabian [ˈfeɪbɪən] Ⓐ ADJ fabianista
Ⓑ N fabianista *mf*
Ⓒ CPD ► **Fabian Society** N Sociedad *f* Fabiana

fable [ˈfeɪbl] N fábula *f*

fabled [ˈfeɪbld] ADJ legendario, fabuloso

fabric [ˈfæbrɪk] Ⓐ N 1 (= *cloth*) tela *f*, tejido *m*; (*gen*) (= *textiles*) tejidos *mpl*
2 (*Archit*) estructura *f*; **the upkeep of the ~** el mantenimiento (estructural) de los edificios
3 (*fig*) **the ~ of society** el tejido social, la estructura de la sociedad; **the ~ of Church and State** los fundamentos de la Iglesia y del Estado
Ⓑ CPD ► **fabric conditioner, fabric softener** N suavizante *m* ► **fabric ribbon** N (*for typewriter*) cinta *f* de tela

fabricate [ˈfæbrɪkeɪt] VT 1 (= *manufacture*) [+ *goods etc*] fabricar
2 (*fig*) inventar; [+ *document, evidence*] falsificar

fabrication [ˌfæbrɪˈkeɪʃən] N 1 (= *manufacture*) fabricación *f*
2 (*fig*) invención *f*; [*of document, evidence*] falsificación *f*; **the whole thing is a ~** todo es pura invención *or* un cuento

fabulous [ˈfæbjʊləs] ADJ 1 (*) (= *incredible*) increíble; (= *wonderful*) fabuloso, estupendo
2 (*liter*) (= *mythical*) [*beast, monster*] fabuloso, de fábula

fabulously [ˈfæbjʊləslɪ] ADV fabulosamente; **~ rich** fabulosamente rico; **it was ~ successful** tuvo un éxito fabuloso

façade [fəˈsɑːd] N (*Archit*) fachada *f*; (*fig*) apariencia *f*

face [feɪs] Ⓐ N 1 (= *part of body*) cara *f*, rostro *m*; **the wind was blowing in our ~s** el viento soplaba de cara; **the bomb blew up in his ~** la bomba estalló delante suyo; **it all blew up in his ~*** (*fig*) le salió el tiro por la culata*; **I could never look him in the ~ again** no tendría valor para mirarle a la cara de nuevo; **to say sth to sb's ~** decirle algo a la cara a algn; **I told him to his ~** se lo dije a la cara; **to bring sb face to face with sb** confrontar algn con algn; **to bring two people face to face** poner a dos personas cara a cara, confrontar a dos personas; **to come face to face with** [+ *person*] encontrarse cara a cara con; [+ *problem, danger*] enfrentarse con; **~ up** boca arriba; ✦**IDIOMS to put a brave** *or* (*US*) **good ~ on it** poner al mal tiempo buena cara; **get out of my ~!‡** ¡déjame en paz!*; **to lose ~** quedar mal, desprestigiarse; **to be off one's ~** (*Brit‡*) estar como una cuba*; **to put one's ~ on*** maquillarse, pintarse; **to save ~** salvar las apariencias, quedar bien; **to set one's ~ against sth** oponerse resueltamente a algo; **to show one's ~** dejarse ver; **shut your ~!‡** ¡cállate la boca!*, ¡calla la boca!*; *see also* **blue A1**, **egg A1**, **laugh B**, **plain A1**, **pretty A1**, **slap A**, **stuff B1**
2 (= *expression*) cara *f*, expresión *f*; **a happy ~** una cara alegre *or* de Pascua; **his ~ fell** puso cara larga; **a long ~** una cara larga; **to make** *or* **pull ~s (at sb)** hacer muecas (a algn); **to pull a (wry) ~** poner mala cara; *see also* **straight A1**
3 (= *person*) cara *f*; **there were plenty of familiar ~s at the party** había muchas caras conocidas en la fiesta; **we need some new** *or* **fresh ~s on the team** el equipo necesita sangre nueva
4 (= *surface*) superficie *f*; [*of dial, watch*] esfera *f*; [*of sundial*] cuadrante *m*; [*of mountain, cliff, coin, playing card*] cara *f*; [*of building*] fachada *f*, frente *m*; ✦**IDIOM it's vanished off the ~ of the earth** ha desaparecido de la faz de la tierra
5 (= *aspect*) **the unacceptable ~ of capitalism** los aspectos inadmisibles del capitalismo; **the changing ~ of modern politics** la cambiante fisonomía de la política actual
6 (= *effrontery*) descaro *m*, cara *f*, caradura *f*; **to have the ~ to do sth** tener el descaro de hacer algo
7 (= *typeface*) tipo *m* de imprenta
8 (*in set expressions*) **~ down(ward)** [*person, card*] boca abajo; **in the ~ of** [+ *enemy*] frente a; [+ *threats, danger*] ante; [+ *difficulty*] en vista de, ante; **on the ~ of it** a primera vista, a juzgar por las apariencias; **~ up(ward)** [*person, card*] boca arriba; ✦**IDIOM to fly in the ~ of reason** oponerse abiertamente a la razón
Ⓑ VT 1 (= *be facing*) [+ *person, object*] estar de cara a; (= *be opposite*) estar enfrente de; **~ the wall!** ¡ponte de cara a la pared!; **turn it to ~ the fire** gíralo para que esté de cara al fuego; **to sit facing the engine** estar sentado de frente a la locomotora; **they sat facing each other** se sentaron uno frente al *or* enfrente del otro; ✦**IDIOM to ~ both ways** dar una de cal y otra de arena
2 [*room, building*] 2·1 (= *overlook*) dar a, tener vista a; **my room ~s the sea** mi cuarto da al mar
2·2 (= *be opposite to*) [+ *building*] estar enfrente de; **the flat ~s the Town Hall** el piso está enfrente del Ayuntamiento
3 (= *confront*) [+ *enemy, danger, problem, situation*] enfrentarse a; [+ *consequences*] hacer frente a, afrontar; **many people are facing redundancy** muchas personas se ven enfrentadas al desempleo; **I can't ~ him** (*ashamed*) no podría mirarle a los ojos; **we are ~d with serious problems** se nos plantean graves problemas; **he ~s a fine of £200 if convicted** le espera una multa de £200 si lo declaran culpable; **he was ~d with a class who refused to cooperate** se encontraba ante una clase que se negaba a cooperar; **~d with the prospect of living on his own, he …** ante la perspectiva de vivir solo, …; **to ~ facts** aceptar los hechos *or* la realidad; **to ~ the fact that …** reconocer que …; **we will ~ him with the facts** le expondremos los hechos *or* la realidad; **let's ~ it!** ¡seamos realistas!, ¡reconozcámoslo!; ✦**IDIOM to ~ the music** afrontar las consecuencias
4 (= *bear, stand*) **I can't ~ breakfast this morning** hoy no podría desayunar nada; **I can't ~ this alone** no me veo capaz de enfrentar esto solo; **I can't ~ changing jobs again** no me veo capaz de volver a cambiar de trabajo
5 (= *clad*) revestir; **a wall ~d with concrete** una pared revestida de hormigón
6 (*Sewing*) (*on inside*) forrar; (*on outside*) recubrir; **the hood is ~d with silk** la capucha está forrada de seda
Ⓒ VI 1 [*person, animal*] (= *look*) mirar hacia; (= *turn*) volverse hacia; **~ this way!** ¡vuélvete hacia aquí!; **right ~!** (*US Mil*) ¡derecha!; **about ~!** (*US Mil*) ¡media vuelta!
2 [*building*] **which way does the house ~?** ¿en qué dirección está orientada la casa?; **it ~s east/towards the east** da al este/mira hacia el este
Ⓓ CPD ► **face card** N (*US*) figura *f* ► **face cloth** N = **face flannel** ► **face cream** N crema *f* para la cara ► **face flannel** N (*Brit*) toallita *f*; (= *glove*) manopla *f* (*para lavarse la cara*) ► **face mask** N mascarilla *f*; (*Cosmetics*) = **face pack** ► **face pack** N mascarilla *f* facial ► **face paint** N *pintura ornamental para la cara* ► **face powder** N polvos *mpl* para la cara ► **face value** N [*of coin, stamp*] valor *m* nominal; ✦**IDIOM to take sb at ~ value** juzgar a algn por las apariencias; **I took his statement at (its) ~ value** tomé lo que dijo en sentido literal

►**face down** VT + ADV (*esp US*) amilanar

►**face on to** VI + PREP dar a, mirar hacia
►**face out** VT + ADV **to ~ it out** afrontar las consecuencias; **to ~ out a crisis** hacer frente a una crisis
►**face up to** VI + PREP [+ *difficulty*] afrontar, hacer frente a; **to ~ up to the fact that …** reconocer *or* admitir (el hecho de) que …; **she ~d up to it bravely** hizo frente a la situación con valentía

-faced [feɪst] ADJ (*ending in compounds*) de cara …; (*eg*) **brown-faced** de cara morena; **long-faced** de cara larga

faceless ['feɪslɪs] ADJ sin rostro; (= *anonymous*) anónimo

facelift ['feɪslɪft] N 1 (*Med*) lifting *m*, estiramiento *m* (facial); **to have a ~** hacerse un lifting
2 (*fig*) reforma *f* (superficial), modernización *f* (ligera); **to give a ~ to** [+ *building*] remozar, mejorar de aspecto; **the building has had a ~** han remozado el edificio

face-off ['feɪsɒf] N confrontación *f*

facer* ['feɪsəʳ] N (*Brit*) problema *m* desconcertante; **that's a ~!** ¡vaya problemazo!*

face-saver ['feɪs,seɪvəʳ] N maniobra *f* para salvar las apariencias

face-saving ['feɪs,seɪvɪŋ] Ⓐ ADJ para salvar las apariencias
Ⓑ N **~ is important** importa salvar las apariencias; **this is a piece of blatant ~** esto es una maniobra descarada para salvar las apariencias

facet ['fæsɪt] N (= *feature*) faceta *f*, aspecto *m*; [*of gem*] lado *m*, faceta *f*

facetious [fə'siːʃəs] ADJ [*person*] ocurrente, ingenioso; [*remark*] jocoso, gracioso; **don't be ~** deja de decir frivolidades

facetiously [fə'siːʃəslɪ] ADV chistosamente; **he said ~** dijo con mucha guasa

facetiousness [fə'siːʃəsnɪs] N guasa *f*, jocosidad *f*

face-to-face [,feɪstə'feɪs] Ⓐ ADJ **a ~ argument** un enfrentamiento *or* una discusión cara a cara
Ⓑ ADV *see* **face**

facia ['feɪʃɪə] = **fascia**

facial ['feɪʃəl] Ⓐ ADJ de la cara, facial
Ⓑ N tratamiento *m* facial

facially ['feɪʃəlɪ] ADV (= *from a facial point of view*) de cara; (= *with the face*) [*express*] con la expresión (de la cara); **to be ~ disfigured** tener la cara desfigurada

facile ['fæsaɪl] ADJ [*remark, expression*] superficial; [*writer*] vulgar; [*victory*] fácil

facilitate [fə'sɪlɪteɪt] VT (= *make easier*) facilitar; (= *assist progress of*) favorecer

facilitator [fə'sɪlɪteɪtəʳ] N facilitador(a) *m/f*

facility [fə'sɪlɪtɪ] N 1 (= *equipment, place*) instalación *f*; **the hotel's facilities are open to non-residents** las instalaciones del hotel están abiertas a los no residentes; **the flat has no cooking facilities** el piso no está equipado para cocinar; **recreational facilities** instalaciones *fpl* recreativas; **sports facilities** instalaciones *fpl* deportivas
2 (= *service, provision*) servicio *m*; **the main ~ is the library** el servicio principal es la biblioteca; **the company offers day-care facilities for children** la empresa ofrece un servicio de guardería para los niños; **toilet facilities** servicios *mpl*, aseos *mpl*; **transport facilities** servicios *mpl* de transporte
3 (*Fin*) **credit facilities** facilidades *fpl* (de pago), crédito *m*; **overdraft ~** crédito *m* al descubierto
4 (= *function*) función *f*; **the oven has an automatic timing ~** el horno dispone de una función de reloj automático; **the watch has a stopwatch ~** el reloj también posee la función de cronómetro; **there's a ~ for storing data** dispone de un servicio de almacenamiento de datos
5 (= *centre*) centro *m*; **a state ~ for women prisoners** un centro penitenciario estatal para mujeres; **a medical ~** un centro médico, un punto de asistencia médica; **a nuclear ~** un complejo nuclear
6 (= *talent, ease*) facilidad *f*; **he had a ~ for languages** tenía facilidad para los idiomas, se le daban bien los idiomas; **he writes with great ~** escribe con gran facilidad
7 (= *ability*) habilidad *f*, facultad *f*; (= *capacity*) capacidad *f*; **humans have lost the ~ to use their sense of smell** los humanos han perdido la habilidad *or* la facultad de utilizar el olfato; **the new model has the ~ to reproduce speech** el nuevo modelo tiene la capacidad de *or* es capaz de reproducir el habla

facing ['feɪsɪŋ] Ⓐ PREP de cara a, frente a
Ⓑ ADJ opuesto, de enfrente; **the houses ~** las casas de enfrente; **on the ~ page** en la página opuesta *or* de enfrente
Ⓒ N (*Archit*) paramento *m*, revestimiento *m*; (*Sew*) guarnición *f*; **facings** (*Sew*) vueltas *fpl*

-facing ['feɪsɪŋ] ADJ (*ending in compounds*) **south-facing** con orientación sur, orientado hacia el sur

facsimile [fæk'sɪmɪlɪ] Ⓐ ADJ facsímil
Ⓑ N facsímile *m*, facsímil *m*
Ⓒ CPD ► **facsimile machine** N máquina *f or* aparato *m* de fax ► **facsimile transmission** N (transmisión *f* por) fax *m*

▼**fact** [fækt] Ⓐ N 1 (= *detail, circumstance*) hecho *m*; **the ~ that …** el hecho de que …; **the ~ that she knew is not the point** el hecho de que ella lo supiera no viene al caso; **he still loved her in spite of the ~ that she had left him** aunque le había dejado él aún la quería; **my family accepts the ~ that I'm a vegetarian** mi familia acepta que sea vegetariano; **their priority is to establish the ~s of the case** su prioridad es esclarecer los hechos *or* lo que ocurrió realmente; **hard ~s** hechos *mpl* innegables; **to stick to the ~s** atenerse a los hechos
2 (= *piece of information*) dato *m*; **~s and figures** datos *mpl*; **the ~s of life** los detalles de la reproducción; **get your ~s right before you start accusing people** infórmate bien antes de empezar a acusar a la gente; **he accused her of getting her ~s wrong** la acusó de no contar con la información correcta
3 (= *reality*) realidad *f*; **the ~ remains that …** la realidad sigue siendo que …; **the ~ (of the matter) is that …** la verdad *or* el hecho es que …; **I accept what he says as ~** acepto lo que dice como cierto; **a story founded on ~** una historia basada en hechos verídicos *or* reales; **it has no basis in ~** carece de base (real); **it's a ~ that …** es un hecho que …; **to face (the) ~s** enfrentarse a la realidad *or* los hechos; **he can't tell ~ from fiction** no es capaz de distinguir la realidad de la ficción; **to know for a ~ that …** saber a ciencia cierta que …; **in ~** de hecho; **it sounds simple, but in ~ it's very difficult** parece sencillo, pero de hecho *or* en realidad es muy difícil; **I don't like it, as a matter of ~ I'm totally against it** no me gusta, de hecho estoy totalmente en contra; **"don't tell me you like it?" — "as a matter of ~ I do"** —no me digas que te gusta —pues sí, la verdad es que sí; **they're very alike, in point of ~ you can't tell the difference** son muy parecidos, de hecho no puedes distinguirlos; **is that a ~!** (*iro*) ¡no me digas!; **he's a dull writer, and that's a ~** es un escritor aburrido, eso no hay quien lo discuta; *see also* **face B3**
4 (*Jur*) (= *event*) **before/after the ~** antes/después de los hechos; *see also* **accessory**
Ⓑ CPD ► **fact sheet** N hoja *f* informativa, informe *m*

fact-finding ['fækt,faɪndɪŋ] ADJ **on a ~ tour/mission** en viaje/misión de reconocimiento; **a ~ committee** una comisión de investigación

faction ['fækʃən] N facción *f*

factional ['fækʃənl] ADJ [*fighting, violence*] entre distintas facciones

factionalism ['fækʃənəlɪzm] N enfrentamientos *mpl* entre distintas facciones

factionalize ['fækʃənlaɪz] Ⓐ VT fragmentar, dividir en facciones
Ⓑ VI dividirse en facciones

factious ['fækʃəs] ADJ faccioso

factitious [fæk'tɪʃəs] ADJ facticio

factitive ['fæktɪtɪv] ADJ factitivo, causativo

▼**factor** ['fæktəʳ] Ⓐ N 1 (= *consideration*) factor *m*; **safety ~** factor *m* de seguridad; **the human ~** el factor humano
2 (*Math*) factor *m*; **highest common ~** máximo común divisor *m*; **to increase by a ~ of five** aumentar cinco veces, multiplicarse por cinco
3 (*Comm*) agente *mf* comisionado/a
Ⓑ VI (*Comm*) comprar deudas
►**factor in** VT + ADV **to ~ sth in** incluir algo como factor a tener en cuenta
►**factor into** VT + PREP **~ it into your decision-making** tenlo en cuenta a la hora de tomar una decisión

factorial [fæk'tɔːrɪəl] Ⓐ ADJ factorial
Ⓑ N factorial *m or f*

factoring ['fæktərɪŋ] N factorización *f*

factory ['fæktərɪ] Ⓐ N fábrica *f*
Ⓑ CPD ► **factory farm** N granja *f* de cría intensiva ► **factory farming** N cría *f* intensiva ► **factory floor** N fábrica *f*; **workers on the ~ floor** trabajadores *mpl* de fábrica; **~ floor opinion** opinión *f* de los obreros ► **factory inspector** N inspector(a) *m/f* de trabajo ► **factory ship** N buque *m* factoría ► **factory work** N trabajo *m* de fábrica ► **factory worker** N obrero/a *m/f* industrial

factotum [fæk'təʊtəm] N factótum *mf*

factual ['fæktjʊəl] ADJ [*report, description*] objetivo, basado en datos objetivos; [*error*] de hecho

factually ['fæktjʊəlɪ] ADV objetivamente; **~ speaking, I would say …** limitándome a los hechos, diría que …

faculty ['fækəltɪ] N 1 (= *power of body, mind*) facultad *f*; **to have** *or* **be in possession of all one's faculties** estar en pleno uso de sus facultades
2 (= *ability*) aptitud *f*, facilidad *f*; **to have a ~ for sth/doing sth** tener aptitud *or* facilidad para algo/hacer algo
3 (*Univ*) facultad *f*; (*esp US Univ*) (= *teaching staff*) profesorado *m* (de facultad *or* universidad)

fad [fæd] N (= *fashion*) moda *f*; **a passing ~** una moda pasajera; **it's just a ~** es la novedad nada más, es una moda pasajera; **the ~ for Italian clothes** la moda de la ropa italiana; **he has his ~s** tiene sus caprichos

faddish ['fædɪʃ] ADJ pasajero, poco duradero

faddy ['fædɪ] ADJ (*Brit*) [*person*] que tiene sus

➤ LANGUAGE IN USE: **fact A3** 26.1, 26.3 **factor A1** 26.1, 26.2

manías, difícil de contentar; [*distaste, desire*] idiosincrático

fade [feɪd] Ⓐ VI 1 (= *lose colour, intensity*) [*fabric*] desteñirse, perder color; [*colour*] perder intensidad; **"guaranteed not to ~"** "no destiñe"; **the black had ~d to grey** el negro se había vuelto gris; **my tan soon ~d** el moreno se me quitó pronto; **the light was fading rapidly** estaba oscureciendo rápidamente, la luz se iba rápidamente; **in the fading light he failed to see her** no la vio en la penumbra
2 (= *melt away*) [*sound*] desvanecerse; [*signal*] debilitarse; [*voice, music*] apagarse; (*Cine, TV*) [*image*] fundirse; **the sound of the engine ~d into the distance** el ruido del motor se desvanecía *or* se perdía en la distancia; **her voice ~d to a whisper** su voz se apagó hasta convertirse en un susurro; **the music ~d** la música se fue apagando; **the laughter ~s and we hear birds singing** las risas se apagan *or* se desvanecen y se oye el canto de unos pájaros; **the image ~d** la imagen se fundió, hubo un fundido; **~s to music, production credits** fundido a música y títulos de créditos
3 (= *deteriorate, decline*) [*flower, beauty*] marchitarse; [*organization, culture*] decaer; [*strength*] debilitarse; [*person*] consumirse; **he was unconscious and fading fast** estaba inconsciente y se consumía por momentos; **the team ~d in the second half** el equipo perdió fuerza en el segundo tiempo
4 (= *begin to disappear*) [*hopes, memories, smile*] desvanecerse; [*appeal*] pasarse; [*scar*] borrarse; **he saw his chances fading** veía como se iban agotando sus posibilidades; **once he became used to it the novelty began to ~** cuando se acostumbró a ello dejó pronto de ser una novedad; **he's the sort of person who always ~s into the background** es el tipo de persona que siempre se queda en un segundo plano; **to ~ from sight** *or* **view** perderse de vista
5 (*Aut*) [*engine*] perder potencia
6 (*Sport*) [*ball*] desviarse; **to ~ to the left/right** desviarse a la izquierda/derecha
Ⓑ VT 1 (= *discolour*) [+ *fabric*] desteñir, hacer perder el color a; [+ *colour*] desteñir; [+ *flower*] marchitar
2 (*Cine, TV*) fundir
Ⓒ N (*Cine*) fundido *m*; **~ to music, closing credits** fundido a música y títulos de créditos finales; **~ to black** fundido en negro

►**fade away** VI + ADV [*sound, music*] apagarse; [*emotion*] irse apagando; [*sick person*] consumirse; **her voice ~d away** su voz se fue apagando; **the applause ~d away** los aplausos se fueron apagando; **we'd watched her fading away in front of our eyes** la veíamos consumirse delante de nuestros propios ojos; **you'll ~ away if you don't eat more** te vas a quedar en los huesos como no comas más

►**fade in** (*Cine, TV*) Ⓐ VT + ADV [+ *image*] meter con un fundido; [+ *sound*] meter poco a poco
Ⓑ VI + ADV [*image*] entrar en fundido (**to** con); [*sound*] entrar (**over** sobre); **a hymn ~s in over the voices** se oye un himno que entra sobre las voces; **we'll ~ in on a view of the island, at dawn** entramos con un fundido de la isla al amanecer

►**fade out** Ⓐ VT + ADV (*Cine, TV*) [+ *image*] cerrar en fundido, fundir; [+ *sound*] apagar lentamente, bajar el volumen de
Ⓑ VI + ADV 1 (*Cine, TV*) [*image*] fundirse (**to** en); [*sound*] apagarse, dejar de oírse
2 (*fig*) **he ~d out of public life when he became ill** al enfermar desapareció de la vida pública

►**fade up** VT + ADV = **fade in A**

faded ['feɪdɪd] ADJ [*garment*] descolorido, desteñido; [*colour*] apagado, desvaído; [*photograph*] desvaído; [*plant, glory*] marchito

fade-in ['feɪdɪn] N (*Cine, TV*) (entrada *f* en) fundido *m*

fade-out ['feɪdaʊt] N (*Cine, TV*) fundido *m* (en negro), (cierre *m* en) fundido *m*

faecal, **fecal** (*US*) ['fiːkəl] ADJ fecal

faeces, **feces** (*US*) ['fiːsiːz] NPL (*frm*) excrementos *mpl*, heces *fpl* (*frm*)

Faeroes ['feərəʊz], **Faeroe Islands** ['feərəʊˌaɪləndz] = **Faroes**

faff* [fæf] VI (*Brit*) **to ~ about** *or* **around** perder el tiempo, ocuparse en bagatelas; **stop ~ing about** *or* **around!** ¡déjate de tonterías!

fag [fæg] Ⓐ N 1 (*Brit**) (= *cigarette*) pitillo* *m*, cigarro *m*
2 (*esp US‡ pej*) (= *homosexual*) marica* *m*
3 (*Brit†**) (= *effort, job*) lata* *f*; **what a ~!** ¡qué lata!; **it's just too much of a ~** la verdad, es mucho trabajo
4 (*Brit Scol*) *alumno joven que trabaja para otro mayor*
Ⓑ VT (*) (*also* **~ out**) (= *exhaust*) dejar rendido; **to be ~ged (out)** estar rendido
Ⓒ VI **to ~ for sb** (*Brit Scol*) trabajar para algn
Ⓓ CPD ► **fag end*** N [*of cigarette*] colilla *f*; (*fig*) (= *remainder*) final *m* ► **fag hag‡** N *mujer a la que le gusta la compañía de hombres homosexuales*

faggot[1], **fagot** (*US*) ['fægət] N 1 (*for fire*) haz *m* de leña
2 (*Brit Culin*) albóndiga *f*

faggot[2]‡ ['fægət] N (*esp US pej*) (= *homosexual*) marica* *m*

fah [fɑː] N (*Mus*) fa *m*

Fahrenheit ['færənhaɪt] Ⓐ N Fahrenheit *m* (*termómetro, grados etc*)
Ⓑ CPD ► **Fahrenheit thermometer** N termómetro *m* de (grados) Fahrenheit

FAI N ABBR = **Football Association of Ireland**

fail [feɪl] Ⓐ VI 1 (= *not succeed*) [*candidate in examination*] suspender; [*plan*] fracasar, no dar resultado; [*show, play*] fracasar; [*business*] quebrar; [*remedy*] fallar, no surtir efecto; [*hopes*] frustrarse, malograrse; **to ~ by five votes** perder por cinco votos; **to ~ in one's duty** faltar a su deber, no cumplir con su obligación
2 [*light*] irse, apagarse; [*crops*] perderse; [*health, sight, voice*] debilitarse; [*strength*] acabarse; [*engine, brakes, mechanism*] fallar, averiarse; [*water supply*] acabarse; [*power supply*] cortarse, fallar; **the light was ~ing** iba anocheciendo
Ⓑ VT 1 [+ *exam, subject*] suspender; [+ *candidate*] suspender (a); **a ~ed painter** un pintor fracasado
2 (= *let down*) [+ *person*] fallar (a); [*memory, strength*] fallar; **don't ~ me!** ¡no me falles!, ¡no faltes!; **his strength ~ed him** le fallaron las fuerzas; **his heart ~ed him** se encontró sin ánimo; **his courage ~ed him** le faltó valor; **words ~ me!** ¡no encuentro palabras!
3 (= *not succeed*) **to ~ to be elected** no lograr ser elegido; **to ~ to win a prize** no obtener un premio
4 (= *omit, neglect*) **to ~ to do sth** no hacer algo, dejar de hacer algo; **don't ~ to visit her** no deje de visitarla
5 (= *be unable*) **I ~ to see why/what** *etc* no veo *or* alcanzo a ver por qué/qué *etc*
Ⓒ N 1 **without ~** sin falta
2 (*Univ*) suspenso *m* (**in** en)

failing ['feɪlɪŋ] Ⓐ PREP a falta de; **~ that, …** de no ser posible, …
Ⓑ N (= *flaw*) falta *f*, defecto *m*; **the plan has numerous ~s** el plan tiene muchos defectos; **it's his only ~** es su único punto débil
Ⓒ ADJ **he was in ~ health** su salud era cada vez más débil; **I had to stop work because of ~ eyesight** tuve que dejar de trabajar porque me fallaba la vista; **we reached the top in ~ light** anochecía cuando llegamos a la cumbre; **a ~ marriage** un matrimonio que anda mal

fail-safe ['feɪlseɪf] ADJ [*device*] de seguridad, a prueba de fallos; [*method*] infalible

failure ['feɪljə[r]] Ⓐ N 1 (= *lack of success*) fracaso *m*; (*in exam*) suspenso *m*; [*of crops*] pérdida *f*; [*of supplies*] corte *m*, interrupción *f*; [*of hopes*] frustración *f*, malogro *m*; **to end in ~** acabar mal, malograrse (*LAm*); **it was a complete ~** fue un fracaso total; **the crop was a total ~** la cosecha se perdió por completo; *see also* **power C**
2 (*Tech*) fallo *m*, avería *f*; (*Med*) crisis *f inv*, ataque *m*; (*Fin*) quiebra *f*; *see also* **heart**
3 (= *person*) fracasado/a *m/f*
4 (= *neglect*) falta *f*; **his ~ to come** su ausencia, el que no viniera; **~ to pay** incumplimiento *m* en el pago, impago *m*
Ⓑ CPD ► **failure rate** N (*in exams*) porcentaje *m* de suspensos; [*of machine*] porcentaje *m* de averías

fain†† [feɪn] ADV (*used only with "would"*) de buena gana

faint [feɪnt] Ⓐ ADJ (*compar* **fainter**; *superl* **faintest**) 1 (= *light, weak*) [*breeze*] débil, ligero; [*outline*] borroso, indistinto; [*trace, mark, line*] tenue; [*colour*] pálido; [*light*] tenue; [*sound*] apagado, débil; [*smell*] tenue, casi imperceptible; [*taste, resemblance*] ligero; [*voice, breathing*] débil; [*hope*] remoto; [*smile*] leve; [*idea, memory*] vago; [*heart*] medroso; **I haven't the ~est idea*** no tengo ni la más remota idea
2 (*Med*) **to feel ~** marearse, tener vahídos; **she was ~ with hunger** estaba que se desmayaba de hambre
Ⓑ N (*Med*) desmayo *m*, desvanecimiento *m*; **to be in a ~** estar desmayado *or* sin conocimiento; **to fall down in a ~** desmayarse
Ⓒ VI (*Med*) (*also* **~ away**) desmayarse, perder el conocimiento (**from** de); **he was ~ing with tiredness** estaba que se caía de cansancio

fainthearted ['feɪnt'hɑːtɪd] ADJ pusilánime, apocado, medroso; **this film is not for the ~** es una película muy fuerte

faintheartedness [ˌfeɪnt'hɑːtɪdnɪs] N pusilanimidad *f*

fainting fit ['feɪntɪŋˌfɪt] N, **fainting spell** ['feɪntɪŋˌspel] N síncope *m*, desvanecimiento *m*

faintly ['feɪntlɪ] ADV 1 (= *lightly, weakly*) [*call, say*] débilmente; [*breathe, shine*] débilmente, ligeramente; [*write, mark, scratch*] levemente, débilmente
2 (= *slightly*) [*disappointed*] ligeramente; **this is ~ reminiscent of …** esto me recuerda vagamente a …

faintness ['feɪntnɪs] N 1 (= *weakness*) [*of light*] tenuidad *f*; [*of outline*] lo indistinto; [*of voice, breathing*] debilidad *f*
2 (*Med*) desmayo *m*, desfallecimiento *m*

fair[1] [feə[r]] Ⓐ ADJ (*compar* **fairer**; *superl* **fairest**) 1 (= *just*) [*person, treatment, wage, exchange*] justo; [*decision, report, hearing*] imparcial; [*comment*] razonable, válido; [*sample*] representativo; [*price*] justo, razonable; [*deal*] justo, equitativo; [*fight, election*] limpio; [*competition*] leal; **that's ~ comment** ésa es una observación razonable *or* válida; **it's not ~!** ¡no es justo!, ¡no hay derecho!; **it's not ~ to expect you to wash up** no es justo pretender que friegues; **it's ~ to say that ...** es cierto que ..., lo cierto es que ...; **be ~, darling, it's not their fault** sé justo *or* razonable, cariño, no es culpa suya; **to be ~ ...** (= *truth to tell*) a decir verdad ..., en honor a la verdad ...; (= *not to be unjust*) para ser justo ...; **~ enough!** ¡vale!, ¡muy bien!; **fair's fair, it's my turn now** vale ya *or* ya basta, ahora me toca a mí; **~ game** (*fig*) blanco *m* legítimo; **it's not ~ on the old** es injusto *or* no es justo para (con) los ancianos; **it's only ~ that ...** lo más justo sería que ...; **as is only ~** como es justo; **~ play** (*in game*) juego *m* limpio; **sense of ~ play** (*fig*) sentido *m* de la justicia; **she's had more than her ~ share of problems in life** ha pasado mucho *or* lo suyo en la vida; **they are not paying their ~ share** no están pagando la cantidad que les corresponde *or* que les toca; **to be ~ to sb** ser justo con algn; **that's not true, you're not being ~ to him** eso no es verdad, no estás siendo justo con él; **~ trade** comercio *m* equitativo; ♦*IDIOM* **by ~ means or foul** por las buenas o por las malas; ♦*PROV* **all's ~ in love and war** todo vale en el amor y la guerra

2 (= *reasonable, average*) [*work*] pasable, regular; **she has a ~ chance** tiene bastantes posibilidades; **you've got to give him a ~ chance** le tienes que dar una oportunidad con todas las de la ley; **I have a ~ idea of what to expect** sé más o menos qué esperar; **~ to middling** regular; **"how are you?" — "~ to middling"** —¿qué tal estás? —regular; **he's been given ~ warning** no puede decir que no se le ha avisado

3 (= *quite large*) [*sum, speed*] considerable; **a ~ amount of** bastante; **this happens in a ~ number of cases** esto sucede en bastantes casos; **we've still got a ~ way to go** aún nos queda un buen trecho que recorrer

4 (= *pale, light-coloured*) [*hair, person*] rubio, güero (*Mex*); [*complexion, skin*] blanco, güero (*Mex*)

5 (= *fine, good*) [*weather*] bueno; **if it's ~ tomorrow** si hace buen tiempo mañana; **~ copy** copia *f* en limpio; **to make a ~ copy of sth** hacer una copia en limpio de algo, pasar algo en limpio; **his legal career seemed set ~** su carrera como abogado parecía tener el éxito asegurado; ♦*IDIOM* **in ~ weather or foul** (*referring to present, future*) haga bueno o malo; (*referring to past*) hiciera bueno o malo

6 (*liter*) (= *beautiful*) bello, hermoso; **this ~ city of ours** esta bella ciudad nuestra; **the ~ sex** el bello sexo

Ⓑ ADV 1 **to play ~** jugar limpio; **to win ~ and square** ganar con todas las de la ley; **it hit the target ~ and square** dio justo en el centro del blanco

2 (†*) (= *positively*) verdaderamente; **we were ~ terrified** estábamos verdaderamente asustados; **it ~ took my breath away** te/os juro que me dejó sin habla*

fair² [fɛəʳ] N 1 (= *market*) feria *f*; **antiques/craft ~** feria *f* de antigüedades/artesanía; **book ~** feria *f* del libro; *see also* **trade D**

2 (*Brit*) (= *funfair*) parque *m* de atracciones

STATE FAIR

En todos los estados de EE.UU. se celebra una feria en otoño llamada **state fair** *a la que acude gran cantidad de gente de todo el estado. Estas ferias son generalmente agrícolas y en ellas se celebran concursos de animales y productos del campo, de gastronomía y de artesanía. También se organizan juegos y se instalan stands en los que fabricantes y comerciantes hacen demostraciones de sus productos. La feria más grande de todo el país es la Feria de Texas, que se celebra cada octubre en Dallas.*

fairground [ˈfɛəgraʊnd] N parque *m* de atracciones

fair-haired [ˈfɛəˈhɛəd] ADJ, **fair-headed** [ˈfɛəˈhedɪd] ADJ [*person*] rubio, güero (*Mex*)

fairly [ˈfɛəlɪ] ADV 1 (= *justly*) justamente, con justicia; (= *impartially*) con imparcialidad; (= *equally*) equitativamente; **our workers are treated ~** tratamos justamente *or* con justicia a nuestros trabajadores; **he always enforced rules ~** siempre aplicó las reglas con imparcialidad; **the blame must be placed ~ and squarely on the shoulders of the government** todo el peso de la culpa debe recaer de lleno sobre el gobierno

2 (= *according to the rules*) [*play*] limpiamente, limpio

3 (= *quite*) bastante; **I'm ~ sure** estoy bastante *or* casi segura; **~ good** bastante bueno

4 (*) (*as intensifier*) verdaderamente; **the literature ~ bulges with illustrations of this** el material publicado está verdaderamente repleto de ilustraciones de esto; **he ~ ran out of the room** poco menos que salió corriendo del cuarto

fair-minded [ˈfɛəˈmaɪndɪd] ADJ imparcial

fair-mindedness [ˌfɛəˈmaɪndɪdnɪs] N imparcialidad *f*

fairness [ˈfɛənɪs] N 1 (= *justice*) justicia *f*; (= *impartiality*) imparcialidad *f*; **in all ~** (= *truth to tell*) a decir verdad, en honor a la verdad; (= *to be fair*) para ser justo; **in all ~, he had to admit that she had a point** para ser justo con ella, tenía que reconocer que llevaba algo de razón; **in (all) ~ to him** para ser justo con él

2 (= *paleness*) [*of hair, person*] lo rubio; [*of complexion, skin*] blancura *f*

3 (*liter*) (= *beauty*) belleza *f*, hermosura *f*

FAIRNESS DOCTRINE

La **Fairness Doctrine** *(Doctrina de la Imparcialidad) es un principio llevado a la práctica en Estados Unidos por la* **Federal Communications Commission** *o* **FCC** *por el que, cuando se trata de noticias importantes de carácter local o nacional, la radio y la televisión deben ofrecer los distintos puntos de vista de forma equilibrada. Este principio, establecido por la* **FCC** *en 1949 con el apoyo del Congreso, no tiene carácter de ley y cuenta entre sus atribuciones con el control equitativo del tiempo en los espacios electorales dedicados a cada uno de los líderes políticos en campaña. También se utilizó en 1967 en la lucha antitabaco, cuando la* **FCC** *estableció que los fabricantes debían dejar claro en sus anuncios los peligros del tabaco, aunque hoy día la* **Fairness Doctrine** *ya ha dejado prácticamente de tener influencia en publicidad.*

⇨ *Ver tb* FCC

fair-sized [ˈfɛəsaɪzd] ADJ bastante grande

fair-skinned [ˌfɛəˈskɪnd] ADJ de tez blanca

fairway [ˈfɛəweɪ] N 1 (*Golf*) calle *f*

2 (*Naut*) canalizo *m*

fair-weather friend [ˌfɛəweðəˈfrend] N amigo/a *m/f* en la prosperidad *or* del buen viento

fairy [ˈfɛərɪ] Ⓐ N 1 (= *creature*) hada *f*

2 (‡ *pej*) (= *homosexual*) maricón‡ *m*, marica* *m*

Ⓑ CPD ► **fairy cycle** N bicicleta *f* de niño ► **fairy footsteps** NPL pasos *mpl* ligeros ► **fairy godmother** N hada *f* madrina ► **fairy lights** NPL bombillas *fpl* de colorines ► **fairy queen** N reina *f* de las hadas ► **fairy story**, **fairy tale** N cuento *m* de hadas; (*fig*) (= *lie*) cuento *m*, patraña *f*

fairyland [ˈfɛərɪlænd] N país *m* de las hadas; (*fig*) país *m* de ensueño; **he's living in ~*** vive en la luna

fairytale [ˈfɛərɪteɪl] Ⓐ ADJ [*castle, world*] fantástico, de ensueño

Ⓑ CPD ► **fairytale romance** N (*fig*) amor *m* de cuento de hadas

fait accompli [ˌfeɪtəˈkɒmplɪ] N hecho *m* consumado

faith [feɪθ] Ⓐ N 1 (*Rel*) fe *f*; (= *doctrine*) creencia *f*, doctrina *f*; (= *sect, confession*) religión *f*; **what ~ does he belong to?** ¿qué religión tiene?

2 (= *trust*) fe *f*, confianza *f*; **to have ~ in sth/sb** tener fe *or* confianza en algo/algn, fiarse de algo/algn; **to put one's ~ in sth/sb** confiar en algo/algn; **to break ~** faltar a la palabra (**with** dada a); **to keep ~** cumplir la palabra (**with** dada a); **in (all) good ~** de buena fe; **in bad ~** de mala fe

Ⓑ CPD ► **faith healer** N curandero/a *m/f* ► **faith healing** N curación *f* por fe

faithful [ˈfeɪθfʊl] Ⓐ ADJ 1 (*also Rel*) fiel (**to** a); [*friend, servant, spouse*] leal

2 (= *trustworthy*) digno de confianza; [*account*] detallado; [*translation*] fiel

Ⓑ NPL **the ~** (*Rel*) los fieles

faithfully [ˈfeɪθfəlɪ] ADV [*serve*] fielmente, lealmente; [*describe, translate*] fielmente, con exactitud; **Yours ~** (*Brit*) (*in letter*) le saluda atentamente

faithfulness [ˈfeɪθfʊlnɪs] N fidelidad *f*

faithless [ˈfeɪθlɪs] ADJ desleal, infiel

faithlessness [ˈfeɪθlɪsnɪs] N infidelidad *f*, deslealtad *f*, perfidia *f*

fake [feɪk] Ⓐ N (= *thing, picture*) falsificación *f*; (= *person*) impostor(a) *m/f*, embustero/a *m/f*; (*as term of abuse*) farsante *mf*

Ⓑ ADJ falso

Ⓒ VT 1 [+ *accounts*] falsificar; **to ~ an illness** fingirse enfermo

2 (*US*) (= *improvise*) improvisar

Ⓓ VI fingir, simular

fakir [ˈfɑːkɪəʳ] N faquir *m*

falcon [ˈfɔːlkən] N halcón *m*

falconer [ˈfɔːlkənəʳ] N halconero/a *m/f*

falconry [ˈfɔːlkənrɪ] N halconería *f*, cetrería *f*

Falklander [ˈfɔːlkləndəʳ], **Falkland Islander** [ˌfɔːlkləndˈaɪləndəʳ] N habitante *mf* de las Islas Malvinas, malvinense *mf*

Falkland Islands [ˈfɔːlklənd‚aɪləndz], **Falklands** [ˈfɔːlkləndz] NPL (Islas *fpl*) Malvinas *fpl*

fall [fɔːl] (*vb: pt* **fell**; *pp* **fallen**) Ⓐ N 1 (= *tumble*) caída *f*; **he had a bad ~** sufrió una mala caída; **the Fall** (*Rel*) la Caída; ♦*IDIOM* **to be heading** *or* **riding for a ~** presumir demasiado

2 [*of building, bridge etc*] derrumbamiento *m*; [*of rocks*] desprendimiento *m*; [*of earth*] corrimiento *m*; **a ~ of snow** una nevada

3 (= *decrease*) disminución *f*; (*in prices, temperature, demand*) descenso *m* (**in** de); (*Fin*) baja *f*

[4] (= *downfall*) caída *f*, ocaso *m*; (= *defeat*) derrota *f*; [*of city*] rendición *f*, caída *f*; (*from favour, power etc*) alejamiento *m*
[5] (= *slope*) [*of ground*] declive *m*, desnivel *m*
[6] **falls** (= *waterfall*) salto *msing* de agua, cascada *fsing*, catarata *fsing*; **Niagara Falls** las cataratas del Niágara
[7] (*US*) (= *autumn*) otoño *m*
Ⓑ VI [1] (= *fall down*) [*person, object*] caerse; **to ~ into the river** caerse al río; **to ~ on one's feet** caer de pie; (*fig*) salir bien parado; **to ~ to** *or* **on one's knees** arrodillarse, caer de rodillas; **✦IDIOMS to ~ on one's ass** (*US***) hacer el ridi*; **to ~ flat** [*joke*] no hacer gracia; [*party*] fracasar; *see also* **flat A6**
[2] (= *drop*) [*leaves, bomb, rain, snow, night*] caer; [*rocks*] desprenderse; **he fell into bed exhausted** se desplomó en la cama, exhausto; **they left as darkness fell** partieron al caer la noche; **to let sth ~** dejar caer algo; **to let ~ that …** soltar que …; **night was ~ing** anochecía, se hacía de noche; **it all began to ~ into place** (*fig*) todo empezó a encajar; **to ~ short of sb's expectations** defraudar las esperanzas de algn; **to ~ short of perfection** no llegar a la perfección; **the arrow fell short of the target** la flecha no alcanzó la diana; **to ~ into temptation** sucumbir a la tentación; **to ~ among thieves** (*esp Bible*) ir a parar entre ladrones
[3] [*person*] (*morally etc*) caer; **to ~ from grace** (*Rel*) perder la gracia; (*fig*) caer en desgracia
[4] (= *slope*) [*ground*] descender, caer en declive
[5] (= *hang*) [*hair, drapery*] caer
[6] (= *decrease*) disminuir; [*price, level, temperature etc*] bajar, descender; [*wind*] amainar; **at a time of ~ing interest rates** en un período cuando bajan los tipos de interés; **he fell in my estimation** perdió mucho a mis ojos
[7] (= *be defeated*) [*government*] caer, ser derrotado; [*city*] rendirse, ser tomado
[8] (*liter*) (= *die*) [*soldier*] caer, morir
[9] (= *become*) **to ~ asleep** quedarse dormido, dormirse; **to ~ to bits** (*Brit*) = **to fall to pieces**; **to ~ due** vencer; **to ~ heir to sth** heredar algo; **to ~ ill** caer enfermo, enfermarse; **to ~ in love (with sth/sb)** enamorarse (de algo/algn); **to ~ open** abrirse; **to ~ to pieces** hacerse pedazos; **to ~ silent** callarse
Ⓒ CPD ► **fall guy*** N (= *easy victim*) víctima *f* (de un truco); (= *scapegoat*) cabeza *f* de turco

►**fall about*** VI + ADV (*Brit*) (*also* **~ about laughing**) morirse *or* partirse de risa

►**fall apart** VI + ADV [*object*] caerse a pedazos, deshacerse; [*empire*] desmoronarse; [*scheme, marriage*] fracasar

►**fall away** VI + ADV [1] (= *slope steeply*) [*ground*] descender abruptamente (**to** hacia)
[2] (= *crumble*) [*plaster*] desconcharse; [*cliff*] desmoronarse; [*stage of rocket, part*] desprenderse
[3] (= *diminish*) [*numbers etc*] bajar, disminuir; [*enthusiasm*] enfriarse; [*trade, interest*] decaer; (*in quality*) empeorar

►**fall back** VI + ADV [1] (= *retreat*) retroceder; (*Mil*) replegarse
[2] **it fell back into the sea** volvió a caer al mar
[3] [*price etc*] bajar
[4] (*fig*) **to ~ back on sth** [+ *remedy etc*] recurrir a algo; **something to ~ back on** algo a lo que recurrir

►**fall backwards** VI + ADV caer hacia atrás

►**fall behind** VI + ADV (*in race etc*) quedarse atrás, rezagarse; (*fig*) (*with work, payments*) retrasarse

►**fall down** Ⓐ VI + ADV [1] [*person*] caerse (al suelo); [*building*] hundirse, derrumbarse; **to ~ down and worship sb** arrodillarse en adoración a algn
[2] (*fig*) (= *fail*) fracasar, fallar; **that is where you fell down** ahí es donde fallaste; **to ~ down on the job** no estar a la altura del trabajo, hacerlo mal
Ⓑ VI + PREP **to ~ down the stairs** caer rodando por la escalera

►**fall for*** VI + PREP [1] (= *feel attracted to*) [+ *person*] enamorarse de; [+ *object, place*] quedarse encantado con; [+ *idea*] interesarse por
[2] (= *be deceived by*) [+ *trick*] dejarse engañar por, tragarse*; **he fell for it** picó*, se lo tragó*

►**fall in** VI + ADV [1] [*person*] caerse (dentro); [*roof, walls*] desplomarse
[2] (*Mil*) formar filas; **~ in!** ¡en filas!

►**fall into** VI + PREP [1] (= *be divided*) **it ~s into four parts** se divide en cuatro partes; **it ~s into this category** está incluido en esta categoría; **his poems ~ into three categories** sus poemas se dividen en tres categorías; *see also* **fall B1**
[2] (*fig*) **to ~ into error/bad habits/bad ways** incurrir en error/adquirir malos hábitos/coger *or* tomar un mal camino; **to ~ into conversation with sb** entablar conversación con algn

►**fall in with** VI + PREP [1] (= *meet*) [+ *person*] encontrarse *or* juntarse con
[2] (= *agree to*) [+ *plan, proposal etc*] aceptar, quedar de acuerdo con; [+ *opinion*] adherirse a

►**fall off** Ⓐ VI + ADV [1] (*gen*) caerse; [*part*] desprenderse
[2] (= *diminish*) (*in amount, numbers*) disminuir; [*interest*] decaer; [*enthusiasm*] enfriarse; [*quality*] empeorar
Ⓑ VI + PREP (*gen*) caerse de; [*part*] desprenderse de

►**fall on, fall upon** VI + PREP [1] [*accent, stress*] recaer en
[2] [*tax etc*] incidir en
[3] (*Mil*) caer sobre
[4] **to ~ on one's food** lanzarse sobre la comida, lanzarse a comer; **people were ~ing on each other in delight** todos se abrazaban de puro contentos
[5] [*birthday, Christmas etc*] caer en
[6] (= *find*) tropezar con, dar con; **to ~ on a way of doing sth** dar por casualidad con la forma de hacer algo
[7] (= *alight on*) **my gaze fell on certain details** me fijé en ciertos detalles
[8] (= *be one's duty*) = **fall to A2**

►**fall out** VI + ADV [1] [*person, object*] caerse (**of** de)
[2] (*Mil*) romper filas
[3] (*fig*) (= *quarrel*) **to ~ out (with sb) (over sth)** enfadarse *or* (*LAm*) enojarse (con algn) (por algo)
[4] (= *happen*) **it fell out that** resultó que; **events fell out (just) as we had hoped** todo salió como habíamos deseado

►**fall over** Ⓐ VI + ADV [*person, object*] caer, caerse
Ⓑ VI + PREP [1] [+ *object*] tropezar con
[2] (*fig*) (*) **he was ~ing over himself** *or* **over backwards to be polite** se desvivía en atenciones; **they were ~ing over each other to get it** se pegaban por conseguirlo

►**fall through** VI + ADV [*plans etc*] fracasar

►**fall to** Ⓐ VI + PREP [1] (= *begin*) **to ~ to doing sth** empezar *or* ponerse a hacer algo; **he fell to wondering if/to thinking (about) …** empezó a preguntarse si/a pensar (en) …
[2] (= *be one's duty*) corresponder a, tocar a; **it ~s to me to say …** me corresponde a mí decir …; **the responsibility ~s to you** la responsabilidad es tuya *or* recae en ti
Ⓑ VI + ADV (= *begin working*) ponerse a trabajar; (= *begin eating*) empezar a comer; **~ to!** ¡a ello!, ¡vamos!

►**fall upon** VI + PREP *see* **fall on**

fallacious [fəˈleɪʃəs] ADJ (= *incorrect*) erróneo; (= *misleading*) engañoso, falaz

fallacy [ˈfæləsɪ] N (= *false belief*) falacia *f*; (= *false reasoning*) sofisma *m*, argucia *f*

fallback [ˈfɔːlbæk] ADJ **~ position** segunda línea *f* de defensa; (*fig*) posición *f* de repliegue

fallen [ˈfɔːlən] Ⓐ PP *of* **fall**
Ⓑ ADJ [1] (*lit*) caído
[2] (*morally*) [*woman*] perdido; [*angel*] caído
Ⓒ NPL **the ~** (*Mil*) los caídos

fallibility [ˌfælɪˈbɪlɪtɪ] N falibilidad *f*

fallible [ˈfæləbl] ADJ falible

falling [ˈfɔːlɪŋ] Ⓐ ADJ que cae; (*Comm*) en baja
Ⓑ CPD ► **falling star** N estrella *f* fugaz

falling-off [ˈfɔːlɪŋˈɒf] N (*in numbers etc*) disminución *f*; (*in standards*) empeoramiento *m*

falling-out* [ˈfɔːlɪŋˈaʊt] N (= *quarrel*) altercado *m*, pelea *f*; **to have a ~** pelear

Fallopian tube [fəˌləʊpɪənˈtjuːb] N trompa *f* de Falopio

fallout [ˈfɔːlaʊt] Ⓐ N [1] [*of radioactivity*] lluvia *f* radiactiva
[2] (*fig*) consecuencias *fpl*, repercusiones *fpl*
Ⓑ CPD ► **fallout shelter** N refugio *m* atómico *or* nuclear

fallow [ˈfæləʊ] Ⓐ ADJ (*Agr*) en barbecho; (*fig*) [*period*] improductivo; **to lie ~** (*Agr*) estar en barbecho; (*fig*) quedar sin utilizar, no ser utilizado
Ⓑ N (*Agr*) barbecho *m*
Ⓒ CPD ► **fallow deer** N gamo *m*

false [fɔːls] Ⓐ ADJ [1] (= *untruthful*) [*statement, accusation*] falso; (= *mistaken*) [*idea, assumption, accusation*] equivocado; **to give a ~ impression** dar una impresión falsa; **~ move** movimiento *m* en falso; **one ~ move and you're dead** un movimiento en falso y te mato; **~ note** nota *f* falsa; **a ~ sense of security** una falsa sensación de seguridad; **~ step** paso *m* en falso; *see also* **lull, true A1**
[2] (= *deceitful*) **under ~ pretences** con engaños, con insidias; **to extort money under ~ pretences** obtener dinero con engaños *or* insidias; **you came here under ~ pretences** viniste aquí con engaños; **to bear ~ witness** (*esp Bible*) levantar falso testimonio
[3] (= *inappropriate, insincere*) **that was ~ economy** fue un mal ahorro; **to give sb ~ hope(s)** dar falsas esperanzas a algn; **to raise ~ hopes** crear falsas esperanzas; **~ modesty** falsa modestia *f*; **~ pride** falso orgullo *m*; **his words rang ~** sus palabras sonaban a falso; **~ smile** sonrisa *f* forzada
[4] (= *artificial*) [*hair, eyelashes*] postizo; **a suitcase with a ~ bottom** una maleta con doble fondo; **he registered in** *or* **under a ~ name** se registró bajo un nombre falso
[5] (†) (= *disloyal*) [*friend*] desleal, pérfido; (= *unfaithful*) [*lover*] infiel
Ⓑ CPD ► **false alarm** N falsa alarma *f* ► **false arrest** N detención *f* ilegal ► **false ceiling** N cielo *m* raso, falso techo *m* ► **false dawn** N (*fig*) espejismo *m* ► **false friend** N (*Ling*) falso amigo *m* ► **false imprisonment** N (*by police*) detención *f* ilegal; (*by criminal*) retención *f* ilegal ► **false start** N (*Sport*) salida *f* nula; (*fig*) comienzo *m* fallido ► **false teeth**

NPL dentadura *fsing* postiza, dientes *mpl* postizos ► **false tooth** N diente *m* postizo

falsehood ['fɔːlshʊd] N (= *falsity*) falsedad *f*; (= *lie*) mentira *f*

falsely ['fɔːlslɪ] ADV [1] (= *untruthfully*) falsamente; (= *mistakenly*) equivocadamente; **she had ~ claimed that ...** había asegurado falsamente que ...; **he was ~ accused of stealing** (= *untruthfully*) se le acusó falsamente de robo; (= *mistakenly*) se le acusó equivocadamente de robo; **they sometimes test ~ positive** algunas veces dan resultados positivos falsos; **she had been ~ diagnosed with cancer** se equivocaron cuando le diagnosticaron cáncer
[2] (= *insincerely*) fingidamente; **he was being ~ enthusiastic about the idea** se mostró fingidamente entusiasmado con la idea; **she sounded ~ cheerful** parecía fingir la alegría, su alegría sonaba falsa

falseness ['fɔːlsnɪs] N [1] (= *incorrectness*) [*of argument, claim*] falsedad *f*; [*of assumption*] lo equivocado
[2] (= *insincerity*) falsedad *f*
[3] (†) (= *disloyalty*) [*of friend*] deslealtad *f*, perfidia *f*; [*of lover*] infidelidad *f*

falsetto [fɔːl'setəʊ] Ⓐ N falsete *m*
Ⓑ ADJ [*voice*] con falsete
Ⓒ ADV [*sing*] con falsete

falsies* ['fɔːlsɪz] NPL rellenos *mpl*

falsification [ˌfɔːlsɪfɪ'keɪʃən] N falsificación *f*

falsify ['fɔːlsɪfaɪ] VT [+ *document*] falsificar; [+ *evidence*] falsificar, falsear; [+ *accounts, figures*] falsear

falsity ['fɔːlsɪtɪ] N falsedad *f*

falter ['fɔːltəʳ] Ⓐ VI (= *waver*) [*person*] vacilar, titubear; [*voice*] entrecortarse, quebrarse; [*steps*] vacilar; [*courage*] fallar, faltar; **without ~ing** sin vacilar
Ⓑ VT decir titubeando

faltering ['fɔːltərɪŋ] ADJ [*voice*] entrecortado, quebrado; [*step*] vacilante

falteringly ['fɔːltərɪŋlɪ] ADV [*say*] con voz entrecortada, con la voz quebrada

fame [feɪm] N fama *f*; **Margaret Mitchell, of "Gone with the Wind" ~** Margaret Mitchell, famosa por su novela "Lo que el viento se llevó"; **~ and fortune** fama *f* y fortuna *f*

famed [feɪmd] ADJ famoso, afamado

familial [fə'mɪlɪəl] ADJ (*frm*) (= *relating to families*) familiar; (= *typical of families*) de familia

familiar [fə'mɪlɪəʳ] ADJ [1] (= *well-known*) [*face, person, place*] conocido, familiar; **his voice sounds ~** me suena (familiar) su voz; **it doesn't sound ~** no me suena; **to be on ~ ground** (*fig*) estar en su elemento, dominar la materia
[2] (= *common*) [*experience, complaint, event*] corriente, común; **it's a ~ feeling** es un sentimiento común
[3] (= *well-acquainted*) **to be ~ with** estar familiarizado con, conocer; **to make o.s. ~ with** familiarizarse con
[4] (= *intimate*) [*tone of voice etc*] íntimo, de confianza; [*language etc*] familiar; (*pej*) (= *over-intimate*) fresco, que se toma demasiadas confianzas; **to be on ~ terms with sb** tener confianza con algn; **he got too ~** se tomó demasiadas confianzas

familiarity [fəˌmɪlɪ'ærɪtɪ] N [1] [*of sight, event etc*] familiaridad *f*
[2] (= *knowledge, acquaintance*) conocimiento *m* (**with** de); ✦**PROV ~ breeds contempt** donde hay confianza hay asco
[3] (= *intimacy*) [*of tone etc*] familiaridad *f*, confianza *f*; (*pej*) frescura *f*, exceso *m* de familiaridad
[4] **familiarities** familiaridades *fpl*, confianzas *fpl*

familiarize [fə'mɪlɪəraɪz] VT familiarizar (**with** con); **to ~ o.s. with** familiarizarse con

familiarly [fə'mɪlɪəlɪ] ADV con demasiada confianza

family ['fæmɪlɪ] Ⓐ N (= *close relatives, group of animals*) familia *f*; **she's one of the ~** es como de la familia; **do you have any ~?** (= *relatives*) ¿tiene usted parientes?; (= *children*) ¿tiene usted hijos?; **to run in the ~** ser cosa de familia; ✦**IDIOM to be in the ~ way**†* estar en estado de buena esperanza; **to get** *or* **put a girl in the ~ way**†* dejar encinta a una joven
Ⓑ CPD [*jewels*] de la familia; [*dinner, resemblance*] de familia; [*Bible*] familiar ► **family allowance** N (*Brit*) (*formerly*) ≈ ayuda *f* familiar ► **family business** N negocio *m* familiar ► **family butcher** N carnicero *m* doméstico ► **family credit** N (*Brit*) ≈ ayuda *f* familiar ► **Family Division** N (*Brit Jur*) *sala del High Court que entiende de derecho de familia* ► **family doctor** N médico/a *m/f* de cabecera ► **family friend** N amigo/a *m/f* de la familia ► **family hotel** N hotel *m* familiar ► **family income** N ingresos *mpl* familiares ► **family life** N vida *f* doméstica ► **family man** N (= *having family*) padre *m* de familia; (= *home-loving*) hombre *m* casero *or* de su casa ► **family name** N apellido *m* ► **family pet** N animal *m* doméstico ► **family planning** N planificación *f* familiar ► **family planning clinic** N centro *m* de planificación familiar ► **family practice** N (*US Med*) (= *work*) medicina *f* general; (= *place*) consulta *f* ► **family therapy** N terapia *f* familiar ► **family tree** N árbol *m* genealógico

family-size(d) ['fæmɪlɪsaɪz(d)] ADJ [*packet*] (tamaño) familiar

famine ['fæmɪn] Ⓐ N (= *hunger*) hambruna *f*; (= *shortage*) escasez *f*
Ⓑ CPD ► **famine relief** N ayuda *f* contra el hambre

famished* ['fæmɪʃt] ADJ famélico; (*fig*) muerto de hambre

famous ['feɪməs] ADJ famoso, célebre (**for** por); (*hum*) dichoso; **~ last words!*** (*hum*) ¡para qué habré dicho nada!, ¡me hubiera callado mejor! (*LAm*)

famously ['feɪməslɪ] ADV [1] **as Wilde ~ remarked** como bien señalara Wilde; **there have been hurricanes in England, most ~ in 1987** ha habido huracanes en Inglaterra, el más famoso ocurrido en 1987
[2] (†*) (= *very well*) **to get on ~** llevarse a las mil maravillas

fan¹ [fæn] Ⓐ N abanico *m*; (*Agr*) aventador *m*; (= *machine*) ventilador *m*; **electric ~** ventilador *m* eléctrico; ✦**IDIOM when the shit hits the ~**** cuando se arme la gorda*
Ⓑ VT [+ *face, person*] abanicar; (*mechanically*) ventilar; (*Agr*) aventar; [+ *flames*] atizar, avivar; (*fig*) avivar, excitar; **to ~ o.s.** abanicarse, darse aire
Ⓒ CPD ► **fan belt** N (*in motor*) correa *f* del ventilador ► **fan heater** N (*Brit*) calentador *m* de aire, estufa *f* eléctrica (de aire caliente) ► **fan vaulting** N (*Archit*) bóveda *f* de abanico

►**fan out** Ⓐ VT + ADV [+ *cards etc*] ordenar en abanico
Ⓑ VI + ADV (*Mil etc*) desplegarse en abanico, avanzar en abanico

fan² [fæn] Ⓐ N (*gen*) aficionado/a *m/f*; (*Sport*) hincha *mf*, forofo/a *m/f* (*Sp*), adicto/a *m/f* (*LAm*); [*of pop star, etc*] fan *mf*, admirador(a) *m/f*; **the ~s** la afición; **I am not one of his ~s** no soy de sus admiradores, yo no soy de los que lo admiran
Ⓑ CPD ► **fan club** N club *m* de admiradores; (*Mus*) club *m* de fans ► **fan mail** N correspondencia *f* de los admiradores

fanatic [fə'nætɪk] Ⓐ ADJ fanático
Ⓑ N fanático/a *m/f*

fanatical [fə'nætɪkəl] ADJ fanático

fanatically [fə'nætɪklɪ] ADV fanáticamente; **they were ~ loyal to their Emperor** su lealtad hacia el emperador llegaba al fanatismo

fanaticism [fə'nætɪsɪzəm] N fanatismo *m*

fanciable* ['fænsɪəbl] ADJ (*Brit*) guapo, bueno*

fancied ['fænsɪd] ADJ [1] (= *imaginary*) imaginario, ficticio
[2] (*Sport*) [*horse, runner*] favorito

fancier ['fænsɪəʳ] N *see* **pigeon**

fanciful ['fænsɪfʊl] ADJ [*drawings*] fantástico; [*ideas, story, account*] descabalado, rocambolesco; [*person*] imaginativo, fantasioso; [*temperament*] caprichoso; [*imagination*] vivo, rico

▼ **fancy** ['fænsɪ] Ⓐ N [1] (= *liking*) **to catch** *or* **take sb's ~** atraer a algn; **they stole anything that took their ~** robaban cualquier cosa que les gustaba *or* atraía; **I eat whatever takes my ~** como lo que me apetece; **to take a ~ to** [+ *person*] (*amorously*) quedarse prendado de, prendarse de; [+ *thing*] encapricharse con; **he had taken a ~ to one of the secretaries** se había quedado prendado *or* se había prendado de una de las secretarias; **he seems to have taken a ~ to you** parece que le gustas
[2] (= *whim*) capricho *m*, antojo *m*; **a passing ~** un capricho pasajero; **when the ~ takes him** cuando se le antoja; **as the ~ takes her** según su capricho; *see also* **tickle**
[3] (= *imagination*) fantasía *f*, imaginación *f*; **in the realm of ~** en el mundo de la fantasía; *see also* **flight¹**
[4] (= *vague idea*) **I have a ~ that he'll be late** tengo *or* me da la sensación de que llegará tarde
Ⓑ ADJ (*compar* **fancier**, *superl* **fanciest**) [1] (= *elaborate*) muy elaborado; **I like good, plain food, nothing ~** me gusta la buena comida, sencilla, nada muy elaborado *or* nada demasiado historiado; **she uses all these ~ words I don't understand** usa todas esas palabrejas que yo no entiendo; **~ footwork** (*in football, dancing*) filigranas *fpl*, florituras *fpl* (*con los pies*); (*fig*) gran habilidad *f*
[2] (= *elegant*) [*restaurant*] de lujo, muy chic; [*house, car*] lujoso; [*clothes*] elegante, chic
[3] (= *exaggerated*) [*price*] desorbitado; [*idea*] estrambótico
Ⓒ VT [1] (= *imagine*) imaginarse, figurarse; **~ that!*** ¡fíjate!, ¡imagínate!; **~ meeting you here!** ¡qué casualidad encontrarte aquí!; **~ him winning!** ¡qué raro que ganara él!; **~ letting him get away with it!** ¡mira que dejarle salirse con la suya!, ¡mira que dejar que se saliese con la suya!; **~ throwing that away, there's nothing wrong with it** ¡a quién se le ocurre tirar eso! está en perfectas condiciones; **he fancied he saw a glint of amusement in her face** le pareció ver una chispa de diversión en su rostro; **I rather ~ he's gone out** me da la impresión *or* se me hace que ha salido, se me antoja que ha salido (*liter*); **he fancies he knows it all** se cree un pozo de sabiduría
[2] (= *like, want*) [2·1] (*at particular moment*) **what do you ~?** ¿qué quieres tomar?, ¿qué te apetece?; **do you ~ an Indian meal?** ¿te apetece *or* (*LAm*) se te antoja un una comida india?

➤ LANGUAGE IN USE: fancy C2 1.1

2·2 (*in general*) **I've always fancied living there** siempre me hubiese gustado vivir allí; **I don't ~ the idea** no me gusta la idea; **he fancies himself*** es un creído *or* un presumido; **he fancies himself as a bit of an actor*** se piensa que es un actor; **he fancies himself as a footballer*** se las da de futbolista; **he fancies himself as the next prime minister*** se cree que va a ser el próximo primer ministro
3 (*esp Brit**) (= *be attracted to*) **I could tell he fancied me** notaba que le gustaba mucho, notaba que se sentía atraído por mí
4 (= *rate*) **I don't ~ his chances of winning** no creo que tenga muchas posibilidades de ganar; **which horse do you ~ for the Grand National?** ¿qué caballo es tu favorito para el Grand National?; **I ~ England to win** yo creo que ganará Inglaterra
Ⓓ CPD ► **fancy dress** N disfraz *m*; **are you going in ~ dress?** ¿vas a ir disfrazado *or* con disfraz?; **they were wearing ~ dress** iban disfrazados ► **fancy dress ball** N baile *m* de disfraces ► **fancy dress party** N fiesta *f* de disfraces ► **fancy goods** NPL (*Comm*) artículos *mpl* de regalo ► **fancy man**†* N (*pej*) **her ~ man** su amante, su amiguito* ► **fancy woman**†* N (*pej*) **his ~ woman** su querida, su amiguita*

fancy-free ['fænsɪ'fri:] ADJ sin compromiso; *see also* **footloose**

fandango [fæn'dæŋgəʊ] N (*pl* **fandangos**) fandango *m*

fanfare ['fænfɛəʳ] N fanfarria *f*

fanfold paper ['fænfəʊld,peɪpəʳ] N papel *m* plegado en abanico *or* acordeón

fang [fæŋ] N colmillo *m*

fanlight ['fænlaɪt] N montante *m* de abanico

Fanny ['fænɪ] N **1** (*familiar form*) *of* **Frances**
2 **sweet ~ Adams** (*Brit**) nada de nada, na' de na'*

fanny ['fænɪ] N **1** (*Brit***) (= *vagina*) coño** *m*, concha *f* (*LAm***)
2 (*US**) (= *buttocks*) culo* *m*

fan-shaped ['fæn,ʃeɪpt] ADJ de *or* en abanico

fantabulous* [fæn'tæbjʊləs] ADJ superguay*

fantasia [fæn'teɪzɪə] N (*Literat, Mus*) fantasía *f*

fantasist ['fæntəzɪst] N fantaseador(a) *m/f*

fantasize ['fæntəsaɪz] VI fantasear, hacerse ilusiones

fantastic [fæn'tæstɪk] ADJ **1** (*) (= *fabulous, terrific*) [*person, achievement, opportunity, news*] fantástico, estupendo, regio (*LAm**), macanudo (*S. Cone**), chévere (*Col, Ven**); **it's ~ to see you again!** ¡qué alegría verte de nuevo!; **you look ~!** (= *healthy*) ¡qué buen aspecto tienes!; (= *attractive*) ¡qué guapo estás!
2 (*) (= *huge*) [*amount, profit, speed*] increíble
3 (= *exotic*) [*creature, world*] fantástico; [*shapes, images*] extraño
4 (= *improbable*) [*story, idea*] fantástico

fantastical [fæn'tæstɪkl] ADJ (*liter*) fabuloso, fantástico

fantastically [fæn'tæstɪkəlɪ] ADV **1** (= *extraordinarily*) [*expensive, complicated*] increíblemente; **~ learned** enormemente erudito
2 (= *imaginatively*) [*wrought, coloured*] maravillosamente

fantasy ['fæntəzɪ] N **1** (= *imagination*) fantasía *f*; **to live in a ~ world** *or* **in ~ land** vivir en un mundo de ensueño
2 (= *fanciful idea, wish*) fantasía *f*, sueño *m*

fanzine ['fænzi:n] N fanzine *m*

FAO N ABBR (= **Food and Agriculture Organization**) OAA *f*, FAO *f*

FAQ Ⓐ ABBR (*Comm*) = **free alongside quay**
Ⓑ N ABBR (*Comput*) = **Frequently Asked Question(s)**; **~ (file)** fichero *m* de preguntas frecuentes

faq ABBR = **of fair average quality**

far [fɑ:ʳ] (*compar* **farther**, **further**; *superl* **farthest**, **furthest**) Ⓐ ADV **1** (*distance*) (*lit, fig*) lejos, a lo lejos; **is it ~ (away)?** ¿está lejos?; **is it ~ to London?** ¿hay mucho hasta Londres?; **it's not ~ (from here)** no está lejos (de aquí); **~ away** *or* **off** lejos; **~ away** *or* **off in the distance** a lo lejos; **not ~ away** *or* **off** no muy lejos; **~ away from one's family** lejos de la familia; **~ beyond** mucho más allá de; **how ~ is it to the river?** ¿qué distancia *or* cuánto hay de aquí al río?; **how ~ have you got with your work/plans?** ¿hasta dónde has llegado en tu trabajo/tus planes?; **to walk ~ into the hills** penetrar profundamente en los montes; **~ into the night** hasta altas horas de la noche; **from ~ and near** de todas partes; **Christmas is not ~ off** la Navidad no está lejos; **he's not ~ off 70** tiene casi 70 años, frisa en los 70 años; **she was not ~ off tears** estaba al borde de las lágrimas; **~ out at sea** en alta mar; **our calculations are ~ out** nuestros cálculos yerran *or* se equivocan por mucho; **so ~** (*in distance*) tan lejos; (*in time*) hasta ahora; **so ~ this year** en lo que va del año; **so ~ so good** por *or* hasta ahora, bien; **in so ~ as ...** en la medida en que ..., en cuanto ...; **so** *or* **thus ~ and no further** hasta aquí, pero ni un paso más; **a bridge too ~** un puente de más; **the plans are too ~ advanced** los proyectos están demasiado adelantados; **~ and wide** por todas partes; **he wasn't ~ wrong** *or* **off** *or* **out** casi acertaba, casi estaba en lo justo
2 **as ~ as** hasta; **as ~ as the eye can see** hasta donde alcanza la vista; **to go as ~ as Milan** ir hasta Milán; **to come from as ~ away as Milan** venir de sitios tan lejanos como Milán; **she climbed as ~ as the rest of the team** escaló tanto como el resto del grupo; **as ~ back as I can remember** hasta donde me alcanza la memoria; **as ~ back as 1945** ya en 1945; **as ~ as possible** en lo posible; **the theory is good as ~ as it goes** la teoría es buena dentro de sus límites; **I will help you as ~ as I can** te ayudaré en lo que pueda; **as** *or* **so ~ as I know** que yo sepa; **as** *or* **so ~ as I am concerned** por lo que a mí se refiere *or* respecta; **I would go as** *or* **so ~ as to say that ...** me atrevería a decir que ...
3 **~ from** [+ *place*] lejos de; **~ from approving it, I ...** lejos de aprobarlo, yo ...; **~ from it!** ¡todo lo contrario!, ¡ni mucho menos!; **he is ~ from well** no está nada bien; **~ be it from me to interfere, but ...** no quiero entrometerme, pero ...; **~ from easy** nada fácil
4 **to go ~**: **how ~ are you going?** ¿hasta dónde vas?; **he'll go ~** (*fig*) llegará lejos; **it doesn't go ~ enough** (*fig*) no va bastante lejos, no tiene todo el alcance que quisiéramos; **he's gone too ~ this time** (*fig*) esta vez se ha pasado; **he's gone too ~ to back out now** (*fig*) ha ido demasiado lejos para echarse atrás *or* retirarse ahora; **it won't go ~** [*money, food*] no alcanzará mucho; **for a white wine you won't go ~ wrong with this** si buscas un vino blanco éste ofrece bastante garantía; ♦**IDIOM** **he was ~ gone*** (= *ill*) estaba muy acabado; (= *drunk*) estaba muy borracho
5 (= *very much*) mucho; **~ better** mucho mejor; **it is ~ better not to go** más vale no ir; **it's ~ and away the best** ◊ **it's by ~ the best** es con mucho el mejor; **she's the prettier by ~** es con mucho la más guapa; **this car is ~ faster (than)** este coche es mucho más rápido (que); **~ superior to** muy superior a
Ⓑ ADJ **the ~ east** *etc* **of the country** el extremo este *etc* del país; **the ~ left/right** (*Pol*) la extrema izquierda/derecha; **at the ~ end of** en el otro extremo de, al fondo de; **on the ~ side of** en el lado opuesto de; ♦**IDIOM** **it's a ~ cry from** tiene poco que ver con
Ⓒ CPD ► **the Far East** N el Extremo *or* Lejano Oriente ► **the Far North** N el Polo Norte

farad ['færəd] N faradio *m*

faraway ['fɑ:rəweɪ] ADJ **1** [*place*] remoto, lejano
2 (*fig*) [*voice*] distraído; [*look*] ausente, perdido

farce [fɑ:s] N **1** (*Theat*) farsa *f*
2 (*fig*) absurdo *m*; **this is a ~** esto es absurdo; **what a ~ this is!** ¡qué follón!; **the trial was a ~** el proceso fue una farsa

farcical ['fɑ:sɪkəl] ADJ absurdo, ridículo

far-distant ['fɑ:'dɪstənt] ADJ lejano, remoto

fare [fɛəʳ] Ⓐ N **1** (= *cost*) precio *m*, tarifa *f*; (= *ticket*) billete *m*, boleto *m* (*LAm*); (*Naut*) pasaje *m*; **"~s please!"** (*on bus*) "¡billetes por favor!"
2 (= *passenger in taxi*) pasajero/a *m/f*
3 (*frm*) (= *food*) comida *f*; *see also* **bill¹**
Ⓑ VI **they ~d badly/well** lo pasaron mal/bien, les fue mal/bien; **how did you ~?** ¿qué tal te fue?; **to ~ alike** correr la misma suerte
Ⓒ CPD ► **fare stage**, **fare zone** (*US*) N (*on bus*) zona *f* de tarifa fija

Far Eastern ['fɑ:r'i:stən] ADJ del Extremo Oriente

farewell [fɛə'wel] Ⓐ N adiós *m*; (= *ceremony*) despedida *f*; **to bid ~ (to sb)** despedirse (de algn); **to say one's ~s** despedirse; **you can say ~ to your wallet** (*fig*) te puedes ir despidiendo de tu cartera
Ⓑ EXCL (*liter*) ¡adiós!
Ⓒ CPD ► **farewell dinner** N cena *f* de despedida ► **farewell party** N fiesta *f* de despedida

far-fetched ['fɑ:'fetʃt] ADJ [*story, explanation*] inverosímil, poco probable; [*idea, scheme*] descabellado

far-flung ['fɑ:flʌŋ] ADJ extenso

farinaceous [,færɪ'neɪʃəs] ADJ farináceo

farm [fɑ:m] Ⓐ N granja *f*, chacra *f* (*LAm*); (= *large*) hacienda *f*, finca *f*, estancia *f* (*LAm*), rancho *m* (*Mex*); [*of mink, oysters etc*] criadero *m*; (= *buildings*) alquería *f*, casa *f* de labranza, quinta *f*, ranchería *f* (*Mex*); *see also* **dairy**
Ⓑ VT cultivar, labrar; **he ~s 300 acres** cultiva 300 acres
Ⓒ VI (*as profession*) ser granjero; **he ~s in Devon** tiene una granja en Devon
Ⓓ CPD agrícola ► **farm labourer**, **farm laborer** (*US*) N jornalero/a *m/f* (del campo), obrero/a *m/f* agrícola ► **farm produce** N productos *mpl* agrícolas ► **farm tractor** N tractor *m* ► **farm worker** N = **farm labourer**

► **farm out*** VT + ADV [+ *work*] mandar hacer fuera (**to sb** a algn); (*hum*) [+ *children*] dejar (**on** a *or* con)

farmer ['fɑ:məʳ] N agricultor(a) *m/f*, granjero/a *m/f*, chacarero/a *m/f* (*LAm*); [*of large farm*] hacendado/a *m/f*, estanciero/a *m/f* (*LAm*), ranchero/a *m/f* (*Mex*)

farmhand ['fɑ:mhænd] N obrero/a *m/f* agrícola, jornalero/a *m/f* (del campo)

farmhouse ['fɑ:mhaʊs] N (*pl* **farmhouses** ['fɑ:mhaʊzɪz]) alquería *f*, casa *f* de labranza, caserío *m* (*Sp*), casa *f* grande (*LAm*), casa *f* de hacienda (*LAm*)

farming ['fɑ:mɪŋ] Ⓐ N (*gen*) agricultura *f*; [*of land*] cultivo *m*; [*of animals*] cría *f*; **good ~**

➤ LANGUAGE IN USE: far A2 26.2

practice técnicas *fpl* agrícolas reconocidas
(B) CPD agrícola ► **the farming community** N los agricultores ► **farming methods** NPL métodos *mpl* de cultivo

farmland [ˈfɑːmlænd] N tierras *fpl* de labranza *or* cultivo

farmstead [ˈfɑːmsted] N alquería *f*, casa *f* de labranza

farmyard [ˈfɑːmjɑːd] N corral *m*

Faroe Islands [ˈfɛərəʊˌaɪləndz], **Faroes** [ˈfɛərəʊz] NPL Islas *fpl* Feroe

far-off [ˈfɑːrˈɒf] ADJ lejano, remoto

far-out* [ˌfɑːrˈaʊt] ADJ [1] (= *odd*) raro, extraño; (= *zany*) estrafalario
[2] (= *modern*) muy moderno, de vanguardia
[3] (= *superb*) guay*, fenomenal*

farrago [fəˈrɑːgəʊ] N (*pl* **farragos** *or* **farragoes**) fárrago *m*

far-reaching [ˈfɑːˈriːtʃɪŋ] ADJ [*effect*] transcendental, de gran alcance

farrier [ˈfærɪəʳ] N (*esp Brit*) herrador(a) *m/f*

farrow [ˈfærəʊ] (A) N lechigada *f* de puercos
(B) VT parir
(C) VI parir (la cerda)

far-seeing [ˈfɑːˈsiːɪŋ] ADJ clarividente, previsor

far-sighted [ˈfɑːˈsaɪtɪd] ADJ [1] (*US Med*) hipermétrope
[2] (*fig*) [*person*] clarividente; [*plan, decision, measure*] con visión de futuro

far-sightedly [ˈfɑːˈsaɪtɪdlɪ] ADV de modo clarividente, con visión de futuro

far-sightedness [ˈfɑːˈsaɪtɪdnɪs] N [1] (*US Med*) hipermetropía *f*, presbicia *f*
[2] (*fig*) clarividencia *f*, visión *f* de futuro

fart‡ [fɑːt] (A) N [1] pedo‡ *m*
[2] **he's a boring old ~** es un tío pesadísimo*, es un pelmazo*
(B) VI tirarse *or* echarse un pedo‡

► **fart about‡**, **fart around‡** VI + ADV *see* **mess about B**

farther [ˈfɑːðəʳ] (A) ADV = **further**
(B) ADJ COMPAR *of* **far**; **she was sitting at the ~ end of the bar** estaba sentada al otro extremo de la barra; **on the ~ side of the lake** al otro lado del lago, en la otra orilla del lago

farthest [ˈfɑːðɪst] SUPERL *of* **far** *see* **furthest**

farthing [ˈfɑːðɪŋ] N cuarto *m* de penique

FAS ABBR = **free alongside ship**

fascia [ˈfeɪʃə] N [1] (*on building*) faja *f* [2] (*for mobile phone*) carcasa *f* [3] (*Brit: Aut*) tablero *m*

fascicle [ˈfæsɪkl] N, **fascicule** [ˈfæsɪkjuːl] N fascículo *m*

fascinate [ˈfæsɪneɪt] VT fascinar; **it ~s me how/why …** me maravilla cómo/por qué …

fascinated [ˈfæsɪneɪtɪd] ADJ fascinado; **to be ~ with sth** estar fascinado por algo

fascinating [ˈfæsɪneɪtɪŋ] ADJ fascinante

fascination [ˌfæsɪˈneɪʃən] N fascinación *f*; **his ~ with the cinema** su fascinación por el cine

fascism [ˈfæʃɪzəm] N fascismo *m*

fascist [ˈfæʃɪst] (A) ADJ fascista
(B) N fascista *mf*

fashion [ˈfæʃən] (A) N [1] (= *manner*) manera *f*, modo *m*; **after a ~** así así, más o menos; **I play after a ~** toco algo; **after the ~ of** a la manera de; **in his usual ~** a su manera *or* modo; **in one's own ~** a su propio modo; **in the Greek ~** a la griega, al estilo griego; **it is not my ~ to pretend** (*frm*) yo no acostumbro fingir
[2] (= *vogue*) (*in clothing, speech etc*) moda *f*; **it's all the ~ now** ahora está muy de moda; **it's no longer the ~** ya no está de moda; **it's the ~ to say that …** es un tópico decir que …; **to be in/out of ~** estar de moda/pasado de moda; **to come into/go out of ~** ponerse de/pasar de moda; **to set a ~ for sth** imponer la moda de algo; **the latest ~** la última moda; **the new Spring ~s** la nueva moda de primavera; **women's/men's ~s** moda para la mujer/el hombre
[3] (= *good taste*) buen gusto *m*; **what ~ demands** lo que impone el buen gusto; **a man of ~** un hombre elegante
(B) VT (= *shape*) formar; (= *make*) fabricar; (= *mould*) moldear; (= *design*) diseñar
(C) CPD ► **fashion designer** N modisto/a *m/f*, diseñador(a) *m/f* de modas ► **fashion editor** N director(a) *m/f* de revista de modas ► **fashion house** N casa *f* de modas ► **fashion magazine** N revista *f* de modas ► **fashion model** N modelo *mf* ► **fashion page** N sección *f* de modas ► **fashion parade** N desfile *m* *or* pase *m* de modelos ► **fashion plate** N figurín *m* de moda ► **fashion show** N = **fashion parade** ► **fashion victim*** N esclavo/a *m/f* de la moda

fashionable [ˈfæʃnəbl] ADJ [1] [*dress etc*] de moda, moderno, a la moda; [*place, restaurant*] de moda; **~ people** gente *f* elegante, gente *f* guapa*; **in ~ society** en la buena sociedad; **it is ~ to do …** está de moda hacer …
[2] (= *popular*) [*writer, subject for discussion*] de moda, popular; **he is hardly a ~ painter now** es un pintor que no está ahora muy de moda

fashionably [ˈfæʃnəblɪ] ADV **to be ~ dressed** ir vestido a la moda

fashion-conscious [ˈfæʃənˌkɒnʃəs] ADJ pendiente de la moda

fast¹ [fɑːst] (A) ADJ (*compar* **faster**; *superl* **fastest**) [1] (= *speedy*) rápido; (*Phot*) [*film*] de alta sensibilidad; **he's a ~ worker** es un trabajador (muy) rápido; **he's a ~ talker*** es un pretencioso; **he was too ~ for me** corrió más que yo; (*fig*) se me adelantó; **~ and furious** vertiginoso; ✦*IDIOM* **to pull a ~ one on sb*** jugar una mala pasada a algn
[2] [*clock*] adelantado; **my watch is five minutes ~** mi reloj está *or* va cinco minutos adelantado
[3] (*Sport*) [*pitch*] seco y firme; [*court*] rápido
[4] (= *dissipated*) [*person*] lanzado, fresco; [*life*] disoluto, disipado
[5] (= *firm*) fijo, firme; **to make sth ~** sujetar algo; **to make a rope ~** atar bien una cuerda; **to make a boat ~** amarrar una barca; **~ friends** íntimos amigos
[6] [*colour, dye*] que no destiñe
(B) ADV [1] (= *quickly*) rápidamente, deprisa; **as ~ as I can** lo más rápido posible; **he ran off as ~ as his legs would carry him** se fue corriendo a toda velocidad; **how ~ can you type?** ¿a qué velocidad escribes a máquina?; **don't speak so ~** habla más despacio; **~er!** ¡más (rápido)!; **not so ~!*** (*interrupting*) ¡un momento!; **he'll do it ~ enough if you offer him money** se dará más prisa si le ofreces dinero; **the rain was falling ~** llovía mucho; **as ~ as I finished them he wrapped them up** a medida que yo los terminaba él los envolvía; ✦*IDIOM* **to play ~ and loose with** jugar con
[2] (= *firmly*) firmemente; **~ asleep** profundamente dormido; **to hold ~** agarrarse bien; (*fig*) mantenerse firme; **to stand ~** mantenerse firme; **tie it ~** átalo bien; **it's stuck ~** está bien pegado; [*door*] está atrancado *or* atascado; **to be stuck ~ in the mud** quedar atascado en el lodo; **to be stuck ~ in a doorway** haberse quedado atascado en una puerta
(C) CPD ► **fast food** N comida *f* rápida, platos *mpl* preparados ► **fast food restaurant** N establecimiento *m* *or* restaurante *m* de comida rápida; (*selling hamburgers*) hamburguesería *f* ► **fast track** N (*fig*) vía *f* rápida; **to be on the ~ track to sth** ir por la vía rápida hacia algo ► **fast train** N tren *m* rápido, ≈ Intercity *m* (*Sp*), ≈ Talgo *m* (*Sp*); *see also* **lane**, **fast-track**

fast² [fɑːst] (A) N ayuno *m*; **to break one's ~** (*frm*) interrumpir el ayuno
(B) VI ayunar
(C) CPD ► **fast day** N día *m* de ayuno

fasten [ˈfɑːsn] (A) VT [1] (= *secure*) [+ *belt, dress, seat belt*] abrochar; [+ *door, box, window*] cerrar; (*with rope*) atar; (*with paste*) pegar; (*with bolt*) echar el cerrojo a; **to ~ two things together** pegar/sujetar dos cosas
[2] (= *attach*) sujetar; (*fig*) atribuir; **to ~ the blame/responsibility (for sth) on sb** echar la culpa/atribuir la responsabilidad (de algo) a algn; **they're trying to ~ the crime on me** tratan de achacarme *or* atribuirme el crimen a mí
(B) VI [*door, box*] cerrarse; [*dress*] abrocharse; **it ~s in front** se abrocha por delante

► **fasten down** VT + ADV [+ *envelope, blind etc*] cerrar

► **fasten on** (A) VT + ADV (= *tie*) atar
(B) VT + PREP *see* **fasten (up)on**
(C) VI + PREP *see* **fasten (up)on**

► **fasten on to** VI + PREP agarrarse de, pegarse a; (*fig*) fijarse en; **he ~ed on to me at once** se fijó en mí en seguida; (*as companion*) se me pegó en seguida; **to ~ on to a pretext** echar mano *or* valerse de un pretexto

► **fasten up** (A) VT + ADV [+ *clothing*] abrochar
(B) VI + ADV **it ~s up in front** se abrocha por delante

► **fasten (up)on** (A) VT + PREP [+ *gaze*] fijar en
(B) VI + PREP [+ *excuse*] valerse de; **to ~ (up)on the idea of doing sth** aferrarse a la idea de hacer algo

fastener [ˈfɑːsnəʳ] N [*of necklace, bag, box*] cierre *m*; (*on dress*) corchete *m*; (*for papers*) grapa *f*; (= *zip fastener*) cremallera *f*

fastening [ˈfɑːsnɪŋ] N = **fastener**

fast forward [ˈfɑːstˈfɔːwəd] (A) N (*also* **~ button**) botón *m* de avance rápido
(B) VT pasar para delante, adelantar
(C) VI avanzar rápidamente

fastidious [fæsˈtɪdɪəs] ADJ [*person*] (*about cleanliness etc*) escrupuloso; (= *touchy*) quisquilloso; [*taste*] fino

fastidiously [fæsˈtɪdɪəslɪ] ADV [*examine, clean, check*] meticulosamente, quisquillosamente

fastidiousness [fæsˈtɪdɪəsnɪs] N meticulosidad *f*, exigencia *f*

fast-moving [ˌfɑːstˈmuːvɪŋ] ADJ rápido, veloz; [*target*] que cambia rápidamente de posición; [*goods*] de venta rápida, que se venden rápidamente; [*plot*] muy movido, lleno de acciones, que se desarrolla rápidamente

fastness [ˈfɑːstnɪs] N (= *stronghold*) fortaleza *f*; [*of mountain etc*] lo más intrincado; **in their Cuban mountain ~** en las espesuras serranas de Cuba

fast-track [ˈfɑːsttræk] ADJ rápido, por la vía rápida

fat [fæt] (A) ADJ (*compar* **fatter**; *superl* **fattest**) [1] (= *plump*) [*person*] gordo; [*face, cheeks, limbs*] relleno, gordo; **to get ~** engordar; **he grew ~ on the proceeds** *or* **profits** (*fig*) se enriqueció con los beneficios; ✦*IDIOM* **it's not over till the ~ lady sings*** mientras hay vida, hay esperanza, hasta el rabo todo es toro*
[2] (= *fatty*) [*meat, pork*] graso; **~ bacon** tocino *m* graso, tocino *m* con mucha grasa

3 (= *thick*) [*book*] grueso
4 (= *substantial*) [*profit*] grande, pingüe; [*salary*] muy elevado, muy alto; **a ~ cheque** un cheque muy cuantioso; **the ~ years** los años de las vacas gordas
5 (*) (= *minimal*) **~ chance!** ¡ni soñarlo!; **a ~ lot he knows about it!** ¡qué sabrá él!; **a ~ lot of good that is!** ¡eso no sirve de nada!, y eso ¿de qué sirve?
Ⓑ N (*on person, in food*) grasa *f*; (*for cooking*) manteca *f*; **he needs to get rid of that excess ~** necesita eliminar toda esa grasa que le sobra; **a short, middle-aged man, tending to ~** un hombre bajito, de mediana edad, más bien gordo; **animal/vegetable ~s** grasas *fpl* animales/vegetales; **beef/chicken ~** grasa *f* de vaca *or* (*Sp*) ternera/de pollo; **fry in deep ~** freír en aceite abundante; **double cream is 48 per cent ~** la nata para montar tiene un 48 por ciento de materia grasa; ✦*IDIOMS* **now the ~'s in the fire** se va a armar la gorda*; **to live off the ~ of the land** vivir a cuerpo de rey; *see also* **body B**
Ⓒ CPD ► **fat cat*** N pez *m* gordo* ► **fat content** N contenido *m* de materia grasa; **it has a very high ~ content** tiene un contenido muy alto de materia grasa ► **fat farm*** N (*US*) clínica *f* de adelgazamiento

fatal ['feɪtl] Ⓐ ADJ 1 (= *causing death*) [*accident, injury*] mortal
2 (= *disastrous*) [*mistake*] fatal; [*consequences*] funesto (**to** para); **it's ~ to mention that** es peligrosísimo mencionar eso
3 (= *fateful*) fatídico
Ⓑ CPD ► **fatal accident enquiry** N (*Scot*) *investigación sobre las causas de un accidente mortal*

fatalism ['feɪtəlɪzəm] N fatalismo *m*

fatalist ['feɪtəlɪst] N fatalista *mf*

fatalistic [ˌfeɪtə'lɪstɪk] ADJ fatalista

fatality [fə'tælɪtɪ] N 1 (= *death*) muerte *f*
2 (= *victim*) muerto/a *m/f*, víctima *f*; **luckily there were no fatalities** por fortuna no hubo víctimas

fatally ['feɪtəlɪ] ADV mortalmente; **~ wounded** herido mortalmente *or* de muerte

fat-cat* ['fætkæt] ADJ **a ~ industrialist** un opulento industrial

fate [feɪt] N 1 (= *destiny*) destino *m*; **what ~ has in store for us** lo que nos guarda *or* depara el destino; **~ decided otherwise** el destino no lo quiso así
2 (= *person's lot*) suerte *f*; **to leave sb to his ~** abandonar a algn a su suerte; **this sealed his ~** esto acabó de perderle; **to meet one's ~** (= *die*) encontrar la muerte; **Italy could suffer the same ~ as India** Italia podría correr la misma suerte que la India, a Italia le podría pasar lo mismo que a la India; **that's a ~ worse than death** no hay cosa peor
3 **the Fates** (*Myth*) las Parcas

fated ['feɪtɪd] ADJ (= *governed by fate*) [*person, project, friendship etc*] predestinado; (= *doomed*) condenado; **to be ~ to do sth** estar predestinado a hacer algo; **it was ~ that ...** era inevitable que ...

fateful ['feɪtfʊl] ADJ [*day, event*] fatídico; [*words*] profético

fat-free ['fætfriː] ADJ [*diet, food*] sin grasa

fathead* ['fæthed] N imbécil *mf*; **you ~!** ¡imbécil!

fat-headed* ['fæt,hedɪd] ADJ imbécil

father ['fɑːðəʳ] Ⓐ N 1 (*gen*) padre *m*; **to talk to sb like a ~** hablar a algn en tono paternal; **to be passed on** *or* **handed down from ~ to son** pasar de padre a hijo; **my ~ and mother** mis padres; ✦*IDIOM* **a ~ and mother of a row*** una bronca fenomenal* *or* de padre y muy señor mío*; ✦*PROV* **like ~ like son** de tal palo, tal astilla
2 **Our Father** (*Rel*) Padre Nuestro; **to say three Our Fathers** rezar tres padrenuestros
3 **Father Brown** (*Rel*) (el) padre Brown
4 (*fig*) (= *founder*) padre *m*; **the ~ of English poetry** el padre de la poesía inglesa; **the Fathers of the Church** los Santos Padres de la Iglesia; *see also* **city B**
Ⓑ VT [+ *child*] engendrar; (*fig*) inventar, producir
Ⓒ CPD ► **Father Christmas** N (*Brit*) Papá *m* Noel ► **father confessor** N (*Rel*) confesor *m*, padre *m or* director *m* espiritual ► **Father's Day** N Día *m* del Padre ► **father figure** N figura *f* paterna ► **(Old) Father Time** N el Tiempo

fatherhood ['fɑːðəhʊd] N paternidad *f*

father-in-law ['fɑːðərɪnlɔː] N (*pl* **fathers-in-law**) suegro *m*

fatherland ['fɑːðəlænd] N patria *f*

fatherless ['fɑːðəlɪs] ADJ huérfano de padre

fatherly ['fɑːðəlɪ] ADJ [*person*] paternal; [*advice, behaviour*] paterno

fathom ['fæðəm] Ⓐ N braza *f*; **water five ~s deep** agua de una profundidad de cinco brazas
Ⓑ VT 1 (*Naut*) sond(e)ar
2 (*fig*) (*also* **~ out**) descifrar, llegar a entender; [+ *mystery*] desentrañar; **I can't ~ why** no me explico por qué; **I can't ~ him/it out at all** no le/lo entiendo en absoluto

fathomless ['fæðəmlɪs] ADJ insondable

fatigue [fə'tiːg] Ⓐ N 1 (= *weariness*) cansancio *m*, fatiga *f*; *see also* **battle D**
2 (*Tech*) fatiga *f*; *see also* **metal**
3 (*Mil*) faena *f*, fajina *f*; **fatigues** traje *msing* de faena
Ⓑ VT fatigar, cansar
Ⓒ CPD ► **fatigue dress** N = **fatigues** ► **fatigue duty** N (*Mil*) servicio *m* de fajina ► **fatigue party** N (*Mil*) destacamento *m* de fajina

fatigued [fə'tiːgd] ADJ fatigado

fatiguing [fə'tiːgɪŋ] ADJ fatigoso

fatless ['fætlɪs] ADJ [*food*] sin grasa

fatness ['fætnɪs] N [*of person*] gordura *f*; [*of meat*] grasa *f*; [*of book*] grosor *m*

fatso* ['fætsəʊ] N (*pl* **fatsos** *or* **fatsoes**) (*pej*) gordo/a *m/f*

fatstock ['fætstɒk] N (*Agr*) animales *mpl* de engorde

fatten ['fætn] Ⓐ VT (*also* **~ up**) [+ *animal*] cebar, engordar
Ⓑ VI engordar

fattening ['fætnɪŋ] Ⓐ ADJ [*food*] que hace engordar; **chocolate is ~** el chocolate engorda
Ⓑ N (*Agr*) engorde *m*

fatty ['fætɪ] Ⓐ ADJ 1 [*food*] graso
2 (*Anat*) [*tissue*] adiposo
Ⓑ N (* *pej*) gordo/a *m/f*; **~!** ¡gordo!
Ⓒ CPD ► **fatty acid** N ácido *m* graso

fatuity [fə'tjuːɪtɪ] N necedad *f*, fatuidad *f*

fatuous ['fætjʊəs] ADJ [*remark*] necio, fatuo; [*smile*] tonto

fatuously ['fætjʊəslɪ] ADV neciamente

fatuousness ['fætjʊəsnɪs] N necedad *f*, fatuidad *f*

fatwa ['fætwə] N fatwa *f*

faucet ['fɔːsɪt] N (*US*) (= *tap*) grifo *m*, llave *f*, canilla *f* (*LAm*)

▼ **fault** [fɔːlt] Ⓐ N 1 (= *defect*) (*in character*) defecto *m*; (*in manufacture*) defecto *m*, falla *f* (*LAm*); (*in supply, machine*) avería *f*; **with all his ~s** con todos sus defectos; **her ~ is excessive shyness** peca de tímida; **generous to a ~** excesivamente generoso; **to find ~** poner reparos; **to find ~ with sth/sb** criticar algo/a algn
2 (= *blame, responsibility*) culpa *f*; **it's all your ~** tú tienes toda la culpa; **it's not my ~** no es culpa mía; **you were at ~ in not telling us** hiciste mal en no decírnoslo; **your memory is at ~** no te acuerdas bien; **you were not at ~** no por culpa suya; **through no ~ of his own** sin falta alguna de su parte; **whose ~ is it (if ...)?** ¿quién tiene la culpa (si ...)?
3 (*Tennis*) falta *f*
4 (*Geol*) falla *f*
Ⓑ VT criticar; **it cannot be ~ed** es intachable; **you cannot ~ him on spelling** su ortografía es impecable

fault-finder ['fɔːlt,faɪndəʳ] N criticón/ona *m/f*

fault-finding ['fɔːlt,faɪndɪŋ] Ⓐ ADJ criticón, reparón
Ⓑ N manía *f* de criticar

faultless ['fɔːltlɪs] ADJ [*person, behaviour*] intachable, impecable; [*appearance, clothing, logic*] impecable; [*work, performance*] perfecto; **Hans's English was ~** Hans hablaba un inglés perfecto

faultlessly ['fɔːltlɪslɪ] ADV [*dress*] impecablemente; [*perform, recite*] perfectamente

faulty ['fɔːltɪ] ADJ (*compar* **faultier**; *superl* **faultiest**) 1 [*machine etc*] defectuoso
2 (= *imperfect*) [*reasoning, argument etc*] imperfecto

faun [fɔːn] N fauno *m*

fauna ['fɔːnə] N (*pl* **faunas** *or* **faunae**) fauna *f*

Faust [faʊst] N Fausto

Faustian ['faʊstɪən] ADJ de Fausto

faux pas ['fəʊ'pɑː] N metedura *f or* (*LAm*) metida *f* de pata*

fava bean ['fɑːvəbiːn] N (*US*) haba *f*

▼ **favour**, **favor** (*US*) ['feɪvəʳ] Ⓐ N 1 (= *kindness*) favor *m*; **I don't expect any ~s in return** no espero que me devuelvas/devuelvan *etc* el favor; **he did it as a ~ (to me)** (me) lo hizo como un favor; **to ask a ~ of sb** pedir un favor a algn; **to do sb a ~** hacer un favor a algn; **do me the ~ of closing the door** ¿me hace el favor de cerrar la puerta?; **do me a ~!*** (*iro*) ¡haz el favor! (*iro*); **do me a ~ and clear off*** ¡haz el favor de largarte!*; **do yourself a ~ and get a haircut** si te cortas el pelo te harás un favor; **those suits you wear do you no ~s** esos trajes que te pones no te favorecen nada
2 (= *approval*) **to curry ~ with sb** tratar de ganar el favor de algn; **to fall from ~** [*person*] caer en desgracia; [*product, style*] perder aceptación; **to find ~ with sb** [*person*] ganarse la aceptación de algn; [*suggestion, product, style*] tener buena acogida por parte de algn, ser bien acogido por algn; **to gain ~ with sb** ganarse la aceptación de algn; **to be in ~ with sb** [*person*] gozar del favor de algn; [*product, style*] gozar de la aceptación de algn; **to lose ~** perder aceptación; **he's currently out of ~ with the prime minister** actualmente no goza del favor del primer ministro; **British companies are clearly out of ~** se ve claramente que las compañías británicas no tienen aceptación; **to fall out of ~** [*person*] caer en desgracia; [*product, style*] perder aceptación; **to win sb's ~** ganarse la aceptación de algn; **his proposals were not looked upon with ~** sus propuestas no fueron consideradas favorablemente

3 (= *support, advantage*) favor *m*; **to be in ~ of (doing) sth** estar a favor de (hacer) algo, ser partidario de (hacer) algo; **he is in ~ of the death penalty** está a favor de *or* es partidario de la pena de muerte; **I am in ~ of selling the house** soy partidario de *or* estoy a favor de vender la casa; **the result of the vote was 111 in ~ and 25 against** el resultado de la votación fue 111 votos a favor y 25 en contra; **the traffic lights are in our ~** los semáforos están a favor nuestro; **it's in our ~ to act now** nos beneficia actuar ahora; **a cheque made out in ~ of** un cheque extendido a nombre de; **the court found in their ~** el tribunal falló a *or* en su favor; **"balance in your favour"** "saldo *m* a su favor"; **that's a point in his ~** es un punto a su favor
4 (= *favouritism*) favoritismo *m*; **to show ~ to sb** favorecer a algn, tratar a algn con favoritismo
5 **your ~ of the 5th inst†** (*Comm*) su atenta del 5 del corriente
6 (*Hist*) (= *token*) prenda *f*, favor† *m*
7 **favours** (*euph*) (*sexual*) favores *mpl*
Ⓑ VT 1 (= *support*) [+ *idea, scheme, view*] estar a favor de, ser partidario de; **he ~s higher taxes** está a favor de *or* es partidario de impuestos más elevados
2 (= *be beneficial to*) favorecer; **the scholarship programme ~s boys** el programa de becas favorece a los chicos; **circumstances that ~ this scheme** circunstancias *fpl* que favorecen este plan, circunstancias *fpl* propicias para este plan
3 (= *prefer, like*) preferir; **they ~ British-made cars** prefieren los coches de fabricación británica
4 (= *treat with favouritism*) tratar con favoritismo
5 (*frm*) (= *honour*) **to ~ sb with sth** honrar a algn con algo; **he eventually ~ed us with a visit** (*hum*) por fin nos honró con su visita, por fin se dignó a visitarnos
6 (= *resemble*) parecerse a, salir a; **he ~s his father** se parece a su padre, sale a su padre
7 (= *protect*) [+ *injured limb*] tener cuidado con
8 (*Sport*) **he is ~ed to win** es el favorito para ganar

favourable, favorable (*US*) [ˈfeɪvərəbl] ADJ [*report*] favorable (**to** para); [*conditions, weather*] propicio, favorable; **to show sb in a ~ light** dar una buena imagen de algn

favourably, favorably (*US*) [ˈfeɪvərəblɪ] ADV favorablemente

favoured, favored (*US*) [ˈfeɪvəd] ADJ [*person, object*] favorito, preferido; **Biarritz was their ~ resort** Biarritz era su lugar de vacaciones favorito *or* preferido; **the ~ method is …** el método preferido es …; **one of the ~ few** uno de los pocos afortunados; **most ~ nation treatment** trato *m* de nación más favorecida

▼ **favourite, favorite** (*US*) [ˈfeɪvərɪt] Ⓐ ADJ favorito, preferido
Ⓑ N 1 (= *object*) favorito/a *m/f*; (= *person*) preferido/a *m/f*, favorito/a *m/f*; (*spoilt*) consentido/a *m/f*; (*at court*) valido *m*, privado *m*; (= *mistress*) querida *f*; **he sang some old ~s** cantó algunas de las viejas y conocidas canciones
2 (*in race, contest, election*) favorito/a *m/f*; **Liverpool are ~s to win** el Liverpool es el gran favorito
Ⓒ CPD ► **favourite son** N (*US Pol*) hijo *m* predilecto

favouritism, favoritism (*US*) [ˈfeɪvərɪtɪzəm] N favoritismo *m*

fawn¹ [fɔːn] Ⓐ N 1 (*Zool*) cervato *m*
2 (= *colour*) pardo *m* claro
Ⓑ ADJ de color pardo claro

fawn² [fɔːn] VI **to ~ (up)on sb** [*animal*] hacer carantoñas a algn; (*fig*) [*person*] adular *or* lisonjear a algn

fawning [ˈfɔːnɪŋ] ADJ adulador, servil

fax [fæks] Ⓐ N (= *document*) fax *m*; (= *machine*) fax *m*, telefax *m*
Ⓑ VT mandar por fax
Ⓒ CPD ► **fax message** N fax *m* ► **fax number** N número *m* de (tele)fax

faze* [feɪz] VT (= *disturb*) perturbar, desconcertar

fazed* [feɪzd] ADJ pasmado, anonadado

FBA N ABBR = **Fellow of the British Academy**

FBI N ABBR (*US*) (= **Federal Bureau of Investigation**) ≈ BIC *f*

FC N ABBR (= **football club**) C. F. *m*

FCA N ABBR 1 = **Fellow of the Institute of Chartered Accountants**
2 (*US*) = **Farm Credit Administration**

FCC N ABBR (*US*) = **Federal Communications Commission**; → FAIRNESS DOCTRINE

> **FCC**
>
> *La* **Federal Communications Commission** *o* **FCC** *es un organismo gubernamental independiente que regula y supervisa las transmisiones de radio, televisión y comunicación por cable y satélite en Estados Unidos. Entre las funciones más importantes de la* **FCC** *están la de conceder la licencia de emisión a las cadenas de radio y televisión privadas, así como la de asignarles sus frecuencias de transmisión. Además, tiene una gran influencia en la programación de las cadenas de televisión, entre las que ha introducido, por ejemplo, un espacio de dos horas para toda la familia por las noches, un límite a la cantidad de programas nacionales que pueden ser transmitidos por una cadena local y una* **Fairness Doctrine** *o doctrina de imparcialidad para los asuntos más polémicos. La comisión se compone de cinco miembros nombrados por el Presidente de EE.UU., y es responsable de sus actividades ante el Congreso.*
>
> ⇨ *Ver tb* FAIRNESS DOCTRINE

FCO N ABBR (*Brit*) (= **Foreign and Commonwealth Office**) ≈ Min. de AA.EE.

FD Ⓐ N ABBR (*US*) = **Fire Department**
Ⓑ ABBR 1 (*Brit*) (= **Fidei Defensor**) Defensor *m* de la Fe
2 (*Comm*) = **free delivered at dock**

FDA N ABBR (*US*) (= **Food and Drug Administration**) *organismo que fija niveles de calidad de los productos alimentarios y farmacéuticos*

> **FDA**
>
> *El* **FDA** *o* **Food and Drug Administration** *es el organismo de atención al consumidor más antiguo de Estados Unidos. Su función es la de analizar los alimentos, aditivos alimentarios, medicinas y cosméticos para asegurarse de que son aptos para el consumo. El* **FDA** *es muy conocido en el extranjero por su papel en el análisis de los nuevos productos, de su efectividad y de sus posibles efectos nocivos, así como en el control de su consumo una vez han sido puestos a la venta.*

FDD N ABBR (*Comput*) = **floppy disk drive**

FDIC N ABBR (*US*) = **Federal Deposit Insurance Corporation**

FDR ABBR = **Franklin Delano Roosevelt**

FE ABBR = **Further Education**

fealty [ˈfiːəltɪ] N (*Hist*) lealtad *f* (feudal)

▼ **fear** [fɪəʳ] Ⓐ N 1 (= *terror*) miedo *m*; **he has overcome his ~ of dogs** ha superado su miedo a los perros; **to be in ~ of** *or* **for one's life** temer por su propia vida; **workers at the plant frequently went in ~ of their lives** a menudo los trabajadores de la fábrica temían por su vida; **to live in ~ of sth/sb** vivir atemorizado por algo/algn; **she lives in ~ of being found out** vive atemorizada de que la descubran; **to have no ~** no tener ningún miedo; **have no ~!††** (= *don't be afraid*) ¡pierde cuidado!; **~ of heights** miedo *m* a las alturas; **~ of flying** miedo *m* a volar; **in ~ and trembling** temblando de miedo; **she was trembling with ~** estaba temblando de miedo; **without ~ or favour** con imparcialidad, imparcialmente; ✦*IDIOM* **to put the ~ of God into sb** meter el miedo en el cuerpo a algn
2 (= *worry*) temor *m*; **his worst ~s were confirmed** sus mayores temores se vieron confirmados; **there are ~s that …** se teme que + *subjun*; **there are ~s that he may be dead** se teme que esté muerto; **there were ~s that he would raise taxes** se temía que subiera los impuestos; **I didn't go in for ~ of disturbing them** no entré por temor *or* miedo a molestarles; **she never goes out for ~ that it will happen again** nunca sale por temor *or* miedo a que suceda de nuevo; **there are grave ~s for their safety** se teme enormemente por su seguridad; **have no ~!** (*freq hum*) (= *don't worry*) ¡no se preocupe!; **you need have no ~ on that score** no tenga miedo en ese sentido
3 (= *chance*) posibilidad *f*; (= *danger*) peligro *m*; **there's not much ~ of his coming** no hay muchas posibilidades de que venga; **there's no ~ of that!** ¡no hay peligro de eso!; **no ~!*** ¡ni hablar!
Ⓑ VT 1 (= *be afraid of*) temer, tener miedo a; **I do not ~ death** no temo a la muerte, no tengo miedo a la muerte; **he was ~ed and hated by his subjects** sus súbditos le temían y odiaban; **to ~ that** temer que + *subjun*; **we ~ed that he would escape** temíamos que se escapara; **they began to ~ that he was dangerous** empezaron a temer que fuera peligroso; **two people are missing and ~ed dead** hay dos personas desaparecidas y se teme que hayan muerto; **to ~ the worst** temer(se) lo peor
2 (= *think regretfully*) temerse; **to ~ that** temerse que; **I ~ that he won't come** me temo que no vendrá; **I ~ that you are right** me temo que tiene razón; **I ~ you may be right** me temo que tenga razón; **I ~ so/not** me temo que sí/no
3 (= *respect*) [+ *God*] temer
Ⓒ VI temer; **to ~ for sth/sb** temer por algo/algn; **she ~ed for her life** temía por su vida; **I ~ for him** temo por él, tengo miedo por él; **never ~** no hay cuidado*

fearful [ˈfɪəfʊl] ADJ 1 (= *frightened*) temeroso (**of** de); **to be ~ that** tener miedo de que + *subjun*
2 (= *frightening*) espantoso
3 (†*) (= *awful*) horrible

fearfully [ˈfɪəfəlɪ] ADV 1 (= *timidly*) [*cower etc*] con miedo; [*say*] tímidamente
2 (†*) (= *very*) terriblemente

➤ LANGUAGE IN USE: **favourite** A 7.2 **fear** A1 17.1

fearfulness ['fɪəfʊlnɪs] N (= *fear*) medrosidad *f*; (= *shyness*) timidez *f*

fearless ['fɪəlɪs] ADJ (= *courageous*) valiente; (= *daring*) audaz; (= *adventurous*) intrépido; **he was a ~ opponent of slavery** era un valiente opositor de la esclavitud; **a ~ warrior** un valiente *or* audaz *or* intrépido guerrero; **she is completely ~** no le tiene miedo a nada; **he entered, ~ of what he might find there** entró, sin temor a lo que podría encontrarse allí

fearlessly ['fɪəlɪslɪ] ADV (= *courageously*) valientemente; (= *adventurously*) intrépidamente; **he's ~ outspoken** no tiene miedo a la hora de expresar su opinión

fearlessness ['fɪəlɪsnɪs] N (= *courage*) valor *m*, valentía *f*; (= *daring*) audacia *f*; (= *spirit of adventure*) intrepidez *f*

fearsome ['fɪəsəm] ADJ [*opponent, reputation, weapon*] temible; [*sight*] espantoso; [*competition*] encarnizado; **he has a ~ serve** tiene un saque temible *or* tremendo

fearsomely ['fɪəsəmlɪ] ADV tremendamente

feasibility [ˌfiːzə'bɪlɪtɪ] Ⓐ N viabilidad *f*; **to doubt the ~ of a scheme** poner en duda la viabilidad de un proyecto, dudar si un proyecto es factible
Ⓑ CPD ► **feasibility analysis** N análisis *m inv* de viabilidad ► **feasibility study** N estudio *m* de viabilidad

▼**feasible** ['fiːzəbl] ADJ 1 (= *practicable*) [*plan, suggestion*] factible, viable; **to make sth ~** posibilitar algo
2 (= *likely*) [*story, theory*] posible, plausible

feasibly ['fiːzəblɪ] ADV de forma factible

feast [fiːst] Ⓐ N 1 (= *meal*) banquete *m*; (*) (= *big meal*) comilona* *f*, tragadera *f* (*Mex**); ✦**IDIOM it's ~ or famine** cuando mucho, cuando nada
2 (*Rel*) fiesta *f*
3 (*fig*) (= *treat*) **the film promises a ~ of special effects** la película promete ser un derroche de efectos especiales
Ⓑ VT († *or liter*) [+ *guest*] agasajar; **to ~ one's eyes on sth/sb** regalarse la vista con algo/algn
Ⓒ VI darse un banquete; **to ~ on sth** darse un banquete con algo
Ⓓ CPD ► **feast day** N (*Rel*) fiesta *f*, día *m* festivo

feat [fiːt] N hazaña *f*, proeza *f*

feather ['feðəʳ] Ⓐ N pluma *f*; ✦**IDIOMS in fine ~**† de excelente humor; **that is a ~ in his cap** es un tanto que se apunta; **you could have knocked me down with a ~*** me quedé de piedra; **as light as a ~** (tan) ligero como una pluma; *see also* **light A1**, **white C**
Ⓑ VT 1 emplumar; ✦**IDIOM to ~ one's nest** hacer su agosto
2 (*Rowing*) [+ *oar*] volver horizontal
Ⓒ CPD [*mattress, pillow*] de plumas ► **feather bed** N colchón *m* de pluma(s) ► **feather duster** N plumero *m*

featherbed ['feðə'bed] VT, VI (*Ind*) *estar expuesto a o imponer "featherbedding"*

featherbedding ['feðəˌbedɪŋ] N (*Ind*) *la práctica de disminuir la producción, duplicar el trabajo o el número de trabajadores al objeto de evitar despidos o crear más puestos de trabajo*

featherbrain ['feðəbreɪn] N cabeza *f* de chorlito*

featherbrained ['feðəbreɪnd] ADJ [*idea*] disparatado, descabellado; **to be ~** [*person*] ser un/una cabeza de chorlito*

feathered ['feðəd] ADJ [*bird*] plumado, con plumas; **our ~ friends** (*hum*) nuestros amigos plumados, nuestros amigos las aves

feathering ['feðərɪŋ] N plumaje *m*

featherweight ['feðəweɪt] Ⓐ N (*Boxing*) peso *m* pluma
Ⓑ CPD ► **featherweight champion** N campeón/ona *m/f* de peso pluma ► **featherweight title** N título *m* de peso pluma

feathery ['feðərɪ] ADJ [*texture*] plumoso; (= *light*) ligero como pluma

feature ['fiːtʃəʳ] Ⓐ N 1 [*of face*] rasgo *m*; **~s** rasgos *mpl*, facciones *fpl*
2 [*of countryside, building*] característica *f*
3 (*Comm, Tech*) elemento *m*, rasgo *m*
4 (*Theat*) número *m*; (*Cine*) película *f*
5 (*Press*) artículo *m* de fondo; **a regular ~** una crónica regular
6 (*Ling*) (*also* **distinctive ~**) rasgo *m* distintivo
Ⓑ VT 1 [+ *actor, news*] presentar; [+ *event*] ocuparse de, enfocar; (*in paper etc*) presentar; **a film featuring Garbo as ...** una película que presenta a la Garbo en el papel de ...
2 (= *be equipped with*) [*machine*] estar provisto de, ofrecer
Ⓒ VI 1 (*gen*) **it ~d prominently in ...** tuvo un papel destacado en ...
2 (*Cine*) figurar, aparecer (**in** en)
Ⓓ CPD ► **feature article** N artículo *m* de fondo ► **feature film** N (película *f* de) largometraje *m* ► **feature writer** N articulista *mf*, cronista *mf*

feature-length ['fiːtʃəleŋ(k)θ] ADJ [*documentary, drama*] especial; **~ film** (película *f* de) largometraje *m*

featureless ['fiːtʃəlɪs] ADJ monótono, anodino

Feb. ABBR (= **February**) feb.

febrile ['fiːbraɪl] ADJ febril

February ['februərɪ] N febrero *m*; *see* **July** *for usage*

fecal ['fiːkəl] ADJ (*US*) = **faecal**

feces ['fiːsiːz] NPL (*US*) = **faeces**

feckless ['feklɪs] ADJ (= *weak*) débil, incapaz; (= *irresponsible*) irresponsable

fecund ['fiːkənd] ADJ fecundo

fecundity [fɪ'kʌndɪtɪ] N fecundidad *f*

Fed [fed] Ⓐ N ABBR 1 (*US**) (= **federal officer**) federal* *mf*
2 (*US Banking*) = **Federal Reserve Board**
Ⓑ ABBR (*esp US*) = **federal, federated, federation**

fed [fed] PT, PP *of* **feed**

federal ['fedərəl] Ⓐ ADJ federal
Ⓑ N (*US Hist*) federal *mf*
Ⓒ CPD ► **Federal Bureau** N (*US*) Departamento *m* de Estado ► **Federal Bureau of Investigation** N (*US*) FBI *m*, ≈ Brigada *f* de Investigación Criminal ► **federal officer** N (*US*) federal *mf* ► **Federal Republic of Germany** N República *f* Federal de Alemania ► **Federal Reserve Bank** N (*US*) banco *m* de la Reserva Federal ► **Federal Reserve Board** N (*US*) junta *f* de gobierno de la Reserva Federal ► **Federal Reserve System** N (*US*) Reserva *f* Federal (*banco central de los EE. UU.*) ► **federal tax** N impuesto *m* federal; → FCC

federalism ['fedərəlɪzəm] N federalismo *m*

federalist ['fedərəlɪst] Ⓐ ADJ federalista
Ⓑ N federalista *mf*

federalize ['fedərəlaɪz] VT federar, federalizar

federate ['fedəreɪt] Ⓐ VT federar
Ⓑ VI federarse

federation [ˌfedə'reɪʃən] N (= *group, system*) federación *f*

fedora [fə'dɔːrə] N sombrero *m* flexible, sombrero *m* tirolés

fed up* [ˌfed'ʌp] ADJ harto; **to be ~ (with sth/sb)** estar harto (de algo/algn); **to be ~ with doing sth** estar harto de hacer algo

fee [fiː] N (= *professional*) honorarios *mpl*, emolumentos *mpl*; (*Comm*) pago *m*; (*for doctor's visit*) precio *m* de visita; **admission ~** precio *m* de entrada; **entrance/membership ~** cuota *f*; **course/tuition/school ~s** matrícula *fsing*; **what's your ~?** ¿cuánto cobra Vd?; **for a small ~** por una pequeña *or* módica cantidad; *see also* **transfer D**

feeble ['fiːbl] ADJ (*compar* **feebler**; *superl* **feeblest**) 1 (= *weak*) [*person, cry, protest*] débil; [*smile, laugh*] lánguido, débil; [*light*] tenue
2 (= *ineffective*) [*effort, attempt, resistance*] débil; [*excuse, argument*] poco convincente, flojo; [*joke*] soso

feeble-minded ['fiːbl'maɪndɪd] ADJ [*person*] bobo, zonzo (*LAm*)

feeble-mindedness [ˌfiːbl'maɪndɪdnɪs] N (*Med*) debilidad *f* mental

feebleness ['fiːblnɪs] N 1 (= *weakness*) [*of person*] debilidad *f*
2 (= *ineffectiveness*) [*of argument*] lo poco convincente, lo flojo

feebly ['fiːblɪ] ADV 1 (= *weakly*) [*move, struggle*] débilmente; [*smile, laugh*] lánguidamente, débilmente; [*shine*] tenuemente
2 (= *ineffectually*) [*protest*] sin fuerzas

feed [fiːd] (*vb: pt, pp* **fed**) Ⓐ VT 1 (*lit*) 1·1 (= *give meal to*) [+ *person, animal*] dar de comer a; [+ *baby*] (= *bottle-feed*) dar el biberón a; (= *breastfeed*) dar de mamar a, dar el pecho a; [+ *plant*] alimentar; **they fed us well at the hotel** nos dieron de comer bien en el hotel; **have you fed the horses?** ¿has dado de comer a los caballos?; **"(please) do not feed the animals"** "prohibido dar de comer a los animales"; **you've made enough food to ~ an army** has hecho comida para un regimiento; **he has just started ~ing himself** acaba de empezar a comer solo
1·2 (= *provide food for*) dar de comer (a), alimentar; **now there was another mouth to ~** ahora había que dar de comer a una boca más, ahora había una boca más que alimentar; **~ing a family can be expensive** dar de comer a *or* alimentar a una familia puede resultar caro; **it is enough to ~ the population for several months** es suficiente para alimentar a la población durante varios meses
1·3 **to ~ sb sth** ◊ **~ sth to sb** dar algo (de comer) a algn; **you shouldn't ~ him that** no deberías darle eso; **he fed her ice cream with a spoon** ◊ **he fed ice cream to her with a spoon** le dio helado con una cuchara; **he was ~ing bread to the ducks** les estaba echando pan a los patos; **what do you ~ your dog on?** ¿qué le das (de comer) a tu perro?; **they have been fed a diet of cartoons and computer games** los han tenido a base de dibujos animados y juegos de ordenador
2 (= *supply*) suministrar; **gas fed through pipelines** gas suministrado a través de tuberías; **the blood vessels that ~ blood to the brain** los vasos sanguíneos que suministran sangre al cerebro; **two rivers ~ this reservoir** dos ríos vierten sus aguas en este embalse; **he stole money to ~ his drug habit** robaba dinero para costear su drogadicción; **to ~ the (parking) meter** echar *or* meter monedas en el parquímetro
3 (= *tell*) **to ~ sb sth** ◊ **~ sth to sb: they fed us details of troop movements in the area** nos facilitaron detalles de movimientos de tropas en la zona; **he was being fed false**

➤ LANGUAGE IN USE: **feasible 1** 12.2

information le estaban pasando información falsa; **he was surrounded by people who fed him lies** estaba rodeado de gente que le llenaba la cabeza de mentiras; **✦IDIOM to ~ sb a line*** contar *or* soltar una bola a algn*

4 (= *insert*) **to ~ sth into sth** meter *or* introducir algo en algo; **I fed a sheet of paper into the typewriter** metí *or* puse una hoja de papel en la máquina de escribir; **to ~ data into a computer** meter *or* introducir datos en un ordenador

5 (= *fuel*) [+ *fire, emotion, feeling*] alimentar; [+ *imagination*] estimular; **these rumours fed his fears** estos rumores alimentaron sus miedos; **to ~ the flames** (*lit, fig*) echar leña al fuego

6 (*Sport*) [+ *ball*] pasar

Ⓑ VI 1 (= *take food*) (*gen*) comer; (*at breast*) mamar; **to ~ on sth** (*lit*) alimentarse de algo, comer algo; (*fig*) alimentarse de algo; **the press ~s on intrigue** la prensa se alimenta de las intrigas

2 (= *lead*) **a river that ~s into the Baltic Sea** un río que desemboca en el mar Báltico; **this road ~s into the motorway** esta carretera va a parar a la autopista; **the money spent by consumers ~s back into industry** el dinero que gastan los consumidores revierte en la industria

Ⓒ N 1 (= *food*) (*for animal*) forraje *m*, pienso *m*; **the six o'clock ~** (*for baby*) (= *breast or bottle feed*) la toma de las seis; (= *baby food*) la papilla de las seis; (= *ordinary food*) la comida de las seis; **it's time for his ~** le toca comer; **to be off one's ~** no tener apetito, estar desganado; *see also* **chicken**

2 (*) (= *meal*) **a good ~** una buena comida

3 (*Tech, Comput*) alimentador *m*; (= *tube*) tubo *m* de alimentación

4 (*Theat**) (= *straight man*) *personaje serio en una pareja cómica*; (= *line*) material *m* (*de un sketch cómico*)

Ⓓ CPD ► **feed bag** N morral *m* ► **feed merchant** N vendedor(a) *m/f* de forraje *or* pienso ► **feed pipe** N tubo *m* de alimentación

►**feed back** VT + ADV [+ *information, results*] proporcionar, facilitar

►**feed in** VT + ADV 1 (= *insert*) [+ *coins, paper*] meter, introducir

2 (*Comput*) [+ *data*] meter, introducir

►**feed up** VT + ADV [+ *person*] engordar; [+ *animal*] cebar, engordar

feedback ['fi:dbæk] N 1 (*from person*) reacción *f*; **we're not getting much ~** no nos tienen demasiado informados de cómo vamos

2 (*from loudspeaker*) realimentación *f*, feedback *m*

feeder ['fi:dəʳ] Ⓐ N 1 (*Mech*) alimentador *m*, tubo *m* de alimentación

2 (*Aut, Rail*) ramal *m*

3 (*Geog*) afluente *m*

4 (*Brit*) (= *bib*) babero *m*

5 (= *device*) (*for birds etc*) comedero *m*

Ⓑ CPD ► **feeder (primary) school** N (*Brit*) *escuela primaria que envía alumnos a un determinado colegio de enseñanza secundaria* ► **feeder service** N (*US*) servicio *m* secundario (de transportes)

feeding ['fi:dɪŋ] Ⓐ N (= *act*) alimentación *f*; (= *meals*) comida *f*

Ⓑ CPD ► **feeding bottle** N (*esp Brit*) biberón *m* ► **feeding frenzy** N **the birds engage in a ~ frenzy** los pájaros inician un frenético festín; **she was caught in a media ~ frenzy** se vio convertida en el centro de una atención febril por parte de los medios de comunicación ► **feeding ground** N (*lit*) fuente *f* de alimentación; (*fig*) mina *f* de oro; **the factory will soon be a ~ ground for lawyers** la fábrica será pronto una mina de oro para los abogados ► **feeding time** N (*at zoo*) hora *f* de comer; (*baby's*) (= *time for breast feed*) hora *f* del pecho; (= *time for bottle feed*) hora *f* del biberón

feedstuffs ['fi:dstʌfs] NPL piensos *mpl*

feel [fi:l] (*vb: pt, pp* **felt**) Ⓐ VT 1 (= *touch*) tocar, palpar; [+ *pulse*] tomar; **I'm still ~ing my way** (*fig*) todavía me estoy familiarizando con la situación/el trabajo *etc*; **to ~ one's way (towards)** (*lit*) ir a tientas (hacia); **we're ~ing our way towards an agreement** estamos tanteando el terreno para llegar a un acuerdo

2 (= *be aware of*) [+ *blow, pain, heat*] sentir; [+ *responsibility*] ser consciente de; **she felt a hand on her shoulder** sintió una mano en el hombro; **I felt something move** sentí que algo se movía; **I felt it getting hot** sentí que se iba calentando; **I do ~ the importance of this** soy plenamente consciente de la importancia de ello

3 (= *experience*) [+ *pity, anger, grief*] sentir; **the consequences will be felt next year** las consecuencias se harán sentir el año próximo; **they are beginning to ~ the effects of the trade sanctions** están empezando a sentir *or* notar los efectos de las sanciones económicas; **I ~ no interest in it** no me interesa en absoluto, no siento ningún interés por ello; **I felt myself blush** noté que me estaba sonrojando; **I felt myself being swept up in the tide of excitement** noté que me estaba dejando llevar por la oleada de entusiasmo; **I felt a great sense of relief** sentí un gran alivio

4 (= *be affected by, suffer from*) ser sensible a; **he doesn't ~ the cold** no es sensible al frío; **don't you ~ the heat?** ¿no te molesta el calor?; **he ~s the loss of his father very deeply** está muy afectado por la muerte de su padre

5 (= *think, believe*) **what do you ~ about it?** ¿qué te parece a ti?; **I ~ that you ought to do it** creo que deberías hacerlo; **I ~ strongly that we should accept their offer** me parece muy importante que aceptemos su oferta; **he felt it necessary to point out that …** creyó *or* le pareció necesario señalar que …

Ⓑ VI 1 (*physically*) sentirse, encontrarse; **how do you ~ now?** ¿qué tal *or* cómo te sientes *or* te encuentras ahora?; **I ~ much better** me siento *or* me encuentro mucho mejor; **you'll ~ all the better for a rest** te sentirás mucho mejor después de descansar; **to ~ cold/hungry/sleepy** tener frío/hambre/sueño; **I felt (as if I was going to) faint** sentí como si fuera a desmayarme; **she's not ~ing quite herself** no se encuentra del todo bien; **to ~ ill** sentirse mal; **to ~ old** sentirse viejo; **do you ~ sick?** ¿estás mareado?; **I ~ quite tired** me siento bastante cansado; **I don't ~ up to a walk just now*** ahora mismo no me encuentro con fuerzas para dar un paseo

2 (*mentally*) **how does it ~ to go hungry?** ¿cómo se siente uno pasando hambre?; **how do you ~ about him/about the idea?** ¿qué te parece él/la idea?; **how do you ~ about going for a walk?** ¿te apetece *or* (*LAm*) se te antoja dar un paseo?; **I ~ as if there is nothing we can do** tengo la sensación de que no hay nada que hacer, me da la impresión de que no podemos hacer nada; **he ~s bad about leaving his wife alone** siente haber dejado sola a su mujer; **I ~ very cross** estoy muy enfadado *or* (*LAm*) enojado; **I ~ for you!** (= *sympathize*) ¡lo siento por ti!, ¡te compadezco!; **we ~ for you in your loss** le acompañamos en el sentimiento; **since you ~ so strongly about it …** ya que te parece tan importante …; **I ~ sure that** estoy seguro de que

3 **to ~ like** 3·1 (= *resemble*) **it ~s like silk** parece seda al tocarlo; **what does it ~ like to do that?** ¿qué se siente al hacer eso?; **it felt like being drunk** parecía como si estuviera uno borracho

3·2 (= *give impression, have impression*) **it ~s like (it might) rain** parece que va a llover; **I felt (like) a fool** me sentí (un) estúpido; **I felt like a new man/woman** me sentí como un hombre nuevo/una mujer nueva

3·3 (= *want*) **I ~ like an apple** me apetece una manzana; **do you ~ like a walk?** ¿quieres dar un paseo?, ¿te apetece dar un paseo?; **I go out whenever I ~ like it** salgo cuando me apetece *or* cuando quiero; **I don't ~ like it** no me apetece, no tengo ganas; **I don't ~ like going out now** no tengo ganas de salir ahora

4 (= *give impression*) **it ~s colder out here** se siente más frío aquí fuera; **the house ~s damp** la casa parece húmeda; **to ~ hard/cold/damp** *etc* (*to the touch*) ser duro/frío/húmedo *etc* al tacto

5 (*also* **~ around**) (= *grope*) tantear, ir a tientas; **to ~ around in the dark** ir a tientas *or* tantear en la oscuridad; **he was ~ing around in the dark for the door** iba tanteando en la oscuridad para encontrar la puerta; **she felt in her pocket for her keys** rebuscó en el bolsillo para encontrar las llaves

Ⓒ N 1 (= *sensation*) sensación *f*; **the ~ of them against his palm** la sensación que producían al tocarlas; **she liked the ~ of the breeze on her face** le gustaba sentir la brisa en la cara; **I don't like the ~ of wool against my skin** no me gusta el contacto de la lana contra la piel; **the fabric has a papery ~** la tela tiene una textura como de papel; **to know sth by the ~ of it** reconocer algo por el tacto

2 (= *sense of touch*) tacto *m*; **to be rough to the ~** ser áspero al tacto

3 (= *act*) **let me have a ~!** ¡déjame que lo toque!

4 (*fig*) (= *impression, atmosphere*) ambiente *m*, aspecto *m*; **the room has a cosy ~** la habitación tiene un ambiente acogedor; **to get the ~ of** (*fig*) [+ *new job, place*] ambientarse a, familiarizarse con; [+ *new car, machine*] familiarizarse con; **repeat this a few times to get the ~ of it** repítelo unas cuantas veces hasta que te acostumbres *or* te cojas el tino; **to get a ~ for** (= *get impression*) hacerse una idea de; **to have a ~ for languages/music** tener talento para los idiomas/la música

►**feel out*** VT + ADV (*fig*) [+ *person*] tantear

►**feel up‡** VT + ADV **to ~ sb up** meter mano a algn*

feeler ['fi:ləʳ] N 1 (*Zool*) [*of insect, snail*] antena *f*

2 (*fig*) sondeo *m*; **✦IDIOM to put out ~s** hacer un sondeo

feelgood ['fi:lgʊd] ADJ **the ~ factor** la sensación de bienestar; **a ~ movie** una película que te hace sentir bien

▼**feeling** ['fi:lɪŋ] N 1 (*physical*) sensación *f*; **a cold ~** una sensación de frío; **to have no ~ in one's arm** ◊ **have lost all ~ in one's arm** no sentir un brazo

2 (= *emotion*) sentimiento *m*; **bad** *or* **ill ~** rencor *m*, hostilidad *f*; **to speak/sing with ~** hablar/cantar con sentimiento; **she showed no ~ for him** se mostró totalmente indiferente con él

3 **feelings** sentimientos *mpl*; **to appeal to**

➤ LANGUAGE IN USE: **feeling 4** 6.2

sb's finer ~s apelar a los sentimientos nobles de algn; **no hard ~s!** ¡todo olvidado!; **to have ~s for sb** querer a algn; **to hurt sb's ~s** herir los sentimientos de algn, ofender a algn; **you can imagine my ~s!** ¡ya te puedes imaginar cómo me sentía!; **~s ran high about it** causó mucha controversia; **to relieve one's ~s** desahogarse; **to spare sb's ~s** no herir los sentimientos de algn; *see also* **fine A3**

[4] (= *impression*) impresión *f*, sensación *f*; **a ~ of security/isolation** una sensación de seguridad/aislamiento; **I have a (funny) ~ that ...** tengo la (extraña) sensación de que ...; **I get the ~ that ...** me da la impresión de que ...

[5] (= *opinion*) opinión *f*; **there was a general ~ that ...** la opinión general era que ...; **our ~s do not matter** nuestras opiniones no valen para nada; **what are your ~s about the matter?** ¿qué opinas tú del asunto?; **my ~ is that ...** creo que ...

[6] (= *sensitivity*) sensibilidad *f*; **a man of ~** un hombre sensible

[7] (= *aptitude*) **to have a ~ for music** tener talento para la música; **he has no ~ for music** no sabe apreciar la música

feelingly ['fiːlɪŋlɪ] ADV con honda emoción

fee-paying ['fiː,peɪɪŋ] Ⓐ ADJ [*pupil*] que paga pensión
Ⓑ CPD ► **fee-paying school** N colegio *m* de pago

feet [fiːt] NPL *of* **foot**

FEFC N ABBR (*Brit*) (= **Further Education Funding Council**) *organismo de financiación de la formación profesional*

feign [feɪn] VT [+ *surprise, indifference*] fingir; **to ~ madness/sleep/death** fingirse loco/dormido/muerto; **to ~ not to know** fingir no saber

feigned [feɪnd] ADJ fingido

feint [feɪnt] Ⓐ N (*Boxing, Fencing*) finta *f*
Ⓑ VI fintar

feisty* ['faɪstɪ] ADJ (*esp US*) (= *lively*) animado; (= *quarrelsome*) pendenciero

feldspar ['feldspɑːʳ] N feldespato *m*

felicitate [fɪ'lɪsɪteɪt] VT (*frm*) felicitar, congratular

felicitations [fɪlɪsɪ'teɪʃənz] NPL (*frm*) felicitaciones *fpl*

felicitous [fɪ'lɪsɪtəs] ADJ (*frm*) feliz, oportuno

felicity [fɪ'lɪsɪtɪ] N (*frm*) felicidad *f*; (= *aptness*) [*of words*] acierto *m*

feline ['fiːlaɪn] Ⓐ ADJ felino
Ⓑ N felino *m*

fell[1] [fel] PT *of* **fall**

fell[2] [fel] VT (*with a blow*) derribar; [+ *tree*] talar, cortar; [+ *cattle*] acogotar

fell[3] [fel] ADJ **with one ~ blow** con un golpe feroz; **at one ~ swoop** de un solo golpe

fell[4] [fel] N (*Brit*) (= *moorland*) páramo *m*, brezal *m*; (= *hill*) (*usu pl*) colina *f* rocosa

fell[5] [fel] N (= *hide, pelt*) piel *f*

fella* ['felə, 'feləʳ] N tipo* *m*, tío *m* (*Sp**)

fellate [fe'leɪt] VT (*frm*) hacer una felación a

fellatio [fɪ'leɪʃɪəʊ] N, **fellation** [fɪ'leɪʃən] N felación *f*

feller* ['feləʳ] N tipo* *m*, tío *m* (*Sp**)

fellow ['feləʊ] Ⓐ N [1] (= *chap*) hombre *m*, tipo* *m*, tío* *m*; **can't a ~ get any peace!** ¡es mucho pedir que le dejen a uno en paz!; **my dear ~!** ¡hombre!; **well, this journalist ~** bueno, el tal periodista; **those journalist ~s** los periodistas esos; **nice ~** buen chico *m*, buena persona *f*; **he's an odd ~** es un tipo raro; **old ~** viejo *m*; **look here, old ~** mira, amigo; **poor ~!** ¡pobrecito!; **young ~** chico *m*; **I say, young ~** oiga, joven

[2] (= *comrade*) compañero *m*

[3] [*of association, society etc*] socio/a *m/f*

[4] (*Brit Univ etc*) *miembro de la junta de gobierno de un colegio universitario*

[5] (*frm*) (= *other half*) pareja *f*; (= *equal*) igual *mf*; **it has no ~** no tiene par

Ⓑ CPD ► **fellow being** N = **fellow creature** ► **fellow citizen** N conciudadano/a *m/f* ► **fellow countryman/-woman** N compatriota *mf*; **"my ~ countrymen, ..."** (*in speech*) —queridos compatriotas, ... ► **fellow creature** N prójimo *m* ► **fellow feeling** N compañerismo *m* ► **fellow member** N consocio/a *m/f* ► **fellow men** NPL prójimos *mpl*, semejantes *mpl* ► **fellow passenger** N compañero/a *m/f* de viaje ► **fellow student** N compañero/a *m/f* de clase *or* curso ► **fellow sufferer** N *persona que tiene la misma enfermedad que algn*; (*fig*) compañero/a *m/f* en la desgracia ► **fellow traveller, fellow traveler** (*US*) N (*lit*) = **fellow passenger** (*Pol*) (*with communists*) simpatizante *mf* ► **fellow worker** N compañero/a *m/f* de trabajo, colega *mf*

fellowship ['feləʊʃɪp] N [1] (= *companionship*) compañerismo *m*

[2] (= *club, society*) asociación *f*

[3] (*Brit Univ*) (= *paid research post*) puesto *m* de becario (de investigación); (*US Univ*) (= *grant*) beca *f* de investigación

felon ['felən] N (*Jur*) criminal *mf*, delincuente *mf* (de mayor cuantía)

felonious [fɪ'ləʊnɪəs] ADJ (*Jur*) criminal, delincuente

felony ['felənɪ] N (*Jur*) crimen *m*, delito *m* grave

felspar ['felspɑːʳ] N feldespato *m*

felt[1] [felt] PT, PP *of* **feel**

felt[2] [felt] Ⓐ N fieltro *m*
Ⓑ CPD ► **felt hat** N sombrero *m* de fieltro

felt-tip ['felttɪp] N (*also* **~ pen**) rotulador *m*

fem. ABBR [1] = **female**
[2] = **feminine**

female ['fiːmeɪl] Ⓐ ADJ [1] [*animal, plant*] hembra; **the ~ hippopotamus** el hipopótamo hembra

[2] [*population*] femenino; [*vote*] de las mujeres; [*slave, subject*] del sexo femenino; **a ~ friend** una amiga; **~ labour** trabajo *m* femenino *or* de mujeres; **the ~ sex** el sexo femenino; **a ~ student** una estudiante; **~ suffrage** derecho *m* de las mujeres a votar; **a ~ voice** una voz de mujer

Ⓑ N [1] (= *animal*) hembra *f*
[2] (*pej*) (= *woman*) chica *f*
Ⓒ CPD ► **female condom** N condón *m* femenino ► **female impersonator** N (*Theat*) *actor que representa a una mujer*

Femidom® ['femɪdɒm] N Femidón® *m*

feminine ['femɪnɪn] Ⓐ ADJ femenino; **~ form** (*Ling*) forma *f* femenina
Ⓑ N (*Ling*) femenino *m*; **in the ~** en femenino

femininity [,femɪ'nɪnɪtɪ] N feminidad *f*

feminism ['femɪnɪzəm] N feminismo *m*

feminist ['femɪnɪst] Ⓐ ADJ feminista
Ⓑ N feminista *mf*

feminize ['femɪnaɪz] VT (*frm*) feminizar

femme [fæm, fem] Ⓐ N (‡) *la que hace de "chica" en una relación lesbiana*
Ⓑ ADJ (‡) (*in lesbian relationship*) femenina
Ⓒ CPD ► **femme fatale** N mujer *f* fatal

femoral ['femərəl] ADJ femoral

femur ['fiːməʳ] N (*pl* **femurs** *or* **femora** ['femərə]) fémur *m*

fen [fen] N (*Brit*) (*often pl*) zona *f* pantanosa, pantano *m*; **the Fens** (*Brit*) *las tierras bajas de Norfolk*

fence [fens] Ⓐ N [1] (*gen*) valla *f*, cerca *f*; (= *wire fence*) alambrada *f*; (*Racing*) valla *f*; ✦*IDIOMS* **to mend one's ~s** (= *restore relations*) mejorar las relaciones; (= *restore reputation*) restablecer la reputación; **to sit on the ~** no comprometerse, mirar los toros desde la barrera

[2] (*) (= *receiver of stolen goods*) perista *mf*

Ⓑ VT [1] [+ *land*] vallar, cercar; **~d area** zona *f* cercada *or* vallada
[2] [+ *machinery etc*] cubrir, proteger
Ⓒ VI [1] (*Sport*) practicar esgrima
[2] (*fig*) defenderse con evasivas

►**fence in** VT + ADV [+ *animals, fig*] encerrar; [+ *land*] vallar, cercar

►**fence off** VT + ADV separar con una valla *or* cerca

fencer ['fensəʳ] N (*Sport*) esgrimista *mf*, esgrimidor(a) *m/f*

fencing ['fensɪŋ] Ⓐ N [1] (*Sport*) esgrima *f*
[2] (= *material*) vallado *m*, cercado *m*
Ⓑ CPD ► **fencing master** N maestro *m* de esgrima ► **fencing match** N encuentro *m* de esgrima

fend [fend] VI **to ~ for o.s.** defenderse solo, arreglárselas por cuenta propia

►**fend off** VT + ADV [+ *attack*] repeler, rechazar; [+ *assailant*] repeler; [+ *blow*] desviar, esquivar; [+ *awkward question*] soslayar, eludir

fender ['fendəʳ] N (*round fire*) guardafuego *m*; (*US Aut*) guardabarros *m inv*, guardafango *m* (*LAm*), salpicadera *f* (*Mex*), tapabarro *m* (*Peru*); (*US Rail*) trompa *f*; (*Naut*) defensa *f*

fenestration [,fenɪs'treɪʃən] N (*Tech*) ventanaje *m*

feng shui [,feŋ'ʃuːɪ] N feng shui *m*

fenland ['fenlənd] N (*Brit*) terreno *m* pantanoso, marisma *f*

fennel ['fenl] N hinojo *m*

FEPC N ABBR (*US*) = **Fair Employment Practices Committee**

feral ['fɪərəl] ADJ (*frm*) silvestre, salvaje

FERC N ABBR (*US*) = **Federal Energy Regulatory Commission**

Ferdinand ['fɜːdɪnænd] N Fernando

ferment ['fɜːment] Ⓐ N [1] (= *leaven*) fermento *m*; (= *process*) fermentación *f*
[2] (*fig*) (= *excitement*) agitación *f*, conmoción *f*; **in a (state of) ~** en un estado de agitación, conmocionado
Ⓑ [fə'ment] VT (*lit*) hacer fermentar; (*fig*) fomentar
Ⓒ [fə'ment] VI (*lit*) fermentar

fermentation [,fɜːmen'teɪʃən] N fermentación *f*

fermium ['fɜːmɪəm] N fermio *m*

fern [fɜːn] N helecho *m*

ferocious [fə'rəʊʃəs] ADJ [1] (= *savage*) [*animal*] fiero, feroz; [*attack*] feroz
[2] (= *intense*) [*storm, wind*] violento; [*fire*] voraz; [*battle*] feroz, encarnizado; [*energy*] tremendo; [*heat*] atroz

ferociously [fə'rəʊʃəslɪ] ADV [*bark, glare*] ferozmente, con ferocidad; [*fight, attack*] ferozmente; **the sun was ~ hot** hacía un calor atroz, el calor era implacable; **he worked ~ hard** trabajaba durísimo

ferociousness [fə'rəʊʃəsnɪs] N = **ferocity**

ferocity [fə'rɒsɪtɪ] N [1] (= *savagery*) [*of person, animal, attack, battle*] ferocidad *f*
[2] (= *intensity*) [*of storm, wind, fire*] furia *f*; [*of feelings*] intensidad *f*; [*of criticism*] dureza *f*

ferret ['ferɪt] Ⓐ N hurón *m*
Ⓑ VI cazar con hurones
► **ferret about, ferret around** VI + ADV hurgar (**in** en)
► **ferret out** VT + ADV [+ *person*] dar con; [+ *secret, truth*] desentrañar
ferric ['ferɪk] ADJ férrico
Ferris wheel ['ferɪswi:l] N (*US*) noria *f*
ferrite ['feraɪt] N ferrito *m*, ferrita *f*
ferro- ['ferəʊ] PREFIX ferro-
ferro-alloy ['ferəʊ'ælɔɪ] N ferroaleación *f*
ferrous ['ferəs] ADJ ferroso
ferrule ['feru:l] N regatón *m*, contera *f*
ferry ['ferɪ] Ⓐ N (*also* **~boat**) barca *f* (de pasaje); (*large*) (*for cars etc*) transbordador *m*, ferry *m*
Ⓑ VT **to ~ sth/sb across** *or* **over** llevar algo/a algn a la otra orilla; **to ~ people to and fro** (*fig*) (*in car etc*) llevar *or* transportar a la gente de un lado para otro
ferryboat ['ferɪbəʊt] N = **ferry**
ferryman ['ferɪmən] N (*pl* **ferrymen**) barquero *m*
fertile ['fɜ:taɪl] ADJ [1] (*Agr*) [*land, valley, soil*] fértil
[2] (*Bio*) [*woman, animal, phase*] fértil; [*egg*] fértil, fecundo
[3] (*fig*) (= *productive*) fértil; (= *creative*) [*imagination, mind*] fecundo, fértil; **this was her most ~ period of writing** como escritora, ésta fue su época más fértil; **this situation provides a ~ breeding ground for racists** esta situación es un caldo de cultivo para el racismo
fertility [fə'tɪlɪtɪ] Ⓐ N [*of land, woman, animal*] fertilidad *f*
Ⓑ CPD ► **fertility drug** N medicamento *m* para el tratamiento de la infertilidad ► **fertility rite** N rito *m* de fertilidad ► **fertility treatment** N tratamiento *m* contra la esterilidad
fertilization [ˌfɜ:tɪlaɪ'zeɪʃən] N fecundación *f*, fertilización *f*
fertilize ['fɜ:tɪlaɪz] VT [1] [+ *egg*] fecundar
[2] (*Agr*) [+ *land, soil*] abonar, fertilizar
fertilizer ['fɜ:tɪlaɪzə^r] N (*for soil, land*) abono *m* (artificial), fertilizante *m*
fervent ['fɜ:vənt] ADJ [*prayer*] ferviente; [*desire*] ardiente; [*belief*] firme; [*supporter*] acérrimo, ferviente; [*denial*] enfático; **he is a ~ believer in neoliberalism** es un acérrimo *or* ferviente partidario del neoliberalismo; **it is my ~ hope that ...** espero fervientemente que ...
fervently ['fɜ:vəntlɪ] ADV [*pray*] con fervor, fervientemente; [*believe*] firmemente; [*hope, desire*] fervientemente, ardientemente; [*deny*] enfáticamente, con vehemencia; [*support*] con fervor, fervorosamente; **he is ~ patriotic** es un patriota acérrimo *or* ferviente; **he was ~ opposed to the war** se oponía enérgicamente a la guerra
fervid ['fɜ:vɪd] ADJ (*frm*) = **fervent**
fervour, fervor (*US*) ['fɜ:və^r] N fervor *m*
fest* [fest] N **film ~** festival *m* de cine; **gore ~** orgía *f* de sangre
fester ['festə^r] VI (*Med*) [*wound, sore*] enconarse; (*fig*) [*anger, resentment*] enconarse
festival ['festɪvəl] N (*Rel etc*) fiesta *f*; (*Mus etc*) festival *m*
festive ['festɪv] ADJ (*gen*) festivo; (= *happy*) alegre; **in (a) ~ mood** muy alegre; **the ~ season** las Navidades
festivity [fes'tɪvɪtɪ] N [1] (= *celebration*) fiesta *f*, festividad *f*; (= *joy*) regocijo *m*
[2] **festivities** festejos *mpl*, fiestas *fpl*
festoon [fes'tu:n] Ⓐ N guirnalda *f*, festón *m*; (*Sew*) festón *m*
Ⓑ VT adornar, engalanar (**with** de); **to be ~ed with** estar adornado *or* engalanado de
FET N ABBR (*US*) = **Federal Excise Tax**
feta ['fetə] N (*also* **~ cheese**) feta *m*
fetal ['fi:tl] ADJ (*US*) = **foetal**
fetch [fetʃ] Ⓐ VT [1] (= *go and get, bring*) [+ *object*] traer; [+ *person*] ir a buscar a; **can you ~ my coat?** ¿me trae el abrigo?; **I'll go and ~ it for you** te lo voy a buscar; **~ (it)!** (*to dog*) ¡busca!; **they're ~ing the doctor** han ido (a) por el médico; **please ~ the doctor** llama al médico; **they ~ed him all that way** le hicieron venir desde tan lejos; **to ~ sb back from Spain** hacer que algn vuelva de España
[2] (= *sell for*) venderse por; **how much did it ~?** ¿por cuánto se vendió?
[3] [+ *blow, sigh*] dar
Ⓑ VI **to ~ and carry** ir de acá para allá, trajinar; **to ~ and carry for sb** ser el sirviente de algn
► **fetch in** VT + ADV [+ *object*] meter; [+ *person*] hacer entrar
► **fetch out** VT + ADV sacar
► **fetch up*** Ⓐ VI + ADV (= *reappear, end up*) [*person, object*] ir a parar (**in** a)
Ⓑ VT + ADV (*Brit*) (= *vomit*) vomitar, arrojar
fetching ['fetʃɪŋ] ADJ (= *attractive*) atractivo
fête [feɪt] Ⓐ N [1] (= *party*) fiesta *f*; **to be en ~** estar de fiesta
[2] (*for charity*) feria *f* benéfica
Ⓑ VT (= *honour*) ensalzar; (= *have a celebration for*) festejar
fetid ['fetɪd] ADJ fétido
fetish ['fetɪʃ] N (= *object of cult, sexual*) fetiche *m*; (*fig*) (= *obsession*) obsesión *f*
fetishism ['fetɪʃɪzəm] N fetichismo *m*
fetishist ['fetɪʃɪst] N fetichista *mf*
fetlock ['fetlɒk] N [1] (*Zool*) (= *joint*) espolón *m*
[2] (= *hair*) cernejas *fpl*
fetter ['fetə^r] VT [+ *person*] encadenar, poner grilletes a; [+ *horse*] trabar; (*fig*) poner trabas a
fetters ['fetəz] NPL grilletes *mpl*; (*fig*) trabas *fpl*
fettle ['fetl] N **in fine ~** (= *condition*) en buenas condiciones; (= *mood*) de muy buen humor
fettuccine [ˌfetə'tʃi:nɪ] N fettuchini *mpl*
fetus ['fi:təs] N (*US*) = **foetus**
feud [fju:d] Ⓐ N enemistad *f* heredada; **a family ~** una disputa familiar
Ⓑ VI pelearse; **to ~ with sb** pelearse con algn
feudal ['fju:dl] Ⓐ ADJ feudal
Ⓑ CPD ► **feudal system** N feudalismo *m*
feudalism ['fju:dəlɪzəm] N feudalismo *m*
fever ['fi:və^r] Ⓐ N [1] (= *disease, high temperature*) fiebre *f*, calentura *f* (*LAm*); **he has a ~** tiene fiebre; **a bout of ~** un ataque de fiebre; **a slight/high ~** un poco de/mucha fiebre
[2] (*fig*) **the gambling ~** la fiebre del juego; **a ~ of excitement/impatience** una emoción/impaciencia febril; **she's in a ~ about the party** la fiesta la tiene muy alterada
Ⓑ CPD ► **fever pitch** N **it reached ~ pitch** se puso al rojo vivo
fevered ['fi:vəd] ADJ = **feverish**
feverish ['fi:vərɪʃ] ADJ [1] (*Med*) febril, calenturiento; **to be ~** tener fiebre
[2] (*fig*) febril
feverishly ['fi:vərɪʃlɪ] ADV febrilmente
feverishness ['fi:vərɪʃnɪs] N (*Med, fig*) febrilidad *f*
few [fju:] ADJ, PRON (*compar* **fewer**, *superl* **fewest**) [1] (= *not many*) pocos/as; **~ books** pocos libros; **~ of them** pocos (de ellos); **only a ~** sólo unos pocos; **only a ~ of them came** sólo vinieron unos pocos; **there are very ~ of us** ◊ **we are very ~** somos muy pocos; **~ (people) managed to do it** muy pocos consiguieron hacerlo; **the ~ who ...** los pocos que ...; **she is one of the ~ (people) who ...** ella es una de los pocos que ...; **such men are ~** hay pocos hombres así; **as ~ as three of them** nada más que tres; **every ~ weeks** cada dos o tres semanas; **with ~ exceptions** con pocas excepciones; **they are ~ and far between** son contados; **the lucky ~** unos pocos *or* unos cuantos afortunados; **in** *or* **over the next ~ days** en *or* durante los próximos días, en estos días (*LAm*); **in** *or* **over the past ~ days** en *or* durante los últimos días; **the last** *or* **remaining ~ minutes** el poco tiempo que queda/quedaba; **too ~** demasiado pocos; **there were three too ~** faltaban tres
[2] (= *some, several*) **a ~** algunos; **a good ~** ◊ **quite a ~** bastantes; **a good ~** *or* **quite a ~ (people) came** vinieron bastantes, vino bastante gente; **he'd had a ~ (drinks)*** llevaba ya una copa de más; **a ~ more** algunos más; **(in) a ~ more days** dentro de unos pocos días; **a ~ of them** algunos de ellos; **quite a ~** *see* **a good few**
fewer ['fju:ə^r] ADJ, PRON, COMPAR *of* **few** menos; **~ than ten** menos de diez; **no ~ than ...** no menos de ...; **they have ~ than I** tienen menos que yo; **the ~ the better** cuantos menos mejor; → LESS THAN, FEWER THAN
fewest ['fju:ɪst] ADJ, PRON, SUPERL *of* **few** los/las menos
fewness ['fju:nɪs] N corto número *m*
fey [feɪ] ADJ vidente
fez [fez] N (*pl* **fezzes**) fez *m*
ff ABBR (= **and the following**) sigs., sgtes.
FFA N ABBR (*US*) = **Future Farmers of America**
FFV ABBR (= **First Families of Virginia**) *descendientes de los primeros colonos de Virginia*
FH N ABBR = **fire hydrant**
FHA N ABBR (*US*) = **Federal Housing Association**
FHSA N ABBR (*Brit*) = **Family Health Services Authority**
fiancé [fɪ'ɑ̃:nseɪ] N novio *m*, prometido *m*
fiancée [fɪ'ɑ̃:nseɪ] N novia *f*, prometida *f*
fiasco [fɪ'æskəʊ] N (*pl* **fiascos, fiascoes**) fiasco *m*, desastre *m*
fiat ['faɪæt] N fíat *m*, autorización *f*
fib* [fɪb] Ⓐ N mentirijilla *f*; **to tell a ~** decir una mentirijilla
Ⓑ VI decir mentirijillas
fibber* ['fɪbə^r] N mentirosillo/a *m/f*
fibre, fiber (*US*) ['faɪbə^r] Ⓐ N [1] (= *thread*) fibra *f*, hilo *m*; (= *fabric*) fibra *f*
[2] (*fig*) nervio *m*, carácter *m*
[3] (*in diet*) fibra *f*
Ⓑ CPD ► **fibre optics, fiber optics** (*US*) NSING transmisión *f* por fibra óptica
fibreboard, fiberboard (*US*) ['faɪbəbɔ:d] N fibra *f* vulcanizada
fibreglass, fiberglass (*US*) ['faɪbəglɑ:s] Ⓐ N fibra *f* de vidrio
Ⓑ CPD de fibra de vidrio
fibre-optic, fiber-optic (*US*) [ˌfaɪbər'ɒptɪk] Ⓐ ADJ de fibra óptica
Ⓑ CPD ► **fibre-optic cable** N cable *m* de fibra óptica
fibre-tip ['faɪbətɪp] N (*also* **~ pen**) (*Brit*) rotulador *m* de punta de fibra
fibroid ['faɪbrɔɪd] N fibroma *m*
fibrositis [ˌfaɪbrə'saɪtɪs] N fibrositis *f inv*
fibrous ['faɪbrəs] ADJ fibroso

fibula ['fɪbjʊlə] N (*pl* **fibulas** *or* **fibulae** ['fɪbjʊliː]) peroné *m*

FIC N ABBR (*US*) = **Federal Information Center**

FICA N ABBR (*US*) = **Federal Insurance Contributions Act**

fickle ['fɪkl] ADJ inconstante, veleidoso, voluble

fickleness ['fɪklnɪs] N inconstancia *f*, veleidad *f*, volubilidad *f*

fiction ['fɪkʃən] N [1] (*Literat*) literatura *f* de ficción, narrativa *f*; **a work of ~** una obra de ficción
[2] (= *untruth*) ficción *f*, invención *f*

fictional ['fɪkʃənl] ADJ ficticio

fictionalize ['fɪkʃənəlaɪz] VT novelar

fictionalized ['fɪkʃənəlaɪzd] ADJ novelado

fictitious [fɪk'tɪʃəs] ADJ [1] = **fictional**
[2] (= *false*) falso

Fid. Def. ABBR = **Fidei Defensor** (= *Defender of the Faith*) Defensor *m* de la Fe

fiddle ['fɪdl] Ⓐ N [1] (= *violin*) violín *m*; **✦IDIOMS to play second ~** desempeñar un papel secundario; **to play second ~ to sb** estar a la sombra de algn; **he's fed up with playing second ~ to his older brother** está harto de estar a la sombra de su hermano mayor
[2] (*esp Brit**) (= *cheat*) trampa *f*, superchería *f*; **it's a ~** aquí hay trampa; **tax ~** evasión *f* fiscal; **to work a ~** hacer trampa; **to be on the ~** dedicarse a hacer chanchullos*
Ⓑ VI [1] (*Mus*) tocar el violín; **✦IDIOM to ~ while Rome burns** perder el tiempo con nimiedades e ignorar el verdadero problema
[2] (= *fidget*) enredar; **do stop fiddling!** ¡deja ya de enredar!; **to ~ (about** *or* **around) with sth** enredar *or* juguetear con algo; **someone has been fiddling (about** *or* **around) with it** alguien lo ha estropeado, alguien ha estado enredando con él
[3] (*esp Brit**) (= *cheat*) hacer trampas
Ⓒ VT (*esp Brit**) [+ *accounts, results, expenses claim etc*] manipular; **to ~ one's income tax** defraudar impuestos

►fiddle about*, fiddle around* VI + ADV perder el tiempo

fiddler ['fɪdləʳ] N [1] (*Mus*) violinista *mf*
[2] (*esp Brit**) (= *cheat*) tramposo/a *m/f*

fiddlesticks* ['fɪdlstɪks] EXCL ¡tonterías!

fiddling ['fɪdlɪŋ] Ⓐ ADJ trivial, insignificante
Ⓑ N (*) (= *cheating*) chanchullos* *mpl*

fiddly ['fɪdlɪ] ADJ (*compar* **fiddlier**; *superl* **fiddliest**) [*job*] complicado, difícil; [*object*] difícil de manejar

FIDE N ABBR (= **Fédération Internationale des Échecs**) FIDE *f*

fidelity [fɪ'delɪtɪ] N (= *faithfulness*) fidelidad *f*; (= *closeness to original*) exactitud *f*, fidelidad *f*

fidget ['fɪdʒɪt] Ⓐ N [1] (= *person*) persona *f* inquieta, azogado/a *m/f*
[2] **to have the ~s** no parar quieto, ser un azogue
Ⓑ VI (*also* **~ about, ~ around**) no parar de moverse; **to ~ with sth** juguetear con algo; **don't ~!** ◊ **stop ~ing!** ¡estáte quieto!

fidgety ['fɪdʒɪtɪ] ADJ nervioso, inquieto; **to be ~** no parar quieto

fiduciary [fɪ'djuːʃɪərɪ] Ⓐ ADJ fiduciario
Ⓑ N fiduciario/a *m/f*

fie†† [faɪ] EXCL **~ on him!** ¡al diablo con él!

fief [fiːf] N feudo *m*

fiefdom ['fiːfdəm] N feudo *m*

field [fiːld] Ⓐ N [1] (*Agr*) campo *m*; (= *meadow*) prado *m*; (*Geol*) yacimiento *m*
[2] (*Sport*) campo *m*, terreno *m* de juego, cancha *f* (*LAm*); (= *participants*) participantes *mpl*; (*for post*) opositores *mpl*, candidatos *mpl*; **is there a strong ~?** ¿se ha presentado gente buena?; **to lead the ~** (*Sport, Comm*) llevar la delantera; **to take the ~** (*Sport*) salir al campo, saltar al terreno de juego; **✦IDIOM to play the ~*** alternar con cualquiera
[3] (= *sphere of activity*) campo *m*, esfera *f*; **~ of activity** esfera *f* de actividades, campo *m* de acción; **my particular ~** mi especialidad; **it's not my ~** no es mi campo *or* especialidad, no es lo mío; **what's your ~?** ¿qué especialidad tiene Vd?; **in the ~ of painting** en el campo *or* mundo de la pintura; **to be the first in the ~** ser líder en su campo
[4] (= *real environment*) **a year's trial in the ~** un año de prueba en el mercado; **to study sth in the ~** estudiar algo sobre el terreno
[5] (*Comput*) campo *m*
[6] (*Mil*) campo *m*; **~ of battle** campo *m* de batalla; **to die in the ~** morir en combate
[7] (*Elec etc*) campo *m*; **~ of vision** campo *m* visual
[8] (*Heraldry*) campo *m*
Ⓑ VI (*Baseball, Cricket*) fildear
Ⓒ VT (*Sport*) [+ *team*] alinear; (*Baseball, Cricket*) [+ *ball*] recoger, fildear; (*fig*) [+ *question*] sortear
Ⓓ CPD ► **field day** N (*Mil*) día *m* de maniobras; **✦IDIOM to have a ~ day** sacar el máximo provecho ► **field event** N concurso *m* (atlético) de salto/lanzamiento ► **field glasses** NPL (= *binoculars*) gemelos *mpl* ► **field gun** N cañón *m* de campaña ► **field hand** N (*US*) jornalero/a *m/f* ► **field hospital** N hospital *m* de campaña ► **field kitchen** N cocina *f* de campaña ► **field marshal** N (*Brit*) mariscal *m* de campo, ≈ capitán *m* general del ejército ► **field officer** N oficial *mf* superior ► **field sports** NPL *la caza y la pesca* ► **field study** N estudio *m* de campo ► **field test**, **field trial** N (*Comm*) prueba *f* de mercado ► **field trip** N viaje *m* *or* excursión *f* de estudios ► **field work** N (*Sociol etc*) trabajo *m* de campo ► **field worker** N investigador(a) *m/f* de campo; *see also* **field-test**

fielder ['fiːldəʳ] N (*Baseball, Cricket*) fildeador(a) *m*; → CRICKET, BASEBALL

fieldfare ['fiːldfeəʳ] N zorzal *m* real

fieldmouse ['fiːldmaʊs] N (*pl* **fieldmice**) ratón *m* de campo

fieldsman ['fiːldzmən] N (*pl* **fieldsmen**) = **fielder**

field-test VT ['fiːld,test] (*Comm*) probar en el mercado

fiend [fiːnd] N [1] (= *devil*) demonio *m*, diablo *m*
[2] (*) (= *person*) malvado/a *m/f*
[3] (*) (= *addict*) **drugs ~** drogadicto/a *m/f*; **sex ~** maníaco *m* sexual

fiendish ['fiːndɪʃ] ADJ (= *fierce*) feroz; (= *mildly wicked*) muy travieso; (= *clever and wicked*) diabólico; (*) (= *difficult and unpleasant*) dificilísimo

fiendishly ['fiːndɪʃlɪ] ADV terriblemente; **~ difficult** terriblemente difícil; **~ expensive** carísimo

fierce [fɪəs] ADJ (*compar* **fiercer**; *superl* **fiercest**)
[1] (= *ferocious*) [*animal*] feroz, fiero; [*gesture, expression*] feroz; [*temper*] temible; **the prime minister came under ~ attack from the opposition** la oposición atacó ferozmente al primer ministro; **she gave me a ~ look** me lanzó una mirada furibunda
[2] (= *intense*) [*competition, argument*] encarnizado; [*storm, wind, opposition, resistance*] violento; [*opponent*] empedernido, acérrimo; [*pride, loyalty*] impasionado; [*heat*] intenso; **~ fighting broke out in the capital** se produjeron enfrentamientos encarnizados en la capital; **the fire was so ~ that it took several hours to put it out** el fuego era tan intenso que se tardaron varias horas en apagarlo

fiercely ['fɪəslɪ] ADV [1] (= *ferociously*) [*look, scowl*] ferozmente, con ferocidad; [*attack*] ferozmente
[2] (= *intensely*) [*independent, competitive, loyal*] tremendamente; [*oppose, resist*] ferozmente; [*fight, compete*] encarnizadamente; **she is a ~ independent woman** es una mujer tremendamente independiente; **it was a ~ contested match** fue un partido extremadamente reñido; **they are ~ protective of their privacy** protegen su intimidad con uñas y dientes; **the building was burning ~** el edificio ardía en llamas; **the storm raged ~ outside** fuera, el temporal rugía con fuerza

fierceness ['fɪəsnɪs] N [1] (= *ferocity*) [*of animal, person*] ferocidad *f*
[2] (= *intensity*) [*of heat, sun, passion*] intensidad *f*; [*of storm*] furia *f*

fiery ['faɪərɪ] ADJ (*compar* **fierier**; *superl* **fieriest**)
[1] [*heat, sun*] abrasador
[2] (*fig*) [*sky, sunset, red*] encendido; [*taste*] picante; [*temperament, speech*] acalorado; [*horse*] fogoso; [*liquor*] fuerte

fiesta [fɪ'estə] N fiesta *f*

FIFA ['fiːfə] N ABBR (= **Fédération Internationale de Football Association**) FIFA *f*

fife [faɪf] N pífano *m*

FIFO ['faɪfəʊ] ABBR (= **first in, first out**) primero en entrar, primero en salir

fifteen [fɪf'tiːn] Ⓐ ADJ quince; **about ~ people** unas quince personas
Ⓑ N quince *m*; (*Rugby*) quince *m*, equipo *m*; *see* **five** *for usage*

fifteenth [fɪf'tiːnθ] Ⓐ ADJ decimoquinto
Ⓑ N (*in series*) decimoquinto/a *m/f*; (= *fraction*) quinceavo *m*, quinceava parte *f*; *see* **fifth** *for usage*

fifth [fɪfθ] Ⓐ ADJ quinto; **he came ~ in the competition** ocupó el quinto lugar *or* terminó quinto en la competición; **in the ~ century** (*in writing*) en el siglo V; (*speaking*) en el siglo quinto *or* cinco; **Henry the Fifth** (*in writing*) Enrique V; (*speaking*) Enrique Quinto; **the ~ of July** ◊ **July the ~** el cinco de julio; **~ form** (*Brit Scol*) quinto *m*, quinto curso
Ⓑ N [1] (*in series*) quinto/a *m/f*; **I was the ~ to arrive** yo fui el quinto en llegar; **I wrote to him on the ~** le escribí el día cinco; *see also* **amendment**
[2] (= *fraction*) quinto *m*, quinta parte *f*
[3] (*Mus*) quinta *f*
Ⓒ CPD ► **fifth column** N (*Pol*) quinta columna *f* ► **fifth columnist** N (*Pol*) quintacolumnista *mf*

fiftieth ['fɪftɪɪθ] Ⓐ ADJ quincuagésimo; **the ~ anniversary** el cincuenta aniversario
Ⓑ N (*in series*) quincuagésimo/a *m/f*; (= *fraction*) quincuagésimo *m*, quincuagésima parte *f*

fifty ['fɪftɪ] Ⓐ ADJ cincuenta; **about ~ people/cars** alrededor de cincuenta personas/coches; **he'll be ~ (years old) this year** cumple *or* va a cumplir cincuenta este año
Ⓑ N cincuenta *m*; **the fifties** (= *1950s*) los años cincuenta; **to be in one's fifties** andar por los cincuenta; **the temperature was in the fifties** hacía más de cincuenta grados; **to do ~ (miles per hour)** (*Aut*) ir a cincuenta (millas por hora)

fifty-fifty ['fɪftɪ'fɪftɪ] Ⓐ ADJ **we have a ~ chance of success** tenemos un cincuenta por ciento de posibilidades de éxito; **it's a ~**

deal es un negocio a medias; **we'll do it on a ~ basis** lo haremos a medias
Ⓑ ADV **to go ~ with sb** ir a medias con algn

fiftyish ['fɪftɪɪʃ] ADJ de unos cincuenta años

fig [fɪg] Ⓐ N [1] (*Bot*) higo *m*; (*early*) breva *f*; (*also* **~ tree**) higuera *f*
[2] **I don't give a ~ for JB!**†* ¡me importa un comino JB!
Ⓑ CPD ► **fig leaf** N hoja *f* de higuera; (*fig*) (*Art*) hoja *f* de parra

fig. ABBR = **figure**; **A7**

fight [faɪt] (*vb: pt, pp* **fought**) Ⓐ N [1] (*between individuals*) [1·1] (*physical, verbal*) pelea *f* (**over** por); **to have a ~ with sb** pelearse con algn, tener una pelea con algn; **to look for a ~** (*physical*) buscar pelea; (*verbal*) querer pelearse; **I'm not looking for a ~ over this issue** no quiero pelearme por este asunto; *see also* **pick B1**, **pick B1**
[1·2] (*Boxing*) combate *m*, pelea *f*
[2] (*Mil*) (*between armies*) lucha *f*, contienda *f*
[3] (= *struggle, campaign*) lucha *f* (**for** por; **against** contra); **the ~ for justice/against inflation** la lucha por la justicia/contra la inflación; **he won't give up without a ~** no se rendirá sin luchar antes; **if he tries to sack me he'll have a ~ on his hands** si intenta despedirme le va a costar lo suyo
[4] (= *fighting spirit*) ánimo *m* de lucha; **there was no ~ left in him** ya no le quedaba ánimo de lucha, ya no tenía ánimo para luchar; **we still had a lot of ~ in us** todavía nos quedaba mucho ánimo para luchar; **to show (some) ~** mostrarse dispuesto a pelear
[5] (= *resistance*) **police believe the victim put up a ~** la policía cree que la víctima opuso resistencia; **they beat us but we put up a good ~** nos vencieron pero nos defendimos bien
Ⓑ VT [1] (*Mil*) [+ *enemy*] luchar contra, combatir contra; (*Boxing*) [+ *opponent*] pelear contra, luchar contra; **to ~ a battle** (*Mil*) librar una batalla; (*fig*) luchar; **I've had to ~ quite a battle to get as far as this** he tenido que luchar mucho para llegar hasta aquí; **I don't ask you to ~ my battles for me** no te pido que libres mis batallas; **to ~ a duel** batirse en duelo; **to ~ sb for sth**: **he fought the council for the right to build on his land** se enfrentó al ayuntamiento por el derecho a edificar en sus tierras; **I'd like to ~ him for the title** me gustaría luchar *or* pelear contra él por el título; **to ~ one's way through a crowd** abrirse paso a la fuerza entre una multitud
[2] (= *combat*) [+ *fire*] combatir; [+ *poverty, inflation, crime*] combatir, luchar contra; [+ *proposal*] oponerse a; **I've made up my mind so don't try and ~ me on it** lo he decidido, así que no intentes oponerte; **I had to ~ the urge to giggle** tuve que esforzarme para no reír, tuve que contener las ganas de reír
[3] (= *try to win*) [+ *campaign*] tomar parte en; [+ *election*] presentarse a; **he says he'll ~ the case all the way to the Supreme Court** dice que si es necesario llevará el caso hasta el Tribunal Supremo; **he fought his case in various courts for ten years** defendió su causa en varios tribunales durante diez años; **he's decided to ~ the seat for a third time** (*Pol*) ha decidido presentarse por tercera vez como candidato para el escaño
Ⓒ VI [1] (= *do battle*) [*troops, countries*] luchar, combatir (**against** contra); [*person, animal*] pelear; (*Boxing*) luchar, pelear; **did you ~ in the war?** ¿luchó usted en la guerra?, ¿tomó usted parte en la guerra?; **the boys were ~ing in the street** los chicos estaban peleándose en la calle; **they'll ~ to the death** lucharán a muerte; **I fought for my country** luché por mi país; **the dogs were ~ing over a bone** los perros estaban peleando por un hueso
[2] (= *quarrel*) discutir, pelear(se) (**with** con); **they usually ~ about** *or* **over who pays the bills** suelen discutir *or* pelear(se) por quién paga las facturas
[3] (= *struggle*) luchar (**for** por; **against** contra); **to ~ against disease/crime** luchar contra la enfermedad/el crimen; **she was ~ing against sleep** luchaba contra el sueño; **to ~ for sth/sb** luchar por algo/algn; **he was ~ing for his life** estaba luchando por su vida; **he was ~ing for breath** le faltaba la respiración, respiraba con enorme dificultad; ✦*IDIOMS* **to go down ~ing** seguir luchando hasta el fin; **to ~ shy of** rehuir, evitar

►**fight back** Ⓐ VI + ADV (= *resist*) (*in fight, argument*) defenderse; (*Sport*) contraatacar; **they fought back from 2-0 down to win 3-2** contraatacaron, pasando de perder por 2-0 a ganar por 3-2
Ⓑ VT + ADV [+ *tears*] contener; [+ *anger, feeling*] contener, reprimir; [+ *despair*] dominar; **I fought back the urge to slap him** reprimí *or* contuve las ganas de darle una bofetada; **I fought back the urge to laugh** contuve las ganas de reír

►**fight down** VT + ADV [+ *anger, feeling*] contener, reprimir; [+ *anxiety*] dominar, reprimir; **she fought down the impulse to run** reprimió el impulso de correr

►**fight off** VT + ADV [1] (= *repel*) [+ *attack, attacker*] repeler, rechazar; **they successfully fought off a takeover bid** consiguieron defenderse contra una oferta de adquisición
[2] (= *resist*) [+ *disease, infection*] combatir; **he was ~ing off sleep** se esforzaba para combatir el sueño; **I had to ~ off an impulse to scream** tuve que reprimir el impulso de gritar

►**fight on** VI + ADV seguir luchando

►**fight out** VT + ADV [1] (*with fists*) resolver a golpes; **they decided to ~ it out in the street** decidieron resolverlo a golpes en la calle
[2] (*fig*) (= *resolve*) resolver; **we'll have to ~ it out in court** tendremos que resolverlo en los tribunales
[3] (= *compete*) **they'll be ~ing it out for the top prize** competirán por el primer premio

fightback ['faɪtbæk] N (*Brit*) contraataque *m*

fighter ['faɪtə^r] Ⓐ N [1] combatiente *mf*; (*Boxing*) boxeador(a) *m/f*, púgil *m*; (= *warrior*) guerrero/a *m/f*, soldado *mf*; (*fig*) luchador(a) *m/f*; **a bonny ~** un valiente guerrero
[2] (= *airplane*) avión *m* de combate, caza *m*
Ⓑ CPD ► **fighter bomber** N cazabombardero *m* ► **fighter command** N jefatura *f* de cazas ► **fighter pilot** N piloto *mf* de caza

fighting ['faɪtɪŋ] Ⓐ N (*between troops, armies*) enfrentamientos *mpl*; (*between individuals*) (*lit, fig*) peleas *fpl*; **he hates ~** odia las peleas; *see also* **street B**
Ⓑ ADJ **we still have a ~ chance of beating them** aún tenemos una buena posibilidad de vencerlos; **this treatment at least gives her a ~ chance** este tratamiento le da al menos una posibilidad
Ⓒ ADV **to be ~ fit** estar en plena forma
Ⓓ CPD ► **fighting bull** N toro *m* de lidia ► **fighting cock** N gallo *m* de pelea ► **fighting dog** N perro *m* de pelea ► **fighting force** N fuerza *f* de combate ► **fighting line** N frente *m* de combate ► **fighting man** N guerrero *m*, soldado *m* ► **fighting spirit** N espíritu *m* de lucha, combatividad *f* ► **fighting strength** N número *m* de soldados (listos para el combate) ► **fighting talk** N **the Prime Minister's ~ talk at the Rome summit** las declaraciones de tono beligerante que hizo el Primer Ministro en la cumbre de Roma; **this is typical ~ talk from the defending champion** ésta es una típica bravuconada del actual campeón

figment ['fɪgmənt] N **a ~ of the imagination** un producto de la imaginación

figurative ['fɪgərətɪv] ADJ [1] [*meaning*] figurado; [*expression*] metafórico
[2] (*Art*) figurativo

figuratively ['fɪgərətɪvlɪ] ADV figuradamente, en sentido figurado; **he was speaking ~** hablaba en sentido figurado; **you should understand this ~** hay que entender esto en sentido figurado

figure ['fɪgə^r] Ⓐ N [1] (= *shape, silhouette*) figura *f*; **a ~ in a blue dress** una figura vestida de azul
[2] (= *bodily proportions*) tipo *m*, figura *f*; **she's got a nice ~** tiene buen tipo *or* una buena figura; **he's a fine ~ of a man** es un hombre con un tipo imponente; **clothes for the fuller ~** tallas *fpl* grandes; **to keep/lose one's ~** guardar/perder la línea *or* el tipo; **to watch one's ~** cuidar la línea *or* el tipo
[3] (= *person*) figura *f*; **a key ~ in twentieth century music** una figura clave en la música del siglo veinte; **a ~ of authority** una figura de autoridad; **he cut a dashing ~ in his new uniform** se veía muy elegante con su nuevo uniforme; **today she cuts a lonely ~** hoy aparece como una figura solitaria; **father ~** figura *f* paterna; **these days he's become a ~ of fun** últimamente se ha convertido en el hazmerreír de todos; **mother ~** figura *f* materna; **public ~** personaje *m* público
[4] (= *numeral*) cifra *f*; **how did you arrive at these ~s?** ¿cómo has llegado a estas cifras?; **he was the only player to reach double ~s** era el único jugador que marcó más de diez tantos; **we want inflation brought down to single ~s** queremos que la inflación baje a menos del diez por cien
[5] **figures** (= *statistics*) estadísticas *fpl*, datos *mpl*; (= *calculations*) cálculos *mpl*; **the latest ~s show that ...** las últimas estadísticas *or* los últimos datos muestran que ...; **he's always been good at ~s** siempre se le han dado bien los números, siempre se le ha dado bien la aritmética
[6] (= *amount*) [*of money*] cifra *f*, suma *f*; (= *number*) [*of items*] cifra *f*, número *m*; **what sort of ~ did you have in mind?** ¿qué cifra *or* suma tenías en mente?; **I wouldn't like to put a ~ on it** no quisiera dar una cifra; **some estimates put the ~ as high as 20,000 dead** algunos cálculos dan una cifra *or* un número de hasta 20.000 muertos
[7] (= *diagram*) figura *f*
[8] (*Art*) figura *f*
[9] (*Geom, Dance, Skating*) figura *f*; **a ~ of eight** ◊ **a ~ eight** (*US*) un ocho
[10] (*Ling*) **~ of speech** figura *f* retórica
Ⓑ VI [1] (= *appear*) figurar (**as** como; **among** entre); **his name doesn't ~ on the list** su nombre no figura en la lista; **this issue ~d prominently in the talks** este tema ocupó un papel prominente en las negociaciones
[2] (*esp US**) (= *make sense*) **it doesn't ~** no tiene sentido, no encaja; **that ~s!** ¡lógico!, ¡obvio!
Ⓒ VT (*esp US*) (= *think*) imaginarse, figurarse; (= *estimate*) calcular; **I ~ they'll come** me imagino *or* me figuro que vendrán; **I ~d**

there'd be about 20 calculé que habría unos 20; **she ~d that they had both learned from the experience** pensaba *or* creía que los dos habían aprendido de la experiencia
Ⓓ CPD ► **figure skating** N patinaje *m* artístico
►**figure in*** VT + ADV (*US*) contar
►**figure on*** VI + PREP (*esp US*) contar con; **he hadn't ~d on the problems that would arise** no había contado con los problemas que surgirían; **the meeting was longer than I'd ~d on** la reunión fue más larga de lo que yo esperaba; **I wasn't figuring on going** no contaba con ir; **are you figuring on going?** ¿piensas ir?
►**figure out*** VT + ADV 1 (= *understand*) [+ *person*] entender; [+ *writing*] entender, descifrar; **I just can't ~ it out!** ¡no me lo explico!, ¡no lo entiendo!
2 (= *work out*) [+ *sum*] calcular; [+ *problem*] resolver; **can you ~ out how to do this?** ¿entiendes cómo se hace esto?; **I couldn't ~ out the answer** no pude encontrar la respuesta *or* solución; **they had it all ~d out** lo tenían todo calculado
►**figure up** VT + ADV (*US*) calcular
-figure ['fɪgəʳ] ADJ (*ending in compounds*) **a four-figure sum** una suma superior a mil (libras *etc*); **a seven-figure sum** un número de siete cifras
figure-conscious ['fɪgə,kɒnʃəs] ADJ **to be ~** cuidar la línea *or* el tipo
figurehead ['fɪgəhed] N (*on ship*) mascarón *m* de proa; (*fig*) testaferro *m*
figure-hugging ['fɪgə,hʌgɪŋ] ADJ ajustado, ceñido al cuerpo
figure-skate ['fɪgə,skeɪt] VI hacer patinaje artístico (sobre hielo)
figurine [fɪgə'riːn] N figurilla *f*, estatuilla *f*
Fiji ['fiːdʒiː] N (*also* **the ~ Islands**) las Islas Fiji
Fijian [fɪ'dʒiːən] Ⓐ ADJ de (las Islas) Fiji
Ⓑ N (= *person*) nativo/a *m/f* de (las Islas) Fiji, habitante *mf* de (las Islas) Fiji
filament ['fɪləmənt] N (*Elec*) filamento *m*
filbert ['fɪlbət] N avellana *f*
filch* [fɪltʃ] VT (= *steal*) birlar*, mangar*
file[1] [faɪl] Ⓐ N (= *tool*) lima *f*; (*for nails*) lima *f* (de uñas)
Ⓑ VT (*also* **~ down, ~ away**) limar
file[2] [faɪl] Ⓐ N 1 (= *folder*) carpeta *f*; (= *dossier*) archivo *m*, carpeta *f*, expediente *m*; (*eg loose-leaf file*) archivador *m*, clasificador *m*; (= *bundle of papers*) legajo *m*; (= *filing system*) fichero *m*; **the ~s** los archivos; **the Lucan ~** el expediente Lucan; **police ~s** archivos policiales; **to close the ~ on sth** dar carpetazo a algo; **to have sth on ~** tener algo archivado; **to have a ~ on sb** tener fichado a algn
2 (*Comput*) fichero *m*, archivo *m*; **to open/close a ~** abrir/cerrar un fichero *or* archivo
Ⓑ VT 1 (*also* **~ away**) [+ *notes, information, work*] archivar; (*under heading*) clasificar
2 (= *submit*) [+ *claim, application, complaint*] presentar; **to ~ a petition for divorce** entablar pleito de divorcio; **to ~ a suit against sb** (*Jur*) entablar pleito *or* presentar una demanda contra algn
Ⓒ CPD ► **file clerk** N (*US*) archivero/a *m/f* ► **file name** N (*Comput*) nombre *m* de fichero, nombre *m* de archivo ► **file server** N (*Jur*) portador(a) *m/f* de notificaciones judiciales
►**file for** VI + PREP (*Jur*) **to ~ for divorce** entablar pleito de divorcio; **to ~ for bankruptcy** presentar una declaración de quiebra; **to ~ for custody (of children)** reclamar la custodia (de los hijos)
file[3] [faɪl] Ⓐ N (= *row*) fila *f*, hilera *f*; **in single ~** en fila india
Ⓑ VI **to ~ in/out** entrar/salir en fila; **to ~ past** desfilar; **they ~d past the general** desfilaron ante el general
filial ['fɪlɪəl] ADJ filial
filiation [,fɪlɪ'eɪʃən] N filiación *f*
filibuster ['fɪlɪbʌstəʳ] (*esp US Pol*) Ⓐ N (= *person*) (*also* **~er**) obstruccionista *mf*; (= *act*) discurso *m* obstruccionista
Ⓑ VI dar un discurso obstruccionista
filibustering ['fɪlɪ,bʌstərɪŋ] N (*Pol*) maniobras *fpl* obstruccionistas, filibusterismo *m*
filigree ['fɪlɪgriː] Ⓐ N (*in metal*) filigrana *f*
Ⓑ ADJ de filigrana
filing ['faɪlɪŋ] Ⓐ N 1 [*of documents*] clasificación *f*; **to do the ~** archivar documentos
2 [*of claim etc*] formulación *f*, presentación *f*
Ⓑ CPD ► **filing cabinet** N fichero *m*, archivador *m* ► **filing clerk** N (*esp Brit*) archivero/a *m/f*
filings ['faɪlɪŋz] NPL limaduras *fpl*
Filipino [fɪlɪ'piːnəʊ] Ⓐ ADJ filipino
Ⓑ N 1 (= *person*) filipino/a *m/f*
2 (*Ling*) tagalo *m*
fill [fɪl] Ⓐ VT 1 (= *make full*) [+ *container*] llenar (**with** de); **~ a saucepan with water** llenar un cazo de agua; **I am ~ed with admiration for her achievements** sus logros me llenan de admiración; **he was ~ed with remorse** estaba lleno de remordimiento; **he was ~ed with despair** estaba desesperado; **the wind ~ed the sails** el viento henchía las velas
2 (= *occupy*) [+ *space*] llenar (**with** de); [+ *time*] ocupar; **his plays always ~ the theatres** sus obras siempre llenan los teatros; **airlines can always ~ seats in the summer** las compañías aéreas siempre logran ocupar las plazas en verano; **rooms ~ed with furniture** habitaciones *fpl* llenas de muebles; **shouts ~ed the air** resonaron unos gritos en el aire; **the house was ~ed with the smell of burning** el olor a quemado invadía la casa; **she needs a routine to ~ her day** le hace falta una rutina que le llene el día; **the text ~s 231 pages** el texto ocupa 231 páginas
3 (= *plug*) [+ *cavity, hole*] rellenar, tapar (**with** con), llenar (**with** de); [+ *tooth*] empastar, emplomar (*S. Cone*) (**with** con); (*fig*) [+ *gap, vacuum*] llenar; **she ~ed a gap in his life** ella llenó un hueco en su vida
4 (= *fulfill*) [+ *need*] cubrir, satisfacer; [+ *requirement*] llenar, satisfacer; [+ *role*] cumplir, desempeñar; *see also* **bill**[1]
5 (= *supply*) [+ *order*] despachar
6 (= *appoint sb to*) [+ *vacancy*] cubrir; [+ *post*] ocupar; **the position is already ~ed** la vacante ya está cubierta; **she was chosen to ~ the post of Education Secretary** la eligieron para ocupar el puesto de Ministra de Educación
Ⓑ VI 1 llenarse (**with** de); **the room ~ed with smoke** la habitación se llenó de humo; **her eyes ~ed with tears** los ojos se le llenaron de lágrimas
2 [*sails*] henchirse
Ⓒ N 1 (= *sufficiency*) **to eat/drink one's ~ (of sth)** comer/beber (algo) hasta saciarse, hartarse de comer/beber (algo); **to have had one's ~ of sth** (*fig*) haberse hartado de algo, estar harto de algo
2 (= *gravel, stones*) relleno *m*
►**fill in** Ⓐ VT + ADV 1 [+ *hole, gap, outline*] rellenar
2 (= *occupy*) [+ *time*] ocupar, pasar; **I had an hour to ~ in before my train** tenía que ocupar *or* pasar una hora de alguna forma hasta que llegase mi tren; **"what are you doing here?" — "just ~ing in time"** —¿qué haces aquí? —pasar el tiempo
3 (= *complete*) [+ *form*] rellenar, llenar; [+ *details*] completar; (= *write*) [+ *one's name*] escribir, poner; **~ in the blanks in the following sentences** rellenar los espacios vacíos en las siguientes frases
4 (= *inform*) **to ~ sb in (on sth)** poner a algn al corriente (de algo); **Jackie will ~ you in on the rest of the office procedures** Jackie te pondrá al corriente de cómo funciona todo lo demás en la oficina
Ⓑ VI + ADV **to ~ in for sb** suplir a algn, sustituir a algn; **can you find someone to ~ in at such short notice?** ¿puedes encontrar a alguien con tan poco tiempo que haga de suplente?
►**fill out** Ⓐ VT + ADV 1 (= *complete*) [+ *form, application*] rellenar, llenar; [+ *details*] completar; (= *write*) [+ *one's name*] escribir, poner
2 (= *occupy all of*) [+ *garment*] llenar
3 (= *make more substantial*) [+ *essay, information*] rellenar
Ⓑ VI + ADV [*person*] engordar; [*face*] rellenarse, redondearse; [*sail*] henchirse
►**fill up** Ⓐ VI + ADV 1 (= *become full*) [*room, hall*] llenarse
2 (*Aut*) (*with petrol*) echar gasolina; (*with diesel*) echar diesel
3 (= *eat*) **he doesn't eat proper meals, he ~s up on snacks** no come como es debido, se llena el estómago picando
Ⓑ VT + ADV [+ *container, suitcase*] llenar (**with** de); **~ it** *or* **her up!*** (*Aut*) ¡llena el tanque!; **I can't drink too much before a meal, it ~s me up** no puedo beber mucho antes de una comida, me llena; **to ~ o.s. up with sth** llenarse (el estómago) de algo; **I do it to ~ up the time** lo hago para pasar el tiempo
filler ['fɪləʳ] Ⓐ N 1 (*for cracks in wood, plaster*) masilla *f*; (*in foodstuffs*) relleno *m*; (*Press*) relleno *m*
2 (= *device*) [*of bottle, tank*] rellenador *m*; (= *funnel*) embudo *m*
Ⓑ CPD ► **filler cap** N tapa *f* del depósito de gasolina
fillet ['fɪlɪt] Ⓐ N [*of meat, fish*] filete *m*
Ⓑ VT [+ *meat, fish*] cortar en filetes
fill-in ['fɪlɪn] N sustituto *m*, suplente *mf*
filling ['fɪlɪŋ] Ⓐ N 1 [*of tooth*] empaste *m*, emplomadura *f* (*S. Cone*)
2 (*Culin*) relleno *m*
Ⓑ ADJ [*food, dish*] que llena mucho; **this dish is very ~** este plato llena mucho
Ⓒ CPD ► **filling station** N = **petrol station**
fillip ['fɪlɪp] N estímulo *m*; **to give a ~ to** estimular
filly ['fɪlɪ] N potra *f*
film [fɪlm] Ⓐ N (= *thin skin*) película *f*; [*of dust*] capa *f*; [*of smoke etc*] velo *m*; (*Cine, Phot*) (= *negatives*) película *f*; (= *roll of film*) carrete *m*, rollo *m*; (*at cinema*) película *f*, film *m*, filme *m*; (*full-length*) largometraje *m*; (*short*) corto(metraje) *m*; **the ~s** el cine; **silent ~** película *f* muda; **to make a ~ of** [+ *book*] llevar al cine, hacer una película de; [+ *event*] filmar
Ⓑ VT [+ *book*] llevar al cine, hacer una película de; [+ *event*] filmar; [+ *scene*] rodar
Ⓒ VI rodar, filmar
Ⓓ CPD [*camera, festival*] cinematográfico, de cine ► **film buff** N cinéfilo/a *m/f* ► **film crew** N equipo *m* cinematográfico ► **film fan** N aficionado/a *m/f* al cine ► **film library** N ci-

nemateca *f* ► **film première** N estreno *m* oficial, premier *f* ► **film producer** N productor(a) *m/f* (cinematográfico) ► **film rights** NPL derechos *mpl* cinematográficos ► **film script** N guión *m* ► **film set** N plató *m* ► **film star** N estrella *f* de cine ► **film strip** N película *f* de diapositivas ► **film studio** N estudio *m* de cine ► **film test** N prueba *f* cinematográfica

►**film over** VI + ADV [*eyes*] empañarse

filmic ['fɪlmɪk] ADJ fílmico

filming ['fɪlmɪŋ] N rodaje *m*, filmación *f*

film-maker ['fɪlmmeɪkəʳ] N cineasta *mf*

film-making ['fɪlmmeɪkɪŋ] N cinematografía *f*

filmography [fɪl'mɒgrəfɪ] N filmografía *f*

filmsetting ['fɪlmsetɪŋ] N fotocomposición *f*

filmy ['fɪlmɪ] ADJ [*fabric, material*] vaporoso

Filofax® ['faɪləʊ,fæks] N agenda *f* de anillas

filter ['fɪltəʳ] Ⓐ N [1] (*gen, Phot*) filtro *m*
[2] (*Brit Aut*) semáforo *m* de flecha de desvío
Ⓑ VT [+ *liquid, air*] filtrar
Ⓒ VI [*liquid, light*] filtrarse; **to ~ to the left** (*Aut*) tomar el carril izquierdo
Ⓓ CPD ► **filter coffee** N (= *powder*) café *m* para filtrar; (= *cup of coffee*) café *m* hecho con cafetera de filtro ► **filter lane** N (*Aut*) carril *m* de giro ► **filter light** N semáforo *m* de flecha de desvío ► **filter paper** N papel *m* de filtro

►**filter back** VI + ADV [*news, rumour*] llegar; [*people*] volver poco a poco

►**filter in** VI + ADV [*light*] filtrarse; [*news, rumour*] llegar; [*people*] entrar (poco a poco)

►**filter out** Ⓐ VT + ADV [+ *impurities*] quitar filtrando
Ⓑ VI + ADV [*news*] trascender, llegar a saberse

►**filter through** VI + ADV = **filter in**

filter-tipped ['fɪltə,tɪpt] ADJ [*cigarette*] con filtro *or* boquilla

filth [fɪlθ] N [1] (*lit*) (= *dirt*) suciedad *f*, mugre *f*; (= *excrement*) heces *fpl*
[2] (*fig*) [2·1] (= *people*) basura *f*; **those people are nothing but ~** esa gente no es más que basura
[2·2] (= *bad language*) groserías *fpl*, obscenidades *fpl*; **I've never read such ~** jamás he leído groserías *or* obscenidades semejantes
[3] (‡) (= *police*) **the ~** la policía, la pasma (*Sp*‡), la bofia (*Sp*‡), la cana (*S. Cone*‡)

filthiness ['fɪlθɪnɪs] N [1] (*lit*) (= *dirtiness*) suciedad *f*, mugre *f*
[2] (*fig*) [*of behaviour*] lo grosero, lo obsceno; (= *bad language*) groserías *fpl*, obscenidades *fpl*; (= *obscenity*) obscenidad *f*

filthy ['fɪlθɪ] Ⓐ ADJ (*compar* **filthier**, *superl* **filthiest**) [1] (*lit*) (= *dirty*) [*hands, room, house*] asqueroso; [*bathtub*] mugriento, mugroso (*LAm*); [*clothes*] muy sucio; [*water*] inmundo
[2] (= *indecent*) [*language, behaviour*] grosero, obsceno; [*joke*] verde; [*sense of humour*] obsceno
[3] (= *despicable*) asqueroso; **she called him a ~ murderer** lo llamó un asesino asqueroso
[4] (*) [*weather*] asqueroso*, de perros*; [*temper*] de perros*, de mil diablos*; **she was in a ~ temper** estaba con un humor de perros *or* de mil diablos*
Ⓑ ADV **the children came home ~ dirty** los niños llegaron a casa sucísimos, los niños llegaron a casa hechos un asco*; **they're ~ rich*** están podridos de dinero*, son unos ricachos*

filtration [fɪl'treɪʃən] N filtración *f*

fin [fɪn] N (*all senses*) aleta *f*

fin. ABBR = **finance**

final ['faɪnl] Ⓐ ADJ [1] (= *last*) (*in series*) último; [*stage*] final, último; (*Univ*) [*exam*] de fin de carrera; **in the ~ stages of her illness** en la fase final *or* en la última fase de su enfermedad; **I'd like to say one ~ word ...** por último me gustaría añadir lo siguiente ...; **~ demand** último aviso *m* de pago; **~ dividend** dividendo *m* complementario; **~ edition** (*Journalism*) última edición *f*; *see also* **analysis**
[2] (= *conclusive*) [*approval*] definitivo; [*result*] final; **the judge's decision is ~** la decisión del juez es inapelable; **and that's ~!** ¡y punto!, ¡y no se hable más!
[3] (= *ultimate*) [*destination*] final
Ⓑ N [1] (*Sport*) final *f*; **she went on to reach the ~** siguió hasta llegar a la final
[2] **finals** (*Univ*) exámenes *mpl* de fin de carrera

finale [fɪ'nɑːlɪ] N (*Mus*) final *m*; (*Theat*) escena *f* final; **the grand ~** el gran final, la gran escena final; (*fig*) el final apoteósico *or* triunfal

finalist ['faɪnəlɪst] N (*Sport*) finalista *mf*

finality [faɪ'nælɪtɪ] N (= *conclusiveness*) [*of death*] lo irreversible; [*of decision*] carácter *m* definitivo; **he said with ~** dijo de modo terminante

finalization [,faɪnəlaɪ'zeɪʃən] N ultimación *f*, conclusión *f*

finalize ['faɪnəlaɪz] VT [+ *preparations, arrangements*] concluir; [+ *agreement, plans, contract*] ultimar; [+ *report, text*] completar; [+ *date*] fijar, acordar; **to ~ a decision** tomar una decisión final

▼**finally** ['faɪnəlɪ] ADV [1] (= *lastly*) por último, finalmente; **~, I would like to say ...** por último *or* finalmente, me gustaría añadir ...
[2] (= *eventually, at last*) por fin; **she ~ decided to accept** por fin decidió aceptar
[3] (= *once and for all*) de manera definitiva; **they decided to separate, ~ and irrevocably** decidieron separarse de manera definitiva e irrevocable

finance [faɪ'næns] Ⓐ N (*gen*) finanzas *fpl*, asuntos *mpl* financieros; (= *funds*) (*also* **~s**) fondos *mpl*; **(the state of) the country's ~s** la situación económica del país; **Minister of Finance** Ministro/a *m/f* de Economía y Hacienda
Ⓑ VT [+ *project*] financiar; **he stole to ~ his drug habit** robaba para costearse su adicción a las drogas
Ⓒ CPD [*company*] financiero; [*page, section*] de economía, de negocios ► **finance director** N director(a) *m/f* financiero/a

financial [faɪ'nænʃəl] Ⓐ ADJ [*services, aid, backing, affairs, security*] financiero; [*policy, resources, problems*] económico; [*page, section*] de economía, de negocios
Ⓑ CPD ► **financial adviser** N asesor(a) *m/f* financiero/a ► **financial institution** N entidad *f* financiera ► **financial management** N gestión *f* financiera ► **financial statement** N estado *m* financiero, balance *m* ► **Financial Times Index** N índice *m* bursátil del Financial Times ► **financial year** N [*of company*] ejercicio *m* (financiero); [*of government*] año *m* fiscal

financially [faɪ'nænʃəlɪ] ADV [*independent, sound*] económicamente; **the scheme was ~ successful** el plan tuvo éxito desde el punto de vista económico; **this is not ~ possible** esto no es posible por razones financieras; **~, he would be much better off** desde el punto de vista económico *or* económicamente, saldría ganando

financier [faɪ'nænsɪəʳ] N financiero/a *m/f*

financing [faɪ'nænsɪŋ] N financiación *f*

finch [fɪntʃ] N pinzón *m*

find [faɪnd] (*vb: pt, pp* **found**) Ⓐ VT [1] (*after losing*) encontrar; **did you ~ your purse?** ¿encontraste tu monedero?; **I looked but I couldn't ~ it** lo busqué pero no pude encontrarlo; **you distracted me, now I can't ~ my place again** me has distraído y ahora no sé por dónde iba; *see also* **foot**, **tongue A1**
[2] (= *locate*) encontrar; **the plant is found all over Europe** la planta se encuentra *or* existe en toda Europa; **did you ~ the man?** ¿encontraste *or* localizaste al hombre?; **the book is nowhere to be found** el libro no se encuentra por ninguna parte; **to ~ one's way**: **can you ~ your (own) way to the station?** ¿sabes llegar a la estación sin ayuda?, ¿puedes encontrar la estación solo?; **this found its way into my drawer** esto vino a parar a mi cajón; **to ~ one's way around** orientarse; **to ~ one's way around a new city** orientarse en una ciudad nueva; **it took me a while to ~ my way around their kitchen** me llevó un rato familiarizarme con su cocina
[3] (= *chance upon*) encontrar; **I found a pound coin in the street** me encontré una moneda de una libra en la calle
Ⓑ N hallazgo *m*; **your new assistant is a real ~** tu nueva ayudante es todo un hallazgo; **that was a lucky ~!** ¡qué buen hallazgo!; **archaeological ~s** hallazgos *mpl* arqueológicos; **to make a ~** realizar un descubrimiento

►**find out** Ⓐ VT + ADV [1] (= *check out*) averiguar; **~ out everything you can about him** averigua todo lo que puedas sobre él; **she phoned to ~ out when the bus left** llamó por teléfono para averiguar cuándo *or* enterarse de cuándo salía el autobús
[2] (= *discover*) descubrir; **they never found out how he escaped** nunca descubrieron cómo se había escapado; **I found out what he was really like** descubrí su verdadera personalidad, me di cuenta de cómo era realmente; **~ out more by writing to ...** infórmese escribiendo a ...; **I found out that she had been lying** descubrí *or* me enteré que había estado mintiendo; **I found out from his teacher that he hadn't been to school** me enteré a través de su profesor de que había faltado al colegio
[3] (= *expose*) **to ~ sb out** descubrir a algn; ✦***PROV*** **(you can) be sure your sins will ~ you out** puedes estar seguro de que tarde o temprano tus mismas acciones te delatarán
[4] (= *realize*) darse cuenta de, descubrir; **they'll be sorry when they ~ out their mistake** se van a arrepentir cuando se den cuenta de su error
Ⓑ VI + ADV [1] (= *become aware*) enterarse; **they'll soon ~ out** pronto se enterarán; **to ~ out about sth** enterarse de algo, descubrir algo; **she was afraid her husband would ~ out about their relationship** le daba miedo que su marido se enterase de *or* descubriese su relación
[2] (= *enquire*) **to ~ out about sth** informarse acerca de algo; **why don't you ~ out about training courses?** ¿por qué no te informas sobre cursos de capacitación?

finder ['faɪndəʳ] N descubridor(a) *m/f*; ✦***IDIOM*** **~s keepers (losers weepers)** quien se lo encuentra se lo queda

finding ['faɪndɪŋ] N [1] (= *discovery*) descubrimiento *m*
[2] (= *conclusion*) resultado *m*
[3] (*Jur*) fallo *m*; **to make a ~** fallar
[4] **findings** (= *conclusions*) conclusiones *fpl*; (= *results*) resultados *mpl*

▼**fine**[1] [faɪn] Ⓐ ADJ (*compar* **finer**, *superl* **finest**) [1] (= *delicate, thin*) [*thread, hair*] fino, delgado; [*rain, point, nib*] fino; [*line*] delgado, tenue; (= *small*) [*particle*] minúsculo; **~-nibbed pen** bolígrafo *m* de punta fina; *see also* **print**

➤ LANGUAGE IN USE: **finally 1** 26.1, 26.2 **fine**[1] **A5** 11.2, 11.3, 13

2 (= *good*) [*performance, example*] excelente; (= *imposing*) [*house, building*] magnífico; (= *beautiful*) [*object*] hermoso; **she's a very ~ musician** es una música verdaderamente excelente; **we use only the ~st ingredients** sólo usamos ingredientes de primerísima calidad; **he's a ~-looking boy** es un muchacho bien parecido; ✦*IDIOM* **he's got it down to a ~ art** lo hace a la perfección; *see also* **chance A2**

3 (= *subtle*) [*distinction*] sutil; **she has a ~ eye for a bargain** tiene mucho ojo *or* muy buen olfato para las gangas; **there's a ~ line between love and hate** la línea que separa el amor del odio es muy tenue, del amor al odio sólo hay un paso; **not to put too ~ a point on it** hablando en plata; **the ~r points of the argument** los puntos más sutiles del argumento

4 (= *refined*) [*taste, manners*] refinado; **he has no ~r feelings whatsoever** no tiene nada de sensibilidad; *see also* **feeling 3**

5 (= *acceptable*) bien; **"is this ok?" — "yes, it's ~"** —¿vale así? —sí, está bien; **~!** ¡de acuerdo!, ¡vale!, ¡cómo no! (*esp LAm*); **that's ~ by me** por mí bien, de acuerdo; **"would you like some more?" — "no, I'm ~, thanks"** —¿quieres un poco más? —no, gracias, con esto me basta; ✦*IDIOM* **~ and dandy**: **everything may look ~ and dandy to you** puede que tú todo lo veas de color de rosa

6 (= *quite well*) muy bien; **he's ~, thanks** está muy bien, gracias

7 (*of weather*) bueno; **if the weather is ~** si hace buen tiempo; **it's a ~ day today** hoy hace buen tiempo; **the weather kept ~ for the match** duró el buen tiempo hasta el partido; **one ~ day, we were out walking** un día que hacia buen tiempo habíamos salido de paseo

8 (*iro*) menudo; **a ~ friend you are!** ¡valiente amigo estás hecho! (*iro*), ¡menudo amigo eres tú! (*iro*); **you're a ~ one to talk!** ¡mira quién habla!; **a ~ thing!** ¡hasta dónde hemos llegado!

9 (= *pure*) [*metal*] puro, fino

Ⓑ ADV 1 (= *well*) bien; **"how did you get on at the dentist's?" — "~"** —¿qué tal te ha ido en el dentista? —bien; **you're doing ~** lo estás haciendo bien; **mother and baby are doing ~** la madre y el bebé están bien; **to feel ~** [*person*] encontrarse bien; **these shoes feel ~** estos zapatos son cómodos; **five o'clock suits me ~** a las cinco me viene bien

2 (= *finely*) **to chop sth up ~** picar algo en trozos menudos, picar algo muy fino; ✦*IDIOM* **to cut it ~** (*of time*) ir con el tiempo justo; (*of money*) calcular muy justo; **we'll be cutting it pretty ~ if we leave at ten** vamos a ir con el tiempo muy justo si salimos a las diez

Ⓒ CPD ► **fine art**, N **the fine arts** NPL las Bellas Artes ► **fine wines** NPL vinos *mpl* selectos

fine² [faɪn] Ⓐ N multa *f*; **to get a ~ (for sth/doing sth)** ser multado (por algo/hacer algo); **I got a ~ for ...** me pusieron una multa por ...

Ⓑ VT **to ~ sb (for sth/doing sth)** multar a algn (por algo/hacer algo)

fine-drawn [ˈfaɪnˈdrɔːn] ADJ [*wire*] muy delgado; [*distinction*] sutil

fine-grained [ˈfaɪnˈɡreɪnd] ADJ de grano fino

finely [ˈfaɪnlɪ] ADV 1 (= *splendidly, well*) [*dressed, written*] con elegancia

2 (= *delicately*) [*carved, woven*] delicadamente; **a ~ detailed embroidery** un bordado trabajado con mucho detalle; **this could upset the whole ~ balanced process** esto podría trastornar el precario equilibrio del proceso

3 (= *very small*) [*chopped*] en trozos muy menudos, muy fino; [*sliced*] en rodajas finas, en lonchas finas

4 (= *with precision*) [*tuned, judged*] con precisión

fineness [ˈfaɪnnɪs] N 1 (= *thinness*) [*of thread, hair*] lo fino, lo delgado

2 (= *excellent quality*) excelente calidad *f*

3 (= *delicacy*) exquisitez *f*, lo delicado; **observe the ~ of detail in the painting** observe la exquisitez de los detalles en el cuadro

4 (= *precision*) precisión *f*

5 (= *purity*) [*of metal*] pureza *f*

finery [ˈfaɪnərɪ] N galas *fpl*; **spring in all its ~** (*liter*) la primavera con todo su esplendor

fine-spun [ˈfaɪnspʌn] ADJ [*yarn*] fino; (*fig*) [*hair*] fino, sedoso

finesse [fɪˈnes] Ⓐ N 1 (*in judgement*) finura *f*, delicadeza *f*; (*in action*) diplomacia *f*, sutileza *f*; (= *cunning*) astucia *f*

2 (*Cards*) impasse *m*

Ⓑ VT hacer el impasse a

fine-tooth comb [ˌfaɪnˌtuːθˈkəʊm] N peine *m* de púas finas; ✦*IDIOM* **to go over** *or* **through sth with a ~** revisar *or* examinar algo a fondo

fine-tune [ˌfaɪnˈtjuːn] VT 1 [+ *engine*] poner a punto

2 (*fig*) [+ *plans, strategy*] afinar, matizar; [+ *economy*] ajustar; [+ *text*] dar los últimos retoques a

fine-tuning [ˌfaɪnˈtjuːnɪŋ] N 1 [*of engine*] puesta *f* a punto

2 (*fig*) [*of plans, strategy*] matización *f*; [*of economy*] ajuste *m*; [*of text*] últimos retoques *mpl*

finger [ˈfɪŋɡəʳ] Ⓐ N 1 (*Anat*) dedo *m*; **I can count on the ~s of one hand the number of times you've taken me out** con los dedos de la mano se pueden contar las veces que me has sacado; **to cross one's ~s** ◊ **keep one's ~s crossed**: **I'll keep my ~s crossed for you** cruzo los dedos (por ti), ojalá tengas suerte; **~s crossed!** (*for someone*) ¡(que tengas) suerte!, ¡buena suerte!; (*for yourself*) ¡deséame suerte!; **index ~** (dedo *m*) índice *m*; **they never laid a ~ on her** no le pusieron la mano encima; **he didn't lift a ~ to help us** no movió un dedo para ayudarnos; **she never lifts a ~ around the house** nunca mueve un dedo para ayudar en la casa; **little ~** (dedo *m*) meñique *m*; **middle ~** (dedo *m*) corazón *m or* medio *m*; **ring ~** (dedo *m*) anular *m*; **to snap one's ~s** chasquear los dedos; **she only has to snap her ~s and he comes running** no tiene más que chasquear los dedos y él viene corriendo; ✦*IDIOMS* **to burn one's ~s** ◊ **get one's ~s burnt** pillarse los dedos; **to get** *or* **pull one's ~ out*** espabilarse; **to have a ~ in every pie** estar metido en todo; **to point the ~ at sb** acusar a algn, señalar a algn; **evidence points the ~ of suspicion at his wife** las pruebas señalan a su mujer como sospechosa; **to put one's ~ on sth**: **there's something wrong, but I can't put my ~ on it** hay algo que está mal, pero no sé exactamente qué; **there was nothing you could put your ~ on** no había nada concreto; **to slip through one's ~s** escapársele de las manos; **to be all ~s and thumbs** ser un/una manazas, ser muy desmañado/a; **he's got her twisted round his little ~** hace con ella lo que quiere; **to put two ~s up at sb** ◊ **give sb the two ~s*** ≈ hacer un corte de mangas a algn*; **to work one's ~s to the bone** dejarse la piel trabajando*; *see also* **pulse**, **twist B1**

2 [*of glove*] dedo *m*

3 (= *shape*) franja *f*; **a ~ of smoke** una franja de humo; **a ~ of land projecting into the sea** una lengua de tierra adentrándose en el mar

4 (= *measure*) [*of drink*] dedo *m*

Ⓑ VT 1 (= *touch*) toquetear

2 (*Brit**) (= *betray, inform on*) delatar

3 (*Mus*) [+ *piano*] teclear; [+ *guitar*] rasguear; [+ *music score*] marcar la digitación de

Ⓒ CPD ► **finger bowl** N lavafrutas *m inv* ► **finger buffet** N buffet *m* de canapés ► **finger food** N (*for babies*) *comida que los bebés pueden agarrar y comer con las manos*; (*US*) canapés *mpl* ► **finger paint** N pintura *f* para pintar con los dedos

fingerboard [ˈfɪŋɡəbɔːd] N (*on piano*) teclado *m*; (*on stringed instrument*) diapasón *m*

fingering [ˈfɪŋɡərɪŋ] N (*Mus*) digitación *f*

fingermark [ˈfɪŋɡəmɑːk] N huella *f*

fingernail [ˈfɪŋɡəneɪl] N uña *f*

finger-paint [ˈfɪŋɡəpeɪnt] VI pintar con los dedos

fingerprint [ˈfɪŋɡəprɪnt] Ⓐ N huella *f* digital *or* dactilar

Ⓑ VT [+ *person*] tomar las huellas digitales *or* dactilares a; (*Med*) identificar genéticamente

fingerstall [ˈfɪŋɡəstɔːl] N dedil *m*

fingertip [ˈfɪŋɡətɪp] N punta *f or* yema *f* del dedo; **to have sth at one's ~s** tener algo a mano; (= *know sth*) saber(se) algo al dedillo

finicky [ˈfɪnɪkɪ] ADJ 1 [*person*] melindroso (**about** con); **she's a ~ eater** ◊ **she is ~ about her food** es muy melindrosa con la comida

2 [*job*] complicado

finish [ˈfɪnɪʃ] Ⓐ N 1 (= *end*) final *m*; **to be in at the ~** presenciar el final; **a fight to the ~** una lucha a muerte; **to fight to the ~** luchar a muerte; **from start to ~** de principio a fin

2 (*Sport*) [*of race*] final *m*; **it's going to be a close ~** va a ser un final reñido; **the replays showed a close ~** la repetición mostraba que habían cruzado la meta casi a la vez

3 (= *appearance*) acabado *m*; **a table with an oak ~** una mesa con un acabado en roble; **gloss(y) ~** acabado *m* brillo; **matt ~** acabado *m* mate; **a surface with a rough/smooth ~** una superficie sin pulir/pulida

4 (= *refinement*) refinamiento *m*; **she's a beautiful model, but she lacks ~** es una modelo bella, pero le falta refinamiento

Ⓑ VT 1 (= *complete*) terminar, acabar; **I've nearly ~ed the ironing** casi he terminado *or* acabado de planchar; **what time do you ~ work?** ¿a qué hora terminas el trabajo?; **I'll be ~ing my course next year** termino *or* acabo el curso el año que viene; **to ~ doing sth** terminar *or* acabar de hacer algo; **as soon as he ~ed eating, he excused himself** en cuanto terminó *or* acabó de comer, se excusó

2 (= *use up, consume*) [+ *food, resources*] terminar, acabar; **~ your soup** termínate la sopa, acábate la sopa; **if you ~ the milk, let me know** si terminas (toda) la leche, dímelo

3 (= *round off*) rematar; **~ the dish with a sprinkling of parsley** remate el plato espolvoreándolo con perejil; **we ~ed the afternoon with tea at the Ritz** rematamos la tarde tomando té en el Ritz

4 (*) (= *defeat, destroy*) acabar con; **that last kilometre nearly ~ed me** el kilómetro final casi acabó conmigo

5 (= *apply surface to*) **~ the wood with wax or varnish** dele un acabado final a la madera con cera o barniz

Ⓒ VI 1 (= *come to an end*) terminar, acabar; **the party was ~ing** la fiesta se estaba termi-

nando *or* acabando; **have you quite ~ed?** ¿has acabado ya?; (= *can I speak now?*) ¿puedo hablar ya?; **she ~ed by saying that ...** terminó *or* acabó diciendo que ...; **I've ~ed with the paper** he acabado el periódico, he terminado con el periódico; **come back, I haven't ~ed with you yet!** ¡vuelve, que todavía no he terminado *or* acabado contigo!
2 (*Sport*) (= *end race*) terminar, acabar; **she ~ed first/last** terminó *or* acabó en primer lugar/en último lugar
3 (= *end association*) romper, terminar (**with** con); **she's ~ed with him** ha roto *or* terminado con él
4 (*Fin*) **our shares ~ed at $70** al cierre de la Bolsa, nuestras acciones se cotizaban a 70 dólares
Ⓓ CPD ► **finish line** N (*US*) = **finishing line**

►**finish off** Ⓐ VT + ADV 1 (= *conclude*) terminar
2 (= *use up, consume*) terminar(se), acabar(se); **he ~ed off the bottle in one swallow** se terminó *or* se acabó la botella de un trago
3 (= *exhaust*) dejar destrozado, dejar hecho polvo*
4 (= *kill*) [+ *victim*] acabar con, liquidar*; [+ *wounded person/animal*] rematar; (= *defeat*) [+ *opponent*] derrotar, vencer
Ⓑ VI + ADV (= *end*) terminar, concluir (*frm*); **I'd like to ~ off by proposing a toast** quisiera terminar *or* (*frm*) concluir proponiendo un brindis; **let's ~ off now** terminemos ahora

►**finish up** Ⓐ VT + ADV (= *use up, consume*) [+ *food, leftovers*] terminarse, acabarse; **~ up your drinks now please** termínense lo que estén bebiendo ahora, por favor
Ⓑ VI + ADV (= *end up*) terminar, acabar; **he ~ed up in Paris** terminó *or* acabó en París; **he'll probably ~ up in jail** probablemente termine *or* acabe en la cárcel

finished ['fɪnɪʃt] ADJ 1 (= *concluded*) terminado; **it's not ~ yet** aún no está terminado *or* acabado; **when will you be ~?** ¿(para) cuándo vas a terminar?; **a half-~ meal** una comida a medio terminar; **he sent off the ~ manuscript/version** envió el manuscrito terminado/la versión final; **he's ~ with politics** ha renunciado a la política; **I'm not ~ with you yet** aún no he terminado *or* acabado contigo
2 (= *completed*) acabado; **the ~ product** el producto acabado *or* final
3 (= *polished*) [*performance, production*] pulido
4 (*) (= *tired*) rendido, hecho polvo*; (= *destroyed*) acabado; **their marriage is ~** su matrimonio está acabado; **as a film star she's ~** como estrella está acabada
5 (= *surfaced*) **walnut-~ kitchen accessories** accesorios *mpl* de cocina con un acabado de nogal; **a building ~ in smoked glass** un edificio acabado con cristales ahumados

finisher ['fɪnɪʃəʳ] N (*esp Brit Ftbl*) rematador(a) *m/f*; (*Cycling, Running*) *persona que llega a la meta*

finishing ['fɪnɪʃɪŋ] Ⓐ N 1 [*of product*] acabado *m*
2 (*esp Brit Ftbl*) capacidad *f* de remate
Ⓑ CPD ► **finishing line** N (*Sport*) línea *f* de meta, meta *f* ► **finishing school** N *escuela privada para señoritas donde se les enseña a comportarse en la alta sociedad* ► **finishing touch** N toque *m* final; **to put the ~ touches to sth** dar los últimos toques a algo

finite ['faɪnaɪt] Ⓐ ADJ 1 (= *limited*) (*of distance*) finito; [*resources*] limitado; **is the universe ~?** ¿el universo es finito?; **to make the best use of ~ resources** hacer el mejor uso posible de recursos limitados; **we have only a ~ amount of money to invest** sólo disponemos de una cantidad limitada de dinero para invertir
2 (*Ling*) [*mood, verb*] conjugado
Ⓑ CPD ► **finite verb** N verbo *m* conjugado

fink* [fɪŋk] N (*US*) (= *informer*) soplón/ona* *m/f*; (= *strikebreaker*) rompehuelgas *mf inv*, esquirol *m*

►**fink out*** VI + ADV (*US*) acobardarse

Finland ['fɪnlənd] N Finlandia *f*

Finn [fɪn] N finlandés/esa *m/f*

Finnish ['fɪnɪʃ] Ⓐ ADJ finlandés
Ⓑ N (*Ling*) finlandés *m*

Finno-Ugrian ['fɪnəʊ'uːgrɪən], **Finno-Ugric** ['fɪnəʊ'uːgrɪk] Ⓐ ADJ fino-húngaro
Ⓑ N (*Ling*) fino-húngaro *m*

fiord [fjɔːd] N = **fjord**

fir [fɜːʳ] Ⓐ N (*also* **~ tree**) abeto *m*
Ⓑ CPD ► **fir cone** N piña *f*

fire [faɪəʳ] Ⓐ N 1 (= *flames*) fuego *m*; **much of the town was destroyed by ~** el fuego causó la destrucción de gran parte de la ciudad; **~ and brimstone** el fuego eterno; **a ~ and brimstone speech** un discurso lleno de referencias apocalípticas; **to catch ~** [*curtains, furniture*] prender fuego; [*house*] incendiarse; [*engine, car*] empezar a arder; **the aircraft caught ~ soon after take off** poco después de despegar se inició un incendio en el avión; **~ damaged goods** mercancías *fpl* dañadas por el fuego; **to be on ~** (*lit*) estar ardiendo; (*fig*) (*with passion, pain*) arder; **to set ~ to sth** ◊ **set sth on ~** prender fuego a algo; **to set o.s. on ~** prenderse fuego; ✦***IDIOMS*** **to fight ~ with ~** pagar con la misma moneda; **to play with ~** jugar con fuego; **to set the world on ~** comerse el mundo; **to go** *or* **come through ~ and water (to do sth)** pasar lo indecible (por hacer algo); *see also* **smoke A1**
2 (*in grate*) fuego *m*, lumbre *f*; **to lay** *or* **make up a ~** preparar el fuego *or* la lumbre; **to light a ~** encender un fuego *or* una lumbre
3 (= *bonfire*) hoguera *f*, fogata *f*; **to make a ~** hacer una hoguera *or* una fogata
4 (= *fireplace*) lumbre *f*, chimenea *f*; **come and sit by the ~** ven y siéntate a la lumbre *or* a lado de la chimenea
5 (*accidental*) incendio *m*; **87 people died in the ~** 87 personas murieron en el incendio; **to be insured against ~** estar asegurado contra incendios; **bush ~** incendio *m* de monte; **forest ~** incendio *m* forestal
6 (= *heater*) estufa *f*; **electric/gas ~** estufa *f* eléctrica/de gas
7 (*Mil*) fuego *m*; **to draw sb's ~** distraer a algn (*disparando a algo que no es el objetivo real*); **to draw ~** (*fig*) provocar críticas; **the proposed tax has already drawn ~ from the opposition** el impuesto propuesto ya ha provocado las críticas de la oposición; **to exchange ~ (with sb)** tirotearse (con algn); **an exchange of ~** un tiroteo; **to hold (one's) ~** (*lit*) no disparar; (*fig*) esperar; **hold your ~!** (*when already firing*) ¡alto al fuego!; **to open ~ (on sth/sb)** abrir fuego (sobre algo/algn); **to return (sb's) ~** responder a los disparos (de algn); [*troops*] responder al fuego enemigo; **to be/come under ~** (*lit*) estar/caer bajo fuego enemigo; (*fig*) ser atacado; **the President's plan came under ~ from the opposition** el plan del presidente fue atacado por la oposición; ✦***IDIOM*** **to hang ~: banks and building societies were hanging ~ on interest rates** los bancos y las sociedades de préstamos hipotecarios dejaron en suspenso los tipos de interés; **several projects were hanging ~ in his absence** varios proyectos quedaron interrumpidos en su ausencia; *see also* **line A11**
8 (= *passion*) ardor *m*; ✦***IDIOM*** **to have ~ in one's belly*** ser muy ardoroso *or* apasionado
Ⓑ VT 1 (= *shoot*) [+ *gun*] disparar; [+ *missile, arrow*] disparar, lanzar; [+ *rocket*] lanzar; [+ *shot*] efectuar; **to ~ a gun at sb** disparar contra algn; **he ~d a question at her** le lanzó una pregunta; **he continued to ~ (off) questions at her** continuó acosándola con preguntas; **to ~ a salute** tirar una salva
2 (= *operate*) **gas/oil ~d central heating** calefacción *f* central a *or* de gas/de petróleo
3 (= *set fire to*) [+ *property, building*] incendiar, prender fuego a
4 (*) (= *dismiss*) echar (a la calle), despedir; **you're ~d!** ¡queda usted despedido!
5 (*in kiln*) [+ *pottery*] cocer
6 (= *stimulate*) [+ *imagination*] estimular; **~d with enthusiasm/determination, the crowd ...** impulsados por el entusiasmo/por la determinación, la multitud ...; **she ~s others with energy** llena a los demás de energía
Ⓒ VI 1 (*Mil*) disparar (**at** a, contra; **on** sobre); **riot police ~d on the crowd** la policía antidisturbios disparó sobre la multitud; **ready, aim, ~!** ¡atención, apunten, fuego!
2 (*Aut*) [*engine*] encenderse, prender (*LAm*)
3 (*) (= *dismiss*) *see* **hire B**
Ⓓ CPD ► **fire alarm** N alarma *f* contra *or* de incendios ► **fire brigade, fire department** (*US*) N cuerpo *m* de bomberos; **we called the ~ brigade** llamamos a los bomberos ► **fire chief** N (*US*) jefe/a *m/f* de bomberos ► **fire curtain** N telón *m* contra incendios ► **fire department** N (*US*) = **fire brigade** ► **fire dog** N morillo *m* ► **fire door** N puerta *f* contra incendios ► **fire drill** N simulacro *m* de incendio ► **fire engine** N coche *m* de bomberos ► **fire escape** N escalera *f* de incendios ► **fire exit** N salida *f* de incendios ► **fire extinguisher** N extintor *m* ► **fire hazard** N **the spilt oil was a ~ hazard** el aceite derramado podía haber provocado un incendio ► **fire hydrant** N boca *f* de incendios ► **fire insurance** N seguro *m* contra incendios ► **fire irons** NPL utensilios *mpl* para la chimenea ► **fire prevention** N prevención *f* de incendios ► **fire regulations** NPL normas *fpl* para la prevención de incendios ► **fire retardant** N ignirretardante *m* ► **fire risk** N = **fire hazard** ► **fire screen** N pantalla *f* de chimenea ► **fire service** N = **fire brigade** ► **fire station** N estación *f or* (*Sp*) parque *m* de bomberos ► **fire tender, fire truck** N (*US*) coche *m* de bomberos ► **fire tower** N (*US*) torre *f* de vigilancia contra incendios ► **fire trap** N *edificio muy peligroso en caso de incendio* ► **fire warden** N (*US*) *persona encargada de la lucha contra incendios*

►**fire away*** VI + ADV **"may I ask you something?" — "sure, ~ away!"** —¿puedo preguntarle algo? —¡adelante! *or* (*LAm*) —¡siga nomás!

►**fire off** VT + ADV *see* **fire B1**

►**fire up** VT + ADV (*fig*) enardecer; **to be/get ~d up about sth** estar enardecido/enardecerse por algo

firearm ['faɪərɑːm] N arma *f* de fuego

fireball ['faɪəbɔːl] N bola *f* de fuego

Firebird ['faɪəbɜːd] N **the ~** (*Mus*) el Pájaro de fuego

firebomb ['faɪəbɒm] Ⓐ N bomba *f* incendiaria

Ⓑ VT colocar una bomba incendiaria en; (*Aer*) bombardear con bombas incendiarias

firebrand ['faɪəbrænd] N [1] tea *f*
[2] (*fig*) agitador(a) *m/f*, revoltoso/a *m/f*

firebreak ['faɪəbreɪk] N cortafuego *m*

firebrick ['faɪəbrɪk] N ladrillo *m* refractario

firebug ['faɪəbʌg] N (*US*) incendiario/a *m/f*, pirómano/a *m/f*

fireclay ['faɪəkleɪ] N (*Brit*) arcilla *f* refractaria

firecracker ['faɪə,krækəʳ] N petardo *m*

firedamp ['faɪədæmp] N grisú *m*

fire-eater ['faɪər,iːtəʳ] N (*lit*) tragafuegos *mf inv*; (*fig*) pendenciero/a *m/f*

firefight ['faɪə,faɪt] N (*Mil*) (*journalese*) tiroteo *m*

firefighter ['faɪə,faɪtəʳ] N bombero/a *m/f*

firefighting ['faɪə,faɪtɪŋ] Ⓐ N lucha *f* por apagar incendios
Ⓑ CPD ► **firefighting equipment** N equipo *m* contra incendios

firefly ['faɪəflaɪ] N luciérnaga *f*

fireguard ['faɪəgɑːd] N pantalla *f* de chimenea

firehouse ['faɪəhaʊs] N (*pl* **firehouses** ['faɪəhaʊzɪz]) (*US*) estación *f or* (*Sp*) parque *m* de bomberos

firelight ['faɪəlaɪt] N luz *f* de la lumbre *or* del hogar; **by ~** a la luz de la lumbre *or* del hogar

firelighter ['faɪə,laɪtəʳ] N pastilla *f* enciendefuegos, *barra de material inflamable que se utiliza para encender fuego en una chimenea*

fireman ['faɪəmən] N (*pl* **firemen**) [*of fire service*] bombero/a *m/f*; (*Rail*) fogonero/a *m/f*; **~'s lift** *manera de llevar a una persona sobre un solo hombro*

fireplace ['faɪəpleɪs] N chimenea *f*, hogar *m*

fireplug ['faɪəplʌg] N (*US*) = **fire hydrant**

firepower ['faɪə,paʊəʳ] N (*Mil*) potencia *f* de fuego

fireproof ['faɪəpruːf] Ⓐ ADJ [*material*] incombustible, ignífugo; [*suit, clothing*] ignífugo, a prueba de fuego; [*safe*] a prueba de fuego; [*dish*] refractario
Ⓑ VT cubrir con material ignífugo

fire-raiser ['faɪə,reɪzəʳ] N (*Brit*) incendiario/a *m/f*, pirómano/a *m/f*

fire-raising ['faɪə,reɪzɪŋ] N (*Brit*) (delito *m* de) incendiar *m*, piromanía *f*

fire-resistant ['faɪərɪ,zɪstənt] ADJ ignífugo

fire-retardant ['faɪərɪ,tɑːdənt] ADJ resistente al fuego

fireside ['faɪəsaɪd] Ⓐ N **by the ~** junto a la chimenea, al amor de la lumbre
Ⓑ CPD hogareño, familiar ► **fireside chair** N sillón *m* cerca de la lumbre ► **fireside chat** N charla *f* íntima

firewall ['faɪəwɔːl] N (*Internet*) cortafuegos *m inv*, firewall *m*

firewater* ['faɪə,wɔːtəʳ] N (*US*) aguardiente *m*

firewood ['faɪəwʊd] N leña *f*

firework ['faɪəwɜːk] Ⓐ N artilugio *m* pirotécnico (*frm*); **a stray ~ fell onto the roof** un cohete perdido cayó en el techo; **fireworks** fuegos *mpl* artificiales; **there'll be ~s at the meeting*** (*fig*) en la reunión se va a armar la gorda*
Ⓑ CPD ► **firework display** N fuegos *mpl* artificiales

firing ['faɪərɪŋ] Ⓐ N [1] (= *bullets*) disparos *mpl*; (= *exchange of fire*) tiroteo *m*
[2] (*Aut*) encendido *m*
[3] [*of bricks, pottery*] cocción *f*
[4] (*esp US**) despido *m*
Ⓑ CPD ► **firing hammer** N = **firing pin** ► **firing line** N línea *f* de fuego; ✦*IDIOM* **to be in the ~ line** (*Mil, fig*) estar en la línea de fuego ► **firing pin** N martillo *m*, percutor *m* ► **firing squad** N pelotón *m* (de fusilamiento)

firm[1] [fɜːm] Ⓐ ADJ (*compar* **firmer**; *superl* **firmest**) [1] (= *solid*) [*base*] firme, sólido; [*mattress, stomach, thighs*] duro; (= *secure*) [*hold*] firme, seguro; **these legends have a ~ basis in fact** estas leyendas están sólidamente basadas en hechos reales; **to be on ~ ground** (*fig*) pisar terreno firme; **as ~ as a rock** (tan) firme como una roca
[2] (= *staunch*) [*belief, support*] firme; [*friends*] íntimo; [*friendship*] sólido; **she's a ~ believer in justice/discipline** cree firmemente en la justicia/la disciplina
[3] (= *resolute, decisive*) [*decision, measures*] firme; [*voice*] seguro, firme; [*steps*] decidido, resuelto; **he was very ~ about it** se mostró muy firme *or* decidido; **we are taking a ~ stand on this issue** mantenemos una postura firme con respecto a esta cuestión
[4] (= *severe*) estricto, firme; **to be ~ with sb** ser estricto *or* firme con algn; **a ~ hand: this horse needs a ~ hand** a este caballo hay que tratarlo con firmeza; **this child needs a ~ hand** este niño necesita mano dura; **he governed the country with a ~ hand** dirigió el país con mano dura
[5] (= *definite*) [*offer, order*] en firme; [*evidence*] concluyente, contundente; **they won't go ahead without a ~ commitment from us** no van a seguir adelante hasta que no les demos una garantía en firme; **they are ~ favourites to win the trophy** son los grandes favoritos para llevarse el trofeo; **chocolate is a ~ favourite with children** el chocolate siempre tiene el éxito asegurado con los niños
[6] (= *set*) firme; **beat the egg whites until ~** bata las claras a punto de nieve
[7] (*Fin*) (= *not subject to change*) [*price*] estable
Ⓑ ADV **to stand ~** mantenerse firme

►**firm up** Ⓐ VT + ADV [1] (= *reinforce*) [+ *structure*] fortalecer, reforzar; [+ *thighs, muscles*] endurecer
[2] (= *make more specific*) [+ *proposal, deal*] concretar
[3] (*Culin*) [+ *mixture*] dar consistencia a
[4] (*Fin*) [+ *prices*] consolidar
Ⓑ VI + ADV (*Culin*) [*mixture*] hacerse consistente

firm[2] [fɜːm] N firma *f*, empresa *f*; **a ~ of accountants** una firma *or* empresa de contabilidad; **she joined a law ~** se incorporó a un bufete de abogados

firmament ['fɜːməmənt] N firmamento *m*

firmly ['fɜːmlɪ] ADV [1] (= *unwaveringly*) [*fixed, entrenched*] firmemente; **she had her eye ~ fixed on the dog** tenía la mirada fija en el perro
[2] (= *staunchly*) [*believe*] firmemente, con firmeza; **the crowd was ~ behind him** tenía todo el apoyo del público, el público le apoyaba firmemente; **they remain ~ opposed/committed to the plan** se mantienen firmes en su oposición/entrega al proyecto
[3] (= *decisively, severely*) [*speak, say*] con firmeza

firmness ['fɜːmnɪs] N [1] (= *hardness*) [*of mattress, muscles, thighs*] dureza *f*
[2] (= *tightness*) [*of grip*] fuerza *f*
[3] (= *determination*) firmeza *f*; **~ of character/purpose** firmeza *f* de carácter/propósito
[4] (= *severity*) firmeza *f*, mano *f* dura

▼**first** [fɜːst] Ⓐ ADJ primero; (*before m sing n*) primer; **I was ~!** ¡yo iba *or* estaba primero!; **during the ~ three months of pregnancy** durante los primeros tres meses de embarazo; **he felt a bit lonely for the ~ few days** los primeros días se sentía un poco solo; **the ~ three correct answers win a prize** las tres primeras respuestas correctas se llevan un premio; **~-past-the-post system** (*Parl*) *sistema de votación por mayoría relativa*; **at ~** al principio; **on the ~ floor** (*Brit*) en el primer piso; (*US*) en la planta baja; **at ~ hand** directamente; **from ~ to last** de principio a fin; **in the ~ place** en primer lugar; **to win ~ place** (*in competition*) conseguir el primer puesto, ganar; **to win ~ prize** ganar el primer premio; **~ strike weapon** arma *f* de primer golpe; **the ~ time** la primera vez; *see also* **instance A2**, **thing A2**
Ⓑ ADV [1] (*in place, priority*) primero; **~ one, then another** primero uno, después otro; **we arrived ~** fuimos los primeros en llegar, llegamos los primeros; **ladies ~** las señoras primero; **women and children ~!** ¡las mujeres y los niños primero!; **~ of all** ante todo, antes que nada; **to come ~** (*in race*) ganar, llegar el primero; (= *have priority*) estar primero, tener prioridad; **the customer/your homework must come ~** el cliente es lo primero/tus deberes son lo primero **~ and foremost** ante todo, antes que nada; **to get in ~** (*in conversation, process*) adelantarse; **you go ~!** ¡tú primero!, ¡pasa tú!; **head ~** de cabeza; **you have to put your children's needs ~** primero están las necesidades de tus hijos; ✦*IDIOM* **~ come, ~ served** el que llega primero tiene prioridad; **free tickets, on a ~-come-~-served basis** entradas gratis, por riguroso orden de llegada
[2] (*in time*) (= *before anything else*) primero, antes de nada; **~, I need a drink** primero *or* antes de nada *or* antes que nada, necesito una copa; **~, I don't like it, second, I haven't got the money** lo primero: no me gusta, lo segundo: no dispongo del dinero; **~ and last** (= *above all*) por encima de todo; **~ off*** primero de todo, antes de nada
[3] (= *for the first time*) por primera vez; **the word was ~ used in 1835** la palabra se usó por primera vez en 1835; **I ~ met him in Paris** lo conocí en París
[4] (= *rather*) primero, antes; **let him in this house? I'd kill him ~!** ¿dejarle pisar esta casa? ¡primero *or* antes lo mato!; **I'd die ~!** ¡antes me muero!
Ⓒ PRON **the ~ of January** el uno de enero, el primero de enero; **it's the ~ I've heard of it** ahora me entero, no lo sabía; **Charles the First** Carlos Primero; **he came in an easy ~** llegó el primero con ventaja; **from the (very) ~** desde el principio; **to be the ~ to do sth** ser el primero en hacer algo; **they were the ~ to arrive** fueron los primeros en llegar, llegaron los primeros
Ⓓ N [1] (*Aut*) primera *f*; **in ~** en primera
[2] (*Brit Univ*) ≈ sobresaliente *m*; **he got a ~ in French** ≈ se ha licenciado en francés con una media de sobresaliente; → DEGREE
Ⓔ CPD ► **first aid** N primeros auxilios *mpl*; **~-aid box** = **first-aid kit**; **~-aid course** curso *m* de primeros auxilios; **~-aid kit** botiquín *m* de primeros auxilios; **~-aid post** ◊ **~-aid station** (*US*) puesto *m* de socorro ► **first base** N (*Baseball*) primera base *f*; ✦*IDIOM* **not to get to ~ base** (*US**) quedar en agua de borrajas ► **first degree** N licenciatura *f* ► **first edition** N primera edición *f*; [*of early or rare book*] edición *f* príncipe ► **first form** *or* **year** N (*Scol*) *primer curso de secundaria*; **~-year student** (*Univ*) estudiante *mf* de primer año (*de carrera universitaria*) ► **first gear** N (*Aut*) primera *f* ► **first lady** N (*US*) primera dama *f*; **the ~ lady of jazz** la gran dama del jazz ► **first language** N (= *mother tongue*) lengua *f* materna; [*of country*] lengua *f* principal ► **first lieuten-**

➤ LANGUAGE IN USE: **first B** 26.1, 26.2, 26.3 **C** 26.1

ant N (*US Aer*) teniente *mf*; (*Brit Naut*) teniente *mf* de navío ► **first light** N amanecer *m*, alba *f*; **at ~ light** al amanecer, al alba ► **first mate** N primer oficial *m*, primera oficial *f* ► **first minister** N (*in Scotland*) ministro/ministra *m/f* principal ► **first name** N nombre *m* (de pila); **to be on ~ name terms with sb** tutear a algn ► **first night** N (*Theat*) estreno *m* ► **first offender** N (*Jur*) delincuente *mf* sin antecedentes penales ► **first officer** N primer oficial *m*, primera oficial *f* ► **first performance** N (*Theat, Mus*) estreno *m* ► **first person** N (*Ling*) primera persona *f* ► **first school** N (*Brit*) *escuela para niños entre cinco y nueve años* ► **first violin** N primer violín *m*, primera violín *f*; *see also* **cousin**

first-born [ˈfɜːstbɔːn] Ⓐ N primogénito/a *m/f*
Ⓑ ADJ primogénito; **the ~ son** el hijo primogénito

first-class [ˈfɜːstklɑːs] Ⓐ ADJ [1] [*passenger, accommodation*] de primera clase; [*travel, compartment, train*] de primera (clase); [*stamp*] *referido a un sello de correos, que asegura mayor rapidez en la entrega*
[2] (= *very good*) [*education, performance*] de primera (calidad)
Ⓑ CPD ► **first-class compartment** N (*Rail*) compartimento *m* de primera ► **first-class honours degree** N (*Univ*) licenciatura *f* con matrícula de honor; *see also* **honour A7** ► **first-class mail**, **first-class post** N *servicio de correos que asegura mayor rapidez en la entrega* ► **first-class ticket** N (*Rail*) billete *m* or (*LAm*) boleto *m* de primera clase
Ⓒ ADV **to travel ~** viajar en primera; **to send a letter ~** *enviar una carta por el sistema de correos que asegura una entrega rápida*

first-day cover [ˌfɜːstdeɪˈkʌvəʳ] N (*Post*) sobre *m* de primer día

first-degree burns [ˌfɜːstdɪgriːˈbɜːnz] NPL quemaduras *fpl* de primer grado

first-degree murder [ˌfɜːstdɪgriːˈmɜːdəʳ] N (*US*) asesinato *m* premeditado

first-ever [ˈfɜːstˌevəʳ] ADJ primerísimo

first-footing [ˌfɜːstˈfʊtɪŋ] N (*Scot*) **to go ~** *ser el primero en visitar a amigos y familiares tras las doce en Nochevieja*; → HOGMANAY

first-generation [ˈfɜːstˌdʒenəˈreɪʃən] ADJ de primera generación; **he's a ~ American** es americano de primera generación

first-hand [ˈfɜːstˈhænd] Ⓐ ADJ [*information, account*] de primera mano; [*experience, knowledge*] de primera mano Ⓑ ADV directamente

firstly [ˈfɜːstlɪ] ADV [1] (= *before anything else*) antes que nada, en primer lugar, primero; **~, we must stop the bleeding** antes que nada *or* en primer lugar *or* primero tenemos que cortar la hemorragia
[2] (= *on the first occasion*) primero; **we went there ~ as tourists, then bought a house there** fuimos allí primero como turistas, luego nos compramos una casa
[3] (= *in the first place*) en primer lugar; **~, it's too small and secondly it's too expensive** en primer lugar, es demasiado pequeño y en segundo lugar, es demasiado caro

first-named [ˌfɜːstˈneɪmd] ADJ **the ~** el primero, la primera

first-nighter [ˈfɜːstˈnaɪtəʳ] N estrenista *mf*

first-rate [ˈfɜːstˈreɪt] ADJ de primera categoría *or* clase; **she is ~ at her work** su trabajo es de primera clase; **~!** ¡magnífico!

first-time [ˈfɜːstˈtaɪm] ADJ **~ buyer** *persona que compra su primera vivienda*

first-timer [ˌfɜːstˈtaɪməʳ] N novato/a *m/f*, principiante *mf*

➤ LANGUAGE IN USE: **firstly 3** 26.2

firth [fɜːθ] N (*Scot*) estuario *m*, ría *f*

FIS N ABBR (*Brit*) (= **Family Income Supplement**) *ayuda estatal familiar*

FISA N ABBR = **Fédération Internationale de l'Automobile**

fiscal [ˈfɪskəl] Ⓐ ADJ [*policy, system, incentive*] fiscal
Ⓑ N (*Scot Jur*) fiscal *mf*
Ⓒ CPD ► **fiscal year** N año *m* fiscal

fish [fɪʃ] Ⓐ N (*pl* **fish** *or* **fishes**) [1] (*alive*) pez *m*; (*as food*) pescado *m*; **~ and chips** pescado *m* frito con patatas fritas; **~ and chip shop** *tienda de comida rápida principalmente de pescado frito y patatas fritas*; ✦*IDIOMS* **neither ~ nor fowl** ni chicha ni limoná; **I've got other ~ to fry*** tengo cosas más importantes que hacer; **there are other ~ in the sea** hay otros peces en el mar; **to be like a ~ out of water** estar como pez fuera del agua
[2] (*) (= *person*) tipo/a* *m/f*, tío/a *m/f* (*Sp**); **odd ~** bicho *m* raro*; **big ~** pez *m* gordo; ✦*IDIOM* **he's a (bit of a) cold ~*** es un tipo frío*
Ⓑ VI pescar; [*trawler*] faenar; **he goes ~ing at weekends** sale a pescar los fines de semana; **I'm going ~ing** voy de pesca; **to go salmon ~ing** ir a pescar salmón; **to ~ for** [+ *trout, salmon etc*] pescar; [+ *compliments, information*] andar a la caza de; **to ~ (around) in one's pocket for sth** buscarse algo en el bolsillo; ✦*IDIOM* **to ~ in troubled waters** pescar en río revuelto
Ⓒ VT [+ *river, pond*] pescar en; [+ *trout, salmon etc*] pescar
Ⓓ CPD ► **fish course** N (plato *m* de) pescado *m* ► **fish factory** N fábrica *f* de pescado ► **fish farm** N piscifactoría *f*, criadero *m* de peces ► **fish farmer** N piscicultor(a) *m/f* ► **fish farming** N piscicultura *f*, cría *f* de peces ► **fish finger** N (*Brit*) palito *m* de pescado empanado ► **fish glue** N cola *f* de pescado ► **fish knife** N cuchillo *m* de pescado ► **fish manure** N abono *m* de pescado ► **fish market** N lonja *f* de pescado (*Sp*) ► **fish meal** N harina *f* de pescado ► **fish seller** N (*US*) = **fishmonger** ► **fish shop** N pescadería *f* ► **fish slice** N pala *f* para el pescado ► **fish soup** N sopa *f* de pescado ► **fish stick** N (*US*) croqueta *f* de pescado ► **fish store** N (*US*) pescadería *f* ► **fish tank** N acuario *m*

►**fish out** VT + ADV (*from water, from box*) sacar; **they ~ed him out of the water** lo sacaron del agua; **she ~ed a handkerchief out of her handbag** sacó un pañuelo del bolso

►**fish up** VT + ADV sacar

fishbone [ˈfɪʃbəʊn] N espina *f*, raspa *f*

fishbowl [ˈfɪʃbəʊl] N pecera *f*

fishcake [ˈfɪʃkeɪk] N croqueta *f* de pescado

fisherman [ˈfɪʃəmən] N (*pl* **fishermen**) pescador *m*

fishery [ˈfɪʃərɪ] Ⓐ N (= *area*) caladero *m*, pesquería *f*; (= *industry*) pesca *f*, industria *f* pesquera; *see also* **agriculture**
Ⓑ CPD ► **fishery policy** N política *f* pesquera ► **fishery protection** N protección *f* pesquera

fish-eye [ˈfɪʃaɪ] Ⓐ N (*in door*) mirilla *f*
Ⓑ CPD ► **fish-eye lens** N (*Phot*) objetivo *m* de ojo de pez

fishhook [ˈfɪʃhʊk] N anzuelo *m*

fishing [ˈfɪʃɪŋ] Ⓐ N pesca *f*; **to go on a ~ expedition** ir de pesca
Ⓑ CPD ► **fishing boat** N barco *m* pesquero *or* de pesca ► **fishing fleet** N flota *f* pesquera ► **fishing grounds** NPL caladeros *mpl*, pesquerías *fpl* ► **fishing industry** N industria *f* pesquera ► **fishing licence**, **fishing permit** N licencia *f* de pesca ► **fishing line** N sedal *m* ► **fishing net** N red *f* de pesca ► **fishing port** N puerto *m* pesquero ► **fishing rod** N caña *f* de pescar ► **fishing tackle** N equipo *m* de pesca

fishmonger [ˈfɪʃmʌŋgəʳ] N (*Brit*) pescadero/a *m/f*; **~'s (shop)** pescadería *f*

fishnet [ˈfɪʃnet] Ⓐ N [1] (*US, Canada*) red *f* de pesca
[2] (= *material*) red *f*
Ⓑ CPD ► **fishnet stockings** NPL medias *fpl* de red *or* malla ► **fishnet tights** NPL leotardo *m* de red

fishpaste [ˈfɪʃpeɪst] N pasta *f* de pescado

fishplate [ˈfɪʃpleɪt] N (*Rail*) eclisa *f*

fishpond [ˈfɪʃpɒnd] N estanque *m* (de peces)

fishwife [ˈfɪʃwaɪf] N (*pl* **fishwives** [ˈfɪʃwaɪvz]) pescadera *f*; (*pej*) verdulera *f*

fishy [ˈfɪʃɪ] ADJ (*compar* **fishier**; *superl* **fishiest**)
[1] [*smell, taste*] a pescado
[2] (*) (= *suspect*) sospechoso; **there's something ~ about him** hay algo en él que resulta sospechoso; **it sounds ~ to me** me huele a chamusquina (*Sp**); **there's something ~ going on here** aquí hay gato encerrado, me huele a chamusquina (*Sp**)

fissile [ˈfɪsaɪl] ADJ físil

fission [ˈfɪʃən] N (*Phys*) fisión *f*; (*Bio*) escisión *f*; **atomic/nuclear ~** fisión *f* atómica/nuclear

fissionable [ˈfɪʃnəbl] ADJ fisionable

fissure [ˈfɪʃəʳ] N hendidura *f*, grieta *f*; (*Anat, Geol, Metal*) fisura *f*

fissured [ˈfɪʃəd] ADJ agrietado

fist [fɪst] Ⓐ N puño *m*; **he banged his ~ on the table** dio un puñetazo en la mesa; **to shake one's ~ at sb** amenazar con el puño a algn; ✦*IDIOM* **to make a poor ~ of sth** hacer algo mal; *see also* **clench**
Ⓑ CPD ► **fist fight** N pelea *f* a puñetazos

fistful [ˈfɪstfʊl] N puñado *m*

fisticuffs [ˈfɪstɪkʌfs] NPL puñetazos *mpl*

fistula [ˈfɪstjʊlə] N (*pl* **fistulas** *or* **fistulae**) fístula *f*

fit¹ [fɪt] ADJ (*compar* **fitter**; *superl* **fittest**) [1] (= *suitable*) adecuado; **he is not ~ company for my daughter** no es compañía adecuada para mi hija; **~ for sth**: **~ for human consumption/habitation** comestible/habitable; **he's not ~ for the job** no sirve para el puesto, no es apto para el puesto; **a meal ~ for a king** una comida digna de reyes; **~ for nothing** inútil; **to be ~ to do sth**: **he's not ~ to teach** no sirve para profesor; **you're not ~ to be seen** no estás presentable, no estás para que te vea la gente; **the meat was not ~ to eat** *or* **to be eaten** (= *unhealthy*) la carne no estaba en buenas condiciones; (= *bad-tasting*) la carne era incomible, la carne no se podía comer; **you're not ~ to drive** no estás en condiciones de conducir
[2] (= *healthy*) (*Med*) sano; (*Sport*) en forma; **to be ~ for duty** (*Mil*) ser apto para el servicio; **to be ~ for work** (*after illness*) estar en condiciones de trabajar; **to get ~** (*Med*) reponerse; (*Sport*) ponerse en forma; **to keep ~** mantenerse en forma; **to pass sb ~** (*after illness, injury*) dar a algn el alta; **she's not yet ~ to travel** todavía no está en condiciones de viajar; ✦*IDIOM* **to be (as) ~ as a fiddle** estar rebosante de salud
[3] (*) (= *ready*) **I'm ~ to drop** estoy que me caigo*; **he was laughing ~ to bust** *or* **burst** se tronchaba *or* desternillaba de risa
[4] (= *right*) **to see/think ~ to do sth**: **you must do as you think ~** debes hacer lo que

estimes conveniente *or* lo que creas apropiado; **she didn't see ~ to mention it** no creyó apropiado mencionarlo

fit^{2} [fɪt] Ⓐ VT 1 (= *be right size*) [*clothes*] quedar bien a; [*key*] entrar en, encajar en; **it ~s me like a glove** me queda como un guante; **he can't find shirts to ~ him** no encuentra camisas que le queden *or* vengan bien; **the key doesn't ~ the lock** la llave no entra *or* encaja en la cerradura
2 (= *measure*) tomar las medidas a; **I went to get ~ted for a suit** fui a que me tomaran las medidas para un traje; **to ~ a dress (on sb)** probar un vestido (a algn)
3 (= *match*) [+ *facts*] corresponderse con; [+ *description*] encajar con; [+ *need*] adecuarse a; **your story doesn't ~ the facts** tu historia no se corresponde con los hechos; **she doesn't ~ the feminine stereotype** no encaja con el estereotipo femenino; **the punishment should ~ the crime** el castigo debe adecuarse al delito; *see also* **bill A6**
4 (= *put*) **he ~ted the shelf to the wall** fijó el estante a la pared; **to ~ sth into place** hacer encajar algo; **I finally began to ~ the pieces together** (*fig*) finalmente empecé a encajar todas las piezas
5 (= *install*) [+ *windows*] instalar, poner; [+ *carpet*] poner; [+ *kitchen, bathroom, domestic appliance*] instalar; **they're having a new kitchen ~ted** les van a instalar una cocina nueva
6 (= *supply*) equipar de; **to be ~ted with sth** estar equipado con algo; **a car ~ted with a catalytic converter** un coche equipado con un conversor catalítico; **all our coaches are ~ted with seat belts** todos nuestros autobuses están equipados con cinturones de seguridad; **he has been ~ted with a new hearing aid** le han puesto un audífono nuevo
7 (*frm*) (= *make suitable*) **to ~ sb for sth/to do sth** capacitar a algn para algo/para hacer algo; **her experience ~s her for the job** su experiencia la capacita para el trabajo
Ⓑ VI 1 [*clothes, shoes*] **the dress doesn't ~ very well** el vestido no le queda muy bien; *see also* **cap**
2 (= *go in/on*) **this key doesn't ~** esta llave no encaja *or* entra; **will the cupboard ~ into the corner?** ¿cabrá el armario en el rincón?; **it ~s in/on here** se encaja aquí; **the lid won't ~ on this saucepan** la tapa no encaja en esta cazuela
3 (= *match*) [*facts, description*] concordar, corresponderse; **it doesn't ~ with what he said to me** no concuerda *or* no se corresponde con lo que me dijo a mí; **it all ~s now!** ¡todo encaja ahora!; *see also* **fit in A1**
4 (*) (= *belong*) encajar; **his face doesn't ~** él no encaja aquí
Ⓒ N **the lycra in the fabric ensures a good ~** la licra de la tela hace que se ajuste perfectamente; **that suit is not a very good ~** ese traje no te queda bien; **when it comes to shoes, a good ~ is essential** en lo que se refiere a los zapatos, es esencial que se ajusten bien *or* que sean el número correcto; **it was a perfect ~** le quedaba perfectamente; **it's rather a tight ~** me está un poco justo *or* apretado; **she put the key into the lock - it was a tight ~** metió la llave en la cerradura - entraba muy justo

►**fit in** Ⓐ VI + ADV 1 (= *correspond*) [*fact, statement*] concordar, cuadrar (**with** con); **that ~s in with what he told me** eso concuerda *or* cuadra *or* se corresponde con lo que me dijo él
2 (= *adapt*) **to ~ in with sb's plans** amoldarse *or* adaptarse a los planes de algn; **I'll ~ in with whatever dates you've agreed on** me amoldaré *or* me adaptaré a las fechas que hayáis acordado; **she was trying to arrange her work to ~ in with her home life** intentaba organizar el trabajo de forma que se adaptara a su vida doméstica
3 (= *belong*) [*person*] **he left because he didn't ~ in** se marchó porque no congeniaba con los demás *or* no encajaba; **she was great with the children and ~ted in beautifully** con los niños era genial, y se adaptó perfectamente
4 (= *go in*) (*into cupboard, car, corner*) caber; (*into jigsaw puzzle*) encajar; **will we all ~ in?** ¿cabremos todos?
Ⓑ VT + ADV 1 (= *make room for*) **can you ~ another book/passenger in?** ¿te cabe otro libro/pasajero más?; **you could ~ an illustration in here** aquí podrías poner una ilustración, aquí tienes sitio para poner una ilustración
2 (= *make time for*) **I could ~ you in next Friday** podría hacerte un hueco el próximo viernes; **I ~ted in a trip to Ávila** logré incluir una excursión a Ávila; **we could ~ in a round of golf before lunch** nos da tiempo a hacer un recorrido de golf antes de comer; **we rushed around trying to ~ everything in** corrimos como locos intentando abarcarlo todo

►**fit out** VT + ADV [+ *ship, expedition*] equipar; [+ *warship*] armar; **to ~ sb out with sth** proveer a algn de algo, equipar a algn con algo; **we need to get you ~ted out with a new wardrobe** tenemos que equiparte con un nuevo vestuario; **the tailor will ~ you out with a new suit for the wedding** el sastre te hará un traje nuevo para la boda

►**fit up** VT + ADV 1 (= *install*) instalar
2 (*Brit*) (= *equip, supply*) equipar; **to ~ sth/sb up with sth** proveer algo/a algn de algo, equipar algo/a algn con algo
3 (*) (= *frame*) **I've been ~ted up!** ¡han hecho que aparezca como el culpable!

fit^{3} [fɪt] N 1 (*Med*) ataque *m*; **epileptic ~** ataque *m* epiléptico; **fainting ~** desmayo *m*; **she had a ~ last night** anoche tuvo un ataque
2 (= *outburst*) **a ~ of anger** un arranque *or* un arrebato *or* (*frm*) un acceso de cólera; **a ~ of coughing** un ataque *or* (*frm*) un acceso de tos; **a ~ of enthusiasm** un arranque de entusiasmo; **I had a ~ of (the) giggles** me dio un ataque de risa; **to have a ~*** ponerse histérico*; **he'd have a ~ if he knew** le daría un síncope si se enterara*, se pondría histérico si se enterara*; **to be in ~s*** partirse de risa*; **she was so funny, she used to have us all in ~s** era tan graciosa, que nos tenía a todos muertos de risa*; **she had a laughing ~** le dio un ataque de risa; **she was in ~s of laughter** se partía de risa*; **he shot her in a ~ of jealous rage** disparó sobre ella en un arranque *or* arrebato de celos y furia; **by** *or* **in ~s and starts** a tropezones, a trompicones*; **to throw a ~*** ponerse histérico*; **she'll throw a ~ if she finds out** le dará un síncope si se entera*, se pondrá histérica si se entera*; **a ~ of weeping** una llorera; *see also* **pique**

fitful [ˈfɪtfʊl] ADJ [*breeze, showers, gunfire*] intermitente; [*breathing, progress*] irregular; **she fell into a ~ sleep** se durmió pero no descansó bien; **I passed a ~ night** dormí muy mal

fitfully [ˈfɪtfəlɪ] ADV [*work*] de manera irregular; [*sleep*] muy mal; **he dozed ~** echó alguna que otra cabezada; **the candle burned ~** la llama de la vela parpadeaba

fitment [ˈfɪtmənt] N 1 (*Brit*) mueble *m*
2 (= *accessory*) [*of machine*] aparejo *m*
3 = **fitting B2**

fitness [ˈfɪtnɪs] Ⓐ N 1 (= *suitability*) (*gen, for post*) aptitud *f*, capacidad *f* (**for** para); **she doubted his ~ to drive** dudaba que se encontrase en condiciones de conducir
2 (= *state of health*) estado *m* físico; (= *good health*) buena forma *f*; **to be at the peak of ~** estar en condiciones óptimas, estar en plena forma
Ⓑ CPD ► **fitness fanatic** N fanático/a *m/f* del mantenimiento físico ► **fitness programme**, **fitness program** (*US*) N programa *m* de mantenimiento físico ► **fitness test** N prueba *f* de estado físico ► **fitness training** N entrenamiento *m*

fitted [ˈfɪtɪd] ADJ 1 (= *made to measure*) [*jacket, shirt*] entallado; [*sheet*] de cuatro picos; **~ carpet** alfombra *f* de pared a pared, moqueta *f* (*Sp*)
2 (= *integral*) [*cupboards*] empotrado; **~ bathroom** cuarto *m* de baño con todos los elementos; **~ kitchen** cocina *f* con armarios empotrados, cocina *f* integral
3 (= *suited*) **to be ~ to do sth** estar capacitado para hacer algo, reunir las cualidades necesarias para hacer algo; **he is well ~ to be king** reune todas las cualidades necesarias para ser rey; **she wasn't ~ for the role of motherhood** no estaba capacitada para desempeñar la labor de madre

fitter [ˈfɪtəʳ] N 1 (*in garage*) mecánico/a *m/f*; *see also* **electrical**, **gas**
2 [*of garment*] probador(a) *m/f*

fitting [ˈfɪtɪŋ] Ⓐ ADJ 1 (= *appropriate*) [*end*] adecuado, apropiado; [*tribute*] digno; **it is ~ that ...** es apropiado que ...; **it seemed ~ to ...** (+ INFIN) parecía apropiado *or* oportuno ... + *infin*
2 (= *worthy*) digno; **that's not ~ for an officer** eso no es digno de un oficial
Ⓑ N 1 (= *trying on*) [*of dress*] prueba *f*; (= *size*) [*of shoe*] número *m*, tamaño *m*
2 **fittings** [*of house*] accesorios *mpl*; [*of shop*] mobiliario *msing*; **bathroom ~s** accesorios *mpl* de baño; **electrical/gas ~s** instalaciones *fpl* eléctricas/de gas; *see also* **fixture A1**, **light E**
Ⓒ CPD ► **fitting room** N (*in shop*) probador *m*

fittingly [ˈfɪtɪŋlɪ] ADV 1 (= *appropriately*) [*named*] apropiadamente; [*dressed*] convenientemente, adecuadamente; **the ~ named Dark Valley** el apropiadamente denominado Valle Oscuro; **her work is most ~ described as minimalist** la calificación más adecuada de su trabajo es la de minimalista; **the speech was ~ solemn** el discurso fue solemne, como correspondía
2 (= *worthily*) dignamente

five [faɪv] Ⓐ ADJ cinco; **she is ~ (years old)** tiene cinco años (de edad); **they live at number ~** viven en el número cinco; **there are ~ of us** somos cinco; **all ~ of them came** vinieron los cinco; **it costs ~ pounds** cuesta *or* vale cinco libras; **~ and a quarter/half** cinco y cuarto/medio; **~-day week** semana *f* inglesa; **it's ~ (o'clock)** son las cinco
Ⓑ N cinco *m*; **to divide sth into ~** dividir algo en cinco; **they are sold in ~s** se venden de cinco en cinco
Ⓒ CPD ► **five spot*** N (*US*) billete *m* de cinco dólares

five-and-ten-cent store [ˌfaɪvənˈtensentˌstɔːʳ] N, **five-and-dime** [ˌfaɪvənˈdaɪm] N,

five-and-ten [ˌfaɪvən'ten] N (*US*) almacén *m* de baratillo

five-a-side ['faɪvəˌsaɪd] ADJ [*team*] de futbito; **~ football** (*outdoors*) futbito *m*; (*indoors*) fútbol *m* sala

five-fold ['faɪvˌfəʊld] Ⓐ ADJ quintuplo
Ⓑ ADV cinco veces

five-o'-clock shadow ['faɪvəklɒk'ʃædəʊ] N barba *f* crecida

fiver* ['faɪvəʳ] N (= *banknote*) (*Brit*) billete *m* de cinco libras; (*US*) billete de cinco dólares; (= *amount*) (*Brit*) cinco libras *fpl*; (*US*) cinco dólares *mpl*

five-star ['faɪvstɑːʳ] ADJ [*hotel*] de cinco estrellas; [*restaurant*] de cinco tenedores

five-year ['faɪv'jɪəʳ] Ⓐ ADJ [*period, term of office*] de cinco años
Ⓑ CPD ► **five-year plan** N plan *m* quinquenal

fix [fɪks] Ⓐ VT [1] (= *position*) fijar, asegurar; **to ~ sth in place** fijar *or* asegurar algo en su sitio; **to ~ a stake in the ground** clavar *or* fijar una estaca en el suelo
[2] (= *attach*) [2·1] (*with nails*) clavar; (*with string*) atar, amarrar; (*with glue*) pegar; **to ~ sth to sth**: **~ the mirror to the wall** fije el espejo a la pared; **I ~ed the hose to the tap** ajusté la manguera al grifo; **the phone is ~ed to the wall** el teléfono está colgado de la pared; **the chairs and desks are ~ed to the floor** las sillas y mesas están sujetas *or* atornilladas al suelo; **they ~ed the two pieces of bone together with a metal plate** unieron los dos trozos de hueso con una placa de metal
[2·2] [+ *bayonet*] calar; **with ~ed bayonets** con bayonetas caladas
[3] (*fig*) (= *set firmly*) **to ~ sth in one's memory/mind** grabar algo en la memoria/la mente; **the image of her was now firmly ~ed in his mind** su imagen estaba ahora firmemente grabada en su mente
[4] (= *lay*) **to ~ the blame on sb** echar la culpa a algn
[5] (= *arrange, settle*) [+ *date, time*] fijar; [+ *meeting*] fijar, convenir; **we must ~ a date to have lunch** tenemos que fijar un día para quedar a comer; **nothing's been ~ed yet** todavía no se ha decidido *or* acordado nada; **I've ~ed it for you to meet her** lo he arreglado para que la conozcas; **how are you ~ed for this evening?** ¿tienes planes para esta noche?; **how are we ~ed for money?** ¿qué tal andamos de dinero?; **how are we ~ed for time?** ¿cómo vamos de tiempo?
[6] (= *set*) [6·1] (*honestly*) [+ *price, rate*] fijar
[6·2] (= *rig*) [+ *fight, race, election*] amañar; [+ *price*] fijar; **they're in a dispute over price ~ing** tienen una disputa por la fijación de los precios
[7] (= *rivet*) [+ *eyes, gaze*] fijar, clavar; [+ *attention*] fijar; **she ~ed her eyes on him** le clavó los ojos, fijó la mirada en él; **he ~ed his gaze on the horizon** miró fijamente al horizonte; **she ~ed him with an angry glare** lo miró fijamente con indignación; **she had ~ed all her hopes on passing the exam** tenía todas sus esperanzas puestas en aprobar el examen
[8] (= *repair*) [+ *car, appliance*] arreglar, reparar; **to get** *or* **have sth ~ed** arreglar *or* reparar algo; **I've got to get my car ~ed this week** tengo que arreglar *or* reparar el coche esta semana, tengo que llevar el coche a arreglar *or* reparar esta semana; **I should have my teeth ~ed** tendría que arreglarme los dientes
[9] (= *solve*) [+ *problem*] solucionar
[10] (*) (= *deal with*) encargarse de*; (= *kill*) cargarse a*; **I'll soon ~ him!** ¡ya me encargo yo de él!*, ¡ya le ajustaré las cuentas!*
[11] (= *prepare*) [+ *meal, drink*] preparar; **I ~ed myself a coffee** me preparé un café
[12] (*esp US*) (= *tidy up*) [+ *hair, makeup*] arreglar; **to ~ one's hair** arreglarse el pelo
[13] (= *make permanent*) [+ *film, colour, dye*] fijar
[14] (*) (= *neuter*) [+ *animal*] operar
Ⓑ VI (*US*) [1] (= *intend*) tener intención de; **I'm ~ing to go to graduate school** tengo intención de *or* tengo pensado hacer estudios de postgraduado
[2] (= *arrange*) **we had already ~ed to go to the theatre** ya habíamos quedado para ir al teatro
Ⓒ N [1] (*) (= *predicament*) apuro *m*, aprieto *m*; **to be in/get into a ~** estar/meterse en un apuro *or* un aprieto
[2] (*) [*of drug*] (*gen*) dosis *f inv*; (*when injected*) pinchazo* *m*, chute *m* (*Sp*‡); **to give o.s. a ~** pincharse*, chutarse (*Sp*‡); **she needs her daily ~ of publicity** necesita su dosis diaria de publicidad
[3] (*Aer, Naut*) posición *f*; **to get a ~ on sth** (*lit*) establecer la posición de algo, localizar algo; **it's been hard to get a ~ on what's going on** (*fig*) ha sido difícil entender lo que pasa
[4] (*) (= *set-up*) tongo* *m*; **the fight/result was a ~** hubo tongo en la pelea/el resultado*
[5] (*) (= *solution*) arreglo *m*, apaño* *m*; **there is no quick-~ solution to this problem** no existe un arreglo *or* apaño* rápido para este problema

►**fix on** Ⓐ VT + ADV [+ *top, lid*] colocar
Ⓑ VI + PREP (= *decide on*) [+ *date, time*] fijar; **they haven't ~ed on a name yet** no se han decidido por un nombre todavía

►**fix up** Ⓐ VT + ADV [1] (= *arrange*) [+ *date*] fijar; [+ *meeting*] fijar, convenir; **I ~ed up an appointment to see her** concerté una cita para verla; **to ~ sth up with sb** quedar con algn en algo, convenir algo con algn
[2] (= *repair*) arreglar; **he buys properties to ~ them up** compra casas para arreglarlas
[3] (= *set up, install*) instalar, poner; **he ~ed up the lighting in my flat** instaló la iluminación de mi piso, puso las luces de mi piso
[4] (= *put in order*) arreglar; **I'll have to ~ the place up a bit before they arrive** tendré que arreglar un poco la casa antes de que lleguen
[5] (= *provide*) **to ~ sb up with sth**: **~ sb up with a job** encontrar *or* conseguir un trabajo para algn; **I can ~ you up with a place to stay** puedo conseguirte un sitio para alojarte
[6] (*) (= *find partner for*) **they're always trying to ~ me up with friends of theirs** siempre están intentando encontrarme un novio entre sus amigos
Ⓑ VI + ADV **to ~ up with sb** arreglarlo con algn; **to ~ up with sb to** (+ INFIN) convenir con algn en + *infin*

fixate [fɪk'seɪt] Ⓐ VT [+ *point*] fijar la atención en
Ⓑ VI **to ~ on sth/sb** obsesionarse con algo/algn

fixated [fɪk'seɪtɪd] ADJ **to be ~ on sth/sb** estar obsesionado con algo/algn, tener una fijación con algo/algn; **to become** *or* **get ~ on** *or* **with sth/sb** obsesionarse con algo/algn; **mother-~** con fijación materna *or* en la madre

fixation [fɪk'seɪʃən] N (*Psych*) (*fig*) obsesión *f*, fijación *f*; **mother ~** fijación *f* materna *or* en la madre

fixative ['fɪksətɪv] N fijador *m*

fixed [fɪkst] Ⓐ ADJ [1] (= *permanent, invariable*) [*amount, number, rate*] fijo; **of no ~ abode** *or* **address** (*Jur*) sin domicilio fijo
[2] (= *prearranged*) establecido; **at a ~ time** a una hora establecida; **there's no ~ agenda** no hay un orden del día fijo
[3] (= *immovable*) [*smile*] inamovible; [*stare*] fijo; **she kept a ~ smile on her face** mantuvo una sonrisa inamovible; **to keep one's eyes ~ on sth** mantener la mirada fija en algo
[4] (= *inflexible*) [*opinion*] firme, rígido; **he has very ~ ideas** es de ideas fijas
Ⓑ CPD ► **fixed assets** NPL activo *msing* fijo ► **fixed charge** N cargo *m* fijo ► **fixed costs** NPL costos *mpl* fijos ► **fixed price** N precio *m* fijo

fixed-interest ['fɪkstˌɪntrɪst] ADJ a interés fijo

fixedly ['fɪksɪdlɪ] ADV fijamente

fixed-price ['fɪkstpraɪs] Ⓐ ADJ [*contract*] a precio fijo
Ⓑ CPD ► **fixed-price menu** N menú *m* del día

fixed-rate ['fɪkstˌreɪt] ADJ (*Fin*) a tipo fijo

fixed-wing aircraft [ˌfɪkstwɪŋ'ɛəkrɑːft] N avión *m* de ala fija

fixer* ['fɪksəʳ] N (= *person*) apañador(ora)* *m/f*, amañador(a) *m/f*; (*Phot*) fijador *m*

fixings ['fɪksɪŋz] NPL (*US Culin*) guarniciones *fpl*

Fixit* ['fɪksɪt] N **Mr ~** Señor *m* Arreglalotodo*

fixture ['fɪkstʃəʳ] Ⓐ N [1] [*of house etc*] **fixtures** instalaciones *fpl* fijas; **the house was sold with ~s and fittings** la casa se vendió totalmente equipada
[2] (*Sport*) encuentro *m*
[3] (= *permanent feature*) elemento *m* fijo; (= *date*) fecha *f* fija; **he's become a permanent ~ in this house** (*hum*) es como si fuera parte del mobiliario de la casa
Ⓑ CPD ► **fixture list** N lista *f* de encuentros

fizz [fɪz] Ⓐ N [1] (= *fizziness*) efervescencia *f*, gas *m*
[2] (= *fizzing noise*) silbido *m*, ruido *m* sibilante
[3] (*) champán *m*; (*US*) (= *soft drink*) gaseosa *f*
[4] (*fig*) chispa *f*; **the ~ had gone out of their relationship** a su relación no le quedaba chispa
Ⓑ VI [*drink*] burbujear; (= *make fizzing noise*) hacer un ruido sibilante, silbar

fizzle ['fɪzl] VI silbar, hacer un ruido sibilante

►**fizzle out** VI + ADV [*fire, firework*] apagarse; [*enthusiasm, interest*] morirse; [*plan*] quedar en agua de borrajas *or* en nada

fizzy ['fɪzɪ] (*esp Brit*) ADJ (*compar* **fizzier**; *superl* **fizziest**) [*drink*] gaseoso, con gas

fjord [fjɔːd] N fiordo *m*

FL ABBR (*US*) = **Florida**

Fla. ABBR (*US*) = **Florida**

flab* [flæb] N gordura *f*

flabbergasted ['flæbəgɑːstɪd] ADJ pasmado, atónito; **I was ~ by the news** la noticia me dejó pasmado *or* atónito

flabbiness ['flæbɪnɪs] N [1] (= *chubbiness*) gordura *f*
[2] (*fig*) [*of speech, argument*] flojedad *f*, debilidad *f*

flabby ['flæbɪ] ADJ (*compar* **flabbier**; *superl* **flabbiest**) (= *soft*) fofo; (= *fat*) gordo; (*fig*) flojo, soso

flaccid ['flæksɪd] ADJ fláccido

flaccidity [flæk'sɪdɪtɪ] N flaccidez *f*

flag[1] [flæg] Ⓐ N [*of country*] bandera *f*; (*Naut*) pabellón *m*; (*for charity*) banderita *f*; (*small, as souvenir, also Sport*) banderín *m*; **~ of convenience** pabellón *m* de conveniencia; **~ of**

truce bandera *f* blanca; **to raise/lower the ~** izar/arriar la bandera; ✦***IDIOMS*** **to keep the ~ flying** mantener alto el pabellón; **to show the ~** hacer acto de presencia; **to wrap o.s.** *or* **drape o.s. in the ~** (*esp US*) escudarse en el patriotismo

Ⓑ VT (*= mark*) [*+ path*] señalar con banderitas; [*+ item, reference*] señalar, marcar; (*also* **~ down**) [*+ taxi*] (hacer) parar

Ⓒ CPD ► **flag bearer** N (*lit, fig*) abanderado/a *m/f* ► **flag day** N *día de colecta de una organización benéfica* ► **Flag Day** N (*US*) día *m* de la Bandera (*14 junio*) ► **flag officer** N (*Naut*) oficial *mf* superior de la marina ► **flag stop** N (*US*) parada *f* discrecional

►**flag down** VT + ADV [*+ taxi*] (hacer) parar; **to ~ sb down** hacer señales a algn para que se detenga

flag[2] [flæg] VI [*strength, person*] flaquear; [*enthusiasm*] enfriarse, decaer; [*conversation*] decaer

flag[3] [flæg] N (*also* **~stone**) losa *f*

flag[4] [flæg] N (*Bot*) falso ácoro *m*, lirio *m*

flagellate ['flædʒəleɪt] VT flagelar

flagellation [,flædʒə'leɪʃən] N flagelación *f*

flageolet [,flædʒə'let] N flageolet *m*, *flauta dulce de seis u ocho agujeros*

flagging ['flægɪŋ] ADJ [*strength*] que flaquea; [*enthusiasm, interest*] que se enfría; [*popularity, conversation*] que decae; **he soon revived their ~ spirits** les levantó el ánimo rápidamente

flagon ['flægən] N (*approx*) jarro *m*; (*as measure*) *botella de unos dos litros*

flagpole ['flægpəʊl] N asta *f* de bandera

flagrant ['fleɪgrənt] ADJ [*violation, breach, injustice*] flagrante; **in ~ defiance of the rules** en un acto de flagrante rebeldía contra las normas; **with ~ disregard for safety/the law** con total desacato a las normas de seguridad/a la ley

flagrantly ['fleɪgrəntlɪ] ADV flagrantemente

flagship ['flægʃɪp] N [1] (*Naut*) buque *m* insignia, buque *m* almirante

[2] (*fig*) punta *f* de lanza; **the newspaper is the ~ of his media empire** el periódico es la punta de lanza de su imperio mediático

flagstaff ['flægstɑːf] N asta *f* de bandera

flagstone ['flægstəʊn] N losa *f*

flag-waving ['flæg,weɪvɪŋ] N (*fig*) patriotismo *m* de banderita

flail [fleɪl] Ⓐ N (*Agr*) mayal *m*

Ⓑ VT [1] (*Agr*) desgranar

[2] (*= beat*) golpear, azotar

[3] (*= agitate*) [*+ arms, legs*] agitar

Ⓒ VI **to ~ (about)** [*arms, legs*] agitarse; [*person*] revolverse; **I tried to grab his ~ing arms** intenté agarrarle los brazos que no paraba de agitar

flair [fleəʳ] N (*= gift*) don *m*; (*= instinct*) instinto *m*; (*= style*) elegancia *f*, estilo *m*; **to have a ~ for languages** tener don de lenguas, tener facilidad para los idiomas; **she had a natural ~ for getting on with people** tenía mano izquierda con la gente *or* don de gentes

flak [flæk] Ⓐ N [1] fuego *m* antiaéreo

[2] (*) (*= criticism*) críticas *fpl*; **to get a lot of ~** ser muy criticado

Ⓑ CPD ► **flak jacket** N chaleco *m* antibalas

flake [fleɪk] Ⓐ N [*of paint*] desconchón *m*; [*of skin, soap*] escama *f*; [*of snow*] copo *m*

Ⓑ VI (*also* **~ off, ~ away**) [*paint*] descascarillarse, desconcharse; [*skin*] pelarse

Ⓒ VT [*+ cooked fish*] desmenuzar

►**flake out*** VI + ADV (*Brit*) (*= faint*) desplomarse; (*= fall asleep*) caer rendido; **I ~d out on the bed** caí rendido en la cama; **to be ~d out*** estar rendido

flaky ['fleɪkɪ] Ⓐ ADJ (*compar* **flakier**, *superl* **flakiest**) [1] [*paintwork*] desconchado; [*skin*] escamoso

[2] (*) [*idea*] descabellado; [*person*] raro

Ⓑ CPD ► **flaky pastry** N (*Culin*) hojaldre *m*

flambé ['flɑːmbeɪ] Ⓐ ADJ flam(b)eado

Ⓑ VT flam(b)ear

flamboyance [flæm'bɔɪəns] N [*of person, behaviour*] extravagancia *f*; [*of clothes, colour*] vistosidad *f*, lo llamativo

flamboyant [flæm'bɔɪənt] ADJ [*person, behaviour, style*] extravagante; [*clothes, colour*] vistoso, llamativo; **he's a ~ dresser** viste con mucha extravagancia

flame [fleɪm] Ⓐ N [1] llama *f*; **to be in ~s** arder or estar en llamas; **to burst into ~s** [*car, plane*] estallar en llamas; **to commit sth to the ~s** echar algo al fuego; **to fan the ~s** avivar el fuego; **he watched the house go up in ~s** miraba cómo la casa era pasto de las llamas

[2] (*) (*= lover*) **old ~*** antiguo amor *m*

Ⓑ VI [1] (*also* **~ up**) [*fire*] llamear; [*passion*] encenderse; [*person*] acalorarse

[2] [*eyes*] brillar; [*sky*] llamear, enrojecerse; **her cheeks ~d with embarrassment** se puso colorada de vergüenza

Ⓒ VT (*Internet*) insultar a través de la Red, abuchear en la Red

Ⓓ CPD ► **flame retardant** N = **fire retardant**

flame-coloured, **flame-colored** (*US*) ['fleɪm,kʌləd] ADJ de un amarillo intenso

flamenco [flə'meŋkəʊ] Ⓐ N flamenco *m*

Ⓑ CPD [*music*] flamenco; [*dancer*] de flamenco

flameproof ['fleɪmpruːf] ADJ ignífugo, a prueba de fuego

flame-retardant ['fleɪmrɪ,tɑːdənt] ADJ = **fire-retardant**

flamethrower ['fleɪm,θrəʊəʳ] N lanzallamas *m inv*

flaming ['fleɪmɪŋ] ADJ [1] [*torch*] llameante; [*vehicle*] en llamas

[2] [*red, orange*] encendido; **she had ~ red hair** tenía el pelo de un rojo encendido

[3] (*Brit**) (*= furious*) **we had a ~ row** tuvimos una acalorada discusión

[4] (‡) condenado*, maldito*

flamingo [flə'mɪŋgəʊ] N (*pl* **flamingos** *or* **flamingoes**) flamenco *m*

flammable ['flæməbl] ADJ inflamable

flan [flæn] N tarta *f*

Flanders ['flɑːndəz] N Flandes *m*

flange [flændʒ] N (*Tech*) (*on wheel*) pestaña *f*; (*on pipe*) reborde *m*

flanged [flændʒd] ADJ [*wheel*] con pestaña; [*coupling*] rebordeado

flank [flæŋk] Ⓐ N [*of person*] costado *m*; [*of animal*] ijar *m*, ijada *f*; (*Mil*) flanco *m*; [*of hill*] ladera *f*, falda *f*

Ⓑ CPD ► **flank attack** N ataque *m* de flanco

Ⓒ VT (*= stand at side of*) [*+ entrance, statue etc*] flanquear (*also Mil*); **it is ~ed by hills** está flanqueado por colinas; **he was ~ed by two policemen** iba escoltado por dos policías

flannel ['flænl] Ⓐ N [1] (*= face flannel*) manopla *f*; (*= fabric*) franela *f*; **flannels** (*= trousers*) pantalones *mpl* de franela

[2] (*Brit**) (*= waffle*) palabrería *f*, paja* *f*

Ⓑ ADJ de franela

Ⓒ VI (*Brit**) (*= waffle*) meter paja*

flannelette [,flænə'let] N franela *f* de algodón

flap [flæp] Ⓐ N [1] [*of pocket, envelope*] solapa *f*; [*of table*] hoja *f* (plegable); [*of counter*] trampa *f*; [*of skin*] colgajo *m*; (*Aer*) alerón *m*

[2] (*= act*) [*of wing*] aletazo *m*; (*= sound*) (ruido *m* del) aleteo *m*

[3] (*Brit**) (*= crisis*) crisis *f inv*; (*= row*) lío* *m*; **there's a big ~ on** se ha armado un buen lío*; **to get into a ~*** ponerse nervioso

Ⓑ VT [*bird*] [*+ wings*] batir; (*= shake*) [*+ sheets, newspaper*] sacudir; [*+ arms*] agitar

Ⓒ VI [1] [*wings*] aletear; [*sails*] agitarse; [*flag*] ondear, agitarse

[2] (*) (*= panic*) ponerse nervioso; **don't ~!** ¡con calma!

flapdoodle* ['flæp,duːdl] N chorrada* *f*

flapjack ['flæpdʒæk] N (*US*) (*= pancake*) torta *f*, panqueque *m* (*LAm*); (*Brit*) *torta de avena*

flapper* ['flæpəʳ] N (*Hist*) joven *f* a la moda (*de los 1920*)

flare [fleəʳ] Ⓐ N [1] (*= blaze*) llamarada *f*; (*= signal*) bengala *f* (*also Mil, for target*); (*on runway*) baliza *f*; **solar ~** erupción *f* solar

[2] (*Sew*) vuelo *m*

[3] **flares** (*= trousers*) pantalones *mpl* de campana

Ⓑ VI [1] [*match, torch*] llamear; [*light*] brillar

[2] (*= widen*) [*skirt*] hacer vuelo; [*trousers, nostrils*] ensancharse

[3] [*riots*] estallar

[4] [*tempers*] caldearse, encenderse

►**flare up** VI + ADV [1] [*fire*] llamear

[2] (*fig*) [*person*] estallar, ponerse furioso (**at** con); [*riots*] estallar; [*epidemic*] declararse

[3] [*wound*] resentirse, volver a dar problemas; [*rash*] recrudecerse

flared [fleəd] ADJ [*skirt*] de mucho vuelo, acampanado; [*trousers*] acampanado; [*nostrils*] ensanchado

flarepath ['fleəpɑːθ] N pista *f* iluminada con balizas

flare-up ['fleər'ʌp] N [*of anger*] arranque *m*; (*= quarrel*) riña *f*; [*of violence*] estallido *m*; [*of illness, acne*] recrudecimiento *m*

flash [flæʃ] Ⓐ N [1] [*of light*] destello *m*; [*of gun*] fogonazo *m*; [*of jewel*] centelleo *m*, destellos *mpl*; **he saw a ~ of green vanishing round the next bend** vio un destello verde que desaparecía en la siguiente curva; **the ~ of expensive jewellery** el centelleo de alhajas costosas; **a ~ of lightning** un relámpago

[2] (*= burst*) **a ~ of anger** un arranque *or* un arrebato de cólera; **a ~ of inspiration** una ráfaga *or* un momento de inspiración; **a ~ of wit** un ramalazo de ingenio; ✦***IDIOM*** **a ~ in the pan** algo pasajero, flor de un día; **the affair was nothing more than a ~ in the pan** el asunto no fue más que algo pasajero *or* flor de un día; **their win was no ~ in the pan** su victoria no se debió a un golpe de suerte, no ganaron por chiripa*

[3] (*= instant*) instante *m*; **in a ~** en un abrir y cerrar de ojos, en un instante; **it all happened in a ~** todo sucedió en un abrir y cerrar de ojos *or* en un instante; **it came to him in a ~** de repente lo vio todo claro; **I'll be back in a ~** vuelvo en un instante; **quick as a ~** como un relámpago *or* un rayo

[4] (*= news flash*) noticia *f* de última hora

[5] (*Phot*) flash *m*

[6] (*= marking*) (*on animal*) mancha *f*

[7] (*Brit Mil*) (*= insignia*) distintivo *m*

[8] (*US*) (*= torch*) linterna *f*

Ⓑ VT [1] (*= direct*) [*+ look*] lanzar; [*+ smile*] dirigir; **he ~ed me a look of surprise** me lanzó una mirada de sorpresa; **she ~ed him a grateful smile** le dirigió una breve sonrisa de agradecimiento

[2] (*= shine*) **he ~ed his torch into the boat** enfocó el barco con la linterna; **she ~ed the**

light in my eyes me enfocó con la luz en los ojos; **to ~ one's (head)lights** (*Aut*) hacer señales con las luces

3 (= *send quickly*) [+ *news, information*] transmitir rápidamente; **the pictures were ~ed around the world** las imágenes circularon rápidamente por todo el mundo

4 (= *display briefly*) mostrar; **the screen ~es a message** aparece brevemente un mensaje en la pantalla, la pantalla muestra brevemente un mensaje; **I ~ed my card at the security guard** le enseñé *or* mostré brevemente mi tarjeta al guardia de seguridad

5 (= *flaunt*) hacer alarde de, fardar de*; **they're rich but they don't ~ their money around** son ricos pero no van fardando de dinero por ahí*, son ricos pero no hacen alarde de su riqueza

Ⓒ VI 1 (= *shine*) [*light, eyes, teeth*] brillar; [*jewels*] brillar, lanzar destellos; **a light was ~ing on the horizon** brillaba una luz en el horizonte; **cameras ~ed as she stepped from the car** las cámaras disparaban los flashes cuando ella salía del coche; **a police car raced past, lights ~ing** pasó un coche de policía a toda velocidad, con las luces lanzando destellos; **his brake lights ~ed** las luces de freno se iluminaron de repente; **a ~ing neon sign** un anuncio de neón intermitente; **lightning was ~ing all around** relampagueaba por todas partes; **headaches accompanied by ~ing lights** dolores *mpl* de cabeza acompañados de destellos de luz en la visión; **her eyes ~ed with anger** se le encendieron los ojos

2 (*Aut*) **I ~ed to let him out** le hice señales con las luces para que pasara

3 (= *move quickly*) **a thought ~ed through my mind** una idea me cruzó la mente como un relámpago; **his whole life ~ed before his eyes** volvió a revivir toda su vida en unos instantes; **a message ~ed up on the screen** apareció brevemente un mensaje en la pantalla; **to ~ by** *or* **past** [*vehicle, person*] pasar a toda velocidad, pasar como un rayo; [*time*] pasar volando; **the landscape ~ed by in a blur** el paisaje iba pasando con velocidad, fundiéndose en una imagen borrosa

4 (*Cine*) **to ~ back to** retroceder a; **to ~ forward to** adelantarse hasta

5 (*) (= *expose o.s.*) exhibirse

Ⓓ ADJ (*) (= *showy*) [*car, clothes*] llamativo, fardón*; **a ~ restaurant** un restaurante ostentoso, un restaurante de esos impresionantes*

Ⓔ CPD ► **flash bulb** N bombilla *f* de flash ► **flash card** N tarjeta *f* ► **flash fire** N fuego *m* repentino ► **flash flood** N riada *f* ► **flash gun** N (*Phot*) disparador *m* de flash ► **flash photography** N fotografía *f* con flash

flashback ['flæʃbæk] N (*Cine*) escena *f* retrospectiva, flashback *m*

flashcube ['flæʃkju:b] N (*Phot*) cubo *m* de flash

flasher* ['flæʃə^r] N 1 (= *man*) exhibicionista *m*
2 (*Brit Aut*) intermitente *m*

flash-freeze [flæʃ'fri:z] VT someter a un proceso de congelación muy rápido

flashily ['flæʃɪlɪ] ADV **to dress ~** vestirse de manera llamativa

flashing ['flæʃɪŋ] N 1 (*on roof*) tapajuntas *m inv* 2 (*) (= *exposing o.s.*) exhibicionismo *m*

flashlight ['flæʃlaɪt] N (*US*) (= *torch*) linterna *f*

flashpoint ['flæʃpɔɪnt] N 1 punto *m* de inflamación 2 (*fig*) punto *m* crítico; **it could prove the ~ for war** podría aún dar lugar al estallido de la guerra

flashy ['flæʃɪ] ADJ (*compar* **flashier**; *superl* **flashiest**) [*jewellery, clothes, car*] llamativo, ostentoso; [*colour*] chillón; [*person*] llamativo

flask [flɑ:sk] N (*for brandy*) petaca *f*; (= *vacuum flask*) termo *m*; (*Chem*) matraz *m*, redoma *f*

flat[1] [flæt] Ⓐ ADJ (*compar* **flatter**; *superl* **flattest**) 1 (= *level*) [*surface, roof*] plano; [*countryside*] llano; **he was lying ~ on the floor** estaba tumbado en el suelo; **he laid his hands ~ on the table** puso las manos extendidas sobre la mesa; **keep your feet ~ on the floor** mantén los pies bien pegados al suelo; **the sea was calm and ~** el mar estaba en calma y no había olas; **lie ~ on your back** túmbate de espaldas en el suelo; **he was ~ on his back for a month after the accident** tuvo que guardar cama durante un mes después del accidente; **to fall ~ on one's face** (*lit*) caer(se) de bruces; **the government's campaign fell ~ on its face** la campaña del gobierno resultó un fracaso; ✦*IDIOM* **~ as a pancake*** liso como la palma de la mano; *see also* **spin**

2 (= *smooth, even*) [*road, surface*] liso, llano; **to smooth sth ~** [+ *paper etc*] alisar algo

3 (= *shallow*) [*dish*] llano; [*box*] plano

4 [*foot, shoe*] plano; [*nose*] chato; **to have ~ feet** tener los pies planos

5 (= *deflated*) [*tyre, ball*] pinchado, desinflado; **we got a ~ tyre** se nos pinchó una rueda, se nos ponchó una llanta (*Mex*); **I had a ~ tyre** tenía una rueda pinchada *or* desinflada, tenía un pinchazo, tenía una ponchada (*Mex*)

6 (= *dull, lifeless*) [*voice, colour*] apagado; [*taste, style*] soso; [*light*] sin contraste; [*drink*] sin burbujas *or* gas; [*battery*] descargado; **the atmosphere at the party was a bit ~** el ambiente de la fiesta estaba un poco apagado; **I've got a ~ battery** se me ha descargado la batería; **I'm feeling rather ~** estoy un poco deprimido; **she meant it as a joke, but it fell ~** lo dijo de broma, pero nadie le vio la gracia; **the champagne has gone ~** al champán se le ha ido la fuerza *or* se le han ido las burbujas

7 (= *inactive*) [*trade, business*] flojo; **sales have been ~ this summer** las ventas han estado flojas este verano, no ha habido mucho movimiento de ventas este verano

8 (= *outright*) [*refusal, denial*] rotundo, terminante; **his suggestion met with a ~ refusal** su sugerencia recibió una negativa rotunda *or* terminante; **he says he's not going and that's ~*** dice que no va y sanseacabó

9 (*Mus*) 9·1 [*voice, instrument*] desafinado; **she/her singing was ~** desafinaba cantando
9·2 (*of key*) bemol; **E ~ major** mi bemol mayor

10 (= *fixed*) [*rate, fee, charge*] fijo

11 (*Horse racing*) **~ jockey** jinete *mf* de carreras sin obstáculos; **the ~ season** la temporada de carreras de caballos sin obstáculos

12 (= *not shiny*) (*of painted surface*) mate, sin brillo

Ⓑ ADV 1 (= *absolutely*) **to be ~ broke*** estar pelado*, estar sin un duro (*Sp**), estar sin un peso (*LAm**)

2 (= *outright*) [*refuse*] rotundamente, terminantemente; **I told her ~ that she couldn't have it** le dije terminantemente que no se lo podía quedar; **to turn sth down ~** rechazar algo rotundamente *or* de plano

3 (= *exactly*) **he did it in ten minutes ~** lo hizo en diez minutos justos *or* exactos

4 (*esp Brit*) **~ out: ~ out, the car can do 140mph** cuando pones el coche a toda máquina, llega a las 140 millas por hora; **to go ~ out** ir a toda máquina; **to go ~ out for sth** intentar conseguir algo por todos los medios; **she went ~ out for the title** intentó por todos los medios conseguir el título; **to work ~ out (to do sth)** trabajar a toda máquina (para hacer algo)

5 (*Mus*) **to play/sing ~** tocar/cantar demasiado bajo, desafinar

Ⓒ N 1 [*of hand*] palma *f*; [*of sword*] cara *f* de la hoja

2 (*Mus*) bemol *m*

3 (*Aut*) pinchazo *m*, ponchada *f* (*Mex*); **we got a ~** se nos pinchó una rueda, se nos ponchó una llanta (*Mex*); **I had a ~** tenía una rueda pinchada *or* desinflada, tenía un pinchazo, tenía una ponchada (*Mex*)

4 **flats** (*Geog*) (= *marshland*) marismas *fpl*; (= *sand*) bancos *mpl* de arena; **mud ~s** marismas *fpl*; **salt ~s** salinas *fpl*

5 (*Theat*) bastidor *m*

6 (*Horse racing*) **the ~** las carreras de caballos sin obstáculos

Ⓓ CPD ► **flat cap** N *gorra de lana con visera* ► **flat pack** N **it comes in a ~ pack** viene en una caja plana para el automontaje ► **flat racing** N carreras *fpl* de caballos sin obstáculos ► **flat screen** N (*TV, Comput*) pantalla *f* plana

flat[2] [flæt] N (*Brit*) apartamento *m*, piso *m* (*Sp*), departamento *m* (*LAm*)

flat-bottomed ['flæt'bɒtəmd] ADJ [*boat*] de fondo plano

flat-chested ['flæt'tʃestɪd] ADJ de pecho plano

flatfish ['flætfɪʃ] N (*pl* **flatfish** *or* **flatfishes**) pez *m* plano; (*Tech*) (pez *m*) pleuronectiforme *m* (*p.ej. platija, lenguado*)

flat-footed ['flæt'fʊtɪd] ADJ 1 de pies planos; **to be ~** tener los pies planos
2 (*) (*fig*) (= *clumsy*) patoso (*Sp**)

flatiron ['flæt,aɪən] N plancha *f*

flatlet ['flætlɪt] N (*Brit*) apartamento *m or* (*Sp*) piso *m or* (*LAm*) departamento *m* pequeño

flatly ['flætlɪ] ADV 1 (= *without emotion*) [*read, recite*] monótonamente; [*say, reply*] de manera inexpresiva
2 (= *categorically, completely*) [*refuse, deny*] terminantemente, rotundamente; [*contradict*] de plano; **we are ~ opposed to it** nos oponemos terminantemente *or* rotundamente a ello

flatmate ['flætmeɪt] N compañero/a *m/f* de apartamento, compañero/a *m/f* de piso (*Sp*), compañero/a *m/f* de departamento (*LAm*)

flatness ['flætnɪs] N 1 [*of land*] llanura *f*, lo llano; [*of surface*] lisura *f*
2 [*of drink*] lo poco gaseoso
3 (*fig*) [*of atmosphere, relationship, voice*] monotonía *f*; **her voice had a weary ~** su voz tenía una monotonía cansina

flat-pack ['flætpæk] ADJ **~ furniture** *muebles automontables embalados en cajas planas*

flatten ['flætn] Ⓐ VT 1 (= *compress, squash*) [+ *road, grass*] allanar, aplanar; [+ *hair, paper, map*] alisar; **~ the dough with a rolling pin** aplanar *or* extender la masa con un rodillo; **I ~ed myself against the wall** me pegué a la pared
2 (= *level out*) [+ *surface*] nivelar
3 (= *knock down*) [+ *building, city*] arrasar; [+ *person*] tumbar; **he could ~ me with one blow** podría tumbarme de un solo golpe
4 (*fig*) (= *defeat, subdue*) desanimar, desalentar; **she felt ~ed** se sintió desalentada

Ⓑ VI 1 (= *lie flat*) **the dog's ears ~ed** el perro bajó las orejas
2 (= *become flat*) [*road, countryside*] nivelarse, allanarse

►**flatten out** Ⓐ VI + ADV 1 (= *become flat*) [*road, countryside*] nivelarse, allanarse
2 (= *increase less rapidly*) **sales have ~ed out** el ritmo de las ventas ha decrecido

Ⓑ VT + ADV [+ *road*] allanar, aplanar; [+ *paper, map*] extender, alisar

flatter ['flætəʳ] VT 1 (= *praise, compliment*) 1·1 (*sincerely*) halagar; **you ~ me!** ¡me halagas!; **to say that she is tactless is to ~ her** (*iro*) decir que no tiene tacto es como echarle un piropo

1·2 (*insincerely*) adular, lisonjear; **he only said it to ~ you** te lo dijo sólo para adularte

2 (= *gratify*) halagar; **I was very ~ed to be asked** me halagó que me lo pidieran; **to feel ~ed** sentirse halagado

3 (= *show to advantage*) favorecer; **that colour ~s you** ese color te favorece; **it's a dress that will ~ any figure** es un vestido que favorece a cualquiera

4 **to ~ o.s.** 4·1 (= *pride o.s.*) **to ~ o.s. on sth/that** enorgullecerse de algo/de que

4·2 (= *deceive o.s.*) **don't ~ yourself, I didn't come all this way just to see you** no te hagas ilusiones, no he venido hasta aquí sólo para verte a ti; **you ~ yourself! what makes you think he fancies you?** ¡no seas engreída! ¿qué te hace pensar que le gustas?

flatterer ['flætərəʳ] N adulador(a) *m/f*

flattering ['flætərɪŋ] ADJ 1 (= *complimentary*) [*remark, words*] halagador; **the play had very ~ reviews** la obra recibió críticas muy halagadoras *or* halagüeñas; **he was very ~ about you** habló muy bien de ti; **that's not very ~ to him!** ¡vaya imagen que pintas de él! (*iro*)

2 (= *gratifying*) **it was ~ to be told how indispensable he was** le halagó que le dijeran lo indispensable que era; **he found the interest in him ~** se sentía halagado por la atención que le prestaban

3 (= *fawning*) adulador; **she was surrounded by ~ admirers** estaba rodeada de admiradores que la adulaban

4 [*photo, clothes*] favorecedor; **that dress isn't ~ at all on you** ese vestido no te favorece nada

flatteringly ['flætərɪŋlɪ] ADV [*speak*] de forma halagadora; **he was ~ attentive** era tan atento que resultaba halagador

flattery ['flætərɪ] N halagos *mpl*, lisonjas *fpl*; **it wasn't just ~, I meant what I said** no eran simplemente halagos *or* lisonjas, lo decía en serio; **~ will get you nowhere!** (*iro*) ¡con halagos *or* lisonjas no vas a conseguir nada!; **~ will get you everywhere!** (*iro*) ¡con halagos *or* lisonjas se consigue todo!; *see also* **imitation**

flatulence ['flætjʊləns] N flatulencia *f*

flatulent ['flætjʊlənt] ADJ flatulento

flatware ['flætwɛəʳ] N (*US*) (= *cutlery*) cubertería *f*

flatworm ['flætwɜːm] N platelminto *m*

flaunt [flɔːnt] VT (*pej*) [+ *wealth, knowledge*] alardear de, hacer alarde de; **to ~ o.s.** pavonearse

flautist ['flɔːtɪst] N (*esp Brit*) flautista *mf*

flavin ['fleɪvɪn] N flavina *f*

flavour, flavor (*US*) ['fleɪvəʳ] Ⓐ N (*gen*) sabor *m*, gusto *m* (**of** a); (= *flavouring*) condimento *m*; (*fig*) sabor *m*, aire *m*; **with a banana ~** con sabor *or* gusto a plátano; **steaming the vegetables retains the maximum ~** cocinando las verduras al vapor se conserva su sabor al máximo; **the decor has a Victorian ~** la decoración tiene un sabor *or* aire victoriano

Ⓑ VT (*Culin*) condimentar, sazonar (**with** con); **the pudding is ~ed with liqueur** el postre tiene licor

flavouring, flavoring (*US*) ['fleɪvərɪŋ] N condimento *m*; **artificial ~** aromatizante *m* artificial; **vanilla ~** esencia *f* de vainilla

flavourless, flavorless (*US*) ['fleɪvəlɪs] ADJ insípido, soso

flaw [flɔː] N (= *defect*) (*in character, system*) defecto *m*, fallo *m*; (*in material, beauty, diamond*) desperfecto *m*, tara *f*; (*in reasoning*) error *m*, fallo *m*; (= *crack*) grieta *f*

flawed [flɔːd] ADJ [*system, goods*] defectuoso; [*theory*] erróneo; **the agreement is fatally ~** el acuerdo presenta fallos que lo condenan al fracaso

flawless ['flɔːlɪs] ADJ [*diamond, skin*] perfecto, sin defectos; [*beauty*] inmaculado; [*plan*] perfecto; [*conduct*] intachable, impecable; **she spoke in ~ English** habló en un inglés perfecto

flax [flæks] Ⓐ N (*Bot*) lino *m*

Ⓑ CPD ► **flax seed** N linaza *f*

flaxen ['flæksən] ADJ (*poet*) [*hair*] muy rubio

flay [fleɪ] VT 1 (= *skin*) desollar; **he'll ~ me alive if I'm late*** si llego tarde, me despelleja vivo

2 (= *criticize*) [+ *person*] despellejar; [+ *book, film*] hacer trizas

3 (= *defeat*) dar una paliza a*

flea [fliː] Ⓐ N pulga *f*; ✦***IDIOM*** **to send sb away with a ~ in his ear*** despachar a algn con cajas destempladas

Ⓑ CPD ► **flea collar** N collar *m* antipulgas *or* antiparasitario ► **flea market** N mercadillo *m*, rastro *m* (*Sp*)

fleabag‡ ['fliːbæg] N (*Brit*) (= *person*) guarro/a *m/f*; (*US*) (= *hotel*) hotelucho *m* de mala muerte*

fleabite ['fliːbaɪt] N picadura *f* de pulga; (*fig*) nada *f*, nimiedad *f*

flea-bitten* ['fliːbɪtn] ADJ (*lit*) [*dog*] pulgoso; (*fig*) miserable

fleapit* ['fliːpɪt] N cine *m* de mala muerte

fleck [flek] Ⓐ N [*of mud, paint, dust*] mota *f*; [*of spit, foam*] salpicadura *f*; [*of colour*] mota *f*; **his eyes are green with ~s of gold** tiene los ojos verdes con motas doradas

Ⓑ VT salpicar (**with** de); **black ~ed with white** negro moteado de blanco *or* con motas blancas

fled [fled] PT, PP *of* **flee**

fledged [fledʒd] ADJ plumado

fledg(e)ling ['fledʒlɪŋ] Ⓐ N (= *young bird*) pajarito *m*; (*fig*) novato/a *m/f*

Ⓑ CPD [*democracy, writer*] en ciernes; [*company, industry*] joven

flee [fliː] (*pt, pp* **fled**) Ⓐ VT huir de; **to ~ the country** huir del país

Ⓑ VI huir (**from** de), darse a la fuga; **they fled to the West/the mountains** huyeron hacia el oeste/las montañas

fleece [fliːs] Ⓐ N 1 (*on sheep*) lana *f*; (*shorn*) vellón *m* 2 (= *jacket*) forro *m* polar

Ⓑ VT [+ *sheep*] esquilar; (*fig*) (*) (= *rob*) desplumar*

fleece-lined [,fliːs'laɪnd] ADJ forrado de corderito *or* vellón

fleecy ['fliːsɪ] ADJ (*compar* **fleecier**, *superl* **fleeciest**) 1 (= *woolly*) lanoso, lanudo

2 [*clouds*] aborregado

fleet[1] [fliːt] N 1 (*Aer, Naut*) flota *f*; **the British ~** la armada británica; **Fleet Air Arm** (*Brit*) Fuerzas *fpl* Aéreas de la Armada

2 [*of cars, coaches etc*] parque *m* (móvil)

fleet[2] [fliːt] (*poet*) ADJ (*compar* **fleeter**, *superl* **fleetest**) (*also* **~-footed, ~ of foot**) veloz

fleeting ['fliːtɪŋ] ADJ 1 (= *brief*) [*impression*] momentáneo; [*visit*] breve; [*moment*] breve, fugaz; **to have** *or* **catch a ~ glimpse of sth/sb** alcanzar a ver algo/a algn fugazmente; **a ~ glance** una breve mirada

2 (= *ephemeral*) [*joy, popularity*] fugaz, efímero; [*beauty*] pasajero

fleetingly ['fliːtɪŋlɪ] ADV [*smile, see, think, recall*] fugazmente; **he wondered ~ if she knew** se preguntó por un instante si ella lo sabía; **the joy they shared so ~** esa alegría tan efímera que compartieron

Fleet Street ['fliːt,striːt] N (*Brit*) (= *street*) Fleet Street, *calle de Londres en la que muchos periódicos tenían sus oficinas*; (= *industry*) *la prensa británica*

Fleming ['flemɪŋ] N flamenco/a *m/f*

Flemish ['flemɪʃ] Ⓐ ADJ flamenco

Ⓑ N (*Ling*) flamenco *m*

flesh [fleʃ] Ⓐ N (*gen*) carne *f*; [*of fruit*] pulpa *f*; **in the ~** en carne y hueso, en persona; **my own ~ and blood** mi propia sangre; **to put on ~** echar carnes; **the sins of the ~** los pecados de la carne; **it's more than ~ and blood can stand** no hay quien lo aguante; ✦***IDIOMS*** **to make sb's ~ crawl** *or* **creep** poner carne de gallina a algn; **to go the way of all ~** pasar a mejor vida; *see also* **press B1**

Ⓑ CPD ► **flesh colour, flesh color** (*US*) N (*gen, Art*) color *m* de la piel ► **flesh wound** N herida *f* superficial

► **flesh out** VT + ADV desarrollar

flesh-coloured, flesh-colored (*US*) ['fleʃ,kʌləd] ADJ del color de la piel

flesh-eating ['fleʃiːtɪŋ] ADJ carnívoro

fleshly ['fleʃlɪ] ADJ (*frm*) [*lusts, desires*] carnal, de la carne

fleshpots ['fleʃpɒts] NPL (*fig*) antros *mpl* de libertinaje

fleshy ['fleʃɪ] ADJ (*compar* **fleshier**, *superl* **fleshiest**) (= *fat*) gordo; (*Bot*) [*fruit*] carnoso

flew [fluː] PT *of* **fly**[2]

flex [fleks] Ⓐ N (*Brit*) [*of lamp, telephone*] cable *m*, cordón *m*

Ⓑ VT [+ *arms, knees*] flexionar, doblar; **to ~ one's muscles** (*in exercises*) hacer ejercicios de calentamiento de músculos; (*to impress*) sacar los músculos; **the government is ~ing its muscles in Europe** el gobierno está haciendo alarde de su poder en Europa

Ⓒ VI doblarse, flexionarse

flexibility [,fleksɪ'bɪlɪtɪ] N flexibilidad *f*

flexible ['fleksəbl] ADJ (*lit, fig*) flexible; **we have to be ~ about this** tenemos que ser flexibles en este asunto; **we have ~ (working) hours** tenemos un horario de trabajo flexible

flexion ['flekʃən] N flexión *f*

flexitime ['fleksɪtaɪm] N (*Brit*) horario *m* flexible

flexor ['fleksəʳ] Ⓐ N flexor *m*, músculo *m* flexor

Ⓑ ADJ flexor

flextime ['flekstaɪm] N (*US*) = **flexitime**

flibbertigibbet ['flɪbətɪ'dʒɪbɪt] N casquivana *f*

flick [flɪk] Ⓐ N 1 [*of tail*] coletazo *m*; [*of finger*] capirotazo *m*, papirotazo *m*; [*of duster*] pasada *f*; [*of whip*] latigazo *m*; **with a ~ of the whip** de un latigazo; **with a ~ of the wrist** con un movimiento rápido de la muñeca; *see also* **switch A1**

2 (*Brit**) película *f*, peli* *f*; **the ~s** el cine

Ⓑ VT (*with finger*) dar un capirotazo a; **she ~ed her hair out of her eyes** se apartó el pelo de los ojos; **to ~ sth away** quitar algo con un movimiento rápido

Ⓒ VI **the snake's tongue ~ed in and out** la víbora metía y sacaba la lengua; **to ~ over the pages** hojear rápidamente las páginas

Ⓓ CPD ► **flick knife** N (*Brit*) navaja *f* automática, navaja *f* de resorte (*Mex*)

►**flick off** VT + ADV [+ *dust, ash*] sacudir; [+ *light, TV*] apagar

►**flick on** VT + ADV [+ *light, TV*] encender

►**flick through** VI + PREP [+ *book, pages*] hojear rápidamente

flicker ['flɪkəʳ] Ⓐ N [1] [*of light, eyelid*] parpadeo *m*; [*of flame*] destello *m*
[2] (= *hint*) **a ~ of amusement crossed his face** por un momento se atisbó en su rostro una expresión divertida; **a ~ of surprise/dismay crossed his face** por un momento en su rostro pudo verse un atisbo de sorpresa/consternación; **she said it without a ~ of expression** lo dijo sin inmutarse; **without a ~ of regret** sin el menor signo de arrepentimiento; **they showed barely a ~ of interest** apenas dieron muestras de interés
Ⓑ VI [*light*] parpadear; [*flame*] vacilar; [*snake's tongue*] vibrar; **the candle ~ed and went out** la vela parpadeó y se apagó

flickering ['flɪkərɪŋ] ADJ [*flame, candle*] tembloroso; (*before going out*) vacilante; [*light*] parpadeante; [*needle*] oscilante

flier ['flaɪəʳ] N [1] aviador(a) *m/f*
[2] (*US*) folleto *m*, volante *m* (*LAm*)

flight¹ [flaɪt] Ⓐ N [1] (*Aer*) [*of bird*] vuelo *m*; [*of bullet*] trayectoria *f*; **how long does the ~ take?** ¿cuánto dura el vuelo?; **in ~** en vuelo; **~s of fancy** (*fig*) ilusiones *fpl*; **to take ~** [*bird*] alzar el vuelo
[2] (= *group*) [*of birds*] bandada *f*; [*of aircraft*] escuadrilla *f*; **in the top ~** (*fig*) de primera categoría
[3] [*of stairs*] tramo *m*; **I walked up six ~s of stairs** subí seis tramos de escaleras; **he lives two ~s up** vive dos pisos más arriba
Ⓑ CPD ► **flight attendant** N auxiliar *mf* de vuelo *or* de cabina, aeromozo/a *m/f* (*LAm*), sobrecargo *mf* (*Mex*), cabinero/a *m/f* (*Col*) ► **flight bag** N bolso *m* de bandolera ► **flight crew** N tripulación *f* ► **flight deck** N (*on aircraft carrier*) cubierta *f* de aterrizaje/despegue; [*of aeroplane*] cubierta *f* de vuelo ► **flight engineer** N mecánico/a *m/f* de vuelo ► **flight lieutenant** N teniente *mf* de aviación ► **flight log** N diario *m* de vuelo ► **flight path** N trayectoria *f* de vuelo ► **flight plan** N plan *m or* carta *f* de vuelo ► **flight recorder** N registrador *m* de vuelo ► **flight sergeant** N (*Brit*) sargento *mf* de aviación ► **flight simulator** N simulador *m* de vuelo ► **flight test** N vuelo *m* de prueba

flight² [flaɪt] N (= *act of fleeing*) fuga *f*, huida *f*; **to put to ~** ahuyentar; (*Mil*) poner en fuga; **to take ~** fugarse, huir; **a picture of a deer in full ~** una foto de un ciervo en plena huida; **the enemy were in full ~** el enemigo huía en desbandada; **the ~ of capital** la fuga de capitales

flightless ['flaɪtlɪs] ADJ [*bird*] no volador

flight-test ['flaɪttest] VT probar en vuelo

flighty ['flaɪtɪ] ADJ (*compar* **flightier**; *superl* **flightiest**) [*idea, remark*] frívolo, poco serio; [*girl*] caprichoso, voluble

flimsily ['flɪmzɪlɪ] ADV [*constructed*] con poca solidez; [*dressed*] muy ligeramente

flimsiness ['flɪmzɪnɪs] N [*of dress, material*] ligereza *f*; [*of structure*] lo endeble, la poca solidez; [*of excuse*] lo pobre; [*of argument, evidence*] lo poco sólido, inconsistencia *f*

flimsy ['flɪmzɪ] Ⓐ ADJ (*compar* **flimsier**; *superl* **flimsiest**) [1] (= *thin*) [*dress*] muy ligero; [*material*] muy ligero, muy delgado; [*paper*] muy fino
[2] (= *weak, insubstantial*) [*structure*] poco sólido, endeble; [*excuse, pretext*] pobre; [*argument, evidence*] poco sólido, inconsistente
Ⓑ N (*Brit*) (= *thin paper*) papel *m* de copiar; (= *copy*) copia *f*

flinch [flɪntʃ] VI [1] (= *shrink back*) estremecerse; **he ~ed at the pain** se estremeció del dolor; **I ~ed when he touched me** cuando me tocó, me estremecí; **he struck her hard but she did not ~** la golpeó con fuerza, pero ni se inmutó; **without ~ing** sin inmutarse
[2] (= *shirk*) **he did not ~ from his responsibilities** no se retrajo de sus obligaciones

fling [flɪŋ] (*vb: pt, pp* **flung**) Ⓐ N [1] **to have one's last ~** echar la última cana al aire; **to have one's ~** ◊ **go on a ~** echar una canita al aire; **to have a ~ at doing sth** intentar algo
[2] (*) aventura *f* amorosa
[3] (*also* **highland ~**) *see* **highland**
Ⓑ VT [+ *stone*] arrojar, lanzar; **to ~ one's arms round sb** echar los brazos al cuello a algn; **the door was flung open** la puerta se abrió de golpe; **she was flung to the ground by her horse** el caballo la lanzó *or* tiró *or* arrojó al suelo; **to ~ sb into jail** meter a algn en la cárcel; **to ~ o.s. over a cliff** despeñarse por un precipicio; **she flung herself at him** se arrojó *or* lanzó *or* tiró sobre él; **to ~ o.s into a chair** dejarse caer de golpe en una silla; **to ~ o.s. into a job** lanzarse a hacer un trabajo; **to ~ off/on one's clothes** quitarse/ponerse la ropa de prisa

►**fling away** VT + ADV (*fig*) (= *waste*) [+ *money, chance*] desperdiciar

►**fling out** VT + ADV [+ *rubbish*] tirar, botar (*LAm*); [+ *remark*] lanzar; [+ *person*] echar

flint [flɪnt] Ⓐ N (*Geol*) (= *material*) sílex *m*; (= *one piece*) pedernal *m*; [*of lighter*] piedra *f*
Ⓑ CPD ► **flint axe** N hacha *f* de sílex

flinty ['flɪntɪ] ADJ [1] [*material*] de sílex; [*soil*] silíceo
[2] (*fig*) [*eyes, gaze, stare*] duro; [*heart*] de piedra

flip¹ [flɪp] Ⓐ N capirotazo *m*; (*Aer**) vuelo *m*
Ⓑ VT (*gen*) tirar; **to ~ a coin** lanzar una moneda al aire, echar cara o cruz; **he ~ped the book open** abrió el libro de golpe; ✦*IDIOM* **to ~ one's lid*** perder los estribos
Ⓒ VI (*) perder la chaveta*
Ⓓ CPD ► **flip chart** N flip chart *m*, *bloc de papel de grandes dimensiones que se monta sobre un armazón y sirve para ilustrar conferencias, charlas, demostraciones, etc.* ► **flip side** N cara *f* B

►**flip out*** VI + ADV perder la chaveta*

►**flip over** Ⓐ VI + ADV (*Aut etc*) capotar, dar una vuelta de campana
Ⓑ VT + ADV [+ *cassette*] dar la vuelta a

►**flip through** VI + PREP [+ *book*] hojear; [+ *records, index cards*] repasar; **I ~ped through the pages/my notes** hojeé las páginas/mis notas

flip²* [flɪp] EXCL ¡porras!*

flip³* [flɪp] ADJ = **flippant**

flip-flop ['flɪpflɒp] Ⓐ N [1] **flip-flops** (= *sandals*) chancletas *fpl*
[2] (*Comput*) circuito *m* basculante *or* biestable, flip-flop *m*
[3] (*fig*) (*US**) cambio *m* radical, golpe *m* de timón
Ⓑ VI (*fig*) (*US**) cambiar radicalmente, dar un golpe de timón

flippancy ['flɪpənsɪ] N ligereza *f*, frivolidad *f*, falta *f* de seriedad; **she was irritated by his ~** estaba molesta por su frivolidad *or* falta de seriedad; **there was a note of ~ in her voice** había un dejo de ligereza *or* frivolidad en su voz

flippant ['flɪpənt] ADJ [*remark, reply*] ligero, frívolo; **sorry, I didn't mean to sound ~** perdona, no era mi intención parecer frívolo; **don't be ~** deja de decir ligerezas *or* frivolidades

flippantly ['flɪpəntlɪ] ADV [*answer, talk*] con poca seriedad; **such words should not be used ~** esas palabras no deberían usarse con ligereza *or* ligeramente

flipper ['flɪpəʳ] N aleta *f*

flipping* ['flɪpɪŋ] ADJ (*Brit*) condenado*

flip-top ['flɪptɒp] ADJ [*bin, pack*] con tapa abatible

flirt [flɜːt] Ⓐ N coqueto/a *m/f*; **he's/she's a great ~** es terriblemente coqueto/a, le gusta muchísimo flirtear
Ⓑ VI coquetear, flirtear (**with** con); **to ~ with death** jugar con la muerte; **to ~ with an idea** acariciar una idea

flirtation [flɜː'teɪʃən] N flirteo *m*, coqueteo *m*

flirtatious [flɜː'teɪʃəs] ADJ [*man*] mariposón; [*woman*] coqueta; [*glance etc*] coqueta

flirty ['flɜːtɪ] ADJ [*person, dress, smile*] coqueto

flit [flɪt] Ⓐ VI [*bat, butterfly*] revolotear; **to ~ in/out** [*person*] entrar/salir precipitadamente; **she ~s from one job to another** salta de un trabajo a otro
Ⓑ N ✦*IDIOM* **to do a (moonlight) ~** (*Brit*) marcharse de una casa a la francesa

flitch [flɪtʃ] N **~ of bacon** hoja *f* de tocino

flitting ['flɪtɪŋ] N (*N Engl, Scot*) mudanza *f*

Flo [fləʊ] N (*familiar form*) of **Florence**

float [fləʊt] Ⓐ N [*of raft, seaplane*] flotador *m*; (*for fishing line*) corcho *m*; (= *swimming aid*) flotador *m*; (*in procession*) carroza *f*; (= *sum of money*) reserva *f*; (*in shop*) fondo *m* de caja, *dinero en caja antes de empezar las ventas del día (para cambios etc)*
Ⓑ VT [1] [+ *boat, logs*] hacer flotar; ✦*IDIOM* **it doesn't ~ my boat*** no me da ni frío ni calor*, no me llama la atención
[2] (= *render seaworthy*) poner a flote
[3] (= *launch*) [+ *company*] fundar, constituir
[4] (*Fin*) [+ *currency*] hacer fluctuar, hacer flotar; [+ *shares*] emitir, lanzar al mercado; [+ *loan*] emitir
[5] **to ~ an idea** sugerir una idea
Ⓒ VI (*gen*) flotar; [*bather*] hacer la plancha; (= *move in wind*) flotar, ondear; **it ~ed to the surface** salió a la superficie; **to ~ downriver** ir río abajo; **we shall let the pound ~** dejaremos que la libra esterlina flote *or* fluctúe

►**float around** VI + ADV [*rumour*] circular, correr

►**float away, float off** VI + ADV (*in water*) ir a la deriva; (*in air*) irse volando

floating ['fləʊtɪŋ] ADJ [*object, assets, currency, debt, dock*] flotante; (*Brit*) [*voter*] indeciso; **the ~ vote** el voto de los indecisos

flock¹ [flɒk] Ⓐ N [*of sheep, goats*] rebaño *m*; [*of birds*] bandada *f*; [*of people*] tropel *m*, multitud *f*; (*Rel*) grey *f*, rebaño *m*; **they came in ~s** acudieron en tropel
Ⓑ VI (= *move in numbers*) ir en tropel; **they ~ed to the station** fueron en tropel hacia la estación; **to ~ around sb** apiñarse en torno a algn; **to ~ together** congregarse, reunirse

flock² [flɒk] N (= *wool*) borra *f*

floe [fləʊ] N (= *ice floe*) témpano *m* de hielo

flog [flɒg] VT [1] (= *whip*) azotar; (= *beat*) dar una paliza a; ✦*IDIOM* **to ~ a dead horse*** predicar en el desierto, machacar en hierro

frío
[2] (*Brit**) (= *sell*) vender

flogger ['flɒgəʳ] N partidario/a *m/f* del restablecimiento de la pena de azotes

flogging ['flɒgɪŋ] N azotes *mpl*, flagelación *f*; **to give sb a ~** azotar *or* flagelar a algn

flood [flʌd] Ⓐ N [*of water*] inundación *f*; (*in river*) avenida *f*; [*of words, tears*] torrente *m*; (= *flood tide*) pleamar *f*; **the Flood** (*Rel*) el Diluvio; **the river is in ~** el río está crecido; **a ~ of letters** una avalancha de cartas; **she was in ~s of tears** lloraba a lágrima viva
Ⓑ VT (*Aut*) (*gen*) inundar; **to ~ the market with sth** inundar *or* saturar el mercado de algo; **we have been ~ed with applications** nos han llovido las solicitudes, nos han inundado de solicitudes; **the room was ~ed with light** el cuarto se inundó de luz
Ⓒ VI [*river*] desbordarse; **the people ~ed into the streets** la gente inundó la calle
Ⓓ CPD ► **flood control** N medidas *fpl* para controlar las inundaciones ► **flood tide** N pleamar *f*, marea *f* creciente

►**flood in** VI + ADV [*people*] entrar a raudales

►**flood out** VT + ADV [+ *house*] inundar completamente; **they were ~ed out** tuvieron que abandonar su casa debido a la inundación

floodgate ['flʌdgeɪt] N compuerta *f*, esclusa *f*

flooding ['flʌdɪŋ] N inundación *f*

floodlight ['flʌdlaɪt] (*vb: pt, pp* **floodlit**) Ⓐ N foco *m*
Ⓑ VT iluminar con focos

floodlighting ['flʌdlaɪtɪŋ] N iluminación *f* con focos

floodlit ['flʌdlɪt] PT, PP *of* **floodlight** ADJ iluminado

floodplain ['flʌdpleɪn] N llanura *f* sujeta a inundaciones de un río

floodwater ['flʌdwɔːtəʳ] N crecida *f*, riada *f*

floor [flɔːʳ] Ⓐ N [1] (*gen*) suelo *m*; [*of room*] suelo *m*, piso *m* (*LAm*); [*of sea*] fondo *m*; (= *dance floor*) pista *f*; **a tiled ~** un suelo embaldosado; **the Floor** (*St Ex*) el parqué; **to cross the ~ (of the House)** cambiar de adscripción política; **to have the ~** [*speaker*] tener la palabra; **to hold the ~** hacer uso de la palabra; **to take the ~** [*dancer*] salir a bailar; ✦***IDIOM*** **to wipe the ~ with sb*** dar un buen repaso a algn*, hacer picadillo a algn*
[2] (= *storey*) [2·1] (*Brit*) piso *m*; **the first ~** el primer piso; **the ground ~** la planta baja; **the second ~** el segundo piso; **the top ~** el último piso
[2·2] (*US*) piso *m*; **the first ~** la planta baja; **the second ~** el primer piso; **the top ~** el último piso
Ⓑ VT [1] [+ *room*] solar (**with** de)
[2] (*) (= *knock down*) [+ *opponent*] derribar
[3] (*) (= *baffle, silence*) dejar sin respuesta
[4] (*US Aut*) [+ *accelerator*] pisar
Ⓒ CPD ► **floor area** N superficie *f* total ► **floor cloth** N bayeta *f* ► **floor covering** N tapiz *m* para el suelo ► **floor exercise** N (*Gymnastics*) ejercicio *m* de suelo ► **floor lamp** N lámpara *f* de pie ► **floor manager** N (*in department store*) jefe/a *m/f* de sección; (*Cine, TV*) jefe/a *mf* de plató ► **floor plan** N plano *m*, planta *f* ► **floor polish** N cera *f* para suelos ► **floor polisher** N enceradora *f* ► **floor show** N cabaret *m* ► **floor space** N espacio *m*

floorboard ['flɔːbɔːd] N tabla *f* del suelo

flooring ['flɔːrɪŋ] N suelo *m*; (= *material*) solería *f*

floorwalker† ['flɔːˌwɔːkəʳ] N (*US*) jefe/a *m/f* de sección

floosie*, **floozie***, **floozy*** ['fluːzɪ] N putilla* *f*

flop [flɒp] Ⓐ N (*) (= *failure*) fracaso *m*; **the film was a ~** la película fue un fracaso
Ⓑ VI [1] (= *fall*) [*person*] dejarse caer (**into, on** en)
[2] (*) (= *fail*) [*play, book*] fracasar

flophouse* ['flɒphaʊs] N (*pl* **flophouses** ['flɒphaʊzɪz]) (*US*) pensión *f* de mala muerte*, fonducha* *f*

floppy ['flɒpɪ] Ⓐ ADJ (*compar* **floppier**, *superl* **floppiest**) [*hat*] flexible; [*doll*] de trapo; **a dog with ~ ears** un perro con las orejas caídas
Ⓑ N = **floppy disc**
Ⓒ CPD ► **floppy disc** *or* **disk** N (*Comput*) disquete *m*, disco *m* flexible

flora ['flɔːrə] N (*pl* **floras** *or* **florae** ['flɔːriː]) flora *f*

floral ['flɔːrəl] Ⓐ ADJ [*display*] de flores, floral; [*fabric, dress*] de flores, floreado; [*fragrance, design, wallpaper, curtains*] de flores
Ⓑ CPD ► **floral arrangement** N arreglo *m* floral ► **floral print** N estampado *m* de flores *or* floreado ► **floral tribute** N ofrenda *f* floral; (*at funeral*) corona *f* de flores

Florence ['flɒrəns] N Florencia *f*

Florentine ['flɒrəntaɪn] Ⓐ ADJ florentino
Ⓑ N florentino/a *m/f*

florescence [flə'resns] N florescencia *f*

floret ['flɒrət] N [*of flower*] flósculo *m*; [*of cauliflower, broccoli*] grumo *m*, cabezuela *f*

florid ['flɒrɪd] ADJ [*complexion*] colorado, rubicundo; [*style*] florido

Florida ['flɒrɪdə] N Florida *f*

florin ['flɒrɪn] N florín *m*; (*Brit*) (*formerly*) florín *m, moneda de dos chelines*

florist ['flɒrɪst] N florista *mf*; **~'s (shop)** floristería *f*, tienda *f* de flores

floss [flɒs] Ⓐ N [1] (*also* **~ silk**) cadarzo *m*
[2] (*for embroidery*) seda *f* floja
[3] (*also* **dental ~**) hilo *m or* seda *f* dental
Ⓑ VT (*Dentistry*) **to ~ one's teeth** limpiarse los dientes con hilo *or* seda dental
Ⓒ VI (*Dentistry*) limpiarse los dientes con hilo *or* seda dental

Flossie ['flɒsɪ] N (*familiar form*) *of* **Florence**

flossy ['flɒsɪ] ADJ [1] [*cloud, hair*] vaporoso, ahuecado
[2] (*US**) (= *showy*) llamativo, espectacular, ostentoso

flotation [fləʊ'teɪʃən] Ⓐ N [1] (*lit*) [*of boat etc*] flotación *f*
[2] (*Fin*) [*of shares, loan etc*] emisión *f*; [*of company*] lanzamiento *m*, salida *f* a bolsa
Ⓑ CPD ► **flotation tank** N tanque *m* de flotación

flotilla [flə'tɪlə] N flotilla *f*

flotsam ['flɒtsəm] N **~ and jetsam** restos *mpl* (de naufragio); (*Tech, frm*) pecios *mpl*

flounce[1] [flaʊns] N (= *frill*) volante *m*

flounce[2] [flaʊns] VI **to ~ in/out** entrar/salir haciendo aspavientos

flounced [flaʊnst] ADJ [*dress*] guarnecido con volantes

flounder[1] ['flaʊndəʳ] N (*pl* **flounder** *or* **flounders**) (= *fish*) platija *f*

flounder[2] ['flaʊndəʳ] VI [1] (*also* **~ about**) (*in water, mud etc*) (= *flap arms*) debatirse; (= *splash*) revolcarse
[2] (*in speech etc*) perder el hilo

flour ['flaʊəʳ] Ⓐ N harina *f*
Ⓑ CPD ► **flour bin** N harinero *m* ► **flour mill** N molino *m* de harina

flourish ['flʌrɪʃ] Ⓐ N (= *movement*) floritura *f*, ademán *m* ostentoso; (*under signature*) rúbrica *f*; (*Mus*) floreo *m*; (= *fanfare*) toque *m* de trompeta; **to do sth with a ~** hacer algo con una floritura *or* con gesto triunfal
Ⓑ VT [+ *weapon, stick etc*] blandir
Ⓒ VI [*plant etc*] crecer; [*person, business, civilization*] florecer, prosperar

flourishing ['flʌrɪʃɪŋ] ADJ [*plant*] lozano; [*person, business*] floreciente, próspero

floury ['flaʊərɪ] ADJ harinoso

flout [flaʊt] VT (= *ignore*) no prestar atención a, ignorar; (= *mock*) burlarse de; [+ *law*] incumplir

flow [fləʊ] Ⓐ N [*of river, tide, Elec*] corriente *f*, flujo *m*; (= *direction*) curso *m*; [*of blood*] (*from wound*) flujo; [*of words etc*] torrente *m*; **the ~ of traffic** la circulación (del tráfico); **to maintain a steady ~** [*of people, vehicles*] mantener un movimiento constante; ✦***IDIOM*** **to go with the ~** dejarse llevar
Ⓑ VI [*river*] fluir, discurrir; [*tide*] subir, crecer; [*blood*] (*from wound*) manar; (*through body*) circular; [*tears*] correr; [*hair*] caer suavemente *or* con soltura; [*words*] fluir; **tears ~ed down her cheeks** le corrían las lágrimas por las mejillas; **the river ~s through the valley** el río fluye *or* discurre por el valle; **the river ~ed over its banks** el río se desbordó; **the river ~s into the sea** el río desemboca en el mar; **water was ~ing from the pipe** el agua brotaba de la tubería; **traffic is now ~ing normally** el tráfico ya circula *or* fluye *or* discurre con normalidad; **money ~ed in** el dinero entraba a raudales; **people are ~ing in** entra la gente a raudales; **to keep the conversation ~ing** mantener viva la conversación; **the town ~ed with wine and food** el pueblo abundaba en vino y comida; *see also* **ebb**
Ⓒ CPD ► **flow chart**, **flow diagram** N organigrama *m* ► **flow sheet** N (*Comput*) diagrama *m* de flujo, ordinograma *m*; (*Admin*) organigrama *m*

flower ['flaʊəʳ] Ⓐ N [1] (*Bot*) flor *f*; **in ~** en flor
[2] (= *best*) **the ~ of the army** la flor y nata del ejército; **she was in the ~ of her youth** estaba en la flor de la vida
Ⓑ VI florecer
Ⓒ CPD ► **flower arrangement** N (= *art*) = **flower arranging** (= *exhibit*) (*on table*) arreglo *m* floral; (*in park*) adorno *m* floral ► **flower arranging** N arte *m* floral ► **flower child** N (= *hippy*) hippy *mf*, hippie *mf* ► **flower garden** N jardín *m* (de flores) ► **flower head** N cabezuela *f* ► **flower people** NPL hippies *mpl* ► **flower power** N filosofía *f* hippy ► **flower seller** N florista *mf*, vendedor(a) *m/f* de flores ► **flower shop** N floristería *f*, tienda *f* de flores ► **flower show** N exposición *f* de flores ► **flower stall** N puesto *m* de flores

flowerbed ['flaʊəbed] N arriate *m*, parterre *m*, cantero *m* (*S. Cone*)

flowered ['flaʊəd] ADJ [*cloth, shirt*] floreado, de flores

flowering ['flaʊərɪŋ] Ⓐ ADJ floreciente, en flor
Ⓑ N floración *f*

flowerpot ['flaʊəpɒt] N maceta *f*, tiesto *m*

flowery ['flaʊərɪ] ADJ [*meadow, field*] florido; [*fragrance, perfume*] de flores; [*fabric, dress, wallpaper*] de flores, floreado; [*language*] florido

flowing ['fləʊɪŋ] ADJ [*movement*] fluido; [*stream*] corriente; [*hair, clothing*] suelto; [*style*] fluido

flown [fləʊn] PP *of* **fly**[2]

fl. oz. ABBR = **fluid ounce**

F/Lt ABBR = **Flight Lieutenant**

flu [fluː] Ⓐ N gripe *f*, gripa *f* (*Col, Mex*); **I've got ~** tengo gripe; **to get** *or* **catch ~** agarrar la

gripe, agriparse (*LAm*)
Ⓑ CPD ► **flu jab*** N vacuna *f* contra la gripe
► **flu vaccine** N vacuna *f* antigripal

fluctuate ['flʌktjʊeɪt] VI [*cost*] oscilar; [*prices, temperature*] fluctuar, oscilar; **to ~ between** [*person*] vacilar entre

fluctuation [ˌflʌktjʊ'eɪʃən] N [*of prices, temperature*] fluctuación *f*, oscilación *f*

flue [fluː] N humero *m*

fluency ['fluːənsɪ] N 1 (*in foreign language*) fluidez *f*, soltura *f*; **she speaks French with great ~** habla francés con mucha fluidez *or* soltura, domina bien el francés; **you need ~ in at least one foreign language** necesita dominar al menos una lengua; **I was impressed by his ~ in English** me impresionó su dominio del inglés
2 (*in speaking, reading, writing*) fluidez *f*, soltura *f*
3 [*of movement*] soltura *f*

fluent ['fluːənt] ADJ 1 (*in foreign language*) **he is a ~ Japanese speaker** *or* **speaker of Japanese** habla japonés con fluidez *or* soltura, domina bien el japonés; **to speak ~ French** ◊ **be ~ in French** hablar francés con fluidez *or* soltura, dominar bien el francés; **to become ~ in French** llegar a hablar francés con fluidez *or* soltura, llegar a tener un buen dominio del francés
2 (= *not hesitant*) [*written style, speech, sentence*] fluido; [*speaker, debater, writer*] desenvuelto; **a ~ reader** una persona que lee con fluidez *or* soltura; **she speaks in ~ sentences** habla con frases fluidas; **rage was making him ~** la ira le hacía hablar sin trabarse
3 (= *graceful*) [*movement, dancing*] fluido

fluently ['fluːəntlɪ] ADV 1 (= *like a native*) **he speaks Russian ~** habla ruso con fluidez *or* soltura, domina bien el ruso
2 (= *without hesitation*) [*speak, write, read*] con fluidez, con soltura
3 (= *gracefully*) [*dance, move*] con soltura, con fluidez

fluey* ['fluːiː] ADJ (*Brit*) griposo; **to feel ~** estar griposo

fluff [flʌf] Ⓐ N (*from blankets etc*) pelusa *f*, lanilla *f*; [*of chicks*] plumón *m*; [*of kittens*] pelo *m*, pelusa *f*
Ⓑ VT 1 (*also* **~ out**) [+ *feathers*] ahuecar; **to ~ up the pillows** mullir las almohadas
2 (*Theat**) [+ *lines*] hacerse un lío con

fluffy ['flʌfɪ] ADJ (*compar* **fluffier**; *superl* **fluffiest**) [*toy*] de peluche; [*material*] mullido; [*bird*] plumoso; [*surface*] lleno de pelusa

fluid ['fluːɪd] Ⓐ ADJ [*substance, movement*] fluido; [*plan, arrangements*] flexible; [*opinions*] variable
Ⓑ N (*Phys*) fluido *m*; (*Physiol*) fluido *m*, líquido *m*; **drink plenty of ~s** tome mucho líquido, beba mucho
Ⓒ CPD ► **fluid ounce** N onza *f* líquida

fluidity [fluː'ɪdɪtɪ] N [*of substance, movement*] fluidez *f*; [*of situation*] inestabilidad *f*

fluke[1] [fluːk] N chiripa *f*, golpe *m* de suerte; **to win by a ~** ganar de *or* por chiripa

fluke[2] [fluːk] N (*Zool*) trematodo *m*; (*Fishing*) *especie de platija*

fluky* ['fluːkɪ] ADJ afortunado

flummox ['flʌməks] VT (= *disconcert*) desconcertar, confundir; (= *startle*) asombrar; **I was completely ~ed** me quedé totalmente desconcertado

flung [flʌŋ] PT, PP *of* **fling**

flunk* [flʌŋk] (*esp US*) Ⓐ VT [+ *student, course, exam*] suspender, catear (*Sp**), reprobar (*LAm*); **I ~ed Maths** suspendí las matemáticas
Ⓑ VI suspender, catear (*Sp**); **I ~ed** suspendí, cateé (*Sp**), me reprobaron (*LAm*)
►**flunk out*** VI + ADV (*US*) salirse del colegio *etc* sin recibir un título

flunkey, **flunky** ['flʌŋkɪ] N (*pej*) (= *servant*) lacayo *m*; (= *servile person*) adulador/a *m/f*, lacayo *m*

fluorescence [flʊə'resns] N fluorescencia *f*

fluorescent [flʊə'resnt] ADJ [*lighting, tube, lamp*] fluorescente

fluoridate ['flʊərɪˌdeɪt] VT fluorizar

fluoridation [ˌflʊərɪ'deɪʃən] N fluoración *f*, fluorización *f*

fluoride ['flʊəraɪd] Ⓐ N fluoruro *m*
Ⓑ CPD ► **fluoride toothpaste** N pasta *f* de dientes con flúor

fluorine ['flʊəriːn] N flúor *m*

flurry ['flʌrɪ] N [*of wind, snow*] racha *f*, ráfaga *f*; [*of rain*] chaparrón *m*; (*fig*) [*of excitement*] frenesí *m*; **to be in a ~** estar nervioso; **a ~ of activity** un frenesí de actividad

flush[1] [flʌʃ] Ⓐ N 1 (= *blush*) **there was a slight ~ on his cheeks** tenía las mejillas un poco coloradas; **she felt a faint ~ of colour rising in her face** notó que se le dibujaba cierto rubor en el rostro; **the pink ~ of dawn spread across the sky** (*liter*) el arrebol del alba se extendía por el cielo (*liter*)
2 (= *glow*) [*of beauty, health*] resplandor *m*
3 (= *surge*) [*of anger, excitement*] arrebato *m*; **she felt a ~ of excitement on hearing this** al oír esto sintió un arrebato de emoción; **in the first ~ of youth** en la flor de la juventud; **in the (first) ~ of victory** con la euforia del triunfo
4 **to have hot ~es** (*Med*) tener sofocos
Ⓑ VI [*person, face*] ponerse colorado, sonrojarse, ruborizarse (*liter*) (**with** de)

flush[2] [flʌʃ] Ⓐ N [*of toilet*] (= *device*) cisterna *f*; (= *sound*) sonido *m* de la cisterna; (= *action*) descarga *f* de agua
Ⓑ VT (*also* **~ out**) [+ *sink, yard*] limpiar con agua, baldear; **to ~ the toilet** *or* **lavatory** tirar de la cadena
►**flush away** VT + ADV (*down sink*) echar al fregadero; (*down lavatory*) echar al váter

flush[3] [flʌʃ] ADJ 1 (= *level*) a ras (**with** de), al mismo nivel (**with** que); (*DIY*) empotrado (**with** con); **a door ~ with the wall** una puerta al mismo nivel que la pared; **to make two things ~** nivelar dos cosas
2 (*) **to be ~ (with money)** estar forrado*, andar muy bien de dinero

flush[4] [flʌʃ] VT (*also* **~ out**) [+ *game, birds*] levantar; (*fig*) [+ *criminal*] sacar de su escondrijo a

flush[5] [flʌʃ] N (*Cards*) color *m*, flux *m inv*

flushed [flʌʃt] ADJ 1 (= *red*) [*face, cheeks*] colorado, rojo; **she arrived looking ~** llegó colorada; **to be ~ from alcohol/sleep** estar colorado por el alcohol/de haber dormido; **to be ~ with anger** estar rojo de ira; **to be ~ with embarrassment** estar rojo de vergüenza, estar sonrojado
2 (= *excited*) **to be ~ with success** estar eufórico por el éxito; **to be ~ with excitement** estar arrebatado de entusiasmo; **to be ~ with victory** estar eufórico por el triunfo
3 (= *tinged*) **white flowers ~ with pink** flores *fpl* blancas teñidas de rosa

Flushing ['flʌʃɪŋ] N Flesinga *m*

fluster ['flʌstəʳ] Ⓐ N aturdimiento *m*, confusión *f*; **to be in a ~** estar aturdido *or* confuso
Ⓑ VT (= *confuse, upset*) aturdir, poner nervioso; **to get ~ed** ponerse nervioso, aturdirse

flute [fluːt] N flauta *f*; (*in Andes, S. Cone*) (= *bamboo*) quena *f*

fluted ['fluːtɪd] ADJ (*Archit*) estriado, acanalado

flutist ['fluːtɪst] N (*US*) flautista *mf*

flutter ['flʌtəʳ] Ⓐ N 1 (= *movement*) [*of wings*] aleteo *m*; [*of eyelashes*] pestañeo *m*
2 (= *tremor*) **to be in a ~** (*fig*) estar nervioso; **to cause a ~** causar revuelo; **to feel a ~ of excitement** estremecerse de la emoción; **there was a ~ of fear in her voice** la voz le temblaba por el miedo
3 (*) (= *bet*) **to have a ~** echar una apuesta; **to have a ~ on a race** apostar a un caballo
Ⓑ VT [+ *wings*] batir; **the sparrow was ~ing its wings** el gorrión batía las alas, el gorrión aleteaba; **to ~ one's eyelashes at sb** hacer ojitos a algn
Ⓒ VI [*bird*] revolotear; [*butterfly*] mover las alas; [*flag*] ondear; [*heart*] palpitar; **a leaf came ~ing down** una hoja cayó balanceándose; **the bird ~ed about the room** el pájaro revoloteaba por la habitación; **a butterfly ~ed away** una mariposa pasó revoloteando

fluty ['fluːtɪ] ADJ [*tone*] aflautado

fluvial ['fluːvɪəl] ADJ fluvial

flux [flʌks] N **to be in a state of ~** estar inestable, estar cambiando continuamente

fly[1] [flaɪ] Ⓐ N 1 (= *insect*) mosca *f*; ✦*IDIOMS* **people were dropping like flies** la gente caía como moscas; **he wouldn't hurt a ~** sería incapaz de matar una mosca; **there are no flies on him** no tiene un pelo de tonto; **the ~ in the ointment** la única pega, el único inconveniente; **I wish I were a ~ on the wall** me gustaría estar allí para ver qué pasa
2 (*on trousers*) (*also* **flies**) bragueta *f*
3 **flies** (*Theat*) peine *msing*, telar *msing*
4 (= *carriage*) calesa *f*
5 ✦*IDIOM* **to do sth on the ~** hacer algo por la vía rápida, hacer algo a la carrera
Ⓑ CPD ► **fly button** N botón *m* de la bragueta ► **fly spray** N (espray) *m* matamoscas *m inv*

fly[2] [flaɪ] (*pt* **flew**; *pp* **flown**) Ⓐ VI 1 (= *be airborne*) [*plane, bird, insect*] volar; [*air passengers*] ir en avión; **"how did you get here?" — "I flew"** —¿cómo llegaste aquí? —en avión; **do you ~ often?** ¿viajas mucho en avión?; **she's ~ing home tomorrow** sale en avión para casa mañana; **I'm ~ing back to New York tonight** esta noche tomo un vuelo de regreso a Nueva York; **we were ~ing at 5,000ft** volábamos a 5.000 pies de altura; **we ~ (with) Iberia** volamos con Iberia; **to ~ into London airport** llegar (en avión) al aeropuerto de Londres; **the plane flew over London** el avión sobrevoló Londres; ✦*IDIOM* **to be ~ing high**: **we were ~ing high after our success in the championship** estábamos como locos tras el éxito en el campeonato; **the company is ~ing high** la empresa va viento en popa; *see also* **bird**
2 (= *fly a plane*) pilotar un avión, volar; **to learn to ~** aprender a pilotar un avión *or* a volar; **to ~ blind** (*lit*) volar a ciegas *or* guiándose sólo por los instrumentos; (*fig*) ir a ciegas
3 (= *flutter, wave*) [*flag*] ondear; **her hair was ~ing in the wind** su pelo ondeaba al viento; *see also* **flag**
4 (= *move quickly*) **the dust flew in our eyes** se nos metió el polvo en los ojos; **my hat flew into the air** se me voló el sombrero, el sombrero salió volando; **her hand flew to her mouth** se llevó la mano a la boca; **the train was ~ing along** el tren iba como una exhalación; **rumours are ~ing around the office that ...** por la oficina corre el rumor de que

…; **to go ~ing**: **the vase went ~ing** el jarrón salió por los aires *or* salió volando; **to let ~** (*fig*) (*verbally*) empezar a despotricar; (*physically*) empezar a repartir golpes *or* tortazos; (*Ftbl*) (= *shoot*) disparar; **he let ~ with a shot from 20 metres** lanzó un disparo desde unos 20 metros; **to let ~ at sb** (*verbally*) empezar a despotricar contra algn, arremeter contra algn; (*physically*) arremeter contra algn, empezar a dar golpes *or* tortazos a algn; **the door flew open** la puerta se abrió de golpe; **he/the ball came ~ing past me** él/la pelota pasó volando junto a mí; **to ~ into a rage** montar en cólera; **the blow sent him ~ing** el golpe hizo que saliera despedido; **she kicked off her shoes and sent them ~ing across the room** de una patada se quitó los zapatos y los mandó volando al otro lado de la habitación; *see also* **spark**

[5] (= *rush*) ir volando, ir corriendo; **I must ~!** ¡me voy volando *or* corriendo!, ¡me tengo que ir volando *or* corriendo!; **she flew upstairs to look for it** subió volando *or* a toda prisa a buscarlo; **to ~ to sb's aid** *or* **assistance** ir volando a socorrer a algn; **to ~ to sb's side** volar al lado de algn; **to ~ at sb** (*physically*) lanzarse sobre algn, arremeter contra algn; (*fig*) ponerse furioso con algn; **the dog flew at him and bit him** el perro se lanzó *or* se abalanzó sobre él y le mordió; ✦*IDIOM* **to ~ in the face of sth** ir en contra de algo, desafiar algo; **ideas that ~ in the face of common sense** ideas que desafían el sentido común; **she has a reputation for ~ing in the face of authority** tiene fama de ir en contra de la autoridad; *see also* **handle**

[6] (= *pass quickly*) [*time*] pasar *or* irse volando; **the years flew by** los años pasaron volando

[7] (†) (= *flee*) huir, escaparse (**from** de)

Ⓑ VT [1] [+ *aircraft*] pilotar, pilotear (*esp LAm*); [+ *passenger*] llevar en avión; [+ *goods*] transportar en avión; [+ *distance*] recorrer (en avión); [+ *flag*] enarbolar; **to ~ the Atlantic** atravesar el Atlántico en avión; **which routes does the airline ~?** ¿qué rutas cubre la aerolínea?; **to ~ a kite** hacer volar una cometa

[2] (= *flee*) [+ *country*] abandonar, huir de; ✦*IDIOMS* **to ~ the nest** echar a volar, dejar *or* abandonar el nido; **to ~ the coop** tomar las de Villadiego, agarrar *or* tomar el portante (y marcharse)

► **fly away** VI + ADV [*bird*] salir volando, emprender el vuelo

► **fly in** Ⓐ VI + ADV [*plane*] llegar; [*person*] llegar en avión; **he flew in from Rome** llegó en avión desde Roma; **a bee flew in through the window** una abeja entró volando por la ventana

Ⓑ VT + ADV [+ *supplies, troops*] (= *take*) llevar en avión; (= *bring*) traer en avión; **the seafood was flown in from Hawaii** el marisco venía en avión desde Hawai

► **fly off** VI + ADV [1] [*bird, plane*] alejarse volando; [*person in plane*] marcharse (en avión) (**to** a); **I'd love to ~ off to a Caribbean island** me encantaría marcharme a una isla del Caribe

[2] (= *come off*) [*hat*] salir volando; [*lid, handle, wheel*] saltar, salir disparado; **sparks flew off in all directions** saltaban chispas por todos lados

► **fly out** Ⓐ VI + ADV [*person in plane*] salir en avión, irse en avión; [*plane*] salir; **… and we're ~ing out two weeks later** y nosotros salimos *or* nos vamos en avión para allá dos semanas después; **I had to ~ out to California to pick him up** tuve que ir en avión a California a recogerlo

Ⓑ VT + ADV [1] (= *take out*) **we shall ~ supplies out to them** les enviaremos provisiones por avión

[2] (= *bring out*) **the hostages have been flown out** han sacado a los rehenes en avión

fly[3] [flaɪ] ADJ (*esp Brit*) avispado, espabilado

flyaway ['flaɪəweɪ] ADJ [1] [*hair*] suelto, lacio [2] (= *frivolous*) frívolo

fly-blown ['flaɪbləʊn] ADJ (*lit*) lleno de cresas; (*fig*) viejo, gastado

flyby ['flaɪ,baɪ] N (*pl* **flybys**) (*esp US*) desfile *m* aéreo

fly-by-night ['flaɪbaɪnaɪt] Ⓐ ADJ informal, poco fiable

Ⓑ N casquivano/a *m/f*

flycatcher ['flaɪ,kætʃəʳ] N (*Orn*) papamoscas *m inv*

flyer ['flaɪəʳ] = **flier**

fly-fishing ['flaɪ,fɪʃɪŋ] N pesca *f* a *or* con mosca

fly-half ['flaɪ,hɑːf] N medio apertura *m*

flying ['flaɪɪŋ] Ⓐ ADJ [*glass, debris*] que vuela por los aires; **he took a ~ leap at the man** dio un salto *or* saltó sobre el hombre; **he launched himself in a ~ tackle and brought the intruder to the ground** se lanzó por el aire *or* se lanzó en plancha y derribó al intruso; **to make a ~ visit** hacer una visita relámpago; ✦*IDIOMS* **to come through (sth) with ~ colours** salir airoso (de algo); **he passed all his exams with ~ colours** aprobó todos sus exámenes con éxito; **to get off to a ~ start** empezar con muy buen pie

Ⓑ N (*gen*) vuelo *m*; (= *aviation*) aviación *f*; **I had done 60 hours of ~** había realizado 60 horas de vuelo; **I don't like ~** no me gusta ir en avión *or* volar; **to have a fear of ~** tener miedo al avión

Ⓒ CPD ► **flying boat** N hidroavión *m* ► **flying bomb** N bomba *f* volante ► **flying buttress** N arbotante *m* ► **flying doctor** N médico/a *m/f* rural (que se traslada en avión) ► **flying fish** N pez *m* volador ► **flying fortress** N fortaleza *f* volante ► **flying fox** N panique *m* ► **flying lesson** N clase *f or* lección *f* de vuelo ► **flying machine** N máquina *f* de volar ► **flying officer** N teniente *mf* de aviación ► **flying picket** N piquete *m* volante *or* móvil ► **flying saucer** N platillo *m* volante ► **flying squad** N (*Brit*) brigada *f* móvil ► **flying suit** N traje *m* de vuelo ► **flying time** N (= *length of journey*) duración *f* del vuelo; (= *hours flown*) horas *fpl* de vuelo ► **flying trapeze** N trapecio *m* volador

flyleaf ['flaɪliːf] N (*pl* **flyleaves**) guarda *f*

flyover ['flaɪ,əʊvəʳ] N (*Brit Aut*) paso *m* elevado, paso *m* a desnivel (*LAm*); (*US*) (= *flypast*) desfile *m* aéreo

flypaper ['flaɪ,peɪpəʳ] N papel *m* matamoscas

flypast ['flaɪpɑːst] N desfile *m* aéreo

fly-posting [,flaɪ'pəʊstɪŋ] N pegada *f* (ilegal) de carteles

flysheet ['flaɪʃiːt] N (*for tent*) doble techo *m*

fly-swat ['flaɪswɒt], **fly-swatter** ['flaɪswɒtəʳ] N matamoscas *m inv*

fly-tipping [,flaɪ'tɪpɪŋ] N descarga *f* (ilegal) de basura *etc*

flyweight ['flaɪweɪt] Ⓐ N peso *m* mosca

Ⓑ CPD ► **flyweight contest** N combate *m* de pesos mosca

flywheel ['flaɪwiːl] N (*Tech*) volante *m*

FM ABBR [1] (*Brit Mil*) = **Field Marshal**

[2] (*Rad*) (= **frequency modulation**) FM *f*, M.F. *f*

[3] = **foreign minister**

FMB N ABBR (*US*) = **Federal Maritime Board**

FMCG, **fmcg** ABBR = **fast-moving consumer goods**

FMCS N ABBR (*US*) (= **Federal Mediation and Conciliation Services**) ≈ IMAC *m*

FO Ⓐ N ABBR (*Brit Pol*) (= **Foreign Office**) Min. de AA.EE.

Ⓑ ABBR (*Aer*) = **Flying Officer**

fo. ABBR (= **folio**) f.º, fol.

foal [fəʊl] Ⓐ N potro *m*

Ⓑ VI [*mare*] parir

foam [fəʊm] Ⓐ N (*gen*) espuma *f*

Ⓑ VI [*sea*] hacer espuma; **to ~ at the mouth** echar espumarajos; (*fig*) subirse por las paredes

Ⓒ CPD ► **foam bath** N baño *m* de espuma ► **foam extinguisher** N lanzaespumas *m inv*, extintor *m* de espuma ► **foam rubber** N gomaespuma *f*

foamy ['fəʊmɪ] ADJ espumoso

FOB, **f.o.b.** ABBR (= **free on board**) f.a.b.

fob [fɒb] Ⓐ VT **to ~ sb off (with sth)**: **I've asked her about it but she ~s me off** se lo he preguntado, pero me da largas; **she wants an answer, she won't be ~bed off** quiere una respuesta, no aceptará más evasivas; **don't be ~bed off with excuses** no te dejes engatusar con excusas

Ⓑ N (†) [1] (= *watch pocket*) faltriquera *f* de reloj

[2] (= *watch chain*) leontina *f*

Ⓒ CPD ► **fob watch** N reloj *m* de cadena *or* de bolsillo

FOC ABBR = **free of charge**

focal ['fəʊkəl] Ⓐ ADJ (*Tech*) focal

Ⓑ CPD ► **focal distance** N distancia *f* focal ► **focal plane** N plano *m* focal ► **focal point** N punto *m* focal; (*fig*) centro *m* de atención

focus ['fəʊkəs] Ⓐ N (*pl* **focuses** *or* **foci** ['fəʊsaɪ]) (*gen*) foco *m*; [*of attention*] centro *m*, foco *m*; **he was the ~ of attention** era el centro *or* foco de atención; **to be in ~** (*Phot*) estar enfocado; **to be out of ~** (*Phot*) estar desenfocado

Ⓑ VT [+ *camera, instrument*] enfocar (**on** a); [+ *attention*] centrar, concentrar (**on** en); **to ~ one's eyes on sth/sb** fijar la mirada en algo/algn; **all eyes were ~sed on her** todos la miraban fijamente

Ⓒ VI **to ~ (on)** [*light*] converger (en); [*heat rays*] concentrarse (en); [*eyes*] fijarse (en); **to ~ on sth** (*Phot*) enfocar algo

fodder ['fɒdəʳ] Ⓐ N pienso *m*, forraje *m*; *see also* **cannon C**

Ⓑ CPD ► **fodder grain** N cereales *mpl* forrajeros

FOE[1], **FoE** N ABBR (*Brit*) (= **Friends of the Earth**) *organización ecologista*

FOE[2] N ABBR (*US*) (= **Fraternal Order of Eagles**) *sociedad benéfica*

foe [fəʊ] N (*poet*) enemigo *m*

foetal, **fetal** (*US*) ['fiːtl] ADJ fetal

foetus, **fetus** (*US*) ['fiːtəs] N feto *m*

fog [fɒg] Ⓐ N [1] (*Met*) niebla *f*

[2] (*fig*) confusión *f*; **to be in a ~** estar confundido *or* desconcertado

Ⓑ VT [1] (*Phot*) velar

[2] (= *confuse*) [+ *matter*] enredar, complicar; [+ *person*] confundir, ofuscar; **to ~ the issue** complicar el asunto

[3] (*also* **to ~ up**) [+ *spectacles, window*] empañar

Ⓒ VI (*also* **to ~ up**) empañarse

Ⓓ CPD ► **fog bank** N banco *m* de niebla ► **fog lamp**, **fog light** N (*Aut*) faro *m* antiniebla ► **fog signal** N aviso *m* de niebla

fogbound ['fɒgbaʊnd] ADJ inmovilizado por la niebla

fogey ['fəʊgɪ] N **old ~*** carroza* *mf*, persona *f* chapada a la antigua

foggy ['fɒgɪ] ADJ (*compar* **foggier**; *superl* **foggiest**) [1] (*Met*) [*weather*] brumoso; [*day*] de niebla, brumoso; **it's ~** hay niebla; **I haven't the foggiest (idea)*** no tengo la más remota idea
[2] (*Phot*) velado

foghorn ['fɒghɔːn] N sirena *f* de niebla; **to have a voice like a ~** tener un vozarrón*

FOIA N ABBR (*US*) = **Freedom of Information Act**; → FREEDOM OF INFORMATION ACT

foible ['fɔɪbl] N manía *f*

foil[1] [fɔɪl] N [1] (*also* **tinfoil**) papel *m* de aluminio, papel *m* de plata
[2] (*fig*) **to act as a ~ to sth/sb** servir de contraste con algo/algn

foil[2] [fɔɪl] N (*Fencing*) florete *m*

foil[3] [fɔɪl] VT (= *thwart*) [+ *person*] desbaratar los planes de; [+ *attempt*] frustrar

foist [fɔɪst] VT **to ~ sth on sb** endosar algo a algn; **the job was ~ed on me** me endosaron el trabajo; **to ~ o.s. on sb** pegarse a algn, insistir en acompañar a *or* ir con algn

fol. ABBR (= **folio**) f.º, fol.

fold[1] [fəʊld] N (*Agr*) redil *m*; **to return to the ~** (*Rel*) volver al redil

fold[2] [fəʊld] Ⓐ N (*in paper etc*) pliegue *m*, doblez *m*; (*Geol*) pliegue *m*
Ⓑ VT [+ *paper, map, sheet, blanket*] doblar; (*esp several times*) plegar; [+ *wings*] recoger; **she ~ed the newspaper in two** dobló en dos el periódico; **to ~ a piece of paper in half** doblar un trozo de papel por la mitad; **to ~ one's arms** cruzar los brazos; **to ~ sb in one's arms** abrazar a algn tiernamente, estrechar a algn contra el pecho
Ⓒ VI [1] (*lit*) [*chair, table*] plegarse, doblarse
[2] (*) (= *fail*) [*business venture*] fracasar, quebrar; [*play*] fracasar

► **fold away** Ⓐ VI + ADV [*table, bed*] plegarse
Ⓑ VT + ADV [+ *clothes, newspaper*] doblar (*para guardar*); [+ *bed*] plegar

► **fold back** VT + ADV doblar hacia abajo, plegar

► **fold down** Ⓐ VT + ADV = **fold back**
Ⓑ VI + ADV **it ~s down at night** de noche se dobla hacia abajo

► **fold in** VT + ADV (*Culin*) [+ *flour, sugar*] mezclar

► **fold over** VT + ADV [+ *paper*] plegar; [+ *blanket*] hacer el embozo con

► **fold up** Ⓐ VI + ADV [1] (*lit*) doblarse, plegarse; **to ~ up (with laughter)*** troncharse de risa*
[2] (*) (= *fail*) [*business venture*] quebrar, fracasar
Ⓑ VT + ADV [+ *paper, map, sheet, blanket*] doblar; [+ *chair*] plegar; **she ~ed the chair up and walked off** plegó la silla y se marchó

-fold [fəʊld] ADJ, ADV (*ending in compounds*) **thirty-fold** (*as adj*) de treinta veces; (*as adv*) treinta veces

foldaway ['fəʊldəweɪ] ADJ plegable, plegadizo

folder ['fəʊldər] N (= *file*) carpeta *f*; (= *binder*) carpeta *f* de anillas

folding ['fəʊldɪŋ] Ⓐ ADJ [*seat, table, ruler*] plegable
Ⓑ CPD ► **folding chair** N silla *f* plegable *or* de tijera ► **folding doors** NPL puertas *fpl* de fuelle *or* plegadizas ► **folding ruler** N regla *f* plegable

fold-up ['fəʊldʌp] ADJ plegable, plegadizo

foliage ['fəʊlɪɪdʒ] N follaje *m*, hojas *fpl*

foliation [ˌfəʊlɪ'eɪʃən] N foliación *f*

folic acid [ˌfəʊlɪk'æsɪd] N ácido *m* fólico

folio ['fəʊlɪəʊ] N (= *sheet*) folio *m*; (= *book*) infolio *m*, libro *m* en folio

folk [fəʊk] Ⓐ N [1] (= *people*) gente *f*; **country/city ~** la gente de campo/ciudad; **ordinary ~** la gente llana; **they're strange ~ here** aquí la gente es algo rara; **the common ~** el pueblo; **my ~s*** (= *parents*) mis viejos* *mpl*; (= *family*) mi familia; **the old ~s** los viejos; **hello ~s!** ¡hola, amigos!
[2] = **folk music**; *see* **B**
Ⓑ CPD ► **folk art** N artesanía *f* popular *or* tradicional ► **folk dance** N baile *m* popular ► **folk dancing** N danza *f* folklórica ► **folk music** N (*traditional*) música *f* tradicional *or* folklórica; (*contemporary*) música *f* folk ► **folk rock** N folk rock *m* ► **folk singer** N cantante *mf* de música folk ► **folk song** N canción *f* tradicional ► **folk tale** N cuento *m* popular ► **folk wisdom** N saber *m* popular

folklore ['fəʊklɔːr] N folklore *m*

folkloric ['fəʊkˌlɔːrɪk] ADJ folklórico, folclórico

folksy* ['fəʊksɪ] ADJ [1] (= *rustic*) [*furniture*] rústico; [*music*] folklórico; [*clothes*] de campesino; **they sold ~ country furniture** vendían muebles rústicos típicos del campo
[2] (*pej*) (= *affected*) de una rusticidad fingida
[3] (*US*) (= *affable*) [*person, manner*] campechano; [*speech, comment*] de estilo campechano

foll. ABBR (= **following**) sig., sigs., sgte., sgtes.

follicle ['fɒlɪkl] N folículo *m*

follow ['fɒləʊ] Ⓐ VT [1] (= *come, go after*) seguir; **~ that car!** ¡siga a ese coche!; **~ me** sígame; **she arrived first, ~ed by the ambassador** ella llegó primero, seguida del embajador; **to ~ sb about** *or* **around** seguir a algn a todas partes; **he ~ed me into the room** entró en la habitación detrás de mí; **I ~ed her out into the garden** salí al jardín detrás de ella; **we ~ed her up the steps** la seguimos escaleras arriba, subimos (las escaleras) detrás de ella; ✦**IDIOM** **to ~ one's nose** (= *go straight on*) ir todo seguido; (= *use one's instinct*) dejarse guiar por el instinto
[2] (= *succeed*) **the days ~ing her death** los días que siguieron a su muerte; **the dinner will be ~ed by a concert** después de la cena habrá un concierto; **he ~ed his father into the business** siguió los pasos de su padre en el negocio; **they ~ed this with threats** tras esto empezaron a amenazarnos; **the bombing ~s a series of recent attacks** los bombardeos se han producido tras una serie de ataques recientes; **~ing our meeting I spoke to the director** tras nuestra reunión hablé con el director; ✦**IDIOM** **as sure(ly) as night ~s day** como dos y dos son cuatro; *see also* **act A3**
[3] (= *pursue*) seguir; **we're being ~ed** nos están siguiendo, nos vienen siguiendo; **she could feel his eyes ~ing her** sentía que la seguía con la mirada; **to have sb ~ed** mandar seguir a algn; **to ~ a lead** seguir una pista
[4] (= *keep to*) [*road, river*] seguir, ir por; **the road ~s the coast** la carretera sigue la costa *or* va por la costa
[5] (= *observe*) [+ *instructions, advice, example, fashion*] seguir; [+ *rules*] obedecer, cumplir; **I wouldn't advise you to ~ that course of action** no le aconsejo que tome ese camino *or* esas medidas; *see also* **pattern A3**, **suit A3**
[6] (= *engage in*) [+ *career*] emprender; [+ *profession*] ejercer; [+ *trade*] dedicarse a; [+ *religion*] profesar, ser seguidor de
[7] (= *be interested in*) [+ *news*] seguir, mantenerse al corriente de; [+ *TV serial*] seguir; [+ *sb's progress*] seguir; **do you ~ football?** ¿eres aficionado al fútbol?; **which team do you ~?** ¿de qué equipo eres?
[8] (= *understand*) [+ *person, argument*] seguir, entender; **do you ~ me?** ¿me sigue?, ¿me entiende?; **I don't quite ~ you** no te acabo de entender; **it was a difficult plot to ~** era un trama difícil de seguir
Ⓑ VI [1] (= *come after*) **they led her in and I ~ed** la llevaron dentro y yo entré detrás; **to ~, there was roast lamb** de segundo había cordero asado; **roast chicken, with apple pie to ~** pollo asado y después de postre un pastel de manzana; **what ~s is an eye-witness account** lo que viene a continuación es la versión de un testigo presencial; **further price rises are sure to ~** no cabe duda de que tras esto los precios subirán aún más; **as ~s**: **the text reads as ~s** el texto dice lo siguiente, el texto dice así; **the winners are as ~s** los ganadores son los siguientes; *see also* **heel A1**, **footstep**
[2] (= *result, ensue*) deducirse; **that doesn't ~** eso no cuadra, de ahí no se puede deducir eso; **it ~s that …** (de lo cual) se deduce que …, se deduce pues que …; **it doesn't ~ that …** no significa que …
[3] (= *understand*) entender; **I don't quite ~** no lo sigo del todo, no lo acabo de entender

► **follow on** VI + ADV [1] (= *come after*) **we'll ~ on behind** nosotros seguiremos, vendremos después
[2] (= *result*) **it ~s on from what I said** es la consecuencia lógica de lo que dije

► **follow out** VT + ADV [+ *idea, plan*] llevar a cabo; [+ *order*] ejecutar, cumplir; [+ *instructions*] seguir

► **follow through** Ⓐ VT + ADV [1] (= *continue to the end*) **~ it through, it might be the only lead we've got** síguela *or* investígala, puede que sea la única pista que tengamos; **that's all you need to make a start and ~ it through** eso es todo lo que hace falta para empezar y seguir adelante; **I was trained as an actress but I didn't ~ it through** estudié arte dramático pero luego no seguí con ello
[2] (*Sport*) [+ *shot*] acompañar
Ⓑ VI + ADV [1] (= *take further action*) continuar, seguir; **he decided to ~ through with his original plan** decidió continuar *or* seguir con lo que tenía pensado en un principio; **to ~ through on** (*US*) [+ *commitment*] cumplir con; [+ *promise*] cumplir; [+ *plan, initiative*] continuar con, seguir con; [+ *threat*] cumplir, llevar a cabo
[2] (*Ftbl*) rematar; (*Golf, Tennis*) acompañar el golpe

► **follow up** Ⓐ VT + ADV [1] (= *investigate*) [+ *case*] investigar; **to ~ up a lead** seguir *or* investigar una pista
[2] (= *take further action on*) [+ *offer*] reiterar; [+ *job application*] hacer un seguimiento de; [+ *suggestion*] investigar
[3] (= *reinforce*) [+ *victory, advantage, success*] consolidar; **they imposed trade sanctions and ~ed that up with an oil embargo** impusieron sanciones comerciales y las consolidaron con un embargo de petróleo; **they ~ed the visit up with a series of talks** consolidaron la visita con una serie de conferencias
Ⓑ VI + ADV (*Ftbl*) rematar

follower ['fɒləʊər] N (= *disciple*) discípulo/a *m/f*, seguidor(a) *m/f*; [*of team*] aficionado/a *m/f*; (*Pol etc*) partidario/a *m/f*; **the ~s of fashion** los que siguen la moda

following ['fɒləʊɪŋ] Ⓐ ADJ [1] (= *next*) siguiente; **the ~ day** el día siguiente; **the ~ day dawned bright and sunny** el día siguiente *or* al día siguiente amaneció con un sol radiante;

we saw him again the ~ day lo volvimos a ver al día siguiente

2 (= *favourable*) [*wind*] en popa; ✦**IDIOM with a ~ wind** con un poco de suerte; **with a ~ wind you could win the competition** con un poco de suerte podrías ganar el torneo

Ⓑ N 1 (= *supporters*) [*of party, movement, person*] seguidores *mpl*, partidarios *mpl*; [*of product, company*] clientes *mpl*; [*of TV programme*] audiencia *f*, seguidores *mpl*; [*of sport*] afición *f*, aficionados *mpl*; **he has a large ~ in the local community** cuenta con numerosos seguidores *or* partidarios entre la población local; **the programme has a huge ~ in the US** el programa tiene una enorme audiencia *or* muchos seguidores en EE.UU.; **football has no ~ here** aquí no hay afición por el fútbol

2 **the ~**: **he said the ~** dijo lo siguiente; **do you use any of the ~?** ¿utiliza alguna de estas cosas?; **as for hardier plants, the ~ are all well worth trying** por lo que respecta a plantas más resistentes, se puede probar con cualquiera de las siguientes

follow-my-leader [ˌfɒləʊmə'liːdəʳ] N *juego en el que los participantes hacen lo que alguien manda*; **to play ~** jugar a lo que haga el rey

follow-the-leader [ˌfɒləʊðə'liːdəʳ] N (*US*) = **follow-my-leader**

follow-through ['fɒləʊ'θruː] N (= *continuation*) continuación *f*; (= *further action*) seguimiento *m*; (*Golf, Tennis*) acompañamiento *m*; **there was no ~ to the training programme we went on** el programa de formación al que asistimos no tuvo continuación; **how can we make sure that there is ~ on this agreement?** ¿cómo podemos asegurarnos de que se realizará un seguimiento del acuerdo?

follow-up ['fɒləʊ'ʌp] Ⓐ N (= *further action*) seguimiento *m* (**to** de); (= *continuation*) continuación *f* (**to** de); **subsequent ~ is an essential part of the program** un seguimiento posterior es parte fundamental del programa; **this is a ~ to the meeting held last Sunday** esto es la continuación de la reunión celebrada el domingo

Ⓑ CPD ► **follow-up appointment** N (*with doctor, dentist, vet*) revisión *f* ► **follow-up (phone) call** N (*Telec*) llamada *f* de reiteración ► **follow-up care** N (*postoperative*) atención *f* pos(t)operatoria; (*following initial treatment*) seguimiento *m* clínico ► **follow-up interview** N entrevista *f* complementaria ► **follow-up letter** N carta *f* recordatoria ► **follow-up study** N estudio *m* de seguimiento ► **follow-up survey** N investigación *f* complementaria ► **follow-up treatment** N (*postoperative*) tratamiento *m* pos(t)operatorio; (*following initial treatment*) tratamiento *m* complementario ► **follow-up visit** N (= *inspection*) visita *f* de inspección *or* comprobación; (*Med*) revisión *f*

folly ['fɒlɪ] N 1 (= *foolishness, act of folly*) locura *f*; **it would be ~ to do it** sería una locura hacerlo

2 (*Archit*) disparate *m*

foment [fəʊ'ment] VT (*frm*) (*also Med*) fomentar; [+ *revolt, violence*] provocar, instigar a

fomentation [ˌfəʊmen'teɪʃən] N (*frm*) instigación *f*

▼**fond** [fɒnd] ADJ (*compar* **fonder**; *superl* **fondest**) 1 **to be ~ of sb** tener cariño a algn, querer mucho a algn; **I am very ~ of Inga** a Inga le tengo mucho cariño *or* la quiero mucho; **they were very ~ of each other** se tenían mucho cariño, se querían mucho; **I've become** *or* **grown ~ of him** me he encariñado con él, le he cogido cariño

2 **to be ~ of sth: she is very ~ of marmalade/shopping** le gusta mucho la mermelada/ir de compras; **she is very ~ of animals** le gustan mucho los animales; **he's very ~ of his old mini** le tiene mucho cariño a su viejo mini; **he is very ~ of handing out advice** (*pej*) es demasiado aficionado a dar consejos; **he became** *or* **grew very ~ of gardening** le cogió gusto a la jardinería

3 (= *affectionate*) [*wife, parent, relative*] cariñoso, afectuoso; **she gave him a ~ smile** le sonrió cariñosa; **they exchanged ~ looks** intercambiaron miradas cariñosas; **to bid sb a ~ farewell** ◊ **bid a ~ farewell to sb** despedirse de algn cariñosamente; *see also* **absence**

4 (= *pleasant*) **to have ~ memories of sth** tener muy buenos recuerdos de algo

5 (= *foolish*) [*belief, hope*] ingenuo, vano; **in the ~ belief that** con la ingenua *or* vana creencia de que

6 (= *fervent*) [*wish*] ferviente

fondant ['fɒndənt] N pasta *f* de azúcar, glaseado *m*

fondle ['fɒndl] VT acariciar

fondly ['fɒndlɪ] ADV 1 (= *affectionately*) [*say, smile*] cariñosamente, con cariño; [*remember*] con cariño

2 (= *foolishly*) [*imagine, believe, hope*] ingenuamente

fondness ['fɒndnɪs] N (*for person*) cariño *m* (**for** por); (*for thing*) afición *f* (**for** a); **his ~ for cooking** su afición a la cocina; **there were rumours about her ~ for alcohol** corrían rumores sobre su afición al alcohol; **he has a ~ for all things Italian** le gusta mucho todo lo italiano, tiene inclinación por todo lo italiano; **I remember my childhood with ~** recuerdo mi infancia con cariño

fondue [fɒn'duː] Ⓐ N fondue *f*

Ⓑ CPD ► **fondue set** N fondue *f*

font [fɒnt] N 1 (*Typ*) fundición *f*; (*Comput*) fuente *f*, tipo *m* de letra

2 (*in church*) pila *f*

fontanelle, **fontanel** [ˌfɒntə'nel] N fontanela *f*

food [fuːd] Ⓐ N (= *things to eat*) comida *f*; (= *food item*) alimento *m*; (*for plants*) abono *m*; **I've no ~ left in the house** no me queda comida en casa; **we need to buy some ~** hay que comprar cosas de comer; **she gave him ~** le dio de comer; **the ~ at the hotel was terrible** la comida en el hotel era fatal; **the ~ is good here** aquí se come bien; **he likes plain ~** le gustan las comidas sencillas; **the cost of ~** el coste de la alimentación; **to send ~ and clothing** enviar alimentos y ropa; **to be off one's ~*** estar desganado; ✦**IDIOM to give ~ for thought** ser motivo de reflexión; *see also* **cat B**

Ⓑ CPD ► **food additive** N aditivo *m* alimenticio ► **food aid** N ayuda *f* alimenticia ► **food chain** N cadena *f* alimenticia ► **food crop** N cosecha *f* de alimentos ► **food mixer** N batidora *f* ► **food parcel** N paquete *m* de alimentos ► **food poisoning** N intoxicación *f* alimenticia ► **food prices** NPL precios *mpl* de los alimentos ► **food processing** N preparación *f* de alimentos ► **food processor** N robot *m* de cocina ► **food product** N producto *m* alimenticio, comestible *m* ► **food rationing** N racionamiento *m* de víveres ► **food science** N ciencia *f* de la alimentación ► **food shop** N tienda *f* de comestibles ► **food stamp** N (*US*) *cupón para canjear por comida que reciben las personas de pocos recursos* ► **food store** N = **food shop** ► **food subsidy** N subvención *f* alimenticia ► **food supplies** NPL víveres *mpl* ► **food supply** N suministro *m* de alimentos ► **food technology** N tecnología *f* de la alimentación ► **food value** N valor *m* nutritivo; → FDA

foodie* ['fuːdɪ] N *persona que se interesa con entusiasmo en la preparación y consumo de los alimentos*

foodstuffs ['fuːdstʌfs] NPL comestibles *mpl*, productos *mpl* alimenticios

fool[1] [fuːl] Ⓐ N 1 (= *idiot*) tonto/a *m/f*, zonzo/a *m/f* (*LAm*); **don't be a ~!** ¡no seas tonto!; **I was a ~ not to go!** ¡qué tonto fui en no ir!; **to act the ~** hacer el tonto; **to be ~ enough to do sth** ser lo bastante tonto como para hacer algo; **to send sb on a ~'s errand** enviar a algn a una misión inútil; **to make a ~ of sb** poner *or* dejar a algn en ridículo; **to make a ~ of o.s.** quedar en ridículo; **I'm nobody's ~** yo no me chupo el dedo, yo no tengo un pelo de tonto; **to play the ~** hacer el tonto; **some ~ of a civil servant** algún funcionario imbécil; **you ~!** ¡idiota!, ¡imbécil!; ✦**IDIOM to live in a ~'s paradise** vivir de ilusiones; ✦**PROVS there's no ~ like an old ~** la cabeza blanca y el seso por venir; **a ~ and his money are soon parted** a los tontos no les dura el dinero; **~s rush in (where angels fear to tread)** la ignorancia es osada

2 (= *jester*) bufón *m*

Ⓑ ADJ (*US*) tonto, zonzo (*LAm*)

Ⓒ VT (= *deceive*) engañar; **you can't ~ me** a mí no me engañas; **"my husband has always been faithful to me" — "you could have ~ed me!"** (*iro*) —mi marido siempre me ha sido fiel —¡qué fiel ni qué ocho cuartos!*; **you had me ~ed there** casi lo creí, por poco me lo trago*; **that ~ed him!** ¡aquello coló!*, ¡se lo tragó!*; **that ~ed nobody** aquello no engañó a nadie, nadie se tragó aquello*

Ⓓ VI hacer el tonto; **no ~ing** en serio; **I was only ~ing** sólo era una broma; **quit ~ing!** ¡déjate de tonterías!

►**fool about**, **fool around** VI + ADV 1 (= *waste time*) perder el tiempo

2 (= *act the fool*) hacer el tonto; **to ~ about with sth** (= *play with*) jugar con algo; (*and damage*) estropear algo; (= *mess with*) [+ *drugs, drink, electricity*] jugar con

3 (= *have an affair*) **to ~ around with sb** tontear con algn

►**fool with** VI + PREP **to ~ with sb** jugar con algn, hacer el tonto con algn

fool[2] [fuːl] N (*Brit Culin*) (*also* **fruit ~**) *puré de frutas con nata o natillas*

foolery ['fuːlərɪ] N bufonadas *fpl*; (= *nonsense*) tonterías *fpl*

foolhardiness ['fuːlˌhɑːdɪnɪs] N temeridad *f*

foolhardy ['fuːlˌhɑːdɪ] ADJ (= *rash*) temerario

foolish ['fuːlɪʃ] ADJ 1 (= *unwise, foolhardy*) [*person*] insensato; [*mistake*] estúpido, tonto; [*decision*] imprudente; **he will be remembered as a ~ man** se le recordará como un insensato; **don't be ~** no seas tonto; **I was ~ but I won't resign** hice una tontería pero no voy a dimitir; **it would be ~ to believe him** sería una tontería *or* una estupidez creerle; **don't do anything ~** no hagas ninguna tontería *or* insensatez; **it was ~ of him to do that** fue una tontería por su parte hacer eso; **it would be ~ of him to resign** sería una tontería que dimitiese; **to do something ~** hacer una tontería *or* insensatez; **what a ~ thing to do!** ¡hacer eso fue una tontería!

2 (= *ridiculous, laughable*) [*person, question*] estúpido, tonto; **to feel ~** sentirse ridículo, sentirse idiota; **to look ~** hacer el ridículo, que-

➤ LANGUAGE IN USE: fond 2 7.4

dar como un idiota*; **to make sb look ~** dejar a algn en ridículo

foolishly ['fu:lɪʃlɪ] ADV tontamente, como un tonto; **he saw me standing there, grinning ~ at him** me vio allí de pie, sonriéndole tontamente *or* como un tonto; **to act ~** hacer el tonto; **to behave ~** portarse como un tonto

foolishness ['fu:lɪʃnɪs] N insensatez *f*, estupidez *f*

foolproof ['fu:lpru:f] ADJ [*mechanism, scheme etc*] infalible

foolscap ['fu:lskæp] Ⓐ N papel *m* de tamaño folio
Ⓑ CPD ► **foolscap envelope** N ≈ sobre *m* tamaño folio ► **foolscap sheet** N ≈ folio *m*

foot [fʊt] Ⓐ N (*pl* **feet**) 1 (*Anat*) pie *m*; [*of animal, chair*] pata *f*; **my feet are aching** me duelen los pies; **to get to one's feet** ponerse de pie, levantarse, pararse (*LAm*); **lady, my ~!*** ¡dama, ni hablar!; **on ~** a pie, andando, caminando (*LAm*); **to be on one's feet** estar de pie, estar parado (*LAm*); **he's on his feet all day long** está trajinando todo el santo día, no descansa en todo el día; **he's on his feet again** ya está recuperado *or* repuesto; **to rise to one's feet** ponerse de pie, levantarse, pararse (*LAm*); **I've never set ~ there** nunca he estado allí; **to set ~ inside sb's door** poner los pies en la casa de algn, pasar el umbral de algn; **to set ~ on dry land** poner el pie en tierra firme; **it's wet under ~** el suelo está mojado; **to trample sth under ~** pisotear algo; **the children are always under my feet** siempre tengo los niños pegados; **to put one's feet up*** descansar; ✦**IDIOMS to put one's best ~ forward** animarse a continuar; **to get cold feet** entrarle miedo a algn; **to get one's ~ in the door** meter el pie en la puerta; **to put one's ~ down** (= *say no*) plantarse; (*Aut*) acelerar; **to drag one's feet** dar largas al asunto, hacerse el roncero; **to fall on one's feet** tener suerte, caer de pie; **to find one's feet** ponerse al corriente; **to have one ~ in the grave** estar con un pie en la sepultura; **to have one's feet on the ground** ser realista; **to put one's ~ in it*** meter la pata*; **to start off on the right ~** entrar con buen pie; **to shoot o.s. in the ~** pegarse un tiro en el pie; **to sit at sb's feet** ser discípulo de algn; **to stand on one's own two feet** volar con sus propias alas; **to sweep a girl off her feet** enamorar perdidamente a una chica; **she never put a ~ wrong** no cometió ningún error; **it all started off on the wrong ~** todo empezó mal
2 [*of mountain, page, stairs, bed*] pie *m*; **at the ~ of the hill** al pie de la colina
3 (= *measure*) pie *m*; **he's six ~ *or* feet tall** mide seis pies, mide un metro ochenta; → IMPERIAL SYSTEM
Ⓑ VT 1 (= *pay*) ✦**IDIOM to ~ the bill (for sth)** pagar (algo), correr con los gastos (de algo)
2 **to ~ it** (= *walk*) ir andando *or* (*LAm*) caminando; (= *dance*) bailar
Ⓒ CPD ► **foot brake** N (*Aut*) freno *m* de pie ► **foot fault** N (*Tennis*) falta *f* de saque ► **foot passenger** N pasajero/a *m/f* de a pie ► **foot pump** N bomba *f* de pie ► **foot rot** N uñero *m* ► **foot soldier** N soldado *mf* de infantería

footage ['fʊtɪdʒ] N (*Cine*) metraje *m*; (= *pictures*) imágenes *fpl*, secuencias *fpl*

foot-and-mouth (disease) ['fʊtən'maʊθ(dɪ'zi:z)] N fiebre *f* aftosa, glosopeda *f*

football ['fʊtbɔ:l] Ⓐ N (*Sport*) fútbol *m*; (= *ball*) balón *m* de fútbol; **to play ~** jugar al fútbol
Ⓑ CPD ► **football coupon** N (*Brit*) boleto *m* de quinielas ► **football ground** N campo *m* or (*LAm*) cancha *f* de fútbol ► **football hooligan** N (*Brit*) hooligan *mf* ► **football hooliganism** N (*Brit*) hooliganismo *m*, violencia *f* en las gradas ► **football league** N liga *f* de fútbol ► **football match** N partido *m* de fútbol ► **football player** N jugador(a) *m/f* de fútbol, futbolista *mf* ► **football pools** NPL quinielas *fpl* ► **football season** N temporada *f* de fútbol ► **football supporter** N hincha *mf* ► **football team** N equipo *m* de fútbol

footballer ['fʊtbɔ:ləʳ] N (*Brit*) futbolista *mf*

footballing ['fʊtbɔ:lɪŋ] ADJ [*career, skills*] futbolístico; **~ countries** países *mpl* en los que se juega al fútbol

footboard ['fʊtbɔ:d] N estribo *m*

footbridge ['fʊtbrɪdʒ] N puente *m* peatonal

-footed ['fʊtɪd] ADJ (*ending in compounds*) **four-footed** cuadrúpedo; **light-footed** rápido, veloz

footer ['fʊtəʳ] N 1 (*Brit**) fútbol *m*
2 (*Typ, Comput*) pie *m* de página

-footer ['fʊtəʳ] N (*ending in compounds*) **he's a six-footer** mide seis pies, mide un metro ochenta

footfall ['fʊtfɔ:l] N paso *m*, pisada *f*

footgear ['fʊtgɪəʳ] N calzado *m*

foothills ['fʊthɪlz] NPL estribaciones *fpl*

foothold ['fʊthəʊld] N asidero *m*, punto *m* de apoyo (*para el pie*); **to gain a ~** (*fig*) lograr establecerse

footing ['fʊtɪŋ] N 1 (= *foothold*) asidero *m*; **to lose one's ~** perder pie
2 (*fig*) (= *basis*) **on an equal ~** en pie de igualdad; **to be on a friendly ~ with sb** tener amistad con algn; **to gain a ~** lograr establecerse; **to put a company on a sound financial ~** enderezar la situación económica de una empresa; **on a war ~** en pie de guerra

footle ['fu:tl] Ⓐ VT **to ~ away** malgastar
Ⓑ VI (= *waste time*) perder el tiempo; (= *act the fool*) hacer el tonto

footlights ['fʊtlaɪts] NPL (*in theatre*) candilejas *fpl*

footling ['fu:tlɪŋ] ADJ trivial, insignificante

footloose ['fʊtlu:s] ADJ **~ and fancy free** libre como el aire

footman ['fʊtmən] N (*pl* **footmen**) lacayo *m*

footmark ['fʊtmɑ:k] N huella *f*, pisada *f*

footnote ['fʊtnəʊt] N nota *f* a pie de página

footpath ['fʊtpɑ:θ] N (= *track*) sendero *m*, vereda *f*; (= *pavement*) acera *f*, vereda *f* (*Andes, S. Cone*), andén *m* (*CAm, Col*), banqueta *f* (*Mex*)

footplate ['fʊtpleɪt] N (*esp Brit*) plataforma *f* del maquinista

footprint ['fʊtprɪnt] N huella *f*, pisada *f*

footrest ['fʊtrest] N [*of wheelchair*] reposapiés *m inv*; [*of motorbike*] estribo *m*

Footsie* ['fʊtsɪ] N = **Financial Times Stock Exchange Index**

footsie* ['fʊtsɪ] N ✦**IDIOM to play ~ with** acariciar con el pie a

footslog* ['fʊtslɒg] VI andar, marchar

footslogger* ['fʊtslɒgəʳ] N peatón(a) *m/f*; (*Mil*) soldado *mf* de infantería

footsore ['fʊtsɔ:ʳ] ADJ **to be ~** tener los pies cansados y doloridos

footstep ['fʊtstep] N paso *m*, pisada *f*; **I can hear ~s on the stairs** oigo pasos *or* pisadas en la escalera; ✦**IDIOM to follow in sb's ~s** seguir los pasos de algn

footstool ['fʊtstu:l] N escabel *m*

footway ['fʊt,weɪ] N acera *f*

footwear ['fʊtweəʳ] N calzado *m*

footwork ['fʊtwɜ:k] N (*Sport*) juego *m* de piernas; *see also* **fancy B1**

fop [fɒp] N petimetre *m*, currutaco *m*

foppish ['fɒpɪʃ] ADJ petimetre, litri*

FOR ABBR (= **free on rail**) franco en ferrocarril

for [fɔ:ʳ]

A PREPOSITION B CONJUNCTION

When **for** *is part of a phrasal verb, eg* **look for, make for, stand for**, *look up the verb. When it is part of a set combination, eg* **as for, a gift for, for sale, eager for**, *look up the other word.*

Ⓐ PREPOSITION

1 *= going to* para; **the train ~ London** el tren para *or* de Londres; **he left ~ Rome** salió para Roma; **the ship left ~ Vigo** el buque partió (con) rumbo a Vigo; **he swam ~ the shore** fue nadando hacia la playa

2 *= intended for* para; **a table ~ two** una mesa para dos; **a cupboard ~ toys** un armario para los juguetes; **a cloth ~ polishing silver** un paño para sacarle brillo a la plata; **it's not ~ cutting wood** no sirve para cortar madera; **there's a letter ~ you** hay una carta para ti; **is this ~ me?** ¿es para mí esto?; **I have news ~ you** tengo que darte una noticia; **hats ~ women** sombreros de señora; **clothes ~ children** ropa infantil; **I decided that it was the job ~ me** decidí que era el puesto que me convenía; **she decided that hang-gliding was not ~ her*** decidió que el vuelo con ala delta no era lo suyo

3 *to express purpose* para; **he went there ~ a rest** fue allí para descansar; **we went to Tossa ~ our holidays** fuimos a pasar las vacaciones a Tossa, fuimos a Tossa para las vacaciones; **what ~?** ¿para qué?; **what's it ~?** ¿para qué es *or* sirve?; **what do you want it ~?** ¿para qué lo quieres?; **what did you do that ~?** ¿por qué hiciste eso?

4 *employment* para; **he works ~ the government** trabaja para el gobierno; **to write ~ the papers** escribir para los periódicos

5 *= on behalf of* **I'll ask him ~ you** se lo preguntaré de tu parte; **I'll go ~ you** iré yo en tu lugar; **"I can't iron this shirt" — "don't worry, I'll iron it ~ you"** —no puedo planchar esta camisa, —no te preocupes, yo te la plancho; **"I still haven't booked the ticket" — "I'll do it ~ you"** —no he reservado el billete todavía —ya lo haré yo; **who is the representative ~ your group?** ¿quién es el representante de vuestro grupo?

6 *= as in* de; **G ~ George** G de Gerona

7 *= in exchange for* por; **I'll give you this book ~ that one** te cambio este libro por ése; **he'll do it ~ £25** lo hará por 25 libras; **~ every one who voted yes, 50 voted no** por cada persona que votó a favor, 50 votaron en contra; **to pay 50 pence ~ a ticket** pagar 50 peniques por una entrada; **pound ~ pound, it's cheaper** es más económico de libra en libra; **the government will match each donation pound ~ pound** el gobierno igualará cada donativo, libra a libra; **I sold it ~ £5** lo vendí por *or* en 5 libras

8 *= to the value of* **a cheque ~ £500** un cheque *or* talón por valor de 500 libras; **how much is the cheque ~?** ¿por cuánto es el cheque?

9 *after adjective* 9·1 (*making comparisons*) para; **he's tall/mature ~ his age** es alto/maduro para su edad *or* para la edad que tiene; **he's nice ~ a policeman** para policía es muy simpático; **it's cold ~ July** para ser julio

➤ LANGUAGE IN USE: **for B** 17.1

hace frío; **it's quite good ~ a six-year-old** está bastante bien para un niño de seis años

9·2 (*specifying*) **it was too difficult ~ her** era demasiado difícil para ella, le era demasiado difícil; **it was difficult ~ him to leave her** le resultó difícil dejarla; **that's easy ~ you to say** para ti es fácil decirlo, a ti te es fácil decirlo; **they made it very easy ~ us** nos lo pusieron muy fácil

10 *= in favour of* a favor de; **I'm ~ the government** yo estoy a favor del gobierno; **I'm ~ helping him** yo estoy a favor de ayudarle; **anyone ~ a game of cards?** ¿alguien se apunta a una partida de cartas?; **are you ~ or against the idea?** ¿estás a favor o en contra de la idea?; **are you ~ or against us?** ¿estás con nosotros o en contra?; **I'm all ~ it** estoy completamente a favor; **the campaign ~ human rights** la campaña pro derechos humanos, la campaña en pro de los derechos humanos; **a collection ~ the poor** una colecta a beneficio de los pobres

11 *= as, by way of* **what's ~ dinner?** ¿qué hay para cenar?; **I had a sandwich ~ lunch** para almorzar me comí un bocadillo

12 *= because of* por; **it's famous ~ its cathedral** es famosa por su catedral; **if it weren't ~ you** si no fuera por ti; **he was sent to prison ~ fraud** lo mandaron a la cárcel por fraude; **she felt better ~ losing a bit of weight** se sentía mejor por haber adelgazado un poco; **I couldn't see her ~ pot plants** no la veía por taparla las plantas; **we chose it ~ its climate** lo escogimos por el clima; **~ fear of being criticized** por miedo a la crítica, por temor a ser criticado; **to shout ~ joy** gritar de alegría

13 *= in spite of* a pesar de; **~ all his wealth** a pesar de su riqueza; **~ all that** a pesar de todo; **~ all he promised to come, he didn't** a pesar de habérmelo prometido, no vino

14 ***in expressions of time*** 14·1 (*future/past duration*)

When translating **for** *and a period of time, it is often unnecessary to translate* **for**, *as in the examples below where* **durante** *is optional:*

she will be away ~ a month estará fuera un mes; **he worked in Spain ~ two years** trabajó dos años en España; **I'm going ~ three weeks** me voy tres semanas, estaré allí tres semanas

Alternatively, translate **for** *using* **durante**, *or, especially when talking about very short periods,* **por**. *Use* **por** *also with the verb* **ir**, *although again it is often optional in this case:*

they waited ~ over two hours estuvieron esperando durante más de dos horas; **~ a moment, he didn't know what to say** por un momento, no supo qué decir; **I'm going to the country ~ a while** me voy al campo (por) una temporada; **I'm going away ~ a few days** me voy (por) unos cuantos días; **he won't be back ~ a couple of hours/days** no regresará hasta dentro de un par de horas/días, tardará un par de horas/días en regresar; **we went to the seaside ~ the day** fuimos a pasar el día en la playa

14·2 (*with English perfect tenses*)

Use **hace...que** *and the present to describe actions and states that started in the past and are still going on. Alternatively use the present and* **desde hace**. *Another option is sometimes* **llevar** *and the gerund. Don't use the present perfect in Spanish to translate phrases like these, unless they are in the negative.*

he has been learning French ~ two years hace dos años que estudia francés, estudia francés desde hace dos años, lleva dos años estudiando francés; **it has not rained ~ 3 weeks** hace 3 semanas que no llueve, no llueve *or* no ha llovido desde hace 3 semanas, lleva 3 semanas sin llover; **I have known her ~ years** hace años que la conozco, la conozco desde hace años; **I haven't seen her ~ two years** hace dos años que no la veo, no la he visto desde hace dos años, no la veo desde hace dos años, llevo dos años sin verla

Notice how the tenses change when talking about something that **had** *happened or* **had been** *happening* **for** *a time:*

he had been learning French ~ two years hacía dos años que estudiaba francés, estudiaba francés desde hacía dos años, llevaba dos años estudiando francés; **I hadn't seen her ~ two years** hacía dos años que no la veía, no la había visto desde hacía dos años, no la veía desde hacía dos años, llevaba dos años sin verla

15 *= by, before* para; **can you do it ~ tomorrow?** ¿lo puedes hacer para mañana?; **when does he want it ~?** ¿para cuándo lo quiere?

16 *= on the occasion of* para; **I'll be home ~ Christmas** estaré en casa para las Navidades; **he asked his daughter what she would like ~ her birthday** le preguntó a su hija qué le gustaría para su cumpleaños

17 *= for a distance of* **there were roadworks ~ five miles** había obras a lo largo de cinco millas; **we walked ~ two kilometres** caminamos dos kilómetros; **you can see ~ miles from the top of the hill** desde lo alto de la colina se puede ver hasta muy lejos

18 ***with infinitive clauses*** **~ this to be possible ...** para que esto sea posible ...; **it's not ~ me to tell him what to do** yo no soy quien para decirle *or* no me corresponde a mí decirle lo que tiene que hacer; **it's not ~ you to blame him** tú no eres quien para culparle; **he brought it ~ us to see** lo trajo para que lo viéramos; **their one hope is ~ him to return** su única esperanza es que regrese; **it's bad ~ you to smoke so much** te perjudica fumar tanto; **it's best ~ you to go** es mejor que te vayas; **there is still time ~ you to do it** todavía tienes tiempo para hacerlo

19 ***in other expressions*** **what's the German ~ "hill"?** ¿cómo se dice "colina" en alemán?; **oh ~ a cup of tea!** ¡lo que daría por una taza de té!; **✦IDIOMS you're ~ it!*** ¡las vas a pagar!*; **I'll be ~ it if he catches me here!*** ¡me la voy a cargar si me pilla aquí!*; **there's nothing ~ it but to jump** no hay más remedio que tirarse; *see also* **example**

Ⓑ CONJUNCTION

(*liter*) pues, puesto que; **she avoided him, ~ he was rude and uncouth** lo eludía puesto que *or* pues era grosero y ordinario

forage ['fɒrɪdʒ] Ⓐ N (*for cattle*) forraje *m*

Ⓑ VI **they ~d for food in the jungle** se adentraron en la selva en busca de alimento

foray ['fɒreɪ] N (*esp Mil*) incursión *f* (**into** en)

forbad(e) [fə'bæd] PT *of* **forbid**

forbear [fɔː'bɛəʳ] (*pt* **forbore**; *pp* **forborne**) VI contenerse; **to ~ to do sth** abstenerse de hacer algo

forbearance [fɔː'bɛərəns] N paciencia *f*

forbearing [fɔː'bɛərɪŋ] ADJ paciente

forbears ['fɔːbɛəz] NPL = **forebears**

forbid [fə'bɪd] (*pt* **forbad(e)**; *pp* **forbidden**) VT

1 (= *not allow*) prohibir; **such actions are ~den by international law** el derecho internacional prohíbe este tipo de acciones; **to ~ sb alcohol** prohibir el alcohol a algn; **to ~ sb to do sth** ◊ **~ sb from doing sth** prohibir a algn hacer algo, prohibir a algn que haga algo; **I forbade her to see him** le prohibí verlo *or* que lo viera; **I ~ you to go** te prohíbo que vayas; **she was ~den to leave** *or* **from leaving the country** se le prohibió salir del país, le estaba prohibido salir del país; **I ~ you to!** ¡te lo prohíbo!

2 (= *prevent*) impedir; **his pride ~s him from asking for help** ◊ **his pride ~s his asking for help** su orgullo le impide pedir ayuda; **custom ~s any modernization** la tradición impide *or* hace imposible cualquier modernización; **God** *or* **Heaven ~!*** ¡Dios nos libre!, ¡Dios no lo quiera!; **God** *or* **Heaven ~ (that) I should do anything illegal** Dios me libre de hacer nada ilegal; **God** *or* **Heaven ~ that he should come here!** ¡quiera Dios *or* Dios quiera que no venga por aquí!

forbidden [fə'bɪdn] Ⓐ PT *of* **forbid**

Ⓑ ADJ 1 (= *not allowed*) [*book, food, love*] prohibido; **to be ~** estar prohibido; **smoking is ~** está prohibido fumar; **abortion is ~ in this country** el aborto es ilegal *or* está prohibido en este país; **to be strictly ~** estar terminantemente prohibido; **it is ~ to** (+ INFIN) está prohibido + *infin*; **preaching was ~ to women** predicar estaba prohibido para las mujeres, predicar les estaba prohibido a las mujeres

2 (= *out of bounds*) [*area, zone*] prohibido, vedado; [*city*] prohibido; **some cities are ~ to foreigners** a los extranjeros se les prohíbe *or* les está prohibido entrar en algunas ciudades; **✦IDIOM that's ~ territory** eso es tabú

3 (= *taboo*) [*word, feeling*] tabú; **a ~ subject** un (tema) tabú

Ⓒ CPD ► **the forbidden city** N la ciudad prohibida ► **forbidden fruit** N fruto *m* prohibido; **✦IDIOM ~ fruits are always the sweetest** el fruto prohibido es siempre el más dulce

forbidding [fə'bɪdɪŋ] ADJ [*person, manner*] severo, intimidante; [*place, building, room*] imponente, intimidante; [*landscape*] inhóspito; [*task*] ingente, arduo

forbore [fɔː'bɔːʳ] PT *of* **forbear**

forborne [fɔː'bɔːn] PP *of* **forbear**

force [fɔːs] Ⓐ N 1 (= *strength*) fuerza *f*; **the building took the full ~ of the blast** el edificio recibió toda la fuerza *or* todo el impacto de la explosión; **to do sth by ~** hacer algo por la fuerza; **they removed him from the bar by ~** lo sacaron del bar a la fuerza *or* por la fuerza; **by ~ of arms** por la fuerza de las armas; **by ~ of circumstance(s)** debido a las circunstancias; **by sheer ~** (*physical*) sólo a base de fuerza; **by (sheer) ~ of numbers** por pura superioridad numérica; **she tried to convert people by ~ of argument** intentaba convencer a la gente a fuerza de *or* a base de argumentos; **by** *or* **through sheer ~ of personality** a fuerza de *or* a base de puro carácter; **from ~ of habit** por la fuerza de la costumbre; **the ~ of gravity** la fuerza de la gravedad; **the police were out in ~** la policía había salido en masa, había un enorme despliegue policial; **to resort to ~** recurrir a la fuerza; **to use ~** hacer uso de la fuerza; *see also* **brute B**

2 (*Met*) **a ~ five wind** un viento de fuerza cinco

3 (= *influence*) fuerza *f*; **the social and economic ~s that influence our decisions** las fuerzas sociales y económicas que influyen en nuestras decisiones; **he is a powerful ~ in the trade union movement** es una persona con mucho peso dentro del movimiento sindi-

➤ LANGUAGE IN USE: **forbid 1** 9.3, 9.5, 10.4 **force B1** 10.1

calista; **the ~s of evil** las fuerzas del mal; **the ~s of nature** las fuerzas de la naturaleza; **Janet is obviously a ~ to be reckoned with** Janet es sin lugar a dudas una persona a (la que hay que) tener en cuenta; *see also* **driving**, **join**, **life**, **market**
[4] (= *legitimacy*) fuerza *f*; **the guidelines do not have the ~ of law** las directrices no tienen fuerza de ley; **to be in ~** [*law, tax*] estar vigente *or* en vigor; **a curfew is in ~** se ha impuesto un toque de queda; **to come into ~** entrar en vigor, hacerse vigente
[5] (= *body of people*) (*Mil*) fuerza *f*; **allied ~s** fuerzas *fpl* aliadas, ejércitos *mpl* aliados; **sales ~** (*Comm*) personal *m* de ventas; **the ~** (= *police force*) la policía, el cuerpo (de policía); **the ~s** (*Brit Mil*) las fuerzas armadas
Ⓑ VT [1] (= *compel*) [+ *person*] obligar, forzar; **she was ~d to the conclusion that …** se vio obligada *or* forzada a concluir que …; **to ~ sb to do sth** obligar *or* forzar a algn a hacer algo; **I am ~d to admit that …** me veo obligado *or* forzado a admitir que …; **I had to ~ myself to pick it up** tuve que obligarme *or* forzarme a recogerlo del suelo; **I had to ~ myself to stay calm** tuve que obligarme *or* forzarme a permanecer sereno; **to ~ sb into doing sth** obligar *or* forzar a algn a hacer algo; **they ~d me into signing the agreement** me obligaron *or* forzaron a firmar el acuerdo; **to ~ sb into a corner** (*fig*) arrinconar a algn; ✦*IDIOM* **to ~ sb's hand** (*intentionally*) apretar las tuercas *or* las clavijas a algn; (*by circumstances*) no dejar a algn más remedio que actuar
[2] (= *impose*) **to ~ sth on sb** imponer algo a algn; **he ~d his views on them** les impuso su punto de vista; **the decision was ~d on him** la decisión le fue *or* le vino impuesta; **to ~ o.s. on sb: I don't want to ~ myself on you, but …** no quisiera importunarte (con mi presencia), pero …; **he ~d himself on one of the girls** (*sexually*) forzó a una de las chicas
[3] (= *push, squeeze*) **he ~d the clothes into the suitcase** metió la ropa en la maleta a la fuerza, embutió la ropa en la maleta; **they ~d their way into the flat** se metieron en el piso a *or* por la fuerza; **the lorry ~d the car off the road** el camión obligó *or* forzó al coche a salirse de la carretera, el camión hizo que el coche se saliera de la carretera; **he was ~d out of office** lo obligaron *or* forzaron a dimitir del cargo; **she ~d her way through the crowd** se abrió paso entre la muchedumbre a *or* por la fuerza; **to ~ a bill through Parliament** hacer que se apruebe un proyecto de ley en el Parlamento
[4] (= *break open*) [+ *lock, door*] forzar; **to ~ sth open** [+ *drawer, door, window*] forzar algo
[5] (= *exert, strain*) [+ *voice*] forzar; **to ~ the pace** (*lit*) forzar el ritmo *or* la marcha; (*fig*) forzar la marcha de los acontecimientos; **don't ~ the situation** no fuerces la situación
[6] (= *produce with effort*) [+ *answer*] forzar; **to ~ a smile** forzar una sonrisa, sonreír de manera forzada
[7] (*Hort, Agr*) [+ *vegetable, fruit*] acelerar el crecimiento de
[8] (= *obtain by force*) conseguir a *or* por la fuerza; **to ~ a confession from** *or* **out of sb** obtener una confesión de algn a *or* por la fuerza; **we ~d the secret out of him** le sacamos el secreto a *or* por la fuerza; **to ~ a vote on sth** forzar una votación sobre algo
Ⓒ CPD ► **force majeure** N fuerza *f* mayor

►**force back** VT + ADV [1] [+ *crowd, enemy*] obligar a retroceder, hacer retroceder (a la fuerza)
[2] [+ *laughter, tears*] contener; **she ~d back her desire to laugh** contuvo las ganas de reírse; **to ~ back one's tears** contener las lágrimas

►**force down** VT + ADV [1] [+ *food*] tragarse a la fuerza; **can you ~ a bit more down?** (*hum*) ¿te cabe un poco más?
[2] [+ *aeroplane*] obligar a aterrizar
[3] [+ *prices*] hacer bajar, hacer que bajen

►**force out** VT + ADV [1] [+ *person*] (*from office*) obligar a dejar el cargo
[2] [+ *words*] conseguir pronunciar; **he ~d out an apology** con un esfuerzo enorme, pidió perdón

►**force up** VT + ADV [+ *prices*] hacer subir, hacer que suban

forced [fɔːst] Ⓐ ADJ [1] (= *obligatory*) [*march*] forzado; [*repatriation*] forzoso; [*marriage*] forzado, por la fuerza
[2] (= *from necessity*) [*landing*] forzoso
[3] (= *contrived, strained*) [*smile*] forzado; **to sound ~** parecer forzado
[4] (*Hort, Agr*) [*vegetable, fruit*] de crecimiento acelerado; **~ lettuces** lechugas *fpl* de crecimiento acelerado
Ⓑ CPD ► **forced entry** N (*Jur*) allanamiento *m* de morada; **there was no sign of ~ entry** no había señales de que hubieran forzado la entrada ► **forced labour** N trabajos *mpl* forzados

force-feed ['fɔːsfiːd] (*pt, pp* **force-fed**) VT alimentar a la fuerza

force-feeding ['fɔːs,fiːdɪŋ] N alimentación *f* a la fuerza

forceful ['fɔːsfʊl] ADJ [*personality*] enérgico, fuerte; [*argument*] contundente, convincente

forcefully ['fɔːsfʊlɪ] ADV [*say, express*] enérgicamente; [*argue*] de forma convincente; [*push, shove*] violentamente; **he condemned the president for not acting more ~** condenó al presidente por no actuar de forma más enérgica *or* contundente; **it ~ struck him that …** le llamó poderosamente la atención que …

forcefulness ['fɔːsfʊlnɪs] N [*of person*] fortaleza *f*; [*of argument*] contundencia *f*

forcemeat ['fɔːsmiːt] N (*Culin*) relleno *m* de carne picada

forceps ['fɔːseps] Ⓐ NPL fórceps *m inv*
Ⓑ CPD ► **forceps delivery** N parto *m* con fórceps

forcible ['fɔːsəbl] ADJ [1] (= *done by force*) [*repatriation, deportation*] forzoso
[2] (= *effective*) [*argument, style*] contundente; **a ~ reminder of sth** un vivo recordatorio de algo

forcibly ['fɔːsəblɪ] ADV [1] (= *by force*) [*remove, restrain, separate*] a la fuerza, por la fuerza
[2] (= *effectively*) [*express, argue*] de forma contundente, convincentemente

forcing-house ['fɔːsɪŋ,haʊs] N (*pl* **forcing-houses** ['fɔːsɪŋ,haʊzɪz]) (*Agr etc*) maduradero *m*; (*fig*) *instituto etc donde se llevan a cabo cursos intensivos*

ford [fɔːd] Ⓐ N vado *m*
Ⓑ VT vadear

fordable ['fɔːdəbl] ADJ vadeable

fore [fɔːʳ] Ⓐ ADV (*Naut*) **~ and aft** de proa a popa
Ⓑ ADJ anterior, delantero; (*Naut*) de proa
Ⓒ N **to come to the ~** empezar a destacar; **to be at the ~** ir delante
Ⓓ EXCL (*Golf*) ¡atención!

forearm ['fɔːrɑːm] N (*Anat*) antebrazo *m*

forebears ['fɔːbɛəz] NPL antepasados *mpl*

forebode [fɔː'bəʊd] VT presagiar, anunciar

foreboding [fɔː'bəʊdɪŋ] N presentimiento *m*; **to have a ~ that …** presentir que …; **to have ~s** tener un presentimiento *or* una corazonada

forecast ['fɔːkɑːst] (*vb: pt, pp* **forecast**) Ⓐ N [1] (*for weather*) pronóstico *m*; **the weather ~** el pronóstico meteorológico *or* del tiempo; **what is the ~ for the weather?** ¿qué tiempo va a hacer?
[2] (= *prediction*) previsión *f*; **according to all the ~s** según todas las previsiones
Ⓑ VT (*gen*) pronosticar

forecaster ['fɔːkɑːstəʳ] N (*Econ, Pol, Sport*) pronosticador(a) *m/f*; (*Met*) meteorólogo/a *m/f*

forecastle ['fəʊksl] N camarote *m* de la tripulación; (*Hist*) castillo *m* de proa

foreclose [fɔː'kləʊz] (*Jur*) Ⓐ VT [+ *mortgage*] extinguir el derecho de redimir
Ⓑ VI extinguir el derecho de redimir una/la hipoteca

foreclosure [fɔː'kləʊʒəʳ] N apertura *f* de un juicio hipotecario

forecourt ['fɔːkɔːt] (*esp Brit*) N (*gen*) entrada *f*; [*of hotel*] patio *m* (delantero), terraza *f*; [*of petrol station*] patio *m* (delantero)

foredoomed [fɔː'duːmd] ADJ (*liter*) **to be ~ to do sth** estar condenado de antemano a hacer algo

forefathers ['fɔː,fɑːðəz] NPL antepasados *mpl*

forefinger ['fɔː,fɪŋgəʳ] N dedo *m* índice, índice *m*

forefoot ['fɔːfʊt] N (*pl* **forefeet** ['fɔːfiːt]) pie *m* delantero, pata *f* delantera

forefront ['fɔːfrʌnt] N **to be in the ~ of** estar en la vanguardia de

foregather [fɔː'gæðəʳ] VI (*liter*) reunirse

forego [fɔː'gəʊ] (*pt* **forewent**; *pp* **foregone**) VT [1] (= *give up*) renunciar a; (= *do without*) pasar sin, privarse de
[2] (= *precede*) preceder

foregoing ['fɔːgəʊɪŋ] ADJ anterior, precedente

foregone ['fɔːgɒn] Ⓐ PP of **forego**
Ⓑ ADJ **it was a ~ conclusion** era un resultado inevitable

foreground ['fɔːgraʊnd] Ⓐ N primer plano *m*, primer término *m*; **in the ~** (*fig*) en primer plano *or* término
Ⓑ VT [+ *object in photo, picture*] traer al primer plano; (*fig*) [+ *issue, problem*] destacar, subrayar

forehand ['fɔːhænd] N (*Tennis*) drive *m*

forehead ['fɒrɪd] N frente *f*

foreign ['fɒrɪn] Ⓐ ADJ [1] (*gen*) [*person, country, language*] extranjero; [*import*] del extranjero; [*debt*] exterior; **this was her first ~ holiday** éstas eran sus primeras vacaciones en el extranjero; **her job involves a lot of ~ travel** su trabajo supone que tiene que viajar a menudo por el extranjero; **~ news** noticias *fpl* internacionales
[2] (*Pol*) [*minister, ministry*] de asuntos exteriores; [*policy, relations*] exterior
[3] (*frm*) (= *extraneous*) [*object, substance*] extraño
[4] **~ to** [4·1] (= *uncharacteristic of*) ajeno a, impropio de; **such behaviour was ~ to his nature** este comportamiento era ajeno a *or* impropio de su carácter
[4·2] (= *unfamiliar to*) ajeno a; **it's an idea which is completely ~ to them** es una idea que les resulta totalmente ajena
Ⓑ CPD ► **foreign affairs** NPL asuntos *mpl* exteriores; **Secretary of State for Foreign Affairs** Secretario/a *m/f* de Estado para Asuntos Exteriores ► **foreign affairs correspondent**

N corresponsal *mf* de asuntos exteriores ► **foreign agent** N agente *mf* extranjero/a ► **foreign aid** N (= *aid to other countries*) ayuda *f* al extranjero, ayuda *f* internacional; (= *aid from abroad*) ayuda *f* internacional ► **foreign body** N (*frm*) cuerpo *m* extraño (*frm*) ► **foreign correspondent** N corresponsal *mf* en el extranjero ► **foreign debt** N deuda *f* externa *or* exterior ► **foreign exchange** N (= *currency*) divisas *fpl*; (= *reserves*) reservas *fpl* de divisas; (= *market*) mercado *m* de divisas; (= *system*) cambio *m* de divisas; **tourism is Thailand's biggest earner of ~ exchange** el turismo es la principal fuente de divisas para Tailandia; **on the ~ exchanges** en los mercados de divisas ► **foreign exchange dealer** N agente *mf* de cambio, operador(a) *m/f* cambiario/a *or* de cambio ► **foreign exchange market** N mercado *m* de divisas ► **foreign exchange reserves** NPL reservas *fpl* de divisas ► **foreign exchange trader** N = **foreign exchange dealer** ► **foreign exchange trading** N operaciones *fpl* de cambio (de divisas) ► **foreign investment** N (*from abroad*) inversión *f* extranjera; (*in other countries*) inversión *f* en el extranjero ► **the Foreign Legion** N la legión extranjera ► **Foreign Minister** N Ministro/a *m/f* de Asuntos Exteriores ► **Foreign Ministry** N Ministerio *m* de Asuntos Exteriores ► **foreign national** N ciudadano/a *m/f* extranjero/a ► **the Foreign Office** N (*Brit*) el Ministerio de Asuntos Exteriores ► **foreign policy** N política *f* exterior ► **Foreign Secretary** N (*Brit*) Ministro/a *m/f* de Asuntos Exteriores ► **foreign trade** N comercio *m* exterior

foreigner ['fɒrɪnəʳ] N extranjero/a *m/f*

foreknowledge [fɔː'nɒlɪdʒ] N presciencia *f*, conocimiento *m* previo; **to have ~ of sth** saber algo de antemano

foreland ['fɔːlənd] N cabo *m*, promontorio *m*

foreleg ['fɔːleg] N pata *f* delantera

forelock ['fɔːlɒk] N guedeja *f*; ✦***IDIOMS*** **to take time by the ~** tomar la ocasión por los pelos; **to tug one's ~ to sb** (*Brit*) (*fig*) doblegarse ante algn

foreman ['fɔːmən] N (*pl* **foremen**) [*of workers*] capataz *m*; (*Constr*) maestro *m* de obras; (*Jur*) [*of jury*] presidente/a *m/f* del jurado

foremast ['fɔːmɑːst] N palo *m* trinquete, trinquete *m*

▼ **foremost** ['fɔːməʊst] ADJ (= *outstanding*) más destacado; (= *main, first*) primero, principal; *see also* **first B1**

forename ['fɔːneɪm] N nombre *m*, nombre *m* de pila

forenoon ['fɔːnuːn] N (*esp Scot*) mañana *f*

forensic [fə'rensɪk] ADJ forense; [*medicine*] legal, forense

forepaw ['fɔːpɔː] N [*of cat, lion*] zarpa *f*; [*of dog, wolf*] uña *f*

foreplay ['fɔːpleɪ] N caricias *fpl* estimulantes

forequarters ['fɔːˌkwɔːtəz] NPL cuartos *mpl* delanteros

forerunner ['fɔːˌrʌnəʳ] N precursor(a) *m/f*

foresail ['fɔːseɪl] N trinquete *m*

foresee [fɔː'siː] (*pt* **foresaw**; *pp* **foreseen**) VT prever

foreseeable [fɔː'siːəbl] ADJ [*opportunity*] previsible; **in the ~ future** en un futuro previsible

foreseeably [fɔː'siːəblɪ] ADV previsiblemente

foreshadow [fɔː'ʃædəʊ] VT anunciar, presagiar

foreshore ['fɔːʃɔːʳ] N playa *f* (*entre pleamar y bajamar*)

foreshorten [fɔː'ʃɔːtn] VT escorzar

foreshortening [fɔː'ʃɔːtnɪŋ] N escorzo *m*

foresight ['fɔːsaɪt] N previsión *f*; **to have** *or* **show ~** ser previsor *or* precavido; **he had the ~ to ...** tuvo la precaución de ...; **lack of ~** imprevisión *f*, falta *f* de previsión

foreskin ['fɔːskɪn] N (*Anat*) prepucio *m*

forest ['fɒrɪst] Ⓐ N (*temperate*) bosque *m*; (*tropical*) selva *f*; *see also* **tree**
Ⓑ CPD ► **forest fire** N incendio *m* forestal ► **forest ranger** N guardabosques *mf inv* ► **forest track, forest trail** N camino *m* forestal

forestall [fɔː'stɔːl] VT (= *anticipate*) [+ *event, accident*] prevenir; [+ *rival, competitor*] adelantarse a; (*Comm*) acaparar

forested ['fɒrɪstɪd] ADJ arbolado, de bosques; **densely** *or* **heavily ~** cubierto de bosques; **only eight per cent of Britain is ~** las áreas forestales de Gran Bretaña se reducen al ocho por ciento del territorio

forester ['fɒrɪstəʳ] N (= *expert*) ingeniero/a *m/f* de montes; (= *keeper*) guardabosques *mf inv*

forestry ['fɒrɪstrɪ] Ⓐ N silvicultura *f*; (*Univ*) ingeniería *f* forestal
Ⓑ CPD ► **Forestry Commission** N (*Brit*) ≈ Comisión *f* del Patrimonio Forestal

foretaste ['fɔːteɪst] N anticipo *m*, muestra *f*

foretell [fɔː'tel] (*pt, pp* **foretold**) VT (= *predict*) predecir, pronosticar; (= *forebode*) presagiar

forethought ['fɔːθɔːt] N previsión *f*

forever [fər'evəʳ] ADV 1 (= *eternally*) para siempre; **he's gone ~** se ha ido para siempre
2 (*) (= *incessantly, repeatedly*) constantemente; **she's ~ complaining** se queja constantemente, siempre se está quejando; *see also* **ever 1**

forewarn [fɔː'wɔːn] VT avisar, advertir; **to be ~ed** estar prevenido; ✦***PROV*** **~ed is forearmed** hombre prevenido *or* precavido vale por dos

forewoman ['fɔːˌwʊmən] N (*pl* **forewomen**) (*Jur*) presidenta *f* del jurado; [*of workers*] capataz *f*, capataza *f*

foreword ['fɔːwɜːd] N prefacio *m*, prólogo *m*

forex ['fɔːreks] N (*Fin*) divisas *fpl*

forfeit ['fɔːfɪt] Ⓐ N (*in game*) prenda *f*; (= *fine*) multa *f*
Ⓑ VT [+ *one's rights etc*] perder; (*Jur*) decomisar

forfeiture ['fɔːfɪtʃəʳ] N pérdida *f*

forgather [fɔː'gæðəʳ] VI = **foregather**

forgave [fə'geɪv] PT *of* **forgive**

forge [fɔːdʒ] Ⓐ N (= *furnace*) fragua *f*, forja *f*; [*of blacksmith*] herrería *f*; (= *factory*) fundición *f*
Ⓑ VT 1 (*lit, fig*) fraguar, forjar
2 (= *falsify*) [+ *document, painting etc*] falsificar; **she ~d his signature** falsificó su firma; **~d money** moneda *f* falsa
Ⓒ VI **to ~ ahead** avanzar a grandes pasos; **to ~ ahead of sb** adelantarse a algn

forger ['fɔːdʒəʳ] N falsificador(a) *m/f*

forgery ['fɔːdʒərɪ] N (= *act, thing*) falsificación *f*; **it's a ~** es falso

forget [fə'get] (*pt* **forgot**; *pp* **forgotten**) Ⓐ VT olvidar, olvidarse de; **to ~ to do sth** olvidarse de hacer algo; **I forgot to close the window** me olvidé de *or* se me olvidó cerrar la ventana; **I forgot to tell you why** se me olvidó decirte por qué; **we shouldn't ~ that ...** no debemos olvidar que ...; **never to be forgotten** inolvidable; **~ it!*** (= *don't worry*) ¡no te preocupes!, ¡no importa!; (= *you're welcome*) de nada, no hay de qué; (= *no way*) ¡ni hablar!, ¡ni se te ocurra!; **and don't you ~ it!** ¡y que no se te olvide esto!; **to ~ o.s.** (= *lose self-control*) pasarse, propasarse
Ⓑ VI (*gen*) olvidar; (= *have a bad memory*) tener mala memoria; **I ~** no recuerdo, me he olvidado; **but I forgot** pero se me olvidó; **I'm sorry, I'd completely forgotten!** ¡lo siento, se me había olvidado por completo!; **I forgot all about it** se me olvidó por completo; **if there's no money, you can ~ (all) about the new car** si no hay dinero, puedes olvidarte del nuevo coche; **let's ~ about it!** (*in annoyance*) ¡olvidémoslo!, ¡basta!; (*in forgiveness*) más vale olvidarlo

FORGET

You can use **olvidar** in 3 ways when translating **to forget**: **olvidar**, **olvidarse de** or the impersonal **olvidársele algo a alguien**.

- When **forgetting** is *accidental*, the impersonal construction with **se me**, **se le**, *etc* is the commonest option - it emphasizes the involuntary aspect. Here, the object of **forget** becomes the subject of **olvidar**:

I forgot
Se me olvidó
I've forgotten what you said this morning
Se me ha olvidado lo que dijiste esta mañana
He forgot his briefcase
Se le olvidó el maletín

NOTE: **Olvidarse de** and **olvidar** would be more formal alternatives:

- In other contexts, use either **olvidarse de** or **olvidar**.

Have you forgotten what you promised me?
¿Te has olvidado de *or* ***Has olvidado lo que me prometiste?***
In the end he managed to forget her
Al final consiguió olvidarse de ella *or* ***consiguió olvidarla***
Don't forget me
No te olvides de mí, No me olvides

For further uses and examples, see main entry.

forgetful [fə'getfʊl] ADJ (= *lacking memory*) olvidadizo; (= *absent-minded*) despistado; (= *neglectful*) (*of one's duties etc*) descuidado; **he's terribly ~** es tremendamente despistado, tiene una memoria pésima; **~ of all else** olvidando todo lo demás, sin hacer caso de todo lo demás

forgetfulness [fə'getfʊlnɪs] N olvido *m*, falta *f* de memoria; (= *absentmindedness*) despiste *m*; (= *neglect*) descuido *m*

forget-me-not [fə'getmɪnɒt] N nomeolvides *m inv*

forgettable [fə'getəbl] ADJ poco memorable

forgivable [fə'gɪvəbl] ADJ perdonable

▼ **forgive** [fə'gɪv] (*pt* **forgave**; *pp* **forgiven**) Ⓐ VT [+ *person, fault*] perdonar, disculpar (*esp LAm*); **I ~ you** te perdono; **to ~ sb for doing sth** perdonar a algn por haber hecho algo; **~ me** (= *excuse me*) perdone, con permiso (*LAm*)
Ⓑ VI perdonar; **why don't you just ~ and forget?** intenta perdonar y olvidarte

forgiven [fə'gɪvn] PP *of* **forgive**

forgiveness [fə'gɪvnɪs] N (= *pardon*) perdón *m*; (= *willingness to forgive*) compasión *f*

forgiving [fə'gɪvɪŋ] ADJ [*person, smile*] compasivo; **to feel ~** estar dispuesto a perdonar

forgo [fɔː'gəʊ] (*pt* **forwent**; *pp* **forgone** ['fɔːgɒn]) VT = **forego 1**

forgot [fə'gɒt] PT *of* **forget**

forgotten [fə'gɒtn] PP *of* **forget**

fork [fɔːk] Ⓐ N (*at table*) tenedor *m*; (*Agr*) horca *f*, horquilla *f*; (*in road*) bifurcación *f*; (*in*

➤ LANGUAGE IN USE: **foremost** 26.2, 26.3 **forgive A** 18.1

river) horcajo *m*; [*of tree*] horcadura *f*
Ⓑ VT (*Agr*) (*also* ~ **over**) cargar con la horca
Ⓒ VI [*road*] bifurcarse; **~ right for Oxford** tuerza a la derecha para ir a Oxford

► **fork out*** Ⓐ VT + ADV [+ *money, cash*] aflojar*
Ⓑ VI + ADV pagar

► **fork over** VT + ADV = **fork B**

► **fork up** VT + ADV 1 [+ *soil*] remover con la horquilla
2 (*) = **fork out A**

forked [fɔːkt] ADJ [*tail*] hendido; [*branch*] bifurcado; [*lightning*] en zigzag; [*tongue*] bífido

fork-lift truck [ˈfɔːklɪftˌtrʌk] N carretilla *f* elevadora

forlorn [fəˈlɔːn] ADJ [*person*] triste, melancólico; (= *deserted*) [*cottage*] abandonado; (= *desperate*) [*attempt*] desesperado; **to look ~** tener aspecto triste; **why so ~?** ¿por qué tan triste?; **a ~ hope** una vana esperanza

forlornly [fəˈlɔːnlɪ] ADV tristemente

form [fɔːm] Ⓐ N 1 (= *shape*) forma *f*; (= *figure, shadow*) bulto *m*, silueta *f*; **the same thing in a different ~** lo mismo pero con otra forma; **~ and content** forma *f* y contenido; **in the ~ of** en forma de; **I'm against hunting in any ~** estoy en contra de cualquier forma de caza; **to take ~** concretarse, tomar *or* cobrar forma; **it took the ~ of a cash prize** consistió en un premio en metálico; **what ~ will the ceremony take?** ¿en qué consistirá la ceremonia?
2 (= *kind, type*) clase *f*, tipo *m*; **a new ~ of government** un nuevo sistema de gobierno; **as a ~ of apology** como disculpa
3 (= *way, means*) forma *f*; **in due ~** en la debida forma; **~ of payment** modo *m* de pago; **what's the ~?** ¿qué es lo que hemos de hacer?; **that is common ~** eso es muy corriente
4 (*Sport, also fig*) forma *f*; **to be in good ~** estar en buena forma; **he was in great ~ last night** estaba en plena forma anoche; **to be on ~** estar en forma; **to be out of ~** estar desentrenado; **in top ~** en plena forma; **true to ~** como de costumbre
5 (= *document*) (*gen*) formulario *m*, impreso *m*; **application ~** solicitud *f*; **to fill in** *or* **out a ~** rellenar un formulario *or* un impreso
6 (*Brit frm*) (= *etiquette*) apariencias *fpl*; **for ~'s sake** por pura fórmula, para guardar las apariencias; **it's bad ~** está mal visto; **it's a matter of ~** es una formalidad
7 (= *bench*) banco *m*
8 (*Brit Scol*) curso *m*, clase *f*; **she's in the first ~** está haciendo primer curso de secundaria *or* primero de secundaria
9 (*Brit Racing*) **to study the ~** estudiar resultados anteriores
Ⓑ VT (= *shape, make*) formar; [+ *clay etc*] modelar, moldear; [+ *company*] formar, fundar; [+ *plan*] elaborar, formular; [+ *sentence*] construir; [+ *queue*] hacer; [+ *idea*] concebir, formular; [+ *opinion*] hacerse, formarse; [+ *habit*] crear; **he ~ed it out of clay** lo modeló *or* moldeó en arcilla; **to ~ a government** formar gobierno; **to ~ a group** formar un grupo; **to ~ part of sth** formar parte de algo
Ⓒ VI tomar forma, formarse; **an idea ~ed in his mind** una idea tomó forma en su mente; **how do ideas ~?** ¿cómo se forman las ideas?
Ⓓ CPD ► **form feed** N (*Comput*) salto *m* de página ► **form letter** N (*US*) carta *f* tipo

► **form up** Ⓐ VT + ADV [+ *troops*] formar
Ⓑ VI + ADV alinearse; (*Mil*) formar

formal [ˈfɔːməl] ADJ [*person*] (= *correct*) correcto; (= *reliable, stiff*) formal; (= *solemn*) [*greeting, language, occasion, announcement*] solemne; [*dress*] de etiqueta; [*visit*] de cumplido; (*Pol*) [*visit*] oficial; [*function*] protocolario; [*garden*] simétrico; (= *official*) [*evidence*] documental; [*acceptance*] por escrito; **in English, "residence" is a ~ term** en inglés, "residence" es un término formal; **don't be so ~!** ¡no te andes con tantos cumplidos!; **there was no ~ agreement** no había un acuerdo en firme; **~ clothes** ropa *f* de etiqueta; **a ~ dinner** una cena de gala; **he has no ~ education** no tiene formación académica; **~ training** formación *f* profesional

► LANGUAGE IN USE: **former B** 26.2

formaldehyde [fɔːˈmældɪhaɪd] N formaldehido *m*

formalin, **formaline** [ˈfɔːməlɪn] N formalina *f*

formalism [ˈfɔːməlɪzəm] N formalismo *m*

formalist [ˈfɔːməlɪst] Ⓐ ADJ formalista
Ⓑ N formalista *mf*

formalistic [fɔːməlɪstɪk] ADJ formalista

formality [fɔːˈmælɪtɪ] N 1 [*of occasion*] lo ceremonioso; [*of person*] (= *stiffness*) formalidad *f*; (= *correctness*) corrección *f*; **with all due ~** en la debida forma
2 (= *matter of form*) **it's a mere ~** no es más que una formalidad; **let's dispense with the formalities** prescindamos de las formalidades
3 **formalities** (*bureaucratic*) trámites *mpl*, gestiones *fpl*; **first there are certain formalities** primero hay ciertos requisitos

formalize [ˈfɔːməlaɪz] VT [+ *plan, agreement*] formalizar

formally [ˈfɔːməlɪ] ADV (*gen*) formalmente; (= *officially*) oficialmente; (= *ceremoniously*) con mucha ceremonia; [*dress etc*] de etiqueta; (= *stiffly*) con formalidad

format [ˈfɔːmæt] Ⓐ N formato *m*
Ⓑ VT (*Comput*) formatear
Ⓒ CPD ► **format line** N (*Comput*) línea *f* de formato

formation [fɔːˈmeɪʃən] Ⓐ N (*gen*) formación *f*; **in battle ~** en formación de combate
Ⓑ CPD ► **formation flying** N vuelo *m* en formación

formative [ˈfɔːmətɪv] Ⓐ ADJ 1 [*influence etc*] formativo; [*years*] de formación
2 (*Gram*) formativo
Ⓑ N (*Gram*) formativo *m*

formatting [ˈfɔːmætɪŋ] N formateado *m*, formateo *m*

▼ **former** [ˈfɔːməʳ] Ⓐ ADJ 1 (= *earlier, previous*) antiguo; [*chairman, wife etc*] ex; **a ~ pupil** un antiguo alumno; **in ~ days** antiguamente; **the ~ president** el ex-presidente; → OLD
2 (*of two*) primero; **your ~ idea was better** tu primera idea fue mejor
Ⓑ PRON **night and day, the ~ dark, the latter light** la noche y el día, aquélla oscura y éste lleno de luz

formerly [ˈfɔːməlɪ] ADV antiguamente

Formica® [fɔːˈmaɪkə] N formica® *f*

formic acid [ˌfɔːmɪkˈæsɪd] N ácido *m* fórmico

formidable [ˈfɔːmɪdəbl] ADJ [*person*] formidable; [*opponent*] temible; [*task, challenge, obstacle*] tremendo, impresionante; [*reputation, team, combination, talents*] formidable, extraordinario; **he has a ~ temper** tiene un genio tremendo; **she was a ~ woman** era una mujer formidable *or* que imponía

formidably [ˈfɔːmɪdəblɪ] ADV tremendamente, enormemente

formless [ˈfɔːmlɪs] ADJ informe

formula [ˈfɔːmjʊlə] N (*pl* **formulas** *or* **formulae** [ˈfɔːmjʊliː]) 1 (*gen*) (*Math, Chem etc*) fórmula *f*; **winning ~** fórmula *f* del éxito; **peace ~** fórmula *f* de paz
2 (= *baby milk*) leche *f* en polvo (para bebés), leche *f* maternizada
3 (*Motor Racing*) fórmula *f*; **Formula One** Fórmula *f* uno; **a ~-one car** un coche de Fórmula uno

formulaic [ˌfɔːmjʊˈleɪɪk] ADJ formulaico, formulario

formulate [ˈfɔːmjʊleɪt] VT [+ *theory, policy*] formular

formulation [ˌfɔːmjʊˈleɪʃən] N (= *act*) [*of idea, theory, policy*] formulación *f*; (= *medicine*) fórmula *f*; (= *form of words*) formulación *f*

fornicate [ˈfɔːnɪkeɪt] VI (*frm*) fornicar

fornication [ˌfɔːnɪˈkeɪʃən] N (*frm*) fornicación *f*

forsake [fəˈseɪk] (*pt* **forsook**; *pp* **forsaken**) VT (= *abandon*) abandonar; (= *give up*) [+ *plan*] renunciar a; [+ *belief*] renegar de

forsaken [fəˈseɪkən] PP *of* **forsake**

forsook [fəˈsʊk] PT *of* **forsake**

forsooth [fəˈsuːθ] (†† *or hum*) Ⓐ ADV en verdad
Ⓑ EXCL **~!** ¡caramba!

forswear [fɔːˈswɛəʳ] (*pt* **forswore**; *pp* **forsworn**) VT (*frm*) abjurar de, renunciar a; **to ~ o.s.** (= *perjure o.s.*) perjurarse

forsythia [fɔːˈsaɪθɪə] N forsitia *f*

fort [fɔːt] Ⓐ N (*Mil*) fortaleza *f*, fuerte *m*; ✦ *IDIOM* **to hold the ~** quedarse a cargo; **hold the ~ till I get back** hazte cargo hasta que yo regrese
Ⓑ CPD ► **Fort Knox** N *lugar donde se guardan las reservas de oro de EE.UU.*; **they've turned their house into Fort Knox** (*fig*) han convertido su casa en un búnker

forte [ˈfɔːtɪ] (*US*) [fɔːt] N (= *strong point*) fuerte *m*; (*Mus*) forte *m*

forth [fɔːθ]

When **forth** *is an element in a phrasal verb, eg* **pour forth, venture forth,** *look up the verb.*

ADV 1 (†) (= *onward*) adelante; **to go ~** marcharse; **from this day ~** de hoy en adelante; *see also* **back**
2 **and so ~** etcétera, y así sucesivamente

forthcoming [fɔːθˈkʌmɪŋ] ADJ 1 (= *future*) [*event, election*] próximo; [*weeks, months*] venidero; [*book*] de próxima publicación; [*film*] de próximo estreno; [*album*] de próxima aparición; **their ~ marriage** su próximo enlace; **"~ titles"** "libros *mpl* en preparación"
2 (= *available*) **no explanation was ~** no dieron ninguna explicación; **he shot her a desperate look but no help was ~** le lanzó una mirada de desesperación pero no obtuvo ninguna ayuda; **no answer was ~** no hubo respuesta; **if funds are ~** si nos facilitan fondos
3 (= *open*) [*person*] comunicativo; **he's not ~ with strangers** no es muy comunicativo *or* abierto con los desconocidos; **you could have been more ~ with information** podrías haber sido más generoso con la información; **to be ~ about** *or* **on sth** mostrarse comunicativo con respecto a algo; **he wasn't very ~ about it** dijo poco sobre el asunto, se mostró poco comunicativo al respecto

forthright [ˈfɔːθraɪt] ADJ [*person, answer etc*] franco, directo

forthwith [ˈfɔːθˈwɪθ] ADV (*frm*) en el acto, de inmediato

fortieth [ˈfɔːtɪɪθ] Ⓐ ADJ cuadragésimo; **the ~ anniversary** el cuarenta aniversario
Ⓑ N 1 (*in series*) cuadragésimo/a *m/f*
2 (= *fraction*) cuarentavo *m*, cuadragésima parte *f*; *see* **fifth** *for usage*

fortification [ˌfɔːtɪfɪˈkeɪʃən] N (= *act, means of defence*) fortificación *f*

fortify [ˈfɔːtɪfaɪ] VT [1] (*Mil*) fortificar; (= *strengthen*) fortalecer
[2] (*fig*) [+ *person*] fortalecer; **to ~ sb in a belief** confirmar la opinión que tiene algn; **to ~ o.s.** fortalecerse
[3] (= *enrich*) [+ *food*] enriquecer; [+ *wine*] encabezar; **fortified wine** vino *m* encabezado

fortitude [ˈfɔːtɪtjuːd] N fortaleza *f*, valor *m*

fortnight [ˈfɔːtnaɪt] N (*Brit*) quince días *mpl*, quincena *f*; **a ~ (from) today** de hoy en quince días

fortnightly [ˈfɔːtnaɪtlɪ] (*Brit*) Ⓐ ADJ quincenal
Ⓑ ADV quincenalmente, cada quince días

FORTRAN [ˈfɔːtræn] N ABBR (*Comput*) (= **formula translator**) FORTRAN *m*

fortress [ˈfɔːtrɪs] N fortaleza *f*, plaza *f* fuerte

fortuitous [fɔːˈtjuːɪtəs] ADJ fortuito, casual

fortuitously [fɔːˈtjuːɪtəslɪ] ADV fortuitamente, por casualidad

fortunate [ˈfɔːtʃənɪt] ADJ [*person, occurrence*] afortunado; [*coincidence*] feliz; **those less ~ than ourselves** los menos afortunados; **he is ~ in having no dependents to worry about** tiene suerte de no tener personas a su cargo por las que preocuparse; **I was ~ enough to escape** yo tuve la suerte de poder escaparme; **that was ~ for you** en eso tuviste suerte; **how ~!** ¡qué suerte!; **it was ~ that no one was injured** fue una suerte que nadie resultara herido

fortunately [ˈfɔːtʃənɪtlɪ] ADV afortunadamente, por suerte

fortune [ˈfɔːtʃən] Ⓐ N [1] (= *luck*) fortuna *f*, suerte *f*; **by good ~** por fortuna; **we had the good ~ to find him** tuvimos la suerte de encontrarlo; **the ~s of war** las vicisitudes *or* las peripecias de la guerra; **he restored the company's ~s** restableció la prosperidad de la empresa, devolvió el éxito a la compañía; **to seek one's ~ elsewhere** buscar fortuna en otro lugar; **to try one's ~** probar fortuna
[2] (= *fate*) suerte *f*, destino *m*; **to tell sb's ~** decir a algn la buenaventura
[3] (= *property, wealth*) fortuna *f*; **to come into a ~** heredar una fortuna; **to marry a ~** casarse con un hombre/una mujer acaudalado/a
[4] (= *huge amount of money*) dineral *m*, platal *m* (*LAm**); **to cost a ~** costar un ojo de la cara*, valer un dineral; **to make a ~** enriquecerse, ganar un dineral; **a small ~** un montón de dinero, un dineral
Ⓑ CPD ► **fortune cookie** N (*esp US*) *galleta china con un mensaje sobre la suerte* ► **fortune hunter** N cazafortunas *mf inv*

fortune-teller [ˈfɔːtʃənˌteləʳ] N adivino/a *m/f*

fortune-telling [ˈfɔːtʃənˌtelɪŋ] N adivinación *f*

forty [ˈfɔːtɪ] Ⓐ ADJ cuarenta; ♦***IDIOM*** **to have ~ winks*** echar un sueñecito
Ⓑ N cuarenta *m*; **the forties** (= *1940s*) los años cuarenta; **to be in one's forties** tener más de cuarenta años, ser cuarentón; *see* **also fifty** *for usage*

fortyish [ˈfɔːtɪɪʃ] ADJ de unos cuarenta años

forum [ˈfɔːrəm] N (*pl* **forums** *or* **fora** [ˈfɔːrə]) foro *m*; (*fig*) tribunal *m*, foro *m*

forward

When **forward** *is an element in a phrasal verb, eg* **bring forward, come forward, step forward,** *look up the verb.*

[ˈfɔːwəd] Ⓐ ADJ [1] (*in position*) delantero; (*in movement*) hacia adelante; (*in time*) adelantado, avanzado; [*position*] (*Mil etc*) avanzado; (*Naut*) de proa
[2] (= *advanced*) [*child*] precoz; [*season, crop*] adelantado
[3] (= *presumptuous*) [*person, remark*] atrevido
Ⓑ ADV (*gen*) adelante, hacia adelante; (*Naut*) hacia la proa; **~!** ¡adelante!; **~ march!** (*Mil*) de frente ¡mar!; **the lever is placed well ~** la palanca está colocada bastante hacia adelante; **from that day ~** desde ese día en adelante, a partir de entonces; **from this time ~** de aquí en adelante; **to come ~** hacerse conocer; **to go ~** ir hacia adelante, avanzar; (*fig*) progresar, hacer progresos; *see also* **look forward**
Ⓒ N (*Sport*) delantero/a *m/f*
Ⓓ VT [1] (= *dispatch*) [+ *goods*] expedir, enviar; (= *send on*) [+ *letter*] remitir; **"please ~"** "remítase al destinatario"
[2] (= *advance*) [+ *career, cause, interests*] promover
Ⓔ CPD ► **forward buying** N (*Comm*) compra *f* a término ► **forward contract** N (*Comm*) contrato *m* a término ► **forward delivery** N (*Comm*) entrega *f* en fecha futura ► **forward exchange** N (*Comm*) cambio *m* a término ► **forward gear** N (*Aut*) marcha *f* de avance ► **forward line** N (*Sport*) delantera *f*; (*Mil*) primera línea *f* de fuego ► **forward market** N (*Comm*) mercado *m* de futuros ► **forward pass** N (*Rugby*) pase *m* adelantado ► **forward planning** N planificación *f* por anticipado ► **forward rate** N (*Comm*) tipo *m* a término ► **forward sales** NPL (*Comm*) ventas *fpl* a término

forwarding [ˈfɔːwədɪŋ] Ⓐ N [*of letter, luggage*] envío *m*
Ⓑ CPD ► **forwarding address** N destinatario *m*; **she left no ~ address** no dejó dirección (a la que mandarle el correo) ► **forwarding agent** N agente *mf* de tránsito

forward-looking [ˈfɔːwədˌlʊkɪŋ] ADJ [*plan, policy*] con miras al futuro; [*person*] previsor; (*Pol*) progresista

forwardness [ˈfɔːwədnɪs] N [1] (= *boldness*) atrevimiento *m*, frescura *f*, descaro *m*
[2] [*of crop etc*] precocidad *f*

forwards [ˈfɔːwədz] ADV (*esp Brit*) = **forward B**

forward-thinking [ˈfɔːwədˌθɪŋkɪŋ] ADJ de criterio avanzado; (*Pol*) progresista

forwent [fɔːˈwent] PT *of* **forgo**

Fosbury flop [ˈfɒzbərɪˌflɒp] N (*Sport*) fosbury-flop *m*

fossil [ˈfɒsl] Ⓐ N fósil *m*
Ⓑ CPD fósil ► **fossil fuel** N hidrocarburo *m*

fossilization [ˌfɒsɪlaɪˈzeɪʃən] N fosilización *f*

fossilized [ˈfɒsɪlaɪzd] ADJ fosilizado

foster [ˈfɒstəʳ] Ⓐ VT [1] [+ *child*] acoger
[2] (= *encourage*) fomentar, promover; (= *aid*) favorecer; [+ *hope*] alentar
Ⓑ CPD [*parent, child*] de acogida ► **foster brother** N hermano *m* de leche ► **foster home** N casa *f* de acogida ► **foster mother** N madre *f* de acogida; (= *wet nurse*) ama *f* de leche

fosterage [ˈfɒstərɪdʒ] N = **fostering**

fostering [ˈfɒstərɪŋ] N acogimiento *m* familiar

fought [fɔːt] PT, PP *of* **fight**

foul [faʊl] Ⓐ ADJ (*compar* **fouler**, *superl* **foulest**)
[1] (= *disgusting*) [*place*] asqueroso; [*smell*] pestilente, fétido; [*taste*] repugnante, asqueroso
[2] (= *bad*) [*water*] sucio, contaminado; [*air*] viciado; [*breath*] fétido
[3] (*) (= *nasty*) [*weather*] de perros*, malísimo; **it's a ~ day** hace un día de perros*, hace un día malísimo; **I've had a ~ day** he tenido un día malísimo, he tenido un día de perros*; **he was in a ~ mood** estaba de un humor de perros*; **you were ~ to me yesterday** ayer te portaste fatal conmigo*; **she has a ~ temper** tiene muy malas pulgas*, tiene un genio de mil demonios*
[4] (= *obscene*) ordinario, grosero; **to use ~ language** decir groserías; ♦***IDIOM*** **to have a ~ mouth*** ser mal hablado
[5] (= *base, immoral*) [*lie, calumny, crime*] vil, terrible
[6] (*Sport*) [*shot, ball*] nulo; [*blow, tackle*] sucio; [*kick*] antirreglamentario
[7] (*in phrases*) **someone is sure to cry ~** es seguro que alguien dice que no hemos jugado limpio; **to fall ~ of sb** ponerse a malas con algn; **to fall ~ of the law** enfrentarse con la justicia, vérselas con la ley*
Ⓑ N (*Sport*) falta *f* (**on** contra)
Ⓒ VT [1] (= *pollute*) [+ *air*] viciar, contaminar; [+ *water*] contaminar; (= *dirty*) ensuciar; **the dog ~ed the pavement** el perro ensució la acera
[2] (*Sport*) [+ *opponent*] cometer una falta contra
[3] (= *entangle*) [+ *fishing line, net, rope*] enredar; **something had ~ed the propellers** algo se había enredado en las hélices; **the boat had ~ed her anchor** el ancla del barco se había atascado
[4] (= *block*) [+ *pipe*] atascar, obstruir
[5] (*Naut*) (= *hit*) chocar contra
Ⓓ VI [1] (*Sport*) cometer faltas
[2] (= *become entangled*) [*fishing line, rope, nets*] enredarse
Ⓔ CPD ► **foul play** N (*Sport*) jugada *f* antirreglamentaria, juego *m* sucio; **the police suspect ~ play** (*Jur*) la policía sospecha que se trata de un crimen

► **foul up*** Ⓐ VT + ADV [1] (= *spoil*) [+ *activity, event, plans*] dar al traste con, echar a perder; **it's the little things that can ~ up your plans** los detalles son los que pueden dar al traste con *or* echar a perder los planes de uno
[2] (= *make a mess of*) **he has ~ed up his exams** los exámenes le han ido mal, ha metido la pata en los exámenes*
Ⓑ VI + ADV meter la pata*

foulmouthed [ˈfaʊlˈmaʊðd] ADJ malhablado

foul-smelling [ˈfaʊlˈsmelɪŋ] ADJ pestilente, fétido

foul-tempered [ˈfaʊlˈtempəd] ADJ **to be ~** (*habitually*) tener un genio de mil demonios*; (*on one occasion*) estar de mal humor, estar de un humor de perros*

foul-up* [ˈfaʊlʌp] N desastre *m*

foul-weather gear [ˌfaʊlweðəˈgɪəʳ] N impermeables *mpl*

found¹ [faʊnd] PT, PP *of* **find**

found² [faʊnd] VT [+ *town, school etc*] fundar; [+ *opinion, belief*] fundamentar, basar (**on** en); **a statement ~ed on fact** una declaración basada en los hechos

found³ [faʊnd] VT (*Tech*) fundir

foundation [faʊnˈdeɪʃən] Ⓐ N [1] (= *act*) fundación *f*, establecimiento *m*
[2] (*fig*) (= *basis*) fundamento *m*, base *f*; **the story is without ~** la historia carece de fundamento
[3] **foundations** (*Archit*) cimientos *mpl*; **to lay the ~s** (*also fig*) echar los cimientos (**of** de)
[4] (= *organization*) fundación *f*
[5] (= *make-up*) maquillaje *m* de fondo, base *f*
Ⓑ CPD ► **foundation course** N curso *m* preparatorio ► **foundation cream** N crema *f* de base ► **foundation garment** N corsé *m*

► **foundation stone** N (*Brit*) primera piedra *f*; (*fig*) piedra *f* angular

founder[1] ['faʊndəʳ] Ⓐ N (= *originator*) fundador(a) *m/f*
Ⓑ CPD ► **founder member** N (*Brit*) miembro *mf* fundador(a)

founder[2] ['faʊndəʳ] VI (*Naut*) hundirse, irse a pique; (*fig*) fracasar (**on** debido a)

founding ['faʊndɪŋ] Ⓐ N fundación *f*
Ⓑ CPD ► **founding fathers** NPL fundadores *mpl*, próceres *mpl* (*LAm*) ► **Founding Fathers** NPL (*US Hist*) Padres *mpl* Fundadores

foundling ['faʊndlɪŋ] Ⓐ N niño/a *m/f* expósito/a, inclusero/a *m/f*
Ⓑ CPD ► **foundling hospital** N inclusa *f*

foundry ['faʊndrɪ] N fundición *f*, fundidora *f* (*LAm*)

fount [faʊnt] N [1] (*poet*) (= *source*) fuente *f*, manantial *m*; **~ of knowledge/wisdom** fuente *f* de sabiduría
[2] (*Brit Typ*) fundición *f*

fountain ['faʊntɪn] Ⓐ N (*natural*) (*also fig*) fuente *f*, manantial *m*; (*artificial*) fuente *f*, surtidor *m*; (= *jet*) chorro *m*; **drinking ~** fuente *f* (de agua potable)
Ⓑ CPD ► **fountain pen** N estilográfica *f*, plumafuente *f* (*LAm*)

fountainhead ['faʊntɪnhed] N fuente *f*, origen *m*; **to go to the ~** acudir a la propia fuente

four [fɔːʳ] Ⓐ ADJ cuatro; *see also* **corner A2**
Ⓑ N [1] cuatro *m*; **to form ~s** formar a cuatro, dividirse en grupos de cuatro; **to make up a ~ for bridge** completar los cuatro para jugar al bridge
[2] **on all ~s** a gatas; **to go on all ~s** ir a gatas; *see* **five** *for usage*

four-colour, **four-color** (*US*) ['fɔː,kʌləʳ] Ⓐ ADJ a cuatro colores
Ⓑ CPD ► **four-colour (printing) process** N cuatricromía *f*

four-cycle ['fɔː,saɪkl] ADJ (*US*) = **four-stroke**

four-door ['fɔː'dɔːʳ] ADJ [*car*] de cuatro puertas

four-engined ['fɔːr'endʒɪnd] ADJ cuatrimotor, tetramotor

four-eyes‡ ['fɔːraɪz] N cuatrojos* *mf inv*

four-figure [,fɔː'fɪgəʳ] ADJ [*number*] de cuatro cifras; **~ sum** cantidad *f* de 1000 libras o más

fourflusher* ['fɔː'flʌʃəʳ] N (*US*) embustero/a *m/f*

fourfold ['fɔːfəʊld] Ⓐ ADJ cuádruple
Ⓑ ADV cuatro veces

four-footed ['fɔː'fʊtɪd] ADJ cuadrúpedo

four-four time [,fɔːfɔː'taɪm] N (*Mus*) compás *m* de cuatro por cuatro

four-handed [,fɔː'hændɪd] ADJ (*Cards*) de cuatro jugadores

four-legged [,fɔː'legɪd] ADJ [*animal*] cuadrúpedo; **our ~ friends** (*hum*) nuestros amigos cuadrúpedos (*hum*)

four-letter word [,fɔːletə'wɜːd] N palabrota *f*, taco *m*, grosería *f*

four-minute [,fɔː'mɪnɪt] ADJ **a ~ egg** un huevo pasado cuatro minutos; **he was the first to run a ~ mile** fue el primero en correr una milla en cuatro minutos

four-part ['fɔːpɑːt] ADJ [*song*] para cuatro voces; **to sing in ~ harmony** cantar a cuatro voces

four-ply ['fɔːplaɪ] ADJ [*wood*] de cuatro capas; [*wool*] de cuatro hebras

four-poster ['fɔː,pəʊstəʳ] N (*also* **~ bed**) cama *f* de columnas

fourscore† ['fɔː'skɔːʳ] ADJ ochenta

four-seater [,fɔː'siːtəʳ] N coche *m* con cuatro asientos

foursome ['fɔːsəm] N grupo *m* de cuatro

foursquare ['fɔːskweəʳ] Ⓐ ADJ (= *firm*) firme; (= *forthright*) franco, sincero
Ⓑ ADV **to stand ~ behind sb** respaldar completamente a algn

four-star ['fɔːstɑːʳ] Ⓐ ADJ [*hotel*] de cuatro estrellas
Ⓑ CPD ► **four-star petrol** N (*Brit*) ≈ gasolina *f* súper

four-stroke ['fɔːstrəʊk] ADJ (*Aut*) de cuatro tiempos

fourteen ['fɔː'tiːn] Ⓐ ADJ catorce
Ⓑ N catorce *m*; *see* **five** *for usage*

fourteenth ['fɔː'tiːnθ] Ⓐ ADJ decimocuarto
Ⓑ N [1] (*in series*) decimocuarto/a *m/f*
[2] (= *fraction*) catorceavo *m*, catorceava parte *f*; *see* **fifth** *for usage*

fourth [fɔːθ] Ⓐ ADJ cuarto
Ⓑ N [1] (*in series*) cuarto/a *m/f*; **the Fourth of July** (*US*) el cuatro de julio
[2] (*US*) (= *fraction*) cuarto *m*, cuarta parte *f*
[3] (*Aut*) (*also* **~ gear**) cuarta *f* (velocidad)
[4] (*Mus*) cuarta *f*
Ⓒ CPD ► **fourth dimension** N cuarta dimensión *f* ► **the fourth estate** N (*hum*) el cuarto poder, la prensa ► **fourth note** N (*US Mus*) cuarta *f*; *see* **fifth** *for usage*

FOURTH OF JULY

*El 4 de julio, Día de la Independencia (***Independence Day***), es la fiesta nacional más importante de Estados Unidos y se celebra para conmemorar el aniversario de la Declaración de Independencia en 1776. Como una auténtica fiesta de cumpleaños del país, las celebraciones presentan un marcado carácter patriótico y la bandera nacional ondea en las casas de muchos norteamericanos, a la vez que tienen lugar acontecimientos públicos por todo el país, con fuegos artificiales, desfiles y comidas en el campo.*

fourthly ['fɔːθlɪ] ADV en cuarto lugar

fourth-rate ['fɔːθ'reɪt] ADJ de cuarta categoría

four-wheel drive [,fɔːwiːl'draɪv] N (= *system*) tracción *f* de cuatro por cuatro, tracción *f* a las cuatro ruedas; (= *car*) todoterreno *m inv*

fowl [faʊl] Ⓐ N [1] (= *hens etc*) (*collective n*) aves *fpl* de corral; (= *one bird*) ave *f* de corral; (*served as food*) ave *f*
[2] (††) (= *bird in general*) ave *f*; **the ~s of the air** las aves
Ⓑ CPD ► **fowl pest** N peste *f* aviar

fowling-piece ['faʊlɪŋ,piːs] N escopeta *f*

fox [fɒks] Ⓐ N [1] (= *dog fox*) zorro *m*; (= *female fox*) zorra *f*
[2] (*fig*) (= *cunning person*) zorro *m*; **he's an old ~** es un viejo zorro
Ⓑ VT (*esp Brit*) (= *deceive*) engañar; (= *puzzle*) dejar perplejo a; **this will ~ them** esto los despistará; **you had me completely ~ed there** eso me tuvo completamente despistado
Ⓒ CPD ► **fox cub** N cachorro *m* (de zorro) ► **fox fur** N piel *f* de zorro ► **fox terrier** N foxterrier *m*, perro *m* raposero *or* zorrero

foxed [fɒkst] ADJ [*book*] manchado

foxglove ['fɒksglʌv] N dedalera *f*

foxhole ['fɒkshəʊl] N madriguera *f* de zorro; (*Mil*) hoyo *m* de protección

foxhound ['fɒkshaʊnd] N perro *m* raposero

foxhunt ['fɒkshʌnt] N cacería *f* de zorro

foxhunting ['fɒks,hʌntɪŋ] N caza *f* del zorro; **to go ~** ir a cazar zorros

foxtrot ['fɒkstrɒt] N fox *m inv*, foxtrot *m*

foxy ['fɒksɪ] ADJ [1] (= *crafty*) astuto
[2] (*esp US**) [*woman*] sexy

foyer ['fɔɪeɪ] N vestíbulo *m*

FP ABBR [1] (*US*) (= **fireplug**) boca *f* de incendio
[2] (*Brit*) = **former pupil**

FPA N ABBR (*Brit*) = **Family Planning Association**

Fr ABBR (*Rel*) [1] (= **Father**) P., P.ᵉ
[2] (= **Friar**) Fr.

fr. ABBR (= **franc(s)**) fr(s).

fracas ['frækɑː] N gresca *f*, reyerta *f*

fractal ['fræktəl] (*Geom*) Ⓐ ADJ fractal
Ⓑ N fractal *m*
Ⓒ CPD ► **fractal geometry** N geometría *f* fractal

fraction ['frækʃən] N [1] (*Math*) fracción *f*, quebrado *m*
[2] (*fig*) pequeña porción *f*, parte *f* muy pequeña; **move it just a ~** muévelo un poquito; **for a ~ of a second** por un instante

fractional ['frækʃənl] ADJ fraccionario; (*fig*) muy pequeño

fractionally ['frækʃnəlɪ] ADV mínimamente

fractious ['frækʃəs] ADJ (= *irritable*) irritable; (= *unruly*) díscolo

fracture ['fræktʃəʳ] Ⓐ N (*Med*) (*gen*) fractura *f*
Ⓑ VT fracturar; **to ~ one's arm** fracturarse el brazo
Ⓒ VI fracturarse

fragile ['frædʒaɪl] ADJ [1] (= *easily broken*) [*glass, china, object*] frágil; **"fragile, handle with care"** "cuidado, frágil"
[2] (= *delicate, fine*) [*plant, beauty, person*] delicado
[3] (= *frail*) [*person*] débil; [*health*] delicado, precario; **I'm feeling rather ~ this morning** (*esp hum*) me siento un poco pachucho esta mañana*
[4] (= *unstable*) [*peace, democracy, relationship*] precario, frágil; **the ~ state of the economy** el precario *or* frágil estado de la economía

fragility [frə'dʒɪlɪtɪ] N [1] (= *breakable nature*) [*of object*] fragilidad *f*
[2] (= *delicacy, fineness*) [*of plant, beauty, person*] delicadeza *f*
[3] (= *frailty*) [*of person*] debilidad *f*; [*of health*] precariedad *f*
[4] (= *instability*) [*of relationship*] fragilidad *f*, precariedad *f*

fragment Ⓐ ['frægmənt] N fragmento *m*
Ⓑ [fræg'ment] VT fragmentar
Ⓒ [fræg'ment] VI [*alliance, group*] fragmentarse; [*glass, china*] hacerse añicos

fragmentary [fræg'mentərɪ] ADJ [*evidence, account*] fragmentario

fragmentation [,frægmen'teɪʃən] Ⓐ N fragmentación *f*
Ⓑ CPD ► **fragmentation grenade** N granada *f* de fragmentación

fragmented [fræg'mentɪd] ADJ fragmentado

fragrance ['freɪgrəns] N (= *smell*) fragancia *f*; (= *perfume*) perfume *m*

fragrant ['freɪgrənt] ADJ fragante, oloroso; (*fig*) [*memory*] dulce

frail [freɪl] ADJ (*compar* **frailer**; *superl* **frailest**) [*person*] débil; [*health*] delicado, frágil; [*chair etc*] frágil; (*fig*) [*hope*] leve; [*relationship*] frágil

frailty ['freɪltɪ] N [*of person*] debilidad *f*; [*of health*] lo delicado, fragilidad *f*; [*of happiness*] lo efímero; [*of character*] flaqueza *f*

frame [freɪm] Ⓐ N [1] (= *framework*) [*of ship, building etc*] armazón *m or f*, estructura *f*; [*of furniture etc*] armadura *f*; [*of spectacles*] montura *f*; [*of bicycle*] cuadro *m*

2 (= *border*) [*of picture, window, door*] marco *m*; (*Sew*) tambor *m*, bastidor *m* para bordar
3 (*TV, Video*) cuadro *m*; (*Cine*) fotograma *m*
4 (= *body*) cuerpo *m*; **his large ~** su cuerpo fornido; **her whole ~ was shaken by sobs** todo su cuerpo se estremecía por los sollozos
5 (*fig*) **~ of mind** estado *m* de ánimo; **when you're in a better ~ of mind** cuando estés de mejor humor; **~ of reference** marco *m* de referencia
(B) VT 1 [+ *picture*] enmarcar, poner un marco a
2 (= *enclose*) enmarcar; (*Phot*) [+ *subject*] encuadrar; **he appeared ~d in the doorway** apareció en el marco de la puerta; **she was ~d against the sunset** el ocaso le servía de marco, tenía la puesta de sol de fondo
3 (= *formulate*) [+ *plan etc*] formular, elaborar; [+ *question*] formular; [+ *sentence*] construir
4 (*) [+ *innocent person*] **to ~ sb** tender una trampa a algn para incriminarlo; **I've been ~d!** ¡me han tendido una trampa!
(C) CPD ► **frame house** N (*US*) casa *f* de madera ► **frame rucksack** N mochila *f* con armazón

framer ['freɪmə'] N (*also* **picture ~**) fabricante *mf* de marcos

frame-up* ['freɪmʌp] N trampa *f*, montaje *m* (para incriminar a algn); **it's a ~** aquí hay trampa, esto es un montaje

framework ['freɪmwɜ:k] (A) N 1 (*lit*) armazón *m or f*, estructura *f*
2 (*fig*) [*of essay, society*] marco *m*; **within the ~ of the constitution** dentro del marco de la constitución
(B) CPD ► **framework agreement** N (*Ind, Pol*) acuerdo *m* marco

framing ['freɪmɪŋ] N 1 (*also* **picture ~**) enmarcado *m*
2 (*Art, Phot*) encuadrado *m*

Fran [fræn] N (*familiar form*) *of* **Frances**

franc [fræŋk] N franco *m*

France [frɑ:ns] N Francia *f*

Frances ['frɑ:nsɪs] N Francisca

franchise ['fræntʃaɪz] (A) N 1 (*Pol*) sufragio *m*
2 (*Comm*) concesión *f*, franquicia *f*
(B) VT (*Comm*) otorgar la concesión de, franquiciar
(C) CPD ► **franchise holder** N franquiciado/a *m/f*, concesionario/a *m/f*

franchisee [ˌfræntʃaɪ'zi:] N franquiciado/a *m/f*, concesionario/a *m/f*

franchising ['fræntʃaɪzɪŋ] N franquiciamiento *m*

franchisor [ˌfræntʃaɪ'zɔ:'] N franquiciador(a) *m/f*, (compañía *f*) concesionaria *f*

Francis ['frɑ:nsɪs] N Francisco

Franciscan [fræn'sɪskən] (A) ADJ franciscano
(B) N franciscano/a *m/f*

francium ['frænsɪəm] N francio *m*

Franco- ['fræŋkəʊ] PREFIX franco-; **~British** franco-británico

franco invoice [ˌfræŋkəʊ'ɪnvɔɪs] N (*Comm*) factura *f* franca

francophile ['fræŋkəʊfaɪl] N francófilo/a *m/f*

francophobe ['fræŋkəʊfəʊb] N francófobo/a *m/f*

frangipane ['frændʒɪpeɪn] N, **frangipani** [ˌfrændʒɪ'pɑ:nɪ] N (*pl* **frangipanis** *or* **frangipani**) (= *perfume, pastry*) frangipani *m*; (= *shrub*) flor *f* de cebo, frangipani *m* blanco, jazmín *m* de las Antillas

franglais [frã'glɛ] N (*hum*) franglés *m*

Frank¹ [fræŋk] N (*Hist*) franco/a *m/f*

Frank² [fræŋk] N (*familiar form*) *of* **Francis**

frank¹ [fræŋk] ADJ (*compar* **franker**, *superl* **frankest**) franco; **to be ~ (with you)** para serte franco, sinceramente

frank² [fræŋk] VT [+ *letter*] franquear

frank³* (*US*) [fræŋk] = **frankfurter**

Frankenstein ['fræŋkənstaɪn] N Frankenstein

frankfurter ['fræŋkˌfɜ:tə'] N salchicha *f* de Frankfurt

frankincense ['fræŋkɪnsens] N incienso *m*

franking machine ['fræŋkɪŋmə'ʃi:n] N (máquina *f*) franqueadora *f*

Frankish ['fræŋkɪʃ] (A) ADJ (*Hist*) fráncico
(B) N (*Ling*) fráncico *m*

frankly ['fræŋklɪ] ADV francamente

frankness ['fræŋknɪs] N franqueza *f*, sinceridad *f*

frantic ['fræntɪk] ADJ [*activity, pace*] frenético; (= *desperate*) [*need, desire, person*] desesperado; **she was ~ with worry** estaba loca de inquietud; **to drive sb ~** sacar a algn de quicio

frantically ['fræntɪkəlɪ] ADV frenéticamente, con frenesí

frat* [fræt] N (*US Univ*) = **fraternity**, → SORORITY/FRATERNITY

fraternal [frə'tɜ:nl] ADJ fraterno

fraternity [frə'tɜ:nɪtɪ] N 1 (= *comradeship*) fraternidad *f*
2 (*US Univ*) círculo *m* estudiantil
3 (= *organization*) hermandad *f*; **the criminal ~** el mundo del hampa; **the yachting ~** los aficionados a la vela; → SORORITY/FRATERNITY

fraternization [ˌfrætənaɪ'zeɪʃən] N fraternización *f*

fraternize ['frætənaɪz] VI (*esp Mil*) confraternizar (**with** con)

fratricide ['frætrɪsaɪd] N 1 (= *act*) fratricidio *m*
2 (= *person*) fratricida *mf*

fraud [frɔ:d] (A) N 1 (*Jur*) fraude *m*
2 (= *trickery*) estafa *f*; (= *trick, con*) engaño *m*, timo *m*
3 (= *person*) impostor(a) *m/f*, farsante *mf*
(B) CPD ► **fraud squad** N brigada *f* de delitos económicos, brigada *f* anticorrupción

fraudster* ['frɔ:dstə'] N defraudador(a) *m/f*

fraudulence ['frɔ:djʊləns] N fraudulencia *f*, fraude *m*

fraudulent ['frɔ:djʊlənt] (A) ADJ fraudulento
(B) CPD ► **fraudulent conversion** N (*Jur*) apropiación *f* ilícita

fraught [frɔ:t] ADJ 1 (= *tense*) tenso; **things got a bit ~** la situación se puso difícil
2 **to be ~ with** [+ *tension*] estar cargado de; [+ *problems*] estar lleno de; **to be ~ with danger** ser peligrosísimo

fray¹ [freɪ] N (= *fight*) combate *m*, lucha *f*; **to be ready for the ~** (*lit, fig*) estar dispuesto a pelear; **to enter the ~** (*fig*) entrar en acción *or* en liza

fray² [freɪ] (A) VI 1 [*cloth, garment, cuff*] deshilacharse; [*rope*] desgastarse
2 (*fig*) **tempers ~ed in the discussion that followed** los ánimos se caldearon en la discusión que siguió
(B) VT 1 [+ *cloth, garment, cuff*] deshilachar, raer; [+ *rope*] desgastar
2 [+ *nerves*] crispar; **the constant tapping was beginning to ~ my nerves** el constante repiqueteo me estaba empezando a crispar los nervios

frayed [freɪd] ADJ 1 [*cloth, garment, cuff,*] deshilachado, raído; [*rope*] desgastado
2 [*nerves*] crispado; **tempers were getting ~** los ánimos se estaban caldeando, la gente estaba perdiendo la paciencia
3 [*person*] (= *strained*) tenso; **he's beginning to look a bit ~ around the edges** (*fig*) ya se le empiezan a notar los años

frazzle* ['fræzl] (A) N **it was burned to a ~** quedó carbonizado; **to beat sb to a ~** (*Sport*) dar una soberana paliza a algn*; **to be worn to a ~** estar hecho un trapo *or* migas*
(B) VT (*US*) agotar, rendir

FRB N ABBR (*US*) = **Federal Reserve Bank**

FRCM N ABBR (*Brit*) = **Fellow of the Royal College of Music**

FRCO N ABBR (*Brit*) = **Fellow of the Royal College of Organists**

FRCP N ABBR (*Brit*) = **Fellow of the Royal College of Physicians**

FRCS N ABBR (*Brit*) = **Fellow of the Royal College of Surgeons**

freak [fri:k] (A) N 1 (= *person*) monstruo *m*, fenómeno *m*; (= *plant, animal*) monstruo *m*; (= *event*) anomalía *f*; **a ~ of nature** un fenómeno de la naturaleza; **the result was a ~** el resultado fue totalmente anómalo
2 (*) (= *enthusiast*) fanático/a *m/f*, adicto/a *m/f*; **health ~** maniático/a *m/f* en cuestión de salud; **peace ~** fanático/a *m/f* de la paz; *see also* **Jesus B**
(B) ADJ (= *abnormal*) [*storm, conditions*] anómalo, anormal; [*victory*] inesperado
(C) VI (‡) = **freak out**
(D) VT (‡) = **freak out**
(E) CPD ► **freak show** N (*at circus etc*) espectáculo *m* de fenómenos de feria; (*fig*) espectáculo *m* de bichos raros*

► **freak out‡** (A) VI + ADV (= *get excited*) flipar‡, alucinar‡; (*on drugs*) viajar‡, flipar‡
(B) VT + ADV (= *frighten*) dejar helado*; *see also* **freak-out**

freakish ['fri:kɪʃ] ADJ 1 [*appearance*] extravagante; [*result*] inesperado
2 (= *changeable*) [*moods, weather*] variable, caprichoso

freak-out‡ ['fri:kaʊt] N desmadre *m*; (= *party*) fiesta *f* loca*; (*on drug*) viaje‡ *m*

freaky* ['fri:kɪ] ADJ raro, estrafalario

freckle ['frekl] N peca *f*

freckled ['frekld] ADJ, **freckly** ['freklɪ] ADJ pecoso, lleno de pecas

Fred [fred], **Freddie**, **Freddy** ['fredɪ] N (*familiar forms*) *of* **Frederick**

Frederick ['fredrɪk] N Federico

free [fri:] (A) ADJ (*compar* **freer**, *superl* **freest**)
1 (= *at liberty*) libre; (= *untied*) libre, desatado; **to break ~** escaparse; **to get ~** escaparse; **to let sb go ~** dejar a algn en libertad; **to pull sth/sb ~** (*from wreckage*) sacar algo/a algn; (*from tangle*) sacar *or* desenredar algo/a algn; **to set ~** [+ *prisoner*] liberar; [+ *slave*] emancipar, liberar; [+ *animal*] soltar; **the screw had worked itself ~** el tornillo se había aflojado
2 (= *unrestricted*) libre; [*choice, translation*] libre; **the fishing is ~** la pesca está autorizada; **she opened the door with her ~ hand** abrió la puerta con la mano que tenía libre; **to have one's hands ~** (*lit*) tener las manos libres; **~ and easy** (= *carefree*) desenfadado; **"can I borrow your pen?" — "feel ~!"** —¿te puedo coger el bolígrafo? —¡por supuesto! *or* —¡claro que sí!; **feel ~ to ask questions** haced las preguntas que queráis; **feel ~ to help yourself** sírvete con toda libertad; **to be ~ to do sth** ser libre de hacer algo, tener libertad para hacer algo; **he is not ~ to choose** no tiene libertad de elección; ✦*IDIOMS* **to give ~ rein to** dar rienda suelta a; **to give sb a ~ hand** dar a algn carta blan-

ca; **to have a ~ hand to do sth** tener carta blanca para hacer algo; **as ~ as a bird** *or* **the air** libre como el viento

3 (= *clear, devoid*) **~ from** *or* **of sth**: **a world ~ of nuclear weapons** un mundo sin armas nucleares; **the area is ~ of malaria** ya no hay paludismo en la región; **to be ~ from pain** no sufrir *or* padecer dolor; **we are ~ of him at last** por fin nos hemos librado de él; **~ of duty** libre de derechos de aduana

4 (*Pol*) (= *autonomous, independent*) [*country, state*] libre; **~ elections** elecciones *fpl* libres; **the right of a ~ press** la libertad de prensa; **it's a ~ country!*** ¡es una democracia!

5 (= *costing nothing*) [*ticket, delivery*] gratuito, gratis; [*sample, offer, transport, health care*] gratuito; **catalogue ~ on request** solicite nuestro catálogo gratuito; **"admission ~"** "entrada *f* libre"; **~ on board** (*Comm*) franco a bordo; **~ of charge** gratis, gratuito; **to get sth for ~** obtener algo gratis; **✦IDIOMS there's no such thing as a ~ lunch** no te regalan nada; **to get a ~ ride*** aprovecharse de la situación; *see also* **tax-free**

6 (= *not occupied*) [*seat, room, person, moment*] libre; [*post*] vacante; [*premises*] desocupado; **is this seat ~?** ¿está libre este asiento?, ¿está ocupado este asiento?; **are you ~ tomorrow?** ¿estás libre mañana?

7 (= *generous, open*) generoso (**with** con); **to make ~ with sth** usar algo como si fuera cosa propia; **to be ~ with one's money** no reparar en gastos, ser manirroto*; **he's too ~ with his remarks** tiene una lengua muy suelta

Ⓑ ADV 1 (= *without charge*) **I got in (for) ~** entré gratis *or* sin pagar; **they'll send it ~ on request** si lo solicita se lo mandarán gratis

2 (= *without restraint*) **animals run ~ in the park** los animales campan a sus anchas por el parque; **he allowed his imagination to run ~** dio rienda suelta a su imaginación

Ⓒ VT 1 (= *release*) [+ *prisoner, people*] liberar, poner en libertad; (*from wreckage etc*) rescatar; (= *untie*) [+ *person, animal*] desatar, soltar; **to ~ one's hand/arm** soltarse la mano/el brazo; **she ~d herself from his embrace** se desligó de sus brazos

2 (= *make available*) [+ *funds, resources*] hacer disponible, liberar; **this will ~ him to pursue other projects** esto lo dejará libre para dedicarse a otros proyectos, esto le permitirá dedicarse a otros proyectos

3 (= *rid, relieve*) **to ~ sb from sth** liberar a algn de algo; **to ~ sb from pain** quitar *or* aliviar a algn el dolor; **their aim is to ~ the country of disease** se han propuesto acabar con la enfermedad en el país; **to ~ o.s. from** *or* **of sth** librarse de algo

Ⓓ N **the land of the ~** el país de la libertad (*Estados Unidos*)

Ⓔ CPD ► **free agent** N persona *f* independiente; **he's a ~ agent** tiene libertad de acción, es libre de hacer lo que quiere ► **free association** N (*Psych*) asociación *f* libre *or* de ideas ► **Free Church** N (*Brit*) Iglesia *f* no conformista ► **free clinic** N (*US Med*) dispensario *m* ► **free collective bargaining** N ≈ negociación *f* colectiva ► **free enterprise** N libre empresa *f*; **~-enterprise economy** economía *f* de libre empresa ► **free fall** N caída *f* libre; **to be in ~ fall** [*currency, share prices*] caer en picado *or* (*LAm*) picada; **to go into ~ fall** empezar a caer en picado *or* (*LAm*) picada ► **free flight** N vuelo *m* sin motor ► **free gift** N obsequio *m*, regalo *m* ► **free house** N (*Brit*) *pub que es libre de vender cualquier marca de cerveza por no estar vinculado a ninguna cervecería en particular* ► **free kick** N (*Ftbl*) tiro *m* libre ► **free labour** N trabajadores *mpl* no sindicados ► **free love** N amor *m* libre ► **free market** N (*Econ*) mercado *m* libre (**in** de); ► **free marketeer** N partidario/a *m/f* del libre mercado ► **free pass** N pase *m* gratuito ► **free period** N (*Scol*) hora *f* libre ► **free port** N puerto *m* franco ► **free radical** N (*Chem*) radical *m* libre ► **free school** N escuela *f* especial libre ► **free speech** N libertad *f* de expresión ► **free spirit** N persona *f* libre de convencionalismos ► **free trade** N libre cambio *m*; **~-trade zone** zona *f* franca ► **free trader** N librecambista *mf* ► **free verse** N verso *m* libre ► **free vote** N (*Brit Parl*) voto *m* de confianza (independiente de la línea del partido) ► **free will** N libre albedrío *m*; **he did it of his own ~ will** lo hizo por voluntad propia ► **the free world** N el mundo libre, los países libres

►**free up** VT + ADV [+ *funds, resources*] hacer disponible, liberar; [+ *staff*] dejar libre

-free [friː] ADJ (*ending in compounds*) **problem-free** fácil, sin problemas; **lead-free** sin plomo; **a meat-free diet** una dieta alimenticia exenta de carne; **stress-free** sin estrés *or* tensiones

freebase* [ˈfriːbeɪs] (*Drugs*) Ⓐ N crack‡ *m*

Ⓑ VT **to ~ cocaine** fumar crack

Ⓒ VI fumar crack

freebie* [ˈfriːbɪ] Ⓐ ADJ gratuito

Ⓑ N comida *f*/bebida *f etc* gratuita; **it's a ~** es gratis

freebooter [ˈfriːbuːtəʳ] N filibustero *m*

freedom [ˈfriːdəm] Ⓐ N 1 (*gen*) libertad *f*; **~ of action** libertad *f* de acción; **~ of association** libertad *f* de asociación; **~ of choice** libertad *f* de elección; **~ of information** libertad *f* de información; **Freedom of Information Act** (*US*) ley *f* del derecho a la información; **~ of the press** libertad *f* de prensa; **~ of speech** libertad *f* de expresión; **~ of worship** libertad *f* de culto; **to give sb the ~ of a city** hacer a algn ciudadano honorífico *or* hijo predilecto de la ciudad

2 (*from care, responsibility etc*) **they want ~ from government control** no quieren estar sometidos al control del gobierno, quieren estar libres del control del gobierno; **she found her sudden ~ from responsibility exhilarating** viéndose de repente liberada de sus responsabilidades, se sentía eufórica

3 (= *liberation*) liberación *f*

Ⓑ CPD ► **freedom fighter** N guerrillero/a *m/f*

FREEDOM OF INFORMATION ACT

El **Freedom of Information Act** *o* **FOIA** *es la ley estadounidense del derecho a la información, que obliga a los organismos federales a proporcionar información sobre sus actividades a cualquiera que lo solicite, lo que resulta muy útil, sobre todo a los periodistas. Esta información debe ser facilitada por el Estado en un plazo de diez días laborables y, en caso de que no se acceda a la solicitud, esta decisión tiene que ser debidamente justificada. Los motivos para retener la información pueden ser varios, entre ellos el que se ponga en peligro la seguridad nacional, se revelen secretos comerciales o que la información afecte a la vida privada de los ciudadanos. Entre otras noticias, el* **FOIA** *ha hecho posible la publicación de información anteriormente catalogada como secreta sobre asuntos de extrema importancia, como la guerra de Vietnam y las actividades de espionaje ilegal del* **FBI**.

free-fire zone [ˌfaɪəfriːˈzəʊn] N (*Mil*) *zona militar sin restricciones para el uso de armas de fuego, explosivos, etc*

free-floating [ˌfriːˈfləʊtɪŋ] ADJ libre, que flota libremente

Freefone® [ˈfriːfəʊn] N = **Freephone**

free-for-all* [ˈfriːfəˈrɔːl] N (= *brawl*) pelea *f*, bronca *f*; (= *argument*) discusión *f* general

free-form [ˈfriːfɔːm] ADJ (*Art, Mus*) de estilo libre

freehand [ˈfriːhænd] ADJ hecho a pulso

freehold [ˈfriːhəʊld] (*Brit*) Ⓐ ADJ [*property, land*] de pleno dominio

Ⓑ N pleno dominio *m*, propiedad *f* absoluta

freeholder [ˈfriːˌhəʊldəʳ] N (*Brit*) titular *mf* del pleno dominio *or* de la propiedad absoluta

freeing [ˈfriːɪŋ] N puesta *f* en libertad

freelance [ˈfriːlɑːns] Ⓐ ADJ independiente, por cuenta propia

Ⓑ VI trabajar por cuenta propia

Ⓒ N = **freelancer**

freelancer [ˈfriːlɑːnsəʳ] N trabajador(a) *m/f* por cuenta propia

freeload* [ˈfriːləʊd] VI gorronear* (**off** de)

freeloader* [ˈfriːləʊdəʳ] N gorrón/ona* *m/f*

freely [ˈfriːlɪ] ADV 1 (= *unrestrictedly*) libremente, con libertad; **they cannot move ~ about the country** no pueden viajar libremente *or* con libertad por el país; **you may come and go ~** puedes ir y venir libremente *or* con toda libertad; **you use that word a little too ~** usas esa palabra con demasiada libertad; **the hens are allowed to roam ~** las gallinas pueden deambular sueltas *or* en libertad; **to be ~ available** ser fácil de conseguir, conseguirse con facilidad

2 (= *openly*) [*speak*] con toda libertad, francamente

3 (= *willingly*) de buen grado; **the contract was ~ entered into** el contrato se firmó de buen grado; **I ~ admit I was wrong** soy el primero en admitir que estaba equivocado

4 (= *generously*) [*give*] generosamente, con liberalidad; [*flow*] copiosamente; **he spent his money ~** gastaba el dinero con liberalidad *or* a manos llenas; **the wine flowed ~** el vino fluía copiosamente

5 (= *loosely*) [*translate*] libremente; **he has ~ adapted the original** ha hecho una adaptación libre del original

freeman [ˈfriːmən] N (*pl* **freemen**) (*Hist*) hombre *m* libre; [*of city*] ciudadano *m* de honor

freemason [ˈfriːˌmeɪsn] N (franc)masón *m*

freemasonry [ˈfriːˌmeɪsnrɪ] N masonería *f*, francmasonería *f*; (*fig*) compañerismo *m*, camaradería *f*

Freephone® [ˈfriːfəʊn] N (*Brit Telec*) teléfono *m* gratuito

freepost [ˈfriːˌpəʊst] N franqueo *m* pagado

free-range [ˈfriːreɪndʒ] ADJ [*hen, eggs*] de corral

free-ranging [ˈfriːˈreɪndʒɪŋ] ADJ [*discussion*] sobre temas muy diversos; [*role*] libre, amplio

freesia [ˈfriːzɪə] N fresia *f*

free-spirited [ˌfriːˈspɪrɪtɪd] ADJ libre de convencionalismos

free-standing [ˈfriːˈstændɪŋ] ADJ independiente

freestyle [ˈfriːstaɪl] Ⓐ N **100 metres ~** (*Swimming*) 100 metros libres

Ⓑ CPD ► **freestyle race** N carrera *f* de estilo libre ► **freestyle wrestling** N lucha *f* libre

freethinker [ˈfriːˈθɪŋkəʳ] N librepensador(a) *m/f*

freethinking [ˈfriːˈθɪŋkɪŋ] Ⓐ ADJ librepensador

Ⓑ N librepensamiento *m*

freeware ['fri:wɜːʳ] N (*Comput*) programas *mpl* de dominio público, software *m* gratuito

freeway ['fri:weɪ] N (*US*) autopista *f*

freewheel ['fri:'wi:l] Ⓐ VI (= *coast*) (*on bicycle*) ir (en bicicleta) sin pedalear; (*in car*) ir en punto muerto

Ⓑ N [*of bicycle*] rueda *f* libre

freewheeling ['fri:ˌwi:lɪŋ] ADJ [*discussion*] desenvuelto; (= *free*) libre, espontáneo; (= *careless*) irresponsable

freeze [fri:z] (*pt* **froze**; *pp* **frozen**) Ⓐ VT [1] (*lit*) [+ *water*] helar; [+ *food*] congelar

[2] (*fig*) [+ *prices, wages, assets*] congelar

Ⓑ VI [1] (*gen*) helarse, congelarse; **it will ~ tonight** esta noche va a caer una helada; **to ~ to death** morirse de frío

[2] (= *be motionless*) quedarse inmóvil; **~!** ¡no te muevas!; **the smile froze on his lips** se le heló la sonrisa en los labios

Ⓒ N [1] (*Met*) helada *f*

[2] [*of prices, wages etc*] congelación *f*

►**freeze out** VT + ADV (*fig*) marginar, excluir

►**freeze over** VI + ADV [*lake, river*] helarse; [*windows, windscreen*] cubrirse de escarcha; **the lake has frozen over** el lago está helado

►**freeze up** Ⓐ VI + ADV [*handle, pipes*] helarse, congelarse; [*windows*] cubrirse de escarcha

Ⓑ VT + ADV **we're frozen up at home** en casa se han helado las cañerías

freeze-dried [ˌfri:z'draɪd] ADJ liofilizado, deshidratado por congelación

freeze-dry [ˌfri:z'draɪ] VT liofilizar, deshidratar por congelación

freezer ['fri:zəʳ] N congelador *m*

freeze-up ['fri:zʌp] N helada *f*, ola *f* de frío

freezing ['fri:zɪŋ] Ⓐ ADJ glacial, helado; **I'm ~** estoy helado; **it's ~ in here** aquí se congela uno, aquí hace un frío que pela*

Ⓑ ADV **it's ~ cold** hace un frío horrible *or* que pela*

Ⓒ N [1] (*also* **~ point**) punto *m* de congelación; **five degrees below ~** cinco grados bajo cero

[2] (= *deep freezing*) (ultra)congelación *f*

[3] (*fig*) [*of prices, wages, assets*] congelación *f*

Ⓓ CPD ► **freezing fog** N niebla *f* helada

freight [freɪt] Ⓐ N (= *goods transported*) flete *m*; (= *load*) carga *f*; (= *goods*) mercancías *fpl*; (= *charge*) flete *m*, gastos *mpl or* costos *mpl* de transporte; **to send sth (by) ~** enviar algo por flete; **~ forward** ◊ **~ collect** (*US Comm*) flete *m or* porte *m* debido; **~ free** (*Comm*) franco de porte; **~ inward** (*Comm*) flete *m* sobre compras; **~ paid** (*Comm*) porte *m* pagado

Ⓑ VT (= *transport*) [+ *goods*] fletar, transportar

Ⓒ CPD ► **freight car** N (*US*) vagón *m* de mercancías ► **freight charges** NPL gastos *mpl or* costos *mpl* de transporte ► **freight forwarder** N (agente *mf*) transitario/a *m/f*, agente *mf* expedidor(a) ► **freight plane** N avión *m* de transporte de mercancías ► **freight terminal** N terminal *f* de mercancías; (*Aer*) terminal *f* de carga ► **freight train** N (*US*) tren *m* de mercancías ► **freight yard** N área *f* de carga

freightage ['freɪtɪdʒ] N flete *m*

freighter ['freɪtəʳ] N [1] (*Naut*) buque *m* de carga, nave *f* de mercancías

[2] (= *person: carrier*) transportista *m*; (= *agent*) fletador *m*

freightliner ['freɪtˌlaɪnəʳ] N tren *m* de mercancías de contenedores

French [frentʃ] Ⓐ ADJ francés; [*ambassador*] de Francia

Ⓑ N [1] (*Ling*) francés *m*; ✦*IDIOM* **pardon my ~*** (*euph*) con perdón (de la expresión)

[2] **the ~** (= *people*) los franceses

Ⓒ CPD ► **French bean** N (*Brit*) judía *f* verde, ejote *m* (*Mex*), poroto *m* verde (*Chile*) ► **French bread** N pan *m* francés ► **French chalk** N jaboncillo *m*, jabón *m* de sastre ► **French doors** NPL (*US*) puertaventana *fsing* ► **French dressing** N (*Culin*) vinagreta *f* ► **French fried potatoes**, **French fries** NPL patatas *fpl* fritas, papas *fpl* fritas (*LAm*) ► **French Guiana** N la Guayana Francesa ► **French horn** N trompa *f* de llaves ► **French kiss** N beso *m* en la boca (con la lengua) ► **French leave** N despedida *f* a la francesa ► **French letter*** N condón *m* ► **French loaf** N barra *f* de pan francés ► **French pastry** N pastelito *m* relleno de nata *or* frutas ► **French polish** N (*Brit*) laca *f* ► **the French Riviera** N la Riviera francesa ► **French stick** N = **French loaf** ► **French toast** N (*Brit*) (= *toast*) tostada *f*; (= *fried bread in egg*) torrija *f* ► **French windows** NPL puertaventana *fsing*

French-Canadian ['frentʃkə'neɪdɪən] Ⓐ ADJ francocanadiense

Ⓑ N [1] (= *person*) francocanadiense *mf*

[2] (*Ling*) francés *m* canadiense

Frenchified* ['frentʃɪfaɪd] ADJ afrancesado

French-kiss [ˌfrentʃ'kɪs] Ⓐ VI besarse en la boca (con la lengua)

Ⓑ VT besar en la boca (con la lengua)

Frenchman ['frentʃmən] N (*pl* **Frenchmen**) francés *m*

French-polish [ˌfrentʃ'pɒlɪʃ] VT (*Brit*) lacar

French-speaking ['frentʃˌspi:kɪŋ] ADJ francófono, francohablante, de habla francesa

Frenchwoman ['frentʃˌwʊmən] N (*pl* **Frenchwomen**) francesa *f*

Frenchy* ['frentʃɪ] N (*pej*) gabacho/a *m/f*, franchute *mf*

frenetic [frɪ'netɪk] ADJ frenético

frenzied ['frenzɪd] ADJ [*effort etc*] frenético; [*crowd etc*] enloquecido

frenzy ['frenzɪ] N frenesí *m*, delirio *m*; **in a ~ of anxiety** enloquecido por la preocupación; *see also* **feeding B**

frequency ['fri:kwənsɪ] Ⓐ N (*gen, Elec*) frecuencia *f*; **this is happening with increasing ~** esto está ocurriendo con cada vez mayor frecuencia; **high/low ~** alta/baja frecuencia

Ⓑ CPD ► **frequency band** N banda *f* de frecuencia ► **frequency distribution** N (*Statistics*) distribución *f* de frecuencia ► **frequency modulation** N frecuencia *f* modulada

frequent ['fri:kwənt] Ⓐ ADJ frecuente; **his ~ absences from home** sus frecuentes ausencias del hogar; **it's a ~ cause of headaches** es una causa frecuente de los dolores de cabeza; **his demands for money became increasingly ~** pedía dinero con cada vez mayor frecuencia; **they stopped at ~ intervals to rest** paraban con frecuencia para descansar; **Fiona was a ~ visitor there** Fiona solía ir allí con frecuencia

Ⓑ [frɪ'kwent] VT frecuentar

frequentative [frɪ'kwentətɪv] (*Gram*) Ⓐ ADJ frecuentativo Ⓑ N frecuentativo *m*

frequenter [frɪ'kwentəʳ] N frecuentador(a) *m/f* (**of** de)

frequently ['fri:kwəntlɪ] ADV con frecuencia, frecuentemente; **all too ~** con demasiada frecuencia

fresco ['freskəʊ] N (*pl* **frescoes** *or* **frescos**) fresco *m*

fresh [freʃ] Ⓐ ADJ (*compar* **fresher**; *superl* **freshest**) [1] (= *not stale, not preserved*) [*fruit, milk etc*] fresco; [*bread*] recién hecho; [*smell, taste*] a fresco; **I need some ~ air** necesito un poco de aire fresco, necesito salir a respirar aire fresco; **to get some ~ air** tomar el fresco; **to let in some ~ air** dejar que entre un poco de aire; **in the ~ air** al aire libre; ✦*IDIOM* **as ~ as a daisy** fresco como una rosa

[2] (= *not salt*) [*water*] dulce

[3] (= *cool*) [*breeze*] fresco; [*wind*] fuerte; **it's quite ~ out** hace bastante fresco fuera

[4] (= *healthy*) [*face, complexion*] lozano, saludable

[5] (= *rested*) [*person*] descansado; **it's better done in the morning when you're ~** se hace mejor por la mañana, cuando estás descansado

[6] (= *clean and new*) [*sheet of paper*] en blanco; [*shirt, sheets*] limpio; **to give sth a ~ coat of paint** dar otra mano de pintura a algo; **"fresh paint"** (*esp US*) "recién pintado"; **we need some ~ faces** necesitamos ver caras nuevas; **to make a ~ start** volver a empezar, empezar de nuevo

[7] (= *further*) [*outbreak, supplies*] nuevo; **he has had a ~ attack** ha sufrido un nuevo ataque

[8] (= *recent*) [*footprints, tracks*] reciente; **while it is still ~ in our minds** mientras lo tenemos fresco en la memoria; **I've just made a ~ pot of coffee** acabo de hacer una cafetera de café; **~ from the oven** recién salido del horno; **the vegetables are ~ from the garden** la verdura está recién traída del huerto; **a teacher ~ from college** un profesor recién salido de la universidad; **milk ~ from the cow** leche *f* recién ordeñada

[9] (*) (= *cheeky*) [*person*] impertinente, descarado; **to get ~ with sb** (= *be cheeky with*) ponerse impertinente con algn, ponerse chulo con algn*; (= *take liberties with*) propasarse con algn; **don't get ~ with me!** ¡no te pongas impertinente conmigo!, ¡no te pongas chulo conmigo!*; **he got a bit ~ with her** se propasó un poco con ella

Ⓑ ADV **~ ground black pepper** pimienta *f* negra recién molida; **I picked the beans ~ this morning** acabo de recoger *or* coger las judías esta mañana; **to be ~ out of sth: we're ~ out of pan scrubs** [*shopkeeper*] acabamos de vender los últimos estropajos, se nos han acabado los estropajos; [*householder*] se nos han acabado los estropajos; **this government is ~ out of ideas** a este gobierno se le han agotado las ideas

fresh-air fiend* [ˌfreʃ'ɛəˌfi:nd] N **he's a ~** siempre quiere estar al aire libre

freshen ['freʃn] Ⓐ VT [1] [+ *air, breath*] refrescar [2] **let me ~ your drink** déjame que te llene la copa

Ⓑ VI [*wind*] arreciar

►**freshen up** Ⓐ VT + ADV (= *wash*) lavar; **to ~ o.s. up** refrescarse, lavarse

Ⓑ VI + ADV (= *wash o.s.*) refrescarse, lavarse

freshener ['freʃnəʳ] N *see* **air D**, **skin C**

fresher* ['freʃəʳ] (*Brit Univ*) Ⓐ N *see* **freshman**

Ⓑ CPD ► **freshers' week** N semana de bienvenida para nuevos universitarios

fresh-faced ['freʃfeɪst] ADJ [1] (= *youthful-looking*) lozano, saludable

[2] (= *inexperienced*) sin experiencia, nuevo

freshly ['freʃlɪ] ADV recién; **~ squeezed orange juice** zumo *m* de naranja recién exprimido; **~ painted** recién pintado; **~ baked** recién salido del horno

freshman ['freʃmən] N (*pl* **freshmen**) [1] (*Univ*) estudiante *mf* de primer año
[2] (*Scol*) (= *beginner*) novato/a *mf*; → GRADE

freshness ['freʃnɪs] N [1] [*of food*] frescura *f*
[2] [*of air*] frescor *m*
[3] [*of face, complexion*] frescura *f*, lozanía *f*
[4] (= *originality, spontaneity*) [*of style*] originalidad *f*, frescura *f*

freshwater ['freʃ,wɔːtəʳ] Ⓐ ADJ de agua dulce
Ⓑ CPD ► **freshwater fish** N pez *m* de agua dulce

fret[1] [fret] Ⓐ VI (= *worry*) preocuparse, apurarse; **don't ~** no te preocupes, no te apures; **the baby is ~ting for its mother** el niño echa de menos a su madre
Ⓑ VT [1] (= *worry*) preocupar; **to ~ the hours away** pasar las horas consumiéndose de inquietud
[2] (= *wear away*) corroer, raer, desgastar
Ⓒ N **to be in a ~** estar muy inquieto; **to get into a ~** apurarse

fret[2] [fret] N (*Mus*) traste *m*

fretful ['fretfʊl] ADJ [*child*] inquieto

fretfully ['fretfəlɪ] ADV (*gen*) inquietamente; [*complain*] fastidiosamente

fretfulness ['fretfʊlnɪs] N inquietud *f*

fretsaw ['fretsɔː] N sierra *f* de calar *or* de marquetería

fretwork ['fretwɜːk] N calado *m*

Freudian ['frɔɪdɪən] Ⓐ ADJ freudiano
Ⓑ N freudiano /a *m/f*
Ⓒ CPD ► **Freudian slip** N lapsus *m inv* linguae

FRG N ABBR (*Hist*) (= **Federal Republic of Germany**) RFA *f*

Fri. ABBR (= **Friday**) vier.

friable ['fraɪəbl] ADJ friable, desmenuzable

friar ['fraɪəʳ] N fraile *m*; (*before name*) fray *m*; **black ~** dominico *m*; **grey ~** franciscano *m*; **white ~** carmelita *m*

friary ['fraɪərɪ] N monasterio *m*

fricassee ['frɪkəsiː] N (*Culin*) estofado *m*

fricative ['frɪkətɪv] Ⓐ ADJ fricativo
Ⓑ N fricativa *f*

friction ['frɪkʃən] Ⓐ N [1] (*Tech*) fricción *f*; (*Med etc*) frote *m*, frotamiento *m*
[2] (*fig*) roces *mpl*, fricción *f* (**about, over** por)
Ⓑ CPD ► **friction feed** N (*on printer*) avance *m* por fricción

Friday ['fraɪdɪ] N viernes *m inv*; *see* **Tuesday** *for usage*; *see also* **good**

fridge [frɪdʒ] (*esp Brit*) Ⓐ N frigorífico *m*, nevera *f*, refrigerador *m*, refrigeradora *f* (*LAm*), heladera *f* (*S. Cone*)
Ⓑ CPD ► **fridge freezer** N frigorífico-congelador *m*, combi *m*

fried [fraɪd] Ⓐ ADJ (*Culin*) frito
Ⓑ CPD ► **fried egg** N huevo *m* frito ► **fried fish** N pescado *m* frito

friend [frend] N amigo/a *m/f*; (*at school, work etc*) compañero/a *m/f*; **~!** (*Mil*) ¡gente de paz!; **a ~ of mine** un amigo mío; **he's no ~ of mine** no es mi amigo, no es amigo mío; **a ~ of the family** un amigo de la familia; **let's be ~s** hagamos las paces; **to be ~s with sb** ser amigo de algn; **we're the best of ~s** somos muy amigos; **we're just good ~s** somos sólo amigos, somos amigos nada más; **to make ~s with sb** hacerse amigo de algn, trabar amistad con algn; **he makes ~s easily** hace amigos con facilidad; **he is no ~ to violence** no es partidario de la violencia; **to have a ~ at court** (*fig*) tener enchufe; **the Society of Friends** (*Rel*) los cuáqueros; **Friends of the Earth** Amigos *mpl* de la Tierra; **Friends of the National Theatre** Asociación *f* de Amigos del Teatro Nacional; ✦*PROV* **a ~ in need is a ~ indeed** en las malas es cuando se conoce a los amigos; *see also* **learned**

friendless ['frendlɪs] ADJ sin amigos

friendliness ['frendlɪnɪs] N [1] (= *warmth*) cordialidad *f*, simpatía *f*
[2] (= *friendship*) cordialidad *f*, amistad *f*

friendly ['frendlɪ] Ⓐ ADJ (*compar* **friendlier**; *superl* **friendliest**) [1] [*person, dog, cat*] simpático; [*atmosphere, place*] agradable; [*smile, gesture*] simpático, cordial; [*relationship, greeting, tone*] amistoso, cordial; **it was an attempt to establish ~ relations** fue un intento de establecer relaciones amistosas *or* cordiales; **I'm giving you a ~ warning** te estoy advirtiendo como amigo, te estoy dando una advertencia de amigo; **let me give you a piece of ~ advice** déjame que te dé un consejo de amigo; **to become ~ with sb** hacerse amigo de algn, trabar amistad con algn; **we became ~** nos hicimos amigos; **it's nice to see a ~ face** es agradable ver una cara conocida; **to get ~ with sb** hacerse amigo de algn; **we remained on ~ terms after we split up** después de cortar, seguimos siendo amigos; **it's important to keep on ~ terms with them** es importante seguir manteniendo una relación amistosa con ellos; **that wasn't a very ~ thing to do** eso no se hace con los amigos; **to be ~ to sb**: **they are not very ~ to strangers** no se muestran muy amables con los extraños; **she wasn't very ~ to me** no estuvo demasiado amable conmigo, no se mostró muy amable conmigo; **Yul and Steve were ~ with one another** Yul y Steve eran amigos; *see also* **environmentally**
[2] (= *not competitive*) [*match, rivalry, argument*] amistoso
[3] (= *not enemy*) [*nation, forces*] amigo
Ⓑ N (*also* **~ match**) (*Ftbl*) partido *m* amistoso
Ⓒ CPD ► **friendly fire** N (*Mil*) fuego *m* amigo ► **friendly society** N ≈ mutualidad *f*, ≈ mutua *f*, ≈ mutual *f* (*LAm*)

-friendly ['frendlɪ] ADJ (*ending in compounds*) **child-friendly facilities in pubs** instalaciones *fpl* para los niños en los pubs; **dolphin-friendly tuna** *atún pescado sin causar daño a los delfines*; *see also* **environment-friendly**, **user-friendly** *etc*

friendship ['frendʃɪp] N amistad *f*; (*at school, work etc*) compañerismo *m*

Friesian ['friːʒən] = **Frisian**

Friesland ['friːzlənd] N Frisia *f*

frieze [friːz] N (*Archit*) friso *m*; (= *painting*) fresco *m*

frig** [frɪg] VI **to ~ about** *or* **around** hacer gilipolleces*, joder**

frigate ['frɪgɪt] N (*Naut*) fragata *f*

frigging** ['frɪgɪŋ] Ⓐ ADJ **do I need to do every ~ thing myself!** ¿por qué porras tengo que hacerlo yo todo?*; **it's a ~ nuisance!** ¡es un coñazo!*
Ⓑ ADV **she's so ~ lazy!** ¡es una vaga de la hostia!*

fright [fraɪt] N [1] (= *sudden fear*) susto *m*, sobresalto *m*; (= *state of alarm*) miedo *m*; **to get a ~** asustarse; **what a ~ you gave me!** ¡qué susto me diste *or* has dado!; **to take ~ (at)** asustarse (de)
[2] (*) (= *person*) espantajo *m*; **she looked a ~** iba hecha un espantajo

frighten ['fraɪtn] VT asustar; **to be ~ed** tener miedo (**of** a); **don't be ~ed!** ¡no te asustes!; **she is easily ~ed** se asusta con facilidad, es asustadiza; **to ~ sb into doing sth** convencer a algn con amenazas de que haga algo; **I was ~ed out of my wits** *or* **to death** estaba aterrorizado
► **frighten away, frighten off** VT + ADV espantar, ahuyentar

frighteners* ['fraɪtnəz] NPL **to put the ~ on sb** meter a algn miedo en el cuerpo, ponérselos de corbata a algn*

frightening ['fraɪtnɪŋ] ADJ espantoso, aterrador

frighteningly ['fraɪtnɪŋlɪ] ADV [*thin*] alarmantemente; [*ugly*] espantosamente; [*expensive, uncertain*] terriblemente

frightful ['fraɪtfʊl] ADJ (= *terrible*) [*tragedy, experience, shame*] horroroso; (= *awful*) [*noise, weather*] espantoso

frightfully†* ['fraɪtfəlɪ] ADV (*Brit*) terriblemente, tremendamente; **it's ~ hard** es terriblemente difícil; **it's ~ good** es la mar de bueno; **I'm ~ sorry** lo siento muchísimo, lo siento en el alma

frightfulness ['fraɪtfʊlnɪs] N horror *m*

frigid ['frɪdʒɪd] ADJ [1] (*sexually*) frígido
[2] (= *unfriendly*) [*atmosphere, look etc*] frío, glacial

frigidity [frɪ'dʒɪdɪtɪ] N [1] (*sexual*) frigidez *f*
[2] (= *unfriendliness*) frialdad *f*

frill [frɪl] N [1] (*on dress etc*) volante *m*
[2] **frills** (*fig*) adornos *mpl*; **a package holiday without ~s** unas vacaciones organizadas de lo más sencillo *or* sin grandes lujos; **~s and furbelows** encajes *mpl* y puntillas *fpl*

frilly ['frɪlɪ] ADJ con volantes, con adornos

Fringe [frɪndʒ] N (*Brit Theat*) (*also* **~ Festival, Festival ~**) *festival alternativo de Edimburgo*; → EDINBURGH FESTIVAL

fringe [frɪndʒ] Ⓐ N [1] [*of shawl, rug*] (ribete *m* de) flecos *mpl*
[2] (*Brit*) [*of hair*] flequillo *m*
[3] (*also* **~s**) [*of forest*] linde *m or f*, lindero *m*; [*of city*] periferia *f*; **on the ~s of the lake** en los bordes del lago; **to live on the ~ of society** vivir al margen de la sociedad
[4] (= *group of people*) elementos *mpl* marginales
Ⓑ CPD ► **fringe benefits** NPL suplementos *mpl*, ventajas *fpl* adicionales ► **fringe group** N grupo *m* marginal ► **fringe meeting** N reunión *f* paralela ► **fringe organization** N organización *f* marginal *or* no oficial ► **fringe theatre** N (*Brit*) teatro *m* experimental

frippery ['frɪpərɪ] N (*esp Brit*) perifollos *mpl*, perejiles *mpl*

Frisbee® ['frɪzbɪ] N disco *m* volador

Frisian ['frɪʒən] Ⓐ ADJ frisio
Ⓑ N [1] (= *person*) frisio/a *m/f*
[2] (*Ling*) frisio *m*
Ⓒ CPD ► **the Frisian Islands** NPL las Islas Frisias

frisk [frɪsk] Ⓐ VT (*) (= *search*) cachear, registrar
Ⓑ VI (= *frolic*) brincar; [*people*] juguetear; [*animals*] retozar

friskiness ['frɪskɪnɪs] N vivacidad *f*

frisky ['frɪskɪ] ADJ (*compar* **friskier**; *superl* **friskiest**) [*person, horse*] juguetón; **he's pretty ~ still** sigue bastante activo

frisson ['friːsɒn] N [*of horror, fear*] repelús *m*; [*of excitement*] escalofrío *m*

fritter[1] ['frɪtəʳ] N (*Culin*) buñuelo *m*; **corn ~** arepa *f* (*Col, Ven*)

fritter[2] ['frɪtəʳ] VT (*also* **~ away**) malgastar, desperdiciar

frivolity [frɪ'vɒlɪtɪ] N (*gen*) frivolidad *f*

frivolous ['frɪvələs] ADJ frívolo

frivolously ['frɪvələslɪ] ADV frívolamente

frizz [frɪz] Ⓐ N rizos *mpl* pequeños y muy apretados
Ⓑ VT [+ *hair*] rizar con rizos pequeños y muy apretados

frizzle [frɪzl] N, VT = **frizz**

frizzy ['frɪzɪ] ADJ (*compar* **frizzier**, *superl* **frizziest**) [*hair*] ensortijado, crespo; **to go ~** ensortijarse, encresparse

fro [frəʊ] ADV **to and ~** de un lado para otro, de aquí para allá

frock [frɒk] Ⓐ N (*woman's*) vestido *m*; [*of monk*] hábito *m*
Ⓑ CPD ► **frock coat** N levita *f*

Frog* [frɒg], **Froggy*** ['frɒgɪ] N (*pej*) gabacho/a *m/f*, franchute *mf*

frog [frɒg] Ⓐ N rana *f*; ✦**IDIOM to have a ~ in one's throat** tener carraspera
Ⓑ CPD ► **frogs' legs** NPL (*Culin*) ancas *fpl* de rana

frogging ['frɒgɪŋ] N alamares *mpl*

frogman ['frɒgmən] N (*pl* **frogmen**) hombre rana *m*

frog-march ['frɒgmɑːtʃ] VT **to ~ sb in/out** meter/sacar a algn por la fuerza

frogspawn ['frɒgspɔːn] N huevas *fpl* de rana

frolic ['frɒlɪk] (*pt, pp* **frolicked**) Ⓐ N (= *prank*) travesura *f*; (= *merrymaking*) fiesta *f*, jolgorio *m*
Ⓑ VI juguetear, brincar

frolicsome ['frɒlɪksəm] ADJ retozón, juguetón; (= *mischievous*) travieso

from [frɒm] PREP [1] (*indicating starting place*) de, desde; **where are you ~?** ¿de dónde eres?; **where has he come ~?** ¿de dónde ha venido?; **he comes ~ Segovia** es de Segovia; **he had gone ~ home** se había ido de su casa; **the train ~ Madrid** el tren de Madrid, el tren procedente de Madrid; **~ London to Glasgow** de Londres a Glasgow; **~ house to house** de casa en casa; **~ A to Z** de A a Z, desde A hasta Z
[2] (*indicating time*) de, desde; **~ now on** de aquí en adelante; **~ that time** desde aquel momento; **~ one o'clock to** *or* **until two** desde la una hasta las dos; **(as) ~ Friday** a partir del viernes; **~ a child** ◊ **~ childhood** desde niño; **~ time to time** de vez en cuando
[3] (*indicating distance*) de, desde; **the hotel is 1km ~ the beach** el hotel está a 1km de la playa; **a long way ~ home** muy lejos de casa; **to be far ~ the truth** estar lejos de la verdad
[4] (*indicating sender etc*) de; **a letter ~ my sister** una carta de mi hermana; **a telephone call ~ Mr Smith** una llamada de parte del Sr. Smith; **a message ~ him** un mensaje de parte de él; **tell him ~ me** dile de mi parte
[5] (*indicating source*) de; **to drink ~ a stream/~ the bottle** beber de un arroyo/de la botella; **we learned it ~ him** lo aprendimos de él; **we learned it ~ a book** lo aprendimos en un libro; **a quotation ~ Shakespeare** una cita de Shakespeare; **to steal sth ~ sb** robar algo a algn; **to pick sb ~ the crowd** escoger a algn de la multitud; **I'll buy it ~ you** te lo compraré; **where did you get that ~?** ¿de dónde has sacado *or* sacaste eso?; **take the gun ~ him!** ¡quítale el revólver!; **one of the best performances we have seen ~ him** uno de los mejores papeles que le hayamos visto; **painted ~ life** pintado del natural
[6] (*indicating price, number etc*) desde, a partir de; **we have shirts ~ £8 (upwards)** tenemos camisas desde *or* a partir de 8 libras; **prices range ~ £10 to £50** los precios varían entre 10 y 50 libras; **there were ~ 10 to 15 people there** había allí entre 10 y 15 personas
[7] (*indicating change*) **things went ~ bad to worse** las cosas fueron de mal en peor; **the interest rate increased ~ 6% to 10%** la tasa de interés ha subido del 6 al 10 por ciento; **he went ~ office boy to director in five years** pasó de ser recadero a director en cinco años
[8] (*indicating difference*) **to be different ~ sb** ser distinto de algn; **he can't tell red ~ green** no distingue entre rojo y verde; **to know good ~ bad** saber distinguir entre el bien y el mal, saber distinguir el bien del mal
[9] (= *because of, on the basis of*) por; **to act ~ conviction** obrar por convicción; **~ sheer necessity** por pura necesidad; **weak ~ hunger** debilitado por el hambre; **~ what I can see** por lo que veo; **~ what he says** por lo que dice, según lo que dice; **~ experience** por experiencia; **to die ~ exposure** morir de frío
[10] (= *away from*) **to shelter ~ the rain** protegerse de la lluvia; **to escape ~ sth/sb** escapar de algo/algn; **to prevent sb ~ doing sth** impedir a algn hacer algo
[11] (*with prep, adv*) **~ above** desde arriba; **~ afar** desde lejos; **~ among the crowd** de entre la multitud; **~ beneath** *or* **underneath** desde abajo; **~ inside/outside the house** desde dentro/fuera de la casa

fromage frais ['frɒmɑːʒ'freɪ] N *queso fresco descremado*

frond [frɒnd] N fronda *f*

front [frʌnt] Ⓐ N [1] (= *exterior*) [*of house, building*] fachada *f*; [*of shirt, dress*] pechera *f*; [*of book*] (= *cover*) portada *f*; **it fastens at the ~** se abrocha por delante; **back to ~** al revés; **her dress had ripped down the ~** el vestido se le había roto por delante; **you've spilled food all down your ~** te has derramado comida por toda la pechera
[2] (= *forepart*) [*of stage, desk, building*] parte *f* de delante, parte *f* delantera; [*of train, bus*] parte *f* delantera; [*of queue*] principio *m*; **there's a dedication at the ~ of the book** hay una dedicatoria al principio del libro; **there are still some seats left at the ~** todavía quedan asientos delante; **he sat at the ~ of the train** se sentó en la parte delantera del tren; **he sat at the ~ of the class** se sentó en la primera fila de la clase; **at the ~ of the line** *or* **queue** al principio de la cola; **I want to sit in the ~** quiero sentarme delante; **he laid the baby on its ~** puso al bebé boca abajo; **the car's out ~** (*US*) el coche está delante *or* enfrente de la casa
[3] **in ~** delante; **to send sb on in ~** enviar a algn por delante; **the car in ~** el coche de delante; **to be in ~** (*gen*) ir primero, ir delante; (*in race*) ir a la cabeza, llevar la delantera; (*in scoring*) llevar (la) ventaja; **in ~ of** delante de; **don't argue in ~ of the children** no discutas delante de los niños; **a car was parked in ~ of the house** había un coche aparcado delante de la casa; **she sat down in ~ of her mirror** se sentó delante del espejo, se sentó frente al espejo
[4] (*Met*) frente *m*; **cold/warm ~** (*Met*) frente *m* frío/cálido
[5] (*Mil, Pol*) frente *m*; **he fought at the ~ during the War** luchó en el frente durante la guerra; **we must present a united ~** debemos parecer un frente unido
[6] (*Brit*) (= *promenade*) paseo *m* marítimo; (= *beach*) playa *f*
[7] (= *area of activity*) materia *f*; **is there any news on the wages ~?** ¿se sabe algo nuevo en materia de salarios?; **we have made progress on a variety of ~s** hemos avanzado en varios campos *or* varias esferas; **on all ~s** en todos los frentes; **the government's failings on the home** *or* **domestic ~** las deficiencias del gobierno a nivel nacional
[8] (= *show*) **it's all just a ~ with him** lo suyo no es más que una fachada *or* no son más que apariencias; **he kept up a brave ~ to the world** delante de todos ponía buena cara
[9] (*) (= *cover-up*) fachada *f*, tapadera *f*; **to be a ~ for sth** servir de fachada *or* tapadera para algo
Ⓑ ADJ [1] (= *foremost*) [*wheel, leg*] delantero, de delante, de adelante (*LAm*); **I was in the ~ seat** yo estaba en el asiento delantero *or* de delante *or* (*LAm*) de adelante; **if we run, we can get a ~ seat** si corremos, podemos pillar un asiento en la parte delantera *or* la parte de delante *or* (*LAm*) la parte de adelante; **he's in the ~ garden** está en el jardín de delante de la casa
[2] (*Phon*) [*vowel*] frontal
Ⓒ VI [1] **to ~ onto sth** [*house, window*] dar a algo
[2] **to ~ for sth** servir de fachada *or* tapadera para algo
Ⓓ VT [1] (= *head*) [+ *organization*] estar al frente de, liderar
[2] [+ *TV show*] presentar
[3] [+ *band, group*] estar al frente de, ser el cantante de
[4] (*frm*) (= *face*) dar a; **the house ~s the river** la casa da al río
Ⓔ CPD ► **front bench** N (*Brit Pol*) *en la Cámara de Diputados británica, escaños de los ministros y sus equivalentes en la oposición* ► **front crawl** N (*Swimming*) crol *m* ► **front desk** N (*US*) recepción *f* (*de un hotel*) ► **front door** N puerta *f* principal ► **front end** N [*of vehicle*] parte *f* delantera ► **front line** N (*Mil*) primera línea *f* ► **front man** N (*for activity*) testaferro *m*; [*of band, group*] líder *m*; (*TV*) presentador *m* ► **front organization** N organización *f* fachada ► **front page** N (*Press*) primera plana *f* ► **front row** N primera fila *f* ► **front runner** N (*in race*) corredor(ora) *m/f* que va en cabeza; (*in election*) favorito/a *m/f* ► **front tooth** N incisivo *m*, paleta* *f* ► **front view** N **the ~ view of the hotel is very impressive** el frente del hotel *or* la parte de delante del hotel es impresionante

> **FRONT BENCH**
> *El término genérico* **front bench** *se usa para referirse a los escaños situados en primera fila a ambos lados del Presidente* (**Speaker**) *de la Cámara de los Comunes del Parlamento británico. Dichos escaños son ocupados por los parlamentarios que son miembros del gobierno a un lado y por los del gobierno en la sombra* (**shadow cabinet**) *al otro y, por esta razón, se les conoce como* **frontbenchers**.
> ⇨ *Ver tb* BACKBENCHER

frontage ['frʌntɪdʒ] N [*of building*] fachada *f*

frontal ['frʌntl] ADJ (*Anat*) frontal; [*attack*] de frente, frontal

frontbencher [ˌfrʌnt'bentʃəʳ] N (*Brit Parl*) *diputado con cargo oficial en el gobierno o la oposición*; → FRONT BENCH

front-end ['frʌntend] ADJ **~ costs** gastos *mpl* iniciales; **~ processor** procesador *m* frontal

frontier ['frʌntɪəʳ] Ⓐ N (= *border, also fig*) frontera *f*; (= *dividing line*) línea *f* divisoria; **to push back the ~s of knowledge** ensanchar *or* ampliar los límites del conocimiento
Ⓑ CPD fronterizo ► **frontier dispute** N con-

flicto *m* fronterizo ► frontier post N puesto *m* fronterizo; *see also* post A3

frontiersman [frʌn'tɪəzmən] N (*pl* frontiersmen) hombre *m* de la frontera

frontispiece ['frʌntɪspiːs] N [*of book*] frontispicio *m*

front-line ['frʌntlaɪn] ADJ [*troops, news*] de primera línea; [*countries, areas*] fronterizo a una zona en guerra

front-loader [ˌfrʌnt'ləʊdəʳ] N (*also* front-loading washing machine) lavadora *f* de carga frontal

front-loading [ˌfrʌnt'ləʊdɪŋ] ADJ de carga frontal

front-page [ˌfrʌnt'peɪdʒ] (A) ADJ de primera página, de primera plana
(B) CPD ► front-page news N noticias *fpl* de primera plana

frontward ['frʌntwəd] ADV de frente, con la parte delantera primero

frontwards ['frʌntwədz] ADV (*esp Brit*) = frontward

front-wheel drive [ˌfrʌntwiːl'draɪv] N tracción *f* delantera

frost [frɒst] (A) N (= *substance*) escarcha *f*; (= *weather*) helada *f*; four degrees of ~ (*Brit*) cuatro grados bajo cero
(B) VT [1] the grass was ~ed over el césped apareció cubierto de escarcha
[2] (*esp US Culin*) escarchar
(C) VI to ~ over *or* up cubrirse de escarcha, escarcharse

frostbelt [frɒstbelt] N (*US Geog*) *estados del norte de Estados Unidos caracterizados por su clima frío*; → SUNBELT

frostbite ['frɒstbaɪt] N congelación *f*

frostbitten ['frɒstˌbɪtn] ADJ congelado

frostbound ['frɒstbaʊnd] ADJ [*field, land*] helado; [*road*] bloqueado por la helada; [*village*] aislado por la helada

frosted ['frɒstɪd] (A) ADJ (*esp US*) [*cake*] escarchado
(B) CPD ► frosted glass N vidrio *m* *or* cristal *m* esmerilado

frostily ['frɒstɪlɪ] ADV (*fig*) glacialmente

frosting ['frɒstɪŋ] N (*esp US*) (= *icing*) escarcha *f*

frosty ['frɒstɪ] ADJ (*compar* frostier; *superl* frostiest) [1] [*weather*] de helada; [*surface*] escarchado; on a ~ morning una mañana de helada; it was ~ last night anoche cayó una helada *or* heló
[2] (*fig*) [*smile*] glacial

froth [frɒθ] (A) N [1] (= *foam*) espuma *f*
[2] (*fig*) (= *frivolous talk*) naderías *fpl*, banalidades *fpl*
(B) VI hacer espuma; (*at the mouth*) echar espumarajos

frothy ['frɒθɪ] ADJ (*compar* frothier; *superl* frothiest) [1] (= *foamy*) espumoso
[2] (*fig*) banal, superficial

frown [fraʊn] (A) N ceño *m*; he said with a ~ dijo frunciendo el ceño *or* entrecejo
(B) VI fruncir el ceño, fruncir el entrecejo; to ~ at mirar con el ceño fruncido

► frown on, frown upon VI + PREP (*fig*) desaprobar

frowning ['fraʊnɪŋ] ADJ (*fig*) ceñudo, amenazador, severo

frowsy, frowzy ['fraʊzɪ] ADJ (= *dirty*) sucio; (= *untidy*) desaliñado; (= *smelly*) fétido, maloliente; (= *neglected*) descuidado

froze [frəʊz] PT *of* freeze

frozen ['frəʊzn] (A) PP *of* freeze
(B) ADJ [1] [*food*] congelado
[2] we're simply ~ estamos totalmente helados; I'm ~ stiff estoy helado, estoy muerto de frío
(C) CPD ► frozen assets NPL (*Fin*) activo *msing* congelado

FRS N ABBR [1] (*Brit*) = Fellow of the Royal Society [2] (*US*) (= Federal Reserve System) *banco central de los EE.UU.*

Frs ABBR (*Rel*) (= Fathers) PP

fructify ['frʌktɪfaɪ] VI (*frm*) fructificar

frugal ['fruːgəl] ADJ frugal

frugality [fruː'gælɪtɪ] N frugalidad *f*

frugally ['fruːgəlɪ] ADV [*give out*] en pequeñas cantidades; [*live*] económicamente, sencillamente

fruit [fruːt] (A) N [1] (*gen, Bot*) fruto *m*; (= *piece of fruit*) fruta *f*; would you like some ~? ¿quieres fruta?; to be in ~ [*tree, bush*] haber dado *or* echado fruto, tener fruta; the ~s of the sea los productos del mar; to bear ~ (*lit, fig*) dar fruto
[2] fruits (*fig*) (= *benefits*) the ~s of one's labour los frutos del trabajo; to enjoy the ~s of one's success disfrutar de los frutos del éxito
[3] (*US‡ pej*) (= *male homosexual*) maricón* *m*
[4] (†*) (*as term of address*) hello, old ~! ¡hola, compadre!*
(B) VI dar fruto
(C) CPD ► fruit basket N frutero *m*, canasto *m* de la fruta ► fruit cocktail N macedonia *f* de frutas ► fruit cup N ≈ sangría *f* ► fruit dish N frutero *m* ► fruit drop N bombón *m* de fruta ► fruit farm N granja *f* frutícola *or* hortofrutícola ► fruit farmer N fruticultor(a) *m/f*, granjero/a *m/f* frutícola *or* hortofrutícola ► fruit farming N fruticultura *f* ► fruit fly N mosca *f* de la fruta ► fruit grower N fruticultor(a) *m/f*, granjero/a *m/f* frutícola *or* hortofrutícola ► fruit growing N fruticultura *f* ► fruit gum N (*Brit*) gominola *f* ► fruit juice N zumo *m or* jugo *m* de frutas ► fruit knife N cuchillo *m* de la fruta ► fruit machine N (*Brit*) máquina *f* tragaperras ► fruit salad N macedonia *f* de frutas ► fruit salts NPL sal *f* de fruta(s) ► fruit tree N árbol *m* frutal

fruitcake ['fruːtkeɪk] N [1] (*Culin*) tarta *f* de frutas [2] (‡) (= *eccentric person*) chiflado/a* *m/f*; ✦IDIOM he's as nutty as a ~ está más loco que una cabra*, está loco de atar*

fruiterer ['fruːtərəʳ] N (*Brit*) frutero/a *m/f*; ~'s (shop) frutería *f*

fruitful ['fruːtfʊl] ADJ [1] (*gen*) fructífero; [*land*] fértil [2] (*fig*) productivo, provechoso

fruitfully ['fruːtfəlɪ] ADV (*fig*) provechosamente, fructíferamente

fruitfulness ['fruːtfʊlnɪs] N [1] [*of soil*] fertilidad *f*, productividad *f*; [*of plant*] fertilidad *f*, fecundidad *f* [2] (*fig*) [*of discussion etc*] utilidad *f*

fruition [fruː'ɪʃən] N [*of plan etc*] cumplimiento *m*; to bring to ~ realizar; to come to ~ [*hope*] cumplirse; [*plan*] realizarse, dar resultado

fruitless ['fruːtlɪs] ADJ (*fig*) infructuoso, inútil

fruitlessly ['fruːtlɪslɪ] ADV infructuosamente, sin resultado

fruity ['fruːtɪ] ADJ (*compar* fruitier; *superl* fruitiest) [1] [*taste*] a fruta; [*wine*] afrutado
[2] [*voice*] pastoso
[3] (*Brit**) (= *lewd*) [*joke*] verde; [*style*] picante

frump [frʌmp] N espantajo *m*, birria *f*

frumpish ['frʌmpɪʃ] ADJ desaliñado

frumpy ['frʌmpɪ] ADJ = frumpish

frustrate [frʌs'treɪt] VT [+ *plan, effort, person*] frustrar; [+ *hope*] defraudar; to feel ~d sentirse frustrado; he's a ~d artist es un artista frustrado

frustrating [frʌs'treɪtɪŋ] ADJ frustrante; how ~! ¡qué frustrante!

frustration [frʌs'treɪʃən] N (*gen*) frustración *f*; (= *disappointment*) decepción *f*; (= *annoyance*) molestia *f*

fry[1] [fraɪ] (A) VT (*Culin*) freír
(B) VI freírse
(C) N fritada *f*

fry[2] [fraɪ] N (*Fishing*) pececillos *mpl*; *see also* small D

fryer ['fraɪəʳ] N [1] (= *pan*) sartén *f* (*m in LAm*); deep-fat ~ freidora *f*
[2] (= *person*) empleado/a *m/f* de una freiduría

frying ['fraɪɪŋ] (A) N there was a smell of ~ olía a frito
(B) CPD ► frying pan N sartén *f* (*m in LAm*); ✦IDIOM to jump out of the ~ pan into the fire salir de Guatemala para entrar en Guatepeor

frypan ['fraɪpæn] N (*US*) sartén *f* (*m in LAm*)

fry-up ['fraɪʌp] N (*Brit*) fritura *f*

FSA N ABBR (*Brit Fin*) (= Financial Services Authority) *organismo de control financiero en el Reino Unido*

FSLIC N ABBR (*US*) = Federal Savings and Loan Insurance Corporation

FT N ABBR (*Brit*) = Financial Times

ft ABBR = foot, feet

F/T ABBR (*US*) = full-time

FTC N ABBR (*US*) = Federal Trade Commission

FTP, ftp N ABBR (*Comput*) = file transfer protocol; anonymous ftp ftp anónimo

FTSE 100 Index [ˌfʊtsɪwʌnˌhʌndred'ɪndeks] N ABBR (*Brit St Ex*) = Financial Times Stock Exchange 100 Index

fuchsia ['fjuːʃə] N fucsia *f*

fuck** [fʌk] (A) N [1] to have a ~ echar un polvo**, joder**; she's a good ~! tiene un buen polvo**
[2] (*US*) (= *stupid person*) you dumb ~! ¡tonto de los cojones!**
[3] like ~ he will! ¡y un huevo!**, ¡por los cojones!**; ~ knows! ¡qué coño sé yo!**
(B) VT [1] (*lit*) joder**, tirarse**, follarse (*Sp***), coger (*LAm***)
[2] ~ (it)! ¡joder!**, ¡carajo! (*LAm***), ¡chinga tu madre! (*Mex***); ~ you! ¡que te den por culo!**, ¡jódete!**, ¡tu madre! (*LAm***); ~ this car! ¡este jodido coche!**, ¡este coche del carajo! (*LAm***), ¡fregado coche! (*LAm***), ¡chingado coche! (*Mex***)
(C) VI joder**, follar (*Sp***), coger (*LAm***)

► fuck about**, fuck around** VI + ADV joder**; to ~ about *or* around with joder**, manosear, estropear

► fuck off** VI + ADV irse a la mierda**; ~ off! ¡vete a tomar por el culo!**, ¡vete al carajo! (*LAm***), ¡vete a la chingada! (*Mex***)

► fuck up** (A) VT + ADV joder**
(B) VI + ADV cagarla‡

fuck-all** [ˌfʌk'ɔːl] (*Brit*) (A) ADJ it's ~ use no sirve para maldita la cosa*
(B) N I know ~ about it no tengo ni puta idea**; he's done ~ today hoy no ha hecho más que tocarse los huevos *or* cojones**, hoy no ha pegado ni golpe*

fucker** ['fʌkəʳ] N hijo/a *m/f* de puta**, cabronazo** *m*

fucking** ['fʌkɪŋ] (A) ADJ de los cojones**, fregado (*LAm***), chingado (*Mex***); ~ hell! ¡joder!**, ¡coño!**
(B) ADV it was ~ awful fue de puta pena**; it's ~ cold! ¡hace un frío del carajo!**; that's no ~ good no vale una puta mierda**; I don't ~

know! ¡no lo sé, coño!✱✱
Ⓒ N joder✱✱ m, jodienda✱✱ f

fuck-up✱✱ [ˈfʌkʌp] N cagada✱✱ f

fuddled [ˈfʌdld] ADJ [1] (= muddled) confuso, aturdido
[2] (*) (= tipsy) borracho; to get ~ emborracharse

fuddy-duddy* [ˈfʌdɪˌdʌdɪ] Ⓐ ADJ (= old) viejo; (= old-fashioned) chapado a la antigua
Ⓑ N carroza* mf

fudge [fʌdʒ] Ⓐ N (Culin) dulce m de azúcar
Ⓑ VT [+ issue, problem] esquivar, eludir
Ⓒ VI eludir la cuestión

fuel [fjʊəl] Ⓐ N [1] (gen) combustible m; (for engine) carburante m; (specifically coal) carbón m; (= wood) leña f
[2] (fig) pábulo m; ✦IDIOM to add ~ to the flames echar leña al fuego
Ⓑ VT [1] [+ furnace etc] alimentar; [+ aircraft, ship etc] repostar
[2] (fig) [+ speculation etc] estimular, provocar; [+ dispute] avivar, acalorar
Ⓒ VI [aircraft, ship] repostar
Ⓓ CPD ► fuel cap N (Aut) tapa f del depósito de gasolina ► fuel crisis N crisis f inv energética ► fuel injection (engine) N motor m de inyección ► fuel needs NPL necesidades fpl energéticas ► fuel oil N fuel oil m, mazut m ► fuel policy N política f energética ► fuel pump N (Aut) surtidor m de gasolina ► fuel tank N depósito m (de combustible)

fuel-saving [ˈfjʊəlˌseɪvɪŋ] ADJ que ahorra combustible

fug [fʌg] N (esp Brit) aire m viciado; what a ~! ¡qué olor!; there's a ~ in here aquí huele a cerrado

fuggy [ˈfʌgɪ] ADJ (esp Brit) [air] viciado, cargado; [room] que huele a cerrado

fugitive [ˈfjuːdʒɪtɪv] Ⓐ ADJ [1] fugitivo
[2] (liter) (= fleeting) efímero, pasajero
Ⓑ N fugitivo/a m/f; (= refugee) refugiado/a m/f; ~ from justice prófugo/a m/f (de la justicia)

fugue [fjuːg] N fuga f

> **FULBRIGHT**
>
> *Las becas **Fulbright** son concedidas por el gobierno de Estados Unidos a licenciados nacionales y extranjeros con el fin de facilitar la ampliación de estudios y el acceso a la investigación o la enseñanza dentro del país. Miles de personas se han beneficiado de estas becas desde que se introdujo el programa **Fulbright** en 1946, como parte de la legislación establecida por el senador J. William Fulbright, un hombre de estado demócrata con gran experiencia en política exterior.*

fulcrum [ˈfʌlkrəm] N (pl fulcrums or fulcra [ˈfʌlkrə]) fulcro m; (fig) piedra f angular, punto m de apoyo

fulfil, fulfill (US) [fʊlˈfɪl] VT [1] (= carry out) [+ duty, promise] cumplir con; [+ role] desempeñar; [+ order] cumplir; [+ plan, task] llevar a cabo, realizar
[2] (= meet) [+ condition, requirement] satisfacer, cumplir; [+ need] satisfacer; [+ hopes] hacer realidad
[3] (= attain) [+ ambition] realizar; [+ potential] alcanzar
[4] (= satisfy) [+ person] satisfacer, llenar; to ~ o.s. realizarse (plenamente)

fulfilling [fʊlˈfɪlɪŋ] ADJ he has a ~ job tiene un trabajo que le satisface or llena

fulfilment, fulfillment (US) [fʊlˈfɪlmənt] N [1] [of duty, promise, order] cumplimiento m
[2] [of condition, requirement, need] satisfacción f
[3] [of ambition, potential] realización f
[4] (= satisfied feeling) realización f, satisfacción f

full [fʊl] Ⓐ ADJ (compar fuller, superl fullest) [1] (= filled) [room, hall, theatre] lleno; [vehicle] completo; [hotel] lleno, completo; "house full" (Theat) "no hay localidades", "completo"; ~ to the brim hasta el tope; ~ to bursting lleno de bote en bote; ~ to overflowing lleno hasta los bordes; we are ~ up for July estamos completos para julio; his heart was ~ (liter) tenía el corazón apenado
[2] to be ~ of ... estar lleno de ...; the papers were ~ of the murders los periódicos no traían más que noticias de los asesinatos; ~ of cares lleno de cuidados; a look ~ of hate una mirada cargada de odio; ~ of hope lleno de esperanza, ilusionado; he's ~ of good ideas tiene muchísimas ideas buenas; to be ~ of o.s. or one's own importance ser muy engreído or creído; to be ~ of life estar lleno de vida; ✦IDIOMS to be ~ of it* (= excited) estar animadísimo; to be ~ of shit✱✱ no tener puñetera idea✱
[3] (= complete) completo, entero; [account] detallado, extenso; [meal] completo; [power] pleno; [price, pay] íntegro, sin descuento; [speed, strength] máximo; [text] íntegro; [uniform] de gala; a ~ three miles tres millas largas; I waited a ~ hour esperé una hora entera; to take ~ advantage of the situation aprovecharse al máximo de la situación; to put one's headlights on ~ beam poner las luces largas or de carretera; in ~ bloom en plena flor; in ~ colour a todo color; in ~ daylight en pleno día; to pay ~ fare pagar la tarifa íntegra; to fall ~ length caer cuán largo se es; he was lying ~ length estaba tumbado todo lo largo que era; he's had a ~ life ha llevado una vida muy completa; the ~ particulars todos los detalles; he was suspended on ~ pay se le suspendió sin reducción de sueldo; to pay ~ price for sth (for goods, tickets) pagar el precio íntegro de algo; in the ~est sense of the word en el sentido más amplio de la palabra; at ~ speed a toda velocidad; ~ speed or steam ahead! (Naut) ¡avance a toda marcha!; at ~ strength [team, battalion] completo; ✦IDIOMS in ~ cry a toda carrera; to go ~ steam ahead ponerse en marcha a todo vapor; in ~ swing en pleno apogeo
[4] (= ample) [face] redondo; [figure] llenito; [lips] grueso; [skirt, sleeves] amplio; clothes for the ~er figure tallas fpl grandes
[5] (= busy) [day, timetable] muy ocupado; I've had a ~ day he estado ocupado todo el día
[6] (Pol etc) [session] pleno, plenario; [member] de pleno derecho
[7] (after eating) I'm ~ (up)* no puedo más, estoy harto or ahíto; you'll work better on a ~ stomach trabajarás mejor con el estómago lleno or después de haber comido
[8] (in titles) ~ colonel coronel(a) m/f; ~ general general mf; ~ professor (US) profesor(a) m/f titular
Ⓑ ADV it hit him ~ in the face le pegó en plena cara; to turn the sound/volume up ~ subir el volumen a tope; to go ~ out to do sth* ir a por todas para hacer algo*; ~ well muy bien, perfectamente; to know ~ well that saber perfectamente que; he understands ~ well that se da cuenta cabal de que
Ⓒ N in ~: name in ~ nombre m y apellidos; text in ~ texto m íntegro; to pay in ~ pagar la deuda entera; to write sth in ~ escribir algo por extenso; to the ~ al máximo
Ⓓ CPD ► full brother N hermano m carnal ► full cost N coste m total ► full dress N traje m de etiqueta or de gala; in ~ dress vestido de etiqueta or de gala ► full employment N pleno empleo m ► full house N (Cards) full m; (Bingo) cartón m; (Theat) lleno m ► full marks NPL puntuación fsing máxima; ~ marks for persistence! (fig) ¡te mereces un premio a la perseverancia! ► full measure N medida f or cantidad f completa ► full moon N luna f llena ► full name N nombre m y apellidos ► full sister N hermana f carnal ► full stop N (Brit Gram) punto m (y seguido); I'm not going, ~ stop! ¡no voy, y punto or y se acabó!; ✦IDIOM to come to a ~ stop pararse, paralizarse, quedar detenido en un punto muerto ► full time N (Brit Sport) final m del partido; see also full-time

fullback [ˈfʊlbæk] N (Ftbl) defensa mf; (Rugby) zaguero m

full-beam [ˈfʊlˈbiːm] ADJ ~ headlights luces fpl largas or de carretera

full-blast [ˈfʊlˈblɑːst] ADV [work] a pleno rendimiento; [travel] a toda velocidad; [play music etc] a todo volumen

full-blooded [ˈfʊlˈblʌdɪd] ADJ [1] (= vigorous) [attack] vigoroso; [character] viril, vigoroso
[2] (= thoroughbred) (de) pura sangre

full-blown [ˈfʊlˈbləʊn] ADJ [doctor etc] hecho y derecho; [attack, invasion etc] a gran escala; he has ~ AIDS tiene el SIDA en su estado más avanzado

full-bodied [ˈfʊlˈbɒdɪd] ADJ [cry] fuerte; [wine] de mucho cuerpo

full-cream milk [ˌfʊlkriːmˈmɪlk] N leche f (con toda la nata)

full-dress [ˌfʊlˈdres] ADJ [function] de etiqueta, de gala

fuller's earth [ˌfʊləzˈɜːθ] N tierra f de batán

full-face [ˌfʊlˈfeɪs] ADJ [portrait] de rostro entero

full-fledged [ˌfʊlˈfledʒd] ADJ (US) = fully-fledged

full-frontal [ˌfʊlˈfrʌntl] Ⓐ ADJ (= unrestrained) desenfrenado
Ⓑ CPD ► full-frontal nude N desnudo m visto de frente ► full-frontal nudity N desnudo m integral

full-grown [ˌfʊlˈgrəʊn] ADJ maduro

full-length [ˌfʊlˈleŋθ] Ⓐ ADJ [portrait, dress] de cuerpo entero; [novel, study] extenso; [swimming pool etc] de tamaño normal; a ~ film un largometraje
Ⓑ ADV he was lying ~ estaba tumbado todo lo largo que era

fullness [ˈfʊlnɪs] N [1] [of detail] abundancia f
[2] [of figure] plenitud f; [of dress] amplitud f
[3] in the ~ of time (liter) (= eventually) con el correr del tiempo; (= at predestined time) a su debido tiempo

full-on* [fʊlˈɒn] ADJ total, en toda regla

full-page [ˌfʊlˈpeɪdʒ] ADJ [advert etc] a toda plana

full-scale [ˌfʊlˈskeɪl] ADJ [plan, model] de tamaño natural; [search, retreat] a gran escala; [study] amplio, extenso; [investigation] de gran alcance

full-sized [ˌfʊlˈsaɪzd] ADJ de tamaño normal

full-throated [ˌfʊlˈθrəʊtɪd] ADJ [cry etc] fuerte, a pleno pulmón

full-time [ˌfʊlˈtaɪm] Ⓐ ADJ [employment] a tiempo completo; [employee] que trabaja una jornada completa, que trabaja a tiempo completo; he's a ~ musician (= professional) es músico profesional; a ~ job un puesto de trabajo a tiempo completo; **a ~ course** un curso de dedicación plena

Ⓑ ADV **to work ~** trabajar a tiempo completo

fully ['fʊlɪ] ADV [1] (= *completely*) **I was not ~ awake** no estaba completamente despierto, no estaba despierto del todo; **he was ~ aware of the problem** se daba perfecta cuenta del problema; **~ booked** todo reservado, completo; **~ dressed** completamente vestido; **I ~ expected to see you there** esperaba verte allí; **a ~ grown tiger** un tigre adulto; **I ~ intended to let you know** tenía la firme intención de decírtelo; **she is a ~ qualified swimming instructor** es profesora de natación diplomada; **when he has ~ recovered** cuando se haya recuperado completamente *or* del todo; **I don't ~ understand** no lo acabo de comprender, no lo entiendo del todo

[2] (= *at least*) por lo menos; **he earns ~ as much as I do** gana por lo menos lo mismo que yo; **it is ~ three miles** son por lo menos tres millas

[3] (= *in detail*) [*describe, explain*] con todo detalle; [*discuss*] a fondo

[4] (= *in full*) [*reimburse*] enteramente

fully-fashioned [ˌfʊlɪ'fæʃnd] ADJ [*stocking*] menguado, de costura francesa

fully-fledged, **full-fledged** (*US*) [ˌfʊlɪ'fledʒd] ADJ (*Brit*) [*bird*] adulto, en edad capaz de volar; (*fig*) hecho y derecho

fully-paid share [ˌfʊlɪpeɪd'ʃɛəʳ] N acción *f* liberada

fulminate ['fʊlmɪneɪt] VI (*frm*) **to ~ against** tronar contra

fulmination [ˌfʊlmɪ'neɪʃən] N (*frm*) invectiva *f*, filípica *f* (**against** contra)

fulsome ['fʊlsəm] ADJ (*pej*) [*praise*] excesivo, exagerado; [*manner*] obsequioso

fumble ['fʌmbl] Ⓐ VT (= *drop*) dejar caer; (= *handle badly*) manosear, coger *or* (*LAm*) agarrar con torpeza; **to ~ one's way along** ir a tientas

Ⓑ VI (*also* **~ about**) hurgar; **to ~ in one's pockets** hurgar en los bolsillos; **to ~ for sth** buscar algo con las manos; **to ~ for a word** titubear buscando una palabra; **to ~ with sth** manejar algo torpemente; **to ~ with a door** forcejear para abrir una puerta

fume [fju:m] Ⓐ VI [1] [*chemicals etc*] humear, echar humo

[2] (= *be furious*) estar furioso, echar humo; **to be fuming at** *or* **with sb** echar pestes de algn

Ⓑ **fumes** NPL (*gen*) humo *msing*, vapores *mpl*; (= *gas*) gases *mpl*

fumigate ['fju:mɪgeɪt] VT fumigar

fumigation [ˌfju:mɪ'geɪʃən] N fumigación *f*

fun [fʌn] Ⓐ N (= *enjoyment*) diversión *f*; (= *merriment*) alegría *f*; **it's great ~** es muy divertido; **he's great ~** es una persona muy divertida; **it's not much ~ for us** para nosotros no es nada divertido; **it's only his ~** está bromeando, te está tomando el pelo; **for** *or* **in ~** en broma; **to do sth for the ~ of it** hacer algo por divertirse; **~ and games** (= *lively behaviour*) travesuras *fpl*; (*fig*) (= *trouble*) jaleo *m*, bronca *f*; **she's been having ~ and games with the washing machine** ha tenido muchos problemas con la lavadora; **to have ~** divertirse; **have ~!** ¡que os divirtáis!, ¡que lo paséis bien!; **what ~ we had!** ¡qué bien lo pasamos!, ¡cómo nos divertimos!; **we had ~ with the passports** (*iro*) nos armamos un lío con los pasaportes; **to make ~ of sb** burlarse de algn, tomar el pelo a algn*; **to poke ~ at** burlarse de; **to spoil the ~** aguar la fiesta

Ⓑ ADJ (*) **it's a ~ thing** es para divertirse; **she's a ~ person** es una persona divertida

Ⓒ CPD ► **fun run** N maratón *m* corto (*de ciudad para los no atletas*)

function ['fʌŋkʃən] Ⓐ N [1] (= *purpose*) [*of machine, person*] función *f*; **it's not part of my ~ to** (+ INFIN) no me corresponde a mí + *infin*

[2] (= *reception*) recepción *f*; (= *official ceremony*) acto *m*

[3] (*Math*) función *f*

Ⓑ VI (= *operate*) funcionar, marchar; **to ~ as** hacer (las veces) de

Ⓒ CPD ► **function key** N tecla *f* de función ► **function word** N palabra *f* funcional

functional ['fʌŋkʃnəl] Ⓐ ADJ [*design, clothes*] funcional

Ⓑ CPD ► **functional analysis** N análisis *m inv* funcional

functionalism ['fʌŋkʃnəlɪzəm] N funcionalismo *m*

functionalist ['fʌŋkʃnəlɪst] (*frm*) Ⓐ ADJ funcionalista

Ⓑ N funcionalista *mf*

functionary ['fʌŋkʃənərɪ] N funcionario/a *m/f*

fund [fʌnd] Ⓐ N (*gen*) fondo *m*; (= *reserve*) reserva *f*; **funds** fondos *mpl*, recursos *mpl*; **to raise ~s** recaudar fondos; **to be in ~s** estar en fondos; **to be a ~ of information** ser una buena fuente de información; **to have a ~ of stories** saber un montón de historias

Ⓑ VT [+ *project*] financiar; [+ *debt*] consolidar

▼**fundamental** [ˌfʌndə'mentl] Ⓐ ADJ [1] (= *basic*) [*question, problem, principle*] fundamental; **they are being denied their ~ human rights** se les está privando de los derechos humanos fundamentales

[2] (= *profound, great*) [*change, difference*] fundamental; **it is a ~ mistake to think that ...** es un error fundamental pensar que ...

[3] (= *essential*) fundamental, esencial; **to be ~ to sth** ser fundamental *or* esencial para algo; **it is ~ to our understanding of the problem** es fundamental *or* esencial para que entendamos el problema

[4] (= *intrinsic*) [*honesty, good sense*] intrínseco

Ⓑ NPL **the ~s** los fundamentos, lo básico

fundamentalism [ˌfʌndə'mentəlɪzəm] N fundamentalismo *m*

fundamentalist [ˌfʌndə'mentəlɪst] Ⓐ ADJ fundamentalista, integrista

Ⓑ N fundamentalista *mf*, integrista *mf*

fundamentally [ˌfʌndə'mentəlɪ] ADV [1] (= *basically*) básicamente, en lo fundamental; **the situation remains ~ the same** básicamente *or* en lo fundamental, la situación no cambia; **~, your children are your responsibility** básicamente, sus hijos son responsabilidad suya; **he is still ~ optimistic about the situation** básicamente sigue sintiéndose optimista en cuanto a la situación

[2] (= *profoundly*) fundamentalmente; **their lifestyle is ~ different to ours** su forma de vida es fundamentalmente distinta a la nuestra; **there is something ~ wrong in what he says** hay un error fundamental en lo que dice; **it is ~ important that this project continues** es de vital importancia *or* es fundamental que el proyecto siga adelante

[3] (= *intrinsically*) intrínsecamente

fund-holding GP [ˌfʌndhəʊldɪŋdʒi:'pi:] N *médico de cabecera con responsabilidad sobre la gestión de fondos presupuestados para su zona*

funding ['fʌndɪŋ] N [1] (= *funds*) fondos *mpl*, finanzas *fpl*; (= *act of funding*) financiación *f*

[2] [*of debt*] consolidación *f*

fund-raiser ['fʌnd,reɪzəʳ] N recaudador(a) *m/f* de fondos

fund-raising ['fʌnd,reɪzɪŋ] N recaudación *f* de fondos

▼**funeral** ['fju:nərəl] Ⓐ N (= *burial*) funeral *m*, entierro *m*; (= *wake*) velatorio *m*; (= *service*) exequias *fpl*; **state ~** entierro *m or* funeral *m* con honores de estado; **that's your ~!*** ¡con tu pan te lo comas!

Ⓑ CPD ► **funeral cortège** N cortejo *m* fúnebre ► **funeral director** N director(a) *m/f* de funeraria ► **funeral home** N (*US*) = **funeral parlour** ► **funeral march** N marcha *f* fúnebre ► **funeral oration** N oración *f* fúnebre ► **funeral parlour** N funeraria *f* ► **funeral procession** N cortejo *m* fúnebre ► **funeral service** N exequias *fpl*

funerary ['fju:nərərɪ] ADJ (*frm*) [*monument*] funerario; [*ceremony*] fúnebre

funereal [fju:'nɪərɪəl] ADJ fúnebre, funéreo

funfair ['fʌnfɛəʳ] N (*Brit*) parque *m* de atracciones

fungal ['fʌŋgl] ADJ [*infection, disease*] micótico, de hongos

fungi ['fʌŋgaɪ] NPL *of* **fungus**

fungicide ['fʌŋgɪsaɪd] N fungicida *m*

fungoid ['fʌŋgɔɪd] ADJ parecido a un hongo, como un hongo; (*Med*) fungoide

fungous ['fʌŋgəs] ADJ fungoso

fungus ['fʌŋgəs] N (*pl* **fungi**) hongo *m*

funicular railway [fju:,nɪkjʊlə'reɪlweɪ] N funicular *m*

funk [fʌŋk] Ⓐ N [1] (*) (= *fear*) **to be in a (blue) ~** estar muerto de miedo

[2] (*Mus*) funk *m*

Ⓑ VT **to ~ it** rajarse; **to ~ doing something** dejar de hacer algo por miedo

funky* ['fʌŋkɪ] ADJ (*compar* **funkier**; *superl* **funkiest**) [*music*] vibrante, marchoso

fun-loving ['fʌn,lʌvɪŋ] ADJ amigo de diversiones

funnel ['fʌnl] Ⓐ N (*for pouring*) embudo *m*; [*of ship, steam engine etc*] chimenea *f*

Ⓑ VT [+ *traffic etc*] canalizar (**through** por); [+ *aid,finance*] encauzar, canalizar (**through** a través de)

funnily ['fʌnɪlɪ] ADV [1] (= *amusingly*) con gracia

[2] (= *oddly*) de forma extraña, de forma rara; **he was behaving rather ~ that day** ese día se estaba comportando de forma extraña *or* rara; **~ enough ...** aunque parezca extraño ...; **~ enough, it doesn't bother her at all** aunque parezca extraño, no le molesta en absoluto

funny ['fʌnɪ] Ⓐ ADJ (*compar* **funnier**; *superl* **funniest**) [1] (= *amusing*) [*person, joke, film, story*] gracioso; **you look so ~ in that costume** tienes una pinta graciosísima con ese disfraz; **it was so ~, I just couldn't stop laughing** era tan gracioso que no podía dejar de reírme; **he's trying to be ~** quiere hacerse el gracioso; **that's not ~** eso no tiene gracia

[2] (= *odd*) raro; **~! I thought he'd left** ¡qué raro! creía que ya se había marchado; **it strikes me as ~** *or* **I find it ~ that ...** me extraña que + *subjun*, me parece raro que + *subjun*; **(it's) ~ you should say that** qué curioso que digas eso; **there's something ~ going on here** aquí hay gato encerrado; **he's ~ that way** tiene esa manía; **I feel ~** (= *unwell*) no me encuentro muy bien; **it felt ~ going there on my own** se me hizo extraño ir allí solo; **I have the ~ feeling I'm going to regret this** tengo la extraña sensación de que me voy a arrepentir de esto; **I've got a ~ feeling in my stomach** tengo una sensación rara en el estómago; **he must be ~ in the head** tiene que estar ido *or* tocado de la cabeza;

children get some very ~ ideas sometimes! ¡a los niños se les ocurre a veces cada idea!; **this smells/tastes ~** esto huele/sabe raro; **the ~ thing about it is that ...** lo curioso *or* extraño del caso es que ...; ✦*IDIOM* **~ peculiar or ~ ha-ha?*** ¿extraño o divertido?
Ⓑ N **the funnies** (*US*) las tiras cómicas
Ⓒ CPD ► **funny bone** N hueso *m* del codo; **the show seems to have tickled everyone's ~bone** (*fig*) el programa parece haberle hecho gracia a todo el mundo ► **funny business** N tejemanejes* *mpl*; **don't try any ~ business** nada de tejemanejes* ► **funny farm*** N (*hum*) loquero* *m* ► **funny man** N cómico *m* ► **funny money*** N (= *large sum*) una millonada; (= *counterfeit money*) dinero *m* falso; (= *ill-gotten money*) dinero *m* mal habido

fur [fɜːʳ] Ⓐ N 1 [*of animal*] pelo *m*, pelaje *m*; (= *single skin*) piel *f*; (= *coat*) abrigo *m* de pieles
2 (*in kettle*) sarro *m*
3 (*on tongue*) saburra *f*
Ⓑ VI [*kettle etc*] (*also* **~ up**) cubrirse de sarro, formar sarro
Ⓒ CPD ► **fur coat** N abrigo *m* de pieles

furbish [ˈfɜːbɪʃ] VT **to ~ up** renovar, restaurar

furious [ˈfjʊərɪəs] ADJ 1 (= *angry*) [*person, reaction*] furioso; **to be ~ (with sb)** estar furioso (con algn); **she'll be ~ if she finds out** se va a poner furiosa si se entera; **to get ~** ponerse furioso
2 (= *violent, unrestrained*) [*argument, struggle*] violento; [*activity*] frenético; [*pace, speed*] vertiginoso; [*storm, sea*] furioso; *see also* **fast**[1] **A1**

furiously [ˈfjʊərɪəslɪ] ADV 1 (= *angrily*) con furia, furiosamente
2 (= *violently, energetically*) [*work, write*] frenéticamente; **he was silent, his mind working ~** estaba callado, su cerebro trabajando frenéticamente

furl [fɜːl] VT (*Naut*) aferrar; [+ *wings*] recoger

furlong [ˈfɜːlɒŋ] N estadio *m* (*octava parte de una milla*)

furlough [ˈfɜːləʊ] N (*US*) permiso *m*

furnace [ˈfɜːnɪs] N horno *m*; **the room was like a ~** la habitación era un horno

furnish [ˈfɜːnɪʃ] VT 1 [+ *room, house*] amueblar (**with** con); **~ing fabric** tela *f* para revestir muebles; **~ed flat** piso *m* amueblado, departamento *m* amoblado (*LAm*)
2 (= *provide*) [+ *excuse, information*] proporcionar, facilitar; [+ *proof*] aducir; **to ~ sb with sth** [+ *supplies*] proveer a algn de algo; [+ *opportunity*] dar *or* proporcionar algo a algn

furnishings [ˈfɜːnɪʃɪŋz] NPL muebles *mpl*, mobiliario *msing*

furniture [ˈfɜːnɪtʃəʳ] Ⓐ N muebles *mpl*, mobiliario *m*; **a piece of ~** un mueble; **part of the ~*** (*fig*) parte *f* de la casa *or* del mobiliario
Ⓑ CPD ► **furniture mover** N (*US*) = **furniture remover** ► **furniture polish** N cera *f* para muebles ► **furniture remover** N compañía *f* de mudanzas ► **furniture shop** N tienda *f* de muebles ► **furniture van** N camión *m* de mudanzas

furore [fjʊəˈrɔːrɪ], **furor** (*US*) [ˈfjʊərɔːʳ] N (= *protests*) ola *f* de protestas, escándalo *m*; (= *excitement*) ola *f* de entusiasmo

furrier [ˈfʌrɪəʳ] N peletero/a *m/f*; **~'s (shop)** peletería *f*

furrow [ˈfʌrəʊ] Ⓐ N (*Agr*) surco *m*; (*on forehead*) arruga *f*; ✦*IDIOM* **to plough a lonely ~** ser el único en estudiar algo
Ⓑ VT [+ *forehead*] arrugar
Ⓒ VI arrugarse; **his brow ~ed** frunció el ceño

furrowed [ˈfʌrəʊd] ADJ **with ~ brow** con ceño fruncido

furry [ˈfɜːrɪ] Ⓐ ADJ [*animal*] peludo; [*teddy bear*] de peluche
Ⓑ CPD ► **furry dice** NPL (*Brit*) dados *mpl* afelpados (*tipo de colgante para el coche*) ► **furry toy** N (juguete *m* de) peluche *m*

further [ˈfɜːðəʳ] Ⓐ ADV COMPAR *of* **far** 1 (*in distance*) **how much ~ is it?** ¿cuánto camino nos queda?; **have you much ~ to go?** ¿le queda mucho camino por hacer?; **let's go ~ north/south** vayamos más al norte/sur; **his car was parked ~ along** su coche estaba aparcado un poco más arriba/abajo; **a crowd was gathering ~ along the street** se estaba congregando una multitud de gente calle arriba/abajo; **we were too tired to go any ~ that day** estábamos demasiado cansados para continuar ese día; **move it ~ away** apártalo un poco más; **we live ~ away from the city centre** vivimos más lejos del centro de la ciudad; **~ back** más atrás; **I think it's ~ down the road** creo que está bajando un poco más la calle; **I was visiting a friend ~ down the street** estaba visitando a un amigo que vive bajando un poco la calle; **I don't think we want to go any ~ down that road** (*fig*) no creo que sea prudente seguir por ese camino (*fig*); **I need to be a bit ~ forward** tengo que ponerme un poco más para delante; **nothing was ~ from my thoughts** nada más lejos de mi intención; **I sank even ~ in** me hundí aún más; **~ on** más adelante; **the track ended a mile ~ on** el camino terminaba una milla más adelante; **the boat drifted ~ out to sea** la barca iba siendo arrastrada mar adentro; **~ to the south** más al sur; **we decided to go ~ up the track** decidimos seguir avanzando por el camino
2 (*in time*) **let's look a little ~ ahead** miremos un poco más adelante; **I never plan anything ~ than a week ahead** nunca planeo nada con más de una semana de antelación; **there is evidence of this even ~ back in history** incluso más antiguamente se ven evidencias de esto; **records go no ~ back than 1960** los archivos sólo se remontan a 1960
3 (= *in progress*) **you'll get ~ with her if you're polite** conseguirás más si se lo pides educadamente; **I got no ~ with him** (*in questioning*) no pude sacarle nada más; **we need to go ~ and address the issues** tenemos que ir más allá y proponer soluciones a los problemas; **he went ~, claiming the man had attacked him** no se quedó ahí, sino que aseguró que el hombre lo había atacado; **this mustn't go any ~** [*confidential matter*] esto que no pase de aquí; **to go ~ into a matter** estudiar una cosa más a fondo; **~ on in this chapter** más adelante en este capítulo; **I think we should take this matter ~** creo que deberíamos proseguir con este asunto
4 (= *more*) más; **they questioned us ~** nos hicieron más preguntas; **this will ~ damage the country's image** esto va a perjudicar más la imagen del país; **I heard nothing ~ from them** no supe más de ellos; **don't trouble yourself any ~** no se moleste más
5 (= *in addition*) además; **and I ~ believe that ...** y creo además que ...
6 (*Comm*) (*in correspondence*) **~ to your letter of the 7th** con *or* en relación a su carta del 7
Ⓑ ADJ COMPAR *of* **far** (= *additional*) más; **I have no ~ comment to make** no tengo nada más que añadir; **after ~ consideration** tras considerarlo más detenidamente; **without ~ delay** sin más demora; **please send me ~ details of your products** le ruego me envíen más información con respecto a sus productos; **we have no ~ need of your services** ya no necesitamos sus servicios; **until ~ notice** hasta nuevo aviso; **he was detained for ~ questioning** lo retuvieron para someterle a un nuevo interrogatorio; **recommendations for ~ reading** sugerencias de lecturas complementarias *or* adicionales
Ⓒ VT (= *promote*) [+ *cause, aim, understanding, career*] promover, fomentar; **she was accused of ~ing her own interests** la acusaron de actuar en beneficio de sus propios intereses
Ⓓ CPD ► **further education** N educación *f* superior, educación *f* postescolar

furtherance [ˈfɜːðərəns] N promoción *f*, fomento *m*

furthermore [ˈfɜːðɜːˈmɔːʳ] ADV además

furthermost [ˈfɜːðəməʊst] ADJ más lejano

furthest [ˈfɜːðɪst] Ⓐ ADV SUPERL *of* **far** 1 (*in distance*) más lejos; **who has the ~ to go home?** ¿quién es el que vive más lejos?; **that's the ~ that anyone has gone** ése es el punto más lejano al que se ha llegado
2 (*in progress*) **that was the ~ the club had ever gone** eso era lo máximo a lo que el club había llegado; **Poland has taken these ideas ~** Polonia ha sido el país que más ha desarrollado estas ideas
3 (= *most*) más; **prices have fallen ~ in the south of England** donde más han bajado los precios ha sido en el sur de Inglaterra
Ⓑ ADJ más lejano; **the ~ point** el punto más lejano; **the seat ~ from the window** el asiento que más lejos está de la ventana; **the ~ recesses of the mind** los recovecos más olvidados de la mente

furtive [ˈfɜːtɪv] ADJ [*glance, action*] furtivo; [*person*] sospechoso

furtively [ˈfɜːtɪvlɪ] ADV furtivamente

fury [ˈfjʊərɪ] N [*of person*] furia *f*, furor *m*; [*of storm etc*] furia *f*; **to be in a ~** estar furioso; **she flew into a ~** se puso furiosa; **she worked herself up into a ~** montó en cólera; **like ~*** con encono; **the Furies** las Furias

furze [fɜːz] N aulaga *f*, tojo *m*

fuse, **fuze** (*US*) [fjuːz] Ⓐ N 1 (*Elec*) plomo *m*, fusible *m*; **to blow a ~** [*equipment*] fundirse un fusible; [*person*] salirse de sus casillas; **there's been a ~ somewhere** ◊ **a ~ has blown somewhere** un fusible se ha fundido en algún sitio
2 [*of bomb*] (= *cord*) mecha *f*; (= *detonating device*) espoleta *f*; ✦*IDIOM* **he has a very short ~*** tiene un genio muy vivo
Ⓑ VT 1 [+ *lights, television etc*] fundir
2 [+ *metals*] fundir
Ⓒ VI 1 (*Elec*) **the lights have ~d** se han fundido los plomos
2 [*metals*] fundirse
Ⓓ CPD ► **fuse box** N caja *f* de fusibles ► **fuse wire** N hilo *m* fusible

fused [fjuːzd] Ⓐ ADJ (*Elec*) con fusible
Ⓑ CPD ► **fused plug** N enchufe *m* con fusible

fuselage [ˈfjuːzəlɑːʒ] N fuselaje *m*

fusilier [ˌfjuːzɪˈlɪəʳ] N (*Brit*) fusilero *m*

fusillade [ˌfjuːzɪˈleɪd] N (*lit*) descarga *f* cerrada; (*fig*) lluvia *f*

fusion [ˈfjuːʒən] N [*of metals, fig*] fusión *f*

fuss [fʌs] Ⓐ N 1 (= *complaints, arguments*) escándalo *m*, alboroto *m*; **to make** *or* **kick up a ~ about sth** armar un escándalo por algo, armar un lío *or* un follón por algo*; **he's always making a ~ about nothing** siempre monta el número por cualquier tontería*; **I think you**

were quite right to make a ~ creo que hiciste bien en protestar; **there's no need to make such a ~** no hay por qué ponerse así, no es para tanto
[2] (= *anxious preparations etc*) conmoción *f*, bulla *f*; **a lot of ~ about nothing** mucho ruido y pocas nueces; **such a ~ to get a passport!** ¡tanta lata para conseguir un pasaporte!*; **what's all the ~ about?** ¿a qué viene tanto jaleo?
[3] **to make a ~ of sb** (*Brit*) (= *spoil*) mimar *or* consentir a algn
Ⓑ VI preocuparse por pequeñeces
Ⓒ VT [+ *person*] molestar, fastidiar; **don't ~ me!** ¡deja ya de fastidiarme!

►**fuss about, fuss around** VI + ADV (= *busy o.s.*) andar de acá para allá; (= *worry unnecessarily*) preocuparse por pequeñeces

►**fuss over** VI + PREP [+ *person*] consentir a

fussbudget* ['fʌs,bʌdʒɪt] N (*US*) = **fusspot**

fussed* [fʌst] ADJ (*Brit*) **I'm not ~** me da igual, me da lo mismo; **I'm not ~ about going to the party** me da igual *or* lo mismo ir a la fiesta que no

fussily ['fʌsɪlɪ] ADV [1] (= *demandingly*) (*pej*) quisquillosamente; (= *scrupulously*) meticulosamente, escrupulosamente
[2] (= *elaborately*) [*designed, dressed*] de manera recargada
[3] (= *nervously*) nerviosamente

fussiness ['fʌsɪnɪs] N [1] (= *exacting nature*) [1·1] (*pej*) **his ~ about food is driving me mad** sus mañías para la comida me están volviendo loco
[1·2] (= *scrupulousness*) meticulosidad *f*, escrupulosidad *f*; **~ about details is an asset in this job** la meticulosidad *or* escrupulosidad en los detalles es un punto a favor para este puesto
[2] (= *elaborateness*) [*of design, clothes*] lo recargado

fusspot* ['fʌspɒt] N quisquilloso/a *m/f*

fussy ['fʌsɪ] ADJ (*compar* **fussier**; *superl* **fussiest**)
[1] (= *exacting*) [*person*] [1·1] (*pej*) quisquilloso; **they'll think you're ~ if you ring them** van a creer que eres quisquilloso *or* difícil si les llamas; **children are often ~ eaters** los niños son a menudo quisquillosos *or* especiales para la comida
[1·2] (= *scrupulous*) **he's very ~ about detail** es muy escrupuloso *or* meticuloso con los detalles
[1·3] (= *selective*) selectivo; **I'm very ~ about the parts I take on** soy muy selectivo a la hora de elegir papeles, no elijo cualquier papel; **I'm very ~ about what I wear** soy muy especial a la hora de vestir; **I'm not ~*** me da igual, me da lo mismo
[2] (= *elaborate*) [*design, clothes*] recargado, con muchos ringorrangos*
[3] (= *nervous*) [*manner*] nervioso

fusty ['fʌstɪ] ADJ (*compar* **fustier**; *superl* **fustiest**) rancio; [*air*] viciado; [*room*] que huele a cerrado

futile ['fju:taɪl] ADJ [*attempt*] vano; [*suggestion*] fútil

futility [fju:'tɪlɪtɪ] N inutilidad *f*, lo inútil

futon ['fu:tɒn] N futón *m*

future ['fju:tʃəʳ] Ⓐ ADJ [1] [*husband, generations*] futuro; [*plans*] para el futuro; **at some ~ date** *or* **time** en un futuro; **his ~ prospects are bleak** sus perspectivas de futuro no son nada halagüeñas; **in ~ years** en los años venideros; *see also* **reference**
[2] (*Gram*) **the ~ perfect** el futuro perfecto; **the ~ tense** el futuro
Ⓑ N [1] futuro *m*; **who knows what the ~ holds?** ¿quién sabe lo que nos depara el futuro?; **they see schoolchildren as their customers of the ~** ven a los niños en edad escolar como sus clientes del futuro; **we must look to the ~** tenemos que mirar al futuro; **in ~** de ahora en adelante; **in the ~** en el futuro; **in the near ~** en un futuro próximo *or* cercano; **in the not too distant ~** en un futuro no muy lejano
[2] (= *prospects*) futuro *m*, porvenir *m*; **her ~ is assured** tiene el futuro *or* el porvenir asegurado; **he believes his ~ lies in comedy** piensa que su futuro *or* su porvenir está en la comedia; **there's no ~ in it** no tiene futuro
[3] (*Gram*) futuro *m*; **in the ~** en futuro
[4] **futures** (*Fin*) futuros *mpl*
Ⓒ CPD ► **the futures market** N (*Fin*) el mercado de futuros

futurism ['fju:tʃərɪzəm] N futurismo *m*

futurist ['fju:tʃərɪst] N [1] (*esp US*) (= *futurologist*) futurólogo/a *m/f*
[2] (*Art*) futurista *mf*

futuristic [,fju:tʃə'rɪstɪk] ADJ [*painting, design*] futurista

futurologist [,fju:tʃər'ɒlədʒɪst] N futurólogo/a *m/f*

futurology [,fju:tʃər'ɒlədʒɪ] N futurología *f*

fuze [fju:z] N (*US*) = **fuse**

fuzz [fʌz] N [1] (*on chin*) vello *m*; (= *fluff*) pelusa *f*
[2] **the ~‡** la poli*, la pasma (*Sp‡*), los tiras (*Chile‡*)

fuzzily ['fʌzɪlɪ] ADV [1] (= *hazily*) borrosamente
[2] (= *confusedly*) confusamente

fuzzy [fʌzɪ] Ⓐ ADJ (*compar* **fuzzier**; *superl* **fuzziest**) [1] [*hair*] rizado; [*material*] velloso
[2] (= *blurred*) [*photo, memory*] borroso; [*ideas, thinking*] confuso
Ⓑ CPD ► **fuzzy logic** N (*Comput*) lógica *f* difusa, lógica *f* borrosa

fwd ABBR (*esp Comm*) = **forward**

f-word ['ef,wɜ:d] N **to say the ~** (*euph of "fuck"*) decir "jo...roba"

fwy ABBR (*US*) = **freeway**

FX* NPL ABBR (*Cine*) = **special effects**

FY ABBR = **fiscal year**

FYI ABBR = **for your information**

Gg

G, g[1] [dʒiː] (A) N [1] (= *letter*) G, g *f*; **G for George** G de Gerona
[2] (*Mus*) **G** sol *m*; **G major/minor** sol mayor/menor; **G sharp/flat** sol sostenido/bemol
(B) ABBR [1] (*Scol*) (= *mark*) (= **Good**) N
[2] (*US Cine*) (= **general audience**) todos los públicos
[3] (*) = **grand** (*Brit*) mil libras *fpl*; (*US*) mil dólares *mpl*

g[2] (A) ABBR (= **gram(s), gramme(s)**) g, gr.
(B) N ABBR (= **gravity**) g; **G-force** fuerza *f* de la gravedad

GA ABBR (*US*) = **Georgia**

g.a. ABBR = **general average**

GAB N ABBR = **General Arrangements to Borrow**

gab* [gæb] (A) N ✦*IDIOM* **to have the gift of the ~** tener mucha labia, tener un pico de oro
(B) VI (= *chatter*) parlotear, cotorrear

gabardine [ˌgæbəˈdiːn] N = **gaberdine**

gabble [ˈgæbl] (A) N torrente *m* de palabras ininteligibles
(B) VT farfullar
(C) VI hablar atropelladamente; **they were gabbling away in French** parloteaban en francés

gabby* [ˈgæbɪ] ADJ hablador, locuaz

gaberdine [ˌgæbəˈdiːn] N (= *cloth, raincoat*) gabardina *f*

gable [ˈgeɪbl] (A) N aguilón *m*, gablete *m*
(B) CPD ► **gable end** N hastial *m* ► **gable roof** N tejado *m* de dos aguas

gabled [ˈgeɪbld] ADJ [*houses, roofs*] (con tejado) a dos aguas

Gabon [gəˈbɒn] N Gabón *m*

Gabriel [ˈgeɪbrɪəl] N Gabriel

gad[1] [gæd] VI **to ~ about** callejear, salir de picos pardos

gad[2]†* [gæd] EXCL (*also* **by ~**) ¡cáspita!

gadabout [ˈgædəbaʊt] N azotacalles *mf inv*, pindonga* *f*

gadfly [ˈgædflaɪ] N tábano *m*

gadget [ˈgædʒɪt] N (= *little thing*) artilugio *m*, chisme *m*; (= *device*) aparato *m*

gadgetry [ˈgædʒɪtrɪ] N chismes *mpl*, aparatos *mpl*

gadolinium [ˌgædəˈlɪnɪəm] N gadolinio *m*

gadwall [ˈgædwɔːl] N ánade *m* friso

Gael [geɪl] N gaélico/a *m/f*

Gaelic [ˈgeɪlɪk] (A) ADJ gaélico
(B) N (*Ling*) gaélico *m*
(C) CPD ► **Gaelic coffee** N café *m* irlandés

gaff[1] [gæf] (A) N (*Fishing*) (= *harpoon*) arpón *m*, garfio *m*
(B) VT arponear, enganchar

gaff[2]* [gæf] N (*Brit*) (= *home*) casa *f*

gaff[3] [gæf] N ✦*IDIOM* **to blow the ~*** irse de la lengua, descubrir el pastel

gaffe [gæf] N plancha *f* (*Sp*), metedura *f or* (*LAm*) metida *f* de pata; **to make a ~** meter la pata, tirarse una plancha (*Sp*)

gaffer [ˈgæfəʳ] N [1] (= *old man*) vejete* *m*
[2] (*Brit*) (= *foreman*) capataz *m*; (= *boss*) jefe *m*
[3] (*Cine, TV*) iluminista *mf*

gag [gæg] (A) N [1] (*over mouth*) mordaza *f*; (*Parl*) clausura *f*; **the new law will effectively put a ~ on the free press** en efecto la nueva ley va a poner una mordaza a la prensa libre
[2] (= *joke*) chiste *m*; (= *hoax*) broma *f*; (= *gimmick*) truco *m* publicitario; **it's a ~ to raise funds** es un truco para recaudar fondos
(B) VT [+ *prisoner*] amordazar; (*fig*) amordazar, hacer callar; (*Parl*) clausurar
(C) VI (= *retch*) tener arcadas; **to ~ on** [+ *food*] atragantarse con; ✦*IDIOM* **to be ~ging for it*** estar calentón *or* cachondo*

gaga* [ˈgɑːˈgɑː] ADJ gagá, lelo, chocho; **to go ~** ◊ **be going ~** (= *senile*) chochear; (= *ecstatic*) caérsele a algn la baba

gage [geɪdʒ] N, VT (*US*) = **gauge**

gaggle [ˈgægl] N [*of geese*] manada *f*; (*hum*) [*of people*] pandilla *f*, grupo *m*

gaiety [ˈgeɪɪtɪ] N [1] [*of occasion, person*] alegría *f*
[2] [*of dress, costumes*] colorido *m*, vistosidad *f*

gaily [ˈgeɪlɪ] ADV [1] (= *brightly*) [*dressed, decorated*] vistosamente, alegremente; **~ coloured cushions** cojines de vistosos *or* alegres colores; **~ painted barges** barcazas pintadas con alegres colores
[2] (= *cheerfully*) [*chatter, sing*] alegremente
[3] (= *thoughtlessly*) alegremente, como si tal cosa; **people who ~ fritter away their time** gente que malgasta alegremente el tiempo *or* que malgasta el tiempo como si tal cosa; **she ~ admitted that she had lied** admitió alegremente que había mentido, admitió que había mentido como si tal cosa

gain [geɪn] (A) VT [1] (= *obtain, win*) [+ *respect*] ganarse; [+ *approval, support, supporters*] conseguir; [+ *experience*] adquirir, obtener; [+ *freedom*] obtener, conseguir; [+ *popularity, time*] ganar; [+ *friends*] hacerse; [+ *qualification*] obtener; **what do you hope to ~ by it?** ¿qué provecho esperas sacar con esto?, ¿qué esperas ganar *or* conseguir con esto?; **there is nothing to be ~ed by feeling bitter** no se gana *or* consigue nada guardando rencores; **he had nothing to ~ by lying to me** no iba a ganar *or* conseguir nada mintiéndome; **Serbia's newly ~ed territories** los territorios recientemente adquiridos por Serbia; **to ~ an advantage over sb** sacar ventaja a algn; **to ~ confidence** adquirir confianza; **to ~ sb's confidence** ◊ **~ the confidence of sb** ganar(se) la confianza de algn; **to ~ control of sth** hacerse con el control de algo; **Kenya ~ed independence from Great Britain in 1963** Kenia obtuvo *or* consiguió la independencia de Gran Bretaña en 1963; **my daughter has just ~ed a place at university** mi hija acaba de obtener una plaza en la universidad; **Jones ~ed possession of the ball** Jones se hizo con el balón; **Labour has ~ed three seats from the Conservatives** los laboristas les han arrebatado tres escaños a los conservadores; *see also* **access, entry, ground, hand A11**
[2] (= *increase*) **the shares have ~ed four points** las acciones han aumentado *or* subido cuatro enteros; **my watch has ~ed five minutes** mi reloj se ha adelantado cinco minutos; **to ~ speed** ganar *or* cobrar velocidad; **to ~ strength** (*physically*) cobrar fuerzas; (*mentally*) hacerse más fuerte; **to ~ weight** engordar, aumentar de peso; **I've ~ed three kilos** he engordado tres kilos
[3] (= *arrive at*) llegar a; **the steamer ~ed port** el vapor llegó a puerto
(B) VI [1] (= *profit*) **to ~ by/from sth** beneficiarse de algo; **who would ~ by *or* from his death?** ¿quién iba a beneficiarse de su muerte?; **no one ~s by putting others down** nadie sale beneficiando humillando a los demás; **I ~ed immensely from the experience** me beneficié mucho de la experiencia, saqué mucho provecho de la experiencia; *see also* **stand C11**
[2] (= *advance*) [*watch*] adelantarse; [*runner*] ganar terreno
[3] (= *increase, improve*) [*shares*] aumentar de valor, subir; **to ~ in sth**: **to ~ in popularity** adquirir mayor popularidad; **to ~ in prestige** ganar prestigio; **his reputation ~ed in stature** su reputación aumentó *or* creció
(C) N [1] (= *increase*) aumento *m*; **a ~ in weight** un aumento de peso; **Labour made ~s in the South** los laboristas ganaron terreno en el sur; **the effect of a modest ~ in the pound** el efecto de una pequeña subida en la libra; **a ~ of eight per cent** un aumento *or* una subida del ocho por ciento; **their shares showed a three-point ~** sus acciones experimentaron una subida de tres enteros; **productivity ~s** aumentos *mpl* en la productividad; *see also* **weight C**
[2] (= *benefit, advantage*) beneficio *m*; **they are using the situation for personal/political ~** están utilizando la situación en beneficio propio/para ganar terreno político; ✦*IDIOM* **their loss is our ~** ellos pierden y nosotros ganamos
[3] (*Fin*) (= *profit*) ganancia *f*, beneficio *m*; **the company reported pre-tax ~s of £759 million** la compañía anunció haber obtenido

unos beneficios *or* unas ganancias brutas de 759 millones de libras; *see also* **capital C**

►**gain (up)on** VI + PREP **to ~ on sb** (*in polls*) ganar terreno a algn; (*in race*) alcanzar a algn; **the police car was ~ing on us fast** el coche de la policía nos estaba alcanzando rápidamente

gainer ['geɪnəʳ] N **to be the ~** salir ganando

gainful ['geɪnfʊl] ADJ [*employment*] remunerado, retribuido

gainfully ['geɪnfəlɪ] ADV **to be ~ employed** tener un trabajo retribuido *or* remunerado; **there was nothing that could ~ be said** no podía decirse nada que pudiera ser de utilidad

gainsay [ˌgeɪn'seɪ] (*pt, pp* **gainsaid**) VT (*liter*) contradecir, negar; **it cannot be gainsaid** es innegable

gait [geɪt] N paso *m*, modo *m* de andar

gaiter ['geɪtəʳ] N polaina *f*

gal* [gæl] N = **girl**

gal. ABBR (*pl* **gal.** *or* **gals.**) = **gallon(s)**

gala ['gɑːlə] Ⓐ N (= *festive occasion*) fiesta *f*; (*Sport*) festival *m*; **swimming ~** festival *m* de natación

Ⓑ CPD ► **gala day** N día *m* de gala ► **gala performance** N función *f* de gala

galactic [gə'læktɪk] ADJ (*Astron*) galáctico; (*Med*) lácteo

Galapagos Islands [gə'læpəgəsˌaɪləndz] NPL Islas *fpl* (de los) Galápagos

Galatians [gə'leɪʃənz] NPL Galateos *mpl*

galaxy ['gæləksɪ] N (*Astron*) galaxia *f*; (*fig*) constelación *f*, pléyade *f*

gale [geɪl] Ⓐ N (= *strong wind*) vendaval *m*, viento *m* fuerte; (= *storm*) (*on land*) temporal *m*; (*at sea*) temporal *m*, tempestad *f*; **~ force ten** vientos *mpl* de fuerza diez; **it was blowing a ~ that night** aquella noche había vendaval, aquella noche soplaban vientos fuertes; *see also* **gale-force**

Ⓑ CPD ► **gale warning** N aviso *m* de temporal

gale-force ['geɪlfɔːs] ADJ **~ winds** vientos *mpl* huracanados; *see also* **gale**

Galen ['geɪlən] N Galeno

Galicia [gə'lɪʃɪə] N [1] (*Spain*) Galicia *f*

[2] (*Central Europe*) Galitzia *f*

Galician [gə'lɪʃɪən] Ⓐ ADJ gallego

Ⓑ N [1] (= *person*) gallego/a *m/f*

[2] (*Ling*) gallego *m*

Galilean [ˌgælɪ'liːən] Ⓐ ADJ (*Bible, Geog*) galileo; (*Astron*) galileico

Ⓑ N galileo/a *m/f*; **the ~** (*Bible*) el Galileo

Galilee ['gælɪliː] N Galilea *f*

gall [gɔːl] Ⓐ N [1] (*Anat*) bilis *f*, hiel *f*

[2] (*Bot*) agalla *f*; (*on animal*) matadura *f*

[3] (*fig*) (= *bitterness*) hiel *f*; (*) (= *cheek*) descaro *m*; **she had the ~ to say that** tuvo el descaro de decir eso

Ⓑ VT molestar, dar rabia a

Ⓒ CPD ► **gall bladder** N vesícula *f* biliar

gall. ABBR (*pl* **gall.** *or* **galls.**) = **gallon(s)**

gallant† Ⓐ ['gælənt] ADJ [1] (= *brave*) [*warrior, officer*] gallardo; [*effort*] valiente, noble

[2] (= *courteous*) galante, cortés

Ⓑ [gə'lænt] N galán *m*

gallantly ['gæləntlɪ] ADV [1] (= *bravely*) valientemente, valerosamente

[2] (= *courteously*) galantemente, cortésmente

gallantry† ['gæləntrɪ] N [1] (= *bravery*) valor *m*, valentía *f*

[2] (= *courtesy*) galantería *f*, cortesía *f*; **gallantries** galanterías *fpl*

galleon ['gælɪən] N galeón *m*

gallery ['gælərɪ] N (*gen*) galería *f* (*also Min, Theat*); (*for spectators*) tribuna *f*; (= *art gallery*) (*state owned*) museo *m* de arte; (*private*) galería *f* de arte; ✦*IDIOM* **to play to the ~** actuar para la galería

galley ['gælɪ] Ⓐ N [1] (= *ship*) galera *f*

[2] (= *ship's kitchen*) cocina *f*, fogón *m*

[3] (*Typ*) galerada *f*, galera *f*

Ⓑ CPD ► **galley proof** N (*Typ*) galerada *f* ► **galley slave** N galeote *m*

Gallic ['gælɪk] ADJ (= *of Gaul*) galo; (= *French*) francés

gallicism ['gælɪsɪzəm] N galicismo *m*

galling ['gɔːlɪŋ] ADJ mortificante

gallium ['gælɪəm] N galio *m*

gallivant [ˌgælɪ'vænt] VI = **gad**[1]

gallon ['gælən] N galón *m* (*Brit = 4,546 litros; US = 3,785 litros*); → IMPERIAL SYSTEM

gallop ['gæləp] Ⓐ N (= *pace*) galope *m*; (= *distance covered*) galopada *f*; **at a ~** al galope; **at full ~** a galope tendido; **to break into a ~** ponerse a galopar

Ⓑ VI [*horse*] galopar; **to ~ up/off** llegar/alejarse al galope; **to ~ past** pasar al galope; (*in procession*) desfilar al galope; **he ~ed through his homework** terminó sus deberes a la carrera

Ⓒ VT hacer galopar

galloping ['gæləpɪŋ] ADJ **~ consumption** (*Med*) tisis *f* galopante; **~ inflation** inflación *f* galopante

gallows ['gæləʊz] Ⓐ NSING (*pl* **gallowses** *or* **gallows**) horca *f*

Ⓑ CPD ► **gallows humour** N (*fig*) humor *m* negro *or* macabro

gallstone ['gɔːlstəʊn] N cálculo *m* biliar

Gallup poll ['gæləpˌpəʊl] N sondeo *m or* encuesta *f* Gallup

galoot* [gə'luːt] N (*esp US*) zoquete* *mf*

galore [gə'lɔːʳ] ADV en cantidad, a porrillo*; **bargains ~** gangas *fpl* a porrillo* *or* en cantidad

galosh [gə'lɒʃ] N chanclo *m* (de goma)

galumph* [gə'lʌmf] VI (*hum*) brincar alegre pero torpemente, brincar como un elefante contento

galvanic [gæl'vænɪk] ADJ galvánico

galvanism ['gælvənɪzəm] N galvanismo *m*

galvanize ['gælvənaɪz] VT [1] [+ *metal*] galvanizar

[2] (*fig*) **to ~ sb into action** mover a algn para que actúe; **to ~ sb into life** sacar a algn de su abstracción

galvanized ['gælvənaɪzd] ADJ galvanizado

galvanizing ['gælvənaɪzɪŋ] ADJ [*influence, force*] galvanizante; [*performance*] electrizante

galvanometer [ˌgælvə'nɒmɪtəʳ] N galvanómetro *m*

Gambia ['gæmbɪə] N **(the) ~** Gambia *f*

Gambian ['gæmbɪən] Ⓐ ADJ gambiano

Ⓑ N gambiano/a *m/f*

gambit ['gæmbɪt] N (*Chess*) gambito *m*; (*fig*) táctica *f*; **opening ~** (*fig*) estrategia *f* inicial

gamble ['gæmbl] Ⓐ N (= *risk*) riesgo *m*; (= *bet*) apuesta *f*; **life's a ~** la vida es una lotería; **the ~ came off** la jugada salió bien; **to have a ~ on** [+ *horse*] jugar dinero a, apostar a; [+ *Stock Exchange*] jugar a; **to take a ~** arriesgarse

Ⓑ VT [+ *money*] jugar, apostar; [+ *one's life*] arriesgar; **to ~ everything/one's future (on sth)** jugarse todo/el porvenir (a algo)

Ⓒ VI (= *bet money*) jugar, apostar; (= *take a chance*) jugársela; **to ~ on sth** confiar en algo, contar con algo; **he ~d on my being there** confiaba en que yo estuviera allí, contaba con que yo estuviera allí; **to ~ on the Stock Exchange** jugar a la Bolsa; **to ~ with others' money** especular con el dinero ajeno

►**gamble away** VT + ADV perder en el juego

gambler ['gæmbləʳ] N jugador(a) *m/f*

gambling ['gæmblɪŋ] Ⓐ N juego *m*; **~ on the Stock Exchange** especulación *f* en la Bolsa

Ⓑ CPD ► **gambling debts** NPL deudas *fpl* de juego ► **gambling den** N garito *m*, casa *f* de juego ► **gambling losses** NPL pérdidas *fpl* de juego ► **gambling man** N **I'm not a ~ man** yo no juego

gambol ['gæmbəl] VI [*lamb, child*] brincar, retozar

game[1] [geɪm] Ⓐ N [1] (*lit*) [1·1] (= *entertainment*) juego *m*; **it's only a ~** no es más que un juego; **a ~ of chance/skill** un juego de azar/de habilidad; ✦*IDIOM* **to play the ~** jugar limpio; *see also* **video**

[1·2] (= *match*) [*of football, rugby, cricket, tennis*] partido *m*; (*within tennis set*) juego *m*; [*of cards, chess, snooker*] partida *f*; **to have** *or* **play a ~ of football** jugar un partido de fútbol; **he plays a good ~ of football** juega bien al fútbol; **to have** *or* **play a ~ of chess** echar *or* jugar una partida de ajedrez; **they were (one) ~ all** (*Tennis*) iban iguales *or* empatados a un juego; **~, set and match** juego, set y partido; **~ to Johnston** juego a Johnston; *see also* **ball**[1], **board**, **card**[1]

[1·3] (= *type of sport*) deporte *m*; **football is not my ~** el fútbol no se me da bien

[1·4] **games** (= *contest*) juegos *mpl*; (*Brit Scol*) deportes *mpl*; **the Olympic Games** los Juegos Olímpicos, las Olimpiadas; **I was no good at ~s** no se me daban bien los deportes; **we have ~s on Thursdays** los jueves tenemos deportes

[1·5] (= *style of play*) **my ~ picked up in the second set** empecé a mejorar el juego en el segundo set; **to be off one's ~** no estar en forma; **to put sb off his/her ~** afectar la forma de jugar de algn, hacer jugar mal a algn

[1·6] (*Hunting*) (= *large animals*) caza *f* mayor; (= *birds, small animals*) caza *f* menor; *see also* **big C**, **fair**[1]

[2] (*fig*) [2·1] (= *scheme*) juego *m*; **I'll play his ~ for a while** voy a seguirle el juego un rato; **we know his little ~** le conocemos el jueguecillo*; **what's your ~?** ¿qué estás tramando?; ✦*IDIOMS* **to beat sb at his/her own ~** ganar a algn con sus propias armas; **to give the ~ away** descubrir el pastel*; **the faces of the two conspirators gave the ~ away** la expresión de su rostro delató a los dos conspiradores, la expresión del rostro de los dos conspiradores hizo que se descubriera el pastel*; **two can play at that ~** donde las dan las toman; **the ~ is up** se acabó el juego*; **the ~ is not worth the candle** la cosa no vale la pena; **the only ~ in town** la mejor alternativa; *see also* **waiting B**

[2·2] (= *joke*) juego *m*; **this isn't a ~** esto no es ningún juego; **don't play ~s with me!** ¡no juegues conmigo!; **he's just playing silly ~s** no está más que jugando; *see also* **fun**

[2·3] (*) (= *business*) negocio *m*; **how long have you been in this ~?** ¿cuánto tiempo llevas metido en este negocio?, ¿cuánto tiempo hace que trabajas en esto?; **she's new to this ~** esto es nuevo para ella; ✦*IDIOM* **to be ahead of the ~** llevar ventaja, llevar la delantera

[2·4] (*) (= *prostitution*) **to be on the ~** hacer la calle*

[2·5] (*) (= *trouble*) lata* *f*; **it was a ~ getting here!** ¡menuda lata para llegar aquí!*

Ⓑ ADJ (= *willing*) **are you ~?** ¿te animas?, ¿te

apuntas?; **I'm ~ if you are** si tú te animas, yo también; **to be ~ to do sth** estar dispuesto a hacer algo; **to be ~ for anything** apuntarse a cualquier cosa *or* a todo
Ⓒ VI (= *gamble*) jugar (*por dinero*)
Ⓓ CPD ► **game bird** N ave *f* de caza ► **game fish** N *pez de agua dulce pescado como deporte* ► **game fishing** N *pesca deportiva de peces de agua dulce* ► **game laws** NPL leyes *fpl* relativas a la caza ► **games master** N profesor *m* de deportes ► **games mistress** N profesora *f* de deportes ► **game park** N parque *m* natural, reserva *f* natural ► **game pie** N *empanada elaborada con una pieza de caza mayor o menor* ► **game plan** N (*Sport*) plan *m* de juego; (*fig*) estrategia *f* ► **game preserve, game reserve** N coto *m* de caza ► **game show** N programa *m* concurso ► **game theory** N teoría *f* de juegos ► **game warden** N guarda *mf* de coto *or* de caza

game² [geɪm] ADJ (= *lame*) **to have a ~ leg** tener una pierna coja

gamebag ['geɪmbæg] N morral *m*

gamecock ['geɪmkɒk] N gallo *m* de pelea

gamekeeper ['geɪm,kiːpəʳ] N guardabosques *mf inv*, guardabosque *mf*

gamely ['geɪmlɪ] ADV 1 (= *bravely*) valientemente, con el mejor de los ánimos
2 (= *sportingly*) animosamente

gamesman ['geɪmzmən] N (*pl* **gamesmen**) jugador *m* astuto

gamesmanship ['geɪmzmənʃɪp] N astucia *f* en el juego; **piece of ~** truco *m* para ganar

gamester ['geɪmstəʳ] N jugador(a) *m/f*, tahúr *mf*

gamete ['gæmiːt] N gameto *m*

gamey ['geɪmɪ] ADJ = **gamy**

gamin ['gæmɛ̃] N golfillo *m*

gamine [gæ'miːn] Ⓐ N *muchacha delgada y con aspecto de chico* Ⓑ CPD ► **gamine haircut** N corte *m* a la garçon

gaming ['geɪmɪŋ] Ⓐ N juego *m*
Ⓑ CPD ► **gaming house** N casa *f* de juego ► **gaming laws** NPL leyes *fpl* reguladoras del juego

gamma ['gæmə] Ⓐ N gamma *f*
Ⓑ CPD ► **gamma radiation** N radiación *f* gamma ► **gamma ray** N rayo *m* gamma

gammon ['gæmən] N (*Brit*) jamón *m*

gammy* ['gæmɪ] ADJ (*Brit*) cojo

gamp†* [gæmp] N (*Brit*) paraguas *m inv*

gamut ['gæmət] N gama *f*; **to run the (whole) ~ of** (*fig*) recorrer toda la gama de

gamy ['geɪmɪ] ADJ [*meat*] *con olor a animal de caza*

gander ['gændəʳ] N 1 (*Zool*) ganso *m* (macho)
2 (*) **to have** *or* **take a ~** echar un vistazo (**at** a)

gang [gæŋ] Ⓐ N [*of thieves*] banda *f*, pandilla *f*; [*of friends, youths*] grupo *m*; (*pej*) pandilla *f*; [*of workmen*] cuadrilla *f*, brigada *f*; **the Gang Of Four** (*Pol, Hist*) la Banda de los Cuatro; **he's one of the ~ now** ya es uno de los nuestros
Ⓑ CPD ► **gang rape** violación *f* en grupo

►**gang together** VI + ADV formar un grupo *or* una pandilla, agruparse

►**gang up** VI + ADV unirse (**with** a); **to ~ up on** *or* **against sb** unirse en contra de algn; **I feel everybody's ~ing up on me** tengo la sensación de que todos se han unido en mi contra

gangbang‡ ['gæŋbæŋ] Ⓐ N violación *f* múltiple *or* colectiva
Ⓑ VT violar colectivamente

gangbanger* ['gæŋbæŋəʳ] N (*US*) (= *gang member*) pandillero *m*

gangbusters ['gæŋbʌstəz] NPL (*US*) **to be going ~** ir viento en popa; **to do sth like ~** hacer algo con paso firme

ganger ['gæŋəʳ] N (*Brit*) capataz *m*

Ganges ['gændʒiːz] N **the ~** el Ganges

gangland ['gæŋlænd] Ⓐ N mundo *m* del crimen
Ⓑ CPD ► **gangland boss** N cabecilla *mf* del mundo del crimen ► **gangland murder** N asesinato *m* en el mundo del crimen, asesinato *m* por ajuste de cuentas entre criminales

gangling ['gæŋglɪŋ] ADJ [*youth*] larguirucho, desgarbado; [*legs*] larguirucho, desproporcionado

ganglion ['gæŋglɪən] N (*pl* **ganglia** ['gæŋglɪə] *or* **ganglions**) ganglio *m*

gangly ['gæŋglɪ] ADJ = **gangling**

gangplank ['gæŋplæŋk] N (*Naut*) plancha *f*

gangrene ['gæŋgriːn] N gangrena *f*

gangrenous ['gæŋgrɪnəs] ADJ gangrenoso

gangster ['gæŋstəʳ] N gán(g)ster *mf*

gangsterism ['gæŋstərɪzəm] N gan(g)sterismo *m*

gangway ['gæŋweɪ] N 1 (*Brit*) (*in theatre, aircraft*) pasillo *m*, pasadizo *m* 2 (*Naut*) (*on ship*) escalerilla *f*, pasarela *f*; (*from ship to shore*) pasarela *f*; **gangway!** ¡abran paso!

ganja‡ ['gændʒə] N maría *f* (*Sp**), marihuana *f*

gannet ['gænɪt] N 1 (= *bird*) alcatraz *m*
2 (*) (= *glutton*) (*fig*) comilón/ona *m/f*

gantlet ['gæntlɪt] N (*US Rail*) vía *f* traslapada, vía *f* de garganta

gantry ['gæntrɪ] N (*gen*) caballete *m*; (*for crane, railway signal*) pórtico *m*; (*for rocket*) torre *f* de lanzamiento

GAO N ABBR (*US*) (= **General Accounting Office**) *oficina general de contabilidad gubernamental*

gaol [dʒeɪl] N (*Brit*) = **jail**

gaoler ['dʒeɪləʳ] N (*Brit*) = **jailer**

gap [gæp] Ⓐ N (*gen, fig*) hueco *m*, vacío *m*; (*in wall etc*) boquete *m*, brecha *f*; (= *mountain pass*) quebrada *f*, desfiladero *m*; (*in traffic, vegetation*) claro *m*; (*between teeth, floorboards*) hueco *m*; (*between bars*) distancia *f*, separación *f*; (= *crack*) hendedura *f*, resquicio *m*; (*in text*) espacio *m* (en blanco); (*fig*) (*in knowledge*) laguna *f*; (*in conversation*) silencio *m*; [*of time*] intervalo *m*; **there's a ~ in the hedge** hay un hueco en el seto; **there is a ~ in the balance of payments** hay un desequilibrio en la balanza de pagos; **to close the ~** cerrar la brecha; **we discerned a ~ in the market** vimos que había un hueco en el mercado; **leave a ~ for the name** deje un espacio para poner el nombre; **to stop up** *or* **fill a ~** (*lit*) tapar un hueco; **to fill a ~** (*fig*) llenar un vacío *or* un hueco; (*in knowledge*) llenar una laguna; **he left a ~ that will be hard to fill** dejó un hueco difícil de llenar
Ⓑ CPD ► **gap year** (*Brit*) año *m* sabático

gape [geɪp] VI 1 [*mouth*] estar abierto; [*hole*] estar muy abierto; **the chasm ~d before him** delante de él se abría la sima; **her blouse ~d at the neck** llevaba una blusa muy abierta por el cuello 2 [*person*] **tourists go there to ~** los turistas van allí y se quedan boquiabiertos; **to ~ (at)** mirar boquiabierto (a); **he ~d at me in amazement** se me quedó mirando boquiabierto

gaping ['geɪpɪŋ] ADJ 1 [*wound, mouth*] abierto; [*hole*] muy abierto, grande
2 [*person*] boquiabierto, embobado

gappy* ['gæpɪ] ADJ [*teeth*] separado

gap-toothed ['gæp'tuːθt] ADJ (= *with gaps between teeth*) con los dientes separados; (= *with teeth missing*) desdentado, con la dentadura llena de huecos, al/a la que le faltan varios dientes

garage ['gærɑːʒ] Ⓐ N [*of house*] garaje *m*; (*for car repairs*) taller *m*; (= *petrol station*) estación *f* de servicio, gasolinera *f*, grifo *m* (*Peru*), bencinera *f* (*Chile*); (= *bus depot*) cochera *f*
Ⓑ VT dejar en garaje
Ⓒ CPD ► **garage band** N (*Mus*) grupo *m* de rock aficionado ► **garage mechanic** N mecánico/a *m/f* ► **garage proprietor** N propietario/a *m/f* de un taller de reparaciones ► **garage sale** N venta *f* de objetos usados (*en el garaje de una casa particular*)

garageman ['gærɑːʒ,mæn] N (*pl* **garagemen**) garajista *m*

garaging ['gærɑːʒɪŋ] N plazas *fpl* de párking *or* garaje; **there was ~ for 15 cars** había 15 plazas de párking *or* garaje

garb [gɑːb] Ⓐ N (*liter*) (= *clothes*) atuendo *m*
Ⓑ VT vestir (**in** de)

garbage ['gɑːbɪdʒ] (*esp US*) Ⓐ N (= *refuse*) basura *f*; (= *waste*) desperdicios *mpl*; (*fig*) (= *goods, film etc*) birria *f*, porquería *f*; (*spoken, written*) bobadas *fpl*, tonterías *fpl*, disparates *mpl*; **he talks a lot of ~** dice muchas bobadas *or* tonterías; **the book is ~** la novela es una basura *or* birria *or* porquería; **~ in, ~ out** (*Comput*) basura entra, basura sale
Ⓑ CPD ► **garbage bag** N bolsa *f* de la basura ► **garbage can** N cubo *m* de la basura ► **garbage collector** N basurero/a *m/f* ► **garbage disposal unit** N triturador *m* de basura ► **garbage dump** N vertedero *m* ► **garbage man** N = **garbage collector** ► **garbage truck** N camión *m* de la basura

garble ['gɑːbl] VT 1 [+ *message, report*] confundir 2 [+ *text*] mutilar, falsear (*por selección*)

garbled ['gɑːbld] ADJ [*message, version, account, explanation*] confuso, incoherente

Garda ['gɑːdə] N (*pl* **Gardaí** ['gɑːdiː]) policía *f* irlandesa

garden ['gɑːdn] Ⓐ N jardín *m*; (= *vegetable garden*) huerto *m*; **the Garden of Eden** el Edén; **(public) ~s** parque *msing*, jardines *mpl*; **✦IDIOM everything in the ~ is lovely** todo va a las mil maravillas
Ⓑ VI trabajar en el jardín *or* el huerto
Ⓒ CPD ► **garden centre** N centro *m* de jardinería, vivero *m* ► **garden city** N (*Brit*) ciudad *f* jardín ► **garden flat** N piso *m* con jardín en planta baja ► **garden furniture** N muebles *mpl* de jardín ► **garden hose** N manguera *f* de jardín ► **garden party** N recepción *f* al aire libre ► **garden path** N sendero *m*; **✦IDIOM to lead sb up the ~ path** embaucar a algn ► **garden produce** N productos *mpl* de la huerta ► **garden seat** N banco *m* de jardín ► **garden shears** NPL tijeras *fpl* de jardín ► **garden tools** NPL útiles *mpl* de jardinería; *see also* **refuse²**

gardener ['gɑːdnəʳ] N (*gen*) jardinero/a *m/f*

gardenia [gɑː'diːnɪə] N gardenia *f*

gardening ['gɑːdnɪŋ] N (*gen*) jardinería *f*; (= *market gardening*) horticultura *f*; **who does the ~?** ¿quién es el jardinero?, ¿quién se encarga del jardín?

garfish ['gɑː,fɪʃ] N (*pl* **garfish** *or* **garfishes**) aguja *f*

gargantuan [gɑː'gæntjʊən] ADJ colosal, gigantesco

gargle ['gɑːgl] Ⓐ N (= *sound*) gárgaras *fpl*; (= *liquid*) gargarismo *m* Ⓑ VI hacer gárgaras, gargarear (*LAm*)

gargoyle ['gɑːgɔɪl] N gárgola *f*

garish ['gɛərɪʃ] ADJ [*colour*] chillón, estridente; [*clothing*] chillón, llamativo, charro (*LAm**)

garishly ['gɛərɪʃlɪ] ADV **~ coloured** con colores chillones *or* estridentes; **~ decorated/painted/dressed** decorado/pintado/vestido con colores chillones *or* con gusto chabacano *or* (*LAm**) de manera charra; **~ lit** estridentemente iluminado

garishness ['gɛərɪʃnɪs] N [*of clothes, décor*] chabacanería *f*, ordinariez *f*, lo charro (*LAm**); [*of colours, light*] estridencia *f*

garland ['gɑːlənd] Ⓐ N guirnalda *f*
Ⓑ VT engalanar (**with** con)

garlic ['gɑːlɪk] Ⓐ N ajo *m*
Ⓑ CPD ► **garlic mayonnaise** N alioli *m* ► **garlic prawns** N gambas *fpl* al ajillo ► **garlic press** N triturador *m* de ajo ► **garlic salt** N sal *f* de ajo ► **garlic sausage** N salchichón *m* al ajo

garlicky ['gɑːlɪkɪ] ADJ [*taste*] a ajo; [*food*] con ajo; [*breath*] con olor a ajo

garment ['gɑːmənt] N prenda *f* (de vestir); **garments** ropa *fsing*, indumentaria *fsing*

garner ['gɑːnəʳ] Ⓐ N (*liter*, †) (= *granary*) granero *m*
Ⓑ VT (*also* **~ in, ~ up**) [+ *grain*] almacenar, entrojar; (*fig*) [+ *support*] conseguir, obtener; [+ *attention, publicity*] conseguir

garnet ['gɑːnɪt] N granate *m*

garnish ['gɑːnɪʃ] Ⓐ N (*Culin*) aderezo *m*, adorno *m*
Ⓑ VT aderezar, adornar (**with** con)

garnishing ['gɑːnɪʃɪŋ] N (*Culin*) aderezo *m*, adorno *m*

Garonne [gə'rɒn] N Garona *m*

garotte [gə'rɒt] N, VT = **garrotte**

garret ['gærɪt] N (= *attic room*) desván *m*, altillo *m* (*LAm*)

garrison ['gærɪsən] Ⓐ N guarnición *f*
Ⓑ VT guarnecer
Ⓒ CPD ► **garrison town** N plaza *f* fuerte ► **garrison troops** NPL tropas *fpl* de guarnición

garrotte [gə'rɒt] Ⓐ N garrote *m*
Ⓑ VT agarrotar

garrulity [gə'ruːlɪtɪ] N garrulidad *f*

garrulous ['gærʊləs] ADJ [*person, manner*] gárrulo, parlanchín

garrulously ['gærʊləslɪ] ADV con garrulería *or* verborrea

garrulousness ['gærʊləsnɪs] N garrulidad *f*

garter ['gɑːtəʳ] Ⓐ N (*for stocking, sock*) liga *f*; (*US*) (= *suspender*) liguero *m*, portaligas *m inv*; **Order of the Garter** Orden *f* de la Jarretera; **Knight of the Garter** Caballero *m* de la Orden de la Jarretera
Ⓑ CPD ► **garter belt** N (*US*) liguero *m*, portaligas *m inv*

gas [gæs] Ⓐ N (*pl* **gas(s)es**) 1 (*gen*) gas *m*; (*as anaesthetic*) gas *m* anestésico; (*in mine*) grisú *m*
2 (*US*) (= *petrol*) gasolina *f*, nafta *f* (*S. Cone*), bencina *f* (*Chile*); **to step on the ~*** acelerar, pisar el acelerador
3 (†*) (= *gab*) **to have a ~** charlar, parlotear*
4 (‡) (= *fun*) **what a ~!** ¡qué divertido!; **he's a ~!** ¡es un tío divertidísimo!*
5 (*esp US Med**) (= *wind*) gases *mpl*, flatulencia *f*
Ⓑ VT [+ *person*] asfixiar con gas; (*Mil*) gasear; **to ~ o.s.** suicidarse con gas
Ⓒ VI (*) (= *gab*) charlar, parlotear*
Ⓓ CPD [*industry, pipe*] de gas ► **gas bracket** N brazo *m* de lámpara de gas ► **gas burner** N mechero *m* de gas ► **gas can** N (*US*) bidón *m* de gasolina ► **gas canister** N = **gas cylinder** ► **gas chamber** N cámara *f* de gas ► **gas cooker** N cocina *f* de *or* a gas ► **gas cylinder** N bombona *f* de gas ► **gas fire** N estufa *f* de gas ► **gas fitter** N fontanero *m* (*especializado en lo relacionado con el gas*) ► **gas fittings** NPL instalación *fsing* de gas ► **gas guzzler*** N chupagasolina* *m inv*, *vehículo que consume mucha gasolina* ► **gas heater** N = **gas fire** ► **gas jet** N llama *f* de mechero de gas ► **gas leak** N escape *m* de gas ► **gas lighter** N encendedor *m* de gas ► **gas lighting** N alumbrado *m* de gas ► **gas main** N cañería *f* maestra de gas ► **gas mantle** N manguito *m* incandescente ► **gas mask** N careta *f* antigás ► **gas meter** N contador *m* de gas, medidor *m* de gas (*LAm*) ► **gas oil** N gasóleo *m* ► **gas oven** N cocina *f* de *or* a gas ► **gas pedal** N (*esp US*) acelerador *m* ► **gas pipe** N tubo *m* de gas ► **gas pipeline** N gasoducto *m* ► **gas pump** N (*US*) (*in car*) bomba *f* de gasolina; (*in gas station*) surtidor *m* de gasolina ► **gas ring** N fuego *m* de gas ► **gas station** N (*US*) gasolinera *f*, estación *f* de servicio, bencinera *f* (*Chile*), grifo *m* (*Peru*) ► **gas stove** N cocina *f* de *or* a gas ► **gas tank** N (*US Aut*) tanque *m or* depósito *m* (de gasolina) ► **gas tap** N llave *f* del gas ► **gas turbine** N turbina *f* de gas ► **gas worker** N trabajador(a) *m/f* de la compañía de gas

gasbag ['gæsbæg] N 1 (*Aer*) bolsa *f* de gas
2 (‡) (= *talkative person*) charlatán/ana *m/f*

Gascon ['gæskən] Ⓐ ADJ gascón
Ⓑ N 1 gascón/ona *m/f*
2 (*Ling*) gascón *m*

Gascony ['gæskənɪ] N Gascuña *f*

gas-cooled reactor [,gæskuːldriː'æktəʳ] N reactor *m* enfriado por gas

gaseous ['gæsɪəs] ADJ gaseoso

gas-fired [,gæs'faɪəd] ADJ de gas, alimentado por gas

gash[1] [gæʃ] Ⓐ N (*in flesh*) tajo *m*; (*from knife*) cuchillada *f*; (*in material*) raja *f*, hendidura *f*
Ⓑ VT [+ *arm, head*] hacer un tajo en; (*with knife*) acuchillar; [+ *seat etc*] rajar

gash[2]‡ [gæʃ] ADJ (*Brit*) (= *spare*) de sobra; (= *free*) gratuito

gasholder ['gæs,həʊldəʳ] N = **gasometer**

gasification [,gæsɪfɪ'keɪʃən] N gasificación *f*

gasket ['gæskɪt] N (*Tech*) junta *f*

gaslight ['gæslaɪt] N luz *f* de gas, alumbrado *m* de gas

gaslit ['gæslɪt] ADJ con alumbrado de gas

gasman ['gæsmæn] N (*pl* **gasmen**) (*gen*) empleado *m* del gas; (= *gas fitter*) fontanero *m* (*especializado en lo relacionado con el gas*)

gasohol ['gæsəʊhɒl] N (*US*) gasohol *m*

gasoline ['gæsəliːn] N (*US*) gasolina *f*, nafta *f* (*S. Cone*), bencina *f* (*Chile*)

gasometer [gæ'sɒmɪtəʳ] N (*Brit*) gasómetro *m*

gasp [gɑːsp] Ⓐ N (*for breath*) boqueada *f*; (= *panting*) jadeo *m*; [*of surprise*] grito *m* ahogado; **she gave a ~ of surprise** dio un grito ahogado de asombro; **to be at one's last ~** (= *dying*) estar agonizando, estar dando las últimas boqueadas
Ⓑ VI (*for air*) respirar con dificultad; (= *pant*) jadear; (*in surprise*) gritar; **he was ~ing for air** *or* **breath** le costaba respirar, le faltaba el aliento; **I was ~ing for a smoke** tenía unas ganas tremendas de fumar
Ⓒ VT (*also* **~ out**) decir con voz entrecortada

gasper‡ ['gɑːspəʳ] N (*Brit*) pito* *m*, pitillo* *m*

gassed‡ [gæst] ADJ (= *drunk*) bebido

gassy ['gæsɪ] ADJ (*compar* **gassier**, *superl* **gassiest**) gaseoso

gastric ['gæstrɪk] Ⓐ ADJ gástrico
Ⓑ CPD ► **gastric flu** N gastroenteritis *f inv* ► **gastric juice** N jugo *m* gástrico ► **gastric ulcer** N úlcera *f* gástrica

gastritis [gæs'traɪtɪs] N gastritis *f inv*

gastro... ['gæstrəʊ] PREFIX gastro…

gastroenteritis [,gæstrəʊ,entə'raɪtɪs] N gastroenteritis *f*

gastronome ['gæstrənəʊm], **gastronomist** [gæs'trɒnəmɪst] N gastrónomo/a *m/f*

gastronomic [,gæstrə'nɒmɪk] ADJ gastronómico

gastronomy [gæs'trɒnəmɪ] N gastronomía *f*

gastropod ['gæstrəpɒd] N gastrópodo *m*

gasworks ['gæswɜːks] NSING OR NPL fábrica *f* de gas

gat†‡ [gæt] N (*US*) (= *gun*) revólver *m*, quitapenas‡ *m*

gate [geɪt] Ⓐ N 1 [*of wood*] puerta *f* (*also of town, castle*); [*of metal*] verja *f*; (= *sluice*) compuerta *f*; [*of field, in station*] barrera *f*; (*Sport*) entrada *f*; **please go to ~ seven** diríjanse a la puerta siete
2 (*Sport*) (= *attendance*) público *m*, concurrencia *f*; (= *entrance money*) taquilla *f*, recaudación *f*
Ⓑ VT (*Brit**) [+ *pupil*] prohibir la salida fuera del recinto escolar (*como castigo*)
Ⓒ CPD ► **gate money** N taquilla *f*, recaudación *f*

gâteau ['gætəʊ] N (*pl* **gâteaux** ['gætəʊz]) torta *f*, pastel *m*, tarta *f* (*Sp*)

gatecrash* ['geɪtkræʃ] Ⓐ VT [+ *party*] colarse en
Ⓑ VI colarse (de gorra)

gatecrasher* ['geɪt,kræʃəʳ] N colado/a *m/f*

gatehouse ['geɪthaʊs] N (*pl* **gatehouses** ['geɪthaʊzɪz]) casa *f* del guarda *or* del portero

gatekeeper ['geɪt,kiːpəʳ] N portero/a *m/f*

gate-leg(ged) table [,geɪtleg(d)'teɪbl] N mesa *f* de alas abatibles

gatepost ['geɪtpəʊst] N poste *m* (de una puerta); ✦*IDIOM* **between you, me, and the ~** en confianza, entre nosotros

gateway ['geɪtweɪ] N (*gen*) puerta *f* (de acceso); **New York, the ~ to America** Nueva York, la puerta a América; **the ~ to success** la puerta al éxito

gather ['gæðəʳ] Ⓐ VT 1 (*also* **~ together**) [+ *people, objects*] reunir, juntar; (*also* **~ up**) [+ *pins, sticks, etc*] recoger; [+ *harvest, crop*] recoger, recolectar; [+ *flowers*] coger, recoger (*LAm*); [+ *information*] reunir, recopilar; [+ *hair*] recoger; (*Sew*) fruncir; [+ *taxes*] recaudar; **we ~ed enough firewood to last the night** reunimos leña suficiente para toda la noche; **to ~ dust** acumular polvo; **to ~ one's thoughts (together)** ordenar sus pensamientos; **she ~ed her coat around her** se envolvió en su abrigo
2 (= *gain*) **to ~ speed** ir ganando *or* adquiriendo velocidad; **to ~ strength** cobrar fuerzas
3 **to ~ that** (= *understand*) tener entendido que; (= *discover*) enterarse de que; **as you will have ~ed …** se habrá dado cuenta de que …; **as far as I could ~** hasta donde pude enterarme; **I ~ from him that …** según lo que me dice …; **what are we to ~ from this?** ¿qué consecuencia sacamos de esto?
Ⓑ VI 1 [*people*] (*also* **~ together**) reunirse, juntarse, congregarse; (= *crowd together*) amontonarse; [*dust*] acumularse; [*clouds*] acumularse, cerrarse; **they ~ed in the doorway**

se apiñaron en la entrada
2 (*Med*) formar pus
Ⓒ N (*Sew*) frunce *m*

►**gather in** VT + ADV [+ *harvest, crops*] recoger, recolectar; [+ *taxes*] recaudar; **to ~ in the harvest/crops** recoger la cosecha, cosechar

►**gather round** VI + ADV, VI + PREP **to ~ round (sb)** agruparse alrededor (de algn); **~ round!** ¡acercaos!

►**gather together** Ⓐ VT + ADV reunir, juntar
Ⓑ VI + ADV reunirse, juntarse, congregarse

►**gather up** VT + ADV recoger

gathered ['gæðəd] ADJ (*Sew*) fruncido

gatherer ['gæðərəʳ] N [*of wood, flowers*] recolector(a) *m/f*; **intelligence ~** recopilador(a) *m/f* de información; *see also* **hunter B**

gathering ['gæðərɪŋ] Ⓐ N 1 (= *assembly*) reunión *f*; (= *persons present*) concurrencia *f*
2 (*Med*) absceso *m*
3 (*Typ*) alzado *m*
Ⓑ ADJ [*force, speed*] creciente, en aumento; **the ~ storm** la tormenta que se aproxima

gator*, **'gator*** ['geɪtəʳ] (*US*) = **alligator**

GATT [gæt] N ABBR (= **General Agreement on Tariffs and Trade**) GATT *m*

gauche [gəʊʃ] ADJ [*person, behaviour*] torpe, desmañado; (*socially*) cohibido, falto de soltura

gaucheness [gəʊʃnɪs] N cohibición *f*, falta *f* de soltura

gaucho ['gaʊtʃəʊ] Ⓐ ADJ gauchesco
Ⓑ N gaucho *m*

gaudily ['gɔːdɪlɪ] ADV **~ coloured** con colores chillones *or* llamativos; **~ decorated/painted/dressed** decorado/pintado/vestido con colores chillones *or* llamativos

gaudy ['gɔːdɪ] ADJ (*compar* **gaudier**; *superl* **gaudiest**) [*colour, clothes*] chillón, llamativo; [*shop, display*] ordinario, chabacano

gauge, **gage** (*US*) [geɪdʒ] Ⓐ N (= *standard measure*) [*of wire, bullet, gun*] calibre *m*; [*of railway track*] ancho *m*, entrevía *f*, trocha *f* (*LAm*); (= *instrument*) indicador *m*; (*fig*) indicación *f*, muestra *f*; **petrol** *or* (*US*) **gas ~** indicador *m* del nivel de gasolina; **oil ~** indicador *m* de(l) aceite; **pressure ~** manómetro *m*; *see also* **narrow E**
Ⓑ VT [+ *temperature, pressure*] medir; (*fig*) [+ *sb's capabilities, character*] estimar, juzgar; **to ~ the distance with one's eye** medir la distancia al ojo; **he knows how to ~ the feeling of the crowd** sabe reconocer los deseos de la multitud; **to ~ the right moment** elegir el momento oportuno

Gaul [gɔːl] N 1 Galia *f*
2 (= *person*) galo/a *m/f*

Gaullist ['gəʊlɪst] Ⓐ ADJ gaulista, golista
Ⓑ N gaulista *mf*, golista *mf*

gaunt [gɔːnt] ADJ 1 [*face*] (= *drawn*) chupado; (= *unhealthy*) demacrado; [*person*] flaco y adusto
2 (*fig*) (= *grim*) [*building*] sobrio, adusto

gauntlet ['gɔːntlɪt] N [*of knight*] guantelete *m*, manopla *f*; [*of motorcyclist etc*] guante *m*; ✦***IDIOMS*** **to run the ~** (*Mil, Hist*) correr baquetas; **he had to run a ~ of abuse as he arrived for the meeting** tuvo que aguantar una sarta de improperios a su llegada a la reunión; **to throw down/take up the ~** arrojar/recoger el guante

gauze [gɔːz] N (*gen*) gasa *f*

gauzy ['gɔːzɪ] ADJ (= *semi-transparent*) vaporoso

gave [geɪv] PT *of* **give**

gavel ['gævl] N martillo *m* (*de presidente de reunión o subastador*)

gavotte [gə'vɒt] N gavota *f*

Gawd* [gɔːd] EXCL (*Brit*) = **god** ¡Dios mío!

gawk* [gɔːk] Ⓐ N papamoscas *mf inv*
Ⓑ VI mirar boquiabierto; **to ~ at** mirar boquiabierto; **he stood there ~ing at her** quedó boquiabierto mirándola

gawky* ['gɔːkɪ] ADJ (*compar* **gawkier**; *superl* **gawkiest**) desgarbado, torpe

gawp* [gɔːp] VI (*Brit*) = **gawk B**

gay [geɪ] Ⓐ ADJ 1 (= *homosexual*) [*man, community, movement*] gay *adj inv*, homosexual; [*woman*] homosexual, lesbiano; [*bar*] gay *adj inv*, de gays; **a centre for lesbians and ~ men** un centro para lesbianas y gays; **~ men and women** hombres y mujeres homosexuales, gays y lesbianas; **~ sex** relaciones *fpl* homosexuales; **the ~ scene** el ambiente gay *or* homosexual
2 (*compar* **gayer**; *superl* **gayest**) (†) (= *cheerful*) [*person, colour, costume*] alegre; [*atmosphere, music, laughter*] alegre, festivo
3 (= *carefree*) **with ~ abandon** despreocupadamente, alegremente; **she's living the ~ life in Paris** se da la gran vida en París, se pega la vida padre en París*
Ⓑ N (= *man*) gay *m*, homosexual *m*; (= *woman*) lesbiana *f*, homosexual *f*
Ⓒ CPD ► **the gay liberation movement**, **gay lib*** N el movimiento de liberación homosexual ► **gay rights** NPL derechos *mpl* de los homosexuales

gayness ['geɪnɪs] N homosexualidad *f*

Gaza Strip ['gɑːzə'strɪp] N franja *f* de Gaza

gaze [geɪz] Ⓐ N mirada *f* (fija); **his ~ met mine** se cruzaron nuestras miradas
Ⓑ VI **to ~ at** mirar fijamente; **to ~ at o.s. in the mirror** mirarse (fijamente) en el espejo; **they ~d into each other's eyes** se miraron fijamente a los ojos; **to ~ into space** mirar distraídamente al vacío

gazebo [gə'ziːbəʊ] (*pl* **gazebos** *or* **gazeboes**) N cenador *m*

gazelle [gə'zel] N (*pl* **gazelles** *or* **gazelle**) gacela *f*

gazette [gə'zet] N (= *newspaper*) gaceta *f*; (= *official publication*) boletín *m* oficial

gazetteer [ˌgæzɪ'tɪəʳ] N diccionario *m* geográfico

gazpacho [gæz'pætʃəʊ] N gazpacho *m*

gazump* [gə'zʌmp] (*Brit*) Ⓐ VT [*buyer*] ofrecer un precio más alto que; [*seller*] *rehusar la venta de una propiedad a la persona con quien se había acordado aceptando una oferta más alta*; **we were ~ed** ofrecieron más que nosotros
Ⓑ VI [*buyer*] ofrecer un precio más alto; [*seller*] *faltar al compromiso de vender una casa aceptando una oferta más alta*

gazumping* [gə'zʌmpɪŋ] N (*Brit*) *subida del precio de una casa tras haber sido apalabrado*

gazunder* [gə'zʌndəʳ] (*Brit*) Ⓐ VT [+ *person*] ofrecer un precio más bajo de lo antes convenido a; **we were ~ed** nos ofrecieron menos de lo antes convenido
Ⓑ VI ofrecer un precio más bajo de lo antes convenido
Ⓒ N *bajada del precio de una casa tras haber sido apalabrado*

GB N ABBR (= **Great Britain**) Gran Bretaña *f*

GBH N ABBR (*Brit Jur*) (= **grievous bodily harm**) graves daños *mpl* corporales

GBP, **gbp** ABBR = **Great British Pounds**

GBS ABBR (*Brit*) = **George Bernard Shaw**

GC N ABBR (*Brit*) (= **George Cross**) *medalla del valor civil*

GCA N ABBR = **ground-controlled approach**

GCE N ABBR (*Brit*) = **General Certificate of Education**

GCH N ABBR = **gas(-fired) central heating**

GCHQ N ABBR (*Brit*) (= **Government Communications Headquarters**) *entidad gubernamental que recoge datos mediante escuchas electrónicas*

GCSE N ABBR (*Brit*) = **General Certificate of Secondary Education**

> **GCSE**
>
> *El* **GCSE** *o* **General Certificate of Secondary Education** *es el certificado académico que se expide en el Reino Unido (con la excepción de Escocia, cuyo equivalente es el* **Standard Grade**) *para cada una de las asignaturas de la Educación Secundaria Obligatoria. Los exámenes tienen lugar cuando el alumno tiene dieciséis años y las calificaciones van de la A a la G, (A es la máxima, G la mínima), y son el resultado de la combinación de una evaluación continua y de la nota de los exámenes finales, que son corregidos por un tribunal ajeno al centro escolar.*
> ⇨ *Ver tb* A LEVELS

GDI ABBR = **gross domestic income**

gdn ABBR = **garden**

Gdns ABBR = **Gardens**

GDP N ABBR (= **gross domestic product**) PIB *m*, PGB *m* (*Chile*), PTB *m* (*Andes*)

GDR N ABBR (*Hist*) (= **German Democratic Republic**) RDA *f*

gear [gɪəʳ] Ⓐ N 1 (*Aut*) marcha *f*, velocidad *f*; **first/second ~** primera *f*/segunda *f* (velocidad); **top** *or* (*US*) **high ~** (= *fifth*) quinta velocidad, superdirecta *f*; (= *fourth*) cuarta velocidad, directa *f*; **to change ~** (*Brit*) cambiar de marcha; **the election campaign moved into high ~ this week** la campaña electoral se intensificó esta semana; **in ~** embragado; **to put a car in ~** meter una marcha; **he left the car in ~** dejó el coche con una marcha metida; **he helped her get her life back into ~ after the divorce** la ayudó a poner su vida de nuevo en marcha tras el divorcio; **to get one's brain into ~** hacer trabajar el cerebro; **out of ~** desembragado; **that threw all his plans out of ~** eso le desbarató todos los planes; **to shift ~** (*US*) = **to change gear**; ✦***IDIOM*** **to get one's arse** *or* (*US*) **ass in ~**** mover el culo*
2 (*) (= *equipment*) equipo *m*; (= *tools*) herramientas *fpl*; (*for fishing*) aparejo *m*; (= *belongings*) cosas *fpl*, bártulos *mpl*; (= *clothing*) ropa *f*
3 (*Mech*) engranaje *m*; (= *machinery*) mecanismo *m*, aparato *m*; *see also* **landing B**
Ⓑ VT (*fig*) (= *adapt*) **the book is ~ed to adult students** el libro está dirigido a estudiantes adultos; **we both ~ed our lives to the children** los dos orientamos nuestras vidas hacia los niños; **the factory was not ~ed to cope with an increase in production** la fábrica no estaba preparada para hacer frente a un aumento de la producción; **the service is ~ed to meet the needs of the disabled** el servicio está pensado para satisfacer las necesidades de los minusválidos
Ⓒ CPD ► **gear change** N (= *act*) cambio *m* de marcha; (*US*) (= *control*) = **gear lever** ► **gear lever**, **gear stick** N palanca *f* de cambios ► **gear ratio** N [*of cycle*] proporción *f* entre plato y piñón

►**gear down** VI + ADV (*Aut*) reducir la marcha

►**gear up** Ⓐ VT + ADV (*fig*) **to ~ o.s. up to do sth** prepararse (psicológicamente) para hacer algo; **we're ~ed up to do it** estamos preparados para hacerlo
Ⓑ VI + ADV prepararse, hacer preparativos; **they are ~ing up to fight** se están preparando para luchar; **the shops were ~ing up for Christmas** las tiendas se estaban preparando para las Navidades

gearbox ['gɪəbɒks] N (*Aut*) caja *f* de cambios *or* velocidades; (*Mech*) caja *f* de engranajes

gearshift ['gɪəʃɪft] (*US*) = **gear lever**; *see* **gear**

gearwheel ['gɪəwiːl] N rueda *f* dentada

gecko ['gekəʊ] N (*pl* **geckos** *or* **geckoes**) geco *m*

GED N ABBR (*US Educ*) = **general equivalency diploma**

geddit‡ ['gedɪt] EXCL **~?** ¿entiendes?, ¿lo pillas? (*Sp**), ¿lo coges? (*Sp**)

gee¹* [dʒiː] EXCL (*esp US*) ¡caramba!; **~ whiz!** ¡córcholis!; **~ up!** ¡arre!

gee²* [dʒiː] = **gee-gee**

gee-gee* ['dʒiːdʒiː] N (*child language*) caballito *m*, jaca *f*

geek* [giːk] N (*esp US*) cretino/a *m/f*

geeky* ['giːkɪ] ADJ (*esp US*) cretino

geese [giːs] NPL *of* **goose**

geezer* ['giːzəʳ] N (*Brit*) (= *fellow*) tío* *m*, colega‡; **(old) ~** viejo* *m*, tío *m* viejo*

Geiger counter ['gaɪgə,kaʊntəʳ] N contador *m* Geiger

geisha ['geɪʃə] N (*pl* **geisha** *or* **geishas**) geisha *f*

gel [dʒel] Ⓐ N gel *m*; **hair ~** fijador *m*
Ⓑ VI [1] (*lit*) gelificarse
[2] (*fig*) [*ideas, plans*] encajar (**with** en)

gelatin(e) ['dʒelətiːn] N gelatina *f*

gelatinous [dʒɪ'lætɪnəs] ADJ gelatinoso

geld [geld] VT castrar, capar

gelding ['geldɪŋ] N caballo *m* castrado

gelignite ['dʒelɪgnaɪt] N gelignita *f*

gelt‡ [gelt] N (*US*) pasta* *f*

gem [dʒem] N (= *jewel*) joya *f*, alhaja *f*; (= *stone*) piedra *f* preciosa *or* semipreciosa, gema *f*; **I must read you this ~*** tengo que leerte esto porque hace época; **my cleaner is a ~** la señora que me hace la limpieza es una joya

Gemini ['dʒemɪniː] N [1] (= *sign, constellation*) Géminis *m*
[2] (= *person*) géminis *mf*; **I'm (a) ~** soy géminis

gemstone ['dʒem,stəʊn] N piedra *f* preciosa *or* semipreciosa, gema *f*

Gen ABBR (*Mil*) (= **General**) Gen., Gral.

gen¹ ABBR [1] = **general, generally**
[2] (= **gender**) gen.
[3] (= **genitive**) gen.

gen²* [dʒen] N (*Brit*) información *f*; **to give sb the ~ on sth** poner a algn al corriente de algo

►**gen up*** (*Brit*) Ⓐ VT + ADV **to ~ sb up (on sth)** poner a algn al corriente (de algo); **I'm thoroughly ~ned up now** ahora estoy bien enterado, ahora estoy completamente al tanto
Ⓑ VI + ADV **to ~ up on sth** informarse acerca de algo

gendarme ['ʒɑ̃ːndɑːm] N gendarme *mf*

gender ['dʒendəʳ] Ⓐ N (*Ling*) género *m*; (= *sex*) sexo *m*
Ⓑ CPD ► **gender gap** N brecha *f* entre los sexos ► **gender stereotype** N estereotipo *m* sexual

gene [dʒiːn] Ⓐ N (*Bio*) gene *m*, gen *m*
Ⓑ CPD ► **gene mapping** N cartografía *f* genética ► **gene splicing** N acoplamiento *m* de genes ► **gene therapy** N terapia *f* génica, terapia *f* de genes

genealogical [,dʒiːnɪə'lɒdʒɪkəl] ADJ genealógico

genealogist [,dʒiːnɪ'ælədʒɪst] N genealogista *mf*

genealogy [,dʒiːnɪ'ælədʒɪ] N genealogía *f*

genera ['dʒenərə] NPL *of* **genus**

general ['dʒenərəl] Ⓐ ADJ [1] (= *overall*) [*appearance, decline, attitude*] general; **the ~ standard of education is very high** el nivel general de educación es muy alto
[2] (= *widespread*) [*view, interest*] general; **there was ~ agreement on this question** hubo un consenso general con respecto a esta cuestión; **contrary to ~ belief** contrariamente a *or* en contra de lo que comúnmente se cree; **there was ~ opposition to the proposal** la oposición a la propuesta fue general *or* generalizada; **for ~ use** para el uso general; **in ~ use** de uso general
[3] (= *vague, non-specific*) general; **beware of making statements which are too ~** ten cuidado de hacer afirmaciones que sean demasiado generales; **the report was too ~** el informe era poco específico; **try to be more ~** intenta no entrar tanto en detalles; **we drove in the ~ direction of Aberdeen** fuimos conduciendo en dirección aproximada a Aberdeen; **please direct any ~ enquiries you may have to my secretary** le ruego solicite a mi secretaria cualquier información de carácter general; **I've got the ~ idea** tengo más o menos una idea; **I'm beginning to get the ~ picture** estoy empezando a hacerme una idea; **a ~ term** un término genérico; **in ~ terms** en líneas *or* términos generales
[4] (= *usual*) **as a ~ rule** por regla general
[5] (= *not specialized*) [*reader, public*] no especializado; **we employ two ~ labourers** empleamos a dos obreros no especializados; **an introduction to psychology for the ~ reader** una introducción a la psicología para el lector no especializado
[6] (*at end of title*) general; **secretary ~** secretario/a *m/f* general
Ⓑ N [1] **in ~** en general; **we discussed work in ~** hablamos sobre el trabajo en general; **in ~ this kind of situation can be controlled** (= *normally*) en general *or* por lo general este tipo de situaciones pueden controlarse
[2] **the particular and the ~** lo particular y lo general
[3] (*Mil*) (= *officer*) general *mf*; **General Croft arrived late** el general Croft llegó tarde; **good morning, General Croft** buenos días, General Croft
Ⓒ CPD ► **general anaesthetic, general anesthetic** (*US*) N anestesia *f* general ► **general assembly** N asamblea *f* general ► **general audit** N auditoría *f* general ► **general cargo** N cargamento *m* mixto ► **General Certificate of Secondary Education** N (*Brit Educ*) → GCSE ► **the General Confession** N (*Church of England*) la oración de confesión colectiva ► **general costs** NPL gastos *mpl* generales ► **general dealer** N (*US*) tienda *f*, almacén *m* (*S. Cone*) ► **general delivery** N (*US, Canada*) lista *f* de correos ► **general election** N elecciones *fpl or* comicios *mpl* generales ► **general headquarters** N (*Mil*) cuartel *msing* general ► **general holiday** N día *m* festivo ► **general hospital** N hospital *m* ► **general knowledge** N cultura *f* general ► **general manager** N director(a) *m/f* general ► **general medicine** N medicina *f* general ► **general meeting** N asamblea *f* general ► **General Officer Commanding** N (*Mil*) Comandante *mf* en Jefe ► **general partnership** N (*Jur*) sociedad *f* regular colectiva ► **General Post Office** N (*Brit Govt*) (*formerly*) Correos *m*; (= *main post office*) oficina *f* de correos ► **general practice** N (*Brit Med*) (= *work*) medicina *f* general; (= *group*) consultorio *m* médico; **I am currently working in ~ practice** actualmente estoy trabajando como médico de medicina general; **to go into ~ practice** entrar a trabajar en medicina general ► **general practitioner** N médico/a *m/f* de medicina general (*frm*), médico/a *m/f* de cabecera ► **the general public** N el público en general, el gran público ► **general science** N (*Scol*) Ciencias *fpl* ► **general science teacher** N profesor(a) *m/f* de Ciencias ► **General Secretary** N Secretario(a) *m/f* General ► **general staff** N estado *m* mayor (general) ► **general store** N (*US*) tienda *f*, almacén *m* (*S. Cone*) ► **general strike** N huelga *f* general

generalissimo [,dʒenərə'lɪsɪməʊ] N generalísimo *m*

generality [,dʒenə'rælɪtɪ] N [*of rule, belief*] generalidad *f*; **to talk in generalities** hablar en términos generales

generalization [,dʒenərəlaɪ'zeɪʃən] N generalización *f*

generalize ['dʒenərəlaɪz] VI generalizar; **to ~ about** generalizar sobre; **to ~ from** generalizar en base a

generally ['dʒenərəlɪ] ADV [1] (= *on the whole*) en general, en líneas generales; **~, the course is okay** en general *or* en líneas generales el curso está bien; **his account was ~ accurate** su relato fue en general *or* en líneas generales exacto; **they broke the toys, fought, and ~ misbehaved** rompieron los juguetes, se pelearon y en general se portaron mal
[2] (= *usually*) generalmente, por lo general; **we ~ meet on Tuesdays** generalmente *or* por lo general nos reunimos los martes
[3] (= *widely*) generalmente; **a ~ accepted definition** una definición generalmente aceptada, una definición aceptada por casi todo el mundo; **it is ~ believed that …** la mayoría de la gente cree que …, generalmente, se cree que …; **it's not yet ~ available** (*on sale*) no está todavía a la venta *or* en el mercado
[4] **~ speaking** por lo general, en términos generales

general-purpose [,dʒenərəl'pɜːpəs] ADJ [*tool, dictionary*] de uso general

generalship ['dʒenərəlʃɪp] N (= *period in office*) generalato *m*; (= *leadership*) dirección *f*, don *m* de mando

generate ['dʒenəreɪt] VT [+ *electricity, heat*] generar; [+ *employment, income, wealth, publicity*] generar; [+ *interest*] suscitar, generar

generating ['dʒenəreɪtɪŋ] CPD ► **generating set** N grupo *m* electrógeno ► **generating station** N central *f* generadora

generation [,dʒenə'reɪʃən] Ⓐ N [1] (= *act*) generación *f*
[2] (= *group of people*) generación *f*; **the younger ~** la nueva generación; **the older ~** los mayores; **first/second/third/fourth ~** (*Comput*) de primera/segunda/tercera/cuarta generación
Ⓑ CPD ► **the generation gap** N la brecha entre las generaciones

generational [,dʒenə'reɪʃənl] ADJ generacional

generative ['dʒenərətɪv] Ⓐ ADJ generativo
Ⓑ CPD ► **generative grammar** N gramática *f* generativa

generator ['dʒenəreɪtəʳ] N generador *m*, grupo *m* electrógeno

generic [dʒɪˈnerɪk] ADJ genérico

generically [dʒɪˈnerɪklɪ] ADV genéricamente, de manera genérica

generosity [ˌdʒenəˈrɒsɪtɪ] N generosidad *f*

generous [ˈdʒenərəs] ADJ 1 (= *not mean*) [*person, mood*] generoso; **she must have been feeling ~** debía sentirse generosa *or* dadivosa; **she was ~ in her praise of him** se deshizo en elogios para con él; **she was ~ in her praise of what he'd done** hizo grandes elogios de lo que había realizado; **that's very ~ of you** eso es muy generoso de tu parte; **he was rather too ~ with the chilli sauce** se pasó un poco con la salsa picante, se le fue un poco la mano con la salsa picante; **to be ~ with one's money** ser generoso *or* desprendido con el dinero; **be ~ with the cream** no escatimes la nata; **he wasn't exactly ~ with the whisky** no fue muy espléndido que digamos con el whisky
2 (= *lavish, sizeable*) [*gift*] espléndido; [*donation*] cuantioso, generoso; [*rise*] importante, generoso; [*pay, offer*] generoso; [*portion*] grande, generoso; [*bosom, figure*] opulento; **very ~ credit terms** unas condiciones de crédito muy favorables; **a ~ amount of sth** una buena cantidad de algo; **a ~ helping of sth** una ración generosa de algo, una buena ración de algo
3 (= *kind*) [*person, gesture*] amable; **it was very ~ of Nigel to say what he did** fue muy amable por parte de Nigel decir lo que dijo; **thank you for your ~ remarks** gracias por sus amables observaciones

generously [ˈdʒenərəslɪ] ADV 1 (= *not meanly*) [*give, donate, reward*] generosamente; **please give ~ to this worthy cause** por favor, contribuyan generosamente a esta noble causa
2 (= *liberally*) **season ~ with salt** condimentar con abundante sal; **~ cut shirts** camisas de corte amplio; **a ~ illustrated book** un libro ampliamente ilustrado; **she was a ~ proportioned woman** era una mujer de opulentas formas
3 (= *kindly*) [*offer, provide*] generosamente; **he ~ offered to cancel the debt** se ofreció generosamente a cancelar la deuda, en un gesto desinteresado, se ofreció a cancelar la deuda; **they very ~ offered to help us move house** se ofrecieron generosamente a ayudarnos a mudarnos de casa

genesis [ˈdʒenɪsɪs] N (*pl* **geneses** [ˈdʒenɪsiːz])
1 génesis *f inv*
2 **Genesis** (*Bible*) Génesis *m*

genet [ˈdʒenɪt] N jineta *f*, gineta *f*

genetic [dʒɪˈnetɪk] Ⓐ ADJ genético
Ⓑ CPD ▸ **genetic code** N código *m* genético ▸ **genetic engineering** N ingeniería *f* genética ▸ **genetic fingerprint** N huella *f* genética ▸ **genetic fingerprinting** N identificación *f* genética ▸ **genetic manipulation** N manipulación *f* genética

genetically [dʒɪˈnetɪkəlɪ] ADV (*gen*) genéticamente; **~ engineered** manipulado genéticamente; **~ modified** transgénico, modificado genéticamente; **~-modified foods** alimentos *mpl* transgénicos

geneticist [dʒɪˈnetɪsɪst] N (*Med*) genetista *mf*

genetics [dʒɪˈnetɪks] NSING genética *f*

Geneva [dʒɪˈniːvə] N Ginebra; **the ~ Convention** la convención de Ginebra

genial [ˈdʒiːnɪəl] ADJ [*manner, welcome*] cordial; [*person*] simpático, afable

geniality [ˌdʒiːnɪˈælɪtɪ] N simpatía *f*, afabilidad *f*

genially [ˈdʒiːnɪəlɪ] ADV afablemente

genie [ˈdʒiːnɪ] N (*pl* **genii**) genio *m*; ✦**IDIOM the ~ is out of the bottle** lo hecho, hecho está, es imposible dar marcha atrás

genital [ˈdʒenɪtl] Ⓐ ADJ genital
Ⓑ N **genitals** (órganos *mpl*) genitales *mpl*
Ⓒ CPD ▸ **genital herpes** N herpes *m* genital

genitalia [ˌdʒenɪˈteɪlɪə] NPL genitales *mpl*

genitive [ˈdʒenɪtɪv] (*Ling*) Ⓐ N genitivo *m*
Ⓑ CPD ▸ **genitive case** N caso *m* genitivo; **in the ~ case** en el genitivo

genius [ˈdʒiːnɪəs] N (*pl* **geniuses**) (= *person*) genio *m*; (= *cleverness*) genialidad *f*; (= *talent*) don *m*; **he's a ~** es un genio, es genial; **you're a ~!** (*iro*) ¡eres un hacha!; **a man of ~** un hombre genial; **she's a mathematical ~** es un genio para las matemáticas; **to have a ~ for (doing) sth** tener un don especial para (hacer) algo; **you have a ~ for forgetting things** tienes un don especial para olvidar las cosas

genned up [ˈdʒendˈʌp] ADJ *see* **gen up**

Genoa [ˈdʒenəʊə] N Génova *f*

genocidal [ˌdʒenəʊˈsaɪdl] ADJ genocida

genocide [ˈdʒenəʊsaɪd] N genocidio *m*

Genoese [ˌdʒenəʊˈiːz] Ⓐ ADJ genovés
Ⓑ N genovés/esa *m/f*

genome [ˈdʒiːnəʊm] N genoma *m*

genotype [ˈdʒenəʊtaɪp] N genotipo *m*

genre [ʒɑ̃ːnr] N género *m*

gent [dʒent] N ABBR 1 (= **gentleman**) caballero *m*; **what will you have, ~s?** (*hum*) ¿qué van a tomar los caballeros?
2 **the ~s*** (= *lavatory*) el servicio (de caballeros), el baño (de señores) (*LAm*); **can you tell me where the ~s is, please?** ¿el servicio de caballeros, por favor?; **"gents"** "caballeros"

genteel [dʒenˈtiːl] ADJ 1 (= *middle-class*) [*person*] elegante, refinado; [*manners*] refinado, fino; [*atmosphere*] elegante; **a ~ resort on the south coast** un elegante centro turístico de la costa del sur; **to live in ~ poverty** vivir modestamente pero con dignidad
2 (*pej*) (= *affected*) afectado

gentian [ˈdʒenʃɪən] Ⓐ N genciana *f*
Ⓑ CPD ▸ **gentian violet** N violeta *f* de genciana

Gentile [ˈdʒentaɪl] Ⓐ ADJ no judío; (= *pagan*) gentil
Ⓑ N no judío/a *m/f*; (= *pagan*) gentil *mf*

gentility [dʒenˈtɪlɪtɪ] N [*of person, family*] refinamiento *m*, elegancia *f*; [*of place*] elegancia *f*

gentle [ˈdʒentl] ADJ (*compar* **gentler**; *superl* **gentlest**) 1 (= *kind, good-natured*) [*person*] de carácter dulce; [*manner, voice*] dulce, delicado; [*eyes, smile*] dulce, tierno; [*hint, reminder, rebuke*] discreto; [*animal*] manso, dócil; **to be ~ with sb/sth** (= *careful*) tener cuidado con algn/algo; **be ~ with him, he's had a terrible shock** ten consideración con él, ha sufrido un golpe muy duro; **to poke ~ fun at sb** burlarse sin malicia de algn, burlarse cariñosamente de algn; **the policy of ~ persuasion had failed** la política de la sutil persuasión había fracasado; **try a little ~ persuasion, he might say yes** intenta persuadirlo un poco, puede que diga que sí; **he needs a ~ push** necesita un pequeño empuje; **the ~** *or* **~r sex**† el bello sexo; ✦**IDIOM as ~ as a lamb** más bueno que el pan, más manso que un cordero
2 (= *mild*) [*shampoo, soap, detergent*] suave; **it is ~ on the skin** no irrita la piel
3 (= *light*) [*touch, pressure, push, breeze*] suave, ligero; **there was a ~ tap at the door** se oyeron unos golpecitos a la puerta
4 (= *moderate*) [*exercise*] moderado; **cook for 30 minutes over a ~ heat** cocinar durante 30 minutos a fuego lento; **we jogged along at a ~ pace** hicimos footing a un ritmo suave; **it was too hot even for a ~ stroll** hacía demasiado calor incluso para pasear lentamente
5 (= *not steep*) [*slope*] suave, poco pronunciado; [*curve*] no muy cerrado; **~ rolling hills** colinas suaves y onduladas
6 (†) (= *noble*) **of ~ birth** de noble cuna; **~ reader** estimado *or* querido lector

gentleman [ˈdʒentlmən] Ⓐ N (*pl* **gentlemen**) (= *man*) señor *m*; (*having gentlemanly qualities*) caballero *m*; (††) (*at court*) gentilhombre *m*; **there's a ~ waiting to see you** hay un señor esperando para verle; **young ~** señorito *m*; **to be a perfect ~** ser un perfecto caballero; **he's no ~** poco caballero es él; **"gentlemen"** (= *lavatory*) "caballeros"
Ⓑ CPD ▸ **gentleman's agreement** N acuerdo *m* entre caballeros ▸ **gentleman farmer** N terrateniente *m* ▸ **gentleman's gentleman** N ayuda *m* de cámara

gentlemanly [ˈdʒentlmənlɪ] ADJ caballeroso

gentleness [ˈdʒentlnɪs] N 1 (= *gentle nature*) [*of person*] dulzura *f* (de carácter); [*of manner, voice*] dulzura *f*, delicadeza *f*; [*of smile*] dulzura *f*, ternura *f*; [*of hint, reminder, rebuke*] lo discreto; [*of animal*] mansedumbre *f*, docilidad *f*
2 (= *care*) (*in handling sth/sb*) cuidado *m*; (= *consideration*) consideración *f*
3 (= *mildness*) [*of shampoo, soap, etc*] suavidad *f*
4 (= *lightness*) [*of movement, touch, breeze*] suavidad *f*, ligereza *f*
5 (= *not steepness*) [*of slope*] suavidad *f*

gentlewoman†† [ˈdʒentlˌwʊmən] N (*pl* **gentlewomen**) (*by birth*) dama *f*, señora *f* de buena familia

gently [ˈdʒentlɪ] ADV 1 (= *softly, kindly*) [*say*] dulcemente, suavemente; [*smile*] dulcemente, con dulzura; [*hint, remind*] con delicadeza
2 (= *carefully*) [*handle*] con cuidado; **~ clean the wound with salt water** limpiar la herida con cuidado usando agua salada; **a lotion that ~ cleanses your skin** una loción que limpia la piel sin irritar; **~ does it!** ¡con cuidado!, ¡despacito!*
3 (= *lightly*) [*blow, touch, push, tap*] ligeramente, suavemente; **I shook her ~ and she opened her eyes** la sacudí ligeramente *or* suavemente y abrió los ojos
4 (= *slowly*) [*pick up speed*] poco a poco; [*simmer, cook*] a fuego lento; **simmer ~ until the sugar dissolves** hervir a fuego lento hasta que el azúcar se disuelva
5 (= *not steeply*) [*slope*] suavemente

gentrification [ˌdʒentrɪfɪˈkeɪʃən] N aburguesamiento *m*

gentrified [ˈdʒentrɪˌfaɪd] ADJ [*area, houses*] aburguesado

gentrify [ˈdʒentrɪfaɪ] VT aburguesar

gentry [ˈdʒentrɪ] N (*Brit*) alta burguesía *f*, pequeña aristocracia *f*; (*pej*) familias *fpl* bien, gente *f* bien; (= *set of people*) gente *f*

genuflect [ˈdʒenjʊflekt] VI (*frm*) hacer una genuflexión

genuflection, **genuflexion** (*US*) [dʒenjʊˈflekʃən] N genuflexión *f*

genuine [ˈdʒenjʊɪn] ADJ 1 (= *authentic*) [*picture, antique*] auténtico; [*claim, refugee*] verdadero; **it is a ~ Renoir** es un Renoir auténtico; **a ~ leather sofa** un sofá de cuero legítimo *or* auténtico; **this is no cheap imitation, it's the ~ article** esto no es una imitación barata, es genuino *or* auténtico; **this dancer is the ~ article** esta es una bailarina de verdad
2 (= *sincere*) [*concern, disbelief, interest, enthu-*

siasm] verdadero, sincero; [*love*] verdadero, de verdad; [*commitment, difficulty*] verdadero, auténtico; [*offer, buyer*] serio; **it was a ~ mistake** fue realmente un error; **if this offer is ~ I will gladly accept it** si esta oferta va en serio *or* es seria la aceptaré con mucho gusto; **she is very ~ and caring** es noble y bondadosa

genuinely [ˈdʒenjʊɪnlɪ] ADV 1 (= *authentically*) [*funny*] realmente, verdaderamente; **he claims, probably quite ~, to be ...** asegura, y probablemente sea cierto, ser ...
2 (= *sincerely*) [*believe*] sinceramente, realmente; [*want*] realmente, de verdad; [*interested, worried, upset*] verdaderamente, realmente; **he ~ wants to change** realmente *or* de verdad quiere cambiar; **they were ~ pleased to see me** se alegraban de verdad de verme; **I'm ~ sorry that Peter has gone** siento de verdad que Peter se haya ido, lamento sinceramente que Peter se haya ido

genuineness [ˈdʒenjʊɪnnɪs] N 1 (= *authenticity*) [*of painting, antique*] autenticidad *f*; [*of claim*] veracidad *f*
2 (= *sincerity*) [*of concern, feelings*] sinceridad *f*, autenticidad *f*
3 (= *honesty*) [*of person*] nobleza *f*

genus [ˈdʒenəs] N (*pl* **genera** *or* **genuses**) (*Bio*) género *m*

geo... [ˈdʒiːəʊ] PREFIX geo...

geochemical [ˌdʒiːəʊˈkemɪkəl] ADJ geoquímico

geochemist [ˌdʒiːəʊˈkemɪst] N geoquímico/a *m/f*

geochemistry [ˌdʒiːeʊˈkemɪstrɪ] N geoquímica *f*

geodesic [ˌdʒɪ(ː)əʊˈdesɪk] ADJ geodésico

geodesy [dʒiːˈɒdɪsɪ] N geodesia *f*

geodetic [ˌdʒiːəʊˈdetɪk] ADJ = **geodesic**

Geoffrey [ˈdʒefrɪ] N Geofredo, Godofredo

geographer [dʒɪˈɒgrəfəʳ] N geógrafo/a *m/f*

geographic [dʒɪəˈgræfɪk] ADJ = **geographical**

geographical [dʒɪəˈgræfɪkəl] ADJ geográfico

geographically [dʒɪəˈgræfɪkəlɪ] ADV geográficamente; **~ speaking** desde el punto de vista geográfico

geography [dʒɪˈɒgrəfɪ] N geografía *f*; **policemen who knew the local ~** policías que conocían bien el lugar

geological [dʒɪəʊˈlɒdʒɪkəl] ADJ geológico

geologically [dʒɪəˈlɒdʒɪkəlɪ] ADV geológicamente; **~ speaking** desde el punto de vista geológico

geologist [dʒɪˈɒlədʒɪst] N geólogo/a *m/f*

geology [dʒɪˈɒlədʒɪ] N geología *f*

geomagnetic [ˌdʒiːəʊmægˈnetɪk] ADJ geomagnético

geomagnetism [ˌdʒiːəʊˈmægnɪˌtɪzəm] N geomagnetismo *m*

geometric [dʒɪəˈmetrɪk] ADJ geométrico

geometrical [dʒɪəˈmetrɪkəl] ADJ = **geometric**

geometrically [dʒɪəˈmetrɪkəlɪ] ADV geométricamente

geometry [dʒɪˈɒmɪtrɪ] N geometría *f*

geomorphic [ˌdʒiːəʊˈmɔːfɪk] ADJ geomórfico

geomorphologic [ˌdʒiːəʊˈmɔːfəˈlɒdʒɪk] ADJ = **geomorphological**

geomorphological [ˌdʒiːəʊˈmɔːfəˈlɒdʒɪkəl] ADJ geomorfológico

geomorphology [ˌdʒiːəʊmɔːˈfɒlədʒɪ] N geomorfología *f*

geophysical [ˌdʒiːəʊˈfɪzɪkəl] ADJ geofísico

geophysicist [ˌdʒiːəʊˈfɪzɪsɪst] N geofísico/a *m/f*

geophysics [dʒɪəʊˈfɪzɪks] NSING geofísica *f*

geopolitical [ˌdʒiːəʊpəˈlɪtɪkəl] ADJ geopolítico

geopolitics [ˈdʒiːəʊˈpɒlɪtɪks] NSING geopolítica *f*

Geordie* [ˈdʒɔːdɪ] N (*Brit*) *nativo/habitante de Tyneside en el NE de Inglaterra*

George [dʒɔːdʒ] N Jorge

Georgia [ˈdʒɔːdʒɪə] N (*US and USSR*) Georgia *f*

Georgian [ˈdʒɔːdʒɪən] ADJ (*Brit*) georgiano

geoscience [ˌdʒiːəʊˈsaɪəns] N geociencia *f*

geoscientist [ˌdʒiːəʊˈsaɪəntɪst] N geocientífico/a *m/f*

geostationary [ˌdʒiːəʊˈsteɪʃənərɪ] ADJ geoestacionario

geostrategic [ˌdʒiːəʊstrəˈtiːdʒɪk] ADJ geoestratégico

geostrategy [ˌdʒiːəʊstrəˈtiːdʒɪ] N geoestrategia *f*

geothermal [ˌdʒiːəʊˈθɜːməl] ADJ geotérmico

geranium [dʒɪˈreɪnɪəm] N geranio *m*

gerbil [ˈdʒɜːbɪl] N gerbo *m*, jerbo *m*

geriatric [ˌdʒerɪˈætrɪk] Ⓐ ADJ 1 geriátrico; **~ home** residencia *f* geriátrica, centro *m* geriátrico; **~ medicine** geriatría *f*
2 (* *pej*) **~ judges** jueces que son unos vejestorios
Ⓑ N 1 (*Med*) persona *f* mayor
2 (* *pej*) vejestorio* *m*

geriatrician [ˌdʒerɪəˈtrɪʃən] N geriatra *mf*

geriatrics [ˌdʒerɪˈætrɪks] NSING geriatría *f*

germ [dʒɜːm] Ⓐ N (*Bio*) (*fig*) germen *m*; (*Med*) microbio *m*, germen *m*; **the ~ of an idea** el germen de una idea
Ⓑ CPD ► **germ carrier** N portador(a) *m/f* de microbios *or* gérmenes ► **germ cell** N célula *f* germinal ► **germ plasm** N germen *m* plasma ► **germ warfare** N guerra *f* bacteriológica

German [ˈdʒɜːmən] Ⓐ ADJ alemán
Ⓑ N 1 (= *person*) alemán/ana *m/f*
2 (*Ling*) alemán *m*
Ⓒ CPD ► **German Democratic Republic** N (*Hist*) República *f* Democrática Alemana ► **German measles** N rubeola *f*, rubéola *f* ► **German shepherd (dog)** N pastor *m* alemán, perro *m* lobo

germane [dʒɜːˈmeɪn] ADJ (*frm*) (= *relevant*) **that's not ~ to the discussion** eso no atañe a la discusión; **the remark is not ~** el comentario no viene al caso

Germanic [dʒɜːˈmænɪk] ADJ germánico

germanium [dʒɜːˈmeɪnɪəm] N germanio *m*

germanophile [dʒɜːˈmænəfaɪl] N germanófilo/a *m/f*

germanophobe [dʒɜːˈmænəfəʊb] N germanófobo/a *m/f*

German-speaking [ˈdʒɜːmənˌspiːkɪŋ] ADJ de habla alemana

Germany [ˈdʒɜːmənɪ] N Alemania *f*; **East ~** Alemania *f* Oriental; **West ~** Alemania *f* Occidental

germ-free [ˌdʒɜːmˈfriː] ADJ estéril; (= *sterilized*) esterilizado

germicidal [ˌdʒɜːmɪˈsaɪdl] ADJ germicida, microbicida

germicide [ˈdʒɜːmɪsaɪd] N germicida *m*

germinate [ˈdʒɜːmɪneɪt] VI [*seed, idea*] germinar

germination [ˌdʒɜːmɪˈneɪʃən] N germinación *f*

germ-killer [ˈdʒɜːmˌkɪləʳ] N germicida *m*

germproof [ˈdʒɜːmpruːf] ADJ a prueba de microbios *or* gérmenes

gerontocracy [ˌdʒerɒnˈtɒkrəsɪ] N gerontocracia *f*

gerontologist [ˌdʒerɒnˈtɒlədʒɪst] N gerontólogo/a *m/f*

gerontology [ˌdʒerɒnˈtɒlədʒɪ] N gerontología *f*

Gerry [ˈdʒerɪ] N (*familiar form*) *of* **Gerald, Gerard**

gerrymander [ˈdʒerɪmændəʳ] Ⓐ VT [+ *voting area*] *dividir de manera favorable a un partido*; (= *manipulate*) manipular
Ⓑ VI *dividir una zona electoral de manera favorable a un partido*

gerrymandering [ˈdʒerɪmændərɪŋ] N manipulaciones *fpl*

gerund [ˈdʒerənd] N (*Latin*) gerundio *m*; (*English*) sustantivo *m* verbal

gerundive [dʒəˈrʌndɪv] Ⓐ ADJ gerundivo
Ⓑ N gerundio *m*

gestalt [gəˈʃtɑːlt] Ⓐ N gestalt *m*
Ⓑ CPD ► **gestalt psychology** N psicología *f* gestalt ► **gestalt therapy** N terapéutica *f* gestáltica

Gestapo [gesˈtɑːpəʊ] N Gestapo *f*

gestate [dʒesˈteɪt] Ⓐ VT 1 (*Bio*) gestar
2 (*fig*) [+ *idea, project*] gestar
Ⓑ VI [*idea, project*] gestarse

gestation [dʒesˈteɪʃən] N (*Bio*) gestación *f* (*also fig*)

gesticulate [dʒesˈtɪkjʊleɪt] VI gesticular

gesticulation [dʒesˌtɪkjʊˈleɪʃən] N gesticulación *f*, manoteo *m*

gestural [ˈdʒestʃərəl] ADJ [*language*] gestual

gesture [ˈdʒestʃəʳ] Ⓐ N 1 (*lit*) ademán *m*, gesto *m*
2 (*fig*) demostración *f*; (= *small token*) muestra *f*, detalle *m*; **what a nice ~!** ¡qué gesto *or* detalle más agradable!; **as a ~ of friendship** en señal de amistad; **as a ~ of support** para demostrar nuestro apoyo; **empty ~** pura formalidad *f*
Ⓑ VI hacer gestos; **he ~d towards the door** señaló *or* apuntó hacia la puerta; **to ~ to sb to do sth** indicar a algn con la mano que haga algo
Ⓒ VT expresar con un ademán

get [get] (*pt, pp* **got**; *US: pp* **gotten**)

> A TRANSITIVE VERB — C PHRASAL VERBS
> B INTRANSITIVE VERB
> *When* **get** *is part of a set combination, eg* **get the sack**, **get hold of**, **get sth right**, *look up the other word.*

Ⓐ TRANSITIVE VERB
1 = ***obtain*** [+ *information, money, visa, divorce*] conseguir; [+ *benefit*] sacar, obtener; **I'll ~ the money somehow** conseguiré el dinero de alguna forma; **he had trouble ~ting a hotel room** tuvo dificultades para conseguir una habitación de hotel; **that's what got him the rise** eso fue lo que le consiguió el aumento; **he got it for me** él me lo consiguió; **you need to ~ permission off‡ *or* from the owner** tienes que conseguir el permiso del dueño; **I got the idea off‡ *or* from a TV programme** saqué la idea de un programa de televisión; **he ~s all his clothes off‡ *or* from his elder brother** hereda toda la ropa de su hermano mayor; **where did you ~ that idea from?** ¿de dónde sacaste esa idea?; **we shan't ~ anything out of him** no lograremos sacarle nada; **you won't ~ any money out of me** no vas a sacarme dinero; **what are you going to ~ out of it?** ¿qué vas a sacar de *or* ganar con ello?; **a good coach knows how to ~ the best out of his players** un buen entrenador sabe cómo sacar lo mejor de sus jugadores; **she ~s a lot of pleasure out of gardening** disfruta mucho con la jardinería; **you may ~ some fun out of it** puede que te resulte divertido
2 = ***have*** tener; **I go whenever I ~ the**

chance voy siempre que tengo ocasión; **to ~ something to eat** comer algo

3 *= receive* 3·1 [+ *letter, phone call*] recibir; [+ *wage*] ganar, cobrar; [+ *TV station, radio station*] coger, captar; **she ~s a good salary** gana *or* cobra un buen sueldo; **not everyone ~s a pension** no todo el mundo cobra una pensión; **I got lots of presents** me hicieron muchos regalos; **I think he got the wrong impression** creo que se ha llevado una impresión equivocada; **how much did you ~ for it?** ¿cuánto te dieron por él?; **he got 15 years for murder** le condenaron a 15 años por asesinato; **he ~s his red hair from his mother** el pelo rojizo lo ha heredado de su madre; **I didn't ~ much from the film** la película no me dijo gran cosa; **I don't ~ much from his lectures** saco poco provecho de sus clases; *see also* **neck A1**

3·2

Some **get** *+ noun combinations are translated using a more specific Spanish verb. If in doubt, look up the noun.*

I never got an answer no me contestaron, no recibí nunca una respuesta; **they ~ lunch at school** les dan de comer en el colegio; **this area doesn't ~ much rain** en esta área no llueve mucho; **I got a shock/surprise** me llevé un susto/una sorpresa; **this room ~s a lot of sun** a esta habitación le da mucho el sol; *see also* **fine[2]**, **sentence A2**

4 *= buy* comprar; **I went out to ~ some milk** salí a comprar leche; **where did you ~ those shoes?** ¿dónde te has comprado esos zapatos?; **I got it cheap in a sale** lo conseguí barato en unas rebajas

5 *= fetch* [+ *glasses, book*] ir a buscar, traer; [+ *person*] ir a buscar, ir a por; (= *pick up*) [+ *goods, person*] recoger; **would you mind ~ting my glasses?** ¿te importaría ir a buscarme *or* traerme las gafas?; **can you ~ my coat from the cleaner's?** ¿puedes recogerme el abrigo de la tintorería?; **I'll ~ some lettuce from the garden** voy a coger un poco de lechuga del jardín; **quick, ~ help!** ¡rápido, ve a buscar ayuda!; **to ~ sth for sb ◊ ~ sb sth** ir a buscar algo a algn, traer algo a algn; **could you ~ me the scissors please?** ¿puedes ir a buscarme *or* me puedes traer las tijeras, por favor?; **can I ~ you a drink?** ¿te apetece beber *or* tomar algo?, ¿quieres beber *or* tomar algo?; **to go/come and ~ sth/sb**: **I'll go and ~ it for you** voy a buscártelo, voy a traértelo; **go and ~ Jane will you?** vete a buscar a Jane, ve a por Jane; **phone me when you arrive and I'll come and ~ you** cuando llegues llama por teléfono y te iré a buscar *or* recoger

6 *= call* [+ *doctor, plumber*] llamar; **please ~ the doctor** por favor llame al médico

7 *= answer* [+ *phone*] contestar; **can you ~ the phone?** ¿puedes contestar el teléfono?; **I'll ~ it!** (*telephone*) ¡yo contesto!; (*door*) ¡ya voy yo!

8 *= gain, win* [+ *prize*] ganar, llevarse, conseguir; [+ *goal*] marcar; [+ *reputation*] ganarse; **she got first prize** ganó *or* se llevó *or* consiguió el primer premio; **correct, you ~ 5 points** correcto, gana *or* consigue 5 puntos; **he's in it for what he can ~** lo único que quiere es sacarle provecho; **Jackie got good exam results** Jackie sacó buenas notas en los exámenes; **he got a pass/an A in French** sacó un aprobado/un sobresaliente en francés; **I have to ~ my degree first** antes tengo que acabar la carrera *or* conseguir mi diplomatura

9 *= find* [+ *job, flat*] encontrar, conseguir; **he got me a job** me encontró *or* consiguió un trabajo; **you ~ all sorts in this job** te encuentras con todo tipo de gente en este trabajo; **you don't ~ bears in this country** en este país no hay osos

10 *= catch* [+ *ball, disease, person*] coger, agarrar (*LAm*); [+ *thief*] coger, atrapar (*LAm*); [+ *bus*] coger, tomar (*LAm*); [+ *fish*] pescar; **I'm ~ting the bus into town** voy a coger el autobús al centro; **got you!*** ¡te pillé!*, ¡te cacé!*, ¡te agarré! (*LAm*); **got you at last!** ¡por fin te he pillado *or* cazado!*; **I've been trying to ~ him alone** he estado intentando verle a solas; **to ~ sb by the throat/arm** agarrar *or* coger a algn de la garganta/del brazo; **I didn't ~ the details** no oí los detalles; **sorry, I didn't ~ your name** perdone, ¿cómo dice que se llama?, perdone, no me he enterado de su nombre; **did you ~ his (registration) number?** ¿viste el número de matrícula?; **you've got me there!*** ahí sí que me has pillado*; **✦IDIOM to ~ it from sb**: **he really got it from the teacher*** el profesor le echó un rapapolvo*; *see also* **bad C**, **religion**

11 *= reach, put through to* **~ me Mr Jones, please** (*Telec*) póngame *or* (*esp LAm*) comuníqueme con el Sr. Jones, por favor; **you'll ~ him at home if you phone this evening** si le llamas esta tarde lo pillarás* *or* encontrarás en casa; **you can ~ me on this number** puedes contactar conmigo en este número; **I've been trying to ~ you all week** he estado intentando hablar contigo toda la semana

12 ** = attack, take revenge on* **I feel like everyone is out to ~ me** siento que todo el mundo va contra mí; **I'll ~ you for that!** ¡esto me lo vas a pagar!; **they're out to ~ him** van a cargárselo*

13 *= hit* [+ *target*] dar en; **the bullet got him in the leg** la bala le dio en la pierna; **it got him on the head** le dio en la cabeza

14 *= finish* **the drink will ~ him in the end** la bebida acabará con él al final

15 *= take, bring* **how can we ~ it home?** (*speaker not at home*) ¿cómo podemos llevarlo a casa?; (*speaker at home*) ¿cómo podemos traerlo a casa?; **I tried to ~ the blood off my shirt** intenté quitar la sangre de mi camisa; **~ the knife off him!** ¡quítale ese cuchillo!; **I couldn't ~ the stain out of the tablecloth** no podía limpiar la mancha del mantel; **to ~ sth past customs** conseguir pasar algo por la aduana; **we'll ~ you there somehow** le llevaremos de una u otra manera; **we can't ~ it through the door** no lo podemos pasar por la puerta; **to ~ sth to sb** hacer llegar algo a algn; **to ~ the children to bed** meter a los niños en la cama; **where will that ~ us?** ¿de qué nos sirve eso?; **✦IDIOMS that will ~ you/him nowhere ◊ that won't ~ you/him anywhere** eso no te/le va a llevar a ningún sitio

16 *= prepare* [+ *meal*] preparar, hacer; **to ~ breakfast** preparar *or* hacer el desayuno

17 (*with adjective*)

This construction is often translated using a specific Spanish verb. Look up the relevant adjective.

he got his leg broken se rompió la pierna; **to ~ one's hands dirty** ensuciarse las manos; **to ~ sb drunk** emborrachar a algn; **to ~ one's feet wet** mojarse los pies; **you're ~ting me worried** estás haciendo que me preocupe

18 (*with infinitive/present participle*) **to ~ sb to do sth** (= *persuade*) conseguir que algn haga algo, persuadir a algn a hacer algo; (= *tell*) decir a algn que haga algo; **we eventually got her to change her mind** por fin conseguimos que cambiase de idea, por fin le persuadimos a cambiar de idea; **I'll ~ him to ring you** le diré que te llame; **can you ~ someone to photocopy these** puedes decirle *or* mandarle a alguien que me haga una fotocopia de estos; **I can't ~ the door to open** no puedo abrir la puerta, no logro que se abra la puerta; **I couldn't ~ the washing machine to work** no pude *or* no logré poner la lavadora en marcha; **I couldn't ~ the car going** *or* **to go** no pude poner el coche en marcha, no pude arrancar el coche; **to ~ a fire going** conseguir encender un fuego; **to ~ a conversation going** conseguir iniciar una conversación

19 *"get sth done" construction* 19·1 (= *do oneself*) **you'll ~ yourself arrested looking like that** vas a acabar en la cárcel con esas pintas; **to ~ the washing/dishes done** lavar la ropa/fregar los platos; **we got no work done that day** no hicimos nada de trabajo ese día; **when do you think you'll ~ it finished?** ¿cuándo crees que lo vas a acabar?; **you'll ~ yourself killed driving like that** te vas a matar si conduces de esa forma

19·2 (= *get someone to do*) **to ~ one's hair cut** cortarse el pelo, hacerse cortar el pelo; **he knows how to ~ things done** sabe organizar muy bien a la gente; **to ~ sth fixed** arreglar *or* reparar algo; **I've got to ~ my car fixed this week** tengo que arreglar *or* reparar el coche esta semana, tengo que llevar el coche a arreglar *or* reparar esta semana; **I should ~ my teeth fixed** tendría que arreglarme los dientes; **we're going to ~ central heating put in** vamos a poner *or* instalar calefacción central; **I must ~ my car serviced** tengo que llevar el coche a una revisión

20 ** = understand* entender; **I don't ~ you** no te entiendo; **(do you) ~ it?** ¿entiendes?; [+ *joke*] ¿lo coges?, ¿ya caes?*; **I've got it!** [+ *joke*] ¡ya caigo!, ¡ya lo entiendo!; [+ *solution*] ¡ya tengo la solución!, ¡ya he dado con la solución!, ¡ya lo tengo!; *see also* **point A7**, **wrong**

21 ** = annoy* molestar, fastidiar; **what ~s me is the way he always assumes he's right** lo que me molesta *or* fastidia es que siempre da por hecho que tiene razón; **what really ~s me is his total indifference** lo que me molesta *or* fastidia es su total indiferencia

22 ** = thrill* chiflar*; **this tune really ~s me** esta melodía me chifla*, esta melodía me apasiona

23 **to have got sth** (*Brit*) (= *have*) tener algo; **what have you got there?** ¿qué tienes ahí?; **I've got toothache** tengo dolor de muelas

(B) INTRANSITIVE VERB

1 *= reach, go* llegar; **how do you ~ there?** ¿cómo se llega?; **he got there late** llegó tarde; **how did you ~ here?** ¿cómo viniste *or* llegaste?; **how did that box ~ here?** ¿cómo ha venido a parar esta caja aquí?; **I've got as far as page 10** he llegado hasta la página 10; **he won't ~ far** no llegará lejos; **to ~ from A to B** ir de A a B, trasladarse de A a B; **to ~ home** llegar a casa; **to ~ to** llegar a; **how do you ~ to the cinema?** ¿cómo se llega al cine?; **I'll make sure it ~s to you by tomorrow** me aseguraré de que te llegue mañana; **where did you ~ to?** (= *where were you?*) ¿dónde estabas?, ¿dónde te habías metido?; **where can he have got to?** ¿dónde se puede haber metido?; **it's a place that's difficult to ~ to** es un lugar de difícil acceso; **✦IDIOMS not to ~ anywhere**: **you won't ~ anywhere with him** no conseguirás nada con él; **you won't ~ anywhere if you behave like that** no vas a conseguir nada comportándote así; **to ~ nowhere**: **we're ~ting absolutely nowhere ◊ we're ~ting nowhere fast** no estamos llegando a ningún sitio; **to ~**

somewhere: **now we're ~ting somewhere** ahora empezamos a hacer progresos; **to ~ there**: **"how's your thesis going?" — "I'm ~ting there"** —¿qué tal va tu tesis? —va avanzando; **to ~ to sb*** (= *affect*) afectar a algn; (= *annoy*) molestar a algn; **don't let it ~ to you*** (= *affect*) no dejes que te afecte; (= *annoy*) no te molestes por eso; **the whisky has got to him*** el whisky le ha afectado; *see also* **lane A3**

2 *= become, be* ponerse, volverse, hacerse

As expressions with **get** *+ adjective, such as* **get old, get drunk**, *etc, are often translated by a specific verb, look up the adjective.*

it's ~ting late se está haciendo tarde; **how did it ~ like that?** ¿cómo se ha puesto así?; **how do people ~ like that?** ¿cómo puede la gente volverse así?; **this is ~ting ridiculous** esto roza los límites de lo ridículo; **how stupid can you ~?** ¿hasta qué punto llega tu estupidez?, ¿cómo puedes ser tan estúpido?; **to ~ used to sth** acostumbrarse a algo; ✦*IDIOM* **to ~ with it*** espabilarse; **you'd better ~ with it or we'll lose this contract*** espabílate o perderemos este contrato; → BECOME, GO, GET

3 (*with past participle*) 3·1 (= *be*) **he often ~s asked for his autograph** a menudo le piden autógrafos; **we got beaten 3-2** perdimos 3 a 2; **several windows got broken** se rompieron varias ventanas; **to ~ killed** morir, matarse; **I saw her the night she got killed** (*accidentally*) la vi la noche que murió *or* se mató; (= *murdered*) la vi la noche que la asesinaron; **do you want to ~ killed!** ¡¿es que quieres matarte?!; **to ~ paid** cobrar; **he got run over as he was coming out of his house** lo atropellaron al salir de casa

3·2 (*reflexive action*) **to ~ shaved** afeitarse; **to ~ washed** lavarse

4 *= begin* (*with gerund*) empezar a + *infin*, ponerse a + *infin*; **let's ~ going** vamos a ponernos en marcha; **~ going!** ¡muévete!, ¡a menearse!; **once she ~s going on that subject she never stops** una vez que empieza con ese tema no para; **after midnight the party really got going** después de medianoche la fiesta empezó a animarse; **let's ~ moving** vamos a ponernos en marcha; **we got talking** empezamos a hablar *or* charlar; **I got to thinking that ...*** me di cuenta de que ..., empecé a pensar que ...

5 *= come* (*with infinitive*) **to ~ to do sth** llegar a hacer algo; **he eventually got to be prime minister** al final llegó a ser primer ministro; **I got to be quite good at it** llegué a hacerlo bastante bien; **when do we ~ to eat?** ¿cuándo comemos?; **to ~ to know sb** llegar a conocer a algn; **he got to like her despite her faults** le llegó a gustar a pesar de sus defectos; **so when do I ~ to meet this friend of yours?** ¿cuándo me vas a presentar a este amigo tuyo?; **I never ~ to drive the car** nunca tengo oportunidad de conducir el coche; **to ~ to see sth/sb** lograr ver algo/a algn

6 ** = go* **get** ¡lárgate!*

7 **to have got to do sth** (*expressing obligation*) tener que hacer algo; **you've got to tell the police** tienes que denunciarlo a la policía; **why have I got to?** ¿por qué tengo que hacerlo?

Ⓒ PHRASAL VERBS

►**get about** VI + ADV 1 [*invalid*] (= *walk*) caminar; (= *move around*) moverse; **he ~s about with a stick/on crutches** camina con un bastón/con muletas; **she's quite frail and can't ~ about very much** está muy delicada y no puede moverse mucho

2 (= *travel*) viajar; **the sort of work I do means I ~ about a fair bit** el tipo de trabajo que hago significa que viajo *or* me desplazo bastante

3 (= *go out*) (*socially*) salir

4 (= *circulate*) [*rumour*] correr; [*story*] saberse, divulgarse; **it soon got about that they were ~ting divorced** al poco tiempo corrió el rumor de que se estaban divorciando; **I don't want it to ~ about** no quiero que se sepa *or* divulgue

►**get above** VI + PREP **to ~ above o.s.** volverse un engreído

►**get across** Ⓐ VI + PREP [+ *road*] cruzar; [+ *river, sea, desert*] cruzar, atravesar

Ⓑ VI + ADV 1 (= *cross road, river, etc*) cruzar

2 (= *be understood*) [*meaning*] ser comprendido; [*person*] hacerse entender; **the message seems to be ~ting across** parece que está empezando a captar el mensaje; **to ~ across to sb** lograr comunicar con algn, hacerse entender por algn

Ⓒ VT + ADV 1 (= *communicate*) [+ *meaning, message*] comunicar, hacer entender; **she was anxious to ~ her point across** le preocupaba que se entendiese bien lo que quería decir

2 (= *transport across*) [+ *people, objects*] cruzar; **we can use one of the big patrolboats to ~ you across** podemos usar uno de esos barcos patrulleros grandes para cruzaros

►**get after** VI + PREP 1 (= *pursue*) perseguir; (= *hunt down*) dar caza a; **~ after him! he's forgotten his wallet** ¡ve y lo alcanzas! ¡que se le ha olvidado la cartera!

2 (*) (= *criticize, nag*) dar la vara a*; **she ~s after me about the way I dress** siempre me está dando la vara por la forma en que visto*

►**get ahead** VI + ADV 1 (*in race*) tomar la delantera; **having got ahead of the other runners, he relaxed** tras tomar la delantera se relajó

2 (= *succeed*) (*by doing better than others*) ir por delante; (= *make progress*) progresar, avanzar; **to ~ ahead of sb** adelantar a algn

3 (*with work*) adelantar (**with** con)

►**get along** Ⓐ VI + ADV 1 (= *leave*) marcharse, irse; **it's time we were ~ting along** ya es hora de que nos marchemos *or* nos vayamos; **~ along with you!** (= *go*) ¡vete ya!, ¡lárgate!; (*) (*expressing disbelief*) ¡venga ya!, ¡anda ya!; (*joking*) ¡no digas bobadas!

2 (= *manage*) arreglárselas*, apañárselas*; **to ~ along without sth/sb** arreglárselas sin algo*, apañárselas sin algo*; **we ~ along (somehow)** vamos tirando

3 (= *progress*) **how is he ~ting along?** ¿qué tal está?, ¿cómo le va? (*LAm*); **try it and see how you ~ along** prueba a ver cómo te va; **we were ~ting along fine until he arrived** la cosa iba perfectamente hasta que llegó él

4 (= *be on good terms*) llevarse bien; **to ~ along well with sb** llevarse bien con algn

Ⓑ VT + ADV **we'll try to ~ him along** trataremos de hacerle venir

►**get around** VI + ADV 1 = **get about**

2 = **get round 2**

►**get at** VI + PREP 1 (= *gain access to*) [+ *object*] alcanzar; [+ *place*] llegar a *or* hasta; **put the sweets somewhere he can't ~ at them** pon los caramelos en un sitio donde él no pueda alcanzarlos; **it was working fine until he got at it** funcionaba perfectamente hasta que cayó en sus manos; **the dog got at the meat** el perro pilló la carne; **as soon as he ~s at the drink ...** en cuanto se pone a beber ...; **just let me ~ at him!** ¡deja que le ponga la mano encima!

2 (= *ascertain*) [+ *facts, truth*] establecer

3 (*Brit**) 3·1 (= *criticize*) meterse con*; **she's always ~ting at her brother** siempre se está metiendo con su hermano*; **I'm not ~ting at you, I just think that ...** no te estoy echando la bronca, simplemente creo que ...*

3·2 (= *nag*) dar la lata a*; **she's always ~ting at me to have my hair cut** siempre me está dando la lata para que me corte el pelo*

4 (*) (= *imply*) querer decir; (*negatively*) insinuar; **I couldn't see what he was ~ting at** no entendía qué quería decir

5 (= *influence unduly*) (*using bribery*) sobornar; (*using pressure*) presionar; **I feel I'm being got at** tengo la impresión de que están intentando influenciarme

►**get away** Ⓐ VI + ADV 1 (= *depart*) salir (**from** de); (*at start of race*) escapar; (= *go away*) irse; **I couldn't ~ away any sooner** (*from work*) no pude salir antes; **I didn't ~ away till seven thirty** no conseguí marcharme hasta las siete y media; **I can't ~ away before the 15th** no puedo escaparme *or* irme antes del 15; **it would be lovely to ~ away somewhere** sería maravilloso irse a algún sitio; **~ away!** (= *go away*) ¡vete ya!, ¡lárgate!; **to ~ away from** [+ *place, person*] escaparse de; **it's time we got away from this idea** es hora de que abandonemos esta idea; ✦*IDIOM* **~ away (with you)!*** (*expressing disbelief*) ¡venga ya!, ¡anda ya!; (*joking*) ¡no digas bobadas!

2 (= *move away*) apartarse (**from** de); **I yelled at him to ~ away from the edge** le chillé que se apartase del borde

3 (= *escape*) escaparse (**from** de); **you let them ~ away!** ¡dejaste que se escapasen!; **he let a golden opportunity ~ away** dejó escapar una oportunidad única; **to ~ away from it all** escapar de todo; **there's no ~ting away from it*** es algo que no podemos más que aceptar, no se lo puede negar; *see also* **get away with**

Ⓑ VT + ADV (= *remove*) **to ~ sth away from sb** (= *remove*) quitar algo a algn; **~ that snake away from me!** ¡quítame esa serpiente de delante!; **to ~ sb away from sth: I can't ~ him away from that computer** no puedo despegarlo del ordenador; **we managed to ~ her away from the party** conseguimos sacarla de la fiesta con grandes esfuerzos; **you must ~ her away to the country** tienes que llevártela al campo

►**get away with** VI + PREP 1 (= *steal*) llevarse

2 (= *go unpunished*) **he got away with an official warning** sólo se llevó una amonestación; **we can ~ away with just repainting it** bastará con volver a pintarlo; **do you think I'd be able to ~ away with a trouser suit?** ¿crees que iré bien con un traje pantalón?, ¿crees que pasará algo si llevo un traje pantalón?; **we mustn't let them ~ away with it** no debemos dejar que salgan impunes; **he broke the law and got away with it** infringió la ley y no le pillaron; **you won't ~ away with it!** (*with past action*) ¡esto no va a quedar así!; (*with possible action*) esto no te lo van a consentir; **he'll never ~ away with it** nunca se va a salir con la suya; *see also* **murder A2**

3 *see* **get away A1**

►**get back** Ⓐ VT + ADV 1 (= *recover*) [+ *possessions, money, spouse*] recuperar; [+ *strength*] recobrar; **he never got the use of his arm back** nunca recuperó el uso de su brazo; **he resigned but we want to try and ~ him back** dimitió, pero queremos intentar que vuelva

2 (= *return*) [+ *object, person*] devolver; **I'll ~ him back to you by 7 pm** te lo devolveré

antes de las 7; *see also* **own B**

Ⓑ VI + ADV [1] (= *return*) volver; **to ~ back (home)** volver a casa; **~ back into bed/the car** vuelve a la cama/al coche; **things are ~ting back to normal** las cosas están volviendo a la normalidad; **to ~ back to the point** volver al tema; **~ back to what you were doing** sigue con lo que estabas haciendo; **let's ~ back to why you didn't come yesterday** volvamos a la cuestión de por qué no viniste ayer; **to ~ back to work** volver al trabajo

[2] (= *talk*) **I'll ~ back to you on that** te daré una respuesta; **can you ~ back to Harry about the flat?** ¿puedes volver a llamar a Harry para lo del piso?

[3] (= *move back*) **~ back!** ¡atrás!

►**get back at*** VI + PREP **to ~ back at sb (for sth)** vengarse de algn (por algo), desquitarse con algn (por algo)

►**get behind** Ⓐ VI + ADV [1] (*with work, payments*) retrasarse (**with** en)

[2] (*in race*) quedarse atrás

Ⓑ VI + PREP [1] (= *move behind, sit behind*) ponerse detrás de; **she got behind the wheel and drove off** se puso al volante y se fue

[2] (= *support*) [+ *team, government*] apoyar

Ⓒ VT + PREP (= *secure support of*) **we must ~ the government behind us** tenemos que conseguir el apoyo del gobierno

►**get by** VI + ADV [1] (= *pass*) pasar

[2] (*) (= *manage*) arreglárselas*, apañárselas*; (*in language*) defenderse; **we'll ~ by** nos las arreglaremos*, nos las apañaremos*; **she manages to ~ by on what her son gives her** se las arregla *or* apaña para vivir con lo que le da su hijo*; **my pension is not enough to ~ by on** mi pensión no me da para vivir; **we'll have to ~ by without him** tendremos que arreglárnoslas sin él*, tendremos que apañárnoslas sin él*

[3] (= *be acceptable*) pasar; **his work is not brilliant but it'll ~ by** su trabajo no es excepcional, pero pasará; **he ~s by because of his charm rather than his ability** se salva por su encanto no por su habilidad

►**get down** Ⓐ VT + ADV [1] (= *take down*) [+ *book, jug*] bajar (**from** de); [+ *hanging object, light*] descolgar (**from** de); **can you ~ that jar down for me?** ¿puedes bajarme esa jarra?; **I want to ~ that picture down from the wall** quiero quitar ese cuadro de la pared

[2] (= *swallow*) tragarse, tragar

[3] (= *note down*) escribir; **to ~ sth down in writing** *or* **on paper** poner algo por escrito

[4] (= *reduce*) [+ *prices*] bajar; **I need to ~ my weight down a bit** tengo que bajar de peso un poco

[5] (*) (= *depress*) deprimir; **don't let it ~ you down** no dejes que eso te deprima; **this weather's ~ting me down** este invierno me está deprimiendo

[6] (*) (= *annoy*) molestar; **what ~s me down is the way they take him for granted** lo que me molesta es que no sepan valorarlo

Ⓑ VI + ADV [1] (= *descend*) bajar (**from, off** de); **~ down from there!** ¡baja de ahí!

[2] (= *reduce*) bajar; **I've got down to 62 kilos** he bajado a 62 kilos; *see also* **get down to**

[3] (= *crouch*) agacharse; **quick, ~ down! they'll see you!** ¡rápido, agáchate, te van a ver!; **to ~ down on one's knees** ponerse de rodillas

[4] (*) (= *leave table*) levantarse de la mesa; **may I ~ down?** ¿puedo levantarme de la mesa?

[5] (= *go*) bajar; **I'll try and ~ down this weekend** intentaré bajar este fin de semana

►**get down to** VI + PREP **to ~ down to doing sth** ponerse a hacer algo; **let's ~ down to business** (= *start work*) pongámonos manos a la obra; (= *get to the point*) vayamos al grano; **when you ~ down to it there's not much difference between them** cuando lo miras bien, no se diferencian mucho; **to ~ down to work** ponerse a trabajar (en serio); *see also* **brass B**, **get down B2**, **nitty-gritty**

►**get in** Ⓐ VT + ADV [1] (= *bring in*) [+ *person, animal*] hacer entrar; [+ *harvest*] recoger; [+ *supplies*] traer; **I'll ~ some beer in for the weekend** compraré cerveza para el fin de semana

[2] (= *hand over*) entregar; (= *post in*) mandar; **did you ~ your essay in on time?** ¿entregaste tu trabajo a tiempo?; **you must ~ your entries in by 5th May** deben mandar sus inscripciones antes del 5 de mayo

[3] (= *plant*) [+ *bulbs etc*] plantar

[4] (= *summon*) [+ *expert etc*] llamar a

[5] (= *insert*) [+ *object, comment*] meter; [+ *blow*] lograr dar; **I can't ~ any more in** no cabe nada más; **he got in a reference to his new book** logró mencionar su nuevo libro; **he managed to ~ in a game of golf** consiguió meter un partido de golf; **it was hard to ~ a word in** era muy difícil meter baza; **when I could ~ a word in I asked how they had found out** cuando pude meter palabra les pregunté cómo se habían enterado

[6] (= *sneak in*) [+ *arms, drugs*] meter, pasar; [+ *visitor*] colar*; **I can ~ you in as a visitor** puedo colarte como visitante*

Ⓑ VI + ADV [1] (= *enter*) entrar, meterse; **how did that dog ~ in here?** ¿cómo ha entrado *or* se ha metido ese perro aquí?; **the rain ~s in through the roof** la lluvia entra *or* se mete por el tejado

[2] (= *arrive*) [*train, bus, plane*] llegar; (= *reach home*) [*person*] llegar (a casa); **what time did you ~ in last night?** ¿a qué hora llegaste (a casa) anoche?; **I got in from Miami at 6 am** llegué de Miami a las 6 de la mañana

[3] (= *be admitted*) (*to club*) ser admitido; (*Pol*) (= *be elected*) ser elegido

[4] (= *intervene*) **you'll have to ~ in there quick or you'll miss your chance** no se retrase o perderá su oportunidad; **he tried to say something but I got in first** intentó decir algo pero yo me adelanté

►**get in on** VI + PREP (= *become involved*) **it's a big market and everyone wants to ~ in on it** es un mercado grande y todos quieren entrar en él; **how can we ~ in on the deal?** ¿cómo podemos entrar a formar parte del trato?; *see also* **act A2**

►**get into** Ⓐ VI + PREP [1] (= *enter*) [+ *house*] entrar en; [+ *vehicle*] subir a; [+ *bed, bath*] meterse en; **earth had got into the wound** se le había metido tierra en la herida; **to ~ into politics** meterse en la política; ✦**IDIOM what's got into him?** ¿qué mosca le ha picado?, ¿pero qué le pasa?; **I don't know what's got into you!** ¡no sé qué mosca te ha picado!, ¡no sé qué demonios te pasa!

[2] (= *reach*) [+ *office, school*] llegar a; **if this document ~s into the wrong hands …** si este documento cae en en manos de quien no debe …

[3] (= *become member of*) [+ *club*] entrar en

[4] (= *put on*) [+ *clothes*] ponerse

[5] (= *become involved in*) [+ *situation, trouble, argument, fight*] meterse en; **I wish I'd never got into this** ojalá no me hubiera metido nunca en esto; **the yacht got into difficulties in a heavy sea** el yate empezó a tener problemas en el mar encrespado; **he got into trouble with the police** se metió en problemas con la policía

[6] (= *acquire*) **to ~ into the habit of doing sth** coger *or* (*LAm*) agarrar la costumbre de hacer algo; *see also* **shape A5**

Ⓑ VT + PREP [1] (= *cause to enter*) meter en; **it took two of us to ~ him into the car** nos llevó a dos personas meterle en el coche; **we got the boat into the water** metimos la barca en el agua; **we need to ~ him into hospital** tenemos que llevarlo al hospital; *see also* **head A2**, **tooth A1**

[2] (= *involve in*) **to ~ sb into sth** meter a algn en algo; **you got me into this** tú me has metido en esto; **he's the one who got me into music** él es quien me aficionó a la música

►**get in with** VI + PREP (= *gain favour with*) congraciarse con; **he tried to ~ in with the headmaster** intentó congraciarse con el director; **he got in with a bad crowd** empezó a andar con malas compañías

►**get off** Ⓐ VT + ADV [1] (= *remove*) [+ *stain, top, lid*] quitar; **to ~ one's clothes off** quitarse la ropa

[2] (= *send off*) [+ *letter, telegram*] mandar (**to** a); **to ~ sb off to school** despachar a algn al colegio; **she got the baby off to sleep** logró dormir al niño

[3] (= *save from punishment*) **his lawyer managed to ~ him off** su abogado logró que se librase del castigo

[4] (= *have as leave*) [+ *day, time*] tener libre; **we ~ a day off on the Queen's birthday** nos dan un día libre en el cumpleaños de la reina

[5] (= *learn*) aprender; **to ~ sth off by heart** aprender algo de memoria

[6] (= *rescue*) rescatar

Ⓑ VT + PREP [1] (= *cause to give up*) **to ~ sb off** [+ *drugs, alcohol, addiction*] hacer que algn deje; *see also* **get A1, A15**

[2] (= *remove*) **~ your dog off me!** ¡quítame al perro de encima!

Ⓒ VI + PREP [1] (= *descend from*) [+ *bus, train, bike, horse*] bajarse de, apearse de (*frm*); ✦**IDIOM to ~ off sb's back**: **I wish he would ~ off my back!*** ¡ojalá me dejara en paz!; *see also* **high A3**

[2] (= *leave*) salir de; **~ off my land!** ¡sal de mis tierras!; **~ off my foot!** ¡deja de pisarme el pie!; **I couldn't ~ off the phone** no podía colgar el teléfono; **what time do you ~ off work/school?** ¿a qué hora sales del trabajo/del colegio?

[3] (= *move away from*) **let's ~ off this subject** cambiemos de tema, dejemos el tema; **we've rather got off the subject** nos hemos alejado bastante del tema

[4] (*) (= *escape*) [+ *chore etc*] escaquearse de*; **she got off the washing-up** se escaqueó de lavar los platos

[5] (= *get up from*) levantarse de; **why don't you ~ off your backside and do some work?‡** ¿por qué no mueves el trasero y te pones a hacer algo de trabajo?‡

[6] (= *give up*) [+ *drugs, alcohol, addiction*] dejar

Ⓓ VI + ADV [1] (*from bus, train, bike, horse*) bajarse, apearse (*frm*); **~ off!** (= *let go*) ¡suelta!; ✦**IDIOM to tell sb where to ~ off*** cantar a algn las cuarenta*

[2] (= *leave*) partir; **we got off at 6am** partimos a las 6 de la mañana; **can you ~ off early tomorrow?** (*from work*) ¿puedes salir del trabajo temprano mañana?

[3] (= *escape injury, punishment*) librarse; **he got off** se libró (del castigo); **you're not go-**

ing to ~ off that lightly! ¡no se va a librar con tan poco!; **he got off lightly, he could have been killed** tuvo suerte, podría haberse matado; **they got off lightly, we should have killed them** no se llevaron lo que se merecían, deberíamos haberlos matado; **he got off with a fine** se libró con una multa
4 **to ~ off (to sleep)** dormirse

►**get off on‡** VT + PREP pirrarse por*; **he loves making fun of people, he really ~s off on it** le encanta reírse de la gente, le chifla *or* se pirra*

►**get off with*** VI + PREP (*Brit*) (= *start relationship with*) enrollarse con*, liarse con*

►**get on** Ⓐ VI + ADV 1 (= *mount*) subir
2 (= *proceed*) seguir; **we must be ~ting on, Sue's waiting for us** tenemos que seguir, Sue nos está esperando; **~ on, man!** ¡sigue!, ¡adelante!; **to ~ on with sth** seguir con algo; **now we can ~ on with our lives again** ahora podemos seguir con nuestras vidas; **~ on with it!** ¡venga!, ¡apúrese! (*LAm*); **~ on with your work, please** seguid trabajando, por favor; **this will do to be ~ting on with** esto basta por ahora; *see also* **get on to**
3 (= *manage*) **I was ~ting on fine till he came along** me iba bien hasta que llegó él; **how did you ~ on?** (*in exam, interview*) ¿qué tal te fue?, ¿cómo te fue?; **how are you ~ting on with him/the new computer?** ¿qué tal *or* cómo te va con él/el ordenador nuevo?; **she's ~ting on very well with Russian** está haciendo muchos progresos con el ruso
4 (= *progress*) progresar; (= *succeed*) tener éxito; **he's keen to ~ on** quiere progresar; **if you want to ~ on in life, you must ...** si quieres tener éxito en la vida, debes ...
5 **to be ~ting on: it's ~ting on for nine** son casi las nueve; **he's ~ting on for 70** está rondando los 70, anda cerca de los 70; **there were ~ting on for 50 people** había casi 50 personas; **her parents are ~ting on a bit** sus padres ya están un poco viejos; **time is ~ting on** se está haciendo tarde
6 (= *be on good terms*) llevarse bien; **I'm afraid we just don't ~ on** me temo que no nos llevamos *or* entendemos bien; **to ~ on (well) with sb** llevarse bien con algn; **I can't ~ on with computers** no me aclaro con los ordenadores, los ordenadores y yo no hacemos migas
Ⓑ VI + PREP 1 (= *mount*) [+ *vehicle*] subir(se) a; [+ *horse, bicycle*] subir(se) a, montar a
2 (= *be appointed/elected to*) [+ *committee*] entrar en
Ⓒ VT + ADV (= *put on*) [+ *clothes*] ponerse; [+ *lid, cover, dinner*] poner; **it's time I got the vegetables on** es hora de poner la verdura

►**get on at*** VI + PREP = **get at 3**

►**get on to, get onto** Ⓐ VI + PREP 1 (= *climb on to*) [+ *bike, horse*] montarse en, subir(se) a; [+ *bus, train*] subir(se) a
2 (= *enter*) **we got on to the motorway at junction 15** entramos en la autopista en el acceso número 15
3 (= *enrol on*) [+ *course*] matricularse en
4 (= *be elected to*) [+ *committee*] ser elegido como miembro de
5 (= *start talking of*) [+ *subject*] empezar a hablar de; (= *move on to*) pasar a; (= *reach*) llegar a; **we got on to the subject of money** empezamos a hablar de dinero; **let's ~ on to the question of complaints** pasemos al tema de las reclamaciones; **by the time they got on to my question there was no time left** cuando llegaron a mi pregunta ya no había tiempo
6 (*Brit*) (= *contact*) ponerse en contacto con; (= *phone*) llamar; (= *talk to*) hablar con
7 (= *deal with*) ocuparse de; **I'll ~ on to it right away** ahora mismo lo hago; **don't let's ~ on to that again** no empecemos con eso otra vez
8 (= *get wise to*) **how did the Russians ~ on to us?** ¿cómo nos descubrieron los rusos?; **how did the press ~ on to this?** ¿cómo se ha enterado la prensa de esto?; **the police got on to him at once** la policía se puso en seguida sobre su pista
9 = **get at 3**
Ⓑ VT + PREP 1 (= *make deal with*) poner a trabajar en; **I'll ~ my men on to it right away** pondré a mis hombres a trabajar en esto enseguida; (= *send*) ahora mismo mando a mis hombres; **I'm going to ~ my dad on to you!*** le voy a decir a mi papá que te arregle las cuentas
2 (= *cause to talk about*) **we got him on to the subject of drugs** logramos que hablase de las drogas; **don't ~ him on to the subject of golf** no le des pie para que se ponga a hablar de golf
3 (= *make a member of*) **we need to ~ some new people on to the committee** necesitamos conseguir gente nueva para el comité, necesitamos meter gente nueva en el comité

►**get out** Ⓐ VI + ADV 1 (*of room*) salir; (*of country*) marcharse; (*of vehicle*) bajarse, apearse (*frm*); **~ out!** ¡fuera de aquí!; **~ out of the way!** ¡apártate!, ¡ponte de un lado!; **to ~ out of bed/one's chair** levantarse de la cama/de la silla; **she wanted to ~ out of teaching** quería dejar la enseñanza; **the company decided to ~ out of England** la compañía decidió dejar Inglaterra
2 (= *escape*) [*animal*] escaparse; [*prisoner*] escaparse, fugarse; **the lion got out of its cage** el león se escapó de la jaula; **you'll never ~ out of this one!** ¡de ésta sí que no te escapas!
3 (= *be released*) [*prisoner*] salir
4 (= *go out*) salir; **you ought to ~ out a bit more** tendrías que salir un poco más
5 [*secret*] llegarse a saber; [*news*] (= *become public*) hacerse público; (= *leak*) filtrarse; **if this ever ~s out we're done for** si esto se llega a saber alguna vez estamos perdidos
Ⓑ VT + ADV 1 (= *remove, bring out*) [+ *object, person, library book, money from bank*] sacar; [+ *tooth*] arrancar; [+ *stain*] quitar; **~ that dog out of here!** ¡saque a ese perro de aquí!; **I can never ~ him out of bed in the morning** por las mañanas no puedo sacarlo de la cama; **~ the cards out and we'll have a game** saca las cartas y echemos una partida; **he got his diary out of his pocket** se sacó la agenda del bolsillo; **I can't ~ it out of my mind** no me lo puedo quitar de la mente *or* de la cabeza; **it ~s me out of the house** me hace salir de casa
2 (= *send for*) [+ *doctor, plumber, electrician*] llamar
3 (= *send out*) [+ *message*] mandar
4 (= *pronounce*) **I couldn't ~ the words out** no me salían las palabras; **I'd hardly got the words out of my mouth before she silenced me** apenas había empezado a hablar cuando me hizo callar
5 (*Cricket*) [+ *batsman*] eliminar

►**get out of** Ⓐ VI + PREP *see also* **get A1** 1 (= *escape*) [+ *duty, punishment*] librarse de; [+ *difficulty*] salir de; **some people will do anything to ~ out of paying taxes** algunas personas hacen lo imposible para librarse de pagar impuestos; **there's no ~ting out of it** no hay más remedio; **how are you going to ~ out of this one?** ¿cómo vas a salir de ésta?
2 (= *lose*) **to ~ out of the habit of doing sth** perder la costumbre de hacer algo
Ⓑ VT + PREP *see* **get out B**

►**get over** Ⓐ VI + PREP 1 (= *cross*) [+ *stream, road*] cruzar, atravesar; [+ *wall, fence*] (= *go over*) pasar por encima de; (= *jump over*) saltar por encima de
2 (= *overcome, recover from*) [+ *problem, serious illness, disappointment*] superar; [+ *cold, virus*] reponerse de; [+ *shock, fright, grief*] sobreponerse a; [+ *surprise*] recuperarse de; [+ *resentment*] olvidar; [+ *shyness*] vencer, dominar; **she got over cancer 5 years ago** superó un cáncer hace 5 años; **she refused! I can't ~ over it!** ¡dijo que no! ¡no me cabe en la cabeza *or* no puedo creerlo!; **I can't ~ over how much he's changed** no puedo creer lo mucho que ha cambiado; **she never really got over him** nunca llegó realmente a olvidarlo
Ⓑ VI + ADV 1 (= *cross sth*) (*stream, road*) cruzar; (*wall, fence*) (= *go over*) pasar por encima; (= *climb over*) saltar por encima
2 (= *come*) venir; (= *go*) ir; **I'll see if I can ~ over later on** veré si puedo ir más tarde
Ⓒ VT + ADV 1 (= *transport across*) [+ *people, objects*] cruzar; (= *lift over*) hacer pasar por encima; **they made a rope bridge to ~ the guns/men over** construyeron un puente de cuerda para pasar las armas/a los hombres al otro lado
2 (= *send*) **I'll ~ the documents over to you tomorrow** te haré llegar los documentos mañana; **~ yourself over here as soon as you can** vente para acá tan pronto como puedas
3 (= *have done with*) acabar de una vez; **let's ~ it over (with)** acabemos de una vez; **I just want to ~ this interview over (with)** lo único que quiero es sacarme de encima esta entrevista
4 (= *communicate*) [+ *idea*] transmitir; **the film ~s its message over very convincingly** la película transmite el mensaje de forma muy convincente; **I was trying to ~ it over to him that it was impossible** estaba intentando hacerle comprender que era imposible
Ⓓ VT + PREP 1 (= *transport across*) **to ~ troops/supplies over a river** pasar tropas/suministros al otro lado del río
2 (= *lift over*) hacer pasar por encima de; **they got him over the gate** le pasaron al otro lado de la verja

►**get round** Ⓐ VI + PREP 1 (= *negotiate*) [+ *corner*] dar la vuelta a
2 (= *overcome*) [+ *problem*] superar
3 (= *avoid*) [+ *regulation*] sortear
4 (= *persuade*) **to ~ round sb** engatusar a algn; **you're not going to ~ round me** no me vas a engatusar
5 (= *congregate at*) **12 of us can't ~ round that table** no podemos sentarnos 12 personas alrededor de esa mesa; **we need to ~ round the table and discuss this** (*fig*) tenemos que juntarnos y discutir esto
6 (= *complete*) [+ *course, circuit*] completar
Ⓑ VI + ADV 1 (= *come*) venir; (= *go*) ir; **how can we ~ round to the back of the house?** ¿cómo podemos ir a la parte de atrás de la casa?; **I got round there as soon as I could** fui tan pronto como pude
2 **to ~ round to (doing) sth: I shan't ~ round to that before next week** no lo podré hacer antes de la semana próxima; **we never seem to ~ round to it** parece que nunca tenemos tiempo para eso; **we never got round to exchanging addresses** al final no llegamos a intercambiarnos las señas

Ⓒ VT + ADV 1 (= *cause to come, go*) **we'll ~ a car round to you for 9am** le mandaremos un coche para las 9 de la mañana; **we got all the neighbours round for a meeting** juntamos a todos los vecinos en casa para una reunión

2 (= *persuade*) convencer; **we soon got him round to our way of thinking** pronto logramos que pensase como nosotros

►**get through** Ⓐ VI + PREP 1 (= *pass through*) [+ *window, door, gap*] pasar por; [+ *crowd*] abrirse paso entre

2 (= *finish*) [+ *book, meal*] terminar; **we've got a lot of work to ~ through** tenemos mucho trabajo para hacer; **she can ~ through a whole box of chocolates at one go** es capaz de terminarse una caja entera de bombones de una vez

3 (= *survive*) aguantar; **how are they going to ~ through the winter?** ¿cómo van a aguantar el invierno?

4 (= *use up*) [+ *money*] gastar; **she ~s through £300 a month on clothes** gasta 300 libras al mes en ropa; **he's got through two pairs of trousers already this term** ya ha gastado dos pares de pantalones este trimestre; **they ~ through three loaves of bread a day** comen tres panes al día

5 (= *pass*) [+ *exam*] aprobar, pasar; (*Sport*) [+ *qualifying round*] superar

Ⓑ VT + PREP **we can't ~ it through the door** no lo podemos pasar por la puerta; **I'll never ~ the car through here** no voy a poder hacer que el coche pase por aquí; **coffee is the only thing that ~s me through the day** el café es lo único que me ayuda a pasar el día; **I got 15 students through this exam** conseguí que 15 de mis alumnos aprobasen este examen; **to ~ a bill through parliament** conseguir que una ley se apruebe en el parlamento; **we have three children to ~ through university** tenemos tres hijos a los que tenemos que pagarles la carrera

Ⓒ VT + ADV 1 (= *cause to succeed*) [+ *student*] conseguir que apruebe; **it was his faith in God that got him through** su creencia en Dios fue lo que le ayudó a salir adelante *or* superar la crisis

2 (= *succeed in sending*) [+ *supplies*] conseguir entregar

3 (= *cause to be understood*) **I can't ~ it through to him that ...** no puedo hacerle entender que ...

4 (*Pol*) [+ *bill*] conseguir que se apruebe, conseguir que sea aprobado

Ⓓ VI + ADV 1 (= *pass through*) abrirse paso; (= *arrive*) [*news, supplies etc*] llegar (a su destino)

2 (*Telec*) (lograr) comunicar (**to** con); **I've been trying to ~ through to Buenos Aires** he estado intentando comunicar con Buenos Aires; ✦***IDIOM*** **to ~ through to sb** hacerse entender por algn; **I can't seem to ~ through to him any more** parece que ya no me entiende; **I think the message is ~ting through to him** creo que está empezando a captar el mensaje

2 (= *pass, succeed*) [*student*] aprobar; (*Sport*) [*team*] pasar; [*bill*] ser aprobado; [*candidate*] ser aceptado

4 (*esp US*) (= *finish*) acabar; **to ~ through with sth** terminar algo

►**get together** Ⓐ VT + ADV [+ *people, money, team*] reunir; [+ *objects*] reunir, juntar; [+ *show, concert*] preparar; [+ *proposal*] elaborar; [+ *thoughts, ideas*] poner en orden; **we couldn't ~ the down payment together** no pudimos reunir el dinero para la entrada; **it won't take me long to ~ my stuff together** no tardaré mucho en recoger mis cosas; **~ yourself together and make sure you're there on time** organízate y asegúrate que estás allí a la hora; *see also* **act A3**

Ⓑ VI + ADV [*friends, group, club*] reunirse; **could we ~ together this evening?** ¿podemos reunirnos esta tarde?; **to ~ together about sth** reunirse para discutir algo; **you'd better ~ together with him before you decide** te conviene hablar con él antes de decidirte

►**get under** Ⓐ VI + ADV (= *pass underneath*) pasar por debajo

Ⓑ VI + PREP **to ~ under a fence/rope** pasar por debajo de una cerca/cuerda; **to ~ under the covers** meterse debajo de las mantas

Ⓒ VT + ADV hacer pasar por debajo

Ⓓ VT + PREP hacer pasar por debajo de; **we couldn't ~ it under the bed** no podíamos meterlo debajo de la cama; *see also* **skin A1**

►**get up** Ⓐ VI + ADV 1 (= *stand*) levantarse, ponerse de pie; (*from bed*) levantarse; **~ up!** ¡levántate!; (*to horse*) ¡arre!

2 (= *climb up*) subir

3 [*wind*] (= *start to blow*) levantarse; (= *become fiercer*) empezar a soplar recio; [*sea*] embravecerse; [*fire*] avivarse

Ⓑ VT + ADV 1 (= *raise*) [+ *person*] (*from chair, floor, bed*) levantar

2 (= *gather*) [+ *courage*] reunir; **I couldn't ~ up the nerve to ask the question** no conseguí reunir el valor necesario para hacer la pregunta; **we couldn't ~ up much enthusiasm for the idea** no conseguimos suscitar *or* despertar mucho entusiasmo entre la gente hacia la idea; **I want to ~ my strength up for this race** quiero ponerme en plena forma (física) para esta carrera, quiero cobrar fuerzas para esta carrera; **to ~ up speed** cobrar velocidad, ganar velocidad

3 (*) (= *organize*) [+ *celebration*] organizar, preparar; [+ *petition*] organizar

4 (*) (= *dress up*) [+ *person*] ataviar (**in** con); **she'd got herself up in all her finery** se había ataviado con sus mejores galas; **beautifully got up** muy bien vestido; **to ~ o.s. up as** disfrazarse de, vestir de

►**get up to** VI + PREP 1 (= *reach*) llegar a; **I've got up to chapter four** he llegado al capítulo cuatro

2 (= *do*) **to ~ up to mischief** hacer travesuras; **I don't want you ~ting up to any mischief** no quiero que hagas ninguna travesura; **what have you been ~ting up to lately?** ¿qué has estado haciendo últimamente?; **you never know what he'll ~ up to next** nunca se sabe qué locura va a hacer luego

get-at-able [get'ætəbl] ADJ accesible

getaway ['getəweɪ] Ⓐ N escape *m*, huida *f*, fuga *f*; **to make one's ~** escaparse

Ⓑ CPD ► **getaway car** N **the thieves' ~ car** el coche en que huyeron los ladrones

get-rich-quick* [ˌget,rɪtʃ'kwɪk] ADJ **~ scheme** plan *m* para hacerse rico pronto, plan *m* para hacer una rápida fortuna

get-together* ['gettəˌgeðər] N (= *meeting*) reunión *f*; (= *regular social gathering*) tertulia *f*; (= *party*) fiesta *f*; **we're having a little ~ on Friday, can you come?** vamos a reunirnos unos amigos el viernes, ¿puedes venir?; **a family ~** una reunión familiar

getup* ['getʌp] N atuendo *m*, traje *m*, atavío *m*

get-up-and-go* [ˌgetʌpənd'gəʊ] N **he's got lots of ~** tiene mucho empuje

get-well card [ˌget'wel,kɑːd] N *tarjeta para un enfermo deseándole que se mejore*

gewgaw† ['gjuːgɔː] N baratija *f*

geyser ['giːzər, (*US*) 'gaɪzər] N (*Geog*) géiser *m*; (= *water heater*) calentador *m* de agua

G-Force ['dʒiːfɔːs] N ABBR = **force of gravity**

Ghana ['gɑːnə] N Ghana *f*

Ghanaian [gɑː'neɪən] Ⓐ ADJ ghanés

Ⓑ N ghanés/esa *m/f*

ghastly ['gɑːstlɪ] ADJ (*compar* **ghastlier**; *superl* **ghastliest**) 1 (*) (= *very bad*) [*person*] inaguantable; [*dress, wallpaper*] horrible; [*situation, experience*] espantoso, horrendo; [*mistake*] funesto; **how ~!** ¡qué horror!; **it must be ~ for her** debe ser horrible para ella

2 (= *horrible*) horroroso

3 (= *pale*) pálido, cadavérico

Ghent [gent] N Gante *m*

gherkin ['gɜːkɪn] N pepinillo *m*

ghetto ['getəʊ] N (*pl* **ghettos** *or* **ghettoes**) gueto *m*; (*Hist*) judería *f*

ghetto-blaster ['getəʊ,blɑːstər] N radiocasete *m* portátil (*muy grande*)

ghettoization [ˌgetəʊaɪ'zeɪʃən] N (*fig*) marginación *f*

ghettoize ['getəʊ,aɪz] VT (*fig*) marginar

ghost [gəʊst] Ⓐ N fantasma *m*, espectro *m*; (*TV*) imagen *f* fantasma; **Holy Ghost** (*Rel*) Espíritu *m* Santo; **he hasn't the ~ of a chance** no tiene la más remota posibilidad; **she managed the ~ of a smile** consiguió esbozar un amago de sonrisa; ✦***IDIOM*** **to give up the ~** (= *die*) entregar el alma; (*hum*) [*car, washing machine, etc*] pasar a mejor vida

Ⓑ VT [+ *book*] escribir por otro; **an autobiography ~ed by Peters** una autobiografía escrita por el negro Peters

Ⓒ CPD ► **ghost image** N (*Cine, TV*) imagen *f* fantasma ► **ghost story** N cuento *m* de fantasmas ► **ghost town** N pueblo *m* fantasma ► **ghost train** N tren *m* fantasma

ghostly ['gəʊstlɪ] ADJ fantasmal, espectral

ghost-write ['gəʊst,raɪt] (*pt* **ghost-wrote**; *pp* **ghost-written**) VT = **ghost B**

ghostwriter ['gəʊst,raɪtər] N negro/a *m/f*

ghoul [guːl] N (= *malevolent spirit*) demonio *m* necrófago; (= *person*) morboso/a *m/f*

ghoulish ['guːlɪʃ] ADJ [*practice, activity*] macabro; [*person, curiosity*] morboso

GHQ N ABBR (= **General Headquarters**) cuartel *m* general

GI* Ⓐ N ABBR (*US*) (= **Government Issue**) propiedad *f* del Estado; (*also* **GI Joe**) soldado *m* (raso) americano

Ⓑ ADJ **GI bride** novia *f or* esposa *f* de un soldado americano

giant ['dʒaɪənt] Ⓐ N 1 (*physically*) gigante/a *m/f*

2 (*fig*) (*in importance, power*) gigante *m*; **Sol, the computer ~** Sol, líder en ordenadores; **he was a ~ among actors** como actor fue un coloso

Ⓑ ADJ [*tree, star*] gigantesco; [*animal, insect, bird, plant*] gigante; [*portion*] gigantesco, enorme; [*packet*] gigante, familiar; [*strides*] de gigante

Ⓒ CPD ► **giant panda** N panda *mf* gigante ► **giant slalom** N slalom *m* gigante

giantess [ˌdʒaɪən'tes] N giganta *f*

giant-killer ['dʒaɪənt,kɪlər] N (*Sport*) matagigantes *m inv*, *equipo que vence a otro muy superior*

giant-killing ['dʒaɪənt,kɪlɪŋ] ADJ (*Sport*) **Scarborough's ~ act against Chelsea** la hazaña de Scarborough de ser el David que venció al Goliat Chelsea; **Spain's ~ French**

Open champion el matagigantes español, campeón en el Open francés

giant-size(d) ['dʒaɪəntsaɪz(d)] ADJ [*packet*] (de tamaño) gigante

Gib* [dʒɪb] N = **Gibraltar**

gibber ['dʒɪbəʳ] VI [*person*] farfullar, hablar atropelladamente; [*monkey*] chillar; **to ~ with rage/fear** farfullar a causa de la ira/del miedo

gibbering ['dʒɪbərɪŋ] ADJ **I must have sounded like a ~ idiot** debí de sonar como un tonto balbuceando

gibberish ['dʒɪbərɪʃ] N galimatías *m inv*, guirigay *m*

gibbet ['dʒɪbɪt] N horca *f*

gibbon ['gɪbən] N gibón *m*

gibe [dʒaɪb] (A) N mofa *f*, burla *f*
(B) VI mofarse, burlarse (**at** de)

giblets ['dʒɪblɪts] NPL menudillos *mpl*, menudencias *fpl* (*Andes, Chile*)

Gibraltar [dʒɪ'brɔːltəʳ] N Gibraltar *m*

Gibraltarian [ˌdʒɪbrɔːl'tɛərɪən] (A) ADJ gibraltareño
(B) N gibraltareño/a *m/f*

giddily ['gɪdɪlɪ] ADV [1] (= *dizzily*) [*spin, twirl*] vertiginosamente; **she struggled ~ to her feet** se esforzó para ponerse en pie, con la cabeza dándole vueltas
[2] (= *light-heartedly*) frívolamente

giddiness ['gɪdɪnɪs] N vértigo *m*

giddy[1] ['gɪdɪ] ADJ (*compar* **giddier**, *superl* **giddiest**) (= *dizzy*) mareado; (= *causing dizziness*) [*height, speed*] vertiginoso; (*of character*) atolondrado, ligero de cascos; **to feel ~** sentirse mareado; **it makes me ~** me marea, me da vértigo

giddy[2] ['gɪdɪ] EXCL **~ up!** (*to horse*) ¡arre!

GIFT [gɪft] N ABBR = **Gamete Intrafallopian Transfer**

gift [gɪft] (A) N [1] (= *present*) regalo *m*, obsequio *m* (*frm*); (*Comm*) (*also* **free ~**) obsequio *m*; (*Jur*) donación *f*; **it's a ~!*** (= *very cheap*) ¡es una ganga!; (= *very easy*) es pan comido, ¡está tirado!*; ✦**PROV don't look a ~ horse in the mouth** a caballo regalado no le mires el dentado
[2] (= *talent*) don *m*, talento *m*; **the ~ of tongues** el don de las lenguas; **he has a ~ for administration** tiene talento para la administración; **to have a ~ for languages** tener mucha facilidad para los idiomas; **he has artistic ~s** tiene dotes artísticas; *see also* **gab**
[3] (= *power to give*) **the office is in the ~ of ...** el cometido está en manos de ...
(B) VT dar, donar; (*Sport*) [+ *goal*] regalar
(C) CPD ► **gift certificate** N (*US*) = **gift token** ► **gift coupon** N cupón *m* de regalo ► **gift shop, gift store** (*US*) N tienda *f* de regalos; **"gift shop"** "artículos *mpl* de regalo" ► **gift tax** N impuesto *m* sobre donaciones ► **gift token, gift voucher** N vale-obsequio *m*

gifted ['gɪftɪd] ADJ talentoso, de talento; **she is a very ~ writer** es una escritora de mucho talento; **the ~ child** el niño superdotado

giftwrap ['gɪftˌræp], **giftwrapping** ['gɪftˌræpɪŋ] N papel *m* de regalo

gift-wrap ['gɪftˌræp] VT envolver en papel de regalo

giftwrapped ['gɪftˌræpt] ADJ envuelto para regalo

gig [gɪg] N [1] (= *carriage*) calesa *f*
[2] (*Naut*) lancha *f*, canoa *f*
[3] (*Mus**) actuación *f*, concierto *m*
[4] (*US*) (= *job*) trabajo *m* temporal

gigabyte ['dʒɪgəˌbaɪt] N gigabyte *m*

gigantic [dʒaɪ'gæntɪk] ADJ gigantesco

gigawatt ['dʒɪgəˌwɒt] N gigavatio *m*

giggle ['gɪgl] (A) N risita *f*; **she got the ~s** le dio la risa tonta; **they did it for a ~** (*Brit*) lo hicieron para reírse
(B) VI reírse tontamente

giggly ['gɪglɪ] ADJ dado a la risa tonta

GIGO ['gaɪgəʊ] N ABBR (*Comput*) (= **garbage in, garbage out**) BEBS

gigolo ['ʒɪgələʊ] N gigoló *m*

gigot ['ʒiːgəʊ, 'dʒɪgət] N (*Culin*) gigot *m*

gild [gɪld] (*pt* **gilded**; *pp* **gilded, gilt**) VT [+ *metal, frame*] dorar; ✦**IDIOM to ~ the lily** embellecer lo perfecto

gilded ['gɪldɪd] ADJ dorado

gilding ['gɪldɪŋ] N doradura *f*, dorado *m*

Giles [dʒaɪlz] N Gil

gill[1] [gɪl] N [*of fish*] branquia *f*, agalla *f*; ✦**IDIOM to look green about the ~s** tener mala cara

gill[2] [dʒɪl] N (= *measure*) cuarta parte *f* de una pinta (= *0,142 litro*)

gillie ['gɪlɪ] N (*Scot*) [1] (*Hunting*) ayudante *mf* de cazador *or* pescador
[2] (†) (= *attendant*) criado *m*

gilt [gɪlt] (A) PP *of* **gild**
(B) N [1] dorado *m*
[2] **gilts** (*Fin*) papel *msing* del Estado, valores *mpl* de máxima confianza
(C) ADJ dorado

gilt-edged ['gɪlt'edʒd] ADJ [1] (*Fin*) **~ securities** papel *msing* del Estado
[2] [*book*] con cantos dorados

gimbal(s) ['dʒɪmbəl(z)] N (*Aut, Naut*) cardán *m*

gimcrack ['dʒɪmkræk] ADJ [*furniture*] de pacotilla

gimlet ['gɪmlɪt] N (*for wood*) barrena *f* de mano; **he had ~ eyes** tenía una mirada muy penetrante

gimme‡ ['gɪmɪ] = **give me**

gimmick ['gɪmɪk] N truco *m* publicitario; (= *gadget*) artilugio *m*; **it's just a sales ~** es un truco para vender más

gimmickry ['gɪmɪkrɪ] N trucos *mpl*

gimmicky ['gɪmɪkɪ] ADJ efectista

gimp* [gɪmp] N (*US*) cojo/a *m/f*

gin[1] [dʒɪn] N (= *drink*) ginebra *f*; **~ and it** (*Brit*) vermú *m* con ginebra; **~ and tonic** gin-tonic *m*

gin[2] [dʒɪn] (A) N [1] (*Brit*) (*also* **~ trap**) trampa *f*
[2] (*Tech*) desmotadera *f* de algodón
(B) CPD ► **gin rummy** N gin rummy *m*

ginger ['dʒɪndʒəʳ] (A) N (= *spice*) jengibre *m*; (*as nickname*) pelirrojo *m*
(B) ADJ [*hair*] rojo; [*cat*] de color melado; **to have ~ hair** ser pelirrojo
(C) CPD ► **ginger ale, ginger beer** N gaseosa *f* de jengibre ► **ginger group** N (*Brit*) grupo *m* de activistas, grupo *m* de presión

►**ginger up** VT + ADV (*Brit*) espabilar, animar

gingerbread ['dʒɪndʒəbred] N pan *m* de jengibre

gingerly ['dʒɪndʒəlɪ] (A) ADJ cauteloso
(B) ADV con cautela

gingery ['dʒɪndʒərɪ] ADJ [*hair*] rojizo

gingham ['gɪŋəm] N (= *material*) guingán *m*

gingivitis [ˌdʒɪndʒɪ'vaɪtɪs] N gingivitis *f*

Ginny ['dʒɪnɪ] N (*familiar form*) *of* **Virginia**

ginormous* [dʒaɪ'nɔːməs] ADJ (*hum*) enorme de grande

ginseng ['dʒɪnseŋ] (A) N ginseng *m*
(B) CPD [*tea, tablets*] de ginseng

gippo‡ ['dʒɪpəʊ] N (*pej*) gitano/a *m/f*, calé *mf*

gipsy ['dʒɪpsɪ] ADJ, N = **gypsy**

giraffe [dʒɪ'rɑːf] N (*pl* **giraffes** *or* **giraffe**) jirafa *f*

gird [gɜːd] (*pt, pp* **girded, girt**) VT (*liter*) ceñir, rodear (**with** de); ✦**IDIOMS to ~ o.s. for the fight** *or* **fray** aprestarse para la lucha; **to ~ (up) one's loins** aprestarse para la lucha; *see also* **loin**

►**gird on** VT + ADV **to ~ on one's sword** ceñirse la espada

girder ['gɜːdəʳ] N viga *f*

girdle ['gɜːdl] (A) N (= *corset*) faja *f*; (= *belt*) cinturón *m* (*also fig*)
(B) VT ceñir, rodear (*also fig*) (**with** con)

girl [gɜːl] (A) N chica *f*, muchacha *f*; (= *small*) niña *f*; (= *young woman*) chica *f*, joven *f*; (= *servant*) criada *f*, chica *f*; (*) (= *girlfriend*) novia *f*, polola *f* (*Chile*); **factory ~** obrera *f*; **shop ~** dependienta *f*; **old ~** (*Brit*) [*of school*] exalumna *f*, antigua alumna *f*; (†*) (= *elderly woman*) señora *f*, abuelita* *f*; **the old ~** (*Brit**) (= *wife*) la parienta*; (= *mother*) la vieja; **now listen to me, my ~!** ¡escúchame, guapa!
(B) CPD ► **girl Friday** N empleada *f* de confianza ► **girl guide, girl scout** (*US*) N exploradora *f*, guía *f*

girlfriend ['gɜːlfrend] N [*of girl*] amiga *f*; [*of boy*] novia *f*, compañera *f*, polola *f* (*Chile*)

girlhood ['gɜːlhʊd] N juventud *f*, mocedad *f*

girlie* ['gɜːlɪ] (A) N (*US*) nena *f*, chiquilla *f*
(B) CPD ► **girlie magazine** N revista *f* de desnudos

girlish ['gɜːlɪʃ] ADJ de niña; (*pej*) [*man, boy*] afeminado

giro ['dʒaɪrəʊ] (*Brit*) (A) N giro *m*; **bank ~** transferencia *f* bancaria; **post-office ~** giro *m* postal; **National Giro** giro *m* postal
(B) CPD ► **giro cheque** N cheque *m* de giro ► **bank giro system** N sistema *m* de giro bancario ► **giro transfer** N **by ~ transfer** mediante giro

Gironde [dʒɪ'rɒnd] N Gironda *m*

girt [gɜːt] PT, PP *of* **gird**

girth [gɜːθ] N [1] (*for saddle*) cincha *f*
[2] (= *measure*) [*of tree*] circunferencia *f*; [*of person's waist*] contorno *m*; **because of its great ~** por su gran tamaño, por lo abultado

gist [dʒɪst] N [*of speech, conversation*] lo esencial; **to get the ~ of sth** captar lo esencial de algo

git‡ [gɪt] N (*Brit*) cretino/a* *m/f*

give [gɪv] (*pt* **gave**; *pp* **given**)

A TRANSITIVE VERB	C NOUN
B INTRANSITIVE VERB	D PHRASAL VERBS

(A) TRANSITIVE VERB

When **give** *is part of a set combination, eg* **give evidence, give a lecture, give a party, give a yawn,** *look up the other word.*

[1] [*+ possession, object*] dar; (*for special occasion*) regalar, obsequiar (*frm*); [+ *title, honour, award, prize*] dar, otorgar (*frm*); [+ *organ, blood*] dar, donar; (*Scol*) [+ *mark*] poner; **he was ~n a gold watch when he retired** le regalaron *or* (*frm*) obsequiaron un reloj de oro cuando se jubiló; **he gave her a dictionary for her birthday** le regaló un diccionario por su cumpleaños; **he was ~n an award for bravery** le dieron *or* otorgaron un galardón por su valentía; **to ~ sb a penalty** (*Sport*) conceder un penalti *or* penalty a algn; **to ~ o.s to sb** entregarse a algn
[2] [*= pass on*] [+ *message*] dar; [+ *goods, document*] dar, entregar (*more frm*); [+ *illness*] contagiar, pegar*; **~ them my regards** *or* **best wishes** dales saludos de mi parte; **can you ~ Mary the keys when you see her?** ¿puedes darle las llaves a Mary cuando la veas?; **to ~**

sb a cold contagiar el resfriado a algn, pegar el resfriado a algn*; **to ~ sth into sb's hands** (*liter*) entregar *or* confiar algo a algn

3 *= offer* [+ *party, dinner*] dar; **to ~ a party for sb** dar *or* ofrecer una fiesta en honor de algn; **why don't you ~ them melon to start with?** ¿por qué no les das melón para empezar?; **she gave us a wonderful meal** nos hizo una comida buenísima; **we can ~ them cava to drink** podemos darles cava para *or* de beber; **what can I ~ him to eat/for dinner?** ¿qué puedo hacerle para comer/cenar?

4 *= provide* [+ *money, information, idea*] dar; [+ *task*] dar, confiar; **can you ~ him something to do?** ¿puedes darle algo para hacer?; **I'll never be able to ~ you a child** nunca podré darte un hijo; **they gave us a lot of help** nos ayudaron mucho; **it gave us a good laugh*** nos hizo reír mucho; ✦*IDIOM* **~ or take …: 12 o'clock, ~ or take a few minutes** más o menos las doce; **in A.D. 500 ~ or take a few years** aproximadamente en el año 500 después de J.C.

5 *= cause* [+ *shock, surprise*] dar, causar; [+ *pain*] causar, provocar; **it ~s me great pleasure to welcome you all** es un gran placer para mí darles la bienvenida a todos; **to ~ sb a kick/push** dar una patada/un empujón a algn; **to ~ sb to believe that …** hacer creer a algn que …; **I was ~n to believe that …** me hicieron creer que …; **to ~ sb to understand that …** dar a entender a algn que …

6 *= grant, allow* 6·1 [+ *permission*] dar, conceder; [+ *chance, time*] dar; **let's ~ him one last chance** vamos a darle una última oportunidad; **can't you ~ me another week?** ¿no me puedes dar otra semana?; **I can ~ you 10 minutes** le puedo conceder 10 minutos; **~ yourself an hour to get there** necesitas una hora para llegar; **I gave myself 10 minutes to do it** me permití 10 minutos para hacerlo; **to ~ sb a choice** dar a elegir a algn; **he's honest, I ~ you that** es honrado, lo reconozco

6·2 (*) (*predicting future*) **how long would you ~ that marriage?** ¿cuánto tiempo crees que durará ese matrimonio?; **the doctors gave him two years to live** los médicos le dieron dos años de vida

7 *= dedicate* [+ *life, time*] dedicar; **he gave his life to helping the needy** dedicó su vida a ayudar a los necesitados; **I've ~n you the best years of my life** te he dado los mejores años de mi vida; **he gave it everything he'd got** dio lo mejor de sí

8 *= sacrifice* [+ *life*] dar; **he gave his life for his country** dio la vida por su país

9 *= pay* dar; **what will you ~ me for it?** ¿qué me das por ello?; **how much did you ~ for it?** ¿cuánto diste *or* pagaste por él?; ✦*IDIOMS* **I'd ~ a lot** *or* **the world** *or* **anything to know …** daría cualquier cosa por saber …; **I don't** *or* **I wouldn't ~ much for his chances** no le doy muchas posibilidades

10 *= put through to* poner con; **could you ~ me Mr Smith/extension 3443?** ¿me podría poner con el Sr. Smith/con la extensión 3443?

11 *= punish with* **the teacher gave him 100 lines** el profesor le castigó a copiar 100 líneas; **the judge gave him five years** el juez le dio cinco años; **to ~ it to sb*** (*= beat*) dar una paliza a algn; (*verbally*) poner a algn como un trapo*

12 *= present* presentar a; **ladies and gentlemen, I ~ you our guest speaker this evening, …** damas y caballeros, les presento a nuestro conferenciante de esta noche, …

13 *in toast* **I ~ you the Queen** brindemos por la Reina

14 *= produce, supply* [+ *milk, fruit*] dar, producir; [+ *light, heat*] dar; [+ *result*] arrojar; [+ *help, advice*] dar, proporcionar; **it ~s a total of 80** arroja un total de 80; **it ~s 6% a year** rinde un 6% al año; **it gave no sign of life** no daba señales de vida

15 *= state* [+ *name, age, address*] dar; (*on form*) poner; **to ~ the right/wrong answer** dar la respuesta correcta/equivocada; **if I may ~ an example** si se me permite dar *or* poner un ejemplo; **he gave the cause of death as asphyxia** señaló la asfixia como causa de la muerte

16 *= care* **I don't ~ a damn*** me importa un comino *or* un bledo*

17 *= make* [+ *speech*] dar, pronunciar (*frm*); [+ *lecture, concert*] dar

18 **to ~ way** 18·1 (*= collapse*) [*bridge, beam, floor, ceiling*] ceder, hundirse; [*cable, rope*] romperse; [*legs*] flaquear; **the ground gave way beneath him** la tierra se hundió bajo sus pies; **the chair gave way under his weight** la silla no soportó su peso, la silla cedió bajo su peso; **after months of stress his health gave way** después de meses de tensión su salud se vió afectada; **his strength gave way** le flaquearon las fuerzas

18·2 (*= break*) [*rope*] romperse

18·3 **to ~ way (to sth)** (*= be replaced*) ser reemplazado (por algo); (*to demands*) ceder (a algo); (*to traffic*) ceder el paso (a algo); **you gave way too easily** cediste con demasiada facilidad; **to ~ way to an impulse** dejarse llevar por un impulso; **she gave way to tears** se deshizo en lágrimas; **he never ~s way to despair** nunca se abandona a la desesperación; **"give way"** (*Brit Aut*) "ceda el paso"; **to ~ way to the left** ceder el paso a la izquierda

19 (*in idiomatic expressions*) **don't ~ me that!*** ¡no me vengas con esas!*; **I'll ~ you something to cry about!*** ¡ya te daré yo razones para llorar!; **holidays? I'll ~ you holidays!*** ¿vacaciones? ya te voy a dar yo a ti vacaciones*, ¿vacaciones? ¡ni vacaciones ni narices!*; **he wants £100? I'll ~ him £100!*** ¿que quiere 100 libras? ¡ni cien libras ni nada!; **I'll ~ him what for!*** ¡se va a enterar!*; **~ me the old songs!** ¡para mí las canciones viejas!; **~ me a gas cooker every time!*** ¡prefiero mil veces una cocina de gas!; **children? ~ me dogs any time!** ¿niños? ¡prefiero mucho antes un perro!; **I wouldn't want it if you gave it to me** eso no lo quiero ni regalado; **he can ~ you 5 years** él tiene la ventaja de ser 5 años más joven que tú

Ⓑ INTRANSITIVE VERB

1 dar; **giving is better than receiving** dar es mejor que recibir; **please ~ generously** por favor, sean generosos; **to ~ to charity** hacer donativos a organizaciones benéficas, dar dinero a organizaciones benéficas; **to ~ and take** hacer concesiones mutuas; ✦*IDIOM* **to ~ as good as one gets** pagar con la misma moneda, devolver golpe por golpe

2 (*also* **~ way**) 2·1 (*= collapse*) [*bridge, beam, floor, ceiling*] ceder, hundirse; [*knees*] flaquear; **the chair gave under his weight** la silla cedió bajo su peso, la silla no soportó su peso

2·2 (*= break*) [*rope*] romperse

2·3 (*= yield*) [*door*] ceder; **the floor gave slightly under his feet** el suelo cedió ligeramente bajo sus pies; ✦*IDIOM* **something's got to ~!*** ¡por algún lado tiene que salir!

3 (*US**) **what ~s?** ¿qué pasa?, ¿qué se cuece por ahí?*

Ⓒ NOUN

= flexibility [*of material*] elasticidad *f*; **there's a lot of ~ in this chair/bed** esta silla/cama es muy mullida; **there's a lot of ~ in this rope** esta cuerda da mucho de sí; **there isn't a lot of ~ in these proposals** estas propuestas no son muy negociables; **how much ~ has there been on their side?** ¿cuánto han cedido ellos?; **~ and take: you won't achieve an agreement without a bit of ~ and take** no vais a conseguir un acuerdo sin hacer concesiones mutuas; **a bit of ~ and take** un poco de toma y daca*

Ⓓ PHRASAL VERBS

►**give away** VT + ADV 1 (*as gift*) [+ *money, goods*] regalar, obsequiar (*frm*); [+ *prizes*] entregar; [+ *bride*] llevar al altar; (*Sport, fig*) regalar; **we've got 200 CDs to ~ away** tenemos 200 CDs para regalar; **we gave away a silly goal** les regalamos un gol de la forma más tonta; **at this price I'm giving it away** a este precio lo estoy regalando

2 (*= reveal*) [+ *secret*] revelar; **he's been accused of giving away company secrets** lo han acusado de revelar secretos de la compañía; **he gave away his secret when he produced the wrong passport** se descubrió a sí mismo al mostrar el pasaporte que no debía; **his face gave nothing away** su rostro no delataba nada; **your taste in colours ~s away a lot about you** tus preferencias en los colores revelan mucho sobre tu personalidad; ✦*IDIOM* **to ~ the game away*** descubrir el pastel*

3 (*= betray*) [+ *person*] (*lit, fig*) delatar; **we mustn't ~ him away** no debemos delatarlo *or* traicionarlo; **the treads on his shoes gave him away** el dibujo de los suelos de los zapatos lo delataron; **to ~ o.s. away** delatarse, descubrirse

►**give back** VT + ADV (*= return*) [+ *sb's property, freedom*] devolver (**to** a); **Peter's ~n her back her confidence** Peter le ha devuelto la confianza en sí misma; **he wants to ~ something back to society** quiere ofrecer algo a *or* hacer algo por la sociedad en compensación

►**give in** Ⓐ VT + ADV (*= hand in*) [+ *form, essay*] entregar; **to ~ in one's name** dar su nombre

Ⓑ VI + ADV (*= surrender*) rendirse; (*= yield*) ceder; (*= agree*) consentir; **I ~ in!** (*in guessing game*) ¡me rindo!, ¡me doy por vencido!; **I went on at my parents until they gave in** les insistí a mis padres hasta que cedieron; **to ~ in to** [+ *threats, pressure*] ceder *or* sucumbir ante; **she always ~s in to him** ella hace siempre lo que él quiere

►**give off** VT + ADV [+ *smell, smoke*] despedir; [+ *heat, radiation*] emitir

►**give onto** VI + PREP [*window, door, house*] dar a

►**give out** Ⓐ VT + ADV 1 (*= distribute*) repartir, distribuir

2 (*= make known*) [+ *news*] anunciar; (*= reveal*) revelar, divulgar; **it was ~n out that …** (*= announced*) anunciaron que …; (*falsely*) hicieron creer que …

3 (*= give off*) [+ *smoke*] despedir

4 (*Rad*) [+ *signal*] emitir

5 (*= let out*) [+ *scream, cry*] dar; **he gave out a scream of pain** dio un grito de dolor

Ⓑ VI + ADV [*supplies*] agotarse; [*strength, patience*] agotarse, acabarse; [*engine*] pararse; [*heart*] fallar; **his legs gave out** le fallaron las piernas

►**give over** VI + ADV (*Brit**) (*= stop*) **~ over!** ¡basta ya!; **~ over arguing!** ¡deja de discutir!

►**give over to** VT + PREP 1 (*= devote to*) dedicar; **mornings were ~n over to physical**

training las mañanas estaban dedicadas al ejercicio físico; **most of the land had been ~n over to wheat-growing** la mayor parte de la tierra estaba destinada a la cultura del trigo; **the front page was ~n over to a report on ...** la primera página estaba dedicada a un informe sobre ...; **to ~ o.s. over to** [+ *activity, pleasure, children, family*] dedicarse a, entregarse a

2 (= *transfer*) [+ *property*] traspasar

3 (= *entrust to*) encomendar, entregar

►**give up** Ⓐ VT + ADV 1 (= *yield up*) [+ *seat, place*] ceder; [+ *authority*] ceder, traspasar; **to ~ o.s. up to the police** entregarse a la policía; **to ~ o.s. up to** [+ *vice*] entregarse a, darse a; **to ~ a child up for adoption** entregar a un hijo para que sea adoptado

2 (= *hand over*) [+ *ticket*] entregar

3 (= *renounce*) [+ *habit*] dejar; [+ *job, post*] renunciar a, dejar; [+ *friend*] dejar de ver; [+ *boyfriend*] dejar, romper con; [+ *beliefs, idea*] abandonar; **to ~ up smoking** dejar de fumar; **I've ~n up trying to persuade her** he dejado de intentar persuadirla *or* convencerla; **eventually he gave up trying** al final dejó de intentarlo; **I gave it up as a bad job*** me di por vencido

4 (= *devote*) [+ *one's life, time*] dedicar (**to** a); **to ~ up one's life to music** dedicar su vida a la música

5 (= *sacrifice*) [+ *one's life*] entregar (**for** por); [+ *career*] renunciar a (**for** por); **they gave up their lives for their country** entregaron *or* sacrificaron sus vidas por la patria; **she gave up her career for her family** renunció a su carrera profesional por su familia

6 (= *abandon hope for*) [+ *patient*] desahuciar; **the doctors had ~n him up** los médicos lo habían desahuciado; **we'd ~n you up** creíamos que ya no venías; **they gave him up for dead** lo dieron por muerto; **to ~ sb up for lost** dar por perdido a algn

Ⓑ VI + ADV (= *stop trying*) rendirse; **I ~ up!** (*trying to guess*) ¡me rindo!, ¡me doy por vencido!; **don't ~ up yet!** ¡no te rindas todavía!

►**give up on** VI + PREP 1 (= *renounce*) [+ *idea*] renunciar a; **I've ~n up on the idea** he renunciado a la idea

2 (= *stop expecting*) [+ *visitor*] **I'd ~n up on you** creía que ya no venías; **I've ~n up on him, he's so unreliable** (= *lost faith in*) no quiero perder más tiempo con él, es muy informal

3 (= *fail*) **the car gave up on us** nos falló el coche

give-and-take* ['gɪvən'teɪk] N toma y daca *m*, concesiones *fpl* mutuas

giveaway ['gɪvəweɪ] Ⓐ N 1 (= *revelation*) revelación *f* involuntaria; **it's a dead ~** (= *obvious*) (eso) lo dice todo

2 (= *gift*) regalo *m*; **the exam was a ~!** ¡el examen estaba tirado!*

Ⓑ CPD ► **giveaway prices** NPL precios *mpl* de regalo

given ['gɪvn] Ⓐ PP *of* **give**

Ⓑ ADJ 1 (= *fixed*) [*time, amount*] determinado; **on a ~ day** en un día determinado; **at any ~ time** en cualquier momento dado

2 **to be ~ to doing sth** ser dado a hacer algo

Ⓒ CONJ **~ (that) ...** dado que ...; **~ the circumstances ...** dadas las circunstancias ...; **~ time, it would be possible** con el tiempo, sería posible

Ⓓ N hecho *m* reconocido, dato *m* conocido

Ⓔ CPD ► **given name** N (*esp US*) nombre *m* de pila

giver ['gɪvəʳ] N donante *mf*, donador(a) *m/f*

gizmo* ['gɪzməʊ] N artilugio *m*, chisme *m*, coso *m* (*LAm*)

gizzard ['gɪzəd] N molleja *f*; **it sticks in my ~** (*fig*) no lo puedo tragar

glacé ['glæseɪ] Ⓐ ADJ [*fruit*] escarchado

Ⓑ CPD ► **glacé icing** N azúcar *m* glaseado

glacial ['gleɪsɪəl] ADJ 1 (*Geol*) [*erosion*] glaciar; [*period*] glacial; (= *cold*) [*weather, wind*] glacial

2 [*person, stare, atmosphere*] glacial

glaciation [,gleɪsɪ'eɪʃən] N glaciación *f*

glacier ['glæsɪəʳ] N glaciar *m*

glaciology [,glæsɪ'ɒlədʒɪ] N glaciología *f*

glad [glæd] ADJ (*compar* **gladder**, *superl* **gladdest**) 1 (= *pleased*) **to be ~** alegrarse; **"I had a great time" — "I'm (so) ~"** —me lo pasé fenomenal —me alegro (mucho); **to be ~ that** alegrarse de que + *subjun*; **I'm ~ that you could come** me alegro de que hayas podido venir; **I'm ~ that I relented in the end** me alegro de haber transigido al final; **to be ~ to do sth** (= *pleased*) alegrarse de hacer algo; (= *willing*) estar encantado de hacer algo; **I was ~ to see him** me alegré de verlo; **I am ~ to hear it** me alegra saberlo; **I'll be ~ to answer any questions** estaré encantado de responder a cualquier pregunta; **our receptionists will be ~ to help you make any theatre reservations** nuestros recepcionistas le ayudarán con el mayor agrado a reservar entradas para el teatro; **I would be only too ~ to take a job like that** me encantaría aceptar un trabajo como ese; **he assured her that he would be only too ~ to help** le aseguró que sería un verdadero placer ayudarla; **to be ~ about sth** alegrarse de algo; **Ralph was ~ of a chance to change the subject** Ralph se alegró de tener la oportunidad de cambiar de tema; **I was ~ of his help** me alegré de que me ayudase; **I'd be very ~ of your advice** le agradecería mucho que me aconseje

2 (*before noun*) (*liter*) (= *joyful*) [*occasion*] feliz; **~ rags†*** trajes *mpl* de fiesta; **~ tidings** (*hum or liter*) buenas nuevas *fpl*; ✦**IDIOM to give sb the ~ eye*** echar a algn una mirada insinuante; *see also* **glad-hand**

gladden ['glædn] (*liter*) VT alegrar, llenar de alegría; **she was ~ed by the news** la noticia la llenó de alegría; **to ~ sb's heart** llenar de alegría el corazón de algn, alegrar el corazón a algn; **it ~ed his heart to see the children play** ver jugar a los niños le llenaba el corazón de alegría *or* le alegraba el corazón

glade [gleɪd] N claro *m*

glad-hand* ['glædhænd] VT (*hum*) estrechar (con entusiasmo fingido) la mano de

gladiator ['glædɪeɪtəʳ] N gladiador *m*

gladiatorial [,glædɪə'tɔːrɪəl] ADJ de gladiadores

gladiolus [glædɪ'əʊləs] N (*pl* **gladiolus** *or* **gladioluses** *or* **gladioli** [,glædɪ'əʊlaɪ]) gladiolo *m*

gladly ['glædlɪ] ADV con mucho gusto, de buena gana; **he ~ accepted their invitation** aceptó con mucho gusto *or* de buena gana su invitación; **I'd ~ help her if I could** la ayudaría con mucho gusto *or* de buena gana si pudiera; **"will you help us?" — "gladly"** —¿nos ayudará? —con mucho gusto; *see also* **suffer A2**

gladness ['glædnɪs] N alegría *f*, gozo *m* (*liter*)

glam* [glæm] Ⓐ VT **to ~ up** [+ *person*] acicalar; [+ *building, area*] mejorar el aspecto de

Ⓑ ADJ = **glamorous**

Ⓒ N = **glamour**

Ⓓ CPD ► **glam rock*** N glam rock *m*

glamor ['glæməʳ] N (*US*) = **glamour**

glamorize ['glæməraɪz] VT hacer parecer más atractivo; **this programme ~s crime** este programa presenta el crimen bajo una luz favorable

glamorous ['glæmərəs] ADJ [*person, dress*] atractivo y sofisticado, glamo(u)roso; [*job*] con mucho glamour, rodeado de gloria *or* grandeza; [*life*] sofisticado; [*place, gathering*] elegante, sofisticado

glamour, **glamor** (*US*) ['glæməʳ] Ⓐ N [*of person, job, place*] glamour *m*

Ⓑ CPD ► **glamour boy** N niño *m* bonito ► **glamour girl** N belleza *f* ► **glamour sport** N deporte *m* rodeado de glamour

glance [glɑːns] Ⓐ N (*at person*) mirada *f*; (*at object*) vistazo *m*, ojeada *f* (**at** a); **at a ~** de un vistazo; **without a backward ~** sin volver la vista atrás; **we exchanged a ~** intercambiamos una mirada; **at first ~** a primera vista; **to steal/take a ~ at sth/sb** echar un vistazo a algo/algn

Ⓑ VI (= *look*) mirar; **she ~d in my direction** miró hacia donde yo estaba; **to ~ at** [+ *person*] lanzar una mirada a; [+ *object*] echar un vistazo a, ojear; **to ~ over** *or* **through a report** hojear un informe

►**glance away** VI + ADV apartar los ojos

►**glance down** VI + ADV echar un vistazo (hacia abajo)

►**glance off** VI + PREP **to ~ off sth** rebotar de algo

►**glance round** Ⓐ VI + ADV (*round about*) echar un vistazo alrededor; (*behind*) echar un vistazo atrás

Ⓑ VI + PREP **he ~d round the room** echó un vistazo por la habitación

►**glance up** VI + ADV (= *raise eyes*) levantar la vista; (= *look upwards*) mirar hacia arriba

glancing ['glɑːnsɪŋ] ADJ [*blow*] oblicuo

gland [glænd] N (*Anat*) glándula *f*; *see also* **lymph**

glandes ['glændiːz] NPL *of* **glans**

glandular ['glændjʊləʳ] Ⓐ ADJ glandular

Ⓑ CPD ► **glandular fever** N mononucleosis *f* infecciosa

glans [glænz] N (*pl* **glandes**) **~ (penis)** glande *m*

glare [glɛəʳ] Ⓐ N 1 [*of light, sun*] luz *f* deslumbradora; (= *dazzle*) deslumbramiento *m*; **because of the ~ of the light in Spain** debido a lo resplandeciente que es la luz en España; **in the full ~ of publicity** bajo los focos de la publicidad

2 (= *look*) mirada *f* feroz

Ⓑ VI 1 [*light*] deslumbrar

2 (= *look*) **to ~ at sb** lanzar una mirada de odio a algn

glaring ['glɛərɪŋ] ADJ 1 (= *dazzling*) [*sun, light*] deslumbrante, resplandeciente; [*colour*] chillón

2 (= *obvious*) [*mistake*] patente, manifiesto

glaringly ['glɛərɪŋlɪ] ADV **to be ~ obvious** estar totalmente claro, saltar a la vista

glasnost ['glæznɒst] N glasnost *f*

glass [glɑːs] Ⓐ N 1 (= *material*) vidrio *m*, cristal *m*; **under ~** [*exhibit*] bajo vidrio, en una vitrina; [*plant*] en invernadero

2 (= *glassware*) cristalería *f*, artículos *mpl* de cristal

3 (= *tumbler, schooner, etc*) (= *drinking vessel for water*) vaso *m*; (*for wine, sherry, champagne*) copa *f*; (*for beer*) caña *f*; (*for liqueur, brandy*) copita *f*

4 (= *glassful*) [*of beer, water, wine*] vaso *m*; [*of liqueur, brandy*] copa *f*

➤ LANGUAGE IN USE: **glad 1** 24.1

5 (= *barometer*) barómetro *m*
6 (= *mirror*) espejo *m*; **to look at o.s. in the ~** mirarse en el espejo
7 (= *spyglass*) catalejo *m*
8 **glasses** (= *spectacles*) gafas *fpl*, lentes *mpl*, anteojos *mpl* (*esp LAm*); (= *binoculars*) gemelos *mpl*
Ⓑ CPD [*bottle, ornament, eye*] de vidrio *or* cristal; [*slipper*] de cristal ► **glass case** N vitrina *f* ► **glass ceiling** N tope *m or* barrera *f* invisible (*que impide ascender profesionalmente a las mujeres o miembros de minorías étnicas*) ► **glass door** N puerta *f* vidriera *or* de cristales ► **glass eye** N ojo *m* de cristal ► **glass fibre**, **glass fiber** (*US*) N fibra *f* de vidrio; (*as modifier*) de fibra de vidrio; **a ~ fibre boat** una embarcación de fibra de vidrio ► **glass house** N ✦**PROV people who live in ~ houses shouldn't throw stones** siempre habla el que más tiene que callar, mira quién fue a hablar ► **glass industry** N industria *f* vidriera ► **glass slipper** N zapatilla *f* de cristal ► **glass wool** N lana *f* de vidrio

glassblower ['glɑːs,bləʊəʳ] N soplador *m* de vidrio

glassblowing ['glɑːs,bləʊɪŋ] N soplado *m* de vidrio

glasscutter ['glɑːs,kʌtəʳ] N (= *tool*) cortavidrios *m inv*; (= *person*) cortador(a) *m/f* de vidrio

glassful ['glɑːsfʊl] N vaso *m*; [*of wine, sherry, champagne*] copa *f*

glasshouse ['glɑːshaʊs] N (*pl* **glasshouses** ['glɑːshaʊzɪz]) (*for plants*) invernadero *m*; (*Brit Mil*✱) cárcel *f* (militar); *see also* **glass B**

glasspaper ['glɑːs,peɪpəʳ] N (*Brit*) papel *m* de vidrio

glassware ['glɑːswɛəʳ] N cristalería *f*, objetos *mpl* de cristal

glassworks ['glɑːswɜːks] N fábrica *f* de vidrio

glassy ['glɑːsɪ] ADJ (*compar* **glassier**; *superl* **glassiest**) [*substance*] vítreo; [*surface*] liso; [*water*] espejado; [*eye, look*] vidrioso

glassy-eyed [,glɑːsɪ'aɪd] ADJ de mirada vidriosa; (*from drugs, drink*) de mirada perdida; (*from displeasure*) de mirada glacial

> **GLASTONBURY**
>
> **Glastonbury** *es una ciudad situada al suroeste de Inglaterra donde, desde 1969, se ha venido celebrando casi todos los veranos un festival de música pop de tres días de duración. El festival es lugar de encuentro para miles de visitantes que acuden a la ciudad para oír a los mejores nombres del pop, y que aprovechan para visitar los lugares que se asocian con la mítica tumba del rey Arturo y con el lugar donde José de Arimatea llevó el Santo Grial.*

Glaswegian [glæz'wiːdʒən] Ⓐ ADJ de Glasgow
Ⓑ N nativo/a *m/f or* habitante *mf* de Glasgow

glaucoma [glɔː'kəʊmə] N glaucoma *m*

glaze [gleɪz] Ⓐ N 1 (*on pottery*) vidriado *m*
2 (*Culin*) (*on cake*) glaseado *m*
Ⓑ VT 1 [+ *window*] poner vidrios *or* cristales a
2 [+ *pottery*] vidriar
3 (*Culin*) glasear
Ⓒ VI **to ~ over** [*eyes*] ponerse vidrioso

glazed [gleɪzd] ADJ 1 [*surface*] vidriado; [*paper*] satinado; [*eye*] vidrioso
2 (*Brit*) [*door, window etc*] con vidrio *or* cristal
3 (*Culin*) glaseado
4 (*US*✱) (= *tipsy*) achispado✱

glazier ['gleɪzɪəʳ] N vidriero/a *m/f*

GLC N ABBR (*Brit*) (*formerly*) (= **Greater London Council**) *antigua corporación metropolitana de Londres*

gleam [gliːm] Ⓐ N 1 [*of light*] rayo *m*, destello *m*; [*of metal, water*] espejeo *m*; **with a ~ in one's eye** con ojos chispeantes
2 (*fig*) **a ~ of hope** un rayo de esperanza
Ⓑ VI [*light*] brillar, lanzar destellos; [*metal, water*] espejear, relucir; [*eyes*] brillar (**with** de)

gleaming ['gliːmɪŋ] ADJ reluciente

glean [gliːn] Ⓐ VT 1 (*Agr*) espigar
2 (*fig*) [+ *information*] recoger; **from what I have been able to ~** por lo que yo he conseguido averiguar
Ⓑ VI espigar

gleaner ['gliːnəʳ] N espigador(a) *m/f*

gleanings ['gliːnɪŋz] NPL (*fig*) fragmentos *mpl* recogidos

glebe [gliːb] N terreno *m* beneficial

glee [gliː] Ⓐ N (= *joy*) regocijo *m*, alegría *f*, júbilo *m*
Ⓑ CPD ► **glee club** N (*Mus*) orfeón *m*, sociedad *f* coral

gleeful ['gliːfəl] ADJ [*smile, laugh*] jubiloso, alegre; (= *malicious*) malicioso

gleefully ['gliːfəlɪ] ADV con júbilo, con regocijo; (= *maliciously*) maliciosamente

glen [glen] N cañada *f*

glib [glɪb] ADJ [*person*] de mucha labia, poco sincero; [*explanation, excuse*] fácil; [*speech*] elocuente pero insincero

glibly ['glɪblɪ] ADV [*speak*] (elocuentemente pero) con poca sinceridad; [*explain*] con una facilidad sospechosa

glibness ['glɪbnɪs] N [*of person*] labia *f*, falta *f* de sinceridad; [*of explanation, excuse*] facilidad *f*

glide [glaɪd] Ⓐ N [*of dancer etc*] deslizamiento *m*; (*Aer*) planeo *m*, vuelo *m* sin motor; (*Mus*) ligadura *f*
Ⓑ VI 1 (= *move smoothly*) deslizarse; **she ~s to the door** se desliza hacia la puerta; **to ~ away** ◊ **to ~ off** escurrirse *or* deslizarse sigilosamente
2 (*Aer*) planear

glider ['glaɪdəʳ] N 1 (*Aer*) planeador *m*; (*towed*) avión *m* remolcado
2 (*US*) (= *swing*) columpio *m*

gliding ['glaɪdɪŋ] N (*Aer*) vuelo *m* sin motor, planeo *m*

glimmer ['glɪməʳ] Ⓐ N 1 [*of light*] luz *f* trémula; [*of water*] espejeo *m*
2 (*fig*) **without a ~ of understanding** sin dar el menor indicio de haber comprendido; **there is a ~ of hope** hay un rayo de esperanza
Ⓑ VI [*light*] brillar con luz trémula; [*water*] espejear

glimpse [glɪmps] Ⓐ N vislumbre *f*, destello *m*; **a ~ into the future** un destello de cómo va a ser el futuro; **to catch a ~ of** vislumbrar; **I only had a fleeting ~ of him** sólo alcancé a verlo fugazmente
Ⓑ VT vislumbrar

glint [glɪnt] Ⓐ N [*of metal etc*] destello *m*, centelleo *m*; **he had a ~ in his eye** le chispeaban los ojos
Ⓑ VI lanzar destellos, centellear

glissando [glɪ'sændəʊ] Ⓐ N glisando *m*
Ⓑ ADV glisando

glisten ['glɪsn] VI [*wet surface*] relucir; [*water*] espejear; [*eyes*] brillar; **her eyes ~ed with tears** le brillaban los ojos de las lágrimas

glitch✱ [glɪtʃ] N fallo *m* técnico

glitter ['glɪtəʳ] Ⓐ N [*of gold etc*] brillo *m*
Ⓑ VI [*gold etc*] relucir, brillar; ✦**PROV all that ~s is not gold** no es oro todo lo que reluce

glitterati✱ [,glɪtə'rɑːtiː] NPL (*hum*) celebridades *fpl* del mundillo literario y artístico

glittering ['glɪtərɪŋ], **glittery** ['glɪtərɪ] ADJ reluciente, brillante (*also fig*); **~ prize** premio *m* rutilante

glitz✱ [glɪts] N ostentación *f*

glitzy✱ ['glɪtsɪ] ADJ (*compar* **glitzier**; *superl* **glitziest**) ostentoso

gloaming ['gləʊmɪŋ] N (*liter*) crepúsculo *m*; **in the ~** al anochecer

gloat [gləʊt] VI relamerse; **to ~ over** [+ *money*] recrearse contemplando; [+ *victory, good news*] recrearse en; [+ *enemy's misfortune*] saborear, regocijarse con

gloating ['gləʊtɪŋ] ADJ **with a ~ smile** sonriendo satisfecho, con una sonrisa satisfecha

glob✱ [glɒb] N (*US*) pegote *m*

global ['gləʊbl] Ⓐ ADJ 1 (= *world-wide*) mundial; **on a ~ scale** a escala mundial; **this has ~ implications** esto tiene consecuencias a nivel global
2 (= *comprehensive*) [*sum, reform, change*] global; **a ~ view** una visión global
Ⓑ CPD ► **the global village** N la aldea global ► **global warming** N calentamiento *m* global, calentamiento *m* del planeta

globalization [,gləʊbəlaɪ'zeɪʃən] N globalización *f*

globalize ['gləʊbəlaɪz] Ⓐ VI globalizarse
Ⓑ VT globalizar

globally ['gləʊbəlɪ] ADV (= *worldwide*) mundialmente; (= *comprehensively*) globalmente

globe [gləʊb] Ⓐ N (= *sphere*) globo *m*, esfera *f*; (= *the world*) mundo *m*; (= *spherical map*) esfera *f* terrestre, globo *m* terráqueo
Ⓑ CPD ► **globe artichoke** N alcachofa *f*

globe-trotter ['gləʊb,trɒtəʳ] N trotamundos *mf inv*

globe-trotting ['gləʊb,trɒtɪŋ] Ⓐ N viajar *m* por todo el mundo
Ⓑ ADJ trotamundos *inv*

globular ['glɒbjʊləʳ] ADJ globular

globule ['glɒbjuːl] N [*of oil, water*] glóbulo *m*

glockenspiel ['glɒkənspiːl] N carillón *m*

gloom [gluːm] N 1 (= *darkness*) penumbra *f*, oscuridad *f*
2 (= *sadness, despondency*) melancolía *f*, tristeza *f*; **it's not all ~ and doom here** aquí no todo son pronósticos de desastre; **she's always full of ~ and doom** siempre lo ve todo negro

gloomily ['gluːmɪlɪ] ADV [*say, look*] con tristeza; [*predict*] con pesimismo

gloomy ['gluːmɪ] ADJ (*compar* **gloomier**; *superl* **gloomiest**) 1 (= *dark*) [*place*] sombrío, lúgubre; [*day, weather*] triste, sombrío
2 (= *sad*) [*atmosphere*] triste, lúgubre; **he's a bit of a ~ character** es un tipo un poco sombrío; **to feel ~** (= *sad*) estar bajo de moral, sentirse deprimido
3 (= *pessimistic*) [*person*] pesimista; [*forecast, assessment*] pesimista, nada prometedor; **to be ~ about sth** ser pesimista acerca de algo; **no wonder shopkeepers are feeling ~** no es de extrañar que los comerciantes se sientan pesimistas; **things are looking ~ for the England team** la cosa no se presenta muy halagüeña para el equipo inglés; **the outlook for next year is ~** las perspectivas para el próximo año no son nada prometedoras; **he paints a very ~ picture** pinta la cosa muy negra; **he takes a ~ view of everything** tiene una visión muy negativa de todo

glorification [ˌglɔːrɪfɪ'keɪʃən] N glorificación *f*

glorify ['glɔːrɪfaɪ] VT (= *exalt*) [+ *God*] alabar; [+ *person*] glorificar; (*pej*) [+ *war, deeds*] embellecer; **it's just a glorified boarding house** es una simple pensión, aunque con pretensiones

glorious ['glɔːrɪəs] ADJ [*career, victory*] glorioso; [*weather, view*] magnífico; **it was a ~ muddle** (*iro*) la confusión era mayúscula

gloriously ['glɔːrɪəslɪ] ADV [1] (= *with glory*) [*win*] gloriosamente
[2] (= *wonderfully*) magníficamente; **it was ~ sunny** hacía un sol magnífico; **we were ~ happy** estábamos contentísimos

glory ['glɔːrɪ] (A) N [1] (= *honour, fame, Rel*) gloria *f*; **~ be!** ¡gracias a Dios!; **she was in her ~** estaba toda ufana; **Rome at the height of its ~** Roma en la cima de su gloria; **she led her team to Olympic ~** condujo a su equipo a la victoria olímpica; ✦*IDIOM* **to go to ~**† subir a los cielos; *see also* **reflect A2**
[2] (= *splendour*) gloria *f*, esplendor *m*
(B) VI **to ~ in** [+ *one's success etc*] enorgullecerse *or* jactarse de; [+ *another's misfortune*] disfrutar maliciosamente de; **the café glories in the name of El Dorado** el café tiene el magnífico nombre de El Dorado
(C) CPD ► **glory hole*** N cuarto *m or* cajón *m etc* en desorden, leonera* *f*; **his room is something of a ~ hole** su habitación parece un trastero

Glos ABBR = **Gloucestershire**

gloss¹ [glɒs] (A) N (= *note*) glosa *f*
(B) VT glosar, comentar
►**gloss over** VI + PREP [1] (= *excuse*) disculpar
[2] (= *play down*) paliar, restar importancia a
[3] (= *cover up*) [+ *mistake etc*] encubrir

gloss² [glɒs] (A) N [1] (= *shine*) brillo *m*, lustre *m*
[2] (*also* **~ paint**) pintura *f* de esmalte
(B) VT lustrar, pulir
(C) CPD ► **gloss finish** N (= *paint*) acabado *m* brillante; (*on photo*) brillo *m* satinado ► **gloss paper** N papel *m* satinado

glossary ['glɒsərɪ] N glosario *m*

glossily ['glɒsɪlɪ] ADV brillantemente; **~ illustrated** elegantemente ilustrado, ilustrado con lujo

glossy ['glɒsɪ] (A) ADJ (*compar* **glossier**; *superl* **glossiest**) [*surface*] brillante, lustroso; [*hair*] brillante; [*cloth, paper*] satinado; **~ magazine** revista *f* de moda
(B) N **the glossies** (*Brit**) las revistas de moda

glottal ['glɒtl] (A) ADJ glotal
(B) CPD ► **glottal stop** N oclusión *f* glotal

glottis ['glɒtɪs] N (*pl* **glottises** *or* **glottides** ['glɒtɪˌdiːz]) glotis *f inv*

Gloucs. ABBR = **Gloucestershire**

glove [glʌv] (A) N guante *m*; ✦*IDIOM* **to fit sb like a ~** sentar a algn como anillo al dedo
(B) CPD ► **glove box, glove compartment** N (*Aut*) guantera *f* ► **glove maker** N guantero/a *m/f* ► **glove puppet** N títere *m* (de guante)

gloved [glʌvd] ADJ [*hand*] enguantado

glover ['glʌvəʳ] N guantero/a *m/f*

glow [gləʊ] (A) N [1] [*of lamp, sunset, fire, bright colour*] brillo *m*, resplandor *m*; [*of cheeks*] rubor *m*; (*in sky*) luz *f* difusa
[2] (*fig*) (= *warm feeling*) sensación *f* de bienestar; **a ~ of satisfaction** una aureola de satisfacción
(B) VI [1] [*lamp, colour, sunset, fire*] brillar, resplandecer
[2] (*fig*) **to ~ with pleasure** estar radiante de felicidad; **to ~ with health** rebosar de salud
(C) CPD ► **glow worm** N luciérnaga *f*

glower ['glaʊəʳ] VI mirar con el ceño fruncido (**at sb** a algn)

glowering ['glaʊərɪŋ] ADJ [*person*] ceñudo; [*sky*] encapotado

glowing ['gləʊɪŋ] ADJ [1] [*light etc*] brillante; [*fire, colour*] vivo; [*complexion, cheeks etc*] encendido
[2] [*person*] (*with health, pleasure*) rebosante
[3] (*fig*) [*report, description etc*] entusiasta

gloxinia [glɒk'sɪnɪə] N gloxínea *f*

glucose ['gluːkəʊs] N glucosa *f*

glue [gluː] (A) N cola *f*, pegamento *m*; (*as drug*) pegamento *m*
(B) VT [1] (*lit*) pegar (**to** a); **to ~ two things together** pegar dos cosas (con goma *etc*)
[2] (*) (*fig*) **her face was ~d to the window** tenía la cara pegada a la ventana; **she was ~d to the television** estaba pegada al televisor; **to be ~d to the spot** quedarse clavado
(C) CPD ► **glue sniffer** N esnifador(a) *m/f* de pegamento, persona *f* que inhala *or* esnifa pegamento ► **glue sniffing** N inhalación *f* de pegamento

gluey ['gluːɪ] ADJ pegajoso, viscoso

glum [glʌm] ADJ (*compar* **glummer**; *superl* **glummest**) [*person*] melancólico; [*mood, expression*] triste; [*tone*] melancólico, sombrío

glumly ['glʌmlɪ] ADV [*walk, shake one's head*] sombríamente; [*answer*] tristemente, sombríamente; [*look, inspect*] taciturnamente, tristemente

glut [glʌt] (A) N superabundancia *f*, exceso *m*; **to be a ~ on the market** inundar el mercado
(B) VT [1] (*Comm*) [+ *market*] inundar
[2] [+ *person*] hartar, saciar; **to ~ o.s.** atracarse (**with** de); **to be ~ted with fruit** haberse atracado de fruta

glutamate ['gluːtəmeɪt] = **monosodium glutamate**

glutamic acid [gluːˌtæmɪk'æsɪd] N ácido *m* glutámico

gluteal [glʊ'tiːəl] ADJ glúteo

gluten ['gluːtən] N gluten *m*

gluten-free [ˌgluːtən'friː] ADJ sin gluten, libre de gluten

glutenous ['gluːtənəs] ADJ glutenoso

gluteus [gluː'tiːəs] N (*pl* **glutei** [gluː'tiːaɪ]) glúteo *m*

glutinous ['gluːtɪnəs] ADJ glutinoso

glutton ['glʌtn] N glotón/ona *m/f*; (*) comilón/ona *m/f*; **~ for work** trabajador(a) *m/f* incansable; **~ for punishment** masoquista *mf*

gluttonous ['glʌtənəs] ADJ glotón, goloso

gluttony ['glʌtənɪ] N glotonería *f*, gula *f*

glycerin(e) [ˌglɪsə'riːn] N glicerina *f*

glycerol ['glɪsərɒl] N glicerol *m*

glycin(e) ['glaɪsiːn] N glicina *f*

glycogen ['glaɪkəʊdʒen] N glicógeno *m*

glycol ['glaɪkɒl] N glicol *m*

GM (A) N ABBR [1] (= **general manager**) director(a) *m/f* general
[2] (*Brit*) (= **George Medal**) *medalla del valor civil*
[3] (*US*) = **General Motors**
(B) ADJ ABBR = **genetically-modified**; **GM foods** alimentos *mpl* transgénicos

gm ABBR (= **gram(me)**) g, gr

G-man ['dʒiːmæn] N (*pl* **G-men**) (*US*) agente *m* del FBI

GMAT N ABBR (*US*) = **Graduate Management Admissions Test**

GM-free [ˌdʒiːem'friː] ADJ [*food*] sin ingredientes transgénicos; [*plant, crop*] no transgénico

gm(s) ABBR (= **gram(s), gramme(s)**) g, gr

GMT N ABBR (= **Greenwich Mean Time**) hora *f* media de Greenwich

GMWU N ABBR (*Brit*) (= **General and Municipal Workers' Union**) *sindicato de trabajadores autónomos y municipales*

gnarled [nɑːld] ADJ [*wood, hands*] nudoso

gnash [næʃ] VT **to ~ one's teeth** rechinar los dientes

gnashing ['næʃɪŋ] (A) N **~ of teeth** rechinamiento *m* de dientes
(B) ADJ rechinante

gnat [næt] N mosquito *m*, jején *m* (*LAm*)

gnaw [nɔː] (A) VT (= *chew, also fig*) roer, carcomer; **~ed by doubts/hunger** atormentado por las dudas/el hambre
(B) VI roer; **to ~ through** roer *or* carcomer haciendo un agujero en; **to ~ at** (*lit, fig*) roer
►**gnaw off** VT + ADV roer

gnawing ['nɔːɪŋ] ADJ [1] [*sound*] persistente
[2] (*fig*) [*remorse, anxiety etc*] corrosivo; [*hunger*] con retortijones; [*pain*] punzante; **I had a ~ feeling that something had been forgotten** me atormentaba la idea de que se había olvidado algo

gneiss [naɪs] N gneis *m*

gnocchi ['nɒkɪ] NPL ñoquis *mpl*

gnome [nəʊm] N gnomo *m*; **the Gnomes of Zurich** (*hum*) los banqueros suizos

gnomic ['nəʊmɪk] ADJ gnómico

gnostic ['nɒstɪk] (A) ADJ gnóstico
(B) N gnóstico/a *m/f*

gnosticism ['nɒstɪˌsɪzəm] N gnosticismo *m*

GNP N ABBR (= **gross national product**) PNB *m*

gnu [nuː] N (*pl* **gnus** *or* **gnu**) ñu *m*

GNVQ N ABBR (*Brit Scol*) (= **General National Vocational Qualification**) *diploma nacional de formación profesional*

go [gəʊ] (*vb: pt* **went**; *pp* **gone**)

[A] INTRANSITIVE VERB	[D] NOUN
[B] TRANSITIVE VERB	[E] ADJECTIVE
[C] MODAL VERB	[F] PHRASAL VERBS

When **go** *is part of a set combination such as* **go cheap, go far, go down the tube**, *look up the other word.*

(A) INTRANSITIVE VERB
[1] **= *move, travel*** ir; **she was going too fast** iba demasiado rápido; **to go and do sth** ir a hacer algo; **I'll go and see** voy a ver; **I'll go and fetch it for you** te lo voy a buscar; **he went and shut the door** cerró la puerta; **now you've gone and done it!*** ¡ahora sí que la has hecho buena!; **to go and see sb** ◊ **go to see sb** ir a ver a algn; **to go along a corridor** ir por un pasillo; **we can talk as we go** podemos hablar por el camino; **add the sugar, stirring as you go** añada el azúcar, removiendo al mismo tiempo, añada el azúcar, sin dejar de remover; **to go at 30 mph** ir a 30 millas por hora; **to go by car/bicycle** ir en coche/bicicleta; **the train goes from London to Glasgow** el tren va de Londres a Glasgow; **to go home** irse a casa; **to go on a journey** ir de viaje; **there he goes!** ¡ahí va!; **to go to a party** ir a una fiesta; **to go to the doctor('s)** ir al médico; **she's gone to the optician('s) for a sight test** ha ido al oculista a graduarse la vista; **she went to the headmaster** fue a ver al director; **the child went to his mother** el niño fue a *or* hacia su madre; **to go to sb for advice** consultar a algn; **where do we go from here?** (*fig*) ¿qué hacemos ahora?; **halt, who goes there?** alto, ¿quién va *or* vive?

[2] [= *depart*] [*person*] irse, marcharse; [*train, coach*] salir; **I'm going now** me voy ya, me marcho ya; **"where's Judy?" — "she's gone"** —¿dónde está Judy? —se ha ido *or* se ha marchado; **"food to go"** (*US*) "comida para llevar"

[3] [*euph* = *die*] irse; **after I've gone** cuando yo me haya ido

[4] [= *disappear*] [*object*] desaparecer; [*money*] gastarse; [*time*] pasar; **the cake is all gone** se ha acabado todo el pastel; **gone are the days when ...** ya pasaron los días cuando ...; **that sideboard will have to go** tendremos que deshacernos de ese aparador; **military service must go!** ¡fuera con el servicio militar!; **there goes my chance of promotion!** ¡adiós a mi ascenso!; **only two days to go** sólo faltan dos días; **eight down and two to go** ocho hechos y dos por hacer; *see also* **missing A1**

[5] [= *be sold*] venderse (**for** por, en); **it went for £100** se vendió por *or* en 100 libras; **it's going cheap** se vende barato; **going, going, gone!** (*at auction*) ¡a la una, a las dos, a las tres!

[6] [= *extend*] extenderse, llegar; **the garden goes down to the lake** el jardín se extiende *or* llega hasta el lago; **a huge sweater that goes down to my knees** un jersey enorme que me llega hasta las rodillas; **money doesn't go far nowadays** hoy día el dinero apenas da para nada; **he went up to £1,000** (*at auction*) llegó a las 1.000 libras

[7] [= *function*] [*machine*] funcionar; **it's a magnificent car but it doesn't go** es un coche magnífico, pero no funciona; **I couldn't get the car to go at all** no podía arrancar el coche; **the washing machine was going so I didn't hear the phone** la lavadora estaba en marcha, así es que no oí el teléfono; **to make sth go** ◊ **get sth going** poner algo en marcha

[8] [= *endure*] aguantar; **I don't know how much longer we can go without food** no sé cuánto tiempo más podremos aguantar sin comida; **to go hungry/thirsty** pasar hambre/sed

[9] [*with activities, hobbies*] **to go fishing/riding/swimming** ir a pescar/montar a caballo/nadar; **to go for a walk** dar un paseo; **to go for a swim** ir a nadar *or* a bañarse

[10] [= *progress*] ir; **the meeting went well** la reunión fue bien; **how did the exam go?** ¿cómo te fue en el examen?; **how's it going?*** ◊ **how goes it?*** ◊ **what goes?** (*US**) ¿qué tal?*, ¿qué tal va?*, ¡qué hubo! (*Mex, Chile**); **we'll see how things go*** veremos cómo van las cosas; **to make a party go (with a swing)** dar ambiente a una fiesta; **the day went slowly** el día pasó lentamente; **all went well for him until ...** todo le fue bien hasta que ...

[11] [= *match, combine with*] [*colours, clothes*] hacer juego, pegar* (**with** con); **mustard and lamb don't go** ◊ **mustard doesn't go with lamb** la mostaza no va bien con el cordero, la mostaza no pega con el cordero*; **cava goes well with anything** el cava va bien *or* combina con todo

[12] [= *become*]

For phrases with **go** *and an adjective, such as* **to go bad, go soft, go pale**, *you should look under the adjective.*

it's just gone seven acaban de dar las siete; **to go red/green** ponerse rojo/verde; **you're not going to go all sentimental/shy/religious on me!** ¡no te me pongas sentimental/tímido/religioso!*, ¡no te hagas el sentimental/tímido/religioso conmigo!; **to go communist** [*constituency, person*] volverse comunista; **to go mad** (*lit, fig*) volverse loco; **to go to sleep** dormirse; → [*BECOME, GO, GET*]

[13] [= *fit*] caber; **it won't go in the case** no cabe en la maleta; **4 into 3 won't go** 3 entre 4 no cabe; **4 into 12 goes 3 times** 12 entre cuatro son tres, 12 dividido entre cuatro son tres

[14] [= *be accepted*] valer; **anything goes*** todo vale; **that goes for me too** (= *applies to me*) eso va también por mí; (= *I agree*) yo también estoy de acuerdo; *see also* **say**

[15] [= *fail*] [*material*] desgastarse; [*chair, branch*] romperse; [*elastic*] ceder; [*fuse, light bulb*] fundirse; [*sight, strength*] fallar; **this jumper has gone at the elbows** este jersey se ha desgastado por los codos; **his health is going** su salud se está resintiendo; **his hearing/mind is going** está perdiendo el oído/la cabeza; **his nerve was beginning to go** estaba empezando a perder la sangre fría; **her sight is going** le está empezando a fallar la vista; **my voice has gone** me he quedado afónico

[16] [= *be kept*] ir; **where does this book go?** ¿dónde va este libro?

[17] [= *be available*] **there are several jobs going** se ofrecen varios puestos; **there's a flat going here** aquí hay un piso libre; **is there any tea going?** (= *is there any left?*) ¿queda té?; (= *will you get me one?*) ¿me haces un té?; **I'll take whatever is going** acepto lo que sea

[18] [= *get underway*] **whose turn is it to go?** (*in game*) ¿a quién le toca?, ¿quién va ahora?; **go!** (*Sport*) ¡ya!; **all systems go** (*Space*) (*also fig*) todo listo; ✦**IDIOMS from the word go*** desde el principio; **there you go again!*** ¡otra vez con lo mismo!*

[19] [= *be destined*] [*inheritance*] pasar; [*fund*] destinarse; **all his money goes on drink** se le va todo el dinero en alcohol; **the inheritance went to his nephew** la herencia pasó a su sobrino; **the money goes to charity** el dinero se destina a obras benéficas; **the prize went to Fiona Lilly** el premio fue para Fiona Lilly; **the qualities which go to make him a great writer** las cualidades que le hacen un gran escritor; **the money will go towards the holiday** el dinero será para las vacaciones

[20] [= *sound*] [*doorbell, phone*] sonar

[21] [= *run*] **how does that song go?** [*tune*] ¿cómo va esa canción?; [*words*] ¿cómo es la letra de esa canción?; **the tune goes like this** la melodía va así; **the story goes that ...** según dicen ...

[22] [= *do*] hacer; **go like that (with your right hand)** haz así (con la mano derecha)

[23] [* = *go to the toilet*] ir al baño; **I need to go** tengo que ir al baño

[24] [*in set expressions*] **it's a fairly good garage as garages go** es un garaje bastante bueno, para como son normalmente los garajes; **he's not bad, as estate agents go** no es un mal agente inmobiliario, dentro de lo que cabe; **let's get going!** (= *be on our way*) ¡vamos!, ¡vámonos!, ¡ándale! (*Mex*); (= *start sth*) ¡manos a la obra!, ¡adelante!; **to get going on** *or* **with sth** ponerse con algo; **I've got to get going on** *or* **with my tax** tengo que ponerme con los impuestos; **once he gets going ...** una vez que se pone ..., una vez que empieza ...; **to keep going** (= *moving forward*) seguir; (= *enduring*) resistir, aguantar; (= *functioning*) seguir funcionando; **to keep sb going: this medicine kept him going** esta medicina le daba fuerzas para seguir; **a cup of coffee is enough to keep him going all morning** una taza de café le basta para funcionar toda la mañana; **enough money to keep them going for a week or two** suficiente dinero para que pudiesen tirar* *or* funcionar una o dos semanas; **to keep sth going: the workers are trying to keep the factory going** los trabajadores están intentando mantener la fábrica en funcionamiento *or* en marcha; **to let sb go** (= *release*) soltar a algn; (*euph*) (= *make redundant*) despedir a algn; **let (me) go!** ¡suéltame!; **we'll let it go at that** por esta vez pase; **you're wrong, but we'll let it go** no llevas razón, pero vamos a dejarlo así; **to let o.s. go** (*physically*) dejarse, descuidarse; (= *have fun*) soltarse el pelo*; **to let go of sth/sb** soltar algo/a algn; *see also* **far A2, A4**

Ⓑ TRANSITIVE VERB

[1] [= *travel*] [+ *route*] hacer; **which route does the number 29 go?** ¿qué itinerario hace el 29?; **which way are you going?** ¿por dónde vais a ir?, ¿qué camino vais a tomar?; **he went his way** siguió su camino; **we had only gone a few kilometres when ...** sólo llevábamos unos kilómetros cuando ...; ✦**IDIOM to go it: the car was really going it*** el coche iba a una buena marcha*; *see also* **distance A1**

[2] [= *make*] hacer; **the car went "bang!"** el coche hizo "bang"

[3] [* = *say*] soltar*; **"shut up!" he goes** —¡cállate! —suelta; **he goes to me, "what do you want?"** va y me dice *or* me suelta: —¿qué quieres?*

[4] [*Gambling*] (= *bet*) apostar; **he went £50 on the red** apostó 50 libras al rojo; **I can only go £15** sólo puedo llegar a 15 libras

[5] (*) ✦**IDIOMS to go one better** ganar el remate; **to go it alone** obrar por su cuenta

Ⓒ MODAL VERB

ir; **I'm going/I was going to do it** voy/iba a hacerlo; **it's going to rain** va a llover; **there's going to be trouble** se va a armar un lío*, va a haber follón*

◆ **to go doing sth: don't go getting upset*** venga, no te enfades; **to go looking for sth/sb** ir a buscar algo/a algn

Ⓓ NOUN (*pl* **goes**)

[1] [= *turn*] **whose go is it?** ¿a quién le toca?; **it's your go** te toca a ti

[2] [= *attempt*] intento *m*; **to have a go (at doing sth)** probar (a hacer algo); **shall I have a go?** ¿pruebo yo?, ¿lo intento yo?; **to have another go** probar otra vez, intentarlo otra vez; **at** *or* **in one go** de un (solo) golpe

[3] [* = *bout*] **he's had a bad go of flu** ha pasado una gripe muy mala; **they've had a rough go of it** lo han pasado mal, han pasado una mala racha

[4] [* = *energy*] empuje *m*, energía *f*; **to be full of go** estar lleno de empuje *or* energía; **there's no go about him** no tiene empuje *or* energía

[5] [* = *success*] **to make a go of sth** tener éxito en algo

[6] ✦**IDIOMS it's all go** aquí no se para nunca; **it's all the go** hace furor; **to have a go at sb*** (*physically*) atacar a algn; (*verbally*) tomarla con algn*; **it's no go** es inútil; **on the go: he's always on the go** nunca para; **to keep sb on the go** tener a algn siempre en danza; **I've got two projects on the go** tengo dos proyectos en marcha

Ⓔ ADJECTIVE [*Space*] **you are go for moonlanding** estás listo para alunizar; **all systems are go** (*lit, fig*) todo listo; → [COME, GO]

Ⓕ PHRASAL VERBS

►**go about** Ⓐ VI + PREP [1] (= *move around*) **he goes about the house with no clothes on** anda *or* va por la casa desnudo
[2] (= *set to work on*) [+ *task*] emprender; [+ *problem*] abordar; **how does one go about joining?** ¿qué hay que hacer para hacerse socio?; **he knows how to go about it** sabe lo que hay que hacer, sabe cómo hacerlo
[3] (= *busy o.s. with*) **to go about one's business** ocuparse de sus cosas
Ⓑ VI + ADV [1] (= *circulate*) [*news, rumour*] correr, circular; [*virus*] rodar; **there's a rumour going about that they're getting married** corre *or* circula el rumor de que se van a casar; **there's a bug going about** hay un virus por ahí rondando; **he goes about in a Rolls** se pasea por ahí en un Rolls; **to go about barefoot/in torn jeans** ir descalzo/con unos vaqueros rotos; **you shouldn't go about bullying people like that?** no deberías ir por ahí intimidando a la gente de esa manera
[2] (*Naut*) (= *change direction*) virar

►**go across** Ⓐ VI + PREP [+ *river, road*] cruzar, atravesar
Ⓑ VI + ADV (= *cross*) cruzar; **she's gone across to Mrs Kelly's** ha ido enfrente *or* ha cruzado a casa de la señora Kelly

►**go after** VI + PREP (= *follow*) seguir; [+ *criminal*] perseguir; [+ *job, record*] andar tras; [+ *girl*] andar tras, perseguir* (*hum*); **we're not going after civilian targets** no vamos a por objetivos civiles

►**go against** VI + PREP [1] (= *be unfavourable to*) [*result, events, evidence*] ir en contra de; **the decision went against him** la decisión iba en contra de él
[2] (= *be contrary to*) [+ *principles, conscience*] ser contrario a
[3] (= *act against*) [+ *sb's wishes*] actuar en contra de

►**go ahead** VI + ADV (= *carry on*) seguir adelante (**with** con); **the exhibition will go ahead as planned** la exposición seguirá adelante tal y como estaba planeado; **go (right) ahead!** ¡adelante!

►**go along** VI + ADV [1] (= *proceed*) seguir; **I'll tell you as we go along** te lo diré de camino; **Cordy's having a party, shall we go along?** Cordy da una fiesta, ¿vamos?; **why don't you go along and see your doctor?*** ¿por qué no vas al médico?; **check as you go along** ve corrigiendo sobre la marcha; **I'm learning as I go along** voy aprendiendo poco a poco; **things are going along nicely*** las cosas marchan bien
[2] **to go along with** (= *accompany*) acompañar; (= *agree with*) [+ *person, idea*] estar de acuerdo con; **we don't go along with that** no estamos de acuerdo con eso

►**go around** Ⓐ VI + ADV [1] = **go round A**
[2] ✦***PROV*** **what goes around comes around** a todos los cerdos les llega su sanmartín
Ⓑ VI + PREP = **go round B**

►**go at*** VI + PREP [1] (= *attack*) atacar, arremeter contra
[2] (= *tackle*) [+ *job etc*] empecinarse en (hacer)

►**go away** VI + ADV [1] [*person*] (= *depart*) irse, marcharse; (*on holiday*) irse de vacaciones; **he's gone away with my keys** se ha ido *or* marchado con mis llaves, se ha llevado mis llaves; **go away!** ¡vete!, ¡lárgate!*, **I think we need to go away and think about this** creo que ahora debemos pensárnoslo un poco; **don't go away with the idea that ...** no te vayas con la idea de que ...
[2] [*pain, problem*] desaparecer

►**go back** VI + ADV [1] (= *return*) volver, regresar (**to** a); **to go back home** volver *or* regresar a casa; **when do the schools go back?** ¿cuándo empieza el colegio?; **the strikers have voted to go back to work** los huelguistas han votado en favor de volver al trabajo; **he's gone back to his wife** ha vuelto con su mujer; **this dress will have to go back (to the shop)** habrá que devolver este vestido; **going back to the point you raised earlier, ...** volviendo al tema que planteaste antes, ...; **to go back to the beginning** volver al principio; *see also* **go back to**
[2] (= *retreat*) volverse atrás; **there's no going back now** ya no podemos volvernos atrás
[3] (= *extend*) extenderse; **the path goes back to the river** el camino llega *or* se extiende hasta el río; **the cave goes back 300 metres** la cueva tiene 300 metros de fondo, la cueva tiene una extensión de 300 metros
[4] (= *date back*) remontarse; **we go back a long way** nos conocemos desde hace mucho; **my memories don't go back so far** mis recuerdos no se remontan tan lejos; **it goes back to Elizabeth I** se remonta a Isabel I; **the controversy goes back to 1929** la controversia se remonta a 1929
[5] (= *change*) **when do the clocks go back?** ¿cuándo hay que atrasar los relojes?; **the clocks go back on Sunday** los relojes se atrasan el domingo

►**go back on** VI + PREP [+ *decision*] volverse atrás en; [+ *promise*] incumplir; **to go back on one's word** faltar a su palabra

►**go back to** VI + PREP (= *revert to*) volver a; **I sold the car and went back to a bicycle** vendí el coche y volví a la bicicleta; **he went back to his former habits** volvió a sus antiguas costumbres; **go back to sleep!** ¡vuelve a dormir!; *see also* **go back**

►**go before** Ⓐ VI + ADV (= *precede*) preceder; **all that has gone before** todo lo que ha pasado antes; **those who are** *or* **have gone before** (*euph*) (= *die*) aquellos que ya pasaron a mejor vida
Ⓑ VI + PREP **the matter has gone before a grand jury** el asunto se ha sometido a un gran jurado

►**go below** VI + ADV (*Naut*) bajar

►**go beyond** VI + PREP ir más allá de; **in this series I have tried to go beyond the basics** en este serie he intentado ir más allá de lo básico *or* esencial; **his interests went beyond political economy** sus intereses iban más allá de la economía política

►**go by** Ⓐ VI + PREP [1] (= *drop by*) pasarse por; **can we go by Sally's house?** ¿podemos pasarnos por casa de Sally?; **did you remember to go by the ironmonger's?** ¿te has acordado de pasarte por la ferretería?
[2] (= *be guided by*) [+ *watch, compass*] guiarse por; **to go by appearances** guiarse por las apariencias; **you can't go by that** no hay que dejarse guiar por eso; **you can't go by what he says** no puedes fiarte de lo que dice
[3] **to go by the name of** llamarse
Ⓑ VI + ADV (= *pass by*) [*opportunity*] pasar; [*time*] pasar, transcurrir; [*person, car*] pasar (cerca); (= *overtake*) adelantar, rebasar (*Mex*); **in days gone by** en tiempos pasados, antaño; **as time goes by** con el tiempo, con el transcurso del tiempo

►**go down** Ⓐ VI + PREP bajar, descender; **to go down a slope** bajar (por) una pendiente; **to go down a mine** bajar a una mina
Ⓑ VI + ADV [1] (= *descend*) [*sun*] ponerse; [*person*] (= *go downstairs*) bajar; **to go down to the coast** bajar a la costa; **go down to the bottom of the page** mira a pie de página
[2] (= *fall*) [*person, horse*] caerse
[3] (= *crash*) [*plane*] estrellarse, caer
[4] (= *sink*) [*ship, person*] hundirse
[5] (= *decrease, decline*) [*price, temperature*] bajar, descender; [*tide, flood, water level*] bajar; **he has gone down in my estimation** ha bajado en mi estima; **the house has gone down in value** la casa ha perdido valor *or* se ha devaluado; **this neighbourhood has really gone down** este barrio ha perdido mucho, este barrio ya no es lo que era; **she's really gone down since I last saw her** [*sick person*] ha dado un buen bajón* *or* ha empeorado mucho desde la última vez que la vi; [*elderly person*] ha perdido muchas facultades desde la última vez que la vi
[6] (= *deflate*) [*balloon, airbed*] desinflarse, deshincharse (*Sp*); **the swelling in my leg has gone down** me ha bajado la hinchazón de la pierna
[7] (= *be defeated*) perder; **Italy went down against Brazil in the semi-final** Italia perdió ante Brasil en la semifinal
[8] (*Comput*) (= *break down*) bloquearse, dejar de funcionar
[9] (= *be remembered*) **to go down in history/to posterity** pasar a la historia/a la posteridad; *see also* **go down as**
[10] (*Brit Univ*) (*at end of term*) marcharse; (*at end of degree*) terminar la carrera, dejar la universidad
[11] (= *be swallowed*) **that omelette went down a treat*** esa tortilla estaba riquísima; **it went down the wrong way** se me atragantó
[12] (= *be accepted, approved*) **to go down well/badly** ser bien/mal recibido; **his speech didn't go down at all well** su discurso fue muy mal recibido; **that should go down well (with him)*** eso le va a gustar; **I wonder how that will go down with her parents** me pregunto cómo les sentará eso a sus padres
[13] (*Theat*) [*curtain*] bajar; [*lights*] apagarse

►**go down as** VI + PREP (= *be regarded as*) considerarse; (= *be remembered as*) pasar a la historia como; **it has to go down as the worst performance of my career** se considerará la peor actuación de mi carrera, pasará a la historia como la peor actuación de mi carrera; **he will go down in history as ...** pasará a la historia como ...

►**go down on**⁑ VI + PREP **to go down on sb** chupárselo *or* chupársela a algn**

►**go down with*** VI + PREP [+ *illness, virus, food poisoning*] pillar*, coger, agarrar (*LAm*)

►**go for** VI + PREP [1] (= *attack*) (*physically, verbally*) atacar; **suddenly the dog went for me** de pronto el perro me atacó *or* fue a por mí; **go for him!** (*to dog*) ¡a él!
[2] (*) (= *like, fancy*) **I don't go for his films very much** no me gustan mucho sus películas; **I don't go for that sort of talk** no me va esa clase de conversación; **I could really go for him!** ¡me gusta muchísimo!, ¡me mola cantidad! (*Sp**); **I go for quiet, unassuming types** me gustan *or* me van más los tipos callados y sin pretensiones
[3] (= *strive for*) dedicarse a obtener; **go for it!*** ¡a por ello!, ¡adelante!; **I decided to go for it*** decidí intentarlo
[4] (= *choose*) escoger, optar por; **I'll go for the cream caramel** para mí flan
[5] ✦***IDIOM*** **to have a lot going for one**: **he**

has a lot going for him tiene mucho a su favor; **the theory has a lot going for it** la teoría cuenta con muchas ventajas

►**go forward** VI + ADV [1] (= *move ahead*) [*person, vehicle*] avanzar
[2] (= *change*) [*clocks*] **when do the clocks go forward?** ¿cuándo se adelantan los relojes?
[3] (*fig*) [3·1] (= *proceed*) (*with sth*) seguir adelante (**with** con); **if we go forward with these radical proposals …** si seguimos adelante con estas propuestas radicales …; **if our present plans go forward, we'll have to take on more staff** si nuestros planes actuales progresan *or* siguen adelante, tendremos que emplear a más personal
[3·2] (= *be put forward*) [*suggestion*] presentarse

►**go in** VI + ADV [1] (= *enter*) entrar; **please do go in** pase, por favor; **they went in by the back door** entraron por la puerta trasera
[2] (= *attack*) atacar; **the troops are going in tomorrow** las tropas atacarán mañana; **British troops will not go in alone** las tropas británicas no serán las únicas en entrar en combate
[3] (= *fit*) caber
[4] [*sun*] ocultarse (**behind** tras, detrás de)
[5] (*Cricket*) entrar a batear

►**go in for** VI + PREP [1] (= *enter for*) [+ *race, competition*] presentarse a; [+ *examination*] presentarse a
[2] (= *take as career*) dedicarse a
[3] (= *be interested in*) [+ *hobby, sport*] interesarse por; **we don't go in for such things here** (*activities*) aquí esas cosas no se hacen
[4] (= *use*) utilizar

►**go into** VI + PREP [1] (= *enter*) (*lit*) entrar en; **she went into the kitchen** entró en la cocina; **to go into politics** entrar en la política, dedicarse a la política; **he doesn't want to go into industry** no quiere dedicarse a la industria; **he's thinking about going into the police force** está pensando entrar en el cuerpo de policía; *see also* **hiding A**
[2] (= *go to*) **Ed has had to go into work** Ed ha tenido que ir a trabajar; **he's had to go into hospital** ha tenido que ingresar en el hospital
[3] (= *embark on*) [+ *explanation, details*] meterse en; (= *investigate, examine*) examinar a fondo; **let's not go into all that now** dejemos todo eso por ahora
[4] (= *fall into*) [+ *trance, coma*] entrar en; **he went into fits of laughter** le entró *or* le dio un ataque de risa
[5] (= *be spent on*) [*money, resources*] dedicarse a; **a lot of money went into the research** se dedicó mucho dinero a la investigación
[6] (*Aut*) **to go into first gear** meter primera velocidad; **they went into the back of a lorry in the ice** resbalaron sobre el hielo y chocaron contra la parte trasera de un camión

►**go in with** VI + PREP asociarse con, unirse con; **we're going in with an American company** nos vamos a unir a una empresa americana; **she went in with her sister to buy the present** entre ella y su hermana compraron el regalo

►**go off** (A) VI + ADV [1] (= *leave*) marcharse, irse; **he went off with the au pair** se largó* *or* se marchó con la chica au pair
[2] (= *stop*) [*TV, light, heating*] apagarse; [*pain*] irse, pasarse
[3] (= *be activated*) [*bomb*] estallar; [*gun*] dispararse; [*alarm clock*] sonar
[4] (= *go bad*) [*food*] echarse a perder; [*milk*] pasarse, echarse a perder
[5] (= *pass off*) salir; **the party went off well** la fiesta salió bien
[6] (*) (*to sleep*) quedarse dormido; **I must have gone off for a few moments** debo haberme quedado dormido unos instantes; **he goes off to sleep the moment his head touches the pillow** en cuanto pone la cabeza en la almohada se queda dormido
(B) VI + PREP (= *no longer like*) [+ *thing*] perder el gusto por; [+ *person*] dejar de querer a; **I've gone off the idea** ya no me gusta la idea

►**go on** (A) VI + PREP [1] (= *be guided by*) [+ *evidence*] basarse en; **there isn't much evidence to go on** no hay muchos indicios en los que basarse, no hay muchas pruebas en las que basarse; **there's nothing to go on** no hay nada en que basarse; **what are you going on?** ¿en qué te basas?; **the police had no clues to go on** la policía no tenía pistas que le sirvieran de guía
[2] (= *like*) **I don't go much on that** eso no me gusta
[3] (= *continue*) **to go on doing sth** seguir haciendo algo, continuar haciendo algo
[4] (*) (= *approach*) **she's going on 50** anda cerca de la cincuentena, va para los cincuenta; **Ann's 25 going on 50** Ann tiene 25 años pero parece que tuviera 50
[5] (= *be spent on*) **most of their money goes on drink** la mayor parte del dinero se les va en bebida
[6] (= *start taking*) [+ *drug*] empezar a tomar; **she's to go on the pill** tiene que empezar a tomar la píldora
(B) VI + ADV [1] (= *fit*) **the lid won't go on** la tapa no le va; **these shoes won't go on** no me entran estos zapatos
[2] (= *continue*) [*war, talks*] seguir, continuar; [*person*] (*on journey*) seguir el camino; **I went on up the road and met Philippa** seguí carretera arriba y me encontré con Philippa; **everything is going on normally** todo sigue con normalidad; **"so," he went on …** —así es que —continuó; **go on!** (= *continue*) sigue, continúa; (*giving encouragement*) ¡venga!; (*showing incredulity*) ¡no digas bobadas!*, ¡anda ya!*, ¡venga ya!*; **go on, tell me what the problem is!** ¡venga, dime cuál es el problema!; **to go on doing sth** seguir *or* continuar haciendo algo; **go on with your work** sigue con tu trabajo; **that'll do to be going on with*** con eso basta por ahora; **I've got enough to be going on with** tengo suficiente por el momento; ✦**IDIOM go on with you!*** (*showing incredulity*) ¡no digas bobadas!*, ¡anda ya!*, ¡venga ya!*
[3] (= *last*) durar; **the concert went on until 11 o'clock at night** el concierto duró hasta las 11 de la noche; **how long will this go on for?** ¿cuánto tiempo durará esto?
[4] (= *proceed*) **to go on to do sth** pasar a hacer algo; **after having taught herself Italian, she went on to learn Arabic** después de haber aprendido italiano por su cuenta, empezó a estudiar árabe; **he went on to say that …** añadió que …
[5] (*) (= *talk*) **he does go on so** habla más que siete*, no para de hablar; **to go on about sth** no parar de hablar de algo, dar la tabarra *or* la matraca con algo*; **she's always going on about it** nunca para de hablar de eso, siempre está con la misma cantinela*; **he's always going on about the government** (= *criticize*) siempre está echando pestes contra el gobierno*; **don't go on about it!** ¡déjalo ya!, ¡deja ya de dar la tabarra *or* la matraca con el tema!*
[6] (*) (= *nag*) **to go on at sb** dar la lata a algn* (**about** con)
[7] (= *happen*) pasar, ocurrir; **it had been going on in her absence** había pasado no estando ella; **there's something odd going on** aquí hay gato encerrado; **what's going on here?** ¿qué pasa *or* ocurre aquí?
[8] (= *pass, go by*) [*time, years*] pasar, transcurrir
[9] (= *come on*) [*lights, machine*] encenderse, prenderse (*LAm*)
[10] (*Theat*) salir (a escena)
[11] (*Sport*) **to go on as a substitute** entrar como suplente
[12] (*) (= *behave*) **what a way to go on!** (*pej*) ¡qué manera de comportarse!

►**go on for** VI + PREP (*with numbers*) **he's going on for 60** anda por los 60; **it's going on for two o'clock** son casi las dos, van a ser las dos; **it's going on for 100km to Vilafranca** Vilafranca está a unos 100km de aquí

►**go out** VI + ADV [1] (= *be extinguished, switch off*) [*fire, light*] apagarse; ✦**IDIOM to go out like a light** dormirse al instante, quedarse frito*
[2] (= *exit*) salir; **to go out of a room** salir de un cuarto; **to go out shopping** salir de compras *or* de tiendas; **to go out for a meal** salir a comer/cenar (fuera); **she goes out to work** trabaja (fuera); **to go out (of fashion)** pasar de moda; **the mail has gone out** ha salido el correo; **there's a lot of money going out on household bills** se gasta mucho dinero en facturas domésticas; **you must go out and get a job** tienes que ponerte a encontrar trabajo; **TV violence incites people to go out and cause trouble** la violencia en la televisión incita a la gente a salir a la calle y causar problemas
[3] (*romantically*) **to go out with sb** salir con algn; **how long have you been going out together?** ¿cuánto tiempo hace que salís juntos?
[4] (= *ebb*) [*tide*] bajar, menguar
[5] (= *travel*) viajar (**to** a); **she went out to Bangkok to join her husband** viajó a Bangkok para reunirse con su esposo
[6] (= *be issued*) [*pamphlet, circular*] salir, publicarse; [*invitation*] mandarse; (= *be broadcast*) [*radio programme, TV programme*] emitirse; **an appeal has gone out for people to give blood** se ha hecho un llamamiento a la población para que done sangre; **the programme goes out on Friday evenings** el programa se emite los viernes por la noche
[7] (*Sport*) (= *be eliminated*) quedar eliminado; **our team went out to a second division side** nuestro equipo fue eliminado por uno de segunda división
[8] (*commiserating*) **my heart went out to him** le compadecí mucho, sentí mucha pena por él; **all our sympathy goes out to you** te damos nuestro más sentido pésame, te acompañamos en el sentimiento

►**go out of** VI + PREP (= *desert*) **all the vitality has gone out of her** se ha quedado sin vitalidad; **the vigour has gone out of the debate** el debate no tiene ya fuerza *or* vigor

►**go over** (A) VI + PREP [1] (= *examine, check*) [+ *report, figures*] examinar, revisar
[2] (= *rehearse, review*) [+ *speech, lesson*] repasar, revisar; **to go over sth in one's mind** repasar algo mentalmente; **let's go over the facts again** repasemos los hechos otra vez
[3] (= *touch up*) retocar
[4] (= *pass over*) [+ *wall*] pasar por encima de; **to go over the same ground: we went over the same ground time and again, trying to sort out the facts** volvimos a lo mismo una y otra vez, intentando esclarecer los hechos

Ⓑ VI + ADV [1] **to go over to** [1·1] (= *cross over to*) cruzar a; (*fig*) (*changing habit, sides etc*) pasarse a; **to go over to America** ir a América; **shall we go over to Inga's?** ¿vamos a casa de Inga?; **to go over to the enemy** pasarse al enemigo
[1·2] (= *approach*) acercarse a, dirigirse a
[2] (= *be received*) recibirse; **how did it go over?** ¿qué tal fue recibido *or* se recibió?; **his speech went over well** su discurso tuvo buena acogida

►**go round** Ⓐ VI + ADV [1] (= *revolve*) girar, dar vueltas; **the wheel was going round very fast** la rueda giraba *or* daba vueltas muy de prisa; **the idea was going round in my head** la idea me daba vueltas en la cabeza; **my head is going round** la cabeza me da vueltas
[2] (= *circulate*) **he goes round in a Rolls** se pasea por ahí en un Rolls; **to go round barefoot/in torn jeans** andar descalzo/con unos vaqueros rotos; **people who go round spreading rumours** la gente que va por ahí esparciendo rumores; **there's a bug going round** hay un virus por ahí rondando; **there's a rumour going round that they're getting married** corre *or* circula el rumor de que se van a casar; **he often goes round with Jimmy** se le ve a menudo con Jimmy
[3] (= *suffice*) alcanzar, bastar; **is there enough food to go round?** ¿hay comida suficiente para todos?
[4] (= *visit*) **let's go round to John's place** vamos a casa de John
[5] (= *make a detour*) dar la vuelta
Ⓑ VI + PREP [1] (= *spin round*) girar alrededor de; **the Earth goes round the sun** la Tierra gira alrededor del sol
[2] (= *visit*) visitar; **we want to go round the museum** queremos visitar el museo; **I love going round the shops** me encanta ir de tiendas; **to go round the world** dar la vuelta al mundo
[3] (= *patrol*) [+ *grounds*] patrullar (por), recorrer
[4] (= *make a detour round*) [+ *obstacle*] dar la vuelta a

►**go through** Ⓐ VI + PREP [1] (= *pass through*) pasar por; (= *cross*) atravesar; **I've never liked going through tunnels** nunca me ha gustado pasar por túneles; **we went through London to get to Brighton** pasamos por *or* atravesamos Londres para llegar a Brighton; **you have to go through the sitting-room to go to the kitchen** para ir a la cocina tienes que pasar por la sala de estar
[2] (= *suffer*) pasar por; (= *bear*) aguantar; **I know what you're going through** sé por lo que estás pasando
[3] (= *examine*) [+ *list, book*] repasar; (= *search through*) [+ *pile, possessions, pockets*] registrar
[4] (= *use up*) [+ *money*] gastar; [+ *food*] comerse; [+ *drink*] beberse; (= *wear out*) [+ *garment*] gastar; **the book went through 8 editions** el libro tuvo 8 ediciones
[5] (= *perform*) [+ *formalities*] cumplimentar; [+ *ceremony*] realizar; **we'll go through some warm-up exercises first** primero haremos algunos ejercicios de calentamiento
Ⓑ VI + ADV [1] (*lit*) pasar; **let's go through to the other room** vamos a pasar a la otra sala; **the bullet went right through** la bala pasó de parte a parte
[2] [*proposal, bill, motion*] ser aprobado, aprobarse; [*deal*] concluirse, hacerse; **it all went through all right** todo se llevó a cabo sin problemas
[3] [*clothing*] romperse *or* agujerearse con el uso; **it has gone through at the elbows** con el uso se ha roto *or* agujereado por los codos

►**go through with** VI + PREP [+ *plan, crime*] llevar a cabo; **I can't go through with it!** ¡no puedo seguir con esto!

►**go to** VI + PREP [1] ✦*IDIOM* **go to it!** ¡adelante!, ¡empieza!; *see also* **go A1**
[2] (= *take*) **you needn't go to the expense of buying a new one** no es preciso que te gastes dinero para comprar uno nuevo; **they went to great expense to send her to a private school** se metieron en *or* (*frm*) incurrieron muchos gastos para mandarla a un colegio privado; **to go to (all) the trouble of doing sth** tomarse la molestia de hacer algo; **I went to a lot of trouble to get it for her** me tomé muchas molestias para conseguírselo

►**go together** VI + ADV [1] (= *harmonize*) [*colours*] hacer juego; [*ideas*] complementarse; **green and mauve go well together** el verde y el malva hacen juego
[2] (= *coincide*) [*events, conditions*] ir de la mano; **poor living conditions and tuberculosis go together** la pobreza y la tuberculosis van siempre de la mano
[3] (*) [*couple*] salir juntos; **Ann and Peter are going together** Ann y Peter salen juntos

►**go toward**, **go towards** (*esp Brit*) VI + PREP (= *contribute to*) **the extra money will go toward a holiday** el dinero extra será para unas vacaciones

►**go under** Ⓐ VI + PREP **he now goes under the name of Curtis** ahora se conoce por Curtis
Ⓑ VI + ADV [1] (= *sink*) [*ship, person*] hundirse
[2] (= *fail*) [*business, firm*] quebrar

►**go up** VI + ADV [1] (= *rise*) [*temperature, price*] subir; **the total goes up to …** el total asciende a …; **Hartlepool should go up this season** (*Sport*) el Hartlepool debería ascender esta temporada
[2] (= *travel*) **to go up to London** ir a Londres
[3] (= *approach*) **to go up to sb** acercarse a algn, abordar a algn
[4] (= *go upstairs*) subir (*a la planta de arriba*)
[5] (= *be built*) [*tower block, building*] levantarse
[6] (= *explode*) estallar; **to go up in flames** arder en llamas, ser pasto de las llamas
[7] (= *be heard*) **a gasp went up from the crowd** la multitud dio un grito entrecortado
[8] (*Brit Univ*) **to go up to university** (*to begin studies*) entrar en la universidad; (*after vacation*) volver a la universidad
[9] (*Theat*) [*curtain*] subir, abrirse, levantarse; [*lights*] encenderse

►**go with** VI + PREP [1] (= *accompany*) ir con, acompañar a; **the house goes with the job** la casa va con el trabajo
[2] (*) (= *go steady with*) salir con
[3] (*sexually*) acostarse con
[4] (*) (= *agree with*) **I'll go with you there** en eso estoy (de acuerdo) contigo, en eso te doy la razón; **yes, I'd go with that** sí, en eso estoy de acuerdo
[5] (*) (= *choose*) escoger, optar por
[6] (= *match*) *see* **go A11**

►**go without** Ⓐ VI + PREP pasar sin, prescindir de
Ⓑ VI + ADV arreglárselas, pasar; **you'll have to go without** tendrás que arreglártelas *or* pasar sin ello

goad [gəʊd] Ⓐ VT [1] (*lit*) aguijonear, picar
[2] (*fig*) incitar, provocar; (= *anger*) irritar; (= *taunt*) provocar con insultos; **to ~ sb into fury** provocar a algn poniéndole furioso; **to ~ sb into doing sth/to do sth** incitar a algn a hacer algo
Ⓑ N [1] (*Agr*) aguijón *m*, puya *f*
[2] (*fig*) estímulo *m*

►**goad on** VT + ADV pinchar, provocar; **to ~ sb on to doing sth** provocar a algn para que haga algo

go-ahead [ˈgəʊəhed] Ⓐ ADJ (*esp Brit*) emprendedor
Ⓑ N **to give sth/sb the ~** autorizar algo/a algn

▼**goal** [gəʊl] Ⓐ N [1] (*Sport*) (= *score*) gol *m*; (= *net etc*) portería *f*, meta *f*, arco *m* (*LAm*); **to keep ~** ◊ **play in ~** ser portero *or* (*LAm*) arquero; **goal!** ¡gol!; **to score a ~** marcar un gol; **they won by two ~s to one** ganaron por dos goles *or* tantos a uno
[2] (= *aim*) (*in life*) meta *f*, objetivo *m*; (*in journey*) fin *m*; **to reach one's ~** llegar a la meta, realizar una ambición
Ⓑ CPD ► **goal area** N área *f* de portería, área *f* de meta ► **goal average** N promedio *m* de goles, golaverage *m* ► **goal kick** N saque *m* de puerta ► **goal line** N línea *f* de portería

goalie* [ˈgəʊlɪ] N = **goalkeeper**

goalkeeper [ˈgəʊlˌkiːpəʳ] N portero/a *m/f*, guardameta *mf*, arquero *m* (*LAm*)

goalkeeping [ˈgəʊlˌkiːpɪŋ] N actuación *f* como portero, actuación *f* del portero

goalless [ˈgəʊllɪs] ADJ sin goles, con empate a cero; **a ~ draw** un empate a cero (goles)

goalmouth [ˈgəʊlmaʊθ] N portería *f*

goalpost [ˈgəʊlpəʊst] N poste *m* (de la portería); ✦*IDIOM* **to move the ~s** cambiar las reglas del juego

goalscorer [ˈgəʊlˌskɔːrəʳ] N goleador(a) *m/f*

goat [gəʊt] Ⓐ N (*gen*) cabra *f*; (*male*) chivo *m*, macho cabrío *m*; ✦*IDIOM* **to get sb's ~*** fastidiar *or* molestar a algn
Ⓑ CPD ► **goat cheese**, **goat's cheese** N queso *m* de cabra

goatee [gəʊˈtiː] N (*short*) perilla *f*; (*long*) barba *f* de chivo

goatherd [ˈgəʊthɜːd] N cabrero *m*

goatskin [ˈgəʊtskɪn] N piel *f* de cabra

gob** [gɒb] Ⓐ N [1] (= *spit*) salivazo *m*
[2] (*Brit*) (= *mouth*) bocaza* *f*
Ⓑ VT (*Brit*) escupir
Ⓒ VI (*Brit*) escupir

gobbet* [ˈgɒbɪt] N [*of food etc*] trocito *m*, pequeña porción *f*; **~s of information** pequeños elementos *mpl* de información

gobble [ˈgɒbl] Ⓐ N gluglú *m*
Ⓑ VT (*also* **~ down, ~ up**) engullir, tragar
Ⓒ VI [*turkey*] gluglutear

gobbledegook*, **gobbledygook*** [ˈgɒbldɪguːk] N jerigonza *f*, galimatías *m inv*

go-between [ˈgəʊbɪˌtwiːn] N intermediario/a *m/f*; (= *pimp*) alcahuete/a *m/f*

Gobi Desert [ˈgəʊbɪˈdezət] N desierto *m* del Gobi

goblet [ˈgɒblɪt] N copa *f*

goblin [ˈgɒblɪn] N duende *m*, trasgo *m*

gobshite** [ˈgɒbʃaɪt] N (= *idiot*) chulo/a *m/f* de mierda**

gobsmacked* [ˈgɒbsmækt] ADJ (*Brit*) **I was ~** me quedé alucinado*

gobstopper* [ˈgɒbˌstɒpəʳ] N (*Brit*) *caramelo grande y redondo*

go-by* [ˈgəʊbaɪ] N **to give sth the ~** pasar algo por alto, omitir algo; **to give a place the ~** dejar de visitar un sitio; **to give sb the ~** desairar a algn (*no haciendo caso de él/ella*), no hacer caso de algn

GOC N ABBR = **General Officer Commanding**

➤ LANGUAGE IN USE: goal A2 8.2

go-cart ['gəʊkɑːt] N cochecito *m* de niño

god [gɒd] N 1 dios *m*; **God** Dios *m*; **(my) God!** ◊ **good God!*** ¡Dios mío!, ¡santo Dios!; **God forbid** ¡Dios me libre!; **he thinks he's God's gift to women*** se cree que lo creó Dios para ser la felicidad de las mujeres; **God help them if that's what they think** que Dios les ayude si piensan así; **I hope to ~ she'll be happy** Dios quiera que sea feliz; **God (only) knows** sólo Dios sabe, sabe Dios; **what in God's name is he doing?** ¿qué demonios está haciendo?; **please God!** ¡quiera Dios!; **for God's sake!** ¡por Dios!; **thank God!** ¡gracias a Dios!; **God willing** si Dios quiere, Dios mediante; **✦PROV God helps those who help themselves** a quien madruga Dios le ayuda; *see also* **forbid 2**
2 **the ~s** (*Theat*) el gallinero, el paraíso

god-awful‡ ['gɒd'ɔːfʊl] ADJ horrible, fatal*

god-botherer* ['gɒd,bɒðərəʳ] N (*pej*) pesado/a *m/f* de la religión

godchild ['gɒdtʃaɪld] N (*pl* **godchildren**) ahijado/a *m/f*

goddam(n)‡ ['gɒd'dæm] (*US*) Ⓐ ADJ (*also* **goddamn(ed)**) maldito, puñetero*
Ⓑ EXCL (*also* **goddammit**) ¡maldición!
Ⓒ N **I don't give a good ~!** ¡me importa un pito!*, ¡me importa un carajo!‡

goddaughter ['gɒd,dɔːtəʳ] N ahijada *f*

goddess ['gɒdɪs] N diosa *f*

godfather ['gɒd,fɑːðəʳ] N padrino *m* (**to** de)

god-fearing ['gɒd,fɪərɪŋ] ADJ temeroso de Dios

godforsaken* ['gɒdfə,seɪkn] ADJ [*place*] olvidado de Dios; [*person*] dejado de la mano de Dios

Godfrey ['gɒdfrɪ] N Godofredo

godhead ['gɒdhed] N divinidad *f*

godless ['gɒdlɪs] ADJ 1 (= *wicked*) [*life*] pecaminoso
2 (= *unbelieving*) ateo

godlike ['gɒdlaɪk] ADJ divino

godliness ['gɒdlɪnɪs] N piedad *f*; *see also* **cleanliness**

godly ['gɒdlɪ] ADJ (*compar* **godlier**; *superl* **godliest**) devoto

godmother ['gɒd,mʌðəʳ] N madrina *f* (**to** de)

godparents ['gɒd,peərənts] NPL padrinos *mpl*

godsend ['gɒdsend] N don *m* del cielo; **it was a ~ to us** nos llegó en buena hora

godson ['gɒdsʌn] N ahijado *m*

Godspeed [,gɒd'spiːd] (††) EXCL **~!** ¡buena suerte!, ¡ande usted con Dios!

-goer ['gəʊəʳ] N (*ending in compounds*) **cinemagoer** asiduo/a *m/f* del cine; *see also* **operagoer, theatre-goer**

goes [gəʊz] 3RD PERS SING PERSENT *of* **go**

go-faster stripes* [gəʊ,fɑːstə'straɪps] NPL (*Aut*) bandas *fpl* laterales decorativas

gofer ['gəʊfeʳ] N recadero/a *m/f*

go-getter* ['gəʊgetəʳ] N ambicioso/a *m/f*

go-getting* ['gəʊgetɪŋ] ADJ dispuesto, resuelto

goggle ['gɒgl] Ⓐ VI **to ~ at** mirar con ojos desorbitados, mirar sin comprender
Ⓑ CPD ► **goggle box*** N (*Brit TV*) caja *f* tonta*

goggle-eyed* ['gɒgl,aɪd] ADJ con ojos desorbitados

goggles ['gɒglz] NPL 1 (*Aut etc*) anteojos *mpl*; [*of diver*] gafas *fpl* de submarinismo
2 (*) (= *glasses*) gafas *fpl*

go-go ['gəʊgəʊ] ADJ 1 [*dancer, dancing*] gogó
2 (*US*) [*market, stocks*] especulativo
3 (*US**) [*team etc*] dinámico

going ['gəʊɪŋ] Ⓐ N 1 (= *departure*) salida *f*, partida *f*; *see also* **coming B**
2 (= *progress*) **it was slow ~** se avanzaba a paso lento; **good ~!** ¡bien hecho!; **that was good ~** eso fue muy rápido; **the climb was hard ~** la subida fue muy dura; **the meeting was hard ~** en la reunión se complicaron bastante las cosas; **the book was heavy ~** la lectura del libro resultó pesada; **it's heavy ~ talking to her** es pesado hablar con ella
3 (= *state of surface etc*) estado *m* del camino; (*Horse racing etc*) estado *m* de la pista; **let's cross while the ~ is good** aprovechemos para cruzar; **we made money while the ~ was good** mientras las condiciones eran favorables ganábamos dinero
Ⓑ ADJ 1 (= *thriving*) [*business, concern*] establecido
2 (= *current*) [*price, rate*] corriente
3 (*) (= *available*) **the best one ~** el mejor que hay

going-over ['gəʊɪŋ'əʊvəʳ] N (*pl* **goings-over**) 1 (= *check*) inspección *f*; **we gave the car a thorough ~** revisamos el coche de arriba a abajo; **we gave the house a thorough ~** (= *search*) registramos la casa de arriba abajo
2 (*) (*fig*) (= *beating*) paliza *f*; **they gave him a ~** le dieron una paliza

goings-on* ['gəʊɪŋz'ɒn] NPL tejemanejes *mpl*

goitre, **goiter** (*US*) ['gɔɪtəʳ] N bocio *m*

go-kart ['gəʊkɑːt] N kart *m*

go-karting ['gəʊ,kɑːtɪŋ] N karting *m*

Golan Heights ['gəʊlæn'haɪts] NPL **the ~** los Altos del Golán

gold [gəʊld] Ⓐ N 1 (= *metal, commodity, currency*) oro *m*; **he paid for it in ~** lo pagó en oro; **to invest in ~** invertir en oro; **she only wears ~** sólo lleva (joyas de) oro; **they stole 12 million pounds worth of ~** robaron oro por valor de 12 millones de libras; **24-carat ~** oro *m* de 24 quilates; **to be made of ~** ser de oro; **pure ~** (*lit*) oro *m* puro; **she's pure ~** (*fig*) es una joya, vale su peso en oro; **solid ~** oro *m* macizo; *see also* **glitter, good A9, heart A2, strike B6, weight**
2 (= *colour*) dorado *m*; **autumnal browns and ~s** los marrones y dorados del otoño
3 (= *gold medal*) medalla *f* de oro; **he won (the) ~ in Barcelona** ganó la medalla de oro en Barcelona; **to go for ~** intentar ganar la medalla de oro
Ⓑ ADJ 1 (= *made of gold*) [*jewellery, coins, tooth*] de oro; *see* **lamé**
2 (= *gold-coloured*) [*paint, lettering, frame*] dorado; [*fabric, dress, shirt*] color oro *inv*, dorado; **the sign was written in ~ letters** el cartel estaba escrito con letras doradas; **she decided to paint it ~** decidió pintarlo color oro *or* dorado; **a green and ~ flag** una bandera verde y oro
Ⓒ CPD ► **gold bar** N barra *f* de oro ► **gold braid** N galón *m* de oro ► **gold card** N tarjeta *f* oro ► **the Gold Coast** N (*Hist*) la Costa de Oro ► **gold digger** N (*lit*) buscador(a) *m/f* de oro; (*fig*) cazafortunas *mf inv* ► **gold disc** N (*Mus*) disco *m* de oro ► **gold dust** N oro *m* en polvo; **✦IDIOM biros are like ~ dust in this office** (*Brit*) (*fig*) en esta oficina no encuentras un bolígrafo ni por casualidad ► **gold fever** N fiebre *f* del oro ► **gold filling** N empaste *m* de oro ► **gold foil** N papel *m* de oro ► **gold leaf** N oro *m* en hojas, pan *m* de oro ► **gold market** N mercado *m* del oro ► **gold medal** N (*Sport*) medalla *f* de oro ► **gold medallist** N medallero/a *m/f* de oro ► **gold mine** N (*lit, fig*) mina *f* de oro ► **gold miner** N minero *m* de oro ► **gold mining** N minería *f* de oro ► **gold plate** N (= *tableware*) vajilla *f* de oro; (= *covering*) baño *m* de oro; **it isn't solid ~ just ~ plate** no es oro puro sino un baño de oro; **doors covered with ~ plate** puertas revestidas de un baño de oro ► **gold reserves** N reservas *fpl* de oro ► **gold rush** N fiebre *f* del oro ► **gold standard** N patrón *m* oro; **to come off** *or* **leave the ~ standard** abandonar el patrón de oro

goldbrick* ['gəʊld'brɪk] (*US*) Ⓐ N 1 (= *worthless thing*) timo* *m*
2 (*Mil*) (= *shirker*) gandul *m*
Ⓑ VI escurrir el bulto

goldcrest ['gəʊldkrest] N reyezuelo *m* (sencillo)

golden ['gəʊldən] Ⓐ ADJ 1 (*in colour*) dorado; **a beautiful girl with bright ~ hair** una chica preciosa con un pelo dorado y brillante; **it gives your face an instant ~ tan** da un tono dorado instantáneo al rostro; **the wine is ~ in colour** el vino es de un color dorado; **fry the chicken pieces until ~** dorar los trozos de pollo
2 (= *made of gold*) de oro
3 (*fig*) (= *outstanding*) [*years, era*] dorado; [*future*] excelente; **this is a ~ opportunity for peace** ésta es una oportunidad de oro para la paz, ésta es una excelente oportunidad para la paz; **the ~ days of …** la época dorada de …
Ⓑ CPD ► **golden age** N edad *f* de oro ► **the Golden Age** N (*in Spanish Literature*) el Siglo de Oro ► **golden boy*** N niño *m* bonito* ► **the golden calf** N el becerro de oro ► **Golden Delicious (apple)** N manzana *f* golden ► **golden eagle** N águila *f* real ► **the Golden Fleece** N el vellocino de oro ► **the Golden Gate** N el Golden Gate ► **golden girl*** N niña *f* bonita* ► **golden goal** N (*Ftbl*) gol *m* de oro ► **golden handcuffs** NPL (*Comm, Ind*) *dinero que una compañía paga a un empleado para inducirle a continuar en la empresa* ► **golden handshake** N (*Comm, Ind*) *dinero que una compañía ofrece a un empleado como gratificación al jubilarlo o al despedirlo* ► **golden hello** N (*Ind*) *dinero que una compañía paga a alguien para inducirle a que trabaje para esa compañía* ► **golden jubilee** N cincuentenario *m*, cincuenta aniversario *m* ► **the golden mean** N el punto medio ► **golden oldie*** N (= *song*) viejo éxito *m*; (= *footballer, singer, etc*) vieja gloria *f* ► **golden parachute** N (*Comm, Ind*) *cláusula del contrato de un alto ejecutivo por el que se le otorgan beneficios especiales en caso de que resulte cesante debido a la adquisición de la empresa por otra* ► **golden retriever** N golden retriever *m* ► **golden rule** N regla *f* de oro ► **golden share** N participación *f* mayoritaria ► **golden syrup** N (*Brit*) miel *f* de caña, melaza *f* de caña ► **the Golden Triangle** N el Triángulo Dorado *or* de Oro ► **golden wedding (anniversary)** N bodas *fpl* de oro

goldenrod ['gəʊldən,rɒd] N vara *f* de oro

goldfield ['gəʊldfiːld] N campo *m* aurífero

gold-filled ['gəʊld,fɪld] ADJ lleno de oro; (*Tech*) revestido de oro, enchapado en oro; [*tooth*] empastado de oro

goldfinch ['gəʊldfɪntʃ] N jilguero *m*

goldfish ['gəʊldfɪʃ] Ⓐ N (*pl* **goldfish** *or* **goldfishes**) pez *m* de colores
Ⓑ CPD ► **goldfish bowl** N pecera *f*; **✦IDIOM to live in a ~ bowl** vivir como en una vitrina

Goldilocks ['gəʊldɪlɒks] N Rubiales

gold-plated [,gəʊld'pleɪtɪd] ADJ chapado en oro; (*fig*) [*deal, contract*] de oro

gold-rimmed [,gəʊld'rɪmd] ADJ [*spectacles*] con montura de oro

goldsmith ['gəʊldsmɪθ] N orfebre *mf*; **~'s (shop)** taller *m* de orfebrería

golf [gɒlf] Ⓐ N golf *m*
Ⓑ VI jugar al golf
Ⓒ CPD ► **golf ball** N pelota *f* de golf; (*Typ*) cabeza *f* de escritura ► **golf buggy** N cochecito *m* de golf ► **golf club** N (= *society*) club *m* de golf; (= *stick*) palo *m* de golf ► **golf course** N campo *m or* (*LAm*) cancha *f* de golf ► **golf links** NPL campo *m* de golf (*junto al mar*); *see also* **professional B3**

golfer ['gɒlfəʳ] N golfista *mf*

golfing ['gɒlfɪŋ] Ⓐ N golf *m*
Ⓑ ADJ [*equipment, trousers*] de golf; [*holiday*] golfístico

Golgotha ['gɒlgəθə] N Gólgota *m*

Goliath [gə'laɪəθ] N Goliat

golliwog ['gɒlɪwɒg] N (*Brit*) muñeco *m* negrito

golly¹* ['gɒlɪ] N (*Brit*) = **golliwog**

golly²†* ['gɒlɪ] EXCL (*Brit*) (*also* **by ~**) ¡caramba!; **and by ~, he's done it too!** ¡vaya si lo ha hecho!, ¡anda que lo ha hecho!

golosh [gə'lɒʃ] N chanclo *m*, galocha *f*

Gomorrah [gə'mɒrə] N Gomorra *f*

gonad ['gɒnæd] N gónada *f*

gondola ['gɒndələ] Ⓐ N 1 (= *boat*) góndola *f*
2 [*of hot-air balloon*] barquilla *f*
Ⓑ CPD ► **gondola car** N (*US Rail*) vagón *m* descubierto, batea *f*

gondolier [ˌgɒndə'lɪəʳ] N gondolero *m*

gone [gɒn] PP *of* **go**

goner‡ ['gɒnəʳ] N **he's a ~** está en las últimas, se nos va

gong [gɒŋ] N 1 gong *m*
2 (*Brit**) (= *medal*) medalla *f*, condecoración *f*; (*in civil service*) cinta *f*, cintajo* *m*

gonna* ['gɒnə] (*esp US*) = **going to**

gonorrhoea, gonorrhea (*US*) [ˌgɒnə'rɪə] N gonorrea *f*

goo* [gu:] N 1 (= *substance*) **why do you put all that ~ on your face?** ¿por qué te pones tanto mejunje en la cara?; **the rice had turned into a heap of ~** el arroz quedó hecho un mazacote
2 (*fig*) (= *sentimentality*) lenguaje *m* sentimental, sentimentalismo *m*

▼ **good** [gʊd]

A ADJECTIVE	C NOUN
B ADVERB	D COMPOUNDS

Ⓐ ADJECTIVE (*compar* **better**, *superl* **best**)

When **good** *is part of a set combination, eg* **in a good temper, a good deal of, good heavens,** *look up the noun.*

The commonest translation of **good** *is* **bueno,** *which must be shortened to* **buen** *before a masculine singular noun.*

1 *= satisfactory* 1·1 bueno; **a ~ book** un buen libro; **at the end of the day, it's a ~ investment** a fin de cuentas es una buena inversión

Note that **bueno/buena** *etc precede the noun in general comments where there is no attempt to compare or rank the person or thing involved:*

if he set his mind to it, he could be a very ~ painter si se lo propusiera podría ser muy buen pintor; **she was a ~ wife and mother** era una buena esposa y madre; **she has a ~ figure** tiene buen tipo

Bueno/buena *etc follow the noun when there is implied or explicit comparison:*

we could make a list of ~ teachers podríamos hacer una lista de profesores buenos; **I'm not saying it's a ~ thing or a bad thing** no digo que sea una cosa buena, ni mala

Use **ser** *rather than* **estar** *with* **bueno** *when translating* **to be good**, *unless describing food:*

the idea is a ~ one la idea es buena; **it's ~ to be aware of the views of intelligent people** es bueno conocer los puntos de vista de la gente inteligente; **the paella was very ~** la paella estaba muy buena

Use **estar** *with the adverb* **bien** *to give a general comment on a situation:*

you've written a book, which is ~ has escrito un libro, lo que está bien; **his hearing is ~** del oído está bien, el oído lo tiene bien

1·2 **she's ~ at maths** se le dan bien las matemáticas, es buena en matemáticas; **she's ~ at singing** canta bien; **she's ~ at putting people at their ease** tiene la capacidad de hacer que la gente se sienta relajada; **that's ~ enough for me** eso me basta; **it's just not ~ enough!** ¡esto no se puede consentir!; **40% of candidates are not ~ enough to pass** el 40% de los candidatos no dan el nivel *or* la talla para aprobar; **to feel ~** sentirse bien; **I started to feel ~ about myself again** empecé a recuperar mi autoestima *or* la moral; **I don't feel very ~ about that*** (= *I'm rather ashamed*) me da bastante vergüenza; **we've never had it so ~!*** ¡nunca nos ha ido tan bien!, ¡jamás lo hemos tenido tan fácil!; **how ~ is her eyesight?** ¿qué tal está de la vista?; **you're looking ~** ¡qué guapa estás!; **things are looking ~** las cosas van bien, la cosa tiene buena pinta*; **you look ~ in that** eso te sienta *or* te va bien; **you can have too much of a ~ thing** lo mucho cansa (y lo poco agrada); **it's too ~ to be true** no puede ser, es demasiado bueno para ser cierto; **he sounds too ~ to be true!** ¡algún defecto tiene que tener!; **she's ~ with cats** entiende bien a los gatos, sabe manejarse bien con los gatos; *see also* **good B4, manner 4.1, mood² A, time A5**

2 *= of high quality* **always use ~ ingredients** utilice siempre ingredientes de calidad *or* los mejores ingredientes; **it's made of ~ leather** está hecho con cuero del bueno

3 *= pleasant* [*holiday, day*] bueno, agradable; [*weather, news*] bueno; **it was as ~ as a holiday** aquello fue como unas vacaciones; **have a ~ journey!** ¡buen viaje!; **how ~ it is to know that ...!** ¡cuánto me alegro de saber que ...!; **it's ~ to see you** me alegro de verte, gusto en verte (*LAm*); **it's ~ to be here** da gusto estar aquí; **have a ~ trip!** ¡buen viaje!; *see also* **alive 1, life A3**

4 *= beneficial, wholesome* [*food*] bueno, sano; [*air*] puro, sano; **it's ~ for burns** es bueno para las quemaduras; **it's ~ for you** *or* **your health** te hace bien; **spirits are not ~ for me** los licores no me sientan bien; **he eats more than is ~ for him** come más de lo que le conviene; **all this excitement isn't ~ for me!** ¡a mí todas estas emociones no me vienen *or* sientan nada bien!; **it's ~ for the soul!** (*hum*) ¡ennoblece el espíritu!, ¡te enriquece (como persona)!; **if you know what's ~ for you you'll say yes** por la cuenta que te tiene dirás que sí; **some children know more than is ~ for them** algunos niños son demasiado listos *or* saben demasiado

5 *= favourable* [*moment, chance*] bueno; **it's a ~ chance to sort things out** es una buena oportunidad de *or* para arreglar las cosas; **I tried to find something ~ to say about him** traté de encontrar algo bueno que decir de él; **it would be a ~ thing** *or* **idea to ask him** no estaría mal *or* no sería mala idea preguntárselo; **this is as ~ a time as any to do it** es tan buen momento como cualquier otro para hacerlo

6 *= useful* **the only ~ chair** la única silla que está bien, la única silla servible *or* sana; **to be ~ for (doing) sth** servir para (hacer) algo; **it'll be ~ for some years** durará todavía algunos años; **he's ~ for ten years yet** tiene todavía por delante diez años de vida; **John's ~ for a few hundred pounds*** John seguramente puede prestarnos unos cientos de libras; **I'm ~ for another mile** todavía puedo aguantar otra milla más; **the ticket is ~ for three months** el billete es válido *or* valedero para tres meses; **he's ~ for nothing** es un inútil, es completamente inútil

7 *= sound, valid* [*excuse*] bueno; **unless you have a ~ excuse** a menos que tengas una buena excusa; **for no ~ reason** sin motivo alguno; **he is a ~ risk** (*financially*) concederle crédito es un riesgo asumible, se le puede prestar dinero; *see also* **word A1**

8 *= kind* **that's very ~ of you** es usted muy amable, ¡qué amable (de su parte)!; **he was so ~ as to come with me** tuvo la amabilidad de acompañarme; **please would you be so ~ as to help me down with my case?** ¿me hace el favor de bajarme la maleta?, ¿tendría la bondad de bajarme la maleta? (*more frm*); **would you be so ~ as to sign here?** ¿me hace el favor de firmar aquí?; **he's a ~ sort** es buena persona *or* gente; **he was ~ to me** fue muy bueno *or* amable conmigo, se portó bien conmigo; *see also* **nature A2**

9 *= well-behaved* [*child*] bueno; **be ~!** (*morally*) ¡sé bueno!; (*in behaviour*) ¡pórtate bien!; (*at this moment*) ¡estáte formal!; ✦***IDIOM*** **to be as ~ as gold*** portarse como un ángel *or* santo

10 *= upright, virtuous* bueno; **he's a ~ man** es una buena persona, es un buen hombre; **I think I'm as ~ as him** yo me considero tan buena persona como él; **the 12 ~ men and true** los doce hombres justos; **yes, my ~ man** sí, mi querido amigo; **send us a photo of your ~ self** (*frm*) tenga a bien enviarnos una foto suya; **she's too ~ for him** ella es más de lo que él se merece; *see also* **lady A5**

11 *= close* bueno; **he's a ~ friend of mine** es un buen amigo mío; **my ~ friend Fernando** mi buen *or* querido amigo Fernando

12 *= middle-class, respectable* **to live at a ~ address** vivir en una buena zona *or* en un buen barrio; **he's got no money but he's of ~ family** no tiene dinero pero es *or* viene de buena familia

13 *= creditable* **he came in a ~ third** llegó en un meritorio tercer puesto

14 *= considerable* [*supply, number*] bueno; **we were kept waiting for a ~ hour/thirty minutes** nos tuvieron esperando una hora/media hora larga, nos tuvieron esperando por lo menos una hora/media hora; **a ~ three hours** tres horas largas; **a ~ 10km** 10kms largos; **a ~ £10** lo menos 10 libras; **a ~ many** *or* **few people** bastante gente

15 *= thorough* [*scolding*] bueno; **to have a ~ cry** llorar a lágrima viva, llorar a moco tendido*; **to have a ~ laugh** reírse mucho; **to take a ~ look (at sth)** mirar bien (algo); **to have a ~ wash** lavarse bien

16 **the ~ ship Domino** el (buque) Domino

17 *in greetings* **~ afternoon/evening** buenas tardes; **~ morning** buenos días; **~ night** buenas noches; **with every ~ wish** ◊ **with all ~ wishes** (*in letter*) saludos, un fuerte abrazo;

➤ LANGUAGE IN USE: **good A2** 16.4 **A18** 13

Robert sends (his) ~ wishes Robert manda recuerdos

18 *in exclamations* **good!** ¡muy bien!; **(that's) ~!** ¡qué bien!, ¡qué bueno! (*LAm*); **very ~, sir** sí, señor; **~ for you!** ¡bien hecho!; (= *congratulations*) ¡enhorabuena!; **~ one!** (= *well done, well said*) ¡muy bien!, ¡sí señor!; *see also* **old A5, A6**

19 *in other set expressions*

◆ **as good as**: **it's as ~ as new** está como nuevo; **I'll soon be as ~ as new** pronto estaré como nuevo; **the job is as ~ as done** el trabajo puede darse por acabado; **it's as ~ as lost** puede darse por perdido; **they're as ~ as beaten** pueden darse por vencidos; **as ~ as saying ...** tanto como decir ...; **she as ~ as told me so** poco menos que me lo dijo; **he as ~ as called me a liar** me llamó poco menos que mentiroso

◆ **to come good**: **things will come ~ eventually*** todo se arreglará al final

◆ **good and ...**: **~ and hot*** bien calentito*; **~ and strong*** bien fuerte; **I'll do it when I'm ~ and ready*** lo haré cuando a mí me parezca

◆ **to hold good** valer (**for** para); **the same advice holds ~ for us** el mismo consejo vale para nosotros

◆ **it's a good job**: **(it's a) ~ job he came!*** ¡menos mal que ha venido!; *see also* **make A3, A10, B, riddance, thing A2**

Ⓑ ADVERB

1 *as intensifier* bien; **a ~ strong stick** un palo bien fuerte; **a ~ long walk** un paseo bien largo, un buen paseo; ✦*IDIOM* **to give as ~ as one gets** pagar con la misma moneda, devolver golpe por golpe

◆ **good and proper**: **they were beaten ~ and proper*** les dieron una buena paliza*; **they were cheated ~ and proper*** les timaron bien timados*, les timaron con todas las de la ley*

2 *esp US* = well* bien; **you did ~** hiciste bien; **"how are you?" — "thanks, I'm ~"** —¿cómo estás? —muy bien, gracias

Ⓒ NOUN

1 = *virtuousness* el bien; **to do ~** hacer (el) bien; **~ and evil** el bien y el mal; **he is a power for ~** su influencia es muy buena *or* beneficiosa, hace mucho bien; **for ~ or ill** para bien o para mal; **there's some ~ in him** tiene algo bueno; **to be up to no ~*** estar tramando algo

2 = *advantage, benefit* bien *m*; **the common ~** el bien común; **if it's any ~ to you** si te sirve de algo; **a rest will do you some ~** un descanso te sentará bien; **the sea air does you ~** el aire del mar le hace *or* sienta a uno bien; **a (fat) lot of ~ that will do you!*** (*iro*) ¡menudo provecho te va a traer!; **much ~ may it do you!** ¡no creo que te sirva de mucho!, ¡para lo que te va a servir!; **it does my heart ~ to see him** verlo me alegra la existencia; **for your own ~** por tu propio bien; **for the ~ of the country** por el bien del país; **to be in ~ with sb** estar a bien con algn; **that's all to the ~!** ¡menos mal!; **what ~ will that do you?** ¿y eso de qué te va a servir?; **what's the ~ of worrying?** ¿de qué sirve *or* para qué preocuparse?

3 = *people of virtue* **the good** los buenos

4 *in set expressions*

◆ **any good**: **is he any ~?** [*worker, singer etc*] ¿qué tal lo hace?, ¿lo hace bien?; **is this any ~?** ¿sirve esto?; **is she any ~ at cooking?** ¿qué tal cocina?, ¿cocina bien?

◆ **for good (and all)** (= *for ever*) para siempre; **he's gone for ~** se ha ido para siempre *or* para no volver

◆ **no good**: **it's no ~** (= *no use*) no sirve; **it's no ~, I'll never get it finished in time** así no hay manera, nunca lo terminaré a tiempo; **it's no ~ saying that** de nada sirve *or* vale decir eso; **it's no ~ worrying** de nada sirve *or* vale preocuparse, no se saca nada preocupándose; **that's no ~** eso no vale *or* sirve; **I'm no ~ at maths** las matemáticas no se me dan nada bien; **that's no ~ to me** eso no me sirve para nada; **to come to no ~** acabar mal

Ⓓ COMPOUNDS

► **the Good Book** N (*Rel*) la Biblia ► **good deeds** NPL = **good works** ► **good faith** N buena fe *f*; **in ~ faith** de buena fe ► **Good Friday** N (*Rel*) Viernes *m* Santo ► **good looks** NPL atractivo *msing* físico ► **good works** NPL buenas obras *fpl*

goodbye ['gʊd'baɪ] Ⓐ EXCL ¡adiós!, ¡hasta luego! Ⓑ N despedida *f*; **to say ~ to** (*lit*) [+ *person*] despedirse de; (*fig*) [+ *thing*] despedirse de, dar por perdido; **you can say ~ to your wallet** ya puedes despedirte de tu cartera, ya no volverás a ver la cartera

good-for-nothing ['gʊdfə'nʌθɪŋ] Ⓐ ADJ inútil Ⓑ N inútil *mf*, gandul(a) *m/f*

good-hearted [,gʊd'hɑːtɪd] ADJ de buen corazón

good-humoured, good-humored (*US*) ['gʊd'hjuːməd] ADJ [*person*] amable, de buen humor; [*remark, joke*] jovial; [*discussion*] de tono amistoso

good-humouredly, good-humoredly (*US*) [,gʊd'hjuːmədlɪ] ADV [*say*] de buen humor; [*tease*] amistosamente

good-looker* [,gʊd'lʊkər] N (= *man*) tío *m* bueno*; (= *woman*) tía *f* buena*; (= *horse etc*) caballo *m etc* de buena estampa

good-looking ['gʊd'lʊkɪŋ] ADJ guapo, bien parecido

goodly ['gʊdlɪ] (*frm*) ADJ 1 (= *fine*) agradable, excelente; (= *handsome*) bien parecido
2 [*sum etc*] importante; [*number*] crecido

good-natured ['gʊd'neɪtʃəd] ADJ [*person*] amable, simpático; [*discussion*] de tono amistoso

good-naturedly [,gʊd'neɪtʃədlɪ] ADV [*complain, joke*] con cordialidad

goodness ['gʊdnɪs] N 1 (= *virtue*) bondad *f*
2 (= *kindness*) amabilidad *f*; **out of the ~ of his heart** de lo bondadoso que es
3 (= *good quality*) calidad *f*
4 (= *essence*) sustancia *f*, lo mejor
5 (*) (*in phrases*) **(my) ~!** ◊ **~ gracious!** ¡Dios mío!; **thank ~!** ¡menos mal!; **for ~' sake!** ¡por Dios!; **I wish to ~ I'd never met him** ojalá nunca lo hubiera conocido

➤**goods** [gʊdz] Ⓐ NPL (= *possessions*) bienes *mpl*; (= *products*) productos *mpl*; (*Comm etc*) géneros *mpl*, mercancías *fpl*; (= *objects*) artículos *mpl*; **leather ~** géneros *mpl* de cuero; **canned ~** conservas *fpl* en lata; **consumer ~** bienes *mpl* de consumo; **~ and chattels** bienes *mpl*; ✦*IDIOM* **to deliver the ~** cumplir con lo prometido
Ⓑ CPD ► **goods siding** N apartadero *m* de mercancías ► **goods station** N estación *f* de mercancías ► **goods train** N tren *m* de mercancías ► **goods vehicle** N vehículo *m* de transporte, camión *m* ► **goods wagon** N vagón *m* de mercancías ► **goods yard** N estación *f* de mercancías

good-tempered ['gʊd'tempəd] ADJ [*person*] amable, de buen humor; [*tone*] afable, amistoso; [*discussion*] sereno, sin pasión

good-time girl* [,guːdtaɪm'gɜːl] N chica *f* alegre

goodwill ['gʊd'wɪl] Ⓐ N 1 buena voluntad *f*; **as a gesture of ~** como muestra de buena voluntad
2 (*Comm*) clientela *f* y renombre *m* comercial
Ⓑ CPD ► **goodwill ambassador** N embajador(a) *m/f* de buena voluntad ► **goodwill mission** N misión *f* de buena voluntad

goody* ['gʊdɪ] Ⓐ ADJ (*esp US*) beatuco*, santurrón Ⓑ EXCL (*also* ~ ~) ¡qué bien!, ¡qué estupendo!*
Ⓒ N 1 (*Culin*) golosina *f*
2 (*Cine*) bueno/a *m/f*; **the goodies** los buenos
Ⓓ CPD ► **goody bag*** N bolsa *f* de regalos

goody-goody* (*pej*) [,gʊdɪ'gʊdɪ] Ⓐ ADJ beatuco*, santurrón Ⓑ N (*pl* **goody-goodies**) santurrón/ona *m/f*

gooey* ['guːɪ] ADJ (*compar* **gooier**; *superl* **gooiest**) pegajoso, viscoso; (= *sweet*) empalagoso

goof* [guːf] Ⓐ N bobo/a *m/f*
Ⓑ VI 1 (= *err*) tirarse una plancha*
2 (*US*) (*also* ~ **off**) gandulear

►**goof around*** VI + ADV (*US*) hacer el tonto

goofy* ['guːfɪ] ADJ (*compar* **goofier**; *superl* **goofiest**) 1 (*esp US*) (= *silly*) bobo
2 [*teeth*] salido, de conejo*

Google® ['guːgl] Ⓐ N Google® *m* Ⓑ VI buscar *or* hacer búsquedas en Google®, buscar *or* hacer búsquedas en Internet Ⓒ VT (= *do search on*) [+ *person*] buscar información *or* hacer una búsqueda en Google® sobre, buscar información en Internet sobre

gook‡ [guːk] N (*US pej*) asiático/a *m/f*

goolies‡‡ ['guːlɪz] N pelotas‡‡ *fpl*, cataplines *mpl* (*Sp*‡‡)

goon [guːn] N 1 (= *fool*) imbécil *mf*
2 (*US*) (= *thug*) gorila *m*, matón/ona *m/f*; (*Hist*) *gorila contratado para sembrar el terror entre los obreros*

goose [guːs] (*pl* **geese**) Ⓐ N (*domestic*) ganso/a *m/f*, oca *f*; (*wild*) ánsar *m*; ✦*IDIOMS* **to cook sb's ~** hacer la santísima a algn; **to kill the ~ that lays the golden eggs** matar la gallina de los huevos de oro
Ⓑ VT (*) (= *prod*) meter mano a
Ⓒ CPD ► **goose bumps** NPL = **gooseflesh** ► **goose pimples** NPL = **gooseflesh**

gooseberry ['gʊzbərɪ] Ⓐ N 1 (*Bot*) grosella *f* espinosa
2 (*Brit*) ✦*IDIOM* **to play ~** hacer de carabina
Ⓑ CPD ► **gooseberry bush** N grosellero *m* espinoso

gooseflesh ['guːsfleʃ] N carne *f* de gallina

goose-step ['guːsstep] Ⓐ N paso *m* de ganso, paso *m* de la oca
Ⓑ VI marchar a paso de ganso *or* de la oca

GOP N ABBR (*US Pol*) (= **Grand Old Party**) Partido *m* Republicano

gopher ['gəʊfər] N 1 (*Zool*) ardillón *m*
2 (*Comput*) gopher *m* 3 = **gofer**

gorblimey‡ [,gɔː'blaɪmɪ] EXCL (*Brit*) ¡puñetas!‡

Gordian ['gɔːdɪən] ADJ ✦*IDIOM* **to cut the ~ knot** cortar el nudo gordiano

gore[1] [gɔːr] N (= *blood*) sangre *f* derramada

gore[2] [gɔːr] VT (= *injure*) cornear

gorge [gɔːdʒ] Ⓐ N 1 (*Geog*) cañón *m*, barranco *m* 2 (*Anat*) garganta *f*; **my ~ rises at it** me da asco Ⓑ VT **to ~ o.s.** atracarse (**with, on** de) Ⓒ VI atracarse (**on** de)

gorgeous ['gɔːdʒəs] ADJ 1 (= *lovely*) [*object, scenery, colour, music*] precioso; [*food, wine*] delicioso, riquísimo; [*weather*] espléndido, magnífico; **she wears the most ~ clothes** lleva

➤ LANGUAGE IN USE: goods A 20.5

una ropa preciosa; **~ silks and jewels** sedas y joyas preciosas *or* espléndidas; **oh! it's absolutely ~!** ¡oh! ¡es una preciosidad!; **the garden looks absolutely ~** el jardín está precioso; **it smells ~** huele delicioso; **this tastes ~** está riquísimo; **the weather was ~** hacía un tiempo espléndido *or* magnífico; **what a ~ day!** ¡hace un día precioso *or* espléndido!

[2] (*) (= *beautiful*) [*woman*] guapísimo, precioso; [*man*] guapísimo; [*child, baby*] riquísimo*, monísimo*; [*eyes, hair*] precioso; **he/she's ~!** ¡es guapísimo/guapísima!; **hello, ~!*** (*to woman*) ¡hola, preciosa!*; (*to man*) ¡hola, guapo!*; **what a ~ hunk!‡** ¡qué tío más bueno!‡; *see also* **drop-dead**

gorgeously ['gɔːdʒəslɪ] ADV [*dressed*] magníficamente, divinamente; [*decorated*] espléndidamente, magníficamente; **it is a ~ decadent work** es una obra fastuosamente decadente

gorgon ['gɔːgən] N [1] **Gorgon** (*Myth*) Gorgona *f*

[2] (*fig*) (= *woman*) pécora *f*

gorilla [gə'rɪlə] N [1] (*Zool*) gorila *m*

[2] (*) (= *thug*) gorila *m*

gormandize ['gɔːməndaɪz] VI (*frm*) glotonear

gormless* ['gɔːmlɪs] ADJ (*Brit*) corto (de entendimiento)*

gorse [gɔːs] N aulaga *f*, tojo *m*

gory ['gɔːrɪ] ADJ (*compar* **gorier**, *superl* **goriest**) [*battle, death*] sangriento; **he told me all the ~ details** (*hum*) me contó todo con pelos y señales

gosh* [gɒʃ] EXCL ¡cielos!; **~ darn!** (*US*) ¡caramba!

goshawk ['gɒshɔːk] N azor *m*

gosling ['gɒzlɪŋ] N ansarino *m*

go-slow ['gəʊ'sləʊ] Ⓐ N (*Brit Ind*) huelga *f* de brazos caídos

Ⓑ VI hacer huelga de celo; (*strictly*) trabajar con arreglo a las bases

gospel ['gɒspəl] Ⓐ N (*Rel*) evangelio *m*; **the Gospel according to St John** el Evangelio según San Juan; ✦*IDIOM* **to take sth as ~*** aceptar algo como si estuviera escrito en el evangelio

Ⓑ CPD ► **gospel music** N música *f* espiritual negra ► **gospel song** N canción *f* espiritual negra ► **gospel truth** N **as though it were ~ truth** como si estuviera escrito en el evangelio

gossamer ['gɒsəməʳ] N (= *web*) telaraña *f*; (= *fabric*) gasa *f*; **~-thin** muy delgado

gossip ['gɒsɪp] Ⓐ N [1] (= *scandal, malicious stories*) cotilleo *m*, chismorreo *m*

[2] (= *chatter*) charla *f*; **we had a good old ~** charlamos un buen rato

[3] (= *person*) cotilla *mf*, chismoso/a *m/f*

Ⓑ VI [1] (= *scandalmonger*) cotillear, chismorrear

[2] (= *chatter*) charlar

Ⓒ CPD ► **gossip column** N ecos *mpl* de sociedad ► **gossip columnist**, **gossip writer** N cronista *mf* de sociedad

gossiping ['gɒsɪpɪŋ] Ⓐ ADJ cotilla, chismoso

Ⓑ N cotilleo *m*, chismorreo *m*

gossipy ['gɒsɪpɪ] ADJ de cotilleo, chismoso; [*style*] familiar, anecdótico

got [gɒt] PT, PP *of* **get**

Goth [gɒθ] N (*Hist*) godo/a *m/f*

Gothic ['gɒθɪk] Ⓐ ADJ [*race*] godo; (*Archit, Typ*) gótico; [*novel etc*] gótico

Ⓑ N (*Archit, Ling etc*) gótico *m*

gotta* ['gɒtə] (*esp US*) = **got to**

gotten ['gɒtn] (*US*) PP *of* **get**

gouache [gʊ'ɑːʃ] N guache *m*, gouache *m*

gouge [gaʊdʒ] Ⓐ N gubia *f*

Ⓑ VT [+ *hole etc*] excavar

►**gouge out** VT + ADV [+ *hole etc*] excavar; **to ~ sb's eyes out** sacar los ojos a algn

goulash ['guːlæʃ] N *especie de guisado húngaro*

gourd [gʊəd] N calabaza *f*

gourmand ['gʊəmənd] N glotón/ona *m/f*

gourmet ['gʊəmeɪ] Ⓐ N gastrónomo/a *m/f*

Ⓑ ADJ [*food, dinner*] de gastronomía; **~ cooking** la gastronomía

gout [gaʊt] N (*Med*) gota *f*

gouty ['gaʊtɪ] ADJ gotoso

gov‡ [gʌv] N ABBR (*Brit*) (= **governor**) jefe *m*, patrón *m*; **yes ~!** ¡sí, jefe!

Gov. ABBR = **Governor**

govern ['gʌvən] Ⓐ VT [1] (= *rule*) [+ *country*] gobernar

[2] (= *control*) [+ *city, business*] dirigir; [+ *choice, decision*] guiar; [+ *emotions*] dominar

[3] (*Ling*) regir

Ⓑ VI (*Pol*) gobernar

governance ['gʌvənəns] N (*frm*) forma *f* de gobierno

governess ['gʌvənɪs] N institutriz *f*, gobernanta *f*

governing ['gʌvənɪŋ] Ⓐ ADJ (*Pol*) [*party*] gobernante, en el gobierno

Ⓑ CPD ► **governing board** N (*Brit Scol*) consejo *m* directivo de escuela ► **governing body** N consejo *m* de administración ► **governing principle** N principio *m* rector

government ['gʌvnmənt] Ⓐ N [1] (*Pol*) gobierno *m*; **the Labour Government** el gobierno *or* la administración laborista; *see also* **local C**

[2] (*Gram etc*) régimen *m*

Ⓑ CPD [*intervention, support, loan*] estatal, del estado; [*responsibility, decision*] gubernamental, del gobierno ► **government body** N ente *m* gubernamental *or* oficial ► **government bonds** NPL bonos *mpl* del Estado ► **government department** N ministerio *m*, departamento *m* gubernamental, secretaría *f* (*Mex*) ► **government expenditure** N = **government spending** ► **government grant** N subvención *f* estatal ► **government health warning** N ≈ advertencia *f* del Ministerio de Sanidad ► **Government House** N (*Brit*) palacio *m* del gobernador/de la gobernadora ► **government issue** N propiedad *f* del Estado ► **government policy** N política *f* gubernamental *or* del gobierno ► **government securities** NPL bonos *mpl* del Estado ► **government spending** N el gasto público ► **government stock** N reservas *fpl* del Estado ► **government subsidy** N subvención *f* estatal, subvención *f* del gobierno

governmental [,gʌvən'mentl] ADJ gubernamental, gubernativo

government-owned [,gʌvənmənt'əʊnd] ADJ [*company, industry*] del Estado, estatal; [*land*] del Estado

governor ['gʌvənəʳ] Ⓐ N [1] [*of colony, state etc*] gobernador(a) *m/f*

[2] (*esp Brit*) [*of prison*] director(a) *m/f*

[3] (*Brit*) [*of school*] miembro *mf* del consejo

[4] (*Brit‡*) (= *boss*) jefe *m*, patrón *m*; (= *father*) viejo* *m*; **thanks, ~!** ¡gracias, jefe!

[5] (*Mech*) regulador *m*

Ⓑ CPD ► **governor general** N (*Brit*) gobernador(a) *m/f* general

governorship ['gʌvənəʃɪp] N gobierno *m*, cargo *m* de gobernador(a)

Govt., **govt.** ABBR (= **government**) gob.^no^

gown [gaʊn] N (= *dress*) vestido *m* largo; (*Jur, Univ*) toga *f*

GP N ABBR (= **general practitioner**) médico/a *m/f* de cabecera

GPA N ABBR (*US*) = **grade-point average**

GPMU (*Brit*) N ABBR (= **Graphical, Paper and Media Union**) *sindicato de trabajadores del sector editorial*

GPO N ABBR [1] (*Brit*) (*formerly*) = **General Post Office**

[2] (*US*) = **Government Printing Office**

gr. ABBR [1] = **gross** (= *12 dozen*) gruesa *f*

[2] (*Comm*) (= **gross**) bto

grab [græb] Ⓐ N [1] (= *snatch*) **to make a ~ at** *or* **for sth** intentar agarrar algo; **it's all up for ~s*** está a disposición de cualquiera

[2] (*esp Brit Tech*) cuchara *f*

Ⓑ VT [1] (= *seize*) coger, agarrar (*LAm*); (*greedily*) echar mano a; **to ~ sth from sb** arrebatarle algo a algn; **to ~ hold of sth/sb** agarrar algo/a algn

[2] (*fig*) [+ *chance etc*] aprovechar; **I'll just ~ a quick shower** me voy a dar una ducha rápida; **we can ~ a sandwich on the way** comeremos un bocadillo por el camino; **I managed to ~ him before he left** conseguí pillarle antes de que se marchara

[3] (*) (= *attract, appeal to*) **how does that ~ you?** ¿qué te parece?; **that really ~bed me** aquello me entusiasmó de verdad; **it doesn't ~ me** no me va

Ⓒ VI **to ~ at** (= *snatch*) tratar de coger *or* (*LAm*) agarrar; (*in falling*) tratar de asir

grace [greɪs] Ⓐ N [1] (= *elegance*) [*of form, movement etc*] gracia *f*, elegancia *f*; [*of style*] elegancia *f*, amenidad *f*

[2] (*Rel*) gracia *f*, gracia *f* divina; **by the ~ of God** por la gracia de Dios; **there but for the ~ of God go I** le podría ocurrir a cualquiera; **to fall from ~** (*Rel*) perder la gracia divina; (*fig*) caer en desgracia

[3] (= *graciousness*) cortesía *f*, gracia *f*; **he had the ~ to apologize** tuvo la cortesía de pedir perdón; **with (a) good ~** de buen talante; **with (a) bad ~** a regañadientes; *see also* **saving B**

[4] **to get into sb's good ~s** congraciarse con algn

[5] (= *respite*) demora *f*; **days of ~** (*Brit Jur*) días *mpl* de gracia; **three days' ~** un plazo de tres días

[6] (= *prayer*) bendición *f* de la mesa; **to say ~** bendecir la mesa

[7] (*in titles*) [7·1] (= *duke*) **His Grace the Duke** su Excelencia el duque; **yes, Your Grace** sí, Excelencia

[7·2] (*Rel*) **His Grace Archbishop Roberts** su Ilustrísima, Arzobispo Roberts; **yes, your Grace** sí, Ilustrísima

Ⓑ VT [1] (= *adorn*) adornar, embellecer

[2] (= *honour*) [+ *occasion, event*] honrar; **he ~d the meeting with his presence** honró a los asistentes con su presencia; *see also* **presence 1**

Ⓒ CPD ► **grace note** N (*Mus*) apoyadura *f* ► **grace period** N (*Jur, Fin*) período *m* de gracia

graceful ['greɪsfʊl] ADJ [1] (= *elegant*) [*person, animal, building*] elegante

[2] (= *flowing*) [*movement*] elegante, airoso; [*lines*] grácil

[3] (= *dignified*) digno; **he was never a ~ loser** nunca supo perder con dignidad

gracefully ['greɪsfəlɪ] ADV [1] (= *elegantly*) [*move*] elegantemente

[2] (= *in a dignified manner*) con dignidad; **to grow old ~** envejecer con dignidad; **he never could lose ~** nunca supo perder con digni-

dad; **she apologized, none too ~** pidió perdón a regañadientes

graceless ['greɪslɪs] ADJ (= *inelegant*) desgarbado, torpe; (= *impolite*) descortés, grosero

gracious ['greɪʃəs] Ⓐ ADJ **1** (= *refined, courteous*) [*person, gesture, smile, letter*] gentil, cortés; [*era*] refinado; **by (the) ~ consent of** (*frm*) por la gracia de; **to be ~ enough to do sth** tener la cortesía de hacer algo; **he was ~ in defeat/victory** era correcto a la hora de la derrota/del triunfo; **he has always been a ~ loser** siempre ha sabido perder con dignidad; **by ~ permission of Her Majesty the Queen** (*frm*) por la gracia de Su Majestad la Reina; **to be ~ to sb** ser gentil *or* cortés con algn
2 (= *merciful*) [*God*] misericordioso
3 (= *elegant, comfortable*) [*place, building*] elegante, refinado; **she loved fine clothes and ~ living** le encantaba la ropa elegante y la vida refinada
Ⓑ EXCL **~!** ◊ **good ~ (me)!** ¡Santo cielo!, ¡Dios mío!; **"you know Jack, don't you?" — "good ~, yes!"** —conoces a Jack, ¿no? —¡por supuesto que sí!; **good ~, what does that matter!** ¡por amor de Dios! ¿qué importancia tiene eso?; *see also* **goodness 5**

graciously ['greɪʃəslɪ] ADV [*wave, smile*] gentilmente, cortésmente; [*accept*] gentilmente; [*live*] con refinamiento; **she has ~ consented to be my wife** (*frm*) ha tenido la gentileza de aceptar mi propuesta de matrimonio; **His Royal Highness has ~ consented to our proposal** (*frm*) Su Alteza se ha dignado aceptar nuestra propuesta

graciousness ['greɪʃəsnɪs] N **1** (= *refinement, courtesy*) [*of person*] gentileza *f*, cortesía *f*; [*of gesture*] gentileza *f*, gracia *f*; **~ in defeat/victory** la corrección a la hora de la derrota/del triunfo
2 [*of God*] misericordia *f*
3 (= *elegance, comfort*) [*of house, room*] elegancia *f*, refinamiento *m*

grad* [græd] (*US*) N = **graduate**

gradate [grə'deɪt] Ⓐ VT degradar
Ⓑ VI degradarse

gradation [grə'deɪʃən] N gradación *f*

grade [greɪd] Ⓐ N **1** (= *level, standard*) (*on scale*) clase *f*, categoría *f*; (*in job*) grado *m*, categoría *f*; **to be promoted to a higher ~** ser ascendido a un grado *or* una categoría superior; ✦*IDIOM* **to make the ~** llegar, alcanzar el nivel
2 (*Mil*) (= *rank*) graduación *f*, grado *m*
3 (= *quality*) clase *f*, calidad *f*; **high-/low-~ material** material *m* de alta/baja calidad
4 (*Scol*) (= *mark*) nota *f*
5 (*US*) (= *school class*) **he's in fifth ~** está en quinto (curso); → [HIGH SCHOOL]
6 (*US*) (= *gradient*) pendiente *f*, cuesta *f*
7 (*US*) (= *ground level*) **at ~** al nivel del suelo
Ⓑ VT **1** [+ *goods, eggs*] clasificar, graduar; [+ *colours*] degradar
2 (*Scol*) (= *mark*) calificar
Ⓒ CPD ► **grade crossing** N (*US Rail*) paso *m* a nivel ► **grade school** N (*US*) escuela *f* primaria

►**grade down** VT + ADV bajar de categoría

►**grade up** VT + ADV subir de categoría

graded ['greɪdɪd] ADJ graduado

grader ['greɪdəʳ] N (*US Scol*) examinador(a) *m/f*

gradient ['greɪdɪənt] N (*esp Brit*) pendiente *f*, cuesta *f*; **a ~ of one in seven** una pendiente del uno por siete

grading ['greɪdɪŋ] N (*gen*) graduación *f*; (*by size*) gradación *f*; (*Scol etc*) calificación *f*

gradual ['grædjʊəl] ADJ **1** (= *slow*) [*change, improvement, decline*] gradual, paulatino
2 (= *not steep*) [*slope, incline*] suave

> **GRADE**
>
> *En Estados Unidos y Canadá, los cursos escolares se denominan* **grades**, *desde el primer año de primaria* **first grade** *hasta el último curso de la enseñanza secundaria* **twelfth grade**. *A los alumnos de los últimos cursos se les suele conocer por un nombre distinto según el curso en el que estén:* **freshmen** *si están en el* **9th grade**, **sophomores** *si están en el* **10th grade**, **juniors** *en el* **11th grade** *y* **seniors** *en el* **12th grade**.
>
> ⇨ *Ver tb* [HIGH SCHOOL]

gradually ['grædjʊəlɪ] ADV **1** (= *slowly*) gradualmente, paulatinamente; **the situation was ~ improving** la situación iba mejorando gradualmente *or* paulatinamente
2 (= *not steeply*) suavemente; **the ground rises ~ to the north** el terreno se va elevando suavemente hacia el norte

gradualism ['grædjʊəlɪzəm] N gradualismo *m*

graduate ['grædjʊɪt] Ⓐ N **1** (*Univ*) licenciado/a *m/f*, graduado/a *m/f*, egresado/a *m/f* (*LAm*)
2 (*US Scol*) bachiller *mf*
Ⓑ ['grædjʊeɪt] VT **1** [+ *thermometer etc*] graduar
2 (*US Scol, Univ*) otorgar el título a
Ⓒ ['grædjʊeɪt] VI **1** (*Univ*) graduarse *or* licenciarse (**from** en), recibirse (*LAm*) (**as** de)
2 (*US Scol*) acabar el bachiller
3 (= *progress*) **to ~ from sth to sth** pasar de algo a algo
Ⓓ ['grædjʊɪt] CPD ► **graduate course** N curso *m* para graduados ► **graduate school** N (*US*) departamento *m* de graduados ► **graduate student** N (*US*) estudiante *mf* de posgrado; → [COLLEGE]

graduated ['grædjʊeɪtɪd] Ⓐ ADJ [*tube, flask, tax etc*] graduado; **in ~ stages** en pasos escalonados
Ⓑ CPD ► **graduated pension** N (*Brit*) pensión *f* escalonada

graduation [ˌgrædjʊ'eɪʃən] N (*Univ etc*) (= *ceremony*) entrega *f* del título universitario; (*US Scol*) entrega *f* del título de bachiller

graffiti [grə'fiːtɪ] Ⓐ NPL graffiti *msing or pl*, pintadas *fpl*
Ⓑ CPD ► **graffiti artist** N artista *mf* de graffiti

graffito [græ'fiːtəʊ] NSING *of* **graffiti**

graft¹ [grɑːft] (*Bot, Med*) Ⓐ N injerto *m*
Ⓑ VT injertar (**in, into, on to** en)

graft² [grɑːft] Ⓐ N **1** (*US*) (= *corruption*) soborno *m*, coima *f* (*Andes, S. Cone*), mordida *f* (*CAm, Mex*)
2 (*Brit**) **hard ~** trabajo *m* muy duro
Ⓑ VI **1** (*Brit**) (= *work*) currar*
2 (= *swindle*) trampear

grafter ['grɑːftəʳ] N **1** (= *swindler etc*) timador(a) *m/f*, estafador(a) *m/f*
2 (*Brit**) (= *hard worker*) persona *f* que trabaja mucho

graham flour ['greɪəm,flaʊəʳ] N (*US*) harina *f* de trigo sin cerner

Grail [greɪl] N **the (Holy) ~** el (Santo) Grial

grain [greɪn] N **1** (= *single particle of wheat, sand etc*) grano *m*
2 (*no pl*) (= *cereals*) cereales *mpl*; (*US*) (= *corn*) trigo *m*
3 (*fig*) [*of sense, truth*] pizca *f*; **there's not a ~ of truth in it** en eso no hay ni pizca de verdad; ✦*IDIOM* **with a ~ of salt** con reservas
4 [*of wood*] fibra *f*, hebra *f*; [*of stone*] veta *f*, vena *f*; [*of leather*] flor *f*; [*of cloth*] granilla *f*; (*Phot*) grano *m*; **against the ~** a contrapelo; **to saw with the ~** aserrar a hebra; ✦*IDIOM* **it goes against the ~** no me pasa, no me entra
5 (*Pharm*) grano *m*

grainy ['greɪnɪ] ADJ (*Phot*) granulado, con grano; [*substance*] granulado

gram [græm] N gramo *m*

grammar ['græməʳ] Ⓐ N **1** gramática *f*; **that's bad ~** eso es gramaticalmente incorrecto
2 (*also* **~ book**) libro *m* de gramática
Ⓑ CPD ► **grammar school** N (*Brit*) instituto *m* de segunda enseñanza (*al que se accede a través de pruebas selectivas*)

> **GRAMMAR SCHOOL**
>
> *En el Reino Unido, una* **grammar school** *es un centro estatal de educación secundaria selectiva que proporciona formación especialmente dirigida a los alumnos que vayan a continuar hasta una formación universitaria. Normalmente no son centros mixtos y para entrar en ellos se exige un examen escrito. Debido a la introducción en los años sesenta y setenta de las* **comprehensive schools** *para las que no hace falta una prueba de acceso, hoy día quedan pocas* **grammar schools**, *aunque sí que continúa el debate sobre si la calidad de la educación en estos centros es mejor o si sólo sirven para favorecer el elitismo en la enseñanza.*
>
> ⇨ *Ver tb* [COMPREHENSIVE SCHOOLS]

grammarian [grə'meərɪən] N gramático/a *m/f*

grammatical [grə'mætɪkəl] ADJ **1** [*rule, structure, error*] gramatical
2 (= *correct*) **in ~ English** en inglés correcto; **that's not ~** eso es gramaticalmente incorrecto

grammaticality [grəˌmætɪ'kælətɪ] N gramaticalidad *f*

grammatically [grə'mætɪkəlɪ] ADV [*write*] bien, correctamente; **~ correct** correcto gramaticalmente; **it's ~ correct to say ...** desde el punto de vista gramático, es correcto decir ...

grammaticalness [grə'mætɪkəlnɪs] N gramaticalidad *f*

gramme [græm] N (*Brit*) gramo *m*

Grammy ['græmɪ] N (*pl* **Grammys** *or* **Grammies**) (*US*) ≈ Premio *m* Grammy

gramophone† ['græməfəʊn] (*Brit*) Ⓐ N gramófono *m*
Ⓑ CPD ► **gramophone needle** N aguja *f* de gramófono ► **gramophone record** N disco *m* de gramófono

Grampian ['græmpɪən] N **the ~ Mountains** ◊ **the ~s** los Montes Grampianos

grampus ['græmpəs] N (*pl* **grampuses**) orca *f*

gran* [græn] N (*Brit*) abuelita *f*

Granada [grə'nɑːdə] N Granada *f*

granary ['grænərɪ] Ⓐ N granero *m*
Ⓑ CPD ► **granary loaf**® N pan *m* con granos enteros

grand [grænd] (*compar* **grander**; *superl* **grandest**) Ⓐ ADJ **1** (= *impressive*) [*building, architecture*] imponente, grandioso; [*clothes*] elegante; [*person*] distinguido; **the job isn't as ~ as it sounds** el trabajo no es de tanta categoría como parece; **I went to a rather ~ dinner** fui a una cena bastante lujosa *or* solemne; **to make a ~ entrance** hacer una entrada solemne; **~ finale** broche *m* de oro; **for the ~ finale ...** como broche de oro ...; **last night diplomats were preparing for the summit's ~ finale** anoche los diplomáticos se preparaban para la apoteosis de la conferencia cum-

bre; **a ~ gesture** (*magnanimous*) un gesto magnánimo; (*ostentatious*) un gesto grandilocuente; **in the ~ manner** por todo lo alto; **it was a very ~ occasion** fue una ocasión muy espléndida; **the ~ old man of English politics** el patriarca de la política inglesa; **~ opening** apertura *f* solemne; **on a ~ scale** a gran escala; **to do sth in ~ style** hacer algo a lo grande *or* por todo lo alto
2 (= *ambitious*) [*scheme, plan, design, strategy*] ambicioso
3 (†*) (= *great*) [*adventure, experience*] maravilloso, fabuloso; [*weather, day, person*] estupendo; **what ~ weather we've been having!** ¡qué tiempo más estupendo nos ha estado haciendo!, ¡qué tiempo tan estupendo hemos tenido!; **we've had some ~ times together, haven't we?** nos lo hemos pasado estupendamente juntos, ¿verdad?; **that's ~!** ¡fabuloso!
4 (*in hotel names*) gran
Ⓑ N 1 (‡) (= *thousand*) **ten ~** (*Brit*) diez mil libras; (*US*) diez mil dólares; **we still need another couple of ~** aún necesitamos otras dos mil
2 (*also* **~ piano**) piano *m* de cola; *see also* **baby C3**
Ⓒ CPD ► **the Grand Canyon** N (*US*) el Gran Cañón del Colorado ► **grand duchess** N gran duquesa *f* ► **grand duchy** N gran ducado *m* ► **grand duke** N gran duque *m* ► **grand jury** N (*esp US Jur*) jurado *m* de acusación (*que decide si hay suficiente causa para llevar a algn a juicio*) ► **grand larceny** N (*US Jur*) hurto *m* de mayor cuantía ► **grand mal** N (*Med*) grand mal *m* ► **grand master** N (*Chess*) gran maestro *m* (de ajedrez) ► **the Grand National** N (*Brit Horse racing*) el Grand National ► **the Grand Old Party** N (*US*) *mote que tiene el partido republicano de Estados Unidos desde 1880* ► **grand opera** N gran ópera *f* ► **grand piano** N piano *m* de cola ► **Grand Prix** N Grand Prix *m*, Gran Premio *m* ► **grand slam** N (*Sport*) gran slam *m*; **to win the ~ slam** ganar el gran slam ► **grand total** N total *m*; **a ~ total of £50** un total de 50 libras ► **grand tour** N (*hum*) (= *trip*) recorrido *m* de rigor (*hum*); **we'll give you a ~ tour of the house** te haremos el recorrido de rigor por la casa ► **the Grand Tour** N (*Hist*) la gran gira europea ► **grand vizier** N (*Hist*) gran visir *m*

GRAND JURY

En el sistema legal estadounidense, un **grand jury** *es un jurado de consulta que decide si debe acusarse a una persona de un delito y llevarla a juicio. Este jurado está compuesto por un número de miembros que oscila entre doce y veintitrés, y normalmente llevan a cabo sus reuniones en secreto. El* **grand jury** *tiene autoridad para citar a testigos a prestar declaración.*
Además del **grand jury**, *existe en la legislación americana otro jurado llamado* **trial jury** *(jurado de juicio) o* **petit jury**, *compuesto de doce miembros, cuya función es la de determinar la inocencia o culpabilidad del acusado ante el tribunal.*

grandchild ['græntʃaɪld] N (*pl* **grandchildren**) nieto/a *m/f*
grand(d)ad* ['grændæd] N abuelo *m*; **yes, ~** sí, abuelo
grand(d)addy* ['grændædɪ] N (*US*) abuelito *m*
granddaughter ['græn,dɔːtəʳ] N nieta *f*
grandee [,græn'diː] N grande *m* (*de España*)

► LANGUAGE IN USE: **grant B1** 9.4, 12.3

grandeur ['grændjəʳ] N [*of occasion, scenery, house etc*] lo imponente; [*of style*] lo elevado
grandfather ['grænd,fɑːðəʳ] Ⓐ N abuelo *m*
Ⓑ CPD ► **grandfather clock** N reloj *m* de pie, reloj *m* de caja
grandiloquence [græn'dɪləkwəns] N altisonancia *f*, grandilocuencia *f*
grandiloquent [græn'dɪləkwənt] ADJ altisonante, grandilocuente
grandiloquently [græn'dɪləkwəntlɪ] ADV con grandilocuencia, con altisonancia
grandiose ['grændɪəʊz] ADJ 1 (= *imposing*) [*style, building etc*] imponente, grandioso
2 (*pej*) [*building etc*] ostentoso, hecho para impresionar; [*scheme, plan*] vasto, ambicioso; [*style*] exagerado, pomposo
grandly ['grændlɪ] ADV 1 (= *impressively*) **to live ~** vivir por todo lo alto; **~ decorated** suntuosamente decorado
2 (= *importantly*) [*announce, proclaim*] (= *solemnly*) solemnemente, con solemnidad; (= *pompously*) pomposamente, en tono pomposo; [*stand, walk*] majestuosamente; **"my daughter's a PhD," he said ~** —mi hija tiene un doctorado —dijo pomposamente *or* en tono pomposo; **what was ~ named "the Palace"** lo que grandiosamente *or* pomposamente llamaban "el Palacio"
grandma* ['grænmɑː], **grandmama** ['grænmə,mɑː] N abuela *f*; **yes, ~** sí, abuela
grandmother ['græn,mʌðəʳ] N abuela *f*; **✦IDIOM stop trying to teach your ~ to suck eggs** (*Brit*) ¿qué me vas a enseñar tú a mí?
grandness ['grændnɪs] N 1 (= *impressiveness*) [*of building, architecture*] lo espléndido, grandiosidad *f*; [*of clothes*] suntuosidad *f*; [*of occasion, spectacle*] solemnidad *f*; [*of person*] distinción *f*
2 (= *pompousness*) [*of manner, behaviour*] pomposidad *f*
grandpa* ['grænpɑː], **grandpapa** ['grænpə,pɑː] N abuelo *m*; **yes, ~** sí, abuelo
grandparents ['græn,peərənts] NPL abuelos *mpl*
grandson ['grænsʌn] N nieto *m*
grandstand ['grændstænd] Ⓐ N (*Sport*) tribuna *f*
Ⓑ VI (*US**) (*fig*) fanfarronear
Ⓒ CPD ► **grandstand view** N **to have a ~ view of** tener una vista magnífica de
grange [greɪndʒ] N (*US Agr*) cortijo *m*, alquería *f*; (*Brit*) casa *f* solariega, casa *f* de señor
granite ['grænɪt] N granito *m*
grannie, granny ['grænɪ] Ⓐ N (*) abuela *f*; **yes, ~** sí, abuela
Ⓑ CPD ► **granny flat*** N (*Brit*) pisito *m* or (*LAm*) departamentito *m* para la abuela ► **granny knot** N nudo *m* corredizo
grant [grɑːnt] Ⓐ N 1 (= *act*) otorgamiento *m*, concesión *f*; (= *thing granted*) concesión *f*; (*Jur*) cesión *f*; (= *gift*) donación *f*
2 (*Brit*) (= *scholarship*) beca *f*; (= *subsidy*) subvención *f*
Ⓑ VT 1 (= *allow*) [+ *request, favour*] conceder; (= *provide, give*) [+ *prize*] otorgar; (*Jur*) ceder
2 (= *admit*) reconocer; **~ed, he's rather old** de acuerdo, es bastante viejo; **~ed** *or* **~ing that ...** en el supuesto de que ...; **I ~ him that** le concedo eso
3 **to take sth for ~ed** dar algo por supuesto *or* sentado; **we may take that for ~ed** eso es indudable; **he takes her for ~ed** no sabe valorarla
grant-aided [,grɑːnt'eɪdɪd] ADJ (*Brit*) subvencionado
grantee [grɑːn'tiː] N cesionario/a *m/f*
grant-in-aid [,grɑːntɪn'eɪd] N (*pl* **grants-in-aid**) subvención *f*
grant-maintained [,grɑːntmeɪn'teɪnd] ADJ (*Brit*) [*school*] *que recibe dinero del gobierno central, y no de la administración local*

GRANT-MAINTAINED SCHOOL

Una **grant-maintained school** *es un colegio público británico financiado por el gobierno central. Este sistema de organización escolar fue establecido para dotar a los colegios de una mayor autonomía y para reducir a la vez el poder de intervención que los ayuntamientos tenían anteriormente en la educación. Aunque muchos centros han preferido seguir adscritos a la autoridad local, los que han optado por el sistema de* **grant-maintained school** *son controlados directamente por un equipo directivo con una representación importante del personal del colegio y de los padres de los alumnos. Este comité se encarga de tomar decisiones tales como la contratación de nuevo personal, el reparto del presupuesto, o el mantenimiento del edificio, asuntos de los que antes se ocupaba la autoridad educativa local.*

grantor [grɑːn'tɔːʳ, 'grɑːntəʳ] N cedente *mf*
granular ['grænjʊləʳ] ADJ granular
granulate ['grænjʊleɪt] VT [+ *salt, sugar, soil, metal*] granular; [+ *surface*] hacer granuloso
granulated ['grænjʊleɪtɪd] Ⓐ ADJ [*paper*] granulado; [*surface*] rugoso
Ⓑ CPD ► **granulated sugar** N azúcar *m or f* granulado *or* granulada
granule ['grænjuːl] N [*of sugar etc*] gránulo *m*
grape [greɪp] Ⓐ N uva *f*; **✦IDIOMS sour ~s!** ¡están verdes de envidia!, ¡pura envidia!; **it's just sour ~s with him** es un envidioso, lo que pasa es que tiene envidia
Ⓑ CPD ► **grape harvest** N vendimia *f* ► **grape hyacinth** N jacinto *m* de penacho ► **grape juice** N (*for making wine*) mosto *m*; (= *drink*) zumo *m or* (*LAm*) jugo *m* de uva
grapefruit ['greɪpfruːt] N (*pl* **grapefruit** *or* **grapefruits**) pomelo *m*, toronja *f* (*esp LAm*)
grapeshot ['greɪpʃɒt] N metralla *f*
grapevine ['greɪpvaɪn] N 1 (*lit*) vid *f*, parra *f*
2 (*) (*fig*) teléfono *m* árabe, radio *f* macuto (*Sp**); **I heard it on** *or* **through the ~** me contó un pajarito, me enteré en radio macuto (*Sp**)
graph [grɑːf] Ⓐ N gráfica *f*, gráfico *m*
Ⓑ CPD ► **graph paper** N papel *m* cuadriculado
grapheme ['græfiːm] N grafema *m*
graphic ['græfɪk] Ⓐ ADJ 1 (= *vivid*) [*description, picture*] muy gráfico; **to describe sth in ~ detail** describir algo con todo lujo de detalles
2 (*Art, Math*) gráfico
Ⓑ CPD ► **graphic artist** N grafista *mf* ► **graphic arts** NPL artes *fpl* gráficas ► **graphic design** N diseño *m* gráfico ► **graphic designer** N grafista *mf* ► **graphic equalizer** N ecualizador *m* gráfico
graphical ['græfɪkəl] Ⓐ ADJ (*gen, also Math*) gráfico
Ⓑ CPD ► **graphical display unit** N (*Comput*) unidad *f* de demostración gráfica ► **graphical user interface** N (*Comput*) interfaz *m* gráfico de usuario, interfaz *f* gráfica de usuario
graphically ['græfɪkəlɪ] ADV 1 (= *vividly*) gráficamente; **their suffering is ~ described** su sufrimiento se describe gráficamente *or* en tér-

minos gráficos
2 (= *with graphics*) gráficamente

graphics [ˈgræfɪks] Ⓐ N 1 (= *art of drawing*) artes *fpl* gráficas
2 (= *graphs*) gráficas *fpl*
3 (*Comput*) gráficos *mpl*
4 (= *pictures*) dibujos *mpl*
Ⓑ CPD ► **graphics environment** N (*Comput*) entorno *m* gráfico ► **graphics pad** N (*Comput*) tablero *m* de gráficos

graphite [ˈgræfaɪt] N grafito *m*

graphologist [græˈfɒlədʒɪst] N grafólogo/a *m/f*

graphology [græˈfɒlədʒɪ] N grafología *f*

grapnel [ˈgræpnəl] N rezón *m*, arpeo *m*

grapple [ˈgræpl] Ⓐ VI [*wrestlers etc*] luchar cuerpo a cuerpo (**with** con); **to ~ with a problem** (*fig*) confrontar un problema
Ⓑ VT asir, agarrar; (*Naut*) aferrar

grappling iron [ˈgræplɪŋ,aɪən] N (*Naut*) rezón *m*

grasp [grɑːsp] Ⓐ N 1 (= *handclasp*) apretón *m*; **to be within sb's ~** estar al alcance de la mano de algn; **he has a strong ~** agarra muy fuerte; **to lose one's ~ on sth** desasirse de algo
2 (*fig*) (= *power*) garras *fpl*, control *m*; (= *range*) alcance *m*; (= *understanding*) comprensión *f*; **it's within everyone's ~** está al alcance de todos; **it is beyond my ~** está fuera de mi alcance; **to have a good ~ of sth** dominar algo
Ⓑ VT 1 (= *take hold of*) agarrar, asir; (= *hold firmly*) sujetar; [+ *hand*] estrechar, apretar; [+ *weapon etc*] empuñar
2 (*fig*) [+ *chance, opportunity*] aprovechar; [+ *power, territory*] apoderarse de
3 (= *understand*) comprender, entender

►**grasp at** VI + PREP 1 (*lit*) [+ *rope etc*] tratar de asir
2 (*fig*) [+ *hope*] aferrarse a; [+ *opportunity*] aprovechar

grasping [ˈgrɑːspɪŋ] ADJ (*fig*) avaro, codicioso

grass [grɑːs] Ⓐ N 1 (*Bot*) hierba *f*, yerba *f*; (= *lawn*) césped *m*, pasto *m* (*LAm*), grama *f* (*LAm*); (= *pasture*) pasto *m*; **"keep off the grass"** "prohibido pisar la hierba"; **to put a horse out to ~** echar un caballo al pasto; ✦*IDIOM* **not to let the ~ grow under one's feet** no dormirse; ✦*PROV* **the ~ is always greener on the other side (of the fence)** nadie está contento con su suerte
2 (‡) (= *marijuana*) marihuana *f*, mota *f* (*LAm**)
3 (*Brit*‡) (= *person*) soplón/ona *m/f*
Ⓑ VI (*Brit*‡) soplar*, dar el chivatazo*; **to ~ on** delatar a
Ⓒ VT (*also* **to ~ over**) cubrir de hierba
Ⓓ CPD ► **grass court** N (*Tennis*) pista *f* de hierba ► **grass cutter** N cortacésped *m* ► **grass roots** NPL (*fig*) base *f*; *see also* **grass-roots** ► **grass snake** N culebra *f* ► **grass widow** N (*esp US*) (*divorced, separated*) mujer *f* separada o divorciada; (*Brit hum*) mujer *f* cuyo marido está ausente ► **grass widower** N (*esp US*) (*divorced, separated*) hombre *m* separado o divorciado; (*Brit hum*) marido *m* cuya mujer está ausente

grass-green [ˈgrɑːs,griːn] ADJ verde hierba

grasshopper [ˈgrɑːs,hɒpəʳ] N saltamontes *m inv*, chapulín *m* (*Mex, CAm*)

grassland [ˈgrɑːslænd] N pradera *f*, pampa *f* (*LAm*)

grass-roots [ˈgrɑːsˈruːts] ADJ [*movement*] de base; [*support, opinion*] de las bases; **~ politics** política *f* donde se trata de los problemas corrientes de la gente; *see also* **grass B**

grassy [ˈgrɑːsɪ] ADJ (*compar* **grassier**; *superl* **grassiest**) herboso, pastoso (*LAm*)

grate¹ [greɪt] N (= *grid*) parrilla *f*; (= *fireplace*) chimenea *f*

grate² [greɪt] Ⓐ VT 1 [+ *cheese etc*] rallar; **~d cheese** queso *m* rallado
2 (= *scrape*) [+ *metallic object, chalk etc*] hacer chirriar; **to ~ one's teeth** hacer rechinar los dientes
Ⓑ VI 1 [*chalk, hinge etc*] chirriar (**on, against** al desplazarse por)
2 (*fig*) **it really ~s (on me)** me pone los pelos de punta; **to ~ on the ear** hacer daño a los oídos; **it ~s on my nerves** me pone los nervios de punta, me destroza los nervios

▼**grateful** [ˈgreɪtfʊl] ADJ (= *thankful*) agradecido; [*smile*] de agradecimiento; **a ~ client** un cliente agradecido; **to be ~ for sth** agradecer algo; **I am ~ for any help I can get** agradezco cualquier ayuda que pueda recibir; **I would be ~ if you would send me ...** le agradecería que me mandase ...; **I should like to extend my ~ thanks to ...** me gustaría extender mi más sincero agradecimiento a ...; **with ~ thanks** con mi más sincero agradecimiento; **to be ~ to sb** estar agradecido a algn; **I am very** *or* **most ~ to you for talking to me** le estoy muy agradecido por hablar conmigo; **I am ~ to Dr Jones for the loan of the book** le estoy agradecido al Dr Jones por prestarme el libro, le agradezco al Dr Jones que me prestase el libro; **she was just ~ to have been released** se sentía agradecida de que la hubiesen liberado; **he was ~ that he was still alive** daba gracias por estar todavía vivo

gratefully [ˈgreɪtfəlɪ] ADV [*accept, say, smile*] con gratitud; **she shook my hand ~** me apretó la mano agradecida *or* con gratitud; **~, I accepted** acepté agradecido; **the contribution of various individuals is ~ acknowledged** agradecemos la colaboración de varias personas; **all contributions/donations will be ~ received** agradecemos todo tipo de colaboración/cualquier donativo

grater [ˈgreɪtəʳ] N (*Culin*) rallador *m*

gratification [,grætɪfɪˈkeɪʃən] N 1 (= *satisfaction*) satisfacción *f*; **to my great ~** con gran satisfacción mía
2 (= *reward*) gratificación *f*, recompensa *f*

gratified [ˈgrætɪfaɪd] ADJ contento, satisfecho

gratify [ˈgrætɪfaɪ] VT [+ *person*] complacer; [+ *desire, whim etc*] satisfacer; **I am gratified to know** me complace saberlo; **he was much gratified** se puso muy contento

gratifying [ˈgrætɪfaɪɪŋ] ADJ grato; **it is ~ to know that ...** me es grato saber que ...; **with ~ speed** con loable prontitud

grating¹ [ˈgreɪtɪŋ] N (*in wall, pavement*) reja *f*, enrejado *m*

grating² [ˈgreɪtɪŋ] ADJ [*tone etc*] áspero

gratis [ˈgrɑːtɪs] Ⓐ ADV gratis
Ⓑ ADJ gratuito

▼**gratitude** [ˈgrætɪtjuːd] N gratitud *f*, agradecimiento *m*; **he expressed his ~ for Britain's support** expresó su gratitud *or* agradecimiento por el apoyo de Gran Bretaña; **he felt a sense of ~ towards her** se sentía agradecido hacia ella; **there's** *or* **that's ~ for you!** (*iro*) ¡así me/te *etc* lo agradecen!

gratuitous [grəˈtjuːɪtəs] ADJ (= *free*) gratuito; (= *needless*) [*violence, sex*] gratuito

gratuitously [grəˈtjuːɪtəslɪ] ADV gratuitamente, de manera gratuita

gratuity [grəˈtjuːɪtɪ] N 1 (*frm*) (= *tip*) propina *f*
2 (*Brit Mil*) gratificación *f*

gravamen [grəˈveɪmen] N (*pl* **gravamina** [grəˈvæmɪnə]) (*Jur*) *fundamento principal de una acusación*

grave¹ [greɪv] ADJ (*compar* **graver**; *superl* **gravest**)
1 (= *serious*) [*danger, problem, mistake*] grave; [*threat, suspicion*] serio; **he expressed ~ concern about the matter** expresó su seria preocupación por el problema; **the situation is very ~** la situación es muy grave; **you do him a ~ injustice** estás cometiendo una grave injusticia con él
2 (= *solemn*) [*face, expression*] grave, serio; [*person*] serio; **his face was ~** su rostro era grave *or* serio

grave² [greɪv] N tumba *f*, sepultura *f*; (*with monument*) sepulcro *m*, tumba *f*; **common ~** fosa *f* común; **from beyond the ~** (*fig*) desde ultratumba; ✦*IDIOM* **he sent her to an early ~** él fue la causa de que muriera tan joven; *see also* **dig B, turn C**

grave³ [grɑːv] ADJ (*Ling*) **~ accent** acento *m* grave

gravedigger [ˈgreɪv,dɪgəʳ] N sepulturero/a *m/f*

gravel [ˈgrævəl] Ⓐ N grava *f*, gravilla *f*
Ⓑ CPD ► **gravel bed** N gravera *f* ► **gravel path** N camino *m* de grava ► **gravel pit** N gravera *f*

gravelled, graveled (*US*) [ˈgrævəld] ADJ de grava, de gravilla

gravelly [ˈgrævəlɪ] ADJ 1 (*lit*) con grava, con gravilla
2 [*voice*] áspero

gravely [ˈgreɪvlɪ] ADV 1 (= *seriously*) [*ill, wounded, injured*] gravemente; **five soldiers were ~ wounded** cinco soldados resultaron gravemente heridos *or* heridos de gravedad; **we are ~ concerned about** *or* **by his decision** estamos muy *or* seriamente preocupados por su decisión
2 (= *solemnly*) [*say, speak*] con gravedad, con seriedad; **he nodded ~** asintió con gravedad

graven [ˈgreɪvən] ADJ (*liter*) **~ image** ídolo *m*; **it is ~ on my memory** lo tengo grabado en la memoria

graveness [ˈgreɪvnɪs] N gravedad *f*

graveside [ˈgreɪvsaɪd] N **at the ~** junto a la tumba

gravestone [ˈgreɪvstəʊn] N lápida *f* (sepulcral)

graveyard [ˈgreɪvjɑːd] Ⓐ N cementerio *m*, camposanto *m*
Ⓑ CPD ► **graveyard shift** N (*esp US*) turno *m* de noche, turno *m* nocturno

graving dock [ˈgreɪvɪŋdɒk] N (*Naut*) dique *m* de carena

gravitas [ˈgrævɪtæs] N (*frm*) gravitas *f*, seriedad *f*; **a certain air of ~** cierto aire de seriedad

gravitate [ˈgrævɪteɪt] VI gravitar; **to ~ towards** (*fig*) (= *be drawn to*) tender hacia; (= *move*) dirigirse hacia

gravitation [,grævɪˈteɪʃən] N (*Phys*) gravitación *f*; (*fig*) tendencia *f* (**towards** a)

gravitational [,grævɪˈteɪʃənl] ADJ gravitatorio, gravitacional

gravity [ˈgrævɪtɪ] Ⓐ N 1 (*Phys*) gravedad *f*; **the law of ~** la ley de la gravedad
2 (= *seriousness*) [*of situation, event*] gravedad *f*; **this is a situation of the utmost ~** ésta es una situación de la mayor gravedad
3 (= *solemnity*) [*of tone, manner*] gravedad *f*
Ⓑ CPD ► **gravity feed** N alimentación *f* por gravedad

gravy [ˈgreɪvɪ] Ⓐ N 1 (*Culin*) salsa *f* de carne, gravy *m*
2 (*US*‡) (= *easy money*) dinero *m* fácil
Ⓑ CPD ► **gravy boat** N salsera *f* ► **gravy**

➤ LANGUAGE IN USE: **grateful** 4, 22 **gratitude** 22

train* N (*fig*) dinero *m* fácil; ✦*IDIOM* **to get on the ~ train** pillar un chollo‡

gray *etc* [greɪ] ADJ (*US*) = **grey** *etc*

graze¹ [greɪz] (*Agr*) Ⓐ VI pacer, pastar
Ⓑ VT [+ *grass, field*] usar como pasto; [+ *cattle*] apacentar, pastar

graze² [greɪz] Ⓐ N (= *injury*) roce *m*
Ⓑ VT 1 (= *touch lightly*) rozar
2 (= *scrape*) [+ *skin*] raspar; **to ~ one's knees** rasparse las rodillas

grazing [ˈgreɪzɪŋ] N 1 (= *land*) pasto *m*
2 (= *act*) pastoreo *m*

GRE N ABBR (*US Univ*) (= **Graduate Record Examination**) *examen de acceso a estudios de posgrado*

grease [griːs] Ⓐ N (= *oil, fat etc*) grasa *f*; [*of candle*] sebo *m*; (= *dirt*) mugre *f*; (= *lubricant*) lubricante *m*
Ⓑ VT [+ *baking tin*] engrasar; (*Aut etc*) engrasar, lubricar; ✦*IDIOMS* **like ~d lightning*** como un relámpago; **to ~ sb's palm** untar la mano a algn
Ⓒ CPD ► **grease gun** N pistola *f* engrasadora, engrasadora *f* a presión ► **grease monkey*** N (*US*) mecánico/a *m/f*, maquinista *mf* ► **grease nipple** N (*Aut*) engrasador *m* ► **grease remover** N quitagrasas *m inv*

greasepaint [ˈgriːspeɪnt] N maquillaje *m*

greaseproof [ˈgriːspruːf] Ⓐ ADJ (*Brit*) a prueba de grasa, impermeable a la grasa
Ⓑ CPD ► **greaseproof paper** N papel *m* encerado

greaser‡ [ˈgriːsəʳ] N 1 (= *mechanic*) mecánico/a *m/f*
2 (†) (= *motorcyclist*) motociclista *mf*
3 (*pej*) (= *ingratiating person*) pelota* *mf*, lameculos* *mf*
4 (*US pej*) (= *Latin American*) sudaca* *mf*

greasiness [ˈgriːsɪnɪs] N [*of substance, hands, clothes*] lo grasiento, lo grasoso (*esp LAm*); [*of hair, skin*] lo graso, lo grasoso (*esp LAm*); [*of food*] lo grasiento; [*of road*] lo resbaladizo

greasy [ˈgriːsɪ] Ⓐ ADJ (*compar* **greasier**, *superl* **greasiest**) 1 (= *oily*) [*substance, hands*] grasiento, grasoso (*esp LAm*); [*clothes*] lleno de grasa, mugriento; [*hair, skin*] graso, grasoso (*esp LAm*); [*food*] grasiento; [*road*] resbaladizo
2 (*) (= *ingratiating*) [*person*] adulón, zalamero
Ⓑ CPD ► **greasy spoon*** N (= *café*) figón *m*

▼ **great** [greɪt] Ⓐ ADJ (*compar* **greater**, *superl* **greatest**) 1 (= *huge*) (*in size*) [*house, room, object*] enorme, inmenso; (*in amount, number*) [*effort, variety*] grande; [*shock, surprise*] verdadero, enorme; **she lived to a ~ age** vivió hasta una edad muy avanzada; **I'll take ~ care of it** lo cuidaré mucho; **he didn't say a ~ deal** no dijo mucho; **a ~ deal of time/money/effort** mucho tiempo/dinero/esfuerzo; **a ~ deal of suffering** mucho sufrimiento; **with ~ difficulty** con gran *or* mucha dificultad; **we had ~ difficulty convincing them** hemos tenido muchas dificultades para convencerlos; **he had ~ difficulty staying awake** le costaba mucho mantenerse despierto; **to a ~ extent** en gran parte; **to an even ~er extent** incluso en mayor parte; **we had ~ fun** lo pasamos fenomenal; **~ heavens!**† ¡Cielo Santo!†, ¡Válgame el cielo!; **to be a ~ help** ser de gran ayuda; **well, you've been a ~ help!** (*iro*) ¡vaya ayuda la tuya!, ¡pues sí que has sido una ayuda!; **I'm in no ~ hurry** ◊ **I'm not in any ~ hurry** no tengo mucha prisa; **you ~ idiot!*** ¡pedazo de idiota!*; **a ~ many people believe he was right** mucha gente cree que tenía razón; **a ~ many of us are uneasy about these developments** a muchos de nosotros estos sucesos nos tienen intranquilos; **it was a ~ pity you didn't come** fue una verdadera pena que no vinieses; **with ~ pleasure** con gran placer; **it's my ~ pleasure to introduce …** es un gran placer para mí presentar a …; **~ progress has been made** se han hecho grandes progresos; **~ Scott!**† ¡Cielo Santo!†, ¡Válgame el cielo!; **the concert was a ~ success** el concierto fue un enorme éxito; *see also* **guns A1**
2 (= *important*) [*achievement, occasion, event*] grande; **the ~ cultural achievements of the past** los grandes logros culturales del pasado; **one of the ~ issues of the day** uno de los temas más importantes del día; **everyone said she was destined for ~ things** todos decían que llegaría lejos; **~ work** (= *masterpiece*) obra *f* maestra
3 (= *outstanding*) [*person, nation, skill*] grande; **one of the ~est engineers of this century** uno de los más grandes ingenieros de este siglo; **a player of ~ ability** un jugador de gran habilidad; **she has a ~ eye for detail** tiene muy buen ojo para los detalles
4 (*with names*) **Frederick/Peter the Great** Federico/Pedro el Grande; **Alexander the Great** Alejandro Magno; **the ~ George Padmore** el gran George Padmore
5 (= *real*) (*as intensifier*) grande; **I am a ~ admirer of his work** soy un gran admirador de su obra; **they are ~ friends** son grandes amigos; **I'm a ~ chocolate-lover** me encanta el chocolate; **he was a ~ womanizer** era un gran mujeriego; **she is a ~ believer in hard work** es una gran partidaria del trabajo duro; **I'm a ~ believer in being frank** soy muy partidario de la franqueza; **she's a ~ one for antique shops** le encantan las tiendas de antigüedades, es una fanática de las tiendas de antigüedades; **he's a ~ one for criticizing others** es único para criticar a los demás, se las pinta solo para criticar a los demás*
6 (*) (= *excellent*) [*person, thing, idea*] estupendo, genial*; **they're a ~ bunch of guys** son un grupo de tíos estupendos *or* geniales*; **you were ~!** ¡estuviste genial!*; **I think she's ~** creo que es genial*; **it's a ~ idea** es una idea estupenda, es una idea genial*; **"how was the movie?" — "it was ~!"** —¿que tal fue la película? —¡genial!*; **(that's) ~!** ¡eso es estupendo!; **I heard a ~ piece of music on the radio** oí en la radio una pieza de música genial*; **wouldn't it be ~ to do that?** ¿no sería fabuloso *or* genial hacer eso?; **camping holidays are ~ for kids** las vacaciones en un camping son estupendas para los críos, las vacaciones en un camping son geniales para los críos*; **she was just ~ about it** se lo tomó muy bien; **he's ~ at football** juega estupendamente al fútbol; **she's ~ at maths** se le dan genial las matemáticas*; **to feel ~** sentirse fenómeno *or* fenomenal*; **you look ~!** (= *attractive*) ¡estás guapísimo!; (= *healthy*) ¡tienes un aspecto estupendo!; **she's ~ on jazz** sabe un montón de jazz*; **the ~ thing is that you don't have to iron it** lo mejor de todo es que no tienes que plancharlo
7 (*Bot, Zool*) grande
Ⓑ EXCL 1 (*) (= *excellent*) **(oh) ~!** ¡fenómeno!*, ¡fenomenal!, ¡qué bien!
2 (*iro*) **(oh) ~! that's all I need!** ¡maravilloso! ¡eso es lo que me faltaba!; **if that's what you want to believe, ~!** si es eso lo que quieres creer, allá tú
Ⓒ ADV **~ big*** grandísimo
Ⓓ N (= *person*) grande *mf*; **the golfing ~s** los grandes del golf; **one of the all-time ~s** uno de los grandes de todos los tiempos; **the ~** los grandes; **history remembers only the ~** la historia recuerda sólo a los grandes; **the ~ and the good** (*hum*) los abonados a las buenas causas
Ⓔ CPD ► **great ape** N antropoide *mf* ► **the Great Australian Bight** N el Gran Golfo Australiano ► **the Great Barrier Reef** N la Gran Barrera de Coral, el Gran Arrecife Coralino ► **the Great Bear** N (*Astron*) la Osa Mayor ► **Great Britain** N Gran Bretaña *f* ► **Great Dane** N gran danés *m* ► **the Great Dividing Range** N la Gran Cordillera Divisoria ► **the Great Lakes** NPL los Grandes Lagos ► **the Great Plains** NPL las Grandes Llanuras ► **the great powers** NPL las grandes potencias ► **great tit** N paro *m* grande, herrerillo *m* grande ► **the Great Wall of China** N la (Gran) Muralla China ► **the Great War** N la Primera Guerra Mundial

> **GREAT, BIG, LARGE**
>
> ### "Grande" shortened to "gran"
>
> • **Grande** must be shortened to **gran** before a singular noun of either gender:
> Great Britain
> ***(La) Gran Bretaña***
>
> ### Position of "grande"
>
> • Put **gran**/**grandes** before the noun in the sense of "great":
> It's a great step forward in the search for peace
> ***Es un gran paso en la búsqueda de la paz***
> He is a (very) great actor
> ***Es un gran actor***
> • In the sense of **big** or **large**, the adjective will precede the noun in the context of a general, subjective comment. However, when there is implicit or explicit comparison with other things or people that are physically bigger or smaller, it will follow the noun:
> It's a big problem
> ***Es un gran problema***
> ...the difference in price between big flats and small ones...
> ***...la diferencia de precio entre los pisos grandes y pequeños...***
> ...a certain type of large passenger plane...
> ***...cierto tipo de avión grande para el transporte de pasajeros...***
> • Compare the following examples:
> ...a great man...
> ***...un gran hombre...***
> ...a big man...
> ***...un hombre grande...***
> *For further uses and examples, see main entries at* ***great***, ***big*** *and* ***large***.

great-aunt [ˈgreɪtˈɑːnt] N tía *f* abuela

greatcoat [ˈgreɪtkəʊt] N gabán *m*; (*Mil etc*) sobretodo *m*

greater [ˈgreɪtəʳ] ADJ COMPAR *of* **great** (*gen, Bot, Zool*) mayor; **Greater London** el gran Londres (*incluyendo los barrios de la periferia*)

greatest [ˈgreɪtɪst] ADJ SUPERL *of* **great** el mayor, la mayor; **Ireland's ~ living poet** el mayor poeta vivo de Irlanda; **with the ~ difficulty** con suma dificultad; **he's the ~!*** ¡es el mejor!

great-grandchild [ˈgreɪtˈgræntʃaɪld] N (*pl* **great-grandchildren**) bisnieto/a *m/f*

great-granddaughter [ˌgreɪtˈgrænd,dɔːtəʳ] N bisnieta *f*

great-grandfather [ˈgreɪtˈgræn,fɑːðəʳ] N bisabuelo *m*

great-grandmother [ˈgreɪtˈgræn,mʌðəʳ] N bisabuela *f*

great-grandparents [ˈgreɪtˈgræn,pɛərənts] NPL bisabuelos *mpl*

➤ LANGUAGE IN USE: **great** A6 13

great-grandson ['greɪt'grændsʌn] N bisnieto *m*

great-great-grandfather ['greɪt'greɪt'græn,fɑːðəʳ] N tatarabuelo *m*

great-great-grandson ['greɪt'greɪt'grænsʌn] N tataranieto *m*

great-hearted ['greɪt'hɑːtɪd] ADJ valiente

greatly ['greɪtlɪ] ADV [1] (*with adj or pp used as adj*) muy; **~ superior** muy superior; **she found him ~ changed** ella lo encontró muy *or* enormemente cambiado; **he was ~ influenced by Debussy** estuvo muy *or* enormemente influenciado por Debussy
[2] (*with verb*) [*contribute, improve, vary, admire, regret*] enormemente, mucho; **I ~ regret having told her about it** me arrepiento mucho *or* enormemente de habérselo dicho; **it is ~ to be regretted** (*frm*) es muy de lamentar

great-nephew ['greɪt,nefjuː] N sobrinonieto *m*

greatness ['greɪtnɪs] N grandeza *f*; **he was destined for ~** su destino era grande

great-niece ['greɪt,niːs] N sobrinanieta *f*

great-uncle ['greɪt,ʌŋkl] N tío *m* abuelo

grebe [griːb] N zampullín *m*, somormujo *m*

Grecian ['griːʃən] ADJ griego

Greece [griːs] N Grecia *f*

greed [griːd] N avaricia *f*, codicia *f*; (*for food*) gula *f*, glotonería *f*

greedily ['griːdɪlɪ] ADV con avidez; [*eat*] con voracidad

greediness ['griːdɪnɪs] N = **greed**

greedy ['griːdɪ] ADJ (*compar* **greedier**; *superl* **greediest**) codicioso (**for** de); (*for food*) goloso; **don't be so ~!** ¡no seas glotón!

greedy-guts* ['griːdɪ,gʌts] N (*Brit hum*) comilón/ona* *m/f*

Greek [griːk] Ⓐ ADJ griego
Ⓑ N [1] (= *person*) griego/a *m/f*
[2] (*Ling*) griego *m*; **ancient ~** griego *m* antiguo; ✦**IDIOM it's all ~ to me*** para mí es chino, no entiendo ni palabra
Ⓒ CPD ► **Greek Orthodox Church** N Iglesia *f* Ortodoxa griega

Greek-Cypriot ['griːk'sɪprɪət] Ⓐ ADJ grecochipriota
Ⓑ N grecochipriota *mf*

green [griːn] Ⓐ ADJ (*compar* **greener**; *superl* **greenest**) [1] (*in colour*) verde; **dark ~** verde oscuro *adj inv*; **light ~** verde claro *adj inv*; **she was wearing a light ~ blouse** llevaba una blusa verde claro; **blue ~** verde azulado *adj inv*; **it's a very ~ city** es una ciudad con muchas zonas verdes; **to turn** *or* **go ~** [*tree*] verdear; **she went ~ at the thought** (= *nauseous*) se puso blanca sólo de pensarlo; ✦**IDIOMS to be ~ with envy** morirse de envidia; **to make sb ~ with envy** ponerle a algn los dientes largos; **she's got ~ fingers** (*Brit*) ◊ **she's got a ~ thumb** (*US*) se le dan muy bien las plantas; **the ~ shoots of recovery** los primeros indicios de la recuperación; *see also* **gill**¹
[2] (= *unripe*) [*banana, tomato, wood*] verde
[3] (*fig*) (= *inexperienced*) novato; (= *naive*) inocente; **I'm not as ~ as I look!** ¡no soy tan inocente como parezco!; ✦**IDIOM he's as ~ as grass** es más inocente que un niño
[4] (= *ecological*) [*movement, vote, person*] verde, ecologista; [*issues, policy, product*] ecologista; **the ~ pound** la libra verde
Ⓑ N [1] (= *colour*) verde *m*
[2] (= *grassy area*) [2·1] (= *lawn*) césped *m*; (= *field*) prado *m*; (*also* **village ~**) césped *m* comunal
[2·2] (*Sport*) (*in Golf*) green *m*; (*for bowls*) pista *f*; *see also* **bowling B**, **putting B**
[3] **greens** (*Culin*) verdura *fsing*; **eat up your ~s!** ¡cómete la verdura!
[4] (*Pol*) **the Greens** los verdes
Ⓒ ADV (*Pol*) **to vote ~** votar por el partido ecologista, votar a los verdes*; **to think ~** pensar en el medio ambiente
Ⓓ CPD ► **green algae** N algas *fpl* verdes ► **green bacon** N tocino *m* sin ahumar, beicon *m* sin ahumar (*Sp*), panceta *f* (*S. Cone*) ► **green bean** N judía *f* verde, ejote *m* (*Mex*), poroto *m* verde (*Andes, S. Cone*), chaucha *f* (*Arg*) ► **green belt** N (*Brit*) zona *f* verde ► **Green Beret** N (*Brit, US*) (= *person*) boina *mf* verde ► **green card** N (*in EC*) (*Aut*) carta *f* verde; (*in US*) *permiso de residencia y trabajo en los EE.UU.* ► **the Green Cross Code** N (*Brit*) código *m* de seguridad vial ► **green goddess*** N (*Brit*) *coche de bomberos del ejército* ► **green light** N luz *f* verde; ✦**IDIOM to give sb/sth the ~ light** dar luz verde a algn/algo ► **green onion** N (*US*) cebolleta *f*, cebollino *m* ► **green paper** N (*Brit Pol*) libro *m* verde ► **the Green Party** N (*Pol*) el partido ecologista, los verdes* ► **green peas** NPL guisantes *mpl* ► **green pepper** N (= *vegetable*) pimiento *m* verde, pimentón *m* verde (*LAm*) ► **green room** N (*Theat*) camerino *m* ► **green salad** N ensalada *f* (*de lechuga, pepino, pimiento verde, etc*) ► **green vegetables** NPL verduras *fpl* de hoja verde

greenback* ['griːnbæk] N (*US*) billete *m* (de banco)

greenery ['griːnərɪ] N follaje *m*

green-eyed ['griːnaɪd] ADJ de ojos verdes; ✦**IDIOM the ~ monster** (*hum*) la envidia

greenfield ['griːn,fiːld] N (*also* **~ site**) solar *m* or terreno *m* sin edificar

greenfinch ['griːnfɪntʃ] N verderón *m*

greenfly ['griːnflaɪ] N (*pl* **greenfly** *or* **greenflies**) pulgón *m*

greengage ['griːngeɪdʒ] N claudia *f*

greengrocer ['griːn,grəʊsəʳ] N (*Brit*) verdulero/a *m/f*; **~'s (shop)** verdulería *f*

greenhorn ['griːnhɔːn] N bisoño *m*, novato *m*

greenhouse ['griːnhaʊs] Ⓐ N (*pl* **greenhouses** ['griːnhaʊzɪz]) invernadero *m*
Ⓑ CPD ► **greenhouse effect** N efecto *m* invernadero ► **greenhouse gas** N gas *m* invernadero

greenish ['griːnɪʃ] ADJ verdoso

Greenland ['griːnlənd] N Groenlandia *f*

Greenlander ['griːnləndəʳ] N groenlandés/esa *m/f*

Greenlandic [,griːn'lændɪk] Ⓐ ADJ groenlandés
Ⓑ N (*Ling*) groenlandés *m*

greenness ['griːnnɪs] N [1] (= *colour*) verdor *m*, lo verde *m*
[2] (= *unripeness*) lo verde
[3] (*fig*) (= *inexperience*) inexperiencia *f*; (= *naivety*) inocencia *f*

greenstuff ['griːnstʌf] N verduras *fpl*, legumbres *fpl*

greensward ['griːnswɔːd] N (*poet*) césped *m*

green-wellie brigade [,griːnwelɪbrɪ'geɪd] N señoritos *m* del campo

GREEN-WELLIE BRIGADE

En el Reino Unido las botas altas de goma verdes **green wellingtons** *se suelen asociar con las clases acomodadas, ya que son las botas que se utilizan normalmente para montar a caballo, ir de caza o de pesca, deportes que han sido tradicionalmente asociados a la clase alta. Por este motivo, el término* **green-wellie brigade** *(que podría traducirse al español por el de* **señoritos del campo**)*, se utiliza a veces despectivamente para referirse a ciertos aspectos negativos del comportamiento de dicha clase social.*

Greenwich mean time [,grenɪtʃ'miːntaɪm] N hora *f* media de Greenwich

greet [griːt] VT (*gen*) saludar; (= *welcome*) recibir; [*sight, smell etc*] [+ *sb, sb's eyes*] presentarse a; **the statement was ~ed with laughter** la declaración fue recibida entre risas; **this was ~ed with relief by everybody** todos recibieron la noticia con gran alivio

greeting ['griːtɪŋ] Ⓐ N [1] (*with words etc*) saludo *m*; (= *welcome*) bienvenida *f*, acogida *f*
[2] **greetings** saludos *mpl*, recuerdos *mpl*; **~s!** ¡bienvenido!
Ⓑ CPD ► **greetings card** N tarjeta *f* de felicitaciones

Greg [greg] N (*familiar form*) *of* **Gregory**

gregarious [grɪ'geərɪəs] ADJ [*animal*] gregario; [*person*] sociable

Gregorian [grɪ'gɔːrɪən] Ⓐ ADJ gregoriano
Ⓑ CPD ► **Gregorian chant** N canto *m* gregoriano

Gregory ['gregərɪ] N Gregorio

gremlin* ['gremlɪn] N duendecillo *m*, diablillo *m*

Grenada [gre'neɪdə] N Granada *f*

grenade [grɪ'neɪd] Ⓐ N (*also* **hand ~**) granada *f*
Ⓑ CPD ► **grenade launcher** N lanzagranadas *m inv*

Grenadian [gre'neɪdɪən] Ⓐ ADJ granadino
Ⓑ N granadino/a *m/f*

grenadier [,grenə'dɪəʳ] N granadero *m*

grenadine ['grenədiːn] N granadina *f*

grew [gruː] PT *of* **grow**

grey, gray (*US*) [greɪ] Ⓐ ADJ (*compar* **greyer**; *superl* **greyest**) [1] (*in colour*) gris; [*face, complexion*] ceniciento; [*hair, beard*] gris, canoso, cano (*liter*); [*horse*] rucio; **the sky was ~** el cielo estaba gris; **dark ~** gris oscuro *adj inv*; **light ~** gris claro *adj inv*; **a light ~ shirt** una camisa gris claro; **he's very ~ for his age** tiene el pelo muy gris *or* canoso para su edad; **to have ~ hair** tener el pelo gris *or* canoso; **to go ~** [*hair*] volverse gris *or* canoso; **she's going ~** le están saliendo canas; **to turn ~** [*person, face*] palidecer
[2] (= *bleak*) [*place, day*] gris; **the future looked ~** el futuro se presentaba sombrío
[3] (= *boring*) [*person*] gris; **people are fed up with stereotype politicians, the men in ~ suits** la gente está cansada de los políticos estereotipados, los personajes incoloros
[4] (*) [*pound, vote*] de la tercera edad
Ⓑ N [1] (= *colour*) gris *m*; **dressed in ~** vestido de gris
[2] (= *horse*) rucio *m*
Ⓒ VI [*hair*] encanecer; **he was ~ing at the temples** se le estaban encaneciendo las sienes
Ⓓ CPD ► **grey area** N (= *unclear area*) área *f* poco definida, área *f* gris; (= *intermediate area*) área *f* intermedia; **it's rather a ~ area** es un área poco definida *or* bastante gris ► **grey friar** N *see* **friar** ► **grey matter** N (*Anat, hum*) materia *f* gris ► **grey mullet** N mújol *m* ► **grey seal** N foca *f* gris ► **grey squirrel** N ardilla *f* gris ► **grey wolf** N lobo *m* gris

greybeard, graybeard (*US*) ['greɪbɪəd] N (*liter*) anciano *m*, viejo *m*

grey-haired, gray-haired (*US*) ['greɪ'heəd] ADJ canoso

Greyhound ['greɪhaʊnd] N (*US*) (*also* **~ bus**) autobús *m* de largo recorrido

greyhound, **grayhound** (*US*) ['greɪhaʊnd] Ⓐ N galgo/a *m/f*
Ⓑ CPD ► **greyhound racing** N carreras *fpl* de galgos ► **greyhound track** N canódromo *m*

GREYHOUND RACING

*Las carreras de galgos son un deporte muy popular en el Reino Unido, sobre todo entre aquellos a quienes les gusta apostar. Los corredores de apuestas (***bookmakers***) tienen mucha clientela con las carreras que llaman* **the dogs**. *El canódromo puede ser ovalado o redondo y los galgos persiguen una liebre mecánica que corre sobre un carril.*

greying, **graying** (*US*) ['greɪɪŋ] ADJ [*hair*] grisáceo, canoso

greyish, **grayish** (*US*) ['greɪɪʃ] ADJ grisáceo; [*hair*] entrecano

greyness, **grayness** (*US*) ['greɪnɪs] N [1] (= *grey colour*) [*of sky, clouds*] lo gris; [*of hair*] lo canoso
[2] (= *bleakness*) [*of situation*] lo deprimente; [*of future*] lo poco prometedor; **the ~ of his suits exactly matched the ~ of his mind** el gris de sus trajes reflejaba lo gris de su mentalidad; **in a world full of ~ this was her only hope** en un mundo tan sombrío ésta era su única esperanza

grid [grɪd] Ⓐ N [1] (= *grating*) (*in wall, pavement*) rejilla *f*
[2] (*Brit Elec, Gas*) (= *network*) red *f*; **the (national) ~** la red nacional
[3] (*on map*) cuadrícula *f*
[4] (*US Sport*) = **gridiron**
Ⓑ CPD ► **grid map** N mapa *m* cuadriculado ► **grid reference** N coordenadas *fpl*

griddle ['grɪdl] Ⓐ N plancha *f*
Ⓑ VT asar a la plancha

gridiron ['grɪd,aɪən] N [1] (*Culin*) parrilla *f*
[2] (*US Sport*) campo *m* de fútbol (americano)

gridlock ['grɪdlɒk] N [1] (*Aut*) embotellamiento *m*
[2] (*fig*) punto *m* muerto

gridlocked ['grɪdlɒkt] ADJ [1] [*road*] paralizado; **traffic is ~ in the cities** el tráfico está paralizado en las ciudades
[2] (*fig*) [*negotiations*] en un punto muerto

grief [gri:f] N [1] (= *sorrow*) pena *f*, dolor *m*; **✦IDIOM to come to ~** fracasar, ir al traste
[2] (= *cause of sorrow*) tristeza *f*
[3] (*Brit**) (= *trouble*) **to give sb ~** dar problemas a algn, dar la vara a algn*
[4] (*as exclamation*) **good ~!** ¡demonio!

grief-stricken ['gri:f,strɪkən] ADJ apesadumbrado

grievance ['gri:vəns] Ⓐ N (= *complaint*) queja *f*; (= *cause for complaint*) motivo *m* de queja; [*of workers*] reivindicación *f*; **to have a ~ against sb** tener queja de algn
Ⓑ CPD ► **grievance procedure** N sistema *m* de trámite de quejas

grieve [gri:v] Ⓐ VT dar pena a, causar tristeza a, afligir; **it ~s me to see ...** me da pena ver ...
Ⓑ VI afligirse, acongojarse (**about, at** por); **to ~ for sb** llorar la pérdida de algn

grieved [gri:vd] ADJ [*tone etc*] lastimoso, apenado

grieving ['gri:vɪŋ] ADJ [*family, relatives*] afligido; **the ~ process** el duelo

grievous ['gri:vəs] Ⓐ ADJ [*loss etc*] doloroso, penoso; [*blow*] severo; [*pain*] fuerte; [*crime, offence, error*] grave; [*task*] penoso
Ⓑ CPD ► **grievous bodily harm** N (*Jur*) daños *mpl* físicos graves, lesiones *fpl* corporales graves

grievously ['gri:vəslɪ] ADV [*hurt, offend*] gravemente; [*err, be mistaken*] lamentablemente; **~ wounded** gravemente herido

griffin ['grɪfɪn] N grifo *m*

griffon ['grɪfən] N (= *dog*) grifón *m*

grifter‡ ['grɪftəʳ] N (*US*) estafador(a) *m/f*, timador(a) *m/f*

grill [grɪl] Ⓐ N [1] (*Brit*) (*on cooker, also restaurant*) parrilla *f*
[2] (= *food*) parrillada *f*; **a mixed ~** una parrillada mixta
[3] = **grille**
Ⓑ VT [1] (*Culin*) asar a la parrilla
[2] (*) (= *interrogate*) interrogar
Ⓒ CPD ► **grill room** N parrilla *f*, grill *m*

grille [grɪl] N rejilla *f*; [*of window*] reja *f*; (= *screen*) verja *f*

grilled [grɪld] ADJ (*Culin*) (asado) a la parrilla

grilling* ['grɪlɪŋ] N (*fig*) interrogatorio *m* intenso; **to give sb a ~** interrogar a algn intensamente

grilse [grɪls] N salmón *m* joven (*que sólo ha estado una vez en el mar*)

grim [grɪm] ADJ (*compar* **grimmer**; *superl* **grimmest**) Ⓐ ADJ [1] (= *gloomy*) [*news, situation, prospect*] desalentador; [*reminder*] duro, crudo; [*building, place, town*] sombrío, lúgubre; **where she made the ~ discovery of a body** donde hizo el macabro descubrimiento de un cadáver; **the situation looked ~** la situación se presentaba muy negra; **to paint a ~ picture of sth** pintar un cuadro muy negro de algo; **the ~ reality** la dura *or* cruda realidad; **the ~ truth** la cruda verdad; **he gave a ~ warning to the British people** hizo una advertencia nada alentadora al pueblo británico; **the weather has been ~** el tiempo ha estado deprimente
[2] (= *stern*) [*person*] adusto; [*face, expression*] serio, adusto; [*smile*] forzado; **she hung** *or* **held on to the rope like ~ death** se agarró *or* aferró a la cuerda como si la vida le fuera en ello; **she walked on with ~ determination** siguió caminando con absoluta determinación; **he looked ~** tenía una expresión seria *or* adusta; **his voice was ~** su voz tenía un tono severo *or* adusto
[3] (= *macabre*) [*humour, joke, story*] macabro
[4] (*) (= *awful*) [*experience, effect*] espantoso*, penoso*; **it was pretty ~** fue bastante espantoso *or* penoso*; **to feel ~** estar *or* encontrarse fatal*
Ⓑ CPD ► **the Grim Reaper** N (*liter*) la Parca, la muerte

grimace [grɪ'meɪs] Ⓐ N mueca *f*
Ⓑ VI hacer muecas

grime [graɪm] N mugre *f*, suciedad *f*

grimly ['grɪmlɪ] ADV (= *gravely*) gravemente; (= *determinedly*) denodadamente; **"he's badly hurt," she said ~** —está muy malherido —dijo gravemente *or* en tono grave, —está gravemente herido —dijo con seriedad; **"this isn't good enough," he said ~** —esto no vale —dijo con seriedad; **he fought ~ to keep afloat** luchó con todas sus fuerzas *or* denodadamente para mantenerse a flote; **his face was ~ determined** tenía una expresión de total determinación; **"I'll be careful," he smiled ~** —tendré cuidado —dijo con una sonrisa forzada

grimness ['grɪmnɪs] N [1] (= *gloominess*) [*of situation, outlook*] lo desalentador, lo funesto; [*of building, place, town*] lo sombrío, lo lúgubre
[2] (= *sternness*) [*of expression, face*] seriedad *f*, gravedad *f*; **there was a ~ in his voice** su voz tenía un tono de seriedad *or* gravedad
[3] (= *sinister quality*) [*of humour, joke, story*] lo macabro

grimy ['graɪmɪ] ADJ (*compar* **grimier**; *superl* **grimiest**) mugriento, sucio

grin [grɪn] Ⓐ N (= *smile*) sonrisa *f*; (*sardonic*) sonrisa *f* burlona; (= *grimace*) mueca *f*
Ⓑ VI sonreír abiertamente (**at** a); **✦IDIOM to ~ and bear it** poner al mal tiempo buena cara

grind [graɪnd] (*pt, pp* **ground**) Ⓐ VT [1] [+ *coffee*] moler; [+ *corn, flour*] moler, machacar; [+ *stone*] pulverizar; (*US Culin*) [+ *meat*] picar; **to ~ sth into** *or* **to a powder** reducir algo a polvo, pulverizar algo; **to ~ sth into the earth** clavar algo en el suelo; **to ~ one's teeth** rechinar los dientes
[2] (= *sharpen*) [+ *knife*] amolar, afilar
[3] (= *polish*) [+ *gem, lens*] esmerilar
Ⓑ VI [*machine etc*] funcionar con dificultad; **to ~ against** ludir ruidosamente con; **to ~ to a halt** *or* **standstill** pararse en seco
Ⓒ N (*) (= *dull hard work*) trabajo *m* pesado; **the work was such a ~** el trabajo era tan pesado; **the daily ~** la rutina diaria

►**grind away*** VI + ADV (= *work hard*) trabajar como un esclavo; (*Mus*) tocar laboriosamente; **to ~ away at grammar** empollar *or* machacar la gramática*

►**grind down** VT + ADV [1] (*lit*) pulverizar; **to ~ sth down to (a) powder** reducir algo a polvo, pulverizar algo
[2] (= *wear away*) desgastar
[3] (= *oppress*) agobiar, oprimir; **to ~ down the opposition** destruir lentamente a la oposición

►**grind on** VI + ADV **the case went ~ing on for months** el pleito se desarrolló penosamente durante varios meses

►**grind out** VT + ADV [+ *tune*] tocar mecánicamente; [+ *essay, novel etc*] producir (*a costa de mucho esfuerzo*)

►**grind up** VT + ADV pulverizar

grinder ['graɪndəʳ] N [1] (= *machine*) (*for coffee*) molinillo *m*; (*US*) (*for meat*) picadora *f* de carne
[2] (*for sharpening*) afiladora *f*
[3] (= *person*) molendero/a *m/f*; (*Tech*) amolador *m*; *see also* **organ-grinder**
[4] **grinders** (= *teeth*) muelas *fpl*

grinding ['graɪndɪŋ] Ⓐ ADJ [1] **~ sound** rechinamiento *m*; **to come to a ~ halt** [*vehicle, traffic*] detenerse en seco; [*work, progress*] llegar a un punto muerto, estancarse
[2] **~ poverty** miseria *f* (absoluta)
Ⓑ N [*of coffee*] molienda *f*; [*of stone*] pulverización *f*; [*of knife*] afilado *m*

grindingly ['graɪndɪŋlɪ] ADV **a ~ familiar routine** una rutina tremendamente monótona; **~ poor** pobrísimo

grindstone ['graɪndstəʊn] N muela *f*; **✦IDIOM to keep one's nose to the ~** batir el yunque

gringo ['grɪŋgəʊ] N (*US pej*) gringo/a *m/f*

grip [grɪp] Ⓐ N [1] (= *handclasp*) apretón *m* (de manos); **he lost his ~ on the branch** se le escapó la rama de las manos, la rama se le fue de las manos
[2] (*fig*) **in the ~ of winter** paralizado por el invierno; **in the ~ of a strike** paralizado por una huelga; **to come to ~s with** luchar a brazo partido con; **to get to ~s with sth/sb** enfrentarse con algo/algn; **he lost his ~ of the situation** la situación se le fue de las manos;

to have a good ~ of a subject entender algo a fondo; **get a ~ (on yourself)!*** ¡cálmate!, ¡contrólate!
3 (= *handle*) asidero *m*, asa *f*; [*of weapon*] empuñadura *f*
4 (= *bag*) maletín *m*, bolsa *f*
Ⓑ VT 1 (= *hold*) agarrar, asir; [+ *weapon*] empuñar; [+ *hands*] apretar, estrechar; **the wheels ~ the road** las ruedas se agarran a la carretera
2 (*fig*) (= *enthrall*) fascinar; [*fear*] apoderarse de; **~ped by fear** presa del pánico
Ⓒ VI [*wheel*] agarrarse

gripe [graɪp] Ⓐ N 1 (*) (= *complaint*) queja *f*
2 (*Med*) (*also* **~s**) retortijón *m* de tripas
Ⓑ VI (*) (= *complain*) quejarse (**about** de)
Ⓒ VT (*) (= *anger*) dar rabia a

griping ['graɪpɪŋ] Ⓐ ADJ [*pain*] retortijante
Ⓑ N (*) quejadumbre *f*

gripping ['grɪpɪŋ] ADJ [*story, novel*] absorbente, muy emocionante

grisly ['grɪzlɪ] ADJ (*compar* **grislier**; *superl* **grisliest**) (= *horrible*) horroroso; (= *horrifying*) horripilante

grist [grɪst] N ✦*IDIOM* **it's all ~ to the mill** de todo hay que sacar provecho

gristle ['grɪsl] N cartílago *m*, ternilla *f*

gristly ['grɪslɪ] ADJ cartilaginoso, ternilloso

grit [grɪt] Ⓐ N 1 (= *gravel*) grava *f*; (*for caged birds, poultry*) arenilla *f* silícea, arena *f*; (= *dust*) polvo *m*
2 (*fig*) (= *courage*) valor *m*, ánimo *m*; (= *firmness of character*) firmeza *f*; (= *endurance*) aguante *m*
3 **grits** (*US Culin*) sémola *fsing*
Ⓑ VT 1 [+ *road*] echar grava a
2 **to ~ one's teeth** apretar los dientes

gritter ['grɪtəʳ] N (= *vehicle*) *vehículo que suelta grava o arena en las carreteras en tiempo de heladas*

gritty ['grɪtɪ] ADJ (*compar* **grittier**; *superl* **grittiest**) 1 (= *grainy*) [*soil, powder, texture*] arenoso; [*surface, floor*] arenoso, granuloso; **the sheets felt ~** las sábanas parecían tener arena
2 (= *courageous*) [*person, display, performance*] enérgico, resuelto; **~ determination** obstinada determinación
3 (= *true to life*) [*drama, story, portrayal*] crudo

grizzle ['grɪzl] VI (*Brit*) (= *whine*) quejumbrar

grizzled ['grɪzld] ADJ [*hair*] entrecano

grizzly ['grɪzlɪ] Ⓐ ADJ 1 (= *grey*) gris, canoso
2 (*) (= *whining*) quejumbroso
Ⓑ N (*also* **~ bear**) oso *m* pardo

groan [grəʊn] Ⓐ N [*of pain, dismay etc*] gemido *m*, quejido *m*; (= *mumble*) gruñido *m*
Ⓑ VI 1 gemir, quejarse; (= *mumble*) gruñir, refunfuñar
2 (= *creak*) [*tree, gate etc*] crujir; **borrowers are ~ing under the burden of high interest rates** los prestatarios están agobiados por la carga de los altos tipos de interés; **the table ~ed under the weight of all the food** la mesa crujía bajo el peso de toda esa comida
Ⓒ VT **"yes," he ~ed** —sí —gimió

groats [grəʊts] NPL avena *fsing* a medio moler

grocer ['grəʊsəʳ] N (*esp Brit*) tendero/a *m/f*, almacenero/a *m/f* (*S. Cone*), abarrotero/a *m/f* (*Andes, Mex, CAm*), bodeguero/a *m/f* (*Andes, Carib, CAm*); **~'s (shop)** tienda *f* de comestibles, almacén *m* (*S. Cone*), tienda *f* de abarrotes (*Andes, Mex, CAm*), bodega *f* (*Andes, Carib, CAm*)

groceries ['grəʊsərɪz] NPL comestibles *mpl*, abarrotes *mpl* (*LAm*)

grocery ['grəʊsərɪ] N (*US*) (*also* **~ store**) tienda *f* de comestibles, tienda de abarrotes (*Andes, Mex, CAm*), almacén *m* (*S. Cone*), bodega *f* (*Andes, Carib, CAm*)

grog [grɒg] N grog *m*

groggily ['grɒgɪlɪ] ADV como atontado, como grogui *or* zombi

groggy ['grɒgɪ] ADJ (*compar* **groggier**; *superl* **groggiest**) (*from blow*) atontado; (*from alcohol*) tambaleante; (*Boxing*) groggy, grogui; **I feel a bit ~** estoy un poco mareado

groin [grɔɪn] N (*Anat*) ingle *f*

groom [gruːm] Ⓐ N 1 (*in stable*) mozo *m* de cuadra
2 (= *bridegroom*) novio *m*
Ⓑ VT 1 [+ *horse*] almohazar, cuidar; **to ~ o.s.** acicalarse; **the cat was ~ing itself** el gato se lamía; **well ~ed** [*person*] muy acicalado
2 (= *prepare*) [+ *person*] **to ~ sb as/to be** preparar a algn para/para ser; **to ~ sb for a post** preparar a algn para un puesto

grooming ['gruːmɪŋ] N 1 (*gen, also well-groomedness*) acicalamiento *m*
2 [*of horse*] almohazamiento *m*; [*of dog*] cepillado *m*

groove [gruːv] Ⓐ N 1 (*in wood, metal etc*) ranura *f*, estría *f*; [*of record*] surco *m*; ✦*IDIOM* **to be (stuck) in a ~** estar metido en una rutina
2 **to be in the ~*** estar en forma
3 (*Mus**) (= *rhythm*) ritmo *m*
Ⓑ VT (= *put groove in*) estriar, acanalar
Ⓒ VI (*) (= *dance*) bailar

grooved [gruːvd] ADJ estriado, acanalado

groovy* ['gruːvɪ] ADJ (= *marvellous*) estupendo*, total*, guay (*Sp**)

grope [grəʊp] Ⓐ VI (*also* **~ around, ~ about**) andar a tientas, tantear; **to ~ for sth** (*lit, fig*) buscar algo a tientas
Ⓑ VT 1 **to ~ one's way (through/towards)** avanzar a tientas (por/hacia)
2 (*) **to ~ sb** (*sexually*) toquetear a algn
Ⓒ N (*) (*sexual*) **they had a ~** se estuvieron toqueteando, se estuvieron metiendo mano*

grosgrain ['grəʊgreɪn] N grogrén *m*, cordellate *m*

gross [grəʊs] (*compar* **grosser**; *superl* **grossest**)
Ⓐ ADJ 1 (= *unacceptable*) [*injustice, inequality, mismanagement*] flagrante; [*exaggeration, simplification*] burdo; **a ~ injustice has been done to him** se ha cometido una flagrante injusticia con él; **~ ignorance** ignorancia *f* supina, crasa ignorancia *f*; **~ incompetence** incompetencia *f* absoluta; **~ violations of human rights** flagrantes violaciones de los derechos humanos; **that is a ~ understatement** eso es quedarse muy corto
2 (= *revolting*) [*person, remark, joke*] ordinario, basto; **he's totally ~*** es de lo más basto; **(how) ~!*** ¡qué asco!*
3 (= *tasteless*) ordinario, de muy mal gusto; **she was wearing really ~ earrings** llevaba unos pendientes de lo más ordinario *or* de un gusto pésimo
4 (= *obese*) gordísimo, cebón*; **after eating so much chocolate she felt really ~*** después de comer tanto chocolate se sentía como una bola *or* foca*
5 (= *total*) [*income, profit, weight*] bruto; **their ~ income is £205 a week** sus ingresos brutos son de 205 libras a la semana; **its ~ weight is 100 grams** su peso bruto es de 100 gramos
Ⓑ ADV (= *in total*) [*earn, pay, weigh*] en bruto; **she earns £30,000 ~ per annum** gana 30.000 libras al año brutas *or* en bruto; **it weighs 12kg ~** pesa 12 kilos brutos *or* en bruto; **how much do you earn ~?** ¿cuánto ganas bruto *or* en bruto?
Ⓒ VT (*Comm*) (*gen*) obtener unos ingresos brutos de; (*from savings, bonds*) obtener unos beneficios brutos de; **the company ~ed $100,000 last year** el año pasado la compañía obtuvo unos beneficios brutos de 100.000 dólares
Ⓓ N 1 (*pl* **grosses**) (= *total income*) ingresos *mpl* brutos
2 (*pl* **gross**) (= *twelve dozen*) doce docenas *fpl*; **he bought them by the ~** los compró en cantidades de doce docenas
Ⓔ CPD ► **gross domestic product** N (*Econ*) producto *m* interno bruto ► **gross indecency** N (*Jur*) ultraje *m* contra la moral pública ► **gross national product** NSING (*Econ*) producto *m* nacional bruto ► **gross negligence** N (*Jur*) culpa *f* grave ► **gross output** N (*Ind*) producción *f* bruta

►**gross out*** VT + ADV (*US*) asquear, dar asco a

►**gross up** VT + ADV (*US*) [+ *salary etc*] recaudar en bruto

grossly ['grəʊslɪ] ADV 1 (= *extremely*) [*unfair, inadequate*] sumamente; [*inaccurate, negligent, inefficient*] sumamente, extremadamente; [*misleading, incompetent, irresponsible, exaggerated*] sumamente, tremendamente; [*mislead*] de forma escandalosa; **he is ~ overweight** está obeso, está gordísimo*; **the police were ~ negligent** la policía incurrió en graves negligencias; **many employees are ~ underpaid** muchos empleados perciben unos sueldos extremadamente bajos
2 (= *crassly*) burdamente; **he didn't put it as ~ as that** no lo puso en términos tan crudos

grossness ['grəʊsnɪs] N 1 (= *fatness*) obesidad *f*, gordura *f*
2 (= *seriousness*) [*of crime, abuse*] crudeza *f*
3 (= *tastelessness*) [*of joke, language, behaviour*] ordinariez *f*

grot* ['grɒt] N (= *dirt*) porquería *f*

grotesque [grəʊ'tesk] Ⓐ ADJ 1 (= *hideous*) [*appearance, idea, sight, spectacle*] grotesco; [*allegation, proposal*] absurdo
2 (*Art*) grotesco
Ⓑ N grotesco *m*

grotesquely [grəʊ'tesklɪ] ADV grotescamente; [*exaggerated*] bestialmente; [*insensitive*] brutalmente; **it was ~ unfair** fue tremendamente injusto

grotto ['grɒtəʊ] N (*pl* **grottos** *or* **grottoes**) gruta *f*

grotty* ['grɒtɪ] ADJ (*compar* **grottier**; *superl* **grottiest**) (*Brit*) asqueroso; **I feel ~** me siento fatal*

grouch* [graʊtʃ] Ⓐ VI refunfuñar, quejarse
Ⓑ N 1 (= *person*) refunfuñón/ona *m/f*, cascarrabias *mf inv*
2 (= *complaint*) queja *f*

grouchiness* ['graʊtʃɪnɪs] N humos *mpl*, malas pulgas *fpl*

grouchy* ['graʊtʃɪ] ADJ malhumorado

▼**ground**[1] [graʊnd] Ⓐ N 1 (= *soil*) tierra *f*, suelo *m*
2 (= *terrain*) terreno *m*; **high/hilly ~** terreno *m* alto/montañoso; **to break new ~** hacer algo nuevo; **common ~** terreno *m* común; **to cover a lot of ~** (*lit*) recorrer una gran distancia; **he covered a lot of ~ in his lecture** abarcó mucho en la clase; **to be on dangerous ~** entrar en territorio peligroso; **to be on firm ~** hablar con conocimiento de causa; **to gain ~** ganar terreno; **to go to ~** [*fox*] meterse en su madriguera; [*person*] esconderse,

➤ LANGUAGE IN USE: ground[1] A9 26.3

refugiarse; **to hold one's ~** (*lit, fig*) = **to stand one's ground**; **to be on (one's) home ~** tratar materia que uno conoce a fondo; **to lose ~** perder terreno; **to run sb to ~** localizar (por fin) a algn, averiguar el paradero de algn; **to shift one's ~** cambiar de postura; **to stand one's ~** (*lit*) no ceder terreno; (*fig*) mantenerse firme; **to be on sure ~** = **to be on firm ground**; ✦*IDIOMS* **to cut the ~ from under sb's feet** quitarle terreno a algn; **it suits me down to the ~** me conviene perfectamente, me viene de perilla; *see also* **prepare A**

3 (= *surface*) suelo *m*, tierra *f*; **above ~** sobre la tierra; **below ~** debajo de la tierra; **to fall to the ~** (*lit*) caerse al suelo; (*fig*) fracasar; **to get off the ~** [*aircraft*] despegar; [*plans etc*] ponerse en marcha; **on the ~** en el suelo; *see also* **raze**

4 (= *pitch*) terreno *m*, campo *m*; **they won on their own ~** ganaron en su propio terreno; *see also* **parade D**, **recreation**

5 (= *estate, property*) tierras *fpl*

6 **grounds** (= *gardens*) jardines *mpl*, parque *msing*

7 (*Art etc*) (= *background*) fondo *m*, trasfondo *m*; **on a blue ~** sobre un fondo azul

8 (*US Elec*) tierra *f*

9 (= *reason*) (*usu pl*) razón *f*, motivo *m*; (= *basis*) fundamento *m*; **~s for complaint** motivos *mpl* de queja; **what ~(s) do you have for saying so?** ¿en qué se basa para decir eso?; **on the ~(s) of ...** con motivo de ..., por causa de ..., debido a ...; **on the ~(s) that ...** a causa de que ..., por motivo de que ...; **on good ~s** con razón; **on medical ~s** por razones de salud

Ⓑ VT 1 [+ *ship*] varar, hacer encallar

2 [+ *plane, pilot*] obligar a permanecer en tierra; **he ordered the planes to be ~ed** ordenó que permaneciesen los aviones en tierra; **to be ~ed by bad weather** no poder despegar por el mal tiempo

3 (*US Elec*) conectar con tierra

4 (= *teach*) **to ~ sb in maths** enseñar a algn los rudimentos de las matemáticas; **to be well ~ed in** tener un buen conocimiento de, estar versado en

5 (*esp US*) [+ *student*] encerrar, no dejar salir

Ⓒ VI (*Naut*) encallar, varar; (*lightly*) tocar (**on** en)

Ⓓ CPD ► **ground attack** N ataque *m* de tierra; (*Aer*) ataque *m* a superficie ► **ground bass** N bajo *m* rítmico ► **ground colour** N fondo *m*, primera capa *f* ► **ground control** N (*Aer*) control *m* desde tierra ► **ground crew** N (*Aer*) personal *m* de tierra ► **ground floor** N (*Brit*) planta *f* baja; **~-floor flat** (*Brit*) piso *m* or (*LAm*) departamento *m* de planta baja; ✦*IDIOM* **he got in on the ~ floor** empezó por abajo ► **ground forces** NPL (*Mil*) fuerzas *fpl* de tierra ► **ground frost** N escarcha *f* ► **ground ivy** N hiedra *f* terrestre ► **ground level** N nivel *m* del suelo ► **ground plan** N plano *m*, planta *f* ► **ground pollution** N contaminación *f* del suelo ► **ground rent** N (*esp Brit*) alquiler *m* del terreno ► **ground rules** NPL reglas *fpl* básicas; **we can't change the ~ rules at this stage** a estas alturas no podemos cambiar las reglas ► **ground staff** N = **ground crew** ► **ground wire** N (*US*) cable *m* de toma de tierra ► **Ground Zero** N zona *f* cero

ground² [graʊnd] Ⓐ PT, PP of **grind**

Ⓑ ADJ [*coffee etc*] molido; [*glass*] deslustrado; (*US*) [*meat*] picado

Ⓒ N **grounds** [*of coffee*] poso *msing*, sedimento *msing*

Ⓓ CPD ► **ground beef** N (*US*) picadillo *m*

groundbait [ˈgraʊnd,beɪt] N cebo *m* de fondo

groundbreaking [ˈgraʊnd,breɪkɪŋ] ADJ [*research, work, book*] revolucionario

groundcloth [ˈgraʊndklɒθ] N (*US*) = **groundsheet**

groundhog [ˈgraʊndhɒg] N (*US*) marmota *f* de América

GROUNDHOG DAY

Groundhog Day, *que literalmente significa* **el día de la marmota**, *es una simpática tradición estadounidense, según la cual se puede predecir la duración del invierno por la observación del comportamiento de este animal. La marmota, en inglés* **groundhog**, *también conocida como* **ground squirrel** *o* **woodchuck**, *supuestamente despierta de su hibernación y abandona su madriguera el 2 de febrero* (**Groundhog Day**). *Si hace sol y la marmota ve su propia sombra, el animal se asusta y vuelve a su madriguera para seguir hibernando durante otras seis semanas, lo cual indica que habrá seis semanas más de invierno. El acontecimiento tiene tal importancia que es televisado a todo el país desde la madriguera más famosa de Punxsutawney, en Pensilvania.*

grounding [ˈgraʊndɪŋ] N 1 (*Naut*) varada *f*

2 (*in education*) conocimientos *mpl* básicos; **to give sb a ~ in** enseñar a algn los rudimentos de

groundkeeper [ˈgraʊnd,kiːpəʳ], **groundskeeper** (*US*) N encargado *m* (*del mantenimiento de una pista de deporte*)

groundless [ˈgraʊndlɪs] ADJ sin fundamento

groundnut [ˈgraʊndnʌt] Ⓐ N (*Brit*) cacahuete *m* (*Sp*), maní *m* (*LAm*), cacahuate *m* (*Mex*)

Ⓑ CPD ► **groundnut oil** N aceite *m* de cacahuete

groundsel [ˈgraʊnsl] N hierba *f* cana

groundsheet [ˈgraʊndʃiːt] N (*in tent*) aislante *m* (de tienda de campaña), suelo *m* (de tienda de campaña)

groundskeeper [ˈgraʊndz,kiːpəʳ] N (*US*) = **groundkeeper**

groundsman [ˈgraʊndzmən] N (*pl* **groundsmen**) (*Brit Sport*) encargado *m* (*del mantenimiento de una pista de deporte*)

groundspeed [ˈgraʊnd,spiːd] N (*Aer*) velocidad *f* respecto a la tierra

groundswell [ˈgraʊndswel] N mar *m* de fondo; (*fig*) marejada *f*

ground-to-air [ˈgraʊndtʊˈɛəʳ] ADJ tierra-aire; **~ missile** misil *m* tierra-aire

ground-to-ground [ˈgraʊndtəˈgraʊnd] ADJ tierra-tierra; **~ missile** misil *m* tierra-tierra

groundwater [ˈgraʊndwɔːtəʳ] N agua *f* subterránea, aguas *fpl* superficiales

groundwork [ˈgraʊndwɜːk] N trabajo *m* preliminar *or* preparatorio; **to do the ~ for sth** poner las bases de algo

group [gruːp] Ⓐ N 1 [*of people, objects*] grupo *m*; (*for specific purpose*) agrupación *f*, asociación *f*; (= *gang*) pandilla *f*, banda *f*; (*Mus*) conjunto *m*, grupo *m*; [*of languages*] familia *f*; **they stood in a ~** estaban en grupo; **ethnic ~** grupo *m* étnico; **family ~** familia *f*, grupo *m* familiar; **a human rights ~** una agrupación *or* asociación pro derechos humanos; *see also* **interest B2**, **support C**

2 (*Comm*) [*of companies*] grupo *m*

Ⓑ VT (*also* **~ together**) agrupar; **we ~ the children by ability** agrupamos a los niños según sus habilidades; **we ~ed ourselves around the piano** nos agrupamos alrededor del piano; **the report's conclusions are ~ed together under one heading** las conclusiones del informe están agrupadas bajo un mismo encabezamiento

Ⓒ VI agruparse; **the children ~ed around her** los niños se agruparon alrededor de ella

Ⓓ CPD ► **group booking** N reserva *f* hecha para un grupo ► **group captain** N (*Brit Aer*) jefe *m* de escuadrilla ► **group discussion** N debate *m* en grupo ► **group dynamics** NPL dinámica *fsing* de grupo ► **group photo** N foto *f* de conjunto ► **group practice** N (*Med*) consultorio *m* (de médicos) ► **group sex** N sexo *m* en grupo ► **group therapy** N terapia *f* de grupo

GROUP

Agreement

- When **grupo** is followed by **de** + PLURAL NOUN, following verbs can be in the plural or, less commonly, in the singular:
  A group of youths came up to him
  Un grupo de jóvenes se le acercaron *or* ***se le acercó***
- Otherwise, use the singular form of the verb:
  The group is *or* are well-known for being aggressive
  El grupo es conocido por su agresividad

For further uses and examples, see main entry.

grouper [ˈgruːpəʳ] N (= *fish*) mero *m*

groupie* [ˈgruːpɪ] N grupi* *mf*, *fan de un grupo pop*

grouping [ˈgruːpɪŋ] N agrupamiento *m*

grouse¹ [graʊs] N (*pl* **grouse** *or* **grouses**) (*Orn*) urogallo *m*; **black ~** gallo *m* lira; **red ~** lagópodo *m* escocés

grouse²* [graʊs] Ⓐ N (= *complaint*) queja *f*

Ⓑ VI quejarse (**about** de)

grout [graʊt] Ⓐ N lechada *f*

Ⓑ VT enlechar

grouting [ˈgraʊtɪŋ] N lechada *f*

grove [grəʊv] N arboleda *f*, bosquecillo *m*; **~ of pines** pineda *f*; **~ of poplars** alameda *f*

grovel [ˈgrɒvl] VI (*lit, fig*) arrastrarse (**to** ante)

grovelling, **groveling** (*US*) [ˈgrɒvlɪŋ] ADJ rastrero, servil

grow [grəʊ] (*pt* **grew**; *pp* **grown**) Ⓐ VI 1 [*plant, hair, person, animal*] crecer; **how you've ~n!** ¡cómo has crecido!; **he has ~n five cms** ha crecido cinco centímetros; **she's letting her hair ~** se está dejando crecer el pelo, se está dejando el pelo largo; **the hair will ~ back eventually** con el tiempo le volverá a crecer el pelo; **that plant does not ~ in Wales** esa planta no crece *or* no se da en Gales; **will it ~ here?** ¿se puede cultivar aquí?; **to ~ to** *or* **into manhood** llegar a la edad adulta; **these sharks can ~ to six metres** estos tiburones pueden llegar a medir hasta seis metros

2 (= *increase*) (*in number, amount*) aumentar; **the number of unemployed has ~n by more than 10,000** el número de parados ha aumentado en más de 10.000; **the economy continues to ~** la economía sigue en su fase de crecimiento; **opposition grew and the government agreed to negotiate** la oposición cobró más fuerza y el gobierno decidió entrar en negociaciones; **the winds grew to gale force** la intensidad del viento aumentó hasta alcanzar velocidades de temporal; **to ~ in popularity** ganar popularidad; **she has ~n in my esteem** se ha ganado mi estima

3 (= *develop*) [*friendship, love*] desarrollarse; [*person*] madurar; **I feel I have ~n immensely**

as a result of the experience siento que he madurado muchísimo como consecuencia de la experiencia; **to ~ spiritually** madurar espiritualmente

[4] (*with adjective*) (= *become*) volverse, ponerse, hacerse (*but often translated by vi or reflexive*); **our eyes gradually grew accustomed to the light** los ojos se nos fueron acostumbrando a la luz; **to ~ angry** enfadarse; **the light grew brighter** la luz se hizo más intensa; **to ~ cold**: **the coffee had ~n cold** el café se había enfriado; **we grew colder as the night wore on** a medida que pasaba la noche nos fue entrando cada vez más frío; **it's ~n a lot colder, hasn't it?** ha enfriado mucho ¿verdad?; **to ~ dark** (*gen*) oscurecer; (*at dusk*) oscurecer, anochecer; **to ~ fat** engordar; **her eyes grew heavy** se le cerraban los ojos; **she has ~n quite knowledgeable on the subject** ha aprendido mucho sobre el tema; **the noise grew louder** el ruido aumentó de volumen; **to ~ old** envejecer(se); **you will realize this as you ~ older** te darás cuenta de esto a medida que te hagas mayor; **he grew tired of waiting** se cansó de esperar; **to ~ used to sth** acostumbrarse a algo; **she grew weaker with each passing day** se fue debilitando día tras día; **to ~ worse**: **the housing shortage is ~ing worse** la escasez de viviendas se está haciendo cada vez mayor; **she grew worse that day and died during the night** ese día se puso peor *or* su condición empeoró y murió durante la noche

[5] **to ~ to like sb** llegar a querer a algn, encariñarse con algn; **he grew to love his work** llegó a tomarle gusto a su trabajo; **in time he grew to accept it** con el tiempo llegó a aceptarlo

Ⓑ VT [1] [+ *plant, crop*] cultivar; **I ~ my own vegetables** tengo mi propio huerto, cultivo mis verduras

[2] [+ *hair, beard, moustache, nails*] dejarse crecer; **she has ~n her hair long** se ha dejado el pelo largo, se ha dejado crecer el pelo; **the lizard grew a new tail** al lagarto le salió una cola nueva

►**grow apart** VI + ADV [*friends*] distanciarse; [*couple*] **he and his wife grew apart** la relación entre él y su mujer se entibió *or* se debilitó; **couples often ~ apart as they get older** a menudo las parejas se van distanciando con la edad

►**grow away from** VI + PREP distanciarse de; **we have ~n away from each other** nos hemos distanciado el uno del otro

►**grow from** VI + PREP [*friendship, theory, idea*] surgir de, nacer de; **I started out with just two clients and the business grew from that** empecé con sólo dos clientes y el negocio surgió *or* nació de ahí

►**grow in** VI + ADV [*nail*] crecer hacia adentro

►**grow into** VI + PREP [1] [+ *clothes*] **the trousers are a bit big but he'll ~ into them** los pantalones son un poco grandes pero ya crecerá y le sentarán bien

[2] (= *get used to*) **to ~ into a job** acostumbrarse a un trabajo

[3] (= *become*) convertirse en; **he's ~n into quite a handsome boy** se ha convertido en un chico muy apuesto; **to ~ into a man** hacerse un hombre

►**grow on** VI + PREP **the tune ~s on you after a while** la melodía te empieza a gustar con el tiempo; **the idea had ~n on her all morning** a medida que avanzó la mañana le fue gustando más la idea

►**grow out** Ⓐ VI + ADV **she let her perm ~ out** se dejó crecer el pelo para cortarse la permanente

Ⓑ VT + ADV [+ *hair*] dejar crecer

►**grow out of** VI + PREP [1] (= *get too big for*) [+ *clothes*] **you've ~n out of your shoes again** se te han vuelto a quedar pequeños los zapatos

[2] (= *stop*) [+ *habit*] **isn't it time you grew out of fighting with your sister?** ¿no te estás haciendo un poco mayor para seguir peleándote con tu hermana?; **most children who stammer ~ out of it** a casi todos los niños el tartamudeo se les quita con la edad; **she grew out of the habit of waiting up for the children** con el tiempo perdió la costumbre de esperar a los niños despierta

[3] (= *arise from*) surgir de

►**grow together** VI + ADV **couples who have ~n together over the years** parejas que han ido uniéndose más con el paso de los años; **there are many ways in which Europe can ~ together** hay muchas formas en las que los países europeos pueden reforzar sus vínculos

►**grow up** VI + ADV [1] (= *become adult*) hacerse mayor; **I watched Tim ~ up** vi a Tim hacerse mayor, vi como Tim se hacía mayor; **when I ~ up I'm going to be a doctor** cuando sea mayor voy a ser médico; **she grew up into a beautiful woman** con el tiempo se convirtió en una mujer hermosa; **~ up!*** ¡no seas niño!

[2] (= *spend young life*) crecer; **we grew up together** crecimos juntos; **she grew up in the country/during the depression** creció *or* se crió en el campo/en los años de la depresión

[3] (= *develop*) [*friendship*] desarrollarse; [*hatred*] crecer; [*town, industry*] desarrollarse, crecer; [*custom*] arraigar, imponerse; **a close friendship had ~n up between us** entre nosotros se había desarrollado una íntima amistad; **a barrier had ~n up between them** se había levantado una barrera entre ellos; **new industries grew up alongside the port** nuevas industrias se desarrollaron alrededor del puerto

growbag ['grəʊbæg] N bolsa *f* de cultivo

grower ['grəʊəʳ] N cultivador(a) *m/f*

growing ['grəʊɪŋ] Ⓐ ADJ [1] (= *developing*) [1·1] (*Bot, Agr*) [*crop, plant*] que está creciendo

[1·2] [*child*] en edad de crecimiento

[2] (= *expanding, increasing*) [*business*] en fase de desarrollo; [*friendship*] creciente; [*population, family*] creciente; **there is ~ concern that he won't be found alive** cada vez es mayor la preocupación de no encontrarlo con vida; **there is a ~ demand for this service** está aumentando la demanda de este servicio; **with ~ horror we realized that ...** cada vez más horrorizados, nos dimos cuenta de que ...; **a ~ number of refugees** un número creciente *or* cada vez mayor de refugiados; **I felt a ~ sense of unease** me sentía cada vez más nervioso

Ⓑ CPD ► **growing pains** NPL (*lit*) dolores *mpl* de crecimiento; (*fig*) problemas *mpl* iniciales ► **growing season** N [*of crop*] época *f* de cultivo; [*of plant*] época *f* de crecimiento

growl [graʊl] Ⓐ N gruñido *m*

Ⓑ VI [*animal*] gruñir; [*person*] refunfuñar; [*thunder*] reverberar

Ⓒ VT **"yes," he ~ed** —sí —refunfuñó

grown [grəʊn] Ⓐ PP *of* **grow**

Ⓑ ADJ (*also* **fully ~**) adulto, maduro

grown-up ['grəʊn'ʌp] Ⓐ ADJ adulto

Ⓑ N adulto/a *m/f*, persona *f* mayor

growth [grəʊθ] Ⓐ N [1] (= *development*) [*of person, animal, plant*] crecimiento *m*; **spiritual ~** desarrollo *m* espiritual

[2] (= *expansion*) [*of city*] crecimiento *m*; (*Econ*) crecimiento *m*, desarrollo *m*; **the ~ of national industries** el desarrollo *or* el crecimiento de las industrias nacionales; *see also* **capital C**

[3] (= *increase*) (*in productivity, profits, demand*) aumento *m*; **population ~** crecimiento *m* demográfico

[4] (*Bot*) (= *vegetation*) vegetación *f*; (= *buds, leaves*) brotes *mpl*; **the pine tree was putting out new ~** el pino estaba echando brotes nuevos

[5] (= *beard*) **with three days' ~ on his face** con barba de tres días

[6] (*Med*) tumor *m*

Ⓑ CPD ► **growth area** N (*Econ*) [*of country*] polo *m* de desarrollo; [*of industry*] sector *m* en crecimiento *or* expansión ► **growth hormone** N hormona *f* del crecimiento ► **growth industry** N industria *f* en crecimiento *or* expansión ► **growth point** N punto *m* de desarrollo ► **growth potential** N potencial *m* de crecimiento ► **growth rate** N (*Econ*) tasa *f* de crecimiento ► **growth shares** NPL (*US*) = **growth stock** ► **growth stock** N acciones *fpl* con perspectivas de valorización ► **growth town** N ciudad *f* en vías de desarrollo

groyne [grɔɪn] N espolón *m*

GRSM N ABBR (*Brit*) = **Graduate of the Royal Schools of Music**

GRT N ABBR (= **gross register tons**) TRB *fpl*

grub [grʌb] Ⓐ N [1] (= *larva*) larva *f*, gusano *m*

[2] (‡) (= *food*) comida *f*; **~('s) up!** ¡la comida está servida!

Ⓑ VI **to ~ about in the earth for sth** remover la tierra buscando algo

Ⓒ CPD ► **Grub Street***† N (*Brit*) *el mundillo de los escritores desconocidos*

►**grub up** VT + ADV arrancar, desarraigar; (= *discover*) desenterrar

grubbiness ['grʌbɪnɪs] N suciedad *f*

grubby ['grʌbɪ] ADJ (*compar* **grubbier**, *superl* **grubbiest**) (= *dirty*) mugriento, sucio, mugroso (*LAm*)

grudge [grʌdʒ] Ⓐ N resentimiento *m*, rencor *m* (**against** a); **to bear sb a ~** ◊ **have a ~ against sb** guardar rencor a algn

Ⓑ VT [1] (= *give unwillingly*) dar de mala gana; **to ~ sb sth** dar algo a algn a regañadientes

[2] (= *envy*) envidiar; **I don't ~ you your success** no te envidio el éxito; **he ~s us our pleasures** mira con malos ojos nuestros placeres

[3] (= *resent*) **to ~ doing sth** hacer algo de mala gana

Ⓒ CPD ► **grudge match*** N (*Sport*) enfrentamiento *m* entre antagonistas, enfrentamiento *m* entre rivales inconciliables; (*fig*) enfrentamiento *m* personal

grudging ['grʌdʒɪŋ] ADJ [*attitude, praise*] reticente; **he earned the ~ admiration/respect of his rivals** se ganó, aunque con reticencias, el respeto/la admiración de sus rivales; **she gave us a ~ apology** se disculpó de mala gana *or* a regañadientes

grudgingly ['grʌdʒɪŋlɪ] ADV de mala gana, a regañadientes

gruel [grʊəl] N gachas *fpl*

gruelling, **grueling** (*US*) ['grʊəlɪŋ] ADJ [*task*] penoso, duro; [*match, race*] agotador

gruesome ['gruːsəm] ADJ espantoso, horrible

gruff [grʌf] ADJ (*compar* **gruffer**, *superl* **gruffest**) [*voice*] ronco; [*manner*] brusco

gruffly ['grʌflɪ] ADV bruscamente

gruffness [ˈgrʌfnɪs] N [*of voice*] ronquera *f*; [*of person, manner*] brusquedad *f*

grumble [ˈgrʌmbl] Ⓐ N 1 (= *complaint*) queja *f*
2 (= *noise*) retumbo *m*
Ⓑ VI 1 (= *complain*) quejarse (**about** de)
2 [*thunder*] retumbar (a lo lejos)

grumbling [ˈgrʌmblɪŋ] Ⓐ N **I couldn't stand his constant ~** no podía soportar que estuviera gruñendo todo el rato
Ⓑ ADJ [*person, tone*] gruñón; **~ sound** gruñido *m*; **a ~ appendix** síntomas *mpl* de apendicitis

grumpily* [ˈgrʌmpɪlɪ] ADV gruñonamente, malhumoradamente

grumpiness* [ˈgrʌmpɪnɪs] N mal humor *m*

grumpy* [ˈgrʌmpɪ] ADJ (*compar* **grumpier**; *superl* **grumpiest**) [*person*] malhumorado, gruñón; [*voice*] de gruñón

grungy* [ˈgrʌndʒɪ] ADJ (*compar* **grungier**; *superl* **grungiest**) (= *dirty*) cutre (*Sp*), roñoso; (*Mus*) de grunge

grunt [grʌnt] Ⓐ N [*of animal, person*] gruñido *m*
Ⓑ VI [*animal, person*] gruñir
Ⓒ VT **"yes," he ~ed** —sí —gruñó

gruppetto [gruːˈpetəʊ] N (*pl* **gruppetti** [gruːˈpetiː]) grupeto *m*

gr. wt. ABBR = **gross weight**

gryphon [ˈgrɪfən] N = **griffin**

GS N ABBR (= **General Staff**) E.M.

GSA N ABBR (*US*) = **General Services Administration**

GSOH* N ABBR (= **good sense of humour**) (buen) sentido *m* del humor

G-string [ˈdʒiːstrɪŋ] N (*Mus*) cuerda *f* de sol; (= *clothing*) tanga *f*, taparrabo *m*

GSUSA N ABBR (*US*) = **Girl Scouts of the United States of America**

GT N ABBR (= **gran turismo**) GT

Gt ABBR = **Great**

GTi N ABBR (= **Gran Turismo injection**) GTi *m*

GU ABBR (*US*) = **Guam**

guacamole [ˌgwɑːkəˈməʊlɪ] N guacamole *m*

Guadeloupe [ˌgwɑːdəˈluːp] N Guadalupe *f*

Guam [gwɑːm] N Guam *f*

guano [ˈgwɑːnəʊ] N guano *m*

guarantee [ˌgærənˈtiː] Ⓐ N 1 (*gen, Comm*) garantía *f*; (= *surety*) caución *f*; **it is under ~** está bajo garantía; **there is no ~ that** no hay seguridad de que + *subjun*; **I give you my ~** se lo aseguro
2 (= *guarantor*) fiador(a) *m/f*
Ⓑ VT (*Comm*) [+ *goods*] garantizar (**against** contra); (= *ensure*) [+ *service, delivery*] asegurar; (= *make o.s. responsible for*) [+ *debt*] ser fiador de; **~d for three months** garantizado durante tres meses; **I ~ that ...** les garantizo que ...; **I can't ~ good weather** no respondo del tiempo; **he can't ~ that he'll come** no está seguro de poder venir

guaranteed [ˌgærənˈtiːd] Ⓐ ADJ [*goods, price, service, delivery*] garantizado
Ⓑ CPD ► **guaranteed bonus** N bonificación *f* garantizada ► **guaranteed loan** N préstamo *m* garantizado

guarantor [ˌgærənˈtɔːʳ] N (*Jur*) garante *mf*, fiador(a) *m/f*; **to act** *or* **stand as ~ for sb** avalar a algn

guaranty [ˈgærəntɪ] N (*Fin*) garantía *f*, caución *f*; (= *agreement*) garantía *f*

guard [gɑːd] Ⓐ N 1 (= *soldier*) guardia *mf*; (= *sentry*) centinela *mf*; (= *squad of soldiers*) guardia *f*; (= *escort*) escolta *f*; **to change (the) ~** relevar la guardia; **he's one of the old ~** pertenece a la vieja guardia; *see also* **advance D**
2 (*Mil*) (*also* **~ duty**) (= *watch*) guardia *f*; (*fig*) (= *watchfulness*) vigilancia *f*; **to drop one's ~** bajar la guardia, descuidarse; **to keep ~** vigilar; **to keep ~ over sth/sb** (*Mil, fig*) vigilar algo/a algn; **to lower one's ~** bajar la guardia, descuidarse; **to mount ~** montar guardia; **to be off one's ~** estar desprevenido; **to catch sb off his ~** coger *or* agarrar a algn desprevenido *or* (*LAm*) de imprevisto; **to be on ~** estar en guardia; **to be on one's ~** (*fig*) estar en guardia (**against** contra); **to put sb on his ~** poner a algn en guardia, prevenir a algn (**against** contra); **to stand ~ over sth** montar guardia sobre algo; **to be under ~** estar vigilado; **to keep sb under ~** vigilar a algn
3 (= *security guard*) guardia *mf* de seguridad
4 (*esp US*) (= *prison guard*) carcelero/a *m/f*
5 (*Brit Rail*) jefe *m* de tren
6 (*Sport*) defensa *mf*
7 (*Fencing*) guardia *f*; **on ~!** ¡en guardia!
8 (= *safety device*) (*on machine*) salvaguardia *f*, resguardo *m*; [*of sword*] guarda *f*, guarnición *f*; (*also* **fireguard**) guardafuego *m*; (= *protection*) protección *f*; **he wears goggles as a ~ against accidents** lleva unas gafas especiales como protección contra accidentes
Ⓑ VT [+ *prisoner, treasure*] vigilar, custodiar; (*while travelling*) escoltar; [+ *secret*] guardar; (= *protect*) [+ *place*] guardar, proteger (**against, from** de); [+ *person*] proteger (**against, from** de); **a closely ~ed secret** un secreto muy bien guardado
Ⓒ CPD ► **guard dog** N perro *m* guardián *or* de guarda ► **guard of honour** N (*Brit*) guardia *f* de honor ► **guard's van** N (*Brit Rail*) furgón *m*

► **guard against** VI + PREP [+ *illness*] guardarse de; [+ *suspicion, accidents*] evitar; **in order to ~ against this** para evitar esto; **to ~ against doing sth** evitar hacer algo

guarded [ˈgɑːdɪd] ADJ [*person*] cauto, comedido; [*reply, tone*] cauteloso; [*optimism*] comedido, moderado; **she was ~ about committing herself** fue cautelosa *or* cauta a la hora de comprometerse

guardedly [ˈgɑːdɪdlɪ] ADV [*say, reply*] cautelosamente, con cautela; **I feel ~ optimistic** me siento comedidamente *or* moderadamente optimista

guardedness [ˈgɑːdɪdnɪs] N cautela *f*, circunspección *f* (*frm*)

guardhouse [ˈgɑːdhaʊs] N (*pl* **guardhouses** [ˈgɑːd,haʊzɪz]) (*for guards*) cuartel *m* de la guardia; (*for prisoners*) cárcel *f* militar

guardian [ˈgɑːdɪən] Ⓐ N 1 protector(a) *m/f*, guardián/ana *m/f*
2 (*Jur*) [*of child*] tutor(a) *m/f*
Ⓑ CPD ► **guardian angel** N ángel *m* custodio, ángel *m* de la guarda

guardianship [ˈgɑːdɪənʃɪp] N tutela *f*, custodia *f*; **she was placed under her mother's ~** quedó sometida a la tutela de su madre

guardrail [ˈgɑːdreɪl] N pretil *m*, baranda *f*

guardroom [ˈgɑːdrʊm] N cuarto *m* de guardia

guardsman [ˈgɑːdzmən] N (*pl* **guardsmen**) (*Brit*) soldado *m* de la guardia real; (*US*) soldado *m* de la guardia (nacional)

Guatemala [ˌgwɑːtɪˈmɑːlə] N Guatemala *f*

Guatemalan [ˌgwɑːtɪˈmɑːlən] Ⓐ ADJ guatemalteco
Ⓑ N guatemalteco/a *m/f*

guava [ˈgwɑːvə] N guayaba *f*

Guayana [gaɪˈɑːnə] N Guayana *f*

gubbins* [ˈgʌbɪnz] N (*Brit*) 1 (= *thing*) chisme *m*, cacharro* *m*
2 (= *silly person*) bobo/a *m/f*

gubernatorial [ˌguːbənəˈtɔːrɪəl] ADJ (*esp US*) de(l) gobernador/de (la) gobernadora; **~ election** elección *f* de gobernador/gobernadora

gudgeon[1] [ˈgʌdʒən] N (= *fish*) gobio *m*

gudgeon[2] [ˈgʌdʒən] N (*Tech*) gorrón *m*

Guernsey [ˈgɜːnzɪ] N Guernesey *m*

guerrilla [gəˈrɪlə] Ⓐ N guerrillero/a *m/f*; **urban ~** guerrillero/a *m/f* urbano/a
Ⓑ CPD ► **guerrilla band** N guerrilla *f* ► **guerrilla warfare** N guerra *f* de guerrillas

guess [ges] Ⓐ N (= *conjecture*) conjetura *f*, suposición *f*; (= *estimate*) estimación *f* aproximada; **to make/have a ~** adivinar; **have a ~** ◊ **I'll give you three ~es** a ver si lo adivinas; **at a (rough) ~** a ojo; **my ~ is that ...** yo creo que ...; **it's anybody's ~** ¿quién sabe?; **your ~ is as good as mine!** ¡vete a saber!
Ⓑ VT 1 [+ *answer, meaning*] acertar; [+ *height, weight, number*] adivinar; **~ what!** ¡a que no lo adivinas!; **~ who!** ¡a ver si adivinas quién soy!; **I ~ed as much** me lo suponía; **you've ~ed it!** ¡has acertado!; **I never ~ed it was so big** nunca supuse que fuera tan grande; **I ~ed him to be about 20** le eché unos 20 años
2 (*esp US*) (= *suppose*) creer, suponer; **I ~ you're right** supongo que tienes razón; **I ~ we'll buy it** me imagino que lo compraremos
Ⓒ VI 1 (= *make a guess*) adivinar; (= *guess correctly*) acertar; **you'll never ~** no lo adivinarás nunca; **he's just ~ing** no hace más que especular; **to keep sb ~ing** mantener a algn a la expectativa; **to ~ at sth** intentar adivinar algo; **all that time we never ~ed** en todo ese tiempo no lo sospechábamos
2 (*esp US*) (= *suppose*) suponer, creer; **I ~ so** creo que sí; **he's happy, I ~** supongo que está contento

guessing game [ˈgesɪŋ,geɪm] N acertijo *m*, adivinanza *f*

guesstimate* [ˈgestɪmɪt] N estimación *f* aproximada

guesswork [ˈgeswɜːk] N conjeturas *fpl*; **it's all ~** son meras conjeturas

guest [gest] Ⓐ N (*at home*) invitado/a *m/f*; (*at hotel, guesthouse*) huésped *mf*; **they had ~s that weekend** tenían invitados *or* visita(s) ese fin de semana; **~ of honour** invitado/a *m/f* de honor; **"do you mind if I sit here?" — "be my ~"*** —¿le importa si me siento aquí? —por supuesto que no; **we were their ~s last summer** nos invitaron a su casa el verano pasado
Ⓑ VI (*US*) aparecer como invitado; **he's ~ing on tonight's show** aparecerá como invitado en el show de esta noche
Ⓒ CPD ► **guest artist** N = **guest star** ► **guest book** N libro *m* de los huéspedes ► **guest room** N cuarto *m* de huéspedes ► **guest speaker** N orador(a) *m/f* invitado/a ► **guest star** N estrella *f* invitada

guesthouse [ˈgesthaʊs] (*pl* **guesthouses** [ˈgesthaʊzɪz]) N 1 (*Brit*) (= *hotel*) pensión *f*, casa *f* de huéspedes
2 (*US*) (*in grounds of large house*) casa *f* de invitados

guff* [gʌf] N chorradas* *fpl*

guffaw [gʌˈfɔː] Ⓐ N carcajada *f*
Ⓑ VI reírse a carcajadas

GUI [ˈguːɪ] N ABBR (*Comput*) = **graphical user interface**

Guiana [gaɪˈɑːnə] N Guayana *f*

guidance [ˈgaɪdəns] N 1 (= *counselling*) consejo *m*; (= *leadership*) dirección *f*; **marriage/**

vocational ~ orientación *f* matrimonial/profesional; **under the ~ of** bajo la dirección de; **I tell you this for your ~** te lo digo para que puedas orientarte
[2] [*of missile*] dirección *f*

guide [gaɪd] Ⓐ N [1] (= *person*) guía *mf*; (= *girl guide*) exploradora *f*, guía *f*; (= *book*) guía *f* turística
[2] (= *fig*) guía *f*; **let conscience be your ~** haz lo que te dicte tu conciencia
Ⓑ VT (*round town, building*) guiar; (*in choice, decision*) orientar; (= *govern*) dirigir, gobernar; **to be ~d by sth/sb** dejarse guiar por algo/algn
Ⓒ CPD ► **guide dog** N perro *m* guía

guidebook ['gaɪdbʊk] N guía *f* turística

guided ['gaɪdɪd] ADJ **~ missile** misil *m* teledirigido; **~ tour** excursión *f* con guía

guideline ['gaɪdlaɪn] N (línea *f*) directriz *f*; (*for writing*) falsilla *f*

guidepost ['gaɪdpəʊst] N poste *m* indicador

guiding ['gaɪdɪŋ] ADJ **~ principle** principio *m* director; **~ star** estrella *f* de guía

guild [gɪld] N gremio *m*

guilder ['gɪldəʳ] N (*pl* **guilders** *or* **guilder**) florín *m* (holandés)

guildhall ['gɪld,hɔːl] N (= *town hall*) ayuntamiento *m*

guile [gaɪl] N astucia *f*

guileful ['gaɪlfəl] ADJ astuto, mañoso

guileless ['gaɪllɪs] ADJ inocente, candoroso

guillemot ['gɪlɪmɒt] N arao *m*

guillotine [,gɪlə'tiːn] Ⓐ N guillotina *f*
Ⓑ VT guillotinar

guilt [gɪlt] Ⓐ N (*gen*) culpa *f*, culpabilidad *f*; (*Jur*) culpabilidad *f*; **feelings of ~** sentimientos *mpl* de culpa *or* de culpabilidad; **to admit one's ~** confesarse culpable; **she was racked with ~** la atormentaba el remordimiento
Ⓑ CPD ► **guilt complex** N complejo *m* de culpabilidad *or* de culpa ► **guilt trip*** N **there's no point in having a ~ trip about it** no merece la pena empezar con sentimientos de culpabilidad, no merece la pena sentirse culpable

guiltily ['gɪltɪlɪ] ADV (= *feeling guilty*) sintiéndose culpable, con sentimiento de culpabilidad; (= *looking guilty*) con aire de culpabilidad

guiltless ['gɪltlɪs] ADJ inocente, libre de culpa; **she was considered ~ of his death** la consideraron inocente de su muerte

guilty ['gɪltɪ] ADJ (*compar* **guiltier**, *superl* **guiltiest**) culpable; **their parents were ~ of gross neglect** sus padres eran culpables de grave negligencia; **he had a ~ look on his face** su rostro reflejaba culpabilidad; **she wondered why the children were looking so ~** se preguntaba por qué los niños tenían esa cara de culpa; **~ conscience** remordimientos *mpl* de conciencia, sentimiento *m* de culpabilidad; **to have a ~ conscience** tener remordimientos (de conciencia), sentirse culpable; **to feel ~ (about sth)** sentirse culpable (por algo); **to find sb ~/not ~** declarar a algn culpable/inocente; **to be ~ of sth** ser culpable de algo; **the ~ party** el/la culpable; **"how do you plead? — ~ or not ~?"** —¿cómo se declara? — ¿culpable o inocente?; **he has a ~ secret** tiene un secreto que le remuerde la conciencia *or* que le hace sentirse culpable; **a ~ smile** una sonrisa de culpabilidad; **a verdict of ~** una sentencia de culpabilidad; **a verdict of not ~** una declaración de inocencia; *see also* **plea A3**, **plead B2**

Guinea ['gɪnɪ] Ⓐ N Guinea *f*
Ⓑ CPD ► **guinea fowl** N gallina *f* de Guinea, pintada *f* ► **guinea pig** N cobayo *m*, cobaya *f*, conejillo *m* de Indias, cuy *m* (*Andes, S. Cone*); (*fig*) conejillo *m* de Indias

guinea ['gɪnɪ] N (*Brit*) (*formerly*) guinea *f* (= *21 chelines*)

Guinea-Bissau ['gɪnɪbɪ'saʊ] N Guinea-Bissau *f*

Guinean ['gɪnɪən] Ⓐ ADJ guineano
Ⓑ N guineano/a *m/f*

Guinevere ['gwɪnɪvɪəʳ] N Ginebra

guise [gaɪz] N **in that ~** de esa manera; **under the ~ of** (= *disguised as*) bajo el disfraz de; (*fig*) con el pretexto de

guitar [gɪ'tɑːʳ] N guitarra *f*; (= *electric guitarist*) guitarra *mf*

guitarist [gɪ'tɑːrɪst] N guitarrista *mf*

Gujarati, **Gujerati** [,gʊdʒjə'rɑːtɪ] Ⓐ ADJ gujarati
Ⓑ N [1] (= *person*) Gujarati *mf*
[2] (*Ling*) gujarati *m*

gulch [gʌlʃ] N (*US*) barranco *m*

gulf [gʌlf] Ⓐ N (= *bay*) golfo *m*; (= *chasm*) (*also fig*) abismo *m*; **the (Persian) Gulf** el Golfo (Pérsico); **the Gulf of Mexico** el Golfo de Méjico *or* (*LAm*) México; **the Gulf of Suez** el Golfo de Suez
Ⓑ CPD ► **the Gulf States** NPL los países del Golfo ► **the Gulf Stream** N la corriente del Golfo

gull [gʌl] Ⓐ N (= *bird*) gaviota *f*
Ⓑ VT estafar, timar

gullet ['gʌlɪt] N esófago *m*, garganta *f*

gulley ['gʌlɪ] = **gully**

gullibility [,gʌlɪ'bɪlɪtɪ] N credulidad *f*, simpleza *f*

gullible ['gʌlɪbl] ADJ crédulo, simplón

gully ['gʌlɪ] N (= *ravine*) barranco *m*; (= *channel*) hondonada *f*

gulp [gʌlp] Ⓐ N trago *m*; **in** *or* **at one ~** de un trago; **"yes," he said with a ~** —sí —dijo tragando saliva
Ⓑ VT (*also* **~ down**) tragarse, engullir
Ⓒ VI (*while drinking*) tragar; (*through fear*) tener un nudo en la garganta; (= *swallow saliva*) tragar saliva

gum[1] [gʌm] N (*Anat*) encía *f*

gum[2] [gʌm] Ⓐ N (*gen*) goma *f*; (= *glue*) goma *f*, pegamento *m*, cemento *m* (*LAm*); (*also* **chewing ~**) chicle *m*; (= *sweet*) pastilla *f* de caramelo
Ⓑ VT (= *stick together*) pegar con goma; (*also* **~ down**) [+ *label, envelope*] pegar
Ⓒ CPD ► **gum arabic** N goma *f* arábiga

►**gum up** VT + ADV (*fig*) estropear, paralizar; ✦*IDIOM* **to ~ up the works*** meter un palo en la rueda

gum[3] [gʌm] EXCL **by ~!** ¡caramba!

gumbo ['gʌmbəʊ] N (*US Culin*) *sopa o estofado espesado con quingombó*

gumboil ['gʌmbɔɪl] N flemón *m*

gumboots ['gʌmbuːts] NPL botas *fpl* altas de goma

gumdrop ['gʌmdrɒp] N pastilla *f* de goma

gummed [gʌmd] ADJ [*envelope, label*] engomado

gummy ['gʌmɪ] ADJ gomoso

gump* [gʌmp] N [1] (= *sense*) sentido *m* común
[2] (= *fool*) tonto/a *m/f*, imbécil *mf*

gumption* ['gʌmpʃən] N (= *initiative*) iniciativa *f*; (*Brit*) (= *common sense*) seso *m*, sentido *m* común

gumshield ['gʌmʃiːld] N (*Sport*) protector *m* de dientes

gumshoe ['gʌmʃuː] N (*US*) [1] (= *overshoe*) zapato *m* de goma
[2] (*) (= *detective*) detective *mf*

gumtree ['gʌmtriː] N (*gen*) árbol *m* gomero; (= *eucalyptus*) eucalipto *m*; ✦*IDIOM* **to be up a ~** (*Brit**) estar en un aprieto

gun [gʌn] Ⓐ N [1] (= *pistol*) pistola *f*, revólver *m*; (= *rifle*) fusil *m*; (= *shotgun*) escopeta *f*; (= *cannon*) cañón *m*; **a 21-~ salute** una salva de 21 cañonazos; **the ~s** (*Mil*) la artillería; **big ~*** pez *m* gordo, espadón *m*; **to draw a ~ on sb** apuntar a algn con un arma; **to jump the ~** salir antes de tiempo; (*fig*) obrar con demasiada anticipación; ✦*IDIOMS* **to be going great ~s** hacer grandes progresos, ir a las mil maravillas; **to stick to one's ~s** mantenerse firme, mantenerse en sus trece
[2] (*Brit*) (= *person*) pistolero/a *m/f*
Ⓑ VT disparar sobre
Ⓒ CPD ► **gun barrel** N cañón *m* ► **gun battle** N tiroteo *m* ► **gun carriage** N cureña *f*; (*at funeral*) armón *m* de artillería ► **gun crew** N dotación *f* de un cañón ► **gun dog** N perro *m* de caza ► **gun law** N (= *rule by the gun*) ley *f* del terror, pistolerismo *m*; (*Jur*) ley *f* que rige la tenencia y uso de armas de fuego ► **gun licence** N licencia *f* de armas ► **gun maker** N armero/a *m/f* ► **gun room** N (*in house*) sala *f* de armas; (*Brit Naut*) sala *f* de suboficiales ► **gun turret** N torreta *f*

►**gun down** VT + ADV abatir a tiros, abalear (*LAm*)

►**gun for** VI + PREP (*fig*) ir a por; **it's really the boss they're ~ning for** en realidad van a por el jefe

gunboat ['gʌnbəʊt] Ⓐ N (*seagoing*) cañonero *m*; (*small*) lancha *f* cañonera
Ⓑ CPD ► **gunboat diplomacy** N diplomacia *f* cañonera

guncotton ['gʌn,kɒtn] N algodón *m* pólvora

gunfight ['gʌnfaɪt] N tiroteo *m*

gunfire ['gʌnfaɪəʳ] N disparos *mpl*; (*from artillery*) cañoneo *m*, fuego *m* de cañón

gunge* [gʌndʒ] Ⓐ N mugre *f*
Ⓑ VT **to ~ up** atascar, obstruir

gung-ho ['gʌŋ'həʊ] ADJ [1] (= *over-enthusiastic*) (tontamente) optimista, (locamente) entusiasta
[2] (= *jingoistic*) patriotero (en exceso), jingoísta

gunk* [gʌŋk] N = **gunge**

gunman ['gʌnmən] N (*pl* **gunmen**) pistolero *m*, gatillero *m* (*LAm*)

gunmetal ['gʌn,metl] N bronce *m* de cañón

gunner ['gʌnəʳ] N artillero/a *m/f*

gunnery ['gʌnərɪ] Ⓐ N [1] (= *art, skill*) puntería *f*; (= *science*) tiro *m*
[2] (= *guns*) artillería *f*
Ⓑ CPD ► **gunnery officer** N oficial *mf* de artillería

gunny ['gʌnɪ] N arpillera *f*; (*also* **~ bag, ~ sack**) saco *m* de yute

gunpoint ['gʌnpɔɪnt] N **at ~** a punta de pistola; **to hold sb at ~** tener a algn a punta de pistola

gunpowder ['gʌn,paʊdəʳ] Ⓐ N pólvora *f*
Ⓑ CPD ► **Gunpowder Plot** N (*Brit*) Conspiración de la Pólvora; → GUY FAWKES NIGHT

gunrunner ['gʌn,rʌnəʳ] N contrabandista *mf* *or* traficante *mf* de armas

gunrunning ['gʌn,rʌnɪŋ] N contrabando *m* *or* tráfico *m* de armas

gunship ['gʌnʃɪp] N helicóptero *m* artillado *or* de combate

gunshot ['gʌnʃɒt] Ⓐ N (= *noise*) disparo *m*; (*from artillery*) cañonazo *m*; (*from shotgun*) escopetazo *m*; **within ~** a tiro de fusil
Ⓑ CPD ► **gunshot wound** N escopetazo *m*

gun-shy ['gʌnʃaɪ] ADJ (*lit*) que se asusta con los disparos; (*fig*) acobardado

gunslinger* ['gʌnslɪŋgəʳ] N pistolero/a *m/f*

gunsmith ['gʌnsmɪθ] N armero/a *m/f*

gunwale ['gʌnl] N borda *f*, regala *f*

guppy ['gʌpɪ] N guppy *m*

gurgle ['gɜːgl] Ⓐ N [*of liquid*] borboteo *m*, gluglú *m*; [*of baby*] gorjeo *m*
Ⓑ VI [*liquid*] borbotear; [*baby*] gorjear

Gurkha ['gɜːkə] N gurkha *mf*, gurja *mf*

gurney ['gɜːnɪ] N (*US*) camilla *f*

guru ['gʊruː] N gurú *mf*

Gus [gʌs] N (*familiar form*) *of* **Angus, Augustus**

gush [gʌʃ] Ⓐ N [1] [*of liquid*] chorro *m*; [*of words*] torrente *m*; [*of feeling*] efusión *f*
[2] (= *sentimentalism*) sentimentalismo *m*
Ⓑ VT [+ *blood*] chorrear, derramar a borbotones; [+ *water*] chorrear, derramar
Ⓒ VI [1] (*also* **~ out**) [*water, blood*] chorrear (**from** de)
[2] (*) (= *enthuse*) hablar con entusiasmo (**about, over** de)

gusher ['gʌʃəʳ] N [1] (= *oilwell*) pozo *m* surtido
[2] **to be a ~** [*person*] ser muy efusivo

gushing ['gʌʃɪŋ] ADJ efusivo

gusset ['gʌsɪt] N escudete *m*

gust [gʌst] Ⓐ N [*of wind*] ráfaga *f*, racha *f*
Ⓑ VI soplar racheado; **the wind ~ed up to 120km/h** el viento soplaba en rachas de hasta 120km/h

gustatory ['gʌstətərɪ] ADJ (*frm*) [*sense*] gustativo; [*delights, pleasures*] gastronómico, del paladar

gusto ['gʌstəʊ] N **with ~** con entusiasmo

gusty ['gʌstɪ] ADJ (*compar* **gustier**; *superl* **gustiest**) [*weather*] borrascoso; [*wind*] racheado

gut [gʌt] Ⓐ N [1] (= *alimentary canal*) intestino *m*; (*for violin, racket*) cuerda *f* de tripa; ✦*IDIOM* **to bust a ~**‡ echar los bofes, echar el hígado
[2] **guts*** (= *innards*) tripas *fpl*; (= *courage*) agallas* *fpl*, coraje *m*; (= *staying power*) aguante *m*, resistencia *f*; (= *moral strength*) carácter *m*; (= *content*) meollo *m*, sustancia *f*; **to have ~s** tener agallas*; **I hate his ~s*** no lo puedo ver ni en pintura; **to spill one's ~s**‡ contar la propia vida y milagros; **to work one's ~s out** echar los bofes, echar el hígado; ✦*IDIOM* **I'll have his ~s for garters!*** ¡le hago trizas!
[3] (*Naut*) estrecho *m*
Ⓑ VT [1] [+ *poultry, fish*] destripar
[2] [+ *building*] no dejar más que las paredes de
Ⓒ CPD ► **gut feeling** N instinto *m* visceral
► **gut reaction** N reacción *f* instintiva

gutless* ['gʌtlɪs] ADJ cobarde, sin agallas*

gutsy* ['gʌtsɪ] ADJ (*compar* **gutsier**; *superl* **gutsiest**) valiente, con agallas*

gutta-percha ['gʌtə'pɜːtʃə] N gutapercha *f*

gutted* ['gʌtɪd] ADJ (*Brit*) (= *disappointed*) **I was ~** me quedé hecho polvo*

gutter[1] ['gʌtəʳ] Ⓐ N (*in street*) arroyo *m*, cuneta *f*, desagüe *m* (*CAm*); (*on roof*) canal *m*, canalón *m*; **the ~** (*fig*) los barrios bajos; (= *underworld*) el hampa; **he rose from the ~** (*fig*) salió de la nada
Ⓑ CPD ► **the gutter press** N (*pej*) la prensa amarilla; → TABLOIDS AND BROADSHEETS

gutter[2] ['gʌtəʳ] VI [*candle*] irse consumiendo

guttering ['gʌtərɪŋ] N canales *mpl*, canalones *mpl*

guttersnipe ['gʌtəsnaɪp] N golfillo *m*

guttural ['gʌtərəl] ADJ [*accent, sound*] gutural

guv [gʌv] N = **governor**; **thanks, ~!** ¡gracias, jefe!

guv'nor* ['gʌvnəʳ] N = **governor**

guy[1]* [gaɪ] Ⓐ N (= *man*) tío* *m*, tipo* *m*, cuate *m* (*Mex*); (= *effigy*) efigie *f*; **he's a nice ~** es un buen tío *or* tipo; **hey, (you) ~s!** ¡eh, amigos!; **are you ~s ready to go?** ¿están todos listos para salir?; *see also* **wise B**
Ⓑ VT (= *make fun of*) ridiculizar; (*Theat*) parodiar

guy[2] [gaɪ] N (*also* **~ rope**) (*for tent*) viento *m*, cuerda *f*

Guy [gaɪ] N Guido; **~ Fawkes Day** ◊ **~ Fawkes Night** (*Brit*) *cinco de noviembre, aniversario de la Conspiración de la Pólvora*

GUY FAWKES NIGHT

La noche del cinco de noviembre, **Guy Fawkes Night** *se celebra en el Reino Unido el fracaso de la conspiración de la pólvora* **Gunpowder Plot**, *un intento fallido de volar el Parlamento de Jaime I en 1605. Esa noche se lanzan fuegos artificiales y se hacen hogueras en las que se queman unos muñecos de trapo que representan a* **Guy Fawkes**, *uno de los cabecillas de la revuelta. Días antes, los niños tienen por costumbre pedir a los transeúntes* **a penny for the guy**, *dinero que emplean en comprar cohetes.*

Guyana [gaɪ'ænə] N Guayana *f*

Guyanese [,gaɪə'niːz] Ⓐ ADJ guyanés
Ⓑ N guyanés/esa *m/f*

guzzle ['gʌzl] Ⓐ VT [1] [+ *food*] engullirse, tragarse; [+ *drink*] soplarse, tragarse (*LAm*)
[2] (* *hum*) [*car*] [+ *petrol*] tragar mucho
Ⓑ VI (= *eat*) engullir, tragar; (= *drink*) soplar, tragar (*LAm*)

guzzler ['gʌzləʳ] N tragon/ona *m/f*, comilón/ona *m/f*; *see also* **gas D**

gym* [dʒɪm] Ⓐ N (= *gymnasium*) gimnasio *m*; (= *gymnastics*) gimnasia *f*
Ⓑ CPD ► **gym shoes** NPL zapatillas *fpl* de gimnasia

gymkhana [dʒɪm'kɑːnə] N gincana *f*

gymnasium [dʒɪm'neɪzɪəm] N (*pl* **gymnasiums** *or* **gymnasia** [dʒɪm'neɪzɪə]) gimnasio *m*

gymnast ['dʒɪmnæst] N gimnasta *mf*

gymnastic [dʒɪm'næstɪk] ADJ gimnástico

gymnastics [dʒɪm'næstɪks] N gimnasia *f*

gymslip ['dʒɪmslɪp] N (*Brit*) túnica *f* de gimnasia

gynaecological, **gynecological** (*US*) [,gaɪnɪkə'lɒdʒɪkəl] ADJ ginecológico

gynaecologist, **gynecologist** (*US*) [,gaɪnɪ'kɒlədʒɪst] N ginecólogo/a *m/f*

gynaecology, **gynecology** (*US*) [,gaɪnɪ'kɒlədʒɪ] N ginecología *f*

gyp[1]‡ [dʒɪp] (*US*) Ⓐ N [1] (= *swindle*) estafa *f*, timo *m*
[2] (= *swindler*) estafador(a) *m/f*, timador(a) *m/f*
Ⓑ VT estafar, timar

gyp[2]* [dʒɪp] N (*Brit*) ✦*IDIOM* **to give sb ~** (= *scold*) echar un rapapolvo de aúpa a algn; **it's giving me ~** (= *hurting*) me duele una barbaridad

gypsum ['dʒɪpsəm] N yeso *m*

gypsy ['dʒɪpsɪ] Ⓐ N gitano/a *m/f*
Ⓑ CPD [*life, caravan, music*] gitano ► **gypsy moth** N lagarta *f*

gyrate [dʒaɪ'reɪt] VI (= *spin*) girar; (= *dance*) bailar enérgicamente

gyration [,dʒaɪ'reɪʃən] N giro *m*, vuelta *f*

gyratory [,dʒaɪ'reɪtərɪ] ADJ giratorio

gyro... ['dʒaɪrəʊ] PREFIX giro...

gyrocompass ['dʒaɪrəʊ'kʌmpəs] N girocompás *m*

gyroscope ['dʒaɪrəskəʊp] N giroscopio *m*, giróscopo *m*

H h

H, h [eɪtʃ] N (= *letter*) H, h *f*; **H for Harry** H de Historia

h. ABBR (= **hour(s)**) h, hs

ha [hɑː] EXCL ¡ah!

habeas corpus ['heɪbɪəs'kɔːpəs] N (*Jur*) hábeas corpus *m*

haberdasher ['hæbədæʃəʳ] N mercero/a *m/f*; (*US*) camisero/a *m/f*; **~'s (shop)** mercería *f*; (*US*) camisería *f*

haberdashery [ˌhæbə'dæʃərɪ] N (= *shop*) mercería *f*; (*US*) camisería *f*; (= *goods*) mercería *f*; (*US*) artículos *mpl* de moda para caballeros

habit ['hæbɪt] N **1** (= *customary behaviour*) costumbre *f*; **a bad ~** un vicio, una mala costumbre; **to get into the ~ of doing sth** acostumbrarse a hacer algo; **to get out of the ~ of doing sth** perder la costumbre de hacer algo; **to have a ~*** (= *drugs*) drogarse habitualmente; **to be in the ~ of doing sth** tener la costumbre de hacer algo, acostumbrar *or* soler hacer algo; **to make a ~ of doing sth** acostumbrarse a hacer algo; **we mustn't make a ~ of arriving late** no debemos acostumbrarnos a llegar tarde; **you can phone me at work as long as you don't make a ~ of it** puedes llamarme al trabajo mientras no lo tomes por costumbre; **let's hope he doesn't make a ~ of it** esperamos que no siga haciéndolo; **I always make a ~ of arriving early** tengo por norma *or* por costumbre llegar siempre pronto; **out of ~** por costumbre; **out of sheer ~** por pura costumbre
2 (= *dress*) [*of monk*] hábito *m*; (= *riding habit*) traje *m* de montar

habitability [ˌhæbɪtə'bɪlɪtɪ] N [*of building, area*] habitabilidad *f*

habitable ['hæbɪtəbl] ADJ habitable

habitat ['hæbɪtæt] N hábitat *m*

habitation [ˌhæbɪ'teɪʃən] N **1** (= *act*) habitación *f*; **to be fit/unfit for (human) ~** estar/no estar en condiciones de habitabilidad; **there was no sign of (human) ~** no había señales de que estuviera habitado
2 (= *dwelling*) residencia *f*, morada *f*; (= *house*) domicilio *m*

habit-forming ['hæbɪtˌfɔːmɪŋ] ADJ que crea hábito

habitual [hə'bɪtjʊəl] ADJ habitual, acostumbrado; [*drunkard, liar etc*] inveterado, empedernido

habitually [hə'bɪtjʊəlɪ] ADV (= *usually*) por costumbre; (= *constantly*) constantemente

habituate [hə'bɪtjʊeɪt] VT acostumbrar, habituar (**to** a)

habitué(e) [hə'bɪtjʊeɪ] N asiduo/a *m/f*, parroquiano/a *m/f*

hacienda [ˌhæsɪ'endə] N (*US*) hacienda *f*

hack¹ [hæk] Ⓐ N (= *cut*) corte *m*, tajo *m*; (= *blow*) (*with axe*) hachazo *m*; (*with machete*) machetazo *m*
Ⓑ VT **1** (= *cut*) cortar; **to ~ one's way through sth** abrirse paso por algo a machetazos *etc*; **to ~ sth to pieces** hacer algo pedazos (a hachazos)
2 **I can't ~ it** (*US**) no puedo hacerlo
Ⓒ VI **1** (= *cut*) dar tajos (**at** a); **he was ~ing at a loaf of bread** estaba dándole tajos a una hogaza de pan
2 (*Comput*) **to ~ into a system** piratear un sistema, conseguir entrar en un sistema

►**hack around*** VI + ADV (*US*) gandulear, vaguear

►**hack down** VT + ADV [+ *tree etc*] derribar a hachazos

hack² [hæk] Ⓐ N **1** (= *old horse*) jamelgo *m*, rocín *m*; (= *hired horse*) caballo *m* de alquiler
2 (= *writer*) escritorzuelo/a *m/f*, plumífero/a *m/f*; (= *journalist*) gacetillero/a *m/f*
3 (*US**) (= *taxi*) taxi *m*
Ⓑ VI **to go ~ing** montar a caballo
Ⓒ CPD ► **hack reporter** N reportero/a *m/f* de poca monta ► **hack writer** N = **hack² A2**

hackberry ['hækberɪ] N almez *m*

hacker ['hækəʳ] N (*Comput*) (= *pirate*) pirata *mf* informático/a

hackery* ['hækərɪ] N **1** = **hackwork**
2 = **hacking²**

hackette* [hæ'ket] N periodista *f*

hacking¹ ['hækɪŋ] ADJ [*cough*] seco

hacking² ['hækɪŋ] N (*Comput*) piratería *f* informática

hacking jacket ['hækɪŋˌdʒækɪt] N chaqueta *f* de montar, saco *m* de montar (*LAm*)

hackles ['hæklz] NPL (*lit*) [*of dog*] (*on back of neck*) pelo *m* del pescuezo; (*on back*) pelo *m* del lomo; **with his ~ up** [*dog*] con el pelo erizado; [*person*] hecho una furia, furioso; ✦***IDIOM* to make sb's ~ rise** poner hecho una furia a algn, enfurecer a algn

hackney cab ['hæknɪ'kæb] N, **hackney carriage** ['hæknɪ'kærɪdʒ] N (*frm*) coche *m* de alquiler; (= *taxi*) taxi *m*

hackneyed ['hæknɪd] ADJ [*saying, expression*] trillado, gastado

hacksaw ['hæksɔː] N sierra *f* para metales

hackwork ['hækwɜːk] N trabajo *m* de rutina; (*iro*) periodismo *m*

had [hæd] PT, PP *of* **have**

haddock ['hædək] N (*pl* **haddock** *or* **haddocks**) eglefino *m*

Hades ['heɪdiːz] N el Hades

hadn't ['hædnt] = **had not**

Hadrian ['heɪdrɪən] N Adriano; **~'s Wall** la Muralla de Adriano

haematological, **hematological** (*US*) [ˌhiːmətə'lɒdʒɪkəl] ADJ hematológico

haematologist, **hematologist** (*US*) [ˌhiːmə'tɒlədʒɪst] N hematólogo/a *m/f*

haematology, **hematology** (*US*) [ˌhiːmə'tɒlədʒɪ] N hematología *f*

haematoma, **hematoma** (*US*) [ˌhiːmə'təʊmə] N (*pl* **haematomas** *or* **haematomata** [ˌhimə'təʊmətə]) hematoma *m*

haemoglobin, **hemoglobin** (*US*) [ˌhiːməʊ'gləʊbɪn] N hemoglobina *f*

haemophilia, **hemophilia** (*US*) [ˌhiːməʊ'fɪlɪə] N hemofilia *f*

haemophiliac, **hemophiliac** (*US*) [ˌhiːməʊ'fɪlɪæk] Ⓐ ADJ hemofílico
Ⓑ N hemofílico/a *m/f*

haemorrhage, **hemorrhage** (*US*) ['hemərɪdʒ] Ⓐ N hemorragia *f*
Ⓑ VI sangrar profusamente

haemorrhoids, **hemorrhoids** (*US*) ['hemərɔɪdz] NPL hemorroides *fpl*

hafnium ['hæfnɪəm] N hafnio *m*

haft [hɑːft] N mango *m*, puño *m*

hag [hæg] N (= *ugly old woman*) vieja *f* fea, bruja *f*; (= *witch*) bruja *f*

haggard ['hægəd] ADJ (*from tiredness*) ojeroso; (= *unwell, unhealthy*) demacrado, macilento

haggis ['hægɪs] N (*Scot Culin*) *asaduras de cordero, avena y especias, cocidas en las tripas del animal*

haggish ['hægɪʃ] ADJ como de bruja, brujeril

haggle ['hægl] VI **1** (= *bargain*) regatear; **to ~ over the price** regatear, regatear el precio
2 (= *argue*) discutir

haggling ['hæglɪŋ] N **1** (*over price*) regateo *m*
2 (= *discussion*) discusión *f*

hagiographer [ˌhægɪ'ɒgrəfəʳ] N hagiógrafo/a *m/f*

hagiography [ˌhægɪ'ɒgrəfɪ] N hagiografía *f*

hag-ridden ['hægrɪdn] ADJ atormentado (*por una pesadilla*); (*) dominado por una mujer

Hague [heɪg] N **The ~** La Haya

hah [hɑː] = **ha**

ha-ha ['hɑː'hɑː] EXCL ¡ja, ja!

hail¹ [heɪl] Ⓐ N **1** (*Met*) granizo *m*, pedrisco *m*
2 (*fig*) [*of bullets*] lluvia *f*; [*of abuse, insults*] sarta *f*, torrente *m*
Ⓑ VI granizar

►**hail down** VI + ADV (*fig*) llover

hail² [heɪl] Ⓐ N (= *call*) grito *m*; (= *greeting*) saludo *m*; **within ~** al alcance de la voz
Ⓑ EXCL (††, *poet*) **~ Caesar!** ¡ave *or* salve, César!; **the Hail Mary** el Ave *f* María
Ⓒ VT **1** (= *acclaim*) aclamar (**as** como); **to ~ sb as king** aclamar a algn (como) rey
2 (= *greet*) saludar

3 (= *call to*) llamar, gritar a
4 (= *signal*) [+ *taxi*] llamar, hacer señas a
Ⓓ VI **to ~ from** [*person*] ser natural de, ser de; **he ~s from Scotland** es (natural) de Escocia; **where does that ship ~ from?** ¿de dónde es ese barco?

hail-fellow-well-met ['heɪl,feləʊ'wel'met] ADJ (demasiado) efusivo, campechano

hailstone ['heɪlstəʊn] N granizo *m*, piedra *f* (de granizo)

hailstorm ['heɪlstɔːm] N granizada *f*

hair [hɛəʳ] Ⓐ N 1 (= *head of hair*) pelo *m*, cabello *m*; (*on legs etc*) vello *m*; [*of animal*] pelo *m*, piel *f*; (= *fluff*) pelusa *f*; **to comb one's ~** peinarse; **to get/have one's ~ cut** cortarse el pelo; **to do one's ~** ◊ **have one's ~ done** arreglarse el pelo; **grey ~** canas *fpl*; **a fine head of ~** una hermosa cabellera; **he still has a full head of ~** aún conserva todo su pelo; **she's got long ~** tiene el pelo largo; **to part one's ~** hacerse la raya; **to remove unwanted ~** depilarse; **to put one's ~ up** recogerse el pelo; **to wash one's ~** lavarse la cabeza *or* el pelo; **white ~** canas *fpl*; ✦**IDIOMS to get in sb's ~** sacar de quicio a algn; **to get sb out of one's ~** quitarse de encima a algn; **keep your ~ on!** (*Brit**) ¡cálmate!; **to let one's ~ down** echar una cana al aire, soltarse la melena, relajarse (*esp LAm*); **to make sb's ~ stand on end** poner los pelos de punta a algn; **it was enough to make your ~ stand on end** te ponía los pelos de punta, era espeluznante; **to tear one's ~ out** ponerse frenético
2 (= *single hair*) pelo *m*; **by a ~'s breadth** por un pelo *or* los pelos; **to be within a ~'s breadth of** estar a dos dedos de; ✦**IDIOMS the ~ of the dog (that bit you)*** una copita para que se te pase la resaca; **what you need is a ~ of the dog that bit you** lo que te hace falta es tomarte otra para que se te pase la resaca; **to put ~s on one's chest**: **this will put ~s on your chest!*** ¡esto te hará la mar de bien!*; **to split ~s** buscarle tres pies al gato, hilar muy fino; **to turn a ~**: **he didn't turn a ~** ni se inmutó, ni siquiera pestañeó
Ⓑ CPD [*follicle, implant, transplant*] capilar; [*lacquer*] para el pelo; [*mattress*] de cerda ► **hair appointment** N **to have/make a ~ appointment** tener/pedir hora en la peluquería ► **hair care** N cuidado *m* del cabello ► **hair clippers** NPL maquinilla *f* para cortar el pelo ► **hair conditioner** N suavizante *m or* (*LAm*) enjuague *m* para el cabello ► **hair curler** N rulo *m*, bigudí *m* ► **hair extension** N postizo *m*; (= *false plait*) trenza *f* postiza ► **hair follicle** N folículo *m* capilar ► **hair gel** N fijador *m* ► **hair implant** N implante *m* capilar ► **hair loss** N pérdida *f* de cabello, caída *f* de pelo; **total ~ loss** pérdida *f* total del cabello, caída *f* total del pelo ► **hair oil** N brillantina *f* ► **hair remover** N depilatorio *m* ► **hair restorer** N loción *f* capilar ► **hair shirt** N cilicio *m* ► **hair slide** N (*Brit*) pasador *m*, hebilla *f* (*S. Cone*) ► **hair specialist** N especialista *mf* capilar ► **hair style** N peinado *m* ► **hair stylist** N peluquero/a *m/f* estilista ► **hair transplant** N trasplante *m* capilar ► **hair trigger** N *gatillo que se dispara con un ligero toque*; *see also* **hair-trigger**

hairball ['hɛəbɔːl] N (*in cats, calves etc*) bola *f* de pelo

hairband ['hɛəbænd] N cinta *f*

hairbrush ['hɛəbrʌʃ] N cepillo *m* (para el pelo)

hair-clip ['hɛəklɪp] N horquilla *f*, clipe *m*

haircream ['hɛəkriːm] N brillantina *f*; (*for setting*) fijador *m*, laca *f*

haircut ['hɛəkʌt] N corte *m* de pelo, corte *m*; **to have** *or* **get a ~** cortarse el pelo

hairdo* ['hɛəduː] N peinado *m*

hairdresser ['hɛə,dresəʳ] N peluquero/a *m/f*; **~'s** (= *salon*) peluquería *f*

hairdressing ['hɛədresɪŋ] Ⓐ N peluquería *f*
Ⓑ CPD ► **hairdressing salon** N salón *m* de peluquería

hairdrier, **hairdryer** ['hɛədraɪəʳ] N secador *m* de pelo

-haired [hɛəd] ADJ (*ending in compounds*) **fair-haired** rubio, güero (*CAm, Mex*), catire/a (*Carib, Col*); **dark-haired** moreno; **long-haired** de pelo largo

hair-grip ['hɛəgrɪp] N (*Brit*) horquilla *f*, clipe *m*

hairless ['hɛəlɪs] ADJ sin pelo, calvo; (= *beardless*) lampiño

hairline ['hɛəlaɪn] Ⓐ N 1 (*on head*) nacimiento *m* del pelo; **to have a receding ~** tener entradas
2 (*Tech*) estría *f* muy delgada
Ⓑ CPD ► **hairline crack** N grieta *f* fina ► **hairline fracture** N fractura *f* fina

hairnet ['hɛənet] N redecilla *f*

hairpiece ['hɛəpiːs] N postizo *m*, tupé *m*; (= *false plait*) trenza *f* postiza

hairpin ['hɛəpɪn] Ⓐ N horquilla *f*
Ⓑ CPD ► **hairpin bend**, **hairpin curve** (*US*) N revuelta *f*, curva *f* muy cerrada

hair-raising ['hɛə,reɪzɪŋ] ADJ [*story, adventure*] espeluznante

hair-splitting ['hɛə,splɪtɪŋ] Ⓐ ADJ nimio; [*discussion*] sobre detalles nimios
Ⓑ N sofismas *mpl*, sofistería *f*

hairspray ['hɛəspreɪ] N laca *f* (para el pelo)

hairspring ['hɛəsprɪŋ] N muelle *m* espiral muy fino (de un reloj)

hair-trigger ['hɛə,trɪgəʳ] ADJ (*fig*) [*temper, reaction*] explosivo; *see also* **hair B**

hairy ['hɛərɪ] ADJ (*compar* **hairier**; *superl* **hairiest**)
1 [*chest, legs, arms*] peludo, velludo; (= *long-haired*) melenudo; **he's got ~ legs** tiene las piernas peludas *or* velludas, tiene mucho pelo *or* vello en las piernas; **a ~ spider** una araña peluda
2 (*) (= *frightening*) [*experience*] horripilante, espeluznante

Haiti ['heɪtɪ] N Haití *m*

Haitian ['heɪʃɪən] Ⓐ ADJ haitiano
Ⓑ N haitiano/a *m/f*

hake [heɪk] N (*pl* **hake** *or* **hakes**) merluza *f*

halal [hə'lɑːl] ADJ *de animales sacrificados conforme a los preceptos musulmanes*

halberd ['hælbəd] N alabarda *f*

halcyon ['hælsɪən] ADJ **~ days** días *mpl* felices

hale [heɪl] ADJ sano, robusto; **~ and hearty** robusto, sano y fuerte

half [hɑːf] N (*pl* **halves**) Ⓐ N 1 (*gen*) mitad *f*; **give me ~** dame la mitad; **~ of my friends** la mitad de mis amigos; **~ man ~ beast** mitad hombre mitad animal; **~ a cup** media taza *f*; **~ a day** medio día *m*; **a pound and a ~** ◊ **one and a ~ pounds** libra *f* y media; **three and a ~ hours** tres horas y media; **we have a problem and a ~** tenemos un problema mayúsculo, vaya problemazo que tenemos; **one's better ~*** (*hum*) su media naranja*; **by ~**: **better by ~** con mucho el mejor; **it has increased by ~** ha aumentado en la mitad; **he's too clever by ~*** se pasa de listo; **he doesn't do things by halves** no hace las cosas a medias; **~ a dollar** (= *value*) medio dólar *m*; **~ a dozen** media docena *f*; **to go halves (with sb) (on sth)** ir a medias (con algn) (en algo); **~ an hour** media hora *f*; **to cut/break sth in ~** cortar/partir algo por la mitad; **~ a moment!** ◊ **~ a second!** ¡un momento!; **one's other ~*** (*hum*) su media naranja*; **they don't know the ~ of it** no saben de la misa la media; **she's asleep ~ the time** (*iro*) se pasa la mitad del tiempo dormida; → AVERAGE, HALF
2 (*Sport*) [*of match*] tiempo *m*; (= *player*) medio *m*; **first/second ~** primer/segundo tiempo *m*
3 [*of beer*] media pinta *f*
4 (= *child's ticket*) billete *m* de niño; **one and two halves, please** un billete normal y dos para niños, por favor
Ⓑ ADJ [*bottle, quantity*] medio; **a ~-point cut in interest rates** una reducción de medio punto en los tipos de interés; **I have a ~ share in the flat** la mitad del piso es mío *or* de mi propiedad; *see also* **halfback**, **half-brother, half-sister**
Ⓒ ADV 1 (*gen*) medio, a medias; **I was ~ afraid that ...** medio temía que ...; **~ as**: **~ as much** la mitad; **~ as big** la mitad de grande; **they paid ~ as much again** pagaron la mitad más; **their garden is ~ as big again** su jardín es la mitad más grande (que éste); **there were only ~ as many people as before** había solamente la mitad de los que había antes; **it wasn't ~ as bad as I had thought** [*interview, trip to the dentist*] no lo pasé ni con mucho *or* ni de lejos tan mal como había imaginado; **~ asleep** medio dormido; **~ done** a medio hacer; **he ~ got up** se levantó a medias; **~ laughing, ~ crying** medio riendo, medio llorando; **I only ~ read it** lo leí sólo a medias; **I was only ~ serious when I said that** aquello sólo lo dije medio en broma; *see also* **half-baked**
2 (*time*) **~ past four** las cuatro y media; **come at ~ three*** ven a las tres y media
3 (*with neg*) (*Brit**) **not ~!** ¡y cómo!, ¡ya lo creo!; **he didn't ~ run** corrió muchísimo, corrió como un bólido; **it didn't ~ rain!** ¡había que ver cómo llovía!; **it wasn't ~ dear** nos costó un riñón, fue carísimo; **it isn't ~ hot** hace un calor de miedo
Ⓓ CPD ► **half fare** N medio pasaje *m*; (*as adv*) **to travel ~ fare** viajar pagando medio pasaje ► **half note** N (*US Mus*) blanca *f* ► **half term** N (*Brit Scol*) vacaciones *fpl* de mediados del trimestre

half-a-crown [,hɑːfə'kraʊn] N = **half-crown**

half-and-half [,hɑːfənd'hɑːf] Ⓐ ADJ [*mixture, solution*] a partes iguales, mitad y mitad
Ⓑ ADV a partes iguales, mitad y mitad; **mix the mayonnaise ~ with yogurt** mezcle la mayonesa a partes iguales *or* mitad y mitad con el yogur; **to split sth ~** dividir algo en dos mitades (a partes iguales)

half-assed‡ ['hɑːfæst] ADJ (*US*) [*person*] que tiene pocas luces; [*idea*] muy poco brillante

halfback ['hɑːfbæk] N (*Ftbl*) medio/a *m/f*

half-baked ['hɑːf'beɪkt] ADJ (*fig*) [*plan, idea*] mal concebido, sin perfilar; [*person*] soso

half board [,hɑːf'bɔːd] N (*Brit*) (*in hotel*) media pensión *f*

half-bred ['hɑːfbred] ADJ mestizo

half-breed ['hɑːfbriːd] N (= *animal*) híbrido *m*; (= *person*) (*pej*) mestizo/a *m/f*

half-brother ['hɑːf,brʌðəʳ] N medio hermano *m*, hermanastro *m*

half-caste ['hɑːfkɑːst] (*often pej*) Ⓐ ADJ mestizo
Ⓑ N mestizo/a *m/f*

half-century [hɑːf'sentjʊrɪ] N (*Cricket*) cincuenta tantos *mpl*

half-circle ['hɑːf'sɜːkl] N semicírculo *m*

half-closed [ˌhɑːf'kləʊzd] ADJ entreabierto

half-cock ['hɑːf'kɒk] N posición *f* de medio amartillado (*de la escopeta etc*); ✦*IDIOM* **to go off at ~** [*person*] hacer las cosas antes de tiempo; [*plan*] irse al garete (por falta de preparación)*

half-cocked [ˌhɑːf'kɒkt] ADJ [*gun*] con el seguro echado; [*plan, scheme*] mal concebido

half-crown ['hɑːf'kraʊn] N (*formerly*) media corona *f*; **a ~** media corona

half-cup ['hɑːfˌkʌp] ADJ [*bra*] de media copa

half-day [ˌhɑːf'deɪ] (A) N medio día *m*, media jornada *f*
(B) CPD ► **half-day closing** N **~ closing is on Mondays** los lunes se cierra por la tarde ► **half-day holiday** N fiesta *f* de media jornada

half-dead ['hɑːf'ded] ADJ medio muerto, más muerto que vivo

half-dozen ['hɑːf'dʌzn] N media docena *f*

half-dressed [ˌhɑːf'drest] ADJ a medio vestir

half-educated [ˌhɑːf'edjʊkeɪtɪd] ADJ con poca cultura; **he is ~** tiene poca cultura

half-empty ['hɑːf'emptɪ] ADJ [*bottle, box, room, train*] medio vacío; [*hall etc*] semidesierto

half-forgotten [ˌhɑːffə'gɒtn] ADJ medio olvidado

half-frozen [ˌhɑːf'frəʊzən] ADJ medio congelado; **he was ~ when they found him** estaba medio congelado cuando lo encontraron, lo encontraron en estado de semicongelación

half-full ['hɑːf'fʊl] ADJ medio lleno, mediado

half-hearted ['hɑːf'hɑːtɪd] ADJ [*effort*] tibio; [*applause*] tímido, poco entusiasta; [*smile*] de conejo, de dientes afuera (*LAm*); **I made a ~ effort to dissuade him** intenté disuadirle sin demasiado entusiasmo, hice un tibio intento de disuadirle

half-heartedly ['hɑːf'hɑːtɪdlɪ] ADV con poco entusiasmo

half-heartedness [ˌhɑːf'hɑːtɪdnɪs] N falta *f* de entusiasmo

half-holiday ['hɑːf'hɒlɪdɪ] N (*Brit Scol*) fiesta *f* de media jornada; (*in shop*) descanso *m*

half-hour ['hɑːf'aʊəʳ] (A) N media hora *f*; **the clock struck the ~** el reloj dio y media *or* dio la media; **on the ~** a y media
(B) CPD [*meeting, session, drive*] de media hora

half-hourly [ˌhɑːf'aʊəlɪ] (A) ADV cada media hora
(B) ADJ **at ~ intervals** cada media hora

half-inch [ˌhɑːf'ɪntʃ] (A) N media pulgada *f*
(B) ADJ **cut into ~ lengths** córtese en trozos de media pulgada de largo, córtese en trozos de algo más de un centímetro de largo

half-length ['hɑːf'leŋθ] ADJ de medio cuerpo

half-life ['hɑːflaɪf] N (*pl* **half-lives**) (*Phys*) media vida *f*

half-light ['hɑːflaɪt] N penumbra *f*

half-marathon ['hɑːf'mærəθən] N medio maratón *m*, media maratón *f*

half-mast ['hɑːf'mɑːst] N **at ~** [*flag*] a media asta; [*trousers*] (= *very short*) muy cortos; (= *halfway down the legs*) medio bajados

half-measures ['hɑːf'meʒəz] NPL paños *mpl* calientes, medias tintas *fpl*; **we don't want any ~** no queremos andarnos con medias tintas *or* paños calientes

half-monthly [ˌhɑːf'mʌnθlɪ] (A) ADJ quincenal
(B) ADV cada quince días

half-moon ['hɑːf'muːn] N media luna *f*

half-naked ['hɑːf'neɪkɪd] ADJ semidesnudo

half-open [ˌhɑːf'əʊpən] ADJ entreabierto, medio abierto

half-panelled, half-paneled (*US*) [ˌhɑːf-'pænəld] ADJ chapado hasta media altura

half-pay ['hɑːf'peɪ] (A) N media paga *f*; **to retire on ~** jubilarse con media paga
(B) CPD ► **half-pay officer** N militar *m* retirado

halfpenny ['heɪpnɪ] N (*pl* **halfpennies** *or* **halfpence** ['heɪpəns]) (*Hist*) medio penique *m*; ✦*IDIOM* **not to have a ~** *or* **two halfpennies to rub together** no tener un céntimo, estar sin blanca

half-pint [ˌhɑːf'paɪnt] N [1] (= *measure*) media pinta *f*
[2] (*) (= *small person*) enano/a *m/f*

half-price ['hɑːf'praɪs] (A) ADV a mitad de precio
(B) ADJ [*ticket etc*] a mitad de precio

half-seas over ['hɑːfsiːz'əʊvəʳ] ADV ✦*IDIOM* **to be ~** estar entre dos velas

half-serious [ˌhɑːf'sɪərɪəs] ADJ entre serio y en broma

half-sister ['hɑːfˌsɪstəʳ] N media hermana *f*, hermanastra *f*

half-size ['hɑːfˌsaɪz] (A) N (*in shoes*) medio número *m*
(B) ADJ [*musical instrument, chair*] de la mitad de tamaño

half-sized [ˌhɑːf'saɪzd] ADJ = **half-size B**

half-timbered [ˌhɑːf'tɪmbəd] ADJ con entramado de madera

half-time ['hɑːf'taɪm] (A) N (*Sport*) descanso *m*; **at ~** en el descanso
(B) ADV **to work ~** trabajar media jornada
(C) CPD ► **half-time score** N marcador *m* en el descanso; **the ~ score was 1-0** el marcador en el descanso era 1-0 ► **half-time work** N trabajo *m* de media jornada

half-tone ['hɑːftəʊn] (A) ADJ **~ illustration** fotograbado *m* a media tinta
(B) N [1] (*Art*) fotograbado *m* a media tinta
[2] (*US Mus*) semitono *m*

half-track ['hɑːf'træk] N camión *m* semi-oruga

half-truth ['hɑːf'truːθ] N (*pl* **half-truths** ['hɑːf'truːðz]) verdad *f* a medias

half-volley ['hɑːf'vɒlɪ] N media volea *f*

halfway ['hɑːf'weɪ] (A) ADV [1] (*lit*) a medio camino; **Reading is ~ between Oxford and London** Reading está a medio camino entre Oxford y Londres; **we're ~ there** estamos a mitad de camino *or* a medio camino; **~ up/down the hill** a media cuesta; **her hair reaches ~ down her back** el pelo le llega hasta la mitad de la espalda; **they've travelled ~ around the world** han recorrido medio mundo; **~ through the film** hacia la mitad de la película, a (la) mitad de la película; **the decision only goes ~ toward giving the strikers what they want** la decisión sólo satisface a medias las demandas de los huelguistas; ✦*IDIOM* **to meet sb ~** llegar a un compromiso con algn
[2] (*fig*) (= *at all, the least bit*) **anything ~ decent will be incredibly expensive** cualquier cosa mínimamente decente va a ser carísima
(B) ADJ [*mark*] a *or* de medio camino; [*stage*] intermedio; (*fig*) (= *incomplete*) a medias
(C) CPD ► **halfway house** N (*for rehabilitation*) centro *m* de reinserción; (*fig*) punto *m* medio, término *m* medio; **it's a ~ house between dance and drama** está a medio camino entre la danza y el teatro

halfwit ['hɑːfwɪt] N imbécil *mf*, tonto/a *m/f*

half-witted ['hɑːf'wɪtɪd] ADJ imbécil, tonto

half-year [ˌhɑːf'jɪəʳ] (A) N medio año *m*, semestre *m*
(B) CPD ► **half-year results** NPL resultados *mpl* semestrales

half-yearly ['hɑːf'jɪəlɪ] (A) ADV semestralmente
(B) ADJ semestral

halibut ['hælɪbət] N (*pl* **halibut** *or* **halibuts**) halibut *m*, hipogloso *m*

halitosis [ˌhælɪ'təʊsɪs] N halitosis *f*

hall [hɔːl] (A) N [1] (= *entrance hall*) hall *m*, entrada *f*; (= *foyer*) vestíbulo *m*; (*US*) (= *passage*) pasillo *m*
[2] (= *large room, building*) sala *f*; **concert ~** sala *f* de conciertos; **dance ~** salón *m* de baile; **church ~** sala *f* parroquial; *see also* **village**
[3] (= *mansion*) casa *f* solariega
[4] (*Brit Univ*) (= *central hall*) paraninfo *m*; (*also* **~ of residence**) residencia *f*, colegio *m* mayor
(B) CPD ► **hall porter** N (*Brit*) portero/a *m/f*, conserje *mf* ► **hall stand** N perchero *m*

hallelujah [ˌhælɪ'luːjə] N, EXCL aleluya *f*

hallmark ['hɔːlmɑːk] N (*on gold, silver*) contraste *m*; (*fig*) sello *m*; **the attack bears all the ~s of the CLF** el atentado lleva el auténtico sello del CLF

hallo [hʌ'ləʊ] EXCL = **hello**

halloo [hə'luː] (A) EXCL ¡sus!, ¡hala!
(B) N grito *m*
(C) VI gritar

hallow ['hæləʊ] VT santificar

hallowed ['hæləʊd] ADJ [*ground etc*] sagrado, santificado

Hallowe'en ['hæləʊ'iːn] N víspera *f* de Todos los Santos

> **HALLOWE'EN**
>
> *La festividad de* **Hallowe'en** *se celebra, tanto en el Reino Unido como en EE.UU., la noche del 31 de octubre. Aunque antes la fiesta se asociaba con la creencia de que las almas de los difuntos regresaban a sus hogares en esa fecha, actualmente* **Hallowe'en** *no es más que un pretexto para la diversión. Los niños se disfrazan de fantasmas y brujas y hacen farolillos con calabazas vacías en cuyo interior colocan una vela. Así vestidos, van de casa en casa por todo el barrio pidiendo caramelos y dinero, una costumbre que se conoce sobre todo en Estados Unidos como* **trick or treat** *porque los niños amenazan con gastarle una broma al dueño de la casa si no reciben los caramelos. También suelen celebrarse en* **Hallowe'en** *fiestas de disfraces para niños y para adultos.*

hallucinate [hə'luːsɪneɪt] VI alucinar, tener alucinaciones

hallucination [həˌluːsɪ'neɪʃən] N alucinación *f*

hallucinatory [hə'luːsɪnətərɪ] ADJ alucinante

hallucinogen [hə'luːsɪnəˌdʒen] N alucinógeno *m*

hallucinogenic [həˌluːsɪnəʊ'dʒenɪk] (A) ADJ alucinógeno
(B) N alucinógeno *m*

hallucinosis [həˌluːsɪ'nəʊsɪs] N alucinosis *f*

hallway ['hɔːlweɪ] N = **hall A1**

halo ['heɪləʊ] N (*pl* **halo(e)s**) halo *m*, aureola *f*

halogen ['heɪləʊdʒɪn] (A) N halógeno *m*
(B) CPD ► **halogen lamp** N lámpara *f* halógena

halogenous [hə'lɒdʒɪnəs] ADJ halógeno

halt [hɔːlt] (A) N [1] (= *stop, standstill*) alto *m*, parada *f*; **to bring sth to a ~** [+ *car*] parar *or* detener algo; [+ *event, process*] interrumpir algo; **to come to a ~** [*car*] pararse, detenerse;

[*train*] hacer alto, detenerse; [*negotiations*] interrumpirse; **to call a ~ (to sth)** (*fig*) poner fin (a algo)

[2] (*Brit*) (= *train stop*) apeadero *m*

Ⓑ VT [+ *vehicle, production*] parar, detener

Ⓒ VI (*gen*) pararse, detenerse; [*train*] hacer alto, detenerse; [*process*] interrumpirse; **~!** (*Mil*) ¡alto!

Ⓓ CPD ► **halt sign** N señal *f* de stop

halter ['hɔːltəʳ] N (*for horse*) cabestro *m*, ronzal *m*; (= *noose*) dogal *m*

halter-neck ['hɔːltəˌnek] Ⓐ N *top sin espalda ni mangas*

Ⓑ ADJ [*dress, top*] sin espalda ni mangas

halting ['hɔːltɪŋ] ADJ (= *hesitant*) [*speech, movement*] titubeante, vacilante

haltingly ['hɔːltɪŋlɪ] ADV [*speak*] titubeando, vacilantemente

halve [hɑːv] Ⓐ VT (= *divide*) partir por la mitad, partir en dos; (= *reduce by half*) reducir a la mitad

Ⓑ VI reducirse a la mitad

halves [hɑːvz] NPL *of* **half**

halyard ['hæljəd] N driza *f*

ham [hæm] Ⓐ N [1] (*Culin*) jamón *m*

[2] **hams** (*Anat*) nalgas *fpl*

[3] (*Theat*) (*also* **~ actor**) comicastro *m*, actor *m* histriónico; (*also* **~ actress**) actriz *f* histriónica

[4] (= *radio ham*) radioaficionado/a *m/f*

Ⓑ VI (*Theat**) actuar de una manera exagerada *or* melodramática

►**ham up*** VT + ADV **to ~ it up*** actuar de manera exagerada *or* melodramática

Hamburg ['hæmbɜːg] N Hamburgo *m*

hamburger ['hæmˌbɜːgəʳ] N hamburguesa *f*; (*US*) (*also* **~ meat**) carne *f* picada

ham-fisted [ˌhæm'fɪstɪd], **ham-handed** [ˌhæm'hændɪd] ADJ torpe, desmañado

Hamitic [hæ'mɪtɪk] ADJ camítico

hamlet ['hæmlɪt] N aldea *f*, caserío *m*

hammer ['hæməʳ] Ⓐ N (= *tool*) martillo *m*; (*Mus*) macillo *m*; [*of firearm*] percusor *m*; **the ~ and sickle** el martillo y la hoz; **to come under the ~** ser subastado; ✦*IDIOM* **to go at it ~ and tongs*** (= *argue*) discutir acaloradamente; (= *fight*) luchar a brazo partido; (= *work*) darle duro*

Ⓑ VT [1] [+ *nail*] clavar; [+ *metal*] martillar, batir; **to ~ a post into the ground** hincar un poste en el suelo a martillazos; **to ~ sth into shape** [+ *metal*] forjar algo a martillazos; (*fig*) [+ *team etc*] forjar algo a golpes; **to ~ a point home** remachar un punto; **to ~ sth into sb** (*fig*) meter algo en la cabeza de algn

[2] (*) (= *defeat, thrash*) dar una paliza a*, machacar*

Ⓒ VI **to ~ on** *or* **at a door** dar golpes en *or* golpear una puerta; **to ~ away at** [+ *subject*] insistir con ahínco en, machacar en; [+ *work*] trabajar asiduamente en; **to ~ away on the piano** aporrear el piano

►**hammer down** VT + ADV [+ *lid etc*] asegurar con clavos; [+ *nail*] meter a martillazos

►**hammer in** VT + ADV meter a martillazos

►**hammer out** VT + ADV [+ *nail*] sacar; [+ *dent*] alisar a martillazos; (*fig*) [+ *solution, agreement*] negociar no sin esfuerzo

►**hammer together** VT + ADV [+ *pieces of wood etc*] clavar

hammerhead ['hæməhed] N (= *shark*) pez *m* martillo

hammering ['hæmərɪŋ] N [1] (*lit*) martilleo *m*

[2] (*) paliza* *f*; **to give sb a ~** dar una paliza a algn*; **to get** *or* **take a ~** recibir una paliza*

hammertoe ['hæmətəʊ] N dedo *m* (en) martillo

hammock ['hæmək] N hamaca *f*; (*Naut*) coy *m*

hammy* ['hæmɪ] ADJ [*actor*] exagerado, melodramático

hamper¹ ['hæmpəʳ] N cesto *m*, canasta *f*

hamper² ['hæmpəʳ] VT (= *hinder*) [+ *efforts, work*] dificultar, entorpecer; [+ *movement*] obstaculizar, impedir; **the investigation was ~ed by their lack of cooperation** la investigación se vio entorpecida por su falta de colaboración

hamster ['hæmstəʳ] N hámster *m*

hamstring ['hæmstrɪŋ] (*vb: pt, pp* **hamstrung**)

Ⓐ N [*of person*] tendón *m* de la corva; [*of animal*] tendón *m* del jarrete

Ⓑ VT (*lit*) desjarretar; (*fig*) paralizar

Ⓒ CPD ► **hamstring injury** N lesión *f* del tendón de la corva

hand [hænd] Ⓐ N [1] (= *part of body*) mano *f*; **to have sth in one's ~** tener algo en la mano; **to be clever** *or* **good with one's ~s** ser hábil con las manos, ser un manitas; **a piece for four ~s** (*Mus*) una pieza para (piano a) cuatro manos; **to hold ~s** [*children*] ir cogidos de la mano, ir tomados de la mano (*LAm*); [*lovers*] hacer manitas; **on (one's) ~s and knees** a gatas; **~s off!*** ¡fuera las manos!, ¡no se toca!; **~s off those chocolates!** ¡los bombones ni tocarlos!; **~s off pensions!** ¡no a la reforma de las pensiones!, ¡dejad las pensiones en paz!; **to keep one's ~s off sth** no tocar algo; **~s up!** (*to criminal*) ¡arriba las manos!; (*to pupils*) ¡que levanten la mano!; ✦*IDIOMS* **~ over fist**: **to be making money ~ over fist** ganar dinero a espuertas; **to be losing money ~ over fist** hacerle agua el dinero; **to be ~ in glove with sb** (= *very close*) ser uña y carne con algn; (= *in cahoots*) estar conchabado con algn; **to work ~ in glove with sb** trabajar en estrecha colaboración con algn; **to live from ~ to mouth** vivir al día; **my ~s are tied** tengo las manos atadas, no puedo hacer nada; **I could do it with one ~ tied behind my back** lo podría hacer con una mano atada a la espalda; **he never does a ~'s turn** no da golpe; ✦*PROV* **many ~s make light work** muchas manos facilitan el trabajo; *see also* **shake B1**

[2] (= *needle*) [*of instrument*] aguja *f*; [*of clock*] manecilla *f*, aguja *f*; **the big ~** la manecilla grande, el minutero; **the little ~** la manecilla pequeña, el horario

[3] (= *agency, influence*) mano *f*, influencia *f*; **his ~ was everywhere** se notaba su influencia por todas partes, su mano se notaba en todo; **to have a ~ in** tomar parte en, intervenir en; **he had no ~ in it** no tuvo arte ni parte en ello

[4] (= *worker*) (*in factory*) obrero/a *m/f*; (= *farm hand*) peón *m*; (= *deck hand*) marinero *m* (de cubierta); **all ~s on deck!** (*Naut*) ¡todos a cubierta!; **to be lost with all ~s** hundirse con toda la tripulación; ✦*IDIOM* **to be an old ~ (at sth)** ser perro viejo (en algo)

[5] (= *help*) mano *f*; **would you like a ~ with moving that?** ¿te echo una mano a mover eso?; **to give** *or* **lend sb a ~** echar una mano a algn; **can you give** *or* **lend me a ~?** ¿me echas una mano?

[6] (= *handwriting*) letra *f*, escritura *f*; **he writes a good ~** tiene buena letra; **in one's own ~** de su (propio) puño y letra

[7] (*Cards*) (= *round*) mano *f*, partida *f*; (= *cards held*) mano *f*; **a ~ of bridge/poker** una mano *or* una partida de bridge/póker

[8] (= *measurement*) [*of horse*] palmo *m*; **he's 15 ~s high** mide 15 palmos de alto

[9] (*) (= *round of applause*) **they gave him a big ~** le aplaudieron calurosamente; **let's have a big ~ for ...!** ¡muchos aplausos para ...!

[10] (*phrases with verb*) **to ask for sb's ~ (in marriage)** pedir la mano de algn; **to change ~s** cambiar de mano *or* de dueño; **just wait till I get my ~s on him!** ¡espera (a) que le ponga la mano encima!; **to lay ~s on** (= *get*) conseguir; (*Rel*) imponer las manos a; **I don't know where to lay my ~s on ...** no sé dónde conseguir ...; **she read everything she could lay her ~s on** leía todo lo que caía en sus manos; **to put** *or* **set one's ~ to sth** emprender algo; **to raise one's** *or* **a ~ to** *or* **against sb** poner a algn la mano encima; **to take a ~ in sth** tomar parte *or* participar en algo; **to try one's ~ at sth** probar algo; ✦*IDIOMS* **to get one's ~ in** adquirir práctica, irse acostumbrando; **to give with one ~ and take away with the other** quitar con una mano lo que se da con la otra; **to keep one's ~ in** conservar *or* no perder la práctica (**at** de); **to sit on one's ~s** (*US**) [*audience*] aplaudir con desgana; [*committee etc*] no hacer nada; **to turn one's ~ to sth** dedicarse a algo; **he can turn his ~ to anything** vale tanto para un barrido como para un fregado; **to wait on sb ~ and foot** desvivirse por algn, ponérselo todo en bandeja a algn; *see also* **eat B**, **force B1**, **join A1**, **show A1, B1**, **throw up B1**, **wash B1**, **win B3, C**

[11] (*phrases with adjective*) **to rule with a firm ~** gobernar con firmeza; **to have a free ~** tener carta blanca; **to give sb a free ~** dar carta blanca a algn; **to have one's ~s full (with sth/sb)** no parar un momento (con algo/algn), estar muy ocupado (con algo/algn); **I've got my ~s full with the kids** con los niños no paro un momento; **I've got my ~s full running the firm while the boss is away** estoy muy ocupado llevando la empresa mientras el jefe está fuera; **don't worry, she's in good ~s** no te preocupes, está en buenas manos; **with a heavy ~** con mano dura; **to give sb a helping ~** echar una mano a algn; **with a high ~** despóticamente; **if this should get into the wrong ~s ...** si esto cayera en manos de quien no debiera ...; ✦*IDIOMS* **to get** *or* **gain the upper ~** empezar a dominar; **to have the upper ~** tener *or* llevar la ventaja

[12] (= *after preposition*) **don't worry, help is at ~** no te preocupes, disponemos de *or* contamos con ayuda; **winter was at ~** se acercaba el invierno; **keep the book close at ~** ten el libro a mano; **we're close at ~ in case she needs help** nos tiene a mano *or* muy cerca si necesita ayuda; **at first ~** de primera mano; **I heard it only at second ~** lo supe sólo de modo indirecto; **at the ~s of** a manos de; **they suffered a series of defeats at the ~s of the French** sufrieron una serie de derrotas a manos de los franceses; **made by ~** hecho a mano; **to raise an animal by ~** criar un animal uno mismo; **to send a letter by ~** enviar una carta en mano; **delivered by ~** entregado en mano; **"by hand"** (*on envelope*) "en su mano"; **to take sb by the ~** coger *or* tomar a algn de la mano; **they were going along ~ in ~** iban cogidos de la mano; **it goes ~ in ~ with** está estrechamente relacionado con; **these plans should go ~ in ~** estos proyectos deben realizarse al mismo ritmo; **gun in ~** el revólver en la mano, empuñando el revólver; **to be in sb's ~s** estar en manos de algn; **it's in his ~s now** depende de él ahora; **I put myself in your ~s** me pongo en tus manos; **to have £50 in ~** tener 50 libras en el haber; **I like to have sth in ~** me

gusta tener algo en reserva; **money in ~** dinero *m* disponible; **the cases I have in ~ at the moment** los casos que tengo entre manos en este momento; **the situation is in ~** tenemos la situación controlada *or* bajo control; **he has them well in ~** sabe manejarlos perfectamente; **let's concentrate on the job in ~** centrémonos en el trabajo que tenemos entre manos; **to take sth in ~** tomar algo a cuestas; **to take sb in ~** (= *take charge of*) hacerse cargo de algn; (= *discipline*) imponer disciplina a algn; **to play into sb's ~s** hacer el juego a algn; **to fall into the ~s of the enemy** caer en manos del enemigo; **to put sth into a lawyer's ~s** poner un asunto en manos de un abogado; **to take justice into one's own ~s** tomar la justicia por su propia mano; **to get sth off one's ~s** (= *get rid of*) deshacerse de algo; (= *finish doing*) terminar de hacer algo; **to take sth off sb's ~s** desembarazar a algn de algo; **the children are off our ~s now** nuestros hijos ya han volado del nido; **on the right/left ~** a derecha/izquierda, a mano derecha/izquierda; **on the one ~ ... on the other ~** por una parte ... por otra parte, por un lado ... por otro lado; **on the other ~, she did agree to do it** pero el caso es que ella (sí) había accedido a hacerlo; **on every ~** ◊ **on all ~s** por todas partes; **there are experts on ~ to give you advice** hay expertos a su disposición para ofrecerle asesoramiento; **I've got him on my ~s all day** está conmigo todo el día; **we've got a difficult job on our ~s** tenemos entre manos una difícil tarea; **he's got time on his ~s** tiene todo el tiempo del mundo; **to have sth left on one's ~s** tener que quedarse con algo; **he was left with the goods on his ~s** tuvo que quedarse con todo el género, el género resultó ser invendible; **to dismiss sth out of ~** descartar algo sin más; **the situation was getting out of ~** la situación se estaba escapando de las manos; **the children were getting out of ~** los niños se estaban desmandando; **to have sth to ~** tener algo a mano; **I don't have the information to ~ just now** ahora mismo no tengo a mano la información; **I hit him with the first thing that came to ~** le golpeé con lo primero que tenía a mano *or* que pillé; **your letter of the 23rd is to ~** (*frm*) he recibido su carta del día 23; *see also* **cap A1**

Ⓑ VT (= *pass*) **to ~ sb sth** ◊ **~ sth to sb** pasar algo a algn; **he ~ed me the book** me pasó el libro; ✦*IDIOM* **you've got to ~ it to him*** hay que reconocérselo

Ⓒ CPD [*lotion, cream*] para las manos ► **hand baggage** N (*US*) = **hand luggage** ► **hand controls** NPL controles *mpl* manuales ► **hand drier**, **hand dryer** N secamanos *m inv* automático ► **hand grenade** N granada *f* (de mano) ► **hand luggage** N equipaje *m* de mano ► **hand print** N manotada *f* ► **hand puppet** N títere *m* ► **hand signal** N (*Aut*) señal *f* con el brazo; **with both indicators broken, he had to rely on ~ signals** con los intermitentes rotos tenía que hacer señales con el brazo *or* la mano; **they had to communicate in ~ signals** tuvieron que comunicarse por señas ► **hand towel** N toalla *f* de manos

►**hand around** VT + ADV = **hand round**

►**hand back** VT + ADV devolver

►**hand down** VT + ADV [+ *suitcase etc*] bajar, pasar; [+ *heirloom*] pasar, dejar en herencia; [+ *tradition*] transmitir; (*US*) [+ *judgement*] dictar, imponer; [+ *person*] ayudar a bajar

►**hand in** VT + ADV [+ *form, homework*] entregar; [+ *resignation*] presentar

►**hand off** VT + ADV (*Rugby*) rechazar

►**hand on** VT + ADV [+ *tradition*] transmitir; [+ *news*] comunicar; [+ *object*] pasar

►**hand out** VT + ADV [+ *leaflets*] repartir, distribuir; [+ *advice*] dar

►**hand over** Ⓐ VT + ADV 1 (= *pass over*) pasar; **can you ~ me over the hammer please?** ¿me pasas el martillo, por favor?

2 (= *hand in*) [+ *driving licence, passport*] entregar; (= *surrender*) [+ *property, business*] traspasar, ceder; [+ *power, government*] ceder

Ⓑ VI + ADV (*to successor*) ceder su puesto a; **I'm now ~ing over to the studio** (*Rad, TV*) ahora devolvemos la conexión al estudio

►**hand round** VT + ADV [+ *information, bottle*] pasar (de mano en mano); [+ *chocolates, biscuits etc*] ofrecer; [+ *photocopies, leaflets, books*] repartir

►**hand up** VT + ADV [+ *person*] subir

handbag [ˈhænd͡bæg] Ⓐ N bolso *m* (de mano), bolsa *f* (de mano), cartera *f* (*LAm*)

Ⓑ VT (*) poner fuera de combate a golpe de bolso, eliminar a bolsazos

handball [ˈhænd͡bɔːl] N 1 (= *game*) balonmano *m*

2 (*Ftbl*) (= *offence*) mano *f*

handbasin [ˈhænd͡ˌbeɪsn] N lavabo *m*

handbell [ˈhænd͡bel] N campanilla *f*

handbill [ˈhænd͡bɪl] N folleto *m*, octavilla *f*

handbook [ˈhænd͡bʊk] N (= *manual*) manual *m*; (= *guide*) guía *f*

handbrake [ˈhænd͡breɪk] N (*Brit*) freno *m* de mano

h. & c. ABBR (= **hot and cold (water)**) con agua caliente y fría

handcart [ˈhænd͡kɑːt] N carretilla *f*, carretón *m*

handclap [ˈhænd͡klæp] N palmada *f*; **to give a player the slow ~** batir palmas a ritmo lento (*para que un jugador se esfuerce más o se dé prisa*)

handclasp [ˈhænd͡klɑːsp] N = **handshake**

handcraft [ˈhænd͡krɑːft] VT (*US*) hacer a mano; **~ed products** productos *mpl* artesanales

handcream [ˈhænd͡kriːm] N crema *f* para las manos

handcuff [ˈhænd͡kʌf] VT poner las esposas a, esposar

handcuffs [ˈhænd͡kʌfs] NPL esposas *fpl*

-handed [ˈhændɪd] ADJ (*ending in compounds*) **two-handed backhand** (*Tennis*) revés *m* a dos manos; **he drove one-handed** conducía con una sola mano; **four-handed game** juego *m* para cuatro personas; *see also* **empty-handed**, **heavy-handed** *etc*

-hander [ˈhændəʳ] N (*ending in compounds*) (*esp Brit*) **two/three-hander** (*TV, Cine*) película *f* con dos/tres personajes; (*Theat*) obra *f* con dos/tres personajes; *see also* **left-hander**, **right-hander**

handful [ˈhænd͡fʊl] N (= *quantity*) manojo *m*, puñado *m*; (= *small number*) puñado *m*; **a ~ of people** un puñado de gente; **that child's a real ~*** ese niño es muy travieso

handgrip [ˈhænd͡grɪp] N = **handle A1** = **grip A1**

handgun [ˈhænd͡gʌn] N (*esp US*) revólver *m*, pistola *f*

hand-held [ˈhændheld] ADJ de mano; (= *portable*) portátil

handicap [ˈhændɪkæp] Ⓐ N 1 (= *disadvantage*) desventaja *f*; (= *impediment*) obstáculo *m*, estorbo *m*

2 (*Sport, Golf*) hándicap *m*; (= *horse race*) hándicap *m*

3 (*Med*) minusvalía *f*, discapacidad *f*

Ⓑ VT (= *prejudice*) perjudicar; (*Sport*) establecer un hándicap para; **he has always been ~ped by his accent** su acento siempre le ha perjudicado *or* le ha supuesto una desventaja

handicapped [ˈhændɪkæpt] Ⓐ ADJ **mentally ~** mentalmente discapacitado, psíquicamente disminuido; **physically ~** minusválido, (físicamente) discapacitado; **to be mentally/physically ~** tener una discapacidad mental/física, ser (un) discapacitado mental/físico

Ⓑ N **the ~** los minusválidos, los discapacitados; **the mentally ~** los discapacitados mentales, los disminuidos psíquicos

handicraft [ˈhændɪkrɑːft] Ⓐ N (= *art, product*) artesanía *f*; (= *skill*) destreza *f* manual

Ⓑ CPD ► **handicraft teacher** N profesor(a) *m/f* de trabajos manuales

handily [ˈhændɪlɪ] ADV 1 (= *conveniently*) [*positioned, situated*] convenientemente, cómodamente

2 (= *dexterously*) con habilidad, con destreza

3 (*US*) (= *easily*) [*win*] fácilmente

handiness [ˈhændɪnɪs] N 1 (= *closeness*) proximidad *f*; **the advantage of this house is its ~ for the school** la ventaja de esta casa es su proximidad a la escuela *or* lo cerca que queda de la escuela; **because of the ~ of the library** debido a que la biblioteca está tan a mano *or* queda tan cerca, porque resulta tan cómodo ir a la biblioteca

2 [*of tool, gadget*] utilidad *f*

3 (= *skill*) habilidad *f*, destreza *f*

handiwork [ˈhændɪwɜːk] N 1 (= *craft*) trabajo *m*

2 (= *action*) obra *f*; **this looks like his ~** (*pej*) parece que es obra de él

handkerchief [ˈhæŋkətʃɪf] N pañuelo *m*; *see also* **pocket C**

hand-knitted [ˌhænd͡ˈnɪtɪd] ADJ tricotado a mano, tejido a mano (*LAm*)

handle [ˈhændl] Ⓐ N 1 [*of knife, brush, spade, saucepan*] mango *m*; [*of broom*] palo *m*; [*of basket, bucket, jug*] asa *f*; [*of drawer*] tirador *m*, manija *f*; [*of door*] (= *round knob*) pomo *m*; (= *lever*) picaporte *m*, manilla *f* (*LAm*); [*of stretcher, wheelbarrow*] brazo *m*; [*of pump*] palanca *f*; (*for winding*) manivela *f*; ✦*IDIOM* **to fly off the ~** perder los estribos, salirse de sus casillas

2 (*fig*) (= *pretext*) excusa *f*, pretexto *m*; (= *opportunity*) oportunidad *f*; **to get a ~ on sth*** llegar a saber cómo lidiar con algo; **to have a ~ on sth*** tener algo controlado

3 (*) (= *title*) título *m*; (= *name*) nombre *m*; **to have a ~ to one's name** (*aristocratic*) tener un título nobiliario

Ⓑ VT 1 (= *touch with hands*) tocar; **"please do not handle the fruit"** "se ruega no tocar la fruta"; **to ~ the ball** (*Ftbl*) tocar la pelota con la mano

2 (= *manipulate, move with hands*) [+ *food*] manipular; **her hands are black from handling newsprint** tiene las manos negras de andar con *or* andar manipulando periódicos; **flowers need to be ~d gently** las flores necesitan que se las trate con cuidado; **"handle with care"** "manéjese *or* trátese con cuidado"; **the police ~d him roughly** la policía lo maltrató; ✦*IDIOM* **to ~ sb with kid gloves** tratar a algn con guantes de seda; *see also* **hot A3**

3 (= *use*) [+ *gun, machine*] manejar; **he knows how to ~ a gun** sabe cómo manejar una pistola; **"not to be taken before handling machinery"** "no ingerir en caso de ir a manejar maquinaria"

4 (= *drive, steer*) [+ *car*] conducir, manejar (*LAm*); [+ *ship*] gobernar; [+ *horse*] manejar

5 (= *tackle*) [+ *situation*] manejar; [+ *people*] tratar; **he ~d the situation very well** manejó *or* llevó muy bien la situación; **I could have ~d it better than I did** podría haberlo manejado mejor de lo que lo hice

6 (= *manage effectively*) [+ *people*] manejar bien; [+ *emotions*] controlar; **she can certainly ~ children** no cabe duda de que maneja bien a *or* sabe manejarse con los niños; **she can't ~ pressure** no puede con la presión; **I don't know if I can ~ the job** no sé si puedo sacar adelante el trabajo

7 (= *be responsible for*) [+ *case, investigation*] llevar, encargarse de; **the solicitor handling your case** el abogado que lleva *or* se encarga de tu caso; **we don't ~ criminal cases** nosotros no nos encargamos *or* ocupamos de las causas penales; **the treasurer ~s large sums of money** el tesorero maneja grandes cantidades de dinero; **I'll ~ this** yo me encargo (de esto)

8 (= *deal in*) [+ *goods*] comerciar con; **we don't ~ that type of product** no comerciamos con ese tipo de productos; **we don't ~ that type of business** no hacemos ese tipo de trabajos; **to ~ stolen goods** comerciar con objetos robados

9 (= *process*) **a computer can store and ~ large amounts of information** un ordenador puede almacenar y trabajar con *or* procesar muchísima información; **can the port ~ big ships?** ¿tiene capacidad el puerto para buques grandes?; **the present system of handling refuse** el actual sistema de recogida y tratamiento de residuos; **there is an extra fee for handling and packing your order** hay un recargo por tramitación y embalaje de su pedido; **we ~ ten per cent of their total sales** movemos *or* trabajamos un diez por ciento del total de sus ventas; **we ~ 2,000 travellers a day** por aquí pasan 2.000 viajeros cada día

Ⓒ VI [*car, plane, horse*] comportarse; [*ship*] gobernarse; **this car ~s like a dream** este coche va *or* se comporta de maravilla

handlebar [ˈhændlbɑːʳ] Ⓐ N manillar *m*, manubrio *m*; **handlebars** manillar *msing*, manubrio *msing* Ⓑ CPD ► **handlebar moustache** N (*hum*) bigote *m* Dalí *or* daliniano

-handled [ˈhændld] ADJ (*ending in compounds*) **a wooden-handled spade** una pala con mango de madera; **a long-handled spoon** una cuchara de mango largo; **a two-handled urn** una urna de dos asas

handler [ˈhændləʳ] N 1 (*Comm*) [*of stock*] tratante *mf*, comerciante *mf*

2 (*also* **dog ~**) adiestrador(a) *m/f*; *see also* **baggage**

handling [ˈhændlɪŋ] Ⓐ N 1 (*lit*) (= *treatment*) trato *m*; (= *manipulation*) manejo *m*; (= *exposure to hands*) manoseo *m*; **the care and ~ of antique textiles** el cuidado y el trato de tejidos antiguos; **the problem of safe ~ of radioactive waste** el problema del manejo seguro de los residuos radiactivos; **all that ~ has not improved the book's condition** tanto manoseo no ha favorecido para nada el estado de conservación del libro; **rough ~** mal trato *m*

2 (= *management*) [*of situation, animal, money*] manejo *m*; [*of person*] trato *m*; **the minister was criticized for his ~ of the economy** el ministro fue criticado por su forma de manejar *or* llevar la economía

3 (*Comm*) porte *m*

4 (*Aut*) [*of car*] conducción *f*, manejo *m* (*LAm*)

Ⓑ CPD ► **handling charges** NPL gastos *mpl* de tramitación

handmade [ˈhændmeɪd] Ⓐ ADJ hecho a mano Ⓑ CPD ► **handmade paper** N papel *m* de tina *or* de mano

handmaid(en) [ˈhændmeɪd(ən)] N (*Hist*) criada *f*; (= *queen's servant*) azafata *f*

hand-me-down* [ˈhændmɪdaʊn] N prenda *f* usada

handout [ˈhændaʊt] N 1 (= *leaflet*) octavilla *f*, panfleto *m*; (= *pamphlet*) folleto *m*; (= *press handout*) nota *f* de prensa; (*at lecture*) hoja *f*

2 (*) (= *money*) limosna *f*

3 (= *distribution*) distribución *f*, repartimiento *m*

handover [ˈhændəʊvəʳ] N (*Pol*) [*of government, power*] entrega *f*, transferencia *f*

hand-picked [ˈhændˈpɪkt] ADJ [*people, staff*] cuidadosamente seleccionado, muy escogido; [*fruit*] cosechado *or* (*LAm*) recogido a mano

handrail [ˈhændreɪl] N (*on staircase etc*) pasamanos *m inv*, barandilla *f*; (*on ship*) barandilla *f*

hand-rear [ˌhændˈrɪəʳ] VT (*with bottle*) criar a biberones, criar con biberón; (*less specific*) criar a mano

handset [ˈhændset] N (*Telec*) aparato *m*, auricular *m*

hands-free [ˌhændzˈfriː] Ⓐ ADJ [*telephone*] manos libres *inv* Ⓑ CPD ► **hands-free kit, hands-free set** N manos libres *m inv*

handshake [ˈhændʃeɪk] N apretón *m* de manos; (*Comput*) coloquio *m*; (*as data signal*) "acuse de recibo"; **she had a firm** *or* **strong ~** estrechaba la mano con fuerza; **she had a weak ~** estrechaba la mano muy débilmente

hands-off [hændzˈɒf] ADJ [*policy, approach*] de no intervención

handsome [ˈhænsəm] ADJ (*compar* **handsomer**; *superl* **handsomest**) 1 (= *attractive*) [*man*] guapo, bien parecido; [*building, house, furniture*] bello, espléndido; **a tall boy with a ~ face** un chico alto y guapo de cara; **a ~ woman** una mujer *or* señora de bandera, una buena moza (*LAm*); **a ~ animal** un magnífico animal

2 (= *considerable*) [*fortune, profit*] cuantioso; [*salary, sum*] generoso, espléndido; [*increase, rise*] importante; **to make a ~ profit (on sth)** conseguir cuantiosos beneficios (de algo)

3 (= *convincing*) [*win, victory*] amplio, holgado

handsomely [ˈhænsəmlɪ] ADV 1 (= *attractively*) [*illustrated, dressed*] espléndidamente

2 (= *generously*) [*pay, reward*] generosamente, espléndidamente

3 (= *convincingly*) [*win, beat*] fácilmente, por un amplio margen; **this strategy has paid off ~** esta estrategia bien ha merecido la pena

hands-on [ˌhændzˈɒn] ADJ [*experience*] práctico; [*knowledge*] personal; **the museum has lots of ~ exhibits** se permite manipular un gran número de los objetos expuestos en el museo

handspring [ˈhændsprɪŋ] N voltereta *f* sobre las manos, salto *m* de paloma

handstand [ˈhændstænd] N **to do a ~** hacer el pino

hand-stitched [ˌhændˈstɪtʃt] ADJ cosido a mano

hand-to-hand [ˈhændtəˈhænd] ADV, ADJ cuerpo a cuerpo

hand-to-mouth [ˈhændtəˈmaʊθ] Ⓐ ADJ [*existence*] precario

Ⓑ ADV **to live ~** vivir precariamente

hand-wash [ˈhændˈwɔːʃ] VT lavar a mano

hand-woven [ˌhændˈwəʊvən] ADJ tejido a mano

handwriting [ˈhændˌraɪtɪŋ] N letra *f*, escritura *f*

handwritten [ˈhændˈrɪtn] ADJ escrito a mano

handy [ˈhændɪ] ADJ (*compar* **handier**; *superl* **handiest**) 1 (= *at hand*) [*scissors, book*] a mano; (= *conveniently close*) [*shops, station*] cerca, a mano; **have you got a pen ~?** ¿tienes un bolígrafo a mano?; **our house is ~ for the shops** nuestra casa está *or* queda cerca de las tiendas; **to keep sth ~** tener algo a mano

2 (= *useful*) [*tool, gadget, hint*] práctico, útil; **credit cards can be ~** las tarjetas de crédito pueden resultar muy prácticas *or* útiles; **it turned out rather ~ that the trip was cancelled** nos vino bastante bien que cancelasen el viaje; **to come in ~** venir muy bien, ser muy útil; **the cheque came in very ~** el cheque nos vino muy bien

3 (= *skilful*) [*carpenter, mechanic*] hábil, diestro; **he's ~ around the home** es un manitas en la casa; **to be ~ with sth: she's ~ with a paint brush/needle** es muy mañosa para la pintura/costura, se le da muy bien la pintura/costura; **to be ~ with a gun** saber manejar una pistola; **to be ~ with one's fists** saber pelear, saber defenderse con los puños

handyman [ˈhændɪmən] N (*pl* **handymen**) manitas *mf* (*Sp, Mex*) (*hombre que tiene dotes prácticas para hacer trabajos de carpintería etc en casa*)

hang [hæŋ] (*pt, pp* **hung**)

A TRANSITIVE VERB	C NOUN
B INTRANSITIVE VERB	D PHRASAL VERBS

Ⓐ TRANSITIVE VERB

1 **= *suspend*** [+ *coat, curtains*] colgar; [+ *picture*] (*on wall*) colgar; (*as exhibit*) exponer; [+ *washing*] tender; [+ *wallpaper*] pegar; [+ *door*] colocar; (*Culin*) [+ *game*] manir; **he hung the rope over the side of the boat** colgó la cuerda de la borda del barco; **are you any good at ~ing wallpaper?** ¿se te da bien empapelar?; ♦***IDIOM*** **to ~ one's head** bajar *or* agachar la cabeza; **he hung his head in shame** bajó *or* agachó la cabeza avergonzado; *see also* **peg A3**, **hung over**

2 **= *decorate*** adornar; **the walls were hung with tapestries** las paredes estaban adornadas con tapices; **trees hung with lights** árboles adornados con luces

3 (*pt, pp* **hanged**) 3·1 [+ *criminal*] ahorcar; **he was ~ed, drawn and quartered** lo ahorcaron, destriparon y descuartizaron; **to ~ o.s.** ahorcarse; ♦***IDIOM*** **I might as well be ~ed for a sheep as a lamb** si me van a castigar que sea por algo gordo, de perdidos al río

3·2 (†*) (= *damn*) **~ the expense!** ¡al diablo (con) los gastos!; **~ it (all) !** ¡qué demonios!; **I'll be ~ed if I know!** ¡que me aspen *or* maten si lo sé!

4 **US = *turn*** **~ a right here** gira *or* dobla *or* tuerce a la derecha aquí

5 **= *hold*** *see* **fire A7**

Ⓑ INTRANSITIVE VERB

1 **= *be suspended*** colgar; **a light-bulb was ~ing from the ceiling** una bombilla colgaba del techo; **I was ~ing from the ledge by my fingertips** estaba colgado de la cornisa sujeto por la punta de los dedos; **his portrait ~s in the National Gallery** su retrato está expuesto en la National Gallery; **let your arms ~ loose at your sides** deje los brazos sueltos *or* caídos; **~ loose!** (*US**) (*fig*) ¡tranqui!*, ¡relájate!; **your coat is ~ing on the hook** tu abrigo está colgado en el perchero; **a picture ~ing on the wall** un cuadro colgado en la pared; ♦***IDIOM*** **and thereby ~s a tale** pero eso es harina de otro costal; *see also* **thread A1**

2 **= *be positioned*** **to ~ open: the door**

hung open (= *not closed*) la puerta estaba abierta; (= *partly off hinges*) la puerta estaba encajada; **her mouth hung open in surprise** se quedó boquiabierta; **to ~ out of the window** [*person*] asomarse por la ventana; [*thing*] colgar de la ventana; **I can't work with you ~ing over me like that** no puedo trabajar contigo pendiente de todo lo que hago

3 *= flow* [*rope, garment, hair*] caer; **her hair ~s down her back** el pelo le cae por la espalda; **it's a fabric that ~s well** es una tela que tiene muy buena caída

4 (*pt, pp* **hanged**) *= be hanged* [*criminal*] morir en la horca; **he'll ~ for it** lo ahorcarán por esto

5 *= hover* [*fog*] flotar; **his breath hung in the icy air** su aliento flotaba en el aire helado; **the hawk hung motionless in the sky** el halcón se cernía inmóvil en el cielo; **the threat ~ing over us** la amenaza que se cierne sobre nosotros; **a question mark ~s over many of their futures** se cierne un *or* una interrogante sobre el porvenir de muchos de ellos

6 ✦*IDIOMS* **to go ~*** pudrirse*; **he can go ~ as far as I'm concerned** por mí que se pudra; **to ~ tough (on/for sth)** (*US*) mantenerse firme (en algo/para conseguir algo); **she hung tough despite the pressure** pese a las presiones no dio su brazo a torcer

Ⓒ NOUN

1 *of garment* caída *f*

2 ✦*IDIOMS* **to get the ~ of sth*** coger el tranquillo a algo*; **I'll never get the ~ of this oven** nunca aprenderé a usar este horno, nunca le cogeré el tranquillo a este horno; **I don't give** *or* **care a ~*** me importa un comino*

Ⓓ PHRASAL VERBS

►**hang about** VI + ADV 1 = **hang around**

2 (= *wait*) esperar; **~ about, you told me she'd agreed to it** (espera) un momento, me dijiste que ella estaba de acuerdo

►**hang around** Ⓐ VI + ADV 1 (= *spend time*) **they always ~ around together** siempre van *or* andan juntos; **to ~ around with sb** juntarse *or* andar con algn

2 (= *loiter*) holgazanear; **they were just ~ing around, with nothing to do** estaban holgazaneando, sin nada que hacer

3 (= *wait*) quedarse a esperar; **I'm not ~ing around to find out** no voy a quedarme (a esperar) para ver qué pasa; **he got sick of ~ing around waiting for me** se hartó de andar de un lado para otro esperándome; **to keep sb ~ing around** hacer esperar a algn, tener a algn esperando

Ⓑ VI + PREP **the usual crowd who hung around the café** el grupo de siempre que frecuentaba el café; **schoolboys who ~ around the streets after school** colegiales que rondan por las calles después de clase

►**hang back** VI + ADV 1 (= *hesitate*) no decidirse; **even his closest advisers believe he should ~ back no longer** incluso sus consejeros más allegados creen que debería decidirse ya *or* que no debería pensárselo más; **she hung back from offering** no tenía claro si debía ofrecerse

2 (= *stay behind*) quedarse atrás; **he hung back shyly in the doorway** se quedó atrás tímidamente en la puerta

►**hang in*** VI + ADV **~ in there!** ¡aguanta!; **I didn't ~ in there long enough to find out for sure** no aguanté *or* seguí allí lo suficiente como para cerciorarme

►**hang on** Ⓐ VI + PREP 1 **she hung on his arm** iba agarrada de su brazo; ✦*IDIOMS* **to ~ on sb's every word** ◊ **~ on sb's words** estar pendiente de todo lo que dice algn, no perder detalle de lo que dice algn

2 (= *depend on*) depender de; **everything ~s on his decision** todo depende de su decisión; **everything ~s on whether he saw her or not** todo depende de si la vio o no

Ⓑ VI + ADV 1 (= *grip, hold*) **to ~ on (to sth)** agarrarse (a *or* de algo); **~ on to the branch** agárrate a *or* de la rama; **~ on tight** agárrate fuerte; ✦*IDIOM* **to ~ on (to sth) for dear life** agarrarse (a algo) como si fuera la vida en ello

2 (*) (= *wait*) esperar; **~ on a minute!** ¡espera (un momento)!; **could you ~ on, please?** (*Telec*) no cuelgue, por favor; **to keep sb ~ing on** hacer esperar a algn, tener a algn esperando

3 (= *hold out*) aguantar; **he managed to ~ on till help came** consiguió aguantar hasta que llegó ayuda; **United hung on to take the cup** el United aguantó el tipo y ganó la copa; **~ on in there!*** ¡aguanta!

►**hang on to***, **hang onto*** VI + PREP (= *keep*) [+ *object*] quedarse (con), guardar; [+ *principle*] aferrarse a; **~ on to it till I see you** quédatelo *or* guárdalo hasta que nos veamos; **the president is trying to ~ on to power** el presidente está intentando aferrarse al poder; **he was unable to ~ on to his lead** no pudo mantener su ventaja

►**hang out** Ⓐ VT + ADV [+ *washing*] tender; [+ *flags, banner*] poner, colgar

Ⓑ VI + ADV 1 [*tongue, shirt tails*] **the dog lay there panting, with his tongue ~ing out** el perro estaba ahí echado, jadeando con la lengua fuera *or* con la lengua colgando; **your shirt is ~ing out** llevas la camisa colgando, tienes la camisa fuera

2 (*) (= *live*) vivir; (= *spend time*) pasar el rato; **he hung out in Paris for several years** pasó *or* vivió varios años en París; **on Saturdays we ~ out in the park** los sábados pasamos el rato en el parque; **I used to ~ out in supermarkets** solía frecuentar los supermercados; **she ~s out with some strange people** anda *or* se junta con gente rara

3 (*) (= *hold out*) **they're ~ing out for more money** siguen exigiendo más dinero, insisten en pedir más dinero

4 ✦*IDIOM* **to let it all ~ out** (*US**) soltarse el pelo *or* la melena

►**hang together*** VI + ADV 1 (= *stay united*) [*people*] mantenerse unidos

2 (*logically*) (= *back one another up*) sostenerse; (= *follow internal logic*) tener coherencia; **his arguments just don't ~ together** sus argumentos no se sostienen; **it all ~s together** todo tiene coherencia; **it doesn't ~ together with what we know** no cuadra *or* no encaja con lo que sabemos

►**hang up** Ⓐ VT + ADV 1 [+ *coat*] colgar; ✦*IDIOM* **to ~ up one's boots** colgar las botas; **he announced he was ~ing up his boots for good** anunció que colgaba las botas para siempre

2 (*) **to be hung up on sth** estar obsesionado por algo; **I've never been hung up on material things** nunca me han obsesionado las cosas materiales; **to be hung up on sb** estar colado por algn

3 (*Telec*) [+ *receiver*] colgar

Ⓑ VI + ADV 1 (= *be suspended*) estar colgado; **his hat was ~ing up in the hall** su sombrero estaba colgado en la entrada

2 (*Telec*) colgar; **don't ~ up!** ¡no cuelgues!; **to ~ up on sb** colgar a algn

hangar [ˈhæŋəʳ] N hangar *m*

hangdog [ˈhæŋdɒg] ADJ (= *guilty*) [*look, expression*] avergonzado; (= *depressed*) abatido

hanger [ˈhæŋəʳ] N (*for clothes*) percha *f*, gancho *m* (*LAm*)

hanger-on* [ˈhæŋərˈɒn] N (*pl* **hangers-on**) parásito/a *m/f*, pegote *mf* (*Sp**)

hang-glide [ˈhæŋˌglaɪd] VI volar con ala delta

hang-glider [ˈhæŋˌglaɪdəʳ] N 1 (= *device*) ala *f* delta

2 (= *person*) piloto *mf* de ala delta

hang-gliding [ˈhæŋˌglaɪdɪŋ] N vuelo *m* con ala delta

hanging [ˈhæŋɪŋ] Ⓐ N 1 (*Jur*) 1·1 (= *death penalty*) (ejecución *f* en) la horca, ahorcamiento *m*; **~ would be too good for them** (la ejecución en) la horca *or* el ahorcamiento sería algo demasiado bueno para ellos

1·2 (= *individual execution*) ejecución *f* en la horca, ahorcamiento *m*; **the last ~ in Britain** la última ejecución en la horca en Gran Bretaña; **~s were commonplace then** entonces los ahorcamientos eran moneda corriente

2 (= *curtain*) colgadura *f*; **wall ~** tapiz *m*

Ⓑ ADJ [*bridge, plant, garden*] colgante; [*lamp*] de techo; [*cupboard*] para colgar; **~ space** espacio *m* para colgar ropa

Ⓒ CPD ► **hanging basket** N macetero *m* colgante ► **hanging committee** N junta *f* seleccionadora (*de una exposición*) ► **hanging judge** N juez(a) *m/f* muy severo/a ► **hanging matter** N (*fig*) **it's not a ~ matter** no es cosa de vida o muerte ► **hanging offence, hanging offense** (*US*) N (*lit*) delito *m* que se castiga con la horca; **prostitution is a ~ offence there** la prostitución allí es un delito que se castiga con la horca; **it's not a ~ offence** (*fig*) no es cosa de vida o muerte

hangman [ˈhæŋmən] N (*pl* **hangmen**) verdugo *m*

hangnail [ˈhæŋneɪl] N padrastro *m*

hang-out* [ˈhæŋaʊt] N (*gen*) lugar *m*; (= *bar*) bar *m* habitual; [*of thieves etc*] guarida *f*

hangover [ˈhæŋˌəʊvəʳ] N 1 (*after drinking*) resaca *f*, cruda *f* (*LAm*)

2 (= *sth left over*) vestigio *m*, reliquia *f*; **it's a ~ from pre-war days** es un vestigio *or* una reliquia de la época de preguerra

hang-up* [ˈhæŋʌp] N 1 (= *problem*) problema *m*, lío* *m*

2 (= *complex*) complejo *m* (**about** con)

hank [hæŋk] N [*of wool*] madeja *f*; [*of hair*] mechón *m*

hanker [ˈhæŋkəʳ] VI **to ~ after** *or* **for sth** añorar *or* anhelar algo

hankering [ˈhæŋkərɪŋ] N añoranza *f* (**for** de), anhelo *m* (**for** por); **to have a ~ for sth** añorar *or* anhelar algo

hankie*, **hanky*** [ˈhæŋkɪ] N pañuelo *m*

hanky-panky* [ˈhæŋkɪˈpæŋkɪ] N 1 (*US*) (= *trickery*) **there's some ~ going on here** aquí hay trampa, esto huele a camelo*

2 (*Brit*) (*sexual*) relaciones *fpl* sospechosas; **we want no ~ with the girls** nada de meterse mano con las chicas*

Hannibal [ˈhænɪbəl] N Aníbal

Hanover [ˈhænəvəʳ] N Hanovre *m*

Hanoverian [ˌhænəʊˈvɪərɪən] Ⓐ ADJ hanoveriano

Ⓑ N hanoveriano/a *m/f*

Hansard [ˈhænsɑːd] N *Actas oficiales de los debates del parlamento británico*

Hanseatic [ˌhænzɪˈætɪk] ADJ **the ~ League** La Liga Hanseática

hansom ['hænsəm] N cabriolé *m* (*con pescante trasero*)

Hants [hænts] N ABBR = **Hampshire**

Hanukkah ['hɑːnəkə] N *celebración judía dedicada al Templo de Jerusalén*

ha'penny* ['heɪpnɪ] N = **halfpenny**

haphazard ['hæp'hæzəd] ADJ [1] (= *random*) [*selection*] al azar; [*manner, method*] poco sistemático; **the town has developed in a ~ way** la ciudad ha crecido sin planificación alguna *or* muy desordenadamente; **their approach to the problem has been rather ~** han abordado el problema de forma poco sistemática
[2] (= *careless*) [*person*] descuidado

haphazardly [ˌhæp'hæzədlɪ] ADV [*arrange*] de cualquier modo; [*select*] al azar

hapless ['hæplɪs] ADJ desventurado

happen ['hæpən] VI [1] (= *occur*) pasar, ocurrir, suceder; **what's ~ing?** ¿qué pasa *or* ocurre *or* sucede?; **how did it ~?** ¿cómo pasó *or* ocurrió *or* sucedió?, ¿cómo fue?; **these things ~** estas cosas pasan, son cosas que pasan; **when did the accident ~?** ¿cuándo ocurrió *or* sucedió el accidente?; **whatever ~s** pase lo que pase; **don't let it ~ again** que no vuelva a ocurrir; **as if nothing had ~ed** como si nada, como si tal cosa; **how does it ~ that ...?** ¿cómo es posible que ...? + *subjun*; **what has ~ed to him?** (= *befall*) ¿qué le ha pasado?; (= *become of*) ¿qué ha sido de él?; **it's the best thing that ever ~ed to me** es lo mejor que me ha pasado en la vida; **if anything should ~ to him ...** si le pasara algo ...; ✦*IDIOM* **it's all ~ing here*** aquí es donde está la movida *or* marcha*; *see also* **accident**
[2] (= *chance*) **it ~ed that I was out that day** dio la casualidad de que *or* resulta que aquel día estuve fuera; **it might ~ that no one turns up** puede ocurrir que no venga nadie; **if you ~ to see John, let him know** si acaso vieras a John *or* si da la casualidad de que ves a John, díselo; **I ~ to know that ...** da la casualidad de que sé que ...; **he just ~s to be here now** da la casualidad de que está aquí ahora; **if anyone should ~ to see you** si acaso alguien te viera; **would you ~ to have a pen?** ¿no tendrá un bolígrafo por casualidad?; **it ~s to be true** da la casualidad de que es verdad; **as it ~s ..., ◊ it (just) so ~s that ...** da la casualidad de que ...; **I do know him, as it ~s** pues da la casualidad de que sí le conozco

► **happen along** VI + ADV aparecer; **who should ~ along but Sheila** quién dirías que apareció, pues Sheila

► **happen on, happen upon** VI + PREP [+ *thing*] dar con, encontrar; [+ *person*] tropezar con, encontrarse con; **we ~ed (up)on this gem of a hotel in Ireland** dimos con *or* encontramos un hotel magnífico en Irlanda; **to ~ (up)on the solution** dar con *or* encontrar la solución

happening ['hæpnɪŋ] Ⓐ N (= *event*) suceso *m*, acontecimiento *m*; (*Theat*) happening *m*
Ⓑ ADJ (*) que es lo último*, de lo último

happenstance ['hæpənstæns] N (*US*) casualidad *f*; **by ~** por casualidad

happily ['hæpɪlɪ] ADV [1] (= *contentedly*) [*smile, say, play*] alegremente, felizmente; **it all ended ~** todo acabó felizmente, todo tuvo un final feliz; **they lived ~ together for many years** vivieron los dos felices durante muchos años; **I'm a ~ married man** soy un hombre feliz en mi matrimonio; **he said he would ~ lend us the money** dijo que nos dejaría el dinero con mucho gusto, dijo que gustosamente nos dejaría el dinero
[2] (= *without difficulty*) sin ningún problema; **Muslims and Catholics live ~ together here** musulmanes y católicos conviven aquí sin ningún problema; **blackberries will grow ~ in any good soil** las moras crecen bien en cualquier tipo de tierra; **she'll ~ spend £100 on a dress** se puede gastar 100 libras en un vestido tan tranquilamente
[3] (= *fortunately*) afortunadamente, por fortuna; **~, no one was hurt** afortunadamente *or* por fortuna, nadie resultó herido

happiness ['hæpɪnɪs] N (= *contentment*) felicidad *f*; (= *cheerfulness*) alegría *f*; **we wish you every ~** te deseamos toda la felicidad del mundo; **if you want to know real ~** si quieres ser verdaderamente feliz

▼ **happy** ['hæpɪ] Ⓐ ADJ (*compar* **happier**; *superl* **happiest**) [1] (= *contented*) feliz; **we've been very ~ here** aquí hemos sido muy felices; **I don't think they're very ~ together** no creo que sean muy felices juntos; **to make sb ~** hacer feliz a algn; **you've just made me a very ~ man!** ¡me acabas de hacer el hombre más feliz del mundo!; ✦*IDIOM* **to be as ~ as Larry** *or* **a lark** *or* **a sandboy** estar como unas pascuas
[2] (= *cheerful*) alegre; **she has always been a ~ little girl** siempre ha sido una niña muy alegre; **he has a ~ temperament** tiene un temperamento alegre
[3] (= *satisfied, pleased*) contento; **the boss is waiting for you and he isn't very ~** te está esperando el jefe y no parece muy contento; **to be ~ to do sth: I'm just ~ to be back running** sólo estoy contento de poder volver a correr; **I am ~ to tell you that ...** tengo mucho gusto en comunicarle que ...; **we'll be ~ to help** estaremos encantados de ayudar; **I'd be ~ to check it for you** no me importa nada comprobártelo, con mucho gusto se lo comprobaré (*more frm*); **yes, I'd be ~ to** sí, con mucho gusto; **he seems quite ~ to let things go on as they are** parece no importarle dejar que las cosas sigan como están; **we are not ~ about the plan** no estamos contentos con el proyecto; **we're very ~ for you** nos alegramos mucho por ti; **to keep sb ~** tener a algn contento; **she wasn't ~ with his work** no estaba contenta con su trabajo
[4] (= *at ease, unworried*) tranquilo; **don't worry about keeping him waiting, he seems quite ~** no te preocupes por hacerle esperar, él parece muy tranquilo; **I'm quite ~ to wait** no me importa esperar
[5] (= *pleasant, joyful*) [*childhood, life, marriage, home*] feliz; [*place, atmosphere*] alegre; **it was the happiest day of my life** fue el día más feliz de mi vida; **they were having such a ~ time splashing around** se lo estaban pasando tan bien chapoteando en el agua; **we spent many ~ hours playing on the beach** pasamos muchas horas maravillosas jugando en la playa; **~ birthday!** ¡feliz cumpleaños!; **~ Christmas!** ¡feliz Navidad!, ¡felices Navidades!; **a ~ ending** un final feliz; **a ~ event** un feliz acontecimiento; **~ New Year!** ¡feliz Año Nuevo!; *see also* **return A1**
[6] (= *felicitous*) [*phrase*] afortunado, oportuno; [*position, chance*] afortunado; [*coincidence, idea*] feliz; **a ~ medium** un término medio; **to strike a ~ medium** encontrar un término medio; *see also* **hunting**
[7] (*) (= *tipsy*) contentillo*, alegre*
Ⓑ CPD ► **happy families** NSING (*Cards*) juego *m* de las familias ► **happy hour** N happy hour *m* (*hora durante la cual se paga menos por la bebida en los bares*)

happy-go-lucky ['hæpɪgəʊ'lʌkɪ] ADJ despreocupado

Hapsburg ['hæpsbɜːg] N Habsburgo

hara-kiri ['hærə'kɪrɪ] N haraquiri *m*

harangue [hə'ræŋ] Ⓐ N arenga *f*
Ⓑ VT arengar

harass ['hærəs] VT acosar, hostigar; (*Mil*) hostilizar, hostigar

harassed ['hærəst] ADJ (= *exhausted*) agobiado; (= *under pressure*) presionado; **to look ~** parecer agobiado

harassment ['hærəsmənt] N acoso *m*; (*Mil*) hostigamiento *m*; **sexual ~** acoso *m* sexual

harbinger ['hɑːbɪndʒəʳ] N (= *person*) heraldo *m*, precursor *m*; (= *sign*) presagio *m*, precursor *m*; **~ of doom** presagio *m* del desastre; **the swallow is a ~ of spring** la golondrina anuncia la venida de la primavera

harbour, harbor (*US*) ['hɑːbəʳ] Ⓐ N puerto *m*
Ⓑ VT (= *retain*) [+ *fear, hope*] abrigar; (= *shelter*) [+ *criminal, spy*] dar abrigo *or* refugio a; (= *conceal*) esconder; **that corner ~s the dust** en ese rincón se amontona el polvo; **to ~ a grudge** guardar rencor
Ⓒ CPD ► **harbour dues** NPL derechos *mpl* portuarios ► **harbour master** N capitán *m* de puerto

hard [hɑːd] Ⓐ ADJ (*compar* **harder**; *superl* **hardest**) [1] (= *not soft*) [*object, substance, cheese, skin*] duro; [*ground, snow*] duro, compacto; **baked ~** endurecido (*al sol o en el horno*); **to become** *or* **go ~** ponerse duro, endurecerse; **the water is very ~ here** aquí el agua es muy dura *or* tiene mucha cal; ✦*IDIOMS* **to be as ~ as nails** [*person*] (*physically*) ser duro como una roca; **(as) ~ as a rock** [*object*] (tan) duro como una piedra; *see also* **nut**
[2] (= *harsh, severe*) [*climate, winter, person*] duro, severo; [*frost*] fuerte; [*words, tone*] duro, áspero; [*expression, eyes, voice*] serio, duro; [*drink, liquor*] fuerte; [*drugs*] duro; [*fact*] concreto; [*evidence*] irrefutable; **a ~ blow** (*fig*) un duro golpe; **to take a long ~ look at sth** examinar algo detenidamente; **to be ~ on sb** ser muy duro con algn, darle duro a algn (*LAm*); **don't be so ~ on him, it's not his fault** no seas tan duro con él, no es culpa suya; **aren't you being a bit ~ on yourself?** ¿no estás siendo un poco duro contigo mismo?; **to be ~ on one's clothes** destrozar la ropa; **the light was ~ on the eyes** la luz hacía daño a los ojos; ✦*IDIOM* **to be as ~ as nails** (*in temperament*) ser muy duro, tener el corazón muy duro; *see also* **feeling**
[3] (= *strenuous, tough*) [*work, day*] duro; [*fight, match*] muy reñido; **gardening is ~ work** arreglar el jardín es un trabajo duro; **phew, that was ~ work!** ¡uf!, ¡ha costado lo suyo!; **he's not afraid of ~ work** el trabajo duro no le asusta; **coping with three babies is very ~ work** tres bebés dan mucha tarea *or* mucho trabajo, arreglárselas con tres bebés es una dura *or* ardua tarea; **it's ~ work getting her to talk about herself** cuesta mucho *or* resulta muy trabajoso hacerla hablar sobre sí misma; **to be a ~ worker** ser muy trabajador(a)
[4] (= *difficult*) [*exam, decision, choice*] difícil; **to be ~ to do: it's ~ to study on your own** es difícil estudiar por tu cuenta; **he found it ~ to make friends** le resultaba difícil hacer amigos; **I find it ~ to believe that ...** me cuesta (trabajo) creer que ...; **bloodstains are ~ to remove** las manchas de sangre son difíciles de quitar; **to be ~ to come by** ser difícil de conseguir; **that is a very ~ question to answer** ésa es una pregunta muy difícil de responder; **to be ~ to deal with** ser de

➤ LANGUAGE IN USE: **happy A3** 14, 24.2 **A5** 23.1, 23.2, 23.3

trato difícil; **to be ~ to please** ser muy exigente *or* quisquilloso; **to be ~ of hearing** ser duro de oído; **he's learning the ~ way** está aprendiendo a base de cometer errores; **we shall have to do it the ~ way** tendremos que hacerlo a pulso; *see also* **bargain**, **play C4**
[5] (= *tough, unpleasant*) [*life, times*] duro; **it's a ~ life!** ¡qué vida más dura!; **those were ~ times to live in** aquellos eran tiempos duros, la vida era dura en aquellos tiempos; **her family had fallen on ~ times** su familia estaba pasando por dificultades económicas; **to have a ~ time** pasarlo mal; **to have a ~ time doing sth** tener problemas para hacer algo; **to give sb a ~ time** hacérselo pasar mal a algn; ✦*IDIOMS* **to take a ~ line against/over sth** adoptar una postura intransigente contra algo/respecto a algo; **~ lines** (*Brit**) mala suerte *f*; **~ lines!** ¡qué mala suerte!, ¡qué mala pata!*; *see also* **going**, **hard-line**, **hard-liner**, **luck**
[6] (= *forceful*) [*push, tug, kick*] fuerte
[7] (*Phon, Ling*) [*sound*] fuerte; [*consonant*] oclusivo
Ⓑ ADV (*compar* **harder**; *superl* **hardest**) [1] (= *with a lot of effort*) [*work*] duro, mucho; [*study*] mucho; **he had worked ~ all his life** había trabajado duro *or* mucho toda su vida; **he works very ~** trabaja muy duro, trabaja mucho; **she works ~ at keeping herself fit** se esfuerza mucho por mantenerse en forma; **he was ~ at work in the garden** estaba trabajando afanosamente *or* con ahínco en el jardín; **he was breathing ~** respiraba con dificultad; **we're saving ~ for our holidays** estamos ahorrando todo lo que podemos para las vacaciones, estamos ahorrando al máximo para las vacaciones; **to try ~**: **she always tries ~** siempre se esfuerza mucho; **I can't do it, no matter how ~ I try** no puedo hacerlo, por mucho que lo intente; **to try one's ~est to do sth** esforzarse al máximo por hacer algo; **maybe you're trying too ~** a lo mejor tienes que tomártelo con más calma; ✦*IDIOM* **to be ~ at it: Bill was ~ at it in the garden*** Bill se estaba empleando a fondo en el jardín, Bill estaba dándole duro al jardín*
[2] (= *with force*) [*hit*] fuerte, duro; [*pull, push, blow*] con fuerza; [*snow, rain*] fuerte, mucho; **she pushed the wardrobe as ~ as she could** empujó el armario con todas sus fuerzas; **the government decided to clamp down ~ on terrorism** el gobierno decidió tomar medidas duras contra el terrorismo; **she was feeling ~ done by** pensaba que la habían tratado injustamente; **~ hit** seriamente afectado; **to hit sb ~** (*fig*) ser un duro golpe para algn; **California has been (particularly) ~ hit by the crisis** California (en particular) se ha visto seriamente afectada por la crisis; **I would be ~ pushed** *or* **put to think of another plan** me resultaría difícil pensar en otro plan; **we'll be ~ pushed** *or* **put to finish this tonight!** ¡nos va a ser difícil terminar esto esta noche!; **to take sth ~** tomarse algo muy mal*; **he took it pretty ~** se lo tomó muy mal, fue un duro golpe para él, le golpeó mucho (*LAm*); **to be ~ up*** estar pelado*, no tener un duro (*Sp**); **to be ~ up for sth** estar falto *or* escaso de algo; *see also* **hard-pressed**
[3] (= *solid*) **to freeze ~** quedarse congelado; **to set ~** [*cement etc*] fraguar, endurecerse
[4] (= *intently*) [*listen*] atentamente; [*concentrate*] al máximo; **to look ~ (at sth)** fijarse mucho (en algo); **think ~ before you make a decision** piénsalo muy bien antes de tomar una decisión; **I thought ~ but I couldn't remember his name** por más que pensé *or* por más vueltas que le di no pude recordar su nombre
[5] (= *sharply*) **~ a-port/a-starboard** (*Naut*) todo a babor/estribor; **to turn ~ left/right** girar todo a la izquierda/derecha
[6] (= *closely*) **~ behind sth** justo detrás de algo; **I hurried upstairs with my sister ~ behind me** subí las escaleras corriendo con mi hermana que venía justo detrás; **~ upon sth** (= *just after*) justo después de algo; **the launch of the book followed ~ upon the success of the film** el lanzamiento del libro se produjo justo después del éxito de la película; *see also* **heel A1**
Ⓒ CPD ► **hard cash** N dinero *m* contante y sonante, (dinero *m* en) efectivo *m* ► **hard centre**, **hard center** (*US*) N relleno *m* duro ► **hard copy** N (*Comput*) copia *f* impresa ► **the hard core** N (= *intransigents*) los incondicionales, el núcleo duro; *see also* **hard-core** ► **hard court** N (*Tennis*) cancha *f* (de tenis) de cemento, pista *f* (de tenis) de cemento ► **hard currency** N moneda *f* fuerte, divisa *f* fuerte ► **hard disk** N (*Comput*) disco *m* duro ► **hard goods** NPL productos *mpl* no perecederos ► **hard hat** N (= *riding hat*) gorra *f* de montar; [*of construction worker*] casco *m*; (= *construction worker*) albañil *mf* ► **hard labour**, **hard labor** (*US*) N trabajos *mpl* forzados ► **hard landing** N aterrizaje *m* duro ► **the hard left** N (*esp Brit*) la extrema izquierda, la izquierda radical ► **hard news** N noticias *fpl* fidedignas ► **hard palate** N paladar *m* ► **hard porn*** N porno *m* duro ► **the hard right** N (*esp Brit*) la extrema derecha, la derecha radical ► **hard rock** N (*Mus*) rock *m* duro ► **hard sell** N venta *f* agresiva; **~ sell tactics** táctica *fsing* de venta agresiva; **~ sell techniques** técnicas *fpl* de venta agresiva ► **hard shoulder** N (*Brit Aut*) arcén *m*, hombrillo *m* ► **hard stuff*** N (= *alcohol*) alcohol *m* duro, bebidas *fpl* fuertes; (= *drugs*) droga *f* dura; **he fancied a drop of the ~ stuff** le apetecía una copita de algo fuerte ► **hard top** N (= *car*) coche *m* no descapotable; (= *car roof*) techo *m* rígido ► **hard water** N agua *f* dura, agua *f* con mucha cal

hard-and-fast ['hɑːdən'fɑːst] ADJ [*rule*] rígido; [*decision*] definitivo, irrevocable

hardback ['hɑːdbæk] Ⓐ N (= *book*) libro *m* encuadernado, libro *m* de tapa dura
Ⓑ ADJ [*edition, book*] de tapa dura

hard-bitten ['hɑːd'bɪtn] ADJ endurecido, amargado

hardboard ['hɑːdbɔːd] N aglomerado *m* (*de madera*)

hard-boiled ['hɑːd'bɔɪld] ADJ [1] (= *hard*) [*egg*] duro
[2] (= *tough, cynical*) duro de carácter, amargado

hard-core ['hɑːdkɔːʳ] ADJ [*pornography*] duro; [*supporter, militant, activist*] acérrimo; [*conservative, communist*] acérrimo, empedernido; *see also* **hard**

hard-cover ['hɑːd,kʌvəʳ] ADJ [*book*] encuadernado, de tapa dura

hard-drinking ['hɑːd'drɪŋkɪŋ] ADJ bebedor

hard-earned ['hɑːd'ɜːnd] ADJ ganado con el sudor de la frente

hard-edged ['hɑːd'edʒd] ADJ (*fig*) [*style, story*] contundente, duro

harden ['hɑːdn] Ⓐ VT [1] (= *make hard*) [+ *substance*] endurecer; [+ *steel*] templar; [+ *skin*] curtir, endurecer
[2] (= *make tough, harsh*) endurecer; **the experience had ~ed her** la experiencia la había endurecido; **to ~ sb to adversity** acostumbrar a algn a hacerse fuerte ante la adversidad; ✦*IDIOM* **to ~ one's heart**: **years of putting up with his violent outbursts had ~ed her heart** después de años de sufrir sus arranques de violencia se le había endurecido el corazón; **she ~ed her heart and refused to have him back** hizo de tripas corazón *or* se hizo fuerte y se negó a aceptarlo de nuevo
[3] (= *make determined*) **these experiences ~ed her resolve** estas experiencias la afianzaron en su propósito; **the workers' behaviour only served to ~ the attitude of the managers** el comportamiento de los obreros sólo contribuyó a reforzar la actitud de la dirección
[4] (*Comm*) (= *stabilize*) estabilizar, consolidar
Ⓑ VI [1] (= *become hard*) [*clay, arteries, icing*] endurecerse; [*cement*] fraguar
[2] (= *become harsh, severe*) [*person, expression, eyes*] endurecerse; **his voice ~ed** el tono de su voz se endureció, adoptó un tono más áspero; **my heart ~ed against her** mi corazón se volvió contra ella; **what happened only caused him to ~ in his determination to continue** lo que sucedió sólo le afianzó más en su propósito de seguir
[3] (*Comm*) (= *stabilize*) [*prices, economy*] estabilizarse, consolidarse

hardened ['hɑːdnd] ADJ [1] [*drinker*] empedernido; [*criminal*] reincidente; **to be ~ to sth** estar acostumbrado a algo; **we are becoming ~ to violence** nos hemos ido acostumbrando a la violencia
[2] (*Tech*) [*steel*] templado

hardening ['hɑːdnɪŋ] N [1] (*lit*) endurecimiento *m*; **~ of the arteries** endurecimiento *m* de las arterias, arteriosclerosis *f*
[2] (*fig*) [*of attitude*] radicalización *f*
[3] (*Comm*) [*of prices, economy*] estabilización *f*, consolidación *f*

hard-faced ['hɑːdfeɪst] ADJ severo, inflexible

hard-fought ['hɑːd'fɔːt] ADJ muy reñido

hard-headed ['hɑːd'hedɪd] ADJ (= *shrewd*) realista, práctico; (= *stubborn*) terco

hard-hearted ['hɑːd'hɑːtɪd] ADJ duro de corazón; **to be ~** tener un corazón de piedra

hard-hit ['hɑːd'hɪt] ADJ muy afectado, muy perjudicado; **small businesses have been particularly ~ by these measures** los pequeños negocios se han visto especialmente afectados *or* perjudicados por estas medidas

hard-hitting ['hɑːd,hɪtɪŋ] ADJ [*speech etc*] contundente

hardiness ['hɑːdɪnɪs] N resistencia *f*

hard-line ['hɑːd'laɪn] ADJ [*communist, conservative*] de línea dura, extremista; [*approach, policy*] radical

hard-liner [,hɑːd'laɪnəʳ] N duro/a *m/f*; (*Pol*) (= *supporter*) partidario/a *m/f* de línea dura; (= *politician*) político/a *m/f* de línea dura; **the ~s of the party** el ala dura del partido

hard-luck story [,hɑːdlʌk'stɔːrɪ] N **he pitched me a ~** me contó sus infortunios *or* su historia tan trágica

hardly ['hɑːdlɪ] ADV apenas; **I ~ know him** apenas lo conozco, casi no lo conozco; **I can ~ believe it** apenas puedo creerlo, casi no puedo creerlo; **I could ~ understand a word** apenas entendí palabra, no pude entender casi nada; **she had ~ any money** apenas tenía dinero, no tenía casi dinero; **~ a day goes by when we don't argue** apenas pasa un día sin que discutamos; **we could ~ refuse** ¿cómo podíamos negarnos?; **she's ~ what you'd call a cordon bleu chef** (*iro*) no es precisamente *or* no es lo que se dice un cocinero de primera; **that can ~ be true** eso difícilmente puede ser verdad; **that is ~ likely**

eso es poco probable; **it's ~ surprising!** ¡no me extraña *or* sorprende!; **"do you think he'll pass?" — "~!"** —¿crees que aprobará? —¡qué va! *or* ¡ni hablar!; **~ anyone** casi nadie; **~ anything** casi nada; **there was ~ anywhere to go** no había casi ningún sitio donde ir; **~ ever** casi nunca

hardness ['hɑ:dnɪs] N 1 (= *not softness*) [*of object, substance, water*] dureza *f*
2 (= *not easiness*) [*of exam, problem*] dificultad *f*; **~ of hearing** dureza *f* de oído
3 (= *harshness*) [*of person, measures*] dureza *f*, severidad *f*; [*of winter, frost*] rigor *m*; **~ of heart** dureza *f* de corazón, insensibilidad *f*

hard-nosed [,hɑ:d'nəʊzd] ADJ (*fig*) duro

hard-on** ['hɑ:dɒn] N empalme *m* (*Sp***), erección *f*; **he had a ~** se le puso dura, se empalmó (*Sp***), se le empinó (*Sp***)

hard-pressed ['hɑ:dprest] ADJ **to be ~** estar en apuros; **our ~ economy** nuestra agobiada economía; **you'd be ~ to find a better deal than that** le va a ser difícil encontrar una oferta mejor

hardship ['hɑ:dʃɪp] Ⓐ N (= *deprivation*) privación *f*; (*financial*) apuro *m*; (= *condition of life*) miseria *f*; **to suffer ~(s)** pasar apuros; **it's no ~ to him (to give up the car)** no le cuesta nada (dejar de usar el coche)
Ⓑ CPD ► **hardship clause** N (*Jur*) cláusula *f* de salvaguarda

hardtack ['hɑ:dtæk] N (*Naut*) galleta *f*

hardware ['hɑ:dwɛəʳ] Ⓐ N (*for domestic use*) ferretería *f*, quincalla *f*; (*Mil*) armas *fpl*, armamento *m*; (*Comput*) hardware *m*, soporte *m* físico
Ⓑ CPD ► **hardware dealer** N ferretero/a *m/f* ► **hardware shop, hardware store** N ferretería *f* ► **hardware specialist** N (*Comput*) especialista *mf* en hardware

hard-wearing ['hɑ:d'wɛərɪŋ] ADJ resistente, duradero

hard-won ['hɑ:d'wʌn] ADJ ganado a duras penas

hardwood ['hɑ:dwʊd] Ⓐ N madera *f* noble *or* dura
Ⓑ CPD ► **hardwood tree** N árbol *m* de hojas caducas

hard-working ['hɑ:d'wɜ:kɪŋ] ADJ trabajador

hardy ['hɑ:dɪ] ADJ (*compar* **hardier**; *superl* **hardiest**) fuerte, robusto; (*Bot*) resistente

hare [hɛəʳ] Ⓐ N (*pl* **hares** *or* **hare**) liebre *f*; ✦***PROV*** **first catch your ~** no hay que empezar por el tejado
Ⓑ VI (*) ir a todo correr*, ir a toda pastilla*; **to ~ away** *or* **off** irse a todo correr *or* a toda pastilla*, salir disparado*; **to ~ in/out/through** (*Brit*) entrar/salir/pasar a todo correr *or* a toda pastilla*; **he went haring past** pasó como un rayo

harebell ['hɛəbel] N campánula *f*

harebrained ['hɛəbreɪnd] ADJ [*idea, scheme*] disparatado, descabellado; [*person*] casquivano

harelip ['hɛə'lɪp] N labio *m* leporino

harelipped [,hɛə'lɪpt] ADJ de labio leporino, labihendido

harem [hɑ:'ri:m] N harén *m*

haricot ['hærɪkəʊ] N (*also* **~ bean**) frijol *m*, judía *f* blanca (*Sp*)

hark [hɑ:k] VI **~!** (*poet*) ¡escucha!; **~ at him!*** ¡qué cosas dice!, ¡quién fue a hablar!; **~ at him singing!** ¡cómo canta!; **to ~ to** escuchar

►**hark back** VI + ADV (= *return to*) volver (**to** a); (= *recall*) recordar; **he's always ~ing back to that** siempre está con la misma canción

➤ LANGUAGE IN USE: **harm** A 18.4

harken ['hɑ:kən] = **hearken**

Harlequin ['hɑ:lɪkwɪn] N Arlequín

Harley Street ['hɑ:lɪstri:t] N (*Brit*) *calle de Londres donde tienen su consulta muchos médicos especialistas prestigiosos*

harlot ['hɑ:lət] N ramera *f*

▼**harm** [hɑ:m] Ⓐ N daño *m*, mal *m*, perjuicio *m*; **to do sb ~** hacer daño a algn; (*fig*) perjudicar a algn; **it does more ~ than good** es peor el remedio que la enfermedad; **the ~ is done now** el daño *or* mal ya está hecho; **don't worry, no ~ done** no te preocupes, no ha sido nada; **there's no ~ in trying** nada se pierde con probar; **I see no ~ in that** no veo nada en contra de eso; **he means no ~** no tiene malas intenciones; **out of ~'s way** a salvo, fuera de peligro; **to keep out of ~'s way** evitar el peligro; **we moved the car out of ~'s way** quitamos el coche de en medio, movimos el coche a un lugar seguro
Ⓑ VT [+ *person*] hacer daño a, hacer mal a; [+ *health, reputation, interests*] perjudicar; [+ *crops*] dañar, estropear
Ⓒ VI sufrir daños; **will it ~ in the rain?** ¿lo estropeará la lluvia?; **it won't ~ for that** eso no le hará daño

harmful ['hɑ:mfʊl] ADJ [*substance, chemical*] dañino, nocivo; [*effects, consequences*] perjudicial, pernicioso; (*to reputation*) perjudicial (**to** para); **tobacco is ~ to the health** el tabaco perjudica seriamente la salud; **the chemical is not ~ to plants** el producto químico no es nocivo para *or* no daña las plantas

harmless ['hɑ:mlɪs] ADJ [*person, animal*] inofensivo; [*substance, chemical*] inocuo; (= *innocent*) inocente

harmlessly ['hɑ:mlɪslɪ] ADV [*remark*] inocuamente, inofensivamente; [*explode, fall*] sin causar daños

harmonic [hɑ:'mɒnɪk] ADJ armónico

harmonica [hɑ:'mɒnɪkə] N armónica *f*

harmonically [hɑ:'mɒnɪklɪ] ADV armónicamente

harmonics [hɑ:'mɒnɪks] N armonía *f*

harmonious [hɑ:'məʊnɪəs] ADJ 1 (*Mus*) [*sound, chord*] armonioso
2 (*fig*) [*colour scheme, architecture, relationship*] armonioso; [*atmosphere*] de armonía

harmoniously [hɑ:'məʊnɪəslɪ] ADV 1 (= *musically*) armoniosamente
2 (= *amicably*) [*live, work*] en armonía; (= *tastefully*) [*blend*] armoniosamente

harmonium [hɑ:'məʊnɪəm] N armonio *m*

harmonization [,hɑ:mənaɪ'zeɪʃən] N armonización *f*

harmonize ['hɑ:mənaɪz] VT, VI armonizar (**with** con)

harmony ['hɑ:mənɪ] N armonía *f*; **to sing/live in ~ with sb** cantar/vivir en armonía con algn

harness ['hɑ:nɪs] Ⓐ N (*for horse*) arreos *mpl*, jaeces *mpl*; (= *safety harness*) (*for walking a child*) andadores *mpl*, correas *fpl*; (*on high chair, baby seat*) correas *fpl* de sujeción *or* seguridad; (*for mountaineer etc*) arnés *m*; **to work in ~ (with)** trabajar conjuntamente (con); ✦***IDIOMS*** **to die in ~** morir con las botas puestas; **to get back in ~** volver al trabajo
Ⓑ VT 1 (*lit*) [+ *horse*] enjaezar, poner los arreos a; (*to carriage*) enganchar; **to ~ a horse to a cart** enganchar un caballo a un carro
2 (*fig*) [+ *resources, energy*] utilizar, aprovechar
Ⓒ CPD ► **harness race** N carrera *f* de trotones

harp [hɑ:p] N arpa *f*

►**harp on*** VI + ADV **to ~ on (about)** estar siempre con la misma historia (de), machacar (sobre)*; **stop ~ing on!** ¡no machaques!*, ¡corta el rollo!*

harpist ['hɑ:pɪst] N arpista *mf*

harpoon [hɑ:'pu:n] Ⓐ N arpón *m*
Ⓑ VT arponear

harpsichord ['hɑ:psɪkɔ:d] N clavicémbalo *m*, clavecín *m*

harpsichordist ['hɑ:psɪkɔ:dɪst] N clavicembalista *mf*

harpy ['hɑ:pɪ] N arpía *f*

harquebus ['hɑ:kwɪbəs] N (*Hist*) arcabuz *m*

harridan ['hærɪdən] N bruja *f*

harried ['hærɪd] ADJ [*expression etc*] agobiado, preocupado

harrier ['hærɪəʳ] N 1 (= *dog*) lebrel *m* (*inglés*)
2 **harriers** (= *cross-country runners*) corredores *mpl* de cross
3 (*Orn*) aguilucho *m*

Harris Tweed [,hærɪs'twi:d] N tweed® *m* producido en la isla de Harris

harrow ['hærəʊ] (*Agr*) Ⓐ N grada *f*, rastra *f*
Ⓑ VT 1 (*Agr*) gradar
2 (*fig*) torturar, destrozar

harrowing ['hærəʊɪŋ] ADJ (= *distressing*) angustioso; (= *awful*) espeluznante, terrible; (= *moving*) conmovedor

Harry ['hærɪ] N (*familiar form*) of **Harold**; ✦***IDIOM*** **to play old ~ with*** endiablar, estropear

harry ['hærɪ] VT (*Mil*) hostilizar, hostigar; [+ *person*] acosar, hostigar

harsh [hɑ:ʃ] ADJ (*compar* **harsher**; *superl* **harshest**) 1 (= *severe*) [*winter, weather, punishment*] duro, riguroso; [*words*] duro, áspero; [*remarks, criticism, conditions*] duro; [*person, sentence*] duro, severo; **to be ~ on sb** ser duro *or* severo con algn
2 (= *too bright*) [*light*] fuerte; [*colour*] chillón, estridente
3 (= *rough*) [*fabric, material*] áspero
4 (= *rough-sounding*) [*voice, sound*] áspero
5 (= *strong*) [*detergent*] fuerte; [*contrast*] violento

harshly ['hɑ:ʃlɪ] ADV [*treat, judge, speak*] con dureza; [*criticize*] duramente; [*say*] con voz áspera; [*laugh*] ásperamente; **a ~ worded attack** un ataque verbal muy duro; **the room was ~ illuminated** la habitación tenía una iluminación desagradable

harshness ['hɑ:ʃnɪs] N [*of climate*] rigor *m*, dureza *f*; [*of conditions, words*] dureza *f*; [*of punishment*] dureza *f*, severidad *f*; [*of light*] crudeza *f*; [*of colour*] estridencia *f*; [*of sound, fabric*] aspereza *f*

hart [hɑ:t] N (*pl* **harts** *or* **hart**) ciervo *m*

harum-scarum ['hɛərəm'skɛərəm] Ⓐ ADJ atolondrado
Ⓑ ADV a tontas y a locas
Ⓒ N (= *person*) tarambana *mf*

harvest ['hɑ:vɪst] Ⓐ N 1 (= *act*) [*of cereals*] siega *f*; [*of fruit, vegetables*] cosecha *f*, recolección *f*; [*of grapes*] vendimia *f*
2 (= *product*) cosecha *f*
3 (*fig*) cosecha *f*
Ⓑ VT 1 (*Agr*) [+ *cereals*] cosechar; [+ *fruit, vegetables*] cosechar, recolectar; [+ *grapes*] vendimiar
2 (*fig*) cosechar
Ⓒ VI cosechar, segar
Ⓓ CPD ► **harvest festival** N fiesta *f* de la cosecha ► **harvest home** N (= *festival*) ≈ fiesta *f* de la cosecha; (= *season*) cosecha *f* ► **harvest moon** N luna *f* llena ► **harvest time** N cosecha *f*, siega *f*

harvester ['hɑːvɪstəʳ] N [1] (= *person*) [*of cereals*] segador(a) *m/f*; [*of fruit, vegetables*] recolector(a) *m/f*; [*of grapes*] vendimiador(a) *m/f*
[2] (= *machine*) cosechadora *f*; (= *combine harvester*) segadora-trilladora *f*

harvesting ['hɑːvɪstɪŋ] N = **harvest A1**

has [hæz] 3RD PERS SING PRESENT *of* **have**

has-been* ['hæzbiːn] N vieja gloria *f*

hash¹ [hæʃ] (A) N [1] (*Culin*) picadillo *m*
[2] (*) lío* *m*, embrollo *m*; **to make a ~ of sth** hacer algo muy mal; **he made a complete ~ of the interview** la entrevista le fue fatal; **✦IDIOM to settle sb's ~** cargarse a algn*
(B) CPD ► **hash browns** NPL *croquetas de patata hervida y cebolla*

hash²* [hæʃ] N (= *hashish*) hachís *m*, chocolate‡ *m* (*Sp*), mota *f* (*CAm**)

hash³ [hæʃ] N (*Typ*) almohadilla *f*

hashish ['hæʃɪʃ] N hachís *m*

hasn't ['hæznt] = **has not**

hasp [hɑːsp] N (*for padlock*) hembrilla *f*; (*on window*) falleba *f*; (*on box, book*) cierre *m*

Hassidic [hə'sɪdɪk] ADJ hasídico

hassle ['hæsl] (A) N (*) (= *problem, difficulty*) lío *m*, problema *m*; **no ~!** ¡no hay problema!; **it's not worth the ~** no vale la pena
(B) VT molestar, fastidiar

hassock ['hæsək] N (*Rel*) cojín *m*

hast†† [hæst] *see* **have**

haste [heɪst] N prisa *f*, apuro *m* (*LAm*); **to do sth in ~** hacer algo precipitadamente *or* de prisa; **to make ~** darse prisa, apurarse (*LAm*); **to make ~ to do sth** apresurarse a hacer algo; **✦PROVS more ~ less speed ◊ make ~ slowly** vísteme despacio que tengo prisa

hasten ['heɪsn] (A) VT [+ *process*] acelerar; [+ *sb's end, downfall*] precipitar; **to ~ sb's departure** acelerar la partida *or* marcha de algn; **to ~ one's steps** apretar el paso; **to ~ death** precipitar *or* adelantar la muerte
(B) VI apresurarse, darse prisa; **to ~ to do sth** apresurarse a hacer algo; **I ~ to add that ...** me apresuro a añadir que ...; **she ~ed to assure me that nothing was wrong** se apresuró a asegurarme que no pasaba nada

►**hasten away** VI + ADV marcharse precipitadamente (**from** de)

►**hasten back** VI + ADV volver con toda prisa

►**hasten on** VI + ADV seguir adelante con toda prisa

hastily ['heɪstɪlɪ] ADV [1] (= *hurriedly*) de prisa, apresuradamente; **I ~ suggested that ...** me apresuré a sugerir que ...
[2] (= *rashly*) [*speak*] precipitadamente; [*judge*] a la ligera

hasty ['heɪstɪ] ADJ (*compar* **hastier**, *superl* **hastiest**) [1] (= *hurried*) apresurado, precipitado
[2] (= *rash*) precipitado; **don't be so ~** no te precipites

hat [hæt] (A) N sombrero *m*; **to raise one's ~** (*in greeting*) descubrirse; **to take off one's ~** quitarse el sombrero; **✦IDIOMS to eat one's ~: I'll eat my ~ if ...** que me maten si ...; **to hang one's ~ up** jubilarse; **my ~!** ¡caramba!; **that's old ~** eso no es nada nuevo; **to pass the ~ round** pasar el platillo; **to take one's ~ off to sb** quitarse el sombrero *or* descubrirse ante algn; **I take my ~ off to him** me descubro ante él; **to talk through one's ~*** decir disparates *or* tonterías; **to keep sth under one's ~** no decir palabra sobre algo; **keep it under your ~** de esto no digas ni pío*; **to wear two ~s** ejercer un doble papel; **now wearing my other ~ as ...** hablando ahora en mi otra calidad de ...; *see also* **ring¹ A4**
(B) CPD ► **hat rack** N perchero *m* ► **hat shop** N sombrerería *f* ► **hat stand, hat tree** (*US*) N perchero *m* ► **hat trick** N (*Ftbl, Rugby etc*) (= *three goals etc*) tres tantos *mpl or* goles *mpl* en un partido; (= *three consecutive wins*) serie *f* de tres victorias, tres triunfos *mpl* seguidos; **to get** *or* **score a ~-trick** marcar tres tantos *or* goles en un partido

hatband ['hætbænd] N cinta *f* de sombrero

hatbox ['hætbɒks] N sombrerera *f*

hatch¹ [hætʃ] N [1] (*Naut*) escotilla *f*
[2] (*Brit*) (= *serving hatch*) ventanilla *f*; *see also* **batten**

hatch² [hætʃ] (A) VT [1] (*lit*) [+ *chick*] empollar; [+ *egg*] incubar
[2] (*fig*) [+ *scheme*] idear; [+ *plot*] tramar
(B) VI [*chick*] salir del huevo; [*insect, larva*] eclosionar (*frm*); **the egg ~ed** el pollo rompió el cascarón y salió; **those eggs never ~ed** esos huevos resultaron ser hueros

hatch³ [hætʃ] VT (*Art*) sombrear

hatchback ['hætʃbæk] N [1] (= *car*) **a ~** un tres/cinco puertas, un coche con puerta trasera
[2] (= *door*) puerta *f* trasera, portón *m*

hat-check girl ['hættʃek,gɜːl] N (*US*) encargada *f* del guardarropa

hatchery ['hætʃərɪ] N criadero *m*, vivero *m*

hatchet ['hætʃɪt] (A) N hacha *f* (pequeña); *see also* **bury**
(B) CPD ► **hatchet job*** N crítica *f* vitriólica; **to do a ~ job on sb** poner por los suelos a algn, poner a algn a caer de un burro *or* a parir* ► **hatchet man*** N (*US*) *ejecutor de faenas desagradables por cuenta de otro*; (= *assassin*) sicario *m*, asesino *m* a sueldo

hatchet-faced ['hætʃɪt,feɪst] ADJ de cara de cuchillo

hatching¹ ['hætʃɪŋ] N [*of egg*] incubación *f*; [*of chick*] salida *f* del huevo; [*of insect, larva*] eclosión *f* (*frm*); (*fig*) [*of scheme*] ideación *f*; [*of plot*] maquinación *f*

hatching² ['hætʃɪŋ] N (*Art*) sombreado *m*

hatchway ['hætʃweɪ] N *see* **hatch¹**

▼ **hate** [heɪt] (A) N odio *m*; *see also* **pet**
(B) VT odiar; **to ~ sb like poison** odiar a algn a muerte; **I ~ having to commute every day** no soporto tener que tomar el tren todos los días para ir a trabajar; **he ~s to be** *or* **he ~s being corrected** no soporta que se le corrija *or* que le corrijan; **I ~ to see him unhappy** me duele mucho *or* no soporto verlo triste; **I ~ to say it, but ...** lamento tener que decirlo, pero ...; **I ~ to trouble you, but ...** siento muchísimo molestarle, pero ...
(C) CPD ► **hate campaign** N campaña *f or* operación *f* de acoso (y derribo); **to mount/wage a ~ campaign against sb** montar/realizar una campaña *or* operación de acoso y derribo contra algn ► **hate mail** N cartas *fpl* amenazantes

hateful ['heɪtfʊl] ADJ odioso

hath†† [hæθ] *see* **have**

hatless ['hætlɪs] ADJ sin sombrero, descubierto

hatpin ['hætpɪn] N alfiler *m* de sombrero

hatred ['heɪtrɪd] N odio *m* (**for** a)

hatter ['hætəʳ] N sombrerero/a *m/f*; *see also* **mad A1.1**

haughtily ['hɔːtɪlɪ] ADV altaneramente, altivamente

haughtiness ['hɔːtɪnɪs] N altanería *f*, altivez *f*

haughty ['hɔːtɪ] ADJ (*compar* **haughtier**, *superl* **haughtiest**) altanero, altivo

haul [hɔːl] (A) N [1] (= *act of pulling*) tirón *m*, jalón *m* (*LAm*) (**on** de)
[2] (= *distance*) recorrido *m*, trayecto *m*; **it's a long ~** hay mucho trecho, hay una buena tirada*; **revitalizing the economy will be a long ~** hay por delante un largo trecho hasta conseguir revitalizar la economía; **over the long ~** a largo plazo
[3] (= *amount taken*) [*of fish*] redada *f*; (*financial*) ganancia *f*; (*from robbery etc*) botín *m*; (= *arms haul, drugs haul*) alijo *m*; **the thieves made a good ~** los ladrones obtuvieron un cuantioso botín
(B) VT [1] (= *drag*) [+ *heavy object*] arrastrar, jalar (*LAm*); **he ~ed himself to his feet** se puso en pie con gran esfuerzo; **they ~ed me out of bed at five o'clock in the morning** me sacaron de la cama a las cinco de la mañana; **he was ~ed before the manager** tuvo que presentarse al gerente; *see also* **coal**
[2] (= *transport*) transportar, acarrear

►**haul down** VT + ADV [+ *flag, sail*] arriar

►**haul in** VT + ADV [+ *fishing net*] ir recogiendo

►**haul up** VT + ADV [1] (*lit*) ir levantando
[2] (*fig*) **he was ~ed up in court** fue llevado ante el tribunal

haulage ['hɔːlɪdʒ] (A) N (= *road transport*) transporte *m*, acarreo *m*; (= *cost*) gastos *mpl* de transporte
(B) CPD ► **haulage company** N compañía *f* de transportes (por carretera) ► **haulage contractor** N transportista *mf*

hauler ['hɔːləʳ] (*US*) = **haulier**

haulier ['hɔːlɪəʳ] N transportista *mf*

haunch [hɔːntʃ] N [*of animal*] anca *f*; [*of person*] cadera *f*; [*of meat*] pierna *f*; **to sit on one's ~es** sentarse en cuclillas

haunt [hɔːnt] (A) N [*of animal, criminals*] guarida *f*; [*of person*] lugar *m* predilecto; **I know his usual/favourite ~s** sé dónde suele ir/cuáles son sus lugares predilectos; **it's a ~ of artists** es lugar de encuentro de artistas
(B) VT [1] [*ghost*] [+ *castle etc*] aparecerse en, rondar; **the house is ~ed** en la casa hay fantasmas, la casa está encantada *or* embrujada
[2] [*person*] [+ *place*] (= *frequent*) frecuentar, rondar
[3] [*idea, fear*] [+ *person*] obsesionar; **he is ~ed by the thought that ...** le obsesiona el pensamiento de que ...; **he is ~ed by memories** le persiguen los recuerdos

haunted ['hɔːntɪd] ADJ [*look*] de angustia, obsesionado; **~ house** casa encantada *or* embrujada

haunting ['hɔːntɪŋ] ADJ [*sight, music*] evocador; [*melody*] inolvidable

hauntingly ['hɔːntɪŋlɪ] ADV **a ~ lovely scene** una escena de una belleza inolvidable

haute couture [otkutyr] N alta costura *f*

haute cuisine [otkwizin] N alta cocina *f*

hauteur [əʊ'tɜː] N (*frm*) = **haughtiness**

Havana [hə'vænə] N La Habana

▼ **have** [hæv] (*3rd pers sing present* **has**; *pt, pp* **had**)

> [A] TRANSITIVE VERB [C] MODAL VERB
> [B] AUXILIARY VERB [D] PHRASAL VERBS
> *When* **have** *is part of a set combination, eg* **have a look, have a good time, have breakfast, had better**, *look up the other word. For* **have** *+ adverb/preposition combinations, see also the phrasal verb section of this entry.*

(A) TRANSITIVE VERB
[1] [= **possess**] tener; **he's got** *or* **he has blue eyes** tiene los ojos azules; **~ you got** *or* **do you ~ 10p?** ¿tienes diez peniques?; **~ you got** *or* **do you ~ any brothers or sisters?**

➤ LANGUAGE IN USE: hate B 7.3

¿tienes hermanos?; **she had her eyes closed** tenía los ojos cerrados; **he hasn't got** *or* **he doesn't ~ any friends** no tiene amigos; **I've got** *or* **I ~ a friend staying next week** tengo a un amigo en casa la semana que viene; **I've got** *or* **I ~ an idea** tengo una idea

Don't translate the **a** *in sentences like* **has he got a girlfriend?, I haven't got a washing-machine** *if the number of such items is not significant since people normally only have one at a time:*

has he got a girlfriend? ¿tiene novia?; **I ~n't got a washing-machine** no tengo lavadora

Do translate the **a** *if the person or thing is qualified:*

he has a Spanish girlfriend tiene una novia española; **all** *or* **everything I ~ is yours** todo lo que tengo es tuyo; **you must give it all** *or* **everything you ~** tienes que emplearte a fondo; **you must put all** *or* **everything you ~ into it** tienes que emplearte a fondo; **can I ~ a pencil please?** ¿me puedes dar un lápiz, por favor?; **the book has no name on it** el libro no lleva *or* tiene el nombre del dueño; **I've got** *or* **I ~ no Spanish** no sé español; **to ~ something to do** tener algo que hacer; **I've got some letters to write** tengo algunas cartas que escribir; **I've got** *or* **I ~ nothing to do** no tengo nada que hacer; **~n't you got anything to do?** ¿no tienes nada que hacer?; **hello, what ~ we here?** vaya, vaya, ¿qué tenemos aquí?; *see also* **handy 1**, **ready A1.1**

2 *= eat, drink* tomar; **what are we having for lunch?** ¿que vamos a comer?; **we had ice-cream for dessert** tomamos helado de postre; **to ~ something to eat/drink** comer/beber algo, tomar algo; **what will you ~?** ¿qué quieres tomar?, ¿qué vas a tomar?; **I'll ~ a coffee** tomaré un café; **will you ~ some more?** ¿te sirvo más?

3 *= receive* recibir; **thank you for having me** gracias por su hospitalidad; **you can ~ my ticket** puedes quedarte con mi billete; **we had some help from the government** recibimos ayuda del gobierno; **I had a letter from John** tuve carta de Juan, recibí una carta de Juan; **I must ~ them by this afternoon** necesito tenerlos para esta tarde; **to ~ no news** no tener noticias; **they had a lot of wedding presents** recibieron *or* les hicieron muchos regalos de boda; **we had a lot of visitors** (*at home*) tuvimos muchas visitas; (*at exhibition etc*) tuvimos muchos visitantes

4 *= obtain* **they can be had for as little as £10 each** pueden conseguirse por tan sólo 10 libras; **it's not to be had anywhere** no se consigue en ninguna parte; **there was no bread to be had** no quedaba pan en ningún sitio, no podía conseguirse pan en ningún sitio

5 *= take* **I'll ~ a dozen eggs, please** ¿me pones una docena de huevos, por favor?; **which one will you ~?** ¿cuál quiere?; **can I ~ your name please?** ¿me da su nombre, por favor?; **you can ~ it** *or* **I'll let you ~ it for £10** te lo dejo en 10 libras, te lo puedes llevar por 10 libras, te lo vendo por 10 libras

6 *= give birth to* [+ *baby, kittens*] tener; **what did she ~?** ¿qué ha tenido?; **she had a boy** ha tenido un niño

7 *= hold, catch* tener; **I ~ him in my power** lo tengo en mi poder; **he had him by the throat** lo tenía agarrado por la garganta; **I ~ it on good authority that ...** me consta que ..., sé a ciencia cierta que, sé de buena tinta que* ...; **I've got it!** ¡ya!; **you ~ me there** ◊ **there you ~ me** ahí sí que me has pillado*

8 *= allow* consentir, tolerar; **we can't ~ that** eso no se puede consentir; **I won't ~ this nonsense** no voy a consentir *or* tolerar estas tonterías; **I won't ~ it!** no lo voy a consentir *or* tolerar; **she won't ~ it said that ...** no consiente *or* tolera que digan que ...; **I won't ~ him risking his neck on that motorbike** no voy a consentir que se juegue el cuello en esa moto

9 *= spend* pasar; **to ~ a pleasant afternoon/evening** pasar una tarde agradable; **~ a nice day!** ¡que pases un buen día!; **I had a horrible day at school today** he tenido un día horrible en el colegio; **what sort of day ~ you had?** ¿qué tal día has tenido?

10 *on telephone* **can I ~ Personnel please?** ¿me puede poner con Personal, por favor?

11 ** = have sex with* acostarse con

12 *= make* **I'll soon ~ it nice and shiny** enseguida lo dejo bien brillante; **he had us confused** nos tenía confundidos

13 *in set structures*

◆ **to have sth done** hacer que se haga algo, mandar hacer algo; **we had our luggage brought up** mandamos subir el equipaje; **I've had the brakes checked** he mandado revisar los frenos; **to ~ a suit made** (mandar) hacerse un traje; **to ~ one's hair cut** cortarse el pelo; **they had him killed** lo mataron

◆ **to have sb do sth** mandar a algn hacer algo; **he had me do it again** me hizo hacerlo otra vez, me hizo que lo hiciese otra vez; **I had him clean the car** le hice limpiar el coche; **what would you ~ me do?**† ¿qué quiere que haga?; **I'll ~ you know that ...** quiero que sepas que ...

◆ **to have sth happen**: **she had her bag stolen** le robaron el bolso; **he had his arm broken** le rompieron el brazo

◆ **to have sb doing sth**: **she soon had them all reading and writing** (= *organized them*) enseguida los puso a leer y a escribir; (= *taught them*) enseguida les habían enseñado a leer y a escribir

14 *in set expressions*

◆ **to be had**: **you've been had!*** ¡te han engañado!

◆ **to have sth against sb/sth** tener algo en contra de algn/algo

◆ **to have had it**: **you've had it now! he knows all about it*** ¡ahora sí que te la has cargado! se ha enterado de todo; **this sofa has had it*** este sofá ya no da para más*; **I've had it up to here with his nonsense*** estoy hasta la coronilla *or* hasta el moño de sus tonterías*

◆ **to have it that**: **he will ~ it that he is right** insiste en que tiene razón; **rumour has it that ...** corre la voz de que ...

◆ **to have to do with** tener que ver con; **that's got** *or* **that has nothing to do with it!** ¡eso no tiene nada que ver!; **you'd better not ~ anything to do with him** más te vale no tener tratos con él

◆ **to let sb have sth** (= *give*) dar algo a algn; (= *lend*) dejar algo a algn, prestar algo a algn; **I'll let you ~ my reply tomorrow** les daré mi respuesta mañana; **let me ~ your address** dame tus señas; **let me ~ your pen for a moment** déjame el boli un momento; **let him ~ it!*** ¡dale!

◆ **what have you**: **... and what ~ you** ... y qué sé yo qué más; *see also* **luck A**

◆ **would have it**: **as ill-luck** *or* **fate would ~ it** desgraciadamente

Ⓑ AUXILIARY VERB

1 haber; **I've already seen that film** ya he visto esa película; **he's been very kind** ha sido muy amable; **has he gone?** ¿se ha ido?; **hasn't he told you?** ¿no te lo ha dicho?; **she said she had spoken to them** dijo que había hablado con ellos; **had you phoned me** (*frm*) *or* **if you had phoned me I would ~ come round** si me hubieras llamado habría venido; **never having seen it before, I ...** como no lo había visto antes, ...; **having finished** *or* **when he had finished, he left** cuando terminó *or* cuando hubo terminado, se fue; *see also* **just 1.3** → SINCE

2 *verb substitute* 2·1 **you've got more than I ~** tienes más que yo; **they've done more than we ~** ellos han hecho más que nosotros; **he hasn't worked as hard as you ~** él no ha trabajado tanto como tú; **"he's already eaten" — "so ~ I"** —él ya ha comido —yo también; **"we ~n't had any news yet" — "neither ~ we"** —no hemos tenido noticias todavía —nosotros tampoco; **"you've made a mistake" — "no I ~n't!"** —has cometido un error —no es verdad *or* cierto; **"we ~n't paid" — "yes we ~!"** —no hemos pagado —¡qué sí!; **"he's got a new job" — "oh has he?"** —tiene un trabajo nuevo —¿ah, sí?; **"you've written it twice" — "so I ~!"** —lo has escrito dos veces —es verdad *or* cierto; **"~ you read the book?" — "yes, I ~"** —¿has leído el libro? —sí; **"has he told you?" — "no, he hasn't"** —¿te lo ha dicho? —no

2·2 (*in question tags*) **he hasn't done it, has he?** no lo ha hecho, ¿verdad?; **you've done it, ~n't you?** lo has hecho, ¿verdad? *or* ¿no?

3 *avoiding repetition of verb* **you've all been there before, but I ~n't** vosotros habéis estado allí antes, pero yo no; **he has never met her, but I ~** él no la ha llegado a conocer, pero yo sí; **~ you ever been there? if you ...** ¿has estado alguna vez allí? si es así ...; **~ you tried it? if you ~n't ...** ¿lo has probado? (porque) si no ...; *see also* **so A5**, **nor 2**

Ⓒ MODAL VERB

= be obliged **to ~ (got) to do sth** tener que hacer algo; **I've got to** *or* **I ~ to finish this work** tengo que terminar este trabajo; **~ we got to** *or* **do we ~ to leave early?** ¿tenemos que salir temprano?; **I ~n't got to** *or* **I don't ~ to wear glasses** no necesito (usar) gafas; **I shall ~ to go and see her** tendré que ir a verla; **it will just ~ to wait till tomorrow** tendrá que esperar hasta mañana; **he had to pay all the money back** tuvo que devolver todo el dinero; **she was having to get up at six each morning** tenía que levantarse a las seis cada mañana; **this has to be a mistake** esto tiene que ser un error; **do you ~ to make such a noise?** ¿tienes que hacer tanto ruido?; **you didn't ~ to tell her!** ¡no tenías por qué decírselo!; **it's nice not to ~ to work on Saturdays** es un gusto no tener que trabajar los sábados; **it has to be done this way** tiene que hacerse de este modo; **does it ~ to be ironed?** ¿hay que plancharlo?

Ⓓ PHRASAL VERBS

►**have around** VT + ADV 1 (= *have available*) tener cerca; (= *to count on*) contar con; **Sarah was a joy to ~ around** era una delicia tener a Sarah cerca; **a great guy to ~ around** un tipo estupendo para tenerlo a tu lado; **the sort of player I'd like to ~ around** el tipo de jugador con el que me gustaría contar

2 (= *invite*) **we're having Mary around tomorrow** hemos invitado a Mary para que venga mañana; **we're having some people around** tenemos invitados

►**have away*** VT + ADV (*Brit*) = **have off 3**

➤ LANGUAGE IN USE: **have B** 10.1, 10.2, 10.3 **A8** 10.4

►**have back** VT + ADV [1] (= *repossess*) **please can I ~ my book back?** ¿me puedes devolver el libro, por favor?
[2] (= *return invitation to*) devolver la invitación a; **we must ~ the Corks back soon** habrá que devolverles la invitación a los Cork dentro de poco; **they never ~ anyone back** nunca devuelven la invitación a nadie
[3] (= *take back*) [+ *lover, partner*] volver a estar con; [+ *employee*] readmitir

►**have down** VT + ADV [1] (*for visit*) invitar a quedarse en casa; **we are having the Smiths down for a few days** los Smith vienen a pasar unos días con nosotros *or* en casa
[2] (= *dismantle*) [+ *building, wall*] tirar, echar abajo; [+ *tent*] quitar, desmontar
[3] (= *move*) [+ *picture*] quitar, descolgar

►**have in** VT + ADV [1] [+ *doctor*] llamar; **to ~ the plumber in** llamar al fontanero; **to ~ visitors in** tener invitados; **let's ~ the next one in** que pase el siguiente
[2] ✦*IDIOM* **to ~ it in for sb*** tenerla tomada con algn*

►**have off** VT + ADV [1] (= *have as holiday*) **I'm having a fortnight off in July** me voy a tomar dos semanas de vacaciones *or* permiso en julio; **the children ~ got a week off for half term** los niños tienen una semana de vacaciones a mitad del trimestre
[2] (= *dislodge*) quitar; **he had the panelling off in no time** quitó las mamparas en un santiamén; **be careful or you'll ~ the pans off!** ¡ten cuidado, no vayas a tirar las cacerolas!
[3] (*Brit*) **to ~ it off**‡ echar un polvo‡; **to ~ it off with sb** tirarse a algn‡

►**have on** VT + ADV [1] (= *wear*) [+ *dress, hat*] llevar; **she had on a beautiful black evening dress** llevaba (puesto) un precioso vestido de noche negro; *see also* **nothing A**
[2] (= *be busy with*) **I've got so much on this week** tengo mucho que hacer esta semana; **~ you anything on tomorrow?** ¿tienes algo que hacer mañana?, ¿tienes compromiso para mañana?
[3] (= *put on*) [+ *wallpaper, roof*] poner; **we'll ~ the paint on in no time** lo tendremos pintado en un santiamén
[4] (*Brit**) (= *tease*) **to ~ sb on** tomar el pelo a algn*; **he's having you on!** te está tomando el pelo*

►**have out** VT + ADV [1] (= *have removed*) **to ~ a tooth out** sacarse una muela; **to ~ one's tonsils out** operarse de las amígdalas; **we had to ~ the old boiler out** tuvimos que quitar la caldera vieja; **we'll ~ the piano out in a trice** enseguida sacamos el piano
[2] **to ~ it out with sb** ajustar cuentas con algn

►**have over** VT + ADV [1] (= *invite*) **we're having Mary over tomorrow** hemos invitado a Mary para que venga mañana; **we're having some people over** tenemos invitados; **we had them over to dinner last week** vinieron a cenar la semana pasada
[2] (= *overturn*) volcar, tirar; **watch out, you'll ~ the coffee over!** ¡cuidado, que vas a volcar *or* tirar el café!

►**have round** VT + ADV = **have around**

►**have up** VT + ADV [1] (*Brit**) **to be had up** (= *be prosecuted*) ser llevado a juicio; **he was had up for assault** le llevaron a juicio por asalto
[2] [+ *guest*] invitar; **why don't we ~ George up for the weekend?** ¿por qué no invitamos a George el fin de semana?

have-a-go hero [ˌhævəˈɡəʊˌhɪərəʊ] N héroe *m* anónimo, héroe *m* por un día

haven [ˈheɪvn] N refugio *m*; (= *port*) puerto *m*

have-nots [ˈhævnɒts] NPL *see* **haves**

haven't [ˈhævnt] = **have not**

haversack [ˈhævəsæk] N mochila *f*, macuto *m* (*LAm*)

haves* [hævz] NPL **the ~ and the have-nots** los ricos y los pobres

havoc [ˈhævək] N estragos *mpl*; **to cause** *or* **create ~** hacer estragos; **this latest decision will cause ~ in the tourist industry** esta última decisión hará estragos *or* provocará grandes trastornos en el sector turístico; **to play ~ with**: **the recession is playing ~ with the government's balance sheets** la recesión está dando al traste con *or* haciendo estragos en los balances de ejercicio del gobierno; **the food in the hotel played ~ with my digestion** la comida del hotel me destrozó el estómago; **the weather played ~ with sporting fixtures this weekend** el mal tiempo arruinó los acontecimientos deportivos del fin de semana; **to wreak ~** hacer estragos; **the slugs are wreaking ~ in the garden** las babosas están arruinando *or* estropeando el jardín; **stress can wreak ~ on the immune system** el estrés puede causar serios trastornos en el sistema inmunológico

haw[1] [hɔː] N baya *f* del espino

haw[2] [hɔː] VI **to hem and ~** ◊ **hum and ~** (= *be indecisive*) vacilar; (= *express reservations*) poner reparos

Hawaii [həˈwaɪiː] N (Islas *fpl*) Hawai *m*

Hawaiian [həˈwaɪjən] Ⓐ ADJ hawaiano
Ⓑ N hawaiano/a *m/f*

hawfinch [ˈhɔːfɪntʃ] N picogordo *m*

hawk[1] [hɔːk] N (*Orn, Pol*) halcón *m*; **he was watching me like a ~** me vigilaba estrechamente, no me quitaba ojo

hawk[2] [hɔːk] VT [+ *goods for sale*] pregonar

hawk[3] [hɔːk] VI (*also* **~ up**) (= *clear one's throat*) carraspear

hawker [ˈhɔːkəʳ] N vendedor(a) *m/f* ambulante *mf*

hawk-eyed [ˌhɔːkˈaɪd] ADJ con ojos de lince

hawkish [ˈhɔːkɪʃ] ADJ (*Pol*) de línea dura

hawser [ˈhɔːzəʳ] N guindaleza *f*, calabrote *m*

hawthorn [ˈhɔːθɔːn] N espino *m*

hay [heɪ] Ⓐ N heno *m*; ✦*IDIOMS* **that ain't ~** (*US**) eso no es moco de pavo*; **to hit the ~*** acostarse; **to make ~ while the sun shines** aprovecharse la ocasión
Ⓑ CPD ► **hay fever** N fiebre *f* del heno, alergia *f* al polen

haycock [ˈheɪkɒk] N montón *m* de heno

hayfork [ˈheɪfɔːk] N bieldo *m*

hayloft [ˈheɪlɒft] N henil *m*, henal *m*

haymaker [ˈheɪmeɪkəʳ] N heneador(a) *m/f*, labrador(a) *m/f* que trabaja en la siega *or* la recolección del heno

haymaking [ˈheɪmeɪkɪŋ] N siega *f* del heno, recolección *f* del heno

hayseed* [ˈheɪsiːd] N (*US*) palurdo/a *m/f*, paleto/a *m/f* (*Sp**)

haystack [ˈheɪstæk] N almiar *m*; ✦*IDIOM* **to be like looking for a needle in a ~** ser como buscar una aguja en un pajar

haywire* [ˈheɪwaɪəʳ] ADJ ✦*IDIOM* **to go ~** [*person*] volverse loco, perder la chaveta*; [*machine*] averiarse, malograrse (*LAm*); [*scheme etc*] irse a pique; **the switchboard went ~** se colapsó la centralita

hazard [ˈhæzəd] Ⓐ N peligro *m*; (*less serious*) riesgo *m*; **this heater is a fire ~** esta estufa puede provocar un incendio; *see also* **health**
Ⓑ VT [1] (= *venture*) [+ *answer, remark*] aventurar; **would you like to ~ a guess?** ¿quieres intentar adivinarlo?
[2] (= *risk*) [+ *one's life*] poner en peligro, arriesgar
Ⓒ CPD ► **hazard lights**, **hazard warning lights** NPL (*Aut*) luces *fpl* de emergencia

hazardous [ˈhæzədəs] ADJ [*waste, chemicals, weather conditions*] peligroso; [*occupation, journey, enterprise*] arriesgado, peligroso; **~ pay** (*US*) prima *f or* plus *m* de peligrosidad; **~ to health** peligroso para la salud

haze[1] [heɪz] N [1] (= *mist*) bruma *f*, neblina *f*; (*in hot weather*) calina *f*, calima *f*; **a ~ of tobacco smoke filled the room** el cuarto estaba lleno de humo de tabaco
[2] (*fig*) **she spent most of her life in a ~ of alcohol** pasaba la mayor parte de su vida embotada por el alcohol; **to be in a ~** (*fig*) andar atontado *or* aturdido

haze[2] [heɪz] VT (*US*) gastar novatadas a

hazel [ˈheɪzl] Ⓐ N (*tree*) avellano *m*
Ⓑ ADJ [*eyes*] color de avellana *adj inv*

hazelnut [ˈheɪzlnʌt] N avellana *f*

hazelwood [ˈheɪzlˌwʊd] N madera *f* de avellano

hazily [ˈheɪzɪlɪ] ADV [*remember*] vagamente; [*think*] de manera confusa

haziness [ˈheɪzɪnɪs] N [1] [*of view, horizon, sky*] nebulosidad *f*; **the ~ of the morning gave the landscape a mysterious air** (*due to mist*) la bruma *or* neblina de la mañana daba al paisaje un aire de misterio; (*due to heat*) la calina de la mañana daba al paisaje un aire de misterio
[2] (*fig*) (= *vagueness*) confusión *f*, vaguedad *f*

hazing [ˈheɪzɪŋ] N (*US*) novatadas *fpl*; → SORORITY/FRATERNITY

hazy [ˈheɪzɪ] ADJ (*compar* **hazier**, *superl* **haziest**)
[1] (= *not clear*) [*sunshine, morning, view, horizon, sky*] (*due to mist*) brumoso, neblinoso; (*due to heat*) calinoso; **it's a bit ~ today** (*due to mist*) hoy hay un poco de neblina *or* bruma; (*due to heat*) hoy hay un poco de calima
[2] (= *confused, uncertain*) [*notion, details*] confuso; [*memory*] vago, confuso; [*ideas*] poco claro, confuso; **I'm a bit ~ about maths** tengo las matemáticas poco claras *or* un poco confusas; **I'm ~ about what happened** tengo solamente una vaga idea de lo que ocurrió, no recuerdo muy bien lo que ocurrió
[3] (= *blurred*) [*outline, vision*] borroso; [*photograph*] nublado

H-bomb [ˈeɪtʃbɒm] N bomba *f* H

HC ABBR (= **hot and cold (water)**) con agua caliente y fría

HCF N ABBR (= **highest common factor**) MCD *m*

HDD N ABBR (*Comput*) = **hard disk drive**

HDTV N ABBR (= **high definition television**) televisión *f* de alta definición

HE ABBR [1] = **high explosive**
[2] (= **His** *or* **Her Excellency**) S.E.
[3] (= **His Eminence**) S.Em.ª

he [hiː] Ⓐ PERS PRON [1] (*emphatic, to avoid ambiguity*) él; **we went to the cinema but he didn't** nosotros fuimos al cine pero él no; **it is he who ...** es él quien ...; **you've got more money than he has** tienes más dinero que él

Don't translate the subject pronoun when not emphasizing or clarifying:

he's very tall es muy alto; **there he is** allí está
[2] (*frm*) **he who wishes to ...** el que desee ..., quien desee ...

Ⓑ N **it's a he*** (= *animal*) es macho; (= *baby*) es un niño, es varón (*LAm*)
Ⓒ CPD macho ► **he-goat** N cabra *f* macho

head [hed] Ⓐ N [1] (= *part of body*) cabeza *f*; **my ~ aches** me duele la cabeza; **the horse won by a (short) ~** el caballo ganó por una cabeza (escasa); **he went ~ first into the ditch/wall** se cayó de cabeza en la zanja/se dio de cabeza contra la pared; **the government is ploughing ~ first into another crisis** el gobierno avanza irremediablemente hacia otra crisis; **from ~ to foot** de pies a cabeza; **to give a horse its ~** soltar las riendas a un caballo; **to give sb his/her ~** dar rienda suelta a algn; **wine goes to my ~** el vino se me sube a la cabeza; **success has gone to his ~** el éxito se le ha subido a la cabeza; **~ of hair** cabellera *f*; **to go ~ over heels** caer de cabeza; **to fall ~ over heels in love with sb** enamorarse perdidamente de algn; **to keep one's ~ down** (*lit*) no levantar la cabeza; (= *work hard*) trabajar de lo lindo; (= *avoid being noticed*) intentar pasar desapercibido; **to nod one's ~** decir que sí *or* asentir con la cabeza; **to shake one's ~** decir que no *or* negar con la cabeza; **he stands ~ and shoulders above the rest** (*lit*) les saca más de una cabeza a los demás; (*fig*) los demás no le llegan a la suela del zapato; **to stand on one's ~** hacer el pino; **I could do it standing on my ~*** lo podría hacer con los ojos cerrados; **she is a ~ taller than her sister** le saca una cabeza a su hermana; **from ~ to toe** de pies a cabeza; **I ought to bang** *or* **knock your ~s together** os voy a dar un coscorrón a los dos*; **he turned his ~ and looked back at her** volvió la cabeza y la miró; ✦*IDIOMS* **I can't get my ~ around that*** no consigo entenderlo, para mí eso es un misterio; **to have one's ~ up one's arse** *or* (*US*) **ass**** (= *be pig-headed*) ser cabezón; (= *be self-obsessed*) mirarse al ombligón; **to bite sb's ~ off** echar un rapapolvo a algn; **to put** *or* **lay one's ~ on the block** jugársela, arriesgarse; **to get one's ~ down** (*to work*) poner manos a la obra; (*to sleep*) acostarse, echarse; **to go over sb's ~**: **they went over my ~ to the manager** pasaron por encima de mí y fueron directamente al gerente; **to hold one's ~ up (high)** ir con la frente bien alta *or* erguida; **with ~ held high** con la frente bien alta *or* erguida; **to laugh one's ~ off** desternillarse de risa*; **to stand** *or* **turn sth on its ~** dar la vuelta a algo; **on your own ~ be it!** ¡allá tú!, tú sabrás lo que haces; **to want sb's ~ on a plate** querer la cabeza de algn; **to turn one's ~ the other way** hacer la vista gorda; **~s will roll** van a rodar cabezas; **to bury** *or* **hide** *or* **stick one's ~ in the sand** seguir la táctica del avestruz; **to scream/shout one's ~ off** desgañitarse; **I can't make ~ nor** *or* **or tail of it** no le encuentro ni pies ni cabeza; **I can't make ~ nor** *or* **or tail of what he's saying** no entiendo nada de lo que dice; **to turn ~s** llamar la atención; **she had the kind of looks that turn ~s** tenía ese tipo de belleza que llama la atención; **to keep one's ~ above water** (*fig*) ir tirando; *see also* **acid C**, **cloud A**, **hang A1**, **knock**, **price A1**, **rear A2**, **swell C1**, **top A11**
[2] (= *intellect, mind*) cabeza *f*; **use your ~!** ¡usa la cabeza!; **you never know what's going on in his ~** nunca sabes lo que le está pasando por la cabeza; **it's gone right out of my ~** se me ha ido de la cabeza, se me ha olvidado; **it was the first thing that came into my ~** fue lo primero que me vino a la cabeza; **it was above their ~s** no lo entendían; **it's better to come to it with a clear ~ in the morning** es mejor hacerlo por la mañana con la cabeza despejada; **it never entered my ~** ni se me pasó por la cabeza siquiera; **you need your ~ examining** *or* **examined** tú estás mal de la cabeza; **to have a ~ for business/figures** ser bueno para los negocios/con los números; **I have no ~ for heights** tengo vértigo; **to do a sum in one's ~** hacer un cálculo mental; **he added it all up in his ~** lo sumó todo mentalmente; **he has got it into his ~ that ...** se le ha metido en la cabeza que ...; **I wish he would get it into his thick ~ that ...** ya me gustaría que le entrara en ese cabezón que tiene que ...; **who put that (idea) into your ~?** ¿quién te ha metido eso en la cabeza?; **don't put ideas into his ~** no le metas ideas en la cabeza; **I can't get that tune out of my ~** no puedo quitarme esa música de la cabeza; **it was over their ~s** no lo entendían; **it went way over my ~** no lo entendí nada; **I'm sure if we put our ~s together we can work something out** estoy seguro de que si intercambiamos ideas encontraremos una solución; **to take it into one's ~ to do sth**: **he took it into his ~ to go to Australia** se le metió en la cabeza ir a Australia; **don't worry your ~ about it** no te preocupes, no le des muchas vueltas; ✦*IDIOMS* **to keep one's ~** mantener la calma; **to lose one's ~** perder la cabeza *or* los estribos; **to be/go off one's ~*** estar/volverse majara*; **you must be off your ~!** ¡estás como una cabra!; **to be out of one's ~*** (= *mad*) haber perdido el juicio, estar mal de la cabeza; (= *drunk*) estar borracho como una cuba*; (= *on drugs*) estar colocadísimo*, estar como una moto*; **he's got his ~ screwed on (the right way)** tiene la cabeza sobre los hombros; **to be soft** *or* **weak in the ~** estar mal de la cabeza; **to go soft in the ~** perder la cabeza; **all that flattery will turn his ~** todos esos halagos se le subirán a la cabeza; ✦*PROV* **two ~s are better than one** cuatro ojos ven más que dos
[3] (= *leader*) [*of firm*] director(a) *m/f*; (*esp Brit*) [*of school*] director(a) *m/f*; **~ of department** (*in school, firm*) jefe/a *m/f* de departamento; **~ of French** el jefe/la jefa del departamento de francés; **~ of (the) household** cabeza *mf* de familia; **~ of state** (*Pol*) jefe/a *m/f* de Estado
[4] (= *top part*) [*of hammer, pin, spot*] cabeza *f*; [*of arrow, spear*] punta *f*; [*of stick, cane*] puño *m*; [*of bed, page*] cabecera *f*; [*of stairs*] parte *f* alta; (*on beer*) espuma *f*; [*of river*] cabecera *f*, nacimiento *m*; [*of valley*] final *m*; [*of mountain pass*] cima *f*; **at the ~ of** [+ *organization*] a la cabeza de; [+ *train*] en la parte delantera de; **to be at the ~ of the class** ser el mejor de la clase; **to be at the ~ of the league** ir a la cabeza de la liga; **to be at the ~ of the list** encabezar la lista; **to be at the ~ of the queue** ser el primero en la cola; **to sit at the ~ of the table** sentarse en la cabecera de la mesa, presidir la mesa
[5] (*Bot*) [*of flower*] cabeza *f*, flor *f*; [*of corn*] mazorca *f*; **a ~ of celery/garlic** una cabeza de apio/ajo; **a ~ of lettuce** una lechuga
[6] (*Tech*) (*on tape-recorder*) cabezal *m*, cabeza *f* magnética; [*of cylinder*] culata *f*; (*Comput*) cabeza *f*; **reading/writing ~** cabeza *f* de lectura/grabación
[7] (= *culmination*) **this will bring matters to a ~** esto llevará las cosas a un punto crítico; **to come to a ~** [*situation*] alcanzar un punto crítico
[8] **heads** (*on coin*) cara *f*; **it came down ~s** salió cara; **~s or tails?** ¿cara o cruz?, ¿águila o sol? (*Mex*); **to toss ~s or tails** echar a cara o cruz; ✦*IDIOM* **~s I win, tails you lose** cara yo gano, cruz tú pierdes
[9] (*no pl*) (= *unit*) **20 ~ of cattle** 20 cabezas de ganado (vacuno); **£15 a** *or* **per ~** 15 libras por cabeza *or* persona
[10] (*Naut*) proa *f*; **~ to wind** con la proa a barlovento *or* de cara al viento
[11] (*Geog*) cabo *m*
[12] (= *pressure*) **~ of steam** presión *f* de vapor; **~ of water** presión *f* de agua
[13] (= *height*) [*of water*] **there has to be a ~ of six feet between the tank and the bath** el tanque tiene que estar a una altura de dos metros con respecto al baño
[14] (= *title*) titular *m*; (= *subject heading*) encabezamiento *m*; **this comes under the ~ of ...** esto viene en el apartado de ...
Ⓑ VT [1] (= *be at front of*) [+ *procession, league, poll*] encabezar, ir a la cabeza de; [+ *list*] encabezar
[2] (= *be in charge of*) [+ *organization*] dirigir; (*Sport*) [+ *team*] capitanear
[3] (= *steer*) [+ *ship, car, plane*] dirigir
[4] (*Ftbl*) [+ *goal*] cabecear; **to ~ the ball** cabecear (el balón)
[5] [+ *chapter*] encabezar
Ⓒ VI **where are you ~ing** *or* **~ed?** ¿hacia dónde vas?, ¿para dónde vas?; **he hitched a ride on a truck ~ing** *or* **~ed west** hizo autostop y lo recogió un camión que iba hacia el oeste; **he ~ed up the hill** se dirigió hacia la cima de la colina; **they were ~ing home/back to town** volvían a casa/a la ciudad
Ⓓ CPD ► **head boy** N (*Brit Scol*) ≈ delegado *m* de la escuela (*alumno*) ► **head buyer** N jefe/a *m/f* de compras ► **head case*** N (*Brit*) majara* *mf*, chiflado/a* *m/f* ► **head cheese** N (*US*) queso *m* de cerdo, cabeza *f* de jabalí (*Sp*), carne *f* en gelatina ► **head clerk** N encargado/a *m/f* ► **head coach** N (*Sport*) primer(a) entrenador(a) *m/f* ► **head cold** N resfriado *m* (de cabeza) ► **head count** N recuento *m* de personas; **to take a ~ count** hacer un recuento de personas ► **head gardener** N jefe/a *m/f* de jardineros ► **head girl** N (*Brit Scol*) ≈ delegada *f* de la escuela (*alumna*) ► **head injury** N herida *f* en la cabeza ► **head nurse** N enfermero/a *m/f* jefe ► **head office** N sede *f* central ► **head prefect** N (*Brit Scol*) ≈ delegado/a *m/f* de la escuela (*alumno/alumna*) ► **head restraint** N (*Aut*) apoyacabezas *m inv*, reposacabezas *m inv* ► **head start** N ventaja *f*; **a good education gives your child a ~ start in life** una buena educación sitúa a su hijo en una posición aventajada en la vida; **to have a ~ start (over** *or* **on sb)** (*Sport, fig*) tener ventaja (sobre algn); **he has a ~ start over other candidates** tiene ventaja sobre *or* les lleva ventaja a otros candidatos; **even if he had a ~ start he couldn't possibly win** ni empezando con ventaja podría ganar ► **head teacher** N director(a) *m/f* ► **head waiter** N maître *m* ► **head wound** N herida *f* en la cabeza

► **head for** VI + PREP [1] [+ *place*] **where are you ~ing for?** ¿hacia dónde vas?, ¿para dónde vas?; **it's time we were ~ing for home** ya es hora de que nos vayamos para casa; **he picked up his coat and ~ed for the door** tomó el abrigo y se dirigió hacia la puerta; **when he comes home he ~s straight for the TV** nada más llegar a casa se va derechito para la televisión; **the car was ~ing straight for us** el coche venía derecho hacia nosotros; **the vessel was ~ing for the port of Basra** el navío iba rumbo al *or* se dirigía al puerto de Basra
[2] (*fig*) **to be ~ing for: you're ~ing for trouble** vas por mal camino; **he's ~ing for a**

disappointment se va a llevar una decepción; **he's ~ing for a fall** va camino del fracaso

► **head off** Ⓐ VI + ADV (= *set out*) marcharse (**for** para, hacia; **toward(s)** hacia); **I watched them ~ off into the sunset** les vi marcharse por donde se ponía el sol
Ⓑ VT + ADV [1] (= *intercept*) [+ *person*] atajar, interceptar
[2] (= *ward off*) [+ *questions, criticism, trouble*] atajar; [+ *person*] distraer (**from** de); **if she asks where we're going, try and ~ her off** si pregunta dónde vamos, intenta distraerla

► **head up** VT + ADV [+ *group, team*] estar a la cabeza de, dirigir

headache ['hedeɪk] N [1] (= *pain*) dolor *m* de cabeza; (= *sick headache*) jaqueca *f*
[2] (= *problem*) quebradero *m* de cabeza, dolor *m* de cabeza; **that's his ~** allá él

headband ['hedbænd] N cinta *f* (para la cabeza), vincha *f* (*Andes, S. Cone*), huincha *f* (*Andes, S. Cone*)

headboard ['hed,bɔːd] N cabecera *f*

headcount ['hedkaʊnt] N [1] (*Ind*) (= *workforce*) personal *m*, plantilla *f* (*Sp*)
[2] (= *count*) recuento *m* de personas; **to take a ~** hacer un recuento de personas

headdress ['heddres] N tocado *m*

headed ['hedɪd] ADJ [*notepaper*] membretado, con membrete

-headed ['hedɪd] ADJ (*ending in compounds*) de cabeza ...; **small-headed** de cabeza pequeña; **red-headed** pelirrojo

header ['hedəʳ] N [1] (*Ftbl*) cabezazo *m*, remate *m* de cabeza [2] (*) (= *fall*) caída *f* de cabeza; (= *dive*) salto *m* de cabeza [3] (*Typ, Comput*) encabezamiento *m*

header-block ['hedə,blɒk] N bloque *m* de encabezamiento, encabezamiento *m*

headgear ['hedgɪəʳ] N (*gen*) tocado *m*; (= *hat*) sombrero *m*; (= *cap*) gorra *f*; (= *helmet*) casco *m*; **workers must wear protective ~** los trabajadores deben llevar casco

headguard ['hedgɑːd] N casco *m* protector; (*on face*) protector *m* facial

headhunt ['hed,hʌnt] Ⓐ VI buscar talentos
Ⓑ VT **he was ~ed by a bank** un banco lo escogió para su plantilla

headhunter ['hed,hʌntəʳ] N (*lit*) cazador *m* de cabezas; (*fig*) cazatalentos *mf inv*

headhunting ['hed,hʌntɪŋ] Ⓐ N (*lit*) caza *f* de cabezas; (*fig*) caza *f* de talentos
Ⓑ CPD ► **headhunting agency** N agencia *f* de caza de talentos

headiness ['hedɪnɪs] N [*of scent*] aroma *m* embriagador; [*of atmosphere*] excitación *f*; **a wine that is characterized by its ~** un vino que se caracteriza por lo fácilmente que se sube a la cabeza

heading ['hedɪŋ] N (= *title*) encabezamiento *m*, título *m*; (= *letterhead*) membrete *m*; (= *section*) sección *f*, apartado *m*; **under various ~s** en varios apartados; **to come under the ~ of** estar incluido en

headlamp ['hedlæmp] N (*Aut*) faro *m*

headland ['hedlənd] N cabo *m*, punta *f*

headless ['hedlɪs] ADJ (*lit*) [*body*] sin cabeza; (= *leaderless*) acéfalo; ✦*IDIOM* **to run around like a ~ chicken** (*Brit*) ir dando palos de ciego, ir de acá para allá sin saber qué hacer

headlight ['hedlaɪt] N = **headlamp**

headline ['hedlaɪn] Ⓐ N (*in newspaper*) titular *m*, cabecera *f*; **the (news) ~s** (*TV, Rad*) el resumen de las noticias; **to hit** *or* **make the ~s** salir en primera plana
Ⓑ VT anunciar con titulares
Ⓒ CPD ► **headline news** N noticia *f* de cabecera; **to be ~ news** ser noticia de cabecera; **to make ~ news** salir en primera plana ► **headline rate** N **the ~ rate of inflation** la tasa de inflación (*calculada con variables como el tipo de interés hipotecario*)

headlock ['hedlɒk] N llave *f* de cabeza; **to get/have sb in a ~** hacer a algn una llave de cabeza

headlong ['hedlɒŋ] Ⓐ ADJ [*fall*] de cabeza; **he made a ~ dive for the ball** se lanzó en plancha a por la pelota; **the ~ rush to the beaches every summer** la salida precipitada hacia las playas todos los veranos
Ⓑ ADV [1] (= *head first*) [*person*] de cabeza; **the lorry ploughed ~ into a wall** el camión se estrelló de frente contra una pared
[2] (= *swiftly*) precipitadamente; **I dashed ~ up the stairs** subí precipitadamente por las escaleras

headman ['hedmæn] N (*pl* **headmen** ['hedmen]) cacique *m*; (*hum*) jefe *m*

headmaster ['hed'mɑːstəʳ] N director *m* (de colegio)

headmistress ['hed'mɪstrɪs] N directora *f* (de colegio)

head-on ['hed'ɒn] Ⓐ ADJ [*collision*] de frente, frontal; **a ~ confrontation** un enfrentamiento directo *or* frontal
Ⓑ ADV [*collide*] de frente, frontalmente; [*clash*] frontalmente; [*meet*] cara a cara; **the two cars collided ~** los dos coches colisionaron de frente *or* frontalmente; **to tackle sth ~** (*fig*) enfrentarse de lleno con algo

headphones ['hedfəʊnz] NPL auriculares *mpl*, audífono(s) *m(pl)*

headquarter ['hedkwɔːtəʳ] VT (*US*) **the company is ~ed in Reno** la compañía tiene su sede en Reno

headquarters ['hed'kwɔːtəz] Ⓐ NPL (*Mil*) cuartel *msing* general; (*police etc*) jefatura *fsing* de policía; [*of party, organization*] sede *fsing*; (*Comm*) oficina *fsing* central, central *fsing*
Ⓑ CPD ► **headquarters staff** N plantilla *fsing* de la oficina central

headrest ['hedrest] N (*Aut*) apoyacabezas *m inv*, reposacabezas *m inv*; (*on chair*) cabezal *m*

headroom ['hedrʊm] N espacio *m* para estar (derecho) de pie; (*under bridge etc*) altura *f* libre; **"2m headroom"** "2m de altura libre"

headscarf ['hedskɑːf] N (*pl* **headscarfs** *or* **headscarves** ['hedskɑːvz]) pañuelo *m*

headset ['hedset] N = **headphones**

headship ['hedʃɪp] N (*gen*) dirección *f*; [*of school*] puesto *m* de director(a)

head-shrinker* ['hed,ʃrɪŋkəʳ] N psiquíatra *mf*, psiquiatra *mf*

headsman† ['hedzmən] N (*pl* **headsmen**) verdugo *m*

headsquare ['hedskwɛəʳ] N pañuelo *m* de cabeza

headstand ['hedstænd] N posición *f* de cabeza; **to do a ~** hacer el pino

headstone ['hedstəʊn] N (*on grave*) lápida *f* (mortuoria)

headstrong ['hedstrɒŋ] ADJ (= *stubborn*) testarudo; (= *determined*) [*action*] decidido

head-to-head [,hedtə'hed] Ⓐ N mano a mano *m inv*
Ⓑ ADJ mano a mano *inv*
Ⓒ ADV mano a mano; **to go head to head against** *or* **with** enfrentarse mano a mano con

headwaters ['hed,wɔːtəz] NPL cabecera *fsing* (*de un río*)

headway ['hedweɪ] N **to make ~** (*Naut*) avanzar; (*fig*) hacer progresos; **we could make no ~ against the current** no lográbamos avanzar contra la corriente, la corriente nos impedía avanzar; **I didn't make much ~ with him** no conseguí hacer carrera con él

headwind ['hedwɪnd] N viento *m* contrario; (*Naut*) viento *m* de proa

headword ['hedwɜːd] N lema *m*, cabeza *f* de artículo

heady ['hedɪ] ADJ (*compar* **headier**; *superl* **headiest**) [1] (= *intoxicating*) [*wine*] que se sube a la cabeza, cabezón*; [*scent*] embriagador; **a ~ brew** (*fig*) una mezcla embriagadora
[2] (= *exhilarating*) [*days, experience*] excitante, emocionante; [*atmosphere*] excitante, embriagador; **to feel ~** sentirse emocionado; **the ~ heights of sth** las vertiginosas alturas de algo

heal [hiːl] Ⓐ VT [+ *wound*] curar; [+ *person*] sanar, curar (**of** de); (*fig*) [+ *differences*] reconciliar; **he tried to ~ the rift with his father** intentó salvar el distanciamiento con su padre
Ⓑ VI (*also* **~ up**) cicatrizar

healer ['hiːləʳ] N curandero(a) *m/f*

healing ['hiːlɪŋ] Ⓐ ADJ curativo, sanativo
Ⓑ N curación *f*

health [helθ] Ⓐ N salud *f*; **to be in good/bad ~** estar bien/mal de salud; **he was granted early retirement on grounds of ill ~** le concedieron la jubilación anticipada por razones de salud; **good ~!** ¡(a tu) salud!; **to drink (to) sb's ~** beber a la salud de algn, brindar por algn; **Minister of Health** Ministro/a *m/f* de Sanidad; **Ministry of Health** Ministerio *m* de Sanidad; **Department of Health and Human Services** (*US*) Ministerio *m* de Sanidad y Seguridad Social
Ⓑ CPD ► **health authority** N administración *f* sanitaria ► **health benefit** N (*US*) subsidio *m* de enfermedad ► **health care** N asistencia *f* sanitaria, atención *f* sanitaria ► **health centre**, **health center** (*US*) N centro *m* de salud, centro *m* médico ► **health club** N gimnasio *m* ► **health education** N educación *f* sanitaria ► **health farm** N centro *m* de adelgazamiento ► **health food(s)** N(PL) alimentos *mpl* dietéticos, alimentos *mpl* naturales ► **health food shop** N tienda *f* de alimentos dietéticos, herbolario *m* ► **health hazard** N peligro *m* para la salud, riesgo *m* para la salud; **it's a ~ hazard** presenta un peligro *or* un riesgo para la salud ► **health insurance** N seguro *m* de enfermedad, seguro *m* médico ► **health problem** N (*personal*) problema *m* de salud; (*public*) problema *m* sanitario ► **health resort** N (= *spa*) balneario *m*; (*in mountains*) sanatorio *m* ► **Health Service** N (*Brit*) Servicio *m* de Sanidad, Servicio *m* de Salud Pública; *see also* **national** ► **Health Service doctor** N médico *m* de la Seguridad Social ► **health spa** N balneario *m* ► **health visitor** N auxiliar *mf* sanitario/a (*en asistencia domiciliaria*); *see also* **professional B2**

healthful ['helθfʊl], **health-giving** ['helθ,gɪvɪŋ] ADJ sano, saludable

healthily ['helθɪlɪ] ADV [*live, eat*] de forma sana, sanamente

healthy ['helθɪ] ADJ (*compar* **healthier**; *superl* **healthiest**) [1] (= *normal*) [*person, plant, cell, mind*] sano; [*skin, hair*] sano, saludable; [*society*] que goza de buena salud; **to be ~** [*person*] tener buena salud, estar sano; **to look ~** tener un aspecto saludable; **to have a ~ appetite** tener buen apetito
[2] (= *beneficial*) [*diet, lifestyle, air, place*] sano, saludable
[3] (= *thriving*) [*economy, company*] próspero

[4] (= *substantial*) [*profit*] pingüe; [*bank account*] sustancioso
[5] (= *sensible*) [*attitude, scepticism*] razonable; **to have a ~ interest in sth** tener un sano interés en algo; **to have a ~ respect for sb/sth** tenerle un respeto sano a algn/algo

heap [hiːp] Ⓐ N [1] (= *pile*) montón *m*, pila *f*; **her clothes lay in a ~ on the floor** su ropa estaba amontonada en el suelo
[2] (*fig*) (*) montón* *m*; **a whole ~ of trouble** un montón de disgustos*; **a whole ~ of people** un montón de gente*, muchísima gente; *see also* **heaps**
[3] (*) (= *old car*) cacharro* *m*
Ⓑ VT (*also* **to ~ up**) [+ *stones etc*] amontonar, apilar; [+ *bricks, coal*] amontonar (**onto** sobre); **to ~ sth together** juntar algo en un montón; **to ~ a plate with food** colmar un plato de comida; **to ~ favours/praise on sb** colmar a algn de favores/elogios; **~ed tablespoonful** (*Culin*) cucharada *f* colmada

►**heap up** VT + ADV [+ *stones etc*] amontonar, apilar; [+ *wealth*] acumular

heaps* [hiːps] Ⓐ NPL (= *lots*) **~ of** montones de, un montón de; **you've had ~ of opportunities** has tenido montones *or* un montón de oportunidades; **~ of times** muchísimas veces; **we have ~ of time** tenemos tiempo de sobra
Ⓑ ADV muchísimo; **~ better** muchísimo mejor

hear [hɪəʳ] (*pt, pp* **heard**) Ⓐ VT [1] (= *perceive*) [+ *voice, sound*] oír; **can you ~ me?** ¿me oyes?; **I can't ~ you** no te oigo; **I can't ~ a thing** no oigo nada; **I ~d someone come in** he oído entrar a alguien; **I ~d you talking to her** te oí hablar con ella; **I never ~d such rubbish!** ¡en mi vida he oído tantos disparates!; **did you ~ what he said?** ¿has oído lo que ha dicho?; **let's ~ it for ...** un aplauso para ...; **I could hardly make myself ~d** apenas pude lograr que se me oyera; **I have ~d it said that ...** ◊ **I've ~d tell that ...** he oído decir que ...; **I can't ~ myself think** el ruido no me deja pensar *or* concentrarme; *see also* **pin**
[2] (= *discover, be told*) oír; **have you ~d the news?** ¿has oído la noticia?, ¿te has enterado de la noticia?; **what's this I ~ about you getting married?** ¿qué es eso que he oído de que te vas a casar?; **from what I ~, she hasn't long to live** por lo que he oído parece que le queda poco tiempo de vida; **I waited to ~ the result** me quedé esperando para enterarme del resultado; **I ~ bad reports of him** no me hablan bien de él; **I'm glad to ~ it** me alegro; **I'm sorry to ~ it** lo siento; **where did you ~ that?** ¿quién te ha dicho eso?; **to ~ that ...** enterarse de que ...; **I ~d you're going away** me he enterado de que te vas; **I ~ you've been ill** me he enterado de que *or* he oído decir que has estado enfermo; **I haven't ~d yet whether I've passed** aún no sé si he aprobado; **have you ~d anything of** *or* **from him since he left?** ¿has sabido algo *or* has tenido noticias de él desde que se fue?; **the first I ~d of it was when ...** lo primero que supe al respecto fue cuando ...; **that's the first I've ~d of it** no tenía ni idea, es la primera noticia que tengo; **you haven't ~d the last of this!** ¡aquí no se acaba esto!; **have you ~d the one about ...?** ¿te sabes el de ...?
[3] (= *listen to*) [+ *radio programme, story*] escuchar, oír; [+ *lecture*] escuchar; **to ~ him (talk) you'd think he was an expert** por la forma en que habla, cualquiera creería *or* diría que es un experto; **I've ~d it all before** ya conozco la historia; **Lord, ~ our prayers** Señor, escucha nuestras plegarias *or* súplicas; **to ~ sb speak** (*in public*) escuchar a algn; **he likes to ~ himself talk** le gusta escucharse a sí mismo
[4] (*Jur*) [+ *case*] ver
[5] (*Rel*) **to ~ mass** oír misa
Ⓑ VI [1] (= *perceive*) oír; **I can't ~** no oigo; **if you don't get out I'll call the police, (do) you ~?** si no te vas llamaré a la policía, ¿me oyes?; **he doesn't** *or* **can't ~ very well** no oye muy bien
[2] **to ~ about sth/sb**: **I ~d about it from Maria** me enteré por María, lo supe a través de María; **did you ~ about Liz?** ¿te enteraste de lo de Liz?; **I don't want to ~ about it** no quiero oír hablar del tema; **to ~ from sb** saber de algn, tener noticias de algn; **have you ~d from him lately?** ¿has sabido algo de él últimamente?, ¿has tenido noticias de él últimamente?; **I ~ from my daughter every week** tengo noticias de mi hija todas las semanas; **hoping to ~ from you** (*in letter*) esperando recibir noticias tuyas; **you will be ~ing from my solicitor** mi abogado se pondrá en contacto con usted; **the police are anxious to ~ from anyone who may know her** la policía pide a todos los que la conozcan que se pongan en contacto con ellos; **what are you ~ing from people there?** ¿qué opina *or* dice allí la gente?; **to ~ of sth** (= *come across*) oír hablar de algo; (= *become aware of*) saber de algo; **many people haven't ~d of reflexology** muchas personas no han oído hablar de la reflexología; **I've never ~d of such a thing!** ¡en mi vida he oído cosa igual!; **I ~d of this school through Leslie** supe de esta escuela por *or* a través de Leslie; **I won't ~ of it!** (= *allow*) ¡ni hablar!; **I offered to pay but she wouldn't ~ of it** me ofrecí a pagar pero dijo que ni hablar; **I always wanted to be an actor but Dad wouldn't ~ of it** siempre quise ser actor pero papá no me dejó; **to ~ of sb** (= *come across*) oír hablar de algn; (= *have news of*) saber de algn, tener noticias de algn; **everyone has ~d of her** todo el mundo ha oído hablar de ella *or* sabe quién es; **he wasn't ~d of for a long time** no se supo nada de él *or* no se tuvieron noticias de él durante mucho tiempo; **he was never ~d of again** nunca se supo más de él
[3] **hear! hear!** (= *bravo*) ¡sí señor!, ¡eso, eso!

►**hear out** VT + ADV [+ *story*] escuchar; **she ~d out their ideas then gave her recommendation** escuchó sus ideas y luego les dio su recomendación; **to ~ sb out** dejar que algn termine de hablar; **let's ~ him out** vamos a dejarle que termine de hablar

heard [hɜːd] PT, PP *of* **hear**

hearer [ˈhɪərəʳ] N oyente *mf*

hearing [ˈhɪərɪŋ] Ⓐ N [1] (= *sense of hearing*) oído *m*; **to have good/poor ~** oír bien/poco; **in my ~** estando yo delante, en mi presencia; **if you must talk about it, do it out of my ~** si tienes que hablar de ello, hazlo sin que yo esté *or* sin que yo me entere; **within/out of ~ (distance)** al alcance/fuera del alcance del oído
[2] (= *chance to speak*) oportunidad *f* de hablar; (*Jur*) vista *f*, audiencia *f*; **he never got a fair ~** en ningún momento se le permitió explicar su punto de vista; (*Jur*) no tuvo un juicio justo; **to give sb a ~** dar a algn la oportunidad de hablar
Ⓑ CPD ► **hearing aid** N audífono *m* ► **hearing problem** N problema *m* de oído; **he has ~ problems** tiene problemas de oído

hearing-assisted [ˈhɪərɪŋəˈsɪstɪd] CPD ► **hearing-assisted telephone** N (*US*) teléfono *m* con sonido aumentado

hearken [ˈhɑːkən] VI (††, *liter*) **to ~ to** escuchar

hearsay [ˈhɪəseɪ] Ⓐ N rumores *mpl*; **it's just ~** son rumores nada más; **by ~** de oídas
Ⓑ CPD ► **hearsay evidence** N testimonio *m* de oídas

hearse [hɜːs] N coche *m or* (*LAm*) carro *m* fúnebre

heart [hɑːt] Ⓐ N [1] (= *organ, symbol of love*) corazón *m*; **she waited with beating ~** le palpitaba el corazón mientras esperaba, esperaba con el corazón palpitante; **to clasp sb to one's ~** abrazar a algn estrechamente; **to have a weak ~** padecer *or* sufrir del corazón
[2] (= *seat of emotions*) corazón *m*; **with all one's ~** de todo corazón, con toda su alma; **at ~** en el fondo; **to have sb's interests at ~** tener presente el interés de algn; **this is an issue which is close to his ~** este es un asunto que le toca muy de cerca; **to one's ~'s content** a gusto; **this is an issue which is dear to his ~** éste es un asunto que le toca muy de cerca; **his words came from the ~** sus palabras salieron del corazón; **it would have done your ~ good** te habría alegrado el corazón; **he knew in his ~ that it was a waste of time** él en el fondo sabía que era una pérdida de tiempo; **you will always have a place in my ~** siempre te llevaré dentro (de mi corazón); ✦**IDIOMS he's a man after my own ~** es un hombre de los que me gustan; **from the bottom of one's ~** con toda sinceridad, de corazón; **to break sb's ~** (*in love*) partir el corazón a algn; (*by behaviour etc*) matar a algn a disgustos; **to break one's ~ over** partirse el corazón por; **to die of a broken ~** morir de pena; **to cut sb to the ~** herir a algn en lo vivo; **to give one's ~ to** enamorarse de; **he has a ~ of gold** tiene un corazón de oro; **have a ~!*** ¡ten un poco de compasión *or* corazón!; **to have no ~** no tener corazón *or* entrañas; **with a heavy ~** apesadumbrado, compungido; **with heavy ~s, we turned our steps homeward** apesadumbrados *or* compungidos, encaminamos nuestros pasos de regreso a casa; **his ~ was not in it** lo hacía sin ganas, no tenía fe en lo que estaba haciendo; **in his ~ of ~s** en lo más íntimo de su corazón; **to lose one's ~ to** enamorarse de; **to open one's ~ to sb** abrir el corazón a algn; **to cry one's ~ out** llorar a lágrima viva; **to sing one's ~ out** cantar a voz en grito; **his ~ is in the right place** tiene buen corazón; **to let one's ~ rule one's head** dejar que el corazón guíe a la cabeza; **to set one's ~ on sth**: **I've set my ~ on that coat I saw yesterday** quiero a toda costa (comprarme) ese abrigo que vi ayer; **she's set her ~ on winning the championship** ha puesto todo su empeño en ganar el campeonato; **she is the ~ and soul of the organization** ella es el alma de la organización; **to throw o.s. into sth ~ and soul** entregarse en cuerpo y alma a algo, meterse de lleno en algo; **to take sth to ~** tomarse algo a pecho; **to wear one's ~ on one's sleeve** llevar el corazón en la mano; **to win sb's ~** enamorar a algn; **she won the ~s of the people** se ganó el corazón *or* el afecto de la gente; *see also* **eat out B**, **sick A1**
[3] (= *courage*) **I did not have the ~** *or* **I could not find it in my ~ to tell her** no tuve valor para decírselo; ✦**IDIOMS to be in good ~** [*person*] estar de buen ánimo; **to lose ~** descorazonarse; **to have one's ~ in one's mouth** tener el alma en un hilo, tener el corazón en un puño; **to put new ~ into sb** infundir nuevos bríos a algn; **my ~ sank** me desco-

razoné, se me cayó el alma a los pies; **to take ~** cobrar ánimos, animarse; **we may take ~ from the fact that ...** que nos aliente el hecho de que ...
[4] (= *centre*) [*of lettuce, celery*] cogollo *m*; [*of place, earth etc*] corazón *m*, seno *m*, centro *m*; **in the ~ of the country** en pleno campo; **the ~ of the matter** lo esencial *or* el meollo *or* el quid del asunto; **in the ~ of winter** en pleno invierno; **in the ~ of the wood** en el centro del bosque
[5] (= *memory*) **to learn/know/recite sth by ~** aprender/saber/recitar algo de memoria
[6] **hearts** (*Cards*) corazones *mpl*; (*in Spanish pack*) copas *fpl*
Ⓑ CPD ► **heart attack** N (*Med*) ataque *m* al corazón, infarto *m* (de miocardio) ► **heart complaint** N enfermedad *f* cardíaca ► **heart condition** N condición *f* cardíaca ► **heart disease** N enfermedad *f* cardíaca ► **heart failure** N (= *attack*) fallo *m* del corazón, paro *m* cardíaco; (*chronic*) insuficiencia *f* cardíaca ► **heart murmur** N soplo *m* en el corazón ► **heart rate** N ritmo *m* del corazón ► **heart surgeon** N cirujano/a *m/f* cardiólogo/a ► **heart surgery** N cirugía *f* cardíaca ► **heart transplant** N trasplante *m* del corazón ► **heart trouble** N problemas *mpl* de corazón, afecciones *fpl* cardíacas; **to have ~ trouble** padecer *or* sufrir del corazón

heartache ['hɑːteɪk] N pena *f*, dolor *m*

heartbeat ['hɑːtbiːt] N (*gen*) latido *m* del corazón

heartbreak ['hɑːtbreɪk] N congoja *f*, sufrimiento *m*

heartbreaking ['hɑːt,breɪkɪŋ] ADJ desgarrador, que parte el corazón

heartbroken ['hɑːt,brəʊkən] ADJ acongojado, desconsolado; **she was ~ about it** estaba desconsolada

heartburn ['hɑːtbɜːn] N (*Med*) acidez *f*, ardor *m*

-hearted ['hɑːtɪd] ADJ (*ending in compounds*) **hard-hearted** duro/a de corazón; **warm-hearted** cariñoso/a; *see also* **broken-hearted**, **open-hearted**

hearten ['hɑːtn] VT alentar, animar

heartening ['hɑːtnɪŋ] ADJ alentador

heartfelt ['hɑːtfelt] ADJ [*sympathy*] sentido; [*thanks, apology*] sincero; **my ~ apologies** mis sinceras disculpas

hearth [hɑːθ] Ⓐ N (*gen, also fig*) hogar *m*; (= *fireplace*) chimenea *f*
Ⓑ CPD ► **hearth rug** N alfombrilla *f*, tapete *m*

heartily ['hɑːtɪlɪ] ADV [1] (= *enthusiastically*) [*laugh*] a carcajadas, de buena gana; [*eat*] con ganas, con apetito; [*say*] efusivamente; [*thank, welcome*] cordialmente, calurosamente
[2] (= *thoroughly*) [*recommend*] encarecidamente; [*agree*] completamente, totalmente; **to be ~ sick of sth** estar completamente *or* realmente harto de algo; **to be ~ glad** alegrarse sinceramente; **he ~ dislikes cabbage** detesta el repollo

heartiness ['hɑːtɪnɪs] N entusiasmo *m*; **he spoke with a ~ he did not feel** habló con un entusiasmo que no sentía; **he shook my hand with exaggerated ~** me estrechó la mano con una efusividad exagerada

heartland ['hɑːtlænd] N [1] (*Geog*) zona *f* central, zona *f* interior; **the ~ of Tibet** el corazón del Tibet
[2] (*fig*) **the conservative ~ in south-east England** el feudo conservador del sudeste de Inglaterra

heartless ['hɑːtlɪs] ADJ despiadado, cruel

heartlessly ['hɑːtlɪslɪ] ADV despiadadamente, cruelmente

heartlessness ['hɑːtlɪsnɪs] N crueldad *f*, inhumanidad *f*

heart-lung machine [,hɑːt'lʌŋmə,ʃiːn] N máquina *f* de circulación extracorpórea

heartrending ['hɑːt,rendɪŋ] ADJ desgarrador, que parte el corazón; **it was ~ to see them** se me partía el corazón de verlos

heart-searching ['hɑːt,sɜːtʃɪŋ] N examen *m* de conciencia

heart-shaped ['hɑːtʃeɪpt] ADJ en forma de corazón

heartstrings ['hɑːtstrɪŋz] NPL ✦*IDIOM* **to pull at** *or* **touch sb's ~** tocar la fibra sensible de algn

heartthrob* ['hɑːtθrɒb] N **he's the ~ of the teenagers** es el ídolo de las quinceañeras; **Bogart was my mother's ~** mi madre idolatraba a Bogart; **we met her latest ~** conocimos a su amiguito del momento

heart-to-heart ['hɑːttə'hɑːt] Ⓐ ADJ íntimo, franco; **to have a ~ talk with sb** tener una conversación íntima con algn
Ⓑ N conversación *f* íntima; **to have a ~ with sb** tener una conversación íntima con algn

heart-warming ['hɑːt,wɔːmɪŋ] ADJ (= *pleasing*) grato, reconfortante; (= *moving*) conmovedor, emocionante

hearty ['hɑːtɪ] (*compar* **heartier**, *superl* **heartiest**) Ⓐ ADJ [1] (= *enthusiastic and friendly*) [*voice, greeting, welcome, thanks*] cordial, caluroso; [*laugh*] efusivo, campechano; [*person*] campechano, sanote; **please accept my ~ congratulations** por favor, acepte mi más cordial felicitación *or* mis más sinceras felicitaciones
[2] (= *hard*) [*slap, kick*] fuerte
[3] (= *substantial*) [*meal*] copioso; [*appetite*] bueno; [*soup*] sustancioso; **the men ate a ~ breakfast** los hombres tomaron un copioso desayuno; *see also* **hale**
Ⓑ N (*) tipo *m* campechano*

heat [hiːt] Ⓐ N [1] (= *warmth*) calor *m*; (*also* **~ing**) calefacción *f*; **in the ~ of the day** en las horas de más calor; **on** *or* **over a low ~** (*Culin*) a fuego lento
[2] (*fig*) (= *excitement*) calor *m*; (= *vehemence*) vehemencia *f*; (= *pressure*) presión *f*; **in the ~ of the moment/battle** en el calor del momento/de la batalla; **he replied with some ~** contestó bastante indignado *or* con bastante acaloramiento; **when the ~ is on** cuando hay presión; **it'll take the ~ off us** esto nos dará un respiro; **to take the ~ out of a situation** reducir la tensión de una situación; ✦*IDIOMS* **to turn on the ~** empezar a ejercer presión; **the ~ is on** ha llegado la hora de la verdad; **we played well when the ~ was on** a la hora de la verdad supimos jugar bien; (*Pol*) crear un ambiente de crisis
[3] (*Sport*) prueba *f* (eliminatoria); **dead ~** empate *m*
[4] (*Zool*) [*of dogs, cats*] celo *m*; **to be in** *or* **on ~** (*Brit*) estar en celo
[5] **the ~** (*US*‡) (= *police*) la poli*, la pasma (*Sp*‡), la cana (*S. Cone*‡)
[6] (*US*) (= *criticism*) **he took a lot of ~ for that mistake** se llevó muchos palos por ese error
Ⓑ VT (= *warm*) calentar; **they ~ their house with coal** su casa tiene calefacción de carbón
Ⓒ VI calentarse
Ⓓ CPD ► **heat exhaustion** N agotamiento *m* por el calor ► **heat haze** N calina *f*, calima *f* ► **heat loss** N pérdida *f* de calor ► **heat rash** N sarpullido *m* ► **heat shield** N escudo *m* contra el calor ► **heat treatment** N tratamiento *m* de calor

►**heat up** Ⓐ VI + ADV (*lit*) calentarse; (*fig*) [*discussion, debate*] acalorarse
Ⓑ VT + ADV (*gen*) calentar; [+ *food*] calentar, recalentar

heated ['hiːtɪd] Ⓐ ADJ [1] (*lit*) [*swimming pool*] climatizado; [*rollers*] caliente
[2] (*fig*) [*discussion*] acalorado; **to grow** *or* **become ~** [*discussion, debate*] acalorarse
Ⓑ CPD ► **heated (swimming) pool** N piscina *f* climatizada ► **heated rear window** N luneta *f* térmica

heatedly ['hiːtɪdlɪ] ADV [*argue, debate*] acaloradamente, con acaloramiento; [*reply, say*] con vehemencia; **"not me!" he replied ~** —¡yo no! —contestó indignado *or* con vehemencia

heater ['hiːtəʳ] N calentador *m*, estufa *f*

heath [hiːθ] N (*esp Brit*) (= *moor etc*) brezal *m*, páramo *m* (*esp LAm*); (*also* **~er**) brezo *m*

heathen ['hiːðən] Ⓐ ADJ (= *pagan*) pagano; (*fig*) (= *uncivilised*) bárbaro, salvaje
Ⓑ N (*pl* **heathens** *or* **heathen**) pagano/a *m/f*; (*fig*) bárbaro/a *m/f*, salvaje *mf*

heathenish ['hiːðənɪʃ] ADJ pagano

heathenism ['hiːðənɪzəm] N paganismo *m*

heather ['heðəʳ] N (= *plant*) brezo *m*

Heath Robinson ['hiːθ'rɒbənsən] ADJ [*device etc*] aparatoso

heating ['hiːtɪŋ] Ⓐ N calefacción *f*; **central ~** calefacción central
Ⓑ CPD ► **heating engineer** N técnico/a *m/f* en calefacciones ► **heating plant** N instalación *m* de calefacción ► **heating power** N poder *m* calorífico ► **heating system** N sistema *m* de calefacción

heatproof ['hiːtpruːf], **heat-resistant** ['hiːtrɪ,zɪstənt] ADJ termorresistente, a prueba de calor; [*ovenware*] refractario

heat-seeking ['hiːt,siːkɪŋ] ADJ [*missile*] termodirigido

heat-sensitive ['hiːt'sensɪtɪv] ADJ sensible al calor

heatstroke ['hiːtstrəʊk] N (*Med*) insolación *f*

heatwave ['hiːtweɪv] N ola *f* de calor

heave [hiːv] Ⓐ N (= *lift*) gran esfuerzo *m* (para levantar *etc*); (= *pull*) tirón *m*, jalón *m* (*LAm*) (**on** de); (= *push*) empujón *m*; (= *throw*) echada *f*, tirada *f*; (= *movement*) [*of waves, sea*] sube y baja *m*; **with a ~ of his shoulders** con un fuerte movimiento de hombros
Ⓑ VT (= *pull*) tirar, jalar (*LAm*); (= *drag*) arrastrar; (= *carry*) llevar; (= *lift*) levantar (con dificultad); (= *push*) empujar; (= *throw*) lanzar, tirar; **they ~d the body off the cliff** lanzaron *or* tiraron el cuerpo por el acantilado; **he ~d himself to a sitting position** se incorporó con gran esfuerzo; **to ~ a sigh** dar *or* echar un suspiro, suspirar; **to ~ a sigh of relief** suspirar aliviado
Ⓒ VI [1] (= *rise and fall*) [*water etc*] subir y bajar; [*chest, bosom*] palpitar
[2] (= *pull*) tirar, jalar (*LAm*) (**at, on** de)
[3] (= *retch*) hacer arcadas; **her stomach was heaving** le daban arcadas, se le revolvía el estómago; **it makes me ~** me da asco
[4] (*Naut*) (*pt, pp* **hove**) (= *move*) virar; (= *pitch*) cabecear; (= *roll*) balancearse; **to ~ in(to) sight** aparecer

►**heave to** VI + ADV ponerse al pairo

►**heave up** VT + ADV (= *vomit*) devolver, arrojar

heave-ho ['hiːv'həʊ] EXCL ¡ahora!; (*Naut*) ¡iza!; ✦*IDIOM* **to give sb the ~*** dar el pasaporte a algn*

heaven ['hevn] N [1] (*Rel, gen*) cielo *m*; **to go to ~** ir al cielo; **(good) ~s!** ¡cielos!; **an injustice that cries out to ~** una injusticia que clama al cielo; **~ forbid!** ¡no lo quiera Dios!; **~ forbid that we end up in the same hotel!** ¡ojalá no *or* quiera Dios que no terminemos en el mismo hotel!; **~ help them if they do** que Dios les ayude si lo hacen; **~ knows why** Dios sabe por qué; **~ knows I tried** no será porque no lo intenté; **what in ~'s name does that mean?** ¿qué demonios significa eso?; **the ~s opened** se abrieron los cielos, las nubes descargaron con fuerza; **for ~'s sake!** ¡por Dios!; **thank ~!** ¡gracias a Dios!, ¡menos mal!; ♦*IDIOMS* **to move ~ and earth to do sth** remover cielo y tierra *or* Roma con Santiago para hacer algo; **to stink to high ~** heder a perro muerto; **to be in seventh ~** estar en el séptimo cielo
[2] (*fig*) paraíso *m*; **this place is just ~** este lugar es el paraíso; **the trip was ~** el viaje fue una maravilla; **isn't he ~?** ¡qué maravilla de hombre!

heavenly ['hevnlɪ] Ⓐ ADJ [1] (*Rel*) celestial; **Heavenly Father** Padre *m* celestial
[2] (*) (= *lovely*) divino
Ⓑ CPD ► **heavenly body** N (*Astron*) cuerpo *m* celeste

heaven-sent ['hevn'sent] ADJ milagroso, (como) llovido del cielo

heavenward ['hevnwəd] ADV hacia el cielo

heavenwards ['hevnwədz] ADV (*esp Brit*) = **heavenward**

heavily ['hevɪlɪ] ADV [1] (= *very much*) [*rain, bleed, sweat*] mucho; [*drink, smoke*] mucho, en exceso; [*criticize*] duramente; [*depend, rely*] en gran medida; [*biased, laden*] muy; **the dangers of drinking or smoking ~** los peligros de beber o fumar mucho *or* en exceso; **she drinks ~/more ~ when she's depressed** bebe mucho/mucho más cuando está deprimida; **he spoke in ~ accented English** hablaba inglés con un acento muy fuerte; **he had to borrow ~** tuvo que pedir grandes cantidades de *or* mucho dinero prestado; **to be ~ in debt** tener muchísimas deudas, estar muy endeudado; **to be ~ defeated** (*in election, war*) sufrir una derrota aplastante; **the book draws ~ on Marxism** el libro se inspira en gran medida en las teorías marxistas; **he was fined ~ by the Football Association** la Asociación de Fútbol le puso una multa muy severa; **to be ~ influenced by sb/sth** estar muy influido por algn/algo; **he's ~ into jazz/football*** le ha dado fuerte por el jazz/el fútbol; **he's ~ into drugs*** está muy metido en las drogas; **he invested ~ in commodities** invirtió grandes cantidades de dinero *or* invirtió mucho en materias primas; **to be ~ involved in** *or* **with sth** estar muy metido en algo*; **to lose ~** (*gambling*) perder grandes cantidades de dinero, perder muchísimo dinero; (*in election, vote, match*) sufrir una derrota aplastante; **she was ~ made up** llevaba muchísimo maquillaje; **a ~ populated area** una zona densamente poblada; **she was ~ pregnant** le quedaba poco para dar a luz, se encontraba en avanzado estado de gestación (*frm*); **~ scented** con un fuerte olor; **~ spiced** con muchas especias, muy condimentado; **each word was ~ underlined** cada palabra estaba subrayada con trazo grueso; **to be ~ weighted against sb/in sb's favour** desfavorecer/favorecer en gran medida a algn
[2] (= *well, strongly*) [*armed*] fuertemente; [*guarded, fortified*] muy bien
[3] (= *deeply*) [*sleep*] profundamente; **to breathe ~** (*from exertion*) resoplar, jadear; **he breathed ~ as he slept** respiraba muy fuerte mientras dormía; **his face was ~ lined** su cara estaba muy marcada de arrugas; **Bernard sighed ~** Bernard exhaló un profundo suspiro
[4] (= *weightily*) [*tread*] con paso pesado; [*move, walk*] pesadamente; [*say*] con gran pesar; **he sat down ~ in his chair** se desplomó en la silla; **he fell ~ and twisted his arm** tuvo una mala caída y se torció el brazo; **~ built** corpulento, fornido; **it weighs ~ on him** (*fig*) le pesa mucho

heaviness ['hevɪnɪs] N [*of object*] lo pesado, peso *m*; [*of subject matter*] lo denso; **always test the ~ of a load** comprueba siempre lo pesada que es una carga *or* el peso de una carga; **I felt a ~ in my legs** sentía pesadez en las piernas; **~ of heart** pesadumbre *f* (*liter*)

heavy ['hevɪ] Ⓐ ADJ (*compar* **heavier**; *superl* **heaviest**) [1] (= *weighty*) pesado; **you mustn't lift ~ weights** no debes levantar cargas pesadas; **to be ~** pesar mucho; **is it ~?** ¿pesa mucho?; **how ~ are you?** ¿cuánto pesas?; **he has his father's ~ build** tiene la misma corpulencia de su padre; **his eyes were ~ (with sleep)** los párpados le pesaban de sueño; **my arms felt so ~** me pesaban tanto los brazos; **the mayor's ~ mob*** los gorilas del alcalde; **the trees were ~ with fruit** los árboles estaban cargados de fruta
[2] (= *considerable*) [*traffic*] denso; [*rain, shower*] fuerte; [*crop*] abundante; [*loss*] considerable, cuantioso; [*fine*] fuerte; [*defeat*] aplastante; [*irony, symbolism*] enorme; [*fighting, fire*] intenso; **there had been a ~ fall of snow** había caído una fuerte nevada; **the news came as a ~ blow** la noticia fue un duro golpe; **a ~ concentration of troops** una gran concentración de tropas; **~ demand has depleted supplies** una intensa *or* enorme demanda ha reducido las existencias; **to be a ~ drinker** beber mucho; **the school places ~ emphasis on languages** la escuela da mucha importancia a los idiomas; **to be ~ on sth: the car is ~ on petrol** el coche consume mucha gasolina; **you've been a bit ~ on the butter** se te ha ido un poco la mano con la mantequilla; **he is under ~ pressure to resign** le están presionando enormemente para que dimita; **the ~ scent of honeysuckle** el intenso *or* fuerte olor a madreselva; **to be a ~ smoker** fumar mucho; *see also* **casualty**, **price**
[3] (= *thick, solid*) [*cloth, coat, line*] grueso; [*features*] tosco; [*meal, food*] fuerte, pesado; [*soil*] arcilloso; [*fog, mist*] espeso, denso; **the going was ~ because of the rain** el terreno estaba muy blando debido a la lluvia; **~ crude (oil)** crudo *m* denso *or* pesado
[4] (= *oppressive, gloomy*) [*atmosphere*] cargado; [*sky*] encapotado; [*burden, responsibility*] pesado; **I found this talk of marriage a bit ~** esa conversación sobre el matrimonio me resultaba algo pesada; **with a ~ heart** apesadumbrado, acongojado; **the air was ~ with scent** el aire estaba cargado de perfume
[5] (= *deep*) [*sigh, sleep, silence*] profundo; **~ breather** (*on telephone*) maníaco *m* telefónico; **~ breathing** (*from exertion*) jadeos *mpl*, resoplidos *mpl*; **his ~ breathing kept me awake** respiraba tan fuerte que no me dejaba dormir, sus jadeos no me dejaban dormir; **to be a ~ sleeper** tener el sueño profundo
[6] (= *arduous*) [*task, work*] pesado; [*schedule*] apretado; **I've had a ~ day** he tenido un día muy liado *or* ajetreado; *see also* **weather**
[7] (= *boring, laboured*) [*book, film, humour*] denso, pesado; **to be ~ going** [*book, film*] ser muy denso; **the conversation was ~ going** era difícil encontrar temas de conversación; **his new album/book is pretty ~ stuff** su nuevo álbum es bastante fuerte
[8] (= *bad*) **to have a ~ cold** estar muy resfriado *or* acatarrado; **he had had a ~ fall** había tenido una mala caída; **to get ~**: **things got a bit ~** (= *nasty*) la cosa se puso fea
[9] (= *rough*) [*sea*] grueso
Ⓑ N [1] (*) (= *thug*) matón* *m*, gorila* *m*
[2] (*) (= *eminent person*) peso *m* pesado
[3] (*) (= *newspaper*) periódico *m* serio
[4] (*Scot*) (*beer*) cerveza *f* tostada
Ⓒ ADV **time hung ~ (on our hands)** las horas/los días *etc* se nos hacían interminables; **the shadow of war hung ~ over the city** la sombra de la guerra pesaba sobre la ciudad; **his son's troubles weighed ~ on his mind** los problemas de su hijo le preocupaban mucho
Ⓓ CPD ► **heavy artillery** N artillería *f* pesada ► **heavy cream** N (*US*) nata *f* para montar (*Sp*), nata *f* enriquecida ► **heavy goods** NPL artículos *mpl* pesados ► **heavy goods vehicle** N vehículo *m* pesado ► **heavy guns** NPL = **heavy artillery** ► **heavy industry** N industria *f* pesada ► **heavy metal** N (*Chem, Ind*) metal *m* pesado; (*Mus*) heavy *m* (metal) ► **heavy type** N negrita *f* ► **heavy water** N (*Phys*) agua *f* pesada

heavy-duty [ˌhevɪ'djuːtɪ] ADJ fuerte, resistente

heavy-handed [ˌhevɪ'hændɪd] ADJ [1] (= *clumsy, tactless*) torpe, patoso
[2] (= *harsh*) severo

heavy-hearted [ˌhevɪ'hɑːtɪd] ADJ apesadumbrado, acongojado

heavy-laden [ˌhevɪ'leɪdn] ADJ lastrado

heavy-set ['hevɪ'set] ADJ (*esp US*) corpulento, fornido

heavyweight ['hevɪweɪt] Ⓐ ADJ pesado, de mucho peso
Ⓑ N (*Boxing, fig*) peso *m* pesado

Hebe* ['hiːbɪ] N (*US pej*) judío/a *m/f*

he-bear ['hiːbɛəʳ] N oso *m* macho

Hebraic [hɪ'breɪɪk] ADJ hebraico

Hebraist ['hiːbreɪɪst] N hebraísta *mf*

Hebrew ['hiːbruː] Ⓐ ADJ hebreo
Ⓑ N [1] (= *person*) hebreo/a *m/f*
[2] (*Ling*) hebreo *m*

Hebrides ['hebrɪdiːz] NPL Hébridas *fpl*; *see also* **outer**

heck* [hek] Ⓐ EXCL ¡jo! (*Sp**), ¡la pucha! (*LAm**)
Ⓑ N **a ~ of a lot** un montón*; **I'm in one ~ of a mess** estoy metido en un lío de narices*; **what the ~ is he doing?** ¿qué narices está haciendo?*; **what the ~ did he mean?** ¿qué narices quiso decir?*; **what the ~!** ¡qué narices!*

heckle ['hekl] Ⓐ VT interrumpir, molestar con preguntas
Ⓑ VI interrumpir, molestar con preguntas

heckler ['hekləʳ] N *persona que interrumpe or molesta a un orador*

heckling ['heklɪŋ] N interrupciones *fpl*, protestas *fpl*

hectare ['hektɑːʳ] N hectárea *f*

hectic ['hektɪk] ADJ (*fig*) agitado; **he has a ~ life** lleva una vida muy agitada; **the ~ pace of modern life** el ritmo agitado de la vida moderna; **we had three ~ days** tuvimos tres días llenos de frenética actividad; **things are pretty ~ here** vamos como locos; **the journey was pretty ~** el viaje era para volverse loco

hectogram ['hektəʊgræm] N hectogramo *m*

hectogramme ['hektəʊgræm] N = **hectogram**

hectolitre, **hectoliter** (*US*) ['hektəʊ,li:təʳ] N hectolitro *m*

Hector ['hektəʳ] N Héctor

hector ['hektəʳ] Ⓐ VT intimidar con bravatas
Ⓑ VI echar bravatas

hectoring ['hektərɪŋ] ADJ [*person*] lleno de bravatas; [*tone, remark*] amedrentador

he'd [hi:d] = **he had**, **he would**

hedge [hedʒ] Ⓐ N [1] (*Hort, Agr*) seto *m* (vivo)
[2] (*fig*) protección *f*; (*Fin*) cobertura *f*; **as a ~ against inflation** como protección contra la inflación
Ⓑ VT [1] (*Agr*) cercar con un seto
[2] (*fig*) **to be ~d with** estar erizado de; **to ~ one's bets** hacer apuestas compensatorias
Ⓒ VI [1] (= *be evasive*) contestar con evasivas; **stop hedging!** ¡dilo sin sofismas!
[2] (*Fin*) **to ~ against inflation** cubrirse contra la inflación
Ⓓ CPD ► **hedge clippers** NPL tijeras *fpl* de podar ► **hedge sparrow** N acentor *m* (común)

► **hedge about** VT + ADV **to be ~d about with** estar erizado de

► **hedge around** VT + ADV = **hedge about**

► **hedge off** VT + ADV separar con un seto

hedgehog ['hedʒhɒg] N erizo *m*

hedgehop ['hedʒhɒp] VI volar a ras de tierra

hedgerow ['hedʒrəʊ] N seto *m* vivo

hedging ['hedʒɪŋ] Ⓐ N [1] (*Bot*) seto *m* vivo
[2] (*fig*) (= *evasions*) evasivas *fpl*
[3] (*Fin*) cobertura *f*
Ⓑ CPD ► **hedging plant** N planta *f* para seto vivo

hedonism ['hi:dənɪzəm] N hedonismo *m*

hedonist ['hi:dənɪst] N hedonista *mf*

hedonistic [,hi:də'nɪstɪk] ADJ hedonista

heebie-jeebies* [,hi:bɪ'dʒi:bɪz] NPL **to have the ~** (= *shaking*) tener un tembleque*; (= *fright, nerves*) estar hecho un flan*; **it gives me the ~** (= *revulsion*) me da asco; (= *fright, apprehension*) me pone los pelos de punta*, me da escalofríos

heed [hi:d] Ⓐ N **to pay (no) ~ to sb** (no) hacer caso a algn; **to take (no) ~ of sth** (no) tener en cuenta algo; **to take ~ to** + INFIN poner atención en + *infin*; **take ~!** ¡ten cuidado!
Ⓑ VT [+ *person*] hacer caso a; [+ *warning*] tomar en cuenta

heedless ['hi:dlɪs] ADJ (= *careless*) descuidado, despreocupado; **to be ~ of ...** no hacer caso a ...

heedlessly ['hi:dlɪslɪ] ADV sin hacer caso

heehaw ['hi:hɔ:] Ⓐ N rebuzno *m*
Ⓑ VI rebuznar

heel¹ [hi:l] Ⓐ N [1] (*Anat*) talón *m*; **to turn on one's ~** dar media vuelta; **to keep to ~** [+ *dog*] seguir de cerca al dueño; ✦*IDIOMS* **to be at** *or* **on sb's ~s** pisar los talones a algn; **to bring sb to ~** sobreponerse a algn, meter a algn en cintura; **to cool one's ~s*** estar plantado *or* de plantón; **I decided to leave him to cool his ~s** decidí hacerle esperar un rato, decidí dejarlo plantado *or* de plantón un rato*; **to dig in one's ~s*** empecinarse; **to drag one's ~s** arrastrar los pies; **to follow hard on sb's ~s** seguir a algn muy de cerca; **to follow hard on the ~s of sth** venir a renglón seguido de algo; **to be hot on sb's ~s** pisar los talones a algn; **to kick one's ~s*** estar plantado *or* de plantón; **to show sb a clean pair of ~s** hacer tragar polvo a algn; **to take to one's ~s*** echar a correr, poner pies en polvorosa*; **to be under the ~ of** estar bajo los talones de
[2] [*of sock*] talón *m*; [*of shoe*] tacón *m*; ✦*IDIOM* **to be down at ~** ir desharrapado; *see also* **down-at-heel**
[3] (†*) (= *person*) sinvergüenza *mf*, canalla *mf*
Ⓑ VT [1] [+ *shoe*] poner tapas a; *see also* **well-heeled**
[2] [+ *ball*] taconear, dar de tacón a
Ⓒ VI **~!** ¡ven aquí!
Ⓓ CPD ► **heel bar** N rápido *m*, tienda *f* de reparación de calzado en el acto

heel² [hi:l] VI (*also* **to ~ over**) (*Naut*) zozobrar, escorar

heft* [heft] (*US*) Ⓐ N peso *m*; (*fig*) influencia *f*; **the ~ of** la mayor parte de
Ⓑ VT [1] (= *lift*) levantar
[2] (= *assess weight of*) sopesar

hefty ['heftɪ] ADJ (*compar* **heftier**, *superl* **heftiest**) [1] (= *large*) [*person*] corpulento, fornido; [*object*] enorme, imponente*; [*increase*] considerable; [*profit, payment*] cuantioso; [*price, salary, fees*] alto; [*bill, debt*] enorme; [*meal*] abundante; [*dose*] grande, mayúsculo*; **a ~ fine** una multa muy cuantiosa, una buena multa*; **a ~ book** un mamotreto*
[2] (= *powerful*) [*kick, punch*] fuerte
[3] (= *heavy*) pesado

hegemony [hɪ'geməni] N hegemonía *f*

hegira [he'dʒaɪərə] N hégira *f*

he-goat ['hi:gəʊt] N macho *m* cabrío

heid* ['hi:d] N (*Scot*) = **head**

heifer ['hefəʳ] N novilla *f*, vaquilla *f*

heigh [heɪ] EXCL ¡oye!, ¡eh!

heigh-ho ['heɪ'həʊ] EXCL ¡ay!

height [haɪt] N [1] (= *measurement*) [*of object*] altura *f*; [*of person*] estatura *f*; **to be 20 metres in ~** medir *or* tener 20 metros de alto, tener una altura de 20 metros; **we are the same ~** tenemos la misma estatura, somos igual de altos; **he was of average ~ and build** era de estatura y constitución media; **he drew himself up to his full ~** se irguió todo lo alto que era; **she's about my ~** tiene mi altura *or* es de mi estatura más o menos; **he sometimes found his ~ a disadvantage** su altura le resultaba a veces una desventaja
[2] (= *altitude*) altura *f*; **~ above sea level** altura *f* or altitud *f* sobre el nivel del mar; **at a ~ of 2,000 m** a una altura *or* altitud de 2.000 m; **to gain/lose ~** ganar/perder altura; **hold your arms out at shoulder ~** levanta los brazos a la altura de los hombros
[3] (= *high place*) cumbre *f*; **to be afraid of ~s** tener miedo a las alturas, tener vértigo; **the ~s** las alturas; *see also* **head A2**
[4] (= *peak, zenith*) cumbre *f*, cima *f*; **at the ~ of her career** en la cumbre *or* la cima de su carrera; **at its ~, the movement had millions of supporters** en su punto más álgido, el movimiento tenía millones de seguidores; **at the ~ of the battle** en los momentos más críticos de la batalla; **the ~ of fashion** la última moda; **at the ~ of summer** en pleno verano; **the dollar has soared to new ~s** el dólar ha escalado a nuevas cotas; *see also* **dizzy**
[5] (= *utmost degree*) colmo *m*; **it is the ~ of arrogance/stupidity** es el colmo de la arrogancia/la estupidez

heighten ['haɪtn] Ⓐ VT [1] (= *increase*) aumentar, acrecentar
[2] (= *enhance*) realzar, hacer destacar
Ⓑ VI (*fig*) aumentarse

heinous ['heɪnəs] ADJ atroz, nefasto

heir [ɛəʳ] N heredero/a *m/f*; **~ apparent** heredero/a *m/f* forzoso/a; **~ at law** (*Jur*) heredero/a *m/f* forzoso/a; **~ to the throne** heredero/a *m/f* al trono; **to be ~ to** (*fig*) ser heredero/a a

heiress ['ɛəres] N (= *wealthy woman*) soltera *f* adinerada; (= *heir*) heredera *f*

heirloom ['ɛəlu:m] N reliquia *f* de familia

heist* [haɪst] Ⓐ N (= *hold-up*) atraco *m* a mano armada
Ⓑ VT robar a mano armada

held [held] PT, PP *of* **hold**

Helen ['helɪn] N Elena, Helena

helical ['helɪkəl] ADJ helicoidal

helices ['helɪsi:z] NPL *of* **helix**

helicopter ['helɪkɒptəʳ] Ⓐ N helicóptero *m*
Ⓑ VT **to ~ troops in** transportar tropas por helicóptero, helitransportar tropas
Ⓒ CPD ► **helicopter gunship** N helicóptero *m* de combate ► **helicopter pad** N = **helipad** ► **helicopter station** N = **heliport**

heliograph ['hi:lɪəʊgrɑ:f] N heliógrafo *m*

heliostat ['hi:lɪəʊstæt] N heliostato *m*

heliotrope ['hi:lɪətrəʊp] N heliotropo *m*

helipad ['helɪpæd] N plataforma *f* de helicóptero, pista *f* de helicóptero

heliport ['helɪpɔ:t] N helipuerto *m*

helium ['hi:lɪəm] N helio *m*

helix ['hi:lɪks] N (*pl* **helixes** *or* **helices** ['helɪ,si:z]) hélice *f*

hell [hel] Ⓐ N [1] (= *underworld, fig*) infierno *m*; **life became ~** la vida se convirtió en un infierno; ✦*IDIOMS* **to be ~ on earth** ser un infierno; **till ~ freezes over** hasta que las ranas críen pelo; **to give sb ~: she gave me ~ when she found out** (= *scold*) me puso de vuelta y media cuando se enteró, me puso como un trapo cuando se enteró*; **my back's giving me ~** esta espalda me está haciendo la vida imposible; **to go through ~** pasar las de Caín; **I've been going through ~, wondering where you were** he estado preocupadísimo, preguntándome dónde estarías; **come ~ or high water** pase lo que pase; **I'm going to finish this come ~ or high water** voy a terminar esto aunque me cueste la vida *or* pase lo que pase; **he's determined to support them come ~ or high water** está decidido a apoyarlos contra viento y marea *or* pase lo que pase; **~ for leather** como un(os) endemoniado(s); **he drove ~ for leather to the airport** condujo hasta el aeropuerto como un endemoniado; **all ~ broke loose** *or* **was let loose** se armó el gran follón *or* la grande; **to play (merry) ~ with sth*** hacer estragos en algo, trastornar algo; **to raise ~ (about sth)*** (= *protest*) armarla (por algo)*, liar un taco (por algo)*; **I'll see you/her** *etc* **in ~ first** antes prefiero morir; **he doesn't stand a snowball** *or* **snowflake in ~'s chance** (*Brit*) no tiene ni la menor posibilidad, lo tiene muy difícil *or* muy crudo*; ✦*PROVS* **~ hath no fury like a woman scorned** no hay mayor peligro que el de una mujer despechada; **the road** *or* **path** *or* **way to ~ is paved with good intentions** el camino del infierno está lleno de buenas intenciones
[2] (*) (*as intensifier*) **(as) ... as ~**: **it was as hot as ~** hacía un calor infernal; **I'm mad as ~** estoy como una cabra* *or* una chota*; **I sure as ~ won't be going back there** pierde cuidado que no volveré a ese sitio; **they did it just for the ~ of it** lo hicieron por puro capricho *or* porque sí; **like ~**: **"I'll go myself" — "like ~ you will!"** —iré yo mismo —¡ni lo sueñes! *or* ¡ni hablar!; **"I swam 100 lengths" — "like ~ you did"** —nadé cien largos —¡eso no te lo crees ni tú!; **to run like ~** correr como un demonio *or* un diablo; **it hurts**

like ~ duele una barbaridad; **a ~ of a: there were a ~ of a lot of people there** había un montañazo de gente; **that's one ~ of a lot of money** eso sí que es un verdadero dineral; **a ~ of a noise** un ruido de todos los demonios, un ruido tremendo; **we had a ~ of a time** (= *good*) lo pasamos en grande *or* (*LAm*) regio; (= *bad*) lo pasamos fatal; **the ~: to beat the ~ out of sb** dar una paliza de padre y muy señor mío a algn*; **to scare the ~ out of sb** darle un susto de muerte a algn; **to ~: I hope to ~ you're right** Dios quiera que tengas razón; **I wish to ~ he'd go** ojalá se fuera de una vez por todas; **what the ~, I've got nothing to lose** ¡qué narices! *or* ¡qué más da! no tengo nada que perder; **what the ~ do you want?** ¿qué demonios *or* diablos quieres?; **who the ~ are you?** ¿quién demonios *or* diablos eres tú?

3 (‡) (*as interjection*) **(oh) ~!** ¡caray!*, ¡mierda!‡; **~'s bells!**† ¡válgame Dios!*; **get the ~ out of here!** ¡vete al diablo!‡; **let's get the ~ out of here!** ¡larguémonos de aquí!*; **go to ~!** ¡vete al diablo!‡; **~, no!** ¡ni lo sueñes!, ¡ni hablar!; **~'s teeth!**† ¡válgame Dios!*; **to ~ with it!** ¡a hacer puñetas!‡; **to ~ with him!** ¡que se vaya a hacer puñetas!‡; *see also* **bloody**

Ⓑ CPD ► **hell's angel** N ángel *m* del infierno

he'll [hiːl] = **he will, he shall**

hellacious* [he'leɪʃəs] ADJ (*US*) infernal

hellbent ['hel'bent] ADJ **to be ~ on doing sth** *or* (*US*) **to do sth** estar totalmente resuelto a hacer algo

hellcat ['helkæt] N harpía *f*, bruja *f*

hellebore ['helɪbɔːʳ] N eléboro *m*

Hellene ['heliːn] N heleno/a *m/f*

Hellenic [he'liːnɪk] ADJ helénico

Hellespont ['helɪspɒnt] N Helesponto *m*

hellfire ['hel'faɪəʳ] N llamas *fpl* del infierno

hellhole ['helhəʊl] N infierno *m*

hellish* ['helɪʃ] Ⓐ ADJ infernal, de muerte

Ⓑ ADV muy, terriblemente

hellishly* ['helɪʃlɪ] ADV muy, terriblemente

hello [hʌ'ləʊ] EXCL 1 (= *greeting*) ¡hola!, ¿qué tal?, ¿qué hubo? (*Mex, Chile*)

2 (*Telec*) (= *answering*) ¡diga!, ¡hola!, ¡bueno! (*Mex*), ¡aló! (*S. Cone*); (= *calling*) ¡oiga!, ¡escuche!

3 (= *surprise*) ¡vaya!, ¡ándale! (*LAm*); **~, what's all this!** ¡vaya *or* hombre!, ¿qué tenemos aquí?

4 (= *attention*) ¡oiga!, ¡escuche!

hell-raiser* ['helreɪzəʳ] N **he has a reputation as a ~** tiene fama de montar siempre la bronca; **he is a real ~** siempre monta la bronca*, es un broncas*

helluva‡ ['heləvə] = **hell of a**; *see* **hell**

helm [helm] N (*Naut*) timón *m*; **to be at the ~** (*lit, fig*) estar al timón

helmet ['helmɪt] N (*gen*) casco *m*; (*Hist*) yelmo *m*

helmsman ['helmzmən] N (*pl* **helmsmen**) timonel *m*

helmswoman ['helmz,wʊmən] N (*pl* **helmswomen**) timonel *f*

▼**help** [help] Ⓐ N 1 (= *assistance*) ayuda *f*; **thanks for your ~** gracias por ayudarme, gracias por tu ayuda; **the books were not much ~** los libros no me sirvieron de mucho; **to ask (sb) for ~** pedir ayuda (a algn); **he is beyond ~** ya no se puede hacer nada por él; **to call for ~** (= *ask for help*) pedir ayuda or auxilio; (= *shout for help*) pedir ayuda *or* auxilio a gritos; **to come to sb's ~** acudir en ayuda *or* auxilio de algn; **financial ~** ayuda *f* económica; **to get ~: he rushed off to get ~** salió corriendo en busca de ayuda; **you'll get no ~ from me** yo no te pienso ayudar; **to go to sb's ~** acudir en ayuda *or* auxilio de algn; **you've been a great ~ to me** me has ayudado muchísimo; **you're a great ~!** (*iro*) ¡valiente ayuda!; **medical ~** asistencia *f* médica; **it's no ~ (to say that)** no sirve de nada (decir eso); **there's no ~ for it but to ...** no hay más remedio que + *subjun*; **to be of ~ to sb** ayudar a algn; **can I be of ~?** ¿puedo ayudar?; **I was glad to be of ~** me alegré de poder ayudar; **you should seek professional ~** deberías consultar a un profesional, deberías pedir asesoramiento; **to shout for ~** pedir ayuda *or* auxilio a gritos; **I could use some ~** una ayudita no me vendría mal; **with the ~ of** con la ayuda de; **with his brother's ~** con la ayuda de su hermano; **with the ~ of a knife** con un cuchillo, ayudándose con un cuchillo

2 (= *helpers*) **we're short of ~ in the shop** nos falta personal en la tienda; **she has no ~ in the house** no tiene a nadie que le ayude en la casa

3 (= *cleaner*) asistenta *f*; *see also* **home C, mother C**

Ⓑ VT 1 (= *aid, assist*) ayudar; **he got his brother to ~ him** consiguió que su hermano lo ayudara; **that won't ~ you** eso no te va a servir de nada, eso no te va a ayudar; **can I ~ you?** (*in shop*) ¿qué deseaba?, ¿en qué le puedo servir?; **to ~ (to) do sth** ayudar a hacer algo; **to ~ sb (to) do sth** ayudar a algn a hacer algo; **to ~ each other/one another** ayudarse el uno al otro; **to ~ sb across the road** ayudar a algn a cruzar la calle; **to ~ sb to their feet** ayudar a algn a levantarse; **to ~ sb on/off with his coat** ayudar a algn a ponerse/quitarse el abrigo; **I couldn't stand so he ~ed me up** no me podía poner de pie así que él me ayudó; **let me ~ you with that suitcase** deja que te ayude *or* que te eche una mano con esa maleta; ✦*IDIOM* **so ~ me God** (*as part of oath*) y que Dios me ayude; **so ~ me, I'll kill him!*** ¡te lo juro que lo mato!*

2 (*at table*) **to ~ sb to soup/vegetables** servir sopa/verdura a algn

3 (= *avoid*) evitar; **"why are you laughing?" — "I can't ~ it"** —¿por qué te ríes? —no lo puedo evitar; **I can't ~ it, I just don't like him** es superior a mí, me cae mal; **"it's rather late now" — "I can't ~ that, you should have come earlier"** —ahora es bastante tarde —no es mi culpa, tenías que haber llegado antes; **it can't be ~ed** no hay más remedio, ¿qué se le va a hacer?; **he won't if I can ~ it** si de mí depende, no lo hará; **can I ~ it if it rains?** ¿es mi culpa si llueve?; **don't spend more than you can ~** no gastes más de lo necesario; **you can't ~ feeling sorry for him** no puede uno (por) menos de sentir lástima por él

4 **to ~ o.s.** 4·1 (= *assist o.s.*) ayudarse a sí mismo; **don't think about ~ing others, think about ~ing yourself** no pienses en ayudar a los demás, piensa en ayudarte a ti mismo; **you won't ~ yourself by keeping silent** no te vas a hacer ningún favor guardando el silencio; ✦*PROV* **God ~s those who ~ themselves** a Dios rogando y con el mazo dando

4·2 (= *serve o.s.*) servirse; **~ yourself!** ¡sírvete!; **she ~ed herself to vegetables** se sirvió verdura

4·3 (= *take sth*) **"can I borrow your pen?" — "~ yourself"** —¿me prestas el bolígrafo? —cógelo

4·4 (*) (= *steal*) **he's ~ed himself to my pencil** me ha mangado el lápiz*

4·5 (= *prevent o.s.*) **I screamed with pain, I couldn't ~ myself** grité del dolor, no lo pude evitar

Ⓒ VI ayudar; **I was only trying to ~** sólo intentaba ayudar; **that doesn't ~ much** eso no sirve de mucho; **it ~s if you plan ahead** resulta más fácil si haces los planes por adelantado; **every little ~s** todo ayuda

Ⓓ EXCL **~!** ¡socorro!, ¡auxilio!

Ⓔ CPD ► **help menu** N (*Comput*) menú *m* de ayuda

►**help along** VT + ADV **she has done much to ~ these negotiations along** ha contribuido considerablemente a que las negociaciones sigan adelante

►**help out** Ⓐ VI + ADV ayudar, echar una mano; **Dad ~ed out with £200** papá ayudó *or* echó una mano con 200 libras

Ⓑ VT + ADV **to ~ sb out** ayudar a algn, echar una mano a algn; **his parents ~ him out financially** sus padres le ayudan *or* le echan una mano económicamente

helper ['helpəʳ] N (*gen*) ayudante *mf*; (= *co-worker*) colaborador(a) *m/f*

helpful ['helpfʊl] ADJ [*person*] atento, servicial; [*suggestion, book, explanation*] útil; [*advice, tip*] útil, práctico; [*medicine, treatment*] eficaz; [*attitude, remark*] positivo; **this cream is ~ in the treatment of allergies** esta pomada es eficaz para tratar alergias; **it would be ~ if you could come** sería de gran ayuda que vinieses; **you have been most ~** ha sido muy amable; **he was very ~ during my illness** me ayudó mucho durante mi enfermedad; **to be ~ to sb** ayudar a algn

helpfully ['helpfəlɪ] ADV [*say, suggest, offer*] amablemente; **they had ~ sent us a map** amablemente, nos habían mandado un mapa; **"it might be here," she said ~** —puede que esté aquí —dijo para ayudar; **the chairs were not very ~ arranged** las sillas no estaban colocadas de una forma muy conveniente

helpfulness ['helpfʊlnɪs] N (= *kindness*) amabilidad *f*; (= *usefulness*) utilidad *f*

helping ['helpɪŋ] Ⓐ ADJ **to give** *or* **lend sb a ~ hand** echarle una mano a algn

Ⓑ N porción *f*, ración *f*; **he came back for second ~s** vino a servirse más

helpless ['helplɪs] ADJ 1 (= *powerless*) [*victim*] indefenso, inerme (*more frm*); [*feeling*] impotente; [*gesture*] de impotencia; (= *incapacitated*) incapacitado; **he is ~ without his crutches** sin las muletas no puede hacer nada; **we were ~ to prevent it** no pudimos hacer nada para impedirlo; **to feel ~** sentirse impotente; **she is a ~ invalid** está inválida y no puede valerse por sí misma; **to be ~ with laughter** estar muerto de (la) risa; **he lay ~ on the ground** yacía indefenso *or* inerme en el suelo

2 (= *vulnerable*) indefenso; **as ~ as a baby** tan indefenso como un bebé

helplessly ['helplɪslɪ] ADV 1 (= *powerlessly*) [*watch, stand by*] sin poder hacer nada; [*struggle*] en vano; [*shrug*] en un gesto de impotencia; **"I can't," he said ~** —no puedo —dijo con una expresión de impotencia

2 (= *uncontrollably*) [*laugh, sob, sneeze*] sin poder contenerse

helplessness ['helplɪsnɪs] N (= *powerlessness*) impotencia *f*; **he threw up his hands in a gesture of ~** alzó las manos en un gesto de impotencia; **the ~ of the situation made her ill with worry** era una situación de impotencia tal que enfermó de preocupación; **our ~ against enemy aircraft** nuestra indefensión ante los aviones enemigos

➤ LANGUAGE IN USE: **help** A1, B1, C 3

helpline ['helplaın] N (*esp Brit*) línea *f* de socorro

helpmate ['helpmeıt] N (= *companion*) buen(a) compañero/a *m/f*; (= *spouse*) esposo/a *m/f*

Helsinki ['helsıŋkı] N Helsinki *m*

helter-skelter ['heltə'skeltəʳ] Ⓐ ADV (= *in a rush*) atropelladamente; (= *in confusion*) a la desbandada
Ⓑ N [1] (*Brit*) (*at fair*) tobogán *m*
[2] (= *rush*) desbandada *f* general

hem [hem] Ⓐ N dobladillo *m*, bastilla *f*
Ⓑ VT (*Sew*) hacer el dobladillo de, coser el dobladillo de

►**hem in** VT + ADV (*lit*) (= *surround*) cercar; (= *corner*) arrinconar; **our forces were ~med in to both east and west** nuestras fuerzas estaban cercadas por el este y el oeste; **I feel ~med in** me siento constreñido *or* limitado

he-man ['hi:mæn] N (*pl* **he-men**) macho *m*

hematological [,hi:mətə'lɒdʒıkəl] ADJ (*US*) = **haematological**

hematologist [,hi:mə'tɒlədʒıst] N (*US*) = **haematologist**

hematology [,hi:mə'tɒlədʒı] N (*US*) = **haematology**

hematoma [,hi:mə'təʊmə] N (*US*) = **haematoma**

hemicycle ['hemısaıkl] N hemiciclo *m*

hemiplegia [hemı'pli:dʒıə] N hemiplejía *f*

hemiplegic [,hemı'pli:dʒık] Ⓐ ADJ hemipléjico
Ⓑ N hemipléjico/a *m/f*

hemisphere ['hemısfıəʳ] N (*Geog*) hemisferio *m*

hemispheric ['hemısferık] ADJ hemisférico

hemistich ['hemıstık] N hemistiquio *m*

hemline ['hemlaın] N (*Sew*) bajo *m* (del vestido)

hemlock ['hemlɒk] N (= *plant, poison*) cicuta *f*

hemo... *etc* ['hi:məʊ] (*US*) = **haemo...** *etc*

hemp [hemp] N [1] (= *plant, fibre*) cáñamo *m*
[2] (= *drug*) hachís *m*

hemstitch ['hemstıtʃ] N vainica *f*

hen [hen] Ⓐ N (= *fowl*) gallina *f*; (= *female bird*) hembra *f*
Ⓑ ADJ **the ~ bird** el pájaro hembra
Ⓒ CPD ► **hen coop** N gallinero *m* ► **hen night** N (*esp Brit**) (= *girls' night*) reunión *f* de mujeres; (*before marriage*) despedida *f* de soltera ► **hen party** N = **hen night**

henbane ['henbeın] N beleño *m*

hence [hens] ADV [1] (= *therefore*) por lo tanto, de ahí; **~ my letter** de allí que le escribiera; **~ the fact that ...** de ahí que ...
[2] (*frm*) (*time*) **five years ~** de aquí a cinco años
[3] (†) (*place*) de *or* desde aquí; **~!** (*poet*) ¡fuera de aquí!

henceforth ['hens'fɔ:θ] ADV (*frm*) (= *from now on*) de hoy en adelante, a partir de hoy; (= *from then on*) en lo sucesivo

henceforward ['hens'fɔ:wəd] ADV = **henceforth**

henceforwards ['hens'fɔ:wədz] ADV (*esp Brit*) = **henceforth**

henchman ['hentʃmən] N (*pl* **henchmen**) (*esp Pol*) (= *follower*) secuaz *m*; (= *guard*) guardaespaldas *m inv*

hendecasyllabic ['hendekəsı'læbık] ADJ endecasílabo

hendecasyllable ['hendekə,sıləbl] N endecasílabo *m*

henhouse ['henhaʊs] N (*pl* **henhouses** ['henhaʊzız]) gallinero *m*

henna ['henə] N alheña *f*

hennaed ['henəd] ADJ [*hair*] alheñado

henpecked ['henpekt] ADJ dominado por su mujer; **a ~ husband*** un marido dominado por su mujer, un calzonazos (*Sp*)

Henry ['henrı] N Enrique

hepatitis [,hepə'taıtıs] N hepatitis *f*

heptagon ['heptəgən] N heptágono *m*

heptagonal [hep'tægənəl] ADJ heptagonal

heptameter [hep'tæmıtəʳ] N heptámetro *m*

heptathlon [hep'tæθlən] N heptatlón *m*

her [hɜ:ʳ] Ⓐ PRON [1] (= *direct object*) la; **I can see ~** la veo; **look at ~!** ¡mírala!; **I have never seen HER** a ella no la he visto nunca
[2] (= *indirect object*) le; (*combined with direct object pron*) se; **you must tell ~ the truth** tienes que decirle la verdad; **yes of course I gave ~ the book** sí, claro que le di el libro; **yes of course I gave them to ~** sí, claro que se los di; **I gave the book to HER not Peter** le di el libro a ella, no a Peter; **I'm speaking to HER not you** le estoy hablando a ella, no a ti; **give it to ~ when you go to Liverpool** dáselo cuando vayas a Liverpool; **I gave it to HER not Peter** se lo di a ella, no a Peter
[3] (*after prep, in comparisons, with verb "to be"*) ella; **he thought of ~** pensó en ella; **without ~** sin ella; **I'm going with ~** voy con ella; **she was carrying it on ~** lo llevaba consigo; **if I were ~** yo que ella; **younger than ~** más joven *or* menor que ella; **it's ~** es ella
Ⓑ POSS ADJ (*with singular noun*) su; (*with plural noun*) sus; **~ book/table** su libro/mesa; **~ friends** sus amigos

Heracles ['herə,kli:z] N Heracles

Heraclitus [,herə'klaıtəs] N Heráclito

herald ['herəld] Ⓐ N (= *messenger*) heraldo *m*; (*fig*) precursor(a) *m/f*
Ⓑ VT (*fig*) anunciar

heraldic [he'rældık] ADJ heráldico

heraldry ['herəldrı] N heráldica *f*

herb [hɜ:b] (*US*) [ɜ:b] Ⓐ N hierba *f*
Ⓑ CPD ► **herb garden** N jardín *m* de hierbas finas ► **herb tea** N infusión *f* de hierbas

herbaceous [hɜ:'beıʃəs] ADJ herbáceo

herbage ['hɜ:bıdʒ] N herbaje *m*, vegetación *f*

herbal ['hɜ:bəl] ADJ de hierbas, herbario; **~ tea** infusión *f* de hierbas

herbalism ['hɜ:bəlızəm] N fitoterapia *f* (*uso de plantas medicinales*)

herbalist ['hɜ:bəlıst] N herbolario/a *m/f*

herbarium [hɜ:'beərıəm] N (*pl* **herbariums** *or* **herbaria** [hɜ:'beərıə]) herbario *m*

herbert†* ['hɜ:bət] N (*Brit*) tipo* *m*, tío* *m*; **some ~ ...** algún tío ...*

herbicide ['hɜ:bısaıd] N herbicida *m*

herbivore ['hɜ:bı,vɔ:ʳ] N herbívoro *m*

herbivorous [hɜ:'bıvərəs] ADJ herbívoro

herculean [,hɜ:kju'li:ən], **Herculean** ADJ hercúleo; **~ task** obra *f* de romanos

Hercules ['hɜ:kjuli:z] N Hércules

herd [hɜ:d] Ⓐ N [*of cattle*] rebaño *m*, manada *f*; [*of goats*] rebaño *m*; [*of elephants*] manada *f*; [*of pigs*] piara *f*; [*of people*] multitud *f*, tropel *m*; **the common ~** el vulgo, las masas
Ⓑ VT (= *drive, gather*) [+ *animals*] llevar en manada; [+ *people*] reunir
Ⓒ CPD ► **herd instinct** N instinto *m* gregario

►**herd together** Ⓐ VI + ADV apiñarse, agruparse
Ⓑ VT + ADV agrupar, reunir

herd-book ['hɜ:dbʊk] N libro *m* genealógico

herdsman ['hɜ:dzmən] N (*pl* **herdsmen**) [*of cattle*] vaquero *m*; [*of sheep*] pastor *m*

here [hıəʳ] Ⓐ ADV [1] (= *in this place*) aquí; **I live ~** vivo aquí; **she's not ~ at the moment** no está (aquí) en este momento; **I'm not ~ to listen to your complaints** no estoy aquí para escuchar tus quejas; **~!** (*at roll call*) ¡presente!; **winter is ~** ha llegado el invierno, ya está aquí el invierno; **my friend ~ will do it** este amigo mío lo hará; **he's well known around ~** es muy conocido por aquí; **in ~, please** aquí (dentro), por favor; *see also* **same B1**, **today**
[2] (= *to this place*) aquí, acá (*esp LAm*); **come ~!** ¡ven aquí *or* (*esp LAm*) acá!; *see also* **look B1**
[3] (*stating or offering sth*) **~ are the books** aquí están los libros; **~ he comes** ya viene; **~'s what I think** esto es lo que pienso; **~ we are, I've found it** aquí está, lo encontré; **~ it is, under the cushion** aquí está, debajo del cojín; **did you want the corkscrew? ~ it is** ¿querías el sacacorchos? aquí lo tienes; **~ you are, you can have my seat** toma, puedes sentarte en mi sitio; **~ you are, I've fixed it** toma *or* aquí lo tienes, lo he arreglado
[4] (= *at this time*) **and ~ he laughed** y entonces se rió; **~ I should remind you that ...** ahora os debería recordar que ...; **it's my job that's at risk ~** lo que me estoy jugando es el trabajo; **what we're talking about ~ is ...** de lo que esto se trata es ...
[5] (= *on this point*) en este punto; **I disagree with you ~** no estoy de acuerdo contigo en este punto
[6] (*in phrases*) **~ we go again!** ¡ya estamos otra vez!; **~ goes!** ¡ahí va!; **~ lies ...** aquí yacen los restos de ...; **whether or not he realized was neither ~ nor there** el que se hubiera dado cuenta o no no venía al caso; **the difference of £5 was neither ~ nor there** las 5 libras de diferencia no iban a ninguna parte; **~ and now** ahora mismo; **I must warn you ~ and now that ...** te tengo que advertir ahora mismo que ...; **I'm out of ~*** me largo*; **~ and there: I do a bit of teaching ~ and there** suelo dar alguna que otra clase; **he could only understand a word ~ and there** sólo entendía palabras sueltas; **~, there and everywhere** en todas partes; **~'s to ...: ~'s to the happy couple!** ¡a la salud de los novios!; **~'s to your new job!** ¡por tu nuevo trabajo!
Ⓑ EXCL **~, you try and open it!** ¡toma, intenta abrirlo tú!; **~, that's my dinner you're eating!** ¡oye tú, que ésa es mi cena!
Ⓒ N **the ~ and now** el presente

hereabouts ['hıərə,baʊts] ADV por aquí (cerca)

hereafter [hıər'ɑ:ftəʳ] Ⓐ ADV (*frm*) a continuación; (= *from now on*) de aquí en adelante, a partir de ahora
Ⓑ N **the ~** el más allá

hereby ['hıə'baı] ADV (*frm*) por este medio; (*in letter, document*) por la presente

hereditaments [,herı'dıtəmənts] NPL herencia *f*, bienes *mpl* por heredar

hereditary [hı'redıtərı] ADJ hereditario; **~ disease** enfermedad *f* hereditaria

heredity [hı'redıtı] N herencia *f*

herein [,hıər'ın] ADV (*frm*) (= *in this matter*) en esto; (= *in this writing*) en ésta

hereinafter [,hıərın'ɑ:ftəʳ] ADV (*Jur*) más adelante, más abajo, a continuación

hereof [,hıər'ɒv] ADV (*frm*) de esto

heresiarch [he'ri:zıɑ:k] N heresiarca *mf*

heresy ['herəsı] N herejía *f*

heretic ['herətık] N hereje *mf*

heretical [hı'retıkəl] ADJ herético

hereto [ˌhɪə'tuː] ADV (*Jur*) a esto; **the parties ~** las partes abajofirmantes

heretofore [ˌhɪətʊ'fɔːʳ] ADV (*frm*) (= *up to specified point*) hasta aquí; (= *up to now*) hasta ahora, hasta este momento; (= *previously*) con anterioridad

hereupon ['hɪərə'pɒn] ADV (*frm*) en ese momento, en esto

herewith ['hɪə'wɪð] ADV (*frm*) (*Comm*) **I enclose ~ a letter** le adjunto (con la presente) una carta

heritable ['herɪtəbl] ADJ [*objects, property*] heredable, hereditable; [*person*] que puede heredar

heritage ['herɪtɪdʒ] Ⓐ N herencia *f*; (*fig*) (*also* **national ~**) patrimonio *m* (nacional)
Ⓑ CPD ► **heritage centre** N (*Brit*) museo *m* (*local, de artesanía etc*)

hermaphrodite [hɜː'mæfrədaɪt] Ⓐ ADJ hermafrodita
Ⓑ N hermafrodita *mf*

hermetic [hɜː'metɪk] ADJ hermético

hermetically [hɜː'metɪkəlɪ] ADV herméticamente; **~ sealed** cerrado herméticamente

hermeticism [hɜː'metɪsɪzəm] N hermetismo *m*

hermit ['hɜːmɪt] Ⓐ N ermitaño/a *m/f*
Ⓑ CPD ► **hermit crab** N ermitaño *m*

hermitage ['hɜːmɪtɪdʒ] N ermita *f*

hernia ['hɜːnɪə] N (*pl* **hernias** *or* **herniae** ['hɜːnɪˌiː]) (*Med*) hernia *f*

hero ['hɪərəʊ] Ⓐ N (*pl* **heroes**) héroe *m*; [*of film, book*] protagonista *mf*, personaje *m* principal
Ⓑ CPD ► **hero worship** N adulación *f*

Herod ['herəd] N Herodes

heroic [hɪ'rəʊɪk] ADJ heroico; **he made a ~ effort to get up** hizo un heroico esfuerzo por levantarse; **a stadium of ~ proportions** un estadio de dimensiones colosales; *see also* **heroics**

heroically [hɪ'rəʊɪkəlɪ] ADV heroicamente

heroics [hɪ'rəʊɪks] NSING (*slightly pej*) (= *deeds*) acciones *fpl* heroicas, actos *mpl* de heroicidad; (= *behaviour*) comportamiento *m* atrevido; (= *language*) lenguaje *m* altisonante; **we don't want any ~** no queremos actos heroicos *or* ninguna heroicidad

heroin ['herəʊɪn] Ⓐ N heroína *f* (*droga*)
Ⓑ CPD ► **heroin addict** N heroinómano/a *m/f* ► **heroin addiction** N adicción *f* a la heroína, dependencia *f* de la heroína, heroinomanía *f* ► **heroin user** N heroinómano/a *m/f*

heroine ['herəʊɪn] N heroína *f*; [*of film, book*] protagonista *f*, personaje *m* principal

heroism ['herəʊɪzəm] N heroísmo *m*

heron ['herən] N garza *f* real

herpes ['hɜːpiːz] N herpes *m*

herring ['herɪŋ] Ⓐ N (*pl* **herrings** *or* **herring**) arenque *m*; **red ~** (*fig*) pista *f* falsa, despiste *m*
Ⓑ CPD ► **herring gull** N gaviota *f* argéntea ► **the herring pond** N (*hum*) el charco; ✦*IDIOM* **to cross the ~ pond** cruzar el charco

herringbone ['herɪŋbəʊn] ADJ **~ pattern** (*on material*) diseño *m* en espiga; (*of floor*) espinapez *m*; **~ stitch** punto *m* de escapulario

hers [hɜːz] POSS PRON (*referring to singular possession*) (el/la) suyo/a; (*referring to plural possession*) (los/las) suyos/as; **this car is ~** este coche es suyo *or* de ella; **is that car ~?** ¿es suyo *or* de ella ese coche?; **"whose is this?" — "it's ~"** —¿de quién es esto? —es de ella; **a friend of ~** un amigo suyo; **my car is much bigger than ~** mi coche es mucho más grande que el suyo *or* el de ella; **"is this her coat?" — "no, ~ is black"** —¿es éste su abrigo? —no, el suyo *or* el de ella es negro; **"is this her scarf?" — "no, ~ is red"** —¿es ésta su bufanda? —no la suya *or* la de ella es roja; **my parents and ~** mis padres y los suyos *or* y los de ella

herself [hɜː'self] PRON 1 (*reflexive*) se; **she washed ~** se lavó
2 (*emphatic*) ella misma; (*after prep*) sí (misma); **she did it ~** lo hizo ella misma; **she went ~** fue ella misma *or* en persona; **she talked mainly about ~** habló principalmente de sí misma; **she said to ~** dijo entre *or* para sí
3 (*phrases*) **she came by ~** vino sola; **she did it by ~** lo hizo ella sola; **she's not ~** no se encuentra nada bien

Herts [hɑːts] N ABBR = **Hertfordshire**

hertz [hɜːts] N hercio *m*, hertzio *m*, hertz *m*

he's [hiːz] = **he is**, **he has**

hesitancy ['hezɪtənsɪ] N = **hesitation**

hesitant ['hezɪtənt] ADJ (*gen*) vacilante; [*character*] indeciso; **to be ~ about doing sth** no decidirse a hacer algo

hesitantly ['hezɪtəntlɪ] ADV indecisamente; [*speak, suggest*] con vacilación

▼**hesitate** ['hezɪteɪt] VI (*gen*) vacilar; (*in speech*) vacilar, titubear; **to ~ to do sth** dudar en hacer algo, vacilar en hacer algo; **I will not ~ to take unpopular decisions** no dudaré *or* vacilaré en tomar decisiones poco populares; **I ~ to call this art** no me atrevo a llamar arte a esto; **don't ~ to ask (me)** no vaciles en pedírmelo, no dejes de pedírmelo; **I ~ to condemn him outright** no me decido a condenarlo del todo; **to ~ before doing sth** dudar antes de hacer algo; **to ~ about** *or* **over doing sth** vacilar en hacer algo; **he ~s at nothing** no vacila ante nada

hesitation [ˌhezɪ'teɪʃən] N vacilación *f*, indecisión *f*; **I have no ~ in saying …** no vacilo en decir …; **without the slightest ~** sin vacilar siquiera, sin pensarlo dos veces

hessian ['hesɪən] (*esp Brit*) Ⓐ N arpillera *f*
Ⓑ ADJ de arpillera

het* [het] ADJ *see* **het up**

hetero* ['hetərəʊ] ADJ, N = **heterosexual**

heterodox ['hetərədɒks] ADJ heterodoxo

heterodoxy ['hetərədɒksɪ] N heterodoxia *f*

heterogeneity ['hetərəʊdʒə'niːətɪ] N heterogeneidad *f*

heterogeneous ['hetərəʊ'dʒiːnɪəs] ADJ heterogéneo

heterosexism ['hetərəʊ'seksɪzm] N *ideología que discrimina contra la homosexualidad*

heterosexual ['hetərəʊ'seksjuəl] Ⓐ ADJ heterosexual
Ⓑ N heterosexual *mf*

heterosexuality ['hetərəʊˌseksjʊ'ælɪtɪ] N heterosexualidad *f*

het up* [ˌhet'ʌp] ADJ **to get ~** acalorarse, emocionarse (**about, over** por); **don't get so ~!** ¡tranquilízate!, ¡no te sulfures!

heuristic [hjʊə'rɪstɪk] ADJ heurístico; **~ search** investigación *f* heurística

HEW N ABBR (*US*) = **Department of Health, Education and Welfare**

hew [hjuː] (*pt* **hewed**; *pp* **hewed, hewn**) VT (= *cut*) cortar; [+ *trees*] talar; (= *shape, work*) labrar, tallar

► **hew down** VT + ADV talar

► **hew out** VT + ADV excavar; **a figure ~n out of the rock** una figura tallada en la roca; **to ~ out a career** hacerse una carrera

hewn [hjuːn] PP *of* **hew**

hex[1]* [heks] (*US*) Ⓐ N 1 (= *spell*) maleficio *m*, mal *m* de ojo
2 (= *witch*) bruja *f*
Ⓑ VT embrujar

hex[2] [heks] ADJ (*Comput*) hexadecimal; **~ code** código *m* hexadecimal

hexadecimal [ˌheksə'desɪməl] ADJ hexadecimal; **~ notation** notación *f* hexadecimal

hexagon ['heksəgən] N hexágono *m*

hexagonal [hek'sægənəl] ADJ hexagonal

hexagram ['heksəˌgræm] N hexagrama *m*

hexameter [hek'sæmɪtəʳ] N hexámetro *m*

hey [heɪ] EXCL ¡oye!, ¡oiga!

heyday ['heɪdeɪ] N auge *m*; **in the ~ of the theatre** cuando el teatro estaba en su apogeo; **in his ~** en sus buenos tiempos

Hezbollah [ˌhezbə'lɑː] N Hezbolá *m*, Hizbulá *m*

HF N ABBR = **high frequency**

hg N ABBR (= **hectogram(s)**) hg

HGV N ABBR (= **heavy goods vehicle**) vehículo *m* pesado

HH ABBR 1 (= **His** *or* **Her Highness**) S.A.
2 (*Rel*) (= **His Holiness**) S.S.

HHS N ABBR (*US*) = **Health and Human Services**

HI ABBR (*US*) = **Hawaii**

hi [haɪ] EXCL ¡oye!; (*greeting*) ¡hola!, ¡qué hubo! (*Mex, Chile*)

hiatus [haɪ'eɪtəs] N (*pl* **hiatuses** *or* **hiatus**) (*Gram*) hiato *m*; (*fig*) vacío *m*, interrupción *f*

hibernate ['haɪbəneɪt] VI hibernar, invernar

hibernation [ˌhaɪbə'neɪʃən] N hibernación *f*, invernación *f*

Hibernia [haɪ'bɜːnɪə] N Hibernia *f*

hibiscus [hɪ'bɪskəs] N (*pl* **hibiscuses**) hibisco *m*

hic [hɪk] EXCL ¡hip!

hiccough, **hiccup** ['hɪkʌp] Ⓐ N 1 hipo *m*; **it gives me ~s** me da hipo, me hace hipar; **to have ~s** tener hipo
2 **a slight ~ in the proceedings** (*fig*) una pequeña dificultad *or* interrupción en los actos
Ⓑ VT decir hipando; **"yes," he ~ed** —sí —dijo hipando
Ⓒ VI hipar

hick* [hɪk] (*US pej*) Ⓐ ADJ rústico, de aldea
Ⓑ N pueblerino/a *m/f*, paleto/a *m/f* (*Sp**)

hickey* ['hɪkɪ] N (*US*) (= *pimple*) grano *m*; (= *love-bite*) mordisco *m* amoroso, chupón* *m*

hickory ['hɪkərɪ] N nuez *f* dura, nogal *m* americano

hid [hɪd] PT *of* **hide**

hidden ['hɪdn] Ⓐ PP *of* **hide**[1]
Ⓑ ADJ escondido; (*fig*) [*meaning, truth*] oculto, secreto; **~ assets** activo *msing* oculto; **~ reserves** reservas *fpl* ocultas

hide[1] [haɪd] (*pt* **hid**; *pp* **hidden**) Ⓐ VT (*gen*) esconder (**from** de); [+ *grief*] ocultar, disimular; **to ~ sth from sb** esconder algo de algn; **to ~ one's face in one's hands** taparse la cara con las manos; **to ~ the truth** encubrir la verdad; **I have nothing to ~** no tengo nada que ocultar
Ⓑ VI esconderse, ocultarse (**from** de); **he's hiding behind his illness** se ampara en su enfermedad; **he's hiding behind his boss** está buscando la protección de su jefe

► **hide away** Ⓐ VI + ADV esconderse
Ⓑ VT + ADV esconder, ocultar

► **hide out**, **hide up** VI + ADV esconderse

hide[2] [haɪd] N (= *skin*) piel *f*, pellejo *m*; (*tanned*) cuero *m*; ✦*IDIOMS* **to save one's ~** salvar el pellejo; **I haven't seen ~ nor hair of him** no le he visto el pelo*; **to tan sb's ~** darle una paliza a algn

➤ LANGUAGE IN USE: **hesitate** 3

hide[3] [haɪd] N (*Hunting*) paranza *f*, trepa *f*; (*Orn*) observatorio *m*

hide-and-seek ['haɪdən'siːk] N escondite *m*; **to play ~** jugar al escondite

hideaway ['haɪdəweɪ] N escondite *m*, escondrijo *m*

hidebound ['haɪdbaʊnd] ADJ rígido, aferrado a la tradición

hideous ['hɪdɪəs] ADJ (*gen*) espantoso, horroroso; (= *repugnant*) repugnante, asqueroso; **a ~ mistake** un error terrible

hideously ['hɪdɪəslɪ] ADV horriblemente; **~ ugly** feísimo

hideout ['haɪdaʊt] N guarida *f*, escondrijo *m*

hidey-hole* ['haɪdɪhəʊl] N escondite *m*, escondrijo *m*

hiding[1] ['haɪdɪŋ] Ⓐ N **to be in ~** estar escondido; **to go into ~** esconderse; (*Pol*) pasar a la clandestinidad
Ⓑ CPD ► **hiding place** N escondite *m*, escondrijo *m*

hiding[2] ['haɪdɪŋ] N (= *beating*) paliza *f*; **to give sb a ~** dar una paliza a algn; ✦**IDIOM to be on a ~ to nothing** llevar todas las de perder

hie [haɪ] (††, *hum*) Ⓐ VT apresurar; **to ~ o.s. home** apresurarse a volver a casa
Ⓑ VI ir volando, correr

hierarchic [,haɪə'rɑːkɪk] ADJ = **hierarchical**

hierarchical [,haɪə'rɑːkɪkəl] ADJ jerárquico

hierarchically [,haɪə'rɑːkɪklɪ] ADV jerárquicamente

hierarchy ['haɪərɑːkɪ] N jerarquía *f*

hieratic [haɪə'rætɪk] ADJ (*frm*) hierático

hieroglyph ['haɪərəglɪf] N jeroglífico *m*

hieroglyphic [,haɪərə'glɪfɪk] Ⓐ ADJ jeroglífico
Ⓑ N jeroglífico *m*; **hieroglyphics** jeroglíficos *mpl*; (*fig*) (*) garabatos *mpl*

hifalutin'* [,haɪfə'luːtɪn] = **highfalutin(g)**

hi-fi ['haɪ'faɪ] Ⓐ ABBR of **high fidelity**
Ⓑ N estéreo *m*
Ⓒ ADJ de alta fidelidad; **~ equipment** equipo *m* de alta fidelidad; **~ system** sistema *m* de alta fidelidad

higgledy-piggledy* ['hɪgldɪ'pɪgldɪ] Ⓐ ADV [*be*] en desorden; [*do*] de cualquier modo, a la buena de Dios
Ⓑ ADJ revuelto, desordenado

high [haɪ] Ⓐ ADJ (*compar* **higher**, *superl* **highest**) [1] (= *tall, elevated*) [*building, mountain*] alto; [*plateau*] elevado; [*altitude*] grande; **a building 60 metres ~** un edificio de 60 metros de alto *or* de altura; **it's 20 metres ~** tiene 20 metros de alto *or* de altura; **at ~ altitudes** a grandes altitudes; **the ceilings are very ~** los techos son muy altos; **~ cheekbones** pómulos *mpl* salientes; **he has a ~ forehead** tiene la frente muy ancha; **how ~ is Ben Nevis/that tree?** ¿qué altura tiene el Ben Nevis/ese árbol?; **economic reform is ~ on the agenda** la reforma económica figura entre los asuntos más importantes a tratar; **the river is ~** el río está crecido; **I've known her since she was so ~*** la conozco desde que era así (de pequeña); **the sun was ~ in the sky** el sol daba de pleno; ✦**IDIOMS ~ and dry** [*boat*] varado; **the boats lay at the river's edge, ~ and dry** los botes estaban en la orilla del río, varados; **to leave sb ~ and dry** (= *in a difficult situation*) dejar a algn en la estacada

[2] (= *considerable, great*) [*level, risk, rent, salary, principles*] alto; [*price, tax, number*] alto, elevado; [*speed*] alto, gran; [*quality*] alto, bueno; [*colour*] subido; [*complexion*] (*characteristically*) rojizo; (*temporarily*) enrojecido; [*wind*] fuerte; **they offered me a ~er salary** me ofrecieron un sueldo más alto; **temperatures were in the ~ 80s** las temperaturas alcanzaron los ochenta y muchos, las temperaturas rondaron los 90 grados; **interest rates are ~** los intereses están muy altos; **we offer education of the ~est quality** ofrecemos una educación de la más alta *or* de la mejor calidad; **to have ~ blood pressure** tener la tensión alta, ser hipertenso; **his team was of the ~est calibre** su equipo era del más alto nivel; **to have ~ hopes of sth: I had ~ hopes of being elected** tenía muchas esperanzas de que me eligieran; **parsley is ~ in calcium** el perejil es rico en calcio; **to have a ~ opinion of sb** (= *think highly of*) tener muy buena opinión *or* concepto de algn; (= *be fond of*) tener a algn en alta estima; **to pay a ~ price for sth** (*lit*) pagar mucho dinero por algo; (*fig*) pagar algo muy caro; **to have a ~ temperature** tener mucha fiebre, tener una fiebre muy alta; ✦**IDIOMS to have a ~ old time*** pasarlo en grande*; **it's ~ time ...*: it's ~ time you were in bed*** ya deberías estar acostado desde hace un buen rato; **it's ~ time we were on our way*** ya deberíamos haber salido hace rato; *see also* **gear**, **priority**, **profile**, **spirit**, **stake**, **high A4**

[3] (= *important, superior*) [*rank, position, office*] alto; **~ and mighty: she's too ~ and mighty** es demasiado engreída; **you needn't act so ~ and mighty with me** no tienes por qué ponerte tan engreído conmigo; **she moves in the circles of the ~ and mighty** se mueve en círculos de los poderosos, se mueve en círculos de gente de mucho fuste (*pej*); **~ official** alto funcionario/a *m/f*; ✦**IDIOMS to get (up) on one's ~ horse** subirse a la parra; **there's no need to get (up) on your ~ horse!** ¡no hace falta que te subas a la parra!; **to come down off** *or* **get off one's ~ horse** bajar los humos; **in ~ places: to have friends in ~ places** tener amigos importantes *or* con influencias; **people in ~ places** gente influyente *or* importante

[4] (= *high-pitched*) [*sound, note*] alto; [*voice*] agudo; **he played another ~er note** tocó otra nota más alta; **she can still hit those ~ notes** todavía llega bien a los agudos; **in a ~ voice** con voz aguda; ✦**IDIOM on a ~ note: he ended his career on a ~ note** terminó su carrera con un gran éxito

[5] (*) (= *intoxicated*) **to be ~ (on)** [+ *drink, drugs*] estar colocado (de)*; **to get ~ (on)** [+ *drink, drugs*] colocarse (de)*; **she was ~ on her latest success** estaba encantada *or* entusiasmada con su último éxito; ✦**IDIOM to be (as) ~ as a kite** (*on drugs, drink*) estar totalmente colocado*; (= *confident*) estar que no se cabe en sí

[6] (*Culin*) (= *mature*) [*game, cheese*] que huele fuerte; (= *rotten*) [*meat*] pasado

Ⓑ ADV (*compar* **higher**, *superl* **highest**) [1] (*in height*) [*fly, rise*] a gran altura; **it rose ~ in the air** se elevó a gran altura; **it sailed ~ over the house** volaba a gran altura por encima de la casa; **~ above: an eagle circled ~ above** un águila circulaba en las alturas; **the town is perched ~ above the river** el pueblo está en un alto, sobre el río; **~ above my head** muy por encima de mi cabeza; **to run ~** [*sea*] estar embravecido; [*river*] estar crecido; **feelings were running ~** los ánimos estaban exaltados; **~ up: his farm was ~ up in the mountains** su granja estaba en lo alto de las montañas; **we saw three birds circling very ~ up** vimos tres pájaros circulando en las alturas; **she had put it too ~ up for me to reach** lo había puesto demasiado alto y no llegaba; **his cousin is someone ~ up in the navy** su primo tiene un cargo importante en la marina; ✦**IDIOMS to hold one's head (up) ~** mantener la cabeza bien alta; **to live ~ on the hog** (*US**) vivir como un rajá; **to hunt** *or* **search ~ and low (for sth/sb)** remover el cielo y la tierra (en busca de algo/algn); *see also* **aim**, **fly A1**, **head A1**, **stand C5**

[2] (*in degree, number, strength*) **the bidding went as ~ as £500** las ofertas llegaron hasta 500 libras

Ⓒ N [1] **on ~** (= *in heaven*) en el cielo, en las alturas; **there's been a new directive from on ~** (*fig*) ha habido una nueva directriz de arriba

[2] (= *peak*) **sales have reached an all-time ~** las ventas han alcanzado cifras récord; ✦**IDIOM to be on a ~*** estar a las mil maravillas

[3] (*Fin*) máximo *m*; **the Dow Jones index reached a ~ of 2503** el índice de Dow Jones alcanzó un máximo de 2.503

[4] (*Met*) zona *f* de altas presiones; (*esp US*) temperatura *f* máxima

[5] (*US Aut*) (= *top gear*) directa *f*; **to be in ~** ir en directa

Ⓓ CPD ► **high altar** N altar *m* mayor ► **high beam** N (*US Aut*) **he had his lights on ~ beam** llevaba las luces largas *or* de cruce ► **high camp** N (*Theat*) amaneramiento *m* ► **high chair** N silla *f* alta (para niño), trona *f* (*Sp*) ► **High Church** N *sector de la Iglesia Anglicana muy cercano a la liturgia y ritos católicos* ► **high comedy** N (*Theat*) comedia *f* de costumbres; **it was ~ comedy** (*fig*) era de lo más cómico ► **high command** N (*Mil*) alto mando *m* ► **high commission** N (= *international body*) alto comisionado *m*; (= *embassy*) embajada *f* (*que representa a uno de los países de la Commonwealth en otro*) ► **high commissioner** N [*of international body*] alto comisario/a *m/f*; (= *ambassador*) embajador(ora) *m/f* (*de un país de la Commonwealth en otro*) ► **High Court** N (*Jur*) Tribunal *m* Supremo; **a ~ court judge** un juez del Tribunal Supremo ► **high definition** N alta definición *f*; *see also* **high-definition** ► **high diving** N saltos *mpl* de trampolín de gran altura ► **high explosive** N explosivo *m* de gran potencia; *see also* **high-explosive** ► **high fidelity** N alta fidelidad *f*; *see also* **high-fidelity** ► **high finance** N altas finanzas *fpl* ► **high flier** N **he's a ~ flier** es ambicioso, tiene talento y promete ► **High German** N alto alemán *m* ► **high ground** N (*fig*) **they believe they have** *or* **occupy the moral ~ ground in this conflict** creen que tienen moralmente la razón de su parte en este conflicto ► **high hat** N sombrero *m* de copa, cilindro* *m*; *see also* **high-hat** ► **high heels** NPL (= *heels*) tacones *mpl* altos; (= *shoes*) zapatos *mpl* de tacón ► **high jinks**†* NPL jolgorio *msing*, jarana *f*; **there were ~ jinks last night** hubo jolgorio *or* jarana anoche; **to get up to ~ jinks** meterse en jarana ► **high jump** N (*Sport*) salto *m* de altura; ✦**IDIOM he's for the ~ jump** (*Brit**) (= *he'll be in trouble*) se la va a cargar, le va a caer una buena; (= *he'll be sacked*) le van a largar ► **high jumper** N (*Sport*) saltador(a) *m/f* de altura ► **the high life** N (*gen*) la buena vida; (*in high society*) la vida de la buena sociedad ► **high living** N la buena vida ► **High Mass** N misa *f* mayor ► **high noon** N (= *midday*) mediodía *m*; (*fig*) (= *peak*) apogeo *m*; (= *critical point*) momento *m* crucial ► **high point** N [*of show, evening*] punto *m* culminante, clímax *m inv*; [*of visit, holiday*] lo más destacado; [*of career*] punto *m* culminante, cenit *m* ► **high priest** N sumo sacerdote *m* ► **high priestess**

N suma sacerdotisa *f* ► **high relief** N alto relieve *m*; **to throw** *or* **bring sth into ~ relief** (*fig*) poner algo de relieve ► **high road** N (*esp Brit*) carretera *f*; **this is the ~ road to disaster** éste es el camino del desastre ► **high roller** N (*US*) (*gen*) derrochón/ona *m/f*; (*gambling*) jugador/ora *m/f* empedernido ► **high school** N (*US, Brit*) instituto *m* de enseñanza secundaria, ≈ liceo *m* (*LAm*); **junior ~ (school)** (*US*) *instituto donde se imparten los dos primeros años de bachillerato* ► **high school diploma** N (*US*) ≈ bachillerato *m* ► **high school graduate** N (*US*) ≈ bachiller *mf* ► **the high seas** NPL alta mar *fsing*; **on the ~ seas** en alta mar ► **high season** N temporada *f* alta; **~ season prices/rates** precios *mpl*/tarifas *fpl* de temporada alta ► **high sign** N seña *f* (*acordada*); **to give sb a ~ sign** hacer la seña a algn ► **high society** N la alta sociedad ► **high spot** N [*of show, evening*] punto *m* culminante, clímax *m inv*; [*of visit, holiday*] lo más destacado; [*of career*] punto *m* culminante, cenit *m* ► **high street** N calle *f* mayor, calle *f* principal; **~ street banks** bancos *mpl* principales; **~ street shops** tiendas *fpl* de la calle principal ► **high summer** N pleno verano *m*, pleno estío *m* ► **high table** N (*gen*) mesa *f* principal, mesa *f* presidencial; (*Univ, Scol*) mesa *f* de los profesores ► **high tea** N (*Brit*) merienda-cena *f* (*que se toma acompañada de té*) ► **high technology** N alta tecnología *f* ► **high tide** N pleamar *f*, marea *f* alta; **at ~ tide** en la pleamar, en marea alta ► **high treason** N alta traición *f* ► **high water** N pleamar *f*, marea *f* alta; *see also* **high-water mark** ► **high wire** N cuerda *f* floja ► **high wire act** N número *m* en la cuerda floja, número *m* de funambulismo

HIGH SCHOOL

En Estados Unidos las **high schools** *son los institutos donde los adolescentes de 15 a 18 años realizan la educación secundaria, que dura tres cursos* (**grades**), *desde el noveno hasta el duodécimo año de la enseñanza; al final del último curso se realiza un libro conmemorativo con fotos de los alumnos y profesores de ese año* **Yearbook** *y los alumnos reciben el diploma de* **high school** *en una ceremonia formal de graduación. Estos centros suelen ser un tema frecuente en las películas y programas de televisión estadounidenses en los que se resalta mucho el aspecto deportivo - sobre todo el fútbol americano y el baloncesto - además de algunos acontecimientos sociales como el baile de fin de curso, conocido como* **Senior Prom**.

⇨ *Ver tb* PROM, YEARBOOK

highball ['haɪbɔːl] N (*US*) (= *drink*) jaibol *m*, whisky *m* con soda

highborn ['haɪbɔːn] ADJ linajudo, de ilustre cuna

highboy ['haɪbɔɪ] N (*US*) cómoda *f* alta

highbrow ['haɪbraʊ] Ⓐ N intelectual *mf*, persona *f* culta; (*pej*) intelectualoide *mf*
Ⓑ ADJ [*book, play, film*] para intelectuales

high-calibre, **high-caliber** (*US*) [ˌhaɪ'kælɪbəʳ] ADJ 1 [*person, staff*] de alto nivel
2 [*weapon, rifle*] de gran calibre

high-class [ˌhaɪ'klɑːs] ADJ (= *of good quality*) de (alta) categoría

high-definition [ˌhaɪdefɪ'nɪʃən] ADJ [*television, video*] de alta definición; *see also* **high D**

high-density [ˌhaɪ'densɪtɪ] ADJ **~ housing** alta densidad *f* de inquilinos

high-energy [ˌhaɪ'enədʒɪ] ADJ **~ particle** partícula *f* de alta energía; **~ physics** física *f* de altas energías

higher ['haɪəʳ] Ⓐ ADJ COMPAR *of* **high** más alto; [*form of life, court*] superior; [*price*] más elevado; [*number, speed*] mayor; **any number ~ than six** cualquier número superior a *or* mayor de seis; **~ interest rates are a possibility** existe la posibilidad de una subida de los tipos de interés; **~ rate tax** impuesto *m* en la banda superior
Ⓑ ADV COMPAR *of* **high** 1 (*lit*) más alto; **I can jump ~ than you** puedo saltar más alto que tú; **to fly ~ than the clouds** volar encima de las nubes; **to fly ~ still** volar a mayor altura todavía; **~ and ~** más y más (alto); **the balloon climbed ~ and ~** el globo se elevaba más y más (alto); **try hanging the picture a bit ~ up** prueba a poner el cuadro un poquito más alto *or* más arriba; **~ up the hill** más arriba en la colina
2 (*fig*) **the dollar closed ~ today** la cotización del dólar ha cerrado más alta hoy; **unemployment is expected to rise even ~** se espera que el desempleo aumente aún más; **prices are rising ~ and ~** los precios están subiendo más y más, los precios son cada vez más altos
Ⓒ N (*Scot Scol*) = **Higher Grade**
Ⓓ CPD ► **higher education** N educación *f* superior, enseñanza *f* superior ► **Higher Grade** N (*Scot Scol*) *examen de estado que se realiza a la edad de 16 años* ► **Higher National Certificate** N (*Brit Scol*) Certificado *m* Nacional de Estudios Superiores ► **Higher National Diploma** N (*Brit Scol*) Diploma *m* Nacional de Estudios Superiores; → A LEVELS

highest ['haɪɪst] Ⓐ ADJ SUPERL *of* **high** el/la más alto/a; **he was a man of the ~ principles** era un hombre de los más altos principios; **the ~ common factor** (*Math*) el máximo común denominador
Ⓑ ADV SUPERL *of* **high**; **the ~ scoring player** el máximo anotador; **Britain's ~ paid company director** el director de empresa mejor pagado de Gran Bretaña

high-explosive ['haɪɪks'pləʊsɪv] ADJ **~ shell** obús *m* de alto explosivo; *see also* **high D**

highfalutin(g) ['haɪfə'luːtɪn] ADJ presuntuoso, pomposo

high-fibre, **high-fiber** (*US*) ['haɪ'faɪbəʳ] ADJ **a ~ diet** una dieta rica en fibra

high-fidelity [ˌhaɪfɪ'delɪtɪ] ADJ de alta fidelidad; *see also* **high D**

high-flown ['haɪfləʊn] ADJ exagerado, altisonante

high-flying ['haɪ'flaɪɪŋ] ADJ 1 [*aircraft*] de gran altura
2 (*fig*) [*aim, ambition*] de altos vuelos; [*executive, businessperson*] (= *promising*) prometedor; (= *in high-calibre job*) bien situado, de prestigio; [*career, student*] prometedor

high-frequency [ˌhaɪ'friːkwənsɪ] ADJ de alta frecuencia

high-grade ['haɪ'greɪd] ADJ de calidad superior

high-handed ['haɪ'hændɪd] ADJ arbitrario, despótico

high-handedly [ˌhaɪ'hændɪdlɪ] ADV arbitrariamente, despóticamente

high-hat* ['haɪ'hæt] ADJ encopetado, esnob*; *see also* **high D**

high-heeled ['haɪhiːld] ADJ [*shoes*] de tacón (alto)

high-intensity [ˌhaɪɪn'tensɪtɪ] ADJ **~ lights** (*Aut*) faros *mpl* halógenos

highjack *etc* ['haɪdʒæk] = **hijack** *etc*

highland ['haɪlənd] ADJ montañés, de montaña; [*region*] montañoso; **Highland dress** *traje tradicional de las Tierras Altas de Escocia*; **Highland fling** *baile escocés*; **Highland Games** juegos *mpl* escoceses; *see also* **highlands**

HIGHLAND GAMES

Los **Highland Games** *se celebran anualmente en distintos lugares de Escocia y en ellos se realizan competiciones de deportes tradicionales celtas, junto con bailes típicos y concursos de gaitas. Probablemente, de todos los juegos, el más famoso es el que tiene lugar en Braemar, cerca de Balmoral, en el noreste de Escocia. Entre las competiciones normalmente asociadas con estos juegos están el lanzamiento de troncos* (**tossing the caber**) *y el lanzamiento de martillo.*

highlander ['haɪləndəʳ] N montañés/esa *m/f*; **Highlander** (*Brit*) *habitante de las tierras altas de Escocia*

highlands ['haɪləndz] NPL tierras *fpl* altas, sierra *fsing* (*LAm*); **the Highlands** (*Brit*) las Tierras Altas de Escocia

high-level ['haɪ'levl] ADJ [*talks*] (*also Comput*) de alto nivel; **~ nuclear waste** desechos *mpl* nucleares de alta radiactividad; **~ language** lenguaje *m* de alto nivel

highlight ['haɪlaɪt] Ⓐ N 1 (*Art*) toque *m* de luz
2 (*fig*) punto *m* culminante; **the ~ of the evening** el punto culminante de la velada; **they showed the ~s of the game on television** mostraron los momentos más interesantes del partido por televisión; (*Ftbl*) mostraron las jugadas más interesantes del partido por televisión
3 **highlights** (*in hair*) reflejos *mpl*
Ⓑ VT poner de relieve, destacar; [+ *hair*] poner reflejos en

highlighter ['haɪlaɪtəʳ] N (= *pen*) rotulador *m* (*Sp*)

highly ['haɪlɪ] ADV 1 (*with adj, pp used as adj*) [*effective, sensitive, controversial*] muy, sumamente; [*qualified, developed, sophisticated*] sumamente, altamente; [*significant*] sumamente, tremendamente; **~ acclaimed** sumamente elogiado; **~ charged** [*atmosphere, occasion, debate*] muy tenso; **~ coloured** [*clothes, picture*] de colores chillones; [*description, account*] muy exagerado; **~ educated** muy culto; **~ intelligent** sumamente inteligente, inteligentísimo; **it is ~ likely that he will win the competition** es muy *or* sumamente probable que gane la competición; **~ paid** [*person, job*] muy bien pagado; **a ~ placed official** un funcionario importante, un alto cargo; **he is ~ placed in the company** está muy bien situado en la compañía; **~ polished** [*shoes, furniture, tiles*] muy brillantes; [*book, film, description*] muy bueno, muy pulido; **~ qualified** muy preparado, muy cualificado; **this book is ~ recommended** este libro está muy recomendado; **she came to the job ~ recommended** vino muy bien recomendada; **a ~ regarded writer** un escritor de mucha reputación; **~ sexed** muy sensual, con mucho apetito sexual; **~ spiced** con muchas especias, muy condimentado; **~ strung** muy nervioso, muy excitable; **a ~ successful businessman** un hombre de negocios de muchísimo éxito; **~ trained soldiers** soldados sumamente adiestrados; **the staff are ~ trained** el personal está altamente capacitado; **it is ~ unlikely that she will see you** es muy poco probable que te reciba
2 (*with verb*) **to praise sb ~** alabar *or* elogiar

mucho a algn; **I can't praise him ~ enough** todo elogio que haga de él es poco; **I don't rate him very ~** no tengo muy buena opinión de él; **his chances of survival are not rated very ~** no se cree que tenga muchas posibilidades de sobrevivir; **he is ~ regarded by all his staff** está muy bien considerado por todo su personal; **these children score very ~ in intelligence tests** estos niños consiguen unas puntuaciones muy altas en los tests de inteligencia; **to speak ~ of sb/sth** hablar muy bien de algn/algo; **to think ~ of sb/sth** tener muy buena opinión de algn/algo; **to value sth ~** apreciar mucho algo

highly-charged [ˌhaɪlɪ'tʃɑːdʒd] ADJ [*atmosphere, debate*] muy tenso, muy crispado

high-minded ['haɪ'maɪndɪd] ADJ [*person*] de nobles pensamientos, magnánimo; [*act*] noble, altruista

high-mindedness [ˌhaɪ'maɪndɪdnɪs] N nobleza *f* de pensamientos, magnanimidad *f*; (= *altruism*) altruismo *m*

high-necked [ˌhaɪ'nekt] ADJ de cuello alto

highness ['haɪnɪs] N altura *f*; **Highness** (*as title*) Alteza *f*; **His/Her/Your Royal Highness** Su Alteza Real; **Your Royal Highnesses** Sus Altezas Reales

high-octane ['haɪˌɒkteɪn] ADJ [1] **~ petrol** gasolina *f* de alto octanaje, supercarburante *m*
[2] (*fig*) [*film, book*] dinámico y con carácter; [*campaign*] dinámico e intenso; [*party scene*] lleno de energía y dinamismo; [*prose*] vigoroso

high-performance [ˌhaɪpə'fɔːməns] ADJ de gran rendimiento

high-pitched ['haɪ'pɪtʃt] ADJ [*sound, voice*] agudo; [*instrument*] de tono agudo, de tono alto

high-powered ['haɪ'paʊəd] ADJ [1] [*engine*] de gran potencia
[2] (*fig*) (= *dynamic*) [*person*] enérgico, dinámico; (= *important*) importante

high-pressure ['haɪ'preʃəʳ] ADJ de alta presión; (*fig*) enérgico, dinámico; **~ salesman** vendedor *m* agresivo; **~ selling** venta *f* agresiva

high-priced [ˌhaɪ'praɪst] ADJ muy caro

high-principled [ˌhaɪ'prɪnsəpld] ADJ [*person*] de principios; [*manner*] íntegro

high-profile [ˌhaɪ'prəʊfaɪl] ADJ **~ activity** actividad *f* prominente

high-protein [ˌhaɪ'prəʊtiːn] ADJ rico en proteínas

high-quality ['haɪ'kwɒlɪtɪ] ADJ de gran calidad, de calidad superior

high-ranking [ˌhaɪ'ræŋkɪŋ] ADJ de categoría; [*official*] de alto rango, de alto grado; (*Mil*) de alta graduación

high-resolution [ˌhaɪrezə'luːʃən] ADJ [*image, screen*] de alta resolución

high-rise ['haɪraɪz] Ⓐ ADJ **~ block** (*residential*) torre *fsing* de pisos; **~ office block** edificio *m* de oficinas (de muchas plantas); **there are too many ~ buildings here** hay demasiados edificios altos aquí
Ⓑ N torre *fsing* de pisos

high-risk [ˌhaɪ'rɪsk] ADJ [*investment, policy*] de alto riesgo

high-sounding [ˌhaɪ'saʊndɪŋ] ADJ altisonante

high-speed [ˌhaɪ'spiːd] ADJ [*vehicle*] de alta velocidad; [*test*] rápido; **~ train** tren *m* de alta velocidad

high-spending [ˌhaɪ'spendɪŋ] ADJ que gasta mucho; (*pej*) derrochador, pródigo

high-spirited [ˌhaɪ'spɪrɪtɪd] ADJ [*person*] animado; [*horse*] fogoso

high-strung [ˌhaɪ'strʌŋ] ADJ (*US*) muy nervioso, muy excitable

hightail* ['haɪteɪl] VT **to ~ it** (*esp US*) darse el piro**, salir pitando*

high-tech* [ˌhaɪ'tek] ADJ al-tec*, de alta tecnología

high-tension [ˌhaɪ'tenʃən] ADJ de alta tensión

high-test [ˌhaɪ'test] ADJ **~ fuel** supercarburante *m*

high-up* ['haɪ'ʌp] Ⓐ ADJ de categoría, importante
Ⓑ N pez *mf* gordo*, mandamás* *mf inv*

high-water mark [ˌhaɪ'wɔːtəmɑːk] N [1] (*lit*) línea *f* de la pleamar
[2] (*fig*) punto *m* culminante

highway ['haɪweɪ] Ⓐ N (= *main road*) carretera *f*; (= *motorway*) autopista *f*; **~s department** administración *f* de carreteras
Ⓑ CPD ► **Highway Code** N Código *m* de la Circulación ► **highway robbery** N salteamiento *m*, atraco *m* (en el camino)

highwayman ['haɪweɪmən] N (*pl* **highwaymen**) salteador *m* de caminos

HIH ABBR (= **His** *or* **Her Imperial Highness**) S.A.I.

hijack ['haɪdʒæk] Ⓐ VT secuestrar; (*fig*) apropiarse de
Ⓑ N secuestro *m*; (*fig*) apropiación *f*

hijacker ['haɪdʒækəʳ] N secuestrador(a) *m/f*

hijacking ['haɪdʒækɪŋ] N secuestro *m*; (*fig*) apropiación *f*

hike¹ [haɪk] Ⓐ VI ir de excursión a pie, dar una caminata
Ⓑ VT **to ~ it** ir a pie
Ⓒ N excursión *f* a pie, caminata *f*; **to go on a ~** hacer una excursión (a pie), dar una caminata; **✦IDIOM take a ~!*** ¡lárgate!*

hike²* [haɪk] Ⓐ N (= *increase*) aumento *m*
Ⓑ VT [+ *prices, rates*] aumentar, subir

►**hike up** VT + ADV [1] [+ *skirt, socks*] subirse
[2] [+ *prices, amounts*] aumentar, subir

hiker ['haɪkəʳ] N excursionista *mf*

hiking ['haɪkɪŋ] N excursionismo *m* (a pie); **to go ~** ir de excursión a pie

hilarious [hɪ'lɛərɪəs] ADJ (= *very funny*) divertidísimo, graciosísimo; (= *merry*) alegre

hilariously [hɪ'lɛərɪəslɪ] ADV [*speak, describe*] con mucha gracia; **it was ~ funny** fue para morirse de risa

hilarity [hɪ'lærɪtɪ] N hilaridad *f*

hill [hɪl] Ⓐ N (*gen*) colina *f*, cerro *m*, loma *f* (*esp LAm*); (*high*) montaña *f*; (= *slope*) cuesta *f*; **a house at the top of a ~** una casa en lo alto de una colina; **I climbed the ~ up to the office** subí la cuesta hasta la oficina; **the hills** la montaña *fsing*, la sierra *fsing*; **✦IDIOMS to be over the ~*** ir cuesta abajo; **to chase sb up ~ and down dale** perseguir a algn por todas partes; **to take to the ~s** echarse al monte; **as old as the ~s** más viejo que Matusalén
Ⓑ CPD ► **hill climb** N (*Sport*) ascensión *f* de montaña ► **hill farmer** N agricultor(a) *m/f* de montaña ► **hill farming** N agricultura *f* de montaña ► **hill walker** N montañero/a *m/f*, senderista *mf* ► **hill walking** N montañismo *m*, senderismo *m*; **to go ~-walking** hacer montañismo, hacer senderismo

hillbilly* ['hɪl'bɪlɪ] (*US*) Ⓐ N rústico/a *m/f* montañés/esa; (*pej*) palurdo/a *m/f*
Ⓑ CPD ► **hillbilly music** N música *f* country

hillfort ['hɪl'fɔːt] N castro *m*

hilliness ['hɪlɪnɪs] N lo montañoso

hillock ['hɪlək] N montículo *m*, altozano *m*

hillside ['hɪlsaɪd] N ladera *f*, falda *f*

hilltop ['hɪltɒp] N cumbre *f*

hilly ['hɪlɪ] ADJ (*compar* **hillier**, *superl* **hilliest**) [*terrain*] montañoso, accidentado; [*road*] con fuertes pendientes

hilt [hɪlt] N puño *m*, empuñadura *f*; **(up) to the ~** hasta el cuello*; **he's in debt (right) up to the ~** está agobiado *or* hasta el cuello* de deudas; **to back sb up to the ~** apoyar a algn incondicionalmente; **to prove sth up to the ~** demostrar algo hasta la saciedad

him [hɪm] PRON [1] (= *direct object*) lo, le (*Sp*); **I saw ~** lo vi; **look at ~!** ¡míralo!; **I have never seen HIM** a él no lo *or* (*also Sp*) le he visto nunca
[2] (= *indirect object*) le; (*combined with direct object pron*) se; **you must tell ~ the truth** tienes que decirle la verdad; **yes of course I gave ~ the book** sí, claro que le di el libro; **yes of course I gave them to ~** sí, claro que se los di; **I gave the book to HIM not his sister** le di el libro a él no a su hermana; **I'm speaking to HIM not you** le estoy hablando a él, no a ti; **give it to ~ when you go to Liverpool** dáselo cuando vayas a Liverpool; **I gave it to HIM not Charlotte** se lo di a él no a Charlotte
[3] (*after prep, in comparisons, with verb "to be"*) él; **she thought of ~** pensó en él; **without ~** sin él; **I'm going with ~** voy con él; **he was carrying it on ~** lo llevaba consigo; **if I were ~** yo que él; **younger than ~** más joven *or* menor que él; **it's ~** es él

Himalayan [ˌhɪmə'leɪən] ADJ del Himalaya, himalayo

Himalayas [ˌhɪmə'leɪəz] NPL **the ~** los montes Himalaya, el Himalaya

himself [hɪm'self] PRON [1] (*reflexive*) se; **he washed ~** se lavó
[2] (*emphatic*) él mismo; (*after prep*) sí (mismo); **he did it ~** lo hizo él mismo; **he went ~** fue él mismo, fue en persona; **he talked mainly about ~** habló principalmente de sí mismo; **he said to ~** dijo entre *or* para sí
[3] (*phrases*) **he came by ~** vino solo; **he did it by ~** lo hizo él solo; **he's not ~** no se encuentra nada bien

hind¹ [haɪnd] ADJ [*leg, foot*] trasero, posterior; **✦IDIOM he could talk the ~ leg(s) off a donkey** (*Brit**) habla hasta por los codos*

hind² [haɪnd] N (*pl* **hinds** *or* **hind**) cierva *f*

hinder¹ ['hɪndəʳ] VT (= *disturb, make difficult*) estorbar, dificultar; (= *prevent*) impedir; (= *obstruct*) obstaculizar, poner dificultades a; (= *slow down*) entorpecer; **to ~ sb from doing sth** impedir a algn hacer algo

hinder² ['haɪndəʳ] ADJ [*part*] trasero, posterior

Hindi ['hɪndiː] N (*Ling*) hindi *m*

hindmost ['haɪndməʊst] ADJ postrero, último

hindquarters ['haɪndˌkwɔːtəz] NPL cuartos *mpl* traseros

hindrance ['hɪndrəns] N (= *obstacle*) obstáculo *m* (**to** para); (= *disturbance*) estorbo *m*; (= *problem*) impedimento *m*; **to be a ~ to sb/sth** ser un estorbo para algn/algo

hindsight ['haɪndsaɪt] N **with the benefit of ~** en retrospectiva

Hindu ['hɪn'duː] Ⓐ ADJ hindú
Ⓑ N hindú *mf*

Hinduism ['hɪnduːɪzəm] N (*Rel*) hinduismo *m*

Hindustan [ˌhɪndʊ'stɑːn] N Indostán *m*

Hindustani ['hɪndʊ'stɑːnɪ] Ⓐ ADJ indostaní, indostánico, indostanés
Ⓑ N (*Ling*) indostaní *m*

hinge [hɪndʒ] Ⓐ N [*of door, window*] bisagra *f*, gozne *m*; [*of shell*] charnela *f* (*also Zool*); (*for stamps*) fijasellos *m inv*; (*fig*) eje *m*
Ⓑ VI moverse sobre goznes; **to ~ on** moverse

sobre, girar sobre; (*fig*) depender de
Ⓒ VT engoznar

hinged [hɪndʒd] ADJ de bisagra, con goznes

hint [hɪnt] Ⓐ N [1] (= *suggestion*) indirecta *f*, insinuación *f*; (= *advice*) consejo *m*; **~s for purchasers** consejos *mpl* a los compradores; **~s on maintenance** instrucciones *fpl* para la manutención; **broad ~** indicación *f* inconfundible; **to drop a ~** soltar *or* tirar una indirecta; **to drop a ~ that …** insinuar que …; **give me a ~** dame una idea; **to take a ~** captar una indirecta; **take a ~ from me** permite que te dé un consejo; **to take the ~** (*unspoken*) tomar algo a corazón; (*spoken*) darse por aludido
[2] (= *trace*) señal *f*, indicio *m*; **without the least ~ of** sin la menor señal de; **with just a ~ of garlic** con un ligerísimo sabor a ajo; **with a ~ of irony** con un dejo de ironía
Ⓑ VT dar a entender, insinuar; **he ~ed that I had a good chance of getting the job** insinuó que tenía muchas posibilidades de conseguir el trabajo
Ⓒ VI soltar indirectas

► **hint at** VI + PREP referirse indirectamente a, hacer alusión a; **what are you ~ing at?** ¿qué estás insinuando?

hinterland ['hɪntəlænd] N hinterland *m*, interior *m*, traspaís *m*

hip¹ [hɪp] Ⓐ N (*Anat*) cadera *f*; **to shoot from the ~** (= *lit*) disparar sin apuntar; (*fig*) (= *act without thinking*) actuar sin pensar; (= *speak without thinking*) hablar sin pensar
Ⓑ CPD ► **hip bath** N baño *m* de asiento, polibán *m* ► **hip flask** N petaca *f* ► **hip joint** N articulación *f* de la cadera ► **hip pocket** N bolsillo *m* de atrás, bolsillo *m* trasero ► **hip replacement (operation)** N operación *f* de trasplante de cadera ► **hip size** N talla *f* de cadera

hip² [hɪp] N (*Bot*) escaramujo *m*

hip³ [hɪp] EXCL **~ ~ hurray!** ¡viva!

hip⁴* [hɪp] ADJ **to be ~** (= *up-to-date*) estar al día; (= *well-informed*) estar al tanto (de lo que pasa), estar enterado

hipbone ['hɪpbəʊn] N hueso *m* de la cadera

hipped¹ [hɪpt] ADJ (*Archit*) a cuatro aguas

hipped²* [hɪpt] (*US*) ADJ [1] (= *annoyed*) enojado, resentido
[2] (= *interested*) **to be ~ on sth** estar obsesionado por algo
[3] (= *depressed*) **to be ~** estar con la depre*

hippie* ['hɪpɪ] = **hippy**

hippo* ['hɪpəʊ] N hipopótamo/a *m/f*

Hippocrates [hɪ'pɒkrətiːz] N Hipócrates

Hippocratic [ˌhɪpəʊ'krætɪk] ADJ **~ oath** juramento *m* hipocrático

hippodrome ['hɪpədrəʊm] N (*Hist*) hipódromo *m*

Hippolytus [hɪ'pɒlɪtəs] N Hipólito

hippopotamus [ˌhɪpə'pɒtəməs] N (*pl* **hippopotamuses** *or* **hippopotami** [ˌhɪpə'pɒtəmaɪ]) N hipopótamo/a *m/f*

hippy* ['hɪpɪ] Ⓐ N hippy* *mf*, hippie* *mf*
Ⓑ ADJ hippy*, hippie*

hipster ['hɪpstəʳ] Ⓐ N [1] **hipsters** (*Brit*) *pantalón que se lleva a la altura de la cadera*
[2] (*US**) entusiasta *mf* del jazz
Ⓑ CPD ► **hipster skirt** N (*Brit*) falda *f* abrochada en la cadera

hire ['haɪəʳ] Ⓐ VT [+ *car, house*] alquilar, arrendar (*LAm*); [+ *employee*] contratar; **they ~d a lawyer** contrataron a un abogado; **~d hand** jornalero/a *m/f*, enganchado/a *m/f*; **~d assassin** *or* **killer** asesino/a *m/f* a sueldo; **~d car** coche *m* de alquiler
Ⓑ VI **she's in charge of hiring and firing at the company** es la encargada de contratar y despedir al personal en la empresa
Ⓒ N [*of car*] alquiler *m*, arriendo *m* (*LAm*); [*of person*] salario *m*, jornal *m*; **for ~** se alquila *or* (*LAm*) arrienda; (*on taxi*) libre; **to be on ~** estar de alquiler; **we've got it on ~ for a week** lo tenemos alquilado para una semana
Ⓓ CPD ► **hire car** N (*Brit*) coche *m* de alquiler ► **hire charges** NPL tarifa *fsing* de alquiler ► **hire purchase** N (*Brit*) compra *f* a plazos; **to buy sth on ~ purchase** comprar algo a plazos ► **hire purchase agreement** N acuerdo *m* de compra a plazos ► **hire purchase finance company** N compañía *f* de crédito comercial

► **hire out** VT + ADV alquilar, arrendar (*LAm*)

hireling ['haɪəlɪŋ] N mercenario *m*

hirsute ['hɜːsjuːt] ADJ hirsuto

his [hɪz] Ⓐ POSS ADJ (*with singular noun*) su; (*with plural noun*) sus; **~ book/table** su libro/mesa; **~ friends** sus amigos; **he took off ~ coat** se quitó el abrigo; **he's washing ~ hair** se está lavando el pelo; **someone stole ~ car** alguien le robó el coche
Ⓑ POSS PRON (*referring to singular possession*) (el/la) suyo/a; (*referring to plural possession*) (los/las) suyos/as; **this book is ~** este libro es suyo *or* de él; **is that car ~?** ¿es suyo *or* de él ese coche?; **"whose is this?" — "it's ~"** —¿de quién es esto? —es de él; **a friend of ~** un amigo suyo; **my car is much bigger than ~** mi coche es mucho más grande que el suyo *or* el de él; **"is this ~ coat?" — "no, ~ is black"** —¿es éste su abrigo? —no, el suyo *or* el de él es negro; **"is this ~ scarf?" — "no, ~ is red"** —¿es ésta su bufanda? —no la suya *or* la de él es roja; **my parents and ~** mis padres y los suyos *or* y los de él

Hispanic [hɪs'pænɪk] Ⓐ ADJ hispánico; (*within US*) hispano Ⓑ N (*within US*) hispano/a *m/f*

hispanicism [hɪs'pænɪsɪzəm] N hispanismo *m*

hispanicist [hɪs'pənɪst] N = **hispanist**

hispanicize [hɪs'pænɪsaɪz] VT españolizar, hispanizar

Hispanism ['hɪspənɪzəm] N hispanismo *m*

hispanist ['hɪspənɪst] N hispanista *mf*

Hispano… [hɪ'spænəʊ] PREFIX hispano…

hispanophile [hɪs'pænəʊfaɪl] N hispanófilo/a *m/f*

hispanophobe [hɪs'pænəʊfəʊb] N hispanófobo/a *m/f*

hiss [hɪs] Ⓐ N siseo *m*, silbido *m*; [*of protest*] silbido *m*, chiflido *m*; (*Elec*) silbido *m*
Ⓑ VI sisear; (*in protest*) silbar, chiflar
Ⓒ VT abuchear, silbar; **to ~ an actor off the stage** abuchear a un actor (hasta que abandone la escena)

histogram ['hɪstəgræm] N histograma *m*

histologist [hɪs'tɒlədʒɪst] N histólogo/a *m/f*

histology [hɪs'tɒlədʒɪ] N histología *f*

historian [hɪs'tɔːrɪən] N historiador(a) *m/f*

historic [hɪs'tɒrɪk] ADJ histórico

historical [hɪs'tɒrɪkəl] ADJ histórico

historically [hɪs'tɒrɪkəlɪ] ADV históricamente

historicism [hɪ'stɒrɪsɪzəm] N historicismo *m*

historicist [hɪ'stɒrɪsɪst] ADJ historicista

historiographer [ˌhɪstɒrɪ'ɒgrəfəʳ] N historiógrafo/a *m/f*

historiography [ˌhɪstɒrɪ'ɒgrəfɪ] N historiografía *f*

history ['hɪstərɪ] N historia *f*; **to go down in ~** pasar a la historia (**as** como); **to make ~** hacer época, marcar un hito; **to know the inner ~ of an affair** conocer el secreto de un asunto; **he has a ~ of psychiatric disorder** tiene antecedentes de problemas psiquiátricos; **the highest salary in television ~** el sueldo más alto de la historia de la televisión; **a piece of ~** un trozo *or* fragmento de la historia; ✦**IDIOMS that's ancient ~** ésa es cosa vieja; **the rest is ~** el resto ya lo sabéis, el resto ya es historia

histrionic [ˌhɪstrɪ'ɒnɪk] ADJ histriónico

histrionics [ˌhɪstrɪ'ɒnɪks] NPL histrionismo *msing*; **I'm tired of his ~** estoy harto de sus payasadas

hit [hɪt] (*vb: pt, pp* **hit**) Ⓐ N [1] (= *blow*) golpe *m*; (*Sport*) (= *shot*) tiro *m*; (*on target*) tiro *m* certero, acierto *m*; (*Baseball*) jit *m*; [*of bomb*] impacto *m* directo; (= *good guess*) acierto *m*; **we made three ~s on the target** dimos tres veces en el blanco; **that was a ~ at me** lo dijo por mí; **he made a ~ at the government** hizo un ataque contra el gobierno
[2] (*Mus, Theat*) éxito *m*; **to be a ~** tener éxito, ser un éxito; **the film was a massive ~** la película fue un éxito enorme; **she's a ~ with everyone*** les cae bien a todos; **to make a ~ with sb** caerle bien a algn
[3] (*Internet*) visita *f*
Ⓑ VT (*vb: pt, pp* **hit**) [1] (= *strike*) [+ *person*] pegar, golpear; (= *come into contact with*) dar con, dar contra; (*violently*) chocar con, chocar contra; [+ *ball*] pegar; [+ *target*] dar en; **to ~ sb a blow** dar un golpe a algn; **to ~ one's head against a wall** dar con la cabeza contra una pared; **the president was ~ by three bullets** el presidente fue alcanzado por tres balas; **the house was ~ by a bomb** la casa sufrió un directo; **I realized my plane had been ~** me di cuenta de que mi avión había sido tocado; **he was ~ by a stone** le alcanzó una piedra; **the car ~ a road sign** el coche chocó con una señal de tráfico; **he was ~ by a car** le pilló un coche; **his father used to ~ him** su padre le pegaba; **a lot of what he said ~ home** gran parte de lo que dijo dio en el blanco *or* hizo mella; ✦**IDIOMS then it ~ me*** (*realization*) entonces caí en la cuenta; **to ~ sb when he's down** rematar a algn; **to ~ the mark** dar en el blanco, acertar; **to ~ one's head against a wall** dar golpes al viento; **to ~ the ground running** dar el do de pecho desde el principio
[2] (= *affect adversely*) dañar; [+ *person*] afectar, golpear; **the news ~ him hard** la noticia le afectó mucho; **the crops were ~ by the rain** las lluvias dañaron los cultivos; **the company has been hard ~** la compañía se ha visto muy afectada
[3] (= *find, reach*) [+ *road*] dar con; [+ *speed*] alcanzar; [+ *difficulty*] tropezar con; (= *achieve, reach*) [+ *note*] alcanzar; (*fig*) (= *guess*) atinar, acertar; **when we ~ the main road** cuando lleguemos a la carretera; ✦**IDIOMS to ~ the bottle*** beber mucho; **to ~ the ceiling*** perder los estribos, enfurecerse; **to ~ the jackpot** sacar el premio gordo; **to ~ the hay** *or* **the sack*** tumbarse; **to ~ somewhere**: **we ~ London at nightfall*** llegamos a Londres al anochecer; **to ~ the road** *or* **the trail*** ponerse en camino *or* en marcha
[4] (*Press*) ✦**IDIOMS to ~ the front page** *or* **the headlines*** salir en primera plana; **to ~ the papers*** salir en el periódico
[5] ✦**IDIOM he ~ me for ten bucks** (*US**) me dio un sablazo de diez dólares*; **how much can we ~ them for?** ¿qué cantidad podremos sacarles?
Ⓒ VI golpear; (= *collide*) chocar; **to ~ against** chocar con, dar contra; **to ~ at** asestar un

golpe a; **to ~ and run** atacar y retirarse
Ⓓ CPD ► **hit list** N (= *death list*) lista *f* de personas a las que se planea eliminar; (= *target list*) lista *f* negra ► **hit parade** N lista *f* de éxitos ► **hit song** N canción *f* éxito ► **hit squad** N escuadrón *m* de la muerte

►**hit back** Ⓐ VI + ADV (*lit, fig*) devolver el golpe
Ⓑ VT + ADV devolver el golpe a

►**hit off** VT + ADV 1 (= *imitate*) imitar
2 **to ~ it off with sb** hacer buenas migas con algn; **they don't ~ it off** no se llevan bien

►**hit on** VI + PREP 1 (= *stumble on*) dar con; **I ~ on the idea of ...** se me ocurrió la idea de ...
2 (*esp US‡*) (= *make advances to*) intentar ligar con

►**hit out** VI + ADV asestar un golpe; (*wildly*) repartir golpes (**at** a); **to ~ out at sb** asestar un golpe a algn; (*fig*) atacar a algn

►**hit upon** = **hit on 1**

hit-and-miss [ˌhɪtənˈmɪs] ADJ = **hit-or-miss**

hit-and-run [ˈhɪtənˈrʌn] Ⓐ ADJ **~ accident** *accidente de carretera en el que el conductor se da a la fuga*; **~ driver** *conductor(a) que atropella a alguien y huye*; **~ raid** ataque *m* relámpago
Ⓑ N *accidente en el que el culpable se da a la fuga*

hitch [hɪtʃ] Ⓐ N 1 (= *impediment, obstacle*) obstáculo *m*, impedimento *m*; **without a ~** sin ningún problema; **there's been a slight ~** ha habido un pequeño contratiempo
2 (= *tug*) tirón *m*, jalón *m* (*LAm*)
3 (= *knot*) vuelta *f* de cabo
Ⓑ VT 1 **to ~ a lift** hacer autoestop, hacer dedo*, pedir aventón (*Mex*); **they ~ed a lift to Rome** llegaron a Roma haciendo autoestop
2 (= *fasten*) atar, amarrar (**to** a); **to ~ a horse to a wagon** enganchar un caballo a un carro
3 **to get ~ed‡** casarse
4 (= *shift*) mover de un tirón; **he ~ed a chair over** acercó una silla a tirones
Ⓒ VI (*) (*also* **~hike**) hacer autoestop, ir a dedo, hacer dedo*, pedir aventón (*Mex*)

►**hitch up** VT + ADV [+ *trousers, sleeves*] remangarse, subirse

hitchhike [ˈhɪtʃhaɪk] VI hacer autoestop, hacer dedo*, pedir aventón (*Mex*)

hitchhiker [ˈhɪtʃhaɪkəʳ] N autoestopista *mf*

hitchhiking [ˈhɪtʃhaɪkɪŋ] N autoestop *m*, autoestopismo *m*

hi-tech* [ˈhaɪˈtek] ADJ al-tec*, de alta tecnología

hither†† [ˈhɪðəʳ] ADV acá; **~ and thither** acá y acullá

hitherto [ˈhɪðəˈtuː] ADV hasta ahora

Hitlerian [hɪtˈlɪərɪən] ADJ hitleriano

hitman [ˈhɪtmæn] N (*pl* **hitmen** [ˈhɪtmen]) sicario *m*, asesino *m* a sueldo

hit-or-miss [ˈhɪtɔːˈmɪs] ADJ al azar; **to have a ~ way of doing things** hacer las cosas al azar *or* sin ton ni son; **the way she painted the room was rather ~** pintó la habitación a la buena de Dios *or* como Dios le dio a entender; **it's all rather ~** es todo un poco a la buena de Dios

Hittite [ˈhɪtaɪt] Ⓐ ADJ heteo, hitita
Ⓑ N 1 (= *person*) heteo/a *m/f*, hitita *mf*
2 (*Ling*) hitita *m*

HIV Ⓐ N ABBR (= **human immunodeficiency virus**) VIH *m*; **~ positive/negative** VIH positivo/negativo
Ⓑ CPD ► **HIV virus** N virus *m* VIH

hive [haɪv] N colmena *f*; **a ~ of activity** (*fig*) un hervidero de actividad; **a ~ of industry** un lugar donde se trabaja muchísimo

►**hive off*** Ⓐ VT + ADV 1 (*Fin*) (= *sell off*) vender (por separado)
2 (= *privatize*) privatizar
Ⓑ VI + ADV (= *split from*) desligarse

hives [haɪvz] NPL (*Med*) urticaria *fsing*

hiya* [ˈhaɪjə] EXCL ¡hola!

Hizbollah, **Hizbullah** [ˌhɪzbəˈlɑː] N = **Hezbollah**

HK ABBR = **Hong Kong**

hl ABBR (= **hectolitre(s)**) hl

HM ABBR (= **Her** *or* **His Majesty**) S.M.

hm ABBR (= **hectometre(s)**) hm

HMG N ABBR (*Brit*) = **Her** *or* **His Majesty's Government**

HMI N ABBR (*Brit*) = **Her** *or* **His Majesty's Inspector**

HMO N ABBR (*US*) (= **health maintenance organization**) *seguro médico global*

HMS N ABBR (*Brit*) (= **Her** *or* **His Majesty's Ship**) *buque de guerra*

HMSO N ABBR (*Brit*) (= **Her** *or* **His Majesty's Stationery Office**) *imprenta del gobierno*

HNC N ABBR (*Brit Scol*) (= **Higher National Certificate**) *título académico*

HND N ABBR (*Brit Scol*) (= **Higher National Diploma**) *título académico*, ≈ Diploma *m* Nacional de Estudios Superiores

HO ABBR 1 (*Comm etc*) = **head office**
2 (*Brit Pol*) = **Home Office**

hoard [hɔːd] Ⓐ N (= *treasure*) tesoro *m*; (= *stockpile*) provisión *f*; **~s of money*** montones *mpl* de dinero
Ⓑ VT 1 (*also* **to ~ up**) (= *accumulate*) amontonar, acumular; [+ *money*] atesorar
2 (= *keep*) guardar

hoarder [ˈhɔːdəʳ] N **to be a ~** ser un acaparador

hoarding¹ [ˈhɔːdɪŋ] N (= *fence*) valla *f*; (*for advertisements*) valla *f* publicitaria

hoarding² [ˈhɔːdɪŋ] N (= *act*) acumulación *f*, retención *f*

hoarfrost [ˈhɔːˈfrɒst] N escarcha *f*

hoarse [hɔːs] ADJ (*compar* **hoarser**; *superl* **hoarsest**) ronco; **to be ~** tener la voz ronca; **in a ~ voice** con voz ronca; **to shout o.s. ~** enronquecer a fuerza de gritar

hoarsely [ˈhɔːslɪ] ADV en voz ronca

hoarseness [ˈhɔːsnɪs] N (*Med*) ronquera *f*; (= *hoarse quality*) ronquedad *f*

hoary [ˈhɔːrɪ] ADJ (*compar* **hoarier**; *superl* **hoariest**) 1 (= *grey-haired*) cano
2 (= *old*) [*myth*] manido; [*joke*] muy viejo

hoax [həʊks] Ⓐ N engaño *m*
Ⓑ VT engañar
Ⓒ CPD ► **hoax call** N *llamada efectuada a la policía, los bomberos, etc. para dar un falso aviso de bomba, incendio, etc*

hoaxer [ˈhəʊksəʳ] N (*esp Brit*) bromista *mf*

hob [hɒb] N (*Brit*) quemador *m*

hobble [ˈhɒbl] Ⓐ N 1 (= *lameness*) cojera *f*; **to walk with a ~** cojear
2 (= *rope*) maniota *f*
Ⓑ VT [+ *horse*] manear
Ⓒ VI (*also* **to ~ along**) cojear, andar cojeando; **to ~ to the door** ir cojeando a la puerta

hobbledehoy†† [ˈhɒbldɪˈhɒɪ] N gamberro *m*

hobby [ˈhɒbɪ] N (= *leisure activity*) hobby *m*, pasatiempo *m* favorito; **it's just a ~** es sólo un pasatiempo; **he began to paint as a ~** empezó a pintar como hobby

hobbyhorse [ˈhɒbɪhɔːs] N 1 (= *toy*) caballito *m* (de niño), caballo *m* mecedor
2 (*fig*) (= *preoccupation*) caballo *m* de batalla, tema *m* preferido; **he's on his ~ again** ya está otra vez con lo mismo

hobbyist [ˈhɒbɪɪst] N *persona que practica un hobby*

hobgoblin [ˈhɒbˌgɒblɪn] N duende *m*, trasgo *m*

hobnail [ˈhɒbneɪl] N clavo *m* (de botas)

hobnailed [ˈhɒbneɪld] ADJ [*boots*] con clavos

hobnob* [ˈhɒbnɒb] VI **to ~ with** codearse con, alternar con

hobo [ˈhəʊbəʊ] N (*pl* **hobo(e)s**) (*US*) vagabundo/a *m/f*

Hobson's choice [ˈhɒbsənzˈtʃɔɪs] N (*Brit*) opción *f* única; **it's ~** o lo tomas o lo dejas

hock¹ [hɒk] N [*of animal*] corvejón *m*

hock² [hɒk] N (= *wine*) vino *m* blanco del Rin

hock³* [hɒk] Ⓐ VT (= *pawn*) empeñar
Ⓑ N **in ~** [*object*] empeñado; [*person*] endeudado

hockey [ˈhɒkɪ] Ⓐ N hockey *m*; (*also* **field ~**) hockey *m* sobre hierba; (*also* **ice ~**) hockey *m* sobre hielo
Ⓑ CPD ► **hockey player** N jugador(a) *m/f* de hockey ► **hockey stick** N palo *m* de hockey

hocus-pocus [ˈhəʊkəsˈpəʊkəs] Ⓐ N (= *trickery*) juego *m* de manos; (= *words*) jerigonza *f*
Ⓑ EXCL abracadabra

hod [hɒd] N capacho *m*

hodgepodge [ˈhɒdʒpɒdʒ] N (*esp US*) = **hotchpotch**

hoe [həʊ] Ⓐ N azada *f*, azadón *m*
Ⓑ VT [+ *earth*] azadonar, trabajar con la azada; [+ *crop*] sachar

hog [hɒg] Ⓐ N 1 (*esp US*) (= *pig*) cerdo *m*, puerco *m*, chancho *m* (*LAm*)
2 (*Brit*) (= *castrated pig*) cerdo *m* castrado; **he's a greedy ~*** es un cerdo*; ✦***IDIOM*** **to go the whole ~*** jugarse el todo por el todo
Ⓑ VT (*) acaparar; **to ~ the limelight** acaparar toda la atención

Hogmanay [ˈhɒgməneɪ] N (*Scot*) Nochevieja *f*

HOGMANAY

***Hogmanay** es el nombre que recibe el día de Nochevieja en Escocia. La gente suele organizar fiestas y, cuando suenan las doce campanadas, cantan* **Auld Lang Syne**, *una canción típica escocesa, y brindan por el nuevo año. Después es costumbre salir a visitar a los amigos para dar juntos la bienvenida al año que comienza. La costumbre de ser los primeros en hacerlo se denomina* **first footing**. *Según la tradición es señal de prosperidad y buena suerte en el nuevo año si la primera persona que llega a la casa después de las doce de la noche es un hombre moreno que lleve algo de comida, bebida y un trozo de carbón.*

⇨ *Ver tb* AULD LANG SYNE

hogshead [ˈhɒgzhed] N *medida de capacidad esp del vino (= 52,5 galones, aprox. 225 litros)*, pipa *f*

hogwash [ˈhɒgwɒʃ] N tonterías *fpl*

ho hum [ˈhəʊˈhʌm] EXCL (*hum*) pues, vaya

hoi polloi [ˌhɔɪpəˈlɔɪ] N **the ~** (*hum, iro*) la plebe, el vulgo

hoist [hɔɪst] Ⓐ VT (*also* **to ~ up**) levantar, alzar; [+ *flag, sail*] izar; **to ~ onto** subir a
Ⓑ N (= *lift*) montacargas *m inv*; (= *crane*) grúa *f*; **to give sb a ~ (up)** ayudar a algn a subir

hoity-toity* [ˈhɔɪtɪˈtɔɪtɪ] Ⓐ ADJ presumido, en-

greído
Ⓑ EXCL ¡tate!

hokey-cokey ['həʊkɪ'kəʊkɪ] N *canto y baile en grupo*

hokum* ['həʊkəm] N (*esp US*) tonterías *fpl*

hold [həʊld] (*vb: pt, pp* **held**) Ⓐ N [1] (= *grasp*) agarro *m*, asimiento *m*; **to catch ~ of** coger, agarrar (*LAm*); **catch ~!** ¡toma!; **to get ~ of** coger, agarrar (*LAm*); (*fig*) (= *take over*) adquirir, apoderarse de; (= *obtain*) procurarse, conseguir; **where can I get ~ of some red paint?** ¿dónde puedo conseguir pintura roja?; **where did you get ~ of that?** ¿dónde has adquirido eso?; **where did you get ~ of that idea?** ¿de dónde te salió esa idea?; **you get ~ of some odd ideas** te formas unas ideas muy raras; **to get ~ of sb** (*fig*) (= *contact*) localizar a algn; **we're trying to get ~ of him** tratamos de ponernos en contacto con él; **to get (a) ~ of o.s.** (*fig*) dominarse; **to have ~ of** estar agarrado a; **to keep ~ of** seguir agarrado a; (*fig*) guardar para sí; **to lay ~ of** coger, agarrar (*LAm*); **on ~**: **to be on ~** (*Telec*) estar en espera; **to put sb on ~** (*Telec*) poner a algn en espera; **to put a plan on ~** suspender temporalmente la ejecución de un plan; **to relax one's ~** desasirse (**on** de); **to seize ~ of** apoderarse de; **to take ~ of** coger, agarrar (*LAm*)
[2] (*Mountaineering*) asidero *m*
[3] (*Wrestling*) presa *f*, llave *f*; **with no ~s barred** (*fig*) sin restricción, permitiéndose todo
[4] (*fig*) (= *control, influence*) (*exerted by person*) influencia *f*, dominio *m* (**on, over** sobre); (*exerted by habit*) arraigo *m* (**on, over** en); **her powerful ~ on her son** su poderosa influencia sobre su hijo; **this broke the dictator's ~** esto acabó con el dominio del dictador; **to gain a firm ~ over sb** llegar a dominar a algn; **to have a ~ on** *or* **over sb** dominar a algn, tener dominado a algn; **drink has a ~ on him** la bebida está muy arraigada en él, está atrapado por la bebida
[5] (*Aer, Naut*) bodega *f*, compartimento *m* de carga
Ⓑ VT [1] (= *grasp*) tener; (= *grasp firmly*) sujetar; (= *take hold of*) coger, agarrar (*LAm*); (= *embrace*) abrazar; **he was ~ing a little mouse in his hand** tenía un ratoncillo en la mano; **she came in ~ing a baby/bunch of flowers** entró con un niño en brazos/con un ramo de flores en las manos; **he was ~ing her in his arms** (*romantically*) la tenía entre sus brazos; **he held my arm** me tuvo por el brazo; **~ the ladder** sujeta la escalera; **~ this for a moment** coge esto un momento; **~ him or he'll fall** sostenle que va a caer; **to ~ sb close** abrazar a algn estrechamente; **to ~ sth in place** sujetar algo en un lugar; **to ~ sth tight** agarrar algo fuertemente; **to ~ sb tight** abrazar a algn estrechamente; **nose A1**
[2] (= *maintain, keep*) [+ *attention, interest*] mantener; [+ *belief, opinion*] tener, sostener; [+ *note*] sostener; **can he ~ an audience?** ¿sabe mantener el interés de un público?; **to ~ one's head high** mantenerse firme; **to ~ the line** (*Telec*) no colgar; **to ~ one's own** defenderse; **to ~ sb to his promise** hacer que algn cumpla su promesa; **this car ~s the road well** este coche se agarra muy bien; **he held us spellbound** nos tuvo embelesados; **to ~ o.s. upright** mantenerse recto
[3] (= *keep back*) retener, guardar; **I will ~ the money for you** guardaré el dinero para ti; **"~ for arrival"** (*US*) (*on letters*) "no reexpedir", "reténgase"; **we are ~ing it pending inquiries** lo guardamos mientras se hagan indagaciones
[4] (= *check, restrain*) [+ *enemy, breath*] contener; **~ it!** ¡para!, ¡espera!; **~ everything!** ¡que se pare todo!; **the police held him for three days** lo detuvo la policía durante tres días; **there was no ~ing him** no había manera de detenerle; **to ~ sb prisoner** tener preso a algn; **to ~ one's tongue** morderse la lengua, callarse la boca
[5] (= *possess*) [+ *post, town, lands*] ocupar; [+ *passport, ticket, shares, title*] tener; (*Fin*) [+ *reserves*] tener en reserva, tener guardado; [+ *record*] ostentar; (*Mil*) [+ *position*] mantenerse en; **to ~ the fort** (*fig*) quedarse a cargo; **he ~s the key to the mystery** él tiene la clave del misterio; **to ~ office** (*Pol*) ocupar un cargo; **to ~ the stage** (*fig*) dominar la escena
[6] (= *contain*) contener, tener capacidad *or* cabida para; **this stadium ~s 10,000 people** este estadio tiene capacidad *or* cabida para 10.000 personas; **this ~s the money** esto contiene el dinero; **this bag won't ~ them all** en este saco no caben todos; **a car that ~s six** un coche de seis plazas; **what the future ~s for us** lo que el futuro guarda para nosotros; **what does the future ~?** ¿qué nos reserva el futuro?
[7] (= *carry on*) [+ *conversation*] mantener; [+ *interview, meeting, election*] celebrar; [+ *event*] realizar; (*formally*) celebrar; **the maths exam is being held today** hoy tiene lugar el examen de matemáticas; **the meeting will be held on Monday** se celebrará la reunión el lunes, la reunión tendrá lugar el lunes; **to ~ a mass** (*Rel*) celebrar una misa
[8] (= *consider, believe*) creer, sostener; **to ~ that …** creer que …, sostener que …; **I ~ that …** yo creo *or* sostengo que …; **it is held by some that …** hay quien cree que …; **to ~ sth dear** apreciar mucho algo; **to ~ sb dear** querer *or* apreciar mucho a algn; **to ~ sb in high esteem** tener a algn en gran *or* alta estima; **to ~ sb guilty** juzgar a algn culpable; **to ~ sb in respect** tener respeto a algn; **to ~ sb responsible for sth** echar la culpa a algn de algo, hacer a algn responsable de algo; **to ~ sth to be true** creer que algo es verdad; *see also* **peace A4**
[9] (= *bear weight of*) soportar
Ⓒ VI [1] (= *stick*) pegarse; (= *not give way*) mantenerse firme, resistir; [*weather*] continuar, seguir bueno; **the ceasefire seems to be ~ing** el cese de fuego parece que se mantiene; **to ~ firm** *or* **fast** mantenerse firme
[2] (= *be valid*) valer, ser valedero; **the objection does not ~** la objeción no vale
[3] (*Telec*) **please ~** no cuelgue, por favor

►**hold against** VT + PREP tener contra; **they held his origins against him** creían que sus orígenes eran deshonrosos para él; **you won't ~ this against me, will you?** ¿verdad que no vas a pensar mal de mí por esto?

►**hold back** Ⓐ VT + ADV (= *keep*) guardar, retener; (= *stop*) [+ *river, flood*] retener; [+ *progress*] refrenar; [+ *information*] ocultar, no revelar; [+ *names*] no comunicar; [+ *emotion, tears*] reprimir, contener; **are you ~ing sth back from me?** ¿me estás ocultando algo?; **to ~ o.s. back from doing sth** refrenarse de hacer algo
Ⓑ VI + ADV refrenarse; (*in doubt*) vacilar; **to ~ back from** refrenarse de; **to ~ back from doing sth** refrenarse de hacer algo

►**hold down** VT + ADV [1] [+ *object*] sujetar
[2] [+ *prices*] mantener bajo
[3] (= *oppress*) oprimir, subyugar
[4] **to ~ down a job** (= *retain*) mantenerse en su puesto; (= *be equal to*) estar a la altura de su cargo; **he can't ~ down a job** pierde todos los trabajos

►**hold forth** VI + ADV hablar largo y tendido (**about, on** de), perorar

►**hold in** VT + ADV [1] (= *squeeze in*) [+ *stomach*] contener
[2] (= *suppress*) [+ *emotion*] contener
[3] **to ~ o.s. in** (*fig*) controlarse, aguantarse

►**hold off** Ⓐ VT + ADV [1] (= *resist*) [+ *attack, enemy*] rechazar; [+ *threat*] apartar; [+ *person*] defenderse contra; [+ *visitor*] (*fig*) hacer esperar
[2] (= *postpone*) aplazar
Ⓑ VI + ADV [1] (= *stand back*) mantenerse a distancia, no tomar parte; [*person*] (= *wait*) esperar
[2] **if the rain ~s off** si no llueve

►**hold on** Ⓐ VI + ADV [1] (= *grip, cling*) agarrarse
[2] (= *persevere*) aguantar, resistir; **~ on!** ¡ánimo!; **can you ~ on?** ¿te animas a continuar?
[3] (= *wait*) esperar, seguir esperando; **~ on!** ¡espera!; (*Telec*) ¡no cuelgue!; **~ on, I'm coming!** ¡espera que ya voy!
Ⓑ VT + ADV sujetar

►**hold on to** VI + PREP [1] (= *grasp*) agarrarse a, agarrarse de
[2] (= *keep*) guardar, quedarse con; (*fig*) (= *retain*) aferrarse a; [+ *post*] retener

►**hold out** Ⓐ VT + ADV [+ *object*] ofrecer, alargar; [+ *hand*] tender, alargar; [+ *arm*] extender; [+ *possibility*] ofrecer; [+ *hope*] dar; **to ~ out sth to sb** ofrecerle algo a algn
Ⓑ VI + ADV [1] (= *resist*) resistir (**against** a), aguantar; **to ~ out for sth** insistir hasta conseguir algo; **he held out for £10** insistió en 10 libras
[2] (= *last*) [*supplies*] durar; [*weather*] seguir bueno

►**hold out on*** VI + PREP **you've been ~ing out on me!** ¡no me habías dicho nada!

►**hold over** VT + ADV [+ *meeting*] aplazar, posponer

►**hold to** VT + PREP atenerse a

►**hold together** Ⓐ VT + ADV [+ *persons*] mantener unidos; [+ *company, group*] mantener la unidad de
Ⓑ VI + ADV [1] [*persons*] mantenerse unidos
[2] [*argument*] ser sólido, ser lógico; [*deal*] mantenerse

►**hold up** Ⓐ VT + ADV [1] (= *support*) sujetar, sostener
[2] (= *raise*) [+ *hand*] levantar, alzar; [+ *head*] mantener erguido; **~ up your hand** levanta la mano; **to ~ sth up to the light** poner algo a contraluz
[3] (= *display*) mostrar, enseñar; **to ~ sth up as a model** presentar algo como modelo; **to ~ sb up to ridicule** poner en ridículo a algn
[4] (= *delay*) [+ *person, traffic*] retrasar; (= *stop*) detener, parar; [+ *work*] interrumpir; [+ *delivery, payment*] suspender; **we were held up by the traffic** nos retrasamos por culpa del tráfico; **I was held up at the office** me entretuvieron en la oficina; **we were held up for three hours** no nos pudimos mover durante tres horas; **the train was held up** el tren sufrió un retraso; **the train was held up by fog** el tren venía con retraso debido a la niebla; **we are being held up by a shortage of bricks** la escasez de ladrillos nos está retrasando, la escasez de ladrillos está entorpeciendo el trabajo
[5] (= *rob*) atracar, asaltar; **to ~ up a bank** atracar un banco
Ⓑ VI + ADV [1] [*weather*] seguir bueno
[2] (= *survive, last*) resistir; **to ~ up under the**

strain soportar bien la presión
[3] (= *remain strong*) mantenerse bien
►**hold with** VI + PREP estar de acuerdo con, aprobar
holdall ['həʊldɔːl] N (*Brit*) bolsa *f* de viaje
holder ['həʊldər] N [1] (= *tenant*) inquilino/a *m/f*
[2] (= *bearer*) [*of letter*] portador(a) *m/f*; [*of bonds*] tenedor(a) *m/f*; [*of title, office*] titular *mf*; [*of record*] poseedor(a) *m/f*
[3] (= *object*) **pen ~** portaplumas *m inv*; **cigarette ~** boquilla *f*; **lamp ~** portalámparas *m inv*
holding ['həʊldɪŋ] Ⓐ N [1] (= *land*) pequeña propiedad *f*, parcela *f*, chacra *f* (*S. Cone*); **holdings** terrenos *mpl*
[2] (*Comm*) valores *mpl* en cartera
[3] (= *act*) tenencia *f*
Ⓑ CPD ► **holding company** N (*Comm*) holding *m* ► **holding operation** N operación *f* de contención
holdout ['həʊldaʊt] N (*US*) **Britain has been the ~ in trying to negotiate** Gran Bretaña es el único que se resiste a negociar
holdup ['həʊldʌp] Ⓐ N [1] (= *robbery*) atraco *m* (a mano armada), asalto *m* (a mano armada); **a bank clerk was injured in the ~** un empleado del banco resultó herido en el atraco *or* asalto
[2] (= *stoppage, delay*) demora *f*, retraso *m*; **no-one explained the reason for the ~** nadie explicó el motivo de la demora *or* del retraso
[3] (= *traffic jam*) embotellamiento *m*, atasco *m*; **a ~ on the motorway** un embotellamiento *or* atasco en la autopista
Ⓑ CPD ► **holdup man** N atracador *m*
hole [həʊl] Ⓐ N [1] (*gen*) agujero *m*, hoyo *m*; (*in road*) bache *m*; (= *gap, opening*) boquete *m*; (*in wall, defences, dam*) brecha *f*; (= *burrow*) madriguera *f*; (*Golf*) hoyo *m*; **through a ~ in the clouds** a través de un claro entre las nubes; **to dig a ~** cavar un hoyo; **these socks are full of ~s** estos calcetines están llenos de agujeros; **his argument is full of ~s** sus argumentos están llenos de fallas; **~ in the heart** soplo *m* cardíaco; **his injury leaves a ~ in the team** su lesión deja un vacío en el equipo; **to make a ~ in sth** hacer un agujero en algo; **buying the car made a ~ in his savings** la compra del coche le costó una buena parte de sus ahorros; **to pick ~s in sth** (*fig*) encontrar defectos en algo; **to wear a ~ in sth** agujerear algo; *see also* **hole-in-the-wall**
[2] (*) (*fig*) (= *difficulty*) aprieto *m*, apuro *m*; **to be in a ~*** estar en un apuro *or* aprieto; **he got me out of a ~*** me sacó de un aprieto *or* apuro
[3] (*) (= *dwelling, room*) cuchitril *m*, tugurio *m* (*esp LAm*); (= *town*) poblacho *m*, pueblo *m* de mala muerte*
Ⓑ VT [1] (= *make hole in*) (*gen*) agujerear; [+ *ship*] abrir una brecha en
[2] [+ *ball*] (*Golf*) meter en el hoyo; (*Snooker*) meter en la tronera
Ⓒ VI (*Golf*) **to ~ in one** hacer un hoyo de un golpe
►**hole up** VI + ADV esconderse
hole-and-corner ['həʊlən'kɔːnər] ADJ furtivo; **to do sth in a ~ way** hacer algo de tapadillo
hole-in-the-wall* ['həʊlɪnðə'wɔːl] N (*Brit*) cajero *m* automático
holey* ['həʊlɪ] ADJ [*shirt, sweater*] lleno de agujeros, lleno de rotos; [*socks*] con muchos tomates*
holiday ['hɒlədɪ] Ⓐ N (*esp Brit*) (= *period*) vacaciones *fpl*; (= *public*) fiesta *f*; (= *day*) día *m* de fiesta, día *m* feriado, feriado *m* (*LAm*); **to be/go on ~** (*Brit*) estar/ir de vacaciones; **to take a ~** tomarse unas vacaciones; **~s with pay** vacaciones *fpl* retribuidas; **tomorrow is a ~** mañana es fiesta; **to declare a day a ~** declarar un día festivo; **it was no ~, I can tell you*** no fue ningún lecho de rosas, te lo aseguro
Ⓑ CPD ► **holiday camp** N (*Brit*) (*at beach*) colonia *f* de veraneo, colonia *f* de vacaciones ► **holiday clothes** NPL (*Brit*) ropa *fsing* de veraneo ► **holiday home** N (*esp Brit*) casa *f or* piso *m etc* para ocupar durante las vacaciones ► **holiday job** N (*Brit*) trabajo *m* para las vacaciones ► **holiday mood** N (*Brit*) **to be in the ~ mood** tener un espíritu festivo ► **holiday pay** N (*esp Brit*) paga *f* de las vacaciones ► **holiday resort** N (*Brit*) lugar *m* de veraneo ► **holiday season** N (*Brit*) época *f* de vacaciones; (*US*) Navidades *fpl* ► **the holiday spirit** N el espíritu festivo ► **holiday traffic** N tráfico *m* de las vacaciones
Ⓒ VI (*Brit*) pasar las vacaciones
holiday-maker ['hɒlədɪ,meɪkər] N (*Brit*) (*gen*) turista *mf*; (*in summer*) veraneante *mf*
holier-than-thou ['həʊlɪəðən'ðaʊ] ADJ (*pej*) [*attitude, tone of voice*] de superioridad moral; **she's always so ~ about everything** siempre está dando lecciones de moralidad sobre todo
holiness ['həʊlɪnɪs] N [*of place, person*] santidad *f*; [*of day*] lo sagrado; **His Holiness (the Pope)** Su Santidad (el Papa)
holistic [həʊ'lɪstɪk] ADJ holístico
Holland ['hɒlənd] N Holanda *f*
hollandaise [,hɒlən'deɪz] ADJ **~ sauce** salsa *f* holandesa
holler* ['hɒlər] (*esp US*) Ⓐ VT gritar
Ⓑ VI gritar
hollow ['hɒləʊ] Ⓐ ADJ [1] [*tree, object*] hueco; [*cheeks, eyes*] hundido; **it's ~ (inside)** está hueco (por dentro); **his eyes were ~** tenía los ojos hundidos; **she had a ~ feeling in her stomach** tenía una sensación de vacío en el estómago; **he felt ~ inside** se sentía vacío por dentro; **look how much you've eaten, you must have ~ legs!** ¡qué barbaridad, lo que has comido! ¡debes de tener la solitaria!
[2] [*gesture, laugh*] falso; [*threat, promise*] vano, falso; [*words*] hueco, vacío; [*person, victory, success*] vacío; **their marriage was a ~ sham** su matrimonio era una pura farsa *or* pantomima; **to ring** *or* **sound ~** sonar (a) falso; **his denial has a ~ ring (to it)** su negativa suena a falso
[3] [*sound, noise*] hueco; **a deep, ~ voice whispered his name** una voz profunda y cavernosa susurró su nombre; **her voice sounded tired and ~** su voz sonaba cansada y apagada
Ⓑ N [1] (= *hole*) hueco *m*
[2] (= *depression*) (*in ground, surface*) hoyo *m*; **the ~ of one's hand** el cuenco *or* (*Mex*) la cuenca de la mano
Ⓒ ADV **to beat sb ~*** dar una paliza a algn*
►**hollow out** VT + ADV ahuecar
hollow-cheeked [,hɒləʊ'tʃiːkt] ADJ de mejillas hundidas
hollow-eyed ['hɒləʊ'aɪd] ADJ de ojos hundidos; (*with fatigue*) ojeroso
hollowly ['hɒləʊlɪ] ADV **she laughed ~** soltó una risa que sonaba a falsa
hollowness ['hɒləʊnɪs] N [1] [*of words, promise*] falsedad *f*; [*of gesture, threat, victory*] vacuidad *f*; [*of laugh*] lo falso
[2] [*of object, surface*] el hecho de ser hueco; [*of cheeks, eyes*] lo hundido; **its ~ means it can float** el hecho de que es hueco significa que puede flotar, al ser hueco puede flotar; **the ~ of her voice** lo apagado de su voz
holly ['hɒlɪ] Ⓐ N acebo *m*
Ⓑ CPD ► **holly berry** N baya *f* de acebo ► **holly tree** N acebo *m*
hollyhock ['hɒlɪhɒk] N malva *f* loca
Hollywood ['hɒlɪ,wʊd] N Hollywood *m*
holmium ['hɒlmɪəm] N holmio *m*
holm oak ['həʊm'əʊk] N encina *f*
holocaust ['hɒləkɔːst] N (*fig*) holocausto *m*
hologram ['hɒləgræm] N holograma *m*
holograph ['hɒləgrɑːf] Ⓐ ADJ ológrafo
Ⓑ N ológrafo *m*
holography [hɒ'lɒgrəfɪ] N holografía *f*
hols* [hɒlz] NPL = **holidays**
holster ['həʊlstər] N funda *f* de pistola
holy ['həʊlɪ] (*compar* **holier**; *superl* **holiest**) Ⓐ ADJ [*place, book*] sagrado, santo; [*church, shrine*] sagrado; [*person*] santo; [*day*] de precepto; **the holiest day in the Jewish calendar** el principal día de precepto *or* la principal fiesta de guardar del calendario judío; ✦***IDIOMS*** **~ cow** *or* **mackerel** *or* **smoke!*** ¡(por) Dios bendito!*; **~ shit!**‡ ¡mierda!‡; **to be a ~ terror** [*child*] ser (más malo que) un demonio
Ⓑ CPD ► **the Holy Bible** N la Santa Biblia ► **the Holy City** N la Ciudad Santa ► **Holy Communion** N Sagrada Comunión *f* ► **the Holy Father** N el Santo Padre ► **the Holy Ghost** N el Espíritu Santo ► **the Holy Grail** N el Santo Grial ► **the Holy Land** N la Tierra Santa ► **holy man** N santón *m* ► **holy matrimony** N santo matrimonio *m* ► **holy oil** N santos óleos *mpl* ► **holy orders** NPL órdenes *fpl* sagradas; **to be in ~ orders** ser sacerdote; **to take ~ orders** ordenarse sacerdote ► **the Holy Roman Empire** N el Sacro Imperio Romano Germánico ► **Holy Saturday** N Sábado *m* Santo ► **the Holy See** N la Santa Sede ► **the Holy Sepulchre** N el Santo Sepulcro ► **the Holy Spirit** N el Espíritu Santo ► **the Holy Trinity** N la Santísima Trinidad ► **holy war** N guerra *f* santa ► **holy water** N agua *f* bendita ► **Holy Week** N Semana *f* Santa ► **Holy Writ**† N Sagradas Escrituras *fpl*; *see also* **Scripture**
homage ['hɒmɪdʒ] N homenaje *m*; **to pay ~ to** rendir homenaje a
homburg ['hɒmbɜːg] N sombrero *m* de fieltro
home [həʊm] Ⓐ N [1] (= *house*) casa *f*; (= *residence*) domicilio *m*; **there's no place like ~** como su casa no hay dos; **this tool has no ~** esta herramienta no tiene lugar propio; **at ~** en casa; **to feel at ~** sentirse como en casa; **make yourself at ~** estás en tu casa; **is Mr Lyons at ~?** ¿está el señor Lyons?; **to make sb feel at ~** hacer que algn se sienta en casa; **the duchess is at ~ on Fridays** la duquesa recibe los viernes; **Lady Rebecca is not at ~ to anyone** Lady Rebecca no recibe a nadie; **at ~ and abroad** dentro y fuera del país; **he is at ~ with the topic** domina bien la materia; **I'm not at ~ in Japanese** apenas me defiendo en japonés, sé muy poco de japonés; **~ from ~** (*Brit*) ◊ **~ away from ~** (*US*) segunda casa; **for us this is a ~ from ~** aquí estamos como en casa, ésta es como una segunda casa para nosotros; **to give sb/sth a ~** dar casa a algn/algo; (= *position, niche*) encontrar sitio para algn/algo; **he comes from a good ~** es de buena familia; **"good home wanted for puppy"** "búscase buen hogar para perrito"; **the puppy went to a good ~** el perrito fue a vivir con una buena familia; **to have a ~ of one's own** tener casa propia; **~ sweet ~** hogar, dulce hogar; ✦***PROV*** **an Englishman's ~**

is his castle para el inglés su casa es como su castillo
[2] (= *refuge*) hogar *m*; (= *hospital, hostel*) asilo *m*; **~ for the aged** residencia *f* de ancianos, asilo *m* de ancianos; **children's ~** centro *m* de acogida de menores; **old people's ~** residencia *f* de ancianos, asilo *m* de ancianos
[3] (= *country*) patria *f*; (= *town*) ciudad *f* natal; (= *origin*) cuna *f*; **we live in Madrid but my ~ is in Jaén** vivimos en Madrid pero nací en Jaén; **Scotland is the ~ of the haggis** Escocia es la patria del haggis; **he made his ~ in Italy** se estableció en Italia; **for some years he made his ~ in France** durante algunos años vivió en Francia
[4] (*Bio*) hábitat *m*
[5] (*Sport*) (= *target area*) meta *f*; (= *home ground*) **to play at ~** jugar en casa; **Villasanta are at ~ to Castroforte** Villasanta recibe en casa a Castroforte; **they lost nine games at ~** perdieron nueve partidos en casa
[6] (*Comput*) punto *m* inicial, punto *m* de partida
Ⓑ ADV [1] (*lit*) (= *at home*) en casa; (= *to home*) a casa; **to be ~** estar en casa; (= *upon return*) estar de vuelta en casa; **I'll be ~ at five o'clock** (*upon return*) estaré en casa a las cinco; **it's a long journey ~** hay mucho camino hasta llegar a casa; **as we say back ~** como decimos en mi tierra; **back ~ in Australia** en mi tierra, (en) Australia; **to come ~** volver a casa; **to be ~ and dry** respirar tranquilo/a; **to get ~** llegar a casa; **to go ~** volver a casa; (*from abroad*) volver a la patria; **he leaves ~ at eight** sale de casa a las ocho; **she left ~ at the age of 17** se marchó de casa cuando tenía 17 años; **that remark came near ~** esa observación le hirió en lo vivo; **to see sb ~** acompañar a algn a su casa; **to send sb ~** mandar a algn a casa; **to stay ~** quedarse en casa; **it's nothing to write ~ about*** no tiene nada de particular
[2] (*fig*) **to bring sth ~ to sb** hacerle ver algo a algn; **it came ~ to me** me di cuenta de ello; **to drive sth ~**: **to drive a point ~** subrayar un punto; **to drive a nail ~** hacer que un clavo entre a fondo; **to strike ~** (= *hit target*) [*shell, bullet*] dar en el blanco; (= *go right in*) [*hammer, nail*] remachar; *see also* **press B7**
Ⓒ VI [*pigeons*] volver a casa
Ⓓ CPD ► **home address** N (*on form*) domicilio *m*; **my ~ address** mi dirección particular, las señas de mi casa ► **home banking** N banco *m* en casa ► **home brew** N (= *beer*) cerveza *f* casera; (= *wine*) vino *m* casero ► **home buying** N compra *f* de vivienda ► **home comforts** NPL comodidades *fpl* domésticas ► **home computer** N ordenador *m* doméstico ► **home computing** N informática *f* doméstica ► **home cooking** N cocina *f* casera ► **the Home Counties** NPL (*Brit*) *los condados alrededor de Londres* ► **home country** N patria *f*, país *m* de origen ► **home economics** NSING (*Scol*) ciencia *f* del hogar ► **home fries** NPL (*US*) *carne picada frita con patatas y col* ► **home front** N frente *m* interno ► **home ground** N (*Sport*) **to play at one's ~ ground** jugar en casa; **to be on ~ ground** (*fig*) estar en su terreno *or* lugar ► **Home Guard** N (*Brit*) *cuerpo de voluntarios para la defensa nacional durante la segunda guerra mundial* ► **home help** N (= *act*) atención *f* domiciliaria, ayuda *f* a domicilio; (*Brit*) (= *person*) asistente/a *m/f* (*especialmente los que, a cargo de la seguridad social, ayudan en las tareas domésticas a personas necesitadas*) ► **home improvements** NPL reformas *fpl* en casa ► **home industries** NPL (*Comm*) industrias *fpl* nacionales ► **home journey** N viaje *m* a casa, viaje *m* de vuelta ► **home leave** N permiso *m* para irse a casa ► **home life** N vida *f* de familia, vida *f* doméstica ► **home loan** N préstamo *m* para la vivienda ► **home market** N (*Comm*) mercado *m* nacional, mercado *m* interior ► **home match** N (*Sport*) partido *m* en casa ► **home movie** N película *f* hecha por un aficionado ► **home news** NSING (*gen*) noticias *fpl* de casa; (*Pol*) información *f* nacional ► **Home Office** N (*Brit*) Ministerio *m* del Interior, Gobernación *f* (*Mex*) ► **home owner** N propietario/a *m/f* de una casa; **~ owners** propietarios *mpl* de viviendas ► **home ownership** N propiedad *f* de viviendas ► **home page** N (*Internet*) página *f* digital, home page *m* ► **home port** N puerto *m* de origen ► **home product** N (*Comm*) producto *m* nacional ► **home rule** N autonomía *f* ► **home run** N (*Baseball*) jonrón *m*; (= *return journey*) [*of ship, truck*] viaje *m* de vuelta ► **home sales** NPL ventas *fpl* nacionales ► **Home Secretary** N (*Brit*) Ministro *m* del Interior ► **home shopping** N venta *f* por correo; (*TV, Telec*) televenta *f* ► **the home side** N (*Sport*) el equipo de casa, el equipo local ► **home straight** N (*Sport*) recta *f* final; **to be in the ~ straight** (*fig*) estar en la última recta ► **home stretch** N = **home straight** ► **the home team** N (*Sport*) el equipo de casa, el equipo local ► **home town** N ciudad *f* natal ► **home trade** N (*Comm*) comercio *m* interior ► **home truths** NPL **to tell sb a few ~ truths** decir cuatro verdades a algn ► **home victory** N (*Sport*) victoria *f* en casa ► **home visit** N visita *f* a domicilio ► **home waters** NPL aguas *fpl* territoriales ► **home win** N (*Sport*) victoria *f* en casa
►**home in on** VI + PREP [1] [*missiles*] dirigirse hacia; **to ~ in on the target** buscar el blanco
[2] (*fig*) concentrarse en

HOME COUNTIES

Los **Home Counties** *son los condados que se encuentran en los alrededores de Londres: Berkshire, Buckinghamshire, Essex, Hertfordshire, Kent y Middlesex, un alto porcentaje de cuya población se encuentra en buena posición económica. De ahí que el término* **Home Counties** *haya adquirido dimensiones culturales y a la gente que vive en ellos se les considere en general personas adineradas de clase media-alta que, además, tienen al hablar un acento muy particular, conocido como* **RP**.
⇨ *Ver tb* ENGLISH

home-baked ['həʊm'beɪkt] ADJ [*bread, cake*] casero
homebody ['həʊmbədɪ] N (*pl* **homebodies**) (*US*) persona *f* hogareña, persona *f* casera
homebound ['həʊmbaʊnd] ADJ **the ~ traveller** el viajero que vuelve a *or* se dirige a casa
homeboy* ['həʊmbɔɪ] N (*US*) chico *m* del barrio
home-brewed ['həʊm'bruːd] ADJ hecho en casa, casero
homecoming ['həʊmkʌmɪŋ] Ⓐ N regreso *m* al hogar
Ⓑ CPD ► **Homecoming Queen** N (*US*) *reina de la fiesta de antiguos alumnos*; → YEARBOOK
homegirl* ['həʊmgɜːl] N (*US*) chica *f* del barrio
home-grown ['həʊm'grəʊn] ADJ de cosecha propia; (= *not imported*) del país
homeland ['həʊmlænd] N [1] (= *home country*) patria *f*, tierra *f* natal
[2] (*South Africa*) territorio *m* nativo
homeless ['həʊmlɪs] Ⓐ ADJ sin hogar, sin vivienda; **the storm left a hundred ~** la tormenta dejó a cien personas sin hogar *or* vivienda; **to be made ~** quedarse sin hogar; **to make ~** (*gen*) dejar sin hogar; [+ *tenant*] desahuciar
Ⓑ NPL **the ~** las personas sin hogar
homelessness ['həʊmlɪsnɪs] N el estar sin hogar; **the increase in ~** el aumento de la cifra de los que no tienen hogar
homeliness ['həʊmlɪnɪs] N llaneza *f*, sencillez *f*
home-lover ['həʊm,lʌvəʳ] N persona *f* hogareña, persona *f* casera
home-loving ['həʊm,lʌvɪŋ] ADJ hogareño, casero
homely ['həʊmlɪ] ADJ (*compar* **homelier**, *superl* **homeliest**) [1] (= *like home*) [*food*] casero; [*atmosphere*] familiar; [*advice*] prosaico; **it's very ~ here** aquí se está como en casa
[2] (*Brit*) [*woman*] sencillo
[3] (*US*) (= *unattractive*) poco atractivo
home-made ['həʊm'meɪd] ADJ hecho en casa
home-maker ['həʊm,meɪkəʳ] N (*US*) ama *f* de casa
homeopath *etc* ['həʊmɪəʊpæθ] N (*US*) = **homoeopath** *etc*
Homer ['həʊməʳ] N Homero
homer* ['həʊməʳ] N (*Brit*) trabajo *m* fuera de hora, chollo‡ *m*
Homeric [həʊ'merɪk] ADJ homérico
homesick ['həʊmsɪk] ADJ **to be ~** tener morriña; **I feel ~** echo de menos mi casa
homesickness ['həʊmsɪknɪs] N nostalgia *f*, morriña *f*
homespun ['həʊmspʌn] ADJ tejido en casa, hecho en casa; (*fig*) llano
homestead ['həʊmsted] N (*esp US*) casa *f*, caserío *m*; (= *farm*) granja *f*
homeward ['həʊmwəd] Ⓐ ADJ de regreso
Ⓑ ADV (*also* **~s**) hacia casa; **~ bound** camino a la casa; (*Naut*) con rumbo al puerto de origen
homewards ['həʊmwədz] ADV (*esp Brit*) = **homeward B**
homework ['həʊmwɜːk] N deberes *mpl*, tarea *f*; **my geography ~** mis deberes de geografía, mi tarea de geografía; **to do one's ~** (= *schoolwork*) hacer los deberes *or* la tarea; (*fig*) documentarse, hacer el trabajo preparatorio; **have you done your ~?** ¿has hecho los deberes?
homeworker ['həʊmwɜːkəʳ] N asalariado/a *m/f* que trabaja desde casa
homeworking ['həʊmwɜːkɪŋ] N trabajo *m* desde casa
homey* ['həʊmɪ] ADJ (*US*) íntimo, cómodo
homicidal [,hɒmɪ'saɪdl] ADJ homicida; **~ maniac** maniaco/a *m/f* con tendencias homicidas; **to feel ~** (*fig*) sentirse capaz de matar a alguien, tener ganas de matar a alguien
homicide ['hɒmɪsaɪd] N [1] (= *act*) homicidio *m*
[2] (= *person*) homicida *mf*
homily ['hɒmɪlɪ] N (*pl* **homilies**) homilía *f*; (*fig*) sermón *m*
homing ['həʊmɪŋ] Ⓐ ADJ [*missile*] buscador, cazador
Ⓑ CPD ► **homing device** N dispositivo *m* buscador de blancos ► **homing instinct** N instinto *m* de volver al hogar ► **homing pigeon** N paloma *f* mensajera
hominid ['hɒmɪnɪd] N homínido *m*
hominy ['hɒmɪnɪ] N (*US*) maíz *m* molido
homo†‡ ['həʊməʊ] N (*pej*) ABBR (= **homosexual**) marica‡ *m*

homoeopath, **homeopath** (*US*) [ˈhəʊmɪəʊpæθ] N homeópata *mf*

homoeopathic, **homeopathic** (*US*) [ˌhəʊmɪəʊˈpæθɪk] ADJ homeopático

homoeopathy, **homeopathy** (*US*) [ˌhəʊmɪˈɒpəθɪ] N homeopatía *f*

homogeneity [ˈhɒməʊdʒəˈniːɪtɪ] N homogeneidad *f*

homogeneous [ˌhɒməˈdʒiːnɪəs] ADJ homogéneo

homogenize [həˈmɒdʒənaɪz] VT homogeneizar

homogenous [həˈmɒdʒɪnəs] = **homogeneous**

homograph [ˈhɒməʊɡrɑːf] N homógrafo *m*

homonym [ˈhɒmənɪm] N homónimo *m*

homophobe [ˌhəʊməʊˈfəʊb] N homófobo/a *m/f*

homophobia [ˈhɒməʊˈfəʊbɪə] N homofobia *f*

homophobic [ˈhɒməʊˈfəʊbɪk] ADJ homofóbico

homophone [ˈhɒməfəʊn] N homófono *m*

homophonic [ˌhɒməˈfɒnɪk] ADJ homófono

homosexual [ˈhɒməʊˈseksjʊəl] Ⓐ ADJ homosexual
Ⓑ N homosexual *mf*

homosexuality [ˈhɒməʊseksjʊˈælɪtɪ] N homosexualidad *f*

hon* [hʌn] N (*US*) (= **honey**) cariño; **hi, ~!** ¡hola, cariño!

Hon. ABBR (*in titles*) = **Honorary** *or* **Honourable**

Honduran [hɒnˈdjʊərən] Ⓐ ADJ hondureño
Ⓑ N hondureño/a *m/f*

Honduras [hɒnˈdjʊərəs] N Honduras *f*

hone [həʊn] Ⓐ VT afilar
Ⓑ N piedra *f* de afilar

▼**honest** [ˈɒnɪst] Ⓐ ADJ [1] (= *frank*) sincero; **to be (perfectly) ~ …** para ser (totalmente) sincero *or* franco …; **to be ~ about sth** ser sincero *or* franco con respecto a algo; **I'd like your ~ opinion** me gustaría que me dieras tu sincera opinión; **that's the ~ truth** eso es la pura verdad; **to be (perfectly) ~ with you** para serle sincero *or* franco, si quiere que le diga la verdad; **I'll be ~ with you** voy a serte sincero; **you haven't been ~ with us** no has sido sincero con nosotros; **be ~ with yourself** sé sincero contigo mismo; ✦*IDIOM* **to make an ~ woman of sb**: **he finally made an ~ woman of her** (*hum*) al final hizo lo que Dios manda y se casó con ella
[2] (= *trustworthy, law-abiding*) [*person*] honrado, honesto; **he's very ~ in money matters** es muy honrado *or* honesto en lo que respecta al dinero; **he hasn't done an ~ day's work in his life** no ha trabajado honradamente en su vida; **to make an ~ living** ganarse la vida honradamente; **by ~ means** de forma honrada; **it was an ~ mistake** no fue un error deliberado; ✦*IDIOM* **to earn an ~ penny** *or* **crust** ganarse el pan honradamente
[3] (= *genuine*) sencillo; **good, ~ country cooking** cocina rústica buena y sencilla
Ⓑ ADV (*) de verdad; **I didn't know about it, ~** no lo sabía, de verdad, de verdad que no lo sabía; **~ to God** *or* **goodness** palabra (de honor), te lo juro; **~ injun†*** palabra, ¡por éstas!

honestly [ˈɒnɪstlɪ] ADV [1] (= *truly*) sinceramente, francamente; **I ~ believe this is the right decision** creo sinceramente *or* francamente que ésta es la decisión correcta; **he cannot ~ call this a good law** no puede, en honor a la verdad, llamar a esto una buena ley; **no, ~, I'm fine** no, de verdad *or* de veras *or* en serio, estoy bien; **I didn't do it, ~** de verdad que no lo hice; **do you ~ expect me to believe that?** ¿de verdad *or* de veras esperas que me lo crea?; **I can ~ say that it doesn't bother me** puedo decir con toda sinceridad *or* franqueza que no me importa; **I can't ~ say I ever knew him well** la verdad es que no puedo decir que lo conociese bien; **can you ~ say you've ever thought about it?** ¿puedes decir sin mentir que has pensado alguna vez en ello?; **I ~ thought you'd be pleased** de verdad *or* de veras pensé que te gustaría
[2] (= *truthfully*) [*speak, answer*] sinceramente, con sinceridad
[3] (= *legally*) honradamente; **if he couldn't get money ~, he stole** si no podía conseguir dinero honradamente, robaba
[4] (*showing exasperation*) vamos, por favor; **"honestly," said Barbara, "that woman …"** —vamos *or* por favor —dijo Barbara —esa mujer …; **oh, ~!** ¡por favor!, ¡anda, anda!

honest-to-God [ˈɒnɪstəˈɡɒd] ADJ cien por cien

honest-to-goodness [ˈɒnɪstəˈɡʊdnɪs] ADJ = **honest-to-God**

honesty [ˈɒnɪstɪ] Ⓐ N [1] (= *sincerity*) sinceridad *f*; **I admire his ~** admiro su sinceridad; **in all ~ …** para ser sincero *or* franco …; ✦*IDIOM* **~ is the best policy** lo mejor es ir con la sinceridad por delante
[2] (= *trustworthiness*) honradez *f*, honestidad *f*
Ⓑ CPD ► **honesty box** N *caja donde se deposita el dinero para pagar algo cuando no hay nadie para recogerlo en persona*

honey [ˈhʌnɪ] Ⓐ N [1] (*from bees*) miel *f*
[2] (*US**) (= *form of address*) cariño *m*; **hi, ~!** ¡hola, cariño!; **is everything ok, ~?** ¿todo bien, cariño *or* mi vida?*; **she's a ~** es un encanto
Ⓑ CPD ► **honey blonde** N rubia *f* miel; *see also* **honey-blonde**

honeybee [ˈhʌnɪbiː] N abeja *f*

honey-blonde [ˌhʌnɪˈblɒnd] ADJ rubio miel; *see also* **honey**

honeybun* [ˈhʌnɪbʌn], **honeybunch*** [ˈhʌnɪbʌntʃ] N (*esp US*) cielito *m*

honeycomb [ˈhʌnɪkəʊm] Ⓐ N panal *m*; (*fig*) laberinto *m*
Ⓑ VT (*fig*) **the hill is ~ed with tunnels** el cerro está lleno de cuevas; **the building is ~ed with passages** hay un laberinto de pasillos en el edificio

honeydew melon [ˈhʌnɪdjuːˈmelən] N melón *m* dulce

honeyed [ˈhʌnɪd] ADJ meloso, melifluo

honeyfuggle* [ˈhʌnɪˌfʌɡəl] VT (*US*) obtener mediante un truco

honeymoon [ˈhʌnɪmuːn] Ⓐ N (*lit, fig*) luna *f* de miel; **to go on ~** irse de luna de miel
Ⓑ VI pasar la luna de miel
Ⓒ CPD ► **the honeymoon couple** N la pareja de recién casados ► **honeymoon period** N (*Pol*) período *m* de gracia, cien días *mpl*

honeymooner [ˈhʌnɪˌmuːnəʳ] N *persona que está en su luna de miel*

honeypot [ˈhʌnɪpɒt] N mielera *f*

honeysuckle [ˈhʌnɪˌsʌkl] N madreselva *f*

Hong Kong [ˌhɒŋˈkɒŋ] N Hong Kong *m*

honk [hɒŋk] Ⓐ VI [*driver*] tocar la bocina, tocar el claxon (*LAm*); [*goose*] graznar
Ⓑ N [*of goose*] graznido *m*; [*of horn*] bocinazo *m*

honkie*, **honky*** [ˈhɒŋkɪ] N (*pl* **honkies**) (*US pej*) blanco/a *m/f*, blancucho/a* *m/f*

honky-tonk* [ˈhɒŋkɪˌtɒŋk] N [1] (*US*) (= *club*) garito *m*
[2] (*Mus*) honky-tonk* *m*

Honolulu [ˌhɒnəˈluːluː] N Honolulú *m*

honor [ˈɒnəʳ] N (*US*) = **honour**

honorable [ˈɒnərəbl] ADJ (*US*) = **honourable**

honorably [ˈɒnərəblɪ] ADV (*US*) = **honourably**

honorarium [ˌɒnəˈreərɪəm] N (*pl* **honorariums** *or* **honoraria** [ˌɒnəˈreərɪə]) honorarios *mpl*

honorary [ˈɒnərərɪ] ADJ [*member, president*] de honor, honorario; [*title*] honorífico; [*secretary*] (= *unpaid*) no remunerado; **an ~ degree** un doctorado "honoris causa"

honorific [ɒnəˈrɪfɪk] Ⓐ ADJ honorífico
Ⓑ N título *m* honorífico

honour, **honor** (*US*) [ˈɒnəʳ] Ⓐ N [1] (= *integrity, good name*) honor *m*; **a man of ~** un hombre de honor; **to be/feel (in) ~ bound to do sth** estar/sentirse moralmente obligado a hacer algo; **it's a matter of ~** es una cuestión de honor; **on my ~!** ¡palabra de honor!; **remember, you are on your ~ to report any irregularities** recuerde, es su deber moral informar de cualquier irregularidad; **to put sb on his/her ~ to do sth** hacer prometer a algn que va a hacer algo; **to have a sense of ~** tener pundonor; **to be an ~ to one's profession** ser un orgullo para su profesión; ✦*PROV* **(there is) ~ among thieves** entre bueyes no hay cornadas; *see also* **debt**, **word A5**
[2] (= *distinction, privilege*) honor *m*; **it's a great ~ for him** es un gran honor para él; **I had the ~ of meeting him** tuve el honor de conocerlo; **may I have the ~ (of this dance)?** ¿me concede este baile?; **would you do me the ~ of having lunch with me?** ¿me haría el honor de almorzar conmigo?; **you do me great ~ by accepting** me concede usted un gran honor al aceptar; **to bury sb with full military ~s** sepultar a algn con todos los honores militares; ✦*IDIOM* **to do the ~s** (*introducing people, serving drinks or food*) hacer los honores; *see also* **guard C**, **guest**, **lap²**, **maid**, **roll A3**
[3] (= *award*) (*by the state*) condecoración *f*; (*in contest*) galardón *m*
[4] (= *homage*) honor *m*; **to do ~ to sb** ◊ **do sb ~** rendir honores a algn; **in ~ of sth/sb** en honor a algo/algn; **he will attend a dinner in his ~** asistirá a una cena en su honor
[5] (*as title*) **His Honour Judge Brodrick** el señor Juez Brodrick; **Your Honour** (*to judge*) su Señoría, señor Juez; (*US*) (*to mayor*) Excelentísimo Señor, su Señoría
[6] (†) (= *chastity, virginity*) honra *f*
[7] **honours** (*Brit Univ*) **she got first/second class ~s in French** ≈ terminó la carrera de francés con matrícula de honor/con notable; **to take ~s in chemistry** ≈ licenciarse en químicas; **to graduate with ~s** ≈ licenciarse (*con nota*)
[8] (*Bridge*) **honours** honores *mpl*
Ⓑ VT [1] (= *compliment*) honrar; **I am ~ed by your confidence in me** su confianza en mí me honra; **I am deeply ~ed to be asked** me siento muy honrado de que me lo pidan; **I should be ~ed if …** sería un honor para mí si …; **~ed guest** invitado/a *m/f* de honor; **to ~ sb with one's presence** (*liter or hum*) honrar a algn con su presencia
[2] (= *respect*) honrar; **thou shalt ~ thy father and thy mother** honrarás a tu padre y a tu madre
[3] (= *pay homage to*) rendir homenaje a
[4] (= *decorate*) [*the state, authorities*] condecorar; (*in contest*) galardonar
[5] (= *fulfil*) [+ *agreement, contract, promise*] cumplir, cumplir con
[6] (= *pay*) [+ *cheque*] aceptar, pagar; [+ *debt*] liquidar, pagar
Ⓒ CPD ► **honor guard** N (*US*) guardia *f* de honor ► **honor roll** N (*US*) cuadro *m* de honor ► **honours degree** N (*Brit Univ*) ≈ licen-

➤ LANGUAGE IN USE: honest A1 6.2

ciatura *f*; **she has an ~s degree in French** es licenciada en filología francesa ► **Honours List** N (*Brit*) lista *f* de condecoraciones; **Birthday Honours List** *lista de condecoraciones que otorga el monarca el día de su cumpleaños*; **New Year Honours List** *lista de condecoraciones que otorga el monarca el día de Año Nuevo*; → DEAN'S LIST, DEGREE

HONOURS LIST

La **Honours List** *es una lista de personas a las que se considera merecedoras de un reconocimiento especial por su labor, tanto en la vida pública como por servicios prestados a la zona en la que viven. Esta lista es elaborada por el Primer Ministro británico con la aprobación del monarca y se publica dos veces al año, la primera en Año Nuevo - la* **New Year's Honours List** *- y la segunda en junio, el día del cumpleaños de la reina -la* **Queen's Birthday Honours List**. *En la mayoría de los casos a estas personas se les reconoce su mérito con la concesión del título de miembro de la Orden del Imperio Británico,* **Member of the Order of the British Empire** *o* **MBE**, *u oficial de la Orden del Imperio Británico* **Officer of the Order of the British Empire** *u* **OBE**.

honourable, **honorable** (*US*) ['ɒnərəbl] ADJ (= *upright*) honrado; [*title*] honorable; **~ mention** mención *f* honorífica; **the ~ member for Woodford** (*Brit Parl*) el señor diputado de Woodford

honourably, **honorably** (*US*) ['ɒnərəblɪ] ADV honradamente

Hons. (*Univ*) ABBR = **Honours**

Hons. ABBR (*Univ*) = **honours degree**

Hon. Sec. ABBR = **Honorary Secretary**

hooch* [huːtʃ] N licor *m* (*esp ilícito*)

hood [hʊd] N [1] [*of cloak, raincoat*] capucha *f*; (*Univ*) muceta *f*
[2] (*Brit Aut*) capota *f*; (*US*) capó *m*
[3] (= *cover*) (*on pram*) capota; (*on cooker*) tapa *f*; (*on chimney pot*) campana *f*
[4] (*esp US**) (= *hoodlum*) matón/ona *m/f*, gorila* *m*

hooded ['hʊdɪd] ADJ encapuchado

hoodlum* ['huːdləm] N matón/ona *m/f*, gorila* *m*

hoodoo ['huːduː] N (= *voodoo*) vudú *m*; (= *jinx*) gafe *m*, mala suerte *f*; **there's a ~ on it** tiene gafe

hoodwink ['hʊdwɪŋk] VT engañar

hooey* ['huːɪ] N música *f* celestial*

hoof [huːf] Ⓐ N (*pl* **hoofs** *or* **hooves**) [1] [*of horse*] casco *m*; [*of other animals*] pezuña *f*; **cloven ~** pata *f* hendida; **cattle on the ~** ganado *m* en pie; **~ and mouth disease** (*US*) fiebre *f* aftosa, glosopeda *f*
[2] (*) [*of person*] (= *foot*) pezuña* *f*, pata* *f*
Ⓑ VT (*) **to ~ it** (= *walk*) ir a pata*; (= *depart*) liar el petate*

hoofed [huːft] ADJ ungulado

hoofer† ['huːfəʳ] N (*esp US*) (= *dancer*) bailarín/ina *m/f*

hoo-ha* ['huːˌhɑː] N [1] (= *fuss*) lío* *m*, marimorena* *f*, follón *m* (*Sp**); **there was a great ~ about it** se armó la marimorena*
[2] (= *noise*) estrépito *m*
[3] (*pej*) (= *publicity*) bombo* *m*

hook [hʊk] Ⓐ N [1] (*gen*) gancho *m*; (*for painting*) alcayata *f*; (= *meat hook*) garfio *m*; (*Fishing*) anzuelo *m*; **the jacket hung from a ~** la chaqueta estaba colgada de un gancho; **he hung the painting on the ~** colgó el cuadro de la alcayata; ✦**IDIOMS by ~ or by crook** por las buenas o por las malas, a como dé lugar (*LAm*); **~, line and sinker**: **he fell for it ~, line and sinker** se tragó el anzuelo; **to get sb off the ~** sacar a algn de un apuro; **to let sb off the ~** dejar escapar a algn; **to sling one's ~**‡ (= *leave*) largarse*
[2] (*Telec*) **to take the phone off the ~** descolgar el teléfono; **to leave the phone off the ~** dejar el teléfono descolgado; ✦**IDIOM the phone was ringing off the ~** (*esp US**) el teléfono echaba humo, el teléfono no paraba de sonar
[3] (= *hanger*) percha *f*, colgadero *m*
[4] (*Sew*) **~s and eyes** corchetes *mpl*, macho y hembra *msing*
[5] (*Boxing*) gancho *m*, crochet *m*
[6] (*Golf*) golpe *m* con efecto a la izquierda
[7] **hooks**‡ manos *fpl*
Ⓑ VT [1] (= *fasten*) enganchar; (*Fishing*) pescar; **to ~ sth to a rope** enganchar algo a una cuerda; **to ~ one's arms/feet around sth** envolver algo con los brazos/los pies; **to ~ a rope round a nail** atar una cuerda a un clavo
[2] (*) (= *catch*) **she finally ~ed him** por fin lo enganchó
[3] ✦**IDIOM to ~ it*** largarse*
Ⓒ VI [1] (= *fasten*) [*dress*] abrocharse; (= *connect*) engancharse
[2] (*US*‡) trabajar como prostituta, hacer la calle*

►**hook on** Ⓐ VI + ADV engancharse (**to** a)
Ⓑ VT + ADV enganchar (**to** a)

►**hook up** Ⓐ VI + ADV [1] [*dress*] abrocharse
[2] (*Rad, TV*) transmitir en cadena
Ⓑ VT + ADV [1] [+ *dress*] abrochar
[2] (*Rad, TV*) conectar

hookah ['hʊkɑː] N narguile *m*

hooked [hʊkt] ADJ [1] (= *having a hook*) ganchudo
[2] (*) (= *addicted*) **to be ~ on sth** estar enganchado a algo*, ser adicto a algo; **to be ~ on drugs** estar enganchado a las drogas*, ser adicto a las drogas; **to get ~ on sth** volverse adicto a algo

hooker ['hʊkəʳ] N [1] (*) (= *prostitute*) puta *f*
[2] (*Sport*) talonador *m*

hookey*, **hooky*** ['hʊkɪ] N (*esp US*) **to play ~** hacer novillos, hacer pirola

hook-nosed [ˌhʊk'nəʊzd] ADJ de nariz ganchuda

hook-up ['hʊkʌp] N (*Rad, TV*) transmisión *f* en cadena; (*Elec*) acoplamiento *m*; **a ~ with Eurovision** una conexión con Eurovisión

hookworm ['hʊkwɜːm] N anquilostoma *m*

hooky* ['hʊkɪ] N = **hookey**

hooligan ['huːlɪgən] N gamberro/a *m/f*

hooliganism ['huːlɪgənɪzəm] N gamberrismo *m*

hoop [huːp] N (*gen*) aro *m*, argolla *f*; [*of barrel*] fleje *m*; (= *croquet hoop*) argolla *f*; ✦**IDIOM to put sb through the ~** hacer pasar penas a algn

hoopoe ['huːpuː] N abubilla *f*

hooray [hʊ'reɪ] Ⓐ EXCL = **hurrah**
Ⓑ CPD ► **Hooray Henry** N (*Brit pej*) señorito *m*

hoot [huːt] Ⓐ N [1] (= *sound*) [*of owl*] ululato *m*; (*esp Brit*) [*of car*] bocinazo *m*; [*of train*] silbato *m*; [*of siren*] toque *m* de sirena; **I don't care a ~*** (no) me importa un comino*
[2] (= *laugh*) risotada *f*; **it was a ~*** ¡era para morirse de (la) risa!
Ⓑ VT [1] [+ *person*] abuchear; **to ~ sb off the stage** echar a algn de la escena a chiflidos
[2] (*esp Brit*) [+ *horn*] tocar; **he ~ed his horn** tocó la bocina *or* (*esp LAm*) el claxon
Ⓒ VI [1] (= *make sound*) [*owl*] ulular; [*person*] (*in scorn*) abuchear; [*ship, train, factory hooter*] silbar; **to ~ with laughter** carcajear
[2] (*esp Brit Aut*) tocar la bocina, tocar el claxon (*esp LAm*)

hooter ['huːtəʳ] (*Brit*) N [1] [*of ship, factory*] sirena *f*; (*Aut*†) bocina *f*, claxon *m* (*esp LAm*)
[2] (*) (= *nose*) napia* *f*

hoover® ['huːvəʳ] Ⓐ N aspiradora *f*
Ⓑ VT pasar la aspiradora por
Ⓒ VI pasar la aspiradora

hooves [huːvz] NPL *of* **hoof**

hop¹ [hɒp] Ⓐ N [1] (= *jump*) salto *m*, brinco *m*; **~, skip and jump** (*Sport*) triple salto *m*; **in one ~** de un salto; ✦**IDIOM to catch sb on the ~** (*Brit**) pillar *or* (*LAm*) agarrar a algn desprevenido; **the uncertainty should keep them on the ~** (*Brit**) la incertidumbre los mantendrá en estado de alerta
[2] (†*) (= *dance*) baile *m*
[3] (*Aer*) vuelo *m* corto; **in one ~** sin hacer escala
Ⓑ VI [*person, bird, animal*] dar saltos, brincar (*LAm*); ✦**IDIOM to be ~ping mad*** echar chispas*
Ⓒ VT **to ~ it** (*Brit**) largarse*; **~ it!** ¡lárgate!*

►**hop along** VI + ADV avanzar a saltos

►**hop off** Ⓐ VI + PREP (= *get down from*) bajar de
Ⓑ VI + ADV [1] (= *get down*) bajar
[2] (*) largarse*; **~ off!** ¡lárgate!*

►**hop on** Ⓐ VI + PREP subir a
Ⓑ VI + ADV subir; **~ on!** ¡sube!

►**hop out** VI + ADV salir de un salto; **to ~ out of bed** saltar de la cama

►**hop over to** VI + PREP darse una vuelta por

hop² [hɒp] Ⓐ N (*Bot*) (*also* **~s**) lúpulo *m*
Ⓑ CPD ► **hop field** N campo *m* de lúpulo
► **hop picking** N recolección *f* del lúpulo

hope [həʊp] Ⓐ N [1] (= *expectation*) esperanza *f*; **where there's life there's ~** mientras hay vida, hay esperanza; **my ~ is that he'll see reason** espero que entre en razón; **to be beyond (all) ~** [*damaged article*] no tener posibilidad de reparación; [*person*] no tener remedio; **to build one's ~s up (about *or* over sth)** hacerse ilusiones (con algo); **to be full of ~** estar lleno de esperanzas *or* ilusión; **to get one's ~s up (about *or* over sth)** hacerse ilusiones (con algo); **don't get your ~s up** no te hagas ilusiones; **to give up ~ (of doing sth)** perder las esperanzas (de hacer algo); **to have ~s of doing sth** tener esperanzas de hacer algo; **I haven't much ~ of succeeding** no tengo muchas esperanzas de conseguirlo; **I had great ~s of *or* for him** tenía muchas esperanzas puestas en él; **he set out with high ~s** empezó lleno de esperanzas *or* ilusión, empezó con muchas esperanzas; **I ignored him in the ~ that he would go away** no le hice caso con la esperanza de que se fuera; **I don't think there's much chance but we live in ~** no creo que haya muchas posibilidades pero la esperanza es lo último que se pierde; **she lives in (the) ~ of seeing her son again** vive con la esperanza de volver a ver a su hijo; **to lose ~ (of doing sth)** perder las esperanzas (de hacer algo); **to be past ~** [*damaged article*] no tener posibilidad de reparación; [*person*] no tener remedio; **to place one's ~(s) in/on sth** depositar las esperanzas en algo; **to raise sb's ~s** dar esperanzas a algn; **don't raise her ~s too much** no le des demasiadas esperanzas; **don't raise your ~s** no te hagas ilusiones; *see also* **false A3**, **forlorn**, **pin B3**

➤ LANGUAGE IN USE: **hope B** 8.3, 23.1, 23.4, 23.5

[2] (= *chance*) posibilidad *f*; **he hasn't much ~ of winning** no tiene muchas posibilidades de ganar; **there is little ~ of reaching an agreement** hay pocas posibilidades *or* esperanzas de llegar a un acuerdo; **you haven't got a ~ in hell*** no tienes la más remota posibilidad; **there's no ~ of that** no hay posibilidad de eso; **not a ~!*** ¡ni en sueños!; **your only ~ is to ...** tu única esperanza es ...; **some ~(s)!***: **"have you got the day off tomorrow?" — "some ~(s)!"** —¿libras mañana? —¡qué va! *or* ¡ya quisiera yo!; **"maybe she'll change her mind" — "some ~(s)!"** —tal vez cambie de idea —¡no caerá esa breva!
[3] (= *person*) esperanza *f*; **he's the bright ~ of the team** es la gran esperanza del equipo; **you are my last/only ~** tú eres mi última/única esperanza
Ⓑ VT esperar; **your mother is well, I ~?** espero que su madre esté bien; **to ~ that ...** esperar que ... + *subjun*; **I ~ he comes soon** espero que venga pronto, ojalá venga pronto; **I was hoping you'd stay** esperaba que te quedaras; **I ~ you don't think I'm going to do it!** ¡no pensarás que lo voy a hacer yo!; **I ~ to God** *or* **hell she remembers*** quiera el cielo que se acuerde; **to ~ to do sth** esperar hacer algo; **what do you ~ to gain from that?** ¿qué esperas ganar *or* conseguir con eso?; **hoping to hear from you** en espera *or* a la espera de recibir noticias tuyas; **let's ~ it doesn't rain** esperemos que no llueva; **I ~ not** espero que no; **I ~ so** espero que sí; **I should ~ so (too)!** ¡eso espero!; **"I washed my hands first" — "I should ~ so too!"** —me he lavado las manos antes —¡eso espero!; **"but I apologized" — "I should ~ so too!"** —pero me disculpé —¡faltaría más!
Ⓒ VI esperar; **to ~ against ~** esperar en vano; **to ~ for sth** esperar algo; **it's the best we can ~ for** no podemos esperar nada mejor; **we're hoping for a boy this time** esta vez esperamos que sea niño; **I shouldn't ~ for too much from this meeting** no depositaría muchas esperanzas en esta reunión; **I always knew it was too much to ~ for** siempre supe que era mucho pedir; **we'll just have to ~ for the best** esperemos que todo salga bien; **I'm just going to enter the competition and ~ for the best** voy a presentarme al concurso y que sea lo que Dios quiera; **to ~ in God** confiar en Dios
Ⓓ CPD ► **hope chest** N (*US*) ajuar *m* (de novia)

hoped-for ['həʊpt,fɔːʳ] ADJ esperado; **their action had the ~ effect** su acción produjo el efecto esperado; **the ~ economic recovery** la tan esperada reactivación económica

hopeful ['həʊpfʊl] Ⓐ ADJ [1] (= *optimistic*) [*person*] esperanzado, optimista; [*face*] esperanzado, lleno de esperanza; **groups of beggars made ~ sorties towards the tourists** grupos de mendigos se dirigían esperanzados hacia los turistas; **he gave the engine a ~ kick** le dio al motor una patada con la esperanza de que eso lo hiciese funcionar; **I'll ask her, but I'm not too ~** le preguntaré, pero no me hago demasiadas ilusiones *or* no tengo muchas esperanzas; **to be ~ that** tener esperanzas de que, esperar que + *subjun*; **to be ~ about sth** tener esperanzas con respecto a algo; **in the ~ anticipation that ...** con la esperanza de que ...; **ever ~, he never gave up the fight** con las esperanzas intactas, nunca abandonó la lucha; **to feel ~** sentirse optimista; **I am ~ of a positive outcome** tengo esperanzas de que las cosas salgan bien; **to be ~ of doing sth** tener esperanzas de hacer algo, esperar poder hacer algo
[2] (= *promising*) [*sign, future, news*] esperanzador(a), prometedor(a)
Ⓑ N aspirante *mf*; **presidential ~s** aspirantes *mpl* a la presidencia; **he enjoys his job as football coach to young ~s** disfruta entrenando a jóvenes promesas del fútbol

hopefully ['həʊpfəlɪ] ADV [1] (= *with feeling of hope*) **"is he coming with us?" I asked ~** —¿viene con nosostros? —pregunté esperanzado; **I looked ~ around the room for a glimpse of my luggage** miré por la habitación con esperanzas de ver mi equipaje; **she smiled at me ~** me dirigió una sonrisa esperanzada
[2] (*) (= *one hopes*) **~ we'll be able to sort something out** con un poco de suerte podremos arreglar algo; **the new legislation, ~, will lead to some improvements** es de esperar que la nueva legislación traiga consigo algunas mejoras; **~, it won't rain** esperemos que no llueva

hopefulness ['həʊpfʊlnɪs] N esperanza *f*

hopeless ['həʊplɪs] ADJ [1] (= *impossible*) [*task*] imposible; [*attempt*] vano; [*cause*] perdido; [*situation, position*] desesperado; [*love*] imposible; **his attempt to swim the river was ~ from the beginning** su tentativa de cruzar el río a nado estaba condenada al fracaso desde el principio; **it's ~!** ¡es inútil!; **a ~ case** (= *person*) un caso perdido; **he's a ~ case!** es un caso perdido, no tiene remedio; **the doctor says it is a ~ case** el médico dice que no tiene salvación, el médico lo ha desahuciado; **a ~ drunk** un borracho empedernido; **to be (in) a ~ mess** *or* **muddle** [*room*] estar hecho un desastre; [*plans*] estar muy embrollado; [*person*] estar hecho un lío; **a ~ romantic** un romántico incorregible
[2] (= *despairing*) [*cry*] de desespración; [*grief*] desesperado; **to feel ~** sentirse desesperanzado; **she gave a ~ sigh** suspiró desesperada
[3] (*) (= *not competent*) **he's completely ~** es un inútil*; **she's a ~ manager** como jefa es una nulidad *or* es penosa*; **the buses round here are ~** los autobuses de por aquí son un desastre; **to be ~ at (doing) sth: he's ~ at football** es un desastre jugando al fútbol, es una nulidad para el fútbol*; **I was ~ at school** era un negado *or* una nulidad para los estudios*; **I'm ~ at maths/cooking** soy un negado para las matemáticas/la cocina; **I'd be ~ at working for somebody else** yo no serviría para trabajar para otros

hopelessly ['həʊplɪslɪ] ADV [1] (= *despairingly*) [*look, speak, continue*] sin esperanza
[2] (*as intensifier*) [*inadequate, confused, lost*] totalmente, completamente; **he is ~ in debt** está totalmente *or* completamente endeudado; **to be ~ in love** estar perdidamente enamorado

hopelessness ['həʊplɪsnɪs] N [1] [*of situation*] lo desesperado
[2] (= *despair*) desesperanza *f*
[3] (= *incompetence*) inutilidad *f*

hopper ['hɒpəʳ] N (= *chute*) tolva *f*

hopscotch ['hɒpskɒtʃ] N infernáculo *m*, rayuela *f* (*LAm*)

Horace ['hɒrɪs] N Horacio

Horatian [hɒ'reɪʃən] ADJ horaciano

horde [hɔːd] N (= *large number, crowd*) multitud *f*; (*Hist*) horda *f*

horizon [hə'raɪzn] N horizonte *m*; (*fig*) horizonte *m*, perspectiva *f*; **a boat on the ~** una barca en el horizonte; **there are new schemes on the ~** hay nuevos planes en perspectiva; **that's over the ~ now** eso queda ya a la espalda

horizontal [,hɒrɪ'zɒntl] Ⓐ ADJ horizontal; **~ integration** integración *f* horizontal
Ⓑ N horizontal *f*

horizontally [,hɒrɪ'zɒntəlɪ] ADV horizontalmente

hormonal [hɔː'məʊnəl] ADJ hormonal

hormone ['hɔːməʊn] Ⓐ N (*Med*) hormona *f*
Ⓑ CPD ► **hormone replacement therapy** N terapia *f* hormonal sustitutiva ► **hormone treatment** N tratamiento *m* de hormonas

horn [hɔːn] N [1] [*of bull*] cuerno *m*, cacho *m* (*LAm*); [*of deer*] asta *f*, cacho *m* (*LAm*); [*of snail*] cuerno *m*; (= *material*) cuerno *m*, carey *m*; **the Horn of Africa** el Cuerno de África; **~ of plenty** cuerno *m* de la abundancia, cornucopia *f*; **to be on the ~s of a dilemma** estar entre la espada y la pared; **to draw in one's ~s** (*fig*) (= *back down*) volverse atrás; (*with money*) hacer economías
[2] (*Mus*) trompa *f*, cuerno *m*; **to play the ~** tocar la trompa *or* el cuerno
[3] (*Aut*) bocina *f*, claxon *m* (*esp LAm*); **to blow** *or* **sound one's ~** tocar la bocina *or* el claxon
[4] (= *shoe horn*) calzador *m*
[5] (*US**) teléfono *m*; **to get on the ~ to sb** llamar a algn (por teléfono)
► **horn in*** VI + ADV (*esp US*) entrometerse (**on** en)

hornbeam ['hɔːnbiːm] N carpe *m*

hornbill ['hɔːnbɪl] N búcero *m*

horned [hɔːnd] ADJ con cuernos, enastado

-horned [hɔːnd] ADJ (*in compounds*) de cuernos ...

hornet ['hɔːnɪt] N avispón *m*; **to stir up a ~'s nest** armar mucho revuelo

hornless ['hɔːnlɪs] ADJ sin cuernos, mocho

hornpipe ['hɔːnpaɪp] N [1] (*Mus*) chirimía *f*
[2] (*Naut*) *cierto baile de marineros*

horn-rimmed ['hɔːnrɪmd] ADJ [*spectacles*] de concha, de carey

horny ['hɔːnɪ] ADJ (*compar* **hornier**; *superl* **horniest**) [1] (= *hard*) [*material*] córneo; [*hands*] calloso
[2] (‡) (= *randy*) caliente*, cachondo (*Sp, Mex**)

horology [hɒ'rɒlədʒɪ] N horología *f*

horoscope ['hɒrəskəʊp] N horóscopo *m*; **to cast a ~** sacar un horóscopo

horrendous [hɒ'rendəs] ADJ [1] (= *horrific*) [*injury, attack, accident*] horrible, horrendo
[2] (*) (= *dreadful*) [*weather, traffic*] horroroso*, espantoso*; [*cost, price*] tremendo; **the company suffered ~ losses** la compañía sufrió enormes pérdidas

horrendously [hɒ'rendəslɪ] ADV [*difficult, expensive*] tremendamente, terriblemente

horrible ['hɒrɪbl] ADJ [1] (*) (= *unpleasant*) [*food, colour, smell, thought*] horroroso*, horrible*; **aren't those dresses ~?** ¿a que esos vestidos son horrorosos?, ¿a que son feísimos esos vestidos?; **he was the most ~ person I've ever met** era la persona más mala que he conocido; **you're ~!** ¡qué malo eres!; **I've got a ~ feeling that ...** tengo la horrible sensación de que ...; **that jumper looks ~ on you** ese jersey te queda horroroso *or* espantoso; **it's all a ~ mess** es un lío horroroso; **we thought something ~ had happened** pensamos que algo horrible había pasado; **the press write some ~ things about him** la prensa cuenta cosas espantosas *or* horribles de él; **what a ~ thought!** ¡qué idea tan horrible!; **to be ~ to sb** tratar fatal a algn*; **she's ~ to her sister** trata fatal a su hermana;

don't be ~ to your brother no seas malo con tu hermano
2 (= *horrific*) [*crime, scream, accident*] horrible, espantoso; **he died a ~ death** tuvo una muerte horrible

horribly ['hɒrɪblɪ] ADV 1 (*) (= *dreadfully*) [*difficult, rich, embarrassed, expensive*] terriblemente, tremendamente; **I was ~ drunk** tenía una borrachera terrible*, estaba borrachísimo; **I felt ~ embarrassed by the whole thing** me sentía terriblemente *or* tremendamente abochornado por todo aquello*; **it's all gone ~ wrong** todo ha salido terriblemente mal
2 (= *horrifically*) [*die, injure, scream*] de una forma horrible; [*mutilated, disfigured*] horriblemente, espantosamente; **they died ~** murieron de una forma horrible, tuvieron una muerte horrible; **men with ~ scarred faces** hombres con unas cicatrices horribles en la cara

horrid ['hɒrɪd] ADJ (= *disagreeable, unpleasant*) horrible; (= *horrifying*) horroroso; (= *unkind*) antipático; **to be ~ to sb** tratar a algn muy mal, portarse muy mal con algn; **don't be ~!** ¡no seas antipático!; **you ~ thing!** ¡qué malo!, ¡qué antipático!

horridly ['hɒrɪdlɪ] ADV [*behave*] tremendamente mal, fatal

horrific [hɒ'rɪfɪk] ADJ [*injury, attack, accident*] horrible, horrendo

horrifically [hɒ'rɪfɪklɪ] ADV espantosamente, terriblemente; **~ injured** con heridas espantosas

horrify ['hɒrɪfaɪ] VT 1 (= *fill with horror*) horrorizar; **I was horrified to discover that …** me horrorizó descubrir que …
2 (= *shock*) escandalizar; **they were all horrified** se escandalizaron todos

horrifying ['hɒrɪfaɪɪŋ] ADJ horroroso, horripilante

horrifyingly ['hɒrɪ,faɪɪŋlɪ] ADV horrorosamente, de manera horripilante

horror ['hɒrəʳ] Ⓐ N 1 (= *terror, dread*) horror *m*, pavor *m*; (= *loathing, hatred*) horror *m*; **to have a ~ of** tener horror a; **to my ~ I discovered I was locked out** descubrí con horror que me había dejado las llaves dentro; **then, to my ~, it moved!** luego ¡qué susto!, se movió; **the ~s of war** los horrores de la guerra; **that gives me the ~s*** eso me pone los pelos de punta*; **~s!** ¡qué horror!
2 (*) diablo *m*; **that child is a little ~** ese niño es un diablillo; **you ~!** ¡bestia!
Ⓑ CPD ► **horror film** N película *f* de terror

horror-stricken ['hɒrə,strɪkən] ADJ horrorizado

horror-struck ['hɒrə,strʌk] ADJ = **horror-stricken**

hors de combat [ɔ:dəkɔ̃ba] ADJ fuera de combate

hors d'oeuvres [ɔ:'dɜ:vr] NPL entremeses *mpl*

horse [hɔ:s] Ⓐ N 1 (*Zool*) caballo *m*; ✦***IDIOMS*** **dark ~** incógnita *f*; **it's a case of ~s for courses** (*Brit*) en cada caso es distinto, a cada cual lo suyo; **to change ~s in midstream** cambiar de política (*or* personal *etc*) a mitad de camino; **a ~ of a different colour** harina *f* de otro costal; **to eat like a ~** comer como una vaca*; **to flog a dead ~** machacar en hierro frío; **to get on one's high ~** ponerse a pontificar; **don't look a gift ~ in the mouth** a caballo regalado, no le mires el diente; **hold your ~s!** ¡para el carro!, ¡despacito!; **to be straight from the ~'s mouth** ser de buena tinta
2 (*in gymnastics*) potro *m*
3 (*carpenter's*) caballete *m*
4 (= *cavalry*) caballería *f*
5 (‡) (= *heroin*) caballo‡ *m*, heroína *f*
Ⓑ CPD ► **horse artillery** N artillería *f* montada ► **horse brass** N jaez *m* ► **horse breaker** N domador(a) *m/f* de caballos ► **horse breeder** N criador(a) *m/f* de caballos ► **horse chestnut** N (*Bot*) (= *tree*) castaño *m* de Indias; (= *fruit*) castaña *f* de Indias ► **horse collar** N collera *f* ► **horse dealer** N chalán *m* ► **horse doctor** N veterinario/a *m/f* ► **Horse Guards** NPL (*Brit*) Guardia *fsing* Montada ► **horse laugh** N risotada *f*, carcajada *f* ► **horse mackerel** N jurel *m* ► **horse manure** N abono *m* de caballo ► **horse meat** N (*Culin*) carne *f* de caballo ► **horse opera** N (*US*) película *f* del Oeste ► **horse race** N carrera *f* de caballos ► **horse racing** N (*gen*) carreras *fpl* de caballos; (*as sport*) hípica *f* ► **horse riding** N (*Brit*) equitación *f* ► **horse sense** N sentido *m* común ► **horse show** N concurso *m* hípico ► **horse trader** N (*Pol*) chalán/ana *m/f* ► **horse trading** N (*Pol*) toma y daca *m*, chalaneo *m* ► **horse trailer** N (*US*) remolque *m* para caballerías ► **horse trials** NPL concurso *m* hípico

► **horse about***, **horse around*** VI + ADV hacer el tonto

horseback ['hɔ:sbæk] Ⓐ N **on ~** a caballo
Ⓑ CPD ► **horseback riding** N (*US*) equitación *f*

horsebox ['hɔ:sbɒks] N (*Brit*) remolque *m* para caballerías; (*Rail*) vagón *m* para caballerías

horse-drawn ['hɔ:sdrɔ:n] ADJ de tracción animal, tirado por caballos

horseflesh ['hɔ:sfleʃ] N 1 (= *horses*) caballos *mpl*
2 (*Culin*) carne *f* de caballo

horsefly ['hɔ:sflaɪ] N (*pl* **horseflies**) tábano *m*

horsehair ['hɔ:shɛəʳ] N crin *f*

horsehide ['hɔ:shaɪd] N cuero *m* de caballo

horseman ['hɔ:smən] N (*pl* **horsemen**) (= *rider*) jinete *m*; (*skilful*) caballista *m*, charro *m* (*Mex*)

horsemanship ['hɔ:smənʃɪp] N (= *activity*) equitación *f*; (= *skill*) manejo *m* del caballo

horseplay ['hɔ:spleɪ] N payasadas *fpl*

horsepower ['hɔ:s,paʊəʳ] N caballo *m* de vapor; **a 20 ~ engine** un motor de 20 caballos

horseradish ['hɔ:s,rædɪʃ] N (= *plant*) rábano *m* picante; (= *sauce*) salsa *f* de rábano

horseshit‡‡ ['hɔ:sʃɪt] N (*lit*) caca‡‡ *f* de caballo; (*fig*) gilipollada‡ *f*

horseshoe ['hɔ:sʃu:] Ⓐ N herradura *f*
Ⓑ CPD ► **horseshoe arch** N arco *m* de herradura

horsewhip ['hɔ:swɪp] Ⓐ VT azotar
Ⓑ N fusta *f*

horsewoman ['hɔ:s,wʊmən] N (*pl* **horsewomen**) amazona *f*, charra *f* (*Mex*)

horsey*, **horsy*** ['hɔ:sɪ] ADJ (*compar* **horsier**; *superl* **horsiest**) [*person*] aficionado a los caballos; [*appearance*] caballuno

horticultural [,hɔ:tɪ'kʌltʃərəl] ADJ hortícola; **~ show** exposición *f* de horticultura

horticulture ['hɔ:tɪkʌltʃəʳ] N horticultura *f*

horticulturist [,hɔ:tɪ'kʌltʃərɪst] N horticultor(a) *m/f*

hose [həʊz] N 1 (*also* **~pipe**) manga *f*, manguera *f*
2 (= *stockings*) medias *fpl*; (= *socks*) calcetines *mpl*; (*Hist*) calzas *fpl*

► **hose down** VT + ADV regar con manguera

► **hose out** VT + ADV regar con manguera

hosepipe ['həʊzpaɪp] N manga *f*, manguera *f*

hosier ['həʊʒɪəʳ] N calcetero/a *m/f*

hosiery ['həʊʒərɪ] N calcetería *f*

hosp ABBR (= **hospital**) Hosp *m*

hospice ['hɒspɪs] N hospicio *m*

hospitable [hɒs'pɪtəbl] ADJ acogedor, hospitalario

hospitably [hɒs'pɪtəblɪ] ADV con hospitalidad

hospital ['hɒspɪtl] Ⓐ N hospital *m*; **maternity ~** casa *f* de maternidad; **mental ~** hospital *m* psiquiátrico, manicomio *m*; **to go into ~** ingresar en el hospital
Ⓑ CPD ► **hospital administration** N administración *f* de hospital ► **hospital administrator** N (*Brit*) administrador(a) *m/f* de hospital; (*US*) director(a) *m/f* de hospital ► **hospital case** N caso *m* clínico; **90% of ~ cases are released within three weeks** el 90% de los casos clínicos son dados de alta en tres semanas ► **hospital doctor** N interno/a *m/f* ► **hospital facilities** NPL instalaciones *fpl* hospitalarias ► **hospital management** N (= *act*) gestión *f* hospitalaria; (= *persons*) dirección *f* del hospital ► **hospital nurse** N enfermera *f* de hospital ► **hospital ship** N buque *m* hospital

hospitality [,hɒspɪ'tælɪtɪ] Ⓐ N hospitalidad *f*; **corporate ~** hospitalidad *f* corporativa
Ⓑ CPD ► **hospitality area** N zona *f* de recepción para invitados importantes ► **hospitality tent** N carpa *f* de recepción para invitados importantes

hospitalization [,hɒspɪtəlaɪ'zeɪʃən] N hospitalización *f*

hospitalize ['hɒspɪtəlaɪz] VT hospitalizar

host[1] [həʊst] Ⓐ N 1 (*to guest*) anfitrión(ona) *m/f*; (*TV, Rad*) presentador(a) *m/f*; [*of inn*] hostelero *m*, mesonero *m*; **I thanked my ~s** di las gracias a los anfitriones *or* a los que me habían invitado; **we were ~s for a week to a Spanish boy** recibimos en casa durante una semana a un joven español
2 (*Bot, Zool*) huésped *m*
3 (*Comput*) (*also* **~ computer**) servidor *m*
Ⓑ VT [+ *TV programme, games*] presentar; [+ *conference*] ser anfitrión de
Ⓒ CPD ► **host country** N país *m* anfitrión

host[2] [həʊst] N 1 (= *crowd*) multitud *f*; **for a whole ~ of reasons** por un sinfín de razones; **I have a ~ of problems** tengo un sinfín *or* un montón de problemas; **they came in ~s** acudieron a millares
2 (††) (= *army*) hueste *f*, ejército *m*

host[3] [həʊst] N (*Rel*) hostia *f*

hostage ['hɒstɪdʒ] N rehén *mf*; **to take sb ~** tomar *or* (*LAm*) agarrar a algn como rehén

hostel ['hɒstəl] N residencia *f*; (= *youth hostel*) albergue *m* juvenil; (*Univ*) residencia *f* de estudiantes

hosteller, **hosteler** (*US*) ['hɒstələʳ] N *persona que va de albergues para jóvenes*

hostelling, **hosteling** (*US*) ['hɒstəlɪŋ] N **to go (youth) ~** viajar de alberguista

hostelry ['hɒstəlrɪ] N (*pl* **hostelries**) (*esp Brit*) mesón *m*

hostess ['həʊstes] N huéspeda *f*, anfitriona *f*; (*in night club*) azafata *f*; (*Aer*) azafata *f*

hostile ['hɒstaɪl] (*US*) ['hɒstəl] ADJ 1 (= *antagonistic*) [*person, question, atmosphere*] hostil; **to get a ~ reception** tener una recepción hostil; **to be ~ to** *or* **towards sth/sb** ser hostil a algo/con algn; **~ witness** (*Law*) testigo *m* hostil *or* desfavorable
2 (*Mil*) [*force, aircraft, territory*] hostil
3 (= *unfavourable*) [*conditions, weather, environment*] adverso, desfavorable
4 (*Econ, Fin*) hostil; **a ~ takeover bid** una OPA hostil

hostility [hɒs'tɪlɪtɪ] N 1 (= *animosity*) hostilidad *f*
2 **hostilities** (*Mil*) hostilidades *fpl*; **to cease/resume hostilities** cesar/reanudar las hostilidades

hostler ['ɒsləʳ] N mozo *m* de cuadra

hot [hɒt] Ⓐ ADJ (*compar* **hotter**; *superl* **hottest**)
1 (*gen*) caliente; [*climate*] cálido; [*day, summer*] caluroso, de calor; [*sun*] abrasador; **with running ~ and cold water** con agua corriente caliente y fría; **it was a very ~ day** fue un día de mucho calor; **it was a ~ and tiring walk** fue una caminata que nos hizo sudar y nos cansó mucho; **a nice ~ bath** un buen baño caliente; **to be ~** [*thing*] estar caliente; [*weather*] hacer calor; [*person*] tener calor; **this room is ~** hace calor en esta habitación; **to be very ~** [*thing*] estar muy caliente; [*weather*] hacer mucho calor; [*person*] tener mucho calor; **I'm too ~** tengo demasiado calor; **it made me go ~ and cold** me dio escalofríos; **to get ~** [*thing*] calentarse; [*weather*] empezar a hacer calor; [*person*] **I'm getting ~** me está entrando calor; **to get (all) ~ and bothered** sofocarse; **you're getting ~** (*fig*) (*when guessing*) caliente, caliente
2 (= *spicy, peppery*) [*taste, food*] picante; **this food is very ~** esta comida es muy picante; **Mexican food's too ~** la comida mejicana es demasiado picante
3 (*fig*) [*contest*] muy reñido; [*temper*] malo; [*dispute*] acalorado; **~ favourite** gran favorito *m*; **to make it ~ for sb** hacerle la vida imposible a algn; **to make a place too ~ for sb** hacer que algn se vaya de un lugar haciéndole la vida imposible; **~ money** dinero *m* caliente; **~ news** noticias *fpl* de última hora; **he's a pretty ~ player** es un jugador experto; **he has a ~ temper** tiene mal genio *or* carácter; **a ~ tip** información *f* de buenas tintas *or* de fuente fidedigna; ✦*IDIOMS* **to be in/get into ~ water** estar/meterse en problemas; **to be ~ under the collar*** estar acalorado; **to get ~ under the collar*** acalorarse; **to be too ~ to handle**: **he's/it's too ~ to handle** es demasiado; **that's a ~ button** *or* **a ~-button issue** (*US*) ése es un asunto polémico, ése es un tema candente; **these accusations have hit a ~ button in the black community** estas acusaciones han levantado ampollas entre la población negra; *see also* **pursuit**
Ⓑ ADV **to be ~ on sb's trail** *or* **heels** pisar los talones a algn; **news ~ from the press** una noticia que acaba de publicarse en la prensa; ✦*IDIOM* **to blow ~ and cold** ser veleta, mudar a todos los vientos
Ⓒ N **he's got the ~s for her*** ella le pone cachondo
Ⓓ CPD ► **hot air** N (*fig*) palabras *fpl* al aire ► **hot cross bun** N *bollo a base de especias y pasas marcado con una cruz y que se come en Viernes Santo* ► **hot dog** N (*Culin*) perrito *m* caliente, hot dog *m*, pancho *m* (*S. Cone*) ► **hot flash** N (*US*) = **hot flush** ► **hot flush** N (*Brit*) sofoco *m* de calor ► **hot goods** NPL artículos *mpl* robados ► **hot line** N teléfono *m* rojo ► **hot potato*** N cuestión *f* muy discutida ► **hot seat*** N **to be in the ~ seat** estar expuesto ► **hot spot*** N (*Pol*) lugar *m* de peligro; (*for amusement*) lugar *m* de diversión; (= *night club*) sala *f* de fiestas ► **hot springs** NPL aguas *fpl* termales ► **hot stuff** N **to be ~ stuff** (= *expert*) ser un hacha*; (= *sexy*) estar como un tren*; **he's pretty ~ stuff at maths*** es un hacha *or* un as para las matemáticas ► **hot tub** N jacuzzi® *m*

►**hot up*** (*esp Brit*) Ⓐ VI + ADV [*party*] animarse; [*competition, battle*] empezar a animarse; [*dispute*] acalorarse
Ⓑ VT + ADV [+ *food*] calentar; [+ *pace*] acelerar, forzar

hot-air balloon [ˌhɒt'ɛəbə'luːn] N globo *m* de aire caliente

hotbed ['hɒtbed] N (*fig*) semillero *m*

hot-blooded ['hɒt'blʌdɪd] ADJ apasionado

hotchpotch ['hɒtʃpɒtʃ] N (*Brit*) mezcolanza *f*

hot-desking [ˌhɒt'deskɪŋ] N *práctica consistente en la asignación variable de mesas en una oficina, de tal forma que nadie ocupa permanentemente la misma*

hotel [həʊ'tel] Ⓐ N hotel *m*
Ⓑ CPD ► **the hotel industry** N el sector hotelero ► **hotel manager** N director(a) *m/f* de hotel ► **hotel receptionist** N recepcionista *mf* de hotel ► **hotel room** N habitación *f* de hotel ► **hotel staff** N plantilla *f* de hotel ► **hotel work** N trabajo *m* de hostelería ► **hotel workers** NPL trabajadores/oras *mpl/fpl* de hostelería

hotelier [həʊ'telɪəʳ], **hotelkeeper** [həʊ'telˌkiːpəʳ] N hotelero/a *m/f*

hotfoot ['hɒt'fʊt] Ⓐ ADV a toda prisa
Ⓑ VT **to ~ it*** ir volando

hothead ['hɒthed] N exaltado/a *m/f*

hot-headed ['hɒt'hedɪd] ADJ impulsivo, impetuoso

hothouse ['hɒthaʊs] N (*pl* **hothouses** ['hɒthaʊzɪz]) invernadero *m*

hotly ['hɒtlɪ] ADV con pasión, con vehemencia; **he was ~ pursued by the policeman** el policía le seguía muy de cerca

hotpants ['hɒtpænts] NPL shorts *mpl*

hotplate ['hɒtpleɪt] N (*on stove*) hornillo *m*; (*for keeping food warm*) calientaplatos *m inv*

hotpot ['hɒtpɒt] N (*Brit Culin*) estofado *m*

hotrod* ['hɒtrɒd] N (*US Aut*) bólido *m*

hotshot* ['hɒtʃɒt] Ⓐ ADJ de primera, de aúpa*
Ⓑ N personaje *m*, pez *m* gordo*

hot-tempered [ˌhɒt'tempəd] ADJ de mal genio, de mal carácter

Hottentot ['hɒtəntɒt] Ⓐ ADJ hotentote
Ⓑ N 1 (= *person*) hotentote *mf*
2 (*Ling*) hotentote *m*

hot-water bottle [hɒt'wɔːtəˌbɒtl] N bolsa *f* de agua caliente

hot-wire* ['hɒtwaɪəʳ] VT hacerle el puente a

hound [haʊnd] Ⓐ N perro *m* de caza; **the ~s** la jauría
Ⓑ VT (*fig*) perseguir, acosar; **they ~ed him for the money** le persiguieron *or* acosaron para conseguir el dinero; **I will not be ~ed into a decision** no permitiré que me presionen para tomar una decisión

►**hound down** VT + ADV perseguir sin descanso

►**hound on** VT + ADV **to ~ sb on (to do sth)** incitar a algn (a hacer algo)

►**hound out** VT + ADV sacar a la fuerza

hour [aʊəʳ] Ⓐ N hora *f*; **after ~s** fuera de horario; **at all ~s (of the day and night)** a cualquier hora; **she's out till all ~s** no regresa hasta muy tarde, vuelve a casa a las tantas; **at 30 miles an ~** a 30 millas por hora; **~s and ~s** horas y horas, horas enteras; **to pay sb by the ~** pagar a algn por horas; **~ by ~** hora tras hora; **he thought his (last) ~ had come** (*fig*) pensó que había llegado su hora; **in the ~ of danger** en el momento de peligro; **in the early ~s** en la *or* de madrugada; **at the eleventh ~** a última hora; **I've been waiting for ~s** llevo horas esperando; **we waited ~s** esperamos horas y horas; **half an ~** media hora; **two and a half ~s** dos horas y media; **to keep late ~s** trasnochar, acostarse a altas horas de la noche; **to work long ~s** trabajar muchas horas; **lunch ~** hora *f* del almuerzo *or* de comer; **on the ~** a la hora en punto; **out of ~s** fuera de horario; **a quarter of an ~** un cuarto de hora; **to keep regular ~s** llevar una vida ordenada; **in the small ~s** en la *or* de madrugada; **to strike the ~** dar la hora; **he took ~s to do it** tardó horas en hacerlo; **she always takes ~s to get ready** siempre se tira horas para arreglarse; **visiting ~s** horas de visita
Ⓑ CPD ► **hour hand** N horario *m*

hourglass ['aʊəglɑːs] N reloj *m* de arena

hourly ['aʊəlɪ] Ⓐ ADJ [*rate, pay, earnings*] por hora; [*bus, train, service*] cada hora; [*news*] de cada hora; **they come at ~ intervals** llegan cada hora; **there are ~ buses** hay autobuses cada hora; **~ rate** *or* **wage** paga *f* por hora
Ⓑ ADV 1 (= *every hour*) cada hora; **trains from Madrid arrive ~** los trenes de Madrid llegan cada hora
2 (= *by the hour*) **she's paid ~** le pagan por horas
3 (= *at any moment*) **we expected him ~** le esperábamos de un momento a otro

hourly-paid [ˌaʊəlɪ'peɪd] ADJ pagado por hora

house Ⓐ [haʊs] N (*pl* **houses** ['haʊzɪz]) 1 (= *building*) casa *f*; **the party's at my/John's ~** la fiesta es en mi casa/en casa de John; **let's go to your ~** vamos a tu casa; **are you handy around the ~?** ¿eres un manitas para la casa?; **~ of cards** castillo *m* de naipes; **the ~ of God** la casa del Señor; **to move ~** mudarse (de casa); **to keep open ~** tener la puerta siempre abierta, recibir a todo el mundo; ✦*IDIOM* **to get on like a ~ on fire*** (= *progress*) ir sobre ruedas*; [*people*] llevarse de maravilla*; *see also* **coffee B**, **eat**, **public**, **safe**, **steak**
2 (= *household*) casa *f*; **the noise woke the whole ~** el ruido despertó a toda la casa; **to keep ~ (for sb)** llevar la casa (a algn); **the children were playing (at) ~** los niños estaban jugando a las casitas; **to set up ~** poner casa; ✦*IDIOM* **to put** *or* **set** *or* **get one's ~ in order** poner sus asuntos en orden; **the government must put its economic ~ in order** el gobierno debe poner en orden la economía
3 (*Pol*) cámara *f*; **the House** (= *House of Commons*) la Cámara de los Comunes; (*US*) la Cámara de Representantes; **the upper/lower ~** la cámara alta/baja; **the House of Commons/Lords** (*Brit*) (= *building, members*) la Cámara de los Comunes/Lores; **the Houses of Parliament** (*Brit*) el Parlamento; **the House of Representatives** (*US*) la Cámara de Representantes; → SPEAKER
4 (*in debate*) asamblea *f*; **this ~ believes that …** esta asamblea cree que …
5 (*Brit Scol*) *subdivisión de alumnos que se crea en algunos colegios para promover la competición entre ellos*
6 (*Theat*) (= *auditorium*) sala *f*; (= *audience*) público *m*; **full ~** (teatro *m*) lleno *m*; **"house full"** "no hay localidades"; **they played to packed ~s** llenaban las salas; **the second ~** la segunda función; ✦*IDIOM* **to bring the ~ down** [*act, scene*] hacer que se venga abajo la sala *or* el teatro; [*joke*] hacer morirse de risa a todos
7 (*Comm*) casa *f*; **banking ~** entidad *f* bancaria; **fashion ~** casa *f* de modas; **finance ~** entidad *f* financiera; **we do our printing in ~** hacemos nuestra propia impresión, hacemos la impresión en la empresa; **it's on the ~** invita la casa; **TV programmes made out of ~** programas de televisión realizados por productoras externas; **publishing ~** (casa *f*) edi-

torial *f*; *see also* **in-house**
[8] (= *family, line*) casa *f*, familia *f*; **the House of Windsor** la casa de los Windsor
[9] (*Cards*) **full ~** full *m*
[10] (*Astrol*) casa *f* (celeste)
Ⓑ [haʊz] VT [1] (= *provide accommodation for*) [+ *person, family*] alojar, dar alojamiento a
[2] (= *have space for, contain*) albergar; **the building will not ~ them all** el edificio no podrá albergarlos a todos, no cabrán todos en el edificio
[3] (= *store*) guardar, almacenar
[4] (*Mech*) encajar
Ⓒ [haʊs] CPD ► **house agent** N (*Brit*) agente *mf* inmobiliario/a ► **house arrest** N arresto *m* domiciliario; **to be under ~ arrest** estar bajo arresto domiciliario ► **house call** N consulta *f* a domicilio ► **house contents insurance** N seguro *m* del contenido de una casa ► **house doctor** N = **house physician** ► **house guest** N invitado/a *m/f* ► **house lights** NPL (*Theat*) luces *fpl* de sala ► **house manager** N (*Theat*) encargado/a *m/f* del teatro ► **house martin** N avión *m* común ► **house officer** N interno/a *m/f* ► **house owner** N propietario/a *m/f* de una casa ► **house painter** N pintor(a) *m/f* (de brocha gorda) ► **house party** N (*event*) *fiesta de varios días en una casa de campo*; (*people*) grupo *m* de invitados (*que pasan varios días en una casa de campo*) ► **house physician** N (*Brit*) médico/a *m/f* interno/a ► **house plant** N planta *f* de interior ► **house prices** NPL el precio de la vivienda ► **house red** N tinto *m* de la casa ► **house sparrow** N gorrión *m* común ► **house style** N estilo *m* de la casa ► **house surgeon** N (*Brit*) cirujano/a *m/f* interno/a ► **house wine** N vino *m* de la casa

houseboat ['haʊsbəʊt] N casa *f* flotante

housebound ['haʊsbaʊnd] ADJ confinado en casa

houseboy† ['haʊsbɔɪ] (*often pej*) N sirviente *m*; (*in former colonies*) mucamo *m*

housebreaker ['haʊs,breɪkəʳ] N ladrón/ona *m/f*

housebreaking ['haʊs,breɪkɪŋ] N allanamiento *m* de morada, invasión *f* de morada

housebroken ['haʊs,brəʊkən] ADJ (*US*) enseñado

housecleaning ['haʊs'kli:nɪŋ] N limpieza *f* de la casa

housecoat ['haʊskəʊt] N bata *f*

housedress ['haʊsdres] N vestido *m* de casa, vestido *m* sencillo

housefather ['haʊs,fɑ:ðəʳ] N *hombre encargado de una residencia de niños*

housefly ['haʊsflaɪ] N (*pl* **houseflies**) mosca *f*

houseful ['haʊsfʊl] N **there was a ~ of people** la casa estaba llena de gente

household ['haʊshəʊld] Ⓐ N (= *home*) casa *f*; (= *family*) familia *f*
Ⓑ CPD ► **household accounts** NPL cuentas *fpl* de la casa ► **Household Cavalry** N (*Mil*) Guardia *f* Real ► **household chores** NPL quehaceres *mpl* domésticos, tareas *fpl* de la casa ► **household expenses** NPL gastos *mpl* de la casa ► **household gods** NPL penates *mpl* ► **household goods** NPL enseres *mpl* domésticos ► **household linen** N ropa *f* blanca ► **household name** N **he's a ~ name** es una persona conocidísima ► **household refuse** N basura *f* doméstica, residuos *mpl* domésticos ► **household soap** N jabón *m* familiar ► **household troops** NPL (*Brit*) guardia *fsing* real ► **household word** N **it's a ~ word** (*fig*) es el pan de cada día

householder ['haʊs,həʊldəʳ] N (= *owner*) propietario/a *m/f*; (= *tenant*) inquilino/a *m/f*; (= *head of house*) cabeza *f* de familia

house-hunt ['haʊshʌnt] VI (*Brit*) buscar casa

house-hunting ['haʊs,hʌntɪŋ] N **to go househunting** ir buscando casa

house-husband ['haʊs,hʌzbənd] N *marido que se ocupa de las tareas de la casa*

housekeeper ['haʊs,ki:pəʳ] N ama *f* de llaves; (*in hotel*) gobernanta *f*

housekeeping ['haʊs,ki:pɪŋ] N (= *administration*) gobierno *m* de la casa; (= *housework*) quehaceres *mpl* domésticos, tareas *fpl* de la casa; (*Comput*) gestión *f* interna; (*esp Brit*) (*also* **~ money**) dinero *m* para gastos domésticos

housemaid ['haʊsmeɪd] N criada *f*

houseman ['haʊsmən] N (*pl* **housemen**) (*Brit*) (*in hospital*) interno/a *m/f*

housemaster ['haʊs,mɑ:stəʳ] N (*Brit Scol*) *profesor a cargo de la subdivisión de un colegio de internado*

housemate ['haʊsmeɪt] N compañero/a *m/f* de piso

housemistress ['haʊs,mɪstrɪs] N (*Brit Scol*) *profesora a cargo de la subdivisión de un colegio de internado*

housemother ['haʊs,mʌðəʳ] N *mujer encargada de una residencia de niños*

house-proud ['haʊspraʊd] ADJ (*esp Brit*) **she's very ~** le gusta tener la casa impecable

houseroom ['haʊsrʊm] N **to give sth ~** guardar algo en su casa; **I wouldn't give it ~*** no lo tendría en casa

house-sit ['haʊssɪt] VI (*pt, pp* **house-sat**) **I'm ~ting for the Sinclairs** vivo en la casa de los Sinclair para vigilarla en ausencia de los dueños

house-to-house ['haʊstə'haʊs] ADJ de casa en casa; **to conduct ~ enquiries** hacer investigaciones de casa en casa

housetop ['haʊstɒp] N tejado *m*; ✦**IDIOM to shout sth from the ~s** pregonar algo a los cuatro vientos

house-train ['haʊstreɪn] VT (*Brit*) educar, enseñar

house-trained ['haʊstreɪnd] ADJ (*Brit*) enseñado

housewares ['haʊsweəz] NPL (*esp US*) artículos *mpl* de uso doméstico, utensilios *mpl* domésticos

house-warming ['haʊs,wɔ:mɪŋ] N (*also* **~ party**) fiesta *f* de estreno de una casa

housewife ['haʊswaɪf] N (*pl* **housewives**) ama *f* de casa

housewifely ['haʊswaɪflɪ] ADJ doméstico

housewifery ['haʊswɪfərɪ] N (= *administration*) gobierno *m* de la casa; (= *housework*) quehaceres *mpl* domésticos, tareas *fpl* de la casa

housewives ['haʊswaɪvz] NPL *of* **housewife**

housework ['haʊswɜ:k] N quehaceres *mpl* domésticos, tareas *fpl* de la casa

housing ['haʊzɪŋ] Ⓐ N [1] (= *houses*) casas *fpl*, viviendas *fpl*; **there's a lot of new ~** hay muchas casas *or* viviendas nuevas
[2] (*gen*) vivienda *f*; **the ~ problem** el problema de la vivienda
[3] (*Mech*) caja *f*, cubierta *f*
Ⓑ CPD ► **housing association** N asociación *f* de la vivienda ► **housing benefit** N (*Brit*) subsidio *m* de vivienda ► **housing cooperative** N cooperativa *f* de la vivienda ► **housing development** N (*US*) = **housing estate** ► **housing estate** N (*Brit*) urbanización *f*, fraccionamiento *m* (*Mex*), reparto *m* (*Mex*); (= *council estate*) urbanización *f or* barrio *m* de viviendas protegidas ► **housing market** N mercado *m* de la vivienda ► **housing policy** N política *f* de la vivienda ► **housing project** N (*US*) urbanización *f or* barrio *m* de viviendas protegidas ► **housing scheme** N (*Scot*) urbanización *f or* barrio *m* de viviendas protegidas ► **housing shortage** N crisis *f inv* de la vivienda ► **housing stock** N total *m* de viviendas ► **housing subsidy** N subsidio *m* por vivienda

hove [həʊv] PT, PP *of* **heave C2**

hovel ['hɒvəl] N casucha *f*, cuchitril *m*, tugurio *m* (*esp LAm*)

hover ['hɒvəʳ] Ⓐ VI [1] [*bird*] planear, cernerse
[2] (*fig*) [*person*] rondar; **a couple of waiters were ~ing near our table** un par de camareros rondaban cerca de nuestra mesa; **she was ~ing in the doorway** andaba rondando por la entrada; **he was ~ing between life and death** se debatía entre la vida y la muerte
Ⓑ CPD ► **hover fly** N mosca *f* de las flores

►**hover about** VI + ADV, VI + PREP = **hover around**

►**hover around** Ⓐ VI + ADV rondar
Ⓑ VI + PREP **to ~ around sb** rondar a algn, girar en torno a algn

hovercraft ['hɒvəkrɑ:ft] N aerodeslizador *m*

hoverport ['hɒvə,pɔ:t] N puerto *m* de aerodeslizadores

how [haʊ]

[A] ADVERB [C] NOUN
[B] CONJUNCTION

Ⓐ ADVERB

[1] ***in direct and indirect questions, reported speech*** [1·1] (*WITH VERB*)

You can usually use **cómo** *to translate* **how** *in questions as well as after report verbs and verbs of (un)certainty and doubt (e.g.* **no sé***):*

cómo; **~ did you do it?** ¿cómo lo hiciste?; **~ can that be?** ¿cómo puede ser eso?; **~ are you?** ¿cómo estás?, ¿cómo *or* qué tal te va? (*LAm**), ¿qué tal (estás)? (*Sp**); **~ was the film?** ¿qué tal la película?; **please tell me ~ to do it** por favor, dígame cómo hacerlo; **I wasn't sure ~ to make soup** no sabía muy bien cómo hacer *or* preparar una sopa; **I explained to her ~ to make a paella** le expliqué cómo se hacía una paella; **I know ~ you did it** ya sé cómo lo hiciste; **to know ~ to do sth** saber hacer algo; **to learn ~ to do sth** aprender a hacer algo, aprender cómo se hace algo; **~ do you like your steak?** ¿cómo le gusta el filete?; **~ do you like the book?** ¿qué te parece el libro?; **~'s that for cheek?** ¿no te parece de una cara dura increíble?; **I can't understand ~ it happened** no entiendo cómo ocurrió

[1·2] (= *to what degree*)

how + ADJECTIVE *in questions can often be translated using* **cómo es/era de** + ADJECTIVE *(agreeing with the noun), but other constructions might be more usual depending on the context:*

~ big is it? ¿cómo es de grande?; **~ difficult was the exam?** ¿cómo fue de difícil el examen?; BUT **~ old are you?** ¿cuántos años tienes?; **~ wide is this bed?** ¿qué anchura tiene esta cama?, ¿cuánto mide de ancho esta cama?

with adverbs various translations are possible depending on the context. A very common construction is PREPOSITION + **qué** + NOUN*:*

~ far away is it? ¿a qué distancia queda?, ¿qué tan lejos queda? (*LAm*); **~ far is it (from here) to Edinburgh?** ¿qué distancia hay de aquí a Edimburgo?; **~ fast can it go?** ¿a qué velocidad puede ir?; **~ soon can you be ready?** ¿cuánto tardas en prepararte?; **~ soon can you come?** ¿cuándo puedes venir?

To translate **how** + **ADJECTIVE/ADVERB** *in reported speech,* **lo** + **ADJECTIVE/ADVERB** *is used. Note that the adjective agrees with the noun.*

you don't know ~ difficult it is no sabes lo difícil que es; **I didn't know ~ expensive the tickets were** no sabía lo caras que eran las entradas; **they've been telling me ~ well you did in your exams** ya me han hablado de lo bien que hiciste los exámenes

◆ **and how!** ¡y cómo!, ¡y tanto!

◆ **how about**: **~ about tomorrow?** ¿qué te parece mañana?; **~ about a cup of tea?** ¿te apetece una taza de té?; **I like it, but ~ about you?** a mí me gusta, pero ¿y a ti?; **~ about going to the cinema?** ¿qué tal si vamos al cine?, ¿y si vamos al cine?

◆ **how long**: **~ long is this bed?** ¿qué longitud tiene esta cama?, ¿cuánto mide de largo esta cama?; **~ long will you be?** ¿cuánto vas a tardar?; **~ long have you been here?** ¿cuánto tiempo llevas aquí?

◆ **how many**: **~ many are there?** ¿cuántos hay?; **~ many cartons of milk did you buy?** ¿cuántos cartones de leche has comprado?

◆ **how much**: **~ much sugar do you want?** ¿cuánto azúcar quieres?; **~ much is it?** ¿cuánto vale?, ¿cuánto es?

◆ **how often**: **~ often do you go?** ¿con qué frecuencia vas?; *see also* **else 2**

2 ***in other statements***

Translate **how** *with verbs other than report ones or verbs of (un)certainty and doubt using* **como** *without an accent:*

como; **this is ~ you do it** así es como se hace; **that was ~ I came to meet him** así es como lo conocí; **I'll do it ~ I like** lo haré como me parezca

3 ***in exclamations***

You can often translate **how** + **ADJECTIVE/ADVERB** *using* **qué** + **ADJECTIVE/ADVERB:**

qué; **~ beautiful!** ¡qué bonito!; **~ strange!** ¡qué raro!; **~ quickly the time passed!** ¡qué de prisa pasó el tiempo!; *BUT* **~ glad I am to see you!** ¡cuánto me alegro de verte!; **~ they talk!** ¡cuánto hablan!; **~ sorry I am!** ¡cuánto lo siento!; **~ she's changed!** ¡cuánto ha cambiado!; **~ kind of you!** es usted muy amable

Ⓑ CONJUNCTION

** = that* que; **she told me ~ she'd seen him last night** me dijo que lo había visto anoche

Ⓒ NOUN

I want to know the ~ and the why of all this quiero saber el cómo y el porqué de todo esto

howdah ['haʊdə] N howdah *f* (*silla para montar elefantes*)

howdy* ['haʊdɪ] EXCL (*US*) ¡hola!

how-d'ye-do ['haʊdjə'du:] N lío *m*; **this is a fine ~!** ¡en buen lío *or* berenjenal nos hemos metido!, ¡vaya lío!

▼**however** [haʊ'evəʳ] Ⓐ ADV 1 (= *nevertheless*) sin embargo, no obstante; **most men, ~, prefer black** la mayoría de los hombres, sin embargo *or* no obstante, prefieren el negro

2 (= *no matter how*) **~ cold it is, we still manage to have fun** por mucho frío que haga, nos las arreglamos para pasarlo bien; **he'll never catch us ~ fast he runs** por muy rápido que vaya *or* por mucho que corra no nos alcanzará; **~ hard she tried, she couldn't remember his name** por mucho *or* más que lo intentaba, no lograba acordarse de su nombre; **wait 10 to 15 minutes, or ~ long it takes** espera 10 ó 15 minutos, o los que sean necesarios; **the 5,000 spectators, or ~ many were there** los 5.000 espectadores, o los que fuesen; **take about a metre of fabric, or ~ much you need** toma un metro de tela o lo que necesites

3 (*in questions*) (= *how*) cómo; **~ did you manage to do that?** ¿cómo te las arreglaste para hacer eso?

Ⓑ CONJ **~ it's done, it has to look right** se haga como se haga, tiene que quedar bien; **~ we add it up, it doesn't come to 83** lo sumemos como lo sumemos, no da 83, hagamos la suma como la hagamos, no da 83; **~ you want** *or* **like** como quieras; **you can do it ~ you want** puedes hacerlo como quieras

HOWEVER

Unlike **however**, **sin embargo** and **no obstante** can never end a sentence; they must always go at the beginning of it or between the clauses:

He has one problem, however
Sin embargo, tiene un problema
He does not expect to come out of the meeting with anything concrete, however
No obstante, no espera salir de la reunión con nada concreto

howitzer ['haʊɪtsəʳ] N obús *m*

howl [haʊl] Ⓐ N [*of animal*] aullido *m*; [*of wind*] rugido *m*; (*fig*) [*of protest*] clamor *m*, grito *m*; **a ~ of pain** un alarido de dolor; **~s of laughter** (*fig*) carcajadas *fpl*; **with a ~ of rage** dando un alarido de furia

Ⓑ VI [*animal*] aullar; [*person*] dar alaridos; [*wind*] rugir, bramar; [*child*] (= *weep*) berrear; **the dog ~ed all night** el perro estuvo aullando toda la noche; **he ~ed with pain** aullaba de dolor, daba alaridos de dolor; **to ~ with laughter** (*fig*) reír a carcajadas; **to ~ with rage** bramar de furia, bramar furioso

Ⓒ VT (= *shout*) gritar

►**howl down** VT + ADV hacer callar a gritos

howler ['haʊləʳ] N falta *f* garrafal

howling ['haʊlɪŋ] ADJ [*success*] clamoroso

howsoever [haʊsəʊ'evəʳ] ADV comoquiera que

hoy [hɔɪ] EXCL ¡eh!, ¡hola!

hoyden† ['hɔɪdn] N marimacho *m*

HP N ABBR 1 (*Brit**) = **hire purchase**
2 (= **horsepower**) C.V. *mpl*

h.p. N ABBR (= **horsepower**) C.V. *mpl*

HQ N ABBR (= **headquarters**) E.M.

HR N ABBR 1 = **Human Resources**
2 (*US*) = **House of Representatives**

hr ABBR (= **hour**) h

HRH N ABBR (= **Her** *or* **His Royal Highness**) S.A.R.

hrs ABBR (= **hours**) hs

HRT N ABBR = **hormone replacement therapy**

HS ABBR (*US*) = **high school**

HST N ABBR 1 (*Brit*) = **high speed train**
2 (*US*) = **Hawaiian Standard Time**

HT N ABBR = **high tension**

ht ABBR (= **height**) alt.

HTML N ABBR (= **hypertext markup language**) HTML *m*

http N ABBR (= **hypertext transfer protocol**) http *m*

HUAC N ABBR (*US Hist*) = **House Un-American Activities Committee**

hub [hʌb] N cubo *m*; (*fig*) eje *m*

hubbub ['hʌbʌb] N algarabía *f*, barahúnda *f*; **a ~ of voices** un barullo de voces

hubby* ['hʌbɪ] N marido *m*, maridito* *m*

hubcap ['hʌbkæp] N (*Aut*) tapacubos *m inv*

hubris ['hju:brɪs] N orgullo *m* desmesurado

huckster ['hʌkstəʳ] N (*US*) vendedor *m* ambulante, buhonero *m*

HUD N ABBR (*US*) = **Department of Housing and Urban Development**

huddle ['hʌdl] Ⓐ N [*of people*] tropel *m*; [*of things*] montón *m*; **to go into a ~*** hacer un corrillo para discutir algo en secreto

Ⓑ VI acurrucarse; **we ~d round the fire** nos arrimamos al fuego; **the chairs were ~d in a corner** las sillas estaban amontonadas en un rincón

►**huddle down** VI + ADV (= *snuggle*) acurrucarse; (= *crouch*) agacharse

►**huddle together** VI + ADV apiñarse; **they were huddling together for warmth** estaban apiñados *or* acurrucados para darse calor

►**huddle up** VI + ADV apretarse (**against** contra)

hue¹ [hju:] N (= *colour*) color *m*; (= *shade*) matiz *m*; **people of every political ~** gente de todos los matices políticos

hue² [hju:] N **~ and cry** [*of protest*] griterío *m*, clamor *m*; **to raise a ~ and cry** levantar protestas; **there was a ~ and cry after him** se le persiguió enérgicamente

huff* [hʌf] Ⓐ N **in a ~** enojado; **to go off in a ~** irse ofendido, picarse; **to take the ~** ofenderse Ⓑ VI **to ~ and puff** (*out of breath*) jadear, resollar; **he ~ed and puffed a lot and then said yes** (*fig*) resopló mucho y luego dijo que bueno

huffed* [hʌft] ADJ enojado

huffily ['hʌfɪlɪ] ADV malhumoradamente; **he said ~** dijo malhumorado

huffiness ['hʌfɪnɪs] N mal humor *m*

huffy ['hʌfɪ] ADJ (*compar* **huffier**; *superl* **huffiest**) (*of character*) enojadizo; (*in mood*) malhumorado, ofendido; **he was a bit ~ about it** se ofendió un tanto por ello

hug [hʌg] Ⓐ N abrazo *m*; **to give sb a ~** dar un abrazo a algn; **give me a ~** dame un abrazo

Ⓑ VT 1 (*lovingly*) abrazar; (= *squeeze*) [*bear*] ahogar, apretar; **they ~ged each other** se abrazaron; **to ~ o.s. to keep warm** acurrucarse para darse calor

2 (= *keep close to*) arrimarse a

huge [hju:dʒ] (*compar* **huger**; *superl* **hugest**) ADJ [*person, building, thing*] enorme, inmenso; [*bill, sum of money, investment*] enorme, astronómico*; [*increase, problem, difference*] enorme, tremendo; **~ amounts of** enormes cantidades de; **~ numbers of** gran número de; **they are making a ~ profit** están sacando enormes beneficios *or* beneficios astronómicos; **the result was human suffering on a ~ scale** el resultado fue sufrimiento humano en proporciones gigantescas; **to be a ~ success** tener un éxito enorme, ser todo un éxito

hugely ['hju:dʒlɪ] ADV 1 (*with adj*) [*expensive, popular, entertaining, important*] tremendamente, enormemente; **a ~ enjoyable book** un libro que se disfruta muchísimo; **a ~ successful film** una película de enorme éxito; **he is a ~ talented songwriter** es un compositor con un talento enorme

2 (*with verb*) [*vary, increase*] enormemente; **she seemed to be enjoying herself ~** parecía que se lo estaba pasando en grande

hugeness ['hju:dʒnɪs] N inmensidad *f*

hugger-mugger ['hʌgə,mʌgəʳ] Ⓐ N confusión *f*; **a ~ of books** un montón de libros en des-

➤ LANGUAGE IN USE: however A1 26.1, 26.3 A2 26.3

orden
Ⓑ ADV desordenadamente
-hugging ['hʌgɪŋ] ADJ (*ending in compounds*) **figure-hugging** ajustado, ceñido al cuerpo
Hugh [hju:] N Hugo, Ugo
Huguenot ['hju:gənəʊ] Ⓐ ADJ hugonote
Ⓑ N hugonote/a *m/f*
huh [hʌ] EXCL ¡eh!
Hula Hoop® ['hu:lə,hu:p] N Hula Hoop *m*
hulk [hʌlk] N 1 (*Naut*) (= *abandoned ship*) casco *m*; (*pej*) (= *clumsy ship*) carraca *f*
2 (= *large, ungainly building*) armatoste *m*; **a great ~ of a man*** un gigantón
hulking* ['hʌlkɪŋ] ADJ pesado; **a ~ great brute** un hombracho
hull [hʌl] Ⓐ N (*Naut*) casco *m*
Ⓑ VT [+ *fruit*] descascarar
hullabaloo* [,hʌləbə'lu:] N (= *noise*) algarabía *f*; (= *fuss*) jaleo *m*, revuelo *m*; **a great ~ broke out** se armó un revuelo tremendo; **that ~ about the money** ese jaleo *or* revuelo que se armó por el dinero*
hullo [hʌ'ləʊ] EXCL = **hello**
hum [hʌm] Ⓐ N (*gen, Elec*) zumbido *m*; [*of voices*] murmullo *m*
Ⓑ VT [+ *tune*] canturrear, tararear
Ⓒ VI 1 [*insect, wire*] zumbar; [*person*] canturrear, tararear una canción
2 (*fig*) (*) (= *be busy*) bullir, hervir; **the market place was ~ming** el mercado era un hervidero (de actividad), el mercado bullía *or* hervía de actividad; **to make things ~** hacer que la cosa marche*; **to ~ with activity** bullir de actividad
3 (*) (= *smell*) oler mal
4 **to ~ and haw** vacilar
human ['hju:mən] Ⓐ ADJ humano; **the ~ voice** la voz humana; **~ feet are made for weight bearing** los pies del ser humano *or* del hombre están hechos para soportar peso; **we bank managers are ~ too** los directores de banco también somos humanos; ✦*IDIOM* **I'm/he's** *etc* **only ~** todos somos humanos
Ⓑ N ser *m* humano
Ⓒ CPD ► **human being** N ser *m* humano ► **human chain** N **to form a ~ chain** formar una cadena humana ► **human consumption** N **to be fit for ~ consumption** ser apto para el consumo humano ► **human error** N error *m* humano; **it was a case of ~ error** fue un (caso de) error humano ► **human interest** N interés *m* humano ► **human interest story** N historia *f* de interés humano ► **human nature** N naturaleza *f* humana; **it's ~ nature to do that** hacer eso es humano ► **the human race** N la raza humana, el género humano ► **human resources** NPL recursos *mpl* humanos ► **human resource manager** N director(a) *m/f* de recursos humanos ► **human rights** NPL derechos *mpl* humanos ► **human rights organization** N organización *f* pro derechos humanos ► **human shield** N **to use sb as a ~ shield** usar a algn como escudo (humano)
humane [hju:'meɪn] Ⓐ ADJ humano, humanitario
Ⓑ CPD ► **humane studies** NPL ciencias *fpl* humanas, humanidades *fpl*
humanely [hju:'meɪnlɪ] ADV humanamente
humaneness [hju:'meɪnnɪs] N humanidad *f*
humanism ['hju:mənɪzəm] N humanismo *m*
humanist ['hju:mənɪst] N humanista *mf*
humanistic [,hju:mə'nɪstɪk] ADJ humanístico
humanitarian [hju:,mænɪ'tɛərɪən] Ⓐ ADJ humanitario
Ⓑ N humanitario/a *m/f*
humanitarianism [hju:,mænɪ'tɛərɪənɪzəm] N humanitarismo *m*
humanity [hju:'mænɪtɪ] N 1 (*gen*) humanidad *f*; **crimes against ~** crímenes *mpl* contra la humanidad *or* de lesa humanidad
2 (*Literat, Art*) **the humanities** las humanidades
3 (*Scol*) **humanities** letras *fpl*, humanidades *fpl*
humanization [,hju:mənaɪ'zeɪʃən] N humanización *f*
humanize ['hju:mənaɪz] VT humanizar
humankind ['hju:mən'kaɪnd] N el género humano
humanly ['hju:mənlɪ] ADV humanamente; **to do everything ~ possible** hacer todo lo humanamente posible; **as quickly/well as is ~ possible** tan deprisa/bien como sea humanamente posible; **as far as is ~ possible** dentro de lo humanamente posible
humanoid ['hju:mənɔɪd] Ⓐ ADJ humanoide
Ⓑ N humanoide *mf*
humble ['hʌmbl] Ⓐ ADJ (*compar* **humbler**, *superl* **humblest**) 1 (= *unassuming*) [*person*] humilde, modesto; [*apology*] humilde; **she was very ~ about her achievements** era muy modesta respecto a sus éxitos; **my ~ apologies for keeping you waiting** (*frm*) mis más humildes disculpas por tenerle esperando; **in my ~ opinion** en mi humilde *or* modesta opinión; **I am** *or* **remain your ~ servant** (*frm*) (*in letters*) su humilde *or* seguro/a servidor(a)
2 (= *lowly*) [*person, origins, background*] humilde; [*house, home*] humilde, modesto; **the ~ maggot** el humilde gusano; **welcome to our ~ abode** (*hum*) bienvenido a nuestra humilde morada
Ⓑ VT 1 (= *make humble*) dar una lección de humildad a; **Ted's words ~d me** Ted me dio una lección de humildad con sus palabras; **it was a humbling experience** fue una lección de humildad; **to ~ o.s. before God** acercarse a Dios con humildad
2 (= *defeat*) humillar
Ⓒ CPD ► **humble pie** N ✦*IDIOM* **to eat ~ pie** morder el polvo
humblebee ['hʌmblbi:] N abejorro *m*
humbleness ['hʌmblnɪs] N humildad *f*
humbly ['hʌmblɪ] ADV 1 (= *meekly*) [*say, act*] humildemente
2 (*frm*) (= *respectfully*) [*ask*] humildemente; [*suggest, propose*] humildemente, modestamente; **to ~ apologise for sth** disculparse humildemente por algo; **I most ~ beg your pardon/thank you** le pido perdón/le doy las gracias con toda humildad
3 (= *modestly*) humildemente; **~ born** de origen humilde
humbug* ['hʌmbʌg] N 1 (= *person*) charlatán/ana *m/f*; **he's an old ~** es un farsante
2 (= *nonsense*) tonterías *fpl*; **~!** ¡bobadas!*
3 (*Brit*) (= *sweet*) caramelo *m* de menta
humdinger ['hʌmdɪŋəʳ] N **it's a ~!*** ¡es una auténtica maravilla!; **a real ~ of a car** una maravilla de coche
humdrum ['hʌmdrʌm] ADJ monótono, rutinario
humerus ['hju:mərəs] N (*pl* **humeri** ['hju:məraɪ]) húmero *m*
humid ['hju:mɪd] ADJ húmedo
humidifier [hju:'mɪdɪfaɪəʳ] N humedecedor *m*
humidify [hju:'mɪdɪfaɪ] VT [+ *room, air*] humidificar
humidity [hju:'mɪdɪtɪ] N humedad *f*
humiliate [hju:'mɪlɪeɪt] VT humillar
humiliating [hju:'mɪlɪeɪtɪŋ] ADJ humillante, vergonzoso
humiliatingly [hju:'mɪlɪeɪtɪŋlɪ] ADV de manera humillante, vergonzosamente; **we were ~ defeated** sufrimos una derrota vergonzosa
humiliation [hju:mɪlɪ'eɪʃən] N humillación *f*
humility [hju:'mɪlɪtɪ] N humildad *f*
humming ['hʌmɪŋ] Ⓐ N [*of insect*] zumbido *m*; [*of person*] tarareo *m*, canturreo *m*
Ⓑ CPD ► **humming top** N trompa *f*
hummingbird ['hʌmɪŋbɜ:d] N colibrí *m*, picaflor *m*
hummock ['hʌmək] N montecillo *m*, morón *m*
hummus, **hummous** ['hʊməs] N *paté de garbanzos originario del Oriente Medio*
humongous* [hju'mɒŋgəs] ADJ **she is such a ~ star** es una superestrella; **we had a ~ row** tuvimos una pelea de órdago*
humor ['hju:məʳ] N, VT (*US*) = **humour**
-humored ['hju:məd] ADJ (*ending in compounds*) (*US*) = **-humoured**
humorist ['hju:mərɪst] N humorista *mf*
humorless ['hju:məlɪs] ADJ (*US*) = **humourless**
humorous ['hju:mərəs] ADJ [*person*] gracioso, divertido; [*book, story*] divertido; [*situation, idea, tone*] cómico, gracioso
humorously ['hju:mərəslɪ] ADV con gracia
humour, **humor** (*US*) ['hju:məʳ] Ⓐ N 1 (= *amusingness*) (*gen*) humor *m*; [*of book, situation*] gracia *f*; **sense of ~** sentido *m* del humor; **to have a sense of ~** tener sentido del humor; **I see no ~ in that** no le veo la gracia a eso
2 (= *mood*) humor *m*; **to be in a good/bad ~** estar de buen/mal humor; **they were in no ~ for fighting** no estaban de humor para pelear; **to be out of ~** estar de mal humor
3 (*Med*) humor *m*
Ⓑ VT complacer, consentir
-humoured, **-humored** (*US*) ['hju:məd] ADJ (*ending in compounds*) de humor …
humourless, **humorless** (*US*) ['hju:məlɪs] ADJ [*person*] arisco; [*joke*] sin gracia
hump [hʌmp] Ⓐ N 1 (*Anat*) joroba *f*
2 [*of camel*] giba *f*
3 (*in ground*) montecillo *m*; **we're over the ~** (*fig*) ya pasamos lo peor
4 (*Brit**) (= *bad mood*) **it gives me the ~** me fastidia, me molesta; **to have the ~** estar de mal humor
Ⓑ VT 1 (= *arch*) encorvar; **to ~ one's back** encorvarse
2 (*) (= *carry*) llevar
3 (**) (= *have sex with*) joder (*Sp***), coger (*LAm***)
Ⓒ VI (**) (= *have sex*) joder**, follar**
humpback ['hʌmpbæk] N 1 (= *person*) jorobado/a *m/f*; **to have a ~** ser jorobado
2 (= *whale*) (*also* **~ whale**) rorcual *m*
humpbacked ['hʌmpbækt] ADJ [*person*] jorobado; **~ bridge** puente *m* encorvado
humph [mm] EXCL ¡bah!
humpy ['hʌmpɪ] ADJ (*compar* **humpier**, *superl* **humpiest**) desigual
humungous* [hju'mʌŋgəs] ADJ = **humongous**
humus ['hju:məs] N (*Bio*) humus *m*
Hun [hʌn] N 1 (*Hist*) huno *m*
2 (*pej*) (= *German*) tudesco *m*, alemán *m*
hunch [hʌntʃ] Ⓐ N 1 (*) (= *idea*) corazonada *f*, presentimiento *m*; **it's only a ~** no es más que una corazonada *or* un presentimiento que tengo; **I had a ~** tuve una corazonada *or* un presentimiento; **the detective had one of his ~es** el detective tuvo una de sus corazo-

nadas
2 (*Anat*) = **hump A1**
Ⓑ VT (*also* ~ **up**) encorvar; **to ~ one's back** encorvarse
Ⓒ VI encorvarse; **to be ~ed up** ser jorobado; **to sit ~ed up** estar sentado con el cuerpo doblado

hunchback ['hʌntʃbæk] N jorobado/a *m/f*

hunchbacked ['hʌntʃbækt] ADJ jorobado

hundred ['hʌndrɪd] Ⓐ N 1 **a** *or* **one ~** (*before noun or used alone*) cien; (*before numbers up to 99*) ciento; **a** *or* **one ~ people** cien personas; **to count up to a** *or* **one ~** contar hasta cien; **a ~ and one/two** ciento uno/dos; **a** *or* **one ~ and ten** ciento diez; **a** *or* **one ~ thousand** cien mil; **two ~** doscientos; **three ~** trescientos; **five ~ people** quinientas personas; **five ~ and one** quinientos uno; **seven ~ euros** setecientos euros; **nine ~ pounds** novecientas libras; **a** *or* **one ~ per cent** cien por cien; **to live to be a ~** llegar a los cien años; **the ~ and first** el centésimo primero 2 (= *figure*) ciento *m* 3 (= *large number*) **in ~s** ◊ **by the ~** a centenares; **for ~s of thousands of years** durante centenares de miles de años; **~s of people** centenares de personas; **I've got ~s of letters to write** tengo que escribir cientos de cartas; **I've told you ~s of times** te lo he dicho cientos *or* centenares de veces; **I've got a ~ and one things to do** tengo la mar de cosas que hacer Ⓑ CPD ► **the Hundred Years' War** N la Guerra de los Cien Años

HUNDRED

"Ciento" or "cien"?

- Use **cien** before a *noun* (even when it follows **mil**):
  ...a *or* one hundred soldiers...
  ...cien soldados...
  ...eleven hundred metres...
  ...mil cien metros...

! Don't translate numbers like **eleven hundred** literally. Translate their equivalent in thousands and hundreds instead.

- Use **cien** before **mil** and **millón**:
  ...a *or* one hundred thousand dollars...
  ...cien mil dólares...
  ...a *or* one hundred million lira...
  ...cien millones de liras...
- But use **ciento** before another *number*:
  ...a *or* one hundred and sixteen stamps...
  ...ciento dieciséis sellos...
- When **hundred** follows another number, use the compound forms (**doscientos, -as, trescientos, -as** *etc*) which must agree with the noun:
  ...two hundred and fifty women...
  ...doscientas cincuenta mujeres...

For further uses and examples, see main entry.

hundredfold ['hʌndrɪdfəʊld] Ⓐ ADJ céntuplo
Ⓑ ADV cien veces

hundredth ['hʌndrɪdθ] Ⓐ ADJ centésimo
Ⓑ N centésimo *m*, centésima parte *f*

hundredweight ['hʌndrɪdweɪt] N (*Brit*) = *112 libras = 50.8 kilogramos*; (*approx*) quintal *m*; (*US*) = *100 libras = 45.4 kilogramos*

hung [hʌŋ] Ⓐ PT, PP *of* **hang**
Ⓑ CPD ► **hung jury** N *jurado cuyos miembros no se pueden poner de acuerdo* ► **hung parliament** N *parlamento en el que ningún partido alcanza mayoría absoluta*

Hungarian [hʌŋ'gɛərɪən] Ⓐ ADJ húngaro
Ⓑ N 1 (= *person*) húngaro/a *m/f*
2 (*Ling*) húngaro *m*

Hungary ['hʌŋgərɪ] N Hungría *f*

hunger ['hʌŋgəʳ] Ⓐ N 1 (*for food*) hambre *f*
2 (*fig*) sed *f*; **to have a ~ for** [+ *adventure, knowledge*] tener hambre *or* sed de, estar hambriento *or* sediento de; **he had a ~ for love** estaba ávido de amor
Ⓑ VI estar hambriento, tener hambre
Ⓒ CPD ► **the hunger marches** NPL (*Brit Hist*) *marchas protagonizadas por los obreros británicos y sus familias durante la Gran Depresión para protestar por sus condiciones de pobreza* ► **hunger strike** N huelga *f* de hambre; **to be on ~ strike** estar haciendo huelga de hambre; **to go on ~ strike** ponerse en huelga de hambre

►**hunger for, hunger after** VI + PREP (*fig*) [+ *adventure, knowledge*] tener hambre *or* sed de, estar hambriento *or* sediento de

hung over* [hʌŋ'əʊvəʳ] ADJ **to be ~** tener resaca

hungrily ['hʌŋgrɪlɪ] ADV 1 [*eat*] ávidamente, con ansia; [*look*] con anhelo
2 (*fig*) (= *eagerly*) ansiosamente; **American businesses are ~ eyeing the British market** las compañías americanas están observando ansiosamente el mercado británico

hungry ['hʌŋgrɪ] ADJ (*compar* **hungrier**; *superl* **hungriest**) 1 (*gen*) [*person, animal*] hambriento; **pictures of ~ children** imágenes de niños hambrientos; **he looked at the cake with ~ eyes** miró el pastel con anhelo; **digging up the road is ~ work** cavar la calle es un trabajo que da hambre *or* abre el apetito; **to be ~** tener hambre; **to feel ~** tener hambre; **to go ~** pasar hambre; **we were late for tea so we had to go ~** llegamos tarde para la cena y tuvimos que quedarnos sin comer; **all this work is making me ~** todo este trabajo me está dando hambre; **talking about food is making me ~** hablando de comida se me está abriendo el apetito
2 (*fig*) (= *eager*) **to be ~ for** [+ *adventure, knowledge*] tener hambre *or* sed de, estar hambriento *or* sediento de; **to be ~ for power** tener sed *or* estar sediento de poder

hunk [hʌŋk] N 1 [*of bread, cheese, cake*] (buen) trozo *m*, pedazo *m* (grande) 2 (*) (= *man*) monumento* *m*, cachas *m inv* (*Sp**)

hunker* ['hʌŋkəʳ] VI (*US*) **to ~ down** agacharse

hunky* ['hʌŋkɪ] ADJ (*compar* **hunkier**; *superl* **hunkiest**) 1 (= *strong*) fuerte, macizo
2 (= *attractive*) bueno*

hunky-dory* [,hʌŋkɪ'dɔːrɪ] ADJ (*esp US*) guay*; **it's all ~** es guay del Paraguay*

hunt [hʌnt] Ⓐ N 1 (*for animals*) caza *f*, cacería *f* (**for** de); (= *huntsmen*) partida *f* de caza, (grupo *m* de) cazadores *mpl*
2 (= *search*) busca *f*, búsqueda *f* (**for** de); (= *pursuit*) persecución *f*; **the ~ for the murderer** la busca *or* búsqueda del asesino; **to be on the ~ for** estar *or* andar a la caza de; **the ~ is on** ha comenzado la búsqueda; **we joined in the ~ for the missing key** ayudamos a buscar la llave perdida
Ⓑ VT 1 [+ *animal*] cazar; [+ *hounds*] emplear en la caza; [+ *area of country*] recorrer de caza, cazar en
2 (= *search for*) buscar; (= *pursue*) perseguir
Ⓒ VI 1 (*Sport*) cazar, ir de cacería; **to go ~ing** ir de caza
2 (= *search*) buscar por todas partes; **to ~ for** buscar; **he ~ed for it in his pocket** lo buscó en el bolsillo; **to ~ about** *or* **around for** buscar por todas partes
Ⓓ CPD ► **hunt ball** N *baile organizado tras una cacería*

►**hunt down** VT + ADV [+ *person*] dar caza a; [+ *thing*] buscar (hasta encontrar)

►**hunt out** VT + ADV buscar (hasta encontrar)

►**hunt up** VT + ADV buscar

hunter ['hʌntəʳ] Ⓐ N 1 (= *person*) cazador(a) *m/f* 2 (= *horse*) caballo *m* de caza Ⓑ CPD ► **hunter gatherer** N cazador-recolector *m*

hunting ['hʌntɪŋ] Ⓐ N (*Sport*) caza *f*, cacería *f*
Ⓑ CPD ► **hunting box** N pabellón *m* de caza ► **the hunting fraternity** N los aficionados a la caza ► **hunting ground** N cazadero *m*; **a happy ~ ground for** (*fig*) un terreno fértil para ► **hunting horn** N cuerno *m* de caza ► **hunting lodge** N pabellón *m* de caza ► **hunting pink** N chaqueta *f* de caza roja ► **hunting season** N época *f* de caza

huntress ['hʌntrɪs] N cazadora *f*

Hunts [hʌnts] N ABBR = **Huntingdonshire**

huntsman ['hʌntsmən] N (*pl* **huntsmen**) (= *hunter*) cazador *m*

hurdle ['hɜːdl] Ⓐ N (*Sport*) valla *f*; (*fig*) obstáculo *m*, barrera *f*; **the 100m ~s** (= *race*) los 100 metros vallas; **the high ~s** las vallas altas; ✦***IDIOM*** **to fall at the first ~** fracasar a las primeras de cambio, no superar el primer escollo
Ⓑ CPD ► **hurdle race** N carrera *f* de vallas

hurdler ['hɜːdləʳ] N vallista *mf*, corredor(a) *m/f* de vallas

hurdling ['hɜːdlɪŋ] N salto *m* de vallas

hurdy-gurdy ['hɜːdɪ,gɜːdɪ] N organillo *m*

hurl [hɜːl] VT (= *throw*) arrojar; **to ~ abuse** *or* **insults at sb** lanzar *or* soltar una sarta de insultos a algn; **to ~ o.s. at sth/sb** abalanzarse sobre algo/algn; **to ~ o.s. into the fray** lanzarse a la batalla; **to ~ o.s. over a cliff** arrojarse por un precipicio

►**hurl back** VT + ADV [+ *enemy*] rechazar

hurley ['hɜːlɪ] N = **hurling**

hurling ['hɜːlɪŋ] N *juego irlandés parecido al hockey*

hurly-burly ['hɜːlɪ'bɜːlɪ] N alboroto *m*, tumulto *m*; **the ~ of politics** la vida tumultuosa de la política

hurrah [hʊ'rɑː], **hurray** [hʊ'reɪ] Ⓐ EXCL ¡hurra!; **~ for Mr Brown!** ¡viva el señor Brown!
Ⓑ N vítor *m*

hurricane ['hʌrɪkən] Ⓐ N (*Met*) huracán *m*
Ⓑ CPD ► **hurricane lamp** N lámpara *f* a prueba de viento

hurried ['hʌrɪd] ADJ [*footsteps*] apresurado; [*visit, meeting*] rápido, cortísimo; [*phone call, conversation*] rápido; **to eat** *or* **have a ~ meal** comer a toda prisa, comer deprisa y corriendo

hurriedly ['hʌrɪdlɪ] ADV [*go, dress*] apresuradamente, a toda prisa; [*study, look at, read*] por encima, rápidamente; [*write*] apresuradamente, a vuela pluma; **Tim ~ made his excuses and left** Tim se excusó atropelladamente y se marchó; **he rose and ~ left** se levantó y se marchó precipitadamente; **"it doesn't matter," she said ~** —no importa —se apresuró a decir ella

hurry ['hʌrɪ] Ⓐ N prisa *f*, apuro *m* (*LAm*); **to be in a ~ (to do sth)** tener prisa *or* (*LAm*) apuro (por hacer algo); **I'm in no ~** ◊ **I'm not in any ~** no tengo prisa; **they were in no ~ to pay us** no se dieron prisa por pagarnos; **are you in a ~ for this?** ¿le corre prisa (esto)?; **in our ~ to leave we left the keys behind** con las prisas de *or* por marcharnos nos dejamos olvidadas las llaves; **to do sth in a ~** hacer algo de prisa; **he won't do that again in a ~*** eso no lo vuelve a hacer; **I shan't come back here in a ~** aquí no pongo los pies nunca más; **is there any ~?** ¿corre prisa?; **there's no (great) ~** no hay *or* corre prisa; **what's the ~?** ¿a qué viene tanta prisa?
Ⓑ VT [+ *person*] meter prisa a, apresurar, apurar (*LAm*); [+ *work, job*] hacer apresuradamen-

te, hacer deprisa y corriendo; **this is a job that cannot be hurried** este es un trabajo que no admite prisas; **he won't be hurried** no le gusta que le metan prisa; **don't let yourself be hurried into making a decision** no te obligues a tomar una decisión precipitada; **they hurried him to a doctor** lo llevaron a toda prisa a un médico; **troops were hurried to the spot** se enviaron tropas con urgencia al lugar
Ⓒ VI darse prisa, apurarse (*LAm*); **~!** ¡date prisa!, ¡apúrate! (*LAm*); **don't ~!** ¡no hay prisa *or* (*LAm*) apuro!; **to ~ to do sth** darse prisa *or* (*LAm*) apurarse en hacer algo, apresurarse a hacer algo; **to ~ after sb** correr detrás de algn; **to ~ back** volver de prisa; **she hurried home** se dio prisa para llegar a casa; **to ~ in** entrar corriendo; **I must ~** tengo que correr *or* darme prisa; **to ~ out** salir corriendo; **he hurried over to us** vino a toda prisa *or* corriendo hasta nosotros

►**hurry along** Ⓐ VI + ADV apresurarse, correr; **~ along now!** ¡vamos, rápido!
Ⓑ VT + ADV [+ *person*] meter prisa a, apresurar, apurar (*LAm*); [+ *work, job*] apurar, acelerar

►**hurry away**, **hurry off** Ⓐ VI + ADV irse corriendo
Ⓑ VT + ADV [+ *object*] llevar a la carrera; **to ~ sb away** *or* **off** llevarse a algn apresuradamente *or* a la carrera; **I wanted to look but the teacher quickly hurried us away** yo quería mirar pero el profesor se apresuró a alejarnos; **the policeman hurried him away** el policía se lo llevó apresuradamente

►**hurry off** VI + ADV, VT + ADV = **hurry away**

►**hurry on** Ⓐ VI + ADV (= *move*) pasar rápidamente; (= *speak*) continuar apresuradamente
Ⓑ VT + ADV = **hurry along B**

►**hurry up** Ⓐ VI + ADV darse prisa, apurarse (*LAm*); **~ up!** ¡date prisa!, ¡apúrate! (*LAm*)
Ⓑ VT + ADV [+ *person*] meter prisa a, apresurar, apurar (*LAm*); [+ *work, job*] apurar, acelerar

hurt [hɜːt] (*pt, pp* **hurt**) Ⓐ VT 1 (= *do physical damage to*) hacer daño a, lastimar (*LAm*); **how did you ~ your finger/leg?** ¿cómo te has hecho daño en el dedo/la pierna?, ¿cómo te has lastimado el dedo/la pierna? (*LAm*); **ten people were ~ in the accident** diez personas resultaron heridas en el accidente; **to ~ o.s.** hacerse daño, lastimarse (*LAm*); **did you ~ yourself?** ¿te has hecho daño?, ¿te has lastimado? (*LAm*); **mind you don't ~ yourself** cuidado no te hagas daño; **he's not badly ~** no está herido de gravedad; **to get ~** resultar herido; **someone is bound to get ~** seguro que alguien resulta herido; ✦*IDIOM* **to ~ a fly**: **he wouldn't ~ a fly** sería incapaz de matar una mosca
2 (= *cause physical pain to*) **did I ~ you?** ¿te he hecho daño?, ¿te he lastimado? (*LAm*); **stop it! you're ~ing me!** ¡para! ¡me estás haciendo daño!, ¡para! ¡me estás lastimando! (*LAm*); **my leg is ~ing me** me duele la pierna; **my feet are ~ing me** me duelen los pies
3 (= *have bad effect on*) 3.1 [+ *person*] **it wouldn't ~ you to try** no pierdes nada intentándolo; **it wouldn't ~ her to try and save some money** no le vendría mal intentar ahorrar algo de dinero; **one little glass of wine won't ~ him** un vasito de vino no le va a hacer daño; **a little hard work never ~ anyone** nadie se ha muerto nunca por trabajar un poco duro, trabajar duro nunca le ha hecho daño a nadie
3.2 [+ *prospects, chances, reputation*] perjudicar; **high interest rates are ~ing small businesses** los tipos de interés altos están perjudicando a las pequeñas empresas
4 (= *cause emotional pain to*) hacer daño a; **I was deeply ~ by his attitude** su actitud me hizo mucho daño; **I didn't mean to ~ you** no era mi intención hacerte sufrir *or* hacerte daño; **this is going to ~ me much more than it's going to ~ you** esto me va a doler mucho más a mí que a ti; **to be easily ~** ser muy susceptible; **you've ~ her feelings** la has ofendido; **his feelings were ~ by what you said** lo que dijiste lo ofendió *or* hirió sus sentimientos; **she was bound to get ~** estaba claro que iba a terminar sufriendo
Ⓑ VI 1 (= *give physical pain*) [*arm, leg, foot, etc*] doler; **my arm ~s** me duele el brazo; **my feet ~** me duelen los pies; **ow, that ~s!** ¡ay! ¡duele!; **it doesn't ~ much** no duele mucho; **it only ~s a little bit** solo duele un poquito; **it ~s when I walk** me duele cuando ando *or* al andar; **does it ~?** ¿te duele?; **where does it ~?** ¿dónde te duele?; **I ~ all over** me duele todo el cuerpo; **my shoes are ~ing** me hacen daño los zapatos; ✦*IDIOM* **to kick/hit sb where it ~s**: **kick him where it ~s!** ¡dale una buena patada donde más les duele (a los hombres)!; **she hit him where it ~s - in his wallet** le dio donde más le duele - en la cartera
2 (= *give emotional pain*) doler; **it ~s to admit it but …** duele *or* cuesta admitirlo pero …; **the truth ~s** la verdad duele
3 (= *do harm*) **it doesn't ~ to ask** por preguntar no se pierde nada; **it wouldn't ~ to let your mum know you'll be late** no te costaría nada avisarle a tu madre que vas a llegar tarde
4 (*esp US**) (= *feel pain*) sufrir
Ⓒ ADJ 1 (= *injured*) [*part of body*] lastimado; **James, are you ~?** James, ¿te has hecho daño?, James, ¿te has lastimado? (*esp LAm*)
2 (= *upset*) [*person, tone*] dolido; **he gave me a slightly ~ look** me miró un poco dolido; **to be/feel ~** estar/sentirse dolido
Ⓓ N (= *emotional pain*) dolor *m*, pena *f*

hurtful [ˈhɜːtfʊl] ADJ [*remark*] hiriente; [*act, behaviour*] ofensivo; [*experience*] doloroso

hurtfully [ˈhɜːtfʊlɪ] ADV de manera hiriente

hurtle [ˈhɜːtl] Ⓐ VI precipitarse; **to ~ along** ir como un rayo *or* a toda velocidad; **the car ~d past** el coche pasó como un rayo *or* a toda velocidad; **the rock ~d over the cliff** la roca cayó estrepitosamente por el precipicio
Ⓑ VT arrojar (violentamente)

husband [ˈhʌzbənd] Ⓐ N marido *m*, esposo *m*
Ⓑ VT [+ *resources*] administrar bien, gestionar bien; **you must ~ your strength** debes dosificar tus fuerzas

husbandry [ˈhʌzbəndrɪ] N 1 (*Agr*) agricultura *f*; **animal ~** cría *f* de animales
2 (= *administration*) (*also* **good ~**) buena administración *f*, buena gestión *f*

hush [hʌʃ] Ⓐ N silencio *m*; **a ~ fell** se hizo un silencio
Ⓑ VI callarse; **~!** ¡cállate!, ¡chitón!
Ⓒ VT [+ *person*] hacer callar
Ⓓ CPD ► **hush money*** N soborno *m*, coima *f* (*Andes, S. Cone*), mordida *f* (*Mex*)

►**hush up** Ⓐ VT + ADV [+ *affair*] encubrir, echar tierra a; [+ *person*] tapar la boca a
Ⓑ VI + ADV (*US*) callarse

hushed [hʌʃt] ADJ [*silence*] profundo; [*tone*] callado, muy bajo; **the room was ~** la sala estaba en silencio; **the atmosphere was ~** el ambiente era silencioso

hush-hush* [ˈhʌʃˈhʌʃ] ADJ muy secreto

husk [hʌsk] Ⓐ N (*gen*) cascarilla *f*, cáscara *f*, cascabillo *m* (*Agr*)
Ⓑ VT quitar la cascarilla a, descascarillar

huskily [ˈhʌskɪlɪ] ADV con voz ronca

huskiness [ˈhʌskɪnɪs] N ronquedad *f*

husky[1] [ˈhʌskɪ] ADJ (*compar* **huskier**; *superl* **huskiest**) 1 [*voice, person*] ronco
2 (= *tough*) [*person*] fornido, fuerte

husky[2] [ˈhʌskɪ] N perro *m* esquimal

hussar [həˈzɑːʳ] N húsar *m*

hussy [ˈhʌsɪ] N fresca* *f*; **she's a little ~** es una fresca

hustings [ˈhʌstɪŋz] NPL (*esp Brit Pol*) campaña *fsing* electoral

hustle [ˈhʌsl] Ⓐ N 1 (= *activity*) bullicio *m*; **~ and bustle** ajetreo *m*, vaivén *m*
2 (*US**) (= *trick*) timo *m*, chanchullo* *m*
Ⓑ VT 1 (= *jostle*) empujar, codear; (= *hurry up*) [+ *person*] dar prisa a; **they ~d him in/out** le hicieron entrar/salir a empujones *or* sin ceremonia; **he was ~d into a car** lo metieron en un coche a empujones *or* sin ceremonia
2 (*fig*) **to ~ things along** llevar las cosas a buen paso; **to ~ sb into making a decision** meter prisa a algn para que tome una decisión; **I won't be ~d into anything** no voy a dejar que me empujen a nada
3 (*US**) **they were paid to ~ drinks out of the customers** les pagaban para sacarles bebidas a los clientes; **they were hustling him for payment of the debt** le apretaban las clavijas para que saldara la deuda
Ⓒ VI 1 (*) (= *hurry*) darse prisa, apresurarse, apurarse (*LAm*)
2 (*) (= *work hard*) trabajar duro, currar (*Sp**)
3 (‡) [*prostitute*] hacer la calle*

hustler* [ˈhʌsləʳ] N 1 (= *go-getter*) persona *f* dinámica
2 (= *swindler*) estafador(a) *m/f*, timador(a) *m/f*
3 (= *prostitute*) puto(a) *m/f*

hut [hʌt] N (= *shed*) cobertizo *m*; (= *small house*) cabaña *f*; (= *hovel*) barraca *f*, choza *f*; (*Mil*) barracón *m*, barraca *f*; **mountain ~** albergue *m* de montaña

hutch [hʌtʃ] N conejera *f*

HV, **h.v.** N ABBR = **high voltage**

HVT N ABBR (= **high-velocity train**) TAV *m*

hyacinth [ˈhaɪəsɪnθ] N (*Bot*) jacinto *m*

hyaena [haɪˈiːnə] N = **hyena**

hybrid [ˈhaɪbrɪd] Ⓐ N 1 (*Bio*) híbrido *m*
2 (= *word*) palabra *f* híbrida
Ⓑ ADJ híbrido

hybridism [ˈhaɪbrɪdɪzəm] N hibridismo *m*

hybridization [ˌhaɪbrɪdaɪˈzeɪʃən] N hibridación *f*

hybridize [ˈhaɪbrɪdaɪz] Ⓐ VT hibridar
Ⓑ VI hibridar

hydra [ˈhaɪdrə] N (*pl* **hydras** *or* **hydrae** [ˈhaɪdriː]) hidra *f*; **Hydra** (*Myth*) Hidra *f*

hydrangea [haɪˈdreɪndʒə] N (*Bot*) hortensia *f*

hydrant [ˈhaɪdrənt] N boca *f* de riego; **fire ~** boca *f* de incendios

hydrate [ˈhaɪdreɪt] Ⓐ N hidrato *m*
Ⓑ VT hidratar

hydraulic [haɪˈdrɒlɪk] Ⓐ ADJ hidráulico
Ⓑ CPD ► **hydraulic brakes** NPL frenos *mpl* hidráulicos ► **hydraulic press** N prensa *f* hidráulica ► **hydraulic suspension** N suspensión *f* hidráulica

hydraulics [haɪˈdrɒlɪks] NSING hidráulica *f*

hydro [ˈhaɪdrəʊ] N (*Brit*) balneario *m*

hydro… [ˈhaɪdrəʊ] PREFIX hidro…

hydrocarbon [ˌhaɪdrəʊˈkɑːbən] N hidrocarburo *m*

hydrocephalus [ˌhaɪdrəʊˈsefələs] N hidrocefalia *f*

hydrochloric [ˌhaɪdrəˈklɒrɪk] ADJ **~ acid** ácido *m* clorhídrico

hydrocyanic [ˌhaɪdrəsaɪˈænɪk] ADJ **~ acid** ácido *m* cianhídrico

hydrodynamics [ˌhaɪdrəʊdaɪˈnæmɪks] NSING hidrodinámica *f*

hydroelectric [ˌhaɪdrəʊɪˈlektrɪk] ADJ [*power*] hidroeléctrico; **~ power station** central *f* hidroeléctrica

hydroelectricity [ˌhaɪdrəʊɪlekˈtrɪsɪtɪ] N hidroelectricidad *f*

hydrofoil [ˈhaɪdrəʊfɔɪl] N hidroala *m*, aliscafo *m*

hydrogen [ˈhaɪdrɪdʒən] Ⓐ N hidrógeno *m*
Ⓑ CPD ► **hydrogen bomb** N bomba *f* de hidrógeno ► **hydrogen chloride** N cloruro *m* de hidrógeno ► **hydrogen peroxide** N agua *f* oxigenada ► **hydrogen sulphide** N ácido *m* sulfhídrico

hydrography [haɪˈdrɒgrəfɪ] N hidrografía *f*

hydrolysis [haɪˈdrɒlɪsɪs] N hidrólisis *f*

hydrolyze [ˈhaɪdrəʊlaɪz] Ⓐ VT hidrolizar
Ⓑ VI hidrolizarse

hydrometer [haɪˈdrɒmɪtəʳ] N areómetro *m*, hidrómetro *m*

hydrophobia [ˌhaɪdrəˈfəʊbɪə] N hidrofobia *f*

hydrophobic [ˌhaɪdrəˈfəʊbɪk] ADJ hidrofóbico

hydroplane [ˈhaɪdrəʊpleɪn] N hidroavión *m*

hydroponic [ˌhaɪdrəʊˈpɒnɪk] ADJ hidropónico

hydroponics [ˌhaɪdrəʊˈpɒnɪks] NSING hidroponia *f*

hydropower [ˈhaɪdrəʊˌpaʊəʳ] N hidrofuerza *f*

hydrotherapy [ˌhaɪdrəʊˈθerəpɪ] N hidroterapia *f*

hydroxide [haɪˈdrɒksaɪd] N hidróxido *m*

hyena [haɪˈiːnə] N hiena *f*; **to laugh like a ~** reírse como una hiena

hygiene [ˈhaɪdʒiːn] N higiene *f*

hygienic [haɪˈdʒiːnɪk] ADJ higiénico

hygienically [haɪˈdʒiːnɪklɪ] ADV higiénicamente

hygienist [haɪˈdʒiːnɪst] N higienista *mf*; *see also* **dental**

hymen [ˈhaɪmen] N himen *m*

hymn [hɪm] Ⓐ N himno *m*
Ⓑ CPD ► **hymn book** N himnario *m*

hymnal [ˈhɪmnəl] N himnario *m*

hype* [haɪp] Ⓐ N exageraciones *fpl*; (*Comm*) bombo *m* publicitario*; **it's just media ~** no es más que una campaña orquestada por los medios de comunicación
Ⓑ VT (*Comm*) dar bombo publicitario a*; **the much-hyped movie: Batman** la tan cacareada película: Batman*

►**hype up*** Ⓐ VT + ADV [+ *product*] dar bombo a*; [+ *claim*] exagerar; [+ *person*] excitar
Ⓑ VI + ADV pincharse*, picarse*

hyper* [ˈhaɪpəʳ] ADJ hiperactivo; **to go ~** desmadrarse*, ponerse hiperactivo

hyper... [ˈhaɪpəʳ] PREFIX hiper...

hyperacidity [ˈhaɪpərəˈsɪdɪtɪ] N hiperacidez *f*

hyperactive [ˌhaɪpərˈæktɪv] ADJ hiperactivo

hyperactivity [ˌhaɪpərækˈtɪvɪtɪ] N hiperactividad *f*

hyperbola [haɪˈpɜːbələ] N (*pl* **hyperbolas** *or* **hyperbole** [haɪˈpɜːbəliː]) hipérbola *f*

hyperbole [haɪˈpɜːbəlɪ] N hipérbole *f*

hyperbolic [ˌhaɪpəˈbɒlɪk] ADJ hiperbólico

hyperbolical [ˌhaɪpəˈbɒlɪkəl] ADJ = **hyperbolic**

hypercorrection [ˌhaɪpəkəˈrekʃən] N hipercorrección *f*, ultracorrección *f*

hypercritical [ˈhaɪpəˈkrɪtɪkəl] ADJ hipercrítico, ultracrítico

hyperglycaemia [ˌhaɪpəglaɪˈsiːmɪə], **hyperglycemia** (*US*) N hiperglucemia *f*

hyperinflation [ˈhaɪpəɪnˈfleɪʃən] N hiperinflación *f*

hyperlink [ˈhaɪpəlɪŋk] N hipervínculo *m*

hypermarket [ˈhaɪpəˌmɑːkɪt] N hipermercado *m*

hypermetropia [ˌhaɪpəmɪˈtrəʊpɪə] N hipermetropía *f*

hypermetropy [ˌhaɪpəˈmetrəpɪ] N = **hypermetropia**

hyperopia [ˈhaɪpərˈəʊpɪə] N hipermetropía *f*

hypersensitive [ˈhaɪpəˈsensɪtɪv] ADJ hipersensible

hypertension [ˈhaɪpəˈtenʃən] N (*Med*) hipertensión *f*

hypertext [ˈhaɪpəˌtekst] N (*Comput*) hipertexto *m*

hypertrophy [haɪˈpɜːtrəfɪ] Ⓐ N hipertrofía *f*
Ⓑ VI hipertrofiarse

hyperventilate [ˌhaɪpəˈventɪleɪt] VI respirar aceleradamente

hyphen [ˈhaɪfən] N guión *m*

hyphenate [ˈhaɪfəneɪt] VT escribir con guión, unir con guión

hypnosis [hɪpˈnəʊsɪs] N (*pl* **hypnoses** [hɪpˈnəʊsiːz]) hipnosis *f*; **she revealed under ~ that ...** bajo los efectos de la hipnosis reveló que ...

hypnotherapist [ˌhɪpnəʊˈθerəpɪst] N hipnoterapeuta *mf*

hypnotherapy [ˌhɪpnəʊˈθerəpɪ] N hipnoterapia *f*

hypnotic [hɪpˈnɒtɪk] Ⓐ ADJ [*state*] hipnótico; [*eyes, rhythm, sound*] hipnótico, hipnotizador
Ⓑ N hipnótico *m*

hypnotism [ˈhɪpnətɪzəm] N hipnotismo *m*

hypnotist [ˈhɪpnətɪst] N hipnotista *mf*

hypnotize [ˈhɪpnətaɪz] VT hipnotizar

hypo [ˈhaɪpəʊ] N (*Phot*) hiposulfito *m* sódico

hypoallergenic [ˌhaɪpəʊˌæləˈdʒenɪk] ADJ hipoalérgeno

hypochondria [ˌhaɪpəʊˈkɒndrɪə] N hipocondría *f*

hypochondriac [ˌhaɪpəʊˈkɒndrɪæk] Ⓐ ADJ hipocondríaco
Ⓑ N hipocondríaco/a *m/f*

hypocrisy [hɪˈpɒkrɪsɪ] N hipocresía *f*

hypocrite [ˈhɪpəkrɪt] N hipócrita *mf*

hypocritical [ˌhɪpəˈkrɪtɪkəl] ADJ hipócrita

hypocritically [ˌhɪpəˈkrɪtɪkəlɪ] ADV hipócritamente

hypodermic [ˌhaɪpəˈdɜːmɪk] Ⓐ ADJ hipodérmico
Ⓑ N (*also* **~ needle**) aguja *f* hipodérmica

hypoglycaemia, **hypoglycemia** (*US*) [ˌhaɪpəʊglaɪˈsiːmɪə] N hipoglucemia *f*

hypoglycaemic, **hypoglycemic** (*US*) [ˌhaɪpəʊglaɪˈsiːmɪk] ADJ hipoglucémico

hyponym [ˈhaɪpənɪm] N hipónimo *m*

hyponymy [haɪˈpɒnɪmɪ] N hiponimia *f*

hypostasis [haɪˈpɒstəsɪs] N (*pl* **hypostases** [haɪˈpɒstəsiːz]) (*Rel*) hipóstasis *f*

hypostatic [ˌhaɪpəʊˈstætɪk] ADJ (*Rel*) hipostático

hypotenuse [haɪˈpɒtɪnjuːz] N (*Math*) hipotenusa *f*

hypothalamus [ˌhaɪpəˈθæləməs] N (*pl* **hypothalami** [ˌhaɪpəˈθæləmaɪ]) hipotálamo *m*

hypothermia [ˌhaɪpəʊˈθɜːmɪə] N hipotermia *f*

▼ **hypothesis** [haɪˈpɒθɪsɪs] N (*pl* **hypotheses** [haɪˈpɒθɪsiːz]) hipótesis *f inv*

hypothesize [haɪˈpɒθɪsaɪz] Ⓐ VI realizar hipótesis, hacer hipótesis; **to ~ about** *or* **(up)on sth** realizar *or* hacer hipótesis sobre algo
Ⓑ VT plantear la hipótesis de

hypothetic [ˌhaɪpəʊˈθetɪk] ADJ = **hypothetical**

▼ **hypothetical** [ˌhaɪpəʊˈθetɪkəl] ADJ hipotético

hypothetically [ˌhaɪpəʊˈθetɪkəlɪ] ADV hipotéticamente

hyssop [ˈhɪsəp] N (*Bot*) hisopo *m*

hysterectomy [ˌhɪstəˈrektəmɪ] N histerectomía *f*; **she had to have a ~** le tuvieron que hacer una histerectomía

hysteria [hɪsˈtɪərɪə] N histeria *f*, histerismo *m*; **mass ~** histeria *f* colectiva

hysterical [hɪsˈterɪkəl] ADJ **1** (*Psych*) histérico
2 (= *out of control*) histérico; **you're being ~** te estás comportando como un histérico; **to get ~** ponerse histérico
3 (= *very funny*) [*situation*] para morirse de (la) risa; [*person*] graciosísimo, desternillante

hysterically [hɪsˈterɪkəlɪ] ADV histéricamente; **to weep/laugh ~** llorar/reír histéricamente; **it was ~ funny** fue para morirse de (la) risa, fue graciosísimo; **"come here!" — she shouted ~** —¡ven acá! —gritó, histérica

hysterics [hɪsˈterɪks] NPL **1** (= *tears, shouts*) histeria *f*, histerismo *m*; **she was in ~** tenía un ataque de histeria, estaba histérica; **to go into** *or* **have ~** ponerse histérico
2 (*) (= *laughter*) ataque *m* de risa; **we were in ~ about it** estábamos muertos de risa

Hz ABBR (*Rad etc*) (= **hertz**) H_z

➤ LANGUAGE IN USE: **hypothesis** 26.2 **hypothetical** 26.3

Ii

I¹, i [aɪ] N (= *letter*) I, i *f*; **I for Isabel** I de Isabel; ✦***IDIOM*** **to dot the i's and cross the t's** poner los puntos sobre las íes

I² [aɪ] PERS PRON (*emphatic, to avoid ambiguity*) yo; **I'm not one to exaggerate** yo no soy de los que exageran; **it is I who ...** soy yo quien ...; **he was frightened but I wasn't** él estaba asustado pero yo no; **if I were you** yo que tú; **Ann and I** Ann y yo; **he is taller than I am** es más alto que yo

Don't translate the subject pronoun when not emphasizing or clarifying:

I've got an idea tengo una idea; **I'll go and see** voy a ver

I. ABBR (*Geog*) (= **Island, Isle**) isla *f*

i. ABBR (*Fin*) = **interest**

IA, Ia. ABBR (*US*) = **Iowa**

IAAF N ABBR = **International Amateur Athletic Federation**

IAEA N ABBR (= **International Atomic Energy Agency**) OIEA *f or m*

iambic [aɪ'æmbɪk] Ⓐ ADJ yámbico
Ⓑ N yambo *m*, verso *m* yámbico
Ⓒ CPD ► **iambic pentameter** N pentámetro *m* yámbico

IATA [aɪ'ɑːtə] N ABBR (= **International Air Transport Association**) AITA *f*

IBA N ABBR (*Brit*) (= **Independent Broadcasting Authority**) *entidad que controla los medios privados de televisión y radio*

Iberia [aɪ'bɪərɪə] N Iberia *f*

Iberian [aɪ'bɪərɪən] Ⓐ ADJ ibero, ibérico
Ⓑ N ibero/a *m/f*
Ⓒ CPD ► **the Iberian Peninsula** N la Península Ibérica

IBEW N ABBR (*US*) = **International Brotherhood of Electrical Workers**

ibex ['aɪbeks] N (*pl* **ibexes** *or* **ibex** *or* **ibices** ['aɪbɪ,siːz]) cabra *f* montés, íbice *m*

ibid ['ɪbɪd] ADV ABBR (= **ibidem**) ibíd., ib.

ibis ['aɪbɪs] N (*pl* **ibises** *or* **ibis**) ibis *f inv*

IBM N ABBR = **International Business Machines**

IBRD N ABBR (= **International Bank for Reconstruction and Development**) BIRD *m*

IBS N ABBR = **irritable bowel syndrome**

i/c ABBR (= **in charge (of)**) encargado (de)

ICA N ABBR [1] (*Brit*) = **Institute of Contemporary Arts**
[2] (*Brit*) = **Institute of Chartered Accountants**
[3] = **International Cooperation Administration**

ICAO N ABBR (= **International Civil Aviation Organization**) OACI *f*

ICBM N ABBR = **intercontinental ballistic missile**

ICC N ABBR [1] (= **International Chamber of Commerce**) CCI *f*
[2] (*US*) = **Interstate Commerce Commission**

ice [aɪs] Ⓐ N [1] (= *frozen water*) hielo *m*; **as cold as ~** (tan) frío como el hielo; **my feet are like ~** tengo los pies helados; ✦***IDIOMS*** **to break the ~** romper el hielo; **to cut no ~**: **arguments like that cut no ~ with him** ese tipo de argumentos lo dejan frío; **to keep/put sth on ~**: **we put the champagne on ~** pusimos el champán a enfriar; **she put her career on ~ for ten years while she had children** dejó su carrera aparcada durante diez años para tener hijos; **to keep money on ~** tener dinero en reserva; **to put a project on ~** posponer un proyecto; **to skate on thin ~** pisar terreno peligroso
[2] (= *ice cream*) helado *m*
Ⓑ VT [1] helar; [+ *drink*] enfriar, echar cubos de hielo a
[2] [+ *cake*] glasear, escarchar
Ⓒ CPD ► **the Ice Age** N la edad de hielo, el periodo glacial; **an ~-age rock/fossil** una roca/un fósil del periodo glacial ► **ice axe, ice ax** (*US*) N piqueta *f* (de alpinista), piolet *m* ► **ice bucket** N cubo *m* del hielo, hielera *f* (*LAm*) ► **ice cream** N helado *m*; **~-cream cone** cucurucho *m* (de helado); **~-cream parlour** heladería *f*; **~-cream soda** soda *f* mezclada con helado ► **ice cube** N cubito *m* de hielo ► **ice dance** N baile *m* sobre hielo ► **ice field** N campo *m* de hielo, banquisa *f* ► **ice floe** N témpano *m* de hielo ► **ice hockey** N hockey *m* sobre hielo ► **ice house** N (*for storing ice*) nave *f* frigorífica (*edificio*); [*of Eskimo*] iglú *m* ► **ice lolly** N (*Brit*) polo *m* (*Sp*), paleta *f* (*LAm*) ► **ice maiden*** N mujer *f* de hielo ► **ice pack** N compresa *f* de hielo ► **ice pick** N (*Culin*) punzón *m* para el hielo ► **ice rink** N pista *f* de patinaje sobre hielo, pista *f* de hielo ► **ice skate** N patín *m* de hielo, patín *m* de cuchilla; *see also* **ice-skate** ► **ice skater** N patinador(a) *m/f* (artístico/a), patinador(a) *m/f* sobre hielo ► **ice skating** N patinaje *m* sobre hielo; **to go ~ skating** ir a patinar sobre hielo ► **ice water, iced water** N agua *f* helada, agua *f* fría (*de la nevera*)

►**ice over, ice up** VI + ADV helarse, congelarse

iceberg ['aɪsbɜːg] Ⓐ N iceberg *m*; ✦***IDIOM*** **that's just the tip of the ~!** no es más que la punta del iceberg
Ⓑ CPD ► **iceberg lettuce** N lechuga *f* repollo

ice-blue [,aɪs'bluː] ADJ azul claro, azul pálido

icebound ['aɪsbaʊnd] ADJ [*road, ship*] bloqueado por el hielo

icebox ['aɪsbɒks] N (*Brit*) (= *part of refrigerator*) congelador *m*; **this room is like an ~** este cuarto es como un congelador; (*US*†) (= *refrigerator*) nevera *f*, refrigeradora *f*, heladera *f* (*S. Cone*)

icebreaker ['aɪs,breɪkəʳ] N rompehielos *m inv*; **we used the video as an ~** el vídeo nos sirvió para romper el hielo

icecap ['aɪskæp] N casquete *m* glaciar, casquete *m* de hielo

ice-cold ['aɪs'kəʊld] ADJ [*hands, drink*] helado

iced [aɪst] ADJ [*water*] helado, frío (*de la nevera*); [*drink*] con hielo; [*cake*] glaseado, escarchado

Iceland ['aɪslənd] Ⓐ N Islandia *f*
Ⓑ CPD ► **Iceland spar** N espato *m* de Islandia

Icelander ['aɪsləndəʳ] N islandés/esa *m/f*

Icelandic [aɪs'lændɪk] Ⓐ ADJ islandés
Ⓑ N (*Ling*) islandés *m*

iceman ['aɪsmæn] N (*pl* **icemen**) [1] (*US*) vendedor *m or* repartidor *m* de hielo
[2] (*Archeol*) hombre *m* de hielo

ice-skate ['aɪsskeɪt] VI patinar sobre hielo

ichthyology [,ɪkθɪ'ɒlədʒɪ] N ictiología *f*

icicle ['aɪsɪkl] N carámbano *m*

icily ['aɪsɪlɪ] ADV [1] (*lit*) glacialmente
[2] (*fig*) [*say, stare*] glacialmente, con mucha frialdad; **he looked at me ~** me dirigió una mirada glacial

iciness ['aɪsɪnɪs] N [1] (*lit*) **problems caused by the ~ of the roads** problemas causados por el hielo en las carreteras; **the ~ of the weather conditions** las condiciones glaciales (del tiempo)
[2] (*fig*) **the ~ of his look** su mirada glacial

icing ['aɪsɪŋ] Ⓐ N (*on plane, car, road, railway*) formación *f* de hielo; (*on cake*) glaseado *m*; ✦***IDIOM*** **this is the ~ on the cake** esto es la guinda que corona la torta; *see also* **butter, glacé**
Ⓑ CPD ► **icing sugar** N azúcar *m* glasé, azúcar *m* en polvo, azúcar *m* flor (*S. Cone*)

ICJ N ABBR (= **International Court of Justice**) CIJ *f*

icky* ['ɪkɪ] ADJ (= *sticky*) todo pegajoso; (*fig*) (= *horrible*) asqueroso

icon ['aɪkɒn] N (*gen, Comput*) icono *m*

iconic [aɪ'kɒnɪk] ADJ [*image*] simbólico; (*Comput, Math*) icónico

iconoclasm [aɪ'kɒnə,klæzəm] N iconoclastia *f*

iconoclast [aɪ'kɒnəklæst] N iconoclasta *mf*

iconoclastic [aɪ,kɒnə'klæstɪk] ADJ iconoclasta

iconographer [,aɪkɒ'nɒgrəfəʳ] N iconógrafo/a *m/f*

iconographic [aɪ,kɒnə'græfɪk] ADJ iconográfico

iconography [,aɪkɒ'nɒgrəfɪ] N iconografía *f*

ICR N ABBR (*US*) = **Institute for Cancer Research**

ICRC N ABBR (= **International Committee of the Red Cross**) CICR *m*

ICT N ABBR (= **information and communications technology**) informática *f*, tecnología *f* de la información

ICU N ABBR (= **intensive care unit**) UVI *f*, UCI *f*, UMI *f*

icy ['aɪsɪ] ADJ (*compar* **icier**; *superl* **iciest**) [1] (= *covered with ice*) [*road, ground*] helado, cubierto de hielo; **the ~ conditions caused accidents** las heladas provocaron accidentes; **I don't like driving when it's ~** no me gusta conducir cuando hiela
[2] (= *freezing*) [*air, wind, weather*] glacial; [*hand, water*] helado; **the water was ~ cold** el agua estaba helada; **it's ~ cold out here** aquí fuera hace un frío glacial
[3] (*fig*) (= *cold*) [*stare, silence, tone, reception*] glacial

ID Ⓐ ABBR (*US*) = **Idaho**
Ⓑ N ABBR = **identification, identity**
Ⓒ CPD [*bracelet, tag, number*] de identidad ► **ID card** N carnet *m* de identidad, ≈ DNI *m* (*Sp*), ≈ cédula *f* (de identidad) (*LAm*), C.I. *f* (*LAm*) ► **ID parade** N (*Brit*) rueda *f* de reconocimiento, rueda *f* de identificación

I'd [aɪd] = **I would, I had**

id [ɪd] N (*Psych*) id *m*

IDA N ABBR (= **International Development Association**) AIF *f*

Ida. ABBR (*US*) = **Idaho**

IDB N ABBR (= **International Development Bank**) BID *m*

IDD N ABBR (*Brit Telec*) (= **international direct dialling**) servicio *m* internacional automático

▼**idea** [aɪ'dɪə] N [1] (= *thought, plan*) idea *f*; **it wasn't my ~** no fue idea mía; **that's the ~** así es; **the ~ is to sell it** la idea *or* el plan es venderlo; **let's forget the whole ~** olvidémonos de todo el asunto; **I can't bear the ~ (of it)** sólo de pensarlo me pongo mala; **it wouldn't be a bad ~ to paint it** no le vendría mal pintarlo; **it might not be a bad ~ to wait a few days** puede que no sea mala idea esperar unos cuantos días; **whose bright ~ was it to come this way?** (*iro*) ¿quién ha tenido la bonita *or* feliz idea de venir por aquí?*; **you'll have to buck up your ~s** tendrás que menearte; **the ~ never entered my head** ni se me pasó esa idea por la cabeza; **to get an ~ for a novel** encontrar una idea para una novela; **don't go getting ~s** (= *build up one's hopes*) no te hagas ilusiones; (= *be presumptuous*) no se te ocurra; **he got the ~ into his head that they didn't like him** se le metió en la cabeza (la idea de) que no les caía bien; **once she gets an ~ into her head there's no stopping her** como se le meta una idea en la cabeza no hay quien se la quite; **to get used to the ~ of sth** hacerse a la idea de algo; **to give sb ~s** meter ideas en la cabeza a algn; **whatever gave you that ~?** ¿como se te ha ocurrido semejante cosa?; **good ~!** ¡buena idea!; **what a good ~!** ¡qué idea más buena!; **to have an ~** tener una idea; **I suddenly had the ~ of going to see her** de repente se me ocurrió ir a verla, de repente tuve la idea de ir a verla; **he hit on the ~ of painting it red** se le ocurrió pintarlo de rojo; **to put ~s into sb's head** meter ideas en la cabeza a algn; **the very ~!** ◊ **what an ~!** ¡qué ocurrencias!
[2] (= *understanding*) idea *f*; **have you any ~ how ridiculous you look?** ¿tienes idea de lo ridículo que estás?; **I haven't the foggiest ~** no tengo ni la menor *or* más remota *or* más mínima idea; **what(ever) gave you that ~?** ¿de dónde sacaste eso?; **to get an ~ of sth** hacerse una idea de algo; **you're getting the ~** (= *understanding*) estás empezando a comprender; (= *getting the knack*) estás cogiendo el tino *or* truco; **I've got the general ~** he comprendido la idea general; **where did you get that ~?** ¿de dónde sacaste eso?; **don't get the wrong ~** no malinterpretes la situación; **many people have got the wrong ~ about him** mucha gente tiene un concepto equivocado de él; **I haven't the least ~** no tengo ni la menor *or* más remota *or* más mínima idea; **I've no ~!** ¡ni idea!; **it was awful, you've no ~** no te puedes hacer una idea de lo horrible que fue; **I had no ~ that …** no tenía ni idea *or* la menor idea de que …; **I haven't the slightest ~** no tengo ni la menor *or* más remota *or* más mínima idea; **he has some ~ of French** tiene algo de idea de francés
[3] (= *conception, notion*) idea *f*; **there may be some truth in the ~ that …** puede que haya algo de cierto en la idea de que …; **she has some odd ~s about how to bring up children** tiene unas ideas muy raras *or* una opinión muy rara de cómo criar a los niños; **it wasn't my ~ of a holiday** no era la idea que yo tengo de unas vacaciones; **if that's your ~ of fun** si eso es lo que tú entiendes por diversión
[4] (= *vague idea*) impresión *f*; **to have an ~ that …** tener la impresión de que …; **I have an ~ that she was going to Paris** tengo la impresión de que se iba a París
[5] (= *purpose*) intención *f*, idea *f*; **the whole ~ of this trip was to relax** la única intención *or* idea de este viaje era relajarse; **we went with the ~ of meeting new people** fuimos con la intención *or* idea de conocer a gente nueva; **what's the big ~?*** ¿a qué viene eso?*
[6] (= *estimate*) idea *f*; **can you give me a rough ~ of how many you want?** ¿puede darme una idea aproximada de cuántos quiere?

ideal [aɪ'dɪəl] Ⓐ ADJ [*opportunity, weight, conditions, solution*] ideal; **we do not live in an ~ world** no vivimos en un mundo ideal; **he is the ~ person for the job** es la persona ideal para el puesto; **an ~ place to live** un sitio ideal para vivir
Ⓑ N ideal *m*

idealism [aɪ'dɪəlɪzəm] N idealismo *m*

idealist [aɪ'dɪəlɪst] N idealista *mf*

idealistic [aɪ,dɪə'lɪstɪk] ADJ idealista

idealization [,aɪdɪəlaɪ'zeɪʃən] N idealización *f*

idealize [aɪ'dɪəlaɪz] VT idealizar

ideally [aɪ'dɪəlɪ] ADV **they're ~ suited** hacen una pareja ideal; **the hotel is ~ situated** el hotel tiene una situación ideal; **~, I'd like a garden** de ser posible, me gustaría tener jardín; **~, it will last forever** en el mejor de los casos, durará siempre; **~, all the children should live together** lo ideal *or* lo mejor sería que todos los hijos vivieran juntos

idée fixe ['iːdeɪ'fiːks] N idea *f* fija

ident* ['aɪdent] N (*also* **station ~**) (*TV, Rad*) identificativo *m*

identical [aɪ'dentɪkəl] Ⓐ ADJ idéntico; **their status is ~ to** *or* **with that of all other citizens** su condición es idéntica a *or* exactamente igual que la de cualquier otro ciudadano
Ⓑ CPD ► **identical twins** NPL gemelos *mpl* idénticos

identically [aɪ'dentɪkəlɪ] ADV idénticamente; **~ sized** de tamaño idéntico, exactamente del mismo tamaño; **they always dress ~** siempre se visten igual

identifiable [aɪ,dentɪ'faɪəbl] ADJ identificable

identification [aɪ,dentɪfɪ'keɪʃən] Ⓐ N identificación *f*; **the state of the body made ~ difficult** el estado del cadáver dificultaba su identificación; **we have a positive ~ of the victim** disponemos ya de la identidad de la víctima; **the ~ of democracy with liberty** la identificación de la democracia con la libertad
Ⓑ CPD ► **identification card** N = **identity card** ► **identification documents, identification papers** NPL documentos *mpl* de identidad, documentación *f* ► **identification mark** N señal *f* de identificación ► **identification parade** N (*Brit*) rueda *f* de reconocimiento, rueda *f* de identificación ► **identification tag** N (*US*) chapa *f* de identificación

identifier [aɪ'dentɪfaɪəʳ] N identificador *m*

identify [aɪ'dentɪfaɪ] Ⓐ VT [+ *person, problem*] identificar; **to ~ o.s.** identificarse; **to ~ o.s. with** identificarse con
Ⓑ VI **to ~ with** identificarse con

Identikit picture [aɪ,dentɪkɪt'pɪktʃəʳ] N retrato-robot *m*

identity [aɪ'dentɪtɪ] Ⓐ N (*all senses*) identidad *f*; **a case of mistaken ~** un caso de identificación errónea; **to withhold sb's ~** silenciar la identidad de algn
Ⓑ CPD ► **identity bracelet** N pulsera *f* identificativa, brazalete *m* identificativo ► **identity card** N carnet *m* de identidad, cédula *f* (de identidad) (*LAm*) ► **identity crisis** N crisis *f inv* de identidad ► **identity disc** N chapa *f* de identidad ► **identity papers** NPL documentos *mpl* de identidad, documentación *f* ► **identity parade** N = **identification parade**

ideogram ['ɪdɪəgræm] N ideograma *m*

ideographic [,ɪdɪə'græfɪk] ADJ ideográfico

ideological [,aɪdɪə'lɒdʒɪkəl] ADJ ideológico

ideologically [,aɪdɪə'lɒdʒɪkəlɪ] ADV ideológicamente

ideologist [,aɪdɪ'ɒlədʒɪst] N ideólogo/a *m/f*

ideologue ['ɪdɪəlɒg] N ideólogo/a *m/f*

ideology [,aɪdɪ'ɒlədʒɪ] N ideología *f*

ides [aɪdz] NPL idus *mpl*

idiocy ['ɪdɪəsɪ] N idiotez *f*, imbecilidad *f*

idiolect ['ɪdɪəʊlekt] N idiolecto *m*

idiom ['ɪdɪəm] N [1] (= *phrase*) modismo *m*, giro *m* [2] (= *style of expression*) lenguaje *m*

idiomatic [,ɪdɪə'mætɪk] ADJ idiomático

idiomatically [,ɪdɪə'mætɪkəlɪ] ADV idiomáticamente

idiosyncrasy [,ɪdɪə'sɪŋkrəsɪ] N idiosincrasia *f*; **Victorian ~** la idiosincrasia victoriana; **it's one of her idiosyncrasies** es una de sus peculiaridades

idiosyncratic [ɪdɪəsɪŋ'krætɪk] ADJ idiosincrásico

idiot ['ɪdɪət] Ⓐ N (= *fool*) tonto/a *m/f*; (= *imbecile*) idiota *mf*, imbécil *mf*; **you (stupid) ~!** ¡imbécil!; **her ~ son** el idiota *or* imbécil de su hijo Ⓑ CPD ► **idiot board*** N (*TV*) chuleta* *f*, autocue *m*

idiotic [,ɪdɪ'ɒtɪk] ADJ [*person*] idiota, imbécil; [*behaviour, laughter, idea*] estúpido, idiota; [*price*] desorbitado; **that was an ~ thing to do!** ¡eso que hiciste fue una idiotez *or* estupidez!

idiotically [,ɪdɪ'ɒtɪkəlɪ] ADV tontamente, estúpidamente; **to laugh ~** reírse como un tonto

idiot-proof* ['ɪdɪətpruːf] ADJ para torpes*, de fácil manejo

idle ['aɪdl] Ⓐ ADJ (*compar* **idler**; *superl* **idlest**) [1] (= *lazy*) perezoso, holgazán, flojo (*LAm*); (= *work-shy*) vago; (= *without work*) parado, desocupado; (= *inactive*) [*machine, factory*] parado; [*moment*] de ocio, libre; **the machine is never ~** la máquina no está nunca parada; **the reduction in orders made 100 workers ~** la

➤ LANGUAGE IN USE: **idea 1** 1.2

caída en el número de pedidos dejó a 100 obreros sin trabajo; **to stand ~** [*factory, machine*] estar parado

[2] [*fear, speculation*] infundado; [*threat*] vano; **he is not one to indulge in ~ boasting/speculation** no es de los que se da a fanfarronear/especular porque sí; **we sat making ~ conversation** pasamos el rato sentados charlando; **I asked out of ~ curiosity** lo pregunté por pura curiosidad; **it's just ~ gossip** no es más que cotilleo; **this is no ~ threat** no es ésta una amenaza hecha a la ligera

(B) VI [1] haraganear, gandulear; **we spent a few days idling in Paris** pasamos unos días ociosos en París; **we ~d over our meal** comimos con calma

[2] (*Tech*) [*engine*] marchar en vacío; **idling speed** velocidad *f* de marcha en vacío

(C) CPD ► **idle capacity** N (*Comm*) capacidad *f* sin utilizar ► **idle money** N (*Comm*) capital *m* improductivo ► **idle time** N (*Comm*) tiempo *m* de paro

►**idle away** VT + ADV [+ *time*] desperdiciar, echar a perder; **he ~s away his days in the garden** se pasa las horas muertas en el jardín

idleness ['aɪdlnɪs] N [1] (= *leisure*) ocio *m*, ociosidad *f*; (= *having nothing to do*) inactividad *f*, desocupación *f*; (= *laziness*) holgazanería *f*, pereza *f*, flojera *f* (*LAm*); (= *unemployment*) paro *m*, desempleo *m* (*LAm*); **to live a life of ~** llevar una vida ociosa; **she was frustrated by her enforced ~** la desesperaba su forzada inactividad

[2] (= *emptiness*) [*of threat, promise*] lo vano; [*of gossip, talk*] banalidad *f*, insustancialidad *f*

idler ['aɪdləʳ] N ocioso/a *m/f*, holgazán/ana *m/f*, vago/a *m/f*

idly ['aɪdlɪ] ADV (= *in a leisurely way*) ociosamente; (= *without doing anything*) sin hacer nada; (= *absentmindedly*) distraídamente; (= *to pass the time*) [*chat*] para pasar el rato; (= *uselessly*) vanamente, inútilmente; **she found it impossible to sit ~ at home** le resultaba imposible sentarse en casa sin hacer nada; **he glanced ~ out of the window** miró distraído por la ventana; **I wondered ~ if he had meant what he said** me preguntaba inadvertidamente si lo que había dicho iba en serio; **to stand** *or* **sit ~ by** estarse de brazos cruzados

idol ['aɪdl] N ídolo *m*

idolater [aɪ'dɒlətəʳ] N idólatra *mf*

idolatrous [aɪ'dɒlətrəs] ADJ idólatra, idolátrico

idolatry [aɪ'dɒlətrɪ] N idolatría *f*

idolize ['aɪdəlaɪz] VT (*fig*) (= *worship blindly*) idolatrar

IDP N ABBR (= **integrated data processing**) PID *m*

idyll ['ɪdɪl] N idilio *m*

idyllic [ɪ'dɪlɪk] ADJ idílico

i.e. ABBR = **id est** (= *that is*) esto es, es decir, i.e.

if [ɪf] (A) CONJ [1] (*conditional*) si; **I'll go if you come with me** yo iré si tú me acompañas; **if you studied harder you would pass your exams** si estudiaras más aprobarías los exámenes; **if they are to be believed** si hacemos caso de lo que dicen; **if you ask me** en lo que a mí se refiere; **if you had come earlier, you would have seen him** si hubieras venido antes, le habrías visto; **if I had known I would have told you** de haberlo sabido te lo habría dicho, si lo sé te lo digo*; **if it hadn't been for you we would have all died** de no ser *or* de no haber sido por ti hubiéramos muerto todos; **you can go if you like** puedes ir si quieres; **if necessary** si es necesario, si hace falta; **if I were you I would go to Spain** yo que tú iría a España, yo en tu lugar iría a España; **if you were to say that you'd be wrong** si dijeras eso te equivocarías; **if it weren't for him, we wouldn't be in this mess!** ¡si estamos metidos en este lío, es por él!*, ¡no estaríamos metidos en este lío de no ser por él!*; **if and when she comes** si (en efecto) viene, en el caso de que venga

[2] (= *whenever*) si, cuando; **if she wants any help she asks me** si *or* cuando necesita ayuda me la pide; **if it was fine we went out for a walk** si *or* cuando hacía buen tiempo dábamos un paseo

[3] (= *although*) aunque, si bien; **it's a nice film if rather long** es una buena película, aunque *or* si bien algo larga; **I will do it, even if it is difficult** lo haré, aunque me resulte difícil; **I'll finish it if** *or* **even if it takes me all day** lo terminaré aunque me lleve todo el día; **even if he tells me himself I won't believe it** ni aunque me lo diga él mismo me lo creo; **I couldn't eat it if I tried** aunque me lo propusiera no lo podría comer

[4] (= *whether*) si; **he asked me if I had eaten** me preguntó si había comido; **I don't know if he's here** no sé si está aquí; **I wonder if it's true** me pregunto si es *or* será verdad

[5] (*in phrases*) **if anything this one is better** hasta creo que éste es mejor, éste es mejor si cabe; **it's no bigger than our last house, if anything, it's even smaller** no es más grande que nuestra última casa si acaso, es incluso más pequeña; **I think you should paint it blue, if anything** en todo caso *or* si acaso, yo lo pintaría de azul; **as if** como si; **she acts as if she were the boss** se comporta como si fuera la jefa; **as if by chance** como por casualidad; **it isn't as if we were rich** no es que seamos precisamente ricos, no es que seamos ricos que digamos; **if at all: they aren't paid enough, if (they are paid) at all** les pagan poco, eso cuando les pagan; **change it to red, if at all** en todo caso *or* si acaso, cámbialo a rojo; **if it isn't old Garfield!** ¡pero si es el bueno de Garfield!, ¡hombre, Garfield, tú por aquí!; **if not** si no; **are you coming? if not, I'll go with Mark** ¿vienes? si no, iré con Mark; **if only I had known!** ¡de haberlo sabido!; **if only I could!** ¡ojalá pudiera!; **if only we had a car!** ¡ojalá tuviéramos coche!, ¡quién tuviera coche!; **I'll come, if only to see him** voy, aunque sólo sea para verlo; **I'll try to be there, if only for a few minutes** trataré de estar allí, aunque sólo sea unos minutos; **if so** si es así, de ser así; **are you coming? if so, I'll wait** ¿vienes? si es así *or* de ser así te espero; *see* **as, even B4**

(B) N **that's** *or* **it's a big if** es un gran pero; **there are a lot of ifs and buts** hay muchas dudas sin resolver

IFAD N ABBR (= **International Fund for Agricultural Development**) FIDA *m*

IFC N ABBR = **International Finance Corporation**

iffy* ['ɪfɪ] ADJ dudoso, incierto

IFTO N ABBR = **International Federation of Tour Operators**

IG N ABBR (*US*) = **Inspector General**

igloo ['ɪgluː] N iglú *m*

Ignatius [ɪg'neɪʃəs] N Ignacio, Íñigo

igneous ['ɪgnɪəs] ADJ ígneo

ignite [ɪg'naɪt] (A) VT encender, prender fuego a (*LAm*)

(B) VI encenderse, prender (*LAm*)

IF

Indicative/Subjunctive after "si"

Si can be followed by both the *indicative* and the *subjunctive*. The *indicative* describes facts and likely situations; the *subjunctive* describes remote or hypothetical situations.

Indicative

- Use **si** + **PRESENT INDICATIVE** to translate **if** + **PRESENT** in English:

If you go on overeating, you'll get fat
Si sigues comiendo tanto, vas a engordar
Don't do it if you don't want to
No lo hagas si no quieres

! Don't use **si** with the **PRESENT SUBJUNCTIVE**.

Subjunctive

- Use **si** + **IMPERFECT SUBJUNCTIVE** to translate **if** + **PAST** for remote or uncertain possibilities and hypotheses:

If we won the lottery, we would never have to work again
Si nos tocase *or* ***tocara la lotería, no tendríamos que trabajar nunca más***
What would you do if I weren't here?
¿Qué harías si yo no estuviese *or* ***estuviera aquí?***

- Use **si** + **PLUPERFECT SUBJUNCTIVE** (= **hubiera** or **hubiese** + **PAST PARTICIPLE**) to translate **if** + **had** + **PAST PARTICIPLE**:

If Paula hadn't lost her ticket, she would have left today
Si Paula no hubiera *or* ***hubiese perdido el billete, habría salido hoy***

NOTE: Alternatively, instead of a clause with **si**, you can often use **de** (**no**) **haber** + **PAST PARTICIPLE**:

If Paula hadn't lost her ticket, she would have left today
De no haber perdido Paula el billete, habría salido hoy

For further uses and examples, see main entry.

---

ignition [ɪg'nɪʃən] (A) N (= *igniting*) ignición *f*; (*Aut*) encendido *m*, arranque *m*; **to switch** *or* **turn on the ~** arrancar el motor, dar al contacto; **to switch** *or* **turn off the ~** apagar el motor, quitar el contacto; **I left the key in the ~** (*intentionally*) dejé la llave de contacto puesta; (*unintentionally*) me dejé la llave de contacto puesta

(B) CPD ► **ignition coil** N (*Aut*) bobina *f* de encendido ► **ignition key** N llave *f* de contacto ► **ignition switch** N interruptor *m* de encendido, interruptor *m* de arranque

ignoble [ɪg'nəʊbl] ADJ (*frm*) innoble, vil

ignominious [,ɪgnə'mɪnɪəs] ADJ [*act, behaviour*] ignominioso, oprobioso; [*defeat*] vergonzoso

ignominiously [,ɪgnə'mɪnɪəslɪ] ADV ignominiosamente; **to be ~ defeated** sufrir una derrota vergonzosa

ignominy ['ɪgnəmɪnɪ] N ignominia *f*, oprobio *m*, vergüenza *f*

ignoramus [,ɪgnə'reɪməs] N ignorante *mf*, inculto/a *m/f*

ignorance ['ɪgnərəns] N ignorancia *f* (**of** de); **to be in ~ of** ignorar, desconocer; **to keep sb in ~ of sth** ocultar algo a algn; **to show one's ~** demostrar su ignorancia

ignorant ['ɪgnərənt] ADJ ignorante; **to be ~ of** ignorar, desconocer; **he can't be ~ of what's going on** seguro que no ignora *or* seguro que sabe lo que está pasando; **they are surprisingly ~ about their own culture** es sorprendente lo poco que saben de su propia cultura, es sorprendente lo poco que conocen su propia cultura; **he's an ~ fool** es un necio ignorante, es un inepto

ignorantly ['ɪgnərəntlɪ] ADV ignorantemente; **we ~ went to the next house** al no saber, fuimos a la casa de al lado

ignore [ɪg'nɔːʳ] VT [+ *person*] (= *disregard*) no hacer caso a; (= *spurn*) ignorar; [+ *remark, danger*] hacer caso omiso de, no hacer caso de; [+ *behaviour, rudeness*] pasar por alto; [+ *awkward fact*] cerrar los ojos ante; **I told him what he should do but he completely ~d me** le dije qué debía hacer pero no me hizo el menor caso; **I smiled but she ~d me** le sonreí pero me ignoró *or* hizo como si no me viera; **just ~ him** no le hagas caso; **we can safely ~ that** eso lo podemos dejar a un lado

iguana [ɪ'gwɑːnə] N iguana *f*

IHS ABBR (= **Jesus**) IHS, JHS

ikon ['aɪkɒn] N = **icon**

IL ABBR (*US*) = **Illinois**

ILA N ABBR (*US*) (= **International Longshoremen's Association**) *sindicato*

ILEA ['ɪlɪə] N ABBR (*Brit Educ*) (*formerly*) (= **Inner London Education Authority**) *organismo que controlaba la enseñanza en la ciudad de Londres*

ileum ['ɪlɪəm] N (*Anat*) íleon *m*

ilex ['aɪleks] N encina *f*

ILGWU N ABBR (*US*) = **International Ladies' Garment Workers Union**

Iliad ['ɪlɪæd] N Ilíada *f*

ilk [ɪlk] N índole *f*, clase *f*; **and others of that ~** y otros así *or* de esa clase, y otros de ese jaez

I'll [aɪl] = **I will, I shall**

ill [ɪl] Ⓐ ADJ (*compar* **worse**; *superl* **worst**) [1] (*Med*) enfermo; **to be ~** estar enfermo; **to be seriously ~** estar gravemente enfermo; **he's ~ with cancer** tiene cáncer, está enfermo de cáncer; **to fall ~** caer *or* ponerse enfermo, enfermarse (*LAm*); **to feel ~** encontrarse mal, sentirse mal; **to look ~** tener mal aspecto *or* mala cara; **to make sb ~** [*food, wine*] sentarle mal a algn; [*lifestyle, diet*] afectar a la salud de algn; **the soup made me ~** la sopa me sentó mal; **all the worry was making me ~** la preocupación estaba afectando a mi salud; **to make o.s. ~** ponerse enfermo, ponerse malo*; **to be taken ~** caer *or* ponerse enfermo, enfermarse (*LAm*); *see also* **mentally**

[2] (= *bad*) [*fortune, luck*] malo; **~ at ease** a disgusto; **~ effects** efectos *mpl* adversos; **with no ~ effects** sin mayores daños; **~ feeling** (= *hostility*) hostilidad *f*; (= *spite*) rencor *m*; **there are no ~ feelings** no quedan rencores; **I have no ~ feelings toward them** no les guardo rencor; **~ health** mala salud *f*; **to be in ~ health** no estar bien (de salud), estar enfermo; **he retired because of ~ health** se retiró por problemas de salud; **~ humour** mal humor *m*; **~ repute** (*liter or hum*) mala reputación *f*; **a house/lady of ~ repute** una casa/mujer de mala reputación; **~ temper** mal genio *m*; **~ will** (= *hostility*) hostilidad *f*; (= *spite*) rencor *m*; **I bear you no ~ will for that** no le guardo rencor por eso; *see also* **wind[1] A1**

Ⓑ ADV mal; **to speak/think ~ of sb** hablar/pensar mal de algn; **we can ~ afford to lose him** mal podemos dejar que se vaya; **we can ~ afford to buy it** no podemos permitirnos el lujo de comprarlo; **it ~ becomes you to criticize** no te sienta bien criticar

Ⓒ N (*fig*) [1] **ills** (*frm*) (= *problems*) males *mpl*; **the ~s of the economy** los males de la economía; **the inevitable ~s of old age** los inevitables males *or* achaques de la vejez

[2] (†) (= *evil*) **no ~ had befallen the child** el niño no había sufrido ningún mal; **to bode** *or* **augur ~** no augurar nada bueno

Ill. ABBR (*US*) = **Illinois**

ill-advised ['ɪləd'vaɪzd] ADJ [*remark*] inoportuno; [*plan*] desacertado; [*attempt*] imprudente; **you would be ~ to go** harías mejor en no ir, sería poco aconsejable que fueras

ill-assorted ['ɪlə'sɔːtɪd] ADJ mal avenido

ill-at-ease ['ɪlət'iːz] ADJ (= *awkward*) molesto, incómodo; (= *uneasy*) inquieto, intranquilo

ill-bred ['ɪl'bred] ADJ mal educado, malcriado

ill-breeding [ˌɪl'briːdɪŋ] N mala educación *f*

ill-considered ['ɪlkən'sɪdəd] ADJ [*plan, remark*] poco pensado, poco meditado; [*act, decision*] apresurado, irreflexivo

ill-defined [ˌɪldɪ'faɪnd] ADJ mal definido

ill-disposed [ˌɪldɪs'pəʊzd] ADJ **to be ~ toward sb** estar predispuesto en contra de algn; **he is ~ toward the idea** no le gusta la idea; **they are ~ to wait any longer** no están muy dispuestos a seguir esperando

illegal [ɪ'liːgəl] Ⓐ ADJ [1] (*Jur*) ilegal; **~ possession of sth** posesión *f* ilegal de algo; **it is ~ to do that** hacer eso es ilegal; **it is ~ for children to buy alcohol** está prohibido que los niños compren alcohol; **to make it ~ to do sth** prohibir hacer algo, prohibir que se haga algo

[2] (*Sport*) [*tackle*] antirreglamentario

[3] (*Comput*) **to perform an ~ operation** realizar una operación ilegal *or* no válida

Ⓑ CPD ► **illegal immigrant** N inmigrante *mf* ilegal ► **illegal substance** N sustancia *f* ilegal

illegality [ˌɪliː'gælɪtɪ] N ilegalidad *f*

illegally [ɪ'liːgəlɪ] ADV [1] (*Jur*) [*act, occupy, fish*] ilegalmente; **they were convicted of ~ using a handgun** se los declaró culpables de la utilización ilegal de un revólver

[2] (*Sport*) [*tackle*] antirreglamentariamente

illegible [ɪ'ledʒəbl] ADJ ilegible

illegibly [ɪ'ledʒəblɪ] ADV de modo ilegible

illegitimacy [ˌɪlɪ'dʒɪtɪməsɪ] N ilegitimidad *f*

illegitimate [ˌɪlɪ'dʒɪtɪmɪt] ADJ ilegítimo

illegitimately [ˌɪlɪ'dʒɪtɪmɪtlɪ] ADV ilegítimamente

ill-equipped ['ɪlɪ'kwɪpt] ADJ [*expedition etc*] mal equipado; **he was ~ for the task** no estaba preparado para esa tarea; **the prisons are ~ to cope with such large numbers** las cárceles carecen del equipamiento necesario para acoger a tanta población reclusa

ill-fated ['ɪl'feɪtɪd] ADJ [*day*] funesto, nefasto; [*expedition, journey, attempt*] desafortunado, malhadado (*liter*)

ill-favoured, ill-favored (*US*) ['ɪl'feɪvəd] ADJ (*liter*) (= *ugly*) mal parecido

ill-formed [ˌɪl'fɔːmd] ADJ mal formado

ill-founded ['ɪl'faʊndɪd] ADJ [*claim, fear*] infundado, sin fundamento

ill-gotten ['ɪl'gɒtn] ADJ **~ gains** (*liter or hum*) ganancias *fpl* ilícitas

ill-humoured, ill-humored (*US*) ['ɪl'hjuːməd] ADJ malhumorado

illiberal [ɪ'lɪbərəl] ADJ (= *bigoted*) intolerante; (= *mean*) avaro, mezquino

illicit [ɪ'lɪsɪt] ADJ ilícito

illicitly [ɪ'lɪsɪtlɪ] ADV ilícitamente

illimitable [ɪ'lɪmɪtəbl] ADJ ilimitado, sin límites

ill-informed ['ɪlɪn'fɔːmd] ADJ [*judgment, criticism*] desinformado, inexacto; [*person*] mal informado

illiquid [ɪ'lɪkwɪd] Ⓐ ADJ falto de liquidez

Ⓑ CPD ► **illiquid assets** NPL activos *mpl* no realizables (a corto plazo)

illiteracy [ɪ'lɪtərəsɪ] N analfabetismo *m*

illiterate [ɪ'lɪtərɪt] Ⓐ ADJ [*person*] (= *unable to read or write*) analfabeto; (= *ignorant*) ignorante, inculto; [*letter, handwriting*] plagado de faltas; **to be functionally ~** ser un analfabeto funcional; **he's sexually ~** en materia sexual está en mantillas

Ⓑ N analfabeto/a *m/f*

ill-judged ['ɪl'dʒʌdʒd] ADJ imprudente

ill-kempt ['ɪl'kempt] ADJ desaliñado, desaseado

ill-mannered ['ɪl'mænəd] ADJ mal educado, sin educación

ill-natured ['ɪl'neɪtʃəd] ADJ desabrido, malhumorado

illness ['ɪlnɪs] N enfermedad *f*, dolencia *f* (*more frm*); **~ prevented her going** una enfermedad le impidió asistir; *see also* **mental**

ill-nourished [ˌɪl'nʌrɪʃt] ADJ malnutrido

illogic [ɪ'lɒdʒɪk] N falta *f* de lógica

illogical [ɪ'lɒdʒɪkəl] ADJ ilógico, falto de lógica

illogicality [ɪˌlɒdʒɪ'kælɪtɪ] N falta *f* de lógica

illogically [ɪ'lɒdʒɪkəlɪ] ADV ilógicamente

ill-omened ['ɪl'əʊmənd] ADJ [*day, event, occurrence*] nefasto, funesto

ill-prepared [ˌɪlprɪ'peəd] ADJ mal preparado

ill-starred ['ɪl'stɑːd] ADJ malhadado, malogrado

ill-suited ['ɪl'suːtɪd] ADJ **as a couple they are ~** como pareja no son compatibles, no hacen buena pareja; **he is ~ to the job** no es la persona indicada para el trabajo

ill-tempered ['ɪl'tempəd] ADJ [*person*] de mal genio; [*remark, tone etc*] malhumorado

ill-timed ['ɪl'taɪmd] ADJ inoportuno, intempestivo

ill-treat ['ɪl'triːt] VT [+ *person, animal*] maltratar, tratar mal

ill-treatment ['ɪl'triːtmənt] N maltrato *m*, malos tratos *mpl*

illuminate [ɪ'luːmɪneɪt] VT [1] (= *light up*) [+ *room, building*] iluminar; [+ *street*] iluminar, alumbrar; **the castle is ~d in summer** en verano el castillo está iluminado; **~d sign** letrero *m* luminoso

[2] (= *clarify*) [+ *problem, question*] aclarar, echar luz sobre

[3] (= *enlighten*) [*person*] iluminar

[4] (*Art*) **~d manuscript** manuscrito *m* iluminado

illuminating [ɪ'luːmɪneɪtɪŋ] ADJ [*remark, observation*] esclarecedor; [*lecture, experience*] instructivo

illumination [ɪˌluːmɪ'neɪʃən] N (*gen*) iluminación *f*; (*Art*) iluminación *f*; (*fig*) aclaración *f*; **illuminations** (*Brit*) (= *decorative lights*) luces *fpl*, iluminaciones *fpl*

illuminator [ɪ'luːmɪneɪtəʳ] N iluminador(a) *m/f*

illumine [ɪ'luːmɪn] VT = **illuminate**

ill-use ['ɪl'juːz] VT maltratar, tratar mal

illusion [ɪ'luːʒən] N [1] (= *deceptive appearance*) ilusión *f*; **optical ~** ilusión *f* óptica; **it gives an ~ of space** crea una ilusión *or* impresión de espacio

[2] (= *misapprehension*) ilusión *f*; **to be under an ~** hacerse falsas ilusiones, estar en un error; **I am under no ~s on that score** sobre ese punto no me hago (falsas) ilusiones; **to be under the ~ that ...** creerse que ...; **he was under the ~ that he would win** se creía que iba a ganar; **he cherishes the ~ that ...** abriga la esperanza de que ... + *subjun*

illusionist [ɪ'luːʒənɪst] N prestidigitador(a) *m/f*, ilusionista *mf*

illusive [ɪ'luːsɪv], **illusory** [ɪ'luːsərɪ] ADJ ilusorio

illustrate [ˈɪləstreɪt] VT 1 [+ *book*] ilustrar; **a book ~d by Ann Miles** un libro ilustrado por Ann Miles, un libro con ilustraciones de Ann Miles
2 (= *exemplify*) [+ *subject*] ilustrar; [+ *point*] demostrar; **I can best ~ this in the following way** esto puede ilustrarse del modo siguiente

illustrated [ˈɪləstreɪtɪd] Ⓐ ADJ [*book, catalogue*] ilustrado
Ⓑ CPD ► **illustrated (news)paper** N (*Hist*) revista *f* gráfica

illustration [ˌɪləsˈtreɪʃən] N (*in book, paper*) ilustración *f*; (= *example*) ejemplo *m*, ilustración *f*; (= *explanation*) explicación *f*; **by way of ~** a modo de ejemplo, a título ilustrativo

illustrative [ˈɪləstrətɪv] ADJ [*drawing*] ilustrativo; [*example*] ilustrativo; **to be ~ of sth** ejemplificar *or* demostrar algo

illustrator [ˈɪləstreɪtəʳ] N ilustrador(a) *m/f*

illustrious [ɪˈlʌstrɪəs] ADJ ilustre

illustriously [ɪˈlʌstrɪəslɪ] ADV ilustremente

ILO N ABBR (= **International Labour Organization**) OIT *f*

ILS N ABBR (*Aer*) = **Instrument Landing System**

ILWU N ABBR (*US*) = **International Longshoremen's and Warehousemen's Union**

IM, i.m. ABBR = **intramuscular(ly)**

I'm [aɪm] = **I am**

image [ˈɪmɪdʒ] Ⓐ N 1 (*gen, Literat, Rel*) (= *representation, symbol*) imagen *f*; **the ~ I had of him was completely different** tenía una imagen de él totalmente distinta; **to make sb in one's own ~** hacer a algn a su imagen; ✦*IDIOM* **to be the very** *or* **the spitting ~ of sb** ser el vivo retrato *or* la viva imagen de algn
2 (= *reflection*) reflejo *m*; **mirror ~** reflejo *m* exacto
3 (= *public image*) imagen *f*; **to have a good/bad ~** [*company, person*] tener buena/mala imagen; **we must improve our ~** tenemos que mejorar nuestra imagen; **the company has changed its ~** la empresa ha cambiado de imagen
Ⓑ CPD ► **image intensifier** N intensificador *m* de imagen ► **image processing** N proceso *m* de imágenes

imager [ˈɪmɪdʒəʳ] N **thermal ~** cámara *f* térmica; **magnetic resonance ~** aparato *m* de resonancia magnética

imagery [ˈɪmɪdʒərɪ] N imágenes *fpl*, imaginería *f*

imaginable [ɪˈmædʒɪnəbl] ADJ imaginable; **the biggest party ~** la fiesta más grande que se pueda imaginar

imaginary [ɪˈmædʒɪnərɪ] ADJ imaginario

imagination [ɪˌmædʒɪˈneɪʃən] N (= *mental ability*) imaginación *f*; (= *inventiveness*) imaginación *f*, inventiva *f*; **it's all in your ~** te lo estás imaginando, son imaginaciones tuyas; **was it my ~ or did I see you there?** ¿me lo he imaginado o te vi allí de verdad?; **to have a vivid ~** tener una imaginación muy viva *or* despierta; **she let her ~ run away with her** se dejó llevar por la imaginación; **her story caught the popular ~** su historia atrapó el interés popular; **it doesn't take much ~ to realize what happened** no hace falta tener mucha imaginación para darse cuenta de lo que ocurrió; **use your ~** usa la imaginación

imaginative [ɪˈmædʒɪnətɪv] ADJ [*person*] imaginativo, lleno de imaginación; [*drawing, story*] imaginativo

imaginatively [ɪˈmædʒɪnətɪvlɪ] ADV con imaginación

imaginativeness [ɪˈmædʒɪnətɪvnɪs] N imaginativa *f*

➤ LANGUAGE IN USE: **illustrate 2** 26.2

imagine [ɪˈmædʒɪn] VT 1 (= *visualize*) imaginarse, figurarse; **~ my surprise** imagínate *or* figúrate mi sorpresa; **you can ~ how I felt!** ¡imagínate *or* figúrate cómo me sentí!; **(just) ~!** ¡imagínate!, ¡figúrate!; **"is he angry?" — "I ~ so!"** —¿está enfadado? —¡me imagino que sí!; **I can't ~ a better end to the evening** la noche no podría acabar mejor; **I (just) can't ~** no me lo puedo imaginar; **what he's done with it I (just) can't ~** no tengo ni idea de qué puede haber hecho con ello; **you can't begin to ~ what it was like** no puedes hacerte (ni) idea de lo que fue aquello; **~ yourself on a Caribbean island** imagínate (que estás) en una isla del Caribe
2 (= *falsely believe*) **you're just imagining things** te lo estás imaginando, son imaginaciones tuyas; **he ~d himself to be the Messiah** se creía *or* se imaginaba que era el Mesías
3 (= *suppose, think*) suponer, creer; **don't ~ that you're going to get it free** no te vayas a pensar *or* no te creas que te va a salir gratis; **she fondly ~s that ...** se hace la ilusión de que ...

imaging [ˈɪmɪdʒɪŋ] N **thermal ~** representación *f* óptica por cámara térmica; **magnetic resonance ~** representación *f* óptica por resonancia magnética

imaginings [ɪˈmædʒɪnɪŋz] NPL (*liter*) imaginaciones *fpl*, figuraciones *fpl*

imam [ɪˈmɑːm] N imán *m*

imbalance [ɪmˈbæləns] N desequilibrio *m*, falta *f* de equilibrio

imbalanced [ɪmˈbælənst] ADJ [*distribution, structure*] desequilibrado

imbecile [ˈɪmbəsiːl] Ⓐ N imbécil *mf*; **you ~!** ¡imbécil!
Ⓑ ADJ imbécil

imbecility [ˌɪmbɪˈsɪlɪtɪ] N imbecilidad *f*

imbibe [ɪmˈbaɪb] Ⓐ VT (*frm*) (= *drink*) beber; (*fig*) [+ *atmosphere*] empaparse de; [+ *information*] imbuirse de (*frm*), empaparse de
Ⓑ VI († *also hum*) beber

imbroglio [ɪmˈbrəʊlɪəʊ] N embrollo *m*, enredo *m*

imbue [ɪmˈbjuː] VT **to ~ sth with** imbuir algo de *or* en (*frm*), empapar algo de; **to ~ sb with sth** [+ *quality, virtue*] infundir *or* conferir algo a algn, imbuir a algn de algo (*frm*); **to be ~d with** estar imbuido (*frm*) *or* empapado de

IMF N ABBR (= **International Monetary Fund**) FMI *m*

IMHO ABBR = **In My Honest Opinion**

imitable [ˈɪmɪtəbl] ADJ imitable

imitate [ˈɪmɪteɪt] VT [+ *person, action, accent*] imitar; (*pej*) remedar; [+ *signature, writing*] reproducir, copiar

imitation [ˌɪmɪˈteɪʃən] Ⓐ N (= *act*) imitación *f*; (*pej*) remedo *m*; (= *copy*) reproducción *f*, copia *f*; **in ~ of** a imitación de; **beware of ~s** desconfíe de las imitaciones; ✦*PROV* **~ is the sincerest form of flattery** no hay mejor halago *or* lisonja que el que te imiten
Ⓑ CPD de imitación ► **imitation fur** N piel *f* sintética ► **imitation gold** N oro *m* de imitación ► **imitation jewellery, imitation jewels** NPL bisutería *f*, joyas *fpl* de imitación ► **imitation leather** N imitación *f* a piel ► **imitation marble** N mármol *m* artificial

imitative [ˈɪmɪtətɪv] ADJ imitativo; **a style ~ of Joyce's** un estilo que imita el de Joyce

imitator [ˈɪmɪteɪtəʳ] N imitador(a) *m/f*

immaculate [ɪmækjʊlɪt] ADJ [*house, clothes*] impecable, inmaculado; [*hair, make-up, performance, taste*] impecable; [*conduct, behaviour*] impecable, intachable; **a hotel where the service is ~** un hotel donde el servicio es impecable; **to be in ~ condition** estar en perfectas condiciones; **to look ~** estar impecable; **the Immaculate Conception** (*Rel*) la Inmaculada Concepción

immaculately [ɪˈmækjʊlɪtlɪ] ADV [*behave*] impecablemente, intachablemente; [*dress*] impecablemente; **~ clean** impecablemente limpio, de un limpio inmaculado; **he was ~ dressed** iba impecablemente vestido, iba vestido de punta en blanco*

immanent [ˈɪmənənt] ADJ inmanente

Immanuel [ɪˈmænjʊəl] N Emanuel

immaterial [ˌɪməˈtɪərɪəl] ADJ 1 (= *irrelevant*) irrelevante; **that is quite ~** eso no tiene ninguna importancia, eso es irrelevante; **the difference between them is ~ to me** la diferencia entre ellos me es indiferente; **it is ~ whether ...** no importa si ...
2 (= *incorporeal*) inmaterial, incorpóreo

immature [ˌɪməˈtjʊəʳ] ADJ 1 (= *childish*) [*person, attitude*] inmaduro
2 (= *half-grown*) [*tree, plant*] joven; [*fruit*] verde, inmaduro

immaturity [ˌɪməˈtjʊərɪtɪ] N inmadurez *f*, falta *f* de madurez; [*of tree, plant*] inmadurez *f*

immeasurable [ɪˈmeʒərəbl] ADJ (= *not measurable*) inconmensurable, imposible de medir; (= *enormous*) [*benefit, value*] inconmensurable, incalculable

immeasurably [ɪˈmeʒərəblɪ] ADV enormemente

immediacy [ɪˈmiːdɪəsɪ] N [*of text, image, style*] inmediatez *f*; (= *urgency*) [*of task*] urgencia *f*

immediate [ɪˈmiːdɪət] ADJ 1 (= *instant*) [*decision, answer, reaction*] inmediato; **~ access** (*Comput*) entrada *f* inmediata; **to take ~ action** actuar inmediatamente *or* de inmediato; **for ~ delivery** para entrega inmediata; **these changes will take place with ~ effect** estos cambios tendrán lugar con un efecto inmediato
2 (= *urgent*) [*needs, problem*] urgente, apremiante; [*danger, threat, crisis, task*] inmediato; **my ~ concern was for Max** Max era mi primera preocupación; **the ~ needs of the refugees** las necesidades urgentes *or* apremiantes de los refugiados; **what are your ~ plans?** ¿cuáles son tus planes más inmediatos?
3 (= *near*) [*future, cause*] inmediato; [*predecessor, successor*] más inmediato; **my ~ family** mi familia más cercana; **in the ~ future** en el futuro inmediato; **my ~ neighbours** mis vecinos de al lado; **to the ~ north/south** directamente al norte/sur; **in the ~ vicinity** en las inmediaciones, en los alrededores

immediately [ɪˈmiːdɪətlɪ] Ⓐ ADV 1 (= *at once*) [*reply, come, agree*] inmediatamente, de inmediato; **do it ~!** ¡hazlo inmediatamente!, ¡hazlo de inmediato!; **the cause of the accident was not ~ apparent** la causa del accidente no se apreciaba a simple vista; **there was no one ~ available** no había nadie disponible en ese momento
2 (= *directly*) [*affect, concern*] directamente; **he is not ~ involved in the project** no está directamente involucrado en el proyecto; **~ above sth** justo *or* justamente encima de algo; **~ after/before sth** inmediatamente después de/antes de algo; **~ behind/below sth** justo *or* justamente detrás de/debajo de algo; **he is ~ below the managing director** (*in rank*) trabaja a las órdenes directas del director general, el director general es su superior más inmediato
Ⓑ CONJ **~ he put the phone down, he remembered** nada más colgar el teléfono se

acordó, en cuanto *or* (*LAm*) no más colgó el teléfono se acordó; **let me know ~ he arrives** avíseme en cuanto llegue, avíseme en el momento en que llegue

immemorial [ˌɪmɪˈmɔːrɪəl] ADJ inmemorial, inmemorable; **from time ~** desde tiempo(s) inmemorial(es)

immense [ɪˈmens] ADJ [*distance, difficulty, effort*] inmenso, enorme; **to his ~ relief/satisfaction** para gran alivio suyo/satisfacción suya; **it has been of ~ benefit to her** le ha resultado enormemente beneficioso

immensely [ɪˈmenslɪ] ADV [*like, enjoy*] muchísimo; [*differ*] enormemente; [*difficult*] sumamente, enormemente; [*powerful*] inmensamente, enormemente; **I was ~ grateful/relieved** me sentía enormemente agradecido/aliviado

immensity [ɪˈmensɪtɪ] N [*of size*] inmensidad *f*; [*of difference, problem etc*] enormidad *f*, inmensidad *f*

immerse [ɪˈmɜːs] VT (*lit*) **to ~ sth in water** sumergir algo en el agua; **to be ~d in sth** (*fig*) estar metido de lleno *or* inmerso en algo; **he was totally ~d in his work** estaba metido de lleno *or* inmerso en su trabajo; **she was ~d in the newspaper** estaba absorta *or* inmersa en la lectura del periódico; **to ~ o.s. in sth** (*fig*) sumergirse en algo; **she ~d herself in the history and culture of the place** se metió de lleno *or* se sumergió en la historia y la cultura del lugar

immersion [ɪˈmɜːʃən] Ⓐ N (*lit*) (*in liquid*) inmersión *f*, sumersión *f*; (*fig*) (*in work, thoughts*) absorción *f*
Ⓑ CPD ► **immersion course** N curso *m* de inmersión ► **immersion heater** N calentador *m* de inmersión

immigrant [ˈɪmɪgrənt] Ⓐ ADJ inmigrante
Ⓑ N inmigrante *mf*
Ⓒ CPD ► **immigrant community** N comunidad *f* de inmigrantes ► **immigrant worker** N trabajador(a) *m/f* inmigrante

immigrate [ˈɪmɪgreɪt] VI inmigrar

immigration [ˌɪmɪˈgreɪʃən] Ⓐ N inmigración *f*
Ⓑ CPD ► **immigration authorities** NPL agencia *f* de inmigración ► **immigration control** N control *m* de inmigración ► **immigration laws** NPL leyes *fpl* inmigratorias ► **immigration quota** N cuota *f* de inmigración

imminence [ˈɪmɪnəns] N inminencia *f*

imminent [ˈɪmɪnənt] ADJ (= *impending*) inminente

immobile [ɪˈməʊbaɪl] ADJ inmóvil

immobiliser [ɪˈməʊbɪlaɪzəʳ] N (*Aut*) inmovilizador *m*

immobility [ˌɪməʊˈbɪlɪtɪ] N inmovilidad *f*

immobilize [ɪˈməʊbɪlaɪz] VT [+ *person, troops, engine*] inmovilizar

immoderate [ɪˈmɒdərɪt] ADJ [*opinion, reaction*] desmesurado; [*demand*] excesivo, inmoderado; [*person*] extremista, radical; **with ~ haste** (*frm*) con excesiva *or* desmesurada celeridad (*frm*)

immoderately [ɪˈmɒdərɪtlɪ] ADV [*hasty, eager*] excesivamente; [*laugh*] exageradamente; [*use*] en exceso; **to drink ~** beber en exceso

immodest [ɪˈmɒdɪst] ADJ (= *indecent*) [*behaviour*] indecoroso, impúdico; [*dress*] poco recatado; [*claim, statement*] poco modesto, presuntuoso

immodestly [ɪˈmɒdɪstlɪ] ADV [*behave*] indecorosamente, impúdicamente; [*dress*] sin recato; [*say, claim*] con presunción

immodesty [ɪˈmɒdɪstɪ] N (= *indecency*) [*of behaviour*] falta *f* de decoro, impudicia *f*; [*of dress*] falta *f* de recato; (= *boastfulness*) falta *f* de modestia, presunción *f*

immolate [ˈɪməʊleɪt] VT inmolar

immoral [ɪˈmɒrəl] ADJ [*person, behaviour, practice*] inmoral; **to live off ~ earnings** vivir del proxenetismo, vivir del lenocinio (*frm*)

immorality [ˌɪməˈrælɪtɪ] N inmoralidad *f*

immorally [ɪˈmɒrəlɪ] ADV inmoralmente, de modo inmoral

immortal [ɪˈmɔːtl] Ⓐ ADJ [*person, god*] inmortal; [*memory, fame*] imperecedero
Ⓑ N inmortal *mf*

immortality [ˌɪmɔːˈtælɪtɪ] N inmortalidad *f*

immortalize [ɪˈmɔːtəlaɪz] VT inmortalizar

immovable [ɪˈmuːvəbl] Ⓐ ADJ [*object*] imposible de mover, inamovible; [*person*] inconmovible; [*feast, post*] inamovible; **he was quite ~** estuvo inflexible
Ⓑ **immovables** NPL inmuebles *mpl*

immune [ɪˈmjuːn] Ⓐ ADJ (*to disease*) inmune (**to** a); (*from tax, regulations*) exento (**from** de); **to be ~ to sth** (*Med*) ser inmune a algo; **she is ~ to measles** es inmune al sarampión; (*fig*) **they seemed ~ to the cold** parecían inmunes al frío; **he is ~ to criticism** es inmune *or* insensible a las críticas, no le afectan las críticas; **no one is ~ from this problem** nadie queda al margen de este problema, nadie es inmune a este problema
Ⓑ CPD ► **immune deficiency** N inmunodeficiencia *f* ► **immune response** N respuesta *f* inmunitaria, respuesta *f* inmunológica ► **immune system** N sistema *m* inmunológico

immunity [ɪˈmjuːnɪtɪ] N (*Med, fig*) inmunidad *f*; (*from tax, regulations*) exención *f* (**from** de); **diplomatic ~** inmunidad *f* diplomática; **parliamentary ~** inmunidad *f* parlamentaria

immunization [ˌɪmjʊnaɪˈzeɪʃən] N (*Med*) inmunización *f*

immunize [ˈɪmjʊnaɪz] VT (*Med*) inmunizar

immunodeficiency [ɪˌmjuːnəʊdɪˈfɪʃənsɪ] N inmunodeficiencia *f*

immunodepressant [ɪˌmjʊnəʊdɪˈpresnt] Ⓐ ADJ inmunodepresor
Ⓑ N inmunodepresor *m*

immunoglobulin [ˌɪmjʊnəʊˈglɒbjʊlɪn] N inmunoglobulina *f*

immunological [ɪˌmjuːnəˈlɒdʒɪkəl] Ⓐ ADJ inmunológico
Ⓑ CPD ► **immunological defences** NPL defensas *fpl* inmunológicas

immunologist [ɪmjʊˈnɒlədʒɪst] N inmunólogo/a *m/f*

immunology [ˌɪmjʊˈnɒlədʒɪ] N inmunología *f*

immunosuppressant [ɪˈmjuːnəʊsəˈpresənt] Ⓐ ADJ inmunosupresor, inmunosupresivo
Ⓑ N inmunosupresor *m*, inmunosupresivo *m*

immunosuppression [ɪˈmjʊːnəʊsəˈpreʃən] N inmunosupresión *f*

immunosuppressive [ɪˈmjʊːnəʊsəˈpresɪv] ADJ inmunosupresor, inmunosupresivo

immunotherapy [ˌɪmjʊnəʊˈθerəpɪ] N inmunoterapia *f*

immure [ɪˈmjʊəʳ] VT enclaustrar, encerrar; (*fig*) encerrar; **to be ~d in** estar encerrado en

immutability [ɪˌmjuːtəˈbɪlɪtɪ] N inmutabilidad *f*, inalterabilidad *f*

immutable [ɪˈmjuːtəbl] ADJ inmutable

immutably [ɪˈmjuːtəblɪ] ADV inmutablemente, inalterablemente

IMO Ⓐ ABBR = **In My Opinion**
Ⓑ N ABBR 1 = **International Miners' Organization**
2 (= **International Maritime Organization**) OMI *f*

imp [ɪmp] N diablillo *m*; (*fig*) diablillo *m*, pillín/ina *m/f*

imp. ABBR = **imperial**

impact [ˈɪmpækt] Ⓐ N 1 (= *force, effect*) impacto *m*; **the book had a great ~ on me** el libro me impactó mucho *or* me causó gran impacto; **the speech made no ~** el discurso no hizo mella; **he wants to make an ~ in the company** pretende causar una buena impresión en la empresa; **the measure would have considerable ~ on consumers** la medida afectaría considerablemente a los consumidores
2 (= *crash*) choque *m*; **on ~** al chocar
Ⓑ VT (*US*) (= *affect*) afectar, tener impacto en
Ⓒ VI 1 (= *make contact*) impactar, hacer impacto
2 (= *have impact*) **to ~ on sth** afectar a algo, tener impacto en algo
Ⓓ CPD ► **impact printer** N impresora *f* de impacto

impacted [ɪmˈpæktɪd] ADJ [*tooth*] incrustado

impair [ɪmˈpɛəʳ] VT [+ *health, relations*] perjudicar, afectar; [+ *sight, hearing*] afectar, dañar; [+ *ability*] mermar; [+ *judgement*] afectar; [+ *visibility*] reducir; **~ed hearing** problemas *mpl* de audición

impairment [ɪmˈpɛəmənt] N [*physical, mental*] discapacidad *f*; (= *deterioration*) deterioro *m*

impala [ɪmˈpɑːlə] N (*pl* **impalas** *or* **impala**) impala *m*

impale [ɪmˈpeɪl] VT (*as punishment*) empalar; (*on sword, spike*) ensartar, atravesar; **to ~ o.s. on** atravesarse con; **the heads of their victims were ~d on spikes** las cabezas de sus víctimas eran ensartadas en postes; **he fell, impaling himself on the dagger** se cayó y se atravesó con la daga

impalpable [ɪmˈpælpəbl] ADJ impalpable; (*fig*) intangible, inaprensible

imparity [ɪmˈpærɪtɪ] N disparidad *f*

impart [ɪmˈpɑːt] VT 1 (= *make known*) [+ *knowledge*] impartir, transmitir; [+ *information*] transmitir; [+ *ideas, values*] transmitir
2 (= *bestow*) [+ *wisdom*] otorgar; [+ *quality, sense*] conferir; [+ *flavour, taste*] dar

impartial [ɪmˈpɑːʃəl] ADJ imparcial

impartiality [ɪmˌpɑːʃɪˈælɪtɪ] N imparcialidad *f*

impartially [ɪmˈpɑːʃəlɪ] ADV imparcialmente, con imparcialidad

impassable [ɪmˈpɑːsəbl] ADJ [*road*] intransitable; [*barrier, river*] infranqueable

impasse [æmˈpɑːs] N punto *m* muerto, impasse *m or f*; **negotiations have reached an ~** las negociaciones han llegado a un punto muerto *or* impasse; **the government is in an ~** el gobierno se halla en un impasse

impassioned [ɪmˈpæʃnd] ADJ [*speech, plea*] apasionado; [*person*] exaltado

impassive [ɪmˈpæsɪv] ADJ impasible, imperturbable

impassively [ɪmˈpæsɪvlɪ] ADV impasiblemente, sin inmutarse; **he listened ~** escuchó impasible *or* sin inmutarse

impatience [ɪmˈpeɪʃəns] N impaciencia *f*

impatiens [ɪmˈpeɪʃɪˌenz] N impatiens *f*

impatient [ɪmˈpeɪʃənt] ADJ 1 (= *irascible*) [*person*] impaciente, sin paciencia; [*gesture*] de impaciencia; **to get ~ (with sth/sb)** perder la paciencia *or* impacientarse (con algo/algn); **to make sb ~** impacientar a algn
2 (= *eager*) impaciente; **to be ~ to do sth** estar impaciente por hacer algo

impatiently [ɪm'peɪʃəntlɪ] ADV con impaciencia, impacientemente

impeach [ɪm'piːtʃ] VT [1] (= *doubt*) [+ *character, motive*] poner en tela de juicio; [+ *witness*] recusar
[2] [+ *public official*] (= *accuse*) acusar de prevaricación; (= *try*) procesar por prevaricación; [+ *president*] someter a un proceso de destitución

impeachable [ɪm'piːtʃəbl] ADJ [*act*] susceptible de acusación por prevaricación; [*witness*] recusable

impeachment [ɪm'piːtʃmənt] Ⓐ N (= *accusation*) acusación *f* de prevaricación; (= *trial*) proceso *m* por prevaricación; [*of president*] proceso *m* de destitución
Ⓑ CPD ► **impeachment hearing** N juicio *m* por destitución ► **impeachment proceedings** NPL proceso *m* de destitución

impeccable [ɪm'pekəbl] ADJ [*appearance, uniform, performance, manners*] impecable; [*behaviour, conduct, service*] impecable, intachable; **she has ~ taste in clothes** tiene un gusto impecable para la ropa; **she speaks ~ English** habla un inglés impecable

impeccably [ɪm'pekəblɪ] ADV impecablemente; **he behaved ~** se comportó impecablemente *or* de manera intachable; **~ clean** impecablemente limpio; **he was ~ dressed** iba impecablemente vestido, iba vestido de punta en blanco*

impecunious [,ɪmpɪ'kjuːnɪəs] ADJ (*frm or hum*) falto de dinero

impedance [ɪm'piːdəns] N (*Elec*) impedancia *f*

impede [ɪm'piːd] VT [+ *progress, movement, growth, development*] dificultar, obstaculizar

impediment [ɪm'pedɪmənt] N [1] (= *obstacle*) obstáculo *m*, impedimento *m* (**to** para); (*Jur*) impedimento *m* (**to** para)
[2] (*Med*) defecto *m*; **speech ~** defecto *m* del habla

impedimenta [ɪm,pedɪ'mentə] NPL impedimenta *f*

impel [ɪm'pel] VT [1] (= *force, compel*) obligar; **I feel ~led to say ...** me veo obligado a decir ...
[2] (= *drive*) impulsar, impeler (*frm*); **hunger ~led him to do it** el hambre lo impulsó a hacerlo

impend [ɪm'pend] VI amenazar, ser inminente, cernerse

impending [ɪm'pendɪŋ] ADJ (*gen*) inminente; **his ~ retirement** su inminente jubilación; **a sign of ~ disaster** una señal de que se avecina un desastre

impenetrability [ɪm,penɪtrə'bɪlɪtɪ] N impenetrabilidad *f*

impenetrable [ɪm'penɪtrəbl] ADJ [1] (= *impassable*) [*jungle, barrier, fortress*] impenetrable
[2] (= *difficult to understand*) [*writing, idea, accent*] incomprensible; [*mystery*] insondable, inescrutable; [*expression*] inescrutable

impenetrably [ɪm'penɪtrəblɪ] ADV **winter brought the fogs, ~ thick** el invierno trajo las nieblas espesas, impenetrables

impenitence [ɪm'penɪtəns] N impenitencia *f*

impenitent [ɪm'penɪtənt] ADJ impenitente

impenitently [ɪm'penɪtəntlɪ] ADV impenitentemente, incorregiblemente

imperative [ɪm'perətɪv] Ⓐ ADJ [1] (= *essential*) imprescindible, fundamental; **it is ~ that he comes** es imprescindible *or* fundamental que venga; **it was ~ to destroy the bridge** era fundamental destruir el puente; **an ~ need** una necesidad imperiosa
[2] (= *authoritative*) [*manner, command*] imperativo, imperioso
[3] (*Ling*) imperativo
Ⓑ N [1] (*frm*) (= *need, drive*) imperativo *m*; **any animal's first ~ is to survive** el primer imperativo de cualquier animal es sobrevivir
[2] (*Ling*) imperativo *m*; **a verb in the ~** un verbo en (el) imperativo
Ⓒ CPD ► **imperative mood** N (*Ling*) modo *m* imperativo

imperatively [ɪm'perətɪvlɪ] ADV imperiosamente

imperceptible [,ɪmpə'septəbl] ADJ (*gen*) imperceptible

imperceptibly [,ɪmpə'septəblɪ] ADV imperceptiblemente

imperfect [ɪm'pɜːfɪkt] Ⓐ ADJ [1] (= *faulty*) [*machine, product*] defectuoso; [*hearing, vision*] deficiente; [*understanding, world, method*] imperfecto; [*knowledge*] incompleto, limitado; [*reasoning*] deficiente, incorrecto
[2] (*Ling*) [*tense*] imperfecto
Ⓑ N (*Ling*) imperfecto *m*; **a verb in the ~** un verbo en imperfecto

imperfection [,ɪmpə'fekʃən] N [1] (= *state of being imperfect*) imperfección *f*
[2] (= *fault*) defecto *m*

imperfectly [ɪm'pɜːfɪktlɪ] ADV [*design, create*] de manera defectuosa; **this process is still ~ understood by scientists** los científicos aún no entienden completamente este proceso, los científicos tienen aún un conocimiento limitado de este proceso; **she spoke English, though ~** hablaba inglés, aunque no perfectamente

imperial [ɪm'pɪərɪəl] Ⓐ ADJ [1] (= *of empire, emperor*) imperial
[2] (= *imperious*) señorial
[3] (*Brit*) [*weights, measures*] británico
Ⓑ CPD ► **imperial gallon** N (*Brit*) galón *m* inglés ► **imperial system** N sistema *m* británico de pesos y medidas

> **IMPERIAL SYSTEM**
>
> *Aunque el sistema métrico decimal se implantó oficialmente en 1971 en el Reino Unido para medidas y pesos y es el que se enseña en los colegios, en el lenguaje cotidiano aún se sigue usando en muchos casos el llamado* **imperial system**. *Por ejemplo, en las tiendas se sigue pesando en libras* (**pounds**) *y la gente suele decir su peso en* **stones** *y* **pounds**. *La cerveza se mide en pintas* (**pints**), *las distancias en millas* (**miles**) *y la longitud, la altura o la profundidad en pies* (**feet**) *y pulgadas* (**inches**).
> *En Estados Unidos el sistema imperial también se usa para todas las medidas y pesos, aunque la capacidad de la onza* (**ounce**), *del galón* (**gallon**) *y de la pinta* (**pint**) *es ligeramente inferior a la del Reino Unido. Por otro lado, en EE.UU. la gente mide su peso sólo en libras* (**pounds**) *y no en* **stones**.

imperialism [ɪm'pɪərɪəlɪzəm] N imperialismo *m*

imperialist [ɪm'pɪərɪəlɪst] Ⓐ ADJ imperialista
Ⓑ N imperialista *mf*

imperialistic [ɪm,pɪərɪə'lɪstɪk] ADJ imperialista

imperil [ɪm'perɪl] VT (*frm*) arriesgar, poner en peligro

imperious [ɪm'pɪərɪəs] ADJ [*tone, manner*] imperioso; (= *urgent*) apremiante

imperiously [ɪm'pɪərɪəslɪ] ADV imperiosamente

imperishable [ɪm'perɪʃəbl] ADJ [*goods*] imperecedero, no perecedero; [*memory*] imperecedero

impermanence [ɪm'pɜːmənəns] N impermanencia *f*

impermanent [ɪm'pɜːmənənt] ADJ impermanente

impermeable [ɪm'pɜːmɪəbl] ADJ impermeable (**to** a)

impersonal [ɪm'pɜːsnl] ADJ impersonal

impersonality [ɪm,pɜːsə'nælɪtɪ] N impersonalidad *f*

impersonally [ɪm'pɜːsnəlɪ] ADV impersonalmente, de manera impersonal

impersonate [ɪm'pɜːsəneɪt] VT hacerse pasar por; (*Theat*) imitar

impersonation [ɪm,pɜːsə'neɪʃən] N (*to commit crime*) suplantación *f*; (*Theat*) imitación *f*; **he does ~s** hace imitaciones

impersonator [ɪm'pɜːsəneɪtəʳ] N imitador(a) *m/f*

impertinence [ɪm'pɜːtɪnəns] N (= *cheek*) impertinencia *f*, insolencia *f*; **what ~!** ◊ **the ~ of it!** ¡qué impertinencia!, ¡habráse visto qué insolencia!; **an ~** una impertinencia; **it would be an ~ to ask** preguntar sería una impertinencia

impertinent [ɪm'pɜːtɪnənt] ADJ [*person, child, behaviour, manner*] impertinente, insolente; **to be ~ to sb** ser impertinente *or* insolente con algn; **don't be ~!** ¡no seas impertinente!

impertinently [ɪm'pɜːtɪnəntlɪ] ADV impertinentemente

imperturbable [,ɪmpə'tɜːbəbl] ADJ [*person, manner*] imperturbable, impasible

impervious [ɪm'pɜːvɪəs] ADJ [1] (*lit*) (*to water*) impermeable (**to** a)
[2] (*fig*) (*to remarks, threats*) inmune, insensible (**to** a); **he is ~ to criticism** es inmune *or* insensible a las críticas, no le afectan las críticas

impetigo [,ɪmpɪ'taɪgəʊ] N impétigo *m*

impetuosity [ɪm,petjʊ'ɒsɪtɪ] N [*of person, behaviour*] impulsividad *f*

impetuous [ɪm'petjʊəs] ADJ [*person*] impetuoso, impulsivo; [*behaviour*] precipitado, impulsivo

impetuously [ɪm'petjʊəslɪ] ADV [*say*] impetuosamente, de forma impetuosa, impulsivamente; [*behave*] precipitadamente, impulsivamente

impetus ['ɪmpɪtəs] N (*lit*) (= *force*) ímpetu *m*; (*fig*) impulso *m*; **to give an ~ to sales** impulsar *or* incentivar las ventas

impiety [ɪm'paɪətɪ] N impiedad *f*

impinge [ɪm'pɪndʒ] VI **to ~ on sth/sb** incidir en algo/algn, afectar a algo/algn; **to ~ on sb's freedom/rights** vulnerar la libertad/los derechos de algn

impingement [ɪm'pɪndʒmənt] N intromisión *f*

impious ['ɪmpɪəs] ADJ impío

impiously ['ɪmpɪəslɪ] ADV impíamente

impish ['ɪmpɪʃ] ADJ [*expression, smile*] pícaro, travieso

impishly ['ɪmpɪʃlɪ] ADV [*say, smile*] pícaramente, socarronamente

implacable [ɪm'plækəbl] ADJ [*enemy, hatred*] implacable

implacably [ɪm'plækəblɪ] ADV implacablemente

implant ['ɪmplɑːnt] Ⓐ N implante *m*
Ⓑ [ɪm'plɑːnt] VT (*Med*) [+ *organ, tissue*] injertar, implantar; (*fig*) [+ *idea, principle*] inculcar

implausible [ɪm'plɔːzəbl] ADJ inverosímil, poco convincente

implausibly [ɪm'plɔːzəblɪ] ADV inverosímilmente, poco convincentemente

implement Ⓐ ['ɪmplɪmənt] N herramienta *f*, instrumento *m*
Ⓑ ['ɪmplɪment] VT [+ *plan, decision, idea*] llevar

a cabo, poner en práctica; [+ *measure*] aplicar, poner en práctica; [+ *law*] aplicar

implementation [ˌɪmplɪmen'teɪʃən] N [*of plan, decision*] ejecución *f*, puesta *f* en práctica; [*of idea*] puesta *f* en práctica; [*of law, measure*] aplicación *f*

implicate ['ɪmplɪkeɪt] VT **to ~ sb in sth** implicar *or* involucrar a algn en algo; **are you ~d in this?** ¿estás implicado en esto?; **he ~d three others** implicó a otros tres

implication [ˌɪmplɪ'keɪʃən] N [1] (= *consequence*) implicación *f*, consecuencia *f*; **we shall have to study all the ~s** tendremos que estudiar las posibles consecuencias *or* repercusiones; **the proposal has major ~s for schools** la propuesta tiene grandes implicaciones *or* acarrea importantes consecuencias para los colegios
[2] (= *inference*) **his ~ was that she was lying** estaba insinuando que ella mentía; **the ~ of this is that ...** esto significa que ...; **he did not realize the full ~s of his words** no se dio cuenta de la trascendencia de sus palabras; **by ~ then ...** de ahí (se deduce) que ...
[3] (*in crime*) implicación *f*

implicit [ɪm'plɪsɪt] ADJ [1] (= *implied*) [*threat, agreement*] implícito; **it is ~ in what you say** se sobreentiende por lo que dices
[2] (= *unquestioning*) [*faith, belief*] incondicional, absoluto

implicitly [ɪm'plɪsɪtlɪ] ADV [1] (= *by implication*) implícitamente
[2] (= *unquestioningly*) [*trust*] sin reservas, incondicionalmente

implied [ɪm'plaɪd] (A) ADJ implícito, tácito; **it is not stated but it is ~** no se declara abiertamente pero se sobreentiende
(B) CPD ► **implied warranty** N garantía *f* implícita

implode [ɪm'pləʊd] (A) VT [1] implosionar
[2] (*Phon*) pronunciar implosivamente
(B) VI implosionar

implore [ɪm'plɔːʳ] VT [+ *person*] suplicar, rogar; [+ *forgiveness*] implorar; **to ~ sb to do sth** suplicar a algn que haga algo; **I ~ you!** ¡se lo suplico!

imploring [ɪm'plɔːrɪŋ] ADJ [*glance, gesture*] suplicante, de súplica

imploringly [ɪm'plɔːrɪŋlɪ] ADV de modo suplicante

implosion [ɪm'pləʊʒən] N implosión *f* (*also Phon*)

imply [ɪm'plaɪ] VT (= *hint, suggest*) insinuar; (= *involve*) suponer, implicar; **are you ~ing that ...?** ¿quieres decir que ...?, ¿insinúas que ...?; **what are you ~ing?** ¿qué insinúas?; **he implied he would do it** dio a entender que lo haría; **it implies a lot of work** supone *or* implica mucho trabajo

impolite [ˌɪmpə'laɪt] ADJ [*person*] mal educado, descortés; [*behaviour*] descortés

impolitely [ˌɪmpə'laɪtlɪ] ADV con descortesía

impoliteness [ˌɪmpə'laɪtnɪs] N [*of person*] falta *f* de educación; [*of remark*] descortesía *f*

impolitic [ɪm'pɒlɪtɪk] ADJ impolítico

imponderable [ɪm'pɒndərəbl] (A) ADJ imponderable
(B) **imponderables** NPL (elementos *mpl*) imponderables *mpl*

import (A) ['ɪmpɔːt] N [1] (*Comm*) (= *article*) artículo *m* importado, artículo *m* de importación; (= *importing*) importación *f*; **luxury ~s** artículos *mpl* de lujo importados *or* de importación; **oil is their biggest ~** lo que más importan es petróleo; **the idea is an American ~** (*fig*) es una idea importada de América
[2] (*frm*) (= *importance*) trascendencia *f*, importancia *f*; (= *meaning*) significado *m*; **to be of great ~** tener mucha trascendencia *or* importancia; **it is of no great ~** no tiene mayor trascendencia *or* importancia; **they were slow to realise the ~ of his speech** tardaron en darse cuenta de la trascendencia de su discurso
(B) [ɪm'pɔːt] VT [1] importar (**from** de; **into** en); *see also* **imported**
[2] (*frm*) (= *mean, imply*) significar, querer decir
(C) ['ɪmpɔːt] CPD [*licence, quota*] de importación ► **import duty** N derechos *mpl* de importación ► **import tax** N derecho *m* de importación ► **import trade** N comercio *m* importador

importance [ɪm'pɔːtəns] N importancia *f*; **to be of great/little ~** ser de gran/escasa importancia, tener mucha/poca importancia; **to attach great ~ to sth** conceder *or* dar mucha importancia a algo; **to be of no ~** carecer de importancia, no tener importancia; **to be full of one's own ~** darse ínfulas, creerse muy importante; **to be of some ~** ser de cierta importancia, tener cierta importancia

important [ɪm'pɔːtənt] ADJ importante; **it is ~ that** es importante que; **it sounds/looks ~** parece importante; **to try to look ~** (*pej*) darse tono *or* importancia; **he told Henry to touch nothing, and more ~, to say nothing** le dijo a Henry que no tocase nada y, lo que era más importante, que no dijese nada; **to become ~** cobrar importancia; **your opinion is equally ~** tu opinión es igualmente importante *or* es de igual importancia; **to make sb feel ~** hacer que algn se sienta importante; **it is ~ for everyone to be here on time** es importante que todo el mundo esté aquí a la hora; **the ~ thing is ...** lo importante es ...; **the most ~ thing in life** lo más importante en la vida; **it was ~ to me to know** para mí era importante saberlo

importantly [ɪm'pɔːtəntlɪ] ADV [1] (= *significantly*) **these weapons figured ~ in the war** estas armas tuvieron un importante papel en la guerra; **this document differs ~ from the original** este documento presenta importantes diferencias respecto al original; **more ~, ...** aún más importante, ...; **I was hungry, and, more ~, my children were hungry** yo tenía hambre y, lo que era aún más importante, mis hijos tenían hambre
[2] (= *arrogantly*) [*enter, walk, talk*] con un aire de importancia; **"I'll go," he said ~** —yo voy —dijo con un aire de importancia *or* dándose importancia

importation [ˌɪmpɔː'teɪʃən] N importación *f*

imported [ɪm'pɔːtɪd] ADJ [*goods*] de importación; **~ beers** cervezas *fpl* de importación

importer [ɪm'pɔːtəʳ] N (*Comm*) importador(a) *m/f*

import-export trade [ˌɪmpɔːt'ekspɔːtˌtreɪd] N comercio *m* de importación y exportación

importing [ɪm'pɔːtɪŋ] ADJ **~ company** empresa *f* de importación; **~ country** país *m* importador

importunate [ɪm'pɔːtjʊnɪt] ADJ [*demand*] importuno; [*person*] pertinaz

importune [ˌɪmpɔː'tjuːn] VT (*frm*) importunar, perseguir; (*Jur*) [*prostitute*] abordar con fines inmorales

importunity [ˌɪmpɔː'tjuːnɪtɪ] N (*frm*) importunidad *f*

impose [ɪm'pəʊz] (A) VT [+ *condition, fine, tax*] imponer (**on** a); (*Jur*) [+ *sentence*] imponer; **troops were brought in to ~ order** se movilizaron tropas para imponer el orden; **he tries to ~ his views on everyone else** intenta imponer sus puntos de vista a los demás; **to ~ o.s. on sb** abusar de la amabilidad de algn; **I couldn't possibly ~ myself on you for dinner** estaría abusando de su amabilidad si me quedara a cenar
(B) VI **to ~ (up)on** (= *take advantage of*) [+ *kindness, hospitality*] abusar de; **I don't wish to ~ (upon you)** no quiero abusar, no quiero molestar(le)

imposing [ɪm'pəʊzɪŋ] ADJ imponente, impresionante

imposition [ˌɪmpə'zɪʃən] N (= *act*) imposición *f*; (= *burden*) molestia *f*; (= *liberty*) abuso *m*; (= *tax*) impuesto *m*; **it's a bit of an ~** me parece un abuso; **I'm afraid it's rather an ~ for you** me temo que le vaya a resultar molesto

impossibility [ɪmˌpɒsə'bɪlɪtɪ] N imposibilidad *f*; **the ~ of doing sth** la imposibilidad de hacer algo; **it's a physical ~** es físicamente imposible

impossible [ɪm'pɒsəbl] (A) ADJ [1] (= *not possible*) [*task, dream*] imposible; **impossible!** ¡imposible!, ¡no es posible!; **it's almost ~ to read her writing** leer su letra es casi imposible, es casi imposible leer su letra; **this cooker is ~ to clean!** ¡esta cocina es imposible de limpiar!, ¡limpiar esta cocina es imposible!; **the fog made it ~ to see very far** la niebla impedía ver a mucha distancia; **it is ~ for me to leave now** me es imposible salir ahora; **it's not ~ that ...** existe la posibilidad de que ...; **to be physically ~** ser físicamente imposible; → EASY, DIFFICULT, IMPOSSIBLE
[2] (= *not tolerable*) [*person*] insufrible, insoportable; [*situation*] insostenible; **to be in an ~ position** hallarse en una situación insostenible; **you're ~!*** ¡eres insufrible *or* insoportable!
(B) N **the ~** lo imposible; **to ask for/do the ~** pedir/hacer lo imposible

impossibly [ɪm'pɒsəblɪ] ADV [1] (= *extremely*) [*late, expensive, small*] increíblemente, tremendamente; **~ difficult** tan difícil que resulta imposible, increíblemente *or* tremendamente difícil
[2] (= *intolerably*) **she was ~ rude to Ann** era grosera con Ann hasta un punto intolerable; **George behaved ~ at the wedding reception** George estuvo insoportable durante el banquete de bodas

impost ['ɪmpəʊst] N impuesto *m*

imposter, impostor [ɪm'pɒstəʳ] N impostor(a) *m/f*

imposture [ɪm'pɒstʃəʳ] N impostura *f*, engaño *m*

impotence ['ɪmpətəns] N (*gen*) impotencia *f*

impotent ['ɪmpətənt] ADJ (*gen*) impotente

impound [ɪm'paʊnd] VT [+ *vehicle*] retener, retirar de la vía pública; [+ *goods*] confiscar, incautar; [+ *dog*] llevar a la perrera municipal; (*Jur*) [+ *evidence*] recoger

impoundment [ɪm'paʊndmənt] N (*US Fin*) embargo *m*

impoverish [ɪm'pɒvərɪʃ] VT empobrecer; [+ *land*] agotar

impoverished [ɪm'pɒvərɪʃt] ADJ [*person*] empobrecido; [*land*] agotado, pobre

impoverishment [ɪm'pɒvərɪʃmənt] N empobrecimiento *m*; [*of land*] agotamiento *m*

impracticability [ɪmˌpræktɪkə'bɪlɪtɪ] N impracticabilidad *f*

impracticable [ɪm'præktɪkəbl] ADJ (= *unrealizable*) impracticable, no factible

➤ LANGUAGE IN USE: **importance** 18.5, 26.1 **important** 26.2, 26.3 **impossible A1** 26.2, 26.3

impractical [ɪmˈpræktɪkəl] ADJ *[person]* poco práctico, falto de sentido práctico; *[plan]* poco factible; **he's so ~** no es nada práctico

impracticality [ɪmˌpræktɪˈkælɪtɪ] N *[of person]* falta *f* de sentido práctico; *[of plan]* lo poco práctico

imprecation [ˌɪmprɪˈkeɪʃən] N imprecación *f*

imprecise [ˌɪmprɪˈsaɪs] ADJ *[information, definition]* impreciso

imprecision [ˌɪmprɪˈsɪʒən] N *[of information, definition]* imprecisión *f*

impregnable [ɪmˈpregnəbl] ADJ *[castle]* inexpugnable; *(lit, fig)* *[position]* invulnerable

impregnate [ˈɪmpregneɪt] VT (= *permeate*) impregnar, empapar (**with** de); (= *fertilise*) [+ *person, animal, egg*] fecundar; **to become ~d with** impregnarse de

impregnation [ˌɪmpregˈneɪʃən] N (= *permeation*) impregnación *f*; *(Bio)* fecundación *f*

impresario [ˌɪmpreˈsɑːrɪəʊ] N empresario/a *m/f*

impress Ⓐ [ɪmˈpres] VT [1] (= *make good impression on*) impresionar; **he does it just to ~ people** lo hace sólo para impresionar a la gente; **he is not easily ~ed** no se deja impresionar fácilmente; **how did she ~ you?** ¿qué impresión te hizo *or* causó?; **he ~ed me quite favourably** me hizo muy buena impresión; **I'm very ~ed!** ¡estoy admirado!; **I was not ~ed** no me hizo buena impresión
[2] (= *mark*) *(lit)* imprimir, estampar; *(fig)* *(in the mind)* grabar; **to ~ sth (up)on sb** *(fig)* convencer a algn de la importancia de algo; **I tried to ~ the importance of the job on him** traté de convencerle de la importancia del trabajo, traté de recalcar lo importante que era el trabajo; **I must ~ upon you that ...** tengo que subrayar que ...; **it ~ed itself upon my mind** se me quedó grabado en la mente
Ⓑ [ɪmˈpres] VI causar buena impresión
Ⓒ [ˈɪmpres] N impresión *f*; *(fig)* marca *f*, huella *f*

▼**impression** [ɪmˈpreʃən] N [1] (= *effect*) impresión *f*; **to make an ~ (on sb)** impresionar (a algn); **she's out to make an ~** quiere impresionar; **to make a good/bad ~ (on sb)** causar buena/mala impresión (a algn); **to make no ~ (on sth)** no tener el menor efecto (sobre algo); **all our arguments seemed to make no ~ on him** nuestros argumentos no parecieron tener efecto alguno en él; **we had been digging for an hour but weren't making any ~** llevábamos una hora cavando pero sin ningún éxito
[2] (= *vague idea, illusion*) impresión *f*; **to be under** *or* **have the ~ that ...** tener la impresión de que ...; **he gives the ~ of knowing a lot** da la impresión de saber mucho; **my ~s of Paris** mis impresiones de París; **I don't want you to get the wrong ~** no quiero que te lleves una falsa impresión; **they used cotton wool to give the ~ of snow** utilizaban algodón para simular la nieve
[3] (= *mark*) impresión *f*; *(fig)* marca *f*, huella *f*
[4] *(esp Brit Typ)* *(for first time)* impresión *f*, tirada *f*; *(thereafter)* reimpresión *f*
[5] *(Theat)* imitación *f*; **to do ~s** hacer imitaciones

impressionable [ɪmˈpreʃnəbl] ADJ *[person]* impresionable, influenciable; **to be at an ~ age** estar en una edad en la que se es muy impresionable *or* influenciable

impressionism [ɪmˈpreʃənɪzəm] N *(Art)* impresionismo *m*

impressionist [ɪmˈpreʃənɪst] Ⓐ ADJ impresionista
Ⓑ N [1] *(Art)* impresionista *mf*
[2] *(Theat)* imitador(a) *m/f*

impressionistic [ɪmˌpreʃəˈnɪstɪk] ADJ impresionista

impressive [ɪmˈpresɪv] ADJ *[achievement, victory, display]* impresionante; **it was an ~ performance** *(Sport, Mus)* fue una actuación impresionante *or* soberbia; **the company has an ~ record in terms of profits** la empresa posee un impresionante *or* excelente historial de beneficios

impressively [ɪmˈpresɪvlɪ] ADV *[play, perform]* admirablemente, extraordinariamente; **he won both tournaments ~** ganó ambos torneos con una actuación impresionante; **she has an ~ long list of awards to her name** su nombre va unido a una lista impresionante de galardones; **she was ~ brave** tuvo un valor admirable *or* extraordinario

imprest system [ˈɪmprestˌsɪstəm] N sistema *m* de fondo fijo

imprimatur [ɪmprɪˈmeɪtəʳ] N *(Publishing)* *(also fig)* imprimátur *m*

imprint Ⓐ [ɪmˈprɪnt] VT [1] (= *mark*) [+ *paper*] imprimir; **to ~ sth on sth** imprimir *or* estampar algo en algo
[2] *(fig)* grabar; **it was ~ed on his mind** lo tenía grabado en la mente
[3] *(Bio, Psych)* imprimir (**on** a)
Ⓑ [ˈɪmprɪnt] N impresión *f*, huella *f*; *(Typ)* pie *m* de imprenta; **under the HarperCollins ~** publicado por HarperCollins

imprinting [ɪmˈprɪntɪŋ] N *(Bio, Psych)* impresión *f*

imprison [ɪmˈprɪzn] VT [+ *criminal*] (= *put in jail*) encarcelar, meter en la cárcel; **he was ~ed for debt/for ten years** lo encarcelaron *or* lo metieron en la cárcel por deudas/durante diez años

imprisonment [ɪmˈprɪznmənt] N (= *act*) encarcelamiento *m*; (= *term of imprisonment*) cárcel *f*, prisión *f*; **he was sentenced to ten years ~** fue condenado a diez años de prisión; **~ without trial** detención *f* sin procesamiento; **life ~** cadena *f* perpetua

improbability [ɪmˌprɒbəˈbɪlɪtɪ] N (= *unlikelihood*) improbabilidad *f*; (= *implausibility*) inverosimilitud *f*

improbable [ɪmˈprɒbəbl] ADJ *[event]* improbable; *[excuse, story]* inverosímil; **it is ~ that it will happen** es improbable *or* poco probable que ocurra

improbably [ɪmˈprɒbəblɪ] ADV [1] (= *surprisingly*) sorprendentemente; **this area is, ~, one of the best in town** en contra de lo que cabría esperar, este barrio es uno de los mejores de la ciudad
[2] (= *implausibly*) increíblemente; **an ~ blue sky** un cielo increíblemente azul

impromptu [ɪmˈprɒmptjuː] Ⓐ ADJ (= *improvised*) *[performance, speech]* improvisado; (= *unexpected*) *[remark]* espontáneo, impremeditado
Ⓑ ADV (= *ad lib*) de improviso, sin preparación; (= *unexpectedly*) *[say]* espontáneamente
Ⓒ N improvisación *f*

improper [ɪmˈprɒpəʳ] ADJ [1] (= *unseemly*) *[behaviour, laughter]* indecoroso, impropio
[2] (= *indecent*) *[remark]* indecoroso; *[suggestion]* deshonesto
[3] (= *incorrect*) *[use]* indebido
[4] (= *illicit*) *[dealings]* deshonesto

improperly [ɪmˈprɒpəlɪ] ADV *[behave, act]* (= *in unseemly way*) incorrectamente, indecorosamente, impropiamente; (= *indecently*) indecentemente; *[use]* indebidamente; (= *illicitly*) deshonestamente; **they threw me out for being ~ dressed** me echaron por ir vestido incorrectamente

impropriety [ˌɪmprəˈpraɪətɪ] N *[of person, behaviour]* (= *unseemliness*) incorrección *f*, falta *f* de decoro; (= *indecency*) indecencia *f*; *[of language]* impropiedad *f*; (= *illicit nature*) deshonestidad *f*

improve [ɪmˈpruːv] Ⓐ VT [1] (= *make better*) [+ *work*] mejorar; [+ *property*] hacer mejoras en; **to ~ o.s.** *or* **one's mind** cultivarse, instruirse; **to ~ o.s.** *(in wealth)* mejorar su situación
[2] (= *favour*) [+ *appearance*] favorecer
[3] (= *perfect*) [+ *skill*] perfeccionar; (= *add value to*) aumentar el valor de; **to ~ one's Spanish** perfeccionar sus conocimientos del español
[4] (= *increase*) [+ *production, yield*] aumentar; **to ~ one's chances of success** aumentar *or* mejorar las posibilidades de éxito; **the management has refused to ~ its offer of 3%** la dirección se ha negado a mejorar su oferta del 3%
Ⓑ VI *[person]* *(in skill etc)* hacer progresos; *(after illness)* mejorar(se); *[health, weather, work, quality]* mejorar; *[production, yield]* aumentar; *[business]* mejorar, prosperar; **to ~ in sth** hacer progresos en algo; **to ~ with age/use** mejorar con el tiempo/el uso

►**improve on**, **improve upon** VI + PREP *(gen)* mejorar; **it cannot be ~d (up)on** es inmejorable; **to ~ (up)on sb's offer** ofrecer más que algn, mejorar la oferta de algn

improvement [ɪmˈpruːvmənt] Ⓐ N *(in quality)* mejora *f*, mejoramiento *m* (**in** de); (= *increase*) aumento *m* (**in** de); (= *progress*) progresos *mpl* (**in** en); *[of the mind]* cultivo *m*; *(Med)* mejoría *f*; **it's an ~ on the old one** supone una mejora con respecto al antiguo; **there is room for ~** podría mejorarse; **there has been some ~ in the patient's condition** el paciente ha mejorado algo; **they made ~s in safety procedures** mejoraron los mecanismos de seguridad; **to make ~s to** [+ *property*] hacer mejoras en
Ⓑ CPD ► **improvement grant** N subvención *f* para modernizar (una casa *etc*)

improvidence [ɪmˈprɒvɪdəns] N imprevisión *f*

improvident [ɪmˈprɒvɪdənt] ADJ *[person]* imprevisor; *[action]* carente de previsión

improvidently [ɪmˈprɒvɪdəntlɪ] ADV imprόvidamente

improving [ɪmˈpruːvɪŋ] ADJ *[book, programme]* edificante, instructivo

improvisation [ˌɪmprəvaɪˈzeɪʃən] N (= *act*) improvisación *f*; (= *improvised speech, music*) improvisación *f*

improvise [ˈɪmprəvaɪz] VI, VT improvisar

imprudence [ɪmˈpruːdəns] N imprudencia *f*

imprudent [ɪmˈpruːdənt] ADJ imprudente

imprudently [ɪmˈpruːdəntlɪ] ADV imprudentemente

impudence [ˈɪmpjʊdəns] N *[of person]* insolencia *f*, descaro *m*; *[of behaviour]* insolencia *f*; **he had the ~ to say that ...** tuvo la insolencia *or* el descaro de decir que ...; **what ~!** ¡qué insolencia *or* descaro!

impudent [ˈɪmpjʊdənt] ADJ *[person]* insolente, descarado; *[behaviour]* insolente

impudently [ˈɪmpjʊdəntlɪ] ADV descaradamente, insolentemente

impugn [ɪmˈpjuːn] VT [+ *integrity, honesty, motives*] poner en duda; [+ *theory*] cuestionar; [+ *testimony*] impugnar

impulse [ˈɪmpʌls] Ⓐ N *(Tech, fig)* impulso *m*; **my first ~ was to hit him** mi primer impulso

➤ LANGUAGE IN USE: impression 2 6.2

fue de golpearlo; **on ~** llevado por un impulso, impulsivamente; **to act on ~** obrar llevado por un impulso, obrar impulsivamente; **I bought it on ~** lo compré impulsivamente; **to yield to a sudden ~** dejarse llevar por un impulso

Ⓑ CPD ► **impulse buy** N compra *f* impulsiva ► **impulse buying** N compras *fpl* impulsivas ► **impulse sales** NPL ventas *fpl* impulsivas

impulsion [ɪm'pʌlʃən] N impulsión *f*

impulsive [ɪm'pʌlsɪv] ADJ [*person, temperament*] impulsivo; [*act, remark*] irreflexivo

impulsively [ɪm'pʌlsɪvlɪ] ADV [*act*] impulsivamente, llevado por un impulso; [*say*] sin pensar, sin reflexión; **~ she patted him on the arm** le dio palmaditas en el brazo impulsivamente

impulsiveness [ɪm'pʌlsɪvnɪs], **impulsivity** [ɪmpʌl'sɪvɪtɪ] (*US*) N impulsividad *f*, carácter *m* impulsivo

impunity [ɪm'pjuːnɪtɪ] N impunidad *f*; **with ~** con impunidad, impunemente

impure [ɪm'pjʊə^r] ADJ (*Chem*) [*substance, drug*] impuro, con impurezas; [*water*] con impurezas, contaminado; (*morally*) [*person, thought*] impuro

impurity [ɪm'pjʊərɪtɪ] N impureza *f*

imputation [,ɪmpjʊ'teɪʃən] N (= *attribution*) imputación *f*; (= *accusation*) imputación *f*, acusación *f*

impute [ɪm'pjuːt] VT **to ~ sth to sb** imputar *or* atribuir algo a algn

IN ABBR (*US*) = **Indiana**

in [ɪn]

A PREPOSITION	C ADJECTIVE
B ADVERB	D NOUN

Ⓐ PREPOSITION

When **in** *is the second element in a phrasal verb, eg* **ask in, fill in, look in**, *etc, look up the verb. When it is part of a set combination, eg* **in the country, in ink, in danger, covered in**, *look up the other word.*

1 *in expressions of place* en; (= *inside*) dentro de; **it's in London/Scotland/Galicia** está en Londres/Escocia/Galicia; **in the garden** en el jardín; **in the house** en casa; (= *inside*) dentro de la casa; **our bags were stolen, and our passports were in them** nos robaron los bolsos, y nuestros pasaportes iban dentro

When phrases like **in Madrid, in Germany** *are used to identify a particular group,* **de** *is the usual translation:*

our colleagues in Madrid nuestros colegas de Madrid; **the chairs in the room** las sillas de la habitación, las sillas que hay en la habitación *or* dentro de la habitación; **in here/there** aquí/allí dentro; **it's hot in here** aquí dentro hace calor

2 *in expressions of time* 2·1 (= *during*) en; **in 1986** en 1986; **in May/spring** en mayo/primavera; **in the eighties/the 20th century** en los años ochenta/el siglo 20; **in the morning(s)/evening(s)** por la mañana/la tarde; **at four o'clock in the morning/afternoon** a las cuatro de la mañana/la tarde

2·2 (= *for*) **she hasn't been here in years** hace años que no viene

2·3 (= *in the space of*) en; **I did it in 3 hours/days** lo hice en 3 horas/días; **it was built in a week** fue construido en una semana

2·4 (= *within*) dentro de; **I'll see you in three weeks' time** *or* **in three weeks** te veré dentro de tres semanas; **he'll be back in a moment/a month** volverá dentro de un momento/un mes

3 *indicating manner, medium* en; **in a loud/soft voice** en voz alta/baja; **in Spanish/English** en español/inglés; **to pay in dollars** pagar en dólares; **it was underlined in red** estaba subrayado en rojo; **a magnificent sculpture in marble and copper** una magnífica escultura de *or* en mármol y cobre

4 *= clothed in* **she opened the door in her dressing gown** abrió la puerta en bata; **they were all in shorts** todos iban en *or* llevaban pantalón corto; **he went out in his new raincoat** salió con el impermeable nuevo; **you look nice in that dress** ese vestido te sienta bien

When phrases like **in the blue dress, in the glasses** *are used to identify a particular person,* **de** *is the usual translation:*

the man in the hat el hombre del sombrero; **the boy in the checked trousers** el chico de los pantalones de cuadros; BUT **the girl in green** la chica vestida de verde; *see also* **dressed**

5 *giving ratio, number* **one person in ten** una persona de cada diez; **one in five pupils** uno de cada cinco alumnos; **he had only a one in fifty chance of survival** sólo tenía una posibilidad entre cincuenta de sobrevivir; **what happened was a chance in a million** había una posibilidad entre un millón de que pasara lo que pasó; **20 pence in the pound** veinte peniques por (cada) libra; **once in a hundred years** una vez cada cien años; **in twos** de dos en dos; **these jugs are produced in their millions** estas jarras se fabrican por millones, se fabrican millones de estas jarras; **people came in their hundreds** acudieron cientos de personas, la gente acudió a centenares

6 *= among* entre; **this is common in children/cats** es cosa común entre los niños/los gatos; **you find this instinct in animals** este instinto se encuentra en *or* entre los animales, los animales poseen este instinto; **in (the works of) Shakespeare** en las obras de Shakespeare

7 *talking about people* **she has it in her to succeed** tiene la capacidad de triunfar; **it's not in him to do that** no es capaz de hacer eso; **I couldn't find it in me to forgive him** no salía de mí perdonarle; **they have a good leader in him** él es buen líder para ellos, en él tienen un buen líder; **a condition rare in a child of that age** una dolencia extraña en *or* para un niño de esa edad; **it's something I admire in her** es algo que admiro de *or* en ella; **he had all the qualities I was looking for in a partner** tenía todas las cualidades que yo buscaba en un compañero

8 *in profession etc* **to be in teaching** dedicarse a la enseñanza; **to be in publishing** trabajar en el mundo editorial; **he's in the motor trade** es vendedor de coches; **he's in the tyre business** se dedica al comercio de neumáticos; *see also* **army**

9 *after superlative* de; **the biggest/smallest in Europe** el más grande/pequeño de Europa

10 *with verb* **in saying this** al decir esto; **in making a fortune he lost his wife** mientras hacía fortuna, perdió su mujer

11 *in set expressions*

◆ **in all** en total

◆ **in itself** de por sí

◆ **in that** (= *since*) puesto que, ya que; **the new treatment is preferable in that ...** es preferible el nuevo tratamiento puesto *or* ya que ...; **in that, he resembles his father** en eso se parece a su padre

◆ **what's in it for me**: **I want to know what's in it for me** quiero saber qué gano yo con eso; *see also* **far A1**

Ⓑ ADVERB

1 **to be in** (= *be at home*) estar (en casa); (= *be at work*) estar; (= *be gathered in*) [*crops, harvest*] estar recogido; (= *be at destination*) [*train, ship, plane*] haber llegado; (= *be alight*) estar encendido, arder; (*Sport*) [*ball, shuttlecock*] entrar; **he wasn't in** no estaba (en casa); **there's nobody in** no hay nadie; **is Mr Eccles in?** ¿está el Sr. Eccles?; **the boss isn't in yet** el jefe no ha llegado aún; **he's in for tests** (*in hospital*) está ingresado para unas pruebas; **he's in for larceny** (*in prison*) está encerrado por ladrón; **he's in for 5 years** cumple una condena de 5 años; **what's he in for?** ¿de qué delito se le acusa?; **when the Tories were in*** (*in power*) cuando los conservadores estaban en el poder; **the screw was not in properly** el tornillo no estaba bien metido; **the essays have to be in by Friday** hay que entregar los trabajos para el viernes; **strawberries are in** es la temporada de las fresas, las fresas están en sazón; **the fire is still in** el fuego sigue encendido *or* aún arde; ✦**IDIOM** **my luck is in** estoy de suerte; *see also* **C1**

◆ **to be in and out**: **to be in and out of work** no tener trabajo fijo; **don't worry, you'll be in and out in no time** no te preocupes, saldrás enseguida

◆ **to be in for sth**: **he's in for a surprise*** le espera una sorpresa; **we're in for a hard time** vamos a pasar un mal rato; **we may be in for some snow** puede que nieve; **you don't know what you're in for!** ¡no sabes lo que te espera!; **he's in for it** lo va a pagar; **to be in for a competition** (= *be entered*) haberse inscrito en un concurso; **to be in for an exam** presentarse a un examen

◆ **to be in on sth** (= *be aware, involved*) **to be in on the plan/secret*** estar al tanto del plan/del secreto; **are you in on it?** ¿estás tú metido en ello?

◆ **to be well in with sb** (= *be friendly*) **to be well in with sb*** llevarse muy bien con algn

2 *with other verbs* **she opened the door and they all rushed in** abrió la puerta y todos entraron *or* se metieron corriendo; **she opened her bag and put the ticket in** abrió el bolso y metió el billete

3 *with time words* **day in, day out** día tras día; **week in, week out** semana tras semana

4 *Sport* **in!** ¡entró!

Ⓒ ADJECTIVE (*)

1 *= fashionable* de moda; **to be in** estar de moda, llevarse; **short skirts were in** la falda corta estaba de moda, se llevaban las faldas cortas; **it's the in thing** es lo que se lleva; **it's the in place to eat** es el restaurante que está de moda; **she wore a very in dress** llevaba un vestido muy a la moda *or* de lo más moderno

2 *= exclusive* **it's an in joke** es un chiste privado, es un chiste que tienen entre ellos/tenemos entre nosotros; **if you're not in with the in crowd ...** si no estás entre los elegidos ...

Ⓓ NOUN

1 **the ins and outs of: the ins and outs of the problem** los pormenores del problema; **the ins and outs of high finance** los entresijos de las altas finanzas; **dietary experts can advise on the ins and outs of dieting** los expertos en alimentación pueden dar información pormenorizada sobre las dietas

2 *US Pol* **the ins*** el partido del gobierno

in... [ɪn] PREFIX in...

in. ABBR = **inch**

inability [ˌɪnəˈbɪlɪtɪ] N incapacidad *f*; **~ to do sth** incapacidad para hacer algo; **his ~ to express himself** su incapacidad para expresarse

in absentia [ˈinæbˈsentiə] ADV in absentia

inaccessibility [ˈɪnækˌsesəˈbɪlɪtɪ] N inaccesibilidad *f*

inaccessible [ˌɪnækˈsesəbl] ADJ inaccesible; **to be ~ by road/land** ser inaccesible por carretera/tierra; **to be ~ to cars** resultar inaccesible en coche; **to be ~ to sb** ser inaccesible para algn; **goods which are ~ to the average citizen** bienes que son inaccesibles para el ciudadano medio

inaccuracy [ɪnˈækjʊrəsɪ] N 1 (= *imprecision*) [*of figures, information, statement*] inexactitud *f*; [*of shot, aim, instrument, method*] falta *f* de precisión, imprecisión *f*
2 (*usu pl*) (= *mistake*) error *m*; **the report contained many inaccuracies** el informe contenía muchos errores

inaccurate [ɪnˈækjʊrɪt] ADJ [*figures, information, reporting, statement*] inexacto, erróneo; [*shot, aim, instrument, method*] impreciso, poco preciso; **the report gave a very ~ picture of the situation** el informe daba una visión muy inexacta *or* errónea de la situación; **the figures are wildly ~** las cifras son totalmente erróneas *or* del todo inexactas; **his estimate was wildly ~** su cálculo era completamente errado

inaccurately [ɪnˈækjʊrɪtlɪ] ADV **he measured the room ~** no midió la habitación correctamente; **a device which measures distance ~** un dispositivo que no mide las distancias con precisión; **he described the event ~** su descripción del suceso fue inexacta

inaction [ɪnˈækʃən] N inacción *f*, inactividad *f*

inactive [ɪnˈæktɪv] ADJ [*person, animal, volcano, life, substance*] inactivo

inactivity [ˌɪnækˈtɪvɪtɪ] N inactividad *f*

inadequacy [ɪnˈædɪkwəsɪ] N 1 (= *insufficiency*) [*of funding, resources, measures, training*] insuficiencia *f*; [*of housing, diet*] lo inadecuado
2 (= *weakness*) [*of person*] incompetencia *f*, ineptitud *f*; [*of system*] deficiencia *f*

inadequate [ɪnˈædɪkwɪt] ADJ 1 (= *insufficient*) [*supply, funding, measures, training*] insuficiente; [*housing, diet*] inadecuado; **the facilities are ~** las instalaciones dejan mucho que desear; **the company had ~ resources to survive the recession** la empresa no tenía recursos suficientes *or* no tenía los recursos adecuados para sobrevivir a la recesión
2 (= *weak*) incompetente, inepto; **he makes me feel totally ~** hace que me sienta totalmente incompetente *or* un verdadero inepto

inadequately [ɪnˈædɪkwɪtlɪ] ADV **the projects were ~ funded** los proyectos adolecían de insuficiencia de fondos; **the police were ~ trained** la policía no estaba lo suficientemente entrenada, la policía no había recibido el entrenamiento adecuado; **I felt ~ prepared** me sentía mal preparada *or* poco preparada

inadmissible [ˌɪnədˈmɪsəbl] ADJ inadmisible

inadvertence [ˌɪnədˈvɜːtəns] N inadvertencia *f*; **by ~** por inadvertencia, por descuido

inadvertent [ˌɪnədˈvɜːtənt] ADJ (= *unintentional*) [*error, oversight*] involuntario; **this had the ~ effect of ...** esto tuvo el efecto no buscado de ...; **they were trying to trap him into an ~ admission** estaban tratando de tenderle una trampa para que lo admitiera sin darse cuenta

inadvertently [ˌɪnədˈvɜːtəntlɪ] ADV sin darse cuenta, sin querer

inadvisability [ˈɪnədˌvaɪzəˈbɪlɪtɪ] N lo poco aconsejable, lo desaconsejable

inadvisable [ˌɪnədˈvaɪzəbl] ADJ poco aconsejable, desaconsejable

inalienable [ɪnˈeɪlɪənəbl] ADJ inalienable

inamorata [ɪnˌæməˈrɑːtə] N amada *f*, querida *f*

inane [ɪˈneɪn] ADJ [*remark*] necio, fatuo, sonso (*LAm*); [*laugh, task, activity*] tonto; [*expression*] (*on face*) estúpido

inanely [ɪˈneɪnlɪ] ADV [*talk*] a lo tonto*; **they chatted on ~ about the weather** siguieron charlando a lo tonto sobre el tiempo*; **he went through the bar grinning ~** pasó por el bar riéndose como un tonto

inanimate [ɪnˈænɪmɪt] ADJ [*object*] inanimado

inanition [ˌɪnəˈnɪʃən] N inanición *f*

inanity [ɪˈnænɪtɪ] N (= *quality*) necedad *f*, fatuidad *f*; **inanities** (= *inane remarks*) estupideces *fpl*, sandeces *fpl*

inapplicable [ɪnˈæplɪkəbl] ADJ inaplicable

inapposite [ɪnˈæpəzɪt] ADJ inapropiado, fuera de lugar

inappropriate [ˌɪnəˈprəʊprɪɪt] ADJ [*action, punishment, treatment*] inadecuado, poco apropiado; [*word, phrase*] inoportuno; [*behaviour*] impropio

inappropriately [ˌɪnəˈprəʊprɪɪtlɪ] ADV [*act*] de manera impropia; [*dressed*] de manera poco adecuada *or* apropiada

inappropriateness [ˌɪnəˈprəʊprɪɪtnɪs] N [*of behaviour*] lo impropio; [*of remark*] lo inoportuno; [*of dress*] lo poco adecuado *or* apropiado

inapt [ɪnˈæpt] ADJ (= *unsuitable*) poco idóneo; (= *inapposite*) no pertinente

inaptitude [ɪnˈæptɪtjuːd] N (= *unsuitability*) falta *f* de idoneidad; (= *inappositeness*) falta *f* de pertinencia

inarticulate [ˌɪnɑːˈtɪkjʊlɪt] ADJ [*person*] con dificultad para expresarse; [*speech*] mal pronunciado; [*noise, sound*] inarticulado; **he was ~ with rage** de lo furioso que estaba no podía pronunciar palabra

inarticulately [ˌɪnɑːˈtɪkjʊlɪtlɪ] ADV **he speaks ~** tiene dificultad para expresarse; **he was mumbling ~** hablaba entre dientes y apenas se le entendía

inartistic [ɪnɑːˈtɪstɪk] ADJ [*work*] poco artístico, antiestético; [*person*] falto de talento artístico

inasmuch [ɪnəzˈmʌtʃ] ADV **~ as** (= *seeing that*) puesto que, ya que, en vista de que; (= *to the extent that*) *see* **insofar**

inattention [ˌɪnəˈtenʃən] N (= *inattentiveness*) falta *f* de atención; (= *neglect*) falta *f* de interés, desinterés *m*

inattentive [ˌɪnəˈtentɪv] ADJ (= *distracted*) desatento, distraído; (= *neglectful*) poco atento; **she accused him of being ~ to her and the children** lo acusó de no prestarles suficiente atención a ella y a los niños

inattentively [ˌɪnəˈtentɪvlɪ] ADV distraídamente

inaudible [ɪnˈɔːdəbl] ADJ inaudible; **he was almost ~** apenas se le podía oír

inaudibly [ɪnˈɔːdəblɪ] ADV de forma *or* modo inaudible; **he spoke almost ~** habló tan bajo que apenas se le podía oír

inaugural [ɪˈnɔːgjʊrəl] ADJ [*lecture, debate*] inaugural; [*speech*] de apertura; **the president's ~ address** el discurso de investidura *or* de toma de posesión del presidente

inaugurate [ɪˈnɔːgjʊreɪt] VT 1 [+ *policy, new era, building*] inaugurar
2 (= *swear in*) [+ *president, official*] investir

inauguration [ɪˌnɔːgjʊˈreɪʃən] Ⓐ N (= *start*) inauguración *f*; (= *opening*) ceremonia *f* de apertura; (= *swearing in*) [*of president*] investidura *f*, toma *f* de posesión
Ⓑ CPD ► **inauguration ceremony** N [*of building*] ceremonia *f* de inauguración; [*of president*] ceremonia *f* de investidura *or* de toma de posesión ► **inauguration speech** N [*of president*] discurso *m* de investidura *or* de toma de posesión

inauspicious [ˌɪnɔːsˈpɪʃəs] ADJ [*occasion*] poco propicio; [*circumstances*] desfavorable; [*moment*] inoportuno, poco propicio; **the campaign got off to an ~ start** la campaña empezó de manera poco propicia

inauspiciously [ˌɪnɔːsˈpɪʃəslɪ] ADV de modo poco propicio, en condiciones desfavorables

in-between [ˈɪnbɪˈtwiːn] ADJ (*gen*) intermedio; **he's rather ~** no es ni una cosa ni la otra

inboard [ˈɪnbɔːd] ADJ [*engine*] interior

inborn [ˈɪnbɔːn] ADJ [*ability, talent*] innato

inbound [ˈɪnbaʊnd] ADJ [*flight*] de llegada; [*passenger*] que llega/llegaba

inbred [ˈɪnbred] ADJ (= *innate*) innato; (= *result of in-breeding*) engendrado por endogamia; **we're too ~ in this company** en esta empresa estamos demasiado cerrados al exterior

inbreeding [ˈɪnˌbriːdɪŋ] N endogamia *f*

inbuilt [ˈɪnbɪlt] ADJ 1 (= *innate*) [*feeling*] innato; [*prejudice*] inherente
2 (= *integral*) incorporado; **an answering machine with ~ fax and printer** un contestador automático con fax e impresora incorporados

Inc. ABBR (*US Comm*) (= **Incorporated**) S.A.

inc. ABBR (= **included, including, inclusive (of)**) inc.

Inca [ˈɪŋkə] Ⓐ ADJ incaico, incásico
Ⓑ N (*pl* **Inca** *or* **Incas**) inca *mf*

incalculable [ɪnˈkælkjʊləbl] ADJ incalculable

Incan [ˈɪŋkən] ADJ inca, incaico

incandescence [ˌɪnkænˈdesns] N incandescencia *f*

incandescent [ˌɪnkænˈdesnt] ADJ incandescente; **she was ~ (with rage)** estaba que trinaba (de rabia)*

incantation [ˌɪnkænˈteɪʃən] N conjuro *m*, ensalmo *m*

incapability [ɪnˌkeɪpəˈbɪlɪtɪ] N incapacidad *f*

incapable [ɪnˈkeɪpəbl] ADJ 1 (= *unable*) **to be ~ of doing sth** ser incapaz de hacer algo; **she is ~ of harming anyone** es incapaz de hacer daño a alguien; **to be ~ of speech/movement** quedarse sin habla/sin poder moverse, no poder hablar/moverse; **a problem ~ of solution** un problema insoluble; **he is ~ of shame** no tiene vergüenza
2 (= *incompetent*) [*worker*] incompetente
3 (= *helpless*) inútil; **he was drunk and ~** estaba totalmente borracho

incapacitate [ˌɪnkəˈpæsɪteɪt] VT [+ *person*] incapacitar; (*Jur*) inhabilitar, incapacitar; **he was ~d by arthritis** estaba incapacitado por la artritis; **he was ~d by alcohol** estaba en un estado de embriaguez; **physically ~d** incapacitado físicamente

incapacitating [ˌɪnkəˈpæsɪteɪtɪŋ] ADJ [*illness*] que incapacita; **the pain is a nuisance but not ~** el dolor es molesto, pero no me incapacita

incapacity [ˌɪnkəˈpæsɪtɪ] N incapacidad *f*

➤ LANGUAGE IN USE: **inadvisable** 2.2 **incapable 1** 16.4

in-car [ˈɪnˌkaːr] ADJ **~ entertainment system/stereo** aparato *m* de música de coche

incarcerate [ɪnˈkɑːsəreɪt] VT encarcelar

incarceration [ɪnˌkaːsəˈreɪʃən] N encarcelamiento *m*, encarcelación *f*

incarnate Ⓐ [ɪnˈkɑːnɪt] ADJ (*Rel*) encarnado; **the word ~** el verbo encarnado; **the devil ~** el diablo personificado, el mismo diablo
Ⓑ [ˈɪnkɑːneɪt] VT encarnar

incarnation [ˌɪnkɑːˈneɪʃən] N (*Rel*) encarnación *f*; **he is the ~ of evil** es la encarnación del mal

incautious [ɪnˈkɔːʃəs] ADJ incauto, imprudente

incautiously [ɪnˈkɔːʃəslɪ] ADV incautamente, imprudentemente

incendiary [ɪnˈsendɪərɪ] Ⓐ ADJ [*bomb, device, speech*] incendiario
Ⓑ N 1 (= *bomb*) bomba *f* incendiaria
2 (= *arsonist*) incendiario/a *m/f*, pirómano/a *m/f*

incense[1] [ˈɪnsens] Ⓐ N incienso *m*
Ⓑ CPD ► **incense burner** N incensario *m*

incense[2] [ɪnˈsens] VT indignar, encolerizar; **their behaviour so ~d him that ...** su comportamiento lo indignó hasta tal punto que ...

incensed [ɪnˈsenst] ADJ [*person*] furioso, furibundo

incentive [ɪnˈsentɪv] Ⓐ N incentivo *m*, estímulo *m*; **an ~ to work harder** un incentivo *or* estímulo para trabajar más; **as an added ~, they paid her airfare** como incentivo adicional, le pagaron el billete de avión; **they have no ~ to get a job** no tienen ningún incentivo para encontrar trabajo; **production ~** incentivo *m* a la producción
Ⓑ CPD ► **incentive bonus** N prima *f* de incentivación ► **incentive payment** N incentivo *m* económico ► **incentive scheme** N plan *m* de incentivos

inception [ɪnˈsepʃən] N comienzo *m*, principio *m*; **from its ~** desde el comienzo, desde el principio, desde los comienzos

incertitude [ɪnˈsɜːtɪtjuːd] N incertidumbre *f*

incessant [ɪnˈsesnt] ADJ [*rain, demands, complaints, fighting*] incesante, constante

incessantly [ɪnˈsesntlɪ] ADV sin cesar, incesantemente

incest [ˈɪnsest] N incesto *m*

incestuous [ɪnˈsestjʊəs] ADJ incestuoso

inch [ɪntʃ] Ⓐ N pulgada *f* (= *2.54 cm*); **inches** (= *height*) [*of person*] estatura *f*; **not an ~ of territory** ni un palmo de territorio; **the car missed me by ~es** faltó poco para que me atropellara el coche; **~ by ~** palmo a palmo; **we searched every ~ of the room** registramos todos los rincones del cuarto; **every ~ of it was used** se aprovechó hasta el último centímetro; **he's every ~ a soldier** es todo un soldado; **he didn't give an ~** no hizo la menor concesión; **to lose a few ~es*** adelgazar un poco; **to be within an ~ of death/disaster** estar a dos dedos de la muerte/del desastre; ✦*IDIOM* **give him an ~ and he'll take a mile** dale un dedo y se toma hasta el codo; → IMPERIAL SYSTEM
Ⓑ CPD ► **inch tape** N cinta *f* en pulgadas (para medir)

►**inch forward** Ⓐ VI + ADV **to ~ forward** [*person, vehicle*] avanzar muy lentamente
Ⓑ VT + ADV [+ *vehicle*] hacer avanzar muy lentamente

►**inch out** Ⓐ VT + ADV [+ *opponent*] derrotar por muy poco
Ⓑ VI + ADV [*vehicle*] avanzar muy despacio

►**inch up** VI + ADV [*prices*] subir poco a poco

inchoate [ˈɪnkəʊeɪt] ADJ [*idea*] que no ha tomado forma definitiva; [*anger*] inexpresado

inchoative [ɪnˈkəʊətɪv] ADJ [*aspect, verb*] incoativo

incidence [ˈɪnsɪdəns] N (= *extent*) [*of crime*] incidencia *f*, índice *m*; [*of disease*] incidencia *f*, frecuencia *f*; **the angle of ~** (*Phys*) el ángulo de incidencia

incident [ˈɪnsɪdənt] Ⓐ N (= *event*) incidente *m*, suceso *m*; (*in book, play etc*) episodio *m*, incidente *m*; (= *confrontation*) incidente *m*; **a life full of ~** una vida azarosa *or* llena de acontecimientos; **the Agadir ~** el episodio de Agadir; **to provoke a diplomatic ~** provocar un incidente diplomático; **the police were called to the scene of the ~** llamaron a la policía para que acudiera al lugar del suceso; **without ~** sin incidentes
Ⓑ CPD ► **incident room** N centro *m* de coordinación

incidental [ˌɪnsɪˈdentl] Ⓐ ADJ 1 (= *related*) [*benefit*] adicional; [*effect*] secundario; **the troubles ~ to any journey** las dificultades que conlleva cualquier viaje; **~ expenses** gastos *mpl* imprevistos; **~ music** música *f* de acompañamiento
2 (= *secondary, minor*) [*details*] incidental, secundario; **but that is ~ to my purpose** (*frm*) pero eso queda al margen de mi propósito
3 (= *accidental, fortuitous*) fortuito
Ⓑ **incidentals** NPL (= *expenses*) (gastos *mpl*) imprevistos *mpl*

incidentally [ˌɪnsɪˈdentəlɪ] ADV 1 (= *by the way*) a propósito, por cierto; **he spoke no English ~** por cierto *or* a propósito, no hablaba inglés
2 (= *in a minor way*) incidentalmente
3 (= *accidentally, fortuitously*) por casualidad, de forma casual

incinerate [ɪnˈsɪnəreɪt] VT [+ *body*] incinerar; [+ *rubbish*] quemar

incineration [ɪnˌsɪnəˈreɪʃən] N incineración *f*

incinerator [ɪnˈsɪnəreɪtəʳ] N incinerador *m*

incipient [ɪnˈsɪpɪənt] ADJ [*infection, illness, democracy, inflation, recession*] incipiente; [*romance, friendship*] incipiente, naciente

incise [ɪnˈsaɪz] VT cortar; (*Art*) grabar, tallar; (*Med*) hacer una incisión en

incision [ɪnˈsɪʒən] N incisión *f*

incisive [ɪnˈsaɪsɪv] ADJ [*mind*] penetrante; [*remark, criticism*] incisivo, mordaz; [*tone*] mordaz; [*wit*] incisivo

incisively [ɪnˈsaɪsɪvlɪ] ADV [*say, criticize*] de forma incisiva, mordazmente; [*express*] de forma incisiva

incisiveness [ɪnˈsaɪsɪvnɪs] N [*of remark, criticism*] lo incisivo, lo mordaz

incisor [ɪnˈsaɪzəʳ] N incisivo *m*

incite [ɪnˈsaɪt] VT [+ *violence, riots, hatred*] incitar, instigar; **to ~ sb to do sth** incitar *or* instigar a algn a hacer algo; **to ~ sb to violence** incitar *or* instigar a algn a la violencia

incitement [ɪnˈsaɪtmənt] N incitación *f*, instigación *f* (**to** a)

incivility [ˌɪnsɪˈvɪlɪtɪ] N descortesía *f*

incl ABBR (= **included, including, inclusive (of)**) inc.

inclemency [ɪnˈklemənsɪ] N inclemencia *f*

inclement [ɪnˈklemənt] ADJ [*weather*] inclemente

inclination [ˌɪnklɪˈneɪʃən] N 1 (= *tendency*) tendencia *f*, inclinación *f*; **his natural ~s** su tendencia *or* inclinación natural; **she has musical ~s** tiene inclinación por *or* hacia la música; **to have an ~ to meanness** tener tendencia a ser tacaño
2 (= *desire*) **I have no ~ to go** no tengo ganas de ir; **I have neither the time nor the ~ to get involved** no tengo ni tiempo ni ganas de meterme en el asunto; **her ~ was to ignore him** prefería no hacerle caso; **I decided to follow my own ~ and stay at home** decidí hacer lo que más me apetecía y quedarme en casa; **I went to the meeting, against my ~** fui a la reunión, aunque no sentía ningún deseo de hacerlo
3 (= *slope, bow*) inclinación *f*

incline Ⓐ [ˈɪnklaɪn] N pendiente *f*, cuesta *f*
Ⓑ [ɪnˈklaɪn] VT 1 (= *bend*) [+ *head*] bajar, inclinar
2 (= *slope*) inclinar
3 (*frm*) (= *dispose*) **to ~ sb to do sth** predisponer a algn a hacer algo; **the factors which ~ us towards particular beliefs** los factores que nos predisponen a tener ciertas creencias
Ⓒ [ɪnˈklaɪn] VI 1 (= *slope*) inclinarse
2 (= *tend*) **I ~ to** *or* **towards the belief/opinion that ...** me inclino a pensar que ...

inclined [ɪnˈklaɪnd] ADJ 1 (= *tilted*) inclinado
2 (= *apt*) **to be ~ to do sth** tener tendencia a hacer algo, tender a hacer algo; **he was ~ to be moody** tenía tendencia *or* tendía a sufrir cambios de humor, era propenso a los cambios de humor; **it is ~ to break** tiene tendencia a romperse
3 (= *disposed*) **to be ~ to do sth: I'm ~ to believe you** estoy dispuesto a creerte; **I'm ~ to agree** yo me inclino a pensar lo mismo; **I'm ~ to think that ...** me inclino a pensar que ...; **to be academically ~** estar dotado para los estudios; **to be artistically ~** tener inclinaciones artísticas; **I didn't feel at all ~ to go out** no me apetecía nada salir, no tenía ninguna gana de salir; **if you feel so ~** si te apetece; (*more formal*) si así lo deseas; **to be musically ~** tener inclinación por *or* hacia la música; **Florence is full of art galleries, if you are that way ~** Florencia está llena de museos, si eso es lo que te interesa; **I'm ~ toward the latter explanation** me inclino por la última explicación; **to be favourably ~ toward sth/sb** ver algo/a algn con buenos ojos

inclose [ɪnˈkləʊz] VT = **enclose**

include [ɪnˈkluːd] VT incluir; (*with letter*) adjuntar, incluir; **facilities ~ a gym, swimming pool and sauna** las instalaciones disponen de gimnasio, piscina y sauna; **your name is not ~d in the list** su nombre no figura en la lista; **does that remark ~ me?** ¿va ese comentario también por mí?; **he sold everything, books ~d** vendió todo, incluso los libros; **service is/is not ~d** el servicio está/no está *or* (*LAm*) va/no va incluido; **all the team members, myself ~d** todos los miembros del equipo, incluido yo

►**include out*** VT + ADV (*hum*) excluir, dejar fuera; **~ me out!** ¡no contéis conmigo!

including [ɪnˈkluːdɪŋ] PREP **terms £80, not ~ service** precio 80 libras, servicio no incluido; **seven ~ this one** siete con éste; **everyone, ~ the President** todos, incluido el Presidente; **that applies to everyone, ~ you** eso va por todos, tú incluido; **up to and ~ chapter seven** hasta el capítulo siete inclusive

inclusion [ɪnˈkluːʒən] N inclusión *f*

inclusive [ɪnˈkluːsɪv] Ⓐ ADJ [*sum, price*] global; **an ~ price of £32.90** un precio global de 32,90 libras, un precio de 32,90 libras (con) todo incluido; **£5,000 fully ~** 5.000 libras con todo incluido; **~ of tax/postage and packing** incluidos los impuestos/los gastos de envío; **to be ~ of sth** incluir algo; **all prices**

are ~ of VAT todos los precios incluyen el IVA

Ⓑ ADV **from the 10th to the 15th ~** del 10 al 15, ambos inclusive *or* ambos incluidos

inclusively [ɪnˈkluːsɪvlɪ] ADV = **inclusive B**

incognito [ɪnˈkɒgnɪtəʊ] Ⓐ ADV [*travel*] de incógnito

Ⓑ ADJ **to remain ~** permanecer en el anonimato

Ⓒ N incógnito *m*

incoherence [ˌɪnkəʊˈhɪərəns] N [*of ideas, policies*] incoherencia *f*, falta *f* de coherencia; **his attempts to explain degenerated into ~** en su intento por dar una explicación cayó en la más absoluta incoherencia

incoherent [ˌɪnkəʊˈhɪərənt] ADJ [*person, words, letter*] incoherente; [*argument*] falto de coherencia, incoherente; [*conversation*] sin sentido, incoherente; **to become ~** volverse incoherente; **he was ~ with rage** estaba tan furioso que casi no podía hablar, balbuceaba de rabia

incoherently [ˌɪnkəʊˈhɪərəntlɪ] ADV [*mumble, ramble, argue, write*] de forma incoherente; [*speak*] con incoherencia, incoherentemente; [*expressed*] de manera incoherente; **he collapsed on the floor, mumbling ~** se desplomó en el suelo, murmurando de forma incoherente *or* murmurando incoherencias

incohesive [ˌɪnkəʊˈhiːsɪv] ADJ sin cohesión

incombustible [ˌɪnkəmˈbʌstəbl] ADJ incombustible

income [ˈɪnkʌm] Ⓐ N (*gen*) ingresos *mpl*; (*from property*) renta *f*; (= *salary*) salario *m*, sueldo *m*; (= *takings*) entradas *fpl*; (= *interest*) réditos *mpl*; (= *profit*) ganancias *fpl*; **gross/net ~** ingresos *mpl* brutos/netos; **private ~** rentas *fpl*; **national ~** renta *f* nacional; **I can't live on my ~** no puedo vivir con lo que gano; **to live beyond one's ~** gastar más de lo que se gana; **to live within one's ~** vivir de acuerdo a los ingresos

Ⓑ CPD ► **income and expenditure account** N cuenta *f* de gastos e ingresos ► **income bracket**, **income group** N categoría *f* económica; **the lower ~ groups** los sectores de ingresos más bajos ► **incomes policy** N política *f* salarial *or* de salarios ► **income support** N (*Brit*) ≈ ayuda *f* compensatoria ► **income tax** N impuesto *m* sobre la renta ► **income tax return** N declaración *f* de impuestos

incomer [ˈɪnˌkʌməʳ] (*Brit*) N recién llegado/a *m/f*; (*to society, group*) persona *f* nueva; (= *immigrant*) inmigrante *mf*

incoming [ˈɪnˌkʌmɪŋ] Ⓐ ADJ [*passenger, flight*] que llega/llegaba; [*president*] entrante; [*tide*] que sube/subía; **all ~ calls are monitored** todas las llamadas que se reciben están sujetas a control; **~ mail** correo *m* de entrada, correspondencia *f* que se recibe

Ⓑ NPL **incomings** ingresos *mpl*

incommensurable [ˌɪnkəˈmenʃərəbl] ADJ (*frm*) inconmensurable

incommensurate [ˌɪnkəˈmenʃərɪt] ADJ (*frm*) desproporcionado; **to be ~ with** no guardar relación con

incommode [ˌɪnkəˈməʊd] VT (*frm*) incomodar, molestar

incommodious [ˌɪnkəˈməʊdɪəs] ADJ (*frm*) (= *cramped*) estrecho, nada espacioso; (= *inconvenient*) poco conveniente

incommunicado [ˌɪnkəmjʊnɪˈkɑːdəʊ] ADJ incomunicado; **to hold sb ~** mantener incomunicado a algn

in-company [ˈɪnkʌmpənɪ] ADJ **~ training** formación *f* en la empresa

incomparable [ɪnˈkɒmpərəbl] ADJ 1 (= *matchless*) [*beauty, skill*] incomparable, sin par; [*achievement*] inigualable, sin par

2 (= *not comparable*) **to be ~ with sth** no poderse comparar con algo

incomparably [ɪnˈkɒmpərəblɪ] ADV incomparablemente; **this product is ~ better** este producto es incomparablemente mejor

incompatibility [ˈɪnkəmˌpætəˈbɪlɪtɪ] N incompatibilidad *f*

incompatible [ˌɪnkəmˈpætəbl] ADJ (*all senses*) incompatible (**with** con)

incompetence [ɪnˈkɒmpɪtəns] N 1 incompetencia *f*; **he was fired for ~** lo despidieron por incompetente; *see also* **gross A1**

2 (*Jur*) incapacidad *f*

incompetent [ɪnˈkɒmpɪtənt] ADJ 1 (= *inept*) [*person*] incompetente; [*attempt*] torpe; [*work*] deficiente; **he's ~** es un incompetente, es incompetente; **he is ~ at his job** es incompetente en su trabajo

2 (= *unqualified*) **Lennox was declared ~** (*Jur*) a Lennox lo declararon incapacitado; **he is ~ to lead the party** no está capacitado para dirigir el partido, es incapaz de dirigir el partido

incompetently [ɪnˈkɒmpɪtəntlɪ] ADV de modo incompetente, de forma incompetente

incomplete [ˌɪnkəmˈpliːt] ADJ (= *partial*) incompleto; (= *unfinished*) inacabado, sin terminar; **the gathering would be ~ without him** sin él la reunión no estaría completa

incompletely [ˌɪnkəmˈpliːtlɪ] ADV de manera *or* forma incompleta; **an ~ formed foetus** un feto no completamente formado

incompleteness [ˌɪnkəmˈpliːtnɪs] N lo incompleto; **because of the ~ of the reforms** a causa de lo incompleto de las reformas

incomprehensible [ɪnˌkɒmprɪˈhensəbl] ADJ incomprensible; **it is ~ to me** me resulta incomprensible

incomprehensibly [ɪnˌkɒmprɪˈhensəblɪ] ADV de modo incomprensible, incomprensiblemente

incomprehension [ˌɪnkɒmprɪˈhenʃən] N incomprensión *f*

inconceivable [ˌɪnkənˈsiːvəbl] ADJ inconcebible

inconceivably [ˌɪnkənˈsiːvəblɪ] ADJ inconcebiblemente

inconclusive [ˌɪnkənˈkluːsɪv] ADJ (= *not decisive*) [*result*] no concluyente; (= *not convincing*) [*argument*] no convincente; [*evidence*] no concluyente; **the investigation was ~** la investigación no dio resultados concluyentes

inconclusively [ˌɪnkənˈkluːsɪvlɪ] ADV de forma no concluyente; **the talks ended ~** las conversaciones finalizaron sin resultados concluyentes

inconclusiveness [ˌɪnkənˈkluːsɪvnɪs] N [*of evidence, verdict, trial*] lo no concluyente; [*of talks*] falta *f* de resultados concluyentes

incongruity [ˌɪnkɒŋˈgruːɪtɪ] N incongruencia *f*

incongruous [ɪnˈkɒŋgrʊəs] ADJ [*pair, alliance, image, sound*] incongruente; **it seems ~ that …** parece extraño que …

incongruously [ɪnˈkɒŋgrʊəslɪ] ADV (*gen*) de manera incongruente; [*dressed*] inapropiadamente; **he wore old jeans, with ~ smart shoes** llevaba unos vaqueros viejos con unos zapatos muy elegantes, lo que resultaba inapropiado

inconsequent [ɪnˈkɒnsɪkwənt] ADJ = **inconsequential**

inconsequential [ɪnˌkɒnsɪˈkwenʃəl] ADJ [*conversation*] sin trascendencia; (= *illogical*) ilógico

inconsequentially [ˌɪnkɒnsɪˈkwenʃəlɪ] ADV [*talk, say*] sin propósito serio

inconsiderable [ˌɪnkənˈsɪdərəbl] ADJ **a not ~ sum** una cifra nada desdeñable *or* despreciable, una suma considerable

inconsiderate [ˌɪnkənˈsɪdərɪt] ADJ [*behaviour, person*] desconsiderado; **how ~ of him!** ¡qué falta de consideración de su parte!; **to be ~ to sb** no tener consideración con algn

inconsistency [ˌɪnkənˈsɪstənsɪ] N 1 (= *inconsistent nature*) [*of behaviour*] carácter *m* contradictorio *or* incongruente; [*of statement, account, evidence, policy*] falta *f* de coherencia; **his worst fault is his ~** su peor defecto es que es un inconsecuente

2 (= *contradiction*) contradicción *f*

inconsistent [ˌɪnkənˈsɪstənt] ADJ 1 (= *erratic*) [*person*] inconsecuente, voluble; [*quality, work, performance*] irregular, desigual; [*behaviour, policies*] contradictorio, incongruente

2 (= *contradictory*) [*actions*] inconsecuente; [*statement, account, evidence*] contradictorio; **to be ~ with sth** (= *contradict*) contradecir algo, no concordar con algo; (= *not correspond with*) no encajar con algo, no concordar con algo

inconsistently [ˌɪnkənˈsɪstəntlɪ] ADV 1 (= *erratically*) [*behave*] de forma contradictoria *or* incongruente *or* desigual; [*work, perform*] de forma irregular

2 (= *contradictorily*) [*argue, reason*] sin congruencia, contradictoriamente

inconsolable [ˌɪnkənˈsəʊləbl] ADJ inconsolable

inconsolably [ˌɪnkənˈsəʊləblɪ] ADV inconsolablemente

inconspicuous [ˌɪnkənˈspɪkjʊəs] ADJ [*person*] que no llama la atención; [*colour*] poco llamativo, que no llama la atención; [*place*] que pasa desapercibido; **she tried to make herself ~** trató de no llamar la atención *or* de pasar desapercibida

inconspicuously [ˌɪnkənˈspɪkjʊəslɪ] ADV [*sit, move*] sin llamar la atención, discretamente; **~ placed** colocado donde no llama la atención, discretamente colocado

inconstancy [ɪnˈkɒnstənsɪ] N inconstancia *f*, veleidad *f*

inconstant [ɪnˈkɒnstənt] ADJ inconstante, veleidoso

incontestable [ˌɪnkənˈtestəbl] ADJ incontestable, incuestionable

incontestably [ɪnkənˈtestəblɪ] ADV incontestablemente, incuestionablemente

incontinence [ɪnˈkɒntɪnəns] N incontinencia *f*

incontinent [ɪnˈkɒntɪnənt] ADJ incontinente; **to be/become ~** tener incontinencia

incontrovertible [ɪnˌkɒntrəˈvɜːtəbl] ADJ [*fact, evidence*] incontrovertible

incontrovertibly [ɪnˌkɒntrəˈvɜːtɪblɪ] ADV de manera incontrovertible; **this is ~ true** ésta es una verdad incontrovertible

▼ **inconvenience** [ˌɪnkənˈviːnɪəns] Ⓐ N 1 (= *awkwardness*) [*of time, location*] inconveniencia *f*; [*of arrangements, house*] incomodidad *f*

2 (= *drawback*) inconveniente *m*; **living so far from the station is a great ~** vivir tan lejos de la estación es un gran inconveniente

3 (= *trouble*) molestias *fpl*, inconvenientes *mpl*; **you caused a lot of ~** causaste muchas molestias *or* muchos inconvenientes; **it makes up for the ~ of having to move** compensa las molestias *or* los inconvenientes de tener que mudarse; **to put sb to great ~** causar muchas molestias *or* muchos inconve-

➤ LANGUAGE IN USE: **inconvenience A3** 18.1

nientes a algn
Ⓑ VT (= *cause problems to*) causar molestias a; (= *disturb*) molestar; **I hope you haven't been ~d by the delay** espero que el retraso no le haya causado molestias; **I'm sorry to ~ you, but ...** perdone que lo moleste, pero ...; **don't ~ yourself** no se moleste

inconvenient [ˌɪnkənˈviːnɪənt] ADJ [*time, appointment*] inoportuno; [*location, design*] poco práctico, incómodo; **it's an ~ place to get to** es un sitio mal comunicado, no es un sitio al que sea fácil llegar; **how ~!** ¡qué trastorno!, ¡vaya trastorno!; **to be ~** venir mal; (*more formal*) resultar inconveniente; **to be ~ for sb** venirle mal a algn; (*more formal*) resultarle inconveniente a algn

inconveniently [ˌɪnkənˈviːnɪəntlɪ] ADV [*arranged, planned*] de modo poco práctico; [*arrive, turn up*] en mal momento, en un momento inoportuno; **to come ~ early** venir demasiado temprano; **the hotel is rather ~ situated** el hotel está mal situado

inconvertibility [ˈɪnkənˌvɜːtɪˈbɪlɪtɪ] N inconvertibilidad *f*

inconvertible [ˌɪnkənˈvɜːtəbl] ADJ inconvertible

incorporate [ɪnˈkɔːpəreɪt] VT (= *include*) incluir, comprender; (= *integrate*) incorporar (**in, into** a); **a product incorporating vitamin Q** un producto que contiene vitamina Q; **to ~ a company** constituir una compañía en sociedad (anónima)

incorporated [ɪnˈkɔːpəreɪtɪd] ADJ (*US Comm*) **Jones & Lloyd Incorporated** Jones y Lloyd Sociedad Anónima

incorporation [ɪnˌkɔːpəˈreɪʃən] N (= *inclusion*) inclusión *f*, incorporación *f*; (= *integration*) incorporación *f*; (*Comm*) constitución *f* en sociedad (anónima)

incorporeal [ˌɪnkɔːˈpɔːrɪəl] ADJ (*liter*) incorpóreo

incorrect [ˌɪnkəˈrekt] ADJ 1 (= *wrong*) [*answer, spelling*] incorrecto; [*information, statement, assumption*] erróneo; **it is ~ to say that ...** es erróneo decir que ...; **that is ~, you are wrong** no es cierto, usted se equivoca
2 (= *bad*) [*posture, diet*] incorrecto, inadecuado
3 (= *improper*) [*behaviour*] incorrecto, impropio; [*dress*] inapropiado

incorrectly [ˌɪnkəˈrektlɪ] ADV 1 (= *wrongly*) [*spell, answer*] mal; (*more formal*) incorrectamente; [*state, conclude, assume, believe*] erróneamente; [*inform*] mal, erróneamente; **an ~ addressed letter** una carta con las señas mal puestas
2 (= *badly*) mal; (*more frm*) incorrectamente; **the doors had been fitted ~** habían puesto las puertas mal
3 (= *improperly*) [*behave*] incorrectamente; [*dress*] de manera inapropiada, de modo inapropiado

incorrigible [ɪnˈkɒrɪdʒəbl] ADJ [*womaniser, optimist*] incorregible, sin remedio; **you're ~!** ¡eres incorregible!, ¡no tienes remedio!

incorrigibly [ɪnˈkɒrɪdʒəblɪ] ADV incorregiblemente

incorruptible [ˌɪnkəˈrʌptəbl] ADJ incorruptible; (= *not open to bribery*) insobornable

increase [ɪnˈkriːs] Ⓐ VI [*number, size, speed, pain*] aumentar; [*prices, temperature, pressure*] subir, aumentar; [*wages, salaries, productivity, popularity*] aumentar; **to ~ in number** aumentar; **to ~ in weight/volume/size/value** aumentar de peso/volumen/tamaño/valor; **to ~ by 100** aumentar en 100; **to ~ from 8% to 10%** aumentar de 8 a 10 por ciento
Ⓑ [ɪnˈkriːs] VT [+ *number, size, speed, pain*] aumentar; [+ *prices, temperature, pressure*] subir, aumentar; [+ *wages, salaries, taxes, interest rates, productivity*] aumentar; **to ~ one's efforts** redoblar sus esfuerzos; **there has been an ~d interest in his work** ha aumentado el interés por su trabajo; **profits were the result of ~d efficiency** los beneficios eran el resultado de una mayor eficiencia
Ⓒ [ˈɪnkriːs] N (*gen*) aumento *m*, incremento *m*; [*of prices*] subida *f*, aumento *m*; **an ~ in size/volume** un aumento de tamaño/volumen; **an ~ of £5/10%** un aumento de 5 libras/del 10 por ciento; **to be on the ~** estar *or* ir en aumento

increasing [ɪnˈkriːsɪŋ] ADJ [*number, amount*] creciente, cada vez mayor; **an ~ number of women are going out to work** un creciente número de mujeres va a trabajar, el número de mujeres que trabajan va en aumento *or* es cada vez mayor; **the president is under ~ pressure to resign** el presidente recibe cada vez más presiones para presentar la dimisión

increasingly [ɪnˈkriːsɪŋlɪ] ADV cada vez más; **he was finding it ~ difficult to make decisions** le resultaba cada vez más difícil tomar decisiones; **Spanish food is becoming ~ popular** la comida española se está volviendo cada vez más popular *or* está alcanzando una popularidad cada vez mayor; **it is becoming ~ obvious that ...** está cada vez más claro que ...; **they are relying ~ on foreign imports** cada vez dependen más de las importaciones extranjeras

incredible [ɪnˈkredəbl] ADJ increíble; **they found it ~ that I was still alive** les pareció increíble que todavía estuviera viva; **~ though it may seem** por increíble que parezca, aunque parezca mentira; **an ~ number of people** una cantidad de gente increíble

incredibly [ɪnˈkredəblɪ] ADV 1 (= *extremely*) [*ugly, rich, intelligent*] increíblemente; **it all happened ~ fast** todo sucedió con una rapidez increíble
2 (= *amazingly*) **~, they did not come** por increíble que parezca, no vinieron, aunque parezca mentira, no llegaron

incredulity [ˌɪnkrɪˈdjuːlɪtɪ] N incredulidad *f*

incredulous [ɪnˈkredjʊləs] ADJ [*expression*] de incredulidad; **I was ~** no lo creí

incredulously [ɪnˈkredjʊləslɪ] ADV con incredulidad

increment [ˈɪnkrɪmənt] N aumento *m*, incremento *m* (**in** de)

incremental [ɪnkrɪˈmentəl] Ⓐ ADJ [*change, process*] gradual; [*costs*] incremental
Ⓑ CPD ► **incremental compiler** N compilador *m* incremental

incriminate [ɪnˈkrɪmɪneɪt] VT incriminar

incriminating [ɪnˈkrɪmɪneɪtɪŋ] ADJ [*evidence, document*] incriminatorio

incrimination [ɪnˌkrɪmɪˈneɪʃən] N incriminación *f*

incriminatory [ɪnˈkrɪmɪnətərɪ] ADJ = **incriminating**

incrust [ɪnˈkrʌst] VT = **encrust**

incrustation [ˌɪnkrʌsˈteɪʃən] N = **encrustation**

incubate [ˈɪnkjʊbeɪt] Ⓐ VT (*gen*) incubar
Ⓑ VI [*egg*] incubarse; [*hen*] empollar; (*fig*) [*idea*] incubarse

incubation [ˌɪnkjʊˈbeɪʃən] Ⓐ N [*of egg, disease*] incubación *f*
Ⓑ CPD ► **incubation period** N período *m* de incubación

incubator [ˈɪnkjʊbeɪtəʳ] N (*for eggs, bacteria, baby*) incubadora *f*

incubus [ˈɪŋkjʊbəs] N (*pl* **incubuses** *or* **incubi** [ˈɪŋkjʊˌbaɪ]) íncubo *m*

inculcate [ˈɪnkʌlkeɪt] VT **to ~ sth in sb** inculcar algo a algn

inculcation [ˌɪnkʌlˈkeɪʃən] N inculcación *f*

incumbency [ɪnˈkʌmbənsɪ] N (*frm*) 1 (= *being in office*) ocupación *f* del cargo; **the benefits of ~** los beneficios de ocupar el cargo
2 (*Rel*) beneficio *m*

incumbent [ɪnˈkʌmbənt] Ⓐ ADJ (*frm*) **to be ~ on sb to do sth** incumbir a algn hacer algo; **I felt it ~ upon me to go** sentí que debía ir
Ⓑ N titular *mf*, poseedor(a) *m/f* (*de un cargo o dignidad*); (*Rel*) beneficiado *m*

incunabula [ˌɪnkjʊˈnæbjʊlə] NPL incunables *mpl*

incur [ɪnˈkɜːʳ] VT [+ *debt, obligation*] contraer; [+ *expense, charges*] incurrir en; [+ *loss*] sufrir; [+ *anger*] provocar; **I wouldn't wish to ~ his wrath** no me gustaría provocar su ira; **I did not wish to ~ his disapproval** no deseaba hacer que se pusiera en desacuerdo

incurable [ɪnˈkjʊərəbl] Ⓐ ADJ 1 (*Med*) incurable
2 (*fig*) [*optimist, romantic*] incorregible
Ⓑ N incurable *mf*

incurably [ɪnˈkjʊərəblɪ] ADV **to be ~ ill** tener una enfermedad incurable; **to be ~ romantic/optimistic** ser un romántico/optimista incurable *or* incorregible

incurious [ɪnˈkjʊərɪəs] ADJ indiferente; **to be ~ about sth** ser indiferente a algo

incuriously [ɪnˈkjʊərɪəslɪ] ADV [*look*] con indiferencia

incursion [ɪnˈkɜːʃən] N incursión *f*

Ind. ABBR (*US*) = **Indiana**

indebted [ɪnˈdetɪd] ADJ 1 (= *owing money*) endeudado; **to be (heavily) ~ (to sb)** estar (muy) endeudado (con algn)
2 (= *grateful*) **I am ~ to you for your help** estoy muy agradecido por su ayuda; **we are greatly ~ to Shakespeare for his contribution to English literature** le debemos mucho a Shakespeare por su contribución a la literatura inglesa

indebtedness [ɪnˈdetɪdnɪs] N 1 (*Fin*) endeudamiento *m*, deuda *f* (**to** con)
2 (*fig*) deuda *f* (**to** con)

indecency [ɪnˈdiːsnsɪ] N indecencia *f*; *see also* **gross E**

indecent [ɪnˈdiːsnt] Ⓐ ADJ 1 (= *obscene*) [*photograph, language, film, gesture, clothes*] indecente; **to make an ~ suggestion** sugerir algo indecente
2 (= *shocking*) escandaloso; **with ~ haste** con una prisa nada decorosa
Ⓑ CPD ► **indecent assault** N (*Jur*) abusos *mpl* deshonestos ► **indecent exposure** N (*Jur*) exhibicionismo *m*

indecently [ɪnˈdiːsntlɪ] ADV 1 (= *obscenely*) indecentemente, de una forma indecente; **~ short skirts** faldas indecentemente cortas; **to ~ assault sb** realizar abusos deshonestos de algn; **to ~ expose o.s.** cometer un acto de exhibicionismo
2 (= *shockingly*) escandalosamente; **she is ~ rich** es asquerosamente rica

indecipherable [ˌɪndɪˈsaɪfərəbl] ADJ indescifrable

indecision [ˌɪndɪˈsɪʒən] N indecisión *f*, falta *f* de decisión, irresolución *f* (*frm*)

indecisive [ˌɪndɪˈsaɪsɪv] ADJ 1 (= *hesitant*) [*person*] indeciso, irresoluto (*frm*)
2 (= *inconclusive*) [*result, vote*] no concluyente, no decisivo; [*battle*] no decisivo

indecisively [ˌɪndɪˈsaɪsɪvlɪ] ADV 1 (= *hesitantly*) con indecisión, con irresolución (*frm*); **we waited as she stood there ~** esperamos mientras ella estaba ahí parada sin decidirse
2 (= *inconclusively*) [*end, conclude*] sin resultados definitivos, sin resultados decisivos

indecisiveness [ˌɪndɪˈsaɪsɪvnɪs] N 1 (= *hesitancy*) indecisión *f*, falta *f* de decisión, irresolución *f* (*frm*)
2 (= *inconclusiveness*) falta *f* de conclusión

indeclinable [ˌɪndɪˈklaɪnəbl] ADJ indeclinable

indecorous [ɪnˈdekərəs] ADJ indecoroso

indecorously [ɪnˈdekərəslɪ] ADV indecorosamente

indecorum [ˌɪndɪˈkɔːrəm] N indecoro *m*, falta *f* de decoro

indeed [ɪnˈdiːd] ADV 1 (= *in fact*) de hecho; **I feel, ~ I know, he is wrong** creo, de hecho sé *or* en realidad sé, que está equivocado; **we have nothing against diversity, ~, we want more of it** no tenemos nada en contra de la diversidad, de hecho queremos que haya más; **if ~ he is wrong** si es que realmente se equivoca, si efectivamente se equivoca; **the document was ~ missing** efectivamente el documento había desaparecido; **it is ~ true that …** es en efecto verdad que …
2 (*as intensifier*) **that is praise ~** eso es todo un elogio, eso sí es una alabanza; **very … ~: to be very good/small/intelligent ~** ser verdaderamente *or* realmente bueno/pequeño/inteligente; **you're doing very well ~** vas realmente bien; **we are taking the matter very seriously ~** nos estamos tomando la cuestión sumamente en serio *or* pero que muy en serio; **thank you very much ~** muchísimas gracias; **I'm very glad ~** me alegro muchísimo
3 (*in answer to a question*) **"isn't it a beautiful day?" — "yes, ~!"** —¿a que es un día precioso? —¡desde luego! *or* —¡y que lo digas! *or* —¡ya lo creo!; **"did you know him?" — "I did ~"** —¿lo conocías? —sí que lo conocía *or* —claro que sí; **"are you Professor Ratburn?" — "~ I am"** *or* **"I am ~"** —¿es usted el profesor Ratburn? —sí, señor *or* —el mismo; **"may I go?" — "~ you may not!"** —¿puedo ir? —¡claro que no! *or* —¡por supuesto que no!
4 (*expressing interest*) **indeed?** ◊ **is it ~?** ◊ **did you ~?** ¿de veras?, ¿de verdad?, ¿ah, sí?
5 (*expressing disbelief, surprise, scorn*) **"I did the best I could" — "indeed!"** —lo hice lo mejor que pude —¡por supuesto! *or* —¡claro, claro! (*iro*); **"he said he would do it" — "did he ~?"** —dijo que lo haría —¿eso dijo? *or* —¿no me digas?; **"he said I was too short" — "too short ~!"** —dijo que era demasiado bajo —¡sí, hombre, bajísimo! (*iro*)

indefatigable [ˌɪndɪˈfætɪgəbl] ADJ incansable, infatigable

indefatigably [ˌɪndɪˈfætɪgəblɪ] ADV incansablemente, infatigablemente

indefensible [ˌɪndɪˈfensəbl] ADJ 1 (= *unjustifiable*) [*conduct, action*] injustificable, inexcusable; [*idea, policy*] indefendible, insostenible
2 (= *vulnerable*) [*town, country*] indefendible

indefensibly [ˌɪndɪˈfensəblɪ] ADV [*behave, act*] de una forma injustificable

indefinable [ˌɪndɪˈfaɪnəbl] ADJ indefinible

indefinably [ˌɪndɪˈfaɪnəblɪ] ADV indefiniblemente

indefinite [ɪnˈdefɪnɪt] Ⓐ ADJ 1 (= *vague*) [*answer*] impreciso; **he was very ~ about it all** no fue muy preciso al respecto; **our plans are somewhat ~ as yet** nuestros planes están todavía por concretar
2 (= *not fixed*) [*time*] indefinido, indeterminado; **it will be closed for an ~ period** estará cerrado por tiempo indefinido; **to be on ~ leave** estar de permiso por tiempo indefinido
3 (*Ling*) indefinido
Ⓑ CPD ► **indefinite article** N artículo *m* indefinido ► **indefinite pronoun** N pronombre *m* indefinido

indefinitely [ɪnˈdefɪnɪtlɪ] ADV (*gen*) por tiempo indefinido; **it will keep ~** se conserva por tiempo indefinido; **we can carry on ~** podemos continuar hasta cuando sea *or* por tiempo indefinido

indelible [ɪnˈdeləbl] ADJ 1 (= *not washable*) [*ink, stain*] indeleble; **~ pen** bolígrafo *m* de tinta indeleble
2 (= *unforgettable*) [*memory, image*] indeleble, imborrable; **it made an ~ impression on me** se me quedó grabado en la memoria

indelibly [ɪnˈdeləblɪ] ADV indeleblemente; **the horrors he experienced are imprinted ~ in his brain** los horrores que sufrió quedaron grabados de forma indeleble en su mente

indelicacy [ɪnˈdelɪkəsɪ] N indecoro *m*, falta *f* de decoro

indelicate [ɪnˈdelɪkɪt] ADJ (= *tactless*) indiscreto, falto de tacto; (= *crude*) indelicado

indemnification [ɪnˌdemnɪfɪˈkeɪʃən] N indemnización *f*

indemnify [ɪnˈdemnɪfaɪ] VT 1 (= *compensate*) **to ~ sb for sth** indemnizar a algn por algo
2 (= *safeguard*) **to ~ sb against sth** asegurar a algn contra algo

indemnity [ɪnˈdemnɪtɪ] N (= *compensation*) indemnización *f*, reparación *f*; (= *insurance*) indemnidad *f*; **double ~** doble indemnización *f*

indent [ɪnˈdent] Ⓐ VT (*Typ*) [+ *word, line*] sangrar; (= *cut into*) dejar marcas en
Ⓑ VI **to ~ for sth** (*Comm*) hacer un pedido de algo, encargar algo; (*Mil*) requisar algo
Ⓒ N (*Brit Comm*) pedido *m*; (*Mil*) requisición *f*

indentation [ˌɪndenˈteɪʃən] N (*in cloth*) muesca *f*; (*in coastline*) entrante *m*; (= *dent*) (*in wood, metal*) hendidura *f*; (*in metal*) abolladura *f*; (*Typ*) sangría *f*

indented [ɪnˈdentɪd] ADJ [*type*] sangrado; [*surface*] abollado; **a deeply ~ coastline** una costa muy accidentada

indenture [ɪnˈdentʃəʳ] N 1 (*Comm*) escritura *f*
2 **indentures** contrato *m* de aprendizaje

indentured [ɪnˈdentʃəd] ADJ [*servant, labourer*] *obligado a trabajar para alguien durante un periodo de tiempo determinado*

independence [ˌɪndɪˈpendəns] Ⓐ N independencia *f*; **war of ~** guerra *f* de independencia; **Zaire gained** *or* **won ~ in 1960** Zaire obtuvo la independencia *or* se independizó en 1960
Ⓑ CPD ► **Independence Day** N Día *m* de la Independencia; → FOURTH OF JULY

independent [ˌɪndɪˈpendənt] Ⓐ ADJ 1 (= *self-supporting*) [*person, country*] independiente; [*income*] propio; **to be ~** ser independiente; **to be ~ of sth/sb** no depender de algo/algn, ser independiente de algo/algn; **to become ~** [*country*] independizarse; **a person of ~ means** una persona con rentas propias *or* con independencia económica
2 (= *unconnected*) [*events*] independiente, no relacionado; (= *impartial*) [*inquiry, investigation*] independiente; [*witness*] imparcial; **you are advised to seek an ~ opinion** le aconsejamos que se haga asesorar por un tercero
3 (= *self-reliant*) [*person, child*] independiente; **he was incapable of ~ thought** era incapaz de pensar por su cuenta; **she has always been very ~ of her parents** siempre ha dependido muy poco de sus padres
4 (= *private*) [*school, sector*] privado; [*broadcasting company, radio station*] privado, independiente
Ⓑ N 1 (= *politician*) independiente *mf*, candidato/a *m/f* independiente
2 (= *company*) compañía *f* independiente
Ⓒ CPD ► **independent clause** N (*Gram*) oración *f* independiente ► **independent school** N (*Brit*) escuela *f* privada, colegio *m* privado ► **independent suspension** N (*Aut*) suspensión *f* independiente

independently [ˌɪndɪˈpendəntlɪ] ADV 1 (= *self-reliantly*) [*live*] independientemente; [*act*] por su cuenta; **each child will work ~** cada niño trabajará de forma independiente *or* por su cuenta *or* sólo; **for a child of six, he behaves very ~** para ser un niño de seis años es muy independiente; **~ of sth/sb** independientemente de algo/algn; **~ of what he may decide** independientemente de lo que él decida
2 (= *separately*) por separado; **we both ~ came up with the same answer** los dos dimos con la misma respuesta por separado
3 (= *by an independent party*) **you ought to get it valued ~** deberías hacer que un tercero te lo tasase

in-depth [ˈɪnˌdepθ] ADJ [*study*] a fondo, exhaustivo; **~ investigation** investigación *f* a fondo *or* en profundidad

indescribable [ˌɪndɪsˈkraɪbəbl] ADJ [*terror, horror*] indescriptible, increíble; [*beauty, joy*] indescriptible

indescribably [ˌɪndɪsˈkraɪbəblɪ] ADV indescriptiblemente; (*pej*) indeciblemente; **~ bad** indescriptiblemente malo

indestructibility [ˌɪndɪstrʌktəˈbɪlɪtɪ] N indestructibilidad *f*

indestructible [ˌɪndɪsˈtrʌktəbl] ADJ indestructible

indeterminable [ˌɪndɪˈtɜːmɪnəbl] ADJ indeterminable

indeterminacy [ˌɪndɪˈtɜːmɪnəsɪ] N carácter *m* indeterminado

indeterminate [ˌɪndɪˈtɜːmɪnɪt] Ⓐ ADJ indeterminado; **of ~ age** de edad indeterminada
Ⓑ CPD ► **indeterminate sentence** N (*US Jur*) condena *f* indeterminada

indeterminately [ˌɪndɪˈtɜːmɪnɪtlɪ] ADV de modo indeterminado

index [ˈɪndeks] Ⓐ N 1 (*pl* **indexes**) (*in book*) índice *m*
2 (*pl* **indices, indexes**) (= *pointer*) índice *m*, señal *m* (**to** de); (*Econ*) índice *m*; **cost of living ~** índice *m* del costo de la vida; **the Index** (*Rel*) el índice expurgatorio; *see also* **retail E**
3 (*Math*) (*pl* **indices**) exponente *m*
Ⓑ VT (= *put index in*) [+ *book*] poner índice a; (= *make index headings for*) [+ *book*] (*in catalogue*) catalogar; [+ *entry, item, subject*] poner en el índice; **it is ~ed under Smith** está clasificado bajo Smith
Ⓒ CPD ► **index card** N ficha *f* ► **index finger** N dedo *m* índice ► **index number** N índice *m*

indexation [ˌɪndekˈseɪʃən], **indexing** [ˈɪndeksɪŋ] N indexación *f*, indización *f*, indiciación *f*

indexed [ˈɪndekst] ADJ = **index-linked**

index-linked [ˌɪndeksˈlɪŋkt] ADJ indexado, indiciado

index-linking [ˌɪndeksˈlɪŋkɪŋ] N indexación *f*, indiciación *f*

index-tracking fund [ˌɪndeksˈtrækɪŋfʌnd] N, **index-tracker (fund)** [ˌɪndeksˈtrækə(fʌnd)]

N (*Fin*) fondo *m* (de inversión) indexado, fondo *m* (de inversión) en índices

India [ˈɪndɪə] Ⓐ N India *f*
Ⓑ CPD ► **India paper** N papel *m* de China, papel *m* biblia ► **India rubber** N caucho *m*

Indian [ˈɪndɪən] Ⓐ ADJ (= *from India*) [*culture, languages, customs*] indio, hindú; (= *American Indian*) indígena, indio
Ⓑ N (*from India*) indio/a *m/f*, hindú *mf*; (= *American Indian*) indígena *mf*, indio/a *m/f*
Ⓒ CPD ► **Indian corn** N = **maize** ► **Indian elephant** N elefante *m* asiático ► **Indian file** N fila *f* india ► **Indian hemp** N cáñamo *m* índico ► **Indian ink** N tinta *f* china ► **the Indian Ocean** N el Océano Índico ► **Indian summer** N (*in northern hemisphere*) veranillo *m* de San Martín; (*in southern hemisphere*) veranillo *m* de San Juan; **the publication of that book gave her career an ~ summer** la publicación de ese libro dio lugar a un éxito tardío en su carrera

indicate [ˈɪndɪkeɪt] Ⓐ VT [1] (= *point out*) [+ *place*] indicar, señalar; (= *register*) [+ *temperature, speed*] marcar
[2] (= *show, suggest*) [+ *change*] ser indicio de; **the gathering clouds ~d a change in the weather** las nubes que se iban acumulando eran indicio de un cambio de tiempo; **the coroner's report ~d drowning as the cause of death** el informe del juez de instrucción indicaba *or* señalaba que murió ahogado
[3] (= *gesture*) indicar; **he ~d that I was to sit down** me indicó que me sentara
[4] (= *recommend, require*) (*usu passive*) **in this particular case, surgery is not ~d** en este caso en particular no es aconsejable operar; **I think a speedy departure is ~d** (*hum*) creo que habría que poner pies en polvorosa*
Ⓑ VI indicar, señalizar; (*esp Brit*) **to ~ left/right** indicar *or* señalizar a la izquierda/derecha

▼ **indication** [ˌɪndɪˈkeɪʃən] N [1] (= *sign*) indicio *m*; **there is every ~ that …** todo hace suponer que …; **there is no ~ that …** no hay indicios de que …; **this is some ~ of …** esto da una idea de …
[2] (= *mark*) señal *f*; (*on gauge*) marca *f*
[3] (*Med*) (*often pl*) indicación *f*

indicative [ɪnˈdɪkətɪv] Ⓐ ADJ [1] **to be ~ of sth** ser indicio de algo
[2] (*Ling*) [*mood*] indicativo
Ⓑ N (*Ling*) indicativo *m*

indicator [ˈɪndɪkeɪtəʳ] N (*gen*) (*also Chem, Econ*) indicador *m*; **indicators** (*Aut*) intermitentes *mpl*, direccionales *mpl* (*LAm*)

indices [ˈɪndɪsiːz] NPL *of* **index**

indict [ɪnˈdaɪt] VT [1] (*esp US*) (= *charge*) acusar; **to ~ sb for murder** acusar a algn de homicidio
[2] (*fig*) condenar, criticar duramente

indictable [ɪnˈdaɪtəbl] ADJ **~ offence** delito *m* procesable

indictment [ɪnˈdaɪtmənt] N [1] (= *charge, document*) acusación *f*; (= *act*) procesamiento *m*; **to bring an ~ against sb** formular cargos contra algn
[2] (*fig*) condenación *f*, crítica *f*; **the report is an ~ of our system** (*fig*) el informe critica duramente nuestro sistema

indie* [ˈɪndɪ] ADJ (*Brit Mus*) [*music, band*] independiente

Indies [ˈɪndɪz] NPL *see* **East D, West D**

indifference [ɪnˈdɪfrəns] N indiferencia *f* (**to** ante); **it is a matter of total ~ to me** no me importa en lo más mínimo, me es totalmente indiferente

indifferent [ɪnˈdɪfrənt] ADJ [1] (= *uninterested*) indiferente; **she seemed ~ to what was happening** parecía que lo que ocurría le resultaba indiferente
[2] (= *unsympathetic*) indiferente; **I could not remain ~ to their suffering** no podía permanecer indiferente a su sufrimiento
[3] (*pej*) (= *mediocre*) mediocre, regular; **a glass of ~ wine** un vaso de un vino mediocre *or* regular; **the book has had ~ reviews** las críticas del libro lo dejan regular
[4] (= *of no importance*) **it is ~ to me** me es igual *or* indiferente

indifferently [ɪnˈdɪfrəntlɪ] ADV [1] (= *uninterestedly*) con indiferencia
[2] (= *unsympathetically*) con indiferencia; **to treat sb ~** tratar a algn con indiferencia
[3] (= *in a mediocre way*) regularmente; **she performed ~** su actuación fue regular nada más
[4] (= *without preference*) indistintamente

indigence [ˈɪndɪdʒəns] N indigencia *f*

indigenous [ɪnˈdɪdʒɪnəs] ADJ [*people, population*] indígena, autóctono; **the elephant is ~ to India** el elefante es autóctono de India

indigent [ˈɪndɪdʒənt] ADJ indigente

indigestible [ˌɪndɪˈdʒestəbl] ADJ [1] (= *difficult to digest*) indigesto; (= *impossible to digest*) no digerible
[2] (*fig*) [*book*] árido, difícil de leer; [*information, style, writing*] difícil de digerir

indigestion [ˌɪndɪˈdʒestʃən] Ⓐ N indigestión *f*; **it's nothing serious, just ~** no es nada serio, sólo indigestión; **lentils give me ~** las lentejas me resultan indigestas
Ⓑ CPD ► **indigestion tablet** N pastilla *f* para la indigestión

indignant [ɪnˈdɪgnənt] ADJ [*person, mood, tone*] indignado; **she wrote an ~ letter to the local newspaper** escribió una carta en tono indignado al periódico local, escribió una carta al periódico local expresando su indignación; **to be ~ at/about sth** estar indignado ante/por algo; **he is ~ at the suggestion that …** está indignado ante la sugerencia de que …; **to become** *or* **get** *or* **grow ~** indignarse; **why is he looking so ~?** ¿por qué tiene esa cara de indignación?

indignantly [ɪnˈdɪgnəntlɪ] ADV [*say, deny*] con indignación; **"that is not true," she said ~** —eso no es verdad —dijo indignada *or* con indignación

indignation [ˌɪndɪgˈneɪʃən] N indignación *f*; **we expressed our ~ at the demands** expresamos *or* mostramos nuestra indignación ante las demandas

indignity [ɪnˈdɪgnɪtɪ] N indignidad *f*, humillación *f*; **to suffer the ~ of losing** sufrir la indignidad *or* humillación de perder

indigo [ˈɪndɪgəʊ] Ⓐ N (*pl* **indigos** *or* **indigoes**) (= *colour*) añil *m*, índigo *m*
Ⓑ ADJ añil *inv*, índigo *inv*
Ⓒ CPD ► **indigo blue** N azul *m* añil *or* índigo

indirect [ˌɪndɪˈrekt] Ⓐ ADJ [*route, criticism, result, costs*] indirecto; **in an ~ way** de una forma indirecta
Ⓑ CPD ► **indirect lighting** N iluminación *f* indirecta ► **indirect object** N (*Gram*) objeto *m* *or* complemento *m* indirecto ► **indirect question** N (*Gram*) oración *f* interrogativa indirecta ► **indirect speech** N (*Gram*) estilo *m* indirecto ► **indirect tax** N impuesto *m* indirecto

indirectly [ˌɪndɪˈrektlɪ] ADV [*cause, refer to*] indirectamente; [*answer*] con evasivas, evasivamente; **to be ~ responsible for sth** ser el responsable indirecto de algo

indirectness [ˌɪndɪˈrektnɪs] N carácter *m* indirecto; **the ~ of his reply made it difficult to …** su respuesta era tan evasiva *or* velada que era difícil …

indiscernible [ˌɪndɪˈsɜːnəbl] ADJ imperceptible

indiscipline [ɪnˈdɪsɪplɪn] N indisciplina *f*

indiscreet [ˌɪndɪsˈkriːt] ADJ [*person, remark, behaviour*] indiscreto; **to be ~ about sth** ser indiscreto respecto a algo; **it was ~ of her to mention it** fue muy indiscreta *or* cometió una indiscreción mencionándolo

indiscreetly [ˌɪndɪsˈkriːtlɪ] ADV indiscretamente

indiscreetness [ˌɪndɪsˈkriːtnɪs] N indiscreción *f*, falta *f* de discreción

indiscretion [ˌɪndɪsˈkreʃən] N [1] (= *lack of discretion*) indiscreción *f*, falta *f* de discreción
[2] (= *indiscreet act, remark*) indiscreción *f*

indiscriminate [ˌɪndɪsˈkrɪmɪnɪt] ADJ [1] (= *random*) [*bombing, killing, violence*] indiscriminado
[2] (= *undiscerning*) [*person*] falto de discernimiento; [*admirer*] ciego; **~ use of pesticides** el uso indiscriminado de pesticidas

indiscriminately [ˌɪndɪsˈkrɪmɪnɪtlɪ] ADV [1] (= *randomly*) [*distribute, vary*] indistintamente, sin distinción; [*bomb, fire, kill*] indiscriminadamente
[2] (= *without discernment*) [*use, view, read*] sin discernimiento, de forma indiscriminada; [*admire*] ciegamente

indispensable [ˌɪndɪsˈpensəbl] ADJ imprescindible, indispensable; **to be ~ for sth** ser imprescindible *or* indispensable para algo; **to be ~ to sth/sb** ser indispensable para algo/algn

indisposed [ˌɪndɪsˈpəʊzd] ADJ (= *ill*) indispuesto; (= *disinclined*) poco dispuesto (**to do sth** a hacer algo)

indisposition [ˌɪndɪspəˈzɪʃən] N indisposición *f*

indisputable [ˌɪndɪsˈpjuːtəbl] ADJ [*evidence*] irrefutable; [*fact*] incuestionable; [*winner*] indiscutible

indisputably [ˌɪndɪsˈpjuːtəblɪ] ADV indiscutiblemente; **it is ~ the best** es el mejor indiscutiblemente *or* sin ningún género de dudas; **oh, ~** claro que sí

indissoluble [ˌɪndɪˈsɒljʊbl] ADJ indisoluble

indissolubly [ˌɪndɪˈsɒljʊblɪ] ADV indisolublemente; **to be ~ linked (with sth)** estar indisolublemente ligado (a algo)

indistinct [ˌɪndɪsˈtɪŋkt] ADJ [1] (= *muted*) [*voice, noise*] indistinto; **her words were ~** no se le entendían las palabras
[2] (= *blurred*) [*figure, shape, outline*] poco definido, borroso; **the boundaries between the work of the two departments were becoming increasingly ~** los límites entre ambos departamentos estaba cada vez menos definidos *or* más borrosos

indistinctly [ˌɪndɪsˈtɪŋktlɪ] ADV (= *without distinction*) indistintamente, sin distinción; [*hear*] con poca claridad; [*see*] con poca claridad, borrosamente

indistinguishable [ˌɪndɪsˈtɪŋgwɪʃəbl] ADJ [1] (= *impossible to differentiate*) indistinguible (**from** de); **the two drawings are ~** los dos dibujos son indistinguibles *or* imposibles de distinguir, es imposible distinguir un dibujo del otro
[2] (= *indiscernible*) [*sound*] indistinguible; **his accent is ~** no se le nota nada de acento

indistinguishably [ˌɪndɪsˈtɪŋgwɪʃəblɪ] ADV sin distinción posible

indite [ɪnˈdaɪt] VT (*liter*) [+ *letter*] endilgar

individual [ˌɪndɪˈvɪdjʊəl] Ⓐ ADJ [1] (= *separate*) individual; **we are not able to comment on ~ cases** no podemos hacer comentarios sobre casos individuales; **we look after the wel-**

➤ LANGUAGE IN USE: **indication 1** 15.2

fare of ~ members nos cuidamos del bienestar de cada miembro individualmente
2 (= *for one*) particular, propio; **each room has its ~ telephone** cada cuarto tiene su teléfono propio
3 (= *personal*) [*tastes*] personal; **the constitution respects ~ rights** la constitución respeta los derechos del individuo; **the programme is tailored to your ~ needs** el programa se adapta a sus necesidades particulares
4 (= *distinctive*) **he has a very ~ style** tiene un estilo muy personal *or* original
Ⓑ N individuo *m*; **how could a single ~ have achieved all this?** ¿cómo podía haber conseguido todo esto un individuo por sí solo?; **he's a thoroughly nasty ~*** es un individuo sumamente desagradable

individualism [ˌɪndɪˈvɪdjʊəlɪzəm] N individualismo *m*

individualist [ˌɪndɪˈvɪdjʊəlɪst] N individualista *mf*

individualistic [ˈɪndɪˌvɪdjʊəˈlɪstɪk] ADJ individualista

individuality [ˌɪndɪˌvɪdjʊˈælɪtɪ] N (= *personality*) individualidad *f*; (= *separateness*) particularidad *f*

individualize [ˌɪndɪˈvɪdjʊəlaɪz] VT individuar, individualizar

individually [ˌɪndɪˈvɪdjʊəlɪ] ADV 1 (= *separately*) por separado; **they're all right ~, but not together** (*of people*) por separado son simpáticos, pero no cuando están juntos; **we do not sell the volumes ~** no vendemos los tomos sueltos *or* por separado
2 (= *for each individual*) **meals are ~ prepared** las comidas se preparan especialmente para cada individuo; **an ~ designed exercise programme** un programa de ejercicios diseñado según las necesidades de cada individuo

indivisibility [ˌɪndɪˌvɪzəˈbɪlətɪ] N indivisibilidad *f*

indivisible [ˌɪndɪˈvɪzəbl] ADJ [*number*] indivisible

indivisibly [ˌɪndɪˈvɪzəblɪ] ADV indivisiblemente; **to be ~ linked to sth** estar indisolublemente ligado a algo

Indo- [ˈɪndəʊ] PREFIX indo-

Indo-China [ˈɪndəʊˈtʃaɪnə] N Indochina *f*

indoctrinate [ɪnˈdɒktrɪneɪt] VT adoctrinar (**with, in** en); **they have been totally ~d by this cult** están totalmente adoctrinados por esta secta

indoctrination [ɪnˌdɒktrɪˈneɪʃən] N adoctrinamiento *m*

Indo-European [ˈɪndəʊˌjʊərəˈpiːən] Ⓐ ADJ indoeuropeo
Ⓑ N 1 indoeuropeo/a *m/f*
2 (*Ling*) indoeuropeo *m*

indolence [ˈɪndələns] N indolencia *f*

indolent [ˈɪndələnt] ADJ indolente

indolently [ˈɪndələntlɪ] ADV indolentemente

indomitable [ɪnˈdɒmɪtəbl] ADJ indómito, indomable

indomitably [ɪnˈdɒmɪtəblɪ] ADV indómitamente, indomablemente

Indonesia [ˌɪndəʊˈniːzɪə] N Indonesia *f*

Indonesian [ˌɪndəʊˈniːzɪən] Ⓐ ADJ indonesio
Ⓑ N 1 indonesio/a *m/f*
2 (*Ling*) indonesio *m*

indoor [ˈɪndɔːʳ] Ⓐ ADJ [*shoes*] para estar por casa; [*plant*] de interior; [*stadium, pool*] cubierto; [*photography*] de interiores; **the house had no electric light or ~ plumbing** la casa no tenía luz eléctrica ni instalación de agua en el interior
Ⓑ CPD ► **indoor aerial** N antena *f* interior ► **indoor athletics** N atletismo *m* en sala *or* en pista cubierta ► **indoor football** N fútbol *m* (en) sala ► **indoor games** NPL juegos *mpl* de salón

indoors [ɪnˈdɔːz] ADV [*be*] dentro; **I like the outside but what's it like ~?** me gusta por fuera, pero ¿cómo es por dentro?; **to go ~** (= *home*) entrar (en la casa); **we had to stay ~ because of the rain** tuvimos que quedarnos dentro a causa de la lluvia; **Her Indoors*** (*hum*) mi media naranja*, la parienta (*Sp**)

indrawn [ˌɪnˈdrɔːn] ADJ **we watched with ~ breath** mirábamos casi sin respirar

indubitable [ɪnˈdjuːbɪtəbl] ADJ (*frm*) indudable

indubitably [ɪnˈdjuːbɪtəblɪ] ADV (*frm*) indudablemente, sin duda

induce [ɪnˈdjuːs] VT 1 (= *persuade*) inducir, persuadir; **to ~ sb to do sth** inducir *or* persuadir a algn a hacer algo; **nothing would ~ me to go** nada me induciría a ir, nada podría hacerme ir; **what on earth ~d him to do it?** ¿qué diablos lo indujo *or* lo llevó a hacerlo?
2 (= *cause*) [+ *sleep*] producir, inducir
3 (*Med*) [+ *birth*] inducir; **I was ~d** me tuvieron que provocar el parto
4 (*Elec*) inducir

inducement [ɪnˈdjuːsmənt] N 1 (= *incentive*) incentivo *m*, aliciente *m*; **to hold out sth to sb as an ~** ofrecer algo a algn como aliciente; **it's no ~ to work harder** no supone ningún incentivo *or* aliciente para trabajar más
2 (*Med*) [*of birth*] inducción *f*

induct [ɪnˈdʌkt] VT (*Rel*) instalar; [+ *new member*] iniciar (**into** en); (*US Mil*) reclutar, quintar (*Sp*)

induction [ɪnˈdʌkʃən] Ⓐ N (*Rel*) instalación *f*; [*of new member, worker*] iniciación *f* (**into** en); (*US Mil*) reclutamiento *m*, quinta *f* (*Sp*); (*Med, Philos*) inducción *f*
Ⓑ CPD ► **induction coil** N carrete *m* de inducción ► **induction course** N curso *m* *or* cursillo *m* introductorio

inductive [ɪnˈdʌktɪv] ADJ [*reasoning*] inductivo

indulge [ɪnˈdʌldʒ] Ⓐ VT (= *give in to*) [+ *desire, appetite*] satisfacer; [+ *whim*] consentir; [+ *person*] complacer; (= *spoil*) [+ *child*] mimar, consentir; **to ~ o.s.** darse un gusto; **go on, ~ yourself!** venga, ¡date ese gustazo *or* capricho!*
Ⓑ VI **to ~ in** permitirse; **everyone ~s in fattening foods once in a while** todo el mundo se permite comer cosas que engordan de vez en cuando; **he is indulging in fantasy/speculation** se está dejando llevar por la fantasía/especulación

indulgence [ɪnˈdʌldʒəns] N 1 (= *gratification*) [*of desire, appetite*] satisfacción *f*
2 (= *spoiling*) complacencia *f*; *see also* **self-indulgence**
3 (= *tolerance*) indulgencia *f*; **she was treated with great ~ as a child** cuando era niña la trataban con mucha indulgencia *or* estaba muy consentida
4 (= *luxury item*) lujo *m*; **I do allow myself the occasional ~** me permito un lujo de vez en cuando
5 (= *bad habit*) vicio *m*
6 (*Rel*) indulgencia *f*

indulgent [ɪnˈdʌldʒənt] ADJ indulgente; **he took an ~ attitude toward their pranks** adoptó una actitud indulgente para con sus travesuras; **to be ~ to** *or* **toward** *or* **with sb** consentir a algn, ser indulgente con algn

indulgently [ɪnˈdʌldʒəntlɪ] ADV indulgentemente

Indus [ˈɪndəs] N **the ~** el Indo

industrial [ɪnˈdʌstrɪəl] Ⓐ ADJ industrial
Ⓑ CPD ► **industrial accident** N accidente *m* laboral *or* de trabajo ► **industrial action** N (*Brit*) medidas *fpl* de presión *or* protesta laboral; **to take ~ action** tomar medidas de presión *or* protesta laboral ► **industrial alcohol** N alcohol *m* de uso industrial ► **industrial archaeology** N arqueología *f* industrial ► **industrial diamond** N diamante *m* natural *or* industrial ► **industrial disease** N enfermedad *f* laboral ► **industrial dispute** N (*Brit*) conflicto *m* laboral ► **industrial engineering** N ingeniería *f* industrial ► **industrial espionage** N espionaje *m* industrial ► **industrial estate** N (*Brit*) zona *f* *or* (*Sp*) polígono *m* industrial ► **industrial goods** NPL bienes *mpl* de producción ► **industrial injury** N lesión *f* por accidente laboral ► **industrial park** N (*US*) zona *f* *or* (*Sp*) polígono *m* industrial ► **industrial relations** NPL relaciones *fpl* laborales; **~ relations legislation** legislación *f* laboral ► **Industrial Revolution** N Revolución *f* Industrial ► **industrial tribunal** N magistratura *f* de trabajo, tribunal *m* laboral ► **industrial unrest** N agitación *f* obrera, conflictos *mpl* laborales ► **industrial waste** N residuos *mpl* industriales

industrialism [ɪnˈdʌstrɪəlɪzəm] N industrialismo *m*

industrialist [ɪnˈdʌstrɪəlɪst] N industrial *mf*

industrialization [ɪnˌdʌstrɪəlɪˈzeɪʃən] N industrialización *f*

industrialize [ɪnˈdʌstrɪəlaɪz] Ⓐ VT [+ *area, region*] industrializar
Ⓑ VI industrializarse

industrially [ɪnˈdʌstrɪəlɪ] ADV industrialmente; **the parts are produced ~** las piezas se producen industrialmente, las piezas se fabrican mediante un procedimiento industrial; **~, the country has advanced enormously** en el aspecto industrial *or* en el terreno industrial *or* desde el punto de vista industrial, el país ha avanzado enormemente

industrial-strength [ɪnˈdʌstrɪəlˈstreŋθ] ADJ 1 [*product*] muy resistente
2 (* *hum*) (= *strong*) [*wine*] peleón*

industrious [ɪnˈdʌstrɪəs] ADJ (= *hardworking*) trabajador, laborioso; (= *studious*) aplicado, diligente

industriously [ɪnˈdʌstrɪəslɪ] ADV [*work*] laboriosamente; [*study*] con aplicación

industriousness [ɪnˈdʌstrɪəsnɪs] N [*of worker*] laboriosidad *f*; [*of student*] aplicación *f*, diligencia *f*

industry [ˈɪndəstrɪ] N 1 industria *f*; **the steel/coal/textile ~** la industria siderúrgica/minera/textil; **the banking/insurance/hotel ~** el sector bancario/de seguros/hotelero; **the tourist ~** el turismo; **a career in ~** una carrera en el sector empresarial; *see also* **heavy D**
2 (= *industriousness*) laboriosidad *f*, aplicación *f*

inebriate (*frm*) Ⓐ [ɪˈniːbrɪɪt] N borracho/a *m/f*
Ⓑ [ɪˈniːbrɪeɪt] VT embriagar, emborrachar
Ⓒ [ɪˈniːbrɪɪt] ADJ = **inebriated**

inebriated [ɪˈniːbrɪeɪtɪd] ADJ (*frm*) ebrio

inebriation [ɪˌniːbrɪˈeɪʃən] N (*frm*) embriaguez *f*

inedible [ɪnˈedɪbl] ADJ (= *unpleasant*) incomible; (= *poisonous*) no comestible

ineducable [ɪnˈedjʊkəbl] ADJ ineducable

ineffable [ɪnˈefəbl] ADJ (*liter*) inefable

ineffably [ɪnˈefəblɪ] ADV (*liter*) **her face was ~**

well-bred su cara era de una distinción indescriptible *or* (*liter*) inefable

ineffaceable [ˌɪnɪˈfeɪsəbl] ADJ imborrable

ineffective [ˌɪnɪˈfektɪv] ADJ [*measure, policy, drug*] ineficaz; [*person, committee*] incompetente, ineficaz; [*effort, attempt*] infructuoso; **the plan proved wholly ~** el proyecto no surtió ningún efecto *or* no dio ningún resultado; **to be ~ in doing sth** [*law, measure, drug*] ser *or* resultar ineficaz a la hora de hacer algo; [*person, committee*] ser incompetente *or* carecer de eficacia a la hora de hacer algo

ineffectively [ˌɪnɪˈfektɪvlɪ] ADV **1** (= *ineffectually*) infructuosamente, inútilmente
2 (= *badly*) [*govern, rule*] ineficazmente, de modo incompetente

ineffectiveness [ˌɪnɪˈfektɪvnɪs] N [*of measure, policy, drug*] ineficacia *f*; [*of person, committee*] incompetencia *f*, ineficacia *f*; [*of effort, attempt*] infructuosidad *f*

ineffectual [ˌɪnɪˈfektjʊəl] ADJ inútil

ineffectually [ˌɪnɪˈfektjʊəlɪ] ADV inútilmente; **"I couldn't help it," she said ~** —no lo pude evitar —dijo inútilmente

inefficacious [ˌɪnefɪˈkeɪʃəs] ADJ (*frm*) ineficaz

inefficacy [ɪnˈefɪkəsɪ] N (*frm*) ineficacia *f*

inefficiency [ˌɪnɪˈfɪʃənsɪ] N [*of method*] ineficiencia *f*; [*of person*] incompetencia *f*

inefficient [ˌɪnɪˈfɪʃənt] ADJ [*method*] ineficiente; [*person*] incompetente; [*factory, mine, industry*] poco productivo

inefficiently [ˌɪnɪˈfɪʃəntlɪ] ADV de forma ineficaz; **the company is ~ run** la compañía está llevada de forma ineficaz

inelastic [ˌɪnɪˈlæstɪk] ADJ [*demand, supply*] inelástico; (*fig*) rígido, poco flexible

inelegant [ɪnˈelɪgənt] ADJ poco elegante, inelegante

inelegantly [ɪnˈelɪgəntlɪ] ADV de manera poco elegante

ineligible [ɪnˈelɪdʒəbl] ADJ inelegible; (*for military service*) no apto; **to be ~ for sth** (*for candidacy, competition*) ser inelegible para algo; (*for benefit*) no tener derecho a algo; **I was ~ for unemployment benefit** no tenía derecho a cobrar el paro; **to be ~ to vote** no tener derecho al voto

ineluctable [ˌɪnɪˈlʌktəbl] ADJ (*frm*) ineluctable, ineludible

inept [ɪˈnept] ADJ **1** (= *unskilful*) [*person*] inepto, incapaz; [*performance*] malo; **their ~ handling of the case** la forma inepta en que llevaron el caso
2 (= *unsuitable*) [*policy*] inadecuado

ineptitude [ɪˈneptɪtjuːd], **ineptness** [ɪˈneptnɪs] N [*of person*] ineptitud *f*, incapacidad *f*; [*of policies*] lo inadecuado

inequality [ˌɪnɪˈkwɒlɪtɪ] N desigualdad *f*; **~ of wealth/between nations** la desigualdad en el reparto de la riqueza/entre naciones

inequitable [ɪnˈekwɪtəbl] ADJ no equitativo

inequity [ɪnˈekwɪtɪ] N injusticia *f*

ineradicable [ˌɪnɪˈrædɪkəbl] ADJ [*prejudice, hatred*] imposible de erradicar; [*differences*] insalvables

inert [ɪˈnɜːt] ADJ (= *inanimate*) [*substance, gas*] inerte; (= *motionless*) inerte, inmóvil; **he lay ~ on the floor** estaba inerte *or* inmóvil en el suelo

inertia [ɪˈnɜːʃə] N **1** [*of person*] inercia *f*, apatía *f*
2 (*Chem, Phys*) inercia *f*; *see also* **moment 2**

inertia-reel [ɪˈnɜːʃəˌriːl] ADJ **~ seat-belt** cinturón *m* de seguridad retráctil

inescapable [ˌɪnɪsˈkeɪpəbl] ADJ [*duty*] ineludible; [*result*] inevitable; [*fact, reality*] que no se puede ignorar; **I have come to the ~ conclusion that ...** he llegado a la inevitable conclusión de que ...

inescapably [ˌɪnɪsˈkeɪpəblɪ] ADV ineludiblemente, incuestionablemente

inessential [ˈɪnɪˈsenʃəl] Ⓐ ADJ no esencial
Ⓑ N cosa *f* no esencial

inestimable [ɪnˈestɪməbl] ADJ [*value, benefit*] inapreciable, inestimable; [*harm*] incalculable

inevitability [ɪnˌevɪtəˈbɪlɪtɪ] N inevitabilidad *f*

inevitable [ɪnˈevɪtəbl] Ⓐ ADJ inevitable; **it was ~ that he would refuse** era inevitable que se negara; **this raised the ~ question of money** esto suscitó la inevitable cuestión del dinero
Ⓑ N **the ~** lo inevitable

inevitably [ɪnˈevɪtəblɪ] ADV inevitablemente, forzosamente; **as ~ happens ...** como siempre ocurre ...

inexact [ˌɪnɪgˈzækt] ADJ inexacto

inexactitude [ˌɪnɪgˈzæktɪtjuːd] N inexactitud *f*

inexactly [ˌɪnɪgˈzæktlɪ] ADV de modo inexacto

inexcusable [ˌɪnɪksˈkjuːzəbl] ADJ [*behaviour, conduct*] imperdonable, inexcusable

inexcusably [ˌɪnɪksˈkjuːzəblɪ] ADV [*behave*] de modo inexcusable, de modo imperdonable; **she had been ~ careless** había cometido un descuido inexcusable *or* imperdonable

inexhaustible [ˌɪnɪgˈzɔːstəbl] ADJ [*supply*] inagotable; **she has ~ energy** tiene una energía inagotable

inexorable [ɪnˈeksərəbl] ADJ inexorable, implacable

inexorably [ɪnˈeksərəblɪ] ADV inexorablemente, implacablemente

inexpedient [ˌɪnɪksˈpiːdɪənt] ADJ inoportuno, inconveniente, imprudente

inexpensive [ˌɪnɪksˈpensɪv] ADJ económico

inexpensively [ˌɪnɪksˈpensɪvlɪ] ADV económicamente; **they are ~ priced** tienen un precio razonable

inexperience [ˌɪnɪksˈpɪərɪəns] N inexperiencia *f*, falta *f* de experiencia

inexperienced [ˌɪnɪksˈpɪərɪənst] ADJ [*player, team*] inexperto; [*staff*] sin experiencia; [*pilot, driver*] sin experiencia, inexperto; **to be ~ in** *or* **at sth/doing sth** no tener experiencia en algo/hacer algo

inexpert [ɪnˈekspɜːt] ADJ inexperto, poco hábil

inexpertly [ɪnˈekspɜːtlɪ] ADV con poca habilidad *or* pericia

inexplicable [ˌɪnɪksˈplɪkəbl] ADJ [*behaviour, event, delay*] inexplicable

inexplicably [ˌɪnɪksˈplɪkəblɪ] ADV inexplicablemente; **I was ~ moved** inexplicablemente, estaba conmovido

inexpressible [ˌɪnɪksˈpresəbl] ADJ [*feelings, thoughts*] inexpresable; [*joy, beauty, sorrow*] inefable, indescriptible

inexpressive [ˌɪnɪksˈpresɪv] ADJ [*style, person, look, face*] inexpresivo

inextinguishable [ˌɪnɪksˈtɪŋgwɪʃəbl] ADJ inextinguible, inapagable

in extremis [ɪnɪksˈtriːmɪs] ADV (*frm*) in extremis

inextricable [ˌɪnɪksˈtrɪkəbl] ADJ inextricable, inseparable

inextricably [ˌɪnɪksˈtrɪkəblɪ] ADV inextricablemente; **our future is now ~ linked with Europe** nuestro futuro está ahora inextricablemente vinculado a Europa

infallibility [ɪnˌfæləˈbɪlɪtɪ] N infalibilidad *f*; **Papal ~** la infalibilidad del Papa

infallible [ɪnˈfæləbl] ADJ (= *unfailing*) [*remedy, method, punctuality*] infalible; **she has the ~ knack of saying the wrong thing at the wrong time** no falla, siempre mete la pata en el momento más inoportuno*

infallibly [ɪnˈfæləblɪ] ADV (= *unfailingly*) infaliblemente; (= *predictably*) indefectiblemente

infamous [ˈɪnfəməs] ADJ [*person*] infame, de mala fama; [*conduct, crime, speech*] infame; **to be ~ for sth** ser infame por algo

infamy [ˈɪnfəmɪ] N infamia *f*

infancy [ˈɪnfənsɪ] N **1** (= *childhood*) infancia *f*, niñez *f*; (*Jur*) minoría *f* de edad; **from ~** desde niño, desde muy pequeño
2 (*fig*) (= *early stage*) infancia *f*; **the project is still in its ~** el proyecto está todavía en mantillas

infant [ˈɪnfənt] Ⓐ N niño/a *m/f*; (*Jur*) menor *mf* de edad; **the ~ Jesus** el niño Jesús
Ⓑ CPD ► **infant class** N clase *f* de párvulos ► **infant mortality** N mortandad *f or* mortalidad *f* infantil ► **infant school** N (*Brit*) *centro de educación primaria (primer ciclo)*

infanta [ɪnˈfæntə] N infanta *f*

infante [ɪnˈfæntɪ] N infante *m*

infanticide [ɪnˈfæntɪsaɪd] N **1** (= *act*) infanticidio *m*
2 (= *person*) infanticida *mf*

infantile [ˈɪnfəntaɪl] Ⓐ ADJ infantil (*also Med*); **don't be so ~!** ¡no seas niño!
Ⓑ CPD ► **infantile paralysis** N parálisis *f inv* infantil

infantilism [ɪnˈfæntɪˌlɪzəm] N infantilismo *m*

infantilize [ɪnˈfæntɪlaɪz] VT infantilizar

infantry [ˈɪnfəntrɪ] N infantería *f*

infantryman [ˈɪnfəntrɪmən] N (*pl* **infantrymen**) soldado *m* de infantería; (*Hist*) infante *m*

infatuated [ɪnˈfætjʊeɪtɪd] ADJ **to be ~ with sb** estar encaprichado con *or* de algn, estar chiflado por algn*; **to become ~ with sb** encapricharse con *or* de algn; **he was ~ with the idea that ...** se había encaprichado con la idea de ...

infatuation [ɪnˌfætjʊˈeɪʃən] N encaprichamiento *m*

infect [ɪnˈfekt] VT [+ *wound, foot*] infectar; [+ *person*] contagiar; [+ *food*] contaminar; **to ~ sb with sth** contagiar algo a algn; **don't ~ us all with your cold!** ¡no nos contagies tu resfriado a todos!, ¡no nos pegues tu resfriado a todos!*; **he's ~ed everybody with his enthusiasm** contagió su entusiasmo a todos; **scientists ~ed mice with the disease** los científicos inocularon la enfermedad a *or* en ratones

infected [ɪnˈfektɪd] ADJ [*wound, foot, blood, needle*] infectado; [*person*] contagiado, infectado; **to be ~** estar infectado; **to become** *or* **get ~** [*wound, eye*] infectarse

infection [ɪnˈfekʃən] N **1** (= *illness*) infección *f*; **she has a slight ~** tiene una pequeña infección
2 (= *process*) contagio *m*; **the risk of ~** el riesgo de contagio

infectious [ɪnˈfekʃəs] Ⓐ ADJ **1** (*Med*) [*disease*] infeccioso, contagioso; **he is no longer ~** ya le ha pasado el periodo del contagio
2 (*fig*) [*person, laugh, enthusiasm, rhythm*] contagioso
Ⓑ CPD ► **infectious hepatitis** N hepatitis *f* infecciosa

infectiousness [ɪnˈfekʃəsnɪs] N **1** (*Med*) lo contagioso, contagiosidad *f*
2 (*fig*) [*of enthusiasm*] lo contagioso

infective [ɪnˈfektɪv] ADJ [*disease, agent*] infeccioso

infelicitous [ˌɪnfɪˈlɪsɪtəs] ADJ (*frm*) poco feliz, inoportuno

infelicity [ˌɪnfɪˈlɪsɪtɪ] N (*frm*) inoportunidad *f*

infer [ɪnˈfɜːʳ] VT 1 (= *deduce*) inferir, deducir (**from** de)
2 (*) (= *imply*) insinuar; **what are you ~ring?** ¿qué estás insinuando?

inference [ˈɪnfərəns] N deducción *f*, inferencia *f*; **by ~** por deducción; **to draw ~s** sacar conclusiones; **to draw an ~ from sth** hacer una deducción de algo

inferential [ˌɪnfəˈrenʃəl] ADJ ilativo, deductivo

inferentially [ˌɪnfəˈrenʃəlɪ] ADV por inferencia, por deducción

inferior [ɪnˈfɪərɪəʳ] (A) ADJ 1 (*in quality, rank*) [*person, status, position*] inferior; [*product, work, service*] de calidad inferior; **to feel ~** sentirse inferior; **of ~ quality** de calidad inferior; **to be ~ to sth/sb** ser inferior a algo/algn
2 (*Anat, Bot*) (= *lower*) inferior
(B) N 1 (= *inferior person*) inferior *mf*
2 (= *person lower in rank*) inferior *mf*, subalterno/a *m/f*

inferiority [ɪnˌfɪərɪˈɒrɪtɪ] (A) N inferioridad *f*; **~ to sth/sb** inferioridad *f* frente a *or* con respecto a algo/algn
(B) CPD ► **inferiority complex** N (*Psych*) complejo *m* de inferioridad

infernal [ɪnˈfɜːnl] ADJ infernal; (*fig*) infernal, del demonio*; **stop that ~ racket!** ¡deja de hacer ese ruido infernal!, ¡deja de hacer ese ruido del demonio!*

infernally [ɪnˈfɜːnəlɪ] ADV **it's ~ awkward** es terriblemente difícil

inferno [ɪnˈfɜːnəʊ] N (= *hell*) infierno *m*; (= *fire*) hoguera *f*; **in a few minutes the house was a blazing ~** en pocos minutos la casa era una hoguera; **it's like an ~ in there** allí dentro hace un calor insoportable

infertile [ɪnˈfɜːtaɪl] ADJ [*land, soil*] yermo, infecundo; [*person, animal*] estéril

infertility [ˌɪnfɜːˈtɪlɪtɪ] N [*of land, soil*] infecundidad *f*; [*of person, animal*] esterilidad *f*

infest [ɪnˈfest] VT infestar; **to be ~ed with sth** estar infestado *or* plagado de algo

infestation [ˌɪnfesˈteɪʃən] N infestación *f*, plaga *f*

infidel [ˈɪnfɪdəl] (A) ADJ infiel, descreído
(B) N infiel *mf*, descreído/a *m/f*; **the Infidel** los descreídos, la gente descreída

infidelity [ˌɪnfɪˈdelɪtɪ] N (*to partner*) infidelidad *f* (**to** a); (*to principle, cause*) deslealtad *f* (**to** para con)

infighting* [ˈɪnfaɪtɪŋ] N (*in organization*) lucha *f* interna; (*Boxing*) lucha *f* cuerpo a cuerpo; **political ~** peleas *fpl* políticas

infill [ˈɪnfɪl] N (*Constr, Geol*) relleno *m*

infiltrate [ˈɪnfɪltreɪt] (A) VT [+ *organization*] infiltrarse en, infiltrar; **to ~ sb into sth** infiltrar a algn en algo
(B) VI infiltrarse

infiltration [ˌɪnfɪlˈtreɪʃən] N (*gen*) infiltración *f*

infiltrator [ˈɪnfɪltreɪtəʳ] N infiltrado/a *m/f*

infinite [ˈɪnfɪnɪt] (A) ADJ infinito; **he took ~ pains over it** lo hizo con el mayor esmero; **an ~ amount of time/money** una infinidad de tiempo/dinero; **in their ~ wisdom they decided to demolish the building** en su infinita sabiduría, decidieron demoler el edificio
(B) N **the ~** el infinito

infinitely [ˈɪnfɪnɪtlɪ] ADV infinitamente; **this is ~ harder** esto es muchísimo más difícil, esto es mil veces más difícil

infiniteness [ˈɪnfɪnɪtnɪs] N infinidad *f*

infinitesimal [ˌɪnfɪnɪˈtesɪməl] ADJ infinitesimal

infinitive [ɪnˈfɪnɪtɪv] (A) ADJ (*Ling*) infinitivo
(B) N infinitivo *m*

infinitude [ɪnˈfɪnɪtjuːd] N infinitud *f*

infinity [ɪnˈfɪnɪtɪ] N (*gen*) infinidad *f*; (*Math*) infinito *m*; **an ~ of** una infinidad de, un sinfín de

infirm [ɪnˈfɜːm] ADJ [*person*] (= *weak*) débil, endeble; (= *sickly*) enfermizo; (= *ill*) enfermo; **the old and ~** los ancianos y enfermos; **~ of purpose** irresoluto

infirmary [ɪnˈfɜːmərɪ] N (= *hospital*) hospital *m*, clínica *f*; (*in school, prison, barracks*) enfermería *f*

infirmity [ɪnˈfɜːmɪtɪ] N (= *state*) debilidad *f*; (= *illness*) enfermedad *f*, achaque *m*, dolencia *f*; (= *moral*) flaqueza *f*; **mental/physical ~** enfermedad *f* mental/física; **the infirmities of (old) age** los achaques de la vejez

infix [ˈɪnfɪks] N infijo *m*

in flagrante delicto [ɪnfləˈgræntɪdɪˈlɪktəʊ] ADV en flagrante

inflame [ɪnˈfleɪm] VT 1 (*Med*) [+ *wound*] inflamar; **to become ~d** inflamarse
2 (*fig*) [+ *person, feelings*] encender, inflamar; [+ *situation*] exacerbar; [+ *conflict*] avivar, exacerbar; **to be ~d with passion/anger/jealousy** estar inflamado de pasión/ira/celos

inflammable [ɪnˈflæməbl] ADJ 1 [*liquid, substance, fabric*] inflamable; **"highly inflammable"** "muy inflamable"
2 (*fig*) [*situation*] explosivo

inflammation [ˌɪnfləˈmeɪʃən] N (*Med*) [*of wound*] inflamación *f*

inflammatory [ɪnˈflæmətərɪ] ADJ (*Med*) inflamatorio; [*speech*] incendiario

inflatable [ɪnˈfleɪtəbl] ADJ [*boat*] inflable, hinchable (*Sp*)

inflate [ɪnˈfleɪt] (A) VT 1 [+ *tyre, balloon*] inflar, hinchar (*Sp*) (**with** de)
2 (*fig*) [+ *prices*] inflar; [+ *currency*] provocar la inflación de; [+ *report*] exagerar; **don't ~ his ego** no le alimentes el ego
(B) VI [*balloon, tyre*] inflarse, hincharse (*Sp*)

inflated [ɪnˈfleɪtɪd] ADJ 1 [*tyre, balloon*] inflado, hinchado (*Sp*); **~ with pride** (*fig*) henchido de orgullo, envanecido
2 (= *exaggerated*) [*price, salary*] inflado; [*report*] exagerado; [*language*] altisonante, rimbombante; **he has an ~ ego** se cree muy importante

inflation [ɪnˈfleɪʃən] (A) N (*Econ*) inflación *f*
(B) CPD ► **inflation accounting** N contabilidad *f* de inflación

inflationary [ɪnˈfleɪʃnərɪ] ADJ inflacionario, inflacionista; **~ pressures are very strong** las presiones inflacionarias *or* inflacionistas son muy fuertes

inflationism [ɪnˈfleɪʃənɪzəm] N inflacionismo *m*

inflationist [ɪnˈfleɪʃənɪst] (A) ADJ inflacionario, inflacionista
(B) N partidario/a *m/f* de la inflación

inflation-proof [ɪnˈfleɪʃənˌpruːf] ADJ resistente a la inflación

inflect [ɪnˈflekt] VT 1 [+ *voice*] modular
2 (*Gram*) [+ *noun*] declinar; [+ *verb*] conjugar

inflected [ɪnˈflektɪd] ADJ [*language*] flexivo

inflection [ɪnˈflekʃən] N inflexión *f*

inflectional [ɪnˈflekʃənl] ADJ con inflexión

inflexibility [ɪnˌfleksɪˈbɪlɪtɪ] N [*of substance, object*] rigidez *f*; (*fig*) [*of person, opinions, rules*] inflexibilidad *f*

inflexible [ɪnˈfleksəbl] ADJ [*substance, object*] rígido; (*fig*) [*person, opinions, rules*] inflexible

inflexion [ɪnˈflekʃən] N inflexión *f*

inflict [ɪnˈflɪkt] VT **to ~ (on)** [+ *wound*] causar (a), inferir (a); [+ *blow*] asestar *or* dar (a); [+ *penalty, tax, punishment*] imponer (a); [+ *pain, suffering, damage*] causar (a), infligir (a); **they ~ed a serious defeat on the enemy** infligieron una grave derrota al enemigo; **I don't wish to ~ my own wishes on anyone else** no quiero imponer mis deseos a nadie; **to ~ o.s. on sb** imponer su presencia a algn

infliction [ɪnˈflɪkʃən] N (= *act*) imposición *f*; (= *penalty etc*) pena *f*, castigo *m*

in-flight [ˈɪnflaɪt] ADJ **~ entertainment** amenidades *fpl* ofrecidas durante el vuelo; **~ meal** comida *f* servida durante el vuelo; **~ movie** película *f* proyectada durante el vuelo; **~ services** servicios *mpl* de a bordo

inflow [ˈɪnfləʊ] (A) N [*of capital, migrants*] afluencia *f*; [*of water*] entrada *f*
(B) CPD ► **inflow pipe** N tubo *m* de entrada

influence [ˈɪnflʊəns] (A) N influencia *f* (**on** sobre); **a man of ~** un hombre influyente; **to have an ~ on sth** [*person*] tener influencia en *or* sobre algo, influir en *or* sobre algo; **to be a good/bad ~ on sb** ejercer buena/mala influencia sobre algn; **to bring every ~ to bear on sb** ejercer todas las presiones posibles sobre algn; **to have ~ with sb** tener influencias con algn, tener enchufe con algn*; **to have ~ over sb** tener influencia *or* ascendiente sobre algn; **to be under the ~ of drink/drugs** estar ebrio/drogado; **under the ~** (*hum*) borracho
(B) VT [+ *person*] influenciar, influir en; [+ *action, decision*] influir en *or* sobre; **what factors ~d your decision?** ¿qué factores influyeron en tu decisión?; **don't let him ~ you** no te dejes influenciar por él; **the novelist has been ~d by Torrente** el novelista ha sufrido la influencia de *or* está influido por Torrente; **to be easily ~d** ser muy influenciable

influential [ˌɪnflʊˈenʃəl] ADJ [*person, ideas*] influyente; [*organization*] prestigioso; **he was ~ in securing the loan** influyó para que se consiguiera el préstamo; **he was ~ in government circles** tenía influencia en círculos gubernamentales

influenza [ˌɪnflʊˈenzə] N gripe *f*

influx [ˈɪnflʌks] N [*of people*] afluencia *f*; [*of objects, ideas*] flujo *m*; (*Mech*) aflujo *m*, entrada *f*

info* [ˈɪnfəʊ] N = **information**

infobahn [ˈɪnfəʊbɑːn] N = **information superhighway**

infomercial [ˈɪnfəʊmɜːʃl] N publirreportaje *m*

▼**inform** [ɪnˈfɔːm] (A) VT (= *give information*) informar, avisar; (= *bring up to date*) poner al corriente; **to ~ sb about** *or* **of sth** informar a algn sobre *or* de algo; **I am pleased to ~ you that ...** tengo el gusto de comunicarle que ...; **keep me ~ed** téngame *or* manténgame al corriente; **why was I not ~ed?** ¿por qué no me informaron *or* avisaron?; **to ~ o.s. about sth** informarse sobre algo; *see also* **well-informed**
(B) VI soplar; **to ~ on** *or* **against sb** delatar *or* denunciar a algn

informal [ɪnˈfɔːməl] ADJ 1 (= *unceremonious*) [*meal, clothes, atmosphere, manner*] informal; [*occasion*] informal, sin etiqueta; [*expression*] coloquial, familiar; [*person*] informal, poco ceremonioso; **dress is ~** vista ropa informal, no es necesaria etiqueta
2 (= *unofficial*) [*meeting, negotiations, visit*] informal

informality [ˌɪnfɔːˈmælɪtɪ] N informalidad *f*, falta *f* de ceremonia

➤ LANGUAGE IN USE: inform A 21.1

informally [ɪn'fɔːməlɪ] ADV [1] (= *without ceremony*) [*speak, greet, welcome*] de manera informal, sin ceremonias; [*dress*] de manera informal; [*write*] con un lenguaje informal, con un estilo familiar
[2] (= *unofficially*) [*meet, discuss, agree*] informalmente; **I have been ~ told that ...** me han dicho de manera informal *or* extraoficial que ...

informant [ɪn'fɔːmənt] N informante *mf*; **my ~** el que me lo dijo; **who was your ~?** ¿quién se lo dijo?

informatics [ˌɪnfɔː'mætɪks] N informática *f*

information [ˌɪnfə'meɪʃən] (A) N información *f*; (= *knowledge*) conocimientos *mpl*; **a piece of ~** un dato; **"information"** "información"; **to ask for ~** pedir información; **to gather ~ about** *or* **on sth** reunir información sobre algo, informarse sobre algo; **to give sb ~ about** *or* **on sth/sb** proporcionar información a algn sobre algo/algn; **who gave you this ~?** ¿quién le dio esta información?; **we weren't given enough ~ about the risks involved** no nos informaron suficientemente sobre los riesgos que entrañaba; **we have no ~ on that point** no tenemos información sobre ese particular; **for your ~** para su información; **for your ~, I asked him to come!** para que te enteres, ¡le pedí que viniera!
(B) CPD ► **information bureau** N oficina *f* de información ► **information desk** N información *f* ► **information office** N = **information bureau** ► **information pack** N (*Brit*) material *m* informativo ► **information processing** N procesamiento *m* de la información ► **information retrieval** N recuperación *f* de la información ► **information science** N informática *f*, gestión *f* de la información ► **information service** N servicio *m* de información ► **information superhighway** N superautopista *f* de la información ► **information technology** N informática *f* ► **information theory** N teoría *f* de la información

informational [ˌɪnfə'meɪʃənl] ADJ [*needs, requirements*] de información; [*television, video*] informativo, didáctico

informative [ɪn'fɔːmətɪv] ADJ informativo; **talking to him was very ~** la conversación que tuve con él resultó muy informativa; **his school report was not very ~** su boletín de calificaciones no era muy revelador

informativity [ɪnˌfɔːmə'tɪvɪtɪ] N informatividad *f*

informed [ɪn'fɔːmd] ADJ [*person*] bien informado; [*debate*] llevado a cabo con conocimiento de causa; **to give (one's) ~ consent (to sth)** (*Med*) dar el consentimiento (para algo) con total conocimiento de causa; **an ~ guess** una conjetura bien fundamentada; **~ opinion is that ...** la opinión de los que saben del tema es que ...

informer [ɪn'fɔːmə^r] N informante *mf*; (*pej*) delator(a) *m/f*, soplón/ona* *m/f*; **police ~** informante *mf* de la policía; **to turn ~** convertirse en delator

infotainment [ˌɪnfəʊ'teɪnmənt] N (*Brit TV*) **~ programme** magazine *m* informativo

infra... ['ɪnfrə] PREFIX infra ...

infraction [ɪn'frækʃən] N infracción *f*, contravención *f*

infra dig†* ['ɪnfrə'dɪg] ADJ ABBR denigrante

infrared ['ɪnfrə'red] ADJ [*rays, light*] infrarrojo

infrasonic ['ɪnfrəˌsɒnɪk] ADJ infrasónico

infrasound ['ɪnfrəˌsaʊnd] N infrasonido *m*

infrastructure ['ɪnfrəˌstrʌktʃə^r] N infraestructura *f*

infrequency [ɪn'friːkwənsɪ] N infrecuencia *f*, poca frecuencia *f*

infrequent [ɪn'friːkwənt] ADJ [*visit, occurrence*] poco frecuente, infrecuente

infrequently [ɪn'friːkwəntlɪ] ADV rara vez, pocas veces; **not ~** no raramente, no pocas veces

infringe [ɪn'frɪndʒ] (A) VT [+ *law, rights, copyright*] infringir, violar
(B) VI **to ~ (up)on** [+ *sb's rights, interests, privacy*] violar

infringement [ɪn'frɪndʒmənt] N [*of law, rule*] infracción *f*, violación *f*; [*of rights*] violación *f*; (*Sport*) falta *f*; **they sued him for ~ of copyright** lo demandaron por no respetar los derechos de autor

infuriate [ɪn'fjʊərɪeɪt] VT enfurecer, poner furioso; **to be/get ~d** estar/ponerse furioso; **this kind of thing ~s me** estas cosas me ponen furioso; **at times you ~ me** hay veces que me sacas de quicio

infuriating [ɪn'fjʊərɪeɪtɪŋ] ADJ (*gen*) exasperante; **it's simply ~** es exasperante, es para volverse loco; **I find his habit ~** esa costumbre suya me saca de quicio

infuriatingly [ɪn'fjʊərɪeɪtɪŋlɪ] ADV **~, I was cut off** se cortó la línea, vamos, como para volverse loco; **his answer was ~ vague** su respuesta fue de una vaguedad exasperante

infuse [ɪn'fjuːz] (A) VT [1] [+ *courage, enthusiasm*] infundir (**into** a); **to ~ courage into sb** infundir ánimo a algn; **they were ~d with a new hope** se les infundió nuevas esperanzas
[2] (*Culin*) [+ *herbs, tea*] hacer una infusión de
(B) VI **to let sth ~** dejar algo en infusión

infusion [ɪn'fjuːʒən] N [*of new talent, money, capital*] inyección *f*; (*Culin*) (= *tea etc*) infusión *f*

ingenious [ɪn'dʒiːnɪəs] ADJ (*gen*) ingenioso; [*idea, scheme*] ingenioso, genial

ingeniously [ɪn'dʒiːnɪəslɪ] ADV ingeniosamente, con inventiva

ingénue [ˌɛːnʒeɪ'njuː] N ingenua *f*

ingenuity [ˌɪndʒɪ'njuːɪtɪ] N [*of person*] ingenio *m*, inventiva *f*; [*of idea, scheme*] lo ingenioso

ingenuous [ɪn'dʒenjʊəs] ADJ (= *naive*) ingenuo; (= *candid*) cándido

ingenuously [ɪn'dʒenjʊəslɪ] ADV (= *naively*) ingenuamente; (= *candidly*) cándidamente

ingenuousness [ɪn'dʒenjʊəsnɪs] N (= *naivety*) ingenuidad *f*; (= *candidness*) candidez *f*

ingest [ɪn'dʒest] VT ingerir

ingestion [ɪn'dʒestʃən] N ingestión *f*

inglenook ['ɪŋglnʊk] N rincón *m* de la chimenea

inglorious [ɪn'glɔːrɪəs] ADJ ignominioso, vergonzoso

in-going ['ɪngəʊɪŋ] ADJ entrante

ingot ['ɪŋgət] (A) N lingote *m*
(B) CPD ► **ingot steel** N acero *m* en lingotes

ingrained ['ɪn'greɪnd] ADJ [1] [*dirt, blood, stain*] incrustado
[2] (*fig*) (= *deep-seated*) [*attitude, ideas, habit, tradition*] arraigado; **to be deeply ~ in sb** estar profundamente arraigado en algn

ingrate ['ɪngreɪt] N (*frm or iro*) ingrato/a *m/f*

ingratiate [ɪn'greɪʃɪeɪt] VT **to ~ o.s. with sb** congraciarse con algn

ingratiating [ɪn'greɪʃɪeɪtɪŋ] ADJ [*smile, speech*] obsequioso; [*person*] halagador, congraciador, zalamero

ingratitude [ɪn'grætɪtjuːd] N ingratitud *f*

ingredient [ɪn'griːdɪənt] N (*Culin*) ingrediente *m*; [*of beauty product, medicine*] componente *m*; (*fig*) elemento *m*, factor *m*; **it is used as an ~ in sunscreen** se utiliza como componente de cremas solares con filtro; **this is the key ~ of her success** éste es el factor clave de su éxito

ingress ['ɪngres] N (*frm*) acceso *m*

in-group ['ɪnˌgruːp] N grupo *m* exclusivista *or* excluyente, camarilla *f*

ingrowing ['ɪnˌgrəʊɪŋ], **ingrown** (*US*) ['ɪnˌgrəʊn] ADJ **~ (toe)nail** uña *f* encarnada

inguinal ['ɪŋgwɪnl] ADJ (*Tech*) inguinal

inhabit [ɪn'hæbɪt] VT [+ *house*] ocupar; [+ *town, country*] vivir en, habitar (*frm*); [*animal*] habitar; **a place ~ed by ghosts** un lugar habitado por fantasmas

inhabitable [ɪn'hæbɪtəbl] ADJ (*gen*) habitable

inhabitant [ɪn'hæbɪtənt] N habitante *mf*

inhabited [ɪn'hæbɪtɪd] ADJ habitado

inhalant [ɪn'heɪlənt] N inhalante *m*

inhalation [ˌɪnhə'leɪʃən] N aspiración *f*; (*Med*) inhalación *f*

inhalator ['ɪnhəleɪtə^r] N inhalador *m*

inhale [ɪn'heɪl] (A) VT (*Med*) [+ *gas*] inhalar, aspirar; [+ *smoke, vomit*] tragar
(B) VI [*smoker*] tragar el humo; (*Med*) aspirar

inhaler [ɪn'heɪlə^r] N inhalador *m*

inharmonious [ˌɪnhɑː'məʊnɪəs] ADJ [*sounds*] inarmónico, disonante; (*fig*) discorde, falto de armonía

inhere [ɪn'hɪə^r] VI (*frm*) ser inherente (**in** a)

inherent [ɪn'hɪərənt] ADJ inherente, intrínseco; **to be ~ in** *or* **to sth** ser inherente a algo; **with all the ~ difficulties** con todas las dificultades que conlleva

inherently [ɪn'hɪərəntlɪ] ADV intrínsecamente

inherit [ɪn'herɪt] VT (*gen*) heredar (**from** de); **we ~ed these problems from the last government** estos problemas son un legado del gobierno anterior

inheritance [ɪn'herɪtəns] (A) N herencia *f*; (*fig*) patrimonio *m*; **she received a small ~ from her aunt** su tía le dejó una pequeña herencia
(B) CPD ► **inheritance law** N ley *f* sucesoria ► **inheritance tax** N impuesto *m* sobre sucesiones

inheritor [ɪn'herɪtə^r] N heredero/a *m/f*

inhibit [ɪn'hɪbɪt] VT (= *check*) inhibir, reprimir; (= *prevent*) impedir; **to ~ sb from doing sth** impedir a algn hacer algo; **don't let my presence ~ the discussion** no quiero que mi presencia detenga la discusión; **we cannot ~ progress** no podemos reprimir el progreso

inhibited [ɪn'hɪbɪtɪd] ADJ [*person*] cohibido, inhibido

inhibition [ˌɪnhɪ'bɪʃən] N inhibición *f*; **to have/have no ~s** tener/no tener inhibiciones; **to lose one's ~s** perder las inhibiciones

inhibitory [ɪn'hɪbɪtərɪ] ADJ inhibitorio

inhospitable [ˌɪnhɒs'pɪtəbl] ADJ [*person*] inhospitalario, poco hospitalario; [*reception, behaviour*] poco hospitalario; [*place, country, terrain, climate*] inhóspito

inhospitably [ˌɪnhɒs'pɪtəblɪ] ADV de modo poco hospitalario

inhospitality ['ɪnˌhɒspɪ'tælɪtɪ] N falta *f* de hospitalidad, inhospitalidad *f*

in-house ['ɪn'haʊs] (A) ADV dentro de la empresa
(B) ADJ [*staff*] interno
(C) CPD ► **in-house training** N formación *f* en la empresa

➤ LANGUAGE IN USE: **information A** 20.2, 21.1, 21.2

inhuman [ɪn'hjuːmən] ADJ inhumano

inhumane [ˌɪnhjʊ(ː)'meɪn] ADJ [*behaviour, treatment*] inhumano; [*person*] cruel

inhumanity [ˌɪnhjuː'mænɪtɪ] N inhumanidad *f*, crueldad *f*; **man's ~ to man** la crueldad del hombre para con sus semejantes

inhumation [ˌɪnhjuː'meɪʃən] N inhumación *f*

inimical [ɪ'nɪmɪkəl] ADJ [*attitude*] hostil; [*influence*] adverso; **to be ~ to sth** ser adverso a algo

inimitable [ɪ'nɪmɪtəbl] ADJ inimitable

inimitably [ɪ'nɪmɪtəblɪ] ADV inimitablemente

iniquitous [ɪ'nɪkwɪtəs] ADJ inicuo, injusto

iniquitously [ɪ'nɪkwɪtəslɪ] ADV inicuamente, injustamente

iniquity [ɪ'nɪkwɪtɪ] N iniquidad *f*, injusticia *f*; **iniquities** [*of system*] injusticias *fpl*, iniquidades *fpl*; [*of person*] excesos *mpl*, desmanes *mpl*

initial [ɪ'nɪʃəl] Ⓐ ADJ [*shock, success, cost, report*] inicial; **my ~ reaction was to ...** mi primera reacción fue ...; **in the ~ stages** al principio, en la etapa inicial, en la primera etapa
Ⓑ N (= *letter*) inicial *f*; **to sign sth with one's ~s** firmar algo con las iniciales
Ⓒ VT [+ *letter, document*] firmar con las iniciales
Ⓓ CPD ► **initial expenses** NPL gastos *mpl* iniciales ► **initial letter** N inicial *f*

initialize [ɪ'nɪʃəlaɪz] VT (*Comput*) inicializar

initially [ɪ'nɪʃəlɪ] ADV al principio, en un principio, inicialmente (*frm*)

initiate Ⓐ VT [ɪ'nɪʃɪeɪt] 1 (= *begin*) iniciar, dar comienzo a; [+ *talks*] entablar; [+ *reform*] poner en marcha; [+ *fashion*] introducir; **to ~ proceedings against sb** (*Jur*) entablar una demanda contra algn
2 **to ~ sb into a society** admitir a algn en una asociación; **to ~ sb into a secret** iniciar a algn en un secreto
Ⓑ [ɪ'nɪʃɪɪt] N iniciado/a *m/f*

initiation [ɪˌnɪʃɪ'eɪʃən] Ⓐ N (= *beginning*) inicio *m*, comienzo *m*; (= *admission*) (*into society, organization*) admisión *f* (**into** en)
Ⓑ CPD ► **initiation ceremony, initiation rite** N ceremonia *f* de iniciación

initiative [ɪ'nɪʃətɪv] N iniciativa *f*; **to use one's ~** obrar por propia iniciativa; **on one's own ~** por iniciativa propia, motu propio; **to take the ~** tomar la iniciativa

initiator [ɪ'nɪʃɪeɪtəʳ] N iniciador(a) *m/f*

inject [ɪn'dʒekt] VT 1 (*Med*) [+ *medicine*] inyectar (**into** en); [+ *person*] poner una inyección a; **to ~ sb with sth** inyectar algo a algn; **he ~ed her with poison** le inyectó veneno
2 (*fig*) **to ~ into** [+ *enthusiasm*] infundir a; [+ *money, capital*] inyectar en; **they've ~ed new life into the club** han infundido un espíritu nuevo al club; **she did her best to ~ some enthusiasm into her voice** hizo lo que pudo para que su voz sonara entusiasta

injection [ɪn'dʒekʃən] N (*gen, Med*) inyección *f*; **to give sb an ~** poner *or* dar una inyección a algn; **to have an ~** ponerse una inyección; **will I have to have an ~?** ¿me tendrán que poner *or* dar una inyección?

injudicious [ˌɪndʒʊ'dɪʃəs] ADJ imprudente, indiscreto

injudiciously [ˌɪndʒʊ'dɪʃəslɪ] ADV imprudentemente, indiscretamente

injunction [ɪn'dʒʌŋkʃən] N (*Jur*) mandamiento *m* judicial; **to seek an ~ (against sth/sb) (to do sth)** obtener un mandamiento judicial (contra algo/algn) (para hacer algo)

injure ['ɪndʒəʳ] VT 1 (*physically*) herir; (*esp Sport*) lesionar; **he was ~d in the accident** resultó herido en el accidente; **two players were ~d** dos jugadores resultaron lesionados; **he was badly/slightly ~d** resultó gravemente/levemente herido; **he ~d his arm** resultó herido en el brazo; (*Sport*) se lesionó el brazo; **to ~ o.s.** (*in an accident*) resultar herido; (*deliberately*) causarse heridas, autolesionarse; (*in a match, race etc*) lesionarse
2 (*fig*) [+ *feelings, pride*] herir; [+ *reputation*] dañar; [+ *trade, chances*] perjudicar

injured ['ɪndʒəd] Ⓐ ADJ 1 (*physically*) [*person, animal, limb*] herido, lesionado; [*player*] lesionado
2 (*fig*) [*tone, look*] dolido; [*feelings*] herido; **to give sb an ~ look** mirar a algn con expresión dolida; **to say sth in an ~ tone** decir algo con tono dolido; **~ pride** orgullo *m* herido
3 (*Jur*) **the ~ party** la parte perjudicada
Ⓑ NPL **there were four ~** hubo cuatro heridos; **the ~** los heridos

injurious [ɪn'dʒʊərɪəs] ADJ (*frm*) perjudicial (**to** para); **~ to health** perjudicial para la salud

injury ['ɪndʒərɪ] Ⓐ N 1 (*physical*) herida *f*; (*esp Sport*) lesión *f*; **he sustained minor injuries to the hands and face** sufrió heridas leves en las manos y la cara; **he was taken to hospital with serious injuries** lo llevaron al hospital herido de gravedad; **to do o.s. an ~*** hacerse daño; **to do sb an ~** hacer daño a algn
2 (*fig*) (*to reputation*) daño *m*, perjuicio *m*; (*to feelings*) agravio *m*
Ⓑ CPD ► **injury time** N (*Brit Sport*) tiempo *m* de descuento; *see also* **insult**

injustice [ɪn'dʒʌstɪs] N injusticia *f*; **you do me an ~** está siendo injusto conmigo

ink [ɪŋk] Ⓐ N tinta *f*; (= *printing ink*) tinta *f* de imprenta; **in ~** con tinta
Ⓑ VT (*Typ*) entintar
Ⓒ CPD ► **ink blot** N borrón *m* de tinta

► **ink in** VT + ADV [+ *name*] (= *write*) escribir con tinta; (*on top of pencil*) repasar a tinta; [+ *line*] trazar con tinta; [+ *blank area*] entintar

► **ink out** VT + ADV tachar con tinta

► **ink over** VT + ADV repasar con tinta

ink-jet printer ['ɪŋkdʒet'prɪntəʳ] N impresora *f* de chorro de tinta

inkling ['ɪŋklɪŋ] N (= *vague idea*) idea *f*; **I had no ~ that ...** no tenía ni la menor idea de que ...; **we had some ~ of it** teníamos una vaga idea; **there was no ~ of the disaster to come** nadie podía imaginarse el desastre que iba a sobrevenir; **to give sb an ~ that ...** insinuar a algn que ...

inkpad ['ɪŋkpæd] N almohadilla *f*, tampón *m* (de entintar)

inkpot ['ɪŋkpɒt] N tintero *m*

inkstain ['ɪŋksteɪn] N mancha *f* de tinta

inkstand ['ɪŋkstænd] N escribanía *f*

inkwell ['ɪŋkwel] N tintero *m*

inky ['ɪŋkɪ] ADJ (*lit*) [*page, fingers*] manchado de tinta; (*fig*) [*darkness*] profundo

INLA ['ɪnlə] N ABBR (*Brit*) = **Irish National Liberation Army**

inlaid ['ɪn'leɪd] Ⓐ ADJ (*with wood, tiles*) taraceado (**with** de); (*with jewels*) incrustado (**with** de)
Ⓑ CPD [*table, box*] de marquetería; [*floor*] con incrustaciones ► **inlaid work** N taracea *f*

inland ['ɪnlənd] Ⓐ ADJ [*town*] del interior; [*trade*] interior
Ⓑ ADV (*in*) tierra adentro; (*towards*) hacia el interior
Ⓒ CPD ► **Inland Revenue** N (*Brit*) ≈ Hacienda *f* ► **inland sea** N mar *m* interior ► **inland waterways** NPL canales *mpl* y ríos *mpl*

in-laws* ['ɪnˌlɔːz] NPL (= *partner's family*) parientes *mpl* políticos; (= *partner's parents*) suegros *mpl*

inlay Ⓐ ['ɪnleɪ] N [*of wood, tiles*] taracea *f*; [*of jewels*] incrustación *f*
Ⓑ [ɪn'leɪ] VT (*pt, pp* **inlaid**) (*with wood*) taracear, embutir; (*with jewels*) incrustar; **a sword inlaid with jewels** una espada incrustada de joyas

inlet ['ɪnlet] Ⓐ N 1 (*Geog*) ensenada *f*, entrante *m*
2 (*Tech*) admisión *f*, entrada *f*
Ⓑ CPD ► **inlet pipe** N tubo *m* de entrada ► **inlet valve** N válvula *f* de admisión *or* entrada

inmate ['ɪnmeɪt] N [*of hospital*] enfermo/a *m/f*; [*of prison*] preso/a *m/f*, presidiario/a *m/f*; [*of asylum*] internado/a *m/f*

inmost ['ɪnməʊst] ADJ [*place, chamber*] más recóndito; [*thoughts, feelings*] más íntimo, más secreto

inn [ɪn] Ⓐ N (= *pub*) taberna *f*; (= *hotel*) hostería *f*; (††) (= *tavern*) posada *f*, mesón *m*
Ⓑ CPD ► **inn sign** N letrero *m* de mesón ► **the Inns of Court** NPL (*Brit Jur*) el Colegio de Abogados (*en Londres*)

innards* ['ɪnədz] NPL tripas* *fpl*

innate [ɪ'neɪt] ADJ innato

innately [ɪ'neɪtlɪ] ADV de manera innata; **it is not ~ evil** no es malo de por sí

inner ['ɪnəʳ] Ⓐ ADJ 1 [*room, wall, door, part*] interior; **~ circle** círculo *m* de personas más allegadas; **the White House's ~ circle** el círculo de personas más allegadas al presidente; **the ~ city** *barrios céntricos pobres de la ciudad que presentan problemas sociales*; **the ~ sanctum** el sanctasanctórum; *see also* **inner-city**
2 [*thoughts, emotions*] íntimo; [*voice, calm, conflict*] interior; **the ~ life** la vida interior; **the ~ man** (= *soul*) el alma; (*hum*) (= *stomach*) el estómago; **one's ~ self** el fuero interno de uno
Ⓑ N (*Archery*) blanco *m*
Ⓒ CPD ► **inner ear** N oído *m* interno ► **Inner London** N el centro de Londres ► **Inner Mongolia** N Mongolia *f* Interior ► **inner sole** N (*in shoe*) plantilla *f* ► **inner spring mattress** N (*US*) colchón *m* de muelles interiores ► **inner tube** N (*in tyre*) cámara *f*, llanta *f* (*LAm*)

inner-city [ˌɪnə'sɪtɪ] ADJ [*schools, problems*] de las zonas céntricas pobres, de los barrios céntricos pobres; **an ~ area** un área pobre del centro

innermost ['ɪnəməʊst] ADJ [*thoughts, feelings*] más íntimo, más secreto; [*place, chamber*] más recóndito

inning ['ɪnɪŋ] N (*US Baseball*) inning *m*, entrada *f*; **innings** (*pl inv*) (*Cricket*) turno *m*, entrada *f*; (*fig*) turno *m*, oportunidad *f*; ✦**IDIOM he's had a good ~s** ha disfrutado de una larga vida, ha vivido sus buenos años

innit‡ ['ɪnɪt] EXCL (*Brit*) **~?** ¿no?

innkeeper ['ɪnkiːpəʳ] N [*of pub*] tabernero/a *m/f*; (††) posadero/a *m/f*, mesonero/a *m/f*

innocence ['ɪnəsns] N inocencia *f*; **in all ~** con toda inocencia, de la forma más inocente

Innocent ['ɪnəsnt] N (= *pope*) Inocencio

innocent ['ɪnəsnt] Ⓐ ADJ 1 (= *not guilty*) inocente; **to find sb ~** declarar inocente a algn; **to be ~ of a crime** ser inocente de un crimen; **he was found ~ of murder** lo declararon inocente de asesinato
2 (= *innocuous*) [*question, remark*] inocente, sin malicia; [*fun*] sin malicia; [*mistake*] inocente

[3] (= *naive*) inocente, ingenuo; **they seemed so young and ~** parecían tan jóvenes e inocentes *or* ingenuos; **she stood facing him with that ~ air she had** estaba frente a él, con ese aire inocente que tenía; *see also* **bystander**

[4] (*liter*) (= *devoid*) **to be ~ of sth**: **he was ~ of any desire to harm her** no tenía ningún deseo de hacerle daño; **a face ~ of any trace of make-up** una cara sin ningún rastro de maquillaje

Ⓑ N inocente *mf*; **he's an ~ when it comes to women** cuando se trata de mujeres es un inocente *or* inocentón; **I'm not a total ~** no soy tan inocente; **the Massacre of the Holy Innocents** la masacre de los Santos Inocentes

innocently [ˈɪnəsntlɪ] ADV [*ask, smile*] inocentemente, con inocencia; **she looked at her father ~** dirigió a su padre una mirada llena de inocencia; **the joke had begun ~ enough** la broma había empezado de una forma muy inocente

innocuous [ɪˈnɒkjʊəs] ADJ [*substance*] inocuo; [*person, remark*] inofensivo

innovate [ˈɪnəʊveɪt] VI innovar

innovation [ˌɪnəʊˈveɪʃən] N (= *act*) innovación *f*; (= *thing*) innovación *f*, novedad *f*

innovative [ˈɪnəʊˌveɪtɪv] ADJ innovador

innovator [ˈɪnəʊveɪtəʳ] N innovador(a) *m/f*

innovatory [ˈɪnəʊˌveɪtərɪ] ADJ (*Brit*) innovador

innuendo [ˌɪnjʊˈendəʊ] N (*pl* **innuendo(e)s**) indirecta *f*, insinuación *f*; **his comments were full of sexual ~** sus comentarios estaban llenos de alusiones *or* connotaciones sexuales

Innuit [ˈɪnjuːɪt] = **Inuit**

innumerable [ɪˈnjuːmərəbl] ADJ innumerable; **she drank ~ cups of tea** se bebió innumerables tazas de té; **there are ~ reasons** hay infinidad de razones; **he helped us in ~ ways** nos ayudó de muy diversas maneras

innumeracy [ɪˈnjuːmərəsɪ] N *incompetencia en matemáticas or en el cálculo*

innumerate [ɪˈnjuːmərɪt] ADJ incompetente en el cálculo aritmético

inoculate [ɪˈnɒkjʊleɪt] VT [+ *person, animal*] vacunar; **to ~ sb against sth** vacunar a algn contra algo; **to ~ sb with sth** inocular algo a algn

inoculation [ɪˌnɒkjʊˈleɪʃən] N inoculación *f*

inoffensive [ˌɪnəˈfensɪv] ADJ inofensivo

inoperable [ɪnˈɒpərəbl] ADJ inoperable

inoperative [ɪnˈɒpərətɪv] ADJ inoperante

inopportune [ɪnˈɒpətjuːn] ADJ inoportuno

inopportunely [ɪnˈɒpətjuːnlɪ] ADV inoportunamente, a destiempo

inordinate [ɪˈnɔːdɪnɪt] ADJ (= *excessive*) excesivo; (= *unrestrained*) desmesurado, desmedido; **he spent an ~ amount of time/money on it** empleó en ello una cantidad excesiva de tiempo/dinero

inordinately [ɪˈnɔːdɪnɪtlɪ] ADV desmesuradamente, excesivamente

inorganic [ˌɪnɔːˈgænɪk] Ⓐ ADJ (*Chem*) inorgánico

Ⓑ CPD ► **inorganic chemistry** N química *f* inorgánica

inpatient [ˈɪnˌpeɪʃənt] N paciente *mf* hospitalizado/a

input [ˈɪnpʊt] Ⓐ N (*Elec*) entrada *f*; (*Comput*) entrada *f*, input *m*; (= *contribution*) contribución *f*, aportación *f*, aporte *m* (*LAm*); (= *effort, time*) inversión *f*; (*Fin*) dinero *m* invertido, inversión *f*; **we want more ~ from the local community** queremos mayor aportación por parte de la comunidad local

Ⓑ VT (*Comput*) [+ *data*] entrar

input-output device [ˌɪnpʊtˈaʊtpʊtdɪˈvaɪs] N dispositivo *m* de entrada y salida

inquest [ˈɪnkwest] N [1] (*Jur*) investigación *f*, pesquisa *f* judicial; (*by coroner*) *investigación llevada a cabo para averiguar las causas de una muerte violente o sospechosa*

[2] (*fig*) **they held an ~ into** *or* **on their election defeat** realizaron un análisis en profundidad de su derrota electoral; **he likes to hold an ~ on every game** le gusta discutir cada partido hasta la saciedad

inquietude [ɪnˈkwaɪətjuːd] N (*frm*) inquietud *f*

inquire [ɪnˈkwaɪəʳ] Ⓐ VT preguntar; **to ~ sth of sb** preguntar algo a algn; **to ~ when/whether ...** preguntar cuándo/si ...; **he ~d the price** preguntó cuánto costaba

Ⓑ VI preguntar; **to ~ about sth** preguntar por algo, informarse de algo; **I am inquiring about your advertisement in today's paper** (*by phone*) llamo para preguntar acerca de su anuncio en el periódico de hoy; **to ~ after** *or* **for** *or* **about sb** preguntar por algn; **she ~d after your health** preguntó por tu salud, preguntó qué tal andabas de salud; **to ~ into sth** investigar *or* indagar algo; **I shouldn't ~ too closely if I were you** yo que tú no haría demasiadas preguntas; **"inquire within"** "infórmese en el interior"; **"inquire at No. 14"** "razón: en el nº 14"

inquirer [ɪnˈkwaɪərəʳ] N (= *asker*) el/la que pregunta; (= *researcher*) investigador(a) *m/f* (**into** de)

inquiring [ɪnˈkwaɪərɪŋ] ADJ [*mind*] inquieto, inquisitivo; [*look*] inquisitivo; **she looked at me with ~ eyes** me miró con expresión inquisitiva *or* de interrogante

inquiringly [ɪnˈkwaɪərɪŋlɪ] ADV [*look etc*] inquisitivamente

inquiry [ɪnˈkwaɪərɪ] Ⓐ N [1] (= *question*) interrogante *m or f*, pregunta *f*; **"Inquiries"** "Información *f*"; **"all inquiries to the secretary"** "para cualquier información diríjanse al secretario"; **on ~** al preguntar; **to make inquiries (about sth)** pedir información *or* informarse (sobre algo); **I'll make some inquiries about flights** me informaré de los vuelos; **I went to make inquiries of his teacher** fui a preguntarle a su profesor; **a look of ~** una mirada inquisitiva

[2] (= *investigation*) investigación *f*, pesquisa *f*; (= *commission*) comisión *f* investigadora, comisión *f* de investigación; **there will have to be an ~** tendrá que llevarse a cabo una investigación; **to hold an ~ into sth** llevar a cabo una investigación sobre algo, investigar algo; **they set up an ~ into the disaster** nombraron a una comisión para investigar el desastre; **the police are making inquiries** la policía está investigando el caso; **the ~ found that ...** la investigación concluyó que ...

[3] (*Comput*) interrogación *f*

Ⓑ CPD ► **inquiry agent**† N investigador(a) *m/f* privado/a ► **inquiry desk** N mesa *f* de información ► **inquiry office** N oficina *f* de información

inquisition [ˌɪnkwɪˈzɪʃən] N inquisición *f*, investigación *f*; **the Spanish Inquisition** la Inquisición, el Santo Oficio

inquisitive [ɪnˈkwɪzɪtɪv] ADJ (= *interested*) curioso; (= *prying*) entrometido, curioso; [*mind*] inquisitivo

inquisitively [ɪnˈkwɪzɪtɪvlɪ] ADV con curiosidad

inquisitiveness [ɪnˈkwɪzɪtɪvnɪs] N curiosidad *f*

inquisitor [ɪnˈkwɪzɪtəʳ] N inquisidor *m*

inquisitorial [ɪnˌkwɪzɪˈtɔːrɪəl] ADJ inquisitorial; **an ~ system of justice** un sistema judicial inquisitorial

inroads [ˈɪnrəʊdz] NPL **the ~ of mass tourism** los efectos del turismo de masas; **she had to make ~ into her savings** tuvo que recurrir a sus ahorros, tuvo que echar mano de sus ahorros*; **they made significant ~ into Chinese territory** realizaron grandes avances dentro del territorio chino; **they are making ~ into the European market** se están adentrando en el mercado europeo; **I can see you've made ~ into that cake** (*hum*) ya veo que le has metido mano a la tarta*; **to make ~ into sb's time** robar el tiempo a algn

inrush [ˈɪnrʌʃ] N [*of mud, water*] tromba *f*; [*of tourists*] afluencia *f*; [*of foreign imports*] avalancha *f*

INS N ABBR (*US*) = **Immigration and Naturalization Service**

ins. ABBR [1] = **insurance**

[2] = **inches**

insalubrious [ˌɪnsəˈluːbrɪəs] ADJ (*frm*) [*conditions*] insalubre, malsano; [*part of town*] deprimido

insane [ɪnˈseɪn] Ⓐ ADJ [1] (= *mad*) loco; **he is quite ~** está completamente loco, es un demente; **the jury decided King was ~ at the time** el jurado decidió que King estaba loco *or* no estaba en su sano juicio en aquel momento; **she had killed him while temporarily ~** lo había matado mientras sufría demencia temporal; **to drive sb ~** enloquecer *or* volver loco a algn; **to go ~** volverse loco; **~ jealousy** celos *mpl* enfermizos

[2] (*) (*fig*) (= *crazy*) [*suggestion, idea*] descabellado; [*act*] insensato; **if I told them that, they'd think I was ~** si les dijese eso, pensarían que estoy completamente loca *or* que no estoy en mi sano juicio; **this idea is totally ~** esta idea es una verdadera locura *or* es totalmente descabellada; **to drive sb ~** sacar a algn de quicio; **it would be ~ to let him go by himself** sería una locura dejarle ir solo

Ⓑ NPL **the ~** los enfermos mentales; *see also* **criminally**

Ⓒ CPD ► **insane asylum** N (*US*) manicomio *m*, psiquiátrico *m*

insanely [ɪnˈseɪnlɪ] ADV **to laugh ~** reírse como un loco; **to be ~ jealous** (*by nature*) ser terriblemente celoso; (*at particular moment*) estar loco de celos

insanitary [ɪnˈsænɪtərɪ] ADJ insalubre, malsano

insanity [ɪnˈsænɪtɪ] N [1] (*Med*) demencia *f*; **to drive sb to ~** volver loco a algn

[2] (= *foolishness*) locura *f*, insensatez *f*; **what he did was sheer ~** lo que hizo fue una verdadera locura *or* insensatez

insatiable [ɪnˈseɪʃəbl] ADJ insaciable

insatiably [ɪnˈseɪʃəblɪ] ADV [*eat*] con un hambre insaciable; [*kiss*] con una pasión insaciable; **to be ~ hungry/curious/greedy** tener un hambre/una curiosidad/una avaricia insaciable

inscribe [ɪnˈskraɪb] VT (= *engrave*) grabar; (= *write*) inscribir; (= *dedicate*) [+ *book*] dedicar; **to ~ sth on sth** grabar algo en algo; **a set of pens ~d with his initials** un juego de plumas con sus iniciales grabadas

inscription [ɪnˈskrɪpʃən] N (*on stone*) inscripción *f*; (*in book*) dedicatoria *f*

inscrutability [ɪnˌskruːtəˈbɪlɪtɪ] N inescrutabilidad *f*

inscrutable [ɪnˈskruːtəbl] ADJ inescrutable

inseam [ˈɪnsiːm] ADJ (*US*) **~ measurement** medida *f* de pernera

➤ LANGUAGE IN USE: **inquire** B 20.2, 21.1 **inquiry** A1 20.2

insect ['ɪnsekt] Ⓐ N insecto *m*; (*fig*) bicho *m* Ⓑ CPD ► **insect bite** N picadura *f* de insecto ► **insect powder** N insecticida *m* en polvo ► **insect repellent** N repelente *m* contra insectos ► **insect spray** N insecticida *m* en aerosol

insecticide [ɪn'sektɪsaɪd] N insecticida *m*

insectivorous [ˌɪnsek'tɪvərəs] ADJ insectívoro

insecure [ˌɪnsɪ'kjʊəʳ] ADJ 1 (= *not confident*) inseguro; **to feel ~** sentirse inseguro; **he feels ~ about their relationship** se siente inseguro acerca de su relación; **she feels ~ about sharing her flat with somebody else** le preocupa la idea de compartir el piso con otra persona; **she is ~ about her performance as a mother** duda de su habilidad como madre
2 (= *not secure*) [*job, position*] poco seguro; **the hospital faces an ~ future** el hospital se enfrenta a un futuro incierto *or* poco seguro; **their lives are ~** hay mucha inseguridad en sus vidas
3 (= *not safe*) [*country, area, building*] poco seguro; [*situation*] inestable
4 (= *not firm*) [*door, ladder, load*] poco seguro

insecurely [ˌɪnsɪ'kjʊəlɪ] ADV de manera poco segura

insecurity [ˌɪnsɪ'kjʊərɪtɪ] N inseguridad *f*

inseminate [ɪn'semɪneɪt] VT inseminar

insemination [ɪnˌsemɪ'neɪʃən] N inseminación *f*

insensate [ɪn'senseɪt] ADJ 1 (= *lacking sensation*) insensato
2 (= *pointless*) [*violence, aggression*] absurdo

insensibility [ɪnˌsensə'bɪlɪtɪ] N 1 insensibilidad *f* (**to** a)
2 (= *unconsciousness*) inconsciencia *f*

insensible [ɪn'sensəbl] ADJ (*frm*) 1 (= *unconscious*) inconsciente, sin conocimiento; **he drank himself ~** bebió hasta perder el conocimiento; **the blow knocked him ~** el golpe le hizo perder el conocimiento
2 (= *insensitive*) **to be ~ to sth** ser insensible a algo; **~ to heat/cold** insensible al calor/al frío; **he seemed ~ to shame** no parecía saber lo que es tener vergüenza
3 (= *unaware*) **to be ~ of sth** no ser consciente de algo, no darse cuenta de algo; **she seemed wholly ~ of the honour done to her** parecía que no era consciente en absoluto del honor que se le hacía, parecía no darse cuenta en absoluto del honor que se le hacía; **to be ~ of danger** no ser consciente del peligro

insensibly [ɪn'sensɪblɪ] ADV (*frm*) [*change, improve, rise*] imperceptiblemente, insensiblemente

insensitive [ɪn'sensɪtɪv] ADJ [*person*] insensible; [*behaviour, remark*] falto de sensibilidad; **to be ~** [*person*] no tener sensibilidad; **to be ~ to sth** ser insensible a algo; **to be ~ to heat/cold/pain** ser insensible al calor/frío/dolor; **she is ~ to other people's feelings** es insensible a los sentimientos de los demás; **he had become ~ to seeing people suffer** se había vuelto insensible al sufrimiento de los demás

insensitively [ɪn'sensɪtɪvlɪ] ADV con falta de sensibilidad

insensitivity [ɪnˌsensɪ'tɪvɪtɪ] N (*physical*) insensibilidad *f*; (*emotional*) falta *f* de sensibilidad; **~ to sth** [+ *cold, pain*] insensibilidad *f* a algo; [+ *people's feelings, problems*] falta *f* de sensibilidad ante algo

inseparable [ɪn'sepərəbl] ADJ inseparable; **the two brothers were ~** los dos hermanos eran inseparables; **the two questions are ~** los dos temas son inseparables; **pain is ~ from love** el dolor es inseparable del amor

inseparably [ɪn'sepərəblɪ] ADV inseparablemente, indisolublemente

insert Ⓐ ['ɪnsɜːt] N (*in book, magazine*) encarte *m*; (*Sew*) entredós *m*
Ⓑ [ɪn'sɜːt] VT (= *put in*) [+ *coin, finger, needle*] introducir, meter; (= *add*) [+ *word, paragraph*] intercalar, insertar; [+ *advertisement*] insertar, poner; (*Comput*) insertar

insertion [ɪn'sɜːʃən] N (*gen*) inserción *f*, introducción *f*; [*of advertisement*] publicación *f*, inserción *f*; (= *advertisement*) anuncio *m*

in-service ['ɪn'sɜːvɪs] ADJ **~ course/training** cursillo *m*/formación *f* en la empresa

inset ['ɪnset] Ⓐ N (*Typ*) recuadro *m*, *grabado or mapa o dibujo etc que se imprime en un ángulo de otro mayor*; (= *page(s)*) encarte *m*
Ⓑ VT (*pt, pp* **inset**) (*Typ*) [+ *diagram, map*] insertar, imprimir como recuadro; [+ *page(s)*] imprimir como encarte; (= *indent*) sangrar

inshore ['ɪn'ʃɔːʳ] Ⓐ ADV [*be, fish*] cerca de la costa; [*sail, blow*] hacia la costa
Ⓑ ADJ costero
Ⓒ CPD ► **inshore fishing** N pesca *f* de bajura

inside ['ɪn'saɪd] Ⓐ N 1 (= *inner part*) interior *m*, parte *f* de dentro; **he wiped the ~ of the glass** limpió el interior *or* la parte de dentro del vaso; **the ~ of the foot** la parte de dentro del pie; **I have a pain in my ~*** me duele el estómago; **from the ~**: **the doors were locked from the ~** las puertas estaban cerradas (con llave) por dentro; **to know sth from the ~** saber algo por experiencia propia; **crisp on the outside and soft on the ~** crujiente por fuera y tierno por dentro; **~ out**: **your jumper's ~ out** llevas el jersey al *or* del revés; **she turned the sock ~ out** le dio la vuelta al calcetín, volvió el calcetín del revés; **they turned the whole place ~ out** lo revolvieron todo, lo registraron todo de arriba abajo; **to know a subject ~ out** conocer un tema de cabo a rabo; **he knows the district ~ out** se conoce el distrito como la palma de la mano
2 (= *lining*) parte *f* de dentro; **the ~ of the jacket is sheepskin** la parte de dentro de la chaqueta es de piel de borrego
3 [*of road*] (*Brit*) lado *m* izquierdo; (*other countries*) lado *m* derecho; **to overtake** *or* **pass (sb) on the ~** (*Brit*) adelantar (a algn) por la izquierda; (*other countries*) adelantar (a algn) por la derecha; **walk on the ~ of the pavement** camina por la parte de dentro de la acera
4 **insides** [*of person, animal, fruit*] tripas *fpl*
Ⓑ ADV 1 (= *in*) dentro, adentro (*LAm*); **once ~, he was trapped** una vez dentro estaba atrapado; **it gives me a lovely warm feeling ~** me produce una sensación muy agradable por dentro; **deep ~ he is worried** en el fondo está preocupado
2 (= *towards the inside*) adentro, dentro; **he opened the car door and shoved her ~** abrió la puerta del coche y la empujó adentro *or* dentro
3 (= *indoors*) dentro, adentro (*LAm*); **wait for me ~** espérame dentro *or* (*LAm*) adentro; **please step ~** pase (usted); **to come/go ~** entrar
4 (*) (= *in prison*) **to be ~** estar en chirona*, estar a la sombra*
Ⓒ PREP (*also* **~ of**) (*esp US*) 1 (*of place*) dentro de, en el interior de (*frm*); **~ the envelope** dentro del sobre, en el interior del sobre (*frm*); **he went ~ the house** entró en la casa; **75% of chief executives come from ~ the company** un 75% de los altos cargos directivos proceden de la propia empresa
2 (*of time*) en menos de; **~ four hours** en menos de cuatro horas; **her time was five seconds ~ the record** superó el récord por cinco segundos
Ⓓ ADJ 1 (= *internal*) interior; **the ~ pages of a newspaper** las páginas interiores de un periódico
2 (= *confidential, from inside*) **an ~ job*** *un crimen cometido en una empresa, organización, etc por alguien que pertenece a la misma*; **it must be an ~ job*** tiene que haber sido alguien de dentro; **the ~ story** la historia (hasta ahora) secreta; **the KGB: the ~ story** la KGB: la historia secreta
Ⓔ CPD ► **inside forward** N delantero/a *m/f* interior, interior *mf* ► **inside information** N información *f* confidencial ► **the inside lane** N (*Aut*) (*Brit*) el carril de la izquierda; (*most countries*) el carril de la derecha; (*Athletics*) la calle interior ► **inside left** N interior *mf* izquierdo/a ► **inside leg (measurement)** N medida *f* de la entrepierna ► **inside pocket** N bolsillo *m* interior ► **inside right** N (*Sport*) interior *mf* derecho/a

insider [ɪn'saɪdəʳ] Ⓐ N [*of firm*] empleado/a *m/f* de la empresa
Ⓑ CPD ► **insider dealing**, **insider trading** N abuso *m* de información privilegiada

insidious [ɪn'sɪdɪəs] ADJ insidioso

insidiously [ɪn'sɪdɪəslɪ] ADV insidiosamente

insight ['ɪnsaɪt] N 1 (= *understanding*) perspicacia *f*; **a person of ~** una persona perspicaz
2 (= *new perception*) nueva percepción *f*; **to gain** *or* **get an ~ into sth** comprender algo mejor, adquirir una nueva percepción de algo; **the visit gave us an ~ into their way of life** la visita nos ofreció la oportunidad de comprender mejor su manera de vivir

insightful ['ɪnˌsaɪtfʊl] ADJ (*US*) penetrante, perspicaz

insignia [ɪn'sɪgnɪə] NPL (*pl* **insignias** *or* **insignia**) insignias *fpl*

insignificance [ˌɪnsɪg'nɪfɪkəns] N insignificancia *f*; *see also* **pale B2**

insignificant [ˌɪnsɪg'nɪfɪkənt] ADJ [*person, number, amount*] insignificante; [*detail*] insignificante, sin importancia; **who left it here is ~, the important thing is …** no tiene importancia quién lo dejó aquí, lo importante es …

insincere [ˌɪnsɪn'sɪəʳ] ADJ insincero, poco sincero

insincerity [ˌɪnsɪn'serɪtɪ] N falta *f* de sinceridad, insinceridad *f*

insinuate [ɪn'sɪnjʊeɪt] VT 1 [+ *object*] introducir (**into** en); **to ~ o.s. into sth** introducirse en algo; **to ~ o.s. into sb's favour** ganarse el favor de algn
2 (= *hint*) insinuar; **to ~ that** insinuar que, dar a entender que; **what are you insinuating?** ¿qué insinúas?

insinuating [ɪn'sɪnjʊeɪtɪŋ] ADJ [*remark*] malintencionado, con segunda intención

insinuation [ɪnˌsɪnjʊ'eɪʃən] N 1 (= *hint*) insinuación *f*; **he made certain ~s** hizo algunas insinuaciones
2 (= *act*) introducción *f*

insipid [ɪn'sɪpɪd] ADJ insípido, soso

insipidity [ˌɪnsɪ'pɪdɪtɪ] N insipidez *f*, sosería *f*, insulsez *f*

insist [ɪn'sɪst] Ⓐ VI insistir; **if you ~** si insistes; **to ~ on sth** (= *repeat*) insistir en algo; (= *demand*) exigir algo; (= *emphasize*) [+ *point, aspect, benefit*] hacer hincapié en algo; **she always ~s on the best** siempre exige lo mejor;

he ~s on his version of events se reafirma en su versión de los hechos; **to ~ on doing sth** insistir en hacer algo; **he ~s on provoking me** insiste *or* se empeña en provocarme
Ⓑ VT **to ~ that** insistir en que; **he ~ed that it was so** insistió en que era así; **I ~ed that it be done** insistí en que se hiciera

insistence [ɪnˈsɪstəns] N insistencia *f*; **~ that** insistencia en que, empeño en que; **his ~ that we should have a drink** su insistencia *or* su empeño en que tomásemos una copa; **his ~ that he had switched the light off** su insistencia *or* su empeño en que había apagado la luz; **at his/her ~** ante su insistencia; **~ on sth** insistencia en algo; **his ~ on punctuality** su insistencia en la puntualidad; **her great ~ on this point** su enorme insistencia *or* su enorme empeño en este punto

insistent [ɪnˈsɪstənt] ADJ [*person, demands, questions*] insistente; **to be ~ that** insistir en que; **he was ~ that we should have a drink** insistió en que tomásemos una copa; **he was ~ that he had switched the light off** insistía en que había apagado la luz; **to be ~ about sth** insistir en algo; **she was ~ about leaving at seven** insistió en salir a las siete; **to be ~ on sth** insistir en algo; **she is most ~ on this point** insiste mucho en este punto; **we could hear the ~ ringing of a telephone in another room** podríamos oír el insistente sonido de un teléfono en otra habitación; **in an ~ tone** con un tono apremiante

insistently [ɪnˈsɪstəntlɪ] ADV [*ask, say, knock, ring*] insistentemente, con insistencia; **he was tugging ~ at his mother's sleeve** tiraba insistentemente *or* con insistencia de la manga de su madre; **he tried very ~ to sell us some toys** intentó con mucha insistencia vendernos unos juguetes

in situ [ɪnˈsɪtjuː] ADV in situ

insofar [ɪnsəˈfɑːʳ] **~ as …** CONJ en la medida en que …; **~ as can be ascertained …** en la medida en que se puede establecer …

insole [ˈɪnsəʊl] N plantilla *f*

insolence [ˈɪnsələns] N insolencia *f*

insolent [ˈɪnsələnt] ADJ insolente

insolently [ˈɪnsələntlɪ] ADV insolentemente

insolubility [ɪnˌsɒljʊˈbɪlətɪ] N insolubilidad *f*

insoluble [ɪnˈsɒljʊbl] ADJ [*substance*] insoluble; [*problem*] sin solución, insoluble

insolvable [ɪnˈsɒlvəbl] ADJ insoluble

insolvency [ɪnˈsɒlvənsɪ] N [*of company*] insolvencia *f*

insolvent [ɪnˈsɒlvənt] ADJ insolvente; **the company was declared ~** la empresa fue declarada insolvente

insomnia [ɪnˈsɒmnɪə] N insomnio *m*

insomniac [ɪnˈsɒmnɪæk] Ⓐ N insomne *mf*
Ⓑ ADJ insomne

insomuch [ˌɪnsəʊˈmʌtʃ] **~ as** CONJ puesto que, ya que, por cuanto que; **~ that** hasta tal punto que

insouciance [ɪnˈsuːsɪəns] N despreocupación *f*

insouciant [ɪnˈsuːsɪənt] ADJ despreocupado

Insp., insp. ABBR = **inspector**

inspect [ɪnˈspekt] VT 1 (= *examine*) [+ *goods, luggage*] inspeccionar, examinar; (*officially*) [+ *premises, building, school*] inspeccionar; [+ *machinery, vehicle*] inspeccionar, revisar; [+ *ticket, document*] revisar; **to ~ a product for flaws** examinar un producto para detectar defectos
2 (*Mil*) [+ *troops*] pasar revista a

inspection [ɪnˈspekʃən] Ⓐ N 1 [*of goods, premises, school*] inspección *f*; [*of ticket, document*] revisión *f*; **on closer ~ it turned out to be a fake** tras un examen más minucioso resultó ser falso
2 (*Mil*) [*of troops*] revista *f*
Ⓑ CPD ► **inspection pit** N (*Aut*) foso *m* de reconocimiento

inspector [ɪnˈspektəʳ] N (= *official*) inspector(a) *m/f*; (*on bus, train*) revisor(a) *m/f*, controlador(a) *m/f* (*LAm*); (*in police, of school*) inspector(a) *m/f*; **~ of schools** (*Brit*) inspector(a) *m/f* de enseñanza; **~ of taxes** ≈ Inspector(a) *m/f* de Hacienda

inspectorate [ɪnˈspektərɪt] N (*esp Brit*) cuerpo *m* de inspectores, inspección *f*

inspiration [ˌɪnspəˈreɪʃən] N 1 (= *motivation*) inspiración *f*; **the war has provided the ~ for many novels** la guerra ha sido fuente de inspiración para muchas novelas; **to find ~ in** inspirarse en; **she has been an ~ to us all** ha sido un gran estímulo para todos nosotros
2 (= *inspired idea*) idea *f* genial; **she had a sudden ~** de pronto tuvo una idea genial

inspirational [ˌɪnspɪˈreɪʃənl] ADJ inspirador

inspire [ɪnˈspaɪəʳ] VT inspirar; **she has the sort of face that ~s terror/respect** tiene un rostro que inspira terror/respeto; **to ~ sb to do sth** mover a algn a hacer algo; **her achievements have ~d me to make more effort** sus logros me han movido a esforzarme más; **whatever ~d him to do that?** ¿qué lo impulsó *or* movió a hacer eso?; **this painting was ~d by Greek mythology** este cuadro está inspirado en la mitología griega; **he was ~d by her beauty to write the song** su belleza lo llevó *or* movió a escribir la canción; **the painting was divinely ~d** el cuadro fue pintado por inspiración divina; **to ~ confidence in sb** ◊ **~ sb with confidence** infundir *or* inspirar confianza a algn

inspired [ɪnˈspaɪəd] ADJ [*musician, poet, artist, sportsman*] genial; [*performance*] inspirado; [*idea*] genial, excelente; **he gave an ~ performance** su actuación estuvo inspirada; **the pianist was playing like a man ~** el pianista tocaba como si los dioses guiasen sus manos; **it was an ~ choice** fue todo un acierto; **to feel ~** sentirse inspirado; **to make an ~ guess** tener una inspiración; **in an ~ moment** en un momento de inspiración

inspiring [ɪnˈspaɪərɪŋ] ADJ **he was a brilliant and ~ speaker** fue un magnífico orador que conseguía inspirar a la gente; **as a teacher he is capable, but not ~** es un profesor competente pero que no consigue estimular a sus alumnos; **it is ~ to work with people like them** es estimulante trabajar con gente como ellos; **it was not an ~ spot** no era un sitio que inspirase

Inst. ABBR = **Institute**

inst. ABBR = **instant** (= *of the present month*) cte., corrte.

instability [ˌɪnstəˈbɪlɪtɪ] N inestabilidad *f*

instal, install (*US*) [ɪnˈstɔːl] VT 1 [+ *central heating, lighting, equipment*] instalar
2 (= *invest*) **to be ~led in office** tomar posesión de su cargo
3 (*Comput*) [+ *program*] instalar

installation [ˌɪnstəˈleɪʃən] N 1 (*Tech, gen*) instalación *f*; **military ~s** instalaciones *f* militares 2 [*of mayor, official*] toma *f* de posesión, investidura *f*

instalment, installment (*US*) [ɪnˈstɔːlmənt] Ⓐ N 1 (*Comm*) (= *part payment*) plazo *m*, cuota *f* (*LAm*); **to pay in ~s** pagar a plazos; **monthly ~** plazo *m* mensual, cuota *f* mensual (*LAm*)
2 [*of serial, in magazine*] fascículo *m*; (*on radio, TV*) episodio *m*
Ⓑ CPD ► **installment plan** N (*US*) plan *m* de financiación; **to buy sth/pay for sth on an ~ plan** comprar/pagar algo a plazos

instance [ˈɪnstəns] Ⓐ N 1 (= *example*) ejemplo *m*; **for ~** por ejemplo
2 (= *case*) caso *m*; **in that ~** en ese caso; **in many ~s** en muchos casos; **in the present ~** en el caso presente; **in the first ~** en primer lugar
3 (*Jur*) **at the ~ of** a instancia *or* petición de
Ⓑ VT (= *exemplify*) citar como ejemplo; **this is perhaps best ~d by …** quizás esto queda mejor ilustrado por …

instant [ˈɪnstənt] Ⓐ ADJ 1 (= *immediate*) [*reply, reaction, success*] instantáneo, inmediato; **~ access to sth** acceso *m* instantáneo *or* inmediato a algo; **he took an ~ dislike to Derek** Derek le cayó mal desde el primer momento; **sweets give ~ energy** los dulces son una fuente instantánea de energía; **his book was an ~ hit** *or* **success** su libro fue un éxito instantáneo *or* inmediato
2 (*Culin*) [*coffee, soup*] instantáneo; **~ mash** puré *m* de patatas instantáneo
3 (*Brit Comm frm*) **on the 1st ~** el primero del corriente; *see also* **inst.**
4 (*Jur*) **in the ~ case** en el presente caso
Ⓑ N instante *m*, momento *m*; **the ~ I heard it** en el instante *or* momento en que lo supe; **an ~ later she was gone** un instante *or* momento después se había ido; **Jed hesitated for an ~** Jed dudó un instante *or* un momento; **in an ~** en un instante *or* momento; **the next ~** un momento después; **put it down this ~!** ¡deja eso ahora mismo!; **at that very ~ the phone rang** en ese mismo instante *or* momento sonó el teléfono
Ⓒ CPD ► **instant access account** N cuenta *f* de acceso instantáneo *or* inmediato ► **instant camera** N cámara *f* de fotos instantánea, polaroid® *f* ► **instant death** N muerte *f* instantánea *or* en el acto ► **instant gratification** N satisfacción *f* inmediata ► **instant messaging** N mensajería *f* instantánea ► **instant replay** N (*Sport*) repetición *f* de la jugada

instantaneous [ˌɪnstənˈteɪnɪəs] ADJ instantáneo

instantaneously [ˌɪnstənˈteɪnɪəslɪ] ADV instantáneamente

instantly [ˈɪnstəntlɪ] ADV [*recognize, know*] inmediatamente, al instante; [*die*] en el acto, instantáneamente; **the songs are ~ recognizable** las canciones se reconocen inmediatamente *or* al instante; **information will be ~ available to customers** los clientes podrán acceder a la información de forma instantánea

instead [ɪnˈsted] Ⓐ ADV **I was tempted to spend the money, but I put it in the bank ~** tuve la tentación de gastar el dinero, pero en lugar de ello *or* en vez de eso, lo metí en el banco; **she wanted to run away, but ~ she carried on walking** quería echar a correr, pero sin embargo siguió andando; **she's allergic to soap, so she uses cleanser ~** es alérgica al jabón, así es que usa una crema limpiadora en su lugar; **he was busy, so I went ~** él estaba ocupado, así es que fui yo en su lugar; **we had expected to make £2,000, ~, we barely made £200** esperábamos sacar unas 2.000 libras y en cambio apenas sacamos 200
Ⓑ PREP **~ of** en vez de, en lugar de; **I used margarine ~ of butter** usé margarina en vez de *or* en lugar de mantequilla; **we decided to walk ~ of taking the bus** decidimos andar en vez de *or* en lugar de tomar el autobús; **he went ~ of me** fue en mi lugar; **this is ~ of a**

Christmas present esto hace las veces de regalo de Navidad

instep [ˈɪnstep] N empeine *m*

instigate [ˈɪnstɪgeɪt] VT [+ *rebellion, strike, crime*] instigar a; [+ *new ideas*] fomentar; [+ *change*] promover

instigation [ˌɪnstɪˈgeɪʃən] N instigación *f*; **at Brown's ~** ◊ **at the ~ of Brown** a instancias de Brown; **at her ~, I went to see him** fui a verlo a instancias suyas

instigator [ˈɪnstɪgeɪtəʳ] N instigador(a) *m/f*

instil, **instill** (*US*) [ɪnˈstɪl] VT **to ~ sth into sb** [+ *fear, confidence, pride*] inspirar *or* infundir algo a algn; [+ *awareness, moral values, responsibility*] inculcar algo a algn

instinct Ⓐ [ˈɪnstɪŋkt] N instinto *m*; **the ~ for self-preservation** el instinto de conservación *or* supervivencia; **by ~** por instinto; **she had an ~ for attracting the wrong type of man** se las pintaba sola para atraer al tipo de hombre que no le convenía*

Ⓑ [ɪnˈstɪŋkt] ADJ (*liter*) **~ with** lleno de, imbuido de

instinctive [ɪnˈstɪŋktɪv] ADJ instintivo

instinctively [ɪnˈstɪŋktɪvlɪ] ADV instintivamente, por instinto

instinctual [ɪnˈstɪŋktjʊəl] ADJ instintivo

institute [ˈɪnstɪtjuːt] Ⓐ N (= *research centre*) instituto *m*; (= *professional body*) colegio *m*, asociación *f*; (*for professional training*) escuela *f*; (*US*) (= *course*) curso *m*, cursillo *m*

Ⓑ VT (= *begin*) [+ *inquiry*] iniciar, empezar; (= *found*) fundar, instituir; (*Jur*) [+ *proceedings*] entablar

institution [ˌɪnstɪˈtjuːʃən] N [1] (= *act*) (= *founding*) fundación *f*, institución *f*; (= *initiation*) iniciación *f*; (*Jur*) [*of proceedings*] entablación *f*

[2] (= *organization*) institución *f*

[3] (= *workhouse*) asilo *m*; (= *madhouse*) manicomio *m*; (= *hospital*) hospital *m*

[4] (= *custom*) institución *f*; **tea is a British ~** el té es una institución en Gran Bretaña; **it is too much of an ~ to abolish** es una costumbre demasiado arraigada para poder abolirla

[5] (= *person*) **he became an ~ at the Daily Star** se convirtió en toda una institución en el Daily Star

institutional [ˌɪnstɪˈtjuːʃənl] Ⓐ ADJ [*structure, resources*] institucional, de las instituciones; [*change, inefficiency*] institucional

Ⓑ CPD ► **the institutional church** N la iglesia institucional ► **institutional investor** N inversor(a) *m/f* institucional

institutionalize [ˌɪnstɪˈtjuːʃnəlaɪz] VT [1] (= *put into institution*) [+ *patient*] internar en una institución

[2] (= *establish officially*) [+ *practices, values*] institucionalizar

institutionalized [ˌɪnstɪˈtjuːʃənəˌlaɪzd] ADJ [1] (= *living in an institution*) **~ elderly people** personas *fpl* mayores internadas en residencias; **~ children** niños *mpl* que están bajo la custodia; **~ mental patients** enfermos *mpl* mentales ingresados en una institución

[2] (= *affected by living in an institution*) **to become ~** (*Psych*) *habituarse al régimen de vida de un hospital, una cárcel u otra institución de forma que se convierte en un modo de vida*

[3] (= *established*) [*custom, practice, value*] institucionalizado; **to become ~** institucionalizarse; **homelessness is becoming ~** el hecho de que exista gente sin hogar se está institucionalizando

in-store [ˈɪnˌstɔːʳ] ADJ en el establecimiento

instruct [ɪnˈstrʌkt] VT [1] (= *teach*) **to ~ sb in sth** enseñar algo a algn, instruir a algn en algo

[2] (= *order*) **to ~ sb to do sth** mandar *or* ordenar a algn que haga algo; **we were ~ed to stay where we were** se nos ordenó que permaneciéramos donde estábamos

[3] (*Brit*) [+ *solicitor, barrister*] dar instrucciones a, instruir

instruction [ɪnˈstrʌkʃən] Ⓐ N [1] (= *teaching*) instrucción *f*, enseñanza *f*; **to give sb ~ in mathematics/fencing** dar clases de matemáticas/esgrima a algn, enseñar matemáticas/esgrima a algn

[2] (= *order*) orden *f*; **to give sb ~s to do sth** dar órdenes *or* instrucciones a algn de que haga algo; **I gave him strict ~s not to touch it** le di órdenes estrictas de que no lo tocara; **we have given ~s for the transfer of funds** hemos cursado órdenes para la transferencia de fondos; **~s for use** modo *msing* de empleo; **on the ~s of** por orden de

[3] (*Comput*) instrucción *f*

Ⓑ CPD ► **instruction book**, **instruction manual** N manual *m* de instrucciones

instructive [ɪnˈstrʌktɪv] ADJ [*experience*] instructivo

instructor [ɪnˈstrʌktəʳ] N instructor(a) *m/f*; (*US Univ*) profesor(a) *m/f* auxiliar; (*also* **ski ~**) monitor(a) *m/f*; **dance ~** profesor(a) *m/f* de baile; **flying ~** monitor(a) *m/f* de vuelo; *see also* **driving C**

instructress [ɪnˈstrʌktrɪs] N instructora *f*; **dance ~** profesora *f* de baile

instrument [ˈɪnstrʊmənt] Ⓐ N [1] (*Mus, gen*) instrumento *m*; **surgical ~s** instrumental *m* quirúrgico; **set of ~s** instrumental *m*; **to fly on ~s** volar por instrumentos

[2] (*fig*) instrumento *m*; **he was nothing more than her ~** él no era más que su instrumento

[3] (*Jur*) instrumento *m*

Ⓑ CPD ► **instrument board**, **instrument panel** N (*Aer*) tablero *m* de instrumentos, cuadro *m* de instrumentos; (*US Aut*) tablero *m* de mandos, salpicadero *m* (*Sp*)

instrumental [ˌɪnstrʊˈmentl] ADJ [1] **to be ~ in** contribuir decisivamente a; **she had been ~ in getting him the job** ella contribuyó decisivamente a que consiguiera el empleo; **I was ~ in bringing Lisa and Danny together** yo hice que Liza y Danny se conocieran

[2] [*music, piece*] instrumental

instrumentalist [ˌɪnstrʊˈmentəlɪst] N instrumentista *mf*

instrumentality [ˌɪnstrʊmenˈtælɪtɪ] N mediación *f*, agencia *f*; **by** *or* **through the ~ of** por medio de, gracias a

instrumentation [ˌɪnstrʊmenˈteɪʃən] N instrumentación *f*

insubordinate [ˌɪnsəˈbɔːdənɪt] ADJ [*person, behaviour*] insubordinado

insubordination [ˈɪnsəˌbɔːdɪˈneɪʃən] N insubordinación *f*

insubstantial [ˌɪnsəbˈstænʃəl] ADJ (*gen*) insustancial; [*meal*] poco sustancioso

insufferable [ɪnˈsʌfərəbl] ADJ [*impertinence, arrogance, smugness*] insufrible, insoportable; [*heat*] insoportable, inaguantable; **he's ~!** ¡es insufrible!, ¡no hay quien lo aguante!

insufferably [ɪnˈsʌfərəblɪ] ADV **it was ~ hot** hacía un calor insoportable *or* inaguantable; **it was ~ boring** fue de un aburrido insoportable; **he was ~ rude/arrogant** fue de lo más grosero/arrogante

insufficiency [ˌɪnsəˈfɪʃənsɪ] N insuficiencia *f*

insufficient [ˌɪnsəˈfɪʃənt] ADJ insuficiente

insufficiently [ˌɪnsəˈfɪʃəntlɪ] ADV insuficientemente; **his troops were ~ equipped** sus tropas iban insuficientemente pertrechadas; **the office is ~ staffed** la oficina no tiene el personal suficiente

insular [ˈɪnsjələʳ] ADJ [1] (*Geog*) [*climate, location*] insular

[2] (*fig*) [*person, attitude*] estrecho de miras

insularity [ˌɪnsjʊˈlærɪtɪ] N insularidad *f*; (*fig*) estrechez *f* de miras

insulate [ˈɪnsjʊleɪt] VT (*gen*) aislar (**from** de)

insulating tape [ˈɪnsjʊleɪtɪŋˌteɪp] N cinta *f* aislante

insulation [ˌɪnsjʊˈleɪʃən] Ⓐ N (*gen*) aislamiento *m*; (*from cold*) aislamiento *m* térmico

Ⓑ CPD ► **insulation material** N material *m* aislante

insulator [ˈɪnsjʊleɪtəʳ] N (= *material*) aislante *m*; (= *appliance*) aislador *m*

insulin [ˈɪnsjʊlɪn] N insulina *f*

insult [ˈɪnsʌlt] Ⓐ N insulto *m*, injuria *f* (*frm*); **they are an ~ to the profession** son un insulto para la profesión; ✦*IDIOM* **and to add ~ to injury** y para colmo de males, y por si esto fuera poco

Ⓑ [ɪnˈsʌlt] VT [+ *person*] insultar, ofender; **he felt ~ed by this offer** tomó esta oferta como un insulto *or* una ofensa; **now don't feel ~ed** no te ofendas

insulting [ɪnˈsʌltɪŋ] ADJ insultante, ofensivo

insultingly [ɪnˈsʌltɪŋlɪ] ADV [*behave, talk*] ofensivamente, de modo insultante; **she was ~ dismissive** su desdén era insultante; **these adverts are ~ sexist** el sexismo de estos anuncios resulta todo un insulto

insuperable [ɪnˈsuːpərəbl] ADJ [*difficulty*] insuperable

insuperably [ɪnˈsuːpərəblɪ] ADV **~ difficult** dificilísimo

insupportable [ˌɪnsəˈpɔːtəbl] ADJ insoportable

insurable [ɪnˈʃʊərəbl] ADJ asegurable

insurance [ɪnˈʃʊərəns] Ⓐ N (*Comm*) seguro *m*; **~ against theft/fire/damage** seguro *m* contra robo/incendio/daños; **comprehensive/third party ~** seguro *m* a todo riesgo/contra terceros; **to take out ~** hacerse un seguro

Ⓑ CPD ► **insurance agent** N agente *mf* de seguros ► **insurance broker** N corredor(a) *m/f* de seguros, agente *mf* de seguros ► **insurance certificate** N certificado *m* de seguro ► **insurance claim** N demanda *f* de seguro ► **insurance company** N compañía *f* de seguros ► **insurance policy** N póliza *f* de seguros ► **insurance premium** N prima *f* del seguro

insure [ɪnˈʃʊəʳ] VT [+ *house, property*] asegurar; **to ~ sb** *or* **sb's life** hacer un seguro de vida a algn; **to ~ o.s.** *or* **one's life** hacerse un seguro de vida; **to ~ sth against fire/theft** asegurar algo contra incendios/robo; **to ~ one's life for £500,000** hacerse un seguro de vida por valor de 500.000 libras; **to be ~d to do sth** tener un seguro que permite hacer algo; **I'm ~d to drive any car** tengo un seguro que me permite conducir cualquier coche; **I'm ~d to drive my husband's car** estoy en el seguro del coche de mi marido

insured [ɪnˈʃʊəd] Ⓐ ADJ [*person, building, vehicle*] asegurado; **are you ~?** ¿estás asegurado?, ¿tienes seguro?; **what is the sum ~?** ¿qué suma cubre el seguro?; **to be ~ against fire/theft** estar asegurado contra incendios/robo; **it's ~ for £5,000** está asegurado en 5.000 libras

Ⓑ N **the ~** el/la asegurado/a

insurer [ɪnˈʃʊərəʳ] N asegurador(a) *m/f*

insurgency [ɪn'sɜːdʒənsɪ] N insurrección *f*

insurgent [ɪn'sɜːdʒənt] Ⓐ N insurgente *mf*, insurrecto/a *m/f*
Ⓑ ADJ insurgente, insurrecto

insurmountable [ˌɪnsə'maʊntəbl] ADJ insuperable

insurrection [ˌɪnsə'rekʃən] N insurrección *f*

insurrectionary [ˌɪnsə'rekʃnərɪ] ADJ rebelde, insurreccional

insurrectionist [ˌɪnsə'rekʃənɪst] N insurgente *mf*, insurrecto/a *m/f*

Int. ABBR = **International**

int. ABBR (*Fin*) = **interest**

intact [ɪn'tækt] ADJ intacto; **not a window was left ~** no quedó cristal sano *or* sin romper; **I managed to keep my sense of humour ~** conseguí mantener intacto *or* no perder mi sentido del humor

intake ['ɪnteɪk] Ⓐ N 1 (*Tech*) [*of air, gas etc*] entrada *f*; [*of water*] toma *f*
2 (= *quantity*) [*of food*] consumo *m*; **what is your student ~?** ¿cuántos alumnos se matriculan (cada año)?
Ⓑ CPD ► **intake valve** N válvula *f* de admisión, válvula *f* de entrada

intangible [ɪn'tændʒəbl] Ⓐ ADJ (*gen*) intangible
Ⓑ CPD ► **intangible assets** NPL activo *msing* intangible

integer ['ɪntɪdʒə^r] N entero *m*, número *m* entero

integral ['ɪntɪgrəl] Ⓐ ADJ (= *essential*) [*part*] integrante, esencial; **it is an ~ part of the plan** es parte integrante *or* esencial del proyecto
Ⓑ N (*Math*) integral *f*
Ⓒ CPD ► **integral calculus** N (*Math*) cálculo *m* integral

integrate ['ɪntɪgreɪt] Ⓐ VT integrar (*also Math*); **to ~ aid with long-term development** integrar la ayuda con el desarrollo a largo plazo; **to ~ a new pupil into the class** integrar a un nuevo alumno en la clase
Ⓑ VI integrarse (**into** en)

integrated ['ɪntɪgreɪtɪd] Ⓐ ADJ [*plan*] integrado, de conjunto; [*personality*] equilibrado; [*population, school*] integrado, sin separación racial; **to become ~ (into)** integrarse (en)
Ⓑ CPD ► **integrated circuit** N (*Comput*) circuito *m* integrado

integration [ˌɪntɪ'greɪʃən] N integración *f* (**in, into** en)

integrator ['ɪntɪgreɪtə^r] N integrador *m*

integrity [ɪn'tegrɪtɪ] N [*of person*] integridad *f*, honradez *f*; (*Comput*) integridad *f*

integument [ɪn'tegjʊmənt] N (*frm*) integumento *m*

intellect ['ɪntɪlekt] N 1 (= *reasoning power*) intelecto *m*, inteligencia *f*
2 (= *person*) cerebro *m*

intellectual [ˌɪntɪ'lektjʊəl] Ⓐ ADJ intelectual *mf*
Ⓑ N intelectual *mf*
Ⓒ CPD ► **intellectual property** N propiedad *f* intelectual

intellectualize [ˌɪntɪ'lektjʊəlaɪz] Ⓐ VT intelectualizar, racionalizar
Ⓑ VI dar razones

intellectually [ˌɪntɪ'lektjʊəlɪ] ADV [*stimulating, demanding, inferior*] intelectualmente; (= *from an intellectual point of view*) intelectualmente, desde el punto de vista del intelecto

intelligence [ɪn'telɪdʒəns] Ⓐ N 1 (= *cleverness*) inteligencia *f*
2 (= *information*) información *f*, inteligencia *f*; **according to our latest ~** según las últimas noticias
Ⓑ CPD ► **intelligence agent** N agente *mf* de inteligencia, agente *mf* secreto ► **Intelligence Corps** N (*Brit Mil*) Cuerpo *m* de Informaciones ► **intelligence officer** N oficial *mf* de informaciones ► **intelligence quotient (IQ)** N cociente *m* intelectual *or* de inteligencia ► **intelligence service** N servicio *m* de información *or* inteligencia ► **intelligence test** N test *m* de inteligencia ► **intelligence work** N trabajo *m* de inteligencia

intelligent [ɪn'telɪdʒənt] ADJ inteligente

intelligently [ɪn'telɪdʒəntlɪ] ADV inteligentemente

intelligentsia [ɪnˌtelɪ'dʒentsɪə] N intelectualidad *f*

intelligibility [ɪnˌtelɪdʒə'bɪlɪtɪ] N inteligibilidad *f*

intelligible [ɪn'telɪdʒəbl] ADJ inteligible, comprensible; **his prose is so laboured it is scarcely ~** su prosa es tan elaborada que resulta apenas inteligible

intelligibly [ɪn'telɪdʒəblɪ] ADV inteligiblemente, de modo inteligible

INTELSAT ['ɪntelˌsæt] N ABBR = **International Telecommunications Satellite Organization**

intemperance [ɪn'tempərəns] N (= *lack of self-restraint*) intemperancia *f*, inmoderación *f*; (= *drunkenness*) exceso *m* en la bebida

intemperate [ɪn'tempərɪt] ADJ [*person*] (= *immoderate*) desmedido, destemplado; (= *drunken*) dado a la bebida, que bebe con exceso; [*climate*] inclemente

▼ **intend** [ɪn'tend] VT 1 (*with noun*) **it's ~ed for John** está destinado a Juan, es para Juan; **no offence was ~ed** ◊ **he ~ed no offence** no tenía intención de ofender a nadie, no fue su intención ofender a nadie; **I ~ no disrespect** no es mi intención faltarle al respeto a nadie; **that remark was ~ed for you** esa observación iba dirigida a ti; **it was ~ed as a compliment** se dijo como un cumplido; **I ~ed no harm** lo hice sin mala intención; **is that what you ~ed?** ¿fue eso lo que se proponía?
2 (*with verb*) **to ~ to do sth** ◊ **~ doing sth** pensar hacer algo; **what do you ~ to do about it?** ¿qué piensas hacer al respecto?; **I ~ him to come too** quiero que venga él también; **this scheme is ~ed to help** este proyecto tiene la finalidad de ayudar; **I ~ that he should see it** quiero que él lo vea; **I fully ~ to punish him** tengo la firme intención de castigarlo

intended [ɪn'tendɪd] Ⓐ ADJ [*effect*] deseado
Ⓑ N († *also hum*) prometido/a *m/f*

intense [ɪn'tens] ADJ 1 (= *extreme*) [*heat, cold, pain*] intenso; [*interest, enthusiasm, happiness*] enorme; [*emotion, fear, anger, hatred*] intenso, profundo; [*gratitude*] profundo; [*colour*] intenso, vivo; [*light*] intenso, fuerte; **this sparked ~ speculation** esto dio pie a mucha especulación
2 (= *concentrated*) [*activity, fighting, negotiations*] intenso; **she wore an expression of ~ concentration** su expresión era de intensa concentración
3 (= *impassioned*) [*person, face, expression*] apasionado, vehemente; [*relationship*] intenso; [*eyes*] penetrante; [*gaze*] intenso, penetrante; **she's very ~** se lo toma todo como si le fuera la vida en ello; **an ~ debate** un intenso debate

intensely [ɪn'tenslɪ] ADV 1 (= *extremely*) [*interesting, boring, competitive*] sumamente; [*irritated*] sumamente, tremendamente; [*grateful, moving*] profundamente, sumamente; **difficulties of an ~ personal nature** dificultades de carácter sumamente personal; **to be ~ angry** estar terriblemente enfadado *or* (*LAm*) enojado, estar enfadadísimo *or* (*LAm*) enojadísimo
2 (= *concentratedly*) [*work, fight, concentrate*] intensamente
3 (= *with passion*) [*look, love*] intensamente; [*discuss*] apasionadamente; [*say*] con pasión; **I dislike it ~** me desagrada profundamente; **why do you dislike her so ~?** ¿por qué te resulta tan antipática?; **he was staring ~ at me** me miraba fija e intensamente; **they argued the point ~** lo discutieron acaloradamente

intensification [ɪnˌtensɪfɪ'keɪʃən] N intensificación *f*

intensifier [ɪn'tensɪˌfaɪə^r] N intensificador *m*

intensify [ɪn'tensɪfaɪ] Ⓐ VI [*desire, frustration, dislike*] intensificarse; [*pain*] agudizarse; [*odour*] hacerse más intenso; [*rain*] arreciar; [*fighting*] recrudecerse, intensificarse
Ⓑ VT [+ *fear*] intensificar, incrementar; [+ *pain*] agudizar; [+ *attack*] recrudecer, intensificar

intensity [ɪn'tensɪtɪ] N 1 (= *strength*) [*of heat, cold, emotion, pain, light*] intensidad *f*
2 (= *passion*) [*of expression, relationship, debate, fighting*] intensidad *f*; [*of person*] vehemencia *f*; **she looked at me with such ~ that ...** me miró con tal intensidad que ..., me miró de una forma tan intensa que ...

intensive [ɪn'tensɪv] Ⓐ ADJ [*course*] intensivo; [*negotiations, bombardment*] intenso; [*study*] profundo, detenido; (*esp for exam*) intensivo
Ⓑ CPD ► **intensive care** N cuidados *mpl* intensivos; **to be in ~ care** estar en cuidados intensivos ► **intensive care unit** N unidad *f* de cuidados intensivos

intensively [ɪn'tensɪvlɪ] ADV [*bombard*] intensamente; [*study*] profundamente, detenidamente; (*esp for exam*) intensivamente

intent [ɪn'tent] Ⓐ ADJ 1 (= *determined*) **to be ~ on doing sth** estar resuelto *or* decidido a hacer algo
2 (= *absorbed*) absorto; **to be ~ on sth** estar absorto en algo
Ⓑ N propósito *m*, intención *f*; **with ~ to** + INFIN con el propósito de + *infin*; **with ~ to kill** con intentos homicidas; **to all ~s and purposes** prácticamente, en efecto

▼ **intention** [ɪn'tenʃən] N intención *f*, propósito *m*; **I have no ~ of going** no tengo la menor intención de ir; **I have every ~ of going** tengo plena intención de ir; **with the best of ~s** con la mejor intención; **what are your ~s?** ¿qué piensas hacer?, ¿qué proyectos tienes?; **his ~s toward the girl were strictly honourable** pensaba casarse con la joven

intentional [ɪn'tenʃənl] ADJ [*lie, insult*] deliberado; [*omission, injury, infliction of pain*] intencionado, deliberado; **if I offended you it wasn't ~** si te ofendí fue sin querer *or* no fue a propósito

intentionally [ɪn'tenʃnəlɪ] ADV [*do, hurt, discriminate*] a propósito, adrede; [*mislead*] intencionadamente; **he believed he had been ~ misled** creía que había sido engañado intencionadamente *or* de forma intencionada; **the figures are ~ misleading** las cifras están presentadas de manera equívoca a propósito

intently [ɪn'tentlɪ] ADV atentamente, fijamente

intentness [ɪn'tentnɪs] N (= *concentration*) atención *f*; [*of gaze*] intensidad *f*; **~ of purpose** resolución *f*

inter [ɪn'tɜː^r] VT enterrar, sepultar

➤ LANGUAGE IN USE: **intend 2** 8.1, 8.2, 8.4 **intention** 8.4

inter... [ˈɪntəʳ] PREFIX inter…, entre…

interact [ˌɪntərˈækt] VI influirse mutuamente, interactuar; **to ~ with sb** relacionarse con algn

interaction [ˌɪntərˈækʃən] N interacción *f*, interrelación *f*

interactive [ˌɪntərˈæktɪv] ADJ (*gen, Comput*) interactivo

interactively [ˌɪntərˈæktɪvlɪ] ADV (*gen, Comput*) interactivamente

inter alia [ˌɪntərˈælɪə] ADV entre otros

inter-bank [ˈɪntəˌbæŋk] Ⓐ ADJ interbancario
Ⓑ CPD ► **inter-bank loan** N préstamo *m* entre bancos ► **inter-bank rate** N tasa *f* de descuento entre bancos

interbreed [ˈɪntəˈbriːd] (*pt, pp* **interbred** [ˈɪntəˈbred]) Ⓐ VT cruzar
Ⓑ VI cruzarse

intercalate [ɪnˈtɜːkəleɪt] VT intercalar

intercalation [ɪnˌtɜːkəˈleɪʃən] N intercalación *f*

intercede [ˌɪntəˈsiːd] VI interceder (**for** por; **with** con); **to ~ on sb's behalf** interceder por algn

intercept [ˌɪntəˈsept] VT (= *interfere with*) [+ *message, missile*] interceptar; (= *stop*) detener; (= *cut off*) atajar, cortar; (*Sport*) [+ *pass*] cortar, interceptar; (*Math*) cortar

interception [ˌɪntəˈsepʃən] N [*of message, missile*] intercepción *f*; (*Sport*) corte *m*, intercepción *f*

interceptor [ˌɪntəˈseptəʳ] N interceptor *m*

intercession [ˌɪntəˈseʃən] N intercesión *f*, mediación *f*

interchange Ⓐ [ˌɪntəˈtʃeɪndʒ] VT [1] (= *exchange*) [+ *views, ideas*] intercambiar, cambiar; [+ *prisoners, publications*] canjear
[2] (= *alternate*) alternar
Ⓑ [ˈɪntətʃeɪndʒ] N [1] [*of views, ideas*] intercambio *m*, cambio *m*; [*of prisoners, publications*] canje *m*
[2] (*on motorway etc*) nudo *m* de carreteras, paso *m* elevado, paso *m* a desnivel (*LAm*)

interchangeable [ˌɪntəˈtʃeɪndʒəbl] ADJ intercambiable

interchangeably [ˌɪntəˈtʃeɪndʒəblɪ] ADV de manera intercambiable, intercambiando los dos *etc*

intercity [ˈɪntəˈsɪtɪ] Ⓐ N (*Brit Rail*) (*also* **~ train**) tren *m* interurbano, tren *m* intercity (*Sp*)
Ⓑ ADJ interurbano, intercity (*Sp*)

intercollegiate [ˈɪntəkəˈliːdʒɪɪt] ADJ interuniversitario

intercom* [ˈɪntəkɒm] N intercomunicador *m*, interfono *m*

intercommunicate [ˌɪntəkəˈmjuːnɪkeɪt] VI [*people, rooms*] comunicarse

intercommunication [ˈɪntəkəˌmjuːnɪˈkeɪʃən] N intercomunicación *f*

intercommunion [ˌɪntəkəˈmjuːnɪən] N intercomunión *f*

inter-company [ˌɪntəˈkʌmpənɪ] ADJ **~ relations** relaciones *fpl* entre compañías

interconnect [ˌɪntəkəˈnekt] Ⓐ VT (*Elec, Comput*) interconectar; **all these problems are ~ed** todos estos problemas están interrelacionados
Ⓑ VI [*concepts*] interrelacionarse; [*trains*] enlazar

interconnecting [ˌɪntəkəˈnektɪŋ] ADJ [*rooms*] comunicados; [*door, tunnel*] de comunicación; [*trains*] con correspondencia

interconnection [ˌɪntəkəˈnekʃən] N interconexión *f*

intercontinental [ˈɪntəˌkɒntɪˈnentl] Ⓐ ADJ intercontinental
Ⓑ CPD ► **intercontinental ballistic missile** N misil *m* balístico intercontinental

intercostal [ˌɪntəˈkɒstl] ADJ intercostal

intercourse [ˈɪntəkɔːs] N [1] (*frm*) relaciones *fpl*, trato *m*; (*Comm*) comercio *m*
[2] (*also* **sexual ~**) acto *m* sexual, coito *m*; **to have (sexual) ~ with sb** tener relaciones sexuales con algn

intercut [ˌɪntəˈkʌt] VT alternar; **to be ~ with** (*Cine*) alternarse con

interdenominational [ˈɪntədɪˌnɒmɪˈneɪʃənl] ADJ interconfesional

interdepartmental [ˈɪntəˌdiːpɑːtˈmentl] ADJ interdepartamental

interdependence [ˌɪntədɪˈpendəns] N interdependencia *f*

interdependent [ˌɪntədɪˈpendənt] ADJ interdependiente

interdict [ˈɪntədɪkt] Ⓐ N entredicho *m*, interdicto *m*
Ⓑ VT (= *stop*) [+ *enemy shipping, aircraft, communications*] interceptar; (= *prohibit*) prohibir

interdiction [ˌɪntəˈdɪkʃən] N (*Rel*) interdicción *f*; (*Mil*) intercepción *f*

interdisciplinary [ˌɪntəˈdɪsɪplɪnərɪ] ADJ interdisciplinario

interest [ˈɪntrɪst] Ⓐ N [1] (= *curiosity*) interés *m*; **to arouse sb's ~** despertar el interés de algn; **to have an ~ in sth** estar interesado en algo; **I have no further ~ in talking to them** ya no estoy interesado en hablar con ellos; **to lose ~ (in sth)** perder el interés (por *or* en algo); **of ~**: **the guidebook describes all the places of ~** la guía describe todos los lugares de interés; **it is of no ~ to us** no nos interesa; **is this of any ~ to you?** ¿te interesa esto?; **I'm doing it just out of ~** lo hago simplemente porque me interesa; **just out of ~, how much did it cost?** por simple curiosidad, ¿cuánto costó?; **to show (an) ~ (in sth/sb)** mostrar interés (por *or* en algo/por algn); **to take an ~ in sth/sb** interesarse por *or* en algo/por algn; **he took no ~ in his children** no se interesaba por sus hijos
[2] (= *hobby*) interés *m*; **my main ~ is reading** mi interés principal *or* mi pasatiempo favorito es la lectura; **what are your ~s?** ¿qué cosas te interesan?; **special ~ holidays** vacaciones *fpl* de grupos con un interés común
[3] (= *profit, advantage*) interés *m*; **a conflict of ~s** un conflicto de intereses; **in sb's ~(s)**: **it is in your own ~ to confess** te conviene confesar; **it is not in his ~ to sell the house** no le conviene vender la casa; **they acted in the best ~s of their members** obraron en el mejor interés de sus miembros; **in the ~s of hygiene** por razones de higiene; **in the ~s of national unity** con el fin de preservar la unidad nacional; *see also* **heart A1**, **public A2**, **vested**
[4] (= *share, stake*) (*gen*) interés *m*; (*in company*) participación *f*; **he has sold his ~ in the company** ha vendido su participación en la empresa; **British ~s in the Middle East** los intereses británicos en el Medio Oriente; **he has business ~s abroad** tiene negocios en el extranjero; **to have a controlling/financial ~ in a company** tener una participación mayoritaria/tener acciones en una compañía; **to have an ~ in sth** (*gen*) tener interés *or* estar interesado en algo; (*in company*) tener participación en algo; **the West has an ~ in promoting democracy there** Occidente tiene interés *or* está interesado en promover allí la democracia
[5] (*Fin*) (*on loan, shares, savings*) interés *m*; **to bear ~** devengar *or* dar intereses; **it bears ~ at 5%** devenga *or* da un interés del 5%; **compound ~** interés *m* compuesto; **to earn ~** cobrar intereses; **the ~ on an investment** los intereses de una inversión; **simple ~** interés *m* simple; **shares that yield a high ~** acciones *fpl* que rinden bien; ✦***IDIOM*** **to repay sth/sb with ~**: **I repaid his bad manners with ~!** ¡le devolví los malos modales con creces!
Ⓑ VT [1] (= *arouse interest*) interesar; **it may ~ you to know that …** puede que te interese saber que …; **can I ~ you in a new car?** ¿estaría interesado en comprar un coche nuevo?
[2] (= *concern*) interesar; **the struggle against inflation ~s us all** la lucha contra la inflación nos interesa a todos
Ⓒ CPD ► **interest charges** NPL intereses *mpl* ► **interest group** N grupo *m* de gente con un mismo interés ► **interest payments** NPL pago *m* de intereses ► **interest rate** N tipo *m* *or* tasa *f* de interés

interest-bearing [ˈɪntrɪstˌbeərɪŋ] ADJ con interés

interested [ˈɪntrɪstɪd] ADJ interesado; **she seems very ~** parece muy interesada; **anyone ~ should apply in writing to …** cualquier persona interesada debe dirigirse por escrito a …; **I've got some books to sell, are you ~?** tengo unos libros que quiero vender, ¿te interesan?; **I'm going to the canteen, if anybody is ~** voy a la cafetería, si alguien se quiere apuntar; **to be ~ in sth**: **he's ~ in buying a car** está interesado en comprar un coche; **I'm not ~ in football** no me interesa el fútbol; **would you be ~ in my old wardrobe?** ¿te interesaría quedarte con mi armario viejo?; **to become** *or* **grow** *or* **get ~ in sth/sb** interesarse por algn/por algo; **to get sb ~ in sth** hacer que algn se interese por algo; **I tried to get him ~ in opera** intenté hacer que se interesase por la ópera; **I soon got her ~ in my idea** pronto conseguí tenerla interesada en mi idea, pronto conseguí que se interesase por mi idea; **the ~ party** la parte interesada; **she was ~ to see what he would do** tenía curiosidad por ver qué es lo que haría; **I'd be ~ to know the outcome** me interesaría saber el resultado

interest-free [ˌɪntrɪstˈfriː] ADJ sin interés

interesting [ˈɪntrɪstɪŋ] ADJ interesante; **it is ~ that** es interesante el hecho de que; **it was ~ for me** me pareció interesante; **that's an ~ point** ése es un punto interesante; **it will be ~ to see what happens** será interesante ver lo que ocurre

interestingly [ˈɪntrɪstɪŋlɪ] ADV [*speak, write*] de manera interesante; **~ enough, I've been there before** curiosamente, ya he estado allí

interface [ˈɪntəfeɪs] [1] N (*Comput*) interfaz *m* *or f*, interface *m or f*
[2] VI **to ~ with** conectar con; (*Comput*) comunicarse mediante interfaz con

interfacing [ˈɪntəfeɪsɪŋ] N (= *interconnection*) interconexión *f*; (*Sew*) entretela *f*

interfere [ˌɪntəˈfɪəʳ] VI [1] (= *pry, intrude*) entrometerse, meterse (**in** en); **he's always interfering** se mete en todo; **who told you to ~?** ¿quién te mete a ti en esto?; **stop interfering!** ¡deja de entrometerte!
[2] (= *meddle*) **to ~ with sth** manosear *or* tocar algo; **who has been interfering with the TV?** ¿quién ha estado tocando la televisión?
[3] (= *hinder*) **to ~ with sth** afectar a algo; **it mustn't ~ with my work** no debe afectar a mi trabajo; **I don't want to ~ with your plans**

no quiero interferir con tus planes
4 (*Rad, TV*) **to ~ with sth** interferir con algo

interference [ˌɪntəˈfɪərəns] N 1 (= *intrusion*) intromisión *f*
2 (*Rad, TV*) interferencia *f*

interfering [ˌɪntəˈfɪərɪŋ] ADJ [*neighbour*] entrometido

interferon [ˌɪntəˈfɪərɒn] N interferón *m*

intergalactic [ˌɪntəgəˈlæktɪk] ADJ intergaláctico

intergovernmental ADJ [ˌɪntəˌgʌvnˈmentl] ADJ intergubernamental

interim [ˈɪntərɪm] Ⓐ N **in the ~** en el ínterin *or* interín
Ⓑ ADJ [*president*] interino, provisional; [*measure, government, report, result*] provisional
Ⓒ CPD ► **interim dividend** N dividendo *m* a cuenta ► **interim payment** N pago *m* a cuenta ► **the interim period** N el ínterin *or* interín ► **interim profits** NPL (*Fin, Comm*) beneficios *mpl* trimestrales

interior [ɪnˈtɪərɪəʳ] Ⓐ ADJ 1 (= *inside*) [*door, wall, decor*] interior
2 (*Geog*) (= *central*) interior
3 (*Pol*) (= *domestic*) [*affairs*] interno; [*minister, department*] del interior
4 (*frm*) (= *inner*) [*life, world*] interior; [*thoughts*] íntimo
Ⓑ N 1 (= *inside*) [*of building, container, car*] interior *m*
2 (*Geog*) (= *centre*) **the ~** el interior (**of** de)
3 (*Pol*) (*in titles*) **Minister of the Interior** Ministro/a *m/f* del Interior; **Ministry of the Interior** Ministerio *m* del Interior, Secretaría *f* de Gobernación (*Mex*)
Ⓒ CPD ► **interior angle** N (*Math*) ángulo *m* interno ► **interior decoration** N interiorismo *m* ► **interior decorator** N interiorista *mf* ► **interior design** N interiorismo *m*, decoración *f* de interiores ► **interior designer** N interiorista *mf* ► **interior light** N (*in car*) luz *f* de dentro ► **interior sprung mattress** N colchón *m* de muelles

interject [ˌɪntəˈdʒekt] VT [+ *question, remark*] interponer; **"that's not true," he ~ed** —eso no es cierto —interpuso él

interjection [ˌɪntəˈdʒekʃən] N (= *exclamation*) exclamación *f*; (*Ling*) interjección *f*; (= *insertion*) interposición *f*

interlace [ˌɪntəˈleɪs] Ⓐ VT entrelazar
Ⓑ VI entrelazarse

interlard [ˌɪntəˈlɑːd] VT **to ~ with** salpicar de, entreverar de

interleave [ˌɪntəˈliːv] VT interfoliar, intercalar; (*Comput*) intercalar

interleaving [ˌɪntəˈliːvɪŋ] N interfoliación *f*, intercalación *f*; (*Comput*) intercalación *f*

inter-library [ˌɪntəˈlaɪbrərɪ] ADJ **~ loan** préstamo *m* interbibliotecario

interline [ˌɪntəˈlaɪn] VT 1 (*Typ*) interlinear, intercalar entre líneas
2 (*Sew*) entretelar

interlinear [ˌɪntəˈlɪnɪəʳ] ADJ interlineal

interlink [ˌɪntəˈlɪŋk] Ⓐ VT [+ *issues, interests*] interrelacionar, vincular; **the two issues are ~ed** las dos cuestiones están interrelacionadas, las dos cuestiones están vinculadas (entre sí)
Ⓑ VI interrelacionarse

interlock [ˌɪntəˈlɒk] Ⓐ VT trabar, entrelazar; [+ *wheels*] endentar, engranar
Ⓑ VI trabarse, entrelazarse; [*wheels*] endentarse, engranar; **the parts of the plan ~** las partes del plan tienen una fuerte trabazón
Ⓒ N 1 (*Mech*) enclavamiento *m*
2 [*of fabric*] **cotton ~ underwear** ropa *f* interior de algodón de punto

interlocutor [ˌɪntəˈlɒkjʊtəʳ] N (*frm*) interlocutor(a) *m/f*

interloper [ˈɪntələʊpəʳ] N intruso/a *m/f*

interlude [ˈɪntəluːd] N intervalo *m*, intermedio *m*; (*in theatre*) intermedio *m*; (= *musical interlude*) interludio *m*

intermarriage [ˌɪntəˈmærɪdʒ] N (*between races*) matrimonio *m* mixto; (*between relatives*) matrimonio *m* entre parientes

intermarry [ˈɪntəˈmærɪ] VI (*gen*) casarse entre sí; [*within family*] casarse entre parientes

intermediary [ˌɪntəˈmiːdɪərɪ] Ⓐ N intermediario/a *m/f*
Ⓑ ADJ intermediario

intermediate [ˌɪntəˈmiːdɪət] Ⓐ ADJ [*stage*] intermedio; **the course is available on three levels: beginner, ~ and advanced** el curso consta de tres niveles: elemental, medio *or* intermedio y avanzado
Ⓑ N intermediario/a *m/f*
Ⓒ CPD ► **intermediate range ballistic missile** N misil *m* balístico de alcance intermedio ► **intermediate range weapon** N arma *f* de alcance medio ► **intermediate stop** N escala *f* ► **intermediate technology** N tecnología *f* media

interment [ɪnˈtɜːmənt] N entierro *m*, sepelio *m*

intermezzo [ˌɪntəˈmetsəʊ] N (*pl* **intermezzos** *or* **intermezzi** [ˌɪntəˈmetsiː]) intermezzo *m*

interminable [ɪnˈtɜːmɪnəbl] ADJ [*speech, rain, journey etc*] interminable

interminably [ɪnˈtɜːmɪnəblɪ] ADV interminablemente

intermingle [ˌɪntəˈmɪŋgl] Ⓐ VT entremezclar
Ⓑ VI entremezclarse

intermission [ˌɪntəˈmɪʃən] N (= *pause*) interrupción *f*, intermisión *f*; (*between events*) intervalo *m*; (*Theat*) intermedio *m*; **it went on without ~** continuó sin interrupción

intermittent [ˌɪntəˈmɪtənt] ADJ intermitente

intermittently [ˌɪntəˈmɪtəntlɪ] ADV a ratos, a intervalos; **it rained ~** llovía a ratos *or* a intervalos; **they worked/met ~** trabajaban/se veían de cuando en cuando

intern Ⓐ [ɪnˈtɜːn] VT internar, recluir
Ⓑ [ˈɪntɜːn] N (*US*) (= *doctor*) interno/a *m/f*; (= *student on placement*) alumno/a *m/f* en prácticas

internal [ɪnˈtɜːnl] Ⓐ ADJ 1 [*wall*] interior; [*affairs, conflict, divisions*] interno
2 (*Med*) [*bleeding, examination, organ, injury*] interno
Ⓑ CPD ► **internal audit** N auditoría *f* interna ► **internal combustion engine** N motor *m* de combustión interna *or* de explosión ► **internal market** N mercado *m* interno *or* interior ► **Internal Revenue Service** N (*US*) ≈ Hacienda *f*

internalization [ɪnˌtɜːnəlaɪˈzeɪʃən] N interiorización *f*

internalize [ɪnˈtɜːnəlaɪz] VT interiorizar

internally [ɪnˈtɜːnəlɪ] ADV 1 (= *within organization, country*) internamente
2 (= *within o.s.*) por dentro, internamente
3 (*Med*) [*bleed*] internamente; **"not to be taken internally"** "sólo para uso externo"

international [ˌɪntəˈnæʃnəl] Ⓐ ADJ (*gen*) internacional
Ⓑ N (*Brit Sport*) (= *match*) partido *m* internacional; (= *player*) internacional *mf*
Ⓒ CPD ► **International Atomic Energy Agency** N Organización *f* Internacional de Energía Atómica ► **the International Brigade** N las Brigadas Internacionales ► **International Court of Justice** N Corte *f* Internacional de Justicia ► **international date line** N línea *f* de cambio de fecha ► **International Labour Organization** N Organización *f* Internacional del Trabajo ► **international law** N derecho *m* internacional ► **International Monetary Fund** N Fondo *m* Monetario Internacional ► **international money order** N giro *m* postal internacional ► **international reply coupon** N cupón *m* de respuesta internacional ► **International Standards Organization** N Organización *f* Internacional de Normalización

Internationale [ˌɪntəˌnæʃəˈnɑːl] N **the ~** la Internacional

internationalism [ɪntəˈnæʃnəlɪzəm] N internacionalismo *m*

internationalist [ˌɪntəˈnæʃnəlɪst] Ⓐ ADJ internacionalista Ⓑ N internacionalista *mf*

internationalize [ˌɪntəˈnæʃnəlaɪz] VT internacionalizar

internationally [ɪntəˈnæʃnəlɪ] ADV [*function, compete*] internacionalmente; [*known, recognized*] mundialmente

internecine [ˌɪntəˈniːsaɪn] Ⓐ ADJ [*strife, feud, warfare*] intestina Ⓑ CPD ► **internecine war** N guerra *f* de aniquilación mutua

internee [ˌɪntɜːˈniː] N prisionero/a *m/f* de guerra (*civil*)

Internet [ˈɪntənet] Ⓐ N **the ~** Internet *m or f*
Ⓑ CPD ► **Internet café** N cibercafé *m* ► **Internet service provider** N servidor *m*, proveedor *m* de servicios de Internet ► **Internet surfer** N internauta *mf*, cibernauta *mf* ► **Internet user** N internauta *mf*, cibernauta *mf*

internment [ɪnˈtɜːnmənt] Ⓐ N internamiento *m*
Ⓑ CPD ► **internment camp** N campo *m* de internamiento

interoperability [ˌɪntərɒpərəˈbɪlɪtɪ] N (*Comput*) interoperabilidad *f*

interpersonal [ˌɪntəˈpɜːsənl] ADJ interpersonal

interphone [ˈɪntəˌfəʊn] N interfono *m*

interplanetary [ˌɪntəˈplænɪtərɪ] ADJ interplanetario

interplay [ˈɪntəpleɪ] N interacción *f*

Interpol [ˈɪntəˌpɒl] N ABBR (= **International Criminal Police Organization**) Interpol *f*

interpolate [ɪnˈtɜːpəleɪt] VT interpolar

interpolation [ɪnˌtɜːpəˈleɪʃən] N interpolación *f*

interpose [ˌɪntəˈpəʊz] VT 1 (= *insert*) interponer; **she tried to ~ herself between them** trató de interponerse entre ellos
2 [+ *remark*] interponer; **"never!" ~d John** —¡jamás! —interpuso John

interpret [ɪnˈtɜːprɪt] Ⓐ VT 1 (= *translate orally*) traducir, interpretar
2 (= *explain, understand*) interpretar; **how are we to ~ that remark?** ¿cómo hemos de interpretar ese comentario?; **that is not how I ~ it** yo no lo entiendo así, yo lo entiendo de otro modo
Ⓑ VI (= *translate*) traducir; (= *work as interpreter*) trabajar de intérprete

interpretation [ɪnˌtɜːprɪˈteɪʃən] N (*gen*) interpretación *f*; (*Ling*) interpretación *f*, traducción *f*; **what ~ am I to place on your conduct?** ¿cómo he de interpretar tu conducta?; **the words bear another ~** las palabras pueden interpretarse de otro modo

interpretative [ɪnˈtɜːprɪtətɪv] ADJ = **interpretive**

interpreter [ɪnˈtɜːprɪtəʳ] N intérprete *mf*

interpreting [ɪnˈtɜːprɪtɪŋ] N interpretación *f*

interpretive [ɪnˈtɜːprɪtɪv] ADJ [*skills, process*] interpretativo

➤ LANGUAGE IN USE: **interpret A2** 26.3

interregnum [ˌɪntəˈregnəm] N (*pl* **interregnums** *or* **interregna** [ˌɪntəˈregnə]) interregno *m*

interrelate [ˌɪntərɪˈleɪt] Ⓐ VT interrelacionar
Ⓑ VI interrelacionarse

interrelated [ɪntərɪˈleɪtɪd] ADJ interrelacionado

interrelation [ˌɪntərɪˈleɪʃən] N interrelación *f*

interrelationship [ˌɪntərɪˈleɪʃənʃɪp] N interrelación *f*

interrogate [ɪnˈterəgeɪt] VT [+ *person*] interrogar, someter a un interrogatorio; (*Comput*) interrogar

interrogation [ɪnˌterəˈgeɪʃən] Ⓐ N interrogatorio *m*; (*Comput*) interrogación *f*
Ⓑ CPD ► **interrogation mark, interrogation point** (*US*) N signo *m* de interrogación, punto *m* de interrogación ► **interrogation room** N sala *f* de interrogatorios

interrogative [ˌɪntəˈrɒgətɪv] Ⓐ ADJ [*look, tone*] interrogador; (*Ling*) [*pronoun*] interrogativo
Ⓑ N (*Ling*) interrogativo *m*; **in the ~** en (forma) interrogativa

interrogatively [ˌɪntəˈrɒgətɪvlɪ] ADV **he looked up/looked at me ~** levantó la mirada/me miró con gesto interrogante

interrogator [ɪnˈterəgeɪtəʳ] N interrogador(a) *m/f*

interrogatory [ˌɪntəˈrɒgətərɪ] ADJ interrogante

interrupt [ˌɪntəˈrʌpt] Ⓐ VT interrumpir
Ⓑ VI interrumpir; **sorry to ~, but ...** perdonen que les interrumpa, pero ..., siento interrumpir, pero ...

interruption [ɪntəˈrʌpʃən] N interrupción *f*; **I need to be able to work without ~** necesito poder trabajar sin interrupciones *or* sin que nadie me interrumpa

intersect [ˌɪntəˈsekt] Ⓐ VT (*Math*) cortar
Ⓑ VI (*Math*) cortarse, intersecarse; [*roads*] cruzarse

intersection [ˌɪntəˈsekʃən] N (= *crossing*) intersección *f*, cruce *m*; (*Math*) intersección *f*

intersperse [ˌɪntəˈspɜːs] VT **a border of begonias ~d with geraniums** un arriate de begonias entremezcladas *or* intercaladas con geranios; **a speech ~d with jokes** un discurso salpicado de chistes; **sunny periods ~d with showers** periodos *mpl* de sol con intervalos de chubascos irregulares

interstate [ˌɪntəˈsteɪt] ADJ [*relations, commerce*] interestatal, entre estados; (*US*) [*highway*] interestatal

interstellar [ˌɪntəˈsteləʳ] ADJ interestelar

interstice [ɪnˈtɜːstɪs] N intersticio *m*

intertextuality [ˌɪntətekstjʊˈælɪtɪ] N intertextualidad *f*

intertwine [ˌɪntəˈtwaɪn] Ⓐ VI [*limbs, fingers, plants*] entrelazarse; [*fates, destinies*] cruzarse, entrecruzarse
Ⓑ VT [+ *limbs, fingers, plants*] entrelazar; [+ *fates, destinies*] cruzar, entrecruzar; [+ *interests*] interrelacionar

interurban [ˌɪntɜːˈɜːbən] ADJ interurbano

interval [ˈɪntəvəl] N 1 (*in time, space*) intervalo *m*; (*Theat*) intermedio *m*; (*more formally*) entreacto *m*; (*Sport*) (= *half time*) descanso *m*; **at ~s** (*in time*) a intervalos; (*in space*) a intervalos, cada cierta distancia; **at regular ~s** (*in time, space*) a intervalos regulares; **baste the meat at ~s of 15 minutes** *or* **at 15-minute ~s** rocíe la carne con su jugo cada 15 minutos; **sunny ~s** claros *mpl*; **there was an ~ for meditation** se hizo una pausa para la meditación
2 (*Mus*) intervalo *m*

intervene [ˌɪntəˈviːn] VI 1 (= *take part*) [*person*] intervenir, tomar parte (**in** en); [*government*] intervenir (**in** en)
2 (= *step in*) [*person*] interponerse; [*fate*] cruzarse, interponerse; **we were to marry but the war ~d** íbamos a casarnos pero se interpuso la guerra; **to ~ (with sb) on sb's behalf** interceder por algn (ante algn)
3 (= *crop up*) surgir, sobrevenir; **if nothing ~s to prevent it** si no surge nada que lo impida

intervening [ˌɪntəˈviːnɪŋ] ADJ intermedio; **in the ~ period** en el ínterin *or* interín; **in the ~ years** en el transcurso de esos años

intervention [ˌɪntəˈvenʃən] Ⓐ N (*gen*) intervención *f*
Ⓑ CPD ► **intervention price** N precio *m* de intervención

interventionism [ˌɪntəˈvenʃənɪzəm] N intervencionismo *m*

interventionist [ˌɪntəˈvenʃənɪst] Ⓐ ADJ intervencionista
Ⓑ N intervencionista *mf*

▼**interview** [ˈɪntəvjuː] Ⓐ N entrevista *f*; (*for press, TV*) entrevista *f*, interviú *f or m*; **to have an ~ with sb** entrevistarse con algn
Ⓑ VT [+ *person*] entrevistar; (*for press, TV*) hacer una entrevista *or* interviú a; **3% of those ~ed did not know that ...** un 3 por cien de los entrevistados ignoraba que ...
Ⓒ VI **they are ~ing for this post tomorrow** mañana realizarán las entrevistas para este puesto; **I don't ~ very well** no se me dan muy bien las entrevistas

interviewee [ˈɪntəˌvjuːˈiː] N entrevistado/a *m/f*

interviewer [ˈɪntəvjuːəʳ] N (*on radio, for job*) entrevistador(a) *m/f*

inter vivos [ˈɪntəˈviːvɒs] ADJ (*Jur*) **~ gift** donación *f* inter vivos

inter-war [ˌɪntəˈwɔːʳ] ADJ **the ~ years** el período de entreguerras

interweave [ˌɪntəˈwiːv] (*pt* **interwove**; *pp* **interwoven**) VT entretejer

intestate [ɪnˈtestɪt] ADJ **to die ~** morir intestado

intestinal [ˌɪntesˈtaɪnl] ADJ [*tract, complaint*] intestinal

intestine [ɪnˈtestɪn] N intestino *m*; **small/large ~** intestino *m* delgado/grueso

intifada [ˌɪntɪˈfɑːdə] N intifada *f*

intimacy [ˈɪntɪməsɪ] N 1 (= *closeness*) intimidad *f*; **I read the letter in the ~ of my bedroom** leí la carta en la intimidad de mi habitación; **there had never been any sexual ~ between them** nunca habían mantenido relaciones íntimas; **the ~ of his knowledge on the subject** su profundo conocimiento de la materia
2 **intimacies** (*spoken*) intimidades *fpl*; (*sexual*) intimidad *f* (física), proximidad *f* (física)

intimate Ⓐ ADJ [ˈɪntɪmɪt] [*relationship, contact, conversation, meal*] íntimo; [*friend*] íntimo, de confianza; [*friendship, connection*] íntimo, estrecho; [*details*] íntimo, personal; **it's an ~ little restaurant** es un pequeño restaurante de ambiente íntimo; **an ~ atmosphere** un ambiente íntimo; **to be/become ~ with sb** (*friendly*) intimar con algn; (*sexually*) tener relaciones (íntimas) con algn; **~ hygiene** (*euph*) higiene *f* íntima; **to have an ~ knowledge of a subject** tener un profundo conocimiento de una materia, conocer una materia a fondo; **he had an ~ knowledge of the city** conocía muy bien la ciudad; **to be on ~ terms with sb** ser íntimo de algn
Ⓑ [ˈɪntɪmeɪt] VT insinuar, dar a entender; **he ~d his approval** insinuó *or* dio a entender que lo aprobaba; **she ~d that she was ready for a change** insinuó *or* dio a entender que estaba lista para un cambio; **he ~d to the president that ...** le insinuó *or* le dio a entender al presidente que ...
Ⓒ [ˈɪntɪmɪt] N amigo/a *m/f* de confianza; (*pej*) compinche *mf*

intimately [ˈɪntɪmɪtlɪ] ADV íntimamente; **to be ~ acquainted with sb** (*in a friendly way*) conocer a algn íntimamente; **to be ~ acquainted with a subject** tener un profundo conocimiento de una materia, conocer una materia a fondo; **to be ~ involved in sth** estar muy involucrado en algo; **Inspector Green was ~ involved in the case** el Inspector Green estaba muy involucrado en el caso *or* estaba metido a fondo en el caso; **to know sb ~** (*as friends*) conocer a algn íntimamente; (*sexually*) tener relaciones íntimas con algn; **musicians whose work she knew ~** músicos *mpl* cuyo trabajo conocía a fondo *or* en profundidad; **to talk ~** tener una conversación íntima

intimation [ˌɪntɪˈmeɪʃən] N 1 (= *suggestion*) indicación *f*; **it was the first ~ we had had of it** fue la primera indicación que tuvimos de ello; **did you have any ~ that this would happen?** ¿hubo algo que te hiciera pensar que esto sucedería?
2 (= *hint*) insinuación *f*; **her ~ that there would be redundancies worried me** su insinuación de que habría despidos me preocupó

intimidate [ɪnˈtɪmɪdeɪt] VT intimidar

intimidating [ˌɪnˈtɪmɪdeɪtɪŋ] ADJ amedrentador, intimidante

intimidation [ɪnˌtɪmɪˈdeɪʃən] N intimidación *f*

intimidatory [ɪnˌtɪmɪˈdeɪtərɪ] ADJ intimidatorio

into [ˈɪntʊ] PREP

*when **into** is an element in a phrasal verb, eg **break into, enter into, look into, walk into**, look up the verb*

1 (*of place*) en, dentro de; **put it ~ the car/bag/cupboard** mételo en el *or* dentro del coche/bolso/armario; **to get ~ bed** meterse a la cama; **to get ~ a car** subir(se) a un coche; **he helped his mother ~ the car** ayudó a su madre a subir al coche; **to go ~ the country** ir al campo; **I poured the milk ~ a cup** vertí la leche en una taza; **he went off ~ the desert** partió hacia el interior del desierto *or* adentrándose en el desierto; **he went further ~ the forest** siguió adentrándose en el bosque; **it fell ~ the lake** se cayó al lago; **they got ~ the plane** subieron al avión; **to come/go ~ a room** entrar en una habitación; **to go ~ town** ir al centro de la ciudad; **to go ~ the wood** adentrarse *or* penetrar en el bosque; *see also* **go into 3**
2 (*of time*) **it continued well** *or* **far ~ 1996** siguió hasta bien entrado 1996; **we talked far ~ the night** charlamos hasta bien entrada la noche; **he's well ~ his fifties** tiene cincuenta y tantos largos
3 (*change in condition etc*) **to change ~ a monster** volverse un *or* convertirse en un monstruo; **to change pounds ~ dollars** cambiar libras por dólares; **the rain changed ~ snow** la lluvia se convirtió en nieve; **they divided ~ two groups** se dividieron en dos grupos; **to translate sth ~ Spanish** traducir algo al español; **it turned ~ a pleasant day** resultó *or* se hizo un día muy agradable; *see also* **burst into, change C, divide, grow A1, translate, turn B5**
4 (*Math*) **to divide 3 ~ 12** dividir doce entre tres; **2 ~ 6 goes 3** seis entre dos son tres
5 **to be ~ sth*: he is really ~ jazz** es un gran aficionado al *or* del jazz; **to be ~ drugs** meterse drogas, andar metido en drogas;

➤ LANGUAGE IN USE: **interview A** 19.3

she's ~ health food le va mucho lo de la comida sana; **what are you ~ now?** ¿a qué te dedicas ahora?; **the children/puppies are ~ everything!** ¡los críos/perritos andan revolviéndolo todo!

▼ **intolerable** [ɪn'tɒlərəbl] ADJ intolerable; **this is ~!** ¡esto es intolerable!; **it is ~ that** es intolerable que + *subjun*, no se puede consentir que + *subjun*

intolerably [ɪn'tɒlərəblɪ] ADV [*ache*] insoportablemente; **he is ~ vain** es tremendamente vanidoso; **it was ~ hot** hacía un calor insoportable

intolerance [ɪn'tɒlərəns] N (*gen*) intolerancia *f*; (= *bigotry*) intransigencia *f*; (*Med*) intolerancia *f* (**to, of** a); **food ~** intolerancia *f* a los alimentos

intolerant [ɪn'tɒlərənt] ADJ (*gen*) intolerante (**of** con *or* para con); (= *bigoted*) intransigente (**of** con); **to be ~ of sth** (*gen*) no tolerar algo; (*Med*) **he is ~ of certain drugs/foods** tiene intolerancia a ciertos medicamentos/alimentos, su cuerpo no tolera ciertos medicamentos/alimentos

intonation [,ɪntəʊ'neɪʃən] N entonación *f*

intone [ɪn'təʊn] VT entonar; (*Rel*) salmodiar

in toto [ɪn'təʊtəʊ] ADV en total, en conjunto

intoxicant [ɪn'tɒksɪkənt] Ⓐ ADJ embriagador
Ⓑ N (= *drink*) bebida *f* alcohólica; (= *drug*) estupefaciente *m*

intoxicate [ɪn'tɒksɪkeɪt] VT 1 (*lit*) (*frm*) [*alcohol*] embriagar; [*poison*] intoxicar
2 (*fig*) (*liter*) [*victory, success, beauty*] embriagar (*liter*)

intoxicated [ɪn'tɒksɪkeɪtɪd] ADJ 1 (*lit*) (*frm*) (= *drunk*) ebrio, en estado de embriaguez; **to become ~** alcanzar un estado de embriaguez
2 (*fig*) (*liter*) embriagado (*liter*), ebrio; **to be ~ by sth** (*by victory, success*) estar embriagado *or* ebrio a causa de algo; **to be ~ with sth** estar embriagado *or* ebrio de algo; **to feel ~** sentirse embriagado

intoxicating [ɪn'tɒksɪkeɪtɪŋ] ADJ 1 (*frm*) (*lit*) [*substance*] narcótico, estupefaciente; **an ~ mixture of gin, vodka and coke** una mezcla de ginebra, vodka y Coca Cola con un efecto narcótico; **~ drink** *or* **liquor** bebida *f* alcohólica
2 (*fig*) (*liter*) [*success, perfume, atmosphere*] embriagador

intoxication [ɪn,tɒksɪ'keɪʃən] N 1 (*frm*) (*lit*) (*by alcohol*) embriaguez *f*, intoxicación *f* etílica (*frm or hum*); (*Med*) (*by toxic substance*) intoxicación *f*
2 (*fig*) (*liter*) embriaguez *f*

intra... ['ɪntrə] PREFIX intra...

intractability [ɪn,træktə'bɪlətɪ] N [*of person*] intratabilidad *f*; [*of situation*] dificultad *f*; [*of problem*] insolubilidad *f*; (*Med*) [*of illness*] incurabilidad *f*

intractable [ɪn'træktəbl] ADJ [*person*] intratable; (= *unruly*) indisciplinado; [*problem*] insoluble, espinoso; [*illness*] incurable

intramural [,ɪntrə'mjʊərəl] ADJ (*US Univ*) dentro de la universidad; (= *within organization, country*) interno

intramuscular [,ɪntrə'mʌskjʊləʳ] ADJ intramuscular

intranet ['ɪntrənet] N (*Comput*) intranet *f*

intransigence [ɪn'trænsɪdʒəns] N intransigencia *f*

intransigent [ɪn'trænsɪdʒənt] ADJ intransigente

intransitive [ɪn'trænsɪtɪv] ADJ (*Ling*) intransitivo

intransitivity [ɪn,trænsɪ'tɪvɪtɪ] N intransitividad *f*

intrauterine [,ɪntrə'juːtəraɪn] Ⓐ ADJ intrauterino
Ⓑ CPD ► **intrauterine device** N dispositivo *m* intrauterino; (*coil-shaped*) espiral *f*

intravenous [,ɪntrə'viːnəs] ADJ intravenoso; **~ drug users** drogadictos *mpl* que se inyectan por vía intravenosa

intravenously [,ɪntrə'viːnəslɪ] ADV por vía intravenosa

in-tray ['ɪn,treɪ] N bandeja *f* de entrada

intrepid [ɪn'trepɪd] ADJ intrépido

intrepidity [,ɪntrɪ'pɪdɪtɪ] N (*frm*) intrepidez *f*

intrepidly [ɪn'trepɪdlɪ] ADV intrépidamente

intricacy ['ɪntrɪkəsɪ] N [*of pattern, design, machinery*] lo intrincado, complejidad *f*; [*of plot, problem*] complejidad *f*; **the intricacies of the law** los entresijos de la ley

intricate ['ɪntrɪkɪt] ADJ [*pattern, design, machinery*] intrincado; [*plot, problem*] complejo

intricately ['ɪntrɪkɪtlɪ] ADV intrincadamente, de modo intrincado

intrigue [ɪn'triːg] Ⓐ N (= *plot*) intriga *f*; (*amorous*) aventura *f* (sentimental), amorío *m*; **a web of ~** una maraña de intriga
Ⓑ VT fascinar; **I am ~d to know whether ...** me intriga saber si ..., estoy intrigado por saber si ...; **we were ~d by a sign outside a shop** nos llamó la atención el letrero de una tienda
Ⓒ VI intrigar (**against** contra)

intriguer [ɪn'triːgəʳ] N intrigante *mf*

intriguing [ɪn'triːgɪŋ] Ⓐ ADJ (= *fascinating*) [*question, problem*] intrigante; [*prospect, possibility*] fascinante; [*personality*] misterioso, enigmático; **a most ~ problem** un problema de lo más intrigante; **an ~ little gadget** un chisme curiosísimo *or* de lo más curioso; **how very ~!** ¡qué raro!, ¡muy interesante!
Ⓑ N intriga *f*

intriguingly [ɪn'triːgɪŋlɪ] ADV **~, this was never confirmed** curiosamente, esto nunca fue confirmado; **~ different** intrigantemente diferente; **~ original** de una originalidad fascinante

intrinsic [ɪn'trɪnsɪk] ADJ intrínseco; **~ value** valor *m* intrínseco; **stress is ~ to the job** el estrés es algo inherente al trabajo; **the harp and fiddle are ~ to Irish music** el arpa y el violín son intrínsecos a *or* característicos de la música irlandesa

intrinsically [ɪn'trɪnsɪklɪ] ADV intrínsecamente

intro* ['ɪntrəʊ] N (*Mus*) (= **introduction**) entrada *f*

intro... ['ɪntrəʊ] PREFIX intro...

introduce [,ɪntrə'djuːs] VT 1 (= *present, make acquainted*) presentar; **to ~ sb to sb** presentar a algn a algn; **may I ~ ...?** permítame presentarle a ..., le presento a ...; **I don't think we've been ~d** creo que no nos han presentado; **to ~ sb to sth** hacer conocer algo a algn, iniciar a algn en algo; **I was ~d to chess at eight** empecé a jugar al ajedrez a los ocho años; **I was ~d to Milton too young** me hicieron leer a Milton demasiado temprano
2 (= *bring in*) [+ *reform*] introducir; (*Pol*) [+ *bill*] presentar; (*TV, Rad*) [+ *programme*] presentar; [+ *product, new fashion*] lanzar; [+ *subject into conversation, idea*] introducir; **be careful how you ~ the subject** ten cuidado a la hora de abordar el tema; **it was you who ~d the subject, not me** fuiste tú el que sacaste el tema, no yo
3 (= *insert*) introducir; **the tube is ~d into the throat** el tubo se introduce por la garganta; **I was ~d into a dark room** me hicieron entrar en un cuarto oscuro
4 (= *write introduction for*) [+ *book*] prologar

introduction [,ɪntrə'dʌkʃən] N 1 [*of person*] presentación *f*; **to give sb an ~ to sb** dar a algn una carta de recomendación para algn; **a letter of ~** una carta de recomendación; **will you do** *or* **make the ~s?** ¿quieres hacer las presentaciones?
2 (= *initiation*) introducción *f*; **this book is a good ~ to his teachings** este libro es una buena introducción a sus enseñanzas; **my ~ to life in Cadiz** mi primera experiencia de la vida en Cádiz; **my ~ to maths** mi iniciación en las matemáticas
3 (*in book*) prólogo *m*, introducción *f*
4 (= *bringing in*) [*of legislation*] introducción *f*; (*Pol*) [*of bill*] presentación *f*
5 (= *insertion*) introducción *f*, inserción *f*

introductory [,ɪntrə'dʌktərɪ] Ⓐ ADJ [*remarks*] preliminar; [*lecture, talk*] introductorio, de introducción; [*course*] introductorio, de iniciación
Ⓑ CPD ► **introductory offer** N oferta *f* de lanzamiento

introit ['ɪntrɔɪt] N introito *m*

introspection [,ɪntrəʊ'spekʃən] N introspección *f*

introspective [,ɪntrəʊ'spektɪv] ADJ introspectivo

introspectiveness [,ɪntrəʊ'spektɪvnɪs] N introspección *f*

introversion [,ɪntrəʊ'vɜːʃən] N introversión *f*

introvert ['ɪntrəʊvɜːt] Ⓐ ADJ introvertido
Ⓑ N introvertido/a *m/f*

introverted [,ɪntrəʊ'vɜːtɪd] ADJ introvertido

intrude [ɪn'truːd] Ⓐ VI 1 (= *intervene*) entrometerse, inmiscuirse (**on, upon** en); (= *disturb*) molestar; **am I intruding?** ¿les molesto?; **to ~ on** *or* **upon sb** molestar a algn; **to ~ on sb's privacy** meterse en la vida privada de algn; **we mustn't ~ on their grief** debemos respetar la intimidad de su dolor
2 (= *encroach*) **sometimes sentimentality ~s** a veces se asoma el sentimentalismo; **it kept intruding into my thoughts** siguió interfiriendo en mis pensamientos
Ⓑ VT [+ *views, opinions*] imponer (**on, upon** a); [+ *subject*] introducir (sin derecho); **I haven't come to ~ myself upon you** no he venido para molestarles con mi presencia

intruder [ɪn'truːdəʳ] N intruso/a *m/f*

intrusion [ɪn'truːʒən] N intrusión *f*; (*on sb's privacy*) intromisión *f*, invasión *f*; **pardon the ~** siento tener que importunarla; **the ~ of sentimentality** la intrusión del sentimentalismo

intrusive [ɪn'truːsɪv] ADJ [*reporter*] entrometido, indiscreto; [*question*] indiscreto; [*noise, presence*] molesto

intuit [ɪn'tjʊɪt] VT (*esp US*) intuir

intuition [,ɪntjuː'ɪʃən] N intuición *f*

intuitive [ɪn'tjuːɪtɪv] ADJ [*knowledge*] intuitivo; [*powers*] de intuición; **she had an ~ grasp of what was needed** intuía qué era lo que hacía falta

intuitively [ɪn'tjuːɪtɪvlɪ] ADV intuitivamente, por intuición

Inuit ['ɪnjuɪt] (*pl* **Inuit, Inuits**) Ⓐ ADJ Inuit *inv*
Ⓑ N Inuit *mf*, esquimal *mf*; **the ~s** los Inuit

inundate ['ɪnʌndeɪt] VT inundar; **we have been ~d with replies** nos hemos visto inundados *or* desbordados por las respuestas

inundation [,ɪnʌn'deɪʃən] N inundación *f*

inure [ɪn'jʊəʳ] VT (= *accustom*) acostumbrar, habituar (**to** a); **to be ~d to sth** estar acostum-

➤ LANGUAGE IN USE: **intolerable** 14

brado *or* habituado a algo; **to become ~d to sth** acostumbrarse *or* habituarse a algo

inv. ABBR (= **invoice**) f.ª

invade [ɪn'veɪd] VT (*Mil*) invadir; [+ *privacy*] invadir; [+ *sb's rights*] usurpar

invader [ɪn'veɪdəʳ] N invasor(a) *m/f*

invading [ɪn'veɪdɪŋ] ADJ invasor

invalid¹ ['ɪnvəlɪd] Ⓐ N inválido/a *m/f*
Ⓑ ADJ inválido
Ⓒ CPD ► **invalid car, invalid carriage** N coche *m* de inválido
►**invalid out** VT + ADV **to ~ sb out of the army** (*esp Brit Mil*) licenciar a algn por invalidez

invalid² [ɪn'vælɪd] ADJ [*contract*] inválido, nulo; [*ticket, request*] inválido; [*theory, results, conclusions*] sin validez; **to become ~** caducar

invalidate [ɪn'vælɪdeɪt] VT [+ *document, argument, theory*] invalidar; [+ *contract*] anular, invalidar

invalidity [,ɪnvə'lɪdɪtɪ] Ⓐ N 1 [*of document, contract*] invalidez *f*, nulidad *f*
2 (= *illness, disablement*) invalidez *f*
Ⓑ CPD ► **invalidity benefit** N (*Brit*) prestación *f* por invalidez ► **invalidity pension** N pensión *f* de invalidez

invaluable [ɪn'væljʊəbl] ADJ inapreciable, inestimable

invariable [ɪn'vɛərɪəbl] ADJ invariable

invariably [ɪn'vɛərɪəblɪ] ADV invariablemente, siempre; **it ~ happens that ...** ocurre siempre que ...; **he is ~ late** siempre llega tarde, llega tarde invariablemente

invasion [ɪn'veɪʒən] N invasión *f*; **~ force** fuerza *f* invasora; **it would be an ~ of privacy to ...** sería una invasión de la intimidad ...

invasive [ɪn'veɪsɪv] ADJ [*surgery, cancer*] invasivo

invective [ɪn'vektɪv] N (= *accusation*) invectiva *f*; (= *abuse*) improperios *mpl*, palabras *fpl* fuertes

inveigh [ɪn'veɪ] VI **to ~ against** vituperar, lanzar invectivas contra

inveigle [ɪn'viːgl] VT **she ~d him up to her room** lo indujo mañosamente a subir a su habitación; **to ~ sb into doing sth** inducir a algn mediante engaño a que haga algo; **he let himself be ~d into it** se dejó inducir a ello; **he was ~d into the duke's service** fue inducido hábilmente a entrar a servir al duque

invent [ɪn'vent] VT inventar

invention [ɪn'venʃən] N 1 (= *act*) invención *f*; (= *machine*) invento *m*, invención *f*
2 (= *inventiveness*) inventiva *f*
3 (= *falsehood*) mentira *f*, invención *f*; **it's pure ~** es pura invención; **it's ~ from start to finish** es mentira desde el principio hasta el fin

inventive [ɪn'ventɪv] ADJ (= *creative*) ingenioso, lleno de inventiva; **to have an ~ mind** tener ingenio *or* inventiva; **he's an ~ cook** es un cocinero con mucha inventiva *or* muy imaginativo; **~ powers** capacidad *f* inventiva, inventiva *f*

inventively [ɪn'ventɪvlɪ] ADV con inventiva *or* imaginación

inventiveness [ɪn'ventɪvnɪs] N inventiva *f*, ingenio *m*

inventor [ɪn'ventəʳ] N inventor(a) *m/f*

inventory ['ɪnvəntrɪ] Ⓐ N inventario *m*; **to draw up an ~ of sth** hacer un inventario de algo
Ⓑ VT inventariar
Ⓒ CPD ► **inventory control** N control *m* de existencias *or* de inventario

inverse ['ɪn'vɜːs] Ⓐ ADJ inverso
Ⓑ N **the ~** lo inverso, lo contrario

inversely [ɪn'vɜːslɪ] ADV a la inversa; **A is ~ proportional to B** A es inversamente proporcional a B; **interest rates and prices are ~ related** las tasas de interés y los precios guardan una relación inversamente proporcional

inversion [ɪn'vɜːʃən] N inversión *f*

invert [ɪn'vɜːt] VT invertir, poner al revés

invertebrate [ɪn'vɜːtɪbrɪt] Ⓐ ADJ invertebrado
Ⓑ N invertebrado/a *m/f*

inverted [ɪn'vɜːtɪd] ADJ **~ commas** (*Brit*) comillas *fpl*; **in ~ commas** entre comillas; **~ snob** *persona que desprecia las actitudes propias de la clase social a la que pertenece, intentando identificarse con gente de una clase supuestamente inferior*; **~ snobbery** esnobismo *m* regresivo

invert sugar ['ɪnvɜːt'ʃʊgəʳ] N azúcar *m* invertido

invest [ɪn'vest] Ⓐ VT 1 [+ *money, capital, funds*] invertir (**in** en); [+ *person*] (*in office*) investir; (*fig*) [+ *time, effort*] dedicar; **~ed capital** capital *m* invertido
2 **to ~ sb with sth** investir a algn de *or* con algo; **he was ~ed with a dignity** lo invistieron con una dignidad; **he ~ed it with a certain mystery** lo revistió de cierto misterio; **he seems to ~ it with some importance** parece que lo reviste de cierta importancia
3 (*Mil†*) sitiar, cercar
Ⓑ VI **to ~ in** [+ *company, project*] invertir dinero en; (*hum*) (= *buy*) comprarse; **I've ~ed in a new pair of rubber gloves** me he comprado un nuevo par de guantes de goma; **to ~ with** [+ *bank, building society*] invertir dinero en

investigate [ɪn'vestɪgeɪt] Ⓐ VT 1 (= *inquire into*) [+ *crime, case*] investigar; [+ *person*] hacer indagaciones sobre; [+ *claim, possibility*] examinar, estudiar; [+ *complaint*] estudiar; **police are investigating two possibilities** la policía está investigando dos posibles pistas
2 (= *inspect*) examinar
3 (= *research*) investigar, llevar a cabo una investigación sobre
Ⓑ VI investigar; **I heard a noise downstairs, I'd better go and ~** he oído un ruido abajo, mejor que vaya a investigar

investigation [ɪn,vestɪ'geɪʃən] N 1 (= *inquiry*) (*by police, authorities, scientist*) investigación *f*; **the ~ into the causes of the accident** la investigación sobre las causas del accidente; **these allegations need further ~** estas acusaciones se tienen que investigar más a fondo
2 (= *inspection, search*) [*of place, site*] inspección *f*; [*of document*] examen *m*; (*Med*) exploración *f*; **doctors carried out a simple ~ under local anaesthetic** los médicos realizaron una simple exploración utilizando anestesia local
3 (= *in-depth study*) estudio *m* (**of, into** de)

investigative [ɪn'vestɪ,geɪtɪv] Ⓐ ADJ investigador
Ⓑ CPD ► **investigative journalism** N periodismo *m* de investigación

investigator [ɪn'vestɪgeɪtəʳ] N investigador(a) *m/f*

investigatory [ɪn'vestɪ,geɪtərɪ] ADJ [*committee, panel*] investigador

investiture [ɪn'vestɪtʃəʳ] N investidura *f*

investment [ɪn'vestmənt] Ⓐ N 1 (*Comm*) inversión *f*
2 (*Mil†*) sitio *m*, cerco *m*
3 (= *investiture*) investidura *f*
Ⓑ CPD ► **investment analyst** N analista *mf* financiero/a ► **investment bank** N banco *m* de inversión ► **investment company** N compañía *f* de inversiones ► **investment grant** N subvención *f* para la inversión ► **investment income** N renta *f* de inversiones ► **investment portfolio** N cartera *f* de valores ► **investment trust** N sociedad *f* de inversiones

investor [ɪn'vestəʳ] N inversionista *mf*

inveterate [ɪn'vetərɪt] ADJ [*gambler*] empedernido; [*laziness, selfishness*] inveterado

invidious [ɪn'vɪdɪəs] ADJ [*job, task*] odioso, ingrato; [*comparison*] injusto; **I find myself in an ~ position** me encuentro en una situación ingrata; **it would be ~ to mention names** sería inapropiado mencionar nombres

invigilate [ɪn'vɪdʒɪleɪt] (*Brit*) Ⓐ VT [+ *examination*] vigilar
Ⓑ VI vigilar (durante los exámenes)

invigilator [ɪn'vɪdʒɪleɪtəʳ] N (*Brit*) celador(a) *m/f* (*en un examen*)

invigorate [ɪn'vɪgəreɪt] VT [+ *person*] vigorizar; [+ *campaign*] dar nuevo ímpetu a; [+ *economy*] estimular; **I felt refreshed, ~d and ready to tackle anything** me sentía descansado, lleno de energía y dispuesto a abordar cualquier tarea

invigorating [ɪn'vɪgəreɪtɪŋ] ADJ [*walk, shower, air*] vigorizante, tonificante; **how ~ she was to talk to!** ¡qué estimulante resultaba su conversación!

invincibility [ɪn,vɪnsɪ'bɪlɪtɪ] N invencibilidad *f*

invincible [ɪn'vɪnsəbl] ADJ [*army, team*] invencible; [*faith, belief*] inquebrantable; **he has an ~ lead over the other runners** les lleva una ventaja insuperable al resto de los corredores

invincibly [ɪn'vɪnsəblɪ] ADV **the army marched ~ across Europe** el ejército cruzó Europa invencible

inviolability [ɪn,vaɪələ'bɪlɪtɪ] N inviolabilidad *f*

inviolable [ɪn'vaɪələbl] ADJ inviolable

inviolably [ɪn'vaɪələblɪ] ADV inviolablemente

inviolate [ɪn'vaɪəlɪt] ADJ [*land, possessions*] intacto; (*liter*) [*woman*] intacto, sin mancillar (*liter*)

invisibility [ɪn,vɪzə'bɪlɪtɪ] N invisibilidad *f*

invisible [ɪn'vɪzəbl] Ⓐ ADJ (*gen, Comm*) invisible
Ⓑ **invisibles** NPL (*Comm*) ingresos *mpl* invisibles
Ⓒ CPD ► **invisible assets** NPL activo *msing* invisible ► **invisible earnings** NPL ingresos *mpl* invisibles ► **invisible exports** NPL exportaciones *fpl* invisibles ► **invisible imports** NPL importaciones *fpl* invisibles ► **invisible ink** N tinta *f* simpática ► **invisible mending** N zurcido *m* invisible

invisibly [ɪn'vɪzɪblɪ] ADV de manera invisible

invitation [,ɪnvɪ'teɪʃən] Ⓐ N invitación *f*; **an ~ to dinner** ◊ **a dinner ~** una invitación para cenar; **I am here at the ~ of the director** he venido por invitación del director; **the house is an ~ to robbers** la casa es toda una atracción para los ladrones
Ⓑ CPD ► **invitation card** N tarjeta *f* de invitación

invitational [,ɪnvɪ'teɪʃənl] ADJ (*Sport*) [*event, tournament*] invitacional (*en el que sólo participan deportistas invitados*)

invite Ⓐ [ɪn'vaɪt] VT 1 [+ *person*] invitar; (*esp to important celebration*) convidar; **to ~ sb to do sth** invitar a algn a hacer algo; **to ~ sb to dinner/lunch** invitar a algn a cenar/almorzar; **to ~ sb to have a drink** invitar a algn a tomar algo; **to ~ sb in/up** invitar a algn a pasar/subir; **to ~ sb out** invitar a algn a salir;

➤ LANGUAGE IN USE: invitation A 25.1, 25.2, 25.3 invite A1 25.3

they ~d me out to dinner me invitaron a cenar (a un restaurante); **I've ~d them over for drinks** los he invitado a tomar unas copas en casa

2 (= *request*) [+ *opinions*] pedir; (*more frm*) solicitar; **they are inviting applications for the post of ...** han abierto el plazo para recibir solicitudes para el puesto de ...

3 (= *provoke*) [+ *discussion, ridicule*] provocar; **to ~ trouble** buscarse problemas; **to do so would be to ~ defeat** hacer eso sería provocar la propia derrota; **A ~s comparison with B** A nos induce a compararlo con B; **she seems to ~ stares** parece que provoca las miradas de la gente

Ⓑ ['ɪnvaɪt] N (*) invitación *f*

inviting [ɪn'vaɪtɪŋ] ADJ 1 (= *appealing*) [*atmosphere, place, room*] acogedor; [*prospect*] atractivo; [*appearance*] (*of person*) atrayente; (*of food*) tentador; [*food*] apetitoso, apetecible; [*smell*] apetitoso; [*book*] que incita a la lectura, que invita a la lectura; **the water looked warm and ~** el agua aparecía cálida y tentadora; **she offered him the plate with an ~ smile** le ofreció el plato animándole a comer con una sonrisa; **with an ~ gesture, she showed him to his room** le hizo un gesto invitándole a seguirla y le enseñó su habitación

2 (= *seductive*) [*smile, look, gesture*] incitante, sugerente

invitingly [ɪn'vaɪtɪŋlɪ] ADV 1 (= *appealingly, welcomingly*) **the food was displayed ~** la comida estaba dispuesta de forma atrayente; **"are you hungry?" she said ~** —¿tienes hambre? —dijo en un tono que invitaba a decir que sí; **"come in," he said ~** —entrad —dijo invitándoles a pasar; **the soup steamed ~** la sopa echaba un vaporcito que invitaba a comerla; **the water was ~ clear** el agua cristalina invitaba a bañarse; **the packet lay ~ open** el paquete estaba abierto de forma tentadora

2 (= *seductively*) [*smile, gesture*] de forma sugerente, de forma incitante; [*say, whisper*] en tono sugerente

in vitro [ɪn'vi:trəʊ] Ⓐ ADJ, ADV in vitro

Ⓑ CPD ► **in vitro fertilization** N fecundación *f* in vitro

invocation [,ɪnvəʊ'keɪʃən] N invocación *f*

▼ **invoice** ['ɪnvɔɪs] Ⓐ N factura *f*; **as per ~** según factura; **to send an ~** pasar *or* presentar factura

Ⓑ VT [+ *goods*] facturar; **to ~ sb for sth** pasar a algn factura por algo; **you will be ~d once the goods have been delivered** le pasaremos factura *or* le mandaremos la factura una vez le haya sido entregada la mercancía

Ⓒ CPD ► **invoice clerk** N facturador(a) *m/f*
► **invoice value** N valor *m* total de factura

invoicing ['ɪnvɔɪsɪŋ] N facturación *f*

invoke [ɪn'vəʊk] VT [+ *law*] recurrir *or* acogerse a, invocar; [+ *principle*] recurrir a, invocar; [+ *aid, protection, god, spirit*] invocar

involuntarily [ɪn'vɒləntərɪlɪ] ADV involuntariamente; **he had ~ hurt her feelings** la había ofendido sin querer

involuntary [ɪn'vɒləntərɪ] ADJ involuntario

involuted [,ɪnvə'lu:tɪd] ADJ [*design, system*] intrincado

▼ **involve** [ɪn'vɒlv] VT 1 (= *implicate, associate*) implicar, involucrar; **a dispute involving a friend of mine** una disputa en la que estaba implicado *or* involucrado un amigo mío; **a crash involving three vehicles** una colisión en la que se vieron envueltos tres vehículos; **to ~ sb (in sth)** involucrar a algn (en algo); **we would prefer not to ~ the children** preferiríamos no meter *or* involucrar a los niños; **they are trying to ~ him in the theft** están intentando implicarlo *or* involucrarlo en el robo; **try to ~ him in your leisure activities** intenta hacer que participe contigo en tus actividades de tiempo libre; **it may ~ you in extra cost** puede acarrearle costos adicionales; **the persons ~d** (*gen*) los interesados; (= *culprits*) los implicados; **to be ~d (in sth)**: **how did he come to be ~d?** ¿cómo llegó a meterse en esto?; **he was ~d in a fight** se vio envuelto en una pelea; **he/his car was ~d in an accident** él/su coche se vio involucrado en un accidente; **she was only ~d in the final stages of the project** sólo tomó parte en las fases finales del proyecto; **I was so ~d in my book that ...** estaba tan absorto en el libro que ...; **to become** *or* **get ~d (in sth)**: **the police became ~d** la policía tomó cartas en el asunto; **I don't want to get ~d** no quiero meterme; **to get ~d in a fight** verse envuelto en una pelea; **to be/become/get ~d with sth/sb**: **she's so ~d with the project she doesn't have time for me** está tan liada* con el proyecto que no tiene tiempo para mí, el proyecto la absorbe tanto que no tiene tiempo para mí; **she became ~d with the resistance movement** se involucró en el movimiento de resistencia; **she got ~d with some really weird people** se mezcló con una gente muy rara; **she likes him but she doesn't want to get ~d** él le gusta, pero no quiere comprometerse

2 (= *entail, imply*) suponer; **it ~d a lot of expense** supuso *or* acarreó muchos gastos; **there's a good deal of work ~d** supone *or* implica bastante trabajo; **the job ~s moving to London** el trabajo requiere que se traslade a Londres; **what does your job ~?** ¿en qué consiste su trabajo?; **how much money is ~d?** ¿cuánto dinero hay en juego?; **a question of principle is ~d** aquí hay principios en juego

involved [ɪn'vɒlvd] ADJ (= *complicated*) complicado, enrevesado

involvement [ɪn'vɒlvmənt] N 1 (= *implication, association*) **we don't know the extent of his ~** no sabemos hasta qué punto está implicado; **a demonstration against US ~ in Vietnam** una manifestación contra la intervención estadounidense en Vietnam; **student ~ in campus affairs** la participación de los estudiantes en los asuntos universitarios; **I knew of his past ~ with drugs** sabía que en el pasado había estado metido en drogas

2 (= *relationship*) relación *f*; **she didn't know about my ~ with Corinne** no sabía de mi relación con Corinne

invulnerability [ɪn,vʌlnərə'bɪlɪtɪ] N invulnerabilidad *f* (**to** a)

invulnerable [ɪn'vʌlnərəbl] ADJ invulnerable (**to** a)

inward ['ɪnwəd] Ⓐ ADJ 1 (= *inner*) [*peace, happiness*] interior; **she gave an ~ sigh** suspiró para sus adentros; **Bridget watched him with an ~ smile** Bridget lo observó sonriendo para sus adentros; **I sighed with ~ relief** suspiré sintiendo gran alivio por dentro

2 (= *incoming*) [*flow, movement*] hacia el interior

Ⓑ ADV = **inwards A**

Ⓒ CPD ► **inward investment** N inversiones *fpl* extranjeras ► **inward investor** N inversor(a) *m/f* extranjero/a

inward-looking ['ɪnwəd,lʊkɪŋ] ADJ [*person*] introvertido; **the country/company is too ~** el país está muy encerrado en sí mismo/la compañía está muy encerrada en sí misma

inwardly ['ɪnwədlɪ] ADV [*think, sigh, groan, smile*] para sus adentros; [*know, struggle*] en su interior; [*feel*] por dentro; **she was ~ furious** por dentro estaba furiosa; **she felt ~ relieved** se sintió aliviada por dentro; **the house was outwardly clean but ~ filthy** la casa estaba limpia por fuera pero asquerosa por dentro

inwards ['ɪnwədz] Ⓐ ADV (*Brit*) hacia dentro; **the soil had subsided, pushing the walls ~** el suelo se había hundido, haciendo que los muros se fueran hacia dentro; **his frustration and anger turned ~** su frustración y su rabia se volvieron hacia su interior; **the door swung ~** la puerta se abrió hacia dentro

Ⓑ NPL ['ɪnədz] (*) = **innards**

in-your-face‡, in-yer-face‡ [,ɪnjə'feɪs] ADJ [*attitude, music, theatre*] agresivo y descarado

I/O Ⓐ ABBR (*Comput*) (= **input/output**) E/S

Ⓑ CPD ► **I/O error** N error *m* de E/S

IOC N ABBR (= **International Olympic Committee**) COI *m*

iodide ['aɪədaɪd] N yoduro *m*

iodine ['aɪədi:n] N yodo *m*

iodoform [aɪ'ɒdəfɔ:m] N yodoformo *m*

IOM ABBR (*Brit*) = **Isle of Man**

ion ['aɪən] N ion *m*

Ionian [aɪ'əʊnɪən] Ⓐ ADJ jonio, jónico

Ⓑ CPD ► **Ionian Sea** N Mar *m* Jónico

Ionic [aɪ'ɒnɪk] ADJ jónico

ionic [aɪ'ɒnɪk] ADJ (*Chem*) iónico

ioniser ['aɪənaɪzəʳ] = **ionizer**

ionize ['aɪənaɪz] VT ionizar

ionizer ['aɪənaɪzəʳ] N ionizador *m*

ionosphere [aɪ'ɒnəsfɪəʳ] N ionosfera *f*

iota [aɪ'əʊtə] N (= *letter*) iota *f*; (*fig*) pizca *f*, ápice *m*; **there's not one ~ of truth in it** eso no tiene ni pizca de verdad; **if he had an ~ of sense** si tuviera un pizca de inteligencia

IOU N ABBR (= **I owe you**) pagaré *m*, vale *m* (*LAm*)

IOW ABBR (*Brit*) = **Isle of Wight**

IPA N ABBR = **International Phonetic Alphabet**

IP address [aɪ'pi:ə,dres] N (*Comput*) (= **Internet Protocol address**) dirección *f* IP

ipecacuanha [,ɪpɪkækjʊ'ænə] N ipecacuana *f*

iPod® ['aɪpɒd] N iPod® *m*

IQ N ABBR (= **intelligence quotient**) C.I. *m*

IR N ABBR (*Brit*) = **Inland Revenue**

IRA N ABBR 1 (= **Irish Republican Army**) IRA *m* 2 (*US*) = **individual retirement account**

Irak [ɪ'rɑ:k] = **Iraq**

Iraki [ɪ'rɑ:kɪ] = **Iraqi**

Iran [ɪ'rɑ:n] N Irán *m*

Iranian [ɪ'reɪnɪən] Ⓐ ADJ iraní

Ⓑ N (*ancient*) iranio/a *m/f*; (*modern*) iraní *mf*

Iraq [ɪ'rɑ:k] N Irak *m*, Iraq *m*

Iraqi [ɪ'rɑ:kɪ] Ⓐ ADJ iraquí Ⓑ N iraquí *mf*

irascibility [ɪ,ræsɪ'bɪlɪtɪ] N irascibilidad *f*

irascible [ɪ'ræsɪbl] ADJ irascible, colérico

irascibly [ɪ'ræsɪblɪ] ADV **he said ~** dijo colérico

irate [aɪ'reɪt] ADJ indignado, furioso; **he got very ~** se indignó mucho, se puso furioso

IRBM N ABBR = **intermediate range ballistic missile**

ire [aɪəʳ] N (*liter*) ira *f*, cólera *f*; **to rouse sb's ~** provocar la ira de algn

Ireland ['aɪələnd] N Irlanda *f*; **Northern ~** Irlanda *f* del Norte; **Republic of ~** República *f* de Irlanda

iridescence [,ɪrɪ'desns] N irisación *f*

► LANGUAGE IN USE: **invoice A** 20.6, 20.7 **involve 2** 26.3

iridescent [ˌɪrɪˈdesnt] ADJ iridiscente, irisado, tornasolado

iridium [ɪˈrɪdɪəm] N iridio *m*

iris [ˈaɪərɪs] N (*pl* **irises**) [1] (*Anat*) iris *m inv*
[2] (*Bot*) lirio *m*

Irish [ˈaɪərɪʃ] (A) ADJ irlandés
(B) N [1] **the ~** (= *people*) los irlandeses
[2] (*Ling*) irlandés *m*
(C) CPD ► **Irish coffee** N café *m* irlandés ► **Irish stew** N estofado *m* irlandés ► **the Irish Free State** N el Estado Libre de Irlanda ► **the Irish Sea** N el Mar de Irlanda ► **Irish setter** N setter *m* irlandés

Irishman [ˈaɪərɪʃmən] N (*pl* **Irishmen**) irlandés *m*

Irishwoman [ˈaɪərɪʃˌwʊmən] N (*pl* **Irishwomen**) irlandesa *f*

irk [ɜːk] VT fastidiar, molestar

irksome [ˈɜːksəm] ADJ [*child, chore*] fastidioso, pesado

IRN N ABBR (*Brit*) (= **Independent Radio News**) *servicio de noticias en las cadenas de radio privadas*

IRO N ABBR [1] (*Brit*) = **Inland Revenue Office**
[2] (*US*) (= **International Refugee Organization**) OIR *f*

iron [ˈaɪən] (A) N [1] (= *metal*) hierro *m*, fierro *m* (*LAm*); **cast ~** hierro *m* colado; **corrugated ~** chapa *f* ondulada; **old ~** chatarra *f*, hierro *m* viejo; **to have an ~ constitution** tener una constitución de hierro; **with an ~ hand** *or* **fist** con mano de hierro; **a man of ~** un hombre de hierro; **a will of ~** una voluntad férrea *or* de hierro; ✦*IDIOMS* **to have a lot of/too many ~s in the fire** tener muchos/demasiados asuntos entre manos; **the ~ fist in the velvet glove** la mano de hierro en guante de terciopelo; **to strike while the ~ is hot** a hierro candente batir de repente
[2] **irons** (= *fetters*) grilletes *mpl*, grillos *mpl*; **to put** *or* **clap sb in ~s** poner grilletes *or* grillos a algn, aherrojar a algn
[3] (*Golf*) hierro *m*
[4] (*for ironing clothes*) plancha *f*
[5] (*for branding*) hierro *m* candente
[6] (*) (= *gun*) pistola *f*
(B) VT [+ *clothes*] planchar
(C) VI [*person*] planchar; **this blouse ~s really well** esta blusa es muy fácil de planchar
(D) CPD [*bridge, bar, tool*] de hierro, de fierro (*LAm*); (*fig*) [*will, determination*] férreo ► **the Iron Age** N la Edad de hierro ► **the iron and steel industry** N la industria siderúrgica ► **Iron Cross** N cruz *f* de hierro ► **the Iron Curtain** N (*Hist, Pol*) el telón de acero, la cortina de hierro (*LAm*); **the Iron Curtain Countries** los países más allá del telón de acero ► **the Iron Duke** N el Duque de Wellington ► **iron foundry** N fundición *f*, fundidora *f* (*LAm*) ► **the Iron Lady** N (*Brit Pol*) la Dama de Hierro ► **iron lung** N (*Med*) pulmón *m* de acero ► **iron ore** N mineral *m* de hierro ► **iron oxide** N óxido *m* de hierro ► **iron pyrites** N pirita *f* ferruginosa ► **iron rations** NPL ración *f or* víveres *mpl* de reserva

► **iron out** VT + ADV [+ *unevenness*] allanar; [+ *crease*] quitar, planchar; [+ *difficulties*] allanar, suprimir; [+ *problems*] resolver; **they managed to ~ out their differences** consiguieron resolver sus diferencias

ironclad [ˈaɪənklæd] (A) ADJ acorazado; (*fig*) [*proof*] irrefutable, incontrovertible; [*alibi*] incontrovertible, incuestionable
(B) N acorazado *m*

ironic [aɪˈrɒnɪk] ADJ irónico

ironical [aɪˈrɒnɪkəl] ADJ = **ironic**

ironically [aɪˈrɒnɪkəlɪ] ADV irónicamente; [*say etc*] con ironía; **~ enough** paradójicamente, como quiso la suerte

ironing [ˈaɪənɪŋ] (A) N (= *act*) planchado *m*; (= *clothes*) (*awaiting ironing*) ropa *f* por planchar; (*ironed*) ropa *f* planchada; **to do the ~** planchar; **to give a dress an ~** planchar un vestido
(B) CPD ► **ironing board** N tabla *f* de planchar

ironist [ˈaɪərənɪst] N ironista *mf*; **the master ~** el maestro de la ironía

ironmonger [ˈaɪənˌmʌŋgəʳ] N (*Brit*) ferretero/a *m/f*, quincallero/a *m/f*; **~'s (shop)** ferretería *f*, quincallería *f*

ironmongery [ˈaɪənˌmʌŋgərɪ] N (*Brit*) (= *ironware*) quincalla *f*, ferretería *f* (*also fig*)

ironstone [ˈaɪənˌstəʊn] N (= *china*) porcelana *f* resistente

ironwork [ˈaɪənwɜːk] N (*on piece of furniture*) herraje *m*; (*on building*) obra *f* de hierro

ironworks [ˈaɪənwɜːks] N (*sing and pl*) fundición *f*

irony [ˈaɪərənɪ] N ironía *f*; **the ~ of fate** las ironías del destino; **life's little ironies** las (pequeñas) ironías de la vida; **the ~ of it is that …** lo irónico es que …

Iroquois [ˈɪrəkwɔɪ] (A) ADJ iroqués
(B) N [1] iroqués/esa *m/f*
[2] (*Ling*) iroqués *m*

irradiate [ɪˈreɪdɪeɪt] VT irradiar

irradiation [ɪˌreɪdɪˈeɪʃən] N irradiación *f*

irrational [ɪˈræʃənl] ADJ [*behaviour, person, belief*] irracional

irrationality [ɪˌræʃəˈnælɪtɪ] N irracionalidad *f*

irrationally [ɪˈræʃnəlɪ] ADV irracionalmente

irreconcilable [ɪˌrekənˈsaɪləbl] ADJ [*enemies*] irreconciliable; [*ideas*] incompatible

irrecoverable [ˌɪrɪˈkʌvərəbl] ADJ irrecuperable; [*debt*] irrecuperable, incobrable

irredeemable [ˌɪrɪˈdiːməbl] ADJ irredimible; (*Fin*) perpetuo, no amortizable

irredeemably [ˌɪrɪˈdiːməblɪ] ADV irremediablemente; **~ lost/ruined** irremediablemente perdido/destruido

irredentism [ˌɪrɪˈdentɪzəm] N (*fig*) irredentismo *m*

irredentist [ˌɪrɪˈdentɪst] ADJ, N (*fig*) irredentista *mf*

irreducible [ˌɪrɪˈdjuːsəbl] ADJ irreducible

irrefutable [ˌɪrɪˈfjuːtəbl] ADJ [*evidence, argument*] irrefutable

irrefutably [ˌɪrɪˈfjuːtəblɪ] ADV irrefutablemente, de forma irrefutable

irregardless [ɪrɪˈgɑːdlɪs] ADV (*US*) (*incorrect usage*) de cualquier modo; **~ of what he says** a pesar de lo que él diga

irregular [ɪˈregjʊləʳ] (A) ADJ [1] (= *uneven*) [*shape, surface, pattern*] irregular; **John had sharp, ~ features** las facciones de John eran duras, irregulares; **an ~ pentagon** (*Geom*) (= *asymmetrical*) un pentágono irregular
[2] (= *spasmodic*) [*attendance, meals, breathing, heartbeat*] irregular; **he is very ~ in his attendance** no asiste de forma regular; **he leads a very ~ life** lleva una vida muy irregular; **I am not usually ~** (*euph*) normalmente voy como un reloj; **to keep ~ hours** tener un horario irregular; **at ~ intervals** a intervalos irregulares
[3] (= *unorthodox*) [*practice*] poco ortodoxo, irregular; [*treatment*] poco ortodoxo; [*action*] poco ortodoxo, contrario a la práctica; [*payment*] irregular; **her behaviour was ~, to say the least** su comportamiento era un tanto irregular, por no decir algo peor; **~ business practices** negocios *mpl* poco ortodoxos; **all this is very ~** todo esto es muy poco ortodoxo; **this is most ~!** ¡esto es totalmente inadmisible!; **it was highly ~ of Blake to do it alone** era totalmente contrario a la práctica que Blake lo hiciese solo
[4] (*Ling*) [*verb, adjective, noun*] irregular
[5] (*Mil*) [*soldiers, forces, troops*] irregular
(B) N soldado *mf* irregular

irregularity [ɪˌregjʊˈlærɪtɪ] N [1] (= *unevenness*) [*of shape, surface, features*] irregularidad *f*
[2] (= *spasmodic nature*) [*of attendance, meals, pulse*] irregularidad *f*
[3] (= *unorthodox nature*) [*of behaviour*] irregularidad *f*; **the ~ of his actions surprised us all** lo poco ortodoxo de su forma de actuar nos sorprendió a todos; **a number of irregularities were observed** se observaron una serie de irregularidades

irregularly [ɪˈregjʊləlɪ] ADV [1] (= *unevenly*) [*distribute, arrange, spread*] irregularmente, de manera irregular; **~ shaped** de forma irregular
[2] (= *spasmodically*) [*eat, occur*] con irregularidad; [*attend*] de forma poco regular; **her heart was beating ~** su corazón latía con irregularidad; **I see her only ~** sólo la veo ocasionalmente
[3] (= *in an unorthodox manner*) de forma poco ortodoxa; **payments had been made ~** se habían realizado pagos, de forma poco ortodoxa; **he had behaved most ~ in signing the paper himself** el que hubiese firmado el papel él mismo era totalmente contrario a la práctica

irrelevance [ɪˈreləvəns] N irrelevancia *f*, intrascendencia *f*; **it highlighted the ~ of the project to the local community** puso de relieve lo intrascendente del proyecto para la comunidad local; **they dismiss religion as an ~** rechazan la religión como algo irrelevante *or* intrascendente

irrelevant [ɪˈreləvənt] ADJ [*details, information*] irrelevante, intrascendente; **what you are saying is ~** lo que dices no viene al caso, lo que dices es irrelevante; **those remarks are ~ to the present discussion** esas observaciones no tienen relación con lo que se está discutiendo; **the proposals are ~ to most of our customers** las propuestas les son indiferentes a la mayoría de nuestros clientes; **he was ~, merely to be disposed of** era una persona superflua de la que se podía prescindir

irrelevantly [ɪˈreləvəntlɪ] ADV [*say, think*] (*with past tense*) sin que viniera al caso

irreligious [ˌɪrɪˈlɪdʒəs] ADJ [*people, behaviour, play*] irreligioso

irremediable [ˌɪrɪˈmiːdɪəbl] ADJ irremediable

irremediably [ˌɪrɪˈmiːdɪəblɪ] ADV irremediablemente

irremovable [ˌɪrɪˈmuːvəbl] ADJ inamovible

irreparable [ɪˈrepərəbl] ADJ irreparable

irreparably [ɪˈrepərəblɪ] ADV irreparablemente

irreplaceable [ˌɪrɪˈpleɪsəbl] ADJ irre(e)mplazable, insustituible

irrepressible [ˌɪrɪˈpresəbl] ADJ [*person*] irrefrenable; [*high spirits, laughter, urge*] incontenible, irreprimible

irrepressibly [ˌɪrɪˈpresəblɪ] ADV [*laugh*] inconteniblemente, irreprimiblemente; **~ cheerful/enthusiastic** con una alegría/un entusiasmo incontenible *or* irreprimible

irreproachable [ˌɪrɪˈprəʊtʃəbl] ADJ [*conduct*] irreprochable, intachable

irresistible [ˌɪrɪˈzɪstəbl] ADJ irresistible; **she had an ~ urge to yawn** le entraron unas ganas irresistibles de bostezar; **she looked ~ in her new dress** estaba irresistible en su vestido nuevo; **he is ~ to women** las mujeres lo encuentran irresistible; **an ~ political force** una fuerza política a la que es imposible resistirse

irresistibly [ˌɪrɪˈzɪstəblɪ] ADV irresistiblemente; **she was drawn ~ to him** se sentía irresistiblemente atraída hacia él; **he found her ~ beautiful** la encontraba de una belleza irresistible

irresolute [ɪˈrezəluːt] ADJ [*person, character*] indeciso, irresoluto

irresolutely [ɪˈrezəluːtlɪ] ADV irresolutamente, indecisamente

irresoluteness [ɪˈrezəluːtnɪs] N irresolución *f*, indecisión *f*

irrespective [ˌɪrɪˈspektɪv] ADJ **~ of** sin tomar en consideración *or* en cuenta; **the same treatment for all, ~ of age or gender** el mismo trato para todos, sin distinción de edad o sexo

irresponsibility [ˈɪrɪsˌpɒnsəˈbɪlɪtɪ] N irresponsabilidad *f*, falta *f* de responsabilidad

irresponsible [ˌɪrɪsˈpɒnsəbl] ADJ [*person, behaviour*] irresponsable

irresponsibly [ˌɪrɪsˈpɒnsəblɪ] ADV irresponsablemente, de modo irresponsable

irretrievable [ˌɪrɪˈtriːvəbl] ADJ [*object*] irrecuperable; [*loss, damage, error*] irreparable

irretrievably [ˌɪrɪˈtriːvəblɪ] ADV irreparablemente; **~ lost** irreparablemente perdido, totalmente perdido

irreverence [ɪˈrevərəns] N irreverencia *f*, falta *f* de respeto

irreverent [ɪˈrevərənt] ADJ [*person, action*] irreverente, irrespetuoso

irreverently [ɪˈrevərəntlɪ] ADV de modo irreverente, irrespetuosamente

irreversible [ˌɪrɪˈvɜːsəbl] ADJ [*process*] irreversible; [*decision*] irrevocable

irreversibly [ˌɪrɪˈvɜːsəblɪ] ADV [*change, affect*] irreversiblemente; [*damage, harm*] irreparablemente

irrevocable [ɪˈrevəkəbl] ADJ [*decision*] irrevocable

irrevocably [ɪˈrevəkəblɪ] ADV irrevocablemente

irrigable [ˈɪrɪgəbl] ADJ regable

irrigate [ˈɪrɪgeɪt] VT (*Agr*) [+ *land, crops*] regar; (*Med*) irrigar; **~d land** tierras *fpl* de regadío

irrigation [ˌɪrɪˈgeɪʃən] Ⓐ N (*Agr*) irrigación *f*, riego *m*; (*Med*) irrigación *f*
Ⓑ CPD ► **irrigation channel** N acequia *f*, canal *m* de riego

irritability [ˌɪrɪtəˈbɪlɪtɪ] N irritabilidad *f*

irritable [ˈɪrɪtəbl] ADJ [1] (= *easily annoyed*) [*person*] irritable; [*temperament*] irascible, colérico; **to get** *or* **become ~** irritarse; **to be in an ~ mood** estar irritable
[2] (= *sensitive*) [*skin*] sensible

irritably [ˈɪrɪtəblɪ] ADV **he said ~** dijo malhumorado

irritant [ˈɪrɪtənt] N (*Med*) agente *m* irritante; (*fig*) molestia *f*

irritate [ˈɪrɪteɪt] VT [1] (= *annoy*) irritar, fastidiar; **to get ~d** irritarse, enfadarse
[2] (*Med*) irritar

irritating [ˈɪrɪteɪtɪŋ] ADJ [1] (= *annoying*) [*person, habit*] irritante; **it's really most ~** es de lo más irritante
[2] (*to skin, eyes*) [*substance*] irritante

irritatingly [ˈɪrɪteɪtɪŋlɪ] ADV **the answer proved ~ elusive** la respuesta fue esquiva hasta el punto de resultar irritante; **a stone was ~ lodged in his shoe** se le había metido una piedra en el zapato y le molestaba; **~, I was none the wiser after reading his book** para mi fastidio, la lectura de su libro no me había aclarado nada

irritation [ˌɪrɪˈteɪʃən] N [1] (= *state*) irritación *f*, enfado *m*; **she could not conceal her ~** no podía disimular su irritación *or* enfado
[2] (= *irritant*) molestia *f*
[3] (*Med*) irritación *f*; **a minor skin ~** una irritación cutánea de poca importancia

irruption [ɪˈrʌpʃən] N irrupción *f*

IRS N ABBR (*US*) = **Internal Revenue Service**

is [ɪz] *see* **be**

Is. ABBR = **Isle(s), Island(s)**

ISA [ˈaɪsə] N ABBR (*Brit Fin*) (= **Individual Savings Account**) *plan de ahorro personal para pequeños inversores con fiscalidad cero*

Isaac [ˈaɪzək] N Isaac

Isabel [ˈɪzəbel] N Isabel

Isaiah [aɪˈzaɪə] N Isaías

ISBN N ABBR (= **International Standard Book Number**) ISBN *f*

ISDN N ABBR (= **Integrated Services Digital Network**) RDSI *f*

...ish [ɪʃ] SUF [1] **blackish** negruzco; **dearish** algo caro; **smallish** más bien pequeño; **coldish** un poco frío
[2] **at fourish** a eso de las cuatro; **she must be fortyish** tendrá alrededor de 40 años

isinglass [ˈaɪzɪŋglɑːs] N cola *f* de pescado

Islam [ˈɪzlɑːm] N Islam *m*

Islamic [ɪzˈlæmɪk] ADJ islámico

Islamicist [ɪzˈlæmɪsɪst] N islamista *mf*

Islamism [ˈɪzləmɪzəm] N islamismo *m*

Islamist [ˈɪzləmɪst] N = **Islamicist**

Islamophobia [ɪzˌlæməˈfəʊbɪə] N islamofobia *f*

island [ˈaɪlənd] Ⓐ N isla *f*; (*in street*) refugio *m*, isla *f* (peatonal); *see also* **desert**[1]
Ⓑ CPD isleño

islander [ˈaɪləndəʳ] N isleño/a *m/f*

isle [aɪl] N (= *poet*) isla *f*

islet [ˈaɪlɪt] N isleta *f*, islote *m*

ism [ˈɪzəm] N (*pej*) ismo *m*

isn't [ˈɪznt] = **is not**

ISO N ABBR (= **International Standards Organization**) OIN *f*

iso- [ˈaɪsəʊ] PREFIX iso-

isobar [ˈaɪsəʊbɑːʳ] N isobara *f*

isolate [ˈaɪsəʊleɪt] VT [1] (= *cut off*) aislar (**from** de); **this policy could ~ China from the rest of the world** esta política podría aislar a China del resto del mundo; **it is difficult to ~ religion from politics** es difícil separar la religión de la política; **to ~ o.s.** aislarse
[2] (= *pinpoint*) [+ *cause, source*] identificar; [+ *problem, virus, gene*] aislar
[3] (*Med*) (= *quarantine*) [+ *person, animal*] aislar (**from** de)

isolated [ˈaɪsəʊleɪtɪd] ADJ [1] (= *remote, cut off*) [*house, village, community*] aislado, apartado; [*person*] aislado; **the islanders were very ~** los habitantes de la isla estaban muy aislados; **she lived a strange, ~ life** vivía una vida extraña y solitaria; **to feel ~** sentirse aislado; **to be ~ from one's family** estar aislado de su familia; **to keep sth/sb ~ from sth/sb** mantener algo/a algn aislado de algo/algn
[2] (= *individual*) [*incident, case, example*] aislado

isolation [ˌaɪsəʊˈleɪʃən] Ⓐ N aislamiento *m*; **the ~ he endured while in captivity** el aislamiento que tuvo que soportar durante su cautividad; **we cannot discuss this in ~** no podemos discutir esto aisladamente; **things like this don't happen in ~** estas cosas no ocurren aisladas; **she's being kept in ~** (*Med*) la mantienen aislada; **we cannot consider this crime in ~ from the others he has committed** no podemos considerar este crimen aislado de los otros que ha cometido; *see also* **splendid**
Ⓑ CPD ► **isolation hospital** N hospital *m* de infecciosos ► **isolation ward** N pabellón *m* de infecciosos

isolationism [ˌaɪsəʊˈleɪʃənɪzəm] N aislacionismo *m*

isolationist [aɪsəʊˈleɪʃənɪst] Ⓐ ADJ aislacionista Ⓑ N aislacionista *mf*

Isolde [ɪˈzɒldə] N Iseo, Isolda

isomer [ˈaɪsəməʳ] N isómero *m*

isometric [ˌaɪsəʊˈmetrɪk] ADJ isométrico; **~ exercises** ejercicios *mpl* isométricos

isometrics [ˌaɪsəʊˈmetrɪks] NSING isométrica *fsing*

isomorphic [ˌaɪsəʊˈmɔːfɪk] ADJ isomorfo

isosceles [aɪˈsɒsɪliːz] ADJ **~ triangle** triángulo *m* isósceles

isotherm [ˈaɪsəʊθɜːm] N isoterma *f*

isothermal [ˌaɪsəʊˈθɜːməl] ADJ isotérmico

isotonic [ˌaɪsəʊˈtɒnɪk] ADJ isotónico

isotope [ˈaɪsəʊtəʊp] N isótopo *m*

ISP N ABBR = **Internet Service Provider**

I-spy [ˈaɪˈspaɪ] N (*Brit*) veo-veo *m*

Israel [ˈɪzreɪl] N Israel *m*

Israeli [ɪzˈreɪlɪ] Ⓐ ADJ israelí
Ⓑ N (*pl* **Israelis** *or* **Israeli**) israelí *mf*

Israelite [ˈɪzrɪəlaɪt] Ⓐ ADJ israelita
Ⓑ N israelita *mf*

ISS N ABBR (= **International Social Service**) SSI *m*

iss. ABBR = **issue**

▼**issue** [ˈɪʃuː] Ⓐ N [1] (= *matter, question*) asunto *m*, cuestión *f*; **until the ~ is decided** hasta que se decida algo sobre el asunto *or* la cuestión *or* el tema; **I was earning a lot of money but that was not the ~** ganaba mucho dinero, pero ésa no era la cuestión; **we need to address this ~** tenemos que tratar este asunto *or* esta cuestión *or* este tema; **the point at ~** el punto en cuestión; **his integrity is not at ~** no se está cuestionando su integridad; **they were at ~ over ...** estuvieron discutiendo (sobre) ...; **to avoid the ~** eludir *or* (*frm*) soslayar el problema; **to cloud** *or* **confuse the ~** crear confusión; **to face the ~** hacer frente a la cuestión *or* al problema, afrontar la situación; **to force the ~** forzar una decisión; **to join ~ with sb** enfrentarse a *or* con algn; **to make an ~ of sth**: **I think we should make an ~ of this** creo que deberíamos insistir en este punto; **do you want to make an ~ of it?** ¿quieres hacer un problema de esto?; **he makes an ~ of every tiny detail** a todo le da mucha más importancia de la que tiene; **the main** *or* **real ~ is ...** lo fundamental es ...; **it's not a political ~** no es una cuestión política; **to take ~ with sth/sb** discrepar de algo/de *or* con algn; **I feel I must take ~ with you on** *or* **over that** permítame que discrepe de usted en *or* sobre eso; *see also* **side C**
[2] [*of shares, stamps, banknotes*] emisión *f*; [*of library book*] préstamo *m*; [*of document*] expedición *f*; [*of rations*] distribución *f*, reparto *m*; **an army ~ blanket** una manta del ejército; **a standard ~ army rifle** un rifle del ejército de fabricación estándar
[3] (= *copy*) [*of magazine*] ejemplar *m*, número *m*; **the March ~** el ejemplar *or* número de

➤ LANGUAGE IN USE: issue A1 26.1

marzo; **back ~** ejemplar *m* or número *m* atrasado
[4] (*frm*) (= *outcome*) resultado *m*, consecuencia *f*
[5] (*Jur*) (= *offspring*) descendencia *f*; **to die without ~** morir sin (dejar) descendencia
[6] (*Med*) flujo *m*
Ⓑ VT [+ *library book*] prestar; [+ *tickets*] emitir; [+ *shares, stamps*] poner en circulación, emitir; [+ *rations*] distribuir, repartir; [+ *order*] dar; [+ *statement, proclamation*] hacer público; [+ *decree*] promulgar; [+ *passport, certificate*] expedir; [+ *licence*] facilitar; [+ *writ, summons*] extender; **a warrant has been ~d for his arrest** se ha ordenado su detención; **to ~ sth to sb** ◊ **~ sb with sth** dar algo a algn; **we were ~d with ten rounds each** nos dieron diez cartuchos a cada uno; **staff will be ~d with new uniforms** se proveerá de uniformes nuevos al personal
Ⓒ VI [1] (= *come forth*) **to ~ from sth** [*blood, water*] brotar or salir de algo; [*sound*] salir de algo; [*report, account*] provenir de algo; **reports issuing from opposition sources say that ...** informes provenientes de fuentes de la oposición afirman que ...
[2] (= *derive*) derivar (**from** de)
[3] (*frm*) (= *have as result*) **to ~ in sth** resultar en algo, dar algo como resultado
Ⓓ CPD ► **issue price** N precio *m* de emisión

issued [ˈɪʃuːd] ADJ **~ capital** capital *m* emitido

issuer [ˈɪʃuːəʳ] N (*Fin, St Ex*) emisor *m*, sociedad *f* emisora

issuing [ˈɪʃuːɪŋ] ADJ [*company, office*] (*for shares*) emisor; (*for passport, official document*) expedidor

Istanbul [ˈɪstænˈbuːl] N Estambul *m*

isthmus [ˈɪsməs] N (*pl* **isthmuses** *or* **isthmi**) istmo *m*

it[1] [ɪt] PRON [1] (*specific*)

It as subject or following a preposition is often not translated.

(*direct object*) lo, la; (*indirect object*) le; (*after prep*) (*if translated*) él *m*, ella *f*; (*neuter*) ello; **it's on the table** está en la mesa; **where is it?** ¿dónde está?; **"here's the book" — "give it to me"** —aquí está el libro —dámelo; **if you have the list, give it to him** si tienes la lista, dásela; **it's a good film, have you seen it?** es una buena película, ¿la has visto?; **give it a kick** dale una patada; **I have no money for it** no tengo dinero para comprarlo; **I doubt it** lo dudo; **there's a wall in front of/behind it** hay una pared delante/detrás (de ello); **she put a plate on top of it** le puso un plato encima, lo tapó con un plato; **it's a she** [*dog, cat etc*] es hembra; **it's a boy** [*baby*] es niño
[2] (*indefinite*)

The indefinite subject is not translated.

it's raining está lloviendo; **it's Friday tomorrow** mañana es viernes; **it's the 10th of October** es el diez de octubre; **it's six o'clock** son las seis; **how far is it?** ¿a qué distancia está?; **it's ten miles to London** son diez millas de aquí a Londres; **I like it here, it's quiet** me gusta aquí, es tranquilo; **it was kind of you** fue muy amable de su parte; **it's easy to talk** hablar no cuesta nada; **it is not in him to do it** no es capaz de hacer eso; **it's me** soy yo; **don't worry, it's only me** soy yo, no te emociones; **it's no use worrying** no vale la pena inquietarse; **it is said that ...** se dice que ...; **I have heard it said that ...** he oído decir que ...; **it was Peter who phoned** fue Peter quien llamó; **what is it?** (= *what's the matter?*) ¿qué pasa?; **who is it?** ¿quién es?

➤ LANGUAGE IN USE: **item** 20.3

[3] (*special uses with "to be"*) **how is it that ...?** ¿cómo es que ...?, ¿cómo resulta que ...?; **that's it for today** eso es todo por hoy; **that's it! just there is fine** ¡eso es! ahí mismo está bien; **that's it! I've had enough of this waiting!** ¡ya está bien! ¡estoy harto de esperar!; **that's it then! we leave on Sunday** ¡muy bien! *or* ¡solucionado! salimos el domingo; **that's just it!** ¡ahí está el problema!; **this is it** (= *it's time*) ya llegó la hora; (= *train, bus etc*) ahí viene
[4] (*referring to situation*) **he won't agree to it** no lo aceptará; **I spoke to him about it** lo hablé con él; **I'm against it** estoy en contra; **I'm (all) for it*** estoy (muy) a favor; **the worst of it is that ...** lo peor del caso es que ...; ✦**IDIOM he's dropped us in it*** nos la ha hecho buena*; *see also* **at 5**, **get A20**
[5] (*in games*) **you're it!** ¡te tocó!
[6] (*) (= *sexual attraction*) **you've either got it or you haven't** ese algo, o se tiene o no, no hay vuelta de hoja
[7] (*) (= *something special*) **she thinks she's just it!*** se las da de maravillosa*

it[2]* [ɪt] N vermú *m* or vermut *m* italiano

IT N ABBR [1] (*Comput*) (= **information technology**) informática *f*
[2] (*Fin*) = **income tax**

ITA N ABBR (*Brit*) (= **Initial Teaching Alphabet**) *alfabeto parcialmente fonético para enseñar lectura*

Italian [ɪˈtæljən] Ⓐ ADJ italiano
Ⓑ N [1] (= *person*) italiano/a *m/f*
[2] (*Ling*) italiano *m*

Italianate [ɪˈtæljənɪt] ADJ de estilo italiano

italic [ɪˈtælɪk] ADJ (*Typ*) en cursiva *or* bastardilla

italicize [ɪˈtælɪsaɪz] VT poner en cursiva *or* bastardilla

italics [ɪˈtælɪks] NPL cursiva *f*, (letra *f*) bastardilla *f*; **in ~** en cursiva, en bastardilla; **my ~** ◊ **the ~ are mine** lo subrayado es mío

Italy [ˈɪtəlɪ] N Italia *f*

ITC N ABBR (*Brit*) = **Independent Television Commission**

itch [ɪtʃ] Ⓐ N picor *m*; (*less frequent*) picazón *f*, comezón *f*; **to have an ~** tener un picor; (*less frequent*) tener una picazón *or* una comezón; **I've got an ~ here, can you scratch it for me?** me pica aquí *or* tengo un picor aquí, ¿me puedes rascar?; **to have an ~ to do sth** (*fig*) rabiar por hacer algo; *see also* **seven**
Ⓑ VI [1] (= *be itchy*) **my leg ~es** me pica la pierna; (*said by older people*) tengo picazón *or* comezón en la pierna; **I was ~ing all over** me picaba todo; **to be ~ing for sth*** (*fig*) estar deseando algo; **he was ~ing for a chance to play against the champion** estaba deseando tener la oportunidad de jugar contra el campeón; **he's ~ing for a fight** tiene ganas de pelea; **to be ~ing to do sth*** (*fig*) rabiar por hacer algo
[2] (= *cause itchiness*) [*sweater, wool*] picar

itchiness [ˈɪtʃɪnɪs] N picor *m*; (*less frequent*) picazón *f*, comezón *f*

itching [ˈɪtʃɪŋ] Ⓐ N picor *m*; (*less frequent*) picazón *f*, comezón *f*
Ⓑ CPD ► **itching powder** N polvos *mpl* de pica-pica

itchy [ˈɪtʃɪ] ADJ (*compar* **itchier**; *superl* **itchiest**)
[1] (= *irritated*) [*eyes, skin, scalp*] irritado; [*rash*] que produce picor; **~ eyes caused by hay fever** ojos *mpl* irritados a causa de la fiebre del heno; **my head is ~** me pica la cabeza; (*less frequent*) tengo picazón *or* comezón en la cabeza; **I've got an ~ nose** me pica la nariz; **she felt all ~** ◊ **she felt ~ all over** le picaba todo; ✦**IDIOMS to have ~ feet** estar muy inquieto; **to have ~ fingers: I was getting ~ fingers, watching the two of them play chess** viéndolos a los dos jugar al ajedrez me estaban entrando ganas a mí; **to have an ~ palm: the chief of police had an ~ palm and allowed himself to be bribed** al jefe de policía le podía su amor por el dinero y se dejaba sobornar
[2] (= *irritating*) [*sweater, material*] que pica; **that jumper is too ~** ese jersey pica mucho

it'd [ˈɪtd] = **it would, it had**

item [ˈaɪtəm] N (*in list, bill, catalogue*) artículo *m*; (*on agenda*) asunto *m* (a tratar), punto *m* (a tratar); (*in programme*) número *m*; (*in newspaper*) artículo *m*; (*TV, Rad*) noticia *f*; **~ of clothing** prenda *f* (de vestir); **what's the next ~?** (*in meeting*) ¿cuál es el siguiente punto *or* asunto a tratar?; **this books is a collector's ~** este libro es una pieza de colección; **basic/luxury food ~s** productos *mpl* alimenticios básicos/suntuarios; **they sell a selection of gift ~s** venden una selección de artículos de regalo; **a news ~** una noticia; **they're something of an ~*** son pareja

itemize [ˈaɪtəmaɪz] VT detallar; **~d bill** (*of customer*) cuenta *f* detallada; (*Comm*) factura *f* detallada

iterative [ˈɪtərətɪv] Ⓐ ADJ iterativo
Ⓑ CPD ► **iterative statement** N (*Comput*) sentencia *f* iterativa

itinerant [ɪˈtɪnərənt] ADJ [*preacher, lecturer, worker*] itinerante; [*salesperson*] ambulante

itinerary [aɪˈtɪnərərɪ] N (= *route*) itinerario *m*; (= *map*) ruta *f*

it'll [ˈɪtl] = **it will, it shall**

ITN N ABBR (*Brit*) (= **Independent Television News**) *servicio de noticias en las cadenas privadas de televisión*

ITO N ABBR (= **International Trade Organization**) OIC *f*

it's [ɪts] = **it is, it has**

its [ɪts] Ⓐ POSS ADJ (*with singular noun*) su; (*with plural noun*) sus; **everything in ~ place** cada cosa en su sitio; **it has ~ advantages** tiene sus ventajas; **the dog is losing ~ hair** el perro está perdiendo el pelo; **the bird was in ~ cage** el pájaro estaba en su jaula
Ⓑ POSS PRON (el/la) suyo/a, (los/las) suyos/as

itself [ɪtˈself] PRON [1] (*reflexive*) se, sí; **skin renews ~ every 28 days** la piel se renueva cada 28 días
[2] (*emphatic*) **Christmas ~ was an anticlimax** las Navidades mismas fueron una decepción; **he is always politeness ~** siempre es la cortesía personificada; **the door closed by ~** la puerta se cerró sola; **I loved him more than life ~** lo quería más que a mi propia vida; **that was an achievement in ~** eso fue un triunfo de por sí

itsy-bitsy* [ˌɪtsɪˈbɪtsɪ], **itty-bitty*** [ˌɪtɪˈbɪtɪ] (*US*) ADJ pequeñito*

ITU N ABBR (= **International Telecommunications Union**) UIT *f*

ITV N ABBR (= **Independent Television**) *cadena privada de televisión*

IU(C)D N ABBR (= **intrauterine (contraceptive) device**) DIU *m*

IV Ⓐ N ABBR = **intravenous** (*also* **IV drip**) gota a gota *m*
Ⓑ ADJ ABBR = **intravenous**

i.v. ABBR = **invoice value**

I've [aɪv] = **I have**

IVF N ABBR (= **in vitro fertilization**) FIV *f*

ivory [ˈaɪvərɪ] Ⓐ N marfil *m*; **ivories*** (= *teeth*) dientes *mpl*; (*Mus*) teclas *fpl*; (*Billiards*) bolas *fpl*; ✦***IDIOM*** **to tickle the ivories*** tocar el piano

Ⓑ ADJ [*cane, box*] de marfil; [*skin*] de color marfil

Ⓒ CPD ► **Ivory Coast** N Costa *f* de Marfil
► **ivory hunter** N cazador (a) *m/f* de marfil
► **ivory tower** N (*fig*) torre *f* de marfil

ivy [ˈaɪvɪ] Ⓐ N (*Bot*) hiedra *f*, yedra *f*

Ⓑ CPD ► **the Ivy League** N (*US*) *grupo de ocho universidades privadas muy prestigiosas de Nueva Inglaterra*

IVY LEAGUE

En el noreste de Estados Unidos, la **Ivy League** *está formada por ocho universidades de gran prestigio tanto académico como social. El término procede de los tiempos en los que estas ocho universidades,* **Harvard**, **Yale**, **Pennsylvania**, **Princeton**, **Columbia** , **Brown**, **Dartmouth** *y* **Cornell** *formaron una liga para impulsar las competiciones deportivas entre ellas y tiene su origen en la hiedra (***ivy***) que cubre los muros de las facultades y colegios universitarios. A los estudiantes de estas universidades se los denomina* **Ivy Leaguers**.

J j

J, j [dʒeɪ] N (= *letter*) J, j *f*; **J for Jack** J de José

JA N ABBR = **judge advocate**

J/A ABBR = **joint account**

jab [dʒæb] Ⓐ N 1 (= *poke*) (*gen*) pinchazo *m*; (*with elbow*) codazo *m*
2 (= *blow*) (*gen*) golpe *m*; (*Boxing*) golpe *m* rápido
3 (= *prick*) pinchazo *m*
4 (*Brit Med**) inyección *f*
5 (‡) [*of drug*] chute‡ *m*
Ⓑ VT **to ~ sth into sth** clavar algo en algo, hundir algo en algo; **he ~bed the knife into the table** clavó el cuchillo en la mesa; **to ~ sb with one's elbow** dar un codazo a algn; **to ~ a finger at sth** señalar algo con el dedo; **he ~bed a gun in my back** me puso un revólver en los riñones; **I ~bed the knife in my arm** me pinché el brazo con el cuchillo; **he ~bed me with his stick** me golpeó con la punta de su bastón
Ⓒ VI **to ~ at** [+ *person*] intentar golpear a; [+ *fire*] atizar; **to ~ at sb with a knife** tratar de acuchillar a algn; **he ~bed at the map with a finger** dio con el dedo en el mapa

jabber ['dʒæbəʳ] Ⓐ N [*of person*] (= *fast talk*) chapurreo *m*, farfulla *f*; (= *chatter*) cotorreo *m*; (= *noise*) algarabía *f*; [*of monkeys*] chillidos *mpl*; **a ~ of French** un torrente de francés; **a ~ of voices** un jaleo de voces
Ⓑ VT farfullar
Ⓒ VI (= *talk fast*) farfullar; (= *chatter*) charlotear, parlotear; [*monkeys*] chillar; **they were ~ing away in Russian** charloteaban *or* parloteaban en ruso

jabbering ['dʒæbərɪŋ] = **jabber A**

jacaranda [ˌdʒækə'rændə] N jacarandá *m*

Jack [dʒæk] Ⓐ N (*familiar form*) *of* **John** Juanito; ✦**IDIOM I'm all right, ~!** ¡y a mí qué!
Ⓑ CPD ► **Jack Frost** N *personificación del hielo* ► **Jack Ketch** N *el verdugo* ► **Jack Robinson** N **before you can say ~ Robinson** en un santiamén, en un decir Jesús ► **Jack Tar** N *el marinero*

jack [dʒæk] Ⓐ N 1 (*Aut, Tech*) gato *m*, gata *f* (*LAm*)
2 (*Elec*) toma *f* de corriente, enchufe *m* hembra
3 (*Bowls*) boliche *m*
4 (*Cards*) (*in ordinary pack of cards*) jota *f*; (*in Spanish pack*) sota *f*
5 (*also* **bootjack**) sacabotas *m inv*
6 (*Naut*) marinero *m*
7 (= *fish*) lucio *m* joven
8 **jacks** (= *game*) cantillos *mpl*
Ⓑ CPD ► **jack plane** N garlopa *f* ► **jack plug** N enchufe *m* de clavija ► **jack rabbit** N (*US*) liebre *f* americana

►**jack in*** VT + ADV (*Brit*) dejar, abandonar

►**jack off**** VI + ADV (*US*) hacerse una paja**

►**jack up** VT + ADV 1 (*Tech*) levantar con el gato
2 (= *increase*) [+ *price, production*] aumentar

jackal ['dʒækɔːl] N chacal *m*

jackanapes ['dʒækəneɪps] N mequetrefe *m*

jackass ['dʒækæs] N (= *donkey*) asno *m*, burro *m*; (*fig*) (= *person*) burro *m*

jackboot ['dʒækbuːt] N bota *f* de montar, bota *f* militar; **under the Nazi ~** bajo el azote *or* la férula del nazismo

jackdaw ['dʒækdɔː] N grajilla *f*

jacket ['dʒækɪt] Ⓐ N 1 (= *garment*) chaqueta *f*, americana *f*, saco *m* (*LAm*)
2 (= *cover*) [*of boiler*] camisa *f*, envoltura *f*; [*of book*] sobrecubierta *f*; (*US*) [*of record*] funda *f*
3 [*of potato*] **potatoes baked in their ~s** (*Brit*) patatas *fpl* asadas con piel, papas *fpl* asadas con cáscara (*LAm*)
Ⓑ CPD ► **jacket potatoes** NPL (*Brit*) patatas *fpl* asadas con piel, papas *fpl* asadas con cáscara (*LAm*)

jackhammer ['dʒækˌhæməʳ] N (*esp US*) taladradora *f*, martillo *m* neumático

jack-in-the-box ['dʒækɪnðəbɒks] N caja *f* sorpresa, caja *f* de resorte

jackknife ['dʒæknaɪf] Ⓐ N (*pl* **jackknives**) navaja *f*, chaveta *f* (*LAm*)
Ⓑ VI [*lorry*] colear
Ⓒ CPD ► **jackknife dive** N salto *m* de la carpa, carpa *f*

jack-of-all-trades ['dʒækəv'ɔːltreɪdz] N (*pl* **jacks of all trades**) factótum *mf*; **he's a ~ and master of none** es de los que mucho abarca y poco aprieta, sabe un poco de todo pero no es experto en nada

jack-o'-lantern ['dʒækəʊ'læntən] N 1 (= *will-o'-the-wisp*) fuego *m* fatuo
2 (*US*) (= *Hallowe'en lantern*) *linterna hecha con una calabaza vaciada*

jackpot ['dʒækpɒt] N premio *m* gordo; **to hit the ~** sacar el premio gordo; (*fig*) ser todo un éxito *or* un exitazo

jackstraw ['dʒækstrɔː] N (*US*) pajita *f*

Jacob ['dʒeɪkəb] N Jacob

Jacobean [ˌdʒækə'biːən] ADJ de la época de Jacobo I (de Inglaterra)

Jacobin ['dʒækəbɪn] Ⓐ ADJ jacobino
Ⓑ N jacobino/a *m/f*

Jacobite ['dʒækəbaɪt] Ⓐ ADJ jacobita
Ⓑ N jacobita *mf*

Jacuzzi® [dʒə'kuːzɪ] N jacuzzi® *m*, baño *m* de burbujas

jade¹ [dʒeɪd] Ⓐ N (= *stone*) jade *m*
Ⓑ ADJ (*also* **~-green**) verde jade
Ⓒ CPD [*statue, carving, necklace*] de jade

jade² [dʒeɪd] N 1 (= *horse*) rocín *m*
2 (†) (= *woman*) mujerzuela *f*

jaded ['dʒeɪdɪd] ADJ hastiado, harto; **to feel ~** estar hastiado *or* harto; **to get ~** hastiarse, hartarse

jade-green ['dʒeɪd'griːn] ADJ verde jade *inv*

jag¹ [dʒæg] N (= *jagged point*) punta *f*, púa *f*

jag² [dʒæg] N (= *binge*) **to go on a ~*** ir de juerga

JAG N ABBR = **Judge Advocate General**

jagged ['dʒægɪd] ADJ dentado

jaguar ['dʒægjʊəʳ] N jaguar *m*, tigre *m* (*LAm*)

jail [dʒeɪl] Ⓐ N cárcel *f*, prisión *f*; **to go to ~** ir a la cárcel; **sentenced to ten years in ~** condenado a diez años de cárcel *or* prisión
Ⓑ VT (*for crime*) encarcelar (**for** por); (*for length of time*) **to ~ sb for two months** condenar a algn a dos meses de cárcel

jailbait* ['dʒeɪlbeɪt] N *menor con la que el mantener relaciones sexuales está penado*

jailbird ['dʒeɪlbɜːd] N presidiario/a *m/f* reincidente, preso/a *m/f* reincidente

jailbreak ['dʒeɪlbreɪk] N fuga *f*, evasión *f* (*de la cárcel*)

jailbreaker ['dʒeɪlˌbreɪkəʳ] N evadido/a *m/f*, fugado/a *m/f* (*de la cárcel*)

jailer ['dʒeɪləʳ] N carcelero/a *m/f*

jailhouse ['dʒeɪlhaʊs] N (*pl* **jailhouses**) cárcel *f*, prisión *f*

jakes†‡ [dʒeɪks] N meadero‡ *m*

jaloppy* [dʒə'lɒpɪ] N = **jalopy**

jalopy* [dʒə'lɒpɪ] N cacharro *m*, armatoste *m*

jalousie ['ʒælʊ(ː)ziː] N celosía *f*

jam¹ [dʒæm] (*Brit*) Ⓐ N 1 (= *food*) mermelada *f*; **strawberry ~** mermelada *f* de fresas; **you want ~ on it!*** (*fig*) ¡y un jamón!; ✦**IDIOM the ~ is spread very thin*** hay cosas buenas pero apenas se notan
2 (*) (= *luck*) chorra* *f*; **look at that for ~!** ¡qué chorra tiene el tío!*
Ⓑ VT hacer mermelada de
Ⓒ CPD ► **jam jar** N (*Brit*) tarro *m* de mermelada, pote *m* de mermelada ► **jam pot** N (*Brit*) = **jam jar** ► **jam roll** N (*Brit*) brazo *m* de gitano con mermelada ► **jam tart** N tarta *f* de mermelada

jam² [dʒæm] Ⓐ N 1 [*of people*] aglomeración *f*; **you never saw such a ~!** ¡había que ver cómo se agolpaba la gente!; **there was a ~ in the doorway** había una aglomeración de gente en la puerta, se había agolpado la gente en la puerta
2 (= *traffic jam*) embotellamiento *m*, atasco *m*; **a 5km ~ of cars** una caravana *or* un atasco de coches de 5km; **there are always ~s here** aquí siempre se atasca el tráfico, aquí siempre hay atascos
3 (= *obstruction*) atasco *m*; **there's a ~ in the pipe** se ha atascado *or* está atascada la cañería

4 (*fig*) (*) (= *difficulty*) apuro *m*, aprieto *m*; **to be in a ~** estar en un aprieto, estar en apuros; **to get into a ~** meterse en un aprieto, meterse en apuros; **to get sb out of a ~** sacar a algn del apuro
Ⓑ VT 1 (= *block*) [+ *mechanism, drawer, pipe*] atascar; [+ *wheel*] trabar; [+ *exit, road*] cerrar, obstruir; **it's got ~med** se ha atascado, no se puede mover/quitar/retirar *etc*
2 (= *cram*) [+ *passage, exit*] atestar, abarrotar; [+ *container*] atestar, llenar; **people ~med the exits** la gente se agolpaba en las salidas; **I ~med my finger in the door** me pillé el dedo con la puerta; **to ~ sth into a box** meter algo a la fuerza en una caja; **we were all ~med together** estábamos todos apiñados; **the room was ~med with people** el cuarto estaba atestado de gente; **streets ~med with cars** calles atascadas por el tráfico
3 (*Telec, Rad*) interferir
Ⓒ VI 1 [*mechanism, drawer, pipe*] atascarse, atorarse (*LAm*); [*nut, part, wheel*] atascarse, atrancarse; [*gun*] encasquillarse; **this part has ~med** esta pieza se ha atascado, no se puede mover esta pieza; **the drawer had ~med (shut/open)** el cajón no se podía abrir/cerrar
2 (*Mus**) improvisar
Ⓓ CPD ► **jam session** N jam session *f* (*actuación improvisada de jazz, rock etc*)
►**jam in** VT + ADV **if we can ~ two more books in** si podemos introducir a la fuerza dos libros más; **there were 15 people ~med in one room** había 15 personas apretadas unas contra otras en un cuarto
►**jam on** VT + ADV 1 **to ~ one's brakes on** frenar en seco, dar un frenazo
2 **he ~med his hat on his head** se encasquetó el sombrero; **with his hat ~med on his head** con el sombrero encasquetado en la cabeza

Jamaica [dʒə'meɪkə] N Jamaica *f*

Jamaican [dʒə'meɪkən] ADJ, N jamaicano/a *m/f*

jamb [dʒæm] N jamba *f*

jamboree [ˌdʒæmbə'riː] N 1 [*of Scouts*] congreso *m* de exploradores
2 (*) francachela *f*, juerga *f*

James [dʒeɪmz] N Jaime, Diego; (*British kings*) Jacobo; **Saint ~** Santiago

jam-full ['dʒæm'fʊl] ADJ (*of people*) abarrotado, atestado; (*of things*) atestado, repleto

jamming ['dʒæmɪŋ] N (*Rad*) interferencia *f*

jammy* ['dʒæmɪ] ADJ (*Brit*) (*compar* **jammier**, *superl* **jammiest**) suertudo*, potrudo*

jam-packed ['dʒæm'pækt] ADJ (*with people*) abarrotado, atestado; (*with things*) atestado, repleto

JAN N ABBR (*US*) = **Joint Army-Navy**

Jan. ABBR (= **January**) ene., en.

Jane [dʒeɪn] N Juana

jangle ['dʒæŋgl] Ⓐ N tintineo *m*
Ⓑ VT [+ *coins, bracelets*] hacer tintinear
Ⓒ VI tintinear

jangling ['dʒæŋglɪŋ] Ⓐ ADJ tintineante
Ⓑ N cencerreo *m*

janitor ['dʒænɪtəʳ] N (= *doorkeeper*) portero/a *m/f*; (= *caretaker*) conserje *mf*

Jansenism ['dʒænsəˌnɪzəm] N jansenismo *m*

Jansenist ['dʒænsənɪst] Ⓐ ADJ jansenista
Ⓑ N jansenista *mf*

January ['dʒænjʊərɪ] Ⓐ N enero *m*; *see* **July** *for usage*
Ⓑ CPD ► **the January sales** NPL las rebajas de enero

Janus ['dʒeɪnəs] N Jano

Jap** [dʒæp] (*offensive*) = **Japanese**

Japan [dʒə'pæn] N el Japón

japan [dʒə'pæn] Ⓐ N laca *f* japonesa
Ⓑ VT charolar con laca japonesa

Japanese [ˌdʒæpə'niːz] Ⓐ ADJ japonés
Ⓑ N (*pl* **Japanese**) 1 (= *person*) japonés/esa *m/f*; **the ~** (= *people*) los japoneses
2 (*Ling*) japonés *m*

jape [dʒeɪp] N burla *f*

japonica [dʒə'pɒnɪkə] N rosal *m* de China, rosal *m* japonés

jar¹ [dʒɑːʳ] N (= *container*) tarro *m*, bote *m*; (= *jug*) (*gen*) jarra *f*; (*large*) tinaja *f*; **to have a ~*** tomar un trago *or* una copa

jar² [dʒɑːʳ] Ⓐ N 1 (= *jolt*) sacudida *f*, choque *m*
2 (*fig*) (= *shock*) conmoción *f*, sorpresa *f* desagradable; **it gave me a ~** me dejó de piedra
Ⓑ VT 1 (= *jog*) tocar; **he must have ~red the camera** ha debido de mover la cámara; **somebody ~red my elbow** alguien me dio en el codo
2 (= *shake*) sacudir, hacer vibrar; **I've ~red my back** me he lastimado la espalda
3 (*fig*) afectar, impresionar
Ⓒ VI (= *clash*) [*colours, sounds*] desentonar; [*opinions*] chocar (**with** con); **to ~ on sb's nerves** poner a algn los nervios de punta; **to ~ on sb's ears** lastimar a algn el oído

jar³ [dʒɑːʳ] N **on the ~** = **ajar**

jargon ['dʒɑːgən] N jerga *f*

jarring ['dʒɑːrɪŋ] ADJ [*sound*] discordante, desafinado; [*opinions*] discordante; [*colour*] discordante, que desentona; **to strike a ~ note** (*fig*) ser la nota discordante, desentonar

Jas. ABBR = **James**

jasmine ['dʒæzmɪn] N jazmín *m*

jasper ['dʒæspəʳ] N jaspe *m*

jaundice ['dʒɔːndɪs] N ictericia *f*

jaundiced ['dʒɔːndɪst] ADJ 1 (*Med*) con ictericia, que tiene ictericia
2 (*fig*) (= *embittered*) [*person*] amargado, resentido; [*attitude*] negativo, pesimista
3 (*fig*) (= *disillusioned*) desilusionado

jaunt [dʒɔːnt] N excursión *f*

jauntily ['dʒɔːntɪlɪ] ADV [*walk*] garbosamente, airosamente; [*dress*] de manera alegre, de manera desenfadada; **he replied ~** contestó alegremente *or* con desenfado

jauntiness ['dʒɔːntɪnɪs] N [*of tone*] desenfado *m*; [*of clothes*] vistosidad *f*; [*of step*] garbo *m*

jaunting car ['dʒɔːntɪŋˌkɑːʳ] N tílburi *m* (irlandés)

jaunty ['dʒɔːntɪ] ADJ (= *relaxed*) [*air, tone*] desenvuelto, desenfadado; (= *cheerful*) [*clothes, hat*] alegre; [*step*] garboso, airoso

Java¹ ['dʒɑːvə] N (= *island*) Java *f*

Java²® ['dʒɑːvə] N (*Comput*) Java *m*

Javanese [ˌdʒɑːvə'niːz] Ⓐ ADJ javanés
Ⓑ N (*pl* **Javanese**) javanés/esa *m/f*

javelin ['dʒævlɪn] Ⓐ N 1 (= *object*) jabalina *f*; **to throw the ~** lanzar la jabalina
2 (= *event*) **she won a gold medal in the ~** ganó la medalla de oro en lanzamiento de jabalina
Ⓑ CPD ► **javelin thrower** N lanzador(a) *m/f* de jabalina ► **javelin throwing** N lanzamiento *m* de jabalina

jaw [dʒɔː] Ⓐ N 1 (*Anat*) [*of person*] mandíbula *f*; [*of animal*] quijada *f*
2 **jaws** [*of animal*] fauces *fpl*; (*Tech*) [*of vice*] mordaza *fsing*; [*of channel*] boca *fsing*, embocadura *fsing*; **the ~s of death** (*fig*) las garras de la muerte
3 (*) (= *chat*) cháchara *f*; **we had a good old ~** charlamos largo y tendido; **it's just a lot of ~** mucho ruido y pocas nueces; **hold your ~!** ¡cállate la boca!
Ⓑ VT (*) soltar el rollo a*
Ⓒ VI (*) charlar

jawbone ['dʒɔːbəʊn] Ⓐ N [*of person*] mandíbula *f*; [*of animal*] quijada *f*
Ⓑ VT (*US**) presionar, ejercer presión sobre

jawbreaker* ['dʒɔːˌbreɪkəʳ] N (*US*) trabalenguas *m inv*, palabra *f* kilométrica

jawline ['dʒɔːlaɪn] N mandíbula *f*

jay [dʒeɪ] N arrendajo *m*

jaywalk ['dʒeɪwɔːk] VI cruzar la calle imprudentemente

jaywalker ['dʒeɪˌwɔːkəʳ] N peatón/ona *m/f* imprudente

jaywalking ['dʒeɪˌwɔːkɪŋ] N imprudencia *f* al cruzar la calle

jazz [dʒæz] Ⓐ N 1 (*Mus*) jazz *m*
2 (*) (= *talk*) palabrería *f*; **and all that ~*** y otras cosas por el estilo; **don't give me that ~!** ¡no me vengas con cuentos!
Ⓑ CPD ► **jazz ballet** N jazz-ballet *m* ► **jazz band** N orquesta *f* de jazz
►**jazz up** VT + ADV 1 (*Mus*) sincopar
2 (*fig*) [+ *party*] animar; [+ *room*] alegrar

jazzy ['dʒæzɪ] ADJ 1 (*Mus*) sincopado
2 (*) (= *showy*) [*dress etc*] de colores llamativos, de colores chillones

JC N ABBR (= **Jesus Christ**) JC *m*

JCB® N ABBR *excavadora para la construcción con pala hidráulica*

JCC N ABBR (*US*) = **Junior Chamber of Commerce**

JCR N ABBR (*Brit Univ*) = **Junior Common Room**

JCS N ABBR (*US*) = **Joint Chiefs of Staff**

jct., jctn ABBR (*Rail*) = **junction**

JD N ABBR (*US*) 1 (*Univ*) = **Doctor of Laws**
2 = **Justice Department**

jealous ['dʒeləs] ADJ 1 [*husband, wife, lover*] celoso; **to be ~ of sb** tener celos de algn; **to make sb ~** dar celos a algn
2 (= *envious*) (*of possessions, qualities*) envidioso; **to be ~ of sth** envidiar algo

jealously ['dʒeləslɪ] ADV 1 (= *enviously*) con envidia; **he was ~ watching the skaters** observaba a los patinadores con envidia
2 (= *protectively*) celosamente; **she ~ guards her family's privacy** guarda celosamente la intimidad de su familia; **she's ~ possessive of him** es celosa y posesiva con él

jealousy ['dʒeləsɪ] N 1 [*of husband, wife, lover*] celos *mpl*
2 (= *envy*) [*of possessions, qualities*] envidia *f*

jeans [dʒiːnz] NPL vaqueros *mpl*, bluejeans *m* (*esp LAm*)

Jeep®, **jeep** [dʒiːp] N jeep® *m*, yip *m*

jeer [dʒɪəʳ] Ⓐ N 1 (*from crowd*) abucheo *m*; (*from individual*) grito *m* de protesta
2 (= *insult*) insulto *m*
Ⓑ VI 1 (= *mock*) burlarse (**at** de)
2 (= *boo*) abuchear (**at** a)
Ⓒ VT 1 (= *mock*) burlarse de
2 (= *boo*) abuchear

jeering ['dʒɪərɪŋ] Ⓐ ADJ [*remark, laughter*] burlón, sarcástico; **he was led through a ~ crowd** le hicieron pasar por una multitud que le llenó de insultos, le hicieron pasar entre una multitud que lo colmó de insultos
Ⓑ N 1 (= *protests*) protestas *fpl*
2 (= *mockery*) burlas *fpl*
3 (= *insults*) insultos *mpl*
4 (= *booing*) abucheo *m*

Jeez* [dʒiːz] EXCL ¡Santo Dios!

jehad [dʒɪ'hæd] N = **jihad**

Jehovah [dʒɪ'həʊvə] N Jehová *m*; **~'s Witness** Testigo *m* de Jehová

jejune [dʒɪˈdʒuːn] ADJ [1] (= *naïve*) cándido
[2] (= *dull*) [*subject*] árido; [*evening*] aburrido
[3] (= *insipid*) insípido, sin sustancia

jell [dʒel] VI = **gel B**

jellabah [ˈdʒeləbə] N chilaba *f*

jellied [ˈdʒelɪd] ADJ [*eels, meat*] en gelatina

jello®, Jell-O® [ˈdʒeləʊ] N (*US*) = **jelly[1] A1**

jelly[1] [ˈdʒelɪ] Ⓐ N [1] (*Brit*) (= *dessert*) jalea *f*, gelatina *f*; **my legs turned to ~** me temblaban las piernas
[2] (*US*) (= *jam*) mermelada *f*
[3] (= *substance*) gelatina *f*
Ⓑ CPD ► **jelly baby** N caramelo *m* de goma (*en forma de niño*)

jelly[2]‡ [ˈdʒelɪ] N = **gelignite**

jellybean [ˈdʒelɪbiːn] N gominola *f*

jellyfish [ˈdʒelɪfɪʃ] N (*pl* **jellyfish** *or* **jellyfishes**) medusa *f*, aguamala *f* (*Mex*), aguaviva *f* (*S. Cone*)

jemmy [ˈdʒemɪ] N (*Brit*) palanqueta *f*

Jennie, Jenny [ˈdʒenɪ] N (*familiar form*) *of* **Jennifer**

jeopardize [ˈdʒepədaɪz] VT (= *endanger*) arriesgar, poner en peligro; (= *compromise*) comprometer

jeopardy [ˈdʒepədɪ] N riesgo *m*, peligro *m*; **to be in ~** estar en peligro; **to put sth in ~** poner algo en peligro

jeremiad [ˌdʒerɪˈmaɪəd] N jeremiada *f*

Jeremiah [ˌdʒerɪˈmaɪə] N Jeremías

Jeremy [ˈdʒerɪmɪ] N Jeremías

Jericho [ˈdʒerɪkəʊ] N Jericó *m*

jerk [dʒɜːk] Ⓐ N [1] (= *shake*) sacudida *f*; (= *pull*) tirón *m*, jalón *m* (*LAm*); (*Med*) espasmo *m* muscular; **physical ~s** (*Brit**) gimnasia *f*, ejercicios *mpl* (físicos); **by ~s** a sacudidas; **he sat up with a ~** se incorporó de golpe; **to put a ~ in it*** menearse
[2] (*US**) imbécil *mf*, gilipollas** *mf inv*, pendejo *m* (*LAm*‡), huevón/ona *m/f* (*Andes, S. Cone***); **what a ~!** ¡menudo imbécil!
Ⓑ VT [1] (= *pull*) dar un tirón a, tirar bruscamente de, jalar bruscamente de (*LAm*); (= *shake*) sacudir, dar una sacudida a; (= *throw*) arrojar con un movimiento rápido; **to ~ sth along** arrastrar algo a tirones; **to ~ o.s. along** moverse a sacudidas, avanzar a tirones; **he ~ed it away from me** me lo quitó de un tirón *or* (*LAm*) jalón; **to ~ o.s. free** soltarse de un tirón *or* (*LAm*) jalón
[2] (*US*) [+ *meat*] atasajar
Ⓒ VI dar una sacudida; **to ~ along** moverse a sacudidas; **the bus ~ed to a halt** el autobús dio unas sacudidas y se paró

►**jerk off**** VI + ADV hacerse una paja**

►**jerk out** VT + ADV [+ *words*] decir con voz entrecortada

jerkily [ˈdʒɜːkɪlɪ] ADV [*move*] a tirones, a sacudidas; [*play, write*] de modo desigual, nerviosamente

jerkin [ˈdʒɜːkɪn] N chaleco *m*

jerkiness [ˈdʒɜːkɪnɪs] N [*of movement*] brusquedad *f*; [*of speech*] lo entrecortado

jerkwater* [ˈdʒɜːkˌwɔːtəʳ] ADJ (*US*) de poca monta; **a ~ town** un pueblucho*

jerky [ˈdʒɜːkɪ] ADJ (*compar* **jerkier**; *superl* **jerkiest**) [*movement, motion*] brusco; [*speech*] entrecortado, vacilante

Jeroboam [ˌdʒerəˈbəʊəm] N Jeroboam

Jerome [dʒəˈrəʊm] N Jerónimo

Jerry[1] [ˈdʒerɪ] N (*familiar form*) *of* **Gerald, Gerard**

Jerry[2]* [ˈdʒerɪ] N (*Brit Mil*) **a ~** un alemán; **~** los alemanes

jerry [ˈdʒerɪ] Ⓐ N (*Brit**) orinal *m*
Ⓑ CPD ► **jerry can** N bidón *m*

jerry-builder [ˈdʒerɪˌbɪldəʳ] N mal constructor *m*, tapagujeros *m inv*

jerry-building [ˈdʒerɪˌbɪldɪŋ] N mala construcción *f*, construcción *f* defectuosa

jerry-built [ˈdʒerɪbɪlt] ADJ mal construido, hecho con malos materiales

Jersey [ˈdʒɜːzɪ] N [1] (*Geog*) Isla *f* de Jersey, Jersey *m*
[2] (*Zool*) vaca *f* de Jersey

jersey [ˈdʒɜːzɪ] N (= *garment*) jersey *m*, suéter *m*; (= *fabric*) tejido *m* de punto

Jerusalem [dʒəˈruːsələm] Ⓐ N Jerusalén *f*
Ⓑ CPD ► **Jerusalem artichoke** N aguaturma *f*, pataca *f*

jessamine [ˈdʒesəmɪn] N jazmín *m*

jest [dʒest] Ⓐ N guasa *f*, broma *f*; **in ~** en broma, de guasa
Ⓑ VI bromear, estar de guasa; **he was only ~ing** lo dijo en broma nada más, sólo estaba de guasa

jester [ˈdʒestəʳ] N bufón *m*

jesting [ˈdʒestɪŋ] Ⓐ ADJ [*person*] chistoso, guasón; [*tone*] guasón; [*reference*] burlón, en broma
Ⓑ N chanzas *fpl*, bromas *fpl*

Jesuit [ˈdʒezjʊɪt] Ⓐ ADJ jesuita
Ⓑ N jesuita *m*

Jesuitical [ˌdʒezjʊˈɪtɪkəl] ADJ jesuítico

Jesus [ˈdʒiːzəs] Ⓐ N Jesús *m*; **~ Christ** Jesucristo *m*; **~ Christ!*** ¡Santo Dios!
Ⓑ CPD ► **Jesus freak*** N (*pej*) *cristiano ferviente evangélico* ► **Jesus sandals** NPL sandalias *fpl* nazarenas

jet[1] [dʒet] Ⓐ N (= *stone*) azabache *m*
Ⓑ CPD ► **jet black** N negro *m* azabache; *see also* **jet-black**

►**jet off*** VI + ADV salir de viaje (*en avión*)

jet[2] [dʒet] Ⓐ N [1] [*of liquid, steam*] chorro *m*; [*of flame*] llamarada *f*
[2] (= *nozzle*) [*of gas burner*] mechero *m*
[3] (*Aer*) (= *plane*) avión *m* a reacción, reactor *m*
Ⓑ VT lanzar en chorro, echar en chorro
Ⓒ VI chorrear, salir a chorro
Ⓓ CPD [*aircraft, fighter, plane*] a reacción, a chorro ► **the jet age** N la época de los jet ► **jet engine** N [*of plane*] motor *m* a reacción, reactor *m* ► **jet lag** N jet lag *m* (*desfase debido a un largo viaje en avión*); **to be suffering from ~ lag** tener jet lag ► **jet propulsion** N propulsión *f* por reacción, propulsión *f* a chorro ► **the jet set** N la jet set (*Sp*), el jet set (*LAm*), la alta sociedad ► **jet ski** N moto *f* acuática; *see also* **jet-ski** ► **jet stream** N corriente *f* en chorro

jet-black [ˈdʒetˈblæk] ADJ negro azabache *inv*

jetlagged [ˈdʒetˌlægd] ADJ **to be ~** tener jet lag, estar desfasado por el viaje en avión

jetliner [ˈdʒetˌlaɪnəʳ] N (*US*) avión *m* de pasajeros

jet-powered [ˈdʒetˈpaʊəd] ADJ = **jet-propelled**

jet-propelled [ˈdʒetprəˈpeld] ADJ a reacción, a chorro

jetsam [ˈdʒetsəm] N echazón *f*, cosas *fpl* desechadas

jet-setter [ˈdʒetˌsetəʳ] N miembro *mf* de la jet set (*Sp*), miembro *mf* del jet set (*LAm*)

jet-setting [ˈdʒetsetɪŋ] ADJ de la jet set (*Sp*), del jet set (*LAm*)

jet-ski [ˈdʒetskiː] VI practicar el motociclismo acuático; **they were ~ing** iban en moto acuática

jettison [ˈdʒetɪsn] VT (*Naut*) echar al mar, echar por la borda; (*Aer*) vaciar; (*fig*) deshacerse de; **we can safely ~ that** bien podemos prescindir de eso

jetty [ˈdʒetɪ] N (= *breakwater*) malecón *m*; (= *pier*) muelle *m*, embarcadero *m*

Jew [dʒuː] Ⓐ N judío/a *m/f*
Ⓑ CPD ► **Jew's harp** N birimbao *m*

jewel [ˈdʒuːəl] Ⓐ N (= *precious stone*) piedra *f* preciosa; (= *ornament*) joya *f*, alhaja *f*; (= *stone in watch*) rubí *m*; (*fig*) (= *person, thing*) joya *f*
Ⓑ CPD ► **jewel case** N joyero *m*

jewelled, jeweled (*US*) [ˈdʒuːəld] ADJ adornado con piedras preciosas; [*watch*] con rubíes

jeweller, jeweler (*US*) [ˈdʒuːələʳ] N joyero/a *m/f*; **~'s (shop)** joyería *f*

jewellery, jewelry (*US*) [ˈdʒuːəlrɪ] Ⓐ N joyas *fpl*, alhajas *fpl*; **a piece of ~** una joya
Ⓑ CPD ► **jewellery box** N joyero *m* ► **jewelry store** N (*US*) joyería *f*

Jewess [ˈdʒuːɪs] N († *gen pej*) judía *f*

Jewish [ˈdʒuːɪʃ] ADJ judío

Jewishness [ˈdʒuːɪʃnɪs] N carácter *m* judaico

Jewry [ˈdʒʊərɪ] N judería *f*, los judíos

Jezebel [ˈdʒezəbel] N Jezabel

JFK N ABBR (*US*) = **John Fitzgerald Kennedy International Airport**

jib[1] [dʒɪb] Ⓐ N (*Naut*) foque *m*; [*of crane*] aguilón *m*, brazo *m*
Ⓑ CPD ► **jib boom** N botalón *m* de foque

jib[2] [dʒɪb] VI [*horse*] plantarse; [*person*] rehusar, negarse; **to ~ at (doing) sth** resistirse a (hacer) algo; **he ~bed at it** se negó a aprobarlo

jibe [dʒaɪb] N, VI = **gibe**

jiffy* [ˈdʒɪfɪ] N momento *m*, segundo *m*; **in a ~** en un santiamén, en un momento, en un segundito (*LAm*); **to do sth in a ~** hacer algo en un santiamén *or* momento; **wait a ~** espera un momentito, un momentito (*LAm*), ahorita voy (*Mex*)

jig [dʒɪg] Ⓐ N [1] (= *dance, tune*) giga *f*
[2] (*Mech*) plantilla *f*; (*Min*) criba *f*; (*Rail*) gálibo *m*
Ⓑ VI (= *dance*) bailar dando brincos; **to ~ along** ◊ **~ up and down** [*person*] moverse a saltitos; **to keep ~ging up and down** no poder estarse quieto

jigger[1]* [ˈdʒɪgəʳ] N [1] (= *whisky measure*) medida *f* (de whisky *etc*)
[2] (*esp US*) (= *thingummy*) chisme *m*

jigger[2] [ˈdʒɪgəʳ] N (*Min*) criba *f*; (*Mech*) aparato *m* vibratorio

jiggered [ˈdʒɪgəd] ADJ **well I'm ~!** (*Brit**) ¡caramba!; **I'm ~ if I will** que me cuelguen si lo hago

jiggery-pokery* [ˈdʒɪgərɪˈpəʊkərɪ] N (*Brit*) trampas *fpl*, embustes *mpl*; **there's some ~ going on** hay gato encerrado

jiggle [ˈdʒɪgl] Ⓐ N zangoloteo *m*
Ⓑ VT zangolotear
Ⓒ VI zangolotearse

jigsaw [ˈdʒɪgsɔː] N [1] (*also* **~ puzzle**) rompecabezas *m inv*, puzzle *m*
[2] (= *tool*) sierra *f* de vaivén

jihad [dʒɪˈhæd] N (*Rel*) jihad *f* (*guerra santa musulmana*)

jilt [dʒɪlt] VT [+ *fiancé*] dejar plantado a; [+ *fiancée*] dejar plantada a; **her ~ed lover** su amante rechazado

Jim [dʒɪm] N (*familiar form*) *of* **James**

jimdandy†* [ˈdʒɪmˈdændɪ] ADJ (*US*) estupendo*, fenomenal*

jimjams[1]‡ [ˈdʒɪmdʒæmz] NPL delírium *m* tremens; **it gives me the ~** me horripila, me da grima

jimjams²* [ˈdʒɪmdʒæmz] NPL (*baby talk*) pijama *msing*, piyama *msing* (*LAm*)

Jimmy [ˈdʒɪmɪ] N (*familiar form*) *of* **James**

jimmy [ˈdʒɪmɪ] N 1 (*US*) = **jemmy**
2 **to have a ~ (Riddle)*** (*hum*) mear*, cambiar *or* mudar el agua al canario*

jingle [ˈdʒɪŋgl] Ⓐ N 1 (= *sound*) tintineo *m*, retintín *m*
2 (*Literat*) poemita *m* popular, rima *f* infantil; (= *advertising jingle*) cancioncilla *f*, musiquilla *f* (de anuncio)
Ⓑ VT [+ *coins, jewellery*] hacer tintinear
Ⓒ VI [*bells*] tintinear

jingo [ˈdʒɪŋgəʊ] N (*pl* **jingoes**) (*pej*) patriotero/a *m/f*; **by ~!** ¡caramba!

jingoism [ˈdʒɪŋgəʊɪzəm] N (*pej*) patriotería *f*

jingoistic [ˌdʒɪŋgəʊˈɪstɪk] ADJ (*pej*) patriotero

jink* [dʒɪŋk] VI (*Brit*) (= *zigzag*) dar un bandazo; **he ~ed out of the way** se salió del camino dando un bandazo

jinks [dʒɪŋks] NPL **high ~†*** jolgorio *msing*, jarana *f*; **we had high ~ last night** anoche nos lo pasamos pipa

jinx [dʒɪŋks] Ⓐ N (= *person*) cenizo/a *m/f*, gafe *mf*; (= *spell*) gafe *m*, maleficio *m*; **there's a ~ on it** está gafado, tiene la negra; **to put a ~ on sth** echar mal de ojo a algo
Ⓑ VT traer mala suerte a, gafar (*Sp**); **to be ~ed** [*person, project*] tener gafe

jitney* [ˈdʒɪtniː] N (*US*) 1 (= *bus*) autobús *m* pequeño, colectivo *m* (*LAm*)
2 (= *coin*) *moneda de cinco centavos*

jitterbug [ˈdʒɪtəbʌg] Ⓐ N (= *dance*) *baile acrobático al ritmo de jazz o bugui-bugui*; (= *person*) *persona aficionada a bailar ritmos de jazz o el bugui-bugui*
Ⓑ VI *bailar ritmos de jazz o el bugui-bugui*

jitters* [ˈdʒɪtəz] NPL **the ~** el canguelo*, los nervios; **to get the ~** ponerse nervioso; **to give sb the ~** poner nervioso a algn; **to have the ~** tener el canguelo*, estar nervioso

jittery* [ˈdʒɪtərɪ] ADJ muy inquieto, nervioso; **to get ~** inquietarse, ponerse nervioso

jiujitsu [dʒuːˈdʒɪtsuː] N = **jujitsu**

jive [dʒaɪv] Ⓐ N 1 (= *music, dancing*) swing *m*
2 (*US**) (= *big talk*) alardes *mpl*, palabrería *f*; (= *nonsense*) chorradas* *fpl*; (= *slang used by Black people*) (*also* **~ talk**) jerga *f* (*de la población negra norteamericana, en especial de los músicos de jazz*); **don't give me all that ~** deja de decir chorradas*
Ⓑ VI 1 (= *dance*) bailar el swing
2 (*) (= *be kidding*) bromear

Jly ABBR (= **July**) jul.

Jnr ABBR (= **junior**) jr

Jo [dʒəʊ] N 1 (*familiar form*) *of* **Josephine**
2 (*familiar form*) *of* **Joanne**

Joan [dʒəʊn] N Juana; **~ of Arc** Juana de Arco

Job [dʒəʊb] N Job; **~'s comforter** *el que queriendo animar a otro le desconsuela todavía más*

▼**job** [dʒɒb] Ⓐ N 1 (= *employment*) trabajo *m*, empleo *m*; **what would the ~ involve?** ¿en qué consistiría el trabajo *or* empleo?; **what's her ~?** ¿de qué trabaja?; **we shall create 1,000 new ~s** vamos a crear 1.000 puestos de trabajo más; **he got a ~ as a clerk** consiguió un trabajo *or* empleo de oficinista; **I think he's the best man for the ~** creo que es el más apropiado para el puesto; **to be in a ~** tener trabajo; **to look for a ~** buscar (un) trabajo *or* empleo; **to lose one's ~** (*gen*) perder el trabajo *or* empleo; (= *be sacked*) ser despedido; **to be out of a ~** estar sin trabajo *or* empleo; **if they go bankrupt we'll all be out of a ~** si se arruinan nos quedaremos todos sin trabajo *or* empleo; **to put sb out of a ~** quitar el trabajo *or* empleo a algn; ✦**IDIOM ~s for the boys** (*Brit** *pej*) amiguismo *m*, enchufes* *mpl*; *see also* **day B**
2 (= *piece of work*) trabajo *m*; **I have a ~ for you** tengo un trabajo para ti; **I'm afraid this is a ~ for a specialist** me parece que para esto hace falta un especialista; **it was a big ~** dio mucho trabajo, era mucho trabajo; **it's a difficult ~** es (un trabajo) muy difícil; **I'm paid by the ~** me pagan a destajo; **I've got a few ~s to do** tengo unas cosillas que hacer; **to do a ~ for sb** hacer un encargo para algn, hacer un recado a algn; **can you do a ~ for me?** ¿te puedo hacer un encargo?, ¿te puedo encargar algo?; **she's doing a good ~** trabaja bien; **he has done a good ~ with the book** el libro le ha salido bien; **we could do a far better ~ of it** podríamos hacer un trabajo muchísimo mejor; **it's not ideal but it'll do the ~** no es lo ideal pero valdrá; **let's get on with the the ~ in hand** vamos a concentrarnos en el trabajo que tenemos entre manos; **to know one's ~** conocer el oficio; **he really knows his ~** es un experto en lo suyo; **you've made a good ~ of painting the doors** has pintado muy bien las puertas; **he's out on a ~ at the moment** en este momento ha salido a hacer un trabajo; **on the ~: he fell asleep on the ~** se quedó dormido trabajando; **there was no formal training - they learned on the ~** no se ofrecía formación específica - aprendían trabajando *or* sobre la marcha; **he quit after five years on the ~** se fue tras haber estado en el trabajo cinco años; **to be on the ~*** (= *having sex*) estar haciéndolo*; ✦**IDIOM to fall down on the ~** demostrar no tener capacidad; ✦**PROV if a ~'s worth doing, it's worth doing well** las cosas hechas bien parecen; *see also* **hatchet, nose D, odd C, repair C**
3 (*Comput*) trabajo *m*
4 (= *duty, responsibility*) **my ~ is to sell them** yo estoy encargado de venderlos; **that's not my ~** eso no me incumbe a mí, eso no me toca a mí; **he's only doing his ~** está cumpliendo con su deber, nada más; **I had the ~ of telling him** a mí me tocó decírselo
5 (*) (= *undertaking*) **it's quite a ~, bringing up five children** es una tarea bastante dura, criar a cinco hijos
6 (*) (= *difficulty*) **to have a (hard) ~ doing/to do sth**: **we're having a hard ~ keeping up with the demand** nos está costando trabajo satisfacer la demanda; **we had quite a ~ getting here!** ¡vaya que nos costó (trabajo) llegar!; **we'll have a (hard) ~ to finish it in time** nos va a costar mucho trabajo terminarlo a tiempo
7 (*) (= *state of affairs*) **it's a bad ~** es una situación difícil; **it's a good ~ he didn't see us** menos mal que no nos vio; **(and a) good ~ too!** ¡menos mal!*; ✦**IDIOMS to make the best of a bad ~** poner al mal tiempo buena cara; **we'll just have to make the best of a bad ~** habrá que poner al mal tiempo buena cara; **to give sth up as a bad ~** dejar algo por imposible; **she gave him up as a bad ~** por imposible rompió con él
8 (*) (= *crime*) golpe* *m*; **he was planning a bank ~** planeaba un golpe en un banco; **he was caught doing a bank ~** lo cogieron *or* (*LAm*) agarraron asaltando un banco; **that warehouse ~** ese robo en el almacén; *see also* **put-up**
9 (*Brit**) (= *thing*) **this machine is just the ~** esta máquina nos viene que ni pintada*, esta máquina nos viene al pelo*; **a holiday in Majorca would be just the ~** unas vacaciones en Mallorca nos vendrían de perlas *or* de maravilla
10 (*Brit**) (*child language*) **to do a ~** hacer caca*
Ⓑ VI 1 (= *do casual work*) hacer trabajos temporales
2 (= *work as middleman*) **to ~ in sth** trabajar de intermediario en la compraventa de algo
Ⓒ CPD ► **job action** N (*US*) movilización *f* (de trabajadores) ► **job analysis** N (*Ind*) análisis *m* del trabajo, análisis *m* ocupacional ► **job application** N solicitud *f* de trabajo *or* empleo ► **Job Centre** N = **Jobcentre** ► **job club** N grupo *m* de asesoramiento para desempleados ► **job control language** N lenguaje *m* de control de trabajo ► **job creation** N creación *f* de empleo, creación *f* de puestos de trabajo ► **job creation scheme** N plan *m* de creación de puestos de trabajo, plan *m* de creación de nuevos empleos ► **job description** N descripción *f* del trabajo ► **job evaluation, job grading** N evaluación *f* de empleos ► **job holder** N empleado/a *m/f* ► **job hunting** N búsqueda *f* de trabajo, búsqueda *f* de empleo; **to go ~ hunting** salir a buscar trabajo *or* empleo ► **job interview** N entrevista *f* de trabajo ► **job losses** NPL pérdida *fsing* de puestos de trabajo; **500 ~ losses** una pérdida de 500 puestos de trabajo ► **job lot** N lote *m*; **to buy/sell sth as a ~ lot** comprar/vender algo en un lote ► **job number** N número *m* del trabajo ► **job offer** N oferta *f* de trabajo *or* empleo ► **job opportunity** N oportunidad *f* de trabajo ► **job queue** N (*Comput*) cola *f* de trabajos ► **job satisfaction** N satisfacción *f* en el trabajo, satisfacción *f* profesional ► **job security** N seguridad *f* en el trabajo ► **job seeker** N demandante *mf* de empleo, persona *f* que busca trabajo ► **job seeker's allowance** N (*Brit*) prestación *f* por desempleo ► **job sharing** N **~ sharing is encouraged here** intentamos fomentar el empleo compartido; **I'm interested in the possibility of ~ sharing** me interesaría poder compartir el empleo con otra persona ► **job title** N (nombre *m* del) puesto *m* ► **job vacancy** N puesto *m* vacante

jobber [ˈdʒɒbəʳ] N (*Brit St Ex*) corredor(a) *m/f* de Bolsa

jobbery [ˈdʒɒbərɪ] N (*Brit*) intrigas *fpl*, chanchullos *mpl*; **piece of ~** intriga *f*, chanchullo *m*; **by a piece of ~** por enchufe

jobbing [ˈdʒɒbɪŋ] Ⓐ ADJ (*Brit*) [*gardener, carpenter*] que trabaja a destajo, destajista; **~ printer** impresor *m* de circulares, folletos *etc*
Ⓑ N (*St Ex*) agiotaje *m*

Jobcentre [ˈdʒɒbsentəʳ] N (*Brit*) oficina *f* de empleo

jobless [ˈdʒɒblɪs] Ⓐ ADJ sin trabajo, desempleado, parado (*Sp*), cesante (*LAm*)
Ⓑ NPL **the ~** los desempleados, los parados (*Sp*), los cesantes (*LAm*)
Ⓒ CPD ► **the jobless figures** NPL las cifras del desempleo, las cifras de desempleados

joblessness [ˈdʒɒblɪsnɪs] N carencia *f* de trabajo

job-share [ˈdʒɒbʃeəʳ] ADJ **we operate a ~ scheme** tenemos en marcha un plan de empleo compartido

jobsworth* [ˈdʒɒbzwɜːθ] N (*Brit*) *empleado excesivamente legalista con respecto a las normativas que rigen su trabajo*

Jock* [dʒɒk] N (*pej*) *el escocés típico*; **the ~s** los escoceses

➤ LANGUAGE IN USE: job A1 19.2

jock [dʒɒk] N [1] = **jockstrap**
[2] (*US*) deportista *m*

jockey ['dʒɒkɪ] Ⓐ N jockey *m*
Ⓑ VT **to ~ sb into doing sth** convencer a algn para hacer algo; **to ~ sb out of sth** quitar algo a algn con artimañas; **to ~ sb out of a post** lograr con artimañas que algn renuncie a un puesto; **to ~ sb out of doing sth** disuadir a algn de hacer algo
Ⓒ VI **to ~ for position** (*fig*) maniobrar para conseguir una posición
Ⓓ CPD ► **Jockey Shorts**® NPL calzoncillos *mpl* de jockey

jockstrap ['dʒɒkstræp] N suspensorio *m*

jocose [dʒə'kəʊs] ADJ = **jocular**

jocular ['dʒɒkjʊləʳ] ADJ [*person*] gracioso; (= *merry*) alegre; [*manner*] bromista, chistoso; [*remark, reply*] jocoso, divertido

jocularity [ˌdʒɒkjʊ'lærɪtɪ] N jocosidad *f*

jodhpurs ['dʒɒdpɜːz] NPL pantalones *mpl* de montar

Joe* [dʒəʊ] Ⓐ N [1] (*familiar form*) *of* **Joseph** Pepe
[2] (*US*) tipo* *m*, tío* *m*; **the average ~** el hombre de la calle; **a good ~** un buen chico
Ⓑ CPD ► **Joe Bloggs*** N (*Brit*) *ciudadano de a pie británico* ► **Joe College*** N (*US*) *típico estudiante norteamericano* ► **Joe Public*** N = **Joe Bloggs** ► **Joe Soap*** N fulano *m*

jog [dʒɒg] Ⓐ N [1] (= *push*) (*gen*) empujoncito *m*; (*with elbow*) codazo *m*
[2] (= *encouragement*) estímulo *m*; **to give sb's memory a ~** refrescar la memoria a algn
[3] (= *pace*) (*also* **~ trot**) trote *m* corto; **to go at a steady ~** andar a trote corto
[4] (= *run*) carrera *f* a trote corto; **to go for a ~** ir a hacer footing *or* jogging
Ⓑ VT [1] (= *push*) empujar (ligeramente); **he ~ged my arm** me dio ligeramente con el codo
[2] (= *encourage*) estimular; **to ~ sb's memory** refrescar la memoria a algn; **to ~ sb into action** motivar a algn
Ⓒ VI [1] (*also* **to ~ along**) (*gen*) andar a trote corto; (*fig*) hacer algunos progresos, avanzar pero sin prisa
[2] (*Sport*) (*also* **to go ~ging**) hacer footing, hacer jogging
Ⓓ CPD ► **jog trot** N **at a ~ trot** a trote corto

►**jog along** VI + ADV [*vehicle*] avanzar despacio, ir sin prisa; (*fig*) **we're ~ging along** vamos tirando; **the work is ~ging along nicely** el trabajo marcha bien

jogger ['dʒɒgəʳ] N corredor(a) *m/f* (de footing)

jogging ['dʒɒgɪŋ] Ⓐ N footing *m*, jogging *m*
Ⓑ CPD ► **jogging shoes** NPL zapatillas *fpl* de deporte ► **jogging suit** N chandal *m*

joggle* ['dʒɒgl] Ⓐ N sacudida *f*; **I gave his arm a ~** le sacudí el brazo, le di una sacudida en el brazo
Ⓑ VT sacudir
Ⓒ VI dar sacudidas

john[1]**:** [dʒɒn] N (*esp US*) (= *lavatory*) **the ~** el váter*, el retrete, el baño (*LAm*)

john[2]**:** [dʒɒn] N (*US*) (= *prostitute's customer*) putero* *m*, cliente *m* de prostituta

John [dʒɒn] Ⓐ N Juan; **Pope ~ Paul II** el Papa Juan Pablo II
Ⓑ CPD ► **John Bull** N *personificación del pueblo inglés* ► **John Doe** N (*US*) fulano *m* ► **John Dory** N gallo *m* (*pez*) ► **John Hancock*** N firma *f*, rúbrica *f* ► **John Henry** N firma *f* ► **John of the Cross** N (*also* **Saint ~ of the Cross**) San Juan de la Cruz ► **John Q Public*** N (*US*) el hombre de la calle ► **John the Baptist** N (*also* **St ~ the Baptist**) San Juan Bautista ► **John the Evangelist** N (*also* **Saint ~ the Evangelist**) San Juan Evangelista

Johnny ['dʒɒnɪ] N Juanito

johnny* ['dʒɒnɪ] N tío* *m*, sujeto *m*

joie de vivre ['ʒwɑːdə'viːvr] N alegría *f* de vivir

join [dʒɔɪn] Ⓐ VT [1] (= *put together, link*) [+ *ends, pieces, parts*] unir, juntar; [+ *tables*] juntar; **to ~ (together) two ends of a chain** unir *or* juntar dos extremos de una cadena; **the island is ~ed to the mainland by a bridge** un puente une *or* conecta la isla a tierra firme; **to ~ A to B ◊ ~ A and B** unir *or* juntar A con B; **~ the dots to form a picture** una los puntos para formar un dibujo; **to ~ hands** cogerse *or* (*LAm*) tomarse de la mano
[2] (= *merge with*) [+ *river*] desembocar en, confluir con; [+ *sea*] desembocar en; [+ *road*] empalmar con; **where does the River Wye ~ the Severn?** ¿a qué altura desemboca el Wye en el Severn?, ¿dónde confluye el Wye con el Severn?; **where the river ~s the sea** en la desembocadura del río en el mar; **where the track ~s the road** donde el camino empalma con la carretera
[3] (= *enter, become part of*) [+ *university, firm, religious order*] ingresar en, entrar en; [+ *club, society*] hacerse socio de; [+ *political party*] afiliarse a, hacerse miembro de; [+ *army, navy*] alistarse en, ingresar en; [+ *queue*] meterse en; [+ *procession, strike, movement*] sumarse a, unirse a; **~ the club!*** ¡bienvenido al club!; **to ~ forces (with sb to do sth)** (*gen*) juntarse (con algn para hacer algo); (*Mil*) aliarse (con algn para hacer algo); (*Comm*) asociarse (con algn para hacer algo); **we ~ed the motorway at junction 15** nos metimos en la autopista por la entrada 15; **to ~ one's regiment** incorporarse a su regimiento; **to ~ one's ship** (= *return to*) volver a su buque; (= *go on board*) embarcar; *see also* **battle A1**, **rank**[1] **A2**
[4] (= *be with, meet*) [+ *person*] acompañar a; **may I ~ you?** (*at table*) ¿les importa que les acompañe?; **will you ~ us for dinner?** ¿nos acompañas a cenar?, ¿cenas con nosotros?; **if you're going for a walk, do you mind if I ~ you?** si vais a dar un paseo, ¿os importa que os acompañe?; **will you ~ me in** *or* **for a drink?** ¿se toma una copa conmigo?; **I'll ~ you later if I can** yo iré luego si puedo; **~ us at the same time next week for ...** (*Rad, TV*) la próxima semana tiene una cita con nosotros a la misma hora en ...; **Paul ~s me in wishing you ...** al igual que yo, Paul te desea ...; **they should ~ us in exposing government corruption** deberían unirse *or* sumarse a nosotros para sacar a la luz la corrupción del gobierno
Ⓑ VI [1] (= *connect*) [*ends, pieces, parts*] unirse, juntarse
[2] (= *merge*) [*roads*] empalmar, juntarse; [*rivers*] confluir, juntarse; [*lines*] juntarse
[3] **to ~ together (to do sth)** (= *meet*) [*people*] reunirse (para hacer algo); (= *unite*) [*groups, organizations*] unirse (para hacer algo); (= *pool resources*) asociarse (para hacer algo); **to ~ with sb in doing sth** unirse a algn para hacer algo; **Moscow and Washington have ~ed in condemning these actions** Moscú y Washington se han unido para protestar por estas acciones; **we ~ with you in hoping that ...** compartimos su esperanza de que ... + *subjun*, al igual que ustedes esperamos que ... + *subjun*
[4] (= *become a member*) (*of club*) hacerse socio; (*of political party*) afiliarse, hacerse miembro
Ⓒ N [*in wood, crockery*] juntura *f*, unión *f*; (*Tech*) junta *f*; **you could hardly see the ~** apenas se notaba la juntura *or* la unión

►**join in** Ⓐ VI + PREP [+ *game, celebration, conversation*] tomar parte en, participar en; [+ *protest*] sumarse a, unirse a; **they all ~ed in the game** todos tomaron parte *or* participaron en el juego; **can anyone ~ in this discussion?** ¿puede participar cualquiera en esta discusión?; **they all ~ed in the last song** todos cantaron la última canción
Ⓑ VI + ADV (*in game, celebration, conversation*) participar; **he doesn't ~ in much** apenas participa; **a couple began to dance and then we all ~ed in** una pareja salió a bailar y detrás fuimos todos; **she started singing, and the audience ~ed in** empezó a cantar, y el público se unió a ella; **~ in everyone!** (*in chorus*) ¡todo el mundo!, ¡todos!

►**join on** Ⓐ VT + ADV [1] (= *attach*) unir; **how do I ~ on the sleeves?** ¿cómo uno las mangas?
[2] (= *add*) [+ *extra piece, building*] añadir
Ⓑ VI + ADV [*part*] unirse, juntarse; **where the muscles ~ on to the bone** donde los músculos se unen a *or* juntan con el hueso

►**join up** Ⓐ VI + ADV [1] (*Mil*) alistarse
[2] (= *meet*) [*people*] reunirse, juntarse; **we ~ed up with him in Málaga** nos reunimos *or* nos juntamos con él en Málaga
[3] (= *merge*) [*roads*] empalmar, juntarse; [*rivers*] confluir, juntarse
[4] [*organizations, groups*] (= *unite, team up*) unirse, asociarse; (= *merge*) fusionarse
Ⓑ VT + ADV [+ *ends, pieces, parts*] unir, juntar; **~ up the dots to form a picture** una los puntos para formar un dibujo; **~ed up writing** escritura *f* cursiva, escritura *f* corrida

joiner ['dʒɔɪnəʳ] N (= *carpenter*) carpintero/a *m/f*

joinery ['dʒɔɪnərɪ] N carpintería *f*

joint [dʒɔɪnt] Ⓐ ADJ [*work, declaration, consultation*] (*between two parties*) conjunto; (*more than two*) colectivo; [*agreement*] mutuo; [*decision*] de común acuerdo; [*responsibility*] compartido; [*committee*] mixto
Ⓑ N [1] (*Tech*) (*in metal*) juntura *f*, junta *f*; (*in wood*) ensambladura *f*; (= *hinge*) bisagra *f*
[2] [*of meat*] cuarto *m*; **we had a ~ of lamb for lunch** comimos asado de cordero
[3] (*Anat*) articulación *f*, coyuntura *f*; **to be out of ~** [*bone*] estar descoyuntado, estar dislocado; (*fig*) estar fuera de quicio; **to put a bone out of ~** dislocar un hueso; **to put sb's nose out of ~*** (*fig*) bajar los humos a algn; **to throw sb's plans out of ~** estropear los planes a algn
[4] (*) (= *place*) garito *m*
[5] (*) (= *cigarette containing cannabis*) porro *m*, canuto *m*
[6] (*Bot*) nudo *m*
Ⓒ VT [1] (*Culin*) despiezar, cortar en trozos
[2] (= *join*) [+ *parts*] juntar, unir; [+ *wood, pipes*] ensamblar
Ⓓ CPD ► **joint account** N cuenta *f* conjunta ► **joint author** N coautor(a) *m/f* ► **joint communiqué** N comunicado *m* conjunto ► **joint consultations** NPL consultas *fpl* bilaterales ► **joint heir** N coheredero/a *m/f* ► **joint interest** N (*Comm*) coparticipación *f* ► **joint liability** N (*Comm*) responsabilidad *f* solidaria ► **joint owners** NPL copropietarios *mpl* ► **joint ownership** N copropiedad *f* ► **joint partner** N copartícipe *mf* ► **joint stock** N fondo *m* social ► **joint stock bank** N banco *m* comercial ► **joint stock company** N sociedad *f* anónima ► **joint venture** N empresa *f* conjunta

jointed [ˈdʒɔɪntɪd] ADJ [*doll*] articulado; [*fishing rod, tent pole*] plegable

jointly [ˈdʒɔɪntlɪ] ADV en común, conjuntamente

joist [dʒɔɪst] N viga *f*, vigueta *f*

jojoba [həʊˈhəʊbə] Ⓐ N jojoba *f*
Ⓑ CPD [*shampoo, conditioner, oil*] de jojoba

▼ **joke** [dʒəʊk] Ⓐ N (= *witticism, story*) chiste *m*; (= *practical joke*) broma *f*; (= *hoax*) broma *f*; (= *person*) hazmerreír *m*; **what sort of a ~ is this?** ¿qué clase de broma es ésta?; **the ~ is that ...** lo gracioso es que ...; **to take sth as a ~** tomar algo a broma; **to treat sth as a ~** tomar algo a broma; **it's (gone) beyond a ~** (*Brit*) esto no tiene nada de gracioso; **to crack a ~** hacer un chiste; **to crack ~s with sb** contarse chistes con algn; **they spent an evening cracking ~s together** pasaron una tarde contándose chistes; **for a ~** en broma; **one can have a ~ with her** tiene mucho sentido del humor; **is that your idea of a ~?** ¿es que eso tiene gracia?; **he will have his little ~** siempre está con sus bromas; **to make a ~** hacer un chiste (**about sth** sobre algo); **he made a ~ of the disaster** se tomó el desastre a risa; **it's no ~** no tiene nada de divertido; **it's no ~ having to go out in this weather** no tiene nada de divertido salir con este tiempo; **the ~ is on you** la broma la pagas tú; **to play a ~ on sb** gastar una broma a algn; **I don't see the ~** no le veo la gracia; **he's a standing ~** es un pobre hombre; **it's a standing ~ here** aquí eso siempre provoca risa; **I can take a ~** tengo mucha correa *or* mucho aguante; **he can't take a ~** no le gusta que le tomen el pelo; **to tell a ~** contar un chiste (**about sth** sobre algo); **why do you have to turn everything into a ~?** ¿eres incapaz de tomar nada en serio?; **what a ~!** (*iro*) ¡qué gracia! (*iro*)
Ⓑ VI (= *make jokes*) contar chistes, hacer chistes; (= *be frivolous*) bromear; **to ~ about sth** (= *make jokes about*) contar chistes sobre algo; (= *make light of*) tomarse algo a risa; **I was only joking** lo dije en broma, no iba en serio; **I'm not joking** hablo en serio; **you're joking!** ◊ **you must be joking!** ¡no lo dices en serio!
Ⓒ CPD ► **joke book** N libro *m* de chistes

joker [ˈdʒəʊkəʳ] N 1 (= *wit*) chistoso/a *m/f*, guasón/ona *m/f*; (= *practical joker*) bromista *mf*
2 (*) (= *idiot*) payaso/a *m/f*; (*stronger*) idiota *mf*; **some ~ will always start singing** siempre hay algún payaso que se pone a cantar
3 (*Cards*) comodín *m*; **he's the ~ in the pack** (*fig*) es el gran desconocido, el la gran incógnita

jokester [ˈdʒəʊkstəʳ] N bromista *mf*

jokey [ˈdʒəʊkɪ] ADJ [*person*] chistoso, guasón; [*reference*] humorístico; [*mood, tone*] guasón

joking [ˈdʒəʊkɪŋ] Ⓐ ADJ [*tone*] burlón; [*reference*] humorístico; **I'm not in a ~ mood** no estoy para bromas
Ⓑ N (= *jokes*) (*practical*) bromas *fpl*; (*verbal*) chistes *mpl*, cuentos *mpl* (*LAm*); **~ apart** *or* **aside ...** fuera de bromas ..., hablando en serio ...

jokingly [ˈdʒəʊkɪŋlɪ] ADV (= *laughingly*) en broma; (= *mockingly*) en son de burla; **he said ~** dijo en broma, dijo guasón

jollification [ˌdʒɒlɪfɪˈkeɪʃən] N 1 (= *merriment*) regocijo *m*, festividades *fpl*
2 (= *party*) fiesta *f*, guateque *m*

jolliness [ˈdʒɒlɪnɪs] N jovialidad *f*

jollity [ˈdʒɒlɪtɪ] N alegría *f*, regocijo *m*

jolly [ˈdʒɒlɪ] Ⓐ ADJ (*compar* **jollier**, *superl* **jolliest**) [*person*] (= *cheerful*) alegre; (= *amusing*) divertido; [*laugh*] gracioso; **it was all very ~** todo fue muy agradable; **it wasn't very ~ for the rest of us** los demás no nos divertimos tanto; **we had a ~ time** lo pasamos muy bien, nos divertimos mucho; **to get ~*** achisparse*
Ⓑ ADV (*Brit**) muy, la mar de, bastante (*LAm*); **we were ~ glad** estábamos la mar de contentos, nos alegramos muchísimo; **it's ~ hard** es terriblemente difícil; **you did ~ well** lo hiciste la mar de bien*; **you've ~ well got to** no tienes otro remedio, no te queda otra (*LAm*); **~ good!** ¡estupendo!, ¡macanudo! (*Peru, S. Cone*)
Ⓒ VT **to ~ sb along** dar ánimos a algn, animar a algn; **to ~ sb into doing sth** engatusar a algn para que haga algo
Ⓓ CPD ► **jolly boat** N esquife *m* ► **Jolly Roger** N bandera *f* pirata

jolt [dʒəʊlt] Ⓐ N (= *jerk*) sacudida *f*; (= *sudden bump*) choque *m*; (*fig*) susto *m*; **to give sb a ~** (*fig*) dar un susto a algn; **it gave me a bit of a ~** me dio un buen susto
Ⓑ VT [*vehicle*] sacudir; [+ *person, elbow*] empujar (ligeramente), sacudir (levemente); (*fig*) afectar mucho; **to ~ sb into (doing) sth** mover a algn a hacer algo; **to ~ sb out of his complacency** hacer que algn se dé cuenta de la necesidad de hacer algo
Ⓒ VI [*vehicle*] traquetear, dar tumbos

jolting [ˈdʒəʊltɪŋ] N [*of vehicle*] traqueteo *m*

jolty [ˈdʒəʊltɪ] ADJ [*vehicle*] que traquetea, que da saltos

Jonah [ˈdʒəʊnə] N Jonás

Jonathan [ˈdʒɒnəθən] N Jonatás

jonquil [ˈdʒɒŋkwɪl] N junquillo *m*

Jordan [ˈdʒɔːdn] N 1 (= *country*) Jordania *f*
2 (= *river*) Jordán *m*

Jordanian [dʒɔːˈdeɪnɪən] Ⓐ ADJ jordano
Ⓑ N jordano/a *m/f*

Joseph [ˈdʒəʊzɪf] N José

Josephine [ˈdʒəʊzɪfiːn] N Josefina

josh* [dʒɒʃ] (*esp US*) Ⓐ VT tomar el pelo a
Ⓑ VI hacer bromas

Joshua [ˈdʒɒʃwə] N Josué

josser* [ˈdʒɒsəʳ] N (*Brit*) tío *m*, individuo *m*

joss stick [ˈdʒɒsstɪk] N pebete *m*

jostle [ˈdʒɒsl] Ⓐ VT empujar
Ⓑ VI empujar, dar empujones; **to ~ against sb** dar empujones a algn; **to ~ for a place** abrirse paso a empujones
Ⓒ N empujón *m*

jot [dʒɒt] Ⓐ N pizca *f*; **there's not a ~ of truth in it** no tiene ni pizca de verdad; *see also* **care C**
Ⓑ VT **to ~ down** apuntar, anotar

jotter [ˈdʒɒtəʳ] N (= *notebook, pad*) bloc *m* (de notas)

jottings [ˈdʒɒtɪŋz] NPL apuntes *mpl*, anotaciones *fpl*

joule [dʒuːl] N julio *m*, joule *m*

journal [ˈdʒɜːnl] Ⓐ N 1 (= *diary*) diario *m*; (*Naut*) diario *m* de navegación
2 (= *periodical*) periódico *m*; (= *magazine*) revista *f*
3 (*Mech*) gorrón *m*, muñón *m*
Ⓑ CPD ► **journal bearing** N cojinete *m*

journalese [ˈdʒɜːnəˈliːz] N (*pej*) jerga *f* periodística

journalism [ˈdʒɜːnəlɪzəm] N periodismo *m*

journalist [ˈdʒɜːnəlɪst] N periodista *mf*, reportero/a *m/f* (*LAm*)

journalistic [ˌdʒɜːnəˈlɪstɪk] ADJ periodístico

journey [ˈdʒɜːnɪ] Ⓐ N (= *trip*) viaje *m*; (= *distance*) trayecto *m*, tramo *m* (*LAm*); **Scott's ~ to the Pole** la expedición de Scott al Polo; **the capsule's ~ through space** el trayecto de la cápsula por el espacio; **have you much ~ left?** ¿le queda mucho camino?; **to break one's ~** hacer una parada; **to reach one's ~'s end** llegar al final de su viaje, llegar a su destino; **at ~'s end** al fin del viaje; **to be on a ~** estar de viaje; **to go on a ~** hacer un viaje; **to send sb on a ~** enviar a algn de viaje; **the outward ~** el viaje de ida; **pleasant ~!** ¡buen viaje!; **the return ~** el viaje de vuelta
Ⓑ VI viajar

journeyman [ˈdʒɜːnɪmən] N (*pl* **journeymen**) oficial *m*

journo* [ˈdʒɜːnəʊ] N (*Brit*) periodista *mf*

joust [dʒaʊst] Ⓐ N justa *f*, torneo *m*
Ⓑ VI justar

Jove [dʒəʊv] N Júpiter; **by ~!** ¡caramba!, ¡por Dios!

jovial [ˈdʒəʊvɪəl] ADJ jovial

joviality [ˌdʒəʊvɪˈælɪtɪ] N jovialidad *f*

jovially [ˈdʒəʊvɪəlɪ] ADV jovialmente

jowl [dʒaʊl] N (*gen pl*) (= *jaw*) quijada *f*; (= *cheek*) carrillo *m*; (= *chin*) barbilla *f*; (*Zool*) papada *f*; **a man with heavy ~s** un hombre mofletudo

-jowled [ˈdʒaʊld] ADJ (*ending in compounds*) **square-jowled** de mandíbulas cuadradas

jowly [ˈdʒaʊlɪ] ADJ de mejillas caídas

joy [dʒɔɪ] N (= *happiness*) alegría *f*; (= *delight*) júbilo *m*, regocijo *m*; (= *source of delight*) deleite *m*, alegría *f*; **to be a ~ to the eye** ser un gozo para los ojos; **it's a ~ to hear him** es un gusto oírlo, da gusto oírlo; **the ~s of opera** los encantos de la ópera; **the ~s of camping** (*lit*) (*also hum*) los placeres del camping; **to be beside o.s. with ~** no caber en sí de gozo; **did you have any ~ in finding it?** ¿tuviste éxito en encontrarlo?; **to jump** *or* **leap for ~** saltar de alegría; **no ~!*** ¡sin resultado!, ¡sin éxito!; **we got no ~ out of it** no logramos nada, no nos sirvió de nada; **to our great ~ ...** para nuestra gran alegría ...; **I wish you ~ of it!** (*iro*) ¡que lo disfrutes!, ¡enhorabuena!

joyful [ˈdʒɔɪfʊl] ADJ (*gen*) feliz; [*event, occasion*] festivo; **to be ~ about sth** alegrarse de algo

joyfully [ˈdʒɔɪfəlɪ] ADV [*sing, play*] alegremente; [*greet, announce*] con júbilo

joyfulness [ˈdʒɔɪfʊlnɪs] N [*of atmosphere*] alegría *f*; [*of event, occasion*] festividad *f*; (*on hearing news*) júbilo *m*

joyless [ˈdʒɔɪlɪs] ADJ sin alegría, triste

joyous [ˈdʒɔɪəs] ADJ (*liter*) = **joyful**

joyously [ˈdʒɔɪəslɪ] ADV (*liter*) = **joyfully**

joyride* [ˈdʒɔɪraɪd] Ⓐ N 1 (= *irresponsible action*) escapada *f*
2 (*in stolen car*) **to go for a ~** dar una vuelta en un coche robado
Ⓑ VI dar una vuelta en un coche robado

joyrider [ˈdʒɔɪraɪdəʳ] N *persona que se da una vuelta en un coche robado*

joyriding [ˈdʒɔɪraɪdɪŋ] N *delito de robar un coche para dar una vuelta en él*

joystick [ˈdʒɔɪstɪk] N (*Aer*) palanca *f* de mando; (*Comput*) palanca *f* de control, joystick *m*

JP N ABBR (*Brit*) = **Justice of the Peace**

Jr ABBR (*US*) (= **junior**) jr

JSA N ABBR (*Brit Admin*) = **job seeker's allowance**

JTPA N ABBR (*US*) (= **Job Training Partnership Act**) *programa gubernamental de formación profesional*

jubilant [ˈdʒuːbɪlənt] ADJ [*crowd*] jubiloso, exultante; [*cry, shout*] de júbilo, alborozado

jubilation [ˌdʒuːbɪˈleɪʃən] N júbilo *m*

➤ LANGUAGE IN USE: **joke B** 12.1

jubilee ['dʒu:bɪli:] N (= *celebration*) jubileo *m*; (= *anniversary*) aniversario *m*; **silver ~** vigésimo quinto aniversario *m*

Judaea [dʒu:'dɪə] N Judea *f*

Judaeo-Christian, **Judeo-Christian** (*US*) [dʒu:,deɪəʊ'krɪstɪən] ADJ judeo-cristiano

Judah ['dʒu:də] N Judá *m*

Judaic [dʒu:'deɪɪk] ADJ judaico

Judaism ['dʒu:deɪɪzəm] N judaísmo *m*

Judaize ['dʒu:deɪaɪz] VI judaizar

Judaizer ['dʒu:deɪ,aɪzəʳ] N judaizante *mf*

Judas ['dʒu:dəs] N (= *name*) Judas; (= *traitor*) judas *m*

judder ['dʒʌdəʳ] (*Brit*) Ⓐ N vibración *f*
Ⓑ VI vibrar

Judeo-Spanish ['dʒu:deɪəʊ'spænɪʃ] Ⓐ ADJ judeoespañol, sefardí
Ⓑ N (*Ling*) judeoespañol *m*, ladino *m*

▼**judge** [dʒʌdʒ] Ⓐ N 1 (*Jur*) juez *mf*, juez(a) *m/f*; **(the Book of) Judges** el Libro de los Jueces; **~ of appeal** juez *mf* de alzadas, juez *mf* de apelaciones; **the ~'s rules** (*Brit*) los derechos del detenido
2 [*of contest*] juez *mf*, miembro *mf* del jurado; (*Sport*) árbitro *m*; (*in races*) juez *mf*
3 (= *knowledgeable person*) conocedor(a) *m/f* (**of** de), entendido/a *m/f* (**of** en); (= *expert*) perito/a *m/f* (**of** en); **he's a fine ~ of horses** es un excelente conocedor de *or* entendido en caballos; **to be a good/bad ~ of character** ser buen/mal psicólogo, tener/no tener psicología para conocer a la gente; **I'm no ~ of wines** no entiendo de vinos; **I'll be the ~ of that** yo decidiré eso, lo juzgaré yo mismo
Ⓑ VT 1 [+ *person, case, contest*] juzgar; [+ *matter*] decidir, resolver; **who can ~ this question?** ¿quién puede resolver esta cuestión?; **he ~d the moment well** escogió el momento oportuno, atinó
2 (*Sport*) arbitrar
3 (= *estimate*) [+ *weight, size, distance*] calcular; **we ~d the distance right/wrong** calculamos bien/mal la distancia
4 (= *consider*) considerar; **I ~ him a fool** considero que es tonto; **I ~d it to be right** lo consideré acertado, me pareció correcto; **they thought that they were going to win easily, but they ~d wrong** creían que iban a ganar con facilidad, pero erraron en el juicio; **she suspected that his intentions were dishonest, and she ~d right** dudaba que sus intenciones fueran honestas, y acertó en el juicio; **as far as can be ~d** a mi modo de ver, según mi juicio; ✦***PROV*** **you can't ~ a book by its cover** no hay que fiarse de las apariencias, las apariencias engañan
Ⓒ VI (= *act as judge*) juzgar, ser juez; **judging from** *or* **to ~ by his expression** a juzgar por su expresión; **to ~ for o.s.** juzgar por sí mismo; **to ~ of** juzgar de, opinar sobre; **who am I to ~?** ¿es que yo soy capaz de juzgar?; **as far as I can ~** por lo que puedo entender, a mi entender; **only an expert can ~** sólo lo puede decidir un experto
Ⓓ CPD ► **judge advocate** N (*Mil*) auditor *m* de guerra

judgement ['dʒʌdʒmənt] N = **judgment**

judgemental [dʒʌdʒ'mentl] ADJ = **judgmental**

judgment ['dʒʌdʒmənt] Ⓐ N 1 (*Jur*) (= *decision*) sentencia *f*, fallo *m*; (= *act*) juicio *m*; **it's a ~ on you** es un castigo; **to pass** *or* **pronounce ~ (on sb/sth)** (*Jur*) pronunciar *or* dictar sentencia (sobre algn/en algo), emitir un fallo (sobre algn/algo); (*fig*) emitir un juicio crítico (sobre algn/algo), dictaminar (sobre algn/algo); **to sit in ~ on sb** decidir sobre la culpabilidad de algn; **to sit in ~ on sth** juzgar algo; **Last Judgment** Juicio *m* Final
2 (= *opinion*) opinión *f*, parecer *m*; **a critical ~ of Auden** un juicio crítico de Auden
3 (= *understanding*) juicio *m*, criterio *m*; **in my ~** a mi juicio; **to the best of my ~** según mi leal saber y entender; **against my better ~** a pesar mío; **to have good** *or* **sound ~** tener buen juicio, tener buen criterio; **she showed excellent ~ in choosing the colour scheme** demostró tener buen gusto al escoger la combinación de colores; *see also* **colour B3**
Ⓑ CPD ► **judgment call** N (*esp US*) *decisión que depende de la conciencia de cada uno*
► **Judgment Day** N Día *m* del Juicio Final
► **judgment seat** N tribunal *m*

judgmental [dʒʌdʒ'mentl] ADJ crítico

judicature ['dʒu:dɪkətʃəʳ] N judicatura *f*

judicial [dʒu:'dɪʃəl] ADJ 1 [*decision, proceedings*] judicial; [*separation*] legal; **~ inquiry** investigación *f* judicial
2 [*mind, faculty*] crítico

judicially [dʒu:'dɪʃəlɪ] ADV [*decide*] judicialmente; [*separate*] legalmente

judiciary [dʒu:'dɪʃɪərɪ] Ⓐ ADJ judicial
Ⓑ N (= *judges*) judicatura *f*; (= *court system*) poder *m* judicial

judicious [dʒu:'dɪʃəs] ADJ (*frm*) sensato, juicioso

judiciously [dʒu:'dɪʃəslɪ] ADV (*frm*) juiciosamente

Judith ['dʒu:dɪθ] N Judit

judo ['dʒu:dəʊ] N judo *m*, yudo *m*

judoka ['dʒu:dəʊ,kɑ:] N judoka *mf*

Judy ['dʒu:dɪ] N (*familiar form*) *of* **Judith**

jug [dʒʌg] Ⓐ N 1 (= *container*) jarro *m*, jarra *f*
2 (‡) (= *prison*) chirona *f*, chirola *f* (*LAm*)
3 **jugs** (*US*‡) (= *breasts*) tetas* *fpl*
Ⓑ VT 1 **~ged hare** *estofado de liebre condimentado y regado con vino*
2 (‡) (= *imprison*) meter a la sombra‡

juggernaut ['dʒʌgənɔ:t] N 1 (*Brit*) (= *lorry*) camión *m* de gran tonelaje
2 (*fig*) (= *large and powerful entity*) monstruo *m*; **the group became a sales ~** el grupo se convirtió en un monstruo en ventas; **the ~ of tradition/religion** la fuerza irresistible de la tradición/religión

juggins‡ ['dʒʌgɪnz] N bobo/a *m/f*

juggle ['dʒʌgl] Ⓐ VI hacer juegos *mpl* malabares (**with** con); (*fig*) darle vueltas (**with** a)
Ⓑ VT [+ *balls, plates*] hacer juegos malabares con; (*fig*) (*pej*) [+ *facts, figures*] amañar, falsear; **to ~ a career and a family** compaginar las responsabilidades profesionales con las familiares

juggler ['dʒʌgləʳ] N malabarista *mf*

jugglery ['dʒʌglərɪ] N = **juggling A**

juggling ['dʒʌglɪŋ] Ⓐ N juegos *mpl* malabares, malabarismo *m*; (*fig*) (*pej*) trampas *fpl*, fraude *m*
Ⓑ CPD ► **juggling act** N (*fig*) malabarismos *mpl*; **balancing the budget is a complex ~ act** hay que hacer malabarismos para nivelar el presupuesto

Jugoslav ['ju:gəʊ'slɑ:v] Ⓐ ADJ yugoslavo
Ⓑ N yugoslavo/a *m/f*

Jugoslavia ['ju:gəʊ'slɑ:vɪə] N Yugoslavia *f*

jugular ['dʒʌgjʊləʳ] Ⓐ ADJ **~ vein** yugular *f*, vena *f* yugular
Ⓑ N yugular *f*, vena *f* yugular

juice [dʒu:s] Ⓐ N 1 [*of fruit, vegetable*] jugo *m*, zumo *m* (*Sp*); [*of meat*] jugo *m*
2 (*) (= *petrol*) gasolina *f*
3 (*) (= *electricity*) corriente *f*
4 (*Anat*) ► **digestive juices** NPL jugos *mpl* digestivos, jugos *mpl* gástricos
Ⓑ CPD ► **juice extractor** N (*Brit*) exprimidor *m* eléctrico

juicer ['dʒu:səʳ] N (*US*) exprimidor *m* eléctrico

juiciness ['dʒu:sɪnɪs] N 1 [*of fruit, meat*] jugosidad *f*
2 (*) [*of story*] lo sabroso, lo picante

juicy ['dʒu:sɪ] ADJ (*compar* **juicier**; *superl* **juiciest**)
1 [*fruit, meat*] jugoso
2 (*fig*) [*story*] sabroso, picante; [*contract*] sustancioso, jugoso

jujitsu [dʒu:'dʒɪtsʊ] N jiu-jitsu *m*

jujube ['dʒu:dʒu:b] N pastilla *f*

jujutsu [dʒu:'dʒɪtsʊ] N jiu-jitsu *m*

jukebox ['dʒu:kbɒks] N máquina *f* de discos, gramola® *f*, rocanola *f* (*LAm*)

Jul. ABBR (= **July**) jul.

julep ['dʒu:lep] N julepe *m*

Julian ['dʒu:lɪən] N Juliano, Julián

Juliet ['dʒu:lɪet] N Julieta

Julius ['dʒu:lɪəs] N Julio; **~ Caesar** Julio César

July [dʒu:'laɪ] N julio *m*; **~ was wet this year** este año llovió mucho en julio; **at the beginning of ~** a principios de julio; **during (the month of) ~** durante el mes de julio; **each ~** cada mes de julio, todos los meses de julio; **at the end of ~** a finales de julio; **every ~** todos los meses de julio; **in (the month of) ~** en (el mes de) julio; **in ~ of next year** en julio del año que viene; **there are 31 days in ~** julio tiene treinta y un días; **in the middle of ~** a mediados de julio; **on the first/eleventh of ~** el primero/once de julio

jumble ['dʒʌmbl] Ⓐ N 1 [*of objects*] revoltijo *m*, batiburrillo *m*; (*fig*) confusión *f*, embrollo *m*; **a ~ of furniture** un batiburrillo de muebles, un montón de muebles revueltos; **a ~ of sounds** unos ruidos confusos
2 (*Brit*) (*at jumble sale*) (= *old clothes*) ropa *f* usada; (= *bric-à-brac*) objetos *mpl* usados
Ⓑ VT (*also* **~ together, ~ up**) mezclar, amontonar; **papers ~d up together** papeles revueltos; **they were just ~d together anyhow** estaban mezclados *or* amontonados de cualquier manera
Ⓒ CPD ► **jumble sale** N (*Brit*) mercadillo *m* benéfico (*venta de objetos usados con fines benéficos*)

jumbo ['dʒʌmbəʊ] Ⓐ N 1 (= *elephant*) elefante/a *m/f*
2 = **jumbo jet**
Ⓑ ADJ (*) *also* **~ sized**) gigante, de tamaño extra
Ⓒ CPD ► **jumbo jet** N jumbo *m*

jump [dʒʌmp] Ⓐ N 1 (*Sport, Parachuting*) salto *m*; (= *leap*) salto *m*, brinco *m*; **what a great ~!** ¡qué gran salto!; **it was a three metre ~ to the other side** había que saltar tres metros para pasar al otro lado; **high ~** salto *m* de altura; **long ~** salto *m* de longitud; **in** *or* **at one ~** de un salto, de un brinco; *see also* **running D**
2 (= *start*) **she gave an involuntary ~** se sobresaltó sin querer; **my heart gave a ~** me dio un vuelco el corazón
3 (= *fence, obstacle*) obstáculo *m*
4 (*fig*) (= *step*) salto *m*; **in one ~ he went from novice to master** de un salto *or* golpe pasó de novicio a maestro; **Taiwan made the ~ from poverty to wealth in a single generation** Taiwán pasó de golpe *or* dio el salto de la pobreza a la riqueza en una sola generación; ✦***IDIOMS*** **to be one ~ ahead (of sb)** llevar ventaja *or* la delantera (a algn); **try to keep one ~ ahead of the competition** intenta llevarle ventaja *or* la delantera a la com-

➤ LANGUAGE IN USE: **judge C** 26.2

petencia; **to keep one ~ ahead of the pack** mantenerse a la cabeza del pelotón; **to get a** *or* **the ~ on sb*** adelantarse a algn

[5] (*= increase*) aumento *m*, subida *f*; **there has been a ~ in prices/unemployment** se ha producido un aumento *or* una subida de precios/del número de parados

(B) VI [1] (*= leap*) (*gen*) saltar; (*from aeroplane*) lanzarse, tirarse; **how far can you ~?** ¿hasta qué distancia puedes saltar?; **how high can you ~?** ¿hasta qué altura puedes saltar?; **did he ~ or was he pushed?** (*lit*) ¿saltó o lo empujaron?, ¿se tiró o lo empujaron?; (*fig*) ¿se fue o lo echaron?; **to ~ across a stream** cruzar un arroyo de un salto, saltar por encima de un arroyo; **he ~ed back in horror** de un salto retrocedió horrorizado; **she ~ed into the river** se tiró al río; **to ~ into bed** meterse en la cama de un salto; **there were plenty of men ready to ~ into bed with me** (*fig*) había muchos hombres dispuestos a acostarse conmigo; **to ~ for joy** saltar de alegría; **to ~ off a bus/train** bajar de un autobús/tren de un salto; **to ~ on a bus/train** subir a un autobús/tren de un salto; **he ~ed out of a third floor window** saltó *or* se tiró desde una ventana del tercer piso; **to ~ out of bed** saltar de la cama; **he ~ed over the fence** saltó (por encima de) la valla; **he ~ed to his feet** se puso de pie de un salto; **~ to it!*** ¡venga, muévete!, ¡rápido!, ¡apúrate! (*LAm*); **to ~ up** ponerse de pie de un salto; **I ~ed up and down to keep warm** me puse a dar saltos para que no me entrara frío

[2] (*= start*) sobresaltarse; **he ~ed at the sound of her voice** se sobresaltó al oír su voz; **to make sb ~** dar un susto a algn, sobresaltar a algn; **you made me ~!** ¡qué susto me diste!; *see also* **skin**

[3] (*fig*) (*with prep, adv*) **to ~ at sth** no dejar escapar algo; **they offered me a really good salary and thought I'd ~ at it** me ofrecieron un sueldo buenísimo y creyeron que no lo dejaría escapar; **he'd ~ at the chance to get out of the office** si tuviera la oportunidad de irse de la oficina no la dejaría escapar; **then the film ~s forward 20 years** luego la película da un salto adelante de 20 años; **to ~ from one subject to another** saltar de un tema a otro; **he ~s on everything I say** le pone faltas a todo lo que digo; *see also* **bandwagon, conclusion, throat**

[4] (*= increase*) [*sales, profits*] subir, aumentar; [*shares*] subir

(C) VT [1] (*lit*) (*also* **~ over**) [*+ ditch, fence*] saltar (por encima de); (*in draughts, chess*) comerse

[2] [*+ horse*] (*= cause to jump*) hacer saltar; (*= enter in competition*) presentar; (*= ride*) montar; **she ~ed her horse over the fence** hizo saltar la valla a su caballo

[3] (*fig*) (*= skip*) saltarse; **the film ~ed the first ten years of his life** la película se saltó los diez primeros años de su vida; **you've ~ed a page** te has saltado una página; **to ~ the lights** (*Aut**) saltarse el semáforo (en rojo); **to ~ the queue** (*Brit*) colarse

[4] (*= leave, escape*) **to ~ bail** (*Jur*) fugarse estando bajo fianza; **to ~ the rails** [*train*] descarrilar, salirse de la vía; **to ~ ship** (*lit*) desertar (de un buque); (*fig*) (*= leave*) marcharse; (*= join rival organization*) irse con la competencia; **my salary was lousy so I ~ed ship** tenía un sueldo mísero así que me marché; **to ~ town** (*US**) abandonar la ciudad

[5] (*= anticipate*) ✦*IDIOM* **to ~ the gun*** precipitarse

[6] (*= board*) **to ~ a train** subirse a un tren sin billete

[7] (*) (*= attack*) echarse encima de; **one of them ~ed him from behind** uno de ellos se le echó encima por detrás

(D) CPD ► **jump jet** N avión *m* de despegue vertical ► **jump leads** NPL (*Brit Aut*) cables *mpl* de arranque (de batería) ► **jump rope** N (*US*) comba *f*, cuerda *f* de saltar ► **jump seat** N (*Aut, Aer*) asiento *m* plegable

►**jump about, jump around** VI + ADV [1] (*lit*) dar saltos, brincar

[2] (*fig*) dar saltos; **the story ~s about a bit** la historia da muchos saltos

►**jump down** VI + ADV bajar de un salto

►**jump in** VI + ADV [1] (*into car*) subirse corriendo; (*into water*) tirarse; **~ in!** ¡sube!, ¡vamos!

[2] (*fig*) (*in situation, conversation*) intervenir; **the government had to ~ in and buy millions of dollars worth of supplies** el gobierno tuvo que intervenir y comprar suministros por valor de millones de dólares

►**jump off** VI + ADV (*Showjumping*) desempatar

►**jump out** VI + ADV (*= appear suddenly*) salir de un salto; (*from vehicle*) bajar de un salto; **he ~ed out from behind a tree** salió de un salto de detrás de un árbol; **it ~s out at you** (*fig*) salta a la vista

jumped-up* [ˈdʒʌmptˈʌp] ADJ (*Brit pej*) presumido

jumper [ˈdʒʌmpəʳ] (A) N [1] (*Sport*) saltador(a) *m/f*

[2] (*Brit*) (*= sweater*) jersey *m*, suéter *m*

[3] (*US*) (*= pinafore dress*) falda *f* tipo mono, pichi *m*

(B) CPD ► **jumper cables** NPL (*US*) = **jump leads**; *see* **jump D**

jumping [ˈdʒʌmpɪŋ] (A) N (*Sport*) pruebas *fpl* de salto

(B) CPD ► **jumping bean** N judía *f* saltadora, fríjol *m* saltador ► **jumping jack** N (*= firework*) buscapiés *m inv*; (*= puppet*) *muñeco que se acciona tirando de un hilo* ► **jumping rope** N (*US*) comba *f*, cuerda *f* de saltar

jumping-off place [ˌdʒʌmpɪŋˈɒfˌpleɪs], **jumping-off point** [ˌdʒʌmpɪŋˈɒfˌpɔɪnt] N punto *m* de partida

jump-off [ˈdʒʌmpɒf] N (*Showjumping*) prueba *f* de desempate, saltos *mpl* de desempate

jump-start [ˈdʒʌmpstɑːt] (A) N (*Aut*) (*pushing*) arranque *m* en frío (*empujando el automóvil*); (*using jump leads*) arranque *m* con puente; **he gave me a ~** (*pushing*) me ayudó a arrancar el coche empujándolo; (*using jump leads*) me ayudó a arrancar el coche haciendo un puente

(B) VT [*+ car*] (*by pushing*) arrancar empujando; (*using jump leads*) arrancar haciendo un puente

jumpsuit [ˈdʒʌmpsuːt] N (*US*) mono *m*

jumpy [ˈdʒʌmpɪ] ADJ (*compar* **jumpier**; *superl* **jumpiest**) nervioso; (*= easily startled*) asustadizo

Jun. ABBR [1] (*=* **June**) jun.

[2] (*=* **junior**) jr

junction [ˈdʒʌŋkʃən] (A) N [1] (*= joining*) [*of bones, pipes*] juntura *f*, unión *f*

[2] (*Brit*) (*= meeting place*) [*of roads*] cruce *m*, crucero *m* (*LAm*); [*of railway lines*] empalme *m*; [*of rivers*] confluencia *f*

(B) CPD ► **junction box** N (*Elec*) caja *f* de empalmes

juncture [ˈdʒʌŋktʃəʳ] N (*fig*) (*= point*) coyuntura *f*; **at this ~** en este momento, a estas alturas

June [dʒuːn] N junio *m*; *see* **July** *for usage*

Jungian [jʊŋɪən] (A) ADJ jungiano

(B) N jungiano/a *m/f*

jungle [ˈdʒʌŋgl] (A) N [1] selva *f*, jungla *f*; (*fig*) maraña *f*, selva *f*; **the law of the ~** (*fig*) la ley de la selva

[2] (*Mus*) jungle *m*, *género de música de baile de ritmo acelerado*

(B) CPD [*animal, bird*] de la selva, selvático; [*law, life, sounds*] de la selva ► **jungle bunny** N (*US***) negrito/a* *m/f* ► **jungle gym** N *armazón de barras para juegos infantiles* ► **jungle warfare** N guerra *f* en la selva

junior [ˈdʒuːnɪəʳ] (A) ADJ [*employee, executive, manager*] (*in age*) más joven; (*in length of service*) de menor antigüedad; (*in position, rank*) subalterno, auxiliar; [*partner*] segundo; [*section*] (*in competition*) juvenil; **Roy Smith, Junior** Roy Smith, hijo

(B) N [1] (*= younger person*) menor *mf*, joven *mf*; (*US**) (*= son*) hijo *m*, niño *m*; **he is my ~ by three years** ◊ **he is three years my ~** tiene tres años menos que yo, le llevo tres años

[2] (*Brit Scol*) alumno/a *m/f* (*de 7 a 11 años*); (*US Univ*) estudiante *mf* de penúltimo año; → GRADE

[3] (*in rank*) subalterno/a *m/f*, auxiliar *mf*; (*= office junior*) recadero *m*

(C) CPD ► **junior college** N (*US*) *centro universitario donde se imparten cursos de dos años* ► **junior high school** N (*US*) ≈ centro de enseñanza secundaria ► **junior minister** N (*Pol*) ≈ secretario/a *m/f* de Estado, ≈ subsecretario/a *m/f* ► **junior school** N (*Brit*) escuela *f* primaria ► **junior size** N talla *f* infantil

juniper [ˈdʒuːnɪpəʳ] (A) N enebro *m*

(B) CPD ► **juniper berries** NPL bayas *fpl* de enebro

junk[1] [dʒʌŋk] (A) N [1] (*= worthless things*) trastos *mpl* viejos, cacharros* *mpl*; (*= bric-à-brac*) cachivaches *mpl*; (*= cheap goods*) baratijas *fpl*; (*= things thrown away*) desperdicios *mpl*, desechos *mpl*; (*= iron*) chatarra *f*

[2] (*) (*= rubbish*) porquería *f*; **the play is a lot of ~** la obra es una chapuza *or* porquería; **this umbrella is a piece of ~** este paraguas es una porquería; **he eats nothing but ~** no come más que porquerías; **he talks a lot of ~** no dice más que tonterías

(B) VT (*) [*+ object*] tirar, tirar a la basura; [*+ idea, theory etc*] desechar

(C) CPD ► **junk bond** N bono *m* basura ► **junk dealer** N vendedor(a) *m/f* de objetos usados ► **junk food** N comida *f* basura ► **junk heap** N **to end up on the ~ heap** terminar en el cubo de la basura ► **junk mail** N propaganda *f* por correo ► **junk room** N trastero *m* ► **junk shop** N tienda *f* de objetos usados

junk[2] [dʒʌŋk] N (*= Chinese boat*) junco *m*

junket [ˈdʒʌŋkɪt] (A) N [1] (*Culin*) dulce *m* de leche cuajada, cajeta *f* (*LAm*)

[2] (*) (*= party*) fiesta *f*

[3] (*US*) (*= excursion at public expense*) *viaje de placer realizado por un funcionario público o miembro de un comité a expensas del contribuyente*

(B) VI ir de juerga*, estar de fiesta

junketing [ˈdʒʌŋkɪtɪŋ] N (*also* **~s**) festividades *fpl*, fiestas *fpl*

junkie* [ˈdʒʌŋkɪ] N (*= drug addict*) yonqui* *mf*; (*esp of heroin*) heroinómano/a *m/f*; **chocolate ~** adicto/a *m/f* al chocolate

junkman [ˈdʒʌŋkmæn] N (*pl* **junkmen**) chatarrero *m*

junkyard [ˈdʒʌŋkjɑːd] N depósito *m* de chatarra, chatarrería *f*

Juno [ˈdʒuːnəʊ] N Juno

Junoesque [ˌdʒuːnəʊˈesk] ADJ [*figure*] imponente, majestuoso; [*woman*] de belleza majestuosa

Junr. ABBR (= **junior**) jr

junta [ˈdʒʌntə] N junta *f* militar

Jupiter [ˈdʒuːpɪtəʳ] N Júpiter *m*

Jurassic [dʒʊˈræsɪk] ADJ jurásico

juridical [dʒʊəˈrɪdɪkəl] ADJ jurídico

jurisdiction [ˌdʒʊərɪsˈdɪkʃən] N jurisdicción *f*; **it falls** *or* **comes within our ~** entra dentro de nuestra jurisdicción, es de nuestra competencia; **it falls** *or* **comes outside our ~** se sale de nuestra jurisdicción, no es de nuestra competencia

jurisdictional [ˌdʒʊərɪsˈdɪkʃənl] ADJ (*US*) [*dispute, rights*] jurisdiccional

jurisprudence [ˌdʒʊərɪsˈpruːdəns] N jurisprudencia *f*; **medical ~** medicina *f* legal

jurist [ˈdʒʊərɪst] N jurista *mf*

juror [ˈdʒʊərəʳ] N (*Jur*) jurado *m*; (*for contest*) juez *m*; **a woman ~** una miembro del jurado

jury [ˈdʒʊərɪ] Ⓐ N jurado *m*; **trial by ~** proceso con jurado; **to serve** *or* **be on a ~** ser miembro de un jurado; ✦*IDIOM* **the ~ is still out on that one** eso está por ver, no hay una opinión clara sobre eso

Ⓑ CPD ► **jury box** N tribuna *f* del jurado ► **jury duty** N **to do ~ duty** actuar como jurado ► **jury rigging** N amaño *m* de un jurado; → GRAND JURY

juryman [ˈdʒʊərɪmən] N (*pl* **jurymen**) miembro *m* del jurado

jurywoman [ˈdʒuːrɪwʊmən] N (*pl* **jurywomen**) miembro *f* (femenino) del jurado

just¹ [dʒʌst] Ⓐ ADJ 1 (= *fair*) [*person, system*] justo; **as is only ~** como es justo, como es de razón

2 (= *deserved*) [*praise, reward*] merecido; [*punishment*] apropiado, justo

3 (= *justified*) [*complaint, criticism*] justificado; [*opinion*] lógico; *see also* **deserts**

4 (= *accurate*) [*account*] correcto; [*assessment*] correcto, exacto

Ⓑ NPL **the ~** los justos

just² [dʒʌst] ADVERB

1 *relating to time* 1·1 (= *at this moment*) ahora mismo; **we're ~ off** nos vamos ahora mismo; **I'm ~ coming!** ¡ya voy!; **"have some tea!" — "actually, I was ~ going"** —tómate un té —en realidad ya me iba

1·2 (= *at that moment*) justo; **he was ~ leaving when the phone rang** estaba justo saliendo cuando sonó el teléfono

1·3 (= *recently, a moment ago*) **we were ~ talking about that** precisamente *or* ahora mismo estábamos hablando de eso; **~ cooked** recién hecho; **it's ~ gone 10 o'clock** acaban de dar las diez; **to have ~ done sth** acabar de hacer algo; **he has ~ left** acaba de irse; **he had ~ left** acababa de irse; **~ married** recién casados; **the book is ~ out** el libro acaba de salir; **it's ~ past 10 o'clock** acaban de dar las diez

1·4 (*in expressions specifying "when"*) **~ after I arrived** poco después de mi llegada; **~ after Christmas** justo después de Navidad; **it's ~ after 9 o'clock** son las nueve un poco pasadas; **~ as I arrived** justo cuando yo llegaba; **~ as it started to rain** justo cuando empezó a llover, en el momento en que empezó a llover; **~ before I arrived** poco antes de mi llegada; **~ before Christmas** justo antes de Navidad; **I saw him ~ this minute** lo he visto hace un momento; **I've ~ this minute finished it** acabo de terminarlo en este momento; **~ at that moment** en ese mismo momento *or* instante; **~ this morning** esta misma mañana; **~ when it was going well ...** precisamente *or* justamente cuando iba bien ...; **~ yesterday** ayer mismo; **"are you leaving?" — "not ~ yet"** —¿te vas? —aún *or* todavía no; *see also* **now A6, recently 2, then A1**

2 = *barely* por poco; **we (only) ~ missed it** lo perdimos por muy poco; **I (only) ~ caught it** lo alcancé por un pelo, por poco lo pierdo; **we had ~ enough money** teníamos el dinero justo; **he missed the train, but only ~** perdió el tren, pero por poco; **he passed, but only ~** aprobó pero por los pelos; **we arrived ~ in time** por poco no llegamos, llegamos justo a tiempo

3 = *slightly* **~ over/under two kilos** un poco más de/menos de dos kilos; **it's ~ over/under two kilos** pasa de/no llega a los dos kilos; **~ to the left/right** un poco más a la izquierda/derecha; **~ to one side** a un lado

4 = *exactly* justo, exactamente; **it's ~ my size** es justo *or* exactamente mi talla; **it's ~ the same** es justo *or* exactamente igual; **~ here/there** aquí/ahí mismo; **~ behind/in front of/next to** *etc* justo detrás/delante de/al lado de *etc*; **it's ~ (on) 10 (o'clock)** son las diez en punto; **it cost ~ (on) £20** me costó veinte libras justas; **~ how many we don't know** no sabemos exactamente cuántos; **that's ~ it!** ¡ahí está!*, ¡ésa es la cuestión!; **he's ~ like his father** (*physically, in behaviour*) es idéntico a su padre; **that's ~ like him, always late** es típico (de él), siempre llega tarde; **they are ~ like brothers** son como hermanos; **they have their problems ~ like the rest of us** tienen sus problemas, exactamente igual que el resto de nosotros; **I can't find £1,000 ~ like that** no puedo conseguir mil libras así sin más; **that's ~ the point!** ¡ahí está!*, ¡ésa es la cuestión!; **he likes everything ~ so*** le gusta que todo esté perfecto; **it's ~ what I wanted** es justo *or* precisamente lo que quería; **that's ~ what I thought** eso es justo *or* precisamente lo que pensé; **~ what did he say?** ¿qué dijo exactamente?; **~ what are you implying?** ¿qué es exactamente lo que estás insinuando?; *see also* **luck A, right A2**

5 = *only* sólo, nomás (*LAm*); **they were ~ 15 when they got married** tenían sólo *or* nada más 15 años cuando se casaron; **he's ~ a lad** no es más que un chaval, es sólo un chaval; **it's ~ a mouse** es sólo un ratón; **don't take any notice of her, she's ~ jealous** no le hagas ni caso, lo que está es celosa *or* lo que pasa es que está celosa; **it's ~ around the corner** está a la vuelta de la esquina; **I ~ asked!** (*hum*) ¡preguntaba nada más!; **~ a few** sólo unos pocos, unos pocos nada más; **~ a little** sólo un poco, un poco nada más; **~ once** una vez nada más, solamente una vez; **it's ~ over there** está ahí mismo; **it's ~ a suggestion** es sólo una sugerencia; **he's ~ teasing** sólo está bromeando, está bromeando, nada más; **~ this once** sólo esta vez; **we went ~ to see the museum** fuimos sólo para ver el museo; **~ the two of us** los dos solos, sólo nosotros dos; **I ~ wanted to say that ...** sólo quería decir que ...; *see also* **friend, note A3**

6 = *simply* sencillamente; **I ~ told him to go away** le dije sencillamente que se fuera; **~ ask the way** simplemente pregunta por dónde se va; **I'm ~ phoning to remind you that ...** sólo llamo para recordarte que ...; **let's ~ wait and see** es mejor esperar a ver (qué pasa); **you should ~ send it back** deberías devolverlo sin más; **he ~ couldn't wait to see them** tenía unas ganas enormes de verlos; **it's ~ one of those things*** son cosas que pasan; **it's ~ that I don't like it** lo que pasa es que no me gusta; **I ~ thought that you would like it** yo pensé que te gustaría; *see also* **because A, imagine 1, 2, wonder B**

7 = *specially* sólo; **I did it ~ for you** lo hice sólo por ti

8 = *conceivably* **it may ~ be possible** puede que sea posible; **it's an old trick, but it could ~ work** es un viejo truco, pero puede que funcione

9 *in comparisons* **~ as** tan; **it's ~ as good as yours** es tan bueno como el tuyo; **you sing ~ as well as he does** cantas tan bien como él; **the new one is ~ as big** el nuevo es igual de grande; **this model goes ~ as fast** este modelo va igual de rápido

10 *in imperatives* **~ let me get my hands on him!*** ¡cómo lo coja!, ¡con que lo agarre! (*LAm*); **~ listen to that rain!** ¡escucha *or* fíjate cómo llueve!; **~ listen a minute, will you?** ¡escúchame un momento!, ¿quieres?; **~ look at this mess!** ¡fíjate qué desorden!; **~ wait a minute!** ¡espera un momento!; **~ you wait, he'll come sure enough** (*reassuringly*) espera hombre, ya verás cómo viene; **~ (you) wait until I tell your father** (*threateningly*) ya verás cuando se lo cuente a tu padre, espera (nomás (*LAm*)) a que se lo cuente a tu padre; **~ you do!*** ◊ **~ you try it!*** ◊ **~ you dare!*** ¡inténtalo si te atreves!

11 *emphatic* **she's ~ amazing!** es una mujer increíble; **"that dress is awful" — "isn't it ~?"*** —ese vestido es francamente horrible —¡y tanto!; **we're managing ~ fine** nos apañamos perfectamente; **it's ~ perfect!** ¡es absolutamente perfecto!; *see also* **plain A3, B1**

12 *imagining something* **I can ~ hear the roars of laughter** me puedo imaginar muy bien *or* perfectamente las carcajadas; **I can ~ imagine her reaction** me imagino muy bien *or* perfectamente su reacción; **I can ~ see her face if I told her** me puedo imaginar muy bien *or* perfectamente la cara que pondría si se lo dijese

13 *in set expressions* **~ about**: **I've ~ about finished this work** estoy a punto de terminar este trabajo; **it's ~ about finished** está casi terminado; **I think that it was ~ about here that I saw him** creo que yo estaba más o menos aquí cuando lo vi; **I've ~ about had enough of this noise!*** ¡estoy ya más que harto de este ruido!; **to be ~ about to do sth** estar a punto de hacer algo; **I was ~ about to phone** estaba a punto de llamar; **come ~ as you are** ven tal como estás; **leave it ~ as it is** déjalo tal como está; **~ as you wish** como usted quiera; **~ as I thought!** ¡ya me lo figuraba *or* imaginaba!, ¡lo que yo me figuraba *or* imaginaba!; **~ in case** por si acaso; **~ in case it rains** por si acaso llueve, por si llueve; **I've prepared some extra food, ~ in case** he preparado comida de más, por si las moscas* *or* por si acaso; **~ a minute!** ◊ **~ one moment!** (= *coming*) ¡un momento, por favor!, ¡voy!; **~ a minute, I don't know if I agree with that ...** un momento, no sé si estoy de acuerdo con eso ...; **~ the same, I'd rather ...** de todas formas, prefiero ...; **that's ~ too bad!** (*iro*) ¡qué lástima!, ¡qué mala pata!*; **it's ~ as well** menos mal; **it's ~ as well it's insured** menos mal que está asegurado; **I wasn't expecting much, which was ~ as well** no esperaba mucho, y menos mal; **it would be ~ as well if we checked the prices** más valdría que comprobásemos los precios; *see also* **happen 2, soon 4**

justice ['dʒʌstɪs] N [1] (*Jur*) justicia *f*; **to bring sb to ~** llevar a algn ante los tribunales
[2] (= *fairness*) justicia *f*; **to do o.s. ~** quedar bien; **to do sb ~** hacer justicia a algn; **this doesn't do him ~** [*photo etc*] no le favorece; **it doesn't do ~ to his skills** no está a la altura de sus capacidades; **to do ~ to a meal** hacer los honores a una comida
[3] (= *person*) juez *mf*; **Justice of the Peace** (*Brit*) juez *mf* de paz; **(Lord) Chief Justice** Presidente *m* del Tribunal Supremo

justifiable ['dʒʌstɪfaɪəbl] ADJ [1] [*anger, pride, concern*] justificado; **that sort of behaviour is not ~** ese tipo de comportamiento no puede justificarse
[2] (*Jur*) **~ homicide** homicidio *m* justificado

justifiably ['dʒʌstɪfaɪəblɪ] ADV justificadamente, con razón; **he was ~ proud/angry** estaba orgulloso/enfadado y con razón, su orgullo/enfado era justificado; **he insisted, quite ~, that …** insistía, justificadamente *or* con toda razón, en que …

justification [ˌdʒʌstɪfɪ'keɪʃən] N justificación *f*; **there's no ~ for it** esto no tiene justificación posible; **in ~ of** *or* **for sth** como justificación de algo

justified ['dʒʌstɪfaɪd] ADJ [1] (*gen*) justificado; **to be ~ in doing sth** tener motivos para hacer algo, tener razón al hacer algo; **am I ~ in thinking that ...?** ¿hay motivo para creer que ...?
[2] (*Jur*) **~ homicide** homicidio *m* justificado
[3] (*Typ*) justificado; **right ~** justificado a la derecha

justify ['dʒʌstɪfaɪ] VT [1] (*gen*) justificar; **he tried to ~ his decision** trató de justificar su decisión; **the future does not ~ the slightest optimism** el futuro no da lugar al más leve optimismo
[2] (*Typ, Comput*) alinear, justificar

justly ['dʒʌstlɪ] ADV (= *fairly*) justamente, con justicia; (= *rightly*) con razón; **it has been ~ said that …** con razón se ha dicho que …

justness ['dʒʌstnɪs] N justicia *f*

jut [dʒʌt] VI (*also* **~ out**) sobresalir

Jute [dʒu:t] N juto/a *m/f*

jute [dʒu:t] N yute *m*

juvenile ['dʒu:vənaɪl] Ⓐ ADJ [*books, sports etc*] juvenil; (*pej*) infantil; (*Jur*) [*court*] de menores; **~ delinquent** delincuente *mf* juvenil; **~ delinquency** delincuencia *f* juvenil
Ⓑ N joven *mf*, menor *mf*

juvenilia [ˌdʒu:vɪ'nɪlɪə] NPL obras *fpl* de juventud

juxtapose ['dʒʌkstəpəʊz] VT yuxtaponer

juxtaposition [ˌdʒʌkstəpə'zɪʃən] N yuxtaposición *f*

➤ LANGUAGE IN USE: **justification** 12.1 **justify 1** 26.3

K k

K[1], **k** [keɪ] N (= *letter*) K, k *f*; **K for Kilo** K de Kilo

K[2] ABBR 1 (= **kilo-**) kilo-
2 (= *thousand*) **he earns 30K** gana 30.000 libras
3 (*Brit*) (= **Knight**) *caballero de una orden*
4 (*Comput*) (= **kilobyte**) K *m*

Kabala [kəˈbɑːlə] N Cábala *f*, Kábala *f*

Kaffir [ˈkæfəʳ] N (*pl* **Kaffirs** *or* **Kaffir**) (*offensive*) cafre *mf*

Kafkaesque [ˌkæfkəˈesk] ADJ kafkiano

kaftan [ˈkæftæn] N caftán *m*

Kaiser [ˈkaɪzəʳ] N káiser *m*

Kalahari Desert [ˌkæləˈhɑːrɪˈdezət] N desierto *m* de Kalahari

kale [keɪl] N (*Bot*) col *f* rizada

kaleidoscope [kəˈlaɪdəskəʊp] N calidoscopio *m*, caleidoscopio *m*

kaleidoscopic [kəˌlaɪdəˈskɒpɪk] ADJ calidoscópico

Kamasutra [ˌkɑːməˈsuːtrə] N Kamasutra *m*

kamikaze [ˌkæmɪˈkɑːzɪ] N kamikaze *m*

Kampala [kæmˈpɑːlə] N Kampala *f*

Kampuchea [ˌkæmpʊˈtʃɪə] N Kampuchea *f*

Kampuchean [ˌkæmpʊˈtʃɪən] (A) ADJ kampucheano
(B) N kampucheano/a *m/f*

Kan. ABBR (*US*) = **Kansas**

kanga [ˈkæŋgə] N *tela con unos diseños muy alegres usada como prenda por las mujeres del este de África*

kangaroo [ˌkæŋgəˈruː] (A) N canguro/a *m/f*
(B) CPD ► **kangaroo court** N tribunal *m* desautorizado

Kans. ABBR (*US*) = **Kansas**

Kantian [ˈkæntɪən] (A) ADJ kantiano
(B) N kantiano/a *m/f*

kaolin [ˈkeɪəlɪn] N caolín *m*

kapok [ˈkeɪpɒk] N capoc *m*

kaput* [kəˈpʊt] ADJ 1 [*object*] kaput; **to be ~** estar kaput
2 [*organization*] **now he's dead the whole company is ~** ahora que ha fallecido, la empresa se ha ido al traste*

karaoke [kɑːrəˈəʊkɪ] N karaoke *m*

karat [ˈkærət] N (*US*) = **carat**

karate [kəˈrɑːtɪ] N karate *m*

karma [ˈkɑːmə] N (*Rel*) karma *m*

kart [kɑːt] (A) N kart *m*
(B) VI hacer kárting; **to go ~ing** ir a hacer kárting

karting [ˈkɑːtɪŋ] N (*Sport*) kárting *m*

kasbah [ˈkæzbɑː] N casba(h) *f*

Kashmir [kæʃˈmɪəʳ] N Cachemira *f*

Kate [keɪt] N (*familiar form*) *of* **Catherine** *etc*

Katharine, **Katherine** [ˈkæθərɪn], **Kathleen** [ˈkæθliːn] N Catalina

kayak [ˈkaɪæk] N kayac *m*, kayak *m*

Kazak(h) [kəˈzɑːk] (A) ADJ kazajo
(B) N kazajo/a *m/f*

Kazakhstan [ˌkæzəksˈtɑːn] N Kazajstán *m*

kazoo [kəˈzuː] N kazoo *m*, chiflato *m*

KB ABBR (= **kilobyte**) K *m*

KBE N ABBR (= **Knight of the British Empire**) *título ceremonial*

KC (A) N ABBR (*Brit*) (= **King's Counsel**) *abogado de categoría superior*
(B) ABBR (*US*) = **Kansas City**

kc ABBR (= **kilocycle(s)**) k/c

kcal [ˈkeɪkæl] ABBR = **kilocalorie**

KCB N ABBR (*Brit*) (= **Knight Commander of the Bath**) *un título ceremonial*

KD, kd ABBR (*US*) (= **knocked down**) desmontado

kebab [kəˈbæb] N kebab *m*, pincho *m* moruno, anticucho *m* (*Peru, Bol, Chile*)

kedge [kedʒ] N anclote *m*

kedgeree [ˌkedʒəˈriː] N (*Brit*) *plato de pescado desmenuzado, huevos y arroz*

keel [kiːl] N (*Naut*) quilla *f*; **on an even ~** (*Naut*) en iguales calados; (*fig*) en equilibrio, estable; ✦***IDIOM*** **to keep sth on an even ~** [+ *economy, company*] estabilizar algo; **they managed to get their marriage back on an even ~** consiguieron volver a estabilizar su matrimonio

►**keel over** VI + ADV (*Naut*) volcar(se), zozobrar; [*building, structure*] derrumbarse, venirse abajo; [*person*] desplomarse

keelhaul [ˈkiːlhɔːl] VT pasar por debajo de la quilla (*como castigo*)

▼**keen** [kiːn] (A) ADJ (*compar* **keener**; *superl* **keenest**) 1 (= *enthusiastic*) [*supporter*] entusiasta; [*student*] aplicado; **she's a ~ photographer/gardener** es muy aficionada a la fotografía/la jardinería; **he's a ~ footballer** es muy aficionado a jugar al fútbol; **he's a ~ cook** le gusta mucho *or* le encanta cocinar; **she's just started and she's still very ~** acaba de empezar y tiene aún mucho entusiasmo; **try not to seem too ~** procura no parecer muy interesado; **to be ~ to do sth** tener interés por hacer algo; **I was ~ to get started** tenía muchas ganas de empezar; **the government is ~ to dismiss these rumours** al gobierno le interesa descartar estos rumores; **he was ~ to point out the financial benefits** tenía sumo interés por hacer resaltar las ventajas económicas, hizo mucho hincapié en las ventajas económicas; **to be ~ on sth** (*Brit*): **I'm not all that ~ on grapes** no me gustan mucho las uvas; **he's ~ on fishing** es muy aficionado a la pesca, le gusta mucho la pesca; **I'm not ~ on the idea** no me entusiasma *or* no me hace mucha gracia la idea; **both companies were ~ on a merger** ambas compañías querían la fusión *or* tenían interés en la fusión; **I'm not very ~ on him** no es santo de mi devoción, no me cae demasiado bien; **to be ~ on doing sth: I'm very ~ on horse riding** (*Brit*) me gusta muchísimo montar a caballo, me encanta montar a caballo; (*as a hobby*) soy muy aficionada a montar a caballo; **I'm not ~ on going** no me apetece mucho ir; ✦***IDIOM*** **to be as ~ as mustard** ser extraordinariamente entusiasta
2 (= *intense*) [*desire*] fuerte, vivo; [*delight*] intenso; [*interest*] vivo, grande; [*competition, match, struggle*] reñido; **his ~ sense of loyalty** su gran sentido de la lealtad
3 (= *sharp*) [*edge, blade*] afilado; [*wind, air*] cortante; [*mind, intelligence*] agudo, penetrante; [*intellect, wit, sense of humour*] agudo; [*eyesight*] agudo, muy bueno; [*hearing*] fino; **to have a ~ appetite** tener buen apetito; **to have a ~ eye for detail** tener buen ojo para los detalles; **to have a ~ nose for sth** tener buen olfato para algo; **to have a ~ sense of smell** tener buen olfato
4 (= *competitive*) [*price, rate*] competitivo
5 (*US**) (= *good*) **he plays a ~ game of squash** juega genial *or* fenomenal al squash*
(B) N (*Irl Mus*) *lamento fúnebre por la muerte de una persona*
(C) VI lamentar

keenly [ˈkiːnlɪ] ADV 1 (= *intensely*) [*discuss, debate*] vivamente, intensamente; [*feel*] profundamente; [*look*] fijamente; [*listen*] con interés; **his loss was ~ felt by all who knew him** todos los que lo conocían sintieron profundamente su muerte; **they're ~ aware that ...** son muy conscientes de que ...; **it was a ~ contested game** fue un partido muy reñido
2 (= *enthusiastically*) con entusiasmo

keenness [ˈkiːnnɪs] N 1 (= *sharpness*) [*of mind, sense of humour, eyesight*] agudeza *f*; [*of blade*] lo afilado; [*of wind*] lo cortante
2 (= *intensity*) intensidad *f*
3 (= *enthusiasm*) entusiasmo *m*

keep [kiːp] (*vb: pt, pp* **kept**)

A TRANSITIVE VERB	C NOUN
B INTRANSITIVE VERB	D PHRASAL VERBS

(A) TRANSITIVE VERB

When ***keep*** *is part of a set combination, eg* ***to keep an appointment. to keep a promise, to keep one's seat****, look up the noun.*

1 = ***retain*** [+ *change, copy*] quedarse con; [+ *receipt*] guardar; [+ *business, customer, colour*] conservar; **you must ~ the receipt** debe guardar el recibo; **you can ~ the change**

➤ LANGUAGE IN USE: **keen A1** 7.2, 7.3, 12.2, 19.2

quédese con la vuelta *or* (*LAm*) el vuelto; **is this jacket worth ~ing?** ¿merece la pena guardar esta chaqueta?; **he is to ~ his job in spite of the incident** va a mantener *or* conservar el trabajo a pesar del incidente; **this material will ~ its colour/softness** este material conservará su color/suavidad; **to ~ sth for o.s.** quedarse con algo; ✦***IDIOM*** **if this is fashion, you can ~ it!*** ¡si esto es moda no la quiero ni regalada!

2 = ***save, put aside*** guardar, reservar; **I'm ~ing this wine in case we have visitors** voy a guardar *or* reservar este vino por si tenemos visitas; **ask the shop to ~ you one** pide en la tienda que te reserven uno; **I was ~ing it for you** lo guardaba para ti

3 = ***have ready*** **I always ~ a torch in the car** siempre tengo una linterna en el coche; **~ this by you in case of emergencies** guárdate eso para un caso de emergencia

4 = ***store, put*** (*gen*) guardar; (*in museum*) conservar; **where do you ~ the sugar?** ¿dónde guardas el azúcar?; **~ it somewhere safe** guárdalo en un sitio seguro; **you must ~ it in a cold place** debes conservarlo en un sitio fresco

5 = ***house*** **the puppies were kept in cramped conditions** tenían a los cachorros hacinados; **the tarantulas were kept in cages** las tarántulas estaban metidas en jaulas; **the prisoners were kept in a dark room** los prisioneros estaban encerrados en una habitación oscura; **he ~s his wives in separate houses** tiene a sus mujeres alojadas en casas separadas

6 = ***detain*** tener; **~ him in bed for a couple of days** tenlo en cama un par de días; **to ~ sb in prison** tener a algn preso; **he was kept in hospital over night** lo tuvieron una noche en el hospital, le hicieron pasar la noche en el hospital; **illness kept her at home** la enfermedad no le permitió salir de casa; **to ~ sb doing sth** tener a algn haciendo algo

7 = ***delay*** entretener; **I mustn't ~ you** no quiero entretenerte; **don't let me ~ you** no le entretengo más; **what kept you?** ¿por qué te has retrasado?; **am I ~ing you from your work?** quizá tienes trabajo y yo te estoy entreteniendo

8 = ***have*** [+ *shop, hotel, house, servant*] tener; [+ *pigs, bees, chickens*] criar; **he ~s a good cellar** tiene una buena bodega

9 = ***stock*** tener; **we don't ~ that model any more** ya no tenemos ese modelo

10 = ***support*** [+ *family, mistress*] mantener; **to ~ o.s.** mantenerse; **the extra money ~s me in beer and cigarettes** el dinero extra me da para (comprar) cerveza y cigarrillos; **our garden ~s us in vegetables all summer** el huerto nos da suficientes verduras para todo el verano

11 = ***fulfil, observe*** [+ *promise, agreement, obligation*] cumplir; [+ *law, rule*] observar; [+ *appointment*] acudir a, ir a; [+ *feast day*] observar; **to ~ the Sabbath** observar el sábado judío

12 = ***not divulge*** **to ~ sth from sb** ocultar algo a algn; **~ it quiet** de esto no digas ni una palabra; **~ it to yourself*** no se lo digas a nadie; **but he kept the news to himself** pero se guardó la noticia, pero no comunicó la noticia a nadie

13 = ***maintain*** 13·1 [+ *accounts*] llevar; [+ *diary*] escribir; **to ~ a record of sth** llevar nota de algo

13·2 (*with adjective*) mantener, tener (*less frm*); **"keep Britain tidy"** "mantenga limpia Gran Bretaña"; **to ~ sth clean** conservar *or* mantener algo limpio, tener algo limpio (*less frm*); **she always ~s the house very clean** tiene la casa siempre muy limpia; **to ~ o.s. clean** no ensuciarse, mantenerse limpio; **cats ~ themselves clean** los gatos son muy limpios; **exercise ~s you fit** haciendo ejercicio te mantienes en forma; **~ the sauce hot** (*in recipe book*) mantener la salsa caliente; **I'll ~ your supper hot** te guardaré la comida caliente; **to ~ inflation as low as possible** mantener la inflación tan baja como sea posible; **to ~ sth safe** guardar algo bien, guardar algo en un lugar seguro; **try to ~ your head still** intenta no mover la cabeza; **to ~ sth warm** mantener algo caliente; **the garden is well kept** el jardín está muy bien cuidado; *see also* **fixed A3**, **happy A3**, **post B4**

13·3 (+ *-ING*) **to ~ the engine running** dejar el motor en marcha; **to ~ sb talking** entretener a algn hablando; **~ him talking while I ...** entretenlo hablando mientras yo ...; **to ~ sb waiting** hacer esperar a algn; **he kept them working all night** los tuvo trabajando toda la noche; *see also* **go A24**

14 = ***hold*** **to ~ sb at it** obligar a algn a seguir trabajando; **I'll ~ you to your promise** haré que cumplas tu promesa; *see also* **counsel A1**

15 = ***prevent*** **to ~ sb from doing sth** impedir que algn haga algo; **what can we do to ~ it from happening again** ¿qué podemos hacer para evitar que se repita?; **to ~ o.s. from doing sth** contener las ganas de hacer algo, aguantarse de hacer algo*

16 † = ***guard, protect*** guardar; **God ~ you!** ¡Dios te guarde!

17 **to ~ o.s. to o.s.** guardar las distancias

Ⓑ INTRANSITIVE VERB

1 = ***remain*** 1·1 (*with adjective*) **try to ~ calm** intenta mantener la calma; **to ~ fit** mantenerse en forma; **it will ~ fresh for weeks** se conservará fresco durante semanas; **to ~ healthy** mantenerse sano; **~ very quiet** no hagas nada de ruido; **you must ~ still** tienes que estarte *or* quedarte muy quieto; **to ~ together** no separarse; **he was jumping up and down to ~ warm** estaba dando saltos para mantener el calor

1·2 (*with preposition/adverb*) **~ in the left lane** sigue por el carril de la izquierda; **she kept inside for three days** no salió en tres días

2 **to ~ doing sth** 2·1 (= *continue*) seguir haciendo algo; **he kept walking** siguió caminando; **I ~ hoping she'll come back** sigo esperando que vuelva; **you must ~ moving** no pares; **~ smiling!*** ¡no te desanimes!; **~ going!** ¡no pares!

2·2 (= *do repeatedly*) no hacer más que hacer algo; **he ~s mentioning his uncle** no hace más que mencionar a su tío; **I ~ thinking I'll wake up in a minute** no hago más que pensar que es todo un sueño; **she ~s bursting into tears** está todo el tiempo echándose a llorar; **he kept interrupting us** no paraba de interrumpirnos; **I ~ forgetting to pay the gas bill** siempre se me olvida pagar la factura del gas; **you mustn't ~ looking at your watch** no debes estar todo el tiempo mirando al reloj

3 ***in directions*** (= *continue*) seguir; **to ~ straight on** seguir todo recto *or* derecho; **~ due north until you come to ...** siga en dirección norte hasta que llegue a ...; **"keep left"** "circule por la izquierda"

4 = ***not go off*** [*food*] conservarse fresco, conservarse bien; **fish doesn't ~ very well** el pescado no se conserva muy bien; **an apple that ~s** una manzana que se conserva bien

5 * = ***wait*** esperar; **the news will ~ till I see you** la noticia puede esperar hasta que nos veamos; **it can ~** puede esperar

6 * ***talking about health*** **how are you ~ing?** ¿qué tal (estás)? (*Sp**), ¿como *or* qué tal te va?*, ¿cómo sigues? (*LAm**), ¿qué hubo? (*Mex, Chile**); **he's not ~ing very well** no está muy bien de salud; **she's ~ing better** está mejor, se encuentra mejor

7 = ***avoid*** **to ~ from doing sth** evitar hacer algo; (= *abstain from*) abstenerse de hacer algo

Ⓒ NOUN

1 = ***livelihood, food*** **I got £30 a week and my ~** me daban 30 libras a la semana y comida y cama; **I pay £50 a week for my ~** la pensión me cuesta 50 libras a la semana; **to earn one's ~** ganarse el sustento; (*fig*) justificar el gasto; **in a poem every word must earn its ~** en un poema cada palabra debe estar justificada

2 ***Archit*** torreón *m*, torre *f* del homenaje

3 = ***permanently*** **for ~s*** para siempre

Ⓓ PHRASAL VERBS

► **keep ahead** VI + ADV (*in market*) mantenerse al frente; (*in race*) mantenerse en cabeza; **to ~ ahead of sb** (*in market, race*) mantenerse por delante de algn

► **keep at** Ⓐ VI + PREP 1 **to ~ at sth*** (= *persevere with*) perseverar en algo; **despite his problems he kept at his studies** a pesar de sus problemas siguió perseverando en los estudios; **~ at it!*** ¡ánimo!, ¡no te aflojes! (*LAm*)

2 **to ~ at sb: she kept at him until she got an interview*** (= *pester*) no paró hasta que le concedió una entrevista; **I kept at them until they paid** seguí insistiendo hasta que me pagaron

Ⓑ VT + PREP **he wanted to rest but I kept him at it until he had run an extra 100 metres** quería parar a descansar pero seguí animándole y corrió otros 100 metros

► **keep away** Ⓐ VT + ADV mantener alejado, mantener a distancia; **the police kept the crowds away** la policía mantuvo a la multitud alejada *or* a distancia; **~ him away!** ¡que no se acerque!; **vitamin C helps ~ colds away** la vitamina C ayuda a no pillar resfriados; **to ~ sb away from sb/sth** mantener a algn alejado de algn/algo; **they kept him away from school** (= *stopped him going*) no le dejaron ir al colegio; (*because ill*) no lo llevaron al colegio, lo tuvieron en casa; **~ medicines away from children** mantener los medicamentos fuera del alcance de los niños

Ⓑ VI + ADV no acercarse; **~ away!** ¡no te acerques!; **~ away from the fire** no te acerques al fuego; **he promised to ~ away from drink** prometió no tocar la bebida; **he seems to be ~ing away from me** parece que me evita; **you ~ away from my daughter!** ¡no te vuelvas a acercar a mi hija!; **he can't ~ away from the subject** siempre vuelve al mismo tema

► **keep back** Ⓐ VT + ADV 1 (= *contain*) [+ *crowds*] contener; [+ *enemy*] no dejar avanzar, tener a raya

2 (= *withhold*) [+ *part of sth given*] guardar, quedarse con; **~ back some of the parsley to garnish** guárdate parte del perejil para adornar

3 (= *restrain*) [+ *tears*] contener, reprimir

4 (= *conceal*) [+ *names of victims*] no comunicar; **to ~ sth back from sb** ocultar algo a algn; **I'm sure he's ~ing sth back** estoy segura de que oculta algo

5 (= *delay*) [+ *person*] retrasar; **I don't want to ~ you back** no quiero retrasarte; **he had been kept back after school** le habían hecho quedarse después del colegio

Ⓑ VI + ADV **~ back, please!** ¡no se acerquen,

por favor!; **~ well back from the bonfire** no te acerques a la fogata; **I kept well back** me mantuve bien alejado

►**keep down** Ⓐ VT + ADV [1] (*= not raise*) **she kept her eyes down** no levantó los ojos; **~ your head down or you'll get shot** no levantes la cabeza o te dispararán; **you'll have to ~ your head down for 48 hours** (*fig*) tendrás que mantener al margen durante 48 horas; *see also* **head A1, A2**

[2] (*= control*) [+ *anger, rebellion*] contener, reprimir; [+ *weeds*] no dejar crecer; [+ *dog*] sujetar

[3] (*= limit*) [+ *prices, spending, temperature*] mantener bajo; [+ *costs, inflation*] mantener al mismo nivel; **could you ~ the noise down?** ¿puedes hacer menos ruido?; **you must try to ~ your weight down** tienes que intentar no subir de peso

[4] (*= hold back*) [4·1] oprimir; **it's just a way to ~ women down** es sólo una forma de oprimir a las mujeres; ✦*PROV* **you can't ~ a good man down** los buenos siempre vuelven [4·2] (*Scol*) **he was kept down another year** tuvo que repetir (año)

[5] (*= oppress*) [+ *spirits*] oprimir

[6] (*= retain*) [+ *food*] **he can't ~ anything down** lo devuelve *or* vomita todo

Ⓑ VI + ADV seguir agachado, no levantar la cabeza

►**keep in** Ⓐ VT + ADV [1] (*= prevent from going out*) impedir que salga, no dejar salir; **to ~ a child in after school** dejar a un niño castigado después de las clases

[2] (*= hold in*) [+ *stomach*] meter; [+ *elbows*] pegar al cuerpo; [+ *anger*] contener; **~ your tummy in!** ¡mete estómago!

[3] (*= keep alight*) [+ *fire*] mantener encendido; *see also* **hand A10**

Ⓑ VI + ADV [1] [*fire*] mantenerse encendido

[2] **to ~ in with sb*** mantener buenas relaciones con algn

►**keep off** Ⓐ VT + ADV (*= keep distant, repel*) **put a cloth over it to ~ the flies off** pon un trapo encima para que no se posen las moscas; **he kept his hat off** no se puso el sombrero; **~ your hands off!*** ¡no toques!

Ⓑ VT + PREP [1] (*= keep away from*) **~ your dog off my lawn** no deje que el perro me pise el césped; **~ your feet off the grass** no pises la hierba; **~ your hands off my daughter** no toques a mi hija; **they want to ~ young people off the streets** quieren evitar que los jóvenes pierdan el tiempo vagabundeando por las calles; **measures to ~ people off the unemployment register** medidas para que la gente no entre en las listas del paro; **he couldn't ~ his eyes off her*** no podía apartar los ojos de ella

[2] (*= prevent from consuming*) **I've been told to ~ him off processed foods** me han dicho que no le de alimentos procesados; **~ her off cheese for the next 10 days** que no tome queso durante los próximos 10 días

[3] (*= steer away from*) **to ~ sb off a subject** evitar que algn toque un tema; **try to ~ him off the subject of budgets** intenta que no toque el tema de los presupuestos

Ⓒ VI + PREP [1] (*= stay away from*) **~ off my land!** ¡fuera de mi propiedad!; **"keep off the grass"** "prohibido pisar el césped"

[2] (*fig*) [+ *food, subject*] evitar; **~ off politics!** ¡no hables de política!

Ⓓ VI + ADV **if the rain ~s off** si no llueve

►**keep on** Ⓐ VT + ADV [1] (*= not take off*) [+ *hat, coat, gloves*] no quitarse

[2] (*= not turn off*) [+ *light*] dejar encendido, dejar prendido (*LAm*)

[3] (*= retain*) [+ *house*] conservar

[4] (*= continue employing*) **they kept him on for years** siguieron empleándole durante muchos años; *see also* **hair A1**

Ⓑ VT + PREP (*= restrict to*) **~ him on light foods for the next few days** que sólo tome alimentos ligeros en los próximos días; **he was kept on bread and water for three days** durante tres días sólo le dieron pan y agua, le tuvieron a pan y agua durante tres días

Ⓒ VI + ADV [1] (*= continue*) seguir, continuar; **to ~ on doing sth** (*ceaselessly*) seguir *or* continuar haciendo algo; (*repeatedly*) no dejar de hacer algo; **he ~s on hoping** no pierde la esperanza, sigue teniendo esperanzas; **~ on along this road until ...** siga por esta carretera hasta ...; **he ~s on ringing me up** no deja de llamarme por teléfono; **she ~s on having migraines** tiene contínuos ataques de migraña

[2] (*) (*= talk*) **she does ~ on** no para de hablar; **she ~s on <u>about</u> how much money they've got** no hace mas que hablar *or* siempre está hablando de todo el dinero que tienen; **he ~s on about her being stupid** no hace más que decir que es una estúpida

[3] (*) (*= nag*) **she does ~ on** es muy machacona*; **he kept on <u>about</u> me being selfish** siguió dale que te pego con que soy egoísta*; **she ~s on <u>at</u> me about my cheap clothes** siempre me está dando la lata con que llevo ropa barata*; **I kept on at him about the leaking tap** le dije una y otra vez lo del grifo que perdía agua; **she ~s on at him to look for a job** le está siempre insistiendo que busque un trabajo

►**keep out** Ⓐ VT + ADV (*= exclude*) [+ *person, dog*] no dejar entrar; **we were kept out of the room** no nos dejaron entrar en la habitación; **to ~ sb out of trouble** evitar que algn se meta en líos; **to ~ sb out of the way** sacar a algn de en medio; **this coat should ~ out the cold** este abrigo tiene que proteger del frío; **have some brandy to ~ out the cold** tómate un coñac para entrar en calor; **let's ~ my mother's behaviour out of this!** no metamos lo del comportamiento de mi madre en esto; **let's try to ~ lawyers out of this** no nos metamos con abogados

Ⓑ VI + ADV (*= not enter*) no entrar, quedarse fuera; **please ~ out of the hall until further notice** por favor no entren en el hall hasta nuevo aviso; **"keep out"** "prohibida la entrada"; **to ~ out of trouble** no meterse en líos; **to ~ out of sb's way** (*= avoid*) evitar encontrarse con algn; (*= try not to annoy*) procurar no molestar a algn; **you ~ out of this!** ¡no te metas en esto!

►**keep to** Ⓐ VI + PREP [+ *promise*] cumplir con; [+ *subject, schedule, text*] ceñirse a; **to ~ to the left/right** circular por la izquierda/derecha, mantenerse por la izquierda/derecha; **to ~ to the main roads** no salir de las carreteras principales; **to ~ to one's room** no salir de su habitación; **to ~ to one's bed** guardar cama; **to ~ to one's diet** no salirse de la dieta; **they ~ to themselves** guardan las distancias

Ⓑ VT + PREP *see* **keep A14**

►**keep together** Ⓐ VT + ADV [+ *team*] mantener unido; [+ *papers, photographs*] mantener juntos; **it has been hard to ~ the team together** ha sido difícil mantener al equipo unido, ha sido difícil hacer que el equipo siguiese junto; **we try to ~ families together** intentamos mantener a las familias unidas

Ⓑ VI + ADV no separarse; **~ together, children** no os separéis, niños

►**keep under** VT + ADV [1] (*= oppress*) [+ *people, race*] mantener sometido

[2] (*= keep anaesthetized*) [+ *patient*] tener anestesiado

►**keep up** Ⓐ VT + ADV [1] (*= hold up*) [+ *shelf*] sostener, sujetar; [+ *stocking, trousers*] sujetar; **to ~ one's spirits** *or* **morale up** mantener la moral alta

[2] (*= continue*) [+ *tradition*] mantener; [+ *correspondence, subscription, standards, pressure*] mantener; [+ *payments*] no retrasarse en; **~ up the good work!** ¡bien hecho!, ¡sigue así!, ¡síguele dando! (*LAm*); **~ it up!** ¡sigue así!, ¡ánimo!; **he'll never ~ it up!** ¡no va a poder seguir así!, ¡no aguanta! (*LAm*); **it's difficult to ~ up a relationship when you're far apart** es difícil mantener una relación cuando se está alejado uno del otro

[3] (*= maintain*) [+ *property*] cuidar, mantener (en buenas condiciones); [+ *payments*] no retrasarse en; **you must try to ~ up your German** deberías intentar seguir con el alemán

[4] (*= keep out of bed*) tener despierto hasta muy tarde, tener en vela, tener desvelado (*LAm*); **I don't want to ~ you up** no quiero entretenerte más

Ⓑ VI + ADV [1] (*= continue*) [*weather*] seguir, mantenerse

[2] (*= maintain level*) (*in race etc*) mantener el ritmo, no quedarse atrás; (*in comprehension*) seguir (el hilo); **share prices have kept up well** los precios de las acciones se han mantenido bien; **to ~ up <u>with</u> sb** (*in race*) seguirle el ritmo a algn; (*in comprehension*) seguirle el hilo a algn; **to ~ up with the class** (*Scol, Univ*) mantenerse al nivel del resto de la clase; **it's important to ~ up with your languages** es importante que mantengas el nivel de los idiomas; **to ~ up with the times** ir con los tiempos, mantenerse al día; **I try to ~ up with the news/with current affairs** intento estar al día de las noticias/los temas de actualidad; **to ~ up with demand** responder a la demanda; **wage increases have kept up with inflation** las subidas salariales se han mantenido al nivel de la inflación; ✦*IDIOM* **to ~ up with the Joneses** no ser menos que el vecino

keeper ['ki:pəʳ] N (*in park, zoo etc*) guarda *mf*, guardián/ana *m/f*; (*= gamekeeper*) guardabosque *mf*, guardabosques *mf inv*; (*in museum, art gallery*) conservador(a) *m/f*; (*= goalkeeper*) portero/a *m/f*, arquero/a *m/f* (*LAm*); **am I my brother's ~?** (*Bible*) ¿acaso soy el guarda de mi hermano?

keep-fit [,ki:p'fɪt] (*Brit*) Ⓐ N gimnasia *f* (para mantenerse en forma)

Ⓑ CPD ► **keep-fit classes** NPL clases *fpl* de gimnasia (para mantenerse en forma) ► **keep-fit exercises** NPL ejercicios *mpl* para mantenerse en forma

keeping ['ki:pɪŋ] N [1] (*= harmony*) **to be in ~ with** estar de acuerdo con, estar en armonía con; **to be out of ~ with** estar en desacuerdo con; **her clothes were totally out of ~ with the elegant setting** la ropa que llevaba desentonaba totalmente con el elegante entorno

[2] (*= care, custody*) **to be in the ~ of X** estar en manos de X; **to be in safe ~** estar en un lugar seguro, estar en buenas manos; **to give sth to sb for safe ~** poner algo al cuidado de algn

keepsake ['ki:pseɪk] N recuerdo *m*

keester* ['ki:stəʳ] N (*US*) trasero* *m*

keg [keg] Ⓐ N barrilete *m*
Ⓑ CPD ► **keg beer** N cerveza *f* de barril

keister* ['kiːstər] N (*US*) = **keester**

keks* [keks] NPL (*Brit*) pantalones *mpl*

kelp [kelp] N (*Bot*) quelpo *m* (de Patagonia)

Kelper* ['kelpəʳ] N nativo/a *m/f* de las Malvinas, habitante *mf* de las Malvinas

Ken [ken] N (*familiar form*) of **Kenneth**

ken [ken] Ⓐ N **to be beyond sb's ~** ser incomprensible para algn
Ⓑ VT (*Scot*) [+ *person*] conocer; [+ *fact*] saber; (= *recognize*) reconocer

Ken. ABBR (*US*) = **Kentucky**

kennel ['kenl] N Ⓐ N (= *doghouse*) caseta *f* de perro; **kennels** (= *dogs' home*) residencia *f* canina; (*for breeding*) criadero *m* de perros; **to put a dog in ~s** poner a un perro en una residencia canina *or* en una perrera
Ⓑ CPD ► **kennel maid** N chica *f* que trabaja en una residencia canina

Kenya ['kenjə] N Kenia *f*

Kenyan ['kenjən] ADJ, N keniano/a *m/f*

kepi ['keɪpɪ] N quepis *m inv*

kept [kept] Ⓐ PT, PP of **keep**
Ⓑ ADJ **~ woman** mantenida *f*

kerb [kɜːb] Ⓐ N (*Brit*) bordillo *m*, cordón *m* (*S. Cone*), cuneta *f* (*Chile*)
Ⓑ CPD ► **kerb crawler** N *conductor que busca prostitutas desde su coche* ► **kerb crawling** N *busca de prostitutas desde el coche* ► **kerb drill** N prácticas *fpl* de cruce ► **kerb market** N mercado *m* no oficial (*que funciona después del cierre de la Bolsa*)

kerbstone ['kɜːbstəʊn] N (*Brit*) piedra *f* del bordillo *etc*

kerchief ['kɜːtʃɪf] N pañuelo *m*, pañoleta *f*

kerfuffle* [kə'fʌfl] N (*Brit*) jaleo* *m*, follón *m* (*Sp**)

kernel ['kɜːnl] N [*of nut*] almendra *f*; (= *seed*) [*of fruit*] pepita *f*, pepa *f* (*LAm*); [*of grain*] grano *m*; (*fig*) [*of matter, question*] meollo *m*, núcleo *m*; **a ~ of truth** un grano de verdad

kerosene ['kerəsiːn] Ⓐ N keroseno *m*, queroseno *m*, querosén *m* (*LAm*)
Ⓑ CPD ► **kerosene lamp** N lámpara *f* de petróleo

kestrel ['kestrəl] N cernícalo *m* (vulgar)

ketch [ketʃ] N queche *m*

ketchup ['ketʃəp] N salsa *f* de tomate, catsup *m*

kettle ['ketl] N hervidor *m*, caldera *f* (*Bol, Uru*), pava *f* (*S. Cone*); **I'll put the ~ on** voy a poner a hervir el agua (*para hacer café/té*); ✦***IDIOM*** **that's a different ~ of fish** eso es harina de otro costal

kettledrum ['ketldrʌm] N timbal *m*

key [kiː] Ⓐ N [1] (*to door, safe, car etc*) llave *f*; (= *can-opener*) abridor *m*, abrelatas *m inv*
[2] [*of typewriter, piano*] tecla *f*; [*of wind instrument*] llave *f*, pistón *m*
[3] (*to code*) clave *f*; **the ~ to success** (*fig*) la clave del éxito
[4] (*to map, diagram*) explicación *f* de los signos convencionales
[5] (*Mus*) clave *f*; **what ~ is it in?** ¿en qué clave está?; **in the ~ of C** en clave de do; **to change ~** cambiar de tonalidad; **to sing/play off ~** cantar/tocar desafinado; **major/minor ~** tono *m* mayor/menor
Ⓑ ADJ (= *crucial*) [*issue, job, role, witness*] clave *adj inv*; **he is a ~ figure in the negotiations** es una figura clave en las negociaciones; **all the ~ positions in the company are held by men** todos los puestos clave de la compañía están ocupados por hombres
Ⓒ VT (*Comput, Typ*) (*also* **~ in, ~ up**) teclear
Ⓓ CPD ► **key card** N (*for hotel room*) tarjeta *f* de acceso ► **key money** N entrada *f* ► **key ring** N llavero *m*

►**key in** VT + ADV (*Comput, Typ*) teclear

►**key up** VT + ADV [1] **to be all ~ed up** (= *tense*) estar nervioso; (= *excited*) estar entusiasmado; **the children were too ~ed up to go to bed** los niños estaban demasiado entusiasmados para acostarse; **they are all ~ed up to make a good impression when she arrives** están nerviosos porque quieren causarle una buena impresión cuando llegue
[2] (*Comput, Typ*) teclear

keyboard ['kiːbɔːd] Ⓐ N teclado *m*; **keyboards** (*Mus*) teclados *mpl*
Ⓑ VT (*Comput*) [+ *text*] teclear
Ⓒ CPD ► **keyboard instrument** N instrumento *m* de teclado ► **keyboard operator** N = **keyboarder** ► **keyboard player** N teclista *mf*

keyboarder ['kiːˌbɔːdəʳ] N teclista *mf*

keyboardist ['kiːbɔːdɪst] N (*Mus*) teclista *mf*

keyhole ['kiːhəʊl] Ⓐ N ojo *m* de la cerradura
Ⓑ CPD ► **keyhole surgery** N cirugía *f* mínimamente invasiva

keying ['kiːɪŋ] N (*Comput*) tecleado *m*

Keynesian ['kiːnzɪən] ADJ, N keynesiano/a *m/f*

keynote ['kiːnəʊt] Ⓐ N (*Mus*) tónica *f*; (*fig*) (= *main emphasis*) tónica *f*, piedra *f* clave
Ⓑ CPD ► **keynote speech** N discurso *m* de apertura, *discurso en que se sientan las bases de una política or programa*

keypad ['kiːpæd] N teclado *m* numérico

key-puncher ['kiːˌpʌntʃəʳ] N teclista *mf*

keystone ['kiːstəʊn] N (*Archit*) dovela *f*; (*fig*) piedra *f* angular

keystroke ['kiːstrəʊk] N pulsación *f* (*de la tecla*)

keyword ['kiːwɜːd] N palabra *f* clave

Kg, kg ABBR (= **kilogram(s), kilogramme(s)**) kg

KGB N (*in former USSR*) KGB *f*

khaki ['kɑːkɪ] Ⓐ N (= *cloth, colour*) caqui *m*; **khakis** (= *military uniform*) uniforme *m* caqui
Ⓑ ADJ caqui *inv*

kharja ['xɑːʒə] N jarcha *f*

Khartoum [kɑː'tuːm] N Jartum *m*

Khmer [kmɛəʳ] Ⓐ N jemer *mf*; **the ~ Rouge** los jemeres rojos
Ⓑ ADJ jemer

Khyber Pass [ˌkaɪbə'pɑːs] N pasaje *m* de Kyber

kHz ABBR (= **kilohertz**) kHz, KHz

kibbutz [kɪ'bʊts] N (*pl* **kibbutzim** [kɪ'bʊtsɪm]) kibutz *m*

kibitzer ['kɪbɪtsəʳ] N (*US*) mirón/ona *m/f*

kibosh ['kaɪbɒʃ] N ✦***IDIOM*** **to put the ~ on sth*** dar al traste con algo*

kick [kɪk] Ⓐ N [1] (*gen*) patada *f*, puntapié *m*; (*Sport*) puntapié *m*, tiro *m*; (*by animal*) coz *f*; **what he needs is a good ~ up the backside*** lo que necesita es una buena patada en el trasero*; **to give sth/sb a ~** dar una patada a algo/algn; **I gave him a ~ in the pants*** le di una patada en el trasero*; **he got** *or* **took a ~ on the leg** le dieron una patada en la pierna; **to take a ~ at goal** tirar a puerta; **it was a ~ in the teeth for him*** (*fig*) le sentó como una patada (en la barriga)*
[2] [*of firearm*] culatazo *m*
[3] (*) [*of drink*] fuerza *f*; **a drink with a ~ to it** una bebida que pega fuerte*
[4] (*) (= *thrill*) **I get a ~ out of seeing her happy** me encanta verla feliz; **he gets a ~ out of teasing her** se refocila tomándole el pelo; **to do something for ~s** hacer algo sólo para divertirse *or* por pura diversión
[5] (*) (= *craze*) **he's on a fishing ~ now** ahora le ha dado por la pesca*
Ⓑ VT [1] [+ *ball etc*] dar una patada *or* un puntapié a; [+ *goal*] marcar; [+ *person*] dar una patada a; [*animal*] dar una coz a; **he ~ed the stone away** apartó la piedra de una patada; **to ~ sb downstairs** echar a algn escaleras abajo de una patada; **to ~ one's legs in the air** agitar las piernas; **I could have ~ed myself*** ¡me hubiera dado de tortas!*; **to ~ sth out of the way** quitar algo de en medio de una patada; **she ~ed the door shut** cerró la puerta de una patada; ✦***IDIOMS*** **to ~ the bucket*** estirar la pata*; **to ~ ass** *or* **butt** (*esp US***) joder al personal**; **to ~ a man when he's down** dar a moro muerto gran lanzada; *see also* **heel A1**
[2] (*fig*) (*) (= *give up*) **to ~ a habit** dejar un hábito; **I've ~ed smoking** ya no fumo
Ⓒ VI [1] [*person*] dar patadas *or* puntapiés; [*baby*] patalear; [*animal*] dar coces, cocear; **to ~ at** dar patadas a; **she dragged the child off ~ing and screaming** se llevó al niño a rastras [2] (*gun*) dar un culetazo, recular
Ⓓ CPD ► **kick boxing** N kick boxing *m* ► **kick turn** N (*Ski*) cambio *m* brusco de marcha

►**kick about, kick around** Ⓐ VT + ADV (*gen*) dar patadas a; [+ *idea*] darle vueltas a; **to ~ a ball about** divertirse dándole puntapiés a un balón de un lado para otro; **to ~ sb around** (*fig*) tratar a algn a patadas*; **he's been ~ed about a lot** le han maltratado mucho
Ⓑ VI + ADV (*) **it's ~ing about here somewhere** anda por aquí en algún sitio; **I ~ed about in London for two years** anduve por Londres durante dos años

►**kick against** VI + PREP rebelarse contra; ✦***IDIOM*** **to ~ against the pricks** (*lit*) dar coces contra el aguijón; (*fig*) tener una actitud rebelde

►**kick back** Ⓐ VI + ADV (*gun*) dar culatazo, recular
Ⓑ VT + ADV [+ *ball*] devolver

►**kick down** VT + ADV derribar *or* echar abajo a patadas

►**kick in** Ⓐ VT + ADV [1] [+ *door*] derribar *or* echar abajo a patadas; (= *break*) romper a patadas; **to ~ sb's teeth in*** romper la cara a algn*
[2] (*US**) (= *contribute*) contribuir, apoquinar (*Sp**)
Ⓑ VI + ADV (*US**) [1] (= *take effect*) surtir efecto
[2] (= *contribute*) contribuir, apoquinar (*Sp**)

►**kick off** VI + ADV (*Ftbl*) hacer el saque inicial; (*fig*) (*) [*meeting etc*] empezar

►**kick out** Ⓐ VI + ADV [*person*] dar patadas (**at** a); [*animal*] dar coces (**at** a); **to ~ out against** *see* **kick against**
Ⓑ VT + ADV (*) echar a patadas*; (*fig*) (*from job, home*) echar, poner de patitas en la calle*

►**kick up*** VT + ADV **to ~ up a row** *or* **a din** (*lit*) armar un jaleo*; **to ~ up a fuss** *or* **stink about** *or* **over sth** armar un escándalo por algo

kickabout ['kɪkəbaʊt] N (*Ftbl*) **to have a ~** pelotear

kickback ['kɪkbæk] N [1] (*) soborno *m*, coima *f* (*S. Cone**), mordida *f* (*Mex**)
[2] (*fig*) reacción *f*, resaca *f*, contragolpe *m*

kicker ['kɪkəʳ] N (*Rugby*) pateador *m*

kickoff ['kɪkɒf] N (*Ftbl*) saque *m* (inicial); (*fig*) comienzo *m*; **I'm not going there, for a ~*** para empezar, no pienso ir

kick-start ['kɪk'stɑːt] Ⓐ N (*also* **~er**) pedal *m* de arranque

Ⓑ VT [+ *engine*] arrancar con el pedal; [+ *economy, market*] activar

kid [kɪd] Ⓐ N [1] (*Zool*) (= *goat*) cabrito *m*, chivo *m*; (= *skin*) cabritilla *f*
[2] (*) (= *child*) chiquillo/a *m/f*, crío/a *m/f*, chaval/a *m/f* (*Sp*), cabro/a *m/f* (*Chile*), chamaco/a *m/f* (*CAm, Mex*), escuincle/a *m/f* (*Mex**), pibe/a *m/f* (*S. Cone**); **when I was a ~** cuando yo era un crío, cuando yo era pequeño *or* (*LAm*) chico; **that's ~'s stuff** (= *childish*) eso es de *or* para niños; (= *easy*) eso es un juego de niños
Ⓑ VT (*) [1] (= *deceive*) engañar; **who do you think you're ~ding?** ¿a quién te crees que estás engañando?; **don't ~ yourself** no te engañes; **I ~ you not** (*hum*) no te engaño
[2] (= *tease*) **to ~ sb about sth** tomar el pelo a algn por algo [3] (= *pretend to*) **to ~ sb that** hacer creer a algn que
Ⓒ VI (*) bromear; **I'm only ~ding** lo digo en broma; **"they're mother and daughter" — "no ~ding?"** —son madre e hija —¿en serio? *or* —¡no me digas!; **really! no ~ding!** ¡en serio!, ¡de verdad!
Ⓓ CPD ► **kid brother*** N hermano *m* menor *or* pequeño *or* (*LAm*) chico ► **kid gloves** NPL guantes *mpl* de cabritilla; ✦*IDIOM* **to handle sth/sb with ~ gloves** tratar algo/a algn con guante blanco ► **kid sister*** N hermana *f* menor *or* pequeña *or* (*LAm*) chica

►**kid along*** = **kid on**

►**kid on*** VT + ADV **he's ~ding you on** te está tomando el pelo*

kiddy* ['kɪdɪ] N chiquillo/a *m/f*

kidnap ['kɪdnæp] VT secuestrar, raptar, plagiar (*Mex*)

kidnapper, kidnaper (*US*) ['kɪdnæpəʳ] N secuestrador(a) *m/f*, raptor(a) *m/f*, plagiador/a *m/f* (*Mex*)

kidnapping, kidnaping (*US*) ['kɪdnæpɪŋ] N secuestro *m*, rapto *m*, plagio *m* (*Mex*)

kidney ['kɪdnɪ] Ⓐ N (*Anat, Culin*) riñón *m*; (*fig*) índole *f*, especie *f*
Ⓑ CPD ► **kidney bean** N (*Culin*) frijol *m*, judía *f* (*Sp*), poroto *m* (*S. Cone*) ► **kidney disease** N enfermedad *f* renal ► **kidney dish** N batea *f* ► **kidney failure** N insuficiencia *m* renal ► **kidney machine** N riñón *m* artificial ► **kidney stone** N cálculo *m* renal ► **kidney transplant** N trasplante *m* renal *or* de riñón

kidney-shaped ['kɪdnɪ,ʃeɪpt] ADJ ariñonado, con forma de riñon

kidology* [kɪ'dɒlədʒɪ] N (*Brit*) guasa* *f*

kike** [kaɪk] N (*US offensive*) judío/a *m/f*

Kilimanjaro [kɪlɪmæn'dʒɑːrəʊ] N Kilimanjaro *m*

kill [kɪl] Ⓐ VT [1] (*gen*) matar, dar muerte a (*frm*); (= *murder*) asesinar, matar; [+ *animal*] matar, sacrificar; **he was ~ed in the explosion** murió en la explosión; **he was ~ed by an enemy agent** lo mató un agente enemigo; **I'll ~ you for this!** ¡te voy a matar!; **to be ~ed in action** *or* **battle** morir en combate, morir luchando; **I'll do it if it ~s me** lo haré aunque me vaya en ello la vida; **the pace is ~ing him** el ritmo de trabajo lo está matando; **this heat is ~ing me*** este calor acabará conmigo*; **my feet are ~ing me*** los pies me están matando*; **to ~ o.s.** matarse; (= *commit suicide*) suicidarse; **he certainly doesn't ~ himself (with work)!** (*fig*) (*hum*) ¡desde luego ese a trabajar no se mata!; **he was ~ing himself laughing*** se moría de (la) risa; ✦*IDIOM* **to ~ two birds with one stone** matar dos pájaros de un tiro
[2] (*fig*) [+ *story*] suprimir; [+ *rumour*] acabar con; [+ *proposal, parliamentary bill*] echar abajo; [+ *feeling, hope*] destruir; [+ *pain*] calmar; [+ *flavour, taste*] matar; [+ *sound*] amortiguar; [+ *engine, motor*] parar, apagar; [+ *lights*] apagar; **to ~ time** matar el rato
[3] (*) hacer morir de risa*; **this will ~ you** te vas a morir de (la) risa*
Ⓑ VI **thou shalt not ~** (*Bible*) no matarás; ✦*IDIOM* **to be dressed to ~** ir despampanante
Ⓒ N (*Hunting, Bullfighting*) muerte *f*; (= *animal killed*) pieza *f*; (= *number of animals killed*) caza *f*; **to go in for the ~** (*lit*) entrar a matar; **to be in at the ~** (*lit*) asistir a la matanza

►**kill off** VT + ADV [1] (*lit*) exterminar, acabar con; **what ~ed off the dinosaurs?** ¿qué exterminó los dinosaurios?, ¿qué acabó con los dinosaurios?; **the recession is ~ing off many small firms** la recesión está acabando con muchas pequeñas empresas; **his character is ~ed off in the first episode** matan *or* eliminan a su personaje en el primer episodio
[2] (*fig*) [+ *rumour*] acabar con; [+ *proposal*] echar abajo; [+ *hopes*] destruir

killer ['kɪləʳ] Ⓐ N [1] (= *murderer*) asesino/a *m/f*; **diphtheria used to be a ~** antiguamente la difteria era una enfermedad mortal
[2] (*) (*fig*) **it's a ~** (= *joke*) es para morirse de risa*; (= *task*) es agotador; (= *question*) es muy difícil, es mortal*
Ⓑ CPD ► **killer application, killer app*** N aplicación *f* rompedora, aplicación *f* de excelente rendimiento ► **killer bee** N abeja *f* asesina ► **killer disease** N enfermedad *f* mortal ► **killer instinct** N (*also fig*) instinto *m* asesino ► **killer punch** N puñetazo *m* mortal ► **killer shark** N tiburón *m* asesino ► **killer whale** N orca *f*

killing ['kɪlɪŋ] Ⓐ ADJ [1] [*blow, disease*] mortal
[2] (*) (= *exhausting*) [*work, journey*] agotador, durísimo
[3] (*) (= *funny*) divertidísimo, para morirse de (la) risa*
Ⓑ N (= *murder*) asesinato *m*; (*large scale, also of animals*) matanza *f*; ✦*IDIOM* **to make a ~*** hacer su agosto

killingly ['kɪlɪŋlɪ] ADV **~ funny** divertidísimo; **it was ~ funny** fue para morirse de (la) risa*

killjoy ['kɪldʒɔɪ] N aguafiestas *mf inv*

kiln [kɪln] N horno *m*

kilo ['kiːləʊ] N kilo *m*

kilobyte ['kɪləʊ,baɪt] N kilobyte *m*, kilobocteto *m*

kilocycle ['kɪləʊ,saɪkl] N kilociclo *m*

kilogram(me) ['kɪləʊgræm] N kilo(gramo) *m*

kilohertz ['kɪləʊ,hɜːts] N kilohercio *m*

kilolitre, kiloliter (*US*) ['kɪləʊ,liːtəʳ] N kilolitro *m*

kilometre, kilometer (*US*) ['kɪləʊmiːtəʳ] N kilómetro *m*

kilometric [,kɪləʊ'metrɪk] ADJ kilométrico

kiloton ['kɪləʊ,tʌn] N kilotón *m*

kilowatt ['kɪləʊwɒt] N kilovatio *m*

kilowatt-hour ['kɪləʊwɒt,aʊə] N kilovatio-hora *m*; **200 ~s** 200 kilovatios-hora

kilt [kɪlt] N falda *f* escocesa

kilted ['kɪltɪd] ADJ [*man*] vestido con falda escocesa; **~ skirt** falda *f* escocesa

kilter ['kɪltəʳ] N **to be out of ~** [*mechanism*] estar descentrado; **business is bad and everything's out of ~** el negocio va mal y todo anda desbaratado

kimono [kɪ'məʊnəʊ] N (*pl* **kimonos**) kimono *m*, quimono *m*

kin [kɪn] N familiares *mpl*, parientes *mpl*; **next of ~** familiar(es) *m(pl)* *or* pariente(s) *m(pl)* más cercano(s)

▼**kind** [kaɪnd] Ⓐ ADJ (*compar* **kinder**; *superl* **kindest**) [*person*] amable, atento; [*act, word, offer*] amable; [*treatment*] bueno, cariñoso; [*voice*] tierno, cariñoso; **thank you for your ~ offer of help** gracias por ofrecerte amablemente a ayudarnos; (*more frm*) gracias por su amable oferta de ayuda; **the ~est thing that can be said about the play is that …** lo menos malo que se puede decir de la obra es que …; **he was ~ enough to help** tuvo la amabilidad de ayudar; **would you be ~ enough to** *or* **would you be so ~ as to close the door?** (*frm*) ¿haría el favor de cerrar la puerta, por favor?, ¿tendría la bondad de cerrar la puerta, por favor? (*frm*); **to have a ~ heart** tener buen corazón; **that's very ~ of you** es usted muy amable; (*more frm*) es muy amable de su parte; **it was very ~ of you to pick us up** fuiste muy amable viniéndonos a recoger; (*more frm*) fue muy amable de su parte el venir a recogernos; **she was very ~ to me** fue muy amable conmigo, se portó muy bien conmigo; **life has been ~ to me** la vida me ha tratado bien; **you must be ~ to animals** hay que tratar bien a los animales; **a washing-up liquid that is ~ to your hands** un lavavajillas que no daña sus manos, un lavavajillas que es suave con sus manos
Ⓑ N [1] (= *type*) clase *f*, tipo *m*; **which ~ do you prefer?** ¿qué tipo prefieres?; **I prefer the ~ with handles** prefiero los que tienen asas; **she hated Lewis and his ~** odiaba a Lewis y a la gente como él; **many ~s of books/cars** muchos tipos de libros/coches; **people of all ~s** gente *f* de todas clases, gente *f* de todo tipo; **all ~s of things** toda clase de cosas; **it can fail for all ~s of reasons** puede fallar por todo tipo de razones; **a ~ of lizard** un tipo de lagarto; **she's the ~ (of person) that …** ella es de las que …; **what ~ of person do you take me for?** ¿por quién me tomas?; **what ~ of an answer is that?** ◊ **what ~ of an answer do you call that?** ¿qué clase de respuesta es ésa?; **I had a ~ of feeling that would happen** tuve el presentimiento de que ocurriría así; **you know the ~ of thing I mean** ya sabes a lo que me refiero; **it's not his ~ of film/thing** no es el tipo de película/cosa que (a él) le gusta; **he's not her ~ of man** no es su tipo de hombre; **it was tea of a ~** (*pej*) se supone que era té (*pej*); **three/four of a ~** (*in card games*) tres/cuatro del mismo palo; **they're two of a ~** son tal para cual; **she's a very unusual woman, one of a ~** es una mujer muy poco corriente, única; **it's the only one of its ~** es único (en su género); **the castle is the largest of its ~** el castillo es el más grande de los de su estilo; **something of the ~** algo por el estilo; **nothing of the ~!** ¡nada de eso!, ¡ni hablar!; **she never said anything of the ~** nunca dijo nada parecido
[2] **in ~**: **payment in ~** pago *m* en especie; **to repay sth in ~** [+ *cruelty, ingratitude etc*] pagar algo con la misma moneda; **we repaid her generosity in ~** respondimos con nuestra generosidad a la suya
[3] **~ of*** (= *rather*) algo; **we're ~ of busy right now** ahora mismo estamos algo ocupados; **I ~ of felt it might happen** tenía el presentimiento de que iba a suceder; **it's ~ of awkward at the moment** ahora mismo me va mal, ahora no es el mejor momento; **it was ~ of sad, really** era un poco triste, la verdad; **she was ~ of cute** tenía cierto atractivo

kinda* ['kaɪndə] = **kind of**; *see* **kind B3**

kindergarten ['kɪndə,gɑːtn] N jardín *m* de infancia, kindergarten *m*, kinder *m* (*LAm**)

➤ LANGUAGE IN USE: **kind A** 4, 22

kind-hearted ['kaɪnd'hɑːtɪd] ADJ [*person, action*] bondadoso, de buen corazón; **to be ~** ser bondadoso, tener buen corazón

kind-heartedness ['kaɪnd'hɑːtɪdnɪs] N bondad *f*

kindle ['kɪndl] Ⓐ VT [+ *wood*] prender fuego a; [+ *fire*] encender; (*fig*) [+ *emotion, interest*] despertar, suscitar
Ⓑ VI [*wood, fire*] prender, encenderse; (*fig*) (*with emotion*) despertarse

kindliness ['kaɪndlɪnɪs] N bondad *f*

kindling ['kɪndlɪŋ] N leña *f* (menuda), astillas *fpl*

kindly ['kaɪndlɪ] Ⓐ ADJ (*compar* **kindlier**; *superl* **kindliest**) [*person*] bondadoso; [*tone of voice*] tierno, cariñoso; [*face, eyes, smile*] afable, dulce; [*remark*] cariñoso; **a ~ soul** un alma caritativa *or* bondadosa
Ⓑ ADV 1 (= *thoughtfully*) amablemente; **"you seem tired this morning, Jenny," she said ~** —pareces cansada esta mañana, Jenny —dijo cariñosamente; **he very ~ helped** tuvo la amabilidad de ayudar; **to look ~ on sth** ver algo con buenos ojos; **to look ~ on sb** ser benévolo con algn; **to take ~ to sth**: **he didn't take very ~ to her suggestion** no acogió muy bien su sugerencia; **the villagers do not take ~ to newcomers** a la gente del pueblo no les gustan mucho los recién llegados; **he doesn't take ~ to being kept waiting** no le hace ninguna gracia que le hagan esperar; **to think ~ of sb** tener un buen concepto de algn
2 (= *please*) (*frm*) **~ wait a moment** haga el favor de esperar un momento, tenga la amabilidad de esperar un momento; **~ mind your own business** haz el favor de no meterte en lo que no te importa

kindness ['kaɪndnɪs] N 1 (= *thoughtfulness*) amabilidad *f*; **he was ~ itself** era la bondad personificada; **they treated him with every ~** lo trataron con todo género de atenciones; **out of the ~ of her heart** por pura amabilidad; **we were touched by her ~ to** *or* **towards us** su amabilidad para con nosotros nos enterneció *or* nos emocionó
2 (= *favour*) favor *m*; **it would be a ~ to tell him** decírselo sería un favor; **to do sb a ~** hacer un favor a algn

kindred ['kɪndrɪd] Ⓐ ADJ (= *related by blood or group*) emparentado; [*language*] de un tronco común; (*fig*) afín, semejante; **~ spirits** almas *fpl* gemelas; **to have a ~ feeling for sb** sentirse hermano de algn
Ⓑ N (= *relations*) familia *f*, parientes *mpl*

kinescope ['kɪnəskəʊp] N (*US*) tubo *m* de rayos catódicos, cinescopio *m*

kinesiology [kɪ,niːsɪ'ɒlədʒɪ] N kinesiología *f*

kinetic [kɪ'netɪk] Ⓐ ADJ cinético
Ⓑ CPD ► **kinetic energy** N energía *f* cinética

kinetics [kɪ'netɪks] NSING cinética *f*

kinfolk ['kɪnfəʊk] NPL = **kinsfolk**

king [kɪŋ] Ⓐ N 1 (*lit, fig*) rey *m*; **the ~ and queen** los reyes; **the Three Kings** los Reyes Magos; **an oil ~** un magnate del petróleo; **I'm the ~ of the castle!** (*child language*) ¡soy el rey!, ¡soy el amo y señor!; **to turn King's evidence** delatar a los cómplices; ✦**IDIOMS they paid a ~'s ransom for it** les costó mucho dinero, les costó un dineral*; **to live like a ~** vivir a cuerpo de rey
2 (*Chess, Cards*) rey *m*; (*Draughts*) dama *f*
Ⓑ CPD ► **king cobra** N cobra *f* real ► **king penguin** N pingüino *m* real ► **King's Bench** N (*Brit Jur*) departamento *m* del Tribunal Supremo ► **King's Counsel** N (*Brit Jur*) abogado *mf* (*de categoría superior*); → QC/KC

kingcup ['kɪŋkʌp] N botón *m* de oro

kingdom ['kɪŋdəm] N reino *m*; **animal/plant ~** reino *m* animal/vegetal; **the Kingdom of Heaven** el reino de los cielos; **till ~ come*** hasta el día del juicio final

kingfisher ['kɪŋfɪʃəʳ] N martín *m* pescador

kingly ['kɪŋlɪ] ADJ [*manner, presence, splendour*] regio; [*gift*] digno de un rey

kingmaker ['kɪŋ,meɪkəʳ] N persona *f* muy influyente

kingpin ['kɪŋpɪn] N (*Tech*) perno *m* real *or* pinzote; (*fig*) (= *person, object*) piedra *f* angular

kingship ['kɪŋʃɪp] N dignidad *f* real, monarquía *f*; **they offered him the ~** le ofrecieron el trono *or* la corona

king-size(d) ['kɪŋsaɪz(d)] Ⓐ ADJ (*gen*) tamaño gigante *or* familiar; [*cigarette*] extra largo
Ⓑ CPD ► **king-size(d) bed** N cama *f* de matrimonio extragrande

kink [kɪŋk] Ⓐ N (*in rope etc*) retorcedura *f*, vuelta *f*; (*in hair*) onda *f*; (*in paper*) arruga *f*, pliegue *m*; (*fig*) (*emotional, psychological*) manía *f*, trauma *m*; (*sexual*) perversión *f*
Ⓑ VI enroscarse; [*hair*] ondularse

kinky ['kɪŋkɪ] ADJ (*compar* **kinkier**; *superl* **kinkiest**) 1 (*) (*sexually*) pervertido
2 (*) (= *eccentric*) [*dress etc*] estrafalario; (*pej*) [*person*] raro, estrafalario
3 (= *curly*) [*hair*] ondulado

kinsfolk ['kɪnzfəʊk] NPL familiares *mpl*, parientes *mpl*

kinship ['kɪnʃɪp] N [*of family*] parentesco *m*; (*fig*) afinidad *f*

kinsman ['kɪnzmən] N (*pl* **kinsmen**) familiar *m*, pariente *m*

kinswoman ['kɪnz,wʊmən] N (*pl* **kinswomen**) familiar *f*

kiosk ['kiːɒsk] N quiosco *m*; **telephone ~** (*Brit*) cabina *f* telefónica

kip* [kɪp] (*Brit*) Ⓐ N (= *sleep*) siestecita* *f*, sueño* *m*; (= *lodging*) alojamiento *m*; (= *bed*) pulguero* *m*; **to have a ~** echar un sueño*
Ⓑ VI dormir; **to ~ down** echarse a dormir

kipper ['kɪpəʳ] N arenque *m* ahumado

Kirbigrip®, **kirbygrip** ['kɜːbɪ,grɪp] N horquilla *f* para el pelo

Kirghizia, **Kirgizia** [,kɜː'gɪzɪə] N Kirguizia *f*

kirk [kɜːk] N (*Scot*) iglesia *f*; **the Kirk** la Iglesia (Presbiteriana) de Escocia

kirsch [kɪəʃ] N kirsch *m*

kiss [kɪs] Ⓐ N beso *m*; (= *light touch*) roce *m*; **to blow sb a ~** tirar un beso a algn, dar un beso volado a algn; **the ~ of death** (*fig*) el golpe de gracia; **to give sb a ~** dar un beso a algn; **the ~ of life** (*Brit*) (= *artificial respiration*) respiración *f* boca a boca; (*fig*) nueva vida *f*, nuevas fuerzas *fpl*
Ⓑ VT besar; **to ~ sb's cheek/hand** besar a algn en la mejilla/besar la mano a algn; **to ~ sb goodbye/goodnight** dar un beso de despedida/de buenas noches a algn; **to ~ away sb's tears** enjugar las lágrimas a algn con besos; ✦**IDIOM to ~ ass** (*esp US***) lamer culos**; **to ~ sb's ass** (*esp US***) lamer el culo a algn**, hacer la pelota a algn*; **~ my ass!** (*esp US***) ¡vete a la mierda!**, ¡vete al carajo! (*esp LAm***)
Ⓒ VI besarse; **they ~ed** se besaron, se dieron un beso; **to ~ and make up** hacer las paces
Ⓓ CPD ► **kiss curl** N (*Brit*) caracol *m*

kissagram ['kɪsə,græm] N besograma *m*

kiss-and-tell [,kɪsən'tel] ADJ **she is about to reveal all in her ~ autobiography** está a punto de desvelarlo todo sobre su romance con una celebridad en su autobiografía

kisser‡ ['kɪsəʳ] N (= *face*) jeta‡ *f*; (= *mouth*) morrera‡ *f*

kiss-off* ['kɪsɒf] (*US*) N **to give sth the ~** tirar algo, despedirse de algo; **to give sb the ~** (= *employee*) poner a algn de patitas en la calle*, despedir a algn; (= *boyfriend*) plantar a algn*, dejar a algn

kissogram ['kɪsə,græm] N = **kissagram**

kissproof ['kɪspruːf] ADJ indeleble

Kit [kɪt] N (*familiar form*) *of* **Catherine** *etc*, **Christopher**

kit [kɪt] Ⓐ N 1 (= *equipment, gear*) avíos *mpl*; (= *instruments, tools*) útiles *mpl*, herramientas *fpl*; (*Mil*) pertrechos *mpl*, petate *m*
2 (*) (= *belongings*) bártulos* *mpl*; (= *clothes*) ropa *f*; (*for sports*) equipo *m*, indumentaria *f*; (= *luggage*) bultos* *mpl*, equipaje *m*; **to get one's ~ off** (*Brit**) ponerse en cueros*, ponerse en pelotas‡, despelotarse*
3 (= *set of items*) equipo *m*, kit *m*; (= *first-aid kit*) botiquín *m*; **sewing ~** costurero *m*, neceser *m* de costura
4 (= *parts for assembly*) (= *toy, model*) maqueta *f*; (= *assembly kit*) kit *m*, juego *m* por piezas para armar; **a computer in ~ form** un ordenador que se vende como kit *or* por piezas (y lo monta uno mismo); *see also* **caboodle**
Ⓑ CPD ► **kit car** N *coche que se vende por piezas y lo arma uno mismo*

►**kit out, kit up** VT + ADV (*Brit*) (*often passive*) equipar (**with** de); **to be ~ted out in** [+ *clothing*] llevar puesto

kitbag ['kɪtbæg] N (*esp Brit*) saco *m* de viaje, macuto *m*; (*Mil*) mochila *f*

kitchen ['kɪtʃɪn] Ⓐ N cocina *f*
Ⓑ CPD [*cupboard, knife, equipment*] de cocina; [*window*] de la cocina ► **kitchen cabinet** N armario *m* de cocina; (*Pol*) grupo *m* de asesores personales; → CABINET ► **kitchen foil** N papel *m* de aluminio ► **kitchen garden** N huerto *m* ► **kitchen maid** N ayudanta *f* de cocina ► **kitchen paper** N toallitas *fpl* de papel ► **kitchen range** N cocina *f* económica ► **kitchen roll** N = **kitchen paper** ► **kitchen salt** N sal *f* de cocina ► **kitchen sink** N fregadero *m*, pila *f*; ✦**IDIOM they took everything but the ~ sink*** (*hum*) se llevaron la casa a cuestas* ► **kitchen sink drama** N obra *f* ultrarrealista ► **kitchen unit** N módulo *m* de cocina

kitchenette [,kɪtʃɪ'net] N cocina *f* pequeña

kitchenware ['kɪtʃɪnweəʳ] N artículos *mpl* de cocina

kite [kaɪt] Ⓐ N 1 (= *toy*) cometa *f*; **to fly a ~** (*fig*) lanzar una idea (para sondear la opinión); **go fly a ~!** (*US**) ¡vete al cuerno!*; *see also* **high A5**
2 (*Orn*) milano *m* real
3 (*US Fin*‡) cheque *m* sin valor
Ⓑ VI (‡) presentar papeles falsos para conseguir dinero
Ⓒ VT (*US*) **to ~ a cheque** presentar un cheque sin fondos
Ⓓ CPD ► **kite mark** N (*Brit*) señal *f* de aprobación (de la BSI)

kith [kɪθ] N **~ and kin** parientes *mpl* y amigos

kitsch [kɪtʃ] Ⓐ ADJ kitsch, cursi
Ⓑ N kitsch *m*, cursilería *f*

kitten ['kɪtn] N gatito/a *m/f*; ✦**IDIOM to have ~s***: **I nearly had ~s when I saw it** casi me da un ataque (de nervios) cuando lo vi

kittenish ['kɪtənɪʃ] ADJ (*fig*) picaruelo, coquetón, retozón

kittiwake ['kɪtɪweɪk] N gaviota *f* tridáctila, gavina *f*

Kitty ['kɪtɪ] N (*familiar form*) *of* **Catherine** *etc*

kitty ['kɪtɪ] N [1] (= *funds*) fondo *m* común; (*Cards*) bote *m*, puesta *f*; **how much have we got in the ~?** ¿cuánto tenemos en el bote?
[2] (*) (= *name for cat*) minino* *m*

kiwi ['ki:wi:] Ⓐ N [1] (*Orn*) kiwi *m*
[2] (*) (= *New Zealander*) neozelandés/esa *m/f*
Ⓑ CPD ► **kiwi fruit** N kiwi *m*

KKK N ABBR (*US*) = **Ku Klux Klan**

Klansman ['klænzmən] N (*pl* **Klansmen**) miembro *m* del Ku Klux Klan

klaxon ['klæksn] N claxon *m*

Kleenex® ['kli:neks] N (*pl* **Kleenex** *or* **Kleenexes**) Kleenex® *m*

kleptomania [,kleptəʊ'meɪnɪə] N cleptomanía *f*

kleptomaniac [,kleptəʊ'meɪnɪæk] N cleptómano/a *m/f*

klutz⁑ [klʌts] N (*US*) patoso/a* *m/f*, torpe *mf*

km ABBR (= **kilometre(s)**) km

kmh, km/h ABBR (= **kilometre(s) per hour**) km/h, k.p.h.

knack [næk] N **it's just a ~** es un truco que se aprende; **to get** *or* **learn the ~ of (doing) sth** agarrar el truco *or* (*Sp*) el tranquillo a (hacer) algo*; **she has the ~ of making people feel at home** tiene el don de hacer que la gente se sienta cómoda a su alrededor; **you have the ~ for drawing animals** tienes mucha habilidad para dibujar animales; **he seems to have the ~ of rubbing people up the wrong way** no sé cómo se las arregla pero siempre acaba cayéndole mal a la gente

knacker ['nækəʳ] (*Brit*) Ⓐ N (*for horses*) matarife *mf* de caballos; (*for ships*) desguazador(a) *m/f*
Ⓑ VT (*) agotar, reventar*; **I'm ~ed** estoy reventado *or* hecho polvo*
Ⓒ CPD ► **knacker's yard** N (*for horses*) matadero *m*; (*for ships*) desguace *m*

knapsack ['næpsæk] N (= *small rucksack*) mochila *f*

knave [neɪv] N (*Hist*) bellaco *m*, bribón *m*; (*Cards*) valet *m*; (*in Spanish pack*) sota *f*

knavery ['neɪvərɪ] N bellaquería *f*

knavish ['neɪvɪʃ] ADJ bellaco, bribón, vil

knead [ni:d] VT [+ *dough*] amasar, sobar; [+ *clay*] amasar, trabajar; [+ *muscle*] masajear, dar masaje a

knee [ni:] Ⓐ N (*Anat*) rodilla *f*; [*of garment*] rodilla *f*; **on one's ~s, on bended ~** de rodillas; **to bow the ~ to** humillarse ante, someterse a; **a sharp pain nearly brought me to my ~s** un dolor agudo hizo que casi me cayera de rodillas; **the embargo has brought the country to its ~s** el embargo ha llevado al país al borde del desastre; **to fall on one's ~s** caer de rodillas; **to go** *or* **get down on one's ~s** arrodillarse, ponerse de rodillas; **to go** *or* **get down on one's ~s to sb** arrodillarse ante algn; **to go to sb on (one's) bended ~s** (*fig*) suplicar a algn de rodillas; **his ~s were knocking** le temblaban las rodillas; *see also* **weak A1**
Ⓑ VT dar un rodillazo a
Ⓒ CPD ► **knee bend** N flexión *f* de piernas ► **knee breeches** NPL calzón *m* corto ► **knee jerk** N reflejo *m* rotular ► **knee joint** N articulación *f* de la rodilla ► **knee sock** N calcetín *m* alto

kneecap ['ni:kæp] Ⓐ N (*Anat*) rótula *f*
Ⓑ VT **to ~ sb** disparar a las rodillas a algn

kneecapping ['ni:,kæpɪŋ] N disparo *m* a las rodillas

knee-deep ['ni:'di:p] Ⓐ ADJ **the water was ~** el agua cubría hasta las rodillas; **to be ~ in** estar metido hasta las rodillas en; (*fig*) estar metido hasta el cuello en; **the place was ~ in paper** había montones de papeles por todos lados
Ⓑ ADV **to go into the water ~** avanzar hasta que el agua llegue a las rodillas

knee-high ['ni:'haɪ] ADJ [*grass*] hasta las rodillas; [*boots*] de caña alta; [*socks*] largo; ✦**IDIOM he's been riding since he was ~ to a grasshopper*** lleva montando a caballo desde que era un renacuajo*

knee-jerk ['ni:dʒɜ:k] ADJ [*reaction*] instintivo, automático; **he's a ~ conservative** es de derecha *or* (*Sp*) de derechas hasta la médula

kneel [ni:l] (*pt, pp* **knelt** *or* **kneeled**) VI (*also* **~ down**) (= *act*) arrodillarse, ponerse de rodillas; (= *state*) estar de rodillas; **to ~ to** (*fig*) hincar la rodilla ante

knee-length ['ni:leŋθ] ADJ [*boots*] de caña alta; [*socks*] largo; [*coat, skirt*] hasta la rodilla

knee-level ['ni:,levl] N altura *f* de la rodilla

kneeling ['ni:lɪŋ] ADJ [*figure*] arrodillado, de rodillas

kneepad ['ni:pæd] N (*for sport, work*) rodillera *f*

kneeroom ['ni:rʊm] N espacio *m* para las piernas

knees-up* ['ni:zʌp] N (*pl* **knees-ups**) (*Brit hum*) baile *m*, fiesta *f*

knell [nel] N toque *m* de difuntos, doble *m*; *see also* **death B**

knelt [nelt] PT, PP *of* **kneel**

knew [nju:] PT *of* **know**

knickerbockers ['nɪkəbɒkəz] NPL pantalones *mpl* cortos; (*US*) pantalones *mpl* de golf, pantalones *mpl* holgados

knickers ['nɪkəz] NPL [1] (*Brit*) bragas *fpl*, calzones *mpl* (*LAm*); **~ to you!**⁑ ¡vete a al porra!*, ¡vete a tomar por saco! (*Sp*⁑); ✦**IDIOM to get one's ~ in a twist*** ponerse nervioso
[2] (††) = **knickerbockers**

knick-knack ['nɪknæk] N chuchería *f*, chisme *m*

knife [naɪf] Ⓐ N (*pl* **knives**) (= *table knife*) cuchillo *m*; (= *pocket knife*) navaja *f*, cortaplumas *m inv*; (= *dagger*) puñal *m*; (= *flick knife*) navaja *f*, chaveta *f* (*LAm*); (= *blade*) cuchilla *f*; **does he use a ~ and fork yet?** ¿ha aprendido ya a usar los cubiertos?; **I'll get the knives and forks out** voy a sacar los cubiertos; ✦**IDIOMS to get one's ~ into sb** tener inquina a algn; **before you could say ~** en un decir Jesús; **to turn the ~ in the wound** hurgar en la herida; **to put** *or* **stick the ~ in** ensañarse, tirar con bala; **like a (hot) ~ through butter** sin problemas, con la gorra*
Ⓑ VT (= *stab*) acuchillar, apuñalar; **to ~ sb to death** matar a algn a navajazos *or* a puñaladas
Ⓒ CPD ► **knife edge** N filo *m* (de cuchillo); ✦**IDIOM to be (balanced) on a ~ edge** [*person*] estar con el alma pendiente de un hilo; [*result*] estar pendiente de un hilo ► **knife grinder** N (= *person*) afilador(a) *m/f* ► **knife sharpener** N (= *tool*) afilador *m* de cuchillos

knifebox ['naɪfbɒks] N portacubiertos *m inv*

knife-point ['naɪfpɔɪnt] N **at ~** a punta de navaja

knifing ['naɪfɪŋ] N ataque *m* con cuchillo *or* navaja; **the motiveless ~ of a young girl** el apuñalamiento sin motivo de una chica joven

knight [naɪt] Ⓐ N (*Hist*) caballero *m*; (*Chess*) caballo *m*; (*modern*) (*Brit*) Sir *m*, *caballero de una orden*; **~ in shining armour** príncipe *m* azul; **Knight (of the Order) of the Garter** (*Brit*) caballero *m* de la orden de la Jarretera
Ⓑ VT (*Hist*) armar caballero; (*modern*) (*Brit*) otorgar el título de Sir a
Ⓒ CPD ► **knight errant** N caballero *m* andante ► **Knight Templar** N caballero *m* templario, templario *m*

knight-errantry ['naɪt'erəntrɪ] N caballería *f* andante

knighthood ['naɪthʊd] N [1] (= *order*) caballería *f*
[2] (= *title*) título *m* de caballero; (*modern*) (*Brit*) título *m* de Sir; **he was given a ~** le otorgaron el título de Sir; (*Hist*) fue armado caballero

knightly ['naɪtlɪ] ADJ caballeroso, caballeresco

knit [nɪt] Ⓐ VT [+ *garment*] hacer (a punto de aguja), tricotar (*Sp*), tejer (*LAm*); **she can ~ up a sweater in a couple of days** puede hacer un jersey en un par de días; **to ~ one's brows** fruncir el ceño; **his task is to ~ the nation back together** su tarea es la de volver a unir a la gente del país; *see also* **close-knit**
Ⓑ VI (*also* **~ together, ~ up**) hacer punto *or* calceta, tricotar (*Sp*), tejer (*LAm*); [*bones*] soldarse; [*wound*] cerrarse, curarse
Ⓒ CPD ► **knit stitch** N punto *m* de media

►**knit together** Ⓐ VI + ADV = **knit B**
Ⓑ VT + ADV (*fig*) juntar, unir

►**knit up** Ⓐ VT + ADV montar
Ⓑ VI + ADV = **knit B**

knitted ['nɪtɪd] ADJ tejido; **~ goods** géneros *mpl* de punto

knitting ['nɪtɪŋ] Ⓐ N (= *activity*) labor *f* de punto; (= *product*) prenda *f* de punto; (= *piece being worked on*) labor *f*; **I think I'll do some ~** creo que voy a ponerme a hacer punto *or* (*LAm*) tejer; **she put her ~ down on the chair** dejó la labor sobre la silla
Ⓑ CPD ► **knitting machine** N tricotosa *f* (*Sp*), máquina *f* de tejer (*LAm*) ► **knitting needle, knitting pin** N aguja *f* de hacer punto *or* (*LAm*) de tejer ► **knitting pattern** N patrón *m*, instrucciones *fpl* para hacer punto, instrucciones *fpl* de tejido (*LAm*) ► **knitting wool** N lana *f* para labores *or* (*LAm*) para tejer

knitwear ['nɪtweəʳ] N géneros *mpl* de punto

knives [naɪvz] NPL *of* **knife**

knob [nɒb] N [1] (= *protuberance*) protuberancia *f*, bulto *m*; (*on treetrunk*) nudo *m*
[2] (= *control*) [*of radio etc*] botón *m*, mando *m*
[3] (= *handle*) [*of door*] pomo *m*, tirador *m*; [*of drawer*] tirador *m*; [*of stick*] puño *m*
[4] (= *piece*) **a ~ of butter** (*Brit*) un pedazo de mantequilla
[5] (*Brit*⁑⁑) (= *penis*) verga⁑⁑ *f*, polla *f* (*Sp*⁑⁑)

knobbly ['nɒblɪ], **knobby** ['nɒbɪ] ADJ (*compar* **knobb(l)ier**, *superl* **knobb(l)iest**) [*stick*] nudoso; [*knees*] huesudo

knock [nɒk] Ⓐ N [1] (*gen*) golpe *m*; (*in collision*) choque *m*; (*on door*) llamada *f*; **a ~ on the head** un golpe en la cabeza; **there was a ~ at the door** llamaron a la puerta; **his pride took a ~** su orgullo sufrió un golpe; **the team took a hard ~ yesterday** ayer el equipo recibió un rudo golpe; **he has had plenty of hard ~s** ha recibido muchos y duros golpes en la vida
[2] (*in engine*) golpeteo *m*
Ⓑ VT [1] (= *strike*) golpear; **to ~ a hole in sth** hacer *or* abrir un agujero en algo; **to ~ a nail into sth** clavar un clavo en algo; **to ~ sb on the head** golpear a algn en la cabeza; **to ~ one's head on/against sth** (*by accident*) dar con la cabeza contra algo; (*deliberately*) dar cabezazos contra algo; **I ~ed my elbow on** *or* **against the table** me di (un golpe) en el codo con la mesa; **to ~ sb to the ground** tirar *or* echar a algn al suelo; **to ~ sb unconscious** *or* **out** *or* **cold** dejar a algn sin sentido; **to ~ sth to the floor** dar con algo en el sue-

lo; **he ~ed the knife out of her hand** le quitó el cuchillo de la mano de un golpe; **I ~ed the ball into the water** tiré la pelota al agua; **to ~ the bottom out of sth** [+ *box*] desfondar algo; (*fig*) [+ *argument*] dejar algo sin fundamentos; ◆*IDIOMS* **to ~ sth on the head** (*Brit**) (= *put paid to*) [+ *idea*] echar algo por tierra; **to ~ some sense into sb*** hacer entrar en razón a algn; **to ~ sb sideways*** dejar de piedra *or* patidifuso a algn*; **to ~ spots off sb*** dar mil vueltas a algn*

2 (*) (= *criticize*) criticar, hablar mal de

Ⓒ VI 1 (*strike*) golpear; (*at door*) llamar a la puerta; **"knock before entering"** "llamar a la puerta antes de entrar"; **he ~ed at the door/on the table** llamó a la puerta/dio un golpe en la mesa; **poverty was ~ing at his door** la pobreza llamaba a su puerta; **I can't give a job to everyone who comes ~ing on my door** no puedo dar trabajo a todos los que vienen pidiéndomelo *or* que llaman a mi puerta

2 (= *bump*) **to ~ into sth/sb** chocar *or* tropezar con algo/algn; **to ~ against sth** chocar *or* dar con *or* contra algo

3 [*engine*] golpetear

►**knock about, knock around** Ⓐ VT + ADV

1 [+ *person*] pegar, maltratar; [+ *object*] golpear, maltratar; **the place was badly ~ed about** el lugar sufrió grandes estragos; **the car was rather ~ed about** el coche estaba en bastante mal estado

2 (= *discuss*) **to ~ an idea around** dar vueltas a una idea

Ⓑ VI + ADV (*) **he's ~ed about (the world) a bit** ha visto mucho mundo; **he's ~ing about somewhere** anda por algún lado; **she ~s around with a bad crowd** anda con malas compañías

►**knock back*** VT + ADV 1 [+ *drink*] beberse (de un trago); **he can certainly ~ them back** sabe darle al trago*

2 (= *cost*) **it ~ed me back £10** me costó 10 libras

3 (= *shock*) asombrar, pasmar*; **the smell ~s you back** el olor echa para atrás*

4 (*) (= *reject*) [+ *offer*] rechazar; [+ *person*] rechazar, dar con la puerta en las narices a

►**knock down** VT + ADV 1 (= *pull, throw to the ground*) [+ *building*] derribar, demoler; [+ *person*] tirar al suelo; [+ *pedestrian*] atropellar; [+ *tree, door etc*] derribar, echar abajo; (*fig*) [+ *argument etc*] echar por tierra

2 (= *reduce*) [+ *price*] rebajar, reducir; **I ~ed him down to £20** conseguí que me rebajara el precio a 20 libras

3 (*at auction*) **it was ~ed down to him for £200** se lo adjudicaron en 200 libras

►**knock in** VT + ADV clavar

►**knock off** Ⓐ VT + ADV 1 (= *make fall*) hacer caer; (*intentionally*) echar abajo

2 (= *deduct*) **he ~ed £5 off** (*from price*) rebajó el precio en 5 libras, hizo un descuento de 5 libras; **to ~ three seconds off the record** mejorar el récord en tres segundos

3 (*) (= *steal*) birlar*

4 (*) (= *do quickly*) [+ *meal*] preparar enseguida; [+ *garment*] hacer enseguida; [+ *novel*] escribir rápidamente

5 (*) (= *stop*) **~ it off!** ¡déjalo ya!

6 (‡) (= *arrest*) detener, agarrar*; (= *kill*) cargarse*

7 (**) [+ *woman*] tirarse a**

Ⓑ VI + ADV (*) **he ~s off at five** sale del trabajo a las cinco; **I ~ off for lunch at one** dejo el trabajo a la una para (salir a) comer

►**knock on*** VI + ADV **he's ~ing on a bit** es bastante viejo; **she's ~ing on for 60** va para los 60

►**knock out** VT + ADV 1 (= *stun*) dejar sin sentido, hacer perder el conocimiento; (*Boxing*) poner fuera de combate, dejar K.O.

2 (= *strike out*) [+ *nails*] extraer, sacar; (*in fight*) [+ *teeth*] romper

3 (*in competition*) eliminar

4 (*) (= *make*) [+ *product*] producir, fabricar; [+ *garment*] hacer; [+ *novel*] escribir

5 (= *destroy*) [+ *enemy target*] destruir; (= *stop*) [+ *electricity supply, telephone lines*] cortar

6 (*) (= *exhaust*) agotar, dejar para el arrastre*

7 (*) (*shock*) dejar pasmado*

►**knock over** VT + ADV [+ *object*] tirar, voltear (*LAm*); [+ *pedestrian*] atropellar

►**knock together** VT + ADV 1 [+ *two objects*] golpear (uno contra otro); **I ought to ~ your heads together!** ¡os debería dar una buena paliza!

2 = **knock up A2**

►**knock up** Ⓐ VT + ADV 1 (*Brit*) (= *waken*) despertar, llamar

2 (= *make hastily*) hacer; [+ *meal*] preparar

3 (*Brit**) (= *tire*) agotar; (= *make ill*) dejar enfermo; **he was ~ed up for a month** estuvo enfermo durante un mes

4 (‡) (= *make pregnant*) dejar embarazada

Ⓑ VI + ADV (*Tennis*) pelotear

knockabout ['nɒkəbaʊt] Ⓐ ADJ (*esp Brit*) bullicioso, tumultuoso; **~ comedy** farsa *f* bulliciosa

Ⓑ N (*Sport*) **to have a ~** pelotear

knockback* ['nɒkbæk] N 1 (= *rejection*) rechazo *m*, feo* *m*; **to get the ~** sufrir un feo*

2 (= *setback*) revés *m*, duro golpe *m*

knockdown ['nɒkdaʊn] ADJ (= *reduced*) [*price*] de ganga, regalado

knocker ['nɒkəʳ] N 1 (*on door*) aldaba *f*

2 (*) (= *critic*) detractor(a) *m/f*, crítico/a *m/f*

3 **knockers**‡ tetas* *fpl*

knocker-up ['nɒkə'rʌp] N (*Brit*) despertador *m*

knock-for-knock ['nɒkfə'nɒk] ADJ **~ agreement** acuerdo *m* de pago respectivo

knocking ['nɒkɪŋ] Ⓐ N (= *sound*) golpes *mpl*, golpeteo *m*; (*at door*) golpe *m*, llamada *f*; (*Aut*) golpeteo *m*

Ⓑ CPD ► **knocking copy** N contrapublicidad *f*, *anuncio destinado a denigrar el producto de otro*

knocking-off time* [,nɒkɪŋ'ɒf,taɪm] N hora *f* de salir del trabajo

knocking-shop* ['nɒkɪŋʃɒp] N casa *f* de putas

knock-kneed ['nɒk'ni:d] ADJ patizambo; (*fig*) débil, irresoluto

knock-on ['nɒk'ɒn] Ⓐ N (*Rugby*) autopase *m*

Ⓑ CPD ► **knock-on effect** N (*Brit*) repercusiones *fpl*; **the rise in interest rates will have a ~ effect on the housing market** la subida en los tipos de interés repercutirá en el mercado inmobiliario

knockout ['nɒkaʊt] Ⓐ N 1 (*Boxing*) knockout *m*, K.O. *m*, nocaut *m*

2 (= *competition*) concurso *m* eliminatorio, eliminatoria *f*

3 (*) (= *stunner*) maravilla *f*; **she's a ~** es una chica alucinante*; **he's a ~!** ¡está buenísimo!*

Ⓑ CPD ► **knockout agreement** N acuerdo *m* secreto para no hacerse competencia ► **knockout blow** N golpe *m* aplastante ► **knockout competition** N concurso *m* eliminatorio, eliminatoria *f* ► **knockout drops*** NPL somnífero *msing*, calmante *msing* ► **knockout punch** N = **knockout blow**

knock-up ['nɒkʌp] N (*Tennis*) (= *practice*) peloteo *m*; **to have a ~** pelotear

knoll [nəʊl] N otero *m*, montículo *m*

knot [nɒt] Ⓐ N 1 (*gen*) nudo *m*; **to tie a ~** hacer un nudo; **her hair was all in ~s** tenía el pelo enredado; ◆*IDIOMS* **to tie sb up in ~s** enredar a algn; **to get tied up** *or* **tie o.s. up in ~s** armarse un lío*; **to tie the ~** casarse

2 (*Naut*) (= *unit of speed*) nudo *m*; *see also* **rate A2**

3 (*in wood*) nudo *m*; (= *group*) [*of people*] grupo *m*, corrillo *m*

Ⓑ VT anudar, atar; **to ~ sth together** anudar algo, atar algo con un nudo; **get ~ted!*** ¡fastídiate!*

Ⓒ VI hacerse un nudo

knothole ['nɒthəʊl] N agujero *m* (que deja un nudo en la madera)

knotted ['nɒtɪd] ADJ [*rope*] anudado, con nudos; [*scarf, tie*] atado con un nudo

knotty ['nɒtɪ] ADJ (*compar* **knottier**; *superl* **knottiest**) [*wood*] nudoso; (*fig*) [*problem*] espinoso

knout [naʊt] N knut *m*

know [nəʊ] (*pt* **knew**; *pp* **known**)

A TRANSITIVE VERB	C NOUN
B INTRANSITIVE VERB	

Ⓐ TRANSITIVE VERB

Look up set combinations such as **know the ropes, know one's stuff, know sth backward** *at the other word.*

1 = ***be aware of*** 1·1 [+ *facts, dates, etc*] saber; **to ~ the difference between …** saber la diferencia entre …; **she ~s a lot about chemistry** sabe mucho de química; **I don't ~ much about history** no sé mucho de historia; **I don't ~ much about that** no sé mucho de eso; **I ~ nothing about it** ◊ **I don't ~ anything about it** no sé nada de eso; **he ~s all the answers** lo sabe todo; **one minute you're leaving school, then before you ~ it, you've got a family to support** dejas el colegio y al minuto siguiente, antes de darte cuenta, tienes una familia que mantener

1·2 (*with clause*) **to ~ that** saber que; **to ~ why/when/where/if** saber por qué/cuándo/dónde/si; **to ~ how to do sth** saber hacer algo; **do you ~ how he did that?** ¿sabes cómo lo hizo?; **you ~ how it is** ya sabes cómo son las cosas; **you don't ~ how glad I am to see you** no sabes cuánto me alegro de verte; **I'll** *or* **I'd have you ~ that …** que sepas que …, para que te enteres, …; **you haven't time, as well he knew** no tienes tiempo, como él bien sabía; **you ~ as well as I do that …** sabes tan bien como yo que …; **to ~ what** saber qué *or* lo que; **I ~ what I said** ya sé qué *or* lo que dije; **he doesn't ~ what to do** no sabe qué hacer; **I don't ~ whether or not you've heard, but …** no sé si has oído o no pero …; ◆*IDIOM* **to ~ what's what** saber cuántas son cinco

1·3 (*in exclamations*) **I knew it!** ¡lo sabía!; **that's all you ~!*** ¡y más que podría yo contarte!; **don't I ~ it!** ¡a mí me lo vas a contar!; **"she's furious" — "don't I ~ it?"** —está furiosa —¡a mí me lo vas a contar!; **how was I to ~ that … ?** ¿cómo iba yo a saber que …?; **I should have ~n you'd mess things up!** debería haberme figurado *or* imaginado que ibas a estropear las cosas; **do you ~ what, I think she did it!** ¿sabes una cosa? creo que lo hizo ella; **I ~ what, let's drop in on Daphne!** ¡ya sé! ¡vamos a pasarnos por casa de Daphne!; **you ~ what you can do with it!*** ¡métela por donde te quepa!‡; **(well,) what do you ~!***

➤ LANGUAGE IN USE: know A6 16.1

¿qué te parece?, ¡fíjate!, ¡mira nomás! (*LAm*); what does he ~ about dictionaries! ¡qué sabrá él de diccionarios!; Peter, wouldn't you ~ it, can't come! Peter, como era de esperar, no puede venir

[1·4] to ~ to do sth*: does he ~ to feed the rabbits? ¿sabe que tiene que dar de comer a los conejos?

[2] [= *be acquainted with*] [+ *person, place*] conocer; [+ *subject*] saber; do you ~ him? ¿lo conoces?; to ~ French saber francés; to ~ one's classics/linguistic theory saberse los clásicos/la teoría lingüística; most of us ~ him only as a comedian la mayoría de nosotros lo conocemos sólo como comediante; civilization as we ~ it la civilización tal y como la conocemos; don't you ~ me better than that! ¿o es que no me conoces?, ¡como si no me conocieras!; to ~ sb by sight/name conocer a algn de vista/de nombre; to ~ sb by reputation haber oído hablar de algn; she knew him for a liar and a cheat sabía que era un mentiroso y un tramposo; they ~ each other from university se conocen de la universidad; if I ~ him, he'll say no me apuesto a que dice que no; she ~s her own mind sabe lo que quiere; ✦PROV it's not what you ~, it's who you ~ lo importante no es lo que sabes sino a quién conoces

[3] [*with infinitive*] I ~ him to be a liar sé que es un mentiroso; he is ~n to have been there se sabe que ha estado allí; I've never ~n him to smile nunca lo he visto sonreír; I've never ~n her to be wrong que yo sepa nunca se ha equivocado; it has never been ~n to happen no se tienen noticias de que haya pasado nunca; I don't ~ him to speak to no lo conozco personalmente

[4] [= *understand*] I don't ~ how you can say that no sé *or* no entiendo cómo puedes decir eso; you ~ what I mean ya me entiendes, ya sabes lo que quiero decir; I ~ the problem! conozco el problema; I ~ the problems that arise when ... sé los problemas que surgen cuando ...

[5] [= *recognize*] reconocer; he knew me at once me reconoció en seguida; I'd have ~n you anywhere te hubiese reconocido en cualquier parte; I knew him by his voice le reconocí por la voz; to ~ right from wrong saber distinguir el bien del mal; ✦IDIOM she ~s a good thing when she sees it* sabe reconocer algo bueno cuando lo ve

[6] [= *be certain*] I don't ~ if it has made things any easier no sé si ha facilitado las cosas; I don't ~ if *or* that it's a very good idea no sé si es una buena idea, no estoy seguro de que sea una buena idea; I don't ~ if I can do it no sé si puedo hacerlo

[7] [†† *sexually*] to ~ sb conocer a algn

[8] [*in set expressions*]

◆ to get to know sb (llegar a) conocer a algn; I'd like to get to ~ you better me gustaría (llegar a) conocerte mejor; we got to ~ each other during military service llegamos a conocernos bien durante la mili

◆ to get to know sth: as you get to ~ the piece better ... cuando conoces mejor la pieza ..., cuando estás más familiarizado con la pieza ...; get to ~ the area before buying a house estudia bien la zona antes de comprar una casa

◆ to let sb know ...: I'll let you ~ the price as soon as I can en cuanto sepa el precio te lo digo; let us ~ if you need help avísanos si necesitas ayuda; let me ~ if you can't come avísame si no puedes venir; let me ~ how you get on ya me contarás cómo te fue

(B) INTRANSITIVE VERB

➤ LANGUAGE IN USE: knowledge 2 15.4

[1] [*gen*] saber; I don't ~ no (lo) sé; yes, I ~ sí, ya lo sé; Mummy ~s best mamá sabe lo que te conviene; he doesn't ~ any better no sabe lo que hace; he thinks he's going to get the job, but I ~ better cree que va a conseguir el trabajo, pero yo sé mejor lo que cabe esperar; you ought to ~ better than to ... ya deberías saber que no se puede ...; Mary ~s better than to risk upsetting me Mary sabe demasiado bien que no le conviene que me enfade; how should I ~? ¿cómo iba yo a saberlo?; I ~, let's ... ya sé, vamos a ...; one never ~s ◊ you never ~ nunca se sabe; there's no (way of) ~ing no hay manera de saberlo; afterwards they just don't want to ~ (*in relationships*) después "si te he visto no me acuerdo"; (*in business*) después no quieren saber nada del asunto; who ~s? ¿quién sabe?; "was she annoyed about it?" — "I wouldn't ~" —¿se enfadó por eso? —¿y yo qué sé?; it's not easy, you ~ no es fácil, sabes; you ~, I think I'm beginning to like Richard ¿sabes? creo que me está empezando a gustar Richard; *see also* all B4

[2] [*in set expressions*]

◆ to know about: to ~ about sth/sb: did you ~ about Paul? ¿te has enterado de *or* sabes lo de Paul?; I didn't ~ about the accident no me había enterado de lo del accidente, no sabía nada de lo del accidente; I'd ~n about his illness for some time sabía lo de su enfermedad hacía tiempo; everything you always wanted to ~ about sex todo lo que siempre ha querido saber sobre el sexo; she ~s about cats ella entiende de gatos; "you must be delighted!" — "I don't ~ about that" ¡debes estar encantado! —no sé qué decirte; "you're a genius!" — "oh, I don't ~ about that" —¡eres un genio! —hombre, no sé qué decirte; "I'm taking tomorrow off" — "I don't ~ about that!" —mañana me tomo el día libre —no sé, habrá que ver; I don't ~ about you, but I think it's terrible a ti no sé, pero a mí me parece terrible

◆ to get to know about sth enterarse de algo

◆ to know of (= *be acquainted with*) conocer; I ~ of a nice little café conozco un pequeño café muy agradable; I don't ~ him but I ~ OF him no lo conozco pero he oído hablar de él; (= *be aware of*) I ~ of no reason why he should have committed suicide que yo sepa no tenía razones para suicidarse; the first I knew of it was when Pete told me lo primero que oí *or* supe del asunto fue lo que me dijo Pete; that was the first I knew of it esa fue la primera noticia que tuve del asunto; not that I ~ of que yo sepa, no

◆ to let sb know: we'll let you ~ ya te diremos lo que sea, ya te avisaremos; I'll let you ~ on Monday te diré lo que sea el lunes; why didn't you let me ~? ¿por qué no me lo dijiste?

(C) NOUN

to be in the know* (= *well-informed*) estar enterado; (= *privy to sth*) estar al tanto *or* al corriente; those not in the ~ los que no lo sabían

knowable ['nəʊəbl] ADJ conocible

know-all ['nəʊɔːl] N (*Brit pej*) sabelotodo *mf inv*, sabihondo/a *m/f*

know-how ['nəʊhaʊ] N (= *knowledge*) conocimientos *mpl*; (= *experience*) experiencia *f*; (= *expertise*) pericia *f*; technical ~ conocimientos *mpl* técnicos

knowing ['nəʊɪŋ] (A) ADJ (= *sharp*) astuto, sagaz; [*look, smile*] de complicidad

(B) N there's no ~ no hay modo de saberlo; there's no ~ what he'll do es imposible adivinar lo que hará

knowingly ['nəʊɪŋlɪ] ADV [1] (= *intentionally*) a sabiendas, adrede

[2] (= *archly*) [*smile, look, nod*] con complicidad

know-it-all ['nəʊɪtɔːl] N (*US pej*) sabelotodo *mf inv*, sabihondo/a *m/f*

➤ **knowledge** ['nɒlɪdʒ] N [1] (= *information, awareness, understanding*) conocimiento *m*; to deny all ~ of sth negar tener conocimiento de algo; to bring sth to sb's ~ poner a algn al tanto de algo; it has come to my ~ that ... me he enterado de que ...; it is common ~ that ... todo el mundo sabe que ..., es del dominio público que ...; to have no ~ of sth no tener conocimiento de algo; to (the best of) my ~ a mi entender, que yo sepa; not to my ~ que yo sepa, no; without my ~ sin saberlo yo

[2] (= *person's range of information*) conocimientos *mpl*; my ~ of Spanish mis conocimientos del español; he has some ~ of computers sabe algo de informática; to have a working ~ of dominar los principios esenciales de; I have a working ~ of Portuguese me defiendo en portugués; to have a thorough ~ of history conocer a fondo la historia

[3] (= *learning*) saber *m*; the pursuit of ~ la búsqueda del saber; the advance of ~ el progreso de la ciencia

knowledgeable ['nɒlɪdʒəbl] ADJ [*person*] (*gen*) informado; (*in specific subject*) entendido (about en); [*remark*] erudito; she's very ~ about antiques es muy entendida en antigüedades, sabe mucho de antigüedades

knowledgeably ['nɒlɪdʒəblɪ] ADV con conocimiento de causa, de manera erudita

known [nəʊn] (A) PP *of* know

(B) ADJ [1] [+ *person, fact*] conocido; he is ~ as Hercules es conocido por el nombre de Hércules; she wishes to be ~ as Jane Beattie quiere que se la conozca como Jane Beattie; he is ~ as a man of great charm tiene fama de tener mucho encanto; it soon became ~ that ... tardó poco en saberse que ...; to be ~ for sth ser conocido por algo; he is best ~ for his fiction se le conoce sobre todo por sus obras de ficción; he let it be ~ that ... dio a entender que ...; to make o.s. ~ to sb presentarse a algn; they made it ~ that they did not intend to prosecute dieron a saber que no tenían intención de interponer una acción judicial; to make one's presence ~ to sb hacer saber a algn que se ha llegado; to make one's wishes ~ hacer que se sepa lo que uno desea; he is ~ to be unreliable tiene fama de no ser una persona en la que se pueda confiar; the most dangerous snake ~ to man la serpiente más peligrosa de todas las conocidas por el hombre; it's well ~ that ... es bien sabido que ..., es de todos conocido que ...; *see also* know A3

[2] (= *acknowledged*) reconocido; a ~ expert un experto reconocido como tal; an internationally ~ expert un experto conocido en todo el mundo

knuckle ['nʌkl] N (*Anat*) nudillo *m*; [*of meat*] jarrete *m*; to rap sb's ~s ◊ rap sb over the ~s echar un rapapolvo a algn*; ✦IDIOM it was a bit near the ~ rayaba en la indecencia

►**knuckle down*** VI + ADV to ~ down (to work) ponerse a trabajar en serio

►**knuckle under** VI + ADV someterse, bajar la cerviz

knucklebone ['nʌkl,bəʊn] N nudillo *m*

knuckleduster ['nʌkl,dʌstəʳ] N puño *m* de hierro

knucklehead* ['nʌkl,hed] N cabeza *mf* hueca

knurl [nɜːl] Ⓐ N nudo *m*, protuberancia *f*; [*of coin*] cordón *m*
Ⓑ VT [+ *coin*] acordonar

knurled [nɜːld] ADJ nudoso; [*coin*] acordonado

KO* Ⓐ N ABBR = **knockout** (*pl* **KO's**) K.O. *m*, nocaut *m*
Ⓑ VT (*vb: pt, pp* **KO'd**) (*gen, Boxing*) dejar K.O., dejar fuera de combate

koala [kəʊ'ɑːlə] N (*also* **~ bear**) koala *m*

kohlrabi [kəʊl'rɑːbɪ] N (*pl* **kohlrabies**) colinabo *m*

kook* [kuːk] N (*US*) majareta *mf* (*Sp**), excéntrico/a *m/f*

kookaburra ['kʊkə,bʌrə] N kookaburra *m*

kookie*, **kooky*** ['kuːkɪ] ADJ (*compar* **kookier**; *superl* **kookiest**) (*US*) [*person*] chiflado*, majareta (*Sp**); [*idea*] descabellado, disparatado

Koran [kɒ'rɑːn] N Corán *m*, Alcorán *m*

Koranic [kɒ'rænɪk] ADJ coránico, alcoránico

Korea [kə'rɪə] N Corea *f*; **North/South ~** Corea *f* del Norte/Sur

Korean [kə'rɪən] Ⓐ ADJ coreano
Ⓑ N coreano/a *m/f*

korma ['kɔːʳmə] N *plato indio con nata y coco*

kosher ['kəʊʃəʳ] ADJ [1] (*lit*) autorizado por la ley judía, kosher
[2] (*) (= *genuine*) legal*

Kosova, **Kosovo** ['kɒsəvəʊ] N Kosovo *m*

Kosovan ['kɒsəvən], **Kosovar** ['kɒsəvɑːʳ] ADJ kosovar; **~ Albanian** albanokosovar *mf*

kowtow ['kaʊ'taʊ] VI (= *bow*) saludar humildemente; (= *be subservient*) **to ~ to sb** bajar la cabeza *or* doblegarse ante algn

KP N ABBR [1] (*US Mil*) = **kitchen police**
[2] (*Med*) = **Kaposi's sarcoma**

kph ABBR (= **kilometres per hour**) km/h, kph

Kraut‡ [kraʊt] (*offensive*) Ⓐ ADJ alemán
Ⓑ N alemán/ana *m/f*

Kremlin ['kremlɪn] N **the ~** el Kremlin

Kremlinologist [,kremlɪ'nɒlədʒɪst] N kremlinólogo/a *m/f*

Kremlinology [,kremlɪ'nɒlədʒɪ] N kremlinología *f*

krill [krɪl] N (*pl* **krill**) camarón *m* antártico

krugerrand ['kruːgə,rænd] N krugerrand *m*

krum(m)horn ['krʌmhɔːn] N cuerno *m*

Kruschev [kruːs'tʃɒf] N Jruschov

krypton [krɪptɒn] N criptón *m*

KS ABBR (*US*) = **Kansas**

Kt ABBR (*Brit*) = **Knight**

Kuala Lumpur ['kwɑːlə'lʊmpʊəʳ] N Kuala Lumpur *m*

kudos ['kjuːdɒs] N prestigio *m*

kummel ['kʊməl] N cúmel *m*, kummel *m*

kumquat ['kʌmkwɒt] N naranja *f* china

kung fu ['kʌŋ'fuː] N kung fu *m*

Kurd [kɜːd] N kurdo/a *m/f*

Kurdish ['kɜːdɪʃ] Ⓐ ADJ kurdo
Ⓑ N (*Ling*) kurdo *m*

Kurdistan [,kɜːdɪ'stæn] N Kurdistán *m*

Kuwait [kʊ'weɪt] N Kuwait *m*

Kuwaiti [kʊ'weɪtɪ] Ⓐ ADJ kuwaití
Ⓑ N kuwaití *mf*

kV, **kv** ABBR (= **kilovolt(s)**) kv

kW, **kw** ABBR (= **kilowatt(s)**) kw

kWh, **kW/h** ABBR (= **kilowatt-hour(s)**) kw/h

KY ABBR (*US*) = **Kentucky**

Kyrgyzstan [,kɜːgɪs'tɑːn] N Kirguizistán *m*

Ll

L, l [el] Ⓐ N (= *letter*) L, l *f*; **L for Lucy** L de Lorenzo
Ⓑ ABBR [1] (*in maps etc*) = **lake**
[2] (*Aut*) = **learner**; **L-plate** (*Brit*) placa *f* de la L (*de conductor en prácticas*); → DRIVING LICENCE/DRIVER'S LICENSE
[3] (= *garment size*) = **large**
[4] (= **left**) izq., izq.º
[5] (= **litre(s)**) l
[6] (*Ling*) = **Latin**

LA ABBR (*US*) [1] = **Los Angeles**
[2] = **Louisiana**

La. ABBR [1] (*US*) = **Louisiana**
[2] = **Lane**

Lab Ⓐ ADJ ABBR, N ABBR (*Brit Pol*) = **Labour**
Ⓑ ABBR (*Canada*) = **Labrador**

lab* [læb] Ⓐ N ABBR (= **laboratory**) laboratorio *m*
Ⓑ CPD ► **lab coat** N bata *f* de laboratorio ► **lab technician** N técnico/a *m/f* de laboratorio

label ['leɪbl] Ⓐ N [1] (*on merchandise, luggage, clothing*) etiqueta *f*; **sticky ~** etiqueta *f* adhesiva; **warning ~** etiqueta *f* de advertencia; *see also* **address C**, **luggage B**
[2] (= *brand*) marca *f*; **these products are sold under our own ~** estos productos se venden como parte de nuestra propia marca; *see also* **designer B**, **own-label**
[3] (*also* **record ~**) sello *m* discográfico; **the LP is on the A & M ~** el elepé es del sello discográfico A & M
[4] (*fig*) (= *classification*) etiqueta *f*; **it was comforting to be able to put a ~ on my illness** era reconfortante el poder ponerle una etiqueta a mi enfermedad
Ⓑ VT [1] (*lit*) etiquetar, poner etiqueta a; **I've just spent a whole day ~ling boxes** me he pasado el día etiquetando cajas *or* poniendo etiquetas a cajas; **the jar was not ~led** el bote no llevaba etiqueta, el bote no estaba etiquetado; **the bottle was ~led "poison"** la botella llevaba una etiqueta que decía "veneno"; **every packet must be clearly ~led** cada paquete debe llevar una etiqueta que indique claramente su contenido
[2] (*fig*) **to ~ sb (as) sth** calificar a algn de algo, tachar a algn de algo (*pej*); **he was ~led (as) a troublemaker** lo calificaron *or* lo tacharon de alborotador

labelling ['leɪbəlɪŋ] N etiquetado *m*, etiquetaje *m*

labia ['leɪbɪə] NPL *of* **labium**

labial ['leɪbɪəl] Ⓐ ADJ labial
Ⓑ N labial *f*

labiodental [,leɪbɪəʊ'dentəl] Ⓐ ADJ labiodental
Ⓑ N labiodental *f*

labiovelar [,leɪbɪəʊ'viːləʳ] Ⓐ ADJ labiovelar
Ⓑ N labiovelar *f*

labium ['leɪbɪəm] N (*pl* **labia**) labio *m*

labor ['leɪbəʳ] (*US*) Ⓐ N, VT, VI = **labour**
Ⓑ CPD ► **Labor Day** N Día *m* del Trabajo *or* de los Trabajadores ► **labor union** N sindicato *m*

> **LABOR DAY**
>
> *El* **Labor Day** *(Día del Trabajo o de los Trabajadores) es una festividad nacional en honor al trabajo, que se celebra en Estados Unidos y en Canadá el primer lunes de septiembre. Fue instaurada en 1894 por el Congreso de los Estados Unidos, después de que los trabajadores la solicitaran durante más de doce años. En la actualidad, ya sin las connotaciones políticas de sus orígenes y coincidiendo con el final del verano y con el principio del curso escolar, se celebran desfiles, mítines y comidas campestres.*

laboratory [lə'bɒrətərɪ, (*US*) 'læbrə,tɔːrɪ] Ⓐ N laboratorio *m*; *see also* **language B**
Ⓑ CPD de laboratorio ► **laboratory animal** N animal *m* de laboratorio ► **laboratory assistant** N ayudante *mf* de laboratorio ► **laboratory coat** N bata *f* de laboratorio ► **laboratory equipment** N equipo *m* de laboratorio ► **laboratory experiment** N experimento *m* de laboratorio ► **laboratory technician** N técnico/a *m/f* de laboratorio ► **laboratory test** N prueba *f* de laboratorio

laborer ['leɪbərəʳ] N (*US*) = **labourer**

laboring ['leɪbərɪŋ] ADJ (*US*) = **labouring**

labor-intensive ['leɪbərɪn'tensɪv] ADJ (*US*) = **labour-intensive**

laborious [lə'bɔːrɪəs] ADJ [*task, work, process*] laborioso; [*written style*] farragoso, poco claro

laboriously [lə'bɔːrɪəslɪ] ADV [*work*] laboriosamente; (*pej*) [*write*] farragosamente

laborite ['leɪbəraɪt] N (*US*) = **labourite**

labor-saving ['leɪbə,seɪvɪŋ] ADJ (*US*) = **labour-saving**

labour, **labor** (*US*) ['leɪbəʳ] Ⓐ N [1] (= *work, toil*) trabajo *m*; **the division of ~** la división del trabajo; **hard ~** (*Jur*) trabajos *mpl* forzados; **five years' hard ~** cinco años de trabajos forzados; **Ministry of Labour** Ministerio *m* de Trabajo; **to withdraw one's ~** ponerse en huelga; *see also* **manual A**
[2] (= *effort*) (*usu pl*) trabajo *m*, esfuerzo *m*; **he is starting to see the fruits of his ~s** está empezando a ver los frutos de su trabajo *or* sus esfuerzos
[3] (= *task*) trabajo *m*, tarea *f*; **a ~ of love** un trabajo realizado con amor, una tarea realizada con amor; **the ~s of Hercules** los trabajos de Hércules
[4] (*Ind*) (= *workers*) obreros *mpl*; (= *workforce*) mano *f* de obra; **capital and ~** la empresa y los obreros; **women were used as a source of cheap ~** se utilizaba a las mujeres como mano de obra barata; *see also* **child B**, **skilled 2**
[5] **Labour** (*Brit Pol*) el Partido Laborista, los laboristas; **to vote Labour** votar a los laboristas
[6] (= *birth*) parto *m*; **to be in ~** estar de parto; **to go into ~** ponerse de parto
Ⓑ VT [+ *point*] insistir en; **I think that's ~ing the point a bit** creo que eso es insistir demasiado en ese punto; **I won't ~ the point** no insistiré en ello
Ⓒ VI [1] (= *work*) trabajar; **to ~ at sth** trabajar en algo; **the ~ing classes** las clases trabajadoras; **a ~ing job** un trabajo de peón; **to ~ to do sth** esforzarse *or* afanarse por hacer algo
[2] (= *struggle*) [*engine*] sonar forzado; **to ~ up a hill** [*person, vehicle*] subir una cuesta con esfuerzo *or* dificultad; **you seem to be ~ing under a misapprehension** me parece que te estás equivocando; **to ~ under the misapprehension** *or* **illusion that** engañarse pensando que, creerse que
Ⓓ CPD ► **labour camp** N campamento *m* de trabajos forzados ► **labour costs** NPL costo *m* de la mano de obra ► **labour day** N Día *m* del Trabajo *or* de los Trabajadores (*en Reino Unido 1 mayo, en EE.UU., Canadá, primer lunes de septiembre*) ► **labour dispute** N conflicto *m* laboral ► **Labour Exchange** N (*Brit*) (*formerly*) Bolsa *f* de Trabajo ► **labour force** N (= *numbers, people*) mano *f* de obra ► **labour law** N (*as study*) derecho *m* laboral ► **labour market** N mercado *m* laboral, mercado *m* del trabajo ► **labour movement** N movimiento *m* obrero ► **labour pains** NPL (= *birth*) dolores *mpl* de parto ► **Labour party** N Partido *m* Laborista ► **labour relations** NPL relaciones *fpl* laborales ► **labour supply** N oferta *f* de mano de obra ► **labour ward** N sala *f* de partos

laboured, **labored** (*US*) ['leɪbəd] ADJ [*breathing*] pesado; [*style*] forzado; [*text*] farragoso, recargado

labourer, **laborer** (*US*) ['leɪbərəʳ] N (*on roads etc*) peón *m*, obrero/a *m/f*; (= *farm labourer*) trabajador(a) *m/f* del campo, peón *m*; (= *day labourer*) jornalero/a *m/f*; (*Agr*) bracero/a *m/f*; **bricklayer's ~** peón *m* de albañil

labouring, **laboring** (*US*) ['leɪbərɪŋ] ADJ *see* **labour C1**

labour-intensive, **labor-intensive** (*US*) ['leɪbərɪn'tensɪv] ADJ que emplea mucha mano de obra; **~ industry** industria *f* que emplea mucha mano de obra

labourite, **laborite** (*US*) ['leɪbəraɪt] N (*pej*) laborista *mf*

labour-saving, **labor-saving** (*US*) ['leɪbə,seɪvɪŋ] ADJ que ahorra trabajo; **~ device** aparato *m* que ahorra trabajo

labrador ['læbrədɔː] N labrador *m*

laburnum [lə'bɜːnəm] N lluvia *f* de oro, codeso *m*

labyrinth ['læbərɪnθ] N laberinto *m*

labyrinthine [,læbə'rɪnθaɪn] ADJ laberíntico

lac [læk] N laca *f*

lace [leɪs] Ⓐ N [1] (= *open fabric*) encaje *m*; (*as trimming*) puntilla *f*; [*of gold, silver*] galón *m*
[2] [*of shoe, corset*] cordón *m*, agujeta *f* (*Mex*)
Ⓑ CPD de encaje
Ⓒ VT [1] (*also* ~ **up**) [+ *shoes*] atar (los cordones de)
[2] (= *fortify with spirits*) [+ *drink*] echar licor a; **a drink ~d with brandy** una bebida con un chorrito de coñac; **a drink ~d with cyanide** una bebida envenenada con *or* con dosis de cianuro
[3] (*fig*) **the story is ~d with irony** la historia tiene una vena irónica, la historia está teñida de ironía

►**lace into*** VI + PREP **to ~ into sb** dar una paliza a algn

lace-maker ['leɪs,meɪkəʳ] N encajero/a *m/f*

lacemaking ['leɪs,meɪkɪŋ] N labor *f* de encaje

lacerate ['læsəreɪt] VT (*Med*) lacerar; [+ *feelings*] herir

laceration [,læsə'reɪʃən] N laceración *f*

lace-up ['leɪsʌp] ADJ (*Brit*) [*shoes etc*] de cordones, con cordones

lace-ups ['leɪsʌps] NPL (*Brit*) (*also* **lace-up shoes**) zapatos *mpl* con cordones

lachrymal ['lækrɪməl] ADJ lagrimal

lachrymose ['lækrɪməʊs] ADJ lacrimoso, lloroso

lack [læk] Ⓐ N falta *f*; (*frm*) carencia *f*; **~ of funds** falta *f* de fondos; **there was no ~ of applicants for the job** no faltaban candidatos al puesto; **there is no ~ of money** no faltaba dinero; **despite his ~ of experience, he got the job** a pesar de su falta de experiencia, consiguió el trabajo; **there was a complete ~ of interest in my proposals** hubo una absoluta falta de interés por mis propuestas; **for ~ of**: **the charges were dropped for ~ of evidence** retiraron la acusación por falta de pruebas; **malevolence, for ~ of a better word** malevolencia, a falta de una palabra mejor; **if I didn't get them to agree it wasn't for ~ of trying** si no conseguí que accedieran no fue por falta de intentarlo
Ⓑ VT **he ~s confidence** le falta confianza en sí mismo, carece de confianza en sí mismo (*frm*); **they ~ the necessary skills** les faltan los requisitos necesarios, carecen de los requisitos necesarios (*frm*); **what he ~s in ability he makes up for in enthusiasm** lo que le falta en habilidad, lo suple con entusiasmo; **he does not ~ talent** talento no le falta, no carece de talento (*frm*)
Ⓒ VI [1] (= *be missing, deficient*) **to be ~ing** faltar; **even if evidence is ~ing** incluso si faltan las pruebas, incluso si se carece de pruebas (*frm*); **this information was ~ing from the report** esta información no figuraba *or* no constaba en el informe; **to be ~ing in sth**: **he is ~ing in confidence** le falta confianza en sí mismo, carece de confianza en sí mismo (*frm*); **he is completely ~ing in imagination** no tiene nada de imaginación, carece completamente de imaginación (*frm*); **I find her singularly ~ing in charm** la encuentro especialmente falta *or* (*frm*) carente de encanto; **it is a quality that we find ~ing in so many politicians today** es una cualidad de la que nos parece que carecen tantos políticos hoy en día; **innovation has been sadly** *or* **sorely ~ing** ha habido una falta absoluta de innovación; **her education is sadly ~ing** su educación es muy deficiente
[2] (= *want*) **they ~ for nothing** no les falta nada, no carecen de nada (*frm*)

lackadaisical [,lækə'deɪzɪkəl] ADJ (= *careless*) descuidado, informal; (= *lazy*) perezoso, flojo (*LAm*); (= *dreamy*) distraído

lackey ['lækɪ] N (*gen*) lacayo *m* (*also fig*)

lacklustre, **lackluster** (*US*) ['læk,lʌstəʳ] ADJ [1] (= *dull*) [*surface*] sin brillo, deslustrado; [*eyes*] apagado
[2] (*fig*) [*performance, style*] mediocre, deslucido; **he fought a ~ election campaign** realizó una campaña electoral mediocre *or* deslucida

laconic [lə'kɒnɪk] ADJ lacónico

laconically [lə'kɒnɪkəlɪ] ADV lacónicamente

lacquer ['lækəʳ] Ⓐ N laca *f*; (*also* **hair** ~) laca *f* (para el pelo); (*for nails*) esmalte *m* (de uñas), laca *f* (de uñas)
Ⓑ VT [+ *wood*] lacar, barnizar con laca; **to ~ one's hair** ponerse *or* echarse laca en el pelo; **to ~ one's nails** darse esmalte en las uñas

lacquered ['lækəd] ADJ [*surface*] lacado, laqueado, barnizado con laca; [*hair*] con laca; [*nails*] con esmalte

lacrosse [lə'krɒs] N lacrosse *m*

lactate ['lækteɪt] VI lactar

lactation [læk'teɪʃən] N lactancia *f*

lacteal ['læktɪəl] ADJ lácteo

lactic ['læktɪk] Ⓐ ADJ láctico
Ⓑ CPD ► **lactic acid** N ácido *m* láctico

lacto-ovo-vegetarian [,læktəʊ,əʊvəʊ,vedʒɪ'teərɪən] N lacto-ovo-vegetariano/a *m/f*

lactose ['læktəʊs] N lactosa *f*

lacto-vegetarian [,læktəʊ,vedʒɪ'teərɪən] N lacto-vegetariano/a *m/f*

lacuna [lə'kjuːnə] N (*pl* **lacunas** *or* **lacunae** [lə'kjuːniː]) laguna *f*

lacustrine [lə'kʌstraɪn] ADJ lacustre

lacy ['leɪsɪ] ADJ (*compar* **lacier**; *superl* **laciest**) (= *of lace*) de encaje; (= *like lace*) como de encaje; **a ~ dress** un vestido lleno de encajes

lad [læd] N (= *young man, boy*) muchacho *m*, chico *m*, chaval *m* (*Sp**), pibe *m* (*S. Cone**), cabro *m* (*Chile**), chavo *m* (*Mex**); (*in stable etc*) mozo *m*; **come on, ~s!** ¡vamos, muchachos!; **when I was a ~** cuando yo era un muchacho, cuando yo era joven; **he's only a ~** no es más que un muchacho, es aún muy joven; **you need some exercise, my ~** tú, chico *or* muchacho, necesitas hacer algo de ejercicio; **he's gone for a drink with the ~s** (*Brit**) ha salido a tomar algo con los muchachos *or* (*Sp*) con sus amiguetes; **he just wants to be one of the ~s** lo que quiere es que su círculo de amigos lo acepte; **he's a bit of a ~** (*Brit*) (*fig*) es un gamberrete, está hecho una buena pieza*

ladder ['lædəʳ] Ⓐ N [1] escalera *f* de mano; *see also* **extension B**, **rope C**
[2] (*fig*) escala *f*, jerarquía *f*; **the social ~** la escala social; **it's a first step up the ~** es el primer peldaño; **it's a first step up the ~ of success** es el primer paso hacia el éxito; **to be at the top of the ~** estar en la cumbre de su profesión *etc*
[3] (*Brit*) (*in stockings*) carrera *f*
Ⓑ VT (*Brit*) [+ *stocking, tights*] hacer una carrera en
Ⓒ VI (*Brit*) [*stocking*] hacerse una carrera

ladderproof ['lædəpruːf] ADJ (*Brit*) [*stocking, tights*] indesmallable

laddie* ['lædɪ] N (*esp Scot*) = **lad**

laddish* ['lædɪʃ] ADJ (*Brit*) macho *adj inv*

lade [leɪd] (*pt* **laded**; *pp* **laden**) Ⓐ VT cargar (**with** de)
Ⓑ VI tomar cargamento

laden ['leɪdn] ADJ **~ with** cargado de; **trucks ~ with arms** camiones *mpl* cargados (hasta los topes) de armas; **plates ~ with food** platos *mpl* hasta arriba de *or* repletos de comida; **she was ~ with shopping** iba cargando con un montón de compra; **the branches were ~ with fruit** las ramas estaban llenas *or* repletas de frutos; **a report heavily ~ with scientific jargon** un informe con una enorme cantidad de jerga científica

la-di-da* ['lɑːdɪ'dɑː] (*pej*) Ⓐ ADJ [*person, voice*] afectado, cursi*, repipi (*Sp**)
Ⓑ ADV [*talk etc*] de manera afectada, con afectación

lading ['leɪdɪŋ] N cargamento *m*, flete *m*; **bill of ~** conocimiento *m* de embarque

ladle ['leɪdl] Ⓐ N (*Culin*) cazo *m*, cucharón *m*
Ⓑ VT (*also* ~ **out**) servir con cucharón

►**ladle out** VT + ADV (*fig*) [+ *money, advice*] repartir generosamente

lady ['leɪdɪ] Ⓐ N [1] (= *woman*) señora *f*, dama *f* (*frm*); **ladies' clothing** ropa *f* de señora; **ladies' hairdresser** peluquero/a *m/f* de señoras; **ladies first** las damas *or* las señoras primero; **ladies and gentlemen!** ¡señoras y señores!, ¡damas y caballeros!; **"ladies only"** "sólo para Señoras"; **cleaning ~** mujer *f or* señora *f* de la limpieza; **First Lady** Primera Dama *f*; **the ~ of the house** la señora de la casa; **leading ~** (*Theat*) primera actriz *f*; (*Cine*) protagonista *f*; **I'm not used to being a ~ of leisure** no estoy acostumbrada a la vida ociosa; **he's a ladies' man** es un donjuán; **an old ~** una señora mayor; **a little old ~** una viejecita; **this is the young ~ who served me** ésta es la señorita *or* la joven que me sirvió; **now listen here, young ~!** ¡escúchame, jovencita!
[2] (= *educated woman, noblewoman*) dama *f*; **she's no ~** no es lo que se dice una dama; **she's a real ~** es toda una dama; **society ~** dama *f* de la alta sociedad
[3] (*in titles*) **Lady Jane Grey** Lady Jane Grey; ✦***IDIOMS*** **she liked to play Lady Bountiful** le gustaba hacerse la rumbosa; **she thinks she's Lady Muck!*** ¡se cree toda una duquesa!
[4] (*US**) (*as form of address*) señora *f*; **what seems to be the trouble, ~?** ¿qué ocurre, señora?
[5] (†) (= *wife*) señora *f*, esposa *f*; **your good ~** su esposa, su señora; **my ~ wife** mi señora esposa
[6] (*Rel*) **Our Lady** Nuestra Señora
[7] **the ladies** (= *lavatory*) el servicio (de señoras), el baño (de señoras) (*LAm*); **"Ladies"** "Señoras", "Damas"
Ⓑ CPD ► **ladies' room** N servicio *m* de señoras, baño *m* de señoras (*LAm*) ► **Lady Chapel** N (*Rel*) capilla *f* de la Virgen ► **Lady Day** N (*Brit*) día *m* de la Anunciación (*25 de marzo*) ► **lady doctor** N doctora *f*, médico *f* ► **lady friend** N amiga *f* ► **lady mayoress** N alcaldesa *f* ► **lady's fingers** NPL (*Bot*) (*with sing or pl vb*) quingombó *m* ► **lady's maid** N doncella *f*

ladybird ['leɪdɪbɜːd], **ladybug** (*US*) ['leɪdɪbʌg] N (= *beetle*) mariquita *f*, vaca *f* de San Antón*

lady-in-waiting ['leɪdɪɪn'weɪtɪŋ] N (*pl* **ladies-in-waiting**) dama *f* de honor

ladykiller ['leɪdɪˌkɪləʳ] N ladrón *m* de corazones, donjuán* *m*, tenorio* *m*

ladylike ['leɪdɪlaɪk] ADJ elegante, fino

lady-love ['leɪdɪlʌv] N (*liter or hum*) amada *f*

ladyship ['leɪdɪʃɪp] N **Her Ladyship/Your Ladyship** su señoría *f*

LAFTA ['læftə] N ABBR (= **Latin-American Free Trade Association**) ALALC *f*

lag[1] [læg] Ⓐ N (*also* **time ~**) (= *delay*) retraso *m*; (= *interval*) lapso *m* de tiempo, intervalo *m*
Ⓑ VI (*also* **~ behind**) (= *not progress*) quedarse atrás; (*in pace*) rezagarse, quedarse atrás; **we ~ behind in space exploration** nos hemos quedado atrás en la exploración del espacio; **English students are ~ging behind their European counterparts** los alumnos ingleses se están quedando atrás con respecto a sus homólogos europeos, los alumnos ingleses van a la zaga de sus homólogos europeos

lag[2] [læg] VT [+ *boiler, pipes*] revestir (**with** de)

lag[3] [læg] N (*esp Brit*) **old ~** (= *old prisoner*) (preso/a *m/f*) veterano/a *m/f*; (= *ex-prisoner*) ex-presidiario/a *m/f*

lager ['lɑːgəʳ] Ⓐ N cerveza *f* rubia
Ⓑ CPD ► **lager lout** N (*Brit**) gamberro *m* borracho, gamberro *m* de la litrona (*Sp*)

laggard ['lægəd] N (= *having fallen behind*) rezagado/a *m/f*; (= *idler*) holgazán/ana *m/f*

lagging ['lægɪŋ] N (*Tech*) revestimiento *m* calorífugo

lagoon [lə'guːn] N laguna *f*

Lagos ['leɪgɒs] N Lagos *m*

lah [lɑː] N (*Mus*) la *m*

lah-di-dah [ˌlɑːdɪ'dɑː] = **la-di-da**

laicize ['leɪɪsaɪz] VT laicizar

laid [leɪd] PT, PP *of* **lay**[1]

laid-back* [ˌleɪd'bæk] ADJ [*person, attitude*] (= *easy-going*) relajado; (= *casual*) despreocupado; [*party*] tranquilo

lain [leɪn] PP *of* **lie**[2]

lair [leəʳ] N guarida *f*, cubil *m*

laird [leəd] N (*Scot*) terrateniente *m*

laissez faire ['leɪseɪ'feəʳ] Ⓐ N laissez-faire *m*, liberalismo *m* económico
Ⓑ ADJ [*attitude, approach, policy*] liberal, liberalista

laity ['leɪɪtɪ] N **the ~** los seglares, los legos

lake[1] [leɪk] Ⓐ N lago *m*; **the Lakes** (*Brit*) = **the Lake District**; **Lake Michigan** el Lago Michigan; **the Great Lakes** los Grandes Lagos; **wine ~** excedentes *mpl* de vino; ✦**IDIOM oh, go and jump in a ~!*** ¡que te zurzan!*, ¡vete a freír espárragos!*
Ⓑ CPD ► **the Lake District** N el País de los Lagos (*región de lagos en el noroeste de Inglaterra*) ► **lake dweller** N (*Hist*) *habitante de una población lacustre* ► **lake dwelling** N vivienda *f* lacustre

lake[2] [leɪk] N (= *colour*) laca *f*

lakeside ['leɪksaɪd] Ⓐ N ribera *f* de(l) lago, orilla *f* de(l) lago
Ⓑ CPD [*restaurant, village, home*] a la orilla del lago, junto al lago

Lallans ['lælənz] N *dialecto y lengua literaria de las Tierras Bajas (Lowlands) de Escocia*

lam[1]* [læm] Ⓐ VT pegar, dar una paliza a
Ⓑ VI **to ~ into sb** dar una paliza a algn

lam[2]* [læm] N **to be on the ~** (*US*) ser fugitivo de la justicia

lama ['lɑːmə] N lama *m*

lamb [læm] Ⓐ N (= *animal*) cordero *m*; (*older*) borrego *m*; (= *meat*) (carne *f* de) cordero *m*; **the Lamb of God** el Cordero de Dios; **my poor ~!** ¡pobrecito!; **he surrendered like a ~** no ofreció la menor resistencia; **he took it like a ~** ni siquiera rechistó; ✦**IDIOM to go like a ~ to the slaughter** ir como borrego al matadero
Ⓑ VI parir
Ⓒ CPD ► **lamb chop** N chuleta *f* de cordero ► **lamb's lettuce** N valeriana *f* ► **lamb's wool** N = **lambswool**

lambada [ˌlæm'bɑːdə] N lambada *f*

lambast(e) [læm'beɪst] VT fustigar, despellejar

lambing ['læmɪŋ] N parición *f* de las ovejas, época *f* del parto de las ovejas; **~ time** ◊ **the ~ season** la parición de las ovejas, la época del parto de las ovejas

lamb-like ['læmlaɪk] ADJ manso como un cordero

lambskin ['læmskɪn] N (piel *f* de) cordero *m*

lambswool ['læmzwʊl] N lambswool *m*, lana *f* de cordero

lame [leɪm] Ⓐ ADJ (*compar* **lamer**; *superl* **lamest**)
[1] (*physically*) cojo; **to be ~** (*permanently*) ser cojo, cojear; (*temporarily*) cojear, estar cojo; **to go ~** [*animal*] (*permanently*) quedar cojo; (*temporarily*) empezar a cojear; **to be ~ in one foot** (*permanently*) ser cojo de un pie, cojear de un pie; (*temporarily*) estar cojo de un pie, cojear de un pie; **to be left ~** quedarse cojo
[2] (= *weak*) [*excuse*] débil, pobre; [*attempt*] patético; [*joke*] malo; [*argument, performance*] flojo, pobre
Ⓑ N **the ~** los lisiados
Ⓒ VT lisiar, dejar lisiado; **to be ~d** quedar lisiado
Ⓓ CPD ► **lame duck** N (= *person*) caso *m* perdido; **the project was a ~ duck** el proyecto estaba condenado al fracaso

lamé ['lɑːmeɪ] N lamé *m*; **gold ~** lamé *m* de oro, lamé *m* dorado

lamely ['leɪmlɪ] ADV [*say*] de forma poco convincente; [*try*] sin convicción

lameness ['leɪmnɪs] N [1] [*of person, horse, leg*] cojera *f*, renquera *f*
[2] (*fig*) pobreza *f*

lament [lə'ment] Ⓐ N (= *poem*) elegía *f*, endecha *f* (**for** por); (= *song*) canción *f* elegíaca, endecha *f*; (= *grief*) lamento *m*
Ⓑ VT [+ *absence, lack, loss*] llorar, lamentar; **she was ~ing her misfortune** se lamentaba de su infortunio; **to ~ sb** llorar la muerte de algn, llorar a algn; **it is much to be ~ed that ...** es de lamentar que ... + *subjun*
Ⓒ VI **to ~ over sth** [+ *passing, loss*] llorar algo, lamentarse de algo; **to ~ for sb** llorar a algn

lamentable ['læməntəbl] ADJ lamentable

lamentably ['læməntəblɪ] ADV lamentablemente; **there is, ~, nothing we can do** lamentablemente, no podemos hacer nada; **to fail ~ to do sth** fracasar estrepitosamente *or* de manera lamentable en el intento de hacer algo; **there are still ~ few women surgeons** es de lamentar *or* es lamentable que todavía existan muy pocas cirujanas

lamentation [ˌlæmən'teɪʃən] N lamentación *f*

laminate Ⓐ ['læmɪneɪt] VT laminar
Ⓑ ['læmɪnɪt] N laminado *m*

laminated ['læmɪneɪtɪd] ADJ [*metal*] laminado; [*glass*] inastillable; [*wood*] contrachapado; [*document*] plastificado

lamp [læmp] Ⓐ N (= *table lamp, floor lamp*) lámpara *f*; (*hand-held*) linterna *f*; (*in street*) farol *m*, farola *f*; (*Aut, Rail etc*) faro *m*; (= *bulb*) bombilla *f*, bombillo *m* (*LAm*), foco *m* (*LAm*)
Ⓑ CPD ► **lamp bracket** N brazo *m* de lámpara ► **lamp chimney, lamp glass** N tubo *m* de lámpara ► **lamp holder** N portalámparas *m inv* ► **lamp standard** N poste *m* de farola

lampblack ['læmpblæk] N negro *m* de humo

lamplight ['læmplaɪt] N luz *f* de (la) lámpara; [*of street lamp*] luz *f* de(l) farol; **by ~** ◊ **in the ~** a la luz de la lámpara/del farol

lamplighter ['læmpˌlaɪtəʳ] N (*Hist*) farolero *m*

lampoon [læm'puːn] Ⓐ N sátira *f*
Ⓑ VT satirizar

lamppost ['læmppəʊst] N farol *m*, farola *f*

lamprey ['læmprɪ] N lamprea *f*

lampshade ['læmpʃeɪd] N pantalla *f* (de lámpara)

LAN [læn] N ABBR (*Comput*) (= **local area network**) RAL *f*

Lancastrian [læŋ'kæstrɪən] Ⓐ ADJ de Lancashire
Ⓑ N nativo/a *m/f* de Lancashire, habitante *mf* de Lancashire

lance [lɑːns] Ⓐ N (= *weapon*) lanza *f*; (*Med*) lanceta *f*
Ⓑ VT (*Med*) abrir con lanceta
Ⓒ CPD ► **lance corporal** N (*Brit*) soldado *mf* de primera

Lancelot ['lɑːnslət] N Lanzarote

lancer ['lɑːnsəʳ] N lancero *m*; **~s** (= *dance*) lanceros *mpl*

lancet ['lɑːnsɪt] Ⓐ N lanceta *f*
Ⓑ CPD ► **lancet arch** N ojiva *f* aguda ► **lancet window** N ventana *f* ojival

Lancs. [læŋks] ABBR (*Brit*) = **Lancashire**

land [lænd] Ⓐ N [1] (= *not sea*) tierra *f*; **~ ho** ◊ **~ ahoy!** ¡tierra a la vista!; **to go/travel by ~** ir/viajar por tierra; **dry ~** tierra *f* firme; **on dry ~** en tierra firme; **to make ~** (*Naut*) tomar tierra; **there was action at sea, on ~, and in the air** se combatió en mar, tierra y aire; **to sight ~** divisar tierra
[2] (*Agr, Constr*) (= *ground*) tierra *f*, tierras *fpl*; **160 acres of ~** 160 acres de tierra; **agricultural ~** tierra(s) *f(pl)* agrícola(s), terreno *m* agrícola; **grazing ~** tierra(s) *f(pl)* de pastoreo, tierra(s) *f(pl)* para pastos; **the lay** *or* **lie of the ~** (*lit*) la configuración del terreno; **a piece/plot of ~** un terreno, una parcela; **the ~** (*Agr*) la tierra; **to live off the ~** vivir de la tierra; **to work on the ~** trabajar *or* cultivar la tierra; **the drift from the ~** el éxodo rural; ✦**IDIOMS to see how the ~ lies** ◊ **get the lie** *or* **lay of the ~** tantear el terreno; *see also* **arable A**
[3] (= *property*) tierras *fpl*; **get off my ~!** ¡fuera de mis tierras!; **to own ~** poseer tierras
[4] (*Geog*) (= *region*) **desert/equatorial/temperate ~s** tierras *fpl* desérticas/ecuatoriales/templadas
[5] (= *nation, country*) país *m*; **a ~ of opportunity/contrasts** un país de oportunidades/contrastes; **throughout the ~** en todo el país; ✦**IDIOMS to be in the ~ of the living** (*hum*) estar en el mundo de los vivos, estar vivito y coleando (*hum*); **the ~ of milk and honey** el paraíso terrenal; **to be in the Land of Nod** (*hum*) estar dormido, estar roque (*Sp**); *see also* **fantasy 1, native C, promise B1**
Ⓑ VI [1] (*after flight*) [*plane*] aterrizar; (*on water*) amerizar, amarizar; (*on moon*) alunizar; **to ~ on sth** [*bird, insect*] posarse en algo; **the Americans were the first to ~ on the moon** los americanos fueron los primeros en llegar a la luna
[2] (*from boat*) [*passenger*] desembarcar
[3] (*after fall, jump, throw*) caer; **I ~ed awkwardly** caí en una mala postura; **the hat ~ed in my lap** el sombrero me cayó en el regazo;

to ~ on one's back caer de espaldas; **to ~ on one's feet** (*lit*) caer de pie; (*fig*) salir adelante

4 (*) (*also* **~ up**) (*in prison, hospital*) ir a parar* (**in** a), acabar (**in** en); **he ~ed in hospital** fue a parar al hospital*, acabó en el hospital

Ⓒ VT 1 (= *disembark, unload*) [+ *passengers*] desembarcar; [+ *cargo*] descargar; **vessels will have to ~ their catch at designated ports** los buques tendrán que descargar la pesca en los puertos designados

2 (= *bring down*) [+ *plane*] hacer aterrizar

3 (= *catch*) [+ *fish*] pescar, conseguir pescar; (*fig*) [+ *job, contract*] conseguir; [+ *prize*] obtener

4 (*) 4·1 (= *put, dump*) **to ~ a blow on sb's chin** ◊ **~ sb a blow on the chin** asestar a algn un golpe en la barbilla; **they ~ed the children on me** me endilgaron *or* endosaron a los niños*

4·2 **to ~ sb in sth**: **his comments ~ed him in court** sus comentarios hicieron que acabara en los tribunales, sus comentarios hicieron que fuera a parar a los tribunales*; **his extravagant lifestyle soon ~ed him in debt** su estilo de vida extravagante pronto hizo que endeudase; **to ~ sb in it*** fastidiar *or* jorobar a algn pero bien*; **it ~ed me in a mess** me metió en un lío*; **to ~ sb in trouble** causar problemas a algn; **to ~ o.s. in trouble** meterse en problemas

4·3 (= *encumber*) **to ~ sb with sth/sb** endilgar algo/a algn a algn*, endosar algo/a algn a algn*; **I got ~ed with the job** me endilgaron *or* endosaron el trabajo*; **I got ~ed with him for two hours** me lo endilgaron *or* endosaron dos horas*; **getting overdrawn could ~ you with big bank charges** girar al descubierto te puede ocasionar enormes intereses bancarios; **how did you ~ yourself with all these debts?** ¿cómo acabaste tan endeudado?; **I've ~ed myself with a bit of a problem** me he metido en un apuro

Ⓓ CPD ► **land agent** N administrador(a) *m/f* de fincas ► **land defences** NPL defensas *fpl* de tierra ► **land forces** NPL fuerzas *fpl* de tierra ► **land management** N administración *f* de fincas ► **land reclamation** N reclamación *f* de tierras ► **land reform** N reforma *f* agraria ► **land register**, **land registry** N (*Brit*) catastro *m*, registro *m* catastral, registro *m* de la propiedad inmobiliaria ► **Land Rover**® N (*Aut*) (vehículo *m*) todo terreno *m* ► **land tax** N contribución *f* territorial ► **land use** N uso *m* de la tierra

►**land up*** Ⓐ VI + ADV (= *end up*) ir a parar*, acabar; **he ~ed up in prison** fue a parar a la cárcel*, acabó en la cárcel; **so eventually we ~ed up in Madrid** así es que al final fuimos a parar a Madrid*, así es que al final acabamos en Madrid

Ⓑ VT + ADV **this sort of behaviour could ~ you up in prison** este tipo de comportamiento puede llevarte a la cárcel

LAND OF HOPE AND GLORY

Land of Hope and Glory *es el título de una canción patriótica británica. Para muchos ciudadanos, sobre todo en Inglaterra, es un símbolo más del país, casi como el himno o la bandera nacional. Se suele entonar al final del congreso anual del Partido Conservador y en la última noche de los* **Proms**, *junto con otras conocidas canciones patrióticas.*

⇨ *Ver tb* PROM

landau [ˈlændɔː] N landó *m*

landed [ˈlændɪd] Ⓐ ADJ [*person*] hacendado, que posee tierras

Ⓑ CPD ► **landed property** N bienes *mpl* raíces *or* inmuebles ► **the landed gentry** N los terratenientes, la aristocracia rural

landfall [ˈlændfɔːl] N (*Naut*) recalada *f*, aterrada *f*

landfill [ˈlændfɪl] Ⓐ N entierro *m* de basuras

Ⓑ CPD ► **landfill site** N vertedero *m* de basuras

landholder [ˈlænd,həʊldəʳ] N terrateniente *mf*

landing [ˈlændɪŋ] Ⓐ N 1 (*Aer*) [*of aircraft, spacecraft*] (*on land*) aterrizaje *m*; (*on sea*) amerizaje *m*, amarizaje *m*; (*on moon*) alunizaje *m*; *see also* **crash E**, **emergency B**, **forced A2**

2 (*Mil*) [*of troops*] desembarco *m*; **the Normandy ~s** (*Hist*) los desembarcos de Normandía

3 (*Archit*) (*in house*) descansillo *m*, rellano *m*

Ⓑ CPD ► **landing card** N tarjeta *f* de desembarque ► **landing craft** N lancha *f* de desembarco ► **landing field** N campo *m* de aterrizaje ► **landing gear** N (*Aer*) tren *m* de aterrizaje ► **landing ground** N campo *m* de aterrizaje ► **landing lights** NPL luces *fpl* de aterrizaje ► **landing net** N (*Fishing*) salabardo *m*, manga *f*, cuchara *f* ► **landing party** N (*Naut*) destacamento *m* de desembarco ► **landing run** N recorrido *m* de aterrizaje ► **landing stage** N (*Naut*) desembarcadero *m* ► **landing strip** N (*Aer*) pista *f* de aterrizaje ► **landing wheels** NPL (*Aer*) ruedas *fpl* de aterrizaje

landlady [ˈlænd,leɪdɪ] N [*of flat*] casera *f*, dueña *f*; (*Brit*) [*of boarding house*] patrona *f*; (*Brit*) [*of pub*] (= *owner*) dueña *f*, patrona *f*; (= *manager*) encargada *f*, jefa *f*

landless [ˈlændlɪs] Ⓐ ADJ [*peasant*] sin tierras

Ⓑ NPL **the ~** los campesinos sin tierra

landlessness [ˈlændlɪsnɪs] N situación *f* de los desposeídos (de tierra)

landlocked [ˈlændlɒkt] ADJ sin acceso al mar

landlord [ˈlændlɔːd] N [*of property, land*] propietario *m*, dueño *m*; [*of flat*] casero *m*, dueño *m*; (*Brit*) [*of boarding house*] patrón *m*; [*of inn*] posadero *m*, mesonero *m*; (*Brit*) [*of pub*] (= *owner*) dueño *m*, patrón *m*; (= *manager*) encargado *m*, jefe *m*

landlubber [ˈlænd,lʌbəʳ] N marinero *m* de agua dulce

landmark [ˈlændmɑːk] N 1 (*Naut*) marca *f*, señal *f* fija; (= *boundary mark*) mojón *m*

2 (= *well-known thing*) punto *m* de referencia

3 (= *important event*) hito *m*; **to be a ~ in history** marcar un hito en la historia, ser un hito histórico; **it was a ~ case** (*Jur*) el caso sentó precedente

landmass [ˈlænd,mæs] N masa *f* continental

landmine [ˈlændmaɪn] N mina *f* terrestre

landowner [ˈlænd,əʊnəʳ] N terrateniente *mf*, hacendado/a *m/f*

landowning [ˈlændəʊnɪŋ] ADJ terrateniente

landscape [ˈlænskeɪp] Ⓐ N 1 (= *scenery*) paisaje *m*

2 (*Art*) paisaje *m*

3 (*fig*) panorama *m*; **the political ~** el panorama político; **the entire ~ of broadcasting has changed** en el mundo de la radio- y tele-difusión el panorama ha cambiado por completo

Ⓑ VT [+ *terrain, grounds*] ajardinar; [+ *park, garden*] diseñar

Ⓒ CPD ► **landscape architect** N arquitecto/a *m/f* paisajista ► **landscape architecture** N arquitectura *f* paisajista ► **landscape format** N (*Typ, Comput, Phot*) formato *m* apaisado; **in ~ format** en formato apaisado ► **landscape gardener** N jardinero/a *m/f* paisajista ► **landscape gardening** N jardinería *f* paisajista ► **landscape painter** N paisajista *mf* ► **landscape painting** N (= *picture*) paisaje *m*

landscaping [ˈlænskeipiŋ] N (= *subject*) arquitectura *f* paisajista; (= *land area*) arquitectura *f* del paisaje

landslide [ˈlændslaɪd] Ⓐ N corrimiento *m* *or* desprendimiento *m* de tierras; (*Pol*) victoria *f* arrolladora *or* aplastante

Ⓑ CPD ► **landslide majority** N mayoría *f* abrumadora; **to win a ~ majority** ganar por mayoría abrumadora ► **landslide victory** N victoria *f* arrolladora *or* aplastante

landslip [ˈlændslɪp] (*esp Brit*) *see* **landslide**

landward [ˈlændwəd] Ⓐ ADJ de hacia tierra, de la parte de la tierra

Ⓑ ADV hacia tierra; **to ~(s)** en la dirección de la tierra

landwards [ˈlændwədz] ADV (*Brit*) = **landward B**

lane [leɪn] Ⓐ N 1 (*in country*) camino *m*; **a quiet country ~** un tranquilo camino *or* sendero rural; *see also* **memory B**

2 (*in town*) callejuela *f*, callejón *m*

3 (*Aut*) carril *m*, vía *f* (*LAm*); **bus ~** carril de autobuses; **to change ~s** cambiar de carril; **cycle ~** carril *m* bici, carril *m* de bicicletas; **the fast ~** (*Brit*) el carril de la derecha; (*most countries*) el carril de la izquierda; **the frenzied pace of life in the fast ~** el ritmo de vida frenético de los que viven a tope; **"get in ~"** "incorpórese al carril"; **the inside ~** (*Brit*) el carril de la izquierda; (*most countries*) el carril de la derecha; **"keep in ~"** "manténgase en su carril"; **the outside ~** (*Brit*) el carril de la derecha; (*most countries*) el carril de la izquierda; **traffic was reduced to a single ~** se pasó a circular por un solo carril; **a three-~ motorway** una autopista de tres carriles; **I'm in the wrong ~** no estoy en el carril donde debería estar

4 (*Naut*) ruta *f*; **sea ~** ruta *f* marítima; **shipping ~** ruta *f* de navegación

5 (*Aer*) (*also* **air ~**) corredor *m* aéreo, ruta *f* aérea

6 (*Sport*) calle *f*; **inside/outside ~** calle *f* de dentro/de fuera

Ⓑ CPD ► **lane closure** N corte *m* de carril; **there will be ~ closures on the M1** habrá carriles cortados en la M1 ► **lane markings** NPL líneas *fpl* divisorias

langlauf [ˈlɑːŋ,laʊf] N esquí *m* nórdico

language [ˈlæŋgwɪdʒ] Ⓐ N 1 (= *faculty, style of speech*) lenguaje *m*; **the tone of his ~ was diplomatic and polite** se expresó de forma diplomática y educada

2 (= *national tongue*) lengua *f*, idioma *m*; **the Spanish ~** la lengua española, el idioma español; **he studies ~s** estudia idiomas *or* lenguas; **she can speak six ~s** habla seis idiomas; **first ~** lengua *f* materna; **modern ~s** lenguas *fpl* modernas; ✦*IDIOM* **we don't talk the same ~** no hablamos el mismo idioma

3 (= *means of expression*) lenguaje *m*; **in plain ~** en lenguaje sencillo; **legal/technical ~** lenguaje *m* jurídico/técnico; **the ~ of violence** el lenguaje de la violencia

4 (*Comput*) lenguaje *m*; **computer ~** lenguaje *m* de ordenador *or* (*LAm*) computador(a)

5 (= *swear words*) **watch your ~** no digas palabrotas; **that's no ~ to use to your mother!** ¡así no se habla a tu madre!; **bad ~** palabrotas *fpl*, lenguaje *m* grosero; *see also* **strong**

A9
Ⓑ CPD ► **language acquisition** N adquisición *f* del lenguaje ► **language barrier** N barrera *f* del idioma ► **language degree** N título *m* en idiomas ► **language development** N desarrollo *m* lingüístico ► **language laboratory** N laboratorio *m* de idiomas ► **language school** N academia *f* de idiomas ► **language skills** NPL (*with foreign languages*) facilidad *f* para los idiomas ► **language student** N estudiante *mf* de idiomas ► **language studies** NPL estudios *mpl* de idiomas ► **language teacher** N profesor(a) *m/f* de idiomas

languid [ˈlæŋgwɪd] ADJ lánguido

languidly [ˈlæŋgwɪdlɪ] ADV lánguidamente

languidness [ˈlæŋgwɪdnɪs] N languidez *f*

languish [ˈlæŋgwɪʃ] VI [1] (= *pine*) languidecer, consumirse [2] (*in prison*) pudrirse; **the results of her research ~ed for years before action was taken** los resultados de su investigación cayeron en el olvido durante años antes de que se tomaran medidas; **they are ~ing at the bottom of the second division** están pasando sus horas más bajas en los últimos puestos de la segunda división

languishing [ˈlæŋgwɪʃɪŋ] ADJ lánguido; [*look*] amoroso, sentimental

languor [ˈlæŋgəʳ] N languidez *f*

languorous [ˈlæŋgərəs] ADJ lánguido

languorously [ˈlæŋgərəslɪ] ADV lánguidamente

lank [læŋk] ADJ [*hair*] lacio; [*grass*] largo

lanky [ˈlæŋkɪ] ADJ (*compar* **lankier**, *superl* **lankiest**) [*person*] larguirucho*

lanolin(e) [ˈlænəʊlɪn] N lanolina *f*

lantern [ˈlæntən] Ⓐ N farol *m*, linterna *f*; (*Archit*) linterna *f*; (*Naut*) faro *m*, farol *m*; [*of lighthouse*] fanal *m*
Ⓑ CPD ► **lantern lecture** N conferencia *f* con diapositivas ► **lantern slide** N diapositiva *f*

lantern-jawed [ˈlæntənˈdʒɔːd] ADJ chupado de cara

lanyard [ˈlænjəd] N acollador *m*

Laos [laʊs] N Laos *m*

Laotian [ˈlaʊʃɪən] Ⓐ ADJ laosiano
Ⓑ N laosiano/a *m/f*

lap¹ [læp] N regazo *m*; **to sit on sb's ~** sentarse en el regazo *or* las rodillas de algn; **with her hands in her ~** con las manos en el regazo; **he expects the money to fall into his ~** espera que el dinero le caiga como llovido del cielo; **they dump everything in my ~ and expect me to deal with it** lo echan todo a mis espaldas y pretenden que me encargue de ello; ✦*IDIOMS* **the outcome is in the ~ of the gods now** del resultado Dios dirá, la suerte está echada y ya veremos qué pasa; **to live in the ~ of luxury** vivir *or* nadar en la abundancia

lap² [læp] Ⓐ N [1] (*Sport*) vuelta *f*; **~ of honour** (*esp Brit*) vuelta *f* de honor; **a ten-~ race** una carrera de diez vueltas
[2] (= *stage*) etapa *f*, fase *f*; **we're on the last ~ now** (*fig*) ya estamos en la recta final
Ⓑ VT **to ~ sb** doblar a algn
Ⓒ VI completar *or* dar una vuelta; **to ~ at 190k.p.h.** completar *or* dar una vuelta a 190km/h
Ⓓ CPD ► **lap record** N récord *m* del circuito

lap³ [læp] Ⓐ N (= *lick*) lengüetada *f*, lametazo *m*; [*of waves*] chapaleteo *m*
Ⓑ VT [1] (= *drink*) [+ *water, milk etc*] beber a lengüetazos
[2] (= *touch*) [*waves, water, tide*] [+ *shore, cliff*] lamer, besar
Ⓒ VI [1] [*waves, water*] chapalear; **to ~ at** *or* **against sth** lamer *or* besar algo
[2] [*animal*] **to ~ at sth** beber algo a lengüetazos
►**lap up** VT + ADV (*lit*) beber a lengüetazos; (*fig*) [+ *compliments, attention*] disfrutar con

laparoscopy [ˌlæpəˈrɒskəpɪ] N laparoscopia *f*

laparotomy [ˌlæpəˈrɒtəmɪ] N laparotomía *f*

La Paz [laeˈpæz] N La Paz

LAPD (*US*) N ABBR = **Los Angeles Police Department**

lapdog [ˈlæpdɒg] N perro *m* faldero

lapel [ləˈpel] Ⓐ N solapa *f*
Ⓑ CPD ► **lapel pin** N insignia *f* de solapa

lapidary [ˈlæpɪdərɪ] Ⓐ ADJ lapidario
Ⓑ N lapidario/a *m/f*

lapis lazuli [ˈlæpɪsˈlæzjʊlaɪ] N lapislázuli *m*

Lapland [ˈlæplænd] N Laponia *f*

Laplander [ˈlæplændəʳ] N lapón/ona *m/f*

Lapp [læp] Ⓐ ADJ lapón
Ⓑ N [1] lapón/ona *m/f*
[2] (*Ling*) lapón *m*

lapping [ˈlæpɪŋ] N [*of waves, water*] chapaleteo *m*

Lappish [ˈlæpɪʃ] N (*Ling*) lapón *m*

lapse [læps] Ⓐ N [1] (= *error*) fallo *m*, lapsus *m inv*; (= *lack*) falta *f*; **she has the occasional ~ of memory** de vez en cuando tiene fallos *or* lapsus de memoria; **it was a ~ of judgement on his part** fue un error de cálculo por su parte; **the accident was caused by a momentary ~ of** *or* **in concentration** el accidente lo provocó un despiste momentáneo, el accidente lo provocó una falta momentánea de concentración
[2] [*of time*] lapso *m*, intervalo *m*, período *m*; **after a ~ of four months** después de un lapso *or* intervalo *or* período de cuatro meses, al cabo de cuatro meses; **there was a momentary ~ in the conversation** hubo un breve silencio en medio de la conversación
Ⓑ VI [1] (= *slip*) **to ~ into one's old ways** volver a las andadas; **he ~d into silence** se calló, se quedó callado; **he ~d into unconsciousness** perdió el conocimiento; **he ~d into the vernacular** recurrió a la lengua vernácula
[2] (= *expire*) [*season ticket*] caducar, vencer
[3] (= *cease to exist*) **our friendship ~d when she moved to London** dejamos de vernos cuando ella se fue a Londres
[4] (= *decline*) [*standards*] entrar en declive
[5] (= *pass*) [*time*] pasar, transcurrir

lapsed [læpst] ADJ (*Rel*) que ya no practica

laptop [ˈlæptɒp] N (*also* **~ computer**) ordenador *m or* (*LAm*) computador(a) *m/f* portátil

lapwing [ˈlæpwɪŋ] N avefría *f*

larboard [ˈlɑːbəd] Ⓐ ADJ de babor
Ⓑ N babor *m*

larceny [ˈlɑːsənɪ] N (*Jur*) hurto *m*, robo *m*; **grand ~** (*US*) hurto *m* mayor; **petty ~** hurto *m* menor

larch [lɑːtʃ] N (*also* **~ tree**) alerce *m*

lard [lɑːd] Ⓐ N manteca *f* de cerdo
Ⓑ VT lardear, mechar; (*fig*) **to ~ sth with** salpicar algo de, adornar algo con

larder [ˈlɑːdəʳ] N despensa *f*

lardy [ˈlɑːdɪ] ADJ mantecoso

large [lɑːdʒ] Ⓐ ADJ (*compar* **larger**, *superl* **largest**) [1] (*in size*) [*house, object, organization*] grande; [*person*] corpulento; [*area*] grande, extenso; **a ~ room** una gran habitación, una habitación grande; **in ~ doses the toxin is fatal** en grandes dosis, la toxina es mortal; **he has very ~ feet** tiene unos pies muy grandes; **do you have (it in) a ~r size?** ¿lo tiene en una talla más grande?; **by and ~** en general; **to grow ~r** crecer; **as ~ as life** en carne y hueso, en persona; **he was a ~r-than-life character** era una persona que se salía de lo corriente; **the central character is a ~r-than-life, cantankerous Italian** el personaje principal es un italiano exuberante y cascarrabias; **to make ~r** hacer más grande; [+ *premises etc*] ampliar, ensanchar; **in ~ part** en gran parte; *see also* **extent 3**, **measure A6**
[2] (*in number*) [*family, group, army*] numeroso, grande; [*sum, amount*] grande, importante; **a ~ group of people** un grupo numeroso *or* grande de personas; **a ~ crowd had gathered** se había formado un gran gentío; **a ~ number of them** un gran número de ellos; **~ numbers of people came** vinieron muchísimas personas, vinieron gran número de personas; **a ~ proportion of** una gran proporción de; **a ~ quantity of** una gran cantidad de
[3] (*Comm*) de tamaño grande; **"large"** (*on clothing label*) "grande"; (*on food packet, washing powder, etc*) "tamaño familiar"; **a dozen ~ envelopes** una docena de sobres de tamaño grande; → GREAT, BIG, LARGE
Ⓑ N **at ~** [1] (= *in general*) **the country/society at ~** el país/la sociedad en general
[2] (= *on the loose*) **to be at ~** [*dangerous person, animal*] andar suelto
Ⓒ ADV *see* **loom² 2**
Ⓓ CPD ► **the large intestine** N (*Anat*) el intestino grueso

largely [ˈlɑːdʒlɪ] ADV [1] (= *mainly*) en gran parte, en gran medida; **the rest of the world has ~ ignored China's environmental problems** el resto del mundo, en gran parte *or* en gran medida, ha hecho caso omiso de los problemas medioambientales de China; **it is a ~ working-class area** es en su mayor parte una zona de clase obrera; **he was elected ~ because …** se le eligió en gran parte porque …; **this is ~ due to …** esto se debe en gran parte *or* medida a …; **to be ~ reponsible for sth** ser en gran parte *or* medida responsable de algo; **~ speaking** hablando en líneas generales
[2] (= *prominently*) **to figure ~ in sth** [*person*] tener un papel destacado en algo; [*theme, subject*] ocupar un papel destacado en algo

largeness [ˈlɑːdʒnɪs] N [*of person, thing*] gran tamaño *m*; [*of group, family*] lo numeroso; **the ~ of the sum** lo cuantioso *or* grande de la suma

large-scale [ˈlɑːdʒˈskeɪl] ADJ a *or* en gran escala

large-size(d) [ˈlɑːdʒˈsaɪz(d)] ADJ de gran tamaño, de tamaño extra

largesse [lɑːˈʒes] N generosidad *f*, liberalidad *f*; (= *gift*) dádiva *f* espléndida

largish [ˈlɑːdʒɪʃ] ADJ bastante grande, más bien grande

largo [ˈlɑːgəʊ] N (*Mus*) largo *m*

lariat [ˈlærɪət] N lazo *m*

lark¹ [lɑːk] N (= *bird*) alondra *f*; **to get up** *or* **rise with the ~** levantarse con las gallinas, madrugar mucho; *see also* **happy A1**

lark² [lɑːk] (*esp Brit*) N [1] (= *joke*) broma *f*; **what a ~!** ¡qué risa!, ¡qué divertido!; **to do sth for a ~** hacer algo por diversión *or* para divertirse; **to have a ~ with sb** gastar una broma *or* tomar el pelo a algn; **sod this for a ~!‡** ¡vaya lío!*
[2] (= *business, affair*) **that ice-cream ~** ese asunto de los helados, ese tinglado de los helados*; **this dinner-jacket ~** esto de ponerse esmoquin

►**lark about***, **lark around*** VI + ADV (*esp Brit*) (= *act foolishly*) hacer el tonto, hacer tonterías; **stop ~ing about!** ¡basta de bromas!; **to ~ about with sth** divertirse con algo, jugar con algo

larkspur ['lɑːkspɜːʳ] N espuela *f* de caballero

larky* ['lɑːkɪ] ADJ guasón*, bromista

Larry ['lærɪ] N (*familiar form*) of **Laurence, Lawrence**

larva ['lɑːvə] N (*pl* **larvae** ['lɑːviː]) larva *f*

laryngitis [,lærɪn'dʒaɪtɪs] N laringitis *f inv*

larynx ['lærɪŋks] N (*pl* **larynxes** *or* **larynges** [lə'rɪndʒiːz]) laringe *f*

lasagna, **lasagne** [lə'zænjə] N lasaña *f*

lascivious [lə'sɪvɪəs] ADJ lascivo

lasciviously [lə'sɪvɪəslɪ] ADV lascivamente

lasciviousness [lə'sɪvɪəsnɪs] N lascivia *f*, lujuria *f*

laser ['leɪzəʳ] Ⓐ N láser *m*
Ⓑ CPD ► **laser beam** N rayo *m* láser ► **laser gun** N pistola *f* de rayos láser ► **laser printer** N impresora *f* láser ► **laser surgery** N cirujía *f* con láser

lash [læʃ] Ⓐ N 1 (= *eyelash*) pestaña *f*
2 (= *thong*) tralla *f*; (= *whip*) látigo *m*; (= *stroke*) latigazo *m*, azote *m*; [*of tail*] coletazo *m*
Ⓑ VT 1 (= *beat*) azotar, dar latigazos a; [+ *animal*] fustigar; [*rain, waves*] (*also* **~ against**) azotar; **the wind ~ed the trees** el viento azotaba los árboles; **the wind ~ed the sea into a fury** el viento encrespó con fuerza el mar; **it ~ed its tail** dio coletazos
2 (= *tie*) atar; (*Naut*) trincar, amarrar (**to** a)
Ⓒ VI **to ~ about** [*person*] agitarse violentamente, dar bandazos; **the rain ~ed against the windows** la lluvia azotaba las ventanas; **he ~ed at the donkey** fustigaba *or* azotaba al burro

►**lash down** Ⓐ VT + ADV sujetar con cuerdas
Ⓑ VI + ADV [*rain*] caer con fuerza

►**lash out** Ⓐ VI + ADV 1 **to ~ out** (*with fists*) repartir golpes a diestro y siniestro; (*with feet*) soltar patadas, tirar coces; **to ~ out at** *or* **against sb** (*lit, fig*) arremeter contra algn
2 (*) (= *spend*) **now we can really ~ out** ahora podemos gastar todo lo que queramos; **he ~ed out and bought himself a Rolls** tiró la casa por la ventana y se compró un Rolls; **I decided to ~ out on a new sofa** decidí tirar la casa por la ventana con un sofá nuevo
Ⓑ VT + ADV (*) (= *spend*) **he had to ~ out £50** tuvo que desembolsar 50 libras

lashing ['læʃɪŋ] N 1 (= *beating*) azotes *mpl*; **to give sb a ~** azotar a algn
2 (= *tying*) atadura *f*; (*Naut*) trinca *f*, amarradura *f*
3 **~s of** (*esp Brit**) montones de*

lash-up* ['læʃʌp] N arreglo *m* provisional, improvisación *f*

lass [læs] N (*esp Scot*) muchacha *f*, chica *f*, chavala *f* (*Sp**), cabra *f* (*Chile**), piba *f* (*S. Cone**), chamaca *f* (*CAm, Mex**); (= *country lass*) moza *f*, zagala *f*

lassie* ['læsɪ] N (*esp Scot*) = **lass**

lassitude ['læsɪtjuːd] N lasitud *f*

lasso [læ'suː] Ⓐ N (*pl* **lassos** *or* **lassoes**) lazo *m*
Ⓑ VT lazar, coger con el lazo

last[1] [lɑːst] Ⓐ ADJ 1 (= *most recent*) último; **I've seen her twice in the ~ week** la he visto dos veces en la última semana; **the ~ few weeks have been hectic** las últimas semanas han sido muy ajetreadas; **over the ~ few months** durante los últimos meses; **he hasn't been seen these ~ two years** no se lo ha visto en los últimos dos años
2 (= *previous*) (*referring to specific occasion*) [*Christmas, Easter*] pasado; [*time, meeting, birthday*] último; **~ Christmas we went to my mother's** las Navidades pasadas fuimos a casa de mi madre; **the ~ time we went, it rained** la última vez que fuimos, llovió; **on Monday ~** (*frm*) el pasado lunes; **~ Friday/month/year** el viernes/el mes/el año pasado; **this time ~ year** el año pasado por estas fechas; **~ week** la semana pasada; **this time ~ week** la semana pasada a estas horas; *see also* **night A1**
3 (= *final*) último; **the ~ Friday of the month** el último viernes del mes; **the ~ Sunday before Christmas** el último domingo antes de Navidad; **the ~ door on the right** la última puerta a la derecha; **the ~ three pages of the book** las tres últimas paginas del libro; **he spent the ~ few years of his life here** pasó los últimos años de su vida aquí; **~ but one** penúltimo; **down to the ~ detail** hasta el más mínimo detalle, hasta el último detalle; **the Last Judg(e)ment** el Juicio Final; **to fight to the ~ man** (*lit, fig*) luchar hasta el último aliento; **I was the ~ person to arrive/to see him alive** fui la última en llegar/la última persona que lo vió vivo; **I'm down to my ~ pound** sólo me queda una libra; **the ~ rites** (*Rel*) la extremaunción; **second to ~** antepenúltimo; **~ thing at night** antes de acostarse; **I'll finish it if it's the ~ thing I do** ¡lo terminaré aunque sea la última cosa que haga en esta vida!; **that was the ~ time I saw him** esa fue la última vez que lo vi; **for the ~ time, shut up!** ¡cállate, y que sea la última vez que te lo digo!; ✦*IDIOM* **to be on it's/one's ~ legs*** estar en las últimas; *see also* **every 1, gasp A, laugh A1, post A2, supper, resort A1, straw A1, word A1**
4 (= *least likely*) **you're the ~ person I'd trust with it** lo confiaría a cualquiera menos a ti, eres la última persona a la que se lo confiaría; **I would be the ~ person to stand in your way** yo soy la que menos me interpondría en tu camino, yo soy la última persona que se interpondría en tu camino; **that was the ~ thing I expected** eso era lo que menos me esperaba; **at 32, retirement is the ~ thing on his mind** con 32 años, jubilarse es lo último en que piensa
Ⓑ PRON 1 (*of series*) último; **he was the ~ of the Tudors** fue el último de los Tudores; **that was the ~ I saw of him** después de aquello no volví a verlo más; **the ~ we heard of him he was in Rio** según las últimas noticias estaba en Río; **if we don't go we shall never hear the ~ of it** si no vamos no dejarán de recordárnoslo; **you haven't heard the ~ of this!** ¡esto no se acaba aquí!, ¡esto no se va a quedar así!; **to be the ~ (one) to do sth** ser el último en hacer algo; **we're always the ~ to know** siempre somos los últimos en enterarnos; **the ~ but one** el/la penúltimo/a; **to leave sth till ~** dejar algo para lo último *or* el final; **to look one's ~ on sth** (*liter*) ver algo por última vez; **to the ~** hasta el final; *see also* **breathe A1**
2 (= *previous one*) **each one is better than the ~** son cada vez mejores; **the night before ~** anteanoche; **the week before ~** la semana anterior a la pasada, la semana pasada no, la anterior; **the Saturday before ~** el sábado anterior al pasado, el sábado pasado no, el anterior; **it was the question before ~ that I found difficult** la pregunta que me resultó difícil fue la penúltima
3 (= *all that remains*) **this is the ~ of the bread/wine** esto es lo que queda de pan/vino; **he was the ~ of his kind, a true professional** fue el último de los de su clase, un verdadero profesional
4 **at ~** por fin; **at long ~ the search was over** por fin la búsqueda había concluido
Ⓒ ADV 1 (= *finally*) **~ of all, take out the screws** por último, saca los tornillos; **~ but not least** por último, pero no por ello menos importante
2 (= *in last place, at the end*) **he was** *or* **came ~ in the 100 metres** terminó en último lugar *or* en última posición en los 100 metros; **to arrive ~** llegar el *or* (*LAm*) al último; **~ in, first out** los últimos en llegar son a los que despiden los primeros
3 (= *most recently*) **when I ~ saw them** la última vez que las vi; **he was ~ seen in Brighton** se lo vio por última vez en Brighton; **I ~ saw her in 1987** la vi por última vez en 1987

last[2] [lɑːst] Ⓐ VI 1 (= *continue*) durar; **it ~s (for) two hours** dura dos horas; **the trial is expected to ~ (for) three weeks** se espera que el juicio dure tres semanas; **the symptoms can ~ (for) up to a week** los síntomas pueden persistir hasta una semana; **nothing ~s forever** nada dura para siempre; **it's too good to ~** ◊ **it can't ~** esto no puede durar
2 (= *survive*) durar; **the previous boss only ~ed a week** el jefe anterior solamente duró una semana; **he wouldn't have ~ed ten minutes in those conditions** no hubiera durado *or* aguantado ni diez minutos en esas condiciones; **he won't ~ the night (out)** no sobrevivirá hasta la mañana
3 (= *be enough*) durar; **how long will the gas ~?** ¿hasta cuándo durará *or* alcanzará el gas?; **the town has enough water to ~ a fortnight** la ciudad tiene agua suficiente para dos semanas; **"only available while stocks ~"** (*Comm*) "sólo hasta que se agoten las existencias"
4 (= *remain usable*) durar; **this material will ~ (for) years** esta tela durará años; **more expensive batteries ~ longer** las pilas más caras duran más; **made to ~** hecho para que dure
Ⓑ VT durar; **this amount should ~ you (for) a week** esta cantidad debería durarte una semana; **it will ~ you a lifetime** te durará toda la vida; **I've had enough publicity to ~ me a lifetime!** ¡me han dado publicidad suficiente para toda una vida!

►**last out** VI + ADV 1 [*money, resources*] alcanzar; **my money doesn't ~ out the month** el dinero no me alcanza para todo el mes
2 [*person*] aguantar; **I can't ~ out without something to eat** ya no aguanto a no ser que coma algo; **he won't ~ out the winter** no sobrevivirá el invierno

last[3] [lɑːst] N (*in shoemaking*) horma *f*; ✦*IDIOM* **(shoemaker) stick to your ~!** ¡zapatero a tus zapatos!

last-ditch ['lɑːst'dɪtʃ] ADJ [*defence, attempt*] último, desesperado

last-gasp ['lɑːst'gɑːsp] ADJ de última hora

lasting ['lɑːstɪŋ] ADJ duradero, perdurable; [*shame*] eterno; [*colour*] sólido

lastly ['lɑːstlɪ] ADV por último, finalmente

last-minute ['lɑːst'mɪnɪt] ADJ de última hora

lat. ABBR = **latitude**

latch [lætʃ] Ⓐ N (= *bar*) cerrojo *m*, pestillo *m*; (= *lock*) pestillo *m*; **to drop the ~** echar el cerrojo *or* pestillo; **the door is on the ~** la puerta no tiene echado el pestillo
Ⓑ VT 1 [+ *door*] echar el pestillo a
2 (= *fix, fasten*) sujetar, asegurar

►**latch on*** VI + ADV (= *understand*) comprender, darse cuenta

➤ LANGUAGE IN USE: lastly 26.2

►**latch onto** VI + PREP [1] (= *cling*) (*to person, group*) pegarse a; **she ~ed onto his arm** se enganchó a su brazo
[2] [+ *idea*] agarrarse a; **the media were quick to ~ onto the story** la prensa no tardó en recoger la noticia

latchkey ['lætʃkiː] Ⓐ N llave *f*
Ⓑ CPD ► **latchkey child** N niño/a *m/f* cuya madre trabaja

late [leɪt] (*compar* **later**; *superl* **latest**) Ⓐ ADV [1] (= *towards end of period, day, month, etc*) **he had arrived ~ the previous evening** había llegado tarde la noche anterior; **~ at night** muy de noche, ya entrada la noche; **~ in the morning** a última hora de la mañana; **~ in the afternoon** a media tarde; **~ in the year** a finales del año; **~ in 1992/May** a finales del año 1992/de mayo; **symptoms appear only ~ in the disease** los síntomas aparecen sólo cuando la enfermedad ya está muy avanzada; **it wasn't until ~ in his career that he became famous** sólo al final de su carrera se hizo famoso, sólo en los últimos años de su carrera se hizo famoso; **they scored ~ in the second half** metieron un gol ya bien entrado el segundo tiempo; **~ into the night** hasta bien entrada la noche; **~ that night I got a phone call** ya entrada la noche recibí una llamada de teléfono; **too ~** demasiado tarde; ✦*IDIOM* **~ in the day** (= *at the last moment*) a última hora; (= *too late*) **it's a bit ~ in the day to be changing your mind** es un poco tarde para cambiar de opinión
[2] (= *after the usual time*) [*get up, go to bed*] tarde; **the chemist is open ~ on Thursdays** la farmacia cierra tarde los jueves; **everything is flowering very ~ this year** todo está floreciendo tardísimo este año; **she came ~ to acting** empezó a actuar ya mayor; **Liz had started learning German quite ~ in life** Liz había empezado a aprender alemán ya mayor; **to sleep ~** levantarse tarde; **to stay up ~** irse a la cama tarde, trasnochar; **to work ~** trabajar hasta tarde
[3] (= *after arranged/scheduled time*) [*arrive*] tarde, con retraso; **he arrived ten minutes ~** llegó con diez minutos de retraso, llegó diez minutos tarde; **they arrived ~ for dinner** llegaron tarde *or* con retraso a la cena; **we're running ~ this morning** llevamos retraso esta mañana; **we're running about 40 minutes ~** llevamos unos 40 minutos de retraso, llevamos un retraso de unos 40 minutos; ✦*PROV* **better ~ than never** más vale tarde que nunca
[4] (= *recently*) **as ~ as** aún en; **as ~ as 1950** aún en 1950; **of ~** (*frm*) últimamente, recientemente; **Jane Smith, ~ of Bristol** (*frm*) Jane Smith, domiciliada hasta hace poco en Bristol
Ⓑ ADJ [1] (= *towards end of period, day, month, etc*) **~ morning** última hora *f* de la mañana; **~ afternoon** media tarde *f*; **~ evening** última hora *f* de la tarde; **~ 1989** finales de 1989; **it was very ~ and I was tired** era muy tarde y estaba cansado; **in ~ September/spring** a finales de septiembre/de la primavera; **in the ~ 1960s** a finales de los años sesenta; **in the ~ 18th century** a fines del siglo XVIII; **to be in one's ~ thirties/forties** rondar los cuarenta/cincuenta, tener cerca de cuarenta/cincuenta años; **it's getting ~** se está haciendo tarde; **~ goal** gol *m* de última hora; **I apologize for arriving at this ~ hour** siento llegar a estas horas; **even at this ~ stage** incluso a estas alturas
[2] (= *after arranged or scheduled time*) **I apologize for my ~ arrival** perdone/perdonen mi retraso; **we apologize for the ~ arrival/departure of this train** les rogamos disculpen el retraso en la llegada/salida de este tren; **it was postponed to allow for ~ arrivals** se aplazó por si alguien llegaba tarde *or* con retraso; **our train was ~ again** nuestro tren se retrasó otra vez, nuestro tren llegó con retraso otra vez; **as usual, Jim was ~** como siempre, Jim llegó tarde *or* con retraso, como siempre, Jim se retrasó; **sorry I'm ~!** ¡siento llegar tarde *or* con retraso!; **you're ~!** ¡llegas tarde!; **the train is 20 minutes ~** el tren llega con 20 minutos de retraso, el tren lleva un retraso de 20 minutos; **she's 20 minutes ~** lleva 20 minutos de retraso; **I was already ten minutes ~** ya llegaba diez minutos tarde, ya llevaba diez minutos de retraso; **both my babies were ~** mis dos hijos nacieron más tarde de la fecha prevista; **he was ~ (in) finishing his essay** terminó la redacción con retraso; **she was ~ (in) returning from work** regresó tarde del trabajo; **I was ~ (in) paying my phone bill** me retrasé en pagar la factura del teléfono; **I'm ~ for my train** voy a perder el tren; **I'm ~ for work** voy a llegar tarde al trabajo; **I was half an hour ~ for my appointment** llegué con media hora de retraso a la cita; **a fault on the plane made us two hours ~** una avería en el avión nos retrasó dos horas; **you're going to make me ~ for my appointment** vas a hacer que llegue tarde a la cita; **we got off to a ~ start** empezamos tarde *or* con retraso; **I was ~ with the payments** me había retrasado en los pagos
[3] (= *after usual or normal time*) [*reservation, booking*] de última hora; [*crop, flowers*] tardío; **we had a ~ breakfast/lunch** desayunamos/comimos tarde; **Easter is ~ this year** la Semana Santa cae tarde este año; **"~ opening till ten pm on Fridays"** "los viernes cerramos a las diez"; **my period is ~** se me está retrasando la regla; **spring is ~ this year** la primavera llega tarde este año; *see also* **night A1**
[4] **too ~** demasiado tarde; **they tried to operate, but it was too ~** intentaron operar, pero era demasiado tarde; **it's too ~ to change your mind** es demasiado tarde para cambiar de opinión; **it's not too ~ (for you) to change your mind** aún estás a tiempo para cambiar de opinión; **it's never too ~ to ...** nunca es demasiado tarde para ...; *see also* **little A1**
[5] (*Hist, Art*) **~ Baroque** barroco *m* tardío; **the ~ Middle Ages** la baja edad media; **a ~ Georgian house** una casa de finales del periodo Georgiano; **Beethoven's ~ symphonies** las últimas sinfonías de Beethoven; **Rembrandt's ~ work** las últimas obras de Rembrandt
[6] (= *dead*) difunto; **the ~ Harry Brown** el difunto Harry Brown
[7] (*frm*) (= *former*) antiguo; **the ~ Prime Minister** el antiguo primer ministro
Ⓒ CPD ► **late edition** N edición *f* de última hora; *see also* **developer 2**

latecomer ['leɪtkʌmə^r] N rezagado/a *m/f*, el/la que llega tarde; **~s will not be admitted** no se permitirá la entrada una vez comenzado el acto/espectáculo; **the firm is a ~ to the industry** la empresa es nueva en el sector, la empresa acaba de establecerse en el sector

lateen [lə'tiːn] N vela *f* latina

late-lamented ['leɪtlə'mentɪd] ADJ malogrado, fallecido

lately ['leɪtlɪ] ADV últimamente, recientemente; **have you heard from her ~?** ¿has sabido algo de ella últimamente?; **(up) until** *or* **till ~** hasta hace poco; **it's only ~ that ...** hace poco que ...

latency ['leɪtənsɪ] N estado *m* latente

lateness ['leɪtnɪs] N [*of person, vehicle*] retraso *m*, tardanza *f*, atraso *m* (*LAm*); [*of hour*] lo avanzado; **he was fined for persistent ~** le sancionaron por llegar constantemente tarde

late-night ['leɪt'naɪt] ADJ **~ film** (*Cine*) película *f* de sesión de noche; (*TV*) película *f* de medianoche; **~ show** *or* **performance** sesión *f* de noche; **~ opening** *or* **shopping is on Thursdays** se abre hasta tarde los jueves; **is there a ~ bus?** ¿hay autobús nocturno?

latent ['leɪtənt] ADJ [*heat*] latente; [*tendency*] implícito; **~ defect** defecto *m* latente

later ['leɪtə^r] Ⓐ ADV [1] más tarde; **the gun was ~ found in his flat** más tarde se encontró la pistola en su piso; **two years/ten minutes ~** dos años/diez minutos después *or* más tarde; **I'll do it ~** lo haré luego *or* más tarde; **~, when all the guests had left** luego *or* más tarde, cuando todos los invitados se habían marchado; **~ I discovered that he had lied** más tarde descubrí que había mentido; **several whiskies ~, I was rather the worse for wear** después de varios whiskies, se me empezaban a notar los efectos; **~ than expected** más tarde de lo esperado; **all essays should be handed in no ~ than Monday** todos los trabajos deben entregarse el lunes a más tardar; **only ~** sólo más tarde; **it was only ~ that I learned the truth** no descubrí la verdad hasta más tarde, sólo más tarde descubrí la verdad; **~ that day** más tarde *or* posteriormente ese día; **~ that morning/night** más tarde *or* posteriormente esa mañana/esa noche; **the results will be available ~ today** los resultados se sabrán hoy mismo más tarde; *see also* **see[1] 2, sooner 1**
[2] **~ on** más tarde, más adelante; **we'll be dealing with this in more detail ~ on** trataremos esto a fondo más tarde *or* más adelante; **~ on that day/night** aquel día/aquella noche más tarde; **~ on in the play/film** más adelante en la obra/película; **~ on in the morning/afternoon/evening** más entrada la mañana/tarde/noche; **~ on in life** más adelante
Ⓑ ADJ [*chapter, version, work*] posterior; **I took a ~ flight/train** tomé un avión/tren que salía más tarde; **we plan to meet at a ~ date** tenemos intención de reunirnos más adelante; **in ~ life** más adelante; **at a ~ stage** más adelante

lateral ['lætərəl] Ⓐ ADJ lateral
Ⓑ CPD ► **lateral thinking** N pensamiento *m* lateral

laterally ['lætərəlɪ] ADV lateralmente

latest ['leɪtɪst] Ⓐ SUPERL *of* **late** ADJ [1] (= *last*) [*flight, train, bus*] último; **the ~ (possible) date** la fecha límite; **the ~ possible moment** el último momento; **the ~ (possible) time** lo más tarde
[2] (= *most recent*) [*figures, boyfriend, book*] último, más reciente; **the ~ in a series of** el último *or* el más reciente en una serie de; **the ~ fashion** la última moda; **it's the ~ model** es el último modelo; **the ~ news** las últimas noticias
Ⓑ N **the ~** [1] (= *news*) **have you heard the ~?** ¿te has enterado de la última noticia?; **for the ~ on where to go and what to do ...** para la información más actualizada acerca de dónde ir y qué hacer ...; **have you heard his ~? he broke his leg jumping off a wall** ¿has oído la última que ha hecho? se rompió una pierna saltando de un muro
[2] (= *most modern type*) **it's the ~ in food processors** es lo último en robots de cocina
[3] (= *last possible time*) lo más tarde; **the ~ he**

can see you is Thursday lo más tarde que puede verte es el jueves; **at the (very) ~** como muy tarde; **it has to be here by Friday at the (very) ~** tiene que estar aquí el viernes como muy tarde
4 (*) (= *boyfriend, girlfriend*) **have you seen her ~?** ¿has visto a su último ligue?*

latex ['leɪteks] N (*pl* **latexes** *or* **latices** ['lætɪsiːz]) látex *m*

lath [lɑːθ] N (*pl* **laths** [lɑːðz]) listón *m*

lathe [leɪð] N torno *m*

lather ['læðəʳ] Ⓐ N espuma *f*; [*of sweat*] sudor *m*; **the horse was in a ~** el caballo estaba empapado en sudor; **✦IDIOM to be in/get into a ~ (about sth)** estar/ponerse frenético (por algo)
Ⓑ VT [+ *one's face*] enjabonarse
Ⓒ VI hacer espuma

latifundia [ˌlætɪ'fʊndɪə] NPL latifundios *mpl*

Latin ['lætɪn] Ⓐ ADJ latino
Ⓑ N 1 (= *person*) latino/a *m/f*; **the ~s** los latinos
2 (*Ling*) latín *m*
Ⓒ CPD ► **Latin lover** N galán *m* latino ► **Latin quarter** N barrio *m* latino

Latin America ['lætɪnə'merɪkə] N América *f* Latina, Latinoamérica *f*, Hispanoamérica *f*

Latin American ['lætɪnə'merɪkən] Ⓐ ADJ latinoamericano
Ⓑ N latinoamericano/a *m/f*

latinism ['lætɪnɪzəm] N latinismo *m*

latinist ['lætɪnɪst] N latinista *mf*

latinity [lə'tɪnɪtɪ] N latinidad *f*

latinization [ˌlætɪnaɪ'zeɪʃən] N latinización *f*

latinize ['lætɪnaɪz] Ⓐ VT latinizar
Ⓑ VI latinizar

latish ['leɪtɪʃ] Ⓐ ADV algo tarde
Ⓑ ADJ algo tardío

latitude ['lætɪtjuːd] N 1 (*Geog*) latitud *f*
2 (*fig*) (= *freedom*) libertad *f*

latitudinal [ˌlætɪ'tjuːdɪnl] ADJ latitudinal

Latium ['leɪʃɪəm] N Lacio *m*

latrine [lə'triːn] N letrina *f*

▼**latter** ['lætəʳ] Ⓐ ADJ 1 (= *last*) último; **the ~ part of the story** la última parte del relato; **in the ~ part of the century** hacia fines *or* finales del siglo
2 (*of two*) segundo
Ⓑ N **the ~** (*sing*) éste/ésta; (*pl*) éstos/éstas; **the former ... the ~ ...** aquél ... éste ...

latter-day ['lætə'deɪ] ADJ moderno, de nuestros días; **the Latter-day Saints** (= *people*) los Mormones; **the Church of (Jesus Christ of) the Latter-day Saints** la Iglesia de Jesucristo de los Santos de los Últimos Días

latterly ['lætəlɪ] ADV últimamente, recientemente

lattice ['lætɪs] Ⓐ N enrejado *m*; (*on window*) reja *f*, celosía *f*
Ⓑ CPD ► **lattice window** N ventana *f* de celosía

latticed ['lætɪst] ADJ [*window*] con reja

latticework ['lætɪswɜːk] N enrejado *m*; (*on window*) celosía *f*

Latvia ['lætvɪə] N Letonia *f*, Latvia *f*

Latvian ['lætvɪən] Ⓐ ADJ letón, latvio
Ⓑ N letón/ona *m/f*, latvio/a *m/f*

laud [lɔːd] VT (*liter*) alabar, elogiar

laudable ['lɔːdəbl] ADJ loable, laudable

laudably ['lɔːdəblɪ] ADV de modo loable

laudanum ['lɔːdnəm] N láudano *m*

laudatory ['lɔːdətərɪ] ADJ laudatorio

laugh [lɑːf] Ⓐ N 1 (*lit*) risa *f*; (*loud*) carcajada *f*, risotada *f*; **he has a very distinctive ~** tiene una risa muy suya; **if you want a ~, read on** si te quieres reír, sigue leyendo; **she gave a little ~** soltó una risita; **to get a ~** hacer reír (a la gente); **to have a (good) ~ about** *or* **over** *or* **at sth** reírse (mucho) de algo; **that sounds like a ~ a minute** (*iro*) suena como para mondarse de risa(* *iro*); **to raise a ~** hacer reír (a la gente); **"I'm not jealous," he said with a ~** —no estoy celoso —dijo riéndose; **✦IDIOM to have the last ~** ser el que ríe el último
2 (*) (= *fun*) **to be a ~**: **he's a ~** es un tío gracioso *or* divertido*, es muy cachondo (*Sp**); **you should come - it'll be a ~** deberías venir - será divertido; **life isn't a bundle of ~s just now** mi vida ahora mismo no es precisamente muy divertida *or* muy alegre; **to do sth for a ~** hacer algo por divertirse; **he's always good for a ~** siempre te ríes *or* te diviertes con él
3 (= *joke*) **the ~ is on you*** te salió el tiro por la culata*; **that's a ~!** ◊ **what a ~!** (*iro*) ¡no me hagas reír!
Ⓑ VI reírse, reír; **I tried not to ~** intenté no reír(me); **I didn't know whether to ~ or cry** no sabía si reír(me) o llorar; **you may ~, but ...** tú te ríes, pero ...; **once we get this contract signed we're ~ing*** (*fig*) una vez que nos firmen este contrato, lo demás es coser y cantar; **to ~ about sth** reírse de algo; **we're still ~ing about the time that ...** todavía nos reímos de cuando ...; **there's nothing to ~ about** no es cosa de risa *or* (*LAm*) reírse; **to ~ at sb/sth** reírse de algn/algo; **he never ~s at my jokes** nunca se ríe de mis chistes; **to burst out ~ing** echarse a reír; **I thought I'd die ~ing** creí que me moría de (la) risa; **to ~ in sb's face** reírse de algn en su cara; **to fall about ~ing** troncharse *or* desternillarse de risa; **you have (got) to ~** hay que reírse; **to ~ like a drain/hyena** reírse como una hiena; **to make sb ~** hacer reír a algn; **don't make me ~** (*iro*) no me hagas reír; **to ~ out loud** reírse a carcajadas; **I ~ed till I cried** *or* **till the tears ran down my cheeks** me reí a más no poder, me tronché de (la) risa; **I ~ed to myself** me reí para mis adentros; **✦IDIOMS they'll be ~ing all the way to the bank** estarán contentísimos contando el dinero; **he'll soon be ~ing on the other side of his face** pronto se le quitarán las ganas de reír; **to ~ up one's sleeve** reírse por detrás; **✦PROVS ~ and the world ~s with you, cry and you cry alone** si ríes todo el mundo te acompaña, pero si lloras nadie quiere saber nada; **he who ~s last ~s longest** *or* **best** quien ríe el último ríe mejor
Ⓒ VT **"don't be silly," he ~ed** —no seas bobo —dijo riéndose; **he ~ed a nervous laugh** se rió nervioso; **to ~ sb to scorn** mofarse de algn; **to ~ o.s. silly** reírse a más no poder; **✦IDIOMS to ~ sth out of court**: **his idea was ~ed out of court** se rieron de su idea; **to ~ one's head off*** partirse *or* desternillarse *or* troncharse de risa
Ⓓ CPD ► **laugh lines** NPL arrugas *fpl* producidas al reír

►**laugh down** VT + ADV ridiculizar

►**laugh off** VT + ADV [+ *pain, accusation, suggestion*] tomarse a risa; **he tried to ~ it off** intentó tomárselo a risa

laughable ['lɑːfəbl] ADJ [*sum, amount*] irrisorio; [*suggestion*] ridículo; **it's really quite ~ that ...** es realmente un poco ridículo *or* irrisorio que ...

laughably ['lɑːfəblɪ] ADV 1 (*with adjective*) **such ideas now seem ~ dated** esas ideas están ahora tan pasadas de moda que resultan ridículas; **the portions were ~ small** las raciones eran de tamaño irrisorio; **it's a ~ small amount of money** es una cantidad irrisoria *or* de risa
2 (*with verb*) ridículamente; **what was ~ called a double room** lo que ridículamente denominaban una habitación doble

laughing ['lɑːfɪŋ] Ⓐ ADJ risueño, alegre; **it's no ~ matter** no tiene ninguna gracia, no es cosa de risa
Ⓑ CPD ► **laughing gas** N gas *m* hilarante ► **laughing stock** N hazmerreír *m*

laughingly ['lɑːfɪŋlɪ] ADV **he said ~** dijo riendo *or* riéndose; **what is ~ called progress** lo que se llama irónicamente el progreso

laughter ['lɑːftəʳ] Ⓐ N (*gen*) risa *f*, risas *fpl*; (= *guffaws*) risotadas *fpl*, carcajadas *fpl*; **their ~ could be heard in the next room** se oían sus risas *or* se les oía reír desde la habitación de al lado; **there was loud ~ at this remark** el comentario provocó carcajadas *or* grandes risas; **she let out a shriek of ~** soltó una sonora carcajada *or* risotada; **to burst into ~** soltar la carcajada; **✦PROV ~ is the best medicine** la risa es el mejor antídoto; *see also* **roar A1, B1**
Ⓑ CPD ► **laughter lines** NPL arrugas *fpl* producidas al reír

Launcelot ['lɑːnslət] N Lanzarote

launch [lɔːntʃ] Ⓐ N 1 (= *boat*) lancha *f*; **motor ~** lancha *f* motora
2 (= *act*) 2·1 (*lit*) [*of ship*] botadura *f*; [*of lifeboat, rocket, satellite*] lanzamiento *m*
2·2 (= *introduction*) [*of campaign, product, book*] lanzamiento *m*; [*of film, play*] estreno *m*; [*of company*] creación *f*, fundación *f*; [*of shares*] emisión *f*
Ⓑ VT 1 (= *lit*) [+ *ship*] botar; [+ *lifeboat*] echar al mar; [+ *rocket, missile, satellite*] lanzar
2 (= *introduce*) [+ *campaign, product, book, attack*] lanzar; [+ *film, play*] estrenar; [+ *company*] crear, fundar; [+ *shares*] emitir
3 (= *start*) **it was this novel that really ~ed him as a writer** fue esta novela la que lo lanzó a la fama como escritor; **to ~ sb on his/her way** iniciar a algn en su carrera; **once he's ~ed on that subject we'll never stop him** en cuanto se ponga a hablar de ese tema no habrá forma de pararlo
4 (= *hurl*) **to ~ o.s. at sth/sb** abalanzarse *or* arrojarse sobre algo/algn; **to ~ o.s. into sth** meterse de lleno en algo, entregarse a algo
Ⓒ VI **to ~ into sth**: **she ~ed into a long speech about patriotism** se puso a soltar *or* empezó un largo discurso sobre el patriotismo; **he ~ed into an attack on the president** emprendió un ataque contra el presidente, se puso a despotricar contra el presidente; **then the chorus ~es into the national anthem** entonces el coro la emprende con el himno nacional
Ⓓ CPD ► **launch attempt** N intento *m* de lanzamiento ► **launch date** N fecha *f* prevista para el lanzamiento ► **launch pad** N (*lit*) rampa *f or* plataforma *f* de lanzamiento; (*fig*) rampa *f or* plataforma *f* de lanzamiento, trampolín *m* ► **launch party** N (*Comm, Media*) fiesta *f* de lanzamiento ► **launch site** N lugar *m* del lanzamiento ► **launch vehicle** N lanzadera *f*

►**launch forth** VI + ADV = **launch C**

►**launch out** VI + ADV 1 (= *set out*) lanzarse; **the company needs to ~ out into new markets** la compañía necesita lanzarse a nuevos mercados; **he had ~ed out on sth for which he was ill-prepared** se había lanzado a algo para lo que no estaba preparado

➤ LANGUAGE IN USE: latter B 26.2

[2] (= *be extravagant*) **now we can afford to ~ out a bit** ahora nos podemos permitir algunos lujos

launcher [ˈlɔːntʃəʳ] N (*also* **rocket ~**) lanzacohetes *m inv*; (*also* **missile ~**) lanzamisiles *m inv*, lanzadera *f* de misiles

launching [ˈlɔːntʃɪŋ] Ⓐ N [*of missile, satellite, lifeboat, company, product*] lanzamiento *m*; [*of ship*] botadura *f*
Ⓑ CPD ► **launching ceremony** N ceremonia *f* de botadura ► **launching pad** N rampa *f or* plataforma *f* de lanzamiento ► **launching site** N lugar *m* del lanzamiento

launder [ˈlɔːndəʳ] Ⓐ VT [1] (*lit*) lavar y planchar
[2] (*fig*) [+ *money*] blanquear, lavar (*LAm*)
Ⓑ VI **this fabric ~s beautifully** esta tela queda muy bien después de lavarla (y plancharla)

launderette [ˌlɔːndəˈret] N lavandería *f* automática

laundering [ˈlɔːndərɪŋ] N [1] (*lit*) colada *f*
[2] (*fig*) [*of money*] blanqueo *m*, lavado *m* (*LAm*); **money ~** blanqueo *m* de dinero, lavado *m* de dinero (*LAm*)

laundress [ˈlɔːndrɪs] N lavandera *f*

Laundromat® [ˈlɔːndrəˌmæt] N (*US*) lavandería *f* automática

laundry [ˈlɔːndrɪ] Ⓐ N [1] (= *clothes*) (= *dirty*) ropa *f* sucia, ropa *f* para lavar; (= *clean*) ropa *f* lavada, colada *f*; **to do the ~** hacer la colada, lavar la ropa
[2] (= *establishment*) lavandería *f*; (*domestic*) lavadero *m*
Ⓑ CPD ► **laundry basket** N cesto *m* de la ropa sucia ► **laundry list** N lista *f* de ropa para lavar ► **laundry mark** N marca *f* de lavandería

laureate [ˈlɔːrɪɪt] N laureado *m*; **the Poet Laureate** (*Brit*) el Poeta Laureado

laurel [ˈlɒrəl] Ⓐ N laurel *m*; ✦*IDIOMS* **to look to one's ~s** no dormirse en los laureles; **to rest on one's ~s** dormirse en los laureles; **to win one's ~s** cargarse de laureles, laurearse
Ⓑ CPD ► **laurel wreath** N corona *f* de laurel

Laurence [ˈlɒrəns] N Lorenzo

Lausanne [ləʊˈzæn] N Lausana *f*

lav* [læv] N = **lavatory**

lava [ˈlɑːvə] Ⓐ N lava *f*
Ⓑ CPD ► **lava flow** N torrente *m or* río *m* de lava

lavatorial [ˌlævəˈtɔːrɪəl] ADJ [*humour*] cloacal, escatológico

lavatory [ˈlævətrɪ] Ⓐ N (= *room*) (*in house*) wáter *m* (*Sp*), baño *m* (*LAm*); (*in public place*) aseos *mpl*, servicio(s) *m(pl)* (*Sp*), baño(s) *m(pl)* (*LAm*); (= *appliance*) inodoro *m*, wáter *m* (*Sp*), taza *f* (*LAm*)
Ⓑ CPD ► **lavatory bowl, lavatory pan** N taza *f* de wáter ► **lavatory paper** N papel *m* higiénico ► **lavatory seat** N asiento *m* de retrete

lavender [ˈlævɪndəʳ] Ⓐ N espliego *m*, lavanda *f*
Ⓑ CPD ► **lavender blue** N azul *m* lavanda ► **lavender water** N lavanda *f*

lavish [ˈlævɪʃ] Ⓐ ADJ [1] (= *sumptuous*) [*apartment, meal, production, costume*] suntuoso; [*lifestyle*] suntuoso, lleno de lujo
[2] (= *generous*) [*gift, hospitality*] espléndido, generoso; [*praise*] profuso, abundante; [*amount*] abundante, generoso; **to be ~ with one's gifts** hacer regalos espléndidos *or* generosos; **to be ~ with one's money** gastar pródigamente el dinero, derrochar el dinero (*pej*); **to be ~ in** *or* **with one's praise** ser pródigo en elogios, no escatimar elogios
Ⓑ VT **to ~ sth on** *or* **upon sb** colmar a algn de algo; **to ~ attention on sb** colmar a algn de atenciones; **to ~ praise on sb** ser pródigo en elogios hacia algn

lavishly [ˈlævɪʃlɪ] ADV [1] (= *sumptuously*) [*decorated, furnished*] suntuosamente, fastuosamente
[2] (= *generously*) [*entertain, pay*] espléndidamente, generosamente; [*praise*] profusamente

lavishness [ˈlævɪʃnɪs] N [1] (= *sumptuousness*) suntuosidad *f*, fastuosidad *f*
[2] (= *generosity*) [*of person*] prodigalidad *f*; **the ~ of his praise** la profusión de sus elogios

law [lɔː] Ⓐ N [1] (= *piece of legislation*) ley *f*; **there's no ~ against it** no hay ley que lo prohíba; ✦*IDIOM* **to be a ~ unto o.s.** dictar sus propias leyes; *see also* **pass B9**
[2] (= *system of laws*) **the ~** la ley; **it's the ~** es la ley; **to be above the ~** estar por encima de la ley; **according to** *or* **in accordance with the ~** según la ley, de acuerdo con la ley; **the bill became ~ on 6th August** el proyecto de ley se hizo ley el 6 de agosto; **by ~** por ley, de acuerdo con la ley; **to be required by ~ to do sth** estar obligado por (la) ley a hacer algo; **civil/criminal ~** derecho *m* civil/penal; **in ~** según la ley; **the ~ of the land** la ley vigente; **officer of the ~** agente *mf* de la ley; **the ~ on abortion** la legislación sobre el aborto; **~ and order** el orden público; **the forces of ~ and order** las fuerzas del orden; **he is outside the ~** está fuera de la ley; **to have the ~ on one's side** tener la justicia de su lado; **to keep** *or* **remain within the ~** obrar legalmente; **his word is ~** su palabra es ley; ✦*IDIOMS* **to lay down the ~*** imponer su criterio, obrar autoritariamente; **to take the ~ into one's own hands** tomarse la justicia por su mano
[3] (= *field of study*) derecho *m*; **to study ~** estudiar derecho
[4] (= *profession*) abogacía *f*; **she is considering a career in ~** está pensando dedicarse a la abogacía; **to practise ~** ejercer de abogado, ejercer la abogacía
[5] (= *legal proceedings*) **court of ~** tribunal *m* de justicia; **to go to ~** recurrir a la justicia *or* a los tribunales; **to take a case to ~** llevar un caso ante los tribunales
[6] (= *rule*) [*of organization, sport*] regla *f*; **the ~s of the game** las reglas del juego; **God's ~** la ley de Dios
[7] (= *standard*) norma *f*; **there seemed to be one ~ for the rich and another for the poor** parecía haber unas normas para los ricos y otras para los pobres
[8] (*Sci, Math*) ley *f*; **the ~s of physics** las leyes de la física; **by the ~ of averages** por la estadística, estadísticamente; **the ~ of gravity** la ley de la gravedad; **the ~ of supply and demand** la ley de la oferta y la demanda; *see also* **nature A4**
[9] (*) (= *police*) **the ~** la policía; **to have the ~ on sb** denunciar a algn a la policía, llevar a algn a los tribunales
Ⓑ CPD ► **law court** N tribunal *m* de justicia ► **law enforcement** N aplicación *f* de la ley ► **law enforcement agency** N *organismo encargado de velar por el cumplimiento de la ley* ► **law enforcement officer** N (*esp US*) policía *mf* ► **Law Faculty** N (*Univ*) facultad *f* de Derecho ► **law firm** N gabinete *m* jurídico, bufete *m* de abogados ► **Law Lord** NPL (*Brit Pol*) juez *mf* lor; **the Law Lords** *jueces que son miembros de la Cámara de los Lores y constituyen el Tribunal Supremo* ► **law reports** NPL repertorio *m* de jurisprudencia ► **law school** N (*US*) facultad *f* de derecho ► **law student** N estudiante *mf* de derecho

law-abiding [ˈlɔːəˌbaɪdɪŋ] ADJ (*lit*) cumplidor de la ley; (*fig*) decente

lawbreaker [ˈlɔːˌbreɪkəʳ] N infractor(a) *m/f or* transgresor(a) *m/f* de la ley

law-breaking [ˈlɔːˌbreɪkɪŋ] Ⓐ ADJ infractor *or* transgresor de la ley
Ⓑ N infracción *f or* transgresión *f* de la ley

lawful [ˈlɔːfʊl] ADJ [*owner, government*] legítimo; [*action, behaviour*] legítimo, lícito; [*contract*] legal, válido; **~ wedded husband** legítimo esposo *m*; **~ wedded wife** legítima esposa *f*

lawfully [ˈlɔːfəlɪ] ADV legalmente; **the children were not ~ theirs** los hijos no eran legalmente suyos; **he was judged to have acted ~** consideraron que había actuado legítimamente

lawgiver [ˈlɔːˌgɪvəʳ] N (*Brit*) legislador(a) *m/f*

lawless [ˈlɔːlɪs] ADJ [*act*] ilegal; [*person*] rebelde, que rechaza la ley; [*country*] ingobernable, anárquico

lawlessness [ˈlɔːlɪsnɪs] N [*of place*] desgobierno *m*, anarquía *f*; [*of act*] ilegalidad *f*, criminalidad *f*

lawmaker [ˈlɔːˌmeɪkəʳ] N (*US*) legislador(a) *m/f*

lawn[1] [lɔːn] Ⓐ N césped *m*, pasto *m* (*LAm*)
Ⓑ CPD ► **lawn tennis** N tenis *m* sobre hierba

lawn[2] [lɔːn] N (= *cloth*) linón *m*

lawnmower [ˈlɔːnˌməʊəʳ] N cortacésped *m* (*Sp*), segadora *f* (*LAm*)

Lawrence [ˈlɒrəns] N Lorenzo

lawrencium [lɒˈrensɪəm] N laurencio *m*

lawsuit [ˈlɔːsuːt] N pleito *m*, juicio *m*; **to bring a ~ against sb** entablar demanda judicial contra algn

lawyer [ˈlɔːjəʳ] N abogado/a *m/f*; **a divorce ~** un abogado matrimonialista

LAWYERS

En el Reino Unido existen dos tipos diferentes de abogados: **solicitors** *y* **barristers** *(estos últimos reciben el nombre de* **advocates** *en Escocia). Los* **solicitors** *defienden a sus clientes ante tribunales de menor importancia y se encargan de asuntos civiles tales como la compra o venta de propiedades, testamentos, divorcios o el cobro de deudas, aunque pueden ser contratados directamente por el cliente para que los representen en casos tanto civiles como penales. Por su parte, los* **barristers** *o* **advocates** *no tratan directamente con sus clientes sino que, en los asuntos legales particulares, asesoran solamente en aquellos casos que les son remitidos por los* **solicitors**, *ya que su formación va más bien dirigida para actuar ante el Tribunal Supremo.*
⇨ *Ver tb* ATTORNEY

lax [læks] ADJ (*compar* **laxer**, *superl* **laxest**) (*pej*) [*person, discipline*] poco estricto, poco riguroso; [*standards, morals*] laxo, relajado; **things are very ~ at the school** en el colegio hay poca disciplina; **to be ~ about** *or* **on punctuality** ser negligente en la puntualidad; **to be morally ~** tener una moral laxa *or* relajada

laxative [ˈlæksətɪv] Ⓐ ADJ laxante
Ⓑ N laxante *m*

laxity [ˈlæksɪtɪ], **laxness** [ˈlæksnɪs] N (*pej*) [*of person, discipline*] falta *f* de rigor; [*of standards*] relajamiento *m*, relajación *f*; **moral ~** relajamiento *m or* relajación *f* de la moral

lay[1] [leɪ] Ⓐ VT (*pp* **laid**) [1] (= *place, put*) poner, colocar; [+ *carpet, lino*] poner, extender; [+ *bricks*] poner, colocar; [+ *pipes*] (*in building*) instalar; [+ *cable, mains, track, trap*] tender; [+ *foundations*] echar; [+ *foundation stone*] colo-

car; [+ *bomb, explosives*] colocar; [+ *mines*] sembrar; **I haven't laid eyes on him for years** hace años que no lo veo; **I didn't ~ a finger on it!** ¡no lo toqué!; **to ~ sth flat** extender algo (sobre la mesa *etc*); **I don't know where to ~ my hands on ...** no sé dónde echar mano a *or* conseguir ...; **to ~ sth over** *or* **on sth** extender algo encima de algo
2 (= *prepare*) [+ *fire*] preparar; [+ *plans*] hacer; **to ~ the table** (*Brit*) poner la mesa; ✦*PROV* **the best laid plans (of mice and men) can go astray** el hombre propone y Dios dispone
3 (= *present*) [+ *plan, proposal*] presentar (**before** a); [+ *accusation, charge*] hacer; [+ *complaint*] formular, presentar; **to ~ a claim before sb** presentar una reivindicación a algn; **to ~ the facts before sb** presentar los hechos a algn; *see also* **charge A1**, **claim A2**
4 (= *attribute*) [+ *blame*] echar; [+ *responsibility*] atribuir (**on** a); **to ~ the blame (for sth) on sb** echar la culpa (de algo) a algn
5 (= *flatten, suppress*) [+ *corn*] abatir, encamar; [+ *dust*] matar; [+ *doubts, fears*] acallar; [+ *ghost*] conjurar
6 (= *cause to be*) **to ~ a town flat** arrasar *or* destruir una ciudad; **he has been laid low with flu** la gripe lo ha tenido en cama; **to ~ o.s. open to attack/criticism** exponerse al ataque/a la crítica; **to be laid to rest** ser enterrado
7 [+ *bet*] hacer; [+ *money*] apostar (**on** a); **I'll ~ you a fiver on it!** ¡te apuesto cinco libras a que es así!; **to ~ that ...** apostar a que ...; **they're ~ing bets on who is going to leave next** hacen apuestas sobre quién será el próximo en marcharse; *see also* **odds 1**
8 [+ *egg*] [*bird, reptile*] poner; [*fish, amphibian, insect*] depositar; **it ~s its eggs on/in ...** [*fish, amphibian, insect*] deposita los huevos *or* desova en ...
9 (**) (= *have sex with*) tirarse a**, follarse a (*Sp***)
Ⓑ VI [*hen*] poner (huevos)
Ⓒ N 1 [*of countryside, district etc*] disposición *f*, situación *f*; **the ~ of the land** (*US*) la configuración del terreno; (*fig*) la situación, el estado de las cosas
2 **hen in ~** gallina *f* ponedora; **to come into ~** empezar a poner huevos; **to go out of ~** dejar de poner huevos
3 (**) **she's an easy ~** es una tía fácil*; **she's a good ~** se lo hace muy bien**
4 (**) (= *act*) polvo** *m*
Ⓓ CPD ► **lay days** NPL (*Comm*) días *mpl* de detención *or* inactividad

►**lay about** VI + PREP **to ~ about one** dar palos de ciego, repartir golpes a diestro y siniestro

►**lay aside** VT + ADV 1 (= *save*) [+ *food, provisions*] guardar; [+ *money*] ahorrar
2 (= *put away*) [+ *book, pen*] dejar, poner a un lado
3 (= *abandon*) [+ *prejudices, differences*] dejar de lado

►**lay away** VT + ADV (*US*) = **lay aside 1**

►**lay by** VT + ADV = **lay aside 1**

►**lay down** Ⓐ VT + ADV 1 (= *put down*) [+ *book, pen*] dejar, poner a un lado; [+ *luggage*] dejar; [+ *burden*] posar, depositar en tierra; [+ *cards*] extender sobre el tapete; (= *lay flat*) [+ *person, body*] acostar, tender; **to ~ o.s. down** tumbarse, echarse
2 [+ *ship*] colocar la quilla de
3 [+ *wine*] poner en bodega, guardar en cava
4 (= *give up*) [+ *arms*] deponer, rendir; **to ~ down one's life for sth/sb** dar su vida por algo/algn
5 (= *establish*) [+ *condition*] establecer; [+ *precedent*] sentar, establecer; [+ *principle*] establecer, formular; [+ *policy*] trazar, formular; [+ *ruling*] dictar; **to ~ it down that ...** asentar que ..., dictaminar que ...; *see also* **law A2**
6 (= *impose*) [+ *condition*] imponer
Ⓑ VI + ADV (*Cards*) poner sus cartas sobre el tapete; (*Bridge*) (*as dummy*) tumbarse

►**lay in** VT + ADV [+ *food, fuel, water*] proveerse de, abastecerse de; (= *amass*) acumular; (= *buy*) comprar; **to ~ in supplies** aprovisionarse; **to ~ in supplies of sth** proveerse *or* abastecerse de algo

►**lay into*** VI + PREP [+ *person*] (*lit, fig*) arremeter contra; [+ *food*] lanzarse sobre, asaltar

►**lay off** Ⓐ VT + ADV [+ *workers*] (= *sack*) despedir; (*temporarily*) despedir *or* suspender (temporalmente por falta de trabajo)
Ⓑ VI + ADV 1 (*Naut*) virar de bordo
2 (*) **~ off, will you?** ¡déjalo!, ¡por Dios!
Ⓒ VI + PREP (*) **to ~ off sb** dejar a algn en paz; **to ~ off cigarettes** dejar de fumar (cigarrillos); **~ off it!** ¡ya está bien!, ¡déjalo por Dios!

►**lay on** VT + ADV 1 (*Brit*) (= *install*) instalar, conectar; **a house with water laid on** una casa con agua corriente
2 (= *provide*) [+ *food, drink*] proporcionar; **you rent the hall and we'll ~ on the refreshments** usted alquila la sala y nosotros nos hacemos cargo de *or* ponemos los refrigerios; **everything's laid on** todo está dispuesto; **they laid on a car for me** pusieron un coche a mi disposición
3 [+ *paint*] poner, aplicar; ✦*IDIOM* **to ~ it on thick** *or* **with a trowel*** (= *exaggerate*) recargar las tintas*
4 [+ *tax, duty*] imponer
5 **to ~ it on sb*** dar una paliza a algn

►**lay out** VT + ADV 1 (= *dispose*) [+ *cloth, rug*] tender, extender; [+ *objects*] disponer, arreglar; [+ *goods for sale*] exponer; [+ *garden, town*] trazar, hacer el trazado de; [+ *page, letter*] presentar, diseñar; [+ *clothes*] preparar; [+ *ideas*] exponer, explicar; **the house is well laid out** la casa está bien distribuida; **the town is well laid out** la ciudad tiene un trazado elegante
2 [+ *corpse*] amortajar
3 [+ *money*] (= *spend*) gastar; (= *invest*) invertir, emplear (**on** en)
4 (*) (= *knock out*) derribar; (*Boxing*) dejar K.O.
5 (*reflexive*) **to ~ o.s. out for sb** hacer lo posible por ayudar/complacer a algn; **he laid himself out to please** se volcó por complacerla/los *etc*

►**lay over** VI + ADV (*US*) pasar la noche, descansar

►**lay up** VT + ADV 1 (= *store*) guardar, almacenar; (= *amass*) acumular; **he's ~ing up trouble for himself** se está creando *or* buscando problemas
2 (= *put out of service*) [+ *ship*] meter en el dique seco; [+ *boat*] amarrar; [+ *car*] encerrar (en el garaje)
3 (*Med*) **to be laid up (with sth)** estar en cama (con algo); **she was laid up for weeks** tuvo que guardar cama durante varias semanas

lay² [leɪ] PT *of* **lie²**

lay³ [leɪ] Ⓐ ADJ (*Rel*) laico, lego, seglar; (= *non-specialist*) lego, profano, no experto
Ⓑ CPD ► **lay brother** N (*Rel*) donado *m*, lego *m*, hermano *m* lego ► **lay person** N (*Rel*) lego/a *m/f*; (= *non-specialist*) profano/a *m/f* ► **lay reader** N (*Rel*) *persona laica encargada de conducir parte de un servicio religioso* ► **lay sister** N (*Rel*) donada *f*, lega *f*

lay⁴ [leɪ] N (*Mus, Literat*) trova *f*, canción *f*

layabout* [ˈleɪəbaʊt] N holgazán/ana *m/f*, vago/a *m/f*

lay-by [ˈleɪbaɪ] N (*Aut*) área *f* de descanso, área *f* de estacionamiento

layer [ˈleɪəʳ] Ⓐ N 1 (*gen*) capa *f*; (*Geol*) estrato *m*; (*Agr*) acodo *m*
2 (= *hen*) gallina *f* ponedora; **to be a good ~** ser buena ponedora; **the best ~** la más ponedora
Ⓑ VT 1 (*Culin*) [+ *vegetables, pasta, pancakes*] poner en capas
2 (*Agr*) acodar

layette [leɪˈet] N canastilla *f*, ajuar *m*

laying [ˈleɪɪŋ] N (= *placing*) colocación *f*; [*of cable, track etc*] tendido *m*; [*of eggs*] puesta *f*, postura *f*; **~ on of hands** imposición *f* de manos

layman [ˈleɪmən] N (*pl* **laymen**) 1 (*Rel*) seglar *mf*, lego/a *m/f*
2 (*fig*) profano(a) *m/f*, lego(a) *m/f*; **in ~'s terms** para entendernos, para los profanos en la materia

lay-off [ˈleɪɒf] N (= *act*) despido *m*; (= *period*) paro *m* (involuntario), baja *f*

layout [ˈleɪaʊt] N [*of building*] plan *m*, distribución *f*; [*of town*] trazado *m*; (*Typ*) composición *f*

layover [ˈleɪəʊvəʳ] N (*US*) parada *f* intermedia; (*Aer*) escala *f*

Lazarus [ˈlæzərəs] N Lázaro

laze [leɪz] VI (*also* **~ about, ~ around**) no hacer nada, descansar; (*pej*) holgazanear, gandulear; **we ~d in the sun for a week** pasamos una semana tirados al sol

lazily [ˈleɪzɪlɪ] ADV 1 (= *without effort*) perezosamente
2 (*fig*) [*drift, float*] perezosamente (*liter*), lentamente

laziness [ˈleɪzɪnɪs] N pereza *f*, flojera *f* (*esp LAm**)

lazy [ˈleɪzɪ] (*compar* **lazier**; *superl* **laziest**) ADJ 1 (= *idle*) perezoso, vago; **to feel ~** tener pereza, tener flojera (*esp LAm**); **to have a ~ eye** (*Med*) tener un ojo vago
2 (*pej*) (= *unconsidered*) [*assumption*] poco meditado; **it's another example of ~ thinking** es otro ejemplo de pensar sin cuestionar las cosas
3 (= *relaxed*) [*smile, gesture*] perezoso; [*meal, day*] relajado; [*holiday*] descansado; **we spent a ~ Sunday on the river** pasamos un domingo de lo más relajado en el río
4 (*liter*) [*river*] lento

lazybones [ˈleɪzɪˌbəʊnz] NSING gandul(a) *m/f*, vago/a *m/f*, flojo/a *m/f* (*LAm*)

lazy Susan [ˌleɪzɪˈsuːzn] N (= *dish*) *bandeja giratoria para servir la comida en la mesa*

LB ABBR (*Canada*) = **Labrador**

lb ABBR (= **pound**) libra *f*

LBO N ABBR (*Fin*) = **leveraged buyout**

lbw ABBR (*Cricket*) (= **leg before wicket**) *expulsión de un jugador cuya pierna ha sido golpeada por la pelota que de otra forma hubiese dado en los palos*

LC N ABBR (*US*) = **Library of Congress**

lc, **l.c.** ABBR (*Typ*) (= **lower case**) min

L/C N ABBR (*Comm*) (= **letter of credit**) cta. cto.

LCD, **lcd** N ABBR 1 (= **liquid crystal display**) VCL *m*
2 = **lowest common denominator**

L-Cpl ABBR *of* **lance corporal**

Ld ABBR *of* **Lord**

LDS N ABBR 1 (*Univ*) = **Licentiate in Dental Surgery**
2 (= **Latter-day Saints**) Iglesia *f* de Jesucristo de los Santos de los Últimos Días

LEA N ABBR (*Brit Educ*) = **Local Education Authority**

lea [liː] N (*poet*) prado *m*

leach [liːtʃ] Ⓐ VT lixiviar
Ⓑ VI lixiviarse

lead[1] [led] Ⓐ N (= *metal*) plomo *m*; (*in pencil*) mina *f*; (*Naut*) sonda *f*, escandallo *m*; **my limbs felt like ~** *or* **as heavy as ~** los brazos y las piernas me pesaban como plomo; **they filled him full of ~*** lo acribillaron a balazos; ✦***IDIOM*** **to swing the ~*** fingirse enfermo, racanear*, hacer el rácano*
Ⓑ CPD de plomo ► **lead acetate** N acetato *m* de plomo ► **lead crystal** N cristal *m* (que contiene óxido de plomo) ► **lead oxide** N óxido *m* de plomo ► **lead paint** N pintura *f* a base de plomo ► **lead pencil** N lápiz *m* ► **lead pipe** N tubería *f* de plomo ► **lead poisoning** N saturnismo *m*, plumbismo *m*, intoxicación *f* por el plomo ► **lead shot** N perdigonada *f*

lead[2] [liːd] (*vb: pt, pp* **led**) Ⓐ N 1 (= *leading position, Sport*) delantera *f*, cabeza *f*; (= *distance, time, points ahead*) ventaja *f*; **to be in the ~** (*gen*) ir a la *or* en cabeza, ir primero; (*Sport*) llevar la delantera; (*in league*) ocupar el primer puesto; **to have two minutes' ~ over sb** llevar a algn una ventaja de dos minutos; **to have a ~ of half a length** tener medio cuerpo de ventaja; **to take the ~** (*Sport*) tomar la delantera; (= *take the initiative*) tomar la iniciativa
2 (= *example*) ejemplo *m*; **to follow sb's ~** seguir el ejemplo de algn; **to give sb a ~** guiar a algn, dar el ejemplo a algn, mostrar el camino a algn
3 (= *clue*) pista *f*, indicación *f*; **the police have a ~** la policía tiene una pista; **to follow up a ~** seguir *or* investigar una pista
4 (*Theat*) papel *m* principal; (*in opera*) voz *f* cantante; (= *person*) primer actor *m*, primera actriz *f*; **to play the ~** tener el papel principal; **to sing the ~** llevar la voz cantante; **with Greta Garbo in the ~** con Greta Garbo en el primer papel
5 (= *leash*) cuerda *f*, traílla *f*, correa *f* (*LAm*); **dogs must be kept on a ~** los perros deben llevarse con traílla
6 (*Elec*) cable *m*
7 (*Cards*) **whose ~ is it?** ¿quién sale?, ¿quién es mano?; **it's my ~** soy mano, salgo yo; **it's your ~** tú eres mano, sales tú; **if the ~ is in hearts** si la salida es a corazones
8 (*Press*) primer párrafo *m*, entrada *f*
Ⓑ VT 1 (= *conduct*) llevar, conducir; **to ~ sb to a table** conducir a algn a una mesa; **kindly ~ me to him** haga el favor de conducirme a su presencia *or* de llevarme donde está; **they led him into the king's presence** lo condujeron ante el rey; **what led you to Venice?** ¿qué te llevó a Venecia?, ¿con qué motivo fuiste a Venecia?; **this road ~s you back to Jaca** por este camino se vuelve a Jaca; **this ~s me to an important point** esto me lleva a un punto importante; **this discussion is ~ing us nowhere** esta discusión no nos lleva a ninguna parte; **to ~ the way** (*lit*) ir primero; (*fig*) mostrar el camino, dar el ejemplo
2 (= *be the leader of*) [+ *government*] dirigir, encabezar; [+ *party*] encabezar, ser jefe de; [+ *expedition, regiment*] mandar; [+ *discussion*] conducir; [+ *team*] capitanear; [+ *league*] ir a la *or* en cabeza de, encabezar, ocupar el primer puesto en; [+ *procession*] ir a la *or* en cabeza de, encabezar; [+ *orchestra*] (*Brit*) ser el primer violín en; (*US*) dirigir
3 (= *be first in*) **to ~ the field** (*Sport*) ir a la cabeza, llevar la delantera; **they ~ the field in this area of research** son los líderes en este campo de la investigación; **Britain led the world in textiles** Inglaterra era el líder mundial en la industria textil
4 (= *be in front of*) [+ *opponent*] aventajar; **Roberts ~s Brown by four games to one** Roberts le aventaja a Brown por cuatro juegos a uno; **they led us by 30 seconds** nos llevaban una ventaja de 30 segundos
5 [+ *life, existence*] llevar; **to ~ a busy life** llevar una vida muy ajetreada; **to ~ a full life** llevar *or* tener una vida muy activa, llevar *or* tener una vida llena de actividades; **to ~ sb a miserable life** amargar la vida a algn; *see also* **dance A1**, **life A3**
6 (= *influence*) **to ~ sb to do sth** llevar *or* inducir *or* mover a algn a hacer algo; **we were led to believe that …** nos hicieron creer que …; **what led you to this conclusion?** ¿qué te hizo llegar a esta conclusión?; **he is easily led** es muy sugestionable; **to ~ sb into error** inducir a algn a error
Ⓒ VI 1 (= *go in front*) ir primero
2 (*in match, race*) llevar la delantera; **he is ~ing by an hour/ten metres** lleva una hora/diez metros de ventaja
3 (*Cards*) ser mano, salir; **you ~** sales tú, tú eres mano; **she led with the three of clubs** salió con el tres de tréboles
4 (= *be in control*) estar al mando; **we need someone who knows how to ~** necesitamos una persona que sepa estar al mando *or* que tenga dotes de mando
5 **to ~ to** [*street, corridor*] conducir a; [*door*] dar a; **this street ~s to the station** esta calle conduce a la estación, por esta calle se va a la estación; **this street ~s to the main square** esta calle sale a *or* desemboca en la plaza principal; **this road ~s back to Burgos** por este camino se vuelve a Burgos
6 (= *result in*) **to ~ to** llevar a; **it led to his arrest** llevó a su detención; **all my enquiries led nowhere** mis indagaciones no llevaron a nada; **it led to war** condujo a la guerra; **it led to a change** produjo un cambio; **one thing led to another …** una cosa nos/los *etc* llevó a otra …; **it all ~s back to the butler** todo nos lleva de nuevo al mayordomo (como sospechoso)
Ⓓ CPD ► **lead singer** N cantante *mf* ► **lead story** N reportaje *m* principal ► **lead time** N plazo *m* de entrega

►**lead along** VT + ADV llevar (por la mano)

►**lead away** VT + ADV (*gen*) llevar; **he was led away by the police** se lo llevó la policía; **we must not be led away from the main issue** no nos apartemos del asunto principal

►**lead in** Ⓐ VT + ADV hacer entrar a
Ⓑ VI + ADV **this is a way of ~ing in** ésta es una manera de introducir (el argumento *etc*); **to ~ in with** empezar con

►**lead off** Ⓐ VT + ADV 1 (= *take away*) llevar
2 (*fig*) (= *begin*) empezar (**with** con)
Ⓑ VI + PREP [*street*] salir de; [*room*] comunicar con; **the streets that ~ off (from) the square** las calles que salen de la plaza; **a room ~ing off (from) another** una habitación que comunica con otra

►**lead on** Ⓐ VT + ADV 1 (= *tease*) engañar, engatusar; (*amorously*) ir dando esperanzas a
2 (= *incite*) **to ~ sb on (to do sth)** incitar a algn (a hacer algo)
Ⓑ VI + ADV ir primero, ir a la cabeza; **you ~ on** tú primero; **~ on!** ¡vamos!, ¡adelante!

►**lead out** VT + ADV (*outside*) llevar *or* conducir fuera; (*onto stage, dance floor*) sacar

►**lead up to** VI + PREP llevar a, conducir a; **what's all this ~ing up to?** ¿a dónde lleva *or* a qué conduce todo esto?, ¿a qué vas con todo esto?; **the years that led up to the war** los años que precedieron a la guerra; **the events that led up to the war** los sucesos que condujeron a la guerra

leaded ['ledɪd] Ⓐ ADJ [*window*] emplomado
Ⓑ CPD ► **leaded lights** N cristales *mpl* emplomados ► **leaded petrol** N gasolina *f* con plomo

leaden ['ledn] ADJ (= *of lead*) de plomo, plúmbeo; (*in colour*) plomizo; (*fig*) [*heart*] triste

leaden-eyed [ˌledn'aɪd] ADJ **to be ~** tener los párpados pesados

leader ['liːdəʳ] Ⓐ N 1 [*of group, party*] líder *m/f*, jefe/a *m/f*; (= *guide*) guía *mf*, conductor(a) *m/f*; [*of rebels*] cabecilla *mf*; (*Mus*) [*of orchestra*] (*Brit*) primer violín *m*; (*US*) director(a) *m/f*; **our political ~s** nuestros líderes políticos; **he's a born ~** ha nacido para mandar; **Leader of the House** (*of Commons*) (*Pol*) Presidente/a *m/f* de la Cámara de los Comunes; (*of Lords*) Presidente/a *m/f* de la Cámara de los Lores; **Leader of the Opposition** jefe/a *m/f* de la oposición
2 (*in race, field etc*) primero/a *m/f*; (*in league*) líder *m*; (= *horse*) caballo *m* que va primero; *see also* **market D**, **world B**
3 (*in newspaper*) editorial *m*
4 (*Comm*) (= *company, product*) líder *m*
Ⓑ CPD ► **leader writer** N (*Brit*) editorialista *mf*

LEADER OF THE HOUSE

Leader of the House *es el término que, en el Reino Unido, hace referencia tanto al presidente de la Cámara de los Comunes como al presidente de la Cámara de los Lores. Ambos pertenecen al gobierno británico y son los encargados de organizar y hacer público el horario semanal de debates y otros asuntos en sus respectivas cámaras, previa consulta con su homólogo de la oposición o* **Shadow Leader of the House** *y con los* **Whips** *de cada partido.*
⇨ *Ver tb* WHIP, SPEAKER

leaderene [ˌliːdə'riːn] N (*hum*) líder *f*

leadership ['liːdəʃɪp] N 1 (= *position*) dirección *f*, liderazgo *m*; **under the ~ of …** bajo la dirección *or* liderazgo de …; **~ qualities** dotes *fpl* de mando; **to take over the ~ (of sth)** asumir la dirección (de algo)
2 (= *leaders*) dirección *f*, jefatura *f*

lead-free [ˌled'friː] ADJ sin plomo

lead-in ['liːd'ɪn] N introducción *f* (**to** a)

leading ['liːdɪŋ] Ⓐ ADJ 1 (= *foremost*) [*expert, politician, writer*] principal, más destacado; (*Ind*) [*producer*] principal; [*company, product, brand*] líder; (*Theat, Cine*) [*part, role*] principal, de protagonista; **one of Britain's ~ writers** uno de los principales *or* más destacados escritores británicos; **to play the ~ role** *or* **part in** [+ *film, play*] interpretar el papel principal *or* de protagonista en
2 (= *prominent*) [*expert, politician, writer*] destacado; **~ scientists believe it will be possible** destacados científicos creen que será posible; **a ~ member of the Sikh community** un miembro destacado de la comunidad sij; **a ~ industrial nation** un país industrializado líder, uno de los principales países industrializados; **to play a ~ role** *or* **part in sth**

(*fig*) jugar un papel importante *or* destacado en algo
3 (*in race*) [*athlete, horse, driver*] en cabeza, que va a la cabeza; (*in procession, convoy*) que va a la cabeza
Ⓑ CPD ► **leading article** N (*Brit Press*) artículo *m* de fondo, editorial *m* ► **leading edge** N (*Aer*) [*of wing*] borde *m* anterior; (= *forefront*) vanguardia *f*; *see also* **leading-edge**; **to be at** *or* **on the ~ edge of** estar a la vanguardia de ► **leading lady** N (*Theat*) primera actriz *f*; (*Cine*) protagonista *f* ► **leading light** N figura *f* principal ► **leading man** N (*Theat*) primer actor *m*; (*Cine*) protagonista *m* ► **leading question** N pregunta *f* capciosa

leading-edge [ˌliːdɪŋˈedʒ] ADJ **~ technology** tecnología *f* de vanguardia, tecnología *f* punta

lead-up [ˈliːdʌp] N período *m* previo (**to** a); **during the ~ to the election ...** durante la precampaña electoral ...; **the ~ to the wedding** los meses antes de la boda

leaf [liːf] Ⓐ N (*pl* **leaves**) 1 [*of plant*] hoja *f*; **to come into ~** echar hojas; *see also* **shake C1**
2 [*of book*] página *f*; ✦**IDIOMS to turn over a new ~** pasar página, hacer borrón y cuenta nueva; **to take a ~ out of sb's book** seguir el ejemplo de algn
3 [*of table*] ala *f*, hoja *f* abatible
Ⓑ CPD ► **leaf bud** N yema *f* ► **leaf mould**, **leaf mold** (*US*) N mantillo *m* (de hojas), abono *m* verde ► **leaf spinach** N hojas *fpl* de espinaca ► **leaf tobacco** N tabaco *m* en rama

►**leaf through** VI + PREP [+ *book*] hojear

leafless [ˈliːflɪs] ADJ sin hojas, deshojado

leaflet [ˈliːflɪt] Ⓐ N (*containing several pages*) folleto *m*; (= *single piece of paper*) octavilla *f*
Ⓑ VI repartir folletos
Ⓒ VT [+ *area, street*] repartir folletos en

leafy [ˈliːfɪ] ADJ (*compar* **leafier**; *superl* **leafiest**) frondoso, con muchas hojas; **the ~ suburbs of the city** los barrios residenciales de la ciudad

league[1] [liːg] N (= *measure*) legua *f*

league[2] [liːg] Ⓐ N liga *f* (*also Sport*), sociedad *f*, asociación *f*, comunidad *f*; **League of Nations** Sociedad *f* de las Naciones; **he's not in the same ~** (*fig*) no está al mismo nivel; **they're not in the same ~** (*fig*) no hay comparación; **to be in ~ with sb** estar de manga con algn, haberse confabulado con algn
Ⓑ CPD ► **league champion(s)** NPL campeón *msing* de liga ► **league leader** N líder *m* de la liga ► **league table** N clasificación *f*

leak [liːk] Ⓐ N 1 (= *hole*) (*in roof*) gotera *f*; (*in pipe, radiator, tank*) rotura *f*; (*in boat*) vía *f* de agua; *see also* **spring B1**
2 (= *escape*) [*of gas, water, chemical*] escape *m*, fuga *f*
3 (*fig*) [*of information, document*] filtración *f*; *see also* **security B**
4 ✦**IDIOM to go for** *or* **have** *or* **take a ~**‡ echar una meada‡, mear‡
Ⓑ VI 1 (= *be leaky*) [*roof*] tener goteras; [*pipe, radiator, tank*] gotear, tener una fuga; [*boat*] hacer agua; [*pen*] perder tinta; **her shoes ~ed** le entraba agua en *or* por los zapatos; **the window is ~ing a bit** entra un poco de agua por la ventana; **my pen has ~ed onto my shirt** me ha caído tinta del bolígrafo en la camisa
2 (= *escape*) **radioactive gas was ~ing from a reactor** había un escape *or* fuga de gas radiactivo en un reactor; **water was ~ing through the roof** entraba agua por el tejado, goteaba agua del tejado
Ⓒ VT 1 [+ *liquid*] (= *discharge*) perder; (= *pour out*) derramar; **a tanker has ~ed oil into the Baltic Sea** un petrolero ha derramado petróleo al mar Báltico; **it is feared that these weapons could ~ plutonium** se teme que se produzca un escape de plutonio de estas armas
2 (*fig*) [+ *information, document*] filtrar (**to** a); **his letter was ~ed to the press** su carta se filtró a la prensa

►**leak in** VI + ADV [*liquid*] entrar

►**leak out** VI + ADV 1 (*lit*) [*gas, liquid*] salirse
2 (*fig*) [*secret, news, information*] filtrarse

leakage [ˈliːkɪdʒ] N 1 (*lit*) [*of gas, liquid*] escape *m*, fuga *f*
2 (*fig*) filtración *f*

leakproof [ˈliːkpruːf] ADJ [*container*] hermético; [*nappy, pants*] impermeable

leaky [ˈliːkɪ] ADJ (*compar* **leakier**; *superl* **leakiest**) [*roof*] con goteras; [*pipe, container*] que gotea, con fugas; [*boat*] que hace agua; [*pen*] que pierde tinta

lean[1] [liːn] Ⓐ ADJ (*compar* **leaner**; *superl* **leanest**) 1 (= *slim*) [*person, body*] delgado, enjuto; [*animal*] flaco; **companies will need to be ~er in order to compete** las compañías tendrán que racionalizarse para ser más competitivas
2 (= *not prosperous*) [*times*] difícil; [*harvest*] pobre; **to have a ~ time of it** pasar por una mala racha; **~ years** años *mpl* de vacas flacas
3 (= *not fatty*) [*meat*] magro, sin grasa
4 (*Aut*) **~ mixture** mezcla *f* pobre
Ⓑ N (*Culin*) magro *m*

lean[2] [liːn] (*pt, pp* **leaned** *or* **leant**) Ⓐ VI 1 (= *slope*) inclinarse, ladearse; **to ~ to(wards) the left/right** (*lit*) estar inclinado hacia la izquierda/derecha; (*fig*) (*Pol*) inclinarse hacia la izquierda/la derecha; **to ~ towards sb's opinion** inclinarse por la opinión de algn
2 (*for support*) apoyarse; **to ~ on/against sth** apoyarse en/contra algo; **to ~ on sb** (*lit*) apoyarse en algn; (*fig*) (= *put pressure on*) presionar a algn; **to ~ on sb for support** (*fig*) contar con el apoyo de algn
Ⓑ VT **to ~ a ladder/a bicycle against a wall** apoyar una escala/una bicicleta contra una pared; **to ~ one's head on sb's shoulder** apoyar la cabeza en el hombro de algn

►**lean back** VI + ADV reclinarse, recostarse

►**lean forward** VI + ADV inclinarse hacia delante

►**lean out** VI + ADV asomarse; **to ~ out of the window** asomarse a *or* por la ventana

►**lean over** Ⓐ VI + ADV inclinarse; **to ~ over backwards to help sb** volcarse *or* desvivirse por ayudar a algn; **we've ~ed over backwards to get agreement** hemos hecho todo lo posible *or* nos hemos volcado para llegar a un acuerdo
Ⓑ VI + PREP inclinarse sobre

Leander [liːˈændəʳ] N Leandro

leaning [ˈliːnɪŋ] Ⓐ N inclinación *f* (**to, towards** hacia), tendencia *f* (**to, towards** a); **she has leftish ~s** tiene inclinaciones *or* tendencias izquierdistas; **he has artistic ~s** tiene inclinaciones artísticas
Ⓑ ADJ inclinado; **the Leaning Tower of Pisa** la Torre Inclinada de Pisa

leanness [ˈliːnnɪs] N 1 [*of person, body*] delgadez *f*; [*of animal*] flacura *f*, flaqueza *f*
2 [*of meat*] lo magro; **the meat is valued for its ~** la carne es muy apreciada por lo magra que es

leant [lent] PT, PP *of* **lean**[2]

lean-to [ˈliːntuː] N (*pl* **lean-tos**) cobertizo *m*

leap [liːp] (*vb: pp, pt* **leaped** *or* **leapt**) Ⓐ N 1 (= *jump*) 1·1 (*lit*) salto *m*; (*showing exuberance*) salto *m*, brinco *m*
1·2 (*fig*) salto *m*; **by ~s and bounds** a pasos agigantados; **a ~ in the dark** un salto al vacío; **his heart gave a ~** le dio un vuelco el corazón; **it doesn't take a great ~ of the imagination to foresee what will happen** no se requiere un gran esfuerzo de imaginación para prever lo que va a pasar; **she successfully made the ~ into films** dio el salto con éxito al mundo del cine; **to make** *or* **take a huge ~ forward** dar un gran salto *or* paso hacia adelante; **to make** *or* **take a ~ of faith** hacer un gran esfuerzo de fe, hacer profesión de fe; **mental ~** salto *m* mental; **a ~ into the unknown** un salto a lo desconocido
2 (= *increase*) subida *f*; **a 6% ~ in profits** una subida de un 6% en las ganancias
Ⓑ VI 1 (= *jump*) 1·1 (*lit*) saltar; (*exuberantly*) brincar, saltar; **to ~ about** dar saltos, brincar; **to ~ about with excitement** dar saltos *or* brincar de emoción; **the dog ~ed at the man, snarling** el perro saltó *or* se arrojó sobre el hombre gruñiendo; **he ~t down from his horse** se bajó del caballo de un salto; **the car ~t forward** el coche dio una sacudida; **he ~t from a moving train** saltó de un tren en marcha; **he ~ed into the river** saltó *or* se tiró al río; **he ~t off/onto the bus** bajó del/subió al autobús de un salto; **he suddenly ~t on top of me** de repente me saltó *or* se me tiró encima; **to ~ out of a car** bajarse *or* saltar de un coche; **she ~t out of bed** se levantó de la cama de un salto, saltó de la cama; **to ~ over** [+ *obstacle*] saltar por encima de; [+ *stream*] cruzar de un salto; **to ~ to one's feet** levantarse de un salto
1·2 (*fig*) **my heart ~ed** me dio un vuelco el corazón; **she ~t at the chance to play the part** no dejó escapar la oportunidad de representar el papel; **to ~ at an offer** aceptar una oferta al vuelo; **he ~t on my mistake** se lanzó sobre mi error; **the tabloids are quick to ~ on such cases** la prensa amarilla está a la que salta con estos casos; **the headline ~t out at her** el titular le saltó a la vista; **he ~t to his brother's defence** enseguida saltó a defender a su hermano
2 (= *increase*) **sales ~t by one third** las ventas se incrementaron repentinamente en un tercio
Ⓒ VT [+ *fence, ditch*] saltar por encima de; [+ *stream, river*] cruzar de un salto
Ⓓ CPD ► **leap year** N año *m* bisiesto

►**leap up** VI + ADV 1 [*person*] levantarse de un salto; [*flame*] subir; **the dog ~t up at him** el perro le saltó *or* se le echó encima
2 (= *increase*) [*profits, sales, prices, unemployment*] subir de repente

leapfrog [ˈliːpfrɒg] Ⓐ N pídola *f*; **to play ~** jugar a la pídola
Ⓑ VI jugar a la pídola; **to ~ over sth/sb** saltar por encima de algo/algn
Ⓒ VT saltar por encima de

leapt [lept] PT, PP *of* **leap**

learn [lɜːn] (*pt, pp* **learned** *or* **learnt**) Ⓐ VT 1 (*by study, practice, etc*) [+ *language, words, skill*] aprender; [+ *instrument*] aprender a tocar; **you can ~ a lot by listening and thinking** se puede aprender mucho escuchando y pensando; **I ~t a lot from her** aprendí mucho de ella; **you must ~ patience** tienes que aprender a tener paciencia; **to ~ (how) to do sth** aprender a hacer algo; **to ~ sth by heart** aprender(se) algo de memoria; ✦**IDIOM to ~ one's lesson** aprender la lección, escarmentar; *see also* **line**[1] **A4**, **rope A**

2 (= *find out*) enterarse de; **to ~ that** enterarse de que

3 (‡) (= *show, teach*) (*incorrect usage*) enseñar; **that'll ~ you** para que escarmientes *or* aprendas, te está bien empleado; **I'll ~ you!** ¡yo te enseñaré!

Ⓑ VI 1 (*by study, practice, etc*) aprender; **it's never too late to ~** nunca es tarde para aprender; **he'll ~!** ¡un día aprenderá!, ¡ya aprenderá!; **we are ~ing about the Romans** estamos estudiando los romanos; **to ~ from experience** aprender por experiencia; **to ~ from one's mistakes** aprender de los errores (cometidos)

2 (= *find out*) **to ~ of** *or* **about sth** enterarse de algo

►**learn off** VT + ADV aprender de memoria

►**learn up** VT + ADV esforzarse por aprender, empollar

learned [ˈlɜːnɪd] Ⓐ ADJ [*person*] docto, erudito; [*remark, speech, book*] erudito; [*profession*] liberal; **my ~ friend** (*frm*) mi distinguido colega

Ⓑ CPD ► **learned body** N academia *f* ► **learned society** N sociedad *f* científica

learnedly [ˈlɜːnɪdlɪ] ADV eruditamente

learner [ˈlɜːnəʳ] Ⓐ N (= *novice*) principiante *mf*; (= *student*) estudiante *mf*; (*also* **~ driver**) (*Brit*) conductor(a) *m/f* en prácticas, aprendiz(a) *m/f* de conductor(a); **to be a slow ~** tener dificultades de aprendizaje; **to be a fast ~** aprender con mucha rapidez

Ⓑ CPD ► **learner driver** N (*Brit*) conductor(a) *m/f* en prácticas, aprendiz(a) *m/f* de conductor(a)

learner-centred, **learner-centered** (*US*) [ˈlɜːnəˌsentəd] ADJ centrado en el alumno

learning [ˈlɜːnɪŋ] Ⓐ N 1 (= *act*) aprendizaje *m*

2 (= *knowledge*) conocimientos *mpl*, saber *m*; (= *erudition*) saber *m*, erudición *f*; **man of ~** sabio *m*, erudito *m*; **seat of ~** centro *m* de estudios

Ⓑ CPD ► **learning curve** N proceso *m* de aprendizaje; **it's a ~ curve** hay que ir aprendiendo poco a poco; **it's going to be a steep ~ curve** va a ser un proceso de aprendizaje rápido ► **learning difficulties** NPL dificultades *fpl* de aprendizaje

learnt [lɜːnt] (*esp Brit*) PT, PP *of* **learn**

lease [liːs] Ⓐ N contrato *m* de arrendamiento; **to take a house on a 99-year ~** alquilar una casa con un contrato de arrendamiento de 99 años; **to let sth out on ~** arrendar algo, dar algo en arriendo; ✦*IDIOMS* **to give sb a new ~ of life** hacer revivir a algn; **to take on a new ~ of life** [*person*] recobrar su vigor; [*thing*] renovarse

Ⓑ VT (= *take*) arrendar (**from** de), tomar en arriendo; (= *rent*) alquilar; (= *give*) (*also* **~ out**) arrendar, alquilar, dar en arriendo

►**lease back** VT + ADV subarrendar

leaseback [ˈliːsbæk] N rearrendamiento *m* al vendedor, subarriendo *m*

leasehold [ˈliːshəʊld] Ⓐ N (= *contract*) derechos *mpl* de arrendamiento; (= *property*) inmueble *m* arrendado

Ⓑ CPD [*property, house, flat*] arrendado, alquilado ► **leasehold reform** N reforma *f* del sistema de arriendos

leaseholder [ˈliːshəʊldəʳ] N arrendatario/a *m/f*

leash [liːʃ] N correa *f*, traílla *f*; *see also* **strain[1] C**

leasing [ˈliːsɪŋ] N (= *option to buy*) alquiler *m* con opción a compra, leasing *m*; (= *renting*) arrendamiento *m*, alquiler *m*; (*Fin*) arrendamiento *m* financiero

➤ LANGUAGE IN USE: **least B1** 26.3

least [liːst] Ⓐ ADJ 1 SUPERL *of* **little[2]** 1·1 (= *minimum, smallest amount of*) menor; **with the ~ possible delay** con el menor retraso posible, a la mayor brevedad posible (*frm*); **choose yoghurts which contain the ~ fat** elija los yogures que contengan la menor cantidad de grasa; **he didn't have the ~ difficulty deciding** no le costó nada decidir

1·2 (= *smallest, slightest*) [*idea, hint, complaint*] más mínimo; **she wasn't the ~ bit jealous** no estaba celosa en lo más mínimo; **we haven't the ~ idea where he is** no tenemos la más mínima *or* la menor idea de dónde está; **the ~ thing upsets her** se ofende a la mínima *or* por lo más mínimo; *see also* **last[1] C1**, **line[1] A11**

2 (*in comparisons*) menos; **he has the ~ money** es el que menos dinero tiene

Ⓑ PRON 1 SUPERL *of* **little[2]** 1·1 (= *the very minimum*) (*gen*) lo menos; (= *amount*) lo mínimo; **"thanks, anyway" — "it was the ~ I could do"** —gracias de todas formas —era lo menos que podía hacer; **what's the ~ you are willing to accept?** ¿qué es lo mínimo que estás dispuesto a aceptar?; **that's the ~ of it** eso es lo de menos; **the ~ said the better** cuanto menos se hable de eso mejor; **accommodation was basic to say the ~** el alojamiento era muy sencillo, por no decir otra cosa; ✦*PROV* **~ said, soonest mended** cuanto menos se diga, antes se arregla

1·2 (*in comparisons*) **the country that spends the ~ on education** el país que menos (se) gasta en materia de enseñanza; **that's the ~ of my worries** eso es lo que menos me preocupa

2 **in the ~**: **I don't mind in the ~** no me importa lo más mínimo; **Pete wasn't in the ~ in love with me** Pete no estaba ni mucho menos enamorado de mí; **"don't you mind?" — "not in the ~"** —¿no te importa? —en absoluto *or* —para nada

3 **at ~** 3·1 (= *not less than*) por lo menos, como mínimo, al menos; **I must have slept for at ~ 12 hours** debo de haber dormido por lo menos *or* como mínimo *or* al menos 12 horas; **he earns at ~ as much as you do** gana por lo menos *or* al menos tanto como tú

3·2 (= *if nothing more*) al menos, por lo menos; **we can at ~ try** al menos *or* por lo menos podemos intentarlo

3·3 (= *for all that*) por lo menos, al menos; **it's rather laborious but at ~ it is not dangerous** requiere bastante trabajo pero por lo menos *or* al menos no es peligroso

3·4 (= *anyway*) al menos, por lo menos; **Etta appeared to be asleep, at ~ her eyes were shut** Etta parecía estar dormida, al menos *or* por lo menos tenía los ojos cerrados

3·5 **at the (very) ~** como mínimo, como poco

Ⓒ ADV menos; **the ~ expensive car** el coche menos caro; **they're the ones who need it the ~** son los que menos lo necesitan; **when ~ expected** cuando menos se espera; **~ of all me** y yo menos, yo menos que nadie; **no one knew, ~ of all me** nadie lo sabía, y yo menos; **for a variety of reasons, not ~ because it is cheap** por toda una serie de razones, entre ellas que es barato

leastways* [ˈliːstweɪz] ADV de todos modos

leastwise [ˈliːstwaɪz] ADV por lo menos

least-worst [ˈliːstwɜːst] ADJ menos malo; **the ~ scenario** el panorama menos malo (de todos)

leather [ˈleðəʳ] Ⓐ N 1 (= *hide*) cuero *m*, piel *f*

2 (= *washleather*) gamuza *f*

3 **leathers** (*for motorcyclist*) ropa *f* de cuero

Ⓑ VT (= *thrash*) zurrar*

Ⓒ CPD de cuero, de piel ► **leather goods** NPL artículos *mpl* de cuero ► **leather jacket** N cazadora *f* de cuero *or* de piel

leather-bound [ˈleðəˌbaʊnd] ADJ encuadernado en cuero

leatherette [ˌleðəˈret] N cuero *m* sintético, piel *f* sintética, polipiel *f*

leathering* [ˈleðərɪŋ] N **to give sb a ~** dar una paliza a algn

leathern (*liter*) [ˈleðə(ː)n] ADJ de cuero

leatherneck* [ˈleðənek] N (*US*) infante *m* de marina

leathery [ˈleðərɪ] ADJ [*meat*] correoso; [*skin*] curtido

leave [liːv] (*vb: pt, pp* **left**) Ⓐ N 1 (*frm*) (= *permission*) permiso *m*; **to ask ~ to do sth** pedir permiso para hacer algo; **by your ~**† con permiso de usted; **without so much as a "by your ~"** sin pedir permiso a nadie; **I take ~ to doubt it** me permito dudarlo

2 (= *permission to be absent*) permiso *m*; (*Mil*) (*brief*) permiso *m*; (*lengthy, compassionate*) licencia *f*; **~ of absence** permiso *m* para ausentarse; **to be on ~** estar de permiso *or* (*S. Cone*) licenciado

3 (= *departure*) **to take (one's) ~ (of sb)** despedirse (de algn); **to take ~ of one's senses** perder el juicio; **have you taken ~ of your senses?** ¿te has vuelto loco?

Ⓑ VT 1 (= *go away from*) dejar, marcharse de; [+ *room*] salir de, abandonar; [+ *hospital*] salir de; [+ *person*] abandonar, dejar; **I'll ~ you at the station** te dejo en la estación; **I must ~ you** tengo que despedirme *or* marcharme; **you may ~ us** (*frm*) puede retirarse (*frm*); **she ~s home at 8am** sale de casa a las ocho; **he left home when he was 18** se fue de casa a los 18 años; **to ~ one's post** (*improperly*) abandonar su puesto; **to ~ the rails** descarrilar, salirse de las vías; **the car left the road** el coche se salió de la carretera; **to ~ school** (= *finish studies*) terminar el colegio; **to ~ the table** levantarse de la mesa; **he has left his wife** ha dejado *or* abandonado a su mujer

2 (= *forget*) dejar, olvidar

3 (= *bequeath*) dejar, legar

4 (= *allow to remain*) dejar; **to ~ two pages blank** dejar dos páginas en blanco; **to ~ things lying about** dejar las cosas de cualquier modo; **it's best to ~ him alone** es mejor dejarlo solo; **to ~ sb alone** *or* **in peace** dejar a algn en paz; **let's ~ it at that** dejémoslo así, ¡ya está bien (así)!; **this left me free for the afternoon** eso me dejó la tarde libre; **to ~ one's greens** no comer las verduras; **to ~ a good impression on sb** producir a algn una buena impresión; **it ~s much to be desired** deja mucho que desear; **to ~ one's supper** dejar la cena sin comer; **take it or ~ it** lo tomas o lo dejas; **~ it to me!** ¡yo me encargo!, ¡tú, déjamelo a mí!; **I'll ~ it up to you** lo dejo a tu criterio; **I ~ it to you to judge** júzguelo usted; **he ~s a wife and a child** le sobreviven su viuda y un hijo, deja mujer y un hijo; **to ~ sth with sb** dejar algo en manos de algn, entregar algo a algn; **I left the children with my mother** dejé los niños con mi madre; **~ it with me** yo me encargaré del asunto

5 **to be left** (= *remain*) quedar; **there's nothing left** no queda nada; **how many are (there) left?** ¿cuántos quedan?; **we were left with four** quedamos con cuatro, nos quedaron cuatro; **nothing was left for me but to sell it** no tuve más remedio que venderlo; **there are three left over** sobran tres; **all the money I have left** todo el dinero que me

queda
[6] (*Math*) **three from ten ~s seven** diez menos tres son siete, de tres a diez van siete
Ⓒ VI (= *go out*) salir; (= *go away*) [*person*] irse, marcharse, partir; [*train, bus*] salir; **the train is leaving in ten minutes** el tren sale dentro de diez minutos

►**leave about**, **leave around** VT + ADV dejar tirado

►**leave aside** VT + ADV dejar de lado; **leaving that aside, let's consider ...** dejando eso de lado, consideremos ...

►**leave behind** VT + ADV [1] (= *not take*) [+ *person*] dejar, no llevar consigo; **we had to ~ the furniture behind** no pudimos llevarnos los muebles; **we have left all that behind us** (*fig*) todo eso ha quedado atrás *or* ya es historia [2] (= *forget*) olvidarse [3] (= *outdistance*) dejar atrás

►**leave in** VT + ADV [+ *passage, words*] dejar tal como está/estaba, conservar; [+ *plug*] dejar puesto

►**leave off** Ⓐ VT + ADV [1] omitir, no incluir
[2] [+ *lid*] no poner, dejar sin poner; [+ *clothes*] no ponerse
[3] [+ *gas*] no poner, no encender; [+ *light*] dejar apagado
[4] (*) (= *stop*) [+ *work*] terminar, suspender; **to ~ off smoking** dejar de fumar; **to ~ off working** dejar *or* terminar de trabajar; **when it ~s off raining** cuando deje de llover; **we'll carry on where we left off last time** continuaremos por donde quedamos la última vez
Ⓑ VI + ADV (*) (= *stop*) parar; **when the rain ~s off** cuando deje de llover; **~ off, will you!** ¡déjalo!

►**leave on** VT + ADV [+ *clothes*] dejar puesto, no quitarse; [+ *light, TV*] dejar encendido *or* (*LAm*) prendido; **to ~ one's hat on** seguir con el sombrero puesto, no quitarse el sombrero

►**leave out** VT + ADV [1] (= *omit*) [+ *word, passage*] (*on purpose*) omitir; (*accidentally*) omitir, saltarse; [+ *person*] dejar fuera, excluir; **nobody wanted to be left out** nadie quería quedar fuera; **he feels left out** se siente excluido; ✦**IDIOM ~ it out!** (*Brit‡*) ¡venga ya!*, ¡no me vengas con esas!*, ¡tírate de la moto! (*Sp‡*) [2] (= *not put back*) no devolver a su lugar, no guardar; (= *leave outside*) dejar fuera; **it got left out in the rain** quedó fuera bajo la lluvia; **the cat was left out all night** el gato pasó toda la noche fuera [3] (= *leave ready*) [+ *food, meal*] dejar preparado

►**leave over** VT + ADV [1] (*after use*) **she saved whatever was left over of her wages** ahorraba lo que le sobraba del sueldo; **there is some wine left over from the party** queda un poco de vino de la fiesta; **these are hang-ups left over from his childhood** eso son traumas de su niñez; *see also* **leave B5**
[2] (= *postpone*) dejar, aplazar

leaven ['levn] Ⓐ N levadura *f*; (*fig*) toque *m*
Ⓑ VT leudar; (*fig*) (= *enliven*) aligerar

leavening ['levnɪŋ] N levadura *f*; (*fig*) toque *m*

leaves [liːvz] NPL *of* **leaf**

leave-taking ['liːv,teɪkɪŋ] N despedida *f*

leaving ['liːvɪŋ] Ⓐ N (= *departure*) salida *f*
Ⓑ CPD [*ceremony, present*] de despedida

leavings ['liːvɪŋz] NPL sobras *fpl*, restos *mpl*

Lebanese [,lebə'niːz] Ⓐ ADJ libanés
Ⓑ N libanés/esa *m/f*

Lebanon ['lebənən] N **the ~** el Líbano

lech* [letʃ] Ⓐ N libidinoso *m*
Ⓑ VI **to ~ after sb**: **he's ~ing after his secretary** se le van los ojos detrás de su secretaria*, se le alegran las pajarillas cuando ve a su secretaria (*hum*)

lecher ['letʃəʳ] N libidinoso *m*

lecherous ['letʃərəs] ADJ lascivo, lujurioso

lecherously ['letʃərəslɪ] ADV lascivamente

lechery ['letʃərɪ] N lascivia *f*, lujuria *f*

lectern ['lektə(ː)n] N atril *m*; (*Rel*) facistol *m*

lector ['lektɔːʳ] N (*Univ*) profesor(a) *m/f* de universidad

lecture ['lektʃəʳ] Ⓐ N [1] (*Univ*) clase *f*; (*by visitor*) conferencia *f*; (*less formal*) charla *f*; **to attend ~s on** dar *or* recibir clases de, seguir un curso sobre *or* de; **to give a ~** dar una conferencia; (*less formal*) dar una charla
[2] (*fig*) sermón *m*; **I gave him a ~ on good manners** le eché un sermón sobre buenos modales
Ⓑ VI **to ~ (in *or* on sth)** dar clases (de algo); **she ~s in Law** da clases de derecho; **he ~s at Princeton** es profesor en Princeton
Ⓒ VT (= *scold*) sermonear
Ⓓ CPD ► **lecture hall** N (*Univ*) aula *f*; (*gen*) sala *f* de conferencias ► **lecture notes** NPL apuntes *mpl* de clase ► **lecture room**, **lecture theatre** N = **lecture hall**

lecturer ['lektʃərəʳ] N (= *visitor*) conferenciante *mf*; (*Brit Univ*) profesor(a) *m/f*

lectureship ['lektʃəʃɪp] N cargo *m or* puesto *m* de profesor (adjunto)

LED N ABBR = **light-emitting diode**

led [led] PT, PP *of* **lead²**

ledge [ledʒ] N (*on wall, of window*) alféizar *m*; (= *shelf*) repisa *f*, anaquel *m*; (*on mountain*) saliente *m*, cornisa *f*

ledger ['ledʒəʳ] N libro *m* mayor

ledger line ['ledʒə,laɪn] N línea *f* suplementaria

lee [liː] Ⓐ N sotavento *m*; (= *shelter*) abrigo *m*, socaire *m*; **in the ~ of** al socaire *or* abrigo de
Ⓑ ADJ de sotavento

leech [liːtʃ] N sanguijuela *f* (*also fig*); ✦**IDIOM to stick to sb like a ~** pegarse a algn como una lapa*

leek [liːk] N puerro *m*

leer [lɪəʳ] Ⓐ N mirada *f* lasciva; **he said with a ~** dijo con una sonrisa lasciva
Ⓑ VI mirar de manera lasciva; **to ~ at sb** lanzar una mirada lasciva a algn

leery ['lɪərɪ] ADJ (= *cautious*) cauteloso; (= *suspicious*) receloso; **to be ~ of sth/sb** recelar de algo/algn

lees [liːz] NPL heces *fpl*, poso *m*

leeward ['liːwəd] Ⓐ ADJ (*Naut*) de sotavento
Ⓑ ADV a sotavento
Ⓒ N (*Naut*) sotavento *m*; **to ~** a sotavento (**of** de)

Leeward Isles ['liːwəd,aɪlz] NPL Islas *fpl* de Sotavento

leeway ['liːweɪ] N (*Naut*) deriva *f*; (*fig*) (= *scope*) libertad *f* de acción; **that doesn't give me much ~** (= *scope*) eso no me deja mucha libertad de acción; (= *time to spare*) eso no me deja mucho margen de tiempo

left¹ [left] PT, PP *of* **leave**

left² [left] Ⓐ ADJ [1] izquierdo; **~ shoe** zapato *m* (del pie) izquierdo; **take a ~ turn** gira a la izquierda; ✦**IDIOM to have two ~ feet*** ser un patoso*
[2] (*Pol*) de izquierda, de izquierdas (*Sp*)
Ⓑ ADV [*turn, look*] a la izquierda; ✦**IDIOMS ~, right and centre** ◊ **~ and right** (*US*) a diestra y siniestra, a diestro y siniestro (*Sp*); **they owe money ~, right and centre** deben dinero a todos, tienen deudas por doquier
Ⓒ N [1] (= *left side*) izquierda *f*; **turn it to the ~** [+ *key, knob*] gíralo a la izquierda; **pictured from ~ to right are ...** de izquierda a derecha vemos a ...; **the third from the ~** el tercero empezando por la izquierda; **on** *or* **to my, your** *etc* **~** a mi, tu *etc* izquierda; **on the ~** a la izquierda; **it's on the ~ as you go in** está a la izquierda según entras; **it's the first/second door on the ~** es la primera/segunda puerta a la izquierda; **to drive on the ~** conducir *or* (*LAm*) manejar por la izquierda; **"keep left"** "manténgase a la izquierda"
[2] (= *left turning*) **take the next ~** toma la próxima a la izquierda
[3] (*Boxing*) (= *left hand*) izquierda *f*; (= *punch*) izquierdazo *m*, golpe *m* de izquierda *or* con la izquierda
[4] **the ~** (*Pol*) la izquierda; **the parties of the ~** los partidos de izquierda *or* (*Sp*) izquierdas
Ⓓ CPD ► **left back** N (*Sport*) (= *player*) lateral *mf* izquierdo/a; (= *position*) lateral *m* izquierdo ► **left field** N (*Baseball*) (= *area*) jardín *m* izquierdo; (= *position*) jardinero/a *m/f* izquierdo/a; **to come out of ~ field** (*esp US**) (*fig*): **his question/decision came out of ~ field** su pregunta/decisión me/le *etc* pilló desprevenido ► **left half** N (*Sport*) (= *player*) lateral *mf* izquierdo/a; (= *position*) lateral *m* izquierdo ► **left wing** N (*Sport*) banda *f* izquierda; (*Pol*) ala *f* izquierda; *see also* **left-wing**

left-click ['leftklɪk] Ⓐ VI cliquear con la parte izquierda del ratón (**on** en)
Ⓑ VT **to ~ an icon** cliquear en un icono con la parte izquierda del ratón

left-hand ['lefthænd] ADJ **~ drive**: **a ~ drive car** un coche con el volante a la izquierda; **is it a ~ drive?** ¿tiene el volante a la izquierda?; **~ page** página *f* izquierda; **~ side** lado *m* izquierdo, izquierda *f*; **the house is on the ~ side** la casa está a la izquierda *or* en el lado izquierdo; **on the ~ side of the road** en el lado izquierdo de la carretera; **~ turn** vuelta *f* a la izquierda; **to make a ~ turn** girar a la izquierda

left-handed ['left'hændɪd] ADJ [*person*] zurdo; [*shot, stroke*] (realizado) con la (mano) izquierda; [*tool*] para zurdos; (*fig*) [*compliment*] con doble sentido, ambiguo

left-hander [,left'hændəʳ] N (= *person*) zurdo/a *m/f*; (= *blow*) izquierdazo *m*

leftie* ['leftɪ] N (*Brit*) izquierdista *mf*

leftism ['leftɪzəm] N izquierdismo *m*

leftist ['leftɪst] ADJ, N izquierdista *mf*

left-luggage ['left'lʌgɪdʒ] Ⓐ N (*also* **~ office**) (*Brit*) consigna *f*
Ⓑ CPD ► **left-luggage locker** N (*Brit*) consigna *f* automática ► **left-luggage office** N consigna *f*

leftover ['leftəʊvəʳ] Ⓐ ADJ sobrante, restante; **we used up the ~ turkey** usamos el pavo que había sobrado
Ⓑ N [1] (= *relic*) **a ~ from another age** una reliquia de otra edad
[2] **leftovers** sobras *fpl*, restos *mpl*

leftward ['leftwəd] Ⓐ ADJ [*movement*] a *or* hacia la izquierda
Ⓑ ADV [*move*] a *or* hacia la izquierda

leftwards ['leftwədz] ADV (*esp Brit*) = **leftward B**

left-wing ['left,wɪŋ] ADJ (*Pol*) de izquierda, izquierdista, de izquierdas (*Sp*)

left-winger ['left'wɪŋəʳ] N (*Pol*) izquierdista *mf*; (*Sport*) delantero/a *m/f* izquierdo/a

lefty* ['leftɪ] N (*Brit Pol*) izquierdista *mf*, rojillo/a *m/f*

leg [leg] (A) N [1] [*of person*] pierna *f*; [*of animal, bird, insect*] pata *f*; (= *central support*) pie *m*; [*of trousers*] pernera *f*; [*of stocking*] caña *f*; **artificial ~** pierna *f* ortopédica *or* artificial; **wooden ~** pierna *f* de madera, pata *f* de palo*; **he was the fastest thing on two ~s** era rápido donde los haya; **to give sb a ~ up** (*Brit**) (*lit*) aupar a algn; (*fig*) dar un empujoncito a algn*, echar un cable a algn*; ✦***IDIOMS* to get one's** *or* **a ~ over**‡ (*hum*) (= *have sex*) darse un revolcón*; **to be on its/one's last ~s*** estar en las últimas; **the company is on its last ~s** la compañía está en las últimas*; **the washing machine is on its last ~s** la lavadora está en las últimas*; **to pull sb's ~** tomar el pelo a algn; **to shake a ~** (= *hurry*) espabilarse; (= *dance*) menear *or* mover el esqueleto*; **show a ~!*** ¡a levantarse!; **he hasn't got a ~ to stand on** (*in case, argument*) no tiene donde agarrarse*; *see also* **arm[1] 1, break B1, hind[1], inside E, last[1] A3, stretch B3**
[2] (*Culin*) [*of lamb, mutton, pork*] pierna *f*; [*of chicken, turkey*] muslo *m*, pata *f*; **frogs' ~s** ancas *fpl* de rana
[3] (= *stage*) [*of journey*] tramo *m*, etapa *f*; [*of race*] etapa *f*, manga *f*; [*of championship*] vuelta *f*
(B) VT (*) **to ~ it** (= *go on foot*) ir a pata*; (= *run*) echarse una carrera*; (= *run away*) salir por piernas *or* patas*
(C) CPD ► **leg bone** N tibia *f* ► **leg iron** N (*Med*) aparato *m* ortopédico ► **leg irons** NPL (*for prisoner*) grilletes *mpl* ► **leg muscles** NPL músculos *mpl* de las piernas ► **leg room** N sitio *m* para las piernas

legacy ['legəsɪ] N legado *m*; (*fig*) legado *m*, herencia *f*; **this inflation is a ~ of the previous government** esta inflación es un legado del gobierno anterior

legal ['liːgəl] (A) ADJ [1] (= *judicial*) [*error*] judicial; [*document*] legal; [*firm*] de abogados; [*question, matter*] legal, jurídico; **to take ~ action** poner una denuncia; **to take ~ action against sb** poner una denuncia a algn, presentar una demanda (judicial) contra algn; **to take ~ advice** consultar a un abogado; **~ adviser** asesor(a) *m/f* jurídico/a; **~ battle** contienda *f* judicial *or* legal, pleito *m*; **~ costs** *or* **fees** costas *fpl*, gastos *mpl* judiciales; **~ department** (*of bank, company*) departamento *m* jurídico; **to be above** *or* **over the ~ limit** estar por encima del límite permitido por ley; **to be below** *or* **under the ~ limit** estar por debajo del límite permitido por ley; **~ loophole** laguna *f* en la legislación, resquicio *m* legal; **~ proceedings** procedimiento *m* jurídico, pleito *m*; **to start** *or* **initiate ~ proceedings against sb** entablar un pleito contra algn; **the ~ process** el proceso judicial *or* jurídico; **the ~ profession** la abogacía; **to enter the ~ profession** hacerse abogado; **they were allowed no ~ representation** no les permitieron que un abogado les representara
[2] (= *lawful*) [*activity, action*] legal, legítimo; [*owner*] legítimo; (= *under the law*) [*right, protection*] legal; **to be ~ to do sth** ser legal hacer algo; **to have the ~ authority to do sth** tener la autoridad *or* el poder legal para hacer algo; **to make sth ~** legalizar algo; **they decided to make it ~*** (= *get married*) decidieron formalizar *or* legalizar su relación
(B) CPD ► **legal aid** N asistencia *f* de un abogado de oficio ► **legal holiday** N (*US*) fiesta *f* oficial, día *m* festivo oficial, (día *m*) feriado *m* (*LAm*) ► **legal system** N sistema *m* jurídico ► **legal tender** N (*Fin*) moneda *f* de curso legal

legalese [ˌliːgə'liːz] N jerga *f* legal

legalistic [ˌliːgə'lɪstɪk] ADJ legalista

legality [lɪ'gælɪtɪ] N legalidad *f*

legalization [ˌliːgəlaɪ'zeɪʃən] N legalización *f*

legalize ['liːgəlaɪz] VT [+ *document, political party*] legalizar; [+ *drugs, euthanasia, abortion*] legalizar, despenalizar; **to ~ one's position** legalizar la situación

legally ['liːgəlɪ] ADV [1] (= *from a legal point of view*) [*obliged, required*] por ley; [*entitled*] legalmente, según la ley; **~, the whole issue is a nightmare** desde el punto de vista legal, toda esa cuestión es una pesadilla; **this contract is ~ binding** el contrato vincula jurídicamente, el contrato implica obligatoriedad jurídica; **to be ~ responsible for sth/sb** ser legalmente responsable *or* el/la responsable legal de algo/algn
[2] (= *lawfully*) legalmente; **their wealth was ~ acquired** consiguieron su riqueza por medios legales *or* legalmente

legate ['legɪt] N legado *m*

legatee [ˌlegə'tiː] N legatario/a *m/f*

legation [lɪ'geɪʃən] N legación *f*

legato [lɪ'gɑːtəʊ] (*Mus*) (A) ADJ ligado
(B) ADV ligado
(C) N ligadura *f*

legend ['ledʒənd] N leyenda *f*; **she was a ~ in her own lifetime** fue una leyenda en su vida, fue un mito viviente

legendary ['ledʒəndərɪ] ADJ legendario

legerdemain ['ledʒədə'meɪn] N juego *m* de manos, prestidigitación *f*

-legged ['legɪd] ADJ (*ending in compounds*) [*person*] de piernas…; [*animal*] de patas…; [*stool*] de tres patas; **long~** de piernas largas, zancudo; **three~** de tres piernas

leggings ['legɪŋz] NPL mallas *fpl*, leotardos *mpl*; (*baby's*) pantalones *mpl* polainas

leggo‡ [le'gəʊ] EXCL = **let go**; *see* **go A24**

leggy ['legɪ] ADJ (*compar* **leggier**, *superl* **leggiest**) [*person*] de piernas largas, patilargo*; (= *attractive*) [*girl*] de piernas bonitas, de piernas atractivas

Leghorn ['leg'hɔːn] N Livorno *m*; (*Hist*) Liorna *f*

legibility [ˌledʒɪ'bɪlɪtɪ] N legibilidad *f*

legible ['ledʒəbl] ADJ legible

legibly ['ledʒəblɪ] ADV legiblemente

legion ['liːdʒən] N legión *f* (*also fig*); **they are ~** son legión, son muchos

> **LEGION**
>
> *La* **American Legion** *es una organización de veteranos de las Fuerzas Armadas estadounidenses. Se fundó después de la Primera Guerra Mundial y se encarga del cuidado y la reintegración de los veteranos de guerra y sus familias. También es un órgano de presión ante el Congreso en favor de los intereses de los veteranos y de un sólido sistema de defensa nacional. A otro nivel, la* **American Legion** *ha creado clubs sociales para sus miembros.*
>
> *En el Reino Unido el equivalente de la* **American Legion** *es la* **British Legion** *que, todos los años en noviembre, recauda fondos mediante la venta de amapolas de papel.*
>
> ⇨ *Ver tb* POPPY DAY

legionary ['liːdʒənərɪ] (A) ADJ legionario
(B) N legionario *m*

legionnaire [ˌliːdʒə'neəʳ] N legionario *m*; **~'s disease** enfermedad *f* del legionario, legionella *f*

legislate ['ledʒɪsleɪt] (A) VI legislar; **one cannot ~ for every case** es imposible legislarlo todo
(B) VT **to ~ sth out of existence** hacer que algo desaparezca a base de legislación

legislation [ˌledʒɪs'leɪʃən] N (= *law*) ley *f*; (= *body of laws*) legislación *f*

legislative ['ledʒɪslətɪv] (A) ADJ legislativo
(B) CPD ► **legislative action** N acción *f* legislativa ► **legislative body** N cuerpo *m* legislativo

legislator ['ledʒɪsleɪtəʳ] N legislador(a) *m/f*

legislature ['ledʒɪslətʃəʳ] N asamblea *f* legislativa, legislatura *f* (*LAm*)

legist ['liːdʒɪst] N legista *mf*

legit* [lə'dʒɪt] ADJ **I checked him out, he's ~** he hecho averiguaciones y es de fiar, he hecho averiguaciones y es un tipo legal (*Sp**); **to go ~** legalizar la situación

legitimacy [lɪ'dʒɪtɪməsɪ] N [1] (= *lawfulness*) [*of government, action, birth*] legitimidad *f*
[2] (= *justifiableness*) [*of concern*] justificación; [*of argument*] validez *f*; **there can be no doubt as to the ~ of such claims** no cabe duda de que estas reclamaciones están justificadas

legitimate [lɪ'dʒɪtɪmɪt] (A) ADJ [1] (= *lawful*) [*government, right, power*] legítimo; [*business*] legal; **he has a ~ claim to the property** tiene el derecho legítimo de reivindicar la propiedad
[2] (= *valid*) [*reason, argument, target*] válido; [*complaint, conclusion*] justificado; [*interest*] legítimo; **it is perfectly ~ to ask questions** preguntar está perfectamente justificado
[3] (*Jur*) [*son, daughter*] legítimo
(B) VT = **legitimize**

legitimately [lɪ'dʒɪtɪmɪtlɪ] ADV [1] (= *lawfully*) legítimamente
[2] (= *justifiably*) [*expect*] justificadamente; **you could ~ argue that …** sería justo *or* estaría justificado argumentar que …; **he can ~ claim to speak for all South Africans** tiene sobradas razones para erigirse en portavoz de todos los sudafricanos; **he has demanded, quite ~, that …** ha exigido, con toda la razón, que …

legitimation [lɪˌdʒɪtɪ'meɪʃn] N legitimación *f*

legitimize [lɪ'dʒɪtɪmaɪz] VT legitimar; [+ *child, birth*] legalizar

legless ['leglɪs] ADJ [1] (= *without legs*) [*person*] sin piernas; [*animal*] sin patas
[2] (*Brit**) (= *drunk*) como una cuba*

legman ['legmæn] N (*pl* **legmen**) reportero/a *m/f*

leg-pull* ['legpʊl] N broma *f*, tomadura *f* de pelo*

leg-puller* ['legpʊləʳ] N bromista *mf*

leg-pulling* ['legˌpʊlɪŋ] N tomadura *f* de pelo*

legume ['legjuːm] N (= *species*) legumbre *f*; (= *pod*) vaina *f*

leguminous [le'gjuːmɪnəs] ADJ leguminoso

legwarmers ['legˌwɔːməz] NPL calentadores *mpl* (de piernas)

legwork ['legwɜːk] N trabajo *m* de campo, preparativos *mpl*; **to do the ~** hacer los preparativos

Leics. ABBR (*Brit*) = **Leicestershire**

leisure ['leʒəʳ] (*US*) ['liːʒəʳ] (A) N ocio *m*; **a life of ~** una vida de ocio, una vida ociosa; **do it at your ~** hazlo cuando tengas tiempo *or* te convenga; **to have the ~ to do sth** disponer de tiempo para hacer algo; *see also* **lady A1**
(B) CPD ► **leisure activities** NPL pasatiempos

mpl ► **leisure centre** N (*Brit*) polideportivo *m* ► **leisure industry** N sector *m* del ocio ► **leisure occupations**, **leisure pursuits** NPL = **leisure activities** ► **leisure suit** N chandal *m* ► **leisure time** N tiempo *m* libre; **in one's ~ time** en sus ratos libres, en los momentos de ocio ► **leisure wear** N ropa *f* de sport

leisured ['leʒəd] ADJ [*pace*] pausado; [*class*] acomodado

leisurely ['leʒəlɪ] Ⓐ ADJ [*stroll, swim, meal*] relajado, sin prisas; **at a ~ pace** sin prisas
Ⓑ ADV despacio, con calma

leitmotiv ['laɪtməʊ,tiːf] N leitmotiv *m*

lemma ['lemə] (*pl* **lemmas** *or* **lemmata** ['lemətə]) N lema *m*

lemmatization [,lemətaɪ'zeɪʃən] N lematización *f*

lemmatize ['lemətaɪz] VT lematizar

lemmatizer ['lemətaɪzəʳ] N lematizador *m*

lemming ['lemɪŋ] N lem(m)ing *m*; **they were jumping over the side of the ship like ~s** se lanzaban por la borda uno tras otro

lemon ['lemən] Ⓐ N 1 (= *fruit*) limón *m*; (= *tree*) limonero *m*; (= *drink*) limonada *f*
2 (*) bobo/a *m/f*; **I felt a bit of a ~** me sentí como un auténtico imbécil; **you ~!** ¡bobo!
Ⓑ ADJ [*colour*] amarillo limón *inv*
Ⓒ CPD ► **lemon cheese**, **lemon curd** N crema *f* de limón ► **lemon grove** N limonar *m* ► **lemon juice** N zumo *m or* (*LAm*) jugo *m* de limón ► **lemon squash** N limonada *f* (*sin burbujas*) ► **lemon sole** N (*Brit*) platija *f* ► **lemon squeezer** N exprimelimones *m inv*, exprimidor *m* ► **lemon tea** N té *m* con limón ► **lemon tree** N limonero *m*

lemonade [,lemə'neɪd] N limonada *f*, gaseosa *f* (*Sp*)

lemur ['liːməʳ] N lémur *m*

Len [len] N (*familiar form*) *of* **Leonard**

lend [lend] (*pt, pp* **lent**) Ⓐ VT 1 (*as favour*) prestar, dejar; **to ~ sb sth** ◊ **~ sth to sb** prestar algo a algn, dejar algo a algn
2 (*Fin*) [*bank, building society*] prestar
3 (= *give*) **to ~ credibility to sth** conceder credibilidad a algo; *see also* **ear A1**, **hand A5**, **name A1**, **weight A3**
4 (*reflexive*) **the system does not ~ itself to rapid reform** el sistema no se presta a una reforma rápida; **he refused to ~ himself to their scheming** se negó a colaborar en sus intrigas, no quiso prestarse a sus intrigas
Ⓑ VI (*Fin*) prestar dinero

► **lend out** VT + ADV prestar

lender ['lendəʳ] N 1 prestador(a) *m/f*; *see also* **borrower 1**
2 (*professional*) (= *person*) prestamista *mf*; (= *bank, building society*) entidad *f* crediticia *or* de crédito; *see also* **mortgage C**

lending ['lendɪŋ] CPD ► **lending library** N biblioteca *f* de préstamo ► **lending limit** N límite *m* de crédito *or* de préstamos ► **lending policy** N política *f* crediticia *or* de préstamos ► **lending rate** N tipo *m* de interés sobre los préstamos

length [leŋ(k)θ] Ⓐ N 1 (= *size*) largo *m*, longitud *f*; **what is its ~?** ◊ **what ~ is it?** ¿cuánto tiene *or* mide de largo?; **two pieces of cable of roughly equal** *or* **the same ~** dos trozos *mpl* de cable de aproximadamente el mismo largo *or* la misma longitud; **the tail was at least twice the ~ of the body** el rabo medía por lo menos el doble que el cuerpo; **his trousers were never the right ~ for him** los pantalones nunca le quedaban bien de largo; **it was two metres in ~** tenía *or* medía dos metros de largo; **they range in ~ from three to six metres** su longitud varía entre los tres y los seis metros; **they vary in ~** son de diferentes medidas; *see also* **measure B1**
2 (= *extent*) 2·1 [*of street, river, house*] **the room runs the ~ of the house** la habitación tiene el largo de la casa; **he walked the ~ of the beach** recorrió toda la orilla de la playa; **I walked the entire ~ of the street** recorrí la calle de una punta a la otra; **I have travelled the ~ and breadth of the country** he viajado a lo largo y ancho del país, he viajado por todo el país; *see also* **arm**[1] **1**
2·2 [*of book, letter, essay*] extensión *f*; **an essay 4,000 words in ~** un ensayo de 4.000 palabras (de extensión)
2·3 ✦*IDIOM* **to go to great ~s to do sth** esforzarse mucho para hacer algo; **I'd go to any ~(s) to protect her** haría cualquier cosa por protegerla; **they went to extraordinary ~s to keep their relationship secret** llegaron a extremos insospechables para mantener su relación en secreto
3 (= *duration*) duración *f*; **a concert two hours in ~** un concierto de dos horas de duración; **~ of service** antigüedad *f*, años *mpl* de servicio; **we must reduce the ~ of time patients have to wait** tenemos que reducir el tiempo de espera de los pacientes; **you couldn't keep that effort up for any ~ of time** un esfuerzo así no se puede mantener (durante) mucho tiempo; **if you were outside for any ~ of time you'd freeze to death** si te quedases en la calle más de un cierto tiempo, morirías congelado
4 **at ~** (= *finally*) finalmente, por fin; (= *in detail*) [*discuss*] detenidamente; [*explain*] con mucho detalle; [*write*] extensamente; (= *for a long time*) largo y tendido; **she spoke at (some) ~** habló largo y tendido; **he would quote Shakespeare at great ~** se recreaba dando interminables citas de Shakespeare
5 (= *piece*) [*of rope, wire, tubing*] trozo *m*, pedazo *m*; [*of cloth*] largo *m*, corte *m*; [*of track, road*] tramo *m*; **dress ~** largo *m* para vestido
6 [*of vowel, syllable*] duración *f*, cantidad *f* (*Tech*)
7 (*Sport*) (*in horse races*) cuerpo *m*; (*in rowing*) largo *m*; [*of pool*] largo *m*; **to win by half a ~/four ~s** ganar por medio cuerpo/cuatro cuerpos
Ⓑ CPD ► **length mark** N (*Ling*) signo *m* de vocal larga

-length [leŋ(k)θ] ADJ (*ending in compounds*) **ankle-length skirt** falda *f* por los tobillos; **elbow-length sleeves** medias mangas *fpl*; *see also* **feature-length**, **knee-length**, **shoulder-length**

lengthen ['leŋ(k)θən] Ⓐ VT [+ *dress, trousers*] alargar; [+ *term, period, life, jail sentence*] prolongar, alargar; (*Ling*) [+ *vowel*] alargar; **to ~ one's stride** alargar el paso
Ⓑ VI [*shadows, queue, skirts, days, nights*] alargarse; [*silence*] prolongarse; **the odds on us succeeding are ~ing** las probabilidades de que lo consigamos están disminuyendo

lengthily ['leŋ(k)θɪlɪ] ADV [*speak*] largo y tendido; [*write*] extensamente

lengthways ['leŋ(k)θ,weɪz], **lengthwise** ['leŋ(k)θ,waɪz] Ⓐ ADV longitudinalmente, a lo largo; **to measure sth ~** medir el largo de algo
Ⓑ ADJ longitudinal, de largo

lengthy ['leŋ(k)θɪ] ADJ (*compar* **lengthier**; *superl* **lengthiest**) 1 (= *long-lasting*) [*war, illness, process*] largo, prolongado; [*investigation*] largo, extenso; **~ delays** retrasos *mpl* considerables; **he still has a ~ wait for his treatment** aún tiene que esperar mucho para su tratamiento
2 (= *extensive*) [*article, speech, interview*] largo, extenso
3 (= *long and boring*) interminable

lenience ['liːnɪəns], **leniency** ['liːnɪənsɪ] N indulgencia *f*, benevolencia *f*; **to show leniency to** *or* **towards sb** ser *or* mostrarse indulgente con *or* hacia algn

lenient ['liːnɪənt] ADJ [*sentence, treatment*] benévolo, poco severo; [*person, attitude*] indulgente, poco severo; **to be ~ with sb** ser indulgente *or* poco severo con algn

leniently ['liːnɪəntlɪ] ADV con indulgencia, con benevolencia

Leningrad ['lenɪngræd] N (*Hist*) Leningrado *m*

Leninism ['lenɪnɪzəm] N leninismo *m*

Leninist ['lenɪnɪst] Ⓐ ADJ leninista
Ⓑ N leninista *mf*

lenitive ['lenɪtɪv] ADJ lenitivo

lens [lenz] Ⓐ N [*of spectacles*] lente *m or f*; [*of camera*] objetivo *m*; (= *handlens*) (*for stamps etc*) lupa *f*; (*Anat*) cristalino *m*; **contact ~** lente *m or f* de contacto, lentilla *f*
Ⓑ CPD ► **lens cap** N tapa *f* de objetivo ► **lens hood** N parasol *m* de objetivo

Lent [lent] N Cuaresma *f*

lent [lent] PT, PP *of* **lend**

Lenten ['lentən] ADJ cuaresmal

lentil ['lentl] Ⓐ N lenteja *f*
Ⓑ CPD ► **lentil soup** N sopa *f* de lentejas

Leo ['liːəʊ] N 1 (= *sign, constellation*) Leo *m*
2 (= *person*) leo *mf*; **she's (a) ~** es leo

Leon ['liːɒn] N León *m*

Leonese [liːə'niːz] Ⓐ ADJ leonés
Ⓑ N 1 (= *person*) leonés/esa *m/f*
2 (*Ling*) leonés *m*

leonine ['liːənaɪn] ADJ leonino

leopard ['lepəd] N leopardo *m*; ✦*PROV* **the ~ cannot change its spots** genio y figura hasta la sepultura

leopardess ['lepədes] N leopardo *m* hembra

leopardskin ['lepədskɪn] N piel *f* de leopardo; **a ~ coat** un abrigo de piel de leopardo

leotard ['lɪətɑːd] N malla *f*

leper ['lepəʳ] N Ⓐ N leproso/a *m/f* (*also fig*)
Ⓑ CPD ► **leper colony** N leprosería *f*, colonia *f* de leprosos

lepidoptera [,lepɪ'dɒptərə] NPL lepidópteros *mpl*

lepidopterist [,lepɪ'dɒptərɪst] N lepidopterólogo/a *m/f*

leprechaun ['leprəkɔːn] N (*Irl*) duende *m*

leprosy ['leprəsɪ] N lepra *f*

leprous ['leprəs] ADJ leproso

lesbian ['lezbɪən] Ⓐ ADJ lesbiano, lésbico
Ⓑ N lesbiana *f*

lesbianism ['lezbɪənɪzəm] N lesbianismo *m*

lèse-majesté, **lese-majesty** ['leɪz'mæʒəstɪ] N lesa majestad *f*

lesion ['liːʒən] N lesión *f*

Lesotho [lɪ'suːtuː] N Lesoto *m*

▼ **less** [les] Ⓐ ADJ COMPAR *of* **little**[2] menos; **now we eat ~ bread** ahora comemos menos pan; **she has ~ time to spare now** ahora tiene menos tiempo libre; **of ~ importance** de menos importancia; **St James the Less** Santiago el Menor; **no ~ a person than the bishop** no otro que el obispo, el mismísimo obispo; **that was told me by the minister no ~** eso me lo dijo el mismo ministro
Ⓑ PRON menos; **it's ~ than you think** es menos de lo que piensas; **can't you let me have it for ~?** ¿no me lo puedes dar en menos?; **~ than £1/a kilo/three metres** menos de una libra/un kilo/tres metros; **at a price of ~**

➤ LANGUAGE IN USE: **less C** 5.3, 5.6

than £1 a un precio inferior *or* menor a una libra; **~ than a week ago** hace menos de una semana; **a tip of £10, no ~!** ¡una propina de 10 libras, nada menos!; **nothing ~ than** nada menos que; **it's nothing ~ than a disaster** es un verdadero *or* auténtico desastre; **the ~ ... the ~ ...** cuanto menos ... menos ...; **the ~ he works the ~ he earns** cuanto menos trabaja menos gana; **the ~ said about it the better** cuanto menos se hable de eso mejor

Ⓒ ADV menos; **to go out ~ (often)** salir menos; **you work ~ than I do** trabajas menos que yo; **grief grows ~ with time** la pena disminuye a medida que pasa el tiempo; **in ~ than an hour** en menos de una hora; **it's ~ expensive than the other one** cuesta menos que el otro; **~ and ~** cada vez menos; **that doesn't make her any ~ guilty** no por eso es menos culpable; **even ~** ◊ **still ~** todavía menos, menos aún; **the problem is ~ one of capital than of personnel** el problema más que de capitales es de personal

Ⓓ PREP menos; **the price ~ 10%** el precio menos 10 por ciento; **the price ~ VAT** el precio excluyendo el IVA; **a year ~ four days** un año menos cuatro días

...less [lɪs] SUFFIX sin; **coat~** sin abrigo; **hat~** sin sombrero

lessee [le'siː] N [*of house*] inquilino/a *m/f*; [*of land*] arrendatario/a *m/f*

lessen ['lesn] Ⓐ VT [+ *risk, danger*] reducir; [+ *pain*] aliviar; [+ *cost, stature*] rebajar; **it will ~ your chances of getting the job** disminuirá las posibilidades que tienes de conseguir el puesto

Ⓑ VI [*noise, anger, love*] disminuir; [*pain*] aliviarse

lessening ['lesnɪŋ] N disminución *f*, reducción *f*

lesser ['lesəʳ] ADJ COMPAR *of* **less** menor; **to a ~ extent** *or* **degree** en menor grado; **he pleaded guilty to the ~ charge** se declaró culpable del cargo menor; **the ~ of two evils** el menor de dos males

lesser-known [ˌlesə'nəʊn] ADJ menos conocido

lesson ['lesn] Ⓐ N [1] (= *class*) clase *f*; **a French/tennis ~** una clase de francés/tenis; **to give swimming/piano ~s** dar clases de natación/piano; **to give (sb) private ~s in maths** dar (a algn) clases particulares de matemáticas; **she's having driving ~s** le están dando clases de conducir

[2] (*in textbook*) lección *f*

[3] (*fig*) lección *f*; **if there is a single ~ to be drawn from this, it is that ...** si hay algo que podemos aprender de esto, es que ...; **there are ~s to be learnt from this terrible tragedy** esta terrible tragedia nos debe servir de lección; **let that be a ~ to you!** ¡que te sirva de lección!, ¡para que aprendas!; **to teach sb a ~** dar una lección a algn; **his courage is a ~ to us all** su valor debe servirnos a todos de lección; *see also* **learn A1**

[4] (*Rel*) lectura *f*

Ⓑ CPD ► **lesson plan** N plan *m* de estudio

lessor [le'sɔːʳ] N arrendador(a) *m/f*

lest [lest] CONJ (*frm or liter*) [1] (= *in order to prevent*) para que no + *subjun*; **~ we forget** para que no nos olvidemos, no sea que nos olvidemos; **~ he catch me unprepared** para que no me coja *or* (*LAm*) agarre desprevenido

[2] (= *in case*) **I feared ~ he should fall** temía que fuera a caerse; **I didn't do it ~ somebody should object** no lo hice por miedo a que alguien pusiera peros

---

LESS THAN, FEWER THAN

"Menos ... que" or "menos ... de"?

• Use **menos** with **que** before nouns and pronouns (provided they are not followed by clauses) as well as before adverbs and prepositions:

He has less money than his sister
Tiene menos dinero que su hermana
He sells less/fewer than I do *or* than me
Vende menos que yo
These days I'm much less shy than before
Hoy en día soy mucho menos tímido que antes

• Use **menos ... de lo que/del que/de la que/de los que/de las que** with following clauses:

He earns less than I thought
Gana menos de lo que yo creía
They have 16 seats - five fewer than they had before these elections
Tienen 16 escaños - cinco menos de los que tenían antes de estas elecciones
It provides the body with fewer calories than it needs
Proporciona al organismo menos calorías de las que necesita

• Use **menos** with **de** before **lo** + **ADJECTIVE/PAST PARTICIPLE**:

The price of wheat went up less than expected
El precio del trigo subió menos de lo previsto

• Use **menos** with **de** in comparisons involving numbers or quantity:

...in less than 8 seconds...
...en menos de 8 segundos...
You won't get it for less than 4,000 euros
No lo conseguirás por menos de 4.000 euros

! But use **que** instead in emphatic expressions like **nada menos que** and **ni más ni menos que** even when followed by numbers:

They offered him no less than 100,000 euros a year!
¡Le ofrecieron nada menos que *or* ***ni más ni menos que 100.000 euros al año!***

A lot less, far fewer

• When translating **a lot less**, **far fewer** *etc* remember to make the **mucho** in **mucho menos** agree with any noun it describes or refers to:

These bulbs use a lot less electricity than conventional ones
Estas bombillas gastan mucha menos electricidad que las normales
They have had far fewer opportunities than wealthy people
Han gozado de muchas menos oportunidades que la gente rica

For further uses and examples, see main entries at ***fewer*** *and* ***less.***

---

let¹ [let] Ⓐ VT (*pt, pp* **let**) [1] (= *allow to*) [1·1] (*gen*) dejar; (*more frm*) permitir; **to ~ sb do sth** dejar *or* (*more frm*) permitir que algn haga algo, dejar *or* (*more frm*) permitir a algn hacer algo; **my parents wouldn't ~ me go out with boys** mis padres no dejaban que saliera con chicos, mis padres no me dejaban salir con chicos; **~ me help you** déjeme ayudarle *or* que le ayude; **~ me take your coat** permítame que tome su abrigo; **~ me think** déjame pensar, a ver que piense; **don't ~ me forget to post the letters** recuérdame que eche las cartas al correo; **she wanted to help but her mother wouldn't ~ her** quería ayudar, pero su madre no la dejaba; **pride wouldn't ~ him talk about the situation** su orgullo no le permitía hablar de la situación; **to ~ o.s. be persuaded** dejarse persuadir; **don't ~ me catch you cheating again!** ¡no quiero volver a pillarte haciendo trampa!, ¡que no vuelva a pillarte haciendo trampa!; **you must ~ me be the judge of that** eso tengo que juzgarlo yo; **don't ~ me keep you** no quiero entretenerle; **now ~ me see** ¿a ver?, déjame que vea; **it's hard work, ~ me tell you** es mucho trabajo, te lo aseguro; *see also* **alone A2.1, be A13, go A24, rip C2**

[1·2] (*in prayers, wishes*) **please don't ~ it rain** por favor, que no llueva; **don't ~ him die, she prayed** no dejes que se muera, le pidió a Dios

[2] (= *cause to*) **when can you ~ me have it?** ¿cuándo me lo puedes dejar?; **I'll ~ you have it back tomorrow** te lo devuelvo mañana; **he really ~ her have it about being late*** le echó una buena bronca por llegar tarde*; **to ~ it be known that** hacer saber que; *see also* **slip B5**

[3] (+ *prep, adv*) **they won't ~ you into the country** no te dejarán entrar en el país; **he ~ himself into the flat** entró en el piso; **he wouldn't ~ me past** no me dejaba pasar; **the barrier rose to ~ the car through** la barrera subió para dejar pasar el coche; **they wouldn't ~ us through the gate** no nos dejaban pasar en la entrada; *see also* **let in, let out, secret B**

[4] (= *forming imperative*) [4·1] (*1st person plural*) **her then boyfriend (~'s call him Dave) ...** el entonces novio suyo (llamémosle *or* vamos a llamarle Dave) ...; **~'s get out here** bajémonos aquí; **~'s go!** ¡vámonos!; **~'s go for a walk** vamos a dar un paseo; **~'s not** *or* **don't ~'s jump to conclusions** no nos precipitemos a sacar conclusiones; **~ us pray** (*frm*) oremos; **if you weigh, ~'s say, 175 pounds ...** si pesas, digamos, 175 libras ...; **~'s say I'm very pleased with the results** digamos que estoy muy satisfecha con los resultados; **~'s see, what was I saying?** a ver *or* déjame ver, ¿qué decía yo?; **"shall we eat now?" — "yes, ~'s"** —¿comemos ahora? —sí, venga *or* —sí, vale; **"shall we go home now?" — "yes, ~'s"** —¿nos vamos a casa ahora? —¡sí, vamos! *or* —¡sí, vámonos!

[4·2] (*forming 3rd-person imperative*) **~ them wait** que esperen; **"people may complain" — "~ them"** —puede que la gente se queje —pues que lo hagan; **~ people say what they will, we know we are right** que la gente diga lo que quiera, nosotros sabemos que tenemos razón; **~ that be a lesson to you!** ¡que eso te sirva de lección!; **~ there be light** hágase la luz; **never ~ it be said that ...** que nunca se diga que ...

[5] (*Math*) **~ X be 6** supongamos que X equivale a 6

[6] (*esp Brit*) (= *rent out*) alquilar, arrendar (**to** a); **"to let"** "se alquila"

[7] (= *put*) **a plaque ~ into a wall** una lápida empotrada en una pared

[8] (*Med*) [+ *blood*] sacar

Ⓑ N **we're converting the barn for holiday ~s** estamos remodelando el granero para alquilarlo durante las vacaciones; **long/short ~** alquiler *m* a corto/largo plazo

► **let away** VT + ADV **to ~ sb away with sth** dejar a algn salirse con la suya, dejar a algn que se salga con la suya

► **let by** VT + ADV dejar pasar

► **let down** VT + ADV [1] (= *lower*) [+ *window*] bajar; [+ *hair*] soltar, dejar suelto; (*on rope*) bajar; ✦***IDIOM*** **to ~ one's hair down** soltarse la

melena*
[2] (= *lengthen*) [+ *dress, hem*] alargar
[3] (= *deflate*) [+ *tyre*] desinflar
[4] (*fig*) [4·1] (= *disappoint*) defraudar; (= *fail*) fallar; **the weather ~ us down** el tiempo nos defraudó; **we all felt ~ down** todos nos sentimos defraudados; **I trusted you and you ~ me down** confié en ti y me fallaste; **I was badly ~ down** me llevé un gran chasco; **this car has never ~ me down yet** hasta ahora este coche nunca me ha fallado; **my backhand ~s me down** el revés me falla; **to ~ o.s. down** quedar mal; ✦*IDIOM* **to ~ the side down**: **she would never ~ the side down** jamás nos haría quedar mal, jamás nos fallaría
[4·2] **to ~ sb down gently** amortiguarle el golpe a algn

►**let in** VT + ADV [1] **to ~ sb in** (= *allow to enter*) dejar entrar a algn; (= *usher in*) hacer pasar a algn; (= *open door to*) abrir la puerta a algn; **who ~ him in?** ¿quién le ha dejado entrar?, ¿quién le ha abierto la puerta?; **~ him in!** ¡que pase!; **your mother ~ me in** tu madre me abrió la puerta
[2] (= *allow to come through*) **shoes which ~ the water in** zapatos que dejan calar el agua; **a glass roof to ~ in the light** un tejado de cristal para dejar entrar la luz
[3] **to ~ sb in on sth: to ~ sb in on a secret** contar un secreto a algn; **to ~ sb in on a deal** dejar que algn participe en un negocio
[4] **to ~ o.s. in for sth: you don't know what you're ~ting yourself in for** no sabes bien a lo que te estás exponiendo, no sabes bien en lo que te estás metiendo; **you may find you've ~ yourself in for a lot of extra work** puede que encuentres que te has expuesto a un montón de trabajo extra
[5] (*Aut*) [+ *clutch*] soltar

►**let off** Ⓐ VT + ADV [1] (= *cause to explode, fire*) [+ *bomb*] hacer explotar; [+ *firework*] tirar; [+ *firearm*] disparar
[2] (= *release*) **to ~ off steam** [*boiler, engine*] soltar vapor; [*person*] (*) (*fig*) (= *release anger*) desahogarse; (= *unwind*) relajarse
[3] (= *allow to leave*) dejar salir; **they ~ the children off early today** hoy han dejado salir a los niños antes de la hora
[4] (= *exempt*) perdonar; **it's your turn to do the washing up but I'll ~ you off this time** te toca fregar a ti pero esta vez te perdono
[5] (= *not punish*) perdonar; **to ~ sb off lightly** ser demasiado blando con algn; **the headmaster ~ him off with a warning** el director le dejó escapar con sólo una advertencia
Ⓑ VT + PREP [1] (= *release from*) **can I ~ the dog off the lead?** ¿puedo soltar al perro?; *see also* **hook A1**
[2] (= *exempt*) perdonar; **I'll ~ you off the £5 you owe me** te perdono las 5 libras que me debes; **the authorities ~ him off National Service** las autoridades le permitieron librarse del servicio militar

►**let on*** Ⓐ VI + ADV (= *say*) **he's not ~ting on** no dice nada; **don't ~ on!** ¡no digas nada!, ¡no te vayas de la lengua!*; **don't ~ on (to her) about what they did** no (le) digas lo que hicieron
Ⓑ VT + ADV [1] **to ~ on that** [1·1] (= *reveal*) decir que; **she didn't ~ on that she'd seen me** no dijo que me había visto
[1·2] (= *pretend*) fingir que; **I ~ on that the tears in my eyes were because of the onions** fingí que las lágrimas que tenía en los ojos se debían a la cebolla
[2] (= *allow on board*) dejar subir

LET

Meaning "allow"

• Translate using either **dejar**, especially in informal contexts, or **permitir**, especially in more formal contexts. Both verbs can be followed either by an infinitive or by **que** + SUBJUNCTIVE:

Let me do it
Déjame hacerlo, Déjame que lo haga
Let her have a look
Deja que ella lo vea, Déjale verlo
We must not let the children see this
No debemos permitir que los niños vean esto *or* ***permitir a los niños ver esto***

Imperative

First person plural

• Translate **let's** and **let us** + VERB using either **vamos a** + INFINITIVE or using the present subjunctive of the main verb. The second construction is used particularly in formal language and when translating **let's not**:

Let's go for a walk!
Vamos a dar un paseo
Let's consider the implications of the Government's decision
Consideremos las implicaciones de la decisión del Gobierno
Let's not waste any more time
No perdamos ya más tiempo

NOTE: To translate **let's go**, use **vamos** or **vámonos** on its own without a following infinitive:

Let's go to the theatre
¡Vamos al teatro!

• When **let's** is used on its own to reply to a suggestion, translate using **vamos** or **vámonos** if the verb in the suggestion was **ir**. Use **vale** or **venga** if not:

"Shall we go?" - "Yes, let's"
"¿Nos vamos?" - "¡Sí, vamos!" *or* ***"¡Sí, vámonos!"***
"Shall we watch the match?" - "Yes, let's"
"¿Vemos el partido?" - "Sí, vale" *or* ***"Sí, venga"***

Third person

• When **let** introduces a command, suggestion or wish in the third person, translate using **que** + SUBJUNCTIVE:

Let him come up!
¡Que suba!
Let there be no misunderstanding about this
¡Que no haya ningún malentendido sobre esto!
Let them do as they like
¡Que hagan lo que quieran!

• Be careful to distinguish between the "permission" sense of **let sb do something** and the "command" sense:

Please let them stay here (*i.e. Please allow them to stay*)
Déjalos que se queden aquí *or* ***Déjalos quedarse aquí, por favor***
Let them stay here! (*i.e. expressing a decision or an order*)
¡Que se queden aquí!

NOTE: When **que** is used in this sense, it never takes an accent.

For further uses and examples, see main entry.

►**let out** VT + ADV [1] (= *allow to leave*) [+ *visitor*] acompañar a la puerta; [+ *prisoner*] poner en libertad; [+ *penned animal*] dejar salir; **I'll ~ you out** te acompaño a la puerta; **the watchman ~ me out** el vigilante me abrió la puerta (para que pudiera salir); **~ me out!** ¡déjenme salir!; **he ~ himself out quietly** salió sin hacer ruido; **can you ~ yourself out?** ¿hace falta que te acompañe a la puerta?; **they are ~ out of school at four** salen de la escuela a las cuatro; **to ~ the air out of a tyre** desinflar *or* deshinchar un neumático; **to ~ the water out of the bath** dejar salir el agua de la bañera; ✦*IDIOM* **to ~ the cat out of the bag** descubrir el pastel
[2] (= *reveal*) [+ *secret, news*] contar, revelar; **don't ~ it out that …** no digas que …, no cuentes que …
[3] (= *release*) dispensar, eximir; **they won't ~ me out of the contract** no me van a dispensar *or* eximir de las obligaciones contractuales
[4] (= *enlarge*) [+ *dress, skirt*] ensanchar; **to ~ out a seam** soltar una costura
[5] (*esp Brit*) (= *rent out*) alquilar
[6] (= *utter*) **to ~ out a cry/sigh** dar un grito/un suspiro
[7] (*Aut*) [+ *clutch*] soltar

►**let up** VI + ADV [1] (= *moderate*) [*bad weather*] mejorar; [*storm, wind*] amainar; **when the rain ~s up** cuando deje de llover tanto
[2] (= *do less*) **in spite of his health, he did not ~ up** a pesar de su salud, no aflojó el ritmo (*del trabajo, de las actividades etc*); **she can't afford to ~ up on her studies** no puede permitirse aflojar en los estudios
[3] (= *stop*) **he never ~s up** (*talking*) no deja de hablar, habla sin parar; (*working*) trabaja sin descanso
[4] (= *show leniency*) **to ~ up on sb: though she protested, her mother would not ~ up on her** aunque ella protestaba, su madre no cedía

let² [let] N [1] (*Tennis*) dejada *f*, let *m*
[2] (*Jur*) **without ~ or hindrance** sin estorbo ni obstáculo

letch* [letʃ] = **lech**

letdown [ˈletdaʊn] N decepción *f*, desilusión *f*

lethal [ˈliːθəl] ADJ [1] (= *deadly*) [*weapon*] mortífero, letal; [*blow*] mortal; [*dose, injection, effects*] mortal, letal; [*force*] letal; **it is ~ to rats** tiene un efecto mortal en las ratas
[2] (*fig*) (= *very dangerous*) [*opponent*] muy peligroso; [*weather conditions*] nefasto; **the roads are ~ in these conditions** las carreteras son nefastas en estas condiciones; **this coffee is ~** (*hum*) este café es un veneno (*hum*); **this schnapps is ~** (*hum*) este aguardiente es mortal (*hum*); **his driving is ~** (*hum*) es un peligro público al volante (*hum*)

lethargic [leˈθɑːdʒɪk] ADJ letárgico, aletargado; [*response*] apático; **to feel ~** [*person*] sentirse somnoliento *or* aletargado; **the market/trading was ~** (*St Ex*) el mercado/el volumen de contratación apenas se movió

lethargy [ˈleθədʒɪ] N letargo *m*

Lethe [ˈliːθiː] N Lete(o) *m*

let-out [ˈletaʊt] Ⓐ N (*Brit*) escapatoria *f*
Ⓑ CPD ► **let-out clause** N cláusula *f* que incluye una escapatoria

Lett [let] = **Latvian**

▼**letter** [ˈletəʳ] Ⓐ N [1] [*of alphabet*] letra *f*; **the ~ G** la letra G; **small ~** (letra *f*) minúscula *f*; **capital ~** (letra *f*) mayúscula *f*; **the ~ of the law** la ley escrita; **to follow instructions to the ~** cumplir las instrucciones al pie de la letra
[2] (= *missive*) carta *f*; **~s of Galdós** (*as published*) epistolario *m* de Galdós; **~ of acknowledgement** carta *f* de acuse de recibo; **~ of advice** carta *f* de aviso, notificación *f*; **~ of application** instancia *f*, carta *f* de solicitud; **~ of appointment** carta *f* de confirmación de un puesto de trabajo; **~ of attorney** *or* **proxy** (carta *f* de) poder *m*; **by ~** por carta, por escrito; **covering ~** carta *f* adjunta; **~s of credence** cartas *fpl* credenciales; **~ of credit** carta *f* de crédito; **documentary/irrevocable ~ of credit** carta *f*

➤ LANGUAGE IN USE: letter A2 20.2, 21.1

de crédito documentaria/irrevocable; **~ of intent** carta *f* de intenciones; **~ of introduction** carta *f* de presentación; **~ of lien** carta *f* de gravamen; **~s patent** título *m* de privilegio, patente *f* (de invención); **~ of protest** carta *f or* escrito *m* de protesta; **~ of recommendation/reference** carta *f* de recomendación

3 **letters** (= *learning*) letras *fpl*; **man of ~s** hombre *m* de letras, literato *m*

Ⓑ VT estampar con letras; **~ed in gold** estampado con letras doradas; **a hand-~ed sign** un cartel escrito a mano; **the boxes were ~ed according to country** las cajas estaban ordenadas por letras según los países

Ⓒ CPD ► **letter bomb** N carta *f* bomba ► **letter card** N (*Brit*) carta-tarjeta *f* ► **letter carrier** N (*US*) cartero/a *m/f* ► **letter opener** N abrecartas *m inv* ► **letter quality printer** N impresora *f* calidad carta ► **letter writer** N corresponsal *mf*; **I'm not much of a ~ writer** apenas escribo cartas

letterbox ['letəbɒks] N (*esp Brit*) buzón *m*

lettered ['letəd] ADJ [*person*] culto

letterfile ['letəfaɪl] N carpeta *f*, guardacartas *m*

letterhead ['letəhed] N membrete *m*

lettering ['letərɪŋ] N letras *fpl*, inscripción *f*

letterpress ['letəpres] N (= *method, printed image*) impresión *f* tipográfica

letting ['letɪŋ] N arrendamiento *m*, alquiler *m*

lettuce ['letɪs] N lechuga *f*

let-up* ['letʌp] N descanso *m*; (*fig*) tregua *f*; (= *reduction*) reducción *f*, disminución *f* (**in** de); **we worked five hours without a ~** trabajamos cinco horas sin descanso *or* sin interrupción; **if there is a ~ in the rain** si deja un momento de llover; **there has been no ~ in the fighting** se ha luchado sin descanso *or* sin tregua

leucocyte ['luːkəˌsaɪt] N leucocito *m*

leukaemia, leukemia (*US*) [luː'kiːmɪə] N leucemia *f*

Levant [lɪ'vænt] N Oriente *m* Medio

Levantine ['levəntaɪn] Ⓐ ADJ levantino

Ⓑ N levantino/a *m/f*

levee[1] ['leveɪ] N (*Hist*) (= *reception*) besamanos *m inv*, recepción *f*

levee[2] ['levɪ] N (= *bank*) ribero *m*, dique *m*

level ['levl] Ⓐ ADJ 1 (*lit*) (= *not sloping*) nivelado; (= *not uneven*) plano, llano; **place on a ~ surface** (= *not sloping*) colocar en una superficie nivelada; (= *not uneven*) colocar en una superficie plana *or* llana; **a ~ spoonful** (*Culin*) una cucharada rasa; ✦**IDIOMS to compete on a ~ playing field** competir en igualdad de condiciones; **to do one's ~ best to do sth*** hacer todo lo posible para hacer algo

2 (= *at same height, position*) **to be ~ (with sb)** (*in race*) estar *or* ir igualado (con algn); (*in league, competition*) estar *or* ir empatado (con algn); **the teams were ~ at the end of extra time** los equipos estaban *or* iban empatados al terminar la prórroga; **to be ~ (with sth)** (= *at same height*) estar a la misma altura (que algo); **to be ~ with the ground** estar a ras del suelo; **she knelt down so that their eyes were ~** se agachó para que sus ojos estuvieran a la misma altura; **to draw ~ with sth/sb** (*esp Brit*) (*gen, also in race*) alcanzar algo/a algn; (*in league, competition*) empatar con algo/algn

3 (= *steady*) [*voice, tone*] sereno; [*gaze*] penetrante; **she spoke in a ~ voice** habló con voz serena, habló sin alterar la voz; **to keep a ~ head** no perder la cabeza

Ⓑ N 1 (= *amount, degree*) nivel *m*; **we have the lowest ~ of inflation for some years** tenemos el nivel de inflación más bajo que hemos tenido en varios años; **the exercises are graded according to their ~ of difficulty** los ejercicios están ordenados por nivel *or* grado de dificultad; **bankruptcies have reached record ~s** el número de bancarrotas ha alcanzado cifras récord; **~ of unemployment** índice *m* de paro; *see also* **poverty B**

2 (= *height*) nivel *m*; **the water reached a ~ of ten metres** el agua alcanzó un nivel de diez metros; **at eye ~** a la altura de los ojos; **to be on a ~ with sth** (*lit*) estar al nivel *or* a la altura de algo; *see also* **ground**[1] **D, sea B**

3 (= *floor*) [*of building*] piso *m*

4 (= *rank, grade*) nivel *m*; **talks at ministerial ~** conversaciones *fpl* a nivel ministerial; **at advanced/elementary ~** a nivel avanzado/elemental; **at local/national/international ~** a nivel local/nacional/internacional; **on one ~** (*fig*) por un lado, de cierta manera; **to be on a ~ with** (*fig*) estar a la altura de; **some people put him on a ~ with von Karajan** algunos lo equiparan con *or* a von Karajan; ✦**IDIOM to come down to sb's ~** rebajarse al nivel de algn; *see also* **high-level, low-level, top-level**

5 (= *flat place*) llano *m*; **on the ~** en superficie plana *or* llana; **a car which can reach speeds of 300 miles per hour on the ~** un coche que puede alcanzar velocidades de unas 300 millas por hora en superficie plana *or* llana; ✦**IDIOM to be on the ~*** [*person*] ser de fiar, ser un tipo cabal*; **it's on the ~** es un negocio serio *or* limpio

6 (*also* **spirit ~**) nivel *m* de burbuja

Ⓒ VT 1 (= *make level*) [+ *ground, site*] nivelar, allanar; ✦**IDIOM to ~ the playing-field** igualar las condiciones

2 (= *raze*) [+ *building, city*] arrasar

3 (*Sport*) (= *equalize*) [+ *match, game*] igualar; **to ~ the score(s)** igualar el marcador

4 (= *direct*) **he has denied the charges ~led against him** ha negado las acusaciones que se han hecho en su contra; **he has not responded to the criticism ~led at him** no ha reaccionado ante las críticas que se le han dirigido; **to ~ a gun at sb** apuntar a *or* contra algn con una pistola

Ⓓ VI (*esp US**) **I'll ~ with you** te voy a hablar con franqueza, te voy a ser franco; **you didn't ~ with me** no has sido franco conmigo

Ⓔ CPD ► **level crossing** N (*Brit*) paso *m* a nivel

► **level down** VT + ADV nivelar (*al nivel más bajo*)

► **level off** Ⓐ VI + ADV [*ground, road*] nivelarse; [*prices, rate of growth*] estabilizarse; [*aircraft*] tomar una trayectoria horizontal, nivelarse

Ⓑ VT + ADV (= *make flat*) nivelar, allanar

► **level out** Ⓐ VI + ADV [*road, ground*] nivelarse; [*prices, rate of growth*] estabilizarse

Ⓑ VT + ADV (= *make flat*) nivelar, allanar

level-headed ['levl'hedɪd] ADJ sensato, equilibrado

leveller, leveler (*US*) ['levələr] N *persona en pro de la igualdad de derechos*

levelling, leveling (*US*) ['levlɪŋ] Ⓐ N nivelación *f*

Ⓑ CPD ► **levelling process** N proceso *m* de nivelación

levelling-off [ˌlevəlɪŋ'ɒf] N nivelación *f*

levelly ['levəlɪ] ADV [*gaze etc*] con compostura, con ecuanimidad, sin emocionarse

level-peg [ˌlevl'peg] VI **they were ~ging** iban empatados

level-pegging [ˌlevl'pegɪŋ] N igualdad *f*, situación *f* de empate; **it's ~ now** van muy iguales, están empatados

lever ['liːvər] Ⓐ N (*gen, fig*) palanca *f*

Ⓑ VT **to ~ sth up/out/off** levantar/sacar/quitar algo con palanca

leverage ['liːvərɪdʒ] N apalancamiento *m*; (*fig*) influencia *f*, palanca *f*

leveraged buy-out [ˌliːvərɪdʒd'baɪaʊt] N *compra de todas las acciones de una compañía pagándolas con dinero prestado a cambio de asegurar que las acciones serán compradas*

leveret ['levərɪt] N lebrato *m*

leviathan [lɪ'vaɪəθən] N (*Bible*) leviatán *m*; (= *ship*) buque *m* enorme

Levi's® ['liːvaɪz] NPL vaqueros *mpl*, levis® *mpl*

levitate ['levɪteɪt] Ⓐ VT elevar por levitación

Ⓑ VI levitar

levitation [ˌlevɪ'teɪʃən] N levitación *f*

Levite ['liːvaɪt] N levita *m*

Leviticus [lɪ'vɪtɪkəs] N Levítico *m*

levity ['levɪtɪ] N (*frm*) (= *frivolity*) ligereza *f*, frivolidad *f*

levy ['levɪ] Ⓐ N 1 (= *act*) exacción *f* (*de tributos*); (= *tax*) impuesto *m*

2 (*Mil*) leva *f*

Ⓑ VT 1 (= *impose*) [+ *tax, fine*] imponer (**on** a); (= *collect*) [+ *contribution*] recaudar

2 (*Mil*) reclutar

lewd [luːd] ADJ (*compar* **lewder**; *superl* **lewdest**) [*person*] lascivo; [*song, story*] verde, colorado (*LAm*)

lewdly ['luːdlɪ] ADV lascivamente

lewdness ['luːdnɪs] N lascivia *f*; [*of song, story*] lo verde

lexeme ['leksiːm] N lexema *m*

lexical ['leksɪkəl] ADJ léxico

lexicalize ['leksɪkəlaɪz] VT lexicalizar

lexicographer [ˌleksɪ'kɒgrəfər] N lexicógrafo/a *m/f*

lexicographical [ˌleksɪkəʊ'græfɪkəl] ADJ lexicográfico

lexicography [ˌleksɪ'kɒgrəfɪ] N lexicografía *f*

lexicologist [ˌleksɪ'kɒlədʒɪst] N lexicólogo/a *m/f*

lexicology [ˌleksɪ'kɒlədʒɪ] N lexicología *f*

lexicon ['leksɪkən] N léxico *m*

lexis ['leksɪs] N vocabulario *m*

Leyden ['laɪdn] Ⓐ N Leiden

Ⓑ CPD ► **Leyden jar** N botella *f* de Leiden

LGV N ABBR (= **Large Goods Vehicle**) *vehículo pesado*

l.h. ABBR (= **left hand**) izq

LI ABBR (*US*) = **Long Island**

liability [ˌlaɪə'bɪlɪtɪ] Ⓐ N 1 (= *responsibility*) responsabilidad *f*; **to admit/deny ~ (for sth)** admitir/negar ser responsable (de algo)

2 (= *obligation, debt*) **tax ~** carga *f* fiscal; **current liabilities** pasivo *msing* circulante; **long-term liabilities** pasivo *msing* (exigible) a largo plazo; **they failed to meet their liabilities** no hicieron frente a sus obligaciones; *see also* **limited B, unlimited B**

3 (= *risk, burden*) **I do not want to be a ~ to you** no quiero ser una carga *or* un estorbo para ti; **this car's a bit of a ~** este coche da muchos problemas

4 (= *propensity*) predisposición *f*, propensión *f* (**to** a); **the patient may have an increased ~ to infection** el paciente puede tener una mayor predisposición *or* propensión a las infecciones

Ⓑ CPD ► **liability insurance** N seguro *m* de daños a terceros, seguro *m* de responsabilidad civil (*Sp*)

liable ['laɪəbl] ADJ 1 (= *likely*) **to be ~ to do sth: he's ~ to do something stupid** puede fácilmente hacer alguna tontería, es muy posible que haga una tontería; **he's ~ to have an accident** es probable que tenga un accidente; **it's ~ to rain at any moment** puede empezar a llover en cualquier momento

[2] (= *prone*) **we are all ~ to make mistakes** todos podemos cometer errores; **some people are more ~ to depression than others** algunas personas son más propensas a la depresión *or* tienen más tendencia a la depresión que otras

[3] (= *responsible*) **to be ~ for** [+ *debt, loan*] ser responsable de, deber responder de; **the company is ~ for damages** la compañía es responsable de los daños, la compañía debe pagar los daños; **to hold sb ~ for sth** considerar a algn responsable de algo

[4] (= *subject*) **to be ~ for/to sth: the programme is ~ to change without notice** el programa puede cambiar sin previo aviso; **to be ~ to duty** (*Comm*) [*goods*] estar sujeto a derechos de aduana, deber pagar impuestos de aduana; **to be ~ for military service** estar obligado a hacer el servicio militar; **to be ~ to prosecution** poder ser procesado; **to be ~ to** *or* **for tax** [*person*] deber pagar impuestos; [*thing*] estar sujeto a impuestos, ser gravable; **any savings you have are ~ for tax** todos sus ahorros están sujetos a impuestos *or* son gravables; **he is not ~ for tax** no tiene que pagar impuestos, está exento de pagar impuestos

liaise [lɪ'eɪz] VI **to ~ with** (*Brit*) trabajar en colaboración con; **police ~d with the customs authorities to make the arrest** la policía trabajó en colaboración con las autoridades aduaneras para efectuar la detención; **the agency will ~ between youth groups and the government** la agencia servirá de puente *or* enlace entre los grupos juveniles y el gobierno

liaison [lɪ'eɪzɒn] Ⓐ N (= *coordination*) enlace *m*, coordinación *f*; (*fig*) (= *relationship*) relación *f*
Ⓑ CPD ► **liaison committee** N comité *m* de enlace ► **liaison officer** N oficial *mf* de enlace

liana [lɪ'ɑːnə] N bejuco *m*, liana *f*

liar ['laɪəʳ] N mentiroso/a *m/f*, embustero/a *m/f*; **liar!** ¡mentira!

Lib. [lɪb] N ABBR (*Pol*) [1] = **Liberal**
[2] = **Liberation**; **Women's ~** (= *Women's Liberation Movement*) Movimiento *m* de Liberación de la Mujer

libation [laɪ'beɪʃən] N libación *f*

libber* ['lɪbəʳ] N **women's ~** feminista *mf*; **animal ~** defensor(a) *m/f* de los animales

libel ['laɪbəl] Ⓐ N (*Jur*) difamación *f*, calumnia *f* (**on** de); (*written*) escrito *m* difamatorio, libelo *m*; **it's a ~!** (*hum*) ¡es mentira!
Ⓑ VT difamar, calumniar
Ⓒ CPD ► **libel action** N pleito *m* por difamación ► **libel laws** NPL leyes *fpl* contra la difamación ► **libel suit** N = **libel action**

libellous, libelous (*US*) ['laɪbələs] ADJ difamatorio, calumnioso

liberal ['lɪbərəl] Ⓐ ADJ [1] (= *tolerant*) [*person, view, education, regime*] liberal
[2] (= *generous*) [*quantity, amount*] abundante, generoso; [*portion*] generoso; **to be ~ with sth** ser generoso con algo; **he is very ~ with his money** es muy generoso con el dinero; **she was rather ~ with the mayonnaise** puso mucha mayonesa; **he is not ~ with his praise** no es muy pródigo con los elogios
[3] (*Brit Pol*) (= *of the Liberal Party*) **Liberal** [*MP*] del partido liberal; [*government, policy*] liberal
[4] (= *free*) [*interpretation, translation*] libre
Ⓑ N [1] (= *broad-minded person*) liberal *mf*
[2] (*Brit Pol*) **Liberal** liberal *mf*
Ⓒ CPD ► **the liberal arts** NPL (*esp US Univ*) las humanidades, las artes liberales ► **Liberal Democrat** N (*Brit Pol*) demócrata *mf* liberal ► **the Liberal Democratic Party** N (*Brit*) el Partido Democrático Liberal ► **the Liberal Party** N (*Brit*) el Partido Liberal ► **liberal studies** NPL (*esp Brit*) *asignatura de letras complementaria para aquellos que estudian ciencias*

liberalism ['lɪbərəlɪzəm] N liberalismo *m*

liberality [ˌlɪbə'rælɪtɪ] N (= *generosity*) liberalidad *f*, generosidad *f*

liberalization [ˌlɪbərəlaɪ'zeɪʃən] N liberalización *f*

liberalize ['lɪbərəlaɪz] VT liberalizar

liberally ['lɪbərəlɪ] ADV [1] (= *generously*) [*give*] generosamente; [*apply, spread, sprinkle*] abundantemente, generosamente; **his language is ~ sprinkled with swear words** su lenguaje está salpicado de abundantes palabrotas
[2] (= *tolerantly*) con tolerancia; **the political prisoners have generally been treated more ~** por lo general, los prisioneros políticos han sido tratados con más tolerancia; **they treated their children too ~** eran demasiado tolerantes con sus hijos
[3] (= *freely*) [*interpret, translate*] libremente

liberal-minded ['lɪbərəl'maɪndɪd] ADJ tolerante, liberal

liberal-mindedness ['lɪbərəl'maɪndɪdnɪs] N tolerancia *f*, amplitud *f* de miras

liberate ['lɪbəreɪt] VT (= *free*) liberar, libertar (**from** de); [+ *prisoner, slave*] poner en libertad; [+ *gas etc*] dejar escapar

liberated ['lɪbəreɪtɪd] ADJ liberado; **a ~ woman** una mujer liberada

liberation [ˌlɪbə'reɪʃən] Ⓐ N liberación *f*
Ⓑ CPD ► **liberation theology** N teología *f* de la liberación ► **Women's Liberation Movement** N movimiento *m* de liberación de la mujer; *see also* **Lib**

liberator ['lɪbəreɪtəʳ] N libertador(a) *m/f*

Liberia [laɪ'bɪərɪə] N Liberia *f*

Liberian [laɪ'bɪərɪən] Ⓐ ADJ liberiano
Ⓑ N liberiano/a *m/f*

libertarian [ˌlɪbə'teərɪən] Ⓐ ADJ libertario
Ⓑ N libertario/a *m/f*

libertarianism [ˌlɪbə'teərɪənɪzəm] N (= *philosophy*) libertarismo *m*, doctrina *f* libertaria; (= *personal philosophy*) ideas *fpl* libertarias

libertinage ['lɪbətɪnɪdʒ] N libertinaje *m*

libertine ['lɪbətiːn] N libertino/a *m/f*

liberty ['lɪbətɪ] Ⓐ N [1] (= *freedom*) libertad *f*; **individual/personal ~** libertad *f* individual/personal; **to be at ~** (= *free*) estar en libertad; **to be at ~ to do sth** tener libertad para hacer algo, ser libre de hacer algo; **I'm not at ~ to say who it was** no puedo decir quién fue
[2] (= *presumption, impertinence*) atrevimiento *m*; **that was rather a ~ on his part** eso fue un atrevimiento por su parte; **what a ~!*** ¡qué atrevimiento *or* descaro!; **to take liberties with sb** (= *be cheeky*) tomarse libertades *or* demasiadas confianzas con algn; (*sexually*) propasarse con algn; **to take the ~ of doing sth** tomarse la libertad de hacer algo
Ⓑ CPD ► **liberty bodice**† N camiseta *f* interior

libidinous [lɪ'bɪdɪnəs] ADJ libidinoso

libido [lɪ'biːdəʊ] N libido *f*

Libor ['liːbəʳ] N ABBR = **London inter-bank offered rate**

Libra ['liːbrə] N [1] (= *sign, constellation*) Libra *f*
[2] (= *person*) libra *mf*; **he's (a) ~** es libra

librarian [laɪ'breərɪən] N bibliotecario/a *m/f*; (*professionally qualified*) bibliotecólogo/a *m/f*

librarianship [laɪ'breərɪənʃɪp] N (*esp Brit*) [1] (= *post*) puesto *m* de bibliotecario
[2] (= *science*) bibliotecología *f*, biblioteconomía *f*

library ['laɪbrərɪ] Ⓐ N (*also Comput*) biblioteca *f*; **newspaper ~** hemeroteca *f*; **public ~** biblioteca *f* pública; *see also* **film D, video C**
Ⓑ CPD ► **library book** N libro *m* de biblioteca ► **library card** N = **library ticket** ► **library pictures** NPL (*TV*) imágenes *fpl* de archivo ► **library science** N = **librarianship 2** ► **library ticket** N carnet *m* de biblioteca

> **LIBRARY OF CONGRESS**
>
> *La Biblioteca del Congreso es la biblioteca nacional de EE.UU. y tiene su sede en Washington D.C. Se fundó en 1800 como fuente de referencia para los miembros del Congreso y actualmente registra también los derechos de autor de todos los libros publicados en Estados Unidos, por lo que recibe dos ejemplares de cada publicación. Posee un fondo inmenso de libros y manuscritos históricos, así como partituras, mapas, películas, grabaciones sonoras y microfilmes.*

librettist [lɪ'bretɪst] N libretista *mf*

libretto [lɪ'bretəʊ] N (*pl* **librettos** *or* **libretti** [lɪ'bretiː]) libreto *m*

Libya ['lɪbɪə] N Libia *f*

Libyan ['lɪbɪən] Ⓐ ADJ libio
Ⓑ N libio/a *m/f*

lice [laɪs] NPL *of* **louse**

licence, license[1] (*US*) ['laɪsəns] Ⓐ N [1] (= *permit*) permiso *m*, licencia *f*; (*Aut*) permiso *m* de conducir, carnet *m* (de conducir); **dog ~** licencia *f* para tener perro; **export ~** permiso *m or* licencia *f* de exportación; **fishing ~** permiso *m or* licencia *f* de pesca; **full ~** (*Aut*) carnet *m or* permiso *m* de conducir (definitivo); **import ~** licencia *f or* permiso *m* de importación; **he lost his ~** (*Aut*) le retiraron el carnet *or* permiso; **provisional ~** (*Aut*) *permiso o licencia de conducir que se obtiene antes de sacarse el carnet definitivo*; **they were married by special ~** se casaron con una licencia especial; **to manufacture sth under ~** fabricar algo bajo licencia; *see also* **driving C, television B**
[2] (= *freedom*) [2·1] (*pej*) **such a policy would give people a ~ to break the law** una política semejante serviría de excusa para que la gente violase la ley; ✦**IDIOMS to give sb a ~ to kill** darle a algn licencia para matar; **it's a ~ to print money** es una mina de oro
[2·2] (*Art, Literat*) licencia *f*; **artistic/poetic ~** licencia artística/poética; **you can allow some ~ in translation** se pueden aceptar algunas libertades al traducir
[3] (= *immorality*) libertinaje *m*
Ⓑ CPD ► **licence fee** N (*Brit TV*) *cuota que debe pagarse para el uso de un televisor* ► **licence holder** N (*Aut*) titular *mf* del carnet *or* permiso de conducir ► **licence number, licence plate** N (*Aut*) matrícula *f*, placa *f*, patente *f* (*S. Cone*)

license[2] ['laɪsəns] Ⓐ VT [1] (= *issue with license*) [+ *drug, medicine*] autorizar la comercialización de; [+ *vehicle*] conceder el permiso de circulación a; [+ *gun*] autorizar la licencia de; [+ *dog, company, operator*] registrar; [+ *surgeon, practitioner*] otorgarle la licencia de ejercer a; **to be ~d to do sth** tener licencia para hacer algo, estar autorizado para hacer algo; **we are**

not ~d to sell alcohol no tenemos licencia para vender bebidas alcohólicas, no estamos autorizados para vender bebidas alcohólicas; **he is ~d to drive this vehicle** está autorizado para conducir este vehículo; **to be ~d to carry a gun** tener licencia para llevar un revólver
[2] (= *authorize*) [+ *sale, use*] autorizar
(B) N (*US*) = **licence**
(C) CPD ► **license plate** N (*US Aut*) matrícula *f*, placa *f*, patente *f* (*S. Cone*)

licensed ['laɪsənst] (A) ADJ [*dealer*] autorizado; [*restaurant, premises*] autorizado para la venta de bebidas alcohólicas
(B) CPD ► **licensed trade** N comercio *m* autorizado, negocio *m* autorizado ► **licensed victualler** N vendedor(a) *m/f* de bebidas alcohólicas

licensee [,laɪsən'siː] N concesionario/a *m/f*; (*Brit*) [*of bar*] patrón/ona *m/f*

licensing ['laɪsənsɪŋ] (A) N [*of drug*] permiso *m* de comercialización; (*Med*) [*of practitioner*] concesión *f* de licencia para el ejercicio; (*Aut*) matrícula *f*
(B) CPD ► **licensing hours** NPL horas *fpl* durante las cuales se permite la venta y consumo de alcohol (*en un bar etc*) ► **licensing laws** NPL (*Brit*) leyes *fpl* reguladoras de la venta y consumo de alcohol

licentiate [laɪ'senʃɪɪt] N (= *person*) licenciado/a *m/f*; (= *title*) licencia *f*, licenciatura *f*

licentious [laɪ'senʃəs] ADJ licencioso

lichee [,laɪ'tʃiː] = **lychee**

lichen ['laɪkən] N liquen *m*

lich gate ['lɪtʃgeɪt] N entrada *f* de cementerio

licit ['lɪsɪt] ADJ lícito

lick [lɪk] (A) VT [1] lamer; **flames were ~ing (at) the door** las llamas empezaron a lamer la puerta; **to ~ one's wounds** (*lit*) lamerse las heridas; (*fig*) curarse las heridas; ✦**IDIOMS to ~ sb's boots*** hacer la pelota *or* dar coba a algn*; **to ~ sth into shape*** poner algo a punto
[2] (*) (= *defeat*) dar una paliza a*
(B) N [1] (*with tongue*) lametazo *m*, lengüetada *f*; ✦**IDIOM a ~ and a promise*** una lavada a la carrera *or* de cualquier manera
[2] (*fig*) **a ~ of paint** una mano de pintura; **a ~ of polish** un poquito de cera
[3] (*) (= *speed*) **to go at a good** *or* **a fair old ~** ir a buen tren*; **at full ~** a todo gas*, a toda mecha*

► **lick off** VT + ADV quitar de un lametazo

► **lick up** VT + ADV beber a lengüetadas

licking ['lɪkɪŋ] N [1] lamedura *f*
[2] (*) paliza* *f*; **to give sb a ~** dar una paliza a algn*

lickspittle* ['lɪkspɪtl] N cobista* *mf*, pelotillero/a* *m/f*

licorice ['lɪkərɪs] N = **liquorice**

lid [lɪd] N [1] tapa *f*; (*) (= *hat*) gorro *m*; ✦**IDIOMS he's flipped his ~*** ha perdido la chaveta*; **that puts the ~ on it!** ¡esto es el colmo *or* el acabóse!; **to take the ~ off** [+ *scandal*] exponer a la luz pública
[2] (= *eyelid*) párpado *m*

lidded ['lɪdɪd] ADJ [1] [*pot etc*] con tapa
[2] **heavily ~ eyes** ojos *mpl* con párpados gruesos

lido ['liːdəʊ] N (*swimming*) piscina *f* (al aire libre), alberca *f* pública (*Mex*), pileta *f* pública (*Arg*); (*boating*) centro *m* de balandrismo; (= *resort*) balneario *m*

lie¹ [laɪ] (A) N mentira *f*; **it's a ~!** ¡(es) mentira!; **to tell ~s** mentir; **white ~** mentira *f* piadosa; ✦**IDIOM to give the ~ to** [+ *report, theory*] desmentir; [+ *person*] dar el mentís a; *see also* **pack A3**
(B) VI mentir
(C) VT **to ~ one's way out of it** salir del apuro mintiendo
(D) CPD ► **lie detector** N detector *m* de mentiras ► **lie-detector test** N prueba *f* con el detector de mentiras

lie² [laɪ] (*pt* **lay**; *pp* **lain**) (A) VI [1] [*person, animal*] (= *act*) echarse, acostarse, tenderse, tumbarse; (= *state*) estar echado *or* acostado *or* tendido *or* tumbado; (*in grave*) yacer, estar enterrado, reposar (*liter*); **don't ~ on the grass** no te eches sobre el césped; **he lay where he had fallen** se quedó donde había caído; **to ~ asleep/in bed** estar dormido/en la cama; **to ~ dead** yacer muerto; **to ~ helpless** estar tumbado sin poder ayudarse; **here ~s ...** aquí yace ...; **to let things ~** dejar estar las cosas como están; **to ~ resting** estar descansando; **to ~ still** quedarse inmóvil; ✦**IDIOM to ~ low** mantenerse a escondidas
[2] (= *be situated*) [*object*] estar; [*town, house*] estar situado, encontrarse, ubicarse (*LAm*); (= *remain*) quedarse; (= *stretch*) extenderse; **the book lay on the table** el libro estaba sobre la mesa; **our road lay along the river** nuestro camino seguía a lo largo del río; **the plain lay before us** la llanura se extendía delante de nosotros; **where does the difficulty ~?** ¿en qué consiste *or* radica la dificultad?; **the factory lay idle** la fábrica estaba parada; **the town ~s in a valley** el pueblo está situado *or* ubicado en un valle; **England ~s in third place** Inglaterra está en tercer lugar *or* ocupa la tercera posición; **the money is lying in the bank** el dinero sigue en el banco; **how does the land ~?** ¿cuál es el estado actual de las cosas?; **obstacles ~ in the way** hay obstáculos por delante; **the problem ~s in his refusal** el problema estriba en su negativa; **the snow lay half a metre deep** había medio metro de nieve; **the snow did not ~** la nieve se derritió; **the book lay unopened** el libro quedaba sin abrir; **the fault ~s with you** la culpa es tuya, tú eres el culpable; **it ~s with you to change things** te corresponde a ti cambiar las cosas
(B) N [*of ball*] posición *f*; **the ~ of the land** (*Geog*) la configuración del terreno; (*fig*) el estado de las cosas

► **lie about, lie around** VI + ADV [*objects*] estar por ahí tirado; [*person*] pasar el tiempo sin hacer nada; **we lay about on our beds** nos quedamos tumbados en las camas; **it must be lying about somewhere** estará por aquí, debe de andar por aquí

► **lie back** VI + ADV recostarse (**against, on** sobre); **~ back and think of England!** ¡relájate y hazlo por la patria!

► **lie behind** VI + PREP (*fig*) **what ~s behind his attitude?** ¿cuál es la verdadera razón de su actitud?; **I wonder what ~s behind all this** me pregunto qué hay detrás de todo esto

► **lie down** VI + ADV echarse, acostarse, tenderse, tumbarse; **~ down!** (*to dog*) ¡échate!; ✦**IDIOMS to ~ down on the job** gandulear; **to take sth lying down** aguantar *or* soportar algo sin rechistar; **he's not one to take things lying down** no es de los que se callan, no es de los que tragan con todo*; **we're not going to take this lying down** no nos vamos a callar con este tema, no vamos a permitir que esto se quede así

► **lie in** VI + ADV (= *stay in bed*) quedarse en la cama hasta tarde

► **lie over** VI + ADV quedar aplazado *or* en suspenso

► **lie to** VI + ADV (*Naut*) (= *act*) ponerse a la capa; (= *state*) estar a la capa

► **lie up** VI + ADV (= *hide*) esconderse; (= *rest*) descansar; (= *be out of use*) quedar fuera de uso; (*Naut*) estar amarrado

lie-abed ['laɪəbed] N dormilón/ona *m/f*

Liechtenstein ['lɪktənstaɪn] N Liechtenstein *m*

lied [liːd] (*pl* **lieder** ['liːdəʳ]) N lied *m*

lie-down [,laɪ'daʊn] N descanso *m*; **I must have a ~** necesito echarme un rato

lief†† [liːf] ADV **I'd as ~ not go** igual me da no ir, de igual gana no voy

liege [liːdʒ] (A) N (= *lord*) señor *m* feudal; (= *vassal*) vasallo *m*; **yes, my ~** sí, (mi) señor
(B) CPD ► **liege lord** N señor *m* feudal

Liège [lɪ'eɪʒ] N Lieja *f*

liegeman ['liːdʒmæn] N (*pl* **liegemen**) vasallo *m*

lie-in [,laɪ'ɪn] N **to have a ~** quedarse en la cama hasta tarde

lien [lɪən] N derecho *m* de retención (**on** de); **banker's ~** gravamen *m* bancario; **general ~** embargo *m* preventivo, gravamen *m* general; **vendor's ~** gravamen *m* del vendedor

lieu [luː] N **in ~ of** en lugar de, en vez de

Lieut. ABBR (= **Lieutenant**) Tte

lieutenant [lef'tenənt] (*US*) [luː'tenənt] (A) N (*Mil*) teniente *mf*; (*Naut*) teniente *mf* de navío; (= *deputy*) lugarteniente *mf*
(B) CPD ► **lieutenant colonel** N teniente *mf* coronel ► **lieutenant commander** N capitán/ana *m/f* de corbeta ► **lieutenant general** N (*Mil*) teniente *mf* general

life [laɪf] (A) N (*pl* **lives**) [1] (= *animate state*) vida *f*; **~ on earth** la vida en la tierra; **bird ~** los pájaros; **there is not much insect ~ here** aquí hay pocos insectos; **plant ~** vida *f* vegetal, las plantas *fpl*; **to bring sb back to ~** resucitar *or* reanimar a algn; **a matter of ~ and death** cosa *f* de vida o muerte; **I don't believe in ~ after death** no creo en la vida después de la muerte; **to risk ~ and limb** jugarse la vida
[2] (= *existence*) vida *f*; **the ~ of an ant** la vida de una hormiga; **how's ~?*** ¿cómo te va (la vida)?, ¿qué hubo? (*Mex, Chile*); **I do have a ~ outside of work, you know** yo hago otras cosas en mi vida aparte de trabajar ¿sabes?; **to begin ~ as ...** empezar la vida como ...; **~ begins at 40** la vida comienza a los 40; **to depart this ~** (*liter*) partir de esta vida; **in early/later ~** en los años juveniles/maduras; **I can't for the ~ of me remember*** por más que lo intento no puedo recordar; **I clung on for dear ~** me agarré como si me fuera la vida en ello; **she was fighting for her ~** se debatía entre la vida y la muerte; **run for your ~!** ¡sálvese quien pueda!; **to be on trial for one's ~** ser acusado de un crimen capital; **you gave me the fright of my ~!** ¡qué susto me diste!; **~ goes on** *or* **must go on** la vida sigue; **to lay down one's ~** dar su vida, entregar su vida; **to lose one's ~** perder la vida; **how many lives were lost?** ¿cuántas víctimas hubo?; **three lives were lost** murieron tres; **never in my ~** en mi vida; **in the next ~** en el más allá, en la otra vida; **to have a ~ of its own** [*object, machine*] tener vida propia; **in real ~** en la vida real; **to see ~** ver mundo; **to spend one's ~ doing sth** pasar la vida haciendo algo; **to take sb's ~** quitar la vida a algn; **to take one's own ~** quitarse la vida, suicidarse; **you'll be taking your ~ in your hands if you climb up there** subir

allí es jugarse la vida; **at my time of ~** a mi edad, con los años que yo tengo; **his ~ won't be worth living** más le valdría morirse; **it's more than my ~'s worth** sería jugarme la vida; *see also* **bed A4**, **private C**, **save[1] A1**

3 (= *way of living*) **country/city ~** la vida de la ciudad/del campo; **the good ~** una vida agradable; (*Rel*) la vida santa; **it's a good ~** es una vida agradable; **I've had a good ~** la vida me ha tratado bien; **it's a hard ~** la vida es muy dura; **to make a new ~ for o.s.** ◊ **to start a new ~** comenzar una vida nueva; **to live one's own ~** ser dueño de su propia vida; **to lead a quiet ~** llevar una vida tranquila; *see also* **Riley**

4 (*in exclamations*) **get a ~!*** ¡espabílate y haz algo!; **(upon) my ~!†** ¡Dios mío!; **not on your ~!*** ¡ni hablar!; **such is ~!** ◊ **that's ~!** ¡así es la vida!; **this is the ~!** ¡esto sí que es vida!, ¡esto es jauja!; **what a ~!** (= *bad*) ¡qué vida ésta!; (= *good*) ¡vaya vida!, ¡eso sí que es vivir bien!

5 (= *liveliness*) vida *f*; **his acting brought the character to ~** su actuación dio vida al personaje; **she brought the party to ~** animó la fiesta; **to come to ~** animarse; **to put** *or* **breathe new ~ into sth/sb** infundir nueva vida a algo/algn; **you need to put a bit of ~ into it** tienes que ponerle un poco de garra; **the ~ and soul of the party** el alma de la fiesta

6 (= *lifespan*) [*of person*] vida *f*; [*of licence*] vigencia *f*, validez *f*; [*of battery*] vida *f*, duración *f*; **during the ~ of this government** durante el mandato de este gobierno; **friends for ~** amigos *mpl* para siempre; **scarred for ~** con una cicatriz de por vida; **a job for ~** un trabajo para toda la vida; **these birds mate for ~** estas aves tienen una sola pareja en su vida; **it was her ~'s work** fue el trabajo de toda su vida

7 (*) (= *life imprisonment*) **to do ~** cumplir una condena de cadena *or* reclusión perpetua; **to get ~** ◊ **be sentenced to ~** ser condenado a cadena *or* reclusión perpetua

8 (*Art*) **to paint from ~** pintar del natural; **true to ~** fiel a la realidad

9 (= *biography*) vida *f*

10 (*US**) [*of prostitute*] **she's in the ~** hace la calle*, es una mujer de la vida

Ⓑ CPD ► **life and death struggle** N lucha *f* a vida o muerte ► **life annuity** N pensión *f or* anualidad *f* vitalicia ► **life assurance** N seguro *m* de vida ► **life class** N (*Art*) clase *f* de dibujo al natural ► **life coach** N *profesional encargado de mejorar la situación laboral y personal de sus clientes* ► **life cycle** N ciclo *m* vital ► **life expectancy** N esperanza *f* de vida ► **life force** N fuerza *f* vital ► **life form** N forma *f* de vida ► **Life Guards** NPL (*Brit Mil*) *regimiento de caballería* ► **life history** N [*of person*] (historia *f* de la) vida *f*; (*hum, iro*) vida *f* y milagros* *mpl*; **the ~ history of the salmon** (la historia de) la vida del salmón ► **life imprisonment** N cadena *f* perpetua ► **life insurance** N = **life assurance** ► **life interest** N usufructo *m* vitalicio ► **life jacket** N chaleco *m* salvavidas ► **life membership** N **to take out a ~ membership** inscribirse como miembro vitalicio *or* de por vida ► **life peer** N (*Brit Parl*) *miembro de la Cámara de los Lores de carácter no hereditario* ► **life preserver** N (*Brit*) cachiporra *f*; (*US*) chaleco *m* salvavidas ► **life president** N presidente *mf* de por vida ► **life raft** N balsa *f* salvavidas ► **life sciences** NPL ciencias *fpl* de la vida ► **life sentence** N condena *f* a perpetuidad ► **life span** N [*of person*] vida *f*; [*of product*] vida *f* útil ► **life story** N biografía *f*

lifebelt ['laɪfbelt] N salvavidas *m inv*, flotador *m*

lifeblood ['laɪfblʌd] N sangre *f* vital; (*fig*) alma *f*, sustento *m*

lifeboat ['laɪfbəʊt] Ⓐ N (*from shore*) lancha *f* de socorro; (*from ship*) bote *m* salvavidas
Ⓑ CPD ► **lifeboat station** N estación *f* de lanchas de socorro

lifeboatman ['laɪfbəʊtmən] N (*pl* **lifeboatmen**) tripulante *mf* de una lancha de socorro

lifebuoy ['laɪfbɔɪ] N boya *f* salvavidas, guindola *f*

life-enhancing ['laɪfɪn'hɑːnsɪŋ] ADJ [*experience*] edificante; [*drug*] que alarga la vida

life-giving ['laɪfgɪvɪŋ] ADJ que da vida, vivificante

lifeguard ['laɪfgɑːd] N (*on beach*) salvavidas *mf inv*, socorrista *mf*

lifeless ['laɪflɪs] ADJ [*body*] sin vida, exánime; [*streets*] sin vida, desolado; [*face, voice, eyes*] apagado, sin vida; [*hair*] sin cuerpo, lacio

lifelessness ['laɪflɪsnɪs] N (*fig*) falta *f* de vida

lifelike ['laɪflaɪk] ADJ natural; (= *seemingly real*) que parece vivo; **her photo is so ~** la foto es el vivo retrato de ella

lifeline ['laɪflaɪn] N cuerda *f* de salvamento; (*fig*) cordón *m* umbilical, sustento *m*

lifelong ['laɪflɒŋ] ADJ de toda la vida

lifer* ['laɪfəʳ] N presidiario *m* de por vida, condenado/a *m/f* a cadena perpetua

life-saver ['laɪf,seɪvəʳ] N salvador(a) *m/f*; (= *lifeguard*) socorrista *mf*

life-saving ['laɪfseɪvɪŋ] Ⓐ N salvamento *m*; (= *training for life-saving*) socorrismo *m*
Ⓑ ADJ [*equipment*] de salvamento, salvavidas; (*Med*) [*operation*] a vida o muerte; **she was rushed to hospital for a ~ operation** la ingresaron de urgencia en el hospital para operarla a vida o muerte

life-size(d) ['laɪf'saɪz(d)] ADJ de tamaño natural

lifestyle ['laɪfstaɪl] N estilo *m* de vida

life-support ['laɪfsə,pɔːt] ADJ **~ system** sistema *m* de respiración artificial (*pulmón artificial etc*)

lifetime ['laɪftaɪm] N 1 (= *lifespan*) vida *f*; **in my ~** durante mi vida, en el curso de mi vida; **in the ~ of this parliament** en el transcurso de esta legislatura; **within my ~** mientras viva; **the chance of a ~** una oportunidad única en la vida; **once in a ~** una vez en la vida; **the work of a ~** el trabajo de toda una vida
2 (*fig*) eternidad *f*; **it seemed a ~** pareció una eternidad

lifework ['laɪf'wɜːk] N trabajo *m* de toda la vida

LIFO ['laɪfəʊ] ABBR (= **last in, first out**) UEPS

lift [lɪft] Ⓐ N 1 (*Brit*) (= *elevator*) ascensor *m*; (*for goods*) montacargas *m inv*
2 (*esp Brit*) (*in car*) **never accept ~s from strangers** nunca te montes en un coche con extraños; **can I give you a ~?** ¿quiere que le lleve (en coche)?, ¿quiere que le dé aventón? (*Mex*), ¿quiere que le dé un aventón? (*Col*); **she gave me a ~ home** me llevó a casa en coche, me acompañó con su coche a casa; *see also* **hitch B1**
3 (*fig*) (= *boost*) **to give sb a ~** (*psychologically*) levantar el ánimo a algn; (*physically*) dar fuerzas a algn
4 (*Aer*) propulsión *f*
Ⓑ VT 1 (= *raise, pick up*) [+ *cover, box, head*] levantar; [+ *phone, receiver*] descolgar, coger (*Sp*); [+ *child*] tomar en brazos, coger en brazos (*Sp*), alzar; [+ *invalid*] mover; **this suitcase is too heavy for me to ~** esta maleta pesa demasiado para que yo la levante; **he ~ed his eyes and looked out of the window** levantó *or* alzó la vista y miró por la ventana; **the wind ~ed the balloon into the air** el viento se llevó el globo por los aires; **he ~ed the lid off the pan** levantó la tapadera de la olla, destapó la olla; **he ~ed the child onto his knee** alzó *or* (*Sp*) cogió al niño y lo sentó en su rodilla; **to ~ sb's spirits** levantar el ánimo a algn; **she ~ed her glass to her lips** se llevó el vaso a los labios; **to ~ weights** (*Sport*) hacer *or* levantar pesas; ✦*IDIOMS* **she never ~s a finger to help** no mueve un dedo para ayudar; **to ~ the lid on sth** destapar algo
2 (= *remove*) [+ *restrictions, sanctions*] levantar
3 (= *dig up*) [+ *potatoes, carrots*] recoger
4 (= *improve*) mejorar; **they need to ~ their game to win** tienen que mejorar su juego si quieren ganar
5 (*) (= *steal*) [+ *goods, money*] mangar*, birlar*; [+ *idea, quotation*] copiar, plagiar; **the article was ~ed from a newspaper** el artículo fue copiado *or* plagiado de un periódico
Ⓒ VI 1 (= *rise*) levantarse, alzarse (*LAm*)
2 (= *raise*) **a bra which ~s and separates** un sujetador que realza y separa el busto
3 (= *disappear*) [*mist, fog*] disiparse; [*depression*] desaparecer; **his mood seemed to have ~ed** parecía estar de mejor humor
4 (= *cheer up*) **his spirits ~ed at the thought of seeing her** se le levantaron los ánimos al pensar que iba a verla
Ⓓ CPD ► **lift attendant** N (*Brit*) ascensorista *mf* ► **lift cage** N (*Brit*) caja *f* de ascensor ► **lift operator** N (*Brit*) = **lift attendant** ► **lift shaft** N (*Brit*) caja *f or* hueco *m* del ascensor

►**lift down** VT + ADV bajar; **to ~ sth down from a shelf** bajar algo de una estantería

►**lift off** Ⓐ VT + ADV [+ *lid, cover*] quitar, levantar
Ⓑ VI + ADV 1 (= *gen*) levantarse; **the top ~s off** la parte de arriba se levanta
2 [*spacecraft*] despegar

►**lift out** VT + ADV 1 (*gen*) sacar; **he ~ed the child out of his playpen** sacó al niño del parque
2 (*Mil*) [+ *troops*] evacuar

►**lift up** Ⓐ VT + ADV [+ *object, cover*] levantar; [+ *head, person*] levantar, alzar; **to ~ up one's eyes** levantar *or* alzar la vista
Ⓑ VI + ADV levantarse; **the seat ~s up to reveal storage space** el asiento se levanta dejando ver un espacio para guardar cosas

lift-off ['lɪftɒf] N despegue *m*

ligament ['lɪgəmənt] N ligamento *m*

ligature ['lɪgətʃəʳ] N (*Med, Mus*) ligadura *f*; (*Typ*) ligado *m*

light[1] [laɪt] (*vb: pt, pp* **lit** *or* **lighted**) Ⓐ N 1 (= *not darkness*) luz *f*; **she was sitting with her back to the ~** *or* **with the ~ behind her** estaba sentada de espaldas a la luz; **the ~ was beginning to fade** estaba empezando a oscurecer; **her hair is almost black in certain ~s** según como le da la luz tiene el pelo casi negro; **against the ~** al trasluz; **to hold sth against the ~** acercar algo a la luz, mirar algo al trasluz; **by the ~ of the moon/a candle** a la luz de la luna/de una vela; **at first ~** al rayar el día; **you're (standing) in my ~** me quitas la luz, me haces sombra; **~ and shade** luz y sombra; (*Art*) claroscuro *m*; **to hold sth up to the ~** acercar algo a la luz, mirar algo al trasluz; ✦*IDIOMS* **to see (a) ~ at the end of the tunnel** ver la salida del túnel, ver una solución al problema; **to bring sth to ~** sacar algo a la luz; **to shed** *or* **throw** *or* **cast ~ on sth** arrojar luz sobre algo; **in the cold ~ of day** a la luz del día; (*fig*) pensándolo con calma; **to come to ~** salir a la luz (pública); **new facts have come to ~** han salido a la luz nuevos datos; **(the) ~ dawned on him/her** se dio cuenta, comprendió; **to hide one's ~ (under a bushel)** quitarse importancia, ser modesto; **he was the ~ of her life** era la niña de sus ojos; **to see the ~** (*Rel*) ver la luz; (= *understand*) abrir los ojos, ver la luz (*hum*); **to see the ~ (of day)** ver la luz (del día); *see also* **leading B**

2 (= *lamp*) luz *f*; **in the distance I could see the ~s of a town** a lo lejos veía las luces de una ciudad; **to switch on** *or* **turn on the ~** encender la luz; **to switch off** *or* **turn off the ~** apagar la luz; **~s out** hora *f* de apagar las luces; **what time is ~s out?** ¿a qué hora se apagan las luces?; ✦*IDIOM* **to go out like a ~*** (= *fall asleep*) dormirse al instante; (= *lose consciousness*) caer (en) redondo*; *see also* **bright C**, **runway C**

3 (= *electricity*) luz *f*; **electric ~** luz *f* eléctrica

4 (*Aut*) (*on vehicle*) luz *f*; **rear** *or* **tail ~s** pilotos *mpl*, luces *fpl* traseras, calaveras *fpl* (*Mex*); **reversing ~s** luces *fpl* de marcha atrás

5 (= *traffic signal*) semáforo *m*; **a red/green/amber ~** un semáforo en rojo/verde/ámbar; **to go through a red ~** saltarse un semáforo en rojo; **the ~s** el semáforo; **the ~s were at** *or* **on red** el semáforo estaba en rojo; **the ~s were against us all the way** nos tocaron todos los semáforos en rojo; *see also* **green D**

6 (= *viewpoint*) **according to** *or* **by sb's ~s** (*frm*) según el parecer de algn; **to see things/look at sth in a different** *or* **new ~** ver las cosas/mirar algo con una perspectiva distinta *or* desde otro punto de vista; **I began to see my friends in a new ~** empecé a ver a mis amigos con otros ojos; **to show** *or* **portray sth/sb in a good/bad ~** dar una buena/mala imagen de algo/algn; **this shows our country in a bad ~** esto da una mala imagen de nuestro país; **in the ~ of what you have said …** en vista de *or* a la luz de lo que has dicho …

7 (= *glint, twinkle*) brillo *m*; **there was a strange ~ in his eye** había un brillo extraño en su mirada

8 (= *flame*) **have you got a ~?** (*for cigarette*) ¿tienes fuego?; **to set ~ to sth** (*Brit*) prender fuego a algo; *see also* **strike B3**

9 (*Archit*) cristal *m*, vidrio *m*

Ⓑ ADJ (*compar* **lighter**; *superl* **lightest**) 1 (= *bright*) [*room, hallway*] con bastante luz; **her house is ~ and airy** su casa tiene bastante luz y ventilación; **~ summer evenings** las claras tardes de verano; **while it's still ~** mientras es de día *or* hay luz; **to get ~** hacerse de día

2 (= *pale*) [*colour*] claro; [*hair*] rubio, güero (*CAm, Mex*); [*skin*] blanco; **~ blue/green** azul/verde claro; **~ in colour** de color claro

Ⓒ VT 1 (= *illuminate*) iluminar; **she appeared at a ~ed window** se asomó a la ventana de una habitación iluminada; **to ~ the way for sb** alumbrar (el camino) a algn

2 (= *ignite*) [+ *match, candle, fire*] encender, prender; [+ *cigarette*] encender

Ⓓ VI (= *ignite*) encenderse, prender; **the fire wouldn't ~** el fuego no se encendía, el fuego no prendía

Ⓔ CPD ► **light bulb** N bombilla *f*, foco *m* (*Andes*), bombillo *m* (*Col, Ven*) ► **light fitting** N *instalación eléctrica donde se colocan bombillas, tubos fluorescentes, etc* ► **light meter** N (*Phot*) fotómetro *m* ► **light pen** N lápiz *m* óptico ► **light show** N espectáculo *m* de luces ► **light switch** N interruptor *m* ► **light wave** N onda *f* luminosa ► **light year** N año *m* luz; **3000 ~ years away** a una distancia de 3000 años luz

►**light out**†* VI + ADV largarse* (**for** para)

►**light up** Ⓐ VI + ADV 1 (*gen*) iluminarse; **her face lit up** se le iluminó la cara

2 (*) (= *light cigarette*) encender un cigarrillo

Ⓑ VT + ADV iluminar

light² [laɪt] Ⓐ ADJ (*compar* **lighter**; *superl* **lightest**) 1 (*in weight*) [*object, clothing, equipment*] ligero, liviano (*LAm*); [*step*] ligero; **I want to be ten pounds ~er** quiero adelgazar diez libras; **I'm ten pounds ~er than I was** peso diez libras menos que antes; **to be ~ on one's feet** ser ligero de pies; **with a ~ heart** (= *cheerfully*) con el corazón alegre; (= *without thinking*) a la ligera; **you need a ~ touch to make good pastry** necesitas manos de seda para conseguir una buena masa; ✦*IDIOM* **as ~ as a feather** ligero como una pluma

2 (= *scanty, slight*) [*breeze*] leve, suave; [*shower*] ligero; **a ~ rain was falling** lloviznaba; **a ~ fall of snow** una ligera nevada; **trading was ~ on the Stock Exchange** hubo poca actividad en la Bolsa; **traffic was ~** había poco tráfico; **the speech was ~ on content** el discurso tenía poco contenido

3 (*Culin*) [*meal, food, cake*] ligero, liviano (*LAm*)

4 (= *low-alcohol*) de bajo contenido alcohólico, de bajo contenido en alcohol; (= *low-calorie*) light, bajo en calorías; (= *low-tar*) light, de bajo contenido en alquitrán

5 (= *soft*) [*sound*] leve; [*voice*] suave; **there was a ~ tapping on the door** se oyeron unos golpecitos a la puerta

6 (= *not demanding*) [*work, duties*] ligero; **she can only manage ~ work** sólo puede realizar tareas ligeras; ✦*IDIOM* **to make ~ work of sth** hacer algo con facilidad

7 (= *not serious*) [*novel, music*] ligero; **to make ~ of sth** quitar importancia a algo; **on a ~er note** hablando de cosas menos serias; **take along some ~ reading** llévate algo fácil de leer

8 (= *not harsh*) [*sentence*] leve

9 (= *shallow*) **she had drifted into a ~ sleep** se había quedado medio dormida; **to be a ~ sleeper** tener el sueño ligero

10 (= *loose*) [*soil*] poco denso

Ⓑ ADV **to travel ~** viajar con poco equipaje

Ⓒ N 1 **lights** (*Culin*†) pulmones *mpl*

2 (= *cigarette*) cigarrillo *m* light, cigarrillo *m* de bajo contenido en alquitrán

Ⓓ CPD ► **light aircraft** N avión *m* ligero ► **light ale** N cerveza *f* rubia, cerveza *f* clara ► **light entertainment** N (*TV*) programas *mpl* de variedades; **a stand-up comedian provided ~ entertainment** un humorista amenizó la velada ► **light industry** N industria *f* ligera ► **light infantry** N infantería *f* ligera ► **light opera** N (= *show*) opereta *f*; (= *genre*) género *m* lírico ► **light verse** N poesías *fpl* festivas

light³ [laɪt] (*pt, pp* **lit** *or* **lighted**) VI **to ~ on sth** (*liter*) dar con algo, tropezar con algo, encontrar algo

light-coloured [ˈlaɪtˈkʌləd] ADJ claro, de color claro

light-emitting diode [ˌlaɪtɪmɪtɪŋˈdaɪəʊd] N diodo *m* luminoso

lighten¹ [ˈlaɪtn] Ⓐ VT [+ *room*] iluminar más; [+ *sky*] iluminar; [+ *color*] hacer más claro

Ⓑ VI [*sky*] clarear; (*Meteo*) relampaguear

lighten² [ˈlaɪtn] Ⓐ VT [+ *load*] aligerar, hacer menos pesado; (*fig*) (= *make cheerful*) [+ *atmosphere*] relajar; [+ *heart*] alegrar; (= *reduce*) [+ *cares*] aliviar

Ⓑ VI [*load*] aligerarse, hacerse menos pesado; [*heart*] alegrarse

lighter¹ [ˈlaɪtəʳ] Ⓐ N (*also* **cigarette ~**) encendedor *m*, mechero *m*

Ⓑ CPD ► **lighter flint** N piedra *f* de mechero ► **lighter fuel** N gas *m* de encendedor

lighter² [ˈlaɪtəʳ] N (*Naut*) gabarra *f*, barcaza *f*

light-fingered [ˈlaɪtˈfɪŋgəd] ADJ con las manos muy largas; **to be ~** tener las manos muy largas, ser muy amigo de lo ajeno

light-footed [ˈlaɪtˈfʊtɪd] ADJ ligero (de pies)

light-haired [ˈlaɪtˈhɛəd] ADJ rubio, güero (*CAm, Mex*)

light-headed [ˈlaɪtˈhedɪd] ADJ (*by temperament*) ligero de cascos*; (= *dizzy*) mareado; (*with fever*) delirante; (*with excitement*) exaltado; **wine makes me ~** el vino se me sube a la cabeza

light-hearted [ˈlaɪtˈhɑːtɪd] ADJ desenfadado, alegre; [*remark*] poco serio, dicho en tono festivo

light-heartedly [ˈlaɪtˈhɑːtɪdlɪ] ADV alegremente

lighthouse [ˈlaɪthaʊs] Ⓐ N (*pl* **lighthouses** [ˈlaɪthaʊzɪz]) faro *m*

Ⓑ CPD ► **lighthouse keeper** N farero/a *m/f*, torrero/a *m/f*

lighting [ˈlaɪtɪŋ] Ⓐ N (= *act*) iluminación *f*; [*of fire*] encendimiento *m*; [*of cigarette*] encendido *m*; (= *system*) alumbrado *m*; (*at pop show*) equipo *m* de luces, iluminación *f*; (*Theat*) iluminación *f*

Ⓑ CPD ► **lighting effects** NPL efectos *mpl* luminosos ► **lighting engineer** N luminotécnico/a *m/f*

lighting-up time [ˌlaɪtɪŋˈʌptaɪm] N hora *f* de encender los faros

lightly [ˈlaɪtlɪ] ADV 1 (= *gently, softly*) [*touch, knock*] suavemente; [*tread, walk*] con paso ligero; **she kissed him ~ on the forehead** le dio un beso con suavidad en la frente; **brush ~ with beaten egg** extienda una ligera capa de huevo batido

2 (= *slightly*) levemente, ligeramente; **~ clad** ligero de ropa, con muy poca ropa; **season ~ with salt and pepper** sazone con un poquito de sal y pimienta; **a ~ boiled egg** un huevo poco cocido, un huevo pasado por agua; **to touch ~ on a matter** mencionar un asunto de paso

3 (= *frivolously*) a la ligera; **this is not a charge to be made ~** este tipo de acusación no se hace a la ligera; **to get off ~** librarse de una buena; **to speak ~ of danger** despreciar el peligro

lightness¹ [ˈlaɪtnɪs] N 1 (= *brightness*) [*of room*] luminosidad *f*

2 (= *paleness*) [*of colour*] claridad *f*

lightness² [ˈlaɪtnɪs] N 1 (*in weight*) ligereza *f*, liviandad *f* (*LAm*); (*Culin*) [*of pastry, mixture*] ligereza *f*, suavidad *f*; **a feeling of ~ came over her** le invadió una sensación de ligereza; **her ~ of step** la ligereza *or* agilidad de sus pasos

2 (= *undemanding nature*) [*of duties*] ligereza *f*

3 [*of tone, voice*] suavidad *f*

4 [*of sentence*] levedad *f*

lightning [ˈlaɪtnɪŋ] Ⓐ N (= *flash*) relámpago *m*; (= *stroke*) rayo *m*; **a flash of ~** un relámpago; **where the ~ struck** donde cayó el rayo; ✦*IDIOMS* **as quick as ~** ◊ **like (greased) ~*** como un rayo; ✦*PROV* **~ never strikes twice in the same place** desgracias así no suelen repetirse

Ⓑ CPD ► **lightning attack** N ataque *m* relámpago ► **lightning conductor, lightning rod** (*US*) N pararrayos *m inv* ► **lightning strike** N huelga *f* relámpago ► **lightning visit** N visita *f* relámpago

lightship ['laɪtʃɪp] N buque-faro *m*

light-skinned [,lait'skɪnd] ADJ de piel blanca

lightweight ['laɪtweɪt] Ⓐ ADJ (*gen*) ligero, de poco peso, liviano (*esp LAm*); (*Boxing*) de peso ligero

Ⓑ N (*Boxing*) peso *m* ligero; (*fig*) (*pej*) persona *f* de poco peso *or* sin importancia

ligneous ['lɪgnɪəs] ADJ leñoso

lignite ['lɪgnaɪt] N lignito *m*

lignum vitae ['lɪgnəm'viːtaɪ] N palo *m* santo; (= *tree*) guayaco *m*

Ligures ['lɪgjʊəz] NPL ligures *mpl*

Ligurian [lɪ'gjʊərɪən] Ⓐ ADJ ligur

Ⓑ N ligur *mf*

likable ['laɪkəbl] = **likeable**

▼ **like**[1] [laɪk] Ⓐ ADJ (*frm*) (= *similar*) parecido, semejante; **snakes, lizards and ~ creatures** serpientes *fpl*, lagartos *mpl* y criaturas *fpl* parecidas *or* semejantes; **to be of ~ mind** tener ideas afines; **she and a group of friends of ~ mind** ella y un grupo de amigos con ideas afines; **he was very intolerant towards people not of a ~ mind** era muy intransigente con las personas que no le daban la razón; ✦*IDIOM* **they are as ~ as two peas (in a pod)** se parecen como dos gotas de agua

Ⓑ PREP [1] (= *similar to*) como; **what's he ~?** ¿cómo es (él)?; **you know what she's ~** ya la conoces, ya sabes cómo es; **what's Spain ~?** ¿cómo es España?; **what's the weather ~?** ¿qué tiempo hace?; **a house ~ mine** una casa como la mía, una casa parecida a la mía; **I found one ~ it** encontré uno parecido *or* igual; **she was ~ a sister to me** fue (como) una hermana para mí; **we heard a noise ~ someone sneezing** nos pareció oír a alguien estornudar, oímos como un estornudo; **I never saw anything ~ it** nunca he visto cosa igual *or* semejante; **what's he ~ as a teacher?** ¿qué tal es como profesor?; **to be ~ sth/sb** parecerse a algo/algn, ser parecido a algo/algn; **you're so ~ your father** (*in looks, character*) te pareces mucho a tu padre, eres muy parecido a tu padre; **this portrait is not ~ him** en este retrato no parece él; **it was more ~ a prison than a house** se parecía más a una cárcel que a una casa; **the figure is more ~ 300** la cifra se acerca más bien a 300; **why can't you be more ~ your sister?** ¿por qué no aprendes de tu hermana?; **that's more ~ it!*** ¡así está mejor!, ¡así me gusta!; **there's nothing ~ real silk** no hay nada como la seda natural; **something ~ that** algo así, algo por el estilo; **I was thinking of giving her something ~ a doll** pensaba en regalarle algo así como una muñeca, pensaba en regalarle una muñeca o algo por el estilo; **they earn something ~ £50,000 a year** ganan alrededor de 50.000 libras al año; **people ~ that can't be trusted** esa clase *or* ese tipo de gente no es de fiar; *see also* **feel B3, look B4, smell C1, sound**[1] **C2.1, taste C**

[2] (= *typical of*) **it's not ~ him to do that** no es propio de él hacer eso; **isn't it just ~ him!** ¡no cambia!, ¡eso es típico de él!; **(it's) just ~ you to grab the last cake!** ¡qué típico que tomes *or* (*Sp*) cojas tú el último pastelito!

[3] (= *similarly to*) como; **he thinks ~ us** piensa como nosotros; **~ me, he is fond of Brahms** igual que a mí, le gusta Brahms; **she behaved ~ an idiot** se comportó como una idiota; **just ~ anybody else** igual que cualquier otro; **~ this/that** así; **it wasn't ~ that** no fue así, no ocurrió así; **I'm sorry to intrude on you ~ this** siento importunarte de este modo; **stop pacing ~ that** deja de dar vueltas; **he got up and left, just ~ that** se levantó y se marchó, así, sin más; ✦*PROV* **~ father ~ son** de tal palo tal astilla; *see also* **anything 5, crazy A1, hell A2, mad A1.2**

[4] (= *such as*) como; **large cities ~ New York** las grandes urbes como Nueva York; **the basic necessities of life, ~ food and drink** las necesidades básicas de la vida, como la comida y la bebida

Ⓒ ADV [1] (= *comparable*) **on company advice, well, orders, more ~** siguiendo los consejos de la empresa, bueno, más bien sus órdenes; **it's nothing ~ as hot as it was yesterday** no hace tanto calor como ayer, ni mucho menos; **£500 will be nothing ~ enough** 500 libras no serán suficientes, ni mucho menos

[2] (= *likely*) **(as) ~ as not: they'll be down the pub (as) ~ as not** lo más probable es que estén en el bar

Ⓓ CONJ (*) [1] (= *as*) como; **~ we used to (do)** como solíamos (hacer); **do it ~ I do** hazlo como yo; **it's just ~ I say** es como yo digo; ✦*IDIOM* **to tell it ~ it is** decir las cosas como son

[2] (* = *as if*) como si; **he behaved ~ he was afraid** se comportaba como si tuviera miedo; **you look ~ you've seen a ghost** parece que acabas de ver un fantasma

Ⓔ N **we shall not see his ~ again** (*frm, liter*) no volveremos a ver otro igual; **the exchange was done on a ~-for-~ basis** el intercambio se hizo basándose en dos cosas parecidas; **did you ever see the ~ (of it)?** ¿has visto cosa igual?; **I've no time for the ~s of him*** no soporto a la gente como él; **sparrows, starlings and the ~** *or* **and such ~** gorriones, estorninos y otras aves por el estilo; **to compare ~ with ~** comparar dos cosas semejantes; ✦*IDIOM* **~ attracts ~** Dios los cría y ellos se juntan

▼ **like**[2] [laɪk] Ⓐ VT [1] (= *find pleasant*) **I ~ dancing/football** me gusta bailar/el fútbol; **I ~ bright colours** me gustan los colores vivos; **which do you ~ best?** ¿cuál es el que más te gusta?; **your father won't ~ it** esto no le va a gustar a tu padre; **I ~ oysters but they don't ~ me*** me gustan las ostras pero no me sientan muy bien; **we ~ it here** nos gusta este sitio; **I ~ him** me cae bien *or* simpático; **I don't ~ him at all** me resulta antipático, no me cae nada bien; **I've come to ~ him** le he llegado a tomar *or* (*Sp*) coger cariño; **don't you ~ me just a little bit?** ¿no me quieres un poquitín?; **you know he ~s you very much** sabes que te tiene mucho cariño *or* que te quiere mucho; **I don't think they ~ each other** creo que no se caen bien; **I don't ~ the look of him** no me gusta su aspecto, no me gusta la pinta que tiene*; **I ~ your nerve!*** ¡qué frescura!, ¡qué cara tienes!; **well, I ~ that!*** (*iro*) ¡será posible!, ¡habráse visto!; **she is well ~d here** aquí se la quiere mucho

[2] (= *feel about*) **how do you ~ Cadiz?** ¿qué te parece Cádiz?; **how do you ~ it here?** ¿qué te parece este sitio?; **how would you ~ to go to the cinema?** ¿te apetece *or* (*LAm*) se te antoja ir al cine?; **how would you ~ it if somebody did the same to you?** ¿cómo te sentirías si alguien te hiciera lo mismo?; **how do you ~ that! I've been here five years and he doesn't know my name** ¡qué te parece!, llevo cinco años trabajando aquí y no sabe ni cómo me llamo

[3] (= *have a preference for*) **I ~ my whisky neat** me gusta el whisky solo; **this plant doesn't ~ sunlight** a esta planta no le gusta la luz; **I ~ to know the facts before I form opinions** me gusta conocer los hechos antes de formarme una opinión; **I ~ to be obeyed** me gusta que me obedezcan; **she ~s him to be home by ten** le gusta que esté en casa antes de las diez; **I ~ to think I'm not prejudiced** creo que no tengo prejuicios; **I ~ to think of myself as a humanitarian** me considero una persona humanitaria

[4] (= *want*) **I didn't ~ to say no** no quise decir que no; (*because embarrassed*) me dio vergüenza decir que no; **take as much as you ~** toma *or* coge todo lo que quieras; **he thinks he can do as he ~s** cree que puede hacer lo que quiera, cree que puede hacer lo que le de la gana*; **whether he ~s it or not** le guste o no (le guste), quiera o no (quiera); **whenever you ~** cuando quieras

[5] **would/should ~** [5·1] (*specific request, offer, desire*) **would you ~ a drink?** ¿quieres tomar algo?; **I'd ~ you to do it** quiero que lo hagas; **would you ~ me to wait?** ¿quiere que espere?; **I'd** *or* **I would** *or* (*frm*) **I should ~ an explanation** quisiera una explicación, me gustaría que me dieran una explicación; **I'd ~ to think we're still friends** quisiera creer que todavía somos amigos; **I'd ~ to take this opportunity to thank you all** quisiera aprovechar esta oportunidad para darles las gracias a todos; **I'd ~ the roast chicken, please** (me trae) el pollo asado, por favor; **I'd ~ three pounds of tomatoes, please** (me da) tres libras de tomates, por favor

[5·2] (*wishes, preferences*) **I'd ~ a bigger flat** me gustaría tener un piso más grande; **he'd ~ to have met her** le hubiera gustado conocerla; **I should ~ to have been there** ◊ **I should have ~d to be there** (*frm*) me hubiera gustado estar allí

Ⓑ VI querer; **as you ~** como quieras; **"shall we go now?" — "if you ~"** —¿nos vamos ya? —si quieres

Ⓒ N **likes** gustos *mpl*; **~s and dislikes** aficiones *fpl* y fobias *or* manías, cosas *fpl* que gustan y cosas que no; **he has distinct ~s and dislikes where food is concerned** con respecto a la comida tiene claras preferencias *or* sabe muy bien lo que le gusta y lo que no (le gusta)

...like, -like [laɪk] SUFFIX parecido a, como; **bird~** como un pájaro; **with queen~ dignity** con dignidad de reina; *see also* **catlike** *etc*

likeable ['laɪkəbl] ADJ simpático, agradable

likeableness ['laɪkəblnɪs] N simpatía *f*

likelihood ['laɪklɪhʊd] N probabilidad *f*; **what is the ~ of a successful outcome?** ¿qué probabilidad hay de que el resultado sea favorable?; **there is no ~ of infection** no hay probabilidad de infección; **there is little/every ~ that he'll come** es poco/muy probable que venga; **there is a strong ~ they'll be elected** es muy probable que salgan elegidos; **in all ~ the explosion was caused by a bomb** lo más probable es que una bomba causase la explosión

▼ **likely** ['laɪklɪ] Ⓐ ADJ (*compar* **likelier**, *superl* **likeliest**) [1] (= *probable*) [*outcome, consequences*] probable; **what kind of changes are ~?** ¿qué tipo de cambios son probables?; **snow is ~ on high ground** es probable que nieve en zonas altas; **it is ~ that** es probable que + *subjun*; **it is ~ to rain later on** es probable que llueva más tarde; **they are not ~ to come** no es probable que vengan; **he's ~ to do anything** puede hacer cualquier cosa;

➤ LANGUAGE IN USE: **like**[1] **B1** 5.3 **D1** 5.2 **like**[2] **A1** 7.1, 7.2, 7.3 **A5** 7.1, 8.3 **likely A1** 15.2, 16.2

he's the man most ~ to win es el que más probabilidades tiene de ganar; **a ~ story** *or* **tale!** (*iro*) ¡menudo cuento!, ¡y yo que me lo creo! (*iro*)

[2] (= *suitable*) **this seems a ~ spot for a picnic** éste parece un buen sitio para hacer un picnic; **she's the most ~ candidate** es la candidata que parece más idónea; **here comes a ~-looking character** aquí viene un tipo que parece adecuado *or* que bien puede servir

LIKE

Verb

"Gustar" better avoided

- While **gustar** is one of the main ways of translating **like**, its use is not always appropriate. Used to refer to people, it may imply sexual attraction. Instead, use expressions like **caer bien** or **parecer/resultar simpático/agradable**. These expressions work like **gustar** and need an indirect object:

I like Francis very much
Francis me cae muy bien *or* ***me parece muy simpático*** *or* ***agradable***
She likes me, but that's all
(A ella) le caigo bien, pero nada más

Like + verb

- Translate **to like doing sth** and **to like to do sth** using **gustar** + INFINITIVE:

Doctors don't like having to go out to visit patients at night
A los médicos no les gusta tener que salir a visitar pacientes por la noche
My brother likes to rest after lunch
A mi hermano le gusta descansar después de comer

- Translate **to like sb doing sth** and **to like sb to do sth** using **gustar** + **que** + SUBJUNCTIVE:

My wife likes me to do the shopping
A mi mujer le gusta que haga la compra
I don't like Irene living so far away
No me gusta que Irene viva tan lejos

"How do you like...?"

- Use **qué** + **parecer** to translate **how do/did you like** when asking someone's opinion:

How do you like this coat?
¿Qué te parece este abrigo?
How did you like the concert?
¿Qué te ha parecido el concierto?

- But use **cómo** + **gustar** when using **how do you like** more literally:

How do you like your steak?
¿Cómo le gusta la carne?

Would like

- When translating **would like**, use **querer** with requests and offers and **gustar** to talk about preferences and wishes:

Would you like a glass of water?
¿Quiere un vaso de agua?
What would you like me to do about the tickets?
¿Qué quieres que haga respecto a los billetes?
I'd very much like to go to Spain this summer
Me gustaría mucho ir a España este verano

NOTE: Literal translations of **I'd like** are better avoided when making requests in shops and restaurants. Use expressions like the following:

I'd like steak and chips
¿Me pone un filete con patatas fritas?, (Yo) quiero un filete con patatas fritas

For further uses and examples, see main entry.

Ⓑ ADV (= *probably*) **she will very** *or* **most ~ arrive late** lo más probable es que llegue tarde; **some prisoners will ~ be released soon** (*US*) es probable que pronto se deje en libertad a algunos prisioneros; **(as) ~ as not he'll arrive early** lo más probable es que llegue pronto, seguramente llegará pronto; **this is more than ~ true** lo más probable *or* seguro es que sea cierto; **"I expect she'll be re-elected" — "yes, more than ~"** —me imagino que la volverán a elegir —si, seguramente; **not ~!*** ¡ni hablar!*

like-minded [ˈlaɪkˈmaɪndɪd] ADJ con ideas afines, de igual parecer

liken [ˈlaɪkən] VT comparar (**to** con)

likeness [ˈlaɪknɪs] N [1] (= *resemblance*) semejanza *f*, parecido *m*; **family ~** aire *m* de familia
[2] (= *appearance*) aspecto *m*; **in the ~ of ...** a imagen y semejanza de ...; **to assume the ~ of ...** tomar la forma de ..., adoptar la apariencia de ...
[3] (= *portrait*) retrato *m*; **it's a good ~** se parece mucho

likewise [ˈlaɪkwaɪz] ADV (= *also*) asimismo, igualmente, también; (= *the same*) lo mismo, igualmente; **~ it is true that ...** asimismo es verdad que ...; **to do ~** hacer lo mismo

liking [ˈlaɪkɪŋ] N (*for thing*) gusto *m* (**for** por), afición *f* (**for** a); (*for person*) simpatía *f*, aprecio *m* (*LAm*); **to have a ~ for sth** ser aficionado *or* tener afición a algo; **to have a ~ for sb** tener simpatía a algn; **to be to sb's ~** ser del gusto de algn; **to take a ~ to sth/to doing sth** tomar *or* coger gusto a algo/a hacer algo; **to take a ~ to sb** tomar *or* coger simpatía a algn; **it's too strong for my ~** para mí es demasiado fuerte, es demasiado fuerte para mi gusto

lilac [ˈlaɪlək] Ⓐ N (*Bot*) lila *f*; (= *colour*) lila *m*, color *m* lila
Ⓑ ADJ de color lila

Lille [liːl] N Lila *f*

Lilliputian [ˌlɪlɪˈpjuːʃɪən] Ⓐ ADJ liliputiense
Ⓑ N liliputiense *mf*

Lilo® [ˈlaɪləʊ] N colchoneta *f* inflable

lilt [lɪlt] N (*in voice*) tono *m* cantarín; (*in song*) ritmo *m* alegre; **a song with a ~ to it** una canción de ritmo alegre

lilting [ˈlɪltɪŋ] ADJ [*voice*] cantarín

lily [ˈlɪlɪ] Ⓐ N lirio *m*, azucena *f*; **~ of the valley** muguete *m*, lirio *m* de los valles
Ⓑ CPD ► **lily pad** N hoja *f* de nenúfar

lily-livered [ˈlɪlɪˈlɪvəd] ADJ cobarde, pusilánime

lily-white [ˈlɪlɪwaɪt] ADJ blanco como la azucena

Lima [ˈliːmə] N Lima *f*

lima bean [ˈliːməˌbiːn] N (*US*) fríjol *m* de media luna, judía *f* de la peladilla

limb [lɪm] N (*Anat*) miembro *m*, extremidad *f*; [*of tree*] rama *f*; **to lose a ~** perder uno de los miembros *or* una de las extremidades; **✦*IDIOMS*** **to be/go out on a ~** (*in danger*) estar/quedar en peligro; (*be isolated*) estar/quedarse aislado; (= *take risk*) correr el riesgo; **to tear sb ~ from ~** despedazar a algn; *see also* **life A1**

-limbed [lɪmd] ADJ (*ending in compounds*) *see* **long-limbed**

limber[1] [ˈlɪmbəʳ] ADJ [*person*] ágil; [*material*] flexible

► **limber up** VI + ADV (*Sport*) entrar en calor, hacer ejercicios preparatorios; (*fig*) entrenarse, prepararse

limber[2] [ˈlɪmbəʳ] N (*Mil*) armón *m* (de artillería)

limbless [ˈlɪmlɪs] ADJ (que está) falto de un brazo *or* una pierna

limbo [ˈlɪmbəʊ] N (*Rel*) (*also* **Limbo**) limbo *m*; (= *dance*) limbo *m*; **✦*IDIOM*** **to be in ~** [*person*] quedarse nadando entre dos aguas

lime[1] [laɪm] Ⓐ N (*Geol*) cal *f*; (*birdlime*) liga *f*
Ⓑ VT (*Agr*) abonar con cal

lime[2] [laɪm] N (*Bot*) (*also* **~ tree**) (= *linden*) tilo *m*

lime[3] [laɪm] Ⓐ N (*Bot*) (= *citrus fruit*) lima *f*; (= *tree*) limero *m*; (= *colour*) verde *m* lima
Ⓑ CPD ► **lime juice** N zumo *m* *or* (*LAm*) jugo *m* de lima

lime-green [ˌlaɪmˈgriːn] ADJ verde lima

limekiln [ˈlaɪmkɪln] N horno *m* de cal

limelight [ˈlaɪmlaɪt] N luz *f* de calcio; **✦*IDIOMS*** **to be in the ~** ser el centro de atención, estar en el candelero; **to hog the ~** acaparar *or* llevarse todo el protagonismo; **he never sought the ~** no trató nunca de acaparar la atención

limerick [ˈlɪmərɪk] N *especie de quintilla jocosa*

LIMERICK

Un **limerick** *es un poema burlón que consta de cinco versos con rima* **aabba**. *Las composiciones suelen ir dirigidas a una persona y el tono es normalmente bastante grosero o surrealista. A menudo comienzan con las palabras* **there was a...** *y contienen dos versos largos seguidos de otros dos cortos más un remate incisivo que puede llevar una rima torpe o inesperada a propósito. A continuación mostramos un ejemplo de* **limerick**: **There once was a man from North Wales, Who bought a trombone in the sales; But he found, when he tried it, There was something inside it: Fifty pence and a packet of nails.**

limestone [ˈlaɪmstəʊn] N (piedra *f*) caliza *f*

limey* [ˈlaɪmɪ] N (*US, Canada pej*) inglés/esa *m/f*

limit [ˈlɪmɪt] Ⓐ N [1] (= *cut-off point, furthest extent*) límite *m*; **there is a ~ to my patience** mi paciencia tiene un límite; **there's a ~ to what doctors can do in such cases** lo que pueden hacer los médicos en estos casos es limitado; **to be at the ~ of one's endurance** ya no poder más; **to be at the ~ of one's patience** haber agotado la paciencia; **behaviour beyond the ~s of acceptability** comportamiento *m* que va más allá de los límites de lo aceptable; **to know no ~s** no tener límite(s); **these establishments are off ~s to ordinary citizens** los ciudadanos de a pie tienen prohibido el acceso a estos establecimientos; **that sort of question is off ~s** ese tipo de pregunta se sale de los límites; **that is outside the ~s of my experience** eso va más allá de los límites de mi experiencia; **it is important that parents set ~s for their children** es importante que los padres les pongan límites a sus hijos; **she tried my patience to the ~** puso mi paciencia a prueba; **it is true within ~s** es verdad dentro de ciertos límites; *see also* **city B**, **sky**, **stretch B7**
[2] (= *permitted maximum*) límite *m*; **there is no ~ on** *or* **to the amount you can import** no existe un límite con respecto a la cantidad que se puede importar; **one glass of wine's my ~** con un vaso de vino me basta y me sobra; **he was three times over the ~** (*Aut*) había ingerido tres veces más de la cantidad de alcohol permitida (para conducir); *see also* **age D**, **credit C**, **speed**, **spending B**, **time C**, **weight C**
[3] **the ~: it's the ~!*** (= *too much*) ¡es el colmo!, ¡es demasiado!; **he's the ~!** ¡es el colmo!, ¡es el no va más!

4 (*Math*) límite *m*
Ⓑ VT [+ *numbers, power, freedom*] limitar; [+ *spending*] restringir; **try to ~ your fat intake** procura limitar el consumo de grasas; **are you ~ed as to time?** ¿tienes el tiempo limitado?; **he ~ed questions to 25 minutes** limitó las preguntas a 25 minutos; **to ~ o.s. to sth** limitarse a algo; **he ~ed himself to a few remarks** se limitó a hacer algunas observaciones; **I ~ myself to ten cigarettes a day** me permito sólo diez cigarrillos al día

limitation [ˌlɪmɪˈteɪʃən] N limitación *f*, restricción *f*; (*Jur*) prescripción *f*; **he has his ~s** tiene sus limitaciones, tiene sus puntos flacos; **there is no ~ on exports** no hay restricción a las exportaciones

limited [ˈlɪmɪtɪd] Ⓐ ADJ 1 (= *small*) [*number, space*] limitado; [*resources*] limitado, escaso; [*range, scope*] limitado, reducido; **we only have a ~ amount of time** sólo contamos con una cantidad de tiempo limitada; **to a ~ extent** hasta cierto punto; **"for a limited period only"** "sólo por un periodo limitado"
2 (= *restricted*) limitado; **she feels very ~ in her job** se siente muy limitada en su trabajo; **he has ~ use of one arm** tiene algo de movilidad en un brazo; **the choice is ~** hay poca elección
3 (*esp Brit Jur, Comm*) (*in company names*) **Hourmont Travel Limited** Hourmont Travel, Sociedad Anónima
Ⓑ CPD ► **limited company** N (*esp Brit Comm, Jur*) sociedad *f* anónima, sociedad *f* limitada ► **limited edition** N [*of book*] edición *f* limitada; [*of picture, record*] tirada *f* limitada; [*of car*] serie *f* limitada ► **limited liability** N (*esp Brit Jur*) responsabilidad *f* limitada ► **limited partnership** N (*Comm*) sociedad *f* limitada, sociedad *f* en comandita; *see also* **public C**

limiting [ˈlɪmɪtɪŋ] ADJ restrictivo

limitless [ˈlɪmɪtlɪs] ADJ ilimitado, sin límites

limo* [ˈlɪməʊ] N = **limousine**

limousine [ˈlɪməziːn] N limusina *f*

limp¹ [lɪmp] Ⓐ N cojera *f*; **to walk with a ~** cojear
Ⓑ VI cojear, renguear (*LAm*); **he ~ed to the door** fue cojeando a la puerta; **the ship managed to ~ to port** el buque llegó con dificultad al puerto

limp² [lɪmp] ADJ (*compar* **limper**, *superl* **limpest**)
1 [*person, body*] sin fuerzas; [*penis*] flácido; [*hair*] lacio; [*handshake*] flojo; **a piece of ~ lettuce** un trozo de lechuga mustia; **she fell ~ at their feet** cayó sin fuerzas a sus pies; **his arms hung ~** los brazos le colgaban muertos *or* como si fueran de trapo; **his body went ~** se le fueron las fuerzas del cuerpo; **she went ~ in his arms** se dejó caer en sus brazos
2 (= *unconvincing*) [*excuse*] pobre, poco convincente
3 (= *soft*) [*book binding*] blando, flexible

limpet [ˈlɪmpɪt] Ⓐ N lapa *f*; **like a ~** como una lapa
Ⓑ CPD ► **limpet mine** N mina *f* lapa

limpid [ˈlɪmpɪd] ADJ [*water*] límpido, cristalino; [*air*] diáfano, puro; [*eyes*] claro

limply [ˈlɪmplɪ] ADV 1 (= *without energy*) [*lie*] sin fuerzas; **his arms hung ~ at his sides** los brazos le colgaban muertos a los lados; **her hair hung ~ over her face** el pelo lacio le caía sin gracia sobre la cara
2 (*fig*) (= *unconvincingly*) [*say*] de manera poco convincente; [*applaud*] sin entusiasmo

limpness [ˈlɪmpnɪs] N [*of body, limb*] flojedad *f*; [*of excuse*] lo pobre, lo poco convincente

limp-wristed* [ˈlɪmpˈrɪstɪd] ADJ inútil; (*pej*) (= *gay*) de la acera de enfrente, sarasa‡

limy [ˈlaɪmɪ] ADJ calizo

linage [ˈlaɪnɪdʒ] N (*Press*) número *m* de líneas; **advertising ~** espacio *m* destinado a publicidad

linchpin [ˈlɪntʃpɪn] N (*lit*) pezonera *f*; (*fig*) eje *m*

Lincs [lɪŋks] ABBR (*Brit*) = **Lincolnshire**

linctus [ˈlɪŋktəs] N (*pl* **linctuses**) jarabe *m* para la tos

linden [ˈlɪndən] N = **lime²**

line¹ [laɪn] Ⓐ N 1 (*gen*) línea *f*; (*drawn*) raya *f*; **to draw a ~** trazar una línea; **there's a fine** *or* **thin ~ between genius and madness** la línea que separa la genialidad de la locura es muy sutil; **~ of latitude/longitude** línea *f* de latitud/longitud; **to put a ~ through sth** tachar *or* (*LAm*) rayar algo; **the Line** (*Geog*) el ecuador; ✦*IDIOMS* **to draw the ~ at sth** no tolerar *or* aceptar algo; **one must draw the ~ somewhere** hay que fijar ciertos límites; **to know where to draw the ~** saber dónde pararse; **to draw a ~ under** [+ *episode, event*] poner punto final a; **to be on the ~: his job is on the ~** su puesto está en peligro, se expone a perder su puesto; **to lay it on the ~** decirlo claramente, hablar con franqueza; **to lay** *or* **put one's reputation on the ~** arriesgar su reputación; **to put one's neck on the ~‡** ◊ **put one's ass on the ~** (*US‡*) jugársela*
2 (= *rope*) cuerda *f*; (= *fishing line*) sedal *m*; (= *clothes line, washing line*) cuerda *f* para tender la ropa; **they threw a ~ to the man in the sea** le lanzaron un cable *or* una cuerda al hombre que estaba en el agua
3 (= *wrinkle*) (*on face etc*) arruga *f*; (*in palmistry*) raya *f*, línea *f*
4 [*of print, verse*] renglón *m*, línea *f*; **"new ~"** (*in dictation*) "otra línea"; **drop me a ~*** (*fig*) escríbeme; **to learn one's ~s** (*Theat*) aprenderse el papel; ✦*IDIOM* **to read between the ~s** leer entre líneas
5 (= *row*) hilera *f*, fila *f*, línea *f*; **~ of traffic** fila *f or* cola *f* de coches; **the traffic stretched for three miles in an unbroken ~** había una caravana *or* cola de coches de tres millas; **a ~ of winning numbers** (*in bingo, lottery etc*) una línea ganadora; **to be in ~ with** estar de acuerdo con, ser conforme a; **to be in ~ for promotion** estar bajo consideración para un ascenso; **public sector pay is in ~ to rise** está previsto que suban los salarios del sector público; **to keep the party in ~** mantener la disciplina del partido; **to keep people in ~** mantener a la gente a raya; **to bring sth into ~ with sth** poner algo de acuerdo con algo; **to fall** *or* **get into ~** (*abreast*) meterse en fila; **to fall into ~ with sb** estar de acuerdo con algn; **to fall into ~ with sth** ser conforme a algo; **to be out of ~ with** no ser conforme con; **he was completely out of ~ to suggest that ...*** estaba totalmente fuera de lugar que propusiera que ...; ✦*IDIOMS* **all along the ~** desde principio a fin; **somewhere along the ~ we went wrong** en algún punto nos hemos equivocado; **to reach** *or* **come to the end of the ~** llegar al final; *see also* **step B1**
6 (= *series*) serie *f*; **the latest in a long ~ of tragedies** la última de una larga serie *or* lista de tragedias
7 (= *lineage*) linaje *m*; **~ of descent** linaje *m*; **the title is inherited through the male/female ~** el título se hereda por línea paterna/materna; **he comes from a long ~ of artists** proviene de un extenso linaje de artistas; **the royal ~** el linaje real
8 (= *hierarchy*) **~ of command** cadena *f* de mando
9 (*Mil*) línea *f*; **~ of battle** línea de batalla; **the (battle) ~s are drawn** (*fig*) la guerra está declarada; **the first ~ of defence** (*lit*) la primera línea de retaguardia; (*fig*) el primer escudo protector; **behind enemy ~s** tras las líneas enemigas; **ship of the ~** navío *m* de línea; *see also* **front E**
10 (*esp US*) (= *queue*) cola *f*; **to form a ~** hacer una cola; **to get into ~** ponerse en la cola *or* a la cola; **to stand in ~** hacer cola
11 (= *direction*) línea *f*; **the main** *or* **broad ~s** [*of story, plan*] las líneas maestras; **along** *or* **on the ~s of** algo por el estilo de; **something along those** *or* **the same ~s** algo por el estilo; **along** *or* **on political/racial ~s** según criterios políticos/raciales; **on the right ~s** por buen camino; **~ of argument** argumento *m*; **~ of attack** (*Mil*) modo *m* de ataque; (*fig*) planteamiento *m*; **in the ~ of duty** en cumplimiento de sus deberes; **it's all in the ~ of duty** es una parte normal del deber; **in the ~ of fire** (*Mil*) en la línea de fuego; **~ of flight** [*of bird*] trayectoria *f* de vuelo; [*of object*] trayectoria *f*; **~ of inquiry** línea *f* de investigación; **~ of sight** *or* **vision** visual *f*; **~ of thought** hilo *m* del pensamiento
12 (*Elec*) (= *wire*) cable *m*; **to be/come on ~** (*Comput*) estar/entrar en (pleno) funcionamiento
13 (*Telec*) línea *f*; **can you get me a ~ to Chicago?** ¿me puede poner con Chicago?; **it's a very bad ~** se oye muy mal; **~s of communication** líneas *fpl* de comunicación; **to keep the ~s of communication open with sb** mantener todas las líneas de comunicación abiertas con algn; **the ~'s gone dead** se ha cortado la línea; **the ~s are down** no hay línea; **the ~ is engaged** *or* (*US*) **busy** está comunicando; **hold the ~ please** no cuelgue, por favor; **Mr. Smith is on the ~ (for you)** El Sr. Smith está al teléfono (y quiere hablar con usted); **the ~s are open from six o'clock onwards** las líneas están abiertas de seis en adelante; *see also* **hot D**
14 (= *pipe*) (*for oil, gas*) conducto *m*
15 (= *shape*) (*usu pl*) **the rounded ~s of this car** la línea redondeada *or* el contorno redondeado de este coche
16 (= *field, area*) **what ~ (of business) are you in?** ¿a qué se dedica?; **we're in the same ~ (of business)** nos dedicamos a lo mismo, trabajamos en el mismo campo; **~ of research** campo *m* de investigación; **it's not my ~** (= *speciality*) no es de mi especialidad; **fishing's more (in) my ~** me interesa más la pesca, de pesca sí sé algo
17 (= *stance, attitude*) actitud *f*; **to take a strong** *or* **firm ~ on sth** adoptar una actitud firme sobre algo; **to take the ~ that ...** ser de la opinión que ...; **what ~ is the government taking?** ¿cuál es la actitud del gobierno?; **to follow** *or* **take the ~ of least resistance** conformarse con la ley del mínimo esfuerzo; **this is the official ~** ésta es la versión oficial; ✦*IDIOM* **to toe the ~** acatar las normas; **to toe** *or* **follow the party ~** conformarse a *or* seguir la línea del partido; *see also* **hard A5**
18 (*Comm*) (= *product*) línea *f*; **a new/popular ~** una línea nueva/popular; **that ~ did not sell at all** esa línea de productos se vendió muy mal; **we have a nice ~ in spring hats** tenemos un bonito surtido de sombreros para primavera; **he's got a nice ~ in rude jokes** lo suyo son los chistes verdes
19 (*Rail*) (= *route*) línea *f*; (= *track*) vía *f*;

down ~ vía descendente; **up ~** vía ascendente; **the ~ to Palencia** el ferrocarril de Palencia, la línea de Palencia; **to cross the ~(s)** cruzar la vía; **to leave the ~(s)** descarrilar

20 (*also* **shipping ~**) (= *company*) naviera *f*; (= *route*) línea *f* marítima, ruta *f* marítima

21 (= *clue, lead*) pista *f*; **to give sb a ~ on sth** poner a algn sobre la pista de algo; **the police have a ~ on the criminal** la policía anda *or* está sobre la pista del delincuente

22 (= *spiel*) ♦*IDIOM* **to feed sb a ~ (about sth)*** soltar un rollo *or* contar un cuento chino a algn (sobre algo)*; *see also* **shoot B4**

23 (*Ind*) (= *assembly line*) línea *f*

24 [*of cocaine etc*] raya *f*

Ⓑ VT (= *cross with lines*) [+ *paper*] rayar; [+ *field*] surcar; [+ *face*] arrugar

Ⓒ CPD ► **line dancing** N *danza folclórica en que los que bailan forman líneas y filas* ► **line drawing** N dibujo *m* lineal ► **line editing** N corrección *f* por líneas ► **line feed** N avance *m* de línea ► **line fishing** N pesca *f* con caña ► **line judge** N (*Tennis*) juez *mf* de fondo ► **line manager** N (*Brit Ind*) jefe/a *m/f* de línea ► **line printer** N impresora *f* de línea

►**line up** Ⓐ VT + ADV 1 (= *stand in line*) poner en fila

2 (= *arrange*) **I wonder what he's got ~d up for us** me pregunto qué nos tendrá preparado; **have you got something ~d up for this evening?** ¿tienes algún plan para esta noche?; **I had a job and house all ~d up, all I needed was my plane ticket** ya tenía un trabajo y una casa esperándome, sólo me faltaba el billete de avión; **have you got someone ~d up for the job?** ¿tienes pensado *or* tienes en mente a alguien para el puesto?

Ⓑ VI + ADV (*in queue*) hacer cola; (*in row*) ponerse en fila; (*behind one another*) formar fila; **they ~d up in opposition to** *or* **against the chairman** hicieron frente común contra el presidente; **they ~d up behind** *or* **with the head** agruparon para apoyar al director

line² [laɪn] VT 1 (= *put lining in*) [+ *garment*] forrar (**with** de); (*Tech*) revestir (**with** de); [+ *brakes*] guarnecer; [*bird*] [+ *nest*] cubrir; **eat something to ~ your stomach** come algo para no tener el estómago vacío; *see also* **pocket A1**

2 (= *border*) **streets ~d with trees** calles *fpl* bordeadas de árboles; **to ~ the route** alinearse a lo largo de la ruta; **to ~ the streets** ocupar las aceras; **portraits ~d the walls** las paredes estaban llenas de retratos

lineage [ˈlɪnɪɪdʒ] N 1 (= *line of descent*) linaje *m*

2 (*Press*) = **linage**

lineal [ˈlɪnɪəl] ADJ lineal, en línea recta; [*descent*] en línea directa

lineament [ˈlɪnɪəmənt] N lineamento *m*

linear [ˈlɪnɪəʳ] ADJ [*design*] lineal; [*measure*] de longitud

linebacker [ˈlaɪnbækəʳ] N (*US*) defensa *mf* (*en fútbol americano*)

lined¹ [laɪnd] ADJ [*paper*] de rayas, pautado; [*face*] arrugado; **to become ~** arrugarse

lined² [laɪnd] ADJ [*garment*] forrado, con forro; (*Tech*) revestido

linen [ˈlɪnɪn] Ⓐ N 1 (= *cloth*) lino *m*

2 (= *household linen*) ropa *f* blanca; (= *bed linen*) ropa *f* de cama; (= *table linen*) mantelería *f*; **clean ~** ropa *f* limpia; **dirty ~** ropa *f* sucia *or* para lavar; ♦*IDIOM* **to wash one's dirty ~ in public** (*Brit*) sacar a relucir los trapos sucios

Ⓑ CPD de lino ► **linen basket** N canasta *f or* cesto *m* de la ropa ► **linen closet, linen cupboard** N armario *m* para la ropa blanca

line-out [ˈlaɪnaʊt] N saque *m* de banda

liner¹ [ˈlaɪnəʳ] N (= *ship*) transatlántico *m*

liner² [ˈlaɪnəʳ] Ⓐ N (= *bin liner*) bolsa *f* (para basura); (= *eyeliner*) lápiz *m* de ojos; (*US*) (= *record sleeve*) portada *f*, funda *f*; *see also* **nappy B**

Ⓑ CPD ► **liner note** N (*US*) *comentario en la portada de un disco*

linesman [ˈlaɪnzmən] N (*pl* **linesmen**) 1 (*Sport*) juez *m* de línea, linier *m*

2 (*Rail, Telec*) guardavía *mf*

3 (*Elec*) celador *m*, recorredor *m* de la línea

line-up [ˈlaɪnʌp] N (*Sport*) formación *f*, alineación *f*; (*Theat, Cine*) [*of actors*] reparto *m*, elenco *m*; (*Mus*) [*of band*] formación *f*, integrantes *mfpl*; (*US*) (= *suspects*) rueda *f* de reconocimiento; (= *queue*) cola *f*

ling¹ [lɪŋ] N (*pl* **ling** *or* **lings**) (= *fish*) abadejo *m*

ling² [lɪŋ] N (*Bot*) brezo *m*

linger [ˈlɪŋgəʳ] VI 1 (= *be unwilling to go*) rezagarse, tardar en marcharse

2 (*also* **~ on**) (*in dying*) tardar en morirse; [*pain*] persistir, durar; [*doubts*] persistir, quedar; [*smell*] persistir, tardar en desaparecer; [*tradition*] sobrevivir; [*memory*] pervivir, seguir vivo

3 (= *take one's time*) **to ~ on a subject** dilatarse con un tema; **I let my eye ~ on the scene** seguía sin apartar los ojos de la escena; **to ~ over doing sth** tardar *or* no darse prisa en hacer algo; **to ~ over a meal** comer despacio

lingerie [ˈlænʒəriː] N lencería *f*, ropa *f* interior femenina

lingering [ˈlɪŋgərɪŋ] ADJ [*smell*] persistente; [*doubt*] persistente, que no se desvanece; [*look*] fijo; [*death*] lento

lingo* [ˈlɪŋgəʊ] N (*pl* **lingoes**) (= *language*) lengua *f*, idioma *m*; (= *specialist jargon*) jerga *f*

lingua franca [ˌlɪŋgwəˈfræŋkə] N (*pl* **lingua francas** *or* **linguae francae** [ˌlɪŋgwiːˈfrænsiː]) lengua *f* franca

linguist [ˈlɪŋgwɪst] N 1 (= *speaker of languages*) **he's an accomplished ~** domina varios idiomas; **I'm no ~** se me dan mal los idiomas, no puedo con los idiomas; **the company needs more ~s** la compañía necesita más gente que sepa idiomas

2 (= *specialist in linguistics*) lingüista *mf*; (*Univ*) estudiante *mf* de idiomas

linguistic [lɪŋˈgwɪstɪk] ADJ [*ability, skills*] lingüístico; **a child with good ~ skills** un niño con mucha aptitud lingüística; **we need people with good ~ skills** necesitamos gente que tenga facilidad para los idiomas

linguistically [lɪŋˈgwɪstɪkəlɪ] ADV [*able, skilled*] desde el punto de vista lingüístico; **she's very gifted ~** tiene mucha facilidad para los idiomas; **~ speaking** lingüísticamente hablando, hablando desde un punto de vista lingüístico

linguistician [ˌlɪŋgwɪsˈtɪʃən] N lingüista *mf*, especialista *mf* en lingüística

linguistics [lɪŋˈgwɪstɪks] NSING lingüística *f*

liniment [ˈlɪnɪmənt] N linimento *m*

lining [ˈlaɪnɪŋ] N [*of garment*] forro *m*; (*Tech*) revestimiento *m*; [*of brake*] guarnición *f*

link [lɪŋk] Ⓐ N 1 [*of chain*] eslabón *m*; **the last ~ in the chain** (*fig*) el último eslabón en la cadena; **the missing ~** (*fig*) el eslabón perdido; **weak ~** (*fig*) punto *m* débil

2 (= *connection*) relación *f*, conexión *f*; **the ~ between smoking and lung cancer** la relación *or* conexión entre el tabaco y el cáncer de pulmón

3 (= *tie, association*) vínculo *m*, lazo *m*; **cultural ~s** vínculos *mpl or* lazos *mpl* culturales; **to have ~s with sth/sb** tener vínculos *or* lazos con algo/algn; **we now have closer ~s with overseas universities** ahora tenemos vínculos *or* lazos más estrechos con universidades extranjeras; **the district has strong ~s with Charles Dickens** la región está muy vinculada a Charles Dickens; **trade ~s** vínculos *mpl or* lazos *mpl* comerciales

4 (*Travel*) enlace *m*, conexión *f*; **rail/air/road ~s** enlaces *mpl* ferroviarios/aéreos/por carretera, conexiones *fpl* ferroviarias/aéreas/por carretera

5 (*Telec, TV, Rad*) **radio/telephone/satellite ~** conexión *f* radiofónica/telefónica/vía satélite; *see also* **links**

6 (*Internet*) enlace *m*

Ⓑ VT 1 (= *join, connect*) [+ *parts, units*] unir (**to** a), conectar (**to** con); [+ *computers*] conectar (**to** con); [+ *towns, buildings*] comunicar, conectar; **the Channel Tunnel ~s Britain and France** el túnel del Canal de la Mancha comunica *or* conecta Gran Bretaña con Francia, el túnel del Canal de la Mancha une a Gran Bretaña y Francia; **to ~ arms** tomarse del brazo, cogerse del brazo (*Sp*); **to be ~ed into a system** (*Comput*) estar conectado a un sistema; **to ~ two machines together** conectar dos máquinas

2 (= *relate*) relacionar; **the evidence ~ing smoking with early death** las pruebas que relacionan *or* que establecen una relación entre el tabaco y las muertes prematuras; **there is evidence ~ing the group to a series of terrorist attacks** hay pruebas que implican al grupo en una serie de atentados terroristas

Ⓒ VI 1 **to ~ together** [*parts, components*] encajar

2 **to ~ into sth** (*Comput*) conectar con algo

►**link up** Ⓐ VI + ADV [*people*] unirse; [*companies*] unir fuerzas; [*spacecraft*] acoplarse; [*railway lines, roads*] empalmar; **this ~s up with another problem** esto tiene relación con otro problema; **to ~ up with sb** juntarse a algn; **we are ~ing up with another firm for this project** vamos a unir fuerzas con otra empresa para llevar a cabo este proyecto

Ⓑ VT + ADV conectar; **to ~ sth up to sth** conectar algo a algo

linkage [ˈlɪŋkɪdʒ] N 1 conexión *f*, enlace *m*

2 (*Tech*) articulación *f*, acoplamiento *m*; (*Comput*) enlace *m*

linked [lɪŋkt] ADJ [*problems, concepts*] relacionado, vinculado

linking verb [ˈlɪŋkɪŋˌvɜːb] N verbo *m* copulativo

linkman [ˈlɪŋkmæn] N (*pl* **linkmen**) (*Rad, TV*) locutor *m* de continuidad

links [lɪŋks] NPL 1 (= *golf links*) campo *msing or* (*LAm*) cancha *fsing* de golf

2 (= *cuff links*) gemelos *mpl*, mancuernas *fpl* (*CAm, Mex*)

linkup [ˈlɪŋkʌp] N conexión *f*, vinculación *f*; (= *meeting*) encuentro *m*, reunión *f*; [*of roads*] empalme *m*; [*of spaceships*] acoplamiento *m*; (*Rad, TV*) conexión *f*, enlace *m*

linnet [ˈlɪnɪt] N pardillo *m* (común)

lino [ˈlaɪnəʊ], **linoleum** [lɪˈnəʊlɪəm] N (*Brit*) linóleo *m*

Linotype® [ˈlaɪnəʊtaɪp] N linotipia *f*

linseed [ˈlɪnsiːd] Ⓐ N linaza *f*

Ⓑ CPD ► **linseed oil** N aceite *m* de linaza

lint [lɪnt] N hilas *fpl*

lintel [ˈlɪntl] N dintel *m*

lion [ˈlaɪən] Ⓐ N león *m*; (*fig*) celebridad *f*; ♦*IDIOMS* **the ~'s share** la parte del león, la mejor parte; **to beard the ~ in his den** en-

trar en el cubil de la fiera; **to put one's head in the ~'s mouth** meterse en la boca del lobo; **to throw sb to the ~s** abandonar a algn a su suerte
Ⓑ CPD ► **lion cub** N cachorro *m* de león ► **lion tamer** N domador(a) *m/f* de leones

lioness ['laɪənɪs] N leona *f*

lion-hearted [ˌlaɪən'hɑːtɪd] ADJ valiente

lionize ['laɪənaɪz] VT **to ~ sb** tratar a algn como una celebridad

lip [lɪp] Ⓐ N [1] (*Anat*) labio *m*; [*of cup, crater*] borde *m*; [*of jug etc*] pico *m*; **to bite one's ~** (*lit*) morderse el labio; (*fig*) morderse la lengua; **to lick** *or* **smack one's ~s** relamerse; **to read sb's ~s** leer en los labios de algn; **my ~s are sealed** (= *I won't tell*) soy una tumba; (= *I can't tell*) no puedo contar nada; ✦***IDIOM*** **to pay ~ service to an ideal** defender un ideal de boquilla; **he's just paying ~ service** todo lo que dice es boquilla; *see also* **stiff A3**
[2] (*) (= *insolence*) impertinencia *f*, insolencia *f*; **none of your ~!** ¡cállate la boca!*
Ⓑ CPD ► **lip gloss** N brillo *m* de labios ► **lip salve** N (*Brit*) vaselina *f*, cacao *m*, protector *m* labial

lipid ['lɪpɪd] N lípido *m*

liposuction ['lɪpəʊˌsʌkʃən] N liposucción *f*

lippy* ['lɪpɪ] ADJ (*Brit*) contestón*, descarado

lip-read ['lɪpriːd] Ⓐ VT leer los labios a
Ⓑ VI leer los labios

lip-reading ['lɪpˌriːdɪŋ] N lectura *f* de labios

lipstick ['lɪpstɪk] N lápiz *m* de labios, barra *f* de labios; **to put (one's) ~ on** pintarse los labios

liquefaction [ˌlɪkwɪ'fækʃən] N licuefacción *f*

liquefy ['lɪkwɪfaɪ] Ⓐ VT licuar
Ⓑ VI licuarse

liqueur [lɪ'kjʊəʳ] Ⓐ N licor *m*
Ⓑ CPD ► **liqueur glass** N copa *f* de licor

liquid ['lɪkwɪd] Ⓐ ADJ [1] (*lit*) líquido; [*measure*] para líquidos; ✦***IDIOM*** **to have a ~ lunch** (*hum*) remojar el gaznate*
[2] (*fig*) [*sound*] claro, puro; (*Phon*) líquido
Ⓑ N líquido *m*; (*Phon*) líquida *f*
Ⓒ CPD ► **liquid assets** NPL (*Fin*) activo *msing* líquido ► **liquid crystal display** N visualizador *m* de cristal líquido ► **Liquid Paper**® N Tipp-Ex® *m* ► **liquid waste** N vertidos *mpl* líquidos

liquidate ['lɪkwɪdeɪt] VT (*all senses*) liquidar

liquidation [ˌlɪkwɪ'deɪʃən] N liquidación *f*; **to go into ~** entrar en liquidación

liquidator ['lɪkwɪdeɪtəʳ] N liquidador(a) *m/f*

liquidity [lɪ'kwɪdɪtɪ] Ⓐ N (*Fin*) liquidez *f*
Ⓑ CPD ► **liquidity ratio** N tasa *f* or coeficiente *m* de liquidez

liquidize ['lɪkwɪdaɪz] Ⓐ VT licuar
Ⓑ VI licuarse

liquidizer ['lɪkwɪdaɪzəʳ] N (*Brit Culin*) licuadora *f*

liquor ['lɪkəʳ] Ⓐ N (*Brit frm*) licores *mpl*; (*US*) alcohol *m*; **hard ~** licores *mpl* espiritosos, bebidas *fpl* fuertes; **to be in ~** estar borracho; **to be the worse for ~** haber bebido más de la cuenta, estar algo borracho
Ⓑ CPD ► **liquor cabinet** N (*US*) mueble *m* bar ► **liquor store** N (*US*) bodega *f*, tienda *f* de bebidas alcohólicas, licorería *f* (*LAm*)

liquorice ['lɪkərɪs] N regaliz *m*, orozuz *m*

lira ['lɪərə] N (*pl* **lire** ['lɪərɪ]) lira *f*

Lisbon ['lɪzbən] N Lisboa *f*

lisle [laɪl] N hilo *m* de Escocia

lisp [lɪsp] Ⓐ N ceceo *m*; **to speak with a ~** cecear
Ⓑ VI cecear
Ⓒ VT decir ceceando

lissom ['lɪsəm] ADJ ágil, flexible

list[1] [lɪst] Ⓐ N (*gen*) lista *f*; (= *catalogue*) catálogo *m*; **price ~** lista *f* de precios; **waiting ~** lista *f* de espera; **to be on the active ~** (*Mil*) estar en activo; **that job is at the top of my ~** para mí ese trabajo es lo primero *or* lo más importante
Ⓑ VT (= *include in list*) poner en una/la lista; (= *make a list of*) hacer una lista de; (*verbally*) enumerar; (*Fin*) cotizar (**at** a); (*Comput*) listar; **it is not ~ed** no aparece en la lista; **he began to ~ all he had been doing** empezó a enumerar todas las cosas que había hecho
Ⓒ CPD ► **list price** N precio *m* de catálogo ► **list renting** N alquiler *m* de listas de posibles clientes

list[2] [lɪst] Ⓐ N (*Naut*) escora *f*; **to have a ~ of 20°** escorar a un ángulo de 20°
Ⓑ VI (*Naut*) escorar (**to port** a babor); **to ~ badly** escorar de modo peligroso

listed ['lɪstɪd] ADJ **~ building** (*Brit*) edificio *m* protegido; **~ company** empresa *f* con cotización; **~ securities** valores *mpl* registrados en bolsa

listen ['lɪsn] Ⓐ VI [1] (= *try to hear*) escuchar; **~! can't you hear something?** ¡escucha! ¿no oyes algo?; **I ~ed outside the bedroom door** me quedé escuchando en la puerta del dormitorio; **we ~ed for footsteps approaching** estuvimos atentos por si oíamos venir a alguien
[2] (= *pay attention*) escuchar; **he wouldn't ~** no quiso escuchar; **~, I finish at one, why don't we have lunch together?** mira, yo termino a la una, ¿por qué no almorzamos juntos?; **~ (here), young lady, I've had enough of your cheek!** ¡escúchame *or* mira jovencita, ya estoy harto de tu cara dura!; **~ carefully, and repeat after me** escuchen con atención y repitan; **to ~ to sth/sb** escuchar algo/a algn; **I like ~ing to music** me gusta escuchar música; **I love ~ing to the rain** me encanta oír el sonido de la lluvia; **the only person she will ~ to is her father** la única persona a la que escucha es a su padre; **now just you ~ to me!** ¡escúchame!; **I don't have to ~ to this!** ¡no tengo por qué escuchar esta bazofia!; **will you ~ to him! who does he think he is?** ¡fíjate cómo habla! ¡quién se habrá creído que es!; **you never ~ to a word I say!** ¡nunca escuchas nada de lo que te digo!, ¡nunca me haces caso!; **~ to yourself, you're getting paranoid!** ¡será posible lo que estás diciendo! ¡te estás volviendo paranoico!; ✦***IDIOM*** **to ~ with both ears** aguzar el oído; *see also* **reason A3**
Ⓑ N **to have a ~ (to sth)*** escuchar (algo)

►**listen in** VI + ADV [1] (*Rad*) **to ~ in to sth** escuchar algo
[2] (= *eavesdrop*) escuchar; **to ~ in on** *or* **to a conversation** escuchar una conversación a hurtadillas
[3] (= *attend, observe*) **I would like to ~ in on** *or* **to your discussion** me gustaría participar en tu discusión en calidad de oyente

►**listen out** VI + ADV **to ~ out for sth/sb: can you ~ out for the postman?** ¿podrías estar atento por si viene el cartero?

listener ['lɪsnəʳ] N (*gen*) oyente *mf*; (*Rad*) radioyente *mf*; **to be a good ~** saber escuchar; **dear ~s!** (*Rad*) ¡queridos radioyentes *or* oyentes!

listening ['lɪsnɪŋ] Ⓐ N **good ~!** ¡que disfruten de la emisión!; **we don't do much ~ now** ahora escuchamos muy poco la radio
Ⓑ CPD ► **listening comprehension test** N ejercicio *m* de comprensión oral ► **listening device** N aparato *m* auditivo ► **listening post** N puesto *m* de escucha

listeria [lɪs'tɪːərɪə] N listeria *f*

listeriosis [lɪsˌtɪərɪ'əʊsɪs] N listeriosis *f*

listing ['lɪstɪŋ] N [1] (*gen, Comput*) listado *m*
[2] (*Comm*) **they have a ~ on the Stock Exchange** cotizan en Bolsa
[3] **listings** (= *publication*) cartelera *f*, guía *fsing* del ocio

listless ['lɪstlɪs] ADJ [1] (= *without energy*) lánguido
[2] (= *without direction*) apático, indiferente

listlessly ['lɪstlɪslɪ] ADV [1] (= *without energy*) lánguidamente
[2] (= *without direction*) con apatía, con desgana

listlessness ['lɪstlɪsnɪs] N [1] (= *lack of energy*) languidez *f*
[2] (= *lack of direction*) apatía *f*, desgana *f*

lists [lɪsts] NPL (*Hist*) liza *f*; **to enter the ~ (against sth/sb)** (*fig*) salir *or* saltar a la palestra (contra algo/algn)

lit [lɪt] PT, PP *of* **light**[1]; **to be ~ up*** estar achispado*

Lit., lit.[1]* [lɪt] N ABBR = **literature**

lit.[2] ABBR = **literal(ly)**

litany ['lɪtənɪ] N letanía *f*

lite* [laɪt] ADJ [1] (*Culin*) (= *low-fat*) bajo en calorías, light *inv*
[2] (*fig*) (= *mild*) descafeinado, light *inv*

liter ['liːtəʳ] N (*US*) = **litre**

literacy ['lɪtərəsɪ] Ⓐ N alfabetismo *m*, capacidad *f* de leer y escribir; **~ is low in Burkina Faso** el grado de alfabetización es bajo en Burkina Faso
Ⓑ CPD ► **literacy campaign** N campaña *f* de alfabetización ► **literacy project, literacy scheme** N programa *m* de alfabetización ► **literacy test** N prueba *f* básica de lectura y escritura

literal ['lɪtərəl] Ⓐ ADJ [1] [*sense, translation*] literal; **they follow a ~ interpretation of the Bible** siguen la Biblia al pie de la letra; **to be ~ about sth** tomar algo al pie de la letra; **he's a very ~ person** es una persona que todo se lo toma al pie de la letra; *see also* **literal-minded**
[2] (*as intensifier*) **a ~ fact** un hecho real; **the ~ truth** la pura verdad
Ⓑ N (*Typ*) errata *f*

literally ['lɪtərəlɪ] ADV [1] (= *actually*) literalmente; **I was quite ~ living on bread and water** estaba literalmente viviendo a base de pan y agua; **he's crazy, I mean ~** está loco, y lo digo en el verdadero sentido de la palabra; **they were quite ~ in fear of their lives** temían realmente por sus vidas; **to take sth ~** tomarse algo al pie de la letra; **she ~ flew out the door** (*as intensifier*) (= *almost*) salió casi volando por la puerta
[2] (= *word for word*) [*translate, mean*] literalmente, palabra por palabra

literal-minded ['lɪtərəl'maɪndɪd] ADJ sin imaginación, poco imaginativo

literary ['lɪtərərɪ] Ⓐ ADJ [*prize, award*] de literatura, literario; **~ circles** círculos *mpl* literarios; **a ~ man** un hombre de letras; **it's a ~ masterpiece** es una obra maestra de la literatura; **the ~ scene** el ambiente literario, los círculos literarios; **a ~ work** una obra literaria *or* de literatura
Ⓑ CPD ► **literary agent** N agente *mf* literario/a ► **literary critic** N crítico/a *m/f* literario/a ► **literary criticism** N crítica *f* lite-

raria ► **literary history** N historia *f* de la literatura ► **literary studies** NPL estudios *mpl* de literatura, estudios *mpl* literarios ► **literary theory** N teoría *f* de la literatura, teoría *f* literaria

literate ['lɪtərɪt] ADJ que sabe leer y escribir; **highly ~** culto; **not very ~** (*fig*) poco culto, que tiene poca cultura

literati [,lɪtə'rɑːtiː] NPL literatos *mpl*

literature ['lɪtərɪtʃəʳ] N 1 (= *writings*) literatura *f*
2 (*) (= *promotional material*) información *f*, publicidad *f*
3 (= *learned studies of subject*) estudios *mpl*, bibliografía *f*

lithe [laɪð] ADJ ágil

lithium ['lɪθɪəm] N litio *m*

litho* ['laɪθəʊ] N ABBR = **lithograph**

lithograph ['lɪθəʊgrɑːf] Ⓐ N litografía *f*
Ⓑ VT litografiar

lithographer [lɪ'θɒgrəfəʳ] N litógrafo/a *m/f*

lithographic [lɪθəʊ'græfɪk] ADJ litográfico

lithography [lɪ'θɒgrəfɪ] N litografía *f*

Lithuania [,lɪθjʊ'eɪnɪə] N Lituania *f*

Lithuanian [,lɪθjʊ'eɪnɪən] Ⓐ ADJ lituano
Ⓑ N 1 (= *person*) lituano/a *m/f*
2 (*Ling*) lituano *m*

litigant ['lɪtɪgənt] N litigante *mf*

litigate ['lɪtɪgeɪt] VI litigar, pleitear

litigation [,lɪtɪ'geɪʃən] N litigio *m*, pleito *m*

litigator ['lɪtɪgeɪtəʳ] N (= *litigant*) litigante *mf*; (= *lawyer*) abogado/a *m/f* litigante

litigious [lɪ'tɪdʒəs] ADJ litigioso

litmus ['lɪtməs] Ⓐ N tornasol *m*
Ⓑ CPD ► **litmus paper** N papel *m* de tornasol ► **litmus test** N prueba *f* de tornasol; (*fig*) prueba *f* de fuego

litre, **liter** (*US*) ['liːtəʳ] N litro *m*

litter ['lɪtəʳ] Ⓐ N 1 (= *rubbish*) basura *f*; (= *papers*) papeles *mpl* (tirados); (= *wrappings*) envases *mpl*; **"no litter"** "prohibido arrojar basura"
2 (= *untidiness*) desorden *m*; **in a ~** en desorden; **a ~ of books** un montón desordenado de libros, un revoltijo de libros
3 (*Zool*) camada *f*
4 (= *vehicle*) litera *f*; (*Med*) camilla *f*
5 (= *bedding*) lecho *m*, cama *f* de paja
6 (*for animal*) lecho *m* de paja; *see also* **cat B**
Ⓑ VT 1 (= *make untidy*) **to ~ the streets** tirar basura por la calle; **to ~ papers about a room** ◊ **~ a room with papers** esparcir papeles por un cuarto, dejar papeles esparcidos por un cuarto; **he ~ed the floor with all his football gear** dejó toda la ropa de fútbol tirada por el suelo; **the lorry ~ed the road with rubbish** el camión dejó basura esparcida por toda la carretera, el camión dejó la carretera sembrada de basura; **a pavement ~ed with papers** una acera sembrada de papeles; **a room ~ed with books** un cuarto con libros por todas partes; **a page ~ed with mistakes** una página plagada de errores
2 (= *provide with bedding*) [+ *animal*] dar cama de paja a
3 (= *give birth to*) [*animal*] parir
Ⓒ VI [*cat*] parir
Ⓓ CPD ► **litter basket**, **litter bin** N (*Brit*) papelera *f* ► **litter box** N (*US*) = **litter tray** ► **litter lout** N *persona que tira papeles o basura a la vía pública* ► **litter tray** N (*esp Brit*) *lecho de arena higiénica para animales domésticos*

litterbug ['lɪtəbʌg] N (*US*) = **litter lout**

little[1] ['lɪtl] Ⓐ ADJ 1 (= *small*) pequeño, chico (*LAm*); **a ~ house** una casa pequeña *or* (*LAm*) chica; **a ~ book** un libro pequeño *or* (*LAm*) chico; **she had a ~ girl yesterday** ayer tuvo una niñita; **when I was ~** cuando era pequeña, de pequeña; **the ~ ones** (= *children*) los pequeños
2 (= *short*) corto; **a ~ walk** un paseo corto; **we went for a ~ holiday** nos fuimos para unas vacaciones cortitas
3 (= *diminutive*) (*in cpds*) -ito; **a ~ book/boat/piece** *etc* un librito/barquito/trocito *etc*; **a ~ house** una casita; **a ~ girl** una niñita, una chiquita; **a ~ fish** un pececillo, un pececito; **a ~ sip** un sorbito; **the ~ woman** (*hum*) (= *wife*) la costilla*, la parienta (*Sp**); **it's the ~ man who suffers** (= *small trader*) el pequeño comerciante es el que sale perdiendo; **it's just a ~ something*** no es más que una cosita de poco valor
4 (= *younger*) **her ~ brother** su hermano menor, su hermanito
Ⓑ CPD ► **little end** N (*Brit Aut*) pie *m* de biela ► **Little Englander** N (*Brit Hist*) *en el siglo XIX, persona con ideas opuestas a la ampliación del imperio británico*; (= *chauvinist*) patriotero/a *m/f*; (= *anti-European*) anti-europeoísta *mf* ► **little finger** N dedo *m* meñique, meñique *m* ► **the little folk** NPL = **the little people** ► **the little people** NPL (*Irl*) (= *fairies*) los duendecillos ► **little toe** N dedo *m* pequeño del pie

little[2] ['lɪtl] (*compar* **less**; *superl* **least**) Ⓐ PRON 1 (= *not much*) poco; **he knows ~** sabe poco; **to see/do ~** ver/hacer poco; **there was ~ we could do** apenas había nada que hacer; **he had ~ to say** poco fue lo que tenía que decir; **that has ~ to do with it!** ¡eso tiene poco que ver!; **as ~ as £5** 5 libras, nada más; **there's very ~ left** queda muy poco; **to make ~ of sth** (= *play down*) quitarle importancia a algo; (= *fail to exploit*) desaprovechar algo; **they made ~ of loading the huge boxes** (= *accomplish easily*) cargaron las enormes cajas como si nada; **~ of what he says is true** poco de lo que dice es verdad; **~ or nothing** poco o nada; **to spend ~ or nothing** gastar poco o nada; **he lost weight because he ate so ~** adelgazó porque comía muy poco; **I know too ~ about him to have an opinion** no lo conozco lo suficiente para poder opinar; **too ~ too late** muy poco y muy tarde
2 (= *some*) **give me a ~** dame un poco; **I had a ~ of everything** comí un poco de todo; **~ by ~** poco a poco; **however ~ you give, we'll be grateful** agradeceremos su donativo, por pequeño que sea; **a ~ less/more milk** un poco menos/más de leche; **a ~ more slowly** un poco más despacio; **the ~ I have seen is excellent** lo poco que he visto me ha parecido excelente; **I did what ~ I could** hice lo poco que pude; *see also* **every 1**
3 (= *short time*) **they'll have to wait a ~** tendrán que esperar un poco; **for a ~** un rato, durante un rato
Ⓑ ADJ 1 (= *not much*) poco; **there is ~ hope of finding them alive** hay pocas esperanzas de encontrarlos con vida; **with ~ difficulty** sin problema *or* dificultad; **so much to do, so ~ time** tanto que hacer y en tan poco tiempo; **I have so ~ time for reading** tengo muy poco tiempo para leer; **he gave me too ~ money** me dio poquísimo dinero; **I have very ~ money** tengo muy poco dinero
2 (= *some*) **a ~ wine** un poco de vino; **I speak a ~ Spanish** hablo un poco de español; **a ~ bit (of)** un poquito (de); **with no ~ trouble** con bastante dificultad, con no poca dificultad
3 (= *short*) **for a ~ time** *or* **while** un ratito
Ⓒ ADV 1 (= *not much*) poco; **he reads ~** lee poco; **they spoke very ~ on the way home** hablaron muy poco de camino para casa; **try to move as ~ as possible** intenta moverte lo menos posible; **(as) ~ as I like him, I must admit that ...** aunque me gusta muy poco, debo admitir que ...; **a ~ known fact** un hecho poco conocido; **~ more than** poco más que; **~ more than a month ago** hace poco más de un mes; **a ~ read book** un libro poco leído, un libro que se lee poco; **it's ~ short of a miracle** es casi un milagro
2 (= *somewhat*) algo; **we were a ~ surprised/happier** nos quedamos algo sorprendidos/más contentos; **a ~ better** un poco mejor, algo mejor; **a ~ less/more than ...** un poco menos/más que ...; **we were not a ~ worried** nos inquietamos bastante, quedamos muy inquietos
3 (= *not at all*) **~ does he know that ...** ◊ **he ~ knows that ...** no tiene la menor idea de que ...
4 (= *rarely*) poco; **I watch television very ~ nowadays** ahora veo la televisión muy poco; **it occurs very ~ in small companies** raramente ocurre *or* es raro que ocurra en empresas pequeñas

littleness ['lɪtlnɪs] N (*in size*) pequeñez *f*; (*fig*) mezquindad *f*

littoral ['lɪtərəl] Ⓐ ADJ litoral
Ⓑ N litoral *m*

liturgical [lɪ'tɜːdʒɪkəl] ADJ litúrgico

liturgy ['lɪtədʒɪ] N liturgia *f*

livable ['lɪvəbl] ADJ [*house*] habitable; [*life*] llevadero

livable-in ['lɪvəbl,ɪn] ADJ habitable

livable-with ['lɪvəbl,wɪð] ADJ [*person*] tratable

live[1] [lɪv] Ⓐ VI 1 (= *exist*) vivir; **the times we ~ in** los tiempos en que vivimos, los tiempos que corremos; **she has only six months to ~** sólo le quedan seis meses de vida; **to ~ from day to day** vivir de día en día; **to ~ in fear** vivir atemorizado; **she ~s in fear of her life/that she may be found out** vive temiendo por su vida/que la descubran; **to ~ for sth**: **I'm living for the day (when) I retire** vivo esperando a que llegue el día en que me jubile; **she ~d for her work** vivía por y para su trabajo; **to ~ for today** *or* **the moment** vivir al día; **I've got nothing left to ~ for** no tengo nada por lo que vivir; ✦*IDIOM* **to ~ and let ~** vivir y dejar vivir; ✦*PROVS* **we should eat to ~, not ~ to eat** deberíamos comer para vivir, y no vivir para comer; **you ~ and learn** nunca te acostarás sin saber una cosa más; *see also* **hand A1**, **happily 1**, **hope A1**, **long**[1] **B1**, **shadow A1**, **style A4**
2 (= *survive*) **the doctor said she would ~** el médico dijo que sobreviviría; **you'll ~!** (*hum*) ¡de ésta no te mueres! (*hum*); **he ~d to a ripe old age/to be 103** llegó a viejo/a cumplir 103 años; **she'll never ~ to see it** no vivirá para verlo; *see also* **regret B2**
3 (= *conduct o.s.*) vivir; **she ~s by her own rules** vive según sus propias normas; **men who ~d by the gun** hombres cuya ley era la pistola; **to ~ modestly/well** vivir modestamente/bien; ✦*IDIOM* **to ~ like a king** *or* **a lord** vivir a cuerpo de rey; *see also* **dangerously**, **sin A**
4 (= *earn one's living*) vivir; **to ~ by hunting** vivir de la caza; *see also* **pen**[1] **A**, **wit**[1] **A1**
5 (= *reside*) vivir; **where do you ~?** ¿dónde vives?; **to ~ in a flat/in London** vivir en un piso/en Londres; **she ~s in Station Road**

vive en Station Road; **this is a nice place to ~** este es un buen sitio para vivir; **this house isn't fit to ~ in** esta casa está en pésimas condiciones

6 (*Brit**) (= *go, belong*) ir, guardarse; **where does the teapot ~?** ¿dónde va *or* se guarda la tetera?

7 (= *enjoy life*) **let's ~ a little!*** ¡vivamos la vida un poquito!*; **she really knows how to ~** sabe disfrutar muy bien de la vida; **if you've never been to an opera, you haven't ~d*** si no has ido nunca a la ópera no sabes lo qué es vivir

Ⓑ VT 1 [+ *life*] (*gen*) vivir; (*in particular way*) llevar; **to ~ life to the full** vivir la vida al máximo; **to ~ a happy life** llevar una vida feliz; **to ~ a life of luxury/crime** llevar una vida de lujos/de delincuencia; **to ~ a life of hardship** vivir pasando penurias; **how you ~ your life is your business** tu vida es cosa tuya

2 (*Theat*) **to ~ the part** vivir el personaje *or* el papel

► **live down** VT + ADV **I thought I'd never ~ it down** pensé que no se iba a olvidar nunca; **he was unable to ~ down his reputation as a drunk** no consiguió librarse de su fama de borracho

► **live in** VI + ADV [*servant, nanny*] vivir en la casa

► **live off** VI + PREP 1 (= *depend financially on*) vivir a costa de; (= *support o.s. on*) vivir de; **he ~s off his uncle** vive a costa de su tío; **she ~s off the income from her investments** vive de las rentas de sus inversiones; *see also* **land A2**

2 (= *eat*) alimentarse de

► **live on** Ⓐ VI + PREP 1 (= *subsist on*) **what does he ~ on?** ¿de qué vive?; **he ~s on £50 a week** vive con 50 libras por semana; **we have just enough to ~ on** tenemos lo justo para vivir; ✦***IDIOM*** **to ~ on borrowed time** tener los días contados

2 (= *feed on*) alimentarse de; **she ~s on cheese** vive sólo a base de queso; **she absolutely ~s on chocolate** no come otra cosa más que chocolate

Ⓑ VI + ADV (= *go on living*) [*person, memory, tradition*] seguir vivo; **his memory ~s on within us** su recuerdo sigue vivo en nosotros; **Lenin ~s on in the minds and hearts of many people** Lenin sigue vivo en las mentes y corazones de muchas personas

► **live out** Ⓐ VI + ADV [*servant*] vivir fuera

Ⓑ VT + ADV 1 (= *live to the end of*) **she won't ~ the year out** no vivirá hasta fin de año, no llegará a fin de año; **the house where he ~d out his last three years** la casa donde vivió sus últimos tres años; **he ~d out the war in the country** mientras duró la guerra vivió en el campo; **he wanted to ~ out his life in his own home** quería vivir *or* pasar el resto de sus días en su propia casa; **he ~d out his days in a mental asylum** acabó sus días en un psiquiátrico

2 (= *act out*) [+ *fantasy*] vivir

► **live through** VI + PREP 1 (= *experience*) vivir; **she has ~d through two world wars** ha vivido dos guerras mundiales

2 (= *survive*) sobrevivir; **he won't ~ through the winter** no sobrevivirá el invierno

► **live together** VI + ADV (*in amity*) convivir; (*as lovers*) vivir juntos

► **live up** VT + ADV ✦***IDIOM*** **to ~ it up*** (= *have fun*) pasárselo en grande*; (= *live in luxury*) darse la gran vida*

► **live up to** VI + PREP 1 (= *be true to*) [+ *principles*] vivir de acuerdo con; [+ *promises*] cumplir

2 (= *be equal to*) [+ *reputation, expectations*] estar a la altura de; **marriage failed to ~ up to her expectations** el matrimonio no estuvo a la altura de *or* defraudó sus expectativas; **his brother's success will give him something to ~ up to** el éxito de su hermano le dará algo que igualar; **the new president has not ~d up to their hopes** el nuevo presidente ha defraudado sus esperanzas; **the product doesn't ~ up to its name** el producto no hace honor a su nombre

► **live with** VI + PREP 1 (= *coexist with*) [+ *person, memory*] vivir con; **he's not an easy person to ~ with** no es una persona con la que se pueda vivir fácilmente; **to ~ with the knowledge that ...** vivir sabiendo que ...; **I'd never be able to ~ with myself if I let that happen** jamás podría vivir tranquila *or* vivir con mi conciencia si dejara que pasara eso

2 (= *accept*) aceptar; **you'll have to learn to ~ with it** tendrás que aprender a aceptarlo

live² [laɪv] Ⓐ ADJ 1 (= *living*) [*animal, person*] vivo; **experiments on ~ animals** experimentos *mpl* con animales vivos; **a real ~ crocodile** un cocodrilo de verdad; **a real ~ duke** un duque de carne y hueso; **9.1 deaths per thousand ~ births** 9,1 muertes por cada mil bebés nacidos vivos

2 (= *topical*) [*issue*] de actualidad, candente

3 (*Rad, TV*) [*broadcast, coverage*] en vivo, en directo; [*performance, show, recording*] en vivo; **the bar has ~ entertainment at weekends** el bar tiene espectáculos en vivo los fines de semana; **performed before a ~ audience** interpretado delante del público

4 (= *not blank*) [*shell, ammunition*] cargado; [*bomb*] sin explotar

5 (= *still burning*) [*coal*] encendido, prendido (*LAm*)

6 (*Elec*) [*cable, wire, appliance*] conectado, con corriente; **is this cable ~?** ¿está conectado *or* tiene corriente este cable?

Ⓑ ADV 1 (*Rad, TV*) en vivo, en directo; **the match is brought to you ~ from Madrid** le ofrecemos el partido en vivo *or* en directo desde Madrid; **here, ~ from New York, is our reporter Malcolm McDonald** aquí tenemos a nuestro corresponsal Malcolm McDonald que nos habla en directo desde Nueva York; **we'll be going ~ to Montreal later on** conectaremos con Montreal en directo más adelante

2 **to go ~** (= *come into operation*) entrar en funcionamiento; **the new computer system will go ~ next week** el nuevo ordenador entrará en funcionamiento la semana que viene

Ⓒ CPD ► **live bait** N (*Fishing*) cebo *m* vivo ► **live coal** N brasa *f*, ascua *f* ► **live export** N [*of livestock*] exportación *f* en pie ► **live oak** N roble *m* de Virginia ► **live rail** N raíl *m* electrizado ► **live weight** N [*of livestock*] peso *m* en pie ► **live wire** N (*Elec*) alambre *m* conectado, alambre *m* con corriente; (*fig*) (*) torbellino* *m*; **he's a real ~ wire!** ¡es un torbellino!*, ¡tiene mucha marcha!* ► **live yoghurt** N yogur *m* con biocultivos

lived-in [ˈlɪvd,ɪn] ADJ **the blinds and cushions give the room a ~ look** las persianas y los cojines le dan un aspecto acogedor a la habitación

live-in [ˈlɪv,ɪn] ADJ **~ lover** compañero/a *m/f*; **~ maid** criada *f* interna

livelihood [ˈlaɪvlɪhʊd] N sustento *m*; **rice is their ~** el arroz es su único sustento; **to earn a** *or* **one's ~** ganarse la vida *or* el sustento

liveliness [ˈlaɪvlɪnɪs] N [*of person, mind, imagination*] vivacidad *f*; [*of atmosphere, party, place*] animación *f*; [*of conversation, discussion*] lo animado; [*of description, account, style*] lo vívido

livelong [ˈlɪvlɒŋ] ADJ **all the ~ day** todo el santo día

lively [ˈlaɪvlɪ] ADJ (*compar* **livelier**, *superl* **liveliest**) 1 (*gen*) [*person, personality*] vivaz, alegre; [*atmosphere, conversation, party, town*] animado; [*bar, street, market*] animado, bullicioso; [*dog*] juguetón; [*tune*] alegre; [*performance*] enérgico; **things are a little livelier in June** la cosa se anima más en junio

2 (= *heated*) [*debate, discussion*] animado; **the meeting promises to be a ~ affair** la reunión promete ser animada; **things were getting quite ~** el ambiente se estaba caldeando

3 (= *fast*) [*pace, speed*] rápido; **look ~!** ¡espabila!

4 (= *keen*) [*mind*] vivaz, inquieto; [*imagination*] vivo; [*sense of humour*] agudo; **she took a ~ interest in everything** ponía un gran interés en todo

5 (= *vivid*) [*description, account, style*] vivo, vívido

liven [ˈlaɪvn] Ⓐ VT **to ~ up** animar

Ⓑ VI **to ~ up** animarse

liver¹ [ˈlɪvəʳ] Ⓐ N (*Anat*) hígado *m*

Ⓑ CPD [*pâté, sausage*] de hígado; [*disease*] hepático, del hígado ► **liver complaint** N mal *m* de hígado, afección *f* hepática ► **liver pâté** N foie gras *m*, paté *m* de hígado ► **liver salts** NPL sal *fsing* de fruta ► **liver sausage** N salchicha *f* de hígado ► **liver spots** NPL manchas *fpl* de la vejez

liver² [ˈlɪvəʳ] N **fast ~** calavera* *m*; **good ~** (= *lover of good food*) gastrónomo/a *m/f*; (= *lover of the good life*) persona *f* que se da buena vida

liveried [ˈlɪvərɪd] ADJ en librea

liverish [ˈlɪvərɪʃ] ADJ **to be** *or* **feel ~** sentirse mal del hígado

Liverpudlian [,lɪvəˈpʌdlɪən] Ⓐ ADJ de Liverpool

Ⓑ N nativo/a *m/f* de Liverpool, habitante *mf* de Liverpool

liverwort [ˈlɪvə,wɜːt] N hepática *f*

liverwurst [ˈlɪvəwɜːst] N (*esp US*) embutido *m* de hígado

livery [ˈlɪvərɪ] Ⓐ N librea *f*; (*liter*) ropaje *m*

Ⓑ CPD ► **livery company** N (*Brit*) gremio *m* (*antiguo de la Ciudad de Londres*) ► **livery stable** N cuadra *f* de caballos de alquiler

lives [laɪvz] NPL *of* **life**

livestock [ˈlaɪvstɒk] N ganado *m*; (*also* **~ farming**) ganadería *f*

livid [ˈlɪvɪd] ADJ 1 (*) (= *furious*) furioso, furibundo*; **to be ~ about** *or* **at sth** estar furioso por algo, estar furibundo por algo*

2 (= *purple*) [*bruise, scar*] amoratado; [*colour, sky*] morado; **his face was ~** su rostro estaba lívido; **to be ~ with rage** estar lívido de rabia; **the sky was a ~ blue** el cielo era de un azul tirando a morado; **the scar was a ~ red** la cicatriz tenía un color rojo amoratado

living [ˈlɪvɪŋ] Ⓐ ADJ 1 (= *alive*) [*person, creature, plant*] vivo; **I have no ~ relatives** no tengo ningún pariente vivo; **Ireland's greatest ~ playwright** el mejor dramaturgo irlandés vivo *or* aún con vida; **a ~ death** (*liter*) un infierno; **~ faith** fe *f* viva; **he's the ~ image of his uncle** es el retrato vivo *or* la imagen viva de su tío; **~ language** lengua *f* viva; **the worst drought in** *or* **within ~ memory** la peor sequía que se recuerda; **the San Francisco earthquake is still within ~ memory** el terremoto de San Francisco tuvo lugar en nuestro tiempo; **~ proof** prueba *f* evidente *or* palpable; **I didn't see a ~ soul** no vi a un alma; **I promised I wouldn't tell a ~ soul** prometí

que no se lo diría a nadie; **there wasn't a ~ thing to be seen** no se veía a ningún ser vivo; *see also* **daylight A**
[2] (= *for living in*) [*area*] destinado a la vivienda; **our ~ accommodation was pretty basic** el lugar donde vivíamos era bastante modesto
(B) N [1] (= *livelihood*) **to earn a ~** ganarse la vida; **what do you do for a ~?** ¿cómo te ganas la vida?, ¿en qué trabajas?; **now he has to work for a ~** ahora tiene que trabajar para ganarse la vida; **to make a ~** ganarse la vida; **he thinks the world owes him a ~** piensa que tiene derecho a que se lo den todo regalado
[2] (= *way of life*) vida *f*; **the quality of urban ~** la calidad de la vida en la ciudad; **clean ~** vida *f* ordenada; **loose ~** vida *f* disipada, vida *f* disoluta; *see also* **cost C, standard C**
(C) NPL **the ~** los vivos
(D) CPD ► **living area** N zona *f* destinada a la vivienda ► **living conditions** NPL condiciones *fpl* de vida ► **living expenses** NPL gastos *mpl* de mantenimiento ► **living quarters** NPL (*for students*) residencia *f*; (*for soldiers, servants, staff*) dependencias *fpl* ► **living room** N sala *f* de estar, living *m* ► **living space** N espacio *m* vital (*also fig*) ► **living standards** NPL nivel *m* de vida; **a fall in ~ standards** un descenso del nivel de vida ► **living wage** N *salario de subsistencia*; **£20 a week isn't a ~ wage** con 20 libras a la semana no se puede vivir ► **living will** N declaración *f* de últimas voluntades (*por la que el declarante se niega a que su vida sea prolongada por medios artificiales en caso de encontrarse enfermo en fase terminal*)

Livy ['lɪvɪ] N Tito Livio

Liz [lɪz] N (*familiar form*) *of* **Elizabeth**

lizard ['lɪzəd] N (*large*) lagarto *m*; (*small*) lagartija *f*

ll. ABBR = **lines**

llama ['lɑːmə] N llama *f*

LLB N ABBR (*Univ*) = **Legum Baccalaureus** (= *Bachelor of Laws*) Ldo/a en Dcho

LLD N ABBR (*Univ*) = **Legum Doctor** (= *Doctor of Laws*) Dr(a). en Dcho

LM N ABBR = **lunar module**

LMS N ABBR = **local management of schools**

LMT N ABBR (*US*) = **Local Mean Time**

LNG N ABBR = **liquefied natural gas**

lo [ləʊ] EXCL **lo and behold the result!** ¡he aquí el resultado!; **and lo and behold there it was** y mira por dónde ahí estaba

loach [ləʊtʃ] N locha *f*

load [ləʊd] (A) N [1] (= *cargo*) carga *f*; (= *weight*) peso *m*; **the lorry had a full ~** el camión iba lleno; **I put another ~ in the washing machine** puse otra colada a lavar *or* en la lavadora; **I had three ~s of coal delivered** me repartieron tres cargas de carbón; **they were forced to carry heavy ~s** les obligaron a cargar con pesos pesados; **"maximum load: 17 tons"** "carga máxima: 17 toneladas"; *see also* **shed[1] 1**
[2] (*fig*) (= *burden*) carga *f*; **he finds his new responsibilities a heavy ~** sus nuevas responsabilidades le resultan una gran carga; **she's taking some of the ~ off the secretaries** está aligerándoles la carga de trabajo a las secretarias; **that's (taken) a ~ off my mind!** ¡eso me quita un peso de encima!; *see also* **caseload, workload**
[3] (*Elec, Tech*) (*also of firearm*) carga *f*
[4] **loads*** cantidad* *f*, un montón*; **we've got ~s of time** tenemos cantidad *or* un montón de tiempo*; **I've got ~s (of them) at home** tengo cantidad *or* un montón en casa*
[5] **a ~ of***: **the book is a ~ of rubbish** el libro es una basura*, el libro no vale nada; **he talks a ~ of rubbish** no dice más que tonterías; **they're just a ~ of kids** no son más que un hatajo *or* una panda de críos*; **get a ~ of this!** (= *look*) ¡échale un vistazo a esto!*, ¡mírame esto!; (= *listen*) ¡escucha esto!
(B) VT [1] [+ *lorry, washing machine, gun, camera*] cargar; **the gun is not ~ed** la pistola no está cargada; **do you know how to ~ this program?** (*Comput*) ¿sabes cómo cargar este programa?
[2] (= *weigh down*) **to be ~ed with sth**: **we're ~ed with debts** estamos cargados *or* agobiados de deudas; **the branch was ~ed with fruit** la rama estaba cargada de fruta; **her words were ~ed with meaning** sus palabras estaban llenas *or* cargadas de significado; **the whole thing is ~ed with problems** el asunto está erizado de dificultades
[3] (= *bias*) **the dice were ~ed** los dados estaban cargados; **the dice are ~ed against him** (*fig*) todo está en su contra; **the situation is ~ed in our favour** la situación se inclina a nuestro favor
(C) VI [1] [*lorry, ship*] cargar; **"loading and unloading"** "permitido carga y descarga"
[2] [*gun, camera*] cargarse; **how does this gun/camera ~?** ¿cómo se carga esta pistola/cámara?
[3] [*person*] cargar; **load!** ¡carguen armas!
(D) CPD ► **load factor** N (*Elec, Aer*) factor *m* de carga ► **load line** N (*Naut*) línea *f* de carga

► **load down** VT + ADV **to be ~ed down with sth**: **she was ~ed down with shopping** iba cargada de bolsas de la compra; **we're ~ed down with work** estamos hasta arriba de trabajo; **he was ~ed down with debt** estaba cargado *or* agobiado de deudas

► **load up** (A) VT + ADV [+ *vehicle, animal, person*] cargar (**with** de)
(B) VI + ADV [*vehicle*] cargarse; [*person*] cargar; **to ~ up on sth** cargarse de algo

load-bearing ['ləʊd,beərɪŋ] ADJ [*beam*] maestro; **a ~ wall** un muro de carga

loaded ['ləʊdɪd] ADJ [1] [*gun, camera, vehicle*] cargado
[2] [*remark, question*] lleno de implicaciones, cargado de implicaciones
[3] (= *weighted*) [*dice*] cargado
[4] (*) (= *rich*) **to be ~** estar forrado de dinero*, estar podrido de dinero*
[5] (*) (= *drunk*) **to be ~** estar como una cuba*, estar tomado (*LAm**)
[6] ✦*IDIOM* **to be ~ for bear** (*US*) estar preparado para el ataque

loader ['ləʊdəʳ] N cargador(a) *m/f*

loading ['ləʊdɪŋ] (A) N (*Insurance*) sobreprima *f*
(B) CPD ► **loading bay, loading dock** N área *m* de carga y descarga

loadstar ['ləʊdstɑːʳ] N = **lodestar**

loadstone ['ləʊdstəʊn] N = **lodestone**

loaf[1] [ləʊf] (A) N (*pl* **loaves**) [1] [*of bread*] (*unsliced*) pan *m* de molde; (*sliced*) pan *m* de molde (en rebanadas); (= *French bread*) barra *f*; **use your ~!** (*Brit**) ¡espabílate!; ✦*PROV* **half a ~ is better than no bread** menos da una piedra, peor es nada; → RHYMING SLANG
[2] [*of sugar*] pan *m*, pilón *m*
(B) CPD ► **loaf sugar** N pan *m* de azúcar ► **loaf tin** N bandeja *f* de horno

loaf[2] [ləʊf] VI (*also* **~ about, ~ around**) holgazanear, flojear (*LAm*)

loafer ['ləʊfəʳ] N [1] (= *person*) gandul(a) *m/f*, vago/a *m/f*
[2] (= *shoe*) mocasín *m*

loam [ləʊm] N marga *f*

loamy ['ləʊmɪ] ADJ margoso

loan [ləʊn] (A) N (= *thing lent between persons*) préstamo *m*; (*from bank*) crédito *m*, préstamo *m*; **it's on ~** está prestado; **I had it on ~ from the company** me lo prestó la empresa; **she is on ~ to another department** presta temporalmente sus servicios en otra sección; **to raise a ~** (= *money*) obtener *or* conseguir un préstamo; **to subscribe a ~** suscribir un préstamo; **I asked for the ~ of the book** le pedí prestado el libro
(B) VT prestar
(C) CPD ► **loan account** N cuenta *f* de crédito ► **loan agreement** N acuerdo *m* de crédito ► **loan capital** N capital *m* en préstamo ► **loan fund** N fondo *m* de crédito para empréstitos ► **loan shark** N prestamista *mf* usurero/a, tiburón *m* ► **loan translation** N calco *m* lingüístico ► **loan word** N préstamo *m*

loath [ləʊθ] ADJ **to be ~ to do sth** estar poco dispuesto a hacer algo, ser reacio a hacer algo; **to be ~ for sb to do sth** no querer en absoluto que algn haga algo; **nothing ~** de buena gana

loathe [ləʊð] VT [+ *thing, person*] detestar, odiar; **I ~ doing it** detesto *or* odio hacerlo; **he ~s being corrected** detesta que se le corrija

loathing ['ləʊðɪŋ] N odio *m*; **it fills me with ~** me repugna; **the ~ which I felt for him** el odio que sentía hacia *or* por él

loathsome ['ləʊðsəm] ADJ [*thing, person*] detestable, odioso; [*smell, disease*] repugnante

loathsomeness ['ləʊðsəmnɪs] N [*of person, thing*] lo detestable, lo odioso; [*of smell, disease*] lo repugnante

loaves [ləʊvz] NPL *of* **loaf[1]**

lob [lɒb] (A) VT [+ *ball*] volear por alto; **to ~ sth over to sb** tirar *or* echar algo a algn
(B) N lob *m*, globo *m*
(C) VI lanzar un globo

lobby ['lɒbɪ] (A) N [1] (= *entrance hall*) vestíbulo *m*; (= *corridor*) pasillo *m*; (= *anteroom*) antecámara *f*; (= *waiting room*) sala *f* de espera
[2] (*Pol*) (*for public*) vestíbulo *m* público, antecámara *f*; (= *division lobby*) (*for voting*) sala *f* de votantes
[3] (= *pressure group*) grupo *m* de presión; **the environmental ~** el grupo de presión ecologista
(B) VT **to ~ one's member of parliament** ejercer presiones sobre su diputado
(C) VI ejercer presiones, presionar; **to ~ for a reform** presionar para conseguir una reforma
(D) CPD ► **lobby correspondent** N (*Brit*) corresponsal *mf* parlamentario/a

lobbyer ['lɒbɪəʳ] N (*US*) = **lobbyist**

lobbying ['lɒbɪɪŋ] N cabildeo *m*

lobbyist ['lɒbɪɪst] N cabildero/a *m/f*

lobe [ləʊb] N lóbulo *m*

lobelia [ləʊ'biːlɪə] N lobelia *f*

lobotomy [ləʊ'bɒtəmɪ] N lobotomía *f*

lobster ['lɒbstəʳ] (A) N (*pl* **lobsters** *or* **lobster**) (*also* **rock ~, spiny ~**) langosta *f*; (*with large pincers*) langosta *f*, bogavante *m* (*Sp*)
(B) CPD ► **lobster pot** N nasa *f*, langostera *f*

local ['ləʊkəl] (A) ADJ [1] (= *in or of the area*) [*custom, newspaper, radio*] local; [*school, shop, doctor*] del barrio; [*bus, train*] urbano; [*news, weather forecast*] regional; **the ~ community** el vecindario, el barrio; (*wider*) la zona, el área; **~ currency** moneda *f* local, moneda *f* del país; **to be of ~ interest** ser de interés local; **he's a ~ man** es de aquí; **~ residents have complained to the council** los residentes del barrio *or* de la zona se han quejado

al ayuntamiento; **~ train services have been cut** han reducido los servicios locales de tren; **whatever you do, don't drink the ~ wine** hagas lo que hagas no bebas el vino del lugar
[2] (= *municipal*) [*administration, taxes, elections*] municipal; **at (the) ~ level** a nivel municipal *or* local
[3] (*Med*) [*pain*] localizado
Ⓑ N [1] (*) (= *local resident*) **the ~s** los vecinos; (*wider*) la gente de la zona; **he's a ~** es de aquí
[2] (*Brit**) (= *pub*) *bar de la zona donde alguien vive*
[3] (*Med**) (= *local anaesthetic*) anestesia *f* local
[4] (*US Rail*) *tren, autobús, etc que hace parada en todas las estaciones*
Ⓒ CPD ► **local anaesthetic, local anesthetic** (*US*) N anestesia *f* local; **under ~ anaesthetic** bajo anestesia local ► **local authority** N (*Brit, New Zealand*) gobierno *m* local; [*of city, town*] ayuntamiento *m* ► **local call** N (*Telec*) llamada *f* local ► **local colour, local color** (*US*) N (*esp Literat, Cine*) ambiente *m* local, ambiente *m* del lugar ► **local council** N ayuntamiento *m*, municipio *m* ► **local education authority** N secretaría *f* municipal de educación ► **local government** N (*Brit*) administración *f* municipal ► **local government elections** NPL elecciones *fpl* municipales ► **local government expenditure** N gastos *mpl* municipales ► **local time** N hora *f* local

locale [ləʊ'kɑːl] N (= *place*) lugar *m*; (= *scene*) escenario *m*

locality [ləʊ'kælɪtɪ] N localidad *f*

localize ['ləʊkəlaɪz] VT localizar

localized ['ləʊkəlaɪzd] ADJ localizado, local

locally ['ləʊkəlɪ] ADV [1] (= *in the area*) [*live, work*] en las cercanías; [*make, produce*] en la región (*or* la zona, la localidad, *etc*); [*buy*] en las tiendas del barrio (*or* la zona, la localidad, *etc*); **to be known ~ as** conocerse localmente como; **she's very well known ~** es muy conocida en el barrio (*or* la zona, la localidad, *etc*); **I prefer to shop ~** prefiero comprar en las tiendas del barrio *or* del pueblo
[2] (= *at local level*) [*decide, vote*] a nivel local; **both nationally and ~** tanto a nivel nacional como regional

locate [ləʊ'keɪt] VT [1] (= *place*) situar, ubicar (*esp LAm*); **to be ~d at** estar situado en, estar ubicado en (*esp LAm*)
[2] (= *find*) localizar; **we ~d it eventually** por fin lo encontramos

location [ləʊ'keɪʃən] N [1] (= *place*) lugar *m*; **the house is set in** *or* **has a beautiful ~** la casa está situada en un lugar precioso
[2] (= *placing*) [*of building*] situación *f*, ubicación *f*; **"central ~ near the sea"** (*in brochure*) "situación *f or* ubicación *f* céntrica próxima al mar"; **this would be an ideal spot for the ~ of the hotel** éste sería un lugar ideal para la ubicación del hotel
[3] (= *exact position*) [*of missing person, suspect*] paradero *m*; [*of airplane, ship*] posición *f*; **what's your ~?** ¿cuál es tu posición?
[4] (= *finding*) localización *f*
[5] (*Cine*) **to be on ~ in Mexico** estar rodando exteriores en México; **to film on ~** filmar en exteriores

locative ['lɒkətɪv] N (*also* **~ case**) locativo *m*

loch [lɒx] N (*Scot*) lago *m*; (= *sea loch*) ría *f*, brazo *m* de mar

loci ['ləʊsaɪ] NPL *of* **locus**

lock¹ [lɒk] N [*of hair*] mecha *f*, mechón *m*; (= *ringlet*) bucle *m*; **locks** (*poet*) cabellos *mpl*

lock² [lɒk] Ⓐ N [1] (*on door, box, safe*) cerradura *f*, chapa *f* (*LAm*); (*Aut*) (*on steering wheel*) tope *m*, retén *m*; (= *bolt*) cerrojo *m*; (*also* **padlock**) candado *m*; [*of gun*] llave *f*; **under ~ and key** bajo siete llaves; **to put sth under ~ and key** guardar algo bajo llave; **~, stock, and barrel** (*fig*) con todo incluido
[2] (*on canal*) esclusa *f*; (= *pressure chamber*) cámara *f* intermedia
[3] (*Aut*) (= *steering lock*) ángulo *m* de giro
[4] (*Wrestling*) llave *f*
Ⓑ VT [1] (*with key*) cerrar con llave; (*with bolt*) cerrar con cerrojo; (*with padlock*) cerrar con candado; **to ~ sth/sb in a place** encerrar algo/a algn en un lugar
[2] (*Mech*) trabar; [+ *steering wheel*] (*to prevent theft*) bloquear, inmovilizar; (= *jam*) bloquear; (*Comput*) [+ *screen*] desactivar
[3] (= *entwine*) (*usu pass*) **they were ~ed in each other's arms** estaban unidos en un abrazo; **the armies were ~ed in combat** los ejércitos luchaban encarnizadamente; ✦***IDIOM*** **to ~ horns with sb** enzarzarse en una disputa *or* pelea con algn
Ⓒ VI [1] (*with key*) [*door, box, safe*] cerrarse con llave
[2] (*Mech*) trabarse; **the front wheels of the car ~ed** las ruedas delanteras se trabaron
Ⓓ CPD ► **lock gate** N puerta *f* de esclusa ► **lock keeper** N esclusero/a *m/f* ► **lock picker** N espadista *m*

►**lock away** VT + ADV (*gen*) guardar bajo llave; [+ *criminal, mental patient*] encerrar

►**lock in** VT + ADV dejar encerrado dentro

►**lock on to** VI + PREP (*Mech*) acoplarse a, unirse a

►**lock out** VT + ADV cerrar la puerta a, dejar fuera con la puerta cerrada; **to find o.s. ~ed out** estar fuera sin llave para abrir la puerta; **the workers were ~ed out** los obreros se quedaron sin trabajo por cierre patronal

►**lock up** Ⓐ VT + ADV [+ *object*] guardar bajo llave; [+ *house*] cerrar con llave; [+ *criminal*] encarcelar; [+ *funds*] inmovilizar; **you ought to be ~ed up!** ¡irás a parar a la cárcel!
Ⓑ VI + ADV echar la llave

locker ['lɒkəʳ] Ⓐ N cajón *m* con llave; (*for left luggage*) casillero *m* (de consigna), consigna *f* automática; (*US*) cámara *f* de frío; [*of gymnasium*] taquilla *f*
Ⓑ CPD ► **locker room** N vestuario *m*

locket ['lɒkɪt] N relicario *m*, guardapelo *m*

locking ['lɒkɪŋ] ADJ [*door, container, cupboard*] que se cierra con llave; **~ petrol cap** (*Aut*) tapón *m* de gasolina con llave

lockjaw ['lɒkdʒɔː] N trismo *m*

locknut ['lɒknʌt] N contratuerca *f*

lockout ['lɒkaʊt] N cierre *m* patronal

locksmith ['lɒksmɪθ] N cerrajero/a *m/f*

lock-up ['lɒkʌp] Ⓐ N [1] (*US*) (= *prison*) cárcel *f*
[2] (*Brit*) (*also* **~ garage**) garaje *m*, cochera *f* (*LAm*)
[3] (*Brit*) (= *shop*) tienda *f* sin trastienda
Ⓑ CPD ► **lock-up stall** N (*US*) garaje *m*, cochera *f* (*LAm*)

loco¹* ['ləʊkəʊ] N = **locomotive**

loco² ['ləʊkəʊ] (*Comm*) Ⓐ CPD ► **loco price** N *precio cotizado en un lugar (aceptando el comprador todos los costos y riesgos al trasladar la mercancía a otro lugar)*
Ⓑ ADV **~ Southampton** *precio cotizado en Southampton, y la mercancía se halla en Southampton como lugar de origen*

locomotion [,ləʊkə'məʊʃən] N locomoción *f*

locomotive [,ləʊkə'məʊtɪv] Ⓐ ADJ locomotor
Ⓑ N (*Rail*) locomotora *f*, máquina *f*

locum ['ləʊkəm] N (*also* **~ tenens**) (*Brit frm*) interino/a *m/f*

locus ['ləʊkəs] N (*pl* **loci**) punto *m*, sitio *m*; (*Math*) lugar *m* (geométrico)

locust ['ləʊkəst] Ⓐ N [1] (*Zool*) langosta *f*
[2] (*Bot*) algarroba *f*
Ⓑ CPD ► **locust tree** N (= *false acacia*) acacia *f* falsa; (= *carob*) algarrobo *m*

locution [lə'kjuːʃən] N locución *f*

locutory ['lɒkjʊtərɪ] N locutorio *m*

lode [ləʊd] N filón *m*, veta *f*

lodestar ['ləʊdstɑːʳ] N estrella *f* polar; (*fig*) norte *m*

lodestone ['ləʊdstəʊn] N piedra *f* imán

lodge [lɒdʒ] Ⓐ N (*at gate of park*) casa *f* del guarda; [*of porter*] portería *f*; (*Freemasonry*) logia *f*; (= *hunting lodge*) pabellón *m* de caza; (*Univ, master's*) rectoría *f*
Ⓑ VT [+ *person*] alojar, hospedar; [+ *object*] colocar, meter; [+ *complaint*] presentar; [+ *statement*] prestar; (*Jur*) [+ *appeal*] interponer; **to ~ sth with sb** dejar algo en manos de algn, entregar algo a algn; **the bullet is ~d in the lung** la bala se ha alojado en el pulmón
Ⓒ VI (= *reside*) alojarse, hospedarse (**with** con, en casa de); [*object*] (= *get stuck*) alojarse, meterse; **where do you ~?** ¿dónde estás alojado?; **the bullet ~d in the lung** la bala se alojó en el pulmón; **a bomb ~d in the engine room** una bomba se penetró en la sala de máquinas

lodger ['lɒdʒəʳ] N inquilino/a *m/f* (*de habitación en una casa particular*), huésped(a) *m/f*; **I was a ~ there once** hace tiempo me hospedé allí; **she takes ~s** alquila habitaciones en su casa

lodging ['lɒdʒɪŋ] Ⓐ N alojamiento *m*, hospedaje *m*; **they gave me a night's ~** me dieron alojamiento; **lodgings** alojamiento *msing*; **to look for ~s** buscar alojamiento; **we took ~s with Mrs P** nos hospedamos en casa de la Sra. P; **are they good ~s?** ¿es buena la pensión?
Ⓑ CPD ► **lodging house** N pensión *f*, casa *f* de huéspedes

loess ['ləʊɪs] N loess *m*

loft [lɒft] Ⓐ N (= *attic*) desván *m*; (= *hay loft*) pajar *m*; (*in church*) galería *f*; (= *apartment*) loft *m*, *aprovechamiento doméstico de un espacio industrial*
Ⓑ VT [+ *ball*] lanzar por lo alto

loftily ['lɒftɪlɪ] ADV [*say, look*] con altivez, con altanería; **"I know what I'm doing," she said ~** —sé lo que estoy haciendo —dijo muy altanera *or* con altivez

loftiness ['lɒftɪnɪs] N [*of ceiling, mountain, tower*] altura *f*; [*of aim, ideal*] nobleza *f*, lo elevado; [*of person, attitude*] altanería *f*, altivez *f*; [*of tone*] ampulosidad *f*, grandilocuencia *f*

lofty ['lɒftɪ] ADJ (*compar* **loftier**, *superl* **loftiest**)
[1] (*liter*) (= *high*) [*ceiling, building, tower*] alto, elevado; [*mountain*] alto; [*room*] de techo alto; **he rose to a ~ position within the organization** ascendió a una posición elevada dentro de la organización
[2] (= *noble*) [*aim, ideal, ambition*] elevado, noble
[3] (= *haughty*) [*person, attitude*] altivo, altanero; **~ air/manner** aire *m* de superioridad, altivez *f*; **~ contempt/disdain** altivo desdén *m*
[4] (= *grandiose*) [*speech, pronouncement, rhetoric*] grandilocuente

log¹ [lɒg] Ⓐ N [1] [*of wood*] tronco *m*, leño *m*; *see also* **sleep C**
[2] = **logbook**
Ⓑ VT [1] (*Naut, Aer*) anotar, apuntar
[2] (*Aut*) (*also* **~ up**) [+ *distance*] recorrer; **we**

~ged 50 kilometres that day ese día recorrimos *or* cubrimos 50 kilómetros
Ⓒ VI cortar (y transportar) troncos
Ⓓ CPD ► **log cabin** N cabaña *f* de troncos *or* de madera ► **log fire** N fuego *m* de leña
►**log in** (*Comput*) Ⓐ VI + ADV acceder al sistema, entrar en el sistema
Ⓑ VT + ADV meter en el sistema
►**log off** VI + ADV, VT + ADV = **log out**
►**log on** VI + ADV, VT + ADV = **log in**
►**log out** (*Comput*) Ⓐ VI + ADV salir del sistema, terminar de operar
Ⓑ VT + ADV sacar del sistema
►**log up** VT + ADV (*Aut*) [+ *distance*] recorrer; **we ~ged up 50 kilometres that day** ese día recorrimos *or* cubrimos 50 kilómetros

log[2] [lɒg] Ⓐ N ABBR (*Math*) (= **logarithm**) logaritmo *m*
Ⓑ CPD ► **log tables** NPL tablas *fpl* de logaritmos

loganberry [ˈləʊgənbərɪ] N (= *fruit*) frambuesa *f* norteamericana; (= *bush*) frambueso *m* norteamericano

logarithm [ˈlɒgərɪθəm] N logaritmo *m*

logbook [ˈlɒgbʊk] N (*Naut*) cuaderno *m* de bitácora, diario *m* de navegación; (*Aer*) diario *m* de vuelo; (*Aut*) documentación *f*; (*Tech*) cuaderno *m* de trabajo

logger [ˈlɒgəʳ] N 1 (= *dealer*) maderero/a *m/f*, negociante *mf* en maderas
2 (*US*) (= *lumberjack*) leñador(a) *m/f*

loggerheads [ˈlɒgəhedz] NPL **to be at ~ with sb** estar a matar con algn, estar picado con algn

loggia [ˈlɒdʒə] N (*pl* **loggias** *or* **loggie** [ˈlɒdʒe]) logia *f*

logging [ˈlɒgɪŋ] N explotación *f* forestal

logic [ˈlɒdʒɪk] Ⓐ N lógica *f*; **I can't see the ~ of it** no le veo la lógica
Ⓑ CPD ► **logic circuit** N (*Comput*) circuito *m* lógico

logical [ˈlɒdʒɪkəl] Ⓐ ADJ lógico; **she's the ~ choice for the job** es lógico que sea ella la elegida para el puesto; **to take sth to its ~ conclusion** llevar algo a su lógica conclusión; **she has a ~ mind** es una persona lógica; **it seemed a ~ step** parecía el paso lógico; **it is ~ that** es lógico que; **he is incapable of ~ thinking** es incapaz de razonar con lógica *or* de manera lógica
Ⓑ CPD ► **logical positivism** N positivismo *m* lógico

logically [ˈlɒdʒɪkəlɪ] ADV 1 (= *by a logical process*) lógicamente
2 (= *rationally*) [*think, speak, act*] de manera lógica, de forma lógica; [*designed, laid out*] con lógica; **I'm not thinking ~** no estoy pensando de manera *or* forma lógica, no estoy pensando con lógica; **~ (enough), the controls are on the right** como es lógico, los controles están a la derecha

logician [lɒˈdʒɪʃən] N lógico/a *m/f*

login [ˈlɒgɪn] N login *m*

logistic [lɒˈdʒɪstɪk] ADJ logístico

logistical [lɒˈdʒɪstɪkəl] ADJ = **logistic**

logistically [lɒˈdʒɪstɪkəlɪ] ADV logísticamente, desde el punto de vista logístico

logistics [lɒˈdʒɪstɪks] NSING logística *f*

logjam [ˈlɒgdʒæm] N (*fig*) atolladero *m*; **to clear the ~** desbloquear la situación, salir del atolladero

logo [ˈləʊgəʊ] N logo *m*, logotipo *m*

log-off [ˈlɒgˈɒf] N (*Comput*) salida *f* del sistema

log-on [ˈlɒgˈɒn] N (*Comput*) entrada *f* al sistema

logrolling [ˈlɒg,rəʊlɪŋ] N (*US*) intercambio *m* de favores políticos, sistema *m* de concesiones mutuas

logy [ˈləʊgɪ] ADJ (*compar* **logier**; *superl* **logiest**) (*US*) torpe, lerdo

loin [lɔɪn] Ⓐ N 1 [*of meat*] lomo *m*
2 **loins** (*Anat liter*) lomos *mpl*; **to gird (up) one's ~s** (*fig*) aprestarse a luchar, apretarse los machos*
Ⓑ CPD ► **loin chop** N (*Culin*) chuleta *f* de lomo

loincloth [ˈlɔɪnklɒθ] N taparrabo *m*, taparrabos *m inv*

Loire [lwɑːr] N Loira *m*

loiter [ˈlɔɪtəʳ] VI (= *idle*) perder el tiempo; (= *lag behind*) rezagarse; (= *dally*) entretenerse; **don't ~ on the way!** ¡no te entretengas!; **to ~ (with intent)** (*Jur*) merodear con fines sospechosos *or* delictivos
►**loiter away** VT + ADV **to ~ away the time** perder el tiempo

loll [lɒl] VI [*head*] colgar, caer; **to ~ against** recostarse en
►**loll about, loll around** VI + ADV repantigarse
►**loll back** VI + ADV **to ~ back on** recostarse en
►**loll out** VI + ADV **his tongue was ~ing out** le colgaba la lengua

lollipop [ˈlɒlɪpɒp] Ⓐ N pirulí *m*, piruleta *f* (*Sp*), chupaleta *f* (*Mex*), chupetín *m* (*River Plate*); (*iced*) polo *m*, paleta *f* helada (*LAm*)
Ⓑ CPD ► **lollipop lady** N (*Brit**) *mujer encargada de ayudar a los niños a cruzar la calle* ► **lollipop man** N (*Brit**) *hombre encargado de ayudar a los niños a cruzar la calle*

> **LOLLIPOP LADY/MAN**
>
> *Se llama* **lollipop man** *o* **lollipop lady** *a la persona encargada de parar el tráfico en las calles cercanas a los colegios en el Reino Unido, para que los niños las crucen sin peligro. Suelen ser personas ya jubiladas, que van vestidas con una gabardina fosforescente y que llevan una señal de stop en un poste portátil, lo que recuerda por su forma a una piruleta, y de ahí su nombre.*

lollop [ˈlɒləp] VI moverse desgarbadamente; **to ~ along** moverse torpemente, arrastrar los pies

lolly [ˈlɒlɪ] N 1 = **lollipop A**
2 (*Brit**) (= *money*) pasta* *f*, lana *f* (*LAm**)

Lombard [ˈlɒmbɑːd] Ⓐ ADJ lombardo
Ⓑ N lombardo/a *m/f*

Lombardy [ˈlɒmbədɪ] Ⓐ N Lombardía *f*
Ⓑ CPD ► **Lombardy poplar** N chopo *m* lombardo

London [ˈlʌndən] Ⓐ N Londres *m*
Ⓑ CPD londinense ► **London pride** N (*Bot*) corona *f* de rey

Londoner [ˈlʌndənəʳ] N londinense *mf*

lone [ləʊn] Ⓐ ADJ (= *solitary*) solitario; **to play a ~ hand** (*fig*) actuar solo; *see also* **lonely**
Ⓑ CPD ► **lone parent** N = **single parent** ► **lone ranger** N llanero *m* solitario ► **lone wolf** N (*fig*) lobo *m* solitario

loneliness [ˈləʊnlɪnɪs] N soledad *f*

lonely [ˈləʊnlɪ] Ⓐ ADJ 1 (*compar* **lonelier**; *superl* **loneliest**) (= *without company*) **he was a sad and ~ man** era un hombre triste y solitario; **to feel ~** sentirse solo; **I was ~ and didn't know what to do** me sentía solo y no sabía qué hacer
2 (= *solitary*) [*life, place, period of time*] solitario; **the ~ hours of the night** las horas nocturnas de soledad, las solitarias horas de la noche; **it's ~ at the top** uno se siente muy solo en la cumbre
3 (= *remote*) [*village, house*] solitario, aislado; [*road*] solitario
4 (*liter*) (= *mournful*) [*sound*] lúgubre y solitario (*liter*)
Ⓑ NPL **the ~** las personas que están solas
Ⓒ CPD ► **lonely hearts club** N club *m* de corazones solitarios ► **lonely hearts (column)** N sección *f* de corazones solitarios

lone-parent [ˈləʊn,peərənt] CPD ► **lone-parent family** N (*Brit*) familia *f* monoparental

loner [ˈləʊnəʳ] N solitario/a *m/f*

lonesome [ˈləʊnsəm] (*esp US*) ADJ [*person*] solo; [*place*] (= *isolated*) aislado, solitario; **to be/feel ~** sentirse solo

long[1] [lɒŋ] (*compar* **longer**; *superl* **longest**) Ⓐ ADJ 1 (*in size*) [*dress, hair, journey*] largo; **it's six metres ~** tiene seis metros de largo; **it's a very ~ book** es un libro muy largo; **he has ~ legs** tiene las piernas largas; **it's a ~ distance from the school** está (muy) lejos del colegio; **to make** *or* **pull a ~ face** poner cara larga; **to get ~er** [*queue*] hacerse más largo; [*hair*] crecer (más); **how ~ is it?** (*table, hallway, piece of material, stick*) ¿cuánto mide de largo?; (*more precisely*) ¿qué longitud tiene?; (*river*) ¿qué longitud tiene?; **how ~ is her hair?** ¿cómo tiene el pelo de largo?; **to be ~ in the leg** [*trousers*] tener piernas largas; **the speech was ~ on rhetoric and short on details** el discurso tenía mucha retórica y pocos detalles; ✦**IDIOMS the ~ arm of the law** el brazo de la ley, el alcance de la ley; **a list as ~ as your arm** una lista larguísima; **not by a ~ chalk** ni con mucho; **he's a bit ~ in the tooth*** es bastante viejo ya; *see also* **suit A3**
2 (*in distance*) **it's a ~ way** está lejos; **it's a ~ way to the shops** las tiendas están lejos; **we walked a ~ way** caminamos mucho
3 (*in time*) [*film*] largo; [*visit*] prolongado; [*wait*] largo, prolongado; **two hours ~** de dos horas; **the course is six months ~** el curso es de seis meses, el curso dura seis meses; **a ~ walk** un paseo largo; **a ~ holiday** unas vacaciones largas; **it has been a ~ day** (*fig*) ha sido un día muy atareado; **there will be ~ delays** habrá grandes retrasos, habrá retrasos considerables; **he took a ~ drink of water** se bebió un vaso grande de agua; **the days are getting ~er** los días se están alargando; **how ~ is the film?** ¿cuánto (tiempo) dura la película?; **how ~ are the holidays?** ¿cuánto duran las vacaciones?; **to be ~ in doing sth** tardar en hacer algo; **the reply was not ~ in coming** la respuesta no tardó en llegar; **it will be a ~ job** será un trabajo que llevará mucho tiempo; **at ~ last** por fin; **to take a ~ look at sth** mirar algo detenidamente; **he has a ~ memory** (*fig*) es de los que no perdonan fácilmente; **in the ~ run** (*fig*) a la larga; **a ~ time ago** hace mucho tiempo; **it takes a ~ time** lleva mucho tiempo; **I've been waiting a ~ time** llevo esperando mucho tiempo; **~ time no see!*** ¡cuánto tiempo sin verte!; **it's a good place to go for a ~ weekend** es un buen sitio para ir durante un fin de semana largo; ✦**IDIOM he's not ~ for this world*** no le queda mucho de vida; *see also* **term A1, long-term, view A5**
4 (*Ling*) [*vowel*] largo
Ⓑ ADV 1 (= *a long time*) **don't be ~!** ¡vuelve pronto!; **I shan't be ~** (*in finishing*) termino pronto, no tardo; (*in returning*) vuelvo pronto, no tardo; **will you be ~?** ¿vas a tardar mu-

cho?; **we didn't stay ~** nos quedamos poco tiempo; **he hasn't been gone ~** no hace mucho que se ha ido; **have you been waiting ~?** ¿hace mucho que espera?; **I have ~ believed that ...** creo desde hace tiempo que ..., hace tiempo que creo que ...; **this method has ~ been used in industry** este método se viene usando desde hace mucho tiempo en la industria; **~ after he died** mucho tiempo después de morir; **he died ~ after his wife** murió mucho tiempo después que su mujer; **~ ago** hace mucho (tiempo); **how ~ ago was it?** ¿cuánto tiempo hace de eso?; **as ~ ago as 1930** ya en 1930; **not ~ ago** no hace mucho (tiempo); **~ before** mucho antes; **not ~ before** poco antes; **~ before now** hace mucho tiempo; **~ before you came** mucho antes de que llegaras; **not ~ before the war** poco antes de la guerra; **not ~ before his wife died** poco antes de que muriera su mujer; **they left before ~** se marcharon muy pronto; **I only had ~ enough to buy a paper** sólo tuve tiempo para comprar un periódico; **we won't stay for ~** nos quedamos un rato nada más; **are you going away for ~?** ¿te vas para mucho tiempo?; **he hesitated, but not for ~** dudó, pero sólo por un instante; **"are you still in London?" — "yes, but not for much ~er"** —¿todavía estás en Londres? —sí, pero por poco tiempo ya; **how ~ will you be?** (*in finishing*) ¿cuánto (tiempo) tardarás?; (*in returning*) ¿cuánto tiempo te quedarás?; **how ~ have you been here?** ¿cuánto tiempo llevas aquí?; **how ~ will it take?** ¿cuánto tiempo llevará?; **how ~ did he stay?** ¿cuánto tiempo se quedó?; **how ~ have you been learning Spanish?** ¿desde cuándo llevas aprendiendo español?; **how ~ is it since you saw her?** ¿cuánto tiempo hace que no la ves?; **it didn't last ~** fue cosa de unos pocos minutos *or* días *etc*; **to live ~** tener una vida larga; **women live ~er than men** las mujeres son más longevas que los hombres; **he hasn't ~ to live** no le queda mucho de vida; **~ live the King!** ¡viva el rey!; **it's not ~ since he died** ◊ **he died not ~ since** no hace mucho que murió, murió hace poco; **~ since dead** muerto hace mucho; **so ~!** (*esp US**) ¡hasta luego!; **it won't take ~** no tardará mucho; **it didn't take him ~ to realize that ...** no tardó en darse cuenta de que ...; **he talked ~ about politics** habló largamente de política

2 **~er** más tiempo; **we stayed ~er than you** quedamos más tiempo que vosotros; **wait a little ~er** espera un poco más; **how much ~er can you stay?** ¿hasta cuándo podéis quedaros?; **how much ~er do we have to wait?** ¿hasta cuándo tenemos que esperar?; **two hours ~er** dos horas más; **I can't stay any ~er** no me puedo quedar por más tiempo; **I can't stand it any ~er** ya no lo aguanto más; **no ~er** ya no; **he no ~er comes** ya no viene

3 **~est: six months at the ~est** seis meses, como máximo *or* como mucho

4 **as ~ as** ◊ **so ~ as** (= *while*) mientras; **as ~ as the war lasts** mientras dure la guerra; **as ~ as I live** mientras viva; **stay (for) as ~ as you like** quédate hasta cuando quieras; **as ~ as (is) necessary** el tiempo que haga falta, lo que haga falta

5 **as ~ as** ◊ **so ~ as** (= *provided that*) siempre que + *subjun*; **you can borrow it as ~ as John doesn't mind** lo puedes tomar prestado siempre que a John no le importe *or* si a John no le importa

6 (= *through*) **all day ~** todo el (santo) día; **all night ~** toda la noche; **all summer ~** todo el verano

Ⓒ N 1 **the ~ and the short of it is that ...** (*fig*) en resumidas cuentas, es que ..., concretamente, es que ...

2 **longs** (*Fin*) valores *mpl* a largo plazo

Ⓓ CPD ► **long division** N (*Math*) división *f* larga ► **long drink** N refresco *m*, bebida *f* no alcohólica ► **long johns** NPL calzoncillos *mpl* largos ► **long jump** N salto *m* de longitud ► **long jumper** N saltador(a) *m/f* de longitud ► **long shot** N (*Cine*) toma *f* a distancia; (*in race*) desconocido/a *m/f*; **it's a ~ shot*** dudo que resulte; ✦*IDIOM* **not by a ~ shot** ni con mucho ► **long sight** N presbicia *f*, hipermetropía *f*; **to have ~ sight** ser présbita ► **the long term** N **in** *or* **over the ~ term** a largo plazo ► **long trousers** NPL (*as opposed to shorts*) pantalones *mpl* largos ► **the long vac*** N = **the long vacation** ► **the long vacation** N (*Brit Univ*) las vacaciones de verano ► **long wave** N (*Rad*) onda *f* larga; (*used as adj*) de onda larga

long² [lɒŋ] VI **to ~ for sth** anhelar algo, desear algo; **to ~ for sb** suspirar por algn, añorar a algn; **to ~ to do sth** tener muchas ganas de hacer algo, estar deseando hacer algo; **to ~ for sb to do sth** desear que algn haga algo

-long [lɒŋ] ADJ (*ending in compounds*) **month~** de un mes de duración

long. ABBR = **longitude**

long-armed [ˈlɒŋˈɑːmd] ADJ de brazos largos

long-awaited [ˈlɒŋəˈweɪtɪd] ADJ largamente esperado

longboat [ˈlɒŋbəʊt] N lancha *f*

longbow [ˈlɒŋbəʊ] N arco *m*

long-dated [ˈlɒŋˈdeɪtɪd] ADJ a largo plazo

long-distance [ˈlɒŋˈdɪstəns] Ⓐ ADJ [*flight*] largo, de larga distancia; [*race, runner*] de fondo; [*train*] de largo recorrido

Ⓑ ADV **to call sb ~** poner una conferencia a algn

Ⓒ CPD ► **long-distance call** N llamada *f* interurbana *or* de larga distancia, conferencia *f* ► **long-distance bus** N autocar *m*, coche *m* de línea ► **long-distance runner** N corredor(a) *m/f* de fondo, fondista *mf*

long-drawn-out [ˈlɒŋdrɔːnˈaʊt] ADJ interminable

long-eared [ˈlɒŋˈɪəd] ADJ orejudo, de orejas largas

longed-for [ˈlɒŋdfɔːʳ] ADJ ansiado

longevity [lɒnˈdʒevɪtɪ] N longevidad *f*

long-forgotten [ˈlɒŋfəˈgɒtn] ADJ olvidado hace mucho tiempo

long-grain [ˈlɒŋgreɪn] ADJ [*rice*] de grano largo

long-haired [ˈlɒŋˈhɛəd] ADJ de pelo largo

longhand [ˈlɒŋhænd] Ⓐ N **in ~** escrito a mano

Ⓑ ADJ escrito a mano

Ⓒ ADV a mano

long-haul [ˈlɒŋˌhɔːl] ADJ [*flight*] de larga distancia

longing [ˈlɒŋɪŋ] Ⓐ N (= *yearning*) (*for place*) nostalgia *f*, añoranza *f*; (*for past time*) añoranza *f*; (*for person, thing*) anhelo *m*; **she felt a ~ for her childhood days** añoraba los días de su infancia; **he felt a ~ for his homeland** sentía nostalgia por su país, añoraba su país; **people have a ~ for normality** la gente anhela la normalidad; **she gazed at him with ~** lo miró con anhelo

Ⓑ ADJ [*look*] anhelante

longingly [ˈlɒŋɪŋlɪ] ADV [*look, gaze*] con anhelo, con ansia; **she thought ~ of those days in Madrid** pensó con nostalgia *or* añoranza en aquellos días en Madrid

longish [ˈlɒŋɪʃ] ADJ bastante largo

longitude [ˈlɒŋgɪtjuːd] N longitud *f*

longitudinal [ˌlɒŋgɪˈtjuːdɪnl] ADJ longitudinal

longitudinally [ˌlɒŋgɪˈtjuːdɪnəlɪ] ADV longitudinalmente

long-lasting [ˈlɒŋˈlɑːstɪŋ] ADJ [*material, memory, effect*] duradero

long-legged [ˈlɒŋˈlegɪd] ADJ [*person*] de piernas largas; [*animal*] de patas largas; [*bird*] zancudo

long-life [ˈlɒŋˈlaɪf] ADJ de larga duración

long-limbed [ˌlɒŋˈlɪmd] ADJ patilargo

long-lived [ˈlɒŋˈlɪvd] ADJ [*person, species*] longevo, de larga vida; [*plant*] duradero; [*rumour*] duradero, persistente; **women are more ~ than men** las mujeres son más longevas que los hombres

long-lost [ˈlɒŋˈlɒst] ADJ perdido hace mucho tiempo

long-playing [ˈlɒŋˈpleɪɪŋ] ADJ **~ record** (*abbr LP*) disco *m* de larga duración, elepé *m*

long-range [ˈlɒŋˈreɪndʒ] ADJ [*gun, missile*] de largo alcance; [*aircraft*] para vuelos de larga distancia; [*weather forecast, plan*] a largo plazo

long-running [ˈlɒŋˈrʌnɪŋ] ADJ [*dispute*] largo; [*play*] taquillero, que se mantiene mucho tiempo en la cartelera; [*programme*] que lleva mucho tiempo en antena

longship [ˈlɒŋʃɪp] N (*Viking*) barco *m* vikingo

longshoreman [ˈlɒŋʃɔːmən] N (*pl* **longshoremen**) (*esp US*) estibador *m*, obrero *m* portuario

long-sighted [ˈlɒŋˈsaɪtɪd] ADJ (*Med*) hipermétrope, présbita; (*fig*) previsor

long-sightedness [ˈlɒŋˈsaɪtɪdnɪs] N (*Med*) presbicia *f*, hipermetropía *f*; (*fig*) previsión *f*, clarividencia *f*

long-sleeved [ˈlɒŋsliːvd] ADJ de manga larga

long-standing [ˈlɒŋˈstændɪŋ] ADJ [*agreement, dispute, friendship*] antiguo

long-stay [ˈlɒŋsteɪ] ADJ [*hospital*] para enfermos de larga duración; [*patient*] de larga duración; [*car park*] para aparcamiento *or* (*LAm*) estacionamiento prolongado

long-suffering [ˈlɒŋˈsʌfərɪŋ] ADJ sufrido

long-term [ˈlɒŋˈtɜːm] Ⓐ ADJ [*effect, investment, care, solution*] a largo plazo; **joining the army is a ~ commitment** entrar en el ejército significa comprometerse a largo plazo; **the drug's ~ effects** los efectos del medicamento a largo plazo; **this will have a ~ effect on unemployment** esto tendrá un efecto a largo plazo sobre el desempleo; **they're in a ~ relationship** llevan tiempo juntos; **I've had several ~ relationships** he tenido varias relaciones sentimentales duraderas; **the ~ unemployed** *las personas que llevan mucho tiempo sin trabajo*; **~ unemployment** el desempleo de larga duración

Ⓑ CPD ► **long-term car park** N parking *m* para aparcamiento *or* (*LAm*) estacionamiento prolongado ► **long-term memory** N memoria *f* a largo plazo

long-time [ˈlɒŋˈtaɪm] ADJ [*friend*] viejo, de muchos años; [*partner*] de muchos años

longways [ˈlɒŋweɪz] ADV a lo largo, longitudinalmente

long-winded [ˈlɒŋˈwɪndɪd] ADJ [*person*] prolijo; [*speech, explanation*] prolijo, interminable

long-windedly [ˈlɒŋˈwɪndɪdlɪ] ADV prolijamente

loo* [luː] N (= *toilet*) retrete *m*, wáter *m* (*Sp*), baño *m* (*LAm*)

loofah [ˈluːfəʳ] N esponja *f* de lufa

look [lʊk] Ⓐ N [1] (= *glance*) mirada *f*, vistazo *m*; **to have a ~ at sth** echar un vistazo a algo; **let me have a ~** déjame ver; **have a ~ at this!** ¡mira esto!, ¡échale un vistazo a esto!; **shall we have a ~ round the town?** ¿damos una vuelta por la ciudad?; **to have a ~ round a house** inspeccionar una casa; **to take a ~ at sth** echar un vistazo a algo; **take a ~ at this!** ¡mira esto!, ¡échale un vistazo a esto!; **to take a good ~ at sth** mirar algo detenidamente; **to take a long hard ~ at o.s.** (*fig*) examinarse a sí mismo detenidamente; **take a long hard ~ before deciding** antes de decidir conviene pensar muchísimo; **do you want a ~?** ¿quieres verlo?

[2] (= *expression*) mirada *f*; **she gave me a dirty ~** me echó una mirada de odio; **he gave me a furious ~** me miró furioso, me lanzó una mirada furiosa; **a ~ of despair** una cara de desesperación; **we got some very odd ~s** la gente nos miró extrañada; **if ~s could kill*** ... si las miradas mataran ...

[3] (= *search*) **to have a ~ for sth** buscar algo; **I've had a good ~ for it already** lo he buscado ya en todas partes; **have another ~!** ¡vuelve a buscar!

[4] (= *air, appearance*) aire *m*, aspecto *m*, pinta* *f*; **there's a mischievous ~ about that child** ese niño tiene pinta de pillo*; **he had a sad ~** tenía un aspecto *or* aire triste; **he had the ~ of a sailor** tenía aire de marinero; **by the ~(s) of it** *or* **things** a juzgar por las apariencias; **by the ~(s) of him ...** viéndole, se diría que ...; **you can't go by ~s alone** es arriesgado juzgar por las apariencias nada más; **to like the ~ of sb/sth**: **I don't like the ~ of him** me cae mal, no me fío de él; **I don't like the ~ of it** no me gusta nada

[5] **looks** (= *attractiveness*) **~s aren't everything** la belleza no lo es todo; **good ~s** belleza *fsing*; **she has kept her ~s** sigue tan guapa como siempre; **she's losing her ~s** no es tan guapa como antes

[6] (= *fashion*) moda *f*, estilo *m*; **the 1999 ~** la moda de 1999; **the new ~** la nueva moda; **I need a new ~** quiero cambiar de imagen

Ⓑ VI [1] (= *see, glance*) mirar; **look!** ¡mira!; **~ here!** ¡oye!; **just ~!** ¡mira!, ¡fíjate!; **I'll ~ and see** voy a ver; **~ how she does it** fíjate cómo lo hace; **~ who's here!** ¡mira quién está aquí!; **to ~ into sb's eyes** mirarle a los ojos a algn; **to ~ the other way** (*lit*) mirar para el otro lado; (*fig*) hacer como que no se da cuenta; **to be ~ing over sb's shoulder** (*fig*) estar siempre vigilando a algn; ✦*IDIOM* **to ~ down one's nose at sth/sb** menospreciar algo/a algn; ✦*PROV* **~ before you leap** mira bien lo que haces

[2] (= *search*) **~ again!** ¡vuelve a buscar!; **you can't have ~ed far** no has mirado mucho; **you should have ~ed more carefully** tendrías que haber mirado mejor

[3] (= *seem, appear*) parecer, verse (*LAm*); **he ~s about 60 (years old)** aparenta tener alrededor de los 60 años; **to ~ one's age** aparentar *or* representar su edad; **she doesn't ~ her age** no aparenta *or* representa la edad que tiene; **it ~s all right to me** me parece que está bien; **it will ~ bad** (*fig*) quedará mal; **he wanted to ~ his best for the interview** quería estar lo mejor (arreglado) posible para la entrevista; **I don't ~ my best first thing in the morning** cuando me levanto por la mañana no estoy muy guapa que digamos; **he just does it to ~ big*** lo hace sólo para impresionar; **they made me ~ a fool** me hicieron quedar como un idiota; **they made me ~ foolish** me hicieron quedar en ridículo; **he ~s good in a uniform** está muy guapo en uniforme; **Manchester United are ~ing good for the championship** el Manchester United tiene muchas posibilidades de ganar el campeonato; **it ~s good on you** te sienta bien; **he ~s happy** parece contento; **she wasn't ~ing herself** parecía otra, no parecía la misma; **how does it ~ to you?** ¿qué te parece?; **how do I ~?** ¿cómo estoy?; **she's 70 but doesn't ~ it** tiene 70 años pero no los aparenta *or* representa; **~ lively!*** ¡muévete!*; **that cake ~s nice** ese pastel tiene buena pinta*; **that hairstyle makes her ~ old** ese peinado la hace parece mayor; **to ~ the part** (*fig*) parecerlo; **she ~ed prettier than ever** estaba más guapa que nunca; **how pretty you ~!** ¡qué guapa estás!; **it ~s promising** parece prometedor; **to make sb ~ small** (*fig*) rebajar a algn; **he ~ed surprised** hizo un gesto de extrañeza; **he ~s tired** parece cansado; **to ~ well** [*person*] tener buena cara; **it ~s well** parece muy bien, tiene buena apariencia

[4] **to ~ like** [4·1] (= *be in appearance*) **what does she ~ like?** ¿cómo es físicamente?

[4·2] **to ~ like sb** (= *resemble*) parecerse a algn; **he ~s like his brother** se parece a su hermano; **this photo doesn't ~ like him** la foto no se le parece, en esta foto no parece él

[4·3] (= *seem*) **it ~s like cheese to me** a mí me parece (que es) queso; **the festival ~s like being lively** la fiesta se anuncia animada; **it ~s like rain** parece que va a llover; **it certainly ~s like it** parece que sí

[5] **to ~ as if** *or* **as though**: **it ~s as if** *or* **as though the train will be late** parece que el tren va a llegar tarde; **try to ~ as if** *or* **as though you're glad to see me** haz como que te alegras de verme; **it doesn't ~ as if** *or* **as though he's coming** parece que no va a venir

[6] (= *face*) **it ~s south** [*house*] mira hacia el sur, está orientada hacia el sur

[7] (= *seek*) **they are ~ing to make a profit** quieren sacar ganancias

Ⓒ VT [1] (= *look at*) mirar; **to ~ sb (straight) in the eye(s)** *or* **in the face** mirar directamente a los ojos de algn; **I would never be able to ~ her in the eye(s)** *or* **face again** no podría resistir su mirada, siempre me avergonzaría al verla; **to ~ sb up and down** mirar a algn de arriba abajo

[2] (= *pay attention to*) **~ what you've done now!** ¡mira lo que has hecho!; **~ where you're going!** ¡fíjate por donde vas!

►**look about** VI + ADV, VI + PREP = **look around**

►**look after** VI + PREP [1] (= *take care of*) [+ *invalid, animal, plant*] cuidar, cuidar de; [+ *one's possessions*] velar por; **he can ~ after himself** sabe cuidar de *or* valerse por sí mismo; **she can't ~ after herself any more** ya no puede valerse por sí misma

[2] (= *mind*) [+ *child*] vigilar, cuidar; [+ *shop, business*] encargarse de

[3] **to ~ after sth for sb** (= *watch over*) [+ *luggage, house*] vigilar algo a algn; (= *keep temporarily*) guardar algo a algn

►**look ahead** VI + ADV (*in front*) mirar hacia delante; (*to future*) hacer proyectos para el futuro

►**look around** Ⓐ VI + ADV echar una mirada alrededor; **to ~ around for sth** buscar algo; **we're ~ing around for a house** estamos buscando casa

Ⓑ VI + PREP **to ~ around one** mirar a su alrededor

►**look at** VI + PREP [1] (= *observe*) mirar; **to ~ hard at** [+ *person*] observar detenidamente; [+ *idea*] estudiar cuidadosamente; **just ~ at this mess!** ¡mira qué desorden!; **to ~ at him you would never think that ...** por la apariencia nunca pensarías que ...; **it isn't much to ~ at** ◊ **it's nothing to ~ at** no es muy bonito; **~ at how she does it** fíjate cómo lo hace

[2] (= *consider*) [+ *alternatives*] considerar, examinar; [+ *problem*] estudiar; **it depends (on) how you ~ at it** depende de cómo se enfoca la cuestión, depende del punto de vista de uno; **whichever way you ~ at it** se mire por donde se mire

[3] (= *check*) [+ *patient, wound, heart*] examinar; [+ *engine, spelling*] revisar; **will you ~ at the engine?** ¿podría revisar el motor?; **I'll ~ at it tomorrow** lo miraré mañana

[4] (= *accept*) **I wouldn't even ~ at the job** no aceptaría el puesto por nada del mundo; **the landlady won't ~ at students** la patrona no aguanta los estudiantes

[5] (*) (= *have in prospect*) **you're ~ing at a minimum of £200** calcula 200 libras como mínimo

►**look away** VI + ADV apartar la mirada (**from** de)

►**look back** VI + ADV [1] (= *look behind*) mirar hacia atrás

[2] (= *remember*) pensar en el pasado; **~ing back, I'm surprised I didn't suspect anything** pensándolo ahora, me sorprende que no hubiera sospechado nada; **to ~ back on** *or* **at** [+ *event, period*] recordar, rememorar; **after that he never ~ed back** (*fig*) desde entonces todo le ha ido sobre ruedas

►**look down** VI + ADV (= *lower eyes*) bajar la mirada; (= *look downward*) mirar hacia abajo; **to ~ down at sb/sth** mirar abajo hacia algn/algo

►**look down on** VI + PREP [1] (*fig*) (= *despise*) despreciar

[2] (= *overlook*) **the castle ~s down on the town** el castillo domina la ciudad

►**look for** VI + PREP [1] (= *seek*) buscar; **to be ~ing for trouble*** andar buscando camorra*

[2] (= *expect*) [+ *praise, reward*] esperar

LOOK FOR

Omission of article

• Don't translate the article "**a**" in sentences like **I'm looking for a flat**, when the number of such things is not significant since people normally only look for one at a time:

I'm looking for a flat
Estoy buscando piso
He's looking for a secretary
Busca secretaria

NOTE: The personal **a** is not used before people when the article is omitted as above.

• ***Do*** translate the article when the thing or person is qualified:

He's looking for a little flat
Busca un piso pequeño

! When translating examples like **I'm looking for someone to...** translate the English to-infinitive using **que** + **subjunctive**:

I'm looking for someone to help with the children
Busco a alguien que me ayude con los niños
I'm looking for a mechanic to repair my car
Busco a un mecánico que me arregle el coche

For further uses and examples, see main entry.

►**look forward** VI + ADV (= *plan for the future*) mirar hacia el futuro

►**look forward to** VI + PREP [+ *event*] esperar con ansia, esperar con impaciencia; **we're ~ing forward to the journey** el viaje nos hace mucha ilusión; **we had been ~ing for-**

➤ LANGUAGE IN USE: look B5 16.2 look forward to 19.3, 21.2, 25.3

ward to it for weeks durante semanas enteras veníamos pensando en eso con mucha ilusión; **I'm really ~ing forward to the holidays** estoy deseando que lleguen las vacaciones; **I'm not ~ing forward to it at all** no me hace ninguna ilusión; **to ~ forward to doing sth** tener muchas ganas de *or* estar deseando hacer algo; **~ing forward to hearing from you ...** (*in letter*) a la espera de sus noticias ...

►**look in** VI + ADV [1] (= *see in*) mirar por dentro [2] (= *visit*) pasar por casa, caer por casa; **to ~ in on sb** pasar a ver a algn

►**look into** VI + PREP (= *examine*) [+ *matter, possibility*] estudiar, investigar

►**look on** Ⓐ VI + ADV mirar (como espectador) Ⓑ VI + PREP (= *consider*) considerar; **I ~ on him as a friend** lo considero un amigo; **we do not ~ on it with favour** no nos merece una buena opinión; **to ~ kindly on sth/sb** mirar algo/a algn con buenos ojos; **to ~ on the bright side (of things)** mirar el lado bueno (de las cosas)

►**look onto** VI + PREP (= *face*) [*building, room*] dar a; **it ~s onto the garden** da al jardín

►**look out** Ⓐ VI + ADV [1] (= *look outside*) mirar fuera; **to ~ out of the window** mirar por la ventana; **it ~s out on to the garden** da al jardín

[2] (= *take care*) tener cuidado; **~ out!** ¡cuidado!, ¡aguas! (*Mex*)

Ⓑ VT + ADV (*Brit*) (= *search for*) buscar; (= *find*) encontrar

►**look out for** VI + PREP [1] (= *watch for*) **to ~ out for sth/sb** esperar algo/a algn, estar atento a algo/algn; **do ~ out for pickpockets** ten mucho ojo con los carteristas; **~ out for special deals** estáte al tanto de las gangas

[2] (*) (= *look after*) [+ *person*] cuidar; **to ~ out for o.s.** cuidar de sí mismo, cuidarse; **he's only ~ing out for himself** (*pej*) sólo mira sus propios intereses; **we ~ out for each other** nos cuidamos el uno al otro, cuidamos el uno del otro

[3] (= *seek*) buscar

►**look over** VT + ADV [+ *document, list*] echar un vistazo a; [+ *person, goods, produce*] echar un vistazo a; (*carefully*) examinar; [+ *town, building*] echar un vistazo a; (*carefully*) inspeccionar

►**look round** Ⓐ VI + ADV [1] (= *look about one*) mirar a su alrededor

[2] (= *turn*) volver la cabeza, volverse; **I called him and he ~ed round** lo llamé y volvió la cabeza, lo llamé y se volvió

[3] (*in shop*) mirar; **we're just ~ing round** estamos mirando solamente; **do you mind if we ~ round?** ¿le importa que echemos un vistazo?

[4] (= *search*) **to ~ round for** buscar

Ⓑ VI + PREP [+ *town, factory*] visitar, recorrer; **to ~ round an exhibition** visitar una exposición; **I like ~ing round the shops** me gusta ir a ver tiendas

►**look through** VI + PREP [1] [+ *window*] mirar por [2] (= *search*) registrar; (= *leaf through*) hojear; (= *examine closely*) examinar detenidamente; (= *re-read*) [+ *notes*] revisar [3] (*fig*) (= *ignore*) **he ~ed right through me** me miró sin verme, me miró como si no existiera

►**look to** VI + PREP [1] (*fig*) (= *turn to*) contar con, recurrir a; **it's no good ~ing to me for help** es inútil recurrir a mí en busca de ayuda; **to ~ to sb to do sth** esperar que algn haga algo, contar con algn para hacer algo

[2] (= *think of*) **we must ~ to the future** tenemos que pensar en el futuro *or* mirar hacia delante

[3] (= *attend to*) ocuparse de, mirar por

►**look up** Ⓐ VI + ADV [1] (= *glance*) levantar la vista, alzar la vista

[2] (= *improve*) mejorar; **things are ~ing up** las cosas van mejor

Ⓑ VT + ADV [1] [+ *information*] buscar; **if you don't know a word, ~ it up in the dictionary** si no conoces una palabra, búscala en el diccionario

[2] (= *visit*) [+ *person*] ir a visitar

►**look upon** VI + PREP = **look on B**

►**look up to** VI + PREP **to ~ up to sb** (*fig*) respetar a algn, admirar a algn

lookalike ['lʊkə,laɪk] N doble *mf*

looked-for ['lʊktfɔːʳ] ADJ esperado, deseado

looker* ['lʊkəʳ] N bombón* *f*

looker-on ['lʊkər'ɒn] N (*pl* **lookers-on**) espectador(a) *m/f*

look-in* ['lʊkɪn] N **to get a ~** (*Brit*) tener una oportunidad, tener chance (*LAm*); **we never got** *or* **had a ~** no nos dejaron participar; [*losers*] nunca tuvimos posibilidades de ganar

-looking ['lʊkɪŋ] ADJ (*ending in compounds*) **strange~** de aspecto raro; **mad~** con pinta de loco*

looking-glass† ['lʊkɪŋglɑːs] N (*frm*) espejo *m*

lookout ['lʊkaʊt] Ⓐ N [1] (= *act*) observación *f*, vigilancia *f*; **to keep a ~ for sth** ◊ **be on the ~ for sth** estar atento a *or* al acecho de algo; **keep a ~ for the postman** estáte atento por si viene el cartero; **to keep a sharp ~** estar ojo avizor

[2] (= *viewpoint*) mirador *m*; (= *person*) centinela *mf*; (= *place*) = **lookout post**

[3] (= *prospect*) perspectiva *f*; **it's a grim** *or* **poor ~ for us/for education** la perspectiva es desalentadora para nosotros/para la educación; **that's his ~!** ¡eso es asunto suyo!, ¡allá él!

Ⓑ CPD ► **lookout post** N atalaya *f*, puesto *m* de observación

look-see* ['lʊksiː] N vistazo *m*; **to have a ~** echar un vistazo

look-up ['lʊkʌp] Ⓐ N consulta *f*

Ⓑ CPD ► **look-up table** N tabla *f* de consulta

loom[1] [luːm] N (*for weaving*) telar *m*

loom[2] [luːm] VI [1] (*also* **~ up**) (= *appear*) surgir, aparecer; **the ship ~ed (up) out of the mist** el barco surgió de la neblina

[2] (= *threaten*) amenazar; **dangers ~ ahead** se vislumbran los peligros que hay por delante; **to ~ large** cernerse, pender amenazadoramente

LOOM N ABBR (*US*) (= **Loyal Order of Moose**) *asociación benéfica*

looming ['luːmɪŋ] ADJ [*danger*] que amenaza, inminente

loon [luːn] N [1] (*) (= *fool*) bobo/a *m/f*

[2] (= *bird*) somorjugo *m*

loony* ['luːnɪ] Ⓐ ADJ (*compar* **loonier**, *superl* **looniest**) loco, chiflado*

Ⓑ N loco/a *m/f*

Ⓒ CPD ► **loony bin** N manicomio *m* ► **the loony left** N (*Brit Pol pej*) la izquierda radical

loop [luːp] Ⓐ N [1] (*in string, ribbon*) lazo *m*, lazada *f*; (*Naut*) gaza *f*; (= *bend*) curva *f*, recodo *m*; **to knock sb for a ~** (*US**) dejar a algn pasmado

[2] (*Comput*) bucle *m*

[3] (*Elec*) circuito *m* cerrado

[4] (= *informed group*) **to be in the ~** estar en el grupo de gente informada; **to be out of the ~** estar fuera del grupo de gente informada

[5] (*Sew*) presilla *f*

[6] (*Aer*) rizo *m*; **to ~ the ~** hacer el rizo, rizar el rizo

Ⓑ VT **to ~ round** dar vuelta a; **to ~ a rope round a post** pasar una cuerda alrededor de un poste

Ⓒ VI [*rope, ribbon, cable*] formar un lazo; [*line, road*] serpentear

Ⓓ CPD ► **loop line** N (*Rail*) desviación *f*

loophole ['luːphəʊl] N [1] (*Mil*) aspillera *f*, tronera *f* [2] (*fig*) escapatoria *f*; (*in law*) laguna *f*, resquicio *m* legal; **every law has a ~** hecha la ley, hecha la trampa

loopy* ['luːpɪ] ADJ (*compar* **loopier**, *superl* **loopiest**) chiflado*

loose [luːs] Ⓐ ADJ (*compar* **looser**, *superl* **loosest**) [1] (= *not firmly attached*) [*thread, wire, screw, brick, page*] suelto; [*handle, knob*] desatornillado; [*tooth*] flojo, que se mueve; **this button is ~** este botón está a punto de caerse; **to come** *or* **get** *or* **work ~** [*thread, wire, brick*] soltarse; [*screw*] aflojarse; [*page*] desprenderse; [*knob, handle*] aflojarse, desatornillarse; *see also* **screw A1**, **connection 1**

[2] (= *not tied back*) [*hair*] suelto; **to wear one's hair ~** llevar el pelo suelto

[3] (= *not tight*) [*clothes*] holgado, amplio; [*bandage, tie*] flojo; **these trousers are too ~ round the waist** estos pantalones son muy anchos de cintura

[4] (= *not taut*) [*skin*] flácido, colgón*

[5] (= *not dense*) [*mixture, soil, powder*] suelto; **to be of a ~ consistency** tener poca consistencia

[6] (= *not tied up*) [*animal*] suelto; **he was chased by a ~ dog** le persiguió un perro que andaba suelto; **to let** *or* **set sth/sb ~** soltar algo/a algn; **when the cub had recovered it was set ~ in the wild** cuando el cachorro se recuperó lo soltaron *or* lo dejaron en libertad; **the affair has let ~ dangerous political forces** el asunto ha desatado fuerzas políticas peligrosas; **inexperienced doctors were let ~ on seriously ill patients** se dejó que médicos sin experiencia trataran a pacientes gravemente enfermos; *see also* **break C7**, **cut C1**, **hell A1**

[7] (= *flexible*) [*alliance, coalition, grouping*] libre; [*organization*] poco rígido; [*arrangement*] flexible; **a ~ confederation of sovereign republics** una confederación libre de repúblicas soberanas

[8] (= *imprecise*) [*meaning, expression*] poco preciso, vago; [*style, interpretation*] libre; [*translation*] aproximado; **he despised ~ thinking** odiaba toda forma de pensar vaga; **in ~ terms, it could be called a religion** haciendo un uso un tanto libre del término, podría llamarse religión

[9] (= *not packaged*) [*carrots, potatoes*] suelto, a granel; (*Comm*) **to buy/sell sth ~** vender algo suelto *or* a granel

[10] (†, *pej*) (= *immoral*) [*behaviour, attitudes*] disoluto; [*morals*] disoluto, libertino; **a ~ woman** una mujer de vida alegre (*pej*), una mujer fácil (†, *pej*); *see also* **living B2**

[11] (*Med*) **to have ~ bowels** tener el vientre suelto

[12] (= *readily available*) [*funds*] disponible; **~ cash** dinero *m* en efectivo; **~ change** dinero *m* suelto

Ⓑ VT [1] (*liter*) (= *release*) [+ *animal*] soltar; [+ *prisoner*] poner en libertad, soltar; **they ~d the dogs on him** le soltaron los perros

[2] (= *fire*) (*also* **~ off**) [+ *arrow, missile*] lanzar; [+ *gun, cannon*] disparar; **to ~ (off) a volley of abuse at sb** soltar una sarta de insultos a algn

[3] (= *unfasten*) **to ~ a boat from its moorings** soltar las amarras de un barco

Ⓒ N **to be on the ~** [*person, gang*] andar

suelto

Ⓓ ADV **stay** *or* **hang ~!** (*US**) ¡tranqui!*, ¡relájate!; *see also* **play**

Ⓔ CPD ► **loose box** N establo *m* móvil ► **loose cannon** N (*fig*) bomba *f* de relojería ► **loose chippings** NPL (*on roadway*) gravilla *fsing* suelta ► **loose connection** N (*Elec*) mala conexión *f* ► **loose cover** N (*Brit*) (*for furniture*) funda *f* lavable, funda *f* que se puede quitar ► **loose end** N (*fig*) cabo *m* suelto; **to tie up ~ ends** atar los cabos sueltos; **to be at a ~ end*** (*fig*) no saber qué hacer ► **loose scrum** N (*Rugby*) melé *f* abierta *or* espontánea ► **loose talk** N palabrería *f* ► **loose tongue** N **to have a ~ tongue** tener la lengua suelta, ser ligero de lengua ► **loose weave** N tejido *m* abierto

►**loose off** Ⓐ VT + ADV (*esp Brit*) [+ *ammunition, bullet*] disparar; **he ~d off two shots at the oncoming car** disparó dos tiros contra el coche que venía

Ⓑ VI + ADV **to ~ off at sb/sth** disparar a *or* contra algn/algo

loose-fitting ['lu:s'fɪtɪŋ] ADJ [*clothes*] holgado

loose-leaf ['lu:s'li:f] Ⓐ ADJ [*book*] de hojas sueltas

Ⓑ CPD ► **loose-leaf binder** N carpeta *f* de anillas ► **loose-leaf folder** N = **loose-leaf binder**

loose-limbed ['lu:s'lɪmd] ADJ ágil

loose-living ['lu:s'lɪvɪŋ] ADJ de vida airada, de vida inmoral

loosely ['lu:slɪ] ADV 1 (= *not tightly*) [*fasten, tie*] con un nudo flojo, ligeramente; [*hold*] sin apretar, ligeramente; **a ~ tied bandage** un vendaje poco apretado; **cover the dish ~ with foil** cubrir la fuente ligeramente con papel de plata; **to hang ~** [*arms*] colgar relajado; [*skin, flesh*] colgar fláccido; **his shirt hung ~ from his shoulders** la camisa le caía ancha de hombros

2 (= *not precisely*) [*translated*] libremente; **a novel ~ based on the life of Shakespeare** una novela basada, en términos generales, sobre la vida de Shakespeare; **it is ~ defined as ...** en términos generales se define como ..., sin ser muy precisos *or* rigurosos se define como ...; **~ speaking** hablando en términos generales; **what is ~ termed socialist realism** lo que se denomina, de forma poco precisa, realismo socialista

3 (= *informally*) [*organized, structured*] sin mucha rigidez, con bastante flexibilidad; **groups ~ connected to the Hizbollah movement** grupos *mpl* que tienen cierta conexión con el movimiento Hezbolá

loosen ['lu:sn] Ⓐ VT 1 (= *slacken*) aflojar; (= *untie*) desatar; **to ~ one's grip on sth** dejar de apretar algo con tanta fuerza

2 [+ *restrictions*] aflojar, reducir

Ⓑ VI (= *come unfastened*) soltarse, desatarse; (= *get slack*) aflojarse

►**loosen up** Ⓐ VI + ADV (*gen*) desentumecerse; (*before game*) desentumecer los músculos, entrar en calor; (*) (= *relax*) soltarse, relajarse; **to ~ up on sb** (*fig*) tratar a algn con menos severidad

Ⓑ VT + ADV [+ *muscles*] desentumecer

looseness ['lu:snɪs] N 1 (*gen*) [*of bandage, tie*] lo flojo; [*of clothes*] holgura *f*, amplitud *f*; [*of soil*] lo suelto; **~ of the bowels** (*Med*) diarrea *f*

2 (= *imprecision*) [*of meaning, expression*] imprecisión *f*; [*of translation*] lo aproximado

3 (= *immorality*) [*of behaviour, morals*] lo disoluto

loot [lu:t] Ⓐ N botín *m*, presa *f*; (*) (= *money*) pasta* *f*, plata *f* (*LAm**)

Ⓑ VT saquear

Ⓒ VI entregarse al saqueo

looter ['lu:tə^r] N saqueador(a) *m/f*

looting ['lu:tɪŋ] N saqueo *m*

lop [lɒp] VT 1 [+ *tree*] mochar, desmochar

2 (*also* **~ away, ~ off**) [+ *branches*] podar; (*fig*) cortar

lope [ləʊp] VI **to ~ along** andar a grandes zancadas, correr dando grandes zancadas; **to ~ off** alejarse con paso largo

lop-eared ['lɒp,ɪəd] ADJ de orejas caídas

lopsided ['lɒp'saɪdɪd] ADJ (*gen*) torcido, ladeado, chueco (*LAm*); [*table*] cojo; (*fig*) [*view*] desequilibrado

loquacious [lə'kweɪʃəs] ADJ (*frm*) locuaz

loquacity [lə'kwæsɪtɪ] N (*frm*) locuacidad *f*

lord [lɔ:d] Ⓐ N 1 (= *nobleman*) señor *m*; (= *British title*) lord *m*; **Lord (John) Smith** (*Brit*) Lord (John) Smith; **the (House of) Lords** (*Brit Pol*) la Cámara de los Lores; **my Lord** (*to bishop*) Ilustrísima; (*to noble*) señor; (*to judge*) señoría, señor juez; **my ~ bishop of Tooting** su Ilustrísima el obispo de Tooting; **~ of the manor** señor *m* feudal; **~ and master** dueño y señor

2 (*Rel*) **the Lord** el Señor; **Our Lord** Nuestro Señor; **good Lord!** ¡Dios mío!; **the Lord's Prayer** el padrenuestro; **Lord knows where ...!*** ¡Dios sabe dónde ...!

Ⓑ VT **to ~ it** mandar despóticamente; **to ~ it over sb*** ser muy mandón con algn

Ⓒ CPD ► **Lord Lieutenant** N *representante de la Corona en un condado* ► **Lord Mayor** N (*Brit*) alcalde *m* ► **Lord Mayor's Show** N (*Brit*) desfile *m* del alcalde de Londres (*el día de su inauguración*) ► **Lord Provost** N (*Scot*) alcalde *m*

LORD

El título de **Lord** *se les da a los miembros masculinos de la nobleza británica, especialmente a los marqueses, condes, vizcondes y barones, personas que ocupan un escaño en la Cámara de los Lores. El término forma parte también del nombre de algunos cargos oficiales: el* **Lord Chancellor** *es la máxima autoridad judicial en Inglaterra y Gales, el* **Lord Chief Justice** *es el cargo inmediatamente inferior, mientras que en Escocia el encargado del sistema judicial es el* **Lord Advocate**. *Por su parte, el* **Lord Chamberlain** *es el encargado del mantenimiento de las residencias oficiales de la realeza británica.*

lordliness ['lɔ:dlɪnɪs] N lo señorial, carácter *m* señorial; (*pej*) altivez *f*, arrogancia *f*

lordly ['lɔ:dlɪ] ADJ (*compar* **lordlier**; *superl* **lordliest**) [*house, vehicle*] señorial, señoril; [*manner*] altivo, arrogante; [*command*] imperioso

lords-and-ladies ['lɔ:dzənd'leɪdɪz] N (*Bot*) aro *m*

lordship ['lɔ:dʃɪp] N señoría *f*; **your Lordship** Señoría

lore [lɔ:^r] N saber *m* popular; **in local ~** según la tradición local; **he knows a lot about plant ~** sabe mucho de plantas

lorgnette [lɔ:'njet] N impertinentes *mpl*

Lorraine [lɒ'reɪn] N Lorena *f*

lorry ['lɒrɪ] (*Brit*) Ⓐ N camión *m*; **it fell off the back of a ~*** (*euph*) es de trapicheo*

Ⓑ CPD ► **lorry driver** N camionero/a *m/f* ► **lorry load** N carga *f*

lose [lu:z] (*pt, pp* **lost**) Ⓐ VT 1 (= *mislay, fail to find*) perder; **he's always losing things** siempre está perdiendo las cosas; **I've lost my pen** he perdido el bolígrafo; **I lost him in the crowd** lo perdí entre la muchedumbre

2 (= *be deprived of*) perder; **you've got nothing to ~** no tienes nada que perder; **you've nothing to ~ by helping him** no vas a perder nada ayudándole; **what have you got to ~?** ¿qué tienes tú que perder?, ¿qué vas a perder?; **he lost £1,000 on that deal** perdió 1.000 libras en ese trato; **I lost my father when I was ten** perdí a mi padre cuando tenía diez años; **I don't want to ~ you** no quiero perderte; **he's lost his licence** le han retirado el carnet; **to ~ one's life** perder la vida; **to ~ a patient** no lograr salvar a un paciente; **to ~ the use of an arm** perder el uso de un brazo; *see also* **breath A1**, **voice A1**

3 (= *fail to keep*) perder; **the poem lost a lot in the translation** el poema perdió mucho en la traducción; **she's lost her figure/her looks** ha perdido la línea/su belleza; ✦*IDIOM* **to ~ it*** perder los papeles, perder el control; *see also* **interest A1**, **rag¹ A1**, **sight A2**, **temper A1**

4 (= *fail to win*) [+ *game, war, election*] perder

5 (= *miss*) **to ~ one's way** (*lit*) perderse; (*fig*) perder el rumbo

6 (= *waste*) perder; **there was not a moment to ~** no había ni un momento que perder; **I wouldn't ~ any sleep over it!** ¡no pierdas el sueño por ello!, ¡no te preocupes por ello!; **to ~ no time in doing sth**: **she lost no time in making up her mind** se decidió enseguida, no le costó nada decidirse; **I lost no time in telling him exactly what I thought of him** no vacilé en decirle exactamente lo que pensaba de él

7 (*) (= *get rid of*) [+ *unwanted companion*] deshacerse de; [+ *pursuers*] zafarse de; **to ~ weight** perder peso, adelgazar; **I lost two kilos** perdí *or* adelgacé dos kilos

8 (= *fall behind*) [*watch, clock*] atrasarse; **this watch ~s five minutes every day** este reloj se atrasa cinco minutos cada día

9 (= *cause loss of*) **it lost him the job/the match** le costó el puesto/el partido, le hizo perder el puesto/el partido; **that deal lost me £5,000** ese negocio me costó *or* me hizo perder 5.000 libras

10 (*) (= *confuse*) confundir; **you've lost me there** ahora sí que me has confundido, ahora sí que no te entiendo

11 **to ~ o.s. in sth** (*a book, music, memories*) ensimismarse en algo

Ⓑ VI 1 [*player, team*] perder; **he's losing (by) two sets to one** va perdiendo (por) dos sets a uno; **they lost (by) three goals to two** perdieron (por) tres goles a dos; **to ~ to sb** perder contra algn; **you can't ~** no tienes pérdida, tienes que forzosamente salir ganando; **he lost on the deal** salió perdiendo en el negocio; **the story did not ~ in the telling** el cuento no perdió en la narración; **it ~s in translation** pierde en la traducción

2 [*watch, clock*] atrasarse

►**lose out** VI + ADV salir perdiendo; **you've never been in love? don't you think you've lost out on something?** ¿nunca has estado enamorada? ¿no piensas que te has perdido algo?; **in the long run CD-ROMs may ~ out to cable television** a largo plazo, es posible que los CD-ROMs vayan perdiendo mercado frente a la televisión por cable

loser ['lu:zə^r] N (= *person*) perdedor(a) *m/f*; (= *card*) carta *f* perdedora; **he's a born ~** siempre sale perdiendo, es un perdedor nato; **to**

be a bad ~ no saber perder, tener mal perder; **to be a good ~** saber perder, tener buen perder; **to come off the ~** salir perdiendo

losing ['lu:zɪŋ] Ⓐ ADJ perdedor; **the ~ team** el equipo perdedor; **to fight a ~ battle** luchar por una causa perdida; **she was fighting a ~ battle against her depression** luchaba en vano *or* sin éxito contra su depresión; **to be on the ~ side** estar en el lado de los perdedores *or* vencidos; **to be on a ~ streak** estar pasando por una racha de mala suerte; **to be on a ~ wicket*** (*fig*) llevar las de perder

Ⓑ N **losings** (= *money*) pérdidas *fpl*

loss [lɒs] Ⓐ N [1] [*of possessions, blood, sight*] pérdida *f*; **the factory closed with the ~ of 300 jobs** la fábrica cerró, con la pérdida de 300 puestos de trabajo; **it's your ~** el que sales perdiendo eres tú; **~ of appetite** pérdida *f* del apetito; **his death was a great ~ to the company** su muerte fue una gran pérdida para la empresa; **he's no great ~** no vamos a perder nada con su marcha; **the army suffered heavy ~es** el ejército sufrió pérdidas cuantiosas; **we want to prevent further ~ of life** queremos evitar que se produzcan más muertes *or* que se pierdan más vidas; **~ of memory** amnesia *f*, pérdida *f* de la memoria; **to feel a sense of ~** sentir un vacío; *see also* **hair B**, **heat D**, **job C**, **weight C**

[2] (*Fin, Comm*) pérdida *f*; **at a ~**: **the factory was operating at a ~** la fábrica estaba funcionando con pérdida de capital; **to sell sth at a ~** vender algo con pérdida; **the company made a ~ in 1999** la empresa tuvo un balance adverso en 1999; **the company made a ~ of £2 million** la empresa sufrió pérdidas de 2 millones de libras; **✦IDIOM to cut one's ~es** cortar por lo sano; *see also* **dead A5**, **profit D**

[3] (= *death*) pérdida *f*, muerte *f*; **our sadness at the ~ of a loved one** nuestra tristeza por la pérdida *or* muerte de un ser querido; **since the ~ of his wife** desde que perdió a su mujer, desde que falleció su mujer

[4] **✦IDIOM to be at a ~**: **they are at a ~ to explain how such a mistake could have been made** no se explican cómo se pudo haber cometido semejante error; **to be at a ~ for words** no encontrar palabras con qué expresarse; **he's never at a ~ for words** tiene mucha facilidad de palabra; **I was at a ~ (as to) what to do next** no sabía qué hacer después

Ⓑ CPD ► **loss adjuster** N (*Insurance*) ajustador(a) *m/f* de pérdidas, tasador(a) *m/f* de pérdidas ► **loss leader** N (*Comm*) artículo *m* de lanzamiento

lossmaker ['lɒs'meɪkəʳ] N (= *business*) negocio *m* nada rentable, negocio *m* deficitario; [*product*] producto *m* nada rentable

lossmaking ['lɒs,meɪkɪŋ] ADJ [*enterprise*] deficitario

lost [lɒst] Ⓐ PP, PT *of* **lose**

Ⓑ ADJ [1] (= *unable to find one's way*) perdido; **I'm ~** me he perdido, estoy perdido; **the ~ child was taken to the security desk** llevaron al niño perdido al mostrador de seguridad; **to get ~** [*person*] perderse; [*issue, fact*] olvidarse; **to tell sb to get ~*** mandar a algn al cuerno *or* a la porra‡; **get ~!*** ¡vete al cuerno!‡, ¡vete a la porra!‡; **✦IDIOM to be ~ for words** no tener palabras, no saber qué decir; **I had thought of so many things I wanted to say, but now I'm ~ for words** había tantas cosas que quería decir, pero ahora no tengo palabras; **I was ~ for words when I heard the news** me quedé mudo cuando me enteré de la noticia

[2] (= *missing, mislaid*) [*thing, animal*] perdido, extraviado; **he was looking for a ~ contact lens** buscaba una lentilla que se le había perdido; **to get ~** perderse, extraviarse; **to give sb up for ~** dar a algn por desaparecido; **to give sth up for ~** dar algo por perdido; **thousands of credit cards are reported ~ each day** cada día se denuncia la pérdida de miles de tarjetas de crédito; **she is ~ to us forever** (*fig*) la hemos perdido para siempre

[3] (= *bewildered*) perdido, desorientado; **I felt ~ and lonely in a strange town** me sentía perdido *or* desorientado y solo en una ciudad desconocida; **it's too difficult to understand, I'm ~** es demasiado difícil de entender, estoy perdido; **with a ~ expression/look** con la confusión pintada en el rostro

[4] (= *completely absorbed*) **to be ~ in sth** estar absorto en algo; **I was ~ in thought** estaba absorto en mis pensamientos; **she was ~ in the music** estaba absorta en la música; **to be ~ to the world** estar en otro mundo

[5] (= *wasted*) [*opportunity, income, output*] perdido; **to catch up on** *or* **make up for ~ time** recuperar el tiempo perdido; **to be ~ on sb**: **the message is often ~ on drug users** el mensaje a menudo no hace eco en los drogadictos; **the meaning of that was ~ on me** no entendí *or* no capté el significado de eso; **an irony/a fact which was not ~ on me** una ironía/un hecho que no se me escapaba

[6] (= *former*) [*youth, job, homeland*] perdido; **he pined for his ~ youth** suspiraba por su juventud perdida

[7] (= *vanished*) [*civilization*] desaparecido; [*skill, art*] desaparecido, perdido

[8] (= *not won*) [*battle, campaign, struggle*] perdido; **all is not ~!** ¡no se ha perdido todo!

[9] (= *dead*) **she grieved for her ~ son** lloraba al hijo que había perdido; **we are all ~!** (*liter*) ¡estamos perdidos!; **to be ~ at sea** desaparecer en el mar

[10] († *euph*) **~ woman** mujer *f* perdida

Ⓒ CPD ► **lost and found** N (*US*) = **lost property** ► **lost cause** N causa *f* perdida ► **the lost generation** N (*liter*) *generación de escritores a la que pertenecieron autores como Scott Fitzgerald y Hemingway y que produjeron sus obras después de la Primera Guerra Mundial* ► **lost property** N (= *belongings*) objetos *mpl* perdidos; (= *office*) oficina *f* de objetos perdidos ► **lost property office** N oficina *f* de objetos perdidos ► **lost sheep** N (*fig*) oveja *f* perdida, oveja *f* descarriada ► **lost soul** N alma *f* perdida

lost-and-found department ['lɒstən'faʊnddɪ,pɑ:tmənt] N (*US*) = **lost property office**

lot [lɒt] N [1] (= *large quantity*) **a ~ of money** mucho dinero; **a ~ of people** mucha gente; **we have ~s of flowers (that we don't want)** nos sobran flores, tenemos flores de sobra; **an awful ~ of things to do** la mar de cosas que hacer; **I'd give a ~ to know** me gustaría muchísimo saberlo; **quite/such a ~ of books** bastantes/tantos libros; **quite/such a ~ of noise** bastante/tanto ruido; **there wasn't a ~ we could do** apenas había nada que pudiéramos hacer

[2] **a ~** (*as adv*) mucho; **I read a ~** leo mucho; **we don't go out a ~** no salimos mucho; **things have changed a ~** las cosas han cambiado mucho; **he drinks an awful ~** bebe una barbaridad; **not a ~**: **"do you like football?" — "not a ~"** —¿te gusta el fútbol? —no mucho; **thanks a ~!** ¡muchísimas gracias!, ¡muy agradecido!

[3] **lots***: **~s of people** mucha gente, cantidad de gente*; **she has ~s of friends** tiene muchos amigos, tiene un montón de *or* (*LAm*) hartos amigos*; **he feels ~s better** se encuentra mucho mejor; **take as much as you want, I've got ~s** llévate cuanto quieras, tengo un montón *or* (*LAm*) harto(s)*

[4] (*) (= *group*) **a fine ~ of students** un buen grupo de estudiantes; **Melissa's friends? I don't like that ~** ¿los amigos de Melissa? no me cae bien ese grupo

[5] **the ~*** (= *all, everything*) todo; **he took the ~** se lo llevó todo; **that's the ~** eso es todo; **the (whole) ~ of them** todos; **big ones, little ones, the ~!** ¡los grandes, los pequeños, todos!

[6] (= *destiny*) suerte *f*, destino *m*; **his ~ was different** su suerte fue otra; **the common ~** la suerte común; **it fell to my ~ (to do sth)** me cayó en suerte (hacer algo); **it falls to my ~ to do it** me corresponde a mí hacerlo; **to throw in one's ~ with sb** unirse a la suerte de algn

[7] (= *random selection*) **to decide sth by ~** determinar algo por sorteo; **to draw ~s (for sth)** echar suertes (para algo)

[8] (*at auction*) lote *m*; **✦IDIOM he's a bad ~** es un mal sujeto; **I'll send it in three ~s** (*Comm*) se lo mando en tres paquetes *or* tandas

[9] (= *plot*) (*esp US*) terreno *m*, solar *m*; (*Cine*) solar *m*

[10] (= *share*) porción *f*, parte *f*; *see also* **fat A5**

loth [ləʊθ] ADJ = **loath**

lotion ['ləʊʃən] N loción *f*

lottery ['lɒtərɪ] N lotería *f*

lotto ['lɒtəʊ] N (= *game*) lotería *f*

lotus ['ləʊtəs] Ⓐ N loto *m*

Ⓑ CPD ► **lotus position** N postura *f* del loto

louche [lu:ʃ] ADJ [*person, place*] de mala fama

loud [laʊd] (*compar* **louder**; *superl* **loudest**) Ⓐ ADJ [1] (= *noisy*) [*music*] alto, fuerte; [*applause, noise, explosion, scream*] fuerte; **she has a ~ voice** tiene una voz muy fuerte; **in a ~ voice** en voz alta; **the music is too ~** la música está demasiado fuerte *or* alta; **he's a bit ~*** (*pej*) es un poco escandaloso; **to be ~ in one's support for sth** dar grandes muestras de apoyo a algo; **to be ~ in one's condemnation of sth** condenar algo enérgicamente

[2] (*pej*) (= *garish*) [*colour*] chillón, llamativo; [*pattern, clothes*] llamativo; **a ~ check jacket** una llamativa chaqueta de cuadros

Ⓑ ADV [*speak*] alto; [*laugh, shout*] fuerte; **you'll have to speak ~er** tendrás que hablar más fuerte *or* alto; **she likes to listen to her music ~** le gusta escuchar la música muy fuerte *or* alta; **"Nevermind" is one of those records you play ~** "Nevermind" es uno de esos discos que tienes que poner a todo volumen; **~ and clear**: **I am reading** *or* **receiving you ~ and clear** (*Telec*) te recibo perfectamente; **I hear you ~ and clear, but I don't agree** te entiendo perfectamente, pero no estoy de acuerdo; **out ~** [*think, wonder, read, laugh*] en voz alta; *see also* **cry out A**

loudhailer ['laʊd'heɪləʳ] N megáfono *m*

loudly ['laʊdlɪ] ADV [1] (= *not quietly*) [*say*] en voz alta; [*talk, speak*] alto, en voz alta; [*sing, shout, scream*] fuerte; [*laugh, knock*] con fuerza; [*complain, proclaim*] enérgicamente; **don't speak so ~!** ¡no hables tan alto!; **he cleared his throat ~** se aclaró la garganta ruidosamente; **a band that plays very ~ and badly** un grupo que toca muy alto y muy mal; **the audience applauded ~** el público aplaudió con fuerza; **she has been ~ applauded for ...** (*fig*) ha recibido grandes muestras de aprobación por …

[2] (= *garishly*) [*dress*] llamativamente

loudmouth* ['laʊdmaʊθ] N bocazas* *mf inv*

loudmouthed ['laʊd'maʊðd] ADJ bocazas*

loudness ['laʊdnɪs] N [1] [*of bang, explosion*] estrépito *m*; **we couldn't hear because of the ~ of the music** la música estaba tan alta que no nos dejaba oír

[2] [*of clothes, colour*] lo llamativo

loudspeaker ['laʊd'spiːkəʳ] N altavoz *m*, altoparlante *m* (*LAm*)

Louis ['luːɪ] N Luis

Louisiana [lʊ,iːziˈænə] N Luisiana *f*

lounge [laʊndʒ] Ⓐ N (*in house*) salón *m*, sala *f* de estar, living *m* (*LAm*); (*at airport*) sala *f*; (*on liner*) salón *m*

Ⓑ VI (= *be idle*) gandulear, pasar el rato sin hacer nada; **we spent a week lounging in Naples** pasamos una semana en Nápoles sin hacer nada; **to ~ against a wall** apoyarse distraídamente en una pared

Ⓒ CPD ► **lounge bar** N salón-bar *m* ► **lounge lizard*** N *persona a la que le gusta frecuentar lugares de postín* ► **lounge suit** N traje *m* de calle, terno *m* de calle (*LAm*)

►**lounge about**, **lounge around** VI + ADV gandulear, holgazanear

►**lounge back** VI + ADV **to ~ back in a chair** repanchigarse en un asiento

lounger ['laʊndʒəʳ] N gandul *m*, haragán/ana *m/f*

louse [laʊs] N (*pl* **lice**) [1] (= *insect*) piojo *m*

[2] (* *pej*) (= *person*) canalla* *mf*, sinvergüenza *mf*

►**louse up*** VT + ADV fastidiar, echar a perder

lousy ['laʊzɪ] ADJ (*compar* **lousier**; *superl* **lousiest**) [1] (= *louse-ridden*) piojoso

[2] (*) (= *very bad*) [*climate, food*] asqueroso*; [*secretary, driver*] malísimo, pésimo; **it was a ~ meal** fue una comida asquerosa; **I'm a ~ player** juego fatal*; **all for a few ~ quid** todo por unas cochinas libras*; **we had a ~ time** lo pasamos fatal*; **what a ~ trick!** ¡qué cerdada!*; **I feel ~** me siento fatal*

[3] **to be ~ with money**‡ (= *rich*) estar forrado*, estar podrido de dinero*

lout [laʊt] N gamberro *m*

loutish ['laʊtɪʃ] ADJ grosero, maleducado

Louvain ['luːveɪn] N Lovaina

louvre, **louver** (*US*) ['luːvəʳ] N (*Archit*) lumbrera *f*; (= *blind*) persiana *f*

louvred, **louvered** (*US*) ['luːvəd] ADJ [*shutters, windows*] de láminas, de listones

lovable ['lʌvəbl] ADJ adorable

▼**love** [lʌv] Ⓐ N [1] (= *affection*) [*of person*] amor *m*; **I no longer feel any ~ for** *or* **towards him** ya no siento amor *or* cariño por él; **it was ~ at first sight** fue amor a primera vista, fue un flechazo; **her ~ for** *or* **of her children** su amor *m* por sus hijos; **her children's ~ for her** el amor de sus hijos por ella; **don't give me any money, I'm doing it for ~** no me des dinero, lo hago por amor al arte (*hum*); **to marry for ~** casarse por amor; **for ~ of her son** ◊ **out of ~ for her son** por amor a su hijo, por el amor que le tiene/tenía a su hijo; **for the ~ of God** *or* **Mike!** ¡por el amor de Dios!; **to be/fall in ~ (with sb)** estar enamorado/enamorarse (de algn); **they are in ~ (with each other)** están enamorados (el uno del otro); **to make ~ (with/to sb)** (*euph*) (= *have sex*) hacer el amor (con algn); **to make ~ to sb**† (= *woo*) hacer la corte *or* el amor a algn; ✦***IDIOMS*** **there is no ~ lost between them** no se pueden ver; **I wouldn't do it for ~ nor money** no lo haría por nada del mundo; **it wasn't to be had for ~ nor money** era imposible conseguirlo

[2] (= *liking*) [*of activity, food, place*] afición *f*, pasión *f*; **her ~ of colour comes out in her garden** su afición *f or* pasión *f* por el colorido se refleja en su jardín; **he studies history for the ~ of it** estudia historia por pura afición

[3] (*in greetings, letters*) **(with) ~ (from) Jim** con cariño (de) Jim, besos (de) Jim; **all my ~, Jim** con todo mi cariño, Jim; **give him my ~** dale *or* mándale recuerdos míos; **lots of ~, Jim** muchos besos, Jim; **he sends (you) his ~** te da *or* manda recuerdos

[4] (= *person loved*) amor *m*; (= *thing loved*) pasión *f*; **she was my first ~** fue mi primer amor; **football was his first ~** el fútbol era su principal pasión; **the theatre was her great ~** el teatro era su gran pasión; **he was the ~ of her life** fue el amor de su vida

[5] (*as term of address*) cariño *m*; **yes, ~** sí, cariño; **thanks, ~** (*to woman*) gracias, guapa *or* (*Sp*) maja; (*to man*) gracias, guapo *or* (*Sp*) majo; (*to child*) gracias, cielo *or* cariño; **my ~** amor mío, mi vida

[6] (= *adorable person*) **he's a little ~** es un cielo, es un encanto; **be a ~ and make us a cup of tea** venga, cielo *or* cariño, prepáranos una taza de té

[7] (*Tennis*) **~ all** cero cero; **15 ~** 15 a cero

Ⓑ VT [1] (= *feel affection for*) querer, amar (*frm*); **you don't ~ me any more** ya no me quieres; **I ~d that boy as if he were my own son** quería a ese chico como si fuera mi hijo; **~ thy neighbour as thyself** ama al prójimo como a ti mismo (*frm*); **she ~s her children/her cat/that car** quiere mucho a *or* siente mucho cariño por sus hijos/su gato/ese coche; **she ~d him dearly** lo quería muchísimo, lo amaba profundamente; **I must ~ you and leave you** (*hum*) me despido que me tengo que marchar; **~ me, ~ my dog** quien quiere a Beltrán quiere a su can; **she ~s me, she ~s me not** me quiere, no me quiere

[2] (= *like very much*) **I ~ strawberries** me encantan las fresas; **I ~ Madrid** me encanta Madrid, me gusta muchísimo Madrid; **"would you like a drink?" — "I'd ~ one"** —¿quieres tomar algo? —¡sí, por favor!; **I'd ~ a beer** daría cualquier cosa por una cerveza; **he ~s swimming** ◊ **he ~s to swim** le encanta nadar, le gusta muchísimo nadar; **I'd ~ to come** me encantaría ir, me gustaría muchísimo ir; **I'd ~ to!** ¡con mucho gusto!, ¡yo, encantado!

Ⓒ CPD ► **love affair** N aventura *f* (sentimental), amorío *m*; (*fig*) pasión *f*; **her ~ affair with France began in 1836** su pasión por Francia comenzó en 1836; **she had a ~ affair with a younger man** tuvo una aventura (sentimental) *or* un amorío con un hombre más joven que ella ► **love child** N hijo/a *m/f* natural ► **love game** N (*Tennis*) juego *m* en blanco ► **love handles**‡ NPL agarraderas‡ *fpl* ► **love letter** N carta *f* de amor ► **love life** N (*emo- tional*) vida *f* sentimental; (*sexual*) vida *f* sexual; **how's your ~ life these days?** ¿qué tal te va la vida últimamente en el campo sentimental *or* romántico? ► **love match** N matrimonio *m* por amor ► **love nest** N nido *m* de amor ► **love potion** N filtro *m* (de amor), bebedizo *m* (de amor) ► **love seat** N confidente *m*, canapé *m* ► **love song** N canción *f* de amor ► **love story** N historia *f* de amor ► **love token** N prenda *f* de amor, prueba *f* de amor ► **love triangle** N triángulo *m* amoroso

LOVE

Love can usually be translated by **querer**.

• With people, pets and native lands, **querer** is the most typical translation:

I love you
Te quiero
Timmy loves his mother more than his father
Timmy quiere más a su madre que a su padre
When he lived abroad he realized how much he loved his country
Cuando vivió en el extranjero, se dio cuenta de lo mucho que quería a su país

• **Querer** is commonly used with **mucho** in statements like the following:

I love my parents
Quiero mucho a mis padres
He loved his cat and was very depressed when it died
Quería mucho a su gato y tuvo una gran depresión cuando murió

• Use **amar**, especially in formal language, to talk about spiritual or elevated forms of love:

To love God above everything else
Amar a Dios sobre todas las cosas
Their duty was to love and respect their parents
Su deber era amar y respetar a sus padres

• Use the impersonal **encantarle a uno** to talk about things and people that you like very much:

He loved playing tennis
Le encantaba jugar al tenis
I love children
(A mí) me encantan los niños

For further uses and examples, see main entry.

lovebird ['lʌvbɜːd] N periquito *m*; **lovebirds** (*fig*) (*hum*) palomitos *mpl*, tórtolos *mpl*

lovebite ['lʌv,baɪt] N mordisco *m* amoroso

-loved [lʌvd] ADJ (*ending in compounds*) **much~** muy querido; **best~** más querido

love-hate ['lʌvheɪt] CPD ► **love-hate relationship** N relación *f* de amor-odio

loveless ['lʌvlɪs] ADJ sin amor

loveliness ['lʌvlɪnɪs] N [*of woman*] hermosura *f*, belleza *f*; [*of thing, place, landscape*] belleza *f*; **a vision of ~** (*liter*) la viva imagen de la belleza

lovelorn ['lʌvlɔːn] ADJ *perdidamente enamorado y sin ser correspondido*; **to be ~** sufrir de mal de amores

lovely ['lʌvlɪ] ADJ (*compar* **lovelier**; *superl* **loveliest**) Ⓐ ADJ [1] (= *beautiful*) [*face, figure, thing*] precioso, muy bonito, lindo (*LAm*); [*woman*] hermoso, bello; [*day*] precioso, bueno; [*morning*] precioso, bonito; [*food, meal*] delicioso, riquísimo; **look at these ~ flowers!** ¡mira que flores más bonitas!; **the house was full of ~ things** la casa estaba llena de detalles preciosos, la casa estaba llena de detalles monísimos*; **she has two ~ sons** tiene dos hijos preciosos; **what ~ children/puppies!** ¡qué niños/cachorros tan preciosos!, ¡qué niños/cachorros más ricos *or* monos!*; **this is a ~ place for a holiday** este es un lugar precioso para venir de vacaciones; **it's a ~ day!** hace un día precioso *or* muy bueno; **it's a ~ day for a walk** hace un día precioso para dar un paseo; **it was a ~ sunny day** hacía un día de sol precioso; **we had a ~ day** pasamos un día muy agradable; **you look ~, Maria** estás preciosa, María; **it's ~ to see you again** que alegría volver a verte; **what a ~ surprise!** ¡qué sorpresa más agradable!; **what ~ weather!** ¡hace un tiempo estupendo *or* buenísimo!

➤ LANGUAGE IN USE: love B2 7.2, 8.3

2 (= *kind*) [*person, family, character*] encantador, amoroso (*LAm*); **he's got a ~ face** tiene una cara muy dulce; **you do say some ~ things** dices unas cosas preciosas
3 (*as intensifier*) **it's ~ and cool in here** hace un fresquito muy agradable aquí dentro; **it's ~ and hot/cold** [*drink, water*] está calentito/fresquito; [*air*] hace calorcito/fresquito
Ⓑ N (*, *liter, hum*) belleza *f*; **swim-suited lovelies** bellezas *fpl* en bañador

lovemaking ['lʌv,meɪkɪŋ] N (= *courting*) galanteo *m*; (= *sexual intercourse*) relaciones *fpl* sexuales

lover ['lʌvəʳ] Ⓐ N 1 (*sexually*) amante *mf*; (*romantically*) enamorado/a *m/f*; **the ~s** los amantes; **we were ~s for two years** durante dos años fuimos amantes; **he became her ~** se hizo su amante; **so she took a ~** así que se echó un amante
2 (= *fan*) aficionado/a *m/f*; **music ~** ◊ **~ of music** aficionado/a *m/f* a la música, amante *mf* de la música; **cinema ~s** los aficionados al cine, los amantes del cine; **he is a great ~ of the violin** es un gran aficionado al *or* amante del violín
Ⓑ CPD ► **lover boy** N (*hum, iro*) macho *m*

lovesick ['lʌvsɪk] ADJ enfermo de amor

lovestruck ['lʌvstrʌk] ADJ perdidamente enamorado

lovey-dovey* [,lʌvɪ'dʌvɪ] ADJ tierno, sentimental

loving ['lʌvɪŋ] Ⓐ ADJ cariñoso, tierno; **with ~ care** con amoroso cuidado; **~ kindness** bondad *f*; **(from) your ~ wife, Elizabeth**† (*in letters*) (de) tu esposa que te quiere, Elizabeth
Ⓑ CPD ► **loving cup** N copa *f* de la amistad (*que circula en una cena en que beben todos*)

-loving ['lʌvɪŋ] ADJ (*ending in compounds*) **money~** amante del dinero, aficionado al dinero

lovingly ['lʌvɪŋlɪ] ADV 1 (= *affectionately*) [*look, speak*] cariñosamente, tiernamente; (*stronger*) amorosamente
2 (= *carefully*) [*cook, prepare, inscribe*] con cariño; **~ restored** cuidadosamente restaurado

low[1] [ləʊ] Ⓐ ADJ (*compar* **lower**; *superl* **lowest**)
1 (*in height*) [*wall, shelf, seat, level*] bajo; [*bow*] profundo; [*blow*] sucio; **on ~ ground** a nivel del mar, en tierras bajas; **a dress with a ~ neckline** un vestido escotado
2 (= *quiet*) [*voice, TV, radio*] bajo
3 (= *low-pitched*) [*voice, musical note*] grave, bajo
4 [*number*] bajo; [*price, income*] reducido, bajo; [*stock, supplies*] escaso; **five at the ~est** cinco como mínimo; **the battery is ~** la batería se está acabando; **fuel is getting ~** está empezando a escasear la gasolina; **stocks are running ~** las existencias empiezan a escasear
5 (*in intensity*) [*light, rate, speed, temperature*] bajo; **the temperature is in the ~ 40s** la temperatura es de 40 grados y alguno más; **to cook on a ~ heat** cocer a fuego lento
6 (= *inferior*) [*standard, quality*] inferior
7 (= *humble*) [*rank*] humilde; [*card*] pequeño
8 (*Aut*) **in ~ gear** en primera *or* segunda
9 [*health*] débil, malo; [*diet*] deficiente; **to feel ~** ◊ **be ~ in spirits** sentirse deprimido, estar bajo de moral
10 [*character, behaviour, opinion*] malo; [*comedian*] grosero; [*character*] vil; [*joke, song*] verde; [*trick*] sucio, malo; *see also* **tide 1**
Ⓑ ADV (*compar* **lower**; *superl* **lowest**) 1 [*aim, fly, sing*] bajo; [*swing*] bajo, cerca de la tierra; **to bow ~** hacer una reverencia profunda; **a dress cut ~ in the back** un vestido muy escotado de espalda; **to fall ~** (*fig*) caer bajo; **England never fell so ~** Inglaterra nunca cayó tan bajo; **to be laid ~ with flu** ser postrado por la gripe; **to lay sb ~** derribar a algn, poner a algn fuera de combate; **to lie ~** (= *hide*) mantenerse escondido; (= *be silent*) mantenerse quieto; **to sink ~** (*fig*) caer bajo
2 [*quietly*] [*say, sing*] bajo, en voz baja
3 **to turn the lights/the volume down ~** bajar las luces/el volumen
4 (*Cards*) **to play ~** poner pequeño
Ⓒ N 1 (*Meteo*) área *f* de baja presión
2 (*Aut*) primera *or* segunda (marcha) *f*
3 (*fig*) (= *low point*) punto *m* más bajo; **to reach a new** *or* **an all-time ~** estar más bajo que nunca; **this represents a new ~ in deceit** ésta es la peor forma de vileza; *see also* **all-time**
Ⓓ CPD ► **low beam headlights** NPL (*US*) luces *fpl* de cruce ► **Low Church** N *sector de la Iglesia Anglicana de tendencia más protestante* ► **low comedy** N farsa *f* ► **the Low Countries** NPL los Países Bajos ► **Low Latin** N bajo latín *m* ► **low mass** N misa *f* rezada ► **low point** N punto *m* (más) bajo ► **low salt** N sal *f* dietética ► **low season** N (*esp Brit*) temporada *f* baja ► **Low Sunday** N Domingo *m* de Cuasimodo ► **low tide** N marea *f* baja ► **low vowel** N vocal *f* grave ► **low water** N bajamar *f* ► **low water mark** N línea *f* de bajamar

low[2] [ləʊ] Ⓐ VI mugir
Ⓑ N mugido *m*

low-alcohol ['ləʊ'ælkəhɒl] ADJ con baja graduación

lowborn ['ləʊ'bɔːn] ADJ de humilde cuna

lowbrow ['ləʊbraʊ] Ⓐ ADJ poco culto
Ⓑ N persona *f* nada intelectual, persona *f* de poca cultura

low-budget [,ləʊ'bʌdʒɪt] ADJ de bajo presupuesto; **~ film** película *f* de presupuesto modesto

low-cal* [,ləʊ'kæl] ADJ = **low-calorie**

low-calorie [,ləʊ'kælərɪ] ADJ [*diet, menu, food*] bajo en calorías, con pocas calorías; [*beer, cola*] light *inv*

low-class ['ləʊ,klɑːs] ADJ de clase baja

low-cost ['ləʊ'kɒst] ADJ económico

low-cut ['ləʊ'kʌt] ADJ [*dress*] escotado

low-density [,ləʊ'densɪtɪ] ADJ de baja densidad

low-down ['ləʊdaʊn] Ⓐ N (*) informes *mpl* confidenciales; **he gave me the ~ on it** me contó todo sobre el tema; **come on, give us the ~** venga, cuéntanos todo lo que sabes
Ⓑ ADJ rastrero, bajo

lower[1] ['ləʊəʳ] Ⓐ ADJ *see also* **low** 1 (= *bottom*) [*part, section, floors, windows*] de abajo, inferior; [*slopes*] inferior, bajo; **the ~ of the two** el de más abajo de los dos; **the ~ bunk** la litera de abajo; **the ~ left corner** la esquina inferior izquierda; **the ~ half/part of** la mitad/parte inferior de, la mitad/parte de abajo de
2 (= *less important*) [*level, rank, caste*] inferior; **the ~ chamber** (*Parl*) la cámara baja; **the ~ court** (*Jur*) los tribunales inferiores; **the ~ middle class(es)** la clase media baja; **a ~ middle-class family** una familia de clase media baja; **soldiers in the ~ ranks** soldados *mpl* de menor rango *or* de rango inferior; **the ~ school** el segundo ciclo
3 (*Anat*) inferior; **the ~ abdomen/back** la parte inferior del abdomen/de la espalda; **she suffered severe cuts on her ~ leg** sufrió cortes de gravedad en la parte inferior de la pierna; **the ~ limbs** los miembros inferiores
4 (*Zool*) inferior
5 (*Geog*) (*in names*) **Lower Egypt** el Bajo Egipto; **the Lower Rhine** el Bajo Rin; **~ Manhattan** el sur de Manhattan; *see also* **reach C2**
Ⓑ VT (*gen*) bajar; [+ *boat*] echar al agua; [+ *flag, sail*] arriar; (= *reduce*) [+ *price*] bajar, rebajar; **to ~ o.s.** (*fig*) rebajarse; **I wouldn't ~ myself to do such a thing** no me rebajaría a hacer algo así; **to ~ one's guard** bajar la guardia; **to ~ one's headlights** (*US*) poner las luces de cruce; **to ~ one's voice** bajar la voz
Ⓒ VI bajar
Ⓓ CPD ► **lower case** N (*Typ*) minúsculas *fpl*; **in ~ case** en minúsculas; *see also* **lower-case** ► **lower class** N **the ~ class** *or* **classes** la clase baja; *see also* **lower-class** ► **lower deck** N [*of bus*] piso *m* de abajo; (*Naut*) (= *part of ship*) cubierta *f* inferior; **the ~ deck*** (= *personnel*) los marineros ► **the Lower House** N (*Parl*) la Cámara Baja ► **lower vertebrates** NPL vertebrados *mpl* inferiores

lower[2] ['laʊəʳ] VI [*person*] fruncir el entrecejo, fruncir el ceño; [*sky*] encapotarse

lower-case ['ləʊə,keɪs] ADJ minúsculo; **~ letter** minúscula *f*; *see also* **lower**[1] **D**

lower-class ['ləʊə,klɑːs] ADJ de (la) clase baja; **a ~ family** una familia de clase baja

lowering ['laʊərɪŋ] ADJ [*expression, glance*] ceñudo; [*sky*] encapotado

lowest ['ləʊɪst] Ⓐ ADJ SUPERL of **low**
Ⓑ N **activity is at its ~** las actividades están en su punto más bajo
Ⓒ CPD ► **lowest common denominator** N (*Math*) mínimo común denominador *m*; (*fig*) **to appeal to the ~ common denominator** dirigirse al estrato social más bajo ► **lowest common multiple** N mínimo común múltiplo *m*

low-fat ['ləʊ'fæt] Ⓐ ADJ [*margarine, cheese*] bajo en grasas; [*milk, yoghurt*] desnatado
Ⓑ CPD ► **low-fat foods** NPL alimentos *mpl* bajos en grasas

low-flying ['ləʊ,flaɪɪŋ] ADJ que vuela bajo

low-grade ['ləʊ,greɪd] ADJ de baja calidad

low-heeled ['ləʊ'hiːld] ADJ [*shoes*] bajos, de tacón bajo

lowing ['ləʊɪŋ] N mugidos *mpl*

low-key* [,ləʊ'kiː] ADJ discreto

lowland ['ləʊlənd] Ⓐ N tierra *f* baja; **the Lowlands** las tierras bajas de Escocia
Ⓑ ADJ de tierra baja

lowlander ['ləʊləndəʳ] N habitante *mf* de tierra baja

low-level ['ləʊ'levl] Ⓐ ADJ de bajo nivel
Ⓑ CPD ► **low-level language** N (*Comput*) lenguaje *m* de bajo nivel

low-life ['ləʊlaɪf] Ⓐ N bajos fondos *mpl*
Ⓑ ADJ de los bajos fondos

lowlights ['ləʊlaɪts] NPL 1 (*Hairdressing*) reflejos *mpl* oscuros, mechas *fpl* oscuras
2 (*gen hum*) [*of TV programme, football match*] momentos *mpl* más aburridos

lowliness ['ləʊlɪnɪs] N humildad *f*

low-loader [,ləʊ'ləʊdəʳ] N (*Aut*) camión *m* de plataforma de carga baja

lowly ['ləʊlɪ] ADJ (*compar* **lowlier**; *superl* **lowliest**) humilde

low-lying ['ləʊ,laɪɪŋ] ADJ bajo

low-minded ['ləʊ'maɪndɪd] ADJ vil, mezquino

low-necked ['ləʊ'nekt] ADJ escotado

lowness ['ləʊnɪs] N [*of shelf, voice, number, temperature*] lo bajo; [*of note*] lo grave; [*of stocks, supplies*] escasez *f*; [*of rank*] lo bajo; [*of character*] vileza *f*, bajeza *f*; [*of joke, song*] lo verde; **~ of spirits** abatimiento *m*

low-paid [,ləʊ'peɪd] Ⓐ ADJ [*work*] mal pagado; (*more frm*) de baja remuneración; [*worker*] mal pagado; (*more frm*) mal remunerado

Ⓑ NPL **the ~** los mal pagados *or* (*more frm*) remunerados

low-pitched [ˈləʊpɪtʃt] ADJ [*note, voice*] bajo; [*campaign, speech*] en tono menor

low-powered [ˈləʊpaʊəd] ADJ de baja potencia

low-pressure [ˈləʊˈpreʃəʳ] ADJ de baja presión

low-priced [ˌləʊˈpraɪst] ADJ barato, económico

low-profile [ˈləʊˈprəʊfaɪl] ADJ [*activity*] discreto

low-ranking [ˌləʊˈræŋkɪŋ] ADJ (*Mil*) [*official*] de baja graduación

low-rent [ˈləʊrent] ADJ [1] (*lit*) [*housing, flat*] de renta baja, de alquiler bajo
[2] (*fig*) (*) de tres al cuarto*, de pacotilla*

low-rise [ˈləʊraɪz] ADJ de baja altura

low-risk [ˌləʊˈrɪsk] ADJ de bajo riesgo

low-slung [ˈləʊslʌŋ] ADJ [*chair*] con el asiento bajo; [*sports car*] con el suelo bajo

low-spirited [ˈləʊˈspɪrɪtɪd] ADJ desanimado

low-tech [ˈləʊtek] ADJ de tecnología poco avanzada

low-tension [ˈləʊˈtenʃən] ADJ de baja tensión

Loya Jirga [ˌlɔːjəˈdʒɜːgə] N (*in Afghanistan*) Loya Jirga *f*

loyal [ˈlɔɪəl] Ⓐ ADJ [*friend, subject, employee, wife, supporter*] leal, fiel; [*customer, reader*] fiel; **a ~ servant of the Party** un leal *or* fiel servidor del partido; **he has a ~ following** tiene seguidores leales *or* fieles; **to be/remain ~ to** [+ *leader, government*] ser/permanecer leal a; [+ *beliefs, principles*] ser/permanecer fiel a
Ⓑ CPD ► **the loyal toast** N (*Brit*) *el brindis por el rey/la reina*

loyalist [ˈlɔɪəlɪst] N (*gen*) partidario/a *m/f* del régimen; (*in Spain 1936*) republicano/a *m/f*; (*N Irl Pol*) unionista *mf*; **~ paramilitaries** (*in Northern Ireland*) paramilitares *mpl* unionistas

loyally [ˈlɔɪəlɪ] ADV lealmente, fielmente; **she ~ continued to support her husband** continuó apoyando lealmente *or* fielmente a su marido

loyalty [ˈlɔɪəltɪ] Ⓐ N [1] (= *quality*) (*to leader, government*) lealtad *f* (**to** a); (*to beliefs, principles*) fidelidad *f* (**to** a)
[2] (*often pl*) (= *feeling*) **he has divided loyalties** tiene un conflicto de lealtades; **she is a woman of fierce loyalties** es una mujer muy leal
Ⓑ CPD ► **loyalty card** N (*Brit Comm*) *tarjeta que reparten los hipermercados a sus clientes, mediante la que se acumulan puntos u otras ventajas*

lozenge [ˈlɒzɪndʒ] N [1] (*Med*) pastilla *f*
[2] (*Math*) rombo *m*; (*Heraldry*) losange *m*

LP N ABBR (*Mus*) ABBR (= **long-playing record**) elepé *m*

L-plate [ˈelpleɪt] N (placa *f* de) la L; → DRIVING LICENCE/DRIVER'S LICENSE

LPN N ABBR (*US Med*) (= **Licensed Practical Nurse**) *enfermero/a practicante*

LPU N ABBR (= **least publishable unit**) cuanto *m* de publicación

LRAM N ABBR (*Brit*) = **Licentiate of the Royal Academy of Music**

LRCP N ABBR (*Brit*) = **Licentiate of the Royal College of Physicians**

LRCS N ABBR (*Brit*) = **Licentiate of the Royal College of Surgeons**

LSAT N ABBR (*US Univ*) = **Law School Admission Test**

LSD N ABBR [1] (*Drugs*) (= **lysergic acid diethylamide**) LSD *m* [2] (*Brit*) (*formerly*) = **librae, solidi, denarii** (= *pounds, shillings and pence*) *antigua moneda británica*

LSE N ABBR (*Brit*) = **London School of Economics**

LSI N ABBR = **large-scale integration**

LST N ABBR (*US*) = **Local Standard Time**

LT ABBR (*Elec*) = **low tension**

Lt ABBR (= **lieutenant**) Tte

Lt.-Col. ABBR = **lieutenant-colonel**

Ltd ABBR (*Brit Comm etc*) (= **limited**) S.A.

Lt.-Gen. ABBR = **lieutenant-general**

lubricant [ˈluːbrɪkənt] Ⓐ ADJ lubricante
Ⓑ N lubricante *m*

lubricate [ˈluːbrɪkeɪt] VT lubricar, engrasar

lubricating [ˈluːbrɪkeɪtɪŋ] Ⓐ ADJ lubricante
Ⓑ CPD ► **lubricating oil** N aceite *m* lubricante

lubrication [ˌluːbrɪˈkeɪʃən] N (*Aut*) lubricación *f*, engrase *m*

lubricator [ˈluːbrɪkeɪtəʳ] N lubricador *m*

lubricious [luːˈbrɪʃəs] ADJ (*frm or liter*) (= *lewd*) lascivo

lubricity [luːˈbrɪsɪtɪ] N (*frm or liter*) (= *lewdness*) lascivia *f*

Lucan [ˈluːkən] N Lucano

lucerne [luːˈsɜːn] N (*esp Brit*) alfalfa *f*

lucid [ˈluːsɪd] ADJ lúcido; **~ interval** intervalo *m* de lucidez

lucidity [luːˈsɪdɪtɪ] N lucidez *f*

lucidly [ˈluːsɪdlɪ] ADV claramente, con claridad

Lucifer [ˈluːsɪfəʳ] N Lucifer

▼**luck** [lʌk] N suerte *f*; **some people have all the ~** los hay con suerte, algunos parece que nacen de pie*; **I couldn't believe my ~** no me podía creer la suerte que tenía; **good/bad ~** buena/mala suerte *f*; **good ~!** ¡(buena) suerte!; **bad** *or* **hard** *or* **tough ~!** ¡(qué) mala suerte!, ¡qué pena!; **to bring (sb) (good) ~/bad ~** traer buena/mala suerte (a algn); **to have the (good) ~/bad ~ to do sth** tener la (buena) suerte/mala suerte de hacer algo; **it's good/bad ~ to see a black cat** cruzarse con un gato negro trae buena/mala suerte; **any ~?** ¿hubo suerte?; **beginner's ~** suerte *f* del principiante; **best of ~!** ¡muchísima suerte!, ¡que tengas suerte!; **and the best of ~!** (*iro*) ¡Dios te la depare buena! (*iro*); **better next time!** ¡a la tercera va la vencida!; **that was a bit of ~!** ¡eso fue un golpe de suerte!; **for ~: to keep sth for ~** guardar algo por si trae suerte; **once more for ~!** ¡una vez más por si trae suerte!; **I think this is going to be a great photo, I'll take one more for ~** creo que éste va a ser una foto bonita, tomaré una más por si acaso; **as ~ would have it ...** quiso la suerte que ...; **his ~ held and no one detected him** siguió con su racha de buena suerte y nadie lo descubrió; **here's ~!** (*in toast*) ¡salud!; **to be in ~** estar de *or* con suerte; **it would be just my ~ to meet the boss** mira que toparme con el jefe ... ¡sólo me pasan a mí estas cosas!; **knowing my ~** con la suerte que tengo; **no such ~!** ¡ojalá!; **if it's money you want you're out of ~** si lo que quieres es dinero, me temo que no estás de suerte; **to push one's ~** tentar a la suerte; **to have ~ on one's side** tener la suerte de su parte; **~ was on their side** la suerte estaba de su parte; **that was a stroke of ~!** ¡eso fue un golpe de suerte!; **to trust to ~** hacer las cosas a la buena de Dios; **wish me ~!** ¡deséame suerte!; **I wish them all the ~ in the world** les deseo toda la suerte del mundo; **with (any) ~** con (un poco de) suerte; **worse ~** desgraciadamente; ✦**IDIOMS** **to have the ~ of the devil** ◊ **have the devil's own ~** tener la suerte de los tontos; **it's the ~ of the draw** es cuestión de suerte; **to be down on one's ~** estar de mala racha; *see also* **try B5**

►**luck out*** VI + ADV (*US*) tener un golpe de suerte

luckily [ˈlʌkɪlɪ] ADV afortunadamente, por suerte; **~ for me, he believed my story** afortunadamente *or* por suerte para mí, creyó mi historia

luckless [ˈlʌklɪs] ADJ desdichado, desafortunado

lucky [ˈlʌkɪ] (*compar* **luckier**; *superl* **luckiest**) Ⓐ ADJ [1] (= *fortunate*) [*person*] afortunado, suertudo (*esp LAm**); [*coincidence, shot*] afortunado; **he's a ~ chap** es un tipo afortunado *or* con suerte; **it was just a ~ guess** acerté de casualidad; **to be ~** [*person*] tener suerte; **I'm ~ to have** *or* **in having an excellent teacher** tengo la suerte de tener un profesor excelente; **he is ~ to be alive** tiene suerte de seguir vivo; **he will be ~ to get £5 for it** con mucha suerte conseguirá 5 libras por ello; **he was ~ that I didn't kill him** tuvo suerte de que no lo matara; **it's ~ (that) it didn't rain** es una suerte *or* menos mal que no haya llovido; **it was ~ for them that ...** afortunadamente para ellos ...; **she's very ~ at cards** tiene mucha suerte jugando a las cartas; **to be born ~** nacer con suerte; **a ~ break** un golpe de suerte; **it's your ~ day** es tu día de suerte; **~ devil!*** ¡qué suertudo!*; **he was ~ enough to get a seat** tuvo la suerte de conseguir un sitio; **to have a ~ escape** salvarse de milagro; **to get ~*** tener suerte; **to be ~ in life** tener suerte en la vida, tener buena estrella*; **to be ~ in love** tener suerte *or* ser afortunado en el amor; **who's the ~ man/woman?*** ¿quién es el afortunado/la afortunada?; **you should be so ~!*** ¡ya quisieras!*, ¡ojalá!*; **~ winner** afortunado/a ganador(a) *m/f*; **~ (old) you!*** ¡qué suerte!, ¡vaya *or* menuda suerte la tuya!*; **you'll be ~!*** ¡sería un milagro!*; *see also* **count B3, strike B6, third A**
[2] (= *bringing luck*) [*number, shirt*] de la suerte; **seven is his ~ number** el siete es su número de la suerte; **a ~ rabbit's foot** un amuleto de pata de conejo; **~ charm** amuleto *m*; *see also* **star A1**
Ⓑ CPD ► **lucky dip** N (*Brit*) (*at fair*) caja *f* de las sorpresas; (*fig*) **taking in lodgers can be something of a ~ dip** tener inquilinos es un poco una lotería

lucrative [ˈluːkrətɪv] ADJ lucrativo

lucre [ˈluːkəʳ] N (= *profit*) lucro *m*; **filthy ~** (*hum*) el vil metal

Lucretia [luːˈkriːʃə] N Lucrecia

Lucretius [luːˈkriːʃəs] N Lucrecio

lucubration [ˌluːkjʊˈbreɪʃən] N lucubración *f*

Lucy [ˈluːsɪ] N Lucía

Luddite [ˈlʌdaɪt] Ⓐ ADJ ludita, ludista
Ⓑ N ludita *mf*, ludista *mf*

ludic [ˈluːdɪk] ADJ lúdico

ludicrous [ˈluːdɪkrəs] ADJ ridículo, absurdo

ludicrously [ˈluːdɪkrəslɪ] ADV ridículamente, absurdamente

ludo [ˈluːdəʊ] N (*Brit*) ludo *m*

luff [lʌf] Ⓐ N orza *f*
Ⓑ VI orzar

luffa [ˈlʌfə] N (*US*) esponja *f* de lufa

lug* [lʌg] Ⓐ VT (= *drag*) arrastrar, jalar (*LAm*); (= *carry*) cargar (*con trabajo*); **I've been ~ging this camera around with me all day** llevo cargando con esta cámara todo el día; **they ~ged him off to the theatre** lo llevaron a rastras al teatro; **he ~ged the cases upstairs** llevó a rastras las maletas al piso de arriba
Ⓑ N [1] (= *projecting part*) oreja *f*, agarradera *f*; (*Tech*) orejeta *f*
[2] (*) (= *ear*) oreja *f*

➤ LANGUAGE IN USE: **luck** 23.5

3 (= *loop*) (*on harness*) *lazada de cuero de los arreos*
4 = **lugsail**

luggage [ˈlʌgɪdʒ] Ⓐ N equipaje *m*
Ⓑ CPD ► **luggage boot** N (*Brit Aut*) maletero *m*, portaequipajes *m inv* ► **luggage car** N (*US*) = **luggage van** ► **luggage carrier** N portaequipajes *m inv*, baca *f* ► **luggage check-room** N (*US*) consigna *f* ► **luggage grid** N = **luggage carrier** ► **luggage handler** N despachador(a) *m/f* de equipaje ► **luggage label** N etiqueta *f* de equipaje ► **luggage locker** N consigna *f* automática ► **luggage rack** N (*on train etc*) rejilla *f*, redecilla *f*; (*Aut*) baca *f*, portaequipajes *m inv* ► **luggage van** N (*Brit*) furgón *m* de equipajes

lugger [ˈlʌgəʳ] N lugre *m*

lughole* [ˈlʌgəʊl] N oreja *f*; (= *inner ear*) oído *m*

lugsail [ˈlʌgsl] N vela *f* al tercio

lugubrious [luːˈguːbrɪəs] ADJ lúgubre

lugubriously [luːˈguːbrɪəslɪ] ADV lúgubremente

lugworm [ˈlʌg,wɜːm] N lombriz *f* de tierra

Luke [luːk] N Lucas

lukewarm [ˈluːkwɔːm] ADJ 1 (= *slightly warm*) [*water, food, coffee*] tibio
2 (*fig*) [*reception, applause, support*] tibio, poco entusiasta; **the report was given a ~ reception** el informe tuvo una tibia acogida *or* una acogida poco entusiasta; **he was ~ about the idea** no le entusiasmaba la idea

lull [lʌl] Ⓐ N (*in storm, wind*) pausa *f*, momento *m* de calma; (*in fighting, bombardment*) tregua *f*; (*in activity*) respiro *m*, pausa *f*; **during a ~ in the conversation** en una pausa de la conversación; ✦***IDIOM*** **this was just the ~ before the storm** esto era sólo la calma que precede a la tempestad
Ⓑ VT [+ *person*] calmar; [+ *fears*] calmar, sosegar; **to ~ sb to sleep** arrullar a algn, adormecer a algn; ✦***IDIOM*** **he was ~ed into a false sense of security** se le inspiró un falso sentimiento de seguridad

lullaby [ˈlʌləbaɪ] N canción *f* de cuna, nana *f*

lumbago [lʌmˈbeɪgəʊ] N lumbago *m*

lumbar [ˈlʌmbəʳ] ADJ lumbar

lumber¹ [ˈlʌmbəʳ] Ⓐ N 1 (= *wood*) (*esp US*) maderos *mpl*
2 (*esp Brit**) (= *junk*) trastos *mpl* viejos
Ⓑ VT 1 (*Brit**) (= *encumber*) **to ~ sb with sth** hacer que algn cargue con algo, endilgar algo a algn; **he got ~ed with the job** le endilgaron el trabajo; **I got ~ed with the girl for the afternoon** tuve que cargar toda la tarde con la chica, me endilgaron a la chica toda la tarde
2 (= *fill*) [+ *space, room*] **to ~ sth with sth** atiborrar algo de algo
Ⓒ VI cortar y aserrar árboles, explotar los bosques
Ⓓ CPD ► **lumber company** N empresa *f* maderera ► **lumber jacket** N chaqueta *f* de leñador ► **lumber mill** N aserradero *m* ► **lumber room** N trastero *m* ► **lumber yard** N (*US*) almacén *m* de madera

lumber² [ˈlʌmbəʳ] VI (*also* **~ about**) moverse pesadamente; (*also* **~ along**) avanzar pesadamente

lumbering¹ [ˈlʌmbərɪŋ] N (*US*) explotación *f* forestal

lumbering² [ˈlʌmbərɪŋ] ADJ [*gait, run*] pesado, torpe

lumberjack [ˈlʌmbədʒæk] N leñador(a) *m/f*

lumberman [ˈlʌmbəmən] N (*pl* **lumbermen**) = **lumberjack**

luminary [ˈluːmɪnərɪ] N lumbrera *f*

luminescence [,luːmɪˈnesns] N luminescencia *f*

luminosity [,luːmɪˈnɒsɪtɪ] N luminosidad *f*

luminous [ˈluːmɪnəs] ADJ luminoso

lumme†* [ˈlʌmɪ] EXCL (*Brit*) = **lummy**

lummox* [ˈlʌməks] N (*US*) bobo/a* *m/f*

lummy†* [ˈlʌmɪ] EXCL (*Brit*) ¡caray!*

lump [lʌmp] Ⓐ N [*of sugar*] terrón *m*; [*of cheese, earth, clay, ice*] trozo *m*, pedazo *m*; (= *swelling*) bulto *m*, hinchazón *f*; (*on surface*) bulto *m*, protuberancia *f*; (= *person*) (**pej*) zoquete* *mf*; **he had a nasty ~ on his head** tenía un buen chichón en la cabeza; **with a ~ in one's throat** con un nudo en la garganta; **I get a ~ in my throat** se me hace un nudo en la garganta
Ⓑ VT (*) (= *endure*) aguantar; **if he doesn't like it he can ~ it** si no le gusta que se aguante
Ⓒ CPD ► **lump sugar** N azúcar *m* en terrones ► **lump sum** N cantidad *f or* suma *f* global

►**lump together** VT + ADV [+ *things*] amontonar; [+ *persons*] agrupar; **these problems can't be ~ed together under any one heading** estos problemas no pueden agruparse *or* englobarse bajo el mismo encabezamiento; **excellent wine is ~ed together with plonk** un vino excelente aparece junto a un vino peleón

lumpen [ˈlʌmpən] (*esp Brit*) ADJ [*person*] necio

lumpish [ˈlʌmpɪʃ] ADJ torpe, pesado

lumpy [ˈlʌmpɪ] ADJ (*compar* **lumpier**, *superl* **lumpiest**) [*sauce*] grumoso, lleno de grumos; [*bed*] desigual; [*soil*] aterronado

lunacy [ˈluːnəsɪ] N (*fig*) locura *f*; **it's sheer ~!** ¡es una locura!

lunar [ˈluːnəʳ] Ⓐ ADJ lunar
Ⓑ CPD ► **lunar eclipse** N eclipse *m* lunar ► **lunar landing** N alunizaje *m*, aterrizaje *m* lunar ► **lunar module** N módulo *m* lunar ► **lunar month** N mes *m* lunar

lunatic [ˈluːnətɪk] Ⓐ N loco/a *m/f*
Ⓑ ADJ [*person*] loco; [*plan, scheme*] descabellado; [*smile, grin*] de loco; **the ~ fringe** el sector más fanático *or* radical
Ⓒ CPD ► **lunatic asylum** N manicomio *m*

lunch [lʌntʃ] Ⓐ N comida *f*, almuerzo *m*, lonche *m* (*Mex*); **to have ~** comer, almorzar; ✦***IDIOM*** **to be out to ~** (*US* hum*) estar como una regadera *or* cabra*
Ⓑ CPD ► **lunch break** N = **lunch hour** ► **lunch counter** N (*US*) (= *café*) *cafetería donde se sirven comidas*; (= *counter*) *mostrador o barra donde se come* ► **lunch hour** N hora *f* de la comida *or* del almuerzo *or* (*Mex*) del lonche

lunchbox [ˈlʌntʃbɒks] N 1 fiambrera *f*, tartera *f*
2 (** hum*) paquete* *m*

luncheon [ˈlʌntʃən] Ⓐ N (*frm*) comida *f*, almuerzo *m*
Ⓑ CPD ► **luncheon meat** N fiambre *m* en conserva ► **luncheon voucher** N (*Brit*) vale *m or* (*LAm*) tíquet *m* de comida

luncheonette [ˈlʌntʃəˈnet] N bar *m* para almuerzos

lunchtime [ˈlʌntʃtaɪm] N hora *f* del almuerzo *or* (*Mex*) del lonche, hora *f* de comer *or* de la comida

lung [lʌŋ] Ⓐ N pulmón *m*
Ⓑ CPD ► **lung cancer** N cáncer *m* de pulmón ► **lung disease** N enfermedad *f* pulmonar

lunge [lʌndʒ] Ⓐ N arremetida *f*, embestida *f*; (*Fencing*) estocada *f*
Ⓑ VI (*also* **~ forward**) arremeter, embestir; (*Fencing*) dar una estocada; **to ~ at sth/sb (with sth)** arremeter contra algo/algn (con algo), lanzarse *or* abalanzarse sobre algo/algn (con algo)

lupin [ˈluːpɪn] N altramuz *m*, lupino *m*

lurch¹ [lɜːtʃ] Ⓐ N sacudida *f*, tumbo *m*; (*Naut*) bandazo *m*; **to give a ~** dar una sacudida *or* un tumbo
Ⓑ VI [*person*] tambalearse; [*vehicle*] (*continually*) dar sacudidas, dar tumbos; (*once*) dar una sacudida, dar un tumbo; (*Naut*) dar un bandazo; **the bus ~ed forward** el autobús avanzó dando tumbos/dando un tumbo; **he ~ed in/out** entró/salió tambaleándose

lurch² [lɜːtʃ] N ✦***IDIOM*** **to leave sb in the ~** dejar a algn en la estacada

lure [ljʊəʳ] Ⓐ N (= *decoy*) señuelo *m*; (= *bait*) cebo *m*; (*fig*) atractivo *m*, aliciente *m*, encanto *m*
Ⓑ VT [+ *person*] atraer; [+ *animal*] atraer (con un señuelo); **to ~ sb into a trap** hacer que algn caiga en una trampa; **they ~d him into the house** consiguieron con artimañas que entrara en la casa; **he was ~d away from the company by a more lucrative offer** dejó la empresa atraído por una oferta más lucrativa

lurex [ˈlʊəreks] N lúrex *m*

lurgy* [ˈlɜːgɪ] N (*Brit hum*) **I've got the dreaded ~ again** he pillado algo malo otra vez

lurid [ˈljʊərɪd] ADJ 1 (= *sordid, prurient*) [*description, novel, photo, crime*] morboso, escabroso; [*imagination, headline*] morboso; **in ~ detail** sin omitir los detalles más escabrosos
2 (= *garish*) [*colour, tie , shirt*] chillón; **a ~ pink dress** un vestido (de color) rosa chillón
3 (= *unnaturally colourful*) [*sky, sunset, light*] refulgente

luridly [ˈljʊərɪdlɪ] ADV 1 (= *pruriently*) con morbosidad, morbosamente
2 (= *garishly*) **~ coloured** (de color) chillón

lurk [lɜːk] VI [*person*] (= *lie in wait*) estar al acecho, merodear; (= *hide*) estar escondido; **I saw him ~ing around the building** lo vi merodeando *or* al acecho por el edificio; **a doubt ~s in my mind** una duda persiste en mi mente; **danger ~s round every corner** el peligro acecha en cada esquina

lurking [ˈlɜːkɪŋ] ADJ [*fear, doubt*] vago, indefinible

luscious [ˈlʌʃəs] ADJ [*scent, breeze, wine*] delicioso; [*fruit*] suculento; [*girl*] deliciosa, atractiva

lusciousness [ˈlʌʃəsnɪs] N exquisitez *f*; [*of fruit*] suculencia *f*

lush [lʌʃ] Ⓐ ADJ (*compar* **lusher**, *superl* **lushest**)
1 (= *luxuriant*) [*vegetation*] exuberante, lozano; [*pastures*] rico
2 (= *opulent*) opulento, lujoso
Ⓑ N (*) (= *alcoholic*) borracho/a *m/f*

lushness [ˈlʌʃnɪs] N 1 (= *luxuriance*) lozanía *f*, exuberancia *f*
2 (= *opulence*) opulencia *f*, lujo *m*

lust [lʌst] N (= *greed*) codicia *f*; (*sexual*) lujuria *f*; **~ for power/revenge** ansia *f or* sed *f* de poder/venganza; **~ for money** codicia *f*

►**lust after, lust for** VI + PREP **to ~ after** *or* **for sth** codiciar algo; **to ~ after sb** desear a algn

luster [ˈlʌstəʳ] N (*US*) = **lustre**

lusterless [ˈlʌstəlɪs] ADJ (*US*) = **lustreless**

lustful [ˈlʌstfʊl] ADJ lujurioso, libidinoso; [*look*] lascivo, lleno de deseo

lustfully [ˈlʌstfəlɪ] ADV lujuriosamente, libidinosamente; [*look*] lascivamente

lustfulness [ˈlʌstfʊlnɪs] N lujuria *f*, lascivia *f*

lustily [ˈlʌstɪlɪ] ADV [*sing*] animadamente

lustre, luster (*US*) [ˈlʌstəʳ] N lustre *m*, brillo *m*

lustreless, lusterless (*US*) [ˈlʌstəlɪs] ADJ [*hair*] deslustrado; [*eyes*] apagado

lustrous [ˈlʌstrəs] ADJ [*hair*] brillante, lustroso; [*eyes*] brillante; [*gold*] reluciente

lusty [ˈlʌstɪ] ADJ (*compar* **lustier**; *superl* **lustiest**) [*person*] vigoroso, lozano; [*cry, cheer*] fuerte; **he has a ~ appetite** tiene buen apetito

lute [luːt] N laúd *m*

lutetium [lʊˈtiːʃɪəm] N lutecio *m*

Luther [ˈluːθəʳ] N Lutero

Lutheran [ˈluːθərən] Ⓐ ADJ luterano
Ⓑ N luterano/a *m/f*

Lutheranism [ˈluːθərənɪzəm] N luteranismo *m*

luv* [lʌv] N (*Brit*) = **love**; **yes, ~** sí, cariño

luvvies* [ˈlʌvɪz] NPL (*Brit pej*) (= *actors*) gente *f* de la farándula

Luxembourg [ˈlʌksəmbɜːg] N Luxemburgo *m*

Luxembourger [ˈlʌksəmbɜːgəʳ] N luxemburgués/esa *m/f*

luxuriance [lʌgˈzjʊərɪəns] N exuberancia *f*

luxuriant [lʌgˈzjʊərɪənt] ADJ exuberante, lozano

luxuriantly [lʌgˈzjʊərɪəntlɪ] ADV exuberantemente, de manera exuberante

luxuriate [lʌgˈzjʊərɪeɪt] VI [*plant*] crecer con exuberancia; [*person*] disfrutar; **to ~ in** disfrutar (de), deleitarse con, entregarse al lujo de

luxurious [lʌgˈzjʊərɪəs] ADJ [*house, apartment, hotel, furnishings*] lujoso, de lujo; [*life*] de lujo

luxuriously [lʌgˈzjʊərɪəslɪ] ADV lujosamente

luxury [ˈlʌkʃərɪ] Ⓐ N (= *opulence*) lujo *m*; (= *extravagance, treat*) lujo *m*; (= *article*) artículo *m* de lujo; **to live in ~** vivir con mucho lujo; **a holiday is a ~ we can't afford** unas vacaciones son un lujo que no nos podemos permitir
Ⓑ CPD [*goods, apartment*] de lujo ► **luxury tax** N impuesto *m* de lujo

LV N ABBR = **luncheon voucher**

LW N ABBR (*Rad*) (= **long wave**) OL *f*

lyceum [laɪˈsiːəm] N liceo *m*

lychee [ˌlaɪˈtʃiː] N lichi *m*

lych gate [ˈlɪtʃgeɪt] N *entrada techada a un cementerio*

Lycra® [ˈlaɪkrə] N licra® *f*

lye [laɪ] N lejía *f*

lying [ˈlaɪɪŋ] Ⓐ ADJ [*statement, story*] falso; **you ~ son-of-a-bitch!**** ¡mentiroso hijo de puta!**
Ⓑ N mentiras *fpl*

lying-in† [ˈlaɪɪŋˈɪn] (*Med*) Ⓐ N (*pl* **lyings-in**) parto *m*
Ⓑ CPD ► **lying-in ward** N sala *f* de maternidad

lymph [lɪmf] Ⓐ N linfa *f*
Ⓑ CPD ► **lymph gland** N ganglio *m* linfático

lymphatic [lɪmˈfætɪk] Ⓐ ADJ linfático
Ⓑ N vaso *m* linfático

lymphocyte [ˈlɪmfəʊˌsaɪt] N linfocito *m*

lynch [lɪntʃ] Ⓐ VT linchar
Ⓑ CPD ► **lynch law** N ley *f* del linchamiento ► **lynch mob** N *muchedumbre dispuesta a linchar a alguien*

lynching [ˈlɪntʃɪŋ] N linchamiento *m*

lynchpin [ˈlɪntʃpɪn] = **linchpin**

lynx [lɪŋks] N (*pl* **lynxes** *or* **lynx**) lince *m*

lynx-eyed [ˈlɪŋksaɪd] ADJ con ojos de lince

Lyons [ˈlaɪənz] N Lyón *m*

lyre [ˈlaɪəʳ] N lira *f*

lyrebird [ˈlaɪəbɜːd] N ave *f* lira

lyric [ˈlɪrɪk] Ⓐ ADJ lírico
Ⓑ N (= *poem*) poema *m* lírico; (= *genre*) lírica *f*; **lyrics** (= *words of song*) letra *fsing*

lyrical [ˈlɪrɪkəl] ADJ (*lit*) lírico; (*fig*) entusiasmado; **to wax** *or* **become ~ about** *or* **over sth** deshacerse en elogios a algo; **he was waxing ~ about my roast beef** se deshacía en elogios a mi rosbif, estaba entusiasmado con mi rosbif

lyrically [ˈlɪrɪkəlɪ] ADV (= *poetically*) [*speak, write, describe*] líricamente, con lirismo

lyricism [ˈlɪrɪsɪzəm] N lirismo *m*

lyricist [ˈlɪrɪsɪst] N letrista *mf*

lysergic acid [lɪˈsɜːdʒɪk ˈæsɪd] N ácido *m* lisérgico

Lysol® [ˈlaɪsɒl] N lisol® *m*

M m

M¹, m¹ [em] N (= *letter*) M, m *f*; **M for Mary** M de Madrid

M², m² ABBR [1] = **million(s)**
[2] = **medium** (= *garment size*) M
[3] (= **married**) se casó con
[4] (= **metre(s)**) m
[5] = **mile(s)**
[6] (= **male**) m
[7] (= **minute(s)**) m
[8] (*Brit*) = **motorway**; **the M8** ≈ la A8

MA (A) N ABBR (*Univ*) = **Master of Arts**; → [DEGREE]
(B) ABBR [1] (*US*) = **Massachusetts**
[2] (*US*) = **Military Academy**

ma* [mɑː] N mamá *f*

ma'am [mæm] N (*esp US*) = **madam**

Maastricht Treaty [ˈmɑːstrɪktˈtriːtɪ] N **the ~** el Tratado de Maastricht

mac* [mæk] N [1] (*Brit*) (= *mackintosh*) impermeable *m*; (= *cagoule*) chubasquero *m*
[2] (*esp US*) **this way, Mac!** ¡por aquí, amigo!

macabre [məˈkɑːbr] ADJ macabro

macadam [məˈkædəm] N macadán *m*

macadamize [məˈkædəmaɪz] VT macadamizar

macaroni [ˌmækəˈrəʊnɪ] (A) N macarrones *mpl*
(B) CPD ► **macaroni cheese** N macarrones *mpl* gratinados (con queso)

macaronic [ˌmækəˈrɒnɪk] ADJ macarrónico

macaroon [ˌmækəˈruːn] N macarrón *m*, mostachón *m*

macaw [məˈkɔː] N guacamayo *m*

mace¹ [meɪs] N (= *ceremonial staff*) maza *f*

mace² [meɪs] N (= *spice*) macis *f*

macebearer [ˈmeɪsˌbeərəʳ] N macero *m*

Macedonia [ˌmæsɪˈdəʊnɪə] N Macedonia *f*

Macedonian [mæsɪˈdəʊnɪən] (A) ADJ macedonio/a *m/f*
(B) N [1] (= *person*) macedonio/a *m/f*
[2] (*Ling*) macedonio *m*

macerate [ˈmæsəreɪt] (A) VT macerar
(B) VI macerar(se)

Mach [mæk] N mach *m*

machete [məˈtʃetɪ] N machete *m*

Machiavelli [ˌmækɪəˈvelɪ] N Maquiavelo

Machiavellian [ˌmækɪəˈvelɪən] ADJ maquiavélico

machinations [ˌmækɪˈneɪʃənz] NPL maquinaciones *fpl*, intrigas *fpl*, manipulaciones *fpl*

machine [məˈʃiːn] (A) N [1] (*gen*) máquina *f*, aparato *m*; (= *machinery*) maquinaria *f*
[2] (*referring to particular appliance*) (= *car, motorbike*) máquina *f*; (= *aeroplane*) aparato *m*; (= *cycle*) bicicleta *f*; (= *washing machine*) lavadora *f*
[3] (*Pol*) organización *f*, aparato *m*
(B) VT (*Tech*) elaborar a máquina; (*Sew*) coser a máquina
(C) CPD mecánico, (hecho) a máquina ► **machine age** N era *f* de las máquinas ► **machine code** N (*Comput*) lenguaje *m* (de) máquina ► **machine error** N error *m* de la máquina ► **machine gun** N ametralladora *f*; *see also* **machine-gun** ► **machine gunner** N ametrallador *m* ► **machine intelligence** N inteligencia *f* artificial ► **machine language** N lenguaje *m* (de) máquina ► **machine operator** N operario/a *m/f*, maquinista *mf* ► **machine pistol** N metralleta *f* ► **machine shop** N taller *m* de máquinas ► **machine time** N tiempo *m* de máquina ► **machine tool** N máquina *f* herramienta ► **machine translation** N traducción *f* automática

machine-gun [məˈʃiːngʌn] VT ametrallar

machine-made [məˈʃiːnmeɪd] ADJ hecho a máquina

machine-readable [məˈʃiːnˈriːdəbl] ADJ legible por máquina; **in ~ form** en forma legible por máquina; **~ code** código *m* legible por máquina

machinery [məˈʃiːnərɪ] N [1] (= *machines*) maquinaria *f*; (= *mechanism*) mecanismo *m*
[2] (*fig*) maquinaria *f*, aparato *m*

machine-stitch [məˈʃiːnˌstɪtʃ] VT coser a máquina

machine-wash [məˈʃiːnwɒʃ] VT lavar a máquina

machine-washable [məˈʃiːnˈwɒʃəbl] ADJ lavable en la lavadora

machinist [məˈʃiːnɪst] N (*Tech*) operario/a *m/f*; (*Sew*) costurero/a *m/f* a máquina

machismo [məˈtʃɪzməʊ] N machismo *m*

macho [ˈmætʃəʊ] (A) ADJ muy de macho, muy masculino; **a ~ man** un tipo muy macho, un macho
(B) N macho *m*

mackerel [ˈmækrəl] (A) N (*pl* **mackerel** *or* **mackerels**) caballa *f*
(B) CPD ► **mackerel sky** N cielo *m* aborregado

mackintosh [ˈmækɪntɒʃ] N impermeable *m*; (= *cagoule*) chubasquero *m*

macramé [məˈkrɑːmɪ] N macramé *m*

macro [ˈmækrəʊ] N (*Comput*) ABBR (= **macro-instruction**) macro *m*

macro... [ˈmækrəʊ] PREFIX macro…

macrobiotic [ˌmækrəʊbaɪˈɒtɪk] ADJ macrobiótico

macrobiotics [ˌmækrəʊbaɪˈɒtɪks] N macrobiótica *f*

macrocosm [ˈmækrəʊkɒzəm] N macrocosmo *m*

macroeconomic [ˌmækrəʊˌiːkəˈnɒmɪk] ADJ macroeconómico

macroeconomics [ˌmækrəʊˌiːkəˈnɒmɪks] NSING macroeconomía *f*

macroeconomy [ˌmækrəʊɪˈkɒnəmɪ] N macroeconomía *f*

macroscopic [ˌmækrəˈskɒpɪk] ADJ macroscópico

> **MACY'S THANKSGIVING PARADE**
>
> **Macy's Thanksgiving Parade** *es una cabalgata anual que tiene lugar en Nueva York el Día de Acción de Gracias, el cuarto jueves de noviembre. Patrocinado por los grandes almacenes* **Macy's**, *este desfile de globos con personajes de dibujos animados, bandas de música y grupos de personas que vienen de todas las partes de EE.UU. recorre las calles de Broadway a la vez que se televisa a todo el país. En el desfile son típicas unas carrozas profusamente adornadas llamadas* **floats**, *en las que van montados cantantes famosos y estrellas de Broadway. A pesar de que se celebra el Día de Acción de Gracias, el tema del desfile es la Navidad y Santa Claus siempre va en la última carroza.*
>
> ⇨ *Ver tb* [THANKSGIVING]

MAD N ABBR (*US Mil*) = **mutual(ly) assured destruction**

mad [mæd] (A) ADJ (*compar* **madder**; *superl* **maddest**) [1] [*person*] [1·1] (= *mentally ill*) loco; **to drive sb ~** (= *make insane*) volver loco a algn; **captivity drives some animals ~** la cautividad vuelve locos a algunos animales; **to go ~** (= *become insane*) volverse loco; *see also* **raving B**, **stark B**
[1·2] (*) (= *crazy, foolish*) loco; **are you ~?** ¿estás loco?; **you must be ~!** ¡tú estás loco *or* mal de la cabeza!; **to drive sb ~** (= *irritate*) volver loco a algn; **she drove me ~ with her constant questions** me volvió loco con sus constantes preguntas; **don't go ~! we've only got £100** ¡no te pases! sólo tenemos 100 libras; **I worked/ran/pedalled like ~** trabajé/corrí/pedaleé como (un) loco; **they fancy her like ~** les gusta horrores *or* una barbaridad*; **to be ~ with grief** estar loco de dolor
[1·3] (*) (= *angry*) furioso; **I was really ~ when I found out** me puse furiosísimo *or* (*Sp*) me enfadé muchísimo *or* (*esp LAm*) me enojé muchísimo cuando me enteré; **to be ~ at sb** estar furioso con algn, estar muy enfadado con algn (*Sp*), estar muy enojado con algn (*esp LAm*); **to get** *or* **go ~** ponerse furioso; **he gets** *or* **goes ~ when he loses** se pone furioso *or* hecho una fiera cuando pierde; **it makes her ~ when you do that** cuando haces eso la sacas de quicio; **to be ~ with sb** estar furioso con algn, estar muy enfadado con algn (*Sp*), estar muy enojado con algn (*esp LAm*); **I was ~ with him for breaking my window** estaba

muy enfadado con él porque me había roto la ventana

1·4 (*) (= *keen*) **to be ~ about sb** estar loco por algn; **to be ~ about** *or* **on sth**: **he's ~ about** *or* **on football** el fútbol le vuelve loco, es un fanático del fútbol; **she's ~ on Chinese food** le pirra *or* le chifla la comida china*; **I can't say I'm ~ about** *or* **on the idea** no es precisamente que la idea me vuelva loco; **to go ~**: **he walked onstage and the audience went ~** salió al escenario y el público se puso como loco

1·5 ✦*IDIOMS* **to be barking ~** estar loco de remate*, estar loco de atar; **to be (as) ~ as a hatter** *or* **March hare** estar más loco que una cabra*; **to be ~ as hell** (= *furious*) estar cabreadísimo‡; *see also* **hop[1] B**

2 [*thing*] 2·1 (= *silly, irresponsible*) [*plan, idea, scheme*] descabellado, de locos; **after the news came through the phones went ~** tras saberse la noticia los teléfonos sonaban como locos; **this is bureaucracy gone ~** esto es la burocracia llevada al extremo del ridículo

2·2 (= *frantic, uncontrolled*) [*race*] desenfrenado; **the daily ~ dash to work** la desenfrenada carrera diaria por llegar al trabajo; **there was a ~ rush for the exit** todo el mundo corrió *or* se lanzó desenfrenado hacia la salida, todo el mundo corrió como loco hacia la salida

Ⓑ ADV (= *very*) **she's ~ keen to go** tiene unas ganas locas de ir; **I can't say I'm ~ keen on the idea** no es precisamente que la idea me vuelva loco

Ⓒ CPD ► **mad cow disease*** N enfermedad *f* de las vacas locas*, encefalopatía *f* espongiforme bovina ► **mad dog** N (*with rabies*) perro *m* rabioso (*con la enfermedad de la rabia*)

-mad [mæd] ADJ (*ending in compounds*) **he's football~** el fútbol le vuelve loco, es un fanático del fútbol; **football~ boys** chicos *mpl* con la manía del fútbol; **pony~ teenagers** quinceañeras *fpl* locas por los caballitos

Madagascar [ˌmædəˈgæskəʳ] N Madagascar *m*

madam [ˈmædəm] N (*pl* **madams** *or* **mesdames** [ˈmeɪdæm]) 1 señora *f*; **yes, ~** sí, señora; *see also* **dear A4**

2 (*Brit**) (= *girl*) niña *f* malcriada, niña *f* repipi

3 [*of brothel*] madama *f*, dueña *f*

madame [ˈmædəm] N (*pl* **mesdames** [ˈmeɪdæm]) 1 madama *f*, señora *f*; **Madame Dupont** la señora de Dupont

2 [*of brothel*] madama *f*, dueña *f*

madcap [ˈmædkæp] Ⓐ ADJ alocado, disparatado

Ⓑ N loculelo/a *m/f*, tarambana *mf*

madden [ˈmædn] VT (= *infuriate*) enfurecer, sacar de quicio; (= *make demented*) enloquecer; **it ~s me** me pone furioso, me enfurece, me saca de quicio; **a ~ed bull** un toro enloquecido

maddening [ˈmædnɪŋ] ADJ [*delay, habit, trait*] exasperante; **she had a ~ smirk on her face** su rostro tenía una sonrisita exasperante; **it's (quite) ~!** ¡es desesperante!, ¡es como para desesperarse!; **he can be absolutely ~ at times** a veces puede sacarte de quicio

maddeningly [ˈmædnɪŋlɪ] ADV [*smile, grin*] de forma exasperante; **progress was ~ slow** se progresaba con una lentitud exasperante *or* desesperante; **he was always ~ punctual** siempre fue de una puntualidad exasperante *or* desesperante

made [meɪd] PT, PP *of* **make**

Madeira [məˈdɪərə] N Madeira *f*; (= *wine*) (vino *m* de) madeira *m*

made-to-measure [ˌmeɪdtəˈmeʒəʳ] ADJ hecho a (la) medida

made-to-order [ˌmeɪdtəˈɔːdəʳ] ADJ (*Brit*) hecho de encargo; (*US*) hecho a (la) medida

made-up [ˈmeɪdˈʌp] ADJ 1 (= *wearing make-up*) [*face*] maquillado; [*eyes*] pintado, maquillado; **she was heavily ~** llevaba mucho maquillaje, iba muy pintada

2 (= *invented*) [*story, character*] inventado, ficticio; [*word*] inventado

3 (= *ready-made*) [*mixture, solution*] preparado

Madge [maedʒ] N (*familiar form*) *of* **Margaret**

madhouse* [ˈmædhaʊs] N (*pl* **madhouses** [ˈmædhaʊzɪz]) manicomio *m*, casa *f* de locos; **this is a ~!** ¡esto es una casa de locos!

madly [ˈmædlɪ] ADV 1 (= *crazily*) [*scream, laugh, wave, rush*] (*one person*) como (un) loco/(una) loca; (*more than one person*) como locos; **my heart was beating ~** mi corazón latía como loco

2 (= *very*) **he was ~ jealous of his sister** estaba terriblemente celoso de su hermana; **they were ~ in love with each other** estaban locamente *or* perdidamente enamorados uno del otro; **she found her new life ~ exciting** su nueva vida le parecía terriblemente excitante; **life is not ~ exciting at the moment** en este momento mi vida no es muy emocionante

madman [ˈmædmən] N (*pl* **madmen**) loco *m*

▼**madness** [ˈmædnɪs] N 1 (= *mental illness*) locura *f*, demencia *f*

2 (= *foolishness*) locura *f*; **it would be sheer ~ to continue** sería una auténtica locura seguir; **it's ~!** ¡es una locura!

Madonna [məˈdɒnə] N Virgen *f*

Madrid [məˈdrɪd] Ⓐ N Madrid *m*

Ⓑ ADJ madrileño

madrigal [ˈmædrɪgəl] N madrigal *m*

madwoman [ˈmædwʊmən] N (*pl* **madwomen**) loca *f*

maelstrom [ˈmeɪlstrəʊm] N torbellino *m*, remolino *m*

maestro [ˈmaɪstrəʊ] N (*pl* **maestros** *or* **maestri** [ˈmaɪstrɪ]) maestro *m*

Mae West [ˈmeɪˈwest] N (*Aer hum*) chaleco *m* salvavidas

MAFF N ABBR (*Brit*) (= **Ministry of Agriculture, Fisheries and Food**) ≈ MAPA *m*

mafia [ˈmæfɪə] N mafia *f*

mafioso [ˌmæfɪˈəʊsəʊ] N (*pl* **mafiosi** [ˌmæfɪˈəʊsɪ]) mafioso *m*

mag* [mæg] N ABBR (*Brit*) (= **magazine**) revista *f*

magazine [ˌmægəˈziːn] N 1 (= *journal*) revista *f*

2 (*TV, Rad*) (*also* **~ programme**) magazine *m*, programa *m* magazine

3 (*in rifle*) recámara *f*; (*in slide projector*) (*round*) carrusel *m*; (*elongated*) carro *m*, bandeja *f*

4 (*Mil*) (= *store*) almacén *m*; (*for powder*) polvorín *m*; (*Naut*) santabárbara *f*

Magdalen [ˈmægdəlɪn] N Magdalena

Magellan [məˈgelən] Ⓐ N Magallanes

Ⓑ CPD ► **Magellan Straits** NPL Estrecho *m* de Magallanes

magenta [məˈdʒentə] Ⓐ N magenta *m*

Ⓑ ADJ magenta *inv*

Maggie [ˈmægɪ] N (*familiar form*) *of* **Margaret**

maggot [ˈmægət] N cresa *f*, gusano *m*

maggoty [ˈmægətɪ] ADJ agusanado, lleno de gusanos

Maghrib [ˈmʌgrəb] N Magreb *m*

Magi [ˈmeɪdʒaɪ] NPL **the ~** los Reyes Magos

magic [ˈmædʒɪk] Ⓐ N (*lit, fig*) magia *f*; **as if by ~** como por arte de magia, como por encanto; **this bath oil works ~ for tired and aching limbs** este aceite de baño es mágico para brazos y piernas doloridos y cansados; **the ~ of Hollywood** la magia de Hollywood; **the old ~ was still there** (*in relationship*) todavía existía algo especial entre ellos/nosotros; *see also* **black D**, **white C**

Ⓑ ADJ 1 (*relating to spells, sorcery*) [*solution, word*] mágico; **you just have to say the ~ word and we'll forget all about it** basta con que digas la palabra mágica y olvidaremos todo el asunto; **there is no ~ formula for success** no existe una fórmula mágica para el éxito

2 (= *captivating*) [*moment*] especial; **he hasn't lost his ~ touch** no ha perdido ese toque especial suyo

3 (*) (= *super*) fabuloso, estupendo; **"did you enjoy it?" — "it was ~"** —¿te gustó? —fue fabuloso *or* estupendo

Ⓒ CPD ► **magic bullet** N (*Med, also fig*) panacea *f* ► **magic carpet** N alfombra *f* mágica ► **magic circle** N círculo *m* mágico ► **magic lantern** N linterna *f* mágica ► **magic mushrooms*** NPL setas *fpl* alucinógenas, hongos *mpl* alucinógenos ► **magic realism** N (*Literat*) realismo *m* mágico ► **magic spell** N hechizo *m*, encanto *m* ► **magic square** N (*Math*) cuadrado *m* mágico ► **magic trick** N truco *m* de magia ► **magic wand** N varita *f* mágica

►**magic away** VT + ADV hacer desaparecer como por arte de magia

►**magic up** VT + ADV hacer aparecer como por arte de magia

magical [ˈmædʒɪkəl] ADJ 1 (*lit*) [*powers, properties*] mágico

2 (*fig*) 2·1 (= *captivating*) [*experience, moment*] mágico

2·2 (= *miraculous*) [*transformation*] milagroso; **she had undergone a ~ transformation** había sufrido una transformación milagrosa

magically [ˈmædʒɪkəlɪ] ADV como por arte de magia; **a bottle of champagne was ~ produced** apareció una botella de champán como por arte de magia

magician [mədʒɪʃən] N 1 (= *sorcerer*) mago/a *m/f*

2 (= *conjuror*) prestidigitador(a) *m/f*

magisterial [ˌmædʒɪsˈtɪərɪəl] ADJ magistral

magistracy [ˈmædʒɪstrəsɪ] N magistratura *f*

magistrate [ˈmædʒɪstreɪt] Ⓐ N magistrado/a *m/f*, juez *mf*

Ⓑ CPD ► **magistrates' court** N (*in England*) juzgado *m* de primera instancia

magma [ˈmægmə] N (*pl* **magmas** *or* **magmata** [ˈmægmətə]) magma *m*

Magna C(h)arta [ˈmægnəˈkɑːtə] N (*Brit*) Carta *f* Magna

magnanimity [ˌmægnəˈnɪmɪtɪ] N magnanimidad *f*

magnanimous [mægˈnænɪməs] ADJ magnánimo (*frm*), generoso; **to be ~ in victory** mostrarse magnánimo con los perdedores; **to be ~ to sb** mostrarse magnánimo con algn (*frm*), mostrarse generoso con algn

magnanimously [mægˈnænɪməslɪ] ADV (*gen*) magnánimamente; [*say*] con magnanimidad, magnánimamente

magnate [ˈmægneɪt] N magnate *mf*, potentado/a *m/f*

magnesia [mægˈniːʃə] N magnesia *f*

magnesium [mægˈniːzɪəm] Ⓐ N magnesio *m*

➤ LANGUAGE IN USE: **madness 2** 2.3, 12.2

Ⓑ CPD ► **magnesium sulphate** N sulfato *m* magnésico

magnet ['mægnɪt] N (*lit, fig*) imán *m*

magnetic [mæg'netɪk] Ⓐ ADJ magnético; (*fig*) carismático
Ⓑ CPD ► **magnetic card reader** N lector *m* de tarjeta magnética ► **magnetic disk** N disco *m* magnético ► **magnetic field** N campo *m* magnético ► **magnetic mine** N mina *f* magnética ► **magnetic needle** N aguja *f* magnética ► **magnetic north** N norte *m* magnético ► **magnetic pole** N polo *m* magnético ► **magnetic stripe** N banda *f* magnética ► **magnetic tape** N cinta *f* magnética

magnetically [mæg'netɪkəlɪ] ADV magnéticamente

magnetism ['mægnɪtɪzəm] N magnetismo *m*; (*fig*) magnetismo *m*, atractivo *m*

magnetizable [ˌmægnɪ'taɪzəbl] ADJ magnetizable

magnetize ['mægnɪtaɪz] VT [1] (*lit*) magnetizar, imantar
[2] (*fig*) magnetizar

magneto [mæg'niːtəʊ] N magneto *f*

magnetometer [ˌmægnɪ'tɒmɪtəʳ] N magnetómetro *m*

magnetosphere [mæg'niːtəʊˌsfɪəʳ] N magnetosfera *f*

Magnificat [mæg'nɪfɪkæt] N Magníficat *m*

magnification [ˌmægnɪfɪ'keɪʃən] N [1] (*Opt*) aumento *m*, ampliación *f*; **high ~** gran aumento *m*; **low ~** pequeño aumento *m*
[2] (*fig*) exageración *f*

magnificence [mæg'nɪfɪsəns] N magnificencia *f*

magnificent [mæg'nɪfɪsənt] ADJ [*display, performance, achievement, animal, view*] magnífico, espléndido; [*building*] espléndido; **he has done a ~ job** ha hecho un trabajo magnífico *or* espléndido; **the princess looked ~** la princesa estaba esplendorosa

magnificently [mæg'nɪfɪsəntlɪ] ADV magníficamente; **they played/performed ~** tocaron/actuaron magníficamente (bien)

magnify ['mægnɪfaɪ] Ⓐ VT [1] (*Opt*) aumentar, ampliar; **to ~ sth seven times** aumentar algo siete veces
[2] (= *exaggerate*) exagerar
Ⓑ CPD ► **magnifying glass** N lupa *f* ► **magnifying power** N aumento *m*

magnitude ['mægnɪtjuːd] N [1] (*gen*) magnitud *f*; (= *importance*) magnitud *f*, envergadura *f*; **in operations of this ~** en operaciones de esta magnitud *or* envergadura
[2] (*Astron*) magnitud *f*; **a star of the first ~** una estrella de primera magnitud

magnolia [mæg'nəʊlɪə] N magnolia *f*

magnox reactor ['mægnɒksriː'æktəʳ] N reactor *m* magnox

magnum ['mægnəm] Ⓐ N (*pl* **magnums**) (= *bottle*) botella *f* doble
Ⓑ ADJ **~ opus** obra *f* maestra

magpie ['mægpaɪ] N urraca *f*, marica *f*

Magyar ['mægjɑːʳ] Ⓐ ADJ magiar
Ⓑ N magiar *mf*

maharajah [ˌmɑːhə'rɑːdʒə] N maharajá *m*

maharani [ˌmɑːhə'rɑːniː] N maharaní *f*

Mahdi ['mɑːdɪ] N mahdi *m*

mahjong(g) [ˌmɑː'dʒɒŋ] N dominó *m* chino

mahogany [mə'hɒgənɪ] Ⓐ N caoba *f*
Ⓑ ADJ de caoba

Mahomet [mə'hɒmɪt] N Mahoma

Mahometan [mə'hɒmɪtən] Ⓐ ADJ mahometano
Ⓑ N mahometano/a *m/f*

maid [meɪd] Ⓐ N [1] (= *servant*) criada *f*, muchacha *f* (*S. Cone*), mucama *f* (*S. Cone*), recamarera *f* (*Mex*); (*in hotel*) camarera *f*; **lady's ~** doncella *f*
[2] († *or poet*) (= *young girl*) doncella *f*; *see also* **old C**
Ⓑ CPD ► **maid of honor** N (*US*) dama *f* de honor

maiden ['meɪdn] Ⓐ N († *or poet*) doncella *f*
Ⓑ ADJ [*flight, speech*] inaugural, de inauguración
Ⓒ CPD ► **maiden aunt** N tía *f* soltera ► **maiden lady**† N soltera *f* ► **maiden name** N apellido *m* de soltera ► **maiden over** N (*Cricket*) *serie de seis lanzamientos en que no se anota ninguna carrera*

maidenhair ['meɪdnhɛəʳ] N (*also* **~ fern**) cabello *m* de Venus, culantrillo *m*

maidenhead ['meɪdnhed] N virginidad *f*, himen *m*

maidenhood ['meɪdnhʊd] N doncellez *f*

maidenly ['meɪdnlɪ] ADJ (= *virginal*) virginal; (= *demure*) recatado, modesto

maid-of-all-work [ˌmeɪdəv'ɔːlˌwɜːk] N chica *f* para todo

maidservant ['meɪdˌsɜːvənt] N criada *f*, sirvienta *f*

mail¹ [meɪl] Ⓐ N [1] (= *postal system*) correo *m*; **by** *or* **through the ~** por correo; *see also* **airmail**
[2] (= *letters*) cartas *fpl*, correspondencia *f*; **is there any ~ for me?** ¿hay alguna carta para mí?
[3] = **e-mail**
Ⓑ VT [1] (*esp US*) (= *post*) echar al correo; (= *send by mail*) enviar por correo
[2] = **e-mail**
Ⓒ CPD ► **mail boat** N vapor *m* correo ► **mail bomb** N (*US*) (= *letter bomb*) carta *f* bomba; (= *parcel bomb*) paquete *m* bomba ► **mail car** N (*US Rail*) furgón *m* postal, vagón *m* correo ► **mail carrier** N (*US*) cartero/a *m/f* ► **mail coach** N (*Hist*) diligencia *f*, coche *m* correo; (*Rail*) furgón *m* postal, vagón *m* correo ► **mail merge** N combinación *f* de correspondencia ► **mail order** N (= *system*) venta *f* por correo; (= *order*) pedido *m* por correo; *see also* **mail-order** ► **mail room** N sala *f* de correo, departamento *m* de registro (de entradas y salidas) ► **mail train** N tren *m* correo ► **mail van** N (*Brit Aut*) camioneta *f* de correos; (*Rail*) furgón *m* postal, vagón *m* correo

mail² [meɪl] N (*Mil*) malla *f*, cota *f* de malla

mailbag ['meɪlbæg] N saca *f* de correos

mailbox ['meɪlbɒks] N (*US*) (*in street*) buzón *m*; (*in office etc*) casilla *f*; (*Comput*) buzón *m*

maildrop ['meɪldrɒp] N (= *act*) entrega *f* de correo; (= *address*) dirección *f* para correo

mailed fist [ˌmeɪld'fɪst] N **the ~** la mano dura

mailing ['meɪlɪŋ] Ⓐ N envío *m*
Ⓑ CPD ► **mailing list** N lista *f* de direcciones; **I'll put you on our ~ list** le incluiré en nuestra lista de direcciones para enviarle información

mailman ['meɪlmæn] N (*pl* **mailmen**) (*US*) cartero *m*

mail-order ['meɪlˌɔːdəʳ] CPD ► **mail-order catalogue, mail-order catalog** (*US*) N catálogo *m* de venta por correo ► **mail-order firm, mail-order house** N empresa *f* de venta por correo; *see also* **mail**

mailshot ['meɪlʃɒt] N (*Brit*) mailing *m*

maim [meɪm] VT mutilar, lisiar; **to be ~ed for life** quedar lisiado de por vida

main [meɪn] Ⓐ ADJ [*reason, problem, aim, concern*] principal, fundamental; [*gate, entrance*] principal; **that was my ~ reason for doing it** ésa fue la razón principal *or* fundamental por (la) que lo hice; **the ~ thing is that no one was hurt** lo principal es que nadie resultó herido; **the ~ thing is not to panic** lo principal es no dejarse llevar por el pánico
Ⓑ N [1] (= *pipe*) cañería *f* principal, conducto *m* principal; (= *cable*) cable *m* principal; **gas/water ~** cañería *or* conducto principal del gas/agua; **the ~s** (*Elec*) la red, la red de suministro; (*Gas, Water*) la red de suministro; **the water in this tap comes from the ~s** el agua de este grifo viene de la red de suministro; **to turn the gas/water off at the ~s** cerrar la llave principal del gas/agua; **to turn the electricity off at the ~s** apagar la electricidad; **this radio works on batteries or off the ~s** esta radio funciona con pilas o conectada a la red
[2] (*liter*) **the ~** (= *open sea*) la mar océana; **the Spanish Main** el Mar Caribe
[3] **in the ~** (= *generally speaking*) por lo general, por regla general, en general; (= *in the majority*) por lo general, en su mayoría, en su mayor parte; **the people she met were, in the ~, wealthier than her** la gente que conoció era, por lo general *or* en su mayoría *or* en su mayor parte, más rica que ella
[4] *see* **might²**
Ⓒ CPD ► **main beam** N (*Archit*) viga *f* maestra; (*Aut*) luces *fpl* largas, luz *f* larga ► **main clause** N (*Gram*) oración *f* principal ► **main course** N plato *m* principal ► **main deck** N (*Naut*) cubierta *f* principal ► **the main drag*** N (*US*) la calle principal ► **main line** N (*Rail*) línea *f* principal; *see also* **mainline** ► **main office** N (= *headquarters of organization*) sede *f*, oficina *f* central ► **main road** N carretera *f* principal ► **main sheet** N (*Naut*) escota *f* mayor ► **main street** N calle *f* mayor ► **the mains supply** N el suministro de la red

mainbrace ['meɪnbreɪs] N braza *f* de mayor

mainframe ['meɪnfreɪm] N (*also* **~ computer**) ordenador *m or* computadora *f* central

mainland ['meɪnlənd] N tierra *f* firme, continente *m*; **they want to move to the ~** [*islanders*] quieren trasladarse a Inglaterra/Francia *etc*

mainline ['meɪn'laɪn] Ⓐ ADJ [1] (*Rail*) [*service, station*] principal, interurbano
[2] (= *mainstream*) tradicional, al uso
Ⓑ VT (*Drugs**) chutarse*, picarse*, inyectarse; **to ~ heroin** chutarse *or* picarse heroína*, meterse un chute *or* pico de heroína*
Ⓒ VI (*Drugs**) chutarse*, inyectarse

mainly ['meɪnlɪ] ADV [1] (= *fundamentally*) principalmente, fundamentalmente; (= *for the greater part*) mayormente, principalmente; **they have stayed together ~ because of their children** han seguido juntos principalmente *or* fundamentalmente por sus hijos; **he lives ~ in Paris** vive mayormente *or* principalmente en París; **it was ~ his idea** fue mayormente *or* principalmente idea suya
[2] (= *in the majority*) en su mayoría, en su mayor parte; **her customers are ~ women** sus clientes son en su mayoría *or* en su mayor parte mujeres

mainmast ['meɪnmɑːst] N palo *m* mayor

mainsail ['meɪnsl] N vela *f* mayor

mainspring ['meɪnsprɪŋ] N [*of watch*] muelle *m* real; (*fig*) motivo *m* principal, principal resorte *m*

mainstay ['meɪnsteɪ] N (*Naut*) estay *m* mayor; (*fig*) sostén *m* principal, pilar *m*

mainstream ['meɪnstriːm] Ⓐ N [*of ideology, philosophy, literature*] corriente *f* principal; **his work diverges sharply from the ~ of English fiction** su trabajo se aparta radicalmente de la corriente principal de la novela inglesa; **our policies aim to bring these young people into the ~ of American life** nuestra política tiene como objetivo hacer que estos jóvenes adopten la forma de vida del ciudadano medio americano; **they remain outside the political ~** permanecen fuera de la escena política mayoritaria
Ⓑ ADJ [*political party*] mayoritario; [*press, media, culture*] dominante; [*fashion*] de masas; [*education*] convencional; **they remain on the margins of ~ society** siguen estando marginados con respecto al ciudadano medio; **the rise of the right in ~ politics** el ascenso de la derecha dentro de la corriente política dominante; **the mindlessness of much ~ cinema** la estupidez de gran parte de la corriente dominante en el cine
Ⓒ VT (*US Scol*) integrar

▼**maintain** [meɪn'teɪn] VT 1 (= *keep up*) [+ *attitude, correspondence, order, speed, advantage*] mantener; [+ *silence*] guardar; [+ *war*] sostener, continuar; **the two countries ~ friendly relations** los dos países mantienen relaciones amistosas; **he ~ed his opposition to the plan** se mantuvo contrario al plan
2 (= *support*) [+ *family, dependents*] mantener; [+ *army*] mantener, costear
3 (= *keep in good condition*) [+ *road, building, car, machine*] mantener en buen estado; **the house costs a fortune to ~** el mantenimiento de la casa cuesta un dineral, cuesta un dineral mantener la casa en buen estado
4 (= *have, retain*) [+ *house, property*] poseer, tener; **as well as his house in London he ~s one in New York and one in France** además de su casa en Londres, posee *or* tiene una en Nueva York y otra en Francia
5 (= *claim*) [+ *one's innocence*] mantener, sostener; **he ~ed that the earth was round** mantenía *or* sostenía que la tierra era redonda

maintained school [meɪn'teɪnd,skuːl] N (*Brit*) colegio *m* estatal *or* público

maintenance ['meɪntɪnəns] Ⓐ N 1 (= *upkeep*) [*of machine, car*] mantenimiento *m*; [*of house, building*] manutención *f*, cuidado *m*
2 (= *money paid to ex-wife and family*) pensión *f* alimenticia
Ⓑ CPD ► **maintenance agreement** N contrato *m* de mantenimiento ► **maintenance allowance** N pensión *f* alimenticia ► **maintenance contract** N = **maintenance agreement** ► **maintenance costs** NPL gastos *mpl* de mantenimiento ► **maintenance crew** N personal *m* de servicios ► **maintenance grant** N (*Univ*) beca *f* ► **maintenance order** N *orden judicial que obliga al pago de una pensión alimenticia* ► **maintenance payments** NPL pago *msing* de la manutención ► **maintenance staff** N personal *m* del servicio de mantenimiento

Mainz [maɪnts] N Maguncia *f*

maisonette [,meɪzə'net] N (*esp Brit*) dúplex *m inv*

maître d' [,metrə'diː] (*pl* **maîtres d'**), **maître d'hôtel** [,metrədəʊ'tel] N (*pl* **maîtres d'hôtel**) maître *mf*

maize [meɪz] Ⓐ N (*Brit*) maíz *m*; **ear of ~** mazorca *f*, elote *m* (*Mex*), choclo *m* (*Andes, S. Cone*)
Ⓑ CPD ► **maize field** N maizal *m*

Maj. ABBR = **Major**

majestic [mə'dʒestɪk] ADJ majestuoso

➤ LANGUAGE IN USE: **maintain 5** 26.1, 26.2

majestically [mə'dʒestɪkəlɪ] ADV majestuosamente

majesty ['mædʒɪstɪ] N majestad *f*; **His/Her Majesty** Su Majestad; **Your Majesty** (Vuestra) Majestad

Maj.-Gen. ABBR = **Major-General**

major ['meɪdʒə^r] Ⓐ ADJ 1 (= *large, important*) [*city, company*] muy importante; [*change, role*] fundamental, muy importante; [*factor*] clave, muy importante, fundamental; [*problem*] serio, grave; [*worry*] enorme; [*breakthrough*] de enorme importancia; **the result was a ~ blow to the government** el resultado fue un duro golpe para el gobierno; **it is a ~ cause of death** causa un enorme número de muertes; **to be a ~ factor in sth** ser un factor clave *or* muy importante *or* fundamental en algo; **of ~ importance** de la mayor importancia; **three ~ issues remained unresolved** quedaron sin resolver tres temas fundamentales *or* tres temas de enorme importancia; **the ~ issues which affect our lives** las principales cuestiones que afectan nuestras vidas, las cuestiones de mayor importancia *or* más importantes que afectan nuestras vidas; **nothing ~ has happened** no ha pasado nada de importancia; **a hysterectomy is a ~ operation** la histerectomía es una operación seria *or* grave; **getting him off to school is a ~ operation** (*hum*) llevarlo al colegio es una operación a gran escala (*hum*); **this represents a ~ step forward** esto representa un enorme paso hacia delante; **he is recovering after ~ surgery** se está recuperando de una operación seria *or* grave
2 (= *principal*) [*cities, political parties*] más importante; **Brazil's ~ cities** las ciudades más importantes de Brasil; **our ~ concern is the welfare of the hostages** nuestra principal preocupación es el bienestar de los rehenes
3 (*Mus*) [*chord, key*] mayor; **C ~** do mayor
4 (*Brit Scol*†) **Jones Major** Jones el mayor
Ⓑ N 1 (*Mil*) comandante *m*, mayor *m* (*LAm*)
2 (*US Univ*) 2·1 (= *subject*) asignatura *f* principal
2·2 (= *student*) **he's a Spanish ~** estudia español como asignatura principal
3 (*US Baseball*) **the ~s** las grandes ligas
Ⓒ VI **to ~ in sth** (*US Univ*) especializarse en algo
Ⓓ CPD ► **major general** N (*Mil*) general *m* de división ► **major league** N (*US*) liga *f* principal; *see also* **major-league** ► **major suit** N (*Bridge*) palo *m* mayor

Majorca [mə'jɔːkə] N Mallorca *f*

Majorcan [mə'jɔːkən] Ⓐ ADJ mallorquín
Ⓑ N 1 (= *person*) mallorquín/ina *m/f*
2 (*Ling*) mallorquín *m*

majordomo [,meɪdʒə'dəʊməʊ] N mayordomo *m*

majorette [,meɪdʒə'ret] N majorette *f*, batonista *f*

majority [mə'dʒɒrɪtɪ] Ⓐ N 1 mayoría *f*; **a two-thirds ~** una mayoría de las dos terceras partes; **they won by a ~** ganaron por mayoría; **in the ~ of cases** en la mayoría *or* la mayor parte de los casos; **such people are in a ~** la mayoría de la gente es así, predomina la gente así; **to be in a ~ of three** formar parte de una mayoría de tres; **the vast ~** la inmensa mayoría; **the great ~ of lecturers** la mayoría *or* la mayor parte de los conferenciantes
2 (*Jur*) **to attain one's ~** llegar a la mayoría de edad
Ⓑ CPD ► **majority decision** N **by a ~ decision** por decisión mayoritaria *or* de la mayoría ► **majority interest** N interés *m* mayoritario ► **majority rule** N gobierno *m* mayoritario, gobierno *m* en mayoría ► **majority (share)holding** N accionariado *m* mayoritario ► **majority verdict** N **by a ~ verdict** por fallo *or* veredicto mayoritario ► **majority vote** N **by a ~ vote** por la mayoría de los votos

MAJORITY, MOST

Singular or plural verb?

When **mayoría** is the subject of a verb, the verb can be in the singular or the plural, depending on the context.

- When translating **majority** rather than **most**, put the verb in the singular if **majority** is seen as a unit rather than a collection of individuals:

  The socialist majority voted against the four amendments
  La mayoría socialista votó en contra de las cuatro enmiendas

- If **la mayoría** is seen as a collection of individuals, particularly when it is followed by **de** + **PLURAL NOUN**, the plural form of the verb is more common than the singular, though both are possible:

  The majority still wear this uniform
  La mayoría siguen vistiendo *or* ***sigue vistiendo este uniforme***
  Most scientists believe it is a mistake
  La mayoría de los científicos creen *or* ***cree que se trata de un error***

- The plural form must be used when **la mayoría** or **la mayoría de** + **PLURAL NOUN** is followed by **ser** or **estar** + **PLURAL COMPLEMENT**:

  Most of them are men
  La mayoría son hombres
  Most of the dead were students
  La mayoría de los muertos eran estudiantes
  Most of the children were black
  La mayoría de los niños eran negros

*For further uses and examples, see main entries at **majority** and **most**.*

major-league [,meɪdʒə'liːg] CPD (*US*) ► **major-league baseball** N béisbol *m* de la liga principal

make [meɪk] (*pt, pp* **made**)

Ⓐ TRANSITIVE VERB Ⓒ NOUN
Ⓑ INTRANSITIVE VERB Ⓓ PHRASAL VERBS

*When **make** is part of a set combination, eg **make an attempt, make a bow, make a case, make sure**, look up the other word.*

Ⓐ TRANSITIVE VERB
1 **= create, prepare** [+ *fire, bed, tea, will, remark, plan, suggestion*] hacer; [+ *dress*] hacer, confeccionar; [+ *shelter*] construir; [+ *meal*] hacer, preparar; [+ *record*] grabar; [+ *film*] rodar; (= *manufacture*) [+ *tool, machine*] fabricar, hacer; **I'm going to ~ a cake** voy a hacer un pastel; **I ~ my bed every morning** me hago la cama cada mañana; **he made it himself** lo hizo él mismo; **God made man** Dios hizo al hombre; **don't ~ a noise** no hagas ruido; **"made in Spain"** [*tool, machine*] "fabricado en España"; [*dress*] "confeccionado en España"; [*nougat, chocolate*] "elaborado en España"; **he's as cunning as they ~ 'em*** es de lo más astuto que hay; **this car isn't made to carry eight people** este coche no está pensado para ocho personas; **they don't ~ songs like that any more** ya no componen canciones como las de antes; **they were made for each other** estaban hechos el uno para el otro; **her shoes weren't made for walking** llevaba unos zapatos poco adecuados para caminar; **we had the curtains made to meas-**

ure nos hicieron las cortinas a medida; **it's made of gold** es de oro, está hecho de oro; *see also* **show B4**

2 *= carry out* [+ *journey, effort*] hacer; [+ *speech*] pronunciar; [+ *payment*] efectuar; [+ *error*] cometer; **I'd like to ~ a phone call** quisiera hacer una llamada; **he made an agreement to pay off the arrears** se comprometió a pagar los atrasos

3 *= earn* ganar; **how much do you ~?** ¿cuánto ganas?; **he ~s £350 a week** gana 350 libras a la semana; **the deal made him £500** ganó 500 libras con el negocio, el negocio le reportó 500 libras; **the film made millions** la película recaudó millones

4 *= reach, achieve* [+ *place*] llegar a; **will we ~ Paris before lunch?** ¿llegaremos a París antes de la hora de comer?; **Lara made a hundred** (*Cricket*) Lara hizo *or* se anotó 100 carreras; **the novel made the bestseller list** la novela entró en las listas de libros más vendidos; **we made it just in time** llegamos justo a tiempo; **can you ~ it by 10?** ¿puedes llegar a las 10?; **sorry, I can't ~ it** lo siento, no puedo *or* no me va bien; **do you think he'll ~ (it to) university?** ¿crees que conseguirá ir a la universidad?; **he made (it into) the first team** consiguió entrar en el primer equipo; **you've got the talent to ~ it** con tu talento llegarás muy lejos; **to ~ it with sb*** (*sexually*) hacérselo con algn*; **to ~ land** (*Naut*) llegar a tierra; **to ~ port** (*Naut*) tomar puerto; ✦*IDIOM* **he's got it made*** tiene el éxito asegurado

5 *= say, agree* **let's ~ it 9 o'clock** pongamos las 9; **another beer, please, no, ~ that two** otra cerveza por favor, no, que sean dos

6 *= cause to succeed* **this film made her** esta película la consagró; **he was made for life** se aseguró un porvenir brillante; ✦*IDIOM* **to ~ or break sth/sb**: **this deal will ~ or break him** con este negocio o fracasa o se asegura el éxito; **sex can ~ or break a relationship** el sexo es determinante en una relación, el sexo puede afianzar una relación o hacer que fracase

7 *= constitute* **this log ~s a good seat** este tronco va muy bien de asiento; **he'll ~ somebody a good husband** va a ser *or* hará un buen marido para algn; **it'll ~ a (nice) change not to have to cook every day** lo de no tener que cocinar cada día estará muy bien, ¡qué descanso, no tener que cocinar cada día!; **they ~ a lovely couple** hacen muy buena pareja; **he'll ~ a good footballer** será buen futbolista; **it ~s pleasant reading** es una lectura amena; **it still doesn't ~ a set** todavía no completa un juego entero; **it made a nice surprise** fue una sorpresa agradable

8 *= equal* **two and two ~ four** dos y dos son cuatro; **this one ~s 20** con éste son *or* hacen 20; **how much does that ~ (altogether)?** ¿a cuánto sube (en total)?; **8 pints ~ a gallon** 8 pintas hacen *or* son un galón

9 *= calculate* calcular; **what do you ~ the total?** ¿cuánto calculas que es el total?; **how many do you ~ it?** ¿cuántos calculas que hay?; **I ~ the total 17** calculo que hay 17 en total; **what time do you ~ it** ◊ **what do you ~ the time?** ¿qué hora tienes?; **I ~ it 6 o'clock** yo tengo las 6

10 *Cards* [+ *trick*] ganar, hacer; (*Bridge*) [+ *contract*] cumplir

11 *in set structures*

◆ **to make sb sth** (= *cause to be*) **to ~ sb king** hacer rey a algn; **he made her his wife** la hizo su esposa; **they've made Owen secretary** han nombrado secretario a Owen; **he made her a star** hizo de ella una estrella

◆ **to make sb/sth + ADJECTIVE/PAST PARTICIPLE**: **to ~ sb happy** hacer feliz a algn; **to ~ sb angry** poner furioso a algn; **to ~ o.s. heard** hacerse oír; **the noise made concentration difficult** *or* **made it difficult to concentrate** con ese ruido era difícil concentrarse; **why ~ things difficult for yourself?** ¿por qué te complicas la vida?; *see also* **ill A1**, **sick A2**, **unhappy 1**, *etc*

◆ **to make sth/sb into sth** convertir algo/a algn en algo; **we made the guest room into a study** convertimos la habitación de los invitados en estudio; **they have made him into a cult figure** lo han convertido en un ídolo; **the fibres are made into rope** con las fibras se hace cuerda

◆ **to make sb do sth** (= *cause to do sth*) hacer a algn hacer algo; (= *force to do sth*) hacer a algn hacer algo, obligar a algn a hacer algo; **to ~ sb laugh/cry** hacer reír/llorar a algn; **now look what you've made me do!** ¡mira lo que me has hecho hacer!; **what made you say that?** ¿cómo se te ocurrió decir eso?, ¿por qué dijiste eso?; **what ~s you do it?** ¿qué es lo que te lleva a hacerlo?; **it ~s you think, doesn't it?** da que pensar ¿no?; **he made me apologize to the teacher** me hizo pedir perdón *or* me obligó a pedir perdón al profesor; **you can't ~ me (do it)** no puedes obligarme (a hacerlo); **I was made to wait for an hour** me hicieron esperar una hora

◆ **to make o.s. do sth** obligarse a hacer algo; **I have to ~ myself (do it)** tengo que obligarme (a hacerlo), tengo que hacer un esfuerzo (por hacerlo); **she made herself look him in the eye** tuvo que obligarse a mirarle a los ojos

◆ **to make sth do, make do with sth** arreglárselas *or* apañárselas con algo; **I'll ~ do with what I've got** me las arreglaré con lo que tengo

12 *in set expressions*

◆ **to make good** [+ *promise*] cumplir; [+ *accusation*] hacer bueno, probar; [+ *claim*] justificar; [+ *loss*] compensar; [+ *damage*] reparar; (= *pay*) pagar; *see also* **make B**

◆ **to make sth of sth** (= *understand*) **I don't know what to ~ of it** no sé qué pensar; **what do you ~ of Anna?** ¿qué piensas de Anna?, ¿qué te parece Anna?; **what do you ~ of this?** ¿qué te parece esto?; **I can't ~ anything of this letter** no entiendo nada de lo que pone esta carta, no saco nada en claro de esta carta; (= *give importance to*) **I think you're making rather too much of what I said** creo que le estás dando demasiada importancia a lo que dije; *see also* **issue A1**

Ⓑ INTRANSITIVE VERB

in set expressions **to ~ after sb** perseguir a algn, correr tras algn; **he made as if to** + *INFIN* hizo como si + *subjun*, hizo ademán de + *infin*; **he made as if to strike me** hizo como si me fuera a pegar, hizo ademán de pegarme; **to ~ good** [*ex-criminal*] rehabilitar, reformar; **he was making like he didn't have any money** (*US**) hacía como si no tuviera dinero; ✦*IDIOM* **it's ~ or break time for the England team** al equipo inglés le ha llegado la hora de la verdad

Ⓒ NOUN

= brand marca *f*; **what ~ of car was it?** ¿qué marca de coche era?; **they are our own ~** son de nuestra propia marca; **they have rifles of Belgian ~** tienen fusiles de fabricación belga; ✦*IDIOM* **to be on the ~*** (*for money*) estar intentando sacar tajada*; (*for power*) ser muy ambicioso; (*for sex*) ir a la caza*, ir de ligoteo*

Ⓓ PHRASAL VERBS

► **make away** VI + ADV = **make off**

► **make away with** VI + PREP (= *murder*) **to ~ away with sb** eliminar a algn; **to ~ away with o.s.** (*euph*, †) quitarse la vida, suicidarse

► **make for** VI + PREP 1 (= *go towards*) [+ *place*] dirigirse hacia *or* a; **he made for the door** se dirigió hacia la puerta; **police think he may be making for Sweden** la policía cree que puede estar de camino a Suecia

2 (= *attack*) **to ~ for sb** atacar a algn, abalanzarse sobre algn

3 (= *contribute to*) contribuir a; (= *lead to*) conducir a; **it ~s for an easy life** contribuye a hacer la vida más fácil; **it doesn't ~ for good customer relations** no conduce a una buena relación con los clientes

► **make off** VI + ADV irse rápidamente, largarse*; **to ~ off with sth** llevarse algo, escaparse con algo, largarse con algo*

► **make out** Ⓐ VT + ADV 1 (= *write out*) [+ *cheque*] hacer, extender; [+ *receipt, list*] hacer; [+ *document*] redactar; (= *fill in*) [+ *form*] llenar; **to ~ a cheque out to somebody** hacer *or* extender un cheque a favor de algn; **the cheque should be made out to Pérez** el cheque debe extenderse a nombre de Pérez

2 (= *see, discern*) [+ *distant object*] distinguir, divisar

3 (= *decipher*) [+ *writing*] descifrar

4 (= *understand*) entender, comprender; **I can't ~ her out at all** no la entiendo *or* comprendo en absoluto; **can you ~ out what they're saying?** ¿entiendes lo que dicen?; **I can't ~ it out at all** no consigo entenderlo

5 (= *claim, imply*) **you ~ him out to be better than he is** lo haces parecer mejor de lo que es en realidad; **he's not as rich as people ~ out** no es tan rico como dice la gente; **the situation is not so bad as you ~ it out to be** la situación no es tan grave como la pintas; **the play ~s him out to be a fool** en la obra aparece como una idiota; **to ~ out that** dar a entender que; **they're making out it was my fault** están dando a entender que fue culpa mía; **all the time he made out he was working** estuvo todo el tiempo haciéndonos creer que estaba trabajando; **she made out it was a wrong number** hizo como que se había equivocado de número

Ⓑ VI + ADV (*) (= *get on*) (*with person*) llevarse; **how do you ~ out with your neighbours?** ¿cómo te llevas con tus vecinos?; **how did you ~ out at the audition?** ¿qué tal te fue en la audición?; **how are you making out on your pension?** ¿cómo te las arreglas con la pensión?; **to ~ out with sb** (*US**) (*sexually*) hacérselo con algn*

► **make over** VT + ADV 1 (= *assign*) ceder, traspasar (**to** a); **he had made over the farm to his son** le había cedido *or* traspasado la granja a su hijo

2 (= *revamp*) [+ *organization*] modernizar, poner al día; **to ~ o.s. over** cambiar de imagen

► **make up** Ⓐ VT + ADV 1 (= *invent*) inventar(se); **he made up the whole story** (se) inventó toda la historia; **you're making it up!** ¡te lo estás inventando!

2 (= *put together, prepare*) [+ *list*] hacer, preparar; [+ *parcel, bed*] hacer; [+ *medicine*] preparar; [+ *collection*] formar, reunir; [+ *sweater, dress*] montar y coser; **I'll ~ up a bed for him on the sofa** le haré una cama en el sofá; **the chemist's where I went to get the prescription made up** la farmacia a la que fui para que me preparasen la medicina; **I made the papers up into bundles** hice paquetes con los periódicos

3 (= *settle*) **to ~ up one's differences (with**

sb) resolver sus diferencias (con algn); **to ~ it up with sb** hacer las paces con algn, reconciliarse con algn; **they'd made up their quarrel** se habían reconciliado
4 (= *complete*) completar; **I paid £200 and my parents made up the difference** pagué 200 libras y mis padres pusieron la diferencia; **we need someone to ~ up the numbers** necesitamos a alguien para completar el grupo
5 (= *decide*) **to ~ up one's mind** decidirse
6 (= *compensate for, replace*) [+ *loss*] compensar; [+ *deficit*] cubrir; **if I take time off I have to ~ up the hours later** si me tomo tiempo libre después tengo que recuperar las horas; **I'd like to ~ it up to him for spoiling his birthday** me gustaría compensarle por haberle estropeado el cumpleaños; **he tried to ~ it up to her by buying her a bunch of flowers** intentó hacerse perdonar comprándole un ramo de flores; **to ~ up (lost) time** recuperar el tiempo perdido
7 (= *constitute*) componer; **women ~ up 13% of the police force** las mujeres componen el 13% del cuerpo de policía; **it is made up of 6 parts** lo componen 6 partes, está compuesto de 6 partes; **the group was made up of parents, teachers and doctors** el grupo lo componían *or* integraban padres, profesores y médicos; **the blood is made up of red and white cells** la sangre se compone de glóbulos rojos y glóbulos blancos
8 (*with cosmetics*) [+ *actor*] maquillar; **to ~ o.s. up** maquillarse, pintarse
9 [+ *fire*] (*with coal*) echar carbón a; (*with wood*) echar madera *or* leña a
Ⓑ VI + ADV 1 (*after quarrelling*) hacer las paces, reconciliarse
2 (= *apply cosmetics*) maquillarse, pintarse
► **make up for** VI + PREP (= *compensate for*) compensar; **her willingness to learn more than made up for her lack of experience** sus ganas de aprender compensaban con creces su falta de experiencia; **we hope this ~s up for the inconvenience caused** esperamos que esto compense los inconvenientes que podamos haberles causado; **to ~ up for lost time** recuperar el tiempo perdido
► **make up on** VI + PREP alcanzar, coger
► **make up to*** VI + PREP **to ~ up to sb** (procurar) congraciarse con algn, (procurar) ganarse el favor de algn

---

make-believe ['meɪkbɪ,liːv] Ⓐ ADJ fingido, simulado; [*world etc*] de ensueño, de fantasía; **~ play/games** juegos *mpl* de fantasía
Ⓑ N **don't worry, it's just ~** no te preocupes, no es de verdad; **a land** *or* **world of ~** un mundo de ensueño *or* fantasía; **to play at ~** jugar a ser personajes imaginarios
Ⓒ VI fingir
Ⓓ VT **to ~ that ...** fingir que ..., hacer que ...

makeover ['meɪkəʊvəʳ] N 1 (*lit*) (*by beautician*) sesión *f* de maquillaje y peluquería
2 (*fig*) lavado *m* de cara

maker ['meɪkəʳ] N 1 (= *craftsman*) creador(a) *m/f*, artífice *mf*
2 (= *manufacturer*) fabricante *mf*
3 (*Rel*) **Maker** Creador *m*, Hacedor *m*; **she has gone to meet her Maker** ha pasado a mejor vida, Dios la ha llamado a su seno; **prepare to meet your Maker** prepárate a morir

makeshift ['meɪkʃɪft] Ⓐ ADJ (= *improvised*) improvisado; (= *provisional*) provisional
Ⓑ N arreglo *m* provisional

make-up ['meɪkʌp] Ⓐ N 1 (= *cosmetics*) maquillaje *m*, pintura *f*; **she touched up her ~** se retocó el maquillaje; **she was wearing hardly any ~** llevaba muy poco maquillaje, iba casi sin maquillar; **to put on one's ~** maquillarse, pintarse
2 (= *composition*) composición *f*; (= *structure*) estructura *f*; (= *character*) carácter *m*, modo *m* de ser; **the racial ~ of a country** la composición racial de un país
3 [*of clothes*] confección *f*
4 (*Typ*) compaginación *f*, ajuste *m*
Ⓑ CPD ► **make-up artist** N maquillador(a) *m/f* ► **make-up bag** N neceser *m* del maquillaje ► **make-up girl** N maquilladora *f* ► **make-up remover** N desmaquillador *m*, desmaquillante *m*

makeweight ['meɪkweɪt] N 1 (= *weight, object*) contrapeso *m*
2 (*fig*) (= *person*) suplente *mf*, sustituto/a *m/f*; (*pej*) parche *m*, elemento *m* de relleno

making ['meɪkɪŋ] N 1 (= *production*) fabricación *f*; (= *preparation*) preparación *f*; (= *cutting and assembling*) [*of clothes*] confección *f*; **I wasn't involved in the ~ of the film** no colaboré en el rodaje de la película; **the building has been five years in the ~** llevan cinco años construyendo el edificio; **it's a disaster in the ~** es un desastre en potencia; **it's history in the ~** esto pasará a la historia; **the mistake was not of my ~** no soy yo el responsable del error; **she was caught in a trap of her own ~** había caído en su propia trampa; **it was the ~ of him** fue lo que lo consagró
2 **makings** elementos *mpl* (necesarios), ingredientes *mpl*; **a chain of events that had all the ~s of a Hollywood epic** una cadena de acontecimientos que tenía todos los elementos *or* ingredientes de una epopeya de Hollywood; **I have the ~s of a meal in the fridge** con lo que tengo en la nevera puedo hacer una comida; **he has the ~s of an actor** tiene madera de actor

Malachi ['mælə,kaɪ] N Malaquías *m*

malachite ['mælə,kaɪt] N malaquita *f*

maladjusted ['mælə'dʒʌstɪd] ADJ (*Psych*) inadaptado

maladjustment ['mælə'dʒʌstmənt] N (*Psych*) inadaptación *f*, desajuste *m*

maladministration ['mæləd,mɪnɪs'treɪʃən] N mala administración *f*

maladroit ['mælə'drɔɪt] ADJ torpe

maladroitly ['mælə'drɔɪtlɪ] ADV torpemente

maladroitness ['mælə'drɔɪtnɪs] N torpeza *f*

malady ['mælədɪ] N mal *m*, enfermedad *f*

Malagasy ['mæləgɑːzɪ] Ⓐ ADJ madagascarí
Ⓑ N madagascarí *mf*

malaise [mæ'leɪz] N malestar *m*

malapropism ['mæləprɒpɪzəm] N lapsus *m inv* linguae, equivocación *f* de palabras

malaria [mə'lɛərɪə] Ⓐ N malaria *f*, paludismo *m*
Ⓑ CPD ► **malaria control** N lucha *f* contra la malaria

malarial [mə'lɛərɪəl] ADJ palúdico

Malawi [mə'lɑːwɪ] N Malawi *m*, Malaui *m*

Malawian [mə'lɑːwɪən] Ⓐ ADJ malawiano, malauiano
Ⓑ N malawiano/a *m/f*, malauiano/a *m/f*

Malay [mə'leɪ] Ⓐ ADJ malayo
Ⓑ N 1 (= *person*) malayo/a *m/f*
2 (*Ling*) malayo *m*

Malaya [mə'leɪə] N (*Hist*) Malaya *f*

Malayan [mə'leɪən] Ⓐ ADJ malayo
Ⓑ N malayo/a *m/f*

Malaysia [mə'leɪzɪə] N Malaisia *f*

Malaysian [mə'leɪzɪən] Ⓐ ADJ malaisio
Ⓑ N malaisio/a *m/f*

malcontent ['mælkən'tent] Ⓐ ADJ malcontento, desafecto, revoltoso
Ⓑ N malcontento/a *m/f*, desafecto/a *m/f*, revoltoso/a *m/f*

Maldives ['mɔːldaɪvz], **Maldive Islands** [,mɔːldaɪv'aɪləndz] NPL (islas *fpl*) Maldivas *fpl*

male [meɪl] Ⓐ N (= *animal, plant*) macho *m*; (= *person*) varón *m*; **white ~s aged 35 to 40** varones de raza blanca de edades comprendidas entre los 35 y 40 años; **I don't need a ~ to support me** no necesito un hombre para que me mantenga
Ⓑ ADJ 1 [*rat, spider, plant*] macho; [*baby, child*] varón; [*friend, worker, colleague*] del sexo masculino; [*population, hormone, sex, attitude, behaviour*] masculino; [*voice*] de hombre, masculino; **please indicate whether you are ~ or female** por favor indique si es hombre *or* mujer
2 (*Tech*) [*plug*] macho
Ⓒ CPD ► **male chauvinism** N machismo *m* ► **male chauvinist** N machista *m* ► **the male member** N (*euph*) el miembro viril, el miembro masculino ► **male menopause** N menopausia *f* masculina, andropausia *f* ► **male model** N modelo *m* del sexo masculino ► **male nurse** N enfermero *m* ► **male prostitute** N prostituto *m* ► **male voice choir** N coro *m* masculino *or* de hombres; *see also* **supremacist**

malediction [,mælɪ'dɪkʃən] N maldición *f*

male-dominated ['meɪl'dɒmɪneɪtɪd] ADJ dominado por los hombres

malefactor ['mælɪfæktəʳ] N (*frm*) malhechor(a) *m/f*

maleness ['meɪlnɪs] N 1 (= *state of being male*) masculinidad *f*
2 (= *masculinity, virility*) masculinidad *f*, virilidad *f*

malevolence [mə'levələns] N malevolencia *f*

malevolent [mə'levələnt] ADJ malévolo

malevolently [mə'levələntlɪ] ADV con malevolencia

malformation ['mælfɔː'meɪʃən] N malformación *f*, deformidad *f*

malformed [,mæl'fɔːmd] ADJ malformado, deforme

malfunction [mæl'fʌŋkʃən] Ⓐ N [*of machine*] fallo *m*, mal funcionamiento *m*
Ⓑ VI funcionar mal

malice ['mælɪs] N 1 (= *grudge*) rencor *m*; (= *badness*) malicia *f*; **to bear sb ~** guardar rencor a algn; **I bear him no ~** no le guardo rencor; **out of ~** por malicia; **with ~ toward none** sin mala intención hacia nadie
2 (*Jur*) intención *f* delictuosa, dolo *m*; **~ aforethought** premeditación *f*

malicious [mə'lɪʃəs] Ⓐ ADJ [*person, remark*] malicioso
Ⓑ CPD ► **malicious damage** N (*Jur*) daños *mpl* intencionados ► **malicious libel** N difamación *f* intencionada, calumnia *f* intencionada

maliciously [mə'lɪʃəslɪ] ADV maliciosamente, con malicia

malign [mə'laɪn] Ⓐ ADJ maligno, malévolo
Ⓑ VT [+ *person, reputation*] calumniar, difamar; **you ~ me** eso no es justo

malignancy [mə'lɪgnənsɪ] N malignidad *f*

malignant [mə'lɪgnənt] ADJ (= *evil*) malvado; (*Med*) maligno

malignity [mə'lɪgnɪtɪ] N malignidad *f*

malinger [mə'lɪŋgəʳ] VI fingirse enfermo, hacer la encorvada*

malingerer [mə'lɪŋgərəʳ] N enfermo/a *m/f* fingido/a

mall [mɔːl] (*US*) [mæl] N 1 (= *avenue*) alameda *f*, paseo *m*
2 (*US*) (= *pedestrian street*) calle *f* peatonal
3 (*also* **shopping ~**) centro *m* comercial

mallard ['mæləd] N (*pl* **mallard(s)**) ánade *m* real

malleability [ˌmælɪə'bɪlɪtɪ] N maleabilidad *f*

malleable ['mælɪəbl] ADJ maleable, dúctil

mallet ['mælɪt] N (*Carpentry, Sport*) mazo *m*

mallow ['mæləʊ] N malva *f*

malnourished [ˌmæl'nʌrɪʃt] ADJ desnutrido

malnutrition ['mælnjʊ'trɪʃən] N desnutrición *f*

malodorous [mæ'ləʊdərəs] ADJ maloliente, hediondo

malpractice ['mæl'præktɪs] Ⓐ N (= *negligence*) negligencia *f* profesional; (= *wrongdoing*) práctica *f* abusiva
Ⓑ CPD ► **malpractice suit** N (*US Jur*) juicio *m* por negligencia profesional

malt [mɔːlt] Ⓐ N malta *f*
Ⓑ VT [+ *barley*] maltear; [+ *drink etc*] preparar con malta
Ⓒ CPD ► **malt extract** N extracto *m* de malta ► **malt liquor** N (*US*) cerveza *f* ► **malt whisky** N (*Brit*) whisky *m* de malta

Malta ['mɔːltə] N Malta *f*

malted ['mɔːltɪd] Ⓐ ADJ malteado
Ⓑ CPD ► **malted barley** N cebada *f* malteada, malta *f* de cebada ► **malted milk** N leche *f* malteada

Maltese ['mɔːl'tiːz] Ⓐ ADJ maltés
Ⓑ N (*pl* **Maltese**) 1 (= *person*) maltés/esa *m/f*
2 (*Ling*) maltés *m*
Ⓒ CPD ► **Maltese Cross** N cruz *f* de Malta

malthusianism [mæl'θjuːzɪəˌnɪzəm] N malt(h)usianismo *m*

malting barley [ˌmɔːltɪŋ'bɑːlɪ] N cebada *f* para maltear

maltreat [mæl'triːt] VT maltratar, tratar mal

maltreatment [mæl'triːtmənt] N maltrato *m*, maltratamiento *m*, malos tratos *mpl*

Malvinas [mæl'viːnəs] N **the ~** las Malvinas

mam* [mæm] N (*Brit dial*) mamá *f*

mama†* [mə'mɑː] N mamá *f*

mamba ['mæmbə] N (*Zool*) mamba *f*

mamma* [mə'mɑː] N (*esp US*) mamá *f*

mammal ['mæməl] N mamífero *m*

mammalian [mæ'meɪlɪən] ADJ mamífero

mammaries ['mæmərɪz] NPL (*hum*) pechos *mpl*

mammary ['mæmərɪ] Ⓐ ADJ mamario
Ⓑ CPD ► **mammary gland** N mama *f*, glándula *f* mamaria

mammogram ['mæməgræm] N mamografía *f*

mammography [mæ'mɒgrəfɪ] N mamografía *f*

Mammon ['mæmən] N Mammón

mammoth ['mæməθ] Ⓐ N (*Zool*) mamut *m*
Ⓑ ADJ descomunal, gigante

mammy ['mæmɪ] N 1 (*) mami *f*, mamaíta *f*, mamacita *f* (*LAm*)
2 (*US*) (= *black nurse*) nodriza *f* negra

man [mæn] Ⓐ N (*pl* **men**) 1 (= *not woman*) hombre *m*; (= *husband*) marido *m*; (= *boyfriend*) novio *m*; (= *servant*) criado *m*; (= *workman*) obrero *m*; (= *ordinary soldier*) soldado *m*; (= *ordinary sailor*) marinero *m*; **he's been a different ~ since he got married** es otro hombre desde que se casó; **the ~ who does the garden** el señor que hace el jardín; **when a ~ needs a wash** cuando uno necesita lavarse; **her ~ is in the army** (*husband*) su marido está en el ejército; (*boyfriend*) su novio está en el ejército; **officers and men** (= *soldiers*) oficiales y soldados; (= *sailors*) oficiales y marineros; **he's not the ~ to do it** él no es la persona adecuada para hacerlo; **I've lived here ~ and boy** vivo aquí desde pequeño; **he's not the ~ for the job** no es el más indicado para esa tarea; **~ of God** religioso *m*, clérigo *m*; **good ~!** ¡bravo!, ¡muy bien!; **my good ~†** buen hombre, amigo mío; **all good men and true** (*liter*) todos los que merecen llamarse hombres; **~ of letters** literato *m*; **it's got to be a local ~** tiene que ser uno de aquí; **to make a ~ of sb** hacer un hombre de algn; **the army will make a ~ out of him** el ejército le hará un hombre; **~ of means** hombre *m* acaudalado; **the ~ in the moon** el rostro de (mujer en) la luna; **to feel (like) a new ~** sentirse como nuevo; **look here, old ~†** mira, amigo; **my old ~*** el viejo*; **the ~ on the Clapham omnibus** el hombre de la calle; **our ~ in Washington** (= *agent*) nuestro agente en Washington; (= *representative*) nuestro representante en Washington; (= *ambassador*) nuestro embajador en Washington; **~ of parts** hombre *m* de talento; **~ of property** hombre *m* acaudalado; **~ of straw** (= *person of no substance*) monigote *m*, títere *m*; (*esp US*) (= *front man*) hombre *m* de paja, testaferro *m*; **the ~ in the street** el hombre de la calle; **the strong ~ of the government** el hombre fuerte del gobierno; **that ~ Jones** aquel Jones; **~ to ~** de hombre a hombre; **he's a ~ about town** es un gran vividor; **~ and wife** marido y mujer; **to live as ~ and wife** vivir como casados *or* en matrimonio; **a ~ of the world** un hombre de mundo; **a young ~** un joven; **her young ~** su novio; **✦IDIOMS this will separate** *or* **sort the men from the boys** con esto se verá quiénes son hombres y quiénes no; **to be ~ enough to do sth** ser lo bastante hombre *or* tener valor suficiente como para hacer algo; **to reach ~'s estate** (*frm*) llegar a la edad viril; *see also* **best E**, **cloth 4**, **grand A1**
2 (= *humanity in general*) (*also* **Man**) el hombre; **✦PROV ~ proposes, God disposes** el hombre propone y Dios dispone
3 (= *individual, person*) persona *f*; **what else could a ~ do?** ¿es que se podía hacer otra cosa?; **men say that …** se dice que …; **any ~** cualquiera, cualquier hombre; **no ~** ninguno, nadie; **as one ~** como un solo hombre; **one ~ one vote** un voto para cada uno; **they agreed to a ~** no hubo voz en contra; **they're communists to a ~** todos sin excepción son comunistas; **then I'm your ~** entonces soy la persona que estás buscando
4 (= *type*) **he's a six pints a night ~** es de los que se beben seis pintas en una noche; **he's a Celtic ~** es del Celtic; **I'm not a drinking ~** yo no bebo; **he's a family ~** (= *with family*) es padre de familia; (= *home-loving*) es muy casero; **I'm not a football ~** no soy aficionado al fútbol, no me gusta mucho el fútbol; **he's a man's ~** es un hombre estimado entre otros hombres; **he's his own ~** es un hombre muy fiel a sí mismo; **I'm a whisky ~ myself** yo prefiero el whisky
5 (*Chess*) pieza *f*; (*Draughts*) ficha *f*
6 (*) (*excl*) **hey ~!** ¡oye, tronco!*; **you can't do that, ~** hombre, no puedes hacer eso; **~, was I startled!** ¡vaya susto que me dio!, ¡qué susto me pegué!
Ⓑ VT [+ *ship*] tripular; [+ *fortress, watchtower*] guarnecer; [+ *guns*] servir; [+ *pumps*] acudir a, hacer funcionar; **the gun is ~ned by four soldiers** cuatro soldados manejan el cañón; **the telephone is ~ned all day** el teléfono está atendido todo el día; *see also* **manned**
Ⓒ CPD ► **man day** N (*Comm, Ind*) día-hombre *m* ► **man Friday** N criado *m* fiel ► **man hour** N (*Comm, Ind*) hora-hombre *f* ► **men's doubles** N (*Tennis*) dobles *mpl* masculinos ► **men's final** N (*Sport*) final *f* masculina ► **men's room** N (*esp US*) lavabo *m* de caballeros

manacle ['mænəkl] Ⓐ N 1 manilla *f*
2 **manacles** esposas *fpl*, grillos *mpl*
Ⓑ VT esposar, poner esposas a; **they were ~d together** iban esposados (juntos); **his hands were ~d** llevaba esposas en las muñecas

manage ['mænɪdʒ] Ⓐ VT 1 (= *direct*) [+ *firm, economy, shop*] dirigir, administrar; [+ *employees, team*] dirigir; [+ *time, property, money*] administrar; [+ *household*] llevar; (*Comput*) [+ *system, network*] gestionar; **he's been managing my affairs for years** lleva años encargándose de mis asuntos, hace años que lleva mis asuntos; **~d currency** moneda *f* controlada *or* dirigida; **~d economy** economía *f* planificada *or* dirigida; **~d fund** fondo *m* controlado *or* dirigido
2 (= *cope with, control*) [+ *situation*] manejar; [+ *suitcases, packages*] poder con; [+ *animal*] dominar; **you ~d the situation very well** manejaste muy bien la situación; **can you ~ the cases?** ¿puedes con las maletas?; **he has no idea how to ~ children** no tiene ni idea de cómo manejar *or* controlar a los niños; **he's clever at managing people** se le da bien manejar a la gente
3 (= *achieve*) **they've ~d only one win this season** sólo han conseguido una victoria esta temporada; **can you ~ two more in the car?** ¿te caben dos más en el coche?; **can you ~ eight o'clock?** ¿puedes estar para las ocho?; **I can't ~ Friday** el viernes no puedo; **to ~ to do sth** lograr hacer algo, conseguir hacer algo; **how did you ~ not to spill it?** ¿cómo lograste *or* conseguiste no derramarlo?; **he ~d not to get his feet wet** logró *or* consiguió no mojarse los pies; **he ~d to annoy everybody** consiguió irritar a todo el mundo; **£20 is all I can ~** 20 libras es todo lo que puedo dar *or* pagar; **can you ~ another cup?** ¿quieres otra taza?; **I couldn't ~ another mouthful** no podría comer ni un bocado más; **£20 is the most I can ~** 20 libras es todo lo que puedo dar *or* pagar
4 (*pej*) (= *manipulate*) [+ *news, election*] manipular
Ⓑ VI 1 (= *cope*) (*with situation*) arreglárselas; (*financially*) arreglarse, arreglárselas; **can you ~?** (= *deal with situation*) ¿puedes arreglártelas?; (= *carry sth*) ¿puedes con eso?; **thanks, I can ~** gracias, yo puedo; **she ~s on her pension/on £60 a week** se (las) arregla con la pensión/con 60 libras a la semana; **to ~ without sth/sb**: **"do you need the car?" — "I can ~ without it"** —¿necesitas el coche? —me (las) puedo arreglar *or* apañar sin él; **I don't know how we'd have ~d without her** no sé cómo nos (las) hubiéramos arreglado *or* apañado sin ella
2 (= *direct, administrate*) dirigir

manageable ['mænɪdʒəbl] ADJ 1 (= *controllable*) [*size, number, level, rate*] razonable; [*situation*] controlable; [*problem*] que se puede solucionar; [*vehicle*] manejable, fácil de maniobrar; [*hair*] dócil; **she reduces complex issues to ~ proportions** reduce cuestiones muy complejas a algo de proporciones manejables
2 (= *achievable*) [*task*] que se puede realizar; **this cycle ride is quite ~, even for children** este recorrido en bicicleta es fácil de realizar, incluso para los niños
3 (= *docile*) [*person, child, animal*] dócil

management ['mænɪdʒmənt] Ⓐ N 1 (= *process*) [*of firm*] dirección *f*, administración *f*, gestión *f*
2 (= *people*) directivos *mpl*; (= *managing body*) [*of firm*] dirección *f*, gerencia *f*; (*Theat*) empresa *f*; **"under new management"** "bajo nueva dirección"; **~ and workers** empresarios y trabajadores; **almost always ~ is at fault** casi siempre lo que falla es la gestión
3 (= *handling*) [*of situation*] manejo *m*
4 (*Univ*) (*also* **~ studies**) administración *f* de empresas
Ⓑ CPD ► **management accounting** N contabilidad *f* de gestión ► **management audit** N evaluación *f* administrativa *or* de gestión ► **management chart** N organigrama *m* de gestión ► **management committee** N comité *m* directivo ► **management consultancy** N consultoría *f* de gestión ► **management consultant** N consultor(a) *m/f* en gestión de empresas ► **management fee** N honorarios *mpl* de dirección ► **management review** N revisión *f* de gestión (de la gerencia) ► **management services** NPL servicios *mpl* de administración ► **management trainee** N ejecutivo/a *m/f* en formación

manager ['mænɪdʒəʳ] N [*of firm, bank, hotel*] director(a) *m/f*, gerente *mf*; [*of estate*] administrador(a) *m/f*; [*of football team*] director(a) *m/f* técnico/a; [*of restaurant, shop*] encargado/a *m/f*; [*of farm*] capataz(a) *m/f*, mayoral(a) *m/f*; [*of actor, singer*] representante *mf*, mánager *mf*; [*of boxer*] mánager *mf*; **she's a good ~** es buena administradora; *see also* **sale B**

manageress [ˌmænɪdʒə'res] N [*of restaurant, shop*] encargada *f*

managerial [ˌmænə'dʒɪərɪəl] ADJ directivo, de gestión; **the ~ class** el empresariado, la patronal; **at ~ level** a nivel directivo; **~ responsibilities** obligaciones *fpl* directivas; **~ staff** personal *m* directivo *or* de gerencia; **~ structure** estructura *f* administrativa; **~ style** estilo *m* de gestión

managing ['mænɪdʒɪŋ] CPD ► **managing director** N (*Brit*) director(a) *m/f* gerente ► **managing editor** N director(a) *m/f* editorial ► **managing partner** N socio *mf* gerente

man-at-arms ['mænət'ɑːmz] N (*pl* **men-at-arms** ['menət'ɑːmz]) hombre *m* de armas

manatee [ˌmænə'tiː] N manatí *m*

Manchuria [mæn'tʃʊərɪə] N Manchuria *f*

Manchurian [mæn'tʃʊərɪən] Ⓐ ADJ manchuriano
Ⓑ N manchuriano/a *m/f*

Mancunian [mæn'kjuːnɪən] Ⓐ ADJ de Manchester
Ⓑ N (= *native*) nativo/a *m/f* de Manchester; (= *inhabitant*) habitante *mf* de Manchester

mandarin ['mændərɪn] N 1 (= *person*) (*lit, fig*) mandarín *m*
2 (*also* **~ orange**) mandarina *f*
3 **Mandarin** (*Ling*) mandarín *m*

mandate ['mændeɪt] Ⓐ N 1 (= *authority*) mandato *m*; **the UN troops have no ~ to intervene in the fighting** las tropas de la ONU no tienen mandato para intervenir en el conflicto; **he does not have a ~ to rule this country** carece de autoridad para gobernar este país
2 (= *country*) territorio *m* bajo mandato
Ⓑ VT 1 (= *authorize*) [+ *person*] encomendar, encargar; [+ *elections*] autorizar
2 [+ *country*] asignar bajo mandato (**to** a)
3 (*US*) (= *make mandatory*) exigir

mandated ['mændeɪtɪd] ADJ 1 [*territory*] bajo mandato
2 [*delegate*] encargado

mandatory ['mændətərɪ] ADJ 1 (= *compulsory*) obligatorio; **each article contained the ~ quota of rude jokes** (*iro*) cada artículo contenía la cuota obligatoria de chistes verdes; **it is ~ that you complete levels one and two** es obligatorio que usted realice los niveles uno y dos, tiene usted que realizar los niveles uno y dos obligatoriamente
2 (*Jur*) [*sentence, penalty, fine*] preceptivo, obligatorio

Mandelbrot set ['mændəlˌbrɒtˌset] N (*Math*) conjunto *m* de Mandelbrot

mandible ['mændɪbl] N mandíbula *f*

mandolin(e) ['mændəlɪn] N mandolina *f*, bandolina *f* (*LAm*)

mandrake ['mændreɪk] N mandrágora *f*

mandrill ['mændrɪl] N mandril *m*

mane [meɪn] N [*of lion, person*] melena *f*; [*of horse*] crin *f*, crines *fpl*

man-eater ['mænˌiːtəʳ] N 1 (= *animal*) fiera *f* devoradora de hombres
2 (*) (= *woman*) devoradora *f* de hombres

man-eating ['mænˌiːtɪŋ] ADJ antropófago

maneuver *etc* [mə'nuːvəʳ] (*US*) = **manoeuvre** *etc*

manful ['mænfʊl] ADJ valiente, resuelto

manfully ['mænfəlɪ] ADV valientemente, resueltamente

manganese [ˌmæŋgə'niːz] Ⓐ N (*Chem*) manganeso *m*
Ⓑ CPD ► **manganese oxide** N óxido *m* de manganeso ► **manganese steel** N acero *m* al manganeso

mange [meɪndʒ] N sarna *f*

mangel(-wurzel) ['mæŋgl('wɜːzl)] N remolacha *f* forrajera

manger ['meɪndʒəʳ] N pesebre *m*

mangetout ['mɒnʒ'tuː] N (*also* **~ pea**) guisante *m*, arveja *f* (*LAm*) (*con vaina comestible*)

mangle¹ ['mæŋgl] Ⓐ N (= *device*) escurridor *m*
Ⓑ VT (= *wring*) pasar por el escurridor

mangle² ['mæŋgl] VT (= *crush*) aplastar; [+ *text etc*] mutilar, estropear

mango ['mæŋgəʊ] N (*pl* **mangoes**) (= *fruit, tree*) mango *m*

mangold(-wurzel) ['mæŋgəld('wɜːzl)] N remolacha *f* forrajera

mangrove ['mæŋgrəʊv] Ⓐ N mangle *m*
Ⓑ CPD ► **mangrove swamp** N manglar *m*

mangy ['meɪndʒɪ] ADJ (*compar* **mangier**; *superl* **mangiest**) roñoso, sarnoso

manhandle ['mænˌhændl] VT 1 (*esp Brit*) (= *move by hand*) mover a base de brazos; **we ~d the dinghy out of the shed** sacamos la barca del cobertizo a base de brazos
2 (*fig*) maltratar; **the police admitted manhandling the prisoners** la policía admitió haber maltratado a los presos; **the men were ~d into the back of the van** metieron a los hombres de muy malos modos en la trasera de la furgoneta

manhole ['mænhəʊl] Ⓐ N boca *f* de alcantarilla, registro *m* de alcantarilla
Ⓑ CPD ► **manhole cover** N tapa *f* de registro, tapa *f* de alcantarilla

manhood ['mænhʊd] N 1 (= *age of majority*) mayoría *f* de edad, madurez *f*; **to reach ~** alcanzar la mayoría de edad, llegar a la madurez
2 (= *manliness*) hombría *f*, virilidad *f*
3 (*frm*) (= *men*) hombres *mpl*; **English ~** ◊ **England's ~** (*liter*) todos los ingleses, todos los hombres de Inglaterra
4 (*euph*) (= *penis*) miembro *m* viril

manhunt ['mænhʌnt] N búsqueda *f* (*de delincuente, desaparecido*)

mania ['meɪnɪə] N manía *f*; **to have a ~ for (doing) sth** tener la manía de hacer algo

maniac ['meɪnɪæk] Ⓐ ADJ maníaco
Ⓑ N 1 maníaco/a *m/f*; **he drives like a ~** conduce como un loco
2 (*fig*) (= *enthusiast*) fanático/a *m/f*, maniático/a *m/f*; **these sports ~s** estos fanáticos *or* maniáticos del deporte

maniacal [mə'naɪəkəl] ADJ maníaco

maniacally [mə'naɪəkəlɪ] ADV [*work, laugh*] (*one person*) como (un) loco/(una) loca; (*more than one person*) como locos

manic ['mænɪk] Ⓐ ADJ 1 (= *insane*) [*person, behaviour*] maníaco; [*smile, laughter, stare*] de maníaco
2 (= *frenetic*) [*activity, energy*] frenético
Ⓑ CPD ► **manic depression** N maniacodepresión *f*; **she suffers from ~ depression** sufre maniacodepresión, es maniacodepresiva ► **manic depressive** N maniacodepresivo/a *m/f*

manically ['mænɪklɪ] ADV [*work, laugh, search*] (*one person*) como (un) loco/(una) loca; (*more than one person*) como locos; **he was pacing ~ up and down** se paseaba arriba y abajo como si estuviera loco; **he is ~ tidy** es un maniático del orden

Manichaean, Manichean [ˌmænɪ'kiːən] Ⓐ ADJ maniqueo
Ⓑ N maniqueo/a *m/f*

Manichaeism, Manicheism [ˌmænɪ'kiːɪzəm] N maniqueísmo *m*

manicure ['mænɪkjʊəʳ] Ⓐ N manicura *f*
Ⓑ VT [+ *person*] hacer la manicura a; [+ *nails*] limpiar, arreglar
Ⓒ CPD ► **manicure case, manicure set** N estuche *m* de manicura

manicured ['mænɪkjʊəd] ADJ 1 [*nails, hands*] muy cuidado
2 [*lawn, garden*] muy cuidado

manicurist ['mænɪkjʊərɪst] N manicuro/a *m/f*

manifest ['mænɪfest] Ⓐ ADJ manifiesto, patente; **to make sth ~** poner algo de manifiesto
Ⓑ VT manifestar; **to ~ itself** manifestarse
Ⓒ N (*Naut, Comm*) manifiesto *m*

manifestation [ˌmænɪfes'teɪʃən] N manifestación *f*

manifestly ['mænɪfestlɪ] ADV evidentemente

manifesto [ˌmænɪ'festəʊ] N (*pl* **manifesto(e)s**) manifiesto *m*

manifold ['mænɪfəʊld] Ⓐ ADJ (= *numerous*) múltiple; (= *varied*) diverso
Ⓑ N (*Aut*) colector *m* de escape

manikin ['mænɪkɪn] N = **mannikin**

Manila [mə'nɪlə] N Manila *f*

manil(l)a [mə'nɪlə] ADJ [*envelope, paper*] manila

manioc ['mænɪɒk] N mandioca *f*, yuca *f*

manipulate [mə'nɪpjʊleɪt] VT 1 [+ *tool, machine, vehicle*] manipular, manejar
2 (*fig*) [+ *facts, figures*] manipular; [+ *public opinion, person*] manipular

manipulation [məˌnɪpjʊ'leɪʃən] N 1 [*of tool, machine, vehicle*] manipulación *f*, manejo *m*
2 (*fig*) [*of facts, figures, public opinion, person*] manipulación *f*

manipulative [mə'nɪpjʊlətɪv] ADJ (*fig*) [*person, behaviour*] manipulador

manipulator [mə'nɪpjʊˌleɪtəʳ] N manipulador(a) *m/f*

mankind [mæn'kaɪnd] N humanidad *f*, género *m* humano

manlike ['mænlaɪk] ADJ 1 (= *manly*) varonil
2 (= *like man*) parecido al hombre

manliness ['mænlɪnɪs] N masculinidad *f*, hombría *f*, virilidad *f*

manly ['mænlɪ] (**manlier, manliest**) ADJ [1] (= *masculine*) [*person, physique*] varonil, viril; [*quality, pursuit*] masculino, varonil; **it wasn't ~ to talk about one's emotions** hablar de los propios sentimientos no era cosa de hombres
[2] (= *courageous*) valiente

man-made ['mæn'meɪd] ADJ [*material*] sintético, artificial; [*lake, island, environment*] artificial; [*gas, chemical*] producido por el hombre; **~ fibres** fibras *fpl* sintéticas; **~ disasters such as Chernobyl** desastres provocados por el hombre como Chernobyl

manna ['mænə] N maná *m*; ✦*IDIOM* **~ from heaven** maná *m* caído del cielo

manned [mænd] ADJ tripulado; **a fully ~ ship** un buque con toda su tripulación *or* dotación

mannequin ['mænɪkɪn] Ⓐ N [1] (= *dressmaker's dummy*) maniquí *m*
[2] (= *fashion model*) modelo *f*, maniquí *f*
Ⓑ CPD ► **mannequin parade** N desfile *m* de modelos

manner ['mænəʳ] N [1] (= *mode, way*) manera *f*, modo *m*; **after** *or* **in this ~** de esta manera; **after** *or* **in the ~ of Van Gogh** a la manera *or* al estilo de Van Gogh; **a princess (as) to the ~ born** una princesa nata; **in like ~** de la misma manera; **~ of payment** modo *m* de pago, forma *f* de pago; **in a ~ of speaking** (= *so to speak*) por así decirlo, como si dijéramos; (= *up to a point*) hasta cierto punto, en cierto modo; **it's a ~ of speaking** es sólo una manera *or* forma de hablar; **in such a ~ that ...** de tal manera que ...
[2] (= *behaviour etc*) forma *f* de ser, comportamiento *m*; **I don't like his ~** no me gusta su forma de ser; **there's something odd about his ~** tiene un aire algo raro; **he had the ~ of an old man** tenía aire de viejo
[3] (= *class, type*) clase *f*; **what ~ of man is he?** ¿qué clase *or* tipo de hombre es?; **all ~ of** toda clase *or* suerte de; **by no ~ of means** de ningún modo; **no ~ of doubt** sin ningún género de duda
[4] **manners** [4·1] [*of person*] modales *mpl*, educación *fsing*; **bad ~s** falta *f* de educación, malos modos *mpl*; **to have bad ~s** ser maleducado; **it's bad ~s to yawn** es de mala educación bostezar; **to forget one's ~s** perder la compostura; **aren't you forgetting your ~s?** (*to child*) no seas maleducado; **good ~s** educación *f*, buenos modales *mpl*; **good ~s demand that ...** la educación exige que ...; **it's good ~s to say "please"** se dice "por favor"; **he's got no ~s** es un maleducado; **road ~s** comportamiento *m* en la carretera; **to teach sb ~s** enseñar a algn a comportarse
[4·2] [*of society*] costumbres *fpl*; **a novel of ~s** una novela costumbrista *or* de costumbres; ✦*PROV* **~s maketh (the) man** la conducta forma al hombre

mannered ['mænəd] ADJ [1] (= *affected*) [*style*] amanerado
[2] (= *camp*) cursi

-mannered ['mænəd] ADJ (*ending in compounds*) de modales ...; *see* **bad-mannered** *etc*

mannerism ['mænərɪzəm] N [1] (= *gesture etc*) gesto *m*
[2] (*Art, Literat*) (*also* **Mannerism**) manierismo *m*; (*pej*) amaneramiento *m*

mannerist ['mænərɪst] Ⓐ ADJ manierista
Ⓑ N manierista *mf*

mannerliness ['mænəlɪnɪs] N (buena) educación *f*, crianza *f*, cortesía *f*

mannerly ['mænəlɪ] ADJ educado, formal

mannikin ['mænɪkɪn] N [1] (= *dressmaker's dummy*) maniquí *m*
[2] (= *fashion model*) modelo *f*, maniquí *f*
[3] (*frm*) (= *dwarf*) enano *m*

manning levels ['mænɪŋlevlz] NPL niveles *mpl* de personal

mannish ['mænɪʃ] ADJ hombruno

manoeuvrability, maneuverability (*US*) [mə,nuːvrə'bɪlɪtɪ] N maniobrabilidad *f*

manoeuvrable, maneuverable (*US*) [mə'nuːvrəbl] ADJ manejable

manoeuvre, maneuver (*US*) [mə'nuːvəʳ] Ⓐ N [1] (*Mil*) maniobra *f*; **to be on ~s** estar de maniobras
[2] (*fig*) (= *clever plan*) maniobra *f*, estratagema *f*; **this leaves us little room for ~** esto apenas nos deja margen de maniobra
Ⓑ VT (*gen*) maniobrar; **to ~ a gun into position** colocar un cañón en posición; **I was ~d into it** me embaucaron para que lo hiciera; **to ~ sb into doing sth** manipular a algn para que haga algo
Ⓒ VI maniobrar

manoeuvring, maneuvering (*US*) [mə'nuːvrɪŋ] N el maniobrar; **political ~s** maniobras *fpl* políticas

man-of-war ['mænəv'wɔːʳ] N (*pl* **men-of-war** ['menəv'wɔːʳ]) N buque *m* de guerra

manometer [mə'nɒmɪtəʳ] N manómetro *m*

manor ['mænəʳ] Ⓐ N [1] (*feudal*) señorío *m*; (*modern*) finca *f*
[2] (*Brit Police**) distrito *m*, barrio *m*
Ⓑ CPD ► **manor house** N casa *f* solariega, casa *f* señorial

manorial [mə'nɔːrɪəl] ADJ señorial

manpower ['mænpaʊəʳ] Ⓐ N mano *f* de obra; (*Mil*) soldados *mpl*
Ⓑ CPD ► **manpower planning** N planificación *f* de recursos humanos *or* mano de obra

manqué ['mɔːŋkeɪ] ADJ **a novelist ~** un novelista frustrado

manse [mæns] N (*esp Brit*) casa *f* del pastor (protestante)

manservant ['mæn,sɜːvənt] N (*pl* **menservants** *or* **manservants** ['men,sɜːvənts]) criado *m*

mansion ['mænʃən] Ⓐ N mansión *f*; [*of ancient family*] casa *f* solariega
Ⓑ CPD ► **Mansion House** N (*Brit*) *residencia del alcalde de Londres*

man-sized ['mænsaɪzd] ADJ [1] (*lit*) de tamaño de hombre
[2] (*fig*) bien grande, grandote

manslaughter ['mæn,slɔːtəʳ] N homicidio *m* involuntario

mantelpiece ['mæntlpiːs] N repisa *f* (de chimenea)

mantelshelf† ['mæntlʃelf] N (*pl* **mantelshelves** ['mæntlʃelvz]) = **mantelpiece**

mantilla [mæn'tɪlə] N mantilla *f*, velo *m*

mantis ['mæntɪs] N (*pl* **mantises** *or* **mantes**) **praying ~** mantis *f inv* religiosa

mantle ['mæntl] Ⓐ N [1] (= *layer*) capa *f*; (= *blanket*) manto *m*; **a ~ of snow** una capa de nieve
[2] (= *gas mantle*) manguito *m* incandescente, camisa *f* incandescente
[3] (††) (= *cloak*) manto *m*
[4] **he accepted the ~ of leader** asumió el liderazgo, aceptó el cargo de líder; **the ~ of responsibility** la plena responsabilidad
Ⓑ VT (*liter*) cubrir (**in** de), envolver (**in** en)

mantlepiece ['mæntlpiːs] N = **mantelpiece**

mantleshelf† ['mæntlʃelf] N = **mantelpiece**

man-to-man ['mæntə'mæn] Ⓐ ADJ de hombre a hombre
Ⓑ ADV de hombre a hombre

mantra ['mæntrə] N mantra *m*

mantrap ['mæntræp] N cepo *m*

manual ['mænjʊəl] Ⓐ ADJ manual; **~ labour** *or* (*US*) **labor** trabajo *m* manual; **~ training** enseñanza *f* de artes y oficios; **~ worker** trabajador(a) *m/f* manual
Ⓑ N [1] (= *book*) manual *m*
[2] (*Mus*) teclado *m*

manually ['mænjʊəlɪ] ADV manualmente, a mano

manufacture [,mænjʊ'fæktʃəʳ] Ⓐ N [1] (= *act*) fabricación *f*
[2] (= *manufactured item*) producto *m* manufacturado
Ⓑ VT [1] (*Ind*) fabricar; **~d goods** productos *mpl* manufacturados
[2] (*fig*) fabricar, inventar

manufacturer [,mænjʊ'fæktʃərəʳ] N fabricante *mf*

manufacturing [,mænjʊ'fæktʃərɪŋ] Ⓐ N fabricación *f*
Ⓑ CPD [*town, city, sector*] industrial, manufacturero/a ► **manufacturing base** N base *f* industrial ► **manufacturing capacity** N capacidad *f* de fabricación ► **manufacturing costs** NPL costes *mpl* de fabricación ► **manufacturing industries** NPL industrias *fpl* manufactureras

manure [mə'njʊəʳ] Ⓐ N estiércol *m*, abono *m*
Ⓑ VT estercolar, abonar
Ⓒ CPD ► **manure heap** N estercolero *m*

manuscript ['mænjʊskrɪpt] Ⓐ N manuscrito *m*; (= *original of book, article*) original *m*
Ⓑ ADJ manuscrito

Manx [mæŋks] Ⓐ ADJ de la Isla de Man
Ⓑ N [1] (*Ling*) lengua *f* de la Isla de Man
[2] **the ~** (= *people*) los nativos de la Isla de Man
Ⓒ CPD ► **Manx cat** N *gato rabón de pelo corto*

Manxman ['mæŋksmən] N (*pl* **Manxmen**) nativo *m* de la Isla de Man

Manxwoman ['mæŋkswʊmən] N (*pl* **Manxwomen**) nativa *f* de la Isla de Man

many ['menɪ] Ⓐ ADJ muchos/as; **~ people** mucha gente, muchas personas; **in ~ cases** en muchos casos; **a good** *or* **a great ~ houses** muchas *or* (*LAm*) bastantes casas; **however ~ books you have** por muchos libros que tengas; **not ~ people** poca gente; **so ~** tantos/as; **so ~ flies** tantas moscas; **ever so ~ people** la mar de gente, tantísimas personas; **~ a time I've seen him act** ◊ **~'s the time I've seen him act** muchas veces lo he visto actuar; **too ~** demasiados/as; **too ~ difficulties** demasiadas dificultades
Ⓑ PRON muchos/as; **~ of them came** muchos (de ellos) vinieron; **he has as ~ as I have** tiene tantos como yo; **he has three times as ~ as I have** tiene tres veces más que yo; **there were as ~ as 100 at the meeting** asistieron a la reunión hasta cien personas; **as ~ again** otros tantos; **and as ~ more** y otros tantos; **how ~ are there?** ¿cuántos hay?; **how ~ there are!** ¡cuántos hay!; **however ~ you have** por muchos que tengas; **not ~ came** vinieron pocos
Ⓒ N **the ~** la mayoría

many-coloured, many-colored (*US*) ['menɪ'kʌləd] ADJ multicolor

many-sided ['menɪ'saɪdɪd] ADJ [1] [*figure*] multilátero
[2] (*fig*) [*talent, personality*] multifacético, polifacético; [*problem*] complicado

Maoism ['maʊɪzəm] N maoísmo *m*

Maoist ['maʊɪst] Ⓐ ADJ maoísta
Ⓑ N maoísta *mf*

Maori ['maʊrɪ] Ⓐ ADJ maorí
Ⓑ N 1 (= *person*) maorí *mf*
2 (*Ling*) maorí *m*

Mao Tse-tung ['maʊtseɪ'tʊŋ] N Mao Zedong

map [mæp] Ⓐ N [*of town*] plano *m*; [*of world, country*] mapa *m*; (= *chart*) carta *f*; ✦*IDIOMS* **this will put us on the ~** esto nos dará a conocer; **it's right off the ~** está en el quinto infierno
Ⓑ VT **to ~ an area** levantar un mapa de una zona

►**map out** VT + ADV 1 (*lit*) indicar en un mapa
2 (= *organize*) [+ *strategy, future*] planificar, planear; [+ *schedule*] elaborar, confeccionar; [+ *plan*] trazar

maple ['meɪpl] Ⓐ N (*also* **~ tree**) arce *m*
Ⓑ CPD ► **maple leaf** N hoja *f* de arce ► **maple sugar** N azúcar *m* de arce ► **maple syrup** N jarabe *m* de arce

mapmaker ['mæp,meɪkəʳ] N cartógrafo/a *m/f*

mapmaking ['mæp,meɪkɪŋ], **mapping** ['mæpɪŋ] N cartografía *f*

mar [mɑːʳ] VT estropear, echar a perder; **to ~ sb's enjoyment** aguar la fiesta a algn

Mar. ABBR (= **March**) mar.

maracas [mər'ækəs] NPL maracas *fpl*

maraschino [,mærəs'kiːnəʊ] Ⓐ N marrasquino *m*
Ⓑ CPD ► **maraschino cherries** NPL guindas *fpl* en conserva de marrasquino

marathon ['mærəθən] Ⓐ N (*Sport*) maratón *m*
Ⓑ ADJ (*fig*) maratoniano
Ⓒ CPD ► **marathon runner** N corredor(a) *m/f* de maratón

maraud [mə'rɔːd] VI merodear

marauder [mə'rɔːdəʳ] N merodeador(a) *m/f*, intruso/a *m/f*

marauding [mə'rɔːdɪŋ] Ⓐ ADJ merodeador, intruso
Ⓑ N merodeo *m*

marble ['mɑːbl] Ⓐ N 1 (= *material*) mármol *m*
2 (= *work in marble*) obra *f* en mármol
3 (= *glass ball*) canica *f*, bolita *f* (*Andes, S. Cone*), metra *f* (*Ven*); **to play ~s** jugar a las canicas; ✦*IDIOM* **to lose one's ~s*** perder la chaveta*
Ⓑ CPD marmóreo, de mármol ► **marble quarry** N cantera *f* de mármol ► **marble staircase** N escalera *f* de mármol

marbled ['mɑːbld] ADJ 1 (= *covered with marble*) [*floor, pillar, room*] revestido de mármol
2 (= *patterned, streaked*) [*paper, tabletop, work surface*] marmolado; [*meat*] con vetas de grasa; [*soap*] con vetas; **~ effect** efecto *m* marmolado

March [mɑːtʃ] N marzo *m*; *see* **July** *for usage*

march¹ [mɑːtʃ] Ⓐ N (*Mil, Mus*) marcha *f*; (*fig*) (= *long walk*) marcha *f*, caminata *f*; **forced ~** marcha *f* forzada; **an army on the ~** un ejército en marcha; **we were on the ~ to the capital** marchábamos hacia *or* sobre la capital; **it's a day's ~ from here** está a un día de marcha desde aquí; (*fig*) eso queda lejísimos; *see also* **quick A1**, **steal A1**
Ⓑ VT 1 [+ *soldiers*] hacer marchar, llevar; **I was ~ed into an office** me llevaron a un despacho, me hicieron entrar en un despacho
2 [+ *distance*] recorrer (marchando)
Ⓒ VI 1 (*Mil*) marchar; **forward ~!** de frente ¡ar!; **quick ~!** al trote ¡ar!; **to ~ past** desfilar; **to ~ past sb** desfilar ante algn
2 (= *demonstrate*) manifestarse, hacer una manifestación
3 (*fig*) **to ~ into a room** entrar resueltamente en un cuarto; **to ~ up to sb** abordar a algn
Ⓓ CPD ► **march past** N (*Mil*) desfile *m*

►**march in** VI + ADV entrar (resueltamente *etc*)

►**march off** Ⓐ VT + ADV **to ~ sb off** llevarse a algn
Ⓑ VI + ADV irse (resueltamente *etc*)

►**march on** Ⓐ VI + PREP marchar sobre
Ⓑ VI + ADV seguir marchando

►**march out** VI + ADV salir (airado, resueltamente *etc*)

march² [mɑːtʃ] N (*Hist*) marca *f*; **the Spanish March** la Marca Hispánica; **the Welsh ~es** la marca galesa

marcher ['mɑːtʃəʳ] N (*on demonstration*) marchista *mf*, manifestante *mf*

marching ['mɑːtʃɪŋ] Ⓐ ADJ [*song*] de marcha
Ⓑ CPD ► **marching orders** NPL (*Mil*) orden *fsing* de ponerse en marcha; ✦*IDIOMS* **to get one's ~ orders*** ser despedido; **to give sb his ~ orders*** despedir a algn, poner a algn en la calle*

marchioness ['mɑːʃənɪs] N marquesa *f*

mare [mɛəʳ] Ⓐ N yegua *f*
Ⓑ CPD ► **mare's nest** N (*fig*) parto *m* de los montes

marg* [mɑːdʒ] N (*Brit*) = **margarine**

Margaret ['mɑːgərɪt] N Margarita

margarine [,mɑːdʒə'riːn] N margarina *f*

margarita [,mɑːgə'riːtə] N (= *drink*) margarita *f*

Marge [mɑːdʒ] N (*familiar form*) of **Margaret, Marjory**

marge* [mɑːdʒ] N (*Brit*) = **margarine**

margin ['mɑːdʒɪn] N 1 (*on page*) margen *m*; **to write sth in the ~** escribir algo al margen
2 (*fig*) margen *m*; **~ of error** margen *m* de error; **~ of safety** margen *m* de seguridad; **to win by a wide/narrow ~** vencer por un amplio/estrecho margen; **they live on the ~(s) of society** viven al margen *or* marginados de la sociedad
3 (*Comm*) (*also* **profit ~, ~ of profit**) margen *m* de beneficios

marginal ['mɑːdʒɪnl] Ⓐ ADJ 1 (= *very small*) [*benefit, improvement, difference, increase*] mínimo, insignificante; [*role*] marginal, menor; **to be of ~ importance** *or* **significance** tener una importancia menor
2 (= *peripheral*) [*issue*] menor; [*character, public figure*] marginal, al margen; **these points are ~ to the issue of sovereignty** estos puntos son tangenciales respecto a la cuestión de la soberanía; **they are made to feel ~ to the rest of society** se les hace sentirse al margen de la sociedad
3 (*Brit Parl*) [*seat*] obtenido con escasa mayoría; **~ constituency** *distrito electoral en la que un determinado partido ha ganado con escasa mayoría*
4 (*Econ*) [*cost, utility, productivity*] marginal; **~ tax rate** tasa *f* impositiva marginal
5 (*Agr*) [*land*] poco rentable
Ⓑ N (*Brit Parl*) (*also* **~ seat**) *escaño obtenido por escasa mayoría*; (*also* **~ constituency**) *distrito electoral en el que un determinado partido ha ganado con escasa mayoría*

> **MARGINAL SEAT**
>
> *En el Reino Unido se llama* **marginal seat** *o* **marginal constituency** *al escaño (y al distrito electoral correspondiente) que se gana por escaso margen, con lo cual en las siguientes elecciones hay muchas posibilidades de que pueda ganarlo a su vez la oposición. Debido a esto, si dicho escaño queda vacante por fallecimiento o dimisión de un parlamentario y se convocan elecciones parciales con carácter excepcional para cubrirlo (***by-election***), el resultado de las mismas será tomado por los medios de comunicación como un indicador de la popularidad del gobierno. Por el contrario, el escaño que un partido suele ganar por amplia mayoría, debido a la homogeneidad en la tendencia política de los electores, se conoce como* **safe seat**.
>
> ⇨ *Ver tb* BY-ELECTION

marginalize [,mɑːdʒɪnəlaɪz] VT marginar

marginally ['mɑːdʒɪnəlɪ] ADV ligeramente; **sales were ~ better in November** las ventas fueron ligeramente mejores en noviembre; **wholemeal loaves are only ~ more expensive than white ones** las barras de pan integral son sólo ligeramente más caras que las de pan blanco; **they were only ~ affected by the war** la guerra apenas los afectó

marguerite [,mɑːgə'riːt] N (*Bot*) margarita *f*

Maria [mə'riːə] N María

Marian ['mɛərɪən] ADJ mariano

Marie Antoinette [mə'riːæntwɑː'net] N María Antonieta

marigold ['mærɪgəʊld] N (*Bot*) maravilla *f*

marijuana, marihuana [,mærɪ'hwɑːnə] N marihuana *f*, mariguana *f*

marimba [mə'rɪmbə] N marimba *f*

marina [mə'riːnə] N puerto *m* deportivo

marinade [,mærɪ'neɪd] Ⓐ N adobo *m*
Ⓑ VT adobar
Ⓒ VI estar en adobo

marinate ['mærɪneɪt] Ⓐ VT adobar
Ⓑ VI estar en adobo

marine [mə'riːn] Ⓐ N 1 (*Mil*) (= *person*) infante *m* de marina; **the Marines** (*Brit*) la infantería de marina; (*US*) los marines; ✦*IDIOM* **tell that to the ~s!†*** ¡a otro perro con ese hueso!*
2 (= *fleet*) marina *f*; **the merchant** *or* **mercantile ~** la marina mercante
Ⓑ ADJ 1 (= *sea*) [*creature, plant, pollution*] marino
2 (= *maritime*) [*law, warfare*] marítimo
Ⓒ CPD ► **marine biologist** N biólogo/a *m/f* marino/a ► **marine biology** N biología *f* marina ► **Marine Corps** N (*US*) Infantería *f* de Marina ► **marine engineer** N ingeniero/a *m/f* naval ► **marine engineering** N ingeniería *f* naval ► **marine insurance** N seguro *m* marítimo ► **marine life** N vida *f* marina, flora y fauna *f* marina ► **marine science** N ciencia *f* marina ► **marine scientist** N científico/a *m/f* marino/a

mariner ['mærɪnəʳ] N marinero *m*, marino *m*

Mariolatry [,mɛərɪ'ɒlətrɪ] N mariolatría *f*

Mariology [,mɛərɪ'ɒlədʒɪ] N mariología *f*

marionette [,mærɪə'net] N títere *m*, marioneta *f*

marital ['mærɪtl] Ⓐ ADJ [*home, bliss*] conyugal; [*problems*] matrimonial, conyugal; **the ~ bed** el lecho conyugal
Ⓑ CPD ► **marital counselling** N orientación *f* sobre problemas matrimoniales ► **marital rape** N violación *f* dentro del matrimonio ► **marital status** N estado *m* civil

maritime ['mærɪtaɪm] Ⓐ ADJ marítimo
Ⓑ CPD ► **maritime law** N derecho *m* marítimo

marjoram ['mɑːdʒərəm] N mejorana *f*, orégano *m*

mark¹ [mɑːk] N (= *currency*) marco *m*

mark² [mɑːk] Ⓐ N 1 (= *stain, spot etc*) mancha *f*; **the ~s of violence** las señales de violencia; **he left the ring without a ~ on his**

body salió del cuadrilátero sin llevar señal alguna en el cuerpo
2 (= *written symbol on paper etc*) señal *f*, marca *f*; (*instead of signature*) signo *m*, cruz *f*; (*fig*) (= *imprint, trace*) huella *f*; **to make one's ~** (*lit*) firmar con una cruz; (*fig*) dejar huella, distinguirse; ✦**IDIOM to make/leave one's ~ on sth** dejar huella en algo; **he has certainly made his ~ on British politics** no cabe duda de que ha dejado huella en la política británica
3 (= *indication*) señal *f*; (= *proof*) prueba *f*; **as a ~ of my disapproval** en señal de mi desaprobación; **as a ~ of our gratitude** en señal de nuestro agradecimiento; **it's the ~ of a gentleman** es señal de un caballero; **it bears the ~ of genius** lleva la marca de un genio
4 (*in exam*) nota *f*, calificación *f*; **52 ~s** 52 puntos, 52 por cien; **to get high ~s in French** sacar buena nota en francés; **to get no ~s at all as a cook** (*fig*) ser un desastre como cocinero; **there are no ~s for guessing** (*fig*) las simples conjeturas no merecen punto alguno; *see also* **full D**, **top¹ B4**
5 (= *target*) blanco *m*; **to hit the ~** (*lit*) alcanzar el objetivo, acertar; (*fig*) dar en el clavo; **to be wide of the ~** (*lit*) errar el tiro; (*fig*) estar lejos de la verdad; ✦**IDIOMS he's way off the ~** no acierta ni con mucho; **he's on the ~** ha dado en el blanco, está en lo cierto
6 (*Sport*) (= *line*) raya *f*; **to be quick/slow off the ~** ser rápido/lento al salir; (*fig*) ser muy vivo/parado; **on your ~s, get set, go!** ¡preparados, listos, ya!
7 (= *level, standard*) **to hit the £1000 ~** alcanzar el total de 1000 libras; **gas ~ 1** (*Culin*) número 1 del gas; ✦**IDIOMS to be up to the ~** [*person*] estar a la altura de las circunstancias; [*work*] alcanzar el nivel necesario; **to come up to the ~** alcanzar el nivel que era de esperar; *see also* **overstep**
8 (= *model*) **a Spitfire Mark 1** un Spitfire (de) primera serie
9 (*Comm*) (= *label*) marca *f*
10 (= *distinction*) **of ~** de categoría, de cierta distinción
Ⓑ VT 1 (= *make a mark on*) marcar; **~ it with an asterisk** ponga un asterisco allí
2 (= *stain*) manchar; **he wasn't ~ed at all** no mostraba señal alguna de golpe
3 [+ *bird, animal*] **a bird ~ed with red** un pájaro manchado de rojo, un pájaro con manchas rojas
4 (= *label*) rotular; (= *price*) indicar el precio de; **this exhibit is not ~ed** este objeto no lleva rótulo; **the chair is ~ed at £12** la silla tiene un precio de 12 libras
5 (= *indicate*) señalar, indicar; (= *characterize*) señalar, distinguir; [+ *anniversary etc*] señalar, celebrar; [+ *birthday*] festejar; **stones ~ the path** unas piedras señalan el camino; **this ~s the frontier** esto marca la frontera; **it ~s a change of policy** indica un cambio de política; **this ~s him as a future star** esto le señala como un as futuro; **it's not ~ed on the map** no está indicado en el mapa; **we must do something special to ~ the occasion** tenemos que hacer algo especial para celebrarlo
6 (= *note down*) apuntar; (= *notice*) advertir, observar; (= *heed*) prestar atención a; **did you ~ where it fell?** (*frm*) ¿has notado dónde cayó?; **~ what I say** escucha lo que te digo; **~ my words!** ¡fíjese *or* acuérdese bien de lo que le digo!, ¡te lo advierto!; **~ you** ahora (bien)
7 [+ *exam*] calificar; [+ *candidate*] dar nota a; **to ~ sth right** aprobar algo; **to ~ sth wrong** rechazar *or* (*LAm*) reprobar algo; **we ~ed him (as) first class** le dimos nota de sobresaliente
8 (*Ftbl*) marcar, doblar
9 (*Mus*) [+ *rhythm*] marcar; **to ~ time** (*Mil*) marcar el paso; (*fig*) estancarse
Ⓒ VI mancharse
Ⓓ CPD ▸ **mark reader, mark scanner** N lector *m* de marcas ▸ **mark reading, mark scanning** N lectura *f* de marcas

▸**mark down** VT + ADV 1 (= *note down*) apuntar, anotar
2 (*Comm*) [+ *prices, goods*] rebajar
3 [+ *student*] bajar la nota a; **you'll be ~ed down for poor handwriting** te van a bajar la nota por mala caligrafía
4 (= *identify*) **he was immediately ~ed down as a troublemaker** enseguida fue identificado como un alborotador; **I had him ~ed down as a friend of hers** pensé que era un amigo suyo, lo tomé por un amigo suyo

▸**mark off** VT + ADV 1 (= *separate*) separar, dividir
2 (= *distinguish*) distinguir, diferenciar; **her clothes ~ed her off from the rest of the delegates** su atuendo la distinguía *or* diferenciaba del resto de los delegados
3 [+ *items on list etc*] (= *tick off*) marcar, poner una señal contra; (= *cross out*) tachar

▸**mark out** VT + ADV 1 [+ *road etc*] marcar, jalonar; **the track is ~ed out by flags** el camino está marcado con *or* jalonado de banderas
2 (= *single out*) señalar; (= *distinguish*) distinguir, señalar; **he's ~ed out for promotion** se le ha señalado para un ascenso; **his red hair ~ed him out from the others** como era pelirrojo se le distinguía claramente de los demás

▸**mark up** VT + ADV 1 (= *write up*) (*on board, paper etc*) apuntar
2 (*Comm*) [+ *price*] subir; [+ *goods*] subir el precio de
3 [+ *student*] subir la nota a

Mark [mɑːk] N Marcos; **~ Antony** Marco Antonio

markdown [ˈmɑːkdaʊn] N (*Comm*) rebaja *f*, reducción *f*

marked [mɑːkt] ADJ 1 (= *noticeable*) [*improvement, increase, deterioration, reduction*] marcado, notable; [*difference, change*] acusado, marcado; [*contrast*] acusado, fuerte; [*accent*] marcado, fuerte; [*effect*] acusado, notable; [*reluctance*] notable, evidente; **the difference has become more ~** la diferencia se ha vuelto más acusada *or* marcada, la diferencia se acusa cada vez más; **he was a quiet boy, in ~ contrast to his raucous brothers** era un chico callado, muy diferente a sus escandalosos hermanos
2 (= *targeted*) **to be a ~ man** ser un hombre marcado

markedly [ˈmɑːkɪdlɪ] ADV 1 (*with adj/adv*) [*different*] notablemente, marcadamente; [*better, worse*] visiblemente, notablemente; **their second album has been ~ more/less successful than their first** su segundo álbum ha tenido notablemente más/menos éxito que el primero
2 (*with verb*) [*increase, improve, decline*] notablemente, sensiblemente; [*differ, change, contrast*] notablemente

marker [ˈmɑːkəʳ] N 1 (= *indicator*) (*gen, Bio*) marcador *m*; (*in field*) jalón *m*; (= *signpost*) poste *m* indicador; **to put down a ~** (*fig*) dejar una señal, marcar un lugar
2 (*also* **~ pen**) rotulador *m*
3 (= *bookmark*) marca *f*, señal *f*
4 (*Ftbl*) (= *person*) marcador(a) *m/f*, secante *mf*
5 (*Scol*) (= *person*) examinador(a) *m/f*
6 (*Billiards etc*) marcador *m*; (*in other games*) ficha *f*
7 (*Comput*) bandera *f*

market [ˈmɑːkɪt] Ⓐ N 1 (= *place*) mercado *m*; **to go to ~** ir al mercado
2 (= *trade*) mercado *m*; **overseas/domestic ~** mercado exterior/nacional; **to corner the ~ in maize** acaparar el mercado del maíz; **to flood the ~ with sth** inundar el mercado de algo; **strawberries are flooding the ~** las fresas inundan el mercado; **to be in the ~ for sth** estar dispuesto a comprar algo; **to be on the ~** estar en venta *or* a la venta; **it's the dearest shirt on the ~** es la camisa más cara del mercado; **to bring** *or* **put a product on(to) the ~** lanzar un producto al mercado; **to come on(to) the ~** salir a la venta *or* al mercado, ponerse en venta; **to rig the ~** manipular la lonja; *see also* **open E**
3 (= *demand*) demanda *f*; **there is a ready ~ for video games** hay una gran demanda de videojuegos; **there's no ~ for pink socks** los calcetines de color rosa no encuentran salida; **to find a ready ~** venderse fácilmente, tener fácil salida
4 (= *stock market*) bolsa *f* (de valores); **to play the ~** jugar a la bolsa
Ⓑ VT 1 (= *sell*) comercializar, poner en venta
2 (= *promote*) publicitar
Ⓒ VI (*esp US*) hacer la compra
Ⓓ CPD ▸ **market analysis** N análisis *m inv* de mercado(s) ▸ **market day** N día *m* de mercado ▸ **market demand** N demanda *f* del mercado ▸ **market economy** N economía *f* de mercado ▸ **market forces** NPL fuerzas *fpl* del mercado, tendencias *fpl* del mercado ▸ **market garden** N (*Brit*) (*small*) huerto *m*; (*large*) huerta *f* ▸ **market gardener** N (*Brit*) hortelano/a *m/f* ▸ **market gardening** N (*Brit*) horticultura *f* ▸ **market intelligence** N información *f* del mercado ▸ **market leader** N líder *m* del mercado ▸ **market opportunity** N oportunidad *f* comercial ▸ **market penetration** N penetración *f* del mercado ▸ **market place** N plaza *f* (del mercado); (= *world of trade*) mercado *m* ▸ **market potential** N potencial *m* comercial ▸ **market price** N precio *m* de mercado ▸ **market rates** NPL precios *mpl* del mercado; (*Fin*) cotizaciones *fpl* ▸ **market research** N estudios *mpl* de mercados ▸ **market researcher** N investigador(a) *m/f* de mercados ▸ **market share** N cuota *f* de mercado ▸ **market study, market survey** N estudio *m* de mercado ▸ **market town** N mercado *m* ▸ **market trends** NPL tendencias *fpl* de mercado ▸ **market value** N valor *m* de mercado

marketability [ˌmɑːkɪtəˈbɪlɪtɪ] N comerciabilidad *f*, vendibilidad *f*

marketable [ˈmɑːkɪtəbl] ADJ 1 (= *saleable*) [*commodity, product*] vendible, comercializable; **of ~ quality** de valor comercial
2 (*fig*) [*skill*] con mucha salida; **the more specialized your skill, the more ~ you are** cuanto más especializado estés, mayores posibilidades tendrás en el mercado laboral; **he is one of our most ~ young actors** es uno de nuestros actores jóvenes con más posibilidades en el mercado cinematográfico

marketeer [ˌmɑːkɪˈtɪəʳ] N (*Brit Pol*) (*also* **pro-Marketeer**) partidario/a *m/f* del Mercado Común; *see also* **black D**

marketing [ˈmɑːkɪtɪŋ] Ⓐ N márketing *m*, mercadotecnia *f*
Ⓑ CPD ▸ **marketing agreement** N acuerdo *m* de comercialización ▸ **marketing department** N departamento *f* de márketing ▸ **marketing director** N jefe/a *m/f* de márke-

ting ► **marketing manager** N director(a) *m/f* de márketing ► **marketing plan** N plan *m* de comercialización ► **marketing strategy** N estrategia *f* de comercialización

market-led ['mɑːkɪt'led] ADJ generado por el mercado

marking ['mɑːkɪŋ] Ⓐ N 1 (= *mark*) señal *f*, marca *f*; (*on animal*) pinta *f*; (= *colouration*) coloración *f*
2 (*Brit Scol*) corrección *f* (*de exámenes, deberes etc*)
3 (*Ftbl*) marcaje *m*
Ⓑ CPD ► **marking ink** N tinta *f* indeleble ► **marking pen** N rotulador *m*

marksman ['mɑːksmən] N (*pl* **marksmen**) tirador *m*

marksmanship ['mɑːksmənʃɪp] N puntería *f*

markswoman ['mɑːksˌwʊmən] N (*pl* **markswomen**) tiradora *f*

mark-up ['mɑːkʌp] N (= *profit*) margen *m* (de beneficio); (= *price increase*) aumento *m* de precio

marl [mɑːl] N marga *f*

marlin ['mɑːlɪn] N (*pl* **marlin** *or* **marlins**) (= *fish*) aguja *f*

marlin(e) ['mɑːlɪn] Ⓐ N (*Naut*) merlín *m*, empalmadura *f*, trincafía *f*
Ⓑ CPD ► **marlin(e) spike** N pasador *m*

marly ['mɑːlɪ] ADJ margoso

marmalade ['mɑːməleɪd] Ⓐ N mermelada *f* (de naranja amarga *or* limón)
Ⓑ CPD ► **marmalade orange** N naranja *f* amarga

marmoreal [mɑː'mɔːrɪəl] ADJ marmóreo

marmoset ['mɑːməzet] N tití *m*

marmot ['mɑːmət] N marmota *f*

maroon[1] [mə'ruːn] Ⓐ ADJ granate
Ⓑ N (= *colour*) granate *m*

maroon[2] [mə'ruːn] VT [+ *castaway*] abandonar (en una isla desierta); (*fig*) aislar, dejar aislado; **we were ~ed by floods** quedamos aislados debido a las inundaciones

maroon[3] [mə'ruːn] N (= *distress signal*) petardo *m*

marque [mɑːk] N marca *f*

marquee [mɑː'kiː] N (*esp Brit*) (= *tent*) carpa *f*; (*open-sided*) entoldado *m*; (*US*) (*over doorway*) marquesina *f*

marquess ['mɑːkwɪs] N marqués *m*

marquetry ['mɑːkɪtrɪ] N marquetería *f*

marquis ['mɑːkwɪs] N = **marquess**

Marrakech, Marrakesh [ˌmærə'keʃ] N Marraquech *m*, Marraqués *m*, Marrakech *m*

▼**marriage** ['mærɪdʒ] Ⓐ N 1 (= *state of being married*) matrimonio *m*; **aunt by ~** tía *f* política; **to be related by ~** estar emparentados; **to become related by ~ to sb** emparentar con algn; **~ of convenience** matrimonio *m* de conveniencia; **to give sb in ~ to** casar a algn con, dar a algn en matrimonio a
2 (= *wedding*) boda *f*, casamiento *m*; (*fig*) unión *f*
Ⓑ CPD ► **marriage bed** N lecho *m* nupcial, tálamo *m* (*frm*) ► **marriage bonds** NPL lazos *mpl* *or* vínculos *mpl* matrimoniales ► **marriage broker** N casamentero/a *m/f* ► **marriage bureau** N agencia *f* matrimonial ► **marriage ceremony** N ceremonia *f* nupcial, matrimonio *m* ► **marriage certificate** N partida *f* matrimonial *or* de matrimonio ► **marriage counseling** N (*US*) = **marriage guidance** ► **marriage counselor** N (*US*) = **marriage guidance counsellor** ► **marriage guidance** N orientación *f* matrimonial ► **marriage guidance counsellor** N consejero/a *m/f* matrimonial ► **marriage licence**, **marriage license** N (*US*) licencia *f* matrimonial ► **marriage lines** NPL (*Brit*) partida *f* matrimonial *or* de matrimonio ► **marriage partner** N cónyuge *mf*, consorte *mf* ► **marriage rate** N (índice *m* de) nupcialidad *f* ► **marriage settlement** N contrato *m* matrimonial; (*Jur*) capitulaciones *fpl* (matrimoniales) ► **marriage vows** NPL votos *mpl* matrimoniales

marriageable ['mærɪdʒəbl] ADJ casadero; **of ~ age** en edad de casarse

married ['mærɪd] Ⓐ ADJ [*person*] casado; [*love*] conyugal; **~ man** (hombre *m*) casado *m*; **~ woman** (mujer *f*) casada *f*; **~ couple** matrimonio *m*; **~ life** vida *f* matrimonial; **the ~ state** el estado matrimonial; **twice-~** casado por segunda vez *or* en segundas nupcias; **"just married"** "recién casados"
Ⓑ CPD ► **married name** N nombre *m* de casada ► **married quarters** N (*Mil*) casa *fsing* cuartel, residencia *fsing* para matrimonios

marrow ['mærəʊ] N 1 (*Anat*) médula *f*, tuétano *m*; (*as food*) tuétano *m* de hueso; ✦**IDIOMS** **a Spaniard to the ~** un español de pura cepa, un español hasta la médula; **to be frozen to the ~** estar helado hasta los huesos
2 (*Brit Bot*) (*also* **vegetable ~**) calabacín *m*; **baby ~** calabacín *m*, calabacita *f*

marrowbone ['mærəʊbəʊn] N hueso *m* con tuétano

▼**marry** ['mærɪ] Ⓐ VT 1 (= *take in marriage*) casarse con; **to be married to sb** estar casado con algn; **we have been married for 14 years** llevamos 14 años (de) casados; **to ~ money** casarse con alguien de dinero
2 (= *give or join in marriage*) casar; **they were married by the village priest** los casó el cura del pueblo; **he has three daughters to ~ (off)** tiene tres hijas por casar
3 (*fig*) conjugar, aunar; **a style which marries beauty and practicality** un estilo que conjuga *or* aúna belleza y pragmatismo; **he's married to his job** vive por y para el trabajo, vive para trabajar *or* para el trabajo
Ⓑ VI (*also* **to get married**) casarse; **to ~ again** volver a casarse, casarse en segundas nupcias; **to ~ beneath one** casarse con alguien de rango inferior; **to ~ into a rich family** emparentar con una familia rica; **to ~ into the peerage** casarse con alguien de la nobleza
►**marry up** VT + ADV (*fig*) conjugar

Mars [mɑːz] N Marte *m*; **~ landing** ◊ **landing on ~** amartizaje *m*

Marseillaise [ˌmɑːsə'leɪz] N **the ~** la Marsellesa

Marseilles [mɑː'seɪlz] N Marsella *f*

marsh [mɑːʃ] Ⓐ N pantano *m*, ciénaga *f*; (= *salt marsh*) marisma *f*
Ⓑ CPD ► **marsh fever** N paludismo *m* ► **marsh gas** N gas *m* de los pantanos, metano *m* ► **marsh marigold** N botón *m* de oro ► **marsh warbler** N papamoscas *m inv*

marshal ['mɑːʃəl] Ⓐ N 1 (*Mil*) mariscal *m*
2 (*at demonstration, meeting*) oficial *m*
3 (*US*) alguacil *m*, oficial *m* de justicia
Ⓑ VT 1 [+ *soldiers, procession*] formar
2 [+ *facts etc*] ordenar; [+ *evidence*] presentar

marshalling yard ['mɑːʃəlɪŋˌjɑːd] N (*Rail*) área *f* de clasificación

marshland ['mɑːʃlænd] N pantanal *m*

marshmallow ['mɑːʃ'mæləʊ] N (*Bot*) malvavisco *m*; (= *sweet*) esponja *f*, dulce *m* de merengue blando

marshy ['mɑːʃɪ] ADJ (*compar* **marshier**, *superl* **marshiest**) pantanoso

marsupial [mɑː'suːpɪəl] Ⓐ ADJ marsupial
Ⓑ N marsupial *m*

mart [mɑːt] N (*esp US*) (= *trade centre*) emporio *m*; (= *market*) mercado *m*; (= *auction room*) martillo *m*; (= *property mart*) (*in newspaper*) bolsa *f* de la propiedad

marten ['mɑːtɪn] N (*pl* **martens** *or* **marten**) marta *f*

Martial ['mɑːʃəl] N Marcial

martial ['mɑːʃəl] Ⓐ ADJ marcial; **~ bearing** porte *m* militar, aire *m* marcial
Ⓑ CPD ► **martial arts** NPL artes *fpl* marciales ► **martial law** N ley *f* marcial

Martian ['mɑːʃɪən] Ⓐ ADJ marciano
Ⓑ N marciano/a *m/f*

Martin ['mɑːtɪn] N Martín

martin ['mɑːtɪn] N avión *m*, vencejo *m*

martinet [ˌmɑːtɪ'net] N ordenancista *mf*, rigorista *mf*

Martini® [mɑː'tiːnɪ] N 1 (= *vermouth*) vermú *m*
2 (= *cocktail*) martini *m* (*vermú seco con ginebra*)

Martinique [ˌmɑːtɪ'niːk] N Martinica *f*

Martinmas ['mɑːtɪnməs] N día *m* de San Martín (*11 noviembre*)

martyr ['mɑːtəʳ] Ⓐ N mártir *mf*; **to be a ~ to arthritis** ser víctima de la artritis
Ⓑ VT martirizar

martyrdom ['mɑːtədəm] N martirio *m*

martyrize ['mɑːtɪraɪz] VT martirizar

marvel ['mɑːvəl] Ⓐ N maravilla *f*; **you're a ~** eres una maravilla; **it's a ~ to me how she does it** no llego a entender cómo lo hace; **if he gets there it will be a ~** si llega será un milagro
Ⓑ VI maravillarse, asombrarse (**at** de)

marvellous, marvelous (*US*) ['mɑːvələs] ADJ maravilloso, estupendo; **marvellous!** ¡magnífico!; **isn't it ~?** (*also iro*) ¡qué bien!

marvellously, marvelously (*US*) ['mɑːvələslɪ] ADV maravillosamente, de maravilla

Marxism ['mɑːksɪzəm] N marxismo *m*

Marxist ['mɑːksɪst] Ⓐ ADJ marxista
Ⓑ N marxista *mf*

Mary ['meərɪ] N María *f*; **~ Magdalen** la Magdalena; **~ Queen of Scots** ◊ **~ Stuart** María Estuardo

marzipan [ˌmɑːzɪ'pæn] N mazapán *m*

masc. ABBR (= **masculine**) m

mascara [mæs'kɑːrə] N rímel® *m*

mascaraed [mæs'kɑːrəd] ADJ pintado con rímel

mascot ['mæskət] N mascota *f*

masculine ['mæskjʊlɪn] Ⓐ ADJ 1 [*qualities, voice etc*] masculino
2 (*esp pej*) [*woman, image, appearance*] masculino, hombruno (*pej*)
3 (*Gram*) masculino
Ⓑ N (*Gram*) masculino *m*

masculinist ['mæskjʊlɪnɪst] ADJ masculino

masculinity [ˌmæskjʊ'lɪnɪtɪ] N masculinidad *f*

masculinization [ˌmæskjʊlɪnaɪ'zeɪʃən] N masculinización *f*

MASH [mæʃ] N ABBR (*US*) (= **mobile army surgical unit**) *unidad quirúrgica móvil del ejército*

mash [mæʃ] Ⓐ N 1 (= *mixture*) mezcla *f*; (= *pulp*) pasta *f*, amasijo *m*
2 (*Brit**) (= *mashed potatoes*) puré *m* de patata(s) *or* (*LAm*) papas
3 (*in brewing*) malta *f* remojada
4 (*for animals*) afrecho *m*
Ⓑ VT 1 (= *crush*) triturar, machacar
2 (= *purée*) [+ *potatoes*] hacer puré de

mashed [mæʃt] ADJ **~ potatoes** puré *m* de patatas, puré *m* de papas (*LAm*)

➤ LANGUAGE IN USE: **marriage** A2 24.4, 25.1 **marry** A2 24.4

mashie ['mæʃɪ] N (*Golf*) hierro *m* número 5

mask [mɑːsk] Ⓐ N [1] (*as disguise, also fig*) máscara *f*; (*just covering eyes and nose*) antifaz *m*; **the man in the ~ produced a gun** el hombre enmascarado *or* que llevaba la máscara sacó una pistola; **his talk is a ~ for his ignorance** habla para enmascarar su ignorancia
[2] (*ornamental, ritual*) máscara *f*, careta *f*
[3] (*also* **face ~**) (*protective, cosmetic*) mascarilla *f*; (*surgeon's*) mascarilla *f*, barbijo *m*; *see also* **death B, face D, gas D, oxygen B**
[4] (*in baseball, fencing, ice-hockey*) careta *f*
Ⓑ VT [1] [+ *person, face*] enmascarar
[2] [+ *object*] ocultar; **a thick grey cloud ~ed the sun** una nube espesa y gris ocultó el sol
[3] (*fig*) [+ *taste, smell*] enmascarar; [+ *truth, feelings, motives*] ocultar, encubrir; [+ *effect of drug*] enmascarar
[4] (*during painting, spraying*) cubrir

masked [mɑːskt] Ⓐ ADJ enmascarado; [*terrorist, attacker*] encapuchado
Ⓑ CPD ► **masked ball** N baile *m* de máscaras

masking tape ['mɑːskɪŋ,teɪp] N cinta *f* adhesiva protectora (*del margen del área a pintar*)

masochism ['mæsəʊkɪzəm] N masoquismo *m*

masochist ['mæsəʊkɪst] N masoquista *mf*

masochistic [,mæsəʊ'kɪstɪk] ADJ masoquista

mason ['meɪsn] N [1] (= *builder*) albañil *mf*; (= *stonework specialist*) mampostero/a *m/f*
[2] (= *monumental mason*) marmolista *mf* (de monumentos funerarios)
[3] (*in quarry*) cantero/a *m/f*
[4] (= *freemason*) masón *m*, francmasón *m*

> **MASON-DIXON LINE**
>
> *La línea* **Mason-Dixon** *o* **Mason and Dixon** *es la línea simbólica que divide el norte y el sur de Estados Unidos y que, hasta el final de la Guerra Civil, marcaba la separación entre aquellos estados en donde existía la esclavitud y aquéllos en los que no. Esta línea de demarcación, que se extiende a lo largo de 377 kilómetros, fue establecida por Charles Mason y Jeremiah Dixon en el siglo XVIII con el fin de solucionar un conflicto que ya duraba 80 años sobre la frontera entre Maryland y Pensilvania. En 1779 la línea se extendió para demarcar la frontera entre Pensilvania y Virginia (hoy Virginia del Oeste); en la actualidad aún sirve como referencia del sur en general y en las canciones de* **country & western** *los cantantes hablan con nostalgia de "cruzar la línea" para volver a sus tierras sureñas.*

masonic [mə'sɒnɪk] ADJ (*also* **Masonic**) masónico

masonry ['meɪsnrɪ] N [1] (= *building trade*) albañilería *f*
[2] (= *stonework*) mampostería *f*
[3] (= *rubble*) escombros *mpl*
[4] (= *freemasonry*) masonería *f*, francmasonería *f*

masque [mɑːsk] N mascarada *f*

masquerade [,mæskə'reɪd] Ⓐ N [1] (= *pretence*) farsa *f*, mascarada *f*
[2] (= *fancy-dress ball*) baile *m* de máscaras, mascarada *f*
Ⓑ VI **to ~ as** hacerse pasar por

mass¹ [mæs] N (*Rel*) misa *f*; **to go to ~** ir a misa, oír misa; **to hear ~** oír misa; **to say ~** decir misa

mass² [mæs] Ⓐ N [1] (= *concentration*) masa *f*; **the garden was a ~ of colour** el jardín era una masa de color; **she had a ~ of auburn hair** tenía una mata de pelo castaño rojizo; **he's a ~ of bruises** está cubierto de cardenales; **the (great) ~ of the population** la (gran) masa de la población; **in the ~** en conjunto; *see also* **air D, critical B**
[2] **masses*** (= *great quantity*) montones* *mpl*, cantidad* *fsing*; **there's ~es of work for her to do** hay montones* *or* cantidad* de trabajo para ella; **~es of people crowded inside** una masa de gente entró en tropel
[3] **the ~es** (= *ordinary people*) las masas
[4] (*Phys*) masa *f*
Ⓑ VT concentrar
Ⓒ VI [*people, crowds, troops*] concentrarse; [*clouds*] agruparse
Ⓓ CPD [*movement, action*] de masas; [*protest, unemployment, support*] masivo; [*hysteria, suicide*] colectivo; [*tourism*] en masa ► **mass exodus** N éxodo *m* masivo *or* en masa ► **mass grave** N fosa *f* común ► **mass killing** N matanza *f*, masacre *f* ► **mass market** N mercado *m* popular ► **mass media** NPL medios *mpl* de comunicación (de masas) ► **mass meeting** N concentración *f* de masas ► **mass murder** N matanza *f*, masacre *f* ► **mass murderer** N autor(a) *m/f* de una matanza *or* masacre ► **mass noun** N sustantivo *m* *or* nombre *m* no contable ► **mass number** N número *m* de masa ► **mass production** N fabricación *f* en serie ► **mass transit** N (*US*) transporte *m* público

Mass. ABBR (*US*) = **Massachusetts**

massacre ['mæsəkəʳ] Ⓐ N [1] (= *killing*) masacre *f*, carnicería *f*
[2] (*) (= *defeat*) derrota *f* aplastante, paliza* *f*
Ⓑ VT [1] (= *kill*) masacrar, aniquilar
[2] (*) (= *defeat*) aplastar, dar una paliza a*

massage ['mæsɑːʒ] Ⓐ N (*lit*) masaje *m*; **"massage"** (*euph*) "Relax"
Ⓑ VT [1] (*lit*) dar un masaje a
[2] (*) [+ *figures*] maquillar*
Ⓒ CPD ► **massage parlour, massage parlor** (*US*) N (*lit*) sala *f* de masaje; (*euph*) sala *f* de relax

massed [mæst] ADJ **the ~ ranks of the enemy** las pobladas filas del enemigo; **~ ranks of reporters** una masa de periodistas; **~ choirs** grandes agrupaciones *fpl* corales

masseur [mæ'sɜːʳ] N masajista *mf*

masseuse [mæ'sɜːz] N masajista *f*

massif [mæ'siːf] N macizo *m*

massive ['mæsɪv] ADJ [*wall*] macizo, sólido; [*boulder, increase, dose, support*] enorme; [*person, head, body*] enorme, gigantesco*; [*explosion, effort*] enorme, grande; [*job losses*] cuantioso; [*intervention, influx*] masivo; **~ heart attack** infarto *m* masivo; **on a ~ scale** a gran escala

massively ['mæsɪvlɪ] ADV [*overweight*] tremendamente; [*popular*] tremendamente, enormemente; [*invest*] a gran escala; [*increase*] enormemente

massiveness ['mæsɪvnɪs] N [*of wall*] solidez *f*, lo macizo; [*of increase, dose, explosion, effort*] enormidad *f*; [*of person, head, body, boulder*] lo gigantesco

mass-produce ['mæsprə'djuːs] VT fabricar en serie, producir en serie

mass-produced ['mæsprə,djuːst] ADJ fabricado en serie, producido en serie

mast¹ [mɑːst] N [1] (*Naut*) mástil *m*, palo *m*; **ten years before the ~** (*liter*) diez años de servicio como marinero
[2] (*Rad*) torre *f*

mast² [mɑːst] N (*Bot*) [*of oak*] bellota *f*; [*of beech*] hayuco *m*

mastectomy [mæ'stektəmɪ] N (*Med*) mastectomía *f*; **she had to have a ~** tuvieron que hacerle una mastectomía

-masted ['mɑːstɪd] ADJ (*ending in compounds*) de ... palos; **three~** de tres palos

master ['mɑːstəʳ] Ⓐ N [1] [*of the house*] señor *m*, amo *m*; [*of dog, servant*] amo *m*; (*in address*) señor *m*; **the ~ is not at home** el señor no está; **the young ~** el señorito; **to be ~ in one's own house** mandar en su propia casa; **to be one's own ~** ser dueño de sí mismo; **I am (the) ~ now** ahora mando yo; **to be ~ of the situation** dominar la situación; **to be ~ of one's fate** decidir su propio destino; ✦***IDIOMS*** **to meet one's ~** ser derrotado por fin, tener que sucumbir por fin; **to serve two ~s** servir a Dios y al diablo
[2] (*Naut*) [*of ship*] capitán *m*
[3] (= *musician, painter etc*) maestro *m*; *see also* **old C**
[4] (= *expert*) experto/a *m/f*; **he is a ~ at (the art of) making money** es un experto en el arte de hacer dinero; *see also* **past C5**
[5] (†) (= *teacher*) (*primary*) maestro *m*; (*secondary*) profesor *m*; **the music ~** el profesor de música
[6] (*Univ*) **Master of Arts/Science** (= *qualification*) master *m* en letras/ciencias; (= *person*) *persona que posee un master en letras/ciencias*; **she's working for her Master's (degree)** está estudiando para sacarse el máster; → DEGREE
Ⓑ VT [+ *subject, situation, technique*] dominar; **to ~ the violin** llegar a dominar el violín
Ⓒ CPD ► **master baker** N maestro *m* panadero ► **master bedroom** N dormitorio *m* principal ► **master builder** N maestro *m* de obras ► **master card** N carta *f* maestra ► **master class** N clase *f* magistral ► **master copy** N original *m* ► **master disk** N disco *m* maestro ► **master file** N fichero *m* maestro ► **master key** N llave *f* maestra ► **master mariner** N capitán *m* ► **master mason** N albañil *mf* maestro/a ► **master of ceremonies** N maestro *m* de ceremonias; [*of show*] presentador *m*, animador *m* ► **master of foxhounds** N cazador *m* mayor ► **Master of the Rolls** N (*Brit*) juez *mf* del tribunal de apelación ► **master plan** N plan *m* maestro, plan *m* rector ► **master sergeant** N (*US*) sargento *mf* mayor ► **master spy** N jefe *mf* de espías, controlador(a) *m/f* de espías ► **master switch** N interruptor *m* general

masterful ['mɑːstəfʊl] ADJ [1] (= *skilful*) [*performance*] magistral; [*swordsman, horseman*] diestro; [*leadership*] capaz
[2] (= *imperious*) imperioso, autoritario; [*personality*] dominante

masterfully ['mɑːstəfəlɪ] ADV magistralmente

masterly ['mɑːstəlɪ] ADJ magistral, genial; **she is ~ in describing life in Victorian London** describe de forma magistral la vida en el Londres de la época victoriana

mastermind ['mɑːstəmaɪnd] Ⓐ N (= *genius*) genio *m*; (*in crime etc*) cerebro *m*
Ⓑ VT dirigir, planear

masterpiece ['mɑːstəpiːs] N obra *f* maestra

Mastersingers ['mɑːstə,sɪŋəz] NPL **"the Mastersingers"** "los maestros cantores"

masterstroke ['mɑːstə,strəʊk] N golpe *m* maestro

masterwork ['mɑːstəwɜːk] N obra *f* maestra

mastery ['mɑːstərɪ] N [1] (= *understanding*) [*of subject, technique*] dominio *m*
[2] (= *skill*) maestría *f*; **his ~ on the football field** su maestría en el terreno de juego
[3] (= *control*) (*over competitors etc*) dominio *m*,

superioridad *f*; **to gain the ~ of** (= *dominate*) llegar a dominar; (= *take over*) hacerse el señor de

masthead ['mɑːsthed] N [1] (*Naut*) tope *m* [2] [*of newspaper*] mancheta *f*

mastic ['mæstɪk] N masilla *f*

masticate ['mæstɪkeɪt] VT masticar

mastiff ['mæstɪf] N mastín *m*, alano *m*

mastitis [mæs'taɪtɪs] N mastitis *f inv*

mastodon ['mæstədən] N mastodonte *m*

mastoid ['mæstɔɪd] Ⓐ ADJ mastoides *inv* Ⓑ N mastoides *f inv*

masturbate ['mæstəbeɪt] Ⓐ VI masturbarse Ⓑ VT masturbar

masturbation [ˌmæstə'beɪʃən] N masturbación *f*

masturbatory ['mæstə'beɪtərɪ] ADJ masturbatorio

mat[1] [mæt] Ⓐ N [1] (*on floor*) estera *f*, esterilla *f*; (*also* **door~**) felpudo *m* [2] (*also* **table~**) (mantel *m*) individual *m*; (*in centre of table*) salvamanteles *m inv* Ⓑ VT enmarañar Ⓒ VI enmarañarse

mat[2] [mæt] ADJ = **matt**

MAT N ABBR (= **machine-assisted translation**) TAO *f*

matador ['mætədɔːʳ] N matador *m*, diestro *m*

match[1] [mætʃ] N (*for lighting*) fósforo *m*, cerilla *f*, cerillo *m* (*Mex*); **a box of ~es** una caja de fósforos *or* cerillas

match[2] [mætʃ] Ⓐ N [1] (*esp Brit Tennis, Cricket*) partido *m*; (*Ftbl*) partido *m*, encuentro *m*; (*Boxing*) combate *m*; (*Fencing*) asalto *m*; **boxing ~** combate *m* de boxeo; *see also* **shooting C, shouting B, test D**
[2] (= *complement*) **the skirt is a good ~ for the jumper** la falda hace juego *or* queda bien con el jersey; **I'm looking for a ~ for these curtains** estoy buscando un color que haga juego con estas cortinas; **the two of them make** *or* **are a good ~** hacen una buena pareja
[3] (= *equal*) **to be a ~/no ~ for sb** estar/no estar a la altura de algn; **he was more than a ~ for Paul** venció fácilmente a Paul; **he's a ~ for anybody** puede competir con el más pintado, está a la altura del más pintado; **to meet one's ~ (in sb)** encontrar la horma de su zapato (en algn)
[4] (= *marriage*) casamiento *m*, matrimonio *m*; (= *potential partner*) partido *m*; **he's a good ~** es un buen partido; **she made a good ~** se casó bien
Ⓑ VT [1] (= *pair off*) emparejar; **they're well ~ed** [*couple*] hacen buena pareja; **the teams were well ~ed** los equipos estaban muy igualados *or* (*esp LAm*) eran muy parejos; **they ~ your skills with employers' requirements** emparejan tus aptitudes con los requisitos de las empresas; **the children were asked to ~ the pictures with the words** se pidió a los niños que emparejaran las imágenes con las palabras; **they ~ed fibres to the suspect's clothes** encontraron fibras que se correspondían con la ropa del sospechoso; *see also* **evenly 2**
[2] (= *equal*) igualar; **her performance would be hard to ~** su actuación sería difícil de igualar; **I can ~ any offer** puedo igualar cualquier oferta; **for sheer cheek there's no one to ~ him** en cuanto a cara dura no hay quien le iguale; **the results did not ~ our expectations** los resultados no estuvieron a la altura de nuestras expectativas
[3] (= *correspond to*) ajustarse a, corresponder a; **a man ~ing the police description** un hombre que se ajustaba a *or* que correspondía a la descripción de la policía
[4] (= *put in opposition to*) enfrentar; **to ~ sth/sb against sth/sb** enfrentar algo/a algn a *or* con algo/algn; **she ~ed her wits against his strength** enfrentó *or* midió su ingenio con la fuerza de él; **Scotland has been ~ed against France in the final** Escocia se enfrentará a *or* con Francia en la final
[5] (= *tone with*) [+ *clothes, colours*] combinar con, hacer juego con
[6] (*also* **~ up**) (= *find sth similar to*) **can you ~ (up) this material?** (*with sth exactly same*) ¿puedes encontrar algo que iguale este tejido?; (*with sth which goes well*) ¿puedes encontrar algo que vaya bien con este tejido?
Ⓒ VI [1] (= *go together*) [*colours*] combinar bien; [*clothes*] hacer juego; **I dyed the shoes to ~** teñí los zapatos para que hicieran juego; **with a skirt to ~** con una falda a tono *or* que hace juego; **he has a vicious tongue and a temper to ~** tiene una lengua viperina y un genio de mil demonios*
[2] (= *be the same*) corresponderse, coincidir
Ⓓ CPD ► **match point** N (*Tennis*) bola *f* de partido, match point *m* ► **match report** N informe *m* sobre el partido

►**match up** Ⓐ VT + ADV (= *bring together*) [+ *two objects*] emparejar, aparear; [+ *two people*] emparejar; (= *group*) [+ *objects, people*] agrupar; [+ *pattern*] hacer coincidir; **to ~ sth up with sth** [+ *pairs*] emparejar *or* aparear algo con algo; [+ *colours*] (= *coordinate*) conjuntar algo con algo; **they ~ up your skills with employers' requirements** emparejan tus aptitudes con los requisitos de las empresas; **they ~ed up fibres to the suspect's clothes** encontraron fibras que se correspondían con la ropa del sospechoso; *see also* **match B6**
Ⓑ VI + ADV [1] (= *be the same, fit*) [*numbers, pattern*] coincidir; **check the numbers against your card to see if they ~ up** compruebe los números con los de su cartón para ver si coinciden; **his fingerprints don't ~ up exactly with the murderer's** sus huellas dactilares no coinciden exactamente con *or* no corresponden exactamente a las del asesino
[2] (= *perform*) responder
[3] (= *compare*) **his record ~es up well against those of previous presidents** su historial se puede comparar al de presidentes anteriores

►**match up to** VI + PREP estar a la altura de

matchbox ['mætʃbɒks] N caja *f* de fósforos *or* cerillas

matching ['mætʃɪŋ] Ⓐ ADJ haciendo juego, a juego (*Sp*); **a blue silk dress with ~ shoes** un vestido de seda azul con zapatos haciendo juego *or* (*Sp*) a juego
Ⓑ CPD ► **matching funds** NPL (*US*) fondos *mpl* de contrapartida

matchless ['mætʃlɪs] ADJ sin par *or* igual, incomparable

matchmaker ['mætʃˌmeɪkəʳ] N casamentero/a *m/f*, alcahuete/a *m/f*

matchmaking ['mætʃˌmeɪkɪŋ] Ⓐ N actividades *fpl* de casamentero Ⓑ ADJ casamentero

matchplay ['mætʃpleɪ] N partido *m* oficial

matchstick ['mætʃstɪk] N fósforo *m*

matchwood ['mætʃwʊd] N astillas *fpl*; **to smash sth to ~** hacer algo añicos; **to be smashed to ~** hacerse añicos

mate[1] [meɪt] (*Chess*) Ⓐ N mate *m* Ⓑ VT dar jaque mate a, matar Ⓒ VI dar jaque mate, matar; **white plays and ~s in two** blanco juega y mata en dos

mate[2] [meɪt] Ⓐ N [1] (*Zool*) (*male*) macho *m*; (*female*) hembra *f*
[2] (* *hum*) (= *husband, wife*) compañero/a *m/f*
[3] (= *assistant*) ayudante *mf*, peón *m*; *see also* **plumber B**
[4] (*Brit Naut*) primer(a) oficial *mf*; (*US*) segundo/a *m/f* de a bordo
[5] (*at work*) compañero/a *m/f*, colega *mf*
[6] (*Brit**) (= *friend*) amigo/a *m/f*, compinche* *mf*, colega* *mf*, cuate/a *m/f* (*Mex*); **John and his ~s*** John y sus amiguetes *or* colegas; **look here, ~*** mire, amigo
Ⓑ VT [1] (*Zool*) aparear [2] (*hum*) unir
Ⓒ VI (*Zool*) aparearse; ✦**PROV age should not ~ with youth** no debe casarse el viejo con la joven

maté ['mɑːteɪ] N mate *m* (cocido), yerba *f* mate; **~ kettle** pava *f*

material [mə'tɪərɪəl] Ⓐ ADJ [1] (= *physical*) [*goods, needs, comforts, benefits, damage*] material; **to do sth for ~ gain** hacer algo para obtener un beneficio material; **~ possessions** bienes *mpl* materiales; **the ~ world** el mundo físico
[2] (= *important*) [*reason*] importante, de peso, fundamental
[3] (*Jur*) (= *relevant*) [*fact*] pertinente; [*witness*] primordial, principal; **~ evidence** pruebas *fpl* sustanciales; **to be ~ to sth** ser pertinente a algo
Ⓑ N [1] (= *cloth*) tela *f*, tejido *m*
[2] (= *substance*) materia *f*, material *m*; **natural ~s** materias *fpl* naturales, materiales *mpl* naturales; **raw ~s** materias *fpl* primas
[3] **materials** (= *equipment, components*) material(es) *m(pl)*; **building ~s** material(es) *m(pl)* de construcción; **teaching ~s** material(es) *m(pl)* didácticos; **writing ~s** artículos *mpl* de escritorio
[4] (= *information*) datos *mpl*, información *f*; **they researched a lot of background ~ for the book** recogieron muchos datos *or* mucha información antes de escribir el libro; **she was busy gathering ~ for her article** estaba ocupada recogiendo datos *or* información para su artículo
[5] (= *potential*) **he is university ~** tiene madera de universitario; **he is not management ~** no tiene madera de jefe

materialism [mə'tɪərɪəlɪzəm] N materialismo *m*

materialist [mə'tɪərɪəlɪst] Ⓐ N materialista *mf* Ⓑ ADJ materialista

materialistic [mə'tɪərɪə'lɪstɪk] ADJ materialista

materialize [mə'tɪərɪəlaɪz] Ⓐ VI [1] (= *come into being*) [*idea, hope etc*] realizarse
[2] (= *appear*) aparecer; **the funds haven't ~d so far** hasta ahora no han aparecido los fondos
[3] [*spirit*] materializarse
Ⓑ VT materializar

materially [mə'tɪərɪəlɪ] ADV [1] (= *physically*) materialmente; **~ and emotionally** material y emocionalmente
[2] (= *importantly*) sustancialmente, sensiblemente; **interest rates now are not ~ different from last year** los tipos de interés actuales no son sustancialmente *or* sensiblemente diferentes de los del año pasado; **they are not ~ different** no hay grandes diferencias entre ellos, no hay diferencias sustanciales *or* fundamentales entre ellos; **that does not ~ alter things** eso no afecta la situación de modo sustancial

materiel [məˌtɪərɪ'el] N (*US*) material *m* bélico

maternal [mə'tɜːnl] ADJ 1 (= *motherly*) [*woman, behaviour, instinct*] maternal; [*feelings, love*] maternal, de madre
2 (= *on the mother's side*) materno (*por parte de madre*); **~ aunt** tía *f* materna (*por parte de madre*); **~ grandfather** abuelo *m* materno (*por parte de madre*)

maternity [mə'tɜːnɪtɪ] Ⓐ N maternidad *f*
Ⓑ CPD ► **maternity allowance** N subsidio *m* de maternidad ► **maternity dress** N vestido *m* premamá ► **maternity home**, **maternity hospital** N maternidad *f* ► **maternity leave** N baja *f* por maternidad ► **maternity ward** N sala *f* de maternidad

mateship ['meɪtʃɪp] N (*esp Australia*) compañerismo *m*, compadreo *m* (*esp LAm*)

matey* ['meɪtɪ] Ⓐ ADJ (*Brit*) [*person*] afable, simpático; [*atmosphere*] acogedor; [*gathering*] informal, familiar; **she's quite ~ with my wife** es bastante amiga con mi mujer
Ⓑ N (*Brit*) (*in direct address*) chico, hijo

math* [mæθ] N ABBR (*US*) = **mathematics** mates* *fpl*

mathematical [ˌmæθə'mætɪkəl] ADJ matemático; **I'm not very ~** no se me dan bien las matemáticas; **he's a ~ genius** es un genio para las matemáticas

mathematically [ˌmæθə'mætɪkəlɪ] ADV matemáticamente

mathematician [ˌmæθəmə'tɪʃən] N matemático/a *m/f*

mathematics [ˌmæθə'mætɪks] NSING matemáticas *fpl*

Mathilda [mə'tɪldə] N = **Matilda**

maths* [mæθs] NSING ABBR (*Brit*) = **mathematics** mates* *fpl*

Matilda [mə'tɪldə] N Matilde

matinée ['mætɪneɪ] Ⓐ N función *f* de tarde, matiné(e) *f* (*S. Cone*)
Ⓑ CPD ► **matinée coat** N (*Brit*) abriguito *m* de lana ► **matinée idol** N ídolo *m* del público ► **matinée jacket** N = **matinée coat**

matiness* ['meɪtɪnɪs] N [*of person*] afabilidad *f*, simpatía *f*; [*of gathering*] ambiente *m* informal, carácter *m* familiar

mating ['meɪtɪŋ] Ⓐ N 1 (*Zool*) apareamiento *m*
2 (*fig*) unión *f*
Ⓑ CPD ► **mating call** N aullido *m*/rugido *m* de la época de celo ► **mating season** N época *f* de celo

matins ['mætɪnz] NSING OR NPL maitines *mpl*

matriarch ['meɪtrɪɑːk] N matriarca *f*

matriarchal [ˌmeɪtrɪ'ɑːkl] ADJ matriarcal

matriarchy ['meɪtrɪɑːkɪ] N matriarcado *m*

matric* [mə'trɪk] N (*Brit*) (*formerly*) = **matriculation 2**

matrices ['meɪtrɪˌsiːz] NPL *of* **matrix**

matricide ['meɪtrɪsaɪd] N 1 (= *act*) matricidio *m*
2 (= *person*) matricida *mf*

matriculate [mə'trɪkjʊleɪt] Ⓐ VT matricular
Ⓑ VI matricularse

matriculation [məˌtrɪkjʊ'leɪʃən] N 1 matriculación *f*
2 (*Brit Univ*) (*formerly*) examen *m* de ingreso

matrimonial [ˌmætrɪ'məʊnɪəl] ADJ [*problems*] matrimonial; [*vow, bed*] de matrimonio; [*life*] conyugal; **the ~ home** el domicilio conyugal

matrimony ['mætrɪmənɪ] N matrimonio *m*

matrix ['meɪtrɪks] N (*pl* **matrixes** *or* **matrices**) (*all senses*) matriz *f*

matron ['meɪtrən] Ⓐ N 1 (*in nursing home*) supervisora *f*
2 (†) (*in hospital*) enfermera *f* jefe
3 (*in school*) enfermera *f*
4 (= *married woman*) matrona *f*
Ⓑ CPD ► **matron of honour** N dama *f* de honor (*casada*)

matronly ['meɪtrənlɪ] ADJ matronal, de matrona; [*figure*] maduro y algo corpulento

matt [mæt] ADJ mate

matted ['mætɪd] ADJ enmarañado y apelmazado; **~ hair** greñas *fpl*, pelo *m* enmarañado y apelmazado; **~ with blood** enmarañado y apelmazado por la sangre

matter ['mætəʳ] Ⓐ N 1 (= *substance*) materia *f*, sustancia *f*
2 (*Typ, Publishing*) material *m*; **advertising ~** material *m* publicitario; **printed ~** impresos *mpl*
3 (*Med*) (= *pus*) pus *m*, materia *f*
4 (*Literat*) (= *content*) contenido *m*; **form and ~** la forma y el contenido
5 (= *question, affair*) asunto *m*, cuestión *f*; **in this ~** en este asunto; **that's quite another ~** ◊ **that's another ~ altogether** esa es otra cuestión, eso es totalmente distinto; **business ~s** negocios *mpl*; **the ~ is closed** el asunto está concluido; **as a ~ of course** automáticamente; **it's a ~ of course with us** con nosotros es cosa de cajón; **that's a very different ~** esa es otra cuestión, eso es totalmente distinto; **it's an easy ~ to phone him** es cosa fácil llamarle; **it will be no easy ~** no será fácil; **as a ~ of fact ...**: **as a ~ of fact I know her very well** de hecho *or* en realidad la conozco muy bien; **I don't like it, as a ~ of fact I'm totally against it** no me gusta, de hecho estoy totalmente en contra; **"don't tell me you like it?" — "as a ~ of fact I do"** —no me digas que te gusta —pues sí, la verdad es que sí; **as a ~ of fact we were just talking about you** precisamente estábamos hablando de ti; **for that ~** en realidad; **it's a ~ of form** es pura formalidad; **the ~ in hand** la cuestión del momento; **money ~s** asuntos *mpl* financieros; **it is no great ~** es poca cosa, no importa; **in the ~ of** en cuanto a, en lo que se refiere; **there's the ~ of my wages** queda el asunto de mi sueldo; **it will be a ~ of a few weeks** será cuestión de unas semanas; **a ~ of minutes** cosa de minutos; **it's a ~ of a couple of hours** es cosa de un par de horas; **in a ~ of ten minutes** en cosa de diez minutos; **it's a ~ of great concern to us** es motivo de gran preocupación para nosotros; **it's a ~ of taste** es cuestión de gusto; **it's a serious ~** es cosa seria; **as ~s stand** tal como están las cosas; **to make ~s worse** para colmo de males; *see also* **laughing A**, **mince B2**
6 (= *importance*) **no ~!** ◊ **it makes no ~** (*frm*) ¡no importa!, ¡no le hace! (*LAm*); **no ~ how you do it** no importa cómo lo hagas; **no ~ how big it is** por grande que sea; **no ~ how hot it is** por mucho calor que haga; **get one, no ~ how** procura uno, del modo que sea; **no ~ what he says** diga lo que diga; **what ~?** (*frm*) ¿qué importa?; **no ~ when** no importa cuándo; **no ~ who goes** quienquiera que vaya
7 (= *difficulty, problem etc*) **what's the ~?** ¿qué pasa?, ¿qué hay?; **what's the ~ with you?** ¿qué te pasa?, ¿qué tienes?; **what's the ~ with Tony?** ¿qué le pasa a Tony?; **something's the ~ with the lights** algo les pasa a las luces, algo pasa con las luces; **what's the ~ with my hat?** ¿qué pasa con mi sombrero?; **what's the ~ with singing?** ¿por qué no se puede cantar?, ¿es que está prohibido cantar?; **nothing's the ~** no pasa nada; **as if nothing were the ~** como si no hubiese pasado nada, como si tal cosa
Ⓑ VI importar; **does it ~ to you if I go?** ¿te importa que yo vaya?; **why should it ~ to me?** ¿a mí qué me importa *or* qué más me da?; **it doesn't ~** (*unimportant*) no importa; (*no preference*) (me) da igual *or* lo mismo; **what does it ~?** ¿qué más da?, ¿y qué?; **some things ~ more than others** algunas cosas son más importantes que otras

matter-of-fact ['mætərəvˈfækt] ADJ [*style*] prosaico; [*person*] (*practical*) práctico

Matthew ['mæθjuː] N Mateo

matting ['mætɪŋ] N estera *f*

mattins ['mætɪnz] NSING OR NPL = **matins**

mattock ['mætək] N azadón *m*

mattress ['mætrɪs] N colchón *m*

maturation [mætjʊə'reɪʃən] N (*frm*) maduración *f*

mature [mə'tjʊəʳ] Ⓐ ADJ (*compar* **maturer**; *superl* **maturest**) 1 (*emotionally*) maduro; **she's very ~ for her age** es muy madura para su edad
2 (*physically*) [*animal, plant*] adulto; **to be physically ~** estar desarrollado; **of ~ years** de edad madura
3 [*wine, whisky*] añejo; [*cheese*] curado
4 (*Fin*) [*insurance policy, investment*] vencido
Ⓑ VI 1 [*person*] (*emotionally*) madurar; [*child, young animal*] (*physically*) desarrollarse; **she had ~d into a self-possessed young woman** se había convertido en una joven dueña de sí misma; **her style had not yet ~d** su estilo aún no había madurado
2 [*wine, whisky*] añejarse; [*cheese*] curarse
3 (*Fin*) [*insurance policy, investment*] vencer
Ⓒ VT [+ *wine, whisky*] añejar; [+ *cheese*] curar
Ⓓ CPD ► **mature student** N estudiante *mf* mayor

maturely [mə'tjʊəlɪ] ADV de manera juiciosa, con madurez

maturity [mə'tjʊərɪtɪ] N 1 (*emotional*) madurez *f*
2 (*physical*) [*of person, animal*] madurez *f*, pleno desarrollo *m*; [*of plant*] pleno desarrollo *m*; **to reach physical ~** alcanzar su pleno desarrollo
3 (*Fin*) [*of insurance policy, bond*] vencimiento *m*

maudlin ['mɔːdlɪn] ADJ (= *weepy*) llorón; (= *sentimental*) sensiblero

maul [mɔːl] Ⓐ VT 1 (*lit*) [*tiger, bear*] atacar y malherir; **to ~ sb to death** atacar y matar a algn
2 (*fig*) [+ *writer, play*] vapulear; [+ *text*] destrozar, arruinar; [+ *team, competitor, candidate*] arrollar; **he got badly ~ed in the press** la prensa lo vapuleó, la prensa lo puso como un trapo*
Ⓑ N (*Rugby*) melé *f* espontánea

maunder ['mɔːndəʳ] VI divagar

Maundy ['mɔːndɪ] CPD ► **Maundy money** N (*Brit*) *dinero que reparte el monarca a los pobres el Jueves Santo* ► **Maundy Thursday** N Jueves *m* Santo

Maurice ['mɒrɪs] N Mauricio

Mauritania [ˌmɔːrɪ'teɪnɪə] N Mauritania *f*

Mauritanian [ˌmɔːrɪ'teɪnɪən] Ⓐ ADJ mauritano
Ⓑ N mauritano/a *m/f*

Mauritian [mə'rɪʃən] Ⓐ ADJ mauriciano
Ⓑ N mauriciano/a *m/f*

Mauritius [mə'rɪʃəs] N Isla *f* Mauricio *m*

mausoleum [ˌmɔːsə'liːəm] N (*pl* **mausoleums** *or* **mausolea** [ˌmɔːsə'lɪə]) mausoleo *m*

mauve [məʊv] Ⓐ ADJ malva
Ⓑ N malva *m*

➤ LANGUAGE IN USE: **matter B** 7.5, 18.5

maverick [ˈmævərɪk] Ⓐ N [1] (*US Agr*) res *f* sin marcar
[2] (= *nonconformist*) inconformista *mf*; (*Pol etc*) disidente *mf*
Ⓑ ADJ (= *nonconformist*) inconformista; (*Pol*) disidente

maw [mɔː] N [1] (*Anat*) estómago *m*; [*of cow etc*] cuajar *m*; [*of bird*] molleja *f*, buche *m*
[2] (*fig*) fauces *fpl*

mawkish [ˈmɔːkɪʃ] ADJ empalagoso, sensiblero, insulso

mawkishness [ˈmɔːkɪʃnɪs] N sensiblería *f*, insulsez *f*

max [mæks] Ⓐ ABBR (= **maximum**) máx.; **a couple of weeks, ~** dos semanas como máximo
Ⓑ N **to do sth to the ~*** hacer algo al máximo, hacer algo a tope*

maxi* [ˈmæksi] N (= *skirt*) maxifalda *f*, maxi* *f*

maxi... [ˈmæksi] PREFIX maxi...

maxilla [mækˈsɪlə] N (*pl* **maxillae** [mækˈsɪliː]) maxilar *m* superior

maxillary [mækˈsɪlərɪ] ADJ (*Anat*) maxilar

maxim [ˈmæksɪm] N máxima *f*

maximization [ˌmæksɪmaɪˈzeɪʃən] N [*of profits, assets, potential*] maximización *f*

maximize [ˈmæksɪmaɪz] VT [+ *profits, assets, potential, opportunities*] maximizar

maximum [ˈmæksɪməm] Ⓐ ADJ [*amount, temperature, speed, load, efficiency*] máximo; **for ~ benefit, use once a week** para obtener un beneficio máximo úsese una vez a la semana; **for ~ effect** para conseguir el máximo efecto; **to use sth to ~ effect** usar algo de manera muy efectiva; **~ expenditure** gasto *m* máximo; **a ~ security prison/hospital** una prisión/un hospital de máxima seguridad; **~ sentence** condena *f* máxima
Ⓑ N (*pl* **maximums** *or* **maxima**) máximo *m*; **20 kilos is the ~** el máximo son 20 kilos; **at the ~** como máximo, a lo sumo; **up to a ~ of £20** hasta 20 libras como máximo; **to the ~** al máximo
Ⓒ ADV como máximo; **you should drink two cups of coffee a day ~** deberías beber dos tazas de café al día como máximo, deberías beber un máximo de dos tazas de café al día

maxi-single [ˈmæksɪˈsɪŋgəl] N (*Mus*) maxisingle *m*

May [meɪ] Ⓐ N mayo *m*; *see* **July** *for usage*
Ⓑ CPD ► **May Day** N el primero de mayo
► **May Queen** N reina *f* de mayo

▼ **may**[1] [meɪ] (*pt, cond* **might**) MODAL AUX VB [1] (*of possibility*) **it ~ rain** puede *or* es posible que llueva; **it ~ be that he has had to go out** puede (ser) que haya tenido que salir; **he ~ not be hungry** a lo mejor no tiene hambre; **they ~ well be related** puede que sean parientes; **that's as ~ be** eso puede ser; **be that as it ~** sea como sea; **they ~ have gone out** puede que hayan salido, a lo mejor han salido; **he ~ not have spoken to her yet** a lo mejor no ha hablado con ella todavía, puede que no haya hablado con ella todavía; **I ~ have said so** es posible que lo haya dicho, puede que lo haya dicho; **yes, I ~** sí, es posible, sí, a lo mejor; **I might have said so** pudiera haberlo dicho; **as you might expect** como era de esperar, según cabía esperar; **who might you be?** ¿quién es usted?; **how old might you be?** ¿cuántos años tendrás?; **such a policy as might bring peace** una política que pudiera traernos la paz
[2] (*of permission*) poder; **yes, you ~** sí, puedes, ¡cómo no!; **if I ~** si me lo permites; **~ I?** ¿me permite?, con permiso; **~ I go now?** ¿puedo irme ya?; **~ I see it?** ¿se puede ver?, ¿puedo verlo?; **~ I come in?** ¿se puede?, con permiso; **you ~ smoke** se permite fumar; **you ~ not smoke** se prohíbe fumar; **if I ~ advise you** si permites que te dé un consejo; **might I suggest that ...?** me permito sugerir que ...
[3] (*in wishes*) **~ you have a happy life together** ¡que seáis felices!; **~ God bless you** ¡Dios te bendiga!; **~ you be forgiven!** ¡que Dios te perdone!; **long ~ he reign!** ¡que reine muchos años!; **or ~ I never eat prawns again** o que no vuelva nunca a comer gambas
[4] (*frm or liter*) **I hope he ~ succeed** espero que tenga éxito; **I hoped he might succeed this time** esperaba que lo lograra esta vez
[5] **might** [5·1] (*suggesting*) **you might try Smith's** podrías probar en la tienda de Smith; **mightn't it be better to ...?** + *infin* ¿no sería mejor ...? + *infin*
[5·2] (*criticizing*) **you might shut the door!** ¡podrías *or* podías cerrar la puerta!; **he might have offered to help** podría haberse prestado a ayudar; **you might have told me!** ¡habérmelo dicho!
[6] (*in phrases*) **we ~** *or* **might as well go** vámonos ya *or* de una vez; **run as he might** por mucho que corriese

may[2] [meɪ] N (*Bot*) (= *blossom*) flor *f* del espino; (*Brit*) (= *tree*) espino *m*

Maya [ˈmaɪjə], **Mayan** [ˈmaɪjən] Ⓐ ADJ maya
Ⓑ N maya *mf*

▼ **maybe** [ˈmeɪbiː] ADV a lo mejor, quizá(s), tal vez; **~ he'll come tomorrow** a lo mejor viene mañana, puede que *or* quizá(s) *or* tal vez venga mañana; **~ I should grow a moustache** a lo mejor debería dejarme bigote; **there were ~ ten people in the room** habría unas diez personas en la habitación; **maybe, maybe not** puede que sí, puede que no, a lo mejor sí, a lo mejor no

Mayday [ˈmeɪdeɪ] N (= *distress call*) socorro *m*, SOS *m*

mayfly [ˈmeɪflaɪ] N cachipolla *f*, efímera *f*

mayhem [ˈmeɪhem] N [1] alboroto *m*, caos *m*
[2] (*US Jur*) mutilación *f* criminal

mayn't [meɪnt] = **may not**

mayo* [ˈmeɪəʊ] N (*US*) = **mayonnaise**

mayonnaise [meɪəˈneɪz] N mayonesa *f*; *see also* **garlic B**

mayor [mɛəʳ] N alcalde *m*, alcaldesa *f*, intendente *mf* (*S. Cone, Mex*), regente *mf* (*Mex*); **Mr Mayor** Señor Alcalde; **Madam Mayor** Señora Alcaldesa

mayoral [ˈmɛərəl] ADJ [*candidate, election*] para alcalde, para la alcaldía

mayoralty [ˈmɛərəltɪ] N alcaldía *f*

mayoress [ˈmɛəres] (*Brit*) N (= *lady mayor, wife of mayor*) alcaldesa *f*, intendente *f* (*S. Cone, Mex*), regente *f* (*Mex*)

maypole [ˈmeɪpəʊl] N mayo *m*

maze [meɪz] N laberinto *m*

MB N ABBR [1] (*Brit Univ*) = **Bachelor of Medicine** [2] (*Canada*) ABBR = **Manitoba**

Mb N ABBR (*Comput*) (= **megabyte**) Mb

MBA N ABBR (*Univ*) = **Master of Business Administration**; → DEGREE

MBBS, **MBChB** N ABBR (*Univ*) = **Bachelor of Medicine and Surgery**

MBE N ABBR (= **Member of the Order of the British Empire**) *título ceremonial británico*; → HONOURS LIST

MBO N ABBR (*Fin*) = **management buyout**

MC N ABBR [1] = **Master of Ceremonies**
[2] (*US*) = **Member of Congress**
[3] (*Brit Mil*) = **Military Cross**

MCAT N ABBR (*US Univ*) = **Medical College Admissions Test**

McCarthyism [məˈkɑːθɪɪzəm] N (*US Pol*) macartismo *m*

McCoy [məˈkɔɪ] N *see* **real A2**

MCP* N ABBR = **male chauvinist pig**; *see* **chauvinist**

m/cycle ABBR = **motorcycle**

MD Ⓐ N ABBR [1] = **Doctor of Medicine**
[2] = **managing director**
[3] (= **MiniDisc®**) minidisc *m*
Ⓑ ABBR [1] = **mentally deficient**
[2] (*US*) = **Maryland**
Ⓒ CPD ► **MD player** minidisc *m*

MDT N ABBR (*US*) = **Mountain Daylight Time**

ME Ⓐ N ABBR [1] = **myalgic encephalomyelitis**
[2] (*US*) = **medical examiner**
Ⓑ ABBR (*US*) = **Maine**

me[1] [miː] PRON [1] (*direct/indirect object*) me; (*after prep*) mí; **he loves me** me quiere; **look at me!** ¡mírame!; **could you lend me your pen?** ¿me prestas tu bolígrafo?; **without me** sin mí; **come with me** ven conmigo; **like me** como yo; **dear me!** ¡vaya!
[2] (*emphatic, in comparisons, after verb "to be"*) yo; **who, me?** ¿quién, yo?; **what, me?** ¿cómo, yo?; **he's taller than me** es más alto que yo; **it's me** soy yo; **it's me, Paul** (*identifying self*) soy Paul

me[2] [miː] N (*Mus*) mi *m*

Me. ABBR (*US*) = **Maine**

mead [miːd] N aguamiel *f*, hidromiel *m*

meadow [ˈmedəʊ] N prado *m*, pradera *f*; (*esp water meadow*) vega *f*

meadowsweet [ˈmedəʊswiːt] N reina *f* de los prados

meagre, **meager** (*US*) [ˈmiːgəʳ] ADJ [*amount, salary, rations*] escaso, exiguo; **he eked out a ~ existence as a labourer** a duras penas se ganaba la vida trabajando de peón; **his salary is a ~ £350 a month** gana unas míseras 350 libras al mes

meagrely [ˈmiːgəlɪ], **meagerly** (*US*) ADV escasamente, pobremente

meal[1] [miːl] Ⓐ N comida *f*; **to go for a ~** ir a comer fuera; **to have a (good) ~** comer (bien); **I don't eat between ~s** no como entre horas; **~s on wheels** servicio *m* de comidas a domicilio (*para ancianos*); ✦**IDIOM** **to make a ~ of sth*** (= *dramatize*) exagerar algo; (= *make the most of*) sacar todo el jugo posible a algo; (= *take time over*) tardar lo suyo en hacer algo
Ⓑ CPD ► **meal ticket** N (*lit*) vale *m* de comida; (*fig*) **she's just looking for a ~ ticket** sólo busca a alguien que la mantenga

meal[2] [miːl] N (= *flour*) harina *f*

mealie meal [ˈmiːlɪmiːl] N harina *f* de maíz, maicena *f* (*Sp*), Maizena® *f* (*Sp*)

mealtime [ˈmiːltaɪm] N hora *f* de comer

mealy [ˈmiːlɪ] ADJ harinoso

mealy-mouthed [ˈmiːlɪˈmaʊðd] ADJ modoso, evasivo; **let us not be ~ about it** hablemos claro sobre esto

mean[1] [miːn] ADJ (*compar* **meaner**, *superl* **meanest**) [1] (= *stingy*) tacaño, agarrado*, amarrete (*Andes, S. Cone**); **you ~ thing!** ¡qué tacaño eres!
[2] (= *nasty*) malo; **don't be ~!** ¡no seas malo!; **you ~ thing!** ¡qué malo eres!; **a ~ trick** una jugarreta, una mala pasada; **that was pretty ~ of them** se han portado bastante mal; **you were ~ to me** te portaste fatal *or* muy mal conmigo

➤ LANGUAGE IN USE: **may**[1] **1** 15.3 **2** 9.1 **maybe** 15.3

3 (= *vicious*) malo
4 (= *of poor quality*) inferior; (= *shabby*) humilde, vil; (= *humble*) [*birth*] humilde, pobre; **the ~est citizen** el ciudadano más humilde; **obvious to the ~est intelligence** obvio para cualquiera con un mínimo de sentido común; **she's no ~ cook** es una cocinera excelente
5 (*US*) formidable, de primera; **he plays a ~ game** juega estupendamente

mean² [miːn] Ⓐ N (= *middle term*) término *m* medio; (= *average*) promedio *m*; (*Math*) media *f*; **the golden** *or* **happy ~** el justo medio
Ⓑ ADJ medio; **~ life** (*Phys*) vida *f* media

mean³ [miːn] (*pt, pp* **meant**) VT 1 [*word, sign*] (= *signify*) significar, querer decir; **what does this word ~?** ¿qué significa *or* quiere decir esta palabra?; **"vest" ~s something different in America** en América "vest" tiene otro significado *or* significa otra cosa; **you know what it ~s to hit a policeman?** ¿usted sabe qué consecuencias trae el golpear a un policía?; **what do you ~ by that?** ¿qué quieres decir con eso?; **it ~s a lot to have you with us** significa mucho tenerte con nosotros; **your friendship ~s a lot to me** tu amistad es muy importante *or* significa mucho para mí; **a pound ~s a lot to her** para ella una libra es mucho dinero; **it ~s a lot of expense for us** supone un gasto muy fuerte para nosotros; **the name ~s nothing to me** el nombre no me suena; **the play didn't ~ a thing to me** no saqué nada en claro de la obra; *see also* **know A4**
2 [*person*] 2·1 (= *imply*) querer decir; (= *refer to*) referirse a; **what do you ~?** ¿qué quieres decir?; **18, I ~ 19** 18, digo 19; **do you ~ me?** ¿te refieres a mí?
2·2 (= *signify*) significar; **don't I ~ anything to you?** ¿no significo yo nada para ti?
2·3 (= *be determined about*) **I ~ what I say** lo digo en serio; **you can't ~ it!** ¡no lo dirás en serio!; **I ~ it** va en serio
2·4 (= *intend*) **to ~ to do sth** pensar hacer algo; **what do you ~ to do?** ¿qué piensas hacer?; **I ~t to help** pensaba ayudar, tenía la intención de ayudar; **I ~ to have it** pienso *or* me propongo obtenerlo; **he didn't ~ to do it** lo hizo sin querer; **I ~ to have you sacked** voy a encargarme de que te despidan; **sorry, I didn't ~ you to do it** lo siento, mi intención no era que lo hicieras tú; **I ~ to be obeyed** insisto en que se me obedezca; **if he ~s to be awkward** si quiere complicar las cosas; **I ~t it as a joke** lo dije en broma; **was the remark ~t for me?** ¿el comentario iba por mí?; **I ~t no harm by what I said** no lo dije con mala intención; **he ~t no offence** no tenía intención de ofender a nadie; **he ~s well** tiene buenas intenciones
3 (= *suppose*) suponer; **to be ~t to do sth**: **it's ~t to be a good car** este coche se supone que es bueno; **parents are ~t to love their children** se supone que los padres quieren a sus hijos; **the teacher is ~t to do it** se supone que el profesor lo debe hacer; **we were ~t to arrive at eight** se suponía que llegaríamos a las ocho; **this picture is ~t to tell a story** este cuadro se propone contar una historia; **this portrait is ~t to be Anne** este retrato es de Anne, aunque no lo parezca; **perhaps you weren't ~t to be a vet** quizá lo tuyo no sea la veterinaria; **I wasn't ~t to work for my living!** ¡yo no estoy hecho para trabajar!; **you're not ~t to drink it!** ¡no es para beber!

meander [mɪˈændəʳ] Ⓐ VI 1 [*river*] serpentear
2 [*person*] (= *roam*) deambular, vagar; (*in speech*) divagar
Ⓑ N meandro *m*; **~s** (*fig*) meandros *mpl*

meandering [mɪˈændərɪŋ] ADJ 1 (*lit*) [*river*] con meandros; [*road*] serpenteante
2 (*fig*) [*account, speech etc*] lleno de digresiones

meanderings [mɪˈændərɪŋz] NPL (*fig*) divagaciones *fpl*

meanie* [ˈmiːnɪ] N **he's an old ~** es un tío agarrado*

meaning [ˈmiːnɪŋ] Ⓐ N 1 (= *sense*) [*of word*] significado *m*, acepción *f*; [*of phrase*] significado *m*; [*of life, work*] sentido *m*; **this word has lots of ~s** esta palabra tiene muchos significados *or* muchas acepciones; **life has no ~ for her now** ahora para ella la vida no tiene sentido; **double ~** doble sentido; **do you get my ~?** ¿me entiendes?, ¿me comprendes?; **he doesn't know the ~ of the word** (*fig*) ni sabe lo que eso significa; **what's the ~ of "hick"?** ¿qué significa "hick"?, ¿qué quiere decir "hick"?; **what's the ~ of this?** (*as reprimand*) ¿se puede saber qué significa esto?
2 (= *intention*) intención *f*, propósito *m*; **a look full of ~** una mirada llena de intención; **to mistake sb's ~** malinterpretar la intención de algn
Ⓑ ADJ [*look etc*] significativo, lleno de intención

meaningful [ˈmiːnɪŋfʊl] ADJ 1 (= *worthwhile*) [*discussion, negotiations*] valioso, positivo; [*experience*] valioso, significativo; [*relationship*] serio, significativo; [*activity*] que merece la pena; [*question, explanation*] coherente, que tiene sentido; [*comment, analogy*] que tiene sentido; **to lead a ~ life** vivir una vida que tenga sentido; **nothing ~ is ever discussed at these meetings** en estas reuniones nunca se discute nada de trascendencia *or* nada que merezca la pena
2 (= *eloquent*) [*smile, look*] significativo, elocuente

meaningfully [ˈmiːnɪŋfəlɪ] ADV 1 (= *in a worthwhile way*) **to spend one's time ~** emplear el tiempo en algo que valga la pena
2 (= *eloquently*) [*smile, look, say*] de manera significativa

meaningless [ˈmiːnɪŋlɪs] ADJ (*gen*) sin sentido; **in this situation it is ~** en esta situación no tiene sentido; **to write "xybj" is ~** escribir "xybj" carece de sentido

meanly [ˈmiːnlɪ] ADV 1 (= *stingily*) mezquinamente
2 (= *nastily*) maliciosamente

meanness [ˈmiːnnɪs] N 1 (= *stinginess*) tacañería *f*, mezquindad *f*
2 (= *nastiness*) maldad *f*, vileza *f*
3 (= *humbleness*) humildad *f*

means [miːnz] Ⓐ N 1 (*with sing vb*) (= *way*) manera *fsing*, modo *msing*; (= *method*) medio *msing*; **by any ~** de cualquier manera, del modo que sea; **not by any ~** de ninguna manera *or* ningún modo; **by any ~ possible** como sea/fuera posible, a como dé/diera lugar (*CAm, Mex*); **there is no ~ of doing it** no hay manera *or* modo de hacerlo; **by some ~ or other** de alguna manera u otra, de algún modo u otro; **by this ~** de esta manera, de este modo; **a ~ to an end** un medio para conseguir algo *or* un fin; **by ~ of** por medio de; **it moves by ~ of a pulley system** se mueve por medio de poleas; **~ of transport** medio *m* de transporte; *see also* **fair¹ A1**
2 (*in phrases*) **by all ~!** ¡claro que sí!, ¡por supuesto!; **by all ~ take one** por favor toma uno; **"is she a friend of yours?" — "by no means"** —¿es amiga suya? —de ninguna manera *or* ningún modo; **they're by no ~ rich** no son ricos, ni mucho menos; **it is by no ~ difficult** no es nada difícil; **by no manner of ~** en absoluto
3 (*with pl vb*) (*Fin*) recursos *mpl*, medios *mpl*; **we haven't the ~ to do it** no contamos con los recursos *or* los medios para hacerlo; **to live beyond one's ~** vivir por encima de sus posibilidades, gastar más de lo que se gana; **a man of ~** un hombre acaudalado; **private ~** rentas *fpl* (particulares); **to live within one's ~** vivir de acuerdo con sus posibilidades
Ⓑ CPD ► **means test** N prueba *f* de haberes (*para determinar si una persona tiene derecho a determinada prestación*); *see also* **means-test**

means-test [ˈmiːnztest] VT **this benefit is ~ed** este subsidio se otorga después de averiguar los recursos económicos del solicitante; *see also* **means**

meant [ment] PT, PP *of* **mean³**

meantime [ˈmiːnˈtaɪm] Ⓐ ADV entretanto, mientras tanto
Ⓑ N **for the ~** (*referring to now*) por ahora, de momento; (*referring to past*) entretanto; **in the ~** (*referring to now*) mientras tanto; (*referring to past*) en el ínterin; **in the ~ she had had two children** en el ínterin había tenido dos hijos

meanwhile [ˈmiːnˈwaɪl] Ⓐ ADV entretanto, mientras tanto
Ⓑ N **in the ~** entretanto, mientras tanto

measles [ˈmiːzlz] NSING sarampión *m*

measly* [ˈmiːzlɪ] ADJ (*compar* **measlier**; *superl* **measliest**) miserable, mezquino

measurable [ˈmeʒərəbl] ADJ 1 (*lit*) mensurable, que se puede medir
2 (= *perceptible*) apreciable, perceptible

measure [ˈmeʒəʳ] Ⓐ N 1 (= *system*) medida *f*; **liquid/dry ~** medida para líquidos/áridos; **a suit made to ~** un traje hecho a (la) medida; ✦**IDIOMS beyond ~**: **our knowledge has increased beyond ~** nuestros conocimientos han aumentado enormemente *or* de manera inconmensurable; **he irritated her beyond ~** la irritaba hasta más no poder; **to have the ~ of sb** tener a algn calado*; **the government had failed to get the ~ of the crisis** el gobierno no había apreciado la magnitud de la crisis; *see also* **made-to-measure**
2 (= *measuring device*) (= *rule*) metro *m*; (= *glass*) probeta *f* graduada; *see also* **tape C**
3 (= *indication*) indicativo *m*; **it is a ~ of how serious the situation is** es un indicativo de lo grave de la situación
4 (= *amount measured*) cantidad *f*; **I poured two equal ~s into the glasses** eché dos cantidades iguales en los vasos; **to give (sb) good** *or* **full ~** dar la medida exacta (a algn); **to give (sb) short ~** dar una medida escasa (a algn); ✦**IDIOM for good ~**: **he gave me a few extra for good ~** me dio unos pocos más por añadidura; **I repeated my question for good ~** repetí la pregunta por si acaso
5 (= *step*) medida *f*; **to take ~s against sb** tomar medidas contra algn; **to take ~s to do sth** tomar medidas para hacer algo; **they took no ~s to avoid the disaster** no tomaron ninguna medida para evitar el desastre
6 (= *extent*) **we had some ~ of success** tuvimos cierto éxito; **it gives a ~ of protection** da cierta protección; **in large ~** en gran parte *or* medida; **this is due in no small ~ to the problems we have had** esto se debe en gran parte *or* medida a los problemas que hemos tenido; **in some ~** hasta cierto punto, en cierta medida
7 [*of spirits*] cantidad *f*; (*sold in pub*) medida *f*
8 (*Mus*) (= *beat*) ritmo *m*; (= *bar*) compás *m*

➤ LANGUAGE IN USE: mean³ 1 26.3 3 18.4

Ⓑ VT [1] [+ *object, speed, length, width, height*] medir; [+ *person*] (*for height*) medir; (*for clothes*) tomar las medidas a; **to ~ the height of sth** medir la altura de algo; **I have to be ~d for my costume** me tienen que tomar las medidas para el traje; **how can you ~ success?** ¿cómo puedes medir el éxito?; **to ~ one's length (on the floor/ground)** caerse todo lo largo que se es (al suelo); *see also* **word A1**
[2] (= *compare*) **to ~ sth/sb against sth/sb** comparar algo/a algn con algo/algn; **I don't like being ~d against other people** no me gusta que se me compare con otra gente; **the competition will be a chance for him to ~ himself against the best** la competición será una ocasión para medirse con los mejores
Ⓒ VI medir; **what does it ~?** ¿cuánto mide?; **the room ~s four metres across** la habitación mide cuatro metros de ancho
► **measure off** VT + ADV medir
► **measure out** VT + ADV [1] [+ *solid ingredients*] pesar; [+ *liquid, piece of ground, length*] medir
[2] (= *give out*) repartir, distribuir
► **measure up** Ⓐ VT + ADV [1] [+ *wood, material*] medir
[2] (= *evaluate*) [+ *sb's intentions*] averiguar; [+ *situation*] evaluar
Ⓑ VI + ADV [1] (= *take measurements*) tomar medidas; **she ~d up for the curtains** tomó medidas para las cortinas
[2] (= *fulfil expectations*) dar la talla, estar a la altura; **to ~ up to sth** estar a la altura de algo

measured ['meʒəd] ADJ [*tread, pace*] acompasado; [*tone, way of talking, statement*] mesurado, comedido

measureless ['meʒəlɪs] ADJ inmensurable, inmenso

measurement ['meʒəmənt] N [1] (= *size*) medida *f*; **bust/hip ~** contorno *m* de pecho/de caderas; **inside leg ~** largo *m* de entrepierna; **waist ~** cintura *f*, talle *m*; **to take sb's ~s** tomar las medidas a algn
[2] (= *act, system*) medición *f*

measuring ['meʒərɪŋ] Ⓐ N medición *f*
Ⓑ CPD ► **measuring chain** N cadena *f* de agrimensor ► **measuring cup** N taza *f* para medir ► **measuring jug** N jarra *f* medidora *or* graduada ► **measuring rod** N vara *f* de medir ► **measuring spoon** N cuchara *f* medidora ► **measuring tape** N cinta *f* métrica, metro *m*

meat [mi:t] Ⓐ N [1] (*gen*) carne *f*; (= *cold meat*) fiambre *m*; ✦*IDIOM* **it's ~ and drink to me** no puedo vivir sin ello; ✦*PROV* **one man's ~ is another man's poison** lo que a uno cura a otro mata
[2] (*fig*) enjundia *f*, sustancia *f*; **a book with some ~ in it** un libro con enjundia *or* sustancia
Ⓑ CPD ► **meat eater** N (= *person*) persona *f* que come carne; (*Zool*) carnívoro/a *m/f*; **we're not ~ eaters** no comemos carne ► **meat extract** N extracto *m* de carne ► **meat grinder** N (*US*) máquina *f* de picar carne ► **meat hook** N gancho *m* carnicero ► **meat industry** N industria *f* cárnica ► **meat loaf** N *rollo de carne picada sazonado, cocido y servido como fiambre* ► **meat pie** N pastel *m* de carne; (*individual*) empanada *f* ► **meat products** N productos *mpl* cárnicos ► **meat safe** N (*Brit*) fresquera *f*

meatball ['mi:t'bɔ:l] N albóndiga *f*

meat-eating ['mi:t,i:tɪŋ] ADJ carnívoro

meatfly ['mi:tflaɪ] N mosca *f* de la carne

meathead* ['mi:thed] N (*US*) idiota *mf*, gilipollas** *mf*

meatless ['mi:tlɪs] ADJ [*diet*] sin carne; **~ day** día *m* de vigilia

meaty ['mi:tɪ] ADJ (*compar* **meatier**; *superl* **meatiest**) [1] [*soup, filling*] con carne; [*flavour*] a carne
[2] (*fig*) [2·1] (= *substantial*) [*argument, book*] sustancioso, enjundioso; [*part, role*] importante, de peso
[2·2] (= *fleshy*) [*arm, hand*] rollizo

Mecca ['mekə] N La Meca; (*fig*) **a ~ for tourists** una de las mecas del turismo

Meccano® [mɪ'kɑ:nəʊ] N (*Brit*) mecano® *m*

mechanic [mɪ'kænɪk] N mecánico/a *m/f*

mechanical [mɪ'kænɪkəl] Ⓐ ADJ [1] [*toy, problem, failure, device*] mecánico
[2] (*fig*) (= *unthinking*) [*behaviour, reply*] mecánico, maquinal
Ⓑ CPD ► **mechanical engineer** N ingeniero/a *m/f* mecánico/a ► **mechanical engineering** N ingeniería *f* mecánica

mechanically [mɪ'kænɪkəlɪ] ADV [1] [*operated, driven*] mecánicamente; **I'm not ~ minded** no se me da muy bien la mecánica, no tengo cabeza para las cosas mecánicas
[2] (*fig*) (= *unthinkingly*) [*behave, reply*] mecánicamente, maquinalmente

mechanics [mɪ'kænɪks] Ⓐ NSING (*Tech, Phys*) mecánica *f*
Ⓑ NPL (= *machinery*) mecanismo *msing*; (*fig*) mecánica *f*

mechanism ['mekənɪzəm] N [1] (*gen*) mecanismo *m*
[2] (*Philos*) mecanicismo *m*

mechanistic [,mekə'nɪstɪk] ADJ [1] (*gen*) mecánico, maquinal
[2] (*Philos*) mecanístico

mechanization [,mekənaɪ'zeɪʃən] N mecanización *f*

mechanize ['mekənaɪz] VT [+ *process, task*] mecanizar; [+ *factory*] automatizar

mechanized ['mekənaɪzd] ADJ [*process*] mecanizado; [*troops, unit*] motorizado

MEd [em'ed] N ABBR (*Univ*) = **Master of Education**

Med* [med] N **the ~** el Mediterráneo

med. ABBR = **medium**

medal ['medl] N medalla *f*; **he deserves a ~ for it** merece que le den una medalla por ello

medallion [mɪ'dæliən] N medallón *m*

medallist, **medalist** (*US*) ['medəlɪst] N medallista *mf*; **Olympic ~** medallista *mf* olímpico/a; **bronze/silver/gold ~** medalla *mf* de bronce/plata/oro

meddle ['medl] VI [1] (= *interfere*) (entro)meterse (**in** en); **who asked you to ~?** ¿quién te manda a ti meterte en esto?; **he's always meddling** es un entrometido
[2] **to ~ with sth** (= *touch*) toquetear algo, manosear algo; (*causing damage*) estropear algo

meddler ['medlə^r] N entrometido/a *m/f*

meddlesome ['medlsəm], **meddling**[1] ['medlɪŋ] ADJ entrometido

meddlesomeness ['medlsəmnɪs] N entrometimiento *m*

meddling[2] ['medlɪŋ] N intromisión *f*

Mede [mi:d] N medo *m*; **the ~s and the Persians** los medos y los persas

media ['mi:dɪə] Ⓐ NPL *of* **medium**; **the ~** los medios de comunicación (de masas)
Ⓑ CPD ► **media analysis** N análisis *m inv* de los medios ► **media coverage** N cobertura *f* informativa ► **media event** N acontecimiento *m* periodístico ► **media man** N (= *journalist*) periodista *m*; (*in advertising*) agente *m* de publicidad ► **media person** N (= *journalist*) periodista *mf*; (*in advertising*) agente *mf* de publicidad; (= *personality*) personaje *mf* de los medios de comunicación ► **media studies** NPL (*Univ*) ciencias *fpl* de la información (*frm*), periodismo* *msing*

mediaeval [,medɪ'i:vəl] ADJ = **medieval**

medial ['mi:dɪəl] ADJ medial

median ['mi:dɪən] Ⓐ ADJ mediano
Ⓑ N [1] (*US*) (*also* **~ strip**) mediana *f*, franja *f* central
[2] (*Math*) (*gen*) mediana *f*; (= *number*) número *m* medio; (= *point*) punto *m* medio

mediate ['mi:dɪeɪt] Ⓐ VI mediar (**between** entre; **in** en)
Ⓑ VT [+ *talks*] mediar en, actuar de mediador en; [+ *dispute*] mediar en, arbitrar; [+ *agreement*] conseguir mediante mediación

mediating ['mi:dɪeɪtɪŋ] ADJ [*role, efforts*] mediador; **to play a ~ role** actuar como mediador, tener un papel de mediador

mediation [,mi:dɪ'eɪʃən] N mediación *f*

mediator ['mi:dɪeɪtə^r] N mediador(a) *m/f*

medic* ['medɪk] N [1] (= *doctor*) médico/a *m/f*
[2] (= *student*) estudiante *mf* de medicina

Medicaid ['medɪ,keɪd] N (*US*) *seguro médico estatal para personas de bajos ingresos*

medical ['medɪkəl] Ⓐ ADJ [*care, facilities, staff, treatment*] médico; [*records*] médico, clínico; [*student*] de medicina; [*problems*] de salud; **to seek ~ advice** consultar a un médico; **he is in urgent need of ~ attention** necesita atención médica urgente; **she suffered from a rare ~ condition** sufría una enfermedad rara *or* poco frecuente; **on ~ grounds** por razones de salud; **the ~ history of a patient** el historial médico *or* clínico de un paciente, la historia clínica de un paciente; **it made ~ history** pasó a la historia de la medicina; **~ opinion is divided on the subject** la opinión médica está dividida con respecto a este tema; **the ~ profession** la profesión médica
Ⓑ N reconocimiento *m* médico, revisión *f* médica, examen *m* médico; **to have a ~** someterse a un reconocimiento médico *or* a un examen médico *or* a una revisión médica
Ⓒ CPD ► **medical board** N (*Mil*) consejo *m* de médicos ► **medical certificate** N certificado *m* médico ► **medical examination** N reconocimiento *m* médico, revisión *f* médica, examen *m* médico ► **medical examiner** N (*US*) médico/a *m/f* forense ► **medical insurance** N seguro *m* médico ► **medical officer** N médico/a *m/f*; (*Mil*) oficial *mf* médico/a; [*of town*] jefe *mf* de sanidad municipal ► **medical practice** N (= *practice of medicine*) práctica *f* de la medicina; (= *place*) consultorio *m* médico ► **medical practitioner** N (*frm*) médico/a *m/f* ► **medical school** N facultad *f* de medicina ► **medical science** N medicina *f*, ciencia *f* médica

medically ['medɪkəlɪ] ADV [*prove, explain, treat*] médicamente; **he was ~ examined** se le hizo un reconocimiento médico *or* un exámen médico *or* una revisión médica; **it is recognized ~ as being a good diet** se considera una buena dieta desde el punto de vista médico; **he was pronounced ~ fit** dictaminaron que estaba sano *or* que su salud era buena; (*for army*) los médicos lo declararon apto; **~ qualified** titulado en medicina; **~ speaking** desde el punto de vista médico

medicament [me'dɪkəmənt] N medicamento *m*

Medicare ['medɪkeə^r] N (*US*) *seguro médico estatal para ancianos y minusválidos*

medicate ['medɪkeɪt] VT [+ *patient*] medicar; [+ *wound*] curar; [+ *dressing, bandage*] impregnar (**with** de)

medicated ['medɪkeɪtɪd] Ⓐ ADJ medicinal
Ⓑ CPD ► **medicated soap** N jabón *m* medicinal ► **medicated shampoo** N champú *m* medicinal ► **medicated cough sweets** NPL caramelos *mpl* para la tos

medication [,medɪ'keɪʃən] N (= *drugs*) medicación *f*

medicinal [me'dɪsɪnl] ADJ medicinal

medicinally [me'dɪsɪnəlɪ] ADV [*use*] con fines médicos

medicine ['medsɪn,'medɪsɪn] Ⓐ N 1 (= *drug*) medicina *f*, medicamento *m*; ✦***IDIOMS*** **to give sb a dose** *or* **taste of his own ~** pagar a algn con la misma moneda; **to take one's ~** cargar con *or* arrostrar las consecuencias
2 (= *science*) medicina *f*
Ⓑ CPD ► **medicine ball** N (*Sport*) balón *m* medicinal ► **medicine box**, **medicine cabinet**, **medicine chest** N botiquín *m* ► **medicine man** N hechicero *m*

medico* ['medɪkəʊ] N médico/a *m/f*

medieval [,medɪ'i:vəl] ADJ medieval

medievalism [,medɪ'i:vəlɪzəm] N medievalismo *m*

medievalist [,medɪ'i:vəlɪst] N medievalista *mf*

mediocre [,mi:dɪ'əʊkəʳ] ADJ mediocre

mediocrity [,mi:dɪ'ɒkrɪtɪ] N 1 (= *quality*) mediocridad *f*
2 (= *person*) mediocre *mf*

meditate ['medɪteɪt] Ⓐ VI (= *think*) reflexionar, meditar (**on** sobre); (*Rel, Health*) meditar
Ⓑ VT meditar

meditation [,medɪ'teɪʃən] N (= *thought*) meditación *f*, reflexión *f*; (*Rel, Health*) meditación

meditative ['medɪtətɪv] ADJ meditabundo

Mediterranean [,medɪtə'reɪnɪən] Ⓐ ADJ mediterráneo; **the ~ Sea** el Mar Mediterráneo
Ⓑ N **the ~** (= *region, sea*) el Mediterráneo

medium ['mi:dɪəm] Ⓐ ADJ 1 (= *not small or large*) [*object*] mediano; [*length, size*] mediano, medio; **available in small, ~ and large** disponible en talla pequeña, mediana y grande; **of ~ build** de constitución mediana *or* media; **cook over a ~ heat** cocinar a fuego medio; **of ~ height** de estatura regular
2 (*Culin*) **a ~ steak** un filete no muy hecho
Ⓑ N 1 (*pl* **media, mediums**) 1·1 (= *means of communication*) medio *m*; **the advertising media** los medios publicitarios *or* de publicidad; **through the ~ of television/the press** por medio de la televisión/la prensa, a través de la televisión/la prensa
1·2 (= *intervening substance*) medio *m*; (= *environment*) medio ambiente *m*; **air is a ~ for sound** el aire es un medio de transmisión del sonido
1·3 (*for growing culture*) caldo *m* de cultivo; (*for preserving specimens*) *sustancia usada para conservar muestras de laboratorio*
1·4 (= *solvent*) diluyente *m*
1·5 (*Art*) (= *technique, materials used*) medio *m*
1·6 (= *midpoint*) **happy ~** término *m* medio
2 (*pl* **mediums**) (= *spiritualist*) médium *mf*
Ⓒ CPD ► **medium wave** N (*Rad*) onda *f* media

medium-dry [,mi:dɪəm'draɪ] ADJ [*wine*] semi seco

medium-fine [,mi:dɪəm'faɪn] ADJ entrefino

medium-priced [,mi:dɪəm'praɪst] ADJ de precio medio

medium-range [,mi:dɪəm'reɪndʒ] ADJ [*missile*] de alcance medio; [*weather forecast*] a medio plazo

medium-size(d) [,mi:dɪəm'saɪz(d)] ADJ de tamaño mediano *or* medio; **~ business** empresa *f* mediana

medium-sweet [,mi:dɪəm'swi:t] ADJ [*wine*] semidulce

medlar ['medləʳ] N (= *fruit, tree*) níspero *m*; **oriental** *or* **Japanese ~** níspero *m* del Japón

medley ['medlɪ] N (= *mixture*) mezcla *f*; (= *miscellany*) miscelánea *f*; (*Mus*) popurrí *m*

medulla [me'dʌlə] N (*pl* **medullas** *or* **medullae** [me'dʌli:]) medula *f*

meek [mi:k] Ⓐ ADJ (*compar* **meeker**; *superl* **meekest**) (= *submissive*) [*person*] sumiso, dócil, manso (*liter*); [*voice, acceptance*] sumiso; ✦***IDIOMS*** **~ and mild** como una malva; **as ~ as a lamb** más manso que un cordero
Ⓑ NPL **the ~** (*Rel*) los mansos; **blessed are the ~** bienaventurados los mansos

meekly ['mi:klɪ] ADV [*say, accept, follow*] sumisamente, dócilmente, mansamente (*liter*)

meekness ['mi:knɪs] N docilidad *f*, mansedumbre *f* (*liter*)

meerschaum ['mɪəʃəm] N 1 (= *material*) espuma *f* de mar
2 (*also* **~ pipe**) pipa *f* de espuma de mar

meet[1] [mi:t] (*pt, pp* **met**) Ⓐ VT 1 (*by arrangement*) quedar con, verse con; (*by chance*) encontrarse con, tropezarse con; **I'm ~ing them for lunch tomorrow** he quedado para almorzar con ellos mañana; **I had arranged to ~ her in town** había quedado con ella en el centro, había acordado en verla en el centro; **I'll ~ you outside the cinema** te veré en la entrada del cine; **you'll never guess who I met on the bus today?** ¿a que no sabes con quién me encontré *or* me tropecé hoy en el autobús?; **we will be ~ing the ambassador tomorrow to discuss the situation** mañana tendremos un encuentro *or* una reunión con el embajador para discutir la situación, mañana nos entrevistaremos *or* nos reuniremos con el embajador para discutir la situación
2 (= *go/come to get*) ir/venir a buscar; (= *welcome*) recibir; **we met her at the station** la fuimos a buscar a la estación; **I'm being met at the airport** me vendrán a buscar al aeropuerto; **she ran out to ~ us** salió corriendo a recibirnos; **to ~ sb off the train** ir a esperar a algn a la estación; **don't bother to ~ me** no os molestéis en venir a esperarme; **the bus for Aix ~s the ten o'clock train** el autobús que va a Aix conecta con el tren de las diez; *see also* **halfway A1**
3 (= *get to know, be introduced to*) conocer; **I never met him** no lo llegué a conocer; **I met my wife in 1988** conocí a mi mujer en 1988; **~ my brother** quiero presentarte a mi hermano; **he's the kindest person I've ever met** es la persona más amable que he conocido jamás; **nice to have met you!** ¡encantado de conocerlo!; **pleased to ~ you!** ¡mucho gusto!, ¡encantado de conocerlo!
4 (= *come together with*) **where the sea ~s the horizon** donde el mar se junta con el horizonte; **the box met the ground with an almighty thud** la caja se estrelló ruidsosamente contra el suelo; **the sound which met his ears** el sonido que llegó a sus oídos; **I could not ~ his eye** no podía mirarle a los ojos; **her eyes met her sister's across the table** tropezó con la mirada de su hermana al otro lado de la mesa; **what a scene met my eyes!** ¡el escenario que se presentó ante mis ojos!; *see also* **eye A1**
5 (= *come across*) [+ *problem*] encontrarse con; **almost all retired people ~ this problem** casi todos los jubilados se encuentran con este problema
6 (= *confront*) [+ *opponent*] enfrentarse con; (*in duel*) batirse con; [+ *problem*] hacer frente a; **he met his death** *or* **his end in 1800** halló *or* encontró la muerte en 1800; **to ~ death calmly** enfrentarse con la muerte con tranquilidad; **to ~ sth head-on** enfrentarse de lleno con algo, hacer frente *or* plantar cara directamente a algo; **this suggestion was met with angry protests** la gente reaccionó con protestas de indignación ante la sugerencia; *see also* **match**[2] **A3**
7 (= *satisfy*) [+ *need*] satisfacer, cubrir; [+ *demand*] atender a, satisfacer; [+ *wish*] satisfacer; [+ *requirement*] cumplir con; [+ *debt*] pagar; [+ *expense, cost*] correr con, hacer frente a; [+ *obligation*] atender a, cumplir con; [+ *target, goal*] alcanzar; [+ *challenge*] hacer frente a; [+ *expectations*] estar a la altura de; **he offered to ~ the full cost of the repairs** se ofreció a correr con *or* hacer frente a todos los gastos de la reparación; **it did not ~ our expectations** no estuvo a la altura de nuestras expectativas; *see also* **deadline**
Ⓑ VI 1 (= *encounter each other*) (*by arrangement*) quedar, verse; (*by chance*) encontrarse; (= *hold meeting*) reunirse; [*ambassador, politician*] (*with interested parties*) entrevistarse, reunirse; **we could ~ for a drink after work** podríamos vernos *or* quedar para tomar una copa después del trabajo; **what time shall we ~?** ¿a qué hora quieres que quedemos *or* nos veamos?; **let's ~ at eight** quedemos para las ocho; **they arranged to ~ at ten** quedaron en verse a las diez; **the two ministers met to discuss the treaty** los dos ministros se entrevistaron *or* se reunieron para discutir el tratado; **to ~ again** volver a verse; **until we ~ again!** ¡hasta la vista!, ¡hasta pronto!
2 (= *convene*) [*Parliament, club, committee*] reunirse; **the society ~s at eight** la sociedad se reúne a las ocho
3 (= *get to know one another, be introduced*) conocerse; **we met in Seville** nos conocimos en Sevilla; **we have met before** nos conocemos ya; **have we met?** ¿nos conocemos de antes?
4 (= *come together, join*) [*two ends*] unirse; [*rivers*] confluir; [*roads*] empalmar; **our eyes met** cruzamos una mirada; **their lips met** sus labios se encontraron; *see also* **end A1**, **twain**
5 (= *confront each other*) [*teams, armies*] enfrentarse; **Bilbao and Valencia will ~ in the final** el Bilbao se enfrentará con el Valencia en la final, Bilbao y Valencia se disputarán la final; **to ~ (sb) in battle** librar batalla (con algn)
Ⓒ N (*Hunting*) cacería *f*; (*esp US Sport*) encuentro *m*

►**meet up** VI + ADV 1 **to ~ up (with sb)** (*by arrangement*) quedar (con algn), verse (con algn); (*by chance*) encontrarse (con algn), tropezarse (con algn); **they promised to ~ up again in a year's time** prometieron volver a verse *or* quedar un año después; **we ~ up for lunch occasionally** de vez en cuando quedamos para almorzar juntos; **where did you two ~ up?** (*for 1st time*) ¿dónde os conocisteis?
2 (= *join*) empalmar; **this road ~s up with the motorway** esta carretera empalma con la autopista

►**meet with** VI + PREP 1 (= *experience*) [+ *hostility*] experimentar; [+ *difficulties*] encontrarse con, tropezar con; [+ *kindness*] encontrarse con; [+ *accident*] tener, sufrir; [+ *success*] tener; **we hope the idea ~s with your approval** esperamos que la idea reciba su aprobación; **the idea met with a cool response** la idea fue acogida *or* recibida con frialdad; **efforts to contact her met with no response** los esfuerzos para ponerse en contacto con ella fracasaron; **attempts to find them have met with failure** los intentos de encontrarlos han fracasado

2 (*esp US*) [+ *person*] (*by arrangement*) quedarse con, verse con; (*by chance*) encontrarse con, tropezarse con; (*formally*) reunirse con; [+ *politician, ambassador*] entrevistarse con, reunirse con

meet² [miːt] ADJ [*liter*] conveniente, apropiado; **it is ~ that ...** conviene que ... + *subjun*; **to be ~ for** ser apto para

meeting [ˈmiːtɪŋ] Ⓐ N 1 (= *assembly, business meeting*) reunión *f*; [*of legislative body*] sesión *f*; (= *popular gathering*) mitin *m*, mitín *m*; **to address a ~** tomar la palabra en una reunión; **to call a ~** convocar una reunión; **I have a ~ at ten** tengo una reunión a las diez; **the Council had a ~ on Thursday** el Consejo se reunió el jueves; **to hold a ~** celebrar una reunión; **I'm afraid Jeremy's in a ~** ahora mismo Jeremy está reunido *or* está en una reunión; **to open a ~** abrir una sesión

2 (*between 2 people*) (*arranged*) cita *f*, compromiso *m*; (*accidental*) encuentro *m*; (*with politician, person in authority*) entrevista *f*, encuentro *m*; **I liked him from our first ~** me gustó desde el día que le conocí *or* desde nuestro primer encuentro; **to have a ~: the minister had a ~ with the ambassador** el ministro se entrevistó con el embajador; **I had a ~ with the headmistress today** hoy he tenido una entrevista *or* reunión con la directora; **a ~ of minds** un encuentro de inteligencias

3 (*Athletics*) competición *f*; (*Horse racing*) jornada *f*; (*between two teams*) encuentro *m*

4 [*of rivers*] confluencia *f*

Ⓑ CPD ► **meeting house** N (*gen*) centro *m* *or* sala *f* de reuniones; (*Rel*) templo *m* (de los cuáqueros) ► **meeting place** N [*of 2 people*] lugar *m* de cita; [*of many*] lugar *m* de reunión *or* encuentro; **this bar was their usual ~ place** solían citarse en este bar, acostumbraban reunirse en este bar ► **meeting point** N (*lit*) punto *m* de reunión, punto *m* de encuentro; (*fig*) punto *m* de convergencia; **the ~ point between East and West** el punto de convergencia entre Oriente y Occidente

Meg [meg] N (*familiar form*) *of* **Margaret**

mega* [ˈmegə] ADJ súper*

mega... [ˈmegə] PREFIX mega...

megabucks* [ˈmegə,bʌks] N (*esp US*) **now he's making ~** ahora está ganando un dineral*, ahora se está forrando*; **we're talking ~** hablamos de un montón *or* porrón de dinero*

megabyte [ˈmegə,baɪt] N (*Comput*) megabyte *m*, mega *m*

megacycle [ˈmegə,saɪkl] N megaciclo *m*

megadeath [ˈmegə,deθ] N muerte *f* de un millón de personas

megahertz [ˈmegə,hɜːts] N (*pl* **megahertz**) megahercio *m*

megalith [ˈmegəlɪθ] N megalito *m*

megalithic [,megəˈlɪθɪk] ADJ megalítico

megalomania [ˈmegələʊˈmeɪnɪə] N megalomanía *f*

megalomaniac [ˈmegələʊˈmeɪnɪæk] N megalómano/a *m/f*

megalopolis [,megəˈlɒpəlɪs] N megalópolis *f inv*

megaphone [ˈmegəfəʊn] N megáfono *m*

megaton [ˈmegətʌn] N megatón *m*

megavolt [ˈmegəvəʊlt] N megavoltio *m*

megawatt [ˈmegəwɒt] N megavatio *m*

meiosis [maɪˈəʊsɪs] N (*pl* **meioses** [maɪˈəʊsiːz]) 1 (*Bio*) meiosis *f*

2 (= *litotes*) lítote *f*

melamine [ˈmeləmiːn] N melamina *f*

melancholia [,melənˈkəʊlɪə] N melancolía *f*

melancholic [,melənˈkɒlɪk] ADJ melancólico

melancholically [,melənˈkɒlɪklɪ] ADV melancólicamente

melancholy [ˈmelənkəlɪ] Ⓐ ADJ [*person, mood*] melancólico; [*duty, sight*] triste

Ⓑ N melancolía *f*

melange, mélange [meˈlɑːnʒ] N mezcla *f*

melanin [ˈmelənɪn] N melanina *f*

melanism [ˈmelənɪzəm] N melanismo *m*

melanoma [,meləˈnəʊmə] N (*pl* **melanomas** *or* **melanomata** [,meləˈnəʊmətə]) melanoma *m*

Melba toast [ˈmelbəˈtəʊst] N tostada *f* delgada

Meldrew [ˈmeldruː] N (*Brit*) *persona frustrada y desilusionada con la sociedad actual* (*apellido de un protagonista de telecomedia*)

melée [ˈmeleɪ] N 1 (= *confusion*) tumulto *m*; **it got lost in the ~** se perdió en el tumulto; **there was such a ~ at the booking office** la gente se apiñaba delante de la taquilla

2 (= *fight*) pelea *f* confusa, refriega *f*

mellifluous [meˈlɪflʊəs] ADJ melifluo

Mellotron® [ˈmelətrɒn] N Mellotron® *m*

mellow [ˈmeləʊ] Ⓐ ADJ (*compar* **mellower**; *superl* **mellowest**) 1 (= *pleasant, smooth*) [*wine, whisky*] suave, añejo; [*fruit*] maduro, dulce; [*colour, light*] suave y dorado, tenue y dorado; [*instrument*] melodioso; [*voice, tone, sound*] dulce, meloso

2 [*person*] 2·1 (= *calm*) apacible, sosegado; **he has grown more ~ over the years** los años le han suavizado el carácter, se ha vuelto más afable con los años

2·2 (= *relaxed*) **to be ~** (*after eating, drinking*) estar relajado; **to get ~*** (= *tipsy*) achisparse*; **to be in a ~ mood** sentirse relajado

Ⓑ VI 1 (= *soften*) **he has ~ed with age** los años le han suavizado el carácter, con los años se ha vuelto más afable 2 (= *relax*) relajarse 3 [*wine, whisky*] añejarse; [*fruit*] madurar; [*colour, light, voice, character*] suavizarse; [*views*] moderarse; **to ~ with age** [*wine, whisky*] mejorar con los años

Ⓒ VT 1 (= *soften*) **old age has ~ed him** la vejez le ha suavizado el carácter *or* lo ha hecho más afable 2 (= *relax*) relajar 3 [+ *wine*] añejar

mellowing [ˈmeləʊɪŋ] N [*of fruit*] maduración *f*; [*of wine*] añejamiento *m*

mellowness [ˈmeləʊnɪs] N (= *smoothness*) [*of wine, brandy*] suavidad *f*, añejez *f*; [*of fruit*] dulzura *f*; [*of colour , light*] suavidad *f*; [*of instrument*] lo melodioso

melodic [mɪˈlɒdɪk] ADJ melódico

melodious [mɪˈləʊdɪəs] ADJ melodioso

melodiously [mɪˈləʊdɪəslɪ] ADV melodiosamente

melodrama [ˈmeləʊ,drɑːmə] N melodrama *m*

melodramatic [,meləʊdrəˈmætɪk] ADJ melodramático

melodramatically [,meləʊdrəˈmætɪklɪ] ADV melodramáticamente

melody [ˈmelədɪ] N melodía *f*

melon [ˈmelən] N melón *m*

melt [melt] Ⓐ VT 1 (*lit*) [+ *snow, chocolate, butter*] derretir, fundir; [+ *metal*] fundir; [+ *chemical*] disolver 2 (*fig*) (= *soften*) ablandar

Ⓑ VI 1 (*lit*) [*snow, chocolate, butter*] derretirse, fundirse; [*metal*] fundirse; [*chemical*] disolverse; **it ~s in the mouth** se deshace en la boca; *see also* **butter A**

2 (*fig*) 2·1 [*person*] (= *soften*) ablandarse; **to ~ into tears** deshacerse en lágrimas; ✦**IDIOM her heart ~ed with pity** se le ablandó el corazón de lástima

2·2 (= *disappear*) **the gunman ~ed into the crowd** el pistolero desapareció entre la multitud; **night ~ed into day** la noche dio paso al día

► **melt away** VI + ADV 1 (*lit*) derretirse

2 (*fig*) [*confidence*] desvanecerse; [*money*] evaporarse; [*crowd*] dispersarse; [*person*] esfumarse, escabullirse

► **melt down** VT + ADV fundir

meltdown [ˈmeltdaʊn] N 1 (*lit*) fusión *f* de un reactor, fundido *m*

2 (*fig*) cataclismo *m*, debacle *f*

melting [ˈmeltɪŋ] Ⓐ ADJ [*look*] tierno, dulce

Ⓑ CPD ► **melting point** N punto *m* de fusión ► **melting pot** N (*lit, fig*) crisol *m*; ✦**IDIOM to be in the ~ pot** (*Brit*) estar sobre el tapete

meltwater [ˈmeltwɔːtəʳ] N agua *f* de fusión de la nieve

member [ˈmembəʳ] Ⓐ N 1 [*of organization, committee*] miembro *mf*; [*of society, club*] miembro *mf*, socio/a *m/f*; [*of political party, trade union*] miembro *mf*, afiliado/a *m/f*; **"members only"** "sólo para socios", "reservado para los socios"; **the ~ for Woodford** el diputado por Woodford; **if any ~ of the audience ...** si cualquiera de los espectadores ..., si cualquier miembro del público ...; **she's a ~ of our church** es una feligresa *or* es miembro de nuestra iglesia; **~ of Congress** (*US*) miembro *mf* del Congreso; **~ of the crew** ◊ **crew ~** tripulante *mf*; **a ~ of the family** ◊ **a family ~** un miembro de la familia; **full ~** miembro *mf* de pleno derecho; **Member of Parliament** (*Brit*) diputado/a *m/f*, parlamentario/a *m/f*; **Member of the European Parliament** diputado/a *m/f* del Parlamento Europeo, eurodiputado/a *m/f*; **a ~ of the public** un ciudadano/una ciudadana; **the library is open to ~s of the public** la biblioteca está abierta al público; **~ of staff** [*of firm*] empleado/a *m/f*; (*Univ, Scol*) miembro *mf* del profesorado; *see also* **private C**; → BY-ELECTION

2 (*Anat, Bot, Math*) miembro *m*; *see also* **male C**

Ⓑ CPD ► **member country** N país *m* miembro ► **member state** N estado *m* miembro

membership [ˈmembəʃɪp] Ⓐ N 1 (= *members*) [*of club, society*] socios *mpl*, miembros *mpl*; [*of political party*] miembros *mpl*, militancia *f*, afiliados *mpl*; [*of trade union*] afiliados *mpl*, miembros *mpl*

2 (= *position*) **~ carries certain rights** el ser socio *or* miembro conlleva ciertos derechos; **~ of the union is compulsory** es obligatorio afiliarse a *or* hacerse miembro del sindicato; **I've paid for a year's ~** he pagado la cuota anual de socio *or* miembro; **to apply for ~** solicitar el ingreso como socio *or* miembro; **Spain's ~ of** *or* (*US*) **in the Common Market** (= *state*) la pertenencia de España al Mercado Común; (= *act*) el ingreso de España en el Mercado Común

3 (= *numbers*) número *m* de miembros *or* socios *etc*, membresía *f* (*Mex*); **a ~ of more than 800** más de 800 socios *or* miembros; **trade union ~ has declined** el número de afiliados a los sindicatos ha disminuido

Ⓑ CPD ► **membership card** N [*of club, society*] tarjeta *f* *or* carné *m* de socio; [*of political party, trade union*] tarjeta *f* *or* carné *m* de afiliación ► **membership fee** N cuota *f* de socio ► **membership list** N relación *f* de socios

membrane [ˈmembreɪn] N membrana *f*

membranous [memˈbreɪnəs] ADJ membranoso

memento [mɪˈmentəʊ] N (*pl* **mementos** *or* **mementoes**) recuerdo *m*

memo* [ˈmeməʊ] Ⓐ N ABBR (= **memorandum**) memo *m*
Ⓑ CPD ► **memo pad** N bloc *m* de notas

memoir [ˈmemwɑːʳ] N [1] **memoirs** (= *autobiography*) memorias *fpl*, autobiografía *fsing*
[2] (= *biographical note*) nota *f* biográfica
[3] (= *essay*) memoria *f*

memorabilia [ˌmemərəˈbɪlɪə] N (= *objects*) recuerdos *mpl*

memorable [ˈmemərəbl] ADJ memorable

memorably [ˈmemərəblɪ] ADV memorablemente

memorandum [ˌmeməˈrændəm] N (*pl* **memorandums** *or* **memoranda** [ˌmeməˈrændə]) memorándum *m*; (= *personal reminder*) apunte *m*, nota *f*

memorial [mɪˈmɔːrɪəl] Ⓐ ADJ conmemorativo
Ⓑ N [1] (= *monument*) monumento *m* conmemorativo
[2] (= *document*) memorial *m*
Ⓒ CPD ► **memorial park** N (*US*) cementerio *m*

memorialize [mɪˈmɔːrɪəlaɪz] VT conmemorar

memorize [ˈmeməraɪz] VT memorizar, aprender de memoria

memory [ˈmemərɪ] Ⓐ N [1] (= *faculty*) memoria *f*; **to commit sth to ~** aprender algo de memoria; **to lose one's ~** perder la memoria; **I have a bad ~ for faces** se me olvida la cara de la gente; **he recited the poem from ~** recitó el poema de memoria; **if my ~ serves me** si mi memoria no me falla, si mal no recuerdo; **to the best of my ~** que yo recuerde; ✦**IDIOM to have a ~ like a sieve** tener malísima memoria
[2] (= *recollection*) recuerdo *m*; **of blessed ~** de feliz recuerdo, de grata memoria; **"Memories of a country childhood"** "Recuerdos de una infancia campestre"; **to have happy memories of sth** tener *or* guardar buenos recuerdos de algo; **to keep sb's ~ alive** guardar el recuerdo de algn, mantener vivo el recuerdo de algn
[3] (= *remembrance*) **in ~ of** ◊ **to the ~ of** en memoria de
[4] (*Comput*) memoria *f*
Ⓑ CPD ► **memory bank** N banco *m* de memoria ► **memory card** N tarjeta *f* de memoria ► **memory chip** N chip *m* de memoria ► **memory lane** N mundo *m* de los recuerdos (sentimentales); ✦**IDIOM to take a trip down ~ lane** adentrarse en el mundo de los recuerdos ► **memory loss** N pérdida *f* de memoria ► **memory management** N gestión *f* de la memoria

memsahib [ˈmemˌsɑːhɪb] N (*India*) mujer *f* casada

men [men] NPL *of* **man**

menace [ˈmenɪs] Ⓐ N [1] (*no pl*) (= *intimidation*) **a voice full of ~** una voz amenazadora
[2] (= *danger*) peligro *m*, amenaza *f*
[3] (= *threat*) amenaza *f*
[4] (*) (= *person*) **he's a ~** (*child*) es un diablillo*; (*adult*) es un peligro público
Ⓑ VT amenazar

menacing [ˈmenɪsɪŋ] ADJ amenazador

menacingly [ˈmenɪsɪŋlɪ] ADV de modo amenazador

ménage [meˈnɑːʒ] N hogar *m*; **~ à trois** trio *m* amoroso, ménage à trois *m*

menagerie [mɪˈnædʒərɪ] N casa *f or* colección *f* de fieras

mend [mend] Ⓐ N (= *patch*) remiendo *m*; (= *darn*) zurcido *m*; ✦**IDIOM to be on the ~** ir mejorando
Ⓑ VT [1] (= *repair*) [+ *watch, toy, wall*] arreglar, reparar; [+ *shoes*] arreglar; (= *darn*) remendar, zurcir
[2] (= *improve*) **to ~ matters** mejorar las cosas; ✦**IDIOM to ~ one's ways** enmendarse
Ⓒ VI (= *improve*) mejorar

mendacious [menˈdeɪʃəs] ADJ (*frm*) mendaz

mendacity [menˈdæsɪtɪ] N (*frm*) mendacidad *f*

mendelevium [ˌmendɪˈliːvɪəm] N mendelevio *m*

Mendelian [menˈdiːlɪən] ADJ mendeliano

Mendelianism [menˈdiːlɪənɪzəm] N, **Mendelism** [ˈmendəlɪzəm] N mendelismo *m*

mendicancy [ˈmendɪkənsɪ] N mendicidad *f*

mendicant [ˈmendɪkənt] (*frm*) Ⓐ ADJ mendicante
Ⓑ N mendicante *mf*

mendicity [menˈdɪsɪtɪ] N (*frm*) mendicidad *f*

mending [ˈmendɪŋ] N [1] (= *act*) reparación *f*, arreglo *m*; [*of clothes*] zurcido *m*; **invisible ~** zurcido *m* invisible
[2] (= *clothes to be mended*) ropa *f* para remendar

Menelaus [ˌmenɪˈleɪəs] N Menelao

menfolk [ˈmenfəʊk] NPL hombres *mpl*

menhir [ˈmenhɪəʳ] N menhir *m*

menial [ˈmiːnɪəl] Ⓐ ADJ (= *lowly*) servil; (= *domestic*) doméstico, de la casa; **~ work** trabajo *m* de baja categoría
Ⓑ N (= *servant*) sirviente/a *m/f*

meningitis [ˌmenɪnˈdʒaɪtɪs] N meningitis *f inv*

meniscus [məˈnɪskəs] N (*pl* **meniscuses** *or* **menisci** [mɪˈnɪsaɪ]) menisco *m*

menopausal [ˌmenəʊˈpɔːzəl] ADJ menopáusico

menopause [ˈmenəʊpɔːz] N menopausia *f*

menorrhagia [ˌmenɔːˈreɪdʒɪə] N menorragia *f*

menses [ˈmensiːz] NPL menstruo *msing*

menstrual [ˈmenstrʊəl] Ⓐ ADJ menstrual
Ⓑ CPD ► **menstrual cycle** N ciclo *m* menstrual

menstruate [ˈmenstrʊeɪt] VI menstruar, tener la menstruación

menstruation [ˌmenstrʊˈeɪʃən] N menstruación *f*

mensuration [ˌmensjʊəˈreɪʃən] N medición *f*, medida *f*, mensuración *f*

menswear [ˈmenzweəʳ] N ropa *f* de caballero

mental [ˈmentl] Ⓐ ADJ [1] (= *not physical*) [*development, health, effort*] mental; **the stigma attached to ~ illness** el estigma vinculado con las enfermedades mentales; **I formed a ~ picture of what he looked like** me formé una imagen mental de cómo era; **to make a ~ note of sth** tomar nota mentalmente de algo
[2] (*Brit**) (= *crazy*) chiflado*; **he must be ~** debe estar chiflado*
Ⓑ CPD ► **mental age** N edad *f* mental ► **mental arithmetic** N cálculos *mpl* mentales ► **mental block** N bloqueo *m* mental ► **mental cruelty** N crueldad *f* mental ► **mental handicap** N retraso *m* mental ► **mental healing** N (*US*) cura *f* mental ► **mental home, mental hospital** N hospital *m* psiquiátrico, manicomio *m* ► **mental institution** N institución *f* para enfermos mentales ► **mental patient** N paciente *mf* psiquiátrico/a ► **mental powers** N poderes *mpl* mentales

mentality [menˈtælɪtɪ] N mentalidad *f*

mentally [ˈmentəlɪ] ADV [1] (= *not physically*) mentalmente; **to be ~ disturbed** estar trastornado; **to be ~ handicapped** ser un disminuido psíquico; **to be ~ ill** tener una enfermedad mental, ser un enfermo mental
[2] (= *in the mind*) [*calculate, formulate*] mentalmente; **~, I tried to picture what the house must have looked like** intenté formarme una imagen mental de cómo debía haber sido la casa

menthol [ˈmenθɒl] Ⓐ N mentol *m*
Ⓑ CPD [*cigarette, sweet*] mentolado

mentholated [ˈmenθəleɪtɪd] ADJ mentolado

mention [ˈmenʃən] Ⓐ N [1] mención *f*; **the mere ~ of his name exasperates me** la sola mención de su nombre me saca de quicio; **at the ~ of food, she looked up** al oír que se mencionaba comida, levantó la vista; **it got a ~ in the news** lo mencionaron en las noticias; **to make ~ of sth/sb** mencionar algo/a algn, hacer mención de algo/algn; **there was no ~ of any surcharge** no se mencionó ningún recargo adicional, no se hizo mención de ningún recargo adicional; *see also* **honourable**
[2] (*Mil*) citación *f*
Ⓑ VT mencionar; **I will ~ it to him** se lo mencionaré, se lo diré; **he ~ed to me that you were coming** me mencionó *or* comentó que venías; **I've never heard him ~ his father** nunca le he oído mencionar *or* mentar a su padre; **too numerous to ~** demasiado numerosos para mencionar; **he has been ~ed as a potential candidate** se ha hecho alusión a él *or* se le ha aludido como posible candidato; **don't ~ it to anyone** no se lo digas a nadie; **don't ~ it!** (*in reply to thanks*) ¡de nada!, ¡no hay de qué!; **I need hardly ~ that …** ni que decir tiene que …, no es necesario decir que …; **just ~ my name** basta con decir mi nombre; **he didn't ~ any names** no dijo *or* dio los nombres; **they make so much mess, not to ~ the noise** lo dejan todo patas arriba, y no digamos ya el ruido que arman; **to ~ sb in one's will** dejar algo a algn en el testamento, legar algo a algn; **it's worth ~ing that …** merece la pena mencionar que …; *see also* **dispatch A2**

mentor [ˈmentɔːʳ] N mentor *m*

menu [ˈmenjuː] N [1] (= *list*) carta *f*; (= *set meal*) menú *m* [2] (*Comput*) menú *m*

menu-driven [ˈmenjuːˌdrɪvn] ADJ (*Comput*) guiado por menú

meow [mɪˈaʊ] Ⓐ N maullido *m*, miau *m*
Ⓑ VI maullar

MEP N ABBR (*Brit*) (= **Member of the European Parliament**) eurodiputado/a *m/f*

Mephistopheles [ˌmefɪsˈtɒfɪliːz] N Mefistófeles

Mephistophelian [ˌmefɪstəˈfiːlɪən] ADJ mefistofélico

mercantile [ˈmɜːkəntaɪl] ADJ mercantil

mercantilism [ˈmɜːkəntɪlɪzəm] N mercantilismo *m*

mercenary [ˈmɜːsɪnərɪ] Ⓐ ADJ mercenario
Ⓑ N mercenario/a *m/f*

▼ **merchandise** [ˈmɜːtʃəndaɪz] N mercancías *fpl*

merchandiser, merchandizer [ˈmɜːtʃəndaɪzəʳ] N (*US*) minorista *mf*, detallista *mf*

merchandize [ˈmɜːtʃəndaɪz] VT comerciar

merchandizing [ˈmɜːtʃəndaɪzɪŋ] N (*esp US*) comercialización *f*

merchant [ˈmɜːtʃənt] Ⓐ N [1] (= *trader, dealer*) comerciante *mf*; (= *retailer*) minorista *mf*, detallista *mf*; **a diamond ~** un comerciante de diamantes; **a wine ~** un vinatero; **"The Merchant of Venice"** "El Mercader de Venecia"
[2] (*) tío* *m*, sujeto *m*
Ⓑ CPD ► **merchant bank** N banco *m* mercantil *or* comercial ► **merchant banker** N

➤ LANGUAGE IN USE: **merchandise** 20.3

(*Brit*) ejecutivo/a *m/f* de un banco mercantil *or* comercial ► **merchant marine** N (*US*) = **merchant navy** ► **merchant navy** N marina *f* mercante ► **merchant seaman** N marino *m* mercante ► **merchant ship** N buque *m* mercante ► **merchant shipping** N marina *f* mercante; (= *ships*) buques *mpl* mercantes

merchantable [ˈmɜːtʃəntəbl] ADJ comercializable; **of ~ quality** de calidad comerciable

merchantman [ˈmɜːtʃəntmən] N (*pl* **merchantmen**) buque *m* mercante

merciful [ˈmɜːsɪfʊl] ADJ [1] (= *compassionate*) [*god*] misericordioso, clemente, compasivo; [*person*] clemente, compasivo; **to be ~ to** *or* **towards sb** ser clemente con algn, mostrarse compasivo con algn
[2] (= *blessed*) **death came as a ~ release** la muerte fue como una bendición

mercifully [ˈmɜːsɪfəlɪ] ADV [1] (= *kindly*) con clemencia, con compasión
[2] (= *fortunately*) afortunadamente, gracias a Dios

merciless [ˈmɜːsɪlɪs] ADJ [*person, attack*] despiadado, cruel; [*killing, beating*] cruel; [*sun, heat*] implacable; **he's famous for his ~ treatment of hecklers** tiene fama de tratar despiadadamente a los que interrumpen con preguntas o comentarios molestos

mercilessly [ˈmɜːsɪlɪslɪ] ADV [*beat, punish, treat*] despiadadamente, sin piedad; **Joe teased his sister ~** Joe se burló de su hermana despiadadamente *or* sin piedad

mercurial [mɜːˈkjʊərɪəl] ADJ [1] (*Chem*) mercúrico, mercurial
[2] (= *lively*) vivo; (= *changeable*) veleidoso, voluble

Mercury [ˈmɜːkjʊrɪ] N (*Astron, Myth*) Mercurio *m*

mercury [ˈmɜːkjʊrɪ] N mercurio *m*, azogue *m*

mercy [ˈmɜːsɪ] Ⓐ N [1] (= *compassion*) misericordia *f*; (= *clemency*) clemencia *f*, piedad *f*; **to beg for ~** pedir clemencia; **to have ~ on sb** tener misericordia *or* piedad de algn, tener clemencia para con algn; **have ~!** ¡por piedad!; **God in His ~** el Señor en su infinita bondad; **to show sb no ~** no mostrarse misericordioso *or* clemente con algn; **no ~ was shown to the rioters** no hubo clemencia para los revoltosos
[2] (= *discretion*) **to be at the ~ of sth/sb** estar a merced de algo/algn; **to be left to the tender mercies of sb** (*esp hum*) quedar a merced de algn; ✦**IDIOM to throw o.s. on sb's ~** ponerse en (las) manos de algn
[3] (= *blessing*) **his death was a ~** su muerte fue una bendición; **it's a ~ that no-one was hurt*** es un milagro que nadie resultara herido, menos mal que nadie resultó herido; **we should be grateful for small mercies** y demos gracias, porque podría haber sido peor; *see also* **thankful**
Ⓑ CPD ► **mercy flight** N vuelo *m* de ayuda (*para ayudar a alguien necesitado en una guerra, etc*) ► **mercy killing** N eutanasia *f*

mere[1] [mɪəʳ] N lago *m*

mere[2] [mɪəʳ] ADJ (*superl* **merest**) mero, simple; **the ~ fact that ...** el mero *or* simple hecho de que ...; **the merest jolt can upset the balance of the wheels** la más mínima sacudida puede desequilibrar las ruedas; **it was sold for a ~ £45** lo vendieron por apenas 45 libras; **a ~ child could do it** incluso un niño podría hacerlo; **I was a ~ child when I married him** no era más que una niña cuando me casé con él, era solamente una niña cuando me casé con él; **a ~ formality** una mera *or* pura *or* simple formalidad; **the merest hint of a smile** apenas un atisbo de sonrisa; **a ~ man** un hombre nada más *or* (*LAm*) nomás; **it's way beyond the abilities of ~ mortals like us** está más allá de la capacidad del común de los mortales como nosotros; **a ~ nothing** casi nada; **the ~ sight of blood is enough to make her faint** sólo con ver la sangre *or* con sólo ver la sangre se desmaya; **the merest suggestion of sth** la mera sugerencia de algo; *see also* **mention A1**

merely [ˈmɪəlɪ] ADV simplemente, solamente; **she's ~ a secretary** es simplemente *or* solamente una secretaria, no es más que una secretaria; **I was ~ suggesting that ...** estaba simplemente *or* solamente sugiriendo que ...; **this ~ aggravates the problem** esto lo único que hace es agravar el problema; **I ~ said that ...** sólo dije que ..., lo único que dije era que ...; **she ~ shrugged** ella se limitó a encogerse de hombros; **she ~ smiled** sonrió nada más, se limitó a sonreír

meretricious [ˌmerɪˈtrɪʃəs] ADJ [*charm, attraction*] superficial, aparente; [*style, writing*] rimbombante

merge [mɜːdʒ] Ⓐ VT [1] (*Comm*) fusionar, unir
[2] (*Comput*) [+ *text, files*] fusionar
Ⓑ VI [1] [*colours, sounds, shapes*] fundirse; [*roads*] empalmar; **to ~ into the background** confundirse con el fondo; **the bird ~d into its background of leaves** el pájaro se confundía *or* mimetizaba con el fondo de hojas; **this question ~s into a bigger one** esta cuestión queda englobada en otra mayor
[2] [*companies, organizations, parties*] fusionarse; **to ~ with another company** fusionarse con otra empresa
Ⓒ N (*Comput*) fusión *f*

merger [ˈmɜːdʒəʳ] N (*Comm*) fusión *f*

meridian [məˈrɪdɪən] N [1] (*Astron, Geog*) meridiano *m*
[2] (*fig*) cenit *m*, auge *m*

meridional [məˈrɪdɪənl] ADJ meridional

meringue [məˈræŋ] N merengue *m*

merino [məˈriːnəʊ] Ⓐ ADJ merino
Ⓑ N (= *sheep, wool*) merino *m*

merit [ˈmerɪt] Ⓐ N mérito *m*; **it has the ~ of being clear** tiene el mérito de ser claro; **to treat a case on its ~s** juzgar un caso según sus propios méritos; **to look** *or* **inquire into the ~s of sth** estudiar los aspectos positivos de algo; **a work of great ~** un trabajo de mucho mérito, un trabajo muy meritorio
Ⓑ VT merecer; **this ~s further discussion** esto (se) merece mayor discusión
Ⓒ CPD ► **merit increase** N aumento *m* por méritos ► **merit pay** N (*US*) plus *m* por méritos

meritocracy [ˌmerɪˈtɒkrəsɪ] N meritocracia *f*

meritocrat [ˈmerɪtəʊkræt] N meritócrata *mf*

meritorious [ˌmerɪˈtɔːrɪəs] ADJ meritorio

meritoriously [ˌmerɪˈtɔːrɪəslɪ] ADV merecidamente

merlin [ˈmɜːlɪn] N esmerejón *m*

mermaid [ˈmɜːmeɪd] N sirena *f*

merman [ˈmɜːmæn] N (*pl* **mermen**) tritón *m*

Merovingian [ˌmerəʊˈvɪndʒɪən] Ⓐ ADJ merovingio
Ⓑ N merovingio/a *m/f*

merrily [ˈmerɪlɪ] ADV [1] (= *cheerfully*) [*laugh, say, dance*] alegremente
[2] (= *blithely*) **she quite ~ wrote out a cheque for £3,000** extendió tranquilamente *or* tan tranquila un cheque por 3.000 libras

merriment [ˈmerɪmənt] N alegría *f*, regocijo *m*; (= *laughter*) risas *fpl*; **at this there was much ~** esto provocó muchas risas

➤ **merry** [ˈmerɪ] ADJ (*compar* **merrier**, *superl* **merriest**) [1] (= *cheerful*) [*laughter, face, tune*] alegre; **they were in a very ~ mood** estaban de muy buen humor; **Robin Hood and his ~ men** Robin Hood y sus valientes compañeros; **Merry Christmas!** ¡Feliz Navidad!; **to make ~** (*liter*) divertirse; ✦**IDIOMS to go one's (own) ~ way**: **whatever advice you give her she just goes her own ~ way** (*iro*) le des el consejo que le des, ella sigue haciendo su santa voluntad*; **to lead sb a ~ dance** (*Brit iro*) enredar a algn; *see also* **hell A1**, **more B2**
[2] (*Brit**) (= *tipsy*) achispado, alegre; **to get ~** achisparse, ponerse alegre

merry-go-round [ˈmerɪgəʊˌraʊnd] N tiovivo *m*, caballitos *mpl*, calesita(s) *f(pl)* (*Andes, S. Cone*)

merrymaker [ˈmerɪˌmeɪkəʳ] N juerguista *mf*, parrandero/a *m/f*

merrymaking [ˈmerɪˌmeɪkɪŋ] N (= *party*) fiesta *f*; (= *enjoyment*) diversión *f*; (= *happiness*) alegría *f*, regocijo *m*

mesa [ˈmeɪsə] N (*US*) colina *f*, baja duna *f*

mescal [ˈmeskæl] N mezcal *m*

mescaline [ˈmeskəlɪn] N mescalina *f*

mesentery [ˈmeːzəntrɪ] N mesenterio *m*

meseta [məˈseɪtə] N meseta *f*

mesh [meʃ] Ⓐ N [1] (= *spacing*) malla *f*
[2] (= *netting*) **wire ~** tela *f* metálica, malla *f* metálica
[3] (= *network, net, also fig*) red *f*
[4] (= *gears etc*) **in ~** engranado
Ⓑ VT **to get ~ed** enredarse (**in** en)
Ⓒ VI (*Tech*) engranar (**with** con)

mesmeric [mezˈmerɪk] ADJ mesmeriano

mesmerism [ˈmezmərɪzəm] N mesmerismo *m*

mesmerize [ˈmezməraɪz] VT hipnotizar; (*fig*) fascinar

mesolith [ˈmesəʊlɪθ] N mesolito *m*

mesolithic [mesəʊˈlɪθɪk] Ⓐ ADJ mesolítico
Ⓑ N **the Mesolithic** el Mesolítico

mesomorph [ˈmesəʊˌmɔːf] N mesomorfo *m*

meson [ˈmiːzɒn] N mesón *m*

Mesopotamia [ˌmesəpəˈteɪmɪə] N Mesopotamia *f*

Mesozoic [ˌmesəʊˈzəʊɪk] Ⓐ ADJ mesozoico
Ⓑ N **the ~** el Mesozoico

mess [mes] Ⓐ N [1] (*untidy*) desorden *m*; (*dirty*) porquería *f*; (= *shambles*) desastre *m*, desbarajuste *m*; (= *predicament*) lío* *m*, follón* *m*; (= *bad job*) chapuza* *f*, desastre *m*; **excuse the ~** perdone el desorden; **to be a ~**: **this place is a ~** esta casa es un desastre; **her hair is a ~** tiene el pelo hecho un desastre; **this page is a ~, rewrite it** esta página es una chapuza* *or* un desastre, vuélvela a escribir; **the economy is a ~** la economía es un desastre; **her life is a ~** su vida es un desastre *or* un desbarajuste; **you can clean that ~ up** ya puedes ir limpiando esta pena; **to be in a ~**: **the house was in a ~** la casa estaba hecha un desastre; **the toys were in a ~** había un desorden de juguetes; **to leave things in a ~** dejarlo todo desordenado *or* hecho un desastre; **the economy is in a ~** la economía es un desastre; **her life is in a ~** su vida es un desastre *or* un desbarajuste; **his face was in a bit of a ~** (*after fight, accident*) tenía la cara que daba pena; **we're in a ~** estamos metidos en un lío *or* un follón*; **to get (o.s.) into a ~** (*fig*) meterse en un lío *or* un follón*; **a fine** *or* **nice ~ you got us into!** ¡en menudo lío *or* follón nos has metido!*; **you look (such) a ~** vas hecho un desastre; **look at the ~ you've made of this room** mira cómo has dejado esta habitación de desordenada; **to make a ~**: **look what a ~ you've made!** ¡mira cómo

lo has puesto todo!; **he made a ~ of his audition** la audición le fue fatal*; **I've made such a ~ of my life** he arruinado *or* echado a perder mi vida; **you've made a real ~ of things haven't you?** has liado bien las cosas ¿no crees?*
2 (*euph*) (= *excrement*) caca *f*; **dog ~** caca *f* de perro; **the cat's made a ~ in the kitchen** el gato ha hecho caca en la cocina
3 (*Mil*) comedor *m*; **officers' ~** comedor *m* de oficiales
Ⓑ VI 1 (*Mil*) (= *eat*) hacer rancho, comer (juntos)
2 (*) **no ~ing!** ¡sin bromas!, ¡nada de tonterías!; **no ~ing?** ¿en serio?
3 (= *soil o.s.*) hacerse caca encima*
Ⓒ VT **to ~ one's pants/trousers** hacerse caca encima*
Ⓓ CPD ► **mess deck** N sollado *m* ► **mess hall** N comedor *m* ► **a mess of pottage** N (*Bible*) un plato de lentejas ► **mess tin** N plato *m* de campaña

►**mess about***, **mess around*** Ⓐ VT + ADV (*Brit*) **all they do is ~ me about, they won't give me a straight answer** no hacen más que jugar conmigo, no me dan una respuesta concreta; **they were ~ing me about so much over the dates that I told them to forget it** me querían cambiar las fechas tantas veces que les dije que se olvidaran del asunto
Ⓑ VI + ADV (= *play the fool*) hacer tonterías; (= *do nothing in particular*) pasar el rato, gandulear; (= *waste time*) perder el tiempo; **"what are you doing?" — "just ~ing about"** —¿qué haces? —nada, pasando el rato; **we ~ed about in Paris for two days** pasamos dos días en París haciendo esto y lo otro; **he enjoys ~ing about in boats** le gusta entretenerse con las barcas; **she's not one to ~ about, she gets on with the job** no es de las que pierde el tiempo, saca el trabajo adelante; **I don't want him ~ing about here** no le quiero fisgoneando por aquí; **stop ~ing about!** ¡déjate de tonterías!; **to ~ about with sb**: **he isn't the kind of guy you ~ about with** no es de los que se deja enredar *or* tomar el pelo; **he ~ed about with some lads from college for a while** salió con unos tíos de la universidad durante un tiempo; **she'd been ~ing about with other men** había estado liada con otros hombres*; **to ~ about with sth**: **he was ~ing about with his watchstrap** estaba jugueteando con la correa del reloj; **who's been ~ing about with the video?** ¿quién ha estado manoseando *or* toqueteando el vídeo?

►**mess up** Ⓐ VT + ADV 1 (= *disarrange*) [+ *books, papers*] descolocar; [+ *hair*] desarreglar; [+ *room, house*] desordenar, desarreglar
2 (= *dirty*) ensuciar
3 (= *ruin*) [+ *plans, arrangements*] estropear, echar por tierra; [+ *piece of work*] estropear
4 (*US*) (= *beat up*) zurrar*, dar una paliza a*
Ⓑ VI + ADV (*) meter la pata*

►**mess with*** VI + PREP 1 (= *challenge, confront*) meterse con*; **if he ever ~es with me again I'll kill him** si vuelve a meterse conmigo lo mato*
2 (= *interfere with*) interferir con; **the system works well so don't ~ with it** el sistema funciona bien así que no interfieras con él
3 (= *get involved with*) **I used to ~ with drugs** estaba metido en drogas*

message ['mesɪdʒ] Ⓐ N recado *m*; (*frm, fig, Comput*) mensaje *m*; **to leave a ~** dejar un recado; **would you like to leave him a ~?** ¿quiere dejarle algún recado?; **a secret ~** un mensaje secreto; **the ~ of the film** el mensaje de la película; ✦**IDIOM to get the ~***: **do you think he got the ~?*** ¿crees que lo comprendió *or* entendió?
Ⓑ CPD ► **message switching** N (*Comput*) conmutación *f* de mensajes

messaging ['mesɪdʒɪŋ] N mensajería *f*

messenger ['mesɪndʒəʳ] Ⓐ N mensajero/a *m/f*
Ⓑ CPD ► **messenger boy** N recadero *m*

Messiah [mɪ'saɪə] N Mesías *m*

messianic [ˌmesɪ'ænɪk] ADJ mesiánico

Messieurs ['mesəz] NPL señores *mpl*

messily ['mesɪlɪ] ADV 1 (= *creating mess*) **babies eat ~** los bebés lo dejan todo perdido *or* lo ensucian todo cuando comen; **try not to write so ~** intenta que lo que escribes te salga más limpio
2 (= *awkwardly*) **the divorce ended ~** el divorcio terminó de mala manera

messmate ['mesmeɪt] N 1 (*in army etc*) compañero *m* de rancho, comensal *m*
2 (= *friend*) amigo *m*

Messrs ['mesəz] NPL ABBR (*Brit*) (= **Messieurs**) Srs., Sres.

mess-up* ['mesʌp] N (*Brit*) follón* *m*, lío* *m*; **we had a ~ with the trains** nos hicimos un lío con los trenes*

messy ['mesɪ] ADJ (*compar* **messier**; *superl* **messiest**) 1 (= *creating mess*) [*person*] desordenado; [*animal, activity, job*] sucio; **he's such a ~ eater** lo deja todo perdido *or* lo ensucia todo cuando come
2 (= *dirty, untidy*) [*place, room*] desordenado; [*clothes*] desarreglado, desordenado; [*hair*] despeinado; **"this is a ~ piece of work," said the teacher** —la presentación de este trabajo es un desastre —dijo el profesor; **she was penalized for ~ work** la castigaron por presentar un trabajo sucio y descuidado
3 (= *confused and awkward*) [*situation, divorce, relationship*] turbio, turbulento; [*process, dispute*] enrevesado, complicado; **she is locked in a ~ legal battle with her landlord** está metida en un pleito muy enrevesado con su casero

mestizo [mɪs'tiːzəʊ] N (*pl* **mestizos** *or* **mestizoes**) (*US*) mestizo/a *m/f*

met [met] PT, PP *of* **meet**

Met. [met] Ⓐ ADJ ABBR (*Brit*) = **meteorological**; **the ~Office** el instituto meteorológico británico
Ⓑ N ABBR 1 (*Brit*) (= **Metropolitan Police**) *la policía de Londres*
2 (*US*) = **Metropolitan Opera**

meta... ['metə] PREFIX meta...

metabolic [ˌmetə'bɒlɪk] ADJ metabólico; **~ rate** ciclo *m* metabólico

metabolism [me'tæbəlɪzəm] N metabolismo *m*

metabolize [me'tæbəlaɪz] VT metabolizar

metacarpal [ˌmetə'kɑːpl] N metacarpiano *m*

metacarpus [ˌmetə'kɑːpəs] N (*pl* **metacarpi** [ˌmetə'kɑːpaɪ]) metacarpo *m*

metal ['metl] Ⓐ N 1 (*Chem, Phys*) metal *m*
2 (*Brit*) (*on road*) grava *f*
3 (*Brit Rail*) **metals** rieles *mpl*
4 (*fig*) = **mettle**
Ⓑ ADJ metálico, de metal
Ⓒ VT (*Brit*) [+ *road*] engravar
Ⓓ CPD ► **metal detector** N detector *m* de metales ► **metal fatigue** N fatiga *f* del metal ► **metal polish** N abrillantador *m* de metales

metalanguage ['metəˌlæŋgwɪdʒ] N metalenguaje *m*

metalinguistic [ˌmetəlɪŋ'gwɪstɪk] ADJ metalingüístico

metalinguistics [ˌmetəlɪŋ'gwɪstɪks] NSING metalingüística *f*

metallic [mɪ'tælɪk] ADJ metálico

metallurgic [ˌmetə'lɜːdʒɪk] ADJ = **metallurgical**

metallurgical [ˌmetə'lɜːdʒɪkəl] ADJ metalúrgico

metallurgist [me'tælədʒɪst] N metalúrgico/a *m/f*

metallurgy [me'tælədʒɪ] N metalurgia *f*

metalwork ['metlwɜːk] N (= *craft*) metalistería *f*

metamorphic [ˌmetə'mɔːfɪk] ADJ metamórfico

metamorphose [ˌmetə'mɔːfəʊz] Ⓐ VT metamorfosear (**into** en)
Ⓑ VI metamorfosearse (**into** en)

metamorphosis [ˌmetə'mɔːfəsɪs] N (*pl* **metamorphoses** [ˌmetə'mɔːfəsiːz]) metamorfosis *f inv*

metaphor ['metəfɔːʳ] N metáfora *f*; *see also* **mixed B**

metaphoric [ˌmetə'fɒrɪk] ADJ = **metaphorical**

metaphorical [ˌmetə'fɒrɪkəl] ADJ metafórico

metaphorically [ˌmetə'fɒrɪkəlɪ] ADV metafóricamente

metaphysical [ˌmetə'fɪzɪkəl] ADJ metafísico

metaphysics [ˌmetə'fɪzɪks] NSING metafísica *f*

metastasis [mɪ'tæstəsɪs] N (*pl* **metastases** [mɪ'tæstəˌsiːz]) metástasis *f inv*

metatarsal [ˌmetə'tɑːsl] N metatarsiano *m*

metatarsus [ˌmetə'tɑːsəs] N (*pl* **metatarsi** [ˌmetə'tɑːsaɪ]) metatarso *m*

metathesis [me'tæθəsɪs] N (*pl* **metatheses** [me'tæθəˌsiːz]) metátesis *f inv*

mete [miːt] VT **to ~ out** [+ *punishment, justice*] imponer; [+ *challenge*] asignar

metempsychosis [ˌmetəmsaɪ'kəʊsɪs] N metempsicosis *f inv*

meteor ['miːtɪəʳ] Ⓐ N meteoro *m*
Ⓑ CPD ► **meteor shower** N lluvia *f* de meteoritos

meteoric [ˌmiːtɪ'ɒrɪk] ADJ 1 (*lit*) meteórico
2 (*fig*) rápido, meteórico

meteorite ['miːtɪəraɪt] N meteorito *m*

meteoroid ['miːtɪərɔɪd] N meteoroide *m*

meteorological [ˌmiːtɪərə'lɒdʒɪkəl] Ⓐ ADJ meteorológico
Ⓑ CPD ► **the Meteorological Office** N (*Brit*) *el instituto meteorológico británico*

meteorologically [ˌmiːtɪərə'lɒdʒɪklɪ] ADV meteorológicamente, en lo que se refiere a la meteorología

meteorologist [ˌmiːtɪə'rɒlədʒɪst] N meteorólogo/a *m/f*

meteorology [ˌmiːtɪə'rɒlədʒɪ] N meteorología *f*

meter[1] ['miːtəʳ] N contador *m*, medidor *m* (*LAm*); (*in taxi*) taxímetro *m*; **gas/electricity ~** contador de gas/de electricidad; **parking ~** parquímetro *m*

meter[2] ['miːtəʳ] N (*US*) = **metre**

meterage ['miːtərɪdʒ] N metraje *m*

metermaid ['miːtəˌmeɪd] N (*US*) controladora *f* de estacionamiento

methadone ['meθəˌdəʊn] N metadona *f*

methamphetamine [ˌmeθæm'fetəmiːn] N metanfetamina *f*

methane ['miːθeɪn] N metano *m*

methanol ['meθənɒl] N metanol *m*

methinks [mɪ'θɪŋks] ADV (††) a mi parecer, a mi entender

method ['meθəd] Ⓐ N 1 (= *manner, way*) método *m*; (= *procedure*) procedimiento *m*; **~ of payment** forma *f* de pago; ✦**IDIOM there's ~ in his madness** no está tan loco como parece
2 (= *technique*) técnica *f*
Ⓑ CPD ► **method actor** N actor *m* adepto

del método Stanislavski ► **method actress** N actriz *f* adepta del método Stanislavski

methodical [mɪˈθɒdɪkəl] ADJ metódico

methodically [mɪˈθɒdɪkəlɪ] ADV metódicamente

Methodism [ˈmeθədɪzəm] N metodismo *m*

Methodist [ˈmeθədɪst] ADJ, N metodista *mf*

methodological [ˌmeθədəˈlɒdʒɪkəl] ADJ metodológico

methodologically [ˌmeθədəˈlɒdʒɪkəlɪ] ADV metodológicamente, desde el punto de vista metodológico

methodology [ˌmeθəˈdɒlədʒɪ] N metodología *f*

meths* [meθs] (*Brit*) Ⓐ N ABBR = **methylated spirit(s)** Ⓑ CPD ► **meths drinker** N bebedor(a) *m/f* de alcohol metilado

Methuselah [mɪˈθjuːzələ] N Matusalén

methylated spirit(s) [ˈmeθɪleɪtɪdˈspɪrɪt(s)] N (*Brit*) alcohol *msing* desnaturalizado

meticulous [mɪˈtɪkjʊləs] ADJ meticuloso

meticulously [mɪˈtɪkjʊləslɪ] ADV meticulosamente

meticulousness [mɪˈtɪkjʊləsnɪs] N meticulosidad *f*

métier [ˈmeɪtɪeɪ] N (= *trade*) oficio *m*; (= *strong point*) fuerte *m*; (= *speciality*) especialidad *f*

met-man* [ˈmetmæn] N (*pl* **met-men**) meteorólogo *m*

metre, **meter** (*US*) [ˈmiːtəʳ] N metro *m*

metric [ˈmetrɪk] Ⓐ ADJ métrico; **to go ~** pasar al sistema métrico Ⓑ CPD ► **metric system** N sistema *m* métrico ► **metric ton** N tonelada *f* métrica (= *1.000kg*)

metrical [ˈmetrɪkəl] ADJ (*Poetry*) métrico

metrication [ˌmetrɪˈkeɪʃən] N conversión *f* al sistema métrico

metrics [ˈmetrɪks] N métrica *f*

metro [ˈmetrəʊ] N metro *m*

metrological [ˌmetrəˈlɒdʒɪkəl] ADJ metrológico

metronome [ˈmetrənəʊm] N metrónomo *m*

metronomic [ˌmetrəˈnɒmɪk] ADJ metronómico

metropolis [mɪˈtrɒpəlɪs] N metrópoli *f*

metropolitan [ˌmetrəˈpɒlɪtən] Ⓐ ADJ metropolitano
Ⓑ CPD ► **the Metropolitan Police** N *la policía de Londres*

metrosexual [ˌmetrəˈseksjʊəl] Ⓐ ADJ metrosexual
Ⓑ N metrosexual *m*

mettle [ˈmetl] N ánimo *m*, valor *m*; **to be on one's ~** estar dispuesto a demostrar su valía; **to put sb on his ~** picar a algn en el amor propio *or* en el orgullo; **to show one's ~** mostrar lo que uno vale

mettlesome [ˈmetlsəm] ADJ animoso, brioso

Meuse [mɜːz] N Mosa *m*

mew [mjuː] Ⓐ N maullido *m*
Ⓑ VI maullar, hacer miau

mewl [mjuːl] VI [*cat*] maullar, hacer miau; [*baby*] lloriquear

mews [mjuːz] (*Brit*) Ⓐ NSING callejuela *f*
Ⓑ CPD ► **mews cottage** N *casa acondicionada en antiguos establos o cocheras*

Mexican [ˈmeksɪkən] Ⓐ ADJ, N mejicano/a *m/f*, mexicano/a *m/f* (*LAm*) Ⓑ CPD ► **Mexican wave** N (*Brit*) ola *f* (mejicana *or* (*LAm*) mexicana)

Mexico [ˈmeksɪkəʊ] Ⓐ N Méjico *m*, México *m* (*LAm*) Ⓑ CPD ► **Mexico City** N (Ciudad *f* de) México *m*

mezzanine [ˈmezəniːn] N entresuelo *m*

mezzo-soprano [ˈmetsəʊsəˈprɑːnəʊ] N (= *singer*) mezzosoprano *f*; (= *voice*) mezzosoprano *m*

mezzotint [ˈmetsəʊtɪnt] N grabado *m* mezzotinto

MF N ABBR = **medium frequency**

MFA N ABBR (*US Univ*) = **Master of Fine Arts**

MFH N ABBR (*Brit*) = **Master of Foxhounds**

MFN N ABBR (*US*) (= **most favored nation**) nación *f* más favorecida; **~ treatment** trato *m* de nación más favorecida

mfr(s) ABBR (= **manufacturer(s)**) fab

mg ABBR (= **milligram(s)**) mg.

Mgr ABBR (*Rel*) (= **Monseigneur** *or* **Monsignor**) Mons.

mgr ABBR = **manager**

MHR N ABBR (*US*) = **Member of the House of Representatives**

MHz ABBR (*Rad*) (= **megahertz**) MHz

MI Ⓐ N ABBR = **machine intelligence**
Ⓑ ABBR (*US*) = **Michigan**

mi [miː] N (*Mus*) mi *m*

MI5 [ˌemaɪˈfaɪv] N ABBR (*Brit*) (= **Military Intelligence 5**) *servicio de inteligencia contraespionaje*

MI6 [ˌemaɪˈsɪks] N ABBR (*Brit*) (= **Military Intelligence 6**) *servicio de inteligencia*

MIA ADJ ABBR (*Mil*) = **missing in action**

miaow [miːˈaʊ] Ⓐ N maullido *m*
Ⓑ VI maullar, hacer miau

miasma [mɪˈæzmə] N (*pl* **miasmas** *or* **miasmata** [mɪˈæzmətə]) miasma *m*

miasmic [mɪˈæzmɪk] ADJ miasmático

mica [ˈmaɪkə] N mica *f*

mice [maɪs] NPL *of* **mouse**

Mich. ABBR (*US*) = **Michigan**

Michael [ˈmaɪkl] N Miguel

Michaelmas [ˈmɪklməs] Ⓐ N fiesta *f* de San Miguel (*29 setiembre*)
Ⓑ CPD ► **Michaelmas daisy** N margarita *f* de otoño ► **Michaelmas term** N (*Brit Jur, Univ*) trimestre *m* de otoño, primer trimestre *m*

Michelangelo [ˌmaɪkəlˈændʒɪləʊ] N Miguel Ángel

Mick [mɪk] N (*familiar form*) *of* **Michael**

Mickey [ˈmɪkɪ] CPD ► **Mickey Finn** N bebida *f* drogada ► **Mickey Mouse** N el ratón Mickey; **it's a ~ Mouse set-up** es una empresa poco seria

mickey* [ˈmɪkɪ] N **to take the ~ (out of sb)** tomar el pelo (a algn)

micro [ˈmaɪkrəʊ] N 1 (*Comput*) microcomputadora *f*, microordenador *m* (*Sp*)
2 (*) (= *microwave*) microondas *m*

micro... [ˈmaɪkrəʊ] PREFIX micro…

microbe [ˈmaɪkrəʊb] N microbio *m*

microbial [maɪˈkrəʊbɪəl] ADJ microbiano

microbiological [ˌmaɪkrəʊbaɪəˈlɒdʒɪkəl] ADJ microbiológico

microbiologist [ˌmaɪkrəʊbaɪˈɒlədʒɪst] N microbiólogo/a *m/f*

microbiology [ˌmaɪkrəʊbaɪˈɒlədʒɪ] N microbiología *f*

microbrewery [ˈmaɪkrəʊˌbruːərɪ] N pequeña fábrica *f* de cerveza

microbus [ˈmaɪkrəʊˌbʌs] N (*Aut*) microbús *m*

microchip [ˈmaɪkrəʊˌtʃɪp] N microchip *m*

microcircuit [ˈmaɪkrəʊˌsɜːkɪt] N microcircuito *m*

microcircuitry [ˈmaɪkrəʊˈsɜːkɪtrɪ] N microcircuitería *f*

microclimate [ˈmaɪkrəʊˌklaɪmɪt] N microclima *m*

microcomputer [ˌmaɪkrəʊkəmˈpjuːtəʳ] N microcomputador *m*, microcomputadora *f*, microordenador *m* (*Sp*)

microcomputing [ˈmaɪkrəʊkəmˈpjuːtɪŋ] N microcomputación *f*

microcosm [ˈmaɪkrəʊkɒzəm] N microcosmo *m*

microcredit [ˈmaɪkrəʊˌkredɪt] N microcrédito *m*

microdot [ˈmaɪkrəʊˌdɒt] N micropunto *m*

microeconomic [ˌmaɪkrəʊˌiːkəˈnɒmɪk] ADJ microeconómico

microeconomics [ˈmaɪkrəʊˌiːkəˈnɒmɪks] NSING microeconomía *f*

microelectronic [ˈmaɪkrəʊˌɪlekˈtrɒnɪk] ADJ microelectrónico

microelectronics [ˈmaɪkrəʊˌɪlekˈtrɒnɪks] NSING microelectrónica *f*

microfibre, **microfiber** (*US*) [ˈmaɪkrəʊˌfaɪbəʳ] N microfibra *f*

microfiche [ˈmaɪkrəʊˌfiːʃ] Ⓐ N microficha *f*
Ⓑ CPD ► **microfiche reader** N lector *m* de microfichas

microfilm [ˈmaɪkrəʊfɪlm] Ⓐ N microfilm *m*
Ⓑ VT microfilmar Ⓒ CPD ► **microfilm reader** N lector *m* de microfilms

microform [ˈmaɪkrəʊˌfɔːm] N microforma *f*

microgravity [ˌmaɪkrəʊˈgrævɪtɪ] N microgravedad *f*

microgroove [ˈmaɪkrəʊgruːv] N microsurco *m*

microlight, **microlite** [ˈmaɪkrəʊˌlaɪt] N (*also* **~ aircraft**) avión *m* ultraligero, ultraligero *m*

micromesh stockings [ˌmaɪkrəʊmeʃˈstɒkɪŋz] NPL medias *fpl* de malla fina

micrometer [maɪˈkrɒmɪtəʳ] N micrómetro *m*

micron [ˈmaɪkrɒn] N (*pl* **microns** *or* **micra** [ˈmaɪkrə]) micrón *m*

microorganism [ˈmaɪkrəʊˈɔːgənɪzəm] N microorganismo *m*

microphone [ˈmaɪkrəfəʊn] N micrófono *m*

microprocessor [ˌmaɪkrəʊˈprəʊsesəʳ] N microprocesador *m*

microprogramming, **microprograming** (*US*) [ˌmaɪkrəʊˈprəʊgræmɪŋ] N microprogramación *f*

micro-scooter [ˈmaɪkrəʊˌskuːtəʳ] N patinete *m*

microscope [ˈmaɪkrəskəʊp] N microscopio *m*

microscopic [ˌmaɪkrəˈskɒpɪk] ADJ microscópico

microscopical [ˌmaɪkrəˈskɒpɪkəl] ADJ = **microscopic**

microscopically [ˌmaɪkrəʊˈskɒpɪklɪ] ADV microscópicamente; **~ small** microscópico; **to examine sth ~** (*with microscope*) examinar algo al microscopio

microscopy [maɪˈkrɒskəpɪ] N microscopía *f*

microsecond [ˈmaɪkrəʊˌsekənd] N microsegundo *m*

microspacing [ˌmaɪkrəʊˈspeɪsɪŋ] N microespaciado *m*

microstructural [ˌmaɪkrəʊˈstrʌktʃərəl] ADJ microestructural

microstructure [ˈmaɪkrəʊˌstrʌktʃəʳ] N microestructura *f*

microsurgery [ˌmaɪkrəʊˈsɜːdʒərɪ] N microcirugía *f*

microsurgical [ˌmaɪkrəʊˈsɜːdʒɪkəl] ADJ microquirúrgico

microtechnology [ˌmaɪkrəʊtekˈnɒlədʒɪ] N microtecnología *f*

microtransmitter [ˌmaɪkrəʊtrænzˈmɪtəʳ] N microtransmisor *m*

microwavable, **microwaveable** [ˈmaɪkrəʊˌweɪvəbl] ADJ apto para microondas

microwave [ˈmaɪkrəʊˌweɪv] Ⓐ N 1 (*Phys*) microonda *f*
2 (*also* **~ oven**) (horno *m*) microondas *m inv*
Ⓑ VT (= *cook*) cocinar con microondas; (= *heat*) calentar en el microondas

micturate ['mɪktjʊəreɪt] VI (frm) orinar

micturition [,mɪktjʊ'rɪʃən] N (frm) micción *f*

mid [mɪd] Ⓐ ADJ **in ~ June** a mediados de junio; **he's in his ~ twenties** tiene unos veinticinco años, tiene veinte y tantos años; **in ~ afternoon** a media tarde; **in ~ channel** en medio del canal; **in ~ course** (*during academic year*) a mitad de curso; (*of degree course*) a mitad de carrera; **in ~ journey** a medio camino; **in ~ morning** a media mañana; **in ~ ocean** en alta mar, en mitad del océano
Ⓑ PREP (*liter, poet*) = **amid**

mid-air ['mɪdɛəʳ] Ⓐ N **to catch sth in ~** agarrar *or* atrapar algo al vuelo; **to refuel in ~** repostar combustible en pleno vuelo; ✦*IDIOM* **to leave sth in ~** dejar algo a medio hacer
Ⓑ ADJ **~ collision** colisión *f* en el aire

Midas ['maɪdəs] N Midas; ✦*IDIOM* **he has the ~ touch** todo lo que toca se convierte en dinero

mid-Atlantic [mɪdət'læntɪk] ADJ [*accent*] de mitad del Atlántico

midbrain ['mɪdbreɪn] N mesencéfalo *m*, cerebro *m* medio

midday ['mɪd'deɪ] Ⓐ N mediodía *m*; **at ~** a(l) mediodía
Ⓑ CPD ▸ **the midday sun** N el sol de(l) mediodía

midden ['mɪdn] N muladar *m*

middle ['mɪdl] Ⓐ N [1] [*of object, area*] centro *m*, medio *m*; **in the ~ of the table/the room** en medio *or* en el centro de la mesa/la habitación; **he was in the ~ of the road** estaba en medio *or* en (la) mitad de la carretera; **the potatoes were raw in the ~** las patatas estaban crudas por el centro; **to cut sth down the ~** cortar algo por el medio *or* por la mitad; **we agreed to split the bill down the ~** acordamos dividir la cuenta por la mitad; **the party is split down the ~ on this issue** el partido está dividido en dos facciones con respecto a este tema; **in the ~ of nowhere** quién sabe dónde, en el quinto pino (*Sp**); **right in the ~** ◊ **in the very ~** (*physically*) en el mismo centro
[2] [*of period*] **in the ~ of the night** en mitad de la noche; **in the ~ of summer** en pleno verano; **in** *or* **about** *or* **towards the ~ of May** a mediados de mayo; **in the ~ of the morning** a media mañana; **the heat in the ~ of the day was intense** el calor del mediodía era intenso; **he was in his ~ thirties** tenía unos treinta y cinco años, tenía treinta y tantos años
[3] [*of activity*] **to be in the ~ of sth** estar en mitad de algo; **we were in the ~ of dinner** estábamos en mitad de la cena; **I'm in the ~ of a conversation** estoy en mitad de una conversación; **to be in the ~ of doing sth: I'm in the ~ of reading it** lo estoy leyendo; **I'm right in the ~ of getting lunch** justo ahora estoy preparando la comida; *see also* **week**
[4] (*) (= *waist*) cintura *f*; **she wore it round her ~** lo llevaba alrededor de la cintura; **he was in the water up to his ~** el agua le llegaba por *or* a la cintura
Ⓑ ADJ [1] (= *central*) **the ~ shelf of the oven** la bandeja del medio del horno; **my ~ daughter** mi segunda hija, mi hija de en medio; **he stared into the ~ distance** miró fijamente a un segundo plano; **~ ground** terreno *m* neutral; **in the ~ years of the nineteenth century** a mediados del siglo diecinueve; **women in their ~ years** mujeres de mediana edad; ✦*IDIOM* **to steer** *or* **take a ~ course** tomar por la calle de en medio
[2] (= *average*) mediano; **a man of ~ size** un hombre de mediana estatura
Ⓒ CPD ▸ **middle age** N madurez *f* ▸ **the Middle Ages** NPL la Edad Media ▸ **Middle America** N (= *Central America*) Mesoamérica *f*, Centroamérica *f*; (*US Geog*) el centro de los Estados Unidos; (*fig*) (*US*) (= *middle class*) la clase media norteamericana ▸ **middle C** N (*Mus*) do *m* (*en medio del piano*) ▸ **the middle class(es)** N(PL) la clase media; **the ~ classes** la clase media; **the upper/lower ~ class(es)** la clase media alta/baja; *see also* **middle-class** ▸ **middle distance** N **in the ~ distance** (*gen*) a una distancia intermedia; (*Art*) en segundo plano; *see also* **middle-distance** ▸ **middle ear** N oído *m* medio ▸ **the Middle East** N el Oriente Medio ▸ **Middle English** N *la lengua inglesa de la edad media* ▸ **middle finger** N dedo *m* corazón ▸ **middle management** N mandos *mpl* medios ▸ **middle manager** N mando *mf* medio ▸ **middle name** N segundo nombre *m* de pila; ✦*IDIOM* **"discretion" is my ~ name** soy la discreción en persona ▸ **middle school** N (*Brit*) *colegio para niños de ocho o nueve a doce o trece años*; (*US*) *colegio para niños de doce a catorce años* ▸ **the Middle West** N (*US*) *la región central de los Estados Unidos*

middle-aged ['mɪdl'eɪdʒd] ADJ de mediana edad

middlebrow ['mɪdlbraʊ] Ⓐ ADJ de *or* para gusto medianamente culto, de gusto entre intelectual y plebeyo
Ⓑ N persona *f* de gusto medianamente culto, persona *f* de cultura mediana

middle-class ['mɪdl'klɑːs] ADJ de (la) clase media; (= *bourgeois*) burgués; *see also* **middle C**

middle-distance [,mɪdl'dɪstəns] CPD ▸ **middle-distance race** N carrera *f* de medio fondo ▸ **middle-distance runner** N mediofondista *mf*

Middle-Eastern [,mɪdl'iːstən] ADJ de Oriente Medio

middle-income [,mɪdl'ɪnkʌm] ADJ [*family*] de ingresos medios

middleman ['mɪdlmæn] N (*pl* **middlemen**) (*Comm*) intermediario/a *m/f*

middle-of-the-road ['mɪdləvðə'rəʊd] ADJ moderado; (*pej*) mediocre

middle-ranking ['mɪdl'ræŋkɪŋ] ADJ [*official*] medio

middle-sized ['mɪdl,saɪzd] ADJ mediano

middleweight ['mɪdlweɪt] Ⓐ N peso *m* medio; **light ~** peso *m* medio ligero
Ⓑ CPD ▸ **middleweight champion** N campeón/ona *m/f* de peso medio, campeón/ona *m/f* de los pesos medios

middling ['mɪdlɪŋ] Ⓐ ADJ mediano; (*pej*) regular; **"how are you?" — "middling"** —¿qué tal estás? —regular; *see also* **fair**[1] **A2**
Ⓑ ADV (*) **~ good** medianamente bueno, regular

Middx ABBR (*Brit*) = **Middlesex**

middy* ['mɪdɪ] N = **midshipman**

midfield ['mɪdfiːld] Ⓐ N centro *m* del campo
Ⓑ CPD ▸ **midfield player** N centrocampista *mf*

midge [mɪdʒ] N mosquito *m* pequeño

midget ['mɪdʒɪt] Ⓐ N enano/a *m/f*
Ⓑ ADJ en miniatura, en pequeña escala; [*submarine*] de bolsillo

midi ['mɪdɪ] Ⓐ ADJ **~ hi-fi** ◊ **~ system** minicadena *f*
Ⓑ N = **midiskirt**

midiskirt ['mɪdɪskɜːt] N midi *m*, midifalda *f*

midland ['mɪdlənd] ADJ del interior, del centro

Midlander ['mɪdləndəʳ] N *nativo or habitante de la región central de Inglaterra*

Midlands ['mɪdləndz] NPL **the ~** *la región central de Inglaterra*

midlife ['mɪd,laɪf] CPD ▸ **midlife crisis** N crisis *f inv* de los cuarenta

mid-morning ['mɪd'mɔːnɪŋ] ADJ de media mañana; **~ coffee** café *m* de media mañana, café *m* de las once

midmost ['mɪdməʊst] ADJ (*liter*) el/la más cercano/a al centro

midnight ['mɪdnaɪt] Ⓐ N medianoche *f*; **at ~** a medianoche; ✦*IDIOM* **to burn the ~ oil** quemarse las pestañas
Ⓑ CPD ▸ **midnight blue** N negro *m* azulado ▸ **midnight mass** N misa *f* del gallo ▸ **the midnight sun** N el sol de medianoche

midpoint ['mɪd,pɔɪnt] N punto *m* medio

midriff ['mɪdrɪf] N estómago *m*; (*Med*) diafragma *m*

midsection ['mɪdsekʃən] N sección *f* de en medio

midshipman ['mɪdʃɪpmən] N (*pl* **midshipmen**) guardia *mf* marina, alférez *mf* de fragata

midships ['mɪdʃɪps] ADV en medio del navío

midsized ['mɪdsaɪzd], **midsize** ['mɪdsaɪz] ADJ mediano

midst [mɪdst] Ⓐ N **in the ~ of** (*place*) en medio de, a mitad de (*LAm*); **in the ~ of the battle** (*fig*) en plena batalla; **in our ~** entre nosotros
Ⓑ PREP (*liter*) = **amidst**

midstream ['mɪd'striːm] Ⓐ N (*lit*) centro *m* de la corriente/del río; **in ~** (*lit*) en el medio de la corriente/del río; (*fig*) antes de terminar, a mitad de camino; **he stopped talking in ~** dejó de hablar a mitad de la frase
Ⓑ ADV en medio de la corriente/del río

midsummer ['mɪd'sʌməʳ] Ⓐ N pleno verano *m*; **in ~** en pleno verano; **"Midsummer Night's Dream"** "El sueño de una noche de verano"
Ⓑ CPD ▸ **Midsummer('s) Day** N Día *m* de San Juan (*24 junio*) ▸ **midsummer madness** N locura *f* pasajera

midterm ['mɪd'tɜːm] ADJ **~ exam** examen *m* de mitad del trimestre; **~ elections** (*US*) elecciones *fpl* a mitad del mandato (presidencial)

midtown ['mɪd,taʊn] Ⓐ N centro *m* de la ciudad
Ⓑ CPD ▸ **midtown shops** NPL tiendas *fpl* del centro de la ciudad

mid-Victorian ['mɪdvɪk'tɔːrɪən] ADJ (*Brit*) de mitades de la época victoriana

midway ['mɪd'weɪ] Ⓐ ADV a mitad de camino, a medio camino; **~ between Edinburgh and Glasgow** a mitad de camino *or* a medio camino entre Edimburgo y Glasgow; **we are now ~** ahora estamos a mitad de camino *or* a medio camino; **~ through the interview, Taggart got up** Taggart se levantó a mitad de la entrevista
Ⓑ ADJ **the ~ point between X and Y** el punto medio entre X y Y
Ⓒ N (*US*) avenida *f* central, paseo *m* central

midweek ['mɪd'wiːk] Ⓐ ADV entre semana
Ⓑ ADJ de entre semana

Midwest ['mɪd'west] N (*US*) mediooeste *m* (*llanura central de EEUU*)

Midwestern ['mɪd,westən] ADJ (*US*) del mediooeste (*de EEUU*)

Midwesterner [mɪd'westənəʳ] N (*US*) *nativo/habitante del Midwest*

midwife ['mɪdwaɪf] N (*pl* **midwives**) comadrona *f*, partera *f*

midwifery ['mɪd,wɪfərɪ] N partería *f*

midwinter ['mɪd'wɪntəʳ] Ⓐ N pleno invierno *m*; **in ~** en pleno invierno
Ⓑ CPD de pleno invierno

mien [mi:n] N (*liter*) aire *m*, porte *m*, semblante *m*

miff* [mɪf] Ⓐ N disgusto *m*
Ⓑ VT disgustar, ofender; **he was pretty ~ed about it** se ofendió bastante por eso

might¹ [maɪt] PT, COND *of* **may**

might² [maɪt] N poder *m*, fuerza *f*; **with all one's ~** con todas sus fuerzas; **with ~ and main** a más no poder, esforzándose muchísimo

might-have-been ['maɪtəv,bi:n] N esperanza *f* no cumplida

mightily ['maɪtɪlɪ] ADV [1] (†) (= *greatly*) [*rejoice*] tremendamente, enormemente; [*impressive*] sumamente; **to be ~ impressed/relieved** estar tremendamente *or* sumamente impresionado/aliviado; **I was ~ surprised** me sorprendí enormemente
[2] (*liter*) (= *powerfully*) [*strike, hit*] con fuerza; **they heaved ~** tiraron con todas sus fuerzas

mightiness ['maɪtɪnɪs] N (= *strength*) fuerza *f*; (= *power*) poder *m*, poderío *m*

mightn't ['maɪtnt] = **might not**

mighty ['maɪtɪ] Ⓐ ADJ (*compar* **mightier**, *superl* **mightiest**) (*liter*) [1] (= *powerful*) [*blow*] tremendo*; [*effort*] grandísimo; [*nation*] poderoso; **he shook his ~ fist** agitó su poderoso puño; **God's ~ power** la omnipotencia de Dios; *see also* **high A3**
[2] (= *loud*) [*bang, roar*] enorme
[3] (= *large*) [*river, fortress, wall*] enorme, inmenso
Ⓑ ADV (*US**) (= *very*) **I'm ~ glad to hear it** me alegro muchísimo de saberlo; **she's a ~ fine-looking woman** es una mujer muy guapa; **we were ~ worried** estábamos la mar de preocupados*; **it's a ~ long way to Southfork** Southfork está tremendamente lejos *or* está lejísimos
Ⓒ NPL **the ~** los poderosos; ✦*IDIOM* **how the ~ have fallen!** ¡cómo han caído los poderosos!

mignonette [,mɪnjə'net] N reseda *f*

migraine ['mi:greɪn] Ⓐ N jaqueca *f*, migraña *f*; **I've got a ~** tengo jaqueca *or* migraña
Ⓑ CPD ► **migraine attack** N ataque *m* de jaqueca *or* migraña ► **migraine sufferer** N **this will benefit ~ sufferers** esto beneficiará a los que padecen de jaqueca *or* migraña

migrant ['maɪgrənt] Ⓐ ADJ migratorio
Ⓑ N emigrante *mf*; (= *bird*) ave *f* migratoria *or* de paso; **economic ~** emigrante *mf* económico/a, emigrante *mf* por razones económicas
Ⓒ ► **migrant worker** N trabajador(a) *m/f* emigrado/a

migrate [maɪ'greɪt] VI [*animals, people*] emigrar

migration [maɪ'greɪʃən] N migración *f*

migratory [maɪ'greɪtərɪ] ADJ migratorio

Mike [maɪk] N (*familiar form*) *of* **Michael**; **for the love of ~!*** ¡por Dios!

mike* [maɪk] N ABBR (= **microphone**) micro *m*

milady [mɪ'leɪdɪ] N miladi *f*

Milan [mɪ'læn] N Milán *m*

milch cow ['mɪltʃkaʊ] N vaca *f* lechera

mild [maɪld] Ⓐ ADJ (*compar* **milder**, *superl* **mildest**) [1] (= *not severe*) [*winter*] moderado, poco frío; [*weather, climate, evening*] templado; **it's very ~ for the time of year** no hace mucho frío para esta época del año
[2] (= *not strong*) [*cheese, cigar, detergent, shampoo, sedative*] suave; [*curry*] suave, no muy picante; [*protest*] moderado; [*criticism*] suave, moderado; **he issued a ~ rebuke to his Republican opponents** reprendió a sus oponentes republicanos con cierta suavidad
[3] (= *not serious*) [*fever*] ligero; [*infection*] pequeño; [*symptoms*] leve; **he had a ~ stroke last year** tuvo un derrame cerebral de poca seriedad el año pasado; **I had a ~ case of food poisoning** tuve una ligera intoxicación
[4] (= *slight*) [*pain*] leve, ligero; **they listened with ~ interest** escuchaban con cierto interés; **he turned to Mona with a look of ~ confusion/surprise** se volvió hacia Mona y la miró ligeramente confundido/sorprendido
[5] (= *pleasant*) [*person, voice*] afable, dulce; [*words*] dulce; [*disposition*] tranquilo, apacible; [*manner*] afable
Ⓑ CPD ► **mild steel** N *acero con bajo contenido carbónico*
Ⓒ N (*Brit*) (= *beer*) *cerveza suave y de color oscuro*

mildew ['mɪldju:] N (*on plants*) añublo *m*; (*on food, leather etc*) moho *m*

mildewed ['mɪldju:d] ADJ mohoso

mildly ['maɪldlɪ] ADV [1] (= *gently*) [*say, reply*] suavemente, con suavidad
[2] (= *slightly*) [*amusing, surprised, interested, irritated*] ligeramente
[3] (= *weakly*) [*protest*] débilmente; [*rebuke*] con suavidad, suavemente; **he was only ~ criticized for his actions** sólo recibió críticas moderadas por sus acciones
[4] **to put it ~: to put it ~, I was cross** decir que estaba enfadado es quedarse corto; **he's a low-down thief, and that's putting it ~** es un cochino ladrón por no decir algo peor

mild-mannered ['maɪld'mænəd] ADJ apacible

mildness ['maɪldnɪs] N [1] (*Met*) [*of weather, climate*] lo templado
[2] (= *weakness*) [*of cigar, detergent, shampoo, rebuke, criticism*] suavidad *f*; [*of symptoms*] levedad *f*
[3] (= *pleasantness*) [*of person, disposition*] afabilidad *f*, placidez *f*; [*of words*] dulzura *f*; [*of manner*] gentileza *f*, afabilidad *f*

mile [maɪl] Ⓐ N [1] milla *f* (= *1609,33m*); **30 ~s a** *or* **to the gallon** 30 millas por galón; **50 ~s per** *or* **an hour** 50 millas por hora; **we walked ~s!*** ¡anduvimos millas y millas!; **people came from ~s around** la gente vino de millas a la redonda; **they live ~s away** viven lejísimos de aquí; **you could see for ~s** se veía hasta lejísimos; ✦*IDIOMS* **to be ~s away: sorry, I was ~s away** lo siento, estaba pensando en otra cosa; **by a ~** ◊ **by ~s: the shot missed by a ~** *or* **by ~s** el disparo falló por mucho; **the best hotel by a ~** *or* **by ~s is the Inglaterra** el mejor hotel con mucho es el Inglaterra; **to go the extra ~** dar el paso siguiente*; **not a million ~s from here** (*hum*) no muy lejos de aquí; **a ~ off: you can smell/see it a ~ off** eso se huele/se ve a la legua; **to run a ~: as soon as he sees me coming, he runs a ~** en cuanto me ve venir sale pitando*; **it stands** *or* **sticks out a ~** salta a la vista, se ve a la legua; *see also* **inch A**, **miss¹ A1**; → IMPERIAL SYSTEM
[2] (*) **miles** (= *very much*) **she's ~s better than I am at maths** las matemáticas se le dan cien mil veces mejor que a mí; **the sleeves are ~s too long** las mangas no me van largas, me van larguísimas
Ⓑ CPD ► **Mile High City** N Denver; → CITY NICKNAMES

-mile [maɪl] ADJ (*ending in compounds*) **a 50-mile bike ride** un paseo en bici de 50 millas

mileage ['maɪlɪdʒ] Ⓐ N [1] distancia *f* en millas; (*on mileometer*) ≈ kilometraje *m*; **what ~ does your car do?** ≈ ¿cuántos kilómetros hace tu coche por galón de gasolina?, ¿cuántas millas hace tu coche por galón de gasolina?; **what ~ has this car done?** ≈ ¿qué kilómetraje tiene este coche?, ¿cuántas millas/cuántos kilómetros tiene este coche?
[2] (*fig*) **there's no ~ in this story** esta historia sólo tiene un interés pasajero; **he got a lot of ~ out of it** le sacó mucho partido
Ⓑ CPD ► **mileage allowance** N dietas *fpl* por desplazamiento en vehículo propio, ≈ dietas *f* por kilometraje ► **mileage indicator** N ≈ cuentakilómetros *m inv* ► **mileage rate** N tarifa *f* por distancia

mileometer [maɪ'lɒmɪtəʳ] N (*Brit Aut*) ≈ cuentakilómetros *m inv*

milepost ['maɪlpəʊst] N (*Hist*) poste *m* miliar, mojón *m*

miler ['maɪləʳ] N corredor(a) *m/f* (*etc que se especializa en las pruebas de una milla*)

milestone ['maɪlstəʊn] N [1] (*on road*) mojón *m*
[2] (*fig*) hito *m*; **these events are ~s in our history** estos acontecimientos marcan un hito en *or* de nuestra historia

milieu ['mi:ljɜ:] (*pl* **milieus** *or* **milieux** ['mi:ljɜ:]) N medio *m*, entorno *m*

militancy ['mɪlɪtənsɪ] N [*of group, trade union*] militancia *f*, combatividad *m*; [*of person, attitude*] combatividad *m*

militant ['mɪlɪtənt] Ⓐ ADJ [*group, trade union*] militante, combativo; [*person, attitude*] combativo; **to be in (a) ~ mood** estar combativo
Ⓑ N militante *mf*; **to be a party ~** militar en un partido

militantly ['mɪlɪtəntlɪ] ADV [*react, behave*] de forma agresiva *or* combativa; [*nationalist*] radicalmente; **to be ~ opposed to sth** oponerse radicalmente a algo

militarily ['mɪlɪtərɪlɪ] ADV [*intervene, respond*] militarmente; [*significant, useful, effective*] desde un punto de vista militar

militarism ['mɪlɪtərɪzəm] N militarismo *m*

militarist ['mɪlɪtərɪst] Ⓐ ADJ militarista
Ⓑ N militarista *mf*

militaristic [,mɪlɪtə'rɪstɪk] ADJ militarista

militarize ['mɪlɪtəraɪz] VT militarizar

military ['mɪlɪtərɪ] Ⓐ ADJ [*intervention, government, history, bearing*] militar; **he retired with full ~ honours** se retiró con todos los honores militares; **to do sth with ~ precision** hacer algo con una precisión militar
Ⓑ NPL **the ~** los militares
Ⓒ CPD ► **military academy** N academia *f* militar ► **military base** N base *f* militar ► **military police** N policía *f* militar ► **military policeman** N policía *m* militar ► **military service** N servicio *m* militar; **to do (one's) ~ sevice** hacer *or* prestar el servicio militar, hacer la mili*

militate ['mɪlɪteɪt] VI **to ~ against** militar en contra de

militia [mɪ'lɪʃə] Ⓐ N milicia(s) *f(pl)*
Ⓑ CPD ► **the militia reserves** NPL (*US*) las reservas (territoriales)

militiaman [mɪ'lɪʃəmən] (*pl* **militiamen**) N miliciano *m*

milk [mɪlk] Ⓐ N leche *f*; **skim(med) ~** leche *f* desnatada; **powdered ~** leche *f* en polvo; **~ of magnesia** (*Med*) leche de magnesia; **the ~ of human kindness** la compasión personificada; ✦*PROV* **it's no good crying over spilt ~** a lo hecho pecho
Ⓑ VT [1] [+ *cow*] ordeñar

2 (*fig*) exprimir; [+ *applause*] arrancar del público, sacar todo el partido a; **they're ~ing the company for all they can get** chupan todo lo que pueden de la compañía
Ⓒ VI dar leche
Ⓓ CPD ► **milk bar** N cafetería *f* ► **milk chocolate** N chocolate *m* con leche ► **milk churn** N lechera *f* ► **milk cow** N vaca *f* lechera ► **milk diet** N dieta *f* láctea ► **milk duct** N (*Anat*) conducto *m* galactóforo ► **milk float** N carro *m* de la leche ► **milk jug** N jarrita *f* para la leche ► **milk pan** N = **milk saucepan** ► **milk products** NPL productos *mpl* lácteos ► **milk pudding** N arroz *m* con leche ► **milk round** N (*lit*) recorrido *m* del lechero; (*Brit Univ*) *recorrido anual de las principales empresas por las universidades para entrevistar a estudiantes del último curso con vistas a una posible contratación* ► **milk run** N (*Aer*) vuelo *m* rutinario ► **milk saucepan** N cazo *m or* cacerola *f* para la leche ► **milk shake** N batido *m*, malteada *f* (*LAm*) ► **milk tooth** N diente *m* de leche ► **milk truck** N (*US*) = **milk float**

milk-and-water [ˈmɪlkənˈwɔːtəʳ] ADJ (*fig*) débil, flojo

milking [ˈmɪlkɪŋ] Ⓐ ADJ lechero, de ordeño
Ⓑ N ordeño *m*
Ⓒ CPD ► **milking machine** N ordeñadora *f* mecánica

milkmaid [ˈmɪlkmeɪd] N lechera *f*

milkman [ˈmɪlkmən] N (*pl* **milkmen**) lechero *m*, repartidor *m* de leche

milksop [ˈmɪlksɒp] N marica *m*

milkweed [ˈmɪlkwiːd] N algodoncillo *m*

milk-white [ˈmɪlkˈwaɪt] ADJ blanco como la leche

milky [ˈmɪlkɪ] (*compar* **milkier**; *superl* **milkiest**)
Ⓐ ADJ 1 (= *pale white*) [*lotion, liquid, eyes, skin*] lechoso; [*green, blue*] blanquecino; **the leaves yield a ~ juice if broken** si se parten las hojas sueltan un jugo lechoso
2 (*containing a lot of milk*) [*tea, coffee*] con mucha leche; **I like my coffee nice and ~** me gusta el café con mucha leche; **this tea is too ~ for my liking** este té tiene mucha leche para mi gusto; **it tastes ~** sabe mucho a leche; **a ~ drink helps you sleep at night** una bebida hecha con leche te ayuda a dormir por la noche
Ⓑ CPD ► **the Milky Way** N (*Astron*) la Vía Láctea

mill [mɪl] Ⓐ N 1 (= *textile factory*) fábrica *f* (de tejidos); (= *sugar mill*) ingenio *m* de azúcar; (= *spinning mill*) hilandería *f*; (= *steel mill*) acería *f*
2 (= *machine*) molino *m*; (*for coffee, pepper*) molinillo *m*; (*Tech*) fresadora *f*; ♦**IDIOM to put sb through the mill: they put me through the ~** me las hicieron pasar canutas *or* moradas
Ⓑ VT moler; [+ *metal*] pulir; (*coin*) acordonar

►**mill about, mill around** Ⓐ VI + ADV arremolinarse
Ⓑ VI + PREP **people were ~ing about the booking office** la gente se apiñaba delante de la taquilla

milled [mɪld] ADJ [*grain*] molido; [*coin, edge*] acordonado

millenary [mɪˈlenərɪ] Ⓐ ADJ milenario
Ⓑ N milenario *m*

millennial [mɪˈlenɪəl] ADJ milenario

millennium [mɪˈlenɪəm] Ⓐ N (*pl* **millenniums** *or* **millennia** [mɪˈlenɪə]) milenio *m*; **the ~** el milenio
Ⓑ CPD ► **the millennium bug** N (*Comput*) el (problema del) efecto 2000 ► **millennium fund** N (*Brit*) *fondo de financiación y desarrollo para el nuevo milenio*

miller [ˈmɪləʳ] N molinero/a *m/f*

millet [ˈmɪlɪt] N mijo *m*

millhand [ˈmɪlhænd] N obrero/a *m/f*, operario/a *m/f*

milli... [ˈmɪlɪ] PREFIX mili...

milliard [ˈmɪlɪɑːd] N (*Brit*) mil millones *mpl*

millibar [ˈmɪlɪbɑːʳ] N milibar *m*

milligram(me) [ˈmɪlɪgræm] N miligramo *m*

millilitre, milliliter (*US*) [ˈmɪlɪˌliːtəʳ] N mililitro *m*

millimetre, millimeter (*US*) [ˈmɪlɪˌmiːtəʳ] N milímetro *m*

milliner [ˈmɪlɪnəʳ] N sombrerero/a *m/f*; **~'s (shop)** sombrerería *f*

millinery [ˈmɪlɪnərɪ] N sombrerería *f*, sombreros *mpl* de señora

milling [ˈmɪlɪŋ] Ⓐ N 1 (= *grinding*) molienda *f*
2 (*on coin*) cordoncillo *m*
Ⓑ CPD ► **milling machine** N fresadora *f*

million [ˈmɪljən] N millón *m*; **four ~ dogs** cuatro millones de perros; **I've got ~s of letters to write*** tengo miles de cartas que escribir; **I've told you ~s of times*** te lo he dicho infinidad de veces; ♦**IDIOMS to feel like a ~ dollars** *or* (*US*) **bucks*** sentirse a las mil maravillas; **she's one in a ~*** es única, es fuera de lo común

millionaire [ˌmɪljəˈnɛəʳ] N millonario/a *m/f*

millionairess [mɪljəˈnɛəres] N millonaria *f*

millionth [ˈmɪljənθ] Ⓐ ADJ millonésimo
Ⓑ N millonésimo *m*

millipede [ˈmɪlɪpiːd] N milpiés *m inv*

millisecond [ˈmɪlɪˌsekənd] N milésima *f* de segundo, milisegundo *m*

millpond [ˈmɪlpɒnd] N represa *f* de molino

millrace [ˈmɪlreɪs] N caz *m*

millstone [ˈmɪlstəʊn] N piedra *f* de molino, muela *f*; **it's a ~ round his neck** es una cruz que lleva a cuestas

millstream [ˈmɪlstriːm] N corriente *f* del caz

millwheel [ˈmɪlwiːl] N rueda *f* de molino

milometer [maɪˈlɒmɪtəʳ] N = **mileometer**

milord [mɪˈlɔːd] N milord *m*

milt [mɪlt] N lecha *f*

mime [maɪm] Ⓐ N (= *acting*) mimo *m*, mímica *f*; (= *play*) teatro *m* de mimo; (= *actor*) mimo *mf*
Ⓑ VT imitar, remedar
Ⓒ VI (= *act*) hacer mímica; **to ~ to a song** cantar una canción haciendo playback
Ⓓ CPD ► **mime artist** N mimo *mf*

Mimeograph® [ˈmɪmɪəgrɑːf] Ⓐ N mimeógrafo® *m*
Ⓑ VT mimeografiar

mimetic [mɪˈmetɪk] ADJ (*frm*) [*dance*] mimético; [*theatre*] de mimo; [*re-enactment*] mímico

mimic [ˈmɪmɪk] Ⓐ N mímico/a *m/f*
Ⓑ VT imitar, remedar

mimicry [ˈmɪmɪkrɪ] N mímica *f*; (*Bio*) mimetismo *m*

mimosa [mɪˈməʊzə] N mimosa *f*

Min. ABBR (*Brit*) (= **Ministry**) Min

min. ABBR 1 (= **minute(s)**) m
2 (= **minimum**) mín

minaret [mɪnəˈret] N alminar *m*, minarete *m*

minatory [ˈmɪnətərɪ] ADJ (*liter*) amenazador

mince [mɪns] Ⓐ N (*Brit Culin*) (*also* **~d meat**) carne *f* picada
Ⓑ VT 1 [+ *meat*] picar
2 (*fig*) **well, not to ~ matters** bueno, para decirlo francamente; ♦**IDIOM not to ~ one's words** no tener pelos en la lengua
Ⓒ VI (*in walking*) andar con pasos medidos; (*in talking*) hablar remilgadamente
Ⓓ CPD ► **mince pie** N pastel *m* de picadillo de fruta

mincemeat [ˈmɪnsmiːt] N (= *dried fruit*) conserva *f* de picadillo de fruta; (*Brit*) (= *minced meat*) carne *f* picada; ♦**IDIOM to make ~ of sb*** hacer picadillo *or* pedazos a algn

mincer [ˈmɪnsəʳ] N (= *machine*) máquina *f* de picar carne

mincing [ˈmɪnsɪŋ] Ⓐ ADJ remilgado, afectado; [*step*] menudito
Ⓑ CPD ► **mincing machine** N máquina *f* de picar carne

▼**mind** [maɪnd]

A NOUN	D COMPOUND
B TRANSITIVE VERB	E PHRASAL VERBS
C INTRANSITIVE VERB	

Ⓐ NOUN
1 [= *brain, head*] mente *f*; **a logical/creative ~** una mente racional/creativa; **he has the ~ of a five-year-old** tiene la edad mental de un niño de cinco años; **it's all in the ~** es pura sugestión; **at the back of my ~ I had the feeling that ...** tenía la remota sensación de que ...; **to bring one's ~ to bear on sth** concentrarse en algo; **it came to my ~ that ...** se me ocurrió que ...; **I'm not clear in my ~ about it** todavía no lo tengo claro *or* no lo llego a entender; **it crossed my ~ (that)** se me ocurrió (que); **yes, it had crossed my ~** sí, eso se me había ocurrido; **does it ever cross your ~ that ...?** ¿piensas alguna vez que ...?; **my ~ was elsewhere** tenía la cabeza en otro sitio; **it never entered my ~** jamás se me pasó por la cabeza; **I can't get it out of my ~** no me lo puedo quitar de la cabeza; **to go over sth in one's ~** repasar algo mentalmente; **a triumph of ~ over matter** un triunfo del espíritu sobre la materia; **it's a question of ~ over matter** es cuestión de voluntad; **to have one's ~ on sth** estar pensando en algo; **I had my ~ on something else** estaba pensando en otra cosa; **to have sth on one's ~** estar preocupado por algo; **what's on your ~?** ¿qué es lo que te preocupa?; **you can put that right out of your ~** conviene no pensar más en eso; **if you put your ~ to it** si te concentras en ello; **knowing that he had arrived safely set my ~ at ease** *or* **rest** el saber que había llegado sano y salvo me tranquilizó; **if you set your ~ to it** si te concentras en ello; **the thought that springs to ~ is ...** lo que primero se le ocurre a uno es ...; **state of ~** estado *m* de ánimo; **that will take your ~ off it** eso te distraerá; **to be uneasy in one's ~** quedarse con dudas; **he let his ~ wander** dejó que los pensamientos se le fueran a otras cosas; ♦**IDIOM ~'s eye** imaginación *f*; **in my ~'s eye I could still see her sitting there** mentalmente todavía la veía allí sentada; **that's a load** *or* **weight off my ~!** ¡eso me quita un peso de encima!; *see also* **blank A2**, **read A3**, **presence 5**
2 [= *memory*] **to bear sth/sb in ~** tener en cuenta algo/a algn; **we must bear (it) in ~ that ...** debemos tener en cuenta que ..., tenemos que recordar que ...; **I'll bear you in ~** te tendré en cuenta; **to keep sth/sb in ~** tener presente *or* en cuenta algo/a algn; **he puts me in ~ of his father** me recuerda a su padre; **to pass out of ~** caer en el olvido; **time out of ~** tiempo *m* inmemorial; **it went right** *or* **clean out of my ~** se me fue por completo de la cabeza; **to bring** *or* **call sth to**

➤ LANGUAGE IN USE: **mind A5** 26.2 **B5** 4 **C3** 4, 9.1

~ recordar algo, traer algo a la memoria; **that calls something else to ~** eso me trae otra cosa a la memoria; *see also* **slip C3, stick B5**

3 *= intention* **you can do it if you have a ~ to** puedes lograrlo si de verdad estás empeñado en ello; **I have a good ~ to do it** ganas de hacerlo no me faltan; **I have half a ~ to do it** estoy tentado *or* me dan ganas de hacerlo; **nothing was further from my ~** nada más lejos de mi intención; **to have sth in ~** tener pensado algo; **she wrote it with publication in ~** lo escribió con la intención de publicarlo; **to have sb in ~** tener a algn en mente; **who do you have in ~ for the job?** ¿a quién piensas darle el puesto *or* tienes en mente para el puesto?; **to have in ~ to do sth** tener intención de hacer algo

4 *= opinion* opinión *f*, parecer *m*; **to change one's ~** cambiar de opinión *or* idea *or* parecer; **to change sb's ~** hacer que algn cambie de opinión; **to have a closed ~** tener una mente cerrada; **to know one's own ~** saber lo que uno quiere; **to make up one's ~** decidirse; **we can't make up our ~s about selling the house** no nos decidimos a vender la casa; **I can't make up my ~ about him** todavía tengo ciertas dudas con respecto a él; **he has made up his ~ to leave home** ha decidido irse de casa, está decidido a irse de casa; **to my ~** a mi juicio; **to be of one ~** estar de acuerdo; **with one ~** unánimemente; **with an open ~** con espíritu abierto *or* mentalidad abierta; **to keep an open ~ on a subject** mantener una mentalidad abierta con relación a un tema; **to have a ~ of one's own** [*person*] (= *think for o.s.*) pensar por sí mismo; (*hum*) [*machine etc*] tener voluntad propia, hacer lo que quiere; **to be of the same ~** ser de la misma opinión, estar de acuerdo; **I was of the same ~ as my brother** yo estaba de acuerdo con mi hermano, yo era de la misma opinión que mi hermano; ✦*IDIOM* **to be in** *or* (*US*) **of two ~s** dudar, estar indeciso; *see also* **piece A1, speak B2**

5 *= mental balance* juicio *m*; **his ~ is going** está perdiendo facultades mentales; **to lose one's ~** perder el juicio; **nobody in his right ~ would do it** nadie que esté en su sano juicio lo haría; **of sound ~** en pleno uso de sus facultades mentales; **of unsound ~** mentalmente incapacitado; ✦*IDIOM* **to be out of one's ~** estar loco, haber perdido el juicio; **you must be out of your ~!** ¡tú debes estar loco!; **we were bored out of our ~s** estábamos muertos de aburrimiento; **to go out of one's ~** perder el juicio, volverse loco; **to go out of one's ~ with worry/jealousy** volverse loco de preocupación/celos

6 *= person* mente *f*, cerebro *m*; **one of the finest ~s of the period** uno de los cerebros privilegiados de la época; ✦*PROV* **great ~s think alike** (*hum*) los sabios siempre pensamos igual

Ⓑ TRANSITIVE VERB

1 *= be careful of* tener cuidado con; **~ you don't fall** ten cuidado, no te vayas a caer; **~ you don't get wet!** ten cuidado, no te vayas a mojar; **~ your head!** ¡cuidado con la cabeza!; **~ how you go!*** (*as farewell*) ¡cuídate!; **~ your language!** ¡qué manera de hablar es ésa!; **~ your manners!** ¡qué modales son ésos!; **~ the step!** ¡cuidado con el escalón!; **~ what you're doing!** ¡cuidado con lo que haces!; **~ where you're going!** ¡mira por dónde vas!; **~ yourself!** ¡cuidado, no te vayas a hacer daño!

2 *= pay attention to* hacer caso de; **~ what I say!** ¡hazme caso!, ¡escucha lo que te digo!; **~ your own business!** ¡no te metas donde no te llaman!; **don't ~ me** por mí no se preocupe; **don't ~ me!** (*iro*) ¡y a mí que me parta un rayo!*; **never ~ that now** olvídate de eso ahora; **never ~ him** no le hagas caso; **~ you, it was raining at the time** claro que *or* te advierto que en ese momento llovía; **it was a big one, ~ you** era grande, eso sí

3 *= oversee* cuidar; **could you ~ the baby this afternoon?** ¿podrías cuidar al niño esta tarde?; **could you ~ my bags for a few minutes?** ¿me cuidas *or* guardas las bolsas un momento?

4 *= dislike, object to* **I don't ~ the cold** a mí no me molesta el frío; **I don't ~ four, but six is too many** cuatro no me importa, pero seis son muchos; **I don't ~ waiting** no me importa esperar; **if you don't ~ my** *or* **me saying so, I think you're wrong** perdona que te diga pero estás equivocado, permíteme que te diga que te equivocas; **I don't ~ telling you, I was shocked** estaba horrorizado, lo confieso; **I wouldn't ~ a cup of tea** no me vendría mal un té

5 *in requests* **do you ~ telling me where you've been?** ¿te importa decirme dónde has estado?; **would you ~ opening the door?** ¿me hace el favor de abrir la puerta?, ¿le importa(ría) abrir la puerta?

6 *dialect = remember* acordarse de, recordar; **I mind the time when ...** me acuerdo de cuando ...

Ⓒ INTRANSITIVE VERB

1 *= be careful* tener cuidado; **~!** ¡cuidado!, ¡ojo!, ¡abusado! (*Mex*)

2 *= make sure* **~ you get there first** procura llegar primero; **~ you do it!** ¡hazlo sin falta!, ¡no dejes de hacerlo!; **he didn't do it, ~** pero en realidad no lo hizo, la verdad es que no lo hizo

3 *= object* **do you ~?** ¿te importa?; **do you ~!** (*iro*) ¡por favor!; **do you ~ if I open the window?** ¿te molesta que abra *or* si abro la ventana?; **do you ~ if I come?** ¿te importa que yo venga?; **I don't ~** me es igual; **"do you ~ if I take this book?" — "I don't ~ at all"** —¿te importa si me llevo *or* que me lleve este libro? —en absoluto; **if you don't ~, I won't come** si no te importa, yo no iré; **please, if you don't ~** si no le importa, si es tan amable; **close the door, if you don't ~** hazme el favor de cerrar la puerta; **"cigarette?" — "I don't ~ if I do"** —¿un cigarrillo? —pues muchas gracias *or* bueno *or* no digo que no; **never ~** (= *don't worry*) no te preocupes; (= *it makes no odds*) es igual, da lo mismo; (= *it's not important*) no importa; **I can't walk, never ~ run** no puedo andar, ni mucho menos correr

Ⓓ COMPOUND

► **mind game** N juego *m* psicológico

Ⓔ PHRASAL VERBS

► **mind out** VI + ADV tener cuidado; **~ out!** ¡cuidado!, ¡ojo!, ¡abusado! (*Mex*)

mind-bender* ['maɪnd,bendəʳ] N (*US*) 1 (= *drug*) alucinogénico *m*, droga *f* alucinogénica

2 (= *revelation*) noticia *f* *or* escena *f* *etc* alucinante*

mind-bending* ['maɪnd,bendɪŋ], **mind-blowing*** ['maɪnd,bləʊɪŋ], **mind-boggling*** ['maɪnd,bɒglɪŋ] ADJ increíble, alucinante*

minded ['maɪndɪd] ADJ **if you are so ~** si estás dispuesto a hacerlo, si quieres hacerlo

-minded ['maɪndɪd] ADJ (*ending in compounds*) **fair-minded** imparcial; **an industrially-minded nation** una nación de mentalidad industrial; **scientifically-minded** con aptitudes científicas; **a romantically-minded girl** una joven con una vena romántica *or* con ideas románticas

minder* ['maɪndəʳ] N 1 guardaespaldas *mf inv*, acompañante *mf*, escolta *mf*

2 (*esp Brit*) = **childminder**

mind-expanding ['maɪndɪks,pændɪŋ] ADJ [*drug*] visionario

mindful ['maɪndfʊl] ADJ **to be ~ of** tener presente *or* en cuenta; **we must be ~ of the risks** hay que tener presentes *or* en cuenta los riesgos

mindless ['maɪndlɪs] ADJ 1 (*Brit*) (= *senseless*) [*violence, vandalism, killing*] sin sentido

2 (= *unchallenging*) [*work, routine, task, repetition*] mecánico; [*entertainment*] sin sentido, absurdo

3 (= *unintelligent*) [*person*] tonto; **they're a bunch of ~ hooligans** son un atajo de gamberros salvajes

4 (= *heedless*) **~ of sth** (*frm*) haciendo caso omiso de algo

mind-reader ['maɪnd,riːdəʳ] N adivinador(a) *m/f* de pensamientos; **I'm not a ~ you know!*** ¿tú te crees que yo soy adivino?*

mind-reading ['maɪnd,riːdɪŋ] N adivinación *f* de pensamientos

mind-set ['maɪndset] N actitud *f*, disposición *f*

mine[1] [maɪn] POSS PRON (*referring to singular possession*) (el/la) mío/a; (*referring to plural possession*) (los/las) míos/as; **that car is ~** ese coche es mío; **is this glass ~?** ¿es mío este vaso?, ¿este vaso es mío?; **a friend of ~** un amigo mío; **"is this your coat?" — "no, ~ is black"** —¿es éste tu abrigo? —no, el mío es negro; **which is ~?** ¿cuál es el mío?; **your parents and ~** tus padres y los míos; **I think that brother of ~ is responsible*** creo que mi hermano es el que tiene la culpa, creo que el responsable es mi hermano; **be ~!** († *or hum*) ¡cásate conmigo!; **the house became ~** la casa pasó a ser mía *or* de mi propiedad; **it's no business of ~** no es asunto mío, no tiene que ver conmigo; **I want to make her ~** quiero que sea mi mujer; **~ and thine** lo mío y lo tuyo; **what's ~ is yours** todo lo mío es tuyo (también)

mine[2] [maɪn] Ⓐ N 1 mina *f*; **a coal ~** una mina de carbón; **to work down the ~** trabajar en la mina; *see also* **diamond B, gold C, salt D**

2 (*Mil, Naut etc*) mina *f*; **to lay ~s** poner minas; **to sweep ~s** dragar *or* barrer minas

3 (*fig*) **the book is a ~ of information** este libro es una mina de información; *see also* **useless 2**

Ⓑ VT 1 [+ *minerals, coal*] extraer; [+ *area*] explotar

2 (*Mil, Naut*) minar, poner minas en

Ⓒ VI extraer mineral; **to ~ for sth** abrir una mina para extraer algo

Ⓓ CPD ► **mine detector** N detector *m* de minas

minefield ['maɪnfiːld] N 1 (*lit*) campo *m* de minas

2 (*fig*) avispero *m*, campo *m* minado

minelayer ['maɪn,leɪəʳ] N minador *m*

miner ['maɪnəʳ] N minero/a *m/f*

mineral ['mɪnərəl] Ⓐ N mineral *m*

Ⓑ CPD ► **mineral deposit** N yacimiento *m* minero ► **mineral rights** NPL derechos *mpl* al subsuelo ► **mineral water** N agua *f* mineral

mineralogist [,mɪnə'rælədʒɪst] N mineralogista *mf*

mineralogy [,mɪnə'rælədʒɪ] N mineralogía *f*

Minerva [mɪ'nɜːvə] N Minerva

mineshaft ['maɪnʃɑːft] N pozo *m* de mina

minestrone [,mɪnɪ'strəʊnɪ] N minestrone *f*; **~ soup** sopa *f* minestrone

minesweeper ['maɪnswiːpəʳ] N dragaminas *m inv*

mingle ['mɪŋgl] Ⓐ VT mezclar
Ⓑ VI 1 (= *mix*) mezclarse
2 (= *become indistinguishable*) [*sounds*] confundirse (**in, with** con); **to ~ with the crowd** perderse entre la multitud
3 (*socially*) **she ~d for a while and then sat down with her husband** alternó con los invitados durante un rato y luego se sentó junto a su marido; **he ~d with people of all classes** se asociaba con personas de todas las clases

mingy* ['mɪndʒɪ] ADJ (*compar* **mingier**; *superl* **mingiest**) [*person*] tacaño; [*amount, portion*] mísero, miserable

Mini ['mɪnɪ] N (*Aut*) Mini *m*

mini ['mɪnɪ] N (= *miniskirt*) minifalda *f*

mini... ['mɪnɪ] PREFIX mini..., micro...

miniature ['mɪnɪtʃəʳ] Ⓐ N miniatura *f*; **in ~** en miniatura
Ⓑ ADJ (= *not full-sized*) (en) miniatura; (= *tiny*) diminuto; **~ clocks** relojes en miniatura; **a ~ bottle of whisky** una botellita de whisky
Ⓒ CPD ► **miniature golf** N minigolf *m* ► **miniature poodle** N caniche *mf* enano/a ► **miniature railway** N ferrocarril *m* en miniatura ► **miniature submarine** N submarino *m* de bolsillo

miniaturization [,mɪnɪtʃəraɪ'zeɪʃən] N miniaturización *f*

miniaturize ['mɪnɪtʃəraɪz] VT miniaturizar

minibar ['mɪnɪbɑːʳ] N minibar *m*

minibudget ['mɪnɪ,bʌdʒɪt] N presupuesto *m* interino

minibus ['mɪnɪbʌs] N microbús *m*, micro *m*

minicab ['mɪnɪkæb] N radiotaxi *m*

minicomputer [,mɪnɪkəm'pjuːtəʳ] N minicomputadora *f*, miniordenador *m* (*Sp*)

minicourse ['mɪnɪ,kɔːs] N (*US*) cursillo *m*

MiniDisc®, minidisc ['mɪnɪdɪsk] Ⓐ N (= *system, disc*) MiniDisc® *m*, minidisc *m*
Ⓑ CPD ► **MiniDisc® player** N (reproductor *m*) MiniDisc® *m or* minidisc *m*

minidress ['mɪnɪdres] N minivestido *m*

minim ['mɪnɪm] N blanca *f*

minimal ['mɪnɪml] ADJ mínimo

minimalism ['mɪnɪməlɪzəm] N minimalismo *m*

minimalist ['mɪnɪməlɪst] ADJ, N minimalista *mf*

minimally ['mɪnɪməlɪ] ADV **he was paid, but only ~** le pagaron, pero sólo lo mínimo; **I was ~ successful** tuve un éxito mínimo, apenas tuve éxito

minimarket ['mɪnɪ,mɑːkɪt], **minimart** ['mɪnɪ,mɑːt] N autoservicio *m*

minimize ['mɪnɪmaɪz] VT 1 (= *reduce*) reducir al mínimo, minimizar 2 (= *belittle*) menospreciar

minimum ['mɪnɪməm] Ⓐ ADJ [*amount, charge, age, temperature*] mínimo
Ⓑ N (*pl* **minimums** *or* **minima**) mínimo *m*; **to reduce sth to a ~** reducir algo al mínimo; **to keep costs down to a** *or* **the ~** mantener los costos al mínimo; **he's someone who always does the bare ~** es una persona que siempre sigue la ley del mínimo esfuerzo; **with a ~ of effort** con un mínimo de esfuerzo; **with the ~ of clothing** sin apenas ropa
Ⓒ CPD ► **minimum lending rate** N tipo *m* de interés mínimo ► **minimum wage** N salario *m* mínimo

mining ['maɪnɪŋ] Ⓐ N 1 minería *f*, explotación *f* de minas 2 (*Mil, Naut*) minado *m*
Ⓑ CPD ► **mining engineer** N ingeniero/a *m/f* de minas ► **mining industry** N industria *f* minera ► **mining town** N población *f* minera

minion ['mɪnjən] N (= *follower*) secuaz *mf*; (= *servant*) paniaguado *m*

minipill ['mɪnɪ,pɪl] N minipíldora *f*

miniscule ['mɪnɪs,kjuːl] = **minuscule**

miniseries ['mɪnɪ,sɪərɪz] N (*pl* **miniseries**) (*TV*) miniserie *f*

miniskirt ['mɪnɪskɜːt] N minifalda *f*

minister ['mɪnɪstəʳ] Ⓐ N 1 (*Pol*) ministro/a *m/f*, secretario/a *m/f* (*Mex*); **Prime Minister** primer(a) ministro/a *m/f*; **the Minister for Education** el/la Ministro/a de Educación
2 (*Rel*) pastor(a) *m/f*, clérigo/a *m/f*; → CHURCHES OF ENGLAND/SCOTLAND
Ⓑ VI **to ~ to sb** atender a algn; **to ~ to sb's needs** atender *or* satisfacer las necesidades de algn

ministerial [,mɪnɪs'tɪərɪəl] ADJ 1 (*Pol*) [*meeting*] del gabinete; [*post, career, duties*] ministerial; [*changes*] en el gabinete; **at ~ level** a nivel ministerial
2 (*Rel*) [*duties, meeting*] pastoral

ministration [,mɪnɪs'treɪʃən] N (*frm*) ayuda *f*, agencia *f*, servicio *m*; (*Rel*) ministerio *m*

ministry ['mɪnɪstrɪ] N 1 (*Pol*) ministerio *m*, secretaría *f* (*Mex*); **Ministry of Transport** Ministerio *m* de Transporte
2 (*Rel*) sacerdocio *m*; **to enter the ~** hacerse sacerdote; (*Protestant*) hacerse pastor

minium ['mɪnɪəm] N minio *m*

mink [mɪŋk] Ⓐ N (*pl* **mink** *or* **minks**) 1 (*Zool*) visón *m* 2 (= *fur*) piel *f* de visón 3 (= *coat*) abrigo *m* de visón
Ⓑ CPD ► **mink coat** N abrigo *m* de visón ► **mink farm** N criadero *m* de visones

Minn. ABBR (*US*) = **Minnesota**

minnow ['mɪnəʊ] N (*pl* **minnow** *or* **minnows**) pececillo *m* (*de agua dulce*)

minor ['maɪnəʳ] Ⓐ ADJ 1 (= *small, unimportant*) [*problem*] de poca importancia; [*adjustment, detail*] menor, de poca importancia; [*change, damage, poet, work*] menor; [*role*] (*in film, play*) secundario; (*in negotiations*) de poca importancia; [*road*] secundario; **of ~ importance** de poca importancia
2 (= *not serious*) [*injury*] leve; [*illness*] poco grave; [*surgery, operation*] de poca importancia
3 (*Mus*) [*chord*] menor; **in F ~** en fa menor; **in a ~ key** en clave menor
4 (*Brit Scol*†) **Smith ~** Smith el pequeño, Smith el menor
Ⓑ N 1 (*Jur*) menor *mf* (de edad)
2 (*US Univ*) asignatura *f* secundaria
Ⓒ VI (*US Univ*) **to ~ in sth** estudiar algo como asignatura secundaria
Ⓓ CPD ► **minor league** N (*Baseball*) liga *f* menor; *see also* **minor-league** ► **minor offence** (*Brit*), **minor offense** (*US*) N delito *m* de menor cuantía

Minorca [mɪ'nɔːkə] N Menorca *f*

minority [maɪ'nɒrɪtɪ] Ⓐ N 1 (= *small number*) minoría *f*; **only a small ~ of children contract the disease** sólo una pequeña minoría de niños contraen la enfermedad; **to be in a** *or* **the ~** ser minoría, estar en minoría; **you're in a ~ of one, there!** (*hum*) ¡te has quedado más sólo que la una!
2 (= *community*) minoría *f*; **ethnic ~** minoría *f* étnica
3 (*Jur*) (= *age*) minoría *f* de edad
Ⓑ ADJ 1 [*group, interest, view, government*] minoritario; **~ language** lengua *f* minoritaria; **~ rights** (*Pol*) derechos *mpl* de las minorías
2 (*Fin*) **~ interest** ◊ **~ stake** participación *f* minoritaria; **~ shareholder** accionista *mf* minoritario; **~ shareholding** accionado *m* minoritario 3 (*US Pol*) **Minority Leader** líder *mf* de la oposición; **House Minority Leader** líder *mf* de la oposición del Congreso; **Senate Minority Leader** líder *mf* de la oposición del Senado

MINORITY

Singular or plural verb?

When **minoría** is the subject of a verb, the verb can be in the singular or the plural, depending on the context:

- Put the verb in the singular if **minority** is seen as a unit rather than a collection of individuals:

 A minority should always be respected, however small it may be
 Una minoría, aunque sea pequeña, debe ser respetada siempre

- If **la minoría** is seen as a collection of individuals, particularly when it is followed by **de** + PLURAL NOUN, the plural form of the verb is more common than the singular, though both are possible:

 ...a minority of agitators want to introduce anarchy
 ...una minoría de agitadores quieren *or* ***quiere traer la anarquía***

- The plural form must be used when **la minoría** or **la minoría de** + PLURAL NOUN is followed by **ser** or **estar** + PLURAL COMPLEMENT:

 Only a minority of the demonstrators were students
 Sólo una minoría de los manifestantes eran estudiantes

For further uses and examples, see main entry.

minor-league CPD ► **minor-league baseball** N (*US*) béisbol *m* de liga menor ► **minor-league criminals** NPL criminales *mpl* de segundo orden, criminales *mpl* de segunda

Minotaur ['maɪnətɔːʳ] N Minotauro *m*

minster ['mɪnstəʳ] N (= *cathedral*) catedral *f*; (= *church*) iglesia *f* de un monasterio

minstrel ['mɪnstrəl] N juglar *m*

minstrelsy ['mɪnstrəlsɪ] N (= *music*) música *f*; (= *song*) canto *m*; (= *art of epic minstrel*) juglaría *f*; (= *art of lyric minstrel*) gaya ciencia *f*

mint¹ [mɪnt] Ⓐ N casa *f* de la moneda; **Royal Mint** (*Brit*) Real Casa *f* de la Moneda; ✦**IDIOM to be worth a ~ (of money)** valer un dineral
Ⓑ ADJ **in ~ condition** como nuevo, en perfecto estado
Ⓒ VT acuñar; **newly ~ed** [*coin*] recién acuñado; (*fig*) [*graduate*] recién salido de la universidad

mint² [mɪnt] Ⓐ N 1 (*Bot*) hierbabuena *f*, menta *f* 2 (= *sweet*) pastilla *f* de menta
Ⓑ CPD ► **mint julep** N (*US*) julepe *m* de menta, (bebida *f* de) whisky *m* con menta ► **mint sauce** N salsa *f* de menta ► **mint tea** N té *m* de menta

minuet [,mɪnjʊ'et] N minué *m*

minus ['maɪnəs] Ⓐ PREP 1 menos; **nine ~ six** nueve menos seis
2 (= *without, deprived of*) sin; **he appeared ~ his trousers** apareció sin pantalón
Ⓑ ADJ [*number*] negativo; **it's ~ 20 outside** fuera hace una temperatura de 20 bajo cero; **I got a B ~ for my French** me pusieron un notable bajo en francés
Ⓒ N (= *sign*) signo *m* menos; (= *amount*) cantidad *f* negativa
Ⓓ CPD ► **minus sign** N signo *m* menos

minuscule ['mɪnəskjuːl] ADJ minúsculo

minute[1] [ˈmɪnɪt] Ⓐ N [1] (= *60 secs*) minuto *m*; **it is twenty ~s past two** son las dos y veinte (minutos); **a 10-~ break** un descanso de 10 minutos; **every ~ counts** no hay tiempo que perder; **it won't take five ~s** es cosa de pocos minutos; **it's a few ~s walk from the station** está a unos minutos de la estación andando; **they were getting closer by the ~** se nos estaban acercando por minutos; **at six o'clock to the ~** a las seis en punto; **her schedule was planned to the ~** su horario estaba planeado hasta el último minuto; **they were on the scene within ~s** llegaron al lugar de los hechos a los pocos minutos; ✦*PROV* **there's one born every ~!*** ¡hay cada tonto por ahí suelto!*

[2] (= *short time*) momento *m*; **I shan't be a ~** (*on going out*) vuelvo enseguida; (*when busy*) termino enseguida; **will you shut up for a ~!** ¿te callas un momento?; **have you got a ~?** ¿tienes un momento?; **I'll come in a ~** ahora voy, vengo dentro de un momento; **just a ~!** ◊ **wait a ~!** ¡espera un momento!, ¡un momento!, ¡momentito! (*LAm*)

[3] (= *instant*) instante *m*; **it was all over in a ~** todo esto ocurrió en un instante; **I haven't had a ~ to myself all day** no he tenido ni un instante *or* momento para mí en todo el día; **we expect him (at) any ~** le esperamos de un momento a otro; **any ~ now he's going to fall off there** se va caer en cualquier momento; **at that ~ the phone rang** en ese momento sonó el teléfono; **I bet you loved every ~ of it!** ¡seguro que te lo pasaste en grande!; **at the last ~** a última hora, en el último momento; **to leave things until the last ~** dejar las cosas hasta última hora *or* hasta el último momento; **one ~ she was there, the next she was gone** estaba allí, y al momento se había ido; **we caught the train without a ~ to spare** cogimos el tren justo a tiempo; **at that ~ my father came in** en ese momento entró mi padre; **tell me the ~ he arrives** avísame en cuanto llegue; **sit down this ~!** ¡siéntate ya!; **I've just this ~ heard** me acabo de enterar; **(at) this very ~** ahora mismo; ✦*IDIOM* **I don't believe him for a** *or* **one ~** no le creo para nada *or* en absoluto; *see also* **soon 2**

[4] (= *official note*) nota *f*, minuta *f*

[5] **minutes** [*of meeting*] acta *f*; **to take the ~s (of a meeting)** levantar (el) acta (de una reunión)

Ⓑ VT [+ *meeting*] levantar (el) acta de; [+ *remark, fact*] registrar; **I want that ~d** quiero que eso conste en acta; **you don't need to ~ that** no hace falta que registres *or* anotes eso

Ⓒ CPD ► **minute book** N libro *m* de actas ► **minute hand** N minutero *m* ► **minute steak** N biftec *m* pequeño (que se hace rápidamente)

minute[2] [maɪˈnjuːt] ADJ [1] (= *very small*) [*amount, change*] mínimo; [*particles*] diminuto

[2] (= *rigorous*) [*examination, scrutiny*] minucioso; **in ~ detail** hasta el mínimo detalle

minutely [maɪˈnjuːtlɪ] ADV [1] (= *in detail*) [*describe*] detalladamente, minuciosamente; [*examine*] minuciosamente; **a ~ detailed account** un relato extremadamente detallado *or* completo hasta en los más pequeños detalles

[2] (= *by a small amount*) [*move, change, differ*] mínimamente; **anything ~ resembling a fish** cualquier cosa mínimamente parecida a un pez

minutiae [mɪˈnjuːʃiː] NPL detalles *mpl* minuciosos

minx [mɪŋks] N picaruela *f*, mujer *f* descarada; **you ~!** ¡lagarta!

Miocene [ˈmaɪəsiːn] Ⓐ ADJ mioceno

Ⓑ N mioceno *m*

MIPS [mɪps] NPL ABBR (= **millions of instructions per second**) MIPS *mpl*

miracle [ˈmɪrəkl] Ⓐ N (*Rel, fig*) milagro *m*; **it's a ~ that you weren't hurt!** ¡fue un milagro que salieras ileso!; **by some ~ he passed his exam** milagrosamente aprobó el examen

Ⓑ CPD ► **miracle cure** N remedio *m* milagroso ► **miracle drug** N medicamento *m* milagro ► **miracle play** N auto *m* sacramental ► **miracle worker** N **I'm not a ~ worker, you know*** yo no puedo hacer milagros

miraculous [mɪˈrækjʊləs] ADJ [1] (*Rel*) [*powers, healing*] milagroso

[2] (= *extraordinary*) [*escape, recovery*] milagroso; [*change, result*] extraordinario; **he made a ~ recovery** tuvo una recuperación milagrosa, se recuperó de forma milagrosa; **his escape was nothing short of ~** la forma en que logró escaparse fue un verdadero *or* auténtico milagro

miraculously [mɪˈrækjʊləslɪ] ADV [*survive, escape, transform*] milagrosamente; **casualties were ~ light** las bajas resultaron ser milagrosamente escasas; **~, he escaped unhurt** milagrosamente, salió ileso

mirage [ˈmɪrɑːʒ] N espejismo *m*

MIRAS [ˈmaɪræs] N ABBR (*Brit*) = **mortgage interest relief at source**

mire [maɪəʳ] Ⓐ N fango *m*, lodo *m*

Ⓑ VT (*US*) **to get ~d in** quedar atascado *or* preso en

mirror [ˈmɪrəʳ] Ⓐ N espejo *m*; **driving ~** retrovisor *m*, espejo *m* retrovisor; **to look at o.s. in the ~** mirarse en el *or* al espejo; **she got in the car and adjusted the ~** entró en el coche y ajustó el retrovisor

Ⓑ VT reflejar

Ⓒ CPD ► **mirror image** N reflejo *m* exacto

mirth [mɜːθ] N (= *good humour*) alegría *f*, júbilo *m*; (= *laughter*) risas *fpl*

mirthful [ˈmɜːθfʊl] ADJ alegre

mirthless [ˈmɜːθlɪs] ADJ triste, sin alegría

miry [ˈmaɪrɪ] ADJ fangoso, lodoso; **~ place** lodazal *m*

MIS N ABBR = **management information system**

misadventure [ˌmɪsədˈventʃəʳ] N desgracia *f*, contratiempo *m*; **death by ~** (*Jur*) muerte *f* accidental

misalliance [ˌmɪsəˈlaɪəns] N casamiento *m* inconveniente

misanthrope [ˈmɪzənθrəʊp] N misántropo *m*

misanthropic [ˌmɪzənˈθrɒpɪk] ADJ misantrópico

misanthropist [mɪˈzænθrəpɪst] N misántropo/a *m/f*

misanthropy [mɪˈzænθrəpɪ] N misantropía *f*

misapplication [ˌmɪsæplɪˈkeɪʃən] N mala aplicación *f*, uso *m* indebido

misapply [ˌmɪsəˈplaɪ] VT (*gen*) usar indebidamente; [+ *funds*] malversar; [+ *efforts, talents*] malgastar

misapprehend [ˌmɪsæprɪˈhend] VT entender mal, comprender mal

misapprehension [ˌmɪsæprɪˈhenʃən] N malentendido *m*; **there seems to be some ~** parece haber algún malentendido; **to be under a ~** estar equivocado

misappropriate [ˌmɪsəˈprəʊprɪeɪt] VT malversar, desfalcar

misappropriation [ˌmɪsəprəʊprɪˈeɪʃən] N malversación *f*, desfalco *m*

misbegotten [ˌmɪsbɪˈgɒtn] ADJ bastardo, ilegítimo; [*plan etc*] descabellado, llamado a fracasar

misbehave [ˌmɪsbɪˈheɪv] VI portarse mal, comportarse mal

misbehaviour, misbehavior (*US*) [ˌmɪsbɪˈheɪvjəʳ] N mala conducta *f*, mal comportamiento *m*

misc. ABBR = **miscellaneous**

miscalculate [ˌmɪsˈkælkjʊleɪt] Ⓐ VT calcular mal

Ⓑ VI calcular mal

miscalculation [ˌmɪskælkjʊˈleɪʃən] N error *m* de cálculo

miscall [ˌmɪsˈkɔːl] VT llamar equivocadamente

miscarriage [ˈmɪsˌkærɪdʒ] N [1] (*Med*) aborto *m* (natural)

[2] **~ of justice** error *m* judicial

miscarry [mɪsˈkærɪ] VI [1] (*Med*) abortar

[2] (= *fail*) [*plans*] fracasar, malograrse (*Peru*)

miscast [ˌmɪsˈkɑːst] (*pt, pp* **miscast**) VT **to ~ sb** (*Theat*) dar a algn un papel que no le va; **he was ~ as Othello** no fue muy acertado darle el papel de Otello

miscegenation [ˌmɪsɪdʒɪˈneɪʃən] N (*frm*) mestizaje *m*, cruce *m* de razas

miscellaneous [ˌmɪsɪˈleɪnɪəs] ADJ [*objects*] variado, de todo tipo; [*writings, collection*] variado; **a ~ collection of objects** una variada colección de objetos; **categorized** *or* **classified as ~** catalogado *or* clasificado en concepto de "varios"; **~ expenses** gastos *mpl* diversos

miscellany [mɪˈselənɪ] N [*of objects*] miscelánea *f*; [*of writings*] antología *f*

mischance [mɪsˈtʃɑːns] N desgracia *f*, mala suerte *f*; **by some ~** por desgracia

mischief [ˈmɪstʃɪf] N [1] (= *naughtiness*) travesura *f*, diablura *f*; **he's up to some ~** está haciendo alguna travesura; **he's always getting into ~** siempre anda haciendo travesuras; **keep out of ~!** (*to child*) ¡no hagas travesuras!; (*to adult*) (*hum*) ¡pórtate bien!; **to keep sb out of ~** evitar que algn haga travesuras

[2] (= *harm*) daño *m*; **to do o.s. a ~*** hacerse daño

[3] (= *malicious behaviour*) **to make ~** causar daño

mischief-maker [ˈmɪstʃɪfˌmeɪkəʳ] N (= *troublemaker*) revoltoso/a *m/f*; (= *gossip*) chismoso/a *m/f*

mischievous [ˈmɪstʃɪvəs] ADJ [1] (= *impish*) [*person, smile*] pícaro; (= *naughty*) [*child, kitten*] travieso; **the ~ tricks the children used to get up to** las travesuras que los niños solían hacer

[2] (= *malicious*) [*person, glance, rumour*] malicioso

mischievously [ˈmɪstʃɪvəslɪ] ADV [1] (= *impishly*) [*say, smile*] con picardía, pícaramente; [*tease*] juguetonamente, pícaramente

[2] (= *maliciously*) [*say, smile*] maliciosamente; [*tease*] con malicia

mischievousness [ˈmɪstʃɪvəsnɪs] N travesuras *fpl*

misconceive [ˌmɪskənˈsiːv] VT entender mal, comprender mal

misconceived [ˌmɪskənˈsiːvd] ADJ **a ~ plan** un proyecto descabellado

misconception [ˌmɪskənˈsepʃən] N malentendido *m*, concepto *m* erróneo; **but this is a ~** pero esta idea es errónea

misconduct Ⓐ [mɪsˈkɒndʌkt] N mala conducta *f*; (*professional*) falta *f* de ética profesional, mala conducta *f* profesional

Ⓑ [ˌmɪskənˈdʌkt] VT manejar mal, dirigir mal; **to ~ o.s.** portarse *or* conducirse mal

misconstruction [ˈmɪskənsˈtrʌkʃən] N (= *misinterpretation*) mala interpretación *f*; (*deliberate*) tergiversación *f*; **words open to ~** palabras *fpl* que se prestan a ser malinterpretadas

misconstrue [ˌmɪskənˈstruː] VT interpretar mal, malinterpretar

miscount [ˌmɪsˈkaʊnt] Ⓐ VT contar mal, equivocarse en la cuenta de
Ⓑ VI contar mal
Ⓒ [ˈmɪskaʊnt] N **there was a ~** hubo un error en el recuento

miscreant [ˈmɪskrɪənt] N sinvergüenza *mf*, bellaco/a *m/f*

misdeal [ˌmɪsˈdiːl] Ⓐ N reparto *m* erróneo
Ⓑ VT [+ *cards*] dar mal, repartir mal

misdeed [ˌmɪsˈdiːd] N fechoría *f*

misdemeanour, **misdemeanor** (*US*) [ˌmɪsdɪˈmiːnəʳ] N fechoría *f*; (*Jur*) delito *m* menor, falta *f*

misdirect [ˌmɪsdɪˈrekt] VT [+ *operation*] manejar mal; [+ *letter*] poner las señas mal en; [+ *person*] informar mal

misdirection [ˌmɪsdɪˈrekʃən] N [*of operation, scheme*] mala dirección *f*; [*of resources*] mala administración *f*, mal manejo *m*

miser [ˈmaɪzəʳ] N avaro/a *m/f*

miserable [ˈmɪzərəbl] ADJ 1 (= *unhappy*) [*person*] abatido, con el ánimo por los suelos; [*face*] triste; **to feel ~** tener el ánimo por los suelos, sentirse abatido *or* deprimido; **Sheila was looking ~** a Sheila se la veía abatida; **don't look so ~!** ¡alegra esa cara!; **to make sb ~** hacer a algn sentirse deprimido; **my job was making me really ~** mi trabajo me estaba deprimiendo
2 (= *depressing*) [*place, life, weather*] deprimente; [*childhood*] desdichado, infeliz; **it was wet and ~ outside** fuera hacía un tiempo lluvioso y deprimente; **it was a ~ business** era un asunto deprimente *or* lamentable; **to make sb's life ~** ◊ **make life ~ for sb** amargar la vida a algn; **to have a ~ time** pasarlo mal, pasarlo fatal*
3 (= *wretched*) [*hovel, shantytown, beggar*] mísero; **the ~ conditions they were living in** la miseria en la que vivían
4 (= *contemptible, mean*) **you ~ (old) thing!** ¡viejo ruin!
5 (= *paltry*) [*offer*] mísero, mezquino; [*pay*] miserable; [*meal*] triste, mísero; **a ~ two pounds** dos miserables libras; **they gave me a ~ piece of bread for lunch** me dieron un triste trozo de pan para comer
6 (= *complete*) **to be a ~ failure** [*attempt, play*] ser un fracaso espantoso *or* rotundo, ser un triste fracaso; [*person*] ser un fracaso total

miserably [ˈmɪzərəblɪ] ADV 1 (= *unhappily*) [*say, think, nod*] tristemente, con desconsuelo
2 (= *depressingly*) [*furnished, decorated*] miserablemente, míseramente; **the supplies were ~ inadequate** los suministros eran miserablemente escasos; **it was ~ cold** hacía un frío deprimente; **our wages are ~ low** nos pagan una miseria
3 (= *completely*) **to fail ~** fracasar rotundamente

misère [mɪˈzɛəʳ] N (*Cards*) nulos *mpl*; **to go ~** jugar a nulos

miserliness [ˈmaɪzəlɪnɪs] N tacañería *f*

miserly [ˈmaɪzəlɪ] ADJ 1 (= *mean*) [*person*] mezquino, ruin, tacaño
2 (= *paltry*) [*sum*] mísero

misery [ˈmɪzərɪ] N 1 (= *sadness*) tristeza *f*, pena *f*
2 (= *poverty*) miseria *f*, pobreza *f*; **to live in ~** vivir en la miseria
3 (= *misfortune*) desgracia *f*; **a life of ~** una vida desgraciada
4 (= *suffering*) sufrimiento *m*, dolor *m*; **to put an animal out of its ~** rematar a un animal (para que no sufra); **to put sb out of his/her ~** (*fig*) sacar a algn de la incertidumbre; **to make sb's life a ~** amargar la vida a algn
5 (*Brit**) (= *person*) aguafiestas *mf inv*

misfile [ˌmɪsˈfaɪl] VT [+ *papers*] archivar incorrectamente

misfire [ˌmɪsˈfaɪəʳ] VI [*plan, engine*] fallar; [*gun*] encasquillarse

misfit [ˈmɪsfɪt] N (= *person*) inadaptado/a *m/f*; **he's always been a ~ here** no se ha adaptado nunca a las condiciones de aquí, en ningún momento ha estado realmente contento aquí

misfortune [mɪsˈfɔːtʃən] N desgracia *f*; **companion in ~** compañero/a *m/f* en la desgracia; **I had the ~ to meet him** tuve la desgracia de conocerlo; **it is his ~ that he is lame** tiene la mala suerte de ser cojo; **that's your ~!** ¡mala suerte!

misgiving [mɪsˈgɪvɪŋ] N recelo *m*, duda *f*; **not without some ~** no sin cierto recelo; **I had ~s about the scheme** tuve mis dudas sobre el proyecto

misgovern [ˌmɪsˈgʌvən] VT, VI gobernar mal

misgovernment [ˌmɪsˈgʌvənmənt] N desgobierno *m*, mal gobierno *m*

misguided [ˌmɪsˈgaɪdɪd] ADJ [*attempt*] torpe; [*belief, view*] equivocado; [*person*] descaminado, desacertado; [*actions*] desacertado, equivocado; **a ~ sense of loyalty** un sentido desacertado *or* equivocado de la lealtad; **in the ~ belief that …** creyendo, equivocadamente *or* erróneamente, que …; **he was ~ enough to believe he could get away with it** era tan insensato como para creer que podría salirse con la suya; **poor ~ fool!** ¡pobre infeliz!

misguidedly [ˌmɪsˈgaɪdɪdlɪ] ADV [*believe*] equivocadamente, erróneamente; [*tell*] erróneamente

mishandle [ˌmɪsˈhændl] VT 1 (= *treat roughly*) [+ *object, goods*] maltratar
2 (= *mismanage*) [+ *situation*] llevar mal, manejar mal; [+ *problem*] no saber tratar

mishandling [ˌmɪsˈhændlɪŋ] N 1 [*of object, goods*] mal trato *m*
2 [*of situation, problem*] mal manejo *m*

mishap [ˈmɪshæp] N contratiempo *m*; **without ~** sin contratiempos; **to have a ~** tener un accidente; **we had a slight ~** tuvimos un pequeño contratiempo

mishear [ˌmɪsˈhɪəʳ] (*pt, pp* **misheard** [ˌmɪsˈhɜːd]) Ⓐ VT oír mal
Ⓑ VI oír mal

mishit Ⓐ [ˈmɪshɪt] N golpe *m* defectuoso
Ⓑ [ˌmɪsˈhɪt] VT golpear mal

mishmash [ˈmɪʃmæʃ] N revoltijo *m*, batiburrillo* *m*

misinform [ˌmɪsɪnˈfɔːm] VT informar mal

misinformation [ˌmɪsɪnfəˈmeɪʃən] N (= *wrong information*) mala información *f*, información *f* errónea; (= *deliberate act*) desinformación *f*

misinterpret [ˌmɪsɪnˈtɜːprɪt] VT interpretar mal, malinterpretar; (*deliberately*) tergiversar

misinterpretation [ˌmɪsɪntɜːprɪˈteɪʃən] N mala interpretación *f*; (*deliberate*) tergiversación *f*

misjudge [ˌmɪsˈdʒʌdʒ] VT 1 (= *miscalculate*) calcular mal; **the driver ~d the bend** el conductor no calculó bien la curva; **she ~d the distance** calculó mal la distancia
2 (= *judge wrongly*) [+ *person*] juzgar mal; **I may have ~d him** a lo mejor lo juzgué mal

misjudgement [ˌmɪsˈdʒʌdʒmənt] N 1 [*of distance etc*] mal cálculo *m*
2 [*of person*] juicio *m* erróneo

mislay [mɪsˈleɪ] (*pt, pp* **mislaid** [mɪsˈleɪd]) VT extraviar, perder; **I've mislaid my glasses** no sé dónde he puesto las gafas

mislead [mɪsˈliːd] (*pt, pp* **misled**) VT 1 (= *give wrong idea*) engañar; **I wouldn't like to ~ you** no quisiera inducirle a error, no me gustaría que se hiciera una idea equivocada; **I'm afraid you have been misled** me temo que le han dado una idea equivocada
2 (= *misdirect*) despistar
3 (= *lead into bad ways*) corromper

misleading [mɪsˈliːdɪŋ] ADJ engañoso

misled [mɪsˈled] PT, PP *of* **mislead**

mismanage [ˌmɪsˈmænɪdʒ] VT [+ *business, estate, shop*] administrar mal; [+ *situation*] llevar mal, manejar mal

mismanagement [ˌmɪsˈmænɪdʒmənt] N [*of business*] mala administración *f*; [*of situation*] manejo *m* inadecuado

mismatch [ˌmɪsˈmætʃ] Ⓐ VT emparejar mal
Ⓑ N **there is a ~ between the skills offered by people and the skills needed by industry** la preparación ofrecida por la gente no coincide con lo que la industria precisa; **a ~ of styles/colours** una falta de armonía en los estilos/colores

misname [ˌmɪsˈneɪm] VT llamar equivocadamente; **this grotesquely ~d society** esta sociedad con su nombre grotescamente inapropiado

misnomer [ˌmɪsˈnəʊməʳ] N nombre *m* equivocado *or* inapropiado; **that is a ~** ese nombre es impropio

misogamist [mɪˈsɒgəmɪst] N misógamo/a *m/f*

misogamy [mɪˈsɒgəmɪ] N misogamia *f*

misogynist [mɪˈsɒdʒɪnɪst] Ⓐ ADJ misógino
Ⓑ N misógino/a *m/f*

misogynistic [mɪˌsɒdʒɪˈnɪstɪk] ADJ misógino

misogyny [mɪˈsɒdʒɪnɪ] N misoginia *f*

misplace [ˌmɪsˈpleɪs] VT perder; **he frequently ~s important documents** con frecuencia traspapela *or* pierde documentos importantes; **I'm sorry, I seem to have ~d the address** perdona, no sé dónde he puesto las señas

misplaced [ˌmɪsˈpleɪst] ADJ 1 (= *inappropriate*) [*confidence, trust*] inmerecido; [*enthusiasm*] que no viene a cuento; [*good humour*] fuera de lugar, inoportuno; **I realize now that my confidence/trust in you was ~** ahora me doy cuenta de que me equivoqué al confiar en ti; **a ~ sense of duty/loyalty** un sentido desacertado *or* equivocado del deber/de la lealtad
2 (= *wrongly positioned*) [*accent, comma*] mal colocado, puesto en el lugar equivocado

misprint Ⓐ [ˈmɪsprɪnt] N error *m* de imprenta, errata *f*
Ⓑ [mɪsˈprɪnt] VT imprimir mal

mispronounce [ˌmɪsprəˈnaʊns] VT pronunciar mal

mispronunciation [ˌmɪsprənʌnsɪˈeɪʃən] N mala pronunciación *f*

misquotation [ˌmɪskwəʊˈteɪʃən] N cita *f* equivocada

misquote [ˌmɪsˈkwəʊt] VT citar incorrectamente; **he was ~d in the press** la prensa no reprodujo con exactitud sus palabras

misread [ˌmɪsˈriːd] (*pt, pp* **misread** [ˌmɪsˈred]) VT (= *read wrongly*) leer mal; (= *misinterpret*) interpretar mal, malinterpretar

misrepresent [ˌmɪsreprɪˈzent] VT [+ *person*] dar una imagen falsa de; [+ *views, situation*] tergiversar; **he was ~ed in the papers** los periódicos tergiversaron sus palabras

misrepresentation [ˌmɪsreprɪzenˈteɪʃən] N [*of facts*] tergiversación *f*, desfiguración *f*; (*Jur*) declaración *f* falsa; **this report is a ~ of what I said** este informe tergiversa mis palabras

misrule [ˌmɪsˈruːl] (A) N desgobierno *m*, mal gobierno *m*
(B) VT desgobernar, gobernar mal

miss¹ [mɪs] (A) N [1] [*of shot*] fallo *m*; **he scored three hits and two ~es** tuvo tres lanzamientos acertados y dos fallos, acertó tres tiros y falló dos; **he had two bad ~es in the first half** falló dos tiros fáciles en el primer tiempo; ✦*PROV* **a ~ is as good as a mile** lo mismo da librarse por poco que por mucho; *see also* **near C1**
[2] ✦*IDIOM* **to give sth a ~: you could give rehearsals a ~ for once** por una vez podrías faltar a los ensayos; **I'll give the wine a ~ this evening** esta noche no tomaré vino
(B) VT [1] (= *fail to hit*) [+ *target*] no dar en; **the arrow ~ed the target** la flecha no dio en el blanco; **the shot just ~ed me** la bala me pasó rozando; **the plane just ~ed the tower** faltó poco para que el avión chocara con la torre
[2] (= *escape, avoid*) evitar; **if we go that way we can ~ Burgos** si tomamos esa ruta podemos evitarnos pasar por Burgos; **it seems we ~ed the bad weather** parece que nos hemos escapado del mal tiempo; **he narrowly ~ed being run over** por poco lo atropellan, faltó poco para que lo atropellaran
[3] (= *fail to find, take, use etc*) [+ *aim, shot*] fallar; [+ *bus, train, plane, flight*] perder; [+ *opportunity, chance*] dejar pasar, perder; [+ *meeting, class, appointment*] faltar a, no asistir a; [+ *film, match*] perderse; **I ~ed the meeting last week** falté a *or* no asistí a la reunión la semana pasada; **I haven't ~ed a rehearsal in five years** no he faltado a un ensayo en cinco años, no me he perdido un solo ensayo en cinco años; **don't ~ this film** no te pierdas *or* no dejes de ver esta película; **we ~ed our lunch because we were late** nos quedamos sin comer porque llegamos tarde; **she ~ed her holiday last year** el año pasado no pudo tomarse las vacaciones; **you haven't ~ed much!** ¡no te has perdido mucho!; **I ~ed you at the station** no te vi en la estación; **I ~ed you by five minutes** si hubiera llegado cinco minutos antes te hubiera visto, si hubiera llegado cinco minutos antes te hubiera cogido (*Sp**); **they ~ed each other in the crowd** no lograron encontrarse entre tanta gente; **to ~ one's cue** (*Theat*) entrar a destiempo; **we ~ed the tide** nos perdimos la pleamar; **to ~ one's vocation** equivocarse de vocación; **to ~ one's way** equivocarse de camino; ✦*IDIOM* **to ~ the boat** *or* **bus*** perder el tren (*fig*)
[4] (= *skip*) [+ *meal*] saltarse; **I think you've ~ed a page** creo que te has saltado una página; **my heart ~ed a beat** me dio un vuelco el corazón
[5] (= *overlook*) **you've ~ed that bit in the corner** se te ha pasado por alto ese trozo en la esquina; **you ~ed our anniversary again** se te volvió a olvidar *or* pasar nuestro aniversario
[6] (= *fail to understand*) no entender, no coger (*Sp*); **she seems to have ~ed the joke** parece que no ha entendido *or* cogido el chiste; **you're ~ing the point** no lo entiendes
[7] (= *fail to hear, see*) **I ~ed what you said** no he oído lo que has dicho; **you don't ~ much do you?** no se te escapa nada ¿verdad?; **you can't ~ the house** la casa no tiene pérdida; **I ~ed the step and fell flat on my face** no vi el escalón y me caí de bruces; **he ~ed the turning** se pasó de cruce; *see also* **trick A2**
[8] (= *long for*) echar de menos, extrañar (*esp LAm*); **I ~ you so (much)** te echo tanto de menos, te extraño tanto; **they're ~ing one another** se echan de menos *or* se extrañan; **he won't be (much) ~ed** no se le echará de menos *or* no se le echará en falta que digamos; **I ~ having a garden** echo de menos tener un jardín
[9] (= *notice absence of*) echar en falta; **then I ~ed my wallet** entonces eché en falta la cartera; **we're ~ing eight dollars** nos faltan ocho dólares
(C) VI [1] (= *not hit*) [*shot*] errar el blanco; [*person*] fallar, errar el tiro; **you can't ~!** ¡es imposible fallar!, ¡es imposible errar el tiro!
[2] (= *not function properly*) [*motor*] fallar
[3] (= *not attend*) faltar; **I've not ~ed once in ten years** en diez años no he faltado ni una sola vez

►**miss out** (A) VT + ADV (*esp Brit*) [+ *word, line, page*] saltarse; **tell me if I ~ anybody out** decidme si me salto a algn; **he was ~ed out in the promotions** en los ascensos le pasaron por encima
(B) VI + ADV **I'm glad you can come, I wouldn't want you to ~ out** me alegro de que puedas venir, no quisiera que te lo perdieras; **don't ~ out, order your copy today** no se lo pierda, pida su ejemplar hoy

►**miss out on** VI + PREP [+ *opportunity*] dejar pasar, perder; **he ~ed out on several good deals** dejó pasar varias ocasiones buenas; **did you think you were ~ing out on something?** ¿creías que te estabas perdiendo algo?

miss² [mɪs] N señorita *f*; (*in address*) Srta.; **Miss Peters wants to see you** la señorita Peters quiere verte; **the Misses Smith**† las señoritas Smith; **Miss Spain** Miss España; **a modern ~** una señorita moderna; **she's a cheeky little ~!** ¡es una niña muy creidita!; → MR, MRS, MISS

Miss. ABBR (*US*) = **Mississippi**

missal [ˈmɪsəl] N misal *m*

misshapen [ˌmɪsˈʃeɪpən] ADJ deforme

missile [ˈmɪsaɪl] (A) N [1] (*Mil*) misil *m*; **guided ~** misil teledirigido
[2] (= *object thrown*) proyectil *m*
(B) CPD ► **missile launcher** N lanzamisiles *m inv*

missing [ˈmɪsɪŋ] (A) ADJ [1] (= *lost*) [*object*] perdido; [*child, cat*] desaparecido, extraviado; [*fisherman, explorer*] desaparecido; **some companies help with ~ luggage** algunas compañías te ayudan cuando se te pierde *or* extravía equipaje; **an important document was found to be ~** se descubrió que faltaba un importante documento; **to go ~** desaparecer
[2] (*Mil*) [*soldier, plane*] desaparecido; **~ (and) presumed dead** desaparecido y dado por muerto; **~ in action** desaparecido en combate; **reported ~** declarado como desaparecido
[3] (= *lacking*) [*piece, button, tooth*] que falta; **fill in the ~ words** complete las palabras que faltan; **to be ~** faltar; **two pieces are ~** faltan dos piezas; **your shirt has a button ~** te falta un botón en la camisa
(B) CPD ► **the missing link** N (*Anthropology, Zool*) el eslabón perdido; (= *detail*) la pieza que faltaba ► **missing person** N desaparecido/a *m/f*; **I want to report a ~ person** quiero denunciar una desaparición

mission [ˈmɪʃən] (A) N [1] (= *duty, purpose etc*) misión *f*; **it's her ~ in life** es su misión en la vida; **to send sb on a secret ~** enviar a algn en misión secreta
[2] (= *people on mission*) misión *f*
[3] (*Rel*) (= *building*) misión *f*
(B) CPD ► **mission control** N centro *m* de control ► **mission controller** N controlador(a) *m/f* de (la) misión ► **mission statement** N (*Comm, Ind*) (*of a business*) declaración *f* de objetivos; (*of an organization*) declaración *f* de intenciones

missionary [ˈmɪʃənrɪ] (A) N (*Rel*) misionero/a *m/f*
(B) CPD ► **missionary position** N (*hum*) postura *f* del misionero ► **missionary society** N sociedad *f* misionera ► **missionary zeal** N fervor *m* apostólico

missis* [ˈmɪsɪz] N **my ~** ◊ **the ~** mi mujer, la parienta (*Sp**), la patrona (*S. Cone**); **John and his ~** John y su mujer; **is the ~ in?** ¿está la señora?

Mississippi [ˌmɪsɪˈsɪpɪ] N Misisipí *m*

missive [ˈmɪsɪv] N misiva *f*

Missouri [mɪˈzʊərɪ] N Misuri *m*

misspell [ˌmɪsˈspel] (*pt, pp* **misspelled, misspelt**) VT escribir mal

misspelling [ˌmɪsˈspelɪŋ] N error *m* de ortografía

misspend [ˌmɪsˈspend] (*pt, pp* **misspent**) VT malgastar, desperdiciar

misspent [ˌmɪsˈspent] ADJ **a ~ youth** una juventud malgastada *or* desperdiciada

misstate [ˌmɪsˈsteɪt] VT declarar erróneamente; (*deliberately*) declarar falsamente

misstatement [ˌmɪsˈsteɪtmənt] N declaración *f* errónea; (*deliberate*) declaración *f* falsa

missus* [ˈmɪsɪz] N = **missis**

missy* [ˈmɪsɪ] N (*hum or pej*) = **miss²**

mist [mɪst] (A) N neblina *f*; (= *rain*) llovizna *f*, garúa *f* (*LAm*); (*at sea*) bruma *f*; (*in liquid*) nube *f*; (*on glass etc*) vaho *m*; **through a ~ of tears** (*fig*) a través de un velo de lágrimas; **lost in the ~s of time** (*liter*) perdido en la noche de los tiempos
(B) VI (*also* **~ over, ~ up**) [*scene, landscape*] nublarse; [*mirror, window*] empañarse; [*eyes*] llenarse de lágrimas

mistakable [mɪsˈteɪkəbl] ADJ confundible

▼**mistake** [mɪsˈteɪk] (*vb: pt* **mistook**; *pp* **mistaken**) (A) N [1] error *m*; **there must be some ~** debe de haber algún error; **by ~: he has been arrested by ~** lo detuvieron por error *or* equivocación; **he fired the gun by ~** disparó la pistola sin querer; **he took my hat in ~ for his** confundió mi sombrero con el suyo; **to make a ~** (*gen*) cometer un error; (= *be mistaken*) equivocarse; **they made the ~ of asking too much** cometieron el error de pedir demasiado; **the doctor must have made a ~** el médico debe de haberse equivocado; **make no ~ about it** ◊ **let there be no ~ about it** y que no quepa la menor duda; **my ~!** ¡la culpa es mía!, es culpa mía; **she's pretty and no ~*** es guapa de verdad *or* con ganas*
[2] (*in piece of work*) error *m*, fallo *m*; **his essay was full of ~s** su trabajo estaba lleno de errores *or* fallos; **if you make a ~, start again** si te equivocas, vuelve a empezar; **spelling ~** falta *f* de ortografía
(B) VT [1] (= *misunderstand*) [+ *meaning, remark*] malinterpretar; **I'm sorry, I mistook your meaning** perdón, te malinterpreté *or* no te entendí bien; **there was no mistaking his intention** su intención estaba clarísima
[2] (= *mix up, confuse*) [+ *time, road*] equivocarse de; **I mistook the turning to your house** me equivoqué al torcer para ir a tu casa; **to ~**

➤ LANGUAGE IN USE: mistake A1 26.3

sth/sb for sth/sb confundir algo/a algn con algo/algn; **he is often ~n for Peter** se le confunde muchas veces con Peter; **she mistook his attention for interest** erróneamente, interpretó su atención como interés; **she could easily be ~n for a boy** se la podría confundir fácilmente con un chico; **there's no mistaking her voice** su voz es inconfundible

mistaken [mɪs'teɪkən] Ⓐ PP *of* **mistake**
Ⓑ ADJ [*belief, idea*] equivocado, falso; **in the ~ belief that ...** creyendo, equivocadamente *or* erróneamente, que ...; **to be ~** equivocarse, estar equivocado; **you must be ~** debes de estar equivocado; **if I'm not ~** si no me equivoco, a no ser que me equivoque; **unless I'm very much ~** si no me equivoco, o mucho me equivoco o ...; **unless I'm very much ~, that's him** si no me equivoco, ése es él, o mucho me equivoco o es él; **I see I was ~ about you** veo que me equivoqué contigo; **he was ~ in his belief that he was irreplaceable** se equivocaba *or* estaba equivocado al creer que era irreemplazable; **~ identity** identificación *f* errónea

mistakenly [mɪs'teɪkənlɪ] ADV 1 (= *wrongly*) [*believe, assume*] equivocadamente, erróneamente
2 (= *accidentally*) por equivocación, por error

mister ['mɪstəʳ] N 1 (*gen abbr Mr*) señor *m* (*gen abbr Sr.*)
2 (*in direct address*) **hey, ~!** ¡oiga, usted!

mistime [mɪs'taɪm] VT **to ~ sth** hacer algo a destiempo

mistiming [,mɪs'taɪmɪŋ] N **the ~ of his statement was spectacular** la inoportunidad de su declaración fue monumental; **the ~ of the attack** la inoportunidad del momento del ataque

mistle thrush ['mɪslθrʌʃ] N zorzal *m* charlo, tordo *m* mayor

mistletoe ['mɪsltəʊ] N muérdago *m*

mistook [mɪs'tʊk] PT *of* **mistake**

mistral [mɪ'strɑːl] N mistral *m*

mistranslate [,mɪstræns'leɪt] VT traducir mal

mistranslation [,mɪstræns'leɪʃən] N mala traducción *f*

mistreat [mɪs'triːt] VT maltratar

mistreatment [mɪs'triːtmənt] N maltrato *m*, malos tratos *mpl*

mistress ['mɪstrɪs] N 1 [*of household, servant*] señora *f*, ama *f*; **to be one's own ~** ser independiente; **to be ~ of the situation** ser dueña de la situación
2 (= *lover*) amante *f*, querida *f*, amasia *f* (*Mex*)
3 (*Brit*†) (= *teacher*) (*in primary school*) maestra *f*; (*in secondary school*) profesora *f*; **our English ~** nuestra profesora de inglés
4 (††) (= *Mrs*) señora *f* de ...

mistrial [,mɪs'traɪəl] N (*US, Brit*) (*invalidated*) juicio *m* viciado de nulidad; (*US*) (*inconclusive*) juicio *m* nulo por desacuerdo del jurado

mistrust [,mɪs'trʌst] Ⓐ N desconfianza *f*
Ⓑ VT desconfiar de

mistrustful [,mɪs'trʌstfʊl] ADJ desconfiado, receloso; **to be ~ of sth/sb** desconfiar de algo/algn

misty ['mɪstɪ] ADJ (*compar* **mistier**; *superl* **mistiest**) [*day, morning*] neblinoso; [*valley, shore*] cubierto de neblina; [*mirror, window*] empañado; [*memories*] vago; [*outline*] borroso, difuso; [*eyes*] empañado, lloroso; **it is ~** (*Met*) hay neblina; (*US*) está lloviznando

misty-eyed ['mɪstɪ,aɪd] ADJ sentimental

misunderstand [,mɪsʌndə'stænd] (*pt, pp* **misunderstood**) VT entender mal; **sorry, I misunderstood you** lo siento, te entendí mal, lo siento, malinterpreté tus palabras; **don't ~ me** entiéndeme, no me entiendas mal

misunderstanding [,mɪsʌndə'stændɪŋ] N (= *confusion*) malentendido *m*; (= *mistake*) equivocación *f*; (= *disagreement*) desacuerdo *m*; **there must be some ~** (= *confusion*) debe de haber algún malentendido; (= *mistake*) debe de haber alguna equivocación

misunderstood [,mɪsʌndə'stʊd] Ⓐ PT, PP *of* **misunderstand**
Ⓑ ADJ incomprendido

misuse [,mɪs'juːs] Ⓐ N [*of power, drug*] abuso *m*; [*of machine*] mal uso *m or* manejo *m*; [*of word, language*] uso *m* incorrecto; [*of funds*] malversación *f*
Ⓑ [,mɪs'juːz] VT [+ *power, drug*] abusar de; [+ *machine*] usar *or* manejar mal; [+ *word, language*] utilizar *or* emplear mal; [+ *funds*] malversar

MIT N ABBR (*US*) = **Massachusetts Institute of Technology**

mite[1] [maɪt] N (= *insect*) ácaro *m*, acárido *m*

mite[2] [maɪt] N 1 (= *small quantity*) pizca *f*; **a ~ of consolation** una pizca de consuelo; **there's not a ~ left** (*scrap*) no queda ni pizca; (*drop*) no queda ni una sola gota; **well, just a ~ then** bueno, un poquitín; **we were a ~ surprised** nos quedamos un tanto sorprendidos
2 (= *child*) chiquillo/a *m/f*, criatura *f*; **poor little ~!** ¡pobrecito!
3 (= *coin*) ardite *m*; (*as contribution*) óbolo *m*

miter ['maɪtəʳ] N (*US*) = **mitre**

Mithraic [mɪθ'reɪɪk] ADJ mitraico

Mithraism ['mɪθreɪɪzəm] N mitraísmo *m*

Mithras ['mɪθræs] N Mitra

mitigate ['mɪtɪgeɪt] VT aliviar, mitigar; **mitigating circumstances** circunstancias *fpl* atenuantes

mitigation [,mɪtɪ'geɪʃən] N mitigación *f*, alivio *m*; **to say a word in ~** decir algo en descargo

mitre, **miter** (*US*) ['maɪtəʳ] Ⓐ N 1 (*Rel*) mitra *f*
2 (*Tech*) (*also* **~ joint**) inglete *m*, ensambladura *f* de inglete
Ⓑ VT (*Tech*) ingletear
Ⓒ CPD ► **mitre box** N caja *f* de ingletes ► **mitre joint** N inglete *m*, ensambladura *f* de inglete

mitt [mɪt] N 1 (*glove*) mitón *m*
2 (= *baseball glove*) guante *m* de béisbol
3 (*) (= *hand*) zarpa* *f*; **get your ~s off my dictionary!** ¡quita tus zarpas de mi diccionario!*; **keep your ~s off my sweets!** ¡no se te ocurra poner tus zarpas en mis caramelos!*

mitten ['mɪtn] N 1 (= *glove*) mitón *m*, manopla *f*
2 (*Boxing*) guante *mpl* de boxeo

mix [mɪks] Ⓐ VT 1 [+ *ingredients, colours, liquids*] mezclar; [+ *concrete, plaster, cocktail*] preparar; [+ *salad*] remover; **~ all the ingredients together** mezcle todos los ingredientes; **never ~ your drinks!** ¡no mezcle nunca bebidas!; **~ the eggs into the sugar** añada los huevos al azúcar y mézclelos; **to ~ and match sth** combinar algo; **~ to a smooth paste** mezcle hasta que se forme una pasta sin grumos; **to ~ sth with *or* and sth** mezclar algo con algo; **~ the cinnamon with the sugar** mezcle la canela con el azúcar; **to ~ business and *or* with pleasure** mezclar los negocios con el placer; ✦*IDIOM* **to ~ it (with sb)** (*Brit**) buscar camorra (con algn)*
2 [+ *recording, sound*] mezclar
Ⓑ VI 1 [*things*] 1·1 (= *combine*) mezclarse; **oil and water don't ~** el aceite y el agua no se mezclan; **politics and sport don't ~** la política y el deporte no hacen buena combinación
1·2 (= *go together well*) [*colours*] combinar (bien), pegar
2 [*people*] (= *socialize*) alternar; **to ~ in high society** alternar con la alta sociedad; **she ~es with all kinds of people** se mezcla con toda clase de gente
Ⓒ N 1 (= *combination*) mezcla *f*; **there was a good ~ of people at the party** había una mezcla variada *or* una buena variedad de gente en la fiesta
2 (= *ingredients*) mezcla *f*; (*commercially prepared*) preparado *m*; **a cake ~** un preparado para pasteles
3 [*of recording, sound*] mezcla *f*

► **mix in** VT + ADV (= *add*) [+ *ingredients*] añadir; (= *intersperse*) mezclar; **pieces of grit ~ed in with the rice** piedrecitas mezcladas con el arroz

► **mix up** VT + ADV 1 (= *prepare*) [+ *paint, paste*] preparar
2 (= *combine*) [+ *ingredients*] mezclar
3 (= *jumble up*) mezclar; **don't ~ up your clothes with mine** no mezcles tu ropa con la mía; **the letter got ~ed up with my things** la carta se mezcló con mis cosas
4 (= *confuse*) [+ *person*] confundir; **you've got me all ~ed up** me has confundido, me has hecho un lío*
5 (= *mistake*) [+ *names, dates, person*] confundir; **she tends to ~ up her words** tiende a equivocar las palabras al hablar; **we got the dates ~ed up** confundimos las fechas; **I'm ~ing you up with somebody else** te estoy confundiendo con otra persona
6 (= *involve*) **to be/get ~ed up in sth** estar metido/meterse en algo; **are you ~ed up in this?** ¿tú andas metido en esto?, ¿tú tienes que ver con esto?; **how could David be ~ed up in a murder?** ¿cómo puede David estar involucrado en un asesinato?; **he's got ~ed up with a bad crowd** se ha mezclado con mala gente, anda con malas compañías; **why did I ever get ~ed up with you?** ¿cómo acabé relacionándome contigo?, ¿cómo acabé liada contigo?*; **to ~ sb up in sth** meter *or* mezclar a algn en algo
7 ✦*IDIOM* **to ~ it up (with sb)** (*US**) (= *cause trouble*) buscar camorra (con algn)*

mixed [mɪkst] Ⓐ ADJ 1 (= *varied*) [*selection*] variado; (= *assorted*) [*biscuits, sweets, vegetables*] surtido, variado; **a ~ crowd turned up** apareció un grupo muy variopinto, apareció un grupo con gente de todo tipo; ✦*IDIOMS* **a ~ bag*** (= *some good, some bad*) un poco de todo, una mezcla de todo; (= *with good variety*) una gran variedad; **a ~ bunch*** un grupo variopinto, un batiburrillo de gente; **my class were a ~ bunch** mi clase era un grupo variopinto
2 (= *both good and bad*) [*reviews, reactions*] diverso; **to be a ~ blessing** tener su lado bueno y su lado malo; **~ feelings** sentimientos *mpl* encontrados; **to have ~ feelings about sth** no tener muy claro algo, tener sus dudas acerca de algo; **the government's proposals have had a ~ reception** las propuestas del gobierno han sido recibidas con reservas *or* han tenido una acogida desigual; **with ~ results** con resultados desiguales *or* diversos; **we had ~ weather** el tiempo fue variable
3 (= *of different races*) [*parentage, marriage*] mixto; **of ~ race** mestizo
4 (= *for both sexes*) [*school, education, bathing*] mixto; **in ~ company** con personas de ambos

sexos; **I wouldn't say it in ~ company** no lo diría delante de personas del otro sexo
Ⓑ CPD ► **mixed ability class** N clase *f* con niveles de aptitud distintos ► **mixed doubles** NPL (*Sport*) (dobles *mpl*) mixtos *mpl* ► **mixed economy** N economía *f* mixta ► **mixed farming** N agricultura *f* mixta ► **mixed fruit** N frutas *fpl* surtidas ► **mixed grill** N (*Brit*) parrillada *f* mixta ► **mixed herbs** NPL surtido *m* de hierbas ► **mixed marriage** N matrimonio *m* mixto (*de esposos de religión o raza distintas*) ► **mixed metaphor** N metáfora *f* disparada ► **mixed salad** N ensalada *f* mixta ► **mixed spice** N mezcla *f* de especias

mixed-up ['mɪkst'ʌp] ADJ [*person, idea*] confuso; [*things*] revuelto; **he's very ~** (= *disturbed*) es una persona con problemas (psicológicos); (= *confused*) está muy confuso; *see also* **mix up**

mixer ['mɪksəʳ] Ⓐ N [1] (*Culin*) batidora *f*
[2] (= *cement mixer*) hormigonera *f*
[3] (*Rad*) mezclador(a) *m/f*
[4] (= *sociable person*) **he's a good ~** tiene don de gentes; **he's not much of a ~** no le gusta alternar, no tiene don de gentes
[5] (= *drink*) refresco *m* (*para mezclar con licores*)
[6] (*US Univ*) fiesta *f* de bienvenida para nuevos estudiantes
Ⓑ CPD ► **mixer tap** N (*Brit*) (grifo *m*) monobloque *m*

mixing bowl ['mɪksɪŋbəʊl] N cuenco *m* grande

mixture ['mɪkstʃəʳ] N (*gen, Culin*) mezcla *f*; (*Med*) preparado *m*, compuesto *m*; **the ~ as before** la misma receta que antes; (*fig*) lo de siempre; *see also* **cough C**

mix-up ['mɪks'ʌp] N lío *m*, confusión *f*; **there was a ~ over the tickets** hubo un lío *or* una confusión con las entradas; **we got in a ~ with the trains** nos hicimos un lío con los trenes

mizzen ['mɪzn] N mesana *f*

mizzenmast ['mɪznmɑːst] N palo *m* de mesana

mizzle* ['mɪzl] (*also dial*) VI lloviznar

Mk, mk ABBR (= **mark**) Mk

mkt ABBR = **market**

ml ABBR (= **millilitre(s)**) ml

MLA N ABBR (*Brit Pol*) (= **Member of the Legislative Assembly**) *miembro de la asamblea legislativa*

MLitt [em'lɪt] N ABBR (*Univ*) [1] = **Master of Literature** [2] = **Master of Letters**

MLR N ABBR = **minimum lending rate**

MLS N ABBR [1] (*St Ex*) = **multiple listing system**
[2] (*US Univ*) (= **Master of Library Science**) *título de bibliotecario*

M'lud [mə'lʌd] N ABBR (*Brit Jur*) = **My Lord**

MM ABBR (= **Messieurs**) Srs., Sres.

mm ABBR (= **millimetre(s)**) mm

mm... [mm] EXCL esto ..., pues ..., vamos a ver ...

MMC N ABBR (*Brit*) = **Monopolies and Mergers Commission**

MME N ABBR (*US Univ*) [1] = **Master of Mechanical Engineering**
[2] = **Master of Mining Engineering**

MMR vaccine [ˌememˈɑːˌvæksiːn] N (*against measles, mumps, rubella*) vacuna *f* triple vírica

MN Ⓐ N ABBR (*Brit*) = **Merchant Navy**
Ⓑ ABBR (*US*) = **Minnesota**

mnemonic [nɪ'mɒnɪk] Ⓐ ADJ mnemotécnico, nemotécnico
Ⓑ N *figura o frase etc mnemotécnica*

mnemonics [nɪ'mɒnɪks] NSING mnemotécnica *f*, nemotécnica *f*

MO Ⓐ N ABBR = **medical officer**
Ⓑ ABBR [1] (*US*) = **Missouri**
[2] (*esp US**) (= **modus operandi**) *manera de actuar*

mo'* [məʊ] N ABBR = **moment**

mo ABBR (= **month**) m.

Mo. ABBR = **Missouri**

m.o. ABBR (= **money order**) g.p., g/

moan [məʊn] Ⓐ N [1] (= *groan*) [*of person, wind, trees*] gemido *m*
[2] (= *complaint*) queja *f*
Ⓑ VI [1] (= *groan*) gemir
[2] (= *complain*) quejarse; **they're ~ing about the food again** han vuelto a quejarse de la comida; **she's always ~ing about something** siempre se está quejando de algo
Ⓒ VT [1] (= *groan*) decir gimiendo, decir con un gemido
[2] (= *complain*) **"why does it always have to be me?" he ~ed** —¿por qué siempre me toca a mí? —se quejó

moaner* ['məʊnəʳ] N protestón/ona* *m/f*

moaning ['məʊnɪŋ] N [1] (= *groans*) gemidos *mpl*
[2] (= *complaints*) quejas *fpl*, protestas *fpl*

moat [məʊt] N foso *m*

moated ['məʊtɪd] ADJ con foso, rodeado de un foso

mob [mɒb] Ⓐ N [1] (= *crowd*) multitud *f*, muchedumbre *f*, bola *f* (*Mex*); (= *rabble*) populacho *m*, turba *f* (*esp LAm*); **some houses were burnt by the ~s** unas casas fueron incendiadas por el populacho; **the army has become a ~** el ejército se ha transformado en una turba incontrolada; **they went in a ~ to the town hall** fueron en tropel al ayuntamiento; **to join the ~** echarse a las calles; **they're a hard-drinking ~** son una pandilla de borrachos
[2] **the ~** (*pej*) (= *the masses*) el populacho
[3] (*) (= *criminal gang*) pandilla *f*; **Joe and his ~** Joe y su pandilla; **the Mob** (*US*) la Mafia
[4] (*Mil*) **which ~ were you in?** ¿en qué regimiento estuviste?
Ⓑ VT [1] (= *attack*) asaltar
[2] (= *surround*) **he was ~bed whenever he went out** al salir siempre se veía acosado por la gente; **the minister was ~bed by journalists** los periodistas se apiñaban en torno al ministro
Ⓒ CPD ► **mob oratory** N demagogia *f* populachera ► **mob rule** N ley *f* de la calle

mobcap ['mɒbkæp] N cofia *f*

mob-handed* [ˌmɒb'hændɪd] ADV en masa, en tropel, con mogollón de gente (*Sp**)

mobile ['məʊbaɪl] Ⓐ ADJ (= *movable*) [*theatre, shop*] ambulante; [*missile launcher*] portátil, transportable; [*workforce*] que tiene movilidad; [*society*] con movilidad; (= *expressive*) [*face, features*] expresivo; **I'm still very ~** todavía me muevo bastante; **now that we're ~*** ahora que tenemos coche, ahora que estamos motorizados*; *see also* **upwardly**
Ⓑ N [1] (*Art*) móvil *m*
[2] (*) (= *mobile phone*) móvil* *m*, teléfono *m* celular (*LAm*)
Ⓒ CPD ► **mobile home** N caravana *f*, casa *f* rodante (*S. Cone, Ven*) ► **mobile library** N biblioteca *f* ambulante, bibliobús *m* ► **mobile phone** N teléfono *m* móvil, teléfono *m* celular (*LAm*) ► **mobile unit** N unidad *f* móvil

mobility [məʊ'bɪlɪtɪ] Ⓐ N [*of person, joint, society*] movilidad *f*; [*of face, features*] expresividad *f*; **~ of labour** movilidad *f* de la mano de obra; **social ~** movilidad *f* social
Ⓑ CPD ► **mobility allowance** N (*Brit*) *subsidio que reciben ciertos minusválidos para cubrir sus gastos de desplazamiento*; *see also* **upward A**

mobilization [ˌməʊbɪlaɪ'zeɪʃən] N movilización *f*

mobilize ['məʊbɪlaɪz] Ⓐ VT movilizar
Ⓑ VI movilizarse

mobster* ['mɒbstəʳ] N (*US*) gángster *m*, pandillero *m*

moccasin ['mɒkəsɪn] N mocasín *m*

mocha ['mɒkə] N moca *m*

mock [mɒk] Ⓐ VT (= *ridicule*) mofarse de, burlarse de; (= *mimic*) imitar, remedar; **you shouldn't ~ other people's beliefs** no hay que mofarse *or* burlarse de las creencias de la gente
Ⓑ VI mofarse, burlarse; **to ~ at sth/sb** mofarse de algo/algn, burlarse de algo/algn
Ⓒ ADJ (= *feigned*) [*solemnity, terror*] fingido, simulado; (= *imitation*) [*leather, fur*] de imitación; **in ~ despair** fingiendo desesperación; **in ~ horror** fingiendo estar horrorizado
Ⓓ N [1] **to make a ~ of sth** poner algo en ridículo
[2] **mocks** (*Brit Scol**) exámenes *mpl* de prueba
Ⓔ CPD ► **mock battle** N simulacro *m* (de batalla) ► **mock exam** N examen *m* de prueba ► **mock orange** N (*Bot*) jeringuilla *f*, celinda *f* ► **mock trial** N juicio *m* de prueba

mocker ['mɒkəʳ] N [1] (= *scoffer*) mofador(a) *m/f*
[2] ✦*IDIOM* **to put the ~s on sth** dar al traste con algo; **to put the ~s on sb‡** hacer que algn fracase

mockery ['mɒkərɪ] N [1] (= *derision*) burla *f*, mofa *f*
[2] (= *farce*) **this is a ~ of justice** esto es una negación de la justicia; **it was a ~ of a trial** fue un simulacro de juicio; **to make a ~ of sth** poner algo en ridículo

mock-heroic ['mɒkhɪ'rəʊɪk] ADJ heroicoburlesco

mocking ['mɒkɪŋ] Ⓐ ADJ burlón, socarrón
Ⓑ N burlas *fpl*

mockingbird ['mɒkɪŋbɜːd] N sinsonte *m*, zenzontle *m* (*LAm*)

mockingly ['mɒkɪŋlɪ] ADV [*say*] en tono burlón, con sorna; [*smile, look*] burlonamente, con sorna

mock-up ['mɒkʌp] N maqueta *f*, modelo *m* a escala

MOD N ABBR (*Brit*) (= **Ministry of Defence**) ≈ Min. de D.

modal ['məʊdl] ADJ modal

modality [məʊ'dælɪtɪ] N modalidad *f*

mod cons* [ˌmɒd'kɒnz] NPL = **modern conveniences**

mode [məʊd] N [1] (= *way, manner*) manera *f*, modo *m*
[2] (= *fashion*) moda *f*
[3] (*Comput*) función *f*, modalidad *f*

model ['mɒdl] Ⓐ N [1] (= *small-scale representation*) modelo *m* a escala, maqueta *f*
[2] (= *example*) modelo *m*; **to hold sth/sb up as a ~** presentar algo/a algn como modelo (a seguir); **a tribunal is to be set up on the ~ of Nuremberg** se constituirá un tribunal según el modelo de *or* a la manera del de Nuremberg
[3] (= *paragon*) modelo *m*; **he is a ~ of good behaviour/patience** es un modelo de buen comportamiento/paciencia
[4] (= *person*) (*Art*) modelo *mf*; (*Fashion*) modelo *mf*, maniquí *mf*

5 (*Comm*) (= *design*) modelo *m*
B ADJ 1 (= *miniature*) [*railway, village*] en miniatura, a escala; **~ aeroplane** aeromodelo *m*
2 (= *prototype*) [*home*] piloto
3 (= *perfect*) modelo *inv*; **a ~ husband/wife** un marido/una esposa modelo
C VT 1 **to ~ sth on sth: their new socialist state is ~led on that of China** su nuevo estado socialista toma como modelo el de China; **the gardens are ~led on those at Versailles** los jardines están inspirados en los de Versalles; **to ~ o.s. on sb** tomar a algn como modelo; **children usually ~ themselves on their parents** los niños normalmente toman como modelo a sus padres; **he ~s himself on James Dean** imita a James Dean, su modelo a imitar es James Dean
2 (*Art*) modelar
3 (*Fashion*) **Jane is ~ling a design by Valentino** Jane luce un modelo de Valentino; **her daughter ~s children's clothes** su hija es modelo de ropa de niños
D VI 1 (*Art*) (= *make models*) modelar
2 (*Phot, Art*) posar; (*Fashion*) ser modelo, trabajar de modelo

modeller, modeler (*US*) ['mɒdləʳ] N modelador(a) *m/f*

modelling, modeling (*US*) ['mɒdlɪŋ] A N 1 (= *making models*) (*by shaping*) modelado *m*; (*by building*) modelismo *m*, construcción *f* de maquetas
2 (= *modelling clothes*) profesión *f* de modelo; **my daughter does ~** mi hija es modelo
B CPD ► **modelling clay** N plastilina® *f*

modem ['məʊdem] N módem *m*

moderate A ['mɒdərɪt] ADJ 1 (= *not excessive*) [*amount, speed, wind, heat, success*] moderado; [*price*] módico; [*ability*] regular, mediano; [*improvement, achievement*] regular; **bake the fish in a ~ oven** hacer el pescado al horno a una temperatura moderada; **she is a ~ drinker** bebe con moderación
2 (*Pol*) (= *not extreme*) [*leader, views, policies*] moderado
B ['mɒdərɪt] N (*Pol*) moderado/a *m/f*
C ['mɒdəreɪt] VT 1 (= *adjust*) [+ *speed, behaviour, language, temperature*] moderar; [+ *anger*] aplacar
2 (= *reduce*) [+ *one's demands*] moderar
3 (= *act as moderator for*) [+ *discussion, debate*] moderar
D ['mɒdəreɪt] VI 1 [*weather*] moderarse; [*anger*] aplacarse; [*wind, storm*] amainar, calmarse
2 (= *arbitrate*) moderar, hacer de moderador

moderately ['mɒdərɪtlɪ] ADV [*good, wealthy*] medianamente; [*drink, eat*] con moderación; **he was a ~ successful actor** fue un actor de cierto *or* relativo éxito; **she did ~ well in her exams** los exámenes le salieron medianamente bien; **~ priced** de precio módico

moderation [ˌmɒdə'reɪʃən] N moderación *f*; **in ~** con moderación

moderator ['mɒdəreɪtəʳ] N 1 (*Brit Univ*) árbitro *mf*, asesor(a) *m/f*
2 **Moderator** (*Rel*) *presidente de la asamblea de la Iglesia Presbiteriana Escocesa y de otras iglesias protestantes*;
→ CHURCHES OF ENGLAND/SCOTLAND

modern ['mɒdən] A ADJ moderno; **"all modern conveniences"** "todo confort"
B CPD ► **modern art** N arte *m* moderno ► **modern history** N historia *f* contemporánea ► **modern languages** NPL (*esp Brit*) lenguas *fpl* modernas ► **modern literature** N literatura *f* contemporánea

modernism ['mɒdənɪzəm] N modernismo *m*

modernist ['mɒdənɪst] A ADJ modernista
B N modernista *mf*

modernistic [ˌmɒdə'nɪstɪk] ADJ modernista

modernity [mɒ'dɜːnɪtɪ] N modernidad *f*

modernization [ˌmɒdənaɪ'zeɪʃən] N modernización *f*

modernize ['mɒdənaɪz] A VT [+ *methods, system*] modernizar, actualizar; [+ *building*] modernizar
B VI modernizarse, actualizarse

modest ['mɒdɪst] ADJ 1 (= *humble*) modesto; **don't be so ~!** ¡no seas tan modesto!; **he's just being ~** está siendo modesto; **to be ~ about sth** ser modesto con algo
2 (= *small*) [*garden, income*] modesto, pequeño; [*amount, sum*] módico, modesto; [*increase, improvement, reform*] moderado; **on a ~ scale** a escala moderada
3 (= *chaste, proper*) [*person, clothes*] púdico, recatado

modestly ['mɒdɪstlɪ] ADV 1 (= *humbly*) modestamente
2 (= *moderately*) con moderación; **~ priced** de precio módico
3 (= *chastely*) pudorosamente, con pudor

modesty ['mɒdɪstɪ] N 1 (= *humbleness*) modestia *f*; **in all ~, I think I could do the job better** modestamente *or* con toda modestia, creo yo que podría hacer mejor el trabajo; **I can't tell you, ~ forbids** no puedo decírtelo, pecaría de poco modesto; *see also* **false A3**
2 (= *propriety*) pudor *m*, recato *m*

modicum ['mɒdɪkəm] N **a ~ of** un mínimo de

modification [ˌmɒdɪfɪ'keɪʃən] N modificación *f* (**to** de)

modifier ['mɒdɪfaɪəʳ] N modificante *m*

modify ['mɒdɪfaɪ] VT 1 (= *change*) modificar
2 (= *moderate*) moderar
3 (*Ling*) modificar

modifying ['mɒdɪfaɪɪŋ] A ADJ [*note, term, factor*] modificador, modificante
B N modificación *f*

modish ['məʊdɪʃ] ADJ muy de moda, sumamente elegante

modishly ['məʊdɪʃlɪ] ADV elegantemente; **to be ~ dressed** ir vestido con suma elegancia

modiste [məʊ'diːst] N modista *f*

Mods* [mɒdz] N ABBR (*at Oxford university*) (= **(Honour) Moderations**) *examen de la licenciatura de la universidad de Oxford*

modular ['mɒdjʊləʳ] A ADJ modular
B CPD ► **modular program(m)ing** N programación *f* modular

modularity [ˌmɒdjʊ'lærɪtɪ] N modularidad *f*

modulate ['mɒdjʊleɪt] VT (*Mus, Phys*) modular

modulated ['mɒdjʊleɪtɪd] ADJ modulado

modulation [ˌmɒdjʊ'leɪʃən] N (*Mus, Phys*) modulación *f*

module ['mɒdjuːl] N 1 (*Space*) módulo *m*
2 (*Brit Univ*) módulo *m*
3 (*Constr*) módulo *m*
4 (*Comput*) módulo *m*

modus operandi ['məʊdəsˌɒpə'rændiː] N modo *m* de proceder, modus operandi *m inv*

modus vivendi ['məʊdəsvɪ'vendiː] N modus *m* vivendi

Mogadishu [ˌmɒgə'dɪʃuː] N Mogadiscio *m*

moggy* ['mɒgɪ] N (*Brit*) gatito/a *m/f*, michino/a* *m/f*

mogul ['məʊgəl] N 1 (*Hist*) mo(n)gol(a) *m/f*; **the Great Mogul** el Gran Mogol
2 (*fig*) magnate *m*; **film ~** magnate *m* de la cinematografía

MOH N ABBR (*Brit*) = **Medical Officer of Health**

mohair ['məʊhɛəʳ] N mohair *m*

Mohammed [məʊ'hæmed] N Mahoma *m*

Mohammedan [məʊ'hæmɪdən] A ADJ mahometano
B N mahometano/a *m/f*

Mohammedanism [məʊ'hæmɪdənɪzəm] N mahometanismo *m*

Mohican [məʊ'hiːkən] N (*pl* **Mohicans** *or* **Mohican**) 1 (= *Native American*) mohicano/a *m/f*
2 (= *hairstyle*) cresta *f* mohicana

moiré ['mwaːreɪ] N muaré *m*

moist [mɔɪst] ADJ (*compar* **moister**; *superl* **moistest**) [*atmosphere, soil, cloth*] húmedo; [*cake*] esponjoso; **~ with sth** húmedo de algo; **his hands were ~ with perspiration** tenía las manos húmedas del sudor; **her eyes were ~ with tears** tenía los ojos llorosos

moisten ['mɔɪsn] A VT (= *wet*) humedecer, mojar; **to ~ one's lips** humedecerse los labios; **~ with olive oil** imprégnese de aceite de oliva
B VI humedecerse, mojarse

moistness ['mɔɪstnɪs] N = **moisture**

moisture ['mɔɪstʃəʳ] N (= *dampness*) humedad *f*; (*on glass, mirror*) vaho *m*

moisturize ['mɔɪstʃəraɪz] VT [+ *skin, face, hands*] hidratar

moisturizer ['mɔɪstʃəraɪzəʳ] N crema *f* hidratante

moisturizing cream ['mɔɪstʃəraɪzɪŋˌkriːm] N crema *f* hidratante

moke* [məʊk] N (*Brit*) burro *m*

molar ['məʊləʳ] N muela *f*

molasses [mə'læsɪz] NSING melaza *f*

mold *etc* [məʊld] (*US*) N = **mould**[1] *etc*

Moldavia [mɒl'deɪvɪə] N (*formerly*) Moldavia *f*

Moldavian [mɒl'deɪvɪən] (*formerly*) A ADJ moldavo
B N moldavo/a *m/f*

Moldova [mɒl'dəʊvə] N Moldova *f*

Moldovan [mɒl'dəʊvən] A ADJ moldavo
B N moldavo/a *m/f*

mole[1] [məʊl] N (*Anat*) lunar *m*

mole[2] [məʊl] N 1 (*Zool*) topo *m*
2 (*fig*) (= *spy*) topo *m*, espía *mf*

mole[3] [məʊl] N (*Naut*) espigón *m*, rompeolas *m inv*

molecular [mə'lekjʊləʳ] A ADJ (*Chem*) molecular
B CPD ► **molecular biology** N biología *f* molecular

molecule ['mɒlɪkjuːl] N (*Chem*) molécula *f*

molehill ['məʊlhɪl] N topera *f*; *see also* **mountain A**

moleskin ['məʊlskɪn] N piel *f* de topo

molest [məʊ'lest] VT 1 (*sexually*) (= *attack*) agredir sexualmente; (= *abuse*) abusar de
2 (= *bother*) importunar, molestar

molestation [ˌməʊles'teɪʃən] N 1 (= *sexual abuse*) abusos *mpl* sexuales, abusos *mpl* deshonestos
2 (= *trouble*) importunidad *f*

molester [mə'lestəʳ] N (*also* **child ~**) *persona que abusa sexualmente de niños*

moll* [mɒl] N **gangster's ~** compañera *f* de gángster

mollify ['mɒlɪfaɪ] VT aplacar, apaciguar; **he was somewhat mollified by this** esto lo aplacó *or* apaciguó un poco, con esto se calmó un poco

mollusc, mollusk (*US*) ['mɒləsk] N molusco *m*

mollycoddle ['mɒlɪkɒdl] VT mimar, sobreproteger

mollycoddling ['mɒlɪ,kɒdlɪŋ] N mimo *m*

Molotov cocktail [,mɒlətɒf'kɒkteɪl] N cóctel *m* Molotov

molt [məʊlt] VI, VT, N (*US*) = **moult**

molten ['məʊltən] ADJ fundido, derretido; [*lava*] líquido

molybdenum [mɒ'lɪbdɪnəm] N molibdeno *m*

mom* [mɒm] (*US*) Ⓐ N mamá* *f*
Ⓑ CPD ► **mom and pop store** N tienda *f* de la esquina, pequeño negocio *m*

moment ['məʊmənt] N 1 (*in time*) momento *m*; **a ~ ago** hace un momento; **they should be arriving any ~ (now)** deberían llegar ahorita (*LAm*) *or* de un momento a otro; **at the ~** en este momento; **I could lose my job at any ~** podría perder mi trabajo en cualquier momento; **at this/that ~** en este/ese momento, en este/ese instante; **at this ~ in time** en este mismo momento; **I shan't be a ~** (*on going out*) vuelvo en seguida, ahorita vuelvo (*LAm*); (*when busy*) termino en un momento, ahorita acabo (*LAm*); **for the ~** por el momento, por lo pronto; **he didn't hesitate for a ~** no vaciló ni un momento *or* instante; **not for a** *or* **one ~ did I believe it** no me lo creí ni por un momento; **I'm not saying for a ~ you're wrong** no digo que no tengas razón ni mucho menos; **not for a ~ did I think that ...** en ningún momento pensaba que ...; **from the ~ I saw him** desde el momento en que lo vi; **from ~ to ~** al momento; **from that ~ on** desde entonces, desde ese *or* aquel momento; **the play has its ~s** la obra tiene sus momentos; **yes, in a ~!** ¡sí en seguida!; **I'll come in a ~** vengo en seguida, vengo dentro de un momento; **it was all over in a ~** todo ocurrió en un instante; **in ~s, I was asleep** en seguida me quedé dormido; **just a ~!** ¡un momento!; **I've just this ~ heard** acabo de enterarme; **at the last ~** a última hora, en el último momento; **to leave things until the last ~** dejar las cosas hasta última hora, dejarlo todo para lo último; **a ~ later** un momento después, al rato; **the next ~ he collapsed** al instante se desplomó; **he was weeping one ~, laughing the next** tan pronto lloraba como se reía; **the man of the ~** el hombre del momento; **one ~!** ¡un momento!; **I was waiting for the right ~ to tell him** estaba esperando el momento adecuado *or* oportuno para decírselo; **it won't take a ~** no tardará ni un momento, es cosa de un momento; **tell me the ~ he arrives** avísame en cuanto llegue; **the ~ of truth** la hora de la verdad; **I did it in a ~ of weakness** lo hice en un momento de debilidad; *see also* **heat A2**, **live[1] A1**, **odd 2**, **psychological B**, **spur A3** → AS SOON AS
2 (*Phys*) momento *m*; **~ of inertia** momento *m* de inercia
3 (*frm*) (= *importance*) importancia *f*; **of great/little ~** de gran/poca importancia

momentarily ['məʊməntərɪlɪ] ADV 1 (= *for a moment*) por un momento, momentáneamente; **he paused ~ to ...** paró un momento para ...
2 (*US*) (= *at any moment*) de un momento a otro, en seguida, ahorita (*LAm*)

momentary ['məʊməntərɪ] ADJ [*hesitation, silence, weakness*] momentáneo; [*feeling*] pasajero; **there was a ~ calm** hubo un momento de calma

momentous [məʊ'mentəs] ADJ trascendental, de gran trascendencia

momentousness [məʊ'mentəsnɪs] N trascendencia *f*, suma importancia *f*

momentum [məʊ'mentəm] N (*pl* **momentums** *or* **momenta** [məʊ'mentə]) (*Phys*) momento *m*; (*fig*) ímpetu *m*, impulso *m*; **to gather** *or* **gain ~** (*lit*) cobrar velocidad; (*fig*) ganar fuerza

momma* ['mɒmə] N (*US*), **mommy*** ['mɒmɪ] N (*US*) mamá* *f*

Mon. ABBR (= **Monday**) lun.

Monaco ['mɒnəkəʊ] N Mónaco *m*

monad ['mɒnæd] N mónada *f*

Mona Lisa ['məʊnə'liːzə] N **the ~** la Gioconda, la Mona Lisa

monarch ['mɒnək] N monarca *mf*

monarchic [mɒ'nɑːkɪk] ADJ = **monarchical**

monarchical [mɒ'nɑːkɪkəl] ADJ monárquico

monarchism ['mɒnəkɪzəm] N (= *system*) monarquía *f*; (= *advocacy of monarchy*) monarquismo *m*

monarchist ['mɒnəkɪst] Ⓐ ADJ monárquico
Ⓑ N monárquico/a *m/f*

monarchy ['mɒnəkɪ] N monarquía *f*

monastery ['mɒnəstrɪ] N monasterio *m*

monastic [mə'næstɪk] Ⓐ ADJ monástico
Ⓑ CPD ► **monastic order** N orden *f* monástica ► **monastic vows** NPL votos *mpl* monásticos

monasticism [mə'næstɪsɪzəm] N monacato *m*, vida *f* monástica

Monday ['mʌndɪ] N lunes *m inv*; *see* **Tuesday** *for usage*

Monegasque [mɒnə'gæsk] Ⓐ ADJ monegasco
Ⓑ N monegasco/a *m/f*

monetarism ['mʌnɪtərɪzəm] N monetarismo *m*

monetarist ['mʌnɪtərɪst] Ⓐ ADJ monetarista
Ⓑ N monetarista *mf*

monetary ['mʌnɪtərɪ] Ⓐ ADJ monetario
Ⓑ CPD ► **monetary policy** N política *f* monetaria ► **monetary reserves** NPL reservas *fpl* monetarias ► **monetary system** N sistema *m* monetario ► **monetary unit** N unidad *f* monetaria

money ['mʌnɪ] Ⓐ N 1 (*gen*) dinero *m*; **Spanish ~** dinero español; **there's ~ in second-hand cars** los coches de segunda mano son (un) buen negocio; **"~ back if not satisfied"** "si no queda satisfecho le devolvemos su dinero"; **to bring in ~** aportar dinero; **to come into ~** heredar dinero; **when do I get my ~?** ¿cuándo me vas a pagar?; **to earn good ~** ganar un buen sueldo, ganar su buen dinero *or* dinerito*, ganar sus buenos dineros *or* dineritos*; **I paid** *or* **gave good ~ for it** pagué un buen dinero por ello; **I'd rather be paid in ~** prefiero que me paguen en dinero; **your ~ or your life!** ¡la bolsa o la vida!; **to make ~** [*person*] ganar dinero; [*business*] rendir, dar dinero; **he made his ~ by dealing in cotton** ganó el dinero que tiene comerciando con algodón; **to put ~ into sth** invertir dinero en algo; **it was ~ well spent** fue dinero bien empleado; ✦**IDIOMS to have ~ to burn** estar cargado *or* podrido de dinero*; **to be in the ~** estar bien de dinero; **to be made of ~** ser millonario, tener un banco; **it's ~ for jam** *or* **~ for old rope** (*Brit**) es dinero regalado*; **for my ~: that's the one for my ~!** ¡yo apostaría por ése!; **I'd put ~ on it: he'll be back, I'd put ~ on it** apuesto (lo que sea) a que volverá; **my ~ is on Fred** yo apuesto por Fred; **to put one's ~ where one's mouth is** predicar con el ejemplo; **to spend ~ like water** tener un agujero en el bolsillo, ser un/una manirroto/a; **to throw one's ~ about** *or* **around** tirar *or* derrochar el dinero; **to throw ~ at a problem** intentar solucionar un problema a base de dinero; **to throw good ~ after bad** echar la soga tras el caldero; **bad ~ drives out good** el dinero malo echa fuera al bueno; **~ isn't everything** el dinero no lo es todo; **~ doesn't grow on trees** el dinero no cae del cielo *or* de los árboles; **to get one's ~'s worth** sacar partido a su dinero; **he certainly gives the audience its ~'s worth** la verdad es que con él el público sale contento; ✦**PROVS ~ can't buy happiness** el dinero no da *or* trae la felicidad; **~ makes ~** dinero llama dinero; **~ makes the world go round** el dinero mueve montañas; **(the love of) ~ is the root of all evil** el dinero es la raíz de todos los males; **~ talks** poderoso caballero es don Dinero; *see also* **burn[1] B1**, **coin B**, **colour A1**, **even A3**, **hand A1**, **A12**, **licence A2.1**, **marry A1**, **ready D**
2 (*Jur*) **monies** *or* **moneys** (*pl*) sumas *fpl* de dinero; **public monies** dinero *m* público
Ⓑ CPD [*worries, problems*] de dinero, económico ► **money back guarantee** N garantía *f* de devolución (del dinero) ► **money belt** N riñonera *f* ► **money economy** N economía *f* monetaria ► **money market** N bolsa *f or* mercado *m* de valores, mercado *m* monetario ► **money matters** NPL asuntos *mpl* financieros ► **money order** N (*US*) giro *m* postal ► **money prize** N premio *m* en metálico ► **money spider** N araña *f* de la suerte ► **the money supply** N la oferta *or* masa monetaria, el volumen de moneda

moneybags* ['mʌnɪbægz] N **he's a ~** está forrado*

moneybox ['mʌnɪbɒks] N hucha *f*

moneychanger ['mʌnɪ,tʃeɪndʒəʳ] N cambista *mf*

moneyed ['mʌnɪd] ADJ adinerado

moneygrubber ['mʌnɪ,grʌbəʳ] N avaro/a *m/f*

money-grubbing ['mʌnɪ,grʌbɪŋ] ADJ avaro

moneylender ['mʌnɪ,lendəʳ] N prestamista *mf*

moneylending ['mʌnɪ,lendɪŋ] N préstamo *m*

moneymaker ['mʌnɪ,meɪkəʳ] N fuente *f* de ganancias

money-making ['mʌnɪ,meɪkɪŋ] Ⓐ ADJ [*business etc*] rentable
Ⓑ N ganancia *f*, lucro *m*

money-spinner ['mʌnɪ,spɪnəʳ] N (*Brit*) = **moneymaker**

-monger ['mʌŋgəʳ] N (*ending in compounds*) **rumour-monger** *persona que se dedica a difundir rumores*; *see also* **fishmonger, warmonger** *etc*

Mongol ['mɒŋgəl] N 1 (= *person*) mongol(a) *m/f*
2 (*Ling*) mongol *m*

mongol ['mɒŋgəl] (*offensive*) Ⓐ N mongólico/a *m/f*
Ⓑ ADJ mongólico

Mongolia [mɒŋ'gəʊlɪə] N Mongolia *f*

Mongolian [mɒŋ'gəʊlɪən] Ⓐ ADJ mongol
Ⓑ N 1 (= *person*) mongol(a) *m/f*
2 (*Ling*) mongol *m*

mongolism ['mɒŋgəlɪzəm] N mongolismo *m*

Mongoloid ['mɒŋgəlɔɪd] ADJ (*Anthropology*) mongólico

mongoloid ['mɒŋgəlɔɪd] ADJ (*Med*†) mongoloide, mongólico

mongoose ['mɒŋguːs] N (*pl* **mongooses**) mangosta *f*

mongrel ['mʌŋgrəl] Ⓐ N (*also* **~ dog**) perro *m* mestizo, perro *m* cruzado
Ⓑ ADJ [*dog*] mestizo, cruzado

monicker‡ ['mɒnɪkəʳ] N (= *name*) nombre *m*; (= *nickname*) apodo *m*; (= *signature*) firma *f*; (= *initials*) iniciales *fpl*

monied ['mʌnɪd] ADJ = **moneyed**

monitor [ˈmɒnɪtəʳ] Ⓐ N 1 (*TV, Comput, Med*) monitor *m*
2 (= *person*) supervisor(a) *m/f*; (*Rad*) radioescucha *mf*; (*Scol*) encargado/a *m/f* (*de la disciplina*); **human rights ~s** supervisores de los derechos humanos
Ⓑ VT 1 (= *control, check*) [+ *progress, process*] seguir (la marcha de), controlar; [+ *elections*] observar; (*with machine*) monitorizar, monitorear; **we are ~ing the situation closely** estamos observando *or* controlando la situación de cerca
2 (*Rad*) [+ *foreign broadcasts, station*] escuchar

monitoring [ˈmɒnɪtərɪŋ] Ⓐ N 1 [*of process, situation*] supervisión *f*, control *m*; [*of patient, elections*] observación *f*; [*of agreement, law*] supervisión *f*
2 (*Electronics*) monitorización *f*
3 (*Rad*) [*of broadcasts, station*] escucha *f*
Ⓑ CPD [*body, responsibility*] de observación, de verificación

monk [mʌŋk] N monje *m*

monkey [ˈmʌŋkɪ] Ⓐ N (*Zool*) mono *m*; (*fig*) (= *child*) diablillo *m*; ✦**IDIOMS I don't give a ~'s**⁑ me importa un rábano*; **to make a ~ out of sb** poner a algn en ridículo
Ⓑ CPD ► **monkey business*** N (*dishonest*) trapisondas *fpl*, tejemanejes *mpl*; (*mischievous*) travesuras *fpl*, diabluras *fpl* ► **monkey nut** N (*Brit*) cacahuete *m*, maní *m* (*LAm*), cacahuate *m* (*Mex*) ► **monkey puzzle** N (*Bot*) araucaria *f* ► **monkey shines** NPL (*US*) = **monkey tricks** ► **monkey suit*** N traje *m* de etiqueta, esmoquin *m* ► **monkey tricks** NPL travesuras *fpl* ► **monkey wrench** N llave *f* inglesa

►**monkey about, monkey around** VI + ADV hacer tonterías; **to ~ about** *or* **~ around with sth** juguetear con algo

monkfish [ˈmʌŋkfɪʃ] (*pl* **monkfish** *or* **monkfishes**) N rape *m*, pejesapo *m*

monkish [ˈmʌnkɪʃ] ADJ monacal, monástico; (*pej*) frailuno

monkshood [ˈmʌŋkshʊd] N acónito *m*

mono [ˈmɒnəʊ] Ⓐ ADJ ABBR (= **monophonic**) mono *inv*, monoaural, monofónico; **~ system** sistema *m* monoaural
Ⓑ N **in ~** en mono

mono... [ˈmɒnəʊ] PREFIX mono…

monochrome [ˈmɒnəkrəʊm] Ⓐ ADJ monocromo
Ⓑ N monocromo *m*

monocle [ˈmɒnəkl] N monóculo *m*

monoculture [ˈmɒnəʊˌkʌltʃəʳ] N monocultivo *m*

monogamist [mɒˈnɒgəmɪst] N monógamo/a *m/f*

monogamous [mɒˈnɒgəməs] ADJ monógamo

monogamy [mɒˈnɒgəmɪ] N monogamia *f*

monogenetic [mɒnəʊdʒɪˈnetɪk] ADJ monogenético

monoglot [ˈmɒnəʊglɒt] Ⓐ ADJ monolingüe
Ⓑ N monolingüe *mf*

monogram [ˈmɒnəgræm] N monograma *m*, iniciales *fpl*

monogrammed [ˈmɒnəgræmd] ADJ con monograma

monograph [ˈmɒnəgræf] N monografía *f*

monohull [ˈmɒnəʊˌhʌl] N monocasco *m*

monokini [ˌmɒnəʊˈkiːniː] N monokini *m*

monolingual [ˌmɒnəʊˈlɪŋgwəl] ADJ monolingüe

monolingualism [ˌmɒnəʊˈlɪŋgwəlɪzəm] N monolingüismo *m*

monolith [ˈmɒnəʊlɪθ] N monolito *m*

monolithic [ˌmɒnəʊˈlɪθɪk] ADJ monolítico

monologue [ˈmɒnəlɒg], **monolog** (*US*) N monólogo *m*

monomania [ˌmɒnəʊˈmeɪnɪə] N monomanía *f*

monomaniac [ˌmɒnəʊˈmeɪnɪæk] Ⓐ ADJ monomaníaco
Ⓑ N monomaníaco/a *m/f*

mononucleosis [ˌmɒnəʊˌnjuːklɪˈəʊsɪs] N (*US*) (*also* **infectious ~**) mononucleosis *f* infecciosa

monophonic [ˌmɒnəʊˈfɒnɪk] ADJ monoaural, monofónico

monoplane [ˈmɒnəpleɪn] N monoplano *m*

monopolist [məˈnɒpəlɪst] N monopolista *mf*

monopolistic [məˌnɒpəˈlɪstɪk] ADJ monopolístico

monopolization [məˌnɒpəlaɪˈzeɪʃən] N monopolización *f*

monopolize [məˈnɒpəlaɪz] VT (*lit, fig*) monopolizar

monopoly [məˈnɒpəlɪ] Ⓐ N (*lit, fig*) monopolio *m*
Ⓑ CPD ► **Monopolies and Mergers Commission** N (*Brit*) *organismo regulador de monopolios y fusiones encargado de velar por la libre competencia*

monopsony [məˈnɒpsənɪ] N monopsonio *m*

monorail [ˈmɒnəʊreɪl] N monocarril *m*, monorraíl *m*

monoski [ˈmɒnəʊˌskiː] N monoesquí *m*

monoskier [ˈmɒnəʊˌskiːəʳ] N monoesquiador(a) *m/f*

monoskiing [ˈmɒnəʊˌskiːɪŋ] N monoesquí *m*

monosodium glutamate [ˈmɒnəʊˌsəʊdɪəmˈgluːtəmeɪt] N glutamato *m* monosódico

monosyllabic [ˈmɒnəʊsɪˈlæbɪk] ADJ 1 (*lit*) [*word*] monosílabo
2 (*fig*) (= *reticent*) lacónico

monosyllable [ˈmɒnəˌsɪləbl] N monosílabo *m*

monotheism [ˈmɒnəʊˌθiːɪzəm] N monoteísmo *m*

monotheist [ˈmɒnəʊˌθiːɪst] N monoteísta *mf*

monotheistic [ˌmɒnəʊθiːˈɪstɪk] ADJ monoteísta

monotone [ˈmɒnətəʊn] N monotonía *f*; **to speak in a ~** hablar en un solo tono

monotonous [məˈnɒtənəs] ADJ monótono; **he gets drunk with ~ regularity** se emborracha con indefectible regularidad

monotonously [məˈnɒtənəslɪ] ADV de forma monótona, monótonamente; **~ reliable** tediosamente fiable; **~ punctual** de una puntualidad religiosa

monotony [məˈnɒtənɪ] N monotonía *f*; **she decided to go away for the weekend, just to break the ~** decidió irse el fin de semana, sólo para romper la monotonía *or* salir de la rutina

Monotype® [ˈmɒnəʊtaɪp] Ⓐ N monotipia® *f*
Ⓑ CPD ► **Monotype machine** N (máquina *f*) monotipo® *m*

monoxide [mɒˈnɒksaɪd] N (*Chem*) monóxido *m*

Mons ABBR (*Rel*) (= **Monseigneur** *or* **Monsignor**) Mons.

monseigneur [ˌmɒnsenˈjɜːʳ] N monseñor *m*

monsignor [mɒnˈsiːnjəʳ] N (*pl* **monsignors** *or* **monsignori**) monseñor *m*

monsoon [mɒnˈsuːn] Ⓐ N monzón *m*
Ⓑ CPD ► **the monsoon rains** NPL las lluvias monzónicas ► **monsoon season** N época *f* monzónica, estación *f* de los monzones

monster [ˈmɒnstəʳ] Ⓐ ADJ (*) (= *enormous*) enorme, gigantesco
Ⓑ N monstruo *m*; (*) (= *big animal, plant, thing*) monstruo *m*, gigante *m*; **a real ~ of a fish** un pez verdaderamente enorme

monstrance [ˈmɒnstrəns] N custodia *f*

monstrosity [mɒnsˈtrɒsɪtɪ] N monstruosidad *f*

monstrous [ˈmɒnstrəs] ADJ 1 (= *huge*) enorme, gigantesco
2 (= *dreadful*) monstruoso; **it is ~ that …** es una verdadera vergüenza *or* un auténtico escándalo que + *subjun*

monstrously [ˈmɒnstrəslɪ] ADV enormemente; **~ unfair** terriblemente injusto

Mont. ABBR (*US*) = **Montana**

montage [mɒnˈtɑːʒ] N montaje *m*

Mont Blanc [ˌmɔ̃ːmˈblɑ̃ːŋ] N el Mont Blanc

Montenegran, Montenegrin [mɒntɪˈniːgrən] Ⓐ ADJ montenegrino
Ⓑ N montenegrino/a *m/f*

Montenegro [mɒntəˈniːgrəʊ] N Montenegro *m*

month [mʌnθ] N mes *m*; **in the ~ of May** en el mes de mayo; **a deposit of two ~s' rent** un depósito equivalente a dos meses de alquiler; **a ~'s unlimited rail travel** uso ilimitado del tren por el periodo de un mes; **an eight-month-old baby** un bebé de ocho meses; **three times a ~** tres veces al mes; **30 dollars a ~** 30 dólares al mes, 30 dólares mensuales; **at the beginning of the ~** a principios de mes; **I get paid by the ~** me pagan mensualmente; **what** *or* **which day of the ~ is it?** ¿a cuántos estamos?; **at the end of the ~** a fin *or* finales de mes; **every ~** todos los meses; **she was here for a ~** estuvo aquí un mes; **it went on for ~s** duró meses y meses; **I was able to walk for the first time in ~s** por primera vez después de meses pude andar; **I'm off to Mexico in a ~'s time** *or* **in a ~** me voy a México dentro de un mes; **last ~** el mes pasado; **a ~ later** al mes, un mes más tarde; **next ~** el mes que viene; **six ~s pregnant** embarazada de seis meses; **in recent ~s** en los últimos meses; **this ~** este mes; **it's that time of the ~*** tiene/tengo la regla; ✦**IDIOM not** *or* **never in a ~ of Sundays** ni de casualidad; *see also* **calendar B**, **lunar B**

monthly [ˈmʌnθlɪ] Ⓐ ADJ [*publication, salary, rainfall*] mensual; **on a ~ basis** mensualmente, todos los meses; **~ instalment** *or* **payment** mensualidad *f*, cuota *f* mensual
Ⓑ ADV [*publish*] mensualmente, todos los meses; [*pay*] mensualmente, por meses; **they meet ~** se reúnen todos los meses *or* cada mes; **twice ~** dos veces al mes
Ⓒ N 1 (= *journal*) publicación *f* mensual
2 **monthlies*** (= *menstruation*) regla *f*, periodo *m*
Ⓓ CPD ► **monthly cycle** N (*menstrual*) ciclo *m* menstrual ► **monthly period** N (*menstrual*) periodo *m* (menstrual)

monty* [ˈmɒntɪ] N **the full ~** todo completo, el paquete *or* lote completo*

monument [ˈmɒnjʊmənt] N monumento *m* (**to** a)

monumental [ˌmɒnjʊˈmentl] Ⓐ ADJ 1 (= *grand*) [*building, sculpture, arch*] monumental
2 (= *huge*) [*task, success, effort*] monumental, colosal; [*blunder, error*] garrafal; **of ~ proportions** de proporciones monumentales; **on a ~ scale** a una escala gigantesca
Ⓑ CPD ► **monumental mason** N marmolista *mf* (funerario/a)

monumentally [ˌmɒnjʊˈmentəlɪ] ADV [*dull, popular*] enormemente, tremendamente; **~ important** enormemente importante, de tremenda importancia

moo [muː] Ⓐ N mugido *m*

Ⓑ VI mugir
Ⓒ EXCL ¡mu!
mooch* [mu:tʃ] VI **to ~ about** *or* **around the shops** pasear por las tiendas; **to ~ about** *or* **around the house** dar vueltas por la casa; **to ~ along** andar arrastrando los pies
moo-cow* ['mu:kaʊ] N (*baby talk*) vaca *f*
mood¹ [mu:d] N (*Ling*) modo *m*
mood² [mu:d] Ⓐ N humor *m*; **that depends on his ~** eso es según el *or* depende del humor que tenga; **to be in the ~ for sth/to do sth** tener ganas de algo/de hacer algo, estar de humor para algo/para hacer algo; **he plays well when he's in the ~** toca bien cuando está en vena *or* por la labor; **are you in a ~ for chess?** ¿te apetece una partida de ajedrez?, ¿quieres jugar al ajedrez?; **I'm not in the ~** no tengo ganas, no me apetece; **I'm not in the ~ for games** no estoy (de humor) para juegos; **he's in a bit of a ~** está de mal humor; **to be in a bad ~** estar de mal humor; **to be in a forgiving ~** estar dispuesto a perdonar; **to be in a generous ~** sentirse generoso; **to be in a good ~** estar de buen humor; **he has ~s** (*angry*) tiene arranques de cólera; (*gloomy*) tiene sus rachas de melancolía; **I'm in no ~ to argue** no tengo ganas de discutir, no estoy (de humor) para discutir; **to be in no laughing ~** *or* **in no ~ for laughing** no tener ganas de reír; **she's in one of her ~s** está de malas, está con un humor de perros; **to be in an ugly ~** [*person*] estar de muy mal humor; [*crowd*] tener los ánimos muy exaltados *or* encendidos
Ⓑ CPD ► **mood music** N música *f* de fondo *or* de ambiente
moodily ['mu:dɪlɪ] ADV malhumoradamente
moodiness ['mu:dɪnɪs] N (= *variability*) humor *m* variable; (= *bad mood*) mal humor *m*
moody ['mu:dɪ] ADJ (*compar* **moodier**; *superl* **moodiest**) (= *variable*) (de carácter) variable, temperamental; (= *bad-tempered*) malhumorado; **he's very ~** es muy temperamental, es de humor muy variable
moola‡, **moolah‡** ['mu:lɑ:] N (*US*) pasta* *f*, parné‡ *m*
moon [mu:n] Ⓐ N luna *f*; **full ~** luna *f* llena; **there's a full ~ tonight** esta noche hay luna llena; **new ~** luna *f* nueva; **there was no ~** no había luna; **by the light of the ~** a la luz de la luna; **many ~s ago** (*liter or hum*) hace mucho tiempo; ✦***IDIOMS*** **to ask for the ~** pedir la luna; **once in a blue ~** de Pascuas a Ramos; **to be over the ~*** estar loco de contento, estar en el séptimo cielo; **to promise the ~** prometer la luna *or* el oro y el moro; *see also* **phase A2**
Ⓑ VI (*) enseñar el culo*
Ⓒ CPD ► **moon buggy** N vehículo *m* lunar
► **moon landing** N alunizaje *m*
►**moon about**, **moon around** VI + ADV mirar a las musarañas
►**moon over** VI + PREP **she was ~ing over the photo** miraba amorosamente la foto, contemplaba extasiada la foto
moonbeam ['mu:nbi:m] N rayo *m* de luna
moonboots ['mu:nbu:ts] NPL botas *fpl* altas acolchadas
Moonie ['mu:nɪ] N miembro *mf* de la Iglesia de la Unificación
moonless ['mu:nlɪs] ADJ sin luna
moonlight ['mu:nlaɪt] Ⓐ N luz *f* de la luna; **by ~** ◊ **in the ~** a la luz de la luna
Ⓑ VI (*) practicar el pluriempleo; **he ~s as a taxi driver** en sus ratos libres trabaja de taxista
Ⓒ CPD ► **moonlight flit** N (*Brit*) mudanza *f* a la chita callando; **to do a ~ flit** largarse a la chita callando*
moonlighter* ['mu:n,laɪtəʳ] N pluriempleado/a *m/f*
moonlighting* ['mu:n,laɪtɪŋ] N pluriempleo *m*
moonlit ['mu:nlɪt] ADJ [*object*] iluminado por la luna; [*night*] de luna
moonrise ['mu:nraɪz] N salida *f* de la luna
moonscape ['mu:n,skeɪp] N paisaje *m* lunar
moonshine ['mu:nʃaɪn] N [1] (= *moonlight*) luz *f* de la luna
[2] (*) (= *nonsense*) pamplinas *fpl*
[3] (*US*) (= *illegal spirits*) licor *m* destilado ilegalmente
moonshiner* ['mu:nʃaɪnəʳ] N (*US*) [1] (= *distiller*) fabricante *mf* de licor ilegal
[2] (= *smuggler*) contrabandista *mf*
moonshot ['mu:nʃɒt] N [1] (= *vessel*) nave *f* espacial con destino a la luna
[2] (= *launch*) lanzamiento *m* de una nave espacial con destino a la luna
moonstone ['mu:nstəʊn] N feldespato *m*, labradorita *f*
moonstruck ['mu:nstrʌk] ADJ chiflado
moony* ['mu:nɪ] ADJ **to be ~** estar distraído, estar soñando despierto
Moor [mʊəʳ] N moro/a *m/f*
moor¹ [mʊəʳ] N (*esp Brit*) páramo *m*, brezal *m*
moor² [mʊəʳ] Ⓐ VT amarrar
Ⓑ VI echar las amarras
moorhen ['mʊəhen] N polla *f* de agua
mooring ['mʊərɪŋ] N [1] (= *place*) amarradero *m*
[2] **moorings** (= *ropes, fixtures*) amarras *fpl*
Moorish ['mʊərɪʃ] ADJ [*person*] moro; [*culture, influence, invasion*] árabe; [*architecture*] morisco
moorland ['mʊələnd] N páramo *m*, brezal *m*
moose [mu:s] N (*pl* **moose**) alce *m*
moot [mu:t] Ⓐ ADJ **it's a ~ point** *or* **question** es un punto discutible
Ⓑ VT **it has been ~ed that ...** se ha sugerido que ...; **when the question was first ~ed** cuando se discutió la cuestión por primera vez
Ⓒ N (*Hist*) junta *f*, asamblea *f*
mop [mɒp] Ⓐ N [1] (*for floor*) fregona *f*, trapeador *m* (*LAm*); (*for dishes*) estropajo *m*
[2] (*) **~ of hair** pelambrera *f*, melena *f*
Ⓑ VT [+ *floor*] fregar, trapear (*LAm*); [+ *brow*] enjugar; **to ~ one's face** enjugarse la cara
►**mop up** Ⓐ VT + ADV [1] [+ *spilt water*] secar; [+ *floor, surface*] limpiar; **you can always ~ up the sauce with your bread** siempre puedes rebañar *or* mojar la salsa con el pan
[2] (*Mil*) acabar con
Ⓑ VI + ADV (= *clean*) limpiar; (*with mop*) pasar la fregona
mope [məʊp] VI quedar abatido; **to ~ for sb** estar triste por la pérdida de algn
►**mope about**, **mope around** VI + ADV andar con cara mustia
moped ['məʊped] N (*esp Brit*) ciclomotor *m*
mopping-up ['mɒpɪŋ,ʌp] Ⓐ N limpieza *f*
Ⓑ CPD ► **mopping-up operation** N (*Mil*) operación *f* de limpieza, barrida *f*; (*after flood, storm*) operaciones *fpl* de limpieza y reconstrucción
moquette [mə'ket] N moqueta *f*
MOR ADJ ABBR (*Mus*) (= **middle-of-the-road**) para el gran público
moraine [mɒ'reɪn] N morena *f*
moral ['mɒrəl] Ⓐ ADJ [*values, principles, issue, dilemma*] moral; **I have a ~ responsibility for what happened** me siento moralmente responsable de lo que ocurrió; **a fall in ~ standards** una decadencia moral; **~ fibre** fibra *f* moral; **on ~ grounds** por razones morales; **the ~ majority** la mayoría moral
Ⓑ N [1] (= *lesson*) moraleja *f*
[2] **morals** moralidad *f*; **he has no ~s** no tiene moralidad
Ⓒ CPD ► **moral support** N apoyo *m* moral; **I went along with her for ~ support** fui con ella para darle apoyo moral
morale [mɒ'rɑ:l] N moral *f*; **~ was at an all-time low** la moral estaba más baja que nunca; **to raise/lower sb's ~** levantar/bajar la moral a algn, animar/desanimar a algn
morale-booster [mɒ'rɑ:lbu:stəʳ] N inyección *f* de ánimo; **his recent win was a great ~** su reciente victoria le levantó mucho la moral
moralist ['mɒrəlɪst] N moralizador(a) *m/f*; (= *philosopher, teacher*) moralista *mf*
moralistic [,mɒrə'lɪstɪk] ADJ moralizador
morality [mə'rælɪtɪ] Ⓐ N moralidad *f*, moral *f*
Ⓑ CPD ► **morality play** N moralidad *f*
moralize ['mɒrəlaɪz] VI moralizar
moralizing ['mɒrəlaɪzɪŋ] Ⓐ ADJ moralizador
Ⓑ N instrucción *f* moral, predicación *f* sobre la moralidad
morally ['mɒrəlɪ] ADV [*superior, responsible*] moralmente; [*right, wrong*] desde el punto de vista moral; [*act, behave*] moralmente, éticamente; **a ~ bankrupt society** una sociedad en bancarrota moral
morass [mə'ræs] N cenagal *m*, pantano *m*; **a ~ of problems** un laberinto de problemas; **a ~ of figures** un mar de cifras
moratorium [,mɒrə'tɔ:rɪəm] N (*pl* **moratoriums** *or* **moratoria** [,mɒrə'tɔ:rɪə]) moratoria *f*
Moravia [mə'reɪvɪə] N Moravia *f*
moray ['mɒreɪ] N (= *fish*) morena *f*
morbid ['mɔ:bɪd] ADJ [1] (= *perverse*) morboso, malsano; **don't be so ~!** ¡no seas morboso!; **~ curiosity** curiosidad *f* malsana
[2] (*Med*) mórbido
morbidity [mɔ:'bɪdɪtɪ] N, N [1] (= *perverseness*) morbosidad *f*, lo malsano
[2] (*Med*) morbosidad *f*
morbidly ['mɔ:bɪdlɪ] ADV [*talk*] morbosamente, con morbo; [*think*] morbosamente
morbidness ['mɔ:bɪdnɪs] N = **morbidity**
mordacity [mɔ:dæsɪtɪ] N mordacidad *f*
mordant ['mɔ:dənt] ADJ mordaz
mordent ['mɔ:dənt] N mordente *m*
▼ **more** [mɔ:ʳ] Ⓐ ADJ más; **there's ~ tea in the cupboard** hay más té en el aparador; **is there any ~ wine in the bottle?** ¿queda vino en la botella?; **a few ~ weeks** unas semanas más; **it'll take a few ~ days** llevará unos cuantos días más; **many ~ people** muchas más personas; **much ~ butter** mucha más mantequilla; **I have no ~ money** no me queda más dinero; **no ~ singing, I can't bear it!** ¡que no se cante más, no lo aguanto!; **do you want some ~ tea?** ¿quieres más té?; **you have ~ money than I** tienes más dinero que yo; **it's two ~ miles to the house** faltan dos millas para llegar a la casa
Ⓑ N, PRON [1] más; **four ~** cuatro más; **we can't afford ~** no podemos pagar más; **is there any ~?** ¿hay más?; **there isn't any ~** ya no hay más; **a bit ~?** ¿un poco más?; **a few ~** algunos más; **a little ~** un poco más; **many ~** muchos más; **much ~** mucho más; **there isn't much ~ to do** no hay *or* queda mucho más que hacer; **there's no ~ left** no queda (nada); **let's say no ~ about it!** ¡no se hable más del asunto!; **she's no ~ a duchess**

➤ LANGUAGE IN USE: **more B1** 5.3 **B2** 5.6 **C1** 5.6

than I am tan duquesa es como mi padre; **he no ~ thought of paying me than of flying to the moon** antes iría volando a la luna que pensar pagarme a mí; **I shall have ~ to say about this** volveré a hablar de esto; **some ~** más; **he's got ~ than me!** ¡él tiene más que yo!; **it's ~ than a job** es (algo) más que un trabajo; **~ than ever** más que nunca; **~ than half** más de la mitad; **~ than one/ten** más de uno/diez; **not ~ than 15** no más de quince; **not much ~ than £20** poco más de 20 libras; **it cost ~ than we had expected** costó más de lo que esperábamos; **and what's ~ ...** y además ...; **there's ~ where that came from!** ¡esto no es más que el principio!

2 **(all) the ~** tanto más; **it makes me (all) the ~ ashamed** tanto más vergüenza me da; **all the ~ so because** *or* **as** *or* **since ...** tanto más cuanto que ...; **the ~ you give him the ~ he wants** cuanto más se le da, (tanto) más quiere; **the ~ he drank the thirstier he got** cuanto más bebía más sed tenía; **the ~ the better** ◊ **the ~ the merrier** cuantos más mejor

Ⓒ ADV 1 más; **~ difficult** más difícil; **~ easily** con mayor facilidad; **more and more** cada vez más; **if he says that any ~** si vuelve a decir eso, si dice eso otra vez; **if he comes here any ~** si vuelve por aquí; **~ or less** más o menos; **neither ~ nor less** ni más ni menos; **"I don't understand it" — "no ~ do I"** —no lo comprendo —ni yo tampoco; **he's ~ intelligent than me** es más inteligente que yo; **the house is ~ than half built** la casa está más que medio construida; **I had ~ than carried out my obligation** había cumplido con creces mi obligación; **it will ~ than meet the demand** satisfará ampliamente la demanda; **he was ~ surprised than angry** más que enfadarse se sorprendió; **it's ~ a short story than a novel** más que novela es un cuento

2 (= *again*) **once ~** otra vez, una vez más

3 (= *longer*) **he doesn't live here any ~** ya no vive aquí; **Queen Anne is no ~** la reina Ana ya no existe; **we shall see her no ~** no la volveremos a ver

moreish* [ˈmɔːrɪʃ] ADJ apetitoso

▼ **moreover** [mɔːˈrəʊvəʳ] ADV además, es más; **he discovered, moreover, that this was not the first time** descubrió, además, que ésta no era la primera vez, es más, descubrió que ésta no era la primera vez; **moreover, there were the children to consider** por otra parte *or* además, había que tener en cuenta a los niños

mores [ˈmɔːreɪz] NPL costumbres *fpl*

morganatic [ˌmɔːgəˈnætɪk] ADJ morganático

morganatically [ˌmɔːgəˈnætɪkəlɪ] ADV **he married her ~** se casó con ella en casamiento morganático

morgue [mɔːg] N depósito *m* de cadáveres, morgue *f* (*esp LAm*)

MORI [ˈmɔːrɪ] N ABBR (= **Market & Opinion Research Institute**) *empresa británica que realiza sondeos de opinión y estudios de mercado*

moribund [ˈmɒrɪbʌnd] ADJ moribundo

Mormon [ˈmɔːmən] Ⓐ ADJ mormón

Ⓑ N mormón/ona *m/f*

Mormonism [ˈmɔːmənɪzəm] N mormonismo *m*

morn [mɔːn] N (*poet*) (= *morning*) mañana *f*; (= *dawn*) alborada *f*

morning [ˈmɔːnɪŋ] Ⓐ N mañana *f*; (*before dawn*) madrugada *f*; **he's generally out ~s*** por las mañanas no suele estar; **the ~ after** (*hum*) la mañana después de la juerga; **good ~!** ¡buenos días!; **in the ~** (= *during the morning*) por la mañana, en la mañana (*LAm*); (*tomorrow*) mañana por la mañana; **early in the ~** a primera hora de la mañana, muy de mañana; **at seven o'clock in the ~** a las siete de la mañana; **at three in the ~** a las tres de la madrugada; **the next ~** la mañana siguiente; **on Saturday ~** el sábado por la mañana; **tomorrow ~** mañana por la mañana; **yesterday ~** ayer por la mañana

Ⓑ CPD ► **morning coat** N chaqué *m* ► **morning dress** N chaqué *m*, traje *m* de etiqueta ► **morning glory** N dondiego *m* de día, ipomea *f* ► **morning mist** N bruma *f* del alba ► **morning paper** N diario *m* or periódico *m* de la mañana ► **morning prayers** NPL oficio *m* matinal ► **morning sickness** N (*Med*) náuseas *fpl* del embarazo ► **morning star** N lucero *m* del alba ► **morning tea** N té *m* mañanero

morning-after [ˈmɔːnɪŋˈɑːftəʳ] CPD ► **the morning-after pill** N la píldora (anticonceptiva) del día después

Moroccan [məˈrɒkən] Ⓐ ADJ marroquí

Ⓑ N marroquí *mf*

Morocco [məˈrɒkəʊ] N Marruecos *m*

morocco [məˈrɒkəʊ] N (*also* **~ leather**) marroquí *m*, tafilete *m*

moron [ˈmɔːrɒn] N (*Med*) retrasado/a *m/f* mental; (* *pej*) imbécil *mf*

moronic [məˈrɒnɪk] ADJ imbécil

morose [məˈrəʊs] ADJ malhumorado

morosely [məˈrəʊslɪ] ADV malhumoradamente, morbosamente

morph [mɔːf] N morfo *m*

morpheme [ˈmɔːfiːm] N morfema *m*

morphemic [mɔːˈfiːmɪk] ADJ morfímico

morphia [ˈmɔːfɪə], **morphine** [ˈmɔːfiːn] N morfina *f*

morphing [ˈmɔːfɪŋ] N (*Cine*) morphing *m*, mutación *f* con efectos especiales

morphological [ˌmɔːfəˈlɒdʒɪkəl] ADJ morfológico

morphologically [ˌmɔːfəˈlɒdʒɪkəlɪ] ADV morfológicamente

morphologist [mɔːˈfɒlədʒɪst] N morfólogo/a *m/f*

morphology [mɔːˈfɒlədʒɪ] N morfología *f*

morphosyntax [ˌmɔːfəʊˈsɪntæks] N morfosintaxis *f inv*

morris dance [ˈmɒrɪsdɑːns] N *baile tradicional inglés de hombres en el que éstos llevan cascabeles en la ropa*

morrow [ˈmɒrəʊ] N **on the ~** (*liter*) al día siguiente

Morse [mɔːs] Ⓐ N morse *m*

Ⓑ CPD ► **Morse code** N alfabeto *m* Morse

morsel [ˈmɔːsl] N [*of food*] bocado *m*; (*fig*) pedazo *m*

mort. ABBR = **mortgage**

mortadella [ˌmɔːtəˈdelə] N mortadela *f*

mortal [ˈmɔːtl] Ⓐ ADJ 1 (= *destined to die*) mortal

2 (*liter*) (= *fatal*) [*wound, blow*] mortal

3 (= *deadly*) [*enemy*] mortal

4 (= *extreme*) [*terror*] espantoso; **she screamed in ~ terror** gritó aterrorizada; **to be in ~ danger** estar en peligro de muerte; **to live in ~ fear that ...** vivir aterrorizado de que ...

Ⓑ N mortal *mf*; **they are now reduced to the status of ordinary ~s** quedan ahora reducidos al estatus de simples mortales; *see also* **mere**[2]

Ⓒ CPD ► **mortal combat** N combate *m* a muerte ► **mortal remains** NPL restos *mpl* mortales ► **mortal sin** N pecado *m* mortal

> **MORE THAN**
>
> **"Más ... que" or "más ... de"?**
>
> • Use **más** with **que** before nouns and personal pronouns (provided they are not followed by clauses) as well as before adverbs and prepositions:
>
> It was much more than a book
> ***Era mucho más que un libro***
> She knows more than I do about such things
> ***Ella sabe más que yo de esas cosas***
> Spain won more medals than ever before
> ***España logró más medallas que nunca***
>
> • Use **más ... de lo que/del que/de la que/de los que/de las que** with following clauses:
>
> It's much more complicated than you think
> ***Es mucho más complicado de lo que te imaginas***
> There's much more violence now than there was in the seventies
> ***Hay mucha más violencia ahora de la que había en los setenta***
>
> • Use **más** with **de** before **lo** + ADJECTIVE/PAST PARTICIPLE:
>
> You'll have to work more quickly than usual
> ***Tendrás que trabajar más rápido de lo normal***
> It was more difficult than expected
> ***Fue más difícil de lo previsto***
>
> • Use **más** with **de** in comparisons involving numbers or quantity:
>
> There were more than twenty people there
> ***Había más de veinte personas allí***
> More than half are women
> ***Más de la mitad son mujeres***
> They hadn't seen each other for more than a year
> ***No se veían desde hacía más de un año***
>
> • But **más ... que** can be used with numbers in more figurative comparisons:
>
> A picture is worth more than a thousand words
> ***Una imagen vale más que mil palabras***
>
> NOTE: **Más ... que** can be used before numbers in the construction **no ... más que**, meaning "only". Compare the following:
>
> ***No gana más que 100.000 ptas al mes***
> He only earns 100,000 pesetas a month
> ***No gana más de 100.000 ptas al mes***
> He earns no more than 100,000 pesetas a month
>
> **A lot more**
>
> • When translating **a lot more**, **far more** *etc* remember to make the **mucho** in **mucho más** agree with any noun it describes or refers to:
>
> We eat much more junk food than we used to
> ***Tomamos mucha más comida basura que antes***
> It's only one sign. There are a lot *or* many more
> ***Sólo es una señal. Hay muchas más***
> A lot more research will be needed
> ***Harán falta muchos más estudios***
>
> *For further uses and examples, see main entry at* ***more***.

mortality [mɔːˈtælɪtɪ] Ⓐ N 1 (= *condition*) mortalidad *f*

2 (= *fatalities*) mortandad *f*, número *m* de víctimas

Ⓑ CPD ► **mortality rate** N tasa *f* de mortalidad ► **mortality table** N tabla *f* de mortalidad

mortally [ˈmɔːtəlɪ] ADV 1 (= *fatally*) **to be ~ wounded** estar herido de muerte, estar mortalmente herido

2 (= *extremely*) **~ afraid** muerto de miedo; **he was ~ embarrassed** estaba terriblemente

➤ LANGUAGE IN USE: **moreover** 26.2

avergonzado, estaba cortadísimo*; **~ offended** profundamente ofendido

mortar [ˈmɔːtəʳ] Ⓐ N [1] (= *cannon*) mortero *m*
[2] (= *cement*) argamasa *f*, mortero *m*; *see also* **brick A1**
[3] (= *bowl*) mortero *m*
Ⓑ VT (*Mil*) bombardear con morteros

mortarboard [ˈmɔːtəbɔːd] N (*Univ*) birrete *m* cuadrado

mortgage [ˈmɔːgɪdʒ] Ⓐ N hipoteca *f*; **to pay off a ~** amortizar *or* liquidar *or* redimir una hipoteca; **to raise a ~** ◊ **take out a ~** obtener una hipoteca (**on** sobre)
Ⓑ VT hipotecar
Ⓒ CPD ► **mortgage bank** N banco *m* hipotecario, sociedad *f* de crédito hipotecario ► **mortgage broker** N especialista *mf* en hipotecas ► **mortgage company** N (*US*) = **mortgage bank** ► **mortgage lender** N sociedad *f* hipotecaria ► **mortgage loan** N préstamo *m* hipotecario ► **mortgage payment** N pago *m* de la hipoteca, plazo *m* de la hipoteca ► **mortgage rate** N tipo *m* de interés hipotecario

mortgageable [ˈmɔːgədʒəbl] ADJ hipotecable

mortgagee [ˌmɔːgəˈdʒiː] N acreedor(a) *m/f* hipotecario/a

mortgager, mortgagor [ˈmɔːgədʒəʳ] N deudor(a) *m/f* hipotecario/a

mortice [ˈmɔːtɪs] N = **mortise**

mortician [mɔːˈtɪʃən] N (*US*) director/a *m/f* de pompas fúnebres

mortification [ˌmɔːtɪfɪˈkeɪʃən] N mortificación *f*, humillación *f*, vergüenza *f*

mortify [ˈmɔːtɪfaɪ] Ⓐ VT avergonzar; **I was mortified (to find that ...)** me moría de vergüenza (al descubrir que ...)
Ⓑ VI (*Med*) gangrenarse

mortifying [ˈmɔːtɪfaɪɪŋ] ADJ humillante

mortise [ˈmɔːtɪs] Ⓐ N mortaja *f*
Ⓑ CPD ► **mortise lock** N cerradura *f* de muesca

mortuary [ˈmɔːtjʊərɪ] Ⓐ N depósito *m* de cadáveres
Ⓑ ADJ mortuorio

Mosaic [məʊˈzeɪɪk] ADJ mosaico

mosaic [məʊˈzeɪɪk] N mosaico *m*

Moscow [ˈmɒskəʊ] N Moscú *m*

Moselle [məʊˈzel] N Mosela *m*

Moses [ˈməʊzɪs] Ⓐ N Moisés
Ⓑ CPD ► **Moses basket** N moisés *m*

mosey [ˈməʊzɪ] VI **to ~ along*** pasearse; **to ~ down to the shops** ir dando un paseo a las tiendas

Moslem [ˈmɒzlem] Ⓐ ADJ musulmán
Ⓑ N musulmán/ana *m/f*

mosque [mɒsk] N mezquita *f*

mosquito [mɒsˈkiːtəʊ] Ⓐ N (*pl* **mosquitoes**) mosquito *m*, zancudo *m* (*LAm*)
Ⓑ CPD ► **mosquito bite** N picadura *f* de mosquito ► **mosquito net** N mosquitero *m*, mosquitera *f*

moss [mɒs] Ⓐ N (*Bot*) musgo *m*; *see also* **rolling A**
Ⓑ CPD ► **moss stitch** N punto *m* de musgo

mossy [ˈmɒsɪ] ADJ musgoso, cubierto de musgo

most [məʊst] Ⓐ ADJ SUPERL [1] (*making comparisons*) más; **who has (the) ~ money?** ¿quién tiene más dinero?; **for the ~ part** por lo general
[2] (= *the majority of*) la mayoría de, la mayor parte de; **~ men** la mayoría de *or* la mayor parte de los hombres; **~ people go out on Friday nights** la mayoría de *or* la mayor parte de la gente sale los viernes por la noche
Ⓑ N, PRON **~ of it** la mayor parte; **~ of them** la mayoría de ellos, la mayor parte de ellos; **~ of the money** la mayor parte del dinero; **~ of the time** la mayor parte del tiempo, gran parte del tiempo; **~ of those present** la mayoría de *or* la mayor parte de los asistentes; **~ of her friends** la mayoría de *or* la mayor parte de sus amigos; **do the ~ you can** haz lo que puedas; **at (the) ~** ◊ **at the very ~** como máximo, a lo sumo; **20 minutes at the ~** 20 minutos como máximo *or* a lo sumo; **to get the ~ out of a situation** sacar el máximo partido a una situación; **to make the ~ of sth** (= *make good use of*) aprovechar algo al máximo, sacar el máximo partido a algo; (= *enjoy*) disfrutar algo al máximo; **to make the ~ of one's advantages** aprovechar al máximo las propias ventajas; **he made the ~ of the story** explotó todas las posibilidades del cuento
Ⓒ ADV [1] (*superl*) más; **he spent ~** él gastó más; **the ~ difficult question** la pregunta más difícil; **which one did it ~ easily?** ¿quién lo hizo con mayor facilidad?
[2] (= *extremely*) sumamente, muy; **~ holy** santísimo; **a ~ interesting book** un libro interesantísimo *or* sumamente interesante; **you have been ~ kind** ha sido usted muy amable; **~ likely** lo más probable; → MAJORITY, MOST

...most [məʊst] SUFFIX más; **centremost** más central; **furthermost** más lejano

mostly [ˈməʊstlɪ] ADV (= *mainly*) en su mayoría, en su mayor parte; **they are ~ women** en su mayoría *or* en su mayor parte son mujeres, la mayoría *or* casi todas son mujeres; **this part of the country is ~ unspoiled** esta zona del país conserva, en su mayor parte, su belleza natural; **owls hunt ~ at night** el búho caza principalmente *or* sobre todo de noche; **~ because ...** principalmente porque ..., sobre todo porque ...; **it's ~ finished** está casi terminado

MOT (*Brit*) Ⓐ N ABBR [1] (= **Ministry of Transport**) ≈ Ministerio *m* de Transportes
[2] (*Aut*) (*also* **~ test**) (= **Ministry of Transport test**) *examen anual de coches obligatorio*, ≈ Inspección *f* Técnica de Vehículos (*Sp*), ≈ ITV *f* (*Sp*); **to pass the ~** (*Aut*) ≈ pasar la ITV (*Sp*); **~ certificate** ≈ certificado *m* de la ITV (*Sp*)
Ⓑ VT **I got my car ~'d last month** ≈ el coche pasó la ITV el mes pasado; **car for sale, ~'d till June** ≈ se vende coche, ITV válida hasta junio

mote [məʊt] N átomo *m*, mota *f*; **to see the ~ in our neighbour's eye and not the beam in our own** ver la paja en el ojo ajeno y no la viga en el propio

motel [məʊˈtel] N motel *m*

motet [məʊˈtet] N motete *m*

moth [mɒθ] N mariposa *f* nocturna; (= *clothes moth*) polilla *f*

mothball [ˈmɒθbɔːl] Ⓐ N bola *f* de naftalina; **in ~s** (*Naut*) en la reserva; **to put sth in ~s** [+ *project*] aparcar algo, dejar algo aparcado
Ⓑ VT [+ *ship*] poner en la reserva; [+ *project*] aparcar, dejar aparcado

moth-eaten [ˈmɒθˌiːtn] ADJ apolillado

mother [ˈmʌðəʳ] Ⓐ N madre *f*; **to be like a ~ to sb** ser como una madre para algn
Ⓑ VT (= *care for*) cuidar como una madre; (= *spoil*) mimar, consentir; (= *give birth to*) parir, dar a luz
Ⓒ CPD ► **mother country** N patria *f*; (*more sentimentally*) madre patria *f* ► **Mother Earth** N la madre tierra ► **mother figure** N figura *f* materna, figura *f* de la madre ► **Mother Goose** N la Oca ► **mother hen** N gallina *f* madre ► **mother love** N amor *m* maternal ► **Mother Nature** N la madre *f* Naturaleza ► **Mother's Day** N Día *m* de la Madre ► **mother's help** N niñera *f* ► **mother ship** N buque *m* nodriza ► **Mother Superior** N madre *f* superiora ► **mother tongue** N lengua *f* materna

motherboard [ˈmʌðəˌbɔːd] N (*Comput*) placa *f* base

mothercraft [ˈmʌðəkrɑːft] N arte *m* de cuidar a los niños pequeños, arte *m* de ser madre

motherfucker** [ˈmʌðəˌfʌkəʳ] N (*US*) hijoputa** *m*, hijaputa** *f*

motherfucking** [ˈmʌðəˌfʌkɪŋ] ADJ (*US*) pijotero*, condenado*

motherhood [ˈmʌðəhʊd] N maternidad *f*; **to prepare for ~** prepararse para ser madre

mothering [ˈmʌðərɪŋ] Ⓐ N cuidados *mpl* maternales
Ⓑ CPD ► **Mothering Sunday** N (*Brit*) fiesta *f* de la Madre

mother-in-law [ˈmʌðərɪnlɔː] N (*pl* **mothers-in-law**) suegra *f*

motherland [ˈmʌðəlænd] N patria *f*; (*more sentimentally*) madre patria *f*

motherless [ˈmʌðəlɪs] ADJ huérfano de madre, sin madre

motherly [ˈmʌðəlɪ] ADJ maternal

mother-of-pearl [ˈmʌðərəvˈpɜːl] Ⓐ N madreperla *f*, nácar *m*
Ⓑ ADJ nacarado

mother-to-be [ˈmʌðətəˈbiː] N (*pl* **mothers-to-be**) futura madre *f*

moth-hole [ˈmɒθhəʊl] N apolilladura *f*

mothproof [ˈmɒθpruːf] ADJ a prueba de polillas

motif [məʊˈtiːf] N (*Art, Mus*) motivo *m*; [*of speech etc*] tema *m*; (*Sew*) adorno *m*

motion [ˈməʊʃən] Ⓐ N [1] (= *movement*) movimiento *m*; **to be in ~** (*lit*) estar en movimiento; **plans are already in ~ for a new opera house** ya hay planes en marcha para la construcción de un nuevo teatro de la ópera; **to set in ~** [+ *mechanism*] poner en marcha; **the strike set in ~ a chain of events which led to his overthrow** la huelga desencadenó una serie de acontecimientos que condujeron a su derrocamiento; **to go through the ~s (of doing sth): he was just going through the ~s of living** estaba viviendo maquinalmente, vivía por inercia; **they went through the ~s of consulting members** siguieron la formalidad de consultar a los miembros; ✦**IDIOM to set the wheels in ~ (to do sth)** poner las cosas en marcha (para hacer algo); *see also* **perpetual B, slow E, time C**
[2] (= *gesture*) gesto *m*, ademán *m*; **he made a chopping ~ with his hand** hizo un gesto como si fuera a cortar algo con la mano, hizo un ademán de cortar algo con la mano
[3] (= *proposal*) moción *f*; **the ~ was carried/defeated** la moción fue aprobada/rechazada; **to propose** *or* (*US*) **make a ~ (that ...)** presentar una moción (para que + *subjun*); **to propose** *or* (*US*) **make a ~ (to do sth)** presentar una moción (para hacer algo); **to vote on a ~** votar una moción
[4] (*US Jur*) petición *f*; **to file a ~ (for sth/to do sth)** presentar una petición (para algo/para hacer algo)
[5] (*Brit frm*) (*also* **bowel ~**) (= *action*) evacuación *f*; (= *stool*) deposición *f*; **to have** *or* **pass a ~** evacuar el vientre
[6] [*of watch, clock*] mecanismo *m*
Ⓑ VT **he ~ed me to a chair/to sit down** con un gesto indicó que me sentara, hizo señas

para que me sentara; **to ~ sb in(side)/out(side)** señalar *or* indicar a algn con un gesto que entre/salga
Ⓒ VI **he ~ed for the doors to be opened** hizo un gesto *or* hizo señas para que se abrieran las puertas; **to ~ to sb to do sth** indicar a algn con un gesto que haga algo, hacer señas a algn para que haga algo
Ⓓ CPD ► **motion picture** N (*esp US*) película *f* ► **motion picture camera** N (*esp US*) cámara *f* cinematográfica, cámara *f* de cine ► **the motion picture industry** N la industria cinematográfica ► **motion picture theater** (*US*) N cine *m* ► **motion sickness** N mareo *m*

motionless [ˈməʊʃənlɪs] ADJ inmóvil; **to remain ~** permanecer inmóvil, permanecer sin moverse

motivate [ˈməʊtɪveɪt] VT motivar; **to be ~d to do sth** tener motivación *or* estar motivado para hacer algo; **he is highly ~d** tiene una fuerte motivación, está muy motivado; **the campaign is politically ~d** la campaña tiene una motivación política

motivation [ˌməʊtɪˈveɪʃən] N motivación *f*

motivational [ˌməʊtɪˈveɪʃənl] Ⓐ ADJ [*problem, factor*] de motivación
Ⓑ CPD ► **motivational research** N estudios *mpl* motivacionales

motive [ˈməʊtɪv] Ⓐ N motivo *m*; (*for crime*) móvil *m*; **what can his ~ have been?** ¿qué motivos habrá tenido?; **my ~s were of the purest** lo hice con la mejor intención
Ⓑ ADJ motor (*fem: motora/motriz*)
Ⓒ CPD ► **motive power** N fuerza *f* motriz

motiveless [ˈməʊtɪvlɪs] ADV sin motivo, inmotivado

motley [ˈmɒtlɪ] Ⓐ ADJ (= *many-coloured*) multicolor, abigarrado; (= *ill-assorted*) [*collection, bunch*] variopinto; **they were a ~ crew** era una pandilla de lo más variopinto
Ⓑ N botarga *f*, traje *m* de colores

motocross [ˈməʊtəkrɒs] N motocross *m*

motor [ˈməʊtəʳ] Ⓐ N [1] (= *engine*) motor *m*
[2] (*) (= *car*) coche *m*, automóvil *m*, carro *m* (*LAm*), auto *m* (*esp LAm*)
Ⓑ VI (†) ir en coche *etc*; **we ~ed down to Ascot** fuimos en coche a Ascot; **we ~ed over to see them** fuimos a visitarlos (en coche)
Ⓒ ADJ (= *giving motion*) [*nerve, muscle*] motor (*fem: motora/motriz*); (= *motorized*) automóvil
Ⓓ CPD ► **motor accident** N accidente *m* de circulación ► **motor insurance** N seguro *m* de automóvil ► **motor launch** N lancha *f* motora ► **motor mechanic** N mecánico/a *m/f* de automóviles ► **motor oil** N aceite *m* para motores ► **motor racing** N (*Sport*) carreras *fpl* de coches, automovilismo *m* ► **motor racing track** N pista *f* de automovilismo, circuito *m* de automovilismo ► **motor scooter** N Vespa® *f*, escúter *m*, motoneta *f* (*LAm*) ► **motor show** N feria *f* de automóviles; **the Paris ~ show** el salón del automóvil de París ► **motor transport** N transporte *m* rodado, transporte *m* motorizado ► **motor vehicle** N automóvil *m* ► **motor vessel** N motonave *f*

motorail [ˈməʊtəreɪl] N motorraíl *m*

motorbike [ˈməʊtəbaɪk] N motocicleta *f*, moto *f*

motorboat [ˈməʊtəbəʊt] N lancha *f* motora, motora *f*

motorcade [ˈməʊtəkeɪd] N desfile *m* de automóviles

motorcar [ˈməʊtəkɑːʳ] N (*frm*) coche *m*, automóvil *m*

motorcoach [ˈməʊtəkəʊtʃ] N autocar *m*, autobús *m*, camión *m* (*Mex*), micro *m* (*Arg*)

motorcycle [ˈməʊtəˌsaɪkl] Ⓐ N motocicleta *f*, moto *f*
Ⓑ CPD ► **motorcycle combination** N motocicleta *f* con sidecar

motorcycling [ˈməʊtəˌsaɪklɪŋ] N motociclismo *m*, motorismo *m*

motorcyclist [ˈməʊtəˌsaɪklɪst] N motociclista *mf*, motorista *mf*

motor-driven [ˈməʊtəˈdrɪvn] ADJ automóvil, propulsado por motor

-motored [ˈməʊtəd] ADJ (*ending in compounds*) **four-motored** cuatrimotor; **petrol-motored** de gasolina

motoring [ˈməʊtərɪŋ] Ⓐ ADJ [*accident*] de tráfico, de circulación; **~ holiday** vacaciones *fpl* en coche; **the ~ public** los automovilistas
Ⓑ N automovilismo *m*; **school of ~** autoescuela *f*, escuela *f* de manejo (*LAm*)

motorist [ˈməʊtərɪst] N conductor(a) *m/f*, automovilista *mf*

motorization [ˌməʊtəraɪˈzeɪʃən] N motorización *f*

motorize [ˈməʊtəraɪz] VT motorizar; **to be ~d** tener coche, estar motorizado*; **now that we're ~d*** ahora que tenemos coche, ahora que estamos motorizados*; **to get ~d** comprarse un coche, motorizarse*

motorized [ˈməʊtəraɪzd] ADJ motorizado

motorman [ˈməʊtəmən] N (*pl* **motormen**) N (*US*) conductor *m* de locomotora eléctrica *etc*, maquinista *m*

motormouth‡ [ˈməʊtəmaʊθ] N cotorra* *f*

motor-mower [ˈməʊtəˌməʊəʳ] N cortacésped *m* a motor

motorway [ˈməʊtəweɪ] Ⓐ N (*Brit*) autopista *f*
Ⓑ CPD ► **motorway madness** N locura *f* en la autopista ► **motorway service area** N área *f* de servicios de autopista ► **motorway services** NPL servicios *mpl* en autopista

mottled [ˈmɒtld] ADJ [*egg*] moteado; [*leaf, colour*] jaspeado; [*marble*] jaspeado, veteado; [*complexion, skin*] con manchas; **~ blue and white** moteado/jaspeado de azul y blanco; **~ with brown** con manchas marrones

motto [ˈmɒtəʊ] N (*pl* **mottoes** *or* **mottos**) [1] [*of family, person*] lema *m*
[2] (*Heraldry*) divisa *f*
[3] (= *watchword*) consigna *f*
[4] (*in cracker*) (= *joke*) chiste *m*

mould¹, **mold** (*US*) [məʊld] N (= *fungus*) moho *m*; (= *iron mould*) orín *m*

mould², **mold** (*US*) [məʊld] Ⓐ N (*Art, Culin, Tech etc*) molde *m*; **cast in a heroic ~** de carácter heroico; ✦*IDIOM* **to break the mould: they broke the ~ when they made him** rompieron el molde después de hacerlo a él
Ⓑ VT [1] (= *fashion*) moldear; (= *cast*) vaciar; **~ed plastics** plásticos *mpl* moldeados
[2] (*fig*) formar; **it is ~ed on ...** está hecho según ...; **to ~ o.s. on sb** tomar a algn como ejemplo

mould³, **mold** (*US*) [məʊld] N (= *soil*) mantillo *m*

moulder, **molder** (*US*) [ˈməʊldəʳ] VI (*also* **to ~ away**) desmoronarse; (*fig*) desmoronarse, decaer

mouldering, **moldering** (*US*) [ˈməʊldərɪŋ] ADJ [*house*] que se está desmoronando; [*leaves*] podrido

mouldiness, **moldiness** (*US*) [ˈməʊldɪnɪs] N moho *m*, lo mohoso

moulding, **molding** (*US*) [ˈməʊldɪŋ] N [1] (*Archit*) moldura *f*
[2] (= *process*) moldeado *m*
[3] (= *cast*) vaciado *m*
[4] (*fig*) amoldamiento *m*, formación *f*

mouldy, **moldy** (*US*) [ˈməʊldɪ] ADJ (*compar* **mouldier**; *superl* **mouldiest**) [1] (= *covered with mould*) [*cheese, bread*] mohoso, enmohecido; [*mattress, clothing*] enmohecido, lleno de moho; **to go ~** enmohecerse, criar moho; **to smell ~** oler a moho *or* a humedad
[2] (*Brit†**) (= *lousy*) cochino*

moult, **molt** (*US*) [məʊlt] Ⓐ VI [*bird*] mudar las plumas; [*mammal*] mudar el pelo; [*snake*] mudar la piel
Ⓑ VT [+ *feathers, hair*] mudar
Ⓒ N muda *f*

mound [maʊnd] N [1] (= *pile*) montón *m*
[2] (= *hillock*) montículo *m*; (= *burial mound*) túmulo *m*; (= *earthwork*) terraplén *m*

mount¹ [maʊnt] N [1] (*liter*) monte *m*; **the Sermon on the Mount** el Sermón de la Montaña
[2] (*in names*) monte *m*; **the Mount of Olives** el Monte de los Olivos; **Mount Sinai** el Monte Sinaí; **Mount Everest** el Everest

mount² [maʊnt] Ⓐ N [1] (= *horse*) montura *f*, caballería *f* (*frm*)
[2] (= *support, base*) [*of machine*] soporte *m*, base *f*; [*of jewel*] engaste *m*, montura *f*; (*for stamps*) fijasellos *m inv*; (*for photograph in album*) fijafotografías *m inv* adhesivo; (*for transparency*) marco *m*; [*of specimen, exhibit*] soporte *m*; (= *microscope slide*) portaobjetos *m inv*; (= *backing for picture*) fondo *m*
Ⓑ VT [1] [+ *horse*] montar; [+ *bicycle*] montar en; [+ *platform, stage, podium, throne*] subir a; [+ *stairs, hill*] subir; **the vehicle ~ed the pavement** el vehículo se subió a la acera
[2] [+ *jewel*] engastar; [+ *stamp, exhibit, specimen, TV, speakers*] fijar; [+ *picture*] poner un fondo a; [+ *gun, engine*] montar
[3] [+ *exhibition, campaign, event*] montar, organizar; [+ *play*] montar, poner en escena; [+ *attack, offensive, defence*] preparar
[4] **to ~ guard (on** *or* **over sth/sb)** montar (la) guardia (para vigilar algo/a algn)
[5] (*in mating*) cubrir, montar
[6] (= *provide with horse*) proveer de caballo
Ⓒ VI [1] (= *climb*) subir; **the blood ~ed to his cheeks** la sangre (se) le subió a los carrillos
[2] (*also* **~ up**) (= *get on horse*) montar
[3] (= *increase*) [*prices, temperature*] subir, aumentar; [*excitement, tension*] crecer, aumentar
[4] (*also* **~ up**) (= *accumulate*) [*bills, debts, problems*] amontonarse

mountain [ˈmaʊntɪn] Ⓐ N (*lit*) montaña *f*; (*fig*) [*of work etc*] montón *m*; **in the ~s** en la montaña; ✦*IDIOM* **to make a ~ out of a molehill** hacer una montaña de un grano de arena
Ⓑ CPD ► **mountain ash** N serbal *m* ► **mountain bike** N bicicleta *f* de montaña ► **mountain chain** N (*large*) cordillera *f*, cadena *f* montañosa; (*smaller*) sierra *f* ► **mountain goat** N cabra *f* montés ► **mountain hut** N albergue *m* de montaña ► **mountain lion** N puma *m* ► **mountain range** N (*large*) cordillera *f*; (*smaller*) sierra *f*; *see also* **pass A7** ► **mountain refuge** N albergue *m* de montaña ► **mountain rescue** N servicio *m* de rescate de montaña ► **mountain sickness** N mal *m* de montaña, puna *f* (*LAm*), soroche *m* (*LAm*)

mountaineer [ˌmaʊntɪˈnɪəʳ] Ⓐ N alpinista *mf*, andinista *mf* (*LAm*)
Ⓑ VI dedicarse al montañismo, hacer alpinismo

mountaineering [ˌmaʊntɪˈnɪərɪŋ] Ⓐ N alpinismo *m*, andinismo *m* (*LAm*)
Ⓑ CPD montañero, alpinista

mountainous ['maʊntɪnəs] ADJ [1] (*lit*) montañoso
[2] (*fig*) gigantesco

mountainside ['maʊntɪn,saɪd] N ladera *f* de montaña, falda *f* de montaña

mountaintop ['maʊntɪntɒp] N cima *f* de la montaña, cumbre *f* de la montaña

mountebank ['maʊntɪbæŋk] N saltabanco *m*, saltimbanqui *m*

mounted ['maʊntɪd] ADJ [1] (*on horseback*) montado; **the ~ police** la policía montada
[2] [*photograph*] montado

Mountie* ['maʊntɪ] N (*Canada*) miembro *m* de la policía montada canadiense; **the ~s** la policía montada canadiense

mounting ['maʊntɪŋ] Ⓐ N [1] (= *act*) [*of machine*] montaje *m*
[2] (= *support, base*) = **mount² A2**
Ⓑ ADJ [*concern, tension, excitement, opposition, unemployment*] creciente; [*debts*] cada vez mayor; **we watched with ~ horror as …** observábamos cada vez más aterrorizados como …; **to be under ~ pressure to do sth** encontrarse cada vez más presionado para hacer algo; **there is ~ evidence that …** hay pruebas, cada vez más concluyentes, de que …

mourn [mɔːn] Ⓐ VT [+ *person*] (= *grieve for*) llorar (la muerte de); (= *be in mourning for*) estar de luto *or* duelo por; [+ *death, loss*] lamentar, sentir; **Conservatives ~ the passing of family values** los conservadores se lamentan de la desaparición de los valores familiares
Ⓑ VI (= *be in mourning*) estar de luto *or* duelo; **when a relative dies one needs time to ~** (= *grieve*) cuando un pariente muere se necesita tiempo para llorarlo *or* llorar su muerte; **to ~ for sb** llorar a algn, llorar la muerte de algn; **it is no use ~ing for what might have been** no sirve de nada lamentarse por lo que podría haber sido; **he was ~ing over his lost love** lloraba por su amor perdido

mourner ['mɔːnəʳ] N doliente *mf*; (*hired*) plañidero/a *m/f*

mournful ['mɔːnfʊl] ADJ [*person*] afligido; [*tone, sound*] triste, lúgubre; [*occasion*] triste, luctuoso

mournfully ['mɔːnfəlɪ] ADV tristemente

mournfulness ['mɔːnfʊlnɪs] N [*of expression, sigh*] tristeza *f*; [*of person*] aflicción *f*

mourning ['mɔːnɪŋ] Ⓐ N luto *m*, duelo *m*; (= *dress*) luto *m*; **to be in ~ (for sb)** estar de luto *or* duelo (por algn); **to wear ~** llevar luto; **to come out of ~** dejar el luto; **to plunge a town into ~** poner de luto a una ciudad
Ⓑ CPD ► **mourning clothes** NPL luto *m*

mouse [maʊs] Ⓐ N (*pl* **mice**) [1] (*Zool*) ratón *m*
[2] (*Comput*) ratón *m*
Ⓑ CPD ► **mouse mat**, **mouse pad** N (*Comput*) alfombrilla *f*, almohadilla *f*
Ⓒ VI cazar ratones

mousehole ['maʊshəʊl] N ratonera *f*

mouser ['maʊsəʳ] N cazador *m* de ratones

mousetrap ['maʊstræp] Ⓐ N ratonera *f*
Ⓑ CPD ► **mousetrap cheese*** N queso *m* corriente

mousey ['maʊsɪ] ADJ = **mousy**

moussaka [mʊ'sɑːkə] N musaka *f*

mousse [muːs] N [1] (*Culin*) mousse *m or f*; **chocolate ~** mousse *m or f* de chocolate
[2] (*for hair*) espuma *f*

moustache, **mustache** (*US*) [məs'tɑːʃ] N bigote *m*; **to wear a ~** tener bigote; **he's got a ~** tiene bigote; **a tall man with a ~** un hombre alto con bigote

moustachioed, **mustachioed** (*US*) [mə'stɑːʃɪəʊd] ADJ bigotudo

mousy ['maʊsɪ] ADJ (*compar* **mousier**; *superl* **mousiest**) [*person*] tímido; [*colour, hair*] pardusco

mouth [maʊθ] Ⓐ N (*pl* **mouths** [maʊðz]) (*Anat*) boca *f*; [*of bottle*] boca *f*, abertura *f*; [*of cave*] entrada *f*; [*of river*] desembocadura *f*; [*of channel*] embocadero *m*; [*of wind instrument*] boquilla *f*; **to foam** *or* **froth at the ~** espumajear; **to open one's ~** (*lit, fig*) abrir la boca; **he never opened his ~ at the meeting** en la reunión no abrió la boca; **she didn't dare to open her ~** no se atrevió a decir ni pío; ✦***IDIOMS*** **he's all ~ and (no) trousers** (*Brit**) se le va (toda) la fuerza por la boca*, es un fanfarrón *or* un fantasma*; **to be down in the ~** estar deprimido; **to shoot one's ~ off*** hablar más de la cuenta; **to keep one's ~ shut*** callarse, no decir ni esta boca es mía; **shut your ~!**‡ ¡cállate ya!; **to stop sb's ~**‡ hacer callar a algn; **watch your ~!**‡ ¡cuidadito con lo que dices!; **to put words into sb's ~** poner palabras en boca de algn; *see also* **big A6**
Ⓑ [maʊð] VT (*insincerely*) soltar; (*affectedly*) pronunciar con afectación, articular con rimbombancia; **"go away!" she ~ed** —¡vete de aquí! —dijo moviendo mudamente los labios
Ⓒ [maʊθ] CPD ► **mouth organ** N (*esp Brit*) armónica *f*

-mouthed [maʊðd] ADJ (*ending in compounds*) de boca …, que tiene la boca …; **big-mouthed** de boca grande

mouthful ['maʊθfʊl] N [*of food*] bocado *m*; [*of drink*] trago *m*; [*of smoke, air*] bocanada *f*; **the name is a bit of a ~** es un nombre kilométrico; **you said a ~** (*US**) ¡y que lo digas!, ¡tú lo has dicho!

mouthpiece ['maʊθpiːs] N [1] (*Mus*) boquilla *f*
[2] [*of telephone*] micrófono *m*
[3] (= *person, publication*) portavoz *mf*

mouth-to-mouth ['maʊθtə'maʊθ] CPD ► **mouth-to-mouth resuscitation** N (respiración *f*) boca a boca *m*

mouthwash ['maʊθwɒʃ] N elixir *m* bucal

mouthwatering ['maʊθ'wɔːtərɪŋ] ADJ muy apetitoso, que hace la boca agua

movable ['muːvəbl] Ⓐ ADJ movible, móvil; **~ feast** fiesta *f* movible; **not easily ~** nada fácil de mover
Ⓑ NPL **~s** muebles *mpl*, mobiliario *msing*; (*Jur*) bienes *mpl* muebles

move [muːv] Ⓐ N [1] (= *movement*) movimiento *m*; **to watch sb's every ~** observar a algn sin perder detalle, acechar a algn cada movimiento; **to get a ~ on (with sth)*** (= *hurry up*) darse prisa *or* (*LAm*) apurarse (con algo); **get a ~ on!*** ¡date prisa!, ¡apúrate! (*LAm*); **to make a ~** (= *start to leave, go*) ponerse en marcha; **it was midnight and no-one had made a ~** era medianoche pero nadie daba señales de irse; **it's time we made a ~** es hora de irnos; **to be on the ~** (= *travelling*) estar de viaje; [*troops, army*] estar avanzando; **to be always on the ~** [*nomads, circus*] andar siempre de aquí para allá; [*animal, child*] no saber estar quieto; **Spain is a country on the ~** España es país en marcha
[2] (*in game*) (= *turn*) jugada *f*; **whose ~ is it?** ¿a quién le toca jugar?; **it's my ~** es mi turno, me toca a mí; **to have the first ~** salir
[3] (*fig*) (= *step, action*); **the government's first ~** la primera gestión del gobierno; **what's the next ~?** ¿qué hacemos ahora?, y ahora ¿qué?; **that was a bad ~** fue una mala decisión; **there was a ~ to defeat the proposal** se tomaron medidas para rechazar la propuesta; **to make a ~/the first ~** dar un/el primer paso; **it's up to him to make the first ~** le toca a él dar el primer paso; **without making the least ~ to** + *infin* sin hacer la menor intención de + *infin*
[4] (= *house removal*) mudanza *f*; (*to different job*) traslado *m*; **it's our third ~ in two years** ésta es la tercera vez en dos años que nos mudamos
Ⓑ VT [1] (= *change place of*) cambiar de lugar, cambiar de sitio; [+ *part of body*] mover; [+ *chess piece etc*] jugar, mover; (= *transport*) transportar, trasladar; **you've ~d all my things!** ¡has cambiado de sitio todas mis cosas!; **if we can ~ the table a few inches** si podemos mover la mesa unos centímetros; **can you ~ your fingers?** ¿puedes mover los dedos?; **to ~ house** mudarse; **~ your chair nearer the fire** acerca *or* arrima la silla al fuego; **~ the cupboard out of the corner** saca el armario del rincón; **he ~d his family out of the war zone** trasladó a su familia fuera de la zona de guerra; **he asked to be ~d to London/to a new department** pidió el traslado a Londres/a otro departamento
[2] (= *cause sth to move*) mover; **the breeze ~d the leaves gently** la brisa movía *or* agitaba dulcemente las hojas; **to ~ one's bowels** hacer de vientre, evacuar; **~ those children off the grass!** ¡quite esos niños del césped!; *see also* **heaven 1**
[3] (= *change timing of*) **to ~ sth forward/back** [+ *event, date*] adelantar/aplazar algo; **we'll have to ~ the meeting to later in the week** tendremos que aplazar la reunión para otro día de la semana
[4] (*fig*) (= *sway*) **he will not be easily ~d** no se dejará convencer; **"we shall not be ~d"** "no nos moverán"
[5] (= *motivate*) **to ~ sb to do sth** mover *or* inducir a algn a hacer algo; **I'll do it when the spirit ~s me** (*hum*) lo haré cuando sienta la revelación divina (*hum*)
[6] (*emotionally*) conmover, emocionar; **to be ~d** estar conmovido; **to be easily ~d** ser impresionable, ser sensible; **to ~ sb to tears/anger** hacer llorar/enfadar a algn; **to ~ sb to pity** provocar la compasión de algn
[7] (*frm*) (= *propose*) **to ~ a resolution** proponer una resolución; **to ~ that …** proponer que …
[8] (*Comm*) [+ *merchandise*] colocar, vender
Ⓒ VI [1] (*gen*) moverse; **she ~s beautifully** se mueve con elegancia; **~!** ¡muévete!, ¡menéate!; **don't ~!** ¡no te muevas!; **I saw something moving in the bushes** vi moverse algo entre los arbustos; **you can't ~ for books in that room*** hay tantos libros en esa habitación que es casi imposible moverse; **to ~ freely** [*piece of machinery*] tener juego; [*person, traffic*] circular libremente; **I won't ~ from here** no me muevo de aquí; **to ~ in high society** frecuentar la buena sociedad; **let's ~ into the garden** vamos al jardín; **he has ~d into another class** se ha cambiado de clase; **they hope to ~ into the British market** quieren introducirse en *or* penetrar el mercado británico; **keep moving!** ¡no te pares!; (*order from traffic policeman*) ¡circulen!; **the policeman kept the traffic moving** el policía mantuvo la circulación fluida; **the procession ~d slowly out of sight** la procesión avanzaba lentamente hasta que desapareció en la distancia; **it's time we were moving** es hora de irnos; **she ~d to the next room** pasó a la habitación de al lado; **he ~d slowly towards the door** avanzó *or* se acercó lentamente hacia la puerta; **to ~ to** *or* **towards in-**

dependence avanzar *or* encaminarse hacia la independencia
2 (= *move house*) mudarse, trasladarse; **the family ~d to a new house** la familia se mudó *or* se trasladó a una casa nueva; **to ~ to the country** mudarse *or* trasladarse al campo; **the company has ~d to larger offices** la empresa se ha trasladado *or* mudado a oficinas mayores
3 (= *travel*) ir; (= *be in motion*) estar en movimiento; **the bus was moving at 50kph** el autobús iba a 50kph; **the car was not moving** el coche no estaba en movimiento; **do not get out while the bus is moving** no se baje mientras el autobús esté en marcha; **he was certainly moving!*** ¡iba como el demonio!
4 (*Comm*) [*goods*] venderse
5 (= *progress*) **things are moving at last** por fin se empiezan a mover las cosas; **he certainly knows how to get things moving** ése sí que sabe poner las cosas en marcha
6 (*in games*) jugar, hacer una jugada; **who ~s next?** ¿a quién le toca jugar?; **it's you to ~** te toca a ti jugar; **white ~s** (*Chess*) blanco juega; **the knight ~s like this** el caballo se mueve así
7 (= *take steps*) dar un paso, tomar medidas; **the government must ~ first** el gobierno ha de dar el primer paso; **the council ~d to stop the abuse** el consejo tomó medidas para corregir el abuso; **we'll have to ~ quickly if we want to get that contract** tendremos que actuar inmediatamente si queremos hacernos con ese contrato

►**move about, move around** Ⓐ VT + ADV 1 (= *place in different position*) cambiar de sitio
2 (= *employee*) trasladar de un sitio a otro
Ⓑ VI + ADV 1 (= *fidget*) moverse
2 (= *walk about*) andar
3 (= *travel*) viajar de un sitio a otro; **to ~ about freely** circular libremente

►**move along** Ⓐ VT + ADV [+ *crowd*] hacer circular
Ⓑ VI + ADV 1 [*crowd*] circular; **~ along there!** ¡circulen!
2 (= *move forward*) avanzar, adelantarse
3 (*on bench etc*) correrse, hacerse a un lado

►**move aside** Ⓐ VT + ADV apartar
Ⓑ VI + ADV apartarse, ponerse a un lado, quitarse de en medio

►**move away** Ⓐ VT + ADV 1 (*gen*) apartar, alejar
2 (= *move to another place*) mover
Ⓑ VI + ADV 1 (= *move aside*) apartarse
2 (= *leave*) irse, marcharse; **to ~ away (from)** marcharse (de)
3 (= *move house*) mudarse

►**move back** Ⓐ VT + ADV 1 [+ *crowd*] hacer retroceder
2 (*to former place*) volver, regresar
3 [+ *employee*] volver a trasladar
4 (= *postpone*) aplazar, posponer; **let's ~ the meeting back to Friday** vamos a aplazar *or* posponer la reunión hasta el viernes
Ⓑ VI + ADV 1 (= *withdraw*) retroceder, retirarse
2 (*to former place*) volver, regresar
3 (= *move house*) **they ~d back to Burgos again** volvieron a mudarse a Burgos

►**move down** Ⓐ VT + ADV 1 [+ *person, object*] bajar
2 (*on bench etc*) hacer correrse
3 (*Scol*) [+ *pupil*] **I may have to ~ you down (a group)** puede que tenga que ponerte en un nivel más bajo
Ⓑ VI + ADV 1 [*person, object*] bajar
2 (*on bench etc*) correrse
3 (*Scol*) [*pupil*] **he has had to ~ down one class** ha tenido que cambiarse al curso inmediatamente inferior
4 (*Sport*) (*in league*) descender (a la división inferior *etc*)

►**move forward** Ⓐ VT + ADV 1 avanzar
2 (= *bring forward*) [+ *date, meeting*] adelantar; **to ~ the clocks forward** adelantar los relojes
Ⓑ VI + ADV adelantarse

►**move in** Ⓐ VT + ADV (= *take inside*) meter, llevar hacia dentro
Ⓑ VI + ADV 1 (*into accommodation*) instalarse; **to ~ in with sb** irse a vivir con algn
2 (= *start operations*) ponerse manos a la obra, intervenir; (*Comm*) (*to new market*) introducirse; **drug dealers soon ~d in** los traficantes de drogas se pusieron rápidamente manos a la obra
3 (= *come closer*) acercarse (**on** a); [*army*] avanzar (**on** sobre)

►**move off** Ⓐ VT + ADV sacar
Ⓑ VI + ADV 1 (= *go away*) irse, marcharse
2 (= *start moving*) ponerse en marcha

►**move on** Ⓐ VT + ADV 1 [+ *crowd etc*] hacer circular
2 [+ *hands of clock*] adelantar
Ⓑ VI + ADV 1 [*person, vehicle*] circular
2 (*fig*) 2·1 [*time*] pasar
2·2 (*to new job*) **this training will prove useful when you want to ~ on** esta formación te resultará útil cuando quieras cambiar de trabajo; **she wanted to ~ on to a bigger company** quería irse a trabajar a una empresa mayor
2·3 (*in discussion*) pasar (**to** a); **let's leave it there and ~ on (to the next point)** dejémoslo aquí y pasemos al punto siguiente
2·4 (= *change*) cambiar; **things have ~d on since your visit** las cosas han cambiado desde tu visita

►**move out** Ⓐ VT + ADV 1 [+ *person, object*] sacar
2 [+ *troops*] retirar
Ⓑ VI + ADV 1 (= *leave accommodation*) mudarse; **to ~ out of an area** marcharse de un barrio; **to ~ out of a flat** mudarse de un piso *or* (*LAm*) departamento
2 (= *withdraw*) [*troops*] retirarse

►**move over** Ⓐ VT + ADV hacer a un lado, correr
Ⓑ VI + ADV 1 (*on bench, seat*) correrse, hacerse a un lado; **~ over!** ¡córrete!
2 (*fig*) **if he can't do the job, he should ~ over to let someone else have a chance** si no sabe hacerlo, debería dejarlo para que otro lo intente; **we should ~ over to a different system** nos convendría cambiar de sistema

►**move up** Ⓐ VT + ADV 1 [+ *object, person*] subir
2 [+ *troops*] trasladar al frente
3 (= *promote*) ascender
Ⓑ VI + ADV 1 (= *make room*) correrse
2 (= *increase*) [*shares, rates etc*] subir
3 (= *be promoted*) ascender, ser ascendido; **to ~ up a class** [*pupil*] pasar de curso, pasar al curso inmediatamente superior

moveable ['mu:vəbl] = **movable**

movement ['mu:vmənt] N 1 (= *motion*) movimiento *m*; [*of part*] juego *m*, movimiento *m*; [*of traffic*] circulación *f*; (*on stock exchange*) actividad *f*; **upward/downward ~** movimiento ascendente/descendente; **to be in ~** estar en movimiento; **there was a ~ towards the door** algunos se dirigieron hacia la puerta; **the police questioned him about his ~s** la policía le pidió informes sobre sus actividades; **~ of capital** movimiento de capitales
2 (= *gesture*) gesto *m*, ademán *m*
3 (*political, artistic etc*) movimiento *m*
4 (*Mech*) mecanismo *m*
5 (*Mus*) tiempo *m*, movimiento *m*
6 (*Med*) (*also* **bowel ~**) evacuación *f*

mover ['mu:vəʳ] N 1 [*of motion*] promotor/a *m/f* 2 (*US*) agente *m* de mudanzas
3 (*) **he's a lovely ~** se mueve con mucho garbo, baila/anda con mucha elegancia

movie ['mu:vɪ] (*esp US*) Ⓐ N película *f*, film(e) *m*; **the ~s** el cine; **to go to the ~s** ir al cine
Ⓑ CPD ► **movie camera** N cámara *f* cinematográfica ► **movie house** N = **movie theatre** ► **the movie industry** N la industria cinematográfica ► **movie star** N estrella *f* de cine ► **movie theatre** N cine *m*

moviegoer ['mu:vɪgəʊəʳ] N (*US*) aficionado/a *m/f* al cine

movieland ['mu:vɪlænd] N (*US*) (= *dreamworld*) mundo *m* de ensueño creado por el cine; (*eg Hollywood*) centro *m* de la industria cinematográfica

moving ['mu:vɪŋ] Ⓐ ADJ 1 (= *not fixed*) móvil; **~ part** pieza *f* móvil
2 (= *not stationary*) [*vehicle*] en marcha, en movimiento; [*target*] móvil, en movimiento
3 (= *touching*) [*book, story, film, sight, event*] conmovedor, emotivo
4 (*fig*) (= *instigating*) motor (*fem: motora/motriz*), impulsor; **the ~ force behind sth** la fuerza motora *or* motriz *or* impulsora de algo; **the ~ spirit behind sth** el espíritu impulsor de algo
Ⓑ N (= *relocation*) **~ is a very stressful experience** mudarse *or* una mudanza de casa es una experiencia muy estresante
Ⓒ CPD ► **moving company** N (*US*) empresa *f* de mudanzas ► **moving pavement**, **moving sidewalk** (*US*) N cinta *f* móvil ► **moving picture**† N película *f* ► **moving staircase** N escalera *f* mecánica ► **moving van** N (*US*) camión *m* de mudanzas ► **moving walkway** N cinta *f* móvil

movingly ['mu:vɪŋlɪ] ADV [*speak, write*] emotivamente, de manera conmovedora

mow [məʊ] (*pt* **mowed**; *pp* **mown**, **mowed**) VT
1 **to ~ the lawn** cortar el césped
2 (*Agr*) segar, cortar; **to ~ sb down** (*fig*) acabar con algn, segar la vida de algn

mower ['məʊəʳ] N 1 (*also* **lawn ~**) cortacésped *m*
2 (*Agr*) (= *machine*) segadora *f*; (= *person*) segador(a) *m/f*

mowing ['məʊɪŋ] Ⓐ N siega *f*
Ⓑ CPD ► **mowing machine** N segadora *f* (mecánica)

mown [məʊn] PP *of* **mow**

moxie‡, **moxy**‡ ['mɒksɪ] N (*US*) (= *courage*) valor *m*; (= *nerve*) sangre fría *f*; (= *vigour*) vigor *m*, dinamismo *m*

Mozambican [ˌməʊzəm'bi:kən] ADJ, N mozambiqueño/a *m/f*

Mozambique [ˌməʊzəm'bi:k] N Mozambique *m*

Mozarab [mɒz'ærəb] N mozárabe *mf*

Mozarabic [mɒz'ærəbɪk] Ⓐ ADJ mozárabe
Ⓑ N mozárabe *m*

mozzarella [ˌmɒtsə'relə] N mozzarella *f*

MP N ABBR 1 (*Brit*) (= **member of parliament**) Dip., diputado/a *m/f*, parlamentario/a *m/f*
2 (*Mil*) (= **military police**) PM *f*
3 (*Canada*) = **mounted police**

MP3 [ˌempi:'θri:] Ⓐ N MP3 *m*
Ⓑ CPD ► **MP3 player** N reproductor *m* MP3

mpg N ABBR (*Aut*) (= **miles per gallon**) ≈ k.p.l.

mph N ABBR (= **miles per hour**) ≈ km/h, ≈ k.p.h.

MPhil [em'fɪl] N ABBR (*Univ*) = **Master of Philosophy**

MPS N ABBR (*Brit*) = **Member of the Pharmaceutical Society**

MPV N ABBR = **multipurpose vehicle**

Mr ['mɪstəʳ] N ABBR (*pl* **Messrs**) (= **Mister**) Sr., señor; **Mr Jones wants to see you** el señor Jones quiere verte; **yes, Mr Brown** sí, señor Brown; *see also* **big A6**, **right A2**

> **MR, MRS, MISS**
>
> **Use of article**
>
> • Use the article with **Sr./señor**, **Sra./señora**, **Srta./señorita** when you are talking *about* someone rather than *to* them:
>
> Mr Smith is not at home
> ***El Sr. Smith no está en casa***
> Mr and Mrs Crespo are on holiday
> ***Los Sres. (de) Crespo están de vacaciones***
> Have you seen Miss Barrios this morning?
> ***¿Ha visto a la Srta. Barrios esta mañana?***
>
> **NOTE:** The abbreviated form is more common than the full form in writing.
>
> • Don't use the article before **Sr./señor**, **Sra./señora**, **Srta./señorita** when addressing someone directly:
>
> Good morning, Mrs Ramírez
> ***Buenos días, Sra. Ramírez***
> Mr López, there's a telephone call for you
> ***Sr. López, le llaman por teléfono***
>
> **Capitalization**
>
> • Write the *full forms* **señor**, **señora** and **señorita** with a small "s", even when using them as titles:
>
> ***El señor Smith no está en casa***
> ***Estaba hablando con la señora (de) Williams***
>
> **Addressing correspondence**
>
> • Use **Sr. Don/Sra. Doña** (**Sr. D./Sra. Dña.**) rather than **Sr./Sra.** when giving both forename and surname. Don't use the article:
>
> Mr Bernardo García
> ***Sr. Don*** *or* ***Sr. D. Bernardo García***
> Mrs Teresa Álvarez Serrano
> ***Sra. Doña*** *or* ***Sra. Dña. Teresa Álvarez Serrano***
>
> ⇨ *See also* APELLIDO, DON
>
> *For further uses and examples, see main entries at* ***miss²***, ***mister*** *and* ***Mrs***.

MRC N ABBR (*Brit*) (= **Medical Research Council**) *depto. estatal que controla la investigación médica*

MRCP N ABBR (*Brit*) = **Member of the Royal College of Physicians**

MRCS N ABBR (*Brit*) = **Member of the Royal College of Surgeons**

MRCVS N ABBR (*Brit*) = **Member of the Royal College of Veterinary Surgeons**

MRD N ABBR = **machine-readable dictionary**

MRI [ˌemɑːr'aɪ] N = **magnetic resonance imaging**

MRP N ABBR = **manufacturer's recommended price**

Mrs ['mɪsɪz] Ⓐ N ABBR (*pl inv*) (= **Mistress**) Sra., señora; **~ Pitt wants to see you** la señora (de) Pitt quiere verte; **yes, ~ Brown** sí, señora Brown; → MR, MRS, MISS
Ⓑ CPD ► **Mrs Mop*** N (*Brit hum*) la maruja*

MRSA N ABBR (= **methicillin-resistant Staphylococcus aureus**) *virus asesino sin tratamiento conocido*

MS Ⓐ N ABBR 1 = **multiple sclerosis**
2 (*US*) = **Master of Science**
Ⓑ ABBR 1 (*US*) = **Mississippi**
2 (*also* **ms**) = **manuscript**

Ms [mɪz, məz] N ABBR (= **Miss** *or* **Mrs**) *prefijo de nombre de mujer que evita expresar su estado civil*; **Ms Sinclair is not at home** la señora Sinclair no está en casa

> **Ms**
>
> *La fórmula de tratamiento* **Ms** *es el equivalente femenino de* **Mr** *y se utiliza frecuentemente en la actualidad para evitar la distinción que los términos tradicionales establecían entre mujer casada (***Mrs***) y soltera (***Miss***). Las formas* **Ms** *y* **Miss** *nunca llevan punto, pero* **Mr** *y* **Mrs** *a veces sí.*

MSA N ABBR (*US Univ*) = **Master of Science in Agriculture**

MSC N ABBR (*Brit*) (*formerly*) = **Manpower Services Commission**

MSc N ABBR (*Brit Univ*) = **Master of Science**; → DEGREE

MS-DOS [ˌemes'dɒs] N ABBR = **Microsoft Disk Operating System**

MSF N ABBR (*Brit*) = **Manufacturing, Science, Finance**

MSG N ABBR = **monosodium glutamate**

Msgr ABBR (= **Monsignor**) Mons.

MSI N ABBR = **medium-scale integration**

MSP N ABBR (*Brit*) = **Member of the Scottish Parliament**

MSS ABBR = **manuscripts**

MST N ABBR (*US*) = **Mountain Standard Time**

MSW N ABBR (*US Univ*) = **Master of Social Work**

MT Ⓐ N ABBR = **machine translation**
Ⓑ ABBR (*US*) = **Montana**

Mt ABBR (*Geog*) (= **Mount, Mountain**) m.

MTB N ABBR = **motor torpedo boat**

mth ABBR (= **month**) m.

MTV N ABBR = **music television**

much [mʌtʃ] Ⓐ ADJ mucho; **there isn't ~ time** no tenemos mucho tiempo, tenemos poco tiempo; **~ crime goes unreported** hay muchos crímenes que no se denuncian; **I haven't got as ~ energy as you** no tengo tanta energía como tú; **how ~ sugar do you want?** ¿cuánto azúcar quieres?; **so ~ tea** tanto té; **she's got so ~ energy** tiene tanta energía; **too ~ jam** demasiada mermelada *f*; **we haven't got too ~ time** no tenemos demasiado tiempo; **very ~** mucho; **we haven't very ~ time** no tenemos mucho tiempo, tenemos poco tiempo; **without ~ money** sin mucho dinero
Ⓑ ADVERB 1 (= *a lot*) mucho; (*before pp*) muy; **she doesn't go out ~** no sale mucho; **it doesn't ~ matter** ◊ **it doesn't matter ~** no importa mucho; **I ~ regret that …** siento mucho que …; **it won't finish ~ before midnight** no terminará mucho antes de la media noche; **~ better** mucho mejor; **he's ~ richer than I am** *or* **than me** es mucho más rico que yo; **~ pleased** muy satisfecho; **~ as I would like to go** a pesar de que me gustaría mucho ir, aunque me gustaría mucho ir; **~ as I should like to** por mucho que quisiera; **~ as I like him** aunque *or* a pesar de que me gusta mucho; **~ as he hated the idea …** a pesar de lo que odiaba la idea …; **~ as I respect her ideas, I still think she's wrong** a pesar de que respeto mucho sus ideas *or* aunque respeto mucho sus ideas, creo que está equivocada; **however ~ he tries** por mucho que se esfuerce; **I hardly know her, ~ less her mother** apenas la conozco, y mucho menos a su madre; **not ~** no mucho; **thank you (ever) so ~** muchísimas gracias, muy agradecido; **I feel ever so ~ better** me siento muchísimo mejor; **~ though I like him** por mucho que él me guste; **~ though he hated the idea, he knew that …** a pesar de lo que odiaba la idea, sabía que …; **he had reservations about the scheme, ~ though he valued Alison's opinions** tenía sus dudas respecto al plan, a pesar de que valoraba mucho las opiniones de Alison; **~ to my astonishment** para gran sorpresa mía; **he talks too ~** habla demasiado; **very ~** mucho; **I enjoyed myself very ~** me divertí mucho
2 (= *by far*) con mucho; **~ the biggest** con mucho el más grande; **I would ~ rather stay** prefiero mucho más quedarme
3 (= *more or less*) más o menos, casi; **they're ~ the same size** tienen más o menos el mismo tamaño; **they are ~ of an age** tienen casi la misma edad
Ⓒ PRONOUN mucho; **there isn't ~ to do** no hay mucho que hacer; **but ~ remains to be done** pero queda mucho que *or* por hacer; **you've got as ~ as she has** tienes tanto como ella; **it didn't cost as ~ as I had expected** no costó tanto como yo me esperaba; **it can cost as ~ as $2,000** puede llegar a costar 2.000 dólares; **that's a bit ~!*** ¡eso es demasiado!; **there isn't ~ in it** (*between alternatives*) no hay mucha diferencia, no va mucho de uno a otro; **how ~ is it a kilo?** ¿cuánto vale el kilo?; **how ~ does it cost?** ¿cuánto cuesta?; **she won but there wasn't ~ in it** ganó, pero no por mucho; **she's not ~ to look at** físicamente no vale mucho; **to make ~ of sth** dar mucha importancia a algo; **~ of this is true** gran parte de esto es verdad; **we don't see ~ of each other** no nos vemos mucho; **we haven't heard ~ of him lately** últimamente apenas sabemos nada de él; **I'm not ~ of a musician** sé muy poco de música, entiendo poco de música; **I'm not ~ of a cook** no cocino muy bien; **he's not ~ of a player** como jugador no vale mucho; **that wasn't ~ of a dinner** eso apenas se podía llamar cena; **we spent so ~** gastamos tanto; **I've got so ~ to do** tengo tantísimo que hacer; **that's too ~** eso es demasiado; **it's not up to ~*** no vale gran cosa

muchness ['mʌtʃnɪs] N **they're much of a ~** son poco más o menos lo mismo

mucilage ['mjuːsɪlɪdʒ] N mucílago *m*

mucilaginous [ˌmjuːsɪ'lædʒɪnəs] ADJ mucilaginoso

muck [mʌk] N 1 (= *dirt*) suciedad *f*, mugre *f*; (= *manure*) estiércol *m*; *see also* **lady A3**
2 (*fig*) porquería *f*

►**muck about***, **muck around*** Ⓐ VT + ADV **to ~ sb about** *or* **around** fastidiar *or* (*LAm**) fregar a algn
Ⓑ VI + ADV 1 (= *lark about*) hacer tonterías; (= *do nothing in particular*) gandulear; **he enjoys ~ing about in boats** le gusta hacer el gandul navegando; **stop ~ing about!** ¡déjate de tonterías!
2 (= *tinker*) manosear

►**muck in*** VI + ADV compartir el trabajo, arrimar el hombro

►**muck out** VT + ADV (*Brit*) limpiar; **to ~ out a stable** limpiar una cuadra

►**muck up*** VT + ADV 1 (= *dirty*) ensuciar
2 (= *spoil*) echar a perder, fastidiar

mucker‡ ['mʌkəʳ] N compinche *m*

muckheap ['mʌk,hiːp] N estercolero *m*

muckiness ['mʌkɪnɪs] N suciedad *f*

muckrake* ['mʌkreɪk] VI (*pej*) (= *dig up past*) revelar los trapos sucios; (= *pry*) buscar y revelar cosas vergonzosas en la vida de otros, escarbar vidas ajenas

muckraker* ['mʌk,reɪkəʳ] N (*pej*) escarbador(a) *m/f* de vidas ajenas

muckraking* ['mʌk,reɪkɪŋ] N (*pej*) (= *digging up the past*) revelación *f* de trapos sucios; (*in journalism*) amarillismo *m*, sensacionalismo *m*

muck-up* ['mʌkʌp] N lío *m* grande; **that ~ with the timetable** ese lío que nos armamos con el horario; **what a ~!** ¡qué faena!*

mucky ['mʌkɪ] ADJ (*compar* **muckier**; *superl* **muckiest**) (= *muddy*) lleno de barro, embarrado; (= *filthy*) sucio, asqueroso, mugroso (*LAm*); **keep your ~ paws off!*** (*hum*) ¡no toques con esas manazas tan sucias!*; **to get ~** (= *muddy*) llenarse de barro, embarrarse; (= *filthy*) ponerse hecho un asco*, ensuciarse; **to get sth ~** (= *muddy*) llenar algo de barro, embarrar algo; (= *filthy*) dejar algo hecho un asco*, ensuciar algo; ✦***IDIOM*** **you're a ~ pup!*** (*hum*) ¡qué cochinote eres!*

mucous ['mjuːkəs] Ⓐ ADJ mucoso
Ⓑ CPD ► **mucous membrane** N mucosa *f*

mucus ['mjuːkəs] N moco *m*

mud [mʌd] Ⓐ N barro *m*, lodo *m*; **to stick in the ~** [*cart*] quedarse atascado en el barro; [*ship*] embarrancar; ✦***IDIOMS*** **(here's) ~ in your eye!*** (*toast*) ¡salud y pesetas!; **to drag sb's name through the ~** ensuciar el nombre de algn; **his name is ~** tiene muy mala fama; **to sling** *or* **throw ~ at sb** vilipendiar *or* insultar a algn, poner a algn como un trapo *or* por los suelos
Ⓑ CPD ► **mud bank** N banco *m* de lodo ► **mud bath** N baño *m* de lodo ► **mud flap** N cortina *f* ► **mud hut** N choza *f* de barro ► **mud pack** N mascarilla *f* de barro ► **mud pie** N bola *f* de barro ► **mud wall** N tapia *f* ► **mud wrestling** N *espectáculo de lucha sobre un cuadrilátero de barro*

muddle ['mʌdl] Ⓐ N (*untidy*) desorden *m*, lío* *m*; (= *tricky situation*) lío* *m*, follón *m* (*Sp**); (= *mix-up*) confusión *f*; **what a ~!** (*looking at mess*) ¡qué desorden!, ¡qué lío!; (*situation*) ¡qué lío!*, ¡qué follón! (*Sp**); **there's been a ~ over the seats** ha habido una confusión con las localidades; **to be in a ~** [*room, books*] estar en desorden, estar revuelto, estar hecho un desbarajuste*; [*person*] estar confuso, estar hecho un lío*; **the arrangements are all in a ~** hay un verdadero lío con los preparativos*; **to get into a ~** [*things*] desordenarse, revolverse; [*person*] hacerse un lío*; **to get sth into a ~** desordenar algo, revolver algo
Ⓑ VT (*also* **~ up**) [1] (= *jumble*) [+ *photos, papers*] revolver, desordenar; **you've ~d (up) all my papers!** ¡has revuelto *or* desordenado todos mis papeles!; **she'd got all the papers ~d (up)** había revuelto todos los papeles; **to get ~d (up)** [*things*] desordenarse, revolverse
[2] (= *confuse*) [+ *person, details*] confundir; **to get ~d (up)** [*person*] confundirse, hacerse un lío*, liarse*; *see also* **muddle up**

►**muddle along** VI + ADV arreglárselas de alguna manera, ir tirando*

►**muddle on** VI hacer las cosas al tuntún

►**muddle through** VI + ADV arreglárselas de alguna manera, ir tirando*; **I expect we shall ~ through** espero que lo logremos de algún modo u otro

►**muddle up** VT + ADV [1] (= *jumble*) *see* **muddle B1**
[2] (= *confuse*) **I kept getting my words ~d up** no hacía más que confundirme al hablar; **the copies had got ~d up with the original documents** las copias se habían mezclado *or* confundido con los documentos originales; **you're getting me ~d up with the other Julie** me estás confundiendo con la otra Julie; *see also* **muddle B2**

muddled ['mʌdld] ADJ [*account, explanation*] confuso, lioso*; [*ideas, article, thinking*] confuso, poco claro; [*person*] confundido, liado*; **I'm afraid I'm a little ~** me temo que estoy un poco confundido, me temo que estoy un poco liado*

muddleheaded ['mʌdl,hedɪd] ADJ [*person*] despistado, atolondrado; [*ideas*] confuso

muddler ['mʌdləʳ] N atolondrado/a *m/f*

muddy ['mʌdɪ] Ⓐ ADJ (*compar* **muddier**; *superl* **muddiest**) [1] (= *covered in mud*) [*clothes, hands, floor, carpet, track, field*] lleno de barro, embarrado; [*water, stream*] turbio
[2] (= *dull*) [*brown, green*] sucio; [*skin, complexion*] terroso
[3] (= *confused*) [*ideas, thinking*] confuso, poco claro
Ⓑ VT [1] (= *make dirty*) [+ *floor, carpet*] llenar de barro; [+ *hands, dress*] manchar de barro; [+ *water, stream*] enturbiar
[2] (= *make confused*) **to ~ the issue** confundir el tema *or* la cuestión, enredar las cosas; ✦***IDIOM*** **to ~ the waters** confundir el tema *or* la cuestión, enredar las cosas

mudflats ['mʌdflæts] NPL marisma *f*

mudguard ['mʌdgɑːd] N guardabarros *m inv*

mudlark ['mʌdlɑːk] N galopín *m*

mudslide ['mʌdslaɪd] N alud *m* de lodo

mudslinging ['mʌd,slɪŋɪŋ] N injurias *fpl*; **there won't be any ~ in this campaign** no habrá ataques personales en esta campaña

muesli ['mjuːzlɪ] N muesli *m*

muezzin [muː'ezɪn] N almuecín *m*, almuédano *m*

muff¹ [mʌf] N (*for hands*) manguito *m*

muff² [mʌf] VT [+ *shot, catch etc*] fallar; (*Theat*) [+ *entrance, lines*] estropear; **to ~ a chance** desperdiciar una oportunidad, echar a perder una oportunidad; **to ~ it** fastidiarla, hacerlo fatal

muffin ['mʌfɪn] N [1] (= *cake*) magdalena *f* (*generalmente con sabor a chocolate o con trocitos de fruta*)
[2] (*eaten with butter*) (*Brit*) ≈ mollete *m*; (*US*) *especie de pan dulce*, ≈ bollo *m*

muffle ['mʌfl] VT [1] (= *deaden*) [+ *sound*] amortiguar
[2] (= *wrap warmly*) (*also* **~ up**) abrigar; **to ~ o.s. (up)** abrigarse
[3] (= *cover*) [+ *oars, drum, hooves*] enfundar (*para amortiguar el ruido*); **he ~d the receiver** (*Telec*) tapó el auricular con la mano

muffled ['mʌfld] ADJ [1] (= *deadened*) [*sound, shot, cry, sob*] sordo, apagado; [*voice*] apagado
[2] (= *warmly wrapped*) envuelto, abrigado; **children ~ up in scarves and woolly hats** niños envueltos *or* abrigados con bufandas y gorros de lana
[3] (= *covered*) [*oars, drum, hooves*] enfundado (*para amortiguar el ruido*)

muffler ['mʌfləʳ] N [1] (= *scarf*) bufanda *f*
[2] (*Mus*) sordina *f*
[3] (*US Aut*) silenciador *m*, mofle *m* (*LAm*)

mufti ['mʌftɪ] N **in ~** (vestido) de paisano

mug [mʌg] Ⓐ N [1] (= *cup*) tazón *m* (*más alto que ancho*); **do you want a cup or a ~?** ¿quieres una taza normal o una taza grande?
[2] (= *glass*) jarra *f*; **a beer ~** una jarra de *or* para cerveza
[3] (‡) (= *dupe*) bobo/a *m/f*, primo/a *m/f*; **what a ~ I've been!** ¡mira que he sido bobo!; **smoking is a ~'s game** fumar es cosa de bobos
[4] (‡) (= *face*) jeta* *f*, careto *m* (*Sp*‡); **what a ~ she's got!** ¡qué jeta tiene!*
Ⓑ VT (= *attack and rob*) atracar, asaltar; **he was ~ged in the city centre** lo atracaron en el centro de la ciudad
Ⓒ CPD ► **mug shot*** N fotografía *f* para las fichas

►**mug up*** VT + ADV [1] (*Brit*) (*also* **~ up on**) empollar
[2] **to ~ it up** (*US*) (= *grimace*) gesticular, hacer muecas; (*Theat*) actuar exagerando

mugger ['mʌgəʳ] N atracador(a) *m/f*, asaltante *mf*

mugging ['mʌgɪŋ] N atraco *m* (callejero)

muggins* ['mʌgɪnz] N (*Brit*) **~ will do it** lo haré yo, como un tonto

muggy ['mʌgɪ] ADJ (*compar* **muggier**; *superl* **muggiest**) [*weather*] bochornoso; **it's ~ today** hoy hace bochorno

mugwump ['mʌgwʌmp] N (*US*) votante *mf* independiente

Muhammad [mʊ'hæməd] N = **Mohammed**

mujaheddin ['muːdʒəhə'diːn] NPL mujaidines *mpl*

mulatto [mjuː'lætəʊ] Ⓐ ADJ mulato
Ⓑ N (*pl* **mulattos** *or* **mulattoes**) mulato/a *m/f*

mulberry ['mʌlbərɪ] N (= *fruit*) mora *f*; (= *tree*) morera *f*, moral *m*

mulch [mʌltʃ] Ⓐ N capote *m*, mantillo *m*
Ⓑ VT cubrir con capote, cubrir con mantillo

mulct [mʌlkt] VT [1] (= *fine*) multar
[2] (= *cheat*) **to ~ sb of sth** quitar algo a algn, privar a algn de algo

mule¹ [mjuːl] Ⓐ N (= *animal*) mulo/a *m/f*; (*fig*) (= *person*) testarudo/a *m/f*; ✦***IDIOM*** **(as) stubborn as a ~** terco como una mula
Ⓑ CPD ► **mule track** N camino *m* de herradura

mule² [mjuːl] N (= *slipper*) babucha *f*

mule³ [mjuːl] N (*Tech*) máquina *f* de hilar intermitente, selfactina *f*

muleteer [,mjuːlɪ'tɪəʳ] N arriero *m*

mulish ['mjuːlɪʃ] ADJ terco, testarudo

mulishness ['mjuːlɪʃnɪs] N terquedad *f*, testarudez *f*

mull [mʌl] VT calentar con especias; **~ed wine** ponche *m*

►**mull over** VT + ADV reflexionar sobre, meditar

mullah ['mʌlə] N mullah *m*

mullet ['mʌlɪt] N **grey ~** mújol *m*; **red ~** salmonete *m*

mulligatawny [,mʌlɪgə'tɔːnɪ] N *especie de caldo de pollo o carne al curry*

mullion ['mʌlɪən] N parteluz *m*

mullioned ['mʌlɪənd] ADJ [*window*] dividido con parteluz

multi... ['mʌltɪ] PREFIX multi…

multi-access [,mʌltɪ'ækses] Ⓐ ADJ (*Comput*) multiacceso *inv*, de acceso múltiple
Ⓑ N acceso *m* múltiple

multicellular [,mʌltɪ'seljʊləʳ] ADJ multicelular

multichannel ['mʌltɪ'tʃænl] ADJ (*TV*) multicanal

multicoloured, **multicolored** (*US*) ['mʌltɪ'kʌləd] ADJ multicolor

multicultural [,mʌltɪ'kʌltʃərəl] ADJ multicultural

multidimensional [,mʌltɪdɪ'menʃənl] ADJ multidimensional

multidirectional [ˌmʌltɪdɪˈrekʃənl] ADJ multidireccional

multidisciplinary [ˌmʌltɪˈdɪsɪplɪnərɪ] ADJ multidisciplinario

multifaceted [ˌmʌltɪˈfæsɪtɪd] ADJ [*person*] multifacético; [*job*] con múltiples aspectos

multifarious [ˌmʌltɪˈfeərɪəs] ADJ múltiple, vario

multiform [ˈmʌltɪfɔːm] ADJ multiforme

multifunctional [ˈmʌltɪˈfʌŋkʃnəl] ADJ polivalente

multigym [ˈmʌltɪdʒɪm] N estación *f* de musculación

multihull [ˈmʌltɪhʌl] N multicasco *m*

multilateral [ˈmʌltɪˈlætərəl] ADJ (*Pol*) multilateral

multilayer [ˌmʌltɪˈleɪə] ADJ = **multilayered**

multilayered [ˌmʌltɪˈleɪəd] ADJ multicapa

multilevel [ˌmʌltɪˈlevl] ADJ (*US*) de muchos pisos

multilingual [ˌmʌltɪˈlɪŋgwəl] ADJ plurilingüe

multilingualism [ˌmʌltɪˈlɪŋgwəlɪzəm] N plurilingüismo *m*, multilingüismo *m*

multimedia [ˈmʌltɪˈmiːdɪə] ADJ [*aids, presentation*] (*also Comput*) multimedia

multimillion [ˈmʌltɪˈmɪljən] ADJ multimillonario

multimillionaire [ˈmʌltɪmɪljəˈnɛəʳ] N multimillonario/a *m/f*

multi-million-pound [ˌmʌltɪˈmɪljənˌpaʊnd] ADJ [*deal, fraud etc*] de (varios) millones de libras, multimillonario

multi-nation [ˈmʌltɪˈneɪʃən] ADJ [*treaty, agreement*] multinacional

multinational [ˌmʌltɪˈnæʃənl] Ⓐ N compañía *f* multinacional, multinacional *f*
Ⓑ ADJ multinacional

multi-pack [ˈmʌltɪpæk] N multipack *m*

multi-party [ˌmʌltɪˈpɑːtɪ] ADJ (*Pol*) [*system, democracy*] multipartidista, multipartidario; **~ talks** conversaciones *fpl* entre partidos

multiple [ˈmʌltɪpl] Ⓐ ADJ múltiple; **he died of ~ injuries** murió tras sufrir heridas múltiples; **~ accident** (*Aut*) colisión *f* múltiple *or* en cadena; **~ birth** parto *m* múltiple
Ⓑ N [1] (*Math*) múltiplo *m*; **lowest common ~** mínimo común múltiplo *m*
[2] (= *shop*) (*also* **~ store**) (sucursal *f* de una cadena de) grandes almacenes *mpl*
Ⓒ CPD ► **multiple choice question** N pregunta *f* de elección múltiple, pregunta *f* tipo test ► **multiple choice test** N examen *m* de elección múltiple, examen *m* tipo test ► **multiple ownership** N multipropiedad *f* ► **multiple personality (disorder)** N (*Psych*) personalidad *f* múltiple ► **multiple sclerosis** N esclerosis *f* múltiple ► **multiple store** N (sucursal *f* de una cadena de) grandes almacenes *mpl*

multiplex [ˈmʌltɪˌpleks] N (*also* **~ cinema**) multicines *mpl*

multiplexor [ˈmʌltɪˌpleksəʳ] N multiplexor *m*

multiplicand [ˌmʌltɪplɪˈkænd] N multiplicando *m*

multiplication [ˌmʌltɪplɪˈkeɪʃən] Ⓐ N multiplicación *f*
Ⓑ CPD ► **multiplication table** N tabla *f* de multiplicar

multiplicity [ˌmʌltɪˈplɪsɪtɪ] N multiplicidad *f*; **for a ~ of reasons** por múltiples razones; **a ~ of solutions** una gran diversidad *or* variedad de soluciones

multiply [ˈmʌltɪplaɪ] Ⓐ VT (*Math*) multiplicar; **to ~ eight by seven** multiplicar ocho por siete
Ⓑ VI [1] (*Math*) multiplicar
[2] (= *reproduce o.s.*) multiplicarse

multiprocessing [ˌmʌltɪˈprəʊsesɪŋ] N multiprocesamiento *m*

multiprocessor [ˌmʌltɪˈprəʊsesəʳ] N multiprocesador *m*

multiprogramming, **multiprograming** (*US*) [ˌmʌltɪˈprəʊgræmɪŋ] N multiprogramación *f*

multipurpose [ˌmʌltɪˈpɜːpəs] ADJ multiuso

multiracial [ˈmʌltɪˈreɪʃəl] ADJ multirracial

multirisk [ˈmʌltɪrɪsk] CPD ► **multirisk insurance** N seguro *m* multirriesgo, seguro *m* a todo riesgo

multistorey [ˌmʌltɪˈstɔːrɪ], **multistoreyed**, **multistoried** (*US*) [ˌmʌltɪˈstɔːrɪd] Ⓐ ADJ de varias plantas, de varios pisos
Ⓑ CPD ► **multistorey car park** N aparcamiento *m* de varias plantas

multistrike [ˈmʌltɪˌstraɪk] CPD ► **multistrike ribbon** N cinta *f* de múltiples impactos

multitask [ˈmʌltɪˈtɑːsk] N = **multitasking**

multitasking [ˈmʌltɪˈtɑːskɪŋ] N multitarea *f*

multitrack [ˈmʌltɪˌtræk] ADJ **~ recording** grabación *f* en bandas múltiples

multitude [ˈmʌltɪtjuːd] N [1] (= *crowd*) multitud *f*, muchedumbre *f*; **they came in ~s** acudieron en tropel; **the ~** (*pej*) las masas, la plebe
[2] (*fig*) **a ~ of problems** una infinidad de problemas, multitud de problemas; **there are a ~ of reasons why we shouldn't do it** hay multitud de razones por las que no deberíamos hacerlo; **for a ~ of reasons** por múltiples razones

multitudinous [ˌmʌltɪˈtjuːdɪnəs] ADJ muy numeroso, numerosísimo

multiuser [ˌmʌltɪˈjuːzəʳ] ADJ multiusuario; **~ system** sistema *m* multiusuario

mum¹* [mʌm] N (*Brit*) (= *mother*) mamá* *f*, mamaíta* *f*, mamacita* *f* (*LAm*); **I'll ask Mum** le preguntaré a mamá; **my ~** mi mamá

mum²* [mʌm] ADJ **to keep ~ (about sth)** guardar silencio (sobre algo); **everybody is keeping ~ about it** nadie suelta prenda sobre el asunto; **~'s the word!** ¡punto en boca!, ¡ni una palabra a nadie!

mumble [ˈmʌmbl] Ⓐ VI mascullar
Ⓑ VT mascullar
Ⓒ N **he said in a ~** masculló, dijo entre dientes

mumbo jumbo [ˈmʌmbəʊˈdʒʌmbəʊ] N (= *nonsense*) galimatías *m inv*

mummer [ˈmʌməʳ] N *actor o actriz enmascarado en una representación teatral tradicional, por lo general mímica*

mummery [ˈmʌmərɪ] N *representación teatral tradicional, por lo general mímica, en que se usan máscaras*

mummification [ˌmʌmɪfɪˈkeɪʃən] N momificación *f*

mummify [ˈmʌmɪfaɪ] Ⓐ VT momificar
Ⓑ VI momificarse

mummy¹ [ˈmʌmɪ] N (= *preserved corpse*) momia *f*

mummy²* [ˈmʌmɪ] N (*Brit*) = **mum¹**

mumps [mʌmps] NSING paperas *fpl*; **my brother's got ~** mi hermano tiene paperas

mumsy* [ˈmʌmzɪ] ADJ [*appearance, hair*] de señora; **she's much more ~ now** se la ve más maternal ahora

munch [mʌntʃ] Ⓐ VT mascar, masticar
Ⓑ VI mascar, masticar

Münchhausen's Syndrome [ˈmʌntʃaʊzənzˈsɪndrəʊm] N síndrome *m* de Munchhausen

munchies* NPL (*US*) [1] (= *snacks*) algo para picar
[2] **to have the ~** tener hambre

mundane [ˈmʌnˈdeɪn] ADJ (= *humdrum*) [*task*] rutinario; [*matter, problem*] trivial; [*existence*] prosaico; **on a more ~ level** a modo de trivialidad

municipal [mjuːˈnɪsɪpəl] ADJ municipal

municipality [mjuːˌnɪsɪˈpælɪtɪ] N (= *place*) municipio *m*

munificence [mjuːˈnɪfɪsns] N munificencia *f*

munificent [mjuːˈnɪfɪsnt] ADJ munífico, munificente

muniments [ˈmjuːnɪmənts] Ⓐ NPL documentos *mpl* (probatorios)
Ⓑ CPD ► **muniments room** N archivos *mpl*

munitions [mjuːˈnɪʃənz] Ⓐ NPL municiones *fpl*
Ⓑ CPD ► **munitions dump** N polvorín *m*, depósito *m* de municiones ► **munitions factory** N fábrica *f* de municiones

mural [ˈmjʊərəl] Ⓐ ADJ mural
Ⓑ N mural *m*, pintura *f* mural

murder [ˈmɜːdəʳ] Ⓐ N [1] asesinato *m*; (*Jur*) homicidio *m*; **accused of ~** acusado de homicidio; **to commit ~** cometer un asesinato *or* un crimen; **first-degree ~** ◊ **~ in the first degree** homicidio *m* premeditado, homicidio *m* en primer grado; **second-degree ~** ◊ **~ in the second degree** homicidio *m* en segundo grado; **the ~ weapon** el arma homicida; ✦**PROV ~ will out** todo termina por saberse; *see also* **attempted**, **mass² D**
[2] (*) **"did you have a good holiday?" — "no, it was ~!"** —¿pasaste unas buenas vacaciones? —¡no, lo pasé fatal* *or* fueron horribles!; **the noise/heat in here is ~** el ruido que hay aquí/el calor que hace aquí es insoportable; **the roads were ~** las carreteras estaban hasta los topes*; ✦**IDIOMS to scream** *or* **shout blue** *or* **bloody ~** poner el grito en el cielo; **to get away with ~**: **she lets the children get away with ~** a los niños les consiente todo, a los niños les deja hacer lo que les da la gana*
Ⓑ VT [1] [+ *person*] asesinar, matar, ultimar (*LAm*); **the ~ed man** el hombre asesinado
[2] (*fig*) (*) [+ *song, music, play, language*] destrozar, cargarse*; [+ *opponent*] aniquilar*
[3] (*) (= *really enjoy*) **I could ~ a beer/a cup of tea** daría cualquier cosa por una cerveza/una taza de té
Ⓒ VI cometer asesinatos, matar
Ⓓ CPD ► **murder case** N caso *m* de asesinato *or* homicidio ► **murder charge** N acusación *f* por asesinato *or* homicidio; **he is wanted on ~ charges** lo buscan por asesinato ► **Murder Squad** N brigada *f* de homicidios ► **murder trial** N juicio *m* por asesinato ► **murder victim** N víctima *f* de un asesinato *or* homicidio

murderer [ˈmɜːdərəʳ] N asesino/a *m/f*; (*as Jur term*) homicida *mf*

murderess [ˈmɜːdərɪs] N asesina *f*; (*as Jur term*) homicida *f*

murderous [ˈmɜːdərəs] ADJ [1] (= *homicidal*) homicida; (*fig*) cruel, feroz, sanguinario; [*look*] asesino, homicida; **I felt ~** (*lit, fig*) me vinieron pensamientos homicidas
[2] (*) (= *terrible*) **this heat is ~** este calor es cruel

murderously [ˈmɜːdərəslɪ] ADV [1] [*glare*] de manera asesina
[2] (*) (= *terribly*) terriblemente; **the bags were ~ heavy** las bolsas pesaban terriblemente *or* de forma matadora

murk [mɜːk] N oscuridad *f*, tinieblas *fpl*

murkiness ['mɜːkɪnɪs, 'mɜːkɪ] N (= *darkness*) oscuridad *f*; (*fig*) lo turbio, tenebrosidad *f*; [*of water, river*] lo turbio

murky ['mɜːkɪ] ADJ (*compar* **murkier**, *superl* **murkiest**) [1] (= *dark and cloudy*) [*night, evening*] tenebroso, oscuro; [*water*] turbio; [*fog*] espeso; [*brown, green*] sucio
[2] (*fig*) [*past*] turbio; **the ~ depths of Soviet politics** los turbios entresijos de la política soviética

murmur ['mɜːməʳ] Ⓐ N (= *soft speech*) murmullo *m*; [*of water, leaves*] murmullo *m*, susurro *m*; [*of distant traffic*] rumor *m*; **there were ~s of disagreement** hubo un murmullo de desaprobación; **without a ~** sin una queja; *see also* **heart B**
Ⓑ VI [*person*] murmurar; [*water*] murmurar, susurrar; **to ~ about sth** (= *complain*) quejarse de algo, murmurar de algo
Ⓒ VT murmurar, decir en voz baja

Murphy ['mɜːfɪ] N **~'s law*** ley *f* de la indefectible mala voluntad de los objetos inanimados

MusB, **MusBac** N ABBR (*Univ*) = **Bachelor of Music**

muscatel [ˌmʌskə'tel] Ⓐ ADJ moscatel
Ⓑ N moscatel *m*

muscle ['mʌsl] N [1] (*Anat*) músculo *m*; **to flex one's ~s** tensar los músculos; **he never moved a ~** ni se inmutó
[2] (*fig*) fuerza *f*; **political ~** poder *m* político
►**muscle in*** VI + ADV **to ~ in (on sth)** meterse por la fuerza (en algo)

musclebound ['mʌslbaʊnd] ADJ exageradamente musculoso

muscleman* ['mʌslmæn] N (*pl* **musclemen**) forzudo *m*

muscle-wasting ['mʌslˌweɪstɪŋ] ADJ **~ disease** enfermedad *f* de desgaste muscular

Muscovite ['mʌskəvaɪt] Ⓐ N moscovita *mf*
Ⓑ ADJ moscovita

muscular ['mʌskjʊləʳ] Ⓐ ADJ [1] (*Med, Physiol*) [*tissue, pain, control*] muscular
[2] (= *brawny*) [*person, body*] musculoso
Ⓑ CPD ► **muscular dystrophy** N distrofia *f* muscular

musculature ['mʌskjʊlətjʊəʳ] N musculatura *f*

MusD, **MusDoc** N ABBR (*Univ*) = **Doctor of Music**

Muse [mjuːz] N musa *f*; **the ~s** las Musas

muse [mjuːz] Ⓐ VI **to ~ on** *or* **about sth** reflexionar sobre algo, meditar algo
Ⓑ VT **"should we?" he ~d** —¿debemos hacerlo? —dijo pensativo

museum [mjuː'zɪəm] Ⓐ N museo *m*
Ⓑ CPD ► **museum piece** N (*lit*) pieza *f* de museo; (*fig*) antigualla *f*, pieza *f* de museo

mush[1] [mʌʃ] N [1] (*Culin*) gachas *fpl*
[2] (*fig*) sensiblería *f*, sentimentalismo *m*

mush[2]‡ [mʊʃ] N [1] (= *face*) jeta* *f*, careto *m* (*Sp‡*)
[2] (*in direct address*) **hey, ~!** ¡hola, tronco!*

mushroom ['mʌʃrʊm] Ⓐ N (*Culin*) (*round-topped*) champiñón *m*; (*flat-topped*) seta *f*; (*Bot*) seta *f*, hongo *m*, callampa *f* (*Chile*); **a great ~ of smoke** un enorme hongo de humo; **to grow like ~s** crecer como hongos; **to spring up like ~s** (*fig*) surgir como hongos
Ⓑ VI [*town etc*] crecer vertiginosamente; **the cloud of smoke went ~ing up** una nube de humo ascendió en forma de hongo
Ⓒ CPD [*salad, omelette etc*] de champiñones ► **mushroom cloud** N hongo *m* nuclear ► **mushroom growth** N crecimiento *m* vertiginoso ► **mushroom town** N ciudad *f* que crece vertiginosamente

mushy ['mʌʃɪ] ADJ (*compar* **mushier**, *superl* **mushiest**) [1] (*lit*) pulposo, mollar; **~ peas** (*Brit*) puré *m* de guisantes *or* (*LAm*) arvejas, chícharos *mpl* aguados (*Mex*)
[2] (*fig*) sensiblero, sentimentaloide

music ['mjuːzɪk] Ⓐ N música *f*; **to set a work to ~** poner música a una obra; **✦IDIOMS it was ~ to my ears** daba gusto escucharlo, me sonaba a música celestial; **to face the ~** afrontar las consecuencias
Ⓑ CPD ► **music box** N (*esp US*) caja *f* de música ► **music centre** N equipo *m* estereofónico ► **music critic** N crítico/a *m/f* musical ► **music director** N director(a) *m/f* musical ► **music festival** N festival *m* de música ► **music hall** N teatro *m* de variedades ► **music lesson** N (*instrumental*) clase *f* de música; (*vocal*) clase *f* de solfeo ► **music lover** N aficionado/a *m/f* a la música, amante *mf* de la música ► **music paper** N papel *m* de música, papel *m* pautado ► **music stand** N atril *m*

musical ['mjuːzɪkəl] Ⓐ ADJ [1] (= *relating to music*) [*career, taste, style, accompaniment, composition*] musical; [*talent, ability*] musical, para la música
[2] (= *musically talented*) [*person, child*] dotado para la música, con aptitudes musicales; **he came from a ~ family** venía de una familia de músicos *or* dotada para la música
[3] (= *melodious*) [*laugh, voice*] musical
Ⓑ N (*Cine, Theat*) musical *m*
Ⓒ CPD ► **musical box** N caja *f* de música ► **musical chairs** N juego *msing* de las sillas, juego *msing* del stop; **to play ~ chairs** jugar a las sillas, jugar al stop ► **musical comedy** N (*esp US*) comedia *f* musical ► **musical director** N = **music director** ► **musical instrument** N instrumento *m* musical ► **musical score** N (= *written music*) partitura *f*; (= *soundtrack*) banda *f* sonora

musicale [ˌmjuːzɪ'kɑːl] N velada *f* musical

musicality [ˌmjuːzɪ'kælɪtɪ] N musicalidad *f*

musically ['mjuːzɪkəlɪ] ADV [1] (= *from a musical point of view*) **I'm ~ trained** tengo formación musical; **she was incredibly gifted ~** tenía un talento increíble para la música, tenía un talento musical increíble; **~, the piece cannot be faulted** desde el punto de vista musical, no se le pueden sacar defectos a la pieza
[2] (= *melodiously*) [*say*] con un tono musical, melodiosamente

musician [mjuː'zɪʃən] N músico/a *m/f*; **he's a ~** es músico

musicianship [mjuː'zɪʃənʃɪp] N maestría *f* musical

musicologist [ˌmjuːzɪ'kɒlədʒɪst] N musicólogo/a *m/f*

musicology [ˌmjuːzɪ'kɒlədʒɪ] N musicología *f*

musingly ['mjuːzɪŋlɪ] ADV [*say etc*] con aire distraído, pensativamente

musings ['mjuːzɪŋz] NPL meditaciones *fpl*

musk [mʌsk] Ⓐ N (= *substance*) almizcle *m*; (= *scent*) perfume *m* de almizcle; (*Bot*) almizcleña *f*
Ⓑ CPD ► **musk ox** N buey *m* almizclado ► **musk rose** N (*Bot*) rosa *f* almizcleña

musket ['mʌskɪt] N mosquete *m*

musketeer [ˌmʌskɪ'tɪəʳ] N mosquetero *m*

musketry ['mʌskɪtrɪ] N (= *muskets*) mosquetes *mpl*; (= *firing*) fuego *m* de mosquetes, tiros *mpl*

muskrat ['mʌskræt] N ratón *m* almizclero

musky ['mʌskɪ] ADJ almizcleño, almizclado; [*smell*] a almizcle

Muslim N ['mʊslɪm] (*pl* **Muslims** *or* **Muslim**) = **Moslem**

muslin ['mʌzlɪn] Ⓐ N muselina *f*
Ⓑ ADJ de muselina

musquash ['mʌskwɒʃ] N [1] (= *animal*) = **muskrat**
[2] (= *fur*) piel *f* de ratón almizclero

muss* [mʌs] VT (*also* **~ up**) [+ *hair*] despeinar; [+ *dress*] arrugar

mussel ['mʌsl] Ⓐ N mejillón *m*
Ⓑ CPD ► **mussel bed** N criadero *m* de mejillones

must[1] [mʌst] N = **mustiness**

▼ **must[2]** [mʌst] Ⓐ MODAL AUX VB [1] (*obligation*) deber, tener que; **I ~ do it** debo hacerlo, tengo que hacerlo; **the patient ~ have complete quiet** el enfermo debe tener *or* tiene que tener *or* requiere silencio absoluto; **I ~ buy some presents** tengo que comprar unos regalos; **you ~ come again next year** tienes que volver el año que viene; **you ~n't forget to send her a card** no te vayas a olvidar de mandarle una tarjeta; **you ~n't touch it** no debes tocarlo; **"must not be switched off"** "no debe apagarse"; **I'll do it if I ~** si me obligan, lo haré, si es necesario; **do it if you ~** hazlo si es necesario; **if you ~ know, I'm Portuguese** para que lo sepa, soy portugués; **one ~ not be too hopeful** no hay que ser demasiado optimista; **I really ~ go now** de verdad que me tengo que ir ya; **I ~ say, he's very irritating** tengo que decir que es muy irritante; **why ~ you always be so rude?** ¿por qué tienes que ser siempre tan maleducado?
[2] (*probability*) deber de; **you ~ be tired** debes de estar cansado; **it ~ be cold up there** debe de hacer frío allí arriba; **he ~ be there by now** ya debe de estar allí; **it ~ be eight o'clock by now** ya deben de ser las ocho; **but you ~ have seen her!** ¡pero debes de haberla visto!; **there ~ be a reason** debe de haber *or* tiene que haber una razón
Ⓑ N (*) **this programme is a ~** no hay que perderse este programa, este programa hay que verlo

must-* [mʌst-] PREFIX **a ~see movie** una película que hay que ver, una película que no puede perderse; **leather jeans are the ~have fashion item of the season** los vaqueros de cuero son la prenda de moda imprescindible de la temporada; **a ~read** un libro obligado; **it's a ~visit** es una visita obligada

mustache ['mʌstæʃ] N (*US*) = **moustache**

mustachioed [mʌs'tæʃɪəʊd] ADJ (*US*) = **moustachioed**

mustang ['mʌstæŋ] N potro *m*, mesteño mustang(o) *m*

mustard ['mʌstəd] Ⓐ N (*Bot, Culin*) mostaza *f*; **✦IDIOM he doesn't cut the ~*** no da la talla
Ⓑ ADJ **a ~ (yellow) dress** un vestido color mostaza
Ⓒ CPD ► **mustard gas** N (*Chem, Mil*) gas *m* mostaza ► **mustard plaster** N sinapismo *m*, cataplasma *f* de mostaza ► **mustard pot** N mostacera *f*

muster ['mʌstəʳ] Ⓐ N (*esp Mil*) revista *f*; **✦IDIOM to pass ~** ser aceptable
Ⓑ VT (= *call together, collect*) reunir; (*also* **~ up**) [+ *courage*] armarse de; [+ *strength*] cobrar; **the club can ~ 20 members** el club cuenta con 20 miembros, el club consta de 20 miembros
Ⓒ VI juntarse, reunirse

mustiness ['mʌstɪnɪs] N [*of room*] olor *m* a cerrado, olor *m* a humedad

mustn't ['mʌsnt] = **must not**; *see* **must[2]**

➤ LANGUAGE IN USE: **must[2] A1** 2.2, 10.1, 10.2 **A2** 15.2

musty [ˈmʌstɪ] ADJ (*compar* **mustier**; *superl* **mustiest**) [*room etc*] que huele a humedad, que huele a cerrado; (*fig*) anticuado

mutability [ˌmjuːtəˈbɪlɪtɪ] N mutabilidad *f*

mutable [ˈmjuːtəbl] ADJ mudable

mutagen [ˈmjuːtədʒən] N mutagene *m*

mutant [ˈmjuːtənt] Ⓐ ADJ mutante
Ⓑ N mutante *mf*

mutate [mjuːˈteɪt] Ⓐ VT (*Bio*) mutar; (= *change*) transformar
Ⓑ VI (*Bio*) mutarse, sufrir mutación; (= *change*) transformarse

mutation [mjuːˈteɪʃən] N mutación *f*

mute [mjuːt] Ⓐ ADJ mudo; **to become ~** enmudecer; **with H ~** con hache muda
Ⓑ N 1 (= *person*) mudo/a *m/f*
2 (*Mus*) sordina *f*
3 (*Ling*) letra *f* muda
Ⓒ VT (*Mus*) poner sordina a; [+ *noise*] amortiguar; [+ *feelings etc*] acallar

muted [ˈmjuːtɪd] ADJ [*noise*] sordo; [*criticism*] callado, silencioso

mutilate [ˈmjuːtɪleɪt] VT mutilar

mutilation [ˌmjuːtɪˈleɪʃən] N mutilación *f*

mutineer [ˌmjuːtɪˈnɪəʳ] N amotinado *m*, amotinador *m*

mutinous [ˈmjuːtɪnəs] ADJ (*lit*) amotinado; (*fig*) rebelde; **we were feeling pretty ~** estábamos hartos ya, estábamos dispuestos a rebelarnos

mutiny [ˈmjuːtɪnɪ] Ⓐ N motín *m*
Ⓑ VI amotinarse

mutt* [mʌt] N 1 (= *fool*) bobo *m*
2 (= *dog*) chucho *m*

mutter [ˈmʌtəʳ] Ⓐ N murmullo *m*; **a ~ of voices** un murmullo de voces
Ⓑ VT murmurar, decir entre dientes; **"yes," he ~ed** —sí —dijo entre dientes
Ⓒ VI (*gen*) murmurar; [*guns, thunder*] retumbar a lo lejos; (= *complain*) quejarse

mutton [ˈmʌtn] Ⓐ N cordero *m*; **a leg of ~** una pierna de cordero; ✦*IDIOM* **~ dressed as lamb** vejestorio *m* emperifollado
Ⓑ CPD ► **mutton chop** N chuleta *f* de cordero

mutual [ˈmjuːtjʊəl] Ⓐ ADJ 1 (= *reciprocal*) [*affection, help*] mutuo; **the feeling is ~** el sentimiento es mutuo; **they had a ~ understanding not to bring up the subject** tenían el mutuo acuerdo de no sacar el tema
2 (= *common*) [*friend, cousin*] común; **they had a ~ interest in rugby** tenían un interés común *or* compartían su interés por el rugby; **it is to our ~ benefit** *or* **advantage** es beneficioso para ambos; **by ~ consent** de mutuo *or* común acuerdo
Ⓑ CPD ► **mutual benefit society** N mutualidad *f*, mutua *f*, mutual *f* (*Chile, Peru, Bol*) ► **mutual fund** N (*US*) fondo *m* de inversión mobiliaria ► **mutual insurance** N seguro *m* mutuo ► **mutual savings bank** N caja *f* mutua de ahorros

mutuality [ˌmjuːtjʊˈælɪtɪ] N mutualidad *f*

mutually [ˈmjuːtjʊəlɪ] ADV 1 (= *reciprocally*) mutuamente; **these views are ~ exclusive** estas opiniones se excluyen mutuamente
2 (= *for/by both parties involved*) **we arranged to meet at a ~ convenient time** acordamos vernos a una hora que nos viniera bien a los dos; **such a move would be ~ beneficial to the two companies** esta medida resultaría beneficiosa para ambas empresas; **we ~ agreed that …** decidimos de mutuo *or* común acuerdo que …

Muzak® [ˈmjuːzæk] N hilo *m* musical

muzzle [ˈmʌzl] Ⓐ N 1 (= *snout*) hocico *m*
2 [*of gun*] boca *f*
3 (= *restraint for dog*) bozal *m*
Ⓑ VT 1 [+ *dog*] poner bozal a
2 (*fig*) [+ *person*] amordazar
Ⓒ CPD ► **muzzle loader** N arma *f* que se carga por la boca ► **muzzle velocity** N velocidad *f* inicial

muzzy [ˈmʌzɪ] ADJ (*compar* **muzzier**; *superl* **muzziest**) [*outline, ideas*] borroso; [*person*] atontado, confuso

MVP N ABBR (*US*) = **most valuable player**

MW N ABBR 1 (*Rad*) (= **medium wave**) OM *f*
2 (*Elec*) = **megawatt(s)**

my [maɪ] Ⓐ POSS ADJ (*with singular noun*) mi; (*with plural noun*) mis; **my friend** mi amigo; **my books** mis libros; **my two best friends** mis dos mejores amigos; **my own car** mi propio coche; **they stole my car** me robaron el coche; **I'm washing my hair** me estoy lavando la cabeza; **I took off my coat** me quité el abrigo
Ⓑ EXCL ¡caramba!

myalgia [maɪˈældʒɪə] N mialgia *f*

myalgic encephalomyelitis [maɪˈældʒɪkenˌsefələʊmaɪəˈlaɪtɪs] N encefalomielitis *f inv* miálgica

Myanmar [ˈmaɪænmaːʳ] N Myanmar *f*

mycology [maɪˈkɒlədʒɪ] N micología *f*

myopia [maɪˈəʊpɪə] N (*frm*) miopía *f*

myopic [maɪˈɒpɪk] ADJ (*frm*) miope

myriad [ˈmɪrɪəd] (*frm*) Ⓐ ADJ **a ~ flies** un sinnúmero *or* una miríada de moscas
Ⓑ N miríada *f*; **the ~ of problems we face** la miríada de problemas a la que nos enfrentamos

myrmidon [ˈmɜːmɪdən] N (*pej, hum*) secuaz *m* fiel, satélite *m*, esbirro *m*

myrrh [mɜːʳ] N mirra *f*

myrtle [ˈmɜːtl] N arrayán *m*, mirto *m*

myself [maɪˈself] PRON 1 (*reflexive*) me; **I've hurt ~** me he hecho daño; **I couldn't see ~ in the mirror** no pude verme en el espejo
2 (*emphatic*) yo mismo/a; (*after prep*) mí, mí mismo/a; **I made it ~** lo hice yo mismo; **I went ~** fui en persona; **I talked mainly about ~** hablé principalmente de mí (mismo)
3 (*phrases*) **by ~** solo/a; **I did it all by ~** lo hice yo solo; **I don't like travelling by ~** no me gusta viajar solo; **don't leave me all by ~!** ¡no me dejes aquí solo!; **a beginner like ~** un principiante como yo; **I'm not ~** no me encuentro nada bien; **I was talking to ~** hablaba solo

mysterious [mɪsˈtɪərɪəs] ADJ 1 (= *puzzling*) [*disappearance, illness, circumstances*] misterioso; **there is nothing ~ about it** no tiene nada de misterioso, no tiene ningún misterio; ✦*PROV* **the Lord moves in ~ ways** los designios del Señor son inescrutables
2 (= *enigmatic*) [*person, object*] misterioso; [*smile*] misterioso, lleno de misterio; **why are you being so ~?** ¿por qué andas con tanto misterio?, ¿a qué viene tanto misterio?

mysteriously [mɪsˈtɪərɪəslɪ] ADV [*say, smile, behave*] misteriosamente, de forma misteriosa; [*disappear, appear, arrive*] misteriosamente

mystery [ˈmɪstərɪ] Ⓐ N 1 (*gen, Rel*) misterio *m*; **there's no ~ about it** no tiene ningún misterio; **to make a great ~ out of a matter** rodear un asunto con un halo de misterio; **it's a ~ to me where it can have gone** no entiendo dónde puede haberse metido; **it's a ~ how I lost it** no entiendo cómo lo pude perder
2 (*Literat*) (*also* **~ story**) novela *f* de misterio
3 (*Rel Theat*) (*also* **~ play**) auto *m* sacramental, misterio *m*
Ⓑ CPD ► **mystery man** N hombre *m* misterioso ► **mystery play** N auto *m* sacramental, misterio *m* ► **mystery ship** N buque *m* misterioso ► **mystery story** N novela *f* de misterio ► **mystery tour, mystery trip** N viaje *m* sorpresa

mystic [ˈmɪstɪk] Ⓐ ADJ místico
Ⓑ N místico/a *m/f*

mystical [ˈmɪstɪkəl] ADJ místico

mysticism [ˈmɪstɪsɪzəm] N misticismo *m*; (= *doctrine, literary genre*) mística *f*

mystification [ˌmɪstɪfɪˈkeɪʃən] N 1 (= *mystery*) misterio *m*; **why all the ~?** ¿por qué tanto misterio?
2 (= *confusion*) perplejidad *f*; **my ~ increased** creció mi perplejidad

mystified [ˈmɪstɪfaɪd] ADJ perplejo, desconcertado; **I was ~** me quedé perplejo *or* desconcertado; **he had a ~ look on his face** se le notaba en la cara que estaba perplejo *or* desconcertado, tenía cara de perplejidad *or* desconcierto

mystify [ˈmɪstɪfaɪ] VT dejar perplejo, desconcertar

mystifying [ˈmɪstɪfaɪɪŋ] ADJ desconcertante

mystique [mɪsˈtiːk] N mística *f*

myth [mɪθ] N (= *story*) mito *m*; (= *imaginary person, thing*) mito *m*, ilusión *f*; **a Greek ~** un mito griego; **that's a ~** eso es un mito; **it's a ~ that boiling water freezes faster than cold water** es un mito que el agua hirviendo se congela más rápidamente que el agua fría; *see also* **urban B**

mythic [ˈmɪθɪk] ADJ = **mythical**

mythical [ˈmɪθɪkəl] ADJ (*Myth*) [*beast, creature*] mítico; (= *imaginary*) imaginario

mythological [ˌmɪθəˈlɒdʒɪkəl] ADJ mitológico

mythology [mɪˈθɒlədʒɪ] N mitología *f*

myxomatosis [ˌmɪksəʊməˈtəʊsɪs] N mixomatosis *f inv*

N n

N¹, n [en] N (= *letter*) N *f*, n *f*; **N for Nellie** N de Navarra; **there are n ways of doing it** hay X maneras de hacerlo; *see also* **nth**

N² ABBR (= **north**) N

'n'* [ən] CONJ = **and**

NA N ABBR (*US*) [1] = **Narcotics Anonymous** [2] = **National Academy**

n/a ABBR [1] (= **not applicable**) no interesa [2] (*Banking*) = **no account** [3] (*Comm*) = **not available**

NAACP N ABBR (*US*) = **National Association for the Advancement of Colored People**

> **NAACP**
>
> *La* **NAACP**, *siglas que corresponden a* **National Association for the Advancement of Colored People** *(Asociación Nacional para el Progreso de la Gente de Color), es una organización voluntaria estadounidense fundada en 1910 que se opone a la discriminación racial y que lucha por conseguir leyes que protejan los derechos de los ciudadanos de color. En 1953, la* **NAACP** *anunció que la integración en las escuelas era su objetivo prioritario, y éste se vio cumplido cuando al año siguiente el Tribunal Supremo de los Estados Unidos prohibió las escuelas segregadas conocidas como* **separate but equal**. *Esta asociación siempre ha propugnado la no violencia y rechazó el* **black power movement** *de los años sesenta. El movimiento cuenta con el apoyo de cientos de miles de estadounidenses, muchos de ellos de raza blanca.*

NAAFI ['næfɪ] N ABBR (*Brit Mil*) (= **Navy, Army and Air Force Institute**) *(servicio de) cantinas, economatos etc para las fuerzas armadas*

nab* [næb] VT (= *grab*) [+ *thing*] agarrar; [+ *person*] pillar*; (= *arrest*) pescar*, coger, agarrar (*LAm*); (= *steal*) robar, mangar (*Sp**)

nabob ['neɪbɒb] N nabab *m*

nacelle [næ'sel] N barquilla *f*, góndola *f*

nacho ['nɑːtʃəʊ] N (*pl* **nachos**) nacho *m*

nacre ['neɪkəʳ] N nácar *m*

nacreous ['neɪkrɪəs] ADJ nacarino, nacarado, de nácar

NACU N ABBR (*US*) = **National Association of Colleges and Universities**

nadir ['neɪdɪəʳ] N (*Astron*) nadir *m*; (*fig*) punto *m* más bajo, nadir *m*

naevus, nevus (*US*) ['niːvəs] N (*pl* **naevi,** (*US*) **nevi** ['niːvaɪ]) nevo *m*

naff* [næf] ADJ (= *in poor taste*) de mal gusto, hortera (*Sp**); (= *inferior*) ordinario, inferior

►**naff off*** VI + ADV **~ off** vete a paseo*, vete al cuerno*

NAFTA ['næftə] N ABBR (= **North American Free Trade Agreement**) TLC *m*

nag¹ [næg] N (= *horse*) rocín *m*, jaco *m*

nag² [næg] (A) VT [1] (= *annoy*) fastidiar, dar la lata a*; **stop ~ging me!** ¡deja ya de fastidiarme, ¡deja ya de darme la lata!*; **she ~s me all day long** se pasa el día fastidiándome, se pasa el día dándome la lata*; **to ~ sb to do sth** ◊ **~ sb into doing sth** fastidiar a algn para que haga algo*, dar la lata a algn para que haga algo*
[2] (= *scold*) regañar; **to ~ sb for doing sth** regañar a algn por hacer algo
[3] (= *torment*) **his conscience was ~ging him** le remordía la conciencia; **he was ~ged by doubts** lo acosaban las dudas
(B) VI [1] (= *annoy*) fastidiar, dar la lata*; **to ~ at sb (to do sth)** fastidiar a algn (para que haga algo), dar la lata a algn (para que haga algo)*
[2] (= *scold*) regañar
(C) N gruñón/ona *m/f*

nagger ['nægəʳ] N gruñón/ona *m/f*

nagging ['nægɪŋ] (A) ADJ [*person*] gruñón; [*pain, doubt, fear*] persistente; [*conscience*] intranquilo
(B) N quejas *fpl*, críticas *fpl*

NAHT N ABBR (*Brit*) (= **National Association of Head Teachers**) *sindicato de profesores*

naiad ['naɪæd] N (*pl* **naiads** *or* **naiades** ['naɪədiːz]) náyade *f*

nail [neɪl] (A) N [1] (*Anat*) uña *f*; **to bite one's ~s** morderse las uñas
[2] (*metal*) clavo *m*; ✦*IDIOMS* **a ~ in sb's coffin**: **this is another ~ in his coffin** éste es otro paso hacia su destrucción; **to hit the ~ on the head** dar en el clavo; **to pay (cash) on the ~** pagar en el acto, pagar a tocateja (*Sp**); *see also* **hard A1**
(B) VT [1] (= *fix with nails*) clavar, sujetar con clavos; **to ~ two things together** fijar *or* unir dos cosas con clavos
[2] (*) (= *catch, get hold of*) agarrar, pillar*
[3] (= *expose*) [+ *lie*] poner al descubierto; [+ *rumour*] demostrar la falsedad de
[4] (= *define*) definir, precisar
(C) CPD ► **nail bomb** N bomba *f* de metralla ► **nail clippers** NPL cortaúñas *m inv* ► **nail enamel** (*US*) N esmalte *m* de uñas ► **nail file** N lima *f* (para las uñas) ► **nail polish** N esmalte *m* de uñas ► **nail polish remover** N quitaesmalte *m* ► **nail scissors** NPL tijeras *fpl* para las uñas ► **nail varnish** N esmalte *m* de uñas ► **nail varnish remover** N quitaesmalte *m*

►**nail down** VT + ADV [1] (= *secure with nails*) clavar, sujetar con clavos
[2] (*fig*) [+ *person*] obligar a concretar; **you can't ~ him down** es imposible hacerle concretar; **we ~ed him down to a date** le forzamos a fijar una fecha

►**nail up** VT + ADV (= *fix*) (*on wall*) clavar; (= *close*) [+ *window*] condenar (*claveteándole tablas*)

nail-biting ['neɪl,baɪtɪŋ] (A) ADJ [*tension*] angustioso; [*contest, finish*] emocionantísimo
(B) N mala costumbre *f* de morderse las uñas

nailbrush ['neɪlbrʌʃ] N cepillo *m* de uñas

Nairobi [naɪ'rəʊbɪ] N Nairobi *m*

▼ **naïve, naive** [naɪ'iːv] ADJ [1] [*person*] ingenuo; [*argument*] simplista; [*attitude, views*] ingenuo, cándido
[2] (*Art*) naif

naïvely, naively [naɪ'iːvlɪ] ADV ingenuamente

naïveté, naivety [naɪ'iːvtɪ] N ingenuidad *f*, candor *m*

naked ['neɪkɪd] ADJ [1] (= *unclothed*) [*person, body, flesh*] desnudo; [*breasts*] desnudo, al descubierto; **visible/invisible to the ~ eye** visible/invisible a simple vista; *see also* **stark, strip B1**
[2] (*fig*) (= *defenceless*) **to go ~ into battle** entrar en combate a cuerpo descubierto
[3] (= *without grass, plants, etc*) [*earth*] pelado, yermo (*liter*); [*tree, branches*] pelado, desnudo (*liter*)
[4] (= *exposed*) [*light bulb*] sin pantalla; [*wire*] pelado; [*sword*] desenvainado; **~ flame** llama *f*
[5] (= *undisguised*) [*hatred, misery*] manifiesto, visible; [*ambition*] patente, ostensible; **the ~ pursuit of power** la carrera manifiesta por el poder; **the ~ truth** la verdad al desnudo, la pura verdad

nakedly ['neɪkɪdlɪ] ADV (= *unashamedly*) (*with adj*) manifiestamente, ostensiblemente; (*with verb*) de manera ostensible

nakedness ['neɪkɪdnɪs] N (*lit*) desnudez *f*; [*of aggression, ambition*] lo patente

NALGO ['nælgəʊ] N ABBR (*Brit*) (*formerly*) (= **National and Local Government Officers' Association**) *sindicato de funcionarios*

NAM N ABBR (*US*) = **National Association of Manufacturers**

namby-pamby ['næmbɪ'pæmbɪ] (A) ADJ soso, ñoño*
(B) N persona *f* sosa, ñoño/a* *m/f*

name [neɪm] (A) N [1] [*of person, firm*] nombre *m*; (= *surname*) apellido *m*; [*of book, film*] título *m*; **what's your ~?** ¿cómo te llamas?; **my ~ is Peter** me llamo Peter; **what ~ shall I say?** (*Telec*) ¿de parte de quién?; (*announcing arrival*) ¿a quién debo anunciar?; **what ~ are they giving the child?** ¿qué nombre le van a poner al niño?; **they married to give the child a ~** se casaron para darle nombre *or* legitimar al niño; **to take sb's ~ and address** apuntar el nombre y las señas de algn; **by ~**

➤ LANGUAGE IN USE: naïve 26.3

de nombre; **I know him by ~ only** lo conozco solamente de nombre; **Pérez by ~** de apellido Pérez, apellidado Pérez; **a lady by the ~ of Dulcinea** una dama llamada Dulcinea; **we know it by another ~** lo conocemos por otro nombre; **to go by the ~ of** ser conocido por el nombre de; **in ~**: **he was king in ~ only** era rey tan sólo de nombre; **it exists in ~ only** no existe más que de nombre; **at least in ~** al menos nominalmente; **she's the boss in all but ~** para jefa sólo le falta el nombre; **in the ~ of peace** en nombre de la paz; **I thank you in the ~ of all those present** le doy las gracias en nombre de todos los presentes; **he signed on in the ~ of Smith** se inscribió en el paro *or* desempleo con el apellido Smith; **open up, in the ~ of the law!** ¡abran en nombre de la ley!; **what's in a ~?** ¿qué importa un nombre?; **to lend one's ~ to** prestar su nombre a; **I'll do it, or my ~'s not Bloggs!** ¡como que me llamo Bloggs que lo haré!; **to put one's ~ down for** [+ *new car etc*] apuntarse para; [+ *school, course*] inscribirse en; **he had his ~ taken** (*Sport*) el árbitro apuntó su nombre; **we know it under another ~** lo conocemos por otro nombre; **to go under the ~ of** ser conocido por el nombre de; **✦IDIOMS that's the ~ of the game*** (= *the norm*) así son las cosas; (= *what's important*) eso es lo importante; **he hasn't a penny to his ~** no tiene donde caerse muerto; *see also* **Christian**, **first E**, **maiden**, **middle C**, **pet B2**

2 **names** (= *insults*) **to call sb ~s** insultar a algn

3 (= *reputation*) reputación *f*, fama *f*; **to get (o.s.) a bad ~** crearse mala reputación *or* fama; **he's giving the place a bad ~** le está dando mala fama al lugar; **he has a ~ for carelessness** tiene fama de descuidado; **the firm has a good ~** la casa tiene buena reputación; **to make a ~ for o.s.** hacerse famoso; **to make one's ~** llegar a ser famoso

4 (= *person*) **big ~*** (gran) figura *f*, personaje *m* importante; **he's one of the big ~s in the business** es uno de los grandes en este negocio; **this show has no big ~s** este show no tiene figuras famosas

Ⓑ VT 1 (= *call*) llamar; [+ *person*] (*at birth*) poner; **a man ~d Jack** un hombre llamado Jack; **they ~d the child Mary** a la niña le pusieron María; **to ~ sth/sb after** *or* (*US*) **for sth/sb: they ~d him Winston after Churchill** le pusieron Winston por Churchill; **she was ~d after her grandmother** la llamaron como a su abuela, le pusieron el nombre de su abuela; **they ~d the street after Nelson Mandela** a la calle le pusieron el nombre de Nelson Mandela

2 (= *mention*) **you were not ~d in the speech** no se te nombró *or* mencionó en el discurso; **he is not ~d in this list** no figura en esta lista; **~ the third president of the USA** diga el nombre del tercer presidente de EE.UU.; **~ 20 British birds** nómbrame 20 pájaros británicos; **first-named** primero; **last-named** último; **you ~ it, we've got it** cualquier cosa que pidas, la tenemos; **to name names** dar *or* mencionar nombres

3 (= *fix*) [+ *date, price*] fijar; **have you ~d the day yet?** ¿han fijado ya la fecha de la boda?; **they're so keen to buy it you can ~ your price** tienen tanto afán por comprarlo que puedes pedirles lo que quieras *or* decir el precio que quieras

4 (= *nominate*) nombrar; **he was ~d ambassador to Warsaw** lo nombraron embajador en Varsovia

Ⓒ CPD ► **name day** N (*Rel*) día *m* del santo, fiesta *f* onomástica; (*Fin*) día *m* de ajuste de cuentas ► **name tape** N etiqueta *f* con el nombre

name-calling [ˈneɪmkɔːlɪŋ] N insultos *mpl*, ofensas *fpl*

namecheck [ˈneɪmtʃek] Ⓐ N alusión *f* directa, referencia *f* directa (*en una canción, película, etc.*); **he gets a ~ in the first song** hay una referencia directa a él en la primera canción

Ⓑ VT aludir directamente a, mencionar

name-dropper [ˈneɪm,drɒpəʳ] N **he's a ~** siempre está mencionando a la gente importante que conoce

name-dropping [ˈneɪmˈdrɒpɪŋ] N **there was a good deal of ~** todo el mundo se las daba de conocer a gente importante

nameless [ˈneɪmlɪs] ADJ 1 (= *anonymous*) anónimo, sin nombre; **someone, who shall be ~ …** cierta persona, cuyo nombre me callo …

2 (= *indefinable*) [*dread, grief*] indescriptible; [*crime*] horrendo, indescriptible

namely [ˈneɪmlɪ] ADV a saber, concretamente; **another possibility, ~ that it was not working** otra posibilidad, a saber, que no funcionaba

nameplate [ˈneɪmpleɪt] N (*on door*) placa *f* (del nombre); (*on goods*) placa *f* del fabricante

namesake [ˈneɪmseɪk] N tocayo/a *m/f*, homónimo/a *m/f*

name-tag [ˈnɛimtæg] N placa *f* de identificación

Namibia [nɑːˈmɪbɪə] N Namibia *f*

Namibian [nɑːˈmɪbɪən] Ⓐ ADJ namibio

Ⓑ N namibio/a *m/f*

nan* [næn], **nana*** [ˈnænə] N (*Brit*) (= *grandmother*) abuelita* *f*, yaya* *f*

nan bread [ˈnɑːnbred] N *pan indio sin apenas levadura*

nance‡ [næns] N, **nancy(-boy)‡** [ˈnænsɪ(bɔɪ)] N (*Brit pej*) maricón‡ *m*

nanny [ˈnænɪ] Ⓐ N 1 (= *childminder*) niñera *f*

2 (*) (= *grandmother*) abuelita* *f*, yaya* *f*

Ⓑ CPD ► **nanny goat** N cabra *f* ► **nanny state** N (*esp Brit*) papá-estado *m*

nannying [ˈnænɪɪŋ] N 1 (= *job*) profesión *f* de niñera

2 (*pej*) (= *mollycoddling*) protección *f* excesiva

nano- [ˈnænəʊ] PREFIX nano-

nanometre [ˈnænəʊ,miːtəʳ] N nanómetro *m*

nanotechnology [,nænəʊtekˈnɒlədʒɪ] N nanotecnología *f*

Naomi [ˈneɪəmɪ] N Naomi

nap¹ [næp] Ⓐ N sueñecito *m*; (*in afternoon*) siesta *f*; **to have** *or* **take a ~** echar un sueñecito/una siesta

Ⓑ VI dormitar; **✦IDIOMS to catch sb ~ping** pillar a algn desprevenido; **to be caught ~ping** estar desprevenido

nap² [næp] N (*on cloth*) lanilla *f*, pelusa *f*

nap³ [næp] N (*Cards*) (= *game*) napolitana *f*; **to go ~** jugarse el todo (**on** a)

NAPA N ABBR (*US*) (= **National Association of Performing Artists**) *sindicato de trabajadores del espectáculo*

napalm [ˈneɪpɑːm] N napalm *m*

nape [neɪp] N (*also* **~ of the neck**) nuca *f*, cogote *m*

naphtha [ˈnæfθə] N nafta *f*

naphthalene [ˈnæfθəliːn] N naftalina *f*

napkin [ˈnæpkɪn] Ⓐ N (= *table napkin*) servilleta *f*; (*Brit*) (*baby's*) pañal *m*; (*US*) (= *sanitary towel*) compresa *f* higiénica, paño *m* higiénico

Ⓑ CPD ► **napkin ring** N servilletero *m*

Naples [ˈneɪplz] N Nápoles *m*

Napoleon [nəˈpəʊlɪən] N Napoleón

Napoleonic [nə,pəʊlɪˈɒnɪk] ADJ napoleónico

napper* [ˈnæpəʳ] N (= *head*) coca* *f*

nappy [ˈnæpɪ] Ⓐ N (*Brit*) pañal *m*; **the baby's got a dirty ~** el niño tiene caca; **leave the dirty nappies to soak** pon los pañales sucios a remojo

Ⓑ CPD ► **nappy liner** N gasa *f* ► **nappy rash** N irritación *f*; **to have ~ rash** estar escaldado

Narbonne [nɑːˈbɒn] N Narbona *f*

narc* [nɑːk] N (*US*) agente* *mf* de la brigada de los narcóticos

narcissi [nɑːˈsɪsaɪ] NPL *of* **narcissus**

narcissism [nɑːˈsɪsɪzəm] N narcisismo *m*

narcissist [ˈnɑːsɪ,sɪst] N narcisista *mf*

narcissistic [,nɑːsɪˈsɪstɪk] ADJ narcisista

Narcissus [nɑːˈsɪsəs] N Narciso

narcissus [nɑːˈsɪsəs] N (*pl* **narcissi** *or* **narcissuses** [nɑːˈsɪsaɪ]) (*Bot*) narciso *m*

narcolepsy [ˈnɑːkəʊlepsɪ] N narcolepsia *f*

narcoleptic [,nɑːkəʊˈleptɪk] Ⓐ ADJ narcoléptico

Ⓑ N narcoléptico/a *m/f*

narcosis [nɑːˈkəʊsɪs] N narcosis *f*, narcotismo *m*

narco-terrorism [,nɑːkəʊˈterərɪzəm] N narcoterrorismo *m*

narcotic [nɑːˈkɒtɪk] Ⓐ N 1 (*Med*) narcótico *m*

2 (*esp US*) (= *illegal drug*) **narcotics** estupefacientes *mpl*, narcóticos *mpl*

Ⓑ ADJ narcótico; **~ drug** narcótico *m*

Ⓒ CPD ► **narcotics agent** N agente *mf* de narcóticos ► **narcotics charge** N **to be on a ~s charge** estar acusado de traficar con drogas ► **narcotics trafficker** N narcotraficante *mf*, traficante *mf* de drogas ► **narcotics trafficking** N narcotráfico *m*, tráfico *m* de estupefacientes *or* drogas

narcotism [ˈnɑːkə,tɪzəm] N narcotismo *m*

narcotize [ˈnɑːkətaɪz] VT narcotizar

narco-trafficker [,nɑːkəʊˈtræfɪkəʳ] N narcotraficante *mf*

narco-trafficking [,nɑːkəʊˈtræfɪkɪŋ] N narcotráfico *m*

nard [nɑːd] N nardo *m*

nark* [nɑːk] Ⓐ N soplón/ona* *m/f*

Ⓑ VT 1 (= *upset*) **to be ~ed** estar cabreado *or* mosqueado*; **to get ~ed** cabrearse*, mosquearse*; **he got really ~ed** se cabreó* *or* mosqueó* de lo lindo

2 (*Brit*) **~ it!** (= *stop it*) ¡déjalo!; (= *go away*) ¡lárgate!*

narky* [ˈnɑːkɪ] ADJ **to get ~** (*Brit*) cabrearse*, mosquearse*

narrate [nəˈreɪt] VT [+ *documentary*] narrar, hacer los comentarios de; [+ *story*] narrar, relatar

narration [nəˈreɪʃən] N [*of documentary*] narración *f*, comentarios *mpl*; [*of story*] narración *f*, relato *m*

narrative [ˈnærətɪv] Ⓐ ADJ narrativo

Ⓑ N (= *act*) narración *f*; (= *story*) narración *f*, relato *m*

narrator [nəˈreɪtəʳ] N [*of story*] narrador(a) *m/f*; [*of documentary*] narrador(a) *m/f*, comentarista *mf*

narrow [ˈnærəʊ] Ⓐ ADJ (*compar* **narrower**; *superl* **narrowest**) 1 (*in width*) [*street, passage, room, stairs*] estrecho, angosto; [*bed, channel, face*] estrecho, angosto (*LAm*); **to become** *or* **get ~(er)** estrecharse, angostarse (*LAm*)

2 (= *limited*) [*range*] reducido, limitado; [*definition*] restringido; **prices rose and fell within a ~ band** los precios subieron y bajaron

dentro de una estrecha banda; **in a ~ sense** en sentido estricto
3 (= *small, slight*) [*margin, majority*] escaso; [*victory, defeat*] por un escaso margen; **to have a ~ escape** salvarse de milagro, salvarse por los pelos*; **to have a ~ lead (over sb)** llevar una pequeña ventaja (a algn)
4 (*usu pej*) (= *restricted*) [*person*] de miras estrechas, intolerante; [*mind*] estrecho de miras; [*view, idea*] cerrado
Ⓑ VI 1 (= *become less wide*) [*road, path, river*] estrecharse, angostarse (*LAm*)
2 (= *almost close*) [*eyes*] entrecerrarse
3 (= *diminish*) [*gap, majority*] reducirse
Ⓒ VT 1 (= *reduce*) [+ *gap*] reducir; [+ *differences*] solventar en cierta medida
2 (= *almost close*) **to ~ one's eyes** entrecerrar los ojos
Ⓓ N 1 *see* **straight C1**
2 **narrows** estrecho *msing*
Ⓔ CPD ► **narrow boat** N (*Brit*) barcaza *f* ► **narrow gauge** N (*Rail*) vía *f* estrecha; (*before noun*) de vía estrecha

►**narrow down** Ⓐ VT + ADV [+ *search, investigation, possibilities*] restringir, limitar; **I've ~ed the guest list down to 30** he reducido la lista de invitados a 30
Ⓑ VI + ADV [*road, path, valley*] estrecharse, angostarse (*LAm*); [*search, investigation*] restringirse; **the list of candidates has ~ed down to four** la lista de candidatos se ha reducido a cuatro

narrowing ['nærəʊɪŋ] N [*of road, path, channel*] estrechamiento *m*; **the ~ of the gap between rich and poor** el acortamiento de la distancia que separa a ricos y pobres

narrowly ['nærəʊlɪ] ADV 1 (= *just*) [*escape, avoid, miss, fail*] por poco; [*defeat*] por un escaso margen; **to be ~ defeated** (*in election*) ser derrotado por un escaso margen; (*Sport*) perder por poco
2 (= *restrictively*) [*define*] de forma restringida; **to be ~ based** [*organization*] tener una base limitada; **these exams are too ~ vocational** estos exámenes tienen un enfoque demasiado vocacional
3 (= *closely*) [*watch*] de cerca; [*observe*] atentamente

narrow-minded ['nærəʊ'maɪndɪd] (*pej*) ADJ [*person*] estrecho de miras, de mentalidad cerrada; [*views*] intolerante, cerrado; [*ideas, outlook*] cerrado

narrow-mindedness ['nærəʊ'maɪndɪdnɪs] N estrechez *f* de miras, intolerancia *f*

narrowness ['nærəʊnɪs] N 1 [*of road, path, channel*] estrechez *f*
2 [*of victory, defeat*] escaso margen *m*
3 [*of attitude*] lo cerrado; **~ of mind** estrechez *f* de miras

narwhal ['nɑːwəl] N narval *m*

NAS N ABBR (*US*) = **National Academy of Sciences**

NASA ['næsə] N ABBR (*US*) (= **National Aeronautics and Space Administration**) NASA *f*

nasal ['neɪzəl] Ⓐ ADJ 1 (*Anat*) nasal
2 (= *twanging*) gangoso
Ⓑ N nasal *f*

nasality [neɪ'zælɪtɪ] N nasalidad *f*

nasalization [,neɪzəlaɪ'zeɪʃən] N nasalización *f*

nasalize ['neɪzəlaɪz] VT nasalizar; (*twangingly*) pronunciar con timbre gangoso

nasally ['neɪzəlɪ] ADV nasalmente, por la nariz; **to speak ~** hablar por la nariz

nascent ['næsnt] ADJ [*industry, democracy*] naciente

Nassau ['næsɔː] N Nassau *m*

nastily ['nɑːstɪlɪ] ADV [*speak, behave*] con maldad

nastiness ['nɑːstɪnɪs] N 1 (= *unpleasantness*) [*of weather, situation*] lo desagradable; [*of taste, smell*] lo desagradable, lo repugnante
2 (= *spitefulness*) maldad *f*

nasturtium [nəs'tɜːʃəm] N (*Bot*) capuchina *f*

nasty ['nɑːstɪ] Ⓐ ADJ (*compar* **nastier**, *superl* **nastiest**) 1 (= *unpleasant*) [*situation, experience, surprise*] desagradable; [*taste, smell*] desagradable, repugnante; [*habit, weather*] desagradable, feo, malo; **it was a ~ business** fue un asunto desagradable; **I've got a ~ feeling that …** tengo la horrible sensación de que …; **history has a ~ habit of repeating itself** la historia tiene la mala costumbre de repetirse; **he had a ~ shock** se llevó un susto terrible; **the situation turned ~** la situación se puso fea; *see also* **taste A2**
2 (= *serious*) [*accident*] serio, grave; [*cut, wound*] feo; [*infection*] fuerte; [*disease*] peligroso; **a ~ case of** un caso grave de; **she had a ~ fall** tuvo una mala caída
3 (= *difficult*) [*question*] difícil; [*bend, junction*] peligroso; [*problem*] complicado; **there was one ~ moment when …** se produjo un momento de tensión cuando …
4 (= *spiteful*) [*person, remark*] cruel, desagradable; [*joke*] de mal gusto, grosero; **a ~-looking individual** un individuo mal encarado; **he's a ~ piece of work** es un canalla*; **to be ~ to sb** ser cruel con algn; **don't be ~ to your little brother** no seas malo con tu hermanito; **a ~ trick** una mala jugada; **he turned ~ and started to shout** se puso agresivo y empezó a gritar
Ⓑ N (*) **there were a few hidden nasties in my bill** había unas cuantas sorpresas desagradables en mi cuenta; *see also* **video C**

NAS/UWT N ABBR (*Brit*) (= **National Association of Schoolmasters/Union of Women Teachers**) *sindicato de profesores*

nat ABBR (= **national**) nal.

Natal [nə'tæl] N Natal *m*

natal ['neɪtl] ADJ natal

natality [nə'tælɪtɪ] N natalidad *f*

natatorium [,neɪtə'tɔːrɪəm] N (*pl* **natatoria** [,neɪtə'tɔːrɪə]) (*US*) piscina *f*

natch‡ [nætʃ] EXCL naturalmente, naturaca‡

NATFHE N ABBR (*Brit*) (= **National Association of Teachers in Further and Higher Education**) *sindicato de la enseñanza superior*

nation ['neɪʃən] Ⓐ N (*Pol*) nación *f*; (= *people*) pueblo *m*, nación *f*
Ⓑ CPD ► **Nation of Islam** N (*US*) Nación *f* del Islam

national ['næʃənl] Ⓐ ADJ 1 (= *of one nation*) nacional
2 (= *nationwide*) [*newspaper, economy*] nacional; [*election, campaign*] a nivel nacional; **the ~ average** la media nacional
Ⓑ N 1 (= *person*) ciudadano/a *m/f*
2 (= *newspaper*) periódico *m* nacional
Ⓒ CPD ► **National Aeronautics and Space Administration** N (*US*) NASA *f* ► **national anthem** N himno *m* nacional ► **National Assistance** N (*Brit*) (*formerly*) *subsidio (al necesitado)* ► **national bank** N (*state-owned*) banco *m* nacional, banco *m* estatal; (*US*) (*commercial*) *banco que forma parte del Sistema de Reservas Federal* ► **national costume** N traje *m* típico nacional ► **National Curriculum** N (*Brit*) *plan de estudios oficial que se sigue en las escuelas de enseñanza pública de Inglaterra y País de Gales* ► **national debt** N deuda *f* pública ► **national dress** N = **national costume** ► **the National Front** N (*Brit*) el Frente Nacional (británico) (*partido político de extrema derecha e ideología racista*) ► **national government** N gobierno *m* nacional ► **national grid** N red *f* eléctrica nacional ► **the National Guard** (*US*) N la Guardia Nacional ► **the National Health (Service)** N (*Brit*) *servicio de asistencia pública sanitaria*; **to have an operation done on the National Health (Service)** ≈ operarse por la Seguridad Social *or* el Seguro ► **national heritage** N patrimonio *m* nacional ► **National Insurance** N (*Brit*) ≈ Seguridad *f* Social; **National Insurance contributions** cotizaciones *fpl* a la Seguridad Social, aportes *mpl* a la Seguridad Social (*S. Cone*); **National Insurance number** número *m* de la Seguridad Social ► **the National Lottery** N (*Brit*) ≈ la lotería primitiva ► **national monument** N monumento *m* nacional ► **national park** N parque *m* nacional ► **National Savings (Bank)** N (*Brit*) ≈ caja *f* postal de ahorros ► **National Savings Certificate** N (*Brit*) ≈ bono *m* del Estado ► **national security** N seguridad *f* nacional ► **the National Security Council** N (*US*) el Consejo para la Seguridad Nacional ► **national service** N (*Mil*) servicio *m* militar; **to do (one's) ~ service** hacer el servicio militar, hacer la mili* ► **National Socialism** N nacionalsocialismo *m* ► **the National Trust** N (*Brit*) ≈ la Dirección General del Patrimonio Nacional

NATIONAL GUARD

La **National Guard** *(Guardia Nacional) es una organización estadounidense que recluta voluntarios no profesionales a los que se prepara para colaborar con el ejército profesional y las fuerzas aéreas en tiempos de crisis. Los requisitos para alistarse son los mismos que para el ejército normal y, aunque su preparación la dirige el gobierno federal, sus miembros pueden ser movilizados para ayudar en situaciones de emergencia, catástrofes naturales y el control de situaciones excepcionales de violencia civil. Los miembros de la* **National Guard** *tienen que prestar juramento de fidelidad a los EE.UU. y al estado al que pertenecen.*

NATIONAL TRUST

El **National Trust** *es una organización benéfica británica que se dedica a la conservación de lugares del patrimonio histórico-artístico o de parajes naturales. Se financia a través de donaciones, aportaciones de los socios, y dinero procedente de la venta de entradas, souvenirs y de las cafeterías o restaurantes que suele haber en muchos de estos lugares.*

nationalism ['næʃnəlɪzəm] N nacionalismo *m*

nationalist ['næʃnəlɪst] Ⓐ ADJ nacionalista
Ⓑ N nacionalista *mf*

nationalistic [,næʃnə'lɪstɪk] ADJ nacionalista

nationality [,næʃə'nælɪtɪ] N 1 (= *citizenship*) nacionalidad *f*, ciudadanía *f*; **she took/adopted French ~** adquirió/adoptó la nacionalidad *or* ciudadanía francesa
2 (= *national group*) nacionalidad *f*; **the city is home to 20 different nationalities** la ciudad alberga hasta 20 nacionalidades distintas

nationalization [,næʃnəlaɪ'zeɪʃən] N nacionalización *f*

nationalize ['næʃnəlaɪz] VT nacionalizar; **~d industry** industria *f* nacionalizada

nationally ['næʃnəlɪ] ADV [*distributed*] por todo el país, a escala nacional; [*available*] en todo el país; **this is the case locally, but not ~** eso es cierto a nivel local, pero no a nivel nacional; **a ~ recognized qualification** una titulación reconocida a nivel nacional *or* en todo el país

nationhood ['neɪʃənhʊd] N carácter *m* de nación; **they have a strong sense of ~** poseen un acusado sentimiento nacionalista; **to achieve ~** llegar a constituir una nación, llegar a tener categoría de nación

nation-state ['neɪʃən'steɪt] N estado-nación *m*

nationwide ['neɪʃənwaɪd] Ⓐ ADJ [*survey, poll*] a nivel nacional; [*campaign, strike, debate*] a escala nacional; [*interest, support*] en todo el país; [*network, referendum*] nacional; [*tour*] por todo el país; **police have initiated a ~ hunt for the killer** la policía ha comenzado una búsqueda del asesino por todo el país
Ⓑ ADV [*deliver*] en todo el territorio nacional, por todo el país; **we now have over 300 branches ~** ya tenemos más de 300 sucursales por todo el país; **the film will be released ~ on 28th** la película se estrena en todo el país el día 28

native ['neɪtɪv] Ⓐ ADJ [1] (= *of one's birth*) [*town, country, soil*] natal; **~ Britons** los nacidos en Gran Bretaña
[2] (= *indigenous*) [2·1] [*inhabitant, culture, population*] indígena; **the ~ peoples of the Amazon** los pueblos indígenas del Amazonas; **to go ~** adoptar las costumbres del lugar
[2·2] [*plant, animal, species*] autóctono, originario del lugar; **to be ~ to** ser originario de
[3] (= *innate*) [*ability, talent*] natural, innato; **~ wit** ingenio *m*
Ⓑ N [1] (*referring to birth or nationality*) nativo/a *m/f*; **he speaks German like a ~** habla alemán como un nativo; **he was a ~ of Seville** nació en Sevilla
[2] (= *member of indigenous people*) (†*freq pej*) indígena *mf*
[3] (= *plant, animal*) **to be a ~ of** ser originario de
Ⓒ CPD ► **native country, native land** N patria *f* ► **native language** N lengua *f* materna ► **native son** N (*liter*) hijo *m* predilecto ► **native speaker** N hablante *mf* nativo/a; **a Spanish ~ speaker** ◊ **a ~ speaker of Spanish** un hablante nativo de español ► **native tongue** N = **native language**

Native American [ˌneɪtɪvə'merɪkən] Ⓐ ADJ americano nativo
Ⓑ N americano/a *m/f* nativo/a

nativity [nə'tɪvɪtɪ] Ⓐ N [1] (*gen*) natividad *f*
[2] (*Rel*) **the Nativity** la Natividad
[3] (*Art*) **Nativity** nacimiento *m*
Ⓑ CPD ► **Nativity play** N auto *m* de Navidad ► **Nativity scene** N belén *m*, nacimiento *m*

NATO ['neɪtəʊ] N ABBR (= **North Atlantic Treaty Organization**) OTAN *f*

NATSOPA [ˌnæt'səʊpə] N ABBR (*Brit*) (= **National Society of Operative Printers, Graphical and Media Personnel**) *sindicato de tipógrafos*

natter* ['nætər] (*Brit*) Ⓐ N charla *f*, plática *f* (*Mex*); **to have a ~** charlar, estar de palique (*Sp**), platicar (*Mex*) (**with** con); **we had a good old ~** estuvimos charlando un buen rato
Ⓑ VI (= *chat*) charlar, platicar (*Mex*); (= *chatter*) parlotear, hablar mucho

natterer* ['nætərər] N charlatán/ana *m/f*, cotorra* *mf*

NATTKE N ABBR (*Brit*) (= **National Association of Television, Theatrical and Kinematographic Employees**) *sindicato de empleados de televisión, teatro y cine*

natty* ['nætɪ] ADJ (*compar* **nattier**; *superl* **nattiest**) [1] (= *smart*) [*suit, tie*] elegante, elegantoso (*esp LAm**); **he looked ~ in his white uniform** iba de lo más elegantoso *or* elegantón con su uniforme blanco*; **to be a ~ dresser** ir siempre muy elegantoso *or* elegantón*
[2] (= *handy*) [*gadget*] ingenioso

natural ['nætʃrəl] Ⓐ ADJ [1] (= *occurring naturally*) [*environment, substance, disaster, remedy*] natural; **she isn't a ~ blonde** no es rubia natural; **he died of ~ causes** murió de muerte natural; **the rest of his ~ life** el resto de sus días; *see also* **die**[1]
[2] (= *understandable*) [*reaction, behaviour, feeling*] natural, normal; [*mistake*] comprensible; [*explanation*] lógico y natural; **it's a perfectly ~ mistake to make** es un error totalmente comprensible; **there is a perfectly ~ explanation** hay una explicación perfectamente lógica y natural; **it's only ~** es normal *or* natural; **it's only ~ that she should be upset** es normal *or* natural que esté disgustada
[3] (= *inborn*) [*ability, talent*] innato; [*reaction, fear*] instintivo; **he had a ~ flair for business** tenía un don innato para los negocios; **she is a ~ leader/athlete** es una líder/atleta innata; **~ instinct** instinto *m* natural
[4] (= *relaxed, unforced*) [*person, manner, charm*] natural; **I was able to be very ~ with him** con él pude ser yo mismo
[5] (= *biological*) [*father, mother, child*] biológico
[6] (*Mus*) natural
Ⓑ N [1] (= *person*) **she's a ~ with computers** tiene un don innato para los ordenadores
[2] (*Mus*) (= *note*) nota *f* natural; (= *sign*) becuadro *m*
Ⓒ CPD ► **natural childbirth** N parto *m* natural ► **natural gas** N gas *m* natural ► **natural history** N historia *f* natural ► **natural law** N ley *f* natural ► **natural number** N (*Math*) número *m* natural ► **natural philosophy** N filosofía *f* natural ► **natural resources** NPL recursos *mpl* naturales ► **natural science** N (*uncount*) ciencias *fpl* naturales; (*count*) ciencia *f* de la naturaleza ► **natural selection** N selección *f* natural; **by ~ selection** por selección natural ► **natural wastage** N (*Brit Ind*) *bajas voluntarias de los empleados de una empresa, y cuyos puestos quedan sin cubrir*; **the jobs will be lost through ~ wastage** los puestos irán desapareciendo a medida que se produzcan bajas voluntarias

naturalism ['nætʃrəlɪzəm] N naturalismo *m*

naturalist ['nætʃrəlɪst] N naturalista *mf*

naturalistic [ˌnætʃrə'lɪstɪk] ADJ naturalista

naturalization [ˌnætʃrəlaɪ'zeɪʃən] Ⓐ N naturalización *f*
Ⓑ CPD ► **naturalization papers** NPL carta *fsing* de ciudadanía

naturalize ['nætʃrəlaɪz] Ⓐ VT [+ *person*] naturalizar; [+ *plant, animal*] aclimatar, establecer; **to become ~d** [*person*] naturalizarse; [*plant, animal*] aclimatarse, establecerse
Ⓑ VI [*person*] naturalizarse; [*plant etc*] aclimatarse, establecerse

naturally ['nætʃrəlɪ] ADV [1] (= *by a natural process*) [*happen, develop*] de forma natural; **beans are ~ high in minerals** las alubias tienen de por sí un alto contenido de minerales; **to die ~** morir de muerte natural; **to give birth ~** tener un parto natural
[2] (= *by nature*) [*cheerful, cautious*] por naturaleza; **her hair is ~ curly** tiene el pelo rizado natural; **he is a ~ gifted singer** es un cantante con un talento innato; **playing the violin seems to come ~ to her** parece que hubiera nacido sabiendo tocar el violín; **I just do what comes ~** simplemente hago lo que me sale; **winning seems to come ~ to him** se diría que ganar no le supone ningún esfuerzo
[3] (= *unaffectedly*) [*behave, speak*] con naturalidad, con espontaneidad
[4] (= *as a consequence*) [*follow, lead*] como consecuencia natural
[5] (= *obviously*) naturalmente, por supuesto; **~, I understand your feelings** naturalmente *or* por supuesto, sé cómo te sientes; **"did you tell him?" — "naturally"** —¿se lo dijiste? —por supuesto; **~ enough** como es natural, lógicamente

naturalness ['nætʃrəlnɪs] N naturalidad *f*

nature ['neɪtʃər] Ⓐ N [1] (= *essential quality*) [*of things*] naturaleza *f*; **the ~ and extent of the damage is still not known** aún se desconoce la naturaleza y el alcance de los daños; **the project is experimental in ~** el proyecto es de carácter experimental; **his comment was in the ~ of a compliment** su comentario fue algo así como un cumplido; **in the ~ of things it's impossible** desde el punto de vista lógico es imposible; **we were unaware of the serious ~ of his illness** ignorábamos que su enfermedad fuera tan grave; **the true ~ of his intentions** sus verdaderas intenciones; **by its very ~** por su propia naturaleza; *see also* **human C**
[2] (= *character*) [*of person*] carácter *m*; **she trusted people, that was her ~** se fiaba de la gente, era así por naturaleza; **to appeal to sb's better ~** apelar al buen corazón de algn; **to be cautious by ~** ser cauteloso por naturaleza; **she took all their teasing with good ~** aceptó todas sus burlas de buen grado; **to take advantage of sb's good ~** abusar de la amabilidad de algn; **it is not in his ~ to lie** mentir no es propio de él; *see also* **second**[1] **A1**
[3] (= *kind, type*) **something of that ~** algo por el estilo; **documents of a technical ~** documentos *mpl* de carácter técnico; **"nature of contents"** (*Comm*) "descripción *f* del contenido"
[4] (= *natural life, environment*) naturaleza *f*; **it's against ~** es antinatural, es contrario a la naturaleza; **the beauties of ~** las maravillas de la naturaleza; **to draw/paint from ~** dibujar/pintar del natural; **to get back to ~** [*person*] volver a la naturaleza; **the laws of ~** las leyes de la naturaleza; **to return to ~** [*area*] volver a su estado natural; **fever is ~'s way of fighting infection** la fiebre es el mecanismo natural para combatir la infección; *see also* **call A4**, **freak**, **mother**
Ⓑ CPD ► **nature conservation** N protección *f* de la naturaleza ► **nature cure** N curación *f* natural ► **nature lover** N amante *mf* de la naturaleza ► **nature reserve** N reserva *f* natural ► **nature study** N estudio *m* de la historia natural, historia *f* natural ► **nature trail** N ruta *f* para el estudio de la naturaleza

-natured ['neɪtʃəd] ADJ (*ending in compounds*) de carácter …; **good-natured** de carácter bondadoso; **ill-natured** de mal carácter

naturism ['neɪtʃərɪzəm] N (*esp Brit*) naturismo *m*

naturist ['neɪtʃərɪst] N (*esp Brit*) naturista *mf*

naturopath ['neɪtʃərəˌpæθ] N naturópata *mf*

naturopathy [ˌneɪtʃə'rɒpəθɪ] N naturopatía *f*

naught [nɔːt] N 1 (*Math*) = **nought**
2 (†, *poet*) (= *nothing*) nada *f*; **all for ~** todo en balde; **to come to ~** [*hopes*] frustrarse; [*project*] malograrse; **to set at ~** no hacer caso de, despreciar; *see also* **nought**

naughtily [ˈnɔːtɪlɪ] ADV 1 (*of child*) traviesamente; [*behave*] mal
2 (*of adult*) [*say*] con picardía

naughtiness [ˈnɔːtɪnɪs] N 1 (= *mischief*) travesuras *fpl*; (= *bad behaviour*) mala conducta *f*
2 (= *risqué character*) atrevimiento *m*; [*of joke, song etc*] lo verde

naughty [ˈnɔːtɪ] ADJ (*compar* **naughtier**, *superl* **naughtiest**) 1 [*child*] travieso, malo; **you've been very ~** has sido muy malo; **that was very ~ of you** ◊ **that was a ~ thing to do** eso ha estado muy feo; **you ~ boy!** (*angrily*) ¡mira que eres malo *or* travieso!; (*indulgently*) ¡anda, pillín *or* picaruelo!*
2 (*of adult*) **I'm going to be very ~ and have two cakes** voy a portarme mal y comerme dos pasteles; **it was a bit ~ of you to leave without telling anyone** no estuvo nada bien que te marcharas sin decir nada
3 (= *risqué*) [*joke, song*] verde, colorado (*LAm*); **she gave me a ~ look** me miró con picardía; **~ bits*** (*hum*) (= *male genitals*) paquete‡ *m*; **the ~ bits*** (*in film etc*) las escenas picantes; **the Naughty Nineties** la Bella Época

nausea [ˈnɔːsɪə] N (*Med*) náusea *f*; **his remarks filled me with ~** (*fig*) sus comentarios me dieron náuseas *or* asco

nauseate [ˈnɔːsɪeɪt] VT (*lit*) dar náuseas a; (*fig*) repugnar, asquear, dar asco a; **I was ~d by her attitude** su actitud me repugnó *or* asqueó

nauseating [ˈnɔːsɪeɪtɪŋ] ADJ [*smell*] nauseabundo; [*crime, violence, hypocrisy*] repugnante, asqueroso; **it was ~ to see it** era repugnante *or* asqueroso verlo

nauseatingly [ˈnɔːsɪeɪtɪŋlɪ] ADV **the film is ~ violent** la película es de una violencia repugnante; **he is ~ virtuous** es tan perfecto que da asco

nauseous [ˈnɔːsɪəs] ADJ 1 (*lit*) **to feel ~** sentir náuseas; **the sight of food made me (feel) ~** sólo de ver la comida me daban náuseas
2 [*colour, smell*] nauseabundo

nautical [ˈnɔːtɪkəl] Ⓐ ADJ [*terms, matters, charts*] náutico, marítimo
Ⓑ CPD ► **nautical almanac** N almanaque *m* náutico ► **nautical mile** N milla *f* marina

nautilus [ˈnɔːtɪləs] N (*pl* **nautiluses** *or* **nautili** [ˈnɔːtɪˌlaɪ]) nautilo *m*

Navaho [ˈnævəhəʊ] Ⓐ ADJ navajo
Ⓑ N 1 (*also* **~ Indian**) Navajo *mf*
2 (*Ling*) Navajo *m*

naval [ˈneɪvəl] Ⓐ ADJ [*warfare, strength, base*] naval; [*affairs, forces*] de la marina; [*officer*] de marina; [*power*] marítimo; **Britain's ~ tradition** la tradición naval británica
Ⓑ CPD ► **naval academy** N escuela *f* naval ► **naval attaché** N agregado *m* naval ► **naval college** N escuela *f* naval

Navarre [nəˈvɑːʳ] N Navarra *f*

Navarrese [ˌnævəˈriːz] Ⓐ ADJ navarro
Ⓑ N 1 navarro/a *m/f*
2 (*Ling*) navarro *m*

nave[1] [neɪv] N (*Archit*) nave *f*

nave[2] [neɪv] N (= *wheel*) cubo *m*; **~ plate** (*Aut*) tapacubos *m inv*

navel [ˈneɪvəl] N ombligo *m*

navel-gazing [ˈneɪvəlgeɪzɪŋ] N (*pej*) ombliguismo *m*, autocontemplación *f*

navigable [ˈnævɪgəbl] ADJ 1 [*river*] navegable
2 [*ship, balloon*] gobernable, dirigible

navigate [ˈnævɪgeɪt] Ⓐ VT 1 [+ *ship, plane*] conducir; (*fig*) conducir, guiar; **to ~ a bill through parliament** lograr que un proyecto de ley se tramite en el parlamento
2 [+ *sea, river*] navegar por
Ⓑ VI 1 (*at sea*) navegar; **navigating officer** oficial *mf* de derrota *or* navegación
2 (*in car*) hacer de copiloto

navigation [ˌnævɪˈgeɪʃən] Ⓐ N 1 (= *act*) [*of ship, plane*] navegación *f*; **to do the ~** (*Aut*) hacer de copiloto
2 (= *science*) náutica *f*, navegación *f*
Ⓑ CPD ► **navigation lights** NPL (*on ship*) luces *fpl* de navegación; (*in harbour*) baliza *f*

navigational [ˌnævɪˈgeɪʃənl] ADJ [*instruments, system*] de navegación; **~ aids** ayudas *fpl* a la navegación

navigator [ˈnævɪgeɪtəʳ] N 1 (*Naut*) (= *officer on ship*) oficial *mf* de derrota, oficial *mf* de navegación; (*Aer*) navegante *mf*; (*Aut*) copiloto *mf*
2 (*Hist*) (= *seafarer*) navegador *m*, navegante *m*

navvy [ˈnævɪ] N (*Brit*) peón *m* caminero

navy [ˈneɪvɪ] Ⓐ N 1 (= *ships*) armada *f*, flota *f*
2 (= *organization*) marina *f* de guerra
3 (= *colour*) (*also* **~ blue**) azul *m* marino
Ⓑ ADJ (= *dark blue*) azul marino
Ⓒ CPD ► **navy blue** N azul *m* marino; *see also* **navy-blue** ► **Navy Department** N (*US*) Ministerio *m* de Marina ► **navy yard** N (*US*) astillero *m* naval

navy-blue [ˈneɪvɪˈbluː] ADJ azul marino

nay [neɪ] Ⓐ ADV (†† *or liter*) (= *no*) no; (= *or rather*) más aún, mejor dicho; **bad, ~ terrible** malo, mejor dicho horrible; **dozens, ~ hundreds** docenas, más aún centenares
Ⓑ N (= *refusal*) negativa *f*; (*in voting*) voto *m* negativo, voto *m* en contra; **to say sb ~** indicar lo contrario a algn; *see also* **yea**

Nazarene [ˌnæzəˈriːn] Ⓐ ADJ nazareno
Ⓑ N nazareno/a *m/f*

Nazareth [ˈnæzərəθ] N Nazaret *m*

Nazi [ˈnɑːtsɪ] Ⓐ ADJ nazi, nazista
Ⓑ N nazi *mf*

Nazism [ˈnɑːtsɪzəm] N nazismo *m*

NB ABBR 1 = **nota bene** (= *note well*) N.B.
2 (*Canada*) = **New Brunswick**

NBA N ABBR 1 (*US*) = **National Basketball Association**
2 (*US*) = **National Boxing Association**
3 (*Brit*) (*formerly*) = **Net Book Agreement**

NBC N ABBR (*US*) = **National Broadcasting Company**

NBS N ABBR (*US*) = **National Bureau of Standards**

NC ABBR 1 (*US*) = **North Carolina**
2 (*Comm etc*) = **no charge**

NCB N ABBR (*Brit*) (*formerly*) = **National Coal Board**

NCC N ABBR 1 (*Brit*) (= **Nature Conservancy Council**) ≈ ICONA *m*, ≈ Icona *m*
2 (*US*) = **National Council of Churches**

NCCL N ABBR (*Brit*) = **National Council for Civil Liberties**

NCO N ABBR (*Mil*) (= **non-commissioned officer**) suboficial *m*

NCV ABBR = **no commercial value**

ND ABBR (*US*) = **North Dakota**

n.d. ABBR (= **no date**) s.f.

N.Dak. ABBR (*US*) = **North Dakota**

NDP N ABBR (= **Net Domestic Product**) PIN *m*

NE ABBR 1 (*Geog*) (= **northeast**) NE
2 (*US*) = **Nebraska**
3 (*US*) = **New England**

NEA N ABBR (*US*) = **National Educational Association**

Neanderthal [nɪˈændətɑːl] Ⓐ N (*Geog*) Neanderthal *m*
Ⓑ ADJ Neanderthal, de Neanderthal; **~ man** hombre *m* de Neanderthal

neap [niːp] N (*also* **~ tide**) marea *f* muerta

Neapolitan [nɪəˈpɒlɪtən] Ⓐ ADJ napolitano; **~ ice-cream** helado *m* napolitano
Ⓑ N napolitano/a *m/f*

near [nɪəʳ] Ⓐ ADV 1 (*in place*) cerca; **he lives quite ~** vive bastante cerca; **don't come any ~er!** ¡no te acerques más!; **so ~ and yet so far**: **the shore was so ~ and yet so far** la orilla estaba al alcance de la mano pero llegar a ella era imposible; **victory was so ~ and yet so far** la victoria parecía estar asegurada pero ese último esfuerzo para obtenerla les resultó imposible
2 (*in time*) **the agreement brings peace a little ~er** este acuerdo nos acerca un poco más a la paz; **winter is drawing ~** el invierno se acerca; **the ~er it gets to the election the more they look like losing** a medida que se acercan las elecciones mayor parece la posibilidad de que pierdan; **to be ~ at hand** [*object*] estar al alcance de la mano; [*event, season*] estar a la vuelta de la esquina
3 (*in level, degree*) **the ~est I ever came to feeling that was when …** la única vez que llegué a sentir algo parecido fue cuando …; **you as ~ as dammit killed me*** no me mataste, pero por un pelo*; **that's ~ enough** (*numbers*) no merece la pena precisar más; (*amount*) con eso vale; **you won't get any ~er than that to what you want** no vas a encontrar otra cosa que se aproxime más a lo que buscas; **the ~est I ever got to winning** lo más cerca que estuve de ganar; **it's nowhere ~ enough*** con eso no basta ni mucho menos; **"have you finished it yet?" — "nowhere ~"** —¿has terminado ya? —qué va, me falta muchísimo; **as ~ as I can recall** que yo recuerde
4 (= *almost*) casi; **I came ~ to telling her everything** llegué casi a decírselo todo; **~ on 3,000 people** casi 3.000 personas; **it's in ~ perfect condition** está casi en perfectas condiciones; **I could hardly see it in the ~ total darkness** apenas lo veía en la oscuridad que era casi total
Ⓑ PREP (*also* **~ to**) 1 (*of place*) cerca de; **I live ~ Liverpool** vivo cerca de Liverpool; **is there a bank ~ here?** ¿hay algún banco por aquí cerca?; **I sat ~ the fire** me senté cerca de la chimenea; **the schools ~ where I live** los colegios de mi barrio; **the person ~est the door** la persona que está más cerca de la puerta; **he won't let anyone ~ his toys** no deja que nadie se acerque a sus juguetes; **we don't live anywhere ~ Lincoln** vivimos bastante *or* muy lejos de Lincoln; **if you come ~ me I'll kill you** como te me acerques, te mato; **nobody comes anywhere ~ him at swimming** en natación nadie le llega ni a la suela del zapato; **the passage is ~ the end of the book** el trozo viene hacia el final del libro; **don't go ~ the edge** no te acerques al borde; **we were nowhere ~ the station** estábamos bastante *or* muy lejos de la estación
2 (*in time*) **her birthday is ~ mine** su cumpleaños cae cerca del mío; **~ the end of the century** hacia fines del siglo
3 (= *almost*) **the sun was ~ to setting** el sol estaba a punto de ponerse; **we were ~ to being drowned** por poco nos morimos ahogados; **she was ~ death** estaba al borde de la muerte, tocaba a su fin (*liter*); **~ to tears** a

punto de llorar

Ⓒ ADJ 1 (*in place*) cercano; **my house is ~ enough to walk** mi casa está muy cerca, se puede ir andando; **where's the ~est service station?** ¿dónde está la gasolinera más cercana?; **these glasses make things look ~er** con estas gafas todo parece estar más cerca; **he had a ~ miss** (*Aer*) por poco se estrelló; (*Aut*) por poco chocó; **it was a ~ miss** (*target*) por poco dio en el blanco; **£250 or ~est offer** 250 libras o precio a discutir; **calculate to the ~est decimal place** para el cálculo sólo utilicen el primer decimal; **he calculated the price to the ~est pound** redondeó el precio a la libra entera

2 (*in time*) próximo; **in the ~ future** en un futuro cercano; **the time is ~ when ...** falta poco cuando ...

3 (*in level, degree*) **it's the ~est thing to heaven I can think of** para mí esto es como estar en el séptimo cielo; **that's the ~est thing to a compliment you'll get from him** (*iro*) eso es lo más parecido a un elogio que vas a conseguir de él; ✦*IDIOM* **a ~ thing**: **she won, but it was a ~ thing** ganó, pero por los pelos

4 [*relative*] cercano; **your ~est and dearest** tus seres más allegados y queridos

Ⓓ VT 1 (*in space*) acercarse a

2 (*in time*) **it was ~ing lunchtime** faltaba poco para la hora de comer; **I'm ~ing the end of my contract** falta poco para que venza mi contrato; **he is ~ing 50** frisa en los 50, tiene casi 50 años

3 (*in level, degree*) **the building is ~ing completion** el edificio está casi terminado; **the country is ~ing total anarchy** el país está al borde de la anarquía total

Ⓔ VI acercarse

Ⓕ CPD ► **the Near East** N el Cercano Oriente ► **near money** N (*Comm*) activos *mpl* realizables

nearby ['nɪə'baɪ] Ⓐ ADV cerca; **there's a church ~** hay una iglesia cerca

Ⓑ ADJ cercano; **we had a drink in a ~ pub** tomamos una copa en un bar cercano *or* que había cerca

near-death experience [ˌnɪədeθɪk'spɪərɪəns] N *experiencia extracorpórea sufrida por una persona que ha estado clínicamente muerta*

nearly ['nɪəlɪ] ADV 1 (= *almost*) casi; **it's ~ three o'clock** son casi las tres; **she's ~ 40** tiene casi 40 años; **it was ~ dark** era casi de noche; **I've ~ finished** casi he terminado; **I ~ fell over** casi me caigo; **she was ~ as tall as he was** era casi tan alta como él; **we are ~ there** casi hemos llegado; **I ~ lost it** casi lo pierdo, por poco lo pierdo; **very ~** casi; **he (very) ~ succeeded** estuvo a punto de conseguirlo

2 (*with negative*) **not ~** ni con mucho, ni mucho menos; **these drugs are not ~ as effective as the others** estos medicamentos no son ni con mucho *or* ni mucho menos tan eficaces como los otros; **that's not ~ enough** eso no es ni mucho menos suficiente; **your work isn't ~ good enough** tu trabajo no es ni con mucho satisfactorio; **it's not ~ ready** falta mucho para que esté listo

nearness ['nɪənɪs] N (*in place*) proximidad *f*, cercanía *f*; (*in time*) proximidad *f*, inminencia *f*; **because of its ~ to the station** por estar tan cerca de la estación, por su cercanía a la estación

nearside ['nɪəsaɪd] (*Aut*) Ⓐ N (*Brit*) lado *m* izquierdo; (*most other countries*) lado *m* derecho

Ⓑ ADJ [*door, verge, lane*] (*Brit*) de la izquierda; (*most other countries*) de la derecha

near-sighted ['nɪə'saɪtɪd] ADJ miope, corto de vista

near-sightedness ['nɪə'saɪtɪdnɪs] N miopía *f*

neat [niːt] ADJ (*compar* **neater**; *superl* **neatest**)

1 (= *tidy in appearance*) [*room, desk, row, pile*] ordenado; [*garden*] bien cuidado; [*appearance*] cuidado, pulcro, prolijo (*S. Cone*); [*clothes*] muy cuidado; [*work*] bien presentado; **everything looks ~ and tidy** todo parece muy ordenado; **she always looks very ~** siempre va muy arreglada; **her hair is always very ~** siempre va muy bien peinada; **he has very ~ handwriting** tiene muy buena letra

2 (= *tidy by nature*) [*person*] ordenado, pulcro, prolijo (*S. Cone*)

3 (= *compact*) [*figure*] bien proporcionado; [*waist, waistline*] delgado; **a ~ little car** un coche pequeño y de línea sencilla

4 (= *clever*) [*solution*] ingenioso, bueno; [*plan*] ingenioso; [*division, category, explanation*] claro

5 (*US**) (= *wonderful*) genial*; **that's a ~ idea** ésa es una idea genial; **those new apartments are really ~** esos nuevos apartamentos son muy chulos*

6 (*Brit*) (= *undiluted*) [*whisky, brandy, etc*] solo; **I take it ~** lo tomo solo; **half a litre of ~ whisky** medio litro de whisky puro

neaten ['niːtn] VT [+ *desk*] arreglar, ordenar; [+ *handwriting*] esmerarse con; **she ~ed her skirt** se alisó la falda; **to ~ one's hair** arreglarse el pelo, retocarse el peinado

'neath [niːθ] PREP (*liter*) = **beneath**

neatly ['niːtlɪ] ADV 1 (= *carefully, tidily*) [*arrange, put, fold*] con cuidado, cuidadosamente, con esmero; [*write, type*] claramente; **she is always very ~ dressed** siempre va muy arreglada; **a ~ kept garden** un jardín bien cuidado

2 (= *cleverly*) [*summarise, explain*] con claridad, bien; [*avoid*] ingeniosamente, con habilidad; **as you so ~ put it** como tú muy bien dijiste; **it was very ~ put** estaba muy bien expresado

3 (= *conveniently*) [*fit*] perfectamente; [*divide*] claramente, fácilmente; **they do not fit ~ into categories** no se los puede encasillar tan fácilmente; **everything worked out very ~** todo se resolvió muy bien

neatness ['niːtnɪs] N 1 (= *tidiness*) [*of room, garden, things*] orden *m*; [*of handwriting, typing*] claridad *f*; [*of person's appearance*] pulcritud *f*, prolijidad *f* (*S. Cone*)

2 (= *cleverness*) habilidad *f*, destreza *f*

3 (= *clarity*) [*of division*] claridad *f*

NEB N ABBR 1 (*Brit*) = **National Enterprise Board**

2 = **New English Bible**

Nebr. ABBR (*US*) = **Nebraska**

Nebuchadnezzar [ˌnebjʊkəd'nezəʳ] N Nabucodonosor

nebula ['nebjʊlə] N (*pl* **nebulas** *or* **nebulae** ['nebjʊliː]) nebulosa *f*

nebulizer ['nebjʊˌlaɪzəʳ] N nebulizador *m*

nebulous ['nebjʊləs] ADJ (*fig*) vago, nebuloso

NEC N ABBR = **National Executive Committee**

necessarily ['nesɪsərɪlɪ] ADV necesariamente, forzosamente; **"you will have to resign" — "not ~"** —tendrás que dimitir —no necesariamente; **it doesn't ~ follow that ...** no implica necesariamente *or* por fuerza que ...; **this is not ~ the case** esto no tiene por qué ser así

necessary ['nesɪsərɪ] Ⓐ ADJ 1 (= *required*) necesario; **is that really ~?** ¿es eso realmente *or* verdaderamente necesario?; **to be ~ to do sth** ser necesario *or* preciso hacer algo; **is it ~ for us to go?** ¿es necesario *or* preciso que vayamos?; **if ~** si es necesario *or* preciso; **don't do more than is ~** no hagas más de lo necesario; **do whatever (is) ~ to find him** haz todo lo posible para encontrarlo; **when/where ~** cuando/donde sea necesario *or* preciso

2 (= *inevitable*) [*consequence, conclusion*] inevitable; **a ~ evil** un mal necesario

Ⓑ N 1 (= *what is required*) **the ~** lo necesario; **I'll do the ~** haré lo que haga falta, haré lo que sea necesario

2 (*) (= *money*) **have you got the ~?** ¿tienes la pasta?*

3 **necessaries** (= *essentials*) **the necessaries of life** las necesidades básicas (de la vida); **there are shops nearby for all the necessaries** hay tiendas cerca para todo lo necesario

necessitate [nɪ'sesɪteɪt] VT requerir, exigir

necessitous [nɪ'sesɪtəs] ADJ (*frm*) necesitado, indigente

necessity [nɪ'sesɪtɪ] N 1 (= *need*) necesidad *f*; **I don't see the ~ of it** no veo la necesidad de eso; **there is no ~ for you to do it** no es necesario que lo hagas; **she works from economic ~** trabaja por necesidad; **of ~** necesariamente, forzosamente, por fuerza; **out of sheer ~** por pura necesidad; ✦*PROV* **~ is the mother of invention** la necesidad agudiza el ingenio

2 (= *necessary thing*) necesidad *f*; **necessities such as food and clothing were in short supply** escaseaban artículos de primera necesidad tales como la comida y la ropa; **the basic necessities of life** las necesidades básicas (de la vida); *see also* **bare A3**

3 (= *unavoidable thing*) **the curfew was seen as a regrettable ~** el toque de queda era visto como un mal necesario

neck [nek] Ⓐ N 1 [*of person*] cuello *m*; [*of animal*] pescuezo *m*, cuello *m*; **the rain ran down my ~** la lluvia me corría por el cuello; **to be ~ and ~** ir parejos; **the back of the ~** la nuca; **to break one's ~** (*lit*) desnucarse; **to break sb's ~** (*fig*) romper *or* partir el cuello a algn; **to win by a ~** ganar por una cabeza; **they threw him out ~ and crop** le pusieron de patitas en la calle*; **she fell on his ~** se le colgó del cuello; **to risk one's ~** jugarse el pellejo *or* el tipo*; **to save one's ~** salvar el pellejo *or* el tipo*; **to be in sth up to one's ~*** (*trouble, plot etc*) estar metido hasta el cuello en algo*; **to be up to one's ~ (in work)*** estar hasta arriba de trabajo*; **to wring sb's ~*** (*fig*) retorcer el pescuezo a algn*; **I'll wring your ~!*** ¡te voy a retorcer el pescuezo!*; **to wring a chicken's ~** retorcer el pescuezo a un pollo; ✦*IDIOMS* **to breathe down sb's ~*** no dejar a algn ni a sol ni a sombra*; **to have sb breathing down one's ~** tener a algn encima; **to get it in the ~*** (= *be punished*) cargársela*; (= *be told off*) llevarse una buena bronca *or* un buen rapapolvo*; **to stick one's ~ out** arriesgarse; *see also* **stiff A3**

2 [*of dress, T-shirt etc*] cuello *m*, escote *m*

3 [*of bottle*] cuello *m*, gollete *m*

4 (*Geog*) [*of land*] istmo *m*; **in your ~ of the woods*** por tu zona; **in this ~ of the woods*** por estos pagos*

5 (*Mus*) [*of guitar*] cuello *m*; [*of violin*] mástil *m*

6 (*Anat*) [*of uterus, bladder*] cuello *m*

7 (*Brit**) = **nerve A4**

Ⓑ VI (*) [*couple*] besuquearse*

neckband ['nekbænd] N tirilla *f*

neckerchief ['nekətʃiːf] N pañuelo *m*

necking* [ˈnekɪŋ] N besuqueo* *m*

necklace [ˈneklɪs] N collar *m*

necklet [ˈneklɪt] N collar *m*

neckline [ˈneklaɪn] N escote *m*; **with a low ~** escotado

necktie [ˈnektaɪ] N corbata *f*

necrological [ˌnekrəʊˈlɒdʒɪkəl] ADJ necrológico

necrology [neˈkrɒlədʒɪ] N necrología *f*

necromancer [ˈnekrəʊmænsəʳ] N nigromante *m*

necromancy [ˈnekrəʊmænsɪ] N nigromancia *f*, nigromancía *f*

necrophile [ˈnekrəʊˌfaɪl] N necrófilo/a *m/f*

necrophilia [ˌnekrəʊˈfɪlɪə] N necrofilia *f*

necrophiliac [ˌnekrəʊˈfɪlɪæk] Ⓐ ADJ necrófilo
Ⓑ N necrófilo/a *m/f*

necropolis [neˈkrɒpəlɪs] N (*pl* **necropolises** *or* **necropoleis** [neˈkrɒpəˌleɪs]) necrópolis *f inv*

necrotising fasciitis [ˈnekrəʊtaɪzɪŋfæʃɪˈaɪtɪs] N (*Med*) fascitis *f* necrotizante

nectar [ˈnektəʳ] N néctar *m*

nectarine [ˈnektəriːn] N nectarina *f*

ned* [ned] N (*esp Scot*) chorizo/a* *m/f*, gamberro/a *m/f*

NEDC N ABBR (*Brit*) (*formerly*) = **National Economic Development Council**

Neddy* [ˈnedɪ] N ABBR (*Brit*) (*formerly*) = **National Economic Development Council**

née [neɪ] ADJ **Mary Green, ~ Smith** Mary Green, de soltera Smith

need [niːd] Ⓐ N 1 (= *necessity*) necesidad *f* (**for, of** de); **I see no ~** no veo la necesidad; **without the ~ to pay so much** sin necesidad de pagar tanto; **staff are always available, in case of ~** siempre hay personal disponible en caso de necesidad; **there is a ~ for qualified staff** hay demanda de personal cualificado; **there is every ~ for discretion in this matter** es muy necesario mantener discreción en este asunto; **a house in ~ of painting** una casa que hace falta pintar; **to be in ~ of** ◊ **have ~ of** ◊ **stand in ~ of** necesitar; **when I'm in ~ of a drink** cuando necesito un trago, cuando me hace falta tomar algo; **there's no ~ to worry** no hay por qué preocuparse; **there's no ~ for you to go** no hace falta *or* no es preciso que vayas; **there's no ~ for that sort of language!** ¡no hay ninguna necesidad de usar ese vocabulario!, ¡no hace falta usar ese vocabulario!; **I have no ~ of advice** no me hacen falta consejos, no necesito consejos; **in times of ~** en momentos de apuro *or* necesidad; *see also* **needs**
2 (= *poverty*) necesidad *f*, indigencia *f*; **to be in ~** estar necesitado
3 (= *thing needed*) necesidad *f*; **the ~s of industry** las necesidades de la industria; **my ~s are few** es poco lo que necesito; **bodily ~s** necesidades *fpl* corporales; **a holiday that caters for every ~** unas vacaciones que satisfacen todas las necesidades; **they tended to my every ~** procuraban que no me faltase de nada; **to supply sb's ~s** proveer lo que necesita algn
Ⓑ VT 1 [*person*] necesitar; **I ~ a bigger car** necesito *or* me hace falta un coche más grande; **I ~ two more to make up the series** me faltan dos para completar la serie; **I ~ to get some petrol** tengo que echar gasolina; **she ~s to go to the toilet** tiene que ir al servicio *or* (*LAm*) al baño; **he ~s to be told everything twice** hay que decírselo todo dos veces; **they don't ~ to be told all the details** no es preciso *or* no hace falta contarles todos los detalles; **you only ~ed to ask** tenía más que pedírmelo; **he ~s watching** hay que vigilarlo; **that's all I ~!** ◊ **that's just what I ~!** (*iro*) ¡sólo me faltaba eso! (*iro*), ¡lo que me faltaba! (*iro*); **it's just what I ~ed** es precisamente lo que necesitaba; **I ~ this like I ~ a hole in the head** esto es lo último que necesitaba; **a much ~ed holiday** unas vacaciones muy necesarias; **he ~ed no asking** no se hizo de rogar; **who ~s more motorways?** ¿para qué queremos más autopistas?
2 (= *require*) [+ *concentration, effort, skill*] requerir; **it ~s care** requiere cuidado; **a visa is ~ed** se requiere un visado; **this room ~s painting** este cuarto hay que *or* hace falta pintarlo; **I gave it a much ~ed wash** le di un buen lavado, que era lo que necesitaba; **the report ~s no comment** el informe no deja lugar a comentarios; **this will ~ some explaining** no va a ser fácil explicar esto
3 (*impersonal*) **it doesn't ~ to be done now** no hace falta hacerlo ahora; **it doesn't ~ me to tell him** no hace falta que yo se lo diga; **it ~ed a war to alter that** fue necesaria una guerra para cambiar eso
Ⓒ AUX VB **~ I go?** ¿es necesario que vaya?, ¿tengo que ir?; **I ~ hardly remind you that …** no hace falta que les recuerde que …; **~ I say that this is untrue?** ni que decir tiene que esto no es cierto; **it ~ not follow that …** lo que no significa necesariamente que …; **I ~n't have bothered** fue trabajo perdido

needful [ˈniːdfʊl] Ⓐ ADJ necesario
Ⓑ N **the ~*** el cumquibus*

neediness [ˈniːdɪnɪs] N necesidad *f*, pobreza *f*

needle [ˈniːdl] Ⓐ N 1 (*for sewing*) aguja *f*; ✦*IDIOMS* **to get the ~*** ponerse negro*; **to give sb the ~*** pinchar a algn, meterse con algn; **it's like looking for a ~ in a haystack** es como buscar una aguja en un pajar; *see also* **knitting, pin A1**
2 (*Bot*) aguja *f*, acícula *f*; **pine ~** aguja *f* de pino
3 (*) rivalidad *f*, pique *m*
4 (‡) (= *drugs*) droga *f*
Ⓑ VT 1 (*) pinchar*, fastidiar
2 (*US‡*) [+ *drink*] añadir alcohol a
Ⓒ CPD ► **needle case** N alfiletero *m* ► **needle exchange** N (centro *m* de) intercambio *m* de jeringuillas ► **needle match** N partido *m* de máxima rivalidad

needlecraft [ˈniːdlkrɑːft] N arte *m* de la costura

needlepoint [ˈniːdlpɔɪnt] N bordado *m* sobre cañamazo, cañamazo *m*

needle-sharp [ˈniːdlˈʃɑːp] ADJ afiladísimo; (*fig*) agudísimo, muy penetrante

needless [ˈniːdlɪs] ADJ innecesario, superfluo; **~ to say …** huelga decir que …, ni qué decir tiene que …; **he was, ~ to say, drunk** ni qué decir tiene que estaba borracho

needlessly [ˈniːdlɪslɪ] ADV innecesariamente; **you worry quite ~** te inquietas sin motivo alguno

needlessness [ˈniːdlɪsnɪs] N [*of action*] carácter *m* innecesario, innecesariedad *f*; [*of remark*] inoportunidad *f*

needlewoman [ˈniːdlˌwʊmən] N (*pl* **needlewomen**) costurera *f*; **to be a good ~** coser bien

needlework [ˈniːdlwɜːk] N (= *sewing*) labor *f* de aguja; (= *embroidery*) bordado *m*; **to do ~** hacer costura

needn't [niːdnt] = **need not**

needs [niːdz] ADV **if ~ be I'll go on my own** si es necesario *or* si hace falta iré solo; **if ~ must** si hace falta; **oh well, ~ must!** ¡qué le vamos a hacer!, ¡qué se le va a hacer!; **one or the other must ~ prevail** uno de los dos habrá de ganar; **we must ~ walk** no tenemos más remedio que ir andando

needy [ˈniːdɪ] Ⓐ ADJ (*compar* **needier**; *superl* **neediest**) necesitado
Ⓑ NPL **the ~** los necesitados

ne'er [nɛəʳ] ADV (*poet*) nunca

ne'er-do-well [ˈnɛədʊˌwel] Ⓐ ADJ inútil
Ⓑ N inútil *mf*

nefarious [nɪˈfɛərɪəs] ADJ nefario, vil, inicuo

nefariousness [nɪˈfɛərɪəsnɪs] N vileza *f*

neg. ABBR = **negative**

negate [nɪˈgeɪt] VT anular, invalidar

negation [nɪˈgeɪʃən] N 1 (*gen, Ling*) negación *f*
2 (= *denial, refusal*) negativa *f*

negative [ˈnegətɪv] Ⓐ ADJ (*all senses*) negativo; **a ~ answer** *or* **reply** *or* **response** una negativa, una respuesta negativa; **the test proved ~** el análisis dio negativo; **~ cash flow** liquidez *f* negativa; **~ feedback** reacción *f* desfavorable
Ⓑ N 1 (= *negative reply*) negativa *f*; **he answered in the ~** contestó negativamente, contestó que no
2 (*Ling*) negación *f*; **in the ~** en negativo
3 (*Phot*) negativo *m*
4 (*Elec*) polo *m* negativo
Ⓒ VT (= *veto*) poner veto a; (= *vote down*) rechazar, desaprobar; [+ *statement*] negar, desmentir; [+ *effect*] anular

negatively [ˈnegətɪvlɪ] ADV 1 [*reply, think, affect*] negativamente; **to answer ~** contestar negativamente, contestar que no
2 (*Phys*) **~ charged** con carga negativa

negativity [ˌnegəˈtɪvɪtɪ] N (*Psych*) negatividad *f*

neglect [nɪˈglekt] Ⓐ N (= *carelessness*) descuido *m*; (= *negligence*) negligencia *f*; (*in appearance*) dejadez *f*; [*of rules, duty*] incumplimiento *m*; (= *neglected state*) abandono *m*; (*towards others*) desatención *f*; **the garden was in a state of ~** el jardín estaba muy descuidado *or* abandonado; **the plants had died of ~** las plantas se habían muerto de no cuidarlas
Ⓑ VT 1 [+ *obligations*] descuidar, desatender; [+ *duty*] no cumplir con, faltar a; [+ *friends, family*] desatender; [+ *opportunity*] desperdiciar, desaprovechar; [+ *work, garden*] descuidar
2 (= *omit*) **to ~ to do sth** omitir hacer algo; **they ~ed to mention this fact** omitieron mencionar este hecho, no mencionaron este hecho

neglected [nɪˈglektɪd] ADJ [*child*] desatendido; [*house, garden*] descuidado, abandonado; [*appearance*] (*of person*) descuidado, desaliñado; [*promise*] incumplido; **he is a much ~ composer** es un compositor insuficientemente *or* poco reconocido

neglectful [nɪˈglektfʊl] ADJ negligente; **to be ~ of** [+ *family, children*] desatender a; [+ *work*] descuidar; [+ *duty*] no cumplir con; **they were ~ of the needs of the community** desatendían las necesidades de la comunidad

neglectfully [nɪˈglektfəlɪ] ADV negligentemente

negligee [ˈneglɪʒeɪ] N 1 (= *nightdress etc*) salto *m* de cama, negligé *m*
2 (= *housecoat*) bata *f*, negligé *m*

negligence [ˈneglɪdʒəns] N 1 (= *carelessness*) negligencia *f*; **through ~** por negligencia
2 (*Jur*) negligencia *f*

negligent [ˈneglɪdʒənt] ADJ 1 (= *careless*) negligente; **to be ~ in doing sth** pecar de negligencia al hacer algo; **she had been ~ of her duties** había faltado a sus deberes
2 (*Liter*) [*gesture*] despreocupado

➤ LANGUAGE IN USE: **need A1** 2.2, 10.3 **B1** 2.3, 10.1, 10.2, 10.3 **C** 10.3

negligently ['neglɪdʒəntlɪ] ADV [1] (= *carelessly*) con negligencia
[2] (= *casually*) despreocupadamente

negligible ['neglɪdʒəbl] ADJ [*amount*] insignificante; [*damage, difference*] insignificante, sin importancia; **a by no means ~ opponent** un adversario nada despreciable

negotiable [nɪ'gəʊʃɪəbl] Ⓐ ADJ [1] (*Comm*) negociable; **this is our position and it is not ~** esta es nuestra postura y no es negociable
[2] [*road etc*] transitable; [*river*] salvable
Ⓑ CPD ► **negotiable instrument** N instrumento *m* negociable

negotiate [nɪ'gəʊʃɪeɪt] Ⓐ VT [1] (= *arrange*) [+ *treaty*] negociar; [+ *loan, deal*] negociar, gestionar
[2] (= *get round, over*) [+ *bend*] tomar; [+ *hill*] subir; [+ *obstacle*] salvar, franquear; [+ *river, stream*] pasar, cruzar
Ⓑ VI negociar; **to ~ for** negociar para obtener; **to ~ for peace** negociar para obtener la paz, entablar negociaciones de paz; **to ~ with sb** negociar con algn

negotiating [nɪ'gəʊʃɪeɪtɪŋ] Ⓐ N negociación *f*
Ⓑ CPD [*strategy*] negociador; [*skills*] de negociación ► **negotiating table** N mesa *f* de negociaciones; **to sit (down) at the ~ table** sentarse a la mesa de negociaciones

negotiation [nɪ,gəʊʃɪ'eɪʃən] N [1] (= *act of negotiating*) negociación *f*; [*of loan, deal*] negociación *f*, gestión *f*; **to be in ~(s) with sb** estar en negociaciones con algn; **the treaty is under ~** el tratado está siendo negociado; **that will be a matter for ~** eso tendrá que ser negociado, eso tendrá que someterse a negociación
[2] **negotiations** (= *talks*) negociaciones *fpl*, tratativas *fpl* (*S. Cone*); **to break off ~s** romper las negociaciones; **to enter into ~s with sb** entrar en negociaciones con algn

negotiator [nɪ'gəʊʃɪeɪtə^r] N negociador(a) *m/f*

Negress ['ni:gres] N (*pej in US*) negra *f*

Negro ['ni:grəʊ] (*pej in US*) Ⓐ ADJ negro
Ⓑ N (*pl* **Negroes**) negro *m*
Ⓒ CPD ► **Negro spiritual** N espiritual *m*

negroid ['ni:grɔɪd] ADJ negroide

neigh [neɪ] Ⓐ N relincho *m*
Ⓑ VI relinchar

neighbour, neighbor (*US*) ['neɪbə^r] Ⓐ N vecino/a *m/f*; (= *fellow being*) prójimo/a *m/f*, semejante *m*; **Israel and its Arab ~s** Israel y sus vecinos árabes; *see also* **next-door**
Ⓑ VI **to ~ (up)on** (= *adjoin*) colindar con, estar contiguo a; (= *be almost*) rayar en; **to ~ with sb** (*US*) comportarse como buen vecino de algn
Ⓒ CPD ► **Good Neighbour Policy** N (*US*) Política *f* del Buen Vecino

neighbourhood, neighborhood (*US*) ['neɪbəhʊd] Ⓐ N [1] (= *area*) barrio *m*, vecindario *m*; **not a very nice ~** un barrio poco atractivo; **somewhere in the ~** por allí
[2] (= *surrounding area*) alrededores *mpl*, cercanías *fpl*; **anyone in the ~ of the crime** cualquier persona que estuviera en las cercancías del lugar del crimen; **in the ~ of £80** alrededor de (las) 80 libras
[3] (= *people*) vecindario *m*, vecinos *mpl*
Ⓑ CPD [*supermarket, chemist*] de(l) barrio; [*policeman*] de barrio ► **neighbourhood watch scheme** N grupo *m* de vigilancia de los (propios) vecinos

neighbouring, neighboring (*US*) ['neɪbərɪŋ] ADJ [*town, villages*] cercano, vecino; [*houses, streets, fields*] cercano, de las proximidades; [*state, country*] vecino; **the people at the ~ table** la gente de la mesa de al lado; **in ~ Latvia** en el país vecino de Letonia

neighbourliness, neighborliness (*US*) ['neɪbəlɪnɪs] N **good ~** buena vecindad *f*

neighbourly, neighborly (*US*) ['neɪbəlɪ] ADJ [*person*] amable; [*attitude*] de buen vecino, amable; **she was full of ~ concern** era de lo más atenta

neighing ['neɪɪŋ] N relinchos *mpl*

▼**neither** ['naɪðə^r] Ⓐ ADV **~ ... nor** ni ... ni; **~ he nor I can go** ni él ni yo podemos ir; **he ~ smokes nor drinks** ni fuma ni bebe; **that's ~ here nor there** (*fig*) eso no viene al caso
Ⓑ CONJ tampoco; **if you aren't going, ~ am I** si tú no vas, yo tampoco; **"I don't like it" — "~ do I"** —a mí no me gusta —a mí tampoco; **~ will he agree to sell it** ni consiente en venderlo tampoco
Ⓒ PRON **~ of them has any money** ninguno de los dos tiene dinero, ni el uno ni el otro tiene dinero; **~ of them saw it** ni el uno ni el otro lo vio
Ⓓ ADJ ninguno de los/las dos; **~ car is for sale** ninguno de los dos coches está a la venta

nelly* ['nelɪ] N **not on your ~!*** ¡ni hablar!*

nelson ['nelsən] N (*Wrestling*) **full ~** llave *f*; **half ~** media llave *f*; **to put a half ~ on sb** (*fig*) ponerle trabas a algn

nem. con. ABBR = **nemine contradicente** (= *no one contradicting*) nemine discrepante

nemesis ['nemɪsɪs] N (*pl* **nemeses**) (justo) castigo *m*; **AIDS is our collective ~** SIDA representa nuestro castigo colectivo

neo... ['ni:əʊ] PREFIX neo...

neoclassical ['ni:əʊ'klæsɪkəl] ADJ neoclásico

neoclassicism ['ni:əʊ'klæsɪsɪzəm] N neoclasicismo *m*

neocolonialism [,ni:əʊkə'ləʊnɪə,lɪzəm] N neocolonialismo *m*

neodymium [,ni:əʊ'dɪmɪəm] N neodimio *m*

neofascism ['ni:əʊ'fæʃɪzəm] N neofascismo *m*

neofascist ['ni:əʊ'fæʃɪst] Ⓐ ADJ neofascista
Ⓑ N neofascista *mf*

neogothic [,ni:əʊ'gɒθɪk] ADJ neogótico

neolithic [,ni:əʊ'lɪθɪk] ADJ neolítico

neological [,nɪə'lɒdʒɪkəl] ADJ neológico

neologism [nɪ'ɒlədʒɪzəm] N neologismo *m*

neomycin [,ni:əʊ'maɪsɪn] N neomicina *f*

neon ['ni:ɒn] Ⓐ N neón *m*
Ⓑ CPD ► **neon light** N luz *f* de neón ► **neon sign** N anuncio *m* de neón

neonatal ['ni:əʊ,neɪtl] ADJ neonatal

neonazi ['ni:əʊ'nɑ:tsɪ] Ⓐ ADJ neonazi, neonazista
Ⓑ N neonazi *mf*

neophyte ['ni:əʊfaɪt] N neófito/a *m/f*

neoplatonic ['ni:əʊplə'tɒnɪk] ADJ neoplatónico

neoplatonism ['ni:əʊ'pleɪtənɪzəm] N neoplatonismo *m*

neoplatonist ['ni:əʊ'pleɪtənɪst] N neoplatonista *mf*

Neozoic [,ni:əʊ'zəʊɪk] ADJ neozoico

Nepal [nɪ'pɔ:l] N Nepal *m*

Nepalese [,nepɔ:'li:z] Ⓐ ADJ nepalés
Ⓑ N nepalés/esa *m/f*

nephew ['nevju:] N sobrino *m*

nephrectomy [nɪ'frektəmɪ] N nefrectomía *f*

nephritic [ne'frɪtɪk] ADJ nefrítico

nephritis [ne'fraɪtɪs] N nefritis *f*

nephrology [nɪ'frɒlədʒɪ] N nefrología *f*

nephrosis [nɪ'frəʊsɪs] N nefrosis *f*

nepotism ['nepətɪzəm] N nepotismo *m*

Neptune ['neptju:n] N Neptuno *m*

neptunium [nep'tju:nɪəm] N neptunio *m*

nerd* [nɜ:d] N pazguato/a *m/f*

nerdy* ['nɜ:dɪ] ADJ pazguato, timorato

nereid ['nɪərɪɪd] N nereida *f*

Nero ['nɪərəʊ] N Nerón

nerve [nɜ:v] Ⓐ N [1] (*Anat, Bot*) nervio *m*; **my ~s are on edge** tengo los nervios de punta; **it/he gets on my ~s** me pone los nervios de punta *or* me saca de quicio; **to be living on one's ~s** vivir en estado de tensión constante; **to have ~s of steel** tener nervios de acero; **to strain every ~ to do sth** hacer un esfuerzo supremo por hacer algo
[2] **nerves** (= *tension*) nerviosismo *m*, nervios *mpl*, excitabilidad *f* nerviosa; **she suffers from ~s** padece de los nervios, sufre trastornos nerviosos; **a fit of ~s** un ataque de nervios; **to be in a state of ~s** estar muy nervioso, estar hipertenso
[3] (= *courage*) valor *m*; **he didn't have the ~ to do it** no tuvo el valor de hacerlo; **I wouldn't have the ~ to do that!** ¡yo no me atrevería a hacer eso!; **to hold** *or* **keep one's ~** mantenerse firme, no amilanarse; **to lose one's ~** perder el valor, rajarse*; **it takes some ~ to do that** hace falta mucho valor *or* mucha sangre fría para hacer eso
[4] (= *cheek*) caradura* *f*, cara* *f*; **of all the ~!** ◊ **the ~ of it!** ◊ **what a ~!** ¡qué caradura!*, ¡qué frescura!*; **you've got a ~!** ¡qué cara tienes!*, ¡eres un caradura!*; **he had the ~ to ask for money** tuvo la cara de pedir dinero*
Ⓑ VT **to ~ o.s. to do sth** armarse de valor para hacer algo
Ⓒ CPD ► **nerve cell** N neurona *f*, célula *f* nerviosa ► **nerve centre, nerve center** (*US*) N centro *m* nervioso; (*fig*) punto *m* neurálgico ► **nerve gas** N gas *m* nervioso ► **nerve specialist** N neurólogo/a *m/f*

nerveless ['nɜ:vlɪs] ADJ (*fig*) [*grasp*] flojo; [*person*] enervado, débil, soso

nerve-racking ['nɜ:v,rækɪŋ] ADJ [*wait, experience*] angustioso; [*drive, journey, interview*] estresante

nerviness ['nɜ:vɪnɪs] N nerviosidad *f*, nerviosismo *m*

nervous ['nɜ:vəs] Ⓐ ADJ [1] (= *tense*) nervioso; **to be/feel ~** estar nervioso; (= *frightened*) tener miedo; **I was ~ about the meeting** estaba nervioso pensando en la reunión, la reunión me tenía nervioso; **I was ~ about speaking in public** me asustaba hablar en público; **to be of a ~ disposition** ser nervioso; **to get ~** ponerse nervioso; **to make sb ~** poner nervioso a algn; (= *frighten*) dar miedo a algn; **to be ~ of sth/sb** tener miedo a algo/algn; **he was in a highly ~ state** estaba muy nervioso, tenía los nervios a flor de piel; **to be a ~ wreck*** (*temporarily*) ser un manojo de nervios; (*more permanently*) estar hecho polvo de los nervios*
[2] (*Med*) nervioso
Ⓑ CPD ► **nervous breakdown** N crisis *f inv* nerviosa ► **nervous collapse** N colapso *m* nervioso ► **nervous exhaustion** N agotamiento *m* nervioso ► **nervous system** N sistema *m* nervioso

nervously ['nɜ:vəslɪ] ADV nerviosamente; **he laughed ~** soltó una risa nerviosa, rió nerviosamente; **I waited ~ in the hall** esperé nervioso en el hall

nervousness ['nɜ:vəsnɪs] N (= *apprehension, timidity*) nerviosismo *m*; (= *fear*) miedo *m*; **his ~ of flying** su miedo a volar

nervy ['nɜ:vɪ] ADJ (*compar* **nervier**; *superl* **nerviest**) [1] (*Brit*) (= *tense*) nervioso
[2] (*US*) (= *cheeky*) descarado, caradura*

nest [nest] Ⓐ N [1] [*of bird*] nido *m*; [*of hen*] nidal *m*; [*of rat, fox*] madriguera *f*; [*of mouse*] ratonera *f*; [*of wasps, hornets*] avispero *m*; [*of ants*] hormiguero *m*; **✦IDIOMS to fly the ~**: **when the children have flown the ~** cuando los hijos dejen el nido; **to feather one's ~** barrer hacia adentro, arrojar piedras al tejado propio; **to foul one's own ~** manchar el propio nido
[2] (*fig*) [*of thieves, spies*] guarida *f*
[3] (= *set*) [*of boxes, tables*] juego *m*
[4] (= *gun emplacement*) **a machine-gun ~** un nido de ametralladoras
Ⓑ VI [1] [*bird*] anidar, hacer su nido
[2] [*collector*] buscar nidos
Ⓒ CPD ► **nest egg** N (*fig*) ahorros *mpl*

nesting ['nestɪŋ] Ⓐ N (*Orn*) nidificación *f*, anidación *f*
Ⓑ CPD ► **nesting box** N (*for hen*) nidal *m*, ponedero *m*; (*for wild bird*) caja *f* anidadera ► **nesting season** N época *f* de puesta, época *f* de nidificación, época *f* de anidación ► **nesting site** N zona *f* de nidificación, zona *f* de anidación

nestle ['nesl] Ⓐ VI **to ~ against** *or* **up to sb** arrimarse *or* acurrucarse junto a algn; **to ~ down in bed** acurrucarse en la cama; **to ~ down among the blankets** hacerse un ovillo entre las mantas; **to ~ among leaves** hacerse un nido entre las hojas; **a village nestling among hills** un pueblo abrigado por las colinas
Ⓑ VT **she ~d the kitten on her lap** le hizo un hueco al gato en su regazo

nestling ['neslɪŋ] N polluelo *m*

net[1] [net] Ⓐ N [1] (*for catching fish, butterflies*) red *f*; (*for hair*) redecilla *f*; (= *fabric*) tul *m*; **✦IDIOMS to cast one's ~ wider** ampliar el campo de acción; **to fall into the ~** caer en la trampa; **to slip through the ~** escapar de la red
[2] (*Tennis, Ftbl*) red *f*
[3] (= *network*) red *f*; **the Net** (= *Internet*) (el *or* la) Internet; **to surf the Net** navegar por Internet
Ⓑ VT [+ *fish*] pescar (con red); [+ *criminal*] atrapar
Ⓒ VI (*Sport*) (= *score goal*) marcar
Ⓓ CPD ► **net curtain** N visillo *m*

net[2] [net] Ⓐ ADJ [1] (*Comm*) [*price, interest, salary*] neto; **~ of tax** deducidos los impuestos; **at a ~ profit of 5%** con un beneficio neto del 5%; **~ weight** peso *m* neto
[2] [*result, effect*] final, global
Ⓑ VT (*Comm*) (= *earn*) ganar en limpio; (= *produce*) producir en limpio; **the new tax will ~ the government £50m** el nuevo impuesto le supondrá al gobierno unos ingresos netos de 50 millones de libras; **the deal ~ted him £50,000** se embolsó 50.000 libras en el negocio
Ⓒ CPD ► **net assets** NPL activo *msing* neto ► **net income** N renta *f* neta ► **net loss** N pérdida *f* neta ► **net payment** N importe *m* neto

NET N ABBR (*US*) = **National Educational Television**

netball ['netbɔːl] N *especie de baloncesto jugado especialmente por mujeres*

nether ['neðə'] ADJ inferior, más bajo; **~ lip** labio *m* inferior; **~ regions** (= *hell*) infierno *m*; (*hum*) (= *buttocks*) trasero *m*, regiones *fpl* donde la espalda pierde su casto nombre (*hum*)

Netherlander ['neðə‚lændə'] N holandés/esa *m/f*, neerlandés/esa *m/f*

Netherlands ['neðələndz] NPL **the ~** los Países Bajos

nethermost† ['neðəməʊst] ADJ SUPERL el más bajo/la más baja

netiquette ['netɪket] N (*Internet*) netiqueta *f*, *normas de conducta oficiosas para navegar por Internet*

nett [net] = **net**[2]

netting ['netɪŋ] N (= *wire*) malla *f*; (= *nets*) redes *fpl*; (*Sew*) malla *f*; *see also* **wire C**

nettle ['netl] Ⓐ N (*Bot*) ortiga *f*; **✦IDIOM to grasp the ~** (*Brit*) agarrar el toro por los cuernos
Ⓑ VT (*) picar*, molestar; **somewhat ~d by this** algo molesto por esto
Ⓒ CPD ► **nettle rash** N urticaria *f* ► **nettle sting** N picadura *f* de ortiga

network ['netwɜːk] Ⓐ N (*gen, Comput*) red *f*; (*Rad, TV*) red *f*, cadena *f*; **the national railway ~** la red nacional de ferrocarriles; **a ~ of spies** una red de espías
Ⓑ VT (*Rad, TV*) difundir por la red de emisoras, emitir en cadena; (*Comput*) conectar a la red
Ⓒ VI hacer contactos (*en el mundo de los negocios*)

networking ['netwɜːkɪŋ] N (*Comput*) conexión *f* de redes; (= *making contacts*) establecimiento *m* de contactos

neural ['njʊərəl] ADJ neural; **~ network** (*Comput*) red *f* neural

neuralgia [njʊə'rældʒə] N neuralgia *f*

neuralgic [njʊ'rældʒɪk] ADJ neurálgico

neurasthenia [‚njʊərəs'θiːnɪə] N neurastenia *f*

neurasthenic [‚njʊərəs'θenɪk] ADJ neurasténico

neuritis [njʊə'raɪtɪs] N neuritis *f*

neuro... ['njʊərəʊ] PREFIX neuro...

neurobiology [‚njʊərəʊbaɪ'ɒlədʒɪ] N neurobiología *f*

neurolinguistic programming ['njʊərəʊlɪŋ'gwɪstɪk'prəʊgræmɪŋ] N programación *f* neurolingüística

neurological [‚njʊərə'lɒdʒɪkəl] ADJ neurológico

neurologist [njʊə'rɒlədʒɪst] N neurólogo/a *m/f*

neurology [njʊə'rɒlədʒɪ] N neurología *f*

neuron ['njʊərɒn] N neurona *f*

neuropath ['njʊərəpæθ] N neurópata *mf*

neuropathic [njʊərə'pæθɪk] ADJ neuropático

neuropathology ['njʊərəʊpə'θɒlədʒɪ] N neuropatología *f*

neuropathy [njʊ'rɒpəθɪ] N neuropatía *f*

neurophysiological [‚njʊərəʊ‚fɪzɪə'lɒdʒɪkəl] ADJ neurofisiológico

neurophysiologist [‚njʊərəʊ‚fɪzɪ'ɒlədʒɪst] N neurofisiólogo/a *m/f*

neurophysiology [‚njʊərəʊ‚fɪzɪ'ɒlədʒɪ] N neurofisiología *f*

neuropsychiatric [‚njʊərəʊ‚saɪkɪ'ætrɪk] ADJ neuropsiquiátrico

neuropsychiatrist [‚njʊərəʊsaɪ'kaɪətrɪst] N neuropsiquiatra *mf*

neuropsychiatry [‚njʊərəʊsaɪ'kaɪətrɪ] N neuropsiquiatría *f*

neuropsychology ['njʊərəʊsaɪ'kɒlədʒɪ] N neuropsicología *f*

neurosis [njʊə'rəʊsɪs] N (*pl* **neuroses** [njʊə'rəʊsiːz]) neurosis *f inv*; **he's got so many neuroses and hang-ups** es un neurótico lleno de complejos

neurosurgeon [‚njʊərəʊ'sɜːdʒən] N neurocirujano/a *m/f*

neurosurgery [‚njʊərəʊ'sɜːdʒərɪ] N neurocirugía *f*

neurosurgical [‚njʊərəʊ'sɜːdʒɪkəl] ADJ neuroquirúrgico

neurotic [njʊ'rɒtɪk] Ⓐ ADJ neurótico
Ⓑ N neurótico/a *m/f*

neurotically [njʊ'rɒtɪkəlɪ] ADV neuróticamente

neuroticism [njʊ'rɒtɪsɪzəm] N neuroticismo *m*

neurotransmitter [‚njʊərəʊtrænz'mɪtə'] N neurotransmisor *m*

neurovascular [‚njʊərəʊ'væskjʊlə'] ADJ neurovascular

neuter ['njuːtə'] Ⓐ ADJ [1] (*Ling*) neutro
[2] [*cat*] castrado
[3] (*Bot*) [*plant*] asexuado
Ⓑ N [1] (*Ling*) neutro *m*; **in the ~** en género neutro
[2] (= *cat*) macho *m* castrado
[3] (= *insect*) insecto *m* asexuado
Ⓒ VT [+ *cat*] castrar, capar

neutral ['njuːtrəl] Ⓐ ADJ [1] (= *impartial*) [*person, country, opinion*] neutral; **to remain ~** permanecer neutral
[2] (= *not controversial*) [*language, term*] neutro; **I kept my questions ~** el tono de mis preguntas era neutro
[3] (= *unemotional*) [*manner, expression, voice*] neutro
[4] (= *indistinct*) [*shade, colour, accent*] neutro; **~ shoe cream** betún *m* incoloro
[5] (*Elec, Chem, etc*) neutro
Ⓑ N [1] (*Pol*) (= *person*) persona *f* neutral; (= *country*) país *m* neutral
[2] (*Aut*) **in ~** en punto muerto

neutralism ['njuːtrəlɪzəm] N neutralismo *m*

neutralist ['njuːtrəlɪst] Ⓐ ADJ neutralista
Ⓑ N neutralista *mf*

neutrality [njuː'trælɪtɪ] N neutralidad *f*

neutralization [‚njuːtrəlaɪ'zeɪʃən] N neutralización *f*

neutralize ['njuːtrəlaɪz] VT neutralizar

neutron ['njuːtrɒn] Ⓐ N neutrón *m*
Ⓑ CPD ► **neutron bomb** N bomba *f* de neutrones ► **neutron star** N estrella *f* de neutrones

Nev. ABBR (*US*) = **Nevada**

▼ **never** ['nevə'] ADV [1] (= *not ever*) nunca; **"have you ever been to Argentina?" "no, ~"** —¿has estado alguna vez en Argentina? —no, nunca; **~ leave valuables in your car** no dejen nunca objetos de valor en el coche; **you ~ saw anything like it** nunca se ha visto nada parecido; **I ~ believed him** nunca le creí; **never!** ¡jamás!; **~ in all my life have I been so embarrassed** en mi vida *or* jamás en la vida he pasado tanta vergüenza; **~ again!** ¡nunca más!; **scenes ~ before shown on TV** imágenes *fpl* nunca vistas con anterioridad en televisión; **it had ~ been tried before** no se había intentado antes; **~, ever do that again!** ¡no vuelvas a hacer eso nunca jamás!; **it's a lesson he'll ~, ever forget** es una lección que nunca jamás olvidará; **I've ~ yet known him to fail** no lo he visto nunca fracasar
[2] (*emphatic negative*) **never!*** ¿en serio?, ¡no puede ser!; **I had a free ticket but I ~ went** tenía una entrada gratis pero no llegué a ir; **I ~ expected to see him again** no contaba con volverlo a ver; **surely you ~ bought it?** ¿pero lo has comprado de verdad?; **you ~ did!*** ¿en serio?, ¡no puede ser!; **~ mind** no importa, no te preocupes; **~ a one** ni uno siquiera; **well I ~!*** ¡no me digas!, ¡no me lo puedo creer!; **~ a word did he say** no dijo ni una sola palabra

never-ending ['nevər'endɪŋ] ADJ [*search, struggle, procession*] interminable, inacabable

never-failing ['nevə'feɪlɪŋ] ADJ [*method*] infalible; [*supply, source*] inagotable

➤ LANGUAGE IN USE: never 1 8.4

nevermore ['nevə'mɔːʳ] ADV nunca más

never-never ['nevə'nevəʳ] Ⓐ N **to buy sth on the ~** (*Brit**) comprar algo a plazos
Ⓑ CPD ► **never-never land** N país *m* del ensueño

▼**nevertheless** [ˌnevəðə'les] ADV sin embargo, no obstante; **~, it is true that ...** ◊ **it is ~ true that ...** sin embargo *or* no obstante es verdad que ...; **he is ~ my brother** sin embargo, es mi hermano; **I don't like him but I appreciate his qualities ~** no me cae bien, pero a pesar de todo sé apreciar

never-to-be-forgotten ['nevətəbiːˌfə'gɒtn] ADJ inolvidable

nevus ['niːvəs] N (*pl* **nevi** ['niːvaɪ]) (*US*) = **naevus**

▼**new** [njuː] Ⓐ ADJ (*compar* **newer**; *superl* **newest**)
[1] (= *unused*) [*purchase, acquisition*] nuevo; **I've bought a ~ house/coat** me he comprado una casa nueva/un abrigo nuevo; **I've put in ~ batteries** he puesto pilas nuevas; **I'll open a ~ packet of biscuits** abriré otro paquete de galletas; **she sold it as ~** lo vendió que parecía nuevo; **~ for old insurance** seguro *m* de valor de nuevo; **it's as good as ~** está como nuevo; **it looks like ~** parece nuevo
[2] (= *novel, different*) [*idea, theory, boyfriend*] nuevo; **it's a ~ way of thinking** es una nueva forma de pensar; **I feel like a ~ man** me siento como nuevo; **she's been a ~ woman since she got divorced** desde que se ha divorciado parece otra; **~ face** (= *person*) cara *f* nueva; (= *image*) **the ~ face of** la nueva imagen de; **that's nothing ~** eso no es ninguna novedad; **there's nothing ~ under the sun** no hay nada nuevo bajo el sol; **that's a ~ one on me!** ¡la primera vez que lo oigo!; **that's something ~!** (*iro*) ¡qué *or* vaya novedad!; **hi, what's ~?*** hola, ¿que hay de nuevo?; **so what's ~?*** (*iro*) ¡qué *or* vaya novedad!
[3] (= *recently arrived*) [*recruit, student, worker*] nuevo; **the ~ people at number five** los nuevos vecinos del número cinco; **~ boy** (*Scol*) alumno *m* nuevo; **~ girl** (*Scol*) alumna *f* nueva; **are you ~ here?** ¿eres nuevo aquí?; **the ~ rich** los nuevos ricos; **I'm ~ to the area** hace poco que vivo aquí; **he's ~ to the office/job** es nuevo en la oficina/el trabajo
[4] (= *freshly produced*) [*bread*] recién hecho; [*wine*] joven; [*crop*] nuevo; **~ potatoes** patatas *f* nuevas; **have you read her ~ book?** ¿has leído el libro que acaba de publicar?
[5] (= *young*) [*shoot, bud*] nuevo
Ⓑ CPD ► **new age** N new age *f*; (*before noun*) [*music, philosophy*] new age *adj inv* ► **New Brunswick** N Nuevo Brunswick *m* ► **New Caledonia** N Nueva Caledonia *f* ► **New Delhi** N Nueva Delhi *f* ► **New England** N Nueva Inglaterra *f* ► **New Englander** N *habitante o nativo de Nueva Inglaterra* ► **New Guinea** N Nueva Guinea *f* ► **New Hampshire** N Nuevo Hampshire *m*, Nueva Hampshire *f* ► **the New Hebrides** NPL las Nuevas Hébridas ► **New Jersey** N Nueva Jersey *f* ► **new man** N *hombre de ideas modernas que se ocupa de tareas tradicionalmente femeninas como el cuidado de la casa y de los niños* ► **New Mexico** N Nuevo Méjico *m* ► **new moon** N luna *f* nueva ► **New Orleans** N Nueva Orleáns *f* ► **New Scotland Yard** N Nuevo Scotland Yard *m* ► **New South Wales** N Nueva Gales *f* del Sur ► **the New Testament** N el Nuevo Testamento ► **new town** N (*Brit*) *ciudad recién creada de la nada* ► **new wave** N nueva ola *f*; (*before noun*) [*music, film*] de la nueva ola ► **the New World** N el Nuevo Mundo ► **New Year** N Año *m* Nuevo; **to bring** *or* **see in the New Year** celebrar el Año Nuevo ► **New Year's Day** N el día de Año Nuevo ► **New Year's Eve** N Nochevieja *f*; **happy New Year!** ¡feliz Año Nuevo! ► **New Year resolutions** NPL buenos propósitos *mpl* del año nuevo ► **New Year's** N (*US**) = **New Year's Eve**, **New Year's Day** ► **New York** N Nueva York *f*; (*before noun*) neoyorquino ► **New Yorker** N neoyorquino/a *m/f* ► **New Zealand** N Nueva Zelanda *f*, Nueva Zelandia *f* (*LAm*); (*before noun*) neocelandés, neozelandés ► **New Zealander** N neocelandés/esa *m/f*, neozelandés/esa *m/f*

> NEW
>
> **Position of "nuevo"**
>
> **Nuevo** tends to follow the noun when it means **new** in the sense of "brand-new" and to precede the noun when it means **new** in the sense of "another", "replacement" or "latest":
>
> ...the sales of new cars...
> ***...las ventas de automóviles nuevos...***
> ...the new prime minister...
> ***...el nuevo primer ministro...***
> ...the new model...
> ***...el nuevo modelo...***
>
> *For further uses and examples, see main entry.*

new... [njuː] PREFIX recién

newbie* ['njuːbɪ] N novato/a *m/f*, principiante *mf*

newborn ['njuːbɔːn] ADJ [*baby*] recién nacido

newcomer ['njuːˌkʌməʳ] N recién llegado/a *m/f*; **they were ~s to the area** eran nuevos en la zona, en la zona eran unos recién llegados

newel ['njuːəl], **newel post** [ˌnjuːəl'pəʊst] N poste *m* (*de una escalera*)

new-fangled ['njuːˌfæŋgld] ADJ (*pej*) [*idea, theory, gadget*] moderno, tan de moda

new-found ['njuːˌfaʊnd] ADJ [*talent*] recién descubierto; [*wealth, freedom*] recién adquirido; [*friend*] nuevo; **his ~ zeal** su recién estrenado entusiasmo

Newfoundland ['njuːfəndlənd] N [1] (*Geog*) Terranova *f*
[2] (*also* **~ dog**) perro *m* de Terranova

Newfoundlander ['njuːfəndləndəʳ] N habitante *mf* de Terranova

newish ['njuːɪʃ] ADJ bastante nuevo

new-laid ['njuː'leɪd] ADJ [*egg*] fresco, recién puesto

new-look [ˌnjuː'lʊk] ADJ nuevo, renovado; **the ~ Labour Party** el nuevo *or* renovado Partido Laborista

newly ['njuːlɪ] ADV (= *recently*) recién; **~ made/arrived/elected** recién hecho/llegado/elegido; **the ~ independent countries of Africa** los países de África que acababan de conseguir la independencia

newlyweds ['njuːlɪwedz] NPL recién casados *mpl*

new-mown ['njuː'məʊn] ADJ recién segado, recién cortado

newness ['njuːnɪs] N [1] [*of car, clothes, etc*] lo nuevo [2] [*of idea, fashion*] novedad *f*
[3] [*of bread*] lo fresco; [*of wine*] lo joven

news [njuːz] Ⓐ NSING [1] **that's wonderful ~!** ¡qué buena noticia!; **some sad ~** ◊ **a sad piece of ~** una triste noticia; **what ~?** ◊ **what's the ~?** ¿qué hay de nuevo?; **a 700th anniversary is ~** un 700 aniversario es noticia; **so you think you're going out tonight? well, I've got ~ for you!** (*iro*) si crees que vas a salir esta noche, te vas a llevar una sorpresa; **to be bad ~*** [*person*] ser un ave de mal agüero; [*thing*] ser mal asunto*; **to break the ~ to sb** dar la noticia a algn; **when the ~ broke** al saberse la noticia; **that's good ~** es una buena noticia; **they're in the ~** son de actualidad; **a piece of ~** una noticia; **it was ~ to me** me pilló de nuevas*; ✦**PROVS bad ~ travels fast** las malas noticias llegan muy rápido; **no ~ is good ~** la falta de noticias es una buena señal
[2] (*Press, Rad, TV*) noticias *fpl*; **the ~** (*Rad*) las noticias, el noticiario; (*TV*) las noticias, el telediario (*Sp*), el noticiero (*LAm*), el noticioso (*Andes*); **the foreign ~ pages** la sección *or* las páginas de noticias internacionales; **News in Brief** (= *section in newspaper*) Noticias *fpl* Breves, Breves *fpl*
Ⓑ CPD ► **news agency** N agencia *f* de noticias ► **news blackout** N apagón *m* informativo ► **news bulletin** N boletín *m* informativo ► **news conference** N rueda *f* de prensa ► **news desk** N redacción *f* ► **news editor** N jefe *mf* de redacción ► **the news headlines** NPL (*TV, Rad*) el resumen de las noticias ► **news item** N noticia *f* ► **news programme**, **news program** (*US*) N programa *m* de actualidad ► **news release** N (*esp US*) = **press release** ► **news sheet** N hoja *f* informativa ► **news vendor** N vendedor(a) *m/f* de periódicos

newsagent ['njuːzˌeɪdʒənt] N (*Brit*) vendedor(a) *m/f* de periódicos; **~'s** tienda *f or* quiosco *m* de periódicos

newsboy ['njuːzbɔɪ] N (= *deliverer*) chico *m* que reparte periódicos; (= *seller*) chico *m* que vende periódicos, voceador *m* (*Mex*)

newscast ['njuːzkɑːst] N noticiario *m*, noticiero *m* (*LAm*), noticioso *m* (*Andes*)

newscaster ['njuːz'kɑːstəʳ] N locutor(a) *m/f*

newscopy ['njuːzkɒpɪ] N (*Press*) texto *m* de la noticia; (*TV, Rad*) resumen *m* de la noticia

newsdealer ['njuːz'diːləʳ] N (*US*) vendedor(a) *m/f* de periódicos

newsflash ['njuːzflæʃ] N flash *m*, noticia *f* de última hora

news-gathering ['njuːzgæðərɪŋ] N recopilación *f* de noticias, recolección *f* de información

newsgroup ['njuːzgruːp] N (*on Internet*) grupo *m* de discusión

newshound* ['njuːzhaʊnd] N reportero/a *m/f*

newsletter ['njuːzˌletəʳ] N boletín *m* informativo

newsman ['njuːzmæn] N (*Press*) periodista *m*, reportero *m*; (*TV, Rad*) locutor *m*

newspaper ['njuːsˌpeɪpəʳ] Ⓐ N (*gen*) periódico *m*; (= *daily*) diario *m*; (= *material*) papel *m* de periódico
Ⓑ CPD ► **newspaper clipping**, **newspaper cutting** N recorte *m* de periódico ► **newspaper office** N redacción *f* (de periódico) ► **newspaper report** N reportaje *m*

newspaperman ['njuːzˌpeɪpəmæn] N (*pl* **newspapermen**) periodista *m*, reportero *m*

newspaperwoman ['njuːzˌpeɪpəwʊmən] N (*pl* **newspaperwomen**) periodista *f*, reportera *f*

newspeak ['njuːspiːk] N neolengua *f*

newsprint ['njuːzprɪnt] N papel *m* prensa, papel *m* continuo; **acres of ~ have been devoted to the subject** han corrido ríos de tinta sobre el asunto

newsreader ['njuːzˌriːdəʳ] N (*Brit TV*) locutor(a) *m/f*

newsreel ['njuːzriːl] N noticiario *m*, documental *m* de actualidades, ≈ Nodo *m* (*Sp*)

newsroom ['njuːzrʊm] N sala *f* de redacción

newsstand ['njuːzstænd] N (*US*) quiosco *m* de periódicos y revistas

➤ LANGUAGE IN USE: nevertheless 26.3 new B 23.2

newsworthy ['nju:z,wɜ:ðɪ] ADJ de interés periodístico; **it's not ~** no es noticia, no tiene interés periodístico

newsy* ['nju:zɪ] ADJ lleno de noticias

newt [nju:t] N tritón *m*; *see also* **pissed**

newton ['nju:tn] N newton *m*, neutonio *m*

Newtonian [nju:'təʊnɪən] ADJ newtoniano

▼ **next** [nekst] Ⓐ ADJ [1] (*of time*) (*in future*) próximo; (*in past*) siguiente; **he retires ~ January** se jubila el enero próximo; **the ~ five days will be crucial** los próximos cinco días serán decisivos; **the ~ five days were very busy** los cinco días siguientes fueron muy ajetreados; **~ month/year** (*in future*) el mes/año que viene, el mes/año próximo, el mes/año entrante (*esp LAm*); **the ~ month/year** (*in past*) el mes/año siguiente; **(the) ~ day/morning** al día/a la mañana siguiente; **unemployment is predicted to fall both this year and ~** se prevé que el desempleo disminuirá este año y el próximo *or* el siguiente; **she'll have been gone six months ~ Friday** el viernes que viene *or* el viernes próximo hará seis meses que se marchó; **on 4th May ~** (*frm*) el 4 de mayo próximo; **the week after ~** la semana que viene no *or* la semana próxima no, la siguiente; **he died ten years ago ~ week** la semana que viene *or* la semana próxima hará diez años que murió *or* se cumplen diez años de su muerte; **the ~ thing I knew he was gone** cuando me quise dar cuenta se había ido; **this time ~ week** la semana que viene a estas horas; **this time ~ year** el año que viene por estas fechas; **~ time** la próxima vez; **(the) ~ time you see him** la próxima vez que lo veas; **from one moment/day to the ~** de un momento/día para otro; *see also* **moment 1**

[2] (*of order*) próximo, siguiente; **I get out at the ~ stop** me bajo en la próxima *or* siguiente parada; **who's ~?** ¿a quién le toca ahora?, ¿quién sigue?; **I'm/you're ~** me/te toca (a mí/ti); **~ please!** ¡el siguiente por favor!; **she was ~ or the ~ person to arrive** ella fue la próxima *or* siguiente en llegar; **I'm as much against violence as the ~ person, but ...** estoy tan en contra de la violencia como cualquiera, pero ...; **he's ~ after me** es el primero después de mí; **it's the ~ road but one** es la segunda calle después de ésta; **the ~ life** la otra vida; **on the ~ page** en la siguiente página; **the ~ size up/down** (*in clothes*) una talla más grande/más pequeña; (*in shoes*) un número más grande/más pequeño

[3] (= *adjacent*) **~ door** (en la casa de) al lado; **~ door's dog** el perro de (los vecinos de) al lado; **I went ~ door to the bathroom** fui al baño que estaba (en el cuarto de) al lado; **(the) ~ door but one** no la puerta de al lado, sino la siguiente; **~ door to** al lado de; **we live ~ door to each other** vivimos uno al lado del otro; **I live ~ door to her** vivo en la casa de al lado de la suya *or* contigua a la suya; **the ~ house** la casa de al lado; **I could hear them talking in the ~ room** les oía hablar en el cuarto de al lado; **she lives in the ~ street to me** vive en la calle contigua a la mía; **✦IDIOM the girl/boy ~ door** la hija/el hijo del vecino

Ⓑ ADV [1] (*in past*) después, luego; **what did he do ~?** ¿qué hizo después *or* luego?; **when I ~ saw him** cuando lo volví a ver; **I ~ saw him in Rome** la siguiente vez que lo vi fue en Roma

[2] (*in future*) **what do we do ~?** ¿y ahora qué hacemos?; **~ we put the salt in** a continuación *or* ahora añadimos la sal; **when you ~ see him ◊ when ~ you see him** cuando lo vuelvas a ver, la próxima vez que lo veas; **whatever ~!** ¡lo que faltaba!

[3] (*of place, order*) **who's the ~ tallest boy?** ¿quién le sigue en altura?; **the ~ smaller size** la talla más pequeña a continuación de ésta; **it's the ~ best thing to having your own swimming pool** si no puedes tener tu propia piscina, esto es lo mejor; **what comes ~?** ¿qué viene ahora?, ¿qué sigue?

[4] **~ to** [4·1] (= *beside*) al lado de; **his room is ~ to mine** su habitación está al lado de la mía; **I was sitting ~ to her** estaba sentada a su lado; **to wear silk ~ to one's skin** llevar seda en contacto directo con la piel

[4·2] (= *after*) después de; **~ to Spain, what country do you like best?** ¿después de España, cuál es tu país preferido?

[4·3] (= *compared to*) al lado de; **~ to her I felt totally inept** al lado de ella, me sentía totalmente inútil

[4·4] (= *second*) **he finished the race ~ to last** terminó la carrera en el penúltimo lugar; **the ~ to last row** la penúltima fila

[4·5] (= *almost*) casi; **it's ~ to impossible** es casi imposible; **I know ~ to nothing about computers** no sé casi nada de ordenadores, sé poquísimo de ordenadores; **we got it for ~ to nothing** lo conseguimos por poquísimo dinero

Ⓒ CPD ► **next of kin** N familiar(es) *m(pl)* más cercano(s), pariente(s) *m(pl)* más cercano(s)

next-door ['neks'dɔ:ʳ] ADJ **~ flat** piso *m* de al lado; **~ neighbour** vecino/a *m/f* de al lado

nexus ['neksəs] N nexo *m*

NF Ⓐ N ABBR (*Brit Pol*) = **National Front**
Ⓑ ABBR (*Canada*) = **Newfoundland**

n/f ABBR (*Banking*) = **no funds**

NFL N ABBR (*US*) = **National Football League**

Nfld. ABBR (*Canada*) = **Newfoundland**

NFS N ABBR (*Brit*) = **National Fire Service**

NFT N ABBR (*Brit*) = **National Film Theatre**

NFU N ABBR (*Brit*) = **National Farmers' Union**

NG ABBR (*US*) = **National Guard**

NGA N ABBR (*Brit*) (= **National Graphical Association**) *sindicato de tipógrafos*

NGO N ABBR (= **non-governmental organization**) ONG *f*

NH ABBR (*US*) = **New Hampshire**

NH(I) ABBR = **National Health (Insurance)**

NHL N ABBR (*US*) = **National Hockey League**

NHS N ABBR (*Brit*) (= **National Health Service**) Sistema *m* Nacional de Salud

NI ABBR [1] = **Northern Ireland**
[2] = **National Insurance**

niacin ['naɪəsɪn] N ácido *m* nicotínico

Niagara [naɪ'ægrə] Ⓐ N Niágara *m*
Ⓑ CPD ► **Niagara Falls** NPL Cataratas *fpl* del Niágara

nib [nɪb] N punta *f*; [*of fountain pen*] plumilla *f*, plumín *m*

nibble ['nɪbl] Ⓐ N [1] (= *little bite*) mordisquito *m*; **I never had a ~ all day** (*Fishing*) el corcho no se movió en todo el día

[2] (= *food*) bocado *m*; **I feel like a ~** me apetece comer algo, no me vendría mal un bocado

[3] **nibbles** (*at party etc*) comida *fsing* para picar

Ⓑ VT [*person*] mordisquear, mordiscar; [*fish*] picar; [*rat, mouse*] roer; [*horse*] rozar

Ⓒ VI **to ~ (at)** [+ *food*] picar; **to ~ at an offer** mostrar cierto interés por una oferta

nibs [nɪbz] N **his ~*** (*hum*) su señoría

NIC N ABBR [1] (*Brit*) (= **National Insurance Contribution**) *contribuciones a la Seguridad Social*

[2] = **newly industrialized** *or* **industrializing country**

NICAM ['naɪkæm] N ABBR = **near-instantaneous companding audio multiplex**

Nicaragua [,nɪkə'rægjʊə] N Nicaragua *f*

Nicaraguan [,nɪkə'rægjʊən] Ⓐ ADJ nicaragüense
Ⓑ N nicaragüense *mf*

Nice [ni:s] N Niza *f*

nice [naɪs] ADJ (*compar* **nicer**, *superl* **nicest**) [1] (= *pleasant*) [*book, holiday, evening*] bueno, agradable, lindo (*LAm*); [*weather*] bueno; [*food, aroma*] rico; **it's very ~ here** se está muy bien aquí; **it would be ~ to speak a foreign language** estaría bien poder hablar otro idioma; **it was ~ to see you** me ha alegrado mucho verte, fue un placer verte (*frm*); **it's not a very ~ day, is it?** (*weather-wise*) no hace un día muy bueno, ¿verdad?; **did you have a ~ day?** (*at work*) ¿qué tal te fue el día?; (*on trip*) ¿lo pasaste bien?; **it's a ~ idea, but ...** es buena idea, pero ...; **it would be ~ if you came too** me gustaría que tú también vinieses; **~ one!*** (*also iro*) ¡estupendo!, ¡genial!*; **it smells ~** huele bien; **it doesn't taste at all ~** no sabe nada bien; **did you have a ~ time at the party?** ¿te lo pasaste bien en la fiesta?

[2] (= *likeable*) simpático, majo*, buena gente*; **he's a really ~ guy** es muy simpático, es muy majo (*Sp**), es muy buena gente (*LAm**)

[3] (= *kind*) amable; **he was very ~ about it** se mostró *or* (*LAm*) se portó muy amable al respecto; **it was ~ of you to help us** fuiste muy amable ayudándonos; **to say ~ things about sb** hablar bien de algn; **to be ~ to sb** ser amable con algn, tratar bien a algn

[4] (= *attractive*) [*person*] guapo, lindo (*LAm*); [*thing, place, house*] bonito, lindo (*LAm*); **~ car!** ¡vaya coche!, ¡qué auto más lindo! (*LAm*); **you look ~!** ¡qué guapa estás!, ¡qué bien te ves! (*LAm*); **she has a ~ smile** tiene una sonrisa muy bonita

[5] (= *polite*) fino, educado; **that's not ~** eso no está bien, eso no se hace; **~ girls don't smoke** las chicas finas *or* bien educadas no fuman; **he has ~ manners** es muy educado; **what a ~ young man** que joven más agradable y educado

[6] (*emphatic*) bien; **a ~ cold drink** una bebida bien fría; **a ~ little house** una casita muy mona*; **it's ~ and convenient** resulta muy conveniente; **~ and early** bien temprano; **just take it ~ and easy** tú tómatelo con calma; **it's ~ and warm here** aquí hace un calorcito muy agradable

[7] (*iro*) (= *not nice*) **that's a ~ thing to say!** ¡hombre, muy amable!; **~ friends you've got, they've just walked off with my radio** vaya amigos que tienes *or* menudos amigos tienes, acaban de llevarse mi radio; **here's a ~ state of affairs!** ¡dónde hemos ido a parar!

[8] (= *subtle*) [*distinction, point*] sutil; [*judgment*] acertado

[9] (†, *liter*) (= *fastidious*) remilgado

nice-looking ['naɪs'lʊkɪŋ] ADJ atractivo, lindo (*LAm*); [*person*] bien parecido, guapo

nicely ['naɪslɪ] ADV [1] (= *well*) bien; **~ browned** bien dorado; **she is coming along ~ at school** en el colegio le va bien; **that will do ~** así está perfecto *or* bien; **your driver's licence will do ~** su carnet de conducir sirve *or* vale; **he's doing very ~ (for himself)** le van muy bien las cosas; **to be ~ placed (to do sth)** estar en buena posición (para hacer algo)

➤ LANGUAGE IN USE: **next B2** 26.1

2 (= *attractively*) [*arranged, decorated, furnished*] bien, con gusto; **she dresses ~** viste con muy buen gusto
3 (= *politely*) [*ask, say*] bien, con educación

niceness ['naɪsnɪs] N 1 (= *pleasantness*) [*of place, thing*] lo agradable
2 (= *likeableness*) [*of person*] simpatía *f*
3 (= *kindness*) amabilidad *f*
4 (= *politeness*) finura *f*
5 (= *subtlety*) sutileza *f*

nicety ['naɪsɪtɪ] N sutileza *f*; **niceties** detalles *mpl*, sutilezas *fpl*; **legal niceties** pormenores *mpl* legales; **she went through the social niceties** realizó las formalidades *or* los cumplidos de rigor; **to judge sth to a ~** juzgar algo con precisión *or* al detalle

niche [niːʃ] N (*Archit*) nicho *m*, hornacina *f*; (*fig*) hueco *m*; **to find a ~ for o.s.** hacerse con una buena posición *or* un huequito*

Nicholas ['nɪkələs] N Nicolás

Nick [nɪk] N (*familiar form*) *of* **Nicholas**; **Old ~** (*hum*) Pedro Botero (* *hum*)

nick [nɪk] Ⓐ N 1 (= *cut*) muesca *f*, mella *f*; (= *crack*) hendedura *f*
2 (*Brit**) (= *prison*) chirona* *f*, trullo *m* (*Sp*‡); (= *police station*) comisaría *f*
3 ✦**IDIOM in the ~ of time** justo a tiempo
4 (*) (= *condition*) **in good ~** en buen estado
Ⓑ VT 1 (= *cut*) hacer una muesca en, mellar; **he ~ed his chin shaving** se hizo un corte en la barbilla afeitándose; **the bullet had ~ed the bone** la bala le había hendido el hueso; **the film does no more than ~ the surface of this thorny issue** la película no hace más que tocar muy de refilón este espinoso asunto; **to ~ o.s.** cortarse
2 (*) (= *steal*) robar, afanar*; (= *arrest*) agarrar*, trincar (*Sp**), apañar (*Mex**); **you're ~ed!** ¡estás detenido!

nickel ['nɪkl] Ⓐ N 1 (= *metal*) níquel *m*
2 (*US*) (= *coin*) moneda *f* de cinco centavos
Ⓑ CPD ► **nickel silver** N plata *f* alemana

nickel-plated ['nɪkl'pleɪtɪd] ADJ niquelado

nicker‡ ['nɪkəʳ] N (*Brit*) libra *f* esterlina

nickname ['nɪkneɪm] Ⓐ N apodo *m*, mote *m*
Ⓑ VT apodar, dar el apodo de; **they ~d him Nobby** le dieron el apodo de Nobby

Nicosia [,nɪkəʊ'siːə] N Nicosia *f*

nicotine ['nɪkətiːn] Ⓐ N nicotina *f*
Ⓑ CPD ► **nicotine poisoning** N nicotinismo *m*

nicotinic [,nɪkə'tɪnɪk] ADJ **~ acid** ácido *m* nicotínico

niece [niːs] N sobrina *f*

niff‡ [nɪf] N (*Brit*) olorcito *m* (**of** a); (*unpleasant*) tufillo *m*

niffy‡ ['nɪfɪ] ADJ (*Brit*) maloliente, apestoso

nifty* ['nɪftɪ] ADJ (*compar* **niftier**; *superl* **niftiest**)
1 (= *excellent*) [*person*] sensacional*, chachi (*Sp**); [*place, car*] chulo*; [*gadget, idea*] ingenioso, chulo*
2 (= *skilful*) diestro, hábil
3 (= *quick*) **you'd better be ~ about it!** ¡ya puedes ir ligerito!, ¡más vale que te des prisa!
4 (= *elegant*) (= *stylish*) [*outfit*] elegante, chulo*

Niger ['naɪdʒəʳ] N (= *country, river*) Níger *m*

Nigeria [naɪ'dʒɪərɪə] N Nigeria *f*

Nigerian [naɪ'dʒɪərɪən] Ⓐ ADJ nigeriano
Ⓑ N nigeriano/a *m/f*

niggardliness ['nɪgədlɪnɪs] N tacañería *f*

niggardly ['nɪgədlɪ] ADJ [*person*] tacaño; [*allowance*] miserable

nigger‡* ['nɪgəʳ] N (*offensive*) negro/a *m/f*; ✦**IDIOM to be the ~ in the woodpile**† ser lo que lo estropea todo

niggle ['nɪgl] Ⓐ VI quejarse
Ⓑ VT preocupar; **it's something that has always ~d me** es algo que siempre me ha tenido inquieto
Ⓒ N (= *complaint*) queja *f*; (= *worry*) preocupación *f*

niggling ['nɪglɪŋ] Ⓐ ADJ [*detail*] engorroso; [*doubt, suspicion*] persistente, constante; [*injury*] molesto, molestoso (*LAm*); [*person*] quisquilloso
Ⓑ N (= *complaints*) quejas *fpl*

nigh† [naɪ] (*liter*) Ⓐ ADJ (= *imminent*) próximo, cercano; **the end is ~** el final se avecina *or* está muy próximo
Ⓑ ADV 1 (= *near*) cerca; **when winter draws ~** cuando se acerca el invierno
2 **~ on** (= *nearly*) casi; **it's ~ on finished** está casi terminado

night [naɪt] Ⓐ N 1 (= *time of day*) noche *f*; **it is ~** (*liter*) es de noche; **Monday ~** el lunes por la noche; **a Beethoven ~** un concierto dedicado a Beethoven; **all ~ (long)** toda la noche; **at ~** por la noche, de noche; **11 o'clock at ~** las 11 de la noche; **last thing at ~** lo último antes de acostarse; **to stay up late at ~** trasnochar; **to have a bad ~** dormir mal, pasar una mala noche; **the ~ before the ceremony** la víspera de la ceremonia; **by ~** de noche, por la noche; **~ and day** noche y día; **to have an early ~** acostarse temprano; **good ~!** ¡buenas noches!; **in the ~** durante la noche; **last ~** (= *late*) anoche; (= *in the evening*) ayer por la tarde; **the ~ before last** anteanoche; **to have a late ~** acostarse muy tarde; **you've had too many late ~s** llevas muchos días acostándote muy tarde; **we decided to make a ~ of it and go to a club afterwards** decidimos prolongar la velada e irnos a una discoteca después; **to have a ~ out** salir por la noche; **I can't sleep ~s** (*US*) no puedo dormir la noche; **to spend the ~** pasar la noche; **to spend the ~ together** (*euph*) (= *to have sex*) pasar la noche juntos; **tomorrow ~** mañana por la noche; **to work ~s** trabajar de noche
2 (*Theat*) **first ~** estreno *m*; **last ~** última representación *f*
Ⓑ CPD ► **night bird** N (*fig*) ave *f* nocturna; ► **night blindness** N ceguera *f* nocturna ► **night fighter** N caza *m* nocturno, cazabombardero *m* nocturno ► **night nurse** N enfermera *f* de noche ► **night owl*** N (*fig*) ave *f* nocturna ► **night porter** N guarda *m* nocturno ► **night safe** N caja *f* de seguridad nocturna ► **night school** N escuela *f* nocturna ► **night shift** N turno *m* nocturno, turno *m* de noche ► **night stand** N (*US*) = **night table** ► **night storage heater** N acumulador *m* eléctrico nocturno ► **night table** N mesita *f* de noche ► **night vision** N visión *f* nocturna; *see also* **night-vision** ► **night watch** N (= *shift*) turno *m* de noche; (*Hist*) ronda *f* nocturna; (= *individual*) = **night watchman** ► **night watchman** N (*in factory*) vigilante *m* nocturno; (*in street*) sereno *m* ► **night work** N trabajo *m* nocturno

nightcap ['naɪtkæp] N 1 (= *hat*) gorro *m* de dormir
2 (= *drink*) *bebida que se toma antes de acostarse*

nightclothes ['naɪt,kləʊðz] N ropa *fsing* de dormir

nightclub ['naɪtklʌb] N club *m* nocturno

nightdress ['naɪtdres] N (*esp Brit*) camisón *m* de noche

nightfall ['naɪtfɔːl] N anochecer *m*; **at ~** al anochecer; **by ~** antes del anochecer

nightgown ['naɪtgaʊn] N (*esp US*) camisón *m* de noche

nighthawk ['naɪthɔːk] N chotacabras *m inv*

nightie* ['naɪtɪ] N = **nightdress**

nightingale ['naɪtɪŋgeɪl] N ruiseñor *m*

nightjar ['naɪtdʒɑːʳ] N chotacabras *m inv*

nightlife ['naɪtlaɪf] N vida *f* nocturna

night-light ['naɪtlaɪt] N lamparilla *f*, mariposa *f*

nightlong ['naɪtlɒŋ] ADJ de toda la noche, que dura toda la noche

nightly ['naɪtlɪ] Ⓐ ADV todas las noches
Ⓑ ADJ de noche, nocturno; (*regular*) de todas las noches

nightmare ['naɪtmɛəʳ] Ⓐ N (*also fig*) pesadilla *f*; ✦**IDIOM to be sb's worst ~** ser la peor pesadilla de algn
Ⓑ CPD ► **nightmare scenario** N **a hung parliament would be the ~ scenario for the market** el peor panorama para el mercado sería un parlamento en el cual ningún partido tiene la mayoría absoluta

nightmarish ['naɪtmɛərɪʃ] ADJ de pesadilla, espeluznante

night-night* ['naɪt,naɪt] EXCL (= *goodnight*) buenas noches

nightshade ['naɪtʃeɪd] N dulcamara *f*, hierba *f* mora; **deadly ~** belladona *f*

nightshirt ['naɪtʃɜːt] N camisa *f* de dormir

night-sight ['naɪtsaɪt] N visor *m* nocturno

nightspot ['naɪt,spɒt] N local *m* nocturno

nightstick ['naɪtstɪk] N (*US*) porra *f* (de policía)

night-time ['naɪttaɪm] Ⓐ N noche *f*; **at ~** por la noche, de noche; **in the ~** durante la noche, por la noche
Ⓑ CPD [*visit, call*] nocturno

night-vision ['naɪtvɪʒən] ADJ [*goggles, binoculars, equipment*] de vigilancia nocturna; *see also* **night B**

nightwear ['naɪtwɛəʳ] N ropa *f* de dormir

nig-nog‡* ['nɪgnɒg] N (*offensive*) negro/a *m/f*

NIH N ABBR (*US*) = **National Institutes of Health**

nihilism ['naɪɪlɪzəm] N nihilismo *m*

nihilist ['naɪɪlɪst] N nihilista *mf*

nihilistic [,naɪɪ'lɪstɪk] ADJ nihilista

Nikkei average [nɪ,keɪ'ævərɪdʒ], **Nikkei index** [nɪ,keɪ'ɪndeks] N índice *m* Nikkei

nil [nɪl] Ⓐ N (= *nothing*) nada *f*; (*Sport*) cero *m*; **Granada beat Murcia two-~** el Granada venció al Murcia dos-cero *or* por dos a cero; **they drew ~-~** empataron a cero; → ZERO
Ⓑ ADJ nulo; **its merits are ~** sus méritos son nulos, no tiene mérito alguno
Ⓒ CPD ► **nil balance** N (*Fin*) balance *m* nulo

Nile [naɪl] N Nilo *m*

nimble ['nɪmbl] ADJ (*compar* **nimbler**; *superl* **nimblest**) [*person, mind*] ágil; [*feet*] ligero; [*fingers*] hábil, diestro; **~-fingered** de dedos hábiles; **~-footed** de pies ligeros

nimbleness ['nɪmblnɪs] N [*of person*] agilidad *f*; [*of feet*] ligereza *f*; [*of fingers*] destreza *f*

nimbly ['nɪmblɪ] ADV 1 [*jump, skip*] ágilmente; [*dance*] con ligereza
2 [*stitch, fasten*] con destreza

nimbostratus [,nɪmbəʊ'streɪtəs] N (*pl* **nimbostrati** [,nɪmbəʊstreɪtaɪ]) nimbostrato *m*

nimbus ['nɪmbəs] N (*pl* **nimbi** *or* **nimbuses**) nimbo *m*

NIMBY ['nɪmbɪ] N ABBR (= **not in my backyard**) *"no al lado de mi casa" (campaña contra el depósito de residuos tóxicos etc en la vecindad)*

nincompoop†* ['nɪŋkəmpu:p] N bobo/a *m/f*

nine [naɪn] Ⓐ ADJ nueve; **~-to-five job** trabajo *m* de nueve a cinco; **~ times out of ten** casi siempre, en el noventa por ciento de los casos; ✦*IDIOM* **a ~ days' wonder** una maravilla de un día
Ⓑ N nueve *m*; ✦*IDIOMS* **to be dressed up to the ~s** (*Brit**) ir de punta en blanco; **to get dressed up to the ~s** ponerse de punta en blanco; *see* **five** *for usage*

9-11, Nine-Eleven [,naɪnɪ'levn] N 11-S

ninepins ['naɪnpɪnz] NPL (= *game*) juego *m* de bolos; (= *objects*) bolos *mpl*; ✦*IDIOM* **to go down like ~** caer como bolos en bolera

nineteen ['naɪn'ti:n] Ⓐ ADJ diecinueve
Ⓑ N diecinueve *m*; ✦*IDIOM* **to talk ~ to the dozen*** hablar por los codos*; *see* **five** *for usage*

nineteenth ['naɪn'ti:nθ] ADJ decimonoveno, decimonono; **the ~ century** el siglo diecinueve; ✦*IDIOM* **the ~ (hole)** (*hum*) el bar; *see* **fifth** *for usage*

ninetieth ['naɪntɪɪθ] ADJ nonagésimo; **the ~ anniversary** el noventa aniversario; *see* **fifth** *for usage*

ninety ['naɪntɪ] Ⓐ ADJ noventa
Ⓑ N noventa *m*; **the nineties** los años noventa; **to be in one's nineties** tener más de noventa años, ser un noventón/una noventona; **temperatures were in the nineties** ≈ las temperaturas superaban los treinta grados centígrados; *see* **five** *for usage*

ninny* ['nɪnɪ] N bobo/a *m/f*

ninth [naɪnθ] Ⓐ ADJ noveno, nono; **Pius IX** Pío Nono; *see* **fifth** *for usage*
Ⓑ N noveno *m*
Ⓒ ADV en novena posición; **to come in ~** llegar el noveno *or* en novena posición

niobium [naɪ'əʊbɪəm] N niobio *m*

Nip* [nɪp] N (*pej*) japonés/esa *m/f*

nip[1] [nɪp] Ⓐ N (= *pinch*) pellizco *m*; (= *bite*) mordisco *m*; **there's a ~ in the air** hace bastante frío; **it was ~ and tuck throughout the match** (= *neck and neck*) el encuentro estuvo muy reñido *or* igualado
Ⓑ VT (= *pinch*) pellizcar, pinchar; (= *bite*) mordiscar, mordisquear; [*frost*] [+ *plant*] quemar; [*wind*] [+ *one's face*] cortar; (*also* **~ off**) [+ *flowers, buds*] cortar; **to ~ one's fingers in a door** pillarse los dedos en una puerta; ✦*IDIOM* **to ~ sth in the bud** cortar algo de raíz
Ⓒ VI (*Brit**) **to ~ inside** entrar un momento; **to ~ in and out of the traffic** colarse por entre el tráfico; **to ~ off/out/down** irse/salir/bajar un momento; **I ~ped round to the shop** hice una escapadita a la tienda; **we were ~ping along at 100kph** íbamos a 100kph

nip[2] [nɪp] N [*of drink*] trago *m*, traguito* *m*

nipper* ['nɪpəʳ] N (*Brit*) chiquillo/a *m/f*

nipple ['nɪpl] N 1 (*Anat*) [*of female*] pezón *m*; [*of male*] tetilla *f*; (*on baby's bottle*) tetina *f*
2 (*Mech*) boquilla *f* roscada, manguito *m* de unión; (*for greasing*) engrasador *m*, pezón *m* de engrase

nippy* ['nɪpɪ] ADJ (*compar* **nippier**; *superl* **nippiest**) 1 (= *quick*) [*person*] ágil, rápido; [*car*] rápido; **be ~ about it!** ¡date prisa!; **we shall have to be ~** tendremos que darnos prisa, tendremos que apurarnos *or* movernos (*LAm*)
2 (= *cold*) [*weather*] fresquito

NIREX ['naɪreks] N ABBR (*Brit*) = **Nuclear Industry Radioactive Waste Executive**

nirvana [nɪə'vɑ:nə] N nirvana *m*

nit [nɪt] N 1 (*Zool*) liendre *f*
2 (*Brit**) (= *idiot*) imbécil *mf*, bobo/a *m/f*, zonzo/a *m/f* (*LAm*); **you ~!** ¡imbécil!

niter ['naɪtəʳ] N (*US*) = **nitre**

nitpick* ['nɪt,pɪk] VI (*pej*) sacarle faltas a todo, buscarle tres pies al gato*

nit-picker* ['nɪt,pɪkəʳ] N criticón/ona *m/f*, quisquilloso/a *m/f*

nit-picking* ['nɪt,pɪkɪŋ] Ⓐ ADJ [*question, criticism*] quisquilloso; [*objection*] puntilloso
Ⓑ N quisquillosidad *f*

nitrate ['naɪtreɪt] N nitrato *m*

nitration [naɪ'treɪʃən] N nitratación *f*, nitración *f*

nitre, niter (*US*) ['naɪtəʳ] N nitro *m*

nitric ['naɪtrɪk] ADJ **~ acid** ácido *m* nítrico; **~ oxide** óxido *m* nítrico

nitrite ['naɪtraɪt] N nitrito *m*

nitro- ['naɪtrəʊ-] PREFIX nitro-

nitrobenzene [,naɪtrəʊben'zi:n] N nitrobenceno *m*

nitrogen ['naɪtrədʒən] Ⓐ N nitrógeno *m*
Ⓑ CPD ► **nitrogen cycle** N ciclo *m* del nitrógeno ► **nitrogen dioxide** N dióxido *m* de nitrógeno ► **nitrogen oxide** N óxido *m* de nitrógeno

nitrogenous [naɪ'trɒdʒɪnəs] ADJ nitrogenado

nitroglycerin(e) ['naɪtrəʊ'glɪsəri:n] N nitroglicerina *f*

nitrous ['naɪtrəs] ADJ nitroso; **~ acid** ácido *m* nitroso; **~ oxide** óxido *m* nitroso

nitty-gritty* [,nɪtɪ'grɪtɪ] N **the ~** lo esencial, el meollo; ✦*IDIOM* **to get down to the ~** ir al grano

nitwit* ['nɪtwɪt] N imbécil *mf*, bobo/a *mf*, zonzo/a *m/f* (*LAm*)

nix‡ [nɪks] Ⓐ N nada Ⓑ EXCL ¡ni hablar!

NJ ABBR (*US*) = **New Jersey**

NLF N ABBR = **National Liberation Front**

NLP N ABBR = **neurolinguistic programming**

NLQ N ABBR (*Comput*) (= **near letter quality**) calidad *f* casi de correspondencia

NLRB N ABBR (*US*) = **National Labor Relations Board**

NM ABBR (*US*) = **New Mexico**

N. Mex. ABBR (*US*) = **New Mexico**

NMR N ABBR = **nuclear magnetic resonance**

NNE ABBR (= **north-northeast**) NNE

NNP N ABBR (= **net national product**) PNN *m*

NNR N ABBR (*Brit*) = **National Nature Reserve**

NNW ABBR (= **north-northwest**) NNO

no [nəʊ] Ⓐ ADV 1 (*answer*) no
2 [*emphatic*] no
3 (*in comparisons*) **I am no taller than you** yo no soy más alto que tú
Ⓑ ADJ 1 (= *not any*) ningún; **they've got no friends in London** no tienen ningún conocido en Londres; **there are no trains after midnight** no hay trenes después de medianoche; **I have no money/furniture** *etc* no tengo dinero/muebles *etc*; **"no admittance"** ◊ **"no entry"** "se prohíbe la entrada"; **"no parking"** "no aparcar", "no estacionarse" (*esp LAm*); **"no smoking"** "prohibido fumar"; **it's no good** es inútil; **details of little or no interest** detalles *mpl* sin interés; **there is no coffee left** no queda café; **we'll be there in no time** llegamos en un dos por tres, no tardamos nada; **it's no trouble** no es molestia; **no two of them are alike** no hay dos iguales; **it's no use** es inútil
2 (= *quite other than*) **he's no film star! that's the man who lives at number 54** ¡ése no es una *or* no es ninguna estrella de cine! es el señor que vive en el número 54; **he's no fool** no es tonto, ni mucho menos, no es ningún tonto; **he's no friend of mine** no es precisamente amigo mío
3 (= *no way of*) **there's no denying it** es imposible negarlo; **there's no getting out of it** no hay posibilidad de evitarlo; **there's no pleasing him** es imposible contentarle; *see* **doubt A**, **end A2, A5, joke A**
Ⓒ N (*pl* **noes**) 1 (= *refusal*) no *m*; **I won't take no for an answer** no acepto un no por respuesta
2 (*Pol*) voto *m* en contra; **the noes have it** se ha rechazado la moción
Ⓓ CPD ► **no throw** N (*Sport*) lanzamiento *m* nulo

No., no. ABBR (= **number**) núm, N.º, n.º; **we live at ~ 23** vivimos en el (número) 23

no-account* ['nəʊə'kaʊnt] (*US*) Ⓐ ADJ insignificante, inútil
Ⓑ N cero *m* a la izquierda

Noah ['nəʊə] N Noé; **~'s ark** arca *f* de Noé

nob[1]‡ [nɒb] N (*Anat*) mollera* *f*, coco* *m*, cholla *f* (*Mex*‡)

nob[2]‡ [nɒb] N (*Brit*) (= *toff, person of importance*) potentado/a *m/f*

nobble* ['nɒbl] (*Brit*) VT 1 [+ *person*] (= *waylay*) pescar*; (= *bribe*) sobornar, comprar
2 (= *drug*) [+ *horse*] drogar
3 (= *arrest*) agarrar, pescar*
4 (= *steal*) birlar*, afanar*

Nobel [nəʊ'bel] CPD ► **Nobel prize** N premio *m* Nobel ► **Nobel prizewinner** N ganador(a) *m/f* del premio Nobel

nobelium [nəʊ'bi:lɪəm] N nobelio *m*

nobility [nəʊ'bɪlɪtɪ] N (*all senses*) nobleza *f*

noble ['nəʊbl] Ⓐ ADJ (*compar* **nobler**, *superl* **noblest**) 1 (*by birth*) noble; [*title*] de nobleza
2 (= *generous, praiseworthy*) magnánimo, generoso
Ⓑ N noble *mf*, aristócrata *mf*; (*Spanish Hist*) hidalgo *m*
Ⓒ CPD ► **the noble art** N el boxeo ► **noble rot** N [*of wine*] podredumbre *f* noble ► **noble savage** N buen salvaje *m*

nobleman ['nəʊblmən] N (*pl* **noblemen**) noble *m*, aristócrata *m*; (*Spanish Hist*) hidalgo *m*

noble-minded [,nəʊbl'maɪndɪd] ADJ generoso, magnánimo

nobleness ['nəʊblnɪs] N nobleza *f*

noblewoman ['nəʊblwʊmən] N (*pl* **noblewomen**) noble *f*, aristócrata *f*

nobly ['nəʊblɪ] ADV noblemente, con nobleza; (*fig*) generosamente, con generosidad

nobody ['nəʊbədɪ] Ⓐ PRON nadie; **~ spoke** nadie habló, no habló nadie; **~ has more right to it than she has** nadie tiene más derecho a ello que ella
Ⓑ N **a mere ~** un don nadie; **I knew him when he was ~** lo conocí cuando no era nadie

no-claim(s) bonus [,nəʊ'kleɪm(z),bəʊnəs], (*US*) **no-claim(s) discount** [,nəʊ'kleɪm(z)-,dɪskaʊnt] N prima *f* de no reclamación

nocturnal [nɒk'tɜ:nl] ADJ nocturno

nocturne ['nɒktɜ:n] N (*Mus*) nocturno *m*

nod [nɒd] Ⓐ N inclinación *f* de la cabeza; **give me a ~ when you want me to start** hazme una señal con la cabeza cuando quieras que empiece; **he gave a ~** (*answering yes*) asintió con la cabeza; **with a ~ (of the head)**: **he answered with a ~** contestó con una inclinación de la cabeza; **he agreed with a ~** asintió con la cabeza; **she greeted me with a ~** me saludó con la cabeza; ✦*IDIOMS* **to give sth/sb the ~** dar luz verde a algo/algn; **to go**

through *or* **be accepted on the ~** ser aprobado sin discusión; **a ~ is as good as a wink (to a blind horse)** a buen entendedor (pocas palabras bastan); **the Land of Nod** el país de los sueños

Ⓑ VT [1] **to ~ (one's) agreement** asentir con la cabeza; **to ~ (one's) approval** hacer un gesto *or* una señal de aprobación con la cabeza; **he ~ded a greeting** nos saludó con la cabeza; **she ~ded her head** inclinó la cabeza; (*saying yes*) asintió con la cabeza; **he was ~ding his head in time to the music** movía la cabeza al son de la música; **the porter ~ded us through** el conserje nos hizo una señal con la cabeza para que pasáramos

[2] (*Sport*) [*+ ball*] cabecear

Ⓒ VI [1] (*= move one's head*) inclinar la cabeza; (*in agreement*) asentir con la cabeza; **she said nothing but simply ~ded** no dijo nada, se limitó a hacer una inclinación de cabeza; **he ~ded in the direction of the house** señaló la casa con la cabeza; **she ~ded to me to come forward** me indicó con la cabeza que me adelantara; **to ~ in agreement** asentir con la cabeza; **to ~ in approval** hacer un gesto *or* una señal de aprobación con la cabeza; **she ~ded to him in greeting** lo saludó con la cabeza

[2] (*= sway*) [*flowers, plumes*] mecerse

[3] (*= doze*) dar cabezadas, cabecear

[4] (*as adj*) **he has a ~ding acquaintance with German** habla un poco de alemán; **he has a ~ding acquaintance with this author** conoce superficialmente las obras de este autor; **we're on ~ding terms** nos conocemos de vista

► **nod off** VI + ADV dormirse, quedarse dormido; **I must have ~ded off for a moment** me he debido dormir *or* quedar dormido un momento; **he was ~ding off (to sleep) in an armchair** estaba dando cabezadas en un sillón

► **nod through** VT + ADV (*Pol*) **the delegates were ~ded through** los delegados fueron aprobados sin votación

noddle* [ˈnɒdl] N mollera* *f*, coco* *m*

node [nəʊd] N (*Anat, Astron, Phys*) nodo *m*; (*Bot*) nudo *m*

nodular [ˈnɒdjʊləʳ] ADJ nodular

nodule [ˈnɒdjuːl] N nódulo *m*

Noel [nəʊˈel] N Navidad *f*

no-fault [ˈnəʊˈfɔːlt] ADJ **~ agreement** acuerdo *m* de pago respectivo; **~ divorce** divorcio *m* en el que no se culpa a ninguno de los esposos; **~ insurance** seguro *m* en el que no entra el factor de culpabilidad

no-frills [ˈnəʊˌfrɪlz] ADJ [*house*] sin adornos, sin lujo; [*wedding*] sencillo

noggin [ˈnɒgɪn] N [1] (*= glass*) vaso *m* pequeño; (*loosely*) vaso *m*, caña *f* (de cerveza); **let's have a ~** (*Brit*) tomemos algo

[2] (*= measure*) *medida de licor (= 1,42 decilitros)*

[3] (*US**) (*= head*) coco* *m*, calabaza‡ *f*

no-go [ˌnəʊˈgəʊ] ADJ **~ area** (*Brit*) zona *f* prohibida

no-good* [ˈnəʊgʊd] ADJ (*US*) inútil

no-growth [ˈnəʊˈgrəʊθ] ADJ **~ economy** economía *f* sin crecimiento *or* de crecimiento cero

no-hoper* [ˈnəʊˌhəʊpəʳ] N nulidad *f*

nohow* [ˈnəʊhaʊ] ADV de ninguna manera

noise [nɔɪz] Ⓐ N [1] (*= sound*) ruido *m*; **she jumps at the slightest ~** el menor ruido la hace sobresaltarse; **I heard a scuffling ~** oí el ruido de algo que correteaba; **I heard a creaking ~** oí un ruido chirriante; **he was making choking ~s in his throat** hacía ruidos con la garganta como si se estuviera ahogando; *see also* **background B**

[2] (*= loud sound*) ruido *m*; **he hates ~** odia el ruido; **stop that ~!** ¡deja de hacer ese ruido!; **to make a ~** hacer ruido; **tell them not to make any ~** diles que no hagan ruido

[3] (*) (*fig*) **to make a ~ about sth** protestar por algo; **they made a lot of ~ about it** protestaron mucho por ello; **she made ~s about wanting to go home early** quería irse pronto a casa y estuvo soltando indirectas; **she showed polite interest and made all the right ~s** se mostró interesada y cortés y dijo todo lo correcto; **I just made sympathetic ~s and said what a shame it was** me limité a mostrarme comprensiva y dije que era una lástima

[4] (*) (*= person*) **a big ~** un pez gordo*

[5] (*Rad, TV, Telec, Comput*) interferencia *f*

Ⓑ VT **to ~ sth about** *or* **abroad** divulgar algo, correr la voz de algo; **we don't want it ~d abroad** no queremos que se corra la voz

Ⓒ CPD ► **noise abatement** N reducción *f* del ruido ► **noise level** N nivel *m* del ruido ► **noise pollution** N contaminación *f* acústica

noiseless [ˈnɔɪzlɪs] ADJ silencioso

noiselessly [ˈnɔɪzlɪslɪ] ADV silenciosamente, en silencio, sin (hacer) ruido

noisemaker [ˈnɔɪzˌmeɪkəʳ] N (*US*) matraca *f*

noisily [ˈnɔɪzɪlɪ] ADV ruidosamente

noisiness [ˈnɔɪzɪnɪs] N ruido *m*, lo ruidoso

noisome [ˈnɔɪsəm] ADJ (*= disgusting*) asqueroso; (*= smelly*) fétido, maloliente; (*= harmful*) nocivo

noisy [ˈnɔɪzɪ] ADJ (*compar* **noisier**; *superl* **noisiest**) [*neighbours, children, crowd*] ruidoso, escandaloso; [*music*] ruidoso, estridente; **it's very ~ here** hay mucho ruido aquí; **don't be too ~** no hagáis mucho ruido

no-jump [ˈnəʊˌdʒʌmp] N salto *m* nulo

nomad [ˈnəʊmæd] N nómada *mf*

nomadic [nəʊˈmædɪk] ADJ nómada

nomadism [ˈnəʊmədɪzəm] N nomadismo *m*

no-man's land [ˈnəʊmænzlænd] N tierra *f* de nadie

nom de plume [ˈnɒmdəˈpluːm] N (*pl* **noms de plume**) seudónimo *m*, nombre *m* artístico

nomenclature [nəʊˈmenklətʃəʳ] N nomenclatura *f*

nomenklatura [ˌnəʊmenkləˈtʊərə] N **the ~** la nomenklatura

nominal [ˈnɒmɪnl] Ⓐ ADJ (*= in name*) [*Christian, Catholic*] solamente de nombre, nominal; (*= token*) [*sum, charge*] simbólico

Ⓑ CPD ► **nominal partner** N socio/a *m/f* nominal ► **nominal value** N valor *m* nominal ► **nominal wage** N salario *m* nominal

nominalism [ˈnɒmɪnəlɪzəm] N nominalismo *m*

nominalist [ˈnɒmɪnəlɪst] Ⓐ ADJ nominalista

Ⓑ N nominalista *mf*

nominalization [ˌnɒm*m*əlaɪˈzeɪʃən] N nominalización *f*

nominalize [ˈnɒmɪnəlaɪz] VT nominalizar

nominally [ˈnɒmɪnəlɪ] ADV nominalmente, sólo de nombre

nominate [ˈnɒmɪneɪt] VT (*= propose*) proponer; (*= appoint*) nombrar; **to ~ sb as** *or* **for chairman** proponer a algn como candidato a la presidencia; **to ~ sb for a job** nombrar a algn para un cargo; **she was ~d for an Oscar** la nominaron para un Oscar

nomination [ˌnɒmɪˈneɪʃən] N (*= proposal*) propuesta *f*; (*= appointment*) nombramiento *m*; **the race for the presidential ~** (*US*) la carrera por la candidatura a la presidencia

nominative [ˈnɒmɪnətɪv] Ⓐ ADJ (*Ling*) nominativo; **~ case** nominativo *m*

Ⓑ N nominativo *m*

nominator [ˈnɒmɪneɪtəʳ] N *persona que propone o nombra a un candidato*

nominee [ˌnɒmɪˈniː] N (*= person proposed*) candidato/a *m/f*; (*= person appointed*) persona *f* nombrada; **the Democratic ~** el candidato propuesto por los demócratas

non- [nɒn] PREFIX no…, des…, in…

non-academic [ˈnonˌækəˈdemɪk] ADJ [*staff*] no docente

non-acceptance [ˈnɒnəkˈseptəns] N rechazo *m*, no aceptación *f*

non-achiever [ˈnɒnəˈtʃiːvəʳ] N *persona que no alcanza lo que se espera de ella*

non-addictive [ˈnɒnəˈdɪktɪv] ADJ que no crea dependencia

nonagenarian [ˌnɒnədʒɪˈneərɪən] Ⓐ ADJ nonagenario

Ⓑ N nonagenario/a *m/f*

non-aggression [ˈnɒnəˈgreʃən] Ⓐ N no agresión *f*

Ⓑ CPD ► **non-aggression pact** N pacto *m* de no agresión

non-alcoholic [ˈnɒnælkəˈhɒlɪk] Ⓐ ADJ no alcohólico

Ⓑ CPD ► **non-alcoholic drink** N bebida *f* no alcohólica

non-aligned [ˈnɒnəˈlaɪnd] ADJ [*country*] no alineado

non-alignment [ˈnɒnəˈlaɪnmənt] N no alineamiento *m*

non-appearance [ˈnɒnəˈpɪərəns] N ausencia *f*; (*Jur*) no comparecencia *f*

non-arrival [ˈnɒnəˈraɪvəl] N ausencia *f*; **the ~ of the mail** el hecho de no haber llegado el correo

non-attendance [ˈnɒnəˈtendəns] N ausencia *f*, no asistencia *f*

non-availability [ˈnɒnəˌveɪləˈbɪlɪtɪ] N no disponibilidad *f*

non-believer [ˈnɒnbɪˈliːvəʳ] N no creyente *mf*

non-belligerent [ˈnɒnbɪˈlɪdʒərənt] Ⓐ ADJ no beligerante

Ⓑ N no beligerante *mf*

non-biological [ˈnɒnbaɪəʊˈlɒdʒɪkl] ADJ no biológico

non-breakable [ˈnɒnˈbreɪkəbl] ADJ irrompible

non-cash [ˈnɒnˈkaeʃ] ADJ **~ assets** activo *m* no líquido; **~ payment** pago *m* no dinerario

non-Catholic [ˈnɒnˈkæθəlɪk] Ⓐ ADJ no católico, acatólico

Ⓑ N no católico/a *m/f*

nonce [nɒns] Ⓐ ADV **for the ~** por el momento

Ⓑ N (‡) (*= sexual offender*) delincuente *mf* sexual

nonce-word [ˈnɒnswɜːd] N hápax *m inv* (*palabra efímera creada para un caso especial*)

nonchalance [ˈnɒnʃələns] N [1] (*= casualness*) despreocupación *f*; **with affected ~** con un descuido afectado

[2] (*= indifference*) falta *f* de interés

nonchalant [ˈnɒnʃələnt] ADJ [1] (*= casual*) [*person, attitude, manner*] despreocupado; **I tried to look ~** intenté adoptar un aire despreocupado; **she gave a ~ wave of her hand** agitó la mano con desenfado

[2] (*= indifferent*) indiferente; **she was very ~ about it** actuó como si no tuviera ninguna importancia para ella

nonchalantly ['nɒnʃələntlɪ] ADV (= *casually*) con aire despreocupado; (= *with indifference*) con indiferencia

non-Christian [,nɒn'krɪstɪən] ADJ, N no cristiano/a *m/f*

non-combatant ['nɒn'kɒmbətənt] ADJ, N no combatiente *mf*

non-combustible ['nɒnkəm'bʌstɪbl] ADJ incombustible

non-commercial ['nɒnkə'mɜːʃl] ADJ no comercial, no lucrativo

non-commissioned ['nɒnkə'mɪʃənd] ADJ ~ **officer** suboficial *mf*

non-committal ['nɒnkə'mɪtl] ADJ [*person*] que no se compromete; [*answer*] evasivo; **he was rather noncommittal** no dijo ni que sí ni que no, no se comprometió a nada; **to be ~ about sth** no definirse con respecto a algo

non-committally [,nɒnkə'mɪtlɪ] ADV sin comprometerse

non-completion ['nɒnkəm'pliːʃən] N incumplimiento *m*

non-compliance ['nɒnkəm'plaɪəns] N incumplimiento *m* (**with** de)

non compos mentis ['nɒn'kɒmpəs'mentɪs] ADJ (*Jur hum*) desposeído de sus facultades mentales

non-conductor ['nɒnkən'dʌktə^r] N (*Elec*) aislante *m*, no conductor *m*, mal conductor *m*

nonconformism ['nɒnkən'fɔːmɪzəm] N inconformismo *m*

nonconformist ['nɒnkən'fɔːmɪst] Ⓐ ADJ inconformista
Ⓑ N inconformista *mf*; **Nonconformist** (*Brit Rel*) no conformista *mf*

nonconformity ['nɒnkən'fɔːmɪtɪ] N inconformismo *m*

non-contagious ['nɒnkən'teɪdʒəs] ADJ no contagioso

non-contributory [,nɒnkən'trɪbjʊtərɪ] ADJ ~ **pension scheme** plan *m* de jubilación no contributivo (*costeado por la empresa*)

non-controversial ['nɒnkɒntrə'vɜːʃl] ADJ no conflictivo, no polémico

non-conventional ['nɒnkən'venʃənəl] ADJ no convencional

non-convertible ['nɒnkən'vɜːtɪbl] ADJ [*currency*] no convertible

non-cooperation ['nɒnkəʊ,ɒpə'reɪʃən] N (*Pol*) no cooperación *f*

non-cooperative [,nɒnkəʊ'ɒpərətɪv] ADJ no cooperativo

non-cumulative ['nɒn'kjuːmjʊlətɪv] ADJ no cumulativo

non-custodial sentence ['nɒnkʌs'təʊdɪəl-'sentəns] N *sentencia que no implica privación de libertad*

non-delivery [,nɒndɪ'lɪvərɪ] N no entrega *f*

non-denominational ['nɒndɪnɒmɪ'neɪʃənl] ADJ aconfesional

nondescript ['nɒndɪskrɪpt] ADJ [*person, clothes, face*] (= *unremarkable*) anodino; (= *uninteresting*) insulso, soso*; [*building, furniture*] corriente; [*colour*] indefinido

non-distinctive [,nɒndɪs'tɪŋktɪv] ADJ (*Ling*) no distintivo

non-drinker ['nɒn'drɪŋkə^r] N no bebedor(a) *m/f*

non-drip ['nɒn'drɪp] ADJ que no gotea

non-durable ['nɒn'djʊərəbl] ADJ perecedero

non-dutiable ['nɒn'djuːtɪəbl] ADJ libre de aranceles, no sujeto a derechos de aduana

none [nʌn] Ⓐ PRON [1] (= *person*) nadie, ninguno; (= *thing*) nada, ninguno; **~ of them** ninguno de ellos; **~ of you can tell me** ninguno de vosotros sabe decirme; **we have ~ of your books** no tenemos ninguno de tus libros *or* ningún libro tuyo; **~ of this is true** nada de esto es verdad; **"any news?" — "none!"** —¿alguna noticia? —¡nada! *or* ¡ninguna!, —¿se sabe algo? —¡nada!; **there are ~ left** no queda ninguno; **I want ~ of your lectures!** ¡no quiero que me sermonees!; **we'll have ~ of that!** ¡vale ya!; **he would have ~ of it, he insisted on paying** no hubo forma de convencerlo, insistió en pagar; **everyone wanted her to win, ~ more so than I** todos querían que ganara, y yo más que nadie; **it was ~ other than the bishop** fue el obispo mismo
[2] (*liter*) **~ can tell** nadie lo sabe; **~ but he knows of this** sólo lo sabe él; **riches have I ~** riqueza no la tengo; **reply came there ~** no hubo respuesta
Ⓑ ADV **I was ~ too comfortable** no me sentía nada cómodo; **he did ~ too well in his exams** los exámenes no le fueron nada bien; **it was ~ too soon** ya era hora; **it's ~ the worse for that** no es peor por eso; *see also* **wise A1, worse A**

nonentity [nɒ'nentɪtɪ] N (= *person*) nulidad *f*, cero *m* a la izquierda

non-essential ['nɒnɪ'senʃəl] Ⓐ ADJ no esencial
Ⓑ N cosa *f* secundaria

nonetheless [,nʌnðə'les] ADV sin embargo, aún así

non-EU [,nɒniː'juː] ADJ [*citizen, passport*] no comunitario; [*imports*] de fuera de la Unión Europea

non-event [,nɒnɪ'vent] N fracaso *m*, fiasco *m*; **it was a ~** fue un fiasco

non-executive [,nɒnɪg'zekjʊtɪv] ADJ ~ **director** vocal *mf*, consejero/a *m/f* (*no ejecutivo*)

non-existence ['nɒnɪg'zɪstəns] N inexistencia *f*, no existencia *f*

non-existent ['nɒnɪg'zɪstənt] ADJ inexistente

non-fattening [,nɒn'fætnɪŋ] ADJ que no engorda

non-ferrous ['nɒn'ferəs] ADJ no ferroso, no férreo

non-fiction ['nɒn'fɪkʃən] N literatura *f* no novelesca

non-finite [,nɒn'faɪnaɪt] ADJ ~ **verb** verbo *m* no conjugado

non-flammable ['nɒn'flæməbl] ADJ ininflamable

non-fulfilment ['nɒnfʊl'fɪlmənt] N incumplimiento *m*

non-governmental ['nɒn,gʌvn'mentl] ADJ no gubernamental

non-infectious ['nɒn,ɪn'fekʃəs] ADJ no infeccioso

non-inflammable ['nɒnɪn'flæməbl] ADJ ininflamable

non-intervention ['nɒn,ɪntə'venʃən] N no intervención *f*

non-iron ['nɒn'aɪən] ADJ que no necesita plancha

non-laddering ['nɒn'lædərɪŋ] ADJ [*stocking*] indesmallable

non-lethal ['nɒn'liːθl] ADJ [*weapon*] no mortífero; [*wound*] no mortal

non-malignant ['nɒnmə'lɪgnənt] ADJ no maligno

non-member ['nɒn,membə^r] N no miembro *mf*

non-metal [,nɒn'metl] ADJ no metálico

non-negotiable [,nɒnnɪ'gəʊʃɪəbl] ADJ [*demand*] innegociable

non-nuclear ['nɒn'njuːklɪə^r] ADJ [*defence, policy*] no nuclear; [*area*] desnuclearizado

no-no* ['nəʊnəʊ] N **that's a ~** (= *undesirable*) eso no se hace; (= *not an option*) no existe tal posibilidad

non-observance ['nɒnəb'zɜːvns] N no observancia *f*, incumplimiento *m*

non obst. ABBR = **non obstante** (= *notwithstanding*) no obstante

no-nonsense [,nəʊ'nɒnsəns] ADJ sensato

non-operational ['nɒn,ɒpə'reɪʃənl] ADJ (= *not working*) que no funciona; (*Mil*) no operacional

nonpareil ['nɒnpərəl] Ⓐ ADJ sin par
Ⓑ N (= *person*) persona *f* sin par; (= *thing*) cosa *f* sin par; (*Typ*) nomparell *m*

non-participating ['nɒnpɑː'tɪsɪpeɪtɪŋ] ADJ no participante

nonpartisan ['nɒn,pɑːtɪ'zæn] ADJ imparcial

non-party ['nɒn'pɑːtɪ] ADJ (*Pol*) independiente

non-paying ['nɒn'peɪɪŋ] ADJ [*member*] que no paga

non-payment ['nɒn'peɪmənt] N falta *f* de pago, impago *m*; **sued for ~ of debts** demandado por no pagar sus deudas

non-person ['nɒn'pɜːsn] N persona *f* que no existe, ser *m* inexistente

non-playing [,nɒn'pleɪɪŋ] ADJ [*captain*] no jugador

nonplus ['nɒn'plʌs] (*pt, pp* **nonplussed**) VT dejar perplejo, desconcertar; **he was completely ~sed** estaba totalmente perplejo *or* desconcertado

non-poisonous [,nɒn'pɔɪznəs] ADJ [*substance*] no tóxico, atóxico; [*snake*] no venenoso

non-political [,nɒnpə'lɪtɪkəl] ADJ apolítico

non-polluting ['nɒnpə'luːtɪŋ] ADJ no contaminante

non-practising ['nɒn'præktɪsɪŋ] ADJ no practicante

non-productive [,nɒnprə'dʌktɪv] ADJ improductivo

non-professional ['nɒnprə'feʃnəl] ADJ no profesional, aficionado

non-profit [,nɒn'prɒfɪt] (*US*) ADJ = **non-profit-making**

non-profit-making ['nɒn'prɒfɪtmeɪkɪŋ] ADJ no lucrativo

non-proliferation treaty [nɒnprəlɪfə-'reɪʃn,triːtɪ] N tratado *m* de no proliferación

non-recurring ['nɒnrɪ'kɜːrɪŋ] Ⓐ ADJ que no se repite, único
Ⓑ CPD ► **non-recurring expenditure** N gasto *m* ocasional

non-resident ['nɒn'rezɪdənt] Ⓐ ADJ [*citizen, population*] no residente, transeúnte; [*status*] de no residente; [*staff, workers*] no fijo
Ⓑ N [*of hotel etc*] no residente *mf*; [*of country*] no residente *mf*, transeúnte *mf*

non-residential ['nɒn,rezɪ'denʃl] ADJ no residencial

non-returnable [,nɒnrɪ'tɜːnəbl] ADJ [*deposit*] no reembolsable; **~ bottle** envase *m* no retornable

non-scheduled ['nɒn'ʃedjuːld] ADJ [*flight, plane*] no regular

non-sectarian ['nɒnsek'teərɪən] ADJ no sectario

nonsense ['nɒnsəns] Ⓐ N tonterías *fpl*; **(what) ~!** ¡tonterías!, ¡qué tontería!; **but that's ~!** ¡eso es absurdo!, ¡eso es ridículo!; **it is ~ to say that …** es absurdo *or* ridículo decir que …; **I've never heard such ~!** ¡vaya (una) tontería!, ¡jamás oí (una) tontería igual!;

to make (a) ~ of [+ *claim, system, law*] quitar sentido a; [+ *pledge*] convertir en papel mojado; **a piece of ~** una tontería; **I'll stand no ~ from you!** ◊ **I won't take any ~ from you!** ¡no voy a tolerar tus tonterías!; **to talk ~** decir tonterías *or* disparates; **stop this ~!** ¡ya vale de tonterías!
Ⓑ CPD ► **nonsense verse** N disparates *mpl* (en verso), versos *mpl* disparatados

nonsensical [nɒn'sensɪkəl] ADJ absurdo

nonsensically [nɒn'sensɪkəlɪ] ADV absurdamente

non seq. ABBR = **non sequitur**

non sequitur [,nɒn'sekwɪtəʳ] N incongruencia *f*, falta *f* de lógica; **it's a ~** es una incongruencia

non-sexist ['nɒn'seksɪst] ADJ no sexista

non-shrink ['nɒn'ʃrɪŋk] ADJ que no encoge

non-skid ['nɒn'skɪd] ADJ [*surface*] antideslizante, antirresbaladizo

non-skilled ['nɒn'skɪld] ADJ [*worker*] no cualificado; [*work*] no especializado

non-slip ['nɒn'slɪp] ADJ = **non-skid**

non-smoker ['nɒn'sməʊkəʳ] N [1] (= *person*) no fumador(a) *m/f*; **I've always been a ~** no he fumado nunca
[2] (*Rail*) compartimiento *m* de no fumadores

non-smoking ['nɒn'sməʊkɪŋ] ADJ [*person*] no fumador; [*compartment, area*] de no fumadores; [*flight*] para no fumadores

non-specialist ['nɒn'speʃəlɪst] N no especialista *mf*

non-specific [,nɒnspə'sɪfɪk] ADJ [1] (*Med*) no específico, sin causa *or* sintomatolgía específica
[2] (= *imprecise*) indeterminado, vago

non-standard [,nɒn'stændəd] ADJ (*Ling*) no estándar

non-starter [,nɒn'stɑːtəʳ] N **that idea is a ~** esa idea es imposible

non-stick [,nɑn'stɪk] ADJ [*pan*] antiadherente, que no se pega; [*coating*] antiadherente

non-stop ['nɒn'stɒp] Ⓐ ADV (= *without a pause*) sin cesar, sin parar; (*Rail*) sin hacer paradas; (*Aer*) sin hacer escalas; **he talks ~** no para de hablar
Ⓑ ADJ (= *without a pause*) continuo; [*flight*] directo; **80 minutes of ~ music** 80 minutos de música ininterrumpida

non-taxable ['nɒn'tæksəbl] ADJ no sujeto a impuestos, exento de impuestos; **~ income** ingresos *mpl* exentos de impuestos

non-teaching ['nɒn'tiːtʃɪŋ] ADJ [*staff*] no docente

non-technical ['nɒn'teknɪkl] ADJ no técnico

non-toxic ['nɒn'tɒksɪk] ADJ no tóxico

non-trading ['nɒn'treɪdɪŋ] ADJ **~ partnership** sociedad *f* no mercantil

non-transferable ['nɒntræns'fɜːrəbl] ADJ intransferible

non-U* [,nɒn'juː] ADJ (*Brit*) (= **non-upper class**) *que no pertenece a la clase alta*

non-union ['nɒn'juːnjən], **non-unionized** ['nɒn'juːnjənaɪzd] ADJ no sindicado

non-verbal ['nɒn'vɜːbl] ADJ sin palabras

non-viable ['nɒn'vaɪəbl] ADJ inviable

non-violence ['nɒn'vaɪələns] N no violencia *f*

non-violent ['nɒn'vaɪələnt] ADJ no violento, pacífico

non-volatile memory ['nɒn,vɒlətaɪl'memərɪ] N (*Comput*) memoria *f* permanente

non-voting [,nɒn'vəʊtɪŋ] ADJ [*delegate*] sin derecho a voto; **~ shares** (*Comm*) acciones *fpl* sin derecho a voto

non-white [,nɒn'waɪt] Ⓐ ADJ de color
Ⓑ N persona *f* de color

non-yielding ['nɒn'jiːldɪŋ] ADJ improductivo

noodle¹* ['nuːdl] N [1] (= *head*) cabeza *f*
[2] (= *fool*) bobo/a *m/f*

noodle² ['nuːdl] Ⓐ NPL **noodles** fideos *mpl*, tallarines *mpl*
Ⓑ CPD ► **noodle soup** N sopa *f* de fideos

nook [nʊk] N rincón *m*; **we looked in every ~ and cranny** buscamos hasta el último rincón

nookie ['nʊkɪ] N **to have a bit of ~**** echarse un polvo**

noon [nuːn] Ⓐ N mediodía *m*; **at ~** a mediodía; **high ~** (= *midday*) mediodía *m*; (*fig*) (= *peak*) apogeo *m*, punto *m* culminante; (= *critical point*) momento *m* crucial
Ⓑ CPD de mediodía

no-one ['nəʊwʌn] PRON = **nobody**

noose [nuːs] Ⓐ N (= *loop*) nudo *m* corredizo; (*for animal, as trap*) lazo *m*; [*of hangman*] soga *f*; **✦IDIOM to put one's head in the ~** ponerse la soga al cuello
Ⓑ VT coger con lazo

no-par securities [,nəʊpɑːsɪ'kjʊərɪtɪz] NPL títulos *mpl* sin valor nominal

nope* [nəʊp] EXCL no

▼ **nor** [nɔːʳ] CONJ [1] (*following "neither"*) ni; **neither Sarah ~ Tamsin is coming to the party** no vienen ni Sarah ni Tamsin a la fiesta, ni Sarah ni Tamsin vienen a la fiesta; **she neither eats ~ drinks** ni come ni bebe; **he was neither fat ~ thin** no estaba ni gordo ni delgado
[2] (*as complement to neg statement*) **"I don't work here" — "~ do I"** —yo no trabajo aquí —ni yo (tampoco) *or* —yo tampoco; **"I didn't like the film" — "~ did I"** —no me gustó la película —a mí tampoco *or* —ni a mí; **"we haven't seen him" — "~ have we"** —no lo hemos visto —nosotros tampoco *or* —ni nosotros; **I don't know, ~ can I guess** ni lo sé, ni (tampoco) lo puedo adivinar, no lo sé y tampoco lo puedo adivinar; **~ does it seem likely** ni tampoco parece probable; **~ was this all** y esto no fue todo

Nordic ['nɔːdɪk] ADJ nórdico

Norf ABBR (*Brit*) = **Norfolk**

norm [nɔːm] N [1] (= *pattern of behaviour, official standard*) norma *f*; **in the West monogamy is the ~** la monogamia es la norma en Occidente; **small families have become the ~** las familias pequeñas han pasado a ser lo normal
[2] (= *average*) **the ~** lo normal; **larger than the ~** más grande de lo normal; (*Bio*) más grande que el tipo

normal ['nɔːməl] Ⓐ ADJ [1] (= *usual*) normal; **it's perfectly ~ to feel that way** es muy normal sentirse así, no hay nada raro en sentirse así; **above/below ~** por encima/debajo de lo normal; **to carry on as ~** seguir haciendo todo como de costumbre; **to get back** *or* **return to ~** [*situation*] normalizarse, volver a la normalidad; **"normal service will be resumed as soon as possible"** "se reanudará la emisión lo antes posible"; **I woke at the ~ time** me desperté a la hora de siempre; **he bought a return ticket instead of the ~ single** compró un billete de ida y vuelta en vez del de sólo ida que solía comprar
[2] (= *well-adjusted*) [*person*] normal
[3] (= *healthy*) [*baby*] normal; [*pregnancy*] sin complicaciones
[4] (*Math, Chem*) normal
Ⓑ CPD ► **normal school** N (*US*†) escuela *f* normal

normalcy ['nɔːməlsɪ] N (*esp US*) normalidad *f*

normality [nɔː'mælɪtɪ] N normalidad *f*

normalization [,nɔːməlaɪ'zeɪʃən] N normalización *f*

normalize ['nɔːməlaɪz] VT normalizar

normally ['nɔːməlɪ] ADV normalmente; **he ~ arrives at seven o'clock** normalmente llega a las siete, suele llegar a las siete; **the trains are running ~** los trenes están funcionando con normalidad

Norman ['nɔːmən] Ⓐ ADJ normando; **the ~ Conquest** la conquista de los normandos; **~ architecture** arquitectura *f* románica
Ⓑ N normando/a *m/f*

Normandy ['nɔːməndɪ] N Normandía *f*

normative ['nɔːmətɪv] ADJ normativo

Norse [nɔːs] Ⓐ ADJ nórdico, escandinavo; **~ mythology** mitología *f* nórdica
Ⓑ N (*Ling*) nórdico *m*

Norseman ['nɔːsmən] N (*pl* **Norsemen**) escandinavo *m*

north [nɔːθ] Ⓐ N norte *m*; **in the ~ of the country** al norte *or* en el norte del país; **to live in the ~** vivir en el norte; **the wind is from the** *or* **in the ~** el viento sopla *or* viene del norte; **North and South** (*Pol*) el Norte y el Sur
Ⓑ ADJ del norte, norteño, septentrional
Ⓒ ADV (= *northward*) hacia el norte; (= *in the north*) al norte, en el norte; **we were travelling ~** viajábamos hacia el norte; **this house faces ~** esta casa mira al norte *or* tiene vista hacia el norte; **my window faces ~** mi ventana da al norte; **~ of the border** al norte de la frontera; **it's ~ of London** está al norte de Londres
Ⓓ CPD ► **North Africa** N África *f* del Norte; *see also* **North African** ► **North America** N Norteamérica *f*, América *f* del Norte; *see also* **North American** ► **North Atlantic Drift** N Corriente *f* del Golfo ► **the North Atlantic Treaty Organization** N la Organización del Tratado del Atlántico Norte ► **North Korea** N Corea *f* del Norte; *see also* **North Korean** ► **the North Pole** N el Polo Norte ► **the North Sea** N el Mar del Norte ► **North Sea gas** N gas *m* del Mar del Norte ► **North Sea oil** N petróleo *m* del Mar del Norte ► **north star** N estrella *f* polar, estrella *f* del norte ► **North Vietnam** N Vietnam *m* del Norte; *see also* **North Vietnamese**

North African ['nɔːθ'æfrɪkən] Ⓐ ADJ norteafricano
Ⓑ N norteafricano/a *m/f*

North American ['nɔːθə'merɪkən] Ⓐ ADJ norteamericano
Ⓑ N norteamericano/a *m/f*

Northants [nɔː'θænts] ABBR (*Brit*) = **Northamptonshire**

northbound ['nɔːθbaʊnd] ADJ [*traffic*] en dirección norte; [*carriageway*] de dirección norte, en dirección norte

north-country ['nɔːθ,kʌntrɪ] ADJ del norte de Inglaterra

Northd ABBR (*Brit*) = **Northumberland**

northeast ['nɔːθ'iːst] Ⓐ N nor(d)este *m*
Ⓑ ADJ [*point, direction*] nor(d)este; [*wind*] del nor(d)este
Ⓒ ADV (= *northeastward*) hacia el nor(d)este; [*situated*] al nor(d)este, en el nor(d)este

northeasterly ['nɔːθ'iːstəlɪ] Ⓐ ADJ [*wind*] del nor(d)este; **we were headed in a north easterly direction** íbamos rumbo al nor(d)este *or* en dirección nor(d)este
Ⓑ N viento *m* del nor(d)este

➤ LANGUAGE IN USE: **nor 1** 26.2

northeastern ['nɔːθ'iːstən] ADJ nor(d)este, del nor(d)este; **in northeastern Spain** al nor(d)este *or* en el nor(d)este de España; **the northeastern coast** la costa nororiental *or* nor(d)este

northeastward ['nɔːθ'iːstwəd] ADV Ⓐ ADJ [*movement, migration*] hacia el nor(d)este, en dirección nor(d)este
Ⓑ (*also* **~s**) hacia el nor(d)este

northeastwards ['nɔːθ'iːstwədz] ADV (*esp Brit*) = **northeastward B**

northerly ['nɔːðəlɪ] Ⓐ ADJ [*wind*] del norte; **the most ~ point in Europe** el punto más al norte *or* más septentrional de Europa; **we were headed in a ~ direction** íbamos hacia el norte *or* rumbo al norte *or* en dirección norte
Ⓑ N viento *m* del norte

northern ['nɔːðən] Ⓐ ADJ del norte, norteño, septentrional; **the ~ part of the island** la parte norte *or* septentrional de la isla; **the ~ coast** la costa septentrional *or* (del) norte; **in ~ Spain** al norte *or* en el norte de España, en la España septentrional
Ⓑ CPD ► **the northern hemisphere** N el hemisferio norte, el hemisferio boreal ► **Northern Ireland** N Irlanda *f* del Norte ► **the northern lights** N la aurora boreal

northerner ['nɔːðənə[r]] N norteño/a *m/f*; (*US Hist*) nordista *mf*; **he's a ~** es del norte; **~s like this sort of thing** a la gente del norte le gusta este tipo de cosas

Northern Irish [ˌnɔːðən'aɪərɪʃ] Ⓐ ADJ norirlandés
Ⓑ NPL **the ~** los norirlandeses

northernmost ['nɔːðənməʊst] ADJ más septentrional, más al norte; **the ~ town in Europe** la ciudad más al norte *or* más septentrional de Europa

north-facing ['nɔːθˌfeɪsɪŋ] ADJ orientado hacia el norte; **~ slope** vertiente *f* norte

North Korean ['nɔːθkə'rɪən] Ⓐ ADJ norcoreano
Ⓑ N norcoreano/a *m/f*

northland ['nɔːθlənd] N (*US*) región *f* septentrional

Northman ['nɔːθmən] N (*pl* **Northmen**) vikingo *m*, escandinavo *m*

north-northeast [ˌnɔːθˌnɔːθ'iːst] Ⓐ N nornor(d)este *m*
Ⓑ ADJ nornor(d)este
Ⓒ ADV (= *toward north-northeast*) hacia el nornor(d)este; [*situated*] al nornor(d)este, en el nornor(d)este

north-northwest [ˌnɔːθˌnɔːθ'west] Ⓐ N nornoroeste *m*
Ⓑ ADJ nornoroeste
Ⓒ ADV (= *toward north-northwest*) hacia el nornoroeste; (*situated*) al nornoroeste, en el nornoroeste

Northumb ABBR (*Brit*) = **Northumberland**

Northumbria [nɔː'θʌmbrɪə] N *región del nordeste de Inglaterra*

Northumbrian [nɔː'θʌmbrɪən] Ⓐ ADJ de Northumbria
Ⓑ N habitante *mf* de Northumbria, nativo/a *m/f* de Northumbria

North Vietnamese ['nɔːθvɪetnə'miːz] Ⓐ ADJ norvietnamita
Ⓑ N norvietnamita *mf*

northward ['nɔːθwəd] Ⓐ ADJ [*movement, migration*] hacia el norte, en dirección norte
Ⓑ ADV (*also* **~s**) hacia el norte, en dirección norte

northwards ['nɔːθwədz] ADV (*esp Brit*) = **northward B**

northwest ['nɔːθ'west] Ⓐ N noroeste *m*
Ⓑ ADJ [*point, direction*] noroeste; [*wind*] del noroeste
Ⓒ ADV (= *northwestward*) hacia el noroeste; (*situated*) al noroeste, en el noroeste

northwesterly ['nɔːθ'westəlɪ] Ⓐ ADJ [*wind*] del noroeste; **we were headed in a northwesterly direction** íbamos hacia el noroeste *or* rumbo al noroeste *or* en dirección noroeste
Ⓑ N viento *m* del noroeste

northwestern ['nɔːθ'westən] ADJ noroeste, del noroeste; **the ~ part of the island** la parte noroeste *or* noroccidental de la isla; **the ~ coast** la costa noroeste *or* noroccidental; **in ~ Spain** en el noroeste *or* al noroeste de España, en la España noroccidental

northwestward ['nɔːθ'westwəd] Ⓐ ADJ [*movement, migration*] hacia el noroeste, en dirección noroeste
Ⓑ ADV (*also* **~s**) hacia el noroeste, en dirección noroeste

northwestwards ['nɔːθ'westwədz] ADV (*esp Brit*) = **northwestward B**

Norway ['nɔːweɪ] Ⓐ N Noruega *f*
Ⓑ CPD ► **Norway lobster** N cigala *f*

Norwegian [nɔː'wiːdʒən] Ⓐ ADJ noruego
Ⓑ N [1] (= *person*) noruego/a *m/f*
[2] (*Ling*) noruego *m*

Nos., nos. ABBR (= **numbers**) núms

no-score draw [ˌnəʊskɔː'drɔː] N empate *m* a cero

nose [nəʊz] Ⓐ N [1] (*Anat*) [*of person*] nariz *f*; [*of animal*] hocico *m*; **his ~ was bleeding** le sangraba la nariz, le salía sangre de la nariz; **to have one's ~ in a book** estar enfrascado en un libro; **get your ~ out of that book and come and help me** deja el libro un momento y ven a ayudarme; **to hold one's ~** (*lit*) taparse la nariz; **to talk** *or* **speak through one's ~** ganguear, hablar con voz gangosa; ✦*IDIOMS* **you wouldn't recognize an opportunity if it bit you on the ~** no reconocerías una buena oportunidad ni aunque te topases con ella de frente; **to keep one's ~ clean*** no meterse en problemas *or* líos*; **to cut off one's ~ to spite one's face** tirar piedras a su tejado; **to get/have one's ~ in front** coger/tener la delantera; **he gets up my ~*** me revienta*; **to keep one's ~ out (of sth)** no entrometerse (en algo); **to lead sb by the ~** tener a algn agarrado por las narices; **you shouldn't let them lead you by the ~** no deberías permitirles que te manejen a su antojo; **to look down one's ~ at sth/sb*** despreciar algo/a algn, mirar a algn por encima del hombro; **(right) on the ~** en el clavo; **that's it! you've hit it on the ~!** ¡eso es! ¡has dado en el clavo!; **to pay through the ~ (for sth)*** pagar un ojo de la cara (por algo)*, pagar un dineral (por algo); **she paid through the ~ (for it)** le costó un ojo de la cara*, pagó un dineral (por ello)*; **to make sb pay through the ~** hacer pagar a algn un dineral*; **to poke** *or* **stick one's ~ into sth*** meter las narices en algo*, meterse en algo; **who asked you to poke your ~ in?** ¿quién te manda meter las narices* *or* meterte en esto?; **he's always poking his ~ (in) where it's not wanted** siempre está metiendo las narices *or* metiéndose en lo que no le incumbe*; **to put sb's ~ out of joint** molestar a algn; **to see no further than the end of one's ~** no ver más allá de sus narices; **to turn up one's ~ at sth** hacerle ascos a algo; **under sb's nose: it's right under your ~** lo tienes delante de las narices*; **she did it under his very ~** *or* **right under his ~** lo hizo delante de sus narices; *see also* **bloody A1**, **blow[2] A2**, **follow A1**, **grindstone**, **joint B3**, **pick B5**, **plain A1**, **thumb B3**
[2] (= *distance*) **to win by a ~** [*horse*] ganar por una nariz; (*fig*) ganar por los pelos
[3] (= *front part*) [*of aeroplane, car*] morro *m*, parte *f* delantera; [*of boat*] proa *f*; **the traffic was ~ to tail** los coches iban pegados unos a otros
[4] (= *sense of smell*) olfato *m*; **I have a sensitive ~** tengo un olfato muy fino
[5] (= *instinct*) **to have a (good) ~ for** tener (buen) olfato para; **she has a keen ~ for facts** tiene buena intuición para saber lo que ha ocurrido realmente; **she's got a (good) ~ for a story** tiene (buen) olfato para lo que es noticia
[6] [*of wine*] aroma *m*, buqué *m*
Ⓑ VI **the car ~d forward** el coche se abrió paso lentamente; **the coach ~d out into the traffic** el autocar se incorporó lentamente al tráfico
Ⓒ VT [1] (= *move*) **he ~d his car into the garage** metió el coche en el garaje maniobrando con cuidado; **a van ~d its way past** una furgoneta pasó despacio
[2] (= *nuzzle, nudge*) **the horse ~d my palm** el caballo me olfateó la palma de la mano; **the dog managed to ~ the door open** el perro consiguió abrir la puerta con el hocico; **they just ~d us into second place** por muy poco nos dejaron en segundo lugar
Ⓓ CPD ► **nose cone** N [*of missile*] ojiva *f*; [*of racing car*] cabeza *f* separable ► **nose drops** NPL gotas *fpl* para la nariz ► **nose job*** N **to have a ~ job** operarse la nariz ► **nose ring** N [*of animal*] argolla *f* (en el hocico); [*of person*] pendiente *m* en la nariz

►**nose about, nose around** Ⓐ VI + ADV curiosear, fisgonear
Ⓑ VI + PREP curiosear por, fisgonear por; **the police came nosing about your house last night** anoche la policía estuvo curioseando *or* fisgoneando por tu casa

►**nose out** VT + ADV [1] (= *smell*) [*dog, fox*] olfatear
[2] (= *discover*) [+ *secret, truth*] averiguar, lograr descubrir; [+ *fugitive*] encontrar

nosebag ['nəʊzbæg] N morral *m*

noseband ['nəʊzbænd] N muserola *f*

nosebleed ['nəʊzbliːd] N hemorragia *f* nasal (*Med*); **to have a ~** sangrar *or* echar sangre por la nariz, tener una hemorragia nasal (*Med*); **you have a ~** estás sangrando *or* echando sangre por la nariz, te está sangrando la nariz

-nosed [nəʊzd] ADJ (*ending in compounds*) de nariz ...; **Roman/snub-nosed** de nariz aguileña/chata; **red-nosed** de nariz colorada*; *see also* **hard-nosed**, **toffee-nosed**

nose-dive ['nəʊzdaɪv] Ⓐ N [1] (*Aer*) picado *m* vertical
[2] (*fig*) caída *f* súbita; **to take a ~** [*profits, shares, sales, reputation*] caer en picado
Ⓑ VI [1] (*Aer*) descender en picado
[2] (*fig*) [*profits, shares, sales, reputation*] caer en picado; **the shares ~d 11p to 511p** las acciones cayeron 11 peniques de golpe y pasaron a cotizar 511 peniques

nosegay ['nəʊzgeɪ] N ramillete *m*

nosewheel ['nəʊzwiːl] N (*Aer*) rueda *f* delantera de aterrizaje

nosey* ADJ ['nəʊzɪ] (*compar* **nosier**; *superl* **nosiest**) entrometido; **don't be so ~!** ¡no seas tan entrometido!

nosey-parker* ['nəʊzɪ'pɑːkə[r]] N metomentodo/a* *m/f*

nosh* [nɒʃ] Ⓐ N (*Brit*) comida *f*, papeo‡ *m*, manduca *f* (*Sp**); **~ up!** ¡a comer!
Ⓑ VI comer, papear‡

no-show ['nəʊ'ʃəʊ] N ausente *mf* (*persona que no ocupa una plaza reservada previamente*)

nosh-up‡ ['nɒʃʌp] N (*Brit*) comilona* *f*, tragadera *f* (*LAm**)

nosily ['nəʊzɪlɪ] ADV entrometidamente

nosiness ['nəʊzɪnɪs] N entrometimiento *m*

no-smoking ['nəʊ,sməʊkɪŋ] ADJ [*area, carriage*] de no fumadores; [*policy*] de prohibición del tabaco

nostalgia [nɒs'tældʒɪə] N nostalgia *f*, añoranza *f*

nostalgic [nɒs'tældʒɪk] ADJ nostálgico

nostril ['nɒstrl] N (*Anat*) [*of person, dog, lion*] ventana *f* de la nariz, orificio *m* nasal (*frm*); [*of horse*] ollar *m*; **~s** narices *fpl*

nostrum ['nɒstrəm] N (= *remedy*) remedio *m* secreto, panacea *f*; (*fig*) panacea *f*

nosy* ['nəʊzɪ] = **nosey**

nosy-parker* ['nəʊzɪ'pɑːkəʳ] N = **nosey-parker**

not [nɒt] ADV [1] (*with vb*)

often contracted to **n't** *on the end of modals, auxiliaries and parts of the verb* **to be** *in everyday language*

no; **I'm ~ sure** no estoy seguro; **he's ~ here** ◊ **he isn't here** no está aquí; **it wasn't me** yo no fui; **it's too late, isn't it?** es demasiado tarde, ¿no?; **you owe me money, don't you?** me debes dinero, ¿verdad? *or* (*esp LAm*) ¿no es cierto?; **she won't go** ◊ **she will ~ go** no irá; **I don't think she'll come now** ya no creo que venga; **he asked me ~ to do it** me pidió que no lo hiciera; **fear ~!** ¡no temas!; **I hope ~** espero que no; **I suppose ~** supongo que no; **to tell sb ~ to do sth** decir a algn que no haga algo; **I think ~** creo que no; **~ thinking that …** sin pensar que …
[2] (*with pronoun etc*) **~ one** ni uno; **~ me/you** *etc* yo/tú *etc* no; **~ I!** ¡yo no!; **~ everybody can do it** no lo puede hacer cualquiera, no todos pueden hacerlo; **~ any more** ya no; *see also* **even B3**
[3] (*in expressions*) **absolutely ~!** ¡en absoluto!; **~ at all** (*after verb*) no ... en absoluto; (*responding to thanks*) ¡de nada!, ¡no hay de qué!; **I don't mind at all** no me importa en absoluto; **it doesn't hurt at all** no duele nada de nada, no duele para nada; **"are you cold?" — "~ at all!"** —¿tienes frío? —¡en absoluto! *or* —¡qué va!; **"you don't mind?" — "~ at all!"** —¿no te importa? —¡en absoluto!; **he's ~ at all selfish** no es nada egoísta; **certainly ~!** ¡en absoluto!; **of course ~!** ¡claro que no!; **~ a few …** no pocos …; **~ for anything (in the world)** por nada (del mundo); **~ guilty** no culpable; **the ~ inconsiderable sum of £30,000** la nada despreciable suma de 30.000 libras; **~ likely!** ¡ni hablar!; **with ~ a little surprise** con no poca sorpresa; **are you coming or ~?** ¿vienes o no?; **whether you go or ~** tanto si vas como si no; **"did you like it?" — "~ really"** —¿te gustó? —no mucho; **big, ~ to say enormous** grande, por no decir enorme; **the young and the ~ so young** los jóvenes y los no tan jóvenes; **I shan't be sorry to see the last of him** no voy a sentirlo cuando lo pierda de vista; **~ that I don't like him** no es que no me guste; **~ that I know of** no que yo sepa; **why ~?** ¿por qué no?; **~ without some regrets** no sin cierto pesar; **~ yet** todavía no; **they haven't arrived yet** todavía no han llegado; *see also* **likely B, mention B, much B1, only B6**

notability [,nəʊtə'bɪlɪtɪ] N [1] [*of person*] notabilidad *f*
[2] (= *person*) notabilidad *f*, personaje *m*

notable ['nəʊtəbl] Ⓐ ADJ [*person*] destacado; **to be ~ for** distinguirse por; **it is ~ that …** es de notar que …
Ⓑ N persona *f* importante, personaje *m*; **~s** personas *fpl* importantes, notables *mpl*

notably ['nəʊtəblɪ] ADV [1] (= *in particular*) particularmente, en particular; **several countries, ~ France and Spain** varios países, particularmente *or* en particular Francia y España; **later religions, most ~ Christianity …** posteriores religiones, muy en particular *or* sobre todo el cristianismo …
[2] (= *noticeably*) notablemente

notarial [nəʊ'tɛərɪəl] ADJ notarial

notarize ['nəʊtəraiz] VT (*US*) dar fe pública de, autenticar mediante acta notarial

notary ['nəʊtərɪ] N (*also* **~ public**) notario/a *m/f*

notate [nəʊ'teɪt] VT (*Mus*) notar

notation [nəʊ'teɪʃən] N (*Math, Mus*) notación *f*

notch [nɒtʃ] Ⓐ N [1] (= *cut*) corte *m*, muesca *f*
[2] (*US*) (= *mountain pass*) desfiladero *m*
Ⓑ VT hacer una muesca en, hacer un corte en

►**notch up** VT + ADV apuntarse

note [nəʊt] Ⓐ N [1] (= *written reminder, record*)
[1·1] (*short*) nota *f*; **keep a ~ of all your expenses** detalla *or* anota todos tus gastos; **to make** *or* **take a ~ of sth** apuntar *or* anotar algo; **I must make a ~ to buy some more** tengo que hacer una nota para que no se me olvide comprar más; *see also* **mental A1**
[1·2] **notes** apuntes *mpl*, notas *fpl*; **to speak from ~s** hablar con la ayuda de apuntes *or* notas; **to make ~s** hacer anotaciones; **to take ~s** tomar apuntes; **to speak without ~s** hablar sin la ayuda de apuntes *or* notas; ✦**IDIOM to compare ~s (about sth)** intercambiar impresiones (acerca de algo); *see also* **lecture D**
[2] (*on text*) anotación *f*, nota *f*; (*more detailed*) comentario *m*; **see ~ 16 on page 223** véase nota número 16 en la página 223; **with an introduction and ~s by …** con introducción y comentarios de …; **author's ~** nota del autor; *see also* **programme D, sleeve**
[3] (= *letter, message*) nota *f*; **I left him a ~ saying where I was** le dejé una nota diciéndole dónde estaba; **just a quick ~ to tell you …** sólo una nota para decirte que …; *see also* **delivery, sick C, suicide**
[4] (*official, diplomatic*) nota *f*
[5] (= *tone*) (*gen*) nota *f*; (*in voice*) dejo *m*, deje *m*; **the only discordant ~ was the bad feeling between his two brothers** la única nota discordante fue la animosidad entre sus dos hermanos; **there was a ~ of nostalgia in her voice** había un dejo *or* deje de nostalgia en su voz; **there was a ~ of bitterness in her voice** había cierto resentimiento en su voz; **the talks ended on a ~ of optimism** las negociaciones se cerraron con una nota de optimismo; **the 1980s/evening ended on a high ~** la década de los ochenta/la velada se cerró con un broche de oro; **on a more positive ~ …** mirando el lado positivo …; **to sound a ~ of caution** llamar a la prudencia; **he tried to strike a ~ of optimism in his speech** intentó que su discurso sonara optimista; **his speech struck the right/wrong ~** su discurso fue/no fue acertado
[6] (*Mus*) (= *sound*) nota *f*; (= *key*) tecla *f*
[7] (= *bank note*) billete *m*; **a five-pound ~** un billete de cinco libras
[8] (= *importance*) **a writer/an artist of ~** un escritor/un artista destacado *or* de renombre; **nothing of ~** nada digno de mención; **this is a first novel of some ~** esta es una primera novela que merece atención
[9] (= *notice*) **to take ~ (of sth/sb)**: **the government should take ~ of this survey** el gobierno debería tomar nota del resultado de esta encuesta; **they will take ~ of what you say** tendrán en cuenta lo que digas; **people began to take ~ of him** la gente empezó a tenerlo en cuenta *or* prestarle atención; **worthy of ~** digno de mención
Ⓑ VT [1] (= *observe*) **~ the statue by Rodin in the entrance hall** tomen nota de *or* fíjense en la estatua de Rodin en el vestíbulo; **to ~ that** notar que; **she ~d that his hands were dirty** notó que tenía las manos sucias, se dio cuenta de que tenía las manos sucias; **please ~ that there are a limited number of tickets** les informamos que el número de entradas es limitado
[2] (= *point out*) **the report ~s that this trend is on the increase** el informe señala *or* indica que esta tendencia se está extendiendo
[3] (= *record officially*) tomar nota de; **your remarks have been ~d** hemos tomado nota de sus observaciones
[4] (= *write down*) anotar, apuntar
Ⓒ CPD ► **note issue** N emisión *f* fiduciaria

►**note down** VT + ADV anotar, apuntar

notebook ['nəʊtbʊk] N [1] (= *notepad, jotter*) libreta *f*, bloc *m*; (= *exercise book*) cuaderno *m*
[2] (*also* **~ computer**) ordenador *m* portátil, computador *m* portátil (*LAm*)

note-case ['nəʊtkeɪs] N (*Brit*) cartera *f*, billetero *m*

noted ['nəʊtɪd] ADJ [*historian, writer*] destacado, renombrado; **to be ~ for sth** ser conocido *or* famoso por algo; **a man not ~ for his generosity** un hombre que no es precisamente conocido *or* famoso por su generosidad

notelet ['nəʊtlɪt] N tarjeta *f* en díptico (*de felicitación, agradecimiento*)

notepad ['nəʊtpæd] N bloc *m*, libreta *f* para notas

notepaper ['nəʊt,peɪpəʳ] N papel *m* de carta

noteworthiness ['nəʊt,wɜːðɪnɪs] N notabilidad *f*

noteworthy ['nəʊt,wɜːðɪ] ADJ notable, digno de atención; **it is ~ that …** es notable que …, es de notar que …

nothing ['nʌθɪŋ] Ⓐ PRON nada *f*; (= *nought*) cero *m*; **I have ~ to give you** no tengo nada que darte; **to have ~ to do with** no tener nada que ver con; **there's ~ mean about him** no tiene nada de tacaño; **~ but** solamente; **to come to ~** parar en nada, quedarse en aguas de borraja; **~ doing!** ¡de ninguna manera!, ¡ni hablar!; **~ else** nada más; **there's ~ to fear** no hay de qué tener miedo; **for ~** (= *free*) gratis; (= *unpaid*) sin sueldo; (= *in vain*) en vano, en balde; **it is not for ~ that …** no es sin motivo que …, por algo será que …; **there was ~ for it but to pay** no había más remedio *or* (*LAm*) no nos quedaba otra que pagar; **to build up a business from ~** crear un negocio de la nada; **he is ~ if not careful** es de lo más cauteloso; **there is ~ in the rumours** los rumores no tienen nada de verdad; **there's ~ in it for us** de esto no vamos a sacar ningún provecho; **there's ~ in it** (*in race*) van muy iguales; **I could make ~ of what he said** no entendí nada *or* no pude sacar nada en claro de lo que dijo; **a mere ~** una nimiedad; **it's ~ more than a rumour** es simplemente un rumor; **~ much** poco, no mucho; **there's ~ much to be said** poco hay que de-

cir; **next to ~** casi nada; **I'm ~ of a swimmer** yo nado bastante mal; **to have ~ on** (= *naked*) estar desnudo; (= *not busy*) estar libre; **it's ~ to be proud of** no es motivo para enorgullecerse; **to say ~ of ...** sin mencionar ..., amén de ...; **to get something for ~** obtener algo gratis; **there's ~ special about it** no tiene nada de particular; **to stop at ~** no pararse en barras; **to stop at ~ to do sth** emplear sin escrúpulo todos los medios para hacer algo; **to think ~ of** tener en poco; **he thinks ~ of walking 30km** para él no tiene importancia *or* no es nada recorrer 30km a pie; **think ~ of it!** ¡no hay de qué!, ¡no tiene cuidado! (*LAm*); **there's ~ to it!** ¡es facilísimo!; **she is ~ to him** ella le es indiferente; **it's ~ to me whether he comes or not** no me importa que venga o no; ✦*IDIOM* **he has ~ on her** (*comparison*) no le llega ni a la suela del zapato*; *see also* **all B4**, **do with**, **kind B1**, **like B1**, **next B4.5**, **short A3**, **sort A1**; → ZERO

Ⓑ ADV **~ daunted** sin inmutarse; **it's ~ like him** el retrato no se le parece en nada; **it was ~ like as expensive as we thought** era mucho menos caro de lo que nos imaginábamos; *see also* **less B**

Ⓒ N **a mere ~** una friolera, una bagatela; **to her he was a ~** para ella él no tenía ningún valor; ✦*IDIOM* **to whisper sweet ~s to sb** decir ternezas a los oídos de algn

nothingness [ˈnʌθɪŋnɪs] N (= *non-existence*) nada *f*; (= *emptiness*) vacío *m*

notice [ˈnəʊtɪs] Ⓐ N 1 (= *intimation, warning*) aviso *m*; **~ to appear** (*Jur*) citación *f* judicial, orden *f* de comparecencia; **we require 28 days' ~ for delivery** se requieren 28 días para la entrega; **until further ~** hasta nuevo aviso; **to give sb ~ to do sth** avisar a algn que haga algo; **~ is hereby given that ...** se pone en conocimiento del público que ...; **at a moment's ~** en seguida, inmediatamente, luego (*Mex*), al tiro (*Chile*); **important decisions often have to be taken at a moment's ~** a menudo las decisiones importantes se han de tomar en seguida *or* inmediatamente; **you must be ready to leave at a moment's ~** tienes que estar listo para salir en cuanto te avisen; **we had no ~ of it** no nos habían avisado; **~ to quit** aviso *or* notificación de desalojo; **at short ~** con poca antelación; **sorry, I know it's short ~, but ...** lo siento, sé que es avisar con poca antelación, pero ...; **to give sb at least a week's ~** avisar a algn por lo menos con una semana de antelación; **I must have at least a week's ~ if you want to ...** me tienes que avisar con una semana de antelación si quieres ...; **without previous ~** sin previo aviso

2 (= *order to leave job etc*) (*by employer*) despido *m*; (*by employee*) dimisión *f*, renuncia *f*; (= *period*) preaviso *m*; **to get one's ~** ser despedido; **to give sb ~** despedir a algn; **to give sb a week's ~** despedir a algn con una semana de preaviso *or* plazo; **to hand in one's ~** dimitir, renunciar; **a week's wages in lieu of ~** el salario de una semana en lugar del plazo *or* de preaviso; **to be under ~** estar despedido; **to dismiss sb without ~** despedir a algn sin preaviso

3 (= *announcement*) (*in press*) anuncio *m*, nota *f*; [*of meeting*] convocatoria *f*, llamada *f*; (= *sign*) letrero *m*; (= *poster*) cartel *m*; **birth/marriage ~** anuncio *m* de nacimiento/matrimonio; **death ~** nota *f* necrológica, esquela *f*; **to give out a ~** anunciar algo, comunicar algo; **the ~ says "keep out"** el letrero dice "prohibida la entrada"

4 (= *review*) [*of play, opera etc*] reseña *f*, crítica *f*

5 (= *attention*) atención *f*; **to attract sb's ~** atraer *or* llamar la atención de algn; **to bring a matter to sb's ~** llamar la atención de algn sobre un asunto; **it has come to my ~ that ...** ha llegado a mi conocimiento que ...; **to escape ~** pasar inadvertido; **to take ~ of sb** hacer caso a algn; **to take no ~ of sth/sb** no hacer caso de algo/a algn, ignorar algo/a algn (*esp LAm*); **to take ~ of sth** hacer caso de algo; **take no ~!** ¡no hagas caso!; **I was not taking much ~ at the time** en ese momento no estaba prestando mucha atención; **a fat lot of ~ he takes of me!*** ¡maldito el caso que me hace!*; **to sit up and take ~** (*fig*) aguzar el oído

6 (= *interest*) interés *m*; **it has attracted a lot of ~** ha suscitado gran interés

Ⓑ VT (= *perceive*) fijarse en, notar; (= *realize*) darse cuenta de; (= *recognize*) reconocer; **did you ~ the bloodstain on the wall?** ¿te fijaste en *or* te diste cuenta de *or* notaste la mancha de sangre que había en la pared?; **I don't ~ such things** no me fijo en tales cosas; **eventually he deigned to ~ me** por fin se dignó a reconocerme; **have you ever ~d how slowly time passes when you're flying?** ¿te has fijado en *or* te has dado cuenta de lo lento que pasa el tiempo cuando vas en avión?; **I ~ you've removed the bookcase** veo que has quitado la estantería

Ⓒ VI fijarse, darse cuenta; **I never ~d** no me había fijado; **don't worry about the mark, he won't ~** no te preocupes por la mancha, no se fijará *or* no se dará cuenta; **yes, so I've ~d!** (*iro*) ¡sí, ya me he dado cuenta *or* ya lo he notado!

Ⓓ CPD ▸ **notice board** N (*esp Brit*) tablón *m* de anuncios

noticeable [ˈnəʊtɪsəbl] ADJ [*difference, change, effect, increase*] sensible, perceptible; **it is ~ that** se nota que, es evidente que, está claro que; **it isn't ~** [*mark, stain*] no se nota; **a ~ smell of burning** un fuerte olor a quemado; **a ~ lack of enthusiasm** una evidente falta de entusiasmo

noticeably [ˈnəʊtɪsəblɪ] ADV [*different, changed, improved*] sensiblemente, perceptiblemente; **the next day it was ~ warmer** al día siguiente se notaba que hacía más calor; **they are ~ less well-off than before** se nota que tienen menos dinero que antes; **she looks ~ worse than when I last saw her** está sensiblemente peor que la última vez que la vi, se la nota peor que la última vez que la vi

notifiable [ˈnəʊtɪfaɪəbl] ADJ de declaración obligatoria

notification [ˌnəʊtɪfɪˈkeɪʃən] N (= *warning, prior notice*) notificación *f*, aviso *m*; (= *announcement*) anuncio *m*

notify [ˈnəʊtɪfaɪ] VT avisar; **you must ~ the police** debes avisar a la policía, debes notificarlo a la policía; **to ~ sb of sth** comunicar *or* notificar algo a algn

notion [ˈnəʊʃən] N 1 (= *idea*) idea *f*; (= *view*) opinión *f*, noción *f*; (= *whim*) capricho *m*; **I have a ~ that ...** tengo la idea de que ...; **I had no ~ that he was planning to leave** no tenía ni idea de que tuviera pensado marcharse; **to have no ~ of** no tener ni idea de; **I haven't the slightest ~** no tengo ni idea; **to have a ~ to do sth** estar inclinado a hacer algo

2 **notions** (*Sew*) artículos *mpl* de mercería, mercería *f*

notional [ˈnəʊʃənl] ADJ 1 (*Fin*) [*value, profit, amount, capital, income*] hipotético, teórico

2 (= *hypothetical*) **it is purely ~** es pura hipótesis *or* teoría *or* especulación

3 (*Ling*) [*word*] nocional

notionally [ˈnəʊʃənəlɪ] ADV teóricamente, en teoría, hipotéticamente

notoriety [ˌnəʊtəˈraɪətɪ] N mala fama *f*, mala reputación *f*; **to achieve** *or* **gain ~** adquirir mala fama *or* reputación

notorious [nəʊˈtɔːrɪəs] ADJ [*criminal*] muy conocido, celebérrimo; [*area, town, prison*] de mala fama, de mala reputación; [*comment, speech*] desgraciadamente famoso; [*case, crime*] muy sonado; **a ~ womanizer** un hombre con fama de donjuán; **she's a ~ flirt** tiene fama de que le gusta flirtear; **Prussia was ~ in this respect** Prusia tenía mala fama en este sentido; **to be ~ as sth** tener fama de ser algo; **to be ~ for sth** ser conocido por algo, tener fama de algo; **he's ~ for cheating at cards** tiene fama de hacer trampas jugando a las cartas

notoriously [nəʊˈtɔːrɪəslɪ] ADJ **anorexia nervosa is ~ difficult to treat** tratar la anorexia nerviosa es de notoria dificultad, es bien sabido que tratar la anorexia nerviosa entraña gran dificultad; **she is ~ difficult to work with** tiene fama de ser una persona con la que resulta difícil trabajar; **he is ~ unreliable** tiene fama de informal

no-trumps [ˈnəʊˈtrʌmps] N **to bid four ~** marcar cuatro sin triunfos

Notts [nɒts] N ABBR (*Brit*) = **Nottinghamshire**

notwithstanding [ˌnɒtwɪðˈstændɪŋ] Ⓐ PREP a pesar de, no obstante; **the weather ~** a pesar del tiempo

Ⓑ ADV sin embargo, no obstante

Ⓒ CONJ (*also* **~ that**) a pesar de que, por más que + *subjun*

nougat [ˈnuːgɑː] N turrón *m*

nought [nɔːt] N 1 (*esp Brit Math*) cero *m*; **~s and crosses** (*Brit*) tres *m* en raya; → ZERO

2 († *liter*) (= *nothing*) nada *f*

noun [naʊn] Ⓐ N (*Ling*) nombre *m*, sustantivo *m*

Ⓑ CPD ▸ **noun clause** N oración *f* sustantiva, cláusula *f* nominal ▸ **noun phrase** N frase *f* nominal

nourish [ˈnʌrɪʃ] VT 1 (*lit*) alimentar, nutrir; **to ~ sb on sth** alimentar a algn con algo

2 (*fig*) fomentar, nutrir

nourishing [ˈnʌrɪʃɪŋ] ADJ nutritivo, alimenticio

nourishment [ˈnʌrɪʃmənt] N 1 (= *food*) alimento *m*; **to derive ~ from** sustentarse de

2 (= *nutrition*) nutrición *f*

nous* [naʊs] N (*Brit*) cacumen* *m*, chirumen* *m*

nouveau riche [ˌnuːvəʊˈriːʃ] N (*pl* **nouveaux riches**) nuevo/a rico/a *m/f*

nouvelle cuisine [ˈnuːvelkwiːˈziːn] N nueva cocina *f*, nouvelle cuisine *f*

Nov. ABBR (= **November**) nov., N.

Nova Scotia [ˈnəʊvəˈskəʊʃə] N Nueva Escocia *f*

Nova Scotian [ˈnəʊvəˈskəʊʃən] Ⓐ ADJ de Nueva Escocia

Ⓑ N habitante *mf* de Nueva Escocia

novel [ˈnɒvəl] Ⓐ ADJ [*idea, suggestion, method*] original, novedoso; **it was a ~ experience for him** era una experiencia nueva para él

Ⓑ N novela *f*

novelette [ˌnɒvəˈlet] N novela *f* corta; (*pej*) novela *f* sentimental, novela *f* sin valor

novelettish [ˌnɒvəˈletɪʃ] ADJ sentimental, romántico

novelist [ˈnɒvəlɪst] N novelista *mf*

novella [nəʊˈvelə] N (*pl* **novellas** *or* **novelle** [nəʊˈveleɪ]) novela *f* corta

novelty [ˈnɒvəltɪ] Ⓐ N (= *quality, thing*) novedad *f*; **once the ~ has worn off** cuando pase la novedad
Ⓑ CPD ▶ **novelty value** N novedad *f*

November [nəʊˈvembəʳ] N noviembre *m*; *see* **July** *for usage*

novena [nəʊˈviːnə] N (*pl* **novenae** [nəʊˈviːniː]) novena *f*

novice [ˈnɒvɪs] Ⓐ N principiante *mf*, novato/a *m/f*; (*Rel*) novicio/a *m/f*; (*Sport*) principiante *mf*, novato/a *m/f*; **he's no ~** no es ningún principiante; **to be a ~ at a job** ser nuevo en un oficio
Ⓑ ADJ **a ~ painter** un pintor principiante, un aspirante a pintor

noviciate, **novitiate** [nəʊˈvɪʃɪɪt] N [1] (*Rel*) (= *period, place*) noviciado *m*
[2] (*fig*) período *m* de aprendizaje

novocaine [ˈnəʊvəʊkeɪn] N novocaína *f*

NOW [naʊ] N ABBR (*US*) = **National Organization for Women**

now [naʊ] Ⓐ ADV [1] (*of present, immediate future*) [1·1] (= *at this time*) ahora; **what shall we do ~?** ¿qué hacemos ahora?; **~ for something completely different** y ahora algo totalmente distinto; **not ~, dear** ahora no, querido; **right ~ all I want to do is …** en este momento *or* ahora mismo, lo único que me apetece es …; **the time is ~ eight o'clock** son las ocho
[1·2] (= *these days*) hoy en día, ahora; **nobody would think of doing that ~** hoy en día *or* ahora a nadie se le ocurriría hacer eso
[1·3] (= *at last, already*) ya; **the fire is ~ under control** el incendio ya está controlado; **can I go ~?** ¿ya me puedo ir?; **I must be off ~** ya me tengo que marchar
[1·4] (= *immediately*) ahora; (*more emphatic*) ya; **if we leave ~, we'll be there by six** si salimos ahora *or* ya, estaremos allí para las seis; **it's ~ or never** es ahora o nunca; **I'll do it right ~** lo haré ahora mismo
[2] (*of duration up to present*) **they've been married ~ for 30 years** ya llevan 30 años casados, hace 30 años que se casaron; **it's some days ~ since I heard anything** hace varios días que no sé nada
[3] (*in accounts of past events*) ahora; **it had once been the pantry but was ~ his office** tiempo atrás había sido la despensa, pero ahora era su estudio
[4] (*after prep*) **as of ~** a partir de ahora; **before ~** (= *already*) ya, antes; (= *in the past*) antes de ahora; (= *till this moment*) hasta ahora, antes; **you should have done that before ~** ya tendrías que haber hecho eso, tendrías que haber hecho eso antes; **I've gone hungry before ~ to feed my children** ya he pasado hambre antes de ahora para poder alimentar a mis hijos; **she should have arrived long before ~** hace tiempo que tenía que haber llegado; **between ~ and next Tuesday** entre hoy y el martes que viene; **by ~: they must be there by ~** ya deben haber llegado; **by ~ it was clear that …** en ese momento ya estaba claro que …; **by ~ everybody was tired** para entonces ya estaban todos cansados; **that will be all for ~** ◊ **that will do for ~** por ahora *or* por el momento basta con eso; **(in) three weeks/100 years from ~** dentro de tres semanas/100 años; **from ~ on** (*with present, future tense*) a partir de ahora, de ahora en adelante; (*with past tense*) a partir de entonces; **till ~** ◊ **until ~** ◊ **up to ~** (= *till this moment*) hasta ahora; (= *till that moment*) hasta entonces; **I've always done it this way up to ~** hasta ahora siempre lo había hecho así
[5] (= *in these circumstances*) [5·1] (*gen*) ya; **it's raining, ~ we won't be able to go** está lloviendo, ya no podemos ir; **it's too late ~** ya es demasiado tarde; **how can I believe you ~?** ¿cómo puedo seguir confiando en ti?; **~ what (do we do)?** ¿y ahora, qué (hacemos)?; **they won't be long ~** no tardarán en venir, al rato vienen (*Mex*)
[5·2] (*emphatic*) **~ you've gone and done it!*** ¡ahora sí que la has hecho buena!*; **~ look what you've done!** ¡mira lo que has hecho!
[6] (*in phrases relating to time*) **(every) ~ and again** de vez en cuando; **any minute** *or* **moment ~** de un momento a otro; **any day ~** cualquier día de estos; **just ~** (= *at this moment*) ahora mismo, en este momento; (= *a moment ago*) hace un momento; **I'm busy just ~** ahora mismo *or* en este momento estoy ocupado; **plums are in season just ~** es temporada de ciruelas; **I saw him come in just ~** lo he visto entrar hace un momento, acabo de verlo entrar; **(every) ~ and then** de vez en cuando; *see also* **here A6**
[7] (*without temporal force*) [7·1] (*introducing new topic*) bien, bueno; **~, as you all know …** bien *or* bueno, como todos sabéis …; **~, some people may disagree but …** bien *or* bueno, puede que algunos no estén de acuerdo pero …
[7·2] (*commenting on previous statement*) **~ there's a coincidence!** ¡eso sí que es una coincidencia!; **~ there's a thought** pues no es mala idea
[7·3] (*asking question*) **~, what's everyone drinking?** a ver, ¿qué queréis tomar?
[7·4] (*remonstrating, pacifying*) **~ Fred, you don't really mean that** vamos Fred, no lo dices en serio; **now, ~, don't get so upset!** ¡venga, no te pongas así!; **now, ~, we'll have none of that!** ¡vale ya, nada de tonterías!; **come ~, you must be hungry** venga ya, no me digas que no tienes hambre; **hush ~, don't cry** shh, no llores; **~ then, what's the trouble?** ¡entonces a ver! ¿cuál es el problema?; **~ then, don't tease!** ¡ya está bien, deja de burlarte!; **well ~, what have we here!** ¡vamos a ver! ¿qué tenemos aquí?
[8] **now …, now …: ~ she dances, ~ she sings** (*liter*) tan pronto está bailando como cantando
Ⓑ PRON **~ is the best time to go to Scotland** ésta es la mejor época para ir a Escocia; **~ is your chance to talk to him** está es tu oportunidad de hablar con él; *see also* **here C**
Ⓒ CONJ **~ (that)** ahora que; **~ that she was retired she had more time** ahora que estaba jubilada disponía de más tiempo; **~ you (come to) mention it** ahora que lo dices
Ⓓ ADJ actual; **the ~ president** el presidente actual

nowadays [ˈnaʊədeɪz] ADV hoy (en) día, en la actualidad

noways* [ˈnəʊweɪz] ADV (*US*) de ninguna manera

nowhere [ˈnəʊwɛəʳ] ADV [1] (*lit*) [*be*] en ninguna parte; [*go*] a ninguna parte; **you're going ~** no vas a ninguna parte; **they have ~ to go** no tienen dónde ir; **there was ~ to hide** no había dónde esconderse; **there is ~ more romantic than Paris** no hay lugar más romántico que París; **it's ~ you know** no es ningún sitio que conoces; **it's ~ you'll ever find it** está en un sitio donde no lo encontrarás nunca; **~ else** en/a ninguna otra parte; **she had ~ else to go** no tenía otro lugar a donde ir; **from ~** de la nada; **~ in Europe** en ninguna parte de Europa; **he was ~ to be seen** ◊ **he was ~ in sight** no se le veía por ninguna parte
[2] (*fig*) **without me he would be ~** sin mí no habría llegado a ninguna parte; **he came from ~ to take the lead in the race** pasó de ir muy a la zaga a tomar la delantera en la carrera; **the party came from ~ to win the election** el partido surgió de la nada y ganó las elecciones; **we're getting ~** no estamos consiguiendo nada; **I'm getting ~ with this analysis** no estoy logrando nada con este análisis; **he got ~ with her** no consiguió nada con ella; **this is getting us ~** esto no nos lleva; **flattery will get you ~** con halagos no vas a conseguir nada; **a fiver goes ~ these days** cinco libras no se hace nada hoy en día; **it's ~ near as big** no es tan grande ni con mucho; **it's ~ near as good** no es tan bueno ni con mucho, dista mucho de ser tan bueno; **£10 is ~ near enough** 10 libras no bastan, ni mucho menos

no-win [ˈnəʊˈwɪn] ADJ **a ~ situation** una situación imposible *or* sin salida

nowise [ˈnəʊwaɪz] ADV (*US*) de ninguna manera

nowt [naʊt] N (*Brit dial*) = **nothing**

noxious [ˈnɒkʃəs] ADJ nocivo

nozzle [ˈnɒzl] N [*of hose, vacuum cleaner etc*] boquilla *f*; [*of spray*] pulverizador *m*; (*Mech*) tobera *f*, inyector *m*

NP N ABBR = **notary public**

n.p. ABBR (= **new paragraph**) punto *m* y aparte

NPD N ABBR (*Comm*) = **new product development**

n.p. or d. ABBR (= **no place or date**) s.l. ni f.

NPV N ABBR (*Fin*) = **net present value**

nr ABBR = **near**

NRA N ABBR [1] (*Brit*) = **National Rivers Authority**
[2] (*US*) = **National Rifle Association of America**

> **NRA**
>
> *La* **National Rifle Association of America** *o* **NRA** *(Asociación Nacional del Rifle) es uno de los grupos de presión más controvertidos y poderosos frente al Congreso de Estados Unidos. Cuenta con varios millones de socios, propietarios de armas de fuego para la caza o el tiro deportivo. La* **NRA** *promueve estos deportes al mismo tiempo que la conservación de la fauna, y organiza competiciones de tiro a nivel nacional. También se encarga de dar clases de seguridad para el uso de armas y apoya el derecho de todo estadounidense a tener armas de fuego para su propia defensa. La* **NRA** *ha recibido bastantes críticas por su oposición a las leyes de control de armas de fuego.*

NRV N ABBR (*Fin*) = **net realizable value**

NS ABBR (*Canada*) = **Nova Scotia**

n/s Ⓐ N ABBR = **nonsmoker**
Ⓑ ADJ ABBR = **nonsmoking**

NSB N ABBR (*Brit*) = **National Savings Bank**

NSC N ABBR [1] (*US Pol*) = **National Security Council**
[2] (*Brit*) = **National Safety Council**

NSF N ABBR (*US*) = **National Science Foundation**

NSPCA N ABBR (*Brit*) = **National Society for the Prevention of Cruelty to Animals**

NSPCC N ABBR (*Brit*) = **National Society for the Prevention of Cruelty to Children**

NSU N ABBR (*Med*) = **nonspecific urethritis**

➤ LANGUAGE IN USE: **now A1** 26.1 **nowadays** 26.1

NSW ABBR = **New South Wales**

NT N ABBR 1 (= **New Testament**) N.T.
2 (*Brit*) = **National Trust**

nth [enθ] ADJ enésimo; **to the ~ power** *or* **degree** a la enésima potencia; **for the ~ time*** por enésima vez

NUAAW N ABBR (*Brit*) = **National Union of Agricultural and Allied Workers**

nuance ['nju:ɑ̃:ns] N matiz *m*

nub [nʌb] N (= *piece*) pedazo *m*, trozo *m*; (= *protuberance*) protuberancia *f*; (*fig*) lo esencial, parte *f* esencial; **that's the ~ of the question** ahí está el quid del asunto

NUBE N ABBR (*Brit*) = **National Union of Bank Employees**

nubile ['nju:baɪl] ADJ [*girl, woman*] núbil; (*hum*) joven y guapa

nuclear ['nju:klɪəʳ] Ⓐ ADJ (*Phys, Mil*) nuclear
Ⓑ CPD ► **nuclear age** N era *f* nuclear ► **nuclear bomb** N bomba *f* nuclear ► **nuclear capability** N capacidad *f* nuclear ► **nuclear deterrent** N fuerza *f* disuasiva nuclear ► **nuclear disarmament** N desarme *m* nuclear ► **nuclear energy** N energía *f* nuclear ► **nuclear family** N familia *f* nuclear ► **nuclear fission** N fisión *f* nuclear ► **nuclear fuel** N combustible *m* nuclear ► **nuclear fusion** N fusión *f* nuclear ► **the nuclear industry** N la industria nuclear ► **Nuclear Non-Proliferation Treaty** N Tratado *m* de No Proliferación Nuclear ► **nuclear physicist** N físico/a *m/f* nuclear ► **nuclear physics** N física *f* nuclear ► **nuclear power** N energía *f* nuclear ► **nuclear power station, nuclear (power) plant** N central *f* nuclear ► **nuclear reaction** N reacción *f* nuclear ► **nuclear reactor** N reactor *m* nuclear ► **nuclear shelter** N refugio *m* antinuclear ► **nuclear submarine** N submarino *m* nuclear ► **nuclear test** N prueba *f* nuclear ► **nuclear testing** N pruebas *fpl* nucleares ► **nuclear war** N guerra *f* nuclear ► **nuclear waste** N desechos *mpl* nucleares ► **nuclear weapon** N arma *f* nuclear ► **nuclear winter** N invierno *m* nuclear

nuclear-free ['nju:klɪə,fri:] Ⓐ ADJ desnuclearizado, no nuclear
Ⓑ CPD ► **nuclear-free zone** N zona *f* desnuclearizada

nuclear-powered [,nju:klɪə'paʊəd] ADJ nuclear

nuclei ['nju:klɪaɪ] NPL *of* **nucleus**

nucleic acid [nju:,kli:ɪk'æsɪd] N acído *m* nucleico

nucleo... ['nju:klɪəʊ] PREFIX nucleo...

nucleus ['nju:klɪəs] N (*pl* **nuclei** *or* **nucleuses** ['nju:klɪaɪ]) núcleo *m*; **the ~ of a library** el núcleo de una biblioteca; **we have the ~ of a crew** tenemos los elementos indispensables para formar una tripulación

NUCPS N ABBR (*Brit*) = **National Union of Civil and Public Servants**

nude [nju:d] Ⓐ ADJ desnudo; **to sunbathe ~** tomar el sol desnudo
Ⓑ N 1 (*Art*) desnudo *m*; **a ~ by Goya** un desnudo de Goya
2 (= *person*) hombre *m* desnudo, mujer *f* desnuda
3 (= *state*) **in the ~** desnudo/a
Ⓒ CPD ► **nude scene** N (*Cine*) desnudo *m*, escena *f* de desnudo ► **nude study** N desnudo *m*

nudge [nʌdʒ] Ⓐ N codazo *m*; **to give sb a ~** dar un codazo a algn; **he said she's his secretary, ~ ~** dijo que era su secretaria, tú ya me entiendes
Ⓑ VT dar un codazo a; **to ~ sb's memory** refrescar la memoria a algn

nudie* ['nju:dɪ] N (*also* **~ magazine**) revista *f* porno*

nudism ['nju:dɪzəm] N nudismo *m*

nudist ['nju:dɪst] Ⓐ N (des)nudista *mf*
Ⓑ CPD ► **nudist camp, nudist colony** N colonia *f* nudista

nudity ['nju:dɪtɪ] N desnudez *f*

nugatory ['nju:gətərɪ] ADJ (*frm*) (= *trivial*) insignificante; (= *useless*) ineficaz, fútil, baladí

nugget ['nʌgɪt] N (*Min*) pepita *f*; **gold ~** pepita de oro

NUGMW N ABBR (*Brit*) = **National Union of General and Municipal Workers**

▼ **nuisance** ['nju:sns] Ⓐ N 1 (= *state of affairs, thing*) fastidio *m*, lata* *f*; **what a ~!** ¡qué lata!*; **it's a ~ having to shave!** ¡qué lata tener que afeitarse!*; **the ~ of having to shave** el fastidio de tener que afeitarse
2 (= *person*) pesado/a *m/f*, latoso/a* *m/f*; **what a ~ you are!** ¡eres un pesado!, ¡eres un latoso!*; **you're being a ~** me estás dando la lata*; **to make a ~ of o.s.** dar la lata*, ponerse pesado
3 (*Jur*) perjuicio *m*; *see also* **public C**
Ⓑ CPD ► **nuisance value** N **he's only of ~ value** no hace más que fastidiar *or* incordiar, sólo vale para crear problemas

NUJ N ABBR (*Brit*) = **National Union of Journalists**

nuke* [nju:k] (*esp US*) Ⓐ VT atacar con arma nuclear
Ⓑ N bomba *f* atómica

null [nʌl] ADJ nulo, inválido; **to render sb's efforts ~** invalidar los esfuerzos de algn; **~ and void** (*Jur*) nulo

nullification [,nʌlɪfɪ'keɪʃən] N anulación *f*, invalidación *f*

nullify ['nʌlɪfaɪ] VT anular, invalidar

nullity ['nʌlɪtɪ] N nulidad *f*

NUM N ABBR (*Brit*) = **National Union of Mineworkers**

numb [nʌm] Ⓐ ADJ 1 (*with cold*) entumecido; **my legs feel ~** (*from bad circulation etc*) se me han dormido las piernas; **my fingers have gone ~** (*gen*) se me han dormido los dedos; (*with cold*) se me han entumecido los dedos; **my feet were ~ with cold** tenía los pies entumecidos de frío
2 (*fig*) (*with fear, shock*) paralizado; **to be ~ with fright** estar paralizado de miedo; **when I heard about the accident I just felt ~** cuando me enteré del accidente me quedé atontado *or* sin poder reaccionar
Ⓑ VT 1 (= *deaden*) (*with injection*) adormecer; **the cold wind ~ed my face** el viento frío me dejó la cara entumecida; **alcohol was the only thing that ~ed the pain** (*fig*) el alcohol era la única cosa que aplacaba el dolor; **repeated images of violence have ~ed people to the reality of war** la contínua exposición a escenas violentas ha insensibilizado a la gente frente a la realidad de la guerra
2 (= *stun*) atontar; **I was ~ed by the news of his death** la noticia de su muerte me dejó atontado *or* sin poder reaccionar

numbed [nʌmd] ADJ 1 (*with cold*) entumecido
2 (*fig*) (*with fear, shock*) paralizado; **after the accident I felt ~** tras el accidente me sentía incapaz de reaccionar

number ['nʌmbəʳ] Ⓐ N 1 (*Math*) número *m*; **think of a ~, any ~** piensa un número, uno cualquiera; **an even/odd ~** un número par/impar; **to do sth by ~s** *or* (*US*) **by the ~s** (*fig*) hacer algo como es debido; **painting by ~s** pintar siguiendo los números; **to play the ~s** (*US**) jugar a la lotería; *see also* **lucky A2, prime D, round A**
2 (= *identification number*) [*of house, room, page, also Telec*] número *m*; [*of car*] (*also* **registration ~**) matrícula *f*; **we live at ~ 15** vivimos en el número 15; **my ~ is 414 3925** mi (número de) teléfono es el 414 3925; **the ~ 49 bus** el autobús número 49; **I don't know her room ~** no sé su número de habitación; **did you get his ~?** ¿has apuntado la matrícula?; **his ~ came up** (*in lottery, raffle*) su número salió premiado; **reference ~** número de referencia; **Number Ten** (*Brit Pol*) *la casa del Primer Ministro británico*; **you've got the wrong ~** (*Telec*) se ha equivocado de número; ✦*IDIOMS* **to have sb's ~**: **I've got his ~ now*** ya lo tengo calado*; **his ~ is up*** le ha llegado la hora; *see also* **registration B, serial, telephone**
3 (*in hierarchy*) **it's (at) ~ three in the charts** está tercero *or* es el número tres en la lista de éxitos; **~ one**: **she's the world ~ one** es la campeona mundial; **the ~ one Spanish player** el mejor jugador español, el número uno de los jugadores españoles; **I'm your ~ one fan** soy su más rendido admirador; **it's my ~ one priority** es lo más importante para mí; **he's my ~ two** es mi inferior inmediato; ✦*IDIOM* **to look after** *or* **look out for ~ one** anteponer el propio interés; **he only thinks of ~ one** sólo piensa en sí mismo; *see also* **opposite C3, public A2**
4 (= *quantity, amount*) número *m*; **equal ~s of women and men** el mismo número de mujeres y hombres; **the slump in student ~s** la caída en picado del número de estudiantes; **a ~ of** (= *several*) varios; **on a ~ of occasions** en varias ocasiones; **a ~ of people have mentioned it** varias personas lo han mencionado; **in a large ~ of cases** en muchos casos, en un gran número de casos; **in a small ~ of cases** en contados *or* unos pocos casos; **I've had a fair/an enormous ~ of letters** he recibido bastantes/muchísimas cartas; **there must be any ~ of people in my position** debe haber gran cantidad de personas en mi situación; **any ~ can play** puede jugar cualquier número de personas; **they were eight/few in ~** eran ocho/pocos; **to make up the ~s** hacer bulto; **times without ~** (*liter*) un sinfín de veces; *see also* **force A1, safety A**
5 (= *group*) **one of their ~** uno de ellos; **I include myself in their ~** me considero uno de ellos
6 (= *edition*) número *m*; **the January ~** el número de enero; *see also* **back F**
7 (= *song, act*) número *m*; **and for my next ~ I shall sing ...** ahora voy a cantar ...; ✦*IDIOM* **to do a ~ on sb** (*US**) hacer una jugada a algn*
8 (*) (= *item of clothing*) modelo *m*; **that little ~ is by Dior** ese modelito es de Dior
9 (*) (= *person*) **she's a nice little ~** está como un tren*, está más buena que el pan*
10 (*) (= *product*) **this wine is a nice little ~** este vino no está nada mal
11 (*) (= *job, situation*) **a cushy ~** un buen chollo (*Sp**)
12 (*Gram*) número *m*
13 **Numbers** (*in Bible*) **(the Book of) Numbers** (el libro de) Números
Ⓑ VT 1 (= *assign number to*) numerar; **they are ~ed from one to ten** están numerados del uno al diez; **~ed (bank) account** cuenta *f* (bancaria) numerada
2 (= *amount to*) **they ~ 700** son 700, hay 700; **the dead ~ed several hundred** el número de muertos ascendía a varios centena-

➤ LANGUAGE IN USE: **nuisance A1** 9.1

res; **the library ~s 30,000 books** la biblioteca cuenta con 30.000 libros

3 (= *include*) contar; **to ~ sb among one's friends** contar a algn entre sus amigos; **he ~ed Beethoven among his pupils** Beethoven era uno de sus discípulos; **to be ~ed among** figurar entre

4 (= *count in numbers*) contar; ✦*IDIOM* **his days are ~ed** tiene los días contados

(C) VI **to ~ among** figurar entre

(D) CPD ► **number cruncher*** N (= *machine*) procesador *m* de números; (= *person*) encargado/a *m/f* de hacer los números* ► **number crunching** N cálculo *m* numérico ► **number plate** N (*Brit Aut*) matrícula *f*, placa *f* (*esp LAm*), chapa *f* (de matrícula) (*S. Cone*) ► **numbers game, numbers racket** (*US*) N (= *lottery*) lotería *f*; (*illegal*) *lotería clandestina*; **to play the ~s game** jugar a la lotería; (*fig*) (*pej*) dar cifras ► **number theory** N teoría *f* numérica

numbering ['nʌmbərɪŋ] (A) N numeración *f*
(B) CPD ► **numbering machine** N numerador *m*

numberless ['nʌmbəlɪs] ADJ innumerable, sin número; **~ friends** un sinfín de amigos

numbhead* ['nʌmhed] N (*US*) tonto/a *m/f*, bobo/a *m/f*

numbly ['nʌmlɪ] ADV [*watch, gaze, say*] aturdido

numbness ['nʌmnɪs] N 1 (*lit*) **I had a feeling of ~ in my legs** se me habían dormido las piernas; (*from cold*) tenía las piernas entumecidas

2 (*fig*) (*from grief, fear, shock*) atontamiento *m*; **a feeling of ~ overcame me** me quedé atontado

numbskull, numskull ['nʌmskʌl] N zoquete* *m*, majadero* *m*; **you ~!** ¡majadero!

numeracy ['nju:mərəsɪ] N conocimientos *mpl* básicos de aritmética

numeral ['nju:mərəl] (A) N número *m*
(B) ADJ numeral

numerate ['nju:mərɪt] ADJ con conocimientos básicos de aritmética; **to be ~** tener conocimientos básicos de aritmética

numeration [,nju:mə'reɪʃən] N numeración *f*

numerator ['nju:məreɪtəʳ] N numerador *m*

numeric [nju'merɪk] (A) ADJ numérico
(B) CPD ► **numeric field** N campo *m* numérico ► **numeric keypad** N teclado *m* numérico

numerical [nju:'merɪkəl] ADJ numérico; **in ~ order** por orden numérico

numerically [nju:'merɪkəlɪ] ADV numéricamente; **~ superior to** con superioridad numérica a, superiores en cuanto a su número a

numerological [,nju:mərə'lɒdʒɪkəl] ADJ numerológico

numerology [,nju:mə'rɒlədʒɪ] N numerología *f*

numerous ['nju:mərəs] ADJ numeroso; **in ~ cases** en numerosos casos; **~ people believe that ...** mucha gente cree que ...

numismatic [,nju:mɪz'mætɪk] ADJ numismático

numismatics [,nju:mɪz'mætɪks] N numismática *f*

numismatist [nju:'mɪzmətɪst] N numismático/a *m/f*, numísmata *mf*

numskull ['nʌmskʌl] N = **numbskull**

nun [nʌn] N monja *f*, religiosa *f*; **to become a ~** hacerse monja, meterse (a) monja*

nunciature ['nʌnʃɪətjʊəʳ] N nunciatura *f*

nuncio ['nʌnʃɪəʊ] N (*also* **papal ~**) nuncio *m* apostólico

nunnery ['nʌnərɪ] N convento *m* de monjas

NUPE ['nju:pɪ] N ABBR (*Brit*) (*formerly*) = **National Union of Public Employees**

nuptial ['nʌpʃəl] ADJ nupcial

nuptials ['nʌpʃəlz] NPL (*hum*) nupcias *fpl*

NUR N ABBR (*Brit*) (*formerly*) = **National Union of Railwaymen**

nurd* [nɜ:d] N = **nerd**

nurse [nɜ:s] (A) N 1 (*in hospital, clinic*) enfermero/a *m/f*; **male ~** enfermero *m*; **student ~** estudiante *mf* de enfermería; **veterinary ~** auxiliar *mf* de veterinaria; *see also* **staff¹ C**

2 (*children's*) niñera *f*; *see also* **wet D**

(B) VT 1 [+ *patient*] cuidar, atender; **she ~d him back to health** lo cuidó hasta que se repuso; **to ~ a cold** curarse de un resfriado

2 [+ *baby*] (= *suckle*) amamantar; (= *cradle*) mecer

3 (*fig*) [+ *anger, grudge*] alimentar; [+ *hope*] abrigar; **to ~ one's constituency** (*Brit Parl*) cuidar de los intereses de los electores de su circunscripción electoral; **to ~ a business along** fomentar un negocio

nursemaid† ['nɜ:smeɪd] N niñera *f*, aya *f*; **to play ~ to sb** hacer de niñera de algn

nursery ['nɜ:srɪ] (A) N 1 (*where small children are looked after*) guardería *f*, jardín *m* de infancia; (= *school*) parvulario *m*, escuela *f* de párvulos, escuela *f* infantil (*Sp*), kínder *m* (*LAm*); (= *room at home*) cuarto *m* del bebé, habitación *f* del bebé

2 (*Agr, Hort*) vivero *m*

3 (*Zool*) criadero *m*

(B) CPD ► **nursery education** N educación *f* preescolar ► **nursery nurse** N puericultor(a) *m/f* ► **nursery rhyme** N canción *f* infantil ► **nursery school** N parvulario *m*, escuela *f* de párvulos, escuela *f* infantil (*Sp*), kínder *m* (*LAm*) ► **nursery schooling** N = **nursery education** ► **nursery school teacher** N = **nursery teacher** ► **nursery slopes** NPL (*Brit Ski*) pistas *fpl* para principiantes ► **nursery teacher** N maestro/a *m/f* de parvulario, maestro/a *m/f* de preescolar

nurseryman ['nɜ:srɪmən] N (*pl* **nurserymen**) horticultor *m*

nursing ['nɜ:sɪŋ] (A) N 1 (= *career, course, profession*) enfermería *f*; **to go in for ~** hacerse enfermero/a, dedicarse a la enfermería

2 (= *care*) [*of patient*] asistencia *f*, cuidado *m*

3 (= *suckling*) lactancia *f*

(B) CPD ► **nursing auxiliary** N (*Brit*) auxiliar *mf* de enfermería ► **nursing college** N escuela *f* de enfermería ► **nursing home** N (*for elderly*) hogar *m* de ancianos; (*for convalescents*) clínica *f* (particular) ► **nursing mother** N madre *f* que amamanta ► **nursing officer** N enfermero/a *m/f* ► **nursing staff** N personal *m* de enfermería

nursling ['nɜ:slɪŋ] N lactante *mf*, niño/a *m/f* de pecho

nurture ['nɜ:tʃəʳ] (A) VT 1 (= *bring up*) criar, educar

2 (= *nourish*) nutrir, alimentar

(B) N 1 (= *bringing-up*) educación *f*, crianza *f*; **nature or ~** naturaleza o educación

2 (= *nourishment*) nutrición *f*

NUS N ABBR (*Brit*) 1 = **National Union of Students**

2 (*formerly*) = **National Union of Seamen**

NUT N ABBR (*Brit*) = **National Union of Teachers**

nut [nʌt] (A) N 1 (*Tech*) tuerca *f*; ✦*IDIOM* **the ~s and bolts of a scheme** los aspectos prácticos de un proyecto

2 (*Bot*) nuez *f*; ✦*IDIOM* **to be a hard** *or* **tough ~: it's a hard** *or* **tough ~ to crack** es un hueso duro de roer; **he's a tough ~** es un tipo duro

3 (*) (= *head*) coco* *m*; ✦*IDIOMS* **to do one's ~** (*Brit*) salirse de sus casillas*; **to be off one's ~** estar chiflado *or* chalado*; **you must be off your ~!** ¿tú estás chalado o qué?*

4 (*) (= *crazy person*) chiflado/a* *m/f*, chalado/a* *m/f*

5 **nuts**** (= *testicles*) cojones** *mpl*, huevos** *mpl*

6 **nuts!*** ¡narices!*

(B) CPD ► **nut chocolate** N chocolate *m* de nueces ► **nut tree** N (= *hazel*) avellano *m*; (= *walnut*) nogal *m*

nut-brown ['nʌt'braʊn] ADJ café avellana *adj inv*; [*hair*] castaño claro

nutcase* ['nʌtkeɪs] N chiflado/a* *m/f*, chalado/a* *m/f*

nutcracker ['nʌtkrækəʳ] N cascanueces *m inv*; **The Nutcracker** (*Mus*) El Cascanueces

nutcrackers ['nʌt,krækəz] NPL cascanueces *m inv*; **a pair of ~** un cascanueces

nuthatch ['nʌthætʃ] N trepador *m*, trepatroncos *m*

nuthouse** ['nʌthaʊs] N (*pl* **nuthouses** ['nʌthaʊzɪz]) manicomio *m*

nutmeg ['nʌtmeg] N nuez *f* moscada

nutrasweet® ['nju:trəswi:t] N edulcorante *m*, sacarina *f*

nutrient ['nju:trɪənt] (A) N nutriente *m*
(B) ADJ nutritivo

nutriment ['nju:trɪmənt] N nutrimento *m*, alimento *m*

nutrition [nju:'trɪʃən] N nutrición *f*, alimentación *f*

nutritional [nju:'trɪʃənl] ADJ [*value*] nutritivo, nutricional

nutritionist [nju:'trɪʃənɪst] N nutricionista *mf*

nutritious [nju:'trɪʃəs], **nutritive** ['nju:trətɪv] ADJ nutritivo, alimenticio

nuts* [nʌts] ADJ chiflado*, chalado*; **to be ~ about sth/sb** estar chiflado por algo/algn*; **to drive sb ~** volver loco a algn; **to go ~** volverse loco

nutshell ['nʌtʃel] N cáscara *f* de nuez; ✦*IDIOM* **in a ~** en pocas palabras; **to put it in a ~** para decirlo en pocas palabras

nutter** ['nʌtəʳ] N (*Brit*) chiflado/a* *m/f*, chalado/a* *m/f*

nutty ['nʌtɪ] ADJ (*compar* **nuttier**, *superl* **nuttiest**) 1 [*cake*] con nueces; [*taste*] a nuez; [*sherry*] almendrado, avellanado; [*colour*] de nuez

2 (*) (= *crazy*) chiflado*; **to be ~ about sth** estar loco por algo*

nuzzle ['nʌzl] (A) VT acariciar con el hocico
(B) VI arrimarse

NV ABBR (*US*) = **Nevada**

NVQ N ABBR (*Brit*) = **National Vocational Qualification**

NVQ

La **National Vocational Qualification** *o* **NVQ** *es una titulación profesional dirigida sobre todo a personas que ya han entrado en el mundo laboral, aunque en algunos casos puede cursarse también durante el período escolar, a la vez que o en vez de algún otro título académico como los* **GCSEs** *o los* **A-levels**. *La evaluación se hace a través del trabajo práctico realizado durante el curso y a través de exámenes orales y escritos. Este sistema funciona en Inglaterra, Gales e Irlanda del Norte, mientras que en Escocia funciona un sistema similar, el llamado* **Scottish Vocational Qualification** *o* **SVQ**.

⇨ *Ver tb* GCSE, ADVANCED LEVELS; *see also* **SVQ**

NW ABBR (= **north-west**) NO

NWT ABBR (*Canada*) = **Northwest Territories**

NY ABBR (*US*) = **New York**

NYC ABBR (*US*) = **New York City**

nylon [ˈnaɪlɒn] Ⓐ N [1] (= *fabric*) nilón *m*, nailon *m*
[2] **nylons** medias *fpl* de nilón *or* nailon
Ⓑ ADJ de nilón, de nailon

nymph [nɪmf] N ninfa *f*

nymphet(te) [nɪmˈfet] N nínfula *f*

nympho* [ˈnɪmfəʊ] Ⓐ ADJ ninfómano
Ⓑ N ninfómana *f*

nymphomania [ˌnɪmfəʊˈmeɪnɪə] N ninfomanía *f*

nymphomaniac [ˌnɪmfəʊˈmeɪnɪæk] Ⓐ N ninfómana *f*
Ⓑ ADJ ninfómano

NYSE N ABBR (*US*) = **New York Stock Exchange**

NZ, **N. Zeal** ABBR = **New Zealand**

O o

O, o [əʊ] Ⓐ N [1] (= *letter*) O, o *f*; **O for Oliver** O de Oviedo
[2] (= *number*) (*Telec etc*) cero *m*
Ⓑ EXCL (*poet*) ¡oh!
Ⓒ CPD ► **O Grade** N (*Scot Scol*) (*formerly*) ≈ bachillerato *m* elemental (*examen oficial que se solía realizar en el cuarto curso de secundaria*) ► **O level** N (*Brit Scol*) (*formerly*) ≈ bachillerato *m* elemental (*examen oficial que se solía realizar en el cuarto curso de secundaria*)

o' [əʊ] PREP (= **of**) de; *see also* **o'clock**

o/a ABBR = **on account**

oaf [əʊf] N zoquete* *mf*

oafish ['əʊfɪʃ] ADJ zafio

oak [əʊk] Ⓐ N roble *m*; (= *evergreen*) encina *f*; ✦*PROV* **great ~s from little acorns grow** *las grandes cosas siempre suelen comenzar de forma modesta*
Ⓑ CPD [*table, furniture*] de roble ► **oak apple** N agalla *f* (de roble)

oaken ['əʊkən] ADJ (*liter*) de roble

oakum ['əʊkəm] N estopa *f* (de calafatear)

oakwood ['əʊkwʊd] N robledo *m*

O & M N ABBR = **Organization and Methods**

OAP N ABBR [1] = **old age pension**
[2] = **old age pensioner**

OAPEC [əʊ'eɪpɛk] N ABBR (= **Organization of Arab Petroleum-Exporting Countries**) OPAEP *f*

oar [ɔːʳ] N [1] (= *paddle*) remo *m*; **to ship the ~s** desarmar los remos; **to lie** *or* **rest on one's ~s** dejar de remar; (*fig*) descansar, dormir sobre sus laureles; ✦*IDIOM* **to put** *or* **shove one's ~ in*** entrometerse, meter las narices*
[2] (= *person*) remero/a *m/f*; **to be a good ~** ser buen remero, remar bien

oared [ɔːd] ADJ (= *having oars*) provisto de remos

-oared [ɔːd] ADJ (*ending in compounds*) de ... remos; **eight-oared** de ocho remos

oarlock ['ɔːlɒk] N (*US*) tolete *m*, escálamo *m*, chumacera *f*

oarsman ['ɔːzmən] N (*pl* **oarsmen**) remero *m*

oarsmanship ['ɔːzmənʃɪp] N arte *m* de remar

oarswoman ['ɔːzˌwʊmən] N (*pl* **oarswomen**) remera *f*

OAS N ABBR (= **Organization of American States**) OEA *f*

oasis [əʊ'eɪsɪs] N (*pl* **oases** [əʊ'eɪsiːz]) (*lit, fig*) oasis *m inv*

oast house ['əʊsthaʊs] N (*pl* **oast houses** ['əʊsthaʊzɪz]) N secadero *m* para lúpulo

oat bran ['əʊt'bræn] N (*US*) salvado *m* de avena

oatcake ['əʊtkeɪk] N torta *f* de avena

oaten ['əʊtn] ADJ de avena

oatfield ['əʊtfiːld] N avenal *m*

oath [əʊθ] N (*pl* **oaths** [əʊðz]) [1] (= *solemn promise etc*) juramento *m*; **under ~** ◊ **on ~** bajo juramento; **to administer an ~ to sb** tomar juramento a algn; **to break one's ~** romper su juramento; **to put sb on ~** hacer prestar juramento a algn; **to swear on (one's) ~** jurar; **to take the ~** prestar juramento; **to take an ~ that ...** jurar que ...; **to take an ~ of allegiance** (*Mil*) jurar la bandera; *see also* **allegiance**
[2] (= *swear word*) palabrota *f*, grosería *f* (*esp LAm*), lisura *f* (*Andes, S. Cone*); (= *curse*) blasfemia *f*, maldición *f*

oatmeal ['əʊtmiːl] Ⓐ N harina *f* de avena
Ⓑ ADJ [*colour*] (color) avena *adj inv*

oats [əʊts] NPL avena *fsing*; ✦*IDIOMS* **to be off one's ~** estar desganado, haber perdido el apetito; **to get one's ~** (*Brit*✱) echarse polvos (con regularidad)✱✱; *see also* **wild A1.2**

OAU N ABBR (= **Organization of African Unity**) OUA *f*

OB N ABBR (*TV*) = **outside broadcast**

ob. ABBR = **obit** (= *died*) m.

Obadiah [ˌəʊbə'daɪə] N Abdías

obbligato [ˌɒblɪ'gɑːtəʊ] (*Mus*) Ⓐ ADJ obligado
Ⓑ N (*pl* **obbligatos** *or* **obbligati**) obligado *m*

obduracy ['ɒbdjʊrəsɪ] N (= *stubbornness*) obstinación *f*, terquedad *f*; (= *inflexibility*) inflexibilidad *f*

obdurate ['ɒbdjʊrɪt] ADJ (= *stubborn*) obstinado, terco; (= *unyielding*) inflexible, firme

OBE N ABBR (*Brit*) (= **Officer of the Order of the British Empire**) *título ceremonial*; → HONOURS LIST

obedience [ə'biːdɪəns] Ⓐ N obediencia *f*; **to command ~** inspirar obediencia; **to owe ~ to sb** (*frm*) deber obediencia a algn; **to show ~ to sb/sth** obedecer a algn/algo; **in ~ to your orders** (*frm*) conforme a *or* en cumplimiento de sus órdenes; **in ~ to your wishes** (*frm*) obedeciendo a sus deseos
Ⓑ CPD ► **obedience training** N adiestramiento *m*

obedient [ə'biːdɪənt] ADJ obediente; **he was a very ~ child** era un niño muy obediente; **to be ~ to sth/sb** obedecer a algo/algn; **to be ~ to sb's wishes** obedecer los deseos de algn; **your ~ servant**† (*frm*) (*in letters*) su humilde servidor (*frm*)

obediently [ə'biːdɪəntlɪ] ADV obedientemente

obeisance [əʊ'beɪsəns] N (*frm*) [1] (= *homage*) homenaje *m*; **to do** *or* **make** *or* **pay ~ to** tributar homenaje a
[2] (= *bow etc*) reverencia *f*; (= *salutation*) saludo *m*

obelisk ['ɒbɪlɪsk] N obelisco *m*

obese [əʊ'biːs] ADJ obeso

obeseness [əʊ'biːsnɪs] N = **obesity**

obesity [əʊ'biːsɪtɪ] N obesidad *f*

obey [ə'beɪ] Ⓐ VT [+ *person*] obedecer; [+ *law*] observar, acatar; [+ *order*] cumplir; [+ *instruction*] seguir; [+ *summons*] acudir a; [+ *need, controls*] responder a; **I like to be ~ed** exijo obediencia
Ⓑ VI obedecer

obfuscate ['ɒbfəskeɪt] VT (*frm*) ofuscar

obit* ['ɒbɪt] N = **obituary A**

obituary [ə'bɪtjʊərɪ] Ⓐ N necrología *f*, obituario *m*
Ⓑ CPD ► **obituary column** N sección *f* necrológica ► **obituary notice** N necrología *f*, esquela *f* de defunción

object[1] ['ɒbdʒɪkt] Ⓐ N [1] (= *item*) objeto *m*; **I was forbidden to lift heavy ~s** tenía prohibido levantar objetos pesados; *see also* **sex C**
[2] (= *focus*) objeto *m*; **the economy was the ~ of heated discussion** la economía fue el objeto de una acalorada discusión; **the ~ of her hatred/love** el objeto de su odio/su amor; **she was an ~ of pity to all** era objeto de conmiseración para todos; **he became an ~ of ridicule** quedó en ridículo
[3] (= *aim*) objetivo *m*; **their main ~ was to make money** su principal objetivo era hacer dinero; **what's the ~ of doing that?** ◊ **what ~ is there in doing that?** ¿de qué sirve hacer eso?; **the ~ of the exercise is to raise money for charity** lo que se persigue con esto es recaudar dinero con fines benéficos; **that's the whole ~ of the exercise** de eso precisamente se trata; **with this ~ in mind** *or* **in view** con este objetivo *or* propósito en mente
[4] (= *obstacle*) **I want the best, money is no ~** quiero lo mejor, no importa cuánto cueste; **I want to have a great holiday, money is no ~** quiero tirarme unas vacaciones estupendas, el dinero no es problema; **money is no ~ to him** el dinero no es problema *or* obstáculo para él
[5] (*Gram*) complemento *m*; **direct/indirect ~** complemento *m* directo/indirecto
Ⓑ CPD ► **object clause** N (*Gram*) proposición *f* en función de complemento ► **object language** N (*Comput*) lengua *f* objeto ► **object lesson** N (*fig*) **it was an ~ lesson in how not to drive a car** fue un perfecto ejemplo de cómo no conducir un coche ► **object pronoun** N (*Gram*) pronombre *m* que funciona como objeto; **direct/indirect ~ pronoun** pronombre *m* que funciona como objeto directo/indirecto

object[2] [əb'dʒekt] Ⓐ VT objetar; **"you can't do that," he ~ed** —no puedes hacer eso —objetó; **he ~ed that there wasn't enough time** puso la objección de que *or* objetó que no tenían suficiente tiempo
Ⓑ VI [1] (= *disapprove*) oponerse; **I won't go**

if you ~ no iré si te opones; **if you don't ~** si no tiene inconveniente; **to ~ to sth: a lot of people will ~ to the book** mucha gente se opondrá al libro; **I wouldn't ~ to a bite to eat** no diría que no a algo que comer; **to ~ to sb: she ~s to my friends** no le gustan mis amigos; **I would ~ to Paul but not to Robert as chairman** me opondría a que Paul fuera presidente, pero no a que lo fuera Robert; **to ~ to sb doing sth: he ~s to her drinking** no le gusta que beba; **do you ~ to my smoking?** ¿le molesta que fume?; **do you ~ to my going?** ¿te importa que vaya?
2 (= *protest*) oponerse, poner objeciones; **he didn't ~ when ...** no su opuso *or* no puso objeciones cuando ...; **he ~ed in the strongest possible terms** se opuso de la manera más enérgica; **I ~!** (*frm*) ¡protesto!; **we ~ed strongly but were outvoted** nos opusimos enérgicamente pero perdimos la votación; **I ~ to that remark!** ¡ese comentario no lo tolero!
3 (*Jur*) **the prosecution ~s to splitting the cases** la acusación se opone a dividir los casos; **the defence can ~ to three jurors** la defensa puede objetar a tres miembros del jurado

▼**objection** [əbˈdʒekʃən] N 1 (= *aversion*) **do you have any ~ to my smoking?** ¿le molesta que fume?; **I have no ~ to people having a celebration, but ...** no tengo nada en contra de que la gente celebre cosas, pero ...
2 (= *opposing view*) objeción *f*; (= *problem*) inconveniente *m*; **are there any ~s?** ¿alguna objeción?, ¿alguien en contra?; **what is your ~?** ¿qué objeción tienes?; **we have no ~ to the plan** no tenemos ninguna objeción al plan; **I have no ~** no tengo inconveniente; **do you have any ~ to my going?** ¿tienes algún inconveniente en que vaya (yo)?; **they had no ~ to our being present** no tuvieron ningún inconveniente en que *or* no pusieron ninguna objeción a que estuviéramos presentes; **she made no ~** no puso ninguna objeción; **it met with no ~** nadie se opuso; **to raise ~s (to sth)** poner objeciones (a algo); **I see no ~** no veo inconveniente
3 (*Jur*) **objection!** ¡protesto!; **~ overruled!** no ha lugar a la protesta; **~ sustained!** ha lugar a la protesta

objectionable [əbˈdʒekʃnəbl] ADJ [*person*] grosero, desagradable; [*behaviour, attitude, remark*] inaceptable; [*language*] (= *indecent*) grosero, soez; (= *offensive*) ofensivo; [*smell*] desagradable, molesto; **the language used in the programme was ~ to many viewers** el lenguaje que se usa en el programa les resultó ofensivo a muchos telespectadores; **I find your tone highly ~** su tono me resulta totalmente inaceptable *or* muy ofensivo

objective [əbˈdʒektɪv] Ⓐ ADJ 1 (= *impartial*) [*person, view, assessment, opinion*] objetivo; **friends may not be able to be ~** puede que los amigos no sean capaces de ser objetivos; **to take an ~ look at sth** mirar algo desde un punto de vista objetivo
2 (= *real*) [*evidence, facts*] objetivo
3 (*Gram*) [*pronoun, genitive*] de complemento directo; **~ case** acusativo *m*
Ⓑ N 1 (= *aim*) objetivo *m*, propósito *m*; **if we achieve our ~** si alcanzamos nuestro objetivo, si conseguimos nuestro propósito; **military ~** objetivo *m* militar
2 (*Phot*) objetivo *m*
3 (*Gram*) acusativo *m*

objectively [əbˈdʒektɪvlɪ] ADV 1 (= *impartially*) objetivamente, de manera objetiva; **stand back and look ~ at the problem** distánciate y estudia el problema objetivamente *or* de manera objetiva; **~, such criticism is hardly fair** objetivamente *or* desde un punto de vista objetivo, críticas semejantes no son lo que se dice justas
2 (= *actually*) realmente; **whether this was ~ true or not, I felt it was** tanto si esto era realmente verdad como si no, yo creí que lo era

objectivism [əbˈdʒektɪvɪzəm] N objetivismo *m*

objectivity [ˌɒbdʒɪkˈtɪvɪtɪ] N objetividad *f*

objector [əbˈdʒektəʳ] N opositor(a) *m/f*; *see also* **conscientious**

objurgate [ˈɒbdʒɜːgeɪt] VT (*frm*) increpar, reprender

objurgation [ˌɒbdʒɜːˈgeɪʃən] N (*frm*) increpación *f*, reprensión *f*

oblation [əʊˈbleɪʃən] N (*Rel*) oblación *f*; (= *offering*) oblata *f*, ofrenda *f*

obligate [ˈɒblɪgeɪt] VT (*frm*) **to ~ sb to do sth** obligar a algn a hacer algo; **to be ~d to do sth** estar obligado a hacer algo

▼**obligation** [ˌɒblɪˈgeɪʃən] N obligación *f*; **without ~** (*in advert*) sin compromiso; **"no obligation to buy"** "sin compromiso a comprar"; **it is your ~ to see that ...** le cumple a usted comprobar que + *subjun*; **to be under an ~ to sb/to do sth** estar comprometido con algn/a hacer algo; **to lay** *or* **put sb under an ~** poner a algn bajo una obligación; **to meet/fail to meet one's ~s** hacer frente a/faltar a sus compromisos; **of ~** (*Rel*) de precepto

obligatory [ɒˈblɪgətərɪ] ADJ obligatorio; **to make it ~ for sb to do sth** hacer obligatorio que algn haga algo

▼**oblige** [əˈblaɪdʒ] VT 1 (= *compel*) obligar, forzar; **to ~ sb to do sth** obligar a algn a hacer algo; **to be ~d to do sth** estar *or* verse obligado a hacer algo; **you are not ~d to do it** no estás obligado a hacerlo
2 (= *gratify*) complacer, hacer un favor a; **he did it to ~ us** lo hizo como favor *or* para complacernos; **to ~ sb with a match** hacer a algn el favor de ofrecerle una cerilla; **anything to ~!*** ¡cualquier cosa!, ¡con mucho gusto!; **to be ~d to sb for sth** (= *grateful*) estarle agradecido a algn por algo; (= *under obligation*) deber un favor a algn por algo; **much ~d!** ¡muchísimas gracias!, ¡muy agradecido!; **I should be much ~d if ...** agradecería que + *subjun*; **I am ~d to you for your help** le agradezco mucho su ayuda

obligee [ˌɒblɪˈdʒiː] N (*Jur*) tenedor(a) *m/f* de una obligación

obliging [əˈblaɪdʒɪŋ] ADJ amable, atento; **she's a very ~ person** es una persona muy amable *or* muy atenta *or* muy solícita; **it was very ~ of them** fue muy amable de su parte

obligingly [əˈblaɪdʒɪŋlɪ] ADV amablemente, atentamente; **he very ~ helped us** nos ayudó muy amablemente *or* atentamente; **he ~ held the door open** sostuvo la puerta con mucha amabilidad; **the baby had been asleep, but he ~ opened his eyes now** el bebé había estado durmiendo, pero ahora amablemente abría los ojos

oblique [əˈbliːk] Ⓐ ADJ 1 [*angle etc*] oblicuo
2 (*fig*) [*reference*] indirecto, tangencial; [*reply*] evasivo
Ⓑ N (*Typ*) oblicua *f*

obliquely [əˈbliːklɪ] ADV (*lit*) oblicuamente; (*fig*) indirectamente

obliqueness [əˈbliːknɪs] N [*of angle*] oblicuidad *f*; (*fig*) [*of reference*] lo indirecto, lo tangencial; [*of reply*] evasividad *f*

obliquity [əˈblɪkwɪtɪ] N = **obliqueness**

obliterate [əˈblɪtəreɪt] VT 1 (= *destroy*) arrasar con, destruir
2 (= *blot out*) borrar; (= *hide*) ocultar

obliteration [əˌblɪtəˈreɪʃən] N 1 (= *destruction*) arrasamiento *m*, destrucción *f*
2 (= *occlusion*) eliminación *f*

oblivion [əˈblɪvɪən] N olvido *m*; **to cast into ~** echar al olvido; **to fall** *or* **sink into ~** caer en el olvido

oblivious [əˈblɪvɪəs] ADJ **~ of** *or* **to** inconsciente de; **he was ~ to the pain he caused** no se daba cuenta *or* era inconsciente del dolor que causaba

oblong [ˈɒblɒŋ] Ⓐ ADJ rectangular, oblongo
Ⓑ N rectángulo *m*

obloquy [ˈɒbləkwɪ] N (*frm*) (= *abuse*) injurias *fpl*, calumnia *f*; (= *shame*) deshonra *f*; **to cover sb with ~** llenar a algn de injurias

obnoxious [əbˈnɒkʃəs] ADJ [*person, behaviour*] odioso, aborrecible; [*smell*] repugnante, asqueroso; **it is ~ to me to** + INFIN me repugna + *infin*, me es odioso + *infin*

o.b.o. ABBR (*US*) (= **or best offer**) abierto ofertas

oboe [ˈəʊbəʊ] N oboe *m*

oboist [ˈəʊbəʊɪst] N oboe *mf*

obscene [əbˈsiːn] Ⓐ ADJ 1 (= *indecent*) [*gesture, language, remark*] obsceno, soez; [*phone call, act*] obsceno, indecente
2 (= *shocking*) [*profit, salary*] escandaloso
Ⓑ CPD ► **obscene publication** N (*Jur*) publicación *f* pornográfica ► **Obscene Publications Act** N (*Brit Jur*) ley *f* de las publicaciones pornográficas ► **Obscene Publications Squad** N (*Brit*) brigada *f* en contra de las publicaciones pornográficas

obscenely [əbˈsiːnlɪ] ADV 1 (= *indecently*) [*gesture, remark*] obscenamente; **to talk/write ~** decir/escribir obscenidades; **he was swearing ~** estaba soltando tacos y obscenidades
2 (= *shockingly*) [*fat*] repugnantemente; [*rich, expensive*] escandalosamente; **she earns ~ large amounts of money** gana unas cantidades de dinero escandalosas

obscenity [əbˈsenɪtɪ] Ⓐ N 1 (= *indecency*) obscenidad *f*, indecencia *f*
2 (= *word*) palabrota *f*, grosería *f* (*esp LAm*), lisura *f* (*Andes, S. Cone*); **to utter obscenities** proferir obscenidades
3 (*fig*) **that thing is an ~** esa cosa es una aberración
Ⓑ CPD ► **the obscenity laws** NPL las leyes de obscenidad

obscurantism [ˌɒbskjʊəˈræntɪzəm] N oscurantismo *m*

obscurantist [ˌɒbskjʊəˈræntɪst] Ⓐ ADJ oscurantista
Ⓑ N oscurantista *mf*

obscure [əbˈskjʊəʳ] Ⓐ ADJ 1 (= *not well-known*) [*book, artist, poet*] poco conocido, oscuro; [*village*] recóndito, perdido; **some ~ disease we had never heard of before** una enfermedad poco conocida de la que nunca habíamos oído hablar antes; **Norris himself has remained relatively ~** el mismo Norris sigue siendo hasta cierto punto un desconocido
2 (= *not obvious*) [*word, jargon, terminology*] de difícil comprensión; [*origins*] oscuro, poco claro; **the meaning is ~** el significado es oscuro *or* poco claro; **for some ~ reason** por alguna extraña razón; **to make ~ references to sth** referirse de forma críptica a algo
3 (= *indistinct*) [*shape, figure*] borroso
Ⓑ VT 1 (= *hide*) [+ *object, face, truth*] ocultar; **some clouds ~d the sun** algunas nubes ocultaron el sol; **the house is ~d by trees** la

➤ LANGUAGE IN USE: **objection 1** 9.2, 11.3 **obligation** 10.3 **oblige 1** 10.1, 10.2, 10.3

casa está escondida detrás de unos árboles; **my view was ~d by a lady in a large hat** una señora con un sombrero enorme no me dejaba ver; **his article ~s the facts** su artículo oscurece los hechos; **this news should not be allowed to ~ the fact that …** no se debería permitir que esta noticia impida ver claramente que …, no se debería permitir que esta noticia vele el hecho de que …
2 (= *complicate*) complicar; **it served only to ~ the matter further** sirvío para complicar aun más el asunto

obscurely [əb'skjʊəlɪ] ADV 1 (= *out of the public eye*) [*live, die*] en la oscuridad
2 (= *cryptically*) [*describe*] de forma poco clara; [*argue, write*] de manera que confunde; [*refer, say*] de forma críptica

obscurity [əb'skjʊərɪtɪ] N 1 (= *the unknown*) oscuridad *f*; **to live in ~** vivir en la oscuridad; **she rose from ~ to be a leading name in fashion** salió de la nada para llegar a ser un nombre destacado del mundo de la moda; **the band faded into ~** el grupo cayó en el olvido
2 (= *complexity*) [*of language, idea*] oscuridad *f*; **obscurities** (*in a book*) puntos *mpl* oscuros
3 (*liter*) (= *darkness*) oscuridad *f*

obsequies ['ɒbsɪkwɪz] NPL (*frm*) exequias *fpl*

obsequious [əb'si:kwɪəs] ADJ servil, sumiso

obsequiously [əb'si:kwɪəslɪ] ADV servilmente, de forma sumisa

obsequiousness [əb'si:kwɪəsnɪs] N servilismo *m*, sumisión *f*

observable [əb'zɜ:vəbl] ADJ [*benefit, consequence, effect*] visible; [*phenomenon*] observable, perceptible; [*rise, fall, improvement, increase*] apreciable, perceptible; **these are ~ facts** estos son hechos visibles; **the ~ universe** el universo visible; **there is no ~ difference** no hay ninguna diferencia apreciable *or* perceptible; **the same pattern is ~ in Georgia** la misma pauta puede apreciarse en Georgia

observably [əb'zɜ:vəblɪ] ADV visiblemente

observance [əb'zɜ:vəns] N 1 [*of rule etc*] observancia *f* (**of** de), cumplimiento *m* (**of** de); [*of customs, rites etc*] práctica *f*
2 (= *rite etc*) práctica *f*; (= *custom*) costumbre *f*; **religious ~s** prácticas *fpl* religiosas

observant [əb'zɜ:vənt] ADJ 1 (= *watchful*) observador; (= *attentive*) atento; **the child is very ~** el niño es muy observador
2 (= *strict in obeying rules*) observante, cumplidor

observation [,ɒbzə'veɪʃən] Ⓐ N 1 (= *perception*) observación *f*; **he is under ~ in hospital** lo tienen en observación en el hospital; **the police are keeping him under ~** la policía lo tiene vigilado; **we can keep the valley under ~ from here** desde aquí dominamos el valle; **powers of ~** capacidad *fsing* de observación; **to escape ~** pasar inadvertido
2 (= *remark*) observación *f*, comentario *m*; **"Observations on Sterne"** "Apuntes *mpl* sobre Sterne"
3 [*of rule etc*] observancia *f*, cumplimiento *m*
Ⓑ CPD ► **observation car** N (*Rail*) vagón-mirador *m*, coche *m* panorámico ► **observation post** N (*Mil*) puesto *m* de observación ► **observation tower** N torre *f* de vigilancia

observatory [əb'zɜ:vətrɪ] N observatorio *m*

observe [əb'zɜ:v] VT 1 (= *see, notice*) observar, ver; **I ~d him steal the duck** vi cómo robaba el pato
2 (= *watch carefully, study*) observar, mirar; [+ *suspect*] vigilar; **now ~ this closely** ahora fijaos bien en esto
3 (= *remark*) observar, comentar; **"it looks like rain" — he ~d** —parece que va a llover —observó *or* comentó él; **I ~d to him that …** le hice observar que …; **as Jeeves ~d** como observó Jeeves
4 (= *obey*) [+ *rule, custom*] observar; [+ *Sabbath, silence*] guardar; **failure to ~ the law** incumplimiento *m* de la ley
5 [+ *anniversary*] celebrar

observer [əb'zɜ:vəʳ] N observador(a) *m/f*

obsess [əb'ses] Ⓐ VT obsesionar
Ⓑ VI obsesionarse (**about, over** con, por)

obsessed [əb'sest] ADJ obsesionado; **you're ~!** ¡estás obsesionado!; **to be ~ with sb/sth** estar obsesionado con algn/algo; **he's ~ with the idea** está obsesionado con la idea, le obsesiona la idea; **he's ~ with cleanliness** está obsesionado con la limpieza, tiene obsesión *or* manía con la limpieza; **she's ~ with becoming rich** está obsesionada con (la idea de) hacerse rica

obsession [əb'seʃən] N obsesión *f*; **to become an ~** convertirse en una obsesión; **to have an ~ about sth** estar obsesionado con algo; **his ~ with her** su obsesión con ella; **his ~ with punctuality** su obsesión *or* manía con la puntualidad; **football is an ~ with him** está obsesionado con el fútbol, el fútbol es una obsesión para él

obsessional [əb'seʃənəl] ADJ [*behaviour, love, hatred, thought*] obsesivo; **to be ~ about sth** estar obsesionado con algo

obsessive [əb'sesɪv] Ⓐ ADJ [*behaviour, jealousy, interest, need*] obsesivo; [*love, gambler*] obsesivo, enfermizo; [*fear*] enfermizo; **his ~ tidiness was driving her crazy** su obsesión *or* manía con *or* por la limpieza la estaba sacando de quicio; **he was an ~ reader** la lectura era una obsesión para él; **to be ~ about sth** estar obsesionado con algo; **to become ~** [*person*] obsesionarse; [*thing*] volverse una obsesión; **to become ~ about sth** obsesionarse con algo; **dieting can become ~** hacer dieta puede volverse una obsesión
Ⓑ N (*Psych*) obsesivo/a *m/f*
Ⓒ CPD ► **obsessive compulsive disorder** N (*Psych*) trastorno *m* obsesivo-compulsivo ► **obsessive neurosis** N (*Psych*) neurosis *f inv* obsesiva

obsessively [əb'sesɪvlɪ] ADV [*work*] de (una) forma obsesiva; [*love, hate*] de (una) forma obsesiva, de (una) forma enfermiza; **to be ~ concerned about sth** estar preocupado de (una) forma obsesiva por algo; **she is ~ tidy** tiene obsesión *or* manía con *or* por la limpieza; **she was ~ devoted to her mother** tenía una devoción obsesiva por su madre

obsidian [ɒb'sɪdɪən] N obsidiana *f*

obsolescence [,ɒbsə'lesns] N caída *f* en desuso, obsolescencia *f*; **planned ~** obsolescencia *f* planificada

obsolescent [,ɒbsə'lesnt] ADJ que está cayendo en desuso; **to be ~** estar cayendo en desuso

obsolete ['ɒbsəli:t] ADJ [*weapon, equipment, machine*] obsoleto; [*attitude, idea, system*] obsoleto, anticuado; [*process, practice, word, law*] obsoleto, en desuso; [*ticket*] caduco; **to become ~** (*gen*) quedarse obsoleto, caer en desuso; [*ticket*] caducar

obstacle ['ɒbstəkl] Ⓐ N obstáculo *m*; (= *hindrance*) estorbo *m*, impedimento *m*; **one of the ~s is money** uno de los obstáculos *or* impedimentos es el dinero; **to be an ~ to sth/sb** ser un obstáculo para algo/algn; **to put an ~ in the way of sth/sb** crear dificultades *or* poner obstáculos a algo/algn; **that is no ~ to our doing it** eso no impide que lo hagamos; **~s to independence** los factores que dificultan la independencia
Ⓑ CPD ► **obstacle course** N pista *f* de obstáculos ► **obstacle race** N (*Sport*) carrera *f* de obstáculos

obstetric [ɒb'stetrɪk] ADJ obstétrico

obstetrical [ɒb'stetrɪkəl] ADJ = **obstetric**

obstetrician [,ɒbstə'trɪʃən] N tocólogo/a *m/f*, obstetra *mf*

obstetrics [ɒb'stetrɪks] NSING obstetricia *f*, tocología *f*

obstinacy ['ɒbstɪnəsɪ] N [*of person*] obstinación *f*, terquedad *f*; [*of resistance*] tenacidad *f*; [*of illness*] persistencia *f*

obstinate ['ɒbstɪnɪt] ADJ 1 (= *stubborn*) [*person*] obstinado, terco; **to be ~ about sth** obstinarse en algo, ser obstinado con algo
2 (= *tenacious*) [*resistance*] tenaz; [*illness*] persistente

obstinately ['ɒbstɪnɪtlɪ] ADV obstinadamente, tercamente

obstreperous [əb'strepərəs] ADJ [*person, behaviour*] escandaloso; **he became ~** empezó a desmandarse

obstreperously [əb'strepərəslɪ] ADV escandalosamente

obstruct [əb'strʌkt] Ⓐ VT 1 (= *block*) obstruir; [+ *pipe*] atascar; [+ *road*] cerrar, bloquear; [+ *view*] tapar
2 (= *hinder*) [+ *person*] estorbar, impedir; [+ *plan, progress etc*] dificultar, obstaculizar; (*Parl, Sport*) obstruir, bloquear
Ⓑ VI estorbar

obstruction [əb'strʌkʃən] N 1 (= *blockage*) obstrucción *f*; (*in pipe, road*) atasco *m*; (*Med*) oclusión *f*; **to cause an ~** estorbar; (*Aut*) obstruir el tráfico
2 (= *obstacle*) (*to progress*) dificultad *f*, obstáculo *m*
3 (*Ftbl*) obstrucción *f*, bloqueo *m*

obstructionism [əb'strʌkʃənɪzəm] N obstruccionismo *m*

obstructionist [əb'strʌkʃənɪst] Ⓐ ADJ obstruccionista
Ⓑ N obstruccionista *mf*

obstructive [əb'strʌktɪv] ADJ obstruccionista; **he's just being ~** está poniendo dificultades nada más

obstructiveness [əb'strʌktɪvnɪs] N obstruccionismo *m*

obtain [əb'teɪn] Ⓐ VT obtener, conseguir; (= *acquire*) adquirir; **his uncle ~ed the job for him** su tío le consiguió el puesto; **oil can be ~ed from coal** se puede extraer aceite del carbón
Ⓑ VI (*frm*) [*price, law*] regir; [*theory*] prevalecer, predominar; **the price which ~s now** el precio que rige ahora; **in the conditions then ~ing** en las condiciones que imperaban entonces; **that did not ~ in my day** en mis tiempos eso no era así

obtainable [əb'teɪnəbl] ADJ (= *on sale*) a la venta; (= *accessible*) asequible; **"obtainable at all chemists"** "de venta en todas las farmacias"; **it is no longer ~** ya no se puede conseguir

obtrude [əb'tru:d] (*frm*) Ⓐ VT [+ *tongue etc*] sacar; **to ~ sth on sb** imponer algo a algn
Ⓑ VI [*person*] entrometerse; **he does not let his opinions ~** no hace gala de sus opiniones, no impone sus opiniones a los demás

obtrusion [əb'tru:ʒən] N (= *imposition*) [*of opinions*] imposición *f*; (= *interference, intrusion*) entrometimiento *m*, importunidad *f*

obtrusive [əb'tru:sɪv] ADJ [*presence, person*] molesto; [*smell*] penetrante; [*colours*] llamativo; [*building*] demasiado prominente; **the back-**

ground music was very ~ la música de fondo resultaba muy molesta; **that lamp/painting is too ~** esa lámpara/ese cuadro es demasiado prominente

obtrusively [əb'tru:sɪvlɪ] ADV [*do sth*] de (una) forma que resulta molesta

obtuse [əb'tju:s] ADJ [1] (*Math*) obtuso
[2] (= *stupid, insensitive*) [*person*] obtuso, torpe; [*remark*] desacertado, poco inteligente; **he can be very ~ at times** a veces puede ser muy obtuso; **now you're just being ~** te empeñas en no comprender

obtuseness [əb'tju:snɪs] N (*fig*) torpeza *f*, obtusidad *f*

obverse ['ɒbvɜ:s] Ⓐ ADJ del anverso
Ⓑ N anverso *m*; (*fig*) complemento *m*

obviate ['ɒbvɪeɪt] VT obviar, evitar; **to ~ the need for sth** evitar *or* ahorrar la necesidad de algo

obvious ['ɒbvɪəs] Ⓐ ADJ [1] (= *clear, perceptible*) [*disadvantage, solution*] obvio, claro; [*danger*] evidente; [*question*] obvio; **to be ~ that** estar claro que, ser obvio *or* evidente que; **it's ~ that he's unhappy/we can't win** está claro *or* es evidente que es infeliz/no podemos ganar; **he isn't going to resign, that much is ~** no va a dimitir, eso está claro *or* es evidente; **it's ~, isn't it?** es obvio, ¿no?; **it was by no means ~ who would win** no estaba claro en absoluto quién iba a ganar; **her confusion was ~** era evidente que estaba confusa; **she made it very ~ that she didn't like him** dejó muy claro que no le gustaba, hizo patente que no le gustaba; **he's the ~ man for the job** es la persona obvia para el puesto; **it was painfully ~ that she hadn't studied for the exam** estaba clarísimo que no había estudiado para el examen; **it's perfectly ~ that he has no intention of coming** está perfectamente claro *or* es más que evidente que no tiene intención de venir; **for ~ reasons** por razones obvias *or* evidentes; **it's the ~ thing to do** está claro que es eso lo que hay que hacer; **it was ~ to everyone that it had been a mistake** todo el mundo se daba cuenta de que había sido un error; **it's not that ~ to me** para mí no está tan claro
[2] (= *unsubtle*) [*ploy*] evidente, obvio; [*lie*] descarado; [*symbolism*] poco sutil; **we mustn't be too ~ about it** no conviene que se nos note demasiado; **her rather ~ charms** sus encantos poco sutiles
Ⓑ N **to state the ~** afirmar lo obvio

obviously ['ɒbvɪəslɪ] ADV [1] (= *clearly*) obviamente; **it's ~ the best** obviamente es el mejor, es evidente que es el mejor; **he was ~ very angry/tired** se notaba que estaba muy enfadado/cansado, estaba claro *or* era evidente *or* era obvio que estaba muy enfadado/cansado; **he was ~ not drunk** estaba claro *or* era evidente *or* era obvio que no estaba borracho; **he was not ~ drunk** no se le notaba que estaba borracho; **~, I am delighted** lógicamente *or* por supuesto, estoy encantado; **obviously!** ¡por supuesto!, ¡lógico!, ¡obvio!; **"aren't they coming?" — "~ not!"** —¿no vienen? —¡evidentemente no *or* obviamente no!; **it's ~ true** está claro que es verdad
[2] (= *unsubtly*) burdamente; **she asked him rather too ~ where he had been** le preguntó sin mucha delicadeza (que) dónde había estado

OC N ABBR (= **Officer Commanding**) jefe *m*

o/c ABBR = **overcharge**

ocarina [,ɒkə'ri:nə] N ocarina *f*

OCAS N ABBR (= **Organization of Central American States**) ODECA *f*

occasion [ə'keɪʒən] Ⓐ N [1] (= *particular time*) ocasión *f*; **(on) the first ~ that it happened** la primera vez que ocurrió; **that was the first ~ that we had met** ésa fue la ocasión en que nos conocimos; **this would be a good ~ to try it out** ésta sería una buena oportunidad *or* ocasión para probarlo; **on ~** de vez en cuando; **on one ~** una vez; **on other ~s** otras veces; **on previous ~s** en ocasiones previas; **on rare ~s** rara vez; **he went back on three separate ~s** volvió en tres ocasiones; **on that ~** esa vez, en aquella ocasión; **on the ~ of his retirement** con motivo de su jubilación; **as (the) ~ requires** si la ocasión lo requiere; **he was waiting for a suitable ~ to apologize** esperaba el momento adecuado para disculparse, esperaba una oportunidad *or* ocasión para disculparse; **to take (the) ~ to do sth** aprovechar la oportunidad para hacer algo
[2] (= *event*) acontecimiento *m*; **it was quite an ~** fue todo un acontecimiento; **what's the ~?** ¿qué se celebra?; **I wasn't dressed for the ~** no estaba vestida de forma adecuada para la ocasión; **to rise** *or* **be equal to the ~** ponerse a la altura de las circunstancias; **I keep it for special ~s** lo guardo para las grandes ocasiones; *see also* **sense A8**
[3] (= *reason*) razón *f*, motivo *m*; **there is no ~ for alarm** ◊ **there is no ~ to be alarmed** no hay razón *or* motivo para alarmarse; **should the ~ arise** ◊ **if the ~ arises** si se da el caso; **to give (sb) ~ to do sth** (= *opportunity*) dar ocasión a algn de hacer algo; (= *reason*) dar motivo a algn para hacer algo; **to give (sb) ~ for sth** (= *opportunity*) dar ocasión a algn para algo; (= *reason*) dar motivo a algn para algo; **to have ~ to do sth** (= *opportunity*) tener ocasión de hacer algo; (= *reason*) tener motivo para hacer algo; **you had no ~ to say that** no había necesidad de que dijeras eso, no había motivo para decir eso
Ⓑ VT (*frm*) ocasionar (*frm*), causar; **losses ~ed by bad weather** pérdidas ocasionadas por el mal tiempo (*frm*), pérdidas causadas por el mal tiempo

occasional [ə'keɪʒənl] Ⓐ ADJ [1] (= *infrequent*) [*lapse, meeting*] esporádico; [*rain, showers*] ocasional, aislado; **she made ~ visits to England** hacía alguna que otra visita a Inglaterra, hacía visitas esporádicas a Inglaterra; **I like the** *or* **an ~ cigarette** me gusta fumar un cigarrillo de vez en cuando; **I have the** *or* **an ~ drink** tomo una copa de vez en cuando; **they had passed the ~ car on the road** de vez en cuando pasaban algún coche en la carretera; **he smokes only the** *or* **a very ~ cigar** sólo muy de vez en cuando *or* muy de tarde en tarde se fuma un puro
[2] (*frm*) (= *created for special event*) [*poem, music*] compuesto especialmente para la ocasión; **it was written as an ~ piece for the Coronation** se escribió la pieza especialmente con ocasión de la coronación
Ⓑ CPD ► **occasional table** N mesa *f* auxiliar ► **occasional worker** N (*US*) jornalero/a *m/f*, temporero/a *m/f*

occasionally [ə'keɪʒnəlɪ] ADV de vez en cuando, a veces, ocasionalmente (*frm*), cada cuando (*LAm*); **he ~ drinks wine but never beer** de vez en cuando *or* a veces bebe vino pero nunca cerveza; **very ~** muy de vez en cuando, muy de tarde en tarde; **we see each other (only) very ~** nos vemos (sólo) muy de vez en cuando *or* muy de tarde en tarde

occident ['ɒksɪdənt] N occidente *m*

occidental [,ɒksɪ'dentl] ADJ occidental

occipital [ɒk'sɪpɪtəl] ADJ occipital

occiput ['ɒksɪpʌt] N (*pl* **occiputs** *or* **occipita**) occipucio *m*

occlude [ɒ'klu:d] VT ocluir

occluded front [ɒ,klu:dɪd'frʌnt] N (*Met*) oclusión *f*, frente *m* ocluido

occlusion [ɒ'klu:ʒən] N oclusión *f*

occlusive [ɒ'klu:sɪv] Ⓐ ADJ oclusivo
Ⓑ N oclusiva *f*

occult [ɒ'kʌlt] Ⓐ ADJ (= *mystic*) oculto; [*reason etc*] oculto, misterioso
Ⓑ N **the ~** lo oculto; **to study the ~** dedicarse al ocultismo, estudiar las ciencias ocultas

occultism ['ɒkəltɪzəm] N ocultismo *m*

occultist ['ɒkəltɪst] N ocultista *mf*

occupancy ['ɒkjʊpənsɪ] N ocupación *f*; (= *tenancy*) inquilinato *m*; [*of post*] tenencia *f*

occupant ['ɒkjʊpənt] N [1] (= *tenant*) inquilino/a *m/f*
[2] [*of boat, car etc*] ocupante *mf*; **all the ~s were killed** perecieron todos los ocupantes *or* pasajeros
[3] [*of job, post*] titular *mf*

occupation [,ɒkjʊ'peɪʃən] N [1] (= *employment*) empleo *m*, profesión *f*; **what is his ~?** ¿cuál es su profesión?; **he's a joiner by ~** es carpintero de profesión; **it gives ~ to 50 men** emplea a 50 hombres, proporciona empleo a 50 hombres
[2] (= *pastime*) pasatiempo *m*; **a harmless enough ~** un pasatiempo inocente; **this will give some ~ to your mind** esto te mantendrá la mente ocupada
[3] (*Mil etc*) ocupación *f*; **army of ~** ejército *m* de ocupación; **the ~ of Paris** la ocupación de París; **under (military) ~** ocupado por el ejército
[4] [*of house etc*] tenencia *f*; **to be in ~** ocupar; **we found them already in ~** vimos que ya se habían instalado allí; **the house is ready for ~** la casa está lista para habitar; **a house unfit for ~** una casa inhabitable, una casa carente de las condiciones mínimas de habitabilidad
[5] [*of post, office*] tenencia *f*

occupational [,ɒkjʊ'peɪʃənl] Ⓐ ADJ (*gen*) profesional
Ⓑ CPD ► **occupational accident** N accidente *m* laboral ► **occupational disease** N enfermedad *f* profesional ► **occupational guidance** N orientación *f* profesional ► **occupational hazard** N [*of job*] riesgo *m* laboral; (*hum*) gaje *m* del oficio ► **occupational pension scheme** N plan *m* de jubilación ► **occupational risk** N = **occupational hazard** ► **occupational therapist** N terapeuta *mf* ocupacional ► **occupational therapy** N terapia *f* ocupacional ► **occupational training** N formación *f* profesional, formación *f* ocupacional

occupier ['ɒkjʊpaɪəʳ] N [*of house, land*] inquilino/a *m/f*; [*of post*] titular *mf*

occupy ['ɒkjʊpaɪ] VT [1] [+ *house*] habitar, vivir en; [+ *office, seat*] ocupar; **is this seat occupied?** ¿está ocupado este asiento?
[2] (*Mil etc*) ocupar; **in occupied France** en la Francia ocupada (por los alemanes)
[3] [+ *post, position*] ocupar
[4] (= *take up, fill*) [+ *space, time*] ocupar; **this job occupies all my time** este trabajo me ocupa *or* absorbe todo el tiempo; **he is occupied in research** se dedica a la investigación
[5] (= *keep busy*) ocupar; **to be occupied with sth/in doing sth** estar ocupado con algo/haciendo algo; **he is very occupied at the moment** está muy ocupado en este mo-

➤ LANGUAGE IN USE: **obvious A1** 15.1

mento; **she occupies herself by knitting** se entretiene haciendo punto

[6] (*US Telec*) **to be occupied** estar comunicando

occur [əˈkɜːʳ] VI [1] (= *happen*) ocurrir, suceder; **to ~ again** volver a suceder, repetirse; **don't let it (ever) ~ again** que no se vuelva a repetir (nunca); **if a vacancy ~s** si se produce una vacante; **if the opportunity ~s** si se presenta la oportunidad

[2] (= *be found*) darse, encontrarse; **the plant ~s all over Spain** la planta se da en todas partes en España

[3] (= *come to mind*) **to ~ to sb** ocurrírsele a algn; **it ~s to me that ...** se me ocurre que ...; **it ~red to me to ask him** se me ocurrió preguntárselo; **such an idea would never have ~red to her** semejante idea jamás se le hubiera ocurrido *or* pasado por la mente

occurrence [əˈkʌrəns] N [1] (= *happening*) suceso *m*, hecho *m*; **it's an everyday ~** es cosa de todos los días, es un hecho cotidiano; **a common ~** un hecho frecuente; **that is a common ~** eso sucede a menudo

[2] (= *existence*) existencia *f*; **its ~ in the south is well known** se sabe que existe en el sur; **its ~ here is unexpected** el hecho de que se dé *or* de que exista aquí es algo insólito

ocean [ˈəʊʃən] Ⓐ N océano *m*; **~s of*** (*fig*) la mar de*

Ⓑ CPD [*climate, region*] oceánico ► **ocean bed** N fondo *m* del océano ► **ocean cruise** N crucero *m* ► **ocean liner** N transatlántico *m*

oceanarium [ˌəʊʃəˈnɛərɪəm] N (*pl* **oceanariums** *or* **oceanaria** [ˌəʊʃəˈnɛərɪə]) oceanario *m*

ocean-going [ˈəʊʃən,gəʊɪŋ] ADJ [*ship*] transatlántico

Oceania [ˌəʊʃɪˈeɪnɪə] N Oceanía *f*

oceanic [ˌəʊʃɪˈænɪk] ADJ oceánico

oceanographer [ˌəʊʃəˈnɒgrəfəʳ] N oceanógrafo/a *m/f*

oceanographic [ˌəʊʃənɒˈgræfɪk] ADJ oceanográfico

oceanography [ˌəʊʃəˈnɒgrəfɪ] N oceanografía *f*

ocelot [ˈəʊsɪlɒt] N ocelote *m*

och [ɒx] EXCL (*Scot*) ¡oh!

ochre, **ocher** (*US*) [ˈəʊkəʳ] N ocre *m*; **red ~** ocre *m* rojo, almagre *m*; **yellow ~** ocre *m* amarillo

ochreous [ˈəʊkrɪəs] ADJ de color ocre

o'clock [əˈklɒk] ADV [1] (*time*) **it is seven ~** son las siete; **it is one ~** es la una; **at nine ~ (exactly)** a las nueve (en punto); **it is just after two ~** son las dos pasadas, son un poco más de las dos; **it is nearly eight ~** son casi las ocho; **the six ~ (train/bus)** el (tren/autobús) de las seis; **the nine ~ news** las noticias de las nueve

[2] (*Aer, Mil*) (*direction*) **aircraft approaching at five ~** se aproxima un aparato a las cinco

OCR N ABBR (*Comput*) [1] (= **optical character reader**) LOC *m*

[2] (= **optical character recognition**) ROC *m*

Oct. ABBR (= **October**) oct.

octagon [ˈɒktəgən] N octágono *m*

octagonal [ɒkˈtægənl] ADJ octagonal

octahedron [ˈɒktəˈhiːdrən] N (*pl* **octahedrons** *or* **octahedra** [ˈɒktəˈhiːdrə]) octaedro *m*

octal [ˈɒktəl] Ⓐ ADJ octal

Ⓑ N octal *m*

octane [ˈɒkteɪn] Ⓐ N octano *m*

Ⓑ CPD ► **octane number**, **octane rating** N grado *m* octánico

octave [ˈɒktɪv] N (*Mus, Poetry*) octava *f*

Octavian [ɒkˈteɪvɪən] N Octavio

octavo [ɒkˈteɪvəʊ] Ⓐ ADJ en octavo

Ⓑ N (*pl* **octavos**) libro *m* en octavo

octet, **octette** [ɒkˈtet] N octeto *m*

October [ɒkˈtəʊbəʳ] N octubre *m*; *see* **July** *for usage*

octogenarian [ˌɒktəʊdʒɪˈnɛərɪən] Ⓐ ADJ octagenario

Ⓑ N octogenario/a *m/f*

octopus [ˈɒktəpəs] N (*pl* **octopuses**) pulpo *m*

octosyllabic [ˈɒktəʊsɪˈlæbɪk] ADJ octosílabo

octosyllable [ˈɒktəʊˈsɪləbl] N octosílabo *m*

ocular [ˈɒkjʊləʳ] ADJ ocular

oculist [ˈɒkjʊlɪst] N oculista *mf*

OD[1], **O/D** ABBR [1] = **on demand**

[2] = **overdraft**

[3] = **overdrawn**

OD[2]* [əʊˈdiː] = **overdose** Ⓐ N sobredosis *f*

Ⓑ VI [1] (*lit*) tomar una sobredosis

[2] (*fig*) (*hum*) **to OD on TV** ver demasiada tele

odalisk, **odalisque** [ˈəʊdəlɪsk] N odalisca *f*

odd [ɒd] Ⓐ ADJ (*compar* **odder**, *superl* **oddest**)

[1] (= *strange*) raro, extraño; **he's got rather ~ lately** recientemente se ha vuelto algo raro; **that's very ~, I could have sworn I'd left my keys here** qué raro *or* qué cosa más rara, juraría que había dejado aquí mis llaves; **how ~!** ¡qué raro!, ¡qué curioso!, ¡qué extraño!; **how ~ that we should meet here** qué raro *or* qué extraño que nos hayamos encontrado aquí; **it was ~ of him to leave suddenly like that** fue raro que se fuese así, tan de repente; **the ~ thing about it is ...** lo raro *or* lo extraño que tiene es que ...; **he says some ~ things** dice cosas muy raras *or* extrañas; → STRANGE, RARE

[2] (= *occasional*) algún que otro; **he has written the ~ article** ha escrito algún que otro artículo; **there will be the ~ shower later** caerá algún que otro chaparrón más tarde; **he enjoys the ~ glass of champagne** le gusta tomar una copa de champán de vez en cuando, le gusta tomar alguna que otra copa de champán; **at ~ moments** en los ratos *or* momentos libres

[3] (*Math*) [*number*] impar; **~ or even** par o impar

[4] (= *unpaired*) [*shoe, sock*] desparejado, sin pareja; **you're wearing ~ socks** llevas los calcetines desparejados, llevas dos calcetines distintos

[5] (= *extra, left over*) **to be the ~ one out** (= *be over*) ser el que sobra, estar de más; (= *be different*) ser distinto; **these clowns are all identical except one, which is the ~ one out?** estos payasos son todos iguales excepto uno, ¿cuál es distinto?; **but everybody will be wearing a tie, I don't want to be the ~ one** *or* **man out** pero todo el mundo va a llevar corbata, yo no quiero ser la excepción; **would you like the ~ penny?** ¿quiere el penique?; **£5 and some ~ pennies** cinco libras y algunos peniques; **any ~ piece of wood** cualquier trozo de madera; **an ~ piece of material** un retal; **an ~ scrap of paper** un trozo de papel

[6] (*) (*with approximate numbers*) **30 ~** treinta y pico, treinta y tantos; **she must be 40 ~** debe tener cuarenta y tantos *or* y pico años; **£20 ~** unas 20 libras; **I haven't seen him for forty ~ years** llevo cuarenta y tantos *or* cuarenta y pico años sin verlo

Ⓑ ADV **he acted a bit ~ when I told him** reaccionó de forma rara cuando se lo dije

Ⓒ CPD ► **odd jobs** NPL trabajillos *mpl*; **he did some ~ jobs around the house for us** nos hizo algunos trabajillos *or* pequeños arreglos en la casa ► **odd lot** N (*St Ex*) cantidad *f* irregular (y normalmente pequeña) de acciones *or* valores

oddball* [ˈɒdbɔːl] Ⓐ N bicho *m* raro*, excéntrico/a *m/f*

Ⓑ ADJ raro, excéntrico

oddbod* [ˈɒd,bɒd] N = **oddball**

oddity [ˈɒdɪtɪ] N [1] (= *odd thing*) cosa *f* rara; (= *odd trait*) manía *f*; **he has his oddities** tiene sus manías; **he's a real ~** es un tipo realmente raro; **one of the oddities of the situation** uno de los aspectos raros de la situación

[2] (= *strangeness*) rareza *f*

odd-job man [ɒdˈdʒɒb,mæn] N (*pl* **odd-job men**) *hombre que se dedica a hacer pequeños trabajos u arreglos*, manitas *m inv* (*Sp, Mex**)

odd-looking [ˈɒd,lʊkɪŋ] ADJ de aspecto singular

oddly [ˈɒdlɪ] ADV [*behave, act*] de (una) manera rara, de (una) manera extraña, en forma extraña (*LAm*); **he's behaving very ~** se está comportando de (una) manera muy rara *or* extraña; **~ attractive/calm** extrañamente atractivo/tranquilo; **an ~ shaped room** una habitación con una forma rara *or* extraña; **they are ~ similar** tienen un extraño parecido; **~ enough, you're right** por extraño que parezca, tienes razón

oddment [ˈɒdmənt] N artículo *m* suelto; (*Brit Comm*) resto *m*; **oddments** [*of fabric*] retazos *mpl*, retales *mpl*

oddness [ˈɒdnɪs] N rareza *f*

odds [ɒdz] NPL [1] (*in betting*) puntos *mpl* de ventaja; **to give ~ of 3 to 1** ofrecer 3 puntos de ventaja a 1; **what ~ will you give me?** ¿cuánta ventaja me da?; **the ~ on the horse are 5 to 1** las apuestas al caballo están a 5 contra 1; **short/long ~** pocas/muchas probabilidades; **to lay ~ on sth** (*fig*) hacer apuestas sobre algo; ✦***IDIOM*** **to pay over the ~** (*Brit*) pagar en demasía

[2] (= *chances for or against*) probabilidades *fpl*; **the ~ are in his favour** lo tiene todo a su favor; **to fight against overwhelming ~** luchar con todo en contra; **to succeed against all the ~** tener éxito en contra de todas las predicciones; **the ~ are that ...** lo más probable es que ...; **the ~ are too great** llevamos mucha desventaja es; **the ~ are against it** es poco probable

[3] (*) (= *difference*) **what's the ~?** ¿qué importa?, ¿qué más da?; **it makes no ~** da lo mismo, da igual; **it makes no ~ to me** me da igual

[4] (= *variance, strife*) **to be at ~ with sb over sth** estar reñido *or* en desacuerdo con algn por algo; **to set two people at ~** enemistar a dos personas

[5] **~ and ends** (= *bits and pieces*) trozos *mpl*, pedacitos *mpl*, corotos *mpl* (*Col, Ven*); [*of cloth etc*] retazos *mpl*, retales *mpl*; [*of food*] restos *mpl*, sobras *fpl*; **there were ~ and ends of machinery** había piezas sueltas de máquinas

[6] **all the ~ and sods‡** todo quisque*, todo hijo de vecina*

odds-on [ˈɒdzˈɒn] Ⓐ ADJ **it's ~ he won't come** lo más probable es que no venga

Ⓑ CPD ► **odds-on favourite** N caballo *m* favorito, caballo *m* con puntos de ventaja; **he's ~ favourite for the job** él tiene las mejores posibilidades de ganar el puesto

odd-sounding [ˈɒd,saʊndɪŋ] ADJ [*name*] raro; **~ words** palabras que suenan raras

ode [əʊd] N oda *f*

odious ['əʊdɪəs] ADJ [*person, task*] odioso, detestable; [*behaviour, crime*] detestable; [*comparison*] odioso
odiously ['əʊdɪəslɪ] ADV odiosamente, de forma detestable
odium ['əʊdɪəm] N (*frm*) odio *m*; **to bring ~ on sb** hacer que algn sea odiado; **to incur the ~ of having done sth** suscitar el odio de la gente por haber hecho algo
odometer [ɒ'dɒmɪtəʳ] N (*US*) cuentakilómetros *m inv*
odontologist [ˌɒdɒn'tɒlədʒɪst] N odontólogo/a *m/f*
odontology [ˌɒdɒn'tɒlədʒɪ] N odontología *f*
odor ['əʊdəʳ] N (*US*) = **odour**
odoriferous [ˌəʊdə'rɪfərəs] ADJ odorífero
odorless ['əʊdəlɪs] ADJ (*US*) = **odourless**
odorous ['əʊdərəs] ADJ oloroso
odour, **odor** (*US*) ['əʊdəʳ] N olor *m* (**of** a); (*fig*) sospecha *f*; **bad ~** mal olor; **~ of sanctity** olor de santidad; ✦***IDIOMS*** **to be in bad ~** (= *bad repute*) tener mala fama; **to be in bad ~ with sb** estar mal con algn
odourless, **odorless** (*US*) ['əʊdəlɪs] ADJ inodoro
Odysseus [ə'dɪsjuːs] N Odiseo
Odyssey ['ɒdɪsɪ] N (*Myth*) Odisea *f*; **odyssey** (*fig*) odisea *f*
OE N ABBR (*Ling*) = **Old English**
OECD N ABBR (= **Organization for Economic Cooperation and Development**) OCDE *f*
oecumenical [ˌiːkjuː'menɪkəl] ADJ ecuménico
oedema [ɪ'diːmə] N (*pl* **oedemata** [ɪ'diːmətə]) edema *m*
oedipal ['iːdɪpl] ADJ [*conflict, situation*] edípico
Oedipus ['iːdɪpəs] Ⓐ N Edipo
Ⓑ CPD ► **Oedipus complex** N (*Psych*) complejo *m* de Edipo
OEEC N ABBR (= **Organization for European Economic Cooperation**) OECE *f*
oenologist, **enologist** (*US*) [iː'nɒlədʒɪst] N enólogo/a *m/f*
oenology, **enology** (*US*) [iː'nɒlədʒɪ] N enología *f*
oenophile, **enophile** (*US*) ['iːnəʊfaɪl] N enófilo/a *m/f*
o'er ['əʊəʳ] (*poet*) = **over**
oesophagus, **esophagus** (*US*) [iː'sɒfəgəs] N esófago *m*
oestrogen, **estrogen** (*US*) ['iːstrəʊdʒən] N estrógeno *m*
oestrous, **estrous** (*US*) ['iːstrəs] Ⓐ ADJ en celo
Ⓑ CPD ► **oestrous cycle** N ciclo *m* de celo
oestrus, **estrus** (*US*) ['iːstrəs] N estro *m*
œuvre ['ɜːvrə] N obra *f*
of [ɒv, əv] PREP [1] (*indicating possession*) de; **the house of my uncle** la casa de mi tío; **the love of God** el amor de Dios; **a friend of mine** un amigo mío; **it's no business of yours** aquí no te metas, no tienes que ver con esto
[2] (*objective genitive*) a, hacia; **hatred of injustice** odio a la injusticia; **love of country** el amor a la patria
[3] (*partitive etc*) de; **a pound of flour** una libra de harina; **how much of this do you need?** ¿cuánto necesitas de eso?; **there were four of them** eran cuatro; **all of them** todos ellos; **of the 12, two were bad** de los 12, dos estaban pasados; **you of all people ought to know** debieras saberlo más que nadie; **most of all** sobre todo, más que nada; **we're the best of friends** somos muy (buenos) amigos; **the book of books** el libro de los libros; **king of kings** rey de reyes
[4] (*indicating cause*) por, de; **out of fear** por temor; **out of anger** de rabia; **of itself** de por sí; **of necessity** por necesidad; **to die of pneumonia** morir de pulmonía
[5] (*agent*) **beloved of all** querido de todos; **it was rude of him to say that** fue de mala educación que dijese eso; **it was nice of him to offer** fue muy amable ofreciéndose; **that was very kind of you** fue muy amable de su parte
[6] (*indicating material*) de; **made of steel/paper** hecho de acero/papel
[7] (*descriptive*) de; **the City of New York** la ciudad de Nueva York; **a boy of eight** un niño de ocho años; **a man of great ability** un hombre de gran talento; **that idiot of a minister** ese idiota de ministro; **by the name of Green** llamado Green; **a real palace of a house** una casa que es un verdadero palacio; **a tragedy of her own making** una tragedia que ella misma había labrado, una tragedia de su propia cosecha; **bright of eye** de ojos claros; **hard of heart** duro de corazón
[8] (= *concerning*) de; **what do you think of him?** ¿qué piensas de él?; **what of it?** ¿y a ti qué (te) importa?, ¿y qué?
[9] (*indicating deprivation, riddance*) **loss of faith** pérdida de fe; **lack of water** falta de agua
[10] (*indicating separation in space or time*) de; **south of Glasgow** al sur de Glasgow; **it's a quarter of six** (*US*) son las seis menos cuarto, falta un cuarto para las seis (*LAm*)
[11] (*in time phrases*) **I go to the pub of an evening*** al pub suelo ir por las noches; **he died of a Friday** (*frm*) murió un viernes; **it was fine of a morning*** por la mañana hacía buen tiempo
[12] (*with certain verbs*) **to dream of sth** soñar con algo; **to judge of sth** juzgar algo, opinar sobre algo; **he was robbed of his watch** le robaron el reloj, se le robó el reloj; **to smell of sth** oler a algo

off [ɒf]

[A] ADVERB	[E] INTRANSITIVE VERB
[B] ADJECTIVE	[F] TRANSITIVE VERB
[C] PREPOSITION	[G] COMPOUNDS
[D] NOUN	

When ***off*** *is the second element in a phrasal verb, eg* ***get off, keep off, take off****, look up the verb. When it is part of a set combination, eg* ***off duty/work, far off****, look up the other word.*

Ⓐ ADVERB
[1] [***= distant***] **a place two miles ~** un lugar a dos millas (de distancia); **it landed not 50 metres ~** cayó a menos de 50 metros; **it's some way ~** está algo lejos; **noises ~** (*gen*) ruidos *mpl* de fondo; (*Theat*) efectos *mpl* sonoros; **a voice ~** una voz de fondo; (*Cine*) una voz en off
[2] [***in time***] **the game is 3 days ~** faltan 3 días para el partido
[3] [***= removed***] **the lid is ~** la tapa está quitada; **there are two buttons ~** faltan dos botones; **he had his coat ~** no llevaba el abrigo puesto; **with his shoes ~** descalzo, sin zapatos; **with his hat ~** con el sombrero quitado; **hats ~!** ¡descúbranse!; **hands ~!** ¡fuera las manos!, ¡sin tocar!; **~ with those wet socks!** ¡quítate esos calcetines mojados!; **~ with his head!** ¡que le corten la cabeza!
[4] [***= departing***] **to be ~** irse, marcharse; **it's time I was ~** es hora de irme, es hora de marcharme; **I must be ~** tengo que irme, tengo que marcharme; **I'm ~** me voy, me marcho; **I'm ~ to Paris** me voy a París, me marcho a París, salgo para París; **where are you ~ to?** ¿a dónde te vas?; **she's ~ at 4** sale del trabajo a las 4; **be ~!** ¡fuera de aquí!, ¡lárgate!; **they're ~!** (*race*) ¡ya salen!; **he's ~ fishing** ha ido a pescar; **~ with you!** (= *go away*) ¡fuera de aquí!, ¡lárgate!; (*affectionately*) ¡vete ya!; **~ we go!** ¡vamos!; **he's ~ on his favourite subject again** está otra vez dale que dale con su tema favorito*
[5] [***= not at work***] **to be ~** (= *away*) estar fuera, no estar; **Ana is ~ sick today** (= *indisposed*) Ana no ha venido a trabajar hoy porque está enferma; (= *with doctor's note*) Ana está de baja hoy; **she's ~ on Tuesdays** los martes no viene (a trabajar); **are you ~ this weekend?** ¿vas a estar fuera este fin de semana?; **to have** *or* **take a day ~** tomarse un día de descanso; **I've got this afternoon ~** tengo esta tarde libre; **he gets two days ~ each week** tiene dos días libres a la semana
[6] [***Elec, Mech, etc***] **to be ~** [*apparatus, radio, TV, light*] estar apagado; [*tap*] estar cerrado; [*water etc*] estar cortado; [*brake*] no estar puesto, estar quitado; [*machinery*] estar parado
[7] [***Comm***] **"10% off"** "descuento del 10 por ciento"; **I'll give you 5% ~** te hago el 5 por ciento de descuento, te hago un descuento del 5 por ciento
[8] [***in phrases***] **~ and on** de vez en cuando, a ratos; **right ~** ◊ **straight ~** inmediatamente, enseguida; **3 days straight ~** 3 días seguidos
Ⓑ ADJECTIVE
[1] [***Brit = bad***] **to be ~** [*fish, yoghurt, meat*] estar malo *or* pasado; [*milk*] estar cortado
[2] [***= cancelled***] **the game is ~** se ha cancelado el partido; **the talks are ~** se han cancelado las conversaciones; **sorry, but the party's ~** lo siento, pero no hay fiesta; **their engagement is ~** han roto el noviazgo; **salmon is ~** (*on menu*) ya no hay salmón, se acabó el salmón
[3] [**** = not right***] **the timing is a bit ~** resulta un poco inoportuno; **it's a bit ~, isn't it?** (*fig*) eso no está muy bien ¿no?; **it was a bit ~, him leaving like that** no estuvo muy bien de su parte marcharse así; **I thought his behaviour was rather ~** me pareció que su forma de comportarse fue una salida de tono *or* estuvo fuera de lugar; **she's feeling rather ~** se siente bastante mal
[4] [***for money, supplies, time***] **how are you ~ for money?** ¿qué tal andas de dinero?; **how are you ~ for bread?** ¿qué tal andas de pan?; **how are we ~ for time?** ¿qué tal vamos de tiempo?; *see also* **badly 6**, **better B**, **well-off**
[5] [***Sport***] = **offside A**
[6] [***Elec, Mech etc***] **in the ~ position** en posición de apagado
Ⓒ PREPOSITION
[1] [***= from***] de; **to fall ~ a table** caer de una mesa; **to fall ~ a cliff** caer por un precipicio; **to eat ~ a dish** comer en un plato; **to dine ~ fish** cenar pescado
[2] [***= near***] **a street ~ the square** una calle que sale de la plaza; **a flat just ~ the high street** un piso junto a la calle mayor
[3] [***= away from***] **a house ~ the main road** una casa algo apartada de la carretera; **height ~ the ground** altura del suelo, altura sobre el suelo; **he ran towards the car and was 5 yards ~ it when …** corrió hacia el coche y estaba a cinco metros de él cuando …
[4] [***Naut***] **~ Portland Bill** a la altura de Portland Bill, frente a Portland Bill
[5] [***= missing from***] **there are two buttons ~ my coat** a mi chaqueta le faltan dos botones; **the lid was ~ the tin** la lata tenía la tapa

quitada

[6] [= *absent from*] **he was ~ work for 3 weeks** estuvo sin poder ir a trabajar tres semanas; **to take 3 days ~ work** tomarse 3 días libres

[7] [*Comm*] **to take 5% ~ the price** rebajar el precio en un cinco por ciento

[8] [= *not taking*] **he's been ~ drugs for a year** hace un año que no prueba las drogas, dejó las drogas hace un año; **I'm ~ coffee** (= *not taking*) he dejado de tomar café; (= *disliking*) tengo aborrecido el café, no puedo ver el café; **to be ~ one's food** no tener apetito

(D) NOUN

[* = *start*] comienzo *m*; (*Sport*) salida *f*; **at the ~** en la salida; **ready for the ~** listos para comenzar; (*Sport*) listos para salir

(E) INTRANSITIVE VERB

[*esp US*‡ = *leave*] largarse*

(F) TRANSITIVE VERB

[*US*‡ = *kill*] cargarse‡, ventilarse‡

(G) COMPOUNDS

► **off day** N **to have an ~ day** tener un día malo ► **off season** N temporada *f* baja; **in the ~ season** fuera de temporada

offal ['ɒfəl] N asaduras *fpl*, menudillos *mpl*

off-beam* [ˌɒf'biːm] ADJ [*statement, person*] desacertado

offbeat ['ɒfˌbiːt] ADJ excéntrico, original

Off-Broadway [ˌɒf'brɔːdweɪ] ADJ *que no pertenece a las superproducciones de Broadway*

OFF-BROADWAY

Off-Broadway *es el término que se utiliza en la jerga del teatro para referirse a las producciones teatrales de Nueva York que no se representan en los famosos escenarios de Broadway. La primera vez que se utilizó esta expresión fue en los años cincuenta, al hablar de obras de bajo presupuesto pero con gran originalidad de dramaturgos como Tennessee Williams o Edward Albee. Estas producciones - tanto las amateur como las más profesionales - suelen representarse en teatros con poco aforo y las entradas suelen ser bastante asequibles. También existe el término* **off-off Broadway**, *para referirse a los teatros que presentan obras aún más vanguardistas.*

off-campus [ˌɒf'kæmpəs] (*Univ*) ADJ, ADV fuera del campus

off-centre, off-center (*US*) [ˌɒf'sentəʳ] ADJ descentrado

off-chance ['ɒftʃɑːns] N **(let's go) on the ~** (vamos) por si acaso; **he bought it on the ~ that it would come in useful** lo compró pensando que tal vez resultaría útil

off-colour, off-color (*US*) [ˌɒf'kʌləʳ] ADJ [1] (*Brit*) (= *ill*) indispuesto, pachucho (*Sp**); **to feel/be ~** sentirse/estar indispuesto

[2] [*joke, remark*] subido de tono

offcut ['ɒfkʌt] N [1] trozo *m*

[2] **offcuts** restos *mpl*, sobras *fpl*

offence, offense (*US*) [ə'fens] N [1] (= *crime*) delito *m*; (*moral*) pecado *m*, falta *f*; (*Sport*) falta *f*; **first ~** primer delito; **second ~** reincidencia *f*; **to commit an ~** cometer un delito; **it is an ~ to ...** está prohibido ..., se prohíbe ...

[2] (= *insult*) ofensa *f*, agravio *m*; **no ~!** ◊ **no ~ meant** sin ánimo de ofender; **no ~ was intended** ◊ **he intended no ~** no tenía intención de ofender a nadie; **it is an ~ to the eye** hace daño a la vista; **to give** *or* **cause ~ (to sb)** ofender (a algn); **to take ~ (at sth)** ofenderse *or* sentirse ofendido (por algo)

▼ **offend** [ə'fend] (A) VT ofender; **to be ~ed** ofenderse; **he is easily ~ed** se ofende fácilmente; **don't be ~ed** no te vayas a ofender; **to be ~ed at or by sth** ofenderse por algo; **to become ~ed** ofenderse; **it ~s my ears/eyes** me hace daño al oído/a la vista; **to feel ~ed** sentirse ofendido; **to look ~ed** poner cara de ofendido; **to ~ reason** ir en contra de la razón; **it ~s my sense of justice** atenta contra mi sentido de la justicia

(B) VI [1] (= *cause offence*) ofender; **scenes that may ~** escenas que pueden ofender; **to ~ against** [+ *good taste*] atentar contra; [+ *law*] infringir; **to ~ against God** pecar contra Dios

[2] (*criminally*) (= *commit an offence*) cometer una infracción; (= *commit offences*) cometer infracciones; **girls are less likely to ~ than boys** las chicas son menos propensas a cometer infracciones que los chicos; **to ~ again** reincidir

offender [ə'fendəʳ] N [1] (= *lawbreaker*) delincuente *mf*; (*against traffic regulations etc*) infractor(a) *m/f*; **first ~** delincuente *mf* sin antecedentes penales

[2] (*moral*) transgresor(a) *m/f*, pecador(a) *m/f*; **regarding air pollution, industry is the worst ~** en lo que se refiere a la contaminación atmosférica, la industria es la mayor culpable

[3] (= *insulter*) ofensor(a) *m/f*

offending [ə'fendɪŋ] (A) ADJ (*esp hum*) **the dentist proceeded to fill the ~ tooth** el dentista procedió a empastar el diente culpable; **the book was withdrawn for the ~ passages to be deleted** el libro fue retirado para eliminar los pasajes responsables de la controversia; **he put the ~ object out of sight** guardó el objeto causante del conflicto; **he put the ~ jacket back in the wardrobe** puso de nuevo en el armario la chaqueta que según parecía era un atentado contra el buen gusto

(B) CPD ► **offending behaviour** N [*of criminal, delinquent*] conducta *f* delictiva

offense [ə'fens] N (*US*) = **offence**

offensive [ə'fensɪv] (A) ADJ [1] (= *causing offence, unpleasant*) [*behaviour, book, joke*] ofensivo; [*remark, language*] ofensivo, insultante; [*smell*] muy desagradable; **to find sth/sb ~** encontrar algo/a algn ofensivo; **he doesn't mean to be ~** no pretende ofender; **to be ~ to sb** ofender a algn

[2] (*Mil*) [*operation, action, capability*] ofensivo

[3] (*Sport*) [*player, play*] de ataque

(B) N (*Comm, Mil, Sport*) ofensiva *f*; **an advertising ~** una ofensiva publicitaria; **to be on the ~** estar a la ofensiva; **to go on the ~** pasar a la ofensiva, pasar al ataque; **to launch an ~** lanzar una ofensiva; **a sales ~** una ofensiva de ventas; **to take the ~** tomar la ofensiva

(C) CPD ► **offensive weapon** N (*Jur*) arma *f* ofensiva; (*Mil*) arma *f* de ataque

offensively [ə'fensɪvlɪ] ADV [1] (= *abusively*) [*behave, shout*] de manera ofensiva, de modo ofensivo; **~ rude/sexist** de un grosero/sexista que ofende

[2] (= *unpleasantly*) **to smell ~** tener un olor muy desagradable; **the music had become ~ loud** la música estaba ya tan alta que molestaba

[3] (*Mil*) **to use/deploy sth ~** usar/hacer uso de algo para atacar; **~, they are superior to us** desde el punto de vista ofensivo, son superiores a nosotros

[4] (*Sport*) **they played ~ in the first half** en la primera mitad realizaron un juego de ataque; **to be good/poor ~** ser bueno/malo en el ataque

▼ **offer** ['ɒfəʳ] (A) N (*gen, Comm*) oferta *f*; **"offers over £25"** "ofertas a partir de 25 libras"; **"£50 or nearest offer"** "50 libras, negociable"; **he has had a good ~ for the house** le han hecho una buena oferta por la casa; **introductory ~** oferta *f* de lanzamiento; **to make (sb) an ~ (for sth)** hacer una oferta (a algn) (por algo); **they made me an ~ I couldn't refuse** me hicieron una oferta que no pude rechazar; **~s of help are flooding in** están lloviendo las ofertas de ayuda; **I accepted his ~ of a lift** acepté cuando se ofreció a llevarme en coche; **~ of marriage** propuesta *f* de matrimonio; **to be on ~** (*Comm*) estar de oferta; **"on offer this week"** "de oferta esta semana"; **it's the only entertainment on ~ in this town** es la única atracción en esta ciudad; **there are so many courses on ~** existe tal oferta de cursillos; **~ of peace** ◊ **peace ~** ofrecimiento *m* de paz; **I might take you up on that ~** puede que acepte tu oferta; **the house is under ~** tenemos una oferta para la casa pendiente de formalizar el contrato; *see also* **job C**, **open A8**, **share**, **special[1] D**

(B) VT [1] (= *invite to*) **can I ~ you sth to drink?** ¿quieres tomar algo?; **"can I get you a drink?" she ~ed** —¿te sirvo algo? —preguntó ofreciéndose

[2] (= *make available*) [+ *help, services, money*] ofrecer; [+ *information, advice*] dar, ofrecer; **to have a lot to ~** tener mucho que ofrecer; **to ~ sb sth** ◊ **~ sth to sb** ofrecer algo a algn; **the island has little to ~ the tourist** la isla no tiene mucho que ofrecer al turista; **I ~ed her a fair price for the land** le ofrecí un buen precio por el terreno; **to ~ to do sth** ofrecerse a hacer algo; **I ~ed to pay for her** me ofrecí a pagar lo suyo; **one of the group ~ed himself as spokesman** uno del grupo se prestó *or* se ofreció a ser el portavoz; **to ~ one's hand** (*to shake*) tender la mano

[3] (= *express, make*) [+ *opinion*] expresar; [+ *comment, remark, suggestion*] hacer; **if I may ~ a suggestion ...** si me permite hacer una sugerencia ...; **to ~ an apology** ofrecer disculpas, disculparse; **he ~ed no explanation** no dio ninguna explicación; **the President has ~ed his sympathy to relatives** el presidente ha expresado sus condolencias a los familiares

[4] (= *afford*) [+ *opportunity, prospect, solution*] ofrecer; **the country ~s a wealth of opportunities for investment** el país ofrece *or* brinda muchas oportunidades de inversión; **the hotel ~s magnificent views over the lake** el hotel tiene unas magníficas vistas al lago; **it seemed to ~ a solution to our problem** parecía ofrecer *or* brindar una solución a nuestro problema

[5] (= *show*) **he ~ed no resistance** no opuso resistencia

[6] (*Rel*) (*also* **~ up**) [+ *sacrifice*] ofrecer; **to ~ (up) a prayer for sb** rezar una oración por algn; **to ~ (up) a prayer to Saint Anthony** ofrecer *or* rezar una oración a San Antonio; **she ~ed (up) a silent prayer of thanks** rezó en silencio dando gracias

(C) VI [1] (= *volunteer*) ofrecerse; **I could have done with some help but no one ~ed** me hubiera venido bien algo de ayuda pero nadie se ofreció

[2] (= *become available*) presentarse; **she promised to do it when opportunity ~ed**

➤ LANGUAGE IN USE: **offend A** 18.4 **offer B2** 3

prometió hacerlo cuando se presentara la oportunidad
Ⓓ CPD ► **offer price** N (*St Ex*) precio *m* de oferta

offering [ˈɒfərɪŋ] N [1] (*gen*) ofrenda *f*; (= *gift*) regalo *m*
[2] (*Rel*) exvoto *m*; (= *sacrifice*) sacrificio *m*

offertory [ˈɒfətərɪ] Ⓐ N (*Rel*) (= *part of service*) ofertorio *m*; (= *collection*) colecta *f*
Ⓑ CPD ► **offertory box** N cepillo *m*

offhand [ɒfˈhænd] Ⓐ ADJ [1] (= *casual*) **he was very ~ about his achievements** no daba importancia a sus logros; **"it was nothing," he said in an ~ manner** —no fue nada —dijo como quitándole importancia; **"it could have been worse," said Hamish, in an ~ tone** —podría haber sido peor —dijo Hamish en tono despreocupado; **his attitude to work/punctuality is very ~** se toma el trabajo/la puntualidad muy a la ligera
[2] (= *cavalier*) displicente; **the next day he was very ~ with her** al día siguiente estuvo muy displicente con ella; **to treat sb in an ~ manner** tratar a algn con displicencia
Ⓑ ADV (= *without some thought*) sin pensarlo; **I can't tell you ~** no te lo puedo decir así de pronto *or* sin pensarlo un poco *or* (*LAm*) así nomás; **~, I'd say that there were around 40** así, a ojo, diría que eran unos cuarenta; **do you know ~ where the copies are kept?** ¿sabes por casualidad dónde se guardan las copias?; **do you know her phone number ~?** ¿te sabes de memoria su número de teléfono?

offhanded [ɒfˈhændɪd] ADJ = **offhand A**

offhandedly [ɒfˈhændɪdlɪ] ADV [1] (= *casually*) a la ligera; **he dealt with the whole matter very ~** trató todo el asunto muy a la ligera; **"we were just playing," I said as ~ as I could** —sólo estábamos jugando —dije en el tono más despreocupado que pude
[2] (= *cavalierly*) [*reply, behave*] displicentemente; **to treat sb ~** tratar a algn con displicencia

offhandedness [ɒfˈhændɪdnɪs] N [1] (= *casualness*) **the ~ with which he handled the matter** la forma tan a la ligera en la que trató el asunto
[2] (= *cavalier manner*) displicencia *f*

office [ˈɒfɪs] Ⓐ N [1] (= *place*) oficina *f*; (= *room*) despacho *m*; [*of lawyer*] bufete *m*; (*US*) [*of doctor*] consultorio *m*
[2] (= *part of organization*) sección *f*, departamento *m*; (= *ministry*) ministerio *m*; (= *branch*) sucursal *f*; *see also* **foreign B**, **head D**
[3] (= *public position*) cargo *m*; (= *duty, function*) función *f*; **it is my ~ to** + *infin* tengo el deber de + *infin*, me incumbe + *infin*; **to perform the ~ of sb** hacer las veces de algn; **to be in/hold ~** [*person*] desempeñar *or* ocupar un cargo; [*political party*] ocupar el poder; **to be out of ~** no estar en el poder; **to come into** *or* **take ~** [*person*] tomar posesión del cargo (**as** de); [*political party*] acceder al poder; **to leave ~** [*person*] dejar el cargo; [*government*] salir del poder; *see also* **remove A6**
[4] **offices** (*frm*) **through his good ~s** mediante sus buenos oficios; **through the ~s of** por mediación *or* medio de
[5] (*Rel*) oficio *m*; **Office for the Dead** oficio de difuntos
Ⓑ CPD de oficina ► **office automation** N ofimática *f*, buromática *f* ► **office bearer** N titular *mf* (de una cartera) ► **office block** N (*Brit*) bloque *m* de oficinas ► **office boy** N recadero *m*, mandadero *m* (*LAm*) ► **office building** N = **office block** ► **office equipment** N mobiliario *m* de oficina ► **office furniture** N mobiliario *m* de oficina ► **office holder** N funcionario/a *m/f* ► **office hours** NPL (*Brit*) horas *fpl* de oficina; (*US*) horas *fpl* de consulta ► **office job** N trabajo *m* de oficina ► **office manager** N gerente *mf* ► **Office of Fair Trading** N (*Brit*) *departamento encargado de mantener las normas comerciales establecidos* ► **office party** N fiesta *f* de la oficina ► **office staff** N personal *m* de oficina ► **office supplies** NPL material *m* de oficina ► **office worker** N (*gen*) oficinista *mf*; (= *civil servant etc*) funcionario/a *m/f*

officer [ˈɒfɪsəʳ] Ⓐ N [1] (*Mil, Naut, Aer*) oficial *mf*; **an ~ and a gentleman** un oficial y un caballero
[2] (= *official*) funcionario/a *m/f*; [*of company*] directivo(a) *m/f*; **the ~s of a company** los directivos *or* la junta directiva de una empresa
[3] (= *police officer*) policía *mf*, agente *mf* de policía; **excuse me, ~** perdone agente
Ⓑ VT (= *command*) mandar; [+ *staff*] proveer de oficiales; **to be well ~ed** tener buena oficialidad
Ⓒ CPD ► **officer of the day** N (*Mil*) oficial *mf* del día ► **officer of the watch** N (*Naut*) oficial *mf* de guardia ► **officers' mess** N comedor *m* de oficiales

official [əˈfɪʃəl] Ⓐ ADJ oficial; **is that ~?** ¿es oficial?, ¿se ha confirmado eso oficialmente?; **it's ~: working mothers are stressed** está confirmado: las madres que trabajan están estresadas; **the phone was answered by an ~ sounding voice** una voz con un tono oficioso contestó el teléfono; **~ channels** conductos *mpl or* vías *fpl* oficiales; **to do sth through (the) ~ channels** hacer algo por los conductos *or* vías oficiales; **"for official use only"** "sólo para uso oficial"
Ⓑ N (*in civil service*) funcionario/a *m/f*; (*elsewhere*) oficial *mf*; **government ~** funcionario/a *m/f* del estado; **trade union ~** representante *mf* sindical
Ⓒ CPD ► **official receiver** N síndico *m* ► **Official Secrets Act** N (*Brit*) *ley relativa a los secretos de Estado* ► **official strike** N huelga *f* oficial

officialdom [əˈfɪʃəldəm] N (*pej*) burocracia *f*

officialese [əˌfɪʃəˈliːz] N (*pej*) jerga *f* burocrática

officially [əˈfɪʃəlɪ] ADV oficialmente

officiate [əˈfɪʃɪeɪt] VI oficiar; **to ~ as Mayor** ejercer las funciones de alcalde; **to ~ at a marriage** oficiar un enlace *or* una boda

officious [əˈfɪʃəs] ADJ oficioso

officiously [əˈfɪʃəslɪ] ADV oficiosamente

officiousness [əˈfɪʃəsnɪs] N oficiosidad *f*

offing [ˈɒfɪŋ] N **to be in the ~** (*Naut*) haber a la vista; (*fig*) haber en perspectiva

off-key [ɒfˈkiː] Ⓐ ADJ desafinado
Ⓑ ADV desentonadamente, fuera de tono

off-licence [ˈɒfˌlaɪsəns] N (*Brit*) (= *shop*) bodega *f*, tienda *f* de licores (*LAm*)

off-limits [ɒfˈlɪmɪts] ADJ [1] (*US Mil*) prohibido, de acceso prohibido
[2] (*fig*) [*activity, substance*] prohibido

off-line [ɒfˈlaɪn] Ⓐ ADJ (*Comput*) off-line, fuera de línea; (= *switched off*) desconectado
Ⓑ ADV fuera de línea, off-line

offload [ˈɒfləʊd] VT [1] [+ *goods*] descargar; [+ *passengers*] desembarcar, hacer bajar
[2] (= *get rid of*) librarse de

off-message [ˈɒfˌmesɪdʒ] ADJ descentrado en cuanto al mensaje; **to be ~** no centrarse en el mensaje adecuado, transmitir el mensaje erróneo

off-peak [ɒfˈpiːk] Ⓐ ADJ (*gen*) fuera de las horas punta (*Sp*), fuera de las horas pico (*LAm*); [*tickets*] de menor demanda; [*holiday*] de temporada baja; [*times*] de tarifa reducida, valle *inv*; [*rate*] reducido, valle *inv*
Ⓑ ADV (*gen*) fuera de las horas punta, en horario de tarifa reducida; [*travel, have holiday*] en temporada baja; [*telephone, consume electricity*] en horas de menor consumo, en horario de tarifa reducida

off-piste [ɒfˈpiːst] ADJ, ADV fuera de pista

offprint [ˈɒfprɪnt] N separata *f*, tirada *f* aparte

off-putting [ˈɒfˌpʊtɪŋ] ADJ (= *dispiriting*) desalentador; (= *unpleasant*) [*taste, smell etc*] desagradable; [*behaviour*] desagradable, chocante; (= *unfriendly*) [*person*] difícil, poco amable; [*reception*] nada amistoso; **it's very ~ to see him do that** es muy desagradable verlo hacer eso

off-road [ˈɒfrəʊd] Ⓐ ADJ [*driving, racing*] todoterreno
Ⓑ CPD ► **off-road vehicle** N vehículo *m* todoterreno

off-roader* [ˈɒfrəʊdəʳ] N todoterreno *m*

off-screen [ˈɒfskriːn] (*Cine, TV*) Ⓐ ADJ real, en la vida privada
Ⓑ ADV fuera de la pantalla, en la vida privada

off-season [ˈɒfˌsiːzn] Ⓐ N temporada *f* baja; **I take my holidays (in the) ~** me voy de vacaciones en temporada baja
Ⓑ ADJ [*rates, prices*] de temporada baja
Ⓒ ADV [*travel, have holiday*] en temporada baja

offset [ˈɒfset] (*vb: pt, pp* **offset**) Ⓐ N [1] (= *counterbalancing factor*) compensación *f*
[2] (*Typ*) offset *m*
[3] (*Hort*) (= *layer*) acodo *m*; (= *bulb*) bulbo *m* reproductor
[4] (*Archit*) retallo *m*
Ⓑ VT [1] (= *compensate for*) compensar; **higher prices will be ~ by wage increases** los aumentos de precios serán compensados por incrementos salariales
[2] (= *counteract*) contrarrestar, contrapesar; **to ~ A against B** contrapesar A y B
Ⓒ CPD ► **offset lithography** N = **offset printing** ► **offset press** N prensa *f* offset ► **offset printing** N impresión *f* con offset

offshoot [ˈɒfʃuːt] N (*Bot*) vástago *m*; (*Comm*) rama *f*; (*fig*) ramificación *f*

offshore [ˌɒfˈʃɔːʳ] Ⓐ ADJ [1] (= *near the shore*) [*island*] cercano a la costa, del litoral; [*waters*] de la costa, del litoral; **~ fishing** pesca *f* de bajura
[2] (= *out at sea*) [*rig, platform, drilling*] offshore *adj inv*, costa afuera; [*well*] submarino; **~ oil** petróleo *m* de costa afuera; **~ oilfield** campo *m* petrolífero submarino
[3] (= *from land*) [*breeze*] que sopla de la tierra, terral
[4] (*Fin*) [*account, fund*] en un paraíso fiscal/en paraísos fiscales, offshore *inv* (*Tech*); **he has an ~ account** tiene una cuenta en un paraíso fiscal, tiene una cuenta offshore (*Tech*); **people with ~ accounts** la gente con cuentas en paraísos fiscales, la gente con cuentas offshore (*Tech*); **~ banking** operaciones *fpl* bancarias en paraísos fiscales; **~ investments** inversiones *fpl* en paraísos fiscales
Ⓑ ADV [1] (= *near the coast*) [*lie, anchor, fish*] cerca de la costa; **they were just ~** estaban en las inmediaciones de la costa
[2] (= *out at sea*) [*drill*] off-shore, costa afuera
[3] (= *away from the shore*) **the current carried him ~** la corriente lo alejaba de la costa *or* hacia el interior del mar; **they were rescued 20 miles ~** los rescataron a 20 millas de la costa

4 (*Fin*) [*invest*] en un paraíso fiscal/en paraísos fiscales; **people who invest ~** la gente que invierte en paraísos fiscales

offside [ˌɒfˈsaɪd] Ⓐ ADJ 1 (*Sport*) [*player, goal*] en fuera de juego; **to be ~** estar fuera de juego, estar orsay *or* offside; **in an ~ position** fuera de juego; **the ~ rule** la regla de fuera de juego; **the ~ trap** la trampa de fuera de juego
2 (*Aut*) [*door, verge, lane*] (= *left-hand*) del lado izquierdo, del lado del conductor; (*Brit*) (= *right-hand*) del lado derecho, del lado del conductor
Ⓑ ADV (*Sport*) en fuera de juego; **Wallace was caught ~** cogieron a Wallace en fuera de juego
Ⓒ N 1 (*Ftbl*) fuera de juego *m*, orsay *m*, offside *m*
2 (*Aut*) (= *left-hand*) lado *m* izquierdo, lado del conductor; (*Brit*) (= *right-hand*) lado *m* derecho, lado *m* del conductor
Ⓓ EXCL ¡fuera de juego!, ¡orsay!, ¡offside!

offspring [ˈɒfsprɪŋ] N (*pl inv*) descendencia *f*, prole* *f*; **to die without ~** morir sin dejar descendencia

offstage [ˌɒfˈsteɪdʒ] Ⓐ ADJ de entre bastidores Ⓑ ADV entre bastidores, fuera del escenario

off-street parking [ˌɒfstriːtˈpɑːkɪŋ] N aparcamiento *m or* estacionamiento *m* fuera de la vía pública

off-the-cuff [ˌɒfðəˈkʌf] Ⓐ ADJ [*remark*] espontáneo, dicho sin pensar; [*speech*] improvisado Ⓑ ADV de improviso

off-the-job training [ˌɒfðədʒɒbˈtreɪnɪŋ] N formación *f* fuera del trabajo

off-the-peg (*Brit*) [ˌɒfðəˈpeg] (*US*), **off-the-rack** [ˈɒfðəˈræk] ADJ confeccionado, de percha

off-the-record [ˌɒfðəˈrekəd] ADJ no oficial, extraoficial

off-the-wall* [ˌɒfðəˈwɔːl] ADJ [*idea etc*] disparatado

off-white [ˌɒfˈwaɪt] ADJ de color hueso *adj inv*, blanquecino

Ofgas [ˈɒfgæs] N ABBR (*Brit*) (= **Office of Gas Supply**) *organismo que controla a las empresas del gas en Gran Bretaña*

Oflot [ˈɒflɒt] N ABBR (*Brit*) (= **Office of the National Lottery**) *organismo regulador de la lotería nacional en Gran Bretaña*, ≈ Organismo Nacional de Loterías y Apuestas del Estado, ≈ ONLAE *m* (*Sp*)

Ofsted [ˈɒfsted] N ABBR = **Office for Standards in Education** (*Brit*) *organismo regulador de los centros escolares*

OFT N ABBR (*Brit*) = **Office of Fair Trading**

oft [ɒft] ADV (*poet*) = **often**; **many a time and ~** repetidas veces

Oftel [ˈɒftel] N ABBR (*Brit*) (= **Office of Telecommunications**) *organismo que controla a las telecomunicaciones británicas*

▼ **often** [ˈɒfən] ADV a menudo, con frecuencia, seguido (*LAm*); **I've ~ wondered why you turned the job down** me he preguntado muchas veces *or* a menudo *or* con frecuencia por qué no aceptaste el trabajo; **it's not ~ that I ask you to help me** no es frecuente que te pida ayuda; **we ~ meet here** solemos reunirnos aquí; **do you ~ argue?** ¿discutís mucho?, ¿discutís muy a menudo?; **we visit her as ~ as possible** la visitamos tanto como nos es posible; **twice as ~ as** dos veces más que; **women consult doctors twice as ~ as men** las mujeres consultan a un médico dos veces más que los hombres; **as ~ as not** la mitad de las veces; **every so ~** (*of time*) de vez en cuando; (*of distance, spacing*) de trecho en trecho, cada cierta distancia; **we see each other every so ~** nos vemos de vez en cuando, nos vemos alguna que otra vez; **how ~?** (= *how many times*) ¿con qué frecuencia?; (= *at what intervals*) ¿cada cuánto?; **how ~ do you see him?** ¿cada cuánto lo ves?, ¿con qué *or* cuánta frecuencia lo ves?; **how ~ have I warned you that this would happen?** ¿cuántas veces te he advertido de que iba a pasar esto?; **how ~ she had asked herself that very question!** ¡cuántas veces se había hecho esa misma pregunta!; **he saw her less ~ now that she had a job** la veía con menos frecuencia ahora que tenía un trabajo; **more ~ than not** la mayoría de las veces, las más de las veces; **he's read it so ~ he knows it off by heart** lo ha leído tantas veces que se lo sabe de memoria; **(all) too ~** con demasiada frecuencia, demasiado a menudo, demasiadas veces; **you've been drunk on duty once too ~** ha estado borracho una y otra vez estando de servicio; **very ~** muchísimas veces, muy a menudo

oft-times [ˈɒftaɪmz] ADV (*liter*) a menudo

Ofwat [ˈɒfwɒt] (*Brit*) N ABBR (= **Office of Water Services**) *organismo que controla a las empresas suministradores de agua en Inglaterra y Gales*

ogival [əʊˈdʒaɪvəl] ADJ ojival

ogive [ˈəʊdʒaɪv] N ojiva *f*

ogle [ˈəʊgl] VT comerse con los ojos

O-grade [ˈəʊgreɪd] N ABBR (*Scot Scol*) (= **Ordinary grade**) ≈ BUP *m*

ogre [ˈəʊgəʳ] N ogro *m*

OH ABBR (*US*) = **Ohio**

oh [əʊ] EXCL 1 (*gen*) ¡ah!; **oh is he?** ¿en serio?; **oh dear, I've spilt the milk!** ¡ay, se me ha caído la leche!; **oh for a horse!** ¡quién tuviera un caballo!; **oh good!** ¡qué bien!; **oh no you don't!** ¡eso sí que no!, ¡de eso nada!; **oh really?** ¿no me digas?, ¿de veras?; **oh really!** ¡no puede ser!; **oh to be in Paris!** ¡ojalá estuviera en París!; **oh what a surprise!** ¡qué sorpresa!; **oh yes?** ¿ah sí?
2 (= *cry of pain*) ¡ay!
3 (*vocative*) **oh king!** ¡oh rey!

ohm [əʊm] N ohmio *m*, ohm *m*

OHMS ABBR (*Brit*) = **On Her** *or* **His Majesty's Service**

OHP N ABBR (= **overhead projector**) retroproyector *m*

oik* [ɔɪk] N (*Brit*) palurdo *m*, patán *m*

oil [ɔɪl] Ⓐ N 1 (*gen, also Aut*) aceite *m*; (= *holy oil*) crisma *f*, santo óleo *m*; **to check the ~** (*Aut etc*) revisar el nivel del aceite; ✦*IDIOMS* **to pour ~ on troubled waters** calmar los ánimos; **to pour ~ on the flames** echar más leña al fuego; *see also* **midnight**
2 (*Geol*) (*as mineral*) petróleo *m*; **to strike ~** encontrar petróleo; (*fig*) encontrar un filón
3 (*Art*) óleo *m*; **an ~ by Rembrandt** un óleo de Rembrandt; **to paint in ~s** pintar al óleo
Ⓑ VT lubricar, engrasar; ✦*IDIOMS* **to ~ the wheels** allanar el terreno; **to be well ~ed*** ir a la vela*
Ⓒ CPD ► **oil change** N (*Aut*) cambio *m* de aceite ► **oil colours** NPL (*Art*) óleos *mpl* ► **oil deposits** NPL (*Geol*) yacimientos *mpl* de petróleo ► **oil filter** N (*Aut*) filtro *m* de aceite ► **oil gauge** N (*Aut*) indicador *m* de(l) aceite ► **oil industry** N industria *f* del petróleo ► **oil lamp** N lámpara *f* de aceite, quinqué *m* ► **oil level** N nivel *m* del aceite ► **oil paint** N (*Art*) óleo *m*, pintura *f* al óleo ► **oil painting** N (*Art*) pintura *f* al óleo; **she's no ~ painting*** no es ninguna belleza ► **oil pipeline** N oleoducto *m* ► **oil platform** N plataforma *f* petrolífera ► **oil pollution** N contaminación *f* petrolífera ► **oil pressure** N (*Aut*) presión *f* del aceite ► **oil refinery** N refinería *f* de petróleo ► **oil rig** N torre *f* de perforación; (*Naut*) plataforma *f* de perforación submarina ► **oil slick** N (*large*) marea *f* negra; (*small*) mancha *f* de petróleo, capa *f* de petróleo (en el agua) ► **oil spill** N (= *act*) fuga *f* de petróleo; (= *substance*) = **oil slick** ► **oil stove** N (*for cooking*) cocina *f* de petróleo; (*for heating*) estufa *f* de petróleo ► **oil tanker** N petrolero *m* ► **oil terminal** N terminal *f* petrolífera ► **oil well** N pozo *m* de petróleo

OFTEN

In statements

- When **often** means "on many occasions", you can usually translate it using **con frecuencia** or **a menudo**:
  He often came to my house
  Venía con frecuencia *or* ***a menudo a mi casa***
  She doesn't often get angry
  No se enfada con frecuencia *or* ***a menudo***
  You are late too often
  Llegas tarde con demasiada frecuencia *or* ***demasiado a menudo***
- In informal contexts, particularly when **often** can be substituted by **a lot** or **much** with no change of meaning, **mucho** is an alternative translation:
  He doesn't often come to see me
  No viene mucho a verme
  He often hangs out in this bar
  Para mucho en este bar
- **Muchas veces** is another possible translation, but it should be used with the present only if the time, place or activity is restricted in some way:
  I've often heard him talk about the need for this law
  Le he oído muchas veces hablar de la necesidad de esta ley
  It can often be difficult to discuss this subject with one's partner
  Muchas veces es difícil hablar con la pareja sobre este tema
- When **often** describes a predictable, habitual or regular action, you can often translate it using the present or imperfect of **soler** as applicable:
  In England it is often cold in winter
  En Inglaterra suele hacer frío en invierno
  I often have a glass of sherry before dinner
  Suelo tomar un jerez antes de cenar
  We often went out for a walk in the evening
  Solíamos salir por la tarde a dar un paseo
- Use **soler** also when **often** means "in many cases":
  This heart condition is often very serious
  Esta enfermedad cardíaca suele ser muy grave

In questions

- You can usually use **con frecuencia** in questions, though there are other possibilities:
  How often do you go to Madrid?
  ¿Con qué frecuencia vas a Madrid?
  Do you often go to Spain?
  ¿Vas a España con frecuencia?, ¿Vas a menudo *or* ***mucho a España?***

For further uses and examples, see main entry.

oil-based [ˈɔɪlbeɪst] ADJ [*product*] derivado del petróleo

oil-burning [ˈɔɪlˌbɜːnɪŋ] ADJ (alimentado) al petróleo, de petróleo

oilcake [ˈɔɪlkeɪk] N torta *f* de borujo, torta *f* de linaza

➤ LANGUAGE IN USE: **often** 26.1

oilcan ['ɔɪlkæn] N aceitera *f*

oilcloth ['ɔɪlklɒθ] N hule *m*, encerado *m*

oildrum ['ɔɪldrʌm] N bidón *m* de aceite

oiler ['ɔɪləʳ] N 1 (= *ship*) petrolero *m*; (= *can*) lata *f* de aceite, lata *f* de lubricante; (= *person*) engrasador/a *m/f*
2 oilers (*US*) (= *clothes*) hule *m*

oilfield ['ɔɪlfiːld] N yacimiento *m* petrolífero

oil-fired ['ɔɪlfaɪəd] Ⓐ ADJ de fuel-oil
Ⓑ CPD ► oil-fired central heating N calefacción *f* central al petróleo ► oil-fired power-station N central *f* térmica de fuel

oiliness ['ɔɪlɪnɪs] N 1 (= *greasiness*) [*of food*] lo aceitoso, lo grasiento; [*of skin, hair*] lo grasiento, lo graso; [*of substance*] oleaginosidad *f*
2 (*pej*) [*of manners, tone*] zalamería *f*, lo empalagoso

oilman ['ɔɪlmæn] N (*pl* oilmen) (= *worker*) petrolero *m*; (= *magnate*) magnate *m* del petróleo

oilpan ['ɔɪlpæn] N (*US Aut*) cárter *m*

oilskin ['ɔɪlskɪn] N 1 (= *oilcloth*) hule *m*, encerado *m*
2 oilskins (*Brit*) (= *clothes*) chubasquero *m*, impermeable *m*

oily ['ɔɪlɪ] Ⓐ ADJ (*compar* oilier; *superl* oiliest)
1 (= *greasy*) [*food*] aceitoso, grasiento, grasoso (*LAm*); [*hands, rag*] grasiento, lleno de aceite; [*skin, hair*] graso, grasoso (*LAm*); [*road, beach*] lleno de aceite; [*substance, liquid*] oleaginoso
2 (= *smarmy*) [*person, voice*] zalamero, empalagoso
Ⓑ CPD ► oily fish N (*Culin*) pescado *m* azul

oink [ɔɪŋk] Ⓐ VI gruñir
Ⓑ EXCL ¡oink!

ointment ['ɔɪntmənt] N ungüento *m*, pomada *f*

OJT N ABBR (*US*) (= on-the-job training) aprendizaje *m* en el trabajo

OK[1]* ['əʊ'keɪ] Ⓐ EXCL (= *all right*) ¡está bien!, ¡okey! (*LAm*); (= *yes*) ¡sí!; (= *understood*) ¡comprendo!; (= *I agree*) ¡vale!; (= *enough*) ¡basta ya!, ¡ya estuvo bueno! (*LAm*); OK, OK! ¡vale, vale!, ¡ya, ya!; OK, the next item on the agenda is … bueno, el siguiente punto en el orden del día es …
Ⓑ ADJ 1 (= *undamaged, in good health*) bien; is the car OK? ¿anda bien el coche?
2 (= *agreed*) it's OK with *or* by me yo estoy de acuerdo, por mí vale; is it OK with you if ...? ¿te importa si ...?, ¿te molesta que ...?; OK it's difficult, but … estoy de acuerdo que es difícil pero …; I'm coming too, OK? vengo yo también, ¿vale *or* (*LAm*) okey?
3 (= *acceptable*) that may have been OK last year eso puede haber estado bien el año pasado
4 (= *well provided for*) are you OK for money/time? ¿andas *or* (*esp LAm*) vas bien de dinero/tiempo?; "do you want another drink?" — "I'm OK, thanks" —¿te apetece otro trago? —no quiero más, gracias
5 (= *likeable*) he's OK ◊ he's an OK guy es un buen tipo*, es un tío majo (*Sp**)
Ⓒ ADV he's doing OK las cosas le van bien
Ⓓ N visto *m* bueno; to give sth the OK dar el visto bueno a algo, aprobar algo
Ⓔ VT dar el visto bueno a, aprobar

OK[2] ABBR (*US*) = Oklahoma

okapi [əʊ'kɑːpɪ] N (*pl* okapis *or* okapi) okapi *m*

okay* [əʊ'keɪ] = OK[1]

okey-doke(y)‡ [ˌəʊkɪ'dəʊk(ɪ)] EXCL bueno, vale*

Okla ABBR (*US*) = Oklahoma

okra ['əʊkrə] N kimbombó *m*

old [əʊld] Ⓐ ADJ (*compar* older; *superl* oldest)
1 (= *not young*) [*person*] viejo; (*more respectful*) mayor, anciano; [*animal*] viejo; [*civilization*] antiguo; an ~ man un viejo, un anciano; an ~ woman una vieja, una anciana; he's a bit of an ~ woman es un poco Doña Remilgos; an ~ lady una señora mayor *or* anciana; a little ~ lady una viejecita, una ancianita; ~ people ◊ ~ folks* los viejos; (*more respectful*) los ancianos, las personas mayores; to live to be ~ llegar a una edad avanzada; if I live to be that ~ si llego a esa edad; to be ~ before one's time hacerse mayor antes de tiempo; to be ~ beyond one's years ser maduro para la edad que se tiene; he's ~ for his age *or* for his years [*child*] es muy maduro para su edad; that dress is too ~ for you ese vestido es para alguien mayor que tú, ese vestido no es apropiado para tu edad; to get *or* grow ~ envejecer; he's afraid of getting *or* growing ~ tiene miedo a envejecer; he's getting ~ se está haciendo viejo; to get ~er envejecer; as we get ~er … según envejecemos …; to look ~ parecer viejo, estar avejentado; she's not as ~ as she looks no es tan vieja como parece; ✦IDIOMS as ~ as Methuselah más viejo que Matusalén; he/she has an ~ head on young shoulders es maduro/a para su edad; *see also* dirty A4, fogey, fool A1, teach A2
2 (*relating to ages*) how ~ are you? ¿cuántos años tienes?, ¿qué edad tienes?; Laura is six weeks/months/years ~ Laura tiene seis semanas/meses/años; she's three years ~ today hoy cumple tres años; he'll be six weeks ~ tomorrow cumplirá seis semanas mañana; a six-week-~ baby un niño de seis semanas; a five-year-~ (child) un niño de cinco años; the building is 300 years ~ el edificio tiene 300 años; the company is a century ~ la compañía existe desde hace un siglo; at ten months ~ she was already walking cuando tenía diez meses ya andaba; she is two years ~er than you tiene dos años más que tú; you'll understand when you are ~er cuando seas mayor lo entenderás; when you are ~er it's harder to change jobs cuando eres mayor es más difícil cambiar de trabajo; their ~est child su hijo mayor; she is the ~est es la mayor; she is the ~est teacher in the school es la profesora de más edad del colegio; to be ~ enough for sth/to do sth tener edad para algo/para hacer algo; she's ~ enough to go alone ya tiene edad para ir sola; he's ~ enough to know better (*to have more sense*) a su edad debería tener más sentido común, ya es mayorcito para saber lo que está bien y lo que está mal; (*to behave better*) a su edad debería portarse mejor; she's ~ enough to be your mother con la edad que tiene, podría ser tu madre; you're as ~ as you feel eres tan viejo como te sientes; *see also* generation
3 (= *not new*) 3-1 (= *antique*) [*painting, book, building*] antiguo; [*wine*] añejo; the ~ part of Glasgow la parte vieja *or* antigua de Glasgow; ✦IDIOMS to be as ~ as the hills ◊ be as ~ as Adam ser de tiempos de Maricastaña, ser más viejo que el mundo; *see also* chip A1
3-2 [*clothes, furniture*] (= *tatty*) viejo; (= *worn*) usado, gastado; it's too ~ to be any use es demasiado viejo para servir de algo
4 (= *long-standing*) viejo; he's an ~ friend of mine es un viejo amigo mío; that's an ~ problem eso no es nada nuevo, eso ya viene de atrás; it's a very ~ tradition/custom es una vieja tradición/costumbre, es una tradición/costumbre antigua; the ~ ways survived in some country areas las viejas costumbres perduraron en algunas partes del campo; an ~ family una familia de abolengo; *see also* score A4
5 (= *former*) antiguo; my ~ flat was very small mi antiguo piso era muy pequeño; the ~ country la madre patria, la patria; in the ~ days antaño, en los viejos tiempos; the good ~ days los viejos tiempos; it's not as good as our ~ one no es tan bueno como el anterior; my ~ school mi antiguo *or* viejo colegio; of the ~ school (*fig*) de la vieja escuela; for ~ times' sake por los viejos tiempos
6 (*) (*expressing affection*) here's ~ Peter coming ahí viene el bueno de Peter; good ~ Mike! ¡este Mike!; come on, ~ man!† ¡venga hombre!; she's a funny ~ thing es rarita; my *or* the ~ lady *or* woman (= *mother*) mi *or* la vieja‡; (= *wife*) la parienta*; my *or* the ~ man (= *father*) mi *or* el viejo‡; (= *husband*) mi marido
7 (*) (*as intensifier*) what a load of ~ rubbish! ¡qué cantidad de chorradas!*; any ~: any ~ thing will do cualquier cosa sirve; it's not just any ~ painting, it's a Rembrandt no es un cuadro cualquiera, es un Rembrandt; just put it any ~ where ponlo en cualquier parte; he leaves his things any ~ how deja sus cosas de cualquier manera; I parked the car any ~ how aparqué el coche de cualquier manera; we had a high ~ time hacía tiempo que no nos divertíamos tanto; it's the same ~ story es la misma historia de siempre
Ⓑ N 1 the ~ los viejos *mpl*, los ancianos *mpl*; their music appeals to ~ and young alike su música gusta tanto a jóvenes como a viejos; the circus appeals to ~ and young alike el circo gusta igualmente a grandes y pequeños
2 (*liter*) of ~: to know sb of ~ conocer a algn desde hace tiempo; knights/legends of ~ los caballeros/las leyendas de antaño (*liter*); in days of ~ antaño (*liter*), en los tiempos antiguos
Ⓒ CPD ► old age N vejez *f*; in one's ~ age en la vejez; perhaps I'm going soft in my ~ age quizá me estoy ablandando al hacerme viejo *or* en la vejez; he is unable to travel much because of ~ age no puede viajar mucho debido a su edad; *see also* ripe ► old age pension N subsidio *m* de la tercera edad, pensión *f* ► old age pensioner N pensionista *mf*, jubilado/a *m/f* ► the Old Bailey N (*Brit*) *el tribunal de lo penal de más alto rango de Inglaterra* ► the Old Bill‡ N (*Brit*) la poli*, la pasma (*Sp‡*) ► old boy N (= *former pupil*) ex-alumno *m*, antiguo alumno *m*; (†*) (= *old chap*) amigo *m* mío; the ~-boy network (*esp pej*) el amiguismo ► the old brigade N los veteranos ► old campaigner N veterano *m* ► old chestnut* N (= *joke*) broma *f* muy pasada; (= *story*) historia *f* muy pasada ► Old Dominion N (*US*) *el estado de Virginia* ► Old English N inglés *m* antiguo; → ANGLO-SAXON ► Old English Sheepdog N perro *m* pastor ovejero inglés ► old flame N antiguo amor *m* ► old folks' home N residencia *f* de ancianos ► old girl N (= *former pupil*) ex-alumna *f*, antigua alumna *f*; (= *elderly woman*) (*†) señora *f*, abuelita* *f* ► Old Glory N (*US*) *bandera de los Estados Unidos* ► old gold N oro *m* viejo ► the old guard N la vieja guardia ► old hand N veterano/a *m/f*; he's an ~ hand at photography es un veterano de la fotografía ► old lag* N (= *old prisoner*) (preso/a *m/f*) veterano/a *m/f*; (= *ex-prisoner*) ex-presidiario/a *m/f* ► old maid N (*pej*) solterona *f*; she'll end up an ~ maid se quedará para vestir santos ► Old Man River N (*US*) *el río Mississippi* ► old master N (= *work*) obra *f* maestra de la

pintura clásica; (= *painter*) gran maestro *m* de la pintura clásica ► **old money** N dinero *m* de familia ► **Old Nick*** N (*hum*) Pedro Botero (* *hum*) ► **old people's home** N residencia *f* de ancianos ► **old salt** N (*Naut*) viejo lobo *m* de mar ► **old school tie** N (*Brit*) (*lit*) *corbata con los colores representativos de la escuela a la que alguien ha asistido*; **the ~ school tie** (*fig*) el amiguismo ► **old soldier** N veterano *m*, excombatiente *m* ► **the Old South** N (*US*) el viejo sur ► **old stager** N veterano/a *m/f* ► **Old Testament** N Antiguo Testamento *m* ► **old wives' tale** N cuento *m* de viejas, patraña *f* ► **the Old World** N el Viejo Mundo, el Viejo Continente; *see also* **old-world**

OLD

Position of "viejo" and "antiguo"

Viejo and **antiguo** can go either before or after the noun, depending on their meaning.

Viejo

- Put **viejo** *after* the noun when you are referring to age:

...boxes full of old clothes...
...cajas llenas de ropa vieja...
Old cars are the ones that pollute the environment most
Son los coches viejos los que más contaminan el medio ambiente

- Put **viejo** *before* the noun when you mean **old** in the sense of "long-standing" or "well-established":

They got in touch with an old friend
Se pusieron en contacto con un viejo amigo
Many of the old customs have changed with the passing of time
Muchas de las viejas costumbres han cambiado con el paso del tiempo

Antiguo

- Generally put **antiguo** *after* the noun to translate **ancient** or **old** in the sense of "ancient":

...one of Canada's most beautiful old houses...
...una de las más bellas casas antiguas de Canadá...
...the old part of the town...
...el barrio antiguo de la ciudad...

- Put **antiguo** *before* the noun to translate **former** or **old** in the sense of "former":

My old colleagues are no longer my friends
Mis antiguos compañeros ya no son mis amigos
...the former British colonies...
...las antiguas colonias británicas...

For further uses and examples, see main entry.

olden ['əʊldən] ADJ (†† *or poet*) antiguo; **in ~ times** *or* **days** antaño (*liter*), antiguamente

old-established ['əʊldɪ'stæblɪʃt] ADJ antiguo

olde-worlde ['əʊldɪ'wɜːldɪ] ADJ (*hum*) viejísimo, antiquísimo; **with ~ lettering** con letras al estilo antiguo; **a very ~ interior** un interior pintoresco de antaño; **Stratford is terribly ~** Stratford tiene sabor arcaico en exceso

old-fashioned ['əʊld'fæʃnd] ADJ [1] (= *outmoded*) [*thing*] anticuado, pasado de moda; [*person, attitude*] anticuado, chapado a la antigua; **good ~ honesty** la honestidad de toda la vida
[2] (*Brit*†) (= *disapproving*) **to give sb an ~ look** mirar a algn con extrañeza

oldie* ['əʊldɪ] N [1] (= *song*) melodía *f* del ayer; (= *joke*) chiste *m* anticuado
[2] (*Brit*) (= *old person*) vejete/a *m/f*

oldish ['əʊldɪʃ] ADJ algo viejo, más bien viejo, que va para viejo

old-looking ['əʊld,lʊkɪŋ] ADJ de aspecto viejo

old-maidish ['əʊld'meɪdɪʃ] ADJ (= *spinsterish*) de solterona; (= *fussy*) remilgado

oldster ['əʊldstəʳ] N (*US*) viejo/a *m/f*, anciano/a *m/f*

old-style ['əʊld'staɪl] ADJ antiguo, al estilo antiguo, a la antigua; **~ calendar** calendario *m* juliano

old-time ['əʊldtaɪm] Ⓐ ADJ de antaño
Ⓑ CPD ► **old-time dancing** N baile *m* antiguo, baile *m* de antaño

old-timer [,əʊld'taɪməʳ] N veterano/a *m/f*; (*US**) (= *old person*) viejo/a *m/f*, anciano/a *m/f*

old-world ['əʊld'wɜːld] ADJ [1] (= *traditional*) antiguo; [*style*] clásico; [*manners*] anticuado; **the ~ charm of Toledo** el sabor antiguo *or* arcaico de Toledo
[2] (*Geog*) del Viejo Mundo; *see also* **old C**

OLE N ABBR (*Comput*) = **object linking and embedding**

oleaginous [əʊlɪ'ædʒɪnəs] ADJ oleaginoso

oleander [,əʊlɪ'ændəʳ] N adelfa *f*

oleo... ['əʊlɪəʊ] PREFIX oleo...

O-level ['əʊ,levl] N (*Brit Scol*) (*formerly*) (= **Ordinary level**) ≈ BUP *m*

olfactory [ɒl'fæktərɪ] ADJ olfativo, olfatorio

oligarchic [,ɒlɪ'gɑːkɪk] ADJ oligárquico

oligarchical [,ɒlɪ'gɑːkɪkəl] ADJ = **oligarchic**

oligarchy ['ɒlɪgɑːkɪ] N oligarquía *f*

oligo... ['ɒlɪgəʊ] PREFIX oligo...

Oligocene ['ɒlɪgəʊsiːn] Ⓐ ADJ oligocénico
Ⓑ N **the ~** el Oligoceno

oligopoly [,ɒlɪ'gɒpəlɪ] N oligopolio *m*

oligopsony [,ɒlɪ'gɒpsənɪ] N oligopsonio *m*

olive ['ɒlɪv] Ⓐ N (= *fruit*) aceituna *f*, oliva *f*; (*also* **~ tree**) olivo *m*; **eating ~** aceituna *f* de mesa
Ⓑ ADJ (*also* **~-green**) [*complexion, skin, shirt, paint*] verde oliva *inv*
Ⓒ CPD ► **olive branch** N rama *f* de olivo; ✦***IDIOM*** **to hold out an ~ branch** hacer un gesto de paz ► **olive green** N verde *m* oliva ► **olive grove** N olivar *m* ► **olive grower** N oleicultor(a) *m/f* ► **olive growing** N oleicultura *f*; *see also* **olive-growing** ► **olive oil** N aceite *m* de oliva ► **olive tree** N olivo *m*

olive-green ['ɒlɪv'griːn] ADJ verde oliva; **~ uniforms** uniformes *mpl* verde oliva

olive-growing ['ɒlɪv,grəʊɪŋ] ADJ **~ region** región *f* olivera; *see also* **olive**

Oliver ['ɒlɪvəʳ] N Oliverio

Olympia [ə'lɪmpɪə] N Olimpia *f*

Olympiad [əʊ'lɪmpɪæd] N olimpíada *f*

Olympian [əʊ'lɪmpɪən] Ⓐ ADJ olímpico
Ⓑ N (*Sport*) olímpico/a *m/f*

Olympic [əʊ'lɪmpɪk] Ⓐ ADJ olímpico
Ⓑ N **the ~s** las Olimpiadas
Ⓒ CPD ► **the Olympic Games** NPL las Olimpiadas ► **Olympic medallist** N medallero/a *m/f* olímpico/a ► **Olympic torch** N antorcha *f* olímpica

Olympus [əʊ'lɪmpəs] N Olimpo *m*

OM N ABBR (*Brit*) (= **Order of Merit**) *título ceremonial*

Oman [əʊ'mɑːn] N Omán *m*

Omani [əʊ'mɑːnɪ] Ⓐ ADJ omaní
Ⓑ N omaní *mf*

OMB N ABBR (*US*) (= **Office of Management and Budget**) *servicio que asesora al presidente en materia presupuestaria*

ombudsman ['ɒmbʊdzmən] N (*pl* **ombudsmen**) ≈ defensor *m* del pueblo

OMBUDSMAN

Se conoce con el nombre de **ombudsman** *al funcionario encargado de investigar las quejas de los ciudadanos contra una institución determinada. En el Reino Unido, el* **ombudsman** *que se ocupa de los casos de administración fraudulenta en los ministerios del gobierno, el* **NHS** *y otros organismos institucionales es el* **Parliamentary Commissioner for Administration**. *Su jurisdicción se limita al área administrativa del gobierno, pero no afecta a su política o legislación. Otros* **ombudsmen** *se nombran para estudiar las quejas que provienen de los clientes de instituciones financieras, como por ejemplo el* **Banking ombudsman**, *el* **Building Societies ombudsman** *o el* **Insurance Ombudsman**. *En Estados Unidos, los* **ombudsmen** *llevan a cabo labores similares de investigación de instituciones, tanto en el sector público como en el privado.*

omega ['əʊmɪgə] N omega *f*

omelet(te) ['ɒmlɪt] N omellete *f*, tortilla *f* francesa, torta *f* de huevos (*Mex*); ✦***PROV*** **you can't make an ~ without breaking eggs** no se puede hacer tortillas sin romper huevos

omen ['əʊmen] N augurio *m*, presagio *m*; **it is a good ~ that ...** es un buen presagio que ...; **bird of ill ~** ave *f* de mal agüero

ominous ['ɒmɪnəs] ADJ [*development, event*] de mal agüero; [*silence*] que no augura nada bueno, que no presagia nada bueno; [*sound*] siniestro; [*cloud*] amenazador; [*tone*] (= *sinister*) amenazador; (= *worrying*) inquietante; **that's ~** eso es una mala señal; **it was an ~ sign** era una señal de mal agüero; **the silence was ~** el silencio no auguraba *or* no presagiaba nada bueno; **to look/sound ~** no augurar *or* presagiar nada bueno

ominously ['ɒmɪnəslɪ] ADV **"we have a problem," she said ~** —tenemos un problema —dijo en un tono que resultaba inquietante; **"I would not do that if I were you," he said ~** —yo que tú no haría eso —dijo con un tono inquietante *or* en tono amenazador; **the men marched ~ up the street** los hombres marchaban calle arriba de una forma que no presagiaba *or* auguraba nada bueno; **the thunder rumbled ~** los truenos retumbaban amenazadores; **Steve was ~ quiet** era inquietante lo tranquilo que estaba Steve; **the deadline was drawing ~ close** la fecha límite se acercaba amenazadora; **this sounded ~ like a declaration of war** esto guardaba un siniestro parecido con una declaración de guerra

omission [əʊ'mɪʃən] N (= *act of omitting*) omisión *f*; (= *mistake*) descuido *m*; **it was an ~ on my part** fue un descuido mío

omit [əʊ'mɪt] VT (*on purpose*) suprimir; (*by accident*) olvidarse de; [+ *person, person's name*] pasar por alto; **to ~ to do sth** (*on purpose*) omitir hacer algo, decidir no hacer algo; (*by accident*) olvidarse de hacer algo

omni... ['ɒmnɪ] PREFIX omni...

omnibus ['ɒmnɪbəs] Ⓐ N [1] (†) (= *bus*) ómnibus *m*, autobús *m*, camión *m* (*Mex*)
[2] (= *book*) antología *f*, tomo *m* de obras escogidas
Ⓑ ADJ general, para todo
Ⓒ CPD ► **omnibus edition** N (*Literat*) edición *f* antológica, edición *f* de obras escogi-

das; (*Brit TV, Rad*) programa *m* especial (*que incluye varios episodios*)

omnidirectional [ˌɒmnɪdɪˈrekʃənəl] ADJ omnidireccional

omnipotence [ɒmˈnɪpətəns] N omnipotencia *f*

omnipotent [ɒmˈnɪpətənt] ADJ omnipotente

omnipresence [ˈɒmnɪˈprezəns] N omnipresencia *f*

omnipresent [ˈɒmnɪˈprezənt] ADJ omnipresente

omniscience [ɒmˈnɪsɪəns] N omnisciencia *f*

omniscient [ɒmˈnɪsɪənt] ADJ omnisciente

omnivore [ˈɒmnɪvɔːʳ] N omnívoro/a *m/f*

omnivorous [ɒmˈnɪvərəs] ADJ omnívoro; **she is an ~ reader** es una lectora insaciable

ON ABBR (*Canada*) = **Ontario**

on [ɒn]

When ***on*** *is the second element in a phrasal verb, eg* ***have on, get on, go on,*** *look up the verb. When it is part of a set combination, such as* ***broadside on, further on,*** *look up the other word.*

Ⓐ PREP [1] (*indicating place, position*) en, sobre; **on the ceiling** sobre el techo; **on the Continent** en Europa; **with her hat on her head** con el sombrero puesto; **on page two** en la página dos; **on the right** a la derecha; **on the high seas** en alta mar; **on all sides** por todas partes, por todos lados; **a house on the square** una casa en la plaza; **on the table** en *or* sobre la mesa; **a meal on the train** una comida en el tren; **hanging on the wall** colgado en la pared

[2] (*indicating time*) **on Friday** el viernes; **on Fridays** los viernes; **on May 14th** el catorce de mayo; **on or about the 8th** el día 8 o por ahí; **on and after the 15th** el día 15 y a partir de la misma fecha; **on a day like this** (en) un día como éste; **on the next day** al día siguiente; **on some days it is** hay días cuando lo es; **on the evening of July 2nd** el 2 de julio por la tarde

[3] (= *at the time of*) **on seeing him** al verlo; **on my arrival** al llegar, a mi llegada; **on my calling to him** al llamarle yo

[4] (= *about, concerning*) sobre, acerca de; **a book on physics** un libro de *or* sobre física; **he lectured on Keats** dio una conferencia sobre Keats; **Eden on the events of 1956** lo que dice Eden acerca de los acontecimientos de 1956; **have you read Purnell on Churchill?** ¿has leído los comentarios de Purnell sobre Churchill?; **have you heard the boss on the new tax?** ¿has oído lo que dice el jefe acerca de la nueva contribución?; **while we're on the subject** como hablamos de esto

[5] (= *towards, against*) **the march on Rome** la marcha sobre Roma; **an attack on the government** un ataque contra el gobierno

[6] (= *earning, receiving*) **he's on £6,000 a year** gana seis mil libras al año; **a student on a grant** un estudiante con beca; **many live on less than that** muchos viven con menos

[7] (= *taking, consuming*) **I'm on a milk diet** sigo un régimen lácteo; **he's back on drugs** ha vuelto a drogarse; **he's on heroin** está enganchado a la heroína; **I'm on three pills a day** tomo tres píldoras al día; *see also* **live on A**

[8] (= *engaged in*) **I'm on a new project** trabajo sobre un nuevo proyecto; **we're on irregular verbs** estamos con los verbos irregulares; **he's away on business** está en viaje de negocios; **to be on holiday** estar de vacaciones; **the company is on tour** la compañía está en gira

[9] (*indicating membership*) **he's on the committee** es miembro del comité; **he's on the permanent staff** es de plantilla

[10] (= *playing*) **with Louis Armstrong on trumpet** con Louis Armstrong a la trompeta; **all the children play on the piano** todos los chicos saben tocar el piano; **he played it on the violin** lo tocó al violín

[11] (*TV, Rad*) **on the radio** en *or* por la radio; **on television** en *or* por (la) televisión; **there's a good film on TV tonight** esta noche dan una buena película en la tele; **on video** en vídeo

[12] (= *about one's person*) **I haven't any money on me** no llevo dinero encima

[13] (= *after, according to*) **on this model** según este modelo

[14] (= *compared to*) **prices are up on last year('s)** los precios han subido frente a los del año pasado

[15] (= *at the expense of*) **this round's on me** esta ronda la pago yo, invito yo; **the tour was on the Council** la gira la pagó el Consejo, corrió el Consejo con los gastos de la gira; ✦***IDIOM*** **it's on the house** la casa invita

[16] (*liter*) **woe on woe** dolor sobre dolor; **snow on snow** nieve y más nieve

[17] (*phrases*) **on account of** a causa de; **on good authority** de buena tinta; **on his authority** con su autorización; **on average** por término medio; **to swear on the Bible** prestar juramento sobre la Biblia; **on a charge of murder** acusado de homicidio; **on foot** a pie; **on horseback** a caballo; **on pain of** so pena de; **on sale** de venta; **on the telephone** por teléfono; **on time** a la hora, a tiempo; *see also* **base B2**

Ⓑ ADV [1] (= *in place*) [*lid etc*] puesto; **the lid is on** la tapa está puesta; **it's not on properly** no está bien puesto; *see also* **screw on**

[2] (*with clothes*) **to have one's boots on** llevar las botas puestas; **to have one's coat on** tener el abrigo puesto; **what's she got on?** ¿qué lleva puesto?, ¿cómo va vestida?; **she had not got much on** iba muy ligera de ropa

[3] (*indicating time*) **from that day on** a partir de aquel día, de aquel día en adelante; **on and off** de vez en cuando, a intervalos; **it was well on in the evening** estaba ya muy entrada la tarde; **well on in June** bien entrado junio; **they talked well on into the night** hablaron hasta bien entrada la noche; **well on in years** entrado en años, que va para viejo; *see also* **further A1**, **later A2**

[4] (*indicating continuation*) **to go/walk on** seguir adelante; **to read on** seguir leyendo; **he rambled on and on** estuvo dale que dale*, estuvo dale y dale (*esp LAm*); **and so on** (= *and the rest*) y demás; (= *etc*) etcétera; **on with the show!** ¡que empiece *or* continúe el espectáculo!; **on with the dancing girls!** ¡que salgan las bailarinas!

[5] (*in phrases*) **what are you on about?*** ¿de qué (me) hablas?; **he's always on at me about it*** me está majando continuamente con eso*; *see also* **go on**

Ⓒ ADJ [1] (= *functioning, in operation*) **to be on** [*engine*] estar encendido, estar en marcha; [*switch*] estar encendido *or* conectado; [*machine*] estar encendido *or* funcionando; [*light*] estar encendido, estar prendido (*LAm*); [*TV set etc*] estar encendido, estar puesto, estar prendido (*LAm*); [*tap*] estar abierto; [*brake etc*] estar puesto, estar echado; **in the on position** [*tap*] abierto, en posición de abierto; (*Elec*) encendido, puesto, prendido (*LAm*)

[2] (= *being performed, shown*) **the show is now on** ha comenzado el espectáculo; **the show is on in London** se ha estrenado el espectáculo en Londres; **the show was on for only two weeks** el show estuvo solamente 15 días en cartelera; **what's on at the cinema?** ¿qué ponen en el cine?; **what's on at the theatre?** ¿qué dan en el teatro?; **"what's on in London"** "cartelera de los espectáculos londinenses"; **the programme is on in a minute** el programa empieza dentro de un minuto; **there's a good film on tonight** hay una película buena esta noche

[3] (= *taking place*) **is the meeting still on tonight?** ¿sigue en pie la reunión de esta noche?, ¿se lleva a cabo siempre la reunión de esta noche? (*LAm*); **the deal is on** se ha cerrado el trato

[4] (= *arranged*) **have you got anything on this evening?** ¿tienes compromiso para esta noche?; **sorry, I've got something on tonight** lo siento, esta noche tengo un compromiso

[5] (= *performing, working*) **to be on** [*actor*] estar en escena; **you're on in five minutes** sales en cinco minutos; **are you on next?** ¿te toca a ti la próxima vez?; **are you on tomorrow?** (= *on duty*) ¿trabajas mañana?, ¿estás de turno mañana?; **to have one day on and the next off** trabajar un día y el otro no

[6] (*) (*indicating agreement, acceptance*) **you're on!** ¡te tomo la palabra!; **are you still on for dinner tomorrow night?** ¿sigo contando contigo para cenar mañana?; **that's not on** (*Brit*) eso no se hace, no hay derecho

Ⓓ EXCL ¡adelante!

onanism [ˈəʊnənɪzəm] N onanismo *m*

on-board [ˌɒnˈbɔːd] ADJ [*computer, entertainment*] de a bordo

ONC N ABBR (*Brit Scol*) (= **Ordinary National Certificate**) *título escolar*

on-campus [ˌɒnˈkæmpəs] (*Univ*) ADJ, ADV en el campus

once [wʌns] Ⓐ ADV [1] (= *on one occasion*) una vez; **you ~ said you'd never do that** una vez dijiste que nunca harías eso; **he walked away without looking back ~** se alejó caminando sin mirar atrás ni una sola vez; **~ a thief, always a thief** quien roba una vez roba veinte; **~ a smoker, always a smoker** el que es fumador no lo deja de ser nunca; **~ a week** una vez a la *or* por semana; **~ again** otra vez, una vez más; **~ and for all** de una vez (por todas); **we were here ~ before** ya estuvimos aquí una vez antes; **~ every two days** una vez cada dos días; **for ~** por una vez; **~ more** otra vez, una vez más; **more than ~** más de una vez; **it never ~ occurred to me** ni se me ocurrió; **~ only** sólo una vez, una sola vez; **~ or twice** un par de veces, una o dos veces; **(every) ~ in a while** de vez en cuando, de cuando en cuando, cada cuando (*LAm*); *see also* **blue A1**

[2] (= *formerly*) antes; **it had ~ been white** antes había sido blanco; **a ~ powerful nation** un país que antes *or* en su día había sido poderoso; **the ~ opulent city** la que en su día fuera una opulenta ciudad, la otrora opulenta ciudad (*frm*); **the ring ~ belonged to my father** el anillo había pertenecido en tiempos a mi padre; **~ when we were young** hace tiempo cuando éramos jóvenes; **Texas was ~ ruled by Mexico** Tejas estuvo en su tiempo gobernada por México; **I knew him ~** le conocí hace tiempo; **~ upon a time there was** (*as start of story*) érase una vez, había una vez; **~ upon a time they used to hang people for stealing sheep** (= *in the old days*) hubo un tiempo en que solían ahorcar a la gente que robaba ovejas

[3] **at ~** [3·1] (= *immediately*) inmediatamente;

(= *now*) ahora mismo; **remove from the heat and serve at ~** retirar del fuego y servir inmediatamente; **he read the letter at ~** leyó la carta inmediatamente *or* en seguida; **we'd better leave at ~** mejor que nos vayamos ahora mismo; **stop it at ~!** ¡deja de hacer eso ahora mismo *or* inmediatamente!

3·2 (= *simultaneously*) a la vez, al mismo tiempo; **everybody was talking at ~** todo el mundo hablaba a la vez *or* al mismo tiempo; **his style is at ~ original and stimulating** su estilo es al mismo tiempo original y estimulante; **all at ~** (= *suddenly*) de repente, de pronto; (= *simultaneously*) a la vez, al mismo tiempo; **all at ~ she felt afraid** de repente *or* de pronto le entró miedo; **a number of things then happened all at ~** una serie de cosas sucedieron a la vez *or* al mismo tiempo; **don't eat it all at ~** no te lo comas todo de un golpe; **you don't have to pay it all at ~** no tienes que pagar todo de un golpe

Ⓑ CONJ una vez que; **~ you give him the chance** una vez que le des la oportunidad, si le das la oportunidad; **~ they finish, we can start** una vez que *or* en cuanto ellos terminen podemos empezar nosotros; **~ the sun had set, the air turned cold** en cuanto se ocultó el sol, el aire se volvió frío; **~ inside her flat, she opened the letter** una vez dentro del piso, abrió la carta

Ⓒ N **I met her just the ~** sólo la he visto una vez; **just this ~** esta vez sólo, esta vez nada más

once-over* ['wʌns,əʊvəʳ] N (= *search etc*) **to give sth/sb the ~** echar un vistazo a algo/algn; **they gave the house the ~** registraron superficialmente la casa

oncologist [ɒŋ'kɒlədʒɪst] N oncólogo/a *m/f*

oncology [ɒŋ'kɒlədʒɪ] N oncología *f*

oncoming ['ɒn,kʌmɪŋ] ADJ 1 [*car, traffic*] que viene en el sentido opuesto

2 [*event*] que se aproxima, venidero

on-costs ['ɒn,kɒsts] NPL (*Brit Comm*) gastos *mpl* generales

OND N ABBR (*Brit Scol*) (= **Ordinary National Diploma**) *título escolar*

one [wʌn] Ⓐ ADJ 1 (= *number*) un/una; **~ man** un hombre; **~ man out of two** uno de cada dos hombres; **the baby is ~ (year old)** el bebé tiene un año; **it's ~ (o'clock)** es la una; **for ~ reason or another** por diferentes razones; **the last but ~** el penúltimo/la penúltima; **~ or two people** algunas personas; **that's ~ way of doing it** ésa es una forma *or* una de las maneras de hacerlo

2 (*indefinite*) un/una; **~ day** un día, cierto día; **~ cold winter's day** un día frío de invierno; **~ hot July evening** una tarde de julio de mucho calor; **~ Pérez** un tal Pérez

3 (= *sole*) único; **his ~ worry** su única preocupación; **the ~ way to do it** la única forma de hacerlo; **no ~ man could do it** ningún hombre podría hacerlo por sí solo; **the ~ and only difficulty** la única dificultad; **the ~ and only Charlie Chaplin** el único e incomparable Charlot

4 (= *same*) mismo; **all in ~ direction** todos en la misma dirección; **it's all ~** es lo mismo; **it's all ~ to me** me da igual, me da lo mismo; **they are ~ and the same** son el mismo; **they are ~ and the same person** son la misma persona; **it is ~ and the same thing** es la misma cosa

5 (= *united*) **God is ~** Dios es uno; **they all shouted as ~** todos gritaron a una; **to become ~** casarse; **to be ~ with sth** formar un conjunto con algo

Ⓑ N (= *figure*) uno *m*; **I belted him ~*** le di un guantazo; **~ and six(pence)** (*Brit*†) un chelín y seis peniques; **to be at ~ (with sb)** estar completamente de acuerdo (con algn); **to be at ~ with o.s.** estar en paz consigo mismo; **to go ~ better than sb** tomar la ventaja *or* la delantera a algn; **but John went ~ better** pero Juan lo hizo mejor; **she's cook and housekeeper in ~** es a la vez cocinera y ama de llaves; **it's made all in ~** está hecho en una sola pieza; **you've got it in ~!*** ¡y que lo digas!*; **in ~s and twos** en pequeños grupos; **they came in ~s and twos** vinieron uno a uno y en parejas; **to be ~ up** (*Sport etc*) llevar un punto/gol *etc* de ventaja; **that puts us ~ up** (*Sport etc*) eso nos da un punto/gol *etc* de ventaja; **to be ~ up on sb** llevar ventaja a algn; *see also* **fast A1**, **quick A3**, **road A2**

Ⓒ PRON 1 (*indefinite*) uno/una; **have you got ~?** ¿tienes uno?; **there is only ~ left** queda uno solamente; **his message is ~ of pessimism** su mensaje es pesimista, el suyo es un mensaje pesimista; **~ after the other** uno tras otro; **~ and all** todos sin excepción, todo el mundo; **~ by ~** uno tras otro, uno a uno; **I for ~ am not going** yo, por mi parte, no voy; **not ~** ni uno; **~ of them** uno de ellos; **any ~ of us** cualquiera de nosotros; **he's ~ of the group** es del grupo, forma parte del grupo; **he's ~ of the family now** ya es de la familia; **the ~ ..., the other ...** uno ..., el otro ...; **you can't buy ~ without the other** no se puede comprar el uno sin el otro; **price of ~** precio *m* de la unidad; **two for the price of ~** dos por el precio de uno; **~ or two** unos pocos

2 (*specific*) **this ~** éste/ésta; **that ~** ése/ésa, aquél/aquélla; **this ~ is better than that ~** éste es mejor que ése; **which ~ do you want?** ¿cuál quieres?; **the white dress and the grey ~** el vestido blanco y el gris; **who wants these red ~s?** ¿quién quiere éstos colorados?; **what about this little ~?** ¿y éste pequeñito *or* (*esp LAm*) chiquito?; **that's a difficult ~** ésa sí que es difícil

3 (*relative*) **the ~ who** ◊ **the ~ that** el/la que; **the ~s who** ◊ **the ~s that** los/las que; **they were the ~s who told us** ellos fueron quienes nos lo dijeron; **he looked like ~ who had seen a ghost** tenía el aspecto del que acababa de ver un fantasma; **to ~ who can read between the lines** para el que sabe leer entre líneas; **the ~ on the floor** el que está en el suelo; **~ more sensitive would have fainted** una persona de mayor sensibilidad se hubiera desmayado

4 (= *person*) **he's a clever ~** es un taimado; **he's the troublesome ~** él es el revoltoso; **you are a ~!** ¡qué cosas dices/haces!; **our dear ~s** nuestros seres queridos; **the Evil One** el demonio; **you're a fine ~!*** ¡menuda pieza estás tú hecho!*; **he's ~ for the ladies** tiene éxito con las mujeres; **he's a great ~ for chess** es muy bueno al ajedrez; **he's a great ~ for arguing** es de los que les encanta discutir; **the little ~s** los pequeños, los chiquillos; **never a ~** ni uno siquiera; **he is not ~ to protest** no es de los que protestan; **he's not much of a ~ for sweets** no le gustan mucho los dulces

5 **~ another**: **they kissed ~ another** se besaron (el uno al otro); **they all kissed ~ another** se besaron (unos a otros); **do you see ~ another much?** ¿se ven mucho?; **it's a year since we saw ~ another** hace un año que no nos vemos

6 (*impers*) uno/una; **~ never knows** nunca se sabe; **~ must eat** hay que comer; **~ has ~'s pride** uno tiene cierto amor propio; **~'s life is not really safe** la vida de uno no tiene seguridad; **~'s opinion does not count** la opinión de uno no cuenta; **to cut ~'s finger** cortarse el dedo

one- [wʌn] PREFIX de un ..., de un solo ..., uni-, un-; **a ~line message** un mensaje de una sola línea; **a ~celled animal** un animal unicelular; **a ~day excursion** (*US*) un billete de ida y vuelta en un día

one-act [wʌn'ækt] ADJ de un solo acto

one-armed ['wʌn'ɑːmd] Ⓐ ADJ manco

Ⓑ CPD ► **one-armed bandit*** N máquina *f* tragamonedas, máquina *f* tragaperras (*Sp*)

one-eyed ['wʌn'aɪd] ADJ tuerto

one-handed ['wʌn'hændɪd] Ⓐ ADV **to catch the ball ~** recoger la pelota con una sola mano

Ⓑ ADJ manco

one-horse ['wʌn'hɔːs] ADJ 1 [*carriage*] de un solo caballo

2 (*) insignificante, de poca monta; **~ town** pueblucho* *m*

3 **a ~ race** (*fig*) una contienda en la que no hay color, un paseo triunfal

one-legged ['wʌn'legɪd] ADJ con una sola pierna

one-liner [,wʌn'laɪnəʳ] N chiste *m* breve

one-man ['wʌn'mæn] Ⓐ ADJ 1 (= *solo*) individual; [*job*] para una sola persona; [*business*] llevado por una sola persona

2 (= *monogamous*) **she's a ~ woman** es (una) mujer de un solo hombre

Ⓑ CPD ► **one-man band** N (*Mus*) hombre *m* orquesta; **it's a ~ band*** (*fig*) lo hace todo uno solo ► **one-man exhibition**, **one-man show** N exposición *f* individual

oneness ['wʌnnɪs] N (= *unity*) unidad *f*; (= *identity*) identidad *f*

one-night stand [,wʌnnaɪt'stænd] N 1 (*Theat*) función *f* de una sola noche, representación *f* única

2 (*fig*) ligue *m* de una noche

one-off* ['wʌnɒf] (*Brit*) Ⓐ N intento *m* único; **it's a ~** es un caso único

Ⓑ ADJ [*appearance, exhibition, show*] aislado; [*payment*] único; **it was just a ~ job, I don't think there will be any more** fue un trabajo aislado, no creo que haya más de ese tipo

one-on-one [wʌnɒn'wʌn] ADJ, ADV (*US*) = **one-to-one**

one-parent family [,wʌnpeərənt'fæmɪlɪ] N familia *f* monoparental

one-party [,wʌn'pɑːtɪ] ADJ [*state etc*] de partido único

one-piece [,wʌn'piːs] Ⓐ ADJ de una pieza

Ⓑ N (= *swimsuit*) bañador *m* de una pieza

onerous ['ɒnərəs] ADJ [*debt*] oneroso; [*task, duty*] pesado

oneself [wʌn'self] PRON 1 (*reflexive*) se; **to wash ~** lavarse

2 (*for emphasis*) uno/a mismo/a; (*after prep*) sí mismo/a; **it's quicker to do it ~** es más rápido si lo hace uno mismo

3 (*phrases*) **to be ~** (= *behave naturally*) conducirse con naturalidad; **to be by ~** estar solo *or* a solas; **to do sth by ~** hacer algo solo *or* por sí solo; **it's nice to have the museum to ~** es agradable tener el museo para uno mismo; **to look out for ~** mirar por sí; **to say to ~** decir para sí, decirse a uno mismo; **to see for ~** ver por sí mismo; **to talk to ~** hablar solo; ✦**IDIOM to come to ~** volver en sí

one-shot* [,wʌnʃɒt] (*US*) N, ADJ = **one-off**

one-sided [,wʌn'saɪdɪd] ADJ [*view etc*] parcial; [*decision*] unilateral; [*contest*] desigual

one-sidedness [ˌwʌnˈsaɪdɪdnɪs] N [*of view etc*] parcialidad *f*; [*of decision*] carácter *m* unilateral; [*of contest*] desigualdad *f*

one-stop shopping [ˌwʌnstɒpˈʃɒpɪŋ] N tiendas *fpl* y servicios *mpl* bajo el mismo techo

one-time [ˈwʌntaɪm] ADJ antiguo, ex; **~ prime minister** ex primer ministro/a *m/f*; **~ butler to Lord Yaxley** antiguo mayordomo *m* de Lord Yaxley; **the ~ revolutionary** el otrora revolucionario

one-to-one [ˈwʌntəˈwʌn], **one-on-one** (*US*) [wʌnɒnˈwʌn] Ⓐ ADJ [*equivalence, correspondence*] exacto; [*relationship, conversation*] de uno a uno; [*meeting*] entre dos; [*teaching*] individual, individualizado; **on a ~ basis** [*teach*] individualmente; [*talk*] de uno a uno
Ⓑ ADV [*discuss, talk*] de uno a uno

one-track [ˈwʌntræk] ADJ (*Rail*) de vía única; **to have a ~ mind** no tener más que una idea en la cabeza

one-two [ˈwʌnˈtuː] N [1] (*Brit Ftbl*) pared *f*; **to play a ~ with sb** hacer la pared con algn
[2] (*Boxing*) un-dos *m*

one-upmanship [wʌnˈʌpmənʃɪp] N arte *m* de aventajar a los demás, arte *m* de llevar siempre la delantera

one-way [ˈwʌnweɪ] ADJ [1] [*street*] de dirección única, de sentido único (*esp LAm*); [*ticket*] de ida, sencillo (*Mex*); **~ journey** viaje *m* sin retorno; **"one-way traffic"** "dirección única", "dirección obligatoria"
[2] (*fig*) [*admiration etc*] no correspondido

one-woman [ˌwʌnˈwʊmən] Ⓐ ADJ [1] (= *solo*) individual; **~ business** empresa *f* dirigida por una sola mujer
[2] (= *monogamous*) **he's a ~ man** es (un) hombre de una sola mujer
Ⓑ CPD ► **one-woman exhibition**, **one-woman show** N exposición *f* individual

one-year [ˈwʌnjɪəʳ] ADJ de *or* para un año; **~ unconditional warranty** garantía *f* incondicional de un año

ongoing [ˈɒnˌgəʊɪŋ] ADJ (= *in progress*) en curso; (= *continuing*) en desarrollo; (= *current*) corriente

onion [ˈʌnjən] Ⓐ N cebolla *f*; ✦**IDIOM to know one's ~s** (*Brit**) conocer a fondo su oficio, conocer el paño*
Ⓑ CPD de cebolla ► **onion dome** N (*Archit*) cúpula *f* bulbosa ► **onion johnny** N vendedor *m* ambulante de cebollas ► **onion rings** NPL aros *mpl* de cebolla rebozados ► **onion skin** N (= *paper*) papel *m* de cebolla ► **onion soup** N sopa *f* de cebolla

onion-shaped [ˈʌnjənʃeɪpd] ADJ acebollado, con forma de cebolla

on-line [ˈɒnlaɪn] Ⓐ ADJ (*Comput*) on-line, en línea; (= *switched on*) conectado
Ⓑ ADV on-line, en línea

onlooker [ˈɒnˌlʊkəʳ] N espectador(a) *m/f*; (*esp pej*) mirón/ona *m/f*; **I was a mere ~** yo era un simple espectador

only [ˈəʊnlɪ] Ⓐ ADJ único; **your ~ hope is to hide** la única posibilidad que te queda es esconderte; **it's the ~ one left** es el único que queda; **"I'm tired" — "you're not the ~ one!"** —estoy cansado —¡no eres el único!; **the ~ thing I don't like about it is ...** lo único que no me gusta de esto es ...; *see also* **pebble**
Ⓑ ADV [1] (= *no more than*) sólo, solamente; **he's ~ ten** sólo *or* solamente tiene diez años; **we ~ have five** sólo *or* solamente tenemos cinco; **what, ~ five?** ¿cómo, cinco nada más?, ¿cómo, sólo *or* solamente cinco?
[2] (= *merely*) **I'm ~ the porter** no soy más que el portero; **I'm ~ a porter** soy un simple portero; **I ~ touched it** no hice más que tocarlo; **it's ~ to be expected** cabe de esperar; **he raced onto the platform ~ to find the train pulling out** llegó corriendo al andén para encontrarse con que el tren estaba saliendo; **you ~ have to ask** ◊ **you have ~ to ask** no tienes más que pedirlo, sólo tienes que pedirlo; **it's ~ fair to tell him** lo mínimo que puedes hacer es decírselo; **I was ~ joking** lo he dicho en broma; **that ~ makes matters worse** eso sólo empeora las cosas; **I will ~ say that ...** diré solamente que ..., sólo diré que ...; **I ~ wish he were here now** ojalá estuviese ahora aquí
[3] (= *exclusively*) sólo; **a ticket for one person ~** un billete para una persona sólo; **"members only"** "sólo socios"; **God ~ knows!**‡ ¡Dios sabe!; **~ time will tell** sólo el tiempo puede decirlo; **a women-~ therapy group** un grupo de terapia sólo para mujeres
[4] (= *not until*) **I've ~ recently met him** hace poco que lo conocí
[5] (= *no longer ago than*) **I saw her ~ yesterday** ayer mismo la vi, la vi ayer nomás (*LAm*), recién ayer la vi (*LAm*); **it seems like ~ yesterday that ...** parece que fue ayer cuando ...
[6] (*in phrases*) **~ just**: **the hole was ~ just big enough** el agujero era lo justo; **I've ~ just arrived** acabo de llegar ahora mismo, no he hecho más que llegar; **it fits him, but ~ just** le cabe pero le queda muy justo; **not ~ ... but also**: **not ~ was he late but he also forgot the tickets** no sólo llegó tarde sino que además olvidó las entradas; **a machine that is not ~ efficient but looks good as well** una máquina que no sólo es eficaz sino también atractiva; **~ too**: **I'd be ~ too pleased to help** estaría encantado de *or* me encantaría poder ayudar(les); **it is ~ too true** por desgracia es verdad *or* cierto; **I knew ~ too well what would happen** sabía demasiado bien lo que iba a pasar; *see also* **if A5**
Ⓒ CONJ sólo que, pero; **it's a bit like my house, ~ nicer** es un poco como mi casa, sólo que *or* pero más bonita; **I would gladly do it, ~ I shall be away** lo haría de buena gana, sólo que *or* pero voy a estar fuera
Ⓓ CPD ► **only child** N hijo/a *m/f* único/a; *see also* **one A3**

on-message [ˈɒnˌmesɪdʒ] ADJ centrado en el mensaje adecuado; **to be ~** centrarse en el mensaje adecuado, transmitir el mensaje adecuado

o.n.o. ABBR (= **or near(est) offer**) abierto ofertas

on-off switch [ˌɒnɒfˈswɪtʃ] N botón *m* de conexión

onomastic [ˌɒnəʊˈmæstɪk] ADJ onomástico

onomastics [ˌɒnəʊˈmæstɪks] NSING onomástica *f*

onomatopoeia [ˌɒnəʊmætəʊˈpiːə] N onomatopeya *f*

onomatopoeic [ˌɒnəʊmætəʊˈpiːɪk] ADJ, **onomatopoetic** [ˌɒnəʊmætəʊpəʊˈetɪk] ADJ onomatopéyico

onrush [ˈɒnrʌʃ] N [*of water*] oleada *f*; (*fig*) oleada *f*, avalancha *f*

onrushing [ˈɒnˌrʌʃɪŋ] ADJ [*vehicle*] embalado, sin freno; [*water*] creciente; **the ~ tide of immigrants** la creciente oleada de inmigrantes

on-screen [ˌɒnˈskriːn] Ⓐ ADJ [1] (*Comput etc*) en pantalla
[2] (*Cine, TV*) [*romance, kiss*] cinematográfico
Ⓑ ADV (*Cine, TV*) en la pantalla

onset [ˈɒnset] N (= *beginning*) principio *m*, comienzo *m*; [*of disease*] aparición *f*; **the ~ of winter** el comienzo del invierno

onshore [ˈɒnʃɔːʳ] Ⓐ ADV tierra adentro
Ⓑ ADJ [*breeze*] que sopla del mar hacia la tierra

onside [ˈɒnsaɪd] Ⓐ ADJ [1] (*Aut*) (*in Britain*) izquierdo; (*in most other countries*) derecho
[2] (*Ftbl etc*) **to be ~** estar en posición correcta
Ⓑ N (*Aut*) (*in Britain*) lado *m* izquierdo; (*in most other countries*) lado *m* derecho

on-site [ˈɒnˌsaɪt] ADJ in situ

onslaught [ˈɒnslɔːt] N (*gen*) ataque *m*, arremetida *f*; **to make a furious ~ on a critic** atacar violentamente a un crítico

on-street parking [ˌɒnstriːtˈpɑːkɪŋ] N aparcamiento *m* en la vía pública

Ont. ABBR (*Canada*) = **Ontario**

on-the-job training [ˌɒnðədʒɒbˈtreɪnɪŋ] N formación *f* en el trabajo, formación *f* sobre la práctica

on-the-spot [ˈɒnðəˈspɒt] ADJ [*decision*] instantáneo; [*investigation*] sobre el terreno; [*report*] inmediato; [*fine*] en el acto; **our ~ reporter** nuestro reportero en el lugar de los hechos

onto [ˈɒntʊ] PREP [1] (= *on top of*) a, sobre, en, arriba de (*LAm*); **he got ~ the table** se subió a la mesa
[2] (= *on track of*) **to be ~ sth** haber encontrado algo, seguir una pista interesante; **he knows he's ~ a good thing** sabe que ha encontrado algo que vale la pena; **the police are ~ the villain** la policía tiene una pista que le conducirá al criminal; **we're ~ them** les conocemos el juego; **they were ~ him at once** le calaron en seguida, le identificaron en el acto
[3] (= *in touch with*) **I'll get ~ him about it** insistiré con él, se lo recordaré

ontological [ˌɒntəˈlɒdʒɪkəl] ADJ ontológico

ontology [ɒnˈtɒlədʒɪ] N ontología *f*

onus [ˈəʊnəs] N (*pl* **onuses**) responsabilidad *f*; **the ~ is upon the makers** la responsabilidad es de los fabricantes; **the ~ is upon him to prove it** es suya la responsabilidad de demostrarlo, le incumbe a él demostrarlo; **the ~ of proof is on the prosecution** le incumbe al fiscal probar la acusación

onward [ˈɒnwəd] Ⓐ ADJ [*march etc*] progresivo, hacia adelante; [*flight, journey*] de conexión; [*connection*] posterior
Ⓑ ADV (*also* **~s**) adelante, hacia adelante; **from that time ~** desde entonces; **from the 12th century ~** desde el siglo doce en adelante, a partir del siglo doce; **~!** ¡adelante!

onwards [ˈɒnwədz] ADV (*esp Brit*) = **onward B**

onyx [ˈɒnɪks] N ónice *m*, ónix *m*

oodles* [ˈuːdlz] NPL **we have ~ (of)** tenemos cantidad *or* montones (de)*

ooh [uː] Ⓐ EXCL ¡oh!
Ⓑ VI exclamar con placer

oolite [ˈəʊəlaɪt] N oolito *m*

oolitic [ˌəʊəˈlɪtɪk] ADJ oolítico

oompah* [ˈuːmpɑː] N chumpa *f*

oomph‡ [ʊmf] N brío *m*, marcha* *f*; **it will put the ~ back into your sex life** dará nuevos bríos a su vida sexual

oophorectomy [ˌəʊəfəˈrektəmɪ] N ooforectomía *f*, ovariotomía *f*

oops* [ʊps] EXCL ¡ay!

ooze [uːz] Ⓐ N cieno *m*, limo *m*; [*of blood*] pérdida *f*, salida *f*
Ⓑ VI [*liquid*] rezumar(se); [*blood*] salir; (= *leak*) gotear

Ⓒ VT rezumar; (*fig*) rebosar; **the wound was oozing blood** la herida sangraba lentamente; **he simply ~s confidence** rebosa confianza

► **ooze away** VI + ADV rezumarse

► **ooze out** VI + ADV rezumarse

op¹* [ɒp] N ABBR (*Med, Mil*) = **operation**

op² ABBR (*Mus*) = **opus**

opacity [əʊˈpæsɪtɪ] N [*of lens, substance*] opacidad *f*; [*of statement etc*] hermetismo *m*, ininteligibilidad *f*

opal [ˈəʊpəl] N ópalo *m*

opalescence [ˌəʊpəˈlesns] N opalescencia *f*

opalescent [ˌəʊpəˈlesnt] ADJ opalescente

opaque [əʊˈpeɪk] ADJ [*glass, lens, substance*] opaco; [*statement etc*] poco claro, ininteligible

op art [ˈɒpɑːt] N op-art *m*

op.cit. [ˈɒpˈsɪt] ABBR = **opere citato** (= *in the work cited*) ob. cit.

OPEC [ˈəʊpek] N ABBR (= **Organization of Petroleum-Exporting Countries**) OPEP *f*

Op-Ed [ˈɒpˈed] (*esp US*) ADJ, N ABBR (*Press*) = **opposite editorial**; **~ (page)** página *f* de tribuna

open [ˈəʊpən] Ⓐ ADJ 1 (*gen*) [*book, grave, pores, wound etc*] abierto; [*bottle, tin etc*] destapado; **the book was ~ at page seven** el libro estaba abierto por la página siete; **the door is ~** la puerta está abierta; **to break a safe ~** forzar una caja fuerte; **to cut a bag ~** abrir una bolsa rajándola; **to fling** *or* **throw a door ~** abrir una puerta de golpe *or* de par en par; **wide ~** (*door etc*) abierto de par en par; ✦*IDIOM* **to welcome sb with ~ arms** dar la bienvenida *or* recibir a algn con los brazos abiertos; *see also* **book A1, arm A1**

2 [*shop, bank etc*] abierto (al público); **the shop is still not ~** la tienda sigue cerrada

3 (= *unfolded*) desplegado; (= *unfastened*) desabrochado; **the map was ~ on the table** el mapa estaba desplegado sobre la mesa; **with his shirt ~** (= *unbuttoned*) con la camisa desabotonada; **a shirt ~ at the neck** una camisa con el cuello desabrochado

4 (= *not enclosed*) descubierto, abierto; [*car*] descapotable; **in the ~ air** al aire libre; **~ country** campo *m* raso; **on ~ ground** en un claro; (= *waste ground*) en un descampado; **~ sea** mar *m* abierto; **with ~ views** con amplias *or* extensas vistas

5 (= *not blocked*) abierto, sin obstáculos; **the way to Paris lay ~** el camino de París quedaba abierto; **the speed permitted on the ~ road** la velocidad permitida circulando en carretera; **road ~ to traffic** carretera abierta al tráfico, vía libre

6 (= *public, unrestricted*) [*championship, race, scholarship, ticket*] abierto; [*trial*] público; **books on ~ access** libros *mpl* en libre acceso; **in ~ court** en juicio público; **to keep ~ house** tener mesa franca *or* casa abierta; **we had an ~ invitation to visit them** nos habían invitado a visitarles cuando quisiéramos; **~ to the public on Mondays** abierto al público los lunes; **the competition is ~ to all** todos pueden participar en el certamen, el certamen se abre a todos; **membership is not ~ to women** la sociedad no admite a las mujeres

7 (= *available, permissible*) **what choices are ~ to me?** ¿qué posibilidades *or* opciones me quedan?; **it is ~ to you to + INFIN** puedes perfectamente + *infin*, tienes derecho a + *infin*

8 (= *not biased or prejudiced*) abierto; **to be ~ to sth: I am ~ to advice** escucho de buena gana los consejos; **I am ~ to offers** estoy dispuesto a recibir ofertas; **I am ~ to persuasion** se me puede convencer

9 (= *declared, frank*) abierto; [*person, admiration*] franco; [*hatred*] declarado; **an ~ enemy of the Church** un enemigo declarado de la Iglesia; **to be in ~ revolt** estar en abierta rebeldía; **it's an ~ secret that ...** es un secreto a voces que ...; **to be ~ with sb** ser franco con algn

10 (= *undecided*) por resolver, por decidir; [*race, contest*] muy abierto, muy igualado; **to leave the matter ~** dejar el asunto pendiente; **~ question** cuestión *f* pendiente *or* sin resolver; **it's an ~ question whether ...** está por ver si ...; *see also* **mind**

11 (= *exposed, not protected*) abierto, descubierto; [*town*] abierto; (*Mil*) expuesto, vulnerable; **to be ~ to sth: it is ~ to criticism on several counts** se le puede criticar por diversas razones, es criticable desde diversos puntos de vista; **to lay o.s. ~ to criticism/attack** exponerse a ser criticado/atacado; **it is ~ to doubt whether ...** queda la duda sobre si ...; **~ to the elements** desprotegido, desabrigado; **~ to influence from advertisers** accesible a la influencia de los anunciantes; **it is ~ to question whether ...** es cuestionable que ...; **~ to every wind** expuesto a todos los vientos

Ⓑ N 1 **(out) in the ~** (= *out of doors*) al aire libre; (= *in the country*) en campo *m* raso *or* abierto; **to sleep (out) in the ~** dormir al raso, dormir a cielo abierto; **to bring a dispute (out) into the ~** hacer que una disputa llegue a ser del dominio público; **their true feelings came (out) into the ~** sus verdaderos sentimientos se dejaron adivinar; **why don't you come (out) into the ~ about it?** ¿por qué no lo declara abiertamente?

2 (*Golf, Tennis*) **the Open** el (Torneo) Abierto, el Open

Ⓒ VT 1 (*gen*) [+ *eyes, case, letter etc*] abrir; [+ *parcel*] abrir, desenvolver; [+ *bottle etc*] destapar; [+ *legs*] abrir, separar; [+ *abscess*] cortar; [+ *pores*] dilatar; **I didn't ~ my mouth** ni abrí la boca, no dije ni pío

2 [+ *shop*] (*for daily business*) abrir; (= *set up*) abrir, poner

3 (= *unfold*) [+ *map*] desplegar, extender; [+ *newspaper*] desplegar

4 (= *unblock*) **to ~ a road to traffic** abrir una carretera al público

5 (= *begin*) [+ *conversation, debate, negotiations*] entablar, iniciar; **to ~ three hearts** (*Bridge*) abrir de tres corazones; **to ~ a bank account** abrir una cuenta en el banco; **to ~ the case** (*Jur*) exponer los detalles de la acusación; **to ~ fire** (*Mil*) romper *or* abrir el fuego

6 (= *declare open, inaugurate*) inaugurar; **the exhibition was ~ed by the Queen** la exposición fue inaugurada por la Reina; **to ~ Parliament** abrir la sesión parlamentaria

7 (= *reveal, disclose*) [+ *mind, heart*] abrir; [+ *feelings, intentions*] revelar; *see also* **mind A4**

8 (= *make*) **to ~ a road through a forest** abrir una carretera a través de un bosque; **to ~ a hole in a wall** hacer un agujero en una pared

Ⓓ VI 1 [*door, flower*] abrirse; [*pores*] dilatarse; **the door ~ed** se abrió la puerta; **this room ~s into a larger one** este cuarto se comunica con *or* se junta con otro más grande; **a door that ~s onto the garden** una puerta que da al jardín; ✦*IDIOM* **the heavens ~ed** se abrieron los cielos

2 (*for business*) [*shop, bank*] abrir; **the shops ~ at nine** las tiendas abren a las nueve

3 (= *begin*) dar comienzo, iniciarse; [*speaker*] comenzar; (*Theat*) [*play*] estrenarse; (*Cards, Chess*) abrir; **the season ~s in June** la temporada comienza en junio; **when we ~ed in Bradford** (*Theat*) cuando dimos la primera representación en Bradford; **to ~ for the Crown** (*Jur*) exponer los detalles de la acusación, presentar los hechos en que se basa la acusación; **the play ~ed to great applause** el estreno de la obra fue muy aplaudido; **the book ~s with a long description** el libro empieza con una larga descripción; **to ~ with two hearts** (*Bridge*) abrir de dos corazones

Ⓔ CPD ► **open cheque** N (*Brit*) cheque *m* sin cruzar ► **open day** N día *m* abierto a todos ► **open letter** N carta *f* abierta ► **open market** N (*in town*) mercado *m* al aire libre; (*Econ*) mercado *m* libre, mercado *m* abierto; **he bought it on the ~ market** lo compró en el mercado público ► **open policy** N (*Insurance*) póliza *f* abierta ► **open prison** N cárcel *f* abierta ► **open sandwich** N sandwich *m* sin tapa, sandwich *m* abierto (*esp LAm*) ► **open shop** N (*Ind*) empresa *f* con personal agremiado y no agremiado ► **Open University** N (*Brit*) ≈ Universidad *f* Nacional de Enseñanza a Distancia ► **open verdict** N (*Jur*) juicio *m* en el que se determina el crimen sin designar el culpable

► **open out** Ⓐ VT + ADV abrir; (= *unfold*) [+ *map*] desplegar, extender

Ⓑ VI + ADV 1 [*flower*] abrirse

2 [*passage, tunnel, street*] ensancharse; [*view, panorama*] extenderse

3 (*fig*) (= *develop, unfold*) desarrollarse; [*new horizons*] abrirse

4 (*Brit*) (*emotionally*) abrirse

► **open up** Ⓐ VT + ADV 1 [+ *box, jacket*] abrir; [+ *map*] extender, desplegar

2 [+ *house, shop*] abrir

3 [+ *new business*] abrir, poner

4 [+ *route*] abrir; [+ *blocked road*] franquear, despejar; [+ *country*] explorar; [+ *secret, new vista*] revelar; [+ *new possibility*] crear; **to ~ up a market** abrirse un mercado, conquistar un mercado; **to ~ up a country for trade** incorporar un país al comercio; **when the oilfield was ~ed up** cuando se empezó a explotar el campo petrolífero

Ⓑ VI + ADV 1 [*flower*] abrirse; [*new shop, business*] abrir, inaugurarse; **~ up!** ¡abran!; (*police order*) ¡abran a la autoridad!

2 (*fig*) [*prospects etc*] abrirse, desplegarse

3 (*emotionally*) abrirse, confiarse

4 (*Mil*) (= *start shooting*) romper el fuego

5 (*) (= *accelerate*) [*car*] acelerar (a fondo)

OPEN UNIVERSITY

La **Open University** *o* **OU** *es el nombre que recibe en el Reino Unido la universidad a distancia para adultos, fundada en 1969. No se exigen requisitos formales de acceso para los primeros cursos y los alumnos estudian desde casa, con el apoyo de algunos programas de radio y televisión emitidos por la* **BBC**, *cursos por correspondencia y tutores en su localidad. Además, sobre todo en verano, se organizan algunos cursos a los que los alumnos tienen que asistir en persona.*

open-air [ˌəʊpnˈɛəʳ] ADJ al aire libre

open-and-shut case [ˌəʊpənənʃʌtˈkeɪs] N caso *m* claro, caso *m* evidente

open-cast [ˈəʊpən,ɑːst] ADJ **~ mining** minería *f* a cielo abierto

open-door [ˌəʊpənˈdɔːʳ] ADJ **~ policy** política *f* de puerta abierta

open-ended [ˌəʊpənˈendɪd] ADJ (*fig*) [*contract,*

offer etc] indefinido, sin plazo definido; [*discussion*] sin desarrollo preestablecido

open-end trust [ˌəʊpənend'trʌst] N (*US*) sociedad *f* inversionista

opener ['əʊpnəʳ] N [1] abridor *m*; (= *bottle opener*) sacacorchos *m inv*; (= *can opener*) abrelatas *m inv*
[2] (*Theat etc*) primer número *m*
[3] **for ~s** (*US**) de entrada

open-eyed [ˌəʊpn'aɪd] ADJ con los ojos abiertos; (= *amazed*) con ojos desorbitados

open-handed [ˌəʊpən'hændɪd] ADJ [1] (= *liberal*) liberal
[2] (= *generous*) generoso

open-handedness [ˌəʊpən'hændɪdnɪs] N (= *liberal attitude*) liberalidad *f*; (= *generosity*) generosidad *f*

open-hearted [ˌəʊpən'hɑːtɪd] ADJ franco, generoso

open-heart surgery [ˌ] N cirugía *f* a corazón abierto

opening ['əʊpnɪŋ] (A) ADJ [*remark*] primer(o); [*ceremony, speech*] de apertura, inaugural; [*price*] inicial
(B) N [1] (= *gap*) abertura *f*; (*in wall*) brecha *f*, agujero *m*; (*in clouds, trees*) claro *m*
[2] (= *beginning*) comienzo *m*, principio *m*; (*Cards, Chess*) apertura *f*; (= *first showing*) (*Theat*) estreno *m*; [*of exhibition*] inauguración *f*; [*of parliament*] apertura *f*
[3] (= *chance*) oportunidad *f*; (= *post*) puesto *m* vacante, vacante *f*; **to give one's opponent an ~** dar una oportunidad *or* (*LAm*) darle chance al adversario; **to give sb an ~ for sth** dar a algn la oportunidad de hacer algo
(C) CPD ► **opening hours** NPL horas *fpl* de abrir ► **opening night** N (*Theat*) noche *f* de estreno; [*of club etc*] inauguración *f* ► **opening price** N cotización *f* de apertura ► **opening stock** N existencias *fpl* iniciales ► **opening time** N hora *f* de apertura

openly ['əʊpənlɪ] ADV (= *frankly*) abiertamente, francamente; (= *publicly*) públicamente

open-minded ['əʊpn'maɪndɪd] ADJ libre de prejuicios, de miras amplias; **I'm still ~ about it** no me he decidido todavía

open-mindedness ['əʊpn'maɪndɪdnɪs] N ausencia *f* de prejuicios, imparcialidad *f*

open-mouthed ['əʊpn'maʊðd] ADJ boquiabierto

open-necked ['əʊpn'nekt] ADJ sin corbata

openness ['əʊpnnɪs] N (= *frankness*) franqueza *f*

open-plan ['əʊpnˌplæn] ADJ [*house, office etc*] sin tabiques, de planta abierta

open-top ['əʊpənˌtɒp] ADJ [*car, bus*] descubierto

openwork ['əʊpnwɜːk] N (*Sew*) calado *m*, enrejado *m*

opera[1] ['ɒpərə] (A) N ópera *f*
(B) CPD ► **opera glasses** NPL gemelos *mpl* de teatro ► **opera hat** N clac *m* ► **opera house** N teatro *m* de la ópera ► **opera singer** N cantante *mf* de ópera

opera[2] ['ɒpərə] NPL *of* **opus**

operable ['ɒpərəbl] ADJ (*Med*) operable

opera-goer ['ɒpərəˌgəʊəʳ] N aficionado/a *m/f* a la ópera

operand ['ɒpərænd] N operando *m*

operate ['ɒpəreɪt] (A) VT [1] (= *work*) [+ *machine, vehicle, switchboard*] manejar; [+ *switch, lever*] accionar; **can you ~ this machine?** ¿sabes manejar esta máquina?; **this switch ~s a fan** este interruptor activa un ventilador
[2] (= *run, manage*) [+ *company*] dirigir; [+ *service*] ofrecer; [+ *system*] aplicar; [+ *mine, oil well, quarry*] explotar; **they ~ a system of flexible working hours** aplican un horario flexible de trabajo
(B) VI [1] (= *function*) [*machine, system, principle, mind*] funcionar; [*person*] actuar, obrar; [*law*] regir; **she knows how to ~ in a crisis** sabe cómo actuar *or* obrar en los momentos difíciles; **we ~ on the principle that ...** partimos del principio de que ...; **special laws ~ in Northern Ireland** en Irlanda del Norte rigen leyes especiales
[2] (= *act, influence*) [*drug, propaganda*] actuar (**on** sobre); [*factors*] intervenir; **advertising ~s on the subconscious** la publicidad actúa sobre el subconsciente
[3] (= *carry on one's business*) [*person*] trabajar; [*company, factory, criminal, service*] operar; [*airport*] funcionar; **we shall be operating under difficult conditions** trabajaremos en unas condiciones difíciles; **we were operating at a loss** estábamos operando con déficit; **an airline operating out of Heathrow** una compañía aérea con base en Heathrow *or* que opera desde Heathrow; **a drug ring operating in New York** una red de narcotráfico que opera en Nueva York; **this service does not ~ on Sundays** este servicio no opera *or* no funciona los domingos; **all flights are operating normally** todos los vuelos están operando con normalidad
[4] (*Med*) operar; **to ~ on sb (for sth)** operar a algn (de algo); **she was ~d on for appendicitis** la operaron de apendicitis; **to ~ on sb's back/eyes** operar a algn de la espalda/de la vista

operatic [ˌɒpə'rætɪk] ADJ operístico

operating ['ɒpəreɪtɪŋ] (A) ADJ [1] (*Comm*) [*budget, assets*] de explotación; **~ costs** *or* **expenses** gastos *mpl* de explotación; **~ loss** pérdida *f* de explotación; **~ profit** beneficio *m* de explotación
[2] (*Comput*) **~ system** sistema *m* operativo
[3] (*Tech*) **~ conditions** condiciones *fpl* de funcionamiento
(B) CPD ► **operating room** N (*US Med*) = **operating theatre** ► **operating table** N (*Med*) mesa *f* de operaciones ► **operating theatre** N (*Med*) quirófano *m*, sala *f* de operaciones

operation [ˌɒpə'reɪʃən] (A) N [1] (= *functioning*) funcionamiento *m*; **to be in ~** [*machine, system, business*] estar en funcionamiento *or* en marcha, estar funcionando; [*law*] ser vigente, estar en vigor; **to come into ~** [*machine, system*] entrar en funcionamiento; [*law*] entrar en vigor; **the system is designed to come into ~ in 2003** está previsto que el sistema entre en funcionamiento en 2003; **to put sth into ~** [+ *plan, factory*] poner algo en funcionamiento *or* en marcha
[2] (= *use*) [*of controls, machine*] manejo *m*; [*of system*] uso *m*
[3] (= *activity*) operación *f*; **United Nations peacekeeping ~s** las operaciones de paz de las Naciones Unidas; **our ~s in Egypt** [*of company*] nuestras operaciones en Egipto; [*of mine, oil well*] nuestras operaciones *or* explotaciones en Egipto; **moving house is an expensive ~** mudarse de casa resulta caro; *see also* **rescue C**
[4] (*Med*) operación *f*, intervención *f* quirúrgica (*frm*); **a liver ~** una operación de hígado; **will I need an ~?** ¿hará falta que me operen?; **to have** *or* (*frm*) **undergo an ~ for appendicitis** operarse de apendicitis; **to have** *or* (*frm*) **undergo an ~ to remove a tumour** someterse a una operación *or* una intervención quirúrgica para extirpar un tumor (*frm*); **to perform an ~ on sb** operar a algn
[5] (*Comm*) (= *business*) operación *f*
[6] (*Mil*) operación *f*; **Operation Torch** Operación Antorcha
[7] (*Fin, St Ex*) (= *transaction*) operación *f*; **~s on the Stock Exchange** las operaciones bursátiles, la actividad bursátil
[8] (*Math, Comput*) operación *f*
(B) CPD ► **operation code** N código *m* de operación ► **operations research** N investigaciones *fpl* operativas *or* operacionales ► **operations room** N (*Police*) centro *m* de coordinación; (*Mil*) centro *m* de operaciones

operational [ˌɒpə'reɪʃənl] ADJ [1] (= *relating to operations*) [*control, plan*] operativo, de operaciones; [*problems, cost, expenses*] de funcionamiento; [*staff*] de servicio; **~ research** investigaciones *fpl* operacionales; **for ~ reasons** por necesidades operativas
[2] (= *ready for use or action*) [*aircraft, service, airport*] en funcionamiento; [*bus, train*] en servicio; [*troops*] operacional; **the bridge could be ~ in three years' time** el puente podría entrar en funcionamiento dentro de tres años; **to be fully ~** estar en pleno funcionamiento

operative ['ɒpərətɪv] (A) ADJ [1] (*gen*) operativo; **the ~ word** la palabra clave
[2] (*Jur*) **to be ~** estar en vigor; **to become ~ from the 9th** entrar en vigor a partir del 9
[3] (*Med*) operatorio
(B) N (= *worker*) obrero/a *m/f*; (*with a special skill*) operario/a *m/f*, obrero/a *m/f* especializado/a

operator ['ɒpəreɪtəʳ] N [1] [*of machine etc*] operario/a *m/f*; (= *machinist*) maquinista *mf*; (*Cine*) operador(a) *m/f*; (*Telec*) telefonista *mf*
[2] (*) (*fig*) **a smooth ~** (*in business*) un tipo hábil; (*in love*) un engatusador; **he's a very clever ~** es un tipo muy vivo*

operetta [ˌɒpə'retə] N zarzuela *f*, opereta *f*

Ophelia [ɒ'fiːlɪə] N Ofelia

ophthalmia [ɒf'θælmɪə] N oftalmía *f*

ophthalmic [ɒf'θælmɪk] ADJ oftálmico

ophthalmologist [ˌɒfθæl'mɒlədʒɪst] N oftalmólogo/a *m/f*

ophthalmology [ˌɒfθæl'mɒlədʒɪ] N oftalmología *f*

ophthalmoscope [ɒf'θælməskəʊp] N oftalmoscopio *m*

opiate ['əʊpɪɪt] N opiata *f*

opine [əʊ'paɪn] VI opinar

opinion [ə'pɪnjən] (A) N [1] (= *belief, view*) opinión *f*; **what's your ~ of him?** ¿qué opinas de él?, ¿qué opinión te merece?; **what's your ~ of this book?** ¿qué opinas de este libro?, ¿qué opinión te merece este libro?; **well, that's my ~** por lo menos eso pienso yo; **to ask sb's ~ (on** *or* **about sth)** pedir a algn su opinión *or* parecer (sobre *or* acerca de algo); **when I want your ~ I'll ask for it!** ¡cuando quiera saber tu opinión, te la pediré!; **if you ask my ~, he's hiding something** mi opinión es que está ocultando algo; **there are differences of ~ as to what happened** hay discordancia *or* discrepancia de opiniones respecto a lo que pasó; **to form an ~ of sth/sb** formarse una opinión sobre algo/algn; **to have** *or* **hold an ~ on** *or* **about sth** tener una opinión sobre *or* acerca de algo; **many people have very strong ~s about this** mucha gente tiene opiniones muy definidas sobre *or* acerca de esto; **she held the ~ that ...** opinaba que ...; **to have a high** *or* **good ~ of sth/sb** tener un alto concepto de algo/algn, tener muy buena opinión de algo/algn; **to have a poor** *or* **low ~ of sth/sb** tener un bajo concepto de algo/algn, tener muy mala opi-

➤ LANGUAGE IN USE: **opinion A1** 6.1, 6.2, 6.3, 11.1, 26.1, 26.2

nión de algo/algn; **she has a very low ~ of herself** tiene un concepto muy bajo de sí misma; **I haven't much of an ~ of him** no tengo un alto concepto de él, no tengo muy buena opinión de él; **in my ~** en mi opinión, a mi juicio; **it's a matter of ~** es cuestión de opiniones; **to be of the ~ that ...** opinar que ...

2 (= *judgment*) opinión *f*; **we need an expert ~** necesitamos la opinión de un experto; **could you give us your professional ~?** ¿nos puede dar su opinión (como) profesional?; **to seek a second ~** pedir una segunda opinión

3 (= *the prevailing view*) opinión *f*; **he is in a position to influence ~** está en una posición en la que puede ejercer influencia sobre las opiniones; **medical ~ was divided over the case** la opinión médica estaba dividida con respecto al caso; **they are trying to turn world ~ against the United States** están intentando poner al mundo entero en contra de Estados Unidos; *see also* **consensus, public C**

Ⓑ CPD ► **opinion poll** N sondeo *m* (de opinión)

opinionated [əˈpɪnjəneɪtɪd] ADJ testarudo

opium [ˈəʊpɪəm] Ⓐ N opio *m*

Ⓑ CPD ► **opium addict** N opiómano/a *m/f* ► **opium addiction** N opiomanía *f* ► **opium den** N fumadero *m* de opio

opossum [əˈpɒsəm] N (*pl* **opossums** *or* **opossum**) zarigüeya *f*

opp. ABBR = **opposite**

opponent [əˈpəʊnənt] N adversario/a *m/f*, contrincante *mf*; (*in debate, discussion*) oponente *mf*, adversario/a *m/f*

opportune [ˈɒpətjuːn] ADJ [*arrival, event, remark*] oportuno; **at an ~ moment** *or* **time** en un momento oportuno

opportunely [ˈɒpətjuːnlɪ] ADV [*remark, intervene*] oportunamente; [*arrive, call*] en un momento oportuno

opportunism [ˌɒpəˈtjuːnɪzəm] N oportunismo *m*

opportunist [ˌɒpəˈtjuːnɪst] Ⓐ ADJ oportunista

Ⓑ N oportunista *mf*

opportunistic [ˌɒpətjʊˈnɪstɪk] ADJ oportunista

opportunity [ˈɒpəˈtjuːnɪtɪ] N oportunidad *f*, ocasión *f*; **at the earliest ~** en la primera oportunidad, cuanto antes; **equality of ~** igualdad *f* de oportunidades; **he criticized her at every ~** la criticaba siempre que se le presentaba la ocasión *or* en cuanto podía; **at the first ~** en la primera oportunidad, cuanto antes; **opportunities for promotion** oportunidades de promoción; **when I get the ~** cuando se me presente la oportunidad *or* la ocasión, cuando tenga ocasión; **we were given no ~ to prepare ourselves** no se nos ofreció la oportunidad *or* la ocasión de prepararnos; **given the ~, he'll watch TV all day** si le dejases, se pasaría el día entero viendo la tele; **to have the/an ~ to do sth** ◊ **have the/an ~ of doing sth** tener la oportunidad de hacer algo; **I haven't had an ~ of talking to him** no he tenido la oportunidad de hablar con él; **to miss one's ~** perder la oportunidad; **he never missed an ~ to criticize her** nunca dejaba pasar la oportunidad de criticarla; **to seize the/one's ~** aprovechar la oportunidad *or* ocasión; **to take the ~ to do sth** ◊ **take the ~ of doing sth** aprovechar la oportunidad *or* la ocasión para hacer algo; *see also* **equal D, job C, photo**

oppose [əˈpəʊz] VT 1 (= *disagree with*) oponerse a, estar en contra de; **67% are in favour of the measure and 33% ~ it** el 67% está a favor de la medida y el 33% restante se opone *or* está en contra; **they ~d the motion** se opusieron a la moción

2 (= *combat*) luchar contra, combatir; **I have no wish to ~ progress** no deseo luchar contra *or* combatir el progreso; **he may decide to ~ him at the next election** puede que decida enfrentarse a él en las próximas elecciones

opposed [əˈpəʊzd] ADJ 1 (= *in disagreement*) **to be ~ to sth** oponerse a algo, estar en contra de algo; **he is strongly ~ to the use of force** se opone enérgicamente al uso de la fuerza, está totalmente en contra del uso de la fuerza; **they have diametrically ~ views on abortion** tienen opiniones diametralmente opuestas sobre el aborto

2 **as ~ to** (= *rather than*) en vez de; (= *compared to*) a diferencia de; **why did you become a Republican, as ~ to a Democrat?** ¿por qué te hiciste republicano, en vez de demócrata?; **savings as ~ to investments** los ahorros a diferencia de las inversiones

opposing [əˈpəʊzɪŋ] ADJ [*views, ideas*] opuesto, contrario; [*team*] contrario; [*army*] enemigo; **we've always had ~ views on politics** nuestras ideas políticas siempre han sido opuestas *or* contrarias; **they found themselves on ~ sides in the war** en la guerra se encontraron luchando en bandos contrarios

opposite [ˈɒpəzɪt] Ⓐ ADV enfrente; **I looked at the director, sitting ~** miré al director que estaba sentado enfrente (de mí); **please fill in the box ~** por favor, rellene la casilla de al lado; **they live directly** *or* **immediately ~** viven justo enfrente

Ⓑ PREP (*also* **~ to**) 1 (= *across from*) frente a, enfrente de; **~ the library** frente a *or* enfrente de la biblioteca; **Lynn was sitting ~ him** Lynn estaba sentada frente a él *or* enfrente de él; **they sat ~ one another** se sentaron uno frente a(l) otro, se sentaron frente a frente

2 (= *next to*) junto a, al lado de; **~ his name was a question mark** junto a *or* al lado de su nombre había una interrogación; **to play ~ sb** (*Theat*) aparecer junto a algn

Ⓒ ADJ 1 (*in position*) de enfrente; **the house ~** la casa de enfrente; **on the ~ bank** en la ribera opuesta; **on the ~ page** en la página opuesta *or* de al lado; **to be facing the ~ way** estar mirando al otro lado, estar de cara al otro lado

2 (= *far*) [*end, corner*] opuesto; **we sat at ~ ends of the sofa** nos sentamos cada uno a un extremo del sofá, nos sentamos en extremos opuestos del sofá

3 (= *contrary*) contrario, opuesto; **in the ~ direction** en dirección contraria *or* opuesta, en sentido contrario *or* opuesto; **it had the ~ effect** produjo el efecto contrario *or* opuesto; **~ number** homólogo/a *m/f*; **the ~ sex** el otro sexo, el sexo opuesto; **they were on ~ sides in the war** lucharon en bandos contrarios *or* opuestos en la guerra; **she presented the ~ view** presentó el punto de vista contrario *or* opuesto; **we take the ~ view** nosotros pensamos lo contrario

Ⓓ N **the ~** lo contrario; **she said the exact ~** ◊ **she said just the ~** dijo exactamente lo contrario; **my brother is just the ~** mi hermano es justo lo contrario; **it's the ~ of what we wanted** es lo contrario de lo que queríamos; **he says the ~ of everything I say** me lleva la contraria en todo; **quite the ~!** ¡todo lo contrario!; **the ~ is true** la verdad es todo lo contrario

opposition [ˌɒpəˈzɪʃən] Ⓐ N 1 (= *resistance*) resistencia *f*, oposición *f*; (= *people opposing*) oposición *f*; (*Sport*) (= *team*) equipo *m* contrario; **to advance a kilometre without ~** avanzar un kilómetro sin encontrar resistencia; **there is a lot of ~ to the new law** hay mucha oposición a la nueva ley; **he made his ~ known** indicó su disconformidad; **to be in ~** estar en la oposición; **in ~ to** (= *against*) en contra de; (= *unlike*) a diferencia de; **to start up a business in ~ to another** montar un negocio en competencia con otro; **to act in ~ to the chairman** obrar en oposición al presidente

2 (*Brit Pol*) **the Opposition** los partidos de la oposición, la oposición; **leader of the Opposition** líder *mf* de la oposición; **the party in ~** el partido de la oposición

Ⓑ CPD [*member, party*] de la oposición ► **the Opposition benches** NPL los escaños de la Oposición, la Oposición

oppositionist [ˌɒpəˈzɪʃənɪst] N (*Pol*) militante *mf* de la oposición clandestina

oppress [əˈpres] VT 1 (*Mil, Pol etc*) oprimir; **the ~ed** los oprimidos

2 [*heat, anxiety etc*] agobiar; **~ed with worry** angustiado/a

oppression [əˈpreʃən] N opresión *f*

oppressive [əˈpresɪv] ADJ 1 (= *unjust*) [*regime, law, system*] opresivo; [*tax*] gravoso

2 (= *stifling*) [*heat, air, atmosphere*] sofocante, agobiante; [*mood, feeling, silence*] opresivo, agobiante; **the little room was ~** la pequeña habitación resultaba opresiva *or* agobiante

oppressively [əˈpresɪvlɪ] ADV 1 (= *unjustly*) [*rule, govern*] de manera opresiva, de modo opresivo

2 (= *stiflingly*) **the room was ~ hot** en la habitación hacía un calor sofocante *or* agobiante; **it was ~ humid** hacía una humedad agobiante; **the city is ~ drab and grey** la ciudad es tan monótona y gris que resulta opresiva *or* agobiante

oppressor [əˈpresəʳ] N opresor(a) *m/f*

opprobrious [əˈprəʊbrɪəs] ADJ (*frm*) oprobioso

opprobrium [əˈprəʊbrɪəm] N (*frm*) oprobio *m*

opt [ɒpt] VI **to ~ for sth** optar por algo; **to ~ to do sth** optar por hacer algo

►**opt out** VI + ADV 1 (= *decide against*) **to ~ out of doing sth** optar por no hacer algo; **I think I'll ~ out of going** creo que optaré por no ir

2 (= *withdraw*) retractarse

optative [ˈɒptətɪv] Ⓐ ADJ optativo

Ⓑ N optativo *m*

optic [ˈɒptɪk] ADJ óptico; **~ nerve** nervio *m* óptico

optical [ˈɒptɪkəl] ADJ óptico; **~ disk** disco *m* óptico; **~ fibre** fibra *f* óptica; **~ illusion** ilusión *f* óptica; **~ (character) reader** lector *m* óptico (de caracteres); **~ character recognition** reconocimiento *m* óptico de caracteres

optician [ɒpˈtɪʃən] N óptico/a *m/f*; **~'s** óptica *f*

optics [ˈɒptɪks] NSING óptica *f*

optimal [ˈɒptɪml] ADJ óptimo

optimally [ˈɒptɪməlɪ] ADV de manera óptima, óptimamente

optimism [ˈɒptɪmɪzəm] N optimismo *m*; **the Prime Minister has expressed ~ about the outcome of the talks** el primer ministro ha expresado su optimismo acerca del resultado de las negociaciones; **there is some cause for ~** hay algunas razones para ser optimistas

optimist [ˈɒptɪmɪst] N optimista *mf*; **he's the eternal ~** es el eterno optimista

optimistic [ˌɒptɪˈmɪstɪk] ADJ optimista; **to be ~ that** ser optimista respecto a que; **to be ~ about sth** ser optimista acerca de *or* con respecto a algo; **to keep** *or* **remain ~** mantener el optimismo; **to be in an ~ mood** sentirse optimista; **to end on an ~ note** terminar con una nota de optimismo; *see also* **cautiously**

optimistically [ˌɒptɪˈmɪstɪklɪ] ADV con optimismo

optimization [ˌɒptɪmaɪˈzeɪʃən] N optimización *f*

optimize [ˈɒptɪmaɪz] VT optimizar

optimum [ˈɒptɪməm] Ⓐ ADJ [*level, number*] óptimo; **in ~ conditions** en las condiciones óptimas *or* más favorables; **within the ~ time** dentro del tiempo ideal; **for ~ health** para gozar de buena salud
Ⓑ N (*pl* **optimums** *or* **optima** [ˈɒptɪmə]) **the ~** lo óptimo, lo mejor; **they are not functioning at their ~** no están funcionando lo mejor que pueden, no están funcionando al nivel óptimo

option [ˈɒpʃən] N [1] (= *choice*) opción *f*; **what are my ~s?** ¿qué opciones tengo?; **you have a number of ~s** tienes varias opciones; **I have no ~** no tengo más *or* otro remedio, no tengo otra opción; **she had no ~ but to leave** no tuvo más remedio que irse; **to have the ~ of doing sth** tener la posibilidad de hacer algo; **imprisonment without the ~ of bail** (*Jur*) prisión *f* preventiva; **to keep one's ~s open** no descartar ninguna posibilidad
[2] (*Comm*) opción *f*; **at the ~ of the purchaser** a opción del comprador; **stock ~** (*Fin*) compra *f* opcional de acciones; **to take out an ~ on another 100** suscribir una opción para la compra de otros 100; **with the ~ to buy** con opción de compra; **with an ~ on ten more aircraft** con opción para la compra de otros diez aviones
[3] (*Scol, Univ*) asignatura *f* optativa; **I'm doing geology as my ~** tengo geología como asignatura optativa

optional [ˈɒpʃənl] ADJ [*course, subject*] optativo, facultativo; [*part, accessory*] opcional; **that is completely ~** eso es completamente opcional; **~ extra** (*Aut*) accesorio *m* opcional, extra *m*; **"dress optional"** "no se requiere (ir de) etiqueta"

optionally [ˈɒpʃənlɪ] ADV opcionalmente

optometrist [ɒpˈtɒmətrɪst] N optometrista *mf*

optometry [ɒpˈtɒmətrɪ] N optometría *f*

opt-out [ˈɒptaʊt] Ⓐ ADJ [1] (*Brit*) [*school, hospital*] autónomo (*transferido de la administración local al gobierno central*)
[2] (*esp Brit*) **~ clause** cláusula *f* de exclusión voluntaria, claúsula *f* de no participación
Ⓑ N (*from agreement, treaty*) opción *f* de exclusión voluntaria, opción *f* de no participación

opulence [ˈɒpjʊləns] N opulencia *f*

opulent [ˈɒpjʊlənt] ADJ opulento

opus [ˈəʊpəs] N (*pl* **opuses** *or* **opera**) (*Mus*) opus *m*

OR Ⓐ ABBR = **operations** *or* **operational research**
Ⓑ ABBR [1] (*US*) = **Oregon**
[2] (*Sport*) = **Olympic record**

or [ɔːʳ] CONJ [1] (*giving alternative*) o; (*before o-, ho-*) u; (*between numerals*) ó; **would you like tea or coffee?** ¿quieres té o café?; **seven or eight** siete u ocho; **men or women** mujeres u hombres; **15 or 16** 15 ó 16; **let me go or I'll scream!** ¡suélteme, o me pongo a gritar!; **hurry up or you'll miss the bus** date prisa, que vas a perder el autobús; **rain or no rain, you've got to go** con lluvia o sin lluvia, tienes que ir; **not ... or ...** no ... ni ...; **he didn't write or telephone** no escribió ni telefoneó; **I don't eat meat or fish** no como carne ni pescado; **she can't dance or sing** no sabe bailar ni cantar; **20 or so** unos veinte, veinte más o menos; **an hour or so** una hora más o menos; **without relatives or friends** sin parientes ni amigos; *see also* **either C, else 4**
[2] (= *that is*) es decir; **botany, or the science of plants** botánica, es decir la ciencia que estudia las plantas; **or rather ...** o mejor dicho ..., o más bien ...

> **OR**
>
> **"U" and "ó" instead of "o"**
>
> • While **or** is usually translated by **o**, use **u** instead before words beginning with **o** and **ho**:
> ...two or three photos...
> ***...dos o tres fotos...***
> ...for one reason or another...
> ***...por un motivo u otro...***
> She was accused of parricide or homicide
> ***Se le acusó de parricidio u homicidio***
> • Write **ó** instead of **o** between numerals to prevent confusion with zero:
> ...5 or 6...
> ***...5 ó 6...***
> **!** Remember to use **ni** with negatives.
> *For further uses and examples, see main entry.*

o.r. ABBR = **at owner's risk**

oracle [ˈɒrəkl] N oráculo *m*

oracular [ɒˈrækjʊləʳ] ADJ profético, fatídico

oral [ˈɔːrəl] Ⓐ ADJ [1] (= *spoken*) [*history, tradition, exam*] oral; (*Jur*) [*agreement, evidence*] verbal
[2] (*Med, Anat*) [*contraceptive, vaccine, sex*] oral; [*hygiene*] bucal
Ⓑ N examen *m* oral

orally [ˈɔːrəlɪ] ADV [1] (= *verbally*) verbalmente, oralmente
[2] (*Med*) por vía oral

orange [ˈɒrɪndʒ] Ⓐ N (= *fruit*) naranja *f*; (*also* **~ tree**) naranjo *m*; (= *colour*) naranja *m*; (= *orangeade*) naranjada *f* (*con burbujas*); (= *orange squash*) naranjada *f* (*sin burbujas*)
Ⓑ ADJ [1] (*in colour*) naranja *inv*, (de) color naranja *inv*; **bright ~** naranja fuerte *or* chillón, (de) color naranja fuerte *or* chillón
[2] (*in taste*) [*flavour*] a naranja
Ⓒ CPD ► **orange blossom** N azahar *m*, flor *f* de naranjo ► **orange box, orange crate** (*US*) N caja *f* de fruta ► **orange drink** N refresco *m* de naranja ► **orange flower water** N agua *f* de azahar ► **orange grove** N naranjal *m* ► **orange juice** N jugo *m* de naranja, zumo *m* de naranja (*Sp*) ► **orange marmalade** N mermelada *f* de naranja ► **orange peel** *or* **rind** N cáscara *f* de naranja ► **orange sauce** N salsa *f* de naranja ► **orange squash** N naranjada *f* (*sin burbujas*) ► **orange stick** N palito *m* de naranjo ► **orange tree** N naranjo *m*

orangeade [ˈɒrɪndʒˈeɪd] N (*natural*) naranjada *f*; (*fizzy*) refresco *m* de naranja

orange-coloured, orange-colored (*US*) [ˈɒrɪndʒˌkʌləd] ADJ naranja *inv*, (de) color naranja *inv*

Orangeman [ˈɒrɪndʒmən] N (*pl* **Orangemen**) *miembro de las logias protestantes de la Orden de Orange*

orangery [ˈɒrɪndʒərɪ] N invernadero *m* de naranjos

orangey [ˈɒrɪndʒɪ] ADJ naranjilla, anaranjado

orang-outang [ɔːˌræŋuːˈtæŋ] N = **orang-utan**

orang-utan [ɔːˌræŋuːˈtæn] N orangután *m*

orate [ɔːˈreɪt] VI (*hum*) perorar

oration [ɔːˈreɪʃən] N (= *speech*) discurso *m*; (= *peroration*) arenga *f*; **funeral ~** oración *f* fúnebre

orator [ˈɒrətəʳ] N orador(a) *m/f*

oratorical [ˌɒrəˈtɒrɪkəl] ADJ oratorio, retórico

oratorio [ˌɒrəˈtɔːrɪəʊ] N (*pl* **oratorios**) (*Mus*) oratorio *m*

oratory[1] [ˈɒrətərɪ] N (= *art of speaking*) oratoria *f*

oratory[2] [ˈɒrətərɪ] N (*Rel*) oratorio *m*

orb [ɔːb] N (= *sphere*) esfera *f*, globo *m*; (*in regalia*) orbe *m*

orbit [ˈɔːbɪt] Ⓐ N órbita *f*; **to be in/go into ~ (round the earth/moon)** estar en/entrar en órbita (alrededor de la tierra/luna); **it's outside my ~** (*fig*) está fuera de mi competencia, que da fuera de mi ámbito
Ⓑ VI [*satellite*] orbitar, girar; [*astronaut*] estar en órbita
Ⓒ VT [+ *earth, moon*] girar alrededor de

orbital [ˈɔːbɪtl] ADJ [1] (*Space*) orbital; **~ space station** estación *f* orbital
[2] (*Brit Aut*) **~ motorway/road** autopista *f*/carrera *f* de circunvalación

orbiter [ˈɔːbɪtəʳ] N (*Space*) orbitador *m*

orchard [ˈɔːtʃəd] N huerto *m*; **apple ~** manzanar *m*, manzanal *m*

orchestra [ˈɔːkɪstrə] Ⓐ N orquesta *f*; **symphony ~** orquesta *f* sinfónica; **string ~** orquesta *f* de cuerdas; **chamber ~** orquesta *f* de cámara
Ⓑ CPD ► **orchestra pit** N foso *m* de orquesta ► **orchestra stalls** NPL (*Theat*) luneta *fsing*, platea *fsing*

orchestral [ɔːˈkestrəl] ADJ orquestal

orchestrate [ˈɔːkɪstreɪt] VT [1] (*Mus*) orquestar
[2] (*fig*) [*rebellion*] tramar; [*campaign*] organizar

orchestration [ˌɔːkɪsˈtreɪʃən] N (*lit, fig*) orquestación *f*

orchid [ˈɔːkɪd] N orquídea *f*

orchis [ˈɔːkɪs] N orquídea *f*

ordain [ɔːˈdeɪn] Ⓐ VT [1] (= *order*) ordenar, decretar; [*God*] mandar, disponer; **it was ~ed that ...** se dispuso que ...
[2] (*Rel*) ordenar; **to ~ sb priest** ordenar a algn sacerdote; **to be ~ed** ordenarse
Ⓑ VI mandar, disponer; **as God ~s** según manda Dios, como Dios manda

ordeal [ɔːˈdiːl] N [1] (= *bad experience*) terrible experiencia *f*; **it was a terrible ~** fue una experiencia terrible; **after such an ~** después de tan terrible experiencia; **exams are an ~ for me** para mí los exámenes son un suplicio
[2] (*Hist*) ordalías *fpl*; **~ by fire** ordalías *fpl* del fuego

order [ˈɔːdəʳ] Ⓐ N [1] (= *sequence*) orden *m*; **in ~** en orden, por orden; **what ~ should these documents be in?** ¿en qué orden deben estar estos documentos?; **in alphabetical ~** por *or* en orden alfabético; **"cast in ~ of appearance"** (*Theat, Cine*) "por orden de aparición"; **in chronological ~** por orden cronológico; **in ~ of merit** ordenado según el mérito; **they are out of ~** están mal ordenados; **to get out of ~** desarreglarse; **put these in the right ~** ponga estos por orden; **in ~ of seniority** por orden de antigüedad; **word ~** orden *m* de las palabras; **they are in the wrong ~** están mal ordenados
[2] (= *system*) orden *m*; **a new political/social ~** un nuevo orden político/social; **she has no ~ in her life** lleva un régimen de vida muy desorganizado; **the old ~ is changing** el viejo orden está cambiando; **it is in the ~ of things** es ley de vida; **a new world ~** un nuevo orden mundial
[3] (= *good order*) buen estado *m*, orden *m*; **in**

~ (*legally*) en regla; [*room*] en orden, ordenado; **his papers are in ~** tiene los papeles en regla; **everything is in ~** todo está en regla; **is this passport in ~?** ¿este pasaporte está en regla?; **to put a matter in ~** arreglar un asunto; **to put one's affairs in ~** poner sus asuntos en orden; **in good ~** en buen estado, en buenas condiciones; **a machine in working** *or* **running ~** una máquina en buen estado; **to be out of ~** [*machine*] estar estropeado *or* (*LAm*) descompuesto; **the line is out of ~** (*Telec*) no hay línea, la línea no funciona; **"out of order"** "no funciona"

[4] (= *peace, control*) orden *m*; **the forces of ~** las fuerzas del orden; **to keep ~** mantener el orden; **she can't keep ~** es incapaz de imponer la disciplina, no puede hacerse obedecer; **to keep children in ~** mantener a los niños en orden

[5] (= *command*) orden *f*; [*of court etc*] sentencia *f*, fallo *m*; **~s are ~s** las órdenes no se discuten; **bankruptcy ~** orden *f* de quiebra; **by ~ of** por orden de; **Order in Council** (*Brit Parl*) Orden *f* Real; **~ of the court** sentencia *f* del tribunal; **deportation ~** orden *f* de deportación; **till further ~s** hasta nueva orden; **to give ~s** dar órdenes; **to give sb ~s to do sth** ordenar *or* mandar a algn hacer algo; **he gave the ~ for it to be done** ordenó que se hiciera; **to obey ~s** cumplir órdenes; **on the ~s of** a las órdenes de; **to take ~s from sb** recibir órdenes de algn; **I don't take ~s from anyone** a mí no me da órdenes nadie; **that's an ~!** ¡es una orden!; **under ~s** bajo órdenes; **we are under ~s not to allow it** tenemos orden de no permitirlo; **to be under the ~s of** estar bajo el mando de; ✦***IDIOM*** **to get one's marching ~s*** ser despedido; *see also* **starter A1**

[6] (= *correct procedure*) (*at meeting, Parliament etc*) orden *m*; **order (order)!** ¡orden!; **to call sb to ~** llamar a algn al orden; **to call the meeting to ~** abrir la sesión; **~ of the day** (*Mil*) orden del día; (*fig*) moda *f*, estilo *m* del momento; **strikes are the ~ of the day** las huelgas están a la orden del día; **to be in ~** [*action, request*] ser procedente; **a beer would be in ~** sería indicado tomarse una cerveza; **it seems congratulations are in ~!** ¡enhorabuena!; **is it in ~ for me to go to Rome?** ¿(le) es inconveniente si voy a Roma?; **it is not in ~ to discuss Ruritania** Ruritania está fuera de la cuestión; **to be out of ~*** (= *unacceptable*) [*remark*] estar fuera de lugar; [*person*] comportarse mal; **to rule a matter out of ~** decidir que un asunto no se puede discutir; **a point of ~** una cuestión de procedimiento

[7] (*Comm*) pedido *m*, encargo *m*; **we have it on ~ for you** está pedido para usted; **we will put it on ~ for you** se lo pediremos para usted al fabricante; **to place an ~ for sth with sb** encargar *or* hacer un pedido de algo a algn; **repeat ~** pedido *m* de repetición; **rush ~** pedido *m* urgente; **made to ~** hecho a medida; **we can't do things to ~** no podemos proveer en seguida todo cuanto se nos pide; ✦***IDIOM*** **that's rather a tall ~** eso es mucho pedir

[8] (*in restaurant*) **the waiter took our ~** el camarero tomó nota de lo que íbamos a comer; **an ~ of French fries** una ración de patatas fritas

[9] **in ~ to do sth** para *or* a fin de hacer algo; **in ~ that he may stay** para que pueda quedarse

[10] [*of society etc*] clase *f*, categoría *f*; (*Bio*) orden *m*; **Benedictine Order** Orden *f* de San Benito; **the present crisis is of a different ~** la crisis actual es de un orden distinto; **talents of the first ~** talentos *mpl* de primer orden; **holy ~s** órdenes *fpl* sagradas; **to be in/take (holy) ~s** ser/ordenarse sacerdote; **the lower ~s** las clases bajas *or* (*LAm*) populares; **of the ~ of 500** del orden de los quinientos; **something in** *or* **of** *or* (*US*) **on the ~ of £3,000** unos 3.000, alrededor de 3.000; **~ of magnitude** magnitud *f*

[11] (*Fin*) libranza *f*; (*postal*) giro *m*; **pay to the ~ of** páguese a la orden de

[12] (*Archit*) orden *m*; **Doric ~** orden *m* dórico

[13] **in short ~** (*US*) rápidamente

[14] (*Mil*) **in battle ~** en orden de batalla; **in close ~** en filas apretadas; **in marching ~** en orden de marchar

Ⓑ VT [1] (= *command*) mandar, ordenar; **to ~ sb to do sth** mandar *or* ordenar a algn hacer algo; **to be ~ed to pay costs** ser condenado en costas; **he was ~ed to be quiet** le ordenaron que se callara; **he ~ed that the army should advance** ordenó que el ejército avanzara, dio órdenes de que el ejército avanzara; **the referee ~ed the player off the field** el árbitro expulsó al jugador del campo; **to ~ sb in/up** *etc* mandar entrar/subir *etc* a algn, hacer entrar/subir *etc* a algn; **are you ~ing me out of my own house?** ¿me estás echando de mi propia casa?

[2] (= *put in order*) ordenar, poner en orden; **they are ~ed by date/size** estan ordenados por fecha/tamaño

[3] (= *organize*) organizar, arreglar; **to ~ one's life properly** organizar bien su vida, vivir de acuerdo a cierto método

[4] [+ *goods, meal, taxi*] pedir, encargar; **to ~ a suit** mandar hacer un traje; **we ~ed steak and chips** pedimos un filete con patatas fritas

Ⓒ VI (*in restaurant*) pedir; **are you ready to ~?** ¿han decidido qué van a pedir?

Ⓓ CPD ► **order book** N (*Comm*) libro *m* de pedidos, cartera *f* de pedidos ► **order department** N (*Comm*) sección *f* de pedidos ► **order form** N (*Comm*) hoja *f* de pedido ► **order number** N (*Comm*) número *m* de pedido ► **order paper** N (*Brit Parl etc*) orden *m* del día; *see also* **garter**

►**order about, order around** VT + ADV dar órdenes a, mandonear*; **she was fed up with being ~ed about** estaba harta de que le dieran órdenes

►**order back** VT + ADV mandar volver

ordered ['ɔːdəd] ADJ ordenado, metódico, disciplinado

ordering ['ɔːdərɪŋ] N (*Comm*) pedido *m*

orderliness ['ɔːdəlɪnɪs] N orden *m*, método *m*, disciplina *f*

orderly ['ɔːdəlɪ] Ⓐ ADJ [*queue, row, room*] ordenado; [*person, mind*] ordenado, metódico; [*crowd*] pacífico; [*class*] obediente, disciplinado; **in an ~ fashion** *or* **way** *or* **manner** de forma *or* manera ordenada

Ⓑ N (*Mil*) ordenanza *mf*; (*Med*) celador(a) *m/f*

Ⓒ CPD ► **orderly room** N (*Mil*) oficina *f*

ordinal ['ɔːdɪnl] Ⓐ ADJ ordinal; **~ number** número *m* ordinal

Ⓑ N ordinal *m*

ordinance ['ɔːdɪnəns] N decreto-ley *m*, reglamento *m*

ordinand ['ɔːdɪnænd] N ordenando *m*

ordinarily [ɔːdɪ'nɛərɪlɪ] ADV por lo común, generalmente

ordinary ['ɔːdnrɪ] Ⓐ ADJ [1] (= *usual, normal*) [*milk, coffee*] normal, corriente; **it has 25 calories less than ~ ice cream** tiene 25 calorías menos que el helado normal *or* corriente; **my ~ doctor** el médico al que voy normalmente; **I'd rather wear my ~ clothes** prefiero usar mi ropa normal; **the heat made ~ life almost impossible** el calor hacía la vida normal casi imposible; **in ~ use** usado normalmente; **in the ~ way** normalmente

[2] (= *unremarkable, average*) normal y corriente; **it was just an ~ weekend for us** para nosotros no era más que un fin de semana cualquiera *or* un fin de semana normal y corriente; **he's a normal, ~ guy** es un tipo normal y corriente; **it's not what you'd call an ~ present** no es lo que se dice un regalo de todos los días; **an ~ citizen** un simple ciudadano, un ciudadano de a pie; **it was no ~ bar** no era un bar corriente; **your life since then must have seemed very ~** tu vida desde entonces debe de haberte parecido demasiado normal; **the meal was very ~** (*pej*) la comida fue bastante mediocre, la comida no fue nada del otro mundo *or* del otro jueves

Ⓑ N **a man above the ~** un hombre fuera de serie, un hombre excepcional; **a cut above the ~** fuera de serie; **out of the ~** fuera de lo común, extraordinario

Ⓒ CPD ► **ordinary degree** N (*Brit Univ*) diploma *m*, *título universitario de categoría inferior al Honours degree*; → DEGREE ► **Ordinary Grade** N (*Scot*) (*formerly*) *nivel medio de la enseñanza secundaria*, ≈ Bachillerato *m* Unificado y Polivalente (*Sp*) ► **Ordinary Level** N (*Brit*) (*formerly*) *nivel medio de la enseñanza secundaria*, ≈ Bachillerato *m* Unificado y Polivalente (*Sp*) ► **Ordinary National Certificate** N (*Brit*) ≈ diploma *m* de técnico especialista ► **Ordinary National Diploma** N (*Brit*) *diploma profesional*, ≈ diploma *m* de técnico especialista ► **ordinary seaman** N (*Brit Navy*) marinero *m* ► **ordinary shares** NPL acciones *fpl* ordinarias

ordination [ˌɔːdɪ'neɪʃən] N (*Rel*) ordenación *f*

ordnance ['ɔːdnəns] (*Mil*) Ⓐ N (= *guns*) artillería *f*; (= *supplies*) pertrechos *mpl* de guerra, material *m* de guerra

Ⓑ CPD ► **Ordnance Corps** N Cuerpo *m* de Armamento y Material ► **ordnance factory** N fábrica *f* de artillería ► **Ordnance Survey** N (*Brit*) *servicio estatal de cartografía* ► **Ordnance Survey map** N (*Brit*) mapa *m* del servicio estatal de cartografía

Ordovician [ˌɔːdəʊ'vɪʃɪən] ADJ ordoviciense

ordure ['ɔːdjʊəʳ] N (*lit, fig*) inmundicia *f*

ore [ɔːʳ] N mineral *m*, mena *f*; **copper ~** mineral *m* de cobre

Ore. ABBR (*US*) = **Oregon**

ore-carrier ['ɔːkærɪəʳ] N mineralero *m*

Oreg. ABBR (*US*) = **Oregon**

oregano [ˌɒrɪ'gɑːnəʊ] (*US*) [ə'regənəʊ] N orégano *m*

organ ['ɔːgən] Ⓐ N [1] (*Mus*) órgano *m*; (= *barrel organ*) organillo *m*

[2] (*Anat*) órgano *m*

[3] (= *mouthpiece*) [*of opinion*] órgano *m*, portavoz *mf*

Ⓑ CPD ► **organ loft** N tribuna *f* del órgano, galería *f* del órgano ► **organ pipe** N cañón *m* de órgano ► **organ stop** N registro *m* de órgano

organdie, organdy (*US*) ['ɔːgəndɪ] N organdí *m*

organ-grinder ['ɔːgən,graɪndəʳ] N organillero/a *m/f*

organic [ɔː'gænɪk] ADJ [1] (= *living*) [*matter, waste*] orgánico; [*fertiliser*] orgánico, natural

[2] (= *not chemical*) [*farmer, farm, methods*] ecológico; [*vegetables, produce*] de cultivo biológico, biológico; [*meat*] ecológico; [*flour*] integral; [*wine, beer*] sin sustancias artificiales; ~

food alimentos *mpl* biológicos, alimentos *mpl* de cultivo biológico; **~ farming** agricultura *f* ecológica *or* biológica; **~ restaurant** restaurante *m* de cocina natural
[3] (*Chem*) orgánico; **~ chemistry** química *f* orgánica
[4] (*frm*) (= *natural*) [*growth, development, change*] natural; (= *united*) [*society, state, community*] orgánico

organically [ɔːˈgænɪkəlɪ] ADV [1] (*Agr*) [*grow, produce, farm*] biológicamente, sin utilizar pesticidas ni fertilizantes artificiales; **~ grown foods** alimentos *mpl* biológicos, alimentos *mpl* de cultivo biológico; **an ~ rich soil** un suelo orgánicamente rico
[2] (*Med*) **the surgeons could find nothing ~ wrong** los cirujanos no encontraban nada que estuviera mal desde el punto de vista físico
[3] (*fig*) [*grow, develop, integrate*] de forma natural

organism [ˈɔːgənɪzəm] N (*Bio*) organismo *m*

organist [ˈɔːgənɪst] N organista *mf*

organization [ˌɔːgənaɪˈzeɪʃən] Ⓐ N [1] (= *act*) organización *f*
[2] (= *body*) organización *f*, organismo *m*
Ⓑ CPD ► **organization chart** N organigrama *m*

organizational [ˌɔːgənaɪˈzeɪʃənl] ADJ organizativo

organize [ˈɔːgənaɪz] Ⓐ VT [1] (= *arrange*) [+ *event, activity*] organizar; **they ~d demonstrations against the closures** organizaron manifestaciones en contra de los cierres; **can you ~ some food for us?** ¿puedes encargarte de nuestra comida?; **I will ~ transport** yo me encargaré del transporte
[2] (= *put in order*) **she tried to ~ her thoughts** intentó ordenar *or* poner en orden sus pensamientos; **she ~s her time very well** administra muy bien su tiempo, se organiza muy bien (el tiempo); **she's always organizing people** siempre le está diciendo a la gente qué hacer; **stop trying to ~ my life** deja de intentar organizar mi vida; **to get (o.s.) ~d** ◊ **~ o.s.** organizarse
[3] (*Ind*) sindicar, organizar en sindicatos
Ⓑ VI [1] (= *make arrangements*) organizar; **we have ~d for every eventuality** lo hemos organizado todo para cualquier eventualidad; **he's ~d for us to meet the director** lo ha organizado para que nos reunamos con el director
[2] (*Ind*) sindicarse

organized [ˈɔːgənaɪzd] ADJ [1] (= *methodical*) [*person*] organizado; **it was ~ chaos** era un caos organizado *or* ordenado
[2] (= *planned*) [*crime, event, tour*] organizado
[3] (*Ind*) **~ labour** trabajadores *mpl or* obreros *mpl* sindicados

organizer [ˈɔːgənaɪzəʳ] N organizador(a) *m/f*

organizing [ˈɔːgənaizɪŋ] Ⓐ ADJ **she has excellent ~ ability** tiene una aptitud excelente para organizar; **the ~ principle** el principio organizador
Ⓑ CPD ► **organizing committee** N comité *m* organizador, comisión *f* organizadora

organophosphate [ɔːˌgənəʊˈfɒsfeɪt] N organofosfato *m*

organza [ɔːˈgænzə] N organza *f*, organdí *m* de seda

orgasm [ˈɔːgæzəm] Ⓐ N orgasmo *m*; **to bring sb to ~** hacer llegar al orgasmo a algn
Ⓑ VI tener un orgasmo, llegar al orgasmo

orgasmic [ɔːˈgæzmɪk] ADJ orgásmico

orgiastic [ˌɔːdʒɪˈæstɪk] ADJ orgiástico

orgy [ˈɔːdʒɪ] N (*lit, fig*) orgía *f*; **an ~ of destruction** una orgía de destrucción

oriel [ˈɔːrɪəl] N mirador *m*

Orient [ˈɔːrɪənt] N Oriente *m*

orient *etc* [ˈɔːrɪənt] VT = **orientate**

oriental [ˌɔːrɪˈentəl] Ⓐ ADJ oriental, de Oriente
Ⓑ N **Oriental**† oriental *mf*

orientalism [ˌɔːrɪˈentəlɪzəm] N orientalismo *m*

orientalist [ˌɔːrɪˈentəlɪst] Ⓐ ADJ orientalista
Ⓑ N orientalista *mf*

orientate [ˈɔːrɪenteɪt] VT orientar; (*fig*) encaminar; **to ~ o.s.** orientarse

-orientated [ˈɔːrɪenteɪtɪd] ADJ (*ending in compounds*) **career-orientated** orientado hacia una carrera; **commercially-orientated** orientado hacia el comercio

orientation [ˌɔːrɪenˈteɪʃən] Ⓐ N orientación *f*
Ⓑ CPD ► **orientation course** N curso *m* de orientación

-oriented [ˈɔːrɪentɪd] ADJ (*ending in compounds*) = **-orientated**

orienteering [ˌɔːrɪənˈtɪərɪŋ] N (= *sport*) carrera *f* con mapa y brújula

orifice [ˈɒrɪfɪs] N orificio *m*

origami [ˌɒrɪˈgɑːmɪ] N papiroflexia *f*

origin [ˈɒrɪdʒɪn] N [*of belief, rumour, language, person*] origen *m*; [*of river*] nacimiento *m*; **country of ~** país *m* de origen *or* de procedencia; **to be of humble ~** ◊ **have humble ~s** ser de origen humilde

original [əˈrɪdʒɪnl] Ⓐ ADJ [1] (= *first, earliest*) [*version, size, colour, owner, intention, idea*] original; [*inhabitants*] primero, primitivo; **of the ~ twenty, only twelve remained** de los veinte iniciales, sólo quedaban doce; **one of the ~ members** uno de los primeros miembros
[2] (= *not copied*) [*document, painting*] original; **an ~ Picasso** un Picasso original
[3] (= *unusual, creative*) [*person, idea*] original; **he's an ~ thinker** es un pensador original; **he has an ~ mind** tiene una mente original
Ⓑ N [1] (= *manuscript, painting, document*) original *m*; **he reads Homer in the ~** lee a Homero en versión original; **in the ~ French** en la versión original francesa
[2] (= *person*) **he was something of an ~** era un tanto original
Ⓒ CPD ► **original sin** N pecado *m* original

originality [əˌrɪdʒɪˈnælɪtɪ] N originalidad *f*

originally [əˈrɪdʒənəlɪ] ADV [1] (= *at first*) originariamente, en un principio; **~ they were in Athens** originariamente *or* en un principio estuvieron en Atenas; **Lucy had ~ intended to be a doctor** Lucy tenía inicialmente la intención de ser médico, Lucy en un principio tenía la intención de ser médico; **he's ~ from Armenia** es originario de Armenia
[2] (= *in an original way*) con originalidad, de manera original; **she dresses very ~** es muy original vistiendo, viste con mucha originalidad *or* de manera muy original; **it is quite ~ written** está escrito con bastante originalidad

originate [əˈrɪdʒɪneɪt] Ⓐ VT producir, originar; [*person*] idear, crear
Ⓑ VI **to ~ (from** *or* **in)** originarse (en), tener su origen (en); (= *begin*) empezar (en *or* con); **where did the fire ~?** ¿dónde se originó el incendio?; **these oranges ~ from Israel** estas naranjas son de Israel; **where do you ~ from?** ¿de dónde eres?; **with whom did the idea ~?** ¿quién tuvo la idea primero?

originator [əˈrɪdʒɪneɪtəʳ] N inventor(a) *m/f*, creador(a) *m/f*

oriole [ˈɔːrɪəʊl] N **golden ~** oropéndola *f*

Orkneys [ˈɔːknɪz], **Orkney Islands** [ˈɔːknɪˌaɪləndz] NPL **the ~** las (Islas) Órcadas

Orlon® [ˈɔːlɒn] N orlón® *m*

ormolu [ˈɔːməʊluː] N similor *m*, bronce *m* dorado

ornament Ⓐ [ˈɔːnəmənt] N (*gen*) adorno *m*, ornamento *m*; (= *vase etc*) objeto *m* de adorno, adorno *m*
Ⓑ [ˈɔːnəment] VT adornar

ornamental [ˌɔːnəˈmentl] ADJ decorativo, de adorno; (*Bot*) ornamental

ornamentation [ˌɔːnəmenˈteɪʃən] N (= *act*) ornamentación *f*, decoración *f*; (= *ornaments*) adornos *mpl*

ornate [ɔːˈneɪt] ADJ [*decor*] ornamentado; [*building, ceiling, vase, architectural style*] ornamentado, ricamente decorado; [*written style, language*] florido, recargado (*pej*); **the room is too ~ for my taste** la habitación está demasiado recargada para mi gusto

ornately [ɔːˈneɪtlɪ] ADV [*carved, painted, designed*] con muchos adornos, de manera elaborada; [*written*] en un estilo florido *or* (*pej*) recargado

ornateness [ɔːˈneɪtnɪs] N [*of decor, ceiling, building, vase*] lo ornamentado; [*of language*] lo florido, estilo *m* florido, recargamiento *m* (*pej*)

ornithological [ˌɔːnɪθəˈlɒdʒɪkəl] ADJ ornitológico

ornithologist [ˌɔːnɪˈθɒlədʒɪst] N ornitólogo/a *m/f*

ornithology [ˌɔːnɪˈθɒlədʒɪ] N ornitología *f*

orphan [ˈɔːfən] Ⓐ N huérfano/a *m/f*
Ⓑ ADJ huérfano
Ⓒ VT **to be ~ed** quedarse huérfano; **she was ~ed at the age of nine** quedó huérfana a los nueve años; **the children were ~ed by the accident** el accidente dejó huérfanos a los niños

orphanage [ˈɔːfənɪdʒ] N [1] (= *institution*) orfanato *m*, orfanatorio *m* (*Mex*)
[2] (= *state*) orfandad *f*

Orpheus [ˈɔːfiuːs] N Orfeo

ortho... [ˈɔːθəʊ] PREFIX orto...

orthodontic [ɔːθəʊˈdɒntɪk] ADJ de ortodoncia, ortodoncista

orthodontics [ˌɔːθəʊˈdɒntɪks] NSING ortodoncia *f*

orthodontist [ˌɔːθəʊˈdɒntɪst] N ortodoncista *mf*

orthodox [ˈɔːθədɒks] ADJ ortodoxo

orthodoxy [ˈɔːθədɒksɪ] N ortodoxia *f*

orthographic [ˌɔːθəˈgræfɪk] ADJ ortográfico

orthographical [ˌɔːθəˈgræfɪkəl] ADJ = **orthographic**

orthography [ɔːˈθɒgrəfɪ] N ortografía *f*

orthopaedic, **orthopedic** (*US*) [ˌɔːθəʊˈpiːdɪk] ADJ ortopédico; **~ surgeon** ortopedista *mf*, traumatólogo/a *m/f*; **~ surgery** cirujía *f* ortopédica

orthopaedics, **orthopedics** (*US*) [ˌɔːθəʊˈpiːdɪks] NSING ortopedia *f*

orthopaedist, **orthopedist** (*US*) [ˌɔːθəʊˈpiːdɪst] N ortopedista *mf*, traumatólogo/a *m/f*

oryx [ˈɒrɪks] N (*pl* **oryxes** *or* **oryx**) orix *m*, órix *m*

OS ABBR [1] (*Brit Geog*) (= **Ordnance Survey**) *servicio oficial de topografía*
[2] (*Brit Navy*) = **Ordinary Seaman**
[3] (*Hist*) (= **old style**) según el calendario juliano

O/S ABBR = **out of stock**

o/s ABBR (*Comm*) (= **outsize**) de tamaño extraordinario

Oscar [ˈɒskəʳ] N (*Cine*) Oscar *m*

oscillate ['ɒsɪleɪt] Ⓐ VI 1 (*Phys*) oscilar; [*compass, needle etc*] oscilar, fluctuar
2 (*fig*) oscilar; **he ~s between boredom and keenness** pasa del aburrimiento al entusiasmo, oscila entre el aburrimiento y el entusiasmo
Ⓑ VT hacer oscilar

oscillating ['ɒsɪleɪtɪŋ] ADJ oscilante

oscillation [ˌɒsɪ'leɪʃən] N 1 (*Phys*) oscilación *f*; [*of prices*] fluctuación *f*
2 (*fig*) oscilación *f*

oscillator ['ɒsɪleɪtəʳ] N oscilador *m*

oscillatory [ˌɒsɪ'leɪtərɪ] ADJ oscilatorio

oscilloscope [ɒ'sɪləˌskəʊp] N osciloscopio *m*

osculate ['ɒskjʊleɪt] (*hum*) Ⓐ VT besar
Ⓑ VI besar, besarse

osculation [ˌɒskjʊ'leɪʃən] N (*hum*) ósculo *m*

OSD ABBR (*Rel*) (= **Order of Saint Dominic**) O.P.

OSHA N ABBR (*US*) = **Occupational Safety and Health Administration**

osier ['əʊʒəʳ] Ⓐ N mimbre *m or f*
Ⓑ CPD ► **osier bed** N mimbrera *f*

Oslo ['ɒzləʊ] N Oslo *m*

osmium ['ɒzmɪəm] N osmio *m*

osmosis [ɒz'məʊsɪs] N ósmosis *f inv*, osmosis *f inv*

osmotic [ɒz'mɒtɪk] ADJ osmótico

osprey ['ɒspreɪ] N pigargo *m*, quebrantahuesos *m inv*

osseous ['ɒsɪəs] ADJ óseo

ossification [ˌɒsɪfɪ'keɪʃən] N osificación *f*

ossify ['ɒsɪfaɪ] Ⓐ VI (*lit*) osificarse; (*fig*) anquilosarse
Ⓑ VT osificar

ossuary ['ɒsjʊərɪ] N osario *m*

OST N ABBR (*US*) = **Office of Science and Technology**

Ostend [ɒs'tend] N Ostende *m*

ostensible [ɒs'tensəbl] ADJ aparente

ostensibly [ɒs'tensəblɪ] ADV aparentemente, en apariencia

ostensive [ɒ'stensɪv] ADJ ostensivo

ostentation [ˌɒsten'teɪʃən] N ostentación *f*, boato *m*

ostentatious [ˌɒsten'teɪʃəs] ADJ [*behaviour, car, clothes*] ostentoso; [*surroundings, style of living*] suntuoso, fastuoso

ostentatiously [ˌɒsten'teɪʃəslɪ] ADV ostentosamente, con ostentación

osteo... ['ɒstɪəʊ] PREFIX osteo...

osteoarthritis ['ɒstɪəʊɑː'θraɪtɪs] N osteoartritis *f*

osteomalacia [ˌɒstɪəʊmə'leɪʃɪə] N osteomalacia *f*

osteomyelitis [ˌɒstɪəʊmaɪ'laɪtɪs] N osteomielitis *f*

osteopath ['ɒstɪəpæθ] N osteópata *mf*

osteopathy [ˌɒstɪ'ɒpəθɪ] N osteopatía *f*

osteoporosis [ˌɒstɪəʊpɔː'rəʊsɪs] N osteoporosis *f inv*

ostler†† ['ɒsləʳ] N (*esp Brit*) mozo *m* de cuadra

ostmark ['ɒstmɑːk] N marco *m* de la antigua RDA

ostracism ['ɒstrəsɪzəm] N ostracismo *m*

ostracize ['ɒstrəsaɪz] VT condenar al ostracismo

ostrich ['ɒstrɪtʃ] N (*pl* **ostriches** *or* **ostrich**) avestruz *m*

OT N ABBR 1 (= **Old Testament**) A.T.
2 (*Med*) = **occupational therapy**

OTB N ABBR (*US*) (= **off-track betting**) *apuestas ilegales hechas fuera del hipódromo*

OTC Ⓐ ADV ABBR (*Comm*) = **over the counter**
Ⓑ N ABBR (*Brit*) = **Officer Training Corps**

OTE NPL ABBR (*Brit*) (= **on-target earnings**) beneficios *mpl* según los objetivos

Othello [ə'θeləʊ] N Otelo

other ['ʌðəʳ] Ⓐ ADJ otro; **all the ~ books have been sold** todos los otros *or* los demás libros se han vendido; **the ~ five** los otros cinco; **the ~ day** el otro día; **every ~ day** cada dos días; **together with every ~ woman** así como todas las mujeres; **if there are no ~ questions ...** si no hay más preguntas ...; **the ~ one** el otro/la otra; **some actor or ~** un actor cualquiera; **~ people** los otros, los demás; **~ people have done it** otros lo han hecho; **some ~ people have still to arrive** todavía no han llegado todos, aún tienen que llegar algunos más; **~ people's property** la propiedad ajena; **~ people's ideas** las ideas ajenas; **on the ~ side of the street** al otro lado de la calle; **among ~ things she is a writer** entre otras cosas es escritora; **some ~ time** en otro momento, en otra ocasión; **there must be some ~ way of doing it** debe haber alguna otra forma de hacerlo
Ⓑ PRON **the ~** el otro/la otra; **the ~s** los otros/las otras, los/las demás; **the ~s are going but I'm not** los demás van, pero yo no; **some do, ~s don't** algunos sí, otros no; **and these five ~s** y estos otros cinco; **we must respect ~s' rights** hay que respetar los derechos ajenos; **one after the ~** uno tras otro; **among ~s** entre otros; **are there any ~s?** (*gen*) ¿hay algún otro?; (= *any unaccounted for*) ¿falta alguno?; (= *anybody unaccounted for*) ¿falta alguien?; **you and no ~** solamente tú; **no book ~ than this** ningún libro que no sea éste; **he had no clothes ~ than those he stood up in** no tenía más ropa que la que llevaba puesta; **it was no ~ than the bishop** fue el obispo en persona; **none ~ than** el mismísimo/la mismísima; **one or ~ of them will come** uno de ellos vendrá; **somebody or ~** alguien, alguno; **some fool or ~** algún tonto; *see also* **every 1**
Ⓒ ADV **somewhere or ~** en alguna parte, en algún lado; **~ than him** aparte de él; **he could not have acted ~ than he did** no le quedaba otro recurso que hacer lo que hizo; **I wouldn't wish him ~ than he is** no quisiera que fuera distinto de como es

otherness ['ʌðənɪs] N alteridad *f*

otherwise ['ʌðəwaɪz] Ⓐ CONJ (= *if not*) si no, de lo contrario; **let's go with them, ~ we shall have to walk** vámonos con ellos, si no *or* de lo contrario tendremos que ir a pie; **of course I'm interested, I wouldn't be here ~** claro que me interesa, si no *or* de lo contrario no estaría aquí
Ⓑ ADV 1 (= *another way, differently*) de otra manera; **it cannot be ~** (*frm*) no puede ser de otra manera; **they may be arrested or ~ persecuted** puede que los detengan o que los persigan de otra manera; **unless your doctor advises ~** a menos que el médico le recomiende otra cosa; **it's true, and nothing you can say will convince me ~** es verdad, y nada que puedas decir me convencerá de lo contrario; **she was ~ engaged** (*frm or hum*) tenía otro compromiso; **Miller, ~ known as Dusty** Miller, también conocido como Dusty; **until proven** *or* **proved ~** hasta que se demuestre lo contrario; **except where** *or* **unless ~ stated** (*frm*) salvo indicación de lo contrario (*frm*), a no ser que se indique lo contrario; **we had no reason to think ~** no teníamos motivo para creer otra cosa
2 (= *in other respects*) aparte de esto, por lo demás; **it's an ~ excellent piece of work** aparte de esto *or* por lo demás es un trabajo excelente; **she was a little thinner, but ~ unchanged** estaba un poco más delgada, pero aparte de eso *or* por lo demás seguía igual
3 (= *in other circumstances*) en otras circunstancias; **people who might ~ have died will live** gente que en otras circunstancias hubiera muerto, vivirá; **it's more expensive than I would ~ have bought** es más caro de lo que hubiera gastado normalmente
4 (= *of another sort*) **he would do it by any means, legal or ~** lo haría por todos los medios, legales o no; **it may not be transmitted by any means, electronic or ~** está prohibida su transmisión por cualquier medio, ya sea electrónico o de otra clase

other-worldly ['ʌðə'wɜːldlɪ] ADJ 1 [*person*] muy espiritual
2 [*experience*] (como) de otro mundo; [*being*] extraterrestre

otiose ['əʊtɪəʊs] ADJ ocioso, inútil

otitis [əʊ'taɪtɪs] N otitis *f*

OTT* ADJ ABBR = **over the top**

otter ['ɒtəʳ] N (*pl* **otters** *or* **otter**) nutria *f*

Otto ['ɒtəʊ] N Otón

Ottoman ['ɒtəmən] Ⓐ ADJ otomano
Ⓑ N otomano/a *m/f*

ottoman ['ɒtəmən] N (*pl* **ottomans**) otomana *f*

OU N ABBR (*Brit*) (= **Open University**) ≈ UNED *f*; → OPEN UNIVERSITY

ouch [aʊtʃ] EXCL ¡ay!

ought¹ [ɔːt] MODAL AUX VB 1 (*moral obligation*) deber; **I ~ to do it** debería hacerlo, debiera hacerlo; **one ~ not to do it** no se debiera hacer; **I ~ to have done it** debiera haberlo hecho; **you ~ to have warned me** me deberías haber avisado; **he ~ to have known** debía saberlo; **I thought I ~ to tell you** me creí en el deber de decírselo; **to behave as one ~** comportarse como se debe
2 (*vague desirability*) **you ~ to go and see it** vale la pena ir a verlo; **you ~ to have seen him!** ¡tenías que haberle visto!
3 (*probability*) deber; **he ~ to win** debería ganar; **that ~ to be enough** con eso debería ser suficiente; **he ~ to have arrived by now** debería de haber llegado ya

ought² [ɔːt] N = **aught**

Ouija® ['wiːdʒə] N (*also* **~ board**) tabla *f* de espiritismo

ounce [aʊns] N 1 (= *measure*) onza *f*; → IMPERIAL SYSTEM
2 (*fig*) pizca *f*; **there's not an ~ of truth in it** en eso no hay ni una pizca de verdad; **if you had an ~ of common sense** si tuvieras una gota de sentido común

our [aʊəʳ] POSS ADJ (*with singular noun*) nuestro/a; (*with plural noun*) nuestros/as; **~ house** nuestra casa; **~ neighbours are very nice** nuestros vecinos son muy simpáticos; **we took off ~ coats** nos quitamos los abrigos; **they stole ~ car** nos robaron el coche

ours [aʊəz] POSS PRON (*referring to singular possession*) (el/la) nuestro/a; (*referring to plural possession*) (los/las) nuestros/as; **this house is ~** esta casa es nuestra; **a friend of ~** un amigo nuestro; **your car is much bigger than ~** vuestro coche es mucho más grande que el nuestro; **"our teachers are strict" — "~ are too"** —nuestros profesores son estrictos —los nuestros también

ourselves [ˌaʊə'selvz] PERS PRON 1 (*reflexive*) nos; **we couldn't see ~ in the photo** no podíamos vernos en la foto; **we really enjoyed**

➤ LANGUAGE IN USE: **ought¹ 1, 2** 2.2

~ nos divertimos mucho

2 (*emphatic*) nosotros/as (mismos/as); (*after prep*) nosotros/as (mismos/as); **we built our garage ~** nos construimos el garaje nosotros mismos; **we went ~** fuimos en persona; **let's not talk about ~ any more** no hablemos más de nosotros (mismos); **we said to ~** nos dijimos

3 (*phrases*) **we were talking among ~** hablábamos entre nosotros; **by ~** solos/as; **we prefer to be by ~** preferimos estar solos; **we did it (all) by ~** lo hicimos nosotros mismos

oust [aʊst] VT (*gen*) expulsar, echar; (*from house*) desahuciar, desalojar; **we ~ed them from the position** les hicimos abandonar su posición; **to ~ sb from a post** hacer que algn renuncie a un puesto

out [aʊt] Ⓐ ADV

When **out** *is the second element in a phrasal verb, eg* **go out, put out, walk out**, *look up the verb.*

1 (= *not in*) fuera, afuera; **it's cold ~** fuera *or* afuera hace frío; **they're ~ in the garden** están fuera *or* afuera en el jardín; **to be ~** (= *not at home*) no estar (en casa); **Mr Green is ~** el señor Green no está *or* (*LAm*) no se encuentra; **he's ~ for the afternoon** no estará en toda la tarde; **he's ~ a good deal** pasa bastante tiempo fuera; **"way out"** "salida"; **to be ~ and about again** estar bien otra vez (*después de una enfermedad*); **to have a day ~** pasar un día fuera de casa; **~ you go!** ¡fuera!; **it's cold ~ here** hace frío aquí fuera; **the journey ~** el viaje de ida; **to have a night ~** salir por la noche (a divertirse); (*drinking*) salir de juerga *or* (*LAm*) de parranda; **to run ~** salir corriendo; **it's dark ~ there** está oscuro ahí fuera; **the tide is ~** la marea está baja; **~ with him!** ¡fuera con él!, ¡que le echen fuera!; *see also* **second¹ C3**

2 (= *on strike*) **the railwaymen are ~** los ferroviarios están en huelga

3 (*indicating distance*) **she's ~ in Kuwait** se fue a Kuwait, está en Kuwait; **the boat was ten km ~** el barco estaba a diez kilómetros de la costa; **three days ~ from Plymouth** (*Naut*) a tres días de Plymouth; **it carried us ~ to sea** nos llevó mar adentro

4 **to be ~**: **when the sun is ~** cuando brilla el sol; **the dahlias are ~** las dalias están en flor; **to come ~**: **when the sun comes ~** cuando sale el sol; **the roses are coming ~** los rosales estan floreciendo

5 (= *in existence*) que hay, que ha habido; **it's the biggest swindle ~*** es la mayor estafa que se ha conocido jamás; **when will the magazine be ~?** ¿cuándo sale la revista?; **the book is ~** se ha publicado el libro, ha salido el libro; **the film is now ~ on video** la película ya ha salido en vídeo

6 (= *in the open*) conocido/a, fuera; **your secret's ~** tu secreto se ha descubierto *or* ha salido a la luz; **~ with it!** ¡desembucha!, ¡suéltalo ya!, ¡suelta la lengua! (*LAm*)

7 (= *to or at an end*) terminado/a; **before the week was ~** antes de que terminara la semana

8 [*lamp, fire, gas*] apagado/a; **all the lights are ~** todas las luces están apagadas; **"lights ~ at ten pm"** "se apagan las luces a las diez"; **my pipe is ~** se me ha apagado la pipa

9 (= *not in fashion*) pasado/a de moda; **long dresses are ~** ya no se llevan los vestidos largos, los vestidos largos estan pasados de moda

10 (= *not in power*) **now that the Liberals are ~** ahora que los liberales están fuera del poder

11 (*Sport*) [*player*] fuera de juego; [*boxer*] fuera de combate; [*loser*] eliminado/a; **that's it, Liverpool are ~** ya está, Liverpool queda eliminado; **you're ~** (*in games*) quedas eliminado; **the ball is ~** el balón está fuera del terreno; **out!** ¡fuera!

12 (*indicating error*) equivocado/a; **he was ~ in his reckoning** calculó mal; **I was not far ~** por poco acierto; **your watch is five minutes ~** su reloj lleva cinco minutos de atraso/de adelanto; **I'm two dollars ~** he perdido dos dólares en el cálculo

13 (*indicating loudness, clearness*) en voz alta, en alto; **speak ~ (loud)!** ¡habla en voz alta *or* fuerte!; *see also* **right B1**, **straight B1**

14 (*indicating purpose*) **he's ~ to make money** lo que busca es hacerse rico; **~ for** en busca de; **to be ~ for sth** buscar algo; **he's ~ for all he can get** busca sus propios fines, anda detrás de lo suyo; **they're ~ for trouble** quieren armar un escándalo

15 **to be ~** (= *unconscious*) estar inconsciente; (= *drunk*) estar completamente borracho; (= *asleep*) estar durmiendo como un tronco; **he was ~ cold** estuvo completamente sin conocimiento; **I was ~ for some minutes** estuve inconsciente durante varios minutos, estuve varios minutos sin conocimiento

16 **~ and away** con mucho

17 (= *worn through*) **the coat is ~ at the elbows** la chaqueta está rota por los codos

Ⓑ **~ of** PREP

When **out** *is part of a set combination, eg* **out of danger, out of proportion, out of sight**, *look up the other word.*

1 (= *outside, beyond*) fuera de; **~ of town** fuera de la ciudad; **he lives ~ of town** vive fuera de la ciudad; **three kilometres ~ of town** a tres kilómetros de la ciudad; **to go ~ of the house** salir de la casa; **to look ~ of the window** mirar por la ventana; **to throw sth ~ of a window** tirar algo por una ventana; **to turn sb ~ of the house** echar a algn de la casa; **we're well ~ of it*** de buena nos hemos librado; **✦IDIOM to feel ~ of it*** sentirse aislado *or* fuera de contacto; *see also* **danger A**, **proportion A1**, **range A5**, **season A2**, **sight A2**

2 (*cause, motive*) por; **~ of curiosity** por curiosidad; **~ of respect for you** por el respeto que te tengo; **to do sth ~ of sympathy** hacer algo por compasión; *see also* **necessity**, **spite**

3 (*origin*) de; **to copy sth ~ of a book** copiar algo de un libro; **to drink sth ~ of a cup** beber algo de una taza; **to take sth ~ of a drawer** sacar algo de un cajón; **a box made ~ of wood** una caja (hecha) de madera; **it was like something ~ of a nightmare** era como de una pesadilla; **a chapter ~ of a novel** un capítulo de una novela; **to read ~ of a novel** leer en una novela

4 (= *from among*) de cada; **one ~ of every three smokers** uno de cada tres fumadores; **in nine cases ~ of ten** en nueve de cada diez casos

5 (= *without*) sin; **we're ~ of petrol** nos hemos quedado sin gasolina; **we're ~ of milk** se nos ha acabado la leche; **it's ~ of stock** (*Comm*) está agotado; **to be ~ of hearts** (*Cards*) tener fallo a corazones; *see also* **breath A1**

6 (*Animal husbandry*) **Blue Ribbon, by Black Rum ~ of Grenada** el caballo Blue Ribbon, hijo de Black Rum y de la yegua Grenada

Ⓒ N *see* **in 3**

Ⓓ VT (= *expose as homosexual*) revelar la homosexualidad de

Ⓔ VI **the truth will ~** se descubrirá la verdad; **murder will ~** el asesinato se descubrirá

outa* ['aʊtə] ABBR (*esp US*) = **out of**

outage ['aʊtɪdʒ] N (*esp US Elec*) apagón *m*, corte *m*

out-and-out ['aʊtən'aʊt] ADJ 1 (= *absolute*) [*liar, villain*] redomado, empedernido; [*defeat, lie*] absoluto

2 (= *dedicated*) acérrimo

outback ['aʊtbæk] N (*in Australia*) despoblado *m*, campo *m*

outbid [aʊt'bɪd] (*pt, pp* **outbid**) VT pujar más alto que

outboard ['aʊtbɔːd] Ⓐ ADJ fuera borda

Ⓑ N **~ (motor)** motor *m* fuera borda *or* bordo

outbound ['aʊt,baʊnd] (*US*) Ⓐ ADV hacia fuera, hacia el exterior

Ⓑ ADJ que va hacia fuera, que va hacia el exterior; [*flight*] de ida

outbox [aʊt'bɒks] VT boxear mejor que

outbreak ['aʊtbreɪk] N [*of war*] declaración *f*; [*of hostilities*] comienzo *m*; [*of disease*] brote *m*; [*of crimes*] ola *f*; [*of violence*] arranque *m*; [*of spots*] erupción *f*; **a salmonella ~** un brote de salmonelosis; **at the ~ of war** al estallar la guerra

outbuilding ['aʊt,bɪldɪŋ] N (= *outhouse*) dependencia *f*; (= *shed*) cobertizo *m*, galpón *m* (*S. Cone*)

outburst ['aʊtbɜːst] N (*gen*) estallido *m*, explosión *f*; [*of anger*] arrebato *m*, arranque *m*; [*of applause*] salva *f*; **forgive my ~ last week** perdona que perdiera los estribos la semana pasada

outcast ['aʊtkɑːst] N (= *rejected person*) paria *mf*; (*in exile*) desterrado/a *m/f*; **he's a social ~** vive marginado por la sociedad

outclass [aʊt'klɑːs] VT aventajar a, superar

outcome ['aʊtkʌm] N (= *result*) resultado *m*; (= *consequences*) consecuencias *fpl*

outcrop ['aʊtkrɒp] Ⓐ N afloramiento *m*

Ⓑ VI aflorar

outcry ['aʊtkraɪ] N (= *protest*) protesta *f*, clamor *m*; (= *noise*) alboroto *m*; **to raise an ~ about sth** levantar fuertes protestas por algo; **there was a great ~** hubo fuertes protestas

outdated ['aʊt'deɪtɪd] ADJ anticuado, pasado de moda

outdistance [aʊt'dɪstəns] VT dejar atrás

outdo [aʊt'duː] (*pt* **outdid** [aʊt'dɪd]; *pp* **outdone** [aʊt'dʌn]) VT **to ~ sb (in sth)** superar a algn (en algo); **he was not to be ~ne** no quiso quedarse atrás; **not to be ~ne, he added …** ni corto ni perezoso, añadió que …

outdoor ['aʊtdɔːʳ] ADJ [*sports, work, market*] al aire libre; [*swimming pool, tennis court*] descubierto, al aire libre; [*clothes, shoes*] de calle; [*plant*] de exterior; **the ~ life** la vida al aire libre; **for ~ use** para uso al aire libre; **she's definitely the ~ type** es definitivamente una persona a la que le gusta estar al aire libre *or* a la que le gustan las actividades al aire libre

outdoors ['aʊt'dɔːz] Ⓐ ADV 1 (= *outside*) fuera; **go and play ~** id a jugar fuera; **to go ~** salir fuera; **~, there are three heated swimming pools** afuera, hay tres piscinas climatizadas

2 (= *in the open air*) [*exercise, bathe*] al aire libre; [*sleep*] al raso

Ⓑ N campo *m* abierto; **the great ~** (*hum*) la naturaleza

outer ['aʊtəʳ] Ⓐ ADJ 1 (= *exterior*) [*layer, surface*] exterior; [*skin, shell*] de fuera; [*wall, door*] exterior, de fuera; [*garment*] externo; **remove the ~ leaves from the cabbage** quite las ho-

jas de la parte de fuera de la col; **the ~ world** el mundo exterior
2 (= *peripheral*) [*edge, limit*] exterior; [*suburbs*] periférico, del extrarradio; **the ~ reaches of the solar system** los extremos del sistema solar
Ⓑ CPD ► **Outer Hebrides** NPL Hébridas *fpl* Exteriores ► **Outer London** N *área administrativa que comprende los barrios situados fuera del centro de Londres* ► **Outer Mongolia** N Mongolia *f* Exterior ► **outer space** N espacio *m* exterior, espacio *m* sideral

outermost [ˈaʊtəməʊst] ADJ [*place*] más extremo, más remoto; [*cover, layer*] más externo, más exterior

outface [aʊtˈfeɪs] VT desafiar

outfall [ˈaʊtfɔːl] N [*of drain*] desagüe *m*, desaguadero *m*; [*of river*] desembocadura *f*

outfield [ˈaʊtfiːld] N (*Sport*) parte *f* más lejana del campo; (*Baseball*) jardín *m*

outfielder [ˈaʊtfiːldəʳ] N (*Baseball, Cricket*) *jugador en el extremo del campo*

outfit [ˈaʊtfɪt] N **1** (= *clothes*) traje *m*; (= *uniform*) uniforme *m*; (= *costume*) conjunto *m*; **a cowboy ~** un traje de vaquero; **why are you wearing that ~?** ¿por qué te has trajeado así?
2 (= *equipment*) equipo *m*; (= *tools*) juego *m* de herramientas; **a complete camper's ~** un equipo completo de campista
3 (*) (= *organization*) grupo *m*, organización *f*; (*Mil*) unidad *f*, cuerpo *m*; **when I joined this ~** cuando vine a formar parte de esta unidad

outfitter [ˈaʊtfɪtəʳ] N camisero *m*; **gentlemen's ~'s** (= *shop*) tienda *f* de ropa para caballero; **sports ~'s** (= *shop*) tienda *f* de artículos deportivos

outflank [aʊtˈflæŋk] VT (*Mil*) flanquear, rebasar; (*fig*) superar en táctica, burlar

outflow [ˈaʊtfləʊ] N efusión *f*; [*of capital etc*] fuga *f*, salida *f*; (*Mech*) tubo *m* de salida

outfox [aʊtˈfɒks] VT ser más listo que

outgeneral [aʊtˈdʒenərəl] VT superar en estrategia, superar en táctica

outgo [ˈaʊtgəʊ] N (*US*) gastos *mpl*

outgoing [ˈaʊtˌgəʊɪŋ] ADJ **1** [*president*] saliente; [*government*] cesante; [*boat, train, mail*] de salida; [*flight*] de ida; [*tide*] que baja
2 [*character*] extrovertido, sociable

outgoings [ˈaʊtˌgəʊɪŋz] NPL gastos *mpl*

outgrow [aʊtˈgrəʊ] (*pt* **outgrew** [aʊtˈgruː]; *pp* **outgrown** [aʊtˈgrəʊn]) VT (*lit*) crecer más que; [+ *habit etc*] perder con la edad; [+ *defect, illness*] curarse de ... con la edad; **to ~ one's clothes** quedarle pequeña la ropa a algn; **she has ~n her gloves** se le han quedado pequeños los guantes; **we've ~n all that** todo eso ha quedado ya atrás

outgrowth [ˈaʊtˌgrəʊθ] N excrecencia *f*; (*fig*) extensión *f*

outguess [aʊtˈges] VT adelantarse a, demostrar ser más rápido que

outgun [ˌaʊtˈgʌn] VT (*Mil*) sobrepasar en potencia de fuego a; (*fig*) vencer

outhouse [ˈaʊthaʊs] N (*pl* **outhouses** [ˈaʊthaʊzɪz]) **1** (*Brit*) = **outbuilding**
2 (*US*) (= *toilet*) retrete *m* fuera de la casa

outing [ˈaʊtɪŋ] N **1** (= *trip*) excursión *f*, paseo *m* (*LAm*); **everyone went on an ~ to Toledo** todos fueron de excursión a Toledo
2 (= *walk*) paseo *m*; **I took a little ~** di un pequeño paseo, di una vuelta

outlandish [aʊtˈlændɪʃ] ADJ [*appearance, clothes*] estrafalario, extravagante; [*behaviour, ideas*] extraño, disparatado; [*prices*] estrafalario

outlast [aʊtˈlɑːst] VT durar más tiempo que; [+ *person*] sobrevivir a

outlaw [ˈaʊtlɔː] Ⓐ N (= *fugitive*) prófugo/a *m/f*, fugitivo/a *m/f*; (= *bandit*) bandido/a *m/f*, matrero/a *m/f* (*Andes, S. Cone*); (*in Westerns*) forajido/a *m/f*
Ⓑ VT proscribir; [+ *drug etc*] ilegalizar; [+ *practice etc*] declarar ilegal

outlawry [ˈaʊtlɔːrɪ] N bandolerismo *m*

outlay [ˈaʊtleɪ] N desembolso *m*, gastos *mpl*

outlet [ˈaʊtlet] Ⓐ N **1** (*for water etc*) salida *f*; (= *drain*) desagüe *m*, distribuidora *f*; [*of river*] desembocadura *f*
2 (*Comm*) (= *shop*) tienda *f*; (= *agency*) sucursal *f*; (= *market*) mercado *m*, salida *f*; **to find an ~ for a product** encontrar una salida *or* un mercado para un producto
3 (*US Elec*) toma *f*
4 (*fig*) (*for emotion, talents etc*) desahogo *m*; **it provides an ~ for his energies** ofrece una válvula de escape para su energía
Ⓑ CPD (*Tech*) de salida; [*drain*] de desagüe; [*valve*] de escape

outline [ˈaʊtlaɪn] Ⓐ N **1** (= *shape*) contorno *m*, perfil *m*
2 (= *draft*) [*of book, film, plan, theory*] esbozo *m*, boceto *m*; (= *summary*) [*of events, facts*] resumen *m*; **parliament gave ~ approval to the new law** el parlamento aprobó en principio el nuevo proyecto de ley; **I'll give you the broad** *or* **general ~ of what we mean to do** te voy a explicar a grandes rasgos lo que pensamos hacer, te voy a resumir lo que pensamos hacer; **in ~, the story goes like this** en resumen, la historia es así
Ⓑ VT **1** (= *sketch*) esbozar, bosquejar; (= *silhouette*) perfilar; **the mountain was ~d against the sky** la montaña se perfilaba *or* recortaba contra el cielo; **she ~s her eyes with a dark pencil** se perfila los ojos con un lápiz de ojos oscuro
2 (= *summarize*) [+ *policy, situation, plan*] resumir, explicar a grandes rasgos
Ⓒ CPD ► **outline drawing** N esbozo *m*, bosquejo *m* ► **outline planning permission** N (*Brit*) (*for building*) permiso *m* provisional de obras ► **outline sketch** N = **outline drawing**

outlive [aʊtˈlɪv] VT sobrevivir a; **the agreement has ~d its original purpose** el acuerdo ha durado más tiempo de lo que se había planeado; **she dropped men as soon as they ~d their usefulness** abandonaba a los hombres tan pronto como dejaban de resultarle útiles

outlook [ˈaʊtlʊk] N **1** (= *view*) vista *f*, perspectiva *f*
2 (= *prospects*) perspectivas *fpl*, panorama *m*; **the ~ for the economy/the wheat crop is good** las perspectivas económicas/de la cosecha de trigo son favorables; **it's a grim ~** las perspectivas no son nada halagüeñas
3 (= *opinion*) punto *m* de vista; (*on life*) actitud *f*; **she has a very positive ~ on life** tiene una actitud muy positiva ante la vida; **his ~ is always pessimistic** su actitud siempre es pesimista; **a person with a broad ~** una persona de amplias miras
4 (*Met*) **the ~ for next Saturday is sunny** la previsión para el próximo sábado es que hará sol

outlying [ˈaʊtˌlaɪɪŋ] ADJ (= *distant*) [*towns, villages*] remoto, lejano; (= *surrounding*) [*areas*] periférico; [*suburb*] periférico, circundante

outmanoeuvre, **outmaneuver** (*US*) [ˌaʊtməˈnuːvəʳ] VT (*Mil*) [+ *enemy*] superar tácticamente; (*fig*) [+ *opposition, competition*] superar a

outmatch [aʊtˈmætʃ] VT superar, aventajar

outmoded [aʊtˈməʊdɪd] ADJ = **outdated**

outnumber [aʊtˈnʌmbəʳ] VT exceder en número, ser más numeroso que; **the actors ~ed the audience** había más actores que público; **we were ~ed ten to one** ellos eran diez veces más que nosotros

out-of-bounds [ˌaʊtəvˈbaʊndz] ADJ *see* **bound**[1]

out-of-court [aʊtəvˈkɔːt] ADJ **an ~ settlement** un arreglo sin acudir a los tribunales

out-of-date [ˈaʊtəvˈdeɪt] ADJ [*ideas*] anticuado; [*clothes*] pasado de moda; [*passport, ticket*] caducado, vencido

out-of-doors [ˈaʊtəvˈdɔːz] ADV = **outdoors A**

out-of-pocket [ˈaʊtəvˈpɒkɪt] ADJ **~ expenses** gastos *mpl* varios

out-of-school [ˌaʊtəvˈskuːl] ADJ **~ activities** actividades *fpl* extraescolares

out-of-the-way [ˈaʊtəvðəˈweɪ] ADJ **1** (= *remote*) remoto, apartado; (= *inaccessible*) inaccesible
2 (= *unusual*) poco conocido, poco común, poco corriente

out-of-towner [ˌaʊtəvˈtaʊnəʳ] N (*US*) forastero/a *m/f*

outpace [aʊtˈpeɪs] VT dejar atrás

outpatient [ˈaʊtˌpeɪʃənt] N paciente *mf* externo/a; **~s' department** sección *f* de pacientes externos *or* no hospitalizados

outperform [ˈaʊtpəˈfɔːm] VT hacer mejor que, superar a; [*shares, investment fund*] dar mayores beneficios que

outplay [aʊtˈpleɪ] VT jugar mejor que; **we were ~ed in every department** ellos resultaron ser mejores que nosotros en todos los aspectos del juego, nos dominaron por completo

outpoint [ˌaʊtˈpɔɪnt] VT (*Boxing*) ganar por puntos a

outpost [ˈaʊtpəʊst] N **1** (*Mil*) avanzada *f*, puesto *m* avanzado
2 (*fig*) avanzada *f*

outpouring [ˈaʊtˌpɔːrɪŋ] N efusión *f*; **an ~ of emotion** una efusión de emoción; **the ~s of a sick mind** los desahogos de una mente enferma

output [ˈaʊtpʊt] Ⓐ N [*of factory*] producción *f*; [*of person, machine*] rendimiento *m*; (*Comput*) salida *f*; (*Elec*) potencia *f* de salida; **to raise ~** aumentar la producción
Ⓑ VT (*Comput*) imprimir
Ⓒ CPD ► **output bonus** N prima *f* por rendimiento ► **output device** N dispositivo *m* de salida

outrage [aʊtˈreɪdʒ] Ⓐ N **1** (= *wicked, violent act*) atrocidad *f*; **bomb ~** atentado *m* (con bomba)
2 (= *indecency*) ultraje *m*, escándalo *m*; (= *injustice*) atropello *m*, agravio *m*; **a public ~** un escándalo público; **an ~ against good taste** un atentado al buen gusto; **it's an ~!** ¡es un escándalo!, ¡qué barbaridad!; **to commit an ~ against** *or* **on sb** [*terrorists*] cometer un atentado contra algn
Ⓑ VT [+ *person*] ultrajar; [+ *standards, decency*] atentar contra; **it ~s justice** es un atentado a la justicia; **to be ~d by sth** indignarse ante algo

outrageous [aʊtˈreɪdʒəs] ADJ **1** (= *shocking, intolerable*) [*conduct, decision, accusation*] escandaloso; [*price, demands*] exorbitante, escandaloso; [*act, crime*] atroz, monstruoso; **it's ~! I won't stand for it** ¡qué barbaridad! *or* ¡es es-

candaloso! no lo pienso consentir; **it is ~ that taxpayers will have to foot the bill** es escandaloso que sean los contribuyentes los que tengan que pagar
2 (= *extravagant*) [*clothes, fashion*] extravagante, estrafalario; [*idea, story*] estrambótico; **she has an ~ sense of humour** su sentido del humor es de escándalo; **he's ~!** ¡es increíble *or* imposible!

outrageously [aʊt'reɪdʒəslɪ] ADV 1 (= *shockingly, intolerably*) [*behave*] de manera escandalosa; **she flirted with him ~** era escandaloso cómo flirteaba con él, flirteaba de manera escandalosa con él
2 (= *extravagantly*) [*dress*] de forma extravagante, de forma estrafalaria
3 (= *extremely*) [*unfair, racist*] terriblemente; [*expensive*] escandalosamente; **his latest comedy is ~ funny** su última comedia es para desternillarse

outran [ˌaʊt'ræn] PT of **outrun**

outrank [aʊt'ræŋk] VT ser de rango superior a

outré ['u:treɪ] ADJ extravagante, estrafalarío

outreach worker ['aʊtri:tʃˌwɜ:kəʳ] N *funcionario dedicado a dar a conocer la existencia de ayudas sociales a las personas o grupos a quienes van dirigidas*

outrider ['aʊtˌraɪdəʳ] N motociclista *mf* de escolta

outrigger ['aʊtˌrɪgəʳ] N (= *beam, spar*) batanga *f*, balancín *m*; (= *rowlock*) portarremos *m* exterior; (= *boat*) bote *m* con batanga, bote *m* con portarremos exterior

outright [aʊt'raɪt] Ⓐ ADJ 1 (= *complete*) [*failure*] completo, total; [*winner, victory*] absoluto; [*lie*] descarado; [*owner*] absoluto (*sin hipotecas*); [*refusal, rejection*] rotundo, absoluto
2 (= *open, forthright*) franco; [*rudeness, hostility*] abierto, franco; [*contempt, scorn*] declarado; [*compliment*] sin ambages
Ⓑ ADV 1 (= *completely*) [*own*] en su totalidad; [*win*] de manera absoluta; [*refuse, reject*] rotundamente, de pleno; **to buy sth ~** comprar algo en su totalidad; **to reject an offer ~** rechazar una oferta de pleno; **they won the cup ~** ganaron la copa indiscutiblemente; **he was killed ~** murió en el acto
2 (= *openly, forthrightly*) abiertamente, francamente; **why don't you tell her ~?** ¿por qué no se lo dices abiertamente *or* francamente?; **to laugh ~ at sth** reírse abiertamente de algo

outrun [aʊt'rʌn] (*pt* **outran**; *pp* **outrun**) VT dejar atrás; (*fig*) exceder, sobrepasar

outsell [ˌaʊtsel] (*pt, pp* **outsold**) VT venderse más que; **this product ~s all the competition** este producto se vende más que todos los competidores

outset ['aʊtset] N principio *m*, comienzo *m*; **at the ~** al principio *or* comienzo; **from the ~** desde el principio *or* comienzo

outshine [aʊt'ʃaɪn] (*pt, pp* **outshone** [aʊt'ʃɒn]) VT (*fig*) eclipsar

outside ['aʊt'saɪd] Ⓐ ADV fuera, afuera (*esp LAm*); **to be/go ~** estar/salir fuera; **seen from ~** visto desde fuera
Ⓑ PREP (*also* **~ of**) 1 (= *not inside*) fuera de, afuera de (*LAm*); (= *beyond*) más allá de; **~ the city** fuera de la ciudad, en las afueras de la ciudad; **it's ~ the normal range** cae fuera del alcance normal; **the car ~ the house** el coche que está frente a la casa; **he waited ~ the door** esperó en la puerta
2 (= *not within*) fuera de; **this matter is ~ their jurisdiction** este asunto queda fuera de su competencia; **that's ~ our terms of reference** eso no entra dentro de nuestro cometido; **it's ~ my experience** no tengo experiencia en eso
Ⓒ ADJ 1 (= *exterior*) [*wall*] exterior; [*door*] que da a la calle; (= *outdoors*) [*patio, swimming pool*] descubierto, al aire libre; (= *alien*) [*influence*] externo; **~ broadcast** (*Rad, TV*) retransmisión *f* desde exteriores; **~ call** llamada *f* de fuera; **the ~ lane** (*Brit Aut*) el carril de la derecha; (*most other countries*) el carril de la izquierda; **~ line** (*Telec*) línea *f* exterior; **an ~ seat** un asiento al lado del pasillo; **his parents shielded him from the ~ world** sus padres le protegieron del mundo exterior
2 (= *unlikely*) **an ~ chance** una posibilidad remota
3 (= *of another organization, person*) **~ contractor** contratista *mf* independiente; **to get an ~ opinion** pedir una opinión independiente
Ⓓ N 1 (= *outer part*) exterior *m*, parte *f* exterior; **judging from the ~** a juzgar por las apariencias; **to open a window from the ~** abrir una ventana desde fuera; **on the ~** por fuera; **to overtake on the ~** (*Brit Aut*) adelantar *or* (*Mex*) rebasar por la derecha; (*most other countries*) adelantar *or* (*Mex*) rebasar por la izquierda
2 (= *maximum*) **at the (very) ~** a lo sumo, como máximo

outside-forward ['aʊtsaɪd'fɔ:wəd] N delantero/a *m/f* extremo/a

outside-left ['aʊtsaɪd'left] N extremo/a *m/f* izquierdo/a

outsider [aʊt'saɪdəʳ] N 1 (= *stranger*) forastero/a *m/f*, desconocido/a *m/f*; (*pej*) intruso/a *m/f*
2 (= *independent*) persona *f* independiente, persona *f* ajena al asunto; **I'm an ~ in these matters** soy un profano en estos asuntos
3 (*in horse race*) caballo *m* que no figura entre los favoritos; (*in election*) candidato *m* poco conocido; (*pej*) segundón *m*

outside-right ['aʊtsaɪd'raɪt] N extremo/a *m/f* derecho/a

outsize ['aʊtsaɪz] ADJ [*clothes*] de talla muy grande; (= *huge*) enorme

outskirts ['aʊtskɜ:ts] NPL [*of town*] afueras *fpl*, alrededores *mpl*; [*of wood*] cercanías *fpl*

outsmart [aʊt'smɑ:t] VT **to ~ sb** ser más listo que algn; (= *deceive*) engañar a algn

outsourcing ['aʊtsɔ:sɪŋ] N (*Comm*) [*of labour*] *contratación de mano de obra que no pertenece a la empresa*; **the ~ of components** la adquisición de componentes de fuentes externas

outspend [aʊt'spend] (*pt, pp* **outspent**) VT **to ~ sb** gastar más que algn

outspoken [aʊt'spəʊkən] ADJ [*criticism*] franco, abierto; [*opponent, critic*] declarado; **to be ~** ser muy franco, no tener pelos en la lengua*

outspokenly [aʊt'spəʊkənlɪ] ADV francamente, abiertamente

outspokenness [aʊt'spəʊkənnɪs] N franqueza *f*

outspread ['aʊt'spred] ADJ [*wings*] extendido, desplegado; [*legs, feet*] extendido; **with ~ arms** con los brazos abiertos

outstanding [aʊt'stændɪŋ] ADJ 1 (= *exceptional*) [*person, achievement, contribution, feature*] destacado; [*beauty, performance, service*] excepcional, extraordinario; [*example*] sobresaliente; **he was the most ~ scientist of his generation** fue el científico más destacado de su generación; **an area of ~ natural beauty** una zona de excepcional belleza natural
2 (= *not settled*) [*issue, problem*] pendiente, por resolver; [*bill*] por cobrar; [*debt, balance, account*] pendiente; [*shares*] en circulación, en manos del público; **a lot of work is still ~** aún queda mucho trabajo pendiente *or* por hacer; **amount ~** saldo *m* pendiente

outstandingly [aʊt'stændɪŋlɪ] ADV [*beautiful, effective, well-written*] excepcionalmente, extraordinariamente; **an ~ gifted musician** un músico de excepcional *or* extraordinario talento; **she performed ~ well in the exam** hizo el examen extraordinariamente bien

outstare [ˌaʊt'stεəʳ] VT **I ~d him** lo miré tan fijamente que tuvo que bajar *or* apartar la vista

outstation ['aʊtˌsteɪʃən] N dependencia *f*

outstay [aʊt'steɪ] VT quedarse más tiempo que; **to ~ one's welcome** quedarse más de lo debido; **I don't want to ~ my welcome** no quiero quedarme más de lo debido, no quiero abusar de su hospitalidad

outstretched ['aʊtstretʃt] ADJ [*arms, legs, hands, wings*] extendido

outstrip [aʊt'strɪp] VT dejar atrás, aventajar; (*fig*) aventajar, adelantarse a

out-take ['aʊtˌteɪk] N trozo *m* de película desechado

out-tray ['aʊtˌtreɪ] N bandeja *f* de salida

outturn ['aʊttɜ:n] N (*US*) rendimiento *m*, producción *f*

outvote [aʊt'vəʊt] VT [+ *proposal*] rechazar (por mayoría de votos); [+ *party, person*] vencer (en la votación); **but I was ~d** pero en la votación perdí

outward ['aʊtwəd] Ⓐ ADJ 1 (= *going out*) [*flight, ship, freight*] de salida, de ida; [*movement*] hacia fuera; **on the ~ journey** en el viaje de ida
2 (= *exterior*) [*appearance etc*] exterior, externo; **with an ~ show of concern** haciendo gala de *or* (*LAm*) luciendo preocupación
Ⓑ ADV hacia fuera; **~ bound (from/for)** saliendo (de/con rumbo a); **the ship was ~ bound from/for Vigo** el barco salía de/iba con rumbo a Vigo

outward-looking ['aʊtwədˌlʊkɪŋ] ADJ [*person, organization, country*] abierto al exterior; [*policy, attitude*] abierto, expansivo

outwardly ['aʊtwədlɪ] ADV por fuera, aparentemente

outwards ['aʊtwədz] ADV (*esp Brit*) = **outward B**

outwear [aʊt'wεəʳ] (*pt* **outwore**; *pp* **outworn**) VT
1 (= *last longer than*) durar más tiempo que
2 (= *wear out*) gastar

outweigh [aʊt'weɪ] VT pesar más que, tener mayor peso que; (*fig*) pesar más que; **the advantages ~ the disadvantages** las ventajas pesan más que *or* superan a las desventajas; **this ~s all other considerations** esto pesa más *or* tiene mayor peso que todos los demás factores

outwit [aʊt'wɪt] VT ser más listo que

outwith [ˌaʊt'wɪθ] PREP (*Scot*) *see* **outside B**

outworker ['aʊtwɜ:kəʳ] N *persona que trabaja en su propio domicilio*

outworn [aʊt'wɔ:n] Ⓐ PP of **outwear**
Ⓑ ADJ [*expression*] trillado, manido; [*idea, custom*] anticuado, caduco; [*joke, slogan*] muy viejo, muy visto; [*superstition*] viejo, antiguo

ouzo ['u:zəʊ] N ouzo *m*

ova ['əʊvə] NPL of **ovum**

oval ['əʊvəl] Ⓐ ADJ oval, ovalado; **the Oval Office** (*US*) el Despacho Oval
Ⓑ N óvalo *m*

ovarian [əʊ'vεərɪən] ADJ ovárico

ovary ['əʊvərɪ] N ovario *m*

ovate ['əʊveɪt] ADJ aovado

ovation [əʊ'veɪʃən] N ovación *f*; **to give sb an ~** ovacionar a algn; **to receive an ~** ser ovacionado; **to give sb a standing ~** ponerse en pie *or* levantarse para ovacionar a algn; **she got a standing ~ from the audience** el público se puso en pie *or* se levantó para ovacionarla, el público puesto en pie la ovacionó

oven ['ʌvn] Ⓐ N horno *m*; **it's like an ~ in there** aquello es un horno
Ⓑ CPD ► **oven glove** N guante *m* para el horno, manopla *f* para el horno ► **oven tray** N bandeja *f* para horno

ovenproof ['ʌvnpru:f] ADJ [*dish*] refractario, (a prueba) de horno

oven-ready [,ʌvn'redɪ] ADJ listo para el horno

ovenware ['ʌvnwɛəʳ] N vajilla *f* refractaria

over ['əʊvəʳ]

A ADVERB	C ADJECTIVE
B PREPOSITION	D NOUN

*When **over** is the second element in a phrasal verb, eg **come over**, **go over**, **start over**, **turn over**, look up the verb.*

Ⓐ ADVERB

1 *= across* por encima, por arriba (*LAm*); **this one goes under and that one goes ~** éste pasa por debajo y ése por encima

2 *= here, there* **I'll be ~ at 7 o'clock** estaré ahí a las 7; **they're ~ for the day** han venido a pasar el día; **when you're next ~ this way** la próxima vez que pases por aquí

*With prepositions and adverbs **over** is usually not translated:*

they're ~ from Canada for the summer han venido desde Canadá a pasar el verano; **~ here** aquí; **how long have you lived ~ here?** ¿cuánto tiempo llevas viviendo aquí?; **when you're next ~ here** la próxima vez que vengas; **he's ~ in the States at the moment** en este momento está en Estados Unidos; **~ in the States, people reacted differently** (allí) en Estados Unidos la gente reaccionó de otra manera; **it's ~ on the other side of town** está al otro lado de la ciudad; **~ there** allí; **how long were you ~ there?** ¿cuánto tiempo estuviste allí?; **the next time you're ~ there** la próxima vez que vayas (allí); **the baby crawled ~ to its mother** el bebé gateó hacia su madre; **to drive ~ to the other side of town** ir en coche al otro lado de la ciudad; **~ to you!** (*to speak*) ¡te paso la palabra!; **so now it's ~ to you** (*to decide*) así que ahora te toca a ti decidir; **now ~ to our Paris correspondent** ahora damos paso a nuestro corresponsal en París

3 *indicating repetition* **it happened all ~ again** volvió a ocurrir, ocurrió otra vez; **to start (all) ~ again** volver a empezar; **~ and ~ (again)** repetidas veces, una y otra vez; **several times ~** varias veces seguidas; **we did it two or three times ~** lo volvimos a hacer dos o tres veces

4 *US = again* otra vez; **to do sth ~** volver a hacer algo, hacer algo otra vez

5 *= remaining* **there are three (left) ~** sobran *or* quedan tres; **there were two slices each and one (left) ~** había dos rebanadas para cada uno y sobraba una; **is there any cake left ~?** ¿queda *or* sobra (algo de) pastel?; **when they've paid the bills there's nothing (left) ~ for luxuries** después de pagar las facturas no les sobra *or* queda nada para caprichos; **4 into 29 goes 7 and 1 ~** 29 dividido entre 4 son 7 y me llevo 1

6 *= more* **sums of £50,000 and ~** cantidades iguales *or* superiores a 50.000 libras; **persons of 21 and ~** las personas de veintiún años para arriba

7 *Telec* **over!** ¡cambio!; **~ and out!** ¡cambio y corto!

8 *in set expressions* **~ against** (*lit*) contra; (*fig*) frente a; **~ against the wall** contra la pared; **the importance of faith ~ against good works** la importancia de la fe frente a las buenas obras; **the (whole) world ~** en *or* por todo el mundo, en el mundo entero

Ⓑ PREPOSITION

1 *indicating position* (= *situated above*) encima de, arriba de (*LAm*); (= *across*) por encima de, por arriba de (*LAm*); **there's a mirror ~ the washbasin** encima del lavabo hay un espejo; **a washbasin with a mirror ~ it** un lavabo con un espejo encima; **the water came ~ his knees** el agua le llegaba por encima de las rodillas; **the ball went ~ the wall** la pelota pasó por encima del muro; **to jump ~ sth** saltar por encima de algo; *BUT* **the bridge ~ the river** el puente sobre el río; **pour some sauce ~ it** échale un poco de salsa por encima; **I put a blanket ~ her** le eché una manta por encima; **she put an apron on ~ her dress** se puso un delantal encima del vestido; **to spread a sheet ~ sth** extender una sábana sobre *or* por encima de algo; *see also* **all C2, head A1, A2, hill A**

2 *= superior to* **he's ~ me (in the company)** está por encima mío (en la empresa)

3 *= on the other side of* **the bar ~ the road** el bar de enfrente; **it's ~ the river** está en la otra orilla del río; **the noise came from ~ the wall** el ruido venía del otro lado de la pared; **~ the page** en la página siguiente

4 *= more than* más de; **~ two hundred** más de doscientos; **well ~ 200 people** bastante más de 200 personas; **he must be ~ 60** debe de tener más de 60 años; **(the) ~-18s** los mayores de 18 años; **an increase of 5% ~ last year** un aumento del 5 por ciento respecto al año pasado; **spending has gone up by 7% ~ and above inflation** el gasto ha aumentado un 7% por encima de la inflación; **this was ~ and above his normal duties** eso iba más allá de sus deberes habituales; **~ and above normal requirements** además de los requisitos normales; **yes, but ~ and above that, we must ...** sí, pero además de eso, debemos ...; **~ and above the fact that ...** además de que ...; *see also* **well A2.1**

5 *= during* durante; **~ the last few years** durante los últimos años; **payments spread ~ some years** pagos espaciados durante varios años; **~ Christmas** durante las Navidades; **~ the winter** durante *or* en el invierno; **why don't we discuss it ~ dinner?** ¿por qué no vamos a cenar y lo hablamos?; **they talked ~ a cup of coffee** hablaron mientras se tomaban un café; **how long will you be ~ it?** ¿cuánto tiempo te va a llevar?; **he took** *or* **spent hours ~ the preparations** dedicó muchas horas a los preparativos; *see also* **linger 3**

6 *= because of* por; **to cry ~ sth** llorar por algo; **they fell out ~ money** se pelearon por una cuestión de dinero

7 *= about* sobre; **the two sides disagreed ~ how much should be spent** ambas partes discrepaban sobre cuánto debería gastarse

8 *= recovered from* **he's not ~ that yet** (*illness*) todavía no se ha repuesto de aquello; (*shock*) todavía no se ha repuesto de *or* sobrepuesto a aquello; **she's ~ it now** (*illness*) se ha repuesto de eso ya; **it'll take her years to get ~ it** (*shock*) tardará años en sobreponerse; **I hope you'll soon be ~ your cold** espero que se te pase pronto el resfriado, espero que te repongas pronto del resfriado; **she's still not ~ her last boyfriend** aún no ha olvidado a su último novio; **we're ~ the worst now** ya pasó lo peor

9 *indicating means of communication* por; **~ the telephone** por teléfono; **~ the loudspeaker** por los altavoces; **I heard it ~ the radio** lo escuché *or* oí por la radio

10 *= contrasted with* **the issue of quality ~ economy** la cuestión de la calidad en contraposición a la rentabilidad

Ⓒ ADJECTIVE

= finished **when** *or* **after the war is ~, we'll go ...** cuando (se) acabe la guerra, nos iremos ...; **I'll be happy when the exams are ~** seré feliz cuando (se) hayan acabado *or* terminado los exámenes; **our troubles are ~** (se) han acabado nuestros problemas; **the danger was soon ~** el peligro pasó pronto; **it's all ~** se acabó; **it's all ~ between us** lo nuestro se acabó; **I'll be glad when it's all ~ and done with** estaré contento cuando todo (se) haya acabado *or* terminado; **for us the incident was ~ and done with** nosotros dábamos el incidente por zanjado; **to get sth ~ and done with: if we've got to tell her, best get it ~ and done with** si tenemos que decírselo, cuanto antes (lo hagamos) mejor

Ⓓ NOUN

Cricket serie *f* de seis lanzamientos

over... ['əʊvəʳ] PREFIX 1 sobre..., super...; (= *too much*) demasiado; **~abundant** sobreabundante, superabundante; **~ambitious** demasiado ambicioso
2 (*with neg*) **I'm not ~keen on Szymanowski's music** no me entusiasma demasiado la música de Szymanowski

overabundance [,əʊvərə'bʌndəns] N sobreabundancia *f*, superabundancia *f*

overabundant [,əʊvərə'bʌndənt] ADJ sobreabundante, superabundante

overachiever [,əʊvərə'tʃi:vəʳ] N *persona que obtiene resultados más altos de lo esperado*

overact [,əʊvər'ækt] VI sobreactuar, exagerar (el papel)

overacting [,əʊvər'æktɪŋ] N sobreactuación *f*, exageración *f* (del papel)

overactive [,əʊvər'æktɪv] ADJ calenturienta; [*thyroid*] hiperactivo

overage ['əʊvərɪdʒ] N (*US Comm*) excedente *m* de mercancías

over-age [,əʊvər'eɪdʒ] ADJ demasiado mayor, mayor de la edad permitida

overall[1] Ⓐ ['əʊvərɔ:l] ADJ [*study, view*] de conjunto, global; [*width, length, cost*] total; **~ dimensions** (*Aut*) dimensiones *fpl* exteriores; **what was your ~ impression?** ¿cuál fue tu impresión general?
Ⓑ [,əʊvər'ɔ:l] ADV en conjunto, en su totalidad; **~, we are well pleased** en términos generales estamos muy contentos

overall[2] ['əʊvərɔ:l] N 1 (*esp Brit*) (= *protective overcoat*) guardapolvo *m*, bata *f*
2 **overalls** (*Brit*) (= *boiler suit*) mono *msing* (*Sp*), overol *msing* (*LAm*); (*US*) (= *dungarees*) peto *msing* (*Sp*), overol *msing* (*LAm*), mameluco *m* (*S. Cone*)

overambitious [,əʊvəræm'bɪʃəs] ADJ demasiado ambicioso

overanxious [,əʊvər'æŋkʃəs] ADJ 1 (= *worried*) demasiado preocupado
2 (= *eager*) **he was ~ to give a good impression** estaba demasiado preocupado por causar buena impresión; **I'm not ~ to go** tengo pocas ganas de ir

overarching [,əʊvər'ɑ:tʃɪŋ] ADJ [*question*] global; [*desire*] general

overarm ['əʊvərɑ:m] ADV [*throw, bowl*] por encima de la cabeza

overate [ˌəʊvəˈreɪt] PT *of* **overeat**

overawe [ˌəʊvərˈɔː] VT intimidar; **I was ~d by his presence** me sentía intimidado en su presencia; **I was ~d by the occasion** me sentía sobrecogido por la ocasión

overbalance [ˌəʊvəˈbæləns] Ⓐ VI [*person*] perder el equilibrio; [*boat, car*] volcar
Ⓑ VT [+ *person*] hacer perder el equilibrio; [+ *thing*] hacer volcar

overbearing [ˌəʊvəˈbɛərɪŋ] ADJ (= *imperious*) imperioso, autoritario; (= *despotic*) despótico

overbid (*vb: pt, pp* **overbid**) Ⓐ [ˈəʊvəbɪd] N (*at auction*) mejor oferta *f*, mejor postura *f*; (*Bridge*) sobremarca *f*
Ⓑ [ˌəʊvəˈbɪd] VT (*at auction*) hacer mejor oferta que, pujar más que; (*Bridge*) marcar más que
Ⓒ [ˌəʊvəˈbɪd] VI (*Bridge*) hacer una sobremarca; (*foolishly*) declarar demasiado

overbill [ˌəʊvəˈbɪl] VT (*US*) = **overcharge A1**

overblown [ˌəʊvəˈbləʊn] ADJ 1 [*flower*] marchito, pasado
2 [*style*] pomposo, pretencioso

overboard [ˈəʊvəbɔːd] ADV (*Naut*) por la borda; **to fall ~** caer al agua *or* por la borda; **man ~!** ¡hombre al agua!; ✦***IDIOM*** **to go ~**: **let's not go ~** no hay que exagerar, no nos pasemos*; **she went ~ with the lace and sequins** se pasó con los encajes y las lentejuelas*; **to go ~ for sb** volverse loco por algn

overbold [ˌəʊvəˈbəʊld] ADJ demasiado atrevido

overbook [ˌəʊvəˈbʊk] VT sobrecontratar

overbooking [ˌəʊvəˈbʊkɪŋ] N overbooking *m* (*reserva de habitaciones en un hotel, plazas en un vuelo etc, que sobrepasa al número real de las mismas*)

overburden [ˌəʊvəˈbɜːdn] VT sobrecargar; (*fig*) agobiar, abrumar; **~ed with worries** abrumado *or* agobiado por las preocupaciones

overcall [ˌəʊvəˈkɔːl] VT, VI = **overbid**

overcame [ˌəʊvəˈkeɪm] PT *of* **overcome**

over-capacity [ˌəʊvəkəˈpæsɪtɪ] N sobrecapacidad *f*

overcapitalization [ˌəʊvəkæpɪtəlaɪˈzeɪʃən] N sobrecapitalización *f*, capitalización *f* inflada

overcapitalize [ˌəʊvəˈkæpɪtəlaɪz] VI sobrecapitalizar

overcast [ˈəʊvəkɑːst] ADJ [*sky*] encapotado, cubierto; [*day*] nublado; **to grow ~** nublarse

overcautious [ˌəʊvəˈkɔːʃəs] ADJ demasiado cauteloso

overcautiousness [ˌəʊvəˈkɔːʃəsnɪs] N excesiva cautela *f*

overcharge [ˌəʊvəˈtʃɑːdʒ] Ⓐ VT 1 **to ~ sb for sth** cobrar a algn de más por algo
2 (*Elec*) sobrecargar, poner una carga excesiva a
Ⓑ VI cobrar más de la cuenta

overcoat [ˈəʊvəkəʊt] N abrigo *m*, sobretodo *m*

overcome [ˌəʊvəˈkʌm] (*pt* **overcame**; *pp* **overcome**) Ⓐ VT 1 (= *conquer*) [+ *enemy, opposition*] vencer; [+ *problem, temptation, inhibitions*] superar, vencer; [+ *rage, fear, disgust*] superar, dominar; **the book is an account of how she overcame cancer** el libro describe cómo superó *or* venció el cáncer; **her curiosity finally overcame her shyness** finalmente, su curiosidad superó *or* venció su timidez
2 (= *overwhelm*) [*feeling*] adueñarse de; [*sleep, fatigue*] vencer; **a sense of total inadequacy overcame him** una sensación de ineptitud total se adueñó de él; **sleep overcame him** lo venció el sueño; **to be ~ by sth**: **I was ~ by the heat** el calor me agobió, me sentí agobiado por el calor; **he was ~ by the smoke** el humo le impidió respirar; **she was quite ~ by the occasion** la ocasión la conmovió mucho; **~ by curiosity, he reached out to touch it** vencido *or* dominado por la curiosidad, extendió la mano para tocarlo; **to be ~ with sth**: **she was ~ with remorse** le abrumaba el remordimiento; **he was ~ with grief** estaba abrumado *or* postrado de dolor; **she was so ~ with emotion she couldn't answer** estaba tan conmovida que no podía responder; **you don't seem exactly ~ with joy** no parece que estés rebosante de alegría
Ⓑ VI vencer, triunfar; **we shall ~!** ¡venceremos!

WE SHALL OVERCOME

We Shall Overcome *(Venceremos) es el título de una canción cantada por los miembros del llamado* **US Civil Rights Movement** *(movimiento por los derechos civiles en Estados Unidos). Se cantaba sobre todo en los años 50 y 60 durante las protestas contra la discriminación racial y aún hoy la usan quienes protestan en contra de la injusticia.*

overcommit [ˌəʊvəkəˈmɪt] VT **to ~ o.s.** (*financially*) contraer cargas financieras en exceso; (*at work*) comprometerse a trabajar más de lo que se puede

overcompensate [ˌəʊvəˈkɒmpenˌseɪt] VI **to ~ for sth** compensar algo en exceso

overcompensation [ˌəʊvəkɒmpenˈseɪʃən] N compensación *f* excesiva

overconfidence [ˌəʊvəˈkɒnfɪdəns] N confianza *f* excesiva, exceso *m* de confianza

overconfident [ˌəʊvəˈkɒnfɪdənt] ADJ demasiado confiado (**of** en); (= *conceited*) presumido

overconsumption [ˌəʊvəkənˈsʌmpʃən] N superconsumo *m*, exceso *m* de consumo

overcook [ˌəʊvəˈkʊk] VT cocer demasiado, recocer

overcritical [ˌəʊvəˈkrɪtɪkəl] ADJ hipercrítico; **let's not be ~** seamos justos en nuestra crítica

overcrowded [ˌəʊvəˈkraʊdɪd] ADJ [*room, bus, train*] atestado de gente; [*road, suburb*] congestionado; [*city, country*] superpoblado; **they live in ~ conditions** viven hacinados

overcrowding [ˌəʊvəˈkraʊdɪŋ] N [*of housing, prison*] hacinamiento *m*; [*of bus, train*] abarrotamiento *m*; [*of town*] superpoblación *f*

overdependence [ˌəʊvədɪˈpendəns] N dependencia *f* excesiva

overdependent [ˌəʊvədɪˈpendənt] ADJ excesivamente dependiente (**on** de)

overdeveloped [ˌəʊvədɪˈveləpt] ADJ (*gen*) excesivamente desarrollado; (*Phot*) sobreprocesado, sobrerrevelado

overdevelopment [ˌəʊvədɪˈveləpmənt] N superdesarrollo *m*

overdo [ˌəʊvəˈduː] (*pt* **overdid** [ˌəʊvəˈdɪd]; *pp* **overdone**) VT 1 (= *exaggerate*) exagerar; (= *use to excess*) pasarse con*; **I overdid the garlic** me he pasado con el ajo*, se me ha ido la mano con el ajo*; **don't ~ the smoking** no fumes demasiado; **she rather ~es the scent** tiende a ponerse demasiado perfume; **to ~ it** *or* **things** (= *work too hard*) trabajar demasiado; (= *exaggerate*) exagerar; (*in description, sentiment etc*) cargar las tintas
2 (= *cook too long*) cocer demasiado, recocer

overdone [ˌəʊvəˈdʌn] Ⓐ PP *of* **overdo**
Ⓑ ADJ (= *exaggerated*) exagerado; (= *overcooked*) recocido, muy hecho

overdose [ˈəʊvədəʊs] N Ⓐ N sobredosis *f inv*
Ⓑ VI tomar una sobredosis (**on** de); **she ~d on the chocolate** comió demasiado chocolate

overdraft [ˈəʊvədrɑːft] Ⓐ N (*Fin*) sobregiro *m*, giro *m* en descubierto; (*on account*) saldo *m* deudor; **to have an ~** tener la cuenta en descubierto
Ⓑ CPD ► **overdraft charges** NPL cargos *mpl* por descubierto ► **overdraft facility** N crédito *m* al descubierto ► **overdraft limit** N límite *m* del descubierto

overdraw [ˌəʊvəˈdrɔː] (*pt* **overdrew** [ˌəʊvəˈdruː]; *pp* **overdrawn** [ˌəʊvəˈdrɔːn]) VT girar en descubierto; **your account is ~n (by £50)** su cuenta tiene un saldo deudor (de 50 libras); **I'm ~n** tengo un descubierto

overdress [ˌəʊvəˈdres] VI vestirse con demasiada elegancia

overdressed [ˌəʊvəˈdrest] ADJ **to be ~** ir demasiado arreglado; **he makes me feel ~** me hace sentir como si fuera demasiado arreglado

overdrive [ˈəʊvədraɪv] N (*Aut*) superdirecta *f*; **to go into ~** (*fig*) ponerse *or* empezar a funcionar a toda marcha; **phones and fax machines went into ~ when the crisis struck** los faxes y teléfonos empezaron a funcionar a toda marcha *or* se dispararon cuando se produjo la crisis

overdue [ˌəʊvəˈdjuː] ADJ [*salary, wages*] atrasado; [*bill*] vencido y no pagado; [*train, plane*] retrasado, con retraso; **the plane was already ~** el avión ya iba retrasado *or* con retraso; **the train is 30 minutes ~** el tren tiene *or* lleva 30 minutos de retraso; **the baby is two weeks ~** el niño tenía que haber nacido hace quince días; **her period was ~** se le había atrasado la regla; **this book is five days ~** el plazo de préstamo de este libro venció hace cinco días; **that change was long ~** ese cambio tenía que haberse hecho hace tiempo; **that coat is long ~ for replacement** hace tiempo que tenía que haber reemplazado ese abrigo por uno nuevo

over-eager [ˌəʊvərˈiːgəʳ] ADJ [*person*] demasiado preocupado; [*efforts*] demasiado entusiasta; **to be ~ (to do sth)** estar demasiado preocupado (por hacer algo); **she was not ~ to help** tenía pocas ganas de ayudar

overeat [ˌəʊvərˈiːt] (*pt* **overate**; *pp* **overeaten** [ˈəʊvərˈiːtn]) VI comer en exceso

overeating [ˌəʊvərˈiːtɪŋ] N comida *f* excesiva

overelaborate [ˌəʊvərɪˈlæbərɪt] ADJ [*instructions, mechanism*] demasiado complicado; [*attempts*] demasiado esforzado; [*analysis*] rebuscado; [*courtesy*] estudiado

overemphasis [ˌəʊvərˈemfəsɪs] N énfasis *m* excesivo

overemphasize [ˌəʊvərˈemfəsaɪz] VT poner demasiado énfasis en

overemphatic [ˌəʊvərɪmˈfætɪk] ADJ demasiado enfático

overemployment [ˌəʊvərɪmˈplɔɪmənt] N superempleo *m*

overenthusiastic [ˌəʊvərɪnθjuːzɪˈæstɪk] ADJ demasiado entusiasta

overenthusiastically [ˌəʊvərɪnθuːzɪˈæstɪkəlɪ] ADV con demasiado entusiasmo

overestimate Ⓐ [ˌəʊvərˈestɪmɪt] N sobre(e)stimación *f*, estimación *f* excesiva; (*Fin*) presupuesto *m* excesivo
Ⓑ [ˌəʊvərˈestɪmeɪt] VT [+ *importance, value, cost, person*] sobre(e)stimar; **to ~ one's strength/ability** creerse uno más fuerte/capaz de lo que es

overexcite [ˌəʊvərɪkˈsaɪt] VT sobreexcitar

overexcited [ˌəʊvərɪk'saɪtɪd] ADJ sobreexcitado; (= *nervous*) muy nervioso

overexcitement [ˌəʊvərɪk'saɪtmənt] N sobre(e)xcitación *f*

overexert [ˌəʊvərɪg'zɜːt] VT **to ~ o.s.** hacer un esfuerzo excesivo

overexertion [ˌəʊvərɪg'zɜːʃən] N (= *effort*) esfuerzo *m* excesivo; (= *weariness*) fatiga *f*, agotamiento *m*

overexpenditure [ˌəʊvəɪks'pendɪtʃəʳ] N gasto *m* excesivo

overexpose [ˌəʊvərɪks'pəʊz] VT (*Phot*) sobreexponer

overexposure [ˌəʊvərɪks'pəʊʒəʳ] N sobre(e)xposición *f*; **~ to the sun** exposición *f* excesiva al sol; **their cause is suffering from ~ in the media** su caso está siendo afectado negativamente por aparecer demasiado en los medios de comunicación

overextended [ˌəʊvərɪk'stendɪd] ADJ [*person, organization*] desbordado (por las obligaciones)

overfamiliar [ˌəʊvəfə'mɪlɪəʳ] ADJ (= *too well-known*) demasiado conocido; **to get ~ with sb** tomarse demasiadas libertades *or* confianzas con algn

overfeed [ˌəʊvə'fiːd] (*pt, pp* **overfed** [ˌəʊvə'fed]) VT sobrealimentar, dar demasiado de comer a

overfeeding [ˌəʊvə'fiːdɪŋ] N sobrealimentación *f*

overfishing [ˌəʊvə'fɪʃɪŋ] N sobrepesca *f*, captura *f* abusiva (*de pescado*)

overflight ['əʊvəflaɪt] N sobrevuelo *m*

overflow Ⓐ ['əʊvəfləʊ] N (= *pipe*) desagüe *m*, tubo *m* de desagüe; (= *outlet, hole*) rebosadero *m*; (= *liquid*) exceso *m* de líquido, líquido *m* derramado; [*of people*] exceso *m*; **they made an extra room available for the ~ from the meeting** acomodaron otra sala para dar cabida al exceso de asistentes a la reunión

Ⓑ [ˌəʊvə'fləʊ] VI [*liquid*] rebosar, derramarse; [*container, room, hall*] rebosar; [*river*] desbordarse; **people ~ed from the hall into the streets outside** la gente desbordó la sala, inundando las calles del alrededor; **to fill a cup to ~ing** llenar una taza hasta rebosar; **the crowd filled the stadium to ~ing** el estadio estaba a rebosar de público; **she was ~ing with joy** estaba rebosante de alegría

Ⓒ [ˌəʊvə'fləʊ] VT [+ *banks*] desbordarse de, salir de; [+ *fields, surrounding area*] inundar

Ⓓ CPD ['əʊvəfləʊ] ► **overflow meeting** N reunión *f* para el exceso de público ► **overflow pipe** N desagüe *m*, tubo *m* de desagüe

overfly [ˌəʊvə'flaɪ] (*pt* **overflew** [ˌəʊvə'fluː]; *pp* **overflown** [ˌəʊvə'fləʊn]) VT sobrevolar

overfond [ˌəʊvə'fɒnd] ADJ **he's rather ~ of criticizing people** le gusta demasiado criticar a la gente; **she is not ~ of dogs** no le dislocan los perros, no se vuelve loca por los perros

overfull [ˌəʊvə'fʊl] ADJ demasiado lleno, rebosante (**of** de)

overgenerous [ˌəʊvə'dʒenərəs] ADJ [*person*] demasiado generoso; [*helping, portion*] excesivamente grande; **they were ~ in their praise of him** lo elogiaron con exceso

overground ['əʊvəgraʊnd] Ⓐ ADJ de superficie Ⓑ ADV por la superficie, a cielo abierto

overgrown [ˌəʊvə'grəʊn] ADJ [1] [*garden*] descuidado, cubierto de malas hierbas; **~ with** cubierto *or* revestido de; **the path is quite ~ now** la senda está ya casi cubierta de vegetación

[2] [*child, adolescent*] demasiado grande para su edad; **he's just an ~ schoolboy** es como un niño grande

overhand ['əʊvəhænd] (*US*) Ⓐ ADJ [*stroke*] dado por encima de la cabeza

Ⓑ ADV por encima de la cabeza

overhang (*vb: pt, pp* **overhung**) Ⓐ ['əʊvəhæŋ] N proyección *f*; [*of roof*] alero *m*; (*in rock climbing*) saliente *m*, extraplomo *m*

Ⓑ [ˌəʊvə'hæŋ] VT sobresalir por encima de; **a beach overhung with palm trees** una playa sobre la que se inclinan las palmeras; **the mists that overhung the valley** la neblina que flotaba sobre el valle

Ⓒ [ˌəʊvə'hæŋ] VI sobresalir

overhanging [ˌəʊvə'hæŋɪŋ] ADJ [*cliff, rock*] saliente; [*branches, trees, balcony*] que sobresale

overhastily [ˌəʊvə'heɪstɪlɪ] ADV apresuradamente, precipitadamente

overhasty [ˌəʊvə'heɪstɪ] ADJ apresurado, precipitado

overhaul Ⓐ ['əʊvəhɔːl] N repaso *m* general, revisión *f*

Ⓑ [ˌəʊvə'hɔːl] VT [1] (= *check*) [+ *machine*] revisar, repasar, dar un repaso general a; [+ *plans etc*] volver a pensar, rehacer, replantear

[2] (= *overtake*) alcanzar, adelantarse a

overhead Ⓐ [ˌəʊvə'hed] ADV por lo alto, en alto, por encima de la cabeza; **a bird flew ~** pasó un pájaro

Ⓑ ['əʊvəhed] ADJ de arriba, encima de la cabeza; [*crane*] de techo; [*railway*] elevado, suspendido; [*camshaft*] en cabeza

Ⓒ ['əʊvəhed] N **~** (*US*) ◊ **~s** (*Brit*) gastos *mpl* generales

Ⓓ ['əʊvəhed] CPD ► **overhead cable** N línea *f* eléctrica aérea ► **overhead expenses** NPL gastos *mpl* generales ► **overhead kick** N chilena *f*, tijereta *f* ► **overhead light** N luz *f* de techo ► **overhead projector** N retroproyector *m*

overhear [ˌəʊvə'hɪəʳ] (*pt, pp* **overheard** [ˌəʊvə'hɜːd]) Ⓐ VT oír (por casualidad); **I couldn't help ~ing their conversation** no pude evitar oír su conversación; **she was ~d complaining** se la oyó quejarse

Ⓑ VI **be careful, someone might ~** ten cuidado, alguien podría oírnos

overheat [ˌəʊvə'hiːt] Ⓐ VT [1] (*lit*) recalentar, sobrecalentar; **to get ~ed** recalentarse

[2] (*Econ, fig*) sobrecalentar

Ⓑ VI recalentarse

overheating [ˌəʊvə'hiːtɪŋ] N recalentamiento *m* (*also fig, Econ*)

overhung [ˌəʊvə'hʌŋ] PT, PP *of* **overhang**

overindulge [ˌəʊvərɪn'dʌldʒ] Ⓐ VT [+ *child*] mimar, consentir; [+ *passion*] dar rienda suelta a, dejarse llevar por

Ⓑ VI excederse; **everyone ~s at Christmas** todo el mundo se excede en Navidades; **to ~ in alcohol** abusar del alcohol

overindulgence [ˌəʊvərɪn'dʌldʒəns] N [1] (= *excess*) abuso *m* (**in** de)

[2] (*with children*) exceso *m* de tolerancia (**towards** con)

overindulgent [ˌəʊvərɪn'dʌldʒənt] ADJ demasiado indulgente, demasiado blando (**toward, with** con)

overinvestment [ˌəʊvərɪn'vestmənt] N sobreinversión *f*

overissue ['əʊvərɪʃuː] (*St Ex*) Ⓐ N emisión *f* excesiva

Ⓑ VT emitir con exceso

overjoyed [ˌəʊvə'dʒɔɪd] ADJ lleno de alegría (**at** por), contentísimo (**at** de); **he was ~ at the news** no cabía en sí de contento con la noticia; **she will be ~ to see you** estará encantada de verte

overkill ['əʊvəkɪl] N [1] (*Mil*) capacidad *f* excesiva de destrucción

[2] (*fig*) **there is a danger of ~ here** corremos peligro de excedernos

overladen [ˌəʊvə'leɪdn] ADJ sobrecargado (**with** de)

overland Ⓐ [ˌəʊvə'lænd] ADV por tierra, por vía terrestre

Ⓑ ['əʊvəlænd] ADJ terrestre

overlap Ⓐ ['əʊvəlæp] N [1] (*lit*) superposición *f* (parcial)

[2] (*fig*) coincidencia *f* (parcial); **there is some ~ between the two categories** las dos categorías coinciden en parte

Ⓑ [ˌəʊvə'læp] VI [1] (*lit*) superponerse (parcialmente); **it is made of ~ping strips of bark** está hecho de tiras de corteza parcialmente superpuestas

[2] (*fig*) coincidir (en parte); **our jobs ~ in some areas** nuestros trabajos coinciden en parte

Ⓒ [ˌəʊvə'læp] VT colocar parcialmente unos sobre otros; **~ the tomato slices as you place them on the plate** coloque las rodajas de tomate en la fuente de manera que queden parcialmente cubiertas unas por otras

overlay (*pt, pp* **overlaid** [ˌəʊvə'leɪd]) Ⓐ [ˌəʊvə'leɪ] VT cubrir (**with** con), revestir (**with** de); **to get overlaid with** formarse una capa de, cubrirse con

Ⓑ ['əʊvəleɪ] N capa *f* sobrepuesta, revestimiento *m*; (= *applied decoration*) incrustación *f*; (*on map etc*) transparencia *f* superpuesta

overleaf [ˌəʊvə'liːf] ADV al dorso; **"see overleaf"** "véase al dorso"

overlie [ˌəʊvə'laɪ] VT recubrir

overload Ⓐ ['əʊvələʊd] N sobrecarga *f*

Ⓑ [ˌəʊvə'ləʊd] VT sobrecargar (**with** de); **to be ~ed with** estar sobrecargado de; (*with work*) estar agobiado de

overlong [ˌəʊvə'lɒŋ] ADJ demasiado largo

overlook [ˌəʊvə'lʊk] VT [1] [*building*] tener vista a, dar a; **the house ~s the park** la casa tiene vistas al parque; **the garden is not ~ed** el jardín no tiene ningún edificio al lado que lo domine

[2] (= *leave out*) pasar por alto; (= *not notice*) pasar por alto, no darse cuenta de; (= *tolerate*) pasar por alto, dejar pasar; (= *turn a blind eye to*) hacer la vista gorda a; **we'll ~ it this time** por esta vez lo pasaremos por alto *or* lo dejaremos pasar; **the plant is easily ~ed** es fácil pasar por alto *or* no ver la planta

[3] (= *watch over*) vigilar; (= *inspect*) inspeccionar, examinar

overlord ['əʊvəlɔːd] N (*feudal*) señor *m*; (= *leader*) jefe *m* supremo

overlordship ['əʊvəlɔːdʃɪp] N (*feudal*) señoría *f*; (= *leadership*) jefatura *f* suprema

overly ['əʊvəlɪ] ADV (*esp US*) demasiado; **he's not ~ fond of cucumber** no le gusta demasiado el pepino, no le vuelve loco el pepino

overman [ˌəʊvə'mæn] VT proveer exceso de mano de obra a; **an ~ned industry** una industria con exceso de mano de obra

overmanning [ˌəʊvə'mænɪŋ] N exceso *m* de mano de obra

overmuch [ˌəʊvə'mʌtʃ] Ⓐ ADV demasiado, en demasía

Ⓑ ADJ demasiado

overnice [ˌəʊvə'naɪs] ADJ melindroso, remilgado

overnight [ˌəʊvə'naɪt] Ⓐ ADV [1] (= *through the night*) **we drove ~** condujimos durante la noche; **we'd like to keep him in ~ for observation** nos gustaría que se quedase la noche en observación; **soak the beans ~** deje las judías a remojo toda la noche; **we stayed ~ in Pisa/at John's place** pasamos la noche en Pisa/en casa de John, hicimos noche en Pisa/ en casa de John

[2] (= *quickly*) [*disappear, spring up*] de la noche a la mañana; **the plants came up almost ~** las plantas salieron prácticamente de la noche a la mañana

Ⓑ ADJ [1] (= *night-time*) **~ accommodation is included** el precio de la estancia por la noche está incluido; **it involved a lot of ~ driving** supuso conducir muchas horas durante la noche; **an ~ journey** un viaje de noche; **to make an ~ journey** viajar de noche; **the operation requires an ~ stay in hospital** esta operación requiere que se quede una noche *or* que haga noche en el hospital; **we arrived in Rio after an ~ stop in Madrid** llegamos a Río tras hacer noche en Madrid

[2] (= *quick*) [*change, transformation*] repentino; **the film that turned her into an ~ sensation** la película que la convirtió en una sensación de la noche a la mañana; **he became an ~ success in America** de la noche a la mañana, se convirtió en una estrella en América

Ⓒ CPD ► **overnight bag** N bolso *m* de viaje

overoptimistic [ˌəʊvərɒptɪˈmɪstɪk] ADJ demasiado optimista

overparticular [ˌəʊvəpəˈtɪkjʊləʳ] ADJ melindroso, escrupuloso en exceso; **he's not ~ about money** le importa poco el dinero; (*pej*) es poco escrupuloso en asuntos de dinero; **he's not ~ about hygiene** no es muy escrupuloso en cuestiones de higiene

overpass [ˈəʊvəpɑːs] N (*US*) paso *m* elevado *or* (*LAm*) a desnivel

overpay [ˌəʊvəˈpeɪ] (*pt, pp* **overpaid** [ˌəʊvəˈpeɪd]) VT [+ *person*] pagar demasiado a

overpayment [ˌəʊvəˈpeɪmənt] N pago *m* excesivo

overplay [ˌəʊvəˈpleɪ] VT [+ *issue, problem*] exagerar; **to ~ (one's hand)** pasarse, ir demasiado lejos

overpopulated [ˌəʊvəˈpɒpjʊleɪtɪd] ADJ superpoblado

overpopulation [ˌəʊvəpɒpjʊˈleɪʃən] N superpoblación *f*

overpower [ˌəʊvəˈpaʊəʳ] VT [1] (= *subdue physically*) dominar; (= *defeat*) [+ *enemy, opponent*] derrotar, vencer; **it took ten guards to ~ him** se necesitaron diez guardas para dominarlo *or* para poder con él

[2] (*fig*) [*heat*] agobiar, sofocar; [*sound*] aturdir; [*emotion*] embargar; [*guilt, shame*] abrumar; [*sleep, tiredness*] vencer; [*flavour*] dominar; **a sudden dizziness ~ed him** un mareo repentino se apoderó de él; **that piece of furniture ~s the room** ese mueble domina la habitación; **I was ~ed by feelings of guilt** me sentía abrumado por un sentimiento de culpabilidad

overpowering [ˌəʊvəˈpaʊərɪŋ] ADJ [1] (= *very strong, intense*) [*smell*] penetrante, intensísimo; [*perfume*] embriagado; [*heat*] asfixiante, sofocante; [*sound*] ensordecedor; [*force*] arrollador; [*flavour*] fortísimo; [*desire*] irresistible; [*need*] acuciante; **the noise was ~** el ruido era ensordecedor

[2] (= *intimidating*) [*person, manner*] apabullante, abrumador

overpraise [ˌəʊvəˈpreɪz] VT elogiar demasiado

overprescribe [əʊvəprɪsˈkraɪb] (*Pharm, Med*) Ⓐ VI recetar demasiados medicamentos Ⓑ VT recetar sin control

overprice [ˌəʊvəˈpraɪs] VT cargar demasiado sobre el precio de; **these goods are ~d** el precio de estas mercancías es excesivo, estas mercancías son demasiado caras para lo que son

overprint [ˌəʊvəˈprɪnt] Ⓐ N sobrecarga *f* Ⓑ VT sobrecargar (**with** de)

overproduce [ˌəʊvəprəˈdjuːs] VT, VI producir demasiado

overproduction [ˌəʊvəprəˈdʌkʃən] N superproducción *f*, exceso *m* de producción

overprotect [ˌəʊvəprəˈtekt] VT proteger demasiado

overprotection [ˌəʊvəprəˈtekʃən] N exceso *m* de protección, sobreprotección *f*

overprotective [ˌəʊvəprəˈtektɪv] ADJ excesivamente protector

overqualified [ˌəʊvəˈkwɒlɪfaɪd] ADJ con titulación que excede la exigida

overran [ˌəʊvəˈræn] PT *of* **overrun**

overrate [ˌəʊvəˈreɪt] VT sobrevalorar, sobre(e)stimar; **I think his success has been ~d** creo que sus logros se han sobrevalorado *or* sobre(e)stimado

overrated [ˌəʊvəˈreɪtɪd] ADJ sobre(e)stimado, sobrevalorado

overreach [ˌəʊvəˈriːtʃ] VT **to ~ o.s.** ir más allá de las propias posibilidades; **the company has ~ed itself and made unwise investments** la compañía ha ido más allá de sus propias posibilidades y ha hecho inversiones poco sensatas

overreact [ˌəʊvərɪˈækt] VI reaccionar de manera exagerada

overreaction [ˌəʊvərɪˈækʃən] N reacción *f* exagerada

overreliance [ˌəʊvərɪˈlaɪəns] N dependencia *f* excesiva (**on** de)

overreliant [ˌəʊvərɪˈlaɪənt] ADJ **to be ~ on sth/sb** depender demasiado de algo/algn

override [ˌəʊvəˈraɪd] (*pt* **overrode**; *pp* **overridden** [ˌəʊvəˈrɪdn]) VT [1] (= *ignore*) hacer caso omiso de, ignorar; (= *cancel*) anular, invalidar; **the court can ~ all earlier decisions** el tribunal puede anular *or* invalidar cualquier toda decisión anterior; **this fact ~s all others** este hecho invalida todos los demás; **our protests were overridden** hicieron caso omiso de nuestras protestas, ignoraron nuestras protestas

[2] (*Tech*) anular, invalidar

overriding [ˌəʊvəˈraɪdɪŋ] ADJ (*gen*) [*need, importance, reason*] primordial; [*principle*] fundamental

overripe [ˌəʊvəˈraɪp] ADJ demasiado maduro, pasado

overrode [ˌəʊvəˈrəʊd] PT *of* **override**

overrule [ˌəʊvəˈruːl] VT [+ *judgment, decision*] anular, invalidar; [+ *request*] denegar, rechazar; [+ *objection*] ignorar; **his suggestion was ~d** denegaron *or* rechazaron su propuesta; **but we were ~d** pero rechazaron nuestra propuesta; **"objection ~d"** (*Jur*) "objeción desestimada"

overrun Ⓐ [ˌəʊvəˈrʌn] (*pt* **overran**; *pp* **overrun**) VT [1] (*Mil*) [+ *country*] invadir; **the field is ~ with weeds** las malas hierbas han invadido el campo, el campo está cubierto de maleza; **the town is ~ with tourists** el pueblo está inundado de turistas

[2] (= *exceed*) [+ *time limit*] rebasar, exceder

Ⓑ [ˌəʊvəˈrʌn] VI [*meeting, speech, TV programme*] exceder el tiempo previsto; **his speech overran by 15 minutes** su discurso se excedió al tiempo previsto en 15 minutos

Ⓒ [ˈəʊvərʌn] N (*on costs*) exceso *m* (en relación a lo previsto); **the project has suffered huge cost ~s** el proyecto ha excedido en mucho los costes previstos

overscrupulous [ˌəʊvəˈskruːpjʊləs] ADJ = **overparticular**

overseas [ˌəʊvəˈsiːz] Ⓐ ADV [*be, live*] en el extranjero, allende el mar (*liter*); **to go ~** ir al extranjero; **to travel ~** viajar por el extranjero; **visitors from ~** visitas *fpl* del extranjero; **to be posted ~** ser destinado al extranjero

Ⓑ ADJ [*student*] extranjero; [*duty, trade*] exterior; (*Mil*) [*service*] en el extranjero, en ultramar; **~ market** mercado *m* exterior; **a company with ~ interests** una empresa con intereses en el extranjero; **she was given an ~ posting/assignment** la destinaron al extranjero

oversee [ˌəʊvəˈsiː] (*pt* **oversaw** [ˌəʊvəˈsɔː]; *pp* **overseen** [ˌəʊvəˈsiːn]) VT supervisar

overseer [ˌəʊvəsɪəʳ] N (= *foreman*) capataz *mf*; (= *supervisor*) supervisor(a) *m/f*

oversell [ˌəʊvəˈsel] (*pt, pp* **oversold**) VT [+ *product*] hacer una propaganda excesiva a favor de; (*fig*) alabar en exceso

oversensitive [ˌəʊvəˈsensɪtɪv] ADJ hipersensible, demasiado susceptible

oversexed [ˌəʊvəˈsekst] ADJ de deseo sexual excesivo; (*hum or pej*) sexualmente obsesionado

overshadow [ˌəʊvəˈʃædəʊ] VT [1] (*lit*) hacer sombra a

[2] (*fig*) eclipsar; **it was ~ed by greater events** fue eclipsado por sucesos de mayor trascendencia; **the event was ~ed by his death** su muerte ensombreció el acontecimiento

overshoe [ˈəʊvəʃuː] N chanclo *m*

overshoot [ˌəʊvəˈʃuːt] (*pt, pp* **overshot** [ˌəʊvəˈʃɒt]) VT [+ *destination*] ir más allá de; [+ *turning*] pasarse de; **to ~ the runway** salirse de la pista de aterrizaje; **we overshot (the target) by 40 tons** producimos 40 toneladas más de lo previsto; ✦**IDIOM to ~ (the mark)** pasarse de la raya, excederse

oversight [ˈəʊvəsaɪt] N [1] (= *omission*) descuido *m*; **it was an ~** fue un descuido; **by an ~** por descuido

[2] (= *supervision*) supervisión *f*

oversimplification [ˌəʊvəsɪmplɪfɪˈkeɪʃən] N simplificación *f* excesiva

oversimplify [ˌəʊvəˈsɪmplɪfaɪ] VT simplificar demasiado

oversize(d) [ˌəʊvəˈsaɪz(d)] ADJ demasiado grande, descomunal; (*US*) [*clothes*] de talla muy grande

oversleep [ˌəʊvəˈsliːp] (*pt, pp* **overslept** [ˌəʊvəˈslept]) VI quedarse dormido, no despertar(se) a tiempo; **I overslept** me quedé dormido, no (me) desperté a tiempo

overspend [ˌəʊvəˈspend] (*pt, pp* **overspent** [ˌəʊvəˈspent]) Ⓐ VT **to ~ one's allowance** gastar más de lo que permite su asignación

Ⓑ VI gastar demasiado *or* más de la cuenta; **we have overspent by 50 dollars** hemos gastado 50 dólares de más *or* más de lo que debíamos

overspending [ˌəʊvəˈspendɪŋ] N gasto *m* excesivo

overspill [ˈəʊvəspɪl] N (= *population*) exceso *m* de población; **an ~ town** una ciudad satélite

overstaffed [ˌəʊvəˈstɑːft] ADJ con exceso de personal, con exceso de plantilla

overstaffing [ˌəʊvəˈstɑːfɪŋ] N exceso *m* de personal, exceso *m* de plantilla

overstate [ˌəʊvəˈsteɪt] VT exagerar; **to ~ one's case** exagerar sus argumentos

overstatement [ˌəʊvəˈsteɪtmənt] N exageración *f*

overstay [ˌəʊvəˈsteɪ] VT **to ~ one's leave** quedarse más tiempo de lo que la licencia permite; **to ~ one's welcome** quedarse más tiempo de lo debido; **I don't want to ~ my welcome** no quiero ser un pesado, no quiero abusar de su hospitalidad

oversteer [ˌəʊvəˈstɪəʳ] VI [*driver*] girar demasiado el volante

overstep [ˌəʊvəˈstep] VT (*fig*) [+ *boundary*] traspasar; [+ *authority*] excederse en el ejercicio de; ✦***IDIOM*** **to ~ the mark** pasarse de la raya, excederse

overstock [ˌəʊvəˈstɒk] VT abarrotar; **to be ~ed with** tener existencias excesivas de

overstrain [ˌəʊvəˈstreɪn] Ⓐ N fatiga *f* excesiva; (*nervous*) hipertensión *f*
Ⓑ VT [+ *person*] (= *tire*) fatigar excesivamente; (= *overstress*) provocar una hipertensión en; [+ *metal*] deformar, torcer; [+ *resources*] estirar; **to ~ o.s.** fatigarse excesivamente

overstretch [ˌəʊvəˈstretʃ] VT [1] (*lit*) [+ *muscles, legs*] forzar demasiado
[2] (*fig*) [+ *resources, budget, finances*] estirar; [+ *abilities*] forzar demasiado; **to ~ o.s.** exigirse demasiado; (*financially*) ponerse en una situación (económica) comprometida

overstrict [ˌəʊvəˈstrɪkt] ADJ [*person*] demasiado estricto; [*regime, schedule*] excesivamente riguroso

overstrike [ˌəʊvəˈstraɪk] Ⓐ N (*on printer*) superposición *f*
Ⓑ VT superponer

overstrung [ˌəʊvəˈstrʌŋ] ADJ [*person*] sobre(e)xcitado, hipertenso; [*piano*] *con dos grupos de cuerdas que se cruzan formando un ángulo oblicuo*

oversubscribed [ˌəʊvəsəbˈskraɪbd] ADJ **the course is heavily ~** existe un exceso enorme de solicitudes para el curso; **the issue was ~** se pidieron más acciones de las que había; **the issue was ~ four times** la solicitud de acciones rebasó cuatro veces la cantidad de títulos ofrecidos

oversupply [ˌəʊvəsəˈplaɪ] VT proveer en exceso (**with** de); **we are oversupplied with cars** tenemos exceso de coches

overt [əʊˈvɜːt] ADJ [*racism, discrimination, hostility*] manifiesto, patente; [*criticism*] abierto, manifiesto; **there were no ~ signs of …** no había signos manifiestos *or* patentes de …

overtake [ˌəʊvəˈteɪk] (*pt* **overtook** [ˌəʊvəˈtʊk]; *pp* **overtaken** [ˌəʊvəˈteɪkən]) Ⓐ VT [1] (= *pass*) [+ *car*] adelantar, rebasar (*Mex*); [+ *runner*] adelantar, dejar atrás; [+ *competition, rival*] tomar la delantera a; **he doesn't want to be ~n** no quiere dejarse adelantar; **you can't ~ that car on the bend** no puedes adelantar ese coche en la curva; **we overtook a lorry near Burgos** cerca de Burgos adelantamos un camión; **Swift has ~n Metmark in steel production** Swift le ha tomado la delantera a Metmark en la producción de acero
[2] (*fig*) pillar desprevenido; **we have been ~n by events** los sucesos nos pillaron desprevenidos *or* de sorpresa
Ⓑ VI (*Aut*) adelantar, rebasar (*Mex*); **"no overtaking"** "prohibido adelantar", "prohibido rebasar" (*Mex*)

overtaking [ˌəʊvəˈteɪkɪŋ] N (*Aut*) adelantamiento *m*, rebase *m* (*Mex*)

overtax [ˌəʊvəˈtæks] VT [1] (*Fin*) gravar en exceso
[2] (*fig*) [+ *strength, patience*] agotar, abusar de; **to ~ o.s.** exigirse demasiado a sí mismo

over-the-counter [ˈəʊvəðəˈkaʊntəʳ] ADJ [*method*] limpio, honrado; **~ drugs** medicamentos *mpl* sin receta; **~ market** (*St Ex*) mercado *m* de acciones no cotizadas en la bolsa

overthrow [ˌəʊvəˈθrəʊ] (*vb: pt* **overthrew** [ˌəʊvəˈθruː]; *pp* **overthrown** [ˌəʊvəˈθrəʊn]) Ⓐ N [*of president, dictator, government*] derrocamiento *m*
Ⓑ VT [+ *system*] echar abajo, derribar; [+ *president, dictator, government*] derrocar

overtime [ˈəʊvətaɪm] Ⓐ N [1] (*Ind*) horas *fpl* extra(s); **to do/work ~** hacer/trabajar horas extra(s); **we shall have to work ~ to catch up** (*fig*) tendremos que esforzarnos al máximo para recuperar lo que hemos perdido; **your imagination has been working ~!** ¡tienes una imaginación demasiado activa!
[2] (*US Sport*) prórroga *f*, tiempo *m* suplementario
Ⓑ CPD ► **overtime ban** N prohibición *f* de horas extra(s) ► **overtime pay** N pago *m* de horas extra(s)

overtired [ˌəʊvəˈtaɪəd] ADJ agotado

overtly [əʊˈvɜːtlɪ] ADV abiertamente

overtone [ˈəʊvətəʊn] N [1] (= *hint, element*) **a speech with a hostile ~** un discurso con cierto tono hostil; **the strike has political ~s** la huelga tiene un trasfondo político; **a play with religious ~s** una obra con connotaciones religiosas; **a wine with citrus ~s** un vino con un cierto sabor cítrico [2] (= *connotation*) [*of word, phrase*] connotación *f* [3] (= *insinuation*) insinuación *f*; **his behaviour was full of sexual ~s** no paraba de insinuarse [4] (*Mus*) armónico *m*

overtop [ˌəʊvəˈtɒp] VT descollar sobre

overtrick [ˈəʊvətrɪk] N baza *f* de más

overtrump [ˌəʊvəˈtrʌmp] VT contrafallar

overture [ˈəʊvətjʊəʳ] N [1] (*Mus*) obertura *f*
[2] (*fig*) **to make ~s to sb** (*Pol, Comm*) hacer una propuesta a algn; (*sexual*) hacer insinuaciones a algn; **they had made ~s to Pan Am, but without success** le hicieron una propuesta a Pan Am, pero no se llegó a nada; **the government made peace ~s to the rebels** el gobierno les hizo una propuesta de paz a los rebeldes

overturn [ˌəʊvəˈtɜːn] Ⓐ VT [+ *car, boat, saucepan*] volcar; [+ *government*] derrocar, derribar; [+ *decision, ruling*] anular; **they managed to have the ruling ~ed** lograron hacer anular la decisión Ⓑ VI [*car*] volcar, dar una vuelta de campana; [*boat*] zozobrar

overuse [ˌəʊvəˈjuːz] VT usar demasiado

overvalue [ˌəʊvəˈvæljuː] VT sobrevalorar

overview [ˈəʊvəvjuː] N visión *f* de conjunto

overweening [ˌəʊvəˈwiːnɪŋ] ADJ arrogante, presuntuoso, altivo; **~ pride** desmesurado orgullo *m*

overweight [ˌəʊvəˈweɪt] Ⓐ ADJ [*person*] gordo; **to be ~** [*parcel, luggage*] pesar demasiado, tener exceso de peso; [*person*] estar demasiado gordo; **he is 8 kilos ~** pesa 8 kilos de más; **the suitcase is a kilo ~** la maleta tiene un exceso de peso de un kilo
Ⓑ N exceso *m* de peso, sobrepeso *m*

overwhelm [ˌəʊvəˈwelm] VT [1] (= *defeat*) [+ *opponent, team*] arrollar, aplastar
[2] (= *overcome*) [*difficulties, fear, loneliness*] abrumar; **sorrow ~ed him** estaba abrumado por el dolor; **try not to let panic ~ you** intenta que el pánico no se apodere de ti; **I felt ~ed by events/her** me sentía abrumado por los acontecimientos/por ella; **he was ~ed by their kindness** su amabilidad le dejó abrumado *or* le conmovió profundamente; **she was ~ed with grief** estaba sumida en la tristeza; **she was ~ed with joy** rebosaba de alegría
[3] (= *inundate, overload*) (*with work*) abrumar, agobiar; (*with questions, requests, information*) atosigar; **you shouldn't ~ the customer with too much information** no deberías atosigar al cliente con demasiada información; **we have been ~ed with offers of help** nos han inundado las ofertas de ayuda

overwhelming [ˌəʊvəˈwelmɪŋ] ADJ [*defeat, victory*] arrollador, aplastante; [*success*] arrollador; [*majority*] abrumador, aplastante; [*heat*] agobiante; [*pressure, urge*] irresistible; [*desire*] irresistible, imperioso; [*emotion*] incontenible; **one's ~ impression is of heat** lo que más impresiona es el calor

overwhelmingly [ˌəʊvəˈwelmɪŋlɪ] ADV **they voted ~ for Blake** una mayoría aplastante *or* arrolladora votó por Blake, la inmensa mayoría votó por Blake; **the proposal was ~ defeated** la propuesta fue rechazada por una mayoría abrumadora *or* aplastante; **the legal profession is ~ male** en la abogacía la inmensa mayoría son hombres

overwind [ˌəʊvəˈwaɪnd] (*pt, pp* **overwound**) VT [+ *watch*] dar demasiada cuerda a

overwork [ˌəʊvəˈwɜːk] Ⓐ N agotamiento *m* por trabajo excesivo
Ⓑ VT [+ *person*] hacer trabajar demasiado; [+ *eye, part of body*] exigir un esfuerzo excesivo a; [+ *word, concept*] desgastar (*a base de utilizarlo en exceso*); **"ecological" has become the most ~ed adjective there is** "ecológico" se ha convertido en el adjetivo más desgastado *or* manido que hay
Ⓒ VI trabajar demasiado

overworked [ˌəʊvəˈwɜːkt] ADJ **we're ~** tenemos demasiado trabajo, nos hacen trabajar demasiado

overwrite [ˌəʊvəˈraɪt] (*pt* **overwrote** [ˌəʊvəˈrəʊt]; *pp* **overwritten** [ˌəʊvəˈrɪtn]) Ⓐ VT [1] exagerar; **this passage is overwritten** este pasaje tiene un estilo recargado
[2] (*Comput*) sobreescribir
Ⓑ VI exagerar

overwrought [ˌəʊvəˈrɔːt] ADJ **to be ~** estar crispado

overzealous [ˌəʊvəˈzeləs] ADJ demasiado entusiasta

Ovid [ˈɒvɪd] N Ovidio

oviduct [ˈəʊvɪdʌkt] N oviducto *m*

oviform [ˈəʊvɪfɔːm] ADJ oviforme

ovine [ˈəʊvaɪn] ADJ ovino

oviparous [əʊˈvɪpərəs] ADJ ovíparo

ovoid [ˈəʊvɔɪd] Ⓐ ADJ ovoide
Ⓑ N ovoide *m*

ovulate [ˈɒvjʊleɪt] VI ovular

ovulation [ˌɒvjʊˈleɪʃən] N ovulación *f*

ovule [ˈəʊvjuːl] N óvulo *m*

ovum [ˈəʊvəm] N (*pl* **ova** [ˈəʊvə]) óvulo *m*

ow [aʊ] EXCL ¡ay!

owe [əʊ] Ⓐ VT (*gen*) deber; **to ~ sb £2** deber dos libras a algn; **I'll ~ it to you** te lo quedo a deber; **to ~ sb for a meal** deber a algn una comida; **he claims he is still ~d for the work** asegura que todavía se le debe dinero por el trabajo; **he ~s his life to a lucky chance** debe su vida a una casualidad; **he ~s his talent to his mother** le debe su talento a su madre; **to what do I ~ the honour of your visit?** ¿a qué debo el honor de su visita?; **you ~ it to yourself to come** venir es un deber que tienes contigo mismo; **I ~ it to**

her to confess mi deber con ella me obliga a confesarlo; **I think I ~ you an explanation** creo que es necesaria una explicación; *see also* **allegiance**

Ⓑ VI tener deudas; **he ~d for three coffees** debía tres cafés

▼**owing** ['əʊɪŋ] Ⓐ ADJ **how much is ~ to you now?** ¿cuánto se le debe ahora?; **I think an explanation is ~** creo que se debe dar una explicación

Ⓑ PREP **~ to** (= *due to*) debido a, a causa de; **~ to the bad weather** debido al mal tiempo; **it is ~ to lack of time** se debe a la falta de tiempo

owl [aʊl] N (= *barn owl*) lechuza *f*; (= *little owl*) mochuelo *m*; (= *long-eared owl*) búho *m*; (= *tawny owl*) cárabo *m*

owlet ['aʊlɪt] N mochuelo *m*

owlish ['aʊlɪʃ] ADJ [*look, eyes*] de búho; [*face*] solemne

own[1] [əʊn] Ⓐ VT [1] (= *possess*) [+ *object, goods*] tener, poseer; [+ *land, house, company*] ser dueño de, poseer; **he ~s two tractors** tiene *or* posee dos tractores; **he ~s three newspapers** es dueño de tres periódicos; **do you ~ your own house?** ¿tienes casa propia?, ¿tienes una casa de tu propiedad?; **who ~s the newspaper?** ¿quién es el propietario *or* dueño del periódico?; **who ~s this pen?** ¿de quién es esta pluma?; **a cat nobody wants to ~** un gato que nadie quiere reclamar; **as if he ~ed the place** como si dueño del lugar; **you don't ~ me!** ¡no te pertenezco!

[2] (= *admit*) reconocer, admitir; **I ~ I was wrong** reconozco *or* admito que me equivoqué; **he ~ed the child as his** reconoció al niño como suyo

Ⓑ VI **to ~ to sth** confesar *or* reconocer algo

►**own up** VI + ADV confesar (**to sth** algo); **~ up!** ¡confiésalo!; **they ~ed up to having stolen the apples** confesaron haber robado las manzanas

own[2] [əʊn] Ⓐ ADJ propio; **the house has its ~ garage** la casa tiene garaje propio; **in her ~ house** en su propia casa; **it's all my ~ money** todo el dinero es mío

Ⓑ PRON **my/his/her** *etc* **~: the house is her ~** la casa es de su propiedad *or* le pertenece; **my time is my ~** dispongo de mi tiempo como quiero; **we all look after our ~** todos cuidamos lo nuestro; **he has a style all his ~** tiene un estilo muy suyo *or* propio; **I'm so busy I can scarcely call my time my ~** estoy tan ocupado que apenas dispongo de mi tiempo; **without a chair to call my ~** sin una silla que pueda decir que es mía; **can I have it for my ~?** ¿puedo quedarme con él?; **he made the theory his ~** hizo suya la teoría, adoptó la teoría; **she has money of her ~** tiene su propio dinero; **a place of one's ~** (una) casa propia; **I'll give you a copy of your ~** te daré una copia para ti; **for reasons of his ~** él sabrá por qué; **to be on one's ~** estar solo; **now we're on our ~** ya estamos solos *or* a solas; **if I can get him on his ~** si puedo hablar con él a solas; **to do sth on one's ~** (= *unaccompanied*) hacer algo por su cuenta; (= *unaided*) hacer algo solo *or* sin ayuda (de nadie); **you'll have a room of your very ~** tendrás una habitación para ti solo; **✦IDIOMS to get one's ~ back (on sb)** vengarse (de algn); **to come into one's ~: women came into their ~ during the Second World War** las mujeres no se hicieron valer hasta la Segunda Guerra Mundial; **his ideas really came into their ~ in the sixties** hasta los años sesenta no se valoraron de verdad sus ideas; **to hold one's ~** defenderse; (= *not give in*) no cejar, mantenerse firme; **he can hold his ~ with the best of them** no le va a la zaga ni al mejor de ellos; **I can hold my ~ in German** me defiendo en alemán; **✦PROV each to his ~** cada uno a lo suyo, cada cual a lo suyo

Ⓒ CPD ► **own brand** N (*Comm*) marca *f* propia (*de un supermercado etc*); *see also* **own-brand** ► **own goal** N (*Brit Sport*) autogol *m*; (*fig*) **the campaign was considered a public relations ~ goal for the government** la campaña se consideró un perjuicio que el gobierno se ha hecho a sí mismo *or* un gol que el gobierno se ha marcado a sí mismo en el ámbito de las relaciones públicas ► **own label** N = **own brand**

own-brand ['əʊn,brænd] ADJ **~ products** productos *mpl* de marca propia (*de un supermercado etc*)

owner ['əʊnəʳ] Ⓐ N [*of goods*] dueño/a *m/f*; [*of land, property, company*] dueño/a *m/f*, propietario/a *m/f*; *see also* **home D**

Ⓑ CPD ► **owner driver** N conductor(a) *m/f* propietario/a ► **owner occupancy** N **there's a growing level of ~ occupancy** hay cada vez más propietarios de la vivienda ► **owner occupier** N ocupante *mf* propietario/a

ownerless ['əʊnəlɪs] ADJ sin dueño

owner-occupied [,əʊnə'ɒkjʊpaɪd] ADJ (*Brit*) [*property, house*] ocupado por el dueño, ocupado por el propietario

ownership ['əʊnəʃɪp] N propiedad *f*; **they abolished private ~ of the means of production** abolieron la propiedad privada de los medios de producción; **the ~ of the land is in dispute** está en disputa la propiedad de la tierra; **"under new ownership"** "nuevo propietario", "nuevo dueño"; **under his ~ the business flourished** el negocio prosperó mientras fue de su propiedad

own-label [,əʊn'leɪbl] ADJ = **own-brand**

ownsome* ['əʊnsəm] N **on one's ~** a solas, solito*

owt [aʊt] N (*Brit dial*) algo, alguna cosa

ox [ɒks] N (*pl* **oxen**) buey *m*

oxalic [ɒk'sælɪk] ADJ **~ acid** ácido *m* oxálico

oxblood ['ɒksblʌd] ADJ de color rojo oscuro

oxbow (lake) ['ɒks,bəʊ('leɪk)] N lago *m* en forma de herradura

Oxbridge ['ɒksbrɪdʒ] N (*Brit*) *Universidades de Oxford y Cambridge*

> **OXBRIDGE**
>
> ***Oxbridge*** *se usa para hacer referencia a las universidades de* ***Oxford*** *y* ***Cambridge****, sobre todo cuando se quiere destacar el ambiente de privilegio al que se las asocia, originado por su posición como las dos universidades más antiguas y prestigiosas del Reino Unido y por el hecho de que muchos licenciados de* ***Oxbridge*** *suelen acabar en puestos muy influyentes del ámbito empresarial, político o diplomático. Muchos número de estudiantes de estas universidades todavía proviene de institutos privados, aunque ambas instituciones tratan de aumentar el número de alumnos de centros estatales.*

oxcart ['ɒkskɑːt] N carro *m* de bueyes

oxen ['ɒksən] NPL *of* **ox**

ox-eye daisy [,ɒksaɪ'deɪzɪ] N margarita *f*

Oxfam ['ɒksfæm] N ABBR = **Oxford Committee for Famine Relief**

> **OXFAM**
>
> ***Oxfam*** *es una organización benéfica cuyas siglas significan en inglés* ***Oxford Committee for Famine Relief****, muy conocida por sus campañas para recaudar fondos, su trabajo de ayuda al Tercer Mundo y su intento de promocionar el uso de tecnología básica y de los recursos locales renovables. Además, el nombre* ***Oxfam*** *se asocia también a una cadena de tiendas gestionadas por esta organización, en las que se puede adquirir ropa y otros artículos de segunda mano, así como objetos hechos en talleres y cooperativas del Tercer Mundo.*

oxford ['ɒksfəd] N (*US*) zapato *m* (de tacón bajo)

oxhide ['ɒkshaɪd] N cuero *m* de buey

oxidation [,ɒksɪ'deɪʃən] N oxidación *f*

oxide ['ɒksaɪd] N óxido *m*

oxidize ['ɒksɪdaɪz] Ⓐ VT oxidar

Ⓑ VI oxidarse

oxlip ['ɒkslɪp] N prímula *f*

Oxon ABBR = **Oxfordshire**

Oxon. ['ɒksən] ADJ ABBR (*Brit*) = **Oxoniensis** (= *of Oxford*) de Oxford

Oxonian [ɒk'səʊnɪən] Ⓐ ADJ oxoniense

Ⓑ N oxoniense *mf*

oxtail ['ɒksteɪl] N **~ soup** sopa *f* de rabo de buey

oxter ['ɒkstəʳ] N (*Scot*) axila *f*

oxyacetylene ['ɒksɪə'setɪliːn] ADJ oxiacetilénico; **~ burner** *or* **lamp** *or* **torch** soplete *m* oxiacetilénico; **~ welding** soldadura *f* oxiacetilénica

oxygen ['ɒksɪdʒən] Ⓐ N oxígeno *m*; **✦IDIOM to give sb the ~ of publicity** hacer propaganda gratuita a algn

Ⓑ CPD ► **oxygen mask** N máscara *f* de oxígeno, mascarilla *f* de oxígeno ► **oxygen tent** N cámara *f* de oxígeno

oxygenate [ɒk'sɪdʒəneɪt] VT oxigenar

oxygenation [,ɒksɪdʒə'neɪʃən] N oxigenación *f*

oxymoron [,ɒksɪ'mɔːrɒn] N (*pl* **oxymora** [,ɒksɪ'mɔːrə]) oxímoron *m*

oyez [əʊ'jez] EXCL ¡oíd!

oyster ['ɔɪstəʳ] Ⓐ N ostra *f*; *see also* **world A1**

Ⓑ CPD ► **oyster farm** N criadero *m* de ostras ► **oyster shell** N concha *f* de ostra

oysterbed ['ɔɪstəbed] N criadero *m* de ostras, vivero *m* de ostras

oystercatcher ['ɔɪstə,kætʃəʳ] N ostrero *m*

oz ABBR = **ounce(s)**

ozone ['əʊzəʊn] Ⓐ N ozono *m*

Ⓑ CPD ► **ozone hole** N agujero *m* de ozono ► **ozone layer** N capa *f* de ozono

ozone-friendly ['əʊzəʊn'frendlɪ] ADJ que no daña la capa de ozono

ozonosphere [əʊ'zəʊnə,sfɪəʳ] N ozonosfera *f*

➤ LANGUAGE IN USE: **owing B** 17.1, 26.3

Pp

P[1], **p**[1] [piː] N (= *letter*) P, p *f*; **P for Peter** P de Pedro; **✦IDIOM to mind** *or* **watch one's Ps and Qs*** cuidarse *or* tener mucho cuidado de no meter la pata*

P[2] ABBR = **parking**

p[2] ABBR [1] = **penny, pence**
[2] (= **page**) p., pág.

P. ABBR [1] (= **president**) P.
[2] (= **prince**) P.

PA (A) N ABBR [1] = **personal assistant**
[2] = **public address system**
[3] = **Press Association**
(B) ABBR [1] (*US*) = **Pennsylvania**
[2] (*Theat etc*) = **personal appearance**

pa* [pɑː] N papá* *m*

p.a. ABBR = **per annum** (= *yearly*) por año, al año

PAC N ABBR (*US*) = **political action committee**

pace[1] [ˈpeɪs] (A) N [1] (= *step*) paso *m*; **I took a couple of ~s forward/back** di un par de pasos hacia delante/atrás; **the tiger was only a few ~s away** el tigre estaba a sólo unos pasos; **to go through one's ~s** [*performer*] demostrar de lo que se es capaz; **to put sb through his/her ~s** poner a algn a prueba; **to put a horse through its ~s** ejercitar un caballo
[2] (= *speed*) [2·1] (*when walking, running*) paso *m*, ritmo *m*; **I could hardly keep ~ (with him)** apenas podía seguirle el ritmo *or* el paso; **to set the ~** (*Sport*) marcar el paso *or* el ritmo; **they walked at a steady ~** ◊ **their ~ was steady** marchaban a un paso *or* ritmo constante; *see also* **quicken, slacken A, snail, walking C**
[2·2] (*fig*) ritmo *m*; **to do sth at one's own ~** hacer algo a su (propio) ritmo; **the economy is growing at a brisk ~** la economía está creciendo a un ritmo rápido; **the ~ of change/life** el ritmo de cambio/vida; **I can't keep ~ with events** no puedo seguir el ritmo de los acontecimientos; **salaries are not keeping ~ with inflation** los sueldos no avanzan al mismo ritmo *or* paso que la inflación, los sueldos no siguen el ritmo de la inflación; **her novels lack ~** el ritmo de sus novelas es demasiado lento; **this company is setting the ~ in new technology** esta empresa está marcando la pauta en nueva tecnología; **he can't stand** *or* **stay the ~** las cosas se desarrollan demasiado rápidamente para él; *see also* **force B5**
(B) VT [1] (*anxiously*) **to ~ the floor** ir *or* andar de un lado para otro; **Harry was pacing the room** Harry iba *or* andaba de un lado para otro de la habitación
[2] (= *set pace of*) **to ~ sb** (*Sport*) marcar el ritmo a algn; **to ~ o.s.: it was a tough race and I had to ~ myself** era una carrera difícil y tuve que tener cuidado de no gastar toda mi energía al principio; **you should ~ yourself and not attempt too much at once** tienes que tomártelo poco a poco y no intentar hacer demasiado de una vez; **he knows how to ~ the action** (*Cine, Theat*) sabe cómo marcar el ritmo de la acción; **a fast-~d world/life** un mundo/una vida de ritmo trepidante; **a well-~d drama** un drama con el ritmo de la acción bien marcado
(C) VI **Alan was pacing nervously** Alan se paseaba nervioso (de un lado para otro), Alan iba *or* andaba de un lado para otro nervioso; **to ~ back and forth** ◊ **~ up and down** ir *or* pasearse de un lado para otro
(D) CPD ► **pace bowler** N (*Cricket*) *jugador de cricket que normalmente lanza la bola rápido* ► **pace bowling** N (*Cricket*) *lanzamiento rápido de la bola*

►**pace out, pace off** VT + ADV [+ *distance*] medir en *or* con pasos; **to ~ out ten metres** medir diez metros en *or* con pasos; **he ~d out the length of the field** midió la longitud del campo en *or* con pasos

pace[2] [ˈpeɪsɪ] PREP (*frm*) según, de acuerdo con

pacemaker [ˈpeɪsˌmeɪkəʳ] N [1] (*Med*) marcapasos *m inv*
[2] (*Sport*) liebre *f*
[3] (*in market, business*) = **pacesetter 2**

pacer [ˈpeɪsəʳ] N (*US Sport*) liebre *f*

pacesetter [ˈpeɪsˌsetəʳ] N [1] (*Sport*) liebre *f*
[2] (*in market, business*) persona *f* que marca la pauta

pacey, pacy [ˈpeɪsɪ] ADJ [1] [*production, thriller*] rápido, con buen ritmo
[2] (*Sport*) [*player*] rápido, con buen ritmo

pachyderm [ˈpækɪdɜːm] N paquidermo *m*

Pacific [pəˈsɪfɪk] (A) ADJ pacífico; **the ~ region** la región del Pacífico
(B) N **the ~ (Ocean)** el (Océano) Pacífico
(C) CPD ► **the Pacific Rim** N los países de la Costa del Pacífico ► **Pacific Standard Time** N (*US*) hora *f* oficial de la región del Pacífico

pacific [pəˈsɪfɪk] ADJ pacífico

pacifically [pəˈsɪfɪkəlɪ] ADV pacíficamente

pacification [ˌpæsɪfɪˈkeɪʃən] N pacificación *f*

pacifier [ˈpæsɪfaɪəʳ] N (*US*) (= *dummy*) chupete *m*

pacifism [ˈpæsɪfɪzəm] N pacifismo *m*

pacifist [ˈpæsɪfɪst] (A) ADJ pacifista
(B) N pacifista *mf*

pacify [ˈpæsɪfaɪ] VT (= *calm*) [+ *person*] apaciguar, calmar; [+ *country*] pacificar; **we managed to ~ him eventually** por fin logramos apaciguarlo *or* calmarlo

pack [pæk] (A) N [1] (= *packet*) (*gen*) paquete *m*; (*esp US*) [*of cigarettes*] paquete *m*, cajetilla *f*; (= *wrapping*) envase *m*; **a six-~ of beer** un paquete de seis cervezas; **she smokes a ~ and a half a day** fuma un paquete y medio *or* una cajetilla y media de tabaco al día; **for sell-by date see back of ~** para la fecha de caducidad ver el reverso del envase; *see also* **economy, information B**
[2] (*traveller's*) (*also* **backpack**) mochila *f*; (*on animal*) fardo *m*
[3] [*of cards*] baraja *f*; **a ~ of cards** una baraja de cartas; **the roof collapsed like a ~ of cards** el tejado se derrumbó como una baraja de cartas; **he told me a ~ of lies** me contó una sarta *or* (*LAm*) bola de mentiras; **it's a ~ of lies!** ¡es una sarta *or* (*LAm*) bola de mentiras!, ¡son todo mentiras!
[4] (= *dressing*) (*Med*) compresa *f*; **cold ~** compresa *f* fría; *see also* **face D, ice C, mud B**
[5] [*of hounds, dogs*] jauría *f*; [*of wolves*] manada *f*; **a ~ of hounds** una jauría (de perros); **a ~ of wolves** una manada de lobos
[6] [*of people*] [6·1] (= *bunch*) [*of tourists, reporters*] manada *f*; [*of idiots, fools*] hatajo *m*; **with a ~ of cameramen in hot pursuit** con una manada de cámaras pisándoles los talones; **they're like a ~ of kids** son como un hatajo de críos*; *see also* **rat C**
[6·2] [*of brownies, cubs*] patrulla *f*
[6·3] [*of runners, cyclists*] pelotón *m*; (*fig*) **they are way ahead of the ~ in electronic gadgetry** están muy a la cabeza del pelotón en materia de aparatos electrónicos
[7] (*Rugby*) **the ~** (= *forwards*) los delanteros; (= *scrum*) el pack
(B) VT [1] (= *put in container*) [1·1] [+ *possessions*] (*in case, bag, etc*) **I decided to ~ a few things** decidí meter algunas cosas en la maleta; **have you ~ed the salt and pepper for the picnic?** ¿has metido *or* puesto la sal y la pimienta para el picnic?; **~ your things and get out!** ¡coge tus cosas *or* haz la maleta (con tus cosas) y lárgate de aquí!*
[1·2] [+ *goods, products for transport*] (*in package*) empaquetar; (*in crate, container*) embalar, empacar (*esp LAm*); **a job ~ing goods in a warehouse** un trabajo empaquetando *or* embalando artículos en un almacén; **he was ~ing plates and wine glasses into** *or* **in boxes** estaba metiendo *or* empaquetando platos y copas en cajas
[1·3] (*Comm*) (*in individual packaging*) envasar; **she spent the summer ~ing apricots** se pasó el verano envasando albaricoques; **they come ~ed in dozens** vienen en cajas de una docena
[2] (= *fill*) [+ *box, crate*] llenar; **he has a job ~ing boxes in a warehouse** trabaja en un almacén llenando cajas; **to ~ one's bags** (*lit*) hacer las maletas; **to ~ one's bags (and go** *or* **leave)** (*fig*) coger sus cosas e irse, coger sus cosas y largarse*; **to ~ one's/a (suit)case** hacer la maleta; **Eleanor was ~ing her trunk** Eleanor estaba metiendo sus cosas en el baúl; **a crate ~ed with books** una caja llena de li-

bros; **~ your shoes with paper so they don't lose their shape** mete papel en los zapatos para que no pierdan la forma

3 (= *fill tightly*) [+ *hall, stadium*] llenar a rebosar; **they ~ed the hall to see him** llenaron la sala a rebosar para verlo; **a fun-~ed holiday** unas vacaciones llenas *or* repletas de diversión; **to ~ a jury** *formar un jurado con personas que simpatizan con el interesado*; **a thrill-~ed evening** una tarde muy emocionante; *see also* **action-packed**

4 (= *press tightly*) **to ~ sth/sb into sth**: **we ~ed the children into the car** apretujamos a los niños en el coche; **they've ~ed enough information into this guide to satisfy every need** han incluído suficiente información en esta guía como para satisfacer las necesidades de todo el mundo; **to ~ sth round sth** encajar algo alrededor de algo; **to ~ earth round a plant** acollar una planta; *see also* **packed**

5 (*) (= *carry*) **he ~s a gun** lleva un revólver; **he ~s a powerful punch** (*lit*) pega duro; **this play ~s a powerful punch** esta es una obra con mucho impacto emocional; **drinks that ~ quite a punch** bebidas *fpl* que pegan fuerte

Ⓒ VI 1 (*lit*) 1·1 (= *do one's packing*) hacer la(s) maleta(s); ✦*IDIOM* **to send sb ~ing*** [+ *visitor, caller*] echar a algn con cajas destempladas; (*from job*) despedir a algn sin contemplaciones

1·2 (= *fit*) caber; **these books will ~ easily into that box** estos libros cabrán bien en esa caja; **do you think all this will ~ into one suitcase?** ¿crees que todo esto cabrá *or* se podrá meter en una maleta?

2 (= *cram*) [*people*] **to ~ into a room/theatre** apiñarse *or* apretujarse en una habitación/un teatro; **the five of us ~ed into her Mini** los cinco nos apiñamos *or* apretujamos en su Mini, los cinco nos metimos apretujados en su Mini; **they ~ed round the speaker** se apiñaron *or* se apretujaron en torno al orador

3 (= *compact*) [*snow*] hacerse una masa compacta

Ⓓ CPD ► **pack animal** N bestia *f or* animal *m* de carga ► **pack ice** N banco *m* de hielo, masa *f* flotante de hielo ► **pack leader** N (*Rugby*) delantero/a *m/f* principal; (*fig*) líder *mf* de la panda *or* del grupo

►**pack away** Ⓐ VT + ADV (*lit*) guardar; **I ~ed the tools away** guardé las herramientas; **he can certainly ~ away food, can't he?*** da buena cuenta de la comida ¿verdad?*

Ⓑ VI + ADV dejarse guardar; **his umbrella wouldn't ~ away correctly** su paraguas no se dejaba guardar bien

►**pack down** Ⓐ VT + ADV (*gen*) apretar, comprimir; (*with feet*) apisonar

Ⓑ VI + ADV (*Rugby*) formar la melé *or* el scrum

►**pack in*** VT + ADV 1 (= *cram*) [+ *people*] **airlines make money by ~ing people in** las compañías aéreas hacen dinero metiendo a un montón de gente en los aviones; **they were ~ed in like sardines** estaban como sardinas en lata; **the show's ~ing them in** el espectáculo llena la sala al completo *or* a rebosar; **we ~ed a lot of sightseeing into those two days** metimos un montón de visitas turísticas en esos dos días

2 (= *stop doing*) [+ *job, activity*] dejar; **it's time we ~ed it in** ya es hora de dejarlo; **let's ~ it in for the day** dejémoslo por hoy; **~ it in!** ¡déjalo ya!

►**pack off** VT + ADV (= *send away*) largar*; **I ~ed him off in a taxi** lo despaché en un taxi, lo largué en un taxi*; **they ~ed him off to London** lo enviaron sin más a Londres; **to ~ a child off to bed/school** mandar a un niño a la cama/al colegio

►**pack out** VT + ADV [+ *stadium, hall*] llenar a rebosar, llenar hasta los topes*

►**pack up** Ⓐ VI + ADV 1 (*) (= *cease to function*) [*washing-machine, car*] estropearse, descomponerse (*esp Mex*); [*battery*] agotarse; [*engine*] averiarse, estropearse

2 (*) [*person*] 2·1 (= *stop activity*) **let's ~ up now** vamos a dejarlo *or* terminar ya

2·2 (= *collect things together*) recoger (mis, tus, sus *etc* cosas); **they just ~ed up and left** recogieron (sus cosas) y se marcharon

Ⓑ VT + ADV 1 (= *put away*) [+ *belongings*] recoger

2 (*) (= *give up*) dejar

package ['pækɪdʒ] Ⓐ N 1 (= *parcel, container*) paquete *m*

2 (*US*) (= *packet*) paquete *m*; **the ingredients were clearly listed on the ~** los ingredientes estaban enumerados claramente en el paquete

3 (*fig*) 3·1 (= *deal*) oferta *f*; **a generous remuneration ~** una generosa oferta de remuneración; **the ~ includes two nights in a hotel** la oferta incluye dos noches en un hotel

3·2 [*of measures, aid*] paquete *m*; **an economic aid ~** un paquete de ayuda económica; *see also* **rescue**

3·3 (= *holiday*) viaje *m* organizado, vacaciones *fpl* organizadas; **the price of a ~ has gone up by 8% since last year** el precio de un viaje organizado *or* de las vacaciones organizadas ha subido un 8% desde el año pasado

4 (*Comput*) paquete *m*; *see also* **software**

Ⓑ VT 1 (*US Comm*) (*also* **~ up**) (*in paper, packet*) empaquetar, embalar, empacar (*LAm*); (*in bottle, jar*) envasar; **~d foods** alimentos *mpl* envasados

2 (*fig*) presentar; **it depends how you ~ the proposal** depende de la forma en que presentes la propuesta

Ⓒ CPD ► **package deal** N (= *holiday*) viaje *m* organizado, vacaciones *fpl* organizadas; (= *deal*) oferta *f*; (= *agreement*) acuerdo *m* global ► **package holiday** (*Brit*), **package vacation** (*US*) N viaje *m* organizado, vacaciones *fpl* organizadas; **to go on** *or* **take a ~ holiday** hacer un viaje organizado ► **package store** N (*US*) *tienda con licencia para vender bebidas alcohólicas* ► **package tour** N viaje *m* organizado

packager ['pækɪdʒəʳ] N (*Publishing, TV*) productora *f*

packaging ['pækɪdʒɪŋ] Ⓐ N 1 (= *packet, box, etc*) embalaje *m*; (= *wrapping*) envoltorio *m*

2 (*Comm*) (= *presentation*) presentación *f*; **if the image and the ~ are right, consumers will buy anything** si la imagen y la presentación son las adecuadas, los clientes comprarán cualquier cosa

Ⓑ CPD ► **packaging company, packaging plant** N envasadora *f* ► **packaging industry** N industria *f* del empaquetado *or* del envase ► **packaging machine** N máquina *f* empaquetadora *or* envasadora ► **packaging material** N material *m* de envasado *or* de empaquetado

packed [pækt] Ⓐ ADJ 1 (= *crowded*) (*with people, vehicles*) lleno, repleto, a rebosar; (*more emph*) atestado; **the bus was ~ (with people)** el autobús estaba lleno *or* repleto *or* a rebosar *or* atestado (de gente); **the lecture was ~** la conferencia llenó la sala a rebosar; **the show played to ~ houses for 12 weeks** el espectáculo tuvo lleno completo durante 12 semanas; **the place was ~ (out)** el local estaba repleto *or* a tope* *or* hasta arriba*; *see also* **jam-packed**

2 (= *filled*) lleno, repleto; **crates ~ with books** cajones *mpl* de embalaje llenos *or* repletos de libros; **the book is ~ with interesting facts** el libro está lleno de datos interesantes; **~ full of sth** repleto de algo, completamente lleno de algo

3 (= *with luggage ready*) **she was ~ and ready to leave** ya había hecho la(s) maleta(s) y estaba lista para irse

4 (= *compressed*) [*snow*] **the snow was ~ hard** la nieve se había convertido en una masa compacta

Ⓑ CPD ► **packed lunch** N bolsa *f* de bocadillos; **I usually take a ~ lunch to work** me suelo preparar algo de comida y llevarla al trabajo, me suelo preparar unos bocadillos y llevarlos al trabajo

packer ['pækəʳ] N empacador(a) *m/f*

packet ['pækɪt] Ⓐ N 1 (= *carton*) cajita *f*; [*of cigarettes*] cajetilla *f*; [*of seeds, needles*] sobre *m*; [*of crisps etc*] bolsa *f*; (= *small parcel*) paquete *m*

2 (*fig*) **a new ~ of proposals** un paquete de nuevas propuestas; **a whole ~ of trouble** la mar de disgustos*

3 (*Brit**) (= *large sum*) dineral *m*; **to make a ~** ganar un dineral *or* una fortuna; **that must have cost a ~** eso habrá costado un dineral

4 (*Naut*) (*also* **~ boat**) paquebote *m*

Ⓑ CPD ► **packet switching** N (*Comput*) conmutación *f* de paquetes

packhorse ['pækhɔːs] N caballo *m* de carga

packing ['pækɪŋ] Ⓐ N 1 (*Comm*) (= *product wrapping, act of packing*) embalaje *m*; *see also* **postage**

2 [*of suitcase*] **to do one's ~** hacer la(s) maleta(s)

Ⓑ CPD ► **packing case** N cajón *m* de embalaje ► **packing density** N (*Comput*) densidad *f* de compacidad ► **packing department** N (*for mail, transport*) departamento *m* de embalaje ► **packing house** N envasadora *f* ► **packing list** N *lista de lo que se va a meter o ya se ha metido en la maleta* ► **packing plant** N envasadora *f* ► **packing slip** N hoja *f* de embalaje

packsaddle ['pæk,sædl] N albarda *f*

pact [pækt] N 1 (*between two people*) pacto *m*; **to make a ~ (with sb)** hacer un pacto (con algn); **to make a ~ with the Devil** hacer un pacto con el diablo; **to make a ~ (not) to do sth** acordar (no) hacer algo, pactar (no) hacer algo; *see also* **suicide**

2 (*Pol, Comm*) pacto *m*; (*esp Econ, Ind*) convenio *m*; **electoral ~** pacto *m* electoral; **non-aggression ~** pacto *m* de no agresión

pacy ['peɪsɪ] ADJ = **pacey**

pad[1] [pæd] Ⓐ N 1 (*to prevent friction etc*) almohadilla *f*, cojinete *m*; (*for ink*) tampón *m*; (= *brake pad*) zapata *f*

2 (= *shoulder pad*) hombrera *f*; (= *knee pad*) rodillera *f*; (= *elbow pad*) codera *f*; (= *shin pad*) espinillera *f*

3 (= *note pad, writing pad*) bloc(k) *m*, cuaderno *m*; (= *blotting pad*) secafirmas *m*

4 (*for helicopter*) plataforma *f*; (= *launch pad*) plataforma *f* de lanzamiento

5 [*of animal's foot*] almohadilla *f*

Ⓑ VT 1 [+ *shoulders etc*] acolchonar, poner hombreras a; [+ *armour*] enguatar

2 (= *stuff*) rellenar; (*fig*) [+ *book, speech etc*] meter paja en

Ⓒ VI **to ~ about** andar *or* (*esp LAm*) caminar sin hacer ruido; **to ~ in** entrar sin hacer ruido

►**pad out** VT + ADV [+ *speech, essay*] meter paja en; **the essay was ~ded out with references to …** el trabajo estaba inflado de referencias a …

pad²* [pæd] N (= *home*) casa *f*; (= *flat*) piso *m*, departamento *m* (*LAm*); (= *room*) agujero‡ *m*, habitación *f*

padded ['pædɪd] Ⓐ ADJ [*bra*] reforzado; [*cell*] acolchonado; [*dashboard etc*] almohadillado; [*armour*] enguatado; [*envelope*] acolchado
Ⓑ CPD ► **padded shoulders** NPL hombreras *fpl*

padding ['pædɪŋ] N 1 (= *material*) relleno *m*, almohadilla *f*
2 (*fig*) (*in speech etc*) paja *f*, borra *f*

paddle ['pædl] Ⓐ N 1 (= *oar*) zagual *m*, pala *f*, remo *m* (*LAm*); (= *blade of wheel*) paleta *f*; (= *wheel*) rueda *f* de paletas
2 (*US*) (= *bat*) raqueta *f*
3 **to go for** *or* **have a ~** ir a chapotear, ir a mojarse los pies
Ⓑ VT 1 [+ *boat*] remar con pala
2 (*US**) (= *spank*) azotar, zurrar*
3 **to ~ one's feet in the sea** mojarse los pies en el mar
Ⓒ VI 1 (*in boat*) remar con pala; **they ~d to the bank** dirigieron el bote a la orilla
2 (= *walk in water*) mojarse los pies
Ⓓ CPD ► **paddle boat**, **paddle steamer** N vapor *m* de ruedas *or* paletas ► **paddle wheel** N rueda *f* de paletas

paddling pool ['pædlɪŋpu:l] N (*Brit*) piscina *f* para niños

paddock ['pædək] N (= *field*) potrero *m*; [*of racecourse*] paddock *m*; (*Motor racing*) parque *m*

paddy¹ ['pædɪ] N (= *rice*) arroz *m*; (= *field*) arrozal *m*

paddy²* ['pædɪ] N (= *anger*) rabieta* *f*; **to get into a ~** coger una rabieta

Paddy ['pædɪ] N 1 (*familiar form*) *of* **Patrick**
2 (*pej*, ‡) irlandés *m*

paddy waggon* ['pædɪˌwægən] N (*US*) coche *m* celular

paddywhack* ['pædɪwæk] N rabieta* *f*

padlock ['pædlɒk] Ⓐ N candado *m*
Ⓑ VT cerrar con candado

padre ['pɑ:drɪ] N (*Mil*) capellán *m* militar; (*Univ*) capellán *m* de colegio; (*in direct address*) padre

paean ['pi:ən] N himno *m* de alegría; **~s of praise** alabanzas *fpl*

paederast ['pedəræst] N = **pederast**

paediatric, **pediatric** (*US*) [ˌpi:dɪ'ætrɪk] Ⓐ ADJ de pediatría, pediátrico
Ⓑ CPD ► **paediatric ward** N sala *f* de pediatría

paediatrician, **pediatrician** (*US*) [ˌpi:dɪə'trɪʃən] N pediatra *mf*

paediatrics, **pediatrics** (*US*) [ˌpi:dɪ'ætrɪks] NSING pediatría *f*

paedological, **pedological** (*US*) [ˌpi:də'lɒdʒɪkl] ADJ pedológico

paedology, **pedology** (*US*) [pɪ'dɒlədʒɪ] N pedología *f*

paedophile, **pedophile** (*US*) ['pi:dəʊfaɪl] N pederasta *mf*, pedófilo/a *m/f*

paedophilia, **pedophilia** (*US*) [ˌpi:dəʊ'fɪlɪə] N pederastia *f*, pedofilia *f*

pagan ['peɪgən] Ⓐ ADJ pagano
Ⓑ N pagano/a *m/f*

paganism ['peɪgənɪzəm] N paganismo *m*

page¹ [peɪdʒ] Ⓐ N [*of book, newspaper, etc*] página *f*; **see ~ 20** véase en la página 20; **a glorious ~ in our history** una página gloriosa de nuestra historia; **back ~** contraportada *f*; **the picture on the facing ~ shows …** el dibujo de la página de en frente muestra …; **financial ~** página *f* de economía *or* de negocios; **front ~** primera plana *f*, primera página *f*; **it made front ~ news** salió en primera plana *or* página; **on ~ 14** en la página 14; **over the ~** en la página siguiente; **a page three girl** (*Brit**) *una chica de las que aparecen en la página tres de los periódicos de prensa amarilla británicos*; *see also* **inside D1**, **title C**, **yellow E**
Ⓑ CPD ► **page break** N (*Comput*) salto *m* de página ► **page proofs** NPL (*Typ*) pruebas *fpl* de página

> **PAGE THREE**
>
> *Durante años, en la página tres del periódico* **The Sun**, *el diario sensacionalista de más venta en el Reino Unido, ha aparecido una foto a toda página de una chica en topless, conocida como la* **page three girl**. *De ahí que el término haya pasado a usarse también, en sentido extenso, para referirse a las modelos que posan semidesnudas en otros periódicos sensacionalistas.*

page² [peɪdʒ] Ⓐ N 1 (*also* **~boy**) (*in hotel*) botones *m inv*
2 (*US*) (*at wedding*) paje *m*
3 (*US*) (*in Congress*) mensajero *m*
4 (*Hist*) escudero *m*
Ⓑ VT **to ~ sb** (*over public address*) llamar a algn por megafonía; (*with pager*) llamar a algn por el busca*

-page [peɪdʒ] ADJ (*ending in compounds*) **a 4-page pamphlet** un folleto de 4 páginas

pageant ['pædʒənt] N (= *show*) espectáculo *m*; (= *procession*) desfile *m*; **a ~ of Elizabethan times** una representación de la época isabelina en una serie de cuadros; **the town held a ~ to mark the anniversary** la ciudad organizó una serie de fiestas públicas para celebrar el aniversario

pageantry ['pædʒəntrɪ] N pompa *f*, boato *m*; **it was celebrated with much ~** se celebró con gran boato; **the ~ of the occasion** lo espectacular *or* vistoso del acontecimiento; **all the ~ of history** todo el esplendor de la historia

pageboy ['peɪdʒbɔɪ] N 1 (*in hotel*) botones *m inv*; (*Brit*) (*at wedding*) paje *m*
2 (*also* **~ hairstyle**) estilo *m* paje

pager ['peɪdʒəʳ] N localizador *m*, busca* *m*

paginate ['pædʒɪneɪt] VT paginar

pagination [ˌpædʒɪ'neɪʃən] N paginación *f*; **without ~** sin paginar

paging ['peɪdʒɪŋ] Ⓐ N (*Comput*) paginación *f*
Ⓑ CPD ► **paging device** N localizador *m*, busca* *m*

pagoda [pə'gəʊdə] N pagoda *f*

pah† [pæ] EXCL ¡bah!

paid [peɪd] Ⓐ PT, PP *of* **pay**
Ⓑ ADJ 1 [*official*] asalariado, que recibe un sueldo; [*work*] remunerado, rentado (*S. Cone*); [*bill, holiday etc*] pagado; **a ~ hack** un escritorzuelo a sueldo*
2 **to put ~ to sth** (*Brit*) acabar con *or* poner fin a algo

paid-up ['peɪd'ʌp] Ⓐ ADJ 1 [*member*] con sus cuotas pagadas *or* al día
2 (*Fin*) [*share*] liberado; **fully ~ share** acción *f* totalmente liberada
Ⓑ CPD ► **paid-up capital** N capital *m* pagado

pail [peɪl] N balde *m*, cubo *m*; (*child's*) cubito *m*

pailful ['peɪlfʊl] N cubo *m*, contenido *m* de un cubo

paillasse ['pælıæs] N jergón *m*

pain [peɪn] Ⓐ N 1 (*physical*) dolor *m*; **she winced with ~** hizo una mueca de dolor; **where is the ~?** ¿dónde le duele?; **in order to ease the ~** para aliviar el dolor; **back/chest/muscle ~** dolor *m* de espalda/pecho/músculos; **I have a ~ in my leg** me duele la pierna; **to be in ~** sufrir dolor(es), tener dolor(es); **I was in excruciating ~** sufría *or* tenía unos dolores horribles; ♦***PROV*** **no ~, no gain** el que algo quiere, algo le cuesta; *see also* **growing B**, **labour D**, **period B**
2 (*mental*) dolor *m*; **his harsh words caused her much ~** sus duras palabras le causaron mucho dolor *or* la hicieron sufrir mucho
3 (*) (= *nuisance*) **to be a ~** [*person*] ser un pesado*; [*situation*] ser una lata*, ser un rollo*; **he's a real ~** es un verdadero pesado*; **don't be such a ~!** ¡no fastidies!*, ¡no seas tan pesada!*; **what a ~!** ¡qué lata!*, ¡qué rollo!*; **he's a ~ in the arse** *or* (*US*) **ass‡** es un coñazo‡; **he's a ~ in the neck*** es insoportable
4 **pains** (= *efforts*) **to be at ~s to do sth** esforzarse al máximo por hacer algo, intentar por todos los medios hacer algo; **for my ~s** después de todos mis esfuerzos; **to take ~s to do sth** poner especial cuidado en hacer algo; **he took infinite ~s with his job** se esmeraba *or* se esforzaba muchísimo en su trabajo; **I had taken great ~s with my appearance** me había esmerado *or* esforzado mucho con mi apariencia
5 (= *penalty*) **on** *or* **under ~ of sth** bajo pena de algo, so pena de algo
Ⓑ VT (*mentally*) doler, hacer sufrir; **it ~s me to think of you struggling all alone** me duele pensar que estás luchando sola, pensar que estás luchando sola me hace sufrir; **it ~s me to tell you** me duele decírtelo; **it ~ed him that his father talked like that** le dolía que su padre hablara así
Ⓒ CPD ► **pain clinic** N unidad *f* del dolor ► **pain relief** N alivio *m* contra el dolor ► **pain threshold** N resistencia *f* al dolor

pained [peɪnd] ADJ [*expression*] dolorido, de dolor; [*voice*] afligido; **Frank gave him a ~ look** Frank le dirigió una mirada dolorida *or* de dolor

painful ['peɪnfʊl] ADJ 1 (*physically*) [*injury, swelling*] doloroso; **a slow and ~ death** una muerte lenta y dolorosa; **my ankle is still ~** todavía me duele el tobillo; **her wrist was ~ to the touch** la muñeca le dolía al tocarla; **was it very ~?** ¿te dolió mucho?; **he received a ~ blow on the back** recibió un golpe en la espalda que le causó un intenso dolor
2 (*mentally*) [*memory, reminder, experience*] doloroso; [*task, decision*] penoso; **it will be a long and ~ process** será un proceso largo y doloroso *or* penoso; **his embarrassment was ~ to witness** daba pena ver lo abochornado que estaba; **it is my ~ duty to tell you that …** es mi penoso deber comunicarle que …, tengo el desagradable deber de comunicarle que …
3 (*) (= *embarrassingly bad*) fatal*, de pena*; **her acting was so bad it was ~ to watch** su actuación era tan mala que daba vergüenza ajena presenciarla, su actuación era de pena*

painfully ['peɪnfəlɪ] ADV 1 (*lit*) **his tooth throbbed ~** la muela le producía un dolor punzante; **he felt the muzzle of the revolver dig ~ into his side** sintió el dolor que le causaba el revólver clavándose en el costado;

I hope he dies slowly and ~ espero que tenga una muerte lenta y dolorosa

2 (*emphatic*) (= *extremely*) **to be ~ aware of sth/that ...** ser plenamente consciente de algo/de que ...; **it was ~ clear that ...** estaba penosamente claro que ...; **she was ~ shy/thin** era tan tímida/delgada que daba pena; **our economic recovery will be ~ slow** nuestra recuperación económica va a ser un proceso lento y penoso *or* doloroso

3 (= *laboriously*) con mucho trabajo *or* esfuerzo

painkiller ['peɪnkɪləʳ] N analgésico *m*

painkilling ['peɪn,kɪlɪŋ] ADJ [*drug*] analgésico

painless ['peɪnlɪs] ADJ 1 (= *without pain*) indoloro, sin dolor; **~ childbirth** parto *m* sin dolor

2 (*fig*) (= *easy*) sin mayores dificultades

painlessly ['peɪnlɪslɪ] ADV (= *without pain*) sin causar dolor; (*fig*) (= *easily*) fácilmente

painstaking ['peɪnz,teɪkɪŋ] ADJ [*task, research etc*] esmerado, concienzudo; [*person*] meticuloso, esmerado

painstakingly ['peɪnz,teɪkɪŋlɪ] ADV laboriosamente, concienzudamente, esmeradamente

paint [peɪnt] Ⓐ N 1 (= *substance*) pintura *f*; **a coat of ~** una mano depintura; **the ~ was flaking off the walls** la pintura de las paredes se estaba descascarillando; **"wet ~"** "(ojo,) recién pintado"; *see also* **face**, **finger C**, **gloss²**, **oil C**, **poster B**, **spray A2, C**

2 **paints** pinturas *fpl*; **a box of ~s** una caja de pinturas

Ⓑ VT 1 (*Art*) [+ *picture, subject*] pintar; [+ *slogan, message*] escribir con pintura

2 (= *apply paint to*) [+ *wall, fence, etc*] pintar; **to ~ sth blue** pintar algo de azul; **✦IDIOM to ~ the town red** irse de juerga *or* parranda*

3 (= *make up*) [+ *nails, lips*] pintarse; **she ~ed her fingernails red** se pintó las uñas rojas *or* de rojo; **to ~ one's face** pintarse, maquillarse

4 (*fig*) (= *portray*) describir, pintar; **to ~ a grim/gloomy/bleak picture of sth** describir algo en términos sombríos/deprimentes/desalentadores, pintar algo muy negro; **pro-democracy activists ~ quite a different picture of the situation** los activistas en pro de la democracia describen la situación en términos muy diferentes; **to ~ a rosy picture of sth** pintar algo de color de rosa; **to ~ a vivid picture of sth** describir algo gráficamente

5 **to ~ sth on** [+ *varnish, dye*] aplicar algo; **~ the solution on with a clean brush** aplicar la solución con un pincel limpio

6 (*Med*) **treatment involves ~ing the sores with iodine solution** el tratamiento requiere aplicar una solución de yodo en las heridas

Ⓒ VI pintar; **to ~ in oils** pintar al óleo; **to ~ in watercolours** pintar con acuarelas

Ⓓ CPD ► **paint remover** N quitapintura *f* ► **paint roller** N rodillo *m* (pintor) ► **paint scraper** N raspador *m* de paredes ► **paint spray** N pistola *f* (rociadora) de pintura ► **paint stripper** N (= *substance*) quitapintura *f*; (= *tool*) raspador *m* de paredes ► **paint thinner** N disolvente *m*

►**paint in** VT + ADV (= *add*) pintar

►**paint out** VT + ADV tapar con pintura

►**paint over** VT + ADV 1 = **paint out**

2 (= *repaint*) pintar otra vez encima, volver a pintar

paintbox ['peɪntbɒks] N caja *f* de pinturas

paintbrush ['peɪntbrʌʃ] N (*Art*) pincel *m*; (*for decorating*) brocha *f*

painter¹ ['peɪntəʳ] N (*Art*) pintor(a) *m/f*; (= *decorator*) pintor(a) *m/f* de brocha gorda

painter² ['peɪntəʳ] N (*Naut*) amarra *f*; **to cut the ~** (*lit*) cortar las amarras; (*fig*) independizarse

painterly ['peɪntəlɪ] ADJ [*style, talents*] pictoricista

painting ['peɪntɪŋ] N 1 (*Art*) (= *picture*) cuadro *m*, pintura *f*; (= *activity, genre*) pintura *f*; **to study ~** estudiar pintura; **French Impressionist ~** la pintura impresionista francesa; *see also* **oil C**

2 (= *decorating*) pintura *f*; **~ and decorating** pintura *f* y decoración

paintpot ['peɪntpɒt] N bote *m* de pintura

paintwork ['peɪntwɜːk] N pintura *f*

pair [peəʳ] Ⓐ N 1 (= *set*) [*of gloves, shoes, socks, etc*] par *m*; **these socks are not a ~** estos calcetines no son del mismo par; **a ~ of binoculars** unos prismáticos; **a ~ of glasses** *or* **spectacles** unas gafas, unos anteojos; **we need another ~ of hands** necesitamos otro par de manos; **I've only got one ~ of hands** sólo tengo dos manos; **a ~ of pyjamas** un pijama; **a ~ of scissors** unas tijeras, un par de tijeras; **six ~s of scissors** seis tijeras; **a ~ of trousers** un pantalón, unos pantalones, un par de pantalones

2 (= *group of 2 things*) pareja *f*; **a ~ of aces** una pareja de ases; **to arrange in ~s** [+ *glasses, chairs*] colocar de dos en dos; [+ *related words, pictures*] colocar en parejas; *see also* **heel¹**

3 [*of people*] (= *group of 2*) par *m*; (= *couple*) pareja *f*; **a ~ of teenage boys were smoking** un par de quinceañeros estaban fumando; **a ~ of identical twins** una pareja de gemelos; **get out of my sight, the ~ of you!** ¡fuera de mi vista, los dos!; **the happy ~** la feliz pareja, los novios; **to do sth in ~s** hacer algo en parejas *or* de dos en dos; **those two make a right ~!** ¡vaya par!, ¡vaya pareja!; **they make an unlikely ~** forman una insólita pareja, hacen *or* forman una extraña pareja

4 [*of animals, birds*] pareja *f*; **a carriage and ~** un carruaje con dos caballos, un landó con dos caballos

5 (= *counterpart*) 5·1 (*gen*) pareja *f*; **can I try on the ~ to this please?** ¿puedo probarme la pareja, por favor?

5·2 (*Brit Parl*) *uno de los dos miembros de partidos opuestos que se ponen de acuerdo para ausentarse de una votación y, de esa forma, anularse mutuamente*

6 (*Sport*) **pairs** dobles *mpl*; **~s skating** patinaje *m* en parejas

Ⓑ VT 1 (*Zool*) aparear

2 (= *put together*) [+ *socks, gloves*] emparejar; **long skirts ~ed with knitted jackets** faldas *fpl* largas a juego *or* haciendo juego con rebecas de punto; **ginger biscuits are delicious ~ed with glasses of lemonade** las galletas de jengibre están buenísimas acompañadas de vasos de limonada; **to ~ sb with sb**: **trainees will be ~ed with experienced managers** a los aprendices se les pondrá formando pareja con gerentes con experiencia; **I was ~ed with Henry in the general knowledge competition** me pusieron formando pareja con *or* de compañero de Henry en el concurso de cultura general

Ⓒ VI 1 (*gen*) formar pareja(s) (**with** con); **when a Y chromosome ~s with an X chromosome** cuando el cromosoma Y forma pareja con el cromosoma X; **beer ~s well with many New Zealand dishes** la cerveza acompaña bien a muchos platos de Nueva Zelanda

2 (*Zool*) aparearse (**with** con), formar pareja(s) (**with** con)

Ⓓ CPD ► **pair bonding** N unión *f* de pareja, emparejamiento *m*

►**pair off** Ⓐ VT + ADV 1 (*as couple*) emparejar; **everyone was ~ed off** todo el mundo estaba emparejado *or* tenía pareja; **they are always trying to ~ her off** siempre están intentando buscarle pareja

2 (= *group in twos*) agrupar por parejas; **people are ~ed off according to their level of competence** se agrupa a las personas por parejas de acuerdo con su nivel de aptitud

Ⓑ VI + ADV 1 (*as a couple, team*) formar pareja(s)

2 (*Zool*) aparearse, formar pareja

►**pair up** Ⓐ VI + ADV formar pareja(s); **~ up with the person next to you** forme pareja con la persona de al lado

Ⓑ VT + ADV [+ *socks, shoes, gloves*] emparejar; [+ *people*] poner formando pareja; **in the final I was ~ed up with a French teacher** me pusieron formando pareja con un profesor de francés para la final

pairing ['peərɪŋ] N 1 (= *team*) pareja *f*, dúo *m*

2 (*Zool*) apareamiento *m*

paisley ['peɪzlɪ] Ⓐ N (= *fabric, design*) cachemira *f*

Ⓑ CPD ► **paisley shawl** N chal *m* de cachemira

pajamas [pə'dʒɑːməz] NPL (*US*) = **pyjamas**

Paki** ['pækɪ] N ABBR (*Brit offensive*) = **Pakistani**

Pakistan [,pɑːkɪs'tɑːn] N Pakistán *m*, Paquistán *m*

Pakistani [,pɑːkɪs'tɑːnɪ] Ⓐ ADJ pakistaní, paquistaní

Ⓑ N pakistaní *mf*, paquistaní *mf*

pakora [pə'kɔːrə] N (*pl* **pakora** *or* **pakoras**) *plato indio consistente en bolas de cebolla fritas en pasta de harina de garbanzos*

PAL [pæl] N ABBR (*TV*) = **phase alternation line**

pal* [pæl] N amigo/a *m/f*, compinche* *mf*, cuate/a *m/f* (*Mex**), pata *mf* (*Peru**); **be a ~!** ¡venga, pórtate como un amigo!; **they're great ~s** son muy amigos; **old ~s' act** acto *m* de amiguismo*

►**pal up*** VI + ADV hacerse amigos; **to ~ up with sb** hacerse amigo de algn

palace ['pælɪs] Ⓐ N (*lit*) palacio *m*; (*fig*) (= *grand house etc*) palacio *m*; **the Palace has refused to comment** (*Brit*) la Casa Real se ha negado a hacer comentarios

Ⓑ CPD ► **palace revolution** N (*fig*) revolución *f* de palacio ► **palace spokesman** N portavoz *mf* de la Casa Real

palaeographer [,pælɪ'ɒgrəfəʳ] N paleógrafo/a *m/f*

palaeography [,pælɪ'ɒgrəfɪ] N paleografía *f*

palaeolithic [,pælɪəʊ'lɪθɪk] Ⓐ ADJ paleolítico

Ⓑ N **the Paleolithic** el Paleolítico

palaeontologist ['pælɪɒn'tɒlədʒɪst] N paleontólogo/a *m/f*

palaeontology [,pælɪɒn'tɒlədʒɪ] N paleontología *f*

Palaeozoic [,pælɪəʊ'zəʊɪk] (*Geol*) Ⓐ ADJ paleozoico

Ⓑ N **the ~** el Paleozoico

palatable ['pælətəbl] ADJ 1 (= *tasty*) sabroso, apetitoso; (= *just passable*) comible

2 (*fig*) aceptable (**to** a); **it may not be ~ to the government** puede no ser del gusto *or* agrado del gobierno

palatal ['pælətl] Ⓐ ADJ palatal

Ⓑ N palatal *f*

palatalize ['pælətəlaɪz] Ⓐ VT palatalizar

Ⓑ VI palatalizarse

palate ['pælɪt] N (*Anat*) paladar *m*; **to have a delicate ~** tener un paladar delicado; **to have no ~ for wine** no tener paladar para el vino; **I have no ~ for that kind of activity** no aguanto *or* no puedo tragar ese tipo de actividad; **hard ~** paladar *m*; **soft ~** velo *m* del paladar

palatial [pə'leɪʃəl] ADJ suntuoso, espléndido

palatinate [pə'lætɪnɪt] N palatinado *m*

palaver* [pə'lɑːvər] Ⓐ N 1 (= *fuss*) jaleo *m*, desmadre* *m*; (= *trouble*) molestias *fpl*, trámites *mpl* engorrosos; (*US*) (= *chatter*) palabrería *f*; **what a ~!** ¡qué jaleo!; **why all the ~!** ¡no es para tanto!; **that ~ about the car** aquel jaleo que se armó con el coche; **can't we do it without a lot of ~?** ¿no podemos hacerlo sin meternos en tantos líos?*
2 (= *conference*) conferencia *f*, parlamento *m*
Ⓑ VI parlamentar

pale¹ [peɪl] Ⓐ ADJ (*compar* **paler**; *superl* **palest**)
1 [*person, face*] (*naturally*) blanco; (*from illness, shock*) pálido; **she had ~ skin** tenía la piel muy blanca; **she looked ~** se la veía pálida; **you look very ~** estás muy pálido; **she was deathly ~** estaba pálida como la muerte; **to go** *or* **grow** *or* **turn ~** [*person*] palidecer, ponerse pálido; **her face went ~ with shock** paledeció *or* se puso pálida del susto
2 (= *not bright*) [*light, daylight*] tenue, pálido; [*moon*] pálido; **the ~ light of dawn** la tenue *or* pálida luz del alba; **a ~ imitation** una burda imitación
3 (= *not dark*) [*colour*] claro; **a ~ blue dress** un vestido azul claro
Ⓑ VI 1 [*person*] palidecer, ponerse pálido; **his face ~d with fear** palideció *or* se puso pálido de miedo
2 (*fig*) (= *seem insignificant*) **it ~s into insignificance beside …** se vuelve insignificante en comparación con *or* al compararse con …; **her beauty ~d beside her mother's** su belleza perdía esplendor al lado de la de su madre
Ⓒ CPD ► **pale ale** N (*Brit*) cerveza *f* rubia suave

pale² [peɪl] N (= *stake*) estaca *f*; ✦**IDIOM to be beyond the ~** ser inaceptable

paleface ['peɪlfeɪs] N rostropálido/a *m/f*; (*US*) blanco/a *m/f*

pale-faced [ˌpeɪl'feɪst] ADJ pálido

paleness ['peɪlnɪs] N palidez *f*; [*of skin*] blancura *f*

paleo- *etc* ['pælɪəʊ] PREFIX = **palaeo-** *etc*

Palestine ['pælɪstaɪn] N Palestina *f*

Palestinian [ˌpæləs'tɪnɪən] Ⓐ ADJ palestino
Ⓑ N palestino/a *m/f*

palette ['pælɪt] Ⓐ N paleta *f*
Ⓑ CPD ► **palette knife** N espátula *f*

palfrey ['pɔːlfrɪ] N palafrén *m*

palimony* ['pælɪmənɪ] N alimentos *mpl* pagados a una ex compañera

palimpsest ['pælɪmpsest] N palimpsesto *m*

palindrome ['pælɪndrəʊm] N palíndromo *m*

paling ['peɪlɪŋ] N (= *stake*) estaca *f*; (= *fence*) estacada *f*, (em)palizada *f*

palisade [ˌpælɪ'seɪd] N 1 palizada *f*, estacada *f*
2 **palisades** (*US*) (= *cliffs*) acantilado *msing*

pall¹ [pɔːl] N 1 (*on coffin*) paño *m* mortuorio; (*Rel*) (= *robe*) palio *m*
2 (*fig*) manto *m*, capa *f*; **a ~ of smoke** una cortina de humo; **to cast a ~ over sth** empañar algo

pall² [pɔːl] VI perder el interés (**on** para), dejar de gustar (**on** a); **it ~s after a time** después de cierto tiempo deja de gustar; **it never ~s** nunca pierde su interés; **I found the book ~ed** encontré que el libro empezaba a aburrirme

palladium [pə'leɪdɪəm] N paladio *m*

pallbearer ['pɔːlˌbɛərər] N portador(a) *m/f* del féretro

pallet ['pælɪt] Ⓐ N 1 (*for goods*) paleta *f*
2 (= *bed*) jergón *m*, catre *m*
Ⓑ CPD ► **pallet truck** N carretilla *f* elevadora de paletas

palletization [pælɪtaɪ'zeɪʃən] N paletización *f*

palliasse ['pælɪæs] N = **paillasse**

palliate ['pælɪeɪt] VT (*frm*) paliar, mitigar

palliative ['pælɪətɪv] Ⓐ ADJ paliativo, lenitivo
Ⓑ N paliativo *m*, lenitivo *m*

pallid ['pælɪd] ADJ pálido

pallidness ['pælɪdnɪs] N = **pallor**

pallor ['pælər] N palidez *f*

pally* ['pælɪ] ADJ (*compar* **pallier**; *superl* **palliest**) **to be ~ with sb** ser muy amigo de algn; **they're very ~** son muy amigos

palm¹ [pɑːm] Ⓐ N (*Bot*) (*also* **~ tree**) palma *f*, palmera *f*; (= *English sallow*) sauce *m*; (*as carried at Easter*) ramo *m*; **coconut ~** cocotero *m*
Ⓑ CPD ► **palm grove** N palmar *m*, palmeral *m* ► **palm oil** N aceite *m* de palma ► **Palm Sunday** N Domingo *m* de Ramos ► **palm tree** N palma *f*, palmera *f*

palm² [pɑːm] Ⓐ N (*Anat*) palma *f*; **to read sb's ~** leer la mano a algn; **you must cross the gipsy's ~ with silver** hay que pagar a la gitana con una moneda de plata; ✦**IDIOMS to grease sb's ~** untar la mano a algn; **to have sb in the ~ of one's hand** tener a algn en la palma de la mano; **to have an itching** *or* **itchy ~** ser muy codicioso; (= *be bribable*) estar dispuesto a dejarse sobornar
Ⓑ VT [+ *card*] escamotear

►**palm off*** VT + ADV **to ~ sth off on sb** encajar algo a algn*; **I managed to ~ the visitor off on John** le encajé la visita a Juan*; **I ~ed him off with the excuse that …** me lo saqué de encima con la excusa de que …

palmcorder ['pɑːmkɔːdər] N videocámara *f* portátil, minicámara *f* de vídeo

palmist ['pɑːmɪst] N quiromántico/a *m/f*, palmista *mf*

palmistry ['pɑːmɪstrɪ] N quiromancia *f*

palmtop ['pɑːmtɒp] N (*also* **~ computer**) ordenador *m* de bolsillo, computador *m or* computadora *f* de bolsillo (*LAm*), palmtop *m*

palmy ['pɑːmɪ] ADJ próspero, feliz; **those ~ days** aquellos días tan prósperos

palomino [pælə'miːnəʊ] N (*pl* **palominos**) *caballo de color tostado con crin y cola blancas*

palpable ['pælpəbl] ADJ 1 (= *tangible*) palpable
2 (*fig*) [*lie, mistake*] obvio, patente

palpably ['pælpəblɪ] ADV 1 (*lit*) palpablemente
2 (*fig*) (= *manifestly*) **a ~ unjust sentence** una condena manifiestamente injusta; **that is ~ untrue** eso es a todas luces falso

palpate ['pælpeɪt] VT (*Med*) palpar

palpitate ['pælpɪteɪt] VI [*heart*] palpitar

palpitating ['pælpɪteɪtɪŋ] ADJ palpitante

palpitation [ˌpælpɪ'teɪʃən] N palpitación *f*; **to have ~s** tener palpitaciones

palsied ['pɔːlzɪd] ADJ paralítico

palsy ['pɔːlzɪ] N perlesía *f*, parálisis *f inv*

paltry ['pɔːltrɪ] (*compar* **paltrier**; *superl* **paltriest**) ADJ ínfimo, miserable; **for a few ~ pennies** por unos miserables peniques; **for some ~ reason** por alguna nimiedad

pampas ['pæmpəs] NPL pampa *fsing*; **the Pampas** la Pampa

pamper ['pæmpər] VT mimar, consentir

pampered ['pæmpəd] ADJ [*child etc*] mimado, consentido; [*life*] regalado; **he had a ~ childhood** se crió entre algodones

pamphlet ['pæmflɪt] N (*informative, brochure*) folleto *m*; (*political, handed out in street*) volante *m*, panfleto *m*; (*Literat*) panfleto *m*

pamphleteer [ˌpæmflɪ'tɪər] N folletista *mf*, panfletista *mf*

pan¹ [pæn] Ⓐ N 1 (*for cooking*) cazuela *f*, cacerola *f*, olla *f* (*LAm*); (= *frying pan*) sartén *f* (*m in LAm*)
2 [*of scales*] platillo *m*; [*of lavatory*] taza *f*; [*of firearm*] cazoleta *f*; ✦**IDIOM to go down the ~**‡ irse al traste*
Ⓑ VT 1 [+ *gold*] lavar con batea
2 (*) (= *criticize*) [+ *play etc*] dejar por los suelos*
Ⓒ VI **to ~ for gold** cribar oro

►**pan out** VI + ADV resultar, salir (bien *etc*); **if it ~s out as we hope** si sale como nosotros lo esperamos; **it didn't ~ out at all well** no dio ningún resultado satisfactorio; **we must wait and see how it ~s out** tenemos que esperar hasta ver cómo sale esto

pan² [pæn] (*Cine*) Ⓐ VI tomar panorámicas *or* vistas pan
Ⓑ VT **a television camera ~ned the stadium** una cámara de televisión recorrió el estadio

pan- [pæn] PREFIX pan-; **~Arabic** panárabe

panacea [ˌpænə'sɪə] N panacea *f*

panache [pə'næʃ] N garbo *m*, gracia *f*; **to do sth with ~** hacer algo con garbo

Pan-African ['pæn'æfrɪkən] ADJ panafricano

Pan-Africanism ['pæn'æfrɪkənɪzəm] N panafricanismo *m*

Panama ['pænəmɑː] Ⓐ N Panamá *m*
Ⓑ CPD ► **Panama Canal** N Canal *m* de Panamá ► **Panama hat** N (sombrero *m* de) jipijapa *f*, panamá *m*

Panamanian [ˌpænə'meɪnɪən] Ⓐ ADJ panameño
Ⓑ N panameño/a *m/f*

Pan-American ['pænə'merɪkən] Ⓐ ADJ panamericano
Ⓑ CPD ► **Pan-American Union** N Unión *f* Panamericana

Pan-Americanism ['pænə'merɪkənɪzəm] N panamericanismo *m*

Pan-Asian ['pæn'eɪʃn] ADJ panasiático

pancake ['pænkeɪk] Ⓐ N tortita *f*, panqueque *m* (*LAm*); *see also* **flat¹**
Ⓑ CPD ► **Pancake Day** N (*Brit*) martes *m inv* de carnaval ► **pancake landing** N (*Aer*) aterrizaje *m* de panza ► **pancake roll** N (*Brit*) rollito *m* de primavera

panchromatic ['pænkrəʊ'mætɪk] ADJ pancromático

pancreas ['pæŋkrɪəs] N páncreas *m*

pancreatic [ˌpæŋkrɪ'ætɪk] ADJ pancreático

panda ['pændə] Ⓐ N panda *m*
Ⓑ CPD ► **panda car** N (*Brit*) coche *m* patrulla

pandemic [pæn'demɪk] Ⓐ ADJ pandémico
Ⓑ N pandemia *f*

pandemonium [ˌpændɪ'məʊnɪəm] N (= *chaos*) jaleo *m*, desmadre* *m*; **at this there was ~** en esto se armó un tremendo jaleo, en esto se armó las de Caín; **it's sheer ~!** ¡es un desmadre!*

pander ['pændər] VI **to ~ to sb** consentir a algn; **to ~ to sb's desire for sth** complacer el deseo de algn por algo; **this is ~ing to the public's worst tastes** esto es condescender con los peores gustos del público

p & h ABBR (*US*) (= **postage and handling**) gastos *mpl* de envío

P & L N ABBR (= **profit and loss**) Pérd. y Gan.

Pandora [pæn'dɔːrə] N **~'s box** caja *f* de Pandora

p & p N ABBR (= **postage and packing**) gastos *mpl* de envío

pandrop ['pændrɒp] N (*Scot*) pastilla *f* de menta

pane [peɪn] N cristal *m*, vidrio *m*

panegyric [,pænɪ'dʒɪrɪk] N panegírico *m*

panel ['pænl] Ⓐ N 1 [*of wall*] panel *m*; [*of door*] entrepaño *m*; [*of ceiling*] artesón *m*
2 [*of instruments, switches*] tablero *m*
3 (*Sew*) paño *m*; (*Art*) tabla *f*
4 [*of judges, in a competition*] jurado *m*; (*TV, Rad*) panel *m*
5 (*Brit Med*) (*formerly*) lista *f* de pacientes
Ⓑ VT [+ *wall, door*] revestir con entrepaños de madera
Ⓒ CPD ► **panel beater** N carrocero/a *m/f* ► **panel beating** N chapistería *f* ► **panel discussion** N mesa *f* redonda ► **panel game** N programa *m* concurso para equipos ► **panel pin** N clavo *m* de espiga

panelled, paneled (*US*) ['pænld] ADJ con paneles

panelling, paneling (*US*) ['pænəlɪŋ] N paneles *mpl*

panellist, panelist (*US*) ['pænəlɪst] N miembro *mf* del jurado/de la mesa redonda

Pan-European ['pæn,jʊərə'piːən] ADJ paneuropeo

pang [pæŋ] N 1 (= *pain*) punzada *f*; **~s of childbirth** dolores *mpl* de parto; **~s of hunger** ◊ **hunger ~s** dolores *mpl* de hambre
2 (*fig*) **I felt a ~ of conscience** me remordió la conciencia; **to feel a ~ of remorse** sentir remordimiento

panhandle ['pænhændl] (*US*) Ⓐ N (*Geog*) *faja angosta de territorio de un estado que entra en el de otro*
Ⓑ VI (*) (= *beg*) mendigar, pedir limosna

panhandler* ['pænhændləʳ] N (*US*) (= *beggar*) pordiosero/a *m/f*

panic ['pænɪk] (*vb: pt, pp* **panicked**) Ⓐ N 1 (= *fear*) pánico *m*; **an earthquake hit the capital, spreading ~ among the population** un terremoto azotó la capital, sembrando el pánico entre la población; **to be in a (state of) ~** ser presa del pánico; **I phoned my mum in a ~** llamé a mi madre muerto de miedo*, llamé a mi madre presa del pánico; **a patient rang me in a state of ~ because her baby had swallowed a key** me llamó una paciente muy asustada porque su hijo se había tragado una llave; **I was in a blind ~** estaba ofuscado por el pánico; **to flee in ~** huir aterrado, huir presa del pánico; **if I asked the simplest question, she would go into** *or* **get into a ~** si le hacía la pregunta más simple le entraba el pánico; **to send** *or* **throw sb into a ~: her sudden arrival threw him into a ~** su inesperada llegado hizo que le entrase el pánico; **the country was thrown into a ~** cundió el pánico en el país; **the explosion threw the crowd into a ~** la explosión provocó el pánico entre la multitud; ✦***IDIOM*** **it was ~ stations*** reinaba el pánico
2 (*) (= *rush*) **there's no ~, tomorrow will do** no es que haya prisa, mañana vale; **we've had a bit of a ~ on here and it slipped my mind till now** hemos ido un poco de cabeza por aquí y se me ha olvidado hasta ahora
Ⓑ VI dejarse llevar por el pánico; **I refused to ~** me negué a dejarme llevar por el pánico; **industry is ~king about the recession** la recesión tiene a la industria presa del pánico; **don't ~!** ¡calma!, ¡cálmate!; **don't ~, sit still and keep calm** no te dejes llevar por el pánico, quédate sentado y mantén la calma
Ⓒ VT [+ *crowd, population*] provocar el pánico entre; [+ *person*] provocar *or* infundir el pánico en, llenar de pánico a; **the sound of the gun ~ked the elephants** el sonido del rifle provocó el pánico en *or* entre los elefantes; **he had been ~ked into the decision** había tomado la decisión impulsado por el pánico
Ⓓ CPD ► **panic attack** N ataque *m* de pánico; **to have a ~ attack** tener *or* sufrir un ataque de pánico ► **panic button** N (*lit*) botón *m* de alarma; **to press** *or* **hit** *or* **push the ~ button** (*fig*) perder el control *or* la calma ► **panic buying** N **~ buying has caused shortages of some foodstuffs** las compras provocadas por el pánico han provocado escasez de algunos alimentos ► **panic measures** NPL medidas *fpl* inducidas por el pánico ► **panic reaction** N reacción *f* motivada por el pánico

panicky ['pænɪkɪ] ADJ [*person, behaviour*] nervioso; [*decision, action*] motivado por el pánico *or* el nerviosismo; [*reaction*] nervioso, motivado por el pánico *or* el nerviosismo; **to get ~** dejarse llevar por el pánico

panic-stricken ['pænɪk,strɪkən] ADJ [*person*] presa del pánico, aterrorizado; [*behaviour*] causado *or* motivado por el pánico; **to be ~** ser presa del pánico, estar aterrorizado

panjandrum [pæn'dʒændrəm] N jefazo *m*, mandamás *m inv*; **he's the great ~** es el archipámpano

pannier ['pænɪəʳ] N (*for horse etc*) cuévano *m*; (*for cycle etc*) (*also* **~ bag**) cartera *f*, bolsa *f*

panoply ['pænəplɪ] N (= *armour*) panoplia *f*; (*fig*) (= *array*) despliegue *m*

panorama [,pænə'rɑːmə] N panorama *m*

panoramic [,pænə'ræmɪk] Ⓐ ADJ panorámico
Ⓑ CPD ► **panoramic screen** N pantalla *f* panorámica ► **panoramic view** N visión *f* panorámica

panpipes ['pænpaɪps] NPL zampoña *f*

pansy ['pænzɪ] N 1 (*Bot*) pensamiento *m*
2 (‡ *pej*) (= *homosexual man*) marica* *m* (*pej*)

pant [pænt] Ⓐ N (= *gasp*) jadeo *m*, resuello *m*
Ⓑ VI jadear, resollar; **to ~ for breath** jadear
Ⓒ VT (*also* **~ out**) decir jadeando, decir de manera entrecortada

►**pant for** VI + PREP (*fig*) suspirar por, anhelar; **he was ~ing for a drink** jadeaba de sed; **to ~ with desire for sth** desear algo ardientemente

pantaloons ['pæntəluːns] NPL (pantalones *mpl*) bombachos *mpl*

pantechnicon [pæn'teknɪkən] N (*Brit*) camión *m* de mudanzas

pantheism ['pænθiːɪzəm] N panteísmo *m*

pantheist ['pænθiːɪst] N panteísta *mf*

pantheistic [,pænθiː'ɪstɪk] ADJ panteísta

pantheon ['pænθɪən] N panteón *m*

panther ['pænθəʳ] N (*pl* **panthers** *or* **panther**) pantera *f*, jaguar *m* (*LAm*)

panties ['pæntɪz] NPL bragas *fpl* (*Sp*), calzones *mpl* (*LAm*); **a pair of ~** unas bragas, unos calzones (*LAm*)

pantihose ['pæntɪhəʊz] NPL = **pantyhose**

panting ['pæntɪŋ] N jadeo *m*

panto* ['pæntəʊ] N ABBR (*Brit Theat*) = **pantomime**

pantomime ['pæntəmaɪm] Ⓐ N 1 (*Theat*) (= *mime*) pantomima *f*; **to explain sth in ~** explicar algo por gestos
2 (*Brit*) (*at Christmas*) revista *f* musical navideña
3 (*Brit*) (*fig*) (= *farce*) **what a ~!** ¡qué farsa!; **it was a real ~** fue una verdadera comedia
Ⓑ CPD ► **pantomime dame** N (*Brit*) *papel femenino en comedia musical navideña, tradicionalmente interpretado por un hombre*

> **PANTOMIME**
>
> *Una* **pantomime**, *abreviada en inglés como* **panto**, *es una obra teatral que se representa normalmente en Navidades ante un público familiar. Suele estar basada en un cuento de hadas u otra historia conocida y en ella nunca faltan personajes como la dama* (**dame**), *papel que siempre interpreta un actor, el protagonista joven* (**principal boy**), *normalmente interpretado por una actriz, y el malvado* (**villain**). *Aunque es un espectáculo familiar dirigido fundamentalmente a los niños, en él se alienta la participación de todo el público y posee una gran dosis de humor para adultos.*

pantry ['pæntrɪ] N despensa *f*

pants [pænts] Ⓐ NPL (*Brit*) (*man's*) calzoncillos *mpl*; (*woman's*) bragas *fpl* (*Sp*), calzones *mpl* (*LAm*); (*US*) pantalones *mpl*; **a pair of ~** (*Brit*) (*man's*) unos calzoncillos; (*woman's*) unas bragas, unos calzones (*LAm*); (*US*) un pantalón, unos pantalones; ✦***IDIOMS*** **to bore the ~ off sb*** aburrir terriblemente a algn; **to catch sb with his ~ down*** pillar a algn desprevenido; **she wears the ~*** ella es la que manda
Ⓑ CPD ► **pants press** N (*US*) prensa *f* para pantalones

pantsuit ['pæntsuːt] N (*US*) traje *m* de chaqueta y pantalón

panty girdle ['pæntɪ,gɜːdl] N faja *f* pantalón

pantyhose ['pæntɪhəʊz] NPL (*esp US*) pantys *mpl*, pantimedias *fpl*

Panzer ['pæntsəʳ] Ⓐ N **the ~s** las tropas motorizadas
Ⓑ CPD motorizado ► **Panzer division** N división *f* motorizada

pap [pæp] N (*Culin*) papilla *f*, gachas *fpl*; (*fig*) (*pej*) bazofia* *f*

papa [pə'pɑː] N papá *m*

papacy ['peɪpəsɪ] N papado *m*, pontificado *m*

papadum ['pæpədəm] N torta *f* india

papal ['peɪpəl] Ⓐ ADJ papal, pontificio
Ⓑ CPD ► **papal nuncio** N nuncio *m* apostólico

paparazzi [,pæpə'rætsiː] N (*pl* **paparazzi**) paparazzi *mpl*

papaya [pə'paɪə] N (= *fruit*) papaya *f*; (= *tree*) árbol *m* de papaya

paper ['peɪpəʳ] Ⓐ N 1 (= *material*) papel *m*; (= *wallpaper*) papel *m* pintado; **a piece of ~** un papel, una hoja (de papel); **to put sth down on ~** ◊ **commit sth to ~** poner algo por escrito; **on ~** (*fig*) en teoría, sobre el papel; **it's not worth the ~ it's written on** no vale para nada
2 (= *newspaper*) periódico *m*, diario *m*; **to write to the ~ about sth** escribir una carta al director de un periódico sobre algo; **the ~s** los periódicos, la prensa; **to write for the ~s** colaborar en los periódicos, escribir artículos para los periódicos; **it came out in the ~s** salió en los periódicos
3 **papers** (= *writings, documents*) papeles *mpl*; (= *identity papers*) documentación *f*, papeles *mpl*; **your ~s, please** la documentación, por favor; **Churchill's private ~s** los papeles personales de Churchill; **his divorce ~s**

➤ LANGUAGE IN USE: **paper** A4 26.1

have just come through han llegado los papeles de su divorcio; **ship's ~s** documentación *f* del barco

4 (*Univ etc*) (= *essay*) ejercicio *m*, ensayo *m*; (= *exam*) examen *m*; **to do a good ~ in maths** hacer un buen examen de matemáticas; **to set a ~ in physics** poner un examen de física

5 (*scholarly*) (*written*) artículo *m*; (*read aloud*) ponencia *f*, comunicación *f*; **we heard a good ~ on place names** escuchamos una buena ponencia sobre toponimia

6 (*Parl*) documento *m* base; **a government ~ on European policy** un documento base gubernamental sobre política europea; *see also* **green D**, **white C**

Ⓑ VT [+ *wall, room*] empapelar, tapizar (*Mex*)

Ⓒ CPD de papel ► **paper advance** N (*on printer*) avance *m* de papel ► **paper bag** N bolsa *f* de papel; ✦*IDIOM* **he couldn't fight his way out of a ~ bag*** (*hum*) es un gallina* ► **paper chain** N cadeneta *f* de papel ► **paper chase** N rallye-paper *m* ► **paper clip** N clip *m*, sujetapapeles *m inv* ► **paper credit** N (*Fin*) papel *m* crédito ► **paper cup** N vaso *m* de cartón ► **paper currency** N papel *m* moneda ► **paper fastener** N grapa *f* ► **paper feed(er)** N alimentador *m* de papel ► **paper handkerchief**, **paper hankie** N pañuelo *m* de papel ► **paper industry** N industria *f* papelera ► **paper knife** N abrecartas *m inv* ► **paper lantern** N farolillo *m* de papel ► **paper loss** N (*Fin*) *pérdida que tiene lugar cuando baja el valor de una acción etc sin venderse ésta* ► **paper mill** N fábrica *f* de papel, papelera *f* ► **paper money** N (*gen*) papel *m* moneda; (= *banknotes*) billetes *mpl* de banco ► **paper profit** N (*Fin*) beneficio *m* no realizado ► **paper qualifications** NPL títulos *mpl* ► **paper round** N reparto *m* de periódicos; **to do a ~ round** repartir periódicos ► **paper shop** N (*Brit*) tienda *f* de periódicos, quiosco *m* ► **paper tape** N cinta *f* de papel ► **paper tiger** N (*fig*) tigre *m* de papel ► **paper tissue** N pañuelo *m* de papel, tisú *m* ► **paper towel** N toallita *f* de papel ► **paper trail** N (*esp US*) pruebas *fpl* documentales

►**paper over** VI + PREP 1 (*lit*) empapelar

2 (*fig*) disimular; ✦*IDIOM* **to ~ over the cracks** (*Brit*) guardar las apariencias; *see also* **crack A1**

paperback ['peɪpəbæk] Ⓐ N libro *m* en rústica; **in ~** en rústica

Ⓑ CPD ► **paperback edition** N edición *f* rústica

paperbacked ['peɪpəbækt] ADJ en rústica

paperbound ['peɪpəbaʊnd] ADJ = **paperbacked**

paperboy ['peɪpəbɔɪ] N repartidor *m* de periódicos

papergirl ['peɪpəgɜːl] N repartidora *f* de periódicos

paperhanger ['peɪpə,hæŋəʳ] N (*Brit*) empapelador(a) *m/f*

paperless ['peɪpəlɪs] ADJ sin papel; **the ~ society** la sociedad sin papel

paper-thin ['peɪpə,θɪn] ADJ [*slice*] muy fino; (*iro*) casi transparente; [*wall*] de papel; (*fig*) [*majority, lead*] estrecho

paperweight ['peɪpəweɪt] N pisapapeles *m inv*

paperwork ['peɪpəwɜːk] N trabajo *m* administrativo; (*pej*) (= *bureaucracy*) papeleo* *m*

papery ['peɪpərɪ] ADJ parecido al papel

papier-mâché ['pæpɪeɪ'mæʃeɪ] Ⓐ N cartón *m* piedra

Ⓑ CPD de cartón piedra

papist ['peɪpɪst] (*pej*) Ⓐ ADJ papista

Ⓑ N papista *mf*

papistry ['peɪpɪstrɪ] N (*pej*) papismo *m*

papoose [pə'puːs] N 1 (= *baby*) niño/a *m/f* indio/a norteamericano/a

2 (= *baby sling*) mochila *f* portabebés

paprika ['pæprɪkə] N pimentón *m*, paprika *f*

Pap smear ['pæp,smɪəʳ], **Pap test** ['pæp,test] N frotis *m* (cervical)

Papua New Guinea ['pæpjʊənjuː'gɪnɪ] N Papúa *f* Nueva Guinea, Nueva Guinea *f* Papúa

Papua New Guinean ['pæpjʊənjuː'gɪnɪən] Ⓐ ADJ de Papúa Nueva Guinea, papú

Ⓑ N papú *mf*

papyrus [pə'paɪərəs] N (*pl* **papyruses** *or* **papyri** [pə'paɪəraɪ]) papiro *m*

par¹ [pɑːʳ] Ⓐ N 1 (*Fin*) par *f*; **to be above/below ~** estar sobre/bajo la par; **to be at ~** estar a la par

2 (*Golf*) par *m*; **two over ~** dos sobre par; **five under ~** cinco bajo par

3 (*fig*) **to be on a ~ with sth/sb** estar en pie de igualdad con algo/algn; **to place sth on a ~ with** parangonar *or* equiparar algo con; **to be under** *or* **below ~** (= *ill*) sentirse mal, estar indispuesto; **not to be up to ~** ser inferior a la calidad normal; ✦*IDIOM* **that's ~ for the course** eso es lo más normal

Ⓑ CPD ► **par value** N (*Fin*) valor *m* a la par

par²* ABBR (*Press*) (= **paragraph**) párr.

para ABBR (= **paragraph**) párr.

parable ['pærəbl] N parábola *f*

parabola [pə'ræbələ] N parábola *f*

parabolic [,pærə'bɒlɪk] Ⓐ ADJ parabólico

Ⓑ CPD ► **parabolic aerial** N antena *f* parabólica

paracetamol [pærə'siːtəmɒl] N paracetamol *m*

parachute ['pærəʃuːt] Ⓐ N paracaídas *m inv*

Ⓑ VT lanzar en paracaídas; **to ~ food to sb** suministrar víveres a algn en paracaídas

Ⓒ VI (*also* **~ down**) lanzarse *or* saltar en paracaídas; **to ~ to safety** salvarse utilizando el paracaídas

Ⓓ CPD ► **parachute drop** N lanzamiento *m* en paracaídas ► **parachute jump** N salto *m* en paracaídas ► **parachute regiment** N regimiento *m* de paracaidistas

parachutist ['pærəʃuːtɪst] N paracaidista *mf*

Paraclete ['pærəkliːt] N **the ~** el Paráclito

parade [pə'reɪd] Ⓐ N 1 (= *procession*) desfile *m*; (*Mil*) desfile *m*, parada *f*; [*of models*] desfile *m*, pase *m*; **to be on ~** (*Mil*) estar en formación; (*fig*) estar a la vista de todos; *see also* **fashion C**

2 (*fig*) **a ~ of** (= *exhibition*) una exibición de; (= *series*) una serie de; **to make a ~ of** (= *show off*) hacer alarde de

3 (*esp Brit*) (= *road*) paseo *m*; **a ~ of shops** una calle de tiendas

Ⓑ VT 1 [+ *troops*] hacer desfilar; [+ *streets*] recorrer, desfilar por; [+ *placard etc*] pasear (**through the streets** por las calles)

2 (= *show off*) [+ *learning, wealth, new clothes*] hacer alarde de, lucir

Ⓒ VI 1 (*Mil etc*) desfilar; **the strikers ~d through the town** los huelguistas desfilaron por la ciudad

2 (*) pasearse; **she ~d up and down with the hat on** se paseaba de un lado a otro con el sombrero puesto, andaba de acá para allá luciendo el sombrero

Ⓓ CPD ► **parade ground** N (*Mil*) plaza *f* de armas

►**parade about***, **parade around*** VI + ADV pavonearse

paradigm ['pærədaɪm] Ⓐ N paradigma *m*

Ⓑ CPD ► **paradigm shift** N cambio *m* de paradigma

paradigmatic [,pærədɪg'mætɪk] ADJ paradigmático

paradise ['pærədaɪs] N paraíso *m*; **this is ~!** ¡esto es el paraíso!; *see also* **fool¹**, **earthly A1**

paradisiacal [,pærədɪ'saɪəkəl] ADJ paradisíaco

paradox ['pærədɒks] N paradoja *f*

paradoxical [,pærə'dɒksɪkəl] ADJ paradójico

paradoxically [,pærə'dɒksɪkəlɪ] ADV paradójicamente

paraffin ['pærəfɪn] Ⓐ N (*Brit*) (*also* **~ oil**) petróleo *m* (de alumbrado), queroseno *m*; (= *wax*) parafina *f*

Ⓑ CPD ► **paraffin heater** N estufa *f* de parafina ► **paraffin lamp** N quinqué *m* ► **paraffin wax** N parafina *f*

paraglider ['pærə,glaɪdəʳ] N 1 (= *person*) parapentista *mf*

2 (= *object*) parapente *m*

paragliding ['pærə,glaɪdɪŋ] N parapente *m*

paragon ['pærəgən] N modelo *m*, dechado *m*; **a ~ of virtue** un dechado de virtudes

paragraph ['pærəgrɑːf] Ⓐ N párrafo *m*, (punto) acápite *m* (*LAm*); (*in law etc*) aparte *m*; (= *short article in newspaper*) suelto *m*; **"new ~"** "(punto y) aparte"

Ⓑ VT dividir en párrafos

Paraguay ['pærəgwaɪ] N Paraguay *m*

Paraguayan [,pærə'gwaɪən] Ⓐ ADJ paraguayo

Ⓑ N paraguayo/a *m/f*

parakeet ['pærəkiːt] N perico *m*, periquito *m*

paralanguage ['pærə,læŋgwɪdʒ] N paralenguaje *m*

paralegal [,pærə'liːgəl] Ⓐ N ayudante *mf* de abogado

Ⓑ ADJ que trabaja como ayudante de abogado

paralinguistic [,pærəlɪŋ'gwɪstɪk] ADJ paralingüístico

parallel ['pærəlel] Ⓐ ADJ 1 (*Geom*) paralelo (**to** a); (*Comput, Elec*) en paralelo; **in a ~ direction to** en dirección paralela a; **to run ~ to** ir en línea paralela a, correr paralelo con

2 (*fig*) análogo (**to** a); **this is a ~ case to the last one** este caso es análogo al anterior

Ⓑ N 1 (*Geom*) paralela *f*; **in ~** (*Elec*) en paralelo

2 (*Geog*) paralelo *m*; **the 49th ~** el paralelo 49

3 (*fig*) **a case without ~** un caso inaudito *or* único; **it has no ~ as far as I know** que yo sepa no tiene paralelo *or* no hay nada parecido; **to draw a ~ between X and Y** establecer un paralelo entre X y Y; **these things occur in ~** estas cosas corren parejas (**with** con), estas cosas ocurren paralelamente

Ⓒ VT (*fig*) (= *compare*) comparar (**with** con); (= *equal*) igualar (**with** a); **it is ~ed by …** es parejo a …, tiene su paralelo en …; **his talent ~s his brother's** su talento es comparable *or* parejo al de su hermano

Ⓓ CPD ► **parallel bars** NPL (*Sport*) paralelas *fpl* ► **parallel printer** N impresora *f* en paralelo ► **parallel processing** N (*Comput*) procesamiento *m* en paralelo

parallelepiped [,pærə,lelə'paɪped] N paralelepípedo *m*

parallelism ['pærəlelɪzəm] N paralelismo *m*

parallelogram [,pærə'leləʊgræm] N paralelogramo *m*

Paralympic [pærə'lɪmpɪk] Ⓐ ADJ paralímpico

Ⓑ **the Paralympics** NPL = **the Paralympic Games**

Ⓒ CPD ► **the Paralympic Games** NPL los juegos paralímpicos

paralysation, **paralyzation** (*US*) [ˌpærəlaɪˈzeɪʃən] N paralización *f*

paralyse, **paralyze** (*US*) [ˈpærəlaɪz] VT (*lit, fig*) paralizar; **to be ~d in both legs** estar paralizado de las dos piernas; **to be ~d with fright** estar paralizado de miedo; **the factory was ~d by the strike** la fábrica quedó paralizada por la huelga

paralysis [pəˈræləsɪs] N (*pl* **paralyses** [pəˈræləsiːz]) (*Med*) parálisis *f inv*; (*fig*) paralización *f*, parálisis *f inv*

paralytic [ˌpærəˈlɪtɪk] Ⓐ ADJ 1 (*Med*) paralítico
2 (*Brit*‡) (= *drunk*) como una cuba*
Ⓑ N paralítico/a *m/f*

paralyzation [ˌpærəlaɪˈzeɪʃən] N (*US*) = **paralysation**

paralyze [ˈpærəlaɪz] VT (*US*) = **paralyse**

paramedic [ˌpærəˈmedɪk] N paramédico/a *m/f*

paramedical [ˌpærəˈmedɪkəl] ADJ paramédico

parameter [pəˈræmɪtəʳ] N parámetro *m*

paramilitary [ˌpærəˈmɪlɪtərɪ] Ⓐ ADJ paramilitar
Ⓑ N paramilitar *mf*

paramount [ˈpærəmaʊnt] ADJ 1 (= *utmost*) sumo; **of ~ importance** de suma importancia
2 (= *of prime importance*) primordial; **solvency must be ~** la solvencia es primordial *or* lo más importante

paramour [ˈpærəmʊəʳ] N (*liter*) amante *mf*, querido/a *m/f*

paranoia [ˌpærəˈnɔɪə] N paranoia *f*

paranoiac [ˌpærəˈnɔɪɪk] Ⓐ ADJ paranoico
Ⓑ N paranoico/a *m/f*

paranoid [ˈpærənɔɪd] Ⓐ ADJ paranoide
Ⓑ N paranoico/a *m/f*

paranormal [ˌpærəˈnɔːməl] Ⓐ ADJ paranormal
Ⓑ N **the ~** lo paranormal

parapet [ˈpærəpɪt] N [*of balcony, roof*] pretil *m*, antepecho *m*; [*of fortification*] parapeto *m*; ✦*IDIOMS* **to put one's head above the ~** (*Brit*) arriesgar el cuello; **to keep one's head below the ~** (*Brit*) mantenerse al margen

paraphernalia [ˈpærəfəˈneɪlɪə] N parafernalia *f*

paraphrase [ˈpærəfreɪz] Ⓐ N paráfrasis *f inv*
Ⓑ VT parafrasear

paraplegia [ˌpærəˈpliːdʒə] N paraplejía *f*

paraplegic [ˌpærəˈpliːdʒɪk] Ⓐ ADJ parapléjico
Ⓑ N parapléjico/a *m/f*

parapsychological [ˌpærəsaɪkəˈlɒdʒɪkəl] ADJ parapsicológico

parapsychologist [ˌpærəsaɪˈkɒlədʒɪst] N parapsicólogo/a *m/f*

parapsychology [ˌpærəsaɪˈkɒlədʒɪ] N parapsicología *f*

Paraquat® [ˈpærəkwɒt] N herbicida *m*

Paras* [ˈpærəz] NPL ABBR (= **Parachute Regiment**) paras* *mpl*, paracas* *mpl*

parascending [ˈpærəsendɪŋ] N *esquí acuático con paracaídas*; **to go ~** *hacer esquí acuático con paracaídas*

parasite [ˈpærəsaɪt] N (*lit, fig*) parásito/a *m/f* (**on** de)

parasitic [ˌpærəˈsɪtɪk] ADJ parásito, parasitario; **to be ~ on** ser parásito de

parasitical [ˌpærəˈsɪtɪkəl] ADJ = **parasitic**

parasitism [ˈpærəsɪtɪzəm] N parasitismo *m*

parasitize [ˈpærəsɪˌtaɪz] VT parasitar (en)

parasitologist [ˌpærəsaɪˈtɒlədʒɪst] N parasitólogo/a *m/f*

parasitology [ˌpærəsɪˈtɒlədʒɪ] N parasitología *f*

parasol [ˈpærəsɒl] N sombrilla *f*, parasol *m*

parasuicide [ˌpærəˈsʊɪsaɪd] N parasuicidio *m*

parataxis [ˌpærəˈtæksɪs] N parataxis *f*

paratrooper [ˈpærətruːpəʳ] N paracaidista *mf*

paratroops [ˈpærətruːps] NPL paracaidistas *mpl*

paratyphoid [ˈpærəˈtaɪfɔɪd] N paratifoidea *f*

parboil [ˈpɑːbɔɪl] VT sancochar, cocer a medias

Parcae [ˈpɑːkiː] NPL **the ~** las Parcas

parcel [ˈpɑːsl] Ⓐ N 1 (= *package*) paquete *m*; **pass the ~** (*Brit*) *juego infantil en que los niños van desenvolviendo un paquete haciéndolo pasar de mano en mano*; *see also* **part A1**
2 [*of land*] parcela *f*, lote *m*
3 (*Brit**) (= *quantity*) **a ~ of nonsense** una sarta de disparates; **a ~ of idiots** una panda de idiotas*
Ⓑ CPD ► **parcel bomb** N paquete-bomba *m* ► **parcel office** N departamento *m* de paquetes ► **parcel post** N servicio *m* de paquetes postales

►**parcel out** VT + ADV repartir; [+ *land*] parcelar

►**parcel up** VT + ADV empaquetar; (*large size*) embalar

parch [pɑːtʃ] Ⓐ VT secar, resecar, agostar
Ⓑ VI secarse

parched [pɑːtʃt] ADJ [*land etc*] abrasado, reseco; (*) (= *thirsty*) reseco, muerto de sed; **I'm ~** me muero de sed

parchment [ˈpɑːtʃmənt] N pergamino *m*

parchment-like [ˈpɑːtʃməntˌlaɪk] ADJ apergaminado

pardon [ˈpɑːdn] Ⓐ N 1 perdón *m*; **to beg sb's ~** pedir perdón a algn; **I do beg your ~!** ¡perdone usted!, ¡disculpe! (*esp LAm*); **I beg your ~, but could you ...?** perdone *or* (*esp LAm*) disculpe la molestia, pero ¿podría usted ...?; **(I beg your) ~?** (= *what?*) ¿perdón?, ¿cómo?, ¿mande? (*Mex*)
2 (*Jur*) indulto *m*; **free ~** indulto *m* absoluto; **general ~** amnistía *f*
Ⓑ VT 1 (= *forgive*) perdonar, disculpar (*esp LAm*); **to ~ sb sth** perdonar algo a algn; **~ me, but could you ...?** perdone *or* (*esp LAm*) disculpe la molestia, pero ¿podría usted ...?; **~ me!** ¡perdone!, ¡ay, perdone!; **~ me?** (*US*) ¿perdón?, ¿cómo?, ¿mande? (*Mex*); **~ my mentioning it** siento tener que decirlo, perdone que se lo diga
2 (*Jur*) indultar

pardonable [ˈpɑːdnəbl] ADJ perdonable, disculpable

pardonably [ˈpɑːdnəblɪ] ADV **he was ~ angry** era fácil disculpar su enojo, se comprende fácilmente que se encolerizara

pare [pɛəʳ] VT [+ *nails*] cortar; [+ *fruit etc*] pelar

►**pare down** VT + ADV reducir; **to ~ sth down to the minimum** reducir algo al mínimo

parent [ˈpɛərənt] Ⓐ N padre *m*/madre *f*; **parents** padres *mpl*
Ⓑ ADJ **the ~ plant** la planta madre
Ⓒ CPD ► **parent company** N casa *f* matriz ► **parent teacher association** N asociación *f* de padres de familia y profesores

parentage [ˈpɛərəntɪdʒ] N familia *f*; **of humble ~** de nacimiento humilde; **of unknown ~** de padres desconocidos

parental [pəˈrentl] Ⓐ ADJ [*care etc*] de los padres
Ⓑ CPD ► **parental guidance** N los consejos de los padres ► **parental authority** N patria potestad *f*

parenteral [pæˈrentərəl] ADJ parenteral

parenthesis [pəˈrenθɪsɪs] N (*pl* **parentheses** [pəˈrenθɪsiːz]) paréntesis *m inv*; **in ~** entre paréntesis

parenthetic [ˌpærənˈθetɪk] ADJ = **parenthetical**

parenthetical [ˌpærənˈθetɪkəl] ADJ entre paréntesis

parenthetically [ˌpærənˈθetɪkəlɪ] ADV entre paréntesis

parenthood [ˈpɛərənthʊd] N paternidad *f*; **planned ~** planificación *f* familiar, paternidad *f* responsable

parenting [ˈpɛərəntɪŋ] N el ser padres; **shared ~** participación *f* conjunta en la vida familiar; **~ is a full-time occupation** el cuidar de los hijos es una labor de plena dedicación

parer [ˈpɛərəʳ] N pelalegumbres *m inv*

par excellence [ˌpɑːrˈeksəlɑ̃ːns] ADV por excelencia

pariah [ˈpærɪə] N paria *mf*

parietal [pəˈraɪɪtl] ADJ parietal

paring knife [ˈpɛərɪŋˌnaɪf] N cuchillo *m* de mondar

parings [ˈpɛərɪŋz] NPL [*of fruit, vegetables*] peladuras *fpl*; [*of nails*] trozos *mpl*

pari passu [ˈpærɪˈpæsuː] ADV a ritmo parecido, al igual; **~ with** a ritmo parecido al de, al igual que

Paris [ˈpærɪs] Ⓐ N París *m*
Ⓑ ADJ parisiense, parisino

parish [ˈpærɪʃ] Ⓐ N parroquia *f*
Ⓑ CPD parroquial, de la parroquia ► **parish church** N iglesia *f* parroquial ► **parish council** N concejo *m* parroquial ► **parish priest** N párroco *m* ► **parish register** N libro *m* parroquial

parishioner [pəˈrɪʃənəʳ] N feligrés/esa *m/f*

parish-pump [ˈpærɪʃˈpʌmp] ADJ (*Brit pej*) pueblerino, de campanario, de aldea; **~ attitude** mentalidad *f* pueblerina, espíritu *m* de campanario; **~ politics** política *f* pueblerina

Parisian [pəˈrɪzɪən] Ⓐ ADJ parisiense, parisino
Ⓑ N parisiense *mf*

parity [ˈpærɪtɪ] N (*Fin etc*) paridad *f*; [*of wages, conditions*] igualdad *f*; **exchange at ~** cambio *m* a la par

park [pɑːk] Ⓐ N 1 (= *public gardens*) parque *m*; *see also* **business B**, **science B**
2 (*Brit Sport**) (= *field*) campo *m*
Ⓑ VT 1 (*Aut*) aparcar (*Sp*), estacionar (*esp LAm*); **can I ~ my car here?** ¿puedo aparcar mi coche aquí?
2 (*) (= *put*) poner, dejar; **she ~ed herself on the sofa** se colocó en el sofá
Ⓒ VI (*Aut*) aparcar (*Sp*), estacionarse (*esp LAm*)
Ⓓ CPD ► **park keeper** N guardián/ana *m/f* (de parque), guardabosque *mf*

parka [ˈpɑːkə] N chaquetón *m* acolchado con capucha, anorak *m*

park-and-ride [ˌpɑːkəndˈraɪd] N *aparcamiento en estaciones periféricas conectadas con el transporte urbano colectivo*

parking [ˈpɑːkɪŋ] Ⓐ N aparcamiento *m* (*Sp*), parking *m*, estacionamiento *m* (*esp LAm*); **"parking for 50 cars"** "parking para 50 coches"; **"no parking"** "prohibido aparcar", "prohibido estacionarse" (*esp LAm*); **"ample parking available"** "amplio aparcamiento *or* (*LAm*) estacionamiento para coches"
Ⓑ CPD ► **parking attendant** N guardacoches *mf inv* ► **parking bay** N área *f* de aparcamiento *or* (*esp LAm*) estacionamiento de coches ► **parking lights** NPL luces *fpl* de estacionamiento ► **parking lot** N (*US*) aparcamiento *m* (*Sp*), (playa *f* de) estacionamiento *m* (*esp LAm*) ► **parking meter** N parquímetro *m* ► **parking offence** N infracción *f* por aparca-

miento *or* (*esp LAm*) estacionamiento indebido ► **parking permit** N permiso *m* de aparcamiento *or* (*esp LAm*) estacionamiento ► **parking place**, **parking space** N aparcamiento *m* (*Sp*), parking *m*, estacionamiento *m* (*esp LAm*) ► **parking ticket** N multa *f* por aparcamiento *or* (*esp LAm*) estacionamiento indebido ► **parking violation** N (*US*) = **parking offence**

Parkinson's disease ['pɑːkɪnsənzdɪˌziːz] N enfermedad *f* de Parkinson

Parkinson's law ['pɑːkɪnsənzˌlɔː] N ley *f* de Parkinson

parkland ['pɑːklænd] N parques *mpl*

park-ride [ˌpɑːk'raɪd] N = **park-and-ride**

parkway ['pɑːkweɪ] N (*US*) alameda *f*

parky* ['pɑːkɪ] ADJ (*Brit*) **it's a bit ~** está haciendo fresco

parlance ['pɑːləns] N lenguaje *m*; **in common ~** en lenguaje corriente; **in technical ~** en lenguaje técnico

parley ['pɑːlɪ] Ⓐ N parlamento *m*
Ⓑ VI parlamentar (**with** con)

parliament ['pɑːləmənt] N parlamento *m*, ≈ Cortes *fpl* (*Sp*), ≈ Congreso *m* (*LAm*); (= *period between elections*) legislatura *f*; **to go into** *or* **enter ~** ser elegido diputado *or* senador

parliamentarian [ˌpɑːləmen'tɛərɪən] Ⓐ ADJ parlamentario
Ⓑ N parlamentario/a *m/f*

parliamentary [ˌpɑːlə'mentərɪ] Ⓐ ADJ parlamentario
Ⓑ CPD ► **parliamentary agent** N agente *mf* parlamentario/a ► **parliamentary democracy** N democracia *f* parlamentaria ► **parliamentary election** N elecciones *fpl* parlamentarias ► **parliamentary government** N gobierno *m* parlamentario ► **parliamentary immunity** N inmunidad *f* parlamentaria ► **parliamentary privilege** N privilegio *m* parlamentario

parlour, **parlor** (*US*) ['pɑːləʳ] Ⓐ N (*in house*) sala *f*, salón *m*; **beauty ~** salón *m* de belleza; **ice-cream ~** heladería *f*
Ⓑ CPD ► **parlor car** N (*US*) coche-salón *m* ► **parlour game**, **parlor game** (*US*) N juego *m* de salón

parlourmaid, **parlormaid** (*US*) ['pɑːləmeɪd] N camarera *f*

parlous ['pɑːləs] ADJ [*state*] lamentable, crítico, pésimo

Parma ham [ˌpɑːmə'hæm] N jamón *m* de Parma

Parma violet [ˌpɑːmə'vaɪəlɪt] N violeta *f* de Parma

Parmesan [ˌpɑːmɪ'zæn] Ⓐ N parmesano *m*
Ⓑ CPD ► **Parmesan cheese** N queso *m* parmesano

Parnassus [pɑː'næsəs] N Parnaso *m*

parochial [pə'rəʊkɪəl] ADJ (*Rel*) parroquial; (*pej*) (= *provincial*) provinciano; (= *narrow-minded*) de miras estrechas

parochialism [pə'rəʊkɪəlɪzəm] N (*pej*) mentalidad *f* provinciana *or* pueblerina

parodic [pə'rɒdɪk] ADJ paródico

parodist ['pærədɪst] N parodista *mf*

parody ['pærədɪ] Ⓐ N parodia *f*
Ⓑ VT parodiar

parole [pə'rəʊl] Ⓐ N (= *word*) palabra *f* (de honor); (*Jur*) libertad *f* condicional; **to be on ~** estar en libertad condicional; **to break one's ~** quebrantar las condiciones impuestas por la libertad condicional; **to put sb on ~** poner a algn en libertad condicional
Ⓑ VT dejar en libertad condicional

paroxysm ['pærəksɪzəm] N paroxismo *m*; **she broke into a ~ of coughing** le dio un ataque muy fuerte de tos; **it sent him into ~s of mirth/rage** le hizo troncharse de risa/le produjo un ataque de ira

parquet ['pɑːkeɪ] N parquet *m*, parqué *m*

parquetry ['pɑːkɪtrɪ] N (= *floor*) entarimado *m*; (= *activity*) obra *f* de entarimado

parricide ['pærɪsaɪd] N [1] (= *act*) parricidio *m*
[2] (= *person*) parricida *mf*

parrot ['pærət] Ⓐ N loro *m*, papagayo *m*; **they repeated it like ~s** lo repitieron como loros; *see also* **sick A3**
Ⓑ VT [+ *words*] repetir como un loro

parrot-cry ['pærətkraɪ] N cantinela *f*, eslogan *m* (*que se repite mecánicamente*)

parrot-fashion ['pærətˌfæʃən] ADV [*learn*] como un loro

parry ['pærɪ] VT (*Fencing*) parar; [+ *blow*] parar, desviar; [+ *attack*] rechazar, defenderse de; (*fig*) esquivar, eludir

parse [pɑːz] VT analizar (sintácticamente)

parsec ['pɑːsek] N parsec *m*

Parsee [pɑː'siː] N parsi *mf*

parser ['pɑːzəʳ] N analizador *m* sintáctico

parsimonious [ˌpɑːsɪ'məʊnɪəs] ADJ parco, excesivamente frugal

parsimoniously [ˌpɑːsɪ'məʊnɪəslɪ] ADV parcamente

parsimony ['pɑːsɪmənɪ] N parquedad *f*, excesiva frugalidad *f*

parsing ['pɑːzɪŋ] N análisis *m inv* sintáctico *or* gramatical

parsley ['pɑːslɪ] N perejil *m*

parsnip ['pɑːsnɪp] N chirivía *f*, pastinaca *f*

parson ['pɑːsn] Ⓐ N clérigo *m*, cura *m*; (*Protestant*) pastor *m*
Ⓑ CPD ► **parson's nose** N [*of chicken*] rabadilla *f*

parsonage ['pɑːsnɪdʒ] N casa *f* del párroco, parroquia *f*

parsonical [pɑː'sɒnɪkəl] ADJ (*hum*) frailuno

part [pɑːt] Ⓐ N [1] (= *portion, proportion*) parte *f*; **the ~s of the body** las partes del cuerpo; **it was all ~ of the job** todo formaba parte del trabajo; **this was only ~ of the story** esta no era la historia completa, esto sólo era parte de la historia; **~ of me wanted to apologize** por un lado quería pedir perdón, una parte de mí quería pedir perdón; **it went on for the best ~ of an hour** continuó durante casi una hora; **you haven't heard the best ~ yet** todavía no has oído lo mejor; **in the early ~ of this century** a principios de este siglo; **the funny ~ of it is that nobody seemed to notice** lo gracioso es que nadie pareció darse cuenta; **a good ~ of sth** gran parte de algo; **in great ~** en gran parte; **in ~** en parte; **the book is good in ~s** hay partes del libro que son buenas, el libro es bueno en partes; **a large ~ of sth** gran parte de algo; **in large ~** en gran parte; **for the most ~** (*proportion*) en su mayor parte; (*number*) en su mayoría; (= *usually*) por lo general; **for the most ~, this is still unexplored terrain** en su mayor parte, este es un territorio aún no explorado; **the locals are, for the most ~, very friendly** los habitantes son, en su mayoría, muy simpáticos; **the work is, for the most ~, quite well paid** el trabajo está, por lo general, bastante bien pagado; ✦***IDIOMS*** **a man of (many) ~s** un hombre de muchas facetas; **to be ~ and parcel of sth** ser parte integrante de algo; **suffering and death are ~ and parcel of life** el sufrimiento y la muerte son parte integrante de la vida; *see also* **furniture**, **private C**, **sum 2**

[2] (= *measure*) parte *f*; **one ~ alcohol to two ~s water** una parte de alcohol por cada dos partes de agua; **mix together equal ~s of salt and flour** mezcle partes iguales de sal y harina

[3] (= *share, role*) **to do one's ~** poner de su parte; **he had no ~ in stealing it** no intervino *or* no participó en el robo; **work plays an important ~ in her life** el trabajo juega un papel importante en su vida; **to take ~ (in sth)** tomar parte (en algo), participar (en algo); **I want no ~ of this** no quiero tener nada que ver con esto

[4] (*Theat, Cine*) papel *m*; **to look the ~** vestir el cargo; **to play the ~ of Hamlet** hacer el papel de Hamlet; **he's just playing a ~** está fingiendo; *see also* **bit B**

[5] (= *region*) [*of city*] parte *f*, zona *f*; [*of country, world*] región *f*; **I don't know this ~ of London very well** no conozco esta parte *or* esta zona de Londres muy bien; **a lovely ~ of the country** una región hermosa del país; **what ~ of Spain are you from?** ¿de qué parte de España eres?; **delegates from all ~s of the country** delegados de todos los rincones del país; **in some ~s of the world** en algunas regiones del mundo; **in this/that ~ of the world** en esta/esa región; **in foreign ~s** en el extranjero; **in** *or* **round these ~s** por aquí, por estos pagos*; **he's not from these ~s** no es de por aquí

[6] (= *side*) **for my ~, I do not agree** en lo que a mí se refiere *or* por mi parte, no estoy de acuerdo; **to take sth in good ~** tomarse algo bien; **it was bad organization on their ~** fue mala organización por su parte; **to take sb's ~** ponerse de parte de algn, tomar partido por algn

[7] (*Mech*) pieza *f*; *see also* **moving**, **replacement B**, **spare D**

[8] (*Gram*) parte *f*; **~ of speech** parte *f* de la oración, categoría *f* gramatical; **what ~ of speech is "of"?** ¿qué parte de la oración es "de"?, ¿a qué categoría gramatical pertenece "de"?

[9] (*Mus*) parte *f*; **the soprano ~** la parte de soprano; **a song in four ~s** ◊ **a four-~ song** una canción a cuatro voces

[10] (= *instalment*) [*of journal*] número *m*; [*of serialized publication*] fascículo *m*; (*TV, Rad*) (= *episode*) parte *f*

[11] (*US*) (*in hair*) raya *f*; **side/center ~** raya *f* al lado/al medio

Ⓑ ADV (= *partly*) en parte; **it is ~ fiction and ~ fact** es en parte ficción y en parte realidad, contiene partes ficticias y partes reales; **the cake was ~ eaten** el pastel estaba empezado *or* medio comido; **she is ~ French** tiene algo de sangre francesa

Ⓒ VT [1] (= *separate*) separar; **it would kill her to be ~ed from him** le mataría estar separada de él; **market traders try to ~ the tourists from their money** los dueños de los puestos en los mercados intentan sacar dinero de los turistas; *see also* **company A2**, **death A1**, **fool A1**

[2] (= *open*) [+ *curtains*] abrir, correr; [+ *legs, lips*] abrir

[3] (= *divide*) **to ~ one's hair on the left/right** peinarse con raya a la izquierda/derecha; **his hair was ~ed at the side/in the middle** tenía raya al lado/al medio

Ⓓ VI [1] (= *separate*) [*people*] separarse; **they couldn't bear to ~** no soportaban la idea de separarse; **we ~ed on good terms** lo dejamos como amigos; **to ~ from sb** separarse de algn

[2] (= *move to one side*) [*crowd, clouds*] apartarse
[3] (= *open*) [*lips, curtains*] abrirse
[4] (= *break*) [*rope*] romperse, partirse
Ⓔ CPD ► **part exchange** N **they take your old car in ~ exchange** aceptan tu coche viejo como parte del pago; **they offer ~ exchange on older vehicles** aceptan vehículos más antiguos como parte del pago de uno nuevo ► **part owner** N copropietario/a *m/f* ► **part payment** N pago *m* parcial; **to accept sth as ~ payment for sth** aceptar algo como parte del pago *or* como pago parcial de algo ► **part song** N canción *f* a varias voces

►**part with** VI + PREP [+ *possession*] desprenderse de, deshacerse de; [+ *person*] separarse de; [+ *money*] gastar, soltar*; **I hate ~ing with it** me duele tener que desprenderme *or* deshacerme de él; **she couldn't bear to ~ with the baby** fue incapaz de separarse del bebé

partake [pɑːˈteɪk] (*pt* **partook**; *pp* **partaken**) VI (*frm*) [1] (= *consume*) **to ~ of** [+ *food*] comer; [+ *drink*] beber
[2] (= *participate*) **to ~ in an activity** tomar parte *or* participar en una actividad; **are you partaking?** ¿va a tomar parte?

parterre [pɑːˈteə] N (= *garden*) parterre *m*

parthenogenesis [ˈpɑːθɪnəʊˈdʒenɪsɪs] N partenogénesis *f inv*

Parthenon [ˈpɑːθənɒn] N Partenón *m*

partial [ˈpɑːʃəl] ADJ [1] (= *not complete*) parcial
[2] (= *biased*) parcial (**towards** hacia)
[3] **to be ~ to sth** (= *like*) tener debilidad por algo; **he's ~ to a cigar after dinner** le gusta fumarse un puro después de cenar

partiality [ˌpɑːʃɪˈælɪtɪ] N [1] (= *bias*) parcialidad *f* (**towards** hacia)
[2] (= *liking*) debilidad *f* (**for, to** por), gusto *m* (**for, to** por)

partially [ˈpɑːʃəlɪ] ADV [1] (= *partly*) parcialmente, en parte
[2] (= *with bias*) con parcialidad

participant [pɑːˈtɪsɪpənt] N (*in debate, fight, argument*) participante *mf*; (*in competition*) concursante *mf*

participate [pɑːˈtɪsɪpeɪt] VI participar, tomar parte (**in** en); **participating countries** países *mpl* participantes; **to ~ in a sport** practicar un deporte

participation [pɑːˌtɪsɪˈpeɪʃən] N participación *f* (**in** en); *see also* **audience**

participative [pɑːˈtɪsɪpətɪv] ADJ [*management, democracy*] participativo

participatory [pɑːtɪsɪˈpeɪtərɪ] ADJ [*democracy, sport*] participativo

participial [ˌpɑːtɪˈsɪpɪəl] ADJ participial

participle [ˈpɑːtɪsɪpl] N participio *m*; **past ~** participio *m* pasado *or* pasivo; **present ~** participio *m* activo *or* (de) presente

particle [ˈpɑːtɪkl] Ⓐ N [1] (*gen*) partícula *f*; [*of dust*] partícula *f*, grano *m*; (*fig*) pizca *f*; **there's not a ~ of truth in it** eso no tiene ni pizca de verdad
[2] (*Fís, Gram*) partícula *f*
Ⓑ CPD ► **particle accelerator** N acelerador *m* de partículas ► **particle board** N (*US*) madera *f* aglomerada ► **particle physics** N física *f* de partículas

parti-coloured, **parti-colored** (*US*) [ˈpɑːtɪˌkʌləd] ADJ de diversos colores, multicolor, abigarrado

▼ **particular** [pəˈtɪkjʊləʳ] Ⓐ ADJ [1] (= *special*) especial; **the flowers had been chosen with ~ care** se habían escogido las flores con especial cuidado; **she's a ~ friend of mine** es muy amiga mía; **is there anything ~ you want?** ¿quieres algo en particular *or* en concreto?; **to pay ~ attention to sth** prestar especial atención a algo; **nothing ~ happened** no pasó nada en especial
[2] (= *specific*) **in this ~ case** en este caso concreto; **at this ~ point in time** en este preciso momento; **is there any ~ food you don't like?** ¿hay algún alimento en particular *or* en especial *or* en concreto que no te guste?; **the people living in a ~ area** la gente que vive en una zona determinada; **for no ~ reason** por ninguna razón especial *or* en particular *or* en concreto
[3] (= *fussy*) **to be ~ about sth**: **he's very ~ about his food** es muy exigente con *or* especial para la comida; **I'm rather ~ about my friends** escojo mis amigos con cierto cuidado; **she's not very ~ about her appearance** no se preocupa mucho por su aspecto; **they weren't too ~ about where the money came from** no les importaba *or* preocupaba mucho de dónde viniera el dinero
[4] (= *insistent*) **he was most ~ that I shouldn't go to any trouble** insistió mucho en que no me tomara ninguna molestia
Ⓑ N [1] (*frm*) (*usu pl*) (= *detail*) detalle *m*; **her account was accurate in every ~** su versión fue exacta en todos los detalles; **please give full ~s** se ruega hacer constar todos los detalles; **for further ~s apply to ...** para más información escriba a ...; **the nurse took her ~s** la enfermera le tomó sus datos personales
[2] **in ~**: **I remember one incident in ~** recuerdo un incidente en particular *or* en concreto; **are you looking for anything in ~?** ¿busca usted algo en particular *or* en concreto?; **"are you doing anything tonight?" — "nothing in ~"** —¿vas a hacer algo esta noche? —nada en particular *or* en especial
[3] **the ~** lo particular; *see* **general B2**

particularity [pəˌtɪkjʊˈlærɪtɪ] N particularidad *f*

particularize [pəˈtɪkjʊləraɪz] Ⓐ VT pormenorizar, especificar
Ⓑ VI entrar en detalles

particularly [pəˈtɪkjʊləlɪ] ADV [1] (= *especially*) especialmente; **in many countries, ~ France** en muchos países, especialmente *or* particularmente en Francia; **he ~ dislikes quiz shows** siente especial aversión por los concursos televisivos; **he was not ~ pleased** no se puso loco de contento que digamos; **"do you want to see it?" — "not ~"** —¿quieres verlo? —no especialmente
[2] (= *specifically*) **do you want it ~ for tomorrow?** ¿lo necesitas expresamente *or* precisamente para mañana?

parting [ˈpɑːtɪŋ] Ⓐ ADJ de despedida; **his ~ words** sus palabras de despedida; **~ shot** (*fig*) golpe *m* de gracia
Ⓑ N [1] (= *separation*) separación *f*, despedida *f*; **the ~ of the ways** (*fig*) la encrucijada, el momento de la separación
[2] (*in hair*) raya *f*; **side/centre ~** raya *f* al lado/al medio

partisan [ˌpɑːtɪˈzæn] Ⓐ ADJ (= *one-sided*) parcial; (= *of party*) partidista; (*Mil*) guerrillero
Ⓑ N partidario/a *m/f* (**of** de); (*Mil*) partisano/a *m/f*, guerrillero/a *m/f*
Ⓒ CPD ► **partisan warfare** N guerra *f* partisana

partisanship [ˌpɑːtɪˈzænʃɪp] N partidismo *m*

partition [pɑːˈtɪʃən] Ⓐ N [1] (= *wall*) tabique *m*
[2] (*Pol*) partición *f*, división *f*
Ⓑ VT [1] (= *divide*) [+ *country*] partir, dividir; (= *share*) repartir (**among** entre)
[2] [+ *room, area*] tabicar, dividir con tabiques

►**partition off** VT + ADV separar con tabiques

partitive [ˈpɑːtɪtɪv] ADJ partitivo

partly [ˈpɑːtlɪ] ADV en parte; **that is only ~ true** eso es verdad sólo en parte; **I am ~ to blame** en parte es culpa mía; **he is ~ responsible for this** en parte él es responsable de esto; **it was ~ destroyed** quedó parcialmente destruido; **the film is ~ a romance, ~ a comedy** la película es en parte romántica y en parte cómica, la película tiene partes románticas y partes cómicas

partner [ˈpɑːtnəʳ] Ⓐ N [1] (*in activity*) compañero/a *m/f*; **work with a ~ for this exercise** realizar este ejercicio con un compañero *or* en pareja; **~(s) in crime** (*lit, hum*) cómplice(s) *m(pl)*
[2] (*in dance, tennis, golf, cards*) pareja *f*; (= *co-driver*) copiloto *mf*
[3] (*Comm, Pol*) socio/a *m/f*; **junior ~** socio/a *m/f* menor; **senior ~** socio/a *m/f* principal, socio/a *m/f* mayoritario/a (*Sp*); *see also* **sleeping, trading B**
[4] (*in relationship*) pareja *f*, compañero/a *m/f*; (*in sex*) pareja *f*; **marriage ~** cónyuge *mf* (*frm*); *see also* **sexual**
Ⓑ VT [1] (= *be partner of*) **to ~ sb in a waltz** bailar un vals con algn; **he ~ed her at bridge** jugó al bridge en pareja con ella, fue su pareja al bridge
[2] (= *pair*) **to ~ sb with sb** juntar a algn con algn (como pareja)

partnership [ˈpɑːtnəʃɪp] Ⓐ N [1] (= *relationship*) asociación *f*; (= *couple*) relación *f* de pareja; **a stable, loving ~** una relación de pareja estable y llena de cariño; **our relationship wasn't just a marriage, it was a ~** nuestra relación no era sólo un matrimonio sino una asociación; **their ~ was based on mutual respect** su relación se basaba en el respeto mutuo; **the ~ between government and industry** la alianza entre el gobierno y la industria
[2] (*Comm*) (= *company*) sociedad *f* colectiva; **to be in ~ with sb** estar asociado con algn; **to go** *or* **enter into ~ (with sb)** asociarse (con algn); **we work in ~ with our clients** trabajamos conjuntamente con nuestros clientes; *see also* **limited**
[3] (= *position as partner*) **they've offered me a ~** me han ofrecido hacerme socio
Ⓑ CPD ► **partnership agreement** N contrato *m* de sociedad

partook [pɑːˈtʊk] PT *of* **partake**

partridge [ˈpɑːtrɪdʒ] N (*pl* **partridges** *or* **partridge**) perdiz *f*

part-time [ˈpɑːtˈtaɪm] Ⓐ ADV a tiempo parcial (*Sp*), medio tiempo (*LAm*); **to work ~** trabajar a tiempo parcial *or* (*LAm*) medio tiempo
Ⓑ ADJ [*worker, job*] de media jornada, a tiempo parcial (*Sp*), de medio tiempo (*LAm*)
Ⓒ N (*Ind*) jornada *f* reducida; **to be on ~** trabajar en horario de jornada reducida

part-timer [ˌpɑːtˈtaɪməʳ] N trabajador(a) *m/f* a tiempo parcial (*Sp*), trabajador(a) *m/f* a medio tiempo (*LAm*)

parturition [ˌpɑːtjʊəˈrɪʃən] N (*frm*) parturición *f*, parto *m*

partway [ˈpɑːtˌweɪ] ADV **~ through the week** a mitad de la semana; **the wood had been sawn ~ through** la madera había sido serrada parcialmente; **I'll walk ~ with you** caminaré un trozo contigo; **it goes ~ toward explaining his strange behaviour** explica en parte su extraño comportamiento; **we're only ~ into** *or* **through the work** hemos hecho sólo una parte del trabajo

▼ **party** [ˈpɑːtɪ] Ⓐ N [1] (= *celebration*) fiesta *f*; **to give** *or* **have** *or* **throw a ~** dar *or* (*frm*) ofrecer

➤ LANGUAGE IN USE: **particular B1** 19.1 **party A1** 25.2, 25.3

una fiesta; ✦*IDIOM* **the ~'s over** se acabó la fiesta; *see also* **house C**

2 (*Pol*) partido *m*; **to join a ~** afiliarse a un partido, hacerse miembro de un partido

3 (= *group*) grupo *m*; **a ~ of tourists** un grupo de turistas; **we were only a small ~** éramos pocos, éramos un grupo pequeño

4 (*in dispute, contract*) parte *f*; **the parties concerned** los interesados, las partes interesadas; **the guilty/injured/innocent ~** la parte culpable/perjudicada/inocente; **to be (a) ~ to sth**: **I will not be a ~ to any violence** no me voy a prestar a la violencia; **to be (a) ~ to an agreement** ser parte en un acuerdo; **to be (a) ~ to a crime** ser cómplice en un delito; **the parties to a dispute** las partes involucradas en una querella; *see also* **third D**, **warring**

Ⓑ VI (*) (= *go to parties*) ir a fiestas; (= *have a good time*) irse de juerga*, irse de marcha (*Sp**); **let's ~!** ¡vámonos de juerga!*, ¡vámonos de marcha! (*Sp**); **where shall we ~ tonight?** ¿a qué fiesta vamos esta noche?

Ⓒ CPD ► **party animal** N fiestero/a *m/f*, juerguista *mf* ► **party dress** N vestido *m* de fiesta ► **party line** N (*Telec*) línea *f* compartida; **the ~ line** (*Pol*) la línea del partido ► **party member** N miembro *m* del partido ► **party piece** N numerito *m* (de fiesta)*; **to do one's ~ piece** hacer su numerito* ► **party politics** NPL (*gen*) política *fsing* de partido; (*pej*) partidismo *msing* (*pej*), politiqueo *msing* (*pej*) ► **party pooper*** N aguafiestas *mf inv* ► **party spirit** N espíritu *m* festivo; **we entered into the ~ spirit** nos empezó a entrar el espíritu festivo ► **party wall** N pared *f* medianera

party-goer [ˈpɑːtɪˌɡəʊəʳ] N (*gen*) asiduo/a *m/f* a fiestas; (*on specific occasion*) invitado/a *m/f*; **I'm not much of a ~** yo voy poco a las fiestas

party-going [ˈpɑːtiˌɡəʊɪŋ] N **he spends his time ~ instead of working** se pasa el tiempo yendo a fiestas en lugar de trabajar

partying* [ˈpɑːtɪɪŋ] N **I'm not a great one for ~** no me gustan mucho las fiestas

party political [ˌpɑːtɪpəˈlɪtɪkəl] ADJ [*advantage, issue*] de(l) partido; **~ broadcast** emisión *f* de propaganda política, ≈ espacio *m* electoral

parvenu [ˈpɑːvənjuː] N advenedizo/a *m/f*

paschal [ˈpɑːskəl] ADJ pascual; **the Paschal Lamb** el cordero pascual

pas de deux [ˈpɑːdəˈdɜː] N paso *m* a dos

pasha [ˈpæʃə] N bajá *m*, pachá *m*

pass [pɑːs] Ⓐ N 1 (= *permit*) (*gen*) pase *m*; (*Mil*) permiso *m*, pase *m*; **bus ~** abono *m or* pase *m* de autobús; **overnight ~** permiso *m or* pase *m* de pernocta; **press ~** pase *m* de prensa; **rail ~** abono *m or* pase *m* de ferrocarril; **security ~** pase *m* de seguridad; **visitor's ~** pase *m* de visitas; **weekend ~** permiso *m or* pase *m* de fin de semana; *see also* **boarding**

2 (*Sport*) pase *m*; **back ~** pase *m* hacia atrás; **forward ~** pase *m* adelantado

3 (*in exam*) aprobado *m*; **a ~ in biology** un aprobado en biología; **to get a ~ (in sth)** aprobar (algo); **she got seven ~es** aprobó siete asignaturas

4 (*by conjuror*) pase *m*; (*by aircraft*) pasada *f*

5 (= *situation*) **things have come to a pretty ~** ¡hasta dónde hemos llegado!; **things had reached such a ~ that …** las cosas habían llegado a tal extremo que …

6 (= *sexual approach*) **to make a ~ at sb*** tirarle a algn los tejos*, intentar ligar con algn*

7 (*Geog*) puerto *m*, paso *m*; (*small*) desfiladero *m*; **mountain ~** puerto *m or* paso *m* de montaña

Ⓑ VT 1 (= *go past*) pasar; (= *go in front of*) pasar por delante de; (= *cross paths with*) cruzarse con; (*Aut*) (= *overtake*) adelantar, pasar, rebasar (*Mex*); **the road ~es a farmyard** la carretera pasa por un corral; **the procession ~ed the royal stand** el desfile pasó por delante de la tribuna de Sus Majestades; **I ~ed them on the stairs** me crucé con ellos en las escaleras; **they ~ed each other on the way** se cruzaron en el camino; **he looked the other way as he ~ed me** miró al otro lado cuando nos cruzamos; **he tried to ~ me on the inside** (*Aut*) intentó adelantarme *or* pasarme por la derecha; (*in UK*) intentó adelantarme *or* pasarme por la izquierda

2 (= *surpass*) superar; **total membership has ~ed the six million mark** el número total de miembros supera los seis millones

3 (= *cross*) [+ *barrier, frontier, customs*] cruzar; **not a word has ~ed my lips** de mí no ha salido una palabra, no he dicho ni una palabra

4 (= *convey, transfer*) (*gen*) pasar; (*Sport*) [+ *ball*] pasar; **the gas is then ~ed along a pipe** el gas luego se pasa por una tubería; **to ~ sth down the line** pasar algo de mano en mano; **to ~ a dish round the table** pasar un plato entre todos los que están a la mesa; **to ~ sb sth ◊ ~ sth to sb** pasar algo a algn; **~ me the salt, please** ¿me pasas *or* alcanzas la sal, por favor?; **my application was ~ed to another department** pasaron mi solicitud a otro departamento; *see also* **buck A3**, **parcel**, **word A4**

5 (= *move in given direction*) pasar; **he ~ed his handkerchief over his face** se pasó el pañuelo por la cara; **to ~ a cloth over sth** limpiar algo con un paño; **he ~ed the rope round the axle/through the ring** pasó la cuerda por el eje/por el aro

6 (= *spend*) [+ *time*] pasar; **it ~es the time** ayuda a pasar el rato; ✦*IDIOM* **to ~ the time of day with sb** charlar un rato con algn

7 (= *not fail*) [+ *exam, essay, candidate*] aprobar; [+ *inspection*] pasar; **he has just ~ed his driving test** acaba de aprobar el examen de conducir; *see also* **fit[1] 2**, **muster**

8 (*Cine*) [+ *film*] [*censor*] aprobar; **the censors felt they could not ~ the film** los censores sintieron que no podían aprobar la película; **the film failed to ~ the censors** la película no consiguió pasar la censura

9 (= *approve*) [+ *law, bill motion*] aprobar

10 (= *express*) [+ *remark, comment*] hacer; **it would be unfair to ~ comment on his private life** no sería justo hacer comentarios sobre su vida privada; **to ~ (an) opinion on sth** expresar una opinión acerca de algo; **to ~ sentence** (*Jur*) fallar, dictar sentencia; **to ~ sentence on sb** sentenciar *or* condenar a algn; *see also* **judgment**

11 (*Med*) [+ *blood*] echar; **to ~ a stone** expulsar un cálculo; **to ~ a stool** realizar una deposición, defecar; **to ~ urine** orinar; **to ~ wind** expulsar ventosidades *or* una ventosidad (*frm*); *see also* **water A3**

12 (*criminally*) [+ *counterfeit money, stolen goods*] pasar

Ⓒ VI 1 (= *go past*) pasar; (*Aut*) (= *overtake*) pasar, adelantar, rebasar (*Mex*); **I stood aside to let her ~** me puse a un lado para dejarle pasar; **we ~ed in the corridor** nos cruzamos en el pasillo; **the procession was still ~ing an hour later** seguían desfilando una hora más tarde; *see also* **ship A1**

2 (= *move, go*) pasar; **to ~ behind/in front of sth/sb** pasar por detrás/por delante de algo/algn; **she ~ed right in front of me** pasó justo por delante mío *or* de mí; **messages ~ed back and forth between them** se intercambiaban mensajes entre sí, se mandaban mensajes el uno al otro; **~ down the bus please!** ¡vayan hacia el fondo del autobús, por favor!; **to ~ into oblivion** pasar al olvido; **control of the business ~ed out of my hands** la dirección de la empresa pasó a otras manos; **to ~ out of sight** perderse de vista; **the bullet ~ed through her shoulder** la bala le atravesó el hombro; **~ through the gate and turn left** cruce la verja y gire a la izquierda; **she knew what was ~ing through his mind** sabía lo que se le estaba pasando por la cabeza; **words ~ed between them** intercambiaron algunas palabras (fuertes)

3 (= *be transferred*) pasar; **the estate ~ed to my brother** la herencia pasó a mi hermano

4 (*Sport*) hacer un pase

5 (= *happen*) **all that ~ed between them** todo lo que hubo entre ellos; **it came to ~ that …** (*liter*) aconteció que … (*liter*)

6 (= *go by*) [*time, deadline*] pasar; **as the years ~ed** a medida que pasaban los años, con el paso de los años; **how time ~es!** ¡como pasa el tiempo!; **the months ~ed into years** los meses se convirtieron en años

7 (= *disappear*) [*storm, pain, danger*] pasar; **it'll ~** eso pasará, eso se olvidará; **once the danger had ~ed** una vez pasado el peligro; **the old order is ~ing** el antiguo orden está desapareciendo; **the rain had ~ed** había dejado de llover

8 (*in exam*) aprobar

9 (= *be approved*) [*bill, amendment*] ser aprobado

10 (= *be accepted*) pasar; **"will this do?" — "oh, it'll ~"** —¿esto servirá? —bueno, pasará; **what ~es in New York may not be good enough here** lo que es aceptable en Nueva York puede no serlo aquí; **to ~ for sth** pasar por algo; **she could easily ~ for 20** podría pasar fácilmente por una chica de 20 años; **or what ~es nowadays for a hat** o lo que pasa por *or* se llama sombrero hoy día; **let it ~** no hagas caso, pásalo por alto; **we can't let that ~!** ¡eso no lo podemos consentir *or* pasar por alto!; *see also* **unnoticed**

11 (*at cards, in quiz*) **(I) pass!** ¡paso!; **I'm afraid I don't know, I'll have to ~ on that one** me temo que no lo sé, no puedo contestar esa pregunta; **I think I'll ~ on the hiking next time*** creo que la próxima vez voy a pasar de la excursión*

Ⓓ CPD ► **pass key** N llave *f* maestra ► **pass mark** N aprobado *m*, nota *f* de aprobado ► **pass rate** N índice *m* de aprobados

►**pass around**, **pass round** VT + ADV **a bottle of whisky was ~ed around** se pasaron una botella de whisky de mano en mano *or* de uno a otro; **you ~ round the biscuits** pasa las galletas entre todos; **to ~ round the hat** pasar la gorra

►**pass away** VI + ADV 1 (*euph*) (= *die*) fallecer

2 (= *disappear*) desaparecer

►**pass by** Ⓐ VI + ADV 1 (= *go past*) pasar; **I was just ~ing by and I saw your car** estaba pasando por aquí y he visto tu coche; **she would beg from the people ~ing by** pedía limosna a la gente que pasaba

2 [*time, occasion*] pasar; **as the hours ~ed by** a medida que pasaban las horas

Ⓑ VT + ADV **life has ~ed her by** la vida se le ha pasado sin enterarse, no ha disfrutado de la vida; **fortune seemed to have ~ed him by** la fortuna parecía haberle dejado de lado; **don't let this opportunity ~ you by** no dejes pasar (por alto) esta oportunidad

Ⓒ VI + PREP pasar por; **I'll ~ by your place to**

pick you up pasaré por tu casa para recogerte

►**pass down** Ⓐ VT + ADV [1] (= *transfer*) [+ *custom, disease, trait*] pasar, transmitir; [+ *inheritance*] pasar; **these beliefs were ~ed down from generation to generation** estas creencias se fueron pasando *or* transmitiendo de generación en generación; **it's been ~ed down through the family** se ha ido heredando en la familia; **the painting was ~ed down to my father and he ~ed it down to me** el cuadro lo heredó mi padre y luego me lo pasó a mí; **my clothes were always ~ed down from my elder sister** yo siempre heredaba la ropa de mi hermana mayor; **when you grow out of this coat you can ~ it down to your brother** cuando este abrigo te quede pequeño se lo puedes pasar *or* dar a tu hermano
[2] (= *convey downwards*) pasar; **he ~ed the bags down to me** me pasó las bolsas
Ⓑ VI + ADV [1] (= *be transferred*) [*custom*] pasar, transmitirse
[2] (= *be inherited*) **the farm ~ed down to me** yo heredé la granja

►**pass off** Ⓐ VI + ADV [1] (= *happen*) transcurrir; **it all ~ed off without incident** todo transcurrió sin percances
[2] (= *wear off*) [*headache, bad mood*] pasarse; **her headache ~ed off after an hour** el dolor de cabeza se le pasó una hora después
Ⓑ VT + ADV [1] (= *present as genuine*) **to ~ sth/sb off as sth** hacer pasar algo/a algn por algo; **he ~ed the girl off as his sister** hizo pasar a la chica por su hermana; **to ~ o.s. off as sth** hacerse pasar por algo; **she tried to ~ herself off as an 18-year-old** intentó hacerse pasar por una chica de 18 años
[2] (= *dismiss*) **he tried to ~ it off as a joke** intentó quitarle importancia haciendo ver que lo había dicho en broma

►**pass on** Ⓐ VT + ADV [1] (= *transfer*) [+ *information*] pasar, comunicar, dar; [+ *message*] (*written*) dar, pasar; (*spoken*) dar, comunicar; [+ *object*] pasar; [+ *disease*] [*person*] contagiar; [*animal*] transmitir; **I didn't want her to ~ her cold on to me** no quería que me contagiara el constipado; **they ~ the increase on to the consumer** hacen que el consumidor cargue con el incremento; **we ~ our savings on to the customer** los ahorros redundan en favor de nuestros clientes; **Sheila's having a party, ~ it on!*** Sheila va a dar una fiesta, ¡corre la voz!
[2] (= *put in contact*) [+ *person*] **to ~ sb on to sb** poner a algn en contacto con algn; (*on telephone*) poner a algn con algn; **I was ~ed on to another doctor** me mandaron a otro médico, me pusieron en contacto con otro médico; **I'll ~ you on to my supervisor** le pongo a mi supervisor
Ⓑ VI + ADV [1] (= *proceed*) pasar (**to** a); **they ~ed on to other matters** pasaron a discutir otros asuntos; **the man lowered his eyes and ~ed on** el hombre bajó la vista y pasó de largo
[2] (*euph*) (= *die*) fallecer

►**pass out** Ⓐ VI + ADV [1] (= *faint*) perder el conocimiento, desmayarse
[2] (*Mil*) graduarse
Ⓑ VT + ADV (= *distribute*) repartir

►**pass over** Ⓐ VI + ADV [1] (= *move overhead*) **a flock of geese ~ed over** una bandada de gansos voló por encima nuestro
[2] (= *cross over*) **we ~ed over into France under cover of night** cruzamos a Francia al amparo de la noche
[3] (*euph*) (= *die*) fallecer
Ⓑ VT + ADV [1] (= *omit*) pasar por alto, omitir; **he had ~ed over an important point** había pasado por alto *or* omitido un punto muy importante; **he was ~ed over for promotion** a la hora de los ascensos lo dejaron de lado
[2] (= *hand over*) dar, pasar; **~ over that butter, will you?** ¿me das *or* pasas la mantequilla?

►**pass round** VT + ADV = **pass around**

►**pass through** Ⓐ VI + ADV [1] (= *not stay*) estar de paso; **I'm just ~ing through** estoy de paso nada más
[2] (= *go through*) pasar; **he wouldn't let me ~ through without identification** no me dejaba pasar sin documentación
Ⓑ VI + PREP [+ *town, country, gap*] pasar por; [+ *phase, crisis*] pasar por, atravesar; [+ *barrier*] pasar

►**pass up** VT + ADV [1] (= *forgo*) echar a perder, desperdiciar; **an opportunity like this was too good to ~ up** una oportunidad así era demasiado buena para echarla a perder *or* desperdiciarla
[2] (*lit*) [+ *object*] pasar

passable ['pɑːsəbl] ADJ [1] (= *tolerable*) pasable
[2] [*road*] transitable

passably ['pɑːsəblɪ] ADV pasablemente; **he spoke ~ good French** hablaba francés bastante bien; **she's doing ~ well at school** los estudios le van bastante bien

passage ['pæsɪdʒ] Ⓐ N [1] (= *corridor*) pasillo *m*; (*between buildings, underground*) pasaje *m*; (= *alley*) callejón *m*; **a house full of secret ~s** una casa llena de pasadizos secretos
[2] (*Anat*) conducto *m*; **nasal ~s** conductos nasales; *see also* **back**
[3] (= *voyage*) travesía *f*, viaje *m*; (= *fare*) pasaje *m*; **to work one's ~** trabajar a bordo a cambio del pasaje
[4] (= *access, way through*) paso *m*; **his bodyguards forced a ~ through the crowds** sus guardaespaldas se abrieron camino *or* paso entre la muchedumbre; **their win has given them an easy ~ to the final** han llegado fácilmente a la final tras esta victoria; **free ~** paso *m* libre; **right of ~** derecho *m* de paso; **safe ~** salvoconducto *m*
[5] (= *progress*) paso *m*; **his ~ through life had not been easy** su paso por la vida no había sido fácil; **the opposition was giving the bill a rough ~ through Parliament** la oposición estaba obstruyendo la aprobación del proyecto de ley en el Parlamento; **the ~ of time** el paso del tiempo; **with the ~ of time** con el (paso del) tiempo; *see also* **bird B**
[6] (= *transition*) paso *m*; **one's ~ into womanhood/manhood** el paso de uno a la edad adulta; **the ~ of summer into autumn** el paso del verano al otoño; **the book charts her ~ into madness** el libro recoge su descenso a la locura; **to ease their ~ from a socialist to a market economy** para facilitar la transición *or* el paso de una economía socialista a una de mercado; *see also* **rite B**
[7] (= *section*) [*of book, music*] pasaje *m*
Ⓑ CPD ► **passage money**† N pasaje *m*

passageway ['pæsɪdʒweɪ] N (*in house*) pasillo *m*, corredor *m*; (*between buildings etc*) pasaje *m*

passbook ['pɑːsbʊk] N libreta *f* de ahorros

passé ['pæseɪ] ADJ pasado de moda

passel ['pæsəl] N (*US*) muchedumbre *f*

passenger ['pæsndʒəʳ] Ⓐ N [1] pasajero/a *m/f*; *see also* **fellow B**, **foot C**
[2] (*pej*) parásito *m*; **I felt like a ~** me sentía como un parásito; **there's no room for ~s in this company** en esta empresa no hay lugar para los gandules
Ⓑ CPD [*jet, ship, train*] de pasajeros
► **passenger door** N (*Aut*) puerta *f* del pasajero ► **passenger list** N lista *f* de pasajeros ► **passenger miles** NPL millas-pasajero *fpl* ► **passenger seat** N (*Aut*) asiento *m* del pasajero

passe-partout ['pæspɑːtuː] N paspartú *m*, passe partout *m*

passer-by ['pɑːsə'baɪ] N (*pl* **passers-by**) transeúnte *mf*

passim ['pæsɪm] ADV passim

passing ['pɑːsɪŋ] Ⓐ ADJ [*fad*] pasajero; [*glance*] rápido, superficial; [*remark*] hecho de paso; **a ~ car** un coche que pasaba; **with each ~ day it gets more difficult** cada día se hace más difícil; **~ fancy** capricho *m*; **the story aroused no more than ~ interest** la noticia no despertó más que un interés pasajero; **the speech made only a ~ reference to the Middle East** el discurso hizo sólo una breve alusión a Oriente Medio; **he bears more than a ~ resemblance to Rock Hudson** su parecido con Rock Hudson es notable
Ⓑ N [1] (= *disappearance*) [*of custom, tradition*] desaparición *f*; (*euph*) (= *death*) fallecimiento *m*; **with the ~ of the years** con el paso de los años, conforme van pasando los años; **to mention sth in ~** mencionar algo de paso *or* pasada
[2] (*US Aut*) adelantamiento *m*
[3] (*Parl*) aprobación *f*
Ⓒ CPD ► **passing bell** N toque *m* de difuntos ► **passing lane** N (*US Aut*) carril *m* de adelantamiento ► **passing place** N (*Brit Aut*) apartadero *m* ► **passing shot** N (*Tennis*) tiro *m* pasado

passing-out [,pɑːsɪŋ'aʊt] Ⓐ N graduación *f*
Ⓑ CPD ► **passing-out parade** N desfile *m* de promoción

passion ['pæʃən] Ⓐ N [1] (= *love*) (*sexual, fig*) pasión *f*; **his ~ for accuracy** su pasión por la exactitud; **I have a ~ for shellfish** el marisco me apasiona; *see also* **crime B**
[2] (= *fervour, emotion*) pasión *f*; **he spoke with great ~** habló con gran pasión; **political ~s are running high** las pasiones políticas están caldeadas; **she has taken to golf with a ~** ha empezado a jugar al golf y le apasiona
[3] (= *anger*) cólera *f*, pasión *f*; **to be in a ~** estar encolerizado; **to do sth in a fit of ~** hacer algo en un arrebato *or* un arranque de cólera *or* pasión; **to fly into a ~** montar en cólera, encolerizarse
[4] (*Rel*) **the Passion** la Pasión; **the St John/St Matthew Passion** la Pasión según San Juan/San Mateo
Ⓑ CPD ► **passion fruit** N granadilla *f* ► **Passion play** N misterio *m* ► **Passion Sunday** N Domingo *m* de Pasión

passionate ['pæʃənɪt] ADJ [*affair, love, kiss*] apasionado; [*believer, supporter*] ardiente, ferviente; [*desire*] ardiente, vehemente; [*speech*] apasionado, vehemente; [*belief*] inquebrantable; [*interest*] enorme; **he is ~ in his desire to achieve this** tiene un deseo ardiente *or* vehemente de conseguir esto; **to be ~ about sth** ser un apasionado de algo; **we're both ~ gardeners** a los dos nos apasiona *or* entusiasma la jardinería; **she has a ~ hatred of conservatism** odia a muerte el conservadurismo

passionately ['pæʃənɪtlɪ] ADV [*love, embrace, kiss*] apasionadamente, con pasión; [*believe, desire*] ardientemente, fervientemente; **she argued ~ in his defence** abogó con vehemencia en su favor, lo defendió con vehemencia; **he was ~ devoted to his sister** sentía una devoción ciega por su hermana; **I was ~ in**

love with him estaba locamente enamorada de él, lo amaba apasionadamente *or* con pasión

passionflower ['pæʃən,flaʊəʳ] N pasionaria *f*

passionless ['pæʃənlɪs] ADJ [*relationship*] sin pasión, frío

passive ['pæsɪv] Ⓐ ADJ (*gen*) pasivo; (= *inactive*) inactivo
Ⓑ N (*Ling*) voz *f* pasiva
Ⓒ CPD ► **passive resistance** N resistencia *f* pasiva ► **passive smoking** N fumar *m* pasivo

passively ['pæsɪvlɪ] ADV pasivamente

passiveness ['pæsɪvnɪs] N, **passivity** [pæ'sɪvɪtɪ] N pasividad *f*

Passover ['pɑːsəʊvəʳ] N Pascua *f* (judía)

passport ['pɑːspɔːt] Ⓐ N pasaporte *m*; **the ~ to fame** el pasaporte a la fama; **the money was his ~ to a new life** el dinero le abrió las puertas a una nueva vida
Ⓑ CPD ► **passport control** N control *m* de pasaportes ► **passport holder** N **British ~ holder** titular *mf* de pasaporte británico ► **passport photo(graph)** N foto *f* de pasaporte

password ['pɑːswɜːd] N (*gen*) contraseña *f*, santo *m* y seña; (*Comput*) contraseña *f* de acceso

past [pɑːst] Ⓐ ADV 1 (*in place*) **she walked slowly ~** pasó despacio; **the days flew ~** los días pasaron volando; **to march ~** desfilar; **to run/rush ~** pasar corriendo/precipitadamente
2 (*in time*) **it's ten ~** son y diez; **I've been waiting since half ~** llevo esperando desde y media
Ⓑ PREP 1 (*in place*) 1·1 (= *passing by*) por delante de; **we went ~ your house** pasamos por delante de tu casa; **we drove ~ a flock of sheep** pasamos al lado de un rebaño de ovejas con el coche
1·2 (= *beyond*) más allá de; **just ~ the town hall** un poco más allá del Ayuntamiento; **it's the first house ~ the park** es la primera casa después del parque; **first you have to get ~ a fierce dog** antes de entrar vas a tener que vértelas con un perro fiero; **we couldn't get ~ the crowds of people** no pudimos abrirnos paso entre la muchedumbre; **she just pushed ~ me** pasó pegándome un empujón; **to run ~ sb** pasar a algn corriendo
2 (*in time*) **quarter/half ~ four** las cuatro y cuarto/media; **at twenty ~ four** a las cuatro y veinte; **it's ~ twelve** son las doce pasadas; **it's long ~ the time he normally gets back** él normalmente hubiese llegado hace tiempo; **it's ~ your bedtime** ya tenías que estar durmiendo
3 (= *beyond the limits of*) **he's ~ 40** tiene más de 40 años; **it's ~ mending** ya no tiene remedio; **it's ~ belief** es increíble; **I'm ~ caring** ya me trae sin cuidado; **it's ~ endurance** es intolerable; ✦**IDIOMS to be ~ it*** [*person*] estar para el arrastre*; **those jeans are a bit ~ it** esos vaqueros ya están como para jubilarlos*; **I wouldn't put it ~ him*** no me extrañaría en él, lo creo capaz hasta de eso
Ⓒ ADJ 1 (= *previous*) [*occasion*] anterior; **~ experience tells me not to trust him** sé por experiencia que no debo fiarme de él; **I'm not interested in his ~ life** no me interesa su pasado; **we must have met in a ~ life** seguro que nos hemos conocido en una vida anterior; **in ~ years** en años anteriores
2 (= *former*) antiguo; **~ president of …** antiguo presidente de …, ex presidente de …; **her ~ and present pupils** sus alumnos de ayer y de hoy
3 (= *most recent, last*) último; **the ~ few weeks have been hell** las últimas semanas han sido un verdadero infierno; **she has got worse in the ~ few days** su condición ha empeorado en los últimos días; **what has happened over the ~ week/year?** ¿qué ha pasado en la última semana/el último año?
4 (= *over*) **all that is ~ now** todo eso ya ha pasado, todo eso ya ha quedado atrás; **what's ~ is ~** lo pasado, pasado (está); **those days are ~ now** aquellos tiempos pasaron ya; **for some time ~** de un tiempo a esta parte; **in times ~** antiguamente, antaño (*liter*)
5 ✦**IDIOM to be a ~ master at (doing) sth** ser un maestro consumado en (hacer) algo
Ⓓ N 1 (= *past times*) **the ~** el pasado; **you mustn't dwell on the ~** no debes pensar demasiado en el pasado; **you can't change the ~** no puedes cambiar el pasado; **in the ~ it was considered bad manners to …** antes *or* antiguamente se consideraba de mala educación hacer …; **I've always done it like this in the ~** yo siempre lo he hecho así; **you're living in the ~** estás viviendo en el pasado; **it's a thing of the ~** pertenece a la historia
2 [*of person*] pasado *m*; [*of place*] historia *f*; **a woman with a ~** una mujer con pasado; **a town with a ~** una ciudad con historia
3 (*Ling*) pasado *m*, pretérito *m*
Ⓔ CPD ► **past participle** N (*Ling*) participio *m* pasado *or* pasivo ► **past perfect** N (*Ling*) pluscuamperfecto *m* ► **past tense** N (*Ling*) (tiempo *m*) pasado *m*

pasta ['pæstə] N pasta(s) *f(pl)*

paste [peɪst] Ⓐ N 1 (= *substance, consistency*) pasta *f*; (*Culin*) pasta *f*; (= *glue*) engrudo *m*, cola *f*; **anchovy ~** pasta *f* de anchoas; **fish ~** paté *m* de pescado; **tomato ~** concentrado *m* de tomate
2 (= *diamond-like material*) estrás *m*; (= *costume jewellery*) bisutería *f*, joyas *fpl* de imitación *or* de fantasía; **it's only ~** es bisutería
Ⓑ VT 1 (= *put paste on*) engomar, encolar; (= *stick with paste*) pegar; **to ~ sth into/onto sth** pegar algo a algo; **to ~ sth to a wall** pegar algo a una pared
2 (*) (= *beat*) pegar; (*Sport*) cascar*, dar una paliza a*
Ⓒ CPD [*jewellery*] (*lit*) de estrás; (*costume*) de fantasía

►**paste up** VT + ADV [+ *notice*] pegar; (*Typ*) armar

pasteboard ['peɪstbɔːd] Ⓐ N cartón *m*
Ⓑ CPD de cartón

pastel ['pæstəl] Ⓐ N 1 (= *crayon, colour*) pastel *m*; (= *drawing*) pintura *f* al pastel
2 **pastels** (= *crayons*) pasteles *mpl*; (= *colours*) colores *mpl* pastel
Ⓑ ADJ [*colour, shade, blue*] pastel; [*drawing*] al pastel

pastern ['pæstɜːn] N cuartilla *f* (del caballo)

pasteurization [,pæstəraɪ'zeɪʃən] N paste(u)rización *f*

pasteurize ['pæstəraɪz] VT paste(u)rizar

pasteurized ['pæstəraɪzd] ADJ paste(u)rizado

pastiche [pæs'tiːʃ] N pastiche *m*, imitación *f*

pastille ['pæstɪl] N pastilla *f*

pastime ['pɑːstaɪm] N pasatiempo *m*

pasting* ['peɪstɪŋ] N paliza *f*; **to give sb a ~** dar una paliza a algn; **the city took a ~ during the war** la ciudad fue muy castigada durante la guerra; **he got a ~ from the critics** los críticos fueron muy duros con él

pastor ['pɑːstəʳ] N pastor(a) *m/f*

pastoral ['pɑːstərəl] Ⓐ ADJ [*care, economy*] pastoral; (*Rel*) pastoral; (*Literat*) pastoril; **~ letter** = **B**
Ⓑ N (*Rel*) pastoral *f*

pastrami [pə'strɑːmɪ] N *especie de embutido ahumado a base de carne de vaca con especias*

pastry ['peɪstrɪ] Ⓐ N (= *dough*) masa *f*; (= *cake*) pastel *m*
Ⓑ CPD ► **pastry board** N tabla *f* de amasar ► **pastry brush** N cepillo *m* de repostería ► **pastry case** N cobertura *f* de pasta ► **pastry cook** N pastelero/a *m/f*, repostero/a *m/f* ► **pastry cutter** N cortador *m* de masa ► **pastry shop** N pastelería *f*, repostería *f*

pasturage ['pɑːstjʊrɪdʒ] N = **pastureland**

pasture ['pɑːstʃəʳ] Ⓐ N (= *field*) pasto *m*, prado *m*; (= *pastureland*) tierra(s) *f(pl)* de pastoreo; **to put animals out to ~** apacentar *or* pastorear el ganado; **they're putting me out to ~** (*fig*) (*hum*) me echan al pasto (como a caballo viejo); ✦**IDIOM to seek ~s new** buscar nuevos horizontes
Ⓑ VT [+ *animals*] apacentar, pastorear; [+ *grass*] comer, pacer
Ⓒ VI pastar, pacer

pastureland ['pɑːstʃəlænd] N pradera *f*, tierra(s) *f(pl)* de pastoreo

pasty[1] ['pæstɪ] N (*Brit*) (= *pie*) pastel *m* (de carne), empanada *f*

pasty[2] ['peɪstɪ] ADJ [*substance*] pastoso; [*complexion*] pálido; **to look ~** estar pálido

pasty-faced ['peɪstɪ,feɪst] ADJ pálido, de cara pálida

pat[1] [pæt] Ⓐ N 1 (= *light blow*) palmadita *f*, golpecito *m*; (= *caress*) caricia *f*; **to give sb a ~ on the back** (*lit*) dar a algn una palmada en la espalda; (*fig*) felicitar a algn; **to give o.s. a ~ on the back** (*fig*) felicitarse a sí mismo
2 [*of butter*] porción *f*
Ⓑ VT (= *touch*) [+ *hair, face etc*] tocar, pasar la mano por; (= *tap*) dar una palmadita en; [+ *child's head, dog*] acariciar

pat[2] [pæt] Ⓐ ADV **he knows it (off) ~** lo sabe al dedillo *or* de memoria; **he always has an excuse just ~** siempre tiene su excusa lista; **the answer came too ~** dio su respuesta con demasiada prontitud; ✦**IDIOM to stand ~** (*US*) mantenerse firme *or* en sus trece
Ⓑ ADJ [*answer*] fácil

Pat [pæt] N (*familiar form*) *of* **Patrick, Patricia**

pat. ABBR (= **patent(ed)**) pat.

Patagonia [,pætə'gəʊnɪə] N Patagonia *f*

Patagonian [,pætə'gəʊnɪən] Ⓐ ADJ patagón, patagónico
Ⓑ N patagón/ona *m/f*

patch [pætʃ] Ⓐ N 1 (= *mend*) (*on clothing*) remiendo *m*, parche *m*; (*on tyre, wound*) parche *m*; ✦**IDIOM this book's not a ~ on the other one*** este libro no tiene ni punto de comparación con el otro
2 (= *stain*) mancha *f*; (= *small area*) pedazo *m*; **a ~ of oil** una mancha de aceite; **a ~ of blue sky** un pedazo de cielo azul, un claro; **a ~ of blue flowers** un área de flores azules; **the team is going through a bad ~** el equipo está pasando por una mala racha; **then we hit a bad ~ of road** dimos luego con un tramo de carretera bastante malo
3 (= *piece of land*) parcela *f*, terreno *m*; *see also* **vegetable B**
4 (*) (= *territory*) territorio *m*; **but this is their ~** pero éste es territorio de ellos; **they must get off our ~** tienen que largarse de nuestro territorio*
5 (*Comput*) ajuste *m*
Ⓑ VT [+ *garment, hole*] remendar, poner re-

miendos a; **a pair of ~ed jeans** unos vaqueros con remiendos

►**patch together** VT + ADV [+ *solution, agreement, coalition, government*] improvisar

►**patch up** VT + ADV [+ *clothes*] remendar provisionalmente; [+ *car, machine*] arreglar provisionalmente; [+ *cut, wound*] vendar; [+ *marriage, relationship*] salvar; **the doctor soon ~ed him up** el doctor enseguida le curó las heridas; **to ~ things up (with sb)** hacer las paces (con algn); **they ~ed up their differences** resolvieron sus diferencias

patchwork ['pætʃwɜːk] Ⓐ N [1] labor *f* de retazos, arpillería *f* (*LAm*)
[2] (*fig*) **a ~ of fields** un mosaico de campos; **their policy is a ~ of half-measures** su política es un conjunto fragmentario de medias tintas
Ⓑ CPD ► **patchwork quilt** N edredón *m* de retazos multicolores

patchy ['pætʃɪ] ADJ (*compar* **patchier**; *superl* **patchiest**) [*performance*] desigual, poco uniforme; [*knowledge*] incompleto; [*clouds*] disperso; [*fog*] discontinuo

pate† [peɪt] N mollera *f*, testa *f*; **bald ~** calva *f*

pâté ['pæteɪ] N paté *m*

patella [pə'telə] N (*pl* **patellae** [pə'teliː]) rótula *f*

paten ['pætən] N patena *f*

patent ['peɪtənt] Ⓐ ADJ [1] (*frm*) (= *obvious*) patente, evidente
[2] (= *patented*) [*invention*] patentado
Ⓑ N patente *f*; **~ applied for** ◊ **~ pending** patente en trámite; **to take out a ~** obtener una patente
Ⓒ VT patentar
Ⓓ CPD ► **patent agent** N agente *mf* de patentes ► **Patent and Trademark Office** N (*US*) = **Patent Office** ► **patent law** N derecho *m* de patentes ► **patent leather** N charol *m* ► **patent medicine** N específico *m* ► **patent office** N oficina *f* de patentes ► **Patent Office** N (*Brit*) *registro de la propiedad industrial* ► **patent rights** NPL derechos *mpl* de patente

patentable ['peɪtəntəbl] ADJ patentable

patentee [,peɪtən'tiː] N poseedor(a) *m/f* de patente

patently ['peɪtəntlɪ] ADV evidentemente; **to be ~ obvious** saltar a la vista, ser evidente; **a ~ untrue statement** una declaración de evidente falsedad

patentor ['peɪtəntəʳ] N *individuo u organismo que otorga una patente*

pater†* ['peɪtəʳ] N (*esp Brit*) **the ~** el viejo*

paterfamilias ['peɪtəfə'mɪlɪæs] N (*pl* **patresfamilias** [,pɑːtreɪzfə'mɪlɪæs]) padre *m* de familia

paternal [pə'tɜːnl] ADJ [1] (= *fatherly*) [*love, feelings*] paterno, paternal; [*authority*] paterno; [*pride*] de padre
[2] (= *on the father's side*) [*grandparent*] por parte de padre, paterno

paternalism [pə'tɜːnəlɪzəm] N paternalismo *m*

paternalist [pə'tɜːnəlɪst] ADJ paternalista

paternalistic [pə,tɜːnə'lɪstɪk] ADJ paternalista

paternally [pə'tɜːnəlɪ] ADV paternalmente; **he said ~** dijo paternal

paternity [pə'tɜːnɪtɪ] Ⓐ N paternidad *f*
Ⓑ CPD ► **paternity leave** N permiso *m* por paternidad, licencia *f* de paternidad ► **paternity suit** N (*Jur*) litigio *m* de paternidad ► **paternity test** N prueba *f* de la paternidad

paternoster ['pætə'nɒstəʳ] N padrenuestro *m*

path [pɑːθ] N (*pl* **paths** [pɑːðz]) [1] (*also* **~way, footpath**) (= *track*) (*surfaced*) camino *m*; (*unsurfaced*) camino *m*, sendero *m*; **feet had worn a ~ in the rock** las pisadas habían formado un camino *or* un sendero sobre la piedra; **they hacked a ~ through the jungle** se abrieron camino a machetazos a través de la jungla; *see also* **cycle C**, **garden C**
[2] (= *course*) [*of person, vehicle*] camino *m*; [*of missile, sun, storm*] trayectoria *f*; **the earth's ~ round the sun** la trayectoria de la tierra alrededor del sol; **the hurricane destroyed everything in its ~** el huracán destruyó todo a su paso; **he stepped into the ~ of an oncoming car** se cruzó en el camino de un coche que se acercaba; *see also* **flight**
[3] (= *way forward*) paso *m*; **a group of reporters blocked his ~** un grupo de periodistas le cerraba el paso
[4] (*fig*) [4·1] (= *route*) camino *m*; **I hope never to cross ~s with him again** espero no volvérmelo a encontrar nunca, espero no volver a toparme con él nunca; **our ~s first crossed in Milan** nuestros caminos se cruzaron por primera vez en Milán, la primera vez que coincidimos fue en Milán; **these measures helped smooth the ~ to independence** estas medidas ayudaron a allanar *or* facilitar el camino hacia la independencia; ✦**IDIOM to beat a ~ to sb's door** asediar a algn; *see also* **garden, primrose C**
[4·2] (= *course of action*) **I wouldn't go down that ~ if I were you** yo en tu lugar no haría eso

pathetic [pə'θetɪk] Ⓐ ADJ [1] (= *piteous*) [*sight*] patético, lastimoso; [*smile*] conmovedor; **it was ~ to see him like that** daba verdadera lástima *or* pena verlo así; **a ~ creature** un pobre infeliz
[2] (*) (= *useless*) [*excuse, attempt*] pobre; **it was a ~ performance** fue una actuación penosa *or* que daba pena; **~, isn't it?** da pena ¿no?
Ⓑ CPD ► **pathetic fallacy** N (*Literat*) engaño *m* sentimental, falacia *f* patética

pathetically [pə'θetɪklɪ] ADV [1] (= *piteously*) [*whimper, moan*] lastimeramente; [*say*] con voz lastimera; **~ thin/weak** tan delgado/débil que da/daba pena; **she was ~ grateful** su gratitud resultaba penosa
[2] (= *uselessly*) [*play, perform*] que da/daba pena; **a ~ inadequate answer** una respuesta patética

pathfinder ['pɑːθ,faɪndəʳ] N explorador(a) *m/f*; (*Mil*) *avión o paracaidista que indica un objetivo militar dejando caer bengalas*

pathogen ['pæθəʊdʒen] N patógeno *m*

pathogenic [pæθə'dʒenɪk] ADJ patógeno

pathological [,pæθə'lɒdʒɪkəl] ADJ (*lit, fig*) patológico

pathologically [,pæθə'lɒdʒɪkəlɪ] ADV patológicamente; **to be ~ jealous** tener celos patológicos

pathologist [pə'θɒlədʒɪst] N patólogo/a *m/f*

pathology [pə'θɒlədʒɪ] N patología *f*

pathos ['peɪθɒs] N patetismo *m*

pathway ['pɑːθweɪ] N camino *m*, sendero *m*; = **path A1**

patience ['peɪʃəns] N [1] paciencia *f*; **my ~ is exhausted** se me ha acabado *or* agotado la paciencia; **you must have ~** hay que tener paciencia; **I have no ~ with you** ya no te aguanto más; **he has no ~ with fools** no soporta a los tontos; **to lose one's ~ (with sth/sb)** perder la paciencia (con algo/algn); **to try sb's ~** poner a prueba la paciencia de algn; ✦**IDIOMS to have the ~ of a saint** tener más paciencia que un santo; **to possess one's soul in ~** armarse de paciencia
[2] (*Brit Cards*) solitario *m*; **to play ~** hacer un solitario

patient¹ ['peɪʃənt] ADJ [*person*] paciente; [*explanation*] detallado; **to be ~** tener paciencia; **you must be ~** hay que tener paciencia; **we have been ~ long enough!** ¡se nos está acabando *or* agotando la paciencia!; **to be ~ with sb** tener paciencia con algn

patient² ['peɪʃənt] Ⓐ N (*on doctor's list*) paciente *mf*; (*having medical treatment*) enfermo/a *m/f*; *see also* **cancer**, **mental**
Ⓑ CPD ► **patient care** N cuidado *m* de los enfermos

patiently ['peɪʃəntlɪ] ADV con paciencia, pacientemente

patina ['pætɪnə] N pátina *f*

patio ['pætɪəʊ] Ⓐ N patio *m*
Ⓑ CPD ► **patio doors** NPL puertas *fpl* que dan al patio

patois ['pætwɑː] N (*pl* **patois**) dialecto *m*, jerga *f*

pat. pend. ABBR = **patent pending**

patriarch ['peɪtrɪɑːk] N (*Rel*) patriarca *m*

patriarchal [,peɪtrɪ'ɑːkəl] ADJ patriarcal

patriarchy ['peɪtrɪ,ɑːkɪ] N patriarcado *m*

Patricia [pə'trɪʃə] N Patricia

patrician [pə'trɪʃən] Ⓐ ADJ patricio
Ⓑ N patricio/a *m/f*

patricide ['pætrɪsaɪd] N (= *crime*) patricidio *m*; (= *person*) patricida *mf*

Patrick ['pætrɪk] N Patricio

patrimony ['pætrɪmənɪ] N patrimonio *m*

patriot ['peɪtrɪət] N patriota *mf*

patriotic [,pætrɪ'ɒtɪk] ADJ patriótico

patriotically ['pætrɪ'ɒtɪkəlɪ] ADV patrióticamente

patriotism ['pætrɪətɪzəm] N patriotismo *m*

patrol [pə'trəʊl] Ⓐ N (*gen*) patrulla *f*; (= *night patrol*) ronda *f*; (*in Scouts*) patrulla *f*; **to be on ~** estar de patrulla
Ⓑ VT [+ *streets*] patrullar por; [+ *frontier*] patrullar; **the frontier is not ~led** la frontera no tiene patrullas
Ⓒ VI patrullar; **he ~s up and down** se pasea de un lado a otro
Ⓓ CPD ► **patrol boat** N patrullero *m*, (lancha *f*) patrullera *f* ► **patrol car** N (*Brit*) coche *m* patrulla ► **patrol leader** N jefe *m* de patrulla ► **patrol wagon** N (*US*) coche *m* celular

patrolman [pə'trəʊlmən] N (*pl* **patrolmen**) [1] (*US*) guardia *m*, policía *m*
[2] (*Aut*) *mecánico del servicio de ayuda en carretera*

patrolwoman [pə'trəʊl,wʊmən] N (*pl* **patrolwomen**) (*US*) mujer *f* policía; (*Brit Aut*) *mecánica del servicio de ayuda en carretera*

patron ['peɪtrən] Ⓐ N [*of charity, society*] patrocinador(a) *m/f*; (*Comm*) [*of shop, hotel*] cliente/a *m/f*; **a ~ of the arts** un mecenas
Ⓑ CPD ► **patron saint** N patrono/a *m/f*

patronage ['pætrənɪdʒ] N (= *support*) patrocinio *m*; (= *clients*) clientela *f*; [*of the arts*] mecenazgo *m*; (*political*) apoyo *m*; (*Rel*) patronato *m*; **under the ~ of** patrocinado por, bajo los auspicios de

patroness ['peɪtrənes] N [*of enterprise*] patrocinadora *f*; [*of the arts*] mecenas *f*

patronize ['pætrənaɪz] VT [1] (= *treat condescendingly*) tratar con condescendencia
[2] (= *be customer of*) [+ *shop*] ser cliente de, comprar en; [+ *hotel, cinema*] frecuentar; [+ *services*] usar, utilizar; **the shop is well ~d** la tienda tiene mucha clientela, la tienda está muy acreditada
[3] (= *support*) [+ *enterprise*] patrocinar, apoyar

patronizing ['pætrənaɪzɪŋ] ADJ *[person, attitude]* condescendiente; **a few ~ remarks** unas cuantas observaciones dichas en tono condescendiente

patronizingly ['pætrənaɪzɪŋlɪ] ADV con condescendencia

patronymic [,pætrə'nɪmɪk] Ⓐ ADJ patronímico Ⓑ N patronímico *m*

patsy* ['pætsɪ] N (*US*) bobo/a *m/f*, primo* *m*

patten ['pætn] N zueco *m*, chanclo *m*

patter¹* ['pætəʳ] Ⓐ N (= *talk*) labia *f*; [*of salesman*] rollo* *m*, discursito* *m*; **the guy has some very clever ~** el tipo *or* (*Sp*) el tío tiene unos argumentos muy hábiles
Ⓑ VI (*also* **to ~ on**) charlar, parlotear (**about** de)

patter² ['pætəʳ] Ⓐ N [*of feet*] golpeteo *m*; [*of rain*] tamborileo *m*; **we shall soon hear the ~ of tiny feet** (*hum*) pronto habrá un niño en la casa
Ⓑ VI [*feet*] golpetear; (*rain*) golpetear, tamborilear; (*also* **to ~ about**) [*person, small animal*] corretear; **he ~ed over to the door** fue con pasos ligeros a la puerta

pattern ['pætən] Ⓐ N 1 (= *design*) dibujo *m*; **a fabric in** *or* **with a floral ~** una tela con un dibujo *or* diseño floral; **to draw a ~** hacer un dibujo
2 (*Sew, Knitting*) patrón *m*, molde *m* (*S. Cone*)
3 (*fig*) (= *system, order*) **a clear ~ began to emerge** empezaron a surgir unas pautas definidas; **behaviour ~** modelo *m* de comportamiento; **a healthy eating ~** unos hábitos alimenticios sanos; **the ~ of events** el curso de los hechos; **to follow a ~** seguir unas pautas; **my daily routine doesn't follow any set ~** mi rutina diaria no sigue unas pautas definidas; **it is following the usual ~** se está desarrollando como siempre *or* según las pautas; **a system of government on the British ~** un sistema de gobierno basado en el modelo británico; **it set a ~ for other conferences** marcó las pautas para otros congresos, creó el modelo para otros congresos; **sleep ~(s)** hábitos *mpl* de dormir; **weather ~(s)** condiciones *fpl* meteorológicas; **work ~(s)** costumbres *fpl* de trabajo
Ⓑ VT 1 (= *model*) **to ~ sth after** *or* **on sth**: **a building ~ed after a 14th century chapel** un edificio modelado sobre una capilla del siglo XIV; **action movies ~ed on Rambo** películas *fpl* de acción que siguen el modelo de Rambo
2 (= *mark*) estampar
Ⓒ CPD ► **pattern book** N [*of wallpaper, fabrics*] muestrario *m*; (*Sew, Knitting*) libro *m* de patrones ► **pattern recognition** N reconocimiento *m* de formas

patterned ['pætənd] ADJ estampado

patterning ['pætənɪŋ] N diseño *m*, dibujo *m*

pattern-maker ['pætən'meɪkəʳ] N carpintero/a *m/f* modelista

patty ['pætɪ] N empanada *f*

paucity ['pɔːsɪtɪ] N escasez *f*, insuficiencia *f*

Paul [pɔːl] N Pablo; (= *Saint*) Pablo; (= *Pope*) Paulo; *see also* **John**

Pauline¹ ['pɔːlaɪn] ADJ **the ~ Epistles** las Epístolas de San Pablo

Pauline² [pɔː'liːn] N Paulina

paunch [pɔːntʃ] N panza* *f*, barriga* *f*; **to have a ~** tener panza*, ser barrigón*

paunchy ['pɔːntʃɪ] ADJ panzudo*, barrigudo*

pauper ['pɔːpəʳ] N pobre *mf*, indigente *mf*; **~'s grave** fosa *f* común

pauperism ['pɔːpərɪzəm] N pauperismo *m*

pauperization [,pɔːpəraɪ'zeɪʃən] N pauperización *f*, empobrecimiento *m*

pauperize ['pɔːpəraɪz] VT pauperizar, empobrecer

pause [pɔːz] Ⓐ N 1 (= *interruption*) pausa *f* (*also Mus*); (= *silence*) silencio *m*; (= *rest*) descanso *m*; **after a moment's ~ he went on speaking** tras una breve pausa continuó hablando; **there was a ~ while the rest came in** se hizo una pausa mientras entraban los demás; **there was a ~ for refreshments** hubo un descanso para tomar refrigerios; **there was an awkward ~ in the conversation** se produjo un silencio incómodo en medio de la conversación; **to give sb ~** ◊ **give ~ to sb** hacer vacilar a algn; **to give sb ~ for thought** dar que pensar a algn; **without (a) ~** sin interrupción
2 (*on cassette-player*) botón *m* de pausa
Ⓑ VI (*in activity*) hacer un descanso; (*when speaking*) callarse (momentáneamente), detenerse; (*when moving*) detenerse; **we ~d for a break half-way through the afternoon** paramos a descansar a media tarde; **let's ~ here** hagamos un descanso aquí; **it made him ~** le hizo vacilar; **to ~ for breath** detenerse para tomar aliento
Ⓒ CPD ► **pause button** N botón *m* de pausa

pave [peɪv] VT (*gen*) pavimentar; (*with flagstones*) enlosar; (*with stones*) adoquinar, empedrar; (*with bricks*) enladrillar; **the streets are ~d with gold** se atan los perros con longaniza; ✦***IDIOM*** **to ~ the way for sth/sb** preparar el terreno para algo/algn

paved [peɪvd] ADJ *[road]* asfaltado, pavimentado; (*with flagstones, tiles*) [*garden, courtyard, path*] enlosado

pavement ['peɪvmənt] Ⓐ N (*Brit*) acera *f*, vereda *f* (*LAm*), andén *m* (*CAm, Col*), banqueta *f* (*Mex*); (*US*) calzada *f*, pavimento *m*; **brick ~** enladrillado *m*; **stone ~** empedrado *m*, adoquinado *m*; **to leave the ~** (*US Aut*) salir de la calzada
Ⓑ CPD ► **pavement artist** N pintor(a) *m/f* callejero/a ► **pavement café** N café *m* con terraza, café *m* al aire libre

pavilion [pə'vɪlɪən] N (*for band*) quiosco *m*; (*Sport*) caseta *f*, vestuario *m*; (*at trade fair*) pabellón *m*

paving ['peɪvɪŋ] Ⓐ N [*of concrete*] pavimento *m*; [*of flagstones*] enlosado *m*; [*of stones*] adoquinado *m*, empedrado *m*; [*of brick*] enladrillado *m*
Ⓑ CPD ► **paving stone** N adoquín *m*, baldosa *f* (*LAm*); (= *flagstone*) losa *f*

Pavlovian [pæv'ləʊvɪən] ADJ pavloviano

paw [pɔː] Ⓐ N 1 [*of animal*] pata *f*; [*of cat*] garra *f*; [*of lion*] zarpa *f*, garra *f*
2 (*) (= *hand*) manaza* *f*
Ⓑ VT 1 [*animal*] tocar con la pata; [*lion*] dar zarpazos a; **to ~ the ground** [*horse*] piafar
2 (*pej*) (= *touch*) [+ *person*] manosear, tocar; (*amorously*) sobar; **stop ~ing me!** ¡fuera las manos!
Ⓒ VI **to ~ at sth** [*animal*] tocar algo con la pata; (*to wound*) dar zarpazos a algo

pawl [pɔːl] N trinquete *m*

pawn¹ [pɔːn] N (*Chess*) peón *m*; (*fig*) instrumento *m*; **they simply used me as a ~** se aprovecharon de mí como mero instrumento; **he was just a ~ in their game** era sólo un títere en sus manos

pawn² [pɔːn] Ⓐ N **to be in ~** estar en prenda, estar empeñado; **the country is in ~ to foreigners** el país está empeñado a extranjeros; **to leave** *or* **put sth in ~** dejar algo en prenda, empeñar algo
Ⓑ VT empeñar
Ⓒ CPD ► **pawn ticket** N papeleta *f* de empeño

pawnbroker ['pɔːn,brəʊkəʳ] N prestamista *mf*; **~'s** = **pawnshop**

pawnshop ['pɔːnʃɒp] N monte *m* de piedad, casa *f* de empeños

pawpaw ['pɔːpɔː] N 1 (*Brit*) = **papaya**
2 (*US*) asimina *f*, chirimoya *f*

pax [pæks] N 1 **pax!** (*Brit*) ¡me rindo!
2 (*Rel*) beso *m* de la paz

pay [peɪ] (*vb: pt, pp* **paid**) Ⓐ N (= *wages*) [*of professional person*] sueldo *m*; [*of worker*] salario *m*, sueldo *m*; [*of day labourer*] jornal *m*; (= *payment*) paga *f*; **the ~'s not very good** no pagan muy bien; **to draw** *or* **get one's ~** cobrar; **to be in sb's ~** estar al servicio de algn; **agents in the enemy's ~** agentes *mpl* al servicio del enemigo
Ⓑ VT 1 [+ *bill, duty, fee*] pagar; [+ *account*] liquidar; [+ *debt*] saldar, liquidar; [+ *employee, worker*] pagar a; **to ~ sb £10** pagar 10 libras a algn; **how much is there to ~?** ¿cuánto hay que pagar?; **to ~ sb to do a job** pagar a algn para que haga un trabajo; **"paid"** (*on receipted bill*) "pagado"; **to ~ sth on account** pagar algo a cuenta; **a badly paid worker** un obrero mal pagado; **to ~ cash (down)** pagar al contado; **I paid £5 for that record** pagué 5 libras por ese disco; **how much did you ~ for it?** ¿cuánto pagaste por él?, ¿cuánto te costó?; **that's what you're paid for** para eso te pagan; **it's a service that has to be paid for** es un servicio que hay que pagar; **to be** *or* **get paid on Fridays** cobrar los viernes; **when do you get paid?** ¿cuándo cobras?; **does your current account ~ interest?** ¿le rinde intereses su cuenta corriente?; **to ~ money into an account** ingresar dinero en una cuenta; **to ~ one's way** pagarse los gastos; *see also* **paid**
2 (= *be profitable to*) **it wouldn't ~ him to do it** (*lit*) no le compensaría hacerlo; (*fig*) no le valdría la pena hacerlo; **but it paid him in the long run** pero a la larga le fue provechoso
3 [+ *attention*] prestar (**to** a); [+ *homage*] rendir (**to** a); [+ *respects*] ofrecer, presentar; **to ~ sb a visit** *or* **call** ◊ **to ~ a visit to** *or* **a call on sb** ir a ver a algn; *see also* **heed**, **penalty A1**, **respect A1**
Ⓒ VI 1 pagar; **don't worry, I'll ~** no te preocupes, lo pago yo; **to ~ in advance** pagar por adelantado; **can I ~ by cheque?** ¿puedo pagar con cheque?; **to ~ for sth** pagar algo; **they paid for her to go** pagaron para que fuera; **to ~ in full** pagarlo todo, pagar la cantidad íntegra; **to ~ in instalments** pagar a plazos
2 [*job*] **his job ~s well** tiene un buen sueldo, el trabajo le paga bien
3 (= *be profitable*) [*business*] rendir, ser rentable; **the business doesn't ~** el negocio no es rentable; **it ~s to advertise** compensa hacer publicidad; **it ~s to be courteous/tell the truth** vale la pena ser cortés/decir la verdad; *see also* **crime**
4 (*fig*) (= *suffer*) pagar; **she paid for it with her life** le costó la vida; **they made him ~ dearly for it** le hicieron pagarlo muy caro; **you'll ~ for this!** ¡me las pagarás!
Ⓓ CPD ► **pay as you earn** (*Brit*), **pay-as-you-go** (*US*) N retención *f* fiscal (hecha por la empresa) ► **pay award** N adjudicación *f* de aumento de salarios ► **pay bargaining** N negociación *f* salarial ► **pay bed** N cama *f* de pago ► **pay cheque** N cheque *m* de la paga; (= *salary*) sueldo *m* ► **pay desk** N caja *f*

► **pay dirt** N (*US*) grava *f* provechosa; ✦*IDIOM* **to hit** *or* **strike ~ dirt** dar con un filón de oro ► **pay envelope** N (*US*) sobre *m* de la paga ► **pay increase** N incremento *m* salarial ► **pay negotiations** NPL negociaciones *fpl* salariales ► **pay office** N caja *f*, pagaduría *f* ► **pay packet** N (*Brit*) sobre *m* de la paga ► **pay pause**† N congelación *f* de sueldos y salarios ► **pay phone** N (*Brit*) teléfono *m* público ► **pay policy** N política *f* salarial ► **pay rise** N incremento *m* salarial ► **pay round** N serie *f* de negociaciones salariales ► **pay scale** N escala *f* salarial ► **pay slip** N nómina *f*, hoja *f* salarial *or* de sueldo ► **pay station** N (*US*) teléfono *m* público ► **pay structure** N estructura *f* salarial ► **pay talks** NPL = **pay negotiations** ► **pay television** N televisión *f* de pago

►**pay back** VT + ADV [1] [+ *money*] devolver; (*frm*) restituir, reintegrar; [+ *loan*] pagar [2] [+ *person*] **to ~ sb back for sth/doing sth**: **I'll ~ you back for the meal tomorrow** te devuelvo el dinero de la comida mañana; **I'll never be able to ~ you back for all you've done** nunca podré corresponderte por todo lo que has hecho; **I'll ~ you back for betraying me!** te voy a hacer pagar caro tu traición; **I'll ~ you back for this!** ¡me las vas a pagar!; ✦*IDIOM* **to ~ sb back in his own coin** pagar a algn con la misma moneda

►**pay in** (A) VT + ADV [+ *money*] ingresar, depositar; [+ *cheque*] ingresar, abonar (B) VI + ADV (*at bank*) ingresar dinero

►**pay off** (A) VT + ADV [1] [+ *debt*] liquidar, saldar; [+ *mortgage*] amortizar; **to ~ sth off in instalments** pagar algo a plazos; **to ~ off old scores** ajustar cuentas [2] (= *discharge*) [+ *workers, crew*] pagar y despedir (B) VI + ADV merecer *or* valer la pena; **the gamble paid off** mereció *or* valió la pena arriesgarse; **his efforts paid off** sus esfuerzos merecieron *or* valieron la pena; **the investment paid off handsomely** la inversión bien mereció la pena *or* dió muy buenos frutos; **when do you think it will begin to ~ off?** ¿cuándo piensas que empezará a dar resultado?

►**pay out** (A) VT + ADV [1] [+ *money*] (*for purchase*) gastar, desembolsar; (*to shareholder, prizewinner*) pagar [2] [+ *rope*] ir soltando [3] (†) (*fig*) desquitarse con; **I'll ~ you out for this!** ¡me las pagarás! (B) VI + ADV **to ~ out on a policy** pagar una póliza

►**pay up** (A) VT + ADV [+ *insurance premiums, subscription*] abonar; **first you must ~ up what you owe** primero debe abonar la deuda; **I was not worried because I knew my insurance policy was paid up** no estaba preocupada porque sabía que los pagos de mi póliza de seguros estaban al día (B) VI + ADV pagar (lo que se debe); **~ up!** ¡a pagar!

payable [ˈpeɪəbl] ADJ pagadero; **~ to bearer** pagadero al portador; **~ on demand** pagadero a presentación *or* a vista; **to make a cheque ~ to sb** extender un cheque a favor de algn

pay-and-display [ˌpeɪəndɪsˈpleɪ] ADJ (*Brit*) [*car park*] de pago (*colocando el ticket en el interior del parabrisas*)

payback [ˈpeɪbæk] (A) N restitución *f* (B) CPD ► **payback period** N período *m* de restitución

paycheck [ˈpeɪtʃek] N (*US*) cheque *m* de la paga; (= *salary*) sueldo *m*

payday [ˈpeɪdeɪ] N día *m* de paga

PAYE N ABBR (*Brit*) = **pay as you earn**; *see* **pay D**

payee [peɪˈiː] N portador(a) *m/f*, tenedor(a) *m/f*; (*on cheque*) beneficiario/a *m/f*; **"account payee only"** (*on cheque*) "cuenta *f* nominal"

payer [ˈpeɪəʳ] N pagador(a) *m/f*; **slow ~** ◊ **bad ~** moroso/a *m/f*

paying [ˈpeɪɪŋ] (A) ADJ provechoso, rentable; **it's a ~ proposition** es un negocio provechoso (B) CPD ► **paying bank** N banco *m* pagador ► **paying guest** N huésped(a) *m/f* (de pago), pensionista *mf*

paying-in slip [ˌpeɪɪŋˈɪnˌslɪp], **pay-in slip** [ˌpeɪˈɪnˌslɪp] N hoja *f* de ingreso

payload [ˈpeɪləʊd] N carga *f* útil

paymaster [ˈpeɪmɑːstəʳ] (A) N [1] (oficial *m*) pagador *m* [2] (*pej*) **the ~s of terrorism** los mecenas del terrorismo (B) CPD ► **Paymaster General** N (*Brit*) *encargado del departamento del ministerio de Hacienda a través del que se paga a los funcionarios públicos*

payment [ˈpeɪmənt] (A) N [1] [*of salary, debt, invoice*] pago *m*; (*for services*) remuneración *f*; **~ of this invoice is now due** ya hay que hacer efectivo el pago de esta factura; **I don't expect ~ for my help** no espero que me paguen por mi ayuda, no espero remuneración por mi ayuda; **as ~ for your help** como pago por tu ayuda; **in ~ for/of** en pago por/de; **to make a ~** efectuar un pago; **to make a ~ into one's account** hacer un depósito *or* (*Sp*) un ingreso en cuenta; **on ~ of £5** mediante pago de cinco libras, pagando cinco libras; **to present sth for ~** presentar algo para el cobro; *see also* **advance D**, **kind B2**, **maintenance B** [2] (= *instalment*) plazo *m*; **ten monthly ~s of £50** diez plazos mensuales *or* diez mensualidades de 50 libras; **to fall behind with one's/the ~s** atrasarse en los pagos; **to keep up one's/the ~s** mantenerse al día con los pagos [3] (*fig*) (= *reward*) recompensa *f*, retribución *f*; **a stream of abuse was the only ~ he received** la única recompensa *or* retribución que recibió fue una sarta de insultos (B) CPD ► **payment card** N tarjeta *f* de pago

payoff* [ˈpeɪɒf] N [1] (= *payment*) pago *m*; [*of debt*] liquidación *f* (total) [2] (= *reward*) recompensa *f*, beneficios *mpl* [3] (= *vengeance*) ajuste *m* de cuentas, castigo *m* [4] (= *bribe*) soborno *m*, coima *f* (*Andes, S. Cone*), mordida *f* (*CAm, Mex*) [5] (= *final outcome, climax*) momento *m* decisivo, desenlace *m*

payola* [peɪˈəʊlə] N (*US*) soborno *m*, coima *f* (*Andes, S. Cone*), mordida *f* (*CAm, Mex*)

payout [ˈpeɪaʊt] N pago *m*; (= *share-out*) reparto *m*; (*in competition*) premio *m* en metálico; (*from insurance*) indemnización *f*

pay-per-click [ˌpeɪpəˈklɪk] (A) N pago *m* por click (B) ADJ de pago por click

pay-per-view [ˌpeɪpəˈvjuː] ADJ de pago; **~ television** televisión *f* de pago

payroll [ˈpeɪrəʊl] (A) N nómina *f* (de sueldos); **to be on a firm's ~** estar en la nómina de una empresa; **he has 1000 people on his ~** tiene una nómina de 1000 empleados (B) CPD ► **payroll tax** N impuesto *m* sobre la nómina

PB ABBR (*Sport*) (= **personal best**) marca *f* personal

PBAB ABBR = **please bring a bottle**

PBS N ABBR (*US*) = **Public Broadcasting Service**

PBX N ABBR (*Telec*) (= **private branch exchange**) *centralita para extensiones*

PC (A) N ABBR [1] (= **personal computer**) PC *m*, OP *m* [2] (*Brit*) (= **police constable**) policía *mf* [3] (*Brit*) = **Privy Councillor** (B) ADJ ABBR (*) = **politically correct**

pc N ABBR = **postcard**

p.c. ABBR (= **per cent**) p.c.

P/C, p/c ABBR [1] (*St Ex*) (= **prices current**) cotizaciones *fpl* [2] (*Comm*) = **petty cash**

PCA N ABBR [1] (*Brit*) = **Police Complaints Authority** [2] = **Professional Chess Association**

PCB N ABBR [1] (= **printed circuit board**) TCI *f* [2] (= **polychlorinated biphenyl**) PCB *m*

PCC N ABBR (*Brit*) = **Press Complaints Commission**

PCFC N ABBR = **Polytechnics and Colleges Funding Council**

PCI N ABBR (= **Peripheral Component Interconnect**) PCI *m*

pcm ADV ABBR (= **per calendar month**) p/mes

PCP® N ABBR [1] (*Drugs*) (= **phencyclidine**) fenciclidina *f* [2] (*Med*) = **pneumocystis carinii pneumonia**

PD N ABBR (*US*) = **police department**

pd ABBR (= **paid**) pgdo.

PDA N ABBR (= **personal digital assistant**) agenda *f* electrónica, PDA *m*

PDF N ABBR (= **Portable Document Format**) PDF *m*

pdq* ADV ABBR = **pretty damn quick**

PDSA N ABBR (*Brit*) = **People's Dispensary for Sick Animals**

PDT N ABBR (*US*) = **Pacific Daylight Time**

PE (A) N ABBR (= **physical education**) ed. física (B) ABBR (*Canada*) = **Prince Edward Island**

pea [piː] (A) N guisante *m* (*Sp*), chícharo *m* (*CAm*), arveja *f* (*LAm*), alverja *f* (*LAm*); **sweet ~** guisante *m* de olor (*Sp*), clarín *m* (*Chile*); *see also* **like¹ A** (B) CPD ► **pea soup** N sopa *f* de guisantes *etc*

peace [piːs] (A) N paz *f*; **to be at ~** (*euph*) (= *dead*) descansar en paz; **Egypt is at ~ with Israel** Egipto está en paz con Israel; **a world at ~** un mundo donde reine la paz *or* donde haya paz; **I am at ~ with my conscience** estoy en paz con mi conciencia; **to be at ~ with o.s.** estar en paz consigo mismo; **we come in ~**† (*also hum*) venimos en son de paz; **to disturb the ~** perturbar la paz; (*Jur*) alterar el orden público; **he gave her no ~ until she agreed** no la dejó tranquila *or* en paz hasta que accedió; **to hold** *or* **keep one's ~** guardar silencio; **speak now or forever hold your ~** hable ahora o calle para siempre; **to keep the ~** (*gen*) mantener la paz *or* el orden; (*Jur*) [*citizen*] respetar el orden público; [*police*] mantener el orden público; **to leave sb in ~** dejar a algn tranquilo *or* en paz; **to live in ~ (with sb)** vivir en paz (con algn); **to make ~ (with sb)** hacer las paces (con algn); **~ of mind** tranquilidad *f* (de espíritu); **anything for the sake of ~ and quiet** lo que sea por un poco de tranquilidad; **the ~ and quiet of the woods** la tranquilidad del bosque; **in times of ~** en tiempos de paz; *see also* **breach A1**, **rest¹ C1** (B) CPD [*agreement, plan, settlement*] de paz; [*campaign, conference*] por la paz ► **peace camp** N campamento *m* por la paz ► **peace campaigner** N *persona que participa en una campaña por la paz* ► **peace conference** N conferencia *f* de paz ► **Peace Corps** N (*US*) Cuerpo *m* de Paz ► **peace dividend** N beneficios *mpl* reportados por la paz ► **peace initiative** N iniciativa *f* de paz ► **peace movement** N movimiento *m* pacifista

➤ LANGUAGE IN USE: **payment A1** 20.1, 20.6, 20.7, 21.4

► **peace offering** N (*fig*) prenda *f* de paz ► **peace pipe** N pipa *f* de la paz ► **the peace process** N el proceso de paz ► **peace settlement** N acuerdo *m* de paz ► **peace sign** N señal *f* de paz ► **peace studies** NPL (*Univ*) estudios *mpl* de la paz ► **peace talks** NPL negociaciones *fpl* por la paz ► **peace treaty** N tratado *m* de paz

peaceable ['pi:səbl] ADJ pacífico

peaceably ['pi:səblɪ] ADV [*live, settle*] pacíficamente

peaceful ['pi:sfʊl] ADJ [1] (= *non-violent*) [*person, tribe, nation*] pacífico; [*demonstration, protest*] pacífico, no violento; **to live in ~ coexistence (with sb)** convivir pacíficamente (con algn); **to change society by** *or* **through ~ means** cambiar la sociedad por medios pacíficos; **to seek a ~ solution to a conflict** buscar una solución pacífica a un conflicto; **the ~ uses of atomic energy** los usos de la energía atómica para fines pacíficos
[2] (= *calm, untroubled*) [*place, life*] tranquilo; **on a ~ June evening** una tranquila tarde de junio; **it's very ~ here** este es un lugar muy tranquilo; **the streets are ~ after yesterday's fighting** las calles están tranquilas después de las confrontaciones de ayer; **they say it's a ~ way to go** dicen que es una forma de morir sin nada de sufrimiento *or* sin sufrir dolores; **she's had a ~ night** ha pasado buena noche

peacefully ['pi:sfəlɪ] ADV [1] (= *non-violently*) [*demonstrate, live, co-exist*] pacíficamente
[2] (= *calmly*) tranquilamente; **he was sleeping ~** dormía tranquilamente; **to die ~** morir sin sufrir

peacefulness ['pi:sfʊlnɪs] N (= *calmness*) tranquilidad *f*, paz *f*; (= *non-violent nature*) carácter *m* pacífico

peacekeeper ['pi:s,ki:pəʳ] N (*Mil*) tropas *fpl* encargadas de mantener la paz; **UN ~s** tropas *fpl* de las Naciones Unidas encargadas de mantener la paz

peace-keeping ['pi:s,ki:pɪŋ] Ⓐ N mantenimiento *m* de la paz
Ⓑ CPD ► **peace-keeping force(s)** N fuerzas *fpl* encargadas de mantener la paz ► **peace-keeping operation** N operación *f* para mantener la paz

peace-loving ['pi:s,lʌvɪŋ] ADJ amante de la paz

peacemaker ['pi:s,meɪkəʳ] N (= *pacifier*) pacificador(a) *m/f*; (= *conciliator*) conciliador(a) *m/f*

peacemaking ['pi:smeɪkɪŋ] Ⓐ N pacificación *f*, negociaciones *mpl* por la paz
Ⓑ ADJ [*efforts, process, role*] pacificador, de conciliación

peacenik* ['pi:snɪk] N pacifista *mf*, milikaka *mf* (*Sp*‡)

peacetime ['pi:staɪm] N tiempos *mpl* de paz

peach [pi:tʃ] Ⓐ N [1] (= *fruit*) melocotón *m* (*Sp*), durazno *m* (*LAm*); (= *tree*) melocotonero *m* (*Sp*), duraznero *m* (*LAm*)
[2] (*) **she's a ~** es un bombón *or* una monada*, es una belleza (*LAm*); **it's a ~ of a job** es un trabajo muy cómodo, es un chollo (*Sp**)
[3] (= *colour*) color *m* (de) melocotón *or* (*LAm*) durazno
Ⓑ ADJ de color melocotón *or* (*LAm*) durazno
Ⓒ CPD ► **peach tree** N melocotonero *m* (*Sp*), duraznero *m* (*LAm*)

peacock ['pi:kɒk] Ⓐ N (*pl* **peacocks** *or* **peacock**) pavo *m* real
Ⓑ CPD ► **peacock blue** N azul *m* (de) pavo real

peacock-blue [,pi:kɒk'blu:] ADJ azul *inv* (de) pavo real

pea-green ['pi:'gri:n] ADJ verde claro

peahen ['pi:hen] N pava *f* real

peak [pi:k] Ⓐ N [1] [*of mountain*] cumbre *f*, cima *f*; (= *mountain itself*) pico *m*; (= *point*) (*also of roof*) punta *f*; (*on graph*) pico *m*; **beat the egg whites until stiff ~s form** bata las claras de huevo a punto de nieve
[2] [*of cap*] visera *f*
[3] (= *high point*) [*of career, fame, popularity*] cumbre *f*, cúspide *f*; **during the ~ of the war in Nicaragua** cuando la guerra en Nicaragua era más intensa; **she died at the ~ of her career** murió cuando estaba en la cumbre *or* la cúspide de su carrera; **to be at the ~ of fitness** estar en condiciones óptimas, estar en plena forma; **coffee is at its ~ just after grinding** cuando mejor está el café es recién molido; **at the ~ of the morning rush hour** en el momento de mayor intensidad de la hora punta matinal; **the heyday of drugs has passed its ~** ya ha pasado la época de máximo apogeo de las drogas; **house prices reached a ~ in 1988** el precio de las viviendas alcanzó su nivel máximo en 1988; **computer technology has not yet reached its ~** la tecnología informática aún no ha alcanzado su cumbre *or* cúspide; **discontent had reached its ~** el descontento había alcanzado su momento crítico; **~s and troughs** auges *mpl* y depresiones *fpl*; *see also* **widow B**
Ⓑ VI [*temperatures*] alcanzar su punto más alto; [*inflation, sales*] alcanzar su nivel máximo; [*crisis*] alcanzar su momento crítico; [*career*] alcanzar su cumbre *or* su cúspide; [*sportsperson*] alcanzar su mejor momento
Ⓒ ADJ (*before noun*) **in ~ condition** (*athlete*) en óptimas condiciones, en plena forma; (*animal*) en óptimas condiciones; **~ hours** (*of traffic*) horas *fpl* punta; (*Elec*) horas *fpl* de mayor consumo; **~ rate** (*Telec*) tarifa *f* alta; **~ season** temporada *f* alta; **~ time** (*TV*) horas *fpl* de máxima audiencia; (*Telec, Elec*) horas *fpl* de máxima demanda; (= *rush hour*) horas *fpl* punta; **it is more expensive to call at ~ times** resulta más caro llamar durante las horas de máxima demanda; **~ viewing time** horas *fpl* de máxima audiencia

peaked[1] [pi:kt] ADJ **~ cap** gorra *f* de visera

peaked[2] [pi:kt] ADJ = **peaky**

peak-time ['pi:ktaɪm] ADJ (*Brit TV*) **a ~ television film** una película que se emite durante las horas de máxima audiencia; (*Telec*) **~ calls** llamadas *fpl* telefónicas durante las horas de máxima demanda

peaky* ['pi:kɪ] ADJ (*compar* **peakier**; *superl* **peakiest**) paliducho*; **to look ~** estar paliducho*

peal [pi:l] Ⓐ N (= *sound of bells*) repique *m*; **a ~ of bells** (= *set*) un carillón; **a ~ of thunder** un trueno; **the ~ of the organ** el sonido del órgano; **~s of laughter** carcajadas *fpl*
Ⓑ VT (*also* **~ out**) repicar, tocar a vuelo
Ⓒ VI [*church bell*] repicar, tocar a vuelo; [*doorbell, organ*] sonar

peanut ['pi:nʌt] Ⓐ N [1] cacahuete *m* (*Sp*), maní *m* (*LAm*), cacahuate *m* (*Mex*)
[2] **peanuts*** (= *very small amount*) una miseria*; **he gets paid ~s** le pagan una miseria
Ⓑ CPD ► **peanut butter** N mantequilla *f* *or* crema *f* de cacahuete (*Sp*), mantequilla *f* de maní (*LAm*), mantequilla *f* de cacahuate (*Mex*) ► **peanut oil** N aceite *m* de cacahuete (*Sp*), aceite *m* de maní (*LAm*), aceite *m* de cacahuate (*Mex*)

peapod ['pi:pɒd] N vaina *f* de guisante (*Sp*), vaina *f* de arveja (*LAm*), vaina *f* de chícharo (*CAm*)

pear [peəʳ] N (= *fruit*) pera *f*; (*also* **~ tree**) peral *m*

pearl [pɜ:l] Ⓐ N perla *f*; (= *mother-of-pearl*) nácar *m*, madreperla *f*; **~ of wisdom** (*fig*) joya *f* de sabiduría; ✦*IDIOM* **to cast ~s before swine** echar margaritas a los cerdos
Ⓑ CPD [*earring, button*] de perla(s); (*in colour*) color de perla ► **pearl barley** N cebada *f* perlada ► **pearl diver** N pescador(a) *m/f* de perlas ► **pearl necklace** N collar *m* de perlas ► **pearl oyster** N ostra *f* perlífera

pearl-grey ['pɜ:l'greɪ] ADJ gris perla

pearly ['pɜ:lɪ] ADJ (*compar* **pearlier**; *superl* **pearliest**) [*teeth*] de perla; [*colour*] color de perla; **~ white/pink** blanco/rosa perla; **the Pearly Gates** (*hum*) las puertas del cielo

pear-shaped ['peəʃeɪpt] ADJ (*lit*) en forma de pera; ✦*IDIOM* **to go ~** (*Brit**) irse a la porra*, fastidiarse*; **things started to go ~** las cosas empezaron a ir mal

peasant ['pezənt] Ⓐ N campesino/a *m/f*; (*pej*) palurdo/a *m/f*; **a ~ revolt** un levantamiento campesino *or* del campesinado
Ⓑ CPD ► **peasant farmer** N campesino *m* ► **peasant woman** N campesina *f*

peasantry ['pezəntrɪ] N campesinado *m*, campesinos *mpl*

peashooter ['pi:ʃu:təʳ] N cerbatana *f*

pea-souper* ['pi:'su:pəʳ] N niebla *f* muy densa

peat [pi:t] Ⓐ N turba *f*
Ⓑ CPD ► **peat bog** N turbera *f*, turbal *m*

peaty ['pi:tɪ] ADJ (*compar* **peatier**; *superl* **peatiest**) turboso

pebble ['pebl] N guijarro *m*; ✦*IDIOM* **you're not the only ~ on the beach*** no eres el único

pebbledash [,pebl'dæʃ] Ⓐ N enguijarrado *m*
Ⓑ VT enguijarrar

pebbly ['peblɪ] ADJ guijarroso

pecan ['pi:kæn] N pacana *f*

peccadillo [,pekə'dɪləʊ] N (*pl* **peccadillos** *or* **peccadilloes**) pecadillo *m*, falta *f* leve

peccary ['pekərɪ] N (*pl* **peccary** *or* **peccaries**) (*Zool*) saíno *m*, pecarí *m* (*LAm*), pécari *m* (*LAm*)

peck[1] [pek] Ⓐ N picotazo *m*; (= *kiss*) besito *m*, beso *m* rápido
Ⓑ VT picotear; (= *kiss*) dar un besito a, dar un beso rápido a
Ⓒ VI picotear; **to ~ at** [*bird*] picar; **he ~ed at his food** picaba la comida (con desgana)

peck[2] [pek] N *medida de áridos (= 9,087 litros)*; (*fig*) montón *m*; **he got himself in a ~ of trouble** se metió en un buen lío*

pecker ['pekəʳ] N [1] (*Brit**) ✦*IDIOM* **to keep one's ~ up** no dejarse desanimar; **keep your ~ up!** ¡ánimo!
[2] (*US***) polla *f* (*Sp***)

pecking order ['pekɪŋ'ɔ:dəʳ] N (*fig*) jerarquía *f*

peckish* ['pekɪʃ] ADJ con ganas de comer algo; **I'm** *or* **I feel a bit ~** tengo ganas de comer algo

pecs* [peks] NPL ABBR (= **pectorals**) pectorales *mpl*

pectin ['pektɪn] N pectina *f*

pectoral ['pektərəl] Ⓐ ADJ pectoral
Ⓑ **pectorals** NPL (músculos *mpl*) pectorales *mpl*

peculate ['pekjʊleɪt] VI desfalcar

peculation [,pekjʊ'leɪʃən] N desfalco *m*, peculado *m*

peculiar [pɪ'kju:lɪəʳ] ADJ [1] (= *strange*) extraño, raro; **it's really most ~** es realmente extraño; **how very ~!** ¡qué extraño!, ¡qué raro!; **I'm feeling a bit ~** me siento algo raro, no me

siento del todo bien; *see also* **funny A2**
[2] (= *exclusive, special*) peculiar; **everyone has their own ~ likes and dislikes** cada uno tiene sus gustos y manías peculiares *or* particulares; **a species ~ to Africa** una especie que existe únicamente en África; **the style of dress ~ to that period in history** la forma de vestir peculiar *or* característica *or* propia de esa época de la historia; **this is not a problem ~ to Britain** éste no es un problema exclusivamente británico; **in his/her own ~ way** a su modo; **in her own ~ way she was very fond of him** a su modo le tenía mucho cariño

peculiarity [pɪˌkjʊlɪˈærɪtɪ] N [1] (= *strangeness*) rareza *f*
[2] (= *specific quality*) peculiaridad *f*; **it's a ~ of hers that she always wears black** ir vestida siempre de negro es una peculiaridad suya; **he has his peculiarities** tiene sus rarezas *or* manías
[3] (= *unusual thing*) rasgo *m* singular; **his only ~ is a missing arm** su único rasgo singular es que le falta un brazo

peculiarly [pɪˈkjuːlɪəlɪ] ADV [1] (= *strangely*) de forma rara; **he's been acting very ~** se ha estado comportando de una forma rarísima
[2] (= *specifically*) típicamente, peculiarmente; **it's a ~ French trait** es un rasgo típicamente *or* peculiarmente francés
[3] (= *unusually, exceptionally*) particularmente, especialmente; **he was ~ quiet that day** ese día estuvo particularmente *or* especialmente callado

pecuniary [pɪˈkjuːnɪərɪ] ADJ (*frm*) [*advantage, benefit*] pecuniario

pedagogic [ˌpedəˈɡɒdʒɪk] ADJ = **pedagogical**

pedagogical [ˌpedəˈɡɒdʒɪkəl] ADJ pedagógico

pedagogically [ˌpedəˈɡɒdʒɪkəlɪ] ADV pedagógicamente

pedagogue, pedagog (*US*) [ˈpedəɡɒɡ] N pedagogo/a *m/f*

pedagogy [ˈpedəɡɒɡɪ] N pedagogía *f*

pedal [ˈpedl] (A) N pedal *m*; **loud ~** (*Mus*) pedal *m* fuerte; **soft ~** (*Mus*) sordina *f*
(B) VI pedalear; **he was ~ling furiously** estaba dándole duro a los pedales
(C) VT [+ *bicycle*] darle a los pedales de
(D) CPD ► **pedal (bi)cycle** N bicicleta *f* a pedales ► **pedal bin** N cubo *m* de la basura con pedal ► **pedal boat** N = **pedalo** ► **pedal car** N cochecito *m* con pedales

pedalo [ˈpedələʊ] N (*pl* **pedalos** *or* **pedaloes**) patín *m* a pedal

pedant [ˈpedənt] N pedante *mf*

pedantic [pɪˈdæntɪk] ADJ pedante

pedantically [pɪˈdæntɪkəlɪ] ADV con pedantería

pedantry [ˈpedəntrɪ] N pedantería *f*

peddle [ˈpedl] VT (= *sell*) ir vendiendo (de puerta en puerta); [+ *drugs*] pasar*; (*fig*) [+ *ideas*] difundir

peddler [ˈpedləʳ] N (*US*) = **pedlar** *see also* **drug C**

pederast [ˈpedəræst] N pederasta *mf*

pederasty [ˈpedəræstɪ] N pederastia *f*

pedestal [ˈpedɪstl] (A) N pedestal *m*, basa *f*; ✦*IDIOMS* **to put sb on a ~** poner a algn sobre un pedestal; **to knock sb off his ~** bajar los humos *or* el copete a algn*
(B) CPD ► **pedestal basin** N lavabo *m or* lavamanos *m inv* con pie central ► **pedestal desk** N escritorio *m* con cajones a ambos lados ► **pedestal lamp** N lámpara *f* de pie

pedestrian [pɪˈdestrɪən] (A) N peatón/ona *m/f*
(B) ADJ (= *dull, commonplace*) [*style, speech*] prosaico, pedestre
(C) CPD ► **pedestrian area** N = **pedestrian precinct** ► **pedestrian crossing** N (*Brit*) paso *m* de peatones ► **pedestrian precinct** N (*Brit*) zona *f* peatonal ► **pedestrian traffic** N circulación *f* de peatones ► **pedestrian zone** N (*US*) = **pedestrian precinct**

pedestrianize [pɪˈdestrɪənaɪz] VT peatonizar; **~d street** calle *f* peatonal

pediatric *etc* [ˌpiːdɪˈætrɪk] (*US*) = **paediatric** *etc*

pedicure [ˈpedɪkjʊəʳ] N pedicura *f*

pedigree [ˈpedɪɡriː] (A) N (= *lineage*) linaje *m*, genealogía *f*; [*of animal*] pedigrí *m*; (= *family tree*) árbol *m* genealógico; (= *document*) certificado *m* de genealogía; (*fig*) (= *record*) historial *m*
(B) CPD (*lit*) de raza, de casta; (*fig*) certificado, garantizado

pediment [ˈpedɪmənt] N frontón *m*

pedlar [ˈpedləʳ] N vendedor(a) *m/f* ambulante, buhonero† *m*

pedological [ˌpiːdəˈlɒdʒɪkl] ADJ (*US*) = **paedological**

pedology [pɪˈdɒlədʒɪ] N (*US*) = **paedology**

pedometer [pɪˈdɒmɪtəʳ] N podómetro *m*

pedophile [ˈpiːdəʊfaɪl] N (*US*) = **paedophile**

pedophilia [ˈpiːdəʊˈfɪlɪə] N (*US*) = **paedophilia**

pee* [piː] (A) N pipí* *m*; **to go for a ~** ir a hacer pipí*; **to have a ~** hacer pipí*
(B) VI hacer pipí*; **the dog ~d on my shoe** el perro se me meó en el zapato*
(C) VT **to ~ one's pants** hacerse pipí encima

peek [piːk] (A) N ojeada *f*, miradita *f*, mirada *f* furtiva; **to take** *or* **have a ~ at** echar una ojeada *or* miradita a; (*furtively*) echar una mirada furtiva a, mirar a hurtadillas
(B) VI (= *glance*) echar una ojeada *or* miradita; (*furtively*) mirar (a hurtadillas); **no ~ing!** ¡sin mirar!; **I opened the door a crack and ~ed in/out** abrí la puerta un poquito y miré (a hurtadillas)

peel [piːl] (A) N (= *skin*) piel *f*; [*of citrus fruit*] cáscara *f*; [*of apple, potato*] piel *f*; (*removed*) [*of citrus fruit*] cáscaras *fpl*; [*of apple, potato*] peladuras *fpl*, mondas *fpl*
(B) VT [+ *fruit, vegetable*] pelar; [+ *layer of paper*] quitar; **to ~ the bark from a tree** descortezar un árbol, quitar la corteza de un árbol
(C) VI [*wallpaper*] despegarse, desprenderse; [*paint*] desconcharse; [*skin, person*] pelarse; **I'm ~ing** me estoy pelando

►**peel away** (A) VI + ADV [*paint*] desconcharse; [*wallpaper*] despegarse, desprenderse; [*skin*] pelarse
(B) VT + ADV quitar, despegar

►**peel back** VT + ADV quitar, despegar

►**peel off** (A) VT + ADV [+ *layer, paper*] quitar, despegar; [+ *clothes*] quitarse rápidamente *or* lisamente
(B) VI + ADV [1] (= *separate*) separarse (**from** de); (= *leave formation*) [*vehicle, plane*] despegarse; **he ~ed off to the east** se desvió hacia el este
[2] (*) desnudarse rápidamente

peeler [ˈpiːləʳ] N [1] (*also* **potato ~**) pelapatatas *m inv*
[2] (*Brit*††*) (= *policeman*) polizonte* *m*

peelie-wally‡ [ˈpiːlɪˈwælɪ] ADJ **to be ~** (*Scot*) tener mala cara

peeling [ˈpiːlɪŋ] N (*Med*) [*of face etc*] descamación *f*; (*cosmetic trade*) peeling *m*; **peelings** [*of apple, potato*] peladuras *fpl*, mondas *fpl*; [*of citrus fruit*] cáscaras *fpl*

peep¹ [piːp] (A) N ojeada *f*, miradita *f*; **to get a ~ at sth** lograr ver algo brevemente; **to take** *or* **have a ~ (at sth)** echar una ojeada *or* miradita (a algo)
(B) VI [1] (= *look*) mirar rápidamente; (*furtively*) mirar furtivamente *or* a hurtadillas; **to ~ at** echar una ojeada *or* miradita a; **I lifted the lid and ~ed inside** levanté la tapa y eché una miradita; **he ~ed through the curtains** se asomó a ver por detrás de las cortinas; **to ~ through the window** asomarse a la ventana para mirar
[2] (= *stick out*) asomar(se); **a head ~ed out** se asomó una cabeza; **the sun ~ed out from behind the clouds** el sol se asomó tras las nubes; **her shoes ~ed from beneath her skirt** los zapatos se le asomaban por debajo de la falda

peep² [piːp] (A) N [1] [*of bird*] pío *m*; [*of whistle*] silbido *m*
[2] (*) **there hasn't been a ~ out of them** no han dicho ni pío*; **we can't get a ~ out of them** no les podemos sacar nada; **I don't want to hear ~ out of you!** ¡tú ni chistar!, ¡tú ni pío!*
(B) VI piar

peepers* [ˈpiːpəz] NPL ojos *mpl*

peephole [ˈpiːphəʊl] N mirilla *f*, atisbadero *m*

Peeping Tom [ˌpiːpɪŋˈtɒm] N mirón *m*

peepshow [ˈpiːpʃəʊ] N (= *device*) mundonuevo *m*; (= *show*) vistas *fpl* sicalípticas, espectáculo *m* deshonesto

peeptoe [ˈpiːptəʊ] ADJ [*sandal, shoe*] abierto

peer¹ [pɪəʳ] (A) N [1] (= *noble*) par *m*, lord *m*; **he was made a life ~** le concedieron un título vitalicio
[2] (= *equal*) (*in status*) par *mf*, igual *mf*; (*in age*) coetáneo/a *m/f*; **as a musician he has no ~** como músico no tiene par *or* igual; **children like to feel accepted by their ~s** a los niños les gusta sentirse aceptados por sus coetáneos
(B) CPD ► **peer evaluation** N = **peer review** ► **peer group** N grupo *m* paritario ► **peer pressure, peer-group pressure** N presión *f* ejercida por los iguales *or* (*frm*) por el grupo paritario ► **peer review** N evaluación *f* por los iguales

peer² [pɪəʳ] VI **to ~ at sth/sb** (*short-sightedly*) mirar algo/a algn con ojos de miope; (*closely*) escudriñar algo/a algn; **the old man ~ed at the book** el anciano miraba el libro con ojos de miope; **he ~ed at his reflection in the water** escudriñaba su reflejo en el agua; **we went up to the window and ~ed in** fuimos hasta la ventana y nos asomamos para ver lo que pasaba dentro; **to ~ into sb's face** escudriñar la cara a algn; **I ~ed over her shoulder** miré por encima de su hombro; **we ~ed over the wall** nos asomamos para mirar por encima de la pared

peerage [ˈpɪərɪdʒ] N nobleza *f*; **he was given a ~** le otorgaron un título de nobleza; **to marry into the ~** casarse con un título; **to be raised to the ~** obtener un título de nobleza

peeress [ˈpɪərɪs] N paresa *f*

peerless [ˈpɪəlɪs] ADJ sin par, incomparable

peeve* [piːv] VT molestar, irritar

peeved* [piːvd] ADJ picado*, molesto

peevish [ˈpiːvɪʃ] ADJ [*look, glance*] malhumorado; [*tone*] de irritación; **he gave her a ~ look** la miró malhumorado

peevishly [ˈpiːvɪʃlɪ] ADV malhumoradamente, con mal humor; **he said ~** dijo malhumorado

peevishness [ˈpiːvɪʃnɪs] N mal humor *m*

peewee* [ˈpiːwiː] ADJ (*US*) diminuto, pequeñito

peewit [ˈpiːwɪt] N avefría *f*

peg [peg] Ⓐ N 1 (*in ground, tent peg*) estaca *f*; (= *clothes peg*) pinza *f*, broche *m* (*LAm*); (*Mus*) (= *tuning peg*) clavija *f*; (*in board game*) ficha *f*; (*in barrel*) estaquilla *f*; (*Croquet*) piquete *m*; (*Climbing*) clavija *f*; ✦*IDIOM* **to take** *or* **bring sb down a ~ (or two)*** bajar los humos *or* el copete a algn*; *see also* **square B1**

2 (*for coat, hat*) gancho *m*, colgador *m*; **off the ~** (*Brit*) confeccionado, de confección; **an off-the-~ suit** un traje confeccionado *or* de confección; **he always buys clothes off the ~** siempre compra ropa confeccionada *or* de confección

3 (= *pretext*) pretexto *m*; **use the new law as a ~ for the question** utiliza la nueva ley como pretexto para hacer la pregunta; **a ~ on which to hang a theory** un punto de apoyo para justificar una teoría

Ⓑ VT 1 (= *secure*) (*gen*) fijar; [+ *clothes*] (*on line*) tender; [+ *tent*] fijar con estacas, sujetar con estacas; *see also* **peg out**

2 (*fig*) 2·1 (= *fix*) [+ *prices, wages*] fijar, estabilizar (**at, to** en); **the Bank wants to ~ rates at 9%** el banco quiere fijar *or* estabilizar las tasas en el 9%

2·2 (= *link*) vincular (**to** a); **they continue to ~ their currencies to the dollar** siguen vinculando su moneda al dólar

2·3 (*) (= *categorize*) [+ *person*] encasillar; **here you're ~ged by what you wear** aquí te encasillan por la ropa que llevas; **his accent ~ged him as an Englishman** su acento lo delataba como inglés

2·4 **to ~ one's hopes on sth** depositar *or* cifrar sus esperanzas en algo

Ⓒ CPD ► **peg leg** N pata *f* de palo

►**peg away*** VI + ADV machacar*; **just keep ~ging away until you feel more confident** sigue machacando hasta que te sientas más seguro*; **to ~ away at sth** machacar algo*, darle duro a algo*

►**peg back** VT + ADV **Villa were ~ged back to a 1-1 draw** Villa perdió su ventaja y terminó empatado a uno

►**peg down** VT + ADV 1 (= *fasten down*) [+ *tent*] fijar con estacas, sujetar con estacas

2 (= *force to agree*) **I ~ged him down to saying how much he wanted for it** conseguí que me dijera exactamente por cuánto lo quería vender; **I ~ged him down to £10 an hour** conseguí que aceptara 10 libras por hora

►**peg out*** Ⓐ VI + ADV (= *die*) estirar la pata*; (= *collapse*) caerse redondo*

Ⓑ VT + ADV (= *mark out*) [+ *area*] marcar con piquetes; (= *secure*) sujetar *or* fijar con estacas; (= *hang out*) [+ *clothes*] tender (con pinzas)

Pegasus ['pegəsəs] N Pegaso *m*

pegboard ['pegbɔːd] N tablero *m* de clavijas

PEI ABBR (*Canada*) = **Prince Edward Island**

peignoir ['peɪnwɑːʳ] N bata *f* (de señora), peinador *m*

pejorative [pɪ'dʒɒrətɪv] ADJ peyorativo, despectivo

pejoratively [pɪ'dʒɒrətɪvlɪ] ADV peyorativamente, de manera peyorativa, despectivamente

peke* [piːk] N pequinés/esa *m/f*

Pekin [piː'kɪn], **Peking** [piː'kɪŋ] N Pekín *m*

pekinese [ˌpiːkɪ'niːz], **pekingese** N pequinés/esa *m/f*

pelagic [pɪ'lædʒɪk] ADJ pelágico

pelican ['pelɪkən] Ⓐ N pelícano *m*

Ⓑ CPD ► **pelican crossing** N semáforo *m* sonoro

pellagra [pə'lægrə] N pelagra *f*

pellet ['pelɪt] N (= *little ball*) bolita *f*; (*for gun*) perdigón *m*; [*of fertilizer*] gránulo *m*; (*Med*) píldora *f*

pell-mell ['pel'mel] ADV [*rush*] en tropel, atropelladamente; **their belongings were piled ~ into the trucks** metieron de cualquier manera sus pertenencias en los camiones

pellucid [pe'luːsɪd] ADJ diáfano, cristalino

pelmet ['pelmɪt] N (*Brit*) galería *f* (para cubrir la barra de las cortinas)

Peloponnese [ˌpeləpə'niːs] N **the ~** el Peloponeso

Peloponnesian [ˌpeləpə'niːʃən] ADJ peloponense

pelota [pɪ'ləʊtə] Ⓐ N pelota *f* (vasca)

Ⓑ CPD ► **pelota player** N pelotari *mf*

pelt[1] [pelt] Ⓐ VT **to ~ sb with eggs** arrojar *or* tirar huevos a algn; **to ~ sb with stones** apedrear a algn; **they ~ed him with questions** lo acribillaron a preguntas

Ⓑ VI 1 (= *fall fast*) **the rain is ~ing down*** está lloviendo a cántaros, está diluviando

2 (*) (= *go fast*) **to go ~ing off** salir como un rayo

Ⓒ N **to go full ~** ir a todo correr, ir a toda pastilla*

pelt[2] [pelt] N (= *fur*) piel *f*; (= *skin*) pellejo *m*

pelvic ['pelvɪk] ADJ pélvico

pelvis ['pelvɪs] N (*pl* **pelvises** *or* **pelves**) pelvis *f*

pen[1] [pen] Ⓐ N (= *fountain pen*) (pluma *f*) estilográfica *f*, pluma *f*, pluma *f* fuente (*LAm*); (= *ballpoint*) bolígrafo *m*; (= *felt tip*) rotulador *m*; **to live by the** *or* **one's ~** ganarse la vida escribiendo; **to put ~ to paper** ponerse a escribir; **to wield a ~** (*liter*) menear cálamo; *see also* **marker, slip A2**

Ⓑ VT [+ *letter, article, book*] escribir; [+ *poem, song*] componer

Ⓒ CPD ► **pen-and-ink drawing** N dibujo *m* a pluma ► **pen friend** N amigo/a *m/f* por correspondencia ► **pen name** N seudónimo *m*, nombre *m* de guerra ► **pen nib** N punta *f* (de pluma) ► **pen pal*** N = **pen friend** ► **pen wiper** N limpiaplumas *m inv*

pen[2] [pen] Ⓐ N 1 (= *enclosure*) (*for cattle*) corral *m*; (*for sheep*) redil *m*, aprisco *m*; (*for bulls*) toril *m*; (= *playpen*) parque *m* (de niño), corral *m*

2 (*US**) (= *prison*) (*also* **penitentiary**) cárcel *f*, chirona *f* (*Sp**)

Ⓑ VT [+ *animal*] encerrar, acorralar; [+ *person*] **I've been ~ned in the kitchen all day** he estado metida en la cocina todo el día

►**pen in** VT + ADV [+ *animal*] encerrar, acorralar; **she was ~ned in by the crowd** se encontraba acorralada por la muchedumbre; **the French had the enemy ~ned in** los franceses tenían al enemigo cercado

►**pen up** VT + ADV [+ *animal*] = **pen in**

pen[3] [pen] N (*Orn*) cisne *m* hembra

penal ['piːnl] Ⓐ ADJ 1 [*reform, policy, system*] penal

2 (= *harsh*) [*rate, charges*] muy gravoso, perjudicial

Ⓑ CPD ► **penal code** N código *m* penal ► **penal colony** N colonia *f* penal ► **penal servitude** N trabajos *mpl* forzados

penalization [ˌpiːnəlaɪ'zeɪʃən] N castigo *m*

penalize ['piːnəlaɪz] VT (= *punish*) castigar; (*by law*) penar; (*accidentally, unfairly*) perjudicar; (*Sport*) sancionar, penalizar; **to be ~d for a foul** ser penalizado por una falta; **we are ~d by not having a car** somos perjudicados por no tener coche; **the decision ~s those who …** la decisión perjudica a quienes …

penalty ['penəltɪ] Ⓐ N 1 (*Jur*) (= *punishment*) pena *f*, castigo *m*; (= *fine*) multa *f*; (*Comm*) recargo *m*; (*fig*) (= *disadvantage*) desventaja *f*; **there is a ~ for paying the loan off early** se cobra un recargo si se paga el préstamo antes de que venza; **"penalty £50"** "multa de 50 libras"; **telling the truth can have its penalties** decir la verdad puede tener sus desventajas; **the ~ for this is death** esto se castiga con la muerte; **on** *or* **under ~ of dismissal** so *or* bajo pena de ser despedido; **to pay the ~ (for** *or* **of sth/for doing sth)** pagar las consecuencias (de algo/de haber hecho algo); **we were paying the ~ of success** estábamos pagando las consecuencias del éxito; *see also* **death B**

2 (*Ftbl*) penalti *m*, penalty *m*; (*Golf*) penalización *f*; (*Bridge*) multa *f*, castigo *m*; **there is a 7-second ~ for each error** se quitan 7 segundos por cada error; **the final was decided on penalties** la final se decidió con penaltis; **to take a ~** lanzar penalti *or* penalty

Ⓑ CPD ► **penalty area, penalty box** N (*Ftbl*) área *f* de castigo *or* de penalti *or* de penalty; (*Ice hockey*) banquillo *m* ► **penalty clause** N cláusula *f* penal ► **penalty corner** N (*Hockey*) córner *m* de penalti *or* penalty ► **penalty goal** N gol *m* de penalti *or* penalty ► **penalty kick** N penalti *m*, penalty *m* ► **penalty point** N (*on driving licence, in showjumping*) punto *m* de castigo ► **penalty shoot-out** N desempate *m* a penaltis ► **penalty spot** N punto *m* de penalti *or* penalty

penance ['penəns] N 1 (= *atonement*) penitencia *f*; **to do ~ for** hacer penitencia por

2 (= *punishment*) castigo *m*

pence [pens] NPL *of* **penny**

penchant [ˌpɑ̃ːŋʃɑ̃ːŋ] N predilección *f* (**for** por), inclinación *f* (**for** hacia, por); **to have a ~ for** tener predilección por

pencil ['pensl] Ⓐ N lápiz *m*, lapicero *m*; (= *propelling pencil*) lapicero *m*; **to draw in ~** dibujar con lápiz; **to write in ~** escribir a lápiz; *see also* **eyebrow B**

Ⓑ VT (*also* **~ in**) escribir a lápiz; **a ~led note** una nota escrita a lápiz

Ⓒ CPD ► **pencil box** N cajita *f* para lápices ► **pencil case** N estuche *m* (para lápices), plumero *m*, plumier *m* (*Sp*) ► **pencil drawing** N dibujo *m* a lápiz ► **pencil sharpener** N sacapuntas *m inv* ► **pencil skirt** N falda *f* tubo ► **pencil torch** N linterna *f* muy fina

►**pencil in** VT + ADV apuntar (con lápiz); (*fig*) [+ *appointment*] apuntar con carácter provisional; **I'll ~ you in for Thursday** de momento te apunto para el jueves

pendant ['pendənt] N colgante *m*

pending ['pendɪŋ] Ⓐ ADJ pendiente; **to be ~** estar pendiente *or* en trámite; **and other matters ~** y otros asuntos todavía por resolver

Ⓑ PREP **~ the arrival of …** hasta que llegue …; **~ your decision** mientras se decida usted; **he has been suspended ~ further investigation** ha sido suspendido en espera de que continúe la investigación

Ⓒ CPD ► **pending tray** N cajón *m* de asuntos pendientes

pendulous ['pendjʊləs] ADJ colgante

pendulum ['pendjʊləm] N péndulo *m*

Penelope [pə'neləpɪ] N Penélope

penes ['piːniːz] NPL *of* **penis**

penetrable ['penɪtrəbl] ADJ penetrable

penetrate ['penɪtreɪt] Ⓐ VT 1 (= *go right through*) [+ *skin, armour*] penetrar (por), traspasar

2 (*Mil*) [+ *defences*] infiltrar, penetrar; [+ *territory*] penetrar en

3 (= *enter, infiltrate*) [+ *organization*] infiltrarse en; (*Comm*) [+ *market*] introducirse en, entrar

en
4 (= *understand*) [+ *mystery*] penetrar; [+ *sb's mind, thoughts*] penetrar en
5 (*during sex*) penetrar
Ⓑ VI (= *go right through*) atravesar; (= *spread, permeate*) [*idea, ideology*] trascender, infiltrarse; (= *get inside*) penetrar; (= *be understood*) entrar, penetrar; **to ~ into** [+ *territory*] penetrar en; **these ideas have ~d into our everyday life** estas ideas han trascendido a *or* se han infiltrado en nuestra vida cotidiana

penetrating [ˈpenɪtreɪtɪŋ] ADJ [*eyes, sound*] penetrante; [*mind*] perspicaz

penetratingly [ˈpenɪtreɪtɪŋlɪ] ADV de manera penetrante, con penetración

penetration [ˌpenɪˈtreɪʃən] N (*gen*) penetración *f*; [*of analysis, observation*] agudeza *f*

penetrative [ˈpenɪtrətɪv] Ⓐ ADJ penetrante
Ⓑ CPD ► **penetrative sex** N relaciones *fpl* sexuales con penetración

penguin [ˈpeŋgwɪn] N pingüino *m*

penholder [ˈpenˌhəʊldəʳ] N portaplumas *m inv*

penicillin [ˌpenɪˈsɪlɪn] N penicilina *f*

penile [ˈpiːnaɪl] ADJ del pene

peninsula [pɪˈnɪnsjʊlə] N península *f*

peninsular [pɪˈnɪnsjʊləʳ] ADJ peninsular; **the Peninsular War** la Guerra de Independencia

penis [ˈpiːnɪs] N (*pl* **penises** *or* **penes**) pene *m*

penitence [ˈpenɪtəns] N penitencia *f*

penitent [ˈpenɪtənt] Ⓐ ADJ arrepentido; (*Rel*) penitente
Ⓑ N penitente *mf*

penitential [ˌpenɪˈtenʃəl] ADJ penitencial

penitentiary [ˌpenɪˈtenʃərɪ] N (*esp US*) (= *prison*) penitenciaria *f*

penitently [ˈpenɪtəntlɪ] N arrepentidamente, compungidamente; (*Rel*) penitentemente

penknife [ˈpennaɪf] N (*pl* **penknives**) navaja *f*, cortaplumas *m inv*

penman [ˈpenmən] N (*pl* **penmen**) calígrafo *m*, pendolista *m*

penmanship [ˈpenmənʃɪp] N caligrafía *f*

Penn, Penna ABBR (*US*) = **Pennsylvania**

pennant [ˈpenənt] N banderín *m*; (*Naut*) gallardete *m*

pennies [ˈpenɪz] NPL *of* **penny**

penniless [ˈpenɪlɪs] ADJ [*aristocrat, immigrant*] sin dinero; **to be ~** no tener un céntimo *or* un centavo; **to be left ~** quedarse sin un céntimo *or* un centavo

Pennine [ˈpenaɪn] N **the ~s** los (Montes) Peninos

pennon [ˈpenən] N pendón *m*

Pennsylvania [ˌpensɪlˈveɪnɪə] N Pensilvania *f*

Penny [ˈpenɪ] N (*familiar form*) *of* **Penelope**

penny [ˈpenɪ] Ⓐ N (= *value*) (*pl* **pence**) (= *coins*) (*pl* **pennies**) (*Brit*) penique *m*; (*US*) (= *cent*) centavo *m*; (*Spanish equivalent*) perra *f* gorda; **it costs five pence** cuesta cinco peniques; **I have five pennies** tengo cinco peniques; **I don't owe you a ~** no te debo nada; **it cost £500 but it was worth every ~** costó 500 libras, pero mereció la pena pagarlas; **£20, not a ~ more, not a ~ less** 20 libras, ni un penique más ni menos; **new ~** *penique del sistema monetario británico actual que es la centésima parte de una libra*; **old ~** *penique del sistema monetario británico antiguo equivalente a 0,4 peniques actuales*; **a ten-pence piece** *or* **coin** una moneda de diez peniques; ✦**IDIOMS he turns up like a bad ~** está hasta en la sopa; **to count the pennies** mirar la peseta (*Sp*), mirar el dinero; **then the ~ dropped** por fin cayó en la cuenta; **he hasn't a ~ to his name** ◊ **he hasn't two pennies to rub together** no tiene dónde caerse muerto; **(a) ~ for your thoughts** ◊ **a ~ for them*** ¿en qué estás pensando?; **for two pence I'd tell her what I think of her** por menos de nada le digo lo que pienso de ella; **to be two** *or* **ten a ~** haberlo a montones; **he thinks jobs are two a ~** cree que hay trabajos a montones; **to watch the pennies** mirar el dinero; ✦**PROVS in for a ~, in for a pound** de perdidos, al río; **take care of the pennies and the pounds will take care of themselves** muchos pocos hacen un montón; **a ~ saved is a ~ gained** si pagas aunque sea sólo un céntimo *or* un poco menos, eso que te ahorras; *see also* **honest A2, pretty A1, spend A1**
Ⓑ CPD ► **penny arcade** N (*US*) galería *f* de máquinas tragaperras ► **penny black** N *primer sello de correos británico, que data del 1830* ► **penny dreadful** N *libro o revista escabroso o sensacionalista* ► **penny farthing** N velocípedo *m* ► **penny whistle** N flauta *f* metálica

penny-a-liner [ˈpenɪəˈlaɪnəʳ] N escritorzuelo/a* *m/f* (*pej*), gacetillero/a *m/f* (*pej*)

penny-in-the-slot machine [ˌpenɪɪnðəˈslɒtməˌʃiːn] N (máquina *f*) tragaperras *f inv*

penny-pinching [ˈpenɪˌpɪntʃɪŋ] Ⓐ N tacañería *f*
Ⓑ ADJ [*person*] tacaño, avaro

pennyweight [ˈpenɪweɪt] N *peso de 24 granos (= 1,555 gramos)*

penny-wise [ˌpenɪˈwaɪz] ADJ **to be ~** mirar el dinero; ✦**IDIOM to be ~ and pound-foolish** mirar tanto el dinero que se acaba gastando un dineral

pennyworth [ˈpenəθ] N (*Hist*) **a ~ of sweets** un penique de caramelos; ✦**IDIOM to put in one's two ~** meter baza*; **you've had your two ~** tú metiste baza*

penologist [piːˈnɒlədʒɪst] N penalista *mf*, criminólogo/a *m/f*

penology [piːˈnɒlədʒɪ] N ciencia *f* penal, criminología *f*

penpusher [ˈpenˌpʊʃəʳ] N (*Brit pej*) chupatintas* *m inv*

pension[1] [ˈpenʃən] Ⓐ N pensión *f*; **to claim/draw one's** *or* **a ~** solicitar/estar cobrando una pensión; **to retire on a ~** jubilarse; **to retire on full ~** retirarse con toda la jubilación; **company ~** plan *m* de pensiones de la empresa; **disability/invalidity ~** pensión *f* de invalidez; **old age ~** (pensión *f* de) jubilación *f*, retiro *m*; **personal** *or* **private ~** plan *m* de pensiones personal; **retirement ~** retiro *m*, (pensión *f* de) jubilación *f*; **state ~** pensión *f* estatal; **war ~** pensión *f* de guerra; **widow's ~** pensión *f* de viudedad
Ⓑ VT (= *allow to retire*) jubilar; (= *give pension*) pagar una pensión a
Ⓒ CPD ► **pension benefits** NPL pensión *f*, *dinero que se cobra de la misma* ► **pension book** N libreta *f* de pensión ► **pension contributions** NPL aportaciones *mpl* a la pensión ► **pension fund** N fondo *m* de pensiones ► **pension plan, pension scheme** N plan *m* de pensiones ► **pension rights** NPL derechos *mpl* de pensión

►**pension off** VT + ADV (*lit*) jubilar; **isn't it time you ~ed off that car of yours?*** ¿no va siendo hora de que jubiles ese coche?*

pension[2] [ˈpɔ̃sjɔ̃] N (= *hotel*) pensión *f*

pensionable [ˈpenʃənəbl] ADJ [*age*] de jubilación; [*post*] con derecho a pensión

pensioner [ˈpenʃənəʳ] N pensionado/a *m/f*, pensionista *mf*; (= *old age pensioner*) jubilado/a *m/f*

pensive [ˈpensɪv] ADJ (*gen*) pensativo, meditabundo

pensively [ˈpensɪvlɪ] ADV pensativamente

pent [pent] ADJ *see* **pent-up**

pentagon [ˈpentəgən] N pentágono *m*; **the Pentagon** (*Washington*) el Pentágono

pentagonal [penˈtægənl] ADJ pentagonal

pentagram [ˈpentəgræm] N estrella *f* de cinco puntas

pentameter [penˈtæmɪtəʳ] N pentámetro *m*

Pentateuch [ˈpentətjuːk] N Pentateuco *m*

pentathlete [penˈtæθliːt] N pentatleta *mf*

pentathlon [penˈtæθlən] N pentatlón *m*

pentatonic [ˌpentəˈtɒnɪk] Ⓐ ADJ pentatónico
Ⓑ CPD ► **pentatonic scale** N escala *f* pentatónica

Pentecost [ˈpentɪkɒst] N (*Rel*) Pentecostés *m*

Pentecostal [ˌpentɪˈkɒstl] ADJ de Pentecostés

Pentecostalism [ˌpentɪˈkɒstlɪzəm] N pentecostalismo *m*

penthouse [ˈpenthaʊs] N (*pl* **penthouses** [ˈpenthaʊzɪz]) ático *m*

Pentium processor® [ˌpentɪəmˈprəʊsesəʳ] N procesador *m* Pentium

pent-up [ˈpentʌp] ADJ [*rage*] contenido, reprimido; [*emotion, frustration, energy*] contenido; **~ demand** demanda *f* reprimida

penult [pɪˈnʌlt] N penúltima *f*

penultimate [pɪˈnʌltɪmɪt] ADJ penúltimo

penumbra [pɪˈnʌmbrə] N (*pl* **penumbras** *or* **penumbrae** [pɪˈnʌmbriː]) penumbra *f*

penurious [pɪˈnjʊərɪəs] ADJ miserable, pobrísimo

penury [ˈpenjʊrɪ] N miseria *f*, penuria *f*; **to live in ~** vivir en la penuria *or* miseria; **to be reduced to ~** quedarse en la miseria

peon [ˈpiːən] N peón *m*

peonage [ˈpiːənɪdʒ] N condición *f* de peón; (*fig*) servidumbre *f*, esclavitud *f*

peony [ˈpɪənɪ] N peonía *f*

people [ˈpiːpl] Ⓐ N 1 (*with pl vb*) 1·1 (*seen as a mass*) gente *f*; **what will ~ think?** ¿qué va a pensar la gente?; **they stole from ~'s houses** robaban las casas de la gente; **the place was full of ~** el local estaba lleno de gente; **country ~** la gente del campo; **I like the ~ here** la gente de aquí me cae bien; **here ~ quarrel a lot** aquí se riñe mucho; **they don't mix much with the local ~** no se tratan mucho con la gente del lugar; **what a lot of ~!** ¡cuánta gente!; **old ~** los ancianos, la gente mayor; **~ say that ...** dicen que ..., la gente dice que ...; **young ~** los jóvenes, la gente joven
1·2 (= *persons, individuals*) personas *fpl*; **20 ~** 20 personas; **millions of ~** millones *mpl* de personas; **~ are more important than animals** las personas son más importantes que los animales; **how many ~ are there in your family?** ¿cuántos sois en tu familia?; **he got a knighthood, him of all ~!** le han nombrado sir, ¡precisamente a él!; **you of all ~ should understand** tú deberías entenderlo mejor que nadie; **the ~ concerned** la gente *or* las personas en cuestión; **English ~** los ingleses; **two English ~** dos ingleses; **the gas ~ are coming tomorrow** los del gas vienen mañana; **~ like you are not welcome** no queremos gente como tú; **many ~ think that ...** mucha gente cree que ..., muchos creen que ...; **most ~ like it** a la mayoría de la gente le gusta; **several ~ have told me** me lo han dicho varias personas; **some ~ are born lucky** hay gente que nace de pie, hay gente con suerte; **they're strange ~** son gente rara;

what do you ~ think? y ustedes ¿qué opinan?; *see also* **little¹ B**

1·3 (= *inhabitants*) habitantes *mpl*; **Madrid has over four million ~** Madrid tiene más de cuatro millones de habitantes; **the ~ of London** los habitantes de Londres, los londinenses; **the ~ of Angola** los habitantes *or* la gente de Angola; **the ~ of this country are fed up** la gente de este país está harta; **a leader who will serve the country and its ~** un líder al servicio del país y de su gente

1·4 (= *citizens, public*) pueblo *m*; **the ~** el pueblo; **the will of the ~** la voluntad popular *or* del pueblo; **the British ~** el pueblo británico; **the king and his ~** el rey y su pueblo *or* sus súbditos; **a ~'s army/democracy/republic** un ejército/una democracia/una república popular; **government by the ~** el gobierno del pueblo; **the ~ at large** el pueblo en general; **a man of the ~** un hombre del pueblo; **power to the ~** poder *m* para el pueblo; **a ~'s tribunal** un tribunal popular; ✦**IDIOM to go to the ~** consultar la opinión popular; *see also* **common A1**

1·5 (= *family*) gente *f*, familia *f*; **my ~ come from the north** mi familia *or* mi gente es del norte; **have you met his ~?** ¿conoces a su familia?

1·6 (= *colleagues*) **I asked one of our ~ in Boston to handle it** pedí a uno de los nuestros en Boston que se encargara de ello

2 (*with sing vb*) (= *ethnic group*) pueblo *m*; **an oppressed ~** un pueblo oprimido; **the ~s of the former Soviet Union** los pueblos de la antigua Unión Soviética; **Spanish-speaking ~s** los pueblos *or* las gentes de habla hispana

Ⓑ VT poblar; **the country is ~d by nomads** el país está poblado *or* habitado por nómadas; **his novels are ~d with outlandish characters** sus novelas están pobladas de personajes extravagantes

Ⓒ CPD ► **people carrier** N monovolumen *m* ► **people mover** N (*US*) cinta *f* transbordadora, pasillo *m* móvil

PEP [pep] N ABBR (*Brit Fin*) = **personal equity plan**

pep* [pep] Ⓐ N energía *f*, dinamismo *m*

Ⓑ CPD ► **pep pill** N estimulante *m* ► **pep rally** N (*US*) *encuentro de motivación* ► **pep talk** N palabras *fpl* que motivan, palabras *fpl* para levantar la moral; **to give sb a ~ talk** hablar a algn para motivarle *or* levantarle la moral

►**pep up** VT + ADV [+ *person*] (= *encourage*) animar, estimular; (= *revive*) dar un nuevo impulso a; [+ *drink*] hacer más fuerte; **how to ~ up your love life** cómo dar un nuevo impulso a su vida amorosa

PEP RALLY

***Pep Rally** es un término usado en Estados Unidos para referirse a las concentraciones que se realizan antes de la celebración de un partido de fútbol americano o baloncesto en los institutos de enseñanza secundaria o en la universidad. En estas celebraciones, que tienen lugar uno o varios días antes del partido, participan animadores de grupo, una banda de música y tanto los jugadores como los entrenadores tienen que pronunciar unas palabras ante los demás. También se emplea a veces el término **Pep Rally** con referencia a los mítines políticos o a encuentros entre los miembros de una empresa para alentar la motivación entre sus afiliados o empleados por medio de la adulación pública o el anuncio de nuevos proyectos o de éxitos futuros.*

pepper [ˈpepəʳ] Ⓐ N 1 (= *spice*) pimienta *f*; **black/white ~** pimienta *f* negra/blanca; *see also* **cayenne**

2 (= *vegetable*) pimiento *m*, pimentón *m* (*S. Cone*); **green ~** pimiento *m* verde, pimentón *m* verde (*LAm*); **red ~** (= *capsicum*) pimiento *m* rojo, pimiento *m* morrón, pimentón *m* rojo (*LAm*); *see also* **chili**

Ⓑ VT 1 (*lit*) echar *or* poner pimienta a, sazonar con pimienta

2 (*fig*) 2·1 (= *bombard*) acribillar; **the walls were ~ed with bullet holes** las paredes habían sido acribilladas a balazos; **to ~ sth/sb with bullets** acribillar algo/a algn a balazos; **to ~ sb with questions** acribillar a algn a preguntas

2·2 (= *sprinkle*) salpicar; **his English is heavily ~ed with Americanisms** su inglés está salpicado de americanismos; **to ~ a work with quotations** salpicar una obra de citas; **his hair is ~ed with grey** tiene el pelo salpicado de canas

Ⓒ CPD ► **pepper mill** N molinillo *m* de pimienta ► **pepper plant** N pimentero *m* ► **pepper pot**, **pepper shaker** (*US*) N pimentero *m* ► **pepper steak** N filete *m* a la pimienta

peppercorn [ˈpepəkɔːn] Ⓐ N grano *m* de pimienta

Ⓑ CPD ► **peppercorn rent** N alquiler *m* nominal

peppermint [ˈpepəmɪnt] N (*Bot*) menta *f*; (= *sweet*) caramelo *m* de menta; (= *lozenge*) pastilla *f* de menta; **~ flavour ice cream** helado *m* con sabor a menta

pepperoni [pepəˈrəʊnɪ] N salchichón *m* a la pimienta, pepperoni *m*

peppery [ˈpepərɪ] ADJ (= *hot, sharp*) picante; (= *tasting of pepper*) con sabor a pimienta; (*fig*) (= *short-tempered*) enojadizo; **~ taste** sabor *m* a pimienta; (*hot, sharp*) sabor *m* picante

pepsin [ˈpepsɪn] N pepsina *f*

peptic [ˈpeptɪk] Ⓐ ADJ péptico

Ⓑ CPD ► **peptic ulcer** N úlcera *f* péptica

peptone [ˈpeptəʊn] N peptona *f*

per [pɜːʳ] PREP por; **~ annum** al año; **we shall proceed as ~ instructions** procederemos de acuerdo con las instrucciones; **as ~ invoice** de acuerdo con *or* según la factura; **£10 ~ dozen** 10 libras la docena; **30 miles ~ gallon** 30 millas por cada galón; **~ head** por cabeza; **~ head of population** por habitante; **60 miles ~ hour** 60 millas por hora; **~ person** por persona; **£15 ~ person ~ night** 15 libras por persona y por noche; **~ se** de por sí; **£7 ~ week** 7 libras a la semana; *see also* **per cent**, **usual A**

perambulate [pəˈræmbjʊleɪt] Ⓐ VT recorrer

Ⓑ VI pasearse, deambular

perambulation [pəˌræmbjʊˈleɪʃən] N (*frm, hum*) (= *stroll*) paseo *m*; (= *journey*) viaje *m*; (= *visit*) visita *f* de inspección

perambulator† [ˈpræmbjʊleɪtəʳ] N (*Brit frm*) cochecito *m* de niño

perborate [pəˈbɔːreɪt] N perborato *m*

per capita [pəˈkæpɪtə] Ⓐ ADV per cápita

Ⓑ CPD ► **per capita consumption** N consumo *m* per cápita; **the ~ consumption of alcohol** el consumo de alcohol per cápita ► **per capita income** N ingresos *mpl* per cápita

perceive [pəˈsiːv] VT 1 (= *see, hear*) percibir; (= *realize*) darse cuenta de, notar; **now I ~ that ...** ahora veo que ...; **do you ~ anything strange?** ¿notas algo raro?; **~d need/interest** necesidad *f*/interés *m* que se ha detectado

2 (= *understand*) comprender; **I do not ~ how it can be done** no comprendo cómo se puede hacer

3 (= *consider*) considerar; **their action may be ~d as a threat** su actuación puede considerarse *or* puede verse como una amenaza; **the things children ~ as being important** las cosas que los niños consideran importantes; **they ~ themselves as rebels** se ven a sí mismos como rebeldes, se consideran a sí mismos rebeldes

per cent [pəˈsent] N por ciento; **20 ~** el 20 por ciento; **it has increased by eight ~** ha aumentado (en) un ocho por ciento; **there's a ten ~ discount** hay un descuento del diez por cien(to), hay un diez por ciento de descuento; **the population is 90 ~ Roman Catholic** el 90 por ciento de la población es católica; **a half (a) ~ cut in interest rates** un recorte de un cero coma cinco por ciento en los tipos de interés; **100 ~** cien por cien; **he's not feeling a hundred ~ today** hoy no se encuentra al cien por cien

percentage [pəˈsentɪdʒ] Ⓐ N 1 (= *proportion*) porcentaje *m*; **what is the ~ of nitrogen in air?** ¿cuál es el porcentaje de nitrógeno en el aire?; **a large ~ of people are immune** un gran porcentaje de la gente es inmune; **the figure is expressed as a ~** la cifra está expresada en tantos por ciento; **on a ~ basis California lost more jobs than any other state** según los porcentajes California perdió más puestos de trabajo que ningún otro estado; **a high ~ are girls** un alto *or* elevado porcentaje son chicas; **in ~ terms** proporcionalmente

2 (= *commission*) porcentaje *m*; **my ~ is deducted beforehand** mi porcentaje se deduce antes; **to get a ~ on all sales** recibir un tanto por ciento sobre todas las ventas; **on a ~ basis** a porcentaje

3 (*) (= *rake-off*) tajada* *f*; **all they're after is their ~** lo único que buscan es llevarse una tajada*

4 (= *advantage, benefit*) **there's no ~ in doing that** haciendo eso no se saca nada; **what ~ is there in it for me?** ¿y yo qué saco?

Ⓑ CPD ► **percentage increase** N aumento *m* porcentual ► **percentage point** N punto *m* porcentual ► **percentage sign** N signo *m* del tanto por ciento

percentile [pəˈsentaɪl] N percentil *m*

perceptible [pəˈseptəbl] ADJ (= *appreciable*) sensible; (= *discernible*) perceptible

perceptibly [pəˈseptəblɪ] ADV (= *appreciably*) sensiblemente; (= *discernibly*) perceptiblemente; **it has improved ~** ha mejorado sensiblemente

perception [pəˈsepʃən] N 1 (= *act*) percepción *f*; **it changes one's ~ of time** cambia la percepción que uno tiene del tiempo; **sense ~** percepción *f* sensorial

2 (= *impression*) impresión *f*; **what is your ~ of the situation?** ¿qué impresión tienes de la situación?; **her ~ was that she had done sth wrong** tenía la impresión de haberse equivocado en algo; **the public ~ is that ...** la gente tiene la impresión de que ...

3 (= *insight*) perspicacia *f*, agudeza *f*

perceptive [pəˈseptɪv] ADJ [*person*] perspicaz; [*remark*] perspicaz, agudo; [*function*] perceptivo

perceptiveness [pəˈseptɪvnɪs] N (= *insight*) perspicacia *f*, agudeza *f*; (= *ability to perceive*) facultad *f* perceptiva

perceptual [pəˈseptjʊəl] ADJ [*skills, problems*] de percepción, perceptual

perch[1] [pɜːtʃ] (A) N [*of bird*] percha *f*; (*fig*) [*of person*] posición *f* elevada; ✦*IDIOM* **to knock sb off his ~** bajar los humos *or* el copete a algn*
(B) VT encaramar; **we ~ed the child on the wall** encaramamos al niño en la tapia; **the village is ~ed on a hilltop** el pueblo está encaramado en lo alto de una colina; **he ~ed his hat on his head** se colocó el sombrero en la cabeza
(C) VI [*bird*] posarse (**on** en); [*person*] (= *sit*) sentarse (**on** en); (*high up*) encaramarse (**on** en); **she ~ed on the arm of my chair** se sentó en el brazo de mi sillón; **we ~ed in a tree to see the procession** nos encaramamos *or* subimos a un árbol para ver el desfile

perch[2] [pɜːtʃ] N (*pl* **perch, perches**) (= *fish*) perca *f*

perch[3] [pɜːtʃ] N *medida de longitud, = 5,029m*

perchance [pəˈtʃɑːns] ADV (*liter*) (= *by chance*) por ventura, acaso; (= *perhaps*) acaso, tal vez; **to sleep, ~ to dream** dormir, acaso *or* tal vez soñar; **are they ~ afraid of me?** ¿acaso les doy miedo?

percipient [pəˈsɪpɪənt] ADJ = **perceptive**

percolate [ˈpɜːkəleɪt] (A) VT filtrar; [+ *coffee*] hacer (*en una cafetera de filtro*); **~d coffee** café *m* (de) filtro
(B) VI [1] (*lit, fig*) filtrarse; **to ~ down to** filtrarse hasta; **to ~ through (sth)** [*water*] filtrarse (por algo); [*ideas*] propagarse (por algo); **these ideas may eventually ~ through to the top of the organization** puede que al final estas ideas se propaguen por la cúpula de la organización
[2] [*coffee*] hacerse (*en una cafetera de filtro*)

percolator [ˈpɜːkəleɪtəʳ] N cafetera *f* de filtro

percussion [pəˈkʌʃən] (A) N [1] (= *impact, noise*) percusión *f*
[2] (*Mus*) percusión *f*; **to play ~** ser percusionista
(B) CPD ► **percussion cap** N cápsula *f* fulminante ► **percussion instrument** N instrumento *m* de percusión ► **percussion section** N percusión *f*, sección *f* de percusión

percussionist [pəˈkʌʃənɪst] N percusionista *mf*

per diem [ˈpɜːˈdiːem] (A) ADV por día
(B) N (= *allowance*) complemento *m* para gastos diarios

perdition [pɜːˈdɪʃən] N (*liter*) perdición *f*

peregrination [ˌperɪgrɪˈneɪʃən] N peregrinación *f*; **peregrinations** (*hum*) periplo *m*, peregrinaje *m*

peregrine [ˈperɪgrɪn] (A) N halcón *m* común, neblí *m*
(B) CPD ► **peregrine falcon** N halcón *m* peregrino

peremptorily [pəˈremptərɪlɪ] ADV [*say, refuse*] en tono perentorio, en tono imperioso; **they were ~ sacked** los despidieron sin más

peremptory [pəˈremptərɪ] ADJ [*tone*] perentorio, imperioso; [*person*] imperioso, autoritario

perennial [pəˈrenɪəl] (A) ADJ (*Bot*) perenne; [*problem*] perenne, eterno; **~ youth** la juventud eterna; **it's a ~ complaint** es una queja constante
(B) N (*Bot*) planta *f* perenne, planta *f* vivaz

perennially [pəˈrenɪəlɪ] ADV perennemente, constantemente; **they are ~ short of staff** les falta personal constantemente

perestroika [perəˈstrɔɪkə] N perestroika *f*

perfect [ˈpɜːfɪkt] (A) ADJ [1] (= *faultless*) perfecto; **nobody is ~** nadie es perfecto; **everything was ~ on the day** ese día todo salió perfecto; **in ~ condition** en perfectas condiciones; **he spoke ~ English** ◊ **his English was ~** hablaba un inglés perfecto; **his Spanish is far from ~** su español dista mucho de ser perfecto; **you're in ~ health** se encuentra perfectamente de salud; *see also* **practice A1**, **word-perfect**
[2] (= *ideal*) [*moment, solution, place*] ideal, perfecto; **a job like that would be ~ for you** un trabajo como ése sería ideal *or* perfecto para ti; **Saturday morning would be ~** el sábado por la mañana sería ideal *or* perfecto; **he's the ~ man for the job** es el hombre idóneo *or* ideal *or* perfecto para el cargo; **his expertise made him the ~ choice** su experiencia hacía de él la persona idónea *or* ideal *or* perfecta; **in a ~ world** en un mundo ideal
[3] (= *exact*) perfecto; **a ~ circle** un círculo perfecto; **a ~ copy** una copia perfecta; **the jacket was a ~ fit** la chaqueta me estaba perfecta *or* me quedaba perfectamente; **my watch keeps ~ time** mi reloj siempre marca la hora exacta
[4] (= *absolute, utter*) **a ~ fool/stranger** un perfecto idiota/desconocido; **I have a ~ right to be here** estoy en el perfecto derecho de estar aquí; **she's a ~ pest** es una verdadera pesada*; **it makes ~ sense to me** me parece completamente *or* totalmente lógico
[5] (*Gram*) perfecto; *see also* **future A2**, **present C**, **past E**
[6] (*Mus*) [*fourth, fifth, octave*] perfecto; **a ~ fifth** una quinta perfecta
(B) [ˈpɜːfɪkt] N (*Gram*) **the ~** el tiempo perfecto; *see also* **future A2**, **present C**, **past E**
(C) [pəˈfekt] VT perfeccionar; **she wanted to ~ her English** quería perfeccionar su inglés; **to ~ the art of doing sth** perfeccionar el arte de hacer algo
(D) [ˈpɜːfɪkt] CPD ► **perfect number** N (*Math*) número *m* perfecto ► **perfect pitch** N (*Mus*) oído *m* perfecto; **to have ~ pitch** tener el oído perfecto

perfectibility [pəˌfektɪˈbɪlɪtɪ] N perfectibilidad *f*

perfectible [pəˈfektəbl] ADJ perfectible

perfection [pəˈfekʃən] N perfección *f*; **the peak of ~** el súmmum de la perfección; **cooked to ~** cocinado a la perfección

perfectionism [pəˈfekʃənɪzm] N perfeccionismo *m*

perfectionist [pəˈfekʃənɪst] N perfeccionista *mf*

perfective [pəˈfektɪv] (A) ADJ [*aspect, verb*] perfectivo
(B) N perfectivo *m*

perfectly [ˈpɜːfɪktlɪ] ADV [1] (= *very well*) perfectamente; **the plan worked ~** el plan salió perfectamente *or* a la perfección; **he is ~ placed to understand the situation** está en la posición perfecta para comprender la situación; **you timed your arrival ~** has llegado en el momento preciso; **one of the most ~ preserved medieval towns in the world** uno de los pueblos medievales mejor conservados del mundo
[2] (= *absolutely, entirely*) [*honest, frank, normal*] totalmente; **to be ~ honest, I hate classical music** si te soy totalmente sincero, odio la música clásica; **I'll be ~ frank with you** te voy a ser totalmente franco; **it's ~ disgusting!** ¡es verdaderamente asqueroso!; **I'm ~ all right** estoy perfectamente; **well, actually, we're ~ happy about it** pues, la verdad, no nos importa en absoluto; **there may be some ~ innocent explanation** puede que esto tenga una explicación totalmente inocente; **it is ~ possible to eat well on a diet** es muy posible alimentarse bien aunque se esté a régimen; **you'll be ~ safe here** aquí no correrás ni el más mínimo peligro; **we're ~ satisfied with this** estamos plenamente satisfechos con esto; **look, it's ~ simple** mira, es de lo más sencillo; **you know ~ well what my answer will be** bien sabes *or* sabes muy bien qué respuesta te voy a dar

perfidious [pɜːˈfɪdɪəs] ADJ (*liter*) pérfido

perfidiously [pɜːˈfɪdɪəslɪ] ADV (*liter*) pérfidamente

perfidy [ˈpɜːfɪdɪ] N (*liter*) perfidia *f*

perforate [ˈpɜːfəreɪt] VT perforar; **to ~ holes in sth** practicar agujeros en algo

perforated [ˈpɜːfəreɪtɪd] (A) ADJ [*stamp*] dentado
(B) CPD ► **perforated line** N línea *f* perforada ► **perforated ulcer** N (*Med*) úlcera *f* perforada

perforation [ˌpɜːfəˈreɪʃən] N (*gen*) perforación *f*; [*of stamp*] perforado *m*

perforce [pəˈfɔːs] ADV (*liter*) forzosamente

perform [pəˈfɔːm] (A) VT [1] (*Theat, Mus*) [+ *play*] representar; [+ *part, piece, song, dance*] interpretar; **it meant a lot to her to have her music ~ed here** significó mucho para ella el que interpretaran su música aquí; **she will ~ a series of sonatas by Mozart** interpretará *or* ejecutará varias sonatas de Mozart
[2] (= *carry out*) [+ *task, experiment, feat*] realizar, llevar a cabo; [+ *operation, autopsy*] practicar, realizar, llevar a cabo; [+ *duty*] cumplir con; [+ *function, role*] desempeñar, cumplir; [+ *rite, ritual, ceremony*] celebrar; [+ *miracle*] realizar, hacer; **they ~ed a great service to their country** prestaron un gran servicio a su país; **to ~ surgery** *or* **an operation on sb** operar a algn, practicar una operación quirúrgica a algn (*frm*)
(B) VI [1] (*Theat, Mus*) [*entertainer, actor*] actuar; [*musician*] tocar; [*orchestra, pop group*] actuar, tocar; [*singer*] cantar; [*dancer*] bailar; [*trained animal*] hacer trucos, realizar trucos; **he ~ed brilliantly as Hamlet** interpretó brillantemente el papel de Hamlet, se lució en el papel de Hamlet; **the band will be ~ing live** el grupo actuará *or* tocará en concierto; **and ~ing for us tonight on the violin is Rebecca Hunt** y esta noche Rebecca Hunt nos tocará el violín
[2] (= *respond, behave*) [*vehicle, machine*] responder, funcionar; [*team, athlete, horse*] responder; [*investment, shares*] rendir; [*metal, material*] comportarse; [*worker*] (= *be productive*) rendir; (= *react*) responder; **how did the company ~ last year?** ¿qué resultados dio la empresa el año pasado?; **the party ~ed abysmally at the last election** el partido obtuvo unos resultados pésimos en las últimas elecciones; **he ~ed well at school** rendía en los estudios; **he did not ~ very well in his exams** no obtuvo muy buenos resultados en los exámenes, los exámenes no le salieron muy bien; **our economy has been ~ing well recently** últimamente, nuestra economía ha estado produciendo buenos resultados
[3] (*) (*esp hum*) (= *go to toilet*) [*child, dog*] hacer sus menesteres
[4] (*) (*sexually*) cumplir*

performance [pəˈfɔːməns] (A) N [1] (*Theat, Mus etc*) [1.1] (= *session*) (*Theat*) función *f*; (*Cine*) sesión *f*; **tonight's ~ will end at 9.45 pm** (*Theat*) la función de esta noche terminará a las 21.45; **the late ~** (*Theat*) la función de noche; (*Cine*) la sesión de noche; **two ~s nightly** (*Theat*) dos funciones *or* representaciones por noche; (*Cine*) dos sesiones por noche; **"no performance tonight"** "esta noche no hay función", "no hay representación esta noche"

1·2 (= *presentation*) [*of play, opera, ballet*] representación *f*; [*of piece of music*] interpretación *f*; **it has not had a ~ since 1950** (*Theat*) no se ha representado desde 1950; (*Mus*) no se ha interpretado desde 1950; **the play ran for over 300 ~s** la obra tuvo más de 300 representaciones; **first ~** estreno *m*; **video footage of the band in ~** unas secuencias en vídeo del grupo en concierto

1·3 (*by actor, singer*) actuación *f*, interpretación *f*; (*by pianist, orchestra*) interpretación *f*; (*by comedian*) actuación *f*; **his ~ as Don Juan was excellent** su actuación en el papel *or* su interpretación del papel de Don Juan fue excelente; **this will be her first ~ at Covent Garden** esta será su primera actuación en Covent Garden; *see also* **gala B**, **virtuoso**

2 (= *effectiveness*) [*of investment, worker*] rendimiento *m*; [*of currency*] comportamiento *m*; [*of team, athlete, racehorse*] actuación *f*; [*of company*] resultados *mpl*; [*of vehicle*] rendimiento *m*, performance *f* (*LAm*); [*of machine*] (= *productivity*) rendimiento *m*; (= *working*) funcionamiento *m*; **the ~ of the pound against the mark** el comportamiento de la libra con respecto al marco; **we judge people on ~ rather than age** juzgamos a las personas por su rendimiento y no por su edad; **the party's disastrous ~ in the elections** los pésimos resultados del partido en las elecciones; **Britain's poor economic ~ in the 1970s** el poco rendimiento de la economía británica en los setenta; **on past ~, an England victory seems unlikely** si nos basamos en las actuaciones anteriores, parece poco probable que Inglaterra vaya a ganar; **her poor ~ in French** su poco rendimiento en francés, sus malos resultados en francés; **he didn't put up a very good ~ in the exams** no obtuvo muy buenos resultados en los exámenes, los exámenes no le salieron muy bien; **the team gave** *or* **put up a poor ~** el equipo tuvo una actuación pobre; *see also* **high-performance**, **performance-related**

3 (= *execution*) [*of task*] realización *f*, ejecución *f*; [*of duty*] cumplimiento *m*; [*of function*] ejercicio *m*; [*of rite, ritual*] práctica *f*, celebración *f*; **she has to rely on others for the ~ of the simplest tasks** tiene que depender de otros para realizar *or* ejecutar las tareas más sencillas; **in the ~ of his duties** en el ejercicio de su cargo

4 (*) (= *bother, rigmarole*) follón* *m*, jaleo* *m*; **it's such a ~ getting here** llegar aquí supone tal follón *or* jaleo*; **what a ~ it is to get a visa!** ¡conseguir un visado es un verdadero follón *or* jaleo!*

5 (*) (= *fuss about nothing*) numero* *m*; **what a ~ she made of making the tea** vaya numero que montó para hacer el té*

6 (*Ling*) actuación *f*

Ⓑ CPD ► **performance art** N performance art *m* ► **performance car** N coche *m* de alto rendimiento ► **performance indicator** N (*Comm, Fin*) indicador *m* del rendimiento ► **performance target** N objetivo *m* de rendimiento

performance-enhancing [pəˈfɔːmənsɪn,hɑːnsɪŋ] ADJ **~ drug** sustancia *f* que potencia el rendimiento

performance-related [pəˈfɔːmənsrɪˈleɪtɪd] ADJ [*bonus, scheme*] en relación con los resultados; **~ pay** remuneración *f* con arreglo al rendimiento

performative [pəˈfɔːmətɪv] N **~ (verb)** (verbo *m*) performativo *m*

performer [pəˈfɔːməʳ] N (*Theat*) actor/actriz *m/f*, artista *mf*; (*Mus*) intérprete *mf*; **a skilled ~ on the piano** un pianista experto; **this fund has been one of the best ~s in recent years** este fondo de inversiones ha sido de los que han dado mejores resultados en los últimos años; **he was a poor ~ at school** no le iba muy bien en el colegio

performing [pəˈfɔːmɪŋ] Ⓐ ADJ [*animal*] amaestrado

Ⓑ CPD ► **performing arts** NPL artes *fpl* de la interpretación

perfume [ˈpɜːfjuːm] Ⓐ N perfume *m*

Ⓑ VT [pəˈfjuːm] perfumar

perfumery [pəˈfjuːmərɪ] N perfumería *f*; (= *perfumes*) perfumes *mpl*

perfunctorily [pəˈfʌŋktərɪlɪ] ADV [*inspect*] superficialmente, someramente; [*reply*] a la ligera; [*kiss*] con indiferencia, mecánicamente

perfunctory [pəˈfʌŋktərɪ] ADJ [*inspection, glance*] superficial, somero; [*reply*] dado a la ligera; [*kiss*] indiferente, mecánico; **he gave a ~ performance** tocó *etc* por cumplir

pergola [ˈpɜːgələ] N pérgola *f*

▼ **perhaps** [pəˈhæps] ADV quizá(s), tal vez; **~ he'll come** quizá *or* tal vez venga, a lo mejor viene; **"will you be seeing her later?" — "perhaps"** —¿la vas a ver después? —a lo mejor *or* —tal vez *or* —puede que sí; **~ not** puede que no; **~ so** puede que sí, puede que así sea, quizá sea así; **there were ~ 50 people there** habría quizás unas 50 personas allí, puede que hubiese unas 50 personas allí

peri... [ˈperɪ] PREFIX peri...

pericardium [,perɪˈkɑːdɪəm] N (*pl* **pericardia** [,perɪˈkɑːdɪə]) pericardio *m*

peridot [ˈperɪdɒt] N peridotita *f*

perigee [ˈperɪdʒiː] N perigeo *m*

peril [ˈperɪl] N riesgo *m*, peligro *m*; **to be in ~** estar en *or* correr peligro; **she was in ~ of her life** su vida estaba en peligro, corría el riesgo *or* peligro de perder la vida; **do it at your ~** hágalo por su cuenta y riesgo

perilous [ˈperɪləs] ADJ peligroso, arriesgado; **it would be ~ to attempt it** sería peligroso *or* arriesgado intentarlo

perilously [ˈperɪləslɪ] ADV peligrosamente; **the film comes ~ close to kitsch** la película roza peligrosamente lo cursi; **he came ~ close to being caught** por poco lo agarran

perimeter [pəˈrɪmɪtəʳ] Ⓐ N perímetro *m*

Ⓑ CPD ► **perimeter fence** N valla *f* que rodea el recinto

perinatal [,perɪˈneɪtl] ADJ perinatal

perineum [,perɪˈniːəm] N (*pl* **perinea**) perineo *m*

period [ˈpɪərɪəd] Ⓐ N 1 (= *length of time*) período *m*; (= *time limit*) plazo *m*; (= *era*) época *f*; (= *stage*) (*in career, development etc*) etapa *f*; (*Sport*) tiempo *m*; **for a ~ of three weeks** durante (un período de) tres semanas; **within a three month ~** en tres meses, dentro de un plazo de tres meses; **for a limited ~** por un periodo limitado; **at that ~ (of my life)** en aquella época (de mi vida); **the holiday ~** el período de vacaciones; **the postwar ~** la posguerra; **the Victorian ~** la época victoriana; **a painting from his early ~** un cuadro de su primera época

2 (*Scol*) clase *f*, hora *f*; **we have two French ~s** tenemos dos clases *or* horas de francés

3 (*Gram*) período *m*; (= *full stop*) (*esp US*) punto *m*; **I said no, ~** he dicho que no, y punto

4 (= *menstruation*) período *m*, regla *f*; **I've got my ~** estoy con la regla

Ⓑ CPD ► **period cost** N costo *m* fijo ► **period dress** N traje(s) *mpl* de época ► **period furniture** N muebles *mpl* de época ► **period instrument** N instrumento *m* de época ► **period pain** N dolores *fpl* menstruales ► **period piece** N (= *film*) película *f* de época; (= *novel*) novela *f* de época

periodic [,pɪərɪˈɒdɪk] Ⓐ ADJ periódico

Ⓑ CPD ► **periodic table** N tabla *f* periódica

periodical [,pɪərɪˈɒdɪkəl] Ⓐ ADJ periódico

Ⓑ N revista *f*, publicación *f* periódica

Ⓒ CPD ► **periodicals library** N hemeroteca *f*

periodically [,pɪerɪˈɒdɪkəlɪ] ADV (= *at regular intervals*) periódicamente; (= *from time to time*) cada cierto tiempo, de vez en cuando

periodicity [,pɪərɪəˈdɪsɪtɪ] N periodicidad *f*

periodontal [perɪˈdɒntl] ADJ periodontal

peripatetic [,perɪpəˈtetɪk] ADJ [*salesman*] ambulante; [*teacher*] con trabajo en varios colegios; (*Philos*) peripatético; **to lead a ~ existence** cambiar mucho de domicilio, no tener residencia fija

peripheral [pəˈrɪfərəl] Ⓐ ADJ 1 (*Med*) [*vision*] periférico

2 (= *outer, surrounding*) [*area*] periférico, de la periferia

3 (= *minor*) [*role, concern*] secundario

Ⓑ N (*Comput*) periférico *m*, unidad *f* periférica

Ⓒ CPD ► **peripheral device** N dispositivo *m* periférico

peripheralize [pəˈrɪfərəlaɪz] VT marginar

periphery [pəˈrɪfərɪ] N periferia *f*

periphrasis [pəˈrɪfrəsɪs] N (*pl* **periphrases** [pəˈrɪfrəsiːz]) perífrasis *f inv*

periphrastic [,perɪˈfræstɪk] ADJ perifrástico

periscope [ˈperɪskəʊp] N periscopio *m*

perish [ˈperɪʃ] Ⓐ VI 1 [*person*] perecer, fallecer; **we shall do it or ~ in the attempt** lo conseguiremos o moriremos intentándolo; **he ~ed at sea** murió en el mar; **~ the thought!** ¡Dios me libre!

2 [*food, material*] deteriorarse, estropearse

Ⓑ VT deteriorar, estropear; **to be ~ed (with cold)*** estar helado*

perishable [ˈperɪʃəbl] Ⓐ ADJ perecedero

Ⓑ N **perishables** productos *mpl* perecederos

perisher†* [ˈperɪʃəʳ] N (*Brit*) tío* *m*; **you little ~!** ¡ay, tunante!*

perishing [ˈperɪʃɪŋ] ADJ 1 (*) (= *freezing*) **it's ~ (cold)** hace un frío de muerte*, hace un frío que pela*; **I'm ~** estoy helado*

2 (*Brit**) condenado*

peristalsis [,perɪˈstælsɪs] N (*pl* **peristalses** [,perɪˈstælsiːz]) peristalsis *f*

peristyle [ˈperɪstaɪl] N peristilo *m*

peritoneum [,perɪtəˈniːəm] N (*pl* **peritoneums** *or* **peritonea** [,perɪtəˈniːə]) peritoneo *m*

peritonitis [,perɪtəˈnaɪtɪs] N peritonitis *f*

periwig [ˈperɪwɪg] N peluca *f*

periwinkle [ˈperɪ,wɪŋkl] N (*Bot*) vincapervinca *f*; (*Zool*) caracol *m* de mar, bígaro *m*

perjure [ˈpɜːdʒəʳ] VT **to ~ o.s.** jurar en falso, perjurar

perjured [ˈpɜːdʒəd] ADJ [*evidence*] falso

perjurer [ˈpɜːdʒərəʳ] N perjuro/a *m/f*

perjury [ˈpɜːdʒərɪ] N perjurio *m*; **to commit ~** cometer perjurio

perk[1]* [pɜːk] N (= *money*) beneficio *m* adicional; **it's one of the ~s of the job** es uno de los incentivos *or* las ventajas del puesto; **there are no ~s in this job** en este puesto no hay nada aparte del sueldo; **company ~s** beneficios *mpl* corporativos

perk²* [pɜːk] VI = **percolate;** [*coffee*] filtrarse

►**perk up** Ⓐ VT + ADV [+ *person*] animar; **this will ~ you up!** ¡esto te animará!; **it ~s up the flavour of frozen vegetables** da vida a *or* anima las verduras congeladas

Ⓑ VI + ADV [*person*] reanimarse; (*in health*) sentirse mejor; **business is ~ing up** el negocio va mejorando; **ears ~ed up when his name was mentioned** todo el mundo aguzó el oído cuando se mencionó su nombre; **share prices ~ed up as a result of the deal** la cotización de las acciones aumentó como resultado del trato

perkiness [ˈpɜːkɪnɪs] N alegría *f,* vida *f;* (= *cheekiness*) frescura *f*

perky [ˈpɜːkɪ] ADJ (*compar* **perkier**; *superl* **perkiest**) (= *cheerful, bright*) alegre, animado; (= *cheeky*) fresco

perm¹* [pɜːm] Ⓐ N (*Brit*) permanente *f*; **she's got a ~** lleva permanente; **to have a ~** hacerse una permanente

Ⓑ VT **to ~ sb's hair** hacer una permanente a algn; **to have one's hair ~ed** hacerse una permanente

perm² [pɜːm] Ⓐ N ABBR = **permutation**

Ⓑ VTI ABBR = **permute**

permafrost [ˈpɜːməfrɒst] N permagel *m*

permanence [ˈpɜːmənəns] N permanencia *f*

permanency [ˈpɜːmənənsɪ] N permanencia *f*; (= *permanent arrangement*) arreglo *m* permanente

permanent [ˈpɜːmənənt] Ⓐ ADJ [1] (= *fixed, unchangeable*) [*limp*] permanente; [*damage*] irreparable; [*finish on steel*] inalterable; **we cannot make any ~ arrangements** no podemos arreglar las cosas de modo definitivo; **on a ~ basis** de forma permanente; **he has become a ~ fixture in her life** se ha convertido en una figura permanente en su vida

[2] (= *stable, lasting*) [*job*] estable, fijo; [*relationship*] estable; **they have made their ~ home in Paris** se han establecido de forma permanente en París; **I'm not ~ here** (*in job*) no estoy fijo aquí

[3] (= *constant*) continuo, permanente; **I lived in a ~ state of fear** vivía en un estado de miedo continuo *or* permanente

Ⓑ N (*US*) = **perm¹**

Ⓒ CPD ► **permanent address** N domicilio *m* permanente ► **permanent magnet** N imán *m* permanente ► **Permanent Secretary** N (*Brit Admin*) Secretario/a *m/f* Permanente (*alto cargo de la Administración en Gran Bretaña*) ► **permanent staff** N personal *m* de plantilla ► **Permanent Under-secretary** N (*Brit Admin*) Subsecretario/a *m/f* Permanente (*alto cargo de la Administración en Gran Bretaña*) ► **permanent wave** N permanente *f*

permanently [ˈpɜːmənəntlɪ] ADV [*live, go away, come back*] permanentemente; [*damage*] irreparablemente, de forma permanente; [*stain, disqualify, ban*] para siempre; **the accident left him ~ brain-damaged** el accidente le produjo un daño cerebral irreparable, el accidente le dejó dañado el cerebro para siempre; **his face seemed to be ~ fixed in a scowl** parecía tener siempre el ceño fruncido; **he is ~ drunk** está siempre *or* permanentemente borracho

permanent-press [ˌpɜːmənəntˈpres] ADJ [*trousers*] de raya permanente; [*skirt*] inarrugable

permanganate [pɜːˈmæŋgənɪt] N permanganato *m*; **~ of potash** permanganato *m* de potasio

permeability [ˌpɜːmɪəˈbɪlɪtɪ] N permeabilidad *f*

permeable [ˈpɜːmɪəbl] ADJ permeable

permeate [ˈpɜːmɪeɪt] Ⓐ VT [1] [*liquid*] penetrar, impregnar; [*smell*] impregnar; [*substance, chemical*] penetrar; **to be ~d with** estar impregnado de

[2] (*fig*) [*ideology, corruption*] estar presente en; **this way of thinking ~s all areas of society** esta forma de pensar está presente en *or* impregna todos los niveles sociales

Ⓑ VI [1] **to ~ through sth** [*liquid*] penetrar a través de algo, impregnar algo; [*smell*] impregnar algo; [*substance, chemical*] penetrar a través de algo

[2] (*fig*) [*ideology, corruption*] extenderse, propagarse (**through** por)

permissible [pəˈmɪsəbl] ADJ lícito; **it is not ~ to do that** no se permite hacer eso; **would it be ~ to say that ...?** ¿podríamos decir que ...?

permission [pəˈmɪʃən] N permiso *m*; **no ~ is needed** no hay que pedir permiso; **I'd like your ~ to go ahead with the deal** me gustaría que me diera permiso *or* su autorización para seguir adelante con el trato; **to ask (sb's) ~ to do sth** pedir permiso (a algn) para hacer algo; **by kind ~ of Pérez Ltd** con el permiso amablemente concedido por Pérez, S. A.; **"reprinted by ~ of the publisher"** reimprimido con permiso *or* autorización de la editorial; **to get ~ from sb (to do sth)** obtener permiso de algn (para hacer algo); **to give** *or* **grant ~ (for sth)** dar *or* conceder permiso (para algo); **to give** *or* **grant sb ~ (to do sth)** dar permiso a algn (para hacer algo); **you have my ~ to use the car** tienes mi permiso para utilizar el coche; **could I have ~ to leave early?** ¿podría salir antes?; **his widow was refused ~ to live in Britain** a su viuda se le negó el permiso de residencia en Gran Bretaña; **to seek ~ (from sb) to do sth** pedir permiso (a algn) para hacer algo; **with your ~** con su permiso; **he borrowed my car/left the country without ~** se llevó mi coche/se marchó del país sin permiso; *see also* **planning B**

permissive [pəˈmɪsɪv] ADJ (= *tolerant*) [*attitude, law*] permisivo; **the ~ society** la sociedad permisiva

permissively [pəˈmɪsɪvlɪ] ADV permisivamente

permissiveness [pəˈmɪsɪvnɪs] N permisividad *f*

permit Ⓐ [ˈpɜːmɪt] N (= *licence*) permiso *m*, licencia *f*; (= *pass*) pase *m*; (= *permission*) permiso *m*; **do you have a ~ to carry that gun?** ¿tienes permiso *or* licencia para llevar esa pistola?; **building ~** permiso *m* de de obras; *see also* **parking B, residence B D**

Ⓑ [pəˈmɪt] VT permitir; **I won't ~ it** no lo permitiré; **is smoking ~ted?** ¿se permite *or* está permitido fumar?, ¿se puede fumar?; **"smoking is not permitted on the car deck"** "está prohibido fumar *or* no se permite fumar en la cubierta de automóviles"; **the law ~s the sale of this substance** la ley autoriza *or* permite la venta de esta sustancia; **he ~ted himself one cigar a day** se permitía (fumar) un cigarro al día; **to ~ sb to do sth** permitir a algn hacer algo, permitir que algn haga algo; **~ me to give you some advice** (*frm*) permítame aconsejarle *or* que le aconseje; **if I may be ~ted to make a suggestion** (*frm*) si se me permite hacer una sugerencia, si me permite que haga una sugerencia

Ⓒ [pəˈmɪt] VI **if time ~s** si hay tiempo (suficiente); **weather ~ting** si el tiempo lo permite; **to ~ of sth** (*frm*) admitir algo, dar posibilidad a algo; **the crime ~s of no defence** el crimen no admite defensa alguna, el crimen no da posibilidad a defensa alguna

Ⓓ [ˈpɜːmɪt] CPD ► **permit holder** N titular *mf* de un permiso

permutation [ˌpɜːmjʊˈteɪʃən] N [1] (*Math*) [*of number*] permutación *f*

[2] (= *variety, combination*) combinación *f*

permute [pəˈmjuːt] VT permutar

pernicious [pɜːˈnɪʃəs] Ⓐ ADJ [1] [*idea, influence*] pernicioso; **the ~ custom of ...** la perniciosa *or* funesta costumbre de ...

[2] (*Med*) pernicioso

Ⓑ CPD ► **pernicious anaemia** N anemia *f* perniciosa

perniciously [pɜːˈnɪʃəslɪ] ADV perniciosamente

pernickety* [pəˈnɪkɪtɪ] ADJ [*person*] quisquilloso, remilgado; [*task*] delicado; **she's ~ about food** es exigente para la comida; **he's terribly ~ about punctuality** tiene la manía de la puntualidad

peroration [ˌperəˈreɪʃən] N (*frm, iro*) perorata *f*

peroxide [pəˈrɒksaɪd] Ⓐ N peróxido *m*

Ⓑ CPD ► **peroxide blonde** N rubia *f* de bote, rubia *f* oxigenada

perpendicular [ˌpɜːpənˈdɪkjʊləʳ] Ⓐ ADJ [1] (*Math*) perpendicular

[2] (*Archit*) *perteneciente al estilo gótico de los siglos XIV y XV en Gran Bretaña*

Ⓑ N perpendicular *f*; **to be out of (the) ~** salir de la perpendicular, no estar a plomo

perpetrate [ˈpɜːpɪtreɪt] VT cometer; (*Jur*) perpetrar

perpetration [ˌpɜːpɪˈtreɪʃən] N comisión *f*; (*Jur*) perpetración *f*

perpetrator [ˈpɜːpɪtreɪtəʳ] N autor(a) *m/f*, responsable *mf*

perpetual [pəˈpetjʊəl] Ⓐ ADJ (= *eternal*) [*youth*] eterno; [*smile, snow*] perpetuo; (= *continuous*) [*complaints*] continuo, constante; **he has a ~ grin on his face** tiene una sonrisa perpetua *or* permanente *or* (*hum*) perenne en la cara; **she is in a state of ~ anxiety** está en un perpetuo estado de preocupación; **it was a ~ reminder of her dependency on him** era un constante recordatorio de su dependencia de él; **his ~ nagging gets on my nerves** sus quejas constantes *or* continuas me ponen de los nervios

Ⓑ CPD ► **perpetual calendar** N calendario *m* perpetuo ► **perpetual motion** N movimiento *m* continuo

perpetually [pəˈpetjʊəlɪ] ADV (= *eternally*) permanentemente; (= *continually*) constantemente, continuamente; **we were ~ hungry** teníamos siempre hambre

perpetuate [pəˈpetjʊeɪt] VT perpetuar

perpetuation [pəˌpetjʊˈeɪʃən] N perpetuación *f*

perpetuity [ˌpɜːpɪˈtjuːɪtɪ] N perpetuidad *f*; **in ~** a perpetuidad

Perpignan [ˈpɜːpiːnjɒn] N Perpiñán *m*

perplex [pəˈpleks] VT (= *puzzle*) dejar perplejo; (= *confuse*) desconcertar, confundir; [+ *situation, issue*] complicar

perplexed [pəˈplekst] ADJ perplejo, confuso; **we were ~** nos quedamos perplejos, estábamos confusos; **to look ~** parecer confuso

perplexedly [pəˈpleksɪdlɪ] ADV perplejamente

perplexing [pəˈpleksɪŋ] ADJ [*person*] desconcertante; [*issue, question, problem*] complicado; **it's all very ~** es todo muy complicado

perplexity [pəˈpleksɪtɪ] N perplejidad *f*, confusión *f*

per pro. ABBR = **per procurationem** (= *by proxy*) p.p.

► LANGUAGE IN USE: **permission** 9.2, 9.4

perquisite ['pɜːkwɪzɪt] N beneficio *m* adicional, gaje *m*; **perquisites** gajes *mpl* y emolumentos *mpl*

perry ['perɪ] N sidra *f* de peras

persecute ['pɜːsɪkjuːt] VT perseguir; (= *harass*) acosar; **they were ~d under the Nazis** sufrieron persecución bajo los nazis; **to ~ sb with questions** acosar a algn con preguntas

persecution [,pɜːsɪ'kjuːʃən] Ⓐ N persecución *f*
Ⓑ CPD ► **persecution complex** N (*Psych*) complejo *m* persecutorio ► **persecution mania** N (*Psych*) manía *f* persecutoria

persecutor ['pɜːsɪkjuːtəʳ] N perseguidor(a) *m/f*

Persephone [pə'sefənɪ] N Perséfone *f*

Perseus ['pɜːsjuːs] N Perseo *m*

perseverance [,pɜːsɪ'vɪərəns] N perseverancia *f*

persevere [,pɜːsɪ'vɪəʳ] VI perseverar, persistir (**in** en); **to ~ with** perseverar con, continuar con

persevering [,pɜːsɪ'vɪərɪŋ] ADJ perseverante, tenaz

perseveringly [,pɜːsɪ'vɪərɪŋlɪ] ADV con perseverancia, perseverantemente

Persia ['pɜːʃə] N (*Hist*) Persia *f*

Persian ['pɜːʃən] Ⓐ ADJ persa
Ⓑ N 1 (= *person*) persa *mf*
2 (*Ling*) persa *m*
Ⓒ CPD ► **Persian carpet** N alfombra *f* persa ► **Persian cat** N gato *m* persa ► **Persian Gulf** N Golfo *m* Pérsico ► **Persian lamb** N (= *animal*) oveja *f* caracul; (= *skin*) caracul *m*

persiflage [,pɜːsɪ'flɑːʒ] N burlas *fpl*, guasa* *f*

persimmon [pɜː'sɪmən] N placaminero *m*, caqui *m*

persist [pə'sɪst] VI 1 (= *continue to exist*) [*belief, rumour, symptoms*] persistir; **this sort of attitude ~s even today** este tipo de actitud persiste incluso hoy en día
2 (= *insist*) **we shall ~ in our efforts to do it** seguiremos esforzándonos por hacerlo; **he ~s in calling me at all hours of the day** se empeña *or* insiste en llamarme a todas horas del día

persistence [pə'sɪstəns], **persistency** [pə'sɪstənsɪ] N 1 (= *tenacity*) perseverancia *f*; **as a reward for her ~** como premio a su perseverancia
2 (= *continuing to exist*) [*of symptoms, disease*] persistencia *f*

persistent [pə'sɪstənt] Ⓐ ADJ 1 (= *tenacious*) [*person*] insistente; **he is most ~** es muy insistente
2 (= *continuing*) [*rumours, rain, headache*] persistente; [*problem*] continuo, que persiste
3 (= *repeated, constant*) [*questions, refusal, denial*] continuo, constante; **despite our ~ warnings** a pesar de nuestras continuas advertencias
Ⓑ CPD ► **persistent offender** N multirreincidente *mf*, delincuente *mf* habitual ► **persistent vegetative state** N estado *m* vegetativo persistente

persistently [pə'sɪstəntlɪ] ADV 1 (= *tenaciously*) persistentemente, con persistencia
2 (= *continually*) constantemente; **he ~ refuses to help** se niega constantemente a prestar su ayuda; **the main problem is ~ high inflation** el principal problema es un nivel de inflación constantemente elevado

persnickety* [pɜː'snɪkɪtɪ] ADJ (*US*) = **pernickety**

person ['pɜːsn] N 1 (*pl* **people** *or* (*frm*) **persons**) (= *individual*) persona *f*; **who would be the best ~ to ask?** ¿quién es la persona más indicada para preguntarle?; **she is a very caring ~** es (una persona) muy comprensiva; **Jane was the last ~ to see him** Jane fue la última (persona) que lo vio; **I don't know of any such ~** no conozco a tal persona; **there is no such ~ as Father Christmas** no hay tal Papá Noel; **who is this Ford ~ she keeps talking about?** ¿quién es este tal Ford del que habla constantemente?; **the right of accused ~s to remain silent** (*frm*) el derecho de los acusados a no declarar; **two-~ households** viviendas *fpl* de dos personas; **I like him as a ~, but not as a politician** me gusta como persona, pero no como político; **a certain ~, who shall be nameless ...** (*hum*) cierta persona, a quien no voy a nombrar ... (*hum*); **to call sb ~ to ~** (*Telec*) llamar a algn de persona a persona; **murder by ~ or ~s unknown** (*Jur*) homicidio *m* a manos de persona *or* personas sin identificar; *see also* **people, per, single C, third D, young A1, person-to-person**
2 (*pl* **persons**) (= *body, physical presence*) persona *f*; **crimes** *or* **offences against the ~** (*Jur*) crímenes *mpl or* ofensas *fpl* contra la persona; **to have a weapon concealed on** *or* **about one's ~** (*frm*) llevar encima una arma oculta; **in ~** en persona; **give it to him in ~** dáselo a él en persona; **he found one new problem in the ~ of Max Steel** encontró un nuevo problema en la persona de Max Steel
3 (*pl* **people**) (*) (= *type*) **I'm not much of a city ~ myself** no soy de los que les gusta la ciudad*; **Steve is a cat ~** Steve es un amante de los gatos
4 (*pl* **persons**) (*Gram*) persona *f*; **the first ~ singular** la primera persona del singular; **in the first/third ~** en primera/tercera persona

persona [pɜː'səʊnə] N (*pl* **personae** [pɜː'səʊnaɪ])
1 (= *character*) personaje *m*
2 (= *image*) imagen *f*
3 **~ grata** persona *f* grata; **~ non grata** persona *f* no grata

personable ['pɜːsnəbl] ADJ bien parecido

personage ['pɜːsnɪdʒ] N personaje *m*

personal ['pɜːsnl] Ⓐ ADJ 1 (= *individual*) personal; **I will give it my ~ attention** me encargaré personalmente; **I know from ~ experience that it's not easy** sé por experiencia personal que no es fácil; **it's an attack on their ~ freedom** es un ataque contra su libertad personal; **he was a ~ friend** era un amigo íntimo *or* personal; **to have/take a ~ interest in sth** tener un interés personal en *or* por algo, interesarse personalmente en *or* por algo; **my ~ opinion is that ...** en mi opinión personal ...; **it is a matter of ~ preference** es una cuestión de preferencia personal; **are you willing to take ~ responsibility for her?** ¿estás dispuesto a responsabilizarte personalmente de ella?; **if you continue with this investigation you do so at great ~ risk** si continúa con esta investigación correrá usted un gran riesgo contra su persona; **to give sth the ~ touch** dar a algo el toque personal
2 (= *private*) personal; **"personal"** (*on letter*) "confidencial"; **~ belongings** efectos *mpl or* cosas *fpl* personales; **they don't allow ~ calls on the office phone** no permiten que se hagan llamadas particulares en el teléfono de la oficina; **she refused to discuss her ~ life** se negó a discutir su vida personal *or* privada; **this was a ~ matter, something between us two** este era un asunto personal, algo entre nosotros dos; **for ~ reasons** por razones personales; **~ space** espacio *m* vital; **to invade sb's ~ space** acercarse demasiado a algn; **two telephones, one for ~ use and the other for business** dos teléfonos, uno para uso personal y el otro para los negocios
3 (= *in person*) [*visit, interview*] en persona; **to make a ~ appearance** hacer acto de presencia
4 (= *against the person*) [*abuse, insult*] de carácter personal; **there's no need to get ~** no hace falta llevar las cosas al terreno personal; **they are suing for ~ injury** van a denunciar por daños contra la persona; **I have nothing ~ against him** no tengo nada personal en contra suya; **to ask ~ questions** hacer preguntas personales *or* de carácter personal; **to make ~ remarks (about sb)** hacer comentarios de carácter personal acerca de *or* sobre algn
5 (= *physical*) personal; **~ appearance** aspecto *m* (físico); **~ cleanliness** aseo *m* personal; **~ hygiene** higiene *f* personal
Ⓑ N (*US Journalism*) (= *advert*) anuncio *m* en la sección de citas
Ⓒ CPD ► **personal account** N (*Fin*) cuenta *f* personal ► **personal allowance** N (*for tax*) desgravación *f* personal ► **personal assets** NPL bienes *mpl* muebles ► **personal assistant** N ayudante *mf* personal (**to** de); ► **personal best** N (*Sport*) marca *f* personal ► **personal column** N (*Brit*) (*for births, deaths and marriages*) (páginas *fpl*) sociales *fpl* (y necrológicas); (*for lonely hearts*) (sección *f* de) anuncios *mpl* personales ► **personal computer** N ordenador *m or* (*LAm*) computadora *f* personal ► **personal effects** NPL efectos *mpl* personales ► **personal foul** N falta *f* personal ► **personal identification number** N número *m* de identificación personal ► **personal income** N ingresos *mpl* personales ► **personal income tax** N impuesto *m* sobre la renta de las personas físicas ► **personal loan** N préstamo *m* personal ► **personal organizer** N (*paper*) agenda *f* personal; (*electronic*) agenda *f* personal electrónica ► **personal pronoun** N pronombre *m* personal ► **personal property** N (*Jur*) bienes *mpl* (muebles); (*private*) cosas *fpl* personales ► **personal secretary** N secretario/a *m/f* personal ► **personal security** N (= *safety*) seguridad *f* personal; (*on loan*) garantía *f* personal ► **personal stereo** N Walkman® *m*, equipo *m* de música personal ► **personal trainer** N preparador(a) *m/f*

personality [,pɜːsə'nælɪtɪ] Ⓐ N 1 (= *nature*) personalidad *f*; **she reached the top through sheer force of ~** alcanzó la cima simplemente gracias a su fuerte personalidad; *see also* **dual B, multiple C, split E**
2 (= *charisma*) personalidad *f*; **a woman of great ~** una mujer de gran personalidad; **some people find him lacking in ~** algunos encuentran que le falta personalidad
3 (= *celebrity*) figura *f*, personalidad *f*; **politicians and other prominent personalities** políticos *mpl* y otras prominentes figuras *or* personalidades; **a well-known TV ~** una conocida figura de la TV; **a sports** *or* **sporting ~** una figura de los deportes
4 (= *remarkable person*) personaje *m*; **the old fellow is a real ~** el viejo es todo un personaje
5 **personalities** (= *personal remarks*) personalismos *mpl*; **the debate degenerated into personalities** el debate degeneró y se entró en personalismos
Ⓑ CPD ► **personality clash** N incompatibilidad *f* de caracteres ► **personality cult** N culto *m* a la personalidad ► **personality disorder** N trastornos *mpl* mentales ► **personality**

test N test *m* psicotécnico ► **personality trait** N rasgo *m* de personalidad

personalize ['pɜːsənəlaɪz] VT 1 [+ *garment, accessory*] marcar con iniciales
2 [+ *argument, issue*] llevar al terreno de lo personal

personalized ['pɜːsənəlaɪzd] ADJ [*garment, accessory*] con las iniciales; [*stationery*] con membrete; [*service*] personalizado, individualizado; **a ~ exercise programme** un programa de ejercicios personalizado; **~ number plate** *matrícula personalizada, que contiene, por ejemplo, las iniciales del propietario*

▼**personally** ['pɜːsnəlɪ] ADV 1 (= *individually*) personalmente; **~ I think that …** personalmente creo que …; **I wasn't referring to you ~** no me estaba refiriendo a ti personalmente; **I know her ~** la conozco personalmente; **I hold you ~ responsible for what has happened/for her safety** lo declaro responsable personalmente de lo que ha ocurrido/de su seguridad
2 (= *in person*) en persona, personalmente; **the manager saw me ~** el gerente habló conmigo en persona *or* personalmente
3 (= *unkindly*) **I didn't mean it ~** no pretendía ofenderte; **don't take it too ~** no te lo tomes a mal

personalty ['pɜːsnltɪ] N bienes *mpl* muebles

personate ['pɜːsəneɪt] VT (= *impersonate*) hacerse pasar por; (*Theat*) hacer el papel de

personification [pɜːˌsɒnɪfɪ'keɪʃən] N personificación *f*; **he is the ~ of evil/kindness** es el mal personificado/la amabilidad personificada, es la personificación del mal/de la amabilidad

personify [pɜː'sɒnɪfaɪ] VT (= *epitomize*) personificar; (= *represent as person*) personificar; **he is greed personified** es la codicia personificada *or* en persona, es la personificación de la codicia; **he personified the spirit of resistance** encarnó el espíritu de la resistencia

personnel [ˌpɜːsə'nel] Ⓐ N 1 (= *staff*) personal *m*
2 (= *department*) departamento *m* de personal, sección *f* de personal; **head of ~** jefe/a *m/f* de personal
3 (*Mil*) personal *m*; **military ~** personal *m* militar; *see also* **antipersonnel**
Ⓑ CPD ► **personnel agency** N agencia *f* de personal ► **personnel carrier** N vehículo *m* militar para transporte de tropas; **armoured** *or* (*US*) **armored ~ carrier** camión *m* blindado ► **personnel department** N departamento *m* de personal, sección *f* de personal ► **personnel director** N director(a) *m/f* de personal ► **personnel file** N historial *m* personal ► **personnel management** N administración *f* de personal, gestión *f* de personal ► **personnel manager** N jefe/a *m/f* de personal ► **personnel officer** N jefe/a *m/f* de personal (*subordinado al "personnel manager" si lo hay*) ► **personnel policy** N política *f* en materia de personal ► **personnel record** N historial *m* personal

person-to-person [ˌpɜːsntə'pɜːsn] ADJ **~ call** (*Telec*) llamada *f* (de) persona a persona

perspective [pə'spektɪv] N 1 (*lit*) 1·1 (*Art*) perspectiva *f*; **to be in/out of ~** estar/no estar en perspectiva
1·2 (= *view*) vista *f*
2 (*fig*) perspectiva *f*; **it has given him a new ~ on life** le ha dado una nueva perspectiva *or* visión de la vida; **I would like to offer a historical ~** me gustaría ofrecer una perspectiva histórica; **from our ~** desde nuestro punto de vista; **let's get things in ~** pongamos las cosas en su sitio; **he gets things out of ~** ve las cosas distorsionadas; **to keep sth in ~** guardar algo en su justa medida; **to look at** *or* **see sth in ~** mirar *or* ver algo en su justa medida; **it helped me put things into ~** me ayudó a ver las cosas con cierta perspectiva *or* en su justa medida; **that puts things in a different ~** eso le da otro cariz a las cosas; **try to keep a sense of ~** trata de ser objetivo

Perspex® ['pɜːspeks] N (*esp Brit*) plexiglás® *m*

perspicacious [ˌpɜːspɪ'keɪʃəs] ADJ (*frm*) perspicaz

perspicacity [ˌpɜːspɪ'kæsɪtɪ] N (*frm*) perspicacia *f*

perspicuity [ˌpɜːspɪ'kjʊːɪtɪ] N (*frm*) perspicuidad *f*

perspicuous [ˌpə'spɪkjʊəs] ADJ (*frm*) perspicuo

perspiration [ˌpɜːspə'reɪʃən] N transpiración *f* (*frm*), sudor *m*; **beads of ~** gotas *fpl* de sudor; **to be bathed in ~** estar bañado en sudor, estar todo sudoroso

perspire [pəs'paɪəʳ] VI transpirar (*frm*), sudar; **to ~ freely** transpirar *or* sudar mucho

perspiring [pəs'paɪərɪŋ] ADJ sudoroso

persuadable [pə'sweɪdəbl] ADJ influenciable, persuasible; **he may be ~** quizá lo podamos persuadir

persuade [pə'sweɪd] VT convencer, persuadir (*frm*); **they would not be ~d** no había quien los convenciera *or* persuadiera; **she is easily ~d** se deja convencer *or* persuadir fácilmente; **she didn't need any persuading** no hizo falta insistirle, no hizo falta que la persuadieran *or* convencieran; **he is not ~d of the need for electoral reform** la necesidad de una reforma electoral no lo convence; **to ~ sb that** convencer a algn de que; **I am ~d that …** estoy convencido de que …; **he tried to ~ himself that it did not matter** intentó convencerse de que no tenía importancia; **to ~ sb to do sth** convencer a algn de que *or* para que haga algo, persuadir a algn para que haga algo; **I wanted to help but they ~d me not to** quise ayudar pero me convencieron de que *or* para que no lo hiciera, quise ayudar pero me persuadieron para que no lo hiciera

persuasion [pə'sweɪʒən] N 1 (= *act*) persuasión *f*; **his powers of ~ were formidable** sus dotes de persuasión *or* convicción eran extraordinarios; **all he needs is a little gentle** *or* **friendly ~** (*lit, fig*) sólo hace falta aplicarle unas suaves técnicas de persuasión; **I wouldn't need much ~ to stop working nights** costaría poco convencerme de *or* para que dejara de trabajar por la noche
2 (= *belief*) (*Rel*) creencia *f*; (*Pol*) ideología *f*; **sport brings people of all races and ~s together** el deporte une a la gente de todas las razas y creencias; **politicians of every ~** políticos *mpl* de todas las ideologías; **I'm not of that ~** no soy de esa opinión, no es ésa mi opinión

persuasive [pə'sweɪsɪv] ADJ [*person, voice, tone*] persuasivo; [*argument, evidence*] convincente

persuasively [pə'sweɪsɪvlɪ] ADV de modo persuasivo

persuasiveness [pə'sweɪsɪvnɪs] N persuasiva *f*

PERT [pɜːt] N ABBR = **programme evaluation and review technique**

pert [pɜːt] ADJ 1 (= *coquettish*) [*young woman, hat*] coqueto
2 (= *neat, firm*) [*nose*] respingón; [*breasts*] levantado
3 (= *rude*) [*reply*] un tanto descarado

pertain [pɜː'teɪn] VI (*frm*) **to ~ to** (= *concern*) concernir a, estar relacionado con; (= *belong to*) pertenecer a; (= *be the province of*) incumbir a; **and other matters ~ing to it** y otros asuntos relacionados

pertinacious [ˌpɜːtɪ'neɪʃəs] ADJ pertinaz

pertinaciously [ˌpɜːtɪ'neɪʃəslɪ] ADV con pertinacia

pertinacity [ˌpɜːtɪ'næsɪtɪ] N pertinacia *f*

pertinence ['pɜːtɪnəns] N pertinencia *f*

pertinent ['pɜːtɪnənt] ADJ [*information, facts*] pertinente; **evidence ~ to the case** pruebas *f* pertinentes al *or* que guardan relación con el caso; **that is not ~ to the discussion** eso no es pertinente a *or* no está relacionado con la discusión; **he asked some very ~ questions** hizo unas preguntas muy pertinentes

pertinently ['pɜːtɪnəntlɪ] ADV [*say, reply*] oportunamente, con tino; **where had he learned all this, or, more ~, why had he remembered it?** ¿dónde había aprendido todo esto, o, lo que es más importante, por qué lo recordó?

pertly ['pɜːtlɪ] ADV [*reply*] descaradamente; [*sit, pose*] con coquetería

pertness ['pɜːtnɪs] N 1 [*of sb's figure*] elegancia *f*
2 [*of reply*] descaro *m*

perturb [pə'tɜːb] VT 1 (= *distress*) inquietar, preocupar; **we are all very ~ed** estamos todos muy inquietos *or* preocupados; **he didn't seem in the least ~ed** no parecía estar inquieto *or* preocupado en lo más mínimo
2 (= *disturb*) [+ *calm, harmony*] perturbar

perturbation [ˌpɜːtɜː'beɪʃən] N 1 (= *distress*) inquietud *f*, preocupación *f*
2 (= *disturbance*) (*esp Phys, Astron*) perturbación *f*

perturbing [pə'tɜːbɪŋ] ADJ inquietante, preocupante

Peru [pə'ruː] N Perú *m*

perusal [pə'ruːzəl] N examen *m*; **after a brief/careful ~ of the document** tras un somero/detenido examen del documento, tras una somera/detenida lectura del documento; **a copy is enclosed for your ~** adjunta se ha enviado una copia para que la examine

peruse [pə'ruːz] VT [+ *book, menu*] leer detenidamente, examinar con detenimiento; [+ *crowd*] examinar con detenimiento; [+ *exhibition*] ver con detenimiento

Peruvian [pə'ruːvɪən] Ⓐ ADJ peruano
Ⓑ N peruano/a *m/f*
Ⓒ CPD ► **Peruvian bark** N quina *f*

perv* [pɜːv] N pervertido/a *m/f*

pervade [pɜː'veɪd] VT [*smell*] extenderse por; [*light*] difundirse por; [*feeling, atmosphere*] impregnar; [*influence, ideas*] extenderse por; **the smell of burnt food ~d the whole house** el olor a comida quemada se extendió por toda la casa; **this prejudice ~s our society** este prejuicio está extendido en nuestra sociedad; *see also* **all-pervading**

pervasive [pɜː'veɪsɪv] ADJ [*smell*] penetrante; [*feeling, influence*] dominante; [*superstition, belief, presence*] generalizado

perverse [pə'vɜːs] ADJ (= *contrary*) retorcido; (= *obstinate*) terco, contumaz; (= *wicked*) perverso; **human nature is ~** el hombre es perverso por naturaleza; **I took a ~ pleasure in his predicament** verlo en un aprieto me producía un placer perverso

perversely [pə'vɜːslɪ] ADV (= *irrationally*) sin ninguna lógica; (= *obstinately*) tercamente; (= *wickedly*) con perversidad

➤ LANGUAGE IN USE: **personally 1** 6.2, 12.1

perverseness [pəˈvɜːsnɪs] N = **perversity**

perversion [pəˈvɜːʃən] N (*Med, Psych*) perversión *f*; [*of justice*] deformación *f*; [*of truth, facts*] tergiversación *f*

perversity [pəˈvɜːsɪtɪ] N (= *contrariness*) contrariedad *f*; (= *obstinacy*) terquedad *f*, contumacia *f*

pervert Ⓐ [pəˈvɜːt] VT [1] (= *corrupt*) pervertir [2] (= *twist*) [+ *words*] torcer, desvirtuar; [+ *facts, truth*] distorsionar, tergiversar; **to ~ the course of justice** (*Jur*) torcer el curso de la justicia
Ⓑ [ˈpɜːvɜːt] N pervertido/a *m/f*

perverted [pəˈvɜːtɪd] ADJ (*all senses*) pervertido

pervious [ˈpɜːvɪəs] ADJ permeable (**to** a)

peseta [pəˈsetə] N peseta *f*

pesky* [ˈpeskɪ] ADJ (*compar* **peskier**; *superl* **peskiest**) (*US*) molesto

peso [ˈpeɪsəʊ] N peso *m*

pessary [ˈpesərɪ] N pesario *m*

pessimism [ˈpesɪmɪzəm] N pesimismo *m*

pessimist [ˈpesɪmɪst] N pesimista *mf*

pessimistic [ˌpesɪˈmɪstɪk] ADJ pesimista; **he is ~ about the future** es pesimista en lo que al futuro se refiere

pessimistically [ˌpesɪˈmɪstɪkəlɪ] ADV con pesimismo

pest [pest] Ⓐ N [1] (*Zool*) plaga *f*; (= *insect*) insecto *m* nocivo; (= *animal*) animal *m* dañino, animal *m* nocivo
[2] (*fig*) (= *person*) pelma *mf* (*Sp**), pelmazo/a *m/f* (*Sp**), fregón/ona *m/f* (*LAm**); (= *thing*) lata* *f*, fastidio *m*; **what a ~ that child is!** ¡cómo me fastidia ese niño!; **it's a ~ having to go** es una lata tener que ir*
Ⓑ CPD ► **pest control** N lucha *f* contra las plagas de insectos y ratas ► **pest control officer** N funcionario/a *m/f* del departamento de lucha contra plagas de insectos y ratas

pester [ˈpestəʳ] VT molestar, fregar (*LAm*); **is this man ~ing you?** ¿la está molestando este hombre?; **he's always ~ing me** siempre me está dando la lata*; **she ~ed me for the book** estuvo dando la lata para que le prestara el libro*; **he ~s me with his questions** me fastidia con sus preguntas; **to ~ sb to do sth** dar la lata a algn para que haga algo*

pesticide [ˈpestɪsaɪd] N pesticida *m*

pestilence [ˈpestɪləns] N pestilencia *f*, peste *f*

pestilent [ˈpestɪlənt] ADJ [1] (= *infected, diseased*) apestado
[2] (*) (= *annoying*) latoso*

pestilential [ˌpestɪˈlenʃəl] ADJ [1] [*disease*] mortal; [*smell*] pestilente
[2] (*) (= *annoying*) latoso*

pestle [ˈpesl] N mano *f* (de mortero)

pesto [ˈpestəʊ] N pesto *m*

pet¹ [pet] Ⓐ N [1] (= *animal*) animal *m* doméstico, mascota *f*; **have you got a ~?** ¿tenéis algún animal en casa?; **family/household ~** animal *m* doméstico; **to keep sth as a ~** tener algo como animal doméstico *or* mascota; **"no pets allowed"** "no se admiten animales"
[2] (= *favourite*) preferido/a *m/f*; **she's teacher's ~** es la preferida de la profesora, es la enchufada de la profesora*
[3] (*) (*as term of address*) cielo *m*, amor *m*; **come here, (my) ~** ven aquí mi cielo *or* amor
[4] (*) (= *lovable person*) cielo *m*; **be a ~ and fetch me my glasses** sé un cielo y alcánzame las gafas; **he's rather a ~** es un cielo
Ⓑ ADJ [1] [*animal*] **she keeps two ~ snakes** tiene dos serpientes en casa; **he had a ~ monkey which had been trained to do tricks** tenía un mono domesticado al que habían enseñado a hacer gracias; **he lives alone with his ~ dog** vive solo con su perro; **he was always hanging around her like a ~ dog** iba siempre con ella como un perro mascota
[2] (= *favourite*) [*theory, project*] preferido, favorito; **once she gets onto her ~ subject there's no stopping her** una vez empieza con su tema preferido *or* predilecto no hay quien la pare; **~ hate** ◊ **~ aversion** pesadilla *f*; **my ~ hate is smoking** lo que más detesto es el tabaco, el tabaco es mi pesadilla; **~ name** nombre *m* cariñoso; (= *short form*) diminutivo *m* cariñoso
Ⓒ VT [1] (= *indulge*) mimar, consentir
[2] (= *fondle*) acariciar
Ⓓ VI (*sexually*) sobarse, acariciarse
Ⓔ CPD ► **pet door** N (*US*) gatera *f* ► **pet food** N comida *f* para animales ► **pet owner** N dueño/a *m/f* de animal ► **pet shop**, **pet store** (*US*) N pajarería *f*

pet² [pet] N **to be in a ~** estar enfurruñado; **to get into a ~** enfurruñarse

petal [ˈpetl] N pétalo *m*

petard [peˈtɑːd] N petardo *m*; ✦*IDIOM* **he was hoist with his own ~** le salió el tiro por la culata*

Pete [piːt] N (*familiar form*) *of* **Peter** Perico; **for ~'s sake!*** ¡por (el amor de) Dios!

peter¹ [ˈpiːtəʳ] VI **to ~ out** [*supply*] irse agotando; [*conversation*] irse acabando; [*road, stream*] perderse, desaparecer; [*interest, excitement*] desvanecerse, decaer; [*plan*] quedar en nada; [*song, noise, voice*] apagarse; **the road ~ed out into a track** la carretera dio paso a un camino, la carretera se transformó en camino

peter²** [ˈpiːtəʳ] N (*US*) verga** *f*, picha** *f*

peter³* [ˈpiːtəʳ] N (= *safe*) caja *f* de caudales; (= *cell*) celda *f*

Peter [ˈpiːtəʳ] N Pedro; **~ the Great** Pedro el Grande; **~ Rabbit** el Conejo Peter; ✦*IDIOM* **to rob ~ to pay Paul** desnudar a un santo para vestir a otro

Peter Pan [ˌpiːtəˈpæn] N Peter Pan *m*, niño *m* eterno

pethidine [ˈpeθɪdiːn] N petidina *f*

petit bourgeois [ˌpetɪˈbʊəʒwɑː] Ⓐ ADJ pequeñoburgués
Ⓑ N pequeñoburgués/esa *m/f*

petite [pəˈtiːt] ADJ chiquita

petite bourgeoisie [pəˌtiːtˌbʊəʒwɑːˈziː] N pequeña burguesía *f*

petit four [ˌpetɪˈfɔː] N pastelito *m* de mazapán

petition [pəˈtɪʃən] Ⓐ N [1] (= *list of names*) petición *f*; **to sign a ~** firmar una petición
[2] (*frm*) (= *request*) solicitud *f*; (*Jur*) demanda *f*; (= *entreaty*) súplica *f*; **~ for divorce** demanda *f* de divorcio; **to file a ~** presentar una demanda
Ⓑ VT [+ *authorities*] solicitar a; (*Jur*) [+ *court*] elevar una petición a; **to ~ sb to do sth** (*Jur*) elevar una petición a algn para que haga algo
Ⓒ VI **to ~ for sth** (*gen*) solicitar algo; (*Jur*) elevar una petición pidiendo algo; **to ~ for divorce** presentar una demanda de divorcio

petitioner [pəˈtɪʃnəʳ] N (*gen*) peticionario/a *m/f*; (*Jur*) demandante *mf*

petits pois [ˈpetiːˈpwɑ] NPL petits pois *mpl*, *guisantes pequeños y dulces*

Petrarch [ˈpetrɑːk] N Petrarca

Petrarchan [peˈtrɑːkən] ADJ petrarquista

Petrarchism [ˈpetrɑːkɪzəm] N petrarquismo *m*

petrel [ˈpetrəl] N petrel *m*, paíño *m*

petrifaction [ˌpetrɪˈfækʃən], **petrification** [ˌpetrɪfɪˈkeɪʃən] N petrificación *f*

petrified [ˈpetrɪfaɪd] ADJ petrificado

petrify [ˈpetrɪfaɪ] Ⓐ VT [1] (*lit*) petrificar; **to become petrified** petrificarse
[2] (*fig*) aterrorizar, horrorizar; **we were petrified** nos quedamos aterrorizados *or* horrorizados; **to be petrified with fear** estar muerto de miedo; **she's petrified of losing** le aterroriza *or* horroriza perder
Ⓑ VI petrificarse

petro... [ˈpetrəʊ] PREFIX petro...

petrochemical [ˌpetrəʊˈkemɪkəl] Ⓐ ADJ petroquímico
Ⓑ N **petrochemicals** productos *mpl* petroquímicos

petrodollar [ˈpetrəʊˌdɒləʳ] N petrodólar *m*

petrol [ˈpetrəl] (*Brit*) Ⓐ N gasolina *f*, nafta *f* (*Arg*), bencina *f* (*Chile*); (*for lighter*) bencina *f*; **4-star ~** gasolina *f* súper; **to run out of ~** quedarse sin gasolina
Ⓑ CPD ► **petrol bomb** N bomba *f* de gasolina ► **petrol can** N bidón *m* de gasolina ► **petrol engine** N motor *m* de gasolina ► **petrol (filler) cap** N tapón *m* del depósito ► **petrol gauge** N indicador *m* de nivel de gasolina ► **petrol pump** N (*at garage*) surtidor *m* de gasolina; (*in engine*) bomba *f* de gasolina ► **petrol station** N gasolinera *f*, estación *f* de servicio, bencinera *f* (*Chile*), surtidor *m* (*Bol*), grifo *m* (*Peru*) ► **petrol tank** N depósito *m* de gasolina ► **petrol tanker** N camión *m* cisterna

petroleum [pɪˈtrəʊlɪəm] Ⓐ N petróleo *m*
Ⓑ CPD ► **petroleum jelly** N vaselina *f* ► **petroleum products** NPL derivados *mpl* del petróleo

petrology [peˈtrɒlɪdʒɪ] N petrología *f*

petticoat [ˈpetɪkəʊt] N enagua(s) *f(pl)*; (= *slip*) combinación *f*

pettifogging [ˈpetɪfɒgɪŋ] ADJ [*detail*] insignificante, nimio; [*lawyer*] pedante; [*suggestion*] hecho para entenebrecer el asunto

pettily [ˈpetɪlɪ] ADV mezquinamente

pettiness [ˈpetɪnɪs] N (= *small-mindedness*) mezquindad *f*, estrechez *f* de miras; (= *triviality*) insignificancia *f*, nimiedad *f*

petting* [ˈpetɪŋ] N caricias *fpl*, manoseo *m* (*pej*), magreo *m* (*Sp** *pej*)

pettish [ˈpetɪʃ] ADJ malhumorado

petty [ˈpetɪ] Ⓐ ADJ (*compar* **pettier**; *superl* **pettiest**) [1] (= *trivial*) [*detail*] insignificante, nimio; [*squabble, rivalry, concerns*] pequeño, trivial
[2] (= *minor*) [*offence*] menor
[3] (= *small-minded, spiteful*) mezquino; **you're being very ~ about it** te estás portando de manera muy mezquina
Ⓑ CPD ► **petty cash** N dinero *m* para gastos menores, caja *f* chica* ► **petty cash book** N libro *m* de caja auxiliar ► **petty crime** N delito *m* menor ► **petty larceny** N robo *m* de menor cuantía ► **petty officer** N suboficial *mf* de marina ► **petty sessions** NPL tribunal *msing* de primera instancia ► **petty theft** N robo *m* de poca monta ► **petty thief** N ladrón/ona *m/f* de poca monta

petulance [ˈpetjʊləns] N mal humor *m*, irritabilidad *f*

petulant [ˈpetjʊlənt] ADJ [*person, voice, tone*] malhumorado, irritable; [*gesture*] malhumorado, de irritación

petulantly [ˈpetjʊləntlɪ] ADV de mal humor, con irritación; **"I'm too busy!" she said ~** —¡estoy demasiado ocupada! —dijo malhumorada *or* irritada

petunia [pɪ'tju:nɪə] N petunia *f*

pew [pju:] N (*in church*) banco *m* (de iglesia); **take a ~!*** (*hum*) ¡siéntate!

pewter ['pju:tə^r] Ⓐ N peltre *m* Ⓑ CPD de peltre

peyote [peɪ'əʊtɪ] N peyote *m*

PFC ABBR (*US Mil*) = **private first class**

pfennig ['fenɪg] N pfennig *m*

PFI N ABBR (*Brit*) (= **private finance initiative**) *plan de incentivos y potenciación de la iniciativa privada en el sector público*

PFLP N ABBR (= **Popular Front for the Liberation of Palestine**) FPLP *m*

PG ABBR [1] (*Cine*) (*film censor's rating*) (= **Parental Guidance**) ≈ menores acompañados [2] = **paying guest**

PG 13 [,pi:dʒi:θɜ:'ti:n] ABBR (*US*) (= **Parental Guidance 13**) no apto para menores de 13 años

PGA N ABBR = **Professional Golfers' Association**

PGCE N ABBR (*Brit*) (= **Postgraduate Certificate in Education**) ≈ C.A.P. *m*

PH ABBR (*US Mil*) (= **Purple Heart**) *decoración otorgada a los heridos de guerra*

pH ABBR (= **potential of hydrogen**) pH *m*

PHA N ABBR (*US*) = **Public Housing Administration**

phagocyte ['fægəʊsaɪt] N fagocito *m*

phalange ['fælændʒ] N falange *f*; **the Phalange** (*in Spain*) la Falange

phalangist [fæ'lændʒɪst] ADJ, N falangista *mf*

phalanx ['fælæŋks] N (*pl* **phalanges** [fæ'lændʒi:z]) falange *f*

phalarope ['fælərəʊp] N falaropo *m*

phallic ['fælɪk] ADJ fálico

phallus ['fæləs] N (*pl* **phalluses** *or* **phalli** ['fælaɪ]) falo *m*

phantasm ['fæntæzəm] N fantasma *m*

phantasmagoria [,fæntæzmə'gɔ:rɪə] N fantasmagoría *f*

phantasmagoric [,fæntæzmə'gɒrɪk] ADJ fantasmagórico

phantasy ['fæntəzɪ] N fantasía *f*

phantom ['fæntəm] Ⓐ N fantasma *m* Ⓑ CPD [*form, shape*] fantasmal; [*bank account*] fantasma ► **phantom limb** N extremidad *f* imaginaria ► **phantom pregnancy** N embarazo *m* psicológico ► **phantom ship** N buque *m* fantasma

Pharaoh ['fɛərəʊ] N Faraón *m*

Pharisaic [,færɪ'seɪɪk], **Pharisaical** [,færɪ'seɪɪkəl] ADJ farisaico

Pharisee ['færɪsi:] N fariseo *m*

pharmaceutical [,fɑ:mə'sju:tɪkəl] Ⓐ ADJ farmacéutico Ⓑ N producto *m* farmacéutico

pharmacist ['fɑ:məsɪst] N farmacéutico/a *m/f*; **to go to the ~'s** ir a la farmacia

pharmacological [,fɑ:məkə'lɒdʒɪkəl] ADJ farmacológico

pharmacologist [,fɑ:mə'kɒlədʒɪst] N farmacólogo/a *m/f*

pharmacology [,fɑ:mə'kɒlədʒɪ] N farmacología *f*

pharmacopoeia, **pharmacopeia** (*US also*) [,fɑ:məkə'pi:ə] N farmacopea *f*

pharmacy ['fɑ:məsɪ] N farmacia *f*

pharyngitis [,færɪn'dʒaɪtɪs] N faringitis *f*

pharynx ['færɪŋks] N (*pl* **pharynxes** *or* **pharynges** [fæ'rɪndʒi:z]) faringe *f*

phase [feɪz] Ⓐ N [1] etapa *f*, fase *f*; **she'll get over it, it's just a ~ (she's going through)** se le pasará, es algo pasajero; **a passing ~** una etapa pasajera; **to be in ~** (*Tech, Elec*) estar en fase; **to be out of ~** (*Tech, Elec*) estar fuera de fase or desfasado; (*fig*) estar desfasado; **their policies were increasingly out of ~ with a rapidly changing society** su política estaba cada vez más desfasada en una sociedad que cambiaba con rapidez [2] (*Astron*) fase *f*; **the ~s of the moon** las fases de la luna Ⓑ VT [1] (= *introduce gradually*) escalonar, llevar a cabo de forma escalonada; **the redundancies will be ~d over two years** los despidos se llevarán a cabo de forma escalonada durante dos años [2] (= *coordinate*) organizar; **~d development** desarrollo *m* por etapas; **~d withdrawal** retirada *f* progresiva

►**phase in** VT + ADV [+ *change, increase*] introducir progresivamente

►**phase out** VT + ADV [+ *machinery, product*] retirar progresivamente; [+ *job*] eliminar por etapas; [+ *subsidy*] eliminar progresivamente; [+ *production*] parar progresivamente; [+ *factory, plant*] cerrar progresivamente

phase-in ['feɪzɪn] N introducción *f* progresiva; **~ period** periodo *m* de introducción progresiva

phase-out ['feɪzaʊt] N retirada *f* progresiva

phatic ['fætɪk] ADJ fático

PhD N ABBR = **Doctor of Philosophy** (= *qualification*) doctorado *m*; (= *person*) doctor(a) *m/f* en filosofía; **to have a ~ in …** tener un doctorado en …; → DEGREE

pheasant ['feznt] N faisán *m*

phenobarbitone ['fi:nəʊ'bɑ:bɪtəʊn] N fenobarbitona *f*

phenol ['fi:nɒl] N fenol *m*

phenomena [fɪ'nɒmɪnə] NPL *of* **phenomenon**

phenomenal [fɪ'nɒmɪnl] ADJ [*memory, success, strength*] extraordinario; [*speed*] espectacular

phenomenally [fɪ'nɒmɪnəlɪ] ADV extraordinariamente; **to be ~ successful** tener un éxito extraordinario

phenomenological [fə,nɒmənə'lɒdʒɪkəl] ADJ fenomenológico

phenomenologist [fə,nɒmə'nɒlədʒɪst] N fenomenólogo/a *m/f*

phenomenology [fɪ'nɒmɪ'nɒlədʒɪ] N fenomenología *f*

phenomenon [fɪ'nɒmɪnən] N (*pl* **phenomenons** *or* **phenomena**) fenómeno *m*

pheromone ['ferəməʊn] N feromona *f*

phew [fju:] EXCL ¡uf!, ¡puf!

phial ['faɪəl] N ampolla *f*, redoma *f*

Phi Beta Kappa [,faɪbeɪtə'kæpə] N (*US Univ*) *asociación de antiguos alumnos sobresalientes*

> **PHI BETA KAPPA**
>
> *La sociedad honorífica* **Phi Beta Kappa** *fue fundada en Estados Unidos en 1776 para estudiantes universitarios con aptitudes académicas sobresalientes. Los miembros se eligen durante el tercer o cuarto año de sus estudios y el nombre proviene de las iniciales griegas que forman el lema de la asociación:* **philosophia biou kubernetes** (**la filosofía como motor de vida**). *A cada miembro se lo conoce como un* **Phi Beta Kappa** *o un* **Phi Beta Kappa student**.

Phil [fɪl] N (*familiar form*) *of* **Philip**

Philadelphia [,fɪlə'delfɪə] N Filadelfia *f*

philander [fɪ'lændə^r] VI flirtear, ejercer de Don Juan (**with** con)

philanderer [fɪ'lændərə^r] N Don Juan *m*, tenorio *m*

philandering [fɪ'lændərɪŋ] Ⓐ ADJ que le gusta flirtear, que le gusta ejercer de Don Juan Ⓑ N flirteo *m*

philanthropic [,fɪlən'θrɒpɪk] ADJ filantrópico

philanthropist [fɪ'lænθrəpɪst] N filántropo/a *m/f*

philanthropy [fɪ'lænθrəpɪ] N filantropía *f*

philatelic [,fɪlə'telɪk] ADJ filatélico

philatelist [fɪ'lætəlɪst] N filatelista *mf*

philately [fɪ'lætəlɪ] N filatelia *f*

...phile [faɪl] SUFFIX ...filo; (*eg*) **francophile** francófilo/a *m/f*

philharmonic [fɪlɑ:'mɒnɪk] ADJ filarmónico; **the Berlin Philharmonic (Orchestra)** la (Orquesta) Filarmónica de Berlín

...philia ['fɪlɪə] SUFFIX ...filia; (*eg*) **francophilia** francofilia *f*

Philip ['fɪlɪp] N Felipe

philippic [fɪ'lɪpɪk] N filípica *f*

Philippine ['fɪlɪpi:n] Ⓐ ADJ filipino Ⓑ N filipino/a *m/f*

Philippines ['fɪlɪpi:nz] NPL **the ~** (las) Filipinas *fpl*; **the Philippine Islands** las Islas Filipinas

Philistine ['fɪlɪstaɪn] Ⓐ ADJ [1] (*lit*) filisteo [2] (*fig*) inculto Ⓑ N [1] (*lit*) filisteo/a *m/f* [2] (*fig*) inculto/a *m/f*

philistinism ['fɪlɪstɪnɪzəm] N filisteísmo *m*

Phillips screw® [,fɪlɪps'skru:] N tornillo *m* de cabeza cruciforme

Phillips screwdriver® [,fɪlɪps'skru:draɪvə^r] N destornillador *m* cruciforme

philological [,fɪlə'lɒdʒɪkəl] ADJ filológico

philologist [fɪ'lɒlədʒɪst] N filólogo/a *m/f*

philology [fɪ'lɒlədʒɪ] N filología *f*

philosopher [fɪ'lɒsəfə^r] N filósofo/a *m/f*; **~'s stone** piedra *f* filosofal

philosophic [,fɪlə'sɒfɪk] ADJ = **philosophical**

philosophical [,fɪlə'sɒfɪkəl] ADJ filosófico; **she was ~ about the delay** se tomó el retraso con filosofía

philosophically [,fɪlə'sɒfɪkəlɪ] ADV [*important, disputable*] filosóficamente; (= *from a philosophical point of view*) desde el punto de vista filosófico; (= *with resignation*) [*accept*] con filosofía; **to be ~ inclined** *or* **minded** tener inclinaciones filosóficas

philosophize [fɪ'lɒsəfaɪz] VI filosofar

philosophy [fɪ'lɒsəfɪ] N filosofía *f*; **her ~ of life** su filosofía de la vida

philtre, **philter** (*US*) ['fɪltə^r] N filtro *m*

phishing ['fɪʃɪŋ] N (*Internet*) phishing *m*

phiz* [fɪz] N jeta* *f*

phlebitis [flɪ'baɪtɪs] N flebitis *f*

phlebotomy [flɪ'bɒtəmɪ] N flebotomía *f*

phlegm [flem] N [1] (*Med*) (= *mucus*) flema *f* [2] (= *equanimity*) flema *f*

phlegmatic [fleg'mætɪk] ADJ flemático

phlegmatically [fleg'mætɪkəlɪ] ADV con flema; **he said ~** dijo flemático

phlox [flɒks] N (*pl* **phlox** *or* **phloxes**) flox *m*

Phnom Penh, **Pnom Penh** ['nɒm'pen] N Phnom Penh *m*

...phobe [fəʊb] SUFFIX ...fobo; (*eg*) **francophobe** francófobo/a *m/f*

phobia ['fəʊbɪə] N fobia *f*

...phobia ['fəʊbɪə] SUFFIX ...fobia; (*eg*) **anglophobia** anglofobia *f*

phobic ['fəʊbɪk] ADJ fóbico

Phoebus ['fi:bəs] N Febo

Phoenicia [fɪ'nɪʃɪə] N Fenicia *f*

Phoenician [fɪ'nɪʃɪən] Ⓐ ADJ fenicio
Ⓑ N fenicio/a *m/f*

phoenix ['fi:nɪks] N fénix *m*

phone [fəʊn] Ⓐ N teléfono *m*; **the ~ hasn't stopped ringing all afternoon** el teléfono no ha dejado de sonar toda la tarde; **he can't come to the ~ just now** ahora no puede ponerse *or* venir al teléfono; **by ~** por teléfono; **to get off the ~** colgar (el teléfono); **to be on the ~** (*Brit*) (= *have a telephone*) tener teléfono; (= *be in conversation*) estar hablando por teléfono; **who was that on the ~?** ¿con quién estabas hablando por teléfono?; **there's someone on the ~ for you** te llama alguien por teléfono, hay alguien al teléfono que quiere hablar contigo; **I spent an hour on the ~ trying to sort things out** me pasé una hora al teléfono intentando resolver las cosas; **Dennis sounded very excited on the ~** Dennis parecía muy entusiasmado por teléfono; **he immediately got on the ~ to his solicitor** llamó por teléfono a su abogado inmediatamente; **I can't talk about it over the ~** no puedo hablar de ello por teléfono; **public ~** teléfono *m* público; **to put down the ~** colgar el teléfono; *see also* **car B**, **mobile**, **pay D**
Ⓑ VT [+ *person*] llamar (por teléfono); [+ *number*] llamar a; **to ~ the hospital/office** llamar al hospital/a la oficina; **I have to ~ Helsinki again** tengo que hablar con Helsinki otra vez; **I tried phoning the emergency number** intenté llamar al número de emergencia; **write to us or ~ 0171 586 4034** escríbanos o llámenos al 0171 586 4034
Ⓒ VI llamar (*por teléfono*); **she ~d to say she would be late** llamó para decir que llegaría tarde; **shall I ~ for a taxi?** ¿llamo a un taxi?, ¿quieres que llame a *or* pida un taxi?
Ⓓ CPD ► **phone bill** N cuenta *f* del teléfono, factura *f* del teléfono; **he ran up a £240 ~ bill** gastó 240 libras de teléfono ► **phone book** N guía *f* (telefónica); **she's not in the ~ book** su número no viene en la guía ► **phone booth** N cabina *f* (telefónica) ► **phone box** N (*Brit*) cabina *f* (telefónica) ► **phone call** N llamada *f* (telefónica); **there's a ~ call for you** tienes una llamada (telefónica); **to make a ~ call** hacer una llamada (telefónica) ► **phone company** N compañía *f* telefónica ► **phone line** N línea *f* de teléfono; **the ~ lines are busy** las líneas de teléfono están ocupadas ► **phone number** N número *m* de teléfono; **we need your daytime ~ number** nos hace falta un número de teléfono en el que se lo pueda contactar durante el día ► **phone tapping** N intervención *f* telefónica, pinchazo *m* de teléfono*

►**phone back** Ⓐ VT + ADV (= *return call of*) llamar; (= *call again*) volver a llamar
Ⓑ VI + ADV (= *return call*) llamar; (= *call again*) volver a llamar; **they asked you to ~ back - urgently** te pidieron que llamaras - urgentemente; **he's not here, could you ~ back tomorrow?** no está aquí, ¿podría volver a llamar mañana?

►**phone down** VI + ADV **just wait while I ~ down to reception** espere un momento mientras llamo (abajo) a la recepción

►**phone in** Ⓐ VI + ADV llamar; **listeners can ~ in with their views** los oyentes pueden llamar para expresar sus puntos de vista; **~ in to base if you change your plans** si cambia de planes, llame por teléfono para comunicárselo a la base; **you could always ~ in sick** siempre podrías llamar diciendo que estás enfermo
Ⓑ VT + ADV **she had ~d in a message for Wade to call her** había llamado dejando un mensaje para Wade de que la llamara; **our reporter ~d in this account of what had happened** nuestro reportero nos mandó por teléfono esta versión de lo ocurrido; **you can ~ in your order on 0898 060606** puede hacer su pedido llamando al 0898 060606

►**phone out** VI + ADV llamar al exterior

►**phone round** Ⓐ VI + ADV llamar a varios sitios
Ⓑ VI + PREP **he ~d round all his friends** llamó a todos sus amigos

►**phone through** Ⓐ VT + ADV **~ through your order on our special credit card line** haga su pedido por teléfono a través de nuestra línea especial para tarjetas de crédito
Ⓑ VI + ADV llamar; **I still haven't managed to ~ through to my wife** aún no he conseguido llamar a mi esposa

►**phone up** Ⓐ VT + ADV llamar; **I must ~ her up tonight** debo llamarla esta noche
Ⓑ VI + ADV llamar

phonecard ['fəʊnkɑ:d] N tarjeta *f* telefónica

phone-in ['fəʊnɪn] N (*also* **~ programme**) (*Brit*) *programa de radio or televisión con participación telefónica del público*

phoneme ['fəʊni:m] N fonema *m*

phonemic [fəʊ'ni:mɪk] ADJ fonémico

phonetic [fəʊ'netɪk] ADJ fonético

phonetically [fəʊ'netɪkəlɪ] ADV fonéticamente

phonetician [,fəʊnɪ'tɪʃən] N fonetista *mf*

phonetics [fəʊ'netɪks] N fonética *f*

phoney*, **phony*** (*US also*) ['fəʊnɪ] Ⓐ ADJ [*moustache*] falso, postizo; [*name, document, smile*] falso; [*accent*] fingido; **there's sth ~ about it** esto huele a camelo*; **the ~ war** (*1939*) la guerra ilusoria
Ⓑ N (*pl* **phoneys**) (= *person*) farsante* *mf*; (= *thing*) falsificación *f*

phonic ['fɒnɪk] ADJ fónico

phono... ['fəʊnəʊ] PREFIX fono...

phonograph ['fəʊnəgrɑ:f] N (*US*) fonógrafo *m*, tocadiscos *m inv*

phonological [,fəʊnə'lɒdʒɪkəl] ADJ fonológico

phonologically [,fəʊnə'lɒdʒɪklɪ] ADV fonológicamente

phonologist [fə'nɒlədʒɪst] N fonólogo/a *m/f*

phonology [fəʊ'nɒlədʒɪ] N fonología *f*

phony ['fəʊnɪ] (*US*) = **phoney**

phooey* ['fu:ɪ] EXCL (= *rubbish*) ¡bobadas!; (*annoyance*) ¡qué tonto soy!; (*disappointment*) ¡ay!

phosgene ['fɒzdʒi:n] N fosgeno *m*

phosphate ['fɒsfeɪt] N fosfato *m*

phosphene ['fɒsfi:n] N fosfeno *m*

phosphide ['fɒsfaɪd] N fosfito *m*

phosphine ['fɒsfi:n] N fosfino *m*

phosphoresce [,fɒsfə'res] VI fosforecer

phosphorescence [,fɒsfə'resns] N fosforescencia *f*

phosphorescent [,fɒsfə'resnt] ADJ fosforescente

phosphoric [fɒs'fɒrɪk] ADJ fosfórico

phosphorous ['fɒsfərəs] ADJ fosforoso

phosphorus ['fɒsfərəs] N fósforo *m*

photo ['fəʊtəʊ] Ⓐ N (*pl* **photos**) foto *f*; **to take a ~** hacer *or* (*esp LAm*) sacar una foto; **I took a ~ of the bride and groom** les hice una foto a los novios
Ⓑ CPD ► **photo booth** N cabina *f* de fotos, fotomatón *m* (*Sp*) ► **photo opportunity**, **photo session** N = **photocall**

photo... ['fəʊtəʊ] PREFIX [1] (= *relating to photography*) foto...; **~-montage** fotomontaje *m*
[2] (= *relating to light*) foto...; **~synthesis** fotosíntesis *f*

photocall ['fəʊtəʊkɔ:l] N sesión *f* de fotos

photochemical [,fəʊtəʊ'kemɪkəl] ADJ fotoquímico

photocompose [,fəʊtəʊkəm'pəʊz] VT fotocomponer

photocomposer [,fəʊtəʊkəm'pəʊzə^r] N fotocomponedora *f*

photocomposition [,fəʊtəʊkɒmpə'zɪʃən] N fotocomposición *f*

photocopier ['fəʊtəʊ'kɒpɪə^r] N fotocopiadora *f*

photocopy ['fəʊtəʊ,kɒpɪ] Ⓐ N fotocopia *f*
Ⓑ VT fotocopiar

photocopying ['fəʊtəʊ,kɒpɪɪŋ] N **to do some ~** hacer algunas fotocopias; **the ~ of this publication is forbidden without prior permission** se prohíbe fotocopiar esta publicación sin permiso previo

photocoverage ['fəʊtəʊ,kʌvərɪdʒ] N reportaje *m* gráfico

photodisk ['fəʊtəʊ,dɪsk] N fotodisco *m*

photoelectric ['fəʊtəʊɪ'lektrɪk] Ⓐ ADJ fotoeléctrico
Ⓑ CPD ► **photoelectric cell** N célula *f* fotoeléctrica

photoelectron [,fəʊtəʊɪ'lektrɒn] N fotoelectrón *m*

photoengrave [,fəʊtəʊɪn'greɪv] VT fotograbar

photoengraving ['fəʊtəʊen'greɪvɪŋ] N fotograbado *m*

photo-finish ['fəʊtəʊ'fɪnɪʃ] N resultado *m* comprobado por fotocontrol; (*fig*) final *m* muy reñido

Photofit® ['fəʊtəʊfɪt] N (*Brit*) (*also* **~ picture**) retrato *m* robot

photoflash ['fəʊtəʊflæʃ] N flash *m*

photogenic [,fəʊtəʊ'dʒenɪk] ADJ fotogénico

photograph ['fəʊtəgræf] Ⓐ N fotografía *f*, foto *f*; **it's a very good ~ of her** es una fotografía muy buena de ella; **to take a ~ (of sth/sb)** hacer *or* (*esp LAm*) sacar una foto (a algo/algn); **he takes a good ~*** (= *is photogenic*) es fotogénico, sale bien en las fotos; *see also* **aerial C**, **black A1**, **passport B**
Ⓑ VT fotografiar, hacer *or* (*esp LAm*) sacar una foto(grafía) a; **I hate being ~ed** odio que me hagan fotos; **"~ed by Paul Smith"** "fotografía de Paul Smith"
Ⓒ VI **to ~ well** ser fotogénico
Ⓓ CPD ► **photograph album** N álbum *m* de fotos

photographer [fə'tɒgrəfə^r] N fotógrafo/a *m/f*; **an amateur ~** un fotógrafo amateur; **he's a keen ~** es muy aficionado a la fotografía; **a ~'s** (= *shop*) una tienda de fotografía; *see also* **press D**

photographic [,fəʊtə'græfɪk] ADJ fotográfico; **to have a ~ memory** tener una memoria fotográfica

photographically [,fəʊtə'græfɪkəlɪ] ADV fotográficamente

photography [fə'tɒgrəfɪ] N fotografía *f*

photogravure [,fəʊtəgrə'vjʊə^r] N fotograbado *m*

photojournalism [,fəʊtəʊ'dʒɜ:nəlɪzəm] N fotoperiodismo *m*

photojournalist [,fəʊtəʊ'dʒɜ:nəlɪst] N fotoperiodista *mf*

photokit ['fəʊtəʊkɪt] N retrato *m* robot

photolitho [,fəʊtəʊ'laɪθəʊ] N fotolito *m*

photolithograph [,fəʊtəʊ'lɪθə,grɑ:f] N grabado *m* fotolitográfico

photolithography [ˌfəʊtəʊlɪˈθɒgrəfɪ] N fotolitografía *f*

photometer [fəˈtɒmətəʳ] N fotómetro *m*

photometric [ˌfəʊtəˈmetrɪk] ADJ fotométrico

photometry [fəʊˈtɒmɪtrɪ] N fotometría *f*

photomontage [ˌfəʊtəʊmɒnˈtɑːʒ] N fotomontaje *m*

photon [ˈfəʊtɒn] N fotón *m*

photosensitive [ˌfəʊtəʊˈsensɪtɪv] ADJ fotosensible

photosensitivity [ˌfəʊtəʊsensɪˈtɪvɪtɪ] N fotosensibilidad *f*

photosensitize [ˌfəʊtəʊˈsensɪˌtaɪz] VT fotosensibilizar

photosetting [ˈfəʊtəʊˌsetɪŋ] Ⓐ N fotocomposición *f*
Ⓑ CPD ► **photosetting machine** N fotocompositora *f*

photostat† [ˈfəʊtəʊstæt] Ⓐ N (= *machine*) fotocopiadora *f*; (= *photocopy*) fotocopia *f*
Ⓑ VT fotocopiar

photosynthesis [ˌfəʊtəʊˈsɪnθəsɪs] N fotosíntesis *f*

phototropism [ˈfəʊtəʊˈtrəʊpɪzəm] N fototropismo *m*

phototype [ˈfəʊtəʊˌtaɪp] N fototipo *m*

phototypesetting [ˌfəʊtəʊˈtaɪpˌsetɪŋ] N (*US Typ*) fotocomposición *f*

phototypography [ˌfəʊtəʊtaɪˈpɒgrəfɪ] N fototipografía *f*

photovoltaic [ˌfəʊtəʊvɒlˈteɪɪk] Ⓐ ADJ fotovoltaico
Ⓑ CPD ► **photovoltaic cell** N célula *f* fotovoltaica

phrasal [ˈfreɪzəl] Ⓐ ADJ frasal
Ⓑ CPD ► **phrasal verb** N verbo *m* con preposición *or* adverbio

phrase [freɪz] Ⓐ N 1 (*Gram, Mus*) frase *f*; **noun/verb ~** frase *f* nominal/verbal
2 (= *expression*) frase *f*; **she had picked up some useful ~s** había aprendido algunas frases útiles; **I think, to use** *or* **to borrow your ~, that …** creo que, usando tus propias palabras, …
3 (= *idiom*) locución *f*, giro *m*; *see also* **catch D, coin B, set B1, stock C2, turn A15**
Ⓑ VT 1 (*orally*) expresar, formular; **I should have ~d that better** debería haberlo expresado *or* formulado mejor
2 (*in writing*) redactar, expresar; **can we ~ that differently?** ¿podemos redactar *or* expresar eso de otro modo?; **a carefully ~d letter** una carta redactada con cuidado
3 (*Mus*) frasear
Ⓒ CPD ► **phrase book** N libro *m* de frases ► **phrase marker** N (*Ling*) marcador *m* de frase ► **phrase structure** N (*Ling*) estructura *f* de frase

phraseology [ˌfreɪzɪˈɒlədʒɪ] N fraseología *f*

phrasing [ˈfreɪzɪŋ] N (= *act*) redacción *f*; [*of question*] formulación *f*; (= *style*) estilo *m*, términos *mpl*; (*Mus*) fraseo *m*; **the ~ is rather unfortunate** la forma en que está expresado es bastante desafortunada

phrenetic [frɪˈnetɪk] ADJ frenético

phrenic [ˈfrenɪk] ADJ (*Anat*) diafragmático

phrenologist [frɪˈnɒlədʒɪst] N frenólogo/a *m/f*

phrenology [frɪˈnɒlədʒɪ] N frenología *f*

phthisis [ˈθaɪsɪs] N tisis *f*

phut* [fʌt] ADJ **to go ~** estropearse, hacer kaput*; (*fig*) fracasar

phyla [ˈfaɪlə] NPL *of* **phylum**

phylactery [fɪˈlæktərɪ] N filacteria *f*

phylloxera [ˌfɪlɒkˈsɪərə] N filoxera *f*

phylum [ˈfaɪləm] N (*pl* **phyla**) (*Bio*) filo *m*, phylum *m*

physic†† [ˈfɪzɪk] N medicina *f*

physical [ˈfɪzɪkəl] Ⓐ ADJ 1 (= *of the body*) [*condition, disability, contact, violence*] físico; [*punishment*] corporal
2 (= *material*) [*properties, characteristics*] físico; [*world*] material; **~ environment** entorno *m* físico; **~ evidence** pruebas *fpl* materiales; **it's a ~ impossibility** es materialmente imposible; **his ~ presence repelled her** su mera presencia le repugnaba
3 (= *involving physical contact, effort*) físico; **he's a very ~ man** es un hombre que recurre mucho al contacto físico; **rugby is a very ~ sport** el rugby es un deporte muy físico *or* con mucho contacto físico; **there was some very ~ play from both teams** hubo mucho juego duro por parte de los dos equipos; **he has been ordered not to do any ~ work** le han dicho que no haga ninguna clase de trabajo que requiera esfuerzo físico; **to get ~** (*sexually*) pasar al plano físico; (= *be rough*) emplear la fuerza física, llegar a las manos*
4 (= *of physics*) físico; **the ~ sciences** las ciencias físicas
Ⓑ N (*also* **~ examination**) reconocimiento *m* físico
Ⓒ CPD ► **physical chemistry** N fisicoquímica *f* ► **physical education** N educación *f* física ► **physical examination** N reconocimiento *m* físico ► **physical exercise** N ejercicio *m* (físico) ► **physical fitness** N (buena) forma *f* física; **a ~ fitness programme** un programa de ejercicios físicos ► **physical geography** N geografía *f* física ► **physical jerks*** NPL (*Brit*) gimnasia *fsing*, ejercicios *mpl* (físicos) ► **physical therapist** N (*US*) fisioterapeuta *mf* ► **physical therapy** N (*US*) fisioterapia *f* ► **physical training** N entrenamiento *m*, ejercicio *m* (físico)

physically [ˈfɪzɪkəlɪ] ADV físicamente; **I don't find him ~ attractive** no me parece físicamente atractivo; **it's very ~ demanding work** es un trabajo que requiere mucho esfuerzo físico; **you need to be ~ fit to attempt this climb** tienes que estar en buena forma (física) para intentar esta escalada; **it's ~ impossible** es materialmente imposible; **he had to be ~ removed from the premises** lo tuvieron que sacar del local por la fuerza; **the thought of food made me ~ sick** sólo pensar en comer me daba náuseas

physician [fɪˈzɪʃən] N médico/a *m/f*

physicist [ˈfɪzɪsɪst] N físico/a *m/f*

physics [ˈfɪzɪks] NSING física *f*

physio* [ˈfɪzɪəʊ] N (*Sport*) = **physiotherapist**; (*Brit*) = **physiotherapy**

physio… [ˈfɪzɪəʊ] PREFIX fisio…

physiognomy [ˌfɪzɪˈɒnəmɪ] N fisonomía *f*

physiological [ˈfɪzɪəˈlɒdʒɪkəl] ADJ fisiológico

physiologically [ˈfɪzɪəˈlɒdʒɪkəlɪ] ADV fisiológicamente

physiologist [ˌfɪzɪˈɒlədʒɪst] N fisiólogo/a *m/f*

physiology [ˌfɪzɪˈɒlədʒɪ] N fisiología *f*

physiotherapist [ˌfɪzɪəˈθerəpɪst] N fisioterapeuta *mf*

physiotherapy [ˌfɪzɪəˈθerəpɪ] N fisioterapia *f*

physique [fɪˈziːk] N físico *m*

phytobiology [ˌfaɪtəʊbaɪˈɒlədʒɪ] N fitobiología *f*

phytofagous [faɪˈtɒfəgəs] ADJ fitófago

phytopathology [ˌfaɪtəʊpəˈθɒlədʒɪ] N fitopatología *f*

pi [paɪ] N (*pl* **pis**) (*Math*) pi *f*

pianist [ˈpɪənɪst] N pianista *mf*

piano [ˈpjɑːnəʊ] Ⓐ N (*pl* **pianos**) piano *m*
Ⓑ CPD ► **piano accordion** N acordeón-piano *m* ► **piano concerto** N concierto *m* para piano ► **piano duet** N pieza *f* para piano a cuatro manos ► **piano lesson** N lección *f* de piano ► **piano piece** N pieza *f* para piano ► **piano player** N pianista *mf* ► **piano stool** N taburete *m* de piano ► **piano teacher** N profesor(a) *m/f* de piano ► **piano tuner** N afinador(a) *m/f* de pianos

pianoforte [ˌpjɑːnəʊˈfɔːtɪ] N = **piano**

pianola® [pɪəˈnəʊlə] N pianola *f*

piastre, piaster (*US*) [pɪˈæstəʳ] N piastra *f*

piazza [pɪˈætsə] N (*US*) pórtico *m*, galería *f*; (= *square*) plaza *f*

pic* [pɪk] (*pl* **pics, pix**) N ABBR 1 = **picture** (= *photo*) foto *f*
2 (= *movie*) película *f*
3 **pics** (= *cinema*) cine *m*; **to go to the ~s** ir al cine

pica [ˈpaɪkə] N (*Med, Vet*) pica *f*; (*Typ*) cícero *m*

picador [ˈpɪkədɔː] N picador *m*

Picardy [ˈpɪkədɪ] N Picardía *f*

picaresque [ˌpɪkəˈresk] ADJ picaresco

picayune* [ˌpɪkəˈjuːn] (*US*) ADJ insignificante, de poca monta

piccalilli [ˈpɪkəˌlɪlɪ] N legumbres *fpl* en escabeche, encurtidos *mpl* picantes

piccaninny† [ˈpɪkəˌnɪnɪ] N negrito/a *m/f*

piccolo [ˈpɪkələʊ] N (*pl* **piccolos**) flautín *m*, píccolo *m*

pick [pɪk] Ⓐ N 1 (= *choice*) **to have one's ~ of sth** escoger *or* elegir lo que uno quiere de algo; **take your ~!** ¡escoja *or* elija lo que quiera!; **take your ~ of** *or* **from ten luxury hotels** escoja *or* elija el que quiera de entre diez hoteles de lujo
2 (= *best*) **the ~ of sth** lo mejor de algo, la flor y nata de algo; **the ~ of the bunch** *or* **the crop** (*fig*) lo mejor de grupo
3 (*also* **~axe**) (= *tool*) pico *m*, piqueta *f*
4 (*US*) (= *plectrum*) púa *f*; *see also* **toothpick**
Ⓑ VT 1 (= *choose*) (*gen*) escoger, elegir; [+ *team, candidate*] seleccionar; **~ a card, any card** escoge *or* elige una carta, cualquiera; **to ~ a fight (with sb)** (*lit*) buscar pelea *or* pleito (con algn); (*fig*) (= *argue*) discutir (con algn); **to ~ one's way through/across sth** abrirse camino cuidadosamente a través de algo; **to ~ a winner** (*lit*) escoger *or* elegir un ganador; (*fig*) escoger bien; **I think she ~ed a winner with her new boyfriend** creo que con su nuevo novio escogió bien; *see also* **quarrel A**
2 (= *gather*) [+ *flowers, fruit, tea, cotton*] coger, recoger (*LAm*); **to go strawberry ~ing** ir a coger fresas
3 (= *lift, remove*) **to ~ sth off the ground** recoger algo del suelo; **let me ~ that bit of fluff off your collar** deja que te quite esa pelusa del cuello; **to ~ o.s. off the floor** *or* **ground** levantarse del suelo; **to ~ names out of a hat** sacar nombres de un sombrero
4 (= *make*) [+ *hole*] hacer; *see also* **hole A1**
5 [+ *scab, spot*] toquetear; [+ *lock*] forzar *or* abrir con ganzúa; [+ *guitar, banjo*] puntear; **to ~ sb's brains** exprimir el coco a algn*; **their bones had been ~ed clean by the birds** los pájaros habían dejado limpios los huesos; **to ~ one's nose** hurgarse la nariz; **to ~ sb's pocket** robar algo a algn del bolsillo; **to ~ one's teeth** mondarse *or* escarbarse los dientes; *see also* **bone A1, piece A1**
Ⓒ VI 1 (= *choose*) escoger, elegir; **to ~ and choose** ponerse a escoger *or* elegir, ser muy exigente; **you can't ~ and choose** no puedes

ponerte a escoger *or* elegir, no puedes ser muy exigente

[2] (= *examine*) **dogs ~ through the garbage on the streets** los perros hurgan en *or* por la basura de las calles; *see also* **pick over**

► **pick at** VI + PREP [1] (= *toy with*) **try not to ~ at your spots** intenta no toquetearte las espinillas; **to ~ at one's food** comer con poca gana, picar la comida

[2] (= *criticize*) **she used to ~ at everything** solía meterse con todo *or* ponerle faltas a todo

[3] (*US**) = **pick on 2**

► **pick off** VT + ADV [1] (= *remove*) [+ *leaves, fluff, paint*] quitar; [+ *scab*] arrancar

[2] (= *shoot*) cargarse*, liquidar*; (= *eliminate*) [+ *opponents*] acabar uno a uno con

► **pick on** VI + PREP [1] (= *choose, single out*) escoger, elegir; **I can't think why he ~ed on that wallpaper** no logro entender por qué escogió *or* eligió ese papel para la pared; **they ~ed on me to go and tell him** me escogieron *or* eligieron a mí para que se lo dijera; **why ~ on me?** ¿por qué yo (y no otro)?

[2] (*) (= *harass*) meterse con*; **stop ~ing on me** deja de meterte conmigo*; **~ on someone your own size!** ¡métete con alguien de tu tamaño!*

► **pick out** VT + ADV [1] (= *choose*) elegir, escoger; **~ out two or three you would like to keep** elige *or* escoge dos o tres con los que te gustaría quedarte

[2] (= *single out*) escoger; **there are so many great pianists it's difficult to ~ one out** hay tantos grandes pianistas que es difícil escoger a uno

[3] (= *draw out*) sacar; **I took the hat and ~ed out a raffle ticket** cogí el sombrero y saqué uno de los boletos de la rifa

[4] (= *discern*) distinguir; **I could just ~ out the letters ALG** sólo podía distinguir y con dificultad, las letras ALG

[5] (= *identify*) reconocer; **can you ~ me out in this photo?** ¿eres capaz de reconocerme en esta foto?

[6] (= *highlight*) resaltar; **the name is ~ed out in gold letters** el nombre está resaltado en letras doradas; **his headlights ~ed out the cyclist in front** los faros de su coche iluminaron al ciclista que tenía delante

[7] (= *play*) [+ *tune*] tocar de oído

► **pick over** VT + ADV **~ over the raspberries** escoge las frambuesas que estén mejor; **she was ~ing over the shirts in the sale** estaba seleccionando las camisas en las rebajas; **it's no good ~ing over the past** de nada sirve remover el pasado

► **pick up** Ⓐ VT + ADV [1] (= *lift*) [+ *box, suitcase, cat*] levantar; [+ *dropped object*] recoger, coger; (= *take hold of*) tomar, coger, agarrar (*LAm*); **I saw her fall and ran to ~ her up** la vi caerse y corrí a levantarla; **that child is always wanting to be ~ed up** ese niño siempre quiere que lo cojan *or* (*LAm*) levanten; **she bent to ~ up her glove** se agachó para recoger *or* coger su guante; **she ~ed up a pencil and fiddled with it** tomó *or* cogió *or* (*LAm*) agarró un lápiz y se puso a enredar con él; **you can't ~ up a newspaper these days without reading about her** últimamente no puedes coger *or* (*LAm*) agarrar un periódico que no hable de ella; **to ~ up the bill** *or* **tab (for sth)*** pagar la cuenta (de algo); **to ~ o.s. up** (*lit*) levantarse, ponerse de pie; (*fig*) recuperarse, reponerse; *see also* **piece A1**

[2] (= *collect*) [+ *person*] recoger, ir a buscar (*esp LAm*); (= *give lift to*) [+ *hitch-hiker, passenger*] recoger, coger; **did you ~ up my laundry?** ¿recogiste mi colada?

[3] (= *learn*) [+ *language, skill*] aprender; [+ *accent, habit*] coger, agarrar (*LAm*), adquirir (*frm*); **you'll soon ~ it up again** pronto lo volverás a aprender; **I ~ed up a bit of news about him today** hoy me enteré de algunas cosas sobre él

[4] (= *buy*) comprar; (= *find*) [+ *bargain*] encontrar; (= *catch*) [+ *disease*] coger, agarrar (*LAm*), pillar*; **an old car he ~ed up for £250** un coche viejo que compró por 250 libras; **I'll ~ up some beer on the way back** compraré unas cervezas a la vuelta; **I may ~ up some useful ideas for my book** puede que encuentre algunas ideas útiles para mi libro

[5] (*) (= *earn, gain*) ganar, sacarse; **she ~s up £400 a week** gana *or* se saca 400 libras a la semana; **it ~ed up the best musical award** ganó *or* se llevó el premio al mejor musical; **to ~ up speed** acelerar, coger velocidad, tomar velocidad (*LAm*)

[6] (*) (*sexually*) ligarse a*; **are you trying to ~ me up?** ¿estás intentando ligar conmigo?

[7] (*Rad, TV*) [+ *station, channel*] captar, coger; (*Tech*) [+ *signal*] captar, registrar; **we can ~ up Italian television** podemos captar *or* coger la televisión italiana

[8] (= *notice, detect*) **he ~ed up ten misprints** encontró diez erratas; **she ~ed up every mistake** no se le escapó ni un error; **I had no difficulty ~ing up the signals he was sending me** (*fig*) no tuve problemas para captar las indirectas que me estaba mandando; *see also* **scent A3**

[9] (= *resume*) [+ *conversation, narrative*] continuar; [+ *relationship*] reanudar; *see also* **thread A1**

[10] (= *focus on*) **I'd like to ~ up the point David made** quisiera volver al punto que planteó David; **the papers ~ed up the story** los periódicos publicaron la historia

[11] (= *reprimand*) reñir, reprender; **she ~ed him up for using bad language** le riñó *or* le reprendió por decir palabrotas

[12] (= *correct*) **he ~ed me up on my grammar** me señaló diversas faltas de gramática; **if I may ~ you up on that point** si me permites corregirte en ese punto

[13] (= *rescue*) recoger, rescatar

[14] (= *arrest*) detener

[15] (= *revive*) [+ *person*] reanimar; **this tonic will soon ~ you up** este tónico te reanimará pronto

[16] (*US**) (= *tidy*) [+ *room, house*] recoger

Ⓑ VI + ADV [1] (= *improve*) [*conditions, weather, sales*] mejorar; [*market, economy*] reponerse; [*business, trade*] ir mejor; [*prices*] volver a subir; **the game ~ed up in the second half** el partido mejoró en el segundo tiempo

[2] (= *increase*) [*wind*] levantarse

[3] (= *continue*) **to ~ up where one left off** [+ *activity, conversation, relationship*] continuar donde se había dejado

[4] (= *notice, react to*) **I was getting nervous and he ~ed up on that** me estaba poniendo nervioso y él lo captó *or* se dió cuenta; **the press did not ~ up on it** la prensa no reaccionó ante la noticia

[5] (*) (= *become involved with*) **to ~ up with sb** juntarse con algn; **she's ~ed up with a bad crowd** se ha juntado con una gente no muy recomendable

[6] (= *tidy up*) **to ~ up after sb** ir recogiendo detrás de algn; **he expects me to ~ up after him** espera que vaya recogiendo detrás suyo

pickaback ['pɪkəbæk] N, ADV = **piggyback**

pick-and-mix [ˌpɪkn'mɪks] ADJ = **pick 'n' mix**

pickaxe, pickax (*US*) ['pɪkæks] N pico *m*, piqueta *f*

picked [pɪkt] ADJ escogido, selecto

picker ['pɪkəʳ] N [*of fruit, tea*] recolector(a) *m/f*

picket ['pɪkɪt] Ⓐ N [1] (= *stake*) estaca *f*

[2] (= *strikers*) piquete *m*; (*Mil*) (= *sentry*) piquete *m*; (= *group*) pelotón *m*

Ⓑ VT [+ *factory*] poner piquetes a la puerta de, piquetear (*LAm*)

Ⓒ VI formar piquetes, piquetear (*LAm*)

Ⓓ CPD ► **picket duty** N **to be on ~ duty** estar de guardia ► **picket fence** N estacada *f*, cerca *f* ► **picket line** N piquete *m*; **to cross a ~ line** no hacer caso de un piquete

picketing ['pɪkɪtɪŋ] N formación *f* de piquetes

picking ['pɪkɪŋ] N [1] [*of fruit etc*] recolección *f*, cosecha *f*; (= *act of choosing*) elección *f*, selección *f*

[2] **pickings** (= *leftovers*) restos *mpl*, sobras *fpl*; (= *profits*) ganancias *fpl*; **there are rich ~s for bargain hunters at these sales** en esta liquidación hay pingües beneficios para los que van a la caza de gangas

pickle ['pɪkl] Ⓐ N [1] (= *condiment*) (*also* **~s**) encurtidos *mpl*; (= *liquid*) escabeche *m*

[2] (*) (= *plight*) lío* *m*, apuro *m*, aprieto *m*; **to be in a ~** estar en un apuro *or* aprieto; **to get into a ~** meterse en un lío*

Ⓑ VT encurtir, escabechar

pickled ['pɪkld] Ⓐ ADJ [1] [*food*] escabechado, encurtido, en conserva

[2] **to be ~*** (= *drunk*) estar jumado*

Ⓑ CPD ► **pickled onions** NPL cebollas *fpl* en vinagre ► **pickled herrings** NPL arenques *mpl* en escabeche ► **pickled walnuts** NPL nueces *fpl* adobadas

picklock ['pɪklɒk] N ganzúa *f*

pick-me-up ['pɪkmiːʌp] N estimulante *m*; (= *drink*) bebida *f* tonificante; (*Med*) tónico *m*, reconstituyente *m*; **he tends to pop into the pub on the way home for a ~** suele pasarse por el pub de camino a casa para ponerse a tono; **this bath oil is the ideal ~ after a hard day at work** esta esencia de baño te deja como nuevo después de un día duro de trabajo

pick 'n' mix [ˌpɪkn'mɪks] ADJ [*selection*] misceláneo; (*also* **~ counter**) *mostrador de caramelos variados*

pickpocket ['pɪkˌpɒkɪt] N carterista *mf*, bolsista *mf* (*Mex*)

pick-up ['pɪkʌp] Ⓐ N [1] (*Mus*) [1·1] (*on instrument*) pastilla *f*; (*on microphone*) toma *f* de sonidos

[1·2] (*also* **~ arm**) brazo *m* (del tocadiscos)

[2] (*also* **~ truck**) furgoneta *f*, camioneta *f*

[3] (= *collection*) **to make a ~** [*truck driver, drug runner*] recoger algo; **the bus made three ~s** el autobús hizo tres paradas para recoger a gente

[4] (= *recovery*) (*in economy, trade, sales*) mejora *f*; (*in prices*) subida *f*

[5] (*) (= *pick-me-up*) estimulante *m*

[6] (*) (*sexual*) **to him it was just a ~** él no quería más que ligar con ella*; **a ~ joint** un garito de ligue*

[7] (*Aut*) (= *acceleration*) facilidad *f* de aceleración

Ⓑ CPD ► **pick-up joint*** N bar *m* de ligoteo* ► **pick-up point** N (*for people*) parada *f*; (*for goods*) punto *m* de recogida

picky* ['pɪkɪ] ADJ (*US*) [1] (= *critical*) criticón

[2] (= *choosy*) melindroso, quisquilloso

picnic ['pɪknɪk] (*vb: pt, pp* **picnicked**) Ⓐ N comida *f* en el campo, picnic *m* (*esp LAm*); **to go on a ~** ir de picnic, ir a comer al campo;

we found a nice place for a ~ encontramos un buen sitio para comer al aire libre; **it was no ~*** (= *unpleasant*) fue muy desagradable; (= *difficult*) no fue nada fácil
Ⓑ VI comer en el campo; **we ~ked by the river** merendamos junto al río
Ⓒ CPD ► **picnic basket** N cesta *f or* (*LAm*) canasta *f* de la merienda *or* comida *etc* ► **picnic site** N lugar *m* destinado para picnics

picnicker ['pɪknɪkəʳ] N excursionista *mf*

Pict [pɪkt] N picto/a *m/f*

Pictish ['pɪktɪʃ] Ⓐ ADJ picto Ⓑ N picto *m*

pictogram ['pɪktəʊgræm] N pictograma *m*

pictograph ['pɪktəgrɑːf] N 1 (= *record, chart*) pictografía *f* 2 (*Ling*) (= *symbol*) pictograma *m*; (= *writing*) pictografía *f*

pictorial [pɪk'tɔːrɪəl] Ⓐ ADJ (*Art*) pictórico; [*record, history*] gráfico; [*magazine*] ilustrado
Ⓑ N revista *f* ilustrada

pictorially [pɪk'tɔːrɪəlɪ] ADV (= *from a pictorial point of view*) pictóricamente; [*represent*] gráficamente, por imágenes

picture ['pɪktʃəʳ] Ⓐ N 1 (*Art*) (= *print, engraving*) cuadro *m*; (= *drawing*) dibujo *m*; (= *painting*) cuadro *m*, pintura *f*; (= *portrait*) retrato *m*; **to draw a ~ (of sth/sb)** hacer un dibujo (de algo/algn); **to paint a ~ (of sth/sb)** pintar un cuadro (de algo/algn); **he painted a black ~ of the future** nos pintó un cuadro muy negro del porvenir; **to paint sb's ~** pintar un retrato de algn, pintar a algn; ✦*PROVS* **every ~ tells a story** detrás de cada imagen hay una historia; **a ~ is worth a thousand words** una imagen vale más que mil palabras; *see also* **pretty A1**
2 (= *photo*) foto *f*, fotografía *f*; **to take a ~ of sth/sb** hacer *or* (*esp LAm*) sacar una foto a algo/algn; **we all had our ~s taken** todos nos hicimos *or* (*esp LAm*) sacamos fotos
3 (= *illustration*) (*in book*) ilustración *f*; (*in magazine*) ilustración *f*, foto *f*
4 (= *personification*) **he looked the ~ of health** era la salud personificada
5 (= *wonderful sight*) **the garden is a ~ in June** el jardín es una preciosidad en junio; **his face was a ~** ¡vaya cara que puso!, ¡vieras *or* hubieras visto su cara! (*LAm*)
6 (= *situation*) panorama *m*; **the overall ~ is encouraging** el panorama general es alentador; **you have to look at the whole ~** tienes que considerar la situación *or* el panorama en conjunto; **where do I come** *or* **fit into the ~?*** ¿qué pinto yo *or* dónde encajo yo en todo esto?*, ¿cuál es mi papel en todo esto?; **to get the ~*** comprender; **I get the ~** ya comprendo; **do you get the ~?** ¿te enteras?*, ¿lo captas?*; **he was a bit unsure in the job at first but he soon got the ~** al principio no se sentía muy seguro de cómo hacer su trabajo pero pronto le cogió el truco*; **to put sb in the ~ (about sth)** poner a algn al corriente *or* al tanto (de algo)
7 (= *idea*) **these figures give the general ~** estas cifras ofrecen una idea general *or* una visión de conjunto; **I have a ~ in my mind of how I want it to look** tengo una imagen mental del aspecto que quiero que tenga
8 (*TV*) imagen *f*
9 (*esp US Cine*) película *f*; (*Brit*†) **the ~s** el cine; **to go to the ~s** ir al cine; *see also* **motion D**
Ⓑ VT 1 (= *imagine*) imaginarse; **I never ~d you as a family man** nunca te imaginé *or* te vi como hombre de familia; **~ the scene** figuraos la escena; **~ yourself lying on the beach** imagínate que estás tumbado en la playa
2 (= *portray*) (*in painting, film, novel*) representar; (*in photograph*) **his wife, ~d with him above** su mujer, que figura con él en la foto de arriba; **the documentary ~d the police as good-natured fools** el documental pintaba a la policía como si fueran un hatajo de tontos con buen corazón, el documental representaba a la policía como un hatajo de tontos con buen corazón
Ⓒ CPD ► **picture book** N libro *m* ilustrado ► **picture frame** N marco *m* ► **picture gallery** N (= *shop*) galería *f* de arte; (= *museum*) museo *m* de pintura, pinacoteca *f*; (*in stately home*) galería *f* de cuadros ► **picture hat** N pamela *f* ► **picture house**† N cine *m* ► **picture message** N mensaje *m* con foto ► **picture messaging** N (envío *m* de) mensajes *mpl* con foto ► **picture palace**† N cine *m* ► **picture phone** N teléfono *m* con cámara ► **picture postcard** N (tarjeta *f*) postal *f* ► **picture rail** N *moldura para colgar cuadros* ► **picture tube** N (*TV*) tubo *m* de imagen ► **picture window** N ventanal *m*

picturegoer ['pɪktʃə,gəʊəʳ] N aficionado/a *m/f* al cine

picture-in-picture [,pɪktʃərɪn'pɪktʃəʳ] N (*TV, Comput*) imagen *f* dentro de la imagen

picture-postcard [,pɪktʃə'pəʊstkɑːd] ADJ [*village*] de postal

picturesque [,pɪktʃə'resk] ADJ (= *quaint*) [*village*] pintoresco; [*name, title*] pintoresco, peculiar; (= *vivid*) [*language*] expresivo, vívido

picturesquely [,pɪktʃə'reskl ɪ] ADV de modo pintoresco

picturesqueness [,pɪktʃə'resknɪs] N [*of village*] lo pintoresco, pintoresquismo *m*; [*of language, description*] expresividad *f*

piddle* ['pɪdl] Ⓐ N **to have a ~** hacer pipí *or* pis* Ⓑ VI hacer pipí*, hacer pis*

piddling* ['pɪdlɪŋ] ADJ ridículo, irrisorio

pidgin ['pɪdʒɪn] N (*also* **~ English**) (*formerly*) *lengua franca (inglés-chino) comercial del Lejano Oriente*; **he used his ~ French to chat up the girls** recurrió a su francés macarrónico para ligar con las chicas*

pie [paɪ] Ⓐ N [*of fruit*] tarta *f*, pay *m* (*LAm*); [*of meat, fish etc*] (= *large*) pastel *m*; (= *small*) empanada *f*; ✦*IDIOMS* **it's as easy as ~*** es pan comido*; **it's all ~ in the sky** son castillos en el aire, es pura ilusión; **to eat humble ~** tragarse el orgullo y pedir perdón, morder el polvo; *see also* **finger A1**
Ⓑ CPD ► **pie chart** N (*Math, Comput*) gráfico *m* de sectores, gráfico *m* circular

piebald ['paɪbɔːld] Ⓐ ADJ pío, picazo
Ⓑ N caballo *m* pío, picazo *m*

piece [piːs] Ⓐ N 1 (= *fragment*) trozo *m*, pedazo *m*; **to come to ~s** hacerse pedazos, romperse; **to fall to ~s** caerse a pedazos, romperse; **my watch lay in ~s on the pavement** mi reloj quedó destrozado en la acera, mi reloj quedó en la acera hecho pedazos; **his life lay in ~s** su vida estaba destrozada; **a ~ of sth**: **a ~ of bread** un trozo *or* un pedazo de pan; **a ~ of cake** una porción *or* un trozo de tarta; **another ~ of cake?** ¿quieres más tarta?; **a ~ of cheese/glass** un trozo de queso/cristal; **a ~ of paper** un trozo *or* una hoja de papel, un papel; **a ~ of string** un trozo de cuerda, un cabo; **a ~ of toast** una tostada; **I've got a ~ of grit in my eye** tengo una mota en el ojo; **(all) in one ~**: **the vase is still in one ~** el jarrón sigue intacto; **we got back all in one ~** llegamos sanos y salvos; **he had a nasty fall but he's still in one ~** sufrió una mala caída pero no le pasó nada; **it is made (all) in one ~** está hecho de una sola pieza; **to pick** *or* **pull sth to ~s** [+ *argument, theory*] echar por tierra algo; **to smash (sth) to ~s**: **the glass fell off the table and smashed to ~s** el vasó se cayó de la mesa y se hizo añicos; **I smashed the vase to ~s** rompí el jarrón en mil pedazos, hice el jarrón añicos; **the boat was smashed to ~s on the rocks** el barco se estrelló contra las rocas y se hizo añicos; ✦*IDIOMS* **to go to ~s** [*person*] (= *break down*) quedar deshecho, quedar hecho pedazos; (= *lose one's grip*) desquiciarse; **she went to ~s when Arnie died** quedó deshecha *or* hecha pedazos cuando Arnie murió; **every time he's faced with a problem he goes to ~s** cada vez que se ve ante un problema se desquicia *or* el pánico se apodera de él; **it's a ~ of cake*** es pan comido*; **to give sb a ~ of one's mind** decir cuatro verdades a algn, cantar las cuarenta a algn*; **he got a ~ of my mind** le dije cuatro verdades, le canté las cuarenta*; **to pick up the ~s**: **they always leave me to pick up the ~s** siempre me toca sacarles las castañas del fuego, siempre dejan que sea yo el que pague los platos rotos; **she never picked up the ~s after her fiancé died** nunca logró superar la muerte de su prometido, nunca rehizo realmente su vida después de la muerte de su prometido; *see also* **action A4, nasty A4, thrill**
2 (= *part, member of a set*) pieza *f*; **~ by ~** pieza por *or* a pieza; **it comes to ~s** se desmonta, es desmontable; **(all) of a ~**: **Dostoyevsky's life and work are of a ~** la vida y las obras de Dostoyevsky son uno y lo mismo; **Amy was putting the ~s together now** ahora Amy estaba juntando *or* atando los cabos; **to take sth to ~s** desmontar *or* desarmar algo
3 (*as suffix*) **a four-~ band** un grupo de cuatro músicos; **a three-~ suit** un traje con chaleco; **a three-~ suite** un juego de sofá y dos butacas, un tresillo (*Sp*); **a fifteen-~ tea set** un juego de té de quince piezas
4 (= *item*) **a ~ of advice** un consejo; **to sell sth by the ~** vender algo suelto; **a ~ of clothing** una prenda (de vestir); **a ~ of equipment** un aparato; **a ~ of evidence** una prueba; **a ~ of furniture** un mueble; **a ~ of information** un dato; **a ~ of legislation** una ley; **you are allowed two ~s of luggage** se le permite llevar dos bultos; **a ~ of news** una noticia; **your essay was a sloppy ~ of work** tu redacción deja mucho que desear; *see also* **history, land A2**
5 (= *instance*) **it was a ~ of luck** fue una suerte; **what a ~ of luck you called round** qué suerte que te hayas pasado por aquí
6 (= *composition*) (*Press*) artículo *m*; (*Mus, Art, Theat*) pieza *f*; **a piano ~** una pieza para piano; ✦*IDIOM* **to say one's ~** decir uno lo que tiene que decir; *see also* **museum, party C, period B**
7 (*Mil*) **artillery ~s** ◊ **~s of artillery** piezas *fpl* de artillería
8 (*in chess*) pieza *f*; (*in draughts, backgammon*) ficha *f*
9 (= *coin*) moneda *f*; **a 10 pence ~** una moneda de 10 peniques; **a ~ of eight** un real de a ocho
10 (*US**) (= *distance*) **his place is down the road a ~** su casa está un poco más allá bajando la calle
11 (†* *offensive*) (= *woman*) tipa* *f*, tía *f* (*Sp**); **a nice little ~** una tía buena (*Sp**), una tipaza*
Ⓑ CPD ► **piece rate** N (*Comm*) tarifa *f* por pieza; **they are on ~ rates** les pagan por pieza *or* a destajo

►**piece together** VT + ADV [+ *jigsaw puzzle, events*] reconstruir; [+ *plan, strategy*] concebir; **she ~d together the torn-up letter** reconstruyó la carta que estaba hecha pedazos; **we eventually ~d together what had happened** por fin logramos atar todos los cabos de lo que había pasado

pièce de résistance [ˌpjɛsdərezɪs'tɑ̃:s] N [*of programme, exhibition*] atracción *f* principal; (*on menu*) plato *m* principal; [*of author, director*] (= *novel, film*) obra *f* maestra; **his ~ was a goal in the 89th minute** dio la campanada con un gol en el minuto 89

piecemeal ['pi:smi:l] Ⓐ ADV (= *gradually*) poco a poco, por partes; (= *unsystematically*) de manera poco sistemática
Ⓑ ADJ [*approach, reform*] poco sistemático; **a ~ solution** una solución de compromiso

piecework ['pi:swɜ:k] N trabajo *m* a destajo; **to be on/do ~** trabajar a destajo

pieceworker ['pi:swɜ:kər] N destajista *mf*

piecrust ['paɪkrʌst] Ⓐ N (= *base*) fondo *m* de masa; (= *top*) tapa *f* de masa
Ⓑ CPD ► **piecrust pastry** N (*US*) pasta *f* quebradiza

pied [paɪd] ADJ [*horse*] pío, picazo; [*bird*] pinto; **the Pied Piper of Hamelin** el flautista de Hamelin

pied-à-terre [ˌpɪeɪdɑ:'tɛər] N (*pl* **pieds-à-terre** [ˌpjeɪdɑ:'tɛər]) segunda vivienda *f* (*en una ciudad*)

Piedmont ['pi:dmɒnt] N Piamonte *m*

Piedmontese [ˌpi:dmɒn'ti:z] Ⓐ ADJ piamontés
Ⓑ N piamontés/esa *m/f*

pie-eyed* ['paɪ'aɪd] ADJ como una cuba*, jumado*

pier [pɪər] N [1] (= *amusement centre*) *paseo marítimo situado como zona de ocio sobre un muelle o malecón*; (= *landing-stage*) embarcadero *m*, muelle *m*
[2] (*Archit*) pilar *m*, columna *f*; [*of bridge*] estribo *m*, pila *f*

pierce [pɪəs] VT (= *puncture*) perforar; (= *go right through*) atravesar, traspasar; (= *make hole in*) agujerear; (*fig*) [*sound*] desgarrar, penetrar; **the broken rib ~d his lung** la costilla rota le perforó el pulmón; **the thorn ~d his heel** la espina se le clavó en el talón; **the dagger ~d her heart/the armour** el puñal le atravesó el corazón/atravesó la armadura; **to ~ a hole in sth** hacer un agujero en algo; **to have one's ears ~d** hacerse los agujeros de las orejas; **a nail ~d the tyre** un clavo pinchó el neumático; **a cry ~d the silence** un grito desgarró *or* penetró el silencio; **a light ~d the darkness** una luz hendió la oscuridad; **the cold ~d their bones** el frío les penetraba hasta los huesos; **the news ~d him to the heart** la noticia le hirió en el alma

piercing ['pɪəsɪŋ] ADJ penetrante, agudo; [*eyes, gaze*] penetrante; [*cry*] desgarrador; [*wind*] cortante; [*cold*] penetrante; [*pain*] punzante

piercingly ['pɪəsɪŋlɪ] ADV [*stare*] de modo penetrante; [*blow*] de modo cortante; **it was ~ cold** el frío se te metía hasta los huesos

pierhead ['pɪəhed] N punta *f* del muelle

pierrot ['pɪərəʊ] N pierrot *m*

pietism ['paɪətɪzəm] N piedad *f*, devoción *f*; (*pej*) beatería *f*, mojigatería *f*

pietistic [paɪə'tɪstɪk] ADJ (*pej*) pietista, beato, mojigato

piety ['paɪətɪ] N piedad *f*, devoción *f*; (= *affected piety*) beatería *f*

piffle* ['pɪfl] N tonterías *fpl*, paparruchas* *fpl*; **piffle!** ¡tonterías!, ¡bobadas!

piffling* ['pɪflɪŋ] ADJ [*dispute, task*] de poca monta, insignificante; [*excuse*] absurdo, ridículo; [*sum, amount*] ridículo, irrisorio

pig [pɪg] Ⓐ N [1] cerdo *m*, chancho *m* (*LAm*); **roast ~** lechón *m* asado *or* al horno; **wild ~** cerdo *m* de monte; ✦**IDIOMS he made a right ~'s ear of it*** le salió muy mal, le salió un verdadero churro (*Sp**), le salió una auténtica cagada‡; **in a ~'s eye!** (*US**) ¡ni hablar!; **when ~s (learn to) fly** cuando las ranas críen pelos; **to buy a ~ in a poke** comprar algo a ciegas; **to sell sb a ~ in a poke** dar gato por liebre a algn
[2] (*) (= *person*) (*dirty, nasty*) cerdo/a* *m/f*, puerco/a* *m/f*, chancho/a* *m/f* (*LAm*); (*greedy*) comilón/ona* *m/f*, tragón/ona* *m/f*; **you ~!** (*hum*) ¡bandido!; ✦**IDIOM to make a ~ of o.s.** darse un atracón*, ponerse las botas*
[3] (‡) (= *policeman*) poli* *m*; **the ~s** la poli*, la pasma (*Sp*‡), la cana (*S. Cone*‡)
[4] (*) (= *sth difficult or unpleasant*) **it was a ~ of a job** fue un trabajo de lo más puñetero*; **this car's a ~ to start** a este puñetero coche le cuesta lo suyo arrancar*
[5] (*Metal*) lingote *m*
Ⓑ VT **to ~ it** vivir como cerdos
Ⓒ CPD ► **pig iron** N hierro *m* en lingotes

►**pig out*** VI + ADV **to ~ out (on sth)** darse un atracón *or* ponerse las botas (de algo)*

pig-breeding ['pɪg,bri:dɪŋ] N cría *f* de cerdos

pigeon ['pɪdʒən] Ⓐ N [1] (*gen*) paloma *f*; (*as food*) pichón *m*; *see also* **clay B**
[2] (*) **that's his ~** allá él; **it's not my ~** eso no tiene que ver conmigo
Ⓑ CPD ► **pigeon fancier** N colombófilo/a *m/f* ► **pigeon fancying** N colombofilia *f* ► **pigeon house, pigeon loft** N palomar *m* ► **pigeon post** N correo *m* de palomas; **by ~ post** por paloma mensajera ► **pigeon shooting** N tiro *m* de pichón

pigeonhole ['pɪdʒənhəʊl] Ⓐ N casilla *f*; (= *set of pigeonholes*) casillero *m*, casillas *fpl*
Ⓑ VT (= *classify*) encasillar, clasificar; (= *store away*) archivar; (= *shelve*) dar carpetazo a

pigeon-toed ['pɪdʒən'təʊd] ADJ **to be ~** tener los pies torcidos hacia dentro

piggery ['pɪgərɪ] N [1] (= *pig farm*) granja *f* porcina
[2] (= *pigsty*) pocilga *f*, porqueriza *f*
[3] (= *greediness*) glotonería *f*

piggish ['pɪgɪʃ] ADJ (*in manners*) cochino, puerco; (= *greedy*) glotón; (= *stubborn*) tozudo, testarudo

piggy ['pɪgɪ] Ⓐ N cerdito *m*, chanchito *m* (*LAm*); **to play ~ in the middle** jugar al balón prisionero; ✦**IDIOM to be ~ in the middle** (= *powerless to act, influence*) estar entre dos fuegos
Ⓑ ADJ **with little ~ eyes** con ojos pequeños como de cerdo
Ⓒ CPD ► **piggy bank** N hucha *f* (*Sp*) (en forma de cerdito), alcancía *f* (*LAm*)

piggyback ['pɪgɪbæk] Ⓐ N **to give sb a ~** llevar a algn a cuestas
Ⓑ ADV **to carry sb ~** llevar a algn a cuestas

pigheaded ['pɪg'hedɪd] ADJ [*person*] terco, testarudo; [*attitude*] obstinado

pigheadedly ['pɪg'hedɪdlɪ] ADV tercamente

pigheadedness ['pɪg'hedɪdnɪs] N terquedad *f*, testarudez *f*

pig-ignorant* [ˌpɪg'ɪgnərənt] ADJ bruto

piglet ['pɪglɪt] N cerdito *m*, lechón *m*, chanchito *m* (*LAm*)

pigman ['pɪgmæn] N (*pl* **pigmen**) porquerizo *m*, porquero *m*

pigmeat ['pɪgmi:t] N carne *f* de cerdo

pigment ['pɪgmənt] N pigmento *m*

pigmentation [ˌpɪgmən'teɪʃən] N pigmentación *f*

pigmented [pɪg'mentɪd] ADJ pigmentado

pigmy ['pɪgmɪ] ADJ, N = **pygmy**

pigpen ['pɪgpen] N (*US*) = **pigsty**

pigskin ['pɪgskɪn] N piel *f* de cerdo, cuero *m* de chancho (*LAm*)

pigsty ['pɪgstaɪ] N pocilga *f*, porqueriza *f*

pigswill ['pɪgswɪl] N bazofia *f* (*also fig*)

pigtail ['pɪgteɪl] N (= *plait*) trenza *f*; (*of Chinese, bullfighter etc*) coleta *f*

pike[1] [paɪk] N (*Mil*) pica *f*

pike[2] [paɪk] N (*pl* **pike** *or* **pikes**) (= *fish*) lucio *m*

pikeman ['paɪkmən] N (*pl* **pikemen**) (*Hist*) piquero *m*

piker‡ ['paɪkər] N (*US*) (= *stingy person*) agarrado/a* *m/f*, roñoso/a* *m/f*; (= *unimportant person*) pelagatos* *mf inv*; (= *coward*) gallina* *mf*

pikestaff ['paɪkstɑ:f] N *see* **plain A1**

pilaf(f) ['pɪlæf] N *plato oriental a base de arroz*

pilaster [pɪ'læstər] N pilastra *f*

Pilate ['paɪlət] N Pilatos

pilau [pɪ'laʊ] N = **pilaf(f)**

pilchard ['pɪltʃəd] N sardina *f*

pile[1] [paɪl] Ⓐ N [1] (= *heap*) [*of books, clothes*] montón *m*; **to put things in a ~** amontonar cosas, juntar cosas en un montón; **the building was reduced to a ~ of rubble** el edificio quedó reducido a un montón *or* una pila de escombros
[2] (*) (= *large amount*) montón* *m*; **I've got ~s of work to do** tengo un montón *or* tengo montones de trabajo que hacer*
[3] (*) (= *fortune*) dineral* *m*, fortuna *f*; **he made a ~ on this deal** ganó un dineral *or* una fortuna con el trato, se hizo de oro con el trato; **he made his ~ in oil** hizo su fortuna con el petróleo
[4] (* *hum*) (= *building*) mole *f* (*hum*); **some stately ~ in the country** una mole de casa *or* un caserón en el campo
[5] (*Phys*) pila *f*; *see also* **atomic**
Ⓑ VT amontonar, apilar; **he ~d the plates onto the tray** amontonó *or* apiló los platos en la bandeja; **we ~d more coal on the fire** echamos más carbón al fuego; **the tables were ~d high with food** en las mesas había montones *or* montañas de comida; **her hair was ~d high on her head** llevaba el pelo recogido con un tocado alto; **I ~d the children into the car*** metí a los niños apretujados en el coche
Ⓒ VI (*) [1] (= *squeeze*) **we all ~d into the car** nos metimos todos apretujados en el coche; **we ~d off the bus** salimos en avalancha *or* en tropel del autobús; **they ~d onto the bus** se metieron apretujados en el autobús
[2] (= *attack*) **they ~d into him** se abalanzaron sobre él
[3] (= *crash*) **his car ~d into the tree** su coche se estrelló contra el árbol; **12 cars had ~d into each other** 12 coches se habían estrellado en cadena

►**pile in*** VI + ADV [1] (= *get in*) **~ in!** ¡súbanse como puedan!
[2] (= *intervene*) lanzarse al ataque

►**pile off*** VI + ADV [*people*] salir en avalancha *or* en tropel

►**pile on*** Ⓐ VI + ADV (= *crowd on*) meterse a empujones, meterse apretujados
Ⓑ VT + ADV **he ~d on more branches** echó más ramas; **they really ~ the work on, don't they?** te dan muchísimo trabajo, ¿ver-

dad?; **to ~ on the agony** multiplicar el martirio*; **he does rather ~ it on*** es un exagerado; **they were piling it on** estaban exagerando; *see also* **pressure A2**

►**pile out*** VI + ADV [*people*] salir en avalancha *or* en tropel

►**pile up** Ⓐ VI + ADV [1] (= *accumulate*) [*work*] amontonarse, acumularse; **black clouds were piling up on the horizon** el horizonte se estaba cargando *or* se llenaba de nubes negras
[2] (= *crash*) [*vehicle*] estrellarse, chocar; [*vehicles*] estrellarse en cadena, chocar en cadena
Ⓑ VT + ADV [1] (= *put in heap*) [+ *books, clothes*] apilar, amontonar
[2] (= *accumulate*) [+ *possessions*] acumular; [+ *debts*] acumular, llenarse de

pile[2] [paɪl] Ⓐ N (*Constr*) pilote *m*, pilar *m*
Ⓑ CPD ► **pile driver** N martinete *m* ► **pile dwelling** N (*Hist*) vivienda *f* construida sobre pilotes

pile[3] [paɪl] N [*of carpet, cloth*] pelo *m*; *see also* **shag**[4]

piles [paɪlz] NPL (*Med*) almorranas *fpl*, hemorroides *fpl*

pile-up* [ˈpaɪlʌp] N (*Aut*) accidente *m* múltiple, choque *m* en cadena; **there was a ~ on the motorway** chocaron varios coches en cadena en la autopista, hubo un accidente múltiple en la autopista

pilfer [ˈpɪlfəʳ] Ⓐ VT ratear*, hurtar, robar; (*esp by servant*) robar, sisar (*Sp**)
Ⓑ VI ratear*, robar cosas

pilferage [ˈpɪlfərɪdʒ] N ratería* *f*, hurto *m*, robo *m*

pilferer [ˈpɪlfərəʳ] N ratero/a* *m/f*, ladronzuelo/a* *m/f*

pilfering [ˈpɪlfərɪŋ] N ratería* *f*, hurto *m*, robo *m*

pilgrim [ˈpɪlgrɪm] Ⓐ N peregrino/a *m/f*, romero/a *m/f*
Ⓑ CPD ► **the Pilgrim Fathers** NPL los primeros colonos de Nueva Inglaterra

> **PILGRIM FATHERS**
>
> *Los* **Pilgrim Fathers** *fueron un grupo de puritanos que abandonaron Inglaterra en 1620 huyendo de las persecuciones religiosas y que, después de cruzar el Atlántico en el* **Mayflower**, *fundaron una colonia en Nueva Inglaterra (New Plymouth, Massachusetts), dando así comienzo a la colonización británica en Norteamérica. Se los considera como los fundadores de Estados Unidos y el éxito de su primera cosecha se conmemora cada año en el Día de Acción de Gracias (***Thanksgiving Day***).*
>
> ⇨ *Ver tb* THANKSGIVING

pilgrimage [ˈpɪlgrɪmɪdʒ] N peregrinación *f*; **to go on a ~** ◊ **make a ~ (to)** ir de peregrinación (a)

piling [ˈpaɪlɪŋ] N (= *post*) pilote *m*

pill [pɪl] Ⓐ N [1] (*Med, fig*) píldora *f*, pastilla *f*; **to take a ~** tomar una píldora; ✦*IDIOM* **to sugar** *or* **sweeten the ~** dorar la píldora; *see also* **bitter A1**, **pop C2**
[2] (= *contraceptive*) **the ~** la píldora (anticonceptiva); **to be on/take the ~** tomar la píldora (anticonceptiva); **to go on/come off the ~** empezar a/dejar de tomar la píldora; **birth control** *or* **contraceptive ~** píldora *f* anticonceptiva
Ⓑ CPD ► **pill bottle** N frasco *m* de pastillas

pillage [ˈpɪlɪdʒ] Ⓐ N pillaje *m*, saqueo *m*
Ⓑ VT, VI saquear

pillar [ˈpɪləʳ] Ⓐ N pilar *m*, columna *f*; **a ~ of smoke** una columna de humo; **the Pillars of Hercules** las Columnas de Hércules; **~ of salt** (*Bible*) estatua *f* de sal; **a ~ of the church** (*fig*) un pilar de la iglesia; ✦*IDIOMS* **to be a ~ of strength** ser firme como una roca; **to go from ~ to post** ir de la Ceca a la Meca
Ⓑ CPD ► **pillar box** N (*Brit*) buzón *m*

pillar-box red [ˌpɪləbɒksˈred] Ⓐ ADJ carmesí *inv*
Ⓑ N carmesí *m*

pillbox [ˈpɪlbɒks] N (*Med*) pastillero *m*; (*Mil*) fortín *m*; (*also* **~ hat**) casquete *m* (*gorro*)

pillion [ˈpɪljən] Ⓐ N (*also* **~ seat**) asiento *m* trasero
Ⓑ ADV **to ride ~** ir en el asiento trasero
Ⓒ CPD ► **pillion passenger** N pasajero/a *m/f* de atrás

pillock‡ [ˈpɪlək] N (*Brit*) imbécil *mf*, gili *mf* (*Sp**)

pillory [ˈpɪlərɪ] Ⓐ N picota *f*
Ⓑ VT poner en ridículo

pillow [ˈpɪləʊ] Ⓐ N almohada *f*
Ⓑ VT apoyar; **she ~ed her head on my shoulder** apoyó la cabeza en mi hombro
Ⓒ CPD ► **pillow fight** N lucha *f* de almohadas ► **pillow talk** N conversaciones *fpl* de alcoba

pillowcase [ˈpɪləʊkeɪs], **pillowslip** [ˈpɪləʊslɪp] N funda *f* de almohada

pilot [ˈpaɪlət] Ⓐ N [1] (*Aer*) piloto *mf*; *see also* **airline B**, **automatic C**, **fighter B**, **test D**
[2] (*Naut*) práctico *mf*, piloto *mf*
[3] = **pilot light**
[4] = **pilot programme**
Ⓑ VT [1] (*Aer, Naut*) pilotar, pilotear (*esp LAm*)
[2] (*fig*) (= *guide*) conducir; (= *test*) [+ *scheme*] poner a prueba; **he ~ed the negotiations through** condujo las negociaciones a buen fin; **to ~ a bill through the House** asegurar la aprobación de un proyecto de ley
Ⓒ CPD [*project, scheme*] piloto *inv*, experimental ► **pilot boat** N barco *m* del práctico ► **pilot episode** N (*TV*) episodio *m* piloto ► **pilot error** N **the airline blamed ~ error for the crash** la compañía achacó el accidente a un error del piloto ► **pilot fish** N pez *m* piloto ► **pilot house** N (*Naut*) timonera *f* ► **pilot's licence** N licencia *f* de piloto ► **pilot light** N piloto *m* ► **pilot officer** N oficial *m* piloto ► **pilot plant** N (*Ind*) planta *f* de prueba, planta *f* piloto ► **pilot programme** N (*TV*) programa *m* piloto ► **pilot study** N estudio *m* piloto ► **pilot whale** N calderón *m* negro

pimento [pɪˈmentəʊ] N (*pl* **pimentos**) pimiento *m*, pimentón *m* morrón (*S. Cone*)

pimp [pɪmp] Ⓐ N proxeneta *m* (*frm*), chulo *m* (de putas) (*Sp**), cafiche *m* (*S. Cone**)
Ⓑ VI **to ~ for sb** ejercer de proxeneta de algn

pimpernel [ˈpɪmpənel] N murajes *mpl*, pimpinela *f*

pimple [ˈpɪmpl] N (*gen*) grano *m*; (*on face*) espinilla *f*; **she came out in ~s** le salieron granos

pimply [ˈpɪmplɪ] ADJ (*compar* **pimplier**; *superl* **pimpliest**) lleno de granos, cubierto de granos; **a ~ youth** (*fig*) un mozalbete, un mocoso (*pej*)

PIMS N ABBR = **personal information management system**

PIN [pɪn] N ABBR = **personal identification number**; **~ number** NPI *m*

pin [pɪn] Ⓐ N [1] (*Sew*) alfiler *m*; (*also* **safety ~**) imperdible *m*, seguro *m* (*CAm, Mex*); (*also* **hairpin**) horquilla *f*; (*also* **hatpin**) alfiler *m* (de sombrero); (= *brooch*) alfiler *m*; (*also* **drawing ~**) chincheta *f*, chinche *m or f* (*LAm*); (*also* **clothes ~**) (*US*) pinza *f* (de la ropa); **~s and needles** hormigueo *msing*; ✦*IDIOMS* **to be on ~s and needles** (*US*) estar hecho un manojo de nervios, estar en *or* sobre ascuas; **you could have heard a ~ drop** se oía el vuelo de una mosca; **like a new ~** ◊ **as neat as a (new) ~** (= *clean*) como una patena, limpio como un espejo; (= *tidy*) pulcro y muy ordenado; **for two ~s I'd knock his head off*** por menos de nada le rompería la crisma; **it doesn't matter two ~s to me** ◊ **I don't care two ~s** me importa un rábano *or* comino*; *see also* **bobby pin**, **lapel**, **panel C**
[2] (*Tech*) [*of metal*] clavija *f*; [*of wood*] espiga *f*, clavija *f*; (= *bolt*) perno *m*; (= *cotter*) chaveta *f*
[3] (*Elec*) [*of plug*] polo *m*; **three-~ plug** clavija *f* de tres polos, clavija *f* tripolar
[4] (*Med*) (*in limb*) clavo *m*
[5] (*on grenade*) anilla *f*
[6] (*Bowls*) bolo *m*; (*Golf*) banderín *m*
[7] **pins** (*hum*, *) (= *legs*) patas* *fpl*, bielas‡ *fpl*
Ⓑ VT [1] [+ *fabric, seam, hem*] prender *or* sujetar con alfileres; **there was a note ~ned on** *or* **to the door** había una nota clavada en la puerta; **to ~ a medal to sb's uniform** prender una medalla al uniforme de algn; **she had ~ned her hair into a bun** se había hecho un moño con horquillas
[2] (*Tech*) (*with bolt*) sujetar (con perno)
[3] (*fig*) **to ~ one's hopes on sth/sb** cifrar *or* depositar sus esperanzas en algo/algn; **the Democrats are ~ning their hopes on the next election** los demócratas tienen cifradas sus esperanzas en las próximas elecciones; **you can't ~ the blame on me** no podéis cargarme con la culpa; **they're trying to ~ the murder on us** tratan de culparnos del asesinato; **there was nothing they could ~ on him** no podían acusarlo *or* culparlo de nada
[4] (= *immobilize*) **two men ~ned him to the floor** dos hombres lo sujetaron en el suelo; **his arms were ~ned to his sides** llevaba los brazos sujetos a los costados; **they ~ned me against the wall** me sujetaron contra la pared
Ⓒ CPD ► **pin money** N dinero *m* para gastos menores ► **pin table** N millón *m*, flíper *m*

►**pin back** VT + ADV [+ *fabric*] doblar hacia atrás y sujetar con alfileres; [+ *hair*] recogerse; [+ *window, door*] sujetar; (*Med*) [+ *ears, skin*] operarse de; ✦*IDIOM* **to ~ one's ears back*** escuchar muy atento

►**pin down** VT + ADV [1] (= *fasten or hold down*) sujetar; **he ~ned me down by my wrists** me sujetó por las muñecas; **I was ~ned down by a fallen tree** quedé atrapado bajo un árbol caído
[2] (*fig*) [2·1] (= *oblige to be specific*) **to ~ sb down** hacer que algn concrete; **she is really hard to ~ down** es difícil hacerla concretar; **the minister refused to be ~ned down on the timing of the reforms** el ministro no quiso comprometerse a dar fechas específicas para las reformas; **you can't ~ him down to a date** es imposible lograr que nos dé una fecha concreta
[2·2] (= *identify*) [+ *problem*] identificar; [+ *concept*] precisar, definir; [+ *reason*] dar con; [+ *date*] precisar; **the idea is rather hard to ~ down** es un concepto difícil de precisar *or* definir; **there's something wrong but I can't ~ it down** algo va mal pero no sé exactamente qué
[3] (*Mil*) [+ *troops*] atrapar; **our men were ~ned down by artillery fire** nuestros hom-

bres se vieron atrapados por fuego de artillería

►**pin on** VT + ADV prender, poner

►**pin together** VT + ADV [+ *fabric pieces, papers*] sujetar, prender

►**pin up** VT + ADV [+ *notice*] poner, pegar; [+ *clothing*] recoger con alfileres; (*with safety pin*) recoger con imperdible; [+ *hem*] sujetar con alfileres; [+ *hair*] recoger (con horquilla)

pina colada ['piːnəkə'lɑːdə] N piña *f* colada

pinafore ['pɪnəfɔːʳ] Ⓐ N (= *overall, apron*) delantal *m*, mandil *m*
Ⓑ CPD ► **pinafore dress** N jumper *m*, pichi *m* (*Sp*)

pinball ['pɪnbɔːl] N (*also* ~ **machine**) millón *m*, flíper *m*; **to play ~** jugar al millón *or* al flíper

pince-nez ['pɛːnsneɪ] NPL quevedos *mpl*

pincer ['pɪnsəʳ] Ⓐ N [1] (*Zool*) pinza *f*
[2] (*Tech*) **pincers** tenazas *fpl*, pinzas *fpl*; **a pair of ~s** unas tenazas
Ⓑ CPD ► **pincer movement** N (*Mil*) movimiento *m* de pinza *or* tenaza

pinch [pɪntʃ] Ⓐ N [1] (*with fingers*) pellizco *m*; **to give sb a ~ on the arm** dar a algn un pellizco en el brazo, pellizcar el brazo a algn
[2] (= *small quantity*) pizca *f*; **a ~ of salt** una pizca de sal; **a ~ of snuff** un polvo de rapé; ✦*IDIOM* **to take sth with a ~ of salt** tomarse algo con reservas, no creerse algo a pies juntillas
[3] (*fig*) apuro *m*; **at a ~** en caso de apuro *or* necesidad; **if it comes to the ~** en un caso extremo; ✦*IDIOM* **to feel the ~** (empezar a) pasar apuros *or* estrecheces; **to feel the ~ of poverty** saber lo que significa ser pobre
Ⓑ VT [1] (*with fingers*) pellizcar; [*shoe*] apretar; **to ~ one's finger in the door** pillarse el dedo en la puerta; **to ~ off** *or* **out** *or* **back a bud** arrancar un brote con los dedos
[2] (*) (= *steal*) robar, birlar*, guindar (*Sp**); **I had my pen ~ed** me robaron la pluma, me birlaron la pluma*; **he ~ed that idea from Shaw** esa idea la robó de Shaw; **he ~ed Mike's girl** le pisó *or* levantó la novia a Mike*
[3] (*) (= *arrest*) pescar*, coger, agarrar (*LAm*); **he got ~ed for a parking offence** lo pescaron en una infracción de aparcamiento*, le metieron un paquete por aparcamiento indebido*
Ⓒ VI [*shoe*] apretar; **to ~ and scrape** privarse de lo necesario; **they ~ed and scraped to send her to college** se privaron de muchas cosas para poder enviarla a la universidad

pinchbeck ['pɪntʃbek] Ⓐ N similor *m*
Ⓑ CPD de similor; (*fig*) falso

pinched ['pɪntʃt] ADJ [1] (= *drawn*) **to look ~** tener un aspecto demacrado; **to be ~ with cold** estar aterido de frío
[2] (= *short*) **to be ~ for money** andar escaso de dinero; **we're very ~ for space** tenemos muy poco espacio

pinch-hit ['pɪntʃhɪt] VI (*US*) batear de suplente; (*fig*) **to ~ for sb** sustituir a algn en un apuro

pinchpenny† ['pɪntʃpenɪ] ADJ tacaño

pincushion ['pɪn,kʊʃən] N acerico *m*, almohadilla *f*

Pindar ['pɪndəʳ] N Píndaro

Pindaric [pɪn'dærɪk] ADJ pindárico

pine¹ [paɪn] Ⓐ N pino *m*
Ⓑ CPD ► **pine cone** N piña *f* ► **pine grove** N pinar *m* ► **pine kernel** N piñón *m* ► **pine marten** N marta *f* ► **pine needle** N aguja *f* de pino ► **pine nut** N piñón *m* ► **pine tree** N pino *m*

pine² [paɪn] VI (*also* **to ~ away**) consumirse, languidecer; **to ~ for sth/sb** suspirar por algo/algn

pineal body ['pɪnɪəl,bɒdɪ], **pineal gland** ['pɪnɪəl,glænd] N glándula *f* pineal

pineapple ['paɪn,æpl] N piña *f*, ananá(s) *m* (*LAm*)

pinewood ['paɪnwʊd] N pinar *m*

ping [pɪŋ] Ⓐ N (*on striking*) sonido *m* metálico; [*of bullet*] silbido *m*; [*of bell*] tintín *m*
Ⓑ VI (*on striking*) producir un sonido metálico; [*bullet*] silbar; [*bell*] tintinear, hacer tintín

ping-pong® ['pɪŋpɒŋ] Ⓐ N ping-pong® *m*, tenis *m* de mesa
Ⓑ CPD ► **ping-pong ball** N pelota *f* de ping-pong

pinhead ['pɪnhed] N [1] (*lit*) cabeza *f* de alfiler
[2] (* *pej*) (= *idiot*) mentecato *m*, cabeza *f* de chorlito*

pinhole ['pɪnhəʊl] Ⓐ N agujero *m* de alfiler
Ⓑ CPD ► **pinhole camera** N cámara *f* de agujero de alfiler

pinion¹ ['pɪnjən] Ⓐ N (*poet*) ala *f*
Ⓑ VT [+ *bird*] cortar las alas a; [+ *person*] atar los brazos a; **he was ~ed against the wall** lo tenían inmovilizado contra la pared

pinion² ['pɪnjən] N (*Mech*) piñón *m*

pink¹ [pɪŋk] Ⓐ N [1] (= *colour*) rosa *m*, rosado *m* (*LAm*); **~ doesn't suit her** el rosa no le sienta bien; ✦*IDIOMS* **to be in the ~** (= *healthy*) rebosar salud; (= *happy*) estar feliz y contento; **to be in the ~ of condition** estar en perfecto estado; *see also* **dusty 2**, **rose B**, **salmon C**, **shocking B**
[2] (*Bot*) clavel *m*, clavelina *f*
[3] (*Snooker*) bola *f* rosa
Ⓑ ADJ (*compar* **pinker**; *superl* **pinkest**) [1] (= *colour*) (*gen*) (color de) rosa, rosado (*LAm*); [*cheeks, face*] sonrosado; **we painted the nursery ~** pintamos el cuarto de los niños de rosa; **their little faces were ~ with excitement** tenían las caritas encendidas de entusiasmo; **his face was ~ with rage** estaba rojo de furia; **his cheeks were flushed ~ from the wine** el vino le había sonrosado las mejillas; **to turn** *or* **go ~** [*person*] (*with embarrassment*) ponerse colorado, sonrojarse; [*sky, liquid*] ponerse rosa; **she turned ~ with pleasure** se sonrojó de placer; *see also* **tickle A3**
[2] (*Pol**) rojillo*
[3] (*) (= *gay*) [*pound, vote*] homosexual, gay *inv*
Ⓒ CPD ► **pink gin** N ginebra *f* con angostura ► **pink grapefruit** N *variedad de pomelo de pulpa rojiza* ► **pink lady** N pink lady *m* ► **pink salmon** N salmón *m* del Pacífico ► **pink slip** N (*US*) notificación *f* de despido

pink² [pɪŋk] Ⓐ VT (*Sew*) rematar con tijeras dentadas; (= *make holes in*) [+ *fabric*] calar; (*Fencing*) herir levemente
Ⓑ VI (*Brit Aut*) [*engine*] picar

pinkeye ['pɪŋkaɪ] N (*Med*) conjuntivitis *f* aguda

pinkie* ['pɪŋkɪ] N (*Scot, US*) (dedo *m*) meñique *m*

pinking ['pɪŋkɪŋ] N (*Brit Aut*) piqueteo *m*

pinking shears ['pɪŋkɪŋ,ʃɪəz] NPL tijeras *fpl* dentadas

pinkish ['pɪŋkɪʃ] ADJ rosáceo; (*Pol*) rojillo*

pinko* ['pɪŋkəʊ] (*Pol pej*) Ⓐ ADJ rojillo*
Ⓑ N (*pl* **pinkos** *or* **pinkoes**) rojillo/a* *m/f*

pinnace ['pɪnɪs] N pinaza *f*

pinnacle ['pɪnəkl] N (*Archit*) pináculo *m*; (= *peak*) [*of rock*] punta *f*; [*of mountain*] cumbre *f*, cima *f*; (*fig*) cumbre *f*, cúspide *f*; **the ~ of fame/success** la cumbre *or* la cúspide de la fama/del éxito

pinny* ['pɪnɪ] N = **pinafore**

Pinocchio [pɪ'nɒkɪəʊ] N Pinocho

pinpoint ['pɪnpɔɪnt] Ⓐ N [*of light*] puntito *m*
Ⓑ VT (= *identify*) [+ *location, source, problem*] identificar, determinar; [+ *cause*] precisar, señalar con precisión; **it's difficult to ~ when it first started happening** resulta difícil precisar cuándo empezó a ocurrir por primera vez; **we ~ed the issues that need priority attention** determinamos qué cuestiones necesitan atención prioritaria

pinprick ['pɪnprɪk] N (*lit*) pinchazo *m*; (*fig*) pequeña molestia *f*

pinstripe ['pɪnstraɪp] Ⓐ ADJ de raya diplomática
Ⓑ N (= *suit*) traje *m* de raya diplomática; (= *fabric*) tela *f* de raya diplomática; (= *stripe*) raya *f* diplomática
Ⓒ CPD ► **pinstripe suit** N traje *m* de raya diplomática

pint [paɪnt] N [1] (= *measure*) pinta *f* ((*Brit*) = *0,57 litros; (US) = 0,47 litros*); → IMPERIAL SYSTEM
[2] (*Brit**) [*of beer*] **a ~** una cerveza; **to go for a ~** salir a tomar una cerveza; **we had a few ~s** bebimos *or* (*LAm*) tomamos unas cervezas, bebimos unas cañas (*Sp*), bebimos *or* (*LAm*) tomamos unas cuantas*

pinta* ['paɪntə] N pinta *f* de leche

pintail ['pɪnteɪl] N ánade *m* rabudo

pinto bean ['pɪntəʊbiːn] N judía *f or* alubia *f* pinta

pint-size(d)* ['paɪntsaɪz(d)] ADJ diminuto, pequeñito*

pin-up ['pɪnʌp] Ⓐ N *foto o póster de un famoso, de una chica atractiva, etc.*
Ⓑ CPD ► **pin-up girl** N chica *f* de revista (*modelo*)

pinwheel ['pɪn,wiːl] N (*esp US*) rueda *f* catalina

pioneer [,paɪə'nɪəʳ] Ⓐ N (= *explorer*) explorador(a) *m/f*, pionero/a *m/f*; (= *early settler*) colonizador(a) *m/f*, pionero/a *m/f*; (= *initiator*) pionero/a *m/f*, precursor(a) *m/f*; (*Mil*) zapador(a) *m/f*; **he was a ~ in the study of bats** fue uno de los primeros en estudiar los murciélagos
Ⓑ VT [+ *technique*] ser el/la primero/a en utilizar; **he ~ed the use of vitamin B in the treatment of mental illness** fue el primero en utilizar la vitamina B para el tratamiento de enfermedades mentales
Ⓒ VI explorar, abrir nuevos caminos
Ⓓ CPD ► **pioneer corps** N cuerpo *m* de zapadores ► **pioneer work** N trabajo *m* pionero

pioneering [,paɪə'nɪərɪŋ] ADJ [*work, research, study, surgeon*] pionero, innovador

pious ['paɪəs] ADJ piadoso, pío; (*pej*) beato; **~ hopes** vanas esperanzas *fpl*

piously ['paɪəslɪ] ADV piadosamente, devotamente; (*pej*) vanamente

pip¹ [pɪp] N [1] (*Bot*) pepita *f*, pepa *f* (*esp LAm*); (*on card, dice*) punto *m*; (*Brit Mil**) (*on uniform*) estrella *f*; (*on radar screen*) señal *f*
[2] (= *sound*) bip *m*, pitido *m*; **the ~s** (*Telec*) la señal; **wait till you hear the ~s** espere a que oiga la señal

pip²†* [pɪp] (*Brit*) N ✦*IDIOM* **to give sb the ~** sacar de quicio a algn; **it's enough to give you the ~** es para volverse loco; **he's got the ~** está de muy mal humor

pip³ [pɪp] VT ✦*IDIOM* **to be ~ped at** *or* **to the post** (*Brit**) perder por un pelo*; **Baby Boy ~ped Omar at** *or* **to the post** Baby Boy le ganó a Omar por un pelo*

pipe [paɪp] Ⓐ N [1] (= *tube*) tubo *m*, caño *m*; (*larger, system of pipes*) tubería *f*, cañería *f*; **a length of copper ~** una tubería de cobre; *see also* **overflow D**, **waste E**

2 (*Mus*) [*of organ*] cañón *m*, tubo *m*; (= *wind instrument*) flauta *f*, caramillo *m*; **pipes** (*also* **bagpipes**) gaita *f*; (*boatswain's*) silbato *m*; **the ~s of Pan** la flauta de Pan; **to play the ~s** tocar la gaita
3 (*smoker's*) pipa *f*, cachimba *f* (*esp LAm*); ✦*IDIOM* **put that in your ~ and smoke it!*** ¡chúpate ésa!*; *see also* **peace B**
Ⓑ VT 1 (= *convey*) [+ *water*] canalizar por tuberías; [+ *gas*] llevar por gasoducto; [+ *oil*] llevar por oleoducto; **sewage from the villages is ~d into the river** las aguas residuales de los pueblos son canalizadas y vertidas al río; **most of the houses here don't have ~d water** la mayoría de las casas aquí no tienen agua corriente; **the oil is ~d across the desert** el petróleo es conducido a través del desierto por un oleoducto
2 (= *broadcast*) [+ *music*] emitir; **~d music** música *f* ambiental, hilo *m* musical (*Sp*)
3 (= *play*) [+ *tune*] tocar (en flauta *or* gaita); **they ~d the admiral aboard** con el silbato avisaron al almirante de que subiera a bordo
4 (*Culin*) [+ *cake*] adornar con manga; [+ *icing, cream*] poner con manga; **to ~ cream on a cake** adornar una tarta con nata *or* (*LAm*) crema usando la manga
5 (*Sew*) ribetear con cordoncillo; **a jacket ~d with blue at the seams** una chaqueta con cordoncillo azul en las costuras
6 (= *say*) decir con voz de pito; (= *sing*) cantar con tono agudo; **"but I want to help," she ~d** —pero es que yo quiero ayudar —dijo ella con voz de pito
Ⓒ VI (*Mus*) tocar el caramillo/la flauta/la gaita; (*Naut*) tocar el silbato; [*bird*] trinar
Ⓓ CPD ► **pipe band** N banda *f* de gaiteros ► **pipe bomb** N *bomba de mano casera en forma de tubo* ► **pipe cleaner** N (escobilla *f*) limpiapipas *m inv* ► **pipe dream** N sueño *m* imposible ► **pipe organ** N órgano *m* de tubos ► **pipe rack** N soporte *m* para pipas ► **pipe smoker** N fumador(a) *m/f* de pipa ► **pipe stem** N cañón *m* de la pipa ► **pipe tobacco** N tabaco *m* de pipa
►**pipe down*** VI + ADV callarse, cerrar el pico*; **~ down, will you!** ¡cerrad ya el pico!*
►**pipe up*** Ⓐ VI + ADV meter baza*, saltar; **then somebody ~d up with another question** y entonces alguien metió baza con otra pregunta*
Ⓑ VT + ADV soltar de sopetón*; **"can I come too?" ~d up a little voice** —¿puedo ir yo también? —soltó de sopetón una vocecilla
pipeclay ['paɪpkleɪ] Ⓐ N albero *m*
Ⓑ VT blanquear con albero
pipefitter ['paɪp,fɪtəʳ] N fontanero/a *m/f*
pipeful ['paɪpfʊl] N pipa *f*; **a ~ of tobacco** una pipa de tabaco
pipeline ['paɪplaɪn] N (*for water*) tubería *f*, cañería *f*; (*for oil*) oleoducto *m*; (*for gas*) gasoducto *m*; ✦*IDIOM* **it's in the ~** está en proyecto, se está tramitando; **a sequel to the series is in the ~** ya hay planes para una segunda parte de la serie
piper ['paɪpəʳ] N (*on bagpipes*) gaitero/a *m/f*; ✦*PROV* **he who pays the ~ calls the tune** quien paga, manda
pipette [pɪ'pet] N pipeta *f*
pipework ['paɪpwɜːk] N tuberías *fpl*, cañerías *fpl*
piping ['paɪpɪŋ] Ⓐ N 1 (*in house, building*) tubería *f*, cañería *f*; **two metres of copper ~** dos metros de tubería de cobre
2 (*Mus*) música *f* de gaita/de flauta, sonido *m* del caramillo; [*of bird*] trinar *m*, trinos *mpl*
3 (*Sew*) ribete *m*, cordoncillo *m*
Ⓑ ADJ [*voice*] agudo
Ⓒ ADV **~ hot** bien caliente
pipistrelle [,pɪpɪ'strel] N pipistrelo *m*
pipit ['pɪpɪt] N bisbita *f*, pitpit *m*
pipkin ['pɪpkɪn] N ollita *f* de barro
pippin ['pɪpɪn] N camuesa *f*, manzana *f* reineta
pipsqueak ['pɪpskwiːk] N fantoche *m*, pintamonas* *mf inv*
piquancy ['piːkənsɪ] N lo fuerte, gusto *m* fuerte; [*of situation*] chispa *f*, gracia *f*
piquant ['piːkənt] ADJ [*taste*] fuerte; [*humour*] corrosivo, ácido; [*situation*] con chispa, con gracia
piquantly ['piːkəntlɪ] ADV (*of taste*) con fuerza; (= *interestingly, provocatively*) con chispa
pique [piːk] Ⓐ N resentimiento *m*; **to be in a ~** estar resentido; **to do sth in a fit of ~** hacer algo por resentimiento *or* por despecho
Ⓑ VT 1 (= *offend*) **I was ~d at his refusal to acknowledge me** me ofendió que se negara a saludarme
2 (= *arouse*) [+ *interest, appetite*] despertar; [+ *curiosity*] picar
piquet [pɪ'ket] N piquet *m*
piracy ['paɪərəsɪ] N (*lit*) piratería *f*; [*of book*] publicación *f* pirata; [*of tape, video, software*] reproducción *f* pirata
piranha [pɪ'rɑːnə] N piraña *f*
pirate ['paɪərɪt] Ⓐ N pirata *mf* (*also in publishing*)
Ⓑ VT [+ *book, tape, video, software*] piratear
Ⓒ CPD pirata *inv* ► **pirate broadcasting, pirate radio** N emisión *f* pirata ► **pirate radio station** N emisora *f* pirata
pirated ['paɪərɪtɪd] ADJ [*book, tape, video, software*] pirata *inv*, pirateado
piratical [paɪ'rætɪkəl] ADJ pirático
pirouette [,pɪrʊ'et] Ⓐ N pirueta *f*
Ⓑ VI piruetear
Piscean ['paɪsɪən] N **to be a ~** ser Piscis
Pisces ['paɪsiːz] N 1 (= *sign, constellation*) Piscis *m*
2 (= *person*) piscis *mf*; **he's (a) ~** es piscis
piss** [pɪs] Ⓐ N (= *urine*) meados** *mpl*; (= *act*) meada** *f*; **to have** *or* **take a ~** mear**, echar una meada**; **to take the ~ out of sb** (*Brit*) tomar el pelo a algn, cachondearse de algn (*Sp**); **it's ~ easy** *or* **a piece of ~** (*Brit*) está tirado*, está chupado (*Sp**)
Ⓑ VI mear**; **it's ~ing with rain** *or* **~ing down** (*Brit*) están cayendo chuzos de punta*
Ⓒ VT **to ~ o.s.** mearse (encima)**; **to ~ o.s. (laughing** *or* **with laughter)** (*Brit*) mearse de (la) risa**
Ⓓ CPD ► **piss artist**** N (*Brit*) borracho/a *m/f*, curda‡ *mf*
►**piss about**, piss around**** Ⓐ VI + ADV 1 (*Brit*) (= *play the fool*) hacer el tonto, hacer el indio (*Sp**)
2 (= *waste time*) perder el tiempo
Ⓑ VT + ADV [+ *treat flippantly*] jugar con; **all they do is ~ me about, I want the truth** no hacen más que jugar conmigo, quiero que me digan la verdad
►**piss off**** Ⓐ VT + ADV reventar*, cabrear‡, joder**; **it really ~es me off when he does that** me revienta cuando hace eso*, me cabrea cuando hace eso‡, me jode cuando hace eso**; **he's feeling ~ed off** (= *depressed*) está fastidiado*, está jodido**; (= *fed up*) está hasta las narices*, está hasta los cojones**; **to be ~ed off (with sth/sb)** estar hasta las narices (de algo/algn)*, estar hasta los cojones (de algo/algn)**, estar cabreado (por algo/con algn)‡
Ⓑ VI + ADV (= *go away*) largarse*; **~ off!** ¡vete a la mierda!**, ¡vete al cuerno!*
pissed‡ [pɪst] ADJ 1 **to be ~** (*Brit*) (= *drunk*) estar mamado‡; **to be as ~ as a newt** *or* **a fart** ◊ **be ~ out of one's mind** tener un buen pedo‡, estar (borracho) como una cuba*
2 (*US*) **to be ~ (at sth/sb)** (= *angry*) estar cabreado (por algo/con algn)‡, estar de mala leche (por algo/con algn)**
piss-take‡ ['pɪsteɪk] N broma *f*, tomadura *f* de pelo*
piss-up** ['pɪsʌp] N (*Brit*) juerga *f* de borrachera; ✦*IDIOM* **he couldn't organize a ~ in a brewery** no tiene ni pajolera idea de cómo organizar algo*
pistachio [pɪs'tɑːʃɪəʊ] N (*pl* **pistachios**) pistacho *m*; (= *tree*) pistachero *m*; (= *colour*) color *m* de pistacho
piste [piːst] N (*Ski*) pista *f*
pistil ['pɪstɪl] N pistilo *m*
pistol ['pɪstl] Ⓐ N pistola *f*, revólver *m*; **at ~ point** a punta de pistola
Ⓑ CPD ► **pistol shot** N pistoletazo *m*; **to be within ~ shot** estar a tiro de pistola
pistol-whip ['pɪstlwɪp] VT golpear con una pistola
piston ['pɪstən] Ⓐ N pistón *m*, émbolo *m*; (*Mus*) pistón *m*, llave *f*
Ⓑ CPD ► **piston engine** N motor *m* a pistón ► **piston ring** N aro *m* *or* segmento *m* de pistón ► **piston rod** N biela *f* ► **piston stroke** N carrera *f* del émbolo
piston-engined ['pɪstən,endʒɪnd] ADJ con motor de pistón
pit[1] [pɪt] Ⓐ N 1 (= *hole in ground*) hoyo *m*, foso *m*; (*as grave*) fosa *f*; (*as trap*) trampa *f*; (*fig*) abismo *m*; **he felt himself in a ~ of despair** se hallaba sumido en un abismo de desesperación; **the ~** (= *hell*) el infierno; **the ~ of hell** lo más profundo del infierno; **the ~ of one's stomach** la boca del estómago; *see also* **bear**[1], **clay**, **gravel**, **snake**
2 (*Min*) mina *f* (de carbón); (= *quarry*) cantera *f*; **to go down the ~(s)** (*lit*) bajar a la mina; (= *start work there*) ir a trabajar a la mina
3 (*Aut*) (*also* **inspection ~**) foso *m* de reparación
4 **the ~s** 4·1 (*Motor racing*) los boxes
4·2 (*US**) **to be in the ~s** [*person, economy*] estar por los suelos*
4·3 (*Brit*) (= *awful*) **this town really is the ~s** este pueblo es para echarse a llorar; **he's the ~s** es insoportable
5 (*Brit Theat*) **the ~** el patio de butacas, la platea; *see also* **orchestra B**
6 (*for cockfighting*) cancha *f*, reñidero *m*
7 (*US St Ex*) parquet *m* de la Bolsa; **the cotton ~** la bolsa del algodón
8 (= *small depression*) [*in metal, glass*] muesca *f*, marca *f*; (*on face*) marca *f*, picadura *f*
9 (*Brit**) (= *bed*) catre* *m*, piltra *f* (*Sp**)
Ⓑ VT 1 (= *mark*) [+ *surface*] picar, marcar; **a car ~ted with rust** un coche con marcas de óxido; **his face was ~ted with pockmarks** tenía la cara picada de viruelas; **the tarmac was ~ted with craters** la calzada estaba llena de hoyos
2 (*fig*) **her argument is ~ted with flaws** su argumento está plagado de defectos
Ⓒ CPD ► **pit bull (terrier)** N pit bull terrier *m*, bull terrier *m* de pelea ► **pit closure** N cierre *m* de pozos (mineros) ► **pit lane** N (*Motor racing*) recta *f* de boxes ► **pit pony** N *poney usado antiguamente en las minas* ► **pit stop** N (*Motor racing*) entrada *f* en boxes; (*) (*on journey*) parada *f* en ruta; **to make a ~**

stop (*Motor racing*) entrar en boxes; (*) (*on journey*) hacer una parada ► **pit worker** N minero/a *m/f*

►**pit against** VT + PREP enfrentar con; **the war ~ted American against American** la guerra enfrentó a americanos con americanos; **salesmen are ~ted against each other** a los vendedores se los enfrenta; **he was ~ting himself against the authorities** se estaba enfrentando a las autoridades; **to ~ one's strength against sb** medir sus fuerzas con algn; **to ~ one's wits against sb** poner a prueba su inteligencia frente a algn; **here is your chance to ~ your wits against the experts** es tu oportunidad de poner a prueba tu inteligencia frente a los expertos

pit² [pɪt] (*US*) Ⓐ N (*US*) (*in fruit*) pepita *f*, hueso *m*, pepa *f* (*esp LAm*)
Ⓑ VT deshuesar, quitar el hueso a

pitapat [ˈpɪtəˈpæt] ADV **to go ~** [*feet, rain*] golpetear; **my heart went ~** el corazón me latía con fuerza

pitch¹ [pɪtʃ] Ⓐ N [1] (*esp Brit Ftbl, Cricket, Hockey*) (= *area of play*) campo *m*, cancha *f* (*LAm*)
[2] (*Baseball*) (= *throw*) lanzamiento *m*, tiro *m*
[3] [*of note, voice, instrument*] tono *m*; *see also* **concert C**, **perfect D**, **queer C**
[4] (*esp Brit*) [*of market trader*] puesto *m*; [*of homeless person*] sitio *m*
[5] (= *height, degree*) extremo *m*, punto *m*; **matters reached such a ~ that ...** las cosas llegaron a tal extremo *or* a tal punto que ...; **excitement is at a high ~** la emoción está al rojo vivo; *see also* **fever B**
[6] (*) (= *sales talk*) rollo* *m*; **she stood up and made her ~** se levantó y soltó su rollo; **he made a ~ for the women's vote** procuró hacerse con *or* acaparar los votos de las mujeres; *see also* **sale B**
[7] (= *slope*) (*gen*) grado *m* de inclinación; [*of roof*] pendiente *f*
[8] (*Naut*) cabezada *f*
Ⓑ VT [1] (= *throw*) [+ *ball*] lanzar; [+ *person*] arrojar; **he was ~ed off his horse** salió disparado del caballo; **the impact ~ed her over the handlebars** el impacto la arrojó por encima del manillar
[2] (*Mus*) [+ *note*] dar; [+ *instrument*] graduar el tono de
[3] (= *present*) **it must be ~ed at the right level for the audience** el tono ha de ajustarse al público; **today he ~ed the plan to business leaders** hoy presentó el plan ante los dirigentes de negocios; **to ~ one's aspirations too high** picar demasiado *or* muy alto; **you're ~ing it a bit high!** *or* **strong!** ¡estás recargando las tintas!
[4] (= *set up*) [+ *tent*] armar, montar; **to ~ camp** acampar, montar el campamento
Ⓒ VI [1] (= *fall*) [*person*] caer, caerse; **he ~ed head-first over the wall** se cayó *or* cayó de cabeza por el muro; **the ball ~ed in front of him** la pelota cayó delante de él *or* vino a parar a sus pies; **the aircraft ~ed into the sea** el avión se precipitó en el mar; **to ~ forward**: **the passengers ~ed forward as the coach stopped** los pasajeros salieron despedidos hacia adelante cuando se paró el autocar; **he went down on his knees, then ~ed forward** se cayó *or* cayó de rodillas y luego de bruces
[2] (*Naut, Aer*) cabecear; **the ship was ~ing and rolling** *or* **tossing** el barco cabeceaba de un lado para otro
[3] (*Baseball*) lanzar; ✦*IDIOM* **to be in there ~ing** (*esp US**) seguir en la brecha*, seguir al pie del cañón*
Ⓓ CPD ► **pitch pipe** N (*Mus*) diapasón *m* ► **pitch shot** N (*Golf*) pitch *m*

►**pitch in*** VI + ADV [1] (= *start to eat*) empezar a comer; **~ in!** ¡venga, a comer!
[2] (= *start work*) **we all ~ed in together** todos nos pusimos manos a la obra, todos nos pusimos a trabajar juntos
[3] (= *cooperate*) echar una mano, arrimar el hombro; **we all ~ed in to help** todos echamos una mano, todos arrimamos el hombro; **the company has ~ed in with a pledge of £50,000** la compañía ha contribuido con un donativo de 50,000 libras

►**pitch into** Ⓐ VI + PREP [1] (= *start*) [+ *food*] atacar; **they ~ed into the work with enthusiasm** se pusieron a trabajar con entusiasmo
[2] (= *attack*) (*physically*) atacar, arremeter contra; (*verbally*) criticar, arremeter contra
Ⓑ VT + PREP **to ~ sb into sth** lanzar a algn a algo; **this ~ed him into the political arena** esto lo lanzó al mundillo de la política

►**pitch up** VI + ADV aparecer

pitch² [pɪtʃ] Ⓐ N (= *tar*) brea *f*, pez *f*; **it was ~ black outside** afuera estaba oscuro como boca de lobo; **his face was ~ black with coal dust** tenía la cara toda tiznada de polvo de carbón
Ⓑ CPD ► **pitch pine** N (= *wood*) pino *m* de tea

pitch-and-putt [ˌpɪtʃənˈpʌt] N minigolf *m*

pitch-and-toss [ˈpɪtʃənˈtɒs] N (juego *m* de) cara *f* o cruz, chapas *fpl*

pitch-black [ˈpɪtʃˈblæk] ADJ [*night*] oscuro como boca de lobo; [*water, sea*] muy oscuro

pitchblende [ˈpɪtʃblend] N pec(h)blenda *f*

pitch-dark [ˈpɪtʃˈdɑːk] ADJ oscuro como boca de lobo

pitched [pɪtʃt] ADJ **~ battle** (*Mil, fig*) batalla *f* campal; **a ~ roof** un tejado a dos aguas

pitcher¹ [ˈpɪtʃəʳ] N (*esp US*) (= *jar*) cántaro *m*, jarro *m*

pitcher² [ˈpɪtʃəʳ] N (*Baseball*) pítcher *mf*, lanzador(a) *m/f*; → BASEBALL

pitchfork [ˈpɪtʃfɔːk] Ⓐ N horca *f*
Ⓑ VT (*fig*) (= *thrust unwillingly or unexpectedly*) **he was ~ed into the job** le encasquetaron el trabajo, lo metieron en el trabajo a la fuerza; **she was ~ed onto the front pages from total obscurity** saltó del más absoluto anonimato a las primeras planas de los periódicos

piteous [ˈpɪtɪəs] ADJ [*cry*] lastimero; [*expression, story*] lastimoso; **it was a ~ sight** daba lástima verlo

piteously [ˈpɪtɪəslɪ] ADV lastimeramente

pitfall [ˈpɪtfɔːl] N (*fig*) (= *danger*) peligro *m*; (= *problem*) dificultad *f*, escollo *m*; **there are many ~s ahead** hay muchos peligros por delante; **it's a ~ for the unwary** es una trampa para los imprudentes; **how to avoid the ~s involved in buying a house** cómo evitar las dificultades *or* los escollos que conlleva la compra de una casa; **"Pitfalls of English"** "Escollos *mpl* del Inglés"

pith [pɪθ] N (*Bot*) *parte interna blanquecina (endocarpo) de la cáscara de los cítricos*, blanco *m* de la cáscara; (*fig*) (= *core*) meollo *m*

pithead [ˈpɪthed] N bocamina *f*

pithiness [ˈpɪθɪnɪs] N (= *terseness*) lo sucinto, concisión *f*

pithy [ˈpɪθɪ] ADJ (*compar* **pithier**, *superl* **pithiest**) (*Bot*) con mucho blanco en la cáscara; (*fig*) (= *terse*) [*statement, comment, style*] sucinto, conciso

pitiable [ˈpɪtɪəbl] ADJ [*condition*] lastimoso; [*attempt*] penoso; **age had reduced him to a ~ figure** la edad lo había reducido a una figura digna de compasión

pitiably [ˈpɪtɪəblɪ] ADV [*low, small, weak*] lamentablemente

pitiful [ˈpɪtɪfʊl] ADJ [1] (= *moving to pity*) [*sight*] lastimoso, penoso; [*cry*] lastimero
[2] (= *contemptible*) [*efforts*] lamentable; [*sum, amount*] irrisorio
[3] (= *dreadful*) pésimo, lamentable; **it was a ~ performance** fue una actuación pésima *or* lamentable

pitifully [ˈpɪtɪfəlɪ] ADV [1] (= *pathetically*) lastimosamente; **she was ~ thin** estaba tan delgada que daba lástima; **she was crying most ~** lloraba que daba lástima
[2] (= *contemptibly*) lamentablemente; **~ inadequate supplies** equipamiento *m* de una pobreza lamentable

pitiless [ˈpɪtɪlɪs] ADJ [*enemy*] despiadado; [*sun, storm*] implacable

pitilessly [ˈpɪtɪlɪslɪ] ADV despiadadamente; [*shine*] [*sun, light*] implacablemente

pitman [ˈpɪtmən] N (*pl* **pitmen**) (*Brit*) minero *m*

piton [ˈpiːtɒn] N pitón *m*, clavija *f* de escala

pit-prop [ˈpɪtprɒp] N puntal *m*, peón *m*

pitta [ˈpɪtə] ADJ (*also* **~ bread**) pan *m* árabe

pittance [ˈpɪtəns] N miseria *f*; **she gets paid a ~** le pagan una miseria

pitted [ˈpɪtɪd] ADJ [1] [*skin*] picado (de viruelas); [*surface*] picado
[2] (*US*) [*fruit*] deshuesado, sin hueso

pitter-patter [ˈpɪtəˈpætəʳ] = **patter²**

pituitary [pɪˈtjuːɪtərɪ] Ⓐ ADJ pituitario
Ⓑ N glándula *f* pituitaria
Ⓒ CPD ► **pituitary gland** N glándula *f* pituitaria

pity [ˈpɪtɪ] Ⓐ N [1] piedad *f*, compasión *f*; **to feel (no) ~ for sb** (no) sentir compasión por algn; **have ~ on us** ten piedad de nosotros; **to move sb to ~** mover a algn a compasión, dar lástima a algn; **I did it out of ~ for him** se lo hice por compasión; **for ~'s sake!** ¡por piedad!; (*less seriously*) ¡por el amor de Dios!; **to take ~ on sb** compadecerse *or* apiadarse de algn
[2] (= *cause of regret*) lástima *f*, pena *f*; **what a ~!** ¡qué lástima!, ¡qué pena!; **what a ~ he didn't see it** ¡qué pena que no lo viera!; **more's the ~** desgraciadamente, pero ¿qué le vamos a hacer?; **it is a ~ that ...** es una lástima que + *subjun*, es una pena que + *subjun*; **it is a ~ that you can't come** es una lástima *or* una pena que no puedas venir; **the ~ of it was that ...** lo lamentable fue que ..., lo peor del caso fue que ...; **it is a thousand pities that ...** es muy de lamentar que + *subjun*
Ⓑ VT compadecer(se de), tener lástima a; **I think he is more to be pitied than feared** yo creo que da más lástima que miedo; **I don't want you to ~ me** no quiero que me tengas lástima; **I ~ you when she finds out!** ¡pobre de ti cuando se entere!

pitying [ˈpɪtɪɪŋ] ADJ (= *compassionate*) [*look, smile*] lleno de compasión, compasivo; (= *contemptuous*) [*look, smile*] de desprecio

pityingly [ˈpɪtɪɪŋlɪ] ADV (= *compassionately*) compasivamente, con lástima; (= *contemptuously*) con desprecio

Pius [ˈpaɪəs] N Pío

pivot [ˈpɪvət] Ⓐ N (*Mil, Tech*) pivote *m*; (*fig*) eje *m* (central); **she is the ~ around which the community revolves** ella es el eje sobre el que gira toda la comunidad
Ⓑ VT (= *mount on pivot*) montar sobre un pivote; (= *cause to turn*) hacer girar; **he ~ed it**

on his hand lo hizo girar sobre la mano
Ⓒ VI girar (**on** sobre); **she ~ed in front of the mirror** se dio una vuelta frente al espejo; **to ~ on sth** (*fig*) girar alrededor de algo, depender de algo

pivotal ['pɪvətl] ADJ (*fig*) central, fundamental

pix* [pɪks] = **pics**

pixel ['pɪksel] N (*Comput*) píxel *m*, punto *m*

pixie ['pɪksɪ] Ⓐ N duendecillo *m*
Ⓑ CPD ► **pixie hat**, **pixie hood** N caperucita *f*

pizza ['piːtsə] N pizza *f*

piz(z)azz* [pə'zæz] N energía *f*, dinamismo *m*

pizzeria [,piːtsə'rɪə] N pizzería *f*

pizzicato [,pɪtsɪ'kɑːtəʊ] ADJ, ADV pizzicato

pkt ABBR (= **packet**) paquete *m*

Pl. ABBR (= **Place**) Plaza *f*

PL a/c ABBR = **profit and loss account**

placard ['plækɑːd] Ⓐ N (*on wall*) cartel *m*; (= *sign, announcement*) letrero *m*; (*carried in demonstration*) pancarta *f*
Ⓑ VT **the wall is ~ed all over** la pared está llena de carteles; **the flats are ~ed as luxury residences** los pisos *or* (*LAm*) los departamentos aparecen anunciados como viviendas de lujo

placate [plə'keɪt] VT aplacar, apaciguar

placatory [plə'keɪtərɪ] ADJ [*act, gesture, smile*] apaciguador

place [pleɪs] Ⓐ N [1] (*gen*) lugar *m*, sitio *m*; **this is the ~** éste es el lugar, aquí es; **we came to a ~ where ...** llegamos a un lugar donde ...; **the furniture was all over the ~** los muebles estaban todos manga por hombro; **we're all over the ~** tenemos un lío que no nos aclaramos; **in another** *or* **some other ~** en otra parte; **any ~ will do** cualquier lugar vale *or* sirve; **it all began to fall into ~** todo empezó a tener sentido; **when the new law/system is in ~** cuando la nueva ley/el nuevo sistema entre en vigor; **a blue suit, worn in ~s** un traje azul, raído a retazos; **the snow was a metre deep in ~s** había tramos *or* trozos en que la nieve cubría un metro; **this is no ~ for you** éste no es sitio para ti; **there was no ~ to hide** no había dónde esconderse; **to run in ~** (*US*) correr en parada; **it must be some ~ else** (*US*) estará en otra parte; **a ~ in the sun** (*fig*) una posición envidiable
[2] (*specific*) lugar *m*; **~ of amusement** lugar *m* de diversión; **~ of birth** lugar *m* de nacimiento; **~ of business** [*of employment*] lugar *m* de trabajo; (= *office*) oficina *f*, despacho *m*; (= *shop*) comercio *m*; **~ of refuge** refugio *m*, asilo *m*; **~ of residence** domicilio *m*, residencia *f*; **~ of worship** templo *m*, lugar *m* de culto
[3] (= *town, area*) lugar *m*, sitio *m*; **it's a small ~** es un pueblo pequeño; **to go ~s** (*US*) (= *travel*) viajar, conocer mundo; **he's going ~s*** (*fig*) llegará lejos; **we like to go ~s at weekends** durante los fines de semana nos gusta salir de excursión; **from ~ to ~** de un sitio a otro; **he drifted from ~ to ~, from job to job** iba de un sitio a otro, de trabajo en trabajo
[4] (= *house*) casa *f*; (= *building*) sitio *m*; **his ~ in the country** su casa de campo; **they have a new ~ now** tienen una nueva casa ya; **we were at Peter's ~** estuvimos en casa de Pedro, estuvimos donde Pedro*; **come to our ~** ven (a visitarnos) a casa; **my ~ or yours?** ¿en mi casa o en la tuya?; **I helped him out when he had no ~ to go** yo le eché una mano cuando no tenía donde ir; **there's a new pizza ~ in town** han abierto un sitio de pizzas en el centro; **I must be mad, working in this ~** debo de estar loca para trabajar en este sitio *or* lugar
[5] (*in street names*) plaza *f*
[6] (= *proper or natural place*) sitio *m*, lugar *m*; **does this have a ~?** ¿tiene esto un sitio determinado?; **this isn't the ~ to discuss politics** no es el lugar más indicado para hablar de política; **his troops were in ~** sus tropas estaban en su sitio; **he checked that his tie was in ~** comprobó que llevaba bien puesta *or* colocada la corbata; **the final arrangements are now in ~** ya se han ultimado los preparativos que faltaban; **everything in its ~** cada cosa en su lugar; **to hold sth in ~** sujetar algo en su lugar; **to put sth back in its ~** devolver algo a su sitio; **to be out of ~** estar fuera de lugar; **it looks out of ~ here** aquí parece que está fuera de (su) lugar; **that remark was quite out of ~** aquella observación estaba fuera de lugar; **I feel rather out of ~ here** me siento como que estoy de más aquí, aquí me siento un poco fuera de lugar; **to laugh in** *or* **at the right ~** reírse en el momento oportuno
[7] (*in book*) página *f*; **to find/lose one's ~** encontrar/perder la página; **to mark one's ~** poner una marca (de por dónde se va) en un libro
[8] (= *seat*) asiento *m*; (*in cinema, theatre*) localidad *f*; (*at table*) cubierto *m*; (*in queue*) turno *m*; (*in school, university, on trip*) plaza *f*; (*in team*) puesto *m*; **are there any ~s left?** ¿quedan plazas?; **is this ~ taken?** ¿está ocupado este asiento?; **he managed to keep his ~ in the team** logró conservar su puesto en el equipo; **a university ~** una plaza en la universidad; **to change ~s with sb** cambiar de sitio con algn; **to give ~ to** dar paso a; **to lay an extra ~ for sb** poner otro cubierto para algn; **to lose one's ~** (*in queue*) perder su turno
[9] (= *job, vacancy*) puesto *m*; **his uncle found him a ~ in the firm** su tío le buscó un puesto en la compañía; **~s for 500 workers** 500 puestos de trabajo; **to seek a ~ in publishing** buscarse una colocación *or* un puesto en una casa editorial
[10] (= *position*) lugar *m*; **it is not my ~ to do it** no me toca a mí hacerlo; **put yourself in my ~** ponte en mi lugar; **if I were in your ~** yo en tu lugar, yo que tú; **your ~ is to obey orders** lo tuyo es obedecer órdenes; **I wouldn't mind changing ~s with her!** ¡no me importaría estar en su lugar!; **friends in high ~s** amigos *mpl* bien situados; **to know one's ~** saber cuál es su lugar; **racism has no ~ here** aquí no hay sitio para el racismo; **she occupies a special ~ in the heart of the British people** ocupa un rincón especial en el corazón del pueblo británico; **to take the ~ of sth/sb** sustituir *or* suplir algo/a algn; **nobody could ever take his ~** nadie sería capaz de sustituirlo; **I was unable to go so Sheila took my ~** yo no pude ir, así que Sheila lo hizo por mí
[11] (*in series, rank*) posición *f*, lugar *m*; **to work sth out to three ~s of decimals** calcular algo hasta las milésimas *or* hasta con tres decimales; **Madrid won, with Bilbao in second ~** ganó Madrid, con Bilbao en segunda posición *or* segundo lugar; **she took second ~ in the race/Latin exam** quedó la segunda en la carrera/el examen de Latín; **he didn't like having to take second ~ to his wife in public** delante de la gente no le gustaba quedar en un segundo plano detrás de su mujer; **for her, money takes second ~ to job satisfaction** para ella un trabajo gratificante va antes que el dinero; ✦**IDIOM to put sb in his ~** poner a algn en su lugar, bajar los humos a algn*
[12] (*other phrases*) **in the first/second ~** en primer/segundo lugar; **in ~ of** en lugar de, en vez de; **to take ~** tener lugar; **the marriage will not now take ~** ahora la boda no se celebrará, ahora no habrá boda; **there are great changes taking ~** están ocurriendo *or* se están produciendo grandes cambios
Ⓑ VT [1] (= *put*) (*gen*) poner; (*more precisely*) colocar; **she ~d the dish on the table** puso el plato en la mesa; **~ the mask over your nose and mouth** colóquese la mascarilla sobre la nariz y la boca; **to ~ a matter in sb's hands** dejar un asunto en manos de algn; **the drought is placing heavy demands on the water supply** la sequía está poniendo en serios apuros al suministro de agua; **his job ~s heavy demands on him** su trabajo le exige mucho; **unemployment ~s a great strain on families** el desempleo somete a las familias a una fuerte presión
[2] (= *give, attribute*) [+ *blame*] echar (**on** a); [+ *responsibility*] achacar (**on** a); [+ *importance*] dar, otorgar (*more frm*) (**on** a); **I had no qualms about placing my confidence in him** no tenía ningún reparo en depositar mi confianza en él; **they ~ too much emphasis on paper qualifications** le dan demasiada importancia a los títulos; **we should ~ no trust in that** no hay que fiarse de eso
[3] (= *situate*) situar, ubicar; **the house is well ~d** la casa está bien situada; **we are better ~d than a month ago** estamos en mejor situación que hace un mes; **he is well ~d to see it all** está en una buena posición para observarlo todo; **we are well ~d to attack** estamos en una buena posición para atacar; **how are you ~d for money?** ¿qué tal andas de dinero?
[4] (*Comm*) [+ *order*] hacer; [+ *goods*] colocar; (*Fin*) [+ *money, funds*] colocar, invertir; **goods that are difficult to ~** mercancías *fpl* que no encuentran salida; **to ~ an advert in a paper** poner un anuncio en un periódico; **to ~ a contract for machinery with a French firm** firmar un contrato con una compañía francesa para adquirir unas máquinas; **to ~ an order (for sth) (with sb)** hacer un pedido (de algo) (a algn); *see also* **bet C1**
[5] (= *find employment for*) [*agency*] encontrar un puesto a, colocar; [*employer*] ofrecer empleo a, colocar; (= *find home for*) colocar; **the child was ~d with a loving family** el niño fue (enviado) a vivir con una familia muy cariñosa
[6] (*of series, rank*) colocar, clasificar; **to be ~d** (*in horse race*) llegar colocado; **they are currently ~d second in the league** actualmente ocupan el segundo lugar de la clasificación; **Vigo is well ~d in the League** Vigo tiene un buen puesto en la Liga; **she was ~d in the top group for maths** en matemáticas la colocaron en el grupo de los mejores
[7] (= *recall, identify*) recordar; (= *recognize*) reconocer; (= *identify*) identificar, ubicar (*LAm*); **I can't ~ her** no recuerdo de dónde la conozco, no la ubico (*LAm*)
Ⓒ VI (*US*) (*in race, competition*) **to ~ second** quedar segundo, quedar en segundo lugar
Ⓓ CPD ► **place card** N *tarjeta que indica el lugar de alguien en la mesa* ► **place kick** N (*Rugby*) puntapié *m* colocado; (*Ftbl*) tiro *m* libre ► **place mat** N bajoplato *m*, salvamanteles *m inv* individual ► **place name** N topónimo *m*; **place names** (*as study, in general*) toponimia *f*; **the ~ names of Aragon** la toponimia aragonesa ► **place setting** N cubierto *m*

placebo [plə'siːbəʊ] Ⓐ N (*pl* **placebos** *or* **placeboes**) placebo *m*
Ⓑ CPD ► **placebo effect** N efecto *m* placebo

placeman ['pleɪsmæn] N (*pl* **placemen**) (*Brit pej*) adlátere *mf*, hombre *m* de confianza

placement ['pleɪsmənt] N (= *positioning*) colocación *f* (*Comm*), emplazamiento *m*; **students come to our company on work ~s** en la empresa tenemos estudiantes en prácticas

placenta [plə'sentə] N (*pl* **placentas** *or* **placentae** [plə'sentiː]) placenta *f*

placid ['plæsɪd] ADJ [*person*] apacible, plácido; [*face*] tranquilo, sosegado; [*water*] apacible, tranquilo

placidity [plə'sɪdɪtɪ] N placidez *f*, apacibilidad *f*, tranquilidad *f*

placidly ['plæsɪdlɪ] ADV [*sit*] plácidamente, apaciblemente; [*say, reply*] tranquilamente, sosegadamente

placing ['pleɪsɪŋ] N (= *act*) colocación *f*; (= *placing in league, rank*) puesto *m*, clasificación *f*

plagal ['pleɪgəl] ADJ plagal

plagiarism ['pleɪdʒɪərɪzəm] N plagio *m*

plagiarist ['pleɪdʒɪərɪst] N plagiario/a *m/f*

plagiarize ['pleɪdʒɪəraɪz] VT plagiar

plague [pleɪg] Ⓐ N (= *disease*) peste *f*; (*fig*) plaga *f*, fastidio *m*; **a ~ of rats** una plaga de ratas; **the ~** la peste; **to avoid sth/sb like the ~** huir de algo/algn como de la peste, evitar algo a toda costa
Ⓑ VT (*lit*) infestar; (*fig*) plagar; [+ *person*] atormentar; **the area is ~d with malaria** la zona está infestada de malaria; **the thought has been plaguing me** la idea me viene atormentando; **the project has been ~d with problems from the beginning** el proyecto se ha visto plagado de problemas desde el comienzo; **a country ~d by recession** un país asolado por la recesión; **to ~ sb with questions** acosar a algn con preguntas

plague-ridden ['pleɪg,rɪdn], **plague-stricken** ['pleɪg,strɪkən] ADJ apestado

plaguey* ['pleɪgɪ] ADJ latoso*, engorroso

plaice [pleɪs] N (*pl* **plaice** *or* **plaices**) platija *f*

plaid [plæd] Ⓐ N (= *cloth*) tela *f* escocesa *or* a cuadros; (= *cloak*) manta *f* escocesa, plaid *m*
Ⓑ CPD [*skirt, trousers, shirt*] escocés

plain [pleɪn] Ⓐ ADJ (*compar* **plainer**; *superl* **plainest**) [1] (= *clear, obvious*) claro, evidente; **it is ~ that** es evidente *or* obvio que, está claro que; **to make sth ~ (to sb)** poner algo de manifiesto (a algn), dejar algo claro; **you have made your feelings ~** has puesto tus sentimientos de manifiesto, has dejado claros tus sentimientos; **her guilt was ~ to see** saltaba a la vista que era culpable; ✦*IDIOM* **it's as ~ as a pikestaff** *or* **as the nose on your face** *or* **as day*** está más claro que el agua
[2] (= *outspoken, honest*) franco; **I shall be ~ with you** le hablaré con toda franqueza, seré franco con usted; **let me be ~ with you** déjeme que le hable claramente *or* sin rodeos, permítame que le hable con franqueza (*frm*); **~ dealing** negocios *mpl* limpios
[3] (= *unadorned*) [*answer*] franco; [*living*] sencillo, sin lujo; [*food, cooking*] sencillo, corriente; [*language, style*] sencillo, llano; [*envelope*] en blanco; [*paper*] liso; [*fabric*] de un solo color, liso; **he drank ~ water** bebió agua nada más; **they're very ~ people** es gente muy sencilla *or* llana; **she used to be ~ Miss Jones** antes se llamaba la Srta. Jones sin más; **it's just ~ common sense** es de sentido común; **in ~ clothes** [*policeman*] (vestido) de civil *or* paisano; **in ~ English** *or* **language** (= *understandably*) en lenguaje claro *or* sencillo; (= *frankly*) (hablando) sin rodeos; **the ~ truth** la verdad lisa y llana; ✦*IDIOM* **it's ~ sailing from now on*** a partir de ahora es pan comido*
[4] (= *not pretty*) poco atractivo; **she's terribly ~** no es nada atractiva; ✦*IDIOM* **to be a ~ Jane** ser una chica poco atractiva, ser más bien fea
Ⓑ ADV [1] (*) (= *completely*) **he's ~ wrong** no tiene razón, y punto; **it's just ~ stupid** es una ridiculez absoluta *or* total
[2] (= *simply*) claramente, con toda claridad; **I can't put it ~er than that** más claramente no lo puedo decir, no lo puedo decir con más claridad; **he told me quite ~ that ...** me dijo claramente *or* con toda claridad que ...
Ⓒ N [1] (*Geog*) llanura *f*, llano *m*; **the Great Plains** (*US*) las Grandes Llanuras
[2] (*Knitting*) punto *m* sencillo
Ⓓ CPD ► **plain chocolate** N chocolate *m* amargo *or* sin leche ► **plain flour** N harina *f* sin levadura

plainchant ['pleɪntʃɑːnt] N = **plainsong**

plain-clothes ['pleɪn'kləʊðz] ADJ **~ policeman** policía *mf* de civil *or* de paisano

plainly ['pleɪnlɪ] ADV [1] (= *clearly*) **I was not welcome** estaba claro *or* era evidente *or* era obvio que no era bienvenido; **I can remember it all quite ~** lo recuerdo con todo detalle *or* perfectamente
[2] (= *frankly*) **to put it ~, he's not wanted** hablando claro *or* sin rodeos, él sobra; **to speak ~ to sb** hablar claro a algn, hablar a algn sin rodeos
[3] (= *simply*) con sencillez, sencillamente; **she dresses ~** viste con sencillez *or* sencillamente

plainness ['pleɪnnɪs] N [1] (= *clarity*) claridad *f*; (= *frankness*) franqueza *f*; (= *simplicity*) sencillez *f*
[2] (= *unattractiveness*) falta *f* de atractivo

plainsman ['pleɪnzmən] N (*pl* **plainsmen**) llanero *m*, hombre *m* de la llanura

plainsong ['pleɪnsɒŋ] N canto *m* llano

plain-spoken ['pleɪn'spəʊkən] ADJ franco, llano

plaintiff ['pleɪntɪf] N demandante *mf*, querellante *mf*

plaintive ['pleɪntɪv] ADJ lastimero, quejumbroso

plaintively ['pleɪntɪvlɪ] ADV lastimeramente, con dolor

plait [plæt] (*esp Brit*) Ⓐ N trenza *f*; **in ~s** trenzado, en trenzas; **she wears her hair in ~s** lleva trenzas
Ⓑ VT trenzar

plan [plæn] Ⓐ N [1] (= *scheme*) proyecto *m*, plan *m*; **~ of action** ◊ **action ~** plan *m* de acción; **~ of attack/campaign** (*Mil, fig*) plan *m* de ataque/de campaña; **to draw up a ~** elaborar un proyecto, hacer *or* redactar un plan; **an exercise ~** una tabla *or* un programa de ejercicios; **a five-year ~** un plan quinquenal; **to make ~s for the future** hacer planes *or* planear para el futuro; **a peace ~** un proyecto *or* un plan de paz; *see also* **business, instalment, master, pension**
[2] (= *idea, intention*) plan *m*; **do you have any ~s for the weekend?** ¿tienes planes para el fin de semana?; **the ~ is to come back later** pensamos volver más tarde; **there are ~s to modernize the building** tienen planeado modernizar el edificio; **if everything goes according to ~** si todo sale como está previsto *or* planeado; **the best ~ is to call first** lo mejor es llamar primero; **a change of ~** un cambio de planes; **to change one's ~s** cambiar de planes
[3] (= *diagram, map*) plano *m*; *see also* **seating**
[4] (= *outline*) [*of story, essay*] esquema *m*
[5] (*Archit, Tech*) (*often pl*) plano *m*
Ⓑ VT [1] (= *organize*) [+ *schedule, event, crime*] planear; [+ *party, surprise*] preparar; [+ *route*] planificar, planear; [+ *essay*] hacer un esquema de, planear; [+ *family*] planificar; **as ~ned** según lo previsto, como estaba planeado; **things didn't work out as ~ned** las cosas no salieron según lo previsto *or* como estaban planeadas
[2] (= *intend*) **I had been ~ning a trip to New York** había estado pensando en *or* planeando un viaje a Nueva York; **how long do you ~ to stay?** ¿cuánto tiempo piensas quedarte?; **what do you ~ to do after college?** ¿qué tienes pensado hacer después de la universidad?, ¿qué te has propuesto hacer después de la universidad?
[3] (= *design*) diseñar; **the art of ~ning a garden** el arte de diseñar un jardín
Ⓒ VI hacer planes; **to ~ ahead** planear con antelación; **to ~ for sth**: **it is advisable to ~ for retirement** es aconsejable que se hagan planes para la jubilación; **to ~ for the future** hacer planes *or* planear para el futuro; **I hadn't ~ned for so many people** no había contado con que viniese tanta gente

► **plan on** VI + PREP [1] (= *intend*) **to ~ on doing sth** tener pensado hacer algo; **I don't ~ on dying just yet** (*iro*) todavía no tengo pensado morirme; **we're ~ning on getting married in July** tenemos pensado casarnos en julio
[2] (= *expect*) contar con; **I hadn't ~ned on the bad weather** no había contado con el mal tiempo

► **plan out** VT + ADV planear detalladamente; **I haven't even ~ned out the route yet** todavía no he planeado la ruta detalladamente; **he's got it all ~ned out** lo tiene todo planeado *or* planificado

planchette [plɑːn'ʃet] N tabla *f* de escritura espiritista

plane [pleɪn] Ⓐ N [1] (= *aeroplane, airplane*) avión *m*; **to go by ~** ir en avión; **to send goods by ~** enviar mercancías por avión
[2] (*Art, Math, Constr*) plano *m*; **vertical/horizontal ~** plano *m* vertical/horizontal
[3] (*fig*) nivel *m*; **he seems to exist on another ~** parece vivir en otro nivel *or* en una esfera distinta; **on the ideological ~** en el plano ideológico; **she tried to lift the conversation onto a higher ~** trató de llevar la conversación a un nivel más elevado
[4] (= *tool*) (= *small*) cepillo *m* (de carpintero); (= *large*) garlopa *f*
[5] (*Bot*) (*also* **~ tree**) plátano *m*
Ⓑ ADJ (*Geom*) plano; **a ~ surface** una superficie plana
Ⓒ VT cepillar; **to ~ sth down** cepillar *or* desbastar algo
Ⓓ VI [*bird, glider*] planear; [*boat, car*] deslizarse
Ⓔ CPD ► **plane crash** N accidente *m* de avión ► **plane geometry** N geometría *f* plana ► **plane ticket** N billete *m* *or* pasaje *m* de avión

planet ['plænɪt] N planeta *m*; **the ~ Earth** el planeta Tierra

planetarium [,plænɪ'teərɪəm] N (*pl* **planetariums** *or* **planetaria** [,plænɪ'teərɪə]) planetario *m*

planetary ['plænɪtərɪ] ADJ planetario

plangent ['plændʒənt] ADJ plañidero

plank [plæŋk] Ⓐ N [1] [*of wood*] tabla *f*, tablón *m*; **deck ~s** tablazón *fsing* de la cubierta; **to walk the ~** pasear por la tabla (sobre los tibu-

➤ LANGUAGE IN USE: plan A1 8.1 B2 8.2

rones); ✦*IDIOM* **to be as thick as two short ~s*** ser más bruto que un arado*
[2] (*fig*) [*of policy*] punto *m*
Ⓑ VT [1] **to ~ sth down** tirar algo violentamente, arrojar algo violentamente; **to ~ o.s. down** sentarse *etc* de modo agresivo
[2] (*Naut*) [+ *hull, deck*] entablar, entarimar

planking ['plæŋkɪŋ] N tablas *fpl*, tablaje *m*; (*Naut*) tablazón *f* de la cubierta

plankton ['plæŋktən] N plankton *m*

planned [plænd] ADJ [*economy*] dirigido; [*development, redundancy*] programado; [*crime, murder*] premeditado; [*pregnancy*] deseado

planner ['plænəʳ] N planificador(a) *m/f*; *see also* **town**

planning ['plænɪŋ] Ⓐ N planificación *f*; **the trip needs careful ~** hay que planear bien el viaje; **we're still in the ~ stage(s)** *or* **at the ~ stage** estamos todavía en la etapa de la planificación; *see also* **family B**, **town B**
Ⓑ CPD [*committee, department, process*] de planificación ► **planning board** N (*US*) comisión *f* planificadora ► **planning officer** N funcionario/a *m/f* de urbanismo ► **planning permission** N permiso *m* de obra ► **planning regulations** N normas *fpl* urbanísticas

plant [plɑːnt] Ⓐ N [1] (*Bot*) planta *f*
[2] (*no pl*) (= *machinery*) maquinaria *f*; (*fixed*) instalaciones *fpl*; **heavy ~** maquinaria *f* pesada
[3] (= *factory*) fábrica *f*, planta *f*; (= *power station*) planta *f*, central *f*
[4] (*) (= *misleading evidence*) **it's a ~** esto es una trampa para incriminarnos
[5] (*) (= *infiltrator*) infiltrado/a *m/f*, espía *mf*
Ⓑ VT [1] (*Bot*) [+ *tree, flower, crop*] plantar; [+ *seed, garden, field*] sembrar; **to ~ sth with sth** sembrar algo de algo; **the field is ~ed with wheat** el campo está sembrado de trigo; **they plan to ~ the area with grass and trees** tienen pensado plantar la zona de árboles y poner césped
[2] (= *put*) **he stood with his feet ~ed apart** se quedó de pie con los pies separados; **he ~ed himself right in her path** se le plantó en el camino*, se plantó en mitad de su camino*; **to ~ an idea in sb's mind** meter a algn una idea en la cabeza; **to ~ a kiss on sb's cheek** plantar un beso en la mejilla a algn*; **she ~ed a punch right on his nose** le plantó un puñetazo en la nariz*
[3] (*furtively*) [+ *bomb, evidence*] colocar, poner; [+ *informer, spy*] poner, infiltrar; **to ~ sth on sb** colocar algo a algn para incriminarle
Ⓒ VI plantar
Ⓓ CPD ► **plant life** N vida *f* vegetal, las plantas ► **plant pot** N maceta *f*, tiesto *m*

►**plant out** VT + ADV [+ *seedlings*] trasplantar

plantain ['plæntɪn] N llantén *m*, plátano *m* (*LAm*)

plantation [plæn'teɪʃən] N [*of tea, sugar etc*] plantación *f*; (= *large estate*) hacienda *f*; [*of trees*] arboleda *f*; [*of young trees*] plantel *m*; (*Hist*) colonia *f*

planter ['plɑːntəʳ] N (= *person*) plantador(a) *m/f*; (= *plantation owner*) hacendado/a *m/f* (*esp LAm*); (*Hist*) (= *settler*) colono/a *m/f*; (= *machine*) plantadora *f*; (= *pot*) tiesto *m*, maceta *f*

planting ['plɑːntɪŋ] Ⓐ N **flooding has delayed ~** las inundaciones han retrasado la plantación
Ⓑ CPD ► **planting season** N estación *f* de plantar

plaque [plæk] N (= *plate*) placa *f*; (*on teeth*) sarro *m*, placa *f* (dental)

plash [plæʃ] (*liter*) = **splash**

plasm ['plæzəm] N = **plasma**

plasma ['plæzmə] Ⓐ N plasma *m*
Ⓑ ADJ [*screen, monitor, television*] de plasma

plaster ['plɑːstəʳ] Ⓐ N [1] (*Constr*) yeso *m*; (= *layer on wall*) enlucido *m*
[2] (*Med*) (*for broken limb*) escayola *f*, yeso *m* (*LAm*); **with his leg in ~** con la pierna escayolada *or* (*LAm*) enyesada
[3] (*Brit*) (= *sticking plaster*) esparadrapo *m*, tirita *f*, curita *f* (*LAm*)
[4] **~ of Paris** yeso *m* mate
Ⓑ VT [1] (*Constr*) enyesar; [+ *wall*] enyesar, enlucir; **to ~ over a hole** llenar *or* tapar un hoyo con yeso
[2] (= *cover*) cubrir, llenar; **to ~ a wall with posters** cubrir *or* llenar una pared de carteles; **the children came back ~ed with mud** los niños volvieron cubiertos de lodo
[3] (= *stick*) pegar; **to ~ posters on a wall** pegar carteles en una pared; **the story was ~ed all over the front page** el reportaje llenaba toda la primera plana
[4] (*) dar una paliza a*
Ⓒ CPD [*model, statue*] de yeso ► **plaster cast** N (*Med*) escayola *f*, enyesado *m* (*LAm*); (= *model, statue*) vaciado *m* de yeso

plasterboard ['plɑːstəbɔːd] N cartón *m* de yeso, pladur® *m* (*Sp*)

plastered* ['plɑːstəd] ADJ (= *drunk*) **to be ~** estar como una cuba*, estar tomado (*LAm**); **to get ~** ponerse como una cuba*

plasterer ['plɑːstərəʳ] N yesero/a *m/f*, enlucidor(a) *m/f*

plastering ['plɑːstərɪŋ] N enlucido *m*

plastic ['plæstɪk] Ⓐ N [1] plástico *m*; **to be made of ~** ser de plástico
[2] **plastics** (materiales *mpl*) plásticos *mpl*
[3] (= *credit cards*) plástico *m*
Ⓑ ADJ [1] [*container etc*] de plástico
[2] (= *flexible*) plástico
[3] (*pej*, *) (= *artificial*) [*smile*] falso, de plástico; [*person*] de plástico, superficial
Ⓒ CPD ► **the plastic arts** NPL las artes plásticas ► **plastic bag** N bolsa *f* de plástico ► **plastic bullet** N bala *f* de goma ► **plastic explosive** N goma *f* dos ► **plastic mac** N (*Brit*) impermeable *m* ► **plastic money** N dinero *m* de plástico ► **plastic sheeting** N plástico *m* en planchas ► **plastics industry** N industria *f* del plástico ► **plastic surgeon** N cirujano/a *m/f* plástico/a ► **plastic surgery** N cirugía *f* plástica *or* estética; **to have ~ surgery** hacerse la cirugía plástica *or* estética ► **plastic wrap** N (*US*) film *m* adherente (*para envolver alimentos*)

Plasticine® ['plæstɪsiːn] N plastelina® *f*, plastilina® *f*, arcilla *f* de modelar

plasticity [plæs'tɪsɪtɪ] N plasticidad *f*

plastinate ['plæstɪneɪt] VT plastinar

Plate [pleɪt] N **the River ~** el Río de la Plata

plate [pleɪt] Ⓐ N [1] (= *flat dish*) plato *m*; [*of metal etc*] lámina *f*, plancha *f*; (*for church collection*) platillo *m*; (= *plateful*) plato *m*; ✦*IDIOMS* **to hand sth to sb on a ~*** ofrecer algo a algn en bandeja (de plata); **to have a lot on one's ~*** estar muy atareado
[2] (*on cooker*) quemador *m*, fuego *m*; (= *warming plate*) plancha *f* (eléctrica)
[3] (= *silverware etc*) vajilla *f*; **gold/silver ~** vajilla *f* de oro/plata
[4] (= *plaque*) (*on wall, door*) placa *f*
[5] [*of microscope*] placa *f*
[6] (*Aut*) (= *number plate*) matrícula *f*, placa *f*
[7] (= *dental plate*) dentadura *f* (postiza)
[8] (= *book illustration*) lámina *f*, grabado *m*
[9] (*Geol*) placa *f*
[10] (*Horse racing*) (= *prize*) premio *m*
[11] (*US Baseball*) plato *m*; **to go to the ~** entrar a batear
[12] **plates** (*Brit‡*) (= *feet*) tachines‡ *mpl*
Ⓑ VT [1] (*with gold*) dorar; (*with silver*) platear; (*with nickel*) niquelar
[2] (*with armour*) blindar
Ⓒ CPD ► **plate armour**, **plate armor** (*US*) N blindaje *m* ► **plate glass** N vidrio *m* cilindrado, cristal *m* cilindrado (*Sp*), luna *f* ► **plate rack** N escurreplatos *m inv* ► **plate tectonics** N (*Geol*) tectónica *f* de placas ► **plate warmer** N calentador *m* de platos

plateau ['plætəʊ] N (*pl* **plateaus** *or* **plateaux** ['plætəʊz]) [1] (*Geog*) meseta *f*; **high ~** (*in LAm*) altiplano *m*
[2] (*fig*) estancamiento *m*, punto *m* muerto

plated ['pleɪtɪd] ADJ [1] [*metal, jewellery*] chapado (**with** en); (*with nickel*) niquelado
[2] (= *armoured*) blindado

plateful ['pleɪtfʊl] N plato *m*

plateholder ['pleɪt,həʊldəʳ] N (*Phot*) portaplacas *m inv*

platelayer ['pleɪt,leɪəʳ] N obrero *m* (de ferrocarriles)

platelet ['pleɪtlɪt] N plaqueta *f*

platen ['plætən] N rodillo *m*

platform ['plætfɔːm] Ⓐ N [1] (*gen*) (= *structure*) plataforma *f*; (*roughly-built*) tarima *f*, tablado *m*; [*of oil rig*] plataforma *f* base; [*of bus*] plataforma *f*; (*for band etc*) estrado *m*; (*at meeting*) plataforma *f*, tribuna *f*; **last year they shared a ~** el año pasado ocuparon la misma tribuna
[2] (*Rail*) andén *m*, vía *f*; **the 5.15 is at** *or* **on ~ eight** el tren de las 5.15 está en la vía número ocho
[3] (*fig*) (*to express one's views*) plataforma *f*
[4] (*Pol*) programa *m*
[5] **platforms*** = **platform shoes**
Ⓑ CPD ► **platform shoes** NPL zapatos *mpl* de plataforma ► **the platform speakers** NPL los oradores de la tribuna ► **platform ticket** N (*Brit Rail*) billete *m* or (*LAm*) boleto *m* de andén

plating ['pleɪtɪŋ] N (= *layer of metal*) capa *f* metálica; **silver ~** plateado *m*; **gold ~** dorado *m*; **nickel ~** niquelado *m*; *see also* **armour C**

platinum ['plætɪnəm] Ⓐ N platino *m*
Ⓑ CPD ► **platinum blonde** N (= *colour*) rubio *m* platino; (= *woman*) rubia *f* platino; **~ blond(e) hair** pelo *m* rubio platino

platitude ['plætɪtjuːd] N tópico *m*, lugar *m* común; **it is a ~ to say that ...** es un tópico decir que ...

platitudinize [,plætɪ'tjuːdɪnaɪz] VI decir tópicos

platitudinous [,plætɪ'tjuːdɪnəs] ADJ [*speech*] lleno de lugares comunes; [*speaker*] aficionado a los lugares comunes, que peca por exceso de tópicos

Plato ['pleɪtəʊ] N Platón

platonic [plə'tɒnɪk] Ⓐ ADJ platónico
Ⓑ CPD ► **platonic love** N amor *m* platónico

Platonism ['pleɪtənɪzəm] N platonismo *m*

Platonist ['pleɪtənɪst] N platonista *mf*

platoon [plə'tuːn] N (*Mil*) pelotón *m*, sección *f*

platter ['plætəʳ] N [1] (*esp US*) (= *dish*) fuente *f*
[2] (= *meal, course*) plato *m*; **a cheese ~** una tabla de quesos
[3] (*US**) (= *record*) disco *m*

platypus ['plætɪpəs] N ornitorrinco *m*

plaudits ['plɔːdɪts] NPL aplausos *mpl*

plausibility [,plɔːzə'bɪlɪtɪ] N [*of argument*] verosimilitud *f*; [*of person*] credibilidad *f*; **his ~ is such that ...** habla tan bien que ...

plausible ['plɔːzəbl] ADJ [*argument etc*] verosímil, plausible; [*person*] convincente

plausibly [ˈplɔːzəblɪ] ADV de modo verosímil, de forma plausible; **he tells it most ~** lo cuenta de la manera más verosímil

play [pleɪ] Ⓐ N [1] (= *recreation*) juego *m*; **to be at ~** estar jugando; **to do/say sth in ~** hacer/decir algo en broma
[2] (*Sport*) juego *m*; (= *move, manoeuvre*) jugada *f*, movida *f*; **neat ~** una bonita jugada; **a clever piece of ~** una hábil jugada; **~ began at three o'clock** el partido empezó a las tres; **to be in ~** [*ball*] estar en juego; **to be out of ~** [*ball*] estar fuera de juego; *see also* **fair**[1], **foul E**
[3] (*Theat*) obra *f* (de teatro), pieza *f*; **plays** teatro *msing*; **the ~s of Lope** las obras dramáticas de Lope, el teatro de Lope; **radio/television ~** obra *f* para radio/televisión; **to be in a ~** [*actor*] actuar en una obra; *see also* **radio**
[4] (*Tech etc*) juego *m*; **there's not enough ~ in the rope** la cuerda no da lo suficiente; **there's too much ~ in the clutch** el embrague tiene demasiada holgura *or* va demasiado suelto
[5] (*fig*) (= *interaction*) **the ~ of light on the water** el rielar de la luz sobre el agua; **the ~ of light and dark in this picture** el efecto de luz y sombra en este cuadro; **the free ~ of market forces** la libre interacción de los mercados; **the ~ of ideas in the film is fascinating** el abanico de ideas en la película es fascinante
[6] (*fig phrases*) **to bring** *or* **call into ~** poner en juego; **to come into ~** entrar en juego; **to make a ~ for sth/sb** intentar conseguir algo/conquistar a algn; **to make (a) great ~ of sth** insistir en algo, hacer hincapié en algo; **a ~ on words** un juego de palabras
Ⓑ VT [1] [+ *football, tennis, chess, bridge, cards, board game etc*] jugar a; [+ *game, match*] jugar, disputar; **do you ~ football?** ¿juegas al fútbol?; **what position does he ~?** ¿de qué juega?; **to ~ centre-forward/centre-half etc** jugar de delantero centro/medio centro etc; **they ~ed him in goal** lo pusieron en la portería; **to ~ a game of tennis** jugar un partido de tenis; **to ~ a game of cards (with sb)** echar una partida de cartas (con algn); **the children were ~ing a game in the garden** los niños estaban jugando (a un juego) en el jardín; **don't ~ games with me!** (*fig*) ¡no me vengas con jueguecitos!, ¡no trates de engañarme!; **✦IDIOMS to ~ the field*** (= *have many girlfriends, boyfriends*) darse al ligue*; **to ~ the game** (= *get involved*) tomar parte, mojarse*; (= *play fair*) acatar las normas
[2] [+ *team, opponent*] jugar contra; **I ~ed him twice** jugué contra él dos veces; **last time we ~ed Sunderland …** la última vez que jugamos contra Sunderland …; **to ~ sb at chess** jugar contra algn al ajedrez; **I'll ~ you for the drinks** quien pierde paga
[3] [+ *card*] jugar; [+ *ball*] golpear; [+ *chess piece etc*] mover; [+ *fish*] dejar que se canse, agotar; **he ~ed the ball into the net** (*Tennis*) estrelló *or* golpeó la pelota contra la red; **to ~ the market** (*St Ex*) jugar a la bolsa; **✦IDIOMS to ~ one's cards right** *or* **well** jugar bien sus cartas; **he ~ed his ace** sacó el as que llevaba escondido en la manga; **to ~ ball (with sb)** (= *cooperate*) colaborar (con algn)
[4] (= *perform*) [+ *role, part*] hacer, interpretar; [+ *work*] representar; (= *perform in*) [+ *town*] actuar en; **what part did you ~?** ¿qué papel tuviste?; **when we ~ed "Hamlet"** cuando representamos "Hamlet"; **when I ~ed Hamlet** cuando hice el papel de Hamlet; **we shall be ~ing the West End** pondremos la obra en el West End; **when we last ~ed Blackpool** cuando actuamos la última vez en Blackpool; **let's ~ it for laughs** hagámoslo de manera burlesca; **to ~ the peacemaker/the devoted husband** (*fig*) hacer el papel de pacificador/de marido amantísimo; **we could have ~ed it differently** (*fig*) podríamos haber actuado de otra forma; **✦IDIOMS to ~ it cool*** mantener el tipo, actuar como si nada; **to ~ (it) safe** obrar con cautela, ser prudente; *see also* **book A1**, **fool A1**, **trick A1**
[5] (*Mus etc*) [+ *instrument, note*] tocar; [+ *tune, concerto*] tocar, interpretar (*more frm*); [+ *tape, CD*] poner, tocar; **to ~ the piano/violin** tocar el piano/el violín; **they ~ed the 5th Symphony** tocaron *or* (*more frm*) interpretaron la Quinta Sinfonía; **they were ~ing Beethoven** tocaban *or* (*more frm*) interpretaban algo de Beethoven; **I can't ~ a note** no tengo ni idea de música
[6] (= *direct*) [+ *light, hose*] dirigir; **to ~ hoses on a fire** dirigir mangueras sobre un incendio; **to ~ a searchlight on an aircraft** dirigir un reflector hacia un avión, hacer de un avión el blanco de un reflector
Ⓒ VI [1] (= *amuse o.s.*) [*child*] jugar; [*puppy, kitten etc*] jugar, juguetear; **to go out to ~** salir a jugar; **to ~ with a stick** juguetear con un palo; **to ~ with an idea** dar vueltas a una idea, barajar una idea; **to ~ with one's food** comiscar; **to ~ with fire** (*fig*) jugar con fuego; **he's got money to ~ with** tiene dinero de sobra; **how much time/money do we have to ~ with?** ¿con cuánto tiempo/dinero contamos?, ¿de cuánto tiempo/dinero disponemos?; **he's just ~ing with you** se está burlando de ti; **to ~ with o.s.*** (*euph*) tocarse, masturbarse
[2] (*Sport, at game, gamble*) jugar; **play!** ¡listo!; **who ~s first?** ¿quién juega primero?; **are you ~ing today?** ¿tu juegas hoy?; **I've not ~ed for a long time** hace mucho tiempo que no juego; **England are ~ing against Scotland in the final** Inglaterra jugará contra *or* se enfrentará a Escocia en la final; **to ~ at chess** jugar al ajedrez; **they're ~ing at soldiers** están jugando a (los) soldados; **he's just ~ing at it** lo hace para pasar el tiempo nada más; **the little girl ~s at being a woman** la niña juega a ser mujer; **what are you ~ing at?*** pero ¿qué haces?, ¿qué te pasa?; **to ~ by the rules** (*fig*) acatar las normas; **to ~ fair** jugar limpio; **he ~s for Liverpool** juega en el Liverpool; **to ~ for money** jugar por dinero; **to ~ for high stakes** (*lit*) apostar muy alto; (*fig*) poner mucho en juego; **to ~ in defence/goal** (*Sport*) jugar de defensa/de portero; **he ~ed into the trees** (*Golf*) mandó la bola a la zona de árboles; **✦IDIOMS to ~ for time** tratar de ganar tiempo; **to ~ into sb's hands** hacer el juego a algn; **to ~ to one's strengths** sacar partido a sus cualidades
[3] (*Mus*) [*person*] tocar; [*instrument, record etc*] sonar; **do you ~?** ¿sabes tocar?; **a record was ~ing in the background** de fondo sonaba un disco; **when the organ ~s** cuando suena el órgano; **will you ~ for us?** ¿nos tocas algo?; **to ~ on the piano** tocar el piano; **to ~ to sb** tocar para algn
[4] (*Theat, Cine*) (= *act*) actuar; **to ~ in a film** trabajar en una película; **we have ~ed all over the South** hemos representado en todas partes del Sur; **the film now ~ing at the Odeon** la película que se exhibe *or* proyecta en el Odeon; **✦IDIOMS to ~ hard to get** hacerse de rogar; [*woman*] hacerse la difícil; **to ~ dead** hacerse el muerto; *see also* **gallery**
[5] (= *move about, form patterns*) correr; **the sun was ~ing on the water** rielaba el sol sobre el agua; **a smile ~ed on his lips** una sonrisa le bailaba en los labios
[6] [*fountain*] correr, funcionar
Ⓓ CPD ► **play clothes** NPL ropa *f* para jugar
► **play reading** N lectura *f* (de una obra dramática)

►**play about** VI + ADV = **play around**

►**play along** Ⓐ VI + ADV **to ~ along (with sb)** (*fig*) seguir el juego (a algn)
Ⓑ VT + ADV **to ~ sb along** (*fig*) dar largas a algn*

►**play around** VI + ADV [1] (*also* **~ about**) [*children*] jugar, divertirse
[2] (*) (= *sleep around*) dormir con cualquiera
[3] **to ~ around** *or* **about with sth** (= *fiddle with*) juguetear con algo; (= *tamper with*) toquetear algo; **I ~ed around with the programme till it worked** ensayé el programa de varias maneras hasta hacerlo funcionar bien; **to ~ around with an idea** dar vueltas a una idea, barajar una idea

►**play back** VT + ADV [+ *tape*] poner

►**play down** VT + ADV (= *downplay*) minimizar, quitar importancia a

►**play in** VT + ADV [1] **the band ~ed the procession in** tocaba la orquesta mientras entraba el desfile
[2] (*Sport etc*) **to ~ o.s. in** acostumbrarse a las condiciones de juego

►**play off** Ⓐ VT + ADV **to ~ one person off against another** enfrentar a una persona con otra
Ⓑ VI + ADV (*Sport*) jugar un partido de desempate

►**play on** Ⓐ VI + PREP (= *take advantage of*) aprovecharse de, explotar; **to ~ on sb's emotions** jugar con las emociones de algn; **to ~ on sb's credulity** explotar la credulidad de algn; **to ~ on words** jugar con las palabras; **to ~ on sb's nerves** (= *be irritating*) afectar los nervios a algn
Ⓑ VI + ADV (*Mus*) seguir tocando; (*Sport*) seguir jugando; **~ on!** ¡adelante!

►**play out** VT + ADV [1] (= *enact*) llevar a cabo; [+ *fantasy etc*] realizar; **they are ~ing out a drama of revenge** están representando un drama de venganza
[2] **to be ~ed out** [*person, argument*] estar agotado
[3] **the organ ~ed the congregation out** el órgano iba tocando mientras salían los fieles

►**play over**, **play through** VT + ADV **to ~ a piece of music over** *or* **through** tocar una pieza entera

►**play up** Ⓐ VI + ADV [1] (*Brit**) (= *cause trouble*) [*children*] dar guerra*; **the car is ~ing up** el coche no anda bien; **my stomach is ~ing up again** el estómago me está dando problemas otra vez, mi estómago vuelve a darme problemas
[2] (*) (= *flatter*) **to ~ up to sb** halagar a algn, dar coba a algn (*Sp**)
[3] (*Sport*†) jugar mejor, jugar con más ánimo; **~ up!** ¡ánimo!, ¡aúpa!
Ⓑ VT + ADV [1] (*Brit**) (= *cause trouble to*) **to ~ sb up** dar la lata a algn (*Sp**), fregar a algn (*LAm**); **the kids ~ her up dreadfully** los chavales *or* (*LAm*) los chicos le dan guerra de mala manera*; **his rheumatism is ~ing him up** el reúma le está fastidiando
[2] (= *exaggerate*) exagerar, encarecer

►**play upon** VI + PREP = **play on A**

play-act [ˈpleɪækt] VI (*lit*) hacer teatro, actuar; (*fig*) (= *pretend*) hacer teatro

play-acting ['pleɪ,æktɪŋ] N (*lit*) actuación *f* teatral; (*fig*) teatro *m*, comedia *f*; **this is mere ~** (*fig*) esto es puro teatro, esto no es más que una comedia

play-actor ['pleɪ,æktəʳ] N (*lit, fig*) actor *m*, actriz *f*

playback ['pleɪbæk] N repetición *f*, reproducción *f*; (*TV etc*) playback *m*, previo *m*

playbill ['pleɪbɪl] N cartel *m*

playboy ['pleɪbɔɪ] N playboy *m*

player ['pleɪəʳ] N [1] (*Sport*) jugador(a) *m/f*; **football ~** jugador(a) *m/f* de fútbol, futbolista *mf*
[2] (*Theat*) actor *m*, actriz *f*
[3] (*Mus*) músico/a *m/f*; **violin/piano ~** violinista *mf*/pianista *mf*

playfellow ['pleɪ,feləʊ] N compañero/a *m/f* de juego

playful ['pleɪfʊl] ADJ [*person*] juguetón; [*mood*] alegre; [*remark*] dicho en broma, festivo

playfully ['pleɪfəlɪ] ADV (= *full of fun*) alegremente; (= *in jest*) en broma; (*as part of game*) jugando, en juego; **he said ~** dijo guasón

playfulness ['pleɪfʊlnɪs] N [*of person*] carácter *m* juguetón; [*of mood*] alegría *f*; [*of remark*] guasa *f*, tono *m* guasón

playgoer ['pleɪ,gəʊəʳ] N aficionado/a *m/f* al teatro; **we are regular ~s** vamos con regularidad al teatro

playground ['pleɪgraʊnd] N (*in school*) patio *m* de recreo; (*fig*) [*of millionaires*] paraíso *m*, lugar *m* favorito

playgroup ['pleɪ,gruːp] N jardín *m* de infancia, guardería *f*, kinder *m* (*LAm*)

playhouse ['pleɪhaʊs] N (*pl* **playhouses** ['plaɪhaʊzɪz]) [1] (= *theatre*) teatro *m*
[2] (*for children*) casa *f* de muñecas

playing ['pleɪɪŋ] Ⓐ N [1] (*Sport*) juego *m*; **~ in the wet is tricky** es difícil jugar cuando llueve
[2] (*Mus*) **the orchestra's ~ of the symphony was uninspired** la interpretación que hizo la orquesta de la sinfonía fue poco inspirada; **there was some fine ~ in the violin concerto** el concierto de violín estuvo muy bien interpretado
Ⓑ CPD ► **playing card** N naipe *m* ► **playing field** N campo *m* or (*LAm*) cancha *f* de deportes

playlet ['pleɪlɪt] N obra *f* corta de teatro

playlist ['pleɪlɪst] N (*Rad*) lista *f* discográfica

playmaker ['pleɪmeɪkəʳ] N (*Sport*) *jugador encargado de facilitar buenas jugadas a sus compañeros*

playmate ['pleɪmeɪt] N compañero/a *m/f* de juego

play-off ['pleɪɒf] N (*Sport*) (partido *m* de) desempate *m*; [*of top teams in league*] liguilla *f*

playpen ['pleɪpen] N parque *m*, corral *m*

playroom ['pleɪrʊm] N cuarto *m* de juego

playschool ['pleɪ,skuːl] N = **playgroup**

plaything ['pleɪθɪŋ] N (*lit, fig*) juguete *m*

playtime ['pleɪtaɪm] N (*Scol*) (hora *f* de) recreo *m*

playwright ['pleɪraɪt] N dramaturgo/a *m/f*

plaza ['plɑːzə] N [1] (= *public square*) plaza *f*
[2] (*US*) (= *motorway services*) zona *f* de servicios; (= *toll*) peaje *m*

PLC, plc N ABBR (*Brit*) (= **public limited company**) S.A.

plea [pliː] Ⓐ N [1] (= *entreaty*) súplica *f*, petición *f*; **he made a ~ for mercy** pidió clemencia
[2] (= *excuse*) pretexto *m*, disculpa *f*
[3] (*Jur*) alegato *m*, defensa *f*; **a ~ of insanity** un alegato de desequilibrio mental; **a ~ of guilty/not guilty** una declaración de culpabilidad/inocencia; **to enter a ~ of innocent** declararse inocente
Ⓑ CPD ► **plea bargaining** N (*Jur*) *acuerdo táctico entre fiscal y defensor para agilizar los trámites judiciales*

plead [pliːd] (*pt, pp* **pleaded, pled** (*esp US*)) Ⓐ VT [1] (= *argue*) **to ~ sb's cause** hablar por algn, interceder por algn; **to ~ sb's case** (*Jur*) defender a algn en juicio
[2] (*as excuse*) aducir, pretextar; **to ~ that** aducir *or* pretextar que; **to ~ ignorance** aducir *or* pretextar desconocimiento; **to ~ poverty** aducir *or* pretextar falta de medios económicos; **he ~ed certain difficulties** adujo *or* pretextó la existencia de ciertas dificultades
Ⓑ VI [1] (= *beg*) suplicar, rogar; **I ~ed and ~ed but it was no use** le supliqué mil veces pero de nada sirvió; **to ~ with sb (to do sth)** suplicar a algn (que haga algo); **to ~ with sb for sth** rogar a algn que conceda algo; **the village has ~ed for a new bridge for ten years** hace diez años que el pueblo viene reclamando un nuevo puente
[2] (*Jur*) (*as defendant*) presentar declaración; (*as barrister*) abogar; **how do you ~?** ¿cómo se declara el acusado?; **to ~ guilty/not guilty** declararse culpable/inocente

pleading ['pliːdɪŋ] Ⓐ N (= *entreaties*) súplicas *fpl*; (*Jur*) alegatos *mpl*; **special ~** argumentos *mpl* especiosos
Ⓑ ADJ [*tone etc*] suplicante, de súplica

pleasant ['pleznt] ADJ [1] (= *agreeable*) [*place, experience, smell, taste, voice*] agradable; [*surprise*] grato, agradable; [*face*] agradable, simpático; **it's very ~ here** aquí se está muy bien; **it made a ~ change from our usual holiday** supuso un agradable cambio respecto a nuestras vacaciones habituales; **~ dreams!** ¡que sueñes con los angelitos!; **~-looking** de aspecto agradable
[2] (= *friendly*) [*person*] agradable, simpático; [*style*] agradable; **he has a ~ manner** es agradable *or* simpático *or* amable; **try and be a bit more ~ to your sister** procura ser un poco más agradable con tu hermana

pleasantly ['plezntlɪ] ADV [*say*] amablemente, en tono agradable; **the evening passed ~ enough** la velada fue bastante agradable; **the room was ~ furnished** la habitación estaba amueblada con gusto; **it was ~ warm** hacía un calor agradable; **we were ~ surprised** fue una grata *or* agradable sorpresa para nosotros; **I was feeling ~ drowsy** tenía una agradable *or* placentera sensación de somnolencia

pleasantness ['plezntnɪs] N (= *agreeableness*) amenidad *f*, lo agradable; (= *friendliness*) simpatía *f*, amabilidad *f*

pleasantry ['plezntrɪ] N [1] (= *joke*) chiste *m*, broma *f*
[2] (= *polite remark*) cumplido *m*; **to exchange pleasantries** intercambiar los cumplidos de rigor

▼**please** [pliːz] Ⓐ EXCL **please!** ¡por favor!; (*as protest*) ¡por Dios!; **(yes,) ~** sí, gracias; **can you pass the salt, ~** me pasas la sal, por favor; **~ don't cry!** ¡no llores, (te lo pido) por favor!; **~ don't interfere, Boris** haz el favor de no meterte, Boris, no te metas, Boris, por favor; **~ be seated** (*said by interviewer, doctor, etc*) siéntese; (*said over intercom, in plane, theatre, etc*) les rogamos tomen asiento; **~ accept this book** le ruego acepte este libro; **oh, ~! not that song again!** ¡oh no! ¡esa canción otra vez no por favor!; **"may I?" — "~ do"** —¿puedo? —¡por supuesto! *or* —¡cómo no!; **"please do not smoke"** "se ruega no fumar"
Ⓑ VI [1] (= *like, prefer*) querer; **he does whatever he ~s** hace lo que quiere *or* lo que le place; **she can live where she ~s** puede vivir donde quiera *or* donde le plazca; **as you ~** como quieras; **do as you ~** haz lo que quieras, haz lo que te dé la gana*; **she came over casually as you ~ and picked up my diary*** se acercó con toda la tranquilidad del mundo y cogió mi agenda; **gentlemen, if you ~!** (*frm*) señores, por favor, señores, si son tan amables; **he wanted ten, if you ~!** quería llevarse diez, ¡a quién se le ocurre!, quería llevarse diez, ¡qué cara!*; **we'll have none of that language if you ~!** ¡mucho cuidadito con usar ese lenguaje!
[2] (= *cause satisfaction*) **we aim to ~** nuestro objetivo es complacer; **to be anxious** *or* **eager to ~** tener muchas ansias de quedar bien; **a gift that is sure to ~** un regalo que siempre gusta, un regalo que de seguro gustará
Ⓒ VT [1] (= *give pleasure to*) agradar, complacer; (= *satisfy*) complacer; **I did it just to ~ you** lo hice únicamente para agradarte *or* complacerte; **you can't ~ all of the people all of the time** no se puede complacer a todo el mundo todo el tiempo; **music that ~s the ear** una música grata al oído; **she is easily ~d** se contenta con cualquier cosa; **he is hard to ~** es difícil de contentar *or* complacer; **there's no pleasing him** no hay manera de contentarlo; **~ yourself!** ¡haz lo que quieras!, ¡haz lo que te dé la gana!*
[2] (*frm*) (= *be the will of*) **may it ~ Your Majesty** sea ésta la voluntad de su Majestad
Ⓓ N **she just took it without so much as a ~ or a thank you** lo cogió sin ni siquiera dignarse a pedirlo por favor ni a dar las gracias

▼**pleased** [pliːzd] ADJ [1] **to be ~** (= *happy*) estar contento; (= *satisfied*) estar satisfecho; **we will be ~ to answer any questions** contestaremos, encantados *or* con mucho gusto, todas sus preguntas; **I am ~ to hear it** me alegra saberlo; **~ to meet you!** mucho gusto (en conocerlo), encantado (de conocerlo); **we are ~ to inform you that …** nos complace *or* nos es grato comunicarle que …; **I'm so ~ you could make it** cómo me alegro de que hayas podido venir; **he wasn't too ~ that I had sold it** no le hizo mucha gracia que lo hubiese vendido; **to be ~ about/at sth**: **I am ~ at the decision** me alegro de la decisión; **we were ~ at the news** la noticia nos alegró; **I'm not very ~ about it** no me hace mucha gracia; **I'm really ~ for you** me alegro mucho por ti; **what are you looking so ~ about?** ¿a qué se debe esa cara de alegría?; **to be ~ with sb/sth** estar contento con algn/algo; **he was ~ with my progress** estaba contento con *or* satisfecho de mis progresos; **he is/looks very ~ with himself** está/parece estar muy satisfecho de sí mismo *or* consigo mismo; **you needn't look so ~ with yourself** esa cara de satisfacción que tienes sobra; *see also* **Punch**
[2] (*with noun*) **he glanced at her with a ~ smile** la miró, sonriendo satisfecho; **there was a look of ~ surprise on her face** se le veía en la cara que se había llevado una grata *or* agradable sorpresa

pleasing ['pliːzɪŋ] ADJ [*manner*] agradable; [*news*] grato; [*result*] satisfactorio; **aesthetically ~** agradable desde el punto de vista estético; **~ to the ear/eye** grato *or* agradable al oído/a la vista

► LANGUAGE IN USE: please A 4 pleased 1 13, 24.1

pleasingly ['pli:zɪŋlɪ] ADV **the surface was ~ smooth to the touch** la superficie era lisa y agradable *or* grata al tacto

pleasurable ['pleʒərəbl] ADJ agradable, grato

pleasurably ['pleʒərəblɪ] ADV agradablemente, deleitosamente; **we were ~ surprised** para nosotros fue una grata sorpresa

▼**pleasure** ['pleʒəʳ] Ⓐ N [1] (= *satisfaction*) placer *m*, gusto *m*; (= *happiness*) alegría *f*; **to be fond of ~** ser amante de los placeres; **sexual ~** placer *m* sexual; **my ~!** ◊ **the ~ is mine!** (*frm*) (*returning thanks*) ¡de nada!, ¡no hay de qué! (*esp LAm*); **what ~ can you find in shooting partridges?** ¿qué placer encuentras en matar perdices?; **to do sth for ~** hacer algo por gusto *or* placer; **is this trip for business or ~?** ¿este viaje es de negocios o de placer?; **to get ~ from sth** disfrutar con algo; **to give sb ~** dar gusto a algn; **if it gives you any ~** si te gusta; **I have much ~ in informing you that ...** tengo el gran placer de comunicarles que ...; **may I have the ~?** (*frm*) (*at dance*) ¿quiere usted bailar?; **Mr and Mrs Brown request the ~ of your company** (*frm*) (*on invitation*) los Sres. Brown tienen el placer de solicitar su asistencia; **to take ~ in books** disfrutar leyendo; **I take great ~ in watching them grow** disfruto muchísimo viéndolos crecer; **to take ~ in teasing sb** disfrutar tomándo el pelo a algn; **with ~** con mucho gusto
[2] (= *source of pleasure*) placer *m*, gusto *m*; **it's a real ~** es un verdadero placer; **all the ~s of London** todos los placeres de Londres; **it's a ~ to see her** da gusto verla; **it's a ~ to know that ...** es un motivo de satisfacción saber que ...
[3] (*frm*) (= *will*) voluntad *f*; **what is your ~, sir?** ¿en qué puedo servirle, señor?, ¿qué manda el señor?; **at sb's ~** según la voluntad de algn; **to be detained during her Majesty's ~** (*Jur*) quedar encarcelado a disposición del Estado
Ⓑ VT (*sexually*) dar placer a; **to ~ o.s.** (*euph*) (= *masturbate*) masturbarse
Ⓒ CPD ► **pleasure boat, pleasure craft** N barco *m* de recreo ► **pleasure cruise** N crucero *m* de recreo ► **pleasure ground** N parque *m* de atracciones ► **pleasure seeker** N hedonista *mf* ► **pleasure steamer** N vapor *m* de recreo ► **pleasure trip** N viaje *m* de placer

pleasure-loving ['pleʒə,lʌvɪŋ], **pleasure-seeking** ['pleʒə,si:kɪŋ] ADJ hedonista

pleat [pli:t] Ⓐ N pliegue *m*, doblez *m*; [*of skirt*] tabla *f*
Ⓑ VT plisar, plegar

pleb* [pleb] (*Brit*) Ⓐ N plebeyo/a *m/f*; **the ~s** la plebe
Ⓑ ADJ plebeyo, aplebeyado

plebeian [plɪ'bi:ən] Ⓐ ADJ plebeyo; (*pej*) ordinario
Ⓑ N plebeyo/a *m/f*

plebiscite ['plebɪsɪt] N plebiscito *m*

plectrum ['plektrəm] N (*pl* **plectrums** *or* **plectra** ['plektrə]) púa *f*, plectro *m*

pled [pled] (*US*) PT, PP *of* **plead**

pledge [pledʒ] Ⓐ N [1] (= *promise, assurance*) (*gen*) compromiso *m*, promesa *f*; [*of money*] promesa *f* de donación; **a company's ~ of satisfaction to its customers** el compromiso *or* la promesa por parte de una empresa de satisfacer a sus clientes; **he received ~s of support from more than 100 MPs** más de 100 parlamentarios se comprometieron a *or* prometieron apoyarlo; **the Pledge of Allegiance** (*US*) ≈ la jura de la bandera; **to break a ~** romper una promesa; **to give (sb) a ~ to do sth** prometer (a algn) hacer algo; **to honour** *or* **keep a ~** cumplir una promesa; **the government will honour its ~s** el gobierno cumplirá sus promesas, el gobierno hará honor a sus compromisos; **to make (sb) a ~ to do sth** prometer (a algn) hacer algo; **he made a ~ not to raise taxes** prometió no subir los impuestos; ♦**IDIOM to sign** *or* **take the ~†*** (*hum*) jurar renunciar al alcohol
[2] (= *token*) **he sent his brother as a ~ of his sincerity** envió a su hermano en señal *or* como muestra de su sinceridad
[3] (= *surety*) prenda *f*, garantía *f*; (*left in pawn*) prenda *f*
[4] (= *toast*) brindis *m inv*
[5] (*US Univ*) *promesa que hace un estudiante universitario en los Estados Unidos para convertirse en miembro de una hermandad*
Ⓑ VT [1] (= *promise*) [+ *money, donation*] prometer; **the government has ~d that it will not increase taxes** el gobierno ha prometido no subir los impuestos; **to ~ to do sth** prometer hacer algo; **to ~ o.s. to do sth** comprometerse a hacer algo; **to ~ (one's) support (for sth/sb)** comprometerse a prestar apoyo (a algo/algn); **I am ~d to secrecy** he jurado *or* prometido guardar (el) secreto; *see also* **allegiance**
[2] (= *give as security*) [+ *property*] entregar como garantía; [+ *one's word*] dar
[3] (= *pawn*) empeñar, dejar en prenda
[4] (*US Univ*) [+ *fraternity*] hacerse miembro de

> **PLEDGE OF ALLEGIANCE**
>
> *El* **Pledge of Allegiance** *es un juramento de lealtad a la nación, considerado como un elemento de gran importancia en la educación norteamericana. Fue escrito en 1892 y desde entonces lo recitan diariamente todos los alumnos estadounidenses (especialmente en los centros de educación primaria) mirando a la bandera y con la mano en el corazón.*

Pleiades ['plaɪədi:z] NPL Pléyades *fpl*

plenary ['pli:nərɪ] Ⓐ ADJ plenario; **in ~ session** en sesión plenaria
Ⓑ N (*also* **~ paper**) ponencia *f* en sesión plenaria, ponencia *f* general

plenipotentiary [,plenɪpə'tenʃərɪ] Ⓐ ADJ plenipotenciario
Ⓑ N plenipotenciario/a *m/f*

plenitude ['plenɪtju:d] N plenitud *f*

plenteous ['plentɪəs] ADJ (*frm*) = **plentiful**

plentiful ['plentɪfʊl] ADJ [*wildlife, game, hair*] abundante; **a ~ supply of ...** un suministro abundante de ...; **eggs are now ~** *or* **in ~ supply** ahora hay abundancia de huevos, ahora abundan los huevos

plentifully ['plentɪfəlɪ] ADV en abundancia, abundantemente

plenty ['plentɪ] Ⓐ N abundancia *f*; **in ~** en abundancia; **the land of ~** la tierra de la abundancia
Ⓑ PRON [1] (= *lots*) **that's ~, thanks** ¡así basta, gracias!; **she's got ~ to do** tiene muchas cosas que hacer, tiene un montón que hacer*; **there are ~ like me** hay mucha gente *or* hay muchos como yo; **there's ~ more where that came from** aún queda más de esto
[2] **~ of** (= *much, a good deal of*) mucho/a; (= *many*) muchos/as; **it takes ~ of courage** requiere mucho valor; **they have ~ of money** tienen mucho dinero; **we've got ~ of time to get there** tenemos tiempo de sobra para llegar; **I've got ~ of work to be getting on with** tengo trabajo más que suficiente para empezar; **drink ~ of fluids** beba muchos líquidos; **there are ~ of them** los hay en cantidad; **~ of people are self-employed nowadays** hoy en día hay mucha gente que trabaja de autónomo; **we see ~ of Mum and Dad** vemos a mis padres con frecuencia, vemos mucho a mis padres
Ⓒ ADV (*esp US**) **it's ~ big enough** es bastante grande; **we like it ~** nos gusta mucho

plenum ['pli:nəm] N (*pl* **plenums** *or* **plena**) pleno *m*

pleonasm ['pli:ənæzəm] N pleonasmo *m*

pleonastic [plɪə'næstɪk] ADJ pleonástico

plethora ['pleθərə] N plétora *f*

plethoric [ple'θɒrɪk] ADJ pletórico

pleurisy ['plʊərɪsɪ] N pleuresía *f*, pleuritis *f*

Plexiglas® ['pleksɪglɑ:s] N plexiglás® *m*

pliability [,plaɪə'bɪlɪtɪ] N (*also fig*) flexibilidad *f*

pliable ['plaɪəbl] ADJ (*also fig*) flexible

pliant ['plaɪənt] ADJ (*fig*) dócil, flexible

pliers ['plaɪəz] NPL alicates *mpl*; **a pair of ~** unos alicates

plight[1] [plaɪt] N situación *f* grave; **the country's economic ~** la grave situación económica del país; **the ~ of the shellfish industry** la crisis de la industria marisquera; **to be in a sad** *or* **sorry ~** estar en un estado lamentable

plight[2]† [plaɪt] VT [+ *word*] dar, empeñar; **to ~ one's troth** prometerse, dar su palabra de casamiento (**to** a)

plimsoll ['plɪmsəl] Ⓐ N (*Brit*) zapatilla *f* de tenis, playera *f*
Ⓑ CPD ► **Plimsoll line, Plimsoll mark** N (*Naut*) línea *f* de máxima carga

plinth [plɪnθ] N plinto *m*

Pliny ['plɪnɪ] N Plinio; **~ the Elder** Plinio el Viejo; **~ the Younger** Plinio el Joven

PLO N ABBR (= **Palestine Liberation Organization**) OLP *f*

plod [plɒd] Ⓐ N [1] **to go at a steady ~** caminar a un ritmo lento pero constante
[2] **it's a long ~ to the village** hay mucho camino hasta llegar al pueblo
Ⓑ VT **we ~ded our way homeward** volvimos penosamente hacia casa
Ⓒ VI [1] (*lit*) andar con paso pesado; **to ~ along** *or* **on** ir andando con paso lento; **keep ~ding!** ¡ánimo!, ¡no os dejéis desanimar!
[2] (*fig*) (*at work etc*) **to ~ away at a task** seguir dándole a un trabajo; **we must ~ on** tenemos que seguir trabajando

plodder* ['plɒdəʳ] N *trabajador diligente pero lento*

plodding ['plɒdɪŋ] ADJ [*pace*] lento y pesado; [*student, worker*] más aplicado que brillante

plonk[1] [plɒŋk] (*esp Brit*) Ⓐ N (= *sound*) golpe *m* seco, ruido *m* seco; **it fell with a ~ to the floor** cayó al suelo con un ruido seco
Ⓑ ADV (*) **he went ~ into the stream** cayó ¡zas! en el arroyo; **it landed ~ on his cheek** le dio de lleno en la mejilla; **~ in the middle** justo en el medio
Ⓒ VT (*) [1] (*Mus*) puntear
[2] (*also* **~ down**) dejar caer; **to ~ o.s. down** dejarse caer
Ⓓ EXCL (*) plaf

plonk[2]* [plɒŋk] N (*Brit*) (= *wine*) vino *m* peleón*

plonker‡ ['plɒŋkəʳ] N (*Brit*) imbécil *mf*, gilipollas *mf inv* (*Sp*‡)

plop [plɒp] Ⓐ N plaf *m*
Ⓑ VI hacer plaf
Ⓒ VT (*also* **to ~ down**) arrojar dejando oír un plaf
Ⓓ EXCL plaf

➤ LANGUAGE IN USE: pleasure A2 3

plosive ['pləʊsɪv] Ⓐ ADJ explosivo
Ⓑ N explosiva *f*

plot¹ [plɒt] N (*Agr*) parcela *f*, terreno *m*; [*of vegetables, flowers etc*] cuadro *m*; **a ~ of grass** un cuadro de césped; **a ~ of land** (*gen*) un terreno; (*for building*) un solar, un lote (*esp LAm*); **a vegetable ~** un cuadro de hortalizas

plot² [plɒt] Ⓐ N [1] (= *conspiracy*) complot *m*, conjura *f*
[2] (*Literat, Theat*) trama *f*, argumento *m*; ✦***IDIOMS*** **to lose the ~*** perderse, perder el hilo; **the ~ thickens** la cosa se complica
Ⓑ VT [1] (*on graph etc*) [+ *progress, course, position*] trazar; **to ~ A against Z** trazar A como función de Z
[2] [+ *downfall, ruin etc*] urdir, fraguar
Ⓒ VI maquinar, conspirar; **to ~ to do sth** conspirar para hacer algo

►**plot out** VT + ADV [+ *course, route*] trazar; [+ *strategy, plan*] marcar, trazar

plotless ['plɒtlɪs] ADJ [*film, play, novel*] sin argumento, carente de argumento

plotter¹ ['plɒtəʳ] N (= *conspirator*) conspirador(a) *m/f*

plotter² ['plɒtəʳ] N (*Comput*) trazador *m* (de gráficos)

plotting ['plɒtɪŋ] Ⓐ N intrigas *fpl*, maquinaciones *fpl*
Ⓑ CPD ► **plotting board** N tablero *m* trazador ► **plotting paper** N (*US*) papel *m* cuadriculado ► **plotting table** N mesa *f* trazadora

plough, plow (*US*) [plaʊ] Ⓐ N (*Agr*) arado *m*; **the Plough** (*Astron*) el Carro, la Osa Mayor
Ⓑ VT [1] (*Agr*) arar
[2] (*fig*) **to ~ money into a project** invertir (grandes cantidades de) dinero en un proyecto; **to ~ one's way through the snow** abrirse paso con dificultad por la nieve; **to ~ one's way through a book** leer un libro con dificultad; **I ~ed my way through it eventually** por fin acabé de leerlo pero resultó pesadísimo
[3] (*Brit Univ*†*) dar calabazas a*, cargar (*Sp**); **I was ~ed in German** ◊ **they ~ed me in German** me dieron calabazas en alemán*
Ⓒ VI [1] (*Agr*) arar
[2] (*fig*) **the car ~ed into the wall** el coche dio fuerte(mente) contra la pared; **the lorry ~ed into the crowd** el camión se metió en la multitud; **to ~ through the mud** abrirse camino con dificultad a través del lodo
[3] (*Brit Univ*†*) **I ~ed again** volvieron a suspenderme *or* (*LAm*) reprobarme, volvieron a cargarme (*Sp**)
Ⓓ CPD ► **plough horse** N caballo *m* de labranza

►**plough back** VT + ADV [+ *profits*] reinvertir

►**plough in, plough under** VT + ADV cubrir arando, enterrar arando

►**plough up** VT + ADV [+ *field*] arar, roturar; [+ *bushes etc*] arrancar con el arado; [+ *pathway*] hacer desaparecer arando; **the train ~ed up the track for 100 metres** el tren destrozó unos 100 metros de vía

ploughing, plowing (*US*) ['plaʊɪŋ] N arada *f*; **~ back of profits** reinversión *f* de ganancias

ploughland, plowland (*US*) ['plaʊlænd] N tierra *f* de labrantío, tierra *f* labrantía

ploughman, plowman (*US*) ['plaʊmən] Ⓐ N (*pl* **ploughmen**) arador *m*, labrador *m*
Ⓑ CPD ► **ploughman's lunch** N (*Brit*) pan *m* con queso y cebolla

ploughshare, plowshare (*US*) ['plaʊʃɛəʳ] N reja *f* del arado

plover ['plʌvəʳ] N chorlito *m*

plow *etc* [plaʊ] (*US*) = **plough** *etc*

ploy [plɔɪ] N truco *m*, estratagema *f*

PLP N ABBR (*Brit*) = **Parliamentary Labour Party**

PLR N ABBR (*Brit Admin*) = **Public Lending Right**

pluck [plʌk] Ⓐ N [1] (= *tug*) tirón *m*
[2] (= *courage*) valor *m*, ánimo *m*; (= *guts*) agallas *fpl*; **it takes ~ to do that** hace falta mucho valor para hacer eso; **he's got plenty of ~** tiene muchas agallas; **I didn't have the ~ to own up** no tuve el valor para confesar
Ⓑ VT [+ *fruit, flower*] (*liter*) arrancar; [+ *bird*] desplumar; [+ *guitar*] pulsar, puntear; **to ~ one's eyebrows** depilarse las cejas; **the helicopter ~ed him from the sea** el helicóptero lo recogió del mar; **it's an idea I've just ~ed out of the air** es una idea que he tenido al vuelo; **he was ~ed from obscurity to star in the show** fue rescatado del anonimato para protagonizar el espectáculo
Ⓒ VI **to ~ at** tirar de, dar un tirón a; **to ~ at sb's sleeve** tirar a algn de la manga

►**pluck off, pluck out** VT + ADV arrancar con los dedos, arrancar de un tirón

►**pluck up** VT + ADV (= *summon up*) **to ~ up (one's) courage** armarse de valor; **to ~ up the courage to do sth** armarse de valor para hacer algo

pluckily ['plʌkɪlɪ] ADV valientemente

pluckiness ['plʌkɪnɪs] N (= *courage*) valor *m*, ánimo *m*; (= *guts*) agallas *fpl*

plucky ['plʌkɪ] ADJ (*compar* **pluckier**; *superl* **pluckiest**) valiente, valeroso

plug [plʌg] Ⓐ N [1] (*in bath, basin, barrel, for leak*) tapón *m*; **a ~ of cotton wool** un tampón (de algodón); ✦***IDIOM*** **to pull the ~ on sth***: **the bank pulled the ~ on my overdraft** el banco me cerró el grifo del descubierto
[2] (*Elec*) (*on flex, apparatus*) enchufe *m*, clavija *f*; (= *socket*) toma *f* de corriente; (*Telec*) clavija *f*; (*Aut*) (= *spark plug*) bujía *f*; **2-/3-pin ~** clavija *f* bipolar/tripolar, clavija *f* de dos/tres polos
[3] [*of tobacco*] rollo *m*, tableta *f* (de tabaco de mascar)
[4] (*) (= *piece of publicity*) publicidad *f*; **to give sth/sb a ~** dar publicidad a algo/algn; **to get/put in a ~ for a product** lograr anunciar un producto (de modo solapado)
Ⓑ VT [1] (*also* **~ up**) [+ *hole*] llenar, tapar; [+ *leak*] cubrir; (*Archit*) rellenar; **~ this cloth into the hole** tapa el agujero con este trapo; **to ~ a tooth** empastar una muela; **to ~ a loophole** (*fig*) cerrar una escapatoria; **to ~ the drain on the reserves** (*fig*) acabar con la pérdida de reservas
[2] (= *insert*) introducir; **to ~ a lead into a socket** enchufar un hilo en una toma
[3] (*) (= *publicize*) dar publicidad a
[4] (*) (= *advocate, put forward*) insistir *or* hacer hincapié en; **he's been ~ging that line for years** hace años que viene diciendo lo mismo
[5] (*‡*) (= *hit*) pegar; (= *shoot*) pegar un tiro a

►**plug away*** VI + ADV **to ~ away (at sth)** perseverar (en algo), darle (a algo)*

►**plug in** Ⓐ VT + ADV (*Elec*) enchufar, conectar; **to ~ in a radio** conectar una radio
Ⓑ VI + ADV [1] (*Elec*) enchufar
[2] (*) (*fig*) ponerse en la onda*; **to ~ in to** ponerse en la onda de*, sintonizar con

►**plug up** VT + ADV (= *fill*) tapar, taponar

plug-and-play [,plʌgən'pleɪ] ADJ (*Comput*) fácil de conectar

plughole ['plʌghəʊl] N desagüe *m*, desaguadero *m*; ✦***IDIOM*** **to go down the ~*** irse al traste; **all that work has gone down the ~** todo ese trabajo se ha ido al traste

plug-in ['plʌg'ɪn] ADJ (*Elec*) enchufable, con enchufe

plug-ugly* [,plʌg'ʌglɪ] ADJ feísimo, horrendo

plum [plʌm] Ⓐ N [1] (= *fruit*) ciruela *f*; (*also* **~ tree**) ciruelo *m*; ✦***IDIOM*** **to speak with** *or* **have a ~ in one's mouth** (*Brit* hum*) hablar muy engoladamente
[2] (= *colour*) color *m* ciruela *or* (*LAm*) guinda
[3] (*fig*) (*) **it's a real ~ (of a) job** es un trabajo fantástico, es un chollo (*Sp**)
Ⓑ CPD ► **plum pudding** N pudín *m or* budín *m* de pasas ► **plum tomato** N tomate *m* pera

plumage ['pluːmɪdʒ] N plumaje *m*

plumb [plʌm] Ⓐ N plomo *m*
Ⓑ ADJ vertical, a plomo
Ⓒ ADV [1] (= *vertically*) verticalmente, a plomo
[2] (*US**) (= *wholly*) totalmente, completamente; **~ crazy** completamente loco; **he's ~ stupid** es un tonto perdido
[3] **~ in the middle** en el mismo *or* (*Mex*) mero centro; **it hit him ~ on the nose** le dio de lleno en las narices
Ⓓ VT [1] (= *descend to*) sondar
[2] (*fig*) sondear; **to ~ the depths of the human mind** penetrar en las profundidades de la mente humana; **to ~ the depths of despair** conocer la mayor desesperación
[3] (= *connect plumbing in*) [+ *building*] instalar la fontanería de, instalar las tuberías de
Ⓔ CPD ► **plumb bob** N plomo *m* ► **plumb line** N plomada *f*

►**plumb in** VT + ADV conectar (con el suministro de agua)

plumbago [plʌm'beɪgəʊ] N (*pl* **plumbagos**) plombagina *f*

plumber ['plʌməʳ] Ⓐ N fontanero/a *m/f*, plomero/a *m/f* (*LAm*), gasfitero/a *m/f* (*Chile*)
Ⓑ CPD ► **plumber's helper** (*US*), **plumber's mate** (*Brit*) N (= *tool*) desatascador *m* de fregaderos; (= *assistant*) ayudante *mf or* aprendiz *mf* de fontanero

plumbic ['plʌmbɪk] ADJ plúmbico, plúmbeo

plumbing ['plʌmɪŋ] N [1] (= *craft*) fontanería *f*, plomería *f* (*LAm*), gasfitería *f* (*Chile*)
[2] (= *piping*) tuberías *fpl*, cañerías *fpl*; (= *bathroom fittings*) aparatos *mpl* sanitarios

plume [pluːm] Ⓐ N (= *feather*) pluma *f*; (*on helmet*) penacho *m*; (*fig*) [*of smoke etc*] columna *f*, hilo *m*
Ⓑ VT **the bird ~s itself** el ave se limpia *or* se arregla las plumas

plumed [pluːmd] ADJ [*hat*] con plumas; [*helmet*] empenachado

plummet ['plʌmɪt] Ⓐ N plomada *f*
Ⓑ VI [*bird, plane etc*] caer en picado *or* (*LAm*) en picada; [*temperature, price, sales*] bajar de golpe; [*spirits, morale*] caer a plomo

plummeting ['plʌmɪtɪŋ] ADJ [*prices, profits, sales*] que cae(n) en picado *or* (*LAm*) en picada; [*popularity*] que se va a pique; [*temperatures*] que baja(n) drásticamente

plummy* ['plʌmɪ] ADJ (*compar* **plummier**; *superl* **plummiest**) (*Brit*) [*voice*] engolado

plump¹ [plʌmp] Ⓐ ADJ (*compar* **plumper**; *superl* **plumpest**) [*person*] relleno, rollizo; [*face*] lleno, rollizo; [*baby*] rechoncho; [*animal*] gordo; [*fruit, vegetable*] gordo, orondo
Ⓑ VT (= *fatten*) engordar; (= *swell*) hinchar

►**plump up** VT + ADV (= *cause to swell*) hinchar; [+ *pillow*] mullir

plump² [plʌmp] Ⓐ ADV de lleno; **it fell ~ on the roof** cayó de lleno en el techo; **to run ~ into sb** dar de cara con algn
Ⓑ VI (= *fall*) caer pesadamente, dejarse caer pesadamente

►**plump down** Ⓐ VT + ADV dejar caer; **to ~ o.s. down** desplomarse, dejarse caer pesadamente
Ⓑ VI + ADV **to ~ down on to a chair** desplomarse en un sillón, dejarse caer pesadamente en un sillón
►**plump for*** VI + PREP (= *choose*) decidirse por, optar por; (= *vote for*) votar por
plumpness ['plʌmpnɪs] N [*of person*] lo rollizo, gordura *f*; [*of face*] lo regordete, lo rollizo; [*of fruit, vegetable*] gordura *f*, lo orondo
plunder ['plʌndəʳ] Ⓐ N (= *act*) pillaje *m*, saqueo *m*; (= *loot*) botín *m*
Ⓑ VT pillar, saquear; [+ *tomb*] robar; [+ *safe*] robar (el contenido de); **they ~ed my cellar** me saquearon la bodega
plunderer ['plʌndərəʳ] N saqueador(a) *m/f*
plundering ['plʌndərɪŋ] N saqueo *m*
plunge [plʌndʒ] Ⓐ N 1 (= *dive*) (*from bank etc*) salto *m*; (*under water*) zambullida *f*; (*by professional diver*) inmersión *f*; (= *bathe*) baño *m*; **the diver rested after each ~** el buzo descansaba después de cada inmersión; **he had a ~ before breakfast** se fue a bañar antes de desayunar
2 (*fig*) [*of currency etc*] caída *f* repentina, desplome *m*; ✦***IDIOM* to take the ~** aventurarse, dar el paso decisivo; (*hum*) (= *get married*) decidir casarse; **I took the ~ and bought it** me armé de valor y lo compré
3 (*) (= *rash investment*) inversión *f* arriesgada
Ⓑ VT 1 (= *immerse*) sumergir, hundir (**into** en); **he ~d his hands into the water** hundió las manos en el agua
2 (= *thrust*) arrojar; **he ~d his hand into his pocket** metió la mano bien dentro del bolsillo; **to ~ a dagger into sb's chest** clavar un puñal en el pecho de algn
3 (*fig*) **to ~ a room into darkness** sumir un cuarto en la oscuridad; **New York was suddenly ~d into darkness** Nueva York se encontró de repente sumida en la oscuridad; **we were ~d into gloom by the news** la noticia nos hundió en la tristeza; **to ~ sb into debt** arruinar a algn
Ⓒ VI 1 (= *dive*) arrojarse, tirarse; (*into water*) lanzarse, zambullirse; **then the submarine ~d** luego el submarino se sumergió; **she ~d into ten metres of water** se zambulló en diez metros de agua
2 (= *fall*) caer, hundirse; [*road, cliff*] precipitarse; **he ~d to his death** tuvo una caída mortal; **he ~d from a fifth storey window** (= *threw himself*) se arrojó desde una ventana del quinto piso; (= *fell*) cayó desde una ventana del quinto piso; **the aircraft ~d into the sea off Dover** el avión cayó al *or* se precipitó en el mar a la altura de Dover
3 [*ship*] cabecear; [*horse*] corcovear
4 [*share prices, currency etc*] desplomarse; **to ~ into debt** sumirse en un mar de deudas
5 (*fig*) (= *rush*) lanzarse, precipitarse; **to ~ forward** precipitarse hacia adelante; **to ~ into one's work** sumirse en el trabajo; **to ~ heedlessly into danger** meterse alegremente en un peligro; **he ~d into a monologue on Plato** se puso a soltar *or* emprendió un monólogo sobre Platón
►**plunge in** Ⓐ VT + ADV [+ *head, hands*] (= *immerse*) sumergir, hundir; (= *thrust*) hundir
Ⓑ VI + ADV 1 (*into water*) zambullirse
2 (*fig*) (= *rush*) lanzarse
plunger ['plʌndʒəʳ] N (*Tech*) émbolo *m*; (*for clearing drain*) desatascador *m*
plunging ['plʌndʒɪŋ] ADJ **~ neckline** escote *m* muy bajo

plunk [plʌŋk] N (*US*) = **plonk¹**
pluperfect ['pluː'pɜːfɪkt] N (*Ling*) pluscuamperfecto *m*
plural ['plʊərəl] Ⓐ ADJ plural; **the ~ form of the noun** la forma del sustantivo en plural
Ⓑ N plural *m*; **in the ~** en (el) plural
pluralism ['plʊərəlɪzəm] N pluralismo *m*
pluralist ['plʊərəlɪst] Ⓐ ADJ pluralista
Ⓑ N pluralista *mf*
pluralistic [ˌplʊərə'lɪstɪk] ADJ pluralista
plurality [ˌplʊə'rælɪtɪ] N pluralidad *f*; **by a ~ of votes** por mayoría (simple) de votos
plus [plʌs] Ⓐ PREP 1 (*Math*) más, y; **3 ~ 4** 3 más 4; **we're ~ 500** (*Bridge*) tenemos una ventaja de 500 puntos
2 (= *in addition to*) **~ what I have to do already** además de lo que ya tengo que hacer
Ⓑ ADJ 1 (*Math, Elec*) positivo; **a ~ factor** (*fig*) un factor a favor
2 **twenty ~** veinte y pico, veintitantos; **two pounds ~** dos libras y algo más, más de dos libras; **on earnings of £40,000 ~** de un sueldo de 40.000 libras en adelante
Ⓒ N 1 (*Math*) (= *plus sign*) signo *m* (de) más, signo *m* de sumar
2 (*fig*) (= *advantage*) punto *m* a favor; **that is a ~ for him** es un punto a su favor
Ⓓ CONJ (= *moreover*) además; **~ we haven't got the money** además, no tenemos el dinero
Ⓔ CPD ► **plus fours** NPL pantalones *mpl* de golf, pantalones *mpl* holgados de media pierna ► **plus sign** N signo *m* (de) más, signo *m* de sumar
plush [plʌʃ] Ⓐ N (= *fabric*) felpa *f*
Ⓑ ADJ afelpado; (*fig*) de mucho lujo
plushy* ['plʌʃɪ] ADJ de mucho lujo
Plutarch ['pluːtɑːk] N Plutarco
Pluto ['pluːtəʊ] N (*Astron, Myth*) Plutón *m*
plutocracy [ˌpluː'tɒkrəsɪ] N plutocracia *f*
plutocrat ['pluːtəʊkræt] N plutócrata *mf*
plutocratic [ˌpluːtəʊ'krætɪk] ADJ plutocrático
plutonium [pluː'təʊnɪəm] N plutonio *m*
pluviometer [ˌpluːvɪ'ɒmɪtəʳ] N pluviómetro *m*
ply [plaɪ] Ⓐ VT 1 [+ *needle, tool*] manejar, emplear; [+ *oars*] emplear; [+ *river, route*] navegar por; (*liter*) [+ *sea*] navegar por, surcar (*liter*); **to ~ one's trade** ejercer su profesión
2 **to ~ sb for information** importunar a algn pidiéndole información; **to ~ sb with questions** acosar a algn con preguntas; **to ~ sb with drink** no parar de ofrecer de beber a algn
Ⓑ VI **to ~ between** ir y venir de; **to ~ for hire** ir en busca de clientes
-ply [plaɪ] ADJ (*ending in compounds*) **three-ply wood** madera *f* de tres capas; **three-ply wool** lana *f* de tres cabos
plywood ['plaɪwʊd] N madera *f* contrachapada
PM N ABBR 1 (*Brit*) = **Prime Minister**
2 (*Jur, Med*) = **post mortem**
pm ADV ABBR (= **post meridiem**) p.m., de la tarde
PMG N ABBR 1 (*Brit*) = **Paymaster General**
2 = **Postmaster General**
PMS N ABBR (= **premenstrual syndrome**) SPM *m*
PMT N ABBR (= **premenstrual tension**) SPM *m*
PN, P/N N ABBR (= **promissory note**) pagaré *m*
PND N ABBR = **postnatal depression**
pneumatic [njuː'mætɪk] Ⓐ ADJ neumático
Ⓑ CPD ► **pneumatic drill** N taladradora *f* neumática

pneumoconiosis [ˌnjuːməʊˌkəʊnɪ'əʊsɪs] N neumoconiosis *f*
pneumonia [njuː'məʊnɪə] N pulmonía *f*, neumonía *f*
Pnom Penh ['nɒm'pen] N = **Phnom Penh**
PO N ABBR 1 (= **Post Office**) oficina *f* de correos; **PO Box** apdo., aptdo., CP (*LAm*)
2 (*Aer*) (= **Pilot Officer**) oficial *m* piloto
3 (*Naut*) (= **Petty Officer**) suboficial *m* de marina
po* [pəʊ] N (*Brit*) orinal *m*
p.o. N ABBR (*Brit*) (= **postal order**) g.p., g/p
POA Ⓐ N ABBR (*Brit*) (= **Prison Officers' Association**) *sindicato de empleados de cárcel*
Ⓑ ABBR (*Comm*) (= **price on application**) el precio a solicitud
poach¹ [pəʊtʃ] VT (*Culin*) [+ *egg*] escalfar; [+ *fish etc*] hervir
poach² [pəʊtʃ] Ⓐ VT 1 (= *hunt*) cazar en vedado; (= *fish*) pescar en vedado
2 (*fig*) (*) (= *steal*) birlar*, quitar
Ⓑ VI (= *hunt*) cazar furtivamente; (= *fish*) pescar furtivamente; ✦***IDIOM* to ~ on sb's preserves** *or* **territory** invadir *or* pisar el terreno a algn
poached [pəʊtʃt] ADJ [*egg*] escalfado; [*fish etc*] hervido
poacher¹ ['pəʊtʃəʳ] N (= *person*) cazador(a) *m/f* furtivo/a; **~ turned gamekeeper** (*Brit*) (*fig*) *persona que abandona una actividad para hacer todo lo contrario*
poacher² ['pəʊtʃəʳ] N (*for eggs*) escalfador *m*
poaching ['pəʊtʃɪŋ] N caza *f*/pesca *f* furtiva
POB ABBR (= **post office box**) apdo
pochard ['pəʊtʃəd] N porrón *m* común
pock [pɒk] N (= *pustule*) pústula *f*; (*also* **~mark**) (= *scar*) picadura *f*, hoyuelo *m*
pocked [pɒkt] ADJ = **pockmarked**
pocket ['pɒkɪt] Ⓐ N 1 (*in trousers etc*) bolsillo *m*, bolsa *f* (*Mex*); **with his hands in his ~s** con las manos (metidas) en los bolsillos; ✦***IDIOMS* to have sth/sb in one's ~** tener algo/a algn en el bolsillo; **to line one's ~s** forrarse; **to live in each other's** *or* **one another's ~s** (*Brit*) vivir el uno para el otro, no dejarse ni a sol ni a sombra; **to put one's hand in one's ~** echar mano al bolsillo; *see also* **pick B5**
2 (*fig*) (= *finances, budget*) **to have deep ~s** tener muchos posibles, tener las espaldas bien cubiertas; **that hurts his ~** eso le duele en el bolsillo; **to be in ~** salir ganando; **to be £5 in ~** haber ganado 5 libras; **to be out of ~** salir perdiendo; **to be £5 out of ~** haber perdido 5 libras
3 (*Billiards*) tronera *f*
4 (*fig*) (= *restricted area, space*) **~ of resistance** foco *m* de resistencia; **~ of warm air** bolsa *f* de aire caliente
Ⓑ VT 1 (*lit*) meter *or* guardar en el bolsillo; ✦***IDIOM* to ~ one's pride** aguantarse, tragarse el orgullo
2 (*Billiards*) entronerar
3 (*fig*) (= *gain, steal*) embolsar; **he ~ed half the takings** se embolsó la mitad de la recaudación
Ⓒ CPD de bolsillo ► **pocket battleship** N acorazado *m* de bolsillo ► **pocket calculator** N calculadora *f* de bolsillo ► **pocket diary** N agenda *f* de bolsillo ► **pocket edition** N edición *f* de bolsillo ► **pocket handkerchief** N pañuelo *m* (de bolsillo) ► **pocket money** N dinero *m* para gastos (personales); (*children's*) dinero *m* de bolsillo
pocketbook ['pɒkɪtbʊk] N 1 (= *notebook*) cuaderno *m*

[2] (*US*) (= *handbag*) bolso *m*, cartera *f* (*LAm*); (= *wallet*) cartera *f*, billetero *m*; (= *purse*) monedero *m*

pocketful ['pɒkɪtfʊl] N (*pl* **pocketfuls**) **a ~ of nuts** un bolsillo (lleno) de nueces

pocketknife ['pɒkɪtnaɪf] N (*pl* **pocketknives**) navaja *f*

pocket-size(d) ['pɒkɪtsaɪz(d)] ADJ de bolsillo

pockmark ['pɒkmɑːk] N picadura *f*, hoyuelo *m*

pockmarked ['pɒkmɑːkt] ADJ [*face*] picado de viruelas; [*surface*] marcado de hoyos; **to be ~ with** estar marcado *or* acribillado de

POD ABBR = **payment on delivery**

pod [pɒd] N vaina *f*

podgy* ['pɒdʒɪ] ADJ (*compar* **podgier**; *superl* **podgiest**) (*esp Brit*) gordinflón*; [*face*] mofletudo*

podiatrist [pɒ'diːətrɪst] N (*US*) pedicuro/a *m/f*

podiatry [pɒ'diːətrɪ] N (*US*) pedicura *f*

podium ['pəʊdɪəm] N (*pl* **podiums, podia** ['pəʊdɪə]) podio *m*

POE ABBR [1] = **port of embarkation**
[2] = **port of entry**

poem ['pəʊɪm] N (*short*) poesía *f*; (*long, narrative*) poema *m*; **Lorca's ~s** las poesías de Lorca, la obra poética de Lorca

poet ['pəʊɪt] Ⓐ N poeta *mf*
Ⓑ CPD ► **poet laureate** N (*pl* **poets laureate**) poeta *mf* laureado/a

POET LAUREATE

El poeta de la Corte, denominado **Poet Laureate**, *ocupa un puesto vitalicio al servicio de la Casa Real británica. Era tradición que escribiera poemas conmemorativos para ocasiones oficiales, aunque hoy día esto es poco frecuente. El primer poeta así distinguido fue Ben Jonson, en 1616.*

poetaster [ˌpəʊɪ'tæstəʳ] N poetastro *m*

poetess† ['pəʊɪtes] N poetisa *f*

poetic [pəʊ'etɪk] Ⓐ ADJ poético
Ⓑ CPD ► **poetic justice** N justicia *f* divina ► **poetic licence, poetic license** (*US*) N licencia *f* poética

poetical [pəʊ'etɪkəl] ADJ poético

poetically [pəʊ'etɪkəlɪ] ADV poéticamente

poeticize [pəʊ'etɪsaɪz] VT (= *enhance*) poetizar, adornar con detalles poéticos; (= *translate into verse*) hacer un poema *or* una versión poética de

poetics [pəʊ'etɪks] NSING poética *f*

poetry ['pəʊɪtrɪ] Ⓐ N poesía *f*; ✦*IDIOM* **~ in motion** poesía *f* en movimiento
Ⓑ CPD ► **poetry magazine** N revista *f* de poesía ► **poetry reading** N recital *m or* lectura *f* de poesías

po-faced* [ˌpəʊ'feɪst] ADJ que mira con desaprobación, severo

pogrom ['pɒgrəm] N pogrom *m*

poignancy ['pɔɪnjənsɪ] N patetismo *m*

poignant ['pɔɪnjənt] ADJ conmovedor, patético

poignantly ['pɔɪnjəntlɪ] ADV [*describe, write, speak*] de modo conmovedor

poinsettia [pɔɪn'setɪə] N flor *f* de pascua

▼**point** [pɔɪnt] Ⓐ N [1] (*Geom*) (= *dot*) punto *m*; (= *decimal point*) punto *m* decimal, coma *f*; **two ~ six (2.6)** dos coma seis (2,6)
[2] (*on scale, thermometer*) punto *m*; **boiling/freezing ~** punto de ebullición/congelación; **the thermometer went up three ~s** el termómetro subió tres grados; **the index is down three ~s** el índice bajó tres enteros; **the shares went down two ~s** las acciones bajaron dos enteros
[3] (*on compass*) cuarta *f*, grado *m*; **from all ~s of the compass** desde los cuatro rincones del mundo
[4] [*of needle, pencil, knife etc*] punta *f*; [*of pen*] puntilla *f*; **to put a ~ on a pencil** sacar punta a un lápiz; **a star with five ~s** una estrella de cinco puntas; **at the ~ of a sword** a punta de espada; **with a sharp ~** puntiagudo; ✦*IDIOM* **not to put too fine a ~ on it** (= *frankly*) hablando sin rodeos
[5] (= *place*) punto *m*, lugar *m*; **he had reached the ~ of resigning** había llegado al punto de la dimisión; **this was the low/high ~ of his career** este fue el momento más bajo/el momento cumbre de su carrera; **at all ~s** por todas partes, en todos los sitios; **delivered free to all ~s in Spain** entrega gratuita en cualquier punto de España; **the train stops at Carlisle and all ~s south** el tren para en Carlisle y todas las estaciones al sur; **at this ~** (*in space*) aquí, allí; (*in time*) en este *or* aquel momento; **when it comes to the ~** en el momento de la verdad; **when it came to the ~ of paying ...** cuando llegó la hora de pagar ..., a la hora de pagar ...; **there was no ~ of contact between them** no existía ningún nexo de unión entre ellos; **to be on** *or* **at the ~ of death** estar a punto de morir; **~ of departure** (*lit, fig*) punto *m* de partida; **~ of entry** (*into a country*) punto *m* de entrada, paso *m* fronterizo; **from that ~ on ...** de allí en adelante ...; **to reach the ~ of no return** (*lit, fig*) llegar al punto sin retorno; **to be on the ~ of doing sth** estar a punto de hacer algo; **abrupt to the ~ of rudeness** tan brusco que resulta grosero; **up to a ~** (= *in part*) hasta cierto punto, en cierta medida; **at the ~ where the road forks** donde se bifurca el camino
[6] (= *counting unit*) (*in Sport, test*) punto *m*; **~s against** puntos *mpl* en contra; **~s for** puntos *mpl* a favor; **to win on ~s** ganar por puntos; **to give sth/sb ~s out of ten** dar a algo/algn un número de puntos sobre diez; **to score ten ~s** marcar diez puntos
[7] (= *most important thing*) **the ~ is that ...** el caso es que ...; **that's the whole ~** ◊ **that's just the ~!** ¡eso es!, ¡ahí está!; **the ~ of the joke/story** la gracia del chiste/cuento; **to be beside the ~** no venir al caso; **it is beside the ~ that ...** no importa que + *subjun*; **do you get the ~?** ¿entiendes por dónde voy *or* lo que quiero decir?; **to miss the ~** no comprender; **that's not the ~** esto no viene al caso, no es eso; **to get off the ~** salirse del tema; **his remarks were to the ~** sus observaciones venían al caso; **an argument very much to the ~** un argumento muy a propósito; **that is hardly to the ~** eso apenas hace al caso; **to come** *or* **get to the ~** ir al grano; **to get back to the ~** volver al tema; **to keep** *or* **stick to the ~** no salirse del tema; **to speak to the ~** (= *relevantly*) hablar acertadamente, hablar con tino
[8] (= *purpose, use*) [*of action, visit*] finalidad *f*, propósito *m*; **it gave ~ to the argument** hizo ver la importancia del argumento; **there's little ~ in telling him** no merece la pena *or* no tiene mucho sentido decírselo; **there's no ~ in staying** no tiene sentido quedarse; **a long story that seemed to have no ~ at all** una larga historia que no parecía venir al caso en absoluto; **to see the ~ of sth** encontrar *or* ver sentido a algo, entender el porqué de algo; **I don't see the ~ of** *or* **in doing that** no veo qué sentido tiene hacer eso; **what's the ~?** ¿para qué?, ¿a cuento de qué?; **what's the ~ of** *or* **in trying?** ¿de qué sirve intentar?
[9] (= *detail, argument*) punto *m*; **the ~s to remember are ...** los puntos a retener son los siguientes ...; **to carry** *or* **gain** *or* **win one's ~** salirse con la suya; **five-~ plan** proyecto *m* de cinco puntos; **to argue ~ by ~** razonar punto por punto; **in ~ of fact** en realidad, el caso es que; **I think she has a ~** creo que tiene un poco de razón; **you've got** *or* **you have a ~ there!** ¡tienes razón!, ¡es cierto! (*LAm*); **the ~ at issue** el asunto, el tema en cuestión; **to make one's ~** convencer; **you've made your ~** nos *etc* has convencido; **he made the following ~s** dijo lo siguiente; **to make the ~ that ...** hacer ver *or* comprender que ...; **to make a ~ of doing sth** ◊ **make it a ~ to do sth** poner empeño en hacer algo; **on this ~** sobre este punto; **on that ~** en cuanto a eso; **on that ~ we agree** sobre eso estamos de acuerdo; **to differ on a ~** no estar de acuerdo en un particular; **to press the ~** insistir (**that** en que); **to stretch a ~** hacer una excepción; **I take your ~** acepto lo que dices; **~ taken!** ¡de acuerdo!
[10] **~ of view** punto *m* de vista; **from the ~ of view of** desde el punto de vista de; **to see** *or* **understand sb's ~ of view** comprender el punto de vista de algn; **to look at a matter from all ~s of view** considerar una cuestión bajo todos sus aspectos; **to come round to sb's ~ of view** adoptar el criterio de algn
[11] (= *matter*) cuestión *f*; **~ of detail** detalle *m*; **~ of honour** cuestión *f or* punto *m* de honor; **~ of interest** punto *m* interesante; **~ of law** cuestión *f* de derecho; **~ of order** cuestión *f* de procedimiento; **a ~ of principle** una cuestión de principios
[12] (= *characteristic*) cualidad *f*; **what ~s should I look for?** ¿qué puntos debo buscar?; **bad ~s** cualidades *fpl* malas; **good ~s** cualidades *fpl* buenas; **he has his ~s** tiene algunas cualidades buenas; **tact isn't one of his strong ~s** la discreción no es uno de sus (puntos) fuertes; **it was always his strong ~** siempre ha sido su punto fuerte; **weak ~** flaco *m*, punto *m* flaco, punto *m* débil
[13] **points** (*Brit Rail*) agujas *fpl*; (*Aut*) platinos *mpl*
[14] (*Brit Elec*) (*also* **power ~**) toma *f* de corriente, tomacorriente *m* (*S. Cone*)
[15] (*Geog*) punta *f*, promontorio *m*, cabo *m*
[16] (*Typ*) (= *punctuation mark*) punto *m*; **9 ~ black** (*Typ*) negritas *fpl* del cuerpo 9
[17] (*Ballet*) (*usu pl*) punta *f*; **to dance on ~s** bailar sobre las puntas
Ⓑ VT [1] (= *aim, direct*) apuntar (**at** a); **to ~ a gun at sb** apuntar a algn con un fusil; **to ~ one's finger at sth/sb** señalar con el dedo algo/a algn; **to ~ one's toes** hacer puntas; **he ~ed the car towards London** puso el coche rumbo a Londres; ✦*IDIOM* **to ~ the finger at sb** señalar con el dedo a algn
[2] (= *indicate, show*) señalar, indicar; **would you ~ me in the direction of the town hall?** ¿me quiere decir dónde está el ayuntamiento?; **we ~ed him in the right direction** le indicamos el camino; **to ~ the moral that ...** subrayar la moraleja de que ...; **to ~ the way** (*lit, fig*) señalar el camino
[3] (*Constr*) [+ *wall*] rejuntar
[4] [+ *text*] puntuar; [+ *Hebrew etc*] puntar
Ⓒ VI [1] (*lit*) señalar; **to ~ at** *or* **towards sth/sb** (*with finger*) señalar algo/a algn con el dedo; **the car isn't ~ing in the right direction** el coche no va en la dirección correcta; **it ~s (to the) north** apunta hacia el norte; **the hands ~ed to midnight** las agujas marcaban las 12 de la noche

➤ LANGUAGE IN USE: **point A5** 26.3 **A9** 26.1 **A11** 26.2

2 (*fig*) (= *indicate*) indicar; **everything ~s that way** todo parece indicarlo; **this ~s to the fact that …** esto indica que …; **the evidence ~s to her** las pruebas indican que ella es la culpable; **everything ~s to his success** todo anuncia su éxito; **everything ~s to the festival being a lively one** el festival se anuncia animado
3 **to ~ to sth** (= *call attention to*) señalar algo
4 [*dog*] mostrar la caza, parar
Ⓓ CPD ► **point duty** N (*Brit Police*) control *m* de la circulación; **to be on ~ duty** dirigir la circulación *or* el tráfico ► **point of reference** N punto *m* de referencia ► **point of sale** N punto *m* de venta ► **points decision** N (*Boxing*) decisión *f* a los puntos ► **points failure** N (*Brit Rail*) fallo *m* en el sistema de agujas ► **points system** N (*gen*) sistema *m* de puntos; (*Aut*) *sistema de penalización por las infracciones cometidas por un conductor que puede llevar a determinadas sanciones (p. ej. la retirada del permiso de conducir)* ► **points victory, points win** N victoria *f* a los puntos; *see also* **point-of-sale**

►**point out** VT + ADV 1 (= *show*) señalar; **to ~ out sth to sb** señalar algo a algn
2 (= *explain*) señalar; **to ~ out sb's mistakes** señalar los errores de algn; **to ~ out that** señalar que; **to ~ out to sb the advantages of a car** señalar *or* hacer notar a algn las ventajas de tener coche; **may I ~ out that …** permítaseme observar que …

►**point up** VT + ADV subrayar, destacar

point-blank [ˈpɔɪntˈblæŋk] Ⓐ ADJ 1 [*shot*] (hecho) a quemarropa; **at ~ range** a bocajarro, a quemarropa
2 [*question*] directo; [*refusal*] rotundo, categórico
Ⓑ ADV [*shoot*] a bocajarro, a quemarropa; [*demand*] tajantemente, categóricamente; [*refuse*] rotundamente, categóricamente; **to ask sb sth ~** preguntar algo a algn a quemarropa

point-by-point [ˈpɔɪntbaɪˈpɔɪnt] ADJ punto por punto

pointed [ˈpɔɪntɪd] ADJ 1 (*lit*) [*chin, nose, shoes*] puntiagudo; [*stick*] de punta afilada; [*hat*] de pico; (*Archit*) [*arch, window, roof*] apuntado, ojival
2 (*fig*) [*remark*] mal intencionado; [*criticism*] mordaz; [*question*] directo; [*look*] penetrante; **the book makes ~ reference to his numerous affairs** el libro hace alusiones directas a sus numerosas aventuras amorosas

pointedly [ˈpɔɪntɪdlɪ] ADV [*say*] intencionadamente; [*ask*] sin rodeos, directamente; **he was staring ~ at the clock** miraba fijamente al reloj sin ocultar su prisa (*or* aburrimiento, *etc*); **she ~ ignored him** lo ignoró intencionadamente *or* aposta; **he was ~ left off the guest list** se lo excluyó de la lista de invitados intencionadamente

pointer [ˈpɔɪntəʳ] N 1 (= *indicator*) indicador *m*, aguja *f*; [*of balance*] fiel *m*
2 (= *stick*) puntero *m*
3 (= *dog*) perro *m* de muestra
4 (= *clue, indication*) indicación *f*, pista *f*; **it is a ~ to a possible solution** es una indicación *or* pista para una posible solución; **there is at present no ~ to the outcome** por ahora nada indica qué resultado tendrá; **this is a ~ to the guilty man** es una pista que conducirá al criminal
5 (= *advice*) consejo *m*

pointillism [ˈpwæntɪlɪzəm] N puntillismo *m*

pointing [ˈpɔɪntɪŋ] N (*Constr*) (= *action*) rejuntado *m*; (= *mortar*) juntas *fpl*

pointless [ˈpɔɪntlɪs] ADJ 1 (= *useless*) inútil; **it is ~ to complain** es inútil quejarse, de nada sirve quejarse
2 (= *motiveless*) sin motivo, inmotivado; **an apparently ~ crime** en apariencia, un crimen inmotivado
3 (= *meaningless*) sin sentido; **a ~ existence** una vida sin sentido, una vida que carece de propósito

pointlessly [ˈpɔɪntlɪslɪ] ADV (= *vainly*) inútilmente; (= *without motive*) sin motivo

pointlessness [ˈpɔɪntlɪsnɪs] N falta *f* de sentido, inutilidad *f*; **the ~ of war** la insensatez de la guerra

point-of-sale [ˌpɔɪntəvˈseɪl] ADJ [*advertising etc*] en el punto de venta

pointsman [ˈpɔɪntsmən] N (*pl* **pointsmen**) (*Rail*) encargado *m* del cambio de agujas

point-to-point [ˈpɔɪnttəˈpɔɪnt] N (*also* **~ race**) *carrera de caballos a campo traviesa*

pointy* [ˈpɔɪntɪ] ADJ [*hat, ears, shoes*] picudo, puntiagudo

poise [pɔɪz] Ⓐ N 1 (= *balance*) equilibrio *m*
2 (= *carriage of head, body*) porte *m*; **she dances with such ~** baila con tal elegancia *or* tal garbo
3 (= *composure or dignity of manner*) elegancia *f*, aplomo *m*; **she does it with great ~** lo hace con el mayor aplomo; **he lacks ~** le falta confianza en sí mismo *or* aplomo
Ⓑ VT 1 (= *hold ready or balanced*) equilibrar, balancear; **the rock was ~d on the edge of the cliff** la roca se balanceaba al borde del precipicio; **the hawk was ~d in the air, about to swoop on its prey** el águila se cernía inmóvil en el aire, a punto de caer sobre su presa; **a waitress approached, pencil ~d** se acercó una camarera, lápicero en ristre; **he remained ~d between life and death** permanecía debatiéndose entre la vida y la muerte
2 **to be ~d** (*fig*) (= *ready, all set*) estar listo; **they are ~d to attack** *or* **for the attack** están listos para atacar

poised [pɔɪzd] ADJ (= *self-possessed*) sereno, ecuánime

poison [ˈpɔɪzn] Ⓐ N (*lit, fig*) veneno *m*; **to die of ~** morir envenenado; **to take ~** envenenarse; **they hate each other like ~** se odian a muerte; ✦***IDIOM*** **what's your ~?*** (*hum*) ¿qué toma?
Ⓑ VT 1 envenenar; (*chemically*) intoxicar; **the wells were ~ed** habían echado sustancias tóxicas a los pozos
2 (*fig*) envenenar, emponzoñar; **to ~ sb's mind (against sth/sb)** envenenar la mente de algn (contra algo/algn); **a ~ed chalice** (*esp Brit*) un arma de doble filo
Ⓒ CPD ► **poison gas** N gas *m* tóxico ► **poison ivy** N (= *plant*) hiedra *f* venenosa; (= *rash*) urticaria *f* ► **poison oak** N (= *plant*) zumaque *m* venenoso; (*loosely*) = **poison ivy** ► **poison pen letter** N anónimo *m* ofensivo

poisoner [ˈpɔɪznəʳ] N envenenador(a) *m/f*

poisoning [ˈpɔɪznɪŋ] N (*lit, fig*) envenenamiento *m*, intoxicación *f*; **to die of ~** morir envenenado *or* intoxicado

poisonous [ˈpɔɪznəs] ADJ 1 [*snake etc*] venenoso; [*substance, plant, fumes etc*] tóxico
2 (*fig*) (= *damaging*) pernicioso; (= *very bad*) horrible, malísimo; **this ~ propaganda** esta propaganda perniciosa; **the play was ~** la obra fue horrible; **he's a ~ individual** es una persona odiosa

poke¹ [pəʊk] Ⓐ N 1 (= *jab*) empujón *m*, empellón *m*; (*with elbow*) codazo *m*; (*with poker*) hurgonada *f*, hurgonazo *m*; **he gave me a ~ in the ribs** (*with finger*) me hincó el dedo en las costillas; (*with elbow*) me dio un codazo en las costillas; **to give the fire a ~** atizar la lumbre, remover la lumbre
2 **to have a ~** (*Brit***) (= *have sex*) echar(se) un polvo**
Ⓑ VT 1 (= *jab with stick, finger etc*) pinchar, clavar; [+ *fire*] hurgar, atizar, remover; **to ~ sb in the ribs** hincar el dedo a algn en las costillas; **to ~ sb with a stick** dar a algn un empujón con un palo; **you nearly ~d me in the eye with that!** ¡casi me saltas un ojo con eso!
2 (= *thrust*) introducir; **to ~ a rag into a tube** meter un trapo en un tubo; **to ~ a stick into a crack** meter un palo en una grieta; **to ~ a stick into the ground** clavar un palo en el suelo; **to ~ one's head out (of a window)** sacar *or* asomar la cabeza (por una ventana); *see also* **nose A1**
3 [+ *hole*] hacer; **to ~ a hole in a picture** hacer un agujero en un cuadro
4 **to ~ fun at sb** reírse de algn
5 (*US**) (= *punch*) pegar un puñetazo a
Ⓒ VI **to ~ at sth with a stick** hurgar algo con un bastón

►**poke about*, poke around*** VI + ADV (*in drawers, attic etc*) fisgonear, hurgar; (*round shops*) curiosear; (*pej*) fisgar, hacer indagaciones a hurtadillas; **we spent a day poking about in the shops** pasamos un día curioseando en las tiendas; **and now you come poking about!** ¡y ahora te metes a husmear!*

►**poke out** Ⓐ VI + ADV (= *stick out*) salir
Ⓑ VT + ADV **you almost ~d my eye out** casi me saltas el ojo

poke² [pəʊk] N (*esp Scot*) (= *bag*) saco *m*, bolsa *f*; *see also* **pig**

poker¹ [ˈpəʊkəʳ] N (*for fire*) atizador *m*, hurgón *m*

poker² [ˈpəʊkəʳ] N (*Cards*) póker *m*, póquer *m*; ✦***IDIOM*** **to have a ~ face** tener una cara impasible, tener una cara de póker; *see also* **stiff A3**

poker-faced [ˈpəʊkəˈfeɪst] ADJ de cara impasible, con cara de póquer; **they looked on ~** miraron impasibles *or* sin expresión

poky [ˈpəʊkɪ] ADJ (*compar* **pokier**, *superl* **pokiest**) (*pej*) **a ~ room** un cuartucho*; **a ~ town** un pueblucho*

Polack** [ˈpəʊlæk] N (*pej*) polaco/a *m/f*

Poland [ˈpəʊlənd] N Polonia *f*

polar [ˈpəʊləʳ] Ⓐ ADJ (*Elec, Geog*) polar
Ⓑ CPD ► **polar bear** N oso *m* polar ► **polar (ice) cap** N casquete *m* polar ► **Polar Circle** N Círculo *m* Polar

polarity [pəʊˈlærɪtɪ] N 1 (*Elec, Phys*) polaridad *f*
2 (*frm*) (*fig*) (*between tendencies, opinions, people*) polaridad *f*

polarization [ˌpəʊləraɪˈzeɪʃən] N 1 (*Elec, Phys*) polarización *f*
2 (*frm*) (*fig*) [*of tendencies, opinions, people*] polarización *f*

polarize [ˈpəʊləraɪz] Ⓐ VT polarizar
Ⓑ VI polarizarse

Polaroid® [ˈpəʊlərɔɪd] Ⓐ ADJ Polaroid®
Ⓑ N 1 (*also* **~ camera**) Polaroid® *f*; (= *photograph*) foto *f* de Polaroid®
2 **Polaroids** (*also* **~ sunglasses**) gafas *fpl* de sol antirreflectantes

pole¹ [pəʊl] Ⓐ N 1 (= *rod*) palo *m*; (= *flag pole*) asta *f*; (= *telegraph pole*) poste *m*; (= *tent-pole*) mástil *m*; (= *curtain pole*) barra *f*; (*for gymnastics*) percha *f*; (*for vaulting, punting*) pértiga *f*, garrocha *f* (*LAm*); (*for fencing*) estaca *f*; [*of cart*] vara *f*, lanza *f*; ✦***IDIOM*** **to be up the**

➤ LANGUAGE IN USE: **point out 2** 26.1, 26.2, 26.3

~†* estar chiflado*

2 (= *archaic measure*) *medida de longitud, equivalente a 5,029 m*

Ⓑ VT [+ *punt etc*] impeler con pértiga

Ⓒ CPD ► **pole bean** N (*US*) judía *f* trepadora ► **pole position** N (*Motor racing*) posición *f* de cabeza en la parrilla de salida, pole *f*; (*fig*) posición *f* de ventaja ► **pole vault** N salto *m* de pértiga ► **pole vaulter** N saltador(a) *m/f* de pértiga, pertiguista *mf* ► **pole vaulting** N salto *m* de pértiga; *see also* **pole-vault**

pole² [pəʊl] Ⓐ N (*Elec, Geog, Astron*) polo *m*; **North/South Pole** Polo *m* Norte/Sur; **from ~ to ~** de polo a polo; ✦**IDIOM to be ~s apart** ser polos opuestos

Ⓑ CPD ► **Pole Star** N Estrella *f* Polar

Pole [pəʊl] N polaco/a *m/f*

poleaxe, poleax (*US*) ['pəʊlæks] VT desnucar; (*) (*fig*) pasmar, aturdir

polecat ['pəʊlkæt] N (*pl* **polecats** *or* **polecat**) (*Brit*) turón *m*; (*US*) mofeta *f*

Pol. Econ., pol. econ. N ABBR = **political economy**

polemic [pɒ'lemɪk] Ⓐ ADJ polémico

Ⓑ N polémica *f*

polemical [pɒ'lemɪkəl] ADJ polémico

polemicist [pɒ'lemɪsɪst] N polemista *mf*

polemics [pɒ'lemɪks] NSING polémica *f*

pole-vault ['pəʊlvɔːlt] VI saltar con pértiga

police [pə'liːs] Ⓐ NPL policía *fsing*; **to join the ~** hacerse policía; **more than a hundred ~ were called in** más de cien policías hicieron acto de presencia

Ⓑ VT [+ *frontier*] vigilar, patrullar por; [+ *area*] mantener el orden público en; [+ *process*] vigilar, controlar; **the frontier is ~d by UN patrols** la frontera la vigilan las patrullas de la ONU; **the area used to be ~d by Britain** la zona estaba antes bajo control de Gran Bretaña

Ⓒ CPD de policía ► **police brutality** N violencia *f* policial ► **police captain** N (*US*) subjefe *mf* ► **police car** N coche *m* de policía ► **police constable** N (*Brit*) guardia *mf*, policía *mf* ► **police court** N tribunal *m* de policía, tribunal *m* correccional ► **police custody** N **in ~ custody** bajo custodia policial ► **police department** N (*US*) policía *f* ► **police dog** N perro *m* policía ► **police escort** N escolta *f* policial ► **police force** N cuerpo *m* de policía ► **police inspector** N inspector(a) *m/f* de policía ► **police officer** N guardia *mf*, policía *mf* ► **police protection** N protección *f* policial ► **police record** N antecedentes *mpl* penales ► **police state** N estado *m* policía ► **police station** N comisaría *f* ► **police work** N trabajo *m* policial *or* de la policía

policeman [pə'liːsmən] N (*pl* **policemen**) guardia *m*, policía *m*

policewoman [pə'liːsˌwʊmən] N (*pl* **policewomen**) mujer *f* policía

policing [pə'liːsɪŋ] N [*of area*] mantenimiento *m* del orden público *or* del servicio de policía; [*of process*] vigilación *f*, control *m*

policy¹ ['pɒlɪsɪ] Ⓐ N 1 (*gen, principles*) política *f*; [*of party, at election*] programa *m*; [*of newspaper*] normas *fpl* de conducta; **it's a matter of ~** es cuestión de política; **that's not my ~** ése no es mi sistema; **to change one's ~** cambiar de táctica; **it is a good/bad ~** es buena/mala táctica; **it would be contrary to public ~ to do this** iría en contra del interés nacional hacer esto

2 (†) (= *prudence, prudent procedure*) discreción *f*; **it is ~ to wait a few days** es prudente esperar unos días

Ⓑ CPD ► **policy decision** N decisión *f* de principio ► **policy statement** N declaración *f* de política

policy² ['pɒlɪsɪ] N (*also* **insurance ~**) póliza *f*; **to take out a ~** sacar una póliza, hacerse un seguro

policy-holder ['pɒlɪsɪˌhəʊldəʳ] N (*Insurance*) asegurado/a *m/f*

policy-maker ['pɒlɪsɪˌmeɪkəʳ] N diseñador(a) *m/f* de políticas

policy-making ['pɒlɪsɪˌmeɪkɪŋ] Ⓐ N elaboración *f* de la política a seguir

Ⓑ ADJ [*body, process*] que organiza la política a seguir; [*role*] en la organización de la política a seguir

polio ['pəʊlɪəʊ] N poliomielitis *f*, polio *f*

poliomyelitis ['pəʊlɪəʊmaɪə'laɪtɪs] N poliomielitis *f*

Polish ['pəʊlɪʃ] Ⓐ ADJ polaco

Ⓑ N 1 (*Ling*) polaco *m*

2 **the ~** (= *people*) los polacos

polish ['pɒlɪʃ] Ⓐ N 1 (= *shoe polish*) betún *m*, bola *f* (*Mex*); (= *furniture polish, floor polish*) cera *f*; (= *metal polish*) líquido *m* para limpiar metales; (= *nail polish*) esmalte *m* *or* laca *f* (para las uñas)

2 (= *act*) **my shoes need a ~** mis zapatos necesitan una limpieza; **to give sth a ~** dar brillo a algo

3 (= *shine*) lustre *m*, brillo *m*; **high ~** lustre *m* brillante; **the buttons have lost their ~** los botones han perdido su brillo *or* se han deslustrado; **to put a ~ on sth** sacar brillo a algo; **the water takes the ~ off** el agua quita el brillo

4 (*fig*) (= *refinement*) refinamiento *m*; [*of artistry etc*] elegancia *f*; **he lacks ~** le falta refinamiento

Ⓑ VT 1 (*gen*) pulir; [+ *shoes*] limpiar, lustrar (*esp LAm*), bolear (*Mex*), embolar (*Chile*); [+ *floor, furniture*] encerar; [+ *pans, metal, silver*] pulir; (*mechanically, industrially*) pulimentar

2 (*fig*) (*also* **~ up**) (= *improve*) perfeccionar; [+ *manners*] refinar; [+ *style etc*] pulir, limar; [+ *one's Spanish etc*] pulir, perfeccionar

►**polish off*** VT + ADV [+ *work, food, drink*] despacharse; [+ *person etc*] liquidar*

►**polish up** VT + ADV = **polish B2**

polished ['pɒlɪʃt] ADJ 1 (*lit*) [*metal, wood*] pulido

2 (*fig*) [*style etc*] pulido, elegante; [*person*] culto, refinado; [*manners*] refinado

polisher ['pɒlɪʃəʳ] N (= *person*) pulidor(a) *m/f*; (= *machine*) enceradora *f*

polishing machine ['pɒlɪʃɪŋməˌʃiːn] N pulidor *m*; (*for floors*) enceradora *f*

Politburo ['pɒlɪtbjʊərəʊ] N Politburó *m*

polite [pə'laɪt] ADJ [*person*] cortés, educado; [*smile*] cortés, amable; [*request*] cortés; **he was very ~ to me** fue muy cortés *or* educado conmigo; **I was too ~ to ask** no pregunté por educación *or* cortesía; **he said he liked it but I think he was just being ~** dijo que le gustaba pero creo que lo hizo sólo por cumplir; **it's ~ to ask permission** es de buena educación pedir permiso; **it's not ~ to stare** es una falta de educación *or* es de mala educación quedarse mirando a la gente; **his speech received ~ applause** su discurso recibió el aplauso de rigor *or* cortesía; **that's not the sort of thing you do in ~ company** ése no es el tipo de cosa que harías entre gente educada *or* fina; **they sat there making ~ conversation** estaban ahí sentados, dando conversación para quedar bien; **he showed a ~ interest in my work** mostró interés en mi trabajo sólo por cumplir; **in ~ society** en la buena sociedad; **that's not a very ~ thing to say** esas cosas no se dicen; **I was trying to think of a ~ way to say no** buscaba una forma de decir "no" sin ofender; **"cosy" is the ~ word for the flat's dimensions** (*iro*) siendo generoso, podría decirse que las dimensiones del piso lo hacen acogedor

politely [pə'laɪtlɪ] ADV 1 (= *courteously*) [*ask, listen, refuse*] cortésmente; [*smile*] cortésmente, amablemente; **I sent them a ~ worded letter** les mandé una carta muy correcta

2 (= *out of politeness*) por cortesía; **I ~ overlooked his bad manners** por cortesía, pasé por alto su falta de educación

politeness [pə'laɪtnɪs] N cortesía *f*, educación *f*; **to do sth out of ~** hacer algo por cortesía

politic ['pɒlɪtɪk] ADJ prudente

political [pə'lɪtɪkəl] Ⓐ ADJ 1 (*gen*) político

2 (= *politically aware*) **she was always very ~** siempre tuvo mucha conciencia política; **I'm not ~** no me interesa mucho la política; **the play is very ~** esta obra tiene mucho contenido político

3 (= *expedient, tactical*) estratégico

Ⓑ CPD ► **political asylum** N asilo *m* político ► **political correctness** N progresismo *m* ideológico ► **political correspondent** N corresponsal *mf* político/a ► **political economy** N economía *f* política ► **political editor** N editor(a) *m/f* político/a ► **political levy** N impuesto *m* político ► **political prisoner** N preso/a *m/f* político/a ► **political process** N proceso *m* político ► **political science** N ciencias *fpl* políticas ► **political scientist** N experto/a *m/f* en ciencias políticas

politically [pə'lɪtɪkəlɪ] ADV políticamente; **~ correct** [*person, attitude, terminology*] políticamente correcto; **~ incorrect** políticamente incorrecto

POLITICALLY CORRECT

Se dice que una persona o su comportamiento es **politically correct** *o* **PC** *cuando sus actitudes o palabras no reflejan ningún desprecio o insulto hacia grupos minoritarios o con algún tipo de desventaja física o social, tales como disminuidos físicos o psíquicos, minorías étnicas, homosexuales, mujeres, etc. Los que propugnan el uso de este tipo de lenguaje y actitud políticamente correctos creen que con ello desafían los valores que la sociedad occidental ha tratado de imponer sobre el resto del mundo a lo largo de la historia. Sin embargo, el término* **politically correct** *se emplea también de forma irónica por las personas que se burlan de este tipo de lenguaje y actitudes por considerarlas excesivas. Entre las expresiones políticamente correctas, algunas de las más conocidas son:* **Native American** *en vez de* **Red Indian** *(indio americano),* **visually impaired** *en vez de* **blind** *(ciego) y* **vertically challenged** *en vez de* **short** *(bajo).*

politician [ˌpɒlɪ'tɪʃən] N político/a *m/f*

politicization [pəˌlɪtɪsaɪ'zeɪʃən] N politización *f*

politicize [pə'lɪtɪsaɪz] VT politizar

politicking ['pɒlɪtɪkɪŋ] N (*pej*) politiqueo *m*

politico* [pə'lɪtɪkəʊ] N (*pl* **politicos**) político *mf*

politics ['pɒlɪtɪks] Ⓐ NSING (= *subject, career*) política *f*; **to go into ~** dedicarse a la política, meterse en política*; **to talk ~** hablar de

política
Ⓑ NPL [1] (= *views*) postura *fsing* política; **office ~** relaciones *fpl* de poder en la oficina; *see also* **sexual B**
[2] (= *political aspects*) **the ~ of health care** la política *or* los aspectos políticos de la asistencia médica

polity ['pɒlɪtɪ] N (= *form of government*) gobierno *m*, forma *f* de gobierno; (= *politically organized state*) estado *m*

polka ['pɒlkə] Ⓐ N (*pl* **polkas**) (= *dance*) polca *f*
Ⓑ CPD ► **polka dot** N dibujo *m* de puntos

poll [pəʊl] Ⓐ N [1] (= *voting*) votación *f*; (= *election*) elecciones *fpl*; **in the ~ of 1945** en las elecciones de 1945; **a ~ was demanded** exigieron una votación, insistieron en que se llevara a cabo una votación; **to head the ~** obtener la mayoría de los votos; **to take a ~ on sth** someter algo a votación; **a ~ was taken among those present** se llevó a cabo una votación entre los asistentes
[2] (= *total votes*) votos *mpl*, votación *f*; **there was a ~ of 84%** el 84% del electorado acudió a las urnas; **the candidate achieved a ~ of 5000 votes** el candidato obtuvo 5000 votos; **the ~ has been a heavy one** ha votado un elevado porcentaje del electorado
[3] **polls** (= *voting place*) urnas *fpl*; **to go to the ~s** acudir a las urnas
[4] (= *opinion poll*) encuesta *f*, sondeo *m*; (*Telec*) interrogación *f*; **to take a ~** hacer una encuesta; *see also* **Gallup poll**
Ⓑ VT [1] [+ *votes*] obtener; **he ~ed only 50 votes** obtuvo solamente 50 votos
[2] (*in opinion poll*) encuestar; **1068 people were ~ed** encuestaron a 1068 personas
[3] (= *remove horns from*) [+ *cattle*] descornar
Ⓒ VI **he ~ed badly** obtuvo pocos votos, tuvo escaso apoyo; **we expect to ~ well** esperamos obtener muchos votos
Ⓓ CPD ► **poll rating** N resultado *m* obtenido en las encuestas ► **poll tax** N (contribución *f* de) capitación *f*; (*Brit*) (*formerly*) impuesto *m* municipal por cabeza

pollack ['pɒlək] N (*pl* **pollacks** *or* **pollack**) abadejo *m*

pollard ['pɒləd] Ⓐ N árbol *m* desmochado
Ⓑ VT desmochar

pollen ['pɒlən] Ⓐ N polen *m*
Ⓑ CPD ► **pollen allergy** N alergia *f* polínica ► **pollen count** N recuento *m* polínico ► **pollen grain** N grano *m* de polen

pollinate ['pɒlɪneɪt] VT polinizar

pollination [,pɒlɪ'neɪʃən] N polinización *f*

pollinator ['pɒlɪneɪtəʳ] N (*Zool*) polinizador(a) *m/f*

polling ['pəʊlɪŋ] Ⓐ N votación *f*; **~ will be on Thursday** las elecciones se celebrarán el jueves, se votará el jueves; **~ has been heavy** ha votado un elevado porcentaje de los electores
Ⓑ CPD ► **polling booth** N cabina *f* electoral ► **polling day** N día *m* de las elecciones ► **polling place** N (*US*) = **polling station** ► **polling station** N centro *m* electoral

polliwog ['pɒlɪwɒg] N (*US Zool*) renacuajo *m*

pollster ['pəʊlstəʳ] N encuestador(a) *m/f*

pollutant [pə'lu:tənt] N contaminante *m*, agente *m* contaminador

pollute [pə'lu:t] VT [1] contaminar, polucionar; **to become ~d** contaminarse (**with** de)
[2] (*fig*) corromper

polluter [pə'lu:təʳ] N contaminador(a) *m/f*

pollution [pə'lu:ʃən] Ⓐ N [1] contaminación *f*, polución *f*
[2] (*fig*) corrupción *f*
Ⓑ CPD ► **pollution control** N control *m* de la contaminación ► **pollution levels** NPL niveles *mpl* de contaminación

Pollyanna [pɒlɪ'ænə] N optimista *mf* redomado/a

pollywog ['pɒlɪwɒg] N = **polliwog**

polo ['pəʊləʊ] Ⓐ N (*Sport*) polo *m*
Ⓑ CPD ► **polo neck (sweater)** N (jersey *m* de) cuello *m* vuelto *or* cisne ► **polo shirt** N polo *m*

polonaise [,pɒlə'neɪz] N polonesa *f*

polo-necked ['pəʊləʊnekt] ADJ con cuello cisne *or* vuelto

polonium [pə'ləʊnɪəm] N polonio *m*

poltergeist ['pɔ:ltəgaɪst] N duende *m*

poltroon†† [pɒl'tru:n] N cobarde *mf*

poly* ['pɒlɪ] N (*Brit*) = **polytechnic**

poly... [pɒlɪ] PREFIX poli…, multi…

polyandrous [,pɒlɪ'ændrəs] ADJ poliándrico

polyandry ['pɒlɪændrɪ] N poliandria *f*

polyanthus [,pɒlɪ'ænθəs] N prímula *f*, primavera *f*, hierba *f* de San Pablo mayor

poly bag* ['pɒlɪbæg] N bolsa *f* de plástico *or* polietileno

polychromatic [,pɒlɪkrəʊ'mætɪk] ADJ policromo

polyester [,pɒlɪ'estəʳ] Ⓐ N poliéster *m*
Ⓑ ADJ de poliéster

polyethylene [,pɒlɪ'eθəli:n] N polietileno *m*

polygamist [pɒ'lɪgəmɪst] N polígamo *m*

polygamous [pɒ'lɪgəməs] ADJ polígamo

polygamy [pɒ'lɪgəmɪ] N poligamia *f*

polygenesis [,pɒlɪ'dʒenɪsɪs] N poligénesis *f*

polyglot ['pɒlɪglɒt] Ⓐ ADJ polígloto
Ⓑ N polígloto/a *m/f*

polygon ['pɒlɪgən] N polígono *m*

polygonal [pɒ'lɪgənl] ADJ poligonal

polygraph ['pɒlɪgrɑ:f] N polígrafo *m*, detector *m* de mentiras

polyhedron [,pɒlɪ'hi:drən] N (*pl* **polyhedrons** *or* **polyhedra** [,pɒlɪ'hi:drə]) poliedro *m*

polymath ['pɒlɪmæθ] N polímata *mf*, erudito/a *m/f*

polymer ['pɒlɪməʳ] N polímero *m*

polymerization ['pɒlɪməraɪ'zeɪʃən] N polimerización *f*

polymorphic [,pɒlɪ'mɔ:fɪk] ADJ polimorfo

polymorphism [,pɒlɪ'mɔ:fɪzəm] N polimorfismo *m*

Polynesia [,pɒlɪ'ni:zɪə] N Polinesia *f*

Polynesian [,pɒlɪ'ni:zɪən] Ⓐ ADJ polinesio
Ⓑ N polinesio/a *m/f*

polynomial [,pɒlɪ'nəʊmɪəl] Ⓐ ADJ polinomio
Ⓑ N polinomio *m*

polyp ['pɒlɪp] N (*Med*) pólipo *m*

Polyphemus [,pɒlɪ'fi:məs] N Polifemo

polyphonic [,pɒlɪ'fɒnɪk] ADJ (*Mus*) polifónico

polyphony [pə'lɪfənɪ] N polifonía *f*

polypropylene [,pɒlɪ'prɒpɪli:n] N polipropileno *m*

polypus ['pɒlɪpəs] N (*pl* **polypi** ['pɒlɪpaɪ]) (*Zool*) pólipo *m*

polysemic [,pɒlɪ'si:mɪk], **polysemous** [pɒ'lɪsəməs] ADJ polisémico

polysemy [pɒ'lɪsəmɪ] N polisemia *f*

polystyrene [,pɒlɪ'staɪri:n] Ⓐ N (*esp Brit*) poliestireno *m*
Ⓑ ADJ de poliestireno

polysyllabic ['pɒlɪsɪ'læbɪk] ADJ polisílabo

polysyllable ['pɒlɪ,sɪləbl] N polisílabo *m*

polytechnic [,pɒlɪ'teknɪk] N (*Brit*) (*formerly*) escuela *f* politécnica, politécnico *m*

polytheism ['pɒlɪθi:ɪzəm] N politeísmo *m*

polytheistic [,pɒlɪθi:'ɪstɪk] ADJ politeísta

polythene ['pɒlɪθi:n] (*Brit*) Ⓐ N polietileno *m*
Ⓑ CPD ► **polythene bag** N bolsa *f* de plástico *or* polietileno

polyunsaturate [,pɒlɪʌn'sætʃərɪt] N poliinsaturado *m*

polyunsaturated [,pɒlɪʌn'sætʃəreɪtɪd] ADJ poliinsaturado

polyurethane [,pɒlɪ'jʊərɪθeɪn] N poliuretano *m*

polyvalent [pə'lɪvələnt] ADJ polivalente

polyvinyl ['pɒlɪvaɪnl] N polivinilo *m*

pom¹* [pɒm] N = **pommy**

pom²* [pɒm] N (= *dog*) perro *m* de Pomerania, lulú *mf* (de Pomerania)

pomade [pə'mɑ:d] N pomada *f*

pomander [pəʊ'mændəʳ] N *recipiente de porcelana que contiene hierbas aromáticas*

pomegranate ['pɒməgrænɪt] N (= *fruit*) granada *f*; (= *tree*) granado *m*

pomelo ['pɒmɪ,ləʊ] N (*pl* **pomelos**) pomelo *m*

Pomeranian [,pɒmə'reɪnɪən] N (= *dog*) pomeranio *m*

pommel ['pʌml] Ⓐ N pomo *m*
Ⓑ VT = **pummel**

pommy* ['pɒmɪ] (*Australia pej*) Ⓐ ADJ inglés
Ⓑ N inglés/esa *m/f*

pomp [pɒmp] N pompa *f*; **~ and circumstance** pompa *f* y solemnidad

Pompeii [pɒm'peɪ] N Pompeya *f*

Pompey ['pɒmpɪ] N Pompeyo

pom-pom ['pɒmpɒm], **pom-pon** ['pɒmpɒn] N (*on hat etc*) borla *f*, pompón *m*

pomposity [pɒm'pɒsɪtɪ] N pomposidad *f*

pompous ['pɒmpəs] ADJ [*person*] pretencioso; [*occasion*] ostentoso; [*language*] ampuloso, inflado

pompously ['pɒmpəslɪ] ADV [*strut, stride*] pomposamente; [*reply, speak*] pomposamente, ampulosamente

ponce‡ [pɒns] (*Brit*) N [1] (= *pimp*) proxeneta *m*, chulo *m* (*Sp**)
[2] (*pej*) (= *homosexual*) marica* *m*

►**ponce about‡, ponce around‡** VI + ADV (*Brit*) chulear*

poncho ['pɒntʃəʊ] N (*pl* **ponchos**) poncho *m*, manta *f*, ruana *f* (*Col, Ven*), sarape *m* (*Mex*), jorongo *m* (*Mex*)

poncy‡ ['pɒnsɪ] ADJ (*Brit*) cursi*

pond [pɒnd] Ⓐ N (= *natural*) charca *f*; (= *artificial*) estanque *m*; ✦*IDIOM* **he's a big fish** *or* (*US*) **big frog in a small ~** es el tuerto en el país de los ciegos, es un reyezuelo (*en algún lugar o en algo poco importante*)
Ⓑ CPD ► **pond life** N fauna *f* de las charcas/estanques ► **pond weed** N planta *f* acuática

ponder ['pɒndəʳ] Ⓐ VT considerar, sopesar
Ⓑ VI reflexionar *or* meditar (**on, over** sobre)

ponderable ['pɒndərəbl] ADJ ponderable

ponderous ['pɒndərəs] ADJ pesado

ponderously ['pɒndərəslɪ] ADV pesadamente; [*say etc*] en tono pesado, lentamente y con énfasis

pone [pəʊn] N (*US*) pan *m* de maíz

pong* [pɒŋ] (*Brit*) Ⓐ N peste *f*
Ⓑ VI apestar

pongy* ['pɒŋɪ] ADJ (*Brit*) foche*, maloliente

poniard ['pɒnjəd] N (= *liter*) puñal *m*

pontiff ['pɒntɪf] N pontífice *m*

pontifical [pɒn'tɪfɪkəl] ADJ pontificio, pontifical; (*fig*) dogmático, autoritario

pontificate Ⓐ [pɒnˈtɪfɪkɪt] N (*Rel*) pontificado *m*
Ⓑ [pɒnˈtɪfɪkeɪt] VI pontificar

Pontius Pilate [ˈpɒnʃəsˈpaɪlət] N Poncio Pilato

pontoon[1] [pɒnˈtuːn] Ⓐ N pontón *m*
Ⓑ CPD ► **pontoon bridge** N puente *m* de pontones

pontoon[2] [pɒnˈtuːn] N (*Brit Cards*) veintiuna *f*

pony [ˈpəʊnɪ] Ⓐ N [1] poney *m*, potro *m*
[2] (*Brit*‡) ≈ 25 libras
[3] (*US**) (*Scol*) chuleta* *f*
Ⓑ CPD ► **pony trekking** N excursión *f* en poney

ponytail [ˈpəʊnɪteɪl] N cola *f* de caballo, coleta *f*

poo‡ [puː] (*Brit baby talk*) Ⓐ N caca‡ *f*; **to do a ~** hacer caca‡
Ⓑ VT **to ~ one's pants** hacerse caca encima*
Ⓒ VI hacer caca*

pooch* [puːtʃ] N perro *m*

poodle [ˈpuːdl] N caniche *mf*

poof‡ [pʊf] N (*Brit pej*) maricón** *m*

poofter‡ [ˈpʊftəʳ] N (*Brit pej*) = **poof**

poofy‡ [ˈpʊfɪ] ADJ (*Brit pej*) de maricón**

pooh [puː] Ⓐ EXCL ¡bah!
Ⓑ N, VT, VI = **poo**

pooh-pooh [puːˈpuː] VT despreciar; [+ *proposal etc*] rechazar con desdén; [+ *danger etc*] menospreciar, negar la importancia de

pool[1] [puːl] Ⓐ N [1] (*natural*) charca *f*; (*artificial*) estanque *m*; (= *swimming pool*) piscina *f*, alberca *f* (*Mex*), pileta *f* (de natación) (*S. Cone*); (*in river*) pozo *m*
[2] [*of spilt liquid*] charco *m*; (*fig*) [*of light*] foco *m*
Ⓑ CPD ► **pool attendant** N encargado/a *m/f* de la piscina

pool[2] [puːl] Ⓐ N [1] (= *common fund*) fondo *m* (común); (*Cards*) polla *f*
[2] (= *supply, source*) reserva *f*; [*of genes etc*] fondo *m*, reserva *f*; **an untapped ~ of ability** una reserva de inteligencia no utilizada; *see also* **car B, typing B**
[3] **the ~s** (*Brit*) (= *football pools*) las quinielas (*Sp*); **to do the (football) ~s** hacer las quinielas
[4] (= *form of snooker*) billar *m* americano; **to shoot ~** (*US*) jugar al billar americano; ✦*IDIOM* **that's dirty ~** (*US**) eso no es jugar limpio
[5] (*Comm*) fondos *mpl* comunes; (*US*) (= *monopoly, trust*) consorcio *m*; **coal and steel ~** comunidad *f* de carbón y acero
Ⓑ VT juntar, poner en común
Ⓒ CPD ► **pool hall, pool room** N sala *f* de billar ► **pool table** N mesa *f* de billar

poop[1] [puːp] (*Naut*) Ⓐ N popa *f*
Ⓑ CPD ► **poop deck** N toldilla *f*, castillo *m* de popa

poop[2]‡ [puːp] N (= *excrement*) caca‡ *f*

poop[3]* [puːp] N (*US*) (= *information*) onda* *f*, información *f*

pooped‡ [puːpt] ADJ **to be ~** (*esp US*) (= *tired*) estar hecho polvo*; (= *drunk*) estar ajumado*

pooper-scooper* [ˈpuːpəˌskuːpəʳ], **poop-scoop*** [ˈpuːpskuːp] N caca-can* *m*

poo-poo‡ [ˈpuːˈpuː] N caca‡ *f*

poor [pʊəʳ] Ⓐ ADJ (*compar* **poorer**; *superl* **poorest**) [1] (= *not rich*) [*person, family, country*] pobre; **a ~ woman** una mujer pobre; **a ~ man** un pobre; **~ people** gente *f* pobre, personas *fpl* pobres; **pewter was the ~ man's silver** el peltre era la plata de los pobres; **they thought that cinema was a** *or* **the ~ relation of theatre** pensaban que el cine era el pariente pobre del teatro; **to be the ~er (for sth)**: **the nation is the ~er for her death** la nación ha sufrido una gran pérdida con su muerte; **it left me £5 the ~er** me dejó con 5 libras de menos; ✦*IDIOM* **to be as ~ as a church mouse** ser más pobre que las ratas
[2] (= *inferior, bad*) [*goods, service*] malo, de mala calidad; **the wine was ~** el vino era malo *or* de mala calidad; **Britain's ~ economic performance** el bajo rendimiento económico obtenido por Gran Bretaña; **she has a very ~ attendance record** su expediente es muy malo en lo que a asistencia se refiere; **they had made a ~ job of it** habían hecho una chapuza*; **to be a ~ imitation of sth** ser una burda *or* pobre imitación de algo; **his decision shows ~ judgment** su decisión denota poco juicio; **to have a ~ opinion of sb** tener un concepto poco favorable de algn; **to come a ~ second (to sth/sb)**: **he came a ~ second in the final race** quedó el segundo en la carrera final, a bastante distancia del primero; **his family comes a ~ second to his career** su familia queda relegada a segundo lugar tras su carrera
[3] (= *deficient*) [*memory*] malo; [*soil*] pobre, estéril; [*harvest*] pobre, escaso; **I had a ~ education** la educación que recibí no fue muy buena; **many people eat a ~ diet** mucha gente tiene una dieta pobre; **"poor"** (*Scol*) (*as mark*) "deficiente"; **soils that are ~ in zinc** suelos que son pobres en zinc *or* que tienen bajo contenido en zinc
[4] (= *untalented*) **he was a ~ actor** era un actor flojo; **I'm a ~ traveller** lo de viajar no lo llevo muy bien; **she was a very ~ swimmer** no era buena nadadora; **to be ~ at maths** no ser muy bueno en matemáticas; **we are ~ at marketing ourselves** no somos muy buenos a la hora de darnos publicidad
[5] (= *unfortunate*) pobre; **the ~ child was hungry** el pobre niño tenía hambre; **~ little thing!** ¡pobrecito!, ¡pobre criaturita!; **~ (old) you!** ◊ **you ~ (old) thing!** ¡pobrecito!; **~ Mary's lost all her money** la pobre María ha perdido todo su dinero; **he's very ill, ~ chap** está grave el pobre; **a ~ little rich girl** una pobre niña rica; *see also* **devil A2**
Ⓑ NPL **the ~** los pobres; **the rural/urban ~** los pobres de las zonas rurales/urbanas
Ⓒ CPD ► **poor box** N cepillo *m* de las limosnas ► **poor law** N (*Hist*) ley *f* de asistencia pública ► **poor white** N (*US*) *persona pobre de raza blanca*; *see also* **relief A4**

> **POOR**
>
> **Position of "pobre"**
>
> You should generally put **pobre** *after* the noun when you mean **poor** in the sense of "not rich" and *before* the noun in the sense of "unfortunate":
>
> It's a poor area
> ***Es una región pobre***
> The poor boy was trembling
> ***El pobre chico estaba temblando***
>
> *For further uses and examples, see main entry.*

poorhouse [ˈpʊəhaʊs] N (*pl* **poorhouses** [ˈpʊəhaʊzɪz]) asilo *m* de los pobres

poorly [ˈpʊəlɪ] Ⓐ ADV [1] (= *badly*) [*designed, equipped*] mal; **the shares have performed ~** el rendimiento de las acciones ha sido bajo; **to do ~**: **she did ~ in history** sacó mala nota en historia; **she did ~ at school** sacaba malas notas en el colegio; **the room/road was ~ lit** la habitación/la carretera estaba mal iluminada; **the job was ~ paid** el trabajo estaba mal pagado; **he was ~ paid** le pagaban poco; **his army was ~ trained** su ejército estaba poco capacitado
[2] (= *meagrely, shabbily*) pobremente; **to be ~ dressed** ir pobremente vestido
Ⓑ ADJ (*esp Brit*) (= *ill*) enfermo; **to be/feel ~** estar/encontrarse mal, estar/encontrarse pachucho *or* malucho*; **to look ~** tener mal aspecto

poorness [ˈpʊənɪs] N [1] (= *poverty*) pobreza *f*
[2] (= *poor quality*) mala calidad *f*; **~ of spirit** apocamiento *m*, mezquindad *f*

poor-spirited [ˈpʊəˈspɪrɪtɪd] ADJ apocado, mezquino

poove‡ [puːv] N (*Brit*) = **poof**

pop[1] [pɒp] Ⓐ N [1] (= *sound*) pequeño estallido *m*; [*of cork*] taponazo *m*; [*of fastener etc*] ruido *m* seco; (= *imitative sound*) ¡pum!
[2] (*) (= *drink*) refresco *m*, gaseosa *f* (*Sp*)
[3] (= *try*) **to have** *or* **take a ~ at (doing) sth*** probar (a hacer) algo
[4] **to have** *or* **take a ~ at sth/sb*** (= *criticize*) criticar algo/a algn
[5] **the drinks go for $3.50 a ~** (*esp US**) las bebidas son a 3.50 dólares cada una
Ⓑ ADV **to go ~** [*balloon*] reventar, hacer ¡pum!; [*cork*] salir disparado, hacer ¡pum!
Ⓒ VT [1] [+ *balloon*] hacer reventar; [+ *cork*] hacer saltar; ✦*IDIOM* **to ~ one's clogs** (*Brit** *hum*) estirar la pata*
[2] (*) (= *put*) poner (rápidamente); **to ~ sth into a drawer** meter algo (rápidamente) en un cajón; **to ~ pills** drogarse (con pastillas); ✦*IDIOM* **to ~ the question** declararse
[3] (‡) (= *pawn*) empeñar
Ⓓ VI [1] [*balloon*] reventar; [*cork*] saltar, salir disparado; **there were corks ~ping all over** los tapones saltaban por todas partes; **to make sb's eyes ~** (*fig*) dejar a algn con los ojos fuera de órbita; **his eyes nearly ~ped out of his head** (*in amazement*) se le saltaban los ojos; **my ears ~ped on landing** al aterrizar se me taponaron los oídos
[2] (*) (= *go quickly or suddenly*) **we ~ped over to see them** fuimos a hacerles una breve visita; **let's ~ round to Joe's** vamos un momento a casa de Joe

►**pop back*** Ⓐ VT + ADV [+ *lid etc*] poner de nuevo, volver a poner
Ⓑ VI + ADV volver un momento

►**pop in*** VI + ADV entrar un momento; **to ~ in to see sb** pasar por casa de algn; **I just ~ped in** no tuve la intención de quedarme; **I just ~ped in to say hello** sólo vine a saludarte

►**pop off*** VI + ADV [1] (= *die*) estirar la pata*
[2] (= *leave*) irse, marcharse

►**pop on*** VT + ADV [+ *light, oven*] poner, encender; [+ *kettle*] poner (a calentar); [+ *clothing*] ponerse (de prisa); **I'll just ~ my hat on** voy a ponerme el sombrero

►**pop out*** Ⓐ VT + ADV **she ~ped her head out** asomó de repente la cabeza
Ⓑ VI + ADV salir un momento; **he ~ped out for some cigarettes** salió un momento a comprar cigarrillos; **he ~ped out from his hiding place** salió de repente de su escondite

►**pop up*** VI + ADV aparecer inesperadamente

pop[2]* [pɒp] = **popular** Ⓐ N (música *f*) pop *m*; **to be top of the ~s** ser el número uno en la lista de éxitos
Ⓑ CPD [*music, song, singer, concert, group*] pop *inv* ► **pop art** N pop-art *m*, arte *f* pop ► **pop star** N estrella *f* de la música pop

pop[3]* [pɒp] N (*esp US*) (= *dad*) papá* *m*

POP ABBR [1] = **publish or perish**
[2] = **Post Office Preferred**

pop. ABBR (= **population**) h.

popcorn [ˈpɒpkɔːn] N palomitas *fpl* de maíz, alborotos *mpl* (*S. Cone, Peru*), cabritas *fpl* (*S. Cone, Peru*)

pope [pəʊp] N papa *m*; **Pope John XXIII** el Papa Juan XXIII

popemobile* [ˈpəʊpməʊˌbiːl] N papamóvil *m*

popery [ˈpəʊpərɪ] N (*pej*) papismo *m*; **no ~!** ¡abajo el papa!, ¡papa no!

pop-eyed [ˈpɒpˈaɪd] ADJ (*permanently*) de ojos saltones *or* desorbitados; **they were ~ with amazement** se les desorbitaron los ojos con el asombro; **they looked at me ~** me miraron con los ojos desorbitados

popgun [ˈpɒpɡʌn] N pistola *f* de juguete (de aire comprimido)

popinjay† [ˈpɒpɪndʒeɪ] N pisaverde *mf*

popish [ˈpəʊpɪʃ] ADJ (*pej*) papista

poplar [ˈpɒpləʳ] N (*black*) chopo *m*, álamo *m*; (*white*) álamo *m* blanco

poplin [ˈpɒplɪn] N popelina *f*

popmobility [ˌpɒpməʊˈbɪlɪtɪ] N gym-jazz *m*

poppa* [ˈpɒpə] N (*US*) papá* *m*

poppadum [ˈpɒpədəm] N = **papadum**

popper [ˈpɒpəʳ] N [1] (*Brit**) (= *press-stud*) corchete *m*
[2] (*Drugs‡*) *cápsula de nitrito amílico*

poppet* [ˈpɒpɪt] N (*Brit*) encanto *m*, cielo *m*; **yes, my ~** sí, hija, sí, querida; **she is a ~** es un cielo; **the boss is a ~** el jefe es un encanto

poppy [ˈpɒpɪ] Ⓐ N amapola *f*
Ⓑ CPD ► **Poppy Day** N (*Brit*) *día en el que se recuerda a las caídos en las dos guerras mundiales* ► **poppy seed** N semilla *f* de amapola

> **POPPY DAY**
>
> **Poppy Day** *es la expresión coloquial para referirise al* **Remembrance Day** *o* **Remembrance Sunday**, *día en que se recuerdan los caídos en las dos grandes guerras mundiales del siglo XX. La celebración se hace el segundo domingo de noviembre y en los días que preceden a este día se venden amapolas de papel con el fin de recaudar fondos destinados a las instituciones de caridad que prestan ayuda a los veteranos de guerra y a sus familias. Las amapolas representan las que florecieron en los campos franceses, donde tantos soldados perecieron durante la Primera Guerra Mundial.*
>
> ⇨ LEGION

poppycock* [ˈpɒpɪkɒk] N paparruchas* *fpl*, tonterías *fpl*; **poppycock!** ¡paparruchas!*

Popsicle® [ˈpɒpsɪkl] N (*US*) polo *m* (*Sp*), paleta *f* (helada) (*LAm*)

popsy‡ [ˈpɒpsɪ] N chica *f*

populace [ˈpɒpjʊlɪs] N (*gen*) pueblo *m*; (= *mob*) populacho *m*, turba *f*

popular [ˈpɒpjʊləʳ] Ⓐ ADJ [1] (= *well-liked*) **the show is proving very ~** el espectáculo está gozando de mucho éxito *or* goza de mucha popularidad; **I'm not very ~ in the office just now** en este momento no gozo de mucha simpatía en la oficina; **this is one of our most ~ lines** (*Comm*) esta es una de nuestras líneas más vendidas; **to be ~ with sb**: **he's ~ with the girls** tiene éxito con las chicas; **I'm not very ~ with her at the moment** en este momento no soy santo de su devoción; **she's very ~ with her colleagues** goza de mucha simpatía entre sus colegas; **the area is ~ with holidaymakers** es una zona muy frecuentada por los turistas
[2] (= *fashionable*) de moda; **long skirts are ~** las faldas largas están de moda
[3] (= *widespread*) [*image, belief*] generalizado; **contrary to ~ belief** *or* **opinion** en contra de *or* contrario a lo que comúnmente se cree; **by ~ demand** *or* **request** a petición del público, respondiendo a la demanda general; **it's a ~ misconception that ...** mucha gente piensa equivocadamente que ...
[4] (= *of the people*) [*unrest, support*] popular; [*uprising*] popular, del pueblo; **he has great ~ appeal** goza del favor del público; **~ feeling is against him** el sentir popular *or* del pueblo está en su contra; **~ opinion** la opinión general
[5] (= *appealing to the layman*) [*culture, music, art, version*] popular
Ⓑ CPD ► **popular front** N frente *m* popular ► **the popular press** N la prensa popular ► **the popular vote** N el voto popular

popularist [ˈpɒpjʊlərɪst] ADJ popularista

popularity [ˌpɒpjʊˈlærɪtɪ] N popularidad *f*; **to gain** *or* **grow in ~** gozar de una popularidad cada vez mayor

popularization [ˈpɒpjʊləraɪˈzeɪʃən] N (= *making well-liked, acceptable*) popularización *f*; (= *making available*) vulgarización *f*

popularize [ˈpɒpjʊləraɪz] VT [1] (= *make well-liked, acceptable*) popularizar
[2] (= *make available to the people*) divulgar

popularly [ˈpɒpjʊləlɪ] ADV [1] (= *generally*) **it is ~ thought that ...** comúnmente se cree que ...; **Albert, ~ known as Bertie** Albert, corrientemente conocido como Bertie
[2] (= *by the people*) **the country's first ~ elected president** el primer presidente del país que ha sido elegido por el pueblo

populate [ˈpɒpjʊleɪt] VT poblar

population [ˌpɒpjʊˈleɪʃən] Ⓐ N [1] (= *inhabitants*) población *f*; **what is the ~ of Mexico?** ¿qué población tiene México?, ¿cuántos habitantes hay en México?; **they go to the cinema more often than the general ~** van al cine con más frecuencia que la población en general; **75% of the male ~** el 75% de la población masculina; **the student ~** la población estudiantil; *see also* **prison B**
[2] (= *settling*) población *f*
Ⓑ CPD ► **population centre** N núcleo *m or* centro *m* de población ► **population control** N control *m* demográfico ► **population density** N densidad *f* de población ► **population explosion** N explosión *f* demográfica ► **population growth** N crecimiento *m* demográfico

populism [ˈpɒpjʊlɪzəm] N populismo *m*

populist [ˈpɒpjʊlɪst] Ⓐ ADJ populista
Ⓑ N populista *mf*

populous [ˈpɒpjʊləs] ADJ populoso; **the most ~ city in the world** la ciudad más populosa del mundo

pop-up [ˈpɒpʌp] Ⓐ ADJ (*Comput*) [*window, menu, advertisement*] emergente
Ⓑ N (*Comput*) ventana *f* emergente, (ventana *f*) pop-up *m*
Ⓒ CPD ► **pop-up book** libro *m* desplegable ► **pop-up menu** menú *m* emergente ► **pop-up toaster** tostador *m* automático

porage [ˈpɒrɪdʒ] N = **porridge**

porcelain [ˈpɔːslɪn] Ⓐ N porcelana *f*
Ⓑ CPD de porcelana

porch [pɔːtʃ] N [*of church*] pórtico *m*; [*of house*] porche *m*, portal *m*; (*US*) (= *veranda*) porche *m*, terraza *f*

porcine [ˈpɔːsaɪn] ADJ porcino, porcuno

porcupine [ˈpɔːkjʊpaɪn] Ⓐ N puerco *m* espín
Ⓑ CPD ► **porcupine fish** N pez *m* globo

pore¹ [pɔːʳ] N (*Anat, Zool*) poro *m*

pore² [pɔːʳ] VI **to ~ over sth** escudriñar algo; **we ~d over it for hours** lo estudiamos durante horas y horas

pork [pɔːk] Ⓐ N carne *f* de cerdo *or* puerco *or* (*LAm*) chancho Ⓑ CPD ► **pork butcher** N charcutero/a *m/f*, chanchero/a *m/f* (*LAm*) ► **pork chop** N chuleta *f* de cerdo *or* puerco ► **pork pie** N (*Culin*) empanada *f* de carne de cerdo; (*Brit‡*) = **porky B** ► **pork sausage** N salchicha *f* de cerdo *or* puerco ► **pork scratchings** NPL chicharrones *mpl*

porker [ˈpɔːkəʳ] N cerdo *m*, cochino *m*

porky [ˈpɔːkɪ] Ⓐ ADJ (*) gordo, gordinflón*
Ⓑ N (*Brit‡*) (= *lie*) (*also* **~ pie**) bola* *f*, mentira *f*

porn* [pɔːn] Ⓐ N pornografía *f*, porno* *m*; **hard/soft ~** pornografía *f* dura/blanda
Ⓑ CPD [*magazine, video, actor*] porno* *inv* ► **porn merchant** N traficante *mf* en pornografía ► **porn shop** N tienda *f* de pornografía

porno* [ˈpɔːnəʊ] ADJ = **porn**

pornographer [pɔːˈnɒɡrəfəʳ] N pornografista *mf*

pornographic [ˌpɔːnəˈɡræfɪk] ADJ pornográfico

pornography [pɔːˈnɒɡrəfɪ] N pornografía *f*

porosity [pɔːˈrɒsɪtɪ] N porosidad *f*

porous [ˈpɔːrəs] ADJ poroso

porousness [ˈpɔːrəsnɪs] N porosidad *f*

porphyria [pɔːˈfɪrɪə] N porfirismo *m*

porphyry [ˈpɔːfɪrɪ] N pórfido *m*

porpoise [ˈpɔːpəs] N (*pl* **porpoise** *or* **porpoises**) marsopa *f*, puerco *m* de mar

porridge [ˈpɒrɪdʒ] Ⓐ N [1] (*Culin*) avena *f* (cocida), ≈ atole *m* (*Mex*); (*baby's*) papilla *f* [2] **to do two years' ~** (*Brit**) pasar dos años a la sombra* Ⓑ CPD ► **porridge oats** NPL copos *mpl* de avena

port¹ [pɔːt] Ⓐ N [1] (= *harbour*) puerto *m*; **to come** *or* **put into ~** tomar puerto; **to leave ~** hacerse a la mar, zarpar; **~ of call** puerto *m* de escala; **his next ~ of call was the chemist's** (*fig*) luego fue a la farmacia; **where is your next ~ of call?** (*fig*) ¿adónde va ahora?; **~ of entry** puerto *m* de entrada; ✦**IDIOM any ~ in a storm** la necesidad carece de ley
[2] (= *city or town with a port*) puerto *m*
Ⓑ CPD portuario ► **port authority** N autoridad *f* portuaria ► **port dues** NPL derechos *mpl* de puerto ► **port facilities** NPL facilidades *fpl* portuarias

port² [pɔːt] (*Naut, Aer*) Ⓐ N (*also* **~ side**) babor *m*; **the sea to ~** la mar a babor; **land to ~!** ¡tierra a babor! Ⓑ ADJ de babor; **on the ~ side** a babor Ⓒ VT **to ~ the helm** poner el timón a babor, virar a babor

port³ [pɔːt] N [1] (*Naut*) (= *porthole*) portilla *f*
[2] (*Comput*) puerta *f*, puerto *m*, port *m*
[3] (*Mech*) lumbrera *f*
[4] (*Mil*††) tronera *f*

port⁴ [pɔːt] N (= *wine*) oporto *m*

portability [ˌpɔːtəˈbɪlɪtɪ] N (*esp Comput*) portabilidad *f*; [*of software*] transferibilidad *f*

portable [ˈpɔːtəbl] Ⓐ ADJ portátil
Ⓑ N máquina *f*/televisor *m etc* portátil

portage [ˈpɔːtɪdʒ] N porteo *m*

Portakabin® [ˈpɔːtəˌkæbɪn] N (*gen*) caseta *f* prefabricada; (= *extension to office etc*) anexo *m* prefabricado; (= *works office etc*) barracón *m* de obras

portal [ˈpɔːtl] N portal *m*

portcullis [pɔːtˈkʌlɪs] N rastrillo *m*

portend [pɔːˈtend] VT (*liter*) augurar, presagiar; **what does this ~?** ¿qué significa esto?

portent [ˈpɔːtent] N [1] (= *omen*) augurio *m*,

presagio *m*; **a ~ of doom** un presagio de la catástrofe
2 (= *prodigy*) portento *m*

portentous [pɔː'tentəs] ADJ 1 (= *ominous, prodigious*) portentoso
2 (= *pompous*) pomposo

portentously [pɔː'tentəslɪ] ADV 1 (= *ominously*) portentosamente
2 (= *pompously*) pomposamente

porter ['pɔːtəʳ] Ⓐ N 1 (*Rail, Aer*) maletero *m*, mozo *m* de cuerda *or* de estación, changador *m* (*S. Cone*); (*US Rail*) mozo *m* de los coches-cama, camarero *m* (*LAm*); (*touting for custom*) mozo *m* de cuerda
2 (*Brit*) [*of hotel, office etc*] portero/a *m/f*
3 (= *Sherpa*) porteador *m*
4 (*in hospital*) camillero/a *m/f*
5 (†) (= *beer*) cerveza *f* negra
Ⓑ CPD ► **porter's lodge** N portería *f*, conserjería *f*

porterage ['pɔːtərɪdʒ] N porte *m*

porterhouse ['pɔːtəhaʊs] N (*pl* **porterhouses** ['pɔːtəhaʊzɪz]) 1 (*Brit*) (*also* **~ steak**) biftec *m* de filete
2 (††) mesón *m*

portfolio [pɔːt'fəʊlɪəʊ] Ⓐ N (*pl* **portfolios**) (= *file*) carpeta *f*; [*of artist, designer*] carpeta *f*, portafolio *m*; [*of business, politician*] cartera *f*; **~ of shares** cartera *f* de acciones; **minister without ~** ministro/a *m/f* sin cartera
Ⓑ CPD ► **portfolio management** N (*Fin*) administración *f* de la cartera de acciones

porthole ['pɔːthəʊl] N portilla *f*

Portia ['pɔːʃə] N Porcia

portico ['pɔːtɪkəʊ] N (*pl* **porticoes** *or* **porticos**) pórtico *m*

portion ['pɔːʃən] Ⓐ N 1 (= *part, piece*) porción *f*, parte *f*; [*of food*] ración *f*; [*of cake*] porción *f*, trozo *m*
2 (= *quantity, in relation to a whole*) porción *f*, porcentaje *m*
3 (*also* **marriage ~**) dote *f*
Ⓑ VT (*also* **~ out**) repartir, dividir

portliness ['pɔːtlɪnɪs] N gordura *f*, corpulencia *f*

portly ['pɔːtlɪ] ADJ grueso, corpulento

portmanteau [pɔːt'mæntəʊ] Ⓐ N (*pl* **portmanteaus, portmanteaux** [pɔːt'mæntəʊz]) baúl *m* de viaje
Ⓑ CPD ► **portmanteau word** N palabra *f* combinada

Porto Rico [ˌpɔːtəʊ'riːkəʊ] *etc* = **Puerto Rico** *etc*

portrait ['pɔːtrɪt] Ⓐ N retrato *m*; **to have one's ~ painted** ◊ **sit for one's ~** hacerse un retrato
Ⓑ CPD ► **portrait format** N (*Comput, Publishing*) formato *m* vertical ► **portrait gallery** N museo *m* de retratos, galería *f* iconográfica ► **portrait painter** N retratista *mf*

portraitist ['pɔːtrɪtɪst] N retratista *mf*

portraiture ['pɔːtrɪtʃəʳ] N (= *portrait*) retrato *m*; (= *portraits collectively*) retratos *mpl*; (= *art of portraiture*) arte *m* de retratar; **Spanish ~ in the 16th century** retratos *mpl* españoles del siglo XVI

portray [pɔː'treɪ] VT 1 (= *paint etc portrait of*) retratar
2 (= *describe, paint etc*) representar, pintar

portrayal [pɔː'treɪəl] N 1 (*Art*) retrato *m*
2 (= *description*) descripción *f*, representación *f*; **a most unflattering ~** una representación nada halagadora *or* favorecedora

portress ['pɔːtrɪs] N portera *f*

Portugal ['pɔːtjʊgəl] N Portugal *m*

Portuguese [ˌpɔːtjʊ'giːz] Ⓐ ADJ portugués
Ⓑ N (*pl* **Portuguese**) 1 (= *person*) portugués/esa *m/f*
2 (*Ling*) portugués *m*
Ⓒ CPD ► **Portuguese man-of-war** N (*Zool*) *especie de medusa*

POS N ABBR (= **point of sale**) punto *m* de venta

pos. ABBR = **positive**

pose [pəʊz] Ⓐ N 1 [*of body*] postura *f*, actitud *f*
2 (*fig*) afectación *f*, pose *f*; **it's only a ~** es pura pose
Ⓑ VT 1 (= *position*) hacer posar; **he ~d the model in the position he wanted** hizo que la modelo posara como él quería
2 [+ *problem, question, difficulty*] plantear; [+ *threat*] representar, encerrar
Ⓒ VI 1 (= *place o.s.*) colocarse; (*for artist etc*) posar; **she once ~d for Picasso** una vez posó para Picasso
2 (*affectedly*) presumir, hacer pose
3 **to ~ as** (= *pretend to be*) hacerse pasar por; (= *disguise o.s. as*) disfrazarse de

Poseidon [pə'saɪdən] N Poseidón

poser* ['pəʊzəʳ] N 1 (= *problem*) problema *m* *or* pregunta *f* difícil
2 (= *person*) = **poseur**

poseur [pəʊ'zɜːʳ] N persona *f* afectada

posh* [pɒʃ] Ⓐ ADJ (*compar* **posher**; *superl* **poshest**) (= *high-class*) elegante, pijo (*Sp**); (= *affected*) [*accent etc*] afectado; [*wedding etc*] de mucho rumbo; [*school*] de buen tono; **a ~ car/hotel** un coche/un hotel de lujo; **~ people** gente *f* bien; **it's a very ~ neighbourhood** es un barrio de lo más elegante
Ⓑ ADV **to talk ~** hablar con acento afectado

►**posh up*** VT + ADV **to ~ a place up** procurar que un local parezca más elegante, renovar la pintura *etc* de un local; **it's all ~ed up** está totalmente renovado, se ha reformado por completo; **to ~ o.s. up** arreglarse, ataviarse, emperejilarse

posing pouch ['pəʊzɪŋˌpaʊtʃ] N tanga *m*, marcapaquete* *m*

posit ['pɒzɪt] VT proponer como principio (**that** que), postular

▼**position** [pə'zɪʃən] Ⓐ N 1 (= *location*) [*of object, person*] posición *f*; [*of house, town*] situación *f*, ubicación *f* (*LAm*); **the ship radioed its ~** el barco transmitió su posición por radio; **the house is in a very exposed ~** la casa está situada *or* (*LAm*) ubicada en un lugar muy expuesto; **to be in ~** estar en su sitio; **to get into ~** ponerse en posición; **the troops are moving into ~** las tropas están ocupando posiciones; **to be out of ~** [*object*] estar desplazado *or* desencajado; (*Sport*) [*player*] estar fuera de sitio; **to take up ~(s)**: **troops have taken up ~s near the border** las tropas se han apostado cerca de la frontera; **he took up his usual ~ in front of the fire** ocupó su sitio *or* lugar habitual frente a la chimenea; **I took up my lookout ~ on the bow** ocupé mi puesto *or* posición de vigilancia en la proa
2 (= *posture*) (*gen*) posición *f*, postura *f*; (*sexual*) postura *f*; **to change (one's) ~** cambiar de posición *or* postura; **he had raised himself to a sitting ~** se había incorporado
3 (*Sport*) **what ~ do you play (in)?** ¿de qué juegas?
4 (*Mil*) [*of troops*] posición *f*; (*for gun*) emplazamiento *m*; **the enemy ~s** las posiciones enemigas *or* del enemigo
5 (*in race, competition*) puesto *m*, posición *f*, lugar *m*; (*in class, league*) puesto *m*; **he finished in third ~** terminó en tercer puesto *or* lugar, terminó en tercera posición; *see also* **pole C**
6 (*in society*) posición *f*; **she gave up career, social ~, everything** renunció a su profesión, a su posición social, a todo
7 (= *post*) (*gen*) puesto *m*; (*high-ranking*) cargo *m*; **a high ~ in government** un alto cargo en el gobierno; **to take up a ~** aceptar un puesto; **a ~ of trust** un puesto de confianza
8 (= *situation, circumstance*) situación *f*; **this is the ~** la situación es ésta; **it puts me in a rather difficult ~** me pone en una situación bastante delicada; **the country's economic ~** la situación económica del país; **put yourself in my ~** ponte en mi lugar; **(if I were) in his ~, I'd say nothing** yo que él *or* yo en su lugar no diría nada; **what is my legal ~?** desde el punto de vista legal, ¿cuál es mi situación?; **we are in a strong negotiating ~** estamos en una buena posición para negociar; **what's the ~ on deliveries/sales?** ¿cuál es la situación respecto a las entregas/ventas?; **they were in a ~ to help** su situación les permitía ayudar; **he's in no ~ to criticize** no es quién para criticar, él no está en condiciones de criticar; *see also* **consider A1**, **jockey C**
9 (= *opinion*) postura *f* (**on** con respecto a); **you must make your ~ clear** tienes que dejar clara tu postura; **what is our ~ on Greece?** ¿cuál es nuestra nuestra política *or* postura con respecto a Grecia?
10 (= *window*) (*in bank, post office*) ventanilla *f*; **"~ closed"** "ventanilla cerrada"
Ⓑ VT 1 (= *place in position*) [+ *furniture, object*] colocar; [+ *police, troops*] apostar; **soldiers have been ~ed around the building** se han apostado soldados rodeando el edificio; **to ~ o.s.** (*lit*) colocarse, situarse; (*fig*) (= *take a stance*) adoptar una postura; **France is ~ing itself for offensive action** Francia está adoptando una postura de ataque
2 (*Sport*) [+ *ball, shuttlecock*] colocar
3 **to be ~ed** (= *located*) 3·1 (*lit*) **the house was strategically ~ed** la casa estaba situada *or* ubicada de forma estratégica; **it was a difficult shot from where she was ~ed** era un tiro difícil desde donde estaba situada *or* colocada
3·2 (*fig*) **he is well ~ed to act as intermediary** está en una buena posición para hacer de intermediario

positive ['pɒzɪtɪv] Ⓐ ADJ 1 (= *sure, certain*) seguro; **you don't sound very ~** no pareces estar muy seguro; **"are you sure?" — "yes, ~"** —¿estás seguro? —segurísimo *or* —no me cabe la menor duda; **he's ~ about it** está seguro de ello; **we have ~ proof that ...** tenemos pruebas concluyentes de que ...; *see* **proof A1**
2 (= *affirmative, constructive*) [*attitude, view, influence*] positivo; [*criticism*] constructivo; [*person*] que tiene una actitud positiva; **she's a ~ sort of person** es una persona que tiene una actitud positiva; **I think this news is a ~ sign** creo que esta noticia es prometedora; **she made a very ~ impression with us** nos causó muy buena impresión; **to take ~ action** tomar medidas firmes; **~ discrimination** discriminación *f* positiva; **on the ~ side** en el lado positivo; **~ vetting** investigación *f* de antecedentes
3 (= *real*) [*disgrace, disadvantage*] verdadero, auténtico; **he's a ~ nuisance** es un verdadero *or* auténtico pelmazo*
4 (*Elec, Phot, Ling*) positivo; (*Med*) [*result*] positivo; (*Math*) [*number*] positivo; **~ cash flow** flujo *m* positivo de caja
Ⓑ N (= *plus point*) aspecto *m* positivo; (*Phot*)

➤ LANGUAGE IN USE: **position A7** 19.1 **A9** 6.2

positivo *m*; (*Math*) número *m* positivo, valor *m* positivo; **the ~s outweigh the negatives** los aspectos positivos tienen más peso que *or* superan a los negativos; **to give a false ~** (*Med*) dar un resultado positivo falso

Ⓒ ADV **to test ~** dar positivo; **you have to think ~** hay que ser positivo

positively ['pɒzɪtɪvlɪ] ADV 1 (= *with certainty*) [*guarantee*] con seguridad; (= *categorically*) [*refuse*] tajantemente; **the body has been ~ identified** se ha hecho una identificación definitiva del cadáver

2 (= *affirmatively*) [*respond, act*] de manera positiva; **most employees view the new system ~** la mayoría de los empleados ha reaccionado favorablemente al nuevo sistema, la mayoría de los empleados ve el nuevo sistema con buenos ojos; **you must think and act ~** debes tener una actitud positiva; **they are contributing ~ to the development of their community** están participando activamente en el desarrollo de su comunidad

3 (*) (= *really, absolutely*) [*amazed, delighted*] realmente, verdaderamente; **the food was ~ disgusting!** ¡la comida daba auténtico *or* verdadero asco!, ¡la comida era realmente *or* verdaderamente asquerosa!; **this is ~ the last time I'm going to tell you** está sí que es la última vez que te lo digo; **Miguel knows ~ nothing about business** Miguel no sabe absolutamente nada de negocios

4 (*Elec*) **a ~ charged ion** un ión con carga positiva

positivism ['pɒzɪtɪvɪzəm] N positivismo *m*

positivist ['pɒzɪtɪvɪst] Ⓐ ADJ positivista

Ⓑ N positivista *mf*

positron ['pɒzɪ,trɒn] N positrón *m*

poss* [pɒs] Ⓐ ADJ ABBR = **possible**; **as soon as ~** cuanto antes, lo más pronto posible

Ⓑ ADV ABBR = **possibly**

posse ['pɒsɪ] N (*esp US*) pelotón *m*

possess [pə'zes] VT 1 (= *have*) tener, poseer; (= *own*) [+ *property*] poseer, ser dueño de; **it ~es many advantages** tiene *or* posee muchas ventajas; **to ~ a large collection** poseer una gran colección; **to ~ o.s. of** (*frm*) tomar posesión de; (*violently*) apoderarse de; ✦**IDIOM to ~ o.s.** *or* **one's soul in patience** (*liter or hum*) armarse de paciencia

2 (= *control, take over*) **to be ~ed by an idea** estar poseído por una idea; **whatever can have ~ed you?** ¿cómo se te ocurrió?; **what can have ~ed you to think like that?** ¿cómo has podido pensar así?

possessed [pə'zest] ADJ poseso, poseído; **to be ~ by demons** estar poseso *or* poseído por los demonios; **like one ~** como un poseído

possession [pə'zeʃən] Ⓐ N 1 (= *act, state*) posesión *f*; **to come into ~ of** adquirir; **to come** *or* **pass into the ~ of** pasar a manos de; **to get ~ of** [+ *building, property*] ganar derecho de entrada a; **to get/have ~ of the ball** (*Sport*) hacerse con/tener el balón; **to have sth in one's ~** tener algo (en su posesión *or* sus manos); **to be in ~ of sth** estar en posesión de algo; **to be in full ~ of one's faculties** estar en pleno uso de sus facultades mentales; **to be in the ~ of** estar en posesión *or* manos de; **to take ~ of sth** (*Jur*) tomar posesión de algo; (*by force*) apoderarse de algo; **a house with vacant ~** una casa (que se vende) desocupada; **"with vacant ~"** "llave en mano"; ✦**PROV ~ is nine points** *or* **tenths of the law** la posesión es lo que cuenta

2 (= *thing possessed*) posesión *f*; **possessions** posesiones *fpl*, bienes *mpl*; **Spain's overseas ~s** las posesiones de España en ultramar

3 (*illegal*) [*of drugs*] posesión *f*; **~ of arms** tenencia *f* de armas

4 (*by devil*) posesión *f*

Ⓑ CPD ► **possession order** N (*Brit Jur*) orden *f* de posesión

possessive [pə'zesɪv] Ⓐ ADJ 1 [*person*] posesivo; [*love etc*] dominante, tiránico; **to be ~ about sth/towards sb** ser posesivo con algo/algn

2 (*Ling*) posesivo

Ⓑ N (*Ling*) posesivo *m*

Ⓒ CPD ► **possessive pronoun** N pronombre *m* posesivo

possessively [pə'zesɪvlɪ] ADV **she slipped her arm into his ~** le tomó del brazo de manera posesiva

possessiveness [pə'zesɪvnɪs] N posesividad *f*

possessor [pə'zesər] N poseedor(a) *m/f*, dueño/a *m/f*; **to be the proud ~ of sth** ser el orgulloso dueño *or* poseedor de algo

▼**possibility** [,pɒsə'bɪlɪtɪ] N 1 (= *chance, likelihood*) posibilidad *f*; **is there any ~ (that) they could help?** ¿hay alguna posibilidad de que nos ayuden?; **there is a strong ~ I'll be late** es muy posible que me retrase, hay muchas posibilidades de que me retrase; **beyond/within the bounds of ~**: **it is within the bounds of ~** está dentro de lo posible; **it is not beyond the bounds of ~ that he'll succeed** cabe dentro de lo posible *or* no es imposible que lo consiga; **there is no ~ of his agreeing to it** no existe ninguna posibilidad de que lo consienta; *see also* **distinct A2**

2 (= *option*) posibilidad *f*; **the possibilities are endless** hay infinidad de posibilidades; **she's a strong ~ for the nomination** tiene muchas posibilidades de ser nominada

3 (*usu pl*) (= *potential*) **the scheme has real possibilities** es un plan que promete, es un plan de gran potencial; **it's a job with great possibilities** es un trabajo con mucho futuro *or* porvenir

▼**possible** ['pɒsəbl] Ⓐ ADJ 1 (= *feasible*) posible; **she scored seven points out of a ~ nine** obtuvo siete puntos de los nueve posibles; **will it be ~ for me to leave early?** ¿hay algún inconveniente en que me vaya antes de la hora?; **as ... as ~**: **try to make the lesson as interesting as ~** trata de que la lección sea lo más interesante posible; **you must practise as much as ~** debes practicar todo lo que puedas *or* todo lo posible; **as soon as ~** cuanto antes, lo antes posible; **we provide the best ~ accommodation for our students** nuestros estudiantes disponen del mejor de los alojamientos; **if (at all) ~** si es posible, a ser posible; **to make sth ~**: **improvements made ~ by new technology** mejoras *fpl* que la nueva tecnología ha hecho posible; **he made it ~ for me to go to Spain** gracias a él pude ir a España; **the new legislation would make it ~ for alcohol to be sold on Sundays** la nueva legislación posibilitaría la venta de alcohol los domingos; **I meant it in the nicest ~ way** lo dije con la mejor de las intenciones; **we will help whenever ~** ayudaremos siempre y cuando sea posible, ayudaremos siempre que podamos; **where ~** ◊ **wherever ~** donde sea posible; **they have joined the job market at the worst ~ time** se han incorporado al mercado de trabajo en el peor momento posible *or* en el peor de los momentos; *see also* **world A1**, **as C**, **far A2**

2 (= *likely*) posible; **a ~ candidate** un posible candidato

3 (= *conceivable*) posible; **what ~ motive could she have?** ¿qué motivo puede tener?; **there is no ~ excuse for his behaviour** su comportamiento no tiene excusa que valga; **it is ~ that he'll come** es posible que venga, puede (ser) que venga; **it's just ~ he may still be there** existe una pequeña posibilidad de que siga allí

Ⓑ N 1 (*) (= *suitable person*) (*for job*) candidato/a *m/f*; **he's a ~ for Saturday's match** es posible que juegue en el partido del sábado

2 **the ~** lo posible

▼**possibly** ['pɒsəblɪ] ADV 1 (= *feasibly, conceivably*) **if I ~ can** si me es posible, si puedo; **I go as often as I ~ can** voy siempre que puedo, voy lo más a menudo posible; **how can I ~ come tomorrow?** ¿cómo voy a poder venir mañana?; **could you ~ come another day?** ¿le sería posible venir otro día?, ¿podría venir otro día?; **I can't ~ eat all this** me es totalmente imposible comer todo esto; **I couldn't ~ allow it** de ninguna manera lo voy a permitir; **it can't ~ be true!** ¡no puede ser verdad!; **she will do everything she ~ can to help you** hará todo lo que esté en su mano *or* todo lo que pueda para ayudarte; **he never does it if he can ~ help it** siempre que puede evitarlo lo evita

2 (= *perhaps*) **"will you be able to come?" — "possibly"** —¿podrás venir? —es posible *or* —puede que sí; **~ not** puede que no; **of the 200 who apply, ~ five may be accepted** de los 200 solicitantes, tal vez se elija a cinco

possum ['pɒsəm] N (*US*) zarigüeya *f*; ✦**IDIOM to play ~** (= *sleeping*) fingir estar dormido; (= *dead*) hacerse el muerto

post¹ [pəʊst] Ⓐ N 1 [*of wood, metal*] poste *m*; (*also* **goalpost**) poste *m* (de la portería); (*for fencing, marking*) estaca *f*; *see also* **bedpost**, **deaf A1**, **doorpost**, **pillar A**

2 (*Sport*) **the starting/finishing ~** el poste de salida/llegada; **the winning ~** la meta; ✦**IDIOM to be left at the ~** quedar muy en desventaja; *see also* **first A**, **pip³**

Ⓑ VT 1 (= *put up*) [+ *bill, notice*] (*also* **~ up**) poner; **"post no bills"** "prohibido fijar carteles"

2 (= *announce*) [+ *exam results*] hacer público, sacar; **to ~ sth/sb (as) missing** dar algo/a algn por desaparecido

3 (*Comm*) (*also* **~ up**) [+ *transaction*] anotar, registrar; (*US St Ex*) [+ *profit, loss*] registrar

4 (= *inform*) **to keep sb ~ed (on** *or* **about sth)** tener *or* mantener a algn al corriente *or* al tanto *or* informado (de algo)

5 (*US Sport*) [+ *time, score*] registrar, obtener

6 (*Internet*) enviar por correo electrónico

Ⓒ CPD ► **post hole** N agujero *m* de poste

▼**post²** [pəʊst] Ⓐ N 1 (*Brit*) (= *mail service*) correo *m*; **by ~** *or* **through the ~** por correo; **first-class ~** correo *m* preferente; **your cheque is in the ~** su cheque está en el correo; **second-class ~** correo *m* normal; *see also* **first-class B**, **registered B**, **return A1**

2 (= *letters*) correo *m*; **is there any ~ for me?** ¿hay correo para mí?

3 (= *office*) correos *m*; (= *mailbox*) buzón *m*; **to drop** *or* **put sth in the ~** echar algo al correo *or* al buzón; **to drop or put sth in the ~ to sb** enviar *or* mandar algo a algn

4 (= *collection*) recogida *f*; (= *delivery*) entrega *f*; **the ~ goes at 8.30** la recogida del correo es a las 8.30, recogen el correo a las 8.30; **the ~ is late** el correo se ha retrasado; **to catch the ~** echar el correo antes de la recogida; **first ~** (= *collection*) primera recogida *f*; (= *delivery*) primer reparto *m*, primera en-

➤ LANGUAGE IN USE: **possibility 1** 15.3 **possible A1** 15.3 **possibly** 16.3 **post² A1** 20.3

trega *f*; **last ~** (= *collection*) última recogida; **to miss the ~** no llegar a tiempo para la recogida del correo; **it will arrive in the second ~** llegue en el segundo reparto
5 (= *cost*) gastos *mpl* de envío; **~ and packing** gastos *mpl* de envío
6 (*Hist*) (= *rider*) correo *m*; (= *coach*) posta *f*
Ⓑ VT (= *send by post*) (*also* **~ off**) mandar *or* enviar por correo; (*Brit*) (= *put in mailbox*) echar al correo *or* al buzón; **this was ~ed on Monday** esto se echó al correo *or* al buzón el lunes; **to ~ sth to sb** mandar *or* enviar algo a algn por correo; **he ~ed a message to a newsgroup** (*Internet*) dejó un mensaje en un grupo de discusión
Ⓒ CPD ► **post horn** N corneta *f* del correo ► **post office** N oficina *f* de correos, correos *m*, correo *m* (*LAm*); **I'm going to the ~ office** voy a correos, voy al correo (*LAm*) ► **the Post Office** N ≈ la Dirección General de Correos ► **post office box** N apartado *m* de correos, casilla *f* (postal *or* de correo(s)) (*LAm*) ► **Post Office Savings Bank** N ≈ Caja *f* Postal de Ahorros ► **post office worker** N empleado/a *m/f* de correos

post³ [pəʊst] Ⓐ N 1 (= *job*) (*gen*) puesto *m*; (*high-ranking*) cargo *m*; **she's been offered a research ~** le han ofrecido un puesto *or* un trabajo de investigadora; **to hold a ~** (*gen*) ocupar un puesto; (*high-ranking*) ocupar un cargo; **to take up one's ~** (*gen*) ocupar el puesto; (*high-ranking*) entrar en funciones, ocupar el cargo; **she resigned to take up a ~ at the university** dimitió porque consiguió un puesto en la universidad
2 (*Mil*) (= *place of duty, stronghold*) puesto *m*; (*for gun*) emplazamiento *m*; **at one's ~** en su puesto; **border** *or* **frontier ~** puesto *m* fronterizo; **first ~** (toque *m* de) diana *f*; **last ~** (toque *m* de) retreta *f*; *see also* **command C**, **customs B**, **observation B**
Ⓑ VT 1 (*Mil*) [+ *sentry, guard*] apostar
2 (*Brit*) (= *send*) [+ *diplomat, soldier*] destinar; **to ~ sb abroad** destinar a algn al extranjero
3 (*US Jur*) [+ *collateral*] pagar; **to ~ bail** pagar la fianza
Ⓒ CPD ► **post exchange** N (*US Mil*) economato *m* militar, cooperativa *f* militar

POST N ABBR = **point-of-sale terminal**

post... [pəʊst] PREFIX post..., pos...

postage ['pəʊstɪdʒ] Ⓐ N franqueo *m*, porte *m*; **~ and packing** gastos *mpl* de envío; **~ due** a pagar; **~ paid** porte *m* pagado
Ⓑ CPD ► **postage meter** N (*US*) franqueadora *f* ► **postage rates** NPL tarifa *fsing* de correo ► **postage stamp** N sello *m* (de correos), estampilla *f* (*LAm*), timbre *m* (*Mex*)

postal ['pəʊstəl] Ⓐ ADJ postal
Ⓑ CPD ► **postal area**, **postal district** N distrito *m* postal ► **postal charges** NPL = **postal rates** ► **postal order** N (*Brit*) giro *m* postal ► **postal rates** NPL tarifa *fsing* de correo ► **postal service** N servicio *m* postal ► **postal survey** N encuesta *f* por correo ► **postal system** N sistema *m* postal, correo *m* ► **postal vote** N voto *m* postal ► **postal worker** N empleado/a *m/f* de correos

postbag ['pəʊstbæg] N (*Brit*) (= *sack*) saco *m* postal; (= *letters*) correspondencia *f*, cartas *fpl*; **it arrived in my ~** llegó en mi correo; **he received a heavy ~** recibió muchas cartas

postbox ['pəʊstbɒks] N (*Brit*) buzón *m*

postcard ['pəʊstkɑːd] N (tarjeta *f*) postal *f*

postcode ['pəʊstkəʊd] Ⓐ N (*Brit*) código *m* postal
Ⓑ CPD ► **postcode prescribing** N *situación arbitraria en la que algunas medicinas se recetan o no por la seguridad social según la zona donde se vive*

post-coital [pəʊst'kəʊɪtəl] ADJ de después del coito

postdate ['pəʊst'deɪt] VT poner una fecha posterior a

postdated ['pəʊst'deɪtɪd] ADJ [*cheque*] con fecha posterior

post-doctoral ['pəʊst'dɒktərəl] Ⓐ ADJ posdoctoral Ⓑ CPD ► **post-doctoral fellow** N becario/a *m/f* posdoctoral ► **post-doctoral fellowship** N beca *f* posdoctoral

poster ['pəʊstəʳ] Ⓐ N cartel *m*, póster *m*, afiche *m* (*LAm*) Ⓑ CPD ► **poster artist**, **poster designer** N cartelista *mf* ► **poster paint** N pintura *f* al agua

poste restante ['pəʊst'restɑːnt] N (*esp Brit*) lista *f* de correos, poste *f* restante (*LAm*)

posterior [pɒs'tɪərɪəʳ] Ⓐ ADJ (*frm*) posterior
Ⓑ N (* *hum*) trasero* *m*

posterity [pɒs'terɪtɪ] N posteridad *f*

postern ['pəʊstɜːn] N postigo *m*

post-free ['pəʊst'friː] ADJ, ADV (con) porte pagado, libre de franqueo

postglacial ['pəʊst'gleɪsɪəl] ADJ posglacial

postgrad* ['pəʊst'græd] = **postgraduate**

postgraduate ['pəʊst'grædjʊɪt] (*Brit*) Ⓐ N posgraduado/a *m/f* Ⓑ CPD ► **postgraduate course** N curso *m* para (pos)graduados ► **postgraduate study**, N **postgraduate studies** NPL estudios *mpl* de posgrado

post-haste† ['pəʊst'heɪst] ADV a toda prisa, con toda urgencia

posthumous ['pɒstjʊməs] ADJ póstumo

posthumously ['pɒstjʊməslɪ] ADV póstumamente, con carácter póstumo

postie* ['pəʊstɪ] N (*Brit*) cartero/a *m/f*

postilion [pəs'tɪlɪən] N postillón *m*

post-imperial ['pəʊstɪm'pɪərɪəl] ADJ posimperial

post-impressionism ['pəʊstɪm'preʃənɪzəm] N posimpresionismo *m*

post-impressionist ['pəʊstɪm'preʃənɪst] ADJ, N posimpresionista *mf*

post-industrial [ˌpəʊstɪn'dʌstrɪəl] ADJ posindustrial

posting ['pəʊstɪŋ] N 1 (*Brit Mil etc*) destino *m*
2 (*Fin*) asiento *m*, traspaso *m* al libro mayor

postman ['pəʊstmən] Ⓐ N (*pl* **postmen**) (*Brit*) cartero *m*
Ⓑ CPD ► **postman's knock** N (= *game*) *juego de niños en que el que se intercambia un beso por una carta imaginaria*

postmark ['pəʊstmɑːk] Ⓐ N matasellos *m inv*; **date as ~** según fecha del matasellos
Ⓑ VT matasellar; **it is ~ed "León"** lleva el matasellos de León

postmaster ['pəʊstˌmɑːstəʳ] Ⓐ N administrador *m* de correos
Ⓑ CPD ► **postmaster general** N (*Brit*) director *m* general de correos

postmistress ['pəʊstˌmɪstrɪs] N administradora *f* de correos

postmodern ['pəʊst'mɒdən] ADJ posmoderno

postmodernism ['pəʊst'mɒdənɪzəm] N posmodernismo *m*

postmodernist ['pəʊst'mɒdənɪst] ADJ, N posmodernista *mf*

post-mortem ['pəʊst'mɔːtəm] N (*gen*) autopsia *f*; **to carry out a ~** practicar una autopsia; **to hold a ~ on sth** (*fig*) analizar los resultados de algo, hacer el balance de algo

post-natal ['pəʊst'neɪtl] Ⓐ ADJ postnatal, pos(t)parto
Ⓑ CPD ► **post-natal depression** N depresión *f* pos(t)parto

post-operative [ˌpəʊst'ɒpərətɪv] ADJ posoperativo

post-paid ['pəʊst'peɪd] ADV porte pagado, franco de porte

postpartum [pəʊst'pɑːtəm] Ⓐ N postparto, posparto
Ⓑ CPD ► **postpartum depression** N depresión *f* pos(t)parto

postpone [pəʊst'pəʊn] VT aplazar, postergar (*LAm*); **mightn't it be better to ~ it?** ¿no sería mejor aplazarlo?; **to ~ sth for a month** aplazar algo por un mes; **it has been ~d till Tuesday** ha sido aplazado hasta el martes

postponement [pəʊst'pəʊnmənt] N aplazamiento *m*

postpositive [pəʊst'pɒzɪtɪv] ADJ pospositivo

postprandial ['pəʊst'prændɪəl] ADJ [*speech, talk etc*] de sobremesa; [*walk etc*] que se da después de comer

postproduction [ˌpəʊstprə'dʌkʃən] Ⓐ N actividad *f* posterior a la producción
Ⓑ CPD [*costs etc*] que sigue a la producción

postscript ['pəʊsskrɪpt] N (*to letter*) posdata *f*; (*fig*) epílogo *m*; **there is a ~ to this story** esta historia tiene epílogo

poststructuralism ['pəʊst'strʌktʃərəlɪzəm] N postestructuralismo *m*

poststructuralist [ˌpəʊst'strʌktʃərəlɪst] Ⓐ ADJ postestructuralista *inv*
Ⓑ N postestructuralista *mf*

post-traumatic stress ['pəʊsttrɔːˌmætɪk'stres] N estrés *m* postraumático

postulant ['pɒstjʊlənt] N postulante/a *m/f*

postulate Ⓐ ['pɒstjʊlɪt] N postulado *m*
Ⓑ ['pɒstjʊleɪt] VT postular

postulation [ˌpɒstjʊ'leɪʃən] N postulación *f*

postural ['pɒstʃərəl] ADJ [*habits, exercises*] postural

posture ['pɒstʃəʳ] Ⓐ N postura *f*, actitud *f*
Ⓑ VI (*pej*) adoptar una postura afectada

posturing ['pɒstʃə'rɪŋ] N pose *f*; **the threat to dispatch troops is mere ~** la amenaza de enviar tropas no es mas que una pose de cara al exterior; **there was a lot of political ~ going on** había mucho de fingimiento en las declaraciones políticas

postviral syndrome [pəʊst'vaɪərəl'sɪndrəʊm] N síndrome *m* posvírico

postvocalic [ˌpəʊstvəʊ'kælɪk] ADJ posvocálico

post-war ['pəʊst'wɔːʳ] ADJ de la posguerra; **the ~ period** la pos(t)guerra

postwoman ['pəʊstˌwʊmən] N (*pl* **postwomen**) (*Brit*) cartera *f*

posy ['pəʊzɪ] N ramillete *m*

pot¹ [pɒt] Ⓐ N 1 (*for cooking*) cazuela *f*, olla *f* (*LAm*); (*for jam*) tarro *m*, pote *m* (*S. Cone*); (*for flowers*) tiesto *m*, maceta *f*; (= *teapot*) tetera *f*; (= *coffee pot*) cafetera *f*; (= *chamber pot*) orinal *m*; (= *piece of pottery*) cacharro *m*; **~s and pans** batería *fsing* de cocina, cacharros *mpl*; ✦**IDIOMS to keep the ~ boiling** (= *earn living*) ganarse la vida; (= *make things progress*) mantener las cosas en marcha; **to go to ~*** irse al traste*; **that's the ~ calling the kettle black** el puchero le dijo a la sartén —apártate que me tiznas
2 (= *potful*) cazuela *f*; **a ~ of coffee for two** café *m* para dos; **to make a ~ of tea** hacer el té
3 (*Cards*) pozo *m*; (*esp US*) (= *kitty*) bote *m*
4 **pots*** (= *lots*) **we have ~s of it** tenemos montones*; **to have ~s of money** estar forrado de dinero*
5 (*Sport**) (= *prize*) copa *f*

➤ LANGUAGE IN USE: **post³ A1** 19.4, 19.5

[6] (*Snooker, Billiards*) billa *f*
[7] (*) (= *shot*) **he took a ~ at the wolf** disparó contra el lobo
[8] (*) (= *stomach*) panza* *f*, barriga *f*
Ⓑ VT [1] [+ *jam, meat, etc*] conservar en tarros
[2] [+ *plant*] poner en tiesto *or* maceta; (*also* **to ~ up**) [+ *seedling*] enmacetar
[3] (*Snooker, Billiards*) meter en la tronera
[4] (*) (= *shoot*) [+ *duck, pheasant*] matar
Ⓒ VI (= *shoot*) **to ~ at sb** disparar sobre algn
Ⓓ CPD ► **pot belly** N (*from overeating*) panza* *f*; (*from malnutrition*) barriga *f* hinchada ► **pot cheese** N (*US*) ≈ requesón *m* ► **pot herb** N hierba *f* aromática ► **pot luck** N **to take ~ luck** conformarse con lo que haya ► **pot plant** N planta *f* de interior ► **pot roast** N carne *f* asada a la cazuela ► **pot shot*** N tiro *m* al azar; **to take a ~ shot at sth** disparar contra algo al azar; *see also* **pot-bellied**, **pot-roast**

pot²‡ [pɒt] N (= *marijuana*) maría* *f*, chocolate* *m*, mota *f* (*LAm**)

potable [ˈpəʊtəbl] ADJ potable

potash [ˈpɒtæʃ] N potasa *f*

potassium [pəˈtæsɪəm] Ⓐ N potasio *m*
Ⓑ CPD ► **potassium cyanide** N cianuro *m* de potasio ► **potassium nitrate** N nitrato *m* de potasio ► **potassium sulphate** N sulfato *m* potásico

potations [pəʊˈteɪʃənz] NPL (*frm*) libaciones *fpl*

potato [pəˈteɪtəʊ] Ⓐ N (*pl* **potatoes**) patata *f*, papa *f* (*LAm*); **baked ~** patata *f* al horno; **~es in their jackets** patatas *fpl* con su piel; *see also* **hot C**, **small A1**, **sweet C**
Ⓑ CPD ► **potato beetle** N dorífora *f*, escarabajo *m* de la patata *or* (*LAm*) papa ► **potato blight** N roña *f* de la patata *or* (*LAm*) papa ► **potato cake** N croqueta *f* de patata *or* (*LAm*) papa ► **potato chip** N (*US*) = **potato crisp** ► **potato crisp** N patata *f* frita, papa *f* frita (*LAm*) ► **potato field** N patatal *m* ► **potato masher** N *utensilio para aplastar las patatas al hacer puré* ► **potato peeler** N pelapatatas *m inv*, pelapapas *m inv* (*LAm*) ► **potato salad** N ensalada *f* de patatas *or* (*LAm*) papas

pot-bellied [ˈpɒt,belɪd] ADJ (*from overeating*) barrigón*; (*from malnutrition*) de vientre hinchado

potboiler [ˈpɒt,bɔɪləʳ] N obra *f* (mediocre) (*escrita para ganar dinero*)

pot-bound [ˈpɒtbaʊnd] ADJ **this plant is ~** esta planta ya no cabe en la maceta, esta planta ha crecido demasiado para esta maceta

poteen [pɒˈtiːn, pɒˈtʃiːn] N aguardiente *m*, whiskey *m* (*irlandés, destilado ilegalmente*)

potency [ˈpəʊtənsɪ] N potencia *f*; [*of drink*] fuerza *f*; [*of remedy*] eficacia *f*; (*Physiol*) potencia *f*

potent [ˈpəʊtənt] ADJ potente, poderoso; [*drink*] fuerte; [*remedy*] eficaz

potentate [ˈpəʊtənteɪt] N potentado *m*

potential [pəˈtenʃəl] Ⓐ ADJ en potencia; **~ earnings** ganancias *fpl* potenciales; **a ~ prime minister** un primer ministro en ciernes; **a ~ threat** una posible amenaza
Ⓑ N [1] (= *possibilities*) potencial *m*; (= *ability*) capacidad *f*; **to have ~** mostrar gran potencial; **the war ~ of this country** el potencial bélico de este país; **our ~ for increasing production** nuestras posibilidades de incrementar la producción; **he hasn't yet realized his full ~** todavía no ha desarrollado plenamente su potencial; **to have the ~ to do sth** [*person*] tener aptitudes *or* capacidad para hacer algo; **the meeting has the ~ to be a watershed** la reunión puede llegar a ser un acontecimiento decisivo
[2] (*Elec, Math, Phys*) potencial *m*

potentiality [pə,tenʃɪˈælɪtɪ] N potencialidad *f*

potentially [pəˈtenʃəlɪ] ADV en potencia, potencialmente

potentiate [pəˈtenʃɪ,eɪt] VT (*frm*) potenciar

pother [ˈpɒðəʳ] N lío *m*; **all this ~!** ¡qué lío!; **to make a ~ about sth** armar un lío a causa de algo

pothole [ˈpɒthəʊl] N [1] (*in road*) bache *m*
[2] (*Geol*) marmita *f* de gigante, gruta *f*; (*loosely*) cueva *f*, caverna *f*, profunda gruta *f*

pot-holed [ˈpɒt,həʊld] ADJ [*road*] lleno de baches

potholer [ˈpɒthəʊləʳ] N (*Brit*) espeleólogo/a *m/f*

potholing [ˈpɒthəʊlɪŋ] N (*Brit*) espeleología *f*; **to go ~** hacer espeleología; (*on specific occasion*) ir de espeleología

pothunter* [ˈpɒthʌntəʳ] N cazador(a) *m/f* de premios

potion [ˈpəʊʃən] N poción *f*, pócima *f*

potpourri [pəʊˈpʊərɪ] N (*pl* **potpourris**) [1] (= *flowers*) flores *fpl* secas aromáticas, popurrí *m*
[2] [*of music, writing*] popurrí *m*

pot-roast [ˈpɒtrəʊst] VT asar

potsherd [ˈpɒt,ʃɜːd] N tiesto *m*, casco *m*

potted [ˈpɒtɪd] ADJ [1] [*food*] conservado en tarros; [*plant*] en tiesto, en maceta
[2] (= *shortened*) [*history, version*] resumido

potter¹ [ˈpɒtəʳ] Ⓐ N alfarero/a *m/f*; (*artistic*) ceramista *mf*
Ⓑ CPD ► **potter's clay** N arcilla *f* de alfarería ► **potter's field** N (*US*) cementerio *m* de pobres ► **potter's wheel** N torno *m* de alfarero

potter² [ˈpɒtəʳ] VI (*Brit*) entretenerse haciendo un poco de todo; **I ~ed round the house all day** estuve todo el día en casa haciendo un poco de todo; **we ~ed round the shops** nos paseamos por las tiendas

► **potter about, potter around** VI + ADV (*Brit*) **he likes ~ing about in the garden** le gusta entretenerse haciendo pequeños trabajos en el jardín

► **potter along** VI + ADV (*Brit*) hacerse el remolón*; **we ~ along** vamos tirando*

pottery [ˈpɒtərɪ] N [1] (= *craft*) alfarería *f*; (= *art*) cerámica *f*
[2] (= *pots*) cerámica *f*; [*of fine quality*] loza *f*; **a piece of ~** una cerámica
[3] (= *workshop*) alfar *m*, alfarería *f*

potting compost [ˈpɒtɪŋ,kɒmpɒst] N compost *m* para macetas

potting shed [ˈpɒtɪŋʃed] N cobertizo *m* de enmacetar

potty¹* [ˈpɒtɪ] N orinal *m* de niño, bacinica *f* (*LAm*)

potty²* [ˈpɒtɪ] ADJ (*compar* **pottier**; *superl* **pottiest**) (*Brit*) [1] (= *mad*) chiflado*; **she's ~ about him** anda loca por él*, se chifla por él*; **you must be ~!** ¡tú estás loco!; **to drive sb ~** volver loco a algn; **it's enough to drive you ~** es para volverse loco
[2] (= *small*) insignificante, miserable

potty-trained [ˈpɒtɪ,treɪnd] ADJ (*Brit*) que ya no necesita pañales

potty-training [ˈpɒtɪtreɪnɪŋ] N (*Brit*) *adiestramiento de los niños pequeños en el uso del orinal para hacer sus necesidades*

pouch [paʊtʃ] N (*for tobacco*) petaca *f*; (*for ammunition*) cartuchera *f*; (*hunter's*) morral *m*; (*Zool, Anat*) bolsa *f*

pouf(fe) [puːf] N [1] (= *seat*) puf(f) *m*
[2] (*Brit‡*) = **poof**

poulterer [ˈpəʊltərəʳ] N (*Brit*) pollero/a *m/f*; **~'s (shop)** pollería *f*

poultice [ˈpəʊltɪs] Ⓐ N cataplasma *f*, emplasto *m*
Ⓑ VT poner una cataplasma a, emplastar (**with** con)

poultry [ˈpəʊltrɪ] Ⓐ N (*alive*) aves *fpl* de corral; (*as food*) aves *fpl*
Ⓑ CPD ► **poultry breeding** N avicultura *f* ► **poultry dealer** N recovero/a *m/f*, pollero/a *m/f* ► **poultry farm** N granja *f* avícola ► **poultry farmer** N avicultor(a) *m/f* ► **poultry farming** N avicultura *f* ► **poultry house** N gallinero *m* ► **poultry keeper** N = **poultry farmer** ► **poultry keeping** N = **poultry farming** ► **poultry shop** N (*US*) pollería *f*

pounce [paʊns] Ⓐ N salto *m*, ataque *m*; (*by bird*) calada *f*
Ⓑ VI abalanzarse (**on** sobre); [*bird*] calarse; **to ~ on sth/sb** (*lit*) abalanzarse sobre algo/algn, echarse encima de algo/algn; **to ~ on sb's mistake** saltar sobre el error de algn

pound¹ [paʊnd] Ⓐ N [1] (= *weight*) libra *f* (= *453,6gr*); **half a ~** media libra; **two dollars a ~** dos dólares la libra; **they sell it by the ~** lo venden por libras; ✦*IDIOM* **to demand one's ~ of flesh** exigir todo lo que le corresponde a uno; → IMPERIAL SYSTEM
[2] (= *money*) libra *f*; **one ~ sterling** una libra esterlina; **the ~** (*Econ*) la libra esterlina
Ⓑ CPD ► **pound coin** N moneda *f* de una libra ► **pound note** N billete *m* de una libra

pound² [paʊnd] Ⓐ VT [1] (*strike*) [1·1] (*with fists*) [+ *door, table*] aporrear, golpear; **he ~ed the table with his fist** aporreó *or* golpeó la mesa con el puño; **to ~ one's fists against sth** golpear algo con los puños; **to ~ sth to pieces (with one's fists)** destrozar algo (a puñetazos *or* con los puños)
[1·2] (*with hammer*) martillear; (*with other instrument*) golpear; **he ~ed the stake into the ground with a rock** clavó la estaca en la tierra golpeándola con una piedra; **to ~ sth to pieces (with a hammer)** destrozar algo (a martillazos); **they ~ed him into a pulp with their sticks** lo molieron a palos
[1·3] [*sea, waves*] azotar, batir contra; **the waves ~ed the boat to pieces** las olas batieron contra el bote hasta destrozarlo
[1·4] (*Mil*) **day after day long-range artillery ~ed the city** día tras día fuego de artillería de largo alcance cayó sobre la ciudad causando estragos; **the bombs ~ed the city to rubble** las bombas redujeron la ciudad a escombros
[2] (*Culin*) [+ *herbs, spices*] machacar; [+ *garlic, mixture*] machacar, majar; [+ *meat*] golpear; [+ *dough*] trabajar
[3] (= *thump*) [+ *piano, typewriter*] aporrear; ✦*IDIOMS* **to ~ the beat*** rondar las calles (como policía); **to ~ the pavement(s)** (*US**) patear las calles*
Ⓑ VI [1] (= *throb, pulsate*) [*head*] estar a punto de estallar; [*heart*] palpitar; [*music*] retumbar; **the blood ~ed in his ears** podía oír el pulso de la sangre en los oídos; **his heart ~ed with fear/joy/excitement** el corazón le palpitaba de miedo/de alegría/de emoción
[2] (= *strike*) **the sea ~ed against** *or* **on the rocks** el mar azotaba las rocas *or* batía contra las rocas; **somebody began ~ing at** *or* **on the door** alguien empezó a aporrear la puerta; **we listened to the rain ~ing on the roof** oíamos la lluvia cayendo con fuerza sobre el tejado
[3] (= *move heavily*) **he was ~ing along the road** corría con paso pesado *or* pesadamente por la carretera; **to ~ up/down the stairs**

subir/bajar las escaleras con paso pesado *or* pesadamente; **the train ~ed past** el tren pasó retumbando

►**pound out** VT + ADV **he was ~ing out a tune on the piano** aporreaba una canción en el piano; **the drums ~ed out the good news** los redobles de los tambores lanzaron a los cuatro vientos la buena noticia

pound[3] [paʊnd] N (= *enclosure*) (*for dogs*) perrera *f*; (*for cars*) depósito *m* de coches

poundage [ˈpaʊndɪdʒ] N *impuesto or comisión que se exige por cada libra esterlina or de peso*

-pounder [ˈpaʊndəʳ] N (*ending in compounds*) **four-pounder** (= *fish*) pez *m* de cuatro libras; **twenty-five-pounder** (*Mil*) cañón *m* de veinticinco

pounding [ˈpaʊndɪŋ] N [1] (= *noise*) [*of feet, hooves*] pisadas *fpl*; [*of guns*] martilleo *m*; [*of sea, waves*] embate *m*; [*of heart*] palpitaciones *fpl*, latidos *mpl* violentos; **suddenly there was a furious ~ on the door** de repente empezaron a aporrear furiosamente la puerta
[2] (= *pummelling*) (*from shells, bombs*) bombardeo *m*; **the city took a ~ last night** la ciudad fue muy castigada en el bombardeo de anoche
[3] (*) (*fig*) (= *thrashing*) **Barcelona gave us a real ~** el Barcelona nos dio una paliza de las buenas*; **to take a ~** sufrir una (dura) derrota

pour [pɔːʳ] (A) VT [1] (= *serve*) servir; **shall I ~ the tea?** ¿sirvo el té?; **to ~ sb a drink** ◊ **~ a drink for sb** servir una copa a algn; **he ~ed himself some coffee** se sirvió café
[2] (= *tip*) [+ *liquid*] verter, echar; [+ *salt, powder*] echar; **I ~ed the milk down the sink** vertí *or* eché la leche por el fregadero; **he ~ed some wine into a glass** vertió *or* echó un poco de vino en un vaso; **~ the sauce over the meat** vierta *or* eche la salsa sobre la carne; *see also* **cold A1**, **oil A1**, **scorn A**
[3] (= *invest*) **they are ~ing millions into the Olympics** están invirtiendo millones en las Olimpiadas; **to ~ money into a project** invertir grandes cantidades de dinero en un proyecto; **we can't go on ~ing money into this project** no podemos seguir invirtiendo ese caudal en este proyecto
(B) VI [1] (= *serve*) servir; **shall I ~?** ¿sirvo?
[2] (= *tip*) **this teapot doesn't ~ very well** es difícil servir con esta tetera
[3] (= *flow*) **water was ~ing down the walls** el agua caía a raudales por las paredes; **tears ~ed down his face** las lágrimas le resbalaban por la cara; **water ~ed from the broken pipe** el agua salía a raudales de la tubería rota; **blood ~ed from the wound** la sangre salía a borbotones de la herida; **water came ~ing into the room** el agua entraba a raudales en el cuarto; **the sweat was ~ing off him** sudaba a chorros
[4] (*Met*) **it's ~ing (with rain)** está lloviendo a cántaros, está diluviando; *see also* **pour down**, **rain B1**
[5] (*fig*) **smoke was ~ing from the window** grandes bocanadas de humo salían de la ventana; **passionate German prose ~ed from her lips** apasionadas palabras de prosa alemana le brotaban de los labios; **refugees ~ed into the country** entraban grandes cantidades de refugiados en el país; **sunshine ~ed into the room** el sol entraba a raudales en la habitación; **cars ~ed off the ferry** muchísimos coches salían del transbordador; **cars are ~ing off the assembly lines** grandes cantidades de coches están saliendo de las cadenas de montaje; *see also* **pour out**

►**pour away** VT + ADV tirar; **he had to ~ the wine away** tuvo que tirar el vino

►**pour down** (A) VI + ADV **it/the rain was ~ing down** llovía a cántaros; **the sun ~ed down on them** el sol les daba de lleno; *see also* **pour B3**
(B) VT + PREP *see* **pour A2**

►**pour forth** (*liter*) (A) VT + ADV (*lit*) [+ *smoke*] echar; (*fig*) [+ *words, abuse*] soltar; **the washing machine was ~ing forth water at an alarming rate** el agua se salía de la lavadora a una velocidad alarmante
(B) VI + ADV (*lit*) [*smoke, gas*] salir en grandes cantidades; [*water, liquid*] salir a raudales; [*blood*] salir a borbotones; (*fig*) [*words, criticisms*] manar

►**pour in** (A) VI + ADV [1] (*lit*) **water was ~ing in** estaba entrando agua a raudales; **sunshine ~ed in from the courtyard** desde el patio el sol entraba a raudales en la habitación
[2] (*fig*) [*people*] (*to country, area*) llegar a raudales; (*to shop, office*) entrar a raudales; **letters ~ed in from their fans** les llovían cartas de sus admiradores, llegaban avalanchas de cartas de sus admiradores; **as the results ~ed in …** a medida que llegaba la avalancha de resultados …
(B) VT + ADV [1] (*lit*) [+ *liquid*] (*into mixture*) añadir; (*into container*) echar; **next, ~ in the milk** luego, añada la leche
[2] (*fig*) **we can't keep ~ing in capital** no podemos seguir invirtiendo tanto capital *or* ese caudal

►**pour off** (A) VT + ADV (= *throw away*) tirar; (= *put aside*) apartar; **~ off the excess fat** tire el exceso de grasa; **~ off half the quantity** aparte la mitad
(B) VI + PREP *see* **pour B3, B5**

►**pour out** (A) VT + ADV [1] (= *serve*) [+ *tea, milk, cornflakes*] servir; **shall I ~ you out some tea?** ◊ **shall I ~ out some tea for you?** ¿te sirvo té?
[2] (= *emit*) [+ *smoke, fumes*] arrojar
[3] (= *produce*) **the factory ~s out hundreds of cars a day** la fábrica produce cientos de coches al día
[4] (*fig*) [+ *anger, emotion*] desahogar; [+ *words, abuse*] soltar; **he ~ed out a torrent of abuse (against them)** (les) soltó un torrente de insultos; **to ~ out one's feelings (to sb)** desahogarse (con algn); **to ~ out one's heart to sb** desahogarse con algn, abrir su corazón a algn; **to ~ it all out** contarlo todo; **to ~ it all out to sb** contárselo todo a algn
(B) VI + ADV [1] (*lit*) [*water, liquid*] salir a raudales; [*blood*] salir a borbotones; **he smashed the window and smoke ~ed out** rompió la ventana y salieron grandes bocanadas de humo
[2] (= *come out in large numbers*) [*people, crowds*] salir en tropel; **the doors opened and thousands of fans ~ed out** las puertas se abrieron y miles de seguidores salieron en tropel; **they ~ed out into the streets** invadieron las calles
[3] (= *gush out*) [*words*] brotar de la boca, manar de la boca; **once she started speaking, the ideas came ~ing out** una vez empezó a hablar, le fluyeron las ideas; **the words came ~ing out** las palabras brotaban *or* manaban de su boca; **once he started to talk it all came ~ing out** una vez empezó a hablar, ya se desahogó del todo

pouring [ˈpɔːrɪŋ] ADJ [1] [*custard, cream etc*] líquido
[2] [*rain*] torrencial; **we queued in the ~ rain for hours** hicimos cola durante horas bajo la lluvia torrencial

pout [paʊt] (A) N puchero *m*, mohín *m*
(B) VI hacer pucheros, hacer un mohín
(C) VT **"never!" she ~ed** —¡nunca! —dijo con gesto mohíno; **to ~ one's lips** hacer pucheros, hacer un mohín

poverty [ˈpɒvətɪ] (A) N [1] (= *state of being poor*) pobreza *f*; **absolute/extreme/relative ~** pobreza *f* absoluta/extrema/relativa; **to live/die in ~** vivir/morir en la pobreza; *see also* **abject 3**, **grinding 2**, **plead A2**, **vow A**
[2] (= *lack*) pobreza *f*, escasez *f*; **~ of resources** pobreza *f or* escasez *f* de recursos; **~ of ideas** pobreza *f* de ideas; **~ of imagination** pobreza *f or* falta *f* de imaginación
[3] (= *poor quality*) [*of soil*] pobreza *f*
(B) CPD ► **poverty line**, **poverty level** (*US*) N umbral *m* de pobreza; **to be** *or* **live above/below the ~ line** *or* **level** vivir por encima/por debajo del umbral de pobreza; **to be** *or* **live on the ~ line** vivir en el umbral de pobreza, vivir al borde de la pobreza ► **poverty trap** N (*Brit*) trampa *f* de la pobreza

poverty-stricken [ˈpɒvətɪˌstrɪkn] ADJ [*person*] muy pobre, indigente; [*area*] muy pobre; **to be ~** estar en la miseria

POW N ABBR = **prisoner of war**

powder [ˈpaʊdəʳ] (A) N polvo *m*; (= *face powder, talcum powder*) polvos *mpl*; (= *gun powder*) pólvora *f*; **a fine white ~** un polvillo blanco; **to grind sth to (a) ~** reducir algo a polvo; ✦***IDIOM*** **to keep one's ~ dry** no gastar la pólvora en salvas, reservarse para mejor ocasión
(B) VT [1] (= *reduce to powder*) pulverizar, reducir a polvo
[2] (= *dust*) (*with face powder, talcum powder*) empolvar; (*Culin*) (*with flour, icing sugar*) espolvorear (**with** de); **to ~ one's nose** (*lit*) empolvarse la nariz; (*euph*) ir al baño; **the ground was ~ed with snow** el terreno estaba salpicado de nieve
(C) VI pulverizarse, hacerse polvo
(D) CPD ► **powder blue** N azul *m* pálido ► **powder compact** N polvera *f* ► **powder horn** N chifle *m*, cuerno *m* de pólvora ► **powder keg** N barril *m* de pólvora; **the country is a ~ keg** el país es un polvorín ► **powder magazine** N santabárbara *f* ► **powder puff** N borla *f* ► **powder room** N tocador *m*, aseos *mpl* (de señora); **"powder room"** "señoras"

powder-blue [ˈpaʊdəˈbluː] ADJ azul pálido

powdered [ˈpaʊdəd] (A) ADJ en polvo
(B) CPD ► **powdered milk** N leche *f* en polvo ► **powdered sugar** N (*US*) azúcar *m* glasé, azúcar *m* en polvo, azúcar *m* flor (*S. Cone*)

powdering [ˈpaʊdərɪŋ] N [*of dust, sawdust*] fina capa *f*; [*of snow*] leve capa *f*

powdery [ˈpaʊdərɪ] ADJ [*substance*] pulverulento; [*snow*] en polvo; [*surface*] polvoriento

power [paʊəʳ] (A) N [1] (= *control*) poder *m*; (*physical strength*) fuerza *f*; **to have ~ over sb** tener poder sobre algn; **to have sb in one's ~** tener a algn en su poder; **to be in sb's ~** estar en poder de algn; **to have the ~ of life and death over sb** tener poder para decidir sobre la vida de algn; ✦***IDIOM*** **more ~ to your elbow!*** ¡qué tengas éxito!
[2] (*Pol*) poder *m*, poderío *m*; **to be in ~** estar en el poder; **to come to ~** subir al poder; **to fall from ~** perder el poder; **~ to the people!** ¡el pueblo al poder!
[3] (*Mil*) (= *capability*) potencia *f*, poderío *m*; **a nation's air/sea ~** la potencia aérea/naval de un país, el poderío aéreo/naval de un país
[4] (= *authority*) poder *m*, autoridad *f*; **she has the ~ to act** tiene poder *or* autoridad para

actuar; **they have no ~ in economic matters** carecen de autoridad en asuntos económicos; **it was seen as an abuse of his ~** se percibió como un abuso de poder por su parte; **~ of attorney** (*Jur*) poder *m*, procuración *f*; **that is beyond** *or* **outside my ~(s)** eso no es de mi competencia; **to exceed one's ~s** excederse en el ejercicio de sus atribuciones *or* facultades; **he has full ~s to negotiate a solution** goza de plenos poderes para negociar una solución; **~ of veto** derecho *m* de veto; **that does not fall within my ~(s)** eso no es de mi competencia

5 (= *ability, capacity*) **it is beyond his ~ to save her** no está dentro de sus posibilidades salvarla, no puede hacer nada para salvarla; **~s of concentration** capacidad *f* de concentración; **to be at the height of one's ~s** estar en plenitud de facultades; **~s of imagination** capacidad *f* imaginativa; **to do all** *or* **everything in one's ~ to help sb** hacer todo lo posible por ayudar a algn; **~s of persuasion** poder *m* de persuasión *or* convicción; *see also* **purchasing B**

6 (= *mental faculty*) facultad *f*; **his ~s are failing** decaen sus facultades; **mental ~s** facultades *fpl* mentales; **the ~ of speech** la facultad del habla

7 (= *nation*) potencia *f*; **the Great Powers** las grandes potencias; **one of the great naval ~s** una de las grandes potencias navales; **the leaders of the major world ~s** los líderes de las principales potencias mundiales

8 (= *person in authority*) **he's a ~ in the land** es de los que mandan en el país; **they are the real ~ in the government** son los que ostentan el auténtico poder en el gobierno; **the Church is no longer the ~ it was** la Iglesia ha dejado de tener el poder que tenía; **the ~s that be** las autoridades, los que mandan; **the ~s of darkness** *or* **evil** las fuerzas del mal; ✦*IDIOM* **the ~ behind the throne** la eminencia gris

9 (= *forcefulness*) [*of argument*] fuerza *f*; **the ~ of love/thought** el poder del amor/del intelecto; **a painting of great ~** un cuadro de gran impacto, un cuadro que causa honda impresión

10 [*of engine, machine*] potencia *f*, fuerza *f*; [*of telescope*] aumento *m*; (= *output*) rendimiento *m*; **microwave on full ~ for one minute** póngalo con el microondas a plena potencia durante un minuto; **engines at half ~** motores *mpl* a medio gas *or* a media potencia; **magnifying ~** capacidad *f* de aumento, número *m* de aumentos; **the ship returned to port under her own ~** el buque volvió al puerto impulsado por sus propios motores

11 (= *source of energy*) energía *f*; (= *electric power*) electricidad *f*; **they cut off the ~** cortaron la corriente; **nuclear ~** energía *f* nuclear

12 (*Math*) potencia *f*; **7 to the ~ (of) 3** 7 elevado a la 3ª potencia, 7 elevado al cubo; **to the nth ~** a la enésima potencia

13 (*) (= *a lot of*) **that holiday did me a ~ of good** esas vacaciones me hicieron mucho bien; **her words did their morale a ~ of good** sus palabras les levantaron un montón la moral; **the new training methods have done their game a ~ of good** el nuevo método de entrenamiento ha supuesto una notable mejoría en su juego

Ⓑ VT **a plane ~ed by four jets** un avión propulsado por cuatro motores a reacción; **a racing car ~ed by a 4.2 litre engine** un coche de carreras impulsado por un motor de 4,2 litros; **a car ~ed by electricity** un coche eléctrico; **the electric lighting is ~ed by a generator** un generador se encarga de alimentar el alumbrado eléctrico; *see also* **-powered**

Ⓒ CPD ► **power base** N base *f* de poder ► **power broker** N (*Pol*) poder *m* en la sombra ► **power cable** N cable *m* de energía eléctrica ► **power cut** N (*Brit*) corte *m* de luz *or* de corriente, apagón *m* ► **power dressing** N moda *f* de ejecutivo ► **power drill** N taladro *m* eléctrico, taladradora *f* eléctrica ► **power failure** N fallo *m* del suministro eléctrico ► **power game** N (*esp Pol*) juego *m* del poder ► **power line** N línea *f* de conducción eléctrica, cable *m* de alta tensión ► **power outage** (*US*) N = **power cut** ► **power pack** N transformador *m* ► **power plant** N (= *generator*) grupo *m* electrógeno; (*US*) = **power station** ► **power play** N (*Sport*) demostración *f* de fuerza (en el juego ofensivo); (*from temporary suspension*) superioridad *f* (en el ataque); (*fig*) (= *use of power*) maniobra *f* de poder, demostración *f* de fuerza; (= *power struggle*) lucha *f* por el poder ► **power point** N (*Brit Elec*) enchufe *m*, toma *f* de corriente ► **power politics** N política *fsing* de fuerza ► **power saw** N motosierra *f*, sierra *f* mecánica ► **power shovel** N excavadora *f* ► **power station** N central *f* eléctrica, usina *f* eléctrica (*S. Cone*) ► **power steering** N (*Aut*) dirección *f* asistida ► **power structure** N estructura *f* del poder ► **power struggle** N lucha *f* por el poder ► **power supply** N suministro *m* eléctrico ► **power surge** N (*Elec*) subida *f* de tensión ► **power tool** N herramienta *f* eléctrica ► **power unit** N grupo *m* electrógeno ► **power workers** NPL trabajadores *mpl* del sector energético

►**power up** VT + ADV [+ *computer etc*] encender, conectar

power-assisted ['paʊərə,sɪstɪd] ADJ **~ brakes** servofrenos *mpl*; **~ steering** dirección *f* asistida

powerboat ['paʊə,bəʊt] N lancha *f* a motor, motora *f*

powerboating ['paʊə,bəʊtɪŋ] N motonáutica *f*

power-driven ['paʊədrɪvn] ADJ [*machinery*] a motor; [*tool*] eléctrico

powered ['paʊəd] ADJ con motor; **the invention of ~ flight** la invención del vuelo a *or* con motor

-powered ['paʊəd] ADJ (*ending in compounds*) **battery-powered** a pilas; **wind-powered** impulsado por el viento, que funciona con energía eólica

powerful ['paʊəfʊl] ADJ 1 (= *influential, controlling*) [*person, government, force, influence*] poderoso; *see also* **all-powerful**

2 (= *physically strong*) [*person*] fuerte, fornido; [*animal, physique, arms, muscles*] fuerte

3 (= *having great force or power*) [*engine, magnet, computer, explosive*] potente; [*kick, explosion, smell*] fuerte; [*voice*] potente, fuerte; [*swimmer*] resistente

4 (= *having a strong effect*) [*drug*] potente; [*emotion*] intenso, profundo; [*argument*] poderoso, convincente; [*performance, film, novel*] impactante, que deja huella; [*speech*] conmovedor; **he gave a ~ performance** su actuación fue impactante *or* de las que deja huella; **we have ~ evidence for this** tenemos pruebas contundentes de esto; **this information is a ~ weapon against the government** esta información es un arma potente contra el gobierno

powerfully ['paʊəfəlɪ] ADV [*affect*] profundamente; [*speak, argue, express*] de forma convincente; [*hit, strike*] con fuerza; **it smelled ~ of sage** tenía un fuerte olor a salvia; **to be ~ built** ser fornido, ser de complexión fuerte

powerhouse ['paʊəhaʊs] N (*pl* **powerhouses** ['paʊəhaʊzɪz]) 1 (*lit*) central *f* eléctrica

2 (*fig*) **the town is the industrial ~ of Germany** el pueblo es el centro neurálgico de la industria alemana; **he's a ~ of ideas** es una fuente inagotable de ideas; **a hulking great ~ of a man** una auténtica mole de hombre*

powerless ['paʊəlɪs] ADJ impotente; **I felt ~ to resist** no tuve fuerzas para resistir, no pude resistir; **we are ~ to help you** no podemos hacer nada para ayudarle; **they are ~ in the matter** no tienen autoridad para intervenir en el asunto

powerlessness ['paʊəlɪsnɪs] N impotencia *f*

power-sharing ['paʊə,ʃɛərɪŋ] Ⓐ N reparto *m* del poder

Ⓑ CPD [*arrangement, agreement*] de reparto del poder; **a ~ government** un gobierno de poder compartido

powwow ['paʊwaʊ] Ⓐ N [*of North American Indians*] *asamblea de indígenas norteamericanos*; (*) (*fig*) asamblea *f*, reunión *f*; **we had a family ~ about it** hubo una asamblea *or* reunión familiar para discutirlo

Ⓑ VI [*North American Indians*] (*also fig*) reunirse en asamblea

pox* [pɒks] N **the ~** (= *VD*) (la) sífilis; (= *smallpox*) (la) viruela; **a ~ on them!**†† ¡malditos sean!

poxy‡ ['pɒksɪ] ADJ (*Brit*) puñetero‡

pp ABBR 1 = **per procurationem** (= *by proxy*) p.p.

2 = **parcel post**

3 = **post paid**

4 = **prepaid**

pp. ABBR (= **pages**) págs.

PPE ABBR (= **philosophy, politics, economics**) *grupo de asignaturas de la Universidad de Oxford*

ppm ABBR (= **parts per million**) ppm

PPP N ABBR = **personal pension plan**

PPS N ABBR 1 (*Brit*) = **Parliamentary Private Secretary**

2 (= **post postscriptum**) posdata *f* adicional

PPV ABBR (= **pay-per-view**) de pago

PQ ABBR (*Canada*) = **Province of Quebec**

PR Ⓐ N ABBR 1 (*Pol*) = **proportional representation**

2 (*Comm*) (= **public relations**) R.P., RRPP *fpl*

Ⓑ ABBR (*US*) = **Puerto Rico**

Pr. ABBR (= **prince**) P.

practicability [,præktɪkə'bɪlɪtɪ] N viabilidad *f*, factibilidad *f*

▼**practicable** ['præktɪkəbl] ADJ practicable, viable, factible

practical ['præktɪkəl] Ⓐ ADJ 1 (= *not theoretical*) práctico; **the ~ applications of this research** las aplicaciones prácticas de estas investigaciones; **I did better in the written exam than in the ~ test** la prueba escrita me salió mejor que la práctica; **for all ~ purposes** a efectos prácticos; **in ~ terms** en términos prácticos; **to put one's knowledge to ~ use** hacer uso de *or* poner en práctica sus conocimientos; **the information was of no ~ use** la información no tenía ninguna utilidad práctica

2 (= *sensible*) [*person*] práctico; **let's be ~ (about this)** seamos prácticos (con respecto a esto)

3 (= *feasible*) factible; **what's the most ~ way of doing this?** ¿cuál es la forma más

➤ LANGUAGE IN USE: practicable 16.3

factible de hacer esto?

4 (= *useful, functional*) [*clothing, suggestion, guide*] práctico; **shoes which are both ~ and stylish** zapatos *mpl* que son prácticos y a la vez tienen estilo; **his clothes weren't very ~ for wet weather** su ropa no era muy práctica *or* apropiada *or* adecuada para la lluvia

5 (= *virtual*) **it's a ~ certainty** es casi seguro

Ⓑ N (*Scol, Univ*) (= *exam*) examen *m* práctico; (= *lesson*) práctica *f*

Ⓒ CPD ► **practical joke** N broma *f*; **to play a ~ joke on sb** gastar una broma a algn ► **practical joker** N bromista *mf* ► **practical nurse** N (*US*) enfermero/a *m/f* práctica *or* sin título

practicality [ˌpræktɪ'kælɪtɪ] N [*of design, model*] utilidad *f*; [*of scheme, project*] lo factible; [*of person*] sentido *m* práctico; **practicalities** detalles *mpl* prácticos

practically ['præktɪklɪ] ADV 1 (= *almost*) casi, prácticamente; **~ everybody** casi todos, prácticamente todos; **the town was ~ deserted** el pueblo estaba casi *or* prácticamente desierto; **there has been ~ no rain** apenas ha llovido, casi no ha llovido; **you've eaten ~ nothing** apenas has comido, casi no has comido; **it ~ killed me** por poco me mata, casi me mata; **this disease has been ~ eliminated** esta enfermedad ha sido erradicada casi completamente

2 (= *sensibly*) con sentido práctico; **"how can we pay for it?" Bertha asked ~** —¿cómo vamos a pagarlo? —preguntó Bertha con sentido práctico

3 (= *in practical terms*) **we are interested in how this might be used ~** nos interesa saber cómo se podría usar en la práctica, estamos interesados en las aplicaciones prácticas de esto; **what this means ~ is unclear** se desconocen las ramificaciones prácticas de esto, se desconoce lo que esto supondría en la práctica; **the work this term is more ~ based** el trabajo de este trimestre es más práctico; **~ speaking** en la práctica

practice ['præktɪs] Ⓐ N 1 (= *custom, tradition*) costumbre *f*, práctica *f*; (= *procedure*) práctica *f*; **ancient pagan ~s** las antiguas costumbres *or* prácticas paganas; **the ~ of sending young offenders to prison** la práctica de enviar a prisión a los menores que han cometido un delito; **it is not our ~ to do that** no tenemos por norma hacer eso; **unfair trade ~s** prácticas *fpl* de comercio desleales; **it is bad ~** no es una práctica recomendable; **these mistakes do not point to bad ~ in general** estos errores no apuntan a deficiencias en los métodos que se practican; **it is common ~ among modern companies to hire all their office equipment** entre las empresas modernas es una práctica muy extendida alquilar todo su material y mobiliario de oficina; **it is good ~ to interview several candidates before choosing one** es una práctica recomendable entrevistar a varios aspirantes antes de decidirse por uno; **to make a ~ of doing sth** acostumbrar a hacer algo; **it is normal *or* standard ~ for newspapers not to disclose such details** los periódicos tienen por norma no revelar ese tipo de detalles; **this procedure has become standard ~ in most hospitals** en la mayoría de los hospitales este procedimiento se ha convertido en norma; *see also* **business B**, **restrictive**, **sharp A3**

2 (= *experience, drilling*) práctica *f*; **I need more ~** (= *practical experience*) necesito más práctica; (= *to practise more*) necesito practicar más; **it takes years of ~** requiere años de práctica; **he does six hours' piano ~ a day** practica el piano seis horas al día; **I haven't got a job yet but the interviews are good ~** aún no tengo trabajo pero las entrevistas me sirven de práctica; **skating's just a matter of ~** aprender a patinar es sólo cuestión de práctica; **to be out of ~** (*at sport*) no estar en forma; **it gets easier with ~** resulta más fácil con la práctica; ✦*PROV* **~ makes perfect** la práctica hace al maestro; *see also* **target C**, **teaching B**

3 (*Sport*) (= *training session*) sesión *f* de entrenamiento, entrenamiento *m*

4 (= *rehearsal*) ensayo *m*; **choir ~** ensayo *m* de coro

5 (= *reality*) práctica *f*; **we must combine theory with ~** tenemos que combinar la teoría con la práctica; **in ~** en la práctica; **to put sth into ~** poner algo en práctica

6 (= *exercise*) 6·1 [*of profession*] ejercicio *m*; **the ~ of medicine** el ejercicio de la medicina; **to be in ~ (as a doctor/lawyer)** ejercer (de médico/abogado); **he is no longer in ~** ya no ejerce; **to go into ~** (*Med*) empezar a ejercer de médico; **to set up in ~** (*Med*) poner consulta; (*Jur*) poner bufete; **to set up in ~ as a doctor/solicitor** establecerse de *or* como médico/abogado

6·2 [*of religion*] práctica *f*

7 (= *premises, firm*) (*Jur*) bufete *m*; (*Med*) consultorio *m*, consulta *f*; (*veterinary, dental*) clínica *f*; **a new doctor has just joined the ~** acaba de llegar un médico nuevo al consultorio; *see also* **family B**, **general C**, **group D**, **private C**

Ⓑ VT, VI (*US*) = **practise**

Ⓒ CPD ► **practice flight** N vuelo *m* de entrenamiento ► **practice match** N partido *m* de entrenamiento ► **practice run** N (*Sport*) carrera *f* de entrenamiento ► **practice session** N (*Sport*) sesión *f* de entrenamiento; (*Scol, Mus*) ensayo *m*

practiced ['præktɪst] ADJ (*US*) = **practised**

practicing ['præktɪsɪŋ] ADJ (*US*) = **practising**

practise, **practice** (*US*) ['præktɪs] Ⓐ VI 1 (*to improve skill*) (*Sport*) entrenar; (*Theat*) ensayar; (*Mus*) practicar; **he ~s for two hours every evening** entrena/ensaya/practica durante dos horas todas las tardes; **I've been practising with a ball on my own** he estado entrenando por mi cuenta con un balón; **I need someone to ~ on** necesito practicar con algn

2 (= *work professionally*) [*lawyer, doctor*] ejercer; **to ~ as a doctor/lawyer** ejercer de *or* como médico/abogado

Ⓑ VT 1 (= *put into practice*) [+ *medicine*] practicar; [+ *law*] ejercer; [+ *self-denial, one's religion, method*] practicar; ✦*IDIOM* **to ~ what one preaches** predicar con el ejemplo

2 (= *work on*) (*Sport*) practicar; [+ *piano, language, technique*] practicar; [+ *song, speech*] ensayar; **I need to ~ my backhand** necesito practicar el revés; **~ giving your speech in front of a mirror** ensaye su discurso delante de un espejo; **I ~d my Spanish on her** practiqué el español con ella

practised, **practiced** (*US*) ['præktɪst] ADJ [*politician, surgeon, climber*] experto; **to be ~ in the art of (doing) sth** ser un experto en el arte de (hacer) algo; **with a ~ eye** con ojo experto

practising, **practicing** (*US*) ['præktɪsɪŋ] ADJ [*lawyer, physician, teacher*] que ejerce como tal; [*Catholic, Muslim*] practicante; **he's a ~ homosexual** mantiene relaciones homosexuales

practitioner [præk'tɪʃənəʳ] N 1 [*of an art, a science*] practicante *mf*

2 (*Med*) médico/a *m/f*; *see also* **general C**

praesidium [prɪ'sɪdɪəm] N (*Pol*) presidio *m*

praetorian [prɪ'tɔːrɪən] Ⓐ ADJ pretoriano

Ⓑ CPD ► **praetorian guard** N guardia *f* pretoriana

pragmatic [præg'mætɪk] ADJ pragmático

pragmatically [præg'mætɪklɪ] ADV pragmáticamente

pragmatics [præg'mætɪks] NSING pragmática *f*; **the ~ of the job in hand** las tareas prácticas del trabajo a realizar

pragmatism ['prægmətɪzəm] N pragmatismo *m*

pragmatist ['prægmətɪst] N pragmatista *mf*

Prague [prɑːg] N Praga *f*

prairie ['prɛərɪ] Ⓐ N pradera *f*, llanura *f*, pampa *f* (*LAm*); **the Prairies** (*US*) las Grandes Llanuras

Ⓑ CPD ► **prairie dog** N perro *m* de las praderas ► **prairie oyster** N (*US*) *huevo crudo y sazonado que se toma en una bebida alcohólica* ► **prairie wolf** N coyote *m*

praise [preɪz] Ⓐ N 1 (= *approval, acclaim*) elogios *mpl*, alabanzas *fpl*; **I have nothing but ~ for her** merece todos mis elogios *or* alabanzas; **it's beyond ~** está por encima de todo elogio; **he is full of ~ for the medical staff** se deshace en elogios para con el personal médico; **let's give ~ where ~ is due** elogiemos a quienes se lo merecen; **to heap ~ on sb** colmar a algn de alabanzas; **that is high ~ indeed** eso sí que es un elogio de verdad; **he spoke in ~ of their achievements** elogió sus logros; **to be loud in ~ of** *or* **in one's ~s of sth** deshacerse en elogios para con algo; *see also* **damn A1**, **lavish A2**, **sing A**

2 (*Rel*) alabanza *f*; **a hymn of ~** un himno de alabanza; **~ be to God!** ¡alabado sea Dios!; **let us give ~ (un)to the Lord** alabemos al Señor

Ⓑ VT 1 (= *applaud*) alabar, elogiar; **to ~ the virtues of sth** alabar *or* elogiar las virtudes de algo; ✦*IDIOM* **to ~ sb to the skies** poner a algn por las nubes *or* los cielos; *see also* **sky**

2 (*Rel*) alabar; **to ~ God** *or* **the Lord** alabar a Dios *or* al Señor

praiseworthily ['preɪzˌwɜːðɪlɪ] ADV loablemente, de modo digno de elogio

praiseworthiness ['preɪzˌwɜːðɪnɪs] N lo loable, mérito *m*

praiseworthy ['preɪzˌwɜːðɪ] ADJ [*conduct, effort, attempt*] loable, digno de elogio

praline ['prɑːliːn] N praliné *m*

pram [præm] N (*Brit*) cochecito *m* (*de niño*)

prance [prɑːns] VI [*horse*] hacer cabriolas; [*person*] (*proudly*) pavonearse; (*gaily*) brincar, saltar; **he came prancing into the room** entró pavoneándose en la habitación

►**prance about**, **prance around** VI + ADV andar pavoneándose; **she was prancing around with nothing on** iba pavoneándose sin nada encima

prang†* [præŋ] VT (*Brit*) (= *crash*) [+ *car*] tener un accidente con; [+ *plane*] estrellar

prank [præŋk] N broma *f*; **a student ~** una broma estudiantil; **a childish ~** una travesura, una diablura; **to play a ~ on sb** gastar una broma a algn

prankish ['præŋkɪʃ] ADJ travieso, pícaro

prankster ['præŋkstəʳ] N bromista *mf*

praseodymium [ˌpreɪzɪəʊ'dɪmɪəm] N praseodimio *m*

prat‡ [præt] (*Brit*) N (= *ineffectual person*) inútil* *mf*; (= *fool*) imbécil *mf*; **you ~!** ¡imbécil!

prate† [preɪt] VI parlotear, charlar; **to ~ about** hablar sin tasa de

pratfall‡ [ˈprætfɔːl] N (*esp US*) culada‡ *f*, caída *f* de culo‡; (*fig*) (= *blunder*) metedura *f* de pata*

prating† [ˈpreɪtɪŋ] ADJ parlanchín

prattle [ˈprætl] Ⓐ N parloteo *m*, cotorreo *m*; (*child's*) balbuceo *m*
Ⓑ VI parlotear, cotorrear; [*child*] balbucear

prawn [prɔːn] Ⓐ N (*esp Brit*) (*medium*) gamba *f*, camarón *m* (*esp LAm*); (*small*) camarón *m*, quisquilla *f* (*Sp*); (= *Dublin Bay prawn, large prawn*) langostino *m*
Ⓑ CPD ► **prawn cocktail** N cóctel *m* de gambas

pray [preɪ] Ⓐ VI (= *say prayers*) rezar, orar; **let us ~** oremos; **to ~ to God** rogar a Dios; **to ~ for sth/sb** rezar *or* rogar por algo/algn; **to ~ for sb's soul** rezar por el alma de algn; **we ~ed for rain** rezamos para que lloviera; **she's past ~ing for!*** ¡con ella ya no hay nada que hacer!, ¡no tiene salvación!
Ⓑ VT rogar, suplicar; **let me go, I ~ you!** (*liter*) ¡suélteme, se lo suplico!; **to ~ sb to do sth** rogar a algn que haga algo; **we ~ that it won't happen** rezamos para que no ocurra; **I was ~ing that he wouldn't notice** le pedía a Dios que no lo notara
Ⓒ EXCL **~ be seated** (*frm*) siéntense, por favor; **~ tell me ...** (*frm*) le ruego decirme ...; **and what, ~, were you doing last night?** (*hum*) ¿y qué estabas tú haciendo anoche, si puede saberse?

prayer [prɛəʳ] Ⓐ N [1] (*Rel*) oración *f*, rezo *m*; (= *entreaty*) oración *f*, plegaria *f*; **a ~ for peace** una oración por la paz; **Lord, hear our ~** Señor, escucha nuestras plegarias *or* súplicas; **the Book of Common Prayer** la liturgia de la Iglesia Anglicana; **to be at one's ~s** estar rezando; **they offered (up) ~s of thanks** ofrecían rezos en acción de gracias; **to say one's ~s** orar, rezar; **say a ~ for me** reza por mí; **he didn't have a ~*** no tenía ni la menor posibilidad
[2] (*as service*) oficio *m*; **morning/evening ~(s)** oficio *m* de maitines/vísperas
Ⓑ CPD ► **prayer beads** NPL rosario *m* ► **prayer book** N devocionario *m*, misal *m* ► **prayer mat** N alfombra *f* de rezo ► **prayer meeting** N reunión *f* de oraciones

praying mantis [ˌpreɪɪŋˈmæntɪs] N mantis *f inv* religiosa

pre... [priː] PREFIX [1] (= *before*) **~-Columbian** precolombino; **I had a ~-breakfast swim** me di un baño antes del desayuno
[2] (= *beforehand*) **a ~-recorded interview** una entrevista pregrabada

preach [priːtʃ] Ⓐ VT [1] (*Rel*) predicar; **to ~ a sermon** dar un sermón; **to ~ the gospel** predicar el Evangelio
[2] [+ *virtues*] predicar; [+ *patience*] aconsejar; *see also* **practise B1**
Ⓑ VI predicar; **to ~ at sb** sermonear a algn, dar un sermón a algn; ✦*IDIOM* **to ~ to the converted** querer convertir a los que ya lo están

preacher [ˈpriːtʃəʳ] N [*of sermon*] predicador(a) *m/f*; (*US*) (= *minister*) pastor(a) *m/f*

preachify* [ˈpriːtʃɪfaɪ] VI sermonear largamente

preaching [ˈpriːtʃɪŋ] N predicación *f*; (*pej*) sermoneo *m*

preachy* [ˈpriːtʃɪ] ADJ [*person*] dado a sermonear; [*style, speech*] de predicador

preamble [priːˈæmbl] N preámbulo *m*

preamplifier [ˌpriːˈæmplɪfaɪəʳ] N preamplificador *m*

prearrange [ˌpriːəˈreɪndʒ] VT arreglar de antemano

prearranged [ˌpriːəˈreɪndʒd] ADJ [*time, location, signal*] convenido; [*meeting*] fijado

prearrangement [ˌpriːəˈreɪndʒmənt] N **by ~** por previo acuerdo

prebend [ˈprebənd] N (= *stipend*) prebenda *f*; (= *person*) prebendado *m*

prebendary [ˈprebəndərɪ] N prebendado *m*

precarious [prɪˈkɛərɪəs] ADJ [*health, position*] precario; **they are in a ~ financial situation** se hallan en una situación económica precaria; **it could upset the ~ balance of the peace negotiations** podría alterar el precario equilibrio de las negociaciones de paz

precariously [prɪˈkɛərɪəslɪ] ADV precariamente

precariousness [prɪˈkɛərɪəsnɪs] N precariedad *f*

precast concrete [ˌpriːkɑːstˈkɒnkriːt] N hormigón *m* precolado

precaution [prɪˈkɔːʃən] N precaución *f*; **as a ~** como precaución, para mayor seguridad; **to take ~s** (*gen*) tomar precauciones; (= *use contraceptive*) usar anticonceptivos, tomar precauciones; **to take the ~ of doing sth** tomar la precaución de hacer algo; **he took the ~ of hiding the letter** tomó la precaución de esconder la carta

precautionary [prɪˈkɔːʃənərɪ] ADJ preventivo, de precaución; **as a ~ measure** como medida preventiva *or* de precaución

precede [prɪˈsiːd] VT (*in space, time, rank*) preceder, anteceder; **he let me ~ him through the door** me dejó pasar por la puerta a mí primero; **the concert was ~d by a talk** el concierto vino precedido de una charla; **his reputation had ~d him** su reputación jugaba en contra de él; **for a month preceding this** durante un mes anterior a esto

precedence [ˈpresɪdəns] N (*in rank*) precedencia *f*; (*in importance*) prioridad *f*; **in order of ~** (= *rank*) por orden de precedencia; (= *importance*) por orden de prioridad; **to take ~ over sth/sb** tener prioridad/precedencia sobre algo/algn; **this question must take ~ over all others** este asunto tiene prioridad con respecto a todos los demás; **they give ~ to people with language skills** le dan prioridad a la gente con idiomas

precedent [ˈpresɪdənt] N precedente *m* (*also Jur*); **according to ~** de acuerdo con los precedentes; **against all ~** contra todos los precedentes; **without ~** sin precedentes; **to break with ~** romper con todo precedente; **to establish** *or* **set a ~ (for sth)** sentar un precedente (para algo)

preceding [prɪˈsiːdɪŋ] ADJ [*day, week, month, year*] anterior; [*chapter, paragraph, sentence*] precedente, anterior

precentor [prɪˈsentəʳ] N chantre *m*

precept [ˈpriːsept] N precepto *m*

preceptor [prɪˈseptəʳ] N preceptor *m*

pre-Christian [priːˈkrɪstʃən] ADJ precristiano

precinct [ˈpriːsɪŋkt] N [1] (= *area*) recinto *m*; (*US Pol*) distrito *m* electoral, circunscripción *f*; (*US*) [*of police*] distrito *m* policial; **shopping ~** centro *m* comercial; **pedestrian ~** zona *f* peatonal
[2] **precincts** (= *grounds, premises*) límites *mpl*; (= *environs*) alrededores *mpl*; [*of cathedral etc*] recinto *msing*; **within the ~s of** dentro de los límites de

preciosity [ˌpreʃɪˈɒsɪtɪ] N (*frm*) preciosidad *f*

precious [ˈpreʃəs] Ⓐ ADJ [1] (= *costly*) [*jewel, stone*] precioso; [*commodity, resource*] preciado; [*possession*] muy valioso; **we're wasting ~ time** estamos desperdiciando un tiempo precioso
[2] (= *treasured*) preciado; **she savoured the ~ moments they spent together** saboreó esos momentos preciados que pasaron juntos; **her friendship is very ~ to me** aprecio *or* valoro mucho su amistad; **the book is very ~ to me** para mí el libro tiene gran valor
[3] (= *artificial, affected*) [*person*] preciosista, afectado; [*style*] rebuscado
[4] (*iro*) **I couldn't care less about your ~ golf clubs** me traen sin cuidado tus queridos palos de golf (*iro*)
Ⓑ ADV (*) **~ little/few** bien poco/pocos; **~ little has been gained** se ha logrado muy poco
Ⓒ N **(my) ~!†** ¡querida!
Ⓓ CPD ► **precious metal** N metal *m* precioso ► **precious stone** N piedra *f* preciosa

precipice [ˈpresɪpɪs] N precipicio *m*, despeñadero *m*

precipitance [prɪˈsɪpɪtəns] N (*frm*) = **precipitancy**

precipitancy [prɪˈsɪpɪtənsɪ] N (*frm*) precipitación *f*

precipitate Ⓐ [prɪˈsɪpɪtɪt] ADJ precipitado, apresurado
Ⓑ [prɪˈsɪpɪteɪt] VT [1] (= *bring on*) precipitar, provocar; **an illness ~d by stress** una enfermedad provocada por el estrés; **the decision ~d her resignation** la decisión precipitó su dimisión
[2] (= *hurl*) lanzar; **the civil war ~d the country into chaos** la guerra civil sumió al país en el caos
[3] (*Chem*) precipitar; (*Met*) condensar
Ⓒ VI [prɪˈsɪpɪteɪt] (*Chem*) precipitarse; (*Met*) condensarse
Ⓓ [prɪˈsɪpɪtɪt] N (*Chem*) precipitado *m*

precipitately [prɪˈsɪpɪtɪtlɪ] ADV precipitadamente

precipitation [prɪˌsɪpɪˈteɪʃən] N (*all senses*) precipitación *f*; **the average annual ~** (*Met*) la media anual de precipitaciones

precipitous [prɪˈsɪpɪtəs] ADJ [1] (= *steep*) escarpado, cortado a pico
[2] (= *hasty*) precipitado, apresurado

precipitously [prɪˈsɪpɪtəslɪ] ADV [1] (= *steeply*) **the road fell away ~** la carretera descendía vertiginosamente; **prices have dropped ~** los precios han caído vertiginosamente
[2] (= *hastily*) precipitadamente, apresuradamente

précis [ˈpreɪsiː] Ⓐ N (*pl* **précis**) resumen *m*
Ⓑ VT hacer un resumen de, resumir

▼**precise** [prɪˈsaɪs] ADJ [1] (= *exact*) [*description, figure, measurements*] exacto; [*instructions*] preciso; [*details, information*] concreto; **he didn't give a ~ date** no precisó la fecha; **the timing had to be very ~** había que calcular el tiempo con mucha precisión; **there were five, to be ~** para ser exacto *or* preciso, fueron cinco; **can you be more ~?** ¿puedes ser más concreto?; **at that ~ moment** en ese preciso instante; **it achieved the ~ opposite of what we intended** con ello se consiguió exactamente *or* justamente lo contrario de lo que queríamos
[2] (= *meticulous*) meticuloso

▼**precisely** [prɪˈsaɪslɪ] ADV [1] (= *exactly*) exactamente; **we have ~ 17 minutes before the train leaves** tenemos exactamente 17 minutos antes de que salga el tren; **at four o'clock ~** ◊ **at ~ four o'clock** a las cuatro en punto; **precisely!** ¡exactamente!, ¡efectivamente!; **~ what was it that you wanted?** ¿qué era lo que quería usted exactamente?
[2] (= *expressly*) precisamente; **he liked her ~ because of her forthrightness** le caía bien

➤ LANGUAGE IN USE: **precise 1** 26.3 **precisely 1** 26.3

precisamente por lo franca que era

3 (= *with precision*) [*calculate, measure*] con precisión

4 (= *meticulously*) meticulosamente

preciseness [prɪˈsaɪsnɪs] N 1 (= *exactness*) precisión *f*, exactitud *f*

2 (= *meticulousness*) meticulosidad *f*, puntualidad *f*

precision [prɪˈsɪʒən] Ⓐ N (*gen*) precisión *f*; [*of calculations*] exactitud *f*; **~-made** [*product, instrument*] hecho con precisión

Ⓑ CPD ► **precision bombing** N bombardeo *m* de precisión ► **precision engineering** N ingeniería *f* de precisión ► **precision instrument** N instrumento *m* de precisión

preclude [prɪˈkluːd] VT (= *prevent*) impedir; [+ *possibility*] excluir; **this does not ~ the possibility of ...** esto no excluye *or* quita la posibilidad de ...; **so as to ~ all doubt** para disipar cualquier duda; **we are ~d from doing that** nos vemos imposibilitados para hacer eso

precocious [prɪˈkəʊʃəs] ADJ precoz

precociously [prɪˈkəʊʃəslɪ] ADV de modo precoz, con precocidad

precociousness [prɪˈkəʊʃəsnɪs], **precocity** [prɪˈkɒsɪtɪ] N precocidad *f*

precognition [ˌpriːkɒgˈnɪʃən] N precognición *f*

pre-Columbian [ˈpriːkəˈlʌmbɪən] ADJ precolombino

preconceived [ˈpriːkənˈsiːvd] ADJ preconcebido

preconception [ˈpriːkənˈsepʃən] N (= *idea*) preconcepción *f*, idea *f* preconcebida

preconcerted [ˈpriːkənˈsɜːtɪd] ADJ preconcertado

precondition [ˈpriːkənˈdɪʃən] N condición *f* previa

precook [ˌpriːˈkʊk] VT precocinar

precooked [ˌpriːˈkʊkt] ADJ precocinado

precool [ˈpriːˈkuːl] VT preenfriar

precursor [priːˈkɜːsər] N precursor(a) *m/f*

precursory [prɪˈkɜːsərɪ] ADJ preliminar

predate [ˈpriːˈdeɪt] VT (= *put earlier date on*) poner fecha anterior a, antedatar; (= *precede*) preceder, ser anterior a

predator [ˈpredətər] N (= *animal*) depredador *m*; (= *bird*) ave *f* de presa, ave *f* rapaz

predatory [ˈpredətərɪ] ADJ [*animal*] depredador; [*bird*] de presa, rapaz; [*person*] rapaz; [*look*] devorador

predecease [ˈpriːdɪˈsiːs] VT (*frm*) morir antes que

predecessor [ˈpriːdɪsesər] N predecesor(a) *m/f*, antecesor(a) *m/f*

predestination [priːˌdestɪˈneɪʃən] N predestinación *f*

predestine [priːˈdestɪn] VT predestinar; **to be ~d to do sth** estar predestinado a hacer algo

predetermination [ˈpriːdɪˌtɜːmɪˈneɪʃən] N predeterminación *f*

predetermine [ˈpriːdɪˈtɜːmɪn] VT (*Philos, Rel*) predeterminar; (= *arrange beforehand*) determinar de antemano

predicament [prɪˈdɪkəmənt] N apuro *m*, aprieto *m*; **to be in a ~** (= *in a fix*) estar en un apuro *or* un aprieto; (= *puzzled*) hallarse en un dilema; **what a ~ to be in!** ¡qué lío!

predicate Ⓐ [ˈpredɪkɪt] N (*Ling*) predicado *m*

Ⓑ [ˈpredɪkeɪt] VT 1 **to be ~d (up)on** estar basado en, partir de

2 (= *imply*) implicar

predicative [prɪˈdɪkətɪv] ADJ predicativo

predicatively [prɪˈdɪkətɪvlɪ] ADV predicativamente

predict [prɪˈdɪkt] VT predecir, pronosticar, prever; **"it'll end in disaster," he ~ed** —será un desastre, —predijo *or* —pronosticó; **the ~ed fall in interest rates has not materialized** la bajada de los tipos de interés que estaba prevista aún no se ha materializado; **the motion was passed, as ~ed** la moción se aprobó como se había previsto *or* pronosticado; **I can't ~ the future** no puedo predecir *or* prever el futuro; **he ~ed a brilliant future for the child** le predijo un futuro brillante al niño; **to ~ that** predecir que, pronosticar que; **nobody can ~ what will happen** nadie puede predecir lo que va a pasar

predictability [prɪdɪktəˈbɪlɪtɪ] N previsibilidad *f*

predictable [prɪˈdɪktəbl] ADJ [*result, outcome*] previsible; **his reaction was ~** su reacción era de esperar; **the contents of the report were entirely ~** el contenido del informe era totalmente previsible; **people were so ~** era tan fácil prever las reacciones de la gente; **you're so ~!** (= *always saying the same*) ¡siempre sales con las mismas!*; (= *always behaving the same*) ¡siempre estás igual!; **you men are so ~** siempre se sabe lo que los hombres vais a hacer/decir *etc*

predictably [prɪˈdɪktəblɪ] ADV [*behave, say, react*] como era de esperar; **his father was ~ furious** ◊ **~, his father was furious** como era de esperar, su padre estaba furioso; **~ enough, share prices fell** de manera previsible *or* como era de esperar, el precio de las acciones bajó

prediction [prɪˈdɪkʃən] N 1 (= *forecast*) (*by expert, layman*) predicción *f*; (*by clairvoyant, oracle*) vaticinio *m*, profecía *f*; **their ~ that house prices would fall** su predicción de que el precio de la vivienda iba a bajar; **there were dire ~s that thousands would die of malnutrition** hubo predicciones alarmantes de que miles de personas morirían por desnutrición; **to make a ~ about sth** pronosticar *or* predecir algo

2 (= *act*) **weather ~ has never been a perfect science** pronosticar el tiempo nunca ha sido una ciencia exacta

predictive [prɪˈdɪktɪv] ADJ [*powers, ability*] de predicción

predictor [prɪˈdɪktər] N indicador *m*

predigested [ˌpriːdaɪˈdʒestɪd] ADJ predigerido

predilection [ˌpriːdɪˈlekʃən] N predilección *f*; **to have a ~ for** tener predilección por

predispose [ˈpriːdɪsˈpəʊz] VT predisponer; **some people are ~d to diabetes** hay gente propensa *or* predispuesta a la diabetes; **I was ~d to believe him** tenía predisposición a creerle

predisposition [ˈpriːˌdɪspəˈzɪʃən] N predisposición *f*

predominance [prɪˈdɒmɪnəns] N 1 (= *dominance*) primacía *f*; [*of flavour*] predominio *m*

2 (= *greater number*) predominio *m*; **the ~ of women in the labour force** el predominio de mujeres entre los trabajadores

predominant [prɪˈdɒmɪnənt] ADJ [*role, opinion, image*] predominante, preponderante; [*flavour, colour*] predominante; **the disease is much more ~ in women** la enfermedad es mucho más predominante en las mujeres

predominantly [prɪˈdɒmɪnəntlɪ] ADV (= *mainly*) predominantemente; (= *in the majority*) en su mayoría; **the emphasis is ~ on languages** se hace hincapié predominantemente en los idiomas; **a population of ~ Italian residents** una población en su mayoría de residentes italianos

predominate [prɪˈdɒmɪneɪt] VI predominar (**over** sobre)

predominately [prɪˈdɒmɪnətlɪ] = **predominantly**

pre-eclampsia [ˌpriːɪˈklæmpsɪə] N pre-eclampsia *f*

preemie* [ˈpriːmɪ] N (*US Med*) bebé *m* prematuro

pre-eminence [priːˈemɪnəns] N preeminencia *f*

pre-eminent [priːˈemɪnənt] ADJ preeminente

pre-eminently [priːˈemɪnəntlɪ] ADV **his family were ~ farmers** su familia era fundamentalmente campesina; **home ownership is a ~ middle-class concern** la adquisición de la vivienda es una inquietud muy propia de la clase media; **it is also, and perhaps ~, a place of recreation** es además, y tal vez principalmente, un lugar de esparcimiento

pre-empt [priːˈempt] VT 1 [+ *person, attack, opposition*] adelantarse a, anticiparse a; **we found they had ~ed us in buying it** encontramos que se nos habían adelantado a comprarlo; **I did it to ~ any family arguments** lo hice para evitar discusiones familiares

2 (*esp US*) [+ *public land*] *ocupar para ejercer la opción de compra prioritaria*

pre-emption [priːˈempʃən] N 1 (*Mil*) prevención *f*, anticipación *f*

2 (*Jur*) derecho *m* preferencial (de compra)

pre-emptive [priːˈemptɪv] Ⓐ ADJ [*measure*] preventivo; [*claim*] por derecho de prioridad, preferente

Ⓑ CPD ► **pre-emptive bid** N oferta *f* hecha con intención de excluir cualquier otra ► **pre-emptive right** N derecho *m* preferencial ► **pre-emptive strike** N ataque *m* preventivo

preen [priːn] VT [+ *feathers*] arreglarse con el pico; **to ~ itself** [*bird*] arreglarse las plumas con el pico; **to ~ o.s.** [*person*] pavonearse, atildarse; **to ~ o.s. on** enorgullecerse de, jactarse de

pre-establish [ˈpriːɪsˈtæblɪʃ] VT establecer de antemano

pre-established [ˈpriːɪsˈtæblɪʃt] ADJ establecido de antemano

pre-exist [ˈpriːɪgˈzɪst] VI preexistir

pre-existence [ˈpriːɪgˈzɪstəns] N preexistencia *f*

pre-existent [ˈpriːɪgˈzɪstənt] ADJ preexistente

prefab* [ˈpriːfæb] N casa *f* prefabricada

prefabricate [ˈpriːˈfæbrɪkeɪt] VT prefabricar

prefabricated [ˈpriːˈfæbrɪkeɪtɪd] ADJ prefabricado

preface [ˈprefɪs] Ⓐ N prólogo *m*, prefacio *m*

Ⓑ VT [+ *book*] prologar; **he ~d this by saying that ...** a modo de prólogo a esto dijo que ..., introdujo este tema diciendo que ...; **the book is ~d by an essay** el libro tiene un ensayo a modo de prólogo; **he has the irritating habit of prefacing his sentences with ...** tiene la molesta costumbre de comenzar las frases con ...

prefaded [ˌpriːˈfeɪdɪd] ADJ [*jeans*] desteñido de origen

prefatory [ˈprefətərɪ] ADJ (*frm*) [*remarks, article, note*] preliminar, introductorio

prefect [ˈpriːfekt] N 1 (*Brit Scol*) monitor(a) *m/f*

2 (*Admin*) (*esp in France*) prefecto *m*

prefecture [ˈpriːfektjʊər] N prefectura *f*

prefer [prɪ'fɜːʳ] Ⓐ VT 1 (= *like better*) preferir (**to** a); **she ~s coffee to tea** prefiere el café al té; **which do you ~?** ¿cuál prefieres?, ¿cuál te gusta más?; **I ~red it the way it was** lo prefería tal como estaba; **"qualifications ~red but not essential"** "ser titulado es una ventaja pero no un requisito"; **to ~ doing sth** preferir hacer algo; **I ~ walking to going by car** prefiero ir andando *or* (*LAm*) caminando a ir en coche; **I'd ~ it if you didn't come with me** preferiría que no vinieras conmigo; **I much ~ Scotland** Escocia me gusta mucho más; **to ~ that** preferir que + *subjun*; **we'd ~ that this visit be kept confidential** preferimos que esta visita se mantenga en secreto; **to ~ to do sth** preferir hacer algo; **"will you do it?" — "I'd ~ not to"** —¿lo harás? —preferiría no hacerlo; **he may ~ to discuss it with friends rather than with his family** puede que prefiera hablarlo con amigos a hacerlo con su familia; **to ~ sb to do sth** preferir que algn haga algo; **would you ~ me to drive?** ¿preferirías que condujera yo?
2 (*Jur*) **to ~ charges (against sb)** presentar cargos (contra algn); **our client may decide to ~ charges of assault** puede que nuestro cliente decida presentar cargos por agresión
3 (*esp Rel*) (= *promote*) ascender; (= *appoint*) nombrar; **he was ~red to the see of Toledo** lo nombraron arzobispo de Toledo
Ⓑ VI preferir; **as you ~** como usted quiera, como usted prefiera; **if you ~, we could leave it till tomorrow** si usted quiere *or* lo prefiere, lo podemos dejar para mañana

preferable ['prefərəbl] ADJ preferible (**to** a)

preferably ['prefərəblɪ] ADV de preferencia, preferentemente; **a large, ~ non-stick, frying pan** una sartén grande, preferentemente *or* a ser posible antiadherente

preference ['prefərəns] Ⓐ N 1 (= *greater liking or favour*) preferencia *f*; **he expressed a ~ for red wine** mostró su preferencia por el vino tinto; **she has a ~ for older men** prefiere a *or* tiene preferencia por los hombres maduros; **for ~** de preferencia; **in ~ to sth** antes que algo, más que algo
2 (= *thing preferred*) **what is your ~?** ¿qué prefieres?; **I have no ~** no tengo preferencia
3 (= *priority*) **to give ~ to sth/sb** dar prioridad a algo/algn; **to give sth ~ over sth else** anteponer algo a otra cosa
Ⓑ CPD ▸ **preference share** N (*Fin*) acción *f* preferente, acción *f* privilegiada

preferential [ˌprefə'renʃəl] ADJ preferente, preferencial; **on ~ terms** con condiciones preferenciales; **to give a country ~ trade status** dar a un país un estatus comercial preferente

preferentially [ˌprefə'renʃəlɪ] ADV de manera preferente, de manera preferencial

preferment [prɪ'fɜːmənt] N (*esp Rel*) (= *promotion*) ascenso *m*, promoción *f*; (= *nomination*) nombramiento *m* (**to** a); **to get ~** ser ascendido

preferred [prɪ'fɜːd] Ⓐ ADJ 1 (*gen*) preferido; **his ~ method of travel** su medio de transporte preferido; **our ~ method of payment is cash** preferimos pagar en efectivo
2 (*Fin*) [*creditor*] privilegiado
Ⓑ CPD ▸ **preferred stock** N (*US Fin*) acciones *fpl* preferentes *or* privilegiadas

prefiguration [ˌpriːfɪgə'reɪʃən] N prefiguración *f*

prefigure [priː'fɪgəʳ] VT prefigurar

prefix ['priːfɪks] Ⓐ N [*of word*] prefijo *m*; [*of phone number*] prefijo *m*
Ⓑ [priː'fɪks] VT 1 (= *introduce*) introducir; **to ~ a statement with …** encabezar una declaración con …
2 (*Ling*) adjuntar un prefijo a

preflight ['priː'flaɪt] ADJ anterior al despegue

preggers* ['pregəz] ADJ **to be ~** estar con bombo*

pregnancy ['pregnənsɪ] Ⓐ N [*of woman*] embarazo *m*; [*of animal*] preñez *f*; *see also* **phantom B**
Ⓑ CPD ▸ **pregnancy test** N prueba *f* del embarazo

pregnant ['pregnənt] ADJ 1 (*lit*) 1·1 [*woman*] embarazada; **to be ~** estar embarazada; **to be six months ~** estar embarazada de seis meses; **to become** *or* **get ~ (by sb)** quedarse embarazada (de algn); **Tina was ~ with their first son** Tina estaba embarazada de su primer hijo; *see also* **heavily 1**
1·2 [*animal*] preñado
2 (*fig*) elocuente, significativo; **a ~ pause** una pausa elocuente *or* significativa; **~ with sth** cargado *or* preñado de algo

preheat ['priː'hiːt] VT precalentar

prehensile [prɪ'hensaɪl] ADJ prensil

prehistoric ['priːhɪs'tɒrɪk] ADJ prehistórico

prehistory ['priː'hɪstərɪ] N prehistoria *f*

preignition [ˌpriːɪg'nɪʃən] N preignición *f*

prejudge ['priː'dʒʌdʒ] VT prejuzgar

prejudice ['predʒʊdɪs] Ⓐ N 1 (= *biased opinion*) prejuicio *m*; **there's a lot of racial ~** hay muchos prejuicios raciales; **~ against women is widespread** los prejuicios machistas son moneda corriente; **to have a ~ against/in favour of sth/sb** estar predispuesto en contra de/a favor de algo/algn; **we all have our ~s** todos tenemos nuestros prejuicios; **he is quite without ~ in this matter** sobre esto no tiene ningún prejuicio
2 (*Jur*) (= *injury, detriment*) perjuicio *m*; **to the ~ of** con perjuicio de, con menoscabo de; **without ~** (*Jur*) sin detrimento de sus propios derechos; **without ~ to** sin perjuicio de
Ⓑ VT 1 (= *bias*) predisponer, prevenir (**against** contra)
2 (= *damage*) perjudicar; **to ~ one's chances** perjudicar sus posibilidades

prejudiced ['predʒʊdɪst] ADJ [*view*] parcial, interesado; **he's very ~** tiene muchos prejuicios; **to be ~ against sth/sb** estar predispuesto en contra de algo/algn; **to be ~ in favour of sth/sb** estar predispuesto a favor de algo/algn

prejudicial [ˌpredʒʊ'dɪʃəl] ADJ perjudicial (**to** para); **it would be ~ to her career** sería perjudicial para *or* perjudicaría a su carrera

prelate ['prelɪt] N prelado *m*

prelim ['priːlɪm] N ABBR = **preliminary**

preliminary [prɪ'lɪmɪnərɪ] Ⓐ ADJ preliminar
Ⓑ N 1 prolegómeno *m*; **a background check is normally a ~ to a presidential appointment** la comprobación del historial personal es normalmente un prolegómeno al nombramiento de presidente; **let's dispense with the preliminaries and get down to business** dejémonos de prolegómenos *or* preámbulos y vayamos al grano
2 (*Sport*) fase *f* previa

prelude ['preljuːd] Ⓐ N preludio *m* (*also Mus*) (**to** de)
Ⓑ VT preludiar

premarital ['priː'mærɪtl] Ⓐ ADJ prematrimonial
Ⓑ CPD ▸ **premarital sex** N relaciones *fpl* prematrimoniales

premature ['premətʃʊəʳ] ADJ [*baby, ageing, baldness*] prematuro; [*ejaculation*] precoz; **it would be ~ to conclude that …** sería prematuro deducir que …; **he was (born) five weeks ~** nació con cinco semanas de antelación; **I think you're being a little ~** creo que te estás adelantando a los acontecimientos

prematurely ['premətʃʊəlɪ] ADV prematuramente, antes de tiempo; **to be born ~** nacer prematuramente

pre-med ['priːmed] Ⓐ N (*Brit*) = **premedication**
Ⓑ ADJ (*US*) = **premedical**; **~ course** curso *m* preparatorio para ingresar en la Facultad de Medicina

premedication [ˌpriːmedɪ'keɪʃən] N premedicación *f*, medicación *f* previa

premeditate [priː'medɪteɪt] VT premeditar

premeditated [priː'medɪteɪtɪd] ADJ premeditado

premeditation [priːˌmedɪ'teɪʃən] N premeditación *f*

premenstrual [ˌpriː'menstrʊəl] Ⓐ ADJ premenstrual
Ⓑ CPD ▸ **premenstrual syndrome** N síndrome *m* premenstrual ▸ **premenstrual tension** N tensión *f* premenstrual

premier ['premɪəʳ] Ⓐ ADJ primero, principal
Ⓑ N (= *prime minister*) primer(a) ministro/a *m/f*; (= *president*) presidente/a *m/f*
Ⓒ CPD ▸ **Premier League** N (*Brit Ftbl*) primera división *f*, división *f* de honor

première [ˌpremɪ'ɛəʳ] Ⓐ N estreno *m*; **world ~** estreno *m* mundial; **the film had its ~** se estrenó la película
Ⓑ VT estrenar

premiership ['premɪəʃɪp] N cargo *m* del primer ministro, puesto *m* de primer ministro; (= *period in office*) mandato *m*

premise ['premɪs] Ⓐ N 1 (= *hypothesis*) premisa *f*
2 **premises** (*gen*) local *msing*; (= *shop, restaurant, hotel*) establecimiento *m*; (= *building*) edificio *m*; **they're moving to new ~s** se trasladan de local; **there is a doctor on the ~s at all times** hay un médico a todas horas en el edificio; **for consumption on the ~s** para consumirse en el local; **licensed ~s** local *msing* autorizado para la venta de bebidas alcohólicas; **to see sb off the ~s** echar a algn del local *or* establecimiento
Ⓑ VT (*frm*) **to be ~d on** estar basado en, tener como premisa

premium ['priːmɪəm] Ⓐ N 1 (*Insurance*) prima *f*
2 (= *surcharge*) recargo *m*; **people will pay a ~ for quality** (*fig*) la gente está dispuesta a pagar más para adquirir calidad
3 (= *bonus*) prima *f*
4 (*US*) (= *gasoline*) súper *f*
5 (*in phrases*) **to be at a ~** (*Comm*) estar por encima de la par; (= *be scarce*) estar muy solicitado; **space is at a ~ in our house** en casa no nos sobra espacio; **to sell sth at a ~** vender algo con prima; **to put** *or* **place a ~ on sth** (= *value*) valorar mucho algo; (= *make valuable*) hacer que suba el valor de algo; (= *make important*) hacer que se dé más importancia a algo; **I put a high ~ on privacy** valoro mucho la intimidad; **population pressure put land at a ~** la presión demográfica hizo que subiera el valor de la tierra; **the risk of disease puts a ~ on hygiene** el riesgo de enfermedad hace que se dé más importancia a la higiene
Ⓑ ADJ 1 (= *top quality*) [*brand, product*] de calidad superior, de primera calidad; **~ gasoline** (*US*) (gasolina *f*) súper *f*
2 (= *higher than normal*) **~ price** precio *m* con prima, precio *m* más elevado; **~ rate** tarifa *f* de primas

➤ LANGUAGE IN USE: prefer A1 7.1, 7.4 premise A1 26.3

Ⓒ CPD ► **premium bond** N (*Brit*) *bono del estado que permite participar en una lotería nacional*

premium-rate ['pri:mɪəm,reɪt] ADJ (*Telec*) con aplicación de la máxima tarifa

premolar [pri:'məʊləʳ] N premolar *m*

premonition [,premə'nɪʃən] N presentimiento *m*, premonición *f*; **to have a ~ that ...** presentir que ...

premonitory [prɪ'mɒnɪtərɪ] ADJ (*frm*) premonitorio

prenatal ['pri:'neɪtl] ADJ prenatal

prenuptial [,pri:'nʌpʃəl] Ⓐ ADJ prematrimonial, prenupcial

Ⓑ CPD ► **prenuptial agreement** N contrato *m* matrimonial

preoccupation [pri:,ɒkjʊ'peɪʃən] N preocupación *f*; **keeping warm was his main ~** su principal preocupación *or* lo que más le preocupaba era no pasar frío; **she was too busy with her own ~s to notice** estaba demasiado ensimismada en sus cosas para darse cuenta; **his incessant ~ with his appearance** su constante obsesión *or* preocupación por el aspecto

preoccupied [pri:'ɒkjʊpaɪd] ADJ (= *worried*) preocupado; (= *absorbed, distracted*) ensimismado, absorto; **he was too ~ to notice** estaba demasiado ensimismado *or* absorto para darse cuenta; **to be ~ about sth** estar preocupado por algo; **to be ~ with sth**: **Britain was ~ with the war in France** a Gran Bretaña le preocupaba la guerra en Francia; **you're too ~ with winning** estás demasiado obsesionado por ganar

preoccupy [pri:'ɒkjʊpaɪ] VT preocupar

pre-op* ['pri:'ɒp] ADJ preoperatorio; **~ medication** medicación *f* preoperatoria

preordain ['pri:ɔ:'deɪn] VT predestinar

preordained ['pri:ɔ:'deɪnd] ADJ predestinado

pre-owned ['pri:'əʊnd] ADJ seminuevo

prep [prep] Ⓐ ABBR (*Brit Scol*) = **preparation** (= *work*) tareas *fpl*, deberes *mpl*; (= *period*) tiempo *m* de estudio, hora *f* de los deberes

Ⓑ VI (*US**) **to ~ for** prepararse para; (*Scol*) hacer el curso de preparación para (*los estudios universitarios*)

Ⓒ VT (*US**) preparar; **to ~ o.s.** prepararse

Ⓓ CPD ► **prep school** N (*Brit*) *see* **preparatory B**

prepack [,pri:'pæk], **prepackage** [,pri:'pækɪdʒ] VT preempaquetar

prepacked [,pri:'pækt], **prepackaged** [,pri:'pækɪdʒd] ADJ (pre)empaquetado

prepaid [,pri:'peɪd] ADJ pagado con antelación; (*Comm*) [*order*] abonado por adelantado, pagado por adelantado; (*Fin*) [*interest*] cobrado por adelantado; [*envelope*] con franqueo pagado; **carriage ~** porte *m* pagado, franco de porte

preparation [,prepə'reɪʃən] N [1] (= *prior activity, development*) preparación *f*; **few things distracted him from the ~ of his lectures** pocas cosas le distraían de la preparación de sus clases; **the person responsible for food ~** la persona encargada de preparar la comida; **education should be a ~ for life** la educación debería servir de preparación para la vida; **her latest novel has been four years in ~** lleva cuatro años preparando su última novela; **he is learning French in ~ for his new job** está aprendiendo francés para prepararse para su nuevo trabajo

[2] **preparations** preparativos *mpl* (**for** para, de **I helped with the ~s for the party** ayudé con los preparativos para *or* de la fiesta; **to make ~s (for sth/to do sth)** hacer preparativos (para algo/para hacer algo); **he'll have to make ~s for the funeral** tendrá que hacer los preparativos del *or* para el funeral

[3] (*Culin, Pharm*) (= *substance*) preparado *m*

[4] (*Brit*) (*in public schools*) (= *homework*) deberes *mpl*

preparatory [prɪ'pærətərɪ] Ⓐ ADJ preparatorio, preliminar; **~ to** como preparación para, antes de

Ⓑ CPD ► **preparatory school** N (*Brit*) *escuela privada para niños de 6 a 13 años*; (*US*) colegio *m* privado

> **PREPARATORY SCHOOL**
>
> *En el Reino Unido una* **preparatory school** *o* **prep school** *es una escuela privada de educación primaria, normalmente no mixta, para alumnos de edades comprendidas entre los 6 y los 13 años. Estos centros exigen uniforme y su objetivo es preparar a los alumnos para que prosigan su formación en centros privados.*
>
> *En Estados Unidos una* **preparatory** *o* **prep school** *es un centro privado de enseñanza secundaria que prepara a sus alumnos para su ingreso en la universidad. Tanto en el Reino Unido como en Estados Unidos las* **preparatory schools** *se asocian con las clases sociales más pudientes y privilegiadas. La palabra* **preppy**, *usada como sustantivo o adjetivo, designa a los alumnos de las* **prep schools** *estadounidenses o la forma de vestir y apariencia pulcra, discreta y conservadora que normalmente se les atribuye.*

prepare [prɪ'peəʳ] Ⓐ VT [+ *meal, lesson, defence*] preparar; [+ *report*] redactar, preparar; [+ *plan, strategy*] idear, preparar; **to ~ sb for sth** preparar a algn para algo; **he had a tutor to ~ him for the exam** tenía un profesor particular para que lo preparara para el examen; **nothing could have ~d me for this** nada hubiera podido ponerme en guardia contra esto; **she tried to ~ her children for her death** intentó preparar a sus hijos para su muerte *or* para que aceptaran su muerte; **to ~ o.s. for sth** prepararse para algo; **~ yourself for a shock** (*good*) prepárate para una sorpresa; (*bad*) prepárate para lo peor; **to ~ sth for sb** preparar algo a algn; **they had ~d a room for him** le habían preparado una habitación; ✦**IDIOM to ~ the ground** *or* **way (for sth/sb)** preparar el terreno (para algo/algn)

Ⓑ VI prepararse; **to ~ for sth** prepararse para algo; **to ~ for an examination** prepararse para un examen; **we must ~ for war** tenemos que prepararnos para la guerra; **I think you'd better ~ for the worst** creo que deberías prepararte para lo peor; **to ~ to do sth** prepararse para hacer algo

➤ **prepared** [prɪ'peəd] ADJ [1] (= *ready*) preparado; **I am ~ for anything** estoy preparado para cualquier eventualidad; **we were ~ for it** íbamos preparados; **we were not ~ for this** esto no lo esperábamos, no contábamos con esto; **"be ~"** (*motto*) ¡siempre listos!; **to be ~ for the worst** estar preparado para lo peor

[2] (= *made earlier*) [2·1] [*statement, answer*] preparado

[2·2] (*Culin*) **supermarkets now stock ~ salads** ahora los supermercados venden ensaladas listas para comer *or* ensaladas preparadas; **~ foods** platos *m* precocinados, productos *mpl* previamente elaborados

[3] (= *willing*) **to be ~ to do sth** estar dispuesto a hacer algo; **he was ~ to be broadminded** estaba dispuesto a ser tolerante

preparedness [prɪ'peərɪdnɪs] N preparación *f*, estado *m* de preparación; **military ~** preparación *f* militar

prepay ['pri:'peɪ] (*pt, pp* **prepaid**) VT (*Comm*) [+ *order*] abonar por adelantado, pagar por adelantado; (*Fin*) [+ *interest*] cobrar por adelantado; [+ *envelope*] emitir con franqueo pagado

prepayment ['pri:'peɪmənt] N pago *m* por adelantado, pago *m* anticipado

preponderance [prɪ'pɒndərəns] N preponderancia *f*, predominio *m*

preponderant [prɪ'pɒndərənt] ADJ preponderante, predominante

preponderantly [prɪ'pɒndərəntlɪ] ADV preponderantemente, predominantemente, de modo predominante

preponderate [prɪ'pɒndəreɪt] VI (*frm*) preponderar, predominar

preposition [,prepə'zɪʃən] N (*Ling*) preposición *f*

prepositional [,prepə'zɪʃənl] ADJ preposicional

prepositionally [,prepə'zɪʃənəlɪ] ADV como preposición

prepossess [,pri:pə'zes] VT (= *preoccupy*) preocupar; (= *bias, impress favourably*) predisponer

prepossessing [,pri:pə'zesɪŋ] ADJ agradable, atractivo; **not very ~** no muy atractivo

preposterous [prɪ'pɒstərəs] ADJ absurdo, ridículo

preposterously [prɪ'pɒstərəslɪ] ADV absurdamente

preposterousness [prɪ'pɒstərəsnɪs] N lo absurdo

preppie*, **preppy*** ['prepɪ] (*US*) Ⓐ ADJ de muy buen tono

Ⓑ N [1] (= *prep school student*) *alumno de colegio secundario privado*

[2] (= *rich kid*) niño/a *m/f* bien, niño/a *m/f* pera*, pijo/a* *m/f*

pre-prandial [,pri:'prændɪəl] ADJ (*frm, hum*) **a ~ drink** un aperitivo

preprepared [,pri:prɪ'peəd] ADJ prepreparado

preproduction [,pri:prə'dʌkʃən] Ⓐ N preproducción *f*

Ⓑ CPD ► **preproduction model** N prototipo *m* ► **preproduction trial** N ensayo *m* con prototipo

preprogramme, **preprogram** (*esp US*) [,pri:'prəʊgræm] VT preprogramar

preprogrammed, **preprogramed** (*US*) [,pri:'prəʊgræmd] ADJ preprogramado

prepubescent [,pri:pju:'besənt] ADJ prepúber

prepuce ['pri:pju:s] N prepucio *m*

prequel ['pri:kwəl] N *película hecha para ser la primera parte de otra aparecida antes*

pre-Raphaelite ['pri:'ræfəlaɪt] Ⓐ ADJ prerrafaelista

Ⓑ N prerrafaelista *mf*

prerecord ['pri:rɪ'kɔ:d] VT grabar de antemano, pregrabar

prerecorded [,pri:rɪ'kɔ:dɪd] ADJ pregrabado, grabado de antemano

pre-release ['pri:rɪ'li:s] Ⓐ ADJ (*Cine*) [*copy*] promocional; [*publicity*] previo al estreno, promocional

Ⓑ CPD ► **pre-release showing** N preestreno *m*

prerequisite ['pri:'rekwɪzɪt] Ⓐ N requisito *m* indispensable, condición *f* previa; **a maths degree is a ~ for the job** la titulación en matemáticas es requisito indispensable para el

➤ LANGUAGE IN USE: **prepared** **3** 3, 12.2

puesto; **it's an essential ~ to success as an actor** es una condición *or* requisito indispensable para triunfar como actor
Ⓑ ADJ previamente necesario

prerogative [prɪˈrɒgətɪv] N prerrogativa *f*; **he can refuse if he wants to, that's his ~** puede negarse si quiere, está en su derecho

Pres ABBR (= **President**) Presidente/a *m/f*

presage [ˈpresɪdʒ] (*liter*) Ⓐ N presagio *m*
Ⓑ VT presagiar

Presbyterian [ˌprezbɪˈtɪərɪən] Ⓐ ADJ presbiteriano
Ⓑ N presbiteriano/a *m/f*

Presbyterianism [ˌprezbɪˈtɪərɪənɪzəm] N presbiterianismo *m*

presbytery [ˈprezbɪtərɪ] N casa *f* parroquial; (*Archit*) presbiterio *m*

preschool [ˈpriːˈskuːl] Ⓐ ADJ preescolar
Ⓑ CPD ► **preschool education** N educación *f* preescolar

prescience [ˈpresɪəns] N clarividencia *f*

prescient [ˈpresɪənt] ADJ [*person, remark*] clarividente; [*dream*] profético

prescribe [prɪˈskraɪb] Ⓐ VT [1] (= *lay down, order*) prescribir, ordenar; **in the ~d way** en conformidad con lo prescrito; **~d books** lecturas *fpl* obligatorias; **the ~d punishment** la pena establecida *or* prescrita
[2] [+ *medicine*] recetar; **to ~ sth for sb** ◊ **~ sb sth** [+ *medicine*] recetar algo a algn; **the doctor ~d a course of antibiotics for me** el médico me recetó antibióticos; **he ~d complete rest** recomendó reposo absoluto; **the ~d dose** la dosis prescrita; **what do you ~?** ¿qué me recomienda?
Ⓑ VI (*Med*) recetar

prescription [prɪˈskrɪpʃən] Ⓐ N [1] (*Med*) receta *f*; **to make up** *or* (*US*) **fill a ~** preparar una receta; **"only available on prescription"** "de venta únicamente bajo receta"; *see also* **write A1**
[2] (*Jur*) prescripción *f*
Ⓑ CPD ► **prescription charges** NPL (*Brit*) precio *msing* de las recetas ► **prescription lenses** NPL (*US*) lentillas *fpl* graduadas

prescriptive [prɪˈskrɪptɪv] ADJ (*Jur*) [*title*] legal; (= *sanctioned by custom*) sancionado por la costumbre; (*Gram*) normativo

prescriptivism [prɪˈskrɪptɪˌvɪzəm] N prescriptivismo *m*

presealed [ˈpriːˈsiːld] ADJ precintado

pre-select [priːsɪˈlekt] VT preseleccionar

presence [ˈprezns] N [1] [*of person*] (*in place*) presencia *f*; (*at function*) asistencia *f* (**at** a); **he was aware of her ~** era consciente de su presencia; **your ~ is requested** se ruega su asistencia; **to grace** *or* **honour sb with one's ~** (*also iro*) honrar a algn con su presencia; **in sb's ~** en presencia de algn, delante de algn; **he said it in the ~ of witnesses** lo dijo en presencia de *or* delante de testigos; **I felt comfortable in her ~** me sentía cómodo en su presencia *or* con ella; **to make one's ~ felt** hacerse notar *or* sentir
[2] (*Mil, Police*) presencia *f*; **military ~** presencia *f* militar; **there was a massive police ~ at the match** hubo una importante presencia policial en el partido
[3] (= *bearing, personality*) presencia *f*; **he had tremendous physical ~** tenía mucha presencia; *see also* **stage C**
[4] [*of thing, substance*] presencia *f*; **the ~ of a carcinogen in the water** la presencia de un carcinógeno en el agua; **metal rusts in the ~ of oxygen** el metal se oxida en presencia de oxígeno
[5] **~ of mind** presencia *f* de ánimo; **to have the ~ of mind to do sth** tener la suficiente presencia de ánimo como para hacer algo, tener la presencia de ánimo de hacer algo
[6] (*ghostly*) presencia *f*

present[1] [ˈpreznt] Ⓐ ADJ [1] [*person*] **to be ~** (*in place*) estar presente; (*at function*) asistir, estar presente; **he insisted on being ~** se empeñó en estar presente *or* en asistir; **the whole family was ~** estaba toda la familia presente; **how many others were ~?** ¿cuántos más había?, ¿cuántos más estuvieron presentes?; **nobody else was ~** no había nadie más, nadie más estuvo presente; **is there a doctor ~?** ¿hay un médico (presente)?; **present!** ¡presente!; **ssh! there are ladies ~** ¡sss! hay señoras delante; **to be ~ at** [+ *function*] asistir a, estar presente en; [+ *scene, accident*] presenciar; **~ company excepted** exceptuando a los presentes; **all ~ and correct** (*Mil*) todos presentes; (*hum*) somos todos los que estamos y estamos todos los que somos; **those ~** los presentes
[2] **to be ~** [*thing, substance*] encontrarse; **in some areas, fluoride is naturally ~ in the water supply** en algunas zonas, el flúor se encuentra de forma natural en el agua; **to be ever ~** estar siempre presente
[3] (= *current*) actual; **how long have you been in your ~ job?** ¿cuánto tiempo llevas en tu puesto actual?; **in its ~ form** en su forma actual; **the ~ government** el actual gobierno; **from Roman times to the ~ day** desde los tiempos romanos hasta nuestros días; **this tradition has continued to the ~ day** esta tradición sigue vigente; **a solution to the problems of the ~ day** una solución a los problemas actuales *or* de nuestros días; **at the ~ time** (= *at this instant*) en este momento; (= *currently*) actualmente, hoy día; **(up) to the ~ time** hasta nuestros días, hasta los tiempos actuales; *see also* **present-day**
[4] (*Gram*) presente
Ⓑ N [1] (= *present time*) **the ~** el presente; **for the ~** de momento, por lo pronto; **that will be all for the ~** de momento *or* por lo pronto esto es todo; **I'll say goodbye for the ~** me despido hasta la próxima; **up to the ~** hasta ahora; ✦*IDIOM* **to live for the ~** vivir el momento; ✦*PROV* **(there's) no time like the ~** no dejes para mañana lo que puedas hacer hoy
[2] **at ~** (= *at this instant*) en este momento; (= *currently*) ahora, actualmente; **Mr Young isn't here at ~** el Sr. Young no está aquí en este momento; **I don't want to get married at ~** de momento no me quiero casar; **as things are at ~** como están las cosas ahora, como están las cosas actualmente
[3] (*Gram*) (tiempo *m*) presente *m*
[4] (*Jur*) **by these ~s** por los aquí presentes
Ⓒ CPD ► **the present continuous** N el presente continuo ► **the present indicative** N el presente de indicativo ► **present participle** N participio *m* activo, participio *m* (de) presente ► **the present perfect** N el pretérito perfecto ► **the present simple** N el presente simple ► **the present subjunctive** N el presente de subjuntivo ► **the present tense** N el (tiempo) presente

present[2] [ˈpreznt] N (= *gift*) regalo *m*, obsequio *m* (*frm*), presente *m* (*frm, liter*); **it's for a ~** es para (un) regalo; **she gave me the book as a ~** me regaló el libro; **it was a ~ from Dad** era un regalo de papá; **to give sb a ~** hacer un regalo a algn; **to make sb a ~ of sth** regalar algo a algn; (*fig*) dar algo a algn medio regalado, servir algo a algn en bandeja; *see also* **birthday, Christmas, wedding**

present[3] [prɪˈzent] Ⓐ VT [1] (= *give*) [1·1] [+ *prize, award*] entregar, hacer entrega de; **to ~ sth to sb** entregar algo a algn, hacer entrega de algo a algn; **they have ~ed a petition to Parliament** han hecho entrega de *or* han presentado una petición al parlamento
[1·2] [+ *gift*] **to ~ sb with sth** ◊ **~ sth to sb** regalar algo a algn, obsequiar a algn con algo (*more frm*), obsequiar algo a algn (*LAm*)
[2] (= *introduce*) presentar; **may I ~ Miss Clark?** ◊ **allow me to ~ Miss Clark** (*frm*) permítame presentarle a *or* le presento a la Srta. Clark; **it gives me great pleasure to ~ ...** es para mí un honor *or* placer presentarles a ...; **he ~ed Jane to his mother** presentó a Jane a su madre; **to be ~ed at court** (*Brit Jur*) ser presentado en la corte
[3] (= *offer formally*) **to ~ one's apologies (to sb)** presentar sus excusas (ante algn); **to ~ one's compliments (to sb)** presentar *or* ofrecer sus saludos (a algn); **to ~ one's credentials (to sb)** [*diplomat*] presentar sus credenciales (ante algn)
[4] (= *show*) [+ *documents, tickets*] presentar, mostrar
[5] (= *put forward, communicate*) [+ *report, proposal, evidence*] presentar; [+ *case, argument*] exponer; (*Parl*) [+ *bill*] presentar; **figures can be ~ed in many ways** hay muchas maneras de presentar las cifras; **the party has to ~ a more professional image** el partido debe presentar *or* proyectar una imagen más profesional; **she ~ed her plan to the meeting** expuso su proyecto a la reunión
[6] (= *pose*) [+ *challenge*] representar; [+ *opportunity*] presentar, ofrecer; [+ *sight*] ofrecer; **if you are old, getting fit can ~ a challenge** si es usted mayor, ponerse en forma puede representar un reto; **the bay ~s a magnificent sight** la bahía ofrece una vista maravillosa; **the boy ~s a problem** el chico nos plantea un problema; **the patrol ~ed an easy target** la patrulla era un blanco fácil
[7] (= *provide, confront*) **to ~ sb with sth: the author ~s us with a vivid chronicle of contemporary America** el autor nos brinda *or* ofrece una vívida crónica de la América contemporánea; **she bought a new car and ~ed me with the bill** se compró un coche nuevo y me pasó la factura; **to ~ sb with a daughter/son** (*frm, hum*) ofrecer a algn una hija/un hijo
[8] (= *represent, portray*) presentar; **the report ~s her in a favourable light** el informe presenta una imagen favorable de ella
[9] (*Comm*) (= *tender, submit*) [+ *bill*] presentar, pasar; [+ *cheque*] presentar; **the cheque was ~ed for payment on 24th** el cheque se presentó para el cobro el día 24
[10] (*Rad, TV*) [+ *programme*] presentar; (*Theat*) [+ *play*] presentar, ofrecer el montaje de; (*Art*) [+ *exhibition*] exponer, presentar; **~ing Garbo as Mimi** con Garbo en el papel de Mimi
[11] (*Mil*) **to ~ arms** presentar las armas; **~ arms!** ¡presenten armas!
[12] **to ~ o.s.** [*person*] presentarse; **how you ~ yourself is extremely important** la manera de presentarse es muy importante; **to ~ o.s. as sth: he ~s himself as a moderate, but he's not** se define a sí mismo como un moderado, pero no lo es; **she's thinking of ~ing herself as a candidate** está pensando en presentarse como candidata; **to ~ o.s. for examination** presentarse a (un) examen; **to ~ o.s. for (an) interview** presentarse a una entrevista

13 to ~ itself [*opportunity, problem*] surgir, presentarse; a problem has ~ed itself ha surgido *or* se ha presentado un problema
Ⓑ VI (*Med*) to ~ with sth [*patient*] presentarse con algo; to ~ with *or* as sth [*condition*] presentarse en forma de algo

presentable [prɪ'zentəbl] ADJ presentable; are you ~? (= *dressed*) ¿estás visible?; to make sth ~ arreglar algo; I must go and make myself ~ voy a arreglarme un poco

presentably [prɪ'zentəblɪ] ADV ~ dressed vestido de manera presentable

presentation [,prezən'teɪʃən] Ⓐ N 1 (= *act of presenting*) presentación *f*; (*Jur*) [*of case*] exposición *f*; on ~ of the voucher al presentar el vale
2 (*TV, Rad*) producción *f*; (*Theat*) representación *f*
3 (= *ceremony*) ceremonia *f* de entrega; (= *gift*) obsequio *m*; to make the ~ hacer la presentación; to make sb a ~ on his retirement hacer un obsequio a algn con ocasión de su jubilación
Ⓑ CPD ► presentation case N estuche *m* de regalo ► presentation copy N ejemplar *m* con dedicatoria del autor

presentational [,prezən'teɪʃənəl] ADJ relativo a la presentación; from a ~ point of view desde el punto de vista de la presentación

present-day ['preznt'deɪ] ADJ actual, de hoy (en día); ~ Spain la España actual *or* de hoy (en día)

presenter [prɪ'zentəʳ] N (*Rad*) locutor(a) *m/f*; (*TV*) presentador/a *m/f*

presentiment [prɪ'zentɪmənt] N presentimiento *m*; to have a ~ about sth tener un presentimiento acerca de algo; to have a ~ that ... tener el presentimiento de que ..., presentir que ...

presently ['prezntlɪ] ADV 1 (= *shortly*) dentro de poco, al rato; you'll feel better ~ enseguida te sentirás mejor; ~, he woke up poco después se despertó
2 (*US*) (= *now*) en este momento, actualmente; they're ~ on tour actualmente están de gira

preservation [,prezə'veɪʃən] Ⓐ N [*of antiquities, food*] conservación *f*; [*of wildlife, land, buildings*] conservación *f*, preservación *f*; [*of order, democracy*] mantenimiento *m*; in a good state of ~ en buen estado, bien conservado
Ⓑ CPD ► preservation order N orden *f* de preservación ► preservation society N (*Brit*) sociedad *f* para la preservación

preservative [prɪ'zɜːvətɪv] Ⓐ N (*Culin*) conservante *m*
Ⓑ CPD [*function, substance*] conservante

preserve [prɪ'zɜːv] Ⓐ VT 1 (= *keep in existence*) [+ *endangered species, jobs, language*] proteger, preservar; [+ *customs, silence, reputation*] conservar, mantener; [+ *sense of humour, memory*] conservar; we will do everything to ~ (the) peace haremos todo lo posible por mantener la paz; as a doctor, it was my duty to ~ life como médico, era mi deber salvar vidas; to ~ sb's anonymity mantener a algn en el anonimato
2 (= *keep from decay*) [+ *object, environment, meat*] conservar; perfectly ~d medieval houses casas *fpl* medievales en perfecto estado; to ~ one's looks conservar el atractivo; to ~ the status quo mantener el statu quo; the body was ~d in ice el cuerpo se conservaba en hielo; *see also* aspic, well-preserved
3 (*esp Brit Culin*) (= *bottle, pickle, etc*) [+ *fruit*] hacer conservas de; [+ *meat, fish*] conservar; peppers and chillies may be ~d in oil los pimientos y los chiles se pueden conservar en aceite; to ~ sth in salt conservar algo en sal
4 (= *protect*) 4·1 (*gen*) proteger; to ~ sth from/against sth proteger algo de algo; paint the metal to ~ it from corrosion pinte el metal para protegerlo de la corrosión
4·2 (*in prayers, wishes*) may God ~ you que Dios os ampare; God *or* Heaven *or* saints ~ us! ¡que Dios nos ampare!; heaven ~ us from little boys (*hum*) que Dios nos proteja de los niños
5 (*for private hunting, fishing*) [+ *game*] proteger
Ⓑ N 1 (*Culin*) 1·1 (= *jam*) mermelada *f*, confitura *f*; (= *bottled fruit, chutney*) conserva *f*; damson ~ mermelada *f* or confitura *f* de ciruela damascena
1·2 preserves conservas *fpl*
2 (= *restricted area*) 2·1 (*Hunting*) coto *m*, vedado *m*; (*for wildlife*) reserva *f*; *see also* game D, wildlife B
2·2 (*fig*) dominio *m*; banking has remained almost exclusively a male ~ la banca sigue siendo casi exclusivamente del dominio masculino; they are poaching on my ~ están invadiendo mi terreno

preserved [prɪ'zɜːvd] ADJ [*fruit, ginger*] en conserva; you can use either fresh or ~ fruit puede usar fruta fresca o en conserva *or* de lata; ~ foods (*in bottles*) comida *f* en conserva; (*in cans*) comida *f* en conserva, comida *f* de lata

preset ['priː'set] (*pt, pp* preset) VT programar

preshrunk ['priː'ʃrʌŋk] ADJ ya lavado

preside [prɪ'zaɪd] VI presidir; to ~ at *or* over a meeting/ceremony presidir una reunión/ceremonia; he ~d over the reunification of Germany condujo la reunificación alemana; a statue of him ~s over the main square of the town una estatua suya preside la plaza mayor de la ciudad; the presiding judge el juez/la jueza presidente de sala

presidency ['prezɪdənsɪ] N 1 (= *office*) [*of country, organization, company*] presidencia *f*; he is to be nominated for the ~ lo van a nombrar candidato a la presidencia
2 (= *period of office*) [*of country*] mandato *m* presidencial, presidencia *f*; [*of organization, company*] presidencia *f*, periodo *m* de gestión en la presidencia

president ['prezɪdənt] N [*of country, company, organization*] presidente/a *m/f*; (*US Univ*) rector(a) *m/f*; ~-elect presidente/a *m/f* electo/a ► President's list N (*US Univ*) lista *f* de honor académica; → DEAN'S LIST

presidential [,prezɪ'denʃəl] Ⓐ ADJ [*palace, adviser, candidate*] presidencial; ~ election(s) elecciones *fpl* presidenciales; he will make his first ~ decision today hoy tomará su primera decisión como presidente; his ~ hopes sus esperanzas de convertirse en presidente
Ⓑ CPD ► presidential guard N guardia *f* presidencial

presidium [prɪ'sɪdɪəm] N (*Pol*) presidio *m*

press [pres]

A NOUN	D COMPOUNDS
B TRANSITIVE VERB	E PHRASAL VERBS
C INTRANSITIVE VERB	

Ⓐ NOUN
1 Publishing 1·1 (= *newspapers collectively*) prensa *f*; to get *or* have a good/bad ~ (*lit, fig*) tener buena/mala prensa; the ~ (= *newspapers, journalists*) la prensa; I saw it in the ~ lo vi en la prensa; the ~ reported that ... la prensa informó que ...; member of the ~ periodista *mf*, miembro *mf* de la prensa; the national/local ~ la prensa nacional/regional; *see also* free A4, gutter B
1·2 (*also* printing ~) imprenta *f*; to go to ~ entrar en prensa; correct at the time of going to ~ correcto en el momento de impresión; hot off the ~(es) recién salido de la imprenta; to be in ~ estar en prensa; to pass sth for ~ aprobar algo para la prensa; to set the ~es rolling poner las prensas en marcha
1·3 (= *publishing firm*) editorial *f*
2 = touch (*with hand*) apretón *m*; at the ~ of a button con sólo apretar un botón
3 with iron to give sth a ~ planchar algo; this skirt needs a ~ esta falda necesita un planchado
4 = apparatus, machine (*for wine, olives, cheese, moulding*) prensa *f*; (*also* trouser ~) prensa *f* para planchar pantalones; (*for racket*) tensor *m*; hydraulic ~ prensa *f* hidráulica; *see also* cider B, printing B
5 = crush apiñamiento *m*, agolpamiento *m*; he lost his hat in the ~ to get out perdió el sombrero en el apiñamiento *or* agolpamiento que se produjo a la salida
6 Weightlifting presa *f*
7 = cupboard armario *m*
Ⓑ TRANSITIVE VERB
1 = push, squeeze 1·1 [+ *button, switch, doorbell*] pulsar, apretar; [+ *hand, trigger*] apretar; [+ *accelerator*] pisar; select the option required, then ~ "enter" escoja la opción que desee, y luego pulse *or* apriete "intro"; he ~ed his face against the window apretó la cara contra el cristal; she ~ed herself against me/the wall se apretó contra mí/contra la pared; she ~ed a note into his hand le metió un billete en la mano; she ~ed the lid on (to) the box cerró la caja apretando la tapa; he ~ed her to him la atrajo hacia sí; Dobbs ~ed his hand to his heart Dobbs se llevó la mano al corazón; he ~ed the revolver to Sally's head le puso a Sally el revólver en la cabeza; he ~ed his fingertips together juntó las yemas de los dedos; ✦IDIOM to ~ the flesh (*US**) ir estrechando manos a diestro y siniestro
1·2 (*painfully*) apretujar; as the crowd moved back he found himself ~ed up against a wall a medida que la multitud retrocedía, se vio apretujado contra una pared
2 using press [+ *grapes, olives, flowers*] prensar
3 = iron [+ *clothes*] planchar
4 Tech (= *make*) [+ *machine part*] prensar; [+ *record, disk*] imprimir
5 = pressurize presionar; he didn't need much ~ing no hubo que presionarle mucho; when ~ed, she conceded the point cuando la presionaron, les dio la razón; to ~ sb for sth exigir algo de algn; to ~ sb for an answer exigir una respuesta de algn; he did not ~ her for further details no le exigió más detalles; to ~ sb for payment insistir en que algn pague, exigir a algn el pago de lo que se debe; to ~ sb into doing sth obligar a algn a hacer algo; I found myself ~ed into playing football with the children me vi obligado a jugar al fútbol con los niños; to ~ sb to do sth (= *urge*) insistir en que algn haga algo; (= *pressurize*) presionar a algn para que haga algo; he ~ed me to have a drink with him insistió en que tomase una copa con él; he didn't ~ her to go back to work no la presionó para que volviera a trabajar; the trade unions are ~ing him to stand firm los sindicatos le están presionando para que se mantenga firme; *see also* pressed

[6] [= *insist*] **don't ~ me on this point** no me insistas sobre este punto; **she smiles coyly when ~ed about her private life** cuando insisten en querer saber sobre su vida privada, sonríe con coquetería; **he was being ~ed by creditors** le acosaban los acreedores

[7] [= *force*] **to ~ sth on sb** insistir en que algn acepte algo; **food and cigarettes were ~ed on him** le estuvieron ofreciendo insistentemente comida y cigarros

[8] **to be ~ed into service**: **we were all ~ed into service** todos tuvimos que ponernos a trabajar; **the town hall has been ~ed into service as a school** se han visto obligados a usar el ayuntamiento como escuela; **Kenny had been ~ed into service to guard the door** habían convencido a Kenny para que vigilara la puerta

[9] [= *pursue*] [+ *claim*] insistir en; [+ *demand*] exigir; **his officials have visited Washington to ~ their case for economic aid** sus representantes han ido a Washington para hacer presión a favor de la ayuda económica; **to ~ charges (against sb)** presentar cargos (contra algn); **the champion failed to ~ home his advantage** el campeón no supo aprovechar su ventaja; **to ~ home an attack** sacar el máximo partido de un ataque; **I shan't ~ the point** no insistiré más sobre eso; *see also* **suit A4**

Ⓒ INTRANSITIVE VERB

[1] [= *exert pressure*] apretar; **does it hurt when I ~ here?** ¿le duele cuando le aprieto aquí?; **I felt something hard ~ into my back** noté la presión de algo duro que se apretaba contra mi espalda; **the bone was ~ing on a nerve** el hueso estaba pinzando un nervio

[2] [= *move, push*] **he ~ed against her** se apretó contra ella; **his leg ~ed against her thigh** su pierna se apretaba contra su muslo; **the crowd ~ed round him** la muchedumbre se apiñó en torno a él; **he ~ed through the crowd** se abrió paso entre la muchedumbre; **the audience ~ed towards the exit** el público se apresuró hacia la salida

[3] [= *urge, agitate*] **to ~ for sth** exigir algo, insistir en algo; **he will ~ for the death penalty in this case** en este caso va a insistir en *or* exigir la pena de muerte; **a protest march in the capital to ~ for new elections** una marcha de protesta en la capital para exigir otras elecciones; **police may now ~ for changes in the law** puede que ahora la policía presione para que cambien las leyes; **to ~ for sb to resign** exigir la dimisión de algn, insistir en que algn dimita; **time is ~ing** el tiempo apremia

[4] [= *weigh heavily*] **to ~ on sb** pesar sobre algn; **the weight of guilt ~ed on her** el sentimiento de culpabilidad pesaba sobre ella

Ⓓ COMPOUNDS

► **press agency** N agencia *f* de prensa
► **press agent** N encargado/a *m/f* de prensa
► **press attaché** N agregado/a *m/f* de prensa
► **press baron** N magnate *m* de la prensa
► **press box** N tribuna *f* de prensa ► **press briefing** N rueda *f* de prensa, conferencia *f* de prensa ► **press card** N pase *m* de periodista, carnet *m* de prensa ► **press clipping** N = **press cutting** ► **press conference** N rueda *f* de prensa, conferencia *f* de prensa; **to call a ~ conference** convocar una rueda *or* una conferencia de prensa; **to hold a ~ conference** celebrar una rueda *or* una conferencia de prensa ► **press corps** N prensa *f* acreditada ► **press coverage** N cobertura *f* periodística; **it's had a lot of ~ coverage** ha tenido mucha cobertura periodística ► **press cutting** N recorte *m* (de periódico) ► **press gallery** N tribuna *f* de prensa ► **press gang** N (*Hist*) leva *f* ► **press office** N oficina *f* de prensa ► **press officer** N agente *mf* de prensa ► **press photographer** N fotógrafo/a *m/f* de prensa ► **press release** N comunicado *m* de prensa; **to issue** *or* **put out a ~ release** publicar un comunicado de prensa ► **press report** N nota *f* de prensa, reportaje *m* de prensa ► **press run** N (*US*) tirada *f* ► **press secretary** N secretario/a *m/f* de prensa ► **press stud** N (*Brit*) automático *m*, broche *m* de presión ► **press view** N preestreno *m* (para prensa)

Ⓔ PHRASAL VERBS

►**press ahead** VI + ADV seguir adelante (**with** con)

►**press back** VT + ADV [+ *crowd, enemy*] obligar a retroceder; **he ~ed himself back against the wall** se apretó contra la pared

►**press down** Ⓐ VT + ADV (= *depress*) [+ *button, knob, switch*] apretar, presionar; (= *flatten*) presionar hacia abajo; **seal the edges by ~ing them down** cierre los lados presionándolos hacia abajo, cierre los lados apretándolos; **he ~ed the lid down tight** apretó la tapa con fuerza

Ⓑ VI + ADV **to ~ down on sth** (*gen*) presionar algo, hacer presión sobre algo; (*on pedal, accelerator*) pisar algo

►**press forward** VI + ADV [1] (= *push forward*) [*crowd*] avanzar en masa; [*individual*] abrirse camino (a base de empujones); [*troops*] avanzar

[2] (= *advance*) seguir adelante (**with** con); **they have decided to ~ forward with their economic reforms** han decidido seguir adelante con las reformas económicas

►**press on** VI + ADV (*with work, journey*) seguir adelante (**with** con), continuar (**with** con)

press-button ['pres,bʌtn] N, ADJ = **push-button**

pressed [prest] ADJ **to be ~ for money/time** andar muy escaso de dinero/tiempo; *see also* **hard-pressed**

press-gang ['presgæŋ] VT **to ~ sb into doing sth** forzar a algn a hacer algo

pressing ['presɪŋ] ADJ [*matter, problem*] urgente; [*request, invitation*] insistente

pressman ['presmæn] N (*pl* **pressmen**) [1] (*Brit*) periodista *m*

[2] (*US*) tipógrafo *m*

pressmark ['presmɑːk] N (*Brit*) signatura *f*

press-up ['presʌp] N (*Brit*) flexión *f*

pressure ['preʃər] Ⓐ N [1] (*lit*) [1·1] (*Phys, Tech, Met*) presión *f*; **a ~ of 200kg to the square metre** una presión de 200kg por metro cuadrado; **oil/water ~** presión *f* del aceite/del agua; **at full ~** (*Tech*) a toda presión; **high/low ~** alta/baja presión *f*; **could you check the tyre ~?** ¿me puede mirar la presión de los neumáticos?; **under ~** a presión; *see also* **atmospheric B**, **blood B**, **diastolic**, **high-pressure**, **systolic**

[1·2] (*from hand, foot, etc*) presión *f*; **he felt the ~ of her hand on his shoulder** notó la presión de su mano en el hombro; **it took a bit of ~ to make the lid close** se tuvo que hacer un poco de fuerza para cerrar la tapa; **to apply** *or* **put ~ (up)on sth** hacer *or* ejercer presión sobre algo

[2] (*fig*) presión *f*; **because of parental ~** debido a la presión de los padres; **I left the job because I couldn't stand the ~** dejé el trabajo porque no aguantaba la presión; **the ~s of modern life** las presiones de la vida moderna; **to bring ~ to bear on sb (to do sth)** (*frm*) ejercer presión sobre algn (para que haga algo); **to put ~ on sb (to do sth)** presionar a algn (para que haga algo); **it will put intense ~ on our already overstretched resources** supondrá una gran carga sobre nuestros recursos, ya apurados al máximo; **to put the ~ on ◊ pile on the ~*** apretar los tornillos*; **it will take some of the ~ off me** me aliviará un poco la carga; **the cut in interest rates will take the ~ off sterling** la reducción de los tipos de interés eliminará la presión existente sobre la libra esterlina; **~ of time prevented her from dealing with all the problems** el apremio del tiempo no le permitió tratar todos los problemas; **they were aware of the ~ of time** eran conscientes de que el tiempo se les echaba encima; **under ~**: **to act/work under ~** obrar/trabajar bajo presión; **he is under ~ to sign the agreement** le están presionando para que firme el acuerdo; **the head resigned under ~ from parents** el director dimitió presionado por los padres; **he's under a lot of ~** está bajo mucha presión, está sometido a mucha presión; **I was unable to go due to ~ of work** no pude ir por razones de trabajo; *see also* **peer B**

Ⓑ VT (= *pressurize*) presionar; **to ~ sb to do sth** presionar a algn para que haga algo; **to ~ sb into doing sth** obligar a algn a hacer algo

Ⓒ CPD ► **pressure cabin** N (*Aer, Space*) cabina *f* presurizada ► **pressure cooker** N (*lit*) olla *f* a presión, olla *f* exprés; (*fig*) polvorín *m*; **the country is a political ~ cooker** el país es un polvorín político ► **pressure feed** N tubo *m* de alimentación a presión ► **pressure gauge** N manómetro *m* ► **pressure group** N grupo *m* de presión ► **pressure pan** N (*US*) = **pressure cooker** ► **pressure point** N (*Anat*) punto *m* de presión ► **pressure suit** N traje *m* de presión compensada

pressure-cook ['preʃə,kʊk] VT cocinar en olla a presión, cocinar en olla exprés

pressurize ['preʃəraɪz] VT [1] (*Phys, Tech*) presurizar

[2] (*fig*) presionar; **to ~ sb to do sth** presionar a algn para que haga algo; **to ~ sb into doing sth** obligar a algn a hacer algo

pressurized ['preʃəraɪzd] ADJ [1] (*lit*) [*cabin, aircraft*] presurizado; [*chamber, container*] cerrado a presión; **~ water reactor** reactor *m* de agua a presión

[2] (*fig*) **the island provides an escape from today's ~ world** la isla permite escapar del cúmulo de tensiones que es el mundo actual; **to feel ~** sentirse presionado

Prestel® ['prestel] N videotex *m*

prestidigitation ['prestɪ,dɪdʒɪ'teɪʃən] N prestidigitación *f*

prestige [pres'tiːʒ] N prestigio *m*

prestigious [pres'tɪdʒəs] ADJ prestigioso

presto ['prestəʊ] ADV **hey ~!** ¡abracadabra!

prestressed ['priː'strest] ADJ **~ concrete** hormigón *m* pretensado

presumably [prɪ'zjuːməblɪ] ADV **~ he'll let us know** supongo *or* me imagino que nos avisará; **"will they be coming later?" — "presumably"** —¿vendrán más tarde? —es de suponer

presume [prɪ'zjuːm] Ⓐ VT [1] (= *suppose*) suponer, presumir; **his death must be ~d** es de suponer que ha muerto, hay que presumir que ha muerto; **to ~ that ...** suponer que ...; **it may be ~d that ...** es de suponer que ...; **to**

~ sb to be innocent suponer que algn es inocente; **Dr Livingstone, I ~** Dr Livingstone según creo

2 (= *venture*) **to ~ to do sth** atreverse a hacer algo; **I wouldn't ~ to question your judgement** no me atrevería a poner en duda su buen criterio; **if I may ~ to advise you** si me permite ofrecerle un consejo

Ⓑ VI 1 (= *suppose*) suponer

2 (= *take liberties*) **to ~ on sb's friendship** abusar de la amistad de algn; **you ~ too much** no sabes lo que pides, pides demasiado

presumption [prɪˈzʌmpʃən] N 1 (= *arrogance*) presunción *f*; (= *liberty-taking*) atrevimiento *m*; **pardon my ~** le ruego perdone mi atrevimiento

2 (= *thing presumed*) suposición *f*, presunción *f*; **the ~ is that ...** se supone que ..., es de suponer que ...

presumptive [prɪˈzʌmptɪv] Ⓐ ADJ [*heir*] presunto

Ⓑ CPD ► **presumptive evidence** N pruebas *fpl* presuntivas

presumptuous [prɪˈzʌmptjʊəs] ADJ atrevido; **in that I was rather ~** en eso fui algo atrevido; **it would be ~ of me to express an opinion** sería osado por mi parte expresar una opinión

presumptuously [prɪˈzʌmptjʊəslɪ] ADV con atrevimiento, con osadía

presumptuousness [prɪˈzʌmptjʊəsnɪs] N (= *arrogance*) presunción *f*; (= *liberty-taking*) atrevimiento *m*

presuppose [ˌpriːsəˈpəʊz] VT presuponer

presupposition [ˌpriːsʌpəˈzɪʃən] N presuposición *f*

pre-tax [ˌpriːˈtæks] ADJ bruto; **~ profits** beneficios *mpl* brutos *or* preimpositivos

pre-teen [ˌpriːˈtiːn] (*US*) Ⓐ ADJ preadolescente

Ⓑ NPL **the ~s** los preadolescentes

pretence, **pretense** (*US*) [prɪˈtens] N 1 (= *make-believe*) fingimiento *m*, simulación *f*; **to make a ~ of doing sth** fingir hacer algo; **it's all a ~** todo es fingido

2 (= *claim*) pretensión *f*; **to make no ~ to learning** no pretender ser erudito

3 (= *pretext*) pretexto *m*; **on** *or* **under the ~ of doing sth** so pretexto de hacer algo; *see also* **false A2**

4 (= *display*) ostentación *f*; **without ~** ◊ **devoid of all ~** sin ostentación

pretend [prɪˈtend] Ⓐ VT 1 (= *feign*) fingir, simular; **to ~ that ...** (querer) hacer creer que ...; **he's ~ing that he can't hear** finge no oír; **let's ~ that I'm the doctor and you're the nurse** (*child language*) yo era el médico y tú eras la enfermera; **to ~ to do sth** fingir hacer algo; **to ~ to be asleep** hacerse el dormido, fingir estar dormido; **to ~ to be mad** fingirse loco; **he ~s to be a poet** se las da de poeta, se dice poeta; **to ~ to go away** fingir marcharse; **to ~ not to be listening** hacerse el distraído; **to ~ not to understand** hacerse el desentendido

2 (= *claim*) pretender; **I don't ~ to know the answer** no pretendo saber la respuesta; **I don't ~ to understand art** no pretendo entender de arte

Ⓑ VI 1 (= *feign*) fingir; **she is only ~ing** es de mentira; **we're only ~ing** (*to child*) es de mentirijillas*; **let's ~** imaginémoslo; **let's not ~ to each other** no nos engañemos uno a otro

2 (= *claim*) **to ~ to the throne** pretender el trono; **to ~ to intelligence** afirmar tener inteligencia, pretender ser inteligente

Ⓒ ADJ (*) de mentira, fingido; **~ money*** dinero *m* de juego

pretended [prɪˈtendɪd] ADJ pretendido

pretender [prɪˈtendər] N pretendiente *mf*; **~ to the throne** pretendiente *mf* al trono; **the Young Pretender** el joven Pretendiente

pretense [prɪˈtens] N (*US*) = **pretence**

pretension [prɪˈtenʃən] N 1 (= *claim*) pretensión *f*; **to have ~s to culture** tener pretensiones de cultura, pretender ser culto

2 (= *pretentiousness*) presunción *f*, pretenciosidad *f*

pretentious [prɪˈtenʃəs] ADJ (= *affected*) pretencioso; (= *ostentatious and vulgar*) cursi

pretentiously [prɪˈtenʃəslɪ] ADV con pretenciosidad

pretentiousness [prɪˈtenʃəsnɪs] N (= *affectedness*) pretenciosidad *f*; (= *vulgar ostentation*) cursilería *f*

preterite [ˈpretərɪt] N (*Ling*) pretérito *m*

preterm [ˌpriːˈtɜːm] Ⓐ ADJ prematuro

Ⓑ ADV prematuramente

preternatural [ˌpriːtəˈnætʃrəl] ADJ preternatural

preternaturally [ˌpriːtəˈnætʃrəlɪ] ADV (*frm*) preternaturalmente

pretext [ˈpriːtekst] N pretexto *m*, excusa *f*; **it's just a ~** no es más que un pretexto *or* una excusa; **on** *or* **under the ~ of doing sth** so pretexto *or* con la excusa de hacer algo

pretorian [prɪˈtɔːrɪən] ADJ = **praetorian**

prettify [ˈprɪtɪfaɪ] VT (*pej*) [+ *person*] emperifollar; [+ *object, place*] engalanar, adornar con mucho boato; [+ *facts, situation*] dulcificar

prettily [ˈprɪtɪlɪ] ADV [*smile, blush*] de forma encantadora; [*sit*] con gracia; [*arrange, lay out*] con elegancia; **~ patterned** con un diseño elegante *or* bonito; **her daughters were always ~ dressed** sus hijas siempre iban muy guapas *or* preciosas

pretty [ˈprɪtɪ] Ⓐ ADJ (*compar* **prettier**, *superl* **prettiest**) 1 (= *attractive*) [*dress, object, baby*] bonito, mono*, lindo (*LAm*); [*girl*] bonito, guapo, lindo (*LAm*); [*name, smile*] bonito, lindo (*LAm*); **what a ~ hat!** ¡qué sombrero más bonito!, ¡qué sombrero más mono!*, ¡qué monada de sombrero!*; **I'm not just a ~ face you know** para que te enteres, no soy tonta; **it'll cost you a ~ penny*** te va a costar un ojo de la cara *or* un dineral; **it was not a ~ sight** no era nada agradable de ver; ✦***IDIOM*** **she was as ~ as a picture** era preciosa; **the garden was as ~ as a picture** el jardín era de foto; *see also* **pass A5**

2 (*) (= *large*) [*sum*] bonito*, importante

3 (*iro*) bueno; **a ~ mess you've got us into!** ¡en vaya *or* menudo *or* buen lío nos has metido!*

Ⓑ ADV bastante; **he got ~ cross** se enfadó bastante; **I have a ~ fair** *or* **good idea who did it** estoy casi seguro de quién lo hizo; **it sounds ~ far-fetched to me** me parece bastante inverosímil; **she got ~ good marks** sacó unas notas bastante buenas; **~ damn** *or* **damned quick*** bien pronto; **he's ~ damn stupid*** es bien estúpido; **it's ~ much the same** es mas o menos igual, es prácticamente lo mismo; **he goes there ~ nearly every day** va allí casi *or* prácticamente todos los días; **~ well**: **I'm ~ well finished** ya casi he terminado; **that's ~ well everything** eso es todo más o menos; *see also* **sit A1**

Ⓒ N (*as excl*) **gee up, my ~!** (*to horse*) ¡arre, caballito!; **I'll get you, my ~!** (*threatening*) ¡de mí no te escapas, preciosa *or* bonita!

►**pretty up** VT + ADV = **prettify**

pretty-pretty* [ˌprɪtɪˈprɪtɪ] ADJ (*pej*) **he's very ~** es un guapito de cara*; **she's very ~** es una niña mona*

pretzel [ˈpretsl] N galleta *f* salada

prevail [prɪˈveɪl] VI 1 (= *gain mastery*) prevalecer; **finally good sense ~ed** por fin se impuso el buen sentido; **eventually peace ~ed** al final se restableció la paz; **to ~ against** *or* **over one's enemies** triunfar sobre los enemigos

2 (= *be current*) [*views, opinions*] predominar; (= *be in fashion*) estar de moda, estar en boga; **the conditions that now ~** las condiciones que ahora imperan

3 (= *persuade*) **to ~ (up)on sb to do sth** convencer a algn para que haga algo; **he was eventually ~ed upon to do it** por fin lograron convencerlo de que lo hiciera; **she could not be ~ed upon** fue imposible persuadirla, no se convenció

prevailing [prɪˈveɪlɪŋ] ADJ [*opinion, wind*] predominante; [*price*] imperante; **the ~ fashion** la moda actual, la moda reinante; **under ~ conditions** bajo las condiciones actuales

prevalence [ˈprevələns] N 1 (= *dominance*) predominio *m*

2 (= *frequency*) frecuencia *f*

prevalent [ˈprevələnt] ADJ 1 (= *dominant*) dominante

2 (= *widespread*) extendido

3 (= *fashionable*) de moda; (= *present-day*) actual

prevaricate [prɪˈværɪkeɪt] VI andar con rodeos

prevarication [prɪˌværɪˈkeɪʃən] N evasivas *fpl*

prevent [prɪˈvent] VT 1 (= *avert*) (*by taking precautions*) [+ *accident, disaster, death, war, pregnancy*] prevenir, evitar; [+ *illness*] prevenir; **we want to ~ a recurrence of yesterday's violence** queremos evitar que la violencia desplegada ayer se repita, queremos prevenir *or* evitar una repetición de la violencia desplegada ayer

2 (= *impede, put a stop to*) [+ *crime, corruption*] impedir; [+ *attempt*] prevenir, impedir; **installations to ~ any attempt to escape** instalaciones *fpl* para prevenir *or* impedir cualquier intento de huida; **bodyguards ~ed his attempt to shoot the president** unos guardaespaldas hicieron fracasar su intento de disparar al presidente; **to ~ the spread of AIDS/nuclear weapons** impedir la propagación del SIDA/la proliferación de las armas nucleares; **to ~ sb (from) doing sth** ◊ **~ sb's doing sth** impedir que algn haga algo; **I can't ~ him (from) leaving the country** ◊ **I can't ~ his leaving the country** no puedo impedir que se vaya del país; **don't let this ~ you from going** no dejes que esto te impida ir; **she bit her lip to ~ herself from crying out** se mordió el labio para no gritar

preventable [prɪˈventəbl] ADJ evitable

preventative [prɪˈventətɪv] = **preventive**

prevention [prɪˈvenʃən] N prevención *f*; **the role of diet in cancer ~** el papel que desempeña la dieta en la prevención del cáncer; **the Government's commitment to crime ~** la dedicación del gobierno a la prevención de la delincuencia; **Society for the Prevention of Cruelty to Children/Animals** Sociedad *f* Protectora de Niños/Animales; ✦***PROV*** **~ is better than cure** más vale prevenir que curar

preventive [prɪˈventɪv] Ⓐ ADJ preventivo

Ⓑ N 1 (*Med*) (= *drug*) *medicamento que previene una enfermedad*

2 (= *measure*) **fasting is sometimes recommended as a ~ against cancer** a veces se recomienda el ayuno como medida preventiva contra el cáncer

Ⓒ CPD ► **preventive dentistry** N odontología *f* preventiva ► **preventive detention** N arresto *m* preventivo ► **preventive measure** N medida *f* preventiva ► **preventive medicine** N medicina *f* preventiva

preview [ˈpriːvjuː] Ⓐ N [*of film*] preestreno *m*; **to give sb a ~ of sth** (*fig*) permitir a algn ver algo de antemano; **to have a ~ of sth** (*fig*) ver algo con anticipación, lograr ver algo antes que otros

Ⓑ VT preestrenar

previous [ˈpriːvɪəs] Ⓐ ADJ 1 (= *former, earlier*) [*night, day, year, page*] anterior; [*experience*] previo; **we met by ~ arrangement** nos reunimos acordando una cita previa *or* mediante cita previa; **I have a ~ engagement** tengo un compromiso previo; **in a ~ incarnation** *or* **life** en una vida anterior; **on ~ occasions** en ocasiones anteriores; **the car has had two ~ owners** el coche ha pasado por dos manos; **in ~ years** los años anteriores; *see also* **conviction 1**

2 (* *hum*) (= *hasty*) prematuro; **this seems somewhat ~** esto parece algo prematuro; **you were a bit ~ in inviting him** te has precipitado un poco invitándole

Ⓑ PREP ► **to: in the five years ~ to 1992** durante los cinco años anteriores a 1992; **~ to that she had worked in London** antes de eso había trabajado en Londres

previously [ˈpriːvɪəslɪ] ADV (= *earlier, formerly*) antes, anteriormente; (= *in advance*) con antelación, previamente; **as ~ mentioned** como se ha mencionado antes *or* anteriormente; **~, the country had been divided in two** antes *or* anteriormente, el país había estado dividido en dos partes; **she read out a ~ prepared speech** leyó un discurso que había preparado con antelación *or* previamente

prewar [ˈpriːˈwɔːʳ] ADJ de antes de la guerra; **the ~ period** la preguerra

prewash [ˈpriːwɒʃ] N prelavado *m*

prey [preɪ] Ⓐ N (*lit, fig*) presa *f*, víctima *f*; **beast of ~** animal *m* de rapiña; **bird of ~** ave *f* de rapiña; **to be (a) ~ to** ser víctima de; **she is ~ to irrational fears** (*fig*) es presa de temores irracionales; **he fell (a) ~ to the disease** fue víctima de la enfermedad

Ⓑ VI **to ~ on** [+ *animals*] (= *attack*) cazar; (= *feed on*) alimentarse de; [+ *person*] vivir a costa de; **rabbits are ~ed on by foxes** los conejos son presa de los zorros; **to ~ on sb's mind** traer preocupado *or* obsesionar a algn; **doubts ~ed on him** le obsesionaban las dudas; **the tragedy so ~ed on his mind that ...** la tragedia le obsesionó de tal modo que ...

prezzie* [ˈprezɪ] N (= *present*) regalo *m*

price [praɪs] Ⓐ N 1 (*Comm*) precio *m*; **an increase in the ~ of petrol** un aumento en el precio de la gasolina; **we pay top ~s for gold and silver** pagamos los mejores precios por el oro y la plata; **who knows what the ~ will be in six months** quién sabe qué precio tendrá dentro de seis meses; **that's my ~, take it or leave it** eso es lo que pido, o lo tomas o lo dejas; **you can get it at a ~** se puede conseguir, pero pagando; **it's not for sale at any ~** no está a la venta a ningún precio; **their loyalty cannot be bought at any ~** su lealtad no tiene precio; **at a reduced ~** a (un) precio reducido, con rebaja; **at today's ~s** a los precios actuales; **it is beyond ~** no tiene precio; **for a ~: he'll do it for a ~** él lo hará, pero será caro, lo hará si le pagan; **you can get anything you want for a ~** puedes conseguir todo lo que quieras pagando; **he would kill a man for the ~ of a packet of cigarettes** mataría a un hombre por el precio de una cajetilla de tabaco; **two for the ~ of one** (*lit, fig*) dos al *or* por el precio de uno; **can you give me a ~ for putting in a new window?** ¿cuánto me cobraría usted por colocar una ventana nueva?; **to go down** *or* **come down** *or* **fall in ~** bajar de precio; **to go up** *or* **rise in ~** subir de precio; **he got a good ~ for it** sacó una buena suma por ello; **everyone has their ~** todos tenemos un precio; **he's got** *or* **there's a ~ on his head** se ha puesto precio a su cabeza; **to name one's ~** fijar el precio, decir cuánto se quiere; **to put a ~ on sth** poner precio a algo; **you can't put a ~ on friendship** la amistad no tiene precio; **if the ~ is right: he is prepared to make a comeback if the ~ is right** está dispuesto a volver si se le paga bien; **as long as the ~ is right, property will sell** si está a un buen precio, la propiedad se vende; **what ~ all his promises now?** (*iro*) ¿de qué sirven todas sus promesas ahora?; *see also* **closing B, cut-price, fixed B, half-price, retail E**

2 (*Fin, St Ex*) (= *quotation*) cotización *f*; **stock ~s fell again on Wall Street** las cotizaciones en bolsa bajaron de nuevo en Wall Street

3 (*Betting*) (= *odds*) puntos *mpl* de ventaja; ✦**IDIOM what ~ ...?*** (= *what's the betting*) ¿qué apuestas ...?; **what ~ she'll change her mind?** ¿qué apuestas a que cambia de opinión?; **what ~ war?** ¿qué apuestas a que estallará la guerra?

4 (= *sacrifice*) precio *m*; **that's the ~ we have to pay for progress** ◊ **that's the ~ of progress** es el precio que tenemos que pagar por el progreso; **to pay the ~ (for sth)** cargar con *or* pagar las consecuencias (de algo); **fame comes at a ~** la fama se paga cara; **he's famous now, but at what a ~!** ahora es famoso, ¡pero a qué precio! *or* ¡pero lo ha pagado caro!; **at any ~** (*with affirmative*) a toda costa; **they want peace at any ~** quieren la paz a toda costa; (*with negative*) **a concert I wasn't going to miss at any ~** un concierto que no me iba a perder por nada del mundo; **to pay a high** *or* **heavy ~ for sth** pagar algo muy caro; **that's a small ~ to pay for independence/for keeping him happy** eso es poco sacrificio a cambio de la independencia/de tenerlo contento

Ⓑ VT 1 (= *fix price of*) **retailers usually ~ goods by adding 100% to the wholesale ~** los minoristas normalmente ponen precio a sus productos añadiendo un cien por cien al precio de coste, los minoristas normalmente cargan un cien por cien al precio de coste de sus productos; **tickets, ~d £20, are now available** las entradas ya están a la venta a un precio de 20 libras; **it was ~d too high/low** su precio era demasiado alto/bajo; **this stylish fryer, competitively ~d at £29.99, can help you create new dishes** por sólo £29.99, esta elegante freidora puede ayudarle a crear nuevos platos; **there is a very reasonably ~d menu** hay un menú a un precio muy razonable; ✦**IDIOM to ~ sb out of the market** hacer que algn pierda competitividad (*rebajando uno sus precios artificialmente*); **the restaurant has ~d itself out of the market** el restaurante ha subido demasiado los precios y ha perdido su competitividad en el mercado; **you'll ~ yourself out of a job if you go on demanding so much money** como sigas exigiendo tanto dinero, pondrás en peligro tu trabajo

2 (= *label with price*) **the tins of salmon weren't clearly ~d** el precio de la latas de salmón no estaba claro *or* claramente indicado; **it was ~d at £15** estaba marcado a un precio de 15 libras

3 (= *estimate value of*) calcular el valor de; **it was ~d at £1,000** estaba valorado en mil libras

4 (= *find out price of*) comprobar el precio de

Ⓒ CPD ► **price bracket** N **he's looking for a property in the £70,000 ~ bracket** está buscando una vivienda que cueste alrededor de las setenta mil libras; **that is the normal ~ bracket for one of his creations** ése es el precio normal de *or* eso es lo que se paga normalmente por una de sus creaciones; **a traditional restaurant in the middle ~ bracket** un restaurante tradicional con precios de un nivel medio (dentro de la escala) ► **price control** N control *m* de precios; **to impose ~ controls** aplicar control de precios ► **price cut** N rebaja *f* ► **price cutting** N reducción *f* de precios ► **price-earnings ratio** N (*Fin*) relación *f* precio ganancias ► **price fixing** N fijación *f* de precios ► **price freeze** N congelación *f* de precios ► **price increase** N subida *f* de precio ► **price index** N (*Brit*) índice *m* de precios; *see also* **consumer B** ► **price inflation** N inflación *f* de los precios ► **price level** N nivel *m* de precios ► **price limit** N tope *m*, precio *m* tope ► **price list** N lista *f* de precios ► **price range** N **there are lots of good products in all ~ ranges** hay gran cantidad de productos de buena calidad en una amplia gama de precios; **in the medium** *or* **middle ~ range** dentro de un nivel medio de la escala de precios; **the upper/lower end of the ~ range** el nivel más alto/bajo en la escala de precios; **(with)in/out of one's ~ range** dentro de/fuera de las posibilidades de uno; **the hotel was somewhat out of my ~ range** el hotel estaba un tanto fuera de mis posibilidades ► **price rigging** N fijación *f* fraudulenta de precios; **they were accused of ~ rigging** se les acusó de amañar los precios ► **price ring** N cártel *m* (para la fijación de precios) ► **price rise** N = **price increase** ► **prices and incomes policy** N política *f* de precios y salarios, política *f* de precios y rentas ► **price support** N subsidio *m* de precios ► **price tag** N (*lit*) etiqueta *f* (del precio); (*fig*) precio *m*; **it doesn't justify the ~ tag of £17.5 million** no justifica un precio de 17,5 millones de libras ► **price war** N guerra *f* de precios

►**price down** VT + ADV rebajar

►**price up** VT + ADV aumentar el precio de

-priced [praɪst] ADJ (*ending in compounds*) **high-priced** muy caro; *see also* **low-priced**

priceless [ˈpraɪslɪs] ADJ 1 [*picture, jewel*] inestimable

2 (*) (= *amusing*) divertidísimo; **it was ~!** ¡fue para morirse de risa!*

pricey* [ˈpraɪsɪ] ADJ (*compar* **pricier**; *superl* **priciest**) (*Brit*) carito*, caro

pricing [ˈpraɪsɪŋ] Ⓐ N fijación *f* de precios

Ⓑ CPD ► **pricing policy** N política *f* tarifaria

prick [prɪk] Ⓐ N 1 (= *act, sensation*) (*with pin, needle*) pinchazo *m*; [*of insect*] picadura *f*; [*of spur*] espolada *f*; (*with goad*) aguijonazo *m*; **~s of conscience** remordimientos *mpl*; ✦**IDIOM to kick against the ~s** dar coces contra el aguijón

2 (**) (= *penis*) polla *f* (*Sp***), picha *f* (*Sp***), pija *f* (*esp LAm***), pinga *f* (*esp LAm***)

3 (**) (= *person*) gilipollas *mf inv* (*Sp**), cojudo/a *m/f* (*Bol, Peru*), boludo/a *m/f* (*Arg, Bol*)

Ⓑ VT 1 (= *puncture*) [*person, needle*] pinchar; [*insect*] picar; (*with spur*) dar con las espuelas a; **to ~ one's finger (with** *or* **on sth)** pin-

charse el dedo (con algo)
2 (= *goad*) aguijar
3 (= *make hole in*) agujerear; (= *mark with holes*) marcar con agujerillos
4 **it ~ed his conscience** le remordía la conciencia
Ⓒ VI = **prickle C**

►**prick out** VT + ADV (*Hort*) plantar

►**prick up** Ⓐ VT + ADV **to ~ up one's ears** (*lit, fig*) aguzar el oído, parar la oreja (*LAm*)
Ⓑ VI + ADV **the dog's ears ~ed up** al perro se le levantaron *or* aguzaron las orejas; **his ears ~ed up** (*fig*) aguzó el oído, pegó la oreja*

pricked [prɪkt] ADJ [*wine*] picado

prickings [ˈprɪkɪŋz] NPL **~ of conscience** remordimientos *mpl*

prickle [ˈprɪkl] Ⓐ N 1 (*on plant, animal*) espina *f*
2 (= *sensation*) picor *m*, comezón *f*
Ⓑ VT picar
Ⓒ VI picar, hormiguear; **my eyes are prickling** me pican los ojos; **I could feel my skin prickling** me escocía la piel

prickly [ˈprɪklɪ] Ⓐ ADJ (*compar* **pricklier**; *superl* **prickliest**) 1 (= *spiky*) espinoso
2 (*fig*) [*person*] enojadizo; **he's rather ~ about that** sobre ese tema es algo quisquilloso
Ⓑ CPD ► **prickly heat** N (*Med*) sarpullido *m* (causado por exceso de calor) ► **prickly pear** N (= *plant*) chumbera *f*, nopal *m* (*LAm*); (= *fruit*) higo *m* chumbo, tuna *f* (*LAm*)

pride [praɪd] Ⓐ N 1 (= *pleasure, satisfaction*) orgullo *m*; **civic/national ~** orgullo *m* cívico/nacional; **it is a source of ~ to us that …** es para nosotros un motivo de orgullo el que …; **to take (a) ~ in sth/in doing sth: he takes a ~ in his appearance** se preocupa mucho por su aspecto; **she could take no ~ in what she had done** no podía enorgullecerse *or* estar orgullosa de lo que había hecho; **we take ~ in offering you the highest standards** nos enorgullecemos *or* estamos orgullosos de ofrecerle la mejor calidad; ✦*IDIOM* **to have** *or* **take ~ of place** (*lit, fig*) ocupar el lugar de honor; **the photo takes ~ of place on the mantlepiece** la foto ocupa el lugar de honor en la repisa de la chimenea
2 (= *conceit*) orgullo *m*, soberbia *f*, arrogancia *f*; ✦*PROV* **~ comes** *or* **goes before a fall** más dura será la caída
3 (= *self-respect*) orgullo *m*, amor *m* propio; **false ~** presuntuosidad *f*; **I wouldn't ask him any favours, I have my ~** no le pediría ningún favor, tengo mi orgullo *or* amor propio; **to hurt** *or* **wound sb's ~** herir a algn en su amor propio; *see also* **swallow A2**
4 (= *source of pride*) orgullo *m*; **he's the ~ of the family** es el orgullo de la familia; **his roses are his ~ and joy** sus rosas son su orgullo
5 [*of lions*] manada *f*
Ⓑ VT **to ~ o.s. on sth: he ~s himself on his punctuality** se precia de ser puntual; **she ~s herself on not owning a TV** está orgullosa de no tener televisor

priest [priːst] N (*gen, pagan*) sacerdote *m*; (*Christian*) sacerdote *m*, cura *m*; **woman ~** diaconisa *f*; *see also* **high D**, **ordain A2**, **parish B**

priestess [ˈpriːstɪs] N sacerdotisa *f*; *see also* **high D**

priesthood [ˈpriːsthʊd] N (= *function*) sacerdocio *m*; (= *priests collectively*) clero *m*; **to enter the ~** ordenarse sacerdote

priestly [ˈpriːstlɪ] ADJ sacerdotal

prig [prɪg] N gazmoño/a *m/f*, mojigato/a *m/f*

priggish [ˈprɪgɪʃ] ADJ gazmoño, mojigato

priggishness [ˈprɪgɪʃnɪs] N gazmoñería *f*, mojigatería *f*

prim [prɪm] ADJ (*compar* **primmer**; *superl* **primmest**) (*also* **~ and proper**) (= *formal*) formal, estirado; (= *demure*) remilgado, cursi; (= *prudish*) mojigato, gazmoño

primacy [ˈpraɪməsɪ] N primacía *f*

prima donna [ˈpriːməˈdɒnə] N (*pl* **prima donna** *or* **prima donnas**) primadonna *f*, diva *f*; (*fig*) persona *f* difícil, persona *f* de reacciones imprevisibles

primaeval [praɪˈmiːvl] ADJ (*Brit*) = **primeval**

prima facie [ˈpraɪməˈfeɪʃɪ] Ⓐ ADV a primera vista
Ⓑ ADJ suficiente a primera vista; **~ evidence** prueba *f* semiplena; **to have a ~ case** (*Jur*) tener razón a primera vista; **he has a ~ case** (*fig*) a primera vista parece que tiene razón; **there are ~ reasons why …** hay suficientes razones que justifican el que + *subjun*

primal [ˈpraɪməl] ADJ (= *first in time*) original; (= *first in importance*) principal; **~ scream** grito *m* primal

primarily [ˈpraɪmərɪlɪ] ADV (= *chiefly*) ante todo, principalmente

primary [ˈpraɪmərɪ] Ⓐ ADJ 1 (= *chief, main*) [*reason, purpose, source*] principal; **our ~ concern is the well-being of our children** nuestra mayor *or* principal preocupación es el bienestar de nuestros hijos; **that is not the ~ reason** ésa no es la razón principal
2 (= *fundamental*) primordial; **to be of ~ importance** ser de primordial importancia
3 (= *first*) primario
4 (*esp Brit Scol*) (= *elementary*) primario
Ⓑ N 1 (*US*) (*also* **~ election**) elección *f* primaria, primaria *f*
2 (= *colour*) color *m* primario
3 = **primary school**
Ⓒ CPD ► **primary colour** N color *m* primario ► **primary education** N (*esp Brit*) enseñanza *f* primaria, educación *f* primaria ► **primary election** N (*US*) elección *f* primaria, primaria *f* ► **primary products** NPL productos *mpl* primarios ► **primary school** N (*Brit*) escuela *f* primaria; (*US*) escuela *f* primaria (de primer ciclo) (*6-9 años*) ► **primary storage** N almacenamiento *m* primario ► **primary teacher** N (*also* **~ school teacher**) (*Brit*) profesor(a) *m/f* de enseñanza primaria, maestro/a *m/f*

> **PRIMARIES**
>
> *Las elecciones primarias* (**primaries**) *sirven para preseleccionar a los candidatos de los partidos demócrata* (**Democratic**) *y republicano* (**Republican**) *durante la campaña que precede a las elecciones a Presidente de Estados Unidos. Se inician en New Hampshire y tienen lugar en 35 estados entre los meses de febrero y junio. El número de votos obtenidos por cada candidato determina el número de delegados que votarán en el congreso general* (**National Convention**) *de julio y agosto, en el que se decide el candidato definitivo de cada partido.*

primate [ˈpraɪmeɪt] N 1 (*Zool*) primate *m*
2 (*Rel*) primado *m*

prime [praɪm] Ⓐ ADJ 1 (= *major, main*) [*cause, objective, target*] principal; **the/a ~ cause of stress in the workplace** la principal causa/una de las principales causas de estrés en el trabajo; **the ~ candidate to take over his job is May Reid** May Reid es la candidata con más posibilidades de sustituirle en el puesto; **our ~ concern is public safety** nuestra mayor *or* principal preocupación es la seguridad ciudadana; **to be of ~ importance** ser de primordial importancia, ser de fundamental importancia; **he's the ~ suspect** es el principal sospechoso
2 (= *top-quality, excellent*) [*real estate, property*] de primera; [*ingredient, cut*] de primera (calidad); **to be in ~ condition** [*cattle, fruit, car*] estar en perfecto estado; [*athlete*] estar en plena forma; **~ quality beef** carne *f* de vaca de primera (calidad); **~ rib(s)** costillas *fpl* de primera (calidad); **a ~ site** un lugar privilegiado
3 (= *classic*) perfecto; **a ~ example of what to avoid** un perfecto ejemplo de lo que se debe evitar
4 (*Math*) [*number*] primo
Ⓑ N 1 (= *best years*) **when trade unionism was in its ~** cuando el sindicalismo estaba en su apogeo; **to be in one's ~** *or* **in the ~ of life** [*person*] estar en la flor de la vida; **to be cut off** *or* **cut down in one's ~** morir en la flor de la vida; **he's past his ~** ya ha dejado atrás los mejores años de su vida; **the hotel was past its ~** (*hum*) el hotel ya había dejado atrás sus días de gloria
2 (*Rel*) prima *f*
Ⓒ VT 1 (*prior to painting*) imprimar, preparar; (*with primer*) aplicar una capa de imprimación a; (*with undercoat*) aplicar una capa de (pintura) base a; (*with anticorrosive*) aplicar una capa de pintura anticorrosiva a
2 (*prior to use*) [+ *gun, pump*] cebar; **he ~d the bomb to go off at ten** cebó la bomba para que explotara a las diez; ✦*IDIOM* **to ~ the pump** sacar las cosas adelante; **he was willing to ~ the pump by offering finance** estaba dispuesto a ofrecerse a financiarlo para que saliera adelante; **public investment is the best way of priming the pump of economic activity** la inversión pública es la mejor forma de promover la actividad económica
3 (= *prepare*) [+ *student, politician, soldier*] preparar; **she came well ~d for the interview** vino a la entrevista bien preparada; **they had been ~d to expect the worst** se les había preparado para lo peor; **to keep troops ~d for combat** tener a las tropas listas para el combate; **he had been ~d to say that** le habían dado instrucciones para que dijera eso
4 (*with drink*) **he arrived well ~d** llegó ya bien bebido; **he ~d himself for the interview with a stiff whisky** se tomó un whisky fuerte como preparación para la entrevista
Ⓓ CPD ► **prime cost** N coste *m* neto, coste *m* de producción ► **prime factor** N factor *m* primordial, factor *m* principal ► **the prime meridian** N (*Geog*) el meridiano de Greenwich ► **prime minister** N primer(a) ministro/a *m/f* ► **prime ministership** N (= *period of office*) mandato *m* como primer ministro; (= *office*) cargo *m* de(l) primer ministro ► **prime mover** N (= *person*) promotor(a) *m/f*; (*Philos*) primer motor *m*; **a ~ mover in Middle East events** una de las promotoras de los acontecimientos en el Oriente Medio ► **prime number** N (*Math*) número *m* primo ► **prime rate** N tipo *m* de interés preferencial; **~ lending rate** tipo *m* de interés preferencial sobre los préstamos ► **prime time** N (*TV*) horas *fpl* de máxima *or* mayor audiencia; **the programme was repeated in ~ time** el programa se repitió a una de las horas de máxima *or* mayor audiencia; *see also* **prime-time**

prime ministerial [ˌpraɪmmɪnɪsˈtɪərɪəl] ADJ [*decision, appointment*] del primer ministro; [*talks*] entre los primeros ministros

primer [ˈpraɪməʳ] N 1 (= *textbook*) manual *m* básico; **a French ~** un manual básico de fran-

cés, un manual de francés elemental
2 (= *basic reader*) abecedario *m*
3 (= *paint*) pintura *f* base, imprimación *f*
4 [*of bomb*] iniciador *m*

prime-time [ˈpraɪmtaɪm] ADJ de máxima audiencia, de mayor audiencia; **the documentary will be broadcast on ~ television** el documental se emitirá por televisión durante las horas de máxima *or* mayor audiencia

primeval [praɪˈmiːvəl] ADJ primitivo

priming [ˈpraɪmɪŋ] Ⓐ N preparación *f*; [*of pump*] cebo *m*; (*Art*) primera capa *f*
Ⓑ CPD ► **priming device** N iniciador *m*

primitive [ˈprɪmɪtɪv] Ⓐ ADJ (*gen*) primitivo; (= *old-fashioned*) anticuado; (= *basic*) rudimentario, básico; (= *uncivilized*) inculto; (= *sordid*) miserable; (*Art*) primitivo
Ⓑ N (*Art*) (= *artist*) primitivista *mf*; (= *work*) obra *f* primitivista

primly [ˈprɪmlɪ] ADV (= *demurely*) remilgadamente, con remilgo; (= *prudishly*) con gazmoñería

primness [ˈprɪmnɪs] N (= *formality*) formalidad *f*, lo estirado; (= *demureness*) remilgo *m*, cursilería *f*; (= *prudishness*) mojigatería *f*, gazmoñería *f*

primogeniture [ˌpraɪməʊˈdʒenɪtʃəʳ] N (*frm*) primogenitura *f*

primordial [praɪˈmɔːdɪəl] ADJ primordial

primp [prɪmp] = **prink**

primrose [ˈprɪmrəʊz] Ⓐ N 1 (*Bot*) primavera *f*
2 (= *colour*) color *m* amarillo pálido
Ⓑ ADJ (*also* ~ **yellow**) amarillo pálido
Ⓒ CPD ► **primrose path** N caminito *m* de rosas

primula [ˈprɪmjʊlə] N (*Bot*) prímula *f*

Primus (stove)® [ˈpraɪməs(stəʊv)] N (*esp Brit*) cocina *f* de camping, camping-gas® *m*

prince [prɪns] Ⓐ N príncipe *m*; **Prince Charles** el príncipe Carlos; **Prince Charming** el Príncipe Azul, el Príncipe Encantador; **the Prince of Darkness** el príncipe de las tinieblas; **the Prince of Wales** el Príncipe de Gales (*heredero del trono del Reino Unido, equivalente al Príncipe de Asturias en España*); *see also* **crown C**
Ⓑ CPD ► **Prince Consort** N príncipe *m* consorte ► **Prince Regent** N príncipe *m* regente

princely [ˈprɪnslɪ] ADJ (*lit*) principesco; (*fig*) magnífico, espléndido; **a ~ gesture** un gesto magnífico, un gesto digno de un príncipe; **the ~ sum of five dollars** (*iro*) la bonita suma de cinco dólares

princess [prɪnˈses] N (= *royal*) princesa *f*; **Princess Victoria** la Princesa Victoria; **the Princess Royal** la princesa real; **the Princess of Wales** la Princesa de Gales; *see also* **crown C**

principal [ˈprɪnsɪpəl] Ⓐ ADJ 1 [*reason, cause, source*] principal; **our ~ concern is the well-being of our children** nuestra mayor *or* principal preocupación es el bienestar de nuestros hijos
2 (*Mus*) primero
3 (*Fin*) **~ amount** capital *m* principal, principal *m*
Ⓑ N 1 [*of school, college*] director(a) *m/f*; (*Univ*) rector(a) *m/f*
2 (*Theat*) protagonista *mf* principal
3 (*Mus*) primer(a) instrumentista *mf*
4 (*Fin*) capital *m*, principal *m*; **~ and interest** el principal y los intereses
Ⓒ CPD ► **principal boy** N (*Brit Theat*) joven héroe *m* (*papel de actriz en la "pantomime" navideña*); → PANTOMIME

principality [ˌprɪnsɪˈpælɪtɪ] N principado *m*

principally [ˈprɪnsɪpəlɪ] ADV principalmente

principle [ˈprɪnsəpl] N (*gen, Sci*) principio *m*; **the basic ~s of physics** los principios básicos de física; **the ~ that ...** el principio según el cual ...; **to lay it down as a ~ that ...** sentar el principio de que ...; **it is** *or* **it goes against my ~s** va (en) contra (de) mis principios; **to go back to first ~s** volver a los principios (fundamentales); **to argue from first ~s** construir un argumento sobre los principios (fundamentales); **to have high ~s** tener principios nobles; **in ~** en principio; **to reach an agreement in ~** llegar a un acuerdo de principio *or* en principio; **I make it a ~ never to lend money** tengo por norma no prestar nunca dinero, yo, por principio, nunca presto dinero; **as a matter of ~** por principio; **it's a matter of ~** es cuestión de principios; **a man/woman of (high) ~s** un hombre/una mujer de principios (nobles); **on ~** por principio, por una cuestión de principios; **it's the ~ of the thing** es cuestión de principios; *see also* **guiding**

principled [ˈprɪnsɪpld] ADJ [*person*] de fuertes principios; [*behaviour, stand*] basado en fuertes principios

prink [prɪŋk] Ⓐ VT acicalar
Ⓑ VI acicalarse

print [prɪnt] Ⓐ N 1 (*Typ*) (= *letters*) letra *f*; (= *printed matter*) texto *m* impreso; **I can't read this ~, it's too small** no puedo leer esta letra, es demasiado pequeña; **columns of tiny ~** columnas *fpl* de letra pequeña *or* menuda; **it presents the reader with solid masses of ~** enfrenta al lector con largos párrafos de texto (impreso) ininterrumpido; **in bold ~** en negrita; **the fine ~** la letra pequeña *or* menuda; **to be in ~** (= *be published*) estar publicado; (= *be available*) estar a la venta; **to appear in ~** [*work*] publicarse; **the first time the term appeared in ~ was in 1530** la primera vez que apareció el término en una publicación fue en 1530; **to get into ~** publicarse; **in large ~** con letra grande; **to be out of ~** estar agotado; **to go out of ~** agotarse; **to rush into ~** lanzarse a publicar; **in small ~** con letra pequeña *or* menuda; **read the small ~ before you sign** lea la letra pequeña *or* menuda antes de firmar
2 (= *mark, imprint*) [*of foot, finger, tyre*] huella *f*, marca *f*; (= *fingerprint*) huella *f* digital, huella *f* dactilar; **to take sb's ~s** tomar las huellas digitales *or* dactilares a algn
3 (= *fabric*) estampado *m*; **a cotton ~** un estampado de algodón; *see also* **floral B**
4 (*Art*) (= *etching, woodcut, lithograph*) grabado *m*; (= *reproduction*) reproducción *f*
5 (*Phot, Cine*) copia *f*; *see also* **contact C**
Ⓑ VT 1 (= *set in print*) [+ *letters, text*] imprimir; [+ *money*] emitir; **they ~ed 300 copies** hicieron una tirada de 300 ejemplares; **~ed in England** impreso en Inglaterra; **~ed by** impreso por; **to ~ sth on** *or* **onto sth** estampar algo en algo
2 (= *write in block letters*) escribir con *or* en letra de imprenta, escribir con *or* en letra de molde; **~ it in block capitals** escríbalo con *or* en mayúsculas
3 (*Phot*) [+ *negative*] imprimir; [+ *photo*] sacar una copia de; [+ *copy*] sacar
4 (*fig*) grabar; **her face was ~ed in my mind** su cara se me había quedado grabada en la mente
Ⓒ VI [*person*] escribir con *or* en letra de imprenta, escribir con *or* en letra de molde; [*machine*] imprimir; [*negative*] salir; **the book is ~ing now** el libro está en la imprenta en este momento
Ⓓ CPD ► **print dress** N vestido *m* estampado ► **print journalist** N periodista *mf* de prensa escrita ► **print media** NPL medios *mpl* de comunicación impresos ► **print reporter** N (*US*) = **print journalist** ► **print run** N tirada *f* ► **print shop** N (*Typ*) imprenta *f*; (= *art shop*) tienda *f* de grabados ► **print union** N sindicato *m* de tipógrafos ► **print worker** N tipógrafo/a *m/f*

►**print off** VT + ADV imprimir

►**print out** VT + ADV (*Comput*) imprimir

printable [ˈprɪntəbl] ADJ imprimible

printed [ˈprɪntɪd] ADJ 1 (*Publishing*) impreso; **the ~ book** el libro impreso; **~ matter** impresos *mpl*; **the ~ page** el impreso; **~ papers** impresos *mpl*; **~ paper rate** (*Brit*) tarifa *f* de impreso; **the ~ word** la palabra impresa
2 (*Textiles*) estampado; **a ~ cotton fabric** una tela de algodón estampada
3 (*Electronics*) **~ circuit** circuito *m* impreso; **~ circuit board** placa *f* de circuito impreso

printer [ˈprɪntəʳ] N 1 (= *person*) impresor(a) *m/f*; **~'s ink** tinta *f* de imprenta; **~'s mark** pie *m* de imprenta
2 (*Comput*) (= *machine*) impresora *f*

printhead [ˈprɪnthed] N cabeza *f* impresora

printing [ˈprɪntɪŋ] Ⓐ N 1 (= *process*) impresión *f*; **fourth ~** cuarta impresión *f*
2 (= *craft, industry*) imprenta *f*; **"16th century ~ in Toledo"** "La imprenta en Toledo en el siglo XVI"
3 (= *block writing*) letras *fpl* de molde; (= *characters, print*) letra *f*
4 (= *quantity printed*) tirada *f*; **a ~ of 500 copies** una tirada de 500 ejemplares
Ⓑ CPD ► **printing frame** N prensa *f* de copiar ► **printing ink** N tinta *f* de imprenta ► **printing office** N imprenta *f* ► **printing press** N prensa *f* ► **printing queue** N cola *f* de impresión ► **printing works** NSING imprenta *f*

printmaking [ˈprɪntmeɪkɪŋ] N grabado *m*

printout [ˈprɪntaʊt] N (*Comput*) copia *f* impresa, listado *m*

prior[1] [ˈpraɪəʳ] Ⓐ ADJ 1 (= *previous*) previo; **I have a ~ engagement** tengo un compromiso previo; **to have a ~ claim to** *or* **on sth/sb**: **there are others who have a ~ claim on my time** hay otros a los que tengo que dedicar mi tiempo que tienen prioridad *or* están antes; **she felt that her past connection with him gave her a ~ claim to him** le parecía que su pasada relación le daba ciertos derechos sobre él; **without ~ notice/warning** sin previo aviso
2 (= *earlier*) [*week, month, year*] anterior; **in ~ years** en años anteriores
Ⓑ ADV (*frm*) **~ to sth** anterior *or* previo a algo; **~ to doing sth** antes de hacer algo; **~ to (his) leaving he hid the money** antes de marchar, escondió el dinero; **in the years ~ to his death** en los años anteriores *or* previos a su muerte; **~ to that day we had not met** antes de ese día no nos conocíamos, hasta ese día no nos conocimos; **~ to this/that** antes de esto/eso
Ⓒ ADV (*US*) antes; **it happened two days ~** ocurrió dos días antes

prior[2] [ˈpraɪəʳ] N (*Rel*) prior *m*

prioress [ˈpraɪərɪs] N priora *f*

prioritize [praɪˈɒrɪtaɪz] VT (*esp US*) priorizar

priority [praɪˈɒrɪtɪ] Ⓐ N 1 (= *precedence*) prioridad *f*; **to give sth/sb** ◊ **give ~ to sth/sb** dar prioridad a algo/algn; **to give sth (a) high/low ~** dar mucha/poca importancia a algo; **to give sth top ~** dar máxima prioridad a algo; **housing must be given top ~** el problema de la vivienda debe tener máxima prioridad; **to have** *or* **take ~ (over sth/sb)** tener

➤ LANGUAGE IN USE: **principle** 26.1 **prior**[1] **A1** 25.2

prioridad (sobre algo/algn); **in (strict) order of ~** por (estricto) orden de prioridad
2 (= *concern, aim*) prioridad *f*; **try to decide what your priorities are** intenta establecer tu orden de prioridades; **it should be a ~ for all of us** tiene que ser prioridad de todos nosotros, debería ser lo más importante *or* lo principal para todos nosotros; **to set spending priorities** repartir los gastos por orden de prioridad; **our first ~ is to cut costs** nuestra máxima prioridad es reducir los gastos; **she made it clear where her priorities lay** dejó bien claro cuáles eran sus prioridades; **to be high/low on sb's list of priorities** ocupar un lugar alto/bajo en el orden de prioridades de algn; **my number one** *or* **top ~** lo más importante para mí; **we must get our priorities right** tenemos que tener claro cuáles son nuestras prioridades, tenemos que tener claro qué es lo más importante *or* lo principal para nosotros
3 (*on highway*) preferencia *f* de paso; **drivers on the right have ~** los conductores de la derecha tienen preferencia de paso
Ⓑ CPD ► **priority case** N caso *m* prioritario ► **priority share** N acción *f* prioritaria ► **priority treatment** N trato *m* preferente

priory ['praɪərɪ] N priorato *m*

prise [praɪz] VT **to ~ sth off** levantar algo haciendo palanca; **to ~ sth open** abrir algo haciendo palanca; **we had to ~ the secret out of him** tuvimos que sacarle el secreto a la fuerza; **to ~ sb out of his post** lograr que algn renuncie a su puesto, desahuciar a algn; **to ~ a lid up** levantar una tapa haciendo palanca

prism ['prɪzəm] N (*Geom, Tech*) prisma *m*

prismatic [prɪz'mætɪk] ADJ prismático

prison ['prɪzn] Ⓐ N 1 (= *place*) cárcel *f*, prisión *f*; **to be in ~** estar en la cárcel, estar en prisión; **to go to ~ for five years** (= *be sentenced*) ser condenado a cinco años de cárcel *or* prisión; (= *be imprisoned*) pasar cinco años en la cárcel *or* en prisión; **to put sb in ~** encarcelar a algn; **to release sb from ~** poner a algn en libertad, excarcelar a algn (*frm*); **to send sb to ~** (= *imprison*) encarcelar a algn; **to send sb to ~ for two years** (= *sentence*) condenar a algn a dos años de prisión; *see also* **maximum A1, open E**
2 (= *imprisonment*) prisión *f*, cárcel *f*; **are there alternatives to ~?** ¿existen alternativas a la prisión *or* cárcel?
Ⓑ CPD ► **prison break** N fuga *f* (de la cárcel) ► **prison camp** N campamento *m* para prisioneros ► **prison cell** N celda *f* de la cárcel *or* prisión ► **prison governor** N director(a) *m/f* de (la) prisión ► **prison life** N vida *f* en la cárcel ► **prison officer** N carcelero/a *m/f* ► **prison population** N número *m* de reclusos ► **prison riot** N motín *m* carcelario ► **prison sentence** N (*Brit*) condena *f*; *see also* **serve A4** ► **the prison service** N los servicios penitenciarios ► **prison system** N sistema *m* penitenciario ► **prison term** N (*US*) = **prison sentence** ► **prison van** N coche *m* celular ► **prison visitor** N visitante *mf* de la prisión ► **prison warden** N (*US*) = **prison governor** ► **prison yard** N patio *m* de (la) cárcel

prisoner ['prɪznəʳ] N 1 (*under arrest*) detenido/a *m/f*; (*in court*) acusado/a *m/f*; (*convicted*) preso/a *m/f*, reo/a *m/f*; (*Mil*) prisionero/a *m/f*; **~ of conscience** preso/a *m/f* de conciencia; **to hold sb ~** detener a algn; **to keep sb (a) ~** tener retenido a algn, tener prisionero a algn; **to take sb ~** tomar preso a algn, hacer prisionero a algn; **~ of war** prisionero/a *m/f* de guerra, preso/a *m/f* de guerra; ✦**IDIOM to take no ~s** no andarse con miramientos, ir a por todas; *see also* **bar A6, political B**
2 (*fig*) preso/a *m/f*, prisionero/a *m/f*

prisoner-of-war camp [ˌprɪznərəvwɔː'kæmp] N campamento *m* para prisioneros de guerra

prissy* ['prɪsɪ] ADJ (*compar* **prissier**, *superl* **prissiest**) remilgado

pristine ['prɪstaɪn] ADJ prístino

prithee†† ['prɪðiː] EXCL le ruego

privacy ['prɪvəsɪ] Ⓐ N intimidad *f*; **they respected each other's ~** cada uno respetaba la intimidad del otro; **there is no ~** no se tiene intimidad; **in ~** en la intimidad; **in the ~ of one's own home** en la intimidad del hogar; **to invade sb's ~** invadir la intimidad *or* privacidad de algn; **lack of ~** falta *f* de intimidad
Ⓑ CPD ► **Privacy Act** N ≈ Ley *f* del Derecho a la Intimidad ► **privacy law** N ley *f* del derecho a la intimidad

private ['praɪvɪt] Ⓐ ADJ 1 (= *not public*) [*conversation, visit, land, matter*] privado; [*letter, reason, opinion*] personal; [*language*] secreto; [*thoughts, grief, fantasy*] íntimo; **it was a ~ wedding** ◊ **the wedding was ~** la boda se celebró en la intimidad; **"private"** (*on door*) "privado"; (*on envelope*) "confidencial"; **"private and confidential"** "confidencial"; **"private fishing"** "coto *m* de pesca"; **"private parking"** "aparcamiento *m* *or* (*LAm*) estacionamiento *m* privado"; **it's a silly ~ joke of ours** es un chiste tonto que sólo nosotras entendemos; **to keep sth ~** [+ *beliefs*] no hablar de algo; [+ *opinions, views, doubts*] guardarse algo, reservarse algo; **I have always kept my political beliefs ~** nunca he hablado de mis ideas políticas; **he was diagnosed with AIDS in 1994 but kept it ~** en 1994 le diagnosticaron SIDA pero lo mantuvo en secreto; **I want to keep this ~** quiero que esto quede entre nosotros; **I've always tried to keep my ~ life ~** [*famous person*] siempre he intentado mantener mi vida privada alejada de la mirada del público; [*ordinary person*] siempre he intentado mantener mi vida privada fuera del alcance de los demás; **to be in ~ ownership** ser propiedad privada; **he's a very ~ person** es una persona muy reservada; *see also* **strictly 3**
2 (= *own, individual*) [*car, house, lesson, room*] particular; [*bank account*] personal; **76 bedrooms, all with ~ bathrooms** 76 habitaciones, cada una con su baño particular; **in a** *or* **one's ~ capacity** a título personal; **for your ~ information** únicamente para su información; **for ~ use** para el uso personal
3 (= *independent*) [*medicine, education, finance*] privado; [*school*] privado, particular; [*patient, tutor, teacher*] particular; **a ~ hospital** una clínica (privada), un hospital privado *or* particular; **he decided to take on ~ pupils** decidió dar clases particulares; **to go ~** [*patient*] ir por lo privado; [*dentist, doctor*] establecerse de forma privada; [*company*] dejar de cotizar en bolsa
4 (= *secluded*) [*place*] retirado; **is there somewhere we can be ~?** ¿hay algún sitio donde podamos hablar en privado?
Ⓑ N 1 (*Mil*) soldado *mf* raso; **Private Jones** el soldado Jones; **Private Jones!** ¡Jones!
2 **in ~: could I talk to you in ~?** ¿te puedo hablar en privado?; **I have been told in ~ that …** me han dicho confidencialmente *or* en confianza que …; **the committee sat in ~** la comisión se reunió a puerta(s) cerrada(s) *or* en privado; **the wedding was held in ~** la boda se celebró en la intimidad; **what people do in ~ is up to them** lo que cada uno haga en su vida privada es asunto suyo
3 **privates*** (*euph, hum*) partes *fpl* pudendas
Ⓒ CPD ► **private citizen** N (*Jur*) particular *mf* ► **private company** N empresa *f* privada, compañía *f* privada ► **private detective** N detective *mf* privado/a ► **private enterprise** N (= *industry*) el sector privado; (= *initiative*) la iniciativa privada; **new employment laws which will hamper ~ enterprise** nuevas leyes *fpl* laborales que van a dificultar el crecimiento del sector privado ► **private enterprise economy** N economía *f* capitalista, economía *f* de mercado ► **private eye** N (*US**) detective *mf* privado/a ► **private finance initiative** N (*Brit*) *plan de incentivos y potenciación de la iniciativa privada en el sector público* ► **private health care** N servicio *m* médico privado ► **private health insurance** N seguro *m* médico privado ► **private hearing** N (*Jur*) vista *f* a puertas cerradas ► **private hotel** N hotel *m* privado ► **private income** N rentas *fpl* ► **private individual** N (*Jur*) particular *mf* ► **private investigator** N investigador(a) *m/f* privado/a ► **private law** N derecho *m* privado ► **private life** N vida *f* privada; **in ~ life** en su vida privada ► **private limited company** N sociedad *f* limitada ► **private line** N (*Telec*) línea *f* particular ► **private means** NPL rentas *fpl*; **a man of ~ means** un hombre que vive de sus rentas ► **private member, Private Member** N (*Brit Parl*) diputado/a *m/f* sin responsabilidades de gobierno ► **Private Member's Bill** N *proyecto de ley presentado por un diputado a título personal*; **to introduce a Private Member's Bill** presentar un proyecto de ley a título personal ► **private parts** NPL (*euph, hum*) partes *fpl* pudendas ► **private patient** N paciente *mf* privado/a ► **private pension** N pensión *f* personal ► **private pension plan** N plan *m* de pensiones personal ► **private pension scheme** N = **private pension plan** ► **private practice** N (*Med*) consulta *f* privada; **to be in ~ practice** (*Med*) ejercer la medicina de forma privada; **he decided to set up in ~ practice** decidió establecerse como médico privado ► **private property** N propiedad *f* privada ► **private property rights** NPL derechos *mpl* de propiedad ► **private prosecution** N (*Jur*) demanda *f* civil; **to bring a ~ prosecution against sb** presentar una demanda civil contra algn ► **private school** N escuela *f* privada, escuela *f* particular ► **private secretary** N secretario/a *m/f* particular ► **the private sector** N el sector privado ► **private soldier** N soldado *mf* raso ► **private view, private viewing** N visita *f* privada (a una exposición)

privateer [ˌpraɪvə'tɪəʳ] N corsario *m*

privately ['praɪvɪtlɪ] ADV 1 (= *not publicly*) en privado; **many politicians ~ admit that …** en privado, muchos políticos admiten que …; **the country may be publicly supporting sanctions while ~ violating them** puede que oficialmente el país esté apoyando las sanciones mientras que extraoficialmente las esté infringiendo; **is there anywhere where we can talk ~?** ¿hay algún sitio donde podamos hablar en privado?; **senior officials from the two sides met ~** altos funcionarios de ambas partes se reunieron en privado *or* a puerta(s) cerrada(s); **~ he was furious at the prime minister's decision** aunque no lo demostró, estaba furioso con la decisión del primer ministro; **I tried to be understanding but ~ I was very angry with her** intenté ser com-

prensiva pero por dentro estaba muy enfadada con ella; **the Foreign Office was ~ appalled** extraoficialmente, el Ministerio de Exterior estaba horrorizado
2 (= *independently*) **one in every four of these operations is now done ~** ahora una de cada cuatro operaciones de este tipo se hace en clínicas privadas; **he is being ~ educated** va a un colegio privado *or* particular; **~ financed projects** proyectos *mpl* de financiación privada; **~ funded organizations** organizaciones *fpl* fundadas por particulares; **~ owned land** tierras *fpl* que son propiedad privada

privation [praɪ'veɪʃən] N 1 (= *poverty*) miseria *f*, estrechez *f*; **to live in ~** vivir en la miseria
2 (= *hardship, deprivation*) privación *f*; **to suffer many ~s** pasar muchos apuros

privative ['prɪvətɪv] ADJ, N privativo *m*

privatization [,praɪvətaɪ'zeɪʃən] N privatización *f*

privatize ['praɪvətaɪz] VT privatizar

privatizing ['praɪvətaɪzɪŋ] N privatización *f*

privet ['prɪvɪt] Ⓐ N alheña *f*
Ⓑ CPD ► **privet hedge** N seto *m* vivo

privilege ['prɪvɪlɪdʒ] Ⓐ N 1 (= *prerogative*) privilegio *m*; (*Jur, Parl*) inmunidad *f*; **members enjoy special ~s** los miembros gozan de privilegios especiales; **as the oldest son, he has certain ~s** como hijo mayor tiene ciertos privilegios; **that's your ~** estás en tu derecho; **to have parliamentary ~** gozar de inmunidad parlamentaria
2 (= *honour*) privilegio *m*, honor *m*; **I had the ~ of meeting her** tuve el privilegio *or* el honor de conocerla
Ⓑ VT 1 (= *favour*) privilegiar
2 **to be ~d to do sth** tener el privilegio *or* el honor de hacer algo; **I am ~d to call him a friend** tengo el privilegio *or* el honor de poder decir que es amigo mío

privileged ['prɪvɪlɪdʒd] Ⓐ ADJ 1 (= *advantaged*) [*position, life*] privilegiado; **for a ~ few** para unos pocos privilegiados *or* afortunados
2 (= *secret*) [*information*] confidencial
3 (*Jur*) [*communication*] privilegiado; [*document*] confidencial
Ⓑ N **the ~** los privilegiados

privily ['prɪvɪlɪ] ADV [*speak*] privadamente, en privado; [*tell*] confidencialmente

privy ['prɪvɪ] Ⓐ ADJ **to be ~ to sth** estar al tanto *or* enterado de algo
Ⓑ N retrete *m*, baño *m* (*LAm*)
Ⓒ CPD ► **Privy Council** N (*Brit*) consejo *m* privado (del monarca), ≈ Consejo *m* de Estado ► **Privy Councillor** N (*Brit*) consejero/a *m/f* privado/a (del monarca), ≈ consejero/a *m/f* de Estado ► **Privy Purse** N (*Brit*) gastos *mpl* personales del monarca

> **PRIVY COUNCIL**
>
> *El consejo de asesores de la Corona, conocido como* **Privy Council**, *tuvo su origen en la época de los normandos, y fue adquiriendo mayor importancia hasta ser substituido en 1688 por el actual Consejo de Ministros* **Cabinet**. *Hoy día sigue existiendo con un carácter fundamentalmente honorífico que se concede de forma automática a los ministros del gobierno, así como a otras personalidades políticas, eclesiásticas y jurídicas.*

prize[1] [praɪz] Ⓐ N 1 (*in competition, lottery*) premio *m*; **to win a ~** (*in competition*) ganar un premio; **she won a ~ in the lottery** le tocó la lotería; **he won first ~** (*in race, competition*) se llevó el primer premio; (*in lottery*) le tocó el gordo; **to carry off the ~** ◊ **win the ~** ganar el premio; *see also* **booby B**, **cash C**, **consolation B**, **Nobel**, **star D**
2 (*Sport*) (= *trophy*) trofeo *m*; (= *money*) premio *m*
3 (*fig*) premio *m*, galardón *m* (*frm*)
4 (*Naut*) presa *f*
Ⓑ ADJ 1 (= *outstanding*) de primera, de primera clase; **a ~ idiot*** un tonto de remate*
2 (= *prizewinning*) [*entry, rose*] galardonado, premiado; (*fig*) digno de premio
Ⓒ VT apreciar mucho, estimar mucho; **to ~ sth highly** estimar algo en mucho; **a ~d possession** un bien preciado
Ⓓ CPD ► **prize court** N (*Naut*) tribunal *m* de presas marítimas ► **prize day** N (*Scol*) día *m* de reparto de premios ► **prize draw** N sorteo *m* con premio, tómbola *f* ► **prize fight** N (*Boxing*) partido *m* (de boxeo) profesional ► **prize fighter** N boxeador *m* profesional ► **prize fighting** N boxeo *m* profesional ► **prize money** N (= *cash*) premio *m* en metálico; (*Boxing*) bolsa *f*; (*Naut*) parte *f* de presa ► **prize ring** N (*Boxing*) ring *m*

prize[2] [praɪz] VT (*US*) = **prise**

prize-giving ['praɪz,gɪvɪŋ] N reparto *m* de premios

prizewinner ['praɪz,wɪnəʳ] N premiado/a *m/f*

prizewinning ['praɪz,wɪnɪŋ] ADJ premiado

pro[1] [prəʊ] Ⓐ PREFIX 1 (= *in favour of*) pro, en pro de; **~-Soviet** pro-soviético; **~-Spanish** hispanófilo; **~-European** europeísta; **they were terribly ~-Franco** eran unos franquistas furibundos, eran partidarios acérrimos de Franco
2 **~ rata** *see* **pro rata**
3 **~ tem** ◊ **~ tempore** *see* **pro tem**
Ⓑ N **the ~s and cons** los pros y los contras; **we are weighing up the ~s and the cons** estamos estudiando los pros y los contras

pro[2]* [prəʊ] N (= *professional*) profesional *mf*

pro[3]* [prəʊ] N (= *prostitute*) puta *f*

PRO N ABBR 1 (= **Public Record Office**) Archivo *m* Nacional
2 = **public relations officer**

pro-abortion [,prəʊə'bɔːʃən] ADJ pro-aborto, proabortista

pro-abortionist [,prəʊə'bɔːʃənɪst] N proabortista *mf*

proactive [prəʊ'æktɪv] ADJ proactivo

probabilistic [,prɒbəbə'lɪstɪk] ADJ probabilístico

probability [,prɒbə'bɪlɪtɪ] N (*also Math*) probabilidad *f*; **the ~ is that ...** es probable que ... + *subjun*; **we calculated the probabilities of it happening** calculamos la probabilidad *or* las probabilidades de que ocurriera; **in all ~ he won't turn up** lo más probable es que no aparezca; **there is little ~ of anyone finding out** es muy poco probable que alguien se entere

probable ['prɒbəbl] ADJ 1 (= *likely*) probable; **wet roads were a ~ cause of the accident** una causa probable del accidente eran las carreteras mojadas; **it is ~ that ...** es probable que ... + *subjun*
2 (= *credible*) verosímil; **her story didn't sound very ~ to me** su historia no me pareció muy verosímil

▼**probably** ['prɒbəblɪ] ADV probablemente; **she ~ forgot** se habrá olvidado, seguramente se ha olvidado, probablemente se haya olvidado; **he will ~ come** es probable que venga; **~ not** puede que no, quizá no; **very ~, but ...** es muy posible *or* bien puede ser, pero ...

probate ['prəʊbɪt] Ⓐ N (*Jur*) validación *f* de un testamento, validación *f* testamentaria; **to value sth for ~** evaluar algo para la validación testamentaria
Ⓑ CPD ► **probate court** N tribunal *m* de testamentarías

probation [prə'beɪʃən] Ⓐ N (*Jur*) libertad *f* condicional; **to be on ~** estar en libertad condicional; (*in employment*) estar a prueba; **to put sb on ~** poner a algn en libertad provisional; (*fig*) asignar a algn un período a prueba; **to take sth on ~** (= *as a trial*) tomar algo a prueba; **release on ~** libertad *f* a prueba
Ⓑ CPD ► **probation officer** N *funcionario que vigila a las personas que están en libertad condicional*

probationary [prə'beɪʃnərɪ] Ⓐ ADJ de prueba
Ⓑ CPD ► **probationary period** N (*Jur*) período *m* de libertad condicional; (*fig*) período *m* de prueba

probationer [prə'beɪʃnəʳ] N (*Jur*) persona *f* en libertad condicional; (*Med*) aprendiz *mf* de ATS (*Sp*), aprendiz *mf* de enfermero/a; (*Rel*) novicio/a *m/f*

probe [prəʊb] Ⓐ N 1 (*Med*) sonda *f*
2 (= *rocket*) cohete *m*, proyectil *m*; (*also* **space ~**) sonda *f* espacial
3 (= *inquiry*) investigación *f*; **a ~ into the drug traffic** una investigación del tráfico de drogas
Ⓑ VT 1 [+ *hole, crack*] (*with instrument, probe*) sondear; (*with hands*) palpar, tantear
2 (*Med*) sondar
3 (= *explore*) explorar
4 (= *investigate*) investigar; **the policeman kept probing me** el policía siguió sondeándome; **to ~ a mystery** investigar un misterio
Ⓒ VI investigar; **to ~ into sb's past** investigar el pasado de algn; **you should have ~d more deeply** deberías haber llevado a cabo una investigación más a fondo

probing ['prəʊbɪŋ] Ⓐ ADJ [*question*] agudo, penetrante
Ⓑ N 1 (*with probe, instrument*) sondeo *m*; (*with hands*) palpación *f*, tanteo *m*
2 (= *investigation*) investigación *f*
3 (= *exploration*) exploración *f*

probity ['prəʊbɪtɪ] N probidad *f*

▼**problem** ['prɒbləm] Ⓐ N (*gen*) (*also Math*) problema *m*; **what's the ~?** ¿cuál es el problema?; **that's your ~** eso es problema tuyo; **it's not my ~** no es problema mío; **loneliness isn't the ~** el problema no está en *or* no es la soledad; **the ~ is that she can't cook** el problema es que no sabe cocinar; **his ~ is that he's never satisfied** su problema es que nunca está satisfecho; **he has a drink ~** tiene problemas con la bebida, bebe demasiado; **she has a serious drug ~** tiene graves problemas con las drogas; **this will not solve America's drug ~** esto no solucionará el problema de las drogas en América; **the real ~ for the police is the lack of funding** el verdadero problema de la policía es la escasez de fondos; **that presents a big ~ for schools** eso supone un gran problema para las escuelas; **he shouldn't have a** *or* **any ~ finding a job** no le será difícil encontrar trabajo; **phone me if you have any ~s** llámame si tienes cualquier problema; **I had no ~ getting a mortgage** no tuve problemas para conseguir una hipoteca; **he's having ~s deciding what subjects to study** le está costando decidir qué asignaturas estudiar; **do you have a ~ with that?*** ¿te molesta?; **I have no ~ with the ordination of women**

➤ LANGUAGE IN USE: **probably** 15.2 **problem A** 13, 26.1, 26.3

no tengo nada en contra de la ordenación de las mujeres; **health ~s** problemas *mpl* de salud; **to have a heart ~** tener problemas de corazón; **the housing ~** el problema de la vivienda; **no ~!*** (= *of course*) ¡claro!, ¡cómo no!; (= *it doesn't matter*) ¡no importa!, ¡no hay problema!; **the ~ of how to fund education** el problema de cómo financiar la enseñanza; **we've still got the ~ of what to give them for lunch** aún nos queda por solucionar el problema de qué darles para comer; **to have a weight ~** tener problemas de peso; **the ~ with men is that ...** lo malo de los hombres es que ...

Ⓑ CPD ► **problem case** N (*Med, Sociol*) caso *m* difícil ► **problem child** N niño/a *m/f* problemático/a ► **problem drinker** N **he's a ~ drinker** tiene problemas con la bebida ► **problem drinking** N **his ~ drinking is wrecking his marriage** sus problemas con la bebida están destrozando su matrimonio ► **problem family** N familia *f* con problemas ► **problem page** N consultorio *m* sentimental ► **problem play** N drama *m* de tesis ► **problem solving** N resolución *f* de problemas

problematic [ˌprɒblɪˈmætɪk] ADJ problemático; **it is ~ whether ...** es dudoso si ...

problematical [ˌprɒblɪˈmætɪkəl] ADJ = **problematic**

proboscis [prəʊˈbɒsɪs] N (*pl* **proboscises** *or* **probocides** [prəʊˈbɒsɪdiːz]) probóscide *f*, trompa *f*; (* *hum*) trompa* *f*

procedural [prəˈsiːdjʊrəl] Ⓐ ADJ relativo al procedimiento; (*Jur*) procesal; **a ~ question** una cuestión de procedimiento

Ⓑ N (*also* **police ~**) (= *novel*) novela *f* policíaca; (= *film*) película *f* policíaca

procedure [prəˈsiːdʒəʳ] N [1] (*gen*) procedimiento *m*; **what is the ~ for emergencies?** ¿cuál es el procedimiento a seguir *or* cómo se procede en caso de emergencia?; **the usual ~ is to write a letter** lo que se hace por lo general es escribir una carta; **the correct ~ would be to ...** lo correcto sería ... + *infin*; *see also* **complain B, disciplinary, selection B**

[2] (*Admin*) trámites *mpl*; **what's the ~ for obtaining a visa?** ¿qué trámites *or* gestiones hay que hacer para conseguir un visado?

proceed [prəˈsiːd] Ⓐ VI [1] (*frm*) (= *go*) [*person, vehicle*] avanzar; [*plan, project*] desarrollarse; [*events*] transcurrir; **he was ~ing along the road** avanzaba por la calle; **things are ~ing according to plan** las cosas se están desarrollando conforme estaban previstas; **the march ~ed without incident** la marcha transcurrió sin incidentes

[2] (= *go on, continue*) seguir, continuar; **proceed!** ¡siga!, ¡continúe!, ¡proceda! (*frm*); **to ~ on one's way** seguir *or* continuar su camino; **before we ~ any further** antes de seguir adelante; **to ~ to sth: let us ~ to the next item** pasemos al siguiente punto; **to ~ to blows** llegar a las manos; (*to place*) **we ~ed to London** proseguimos viaje a Londres; **we ~ed to the bar** nos dirigimos al bar; **to ~ to do sth** pasar a hacer algo; **she ~ed to outline my duties** pasó a hacerme un esquema de mis obligaciones; **he ~ed to drink the lot** acto seguido comenzó a bebérselo todo; **to ~ with sth** seguir adelante con algo; **they did not ~ with the charges against him** no siguieron adelante con los cargos contra él; **~ with your work** sigan con su trabajo

[3] (= *act*) proceder, obrar; **we should ~ with caution** debemos proceder *or* obrar con precaución

[4] (*frm*) (= *arise*) **to ~ from sth**: **sounds ~ed from the box** unos ruidos procedían *or* provenían *or* venían de la caja; **this ~s from ignorance** esto proviene de la ignorancia

[5] (*Jur*) **to ~ against sb** demandar a algn

Ⓑ VT (= *say*) proseguir; **"well," she ~ed** —bueno —prosiguió

proceeding [prəˈsiːdɪŋ] N [1] (= *action, course of action*) proceder *m*; **a somewhat dubious ~** un proceder sospechoso

[2] (*Jur*) proceso *m*; **a criminal ~** un proceso criminal

[3] **proceedings** (= *event*) acto *msing*; (= *record*) [*of learned society*] actas *fpl*; **the ~s began at seven o'clock** el acto comenzó a las siete; **hecklers attempted to disrupt the ~s** hubo gente que intentó perturbar el desarrollo del acto *or* de la reunión; **Proceedings of the Royal Society** Actas *fpl* de la Real Sociedad

[4] **proceedings** (*esp Jur*) (= *measures*) medidas *fpl*; **legal ~s** proceso *msing*; **to take ~s (to do sth)** (*Jur*) abrir un proceso (para hacer algo); **to start (legal) ~s (against sb)** (*Jur*) entablar pleito *or* una demanda (contra algn); *see also* **divorce D, institute B**

proceeds [ˈprəʊsiːdz] NPL [*of sale, transaction*] ganancias *fpl*; [*of insurance policy*] dinero *m* de una póliza; **all ~ will go to charity** toda la recaudación se destinará a obras benéficas; **he stole a wallet and got drunk on the ~** robó una cartera y se emborrachó con lo que sacó

process[1] [ˈprəʊses] Ⓐ N [1] (= *series of developments*) proceso *m*; **the production ~** el proceso de producción; **the ~es of government** los trámites gubernamentales; **the ageing ~** el envejecimiento; **I got what I wanted but made a lot of enemies in the ~** conseguí lo que quería pero a costa de crearme muchos enemigos; **in the ~ of: it is in (the) ~ of construction** está en (vías de) construcción; **we are in the ~ of moving house** estamos en medio de una mudanza; *see also* **due A3, elimination A**

[2] (= *specific method*) proceso *m*, procedimiento *m*; **the Bessemer ~** el proceso de Bessemer

[3] (*Jur*) (= *action*) proceso *m*; (= *summons*) citación *f*; **to bring a ~ against sb** demandar a algn; **to serve a ~ on sb** notificar una citación a algn

[4] (*Anat, Bot, Zool*) protuberancia *f*

Ⓑ VT [1] (= *treat*) [+ *raw materials*] procesar; [+ *food*] (*industrially*) procesar, tratar; (*with food processor*) pasar por el robot de cocina; **to ~ sth into sth** procesar algo para convertirlo en algo

[2] (= *deal with*) [+ *application, claim, order*] tramitar; [+ *applicants*] atender

[3] (*Comput*) procesar

[4] (*Phot*) revelar

Ⓒ CPD ► **process server** N agente *mf* judicial

process[2] [prəˈses] VI (*Brit frm*) (= *go in procession*) desfilar; (*Rel*) ir en procesión

processed [ˈprəʊsest], **process** (*US*) [ˈprəʊses] Ⓐ ADJ [*food*] procesado

Ⓑ CPD ► **processed** *or* (*US*) **process cheese** N queso *m* fundido

processing [ˈprəʊsesɪŋ] Ⓐ N [*of raw materials*] procesamiento *m*, tratamiento *m*; [*of food*] procesamiento *m*; [*of application, claim, order*] tramitación *f*; (*Comput*) procesamiento *m*; (*Phot*) revelado *m*

Ⓑ CPD ► **processing plant** N planta *f* de procesamiento ► **processing unit** N unidad *f* de proceso

procession [prəˈseʃən] N [*of people, cars etc*] desfile *m*; (= *ceremonial, funeral*) cortejo *m*; (*Rel*) procesión *f*; **to go** *or* **walk in ~** desfilar; (*Rel*) ir en procesión

processional [prəˈseʃənl] ADJ procesional

processor [ˈprəʊsesəʳ] N (*Comput*) procesador *m*, unidad *f* de proceso; (*also* **food ~**) robot *m* de cocina

pro-choice [ˌprəʊˈtʃɔɪs] ADJ en favor de la libertad de elección

proclaim [prəˈkleɪm] VT [1] (= *announce*) [+ *independence*] proclamar, declarar; **to ~ sb king** proclamar a algn rey; **to ~ one's innocence** declararse inocente; **to ~ one's loyalty to sb** declararse leal a algn; **to ~ one's support for sb** declarar que se apoya a algn

[2] (= *reveal*) revelar, anunciar; **their faces ~ed their guilt** su culpabilidad se revelaba en las caras

proclamation [ˌprɒkləˈmeɪʃən] N (= *act*) proclamación *f*; (= *document*) proclama *f*

proclivity [prəˈklɪvɪtɪ] N propensión *f*, proclividad *f* (**for, towards** a); **sexual proclivities** tendencias *fpl* sexuales

proconsul [ˌprəʊˈkɒnsəl] N procónsul *m*

procrastinate [prəʊˈkræstɪneɪt] VI dejar las cosas para más tarde, aplazar las cosas; **to ~ over a decision** aplazar una decisión, buscar pretextos para no tomar una decisión; **stop procrastinating!** ¡hazlo ya!, ¡deja de buscar pretextos para no hacerlo!

procrastination [prəʊˌkræstɪˈneɪʃən] N indecisión *f*, falta *f* de resolución; **after months of ~** tras meses de indecisión

procrastinator [prəʊˌkræstɪˈneɪtəʳ] N **he's too much of a ~** tiene una tendencia exagerada a dejar las cosas para más tarde

procreate [ˈprəʊkrɪeɪt] VT, VI procrear

procreation [ˌprəʊkrɪˈeɪʃən] N procreación *f*

Procrustean [prəʊˈkrʌstɪən] ADJ de Procusto

Procrustes [prəʊˈkrʌstiːz] N Procusto

proctor [ˈprɒktəʳ] Ⓐ N (*Jur*) procurador(a) *m/f*; (*Brit Univ*) censor(a) *m/f* (*oficial que cuida de la disciplina*); (*US Univ*) (= *invigilator*) celador(a) *m/f*

Ⓑ VT, VI (*US*) (= *invigilate*) vigilar

procurable [prəˈkjʊərəbl] ADJ (*frm*) asequible; **easily ~** muy asequible

procurator [ˈprɒkjʊreɪtəʳ] Ⓐ N procurador(a) *m/f*

Ⓑ CPD ► **Procurator Fiscal** N (*Scot*) fiscal *mf*

procure [prəˈkjʊəʳ] Ⓐ VT [1] (*frm*) (= *obtain*) obtener, conseguir; **to ~ sb sth** ◊ **~ sth for sb** conseguir *or* procurar algo para algn; **to ~ some relief** conseguir cierto alivio

[2] (*frm*) (= *achieve*) [+ *freedom*] lograr, gestionar; **to ~ sb's release** lograr *or* gestionar la liberación de algn

[3] (*for prostitution*) procurar

Ⓑ VI dedicarse al proxenetismo

procurement [prəˈkjʊəmənt] Ⓐ N obtención *f*

Ⓑ CPD ► **procurement agency** N agencia *f* de aprovisionamiento ► **procurement price** N precio *m* al productor

procurer [prəˈkjʊərəʳ] N proxeneta *m*, alcahuete *m*

procuress [prəˈkjʊərɪs] N alcahueta *f*, proxeneta *f*

procuring [prəˈkjʊərɪŋ] N proxenetismo *m*

prod [prɒd] Ⓐ N [1] (= *push*) empujón *m*; (*with elbow*) codazo *m*; (= *jab*) pinchazo *m*; **to give sb a ~** dar un pinchazo a algn; **he needs an occasional ~** (*fig*) hay que darle un empujón de vez en cuando

[2] (*also* **cattle ~**) aguijada *f*, picana *f* (*LAm*)

Ⓑ VT (= *push*) empujar; (*with elbow*) codear, dar un codazo a; (= *jab*) pinchar, punzar; (*with goad*) agujar; **he needs to be ~ded all the time** (*fig*) hay que pincharlo *or* empujarlo constantemente; **to ~ sb into doing sth** instar a algn a hacer algo

Ⓒ VI **he ~ded at the fire with a stick** atizó el fuego con un palo; **she ~ded gingerly at the sleeping dog** sacudió levemente y con cautela al perro que dormía

prodigal [ˈprɒdɪgəl] Ⓐ ADJ pródigo; **~ of** (*frm*) pródigo con; **the ~ son** el hijo pródigo

Ⓑ N despilfarrador(a) *m/f*

prodigality [ˌprɒdɪˈgælɪtɪ] N prodigalidad *f*

prodigious [prəˈdɪdʒəs] ADJ [*amount, quantity*] enorme, ingente; [*appetite*] enorme; [*memory, energy*] prodigioso; **she is a ~ reader** lee una barbaridad*

prodigiously [prəˈdɪdʒəslɪ] ADV [*grow, read, eat*] una barbaridad*; **to be ~ talented** tener un talento prodigioso

prodigy [ˈprɒdɪdʒɪ] N prodigio *m*; **child ~ ◊ infant ~** niño/a *m/f* prodigio

produce Ⓐ [prəˈdjuːs] VT 1 (= *yield*) [+ *coal, crop, electricity, sound*] producir; [+ *milk*] [*farm*] producir; [*cow*] dar; [+ *interest*] rendir, producir; [+ *profit, benefits*] producir, reportar; **the plant ~s three harvests a year** la planta da tres cosechas al año; **friction ~s heat** la fricción produce calor; **oil-producing countries** países *mpl* productores de petróleo

2 (= *manufacture*) [+ *cars, weapons, drugs*] fabricar, producir

3 (= *create*) [+ *novel*] escribir; [+ *magazine*] publicar; [+ *musical work*] componer; **she has ~d consistently good work at school** su trabajo escolar siempre ha sido bueno; **he is the most creative novelist this century has ~d** es el novelista más creativo que nos ha dado este siglo; **with this symphony he has ~d a masterpiece** ha compuesto una obra maestra con esta sinfonía

4 (= *give birth to*) [+ *offspring*] [*animal*] parir; [*woman*] tener, dar a luz a; [*parents*] tener

5 (= *bring out, supply*) [+ *gift, handkerchief, gun*] sacar; [+ *ticket, documents, evidence, proof*] presentar; [+ *argument*] dar, presentar; [+ *witness*] nombrar; [+ *meal*] preparar; **when challenged he ~d a knife** cuando se le paró sacó una navaja

6 (*Cine, Theat*) [+ *film, play, show*] producir; (*TV, Rad*) realizar; (*Publishing*) [+ *magazine*] publicar; (*Mus*) [+ *record*] producir

7 (= *cause*) [+ *symptoms*] producir, causar; [+ *response*] provocar, producir; **it ~d a sensation of drowsiness** producía *or* causaba una sensación de somnolencia; **the photographer used a special lens to ~ that effect** el fotógrafo usó una lente especial para producir ese efecto; **by combining the two kinds of paint you can ~ some interesting effects** combinando las dos clases de pintura puedes conseguir efectos interesantes; **you may find that just threatening this course of action will ~ the desired effect** puedes encontrarte con que amenazar este procedimiento producirá el efecto deseado; **she is optimistic that his visit could ~ results** piensa que su visita podría surtir efecto

8 (*Geom*) [+ *line, plane*] prolongar

Ⓑ [prəˈdjuːs] VI 1 [*mine, oil well, factory*] producir; [*land, tree*] dar fruto(s); [*cow*] dar leche; [*person*] rendir

2 (*Theat, Cine*) producir; (*TV, Rad*) realizar

Ⓒ [ˈprɒdjuːs] N (*Agr*) productos *mpl* agrícolas, productos *mpl* del campo; **"produce of Turkey"** "producto *m* de Turquía"; **"produce of more than one country"** "producto *m* elaborado en varios países"; *see also* **dairy B**, **farm D**

Ⓓ [ˈprɒdjuːs] CPD ► **produce counter** N (*US*) mostrador *m* de verdura ► **produce store** N (*US*) verdulería *f*

producer [prəˈdjuːsəʳ] N 1 [*of oil, coal, ore, crop*] productor(a) *m/f*; [*of product*] fabricante *mf*

2 (*Theat*) director(a) *m/f* de escena; (*Cine*) productor(a) *m/f*; (*TV*) realizador(a) *m/f*, productor(a) *m/f*

-producing [prəˈdjʊsɪŋ] ADJ (*ending in compounds*) productor de ...; **oil-producing** productor de petróleo

product [ˈprɒdʌkt] Ⓐ N 1 (*Comm, Ind*) producto *m*; **consumer ~s** productos *mpl* de consumo; **food ~s** productos *mpl* alimenticios; *see also* **end D**, **finished 2**, **gross E**, **waste E**

2 (*fig*) producto *m*, fruto *m*; **it is the ~ of his imagination** es producto de su imaginación; **she is the ~ of a broken home** es el clásico producto de un hogar deshecho

3 (*Math, Chem*) producto *m*

Ⓑ CPD ► **product development** N creación *f* de nuevos productos ► **product liability** N responsabilidad *f* del fabricante ► **product line** N línea *f* de productos ► **product manager** N product manager *mf* ► **product placement** N emplazamiento *m* ► **product range** N gama *f* de productos ► **product research** N investigación *f* del producto ► **product specification** N descripción *f* del producto

production [prəˈdʌkʃən] Ⓐ N 1 (= *making*) producción *f*; (= *manufacture*) producción *f*, fabricación *f*; **the factory is in full ~** la fábrica trabaja a plena capacidad; **the car is due to go into ~ later this year** está previsto que el coche empiece a fabricarse este año; **this model went out of ~ in 1974** este modelo dejó de fabricarse en 1974; **to put sth into ~** lanzar algo a la producción; **to take sth out of ~** [+ *product*] dejar de fabricar algo; [+ *land*] dejar de cultivar algo; *see also* **mass² D**

2 (= *output*) (*Ind, Agr*) producción *f*; (*Art, Literat*) obra *f*; **the firm exports 90% of its ~** la empresa exporta el 90% de lo que produce *or* de su producción; **industrial/oil ~** producción *f* industrial/de aceite

3 (= *act of showing*) presentación *f*; **on ~ of this card** al presentar esta tarjeta

4 (*Media*) 4·1 (= *act of producing*) (*Theat*) producción *f*, puesta *f* en escena; (*Cine, TV, Rad*) realización *f*; **the series goes into ~ in March** la serie empezará a realizarse en marzo

4·2 (= *play, film, programme*) (*Theat*) representación *f*, montaje *m*; (*Cine, TV*) producción *f*; **the opera has yet to receive its first ~** no se ha hecho nunca una representación *or* montaje de la ópera, la ópera nunca se ha representado; ✦**IDIOM to make a ~ out of sth*** montar un show por algo*; **he made a real ~ out of it!** ¡montó un verdadero show!*

Ⓑ CPD [*process, department, costs, quota*] de producción ► **production agreement** N (*US*) acuerdo *m* de productividad ► **production assistant** N (*Cine, TV*) ayudante *mf* de realización ► **production company** N (*TV*) (compañía *f*) productora *f* ► **production line** N cadena *f* de fabricación *or* montaje ► **production manager** N (*Ind*) jefe/a *m/f* de producción; (*Cine, TV*) jefe/a *m/f* de realización ► **production run** N serie *f* de producción

productive [prəˈdʌktɪv] ADJ 1 (= *efficient*) [*worker, land, industry*] productivo; **the factory is not yet fully ~** la fábrica todavía no trabaja a plena capacidad; **to be ~ of sth** (*frm*) producir algo, generar algo

2 (= *fruitful*) [*meeting, discussion*] fructífero; **I spent a ~ morning in the library** he tenido una mañana muy fructífera *or* provechosa en la biblioteca

productively [prəˈdʌktɪvlɪ] ADV [*use resources*] de manera productiva; [*spend time*] provechosamente

productivity [ˌprɒdʌkˈtɪvɪtɪ] Ⓐ N productividad *f*

Ⓑ CPD ► **productivity agreement**, **productivity deal** N (*Brit*) acuerdo *m* sobre productividad ► **productivity bonus** N prima *f* de productividad *or* rendimiento

Prof., **prof.¹** [prɒf] N ABBR (= **professor**) Prof.

prof.² ADJ ABBR = **professional**

prof* [prɒf] N profe* *mf*

profanation [ˌprɒfəˈneɪʃən] N profanación *f*

profane [prəˈfeɪn] Ⓐ ADJ 1 (= *secular*) profano

2 (= *irreverent*) [*person, language*] blasfemo

Ⓑ VT profanar

profanity [prəˈfænɪtɪ] N (= *blasphemy*) blasfemia *f*; (= *oath*) blasfemia *f*; **to utter a string of profanities** soltar una sarta de blasfemias

profess [prəˈfes] VT 1 (*Rel*) [+ *faith, religion*] profesar

2 (= *state*) [+ *innocence*] declarar; [+ *regret, surprise*] manifestar; [+ *ignorance*] confesar; **he ~es a belief in the equality of women** se precia *or* presume de creer en la igualdad de las mujeres

3 (= *claim*) pretender; **I do not ~ to be an expert** no pretendo ser experto; **he ~es to be 25** dice *or* afirma tener 25 años; **he ~es to know all about it** afirma estar enterado de ello; **to ~ o.s. satisfied** declararse satisfecho; **to ~ o.s. unable to do sth** declararse incapaz de hacer algo

professed [prəˈfest] ADJ (*Rel*) profeso; (= *self-declared*) declarado; (*pej*) (= *supposed*) supuesto, ostensible

professedly [prəˈfesɪdlɪ] ADV (= *openly*) declaradamente; (*pej*) (= *supposedly*) supuestamente

profession [prəˈfeʃən] N 1 (= *calling*) profesión *f*, oficio *m*; **by ~** de profesión; **he is an engineer by ~** es ingeniero de profesión; **the oldest ~** (*euph*) el oficio más viejo

2 (= *body of people*) profesión *f*, cuerpo *m* profesional; **the ~s** las profesiones, los cuerpos profesionales; **to enter** *or* **join a ~** entrar a formar parte de una profesión *or* un cuerpo profesional; **the legal ~** el cuerpo de abogados; **the liberal ~s** las profesiones liberales; **the medical ~** la profesión médica, el cuerpo médico; **the teaching ~** el cuerpo docente; **a member of the teaching ~** un miembro del cuerpo docente; **to enter the teaching ~** entrar en la docencia *or* la enseñanza; *see also* **caring A**

3 (= *declaration*) declaración *f*, manifestación *f*; **~ of faith** profesión *f* de fe

professional [prəˈfeʃənl] Ⓐ ADJ 1 (= *non-amateur*) [*sport, sportsperson, musician*] profesional; [*soldier*] de carrera; **she's a ~ singer** es cantante profesional; **he plays ~ football** se dedica al fútbol profesional; **that boy's a ~ trouble-maker*** (*iro, hum*) ese niño es un alborotador profesional; **to seek** *or* **take ~ advice** consultar a un profesional; **before spending any money you ought to seek ~ advice** deberías consultar a un profesional antes de gastar nada de dinero; **I have sought ~ advice and have been advised to go ahead with the case** he consultado a un abogado y me ha aconsejado seguir adelante con el caso; **she needs ~ help for her depression** necesita ayuda de un profesional para superar su depresión; **to turn** *or* **go ~** hacerse profesional, profesionalizarse

2 (= *employed in a profession*) **the flat is ideal for the ~ single person** el piso es idóneo para el profesional soltero

3 (= *relating to a profession*) profesional; **he began his ~ life as an accountant** se inició en su vida profesional como contable; **his ~ conduct has come under scrutiny** se está investigando su conducta profesional

4 (= *appropriate to a professional*) **I was impressed by his ~ approach** su profesionalidad me causó muy buena impresión; **that wasn't a very ~ thing to do** eso no fue propio de un profesional, eso fue una falta de profesionalidad

5 (= *competent, skilled*) **it was a very ~ performance** fue una representación hecha con mucha profesionalidad; **a ~ job** obra *f* de un profesional *or* experto; **you could tell the burglary was a ~ job** se veía que el robo fue obra de un profesional *or* de un experto; **you've done a really ~ job of the decorating** has pintado la casa como un verdadero profesional *or* experto

Ⓑ N 1 (= *non-amateur*) profesional *mf*

2 (= *person employed in a profession*) profesional *mf*; **health ~** profesional *mf* de la medicina

3 (= *expert*) profesional *mf*, experto/a *m/f*; **the killing was the work of a ~** el asesinato fue obra de un profesional *or* de un experto; **Brenner was no ordinary thief, but a true ~** Brenner no era un ladrón cualquiera, sino un verdadero profesional *or* experto; **golf ~** golfista *mf* profesional

Ⓒ CPD ► **professional charges** NPL honorarios *mpl* profesionales ► **the professional classes** NPL la gente de carrera ► **professional fees** NPL honorarios *mpl* profesionales ► **professional foul** N falta *f* profesional ► **professional liability** N responsabilidad *f* profesional ► **professional misconduct** N falta *f* de ética profesional; **he was found guilty of ~ misconduct** se le declaró culpable de falta de ética profesional ► **professional practice** N (= *method*) práctica *f* profesional; (= *career*) vida *f* profesional; **the ~ practice of homoeopathy** la práctica profesional de la homeopatía; **in his ~ practice he had come across many patients with similar symptoms** en su vida profesional había atendido a muchos pacientes con síntomas parecidos; **it is not good ~ practice** no es apropiado en el ejercicio de la profesión ► **professional qualification** N título *m* profesional ► **professional school** N (*US*) escuela *f* profesional superior ► **professional services** NPL servicios *mpl* prestados por profesionales ► **professional skills** NPL técnicas *fpl* de la profesión ► **professional standing** N reputación *f* profesional ► **professional training** N formación *f* profesional

professionalism [prəˈfeʃnəlɪzəm] N profesionalismo *m*

professionally [prəˈfeʃnəlɪ] ADV 1 (*Sport, Mus*) [*play, sing*] profesionalmente; **he is known ~ as X** se le conoce profesionalmente como X

2 (= *in a professional capacity*) profesionalmente; **I only knew her ~** sólo la traté profesionalmente; **to be ~ qualified** tener el título profesional

3 (= *expertly*) con profesionalidad, profesionalmente

4 (= *by an expert*) [*made, built*] por un profesional *or* un experto; **I advise you to have it done ~** te aconsejo que lo dejes en manos de un profesional *or* experto

5 (= *as befits a professional*) con profesionalidad; **she conducts her business very ~** lleva sus negocios con mucha profesionalidad

professor [prəˈfesəʳ] N 1 (*Brit, US Univ*) catedrático/a *m/f* (*de universidad*); **Professor Cameron** el catedrático Cameron; **he is a ~ of economics** es catedrático de economía; **full ~** catedrático/a *m/f* (*de universidad*); *see also* **assistant B**, **associate E**

2 (*US*) (= *teacher*) profesor(a) *m/f* (universitario/a); **a science ~** un profesor de ciencias

professorial [ˌprɒfəˈsɔːrɪəl] ADJ [*post, career*] de catedrático; [*tone, manner*] magistral

professorship [prəˈfesəʃɪp] N cátedra *f*; **to be appointed to a ~** ser nombrado a *or* obtener una cátedra

proffer [ˈprɒfəʳ] VT [+ *gift*] ofrecer; [+ *advice, help*] brindar, ofrecer; [+ *congratulations*] dar; **he ~ed his hand** me/le alargó la mano

proficiency [prəˈfɪʃənsɪ] Ⓐ N habilidad *f*, competencia *f*; **reading ~** habilidad *f or* competencia *f* como lector; **language ~** dominio *m* del idioma; **Cambridge Certificate of Proficiency** *diploma de inglés como lengua extranjera*

Ⓑ CPD ► **proficiency test** N prueba *f* de aptitud

proficient [prəˈfɪʃənt] ADJ competente (**at, in** en); **as you become more ~** según te vas haciendo más competente; **she was already ~ in German** tenía ya un gran dominio del alemán, dominaba ya el alemán

profile [ˈprəʊfaɪl] Ⓐ N 1 (= *side view, outline*) perfil *m*; **in ~** de perfil

2 (= *description, portrait*) reseña *f*, perfil *m*; (*TV programme*) perfil *m*; *see also* **customer B**

3 (= *public image*) **her work with the Fund has given her a very high ~** la labor que ha realizado para el Fondo ha dado gran relieve a su figura *or* la ha lanzado a un primer plano; **military men continued to have a high ~ in the administration** los militares seguían ocupando una posición destacada en la administración; **to keep** *or* **maintain a low ~** tratar de pasar desapercibido; **to raise the ~ of sth/sb** realzar la imagen de algo/algn; *see also* **high-profile**

Ⓑ VT 1 (= *show in profile*) perfilar

2 (= *describe*) [+ *situation, candidate*] describir; [+ *person's life*] hacer un perfil de

profit [ˈprɒfɪt] Ⓐ N 1 (*Comm*) ganancias *fpl*, beneficios *mpl*, utilidades *fpl* (*LAm*); **a 32% rise in ~s** un aumento del 32% en las ganancias *or* los beneficios; **at a ~**: **to operate at a ~** ser rentable; **to sell (sth) at a ~** vender (algo) obteniendo una ganancia; **to make a ~** obtener ganancias *or* beneficios; **they made a ~ of two million** obtuvieron unas ganancias *or* unos beneficios de dos millones; **to make a ~ on** *or* **out of sth** obtener beneficios de algo; **to show a ~** registrar beneficios *or* ganancias; **to turn a ~** obtener ganancias *or* beneficios; **with ~s policy** (*Insurance*) póliza *f* con beneficios; *see also* **interim C**, **trading B**

2 (*fig*) utilidad *f*, beneficio *m*; **I could see no ~ in antagonizing them** no veía qué utilidad *or* beneficio tenía el enfadarles; **to turn sth to (one's) ~** sacar provecho *or* beneficio de algo

Ⓑ VI 1 (*financially*) obtener ganancia, obtener beneficio

2 (*fig*) **to ~ by** *or* **from sth** aprovecharse de algo; **we do not want to ~ from someone else's misfortunes** no queremos aprovecharnos de las desgracias de otros; **I can't see how he hopes to ~ (by it)** no veo qué espera sacar (de ello)

Ⓒ VT († *also frm or liter*) **it will ~ him nothing** no le servirá de nada

Ⓓ CPD ► **profit and loss account** N cuenta *f* de pérdidas y ganancias ► **profit margin** N margen *m* de beneficios ► **profit motive** N afán *m* de lucro

profitability [ˌprɒfɪtəˈbɪlɪtɪ] N rentabilidad *f*

profitable [ˈprɒfɪtəbl] ADJ (*Comm*) lucrativo; (= *economic to run*) rentable; (*fig*) (= *beneficial*) provechoso; **a ~ investment** una inversión lucrativa; **the line is no longer ~** la línea ya no es rentable; **a most ~ trip** un viaje sumamente provechoso; **you would find it ~ to read this** te beneficiarías de leer esto, te sería útil leer esto

profitably [ˈprɒfɪtəblɪ] ADV (*Comm*) [*run*] de forma rentable, obteniendo beneficios; [*sell*] con ganancia; (*fig*) (= *beneficially*) provechosamente

profiteer [ˌprɒfɪˈtɪəʳ] Ⓐ N especulador(a) *m/f*; **war ~** *persona que especula en tiempo de guerra*

Ⓑ VI especular, obtener ganancias excesivas

profiteering [ˌprɒfɪˈtɪərɪŋ] N especulación *f*

profitless [ˈprɒfɪtlɪs] ADJ inútil

profitlessly [ˈprɒfɪtlɪslɪ] ADV inútilmente

profit-making [ˈprɒfɪtˌmeɪkɪŋ] ADJ (= *profitable*) rentable; (= *aiming to make profit*) [*organization*] con fines lucrativos; *see also* **non-profit-making**

profit-related [ˈprɒfɪtrəˈleɪtɪd] ADJ [*pay, bonus*] proporcional a los beneficios

profit-seeking [ˈprɒfɪtˌsiːkɪŋ] ADJ [*activity*] con fines lucrativos

profit-sharing [ˈprɒfɪtˌʃeərɪŋ] N reparto *m* de los beneficios

profit-taking [ˈprɒfɪtˌteɪkɪŋ] N (*St Ex*) venta *f* con beneficios, *venta de acciones tras una subida de precios en el mercado o antes de que se produzca una bajada de los mismos*

profligacy [ˈprɒflɪgəsɪ] N (= *dissoluteness*) libertinaje *m*; (= *extravagance*) prodigalidad *f*, despilfarro *m*

profligate [ˈprɒflɪgɪt] Ⓐ ADJ (= *dissolute*) libertino, disoluto; (= *extravagant*) despilfarrador, derrochador

Ⓑ N (= *degenerate*) libertino/a *m/f*; (= *spendthrift*) despilfarrador(a) *m/f*

pro-form [ˈprəʊˌfɔːm] N (*Ling*) pro forma *f*

pro forma [ˌprəʊˈfɔːmə] Ⓐ ADJ [*compliance, implementation*] puramente formal

Ⓑ CPD ► **pro forma invoice** N factura *f* detallada que precede a la entrega ► **pro forma letter** N carta *f* estándar

profound [prəˈfaʊnd] ADJ 1 (= *deep, intense*) [*emotion, silence*] profundo; [*effect, influence, changes*] profundo, grande

2 (= *meaningful*) [*ideas, thoughts*] profundo; [*person*] de ideas profundas; [*book, writing*] profundo; **her first novel is very ~** su primera novela es muy profunda

profoundly [prəˈfaʊndlɪ] ADV profundamente; **I was ~ affected by her ideas/her death** sus ideas me afectaron/su muerte me afectó profundamente; **he apologized ~ when he discovered his mistake** se deshizo en disculpas cuando se dio cuenta de su error; **to be ~ deaf** ser totalmente sordo; **I am ~ grateful to all the people who helped us** les estoy profundamente agradecido a todos los que nos ayudaron; **people are ~ ignorant about the law** la gente no sabe absolutamente nada acerca de la legislación

profundity [prəˈfʌndɪtɪ] N (*frm*) profundidad *f*

profuse [prəˈfjuːs] ADJ [*vegetation*] profuso, abundante; [*sweating*] copioso; [*bleeding*] intenso; **to be ~ in one's apologies** deshacerse en disculpas

profusely [prəˈfjuːslɪ] ADV [*grow*] con profusión, en abundancia; **he apologized ~** se deshizo en disculpas; **she thanked me ~** me dio las gracias efusivamente; **to sweat/bleed ~** sudar/sangrar profusamente *or* copiosamente

profusion [prəˈfjuːʒən] N profusión *f*, abundancia *f*; **there was a ~ of wines to choose from** había una gran profusión *or* abundancia de vinos de entre los que elegir; **orchids bloomed in ~** las orquídeas florecieron profusamente *or* en abundancia; **a ~ of colour** un derroche de color, una gran profusión de color

prog.* [prɒg] (*Brit TV etc*) N ABBR (= **programme**) programa *m*

progenitor [prəʊˈdʒenɪtəʳ] N progenitor *m*

progeny [ˈprɒdʒɪnɪ] N progenie *f*

progesterone [prəʊˈdʒestərəʊn] N progesterona *f*

prognosis [prɒgˈnəʊsɪs] N (*pl* **prognoses** [prɒgˈnəʊsiːz]) (*Med*) pronóstico *m*

prognostic [prɒgˈnɒstɪk] N pronóstico *m*

prognosticate [prɒgˈnɒstɪkeɪt] VT pronosticar

prognostication [prɒg,nɒstɪˈkeɪʃən] N (= *act, art*) pronosticación *f*; (= *forecast*) pronóstico *m*

program, programme [ˈprəʊgræm] (*Comput*)
Ⓐ N programa *m*
Ⓑ VT programar; **to ~ sth to do sth** programar algo para que haga algo
Ⓒ VI programar

programmable [prəʊˈgræməbl] ADJ programable

programme, program (*esp US*) [ˈprəʊgræm]
Ⓐ N 1 (= *plan, schedule*) programa *m*; **Iraq's nuclear weapons ~** el programa iraquí de armamento nuclear; **a training ~ for the unemployed** un programa de formación para los parados; **a ~ of meetings, talks and exhibitions** un programa de reuniones, discursos y exposiciones; **what's (on) the ~ for today?** ¿qué planes *or* programa tenemos para hoy?; *see also* **detoxification B, space C**
2 (*US Univ*) (= *syllabus*) plan *m* de estudios, programa *m*; (= *course*) curso *m*
3 (*TV, Rad*) programa *m*; **television ~** programa *m* de televisión; *see also* **magazine 2**
4 (= *performance details*) programa *m*; **they've put together an interesting ~ for tonight's concert** han conseguido reunir los elementos necesarios para un interesante programa de concierto esta noche; **can I have a look at the ~?** ¿puedo echarle un vistazo al programa?
5 (*Comput*) = **program**
6 (*on washing machine*) programa *m*
Ⓑ VT 1 (= *arrange*) programar, planear; **the broadcast was ~d for Sunday** la emisión estaba programada para el domingo
2 (*Comput*) = **program**
3 (*Elec, fig*) programar; **to ~ sth to do sth** programar algo para que haga algo; **to be ~d (to do sth)** [*machine, person*] estar programado (para hacer algo)
Ⓒ VI (*Comput*) = **program**
Ⓓ CPD ► **programme maker** N (*TV*) realizador(a) *m/f* de televisión ► **programme music** N música *f* de programa ► **programme notes** NPL descripción *f* del programa (*en un concierto*)

programmed, programed (*US*) [ˈprəʊgræmd] Ⓐ ADJ programado
Ⓑ CPD ► **programmed learning, programmed teaching** N enseñanza *f* programada

programmer, programer (*US*) [ˈprəʊgræməʳ] N programador(a) *m/f*

programming, programing (*US*) [ˈprəʊgræmɪŋ] Ⓐ N programación *f*
Ⓑ CPD ► **programming environment** N entorno *m* de programación ► **programming language** N lenguaje *m* de programación

progress Ⓐ [ˈprəʊgres] N 1 (= *forward movement*) avance *m*; **heavy snow slowed our ~** la espesa capa de nieve dificultó nuestro avance *or* nos retrasó; **we are making good ~** estamos avanzando rápidamente
2 (= *development*) [*of activity, student*] progresos *mpl*; [*of events*] marcha *f*, desarrollo *m*; [*of patient*] evolución *f*; [*of disease*] curso *m*, evolución *f*; **he briefed us on the ~ of the talks** nos informó sobre la marcha *or* el desarrollo de las negociaciones; **keep me informed on the patient's ~** manténganme informado de la evolución del paciente; **he came in to check on my ~** vino para ver cómo iba progresando; **to make ~** (*gen*) hacer progresos, progresar; [*patient*] mejorar; **China has made significant ~ in human rights** China ha hecho muchos progresos en lo que respecta a derechos humanos; **the two sides have made little ~ towards agreement** las dos partes apenas han avanzado hacia un acuerdo; **to make good/slow ~** avanzar rápidamente/lentamente; *see also* **chart B**
3 (= *innovation*) progreso *m*; **it was all done in the name of ~** todo se hizo con la excusa del progreso
4 (= *course*) **in ~**: **the game was already in ~** había comenzado ya el partido; **negotiations are still in ~** aún se están manteniendo las negociaciones; **I went to see the work in ~** fui a ver cómo marchaba el trabajo; **"silence: exam in progress"** "silencio: examen"
Ⓑ [prəˈgres] VI 1 (= *go forward*) [*work*] avanzar; [*events*] desarrollarse; [*disease*] evolucionar; **things are ~ing slowly** las cosas avanzan lentamente; **as the game ~ed** a medida que avanzaba *or* iba desarrollándose el partido; **as the evening ~ed** a medida que avanzaba la noche; **to ~ to sth**: **he started sketching, then ~ed to painting** empezó haciendo bosquejos para luego pasar a pintar; **she has ~ed to a senior nursing position** ha ascendido a enfermera de rango superior
2 (= *improve*) [*student*] hacer progresos; [*patient*] mejorar; **her French is ~ing in leaps and bounds** avanza a pasos agigantados en francés
Ⓒ [prəˈgres] VT (= *advance*) seguir adelante con
Ⓓ [ˈprəʊgres] CPD ► **progress report** N (*Admin*) informe *m* sobre la marcha del trabajo; (*Med*) informe *m* médico; (*Scol*) informe *m* sobre el progreso del alumno

progression [prəˈgreʃən] N 1 [*of disease, career*] evolución *f*; [*of events*] desarrollo *m*; **arithmetical/geometric ~** progresión *f* aritmética/geométrica; **her ~ from awkward teenager to superstar** su evolución *or* paso de adolescente difícil a superestrella; **it's a natural ~** es lógico
2 (*Mus*) progresión *f*; **chord ~** progresión *f* de acordes

progressive [prəˈgresɪv] Ⓐ ADJ 1 (= *increasing*) progresivo
2 (*Pol*) progresista
Ⓑ N (= *person*) progresista *mf*

progressively [prəˈgresɪvlɪ] ADV progresivamente, poco a poco; **it diminishes ~** disminuye progresivamente *or* poco a poco; **it's getting ~ better** va mejorando poco a poco

progressiveness [prəˈgresɪvnɪs] N carácter *m* progresista

prohibit [prəˈhɪbɪt] VT 1 (= *forbid*) prohibir; **to ~ sb from doing sth** prohibir a algn hacer algo; **"it is prohibited to feed the animals"** "se prohíbe dar de comer a los animales"; **"smoking prohibited"** "se prohíbe *or* está prohibido fumar"; **~ed area** zona *f* prohibida
2 (= *prevent*) **to ~ sb from doing sth** impedir a algn hacer algo; **his health ~s him from swimming** su salud le impide nadar

prohibition [,prəʊɪˈbɪʃən] N prohibición *f*; **Prohibition** (*US*) la ley seca, la Prohibición

prohibitionism [,prəʊɪˈbɪʃənɪzəm] N prohibicionismo *m*

prohibitionist [,prəʊɪˈbɪʃənɪst] Ⓐ ADJ prohibicionista
Ⓑ N prohibicionista *mf*

prohibitive [prəˈhɪbɪtɪv] ADJ prohibitivo

prohibitively [prəˈhɪbɪtɪvlɪ] ADV **the car is ~ expensive** el precio del coche es prohibitivo, el coche es imposiblemente caro

prohibitory [prəˈhɪbɪtərɪ] ADJ prohibitorio

project Ⓐ [ˈprɒdʒekt] N 1 (= *scheme, plan*) proyecto *m*
2 (*Scol, Univ*) trabajo *m*
3 (*also* **housing ~**) (*US*) urbanización *f or* barrio *m* de viviendas protegidas; *see also* **housing B**
Ⓑ [prəˈdʒekt] VT 1 (= *estimate*) [+ *costs, expenditure*] hacer una proyección de
2 (= *forecast*) prever; **the population of Britain is ~ed to rise slowly over the next ten years** se prevé que la población de Gran Bretaña aumentará lentamente durante los próximos diez años; **a ~ed deficit of 2 million dollars** un déficit previsto de 2 millones de dólares
3 (= *plan*) (*usu passive*) **there were demonstrations against his ~ed visit** hubo manifestaciones en contra de su programada *or* prevista visita; **it stood in the path of a ~ed motorway** estaba situado en un lugar por donde estaba previsto que pasara una autopista
4 (= *throw, send forward*) [+ *object*] (*frm*) lanzar; [+ *light*] proyectar; **the impact ~ed him forward onto the windscreen** con el impacto salió despedido contra el parabrisas; **to ~ one's voice** [*singer, actor*] proyectar la voz
5 (= *show*) [+ *slide, image*] proyectar
6 (= *communicate, represent*) [+ *image, personality*] proyectar; **he ~ed himself as the ideal family man** daba la imagen del hombre de familia ideal
7 (*Psych*) **I ~ my own rage/fear onto the children** proyecto mi propia cólera/mi propio miedo en los niños
8 (*Math*) proyectar
Ⓒ [prəˈdʒekt] VI 1 (= *jut out*) sobresalir; **a spit of land ~ed out from the shore** una lengua de tierra sobresalía de la orilla
2 (= *communicate, enunciate*) proyectarse; **his voice ~s very well** su voz se proyecta muy bien
Ⓓ [ˈprɒdʒekt] CPD ► **project management** N administración *f* de proyectos ► **project manager** N director(a) *m/f* de proyecto

projectile [prəˈdʒektaɪl] N proyectil *m*

projecting [prəˈdʒektɪŋ] ADJ [*nail, branch*] saliente; [*cheekbones*] marcado, prominente; [*teeth*] salido, hacia fuera

projection [prəˈdʒekʃən] Ⓐ N [1] [*of image, voice*] proyección *f*; *see also* **astral B**
[2] (= *overhang*) saliente *m*, resalto *m*; (= *knob*) protuberancia *f*
[3] (= *forecast*) (*Fin*) pronóstico *m*
[4] (*in cartography*) proyección *f*
[5] (*Psych*) proyección *f*
Ⓑ CPD ► **projection room** N (*Cine*) cabina *f* de proyección

projectionist [prəˈdʒekʃnɪst] N (*Cine*) operador(a) *m/f* (de proyector), proyeccionista *mf*

projector [prəˈdʒektəʳ] N (*Cine*) proyector *m*

prolapse [ˈprəʊlæps] N (*Med*) prolapso *m*

prole* [prəʊl] N (*Brit*) proletario/a *m/f*; **the ~s** los proletarios

proletarian [ˌprəʊləˈtɛərɪən] Ⓐ ADJ proletario
Ⓑ N proletario/a *m/f*

proletarianize [ˌprəʊləˈtɛərɪənaɪz] VT proletarizar

proletariat [ˌprəʊləˈtɛərɪət] N proletariado *m*

pro-life [ˌprəʊˈlaɪf] ADJ pro-vida

proliferate [prəˈlɪfəreɪt] VI proliferar

proliferation [prəˌlɪfəˈreɪʃən] N proliferación *f*; **nuclear ~** proliferación *f* de armas nucleares

prolific [prəˈlɪfɪk] ADJ prolífico

prolix [ˈprəʊlɪks] ADJ prolijo

prolixity [prəʊˈlɪksɪtɪ] N prolijidad *f*

prologue, prolog (*US*) [ˈprəʊlɒg] N (*lit, fig*) prólogo *m* (**to** de)

prolong [prəˈlɒŋ] VT [+ *visit, life, war, recession*] prolongar, alargar; ✦***IDIOM*** **to ~ the agony**: **this is just ~ing the agony** esto es sólo prolongar la agonía

prolongation [ˌprəʊlɒŋˈgeɪʃən] N prolongación *f*

prolonged [prəˈlɒŋd] ADJ [*absence, silence, period, struggle, exposure*] prolongado; **~ use of the drug may lead to liver damage** un prolongado uso del medicamento puede ocasionar una lesión hepática; **there was ~ applause** el público aplaudió durante varios minutos

PROM N ABBR (*Comput*) = **Programmable Read Only Memory**

prom [prɒm] N [1] (*Brit**) (= *promenade*) paseo *m* marítimo
[2] (*Brit**) = **promenade concert**
[3] (*US*) *baile de gala bajo los auspicios de los alumnos de un colegio*

PROM

En Gran Bretaña el término **prom** *es la forma abreviada de* **promenade concert**, *y hace referencia a un concierto de música clásica en el que una parte del público permanece de pie en una zona del auditorio reservada al efecto. La serie de conciertos de este tipo más conocida es la que se celebra cada verano en el* **Royal Albert Hall** *de Londres, y que tuvo su origen en 1895 a partir de una idea del director de orquesta Henry Wood. Actualmente convertidos en una institución nacional, destaca entre todas las actuaciones la llamada* **Last Night of the Proms** *en la que se interpretan piezas de carácter patriótico, entre otras de repertorio. En Estados Unidos un* **prom** *es un baile de gala que se celebra para los alumnos de un centro de educación secundaria o universitaria. De todos estos bailes el más famoso es el* **senior prom**, *al que asisten los alumnos del último año de una* **high school** *y que se considera un acontecimiento de gran importancia para los adolescentes estadounidenses. Los alumnos acuden normalmente con su pareja y visten de etiqueta: esmoquin los chicos y traje de noche las chicas.*

promenade [ˌprɒmɪˈnɑːd] Ⓐ N [1] (= *act*) paseo *m*
[2] (= *avenue*) paseo *m*, avenida *f*
[3] (*at seaside*) paseo *m* marítimo
Ⓑ VI pasearse
Ⓒ VT pasear
Ⓓ CPD ► **promenade concert** N *concierto en el que una parte del público permanece de pie*
► **promenade deck** N cubierta *f* de paseo

Prometheus [prəˈmiːθjuːs] N Prometeo

prominence [ˈprɒmɪnəns] N [1] (= *importance*) importancia *f*; **to bring sth/sb to ~** hacer que algo/algn destaque *or* resalte; **to come (in)to** *or* **rise to ~** [*idea, subject*] adquirir importancia; [*person*] empezar a ser conocido; **he came to ~ in the Cuba affair** se le empezó a conocer cuando lo de Cuba; **to give ~ to sth** hacer que algo destaque *or* resalte
[2] (= *conspicuousness*) prominencia *f*; **it was set in bold type to give it ~** para que destacara, aparecía en negrita
[3] (= *hill*) prominencia *f*

prominent [ˈprɒmɪnənt] ADJ [1] (= *projecting*) [*nose*] prominente; [*cheekbones*] marcado, prominente; [*teeth*] salido, hacia fuera; [*eyes*] saltón
[2] (= *conspicuous*) destacado, prominente; **put it in a ~ place** ponlo en un lugar destacado *or* prominente, ponlo donde salte a la vista; **the question of Bosnia was very ~ in their minds** la cuestión de Bosnia estaba muy presente en sus mentes
[3] (= *important*) [*person*] destacado, prominente; [*position, role*] prominente, importante, destacado; **she is ~ in London society** es una figura destacada *or* prominente en la buena sociedad londinense; **to play a ~ part** *or* **role in sth** jugar un papel prominente *or* importante *or* destacado en algo

prominently [ˈprɒmɪnəntlɪ] ADV [1] (= *conspicuously*) **to display sth ~** exponer algo muy a la vista; **the newspapers had carried the story ~** los periódicos habían publicado la historia en grandes titulares
[2] (= *outstandingly*) **he figured ~ in the case** desempeñó un papel prominente *or* importante *or* destacado en el juicio

promiscuity [ˌprɒmɪsˈkjuːɪtɪ] N promiscuidad *f*

promiscuous [prəˈmɪskjʊəs] ADJ promiscuo

promiscuously [prəˈmɪskjʊəslɪ] ADV promiscuamente

promise [ˈprɒmɪs] Ⓐ N [1] (= *pledge*) promesa *f*; **a ~ is a ~** lo prometido es deuda; **~s, ~s!** (*iro*) ¡mucho prometer y poco hacer!; **is that a ~?** ¿me lo prometes?; **to break one's ~** no cumplir su promesa, faltar a su promesa; **to hold** *or* **keep sb to his ~** obligar a algn a cumplir su promesa, hacer que algn cumpla su promesa; **to keep a/one's ~** cumplir una/su promesa; **to make (sb) a ~** hacer una promesa (a algn); **I made him a ~ that I'd come and visit him** le hice la promesa de que *or* le prometí que vendría a visitarlo; **I might do it but I'm not making any ~s** puede que lo haga, pero no prometo nada; **~ of marriage** palabra *f* de matrimonio; **to release sb from his ~** absolver a algn de su promesa; **the party has received many ~s of support** al partido se le ha prometido mucho apoyo; *see also* **lick B**
[2] (= *hope, prospect*) **full of ~** muy prometedor; **she fulfilled** *or* **lived up to the ~ she'd shown in the '84 Olympics** demostró estar a la altura de lo que prometía en las Olimpiadas del 84; **America held (out) the ~ of a new life** América representaba la promesa de una nueva vida, América daba esperanzas de una nueva vida; **a young man of ~** un joven que promete; **she showed considerable ~ as a pianist** prometía mucho como pianista
Ⓑ VT [1] (= *pledge*) prometer; **the ~d aid had not been sent** no se había enviado la ayuda prometida; **to ~ (sb) that** prometer (a algn) que; **I ~d that I'd go** prometí que iría; **~ me you won't tell her** prométeme que no se lo dirás; **to ~ (sb) to do sth** prometer (a algn) hacer algo; **you must ~ me to do as I say** tienes que prometerme que harás lo que yo te diga; **he ~d faithfully to return it** dio su palabra de que lo devolvería; **I ~d myself I would go and visit her** me prometí que iría a visitarla; **buy that new dress you've been promising yourself** cómprate ese nuevo vestido que te habías hecho el propósito de comprarte; **she telephoned, as ~d** llamó, tal y como había prometido; **to ~ sb sth** ◊ **~ sth to sb** prometer dar algo a algn; ✦***IDIOMS*** **to ~ sb the earth** *or* **the moon** prometer el oro y el moro a algn; **the Promised Land** la Tierra Prometida
[2] (= *forecast, augur*) augurar; **their policies ~ little for the future** su política no augura un futuro muy prometedor; **those clouds ~ rain** esas nubes amenazan lluvia; **it ~s to be hot today** el día se presenta caluroso; **the debate ~s to be lively** el debate se presenta animado
[3] (= *assure*) prometer, jurar; **there's no-one here, I ~ you** no hay nadie aquí, te lo prometo *or* juro
Ⓒ VI [1] (= *pledge*) prometer; **"(do you) ~?" — "all right, I ~"** —¿lo prometes? —bueno, lo prometo; **I can't ~ but I'll try** no te prometo nada, pero haré lo que pueda; **"I can't make it" — "but you ~d!"** —no puedo —¡pero lo habías prometido!
[2] (= *augur*) **to ~ well**: **such a good beginning ~s well for the future** un principio tan bueno resulta muy prometedor *or* augura un buen futuro

promising [ˈprɒmɪsɪŋ] ADJ [*student*] prometedor; [*future, prospect*] esperanzador, halagüeño; **a ~ young man** un joven que promete; **two ~ candidates** dos candidatos buenos; **it doesn't look very ~** no promete mucho, no parece muy prometedor

promisingly [ˈprɒmɪsɪŋlɪ] ADV de manera prometedora; **United began ~, with a goal in the second minute** el United tuvo un principio prometedor, con un gol en el segundo minuto

promissory note [ˈprɒmɪsərɪˌnəʊt] N (*esp US*) pagaré *m*

promontory [ˈprɒməntrɪ] N promontorio *m*

promote [prəˈməʊt] VT [1] (*in rank*) [1·1] [+ *employee*] ascender; **to be ~d** ser ascendido; **I got ~d from editor to editorial director** me ascendieron de redactor a jefe de redacción
[1·2] (*Mil*) ascender; **he was ~d (to) colonel** *or* **to the rank of colonel** lo ascendieron a coronel
[1·3] (*Sport*) [+ *team*] ascender; **Tarifa was ~d to the first division** el Tarifa subió *or* ascendió a primera división
[1·4] (*US Scol*) [+ *pupil*] **I failed to get ~d and had to redo my year** no conseguí aprobar y tuve que repetir el curso
[2] (= *encourage*) [+ *trade, cooperation, peace*] promover, fomentar; [+ *growth*] estimular; [+ *sales, campaign, project, cause*] promover; (*Parl*)

[+ *bill*] presentar; **he has spent much of his fortune promoting the arts** ha gastado gran parte de su fortuna promoviendo las artes; **he was accused of promoting his own interests** se le acusó de promover sus propios intereses

3 (= *advertise*) [+ *product*] promocionar, dar publicidad a; **they will do a British tour to ~ their second album** harán una gira por Gran Bretaña para promocionar su segundo álbum; **the island is being ~d as a tourist destination** se está dando publicidad a la isla como centro de interés turístico

4 (= *organize, put on*) [+ *concert, event*] organizar

5 (*Chem*) [+ *reaction*] provocar

promoter [prəˈməʊtəʳ] N (*gen*) promotor(a) *m/f*; (= *backer*) patrocinador(a) *m/f*; (*Boxing*) empresario/a *m/f*

promotion [prəˈməʊʃən] Ⓐ N 1 (*in rank*) 1·1 [*of employee*] ascenso *m*, promoción *f*; **to get ~** ser ascendido (**to** a); **if I get ~, I have to move offices** si me ascienden, tengo que trasladarme de oficina; **to move up the ~ ladder** subir en el escalafón

1·2 (*Sport*) ascenso *m*; **they narrowly missed ~** por muy poco no han ascendido a otra división; **to win ~** ser promovido, ascender

1·3 (*US Scol*) ascenso *m*

2 (= *encouragement*) [*of trade, peace*] fomento *m*, promoción *f*; [*of campaign, project*] apoyo *m*

3 (= *organization*) [*of concert, event*] organización *f*

4 (= *publicity, advertising*) promoción *f*; (= *advertising campaign*) campaña *f* (de promoción); **special ~** oferta *f* de promoción; *see also* **sales B**

Ⓑ CPD ► **promotion prospects** NPL perspectivas *fpl* de ascenso ► **promotions manager** *or* **director** N director(a) *m/f* encargado/a de promoción

promotional [prəˈməʊʃənl] ADJ promocional, de promoción

prompt [prɒmpt] Ⓐ ADJ 1 (= *speedy*) [*delivery, reply, service*] rápido; **it is not too late, but ~ action is needed** no es demasiado tarde pero hay que actuar inmediatamente *or* es necesario tomar medidas inmediatas; **if it hadn't been for her ~ action, we would all have drowned** si no hubiera sido porque reaccionó con mucha rapidez, nos hubiéramos ahogado todos; **they were ~ to offer their services** ofrecieron sus servicios inmediatamente *or* rápidamente; **the company was ~ in its response to these accusations** la empresa reaccionó inmediatamente ante estas acusaciones, la empresa reaccionó con prontitud a estas acusaciones

2 (= *punctual*) puntual; **she is always ~ and efficient** siempre es puntual y eficiente; **please be ~** se ruega puntualidad; **there is a discount for ~ payment** se hace un descuento por prontitud en el pago

Ⓑ ADV [*start, arrive*] puntualmente; **at two o'clock ~** a las dos en punto

Ⓒ VT 1 (= *motivate*) empujar; **I was ~ed by a desire to see justice done** me movía el deseo de ver que se hiciera justicia; **to ~ sb to do sth** mover *or* incitar a algn a hacer algo; **what ~ed you to do it?** ¿qué te movió *or* incitó a hacerlo?; **I felt ~ed to protest** me vi forzado *or* empujado a protestar

2 (= *give rise to*) [+ *thought, question*] dar lugar a; [+ *reply, reaction, speculation*] provocar, dar lugar a; **it has ~ed questions about his suitability** ha dado lugar a que se cuestione su idoneidad; **what ~ed that question?** ¿cuál fue el motivo de esa pregunta?; **my choice was ~ed by a number of considerations** hay varias consideraciones que han influido en mi elección

3 (= *help with speech*) apuntar; **don't ~ her!** ¡no le apuntes!, ¡no le soples cosas al oído!*

4 (*Theat*) apuntar; **she had to be ~ed three times** tuvieron que apuntarle tres veces

Ⓓ VI (*Theat*) apuntar

Ⓔ N 1 (= *suggestion, reminder*) apunte *m*, palabra *f* clave (*que ayuda a recordar*)

2 (*Theat*) (= *person*) apuntador(a) *m/f*; **to give sb a ~** apuntar a algn; **I had to be given a ~** me tuvieron que apuntar

3 (*Comput*) aviso *m*

Ⓕ CPD ► **prompt box** N (*Theat*) concha *f* (del apuntador) ► **prompt side** N (*Theat*) lado *m* izquierdo (del actor)

prompter [ˈprɒmptəʳ] N (*Theat*) apuntador(a) *m/f*

prompting [ˈprɒmptɪŋ] N **without ~** (*lit*) sin tener que consultar el texto; (= *on one's own initiative*) por iniciativa propia, motu propio; **the ~s of conscience** los escrúpulos de la conciencia

promptitude [ˈprɒmptɪtjuːd] N = **promptness**

promptly [ˈprɒmptlɪ] ADV (= *immediately*) inmediatamente; (= *fast*) [*pay, deliver, reply*] rápidamente, con prontitud; (= *punctually*) [*start, arrive*] en punto, puntualmente; **they left ~ at six** partieron a las seis en punto; **he flopped onto the sofa and ~ fell asleep** se dejó caer en el sofá y se durmió inmediatamente

promptness [ˈprɒmptnɪs] N (= *punctuality*) puntualidad *f*; (= *speed*) rapidez *f*, prontitud *f*

promulgate [ˈprɒməlgeɪt] VT [+ *law, decree, constitution*] promulgar; [+ *idea, doctrine*] promulgar

promulgation [ˌprɒməlˈgeɪʃən] N [*of law, decree, constitution*] promulgación *f*; [*of idea, doctrine*] promulgación *f*

prone [prəʊn] ADJ 1 (= *face down*) **to be ~** estar postrado (boca abajo)

2 (= *liable*) **to be ~ to do sth** ser propenso *or* tener tendencia a hacer algo; **to be ~ to sth** ser propenso a algo

proneness [ˈprəʊnnɪs] N propensión *f*, predisposición *f* (**to** a)

prong [prɒŋ] N [*of fork*] punta *f*, diente *m*

-pronged [prɒŋd] ADJ (*ending in compounds*) **three-pronged** [*fork*] de tres puntas *or* dientes; [*attack*] por tres flancos

pronominal [prəʊˈnɒmɪnl] ADJ pronominal

pronoun [ˈprəʊnaʊn] N (*Ling*) pronombre *m*

pronounce [prəˈnaʊns] Ⓐ VT 1 [+ *letter, word*] pronunciar; **how do you ~ it?** ¿cómo se pronuncia?; **the "k" in "knee" is not ~d** la "k" de "knee" no se pronuncia

2 (= *declare*) declarar; **they ~d him unfit to plead** lo declararon incapaz de defenderse; **he was ~d dead** se dictaminó que estaba muerto; **"I now ~ you man and wife"** —y ahora os declaro marido y mujer; **to ~ o.s. for/against sth** declararse a favor de/en contra de algo; **to ~ sentence** (*Jur*) pronunciar *or* dictar sentencia

Ⓑ VI **to ~ in favour of/against sth** pronunciarse a favor de/en contra de algo; **to ~ on sth** pronunciarse sobre algo

pronounceable [prəˈnaʊnsəbl] ADJ pronunciable

pronounced [prəˈnaʊnst] ADJ (= *marked*) [*tendency, influence*] marcado; [*limp*] fuerte, pronunciado; [*accent*] fuerte

pronouncement [prəˈnaʊnsmənt] N declaración *f*

pronto* [ˈprɒntəʊ] ADV en seguida

pronunciation [prəˌnʌnsɪˈeɪʃən] N pronunciación *f*

proof [pruːf] Ⓐ N 1 (= *evidence*) prueba(s) *f(pl)*; **do you have any ~ of this?** ¿tienes pruebas de esto?; **it is ~ that he is innocent** eso prueba su inocencia; **as (a)** *or* **in ~ of** como *or* en prueba de; **the burden of ~ is** *or* **falls on him** sobre él recae la tarea de demostrar su inocencia; **by way of ~** a modo de prueba; **to give** *or* **show ~ of sth/that …** demostrar algo/que …; **you will need ~ of identity** necesitará algo que acredite su identidad; **to be living ~ of sth** ser prueba viviente de algo; **~ positive** prueba *f* concluyente; **to obtain a refund you must produce ~ of purchase** para cualquier devolución necesitará el comprobante de compra

2 (= *test, trial*) prueba *f*; **to put sth to the ~** poner algo a prueba; ✦***PROV* the ~ of the pudding (is in the eating)** para saber si algo es bueno hay que probarlo

3 (*Typ, Phot*) prueba *f*; **to correct** *or* **read the ~s** corregir las pruebas; *see also* **galley B, page[1] B**

4 [*of alcohol*] graduación *f* (alcohólica); **it is 70 degrees ~** tiene una graduación del 40%; (*US*) tiene una graduación del 35%; **over ~** con una graduación alcohólica superior al 57,1%; **under** *or* **below ~** con una graduación alcohólica inferior al 57,1%

5 (= *security, safeguard*) protección *f* (**against** contra); **knowledge is no ~ against certain kinds of disaster** el saber no es protección contra ciertas clases de desastre

6 (*Math, Geom*) prueba *f*

Ⓑ ADJ 1 [*alcohol*] de graduación normal

2 (= *secure*) **to be ~ against sth** estar a prueba de algo; **it is ~ against moisture** está a prueba de la humedad; **I'm not ~ against temptation** no soy insensible a la tentación

Ⓒ VT 1 [+ *fabric, tent*] impermeabilizar

2 (= *proofread*) corregir las pruebas de

Ⓓ CPD ► **proof copy** N copia *f* para la lectura de pruebas ► **proof sheet** N (*Typ, Phot*) prueba *f* ► **proof spirit** N (*Brit, Canada*) licor *m* de graduación normal ► **proof stage** N fase *f* de lectura de pruebas; **to be at ~ stage** estar en la fase de lectura de pruebas

-proof [pruːf] ADJ (*ending in compounds*) **bomb~** a prueba de bombas; **bullet~** a prueba de balas; **inflation~ pension** pensión *f* que no se ve afectada por la inflación; *see also* **childproof, fireproof, foolproof** *etc*

proofread [ˈpruːfriːd] (*pt, pp* **proofread** [ˈpruːfred]) VT corregir las pruebas de

proofreader [ˈpruːfˌriːdəʳ] N corrector(a) *m/f* de pruebas

proofreading [ˈpruːfˌriːdɪŋ] N corrección *f* de pruebas

prop[1] [prɒp] Ⓐ N 1 (*lit*) (*Archit, Min*) puntal *m*; (*for clothesline*) palo *m*; (*Naut*) escora *f*; (*) (*Aer*) (*also* **propeller**) hélice *f*; (*Rugby*) (*also* **~ forward**) pilier *m*; (*Theat*) (*also* **property**) accesorio *m*; **props** accesorios *mpl*, at(t)rezzo *msing*

2 (*fig*) sostén *m*, apoyo *m*

Ⓑ VT (= *support*) apuntalar; (= *rest, lean*) apoyar; (*fig*) sostener, apoyar; **to ~ a ladder against a wall** apoyar una escalera contra una pared; **the door was ~ped open with a bucket** habían puesto un cubo para que no se cerrara la puerta

Ⓒ CPD ► **prop shaft*** N (*Aer*) (*also* **propeller shaft**) árbol *m* de la hélice

►**prop up** VT + ADV [1] (*lit*) [+ *roof, structure*] apuntalar; **I ~ped him up with pillows** le puse almohadas para que se recostara; **she ~ped herself up on one elbow** se enderezó apoyándose en el codo; **he can usually be found ~ping up the bar** (*hum*) te lo encuentras siempre en el bar empinando el codo*
[2] (*fig*) [+ *economy, currency, regime*] respaldar; **the company was ~ped up by a big loan** la compañía recibió el apoyo *or* el respaldo de un préstamo cuantioso, se respaldó a la compañía con un préstamo cuantioso

prop² ABBR (*Comm*) = **proprietor**

propaganda [ˌprɒpəˈgændə] Ⓐ N propaganda *f*
Ⓑ CPD [*leaflet, campaign*] de propaganda

propagandist [ˌprɒpəˈgændɪst] N propagandista *mf*

propagandize [prɒpəˈgændaɪz] Ⓐ VT [+ *doctrine*] propagar; [+ *person*] hacer propaganda a
Ⓑ VI hacer propaganda

propagate [ˈprɒpəgeɪt] Ⓐ VT propagar
Ⓑ VI propagarse

propagation [ˌprɒpəˈgeɪʃən] N propagación *f*

propane [ˈprəʊpeɪn] N propano *m*

propel [prəˈpel] VT [+ *vehicle, rocket*] impulsar, propulsar; **to ~ sth/sb along** impulsar algo/a algn; **they ~led him into the room** lo llevaron dentro de la habitación; (*more violently*) lo metieron en la habitación de un empujón

propellant, **propellent** [prəˈpelənt] N propulsor *m*; (= *aerosol etc*) propelente *m*

propeller [prəˈpeləʳ] Ⓐ N hélice *f*
Ⓑ CPD ► **propeller shaft** N (*Aer*) árbol *m* de la hélice; (*Aut*) árbol *m or* eje *m* de transmisión; (*Naut*) eje *m* portahélice

propelling pencil [prəˈpelɪŋˈpensl] N lapicero *m*, portaminas *m inv*

propensity [prəˈpensɪtɪ] N propensión *f* (**to** a)

proper [ˈprɒpəʳ] Ⓐ ADJ [1] (= *right, suitable*) [*equipment, tools*] apropiado, adecuado; **that's not really the ~ tool for the job** ésa no es la herramienta apropiada *or* adecuada para el trabajo; **at the ~ time** en el momento oportuno; **that's not the ~ way to do it** así no se hace; **you'll have to apply for a permit in the ~ way** tendrás que solicitar el permiso por las vías establecidas
[2] (= *correct*) **it was the ~ thing to say** fue lo que había que decir; **do as you think ~** haz lo que te parezca bien; **I thought it ~ to inform you** pensé que debía informarte; *see also* **right A1**
[3] (= *actual, real*) propiamente dicho; **in the city ~** en la ciudad propiamente dicha, en la ciudad en sí; **he's never had a ~ job** nunca ha tenido un trabajo serio; **forget nouvelle cuisine, give me ~ food, any day** olvida la nueva cocina, dame todos los días comida como Dios manda; **in the ~ sense of the word** en el sentido estricto de la palabra
[4] (*) (= *complete, downright*) verdadero; **I felt a ~ idiot** me sentí como un perfecto *or* verdadero idiota; **we got a ~ beating** nos dieron una paliza de las buenas
[5] (= *seemly*) [*person, behaviour*] correcto; **it wasn't considered ~ for a man to show his emotions** no se consideraba correcto *or* no estaba bien visto que un hombre mostrase sus emociones
[6] (= *prim and proper*) correcto y formal
[7] (= *peculiar, characteristic*) propio (**to** de)
Ⓑ ADV (*Brit**) **he was ~ upset about it** estaba verdaderamente *or* realmente disgustado por ello; **she's a ~ stuck-up young lady** es una joven bien creída; *see also* **good A19**
Ⓒ CPD ► **proper fraction** N (*Math*) fracción *f* propia ► **proper name**, **proper noun** N nombre *m* propio

properly [ˈprɒpəlɪ] ADV [1] (= *suitably, adequately*) adecuadamente, apropiadamente; **the staff are not ~ trained** el personal no está adecuadamente *or* apropiadamente capacitado; **not ~ dressed** (*for occasion*) no vestido de la manera adecuada; (*for activity*) no vestido de la manera apropiada; **I had not eaten ~ for the past few days** hacía unos días que no comía como es debido
[2] (= *correctly*) [*function, work*] bien; **sit up ~!** (*to child*) ¡siéntate como es debido!; **if you don't sit up ~ you can damage your back** si no te sientas correctamente, puedes fastidiarte la espalda; **if you can't behave ~ I'll have to take you home** si no te portas bien, tendremos que irnos a casa; **to do sth ~** hacer algo bien *or* como es debido; **we haven't got the money to do the job ~** no tenemos dinero para hacer bien el trabajo *or* para hacer el trabajo como es debido; **~ speaking** hablando con propiedad, propiamente dicho; **the process is not ~ understood** no se sabe exactamente en qué consiste el proceso
[3] (= *in seemly fashion*) correctamente; **to behave ~** portarse correctamente; **she very ~ refused** se negó a ello e hizo bien
[4] (*) (= *really, thoroughly*) verdaderamente; **we were ~ ashamed/puzzled** estábamos verdaderamente avergonzados/confundidos

propertied [ˈprɒpətɪd] ADJ adinerado, acaudalado; **the ~ classes** la clase acaudalada

property [ˈprɒpətɪ] Ⓐ N [1] (= *possession*) propiedad *f*; **whose ~ is this?** ¿de quién es esto?, ¿a quién pertenece esto?; **it doesn't seem to be anyone's ~** no parece que tenga dueño; **she left her ~ to her daughter** dejó sus bienes a su hija; **common ~** propiedad *f* de todos; **government ~** propiedad *f* del gobierno; **personal ~** efectos *mpl or* objetos *mpl* personales; **you treat me as your personal ~** me tratas como si fuera de tu propiedad; **public ~** (= *land*) bien *m* público; **her success made her public ~ overnight** su éxito la convirtió en un personaje público de la noche a la mañana; **that news is public ~** eso lo saben todos ya, esa noticia es ya del dominio público; **he was charged with receiving stolen ~** se le acusó de comerciar con objetos robados; *see also* **intellectual C**, **lost C**
[2] (= *land*) [2·1] (= *piece of land*) propiedad *f*, terreno *m*; **get off my ~** salga de mi propiedad; **"private property"** "propiedad *f* privada"
[2·2] (= *real estate*) propiedades *fpl*; **he owns ~ in Ireland** tiene propiedades en Irlanda; **a man/woman of ~** un hombre/una mujer acomodado/a; *see also* **real D**
[3] (= *building*) propiedad *f*, inmueble *m*
[4] (= *ownership*) propiedad *f*
[5] (= *phenomenon*) fenómeno *m*, estrella *f*; **he has become the hottest ~ in football** se ha convertido en el fenómemo futbolístico más importante
[6] (*Theat*) accesorio *m*; **properties** accesorios *mpl*, at(t)rezzo *msing*
[7] (= *quality*) (*gen pl*) propiedad *f*; **this plant has healing properties** esta planta tiene propiedades curativas
Ⓑ CPD ► **property company** N compañía *f* inmobiliaria ► **property developer** N promotor(a) *m/f* inmobiliario/a ► **property insurance** N seguro *m* inmobiliario ► **property law** N ley *f* de la propiedad inmobiliaria ► **property manager** N (*Theat*) accesorista *mf*, at(t)rezzista *mf* ► **property market**, **property mart** N mercado *m* inmobiliario ► **property mistress** N (*Theat*) accesorista *f*, at(t)rezzista *f* ► **property owner** N (*rural*) terrateniente *mf*; (*urban*) dueño/a *m/f* de propiedades ► **property page(s)** N(PL) sección *f* de ventas de inmuebles y viviendas (*de un periódico*) ► **property rights** NPL derechos *mpl* sobre la propiedad ► **property speculation** N especulación *f* inmobiliaria ► **property speculator** N especulador(a) *m/f* inmobiliario/a ► **property tax** N impuesto *m* sobre la propriedad

prophecy [ˈprɒfɪsɪ] N profecía *f*

prophesy [ˈprɒfɪsaɪ] VT (= *foretell*) profetizar; (= *predict*) predecir, vaticinar

prophet [ˈprɒfɪt] N profeta *m*; **a ~ of doom** (*fig*) un(a) catastrofista, un(a) agorero/a*

prophetess [ˈprɒfɪtɪs] N profetisa *f*

prophetic [prəˈfetɪk] ADJ profético

prophetically [prəˈfetɪkəlɪ] ADV proféticamente

prophylactic [ˌprɒfɪˈlæktɪk] Ⓐ ADJ profiláctico
Ⓑ N (= *contraceptive*) profiláctico *m*

prophylaxis [ˌprɒfɪˈlæksɪs] N profilaxis *f*

propinquity [prəˈpɪŋkwɪtɪ] N (*frm*) (= *nearness*) propincuidad *f*; (= *kinship*) consanguinidad *f*, parentesco *m*

propitiate [prəˈpɪʃɪeɪt] VT propiciar

propitiation [prəˌpɪʃɪˈeɪʃən] N propiciación *f*

propitiatory [prəˈpɪʃɪətərɪ] ADJ propiciatorio, conciliatorio

propitious [prəˈpɪʃəs] ADJ propicio, favorable

propitiously [prəˈpɪʃəslɪ] ADV de modo propicio, bajo signo propicio, favorablemente

proponent [prəˈpəʊnənt] N defensor(a) *m/f*

proportion [prəˈpɔːʃən] Ⓐ N [1] (= *ratio*) proporción *f*; **the ~ of blacks to whites** la proporción entre negros y blancos; **in/out of ~** proporcionado/desproporcionado; **to be in/out of ~ (to one another)** estar en/no guardar proporción (el uno con el otro); **to be in/out of ~ to** *or* **with sth** estar en/no guardar proporción con algo; **and the rest in ~** y lo demás en proporción; (*Comm*) y lo demás a prorrata; **in due ~** en su justa medida; **in ~ as** a medida que; **to see sth in ~** (*fig*) ver algo en su justa medida; **it has been magnified out of all ~** (*fig*) se ha exagerado mucho; **sense of ~** (*fig*) sentido *m* de la medida
[2] (= *part, amount*) parte *f*; **in equal ~s** por partes iguales; **what ~ is in private hands?** ¿qué porción queda en manos de particulares?
[3] **proportions** (= *size*) dimensiones *fpl*
Ⓑ VT **to ~ sth to sth** [+ *charge, cost*] adecuar algo a algo; **well-~ed** [*room*] de buenas proporciones; [*woman's figure*] bien proporcionado; [*man's figure*] bien armado

proportional [prəˈpɔːʃənl] Ⓐ ADJ proporcional (**to** a), en proporción (**to** con); **X is not ~ to Y** X no guarda proporción con Y
Ⓑ CPD ► **proportional representation** N (*Pol*) representación *f* proporcional ► **proportional spacing** N (*on printer*) espaciado *m* proporcional

proportionality [ˌprəpɔːʃəˈnælɪtɪ] N proporcionalidad *f*

proportionally [prəˈpɔːʃnəlɪ] ADV proporcionalmente

proportionate [prəˈpɔːʃnɪt] ADJ proporcionado (**to** a)

proportionately [prəˈpɔːʃnɪtlɪ] ADV proporcionadamente, en proporción

proposal [prəˈpəʊzl] N [1] (= *offer, suggestion*) (*gen*) propuesta *f*, proposición *f*; (= *written submission*) propuesta *f*; **they have rejected the latest peace ~** han rechazado la última propuesta de paz; **to make sb an indecent ~** hacer una proposición deshonesta a algn; **let me make a ~** permítame hacer una propuesta *or* proposición; **I made the ~ that we should adjourn the meeting** propuse que levantásemos la sesión; **to put forward a ~** presentar una propuesta; **an advert asking for writers to submit ~s for a new TV series** un anuncio pidiendo a los escritores que mandaran propuestas para una nueva serie televisiva

2 (*also* **~ of marriage**) proposición *f* de matrimonio, propuesta *f* de matrimonio

propose [prəˈpəʊz] Ⓐ VT 1 (= *suggest*) 1·1 (*gen*) proponer; **the idea was first ~d in 1789** la idea se propuso por primera vez en 1789; **what do you ~?** ¿qué propones?; **to ~ sth to sb** proponer algo a algn; **to ~ doing sth**: **I ~ writing her a letter** (= *I suggest I write*) me propongo escribirle una carta; (= *I suggest that someone writes*) yo propongo que se le escriba una carta; **to ~ that** proponer que + *subjun*; **I ~ that we go and see her** propongo que vayamos a verla

1·2 (*in meeting, parliament*) [+ *amendment*] proponer; [+ *motion*] presentar

1·3 **to ~ marriage to sb** proponer a algn en matrimonio, hacer una proposición *or* propuesta de matrimonio a algn

1·4 **to ~ sb's health** beber a la salud de algn, brindar por algn; **to ~ a toast (to sb)** proponer un brindis (por algn)

2 (= *nominate*) **he ~d Smith as** *or* **for chairman** propuso a Smith como presidente; **to ~ sb for membership of a club** proponer a algn como socio de un club

3 (= *intend*) **to ~ to do sth** ◊ **~ doing sth** pensar hacer algo; **I do not ~ to discuss this matter any further** no pienso hablar más de este asunto; **what do you ~ doing?** ¿qué piensas hacer?

Ⓑ VI 1 (= *offer marriage*) **to ~ to sb** proponer a algn en matrimonio, hacer una proposición de matrimonio a algn; **have you ~d yet?** ¿le has propuesto en matrimonio ya?, ¿le has hecho una proposición de matrimonio ya?

2 ✦ *PROV* **man ~s, God disposes** el hombre propone y Dios dispone

proposed [prəˈpəʊzd] ADJ **the ~ motorway** la autopista que se propone, la autopista propuesta; **your ~ solution** la solución que propusiste

proposer [prəˈpəʊzəʳ] N [*of motion*] proponente *mf*

proposition [ˌprɒpəˈzɪʃən] Ⓐ N 1 (= *proposal*) proposición *f*, propuesta *f*; **to make sb a ~** proponer algo a algn

2 (= *enterprise*) proposición *f*; **working as a freelance can be an attractive ~** trabajar por cuenta propia puede ser una proposición atractiva; **economically, it is not a viable ~** desde el punto de vista económico, no es una proposición viable

3 (= *opponent*) adversario/a *m/f*, contrincante *mf*; **he's a tough ~** es un adversario *or* contrincante fuerte

4 (*sexual*) **she had received a number of unwanted sexual ~s** había sido objeto de varias proposiciones sexuales no deseadas

5 (*Math, Logic*) proposición *f*

Ⓑ VT hacer proposiciones deshonestas a

propound [prəˈpaʊnd] VT (*frm*) [+ *ideas etc*] exponer, plantear

proprietary [prəˈpraɪətərɪ] Ⓐ ADJ propietario; (*Comm*) patentado

Ⓑ CPD ► **proprietary brand** N marca *f* comercial ► **proprietary goods** NPL artículos *mpl* de marca ► **proprietary interest** N interés *m* patrimonial ► **proprietary name** N nombre *m* propietario

proprietor [prəˈpraɪətəʳ] N [*of shop, hotel etc*] dueño/a *m/f*; [*of land*] propietario/a *m/f*

proprietorial [prəˌpraɪəˈtɔːrɪəl] ADJ [*attitude etc*] protector

proprietorship [prəˈpraɪətəʃɪp] N propiedad *f*, posesión *f*

proprietress [prəˈpraɪətrɪs] N [*of shop, hotel etc*] dueña *f*

propriety [prəˈpraɪətɪ] N 1 (= *decency*) decoro *m*, decencia *f*; **breach of ~** ofensa *f* contra el decoro, incorrección *f*; **the proprieties** los cánones sociales; **to observe the proprieties** atenerse a los cánones sociales

2 (= *appropriateness*) conveniencia *f*

propulsion [prəˈpʌlʃən] N propulsión *f*; *see also* **jet D**

pro rata [ˌprəʊˈrɑːtə] Ⓐ ADV a prorrateo; **the money will be shared out ~** el dinero será repartido a prorrateo, se prorrateará el dinero

Ⓑ ADJ a prorrateo; **a ~ agreement** (*US*) un acuerdo a prorrateo

prorate [ˈprəʊreɪt] (*US*) Ⓐ N prorrata *f*

Ⓑ VT prorratear

prorogation [ˌprəʊrəˈgeɪʃən] N prorrogación *f*

prorogue [prəˈrəʊg] VT prorrogar

prosaic [prəʊˈzeɪɪk] ADJ (= *dull*) prosaico

prosaically [prəʊˈzeɪɪkəlɪ] ADV prosaicamente

Pros. Atty. ABBR (*US*) = **prosecuting attorney**

proscenium [prəʊˈsiːnɪəm] Ⓐ N (*pl* **prosceniums** *or* **proscenia** [prəʊˈsiːnɪə]) proscenio *m*

Ⓑ CPD ► **proscenium arch** N embocadura *f* ► **proscenium box** N palco *m* de proscenio

proscribe [prəʊsˈkraɪb] VT proscribir

proscription [prəʊsˈkrɪpʃən] N proscripción *f*

prose [prəʊz] Ⓐ N 1 (*Literat*) prosa *f*

2 (*Scol*) (*also* **~ translation**) texto *m* para traducir; (*also* **~ composition**) traducción *f* inversa

Ⓑ CPD ► **prose poem** N poema *m* en prosa ► **prose writer** N prosista *mf*

prosecute [ˈprɒsɪkjuːt] Ⓐ VT 1 (*Jur*) (= *try*) procesar, enjuiciar; (= *punish*) sancionar; [+ *claim*] demandar en juicio; [+ *case*] llevar a los tribunales; **to ~ sb for theft** procesar a algn por robo; **to be ~d for a traffic offence** ser procesado por una infracción de tráfico; **"trespassers will be prosecuted"** "se procederá contra los intrusos"; **the lawyer who will ~ the case** el/la fiscal

2 (*frm*) (= *carry on*) proseguir, llevar adelante

Ⓑ VI (*Jur*) interponer una acción judicial; **prosecuting attorney** (*US*) fiscal *mf*; **prosecuting counsel** (*Brit*) fiscal *mf*

prosecution [ˌprɒsɪˈkjuːʃən] Ⓐ N 1 (*Jur*) (= *act, proceedings*) proceso *m*, juicio *m*; (*in court*) (= *case, side*) acusación *f*; **counsel for the ~** fiscal *mf*; **to bring** *or* **start a ~ against sb** entablar juicio *or* una acción judicial contra algn

2 (*frm*) (= *furtherance*) prosecución *f*; **in the ~ of his duty** en el cumplimiento de su deber

Ⓑ CPD ► **prosecution witness** N testigo *mf* de cargo

prosecutor [ˈprɒsɪkjuːtəʳ] N (*Jur*) abogado/a *m/f* de la acusación; (*also* **public ~**) fiscal *mf*

proselyte [ˈprɒsɪlaɪt] Ⓐ N prosélito/a *m/f*

Ⓑ VT, VI (*US*) = **proselytize**

proselytism [ˈprɒsɪlɪtɪzəm] N proselitismo *m*

proselytize [ˈprɒsɪlɪtaɪz] Ⓐ VI ganar prosélitos

Ⓑ VT [+ *person*] convertir

prosody [ˈprɒsədɪ] N métrica *f*

prospect Ⓐ [ˈprɒspekt] N 1 (= *outlook*) perspectiva *f*; **it was a daunting/pleasant ~** era una perspectiva desalentadora/agradable; **the ~s look grim** las perspectivas son desalentadoras; **~s for the harvest are poor** el panorama se anuncia más bien negro para la cosecha; **she was excited at the ~ of the China trip** estaba entusiasmada con la perspectiva de irse a China; **he was terrified at the ~** la perspectiva le aterraba; **to face the ~ of sth** ◊ **be faced with the ~ of sth** verse ante la perspectiva de algo; **faced with the ~ of bankruptcy he committed suicide** ante la perspectiva de la ruina, se suicidó; **in ~** en perspectiva; **to have sth in ~** tener algo en perspectiva

2 (= *possibility*) posibilidad *f*; **the job held out the ~ of rapid promotion** el trabajo ofrecía la posibilidad de ascender con rapidez; **there is little ~ of his coming** hay pocas posibilidades de que venga; **he has little ~ of success/of succeeding** tiene pocas posibilidades de tener éxito; **I see no ~ of that (happening)** eso no lo creo probable; **he didn't relish the ~ of having to look for another job** no le entusiasmaba la posibilidad de tener que buscar otro trabajo

3 **prospects** (= *future possibilities*) porvenir *m*, futuro *m*; **a job with no ~s** un trabajo sin porvenir, un trabajo sin (perspectivas de) futuro; **what are his ~s?** ¿qué perspectivas de futuro tiene?; **job/promotion ~s** perspectivas *fpl* de trabajo/ascenso; **future ~s** perspectivas *fpl* de futuro; **she has good ~s** tiene buen porvenir *or* un buen futuro

4 (†) (= *view*) panorama *m*, vista *f*; **a ~ of Toledo** un panorama de Toledo, una vista de Toledo

5 (= *prospective candidate, champion, etc*) **the company is not an attractive ~ for shareholders** la empresa no representa una opción *or* posibilidad atractiva para los accionistas; **the man who is Britain's best ~ for a gold medal in the Olympics** el hombre que tiene mayores posibilidades de conseguir una medalla de oro para Gran Bretaña en las Olimpiadas; **Steve is a great ~ for the future of British chess** Steve promete muchísimo para el futuro del ajedrez británico; **a salesman who considers everybody a ~** un vendedor que considera a todo el mundo como un potencial comprador

6 (= *marriage partner*) partido *m*; **he's/she's not much of a ~ for her/him** no es muy buen partido para ella/él

7 (*Min*) *zona donde es probable que haya yacimientos de minerales*

Ⓑ [prəsˈpekt] VT [+ *area, land*] hacer prospecciones en, prospectar

Ⓒ [prəsˈpekt] VI hacer prospecciones, prospectar; **oil companies are ~ing near here** las compañías petrolíferas están haciendo prospecciones *or* prospectando cerca de aquí; **to ~ for gold** buscar oro

prospecting [prəsˈpektɪŋ] N (*Min*) prospección *f*

prospective [prəsˈpektɪv] ADJ 1 (= *likely, possible*) [*customer, candidate*] posible

2 (= *future*) [*son-in-law, home, legislation*] futuro; [*heir*] presunto

prospector [prəsˈpektəʳ] N buscador(a) *m/f*, cateador(a) *m/f* (*LAm*); **gold ~** buscador(a) *m/f* de oro; **oil ~s** prospectores *mpl* petroleros

prospectus [prəsˈpektəs] N prospecto *m*

prosper [ˈprɒspəʳ] Ⓐ VI prosperar, medrar

Ⓑ VT (*frm*) favorecer, fomentar

prosperity [prɒsˈperɪtɪ] N prosperidad *f*

▼**prosperous** ['prɒspərəs] ADJ próspero

prosperously ['prɒspərəslɪ] ADV prósperamente

prostaglandin [ˌprɒstə'glændɪn] N prostaglandina *f*

prostate ['prɒsteɪt] N (*also* **~ gland**) próstata *f*

prosthesis [prɒs'θiːsɪs] N (*pl* **prostheses** [prɒs'θiːsiːz]) prótesis *f*

prosthetic [prɒs'θetɪk] ADJ prostético

prostitute ['prɒstɪtjuːt] Ⓐ N prostituto/a *m/f*; **to become a ~** prostituirse
Ⓑ VT (*fig*) prostituir; **to ~ o.s.** prostituirse

prostitution [ˌprɒstɪ'tjuːʃən] N (*lit, fig*) prostitución *f*

prostrate Ⓐ ['prɒstreɪt] ADJ [1] (*lit*) boca abajo, postrado; (*Bot*) procumbente
[2] (*fig*) [*nation, country etc*] abatido; (= *exhausted*) postrado, abatido (**with** por)
Ⓑ [prɒs'treɪt] VT (*lit*) postrar; (*fig*) postrar, abatir; **to be ~d by grief** estar postrado por el dolor; **to ~ o.s.** (*lit, fig*) postrarse

prostration [prɒs'treɪʃən] N postración *f*; (*fig*) postración *f*, abatimiento *m*

prosy ['prəʊzɪ] ADJ (*compar* **prosier**; *superl* **prosiest**) prosaico, aburrido, monótono

Prot*, **prot*** [prɒt] N ABBR (*pej*) = **Protestant**

protagonist [prəʊ'tægənɪst] N protagonista *mf*

protean ['prəʊtɪən] ADJ proteico

protect [prə'tekt] VT proteger (**against** contra; **from** de); **~ed species** especie *f* protegida

protection [prə'tekʃən] Ⓐ N [1] (*gen*) protección *f*, amparo *m*; **to be under sb's ~** estar bajo la protección de algn, estar amparado por algn
[2] (*Insurance, Ind, Jur*) protección *f*; **the policy offers ~ against ...** la póliza protege contra ...
[3] (= *contraception*) anticonceptivo *m*; **they didn't use any ~** no usaron ningún anticonceptivo, no se han cuidado
Ⓑ CPD ► **protection factor** N [*of sun cream*] factor *m* de protección ► **protection money** N **he pays 200 dollars a week ~ money** paga 200 dólares de protección a la semana ► **protection racket** N chantaje *m*

protectionism [prə'tekʃənɪzəm] N proteccionismo *m*

protectionist [prə'tekʃənɪst] Ⓐ ADJ proteccionista
Ⓑ N proteccionista *mf*

protective [prə'tektɪv] Ⓐ ADJ [1] (*physically*) [*layer, covering*] protector; [*clothing*] de protección
[2] (*emotionally*) [*attitude, gesture*] protector; **Becky's fiercely ~ father, John** John, el padre de Becky, que tiene/tenía una actitud terriblemente protectora hacia ella; **to be ~ of sth** proteger algo; **to be/feel ~ towards** *or* **of sb** tener una actitud protectora hacia algn; **he's very ~ towards his little sister** tiene una actitud muy protectora hacia su hermanita, protege mucho a su hermanita
[3] (*Econ*) [*tariffs*] proteccionista
Ⓑ CPD ► **protective cream** N crema *f* protectora ► **protective custody** N detención *f* preventiva

protectively [prə'tektɪvlɪ] ADV en actitud protectora, en actitud de protección

protectiveness [prə'tektɪvnɪs] N actitud *f* protectora

protector [prə'tektəʳ] N [1] (= *defender*) protector(a) *m/f*
[2] (= *protective wear*) protector *m*

protectorate [prə'tektərɪt] N protectorado *m*

protectress [prə'tektrɪs] N protectora *f*

protégé ['prɒteʒeɪ] N protegido *m*, ahijado *m*

protégée ['prɒteʒeɪ] N protegida *f*, ahijada *f*

protein ['prəʊtiːn] Ⓐ N proteína *f*
Ⓑ CPD ► **protein content** N contenido *m* proteínico

protein-rich ['prəʊtiːnrɪtʃ] ADJ rico en contenido proteínico

pro tem ['prəʊ'tem], **pro tempore**† ['prəʊ'tempərɪ] Ⓐ ADV provisionalmente; **he's replacing the chairman ~** sustituye provisionalmente al presidente
Ⓑ ADJ interino; **the ~ chairman** el presidente interino; **on a ~ basis** de manera provisional

▼**protest** Ⓐ ['prəʊtest] N (*gen*) protesta *f*; (= *complaint*) queja *f*; **under ~** bajo protesta; **I'll do it but under ~** lo haré pero que conste mi protesta; **to make a ~** hacer una protesta
Ⓑ [prə'test] VT [1] (= *complain*) protestar; **to ~ that** protestar diciendo que
[2] (*US*) (= *complain about*) protestar de
[3] (= *dispute*) poner reparos a
[4] (= *affirm*) [+ *one's love*] declarar, afirmar; **he ~ed his innocence** declaró enérgicamente su inocencia
Ⓒ [prə'test] VI protestar; **to ~ at** *or* **against** protestar de
Ⓓ ['prəʊtest] CPD ► **protest demonstration**, **protest march** N manifestación *f* *or* marcha *f* (de protesta) ► **protest movement** N movimiento *m* de protesta, movimiento *m* contestatario ► **protest song** N canción *f* (de) protesta ► **protest vote** N voto *m* de protesta

Protestant ['prɒtɪstənt] Ⓐ ADJ protestante
Ⓑ N protestante *mf*

Protestantism ['prɒtɪstəntɪzəm] N protestantismo *m*

protestation [ˌprɒtes'teɪʃən] N [1] (= *affirmation*) [*of love, loyalty etc*] afirmación *f*, declaración *f*
[2] (= *protest*) protesta *f*

protester, **protestor** [prə'testəʳ] N protestador(a) *m/f*; (*on march, in demonstration etc*) manifestante *mf*

proto... ['prəʊtəʊ] PREFIX proto...

protocol ['prəʊtəkɒl] N protocolo *m*

proton ['prəʊtɒn] N protón *m*

protoplasm ['prəʊtəʊplæzəm] N protoplasma *m*

prototype ['prəʊtəʊtaɪp] N prototipo *m*

prototypical [ˌprəʊtə'tɪpɪkəl] ADJ prototípico

protozoan [ˌprəʊtə'zəʊən] Ⓐ N (*pl* **protozoa** [ˌprəʊtə'zəʊə]) (*Bio*) protozoo *m*
Ⓑ ADJ protozoico

protozoon [ˌprəʊtə'zəʊən] N = **protozoan A**

protract [prə'trækt] VT prolongar

protracted [prə'træktɪd] ADJ prolongado, (excesivamente) largo

protraction [prə'trækʃən] N prolongación *f*

protractor [prə'træktəʳ] N transportador *m*

protrude [prə'truːd] Ⓐ VI salir, sobresalir
Ⓑ VT sacar fuera

protruding [prə'truːdɪŋ] ADJ saliente, sobresaliente; [*eye, tooth*] saltón

protrusion [prə'truːʒən] N saliente *m*, protuberancia *f*

protuberance [prə'tjuːbərəns] N protuberancia *f*, saliente *m*

protuberant [prə'tjuːbərənt] ADJ protuberante, saliente; [*eye, tooth*] saltón

proud [praʊd] ADJ (*compar* **prouder**; *superl* **proudest**) [1] (= *satisfied*) [*person*] orgulloso; [*expression, smile*] de orgullo; **he is the ~ father of a baby girl** es el orgulloso padre de una nena; **to be ~ that** estar *or* sentirse orgulloso de (que); **I'm ~ that I did it on my own** estoy *or* me siento orgulloso de haberlo hecho solo; **to be ~ to do sth: I'm ~ to call her my friend** me enorgullece que sea mi amiga; **we are ~ to present ...** tenemos el honor de presentarles ...; **it was his ~ boast that he had never had a proper job** era un motivo de muchísimo orgullo para él el no haber tenido nunca un trabajo serio, presumía orgulloso de no haber tenido nunca un trabajo serio; **it makes you ~ to be a parent, doesn't it?** te hace sentirte orgulloso de ser padre, ¿verdad?; **to be ~ of sth/sb** estar orgulloso de algo/algn; **I'm working-class and ~ of it** soy de clase obrera y estoy orgulloso de ello; **that's nothing to be ~ of!** ¡esto no es motivo de orgullo!; **I'm not very ~ of myself** no estoy muy orgulloso *or* satisfecho de mí mismo; **I hope you're ~ of yourself!** (*iro*) ¡estarás orgulloso!; **✦IDIOM to do sb/o.s. ~***: **the team have done their country ~** el equipo ha sido motivo de orgullo para su país; **his honesty did him ~** su honradez decía mucho en su favor; **the hotel did them ~** el hotel los trató a cuerpo de rey; **she did herself ~ in the piano competition** se lució en el concurso de piano
[2] (= *self-respecting*) [*people, nation*] digno
[3] (*pej*) (= *arrogant*) orgulloso, soberbio; **she's ~ and stubborn** es orgullosa *or* soberbia y terca; **he was flustered, but too ~ to show it** estaba nervioso pero era demasiado orgulloso para demostrarlo; **don't be too ~ to ask for help** no dejes que el orgullo te impida pedir ayuda; **I don't mind sitting on the floor, I'm not ~** no me importa sentarme en el suelo, no soy orgulloso, no me importa sentarme en el suelo, no se me caen los anillos*
[4] (= *causing pride*) [*day, moment*] glorioso, de orgullo; [*history, reputation*] glorioso; [*possession, tradition*] preciado; **the locket was my ~est possession** el guardapelo era mi bien más preciado *or* mi mayor tesoro
[5] (= *splendid, imposing*) espléndido, imponente
[6] (*Brit*) (= *protruding*) **to be/stand ~ (of sth)** sobresalir (de algo); **that screw's still a bit ~ of the surface** ese tornillo aún sobresale un poco de la superficie

proudly ['praʊdlɪ] ADV (= *with satisfaction*) con orgullo; (= *arrogantly*) arrogantemente, con arrogancia; (= *splendidly, impressively*) de forma imponente; **he ~ showed me his drawing** orgulloso, me enseñó su dibujo, me enseñó con orgullo su dibujo

prove [pruːv] (*pt* **proved**; *pp* **proved** *or* **proven**)
Ⓐ VT [1] (= *give proof of*) [+ *theory, statement*] demostrar, probar; (*one's love, loyalty, strength*) demostrar; **my son was murdered, and I'm going to ~ it** a mi hijo lo asesinaron, y voy a demostrarlo *or* probarlo; **can you ~ it?** ¿lo puede demostrar *or* probar?; **statistics never ~ anything** las estadísticas nunca prueban *or* demuestran nada; **you say you love me, so ~ it** dices que me quieres, pues demuéstralo *or* pruébalo; **he wanted to ~ his love for her** quería demostrar su amor por ella; **you can't ~ anything against me** usted no tiene ninguna prueba en mi contra, usted no puede demostrar *or* probar nada en mi contra; **it just ~s how stupid he is** simplemente demuestra *or* prueba lo tonto que es; **to ~ sb's innocence ◊ ~ sb innocent** demostrar *or* probar la inocencia de algn; **to ~ one's point** demostrar que uno está en lo cierto *or* tiene razón; **she took him to court just to ~ a point** lo llevó a los tribunales simplemente para demostrar *or* probar que estaba en lo cierto *or* que ella tenía razón; **to ~ sb right** demostrar que algn tiene razón; **he was ~d**

➤ LANGUAGE IN USE: **prosperous** 23.2 **protest C** 14

right in the end al fin se demostró que tenía razón; **it's been scientifically ~n** *or* **~d** se ha probado *or* demostrado científicamente, ha sido probado *or* demostrado científicamente; **to ~ that** demostrar que, probar que; **that ~s that she did it** eso demuestra *or* prueba que ella lo hizo; **she wants to ~ to herself that she can still hold down a job** quiere demostrarse a sí misma que todavía puede mantener un trabajo; **what are you trying to ~?** ¿qué intentas demostrar *or* probar?; **it's difficult to ~ what's going on** es difícil demostrar *or* probar lo que está pasando; **whether he was right remains to be ~d** aún falta por demostrar *or* probar si tenía razón; **to ~ sb wrong** demostrar que algn está equivocado; **everyone said that we would fail but we ~d them wrong** todo el mundo decía que fracasaríamos, pero demostramos que estaban equivocados; **she attempted to ~ their theory wrong** intentó encontrar pruebas que demostraran que su teoría estaba equivocada; ✦*IDIOM* **the exception ~s the rule** la excepción confirma la regla

2 (= *verify*) comprobar; **you can ~ how effective this method is by trying it out yourself** puede comprobar la eficacia de este método probándolo usted mismo

3 **to ~ o.s.** demostrar lo que uno vale; **you don't need to ~ yourself** no tienes que demostrar lo que vales; **he has ~d himself worthy of our trust** ha demostrado ser digno de nuestra confianza; **he has ~d himself to be a successful manager** ha demostrado ser un gerente eficaz

4 (= *test out*) poner a prueba, someter a prueba

5 (*Jur*) **to ~ a will** homologar un testamento

Ⓑ VI 1 (= *turn out*) resultar; **it ~d (to be) useful** resultó (ser) útil; **if it ~s (to be) otherwise** si resulta (ser) lo contrario; **it may ~ difficult to secure funding** puede que resulte difícil conseguir fondos; **the news ~d false** resultó que la noticia era falsa; **the temptation ~d too much for her** la tentación resultó demasiado grande para ella, no pudo resistir la tentación

2 (*Culin*) [*dough*] leudarse

proven [ˈpruːvən] Ⓐ PP *of* **prove**

Ⓑ ADJ 1 (*gen*) [*formula, method*] de eficacia probada; [*abilities*] probado; **it's a ~ fact that …** está probado *or* demostrado que …, es un hecho comprobado que …

2 [ˈprəʊvən] (*Scot Jur*) **the case was found not ~** el acusado fue absuelto por falta de pruebas

provenance [ˈprɒvɪnəns] N procedencia *f*

Provençal [ˌprɒvɑːnˈsɑːl] Ⓐ ADJ provenzal

Ⓑ N 1 (= *person*) provenzal *mf*

2 (*Ling*) provenzal *m*

Provence [prɒˈvɑːns] N Provenza *f*

provender [ˈprɒvɪndəʳ] N (*frm*) forraje *m*; (*hum*) provisiones *fpl*, comida *f*

proverb [ˈprɒvɜːb] N refrán *m*, proverbio *m*

proverbial [prəˈvɜːbɪəl] ADJ proverbial

proverbially [prəˈvɜːbɪəlɪ] ADV proverbialmente

provide [prəˈvaɪd] Ⓐ VT 1 (= *supply*) 1·1 [+ *materials, food*] proporcionar, suministrar; [+ *money, information, evidence*] proporcionar, facilitar; [+ *service*] prestar; **please place your litter in the receptacle ~d** por favor hagan uso de los recipientes que les hemos proporcionado *or* suministrado para depositar la basura; **the meeting ~d an opportunity to talk** la reunión les brindó *or* ofreció la oportunidad de hablar; **candidates must ~ their own pencils** los candidatos deben traer sus propios lápices; **to ~ sth for sb/sth**: **I will ~ food for everyone** proveeré a todo el mundo de comida, proporcionaré *or* daré comida a todo el mundo; **it ~s accommodation for five families** provee a cinco familias de alojamiento, da *or* proporciona alojamiento a cinco familias; **the company ~s free health care for its employees** la empresa presta asistencia médica gratis a sus empleados; **it ~s shade for the cows** les da sombra a las vacas; **they've asked the United Nations to ~ protection for civilians** han pedido a las Naciones Unidas que faciliten protección a la población civil; **to ~ funding/money for sth** proporcionar *or* facilitar fondos/dinero para algo; **to ~ a solution (to sth)** ofrecer una solución (a algo)

1·2 **to ~ sb with sth** [+ *materials, food*] proveer a algn de algo, suministrar algo a algn; [+ *money, information, details*] proporcionar *or* facilitar algo a algn; [+ *service*] proporcionar algo a algn; [+ *means*] facilitar algo a algn; [+ *opportunity*] brindar algo a algn; **it ~s the plant with a continuous flow of nutrients** provee a la planta de *or* suministra a la planta un flujo continuo de nutrientes; **it ~d her with the opportunity she needed** le brindó la oportunidad que necesitaba

1·3 **to ~ o.s. with sth** proveerse de algo; **plants produce sugars and starch to ~ themselves with energy** las plantas producen azúcares y almidón para proveerse de energía; **he had forgotten to ~ himself with an alibi** se le había olvidado buscarse una coartada

2 (= *have available*) estar provisto de; **the field ~s plenty of space for a car park** el campo está provisto de muchísimo espacio para un aparcamiento de coches; **the car is ~d with a heater** el coche está provisto de un calentador

3 (= *stipulate*) **the law ~s that …** la ley estipula *or* dispone que …

Ⓑ VI ✦*IDIOM* **the Lord will ~** Dios proveerá; *see also* **provide for**

►**provide against** VI + PREP (*frm*) [*person*] tomar precauciones contra, precaverse de; [*policy, insurance*] proporcionar protección contra, proporcionar cobertura contra

►**provide for** VI + PREP 1 (*financially*) 1·1 (= *support*) [+ *person, family*] mantener; **parents are expected to ~ for their children** se espera que los padres mantengan a sus hijos

1·2 (= *make provision for*) **he wanted to see that the children were well ~d for** quería asegurarse de que las necesidades de los niños estaban bien cubiertas; **his wife was left well ~d for in his will** en el testamento dejó a su mujer bien asegurado; **they are well ~d for** tienen medios de sobra; **individuals are encouraged to ~ for themselves by buying private insurance** se anima a las personas a que se aseguren el futuro *or* que hagan previsiones para el futuro comprando un seguro privado

2 (= *take care of*) prever; **the 50 employers which best ~ for the needs of women** los 50 empresarios que mejor preven las necesidades de las mujeres; **we have ~d for that** eso lo hemos previsto; **it's impossible to ~ for all eventualities** es imposible prever todas las eventualidades *or* tomar precauciones contra toda eventualidad

3 (*Jur*) (= *make possible*) **the accord ~s for greater police co-operation** en el acuerdo se prevé una mayor colaboración por parte de la policía; **the Act ~s for financial penalties to be imposed on all offenders** la ley estipula que se impongan multas a todos los transgresores; **as ~d for in the 1990 contract** de acuerdo con lo estipulado en el contrato de 1990

provided [prəˈvaɪdɪd] CONJ **~ (that)** con tal (de) que, a condición de que

providence [ˈprɒvɪdəns] N providencia *f*; **Providence** Divina Providencia *f*

provident [ˈprɒvɪdənt] Ⓐ ADJ providente, previsor, próvido

Ⓑ CPD ► **provident fund** N fondo *m* de previsión ► **provident society** N (*Brit*) sociedad *f* de socorro mutuo, mutualidad *f*

providential [ˌprɒvɪˈdenʃəl] ADJ providencial; (= *fortunate*) afortunado, milagroso

providentially [ˌprɒvɪˈdenʃəlɪ] ADV providencialmente; (= *fortunately*) afortunadamente, milagrosamente

providently [ˈprɒvɪdəntlɪ] ADV próvidamente

provider [prəˈvaɪdəʳ] N proveedor(a) *m/f*

providing [prəˈvaɪdɪŋ] CONJ = **provided**

province [ˈprɒvɪns] N 1 (*Geog*) provincia *f*; **they live in the ~s** viven en provincias

2 (*fig*) (= *area of knowledge, activity etc*) esfera *f*, campo *m*; (= *jurisdiction etc*) competencia *f*; **it's not within my ~** no es de mi competencia

3 (*Rel*) arzobispado *m*

provincial [prəˈvɪnʃəl] Ⓐ ADJ provincial, de provincia; (*pej*) pueblerino, provinciano

Ⓑ N (*usu pej*) provinciano/a *m/f*

provincialism [prəˈvɪnʃəlɪzəm] N provincialismo *m*

proving ground [ˈpruːvɪŋˌgraʊnd] N terreno *m* de prueba

provision [prəˈvɪʒən] Ⓐ N 1 (= *act of providing*) [*of funds, accommodation, jobs*] provisión *f*; [*of food, water*] suministro *m*, abastecimiento *m*; [*of service, care*] prestación *f*; **~ of adequate toilet facilities on the site is essential** es esencial que la obra esté provista de aseos adecuados; **the ~ of care for the elderly** la prestación de asistencia social a los ancianos; **to get in** *or* **lay in a ~ of coal** abastecerse de carbón

2 (= *amount, number provided*) **nursery ~ is usually poor in country areas** la provisión de guarderías es generalmente escasa en las zonas rurales, suele haber pocas guarderías en las zonas rurales; **there is inadequate housing ~ for the poor** la provisión de viviendas para los pobres es insuficiente; **they have cut their ~ of grants to research students** han reducido la cantidad de ayudas destinadas a la investigación; **recent government policies have squeezed welfare ~** las recientes medidas gubernamentales han reducido las prestaciones en materia de bienestar social

3 (= *arrangements*) 3·1 (*gen*) previsiones *fpl*; **to make ~ for sth/sb** hacer previsiones para algo/algn; **the government had made no ~ for the refugees** el gobierno no había hecho previsiones para los refugiados

3·2 (= *financial arrangements*) provisiones *fpl*; **to make ~ for sth/sb**: **you must make ~ for your old age** debes hacer provisiones para la vejez; **to make ~ for one's family** asegurar el porvenir de su familia; **she would find some way of making proper ~ for her baby** ya encontraría alguna manera de proveer para su bebé; **he has made financial ~ for his son's education** ha hecho provisiones económicas para la educación de su hijo; **the state makes ~ for people without alternative resources** el estado hace provisiones para la gente que no tiene otras fuentes de ingreso; **he made no ~ in his will for his only child**

Violet no incluyó a su única hija, Violet, en el testamento
[4] **provisions** (= *food*) provisiones *fpl*, víveres *mpl*
[5] (= *stipulation*) estipulación *f*, disposición *f*; **under** *or* **according to the ~s of the treaty** en virtud de las estipulaciones *or* disposiciones del tratado; **there is no ~ for this in the rules** ◊ **the rules make no ~ for this** las reglas no disponen en previsión de esto; **it comes within the ~s of this law** está comprendido dentro de lo estipulado por esta ley, está comprendido dentro de las estipulaciones *or* disposiciones de esta ley
[6] (= *condition, proviso*) condición *f*; **with the ~ that** con la condición de que; **she approved, with one ~: that …** dio su aprobación con una condición: que …
Ⓑ VT aprovisionar, abastecer; **to be ~ed with sth** (*frm*) estar provisto de algo

provisional [prəˈvɪʒənl] Ⓐ ADJ provisional, provisorio (*LAm*)
Ⓑ N **Provisional** (*Pol*) (*in Ireland*) Provisional *mf* (*miembro de la tendencia activista del IRA*); **the Provisionals** = **the Provisional IRA**
Ⓒ CPD ► **provisional driving licence** N (*Brit*) permiso *m* de conducción provisional (*Sp*), licencia *f* provisional (*esp LAm*); → DRIVING LICENCE/DRIVER'S LICENSE ► **the Provisional IRA** N el IRA provisional

provisionally [prəˈvɪʒnəlɪ] ADV provisionalmente

proviso [prəˈvaɪzəʊ] N (*pl* **provisos** *or* **provisoes**) (*gen*) salvedad *f*; **with the ~ that …** a condición de que …

Provo* [ˈprəʊvəʊ] N = **provisional B**

provocation [ˌprɒvəˈkeɪʃən] N provocación *f*; **she acted under ~** reaccionó a una provocación; **to suffer great ~** sufrir una gran provocación

provocative [prəˈvɒkətɪv] ADJ [1] (= *inflammatory*) [*remark, behaviour*] provocador; [*act*] de provocación, provocador
[2] (= *thought-provoking*) [*book, film*] sugestivo, que hace reflexionar; [*title*] sugestivo
[3] (= *seductive*) [*person*] seductor; [*clothing, look, smile*] provocativo

provocatively [prəˈvɒkətɪvlɪ] ADV [1] (= *aggressively*) [*act, behave*] de modo provocador; [*say*] provocadoramente
[2] (= *seductively*) [*dress, smile*] de forma provocativa

provoke [prəˈvəʊk] VT [1] (= *cause*) [+ *reaction, response*] provocar; [+ *violence*] provocar, causar; [+ *crisis*] causar
[2] (= *rouse, move*) incitar, mover (**to** a); **it ~d us to action** nos incitó a obrar; **it ~d the town to revolt** incitó la ciudad a sublevarse; **to ~ sb into doing sth** incitar a algn a hacer algo
[3] (= *anger*) provocar, irritar; **he is easily ~d** se irrita por cualquier cosa, se le provoca fácilmente

provoking [prəˈvəʊkɪŋ] ADJ irritante; **how very ~!** ¡qué fastidio!

provost [ˈprɒvəst] Ⓐ N (*Univ*) rector(a) *m/f*; (*Scot*) alcalde/esa *m/f*
Ⓑ CPD ► **provost marshal** N capitán *m* preboste

prow [praʊ] N (*Naut*) proa *f*

prowess [ˈpraʊɪs] N [1] (= *skill*) habilidad *f*, capacidad *f*
[2] (= *courage*) valor *m*

prowl [praʊl] Ⓐ N ronda *f* (en busca de presa, botín *etc*); **to be on the ~** merodear, rondar
Ⓑ VI (*also* **~ about** *or* **around**) rondar, merodear; **he ~s round the house at night** (*outside*) ronda la casa de noche; (*inside*) se pasea por la casa de noche
Ⓒ VT **to ~ the streets** rondar las calles
Ⓓ CPD ► **prowl car** N (*US Police*) coche-patrulla *m*

prowler [ˈpraʊlər] N merodeador(a) *m/f*

prox. ABBR (= **proximo**) pr.fr.

proximity [prɒkˈsɪmɪtɪ] N proximidad *f*; **in ~ to** cerca *or* en las cercanías de

proximo [ˈprɒksɪməʊ] ADV (*Comm*) del mes próximo; **before the 7th ~** antes del 7 del mes que viene

proxy [ˈprɒksɪ] Ⓐ N (= *power*) poder *m*; (= *person*) apoderado/a *m/f*; **by ~** por poderes; **to be married by ~** casarse por poderes
Ⓑ CPD ► **proxy vote** N voto *m* por poderes

Prozac® [ˈprəʊzæk] N Prozac® *m*

PRP N ABBR (*Brit*) [1] (= **performance-related pay**) *sistema salarial que incluye un plus de productividad*
[2] (= **profit-related pay**) *sistema salarial en el que los empleados reciben un porcentaje de los beneficios de la empresa*

PRS N ABBR (= **Performing Rights Society**) *sociedad de derechos de autor*, ≈ SGAE *f*

prude [pruːd] N gazmoño/a *m/f*, mojigato/a *m/f*

prudence [ˈpruːdəns] N prudencia *f*

prudent [ˈpruːdənt] ADJ cauteloso, prudente

prudential [prʊˈdenʃəl] ADJ prudencial

prudently [ˈpruːdəntlɪ] ADV prudentemente, con prudencia

prudery [ˈpruːdərɪ] N remilgo *m*, mojigatería *f*, gazmoñería *f*

prudish [ˈpruːdɪʃ] ADJ gazmoño, remilgado

prudishness [ˈpruːdɪʃnɪs] N = **prudery**

prune[1] [pruːn] N [1] (= *fruit*) ciruela *f* pasa
[2] (*) (= *person*) bobo/a *m/f*, majadero/a* *m/f*

prune[2] [pruːn] VT [+ *tree, branches*] podar; (*fig*) reducir, recortar

►**prune away** VT + ADV [+ *branches*] podar; (*fig*) [+ *words*] cortar

pruning [ˈpruːnɪŋ] Ⓐ N [*of tree, branches*] poda *f*
Ⓑ CPD ► **pruning hook** N, **pruning knife** N, **pruning shears** NPL podadera *f*

prurience [ˈprʊərɪəns] N salacidad *f*, lascivia *f*

prurient [ˈprʊərɪənt] ADJ salaz, lascivo

Prussia [ˈprʌʃə] N Prusia *f*

Prussian [ˈprʌʃən] Ⓐ ADJ prusiano
Ⓑ N prusiano/a *m/f*
Ⓒ CPD ► **Prussian blue** N azul *m* de Prusia

prussic acid [ˌprʌsɪkˈæsɪd] N ácido *m* prúsico

pry[1] [praɪ] VI (= *snoop*) fisgonear, curiosear; (= *spy*) atisbar; **to ~ into sb's affairs** (entro)meterse en los asuntos de algn; **to ~ into sb's secrets** curiosear en los secretos de algn

pry[2] [praɪ] VT (*US*) = **prise**

prying [ˈpraɪɪŋ] ADJ (= *nosy*) fisgón; (= *meddling*) entrometido

PS N ABBR [1] (= **postscript**) P.D.
[2] = **private secretary**

psalm [sɑːm] N salmo *m*

psalmist [ˈsɑːmɪst] N salmista *m*

psalmody [ˈsælmədɪ] N salmodia *f*

psalter [ˈsɔːltər] N salterio *m*

PSAT N ABBR (*US*) = **Preliminary Scholastic Aptitude Test**

PSBR N ABBR (*Econ*) (= **public sector borrowing requirement**) *necesidades de endeudamiento del sector público*

psephologist [seˈfɒlədʒɪst] N psefólogo/a *m/f*

psephology [seˈfɒlədʒɪ] N psefología *f*

pseud* [sjuːd] N (*Brit*) farsante *mf*

pseudo* [ˈsjuːdəʊ] ADJ farsante, fraudulento; [*person*] fingido; [*person's character*] artificial, afectado

pseudo… [ˈsjuːdəʊ] PREFIX seudo…; **a ~-artist** un seudo artista

pseudonym [ˈsjuːdənɪm] N seudónimo *m*

pseudonymous [sjuːˈdɒnɪməs] ADJ seudónimo

pshaw† [pʃɔː] EXCL ¡bah!

psi[1] ABBR (= **pounds per square inch**) ≈ kg/cm^2

psi[2] [saɪ] NPL (= *psychic phenomena*) fenómenos *mpl* paranormales

psittacosis [ˌsɪtəˈkəʊsɪs] N psitacosis *f*

psoriasis [səˈraɪəsɪs] N soriasis *f*

psst [pst] EXCL ¡oye!, ¡eh!

PST N ABBR (*US*) = **Pacific Standard Time**

PSV N ABBR (= **public service vehicle**) vehículo *m* de servicio público

psych* [saɪk] VT [1] (= *make uneasy*) (*also* **~ out**) poner nervioso; **that doesn't ~ me** no me da ni frío ni calor, me tiene sin cuidado
[2] (= *prepare psychologically*) (*also* **~ up**) mentalizar
[3] (= *guess, anticipate*) [+ *reactions etc*] adivinar, anticipar

►**psych out*** VT + ADV [1] (= *make uneasy*) poner nervioso
[2] (*US*) (= *analyse, work out*) [+ *person*] calar*; **I ~ed it all out for myself** me di cuenta de por dónde iban los tiros*

►**psych up*** VT + ADV **to get o.s. ~ed up for sth** mentalizarse para algo; **he was all ~ed up to start, when …** ya estaba mentalizado para empezar, cuando …

psych… [saɪk] PREFIX psic…, psiqu…, sic…, siqu…

Psyche [ˈsaɪkɪ] N Psique *f*

psyche [ˈsaɪkɪ] N (*Psych*) psique *f*, psiquis *f*

psychedelic [ˌsaɪkəˈdelɪk] ADJ psicodélico

psychiatric [ˌsaɪkɪˈætrɪk] ADJ psiquiátrico

psychiatrist [saɪˈkaɪətrɪst] N psiquiatra *mf*

psychiatry [saɪˈkaɪətrɪ] N psiquiatría *f*

psychic [ˈsaɪkɪk] Ⓐ ADJ (*also* **~al**) [1] (= *supernatural*) psíquico
[2] (= *telepathic*) telepático; **you must be ~!*** ¿cómo lo adivinaste?; **I'm not ~!*** ¡no soy adivino!*
[3] (*Psych*) psíquico
Ⓑ N (= *person*) vidente *mf*

psychical [ˈsaɪkɪkəl] ADJ = **psychic A**

psycho* [ˈsaɪkəʊ] N psicópata *mf*

psycho… [ˈsaɪkəʊ] PREFIX psico…

psychoactive [ˌsaɪkəʊˈæktɪv] ADJ **~ drug** droga *f* psicoactiva

psychoanalyse, psychoanalyze (*US*) [ˌsaɪkəʊˈænəlaɪz] VT psicoanalizar

psychoanalysis [ˌsaɪkəʊəˈnælɪsɪs] N psicoanálisis *m*

psychoanalyst [ˌsaɪkəʊˈænəlɪst] N psicoanalista *mf*

psychoanalytic [ˌsaɪkəʊænəˈlɪtɪk] ADJ psicoanalítico

psychoanalytical [ˌsaɪkəʊænəˈlɪtɪkəl] ADJ = **psychoanalytic**

psychoanalyze [ˌsaɪkəʊˈænəlaɪz] VT (*US*) = **psychoanalyse**

psychobabble* [ˈsaɪkəʊˌbæbl] N verborrea *f*, jerga *f* de psicólogos

psychodrama [ˈsaɪkəʊˌdrɑːmə] N psicodrama *m*

psychodynamics [ˌsaikəʊdaɪˈnæmiks] NSING psicodinámica *f*

psychokinesis [ˌsaɪkəʊkɪˈniːsɪs] N psicoquinesis *f*

psychokinetic [ˌsaɪkəʊkɪˈnetɪk] ADJ psicoquinético

psycholinguistic [ˌsaɪkəʊlɪŋˈgwɪstɪk] ADJ psicolingüístico

psycholinguistics [ˌsaɪkəʊlɪŋˈgwɪstɪks] NSING psicolingüística *f*

psychological [ˌsaɪkəˈlɒdʒɪkəl] Ⓐ ADJ psicológico; **it's only ~*** son cosas de la imaginación*
Ⓑ CPD ► **psychological block** N bloqueo *m* psicológico ► **psychological make-up** N perfil *m* psicológico ► **psychological moment** N momento *m* psicológico ► **psychological profile** N perfil *m* psicológico ► **psychological profiling** N trazado *m* del perfil psicológico ► **psychological warfare** N guerra *f* psicológica

psychologically [ˌsaɪkəˈlɒdʒɪkəlɪ] ADV psicológicamente

psychologist [saɪˈkɒlədʒɪst] N psicólogo/a *m/f*

psychology [saɪˈkɒlədʒɪ] N psicología *f*

psychometric [ˈsaɪkəʊˈmetrɪk] ADJ psicométrico

psychometrics [ˈsaɪkəʊˈmetrɪks] NSING psicometría *f*

psychometry [saɪˈkɒmɪtrɪ] N psicometría *f*

psychomotor [ˈsaɪkəʊˈməʊtəʳ] ADJ psicomotor

psychoneurosis [ˈsaɪkəʊnjʊəˈrəʊsɪs] N (*pl* **psychoneuroses** [ˈsaɪkəʊnjʊəˈrəʊsiːz]) psiconeurosis *f inv*

psychopath [ˈsaɪkəʊpæθ] N psicópata *mf*

psychopathic [ˌsaɪkəʊˈpæθɪk] ADJ psicopático

psychopathology [ˈsaɪkəʊpəˈθɒlədʒɪ] N psicopatología *f*

psychosexual [ˌsaɪkəʊˈseksjʊəl] ADJ psicosexual

psychosis [saɪˈkəʊsɪs] N (*pl* **psychoses** [saɪˈkəʊsiːz]) psicosis *f inv*

psychosocial [ˈsaɪkəʊˈsəʊʃəl] ADJ psicosocial

psychosociological [ˈsaɪkəʊˌsəʊsɪəˈlɒdʒɪkəl] ADJ psicosociológico

psychosomatic [ˈsaɪkəʊsəʊˈmætɪk] ADJ psicosomático

psychosurgery [ˌsaɪkəʊˈsɜːdʒərɪ] N psicocirugía *f*

psychotherapist [ˌsaɪkəʊˈθerəpɪst] N psicoterapeuta *mf*

psychotherapy [ˌsaɪkəʊˈθerəpɪ] N psicoterapia *f*

psychotic [saɪˈkɒtɪk] Ⓐ ADJ psicótico
Ⓑ N psicótico/a *m/f*

psychotropic [ˌsaɪkəʊˈtrɒpɪk] ADJ psicotrópico

PT† N ABBR (= **physical training**) gimnasia *f*, cultura *f* física

Pt ABBR (*Geog*) (= **Point**) Pta.

pt ABBR [1] = **part**
[2] = **pint(s)**
[3] = **point**
[4] (*Comm*) = **payment**

P/T ABBR = **part-time**

PTA N ABBR [1] (= **Parent-Teacher Association**) ≈ APA *f*
[2] (*Brit*) (= **Prevention of Terrorism Act**) *ley antiterrorista*

ptarmigan [ˈtɑːmɪgən] N (*pl* **ptarmigans** *or* **ptarmigan**) perdiz *f* blanca

Pte ABBR (*Mil*) = **Private**

pterodactyl [ˌterəʊˈdæktɪl] N pterodáctilo *m*

PTO ABBR (= **please turn over**) sigue

Ptolemaic [ˌtɒləˈmeɪɪk] ADJ **~ system** sistema *m* de Tolomeo, sistema *m* tolemaico

Ptolemy [ˈtɒləmɪ] N Tolomeo

ptomaine [ˈtəʊmeɪn] Ⓐ N (p)tomaína *f*
Ⓑ CPD ► **ptomaine poisoning** N envenenamiento *m* (p)tomaínico

PTSD N ABBR = **post-traumatic stress disorder**

PTV N ABBR (*US*) [1] = **pay television**
[2] = **public television**

pub [pʌb] (*Brit*) Ⓐ N pub *m*, bar *m*
Ⓑ CPD ► **pub crawl** N **to go on a ~ crawl*** ir de chateo *or* de parranda (de bar en bar)*

pub. ABBR = **published**

puberty [ˈpjuːbətɪ] N pubertad *f*

pubes¹ [ˈpjuːbiːz] NPL vello *m* púbico

pubescence [pjuːˈbesəns] N pubescencia *f*

pubescent [pjuːˈbesənt] Ⓐ ADJ pubescente
Ⓑ N pubescente *mf*

pubic [ˈpjuːbɪk] Ⓐ ADJ púbico
Ⓑ CPD ► **pubic hair** N vello *m* púbico

pubis [ˈpjuːbɪs] N (*pl* **pubes**) pubis *m inv*

public [ˈpʌblɪk] Ⓐ ADJ [1] (= *of the State*) público; **they can hire expensive lawyers at ~ expense** pueden contratar abogados caros a costa de los contribuyentes; **to run for/hold ~ office** presentarse como candidato a/ostentar un cargo público; **the ~ purse** el erario público
[2] (= *of, for, by everyone*) público; **they want to deflect ~ attention from the real issues** quieren desviar la opinión pública de los verdaderos problemas; **to be in the ~ eye** ser objeto del interés público; **he has kept his family out of the ~ eye** ha mantenido a su familia alejada de la atención pública; **I have decided to resign in the ~ interest** en el interés de los ciudadanos, he decidido dimitir; **in a bid to gain ~ support** en un intento de hacerse con el apoyo de la gente; ✦*IDIOM* **~ enemy number one** enemigo *m* público número uno
[3] (= *open, not private*) [*statement, meeting*] público; [*appearance*] en público; **it's too ~ here** aquí estamos demasiado expuestos al público, aquí no tenemos intimidad; **can we talk somewhere less ~?** ¿podemos hablar en algún sitio más privado *or* menos expuesto al público?; **to become ~** [*news, fact*] hacerse público; **to be in the ~ domain** (= *not secret*) ser de dominio público; **to go ~** (*Comm*) empezar a cotizar en bolsa; **they decided to go ~ about their relationship*** decidieron revelar su relación a la prensa *or* al público; **it is ~ knowledge** ya es de dominio público; **to retire from ~ life** retirarse de la vida pública; **to lead an active ~ life** llevar una vida pública activa; **to make sth ~** hacer público algo, publicar algo
[4] (= *well-known*) **a ~ figure** un personaje público
Ⓑ N [1] (= *people*) **the ~** el público; **the house is open to the ~** la casa está abierta al público; **the general ~** el gran público; **a member of the ~** un ciudadano
[2] (= *open place*) **in ~** en público
[3] (= *devotees*) público *m*; **she couldn't disappoint her ~** no podía decepcionar a su público; **the reading/sporting ~** los aficionados a la lectura/al deporte; **the viewing ~** los telespectadores
Ⓒ CPD ► **public access television** N (*US*) *televisión abierta al público* ► **public address system** N (sistema *m* de) megafonía *f*, altavoces *mpl*, altoparlantes *mpl* (*LAm*) ► **public affairs** NPL actividades *fpl* públicas ► **public assistance** N (*US*) asistencia *f* pública; **to be on ~ assistance** recibir asistencia pública ► **public bar** N bar *m* ► **public body** N organismo *m* público ► **public company** N empresa *f* pública ► **public convenience** N (*Brit frm*) servicios *mpl*, aseos *mpl* públicos ► **public debt** N deuda *f* pública, deuda *f* del Estado ► **public defender** N (*US*) defensor(a) *m/f* de oficio ► **public enquiry** N (*Brit*) = **public inquiry** ► **public expenditure** N gasto *m* (del sector) público ► **public health** N salud *f* pública, sanidad *f* pública ► **public health inspector** N inspector/a *m/f* de salud *or* sanidad pública ► **Public Health Service** N (*US*) ≈ Seguridad *f* Social, *servicio público de asistencia sanitaria* ► **public holiday** N fiesta *f* nacional, fiesta *f* oficial, (día *m*) feriado *m* (*LAm*) ► **public house** N (*Brit frm*) bar *m* ► **public inquiry** N investigación *f* oficial ► **public law** N (= *discipline, body of legislation*) derecho *m* público; (*US*) (= *piece of legislation*) ley *f* pública ► **public library** N biblioteca *f* pública ► **public limited company** N sociedad *f* anónima ► **public nuisance** N (*Jur*) molestia *f* pública; **he's a ~ nuisance** siempre está causando problemas *or* molestias; **to cause a ~ nuisance** alterar el orden público ► **public opinion** N opinión *f* pública ► **public opinion poll** N sondeo *m* (de la opinión pública) ► **public property** N (= *land, buildings*) dominio *m* público; (*fig*) **he couldn't handle being ~ property** no podía soportar ser un personaje público; **his private life is ~ property** su vida privada es de dominio público ► **public prosecutor** N fiscal *mf*; **the Public Prosecutor's Office** la fiscalía; → ATTORNEY ► **Public Record Office** N (*Brit*) archivo *m* nacional ► **public relations** NPL relaciones *fpl* públicas; **the police action was a ~ relations disaster** la actuación de la policía fue desastrosa para su imagen; **it's just a ~ relations exercise** es sólo una operación publicitaria *or* de relaciones públicas ► **public relations officer** N encargado/a *m/f* de relaciones públicas ► **public school** N (*Brit*) colegio *m* privado; (= *boarding school*) internado *m* privado; (*US*) escuela *f* pública ► **the public sector** N el sector público; **60,000 ~-sector jobs must be cut** se deben eliminar 60.000 puestos de funcionario *or* en el sector público ► **public servant** N funcionario/a *m/f* ► **public service** N (= *Civil Service*) administración *f* pública; (*usu pl*) (= *community facility*) servicio *m* público; **she will be remembered for a lifetime of ~ service** se la recordará por cómo entregó su vida al servicio de la comunidad; **in doing this they were performing a ~ service** con esto estaban haciendo un servicio a la comunidad; **~ service announcement** comunicado *m* de interés público; **~ service jobs** puestos *mpl* de funcionario *or* en el sector público; **~ service vehicle** vehículo *m* de servicio público; **~ service worker** funcionario/a *m/f* ► **public speaker** N orador(a) *m/f*; **she is a good ~ speaker** habla muy bien en público, es una buena oradora ► **public speaking** N oratoria *f* ► **public spending** N gasto *m* (del sector) público ► **public television** N (*US*) cadenas *fpl* públicas (de televisión) ► **public transport**, **public transportation** (*US*) N transporte(s) *m(pl)* público(s); **to ban smoking on ~ transport** prohibir fumar en los medios de transporte público ► **public utility** N empresa *f* del servicio público ► **public works** NPL obras *fpl* públicas

PUBLIC ACCESS TELEVISION

En Estados Unidos, el término **Public Access Television** *hace referencia a una serie de cadenas no comerciales de televisión por cable* *que emiten programas de ámbito local o programas dedicados a organizaciones humanitarias sin ánimo de lucro. Entre sus emisiones se incluyen charlas sobre actividades escolares, programas sobre aficiones diversas e incluso discursos de organizaciones racistas. Estas emisiones de acceso público se crearon para dar cabida a temas de interés local e impedir que los canales por cable estuvieran dominados por unos cuantos privilegiados. En virtud de la Ley de Emisiones por Cable, el* **Cable Act** *de 1984, cualquier población en que haya algún canal por cable puede obligar a los propietarios de dicho canal a que instalen una cadena adicional de acceso público y provean el equipo, el estudio, los medios técnicos y el personal necesarios para la emisión.*

publican ['pʌblɪkən] N 1 (*Brit*) dueño/a *m/f or* encargado/a *m/f* de un pub *or* bar
2 (*Bible*) publicano *m*

publication [ˌpʌblɪ'keɪʃən] Ⓐ N (= *act*) publicación *f*, edición *f*; (= *published work*) publicación *f*; **this is not for ~** esto no está destinado a la publicación
Ⓑ CPD ► **publication date** N fecha *f* de publicación ► **publication details** NPL detalles *mpl* de publicación

publicist ['pʌblɪsɪst] N publicista *mf*

publicity [pʌb'lɪsɪtɪ] Ⓐ N 1 publicidad *f*
2 (*Comm*) (= *advertising, advertisements*) publicidad *f*, propaganda *f*
Ⓑ CPD ► **publicity agent** N agente *mf* de publicidad ► **publicity campaign** N campaña *f* publicitaria ► **publicity manager** N director(a) *m/f* de publicidad ► **publicity stunt** N truco *m* publicitario

publicity-seeking [pʌb'lɪsɪtɪˌsiːkɪŋ] Ⓐ ADJ [*stunt, ruse*] publicitario; [*person*] con motivos publicitarios
Ⓑ N **she accused the lawyers of ~** acusó a los abogados de albergar motivos publicitarios

publicity-shy [pʌb'lɪsɪtɪˌʃaɪ] ADJ reacio a la publicidad

publicize ['pʌblɪsaɪz] VT 1 (= *make public*) publicar, divulgar
2 (= *advertise*) anunciar, hacer propaganda de

publicly ['pʌblɪklɪ] ADV [*acknowledge, criticize, accuse*] públicamente, en público; [*announce, state, humiliate*] públicamente; [*funded*] con fondos públicos; **land and buildings that are ~ owned** tierras *fpl* y edificios *mpl* que son propiedad pública *or* del Estado; **this information should be made ~ available** esta información se debería hacer pública

public-spirited ['pʌblɪk'spɪrɪtɪd] ADJ [*act*] de espíritu cívico, solidario; [*person*] lleno de civismo, consciente del bien público

publish ['pʌblɪʃ] VT 1 [*newspaper*] [+ *article, photograph*] publicar; [*publisher*] [+ *book*] publicar, editar; [*publisher*] [+ *author*] publicar las obras de; [*author*] [+ *book*] publicar; **"~ed weekly"** "semanario"
2 (= *make public*) [+ *list, information*] divulgar, hacer público

publisher ['pʌblɪʃə^r] N (= *person*) editor(a) *m/f*; (= *firm*) editorial *f*

publishing ['pʌblɪʃɪŋ] Ⓐ N (= *trade*) industria *f* editorial; **he's in ~** publica libros, está con una casa editorial
Ⓑ CPD ► **publishing company, publishing house** N (casa *f*) editorial *f*

puce [pjuːs] Ⓐ N color *m* castaño rojizo
Ⓑ ADJ de color castaño rojizo; (*with shame etc*) colorado

puck[1] [pʌk] N (= *imp*) duende *m* (malicioso)

puck[2] [pʌk] N (*Sport*) puck *m*, disco *m*

pucker ['pʌkə^r] Ⓐ N arruga *f*; (*Sew*) frunce *m*, fruncido *m*; (*accidentally formed*) buche *m*
Ⓑ VT (*also* **to ~ up**) arrugar; [+ *brow, material*] fruncir
Ⓒ VI (*also* **to ~ up**) arrugarse, formar buches

puckish ['pʌkɪʃ] ADJ malicioso, juguetón

pud* [pʊd] N (*Brit*) = **pudding**

pudding ['pʊdɪŋ] Ⓐ N (= *steamed pudding*) pudín *m*, budín *m*; (*Brit*) (= *dessert*) postre *m*; *see also* **black D**
Ⓑ CPD ► **pudding basin** N (*Brit*) cuenco *m* ► **pudding rice** N arroz *m* redondo

puddingstone ['pʊdɪŋstəʊn] N (*Geol*) pudinga *f*

puddle ['pʌdl] Ⓐ N charco *m*
Ⓑ VT (*Tech*) pudelar

pudenda [pjuː'dendə] NPL (*frm*) partes *fpl* pudendas

pudgy ['pʌdʒɪ] ADJ = **podgy**

puerile ['pjʊəraɪl] ADJ pueril

puerility [pjʊə'rɪlɪtɪ] N puerilidad *f*

puerperal [pjʊ(ː)'ɜːpərəl] Ⓐ ADJ puerperal
Ⓑ CPD ► **puerperal fever** N fiebre *f* puerperal ► **puerperal psychosis** N psicosis *f inv* puerperal

Puerto Rican ['pwɜːtəʊ'riːkən] Ⓐ ADJ puertorriqueño
Ⓑ N puertorriqueño/a *m/f*

Puerto Rico ['pwɜːtəʊ'riːkəʊ] N Puerto Rico *m*

puff [pʌf] Ⓐ N 1 [*of breathing, engine*] resoplido *m*; [*of air*] soplo *m*; [*of wind*] racha *f*, ráfaga *f*; [*of smoke*] bocanada *f*; (*on cigarette, pipe*) chupada *f*; **I'm out of ~*** estoy sin aliento
2 (= *powder puff*) borla *f*
3 (*Culin*) **cream ~** petisú *m*, pastel *m* de crema
4 (*) (= *advert*) bombo* *m*
5 (*Drugs*‡) canabis *m*
Ⓑ VT 1 (= *blow*) soplar; [+ *pipe etc*] chupar; **to ~ smoke** echar bocanadas de humo; **to ~ smoke in sb's face** echar humo a la cara de algn
2 (*also* **~ up**) (= *inflate*) hinchar, inflar (*LAm*)
Ⓒ VI 1 (= *breathe heavily*) jadear, resoplar; **to ~ (away) at** *or* **on one's pipe** chupar la pipa
2 **the train ~ed into/out of the station** el tren entró en/salió de la estación echando humo
Ⓓ CPD ► **puff adder** N víbora *f* puff ► **puff paste** N (*US*) = **puff pastry** ► **puff pastry** N hojaldre *m* ► **puff sleeves** NPL mangas *fpl* filipinas

►**puff along** VI + ADV [*train*] avanzar bufando; [*person*] correr jadeando

►**puff away** VI + ADV *see* **puff C**

►**puff out** VT + ADV 1 [+ *smoke etc*] echar, arrojar, despedir
2 [+ *cheeks, chest, sails*] hinchar, inflar (*LAm*); [+ *feathers*] erizar

►**puff up** Ⓐ VT + ADV 1 (= *inflate*) [+ *tyre etc*] hinchar, inflar (*LAm*)
2 = **puff out 2**
3 (*) (*fig*) dar bombo a; **to ~ o.s. up** darse bombo, engreírse
Ⓑ VI + ADV hincharse

puffball ['pʌfbɔːl] N bejín *m*, pedo *m* de lobo

puffed [pʌft] ADJ 1 (*also* **~ up**) [*eye*] hinchado; **his face was all ~ (up)** tenía la cara hinchada; **to be ~ up with pride** (*fig*) hincharse de orgullo
2 **I'm ~ (out)*** (= *out of breath*) me quedé sin aliento

puffer* ['pʌfə^r] N locomotora *f*

puffin ['pʌfɪn] N frailecillo *m*

puffiness ['pʌfɪnɪs] N hinchazón *f*

puffy ['pʌfɪ] ADJ (*compar* **puffier**; *superl* **puffiest**) [*eye etc*] hinchado

pug [pʌg] Ⓐ N (*also* **~ dog**) doguillo *m*
Ⓑ CPD ► **pug nose** N nariz *f* chata; *see also* **pug-nosed**

pugilism ['pjuːdʒɪlɪzəm] N pugilato *m*, pugilismo *m*

pugilist ['pjuːdʒɪlɪst] N púgil *m*, pugilista *m*

pugnacious [pʌg'neɪʃəs] ADJ pugnaz, agresivo

pugnaciously [pʌg'neɪʃəslɪ] ADV con pugnacidad, agresivamente

pugnacity [pʌg'næsɪtɪ] N pugnacidad *f*, agresividad *f*

pug-nosed ['pʌg'nəʊzd] ADJ de nariz chata

puke‡ [pjuːk] Ⓐ N 1 (= *vomited matter*) vómito *m*
2 **to have a ~** = **B**
Ⓑ VI (*also* **~ up**) devolver; **it makes me (want to) ~** (*fig*) me da asco
Ⓒ VT (*also* **~ up**) devolver*, vomitar

pukka* ['pʌkə] ADJ (*Brit*) (= *real*) auténtico, genuino; (= *posh*) esnob, elegante, lujoso

pulchritude ['pʌlkrɪtjuːd] N (*frm, liter*) belleza *f*

pulchritudinous [ˌpʌlkrɪ'tjuːdɪnəs] ADJ (*frm or liter*) bello

PULITZER

Los premios **Pulitzer** *se conceden anualmente en Estados Unidos a trabajos periodísticos, literarios y musicales excepcionales, y gozan de un enorme prestigio. En periodismo se conceden trece premios, entre ellos los destinados al periodismo de investigación y crítica. En literatura existen seis categorías, entre las que destacan las de novela, poesía y teatro. Los premios llevan el nombre del editor periodístico norteamericano* **Joseph Pulitzer** *(1847—1911), quien inicialmente aportó el dinero de los premios.*

pull [pʊl] Ⓐ N 1 (= *tug*) tirón *m*, jalón *m* (*LAm*); (*with oar etc*) golpe *m*; **give the rope a ~** tira de la cuerda; **suddenly it gave a ~** de repente dio un tirón
2 [*of moon, magnet, sea etc*] (fuerza *f* de) atracción *f*; [*of current*] fuerza *f*, ímpetu *m*; (*fig*) (= *attraction*) atracción *f*; **the ~ of the south** la atracción del Sur, lo atractivo del Sur
3 (*) (= *influence*) enchufe* *m*, palanca *f* (*LAm**); (= *advantage*) ventaja *f*; **he has ~ in the right places** tiene influencia donde hace falta; **they have a ~ over us now** ahora nos llevan ventaja; **he has a slight ~** tiene una pequeña ventaja
4 (*at pipe, cigarette*) chupada *f*; (*at drink*) trago *m*; **he took a ~ at his pipe** le dio una chupada a la pipa; **he took a ~ from the bottle** tomó un trago de la botella, dio un tiento a la botella (*Sp*)
5 (= *journey, drive etc*) **it was a long ~** fue mucho camino *or* trecho; **we had a long ~ up the hill** nos costó mucho trabajo subir la cuesta
6 (= *handle of drawer etc*) tirador *m*; [*of bell*] cuerda *f*
7 (*Typ*) primeras pruebas *fpl*
8 (*Brit**) **to be on the ~** estar de ligue (*Sp**), estar chequeando (*LAm**)
Ⓑ VT 1 (= *draw, drag*) tirar de, jalar (*LAm*); **to ~ a door shut/open** cerrar/abrir una puerta de un tirón *or* (*LAm*) jalón; **the engine ~s six coaches** la locomotora arrastra seis vagones; **~ your chair over** acerca la silla; **his**

ideas ~ed me the same way sus ideas me llevaron por el mismo camino; *see also* **punch A2**, **weight A1**

2 (= *tug*) tirar de, jalar (*LAm*); [+ *trigger*] apretar; [+ *oar*] tirar de; [+ *boat*] remar; (*Naut*) [+ *rope*] halar, jalar; [+ *tooth*] sacar; [+ *weeds*] arrancar; **to ~ sb's hair** tirar *or* (*LAm*) jalar de los pelos a algn; ✦*IDIOM* **~ the other one (it's got bells on)!**‡ ¡cuéntaselo a tu abuela!*; *see also* **leg A1**

3 (= *extract, draw out*) sacar, arrancar; [+ *beer*] servir; **to ~ a gun on sb** amenazar a algn con una pistola; *see also* **rank A1**

4 (= *injure*) **to ~ a muscle** sufrir un tirón en un músculo

5 [+ *ball*] (*at golf, etc*) golpear oblicuamente (a la izquierda)

6 (*Typ*) imprimir

7 (*) (= *cancel*) [+ *TV programme*] suspender

8 (*) (= *carry out, do*) **what are you trying to ~?** ¿qué quieres conseguir?, ¿qué es lo que pretendes con esto?; **to ~ a fast one** *or* **a trick on sb** jugar una mala pasada a algn

9 (*) (= *attract*) **this will really ~ the punters** esto seguramente atraerá clientela; **he knows how to ~ the birds** (*Brit*) sabe ligar con las chicas*

Ⓒ VI 1 tirar, jalar (*LAm*); **to ~ at** *or* **on a rope** tirar de una cuerda; **the car is ~ing to the right** el coche tira hacia la derecha; **the car isn't ~ing very well** el coche no tira

2 **to ~ at** *or* **on one's pipe** dar chupadas a la pipa; **to ~ at a bottle** tomar un trago *or* (*Sp*) dar un tiento a una botella

3 (= *move*) [*vehicle*] ir; [*oarsmen etc*] remar; **he ~ed sharply to one side to avoid the lorry** torció bruscamente a un lado para no chocar con el camión; **the car ~ed slowly up the hill** el coche subía despacio la cuesta; **the train ~ed into the station** el tren entró en la estación; **he ~ed alongside the kerb** se acercó al bordillo; **it ~ed to a stop** se paró; **we ~ed for the shore** remamos hacia la orilla

4 (*Brit**) ligar*, pillar (cacho) (*Sp*‡)

Ⓓ CPD ► **pull ring**, **pull tab** N anilla *f*

► **pull about** VT + ADV (= *handle roughly*) maltratar, manosear

► **pull ahead** VI + ADV (*in race etc*) tomar la delantera; (*in poll, contest*) ponerse por delante; **to ~ ahead of sth/sb** (*in race etc*) tomar la delantera a algo/algn, dejar atrás algo/a algn; (*in poll, contest*) ponerse por delante de algo/algn

► **pull along** VT + ADV arrastrar; **to ~ o.s. along** arrastrarse

► **pull apart** Ⓐ VT + ADV 1 (= *separate*) separar; (= *take apart*) desmontar

2 (*fig*) (*) (= *search thoroughly*) registrar de arriba abajo, revolver

3 (*fig*) (*) (= *criticize*) deshacer, hacer pedazos

Ⓑ VI + ADV **they ~ apart easily** se separan fácilmente

► **pull away** Ⓐ VT + ADV arrancar, quitar

Ⓑ VI + ADV 1 [*vehicle*] (= *move off*) salir, arrancar; **he soon ~ed away from the others** (*in race*) pronto dejó atrás a los demás

2 (= *draw back*) **to ~ away from sb** apartarse bruscamente de algn

3 **to ~ away at the oars** tirar (enérgicamente) de los remos

► **pull back** Ⓐ VT + ADV 1 [+ *lever etc*] tirar hacia sí; [+ *curtains*] descorrer

2 (*Sport**) **to ~ one back** remontar un gol

Ⓑ VI + ADV 1 (= *refrain*) contenerse

2 (*Mil*) (= *withdraw*) retirarse

► **pull down** VT + ADV 1 (= *lower*) [+ *blinds etc*] bajar; **he ~ed his hat down** se caló el sombrero, se encasquetó el sombrero*

2 (= *cause to fall*) [+ *person*] hacer caer, tumbar

3 (= *demolish*) derribar, demoler; (*fig*) [+ *government*] derribar

4 (= *weaken*) debilitar; **the mark in chemistry ~s her down** la nota de química es la que la perjudica *or* la que le baja la media

5 (*US**) (= *earn*) ganar

► **pull in** Ⓐ VT + ADV 1 [+ *claws*] retraer; [+ *net*] recoger; [+ *rope*] cobrar

2 (= *rein in*) [+ *horse*] sujetar

3 (*) (= *attract*) [+ *crowds*] atraer; **the film is ~ing them in** la película atrae un público numeroso, la película es muy popular; **this will ~ them in** esto les hará venir en masa

4 (*) (= *take into custody*) detener

5 (*) (= *earn*) ganar

Ⓑ VI + ADV (= *enter*) (*into station, harbour*) llegar; (*into driveway*) entrar; (= *stop, park*) parar

► **pull off** Ⓐ VT + ADV 1 (= *remove*) quitar, arrancar; [+ *clothes*] quitarse (de prisa)

2 (*) (= *cause to succeed*) [+ *plan etc*] llevar a cabo, conseguir; [+ *deal*] cerrar, concluir con éxito; **to ~ it off** lograrlo

Ⓑ VI + ADV **we ~ed off into a lay-by** (*Aut*) salimos de la carretera y paramos en un apartadero

Ⓒ VT + PREP **the buses were ~ed off the road at once** en seguida los autobuses dejaron de circular

Ⓓ VI + PREP **we ~ed off the road into a lay-by** salimos de la carretera y paramos en un apartadero

► **pull on** VT + ADV [+ *gloves etc*] ponerse (de prisa)

► **pull out** Ⓐ VT + ADV 1 (= *take out*) (*from pocket, drawer*) sacar; (*from ground*) arrancar; [+ *tooth*] sacar, extraer; (= *pull outwards*) [+ *lever etc*] tirar hacia fuera; **to ~ sb out of a river** sacar a algn de un río; **to ~ sb out of a hole** sacar a algn de un hoyo (a estirones)

2 (= *withdraw*) retirar; **everybody was ~ed out on strike** todos fueron llamados a la huelga

Ⓑ VI + ADV 1 (*Aut, Rail*) (= *come out*) salir; **the red car ~ed out from behind that black one** el coche rojo salió de detrás de aquel negro; **he ~ed out and disappeared into the traffic** arrancó y se perdió en el tráfico

2 (*Mil*) (= *withdraw*) retirarse (**from** de)

3 (= *leave*) salir, partir; **we're ~ing out** nos marchamos ya

4 **it ~s out easily** [*drawer etc*] sale fácilmente

► **pull over** Ⓐ VT + ADV 1 (= *bring closer*) [+ *chair*] acercar

2 (= *topple*) volcar

3 (*Police*) [+ *car, driver*] parar

Ⓑ VI + ADV (*Aut*) hacerse a un lado

► **pull round** Ⓐ VT + ADV **to ~ sb round** [+ *unconscious person*] reanimar a algn

Ⓑ VI + ADV [*unconscious person*] reanimarse, volver en sí

► **pull through** Ⓐ VI + ADV (*from illness*) reponerse, recobrar la salud; (*from difficulties etc*) reponerse

Ⓑ VT + ADV **to ~ sb through** [+ *crisis*] sacar a algn del apuro; [+ *illness*] ayudar a algn a reponerse

► **pull together** Ⓐ VT + ADV 1 **let me ~ together the threads of my argument** permítanme atar los cabos de mi razonamiento; **he has ~ed the team together** gracias a él los jugadores han recuperado su espíritu de equipo

2 **to ~ o.s. together** calmarse, tranquilizarse; **~ yourself together!** ¡cálmate!

Ⓑ VI + ADV (*fig*) (= *cooperate*) ir todos a una

► **pull up** Ⓐ VT + ADV 1 (= *raise by pulling*) levantar, subir; [+ *socks etc*] subir

2 (= *bring closer*) [+ *chair*] acercar

3 (= *uproot*) sacar, arrancar; ✦*IDIOM* **to ~ up one's roots** desarraigarse

4 (= *stop*) parar; [+ *horse*] refrenar; **the police ~ed him up for speeding** la policía lo paró por sobrepasar el límite de velocidad

5 (= *scold*) regañar

6 (= *strengthen*) fortalecer; **it has ~ed the pound up** ha fortalecido la libra; **his mark in French has ~ed him up** la nota de francés le ha subido la media

Ⓑ VI + ADV 1 (= *stop*) detenerse, parar; (*Aut*) parar(se)

2 (= *restrain o.s.*) contenerse

pull-back [ˈpʊlbæk] N (*Mil*) retirada *f*

pull-down [ˈpʊl,daʊn] ADJ **~ menu** menú *m* desplegable

pullet [ˈpʊlɪt] N polla *f*, pollita *f*

pulley [ˈpʊlɪ] N polea *f*

pull-in [ˈpʊl,ɪn] N (*Brit Aut*) (= *lay-by*) apartadero *m*; (*for food*) café *m* de carretera, restaurante *m* de carretera

Pullman® [ˈpʊlmən] N (*pl* **Pullmans**) 1 (*Brit*) (*also* **~ carriage**) vagón *m* de primera clase

2 (*US*) (*also* **~ car**) coche *m* cama

pull-off [ˈpʊlɒf] N (*US Aut*) apartadero *m*

pull-out [ˈpʊlaʊt] Ⓐ N 1 (*in magazine*) suplemento *m* separable

2 (*Mil etc*) retirada *f*

Ⓑ CPD [*magazine section*] separable; [*table leaf etc*] extensible

pullover [ˈpʊləʊvəʳ] N (*esp Brit*) jersey *m*, suéter *m*, chompa *f* (*Peru, Bol*)

pullulate [ˈpʌljʊleɪt] VI pulular

pull-up [ˈpʊlʌp] N 1 (*Brit*) = **pull-in**

2 (*US*) = **press-up**

pulmonary [ˈpʌlmənərɪ] ADJ pulmonar

pulp [pʌlp] Ⓐ N 1 (= *paper pulp, wood pulp*) pasta *f*, pulpa *f*; (*for paper*) pulpa *f* de madera; **to reduce sth to ~** hacer algo papilla; **a leg crushed to ~** (*fig*) una pierna hecha trizas; **to beat sb to a ~*** (*fig*) dar a algn una tremenda paliza, hacer a algn papilla*

2 [*of fruit, vegetable*] pulpa *f*

Ⓑ VT reducir a pulpa

Ⓒ CPD ► **pulp literature** N literatura *f* barata

► **pulp magazine** N revista *f* amarilla

pulping [ˈpʌlpɪŋ] N reducción *f* a pulpa

pulpit [ˈpʊlpɪt] N púlpito *m*

pulpy [ˈpʌlpɪ] ADJ 1 pulposo

2 (*) [*literature*] para tirar, de bajísima calidad

pulsar [ˈpʌlsɑːʳ] N pulsar *m*

pulsate [pʌlˈseɪt] VI vibrar, palpitar

pulsating [pʌlˈseɪtɪŋ] ADJ 1 [*heart*] palpitante; [*music*] vibrante

2 (*fig*) (= *exciting*) palpitante, excitante

pulsation [pʌlˈseɪʃən] N pulsación *f*, latido *m*

pulse[1] [pʌls] Ⓐ N (*Anat*) pulso *m*; (*Phys*) pulsación *f*; (*fig*) [*of drums, music*] ritmo *m*, compás *m*; **to take sb's ~** tomar el pulso a algn; ✦*IDIOM* **he keeps his finger on the company's ~** está tomando constantemente el pulso a la compañía, se mantiene al tanto de lo que pasa en la compañía

Ⓑ VI pulsar, latir

Ⓒ CPD ► **pulse beat** N latido *m* del pulso ► **pulse rate** N frecuencia *f* del pulso

pulse² [pʌls] N (*Bot, Culin*) legumbre *f*

pulverization [ˌpʌlvəraɪˈzeɪʃən] N pulverización *f*

pulverize [ˈpʌlvəraɪz] VT pulverizar; (*fig*) hacer polvo; (*) (= *thrash*) hacer polvo a*

puma [ˈpjuːmə] N puma *m*

pumice [ˈpʌmɪs], **pumice stone** [ˈpʌmɪsstəʊn] N piedra *f* pómez

pummel [ˈpʌml] VT aporrear, apalear

pummelling, **pummeling** (*US*) [ˈpʌməlɪŋ] N **to take a ~** (*lit*) recibir una paliza, llevarse una paliza; (*fig*) (*in debate etc*) recibir un vapuleo; (*in match etc*) recibir una paliza*

pump¹ [pʌmp] Ⓐ N [1] (*for liquid, gas, air*) bomba *f*; **foot/hand ~** bomba *f* de pie/de mano; *see also* **bicycle B**, **bilge B**, **petrol B**, **suction B**

[2] (*also* **petrol ~**) surtidor *m* de gasolina

[3] (= *act of pumping*) **I gave the tyre a quick ~** le metí un poco de aire al neumático, inflé un poco el neumático; **after a few ~s water came gushing forth** después de darle a la bomba un par de veces, empezó a salir agua a borbotones

Ⓑ VT [1] (*lit*) [1·1] (*with a pump*) bombear; **gas is ~ed from under the sea bed** el gas se bombea desde el fondo del mar; **to ~ sth dry** [+ *well, river, lake*] secar algo, dejar algo seco; **the tank was ~ed full of water each day** el tanque se llenaba de agua todos los días; **to ~ gas** (*US*) echar *or* meter gasolina; **oil is ~ed into the house from a tank outside** el combustible se bombea a la casa desde un depósito que hay fuera; **a respirator ~ed oxygen into her lungs** un respirador le bombeaba oxígeno a los pulmones; **to ~ air into a tyre** inflar un neumático; **the factory just ~s its waste into the river** la fábrica simplemente vierte sus residuos al río; **they are ~ing oil out of the wrecked tanker** están bombeando el petróleo del buque cisterna siniestrado; **the heart ~s blood round the body** el corazón hace circular la sangre por el cuerpo; **to ~ sb's stomach** hacer un lavado de estómago a algn; ✦*IDIOM* **to ~ sb dry** dejar a algn seco

[1·2] (*Naut*) **to ~ (out) the bilges** achicar la sentina

[2] (*fig*) **we can't go on ~ing money into this project** no podemos seguir metiendo tanto dinero en *or* inyectándole tanto dinero a este proyecto; **he ~ed five bullets into her head** le metió cinco balas en la cabeza; **to ~ sb full of drugs** atiborrar a algn de drogas; **to ~ sb full of lead*** acribillar *or* coser a algn a balazos*; *see also* **prime C2**

[3] (= *move up and down*) [+ *pedal*] pisar repetidamente; [+ *handle*] darle repetidamente a; **he ~ed the accelerator** pisó repetidamente el pedal del acelerador, se puso a darle al pedal del acelerador; **to ~ sb's hand/arm** dar un fuerte apretón de manos a algn; ✦*IDIOM* **to ~ iron*** hacer pesas

[4] (*) (= *question*) **I ~ed him discreetly about his past** le sonsaqué discretamente todo lo que pude acerca de su pasado, le tiré de la lengua discretamente acerca de su pasado*; **to ~ sb for information** sonsacar información a algn

Ⓒ VI [1] [*person*] [1·1] (*at pump*) **here's a bucket, get ~ing!** aquí tienes un balde, ¡a trabajar la bomba!

[1·2] (*on lever*) **he was ~ing away on the lever** estaba moviendo la palanca de arriba abajo sin parar

[1·3] (*on pedal*) **he was ~ing away, trying to get the car to start** pisaba repetidamente el pedal, intentando arrancar el coche

[2] [*pump, machine*] **the machine is ~ing (away) all the time** la máquina de bombeo está en funcionamiento constantemente; **the piston was ~ing up and down** el émbolo subía y bajaba

[3] [*heart*] (= *circulate blood*) bombear la sangre; (= *beat*) latir; [*blood, adrenaline*] correr por las venas

[4] [*liquid*] **the oil was ~ing along the pipeline** el petróleo corría por el tubo; **blood ~ed from the severed artery** la sangre salía a borbotones de la arteria cortada

Ⓓ CPD ► **pump attendant** N encargado/a *m/f* de la gasolinera ► **pump house** N sala *f* de bombas ► **pump price** N [*of petrol*] precio *m* de la gasolina ► **pump room** N sala *f* de bombas

►**pump in** VT + ADV [1] (*lit*) (*with pump*) bombear, meter *or* introducir con una bomba; (*with other device*) bombear; **~ some more air in** bombea más aire, introduce *or* mete más aire (con la bomba); **they are having water ~ed in from surrounding areas** se les está bombeando agua de las zonas colindantes

[2] (*fig*) [+ *money*] inyectar

►**pump out** Ⓐ VT + ADV [1] (= *extract, remove*) [+ *oil, water*] bombear, extraer *or* sacar con una bomba

[2] (= *empty*) [+ *boat*] achicar el agua de; [+ *flooded cellar, building*] sacar el agua de; **it's no fun having your stomach ~ed out** un lavado de estómago no es nada divertido

[3] (= *produce, emit*) [3·1] (*lit*) despedir; **the pipe was ~ing out raw sewage** el tubo estaba despidiendo aguas residuales sin tratar; **cars which ~ out deadly exhaust fumes** los coches que despiden gases letales

[3·2] (*fig*) (*) **the country is investing a lot of money into ~ing out more oil** el país está invirtiendo mucho dinero para producir más petróleo; **this station ~s out music 24 hours a day** esta cadena emite música las veinticuatro horas del día; **he ~s out articles each week** cada semana saca un artículo detrás de otro como si nada

Ⓑ VI + ADV manar; **oil was ~ing out from the ruptured tanks** el petróleo manaba de las cisternas rotas

►**pump up** VT + ADV [1] (= *inflate*) [+ *tyre*] hinchar, inflar (*LAm*)

[2] (= *carry up*) [+ *water, oil*] bombear; **water is ~ed up from springs** se bombea el agua de los manantiales

[3] (*) (= *increase*) [+ *prices, profits*] inflar; **to ~ up the economy** reactivar la economía

[4] (= *enhance*) mejorar; **we need to ~ up his image** tenemos que mejorar su imagen

[5] (= *inspire*) [+ *person*] animar; [+ *morale*] subir, levantar

pump² [pʌmp] N (*esp Brit*) (= *sports shoe*) zapatilla *f*; (*esp US*) (= *dancing shoe*) bailarina *f*; (= *slip-on shoe*) zapato *m* de salón

pump-action shotgun [ˌpʌmpækʃənˈʃɒtgʌn] N escopeta *f* de pistón

pumper [ˈpʌmpəʳ] N (*US*) coche *m* bomba

pumpernickel [ˈpʌmpənɪkl] N pan *m* de centeno entero

pumping station [ˈpʌmpɪŋˌsteɪʃən] N (*for water*) estación *f* de bombeo; (*for oil*) estación *f* de bombeo de crudo

pumpkin [ˈpʌmpkɪn] N (= *vegetable*) calabaza *f*, zapallo *m* (*Andes, S. Cone*); (= *plant*) calabacera *f*

pump-priming [ˈpʌmpˈpraɪmɪŋ] N (*fig*) inversión *f* inicial con carácter de estímulo; (*US*) *inversión estatal en nuevos proyectos que se espera beneficien la economía*

pun [pʌn] Ⓐ N juego *m* de palabras (**on** sobre), retruécano *m*, albur *m* (*Mex*)

Ⓑ VI hacer un juego de palabras (**on** sobre), alburear (*Mex*)

Punch [pʌntʃ] Ⓐ N (*Theat*) Polichinela *m*; ✦*IDIOM* **to be as pleased as ~** estar como unas pascuas

Ⓑ CPD ► **Punch and Judy show** N teatro *m* de títeres

punch¹ [pʌntʃ] Ⓐ N [1] (= *tool*) [1·1] (*for making holes*) (*in leather, etc*) punzón *m*; (*in paper*) perforadora *f*; (*in ticket*) máquina *f* de picar

[1·2] (*for stamping design*) troquel *m*, cuño *m*

[1·3] (*for driving in nails*) clavadora *f*

[2] (= *blow*) puñetazo *m*; **he floored him with one ~** lo derribó de un solo puñetazo; **body ~** (*Boxing*) puñetazo *m* en el cuerpo; **a ~ in the face** un puñetazo en la cara; **to land a ~** asestar un puñetazo; **a ~ on** *or* **in the nose** un puñetazo en la nariz; **he packs a ~*** pega duro*; **to swing** *or* **throw a ~** soltar un puñetazo; **to take a ~** recibir un puñetazo; ✦*IDIOM* **to pull one's ~es** andarse con miramientos; **he didn't pull any ~es** no se mordió la lengua; *see also* **knockout B**

[3] (*fig*) (= *vigour*) empuje *m*, garra *f*; **he has ~** tiene empuje *or* garra; **think of a phrase that's got some ~ to it** piensa una frase que tenga garra

Ⓑ VT [1] (= *perforate*) (*with tool*) [+ *paper, card, metal*] perforar; [+ *leather*] punzar; [+ *ticket*] picar; (*also* ~ **out**) (*with die*) troquelar; (= *stamp*) [+ *design*] estampar; **~ed card** tarjeta *f* perforada; **to ~ the clock** fichar; **to ~ a hole in sth** (*in leather, paper, metal*) hacer un agujero a algo; **they ~ed holes in Arsenal's defence** encontraron huecos en la defensa del Arsenal; **~ed tape** cinta *f* perforada

[2] (= *hit*) (*with fist*) dar un puñetazo a; **to ~ sb in the stomach/on the nose** dar un puñetazo a algn en el estómago/la nariz; **to ~ sb in the face** ◊ **~ sb's face** dar un puñetazo a algn en la cara; **she ~ed the air in triumph** agitaba los brazos, triunfante; **I ~ed the ball into the net** metí el balón en la red de un manotazo; **he ~ed his fist through the glass** atravesó el cristal de un puñetazo; **he ~ed the wall angrily** golpeó la pared furioso

[3] (= *press*) [+ *button, key*] presionar

[4] (*US*) **to ~ cattle** aguijonear al ganado

Ⓒ VI pegar (puñetazos); **come on, you can ~ harder than that!** ¡venga, que puedes pegar con más fuerza!; **to ~ at sb** dar *or* pegar un puñetazo a algn

Ⓓ CPD ► **punch bag** N (*Brit*) saco *m* de arena ► **punch card** N tarjeta *f* perforada ► **punch line** N remate *m* ► **punch operator** N operador(a) *m/f* de máquina perforadora

►**punch in** Ⓐ VT + ADV [1] (= *beat up*) **to ~ sb's face/head in*** romper la cara/la crisma a algn*

[2] (= *key in*) [+ *code, number*] teclear; **you have to ~ the code in first** primero hay que teclear *or* introducir el código

Ⓑ VI + ADV (*on time clock*) fichar

►**punch out** Ⓐ VT + ADV [1] (*with tool*) [+ *hole*] perforar; (*with die*) [+ *machine parts*] troquelar

[2] [+ *number, code*] teclear; **I picked up the phone and ~ed out a number** descolgué el teléfono y tecleé un número

[3] (*) (*with fist*) [+ *person*] pegar

Ⓑ VI + ADV (*on time clock*) fichar al salir

punch² [pʌntʃ] N (= *drink*) ponche *m*

punchball ['pʌntʃbɔːl] N 1 (*Brit*) pera *f*, punching-ball *m*
2 (*US*) (= *game*) *tipo de béisbol que se juega sin bate*

punchbowl ['pʌntʃbəʊl] N ponchera *f*

punch-drunk ['pʌntʃ'drʌŋk] ADJ (*fig*) aturdido; **to be ~** estar grogui*

puncher ['pʌntʃəʳ] N 1 (= *tool*) perforadora *f*; (*for leather*) punzón *m*
2 (= *boxer etc*) **he's a hard ~** pega fuerte

punching bag ['pʌntʃɪŋbæg] N (*US*) = **punch bag**

punch-up* ['pʌntʃʌp] N (*Brit*) pelea *f*, refriega *f*

punchy* ['pʌntʃɪ] ADJ (*compar* **punchier**; *superl* **punchiest**) [*person etc*] de empuje, con garra; [*phrase*] con garra; [*remark*] incisivo, contundente; [*style*] vigoroso

punctilio [pʌŋk'tɪlɪəʊ] N (*pl* **punctilios**) (*frm*) puntillo *m*, etiqueta *f*

punctilious [pʌŋk'tɪlɪəs] ADJ puntilloso, quisquilloso

punctiliously [pʌŋk'tɪlɪəslɪ] ADV de modo puntilloso

punctual ['pʌŋktjʊəl] ADJ puntual; **you're very ~** (*now*) llegaste en punto; (*usually*) siempre llegas puntual; **"please be ~"** "se ruega la mayor puntualidad"

punctuality [,pʌŋktjʊ'ælɪtɪ] N puntualidad *f*

punctually ['pʌŋktjʊəlɪ] ADV puntualmente, en punto; **the bus arrived ~** el autobús llegó puntualmente *or* a la hora; **~ at six o'clock** a las seis en punto

punctuate ['pʌŋktjʊeɪt] VT (*Ling*) puntuar; **his speech was ~d by applause** los aplausos interrumpieron repetidamente su discurso

punctuation [,pʌŋktjʊ'eɪʃən] Ⓐ N (*Ling*) puntuación *f*
Ⓑ CPD ► **punctuation mark** N signo *m* de puntuación

puncture ['pʌŋktʃəʳ] Ⓐ N (*in tyre, balloon*) pinchazo *m*, ponchadura *f* (*Mex*); (*in skin*) perforación *f*; (*Aut*) pinchazo *m*, ponchadura *f* (*Mex*); **I have a ~** se me ha pinchado *or* (*Mex*) ponchado un neumático *or* (*esp LAm*) una llanta; **I had a ~ on the motorway** tuve un pinchazo en la autopista
Ⓑ VT [+ *tyre*] pinchar, ponchar (*Mex*); [+ *skin*] perforar; **this ~d his confidence** esto destruyó su confianza; **we'll see if it ~s his pride** veremos si esto le baja los humos
Ⓒ VI pincharse, poncharse (*Mex*)

pundit ['pʌndɪt] N experto/a *m/f*

pungency ['pʌndʒənsɪ] N [*of smell, flavour*] acritud *f*; [*of remark*] mordacidad *f*

pungent ['pʌndʒənt] ADJ [*smell, flavour*] acre; [*remark, style*] mordaz

pungently ['pʌndʒəntlɪ] ADV [*smell*] acremente; [*remark, write*] mordazmente

Punic ['pjuːnɪk] Ⓐ ADJ púnico
Ⓑ N púnico *m*

punish ['pʌnɪʃ] VT 1 castigar; **to ~ sb for sth/for doing sth** castigar a algn por algo/por hacer algo; **they were severely ~ed for their disobedience** los castigaron severamente por su desobediencia
2 (*fig*) (*) maltratar

punishable ['pʌnɪʃəbl] ADJ (*gen*) punible; (*Jur*) punible, sancionable; **a ~ offence** una infracción penada *or* sancionada por la ley; **a crime ~ by death** un delito castigado con la pena de muerte

punishing ['pʌnɪʃɪŋ] Ⓐ ADJ [*race, schedule*] duro, agotador
Ⓑ N castigo *m*; (*fig*) castigo *m*, malos tratos *mpl*; **to take a ~** recibir una paliza*; [*car, furniture etc*] recibir muchos golpes

punishment ['pʌnɪʃmənt] N 1 (= *punishing, penalty*) castigo *m*; **to make the ~ fit the crime** determinar un castigo acorde con la gravedad del crimen; **to take one's ~** aceptar el castigo
2 (*fig*) (*) malos tratos *mpl*; **to take a lot of ~** (*Sport*) recibir una paliza*; [*car, furniture etc*] recibir muchos golpes

punitive ['pjuːnɪtɪv] ADJ punitivo; (*Jur*) [*damages*] punitorio

Punjabi [pʌn'dʒɑːbɪ] Ⓐ ADJ punjabí
Ⓑ N 1 (*Ling*) punjabí *m*
2 (= *person*) punjabí *mf*

punk [pʌŋk] Ⓐ N 1 (= *person*) (*also* **~ rocker**) punki *mf*, punk *mf*; (= *music*) (*also* **~ rock**) música *f* punk, punk *m*
2 (*US**) (= *hoodlum*) rufián *m*, matón *m* (*LAm*)
Ⓑ CPD ► **punk rock** N música *f* punk, punk *m*; **a ~ rock band** un grupo punk

punnet ['pʌnɪt] N (*Brit*) canastilla *f*

punster ['pʌnstəʳ] N persona *f* aficionada a los juegos de palabras, equivoquista *mf*

punt¹ [pʌnt] Ⓐ N (= *boat*) batea *f*
Ⓑ VT [+ *boat*] impulsar (con percha); [+ *ball*] dar un puntapié a
Ⓒ VI **to go ~ing** ir a pasear en batea

punt² [pʌnt] VI (= *bet*) apostar

punt³ [pʌnt] Ⓐ N puntapié *m* de volea
Ⓑ VT dar un puntapié de volea a

punt⁴ [pʊnt] N (= *currency*) libra *f* (irlandesa)

punter ['pʌntəʳ] (*esp Brit*) N 1 (*Brit Racing*) (= *gambler*) jugador(a) *m/f*, apostador(a) *m/f*
2 (*) (= *customer*) cliente *mf*; [*of prostitute*] cliente *mf*; **the ~(s)** (*Brit*) (= *customer, member of public*) el público

puntpole ['pʌntpəʊl] N percha *f*, pértiga *f* (de batea)

puny ['pjuːnɪ] ADJ (*compar* **punier**; *superl* **puniest**) enclenque, endeble

PUP N ABBR (*Brit*) = **Progressive Unionist Party**

pup [pʌp] Ⓐ N (= *young*) [*of dog*] cachorro/a *m/f*; [*of other animal*] cría *f*; **seal ~** cría *f* de foca; ✦**IDIOM to sell sb a ~** dar a algn gato por liebre
Ⓑ VI [*bitch*] parir

pupa ['pjuːpə] N (*pl* **pupae** ['pjuːpiː]) crisálida *f*

pupate ['pjuːpeɪt] VI crisalidar

pupil¹ ['pjuːpl] N 1 (*in school*) alumno/a *m/f*, educando/a *m/f* (*frm*); **last year ~ numbers increased by 46,100** el año pasado hubo un aumento de 46.100 en el número total de alumnos; **~-teacher ratio** proporción *f* de alumnos por maestro; *see also* **teacher-pupil ratio**
2 [*of musician, artist etc*] alumno/a *m/f*, discípulo/a *m/f*

pupil² ['pjuːpl] N (*Anat*) pupila *f*

puppet ['pʌpɪt] Ⓐ N (*lit*) títere *m*, marioneta *f*; (*fig*) títere *m*
Ⓑ CPD ► **puppet government**, **puppet régime** N gobierno *m* títere ► **puppet show** N teatro *m* de títeres *or* marionetas ► **puppet theatre**, **puppet theater** (*US*) N = **puppet show**

puppeteer [,pʌpɪ'tɪəʳ] N titiritero/a *m/f*

puppetry ['pʌpɪtrɪ] N títeres *mpl*, arte *m* del titiritero

puppy ['pʌpɪ] Ⓐ N cachorro/a *m/f*, perrito/a *m/f*
Ⓑ CPD ► **puppy fat** N gordura *f* infantil ► **puppy love** N amor *m* juvenil

purblind ['pɜːblaɪnd] ADJ cegato; (*fig*) ciego, falto de comprensión

purchase ['pɜːtʃɪs] Ⓐ N 1 (= *act, object*) compra *f*, adquisición *f*; **to make a ~** hacer una compra, efectuar una adquisición (*frm*)
2 (= *grip*) agarre *m*, asidero *m*; (= *leverage*) palanca *f*; **I got a ~ on the rope and pulled** me agarré de la cuerda y tiré; **I was trying to get a ~ on the cliff face** estaba intentando agarrarme a la pared del acantilado; **the wheels can't get a ~ on this surface** los neumáticos no se adhieren bien a esta superficie
Ⓑ VT (*frm*) comprar, adquirir; **to ~ sth from sb** comprar algo a algn; **he ~d his freedom at a great price** pagó muy cara su libertad
Ⓒ CPD ► **purchase order** N orden *f* de compra ► **purchase price** N precio *m* de compra ► **purchase tax** N (*Brit*) (*formerly*) impuesto *m* sobre la venta

purchaser ['pɜːtʃɪsəʳ] N comprador(a) *m/f*

purchasing ['pɜːtʃɪsɪŋ] Ⓐ N compra *f*
Ⓑ CPD ► **purchasing department** N departamento *m* de compras ► **purchasing officer** N agente *mf* de compra ► **purchasing power** N [*of person, currency*] poder *m* adquisitivo

purdah ['pɜːdə] N (*in India etc*) reclusión *f* femenina; **to be in ~** (*fig*) estar en cuarentena

pure [pjʊəʳ] Ⓐ ADJ (*compar* **purer**; *superl* **purest**)
1 (= *unadulterated*) [*wool, alcohol, substance*] puro; [*silk*] natural; **a ~ wool jumper** un jersey de lana pura; **it's blackmail, ~ and simple** esto es chantaje, lisa y llanamente
2 (= *clean, clear*) [*air, water, sound, light*] puro
3 (= *sheer*) [*pleasure, luck, coincidence, speculation*] puro; **the whole story was ~ invention** todo fue puro cuento; **by ~ chance** por pura casualidad
4 (= *theoretical*) puro; **~ mathematics/science** matemáticas *fpl*/ciencias *fpl* puras
5 (= *virgin, blameless*) puro; **~ in** *or* **of heart** (*liter*) limpio de corazón; **~ in mind and body** de mente y cuerpo puros; ✦**IDIOM as ~ as the driven snow** puro como la nieve
Ⓑ CPD ► **pure vowel** N vocal *f* simple

> **PURE**
>
> **Position of "puro"**
>
> You should generally put **puro** after the noun when you mean **pure** in the sense of "uncontaminated" or "unadulterated" and before the noun in the sense of "sheer" or "plain":
>
> ...pure olive oil...
>
> ***...aceite puro de oliva...***
>
> It's pure coincidence
>
> ***Es pura coincidencia***
>
> *For further uses and examples, see main entry.*

purebred ['pjʊə'bred] Ⓐ ADJ [*horse*] de pura sangre; [*dog*] de raza
Ⓑ N animal *m* de raza; (= *horse*) pura sangre *mf*, purasangre *mf*

purée ['pjʊəreɪ] N (*Culin*) puré *m*; **apple ~** puré *m* de manzana; **tomato ~** puré *m* de tomate, concentrado *m* de tomate

purely ['pjʊəlɪ] ADV (= *wholly*) puramente; **their relationship was ~ physical** su relación era puramente física; **it is not a ~ physical illness** no es simplemente una enfermedad orgánica; **we met ~ by accident** nos conocimos por pura casualidad; **~ and simply** lisa y llanamente

pure-minded ['pjʊə'maɪndɪd] ADJ de mente pura

pureness ['pjʊənɪs] N pureza *f*

purgation [pɜː'geɪʃən] N purgación *f*

purgative ['pɜːgətɪv] Ⓐ ADJ (*Med*) purgante,

purgativo
Ⓑ N (*Med*) purgante *m*

purgatory ['pɜːgətərɪ] N (*Rel, fig*) purgatorio *m*; **it was ~!** ¡fue un purgatorio!

purge [pɜːdʒ] Ⓐ N (*all senses*) purga *f*, depuración *f*
Ⓑ VT (*all senses*) purgar, depurar

purification [ˌpjʊərɪfɪ'keɪʃən] N [*of air*] purificación *f*; [*of water*] depuración *f*

purifier ['pjʊərɪfaɪəʳ] N [*of air*] purificador *m*; [*of water*] depurador *m*

purify ['pjʊərɪfaɪ] VT [+ *air*] purificar; [+ *water*] depurar; [+ *metal*] acrisolar, refinar

purism ['pjʊərɪzəm] N purismo *m*

purist ['pjʊərɪst] N purista *mf*

puritan ['pjʊərɪtən] Ⓐ ADJ puritano
Ⓑ N puritano/a *m/f*

puritanical [ˌpjʊərɪ'tænɪkəl] ADJ puritano

puritanism ['pjʊərɪtənɪzəm] N puritanismo *m*

purity ['pjʊərɪtɪ] N pureza *f*

purl [pɜːl] Ⓐ N punto *m* del revés
Ⓑ VT hacer punto del revés; **"~ two"** "dos del revés"

purler* ['pɜːləʳ] N **to come a ~** caer pesadamente, caer aparatosamente; (*fig*) fracasar estrepitosamente, darse un batacazo*

purlieus ['pɜːljuːz] NPL (*frm, hum*) alrededores *mpl*, inmediaciones *fpl*

purloin [pɜː'lɔɪn] VT (*frm or hum*) robar

purple ['pɜːpl] Ⓐ ADJ morado; **to go ~ (in the face)** enrojecer; **Purple Heart** (*US Mil*) *decoración otorgada a los heridos de guerra*; **~ heart** (píldora *f* de) anfetamina *f*; **~ prose** prosa *f* de estilo inflado
Ⓑ N (= *colour*) púrpura *f*, morado *m*
Ⓒ VT purpurar

purplish ['pɜːplɪʃ] ADJ purpurino, algo purpúreo

purport (*frm*) Ⓐ ['pɜːpət] N 1 (= *meaning*) significado *m*, sentido *m*
2 (= *purpose*) intención *f*
Ⓑ [pɜː'pɔːt] VT **to ~ to be** pretender ser

purportedly [pɜː'pɔːtɪdlɪ] ADV supuestamente

▼ **purpose** ['pɜːpəs] Ⓐ N 1 (= *intention*) propósito *m*, objetivo *m*; **we all shared a common ~** todos teníamos el mismo propósito *or* objetivo; **she has a ~ in life** tiene un objetivo *or* una meta *or* un norte en la vida; **what was your ~ in going?** ¿con qué intención fuiste?; **"purpose of visit"** (*on official form*) "motivo *m* del viaje"; **I put that there for a ~** he puesto eso ahí a propósito *or* por una razón; **this is good enough for our ~s** esto sirve para nuestros fines; **he exploited her talent for his own ~s** explotó su talento en beneficio propio; **for all practical ~s** en la práctica; **for the ~s of this meeting** para los fines de esta reunión; **for the ~ of doing sth** con el fin de hacer algo; **on ~** a propósito, adrede; **with the ~ of** con el fin de; *see also* **intent B**
2 (= *use*) uso *m*, utilidad *f*; **what is the ~ of this tool?** ¿qué uso *or* utilidad tiene esta herramienta?; **it wasn't designed for this ~** no se diseñó para este fin *or* uso; **to good ~** provechosamente; **it was all to no ~** todo fue inútil *or* en vano; **you can adapt it to your own ~s** lo puede adaptar a sus necesidades; **it serves no useful ~** no tiene uso práctico, no tiene utilidad práctica; *see also* **serve A2**
3 (= *determination*) resolución *f*, determinación *f*; **to have a sense of ~** tener un rumbo en la vida; **he has no sense of ~** no tiene rumbo en la vida; **she has great strength of ~** tiene muchísima resolución *or* determinación, es muy resuelta; *see also* **infirm**
Ⓑ VT (†) **to ~ doing sth/to do sth** proponerse *or* planear hacer algo

purpose-built [ˌpɜːpəs'bɪlt] ADJ construido especialmente

purposeful ['pɜːpəsfʊl] ADJ [*look, expression*] de determinación; [*manner, walk*] resuelto, decidido; [*work, activity*] con sentido

purposefully ['pɜːpəsfəlɪ] ADV resueltamente

purposefulness ['pɜːpəsfʊlnɪs] N resolución *f*

purposeless ['pɜːpəslɪs] ADJ [*person's character*] irresoluto; [*person's state*] indeciso; [*act*] sin propósito, sin objeto, sin finalidad

purposely ['pɜːpəslɪ] ADV a propósito, adrede, expresamente; **a ~ vague statement** una declaración realizada en términos vagos a propósito *or* adrede *or* expresamente

purposive ['pɜːpəsɪv] ADJ = **purposeful**

purr [pɜːʳ] Ⓐ N ronroneo *m*
Ⓑ VI [*cat, engine*] ronronear
Ⓒ VT (= *say*) susurrar, decir suavemente

purse [pɜːs] Ⓐ N 1 (*Brit*) (*for money*) monedero *m*; **a well-lined ~** una bolsa llena; **it is beyond my ~** mis recursos no llegan a tanto, está fuera de mi alcance; ✦**IDIOM to hold the ~ strings** administrar el dinero; *see also* **public A1, silk C**
2 (*US*) (= *handbag*) bolso *m*, cartera *f* (*LAm*)
3 (= *sum of money as prize*) premio *m* en metálico
Ⓑ VT **to ~ one's lips** fruncir los labios
Ⓒ CPD ► **purse snatcher** N (*US*) carterista *mf*

purser ['pɜːsəʳ] N (*Naut*) comisario/a *m/f*

pursuance [pə'sjuːəns] N (*frm*) **in ~ of** [+ *plan, goal*] para la consecución de; [+ *duty*] en cumplimiento de

pursuant [pə'sjuːənt] ADV (*frm*) **~ to** de acuerdo con, conforme a

pursue [pə'sjuː] VT 1 (= *chase*) perseguir, seguir; **they were being ~d by enemy planes** los aviones enemigos los perseguían *or* los seguían; **she was often ~d by fans** a menudo la perseguían *or* la acosaban sus admiradores; **he has been ~d by bad luck all his life** se ha visto perseguido por la mala suerte toda su vida
2 (= *engage in*) [+ *interests, career*] dedicarse a; [+ *studies, war, talks*] proseguir; [+ *profession*] ejercer, dedicarse a
3 (= *continue with*) [+ *course of action*] seguir; [+ *policy, reform*] aplicar; **he had been pursuing his own inquiries** había estado haciendo sus propias averiguaciones; **we have decided not to ~ the matter further** hemos decidido no seguir adelante con el asunto
4 (= *strive for*) [+ *aim, objective, peace*] luchar por; [+ *happiness, pleasure*] buscar; [+ *success, fame*] perseguir, buscar; [+ *rights*] reivindicar

pursuer [pə'sjuːəʳ] N perseguidor(a) *m/f*

pursuit [pə'sjuːt] Ⓐ N 1 (= *chase*) caza *f*, persecución *f*; (*fig*) [*of pleasure, happiness, knowledge*] busca *f*, búsqueda *f*; **the ~ of wealth** el afán de riqueza; **in (the) ~ of sth/sb** en busca de algo/algn; **to set out in ~ of sb** salir en busca de algn; **with two policemen in hot ~** con dos policías pisándole los talones
2 (= *occupation*) **outdoor ~s** actividades *fpl* al aire libre; **literary ~s** intereses *mpl* literarios, actividades *fpl* literarias; **leisure ~s** pasatiempos *mpl*
Ⓑ CPD ► **pursuit plane** N avión *m* de caza

purulence ['pjʊərʊləns] N purulencia *f*

purulent ['pjʊərʊlənt] ADJ purulento

purvey [pɜː'veɪ] VT (*frm*) proveer, suministrar, abastecer

purveyance [pɜː'veɪəns] N (*frm*) provisión *f*, suministro *m*, abastecimiento *m*

purveyor [pɜː'veɪəʳ] N (*frm*) proveedor(a) *m/f*, abastecedor(a) *m/f*

purview ['pɜːvjuː] N (*frm*) ámbito *m*, esfera *f*; **it comes within the ~ of the law** esta dentro del ámbito *or* la esfera de la ley

pus [pʌs] N pus *m*

push [pʊʃ] Ⓐ N 1 (= *shove*) empujón *m*; **with one ~** de un empujón; **the car needs a ~** hay que empujar el coche; **at the ~ of a button** con sólo apretar *or* pulsar un botón; **to give sth/sb a ~** dar a algo/algn un empujón
2 (*Brit**) **to get the ~**: **he got the ~** [*worker*] lo pusieron de patitas en la calle*, lo echaron; [*lover*] ella lo plantó*, ella lo dejó; **to give sb the ~** [+ *worker*] poner a algn de patitas en la calle*, echar a algn; [+ *lover*] plantar a algn*, dejar a algn
3 (= *effort*) esfuerzo *m*; **in its ~ for economic growth …** en su esfuerzo por desarrollar la economía …
4 (= *encouragement*) empujoncito* *m*; **we need a ~ to take the first step** necesitamos un empujoncito para dar el primer paso*
5 (*Mil*) (= *offensive*) ofensiva *f*; **the allied ~ into occupied Kuwait** la ofensiva de los aliados en la zona ocupada de Kuwait
6 (*) **at a ~** a duras penas; **if** *or* **when it comes to the ~** en último caso, en el peor de los casos; ✦**IDIOM when ~ comes to shove** a la hora de la verdad
7 (= *dynamism*) dinamismo *m*, empuje *m*, energía *f*; **he's got no ~** no tiene empuje, le falta energía; **he's a man with plenty of ~** es hombre de empuje
Ⓑ VT 1 (= *shove, move by pushing*) empujar; **don't ~ me!** ¡no me empujes!; **to ~ sb against a wall** empujar a algn contra una pared; **she ~ed him down the stairs** lo empujó escaleras abajo; **to ~ sb into a room** hacer entrar a algn en una habitación de un empujón; **to ~ a car into the garage** empujar un coche dentro del garaje; **to ~ one's finger into a hole** introducir el dedo en un agujero; **he ~ed the book into my hand** me metió el libro en la mano; **to ~ sb off the pavement** echar a algn de la acera a empujones; **he ~ed the books off the table** tiró los libros de la mesa de un empujón; **they ~ed the car off the cliff** empujaron el coche por el acantilado; **to ~ a door open/shut** abrir/cerrar una puerta empujándola *or* de un empujón; **he ~ed the thought to the back of his mind** intentó quitárselo de la cabeza; **to ~ one's way through the crowd** abrirse paso a empujones por la multitud; **he ~ed his head in through the window** metió la cabeza por la ventana; **he ~ed the box under the table** empujó *or* metió la caja debajo de la mesa
2 (= *press*) [+ *button etc*] apretar, pulsar
3 (*fig*) 3·1 (= *press, advance*) [+ *trade*] fomentar; [+ *product*] promover; **to ~ home one's advantage** aprovechar la ventaja; **don't ~ your luck!*** ¡no te pases!*, ¡no desafíes a la suerte!
3·2 (= *put pressure on*) **when we ~ed her, she explained it all** cuando la presionamos, nos lo explicó todo; **don't ~ her too far** no te pases con ella*; **to ~ sb for payment** ejercer presión sobre algn para que pague; **to ~ sb into doing sth** obligar a algn a hacer algo; **I was ~ed into it** me obligaron a ello; **that's ~ing it a bit*** eso es pasarse un poco*, eso es demasiado; **to ~ o.s.** (*in exercise, work etc*) esforzarse; **to be ~ed for time/money** andar justo de tiempo/escaso de dinero; **to ~ sb to do sth** presionar a algn para que haga algo; **we'll be (hard) ~ed to finish it** tendremos grandes dificultades para terminarlo
4 (*) [+ *drugs*] pasar*
5 (*) **he's ~ing 50** raya en los 50

➤ LANGUAGE IN USE: **purpose A1** 18.4

Ⓒ VI 1 (= *press*) empujar; **don't ~!** ¡no empujes!; **"push"** (*on door*) "empujar"; (*on bell*) "pulsar"; **he ~ed past me** pasó por mi lado dándome un empujón; **she ~ed through the crowd** se abrió paso entre la multitud a empujones
2 (*fig*) (= *make demands*) **he ~es too much** insiste demasiado; **they're ~ing for better conditions** hacen campaña para mejorar sus condiciones (de trabajo)
3 (*Mil*) avanzar; **to ~ into enemy territory** avanzar en territorio enemigo

►**push about***, **push around*** VT + ADV (*fig*) (= *bully*) intimidar; **he's not one to be ~ed around** no se deja intimidar, no se deja mandonear*; **he likes ~ing people around** le gusta mandonear*, le gusta dar órdenes a la gente

►**push ahead** VI + ADV (= *make progress*) seguir adelante; **to ~ ahead with a plan** seguir adelante con un proyecto

►**push along** Ⓐ VT + ADV 1 [+ *object*] empujar
2 [+ *work*] acelerar, agilizar
Ⓑ VI + ADV (*) (= *leave*) marcharse

►**push aside** VT + ADV [+ *person, chair*] apartar, hacer a un lado; (*fig*) [+ *objection, suggestion*] hacer caso omiso de

►**push at** VI + PREP [+ *door etc*] empujar

►**push away** VT + ADV [+ *plate*] apartar; [+ *person*] apartar a un lado; (*more violently*) apartar de un empujón

►**push back** VT + ADV [+ *hair etc*] echar hacia atrás; [+ *enemy, crowd*] hacer retroceder; **he's ~ing back the frontiers of knowledge** está ampliando las fronteras del saber

►**push down** Ⓐ VI + ADV (= *press down*) apretar
Ⓑ VT + ADV 1 (= *press down*) apretar
2 (= *knock over*) derribar
3 (*fig*) [+ *prices, value*] hacer bajar

►**push forward** Ⓐ VI + ADV 1 (*Mil*) avanzar
2 **to ~ forward with a plan** seguir adelante con un proyecto
Ⓑ VT + ADV [+ *person, object*] empujar hacia adelante; [+ *plan, work*] llevar adelante; **he tends to ~ himself forward** (*fig*) suele hacerse notar

►**push in** Ⓐ VT + ADV 1 [+ *screw etc*] introducir (a la fuerza)
2 (= *break*) [+ *window, door*] romper
3 [+ *person*] (*in lake etc*) empujar al agua
Ⓑ VI + ADV 1 (*in queue*) colarse
2 (*fig*) (= *interfere*) entrometerse

►**push off** Ⓐ VT + ADV 1 [+ *top etc*] quitar a la fuerza; [+ *person*] (*off wall etc*) hacer caer; [+ *object*] (*involuntarily*) tirar; (*intentionally*) hacer caer
2 (*Naut*) desatracar
Ⓑ VI + ADV 1 (*Naut*) desatracarse
2 (*) (= *leave*) marcharse; **~ off!** ¡lárgate!*
3 **the top ~es off** la tapa se quita empujando

►**push on** Ⓐ VI + ADV (= *carry on*) continuar; (*on journey*) seguir adelante; **to ~ on with sth** continuar con algo; **we ~ed on to the camp** seguimos hasta el campamento; **they ~ed on another five km** avanzaron cinco km más; **it's time we were ~ing on** es hora de ponernos en camino
Ⓑ VT + ADV 1 [+ *lid etc*] poner a la fuerza
2 (*fig*) (= *incite, urge on*) animar, alentar

►**push out** Ⓐ VT + ADV 1 (*of room, house*) echar a empujones; (*of car*) sacar a empujones
2 (*fig*) [+ *employee, member*] echar, expulsar
3 [+ *tentacle etc*] sacar, extender
4 (*) (= *produce*) [+ *information, products*] producir
5 (*Naut*) [+ *boat*] desatracar
Ⓑ VI + ADV [*root etc*] extenderse

►**push over** VT + ADV 1 (= *cause to fall*) hacer caer, derribar
2 (= *knock over*) [+ *chair, table*] volcar

►**push through** Ⓐ VT + ADV 1 (*through door, hole*) introducir, meter; **I ~ed my way through** me abrí paso a empujones
2 (= *get done quickly*) [+ *deal*] expeditar, apresurar; (*Parl*) [+ *bill*] hacer aprobar
Ⓑ VT + PREP 1 (*lit*) **he ~ed me through the door** me hizo entrar/salir (por la puerta) de un empujón; **he ~ed his hand through the bars** sacó la mano por entre los barrotes; **to ~ one's way through the crowd** abrirse paso a empujones entre la multitud
2 (*Parl*) **the government ~ed the bill through Parliament** el gobierno hizo que el parlamento aprobara el proyecto de ley
Ⓒ VI + ADV [*plant*] abrirse paso
Ⓓ VI + PREP (*through crowd*) abrirse paso por

►**push to** VT + ADV [+ *door*] cerrar

►**push up** VT + ADV 1 [+ *lever, window*] levantar, subir; *see also* **daisy A**
2 (*fig*) (= *raise, increase*) [+ *price, value*] hacer subir

push-bike [ˈpʊʃbaɪk] N (*Brit*) bicicleta *f*, bici* *f*

push-button [ˈpʊʃˌbʌtn] Ⓐ N pulsador *m*, botón *m* (de control *etc*)
Ⓑ CPD de mando de botón; **with ~ control** con mando de botón ► **push-button warfare** N guerra *f* a control remoto

pushcart [ˈpʊʃkɑːt] N carretilla *f* de mano

pushchair [ˈpʊʃtʃɛəʳ] N (*Brit*) sillita *f* de paseo

pusher* [ˈpʊʃəʳ] N 1 [*of drugs*] camello* *mf*, traficante *mf*
2 (= *ambitious person*) ambicioso/a *m/f*

pushful [ˈpʊʃfʊl] ADJ (= *dynamic*) emprendedor, dinámico, enérgico; (= *ambitious*) ambicioso; (*pej*) agresivo

pushfulness [ˈpʊʃfʊlnɪs] N (= *dynamism*) empuje *m*, dinamismo *m*, espíritu *m* emprendedor; (= *ambition*) ambición *f*; (*pej*) agresividad *f*

pushing [ˈpʊʃɪŋ] ADJ = **pushful**

pushover* [ˈpʊʃˌəʊvəʳ] N **it's a ~** está tirado*; **he was a ~** era fácil convencerlo *or* sonsacarlo *etc*; **I'm a ~ when a woman asks me** no resisto cuando me lo pide una mujer

push-pull circuit [ˌpʊʃpʊlˈsɜːkɪt] N circuito *m* de contrafase, circuito *m* equilibrado

push-rod [ˈpʊʃrɒd] N (*Aut*) barra *f* de presión

push-up [ˈpʊʃʌp] N (*US*) = **press-up**

pushy* [ˈpʊʃɪ] ADJ (*pej*) agresivo, avasallador, prepotente (*esp LAm*)

pusillanimity [ˌpjuːsɪləˈnɪmɪtɪ] N pusilanimidad *f*

pusillanimous [ˌpjuːsɪˈlænɪməs] ADJ pusilánime

puss* [pʊs] N (= *cat*) minino* *m*, gatito *m*; **Puss in Boots** El Gato con Botas

pussy [ˈpʊsɪ] Ⓐ N 1 (*also* **~cat**) (* *child language*) minino* *m*, gatito *m*
2 (**) (= *female genitals*) coño** *m*
Ⓑ CPD ► **pussy willow** N sauce *m*

pussycat [ˈpʊsɪkæt] N (*child language*) minino* *m*, gatito *m*

pussyfoot* [ˈpʊsɪfʊt] VI (*esp US*) (*also* **~ around**) andar sigilosamente; (*fig*) no decidirse

pustule [ˈpʌstjuːl] N pústula *f*

put [pʊt] (*pt, pp* **put**)

A TRANSITIVE VERB	C COMPOUND
B INTRANSITIVE VERB	D PHRASAL VERBS

Ⓐ TRANSITIVE VERB

For set combinations consisting of ***put*** *+ noun, eg* ***put a price on, put a strain on, put an end to, put at risk, put out of business, put in touch with*** *look up the noun. For* ***put*** *+ adverb/preposition combinations, see also phrasal verbs.*

1 **= *place, thrust*** 1·1 (*physically*) poner; (*with precision*) colocar; (= *insert*) meter, introducir (*more frm*); (= *leave*) dejar; **I ~ a serviette by each plate** puse *or* coloqué una servilleta junto a cada plato; **~ it in the drawer** ponlo en el cajón; **she ~ the chairs in a circle** puso *or* colocó las sillas en círculo; **shall I ~ milk in your coffee?** ¿te pongo leche en el café?; **you haven't ~ any salt in it** no le has puesto nada de sal; **to ~ an advertisement in the paper** poner un anuncio en el periódico; **he ~ a coin in the slot** puso *or* metió *or* (*more frm*) introdujo una moneda en la ranura; **he ~ the letter in his pocket** se metió la carta en el bolsillo; **he ~ the ball in the net** metió el balón en la red; **to ~ sb in a home** ingresar a algn en una residencia; **you should ~ your money in a bank** deberías poner *or* (*more frm*) depositar el dinero en un banco; **I ~ a sheet of paper into the typewriter** puse *or* coloqué una hoja de papel en la máquina de escribir; **I ~ my hand into the sack** metí la mano en el saco; **he ~ his keys on the table** puso *or* dejó las llaves en la mesa; **I ~ some more coal on the fire** puse *or* eché más carbón en el fuego; **she ~ her head on my shoulder** apoyó *or* recostó la cabeza en mi hombro; **my brother ~ me on the train** mi hermano me dejó en el tren; **to ~ a button on a shirt** coser un botón en una camisa; **she ~ her head out of the window** asomó la cabeza por la ventana; **he ~ his hand over his mouth** se tapó la boca con la mano, se puso la mano en la boca; **he ~ his head round the door** asomó la cabeza por la puerta; **~ it there!*** (*handshake*) ¡chócala!*; **I ~ my fist through the window** rompí la ventana con el puño; **she ~ a bullet through his head** le metió una bala por la cabeza; **he ~ the shell to his ear** se puso *or* se acercó la concha al oído; ✦***IDIOMS*** **~ yourself in my place** ponte en mi lugar; **I didn't know where to ~ myself*** creí que me moría de vergüenza, no sabía dónde meterme; *see also* **bed A1**, **flight²**, **stay A1.1**
1·2 (*with abstract nouns*)

Some ***put*** *+ noun combinations require a more specific Spanish verb. For very set combinations look up the noun.*

the syllabus ~s a lot of emphasis on languages el programa (de estudios) hace *or* pone mucho énfasis en los idiomas; **I wouldn't ~ any faith in what he says** yo no creería lo que dice, yo no tendría ninguna confianza en lo que dice; **you can ~ that idea out of your head** ya te puedes quitar esa idea de la cabeza; **this ~s the responsibility on drivers to be aware of the law** esto responsabiliza a los conductores de estar enterados de la ley; *see also* **blame A**, **figure A6**, **trust A1**, **tax A1**
2 **= *cause to be*** poner; **to ~ sb in a good/bad mood** poner a algn de buen/mal humor; **this ~s me in a very awkward position** esto me pone *or* deja en una situación muy difícil; **his win today ~s him in second place overall** la victoria de hoy le pone *or* coloca en segunda posición en la clasificación general; **to ~ sb in charge of sth** poner a algn a cargo de algo; **to ~ sb on a diet** poner a algn a dieta *or* a régimen; **the doctor has ~ me on**

antibiotics el doctor me ha recetado antibióticos

3 = *cause to undertake* **to ~ sb to sth: it ~ us to a lot of extra expense** nos supuso muchos gastos adicionales; **I don't want to ~ you to any trouble** no quiero causarte ninguna molestia; **she ~ him to work immediately** lo puso a trabajar en seguida

4 = *express* decir; **I don't quite know how to ~ this** la verdad, no sé cómo decir esto; **you can ~ all that in two words** todo eso se puede decir en dos palabras; **as Shakespeare ~s it** como dice Shakespeare; **to ~ it bluntly** para decirlo claramente, hablando en plata*; **I find it hard to ~ into words** me resulta difícil expresarlo con palabras; **to ~ sth into French** traducir algo al francés; **how shall I ~ it?** ¿cómo lo diría?; **let me ~ it this way ...** digámoslo de esta manera ..., por decirlo de alguna manera ...; **to ~ it another way, it'll save you three hours** por decirlo de otra manera, te ahorrará tres horas; **try ~ting it another way** trata de decirlo de otra manera; **to ~ it simply** para decirlo sencillamente

5 = *write* poner, escribir; **what do you want me to ~?** ¿qué quieres que ponga *or* escriba?; **~ your name at the top of the paper** ponga *or* escriba su nombre en la parte superior del papel; **~ the title in capital letters** pon *or* escribe el título en letras mayúsculas; **to ~ sth in writing** poner algo por escrito; **I've ~ you on the waiting list** le he puesto en la lista de espera; **~ it on my account** (*Comm*) cárguelo a mi cuenta; **he ~ a line through the offending paragraph** tachó el párrafo controvertido; **to ~ one's signature to sth** firmar algo

6 = *invest* invertir; **to ~ money into a company** invertir dinero en una compañía; **he ~ all his savings into the project** invirtió todos sus ahorros en el proyecto; **I ~ most of the money into shares** invertí la mayor parte del dinero en acciones; **I've ~ a lot of time and effort into this** he invertido un montón de tiempo y esfuerzo en esto, le he dedicado a esto mucho tiempo y esfuerzo; **she has ~ a lot into the relationship** se ha esforzado mucho en su relación; **"I'm not getting much out of this course" — "well, you're not ~ting much into it, are you?"** —no estoy sacando mucho de este curso —tampoco es que te estés esforzando mucho, ¿no?

7 = *contribute* **to ~ sth towards sth** contribuir (con) algo hacia algo; **I'll pay for the bike but you'll have to ~ something towards it** yo pagaré la bici pero tú tienes que contribuir con algo; **I'm going to ~ the money towards a holiday** voy a poner *or* guardar el dinero para unas vacaciones

8 = *expound, submit* [+ *views*] expresar, exponer; **this will give people an opportunity to ~ their views** esto dará a la gente la oportunidad de expresar *or* exponer sus puntos de vista; **he ~s the case for a change in the law** plantea *or* expone argumentos a favor de un cambio en la ley; **she ~s a convincing case** presenta *or* da argumentos convincentes; **the proposal was ~ before Parliament** la propuesta se presentó ante el parlamento; **to ~ sth to sb**: **how will you ~ it to him?** ¿cómo se lo vas a decir *or* comunicar?; **~ it to him gently** díselo suavemente; **I ~ it to you that ...** les sugiero que ...; **to ~ a question to sb** hacer una pregunta a algn; **the chairman ~ the proposal to the committee** el presidente sometió la propuesta a votación en el comité; **we shall have to ~ it to our members** tendremos que someterlo a la votación de nuestros miembros

9 = *estimate* **they ~ the loss at around £50,000** calcularon *or* valoraron las pérdidas en unas 50.000 libras; **his fortune is ~ at 3 billion** se calcula *or* valora su fortuna en 3 billones; **the number of dead was ~ at 6,000** se calculó *or* estimó el número de muertos en 6.000; **I would ~ him at 40** diría que tiene unos 40 años; **some ~ the figure as high as 20,000** algunos estiman que la cifra llega hasta 20.000

10 = *rank* **he ~ himself above the law** creía estar por encima de la ley; **I wouldn't ~ him among the greatest poets** yo no le pondría entre los más grandes poetas; **we should never ~ money before happiness** no deberíamos nunca anteponer el dinero a la felicidad; **I ~ the needs of my children before anything else** para mí las necesidades de mis hijos van por delante de todo lo demás *or* son más importantes que todo lo demás; **she has always ~ her career first** para ella su carrera siempre ha sido lo primero

11 = *set* **she ~ my brother against me** puso a mi hermano en contra mía; **to ~ a watch to the right time** poner un reloj en hora; **to ~ the words to music** poner música a la letra

12 = *throw* **to ~ the shot** (*Sport*) lanzar el peso

13 *St Ex* (= *offer to sell*) [+ *stock, security*] declararse vendedor de

14 = *bet* *see* **put on**

Ⓑ INTRANSITIVE VERB

Naut **to ~ into port** entrar a puerto; **the ship ~ into Southampton** el barco entró a *or* en Southampton; **to ~ to sea** hacerse a la mar

Ⓒ COMPOUND

► **put option** N (*St Ex*) opción *f* de venta a precio fijado

Ⓓ PHRASAL VERBS

►**put about** Ⓐ VT + ADV 1 (*esp Brit*) [+ *rumour*] hacer correr; **to ~ it about that ...** hacer correr el rumor de que ...

2 (*Naut*) [+ *ship*] hacer virar

3 (*) **he's ~ting it about a bit** (*sexually*) se está ofreciendo a todo quisque*; **to ~ o.s. about** (= *make o.s. noticed*) hacerse notar

Ⓑ VI + ADV (*Naut*) cambiar de rumbo, virar

►**put across** VT + ADV 1 (= *communicate*) [+ *idea*] comunicar; [+ *meaning*] hacer entender; **he finds it hard to ~ his ideas across** le cuesta comunicar sus ideas; **the play ~s the message across very well** la obra transmite el mensaje muy bien; **to ~ o.s. across** (= *present o.s.*) presentarse; **it all depends on how you ~ yourself across** todo depende de cómo te presentes a ti mismo; **to ~ o.s. across well** saber presentarse bien; **he ~s himself across as a sympathetic, caring person** da la impresión de ser una persona comprensiva, compasiva; **to ~ sth across to sb** (= *explain*) explicar algo a algn; (= *convey*) hacer entender algo a algn

2 **to ~ one across on sb*** engañar a algn

►**put aside** VT + ADV 1 (= *lay down*) dejar a un lado, poner a un lado; **he ~ the letter aside to read later** dejó *or* puso a un lado la carta para leerla más tarde

2 (= *save*) [+ *money*] ahorrar, guardar; [+ *time*] reservar; [+ *food*] apartar; **to have money ~ aside** tener ahorros

3 (*in shop*) [+ *goods*] guardar, reservar, apartar; **could you ~ one aside for me?** ¿me podría guardar *or* reservar *or* apartar uno?

4 (= *ignore*) [+ *differences, feelings*] dejar de lado; [+ *fears*] apartar, desechar

5 (= *sacrifice*) [+ *career, personal interest*] sacrificar

►**put away** VT + ADV 1 (*in proper place*) [+ *clothes, toys, books*] guardar, poner en su sitio; [+ *shopping*] guardar, colocar; [+ *car*] poner en el garaje; **~ that knife away!** ¡pon ese cuchillo en su sitio!

2 (*) (= *confine*) (*in prison*) meter en la cárcel, encerrar; (*in asylum*) encerrar en un manicomio

3 (= *save*) [+ *money*] ahorrar, guardar

4 (*) (= *consume*) [+ *food, drink*] tragarse*, zamparse*; **he can certainly ~ it away** ése sí sabe comer

5 (= *reject*) [+ *thought*] desechar, descartar; [+ *wife*] repudiar

6 (*Sport*) (= *score with*) [+ *ball*] meter, marcar; (*US*) (= *beat*) ganar a

7 = **put down A10**

►**put back** Ⓐ VT + ADV 1 (= *replace*) poner otra vez en su sitio; (*in pocket, drawer etc*) volver a guardar; **~ it back when you've finished** ponlo otra vez en su sitio cuando hayas terminado; **~ that back!** ¡deja eso en su sitio *or* donde estaba!; **the fresh air will ~ the colour back in your cheeks** el aire fresco te devolverá el color a las mejillas

2 (= *postpone*) aplazar, posponer; **the meeting has been ~ back till 2 o'clock** la reunión ha sido aplazada hasta las 2

3 (= *delay*) [+ *development, progress*] retrasar, atrasar; **this will ~ us back 10 years** esto nos retrasará 10 años; **he has been ~ back a class** *or* **year** (*Scol*) tiene que repetir el curso

4 (= *change*) [+ *clock*] **to ~ a clock back one hour** atrasar *or* retrasar un reloj una hora; **don't forget to ~ your clocks back on Saturday** el sábado no olviden atrasar *or* retrasar los relojes; ✦*IDIOM* **you can't ~ the clock back** no se puede volver al pasado

5 (= *move back*) **he ~ his head back and roared with laughter** echó hacia atrás la cabeza y se puso a reír a carcajadas

6 (= *reinvest*) [+ *money, profits*] reinvertir (**into** en); **the government didn't ~ enough money back into the economy** el gobierno no reinvirtió suficiente dinero en la economía

7 (*) (= *drink*) beber, beberse; **he's already ~ back seven gins** se ha bebido ya siete copitas de ginebra

Ⓑ VI + ADV (*Naut*) volver, regresar; **to ~ back to port** volver *or* regresar a puerto

►**put back on** VT + ADV [+ *clothes, glasses*] volver a ponerse; **he ~ his trousers back on** volvió a ponerse los pantalones

►**put behind** VT + PREP 1 (*and forget*) **you must ~ all that behind you now** ahora debes olvidar todo eso

2 (*providing support*) **they're ~ting their money and expertise behind the scheme** están apoyando el plan con dinero y experiencia

►**put by** VT + ADV 1 (= *save*) ahorrar; **to have money ~ by** tener ahorros

2 (*in shop*) guardar, reservar, apartar; **I had it ~ by for you** se lo tenía guardado *or* reservado *or* apartado

►**put down** Ⓐ VT + ADV 1 [+ *object*] (= *leave*) dejar; (= *let go of*) soltar; [+ *telephone*] colgar; [+ *passenger*] dejar (bajar), dejar (apearse); **she ~ her glass down and stood up** dejó el vaso y se levantó; **I'll ~ these bags down for a minute** voy a dejar estas bolsas en el suelo un momento; **~ it down!** ¡déjalo!, ¡suéltalo!; **once I started the book I couldn't ~ it down** una vez que empecé el libro no podía dejarlo *or* dejar de leerlo; **~ me down!** ¡bájame!; **the pilot wanted to ~ the plane down**

in Boston el piloto quería aterrizar en Boston; *see also* **foot A1**, **root A3**
2 (= *lay*) [+ *carpets, poison, trap*] poner, colocar
3 (= *lower*) [+ *blinds, hand*] bajar
4 (= *close*) [+ *umbrella, parasol*] cerrar
5 (= *write down*) [+ *ideas*] anotar, apuntar; [+ *name on list*] poner, inscribir; **I've ~ down a few ideas** he anotado *or* apuntado algunas ideas; **I've ~ you down as unemployed** lo he inscrito *or* apuntado como desempleado; **~ me down for £15** apúntame 15 libras; **~ me down for two, please** por favor, apúntame dos; **he's ~ his son down for Eton** ha inscrito a su hijo en Eton (*internado privado*); **I'll ~ you down for the interview on Radio 4, ok?** te apunto para la entrevista en Radio 4, ¿vale?; **I've ~ myself down for the computer course** me he inscrito para el curso de informática; **to ~ sth down in writing** *or* **on paper** poner algo por escrito; **~ it down on my account** (*Comm*) cárguelo a mi cuenta
6 (= *suppress*) [+ *revolt*] reprimir, sofocar
7 (= *reduce in rank*) degradar; (*Sport etc*) pasar a una división inferior
8 (*) (= *criticize, snub*) hacer de menos, rebajar; **he's always ~ting me down in front of my friends** siempre me está haciendo de menos *or* rebajando delante de mis amigos; **to ~ o.s. down** hacerse de menos, rebajarse; **you must stop ~ting yourself down** debes dejar de hacerte de menos *or* rebajarte
9 (= *pay*) **to ~ down a deposit** dejar un depósito; **she ~ down £500 on the car** dejó una señal *or* un anticipo de 500 libras para el coche
10 (*Brit euph*) **to have an animal ~ down** sacrificar a un animal
11 (= *put to bed*) [+ *baby*] acostar, poner a dormir
12 (= *table*) [+ *motion, amendment*] presentar
13 (= *store in cellar*) [+ *wine*] poner en cava
Ⓑ VI + ADV (*Aer*) aterrizar

►**put down as** VT + PREP **to ~ sb down as sth** catalogar a algn como algo; **I had ~ him down as a complete fool** lo tenía catalogado como un tonto perdido; **I would ~ her down as about 30** le daría unos 30 años, debe tener unos 30 años

►**put down to** VT + PREP **to ~ sth down to sth** atribuir algo a algo; **I ~ it down to his inexperience** lo atribuí a su inexperiencia

►**put forth** VT + ADV 1 (*liter*) [+ *leaves, roots, buds*] echar; [+ *hand*] tender, extender
2 (*frm*) = **put forward 1**

►**put forward** VT + ADV 1 (= *propose*) [+ *theory, idea*] presentar; [+ *plan, proposal*] presentar, proponer; [+ *suggestion*] hacer; [+ *argument*] presentar; [+ *opinion*] dar; [+ *name, candidate*] proponer; **to ~ o.s. forward for a job** presentarse como candidato para un puesto
2 (= *make earlier*) [+ *clock, meeting, starting time*] adelantar; **to ~ a clock forward one hour** adelantar un reloj una hora; **don't forget to ~ your clocks forward tonight** esta noche no olviden adelantar sus relojes; **the meeting was ~ forward (by half an hour) to 2 pm** la reunión se adelantó (media hora) a las 2 de la tarde

►**put in** Ⓐ VT + ADV 1 (*inside box, drawer, room*) meter; **she packed the camera but forgot to ~ the film in** cogió la cámara pero se le olvidó (meter) la película; **he ~ his head in at the window** metió la cabeza por la ventana; **I'll ~ some more sugar in** voy a poner más azúcar
2 (= *plant*) [+ *plants*] plantar; [+ *seeds*] sembrar
3 (*to garage, repair shop*) [+ *car*] **I've ~ the car in for repairs** he llevado el coche a que lo reparen
4 (= *install*) [+ *central heating, double glazing*] instalar, poner
5 (= *include*) (*in book, speech*) incluir; (= *add*) agregar; **why don't you ~ a few jokes in?** ¿por qué no incluyes algunos chistes?; **did you ~ in your reasons for wanting to go?** ¿pusiste *or* incluiste las razones por las que quieres irte?
6 (= *interject*) interponer; **"I can't go either," ~ in James** —yo tampoco puedo ir —interpuso James
7 (= *submit*) [+ *request*] presentar; **to ~ in a claim for damages/expenses** presentar una demanda por daños/gastos; **to ~ sb in for an award** proponer a algn para un premio; **to ~ one's name in for sth** inscribirse para algo; **to ~ in a plea of not guilty** declararse inocente; *see also* **appearance A1**
8 (*Pol*) [+ *party, government, candidate*] elegir, votar a
9 (= *devote, expend*) [+ *time*] dedicar; **she ~s in an hour a day at the piano** le dedica al piano una hora al día; **I've ~ in a lot of time on it** le he dedicado mucho tiempo a esto, he empleado mucho tiempo en esto; **I ~ in a couple of hours gardening** dediqué un par de horas a trabajar en el jardín, me pasé un par de horas trabajando en el jardín
10 (= *work*) trabajar; **can you ~ in a few hours at the weekend?** ¿puede trabajar unas horas el fin de semana?; **he ~s in at least 40 hours a week** trabaja por lo menos 40 horas a la semana; **you've ~ in a good day's work** has trabajado bien hoy
Ⓑ VI + ADV (*Naut*) hacer escala (**at** en)
Ⓒ VT + PREP *see* **put A**

►**put in for** VI + PREP [+ *promotion, transfer, pay rise, divorce*] solicitar; **I've ~ in for a new job** he solicitado otro empleo

►**put off** Ⓐ VT + ADV 1 (= *postpone, delay*) [+ *departure, appointment, meeting, decision*] aplazar, posponer; **he ~ off writing the letter** pospuso *or* aplazó el escribir la carta; **I keep ~ting it off** no hago más que aplazarlo; **we shall have to ~ the guests off** tendremos que decir a los invitados que no vengan; **it's no good ~ting it off** (*sth unwelcome*) no tiene sentido eludirlo más; ✦**PROV don't ~ off until tomorrow what you can do today** no dejes para mañana lo que puedes hacer hoy
2 (= *discourage*) **her brusque manner ~s some people off** desanima a la gente con sus maneras tan bruscas; **he's not easily ~ off** no es fácil apartarlo de su propósito, no es de los que se desaniman fácilmente
3 (= *distract*) distraer; **stop ~ting me off!** ¡deja ya de distraerme!
4 (= *dissuade*) disuadir
5 (= *fob off*) dar largas a; **to ~ sb off with an excuse** dar largas a algn con excusas; **she ~ him off with vague promises** le dio largas con vagas promesas
6 (= *switch off*) apagar
7 (= *set down*) [+ *passenger*] dejar; (*forcibly*) hacer bajar
8 (*esp liter*) (= *cast off*) **once you ~ off that uniform you'll need a job** en cuanto dejes ese uniforme necesitarás un trabajo
Ⓑ VT + PREP 1 (= *cause not to like, want*) **it almost ~ me off opera for good** casi mató mi gusto por la ópera para siempre; **you quite ~ me off my meal** me has quitado el apetito; **it ~ me off going to Greece** me quitó las ganas de ir a Grecia
2 (= *dissuade from*) **we tried to ~ him off the idea** intentamos quitarle la idea de la cabeza, intentamos disuadirlo; **I tried to ~ her off going by herself** intenté convencerla de que no fuera sola
3 (*Brit*) (= *distract from*) *see* **stroke A5**, **scent A3**
Ⓒ VI + ADV (*Naut*) hacerse a la mar, salir (**from** de)

►**put on** Ⓐ VT + ADV 1 [+ *one's coat, socks, hat*] ponerse; [+ *ointment, cream*] ponerse, aplicarse (*more frm*); **to ~ on one's make-up** ponerse maquillaje, maquillarse
2 (= *add, increase*) **he's ~ on 3 kilos** ha engordado 3 kilos; **to ~ on speed** acelerar, cobrar velocidad; **to ~ on weight** engordar; **he has ~ on a lot of weight** ha engordado mucho
3 (= *organize*) [+ *concert*] presentar; [+ *exhibition*] montar; [+ *play*] representar, poner en escena; [+ *extra bus, train*] poner; **we're ~ting on "Bugsy Malone"** vamos a representar "Bugsy Malone"
4 (= *assume*) [+ *expression, air*] adoptar; **to ~ on a French accent** fingir (tener) un acento francés; **there's no need to ~ on an act, just be yourself** no tienes por qué fingir, sé tú mismo; **to ~ on an innocent expression** poner cara de inocente; **she's not ill, she's just ~ting it on** no está enferma, es puro teatro *or* está fingiendo; **she ~ on a show of enthusiasm** fingió entusiasmo; **the party ~ on a show of unity** el partido presentó una fachada de unidad; *see also* **air A3**
5 (*Telec*) **"is John there, please?" — "I'll ~ him on"** —¿por favor, está John? —le pongo; **can you ~ me on to Mr Smith please** póngame con *or* (*esp LAm*) me comunica con el Sr. Smith, por favor
6 (= *switch on, start*) [+ *light, radio*] encender, prender (*LAm*); [+ *CD, tape, music*] poner; [+ *vegetables*] (= *begin to cook*) poner (a cocer); (= *begin to heat*) poner (a calentar); **shall I ~ the heating on?** ¿enciendo la calefacción?; **to ~ the brakes on** frenar; **to ~ the kettle on** poner agua a hervir
7 [+ *clock*] adelantar; **to ~ a clock on one hour** adelantar un reloj una hora; **don't forget to ~ the clocks on tonight** esta noche no olviden adelantar los relojes
8 (*esp US**) (= *deceive*) engañar; **you're ~ting me on, aren't you?** me estás tomando el pelo, ¿verdad?
Ⓑ VT + PREP 1 (= *add to*) **the proposal would ~ 5p on (to) a litre of petrol** la propuesta aumentaría en 5 peniques el litro de gasolina; **they ~ £2 on (to) the price** añadieron 2 libras al precio
2 (= *bet on*) **to ~ money on a horse** apostar dinero a un caballo, jugarse dinero en un caballo; **he ~ £20 on Black Beauty to win** apostó *or* se jugó 20 libras a que Black Beauty ganaba; ✦**IDIOMS I wouldn't ~ money on it!** yo no apostaría dinero; **he'll be back, I'd ~ money on it** volverá, me apuesto lo que quieras

►**put onto, put on to** VT + PREP **to ~ sb onto sth/sb** 1 (= *inform about*) **who ~ the police onto him?** ¿quién lo denunció a la policía?; **somebody ~ the Inland Revenue onto his tax evasion** alguien informó a Hacienda de su evasión de impuestos
2 (= *put in touch with*) **can you ~ me onto a good dentist?** ¿me puede recomendar un buen dentista?; **Sue ~ us onto you** Sue nos dio su nombre; **a fellow journalist ~ me onto the story** un compañero periodista me informó *or* me dio la pista de la historia; *see also* **put on A5**

►**put out** Ⓐ VT + ADV 1 (= *place outside*) [+ *rubbish*] sacar; [+ *cat*] sacar fuera, dejar afuera; **he ~ the cat out for the night** sacó al gato a que pasara la noche fuera, dejó al gato fuera para que pasara la noche; **to ~ the clothes out to dry** sacar la ropa a secar; *see also* **pasture A**
2 (= *eject*) [+ *squatter, tenant, troublemaker*] echar, expulsar
3 (= *stretch out, push out*) [+ *hand*] alargar, tender; [+ *arm*] alargar, extender; [+ *tongue, claws, horns*] sacar; [+ *leaves, shoots*] echar; **he ~ out his arm to protect himself** se protegió con el brazo, puso el brazo para protegerse; **to ~ one's head out of a window** asomar la cabeza por una ventana; *see also* **feeler**
4 (= *lay out in order*) [+ *cards, chessmen, chairs*] disponer, colocar; [+ *clothes, best china*] sacar, poner
5 (= *publish*) [+ *book*] publicar, sacar; [+ *record*] sacar; [+ *appeal, statement, propaganda*] hacer; [+ *warning*] dar; (= *broadcast*) [+ *programme*] transmitir; (= *circulate*) [+ *rumour*] hacer circular, hacer correr; **they have ~ out a press release denying the allegations** han desmentido las alegaciones en un comunicado de prensa, han emitido un comunicado de prensa negando las alegaciones
6 (= *extinguish*) [+ *light, cigarette, fire*] apagar; **it took them five hours to ~ out the fire** tardaron cinco horas en apagar el incendio
7 (= *annoy, upset*) enfadar, enojar (*LAm*); **he was very ~ out at finding her there** se enfadó mucho al encontrarla allí; **she looked very ~ out** parecía muy enfadada; **he's a bit ~ out that nobody came** le sentó mal que no viniera nadie
8 (= *disconcert*) desconcertar; **he didn't seem at all ~ out by the news** no parecía estar en absoluto desconcertado por las noticias
9 (= *inconvenience*) molestar; **to ~ o.s. out**: **she really ~ herself out for us** se tomó muchas molestias por nosotros; **don't ~ yourself out, will you!** (*iro*) ¡tú, sobre todo, no hagas nada!; **I don't want to ~ you out** no quiero molestarle; **you mustn't ~ yourself out** no debes molestarte; **are you sure I'm not ~ting you out?** ¿está seguro de que no le causo ningún inconveniente?
10 (= *render incorrect*) [+ *calculations*] desbaratar, echar por tierra
11 (*Sport*) (= *eliminate*) [+ *team, contestant*] eliminar (**of** de); **a knee injury ~ him out of the first two games** una lesión de rodilla lo eliminó de los primeros dos partidos
12 (= *dislocate*) [+ *shoulder, knee*] dislocar; **I ~ my back out lifting that box** me he hecho polvo la espalda levantando esa caja
13 (= *give anaesthetic to*) anestesiar, dormir
14 (= *lend*) [+ *money*] prestar; **to ~ money out at interest** prestar dinero con intereses
15 (= *subcontract*) **to ~ sth out to tender** sacar algo a concurso *or* a licitación; **to ~ work out to contract** sacar una obra a contrata
16 (*Naut*) [+ *boat*] echar al mar
Ⓑ VI + ADV 1 (*Naut*) salir, zarpar (**from** de); **to ~ out to sea** hacerse a la mar
2 (*US‡*) (= *agree to sex*) acceder, consentir

►**put over** VT + ADV 1 = **put across 1**
2 **to ~ one over on sb*** (= *deceive*) engañar a algn, dar a algn gato por liebre*

►**put through** Ⓐ VT + ADV 1 (= *make, complete*) [+ *plan, reform, change*] llevar a cabo; [+ *deal*] cerrar; [+ *proposal*] hacer aceptar; **we ~ through 2,000 orders a week** despachamos 2.000 pedidos a la semana
2 (*Telec*) (= *connect*) [+ *call, caller*] pasar; **don't ~ any calls through for the next hour** no pases ninguna llamada en la próxima hora; **I'm ~ting you through now** ahora le paso *or* pongo; **who? Martha? all right, ~ her through** ¿quién? ¿Marta? bueno, ponme con ella; **can you ~ me through to Miss Blair, please** por favor, póngame *or* (*esp LAm*) me comunica con la Srta. Blair
Ⓑ VT + PREP 1 (*by providing finance*) **she ~ two sons through university** mandó a dos hijos a la universidad
2 (= *make suffer*) **she didn't want to ~ him through another ordeal like that** no quiso hacerle pasar por otra prueba tan dura como esa; **they really ~ him through it at the interview** se las hicieron pasar mal en la entrevista, se las hicieron pasar canutas en la entrevista*; ✦*IDIOM* **to ~ sb through hell*** hacérselas pasar canutas a algn*; *see also* **pace A1**

►**put together** VT + ADV 1 (= *place together*) poner juntos, juntar; **~ your feet together** pon los pies juntos, junta los pies; **don't ~ those two together, they fight** no pongas a esos dos juntos que se pelean; **if all the cigars in the world were ~ together end to end** si se unieran uno tras otro todos los puros del mundo; **~ your hands together now for ...** démosle una calurosa bienvenida a ...; ✦*IDIOM* **she's worth more than all the others ~ together** vale más que todos los demás juntos; *see also* **head A2**, **two B**
2 (= *assemble*) [+ *model kit, piece of furniture*] armar, montar; [+ *meal*] preparar; [+ *collection*] juntar, reunir; [+ *team*] reunir, formar; **he took it apart piece by piece and ~ it back together again** lo desmontó pieza a pieza y lo volvió a montar otra vez; **the furniture had been ~ together out of old crates** habían hecho los muebles con viejos cajones de embalaje
3 (= *formulate*) [+ *plan, scheme*] formular, preparar; [+ *publication*] preparar; **she ~ together a convincing defence of her client** preparó una defensa de su cliente muy convincente; **he can't even ~ two sentences together** no sabe ni siquiera enhilar dos frases seguidas; **I need a few minutes to ~ my thoughts together** necesito unos minutos para pensarme las cosas un poco

►**put up** Ⓐ VT + ADV 1 (= *raise, lift up*) [+ *window, blinds*] subir; [+ *hand*] levantar; [+ *flag, sail*] izar; [+ *collar*] subirse; **if you have any questions, ~ your hand up** quien tenga alguna pregunta que levante la mano; **~ 'em up!*** [+ *hands*] (*in surrender*) ¡manos arriba!; [+ *fists*] ¡pelea!; *see also* **back A1.2**, **foot 1**
2 (= *hang up*) [+ *picture, decorations*] colgar; [+ *notice, sign*] poner
3 (= *erect*) [+ *building, wall*] construir, levantar; [+ *statue, monument*] erigir, levantar; [+ *fence, barrier*] poner; [+ *tent*] montar; [+ *umbrella*] abrir; [+ *ladder*] montar, poner; **to ~ one's hair up** recogerse el pelo; (*stylishly*) hacerse un peinado alto
4 (= *send up*) [+ *satellite*] lanzar, mandar
5 (= *increase*) [+ *price, tax, sb's temperature, blood pressure*] aumentar, subir; **that ~s the total up to over 1,000** con eso el total asciende a más de 1.000
6 (= *offer*) [+ *reward, prize, prayer*] ofrecer; [+ *resistance*] oponer; **the horse ~ up an excellent performance in today's race** el caballo hizo un papel excelente en la carrera de hoy; **he didn't ~ up much of a fight or struggle** no se resistió mucho, no opuso mucha resistencia; **to ~ sth up for sale/auction** poner algo a la venta/a subasta, vender/subastar algo; **to ~ a child up for adoption** ofrecer un niño en adopción
7 (= *provide*) [+ *money*] poner, dar; **to ~ up the money for sth** poner *or* dar el dinero para algo
8 (= *give accommodation to*) alojar, hospedar; **we need volunteers to ~ up the visitors** se necesitan voluntarios para alojar *or* hospedar a los visitantes; **can you ~ me up for the night?** ¿me puedo quedar (en tu casa) esta noche?
9 (= *present, put forward*) [+ *plan, petition*] presentar; [+ *proposal, suggestion*] hacer; [+ *argument, case, defence*] presentar; [+ *candidate*] proponer (**for** para); **he ~ up a spirited defence of the bill in Parliament** hizo una vehemente defensa del proyecto de ley en el parlamento; **we ~ him up for chairman** lo propusimos para presidente
10 (= *preserve*) [+ *fruit*] conservar
Ⓑ VI + ADV 1 (= *stay*) hospedarse, alojarse; **we ~ up for the night at a hotel** esa noche nos alojamos *or* hospedamos en un hotel
2 (*Pol*) (= *offer o.s.*) **to ~ up for president** presentarse a presidente; **to ~ up for the Greens** presentarse como candidato de los Verdes

►**put upon** VI + PREP **to ~ upon sb** (= *inconvenience*) molestar a algn, incomodar a algn; (= *impose on*) abusar de la amabilidad de algn

►**put up to** VT + PREP (= *incite*) **to ~ sb up to sth: they said that she had ~ him up to the murder** dijeron que ella le había incitado *or* instigado al asesinato; **somebody must have ~ him up to it** alguien ha debido sugerírselo; **who ~ you up to this?** ¿quién te ha hecho hacer esto?

▼►**put up with** VI + PREP aguantar; **I can't ~ up with it any longer** ya no (lo) aguanto más; **you'll just have to ~ up with it** tendrás que aguantarte; **he has a lot to ~ up with** tiene que aguantar un montón; **she ~s up with a lot** es muy tolerante, tiene mucho aguante

putative ['pju:tətɪv] ADJ supuesto; [*relation*] putativo

put-down* ['pʊt,daʊn] N (= *act*) humillación *f*; (= *words*) frase *f* despectiva

put-in ['pʊt,ɪn] N (*Rugby*) introducción *f*

put-on* ['pʊt,ɒn] Ⓐ ADJ (= *feigned*) fingido
Ⓑ N (= *pretence*) teatro* *m*; (= *hoax*) broma *f* (de mal gusto)

putrefaction [,pju:trɪ'fækʃən] N putrefacción *f*

putrefy ['pju:trɪfaɪ] Ⓐ VI pudrirse
Ⓑ VT pudrir

putrescence [pju:'tresns] N pudrición *f*

putrescent [pju:'tresnt] ADJ putrefacto

putrid ['pju:trɪd] ADJ 1 (= *rotten*) putrefacto, podrido
2 [*stench*] hediondo, pestilente

putsch [pʊtʃ] N golpe *m* de estado

putt [pʌt] Ⓐ N putt *m*
Ⓑ VT golpear
Ⓒ VI golpear la bola

putter¹ ['pʌtəʳ] N putter *m*

putter² ['pʌtəʳ] VI (*US*) = **potter²**

putting ['pʌtɪŋ] Ⓐ N minigolf *m*
Ⓑ CPD ► **putting green** N (= *miniature golf*) campo *m* de minigolf; (*on golf course*) green *m*

putty ['pʌtɪ] Ⓐ N masilla *f*; ✦*IDIOM* **to be ~ in sb's hands** ser el muñeco de algn
Ⓑ CPD ► **putty knife** N espátula *f* para masilla

put-up ['pʊtʌp] ADJ **~ job*** chanchullo* *m*; **it**

➤ LANGUAGE IN USE: **put up with** 14

was a ~ job to give him the post fue un chanchullo para darle el puesto*

put-upon ['pʊtə,pɒn] ADJ **she's feeling very ~** cree que los demás la están explotando

put-you-up ['pʊtjʊ,ʌp] N (*Brit*) cama *f* plegable, sofá-cama *m*

puzzle ['pʌzl] Ⓐ N 1 (= *game, jigsaw*) rompecabezas *m inv*; (= *crossword*) crucigrama *m*
2 (= *mystery*) misterio *m*, enigma *m*; (= *riddle*) acertijo *m*, adivinanza *f*; **it's a real ~** es un verdadero misterio *or* enigma
Ⓑ VT dejar perplejo, desconcertar; **that properly ~d him** eso lo dejó totalmente perplejo
Ⓒ VI **to ~ about** *or* **over** dar vueltas (en la cabeza) a
Ⓓ CPD ► **puzzle book** N libro *m* de puzzles
►**puzzle out** VT + ADV **to ~ sth out** descifrar algo; **we're still trying to ~ out why he did it** seguimos tratando de comprender por qué lo hizo

puzzled ['pʌzld] ADJ perplejo; **you look ~!** ¡te has quedado perplejo!; **he gave her a ~ look** la miró perplejo; **to be ~ about sth** no entender algo; **I am ~ to know why** no llego a comprender por qué, no acabo de entender por qué

puzzlement ['pʌzlmənt] N perplejidad *f*

puzzler ['pʌzləʳ] N misterio *m*, enigma *m*

puzzling ['pʌzlɪŋ] ADJ desconcertante; **it is ~ that …** es raro *or* curioso que …

PVC N ABBR (= **polyvinyl chloride**) PVC *m*

PVS N ABBR 1 = **postviral syndrome**
2 (= **persistent vegetative state**) estado *m* vegetativo persistente

Pvt. ABBR (*US Mil*) = **Private**

PW N ABBR 1 (*US Mil*) = **prisoner of war**
2 (*Brit*) = **policewoman**

pw ABBR (= **per week**) por semana, a la semana

PWR N ABBR = **pressurized water reactor**

PX N ABBR (*US Mil*) (= **Post Exchange**) *economato militar*

pygmy ['pɪgmɪ] Ⓐ N pigmeo/a *m/f*; (*fig*) enano/a *m/f*
Ⓑ CPD pigmeo; (*fig*) miniatura, minúsculo

pyjamas [pɪ'dʒɑːməz] NPL pijama *msing*, piyama *msing* (*LAm*); **a pair of ~** un pijama

pylon ['paɪlən] N (*Elec*) torre *f* de conducción eléctrica

pyorrhoea, **pyorrhea** (*US*) [,paɪə'rɪə] N piorrea *f*

pyramid ['pɪrəmɪd] Ⓐ N pirámide *f*
Ⓑ CPD ► **pyramid selling** N venta *f* piramidal

pyramidal [pɪ'ræmɪdl] ADJ piramidal

pyre ['paɪəʳ] N pira *f*; (*fig*) hoguera *f*

Pyrenean [,pɪrə'niːən] ADJ pirenaico, pirineo

Pyrenees [,pɪrə'niːz] NPL **the ~** el Pirineo, los Pirineos

pyrethrum [paɪ'riːθrəm] N piretro *m*

pyretic [paɪ'retɪk] ADJ pirético

Pyrex® ['paɪreks] Ⓐ N pyrex® *m*, pirex® *m*
Ⓑ CPD [*bowl, dish*] de pyrex® *or* pirex®

pyrites [paɪ'raɪtiːz] N (*pl* **pyrites**) pirita *f*

pyro... ['paɪərəʊ] PREFIX piro…

pyromania [,paɪərəʊ'meɪnɪə] N piromanía *f*

pyromaniac [,paɪərəʊ'meɪnɪæk] N pirómano/a *m/f*

pyrotechnic [,paɪərəʊ'teknɪk] ADJ pirotécnico

pyrotechnics [,paɪərəʊ'teknɪks] NSING pirotecnia *f*

Pyrrhic ['pɪrɪk] ADJ **~ victory** victoria *f* pírrica

Pyrrhus ['pɪrəs] N Pirro

Pythagoras [paɪ'θægərəs] N Pitágoras

Pythagorean [paɪ,θægə'riːən] ADJ pitagóreo

python ['paɪθən] N pitón *f*

Pythonesque [,paɪθə'nesk] ADJ pitonesco, del estilo de Monty Python

pyx [pɪks] N píxide *f*

pzazz* [pə'zæz] N = **piz(z)azz**

Q q

Q[1], **q** [kjuː] N (= *letter*) Q, q *f*; **Q for Queen** Q de Quebec

Q[2] ABBR 1 = **Queen**
2 (= **question**) P

Qatar [kæ'tɑːʳ] N Qatar *m*, Katar *m*

QC N ABBR (*Brit*) = **Queen's Counsel**

> **QC/KC**
>
> ***QC** o **KC**, abreviaturas de **Queen's** o **King's Counsel**, es el título que se les da a los abogados de más alto rango en el Reino Unido. Los letrados denominados **barristers** (o **advocates** en Escocia) que hayan practicado la abogacía durante al menos diez años pueden solicitar este título al **Lord Chancellor**, quien a su vez los recomienda a la Corona para su designación. Pasar a ser un **QC** o **KC** se conoce como **taking silk** (recibir la seda), haciendo referencia al material de la túnica que llevan estos letrados.*
>
> ⇨ *Ver tb* LAWYERS

QE2 [ˌkjuːiː'tuː] N ABBR (*Brit Naut*) = **Queen Elizabeth II**

QED ABBR (*Math*) (= **quod erat demonstrandum**) QED

QM ABBR = **Quartermaster**

qr ABBR = **quarter(s)**

qt ABBR = **quart(s)**

q.t.* [kjuː'tiː] ABBR = **quiet**; **on the ~** a hurtadillas

qty ABBR (= **quantity**) ctdad

Qu. ABBR = **Queen**

qua [kweɪ] PREP (*frm*) en cuanto, como; **let us consider man ~ animal** consideremos al hombre en cuanto animal

quack[1] [kwæk] Ⓐ N [*of duck*] graznido *m*
Ⓑ VI [*duck*] graznar

quack[2]* [kwæk] Ⓐ N charlatán/ana *m/f*; (= *doctor*) curandero/a *m/f*; (*pej*) matasanos* *mf inv*
Ⓑ CPD [*remedy*] de curandero ► **quack doctor** N medicucho/a* *m/f*, curandero/a *m/f*

quackery ['kwækərɪ] N charlatanismo *m*; (*Med*) curanderismo *m*

quack-quack ['kwæk'kwæk] N cuac cuac *m*

quad [kwɒd] Ⓐ ABBR 1 (*Archit**) *see* **quadrangle 2**
2 (*) = **quadruplet**
3 = **quadruple**
4 (*Typ*) cuadratín *m*
Ⓑ CPD ► **quad bike** N *motocicleta de cuatro ruedas*

Quadragesima [ˌkwɒdrə'dʒesɪmə] N Cuadragésima *f*

quadrangle ['kwɒdræŋgl] N 1 (*Geom*) (*with 4 angles*) cuadrilátero *m*, cuadrángulo *m*
2 (= *courtyard*) patio *m*

quadrangular [kwɒ'dræŋgjʊləʳ] ADJ cuadrangular

quadrant ['kwɒdrənt] N cuadrante *m*

quadraphonic [ˌkwɒdrə'fɒnɪk] ADJ cuatrifónico

quadratic [kwɒ'drætɪk] ADJ [*equation*] cuadrático, de segundo grado

quadrature ['kwɒdrətʃəʳ] N cuadratura *f*

quadrennial [kwɒ'drenɪəl] ADJ cuatrienal

quadrilateral [ˌkwɒdrɪ'lætərəl] Ⓐ ADJ cuadrilátero
Ⓑ N cuadrilátero *m*

quadrille [kwə'drɪl] N cuadrilla *f*

quadripartite ['kwɒdrɪ'pɑːtaɪt] ADJ cuadripartido

quadriplegia [ˌkwɒdrɪ'pliːdʒə] N cuadriplegia *f*, tetraplegia *f*

quadriplegic [ˌkwɒdrɪ'pliːdʒɪk] Ⓐ ADJ cuadriplégico, tetrapléjico
Ⓑ N cuadripléjico/a *m/f*, tetrapléjico/a *m/f*

quadrivium [kwɒ'drɪvɪəm] N cuadrivio *m*

quadroon [kwɒ'druːn] N cuarterón *m*

quadrophonic [ˌkwɒdrə'fɒnɪk] ADJ = **quadraphonic**

quadruped ['kwɒdrʊped] N cuadrúpedo *m*

quadruple Ⓐ ['kwɒdrʊpl] ADJ cuádruple, cuádruplo; **in ~ time** (*Mus*) en compás de cuatro por cuatro
Ⓑ ['kwɒdrʊpl] N cuádruple *m*, cuádruplo *m*
Ⓒ [kwɒ'druːpl] VT cuadruplicar
Ⓓ [kwɒ'druːpl] VI cuadruplicarse

quadruplet [kwɒ'druːplɪt] N cuatrillizo/a *m/f*

quadruplicate Ⓐ [kwɒ'druːplɪkɪt] ADJ cuadruplicado
Ⓑ [kwɒ'druːplɪkɪt] N **in ~** por cuadruplicado
Ⓒ [kwɒ'druːplɪkeɪt] VT cuadruplicar

quaestor, **questor** (*US*) ['kwiːstəʳ] N cuestor *m*

quaff [kwɒf] VT († *or hum*) beber(se), zamparse*

quagmire ['kwægmaɪəʳ] N cenagal *m*, lodazal *m*; (*fig*) atolladero *m*, cenagal *m*

quail[1] [kweɪl] N (*pl* **quail** *or* **quails**) (= *bird*) codorniz *f*

quail[2] [kweɪl] VI (= *cower*) temblar (**at** ante); **her heart ~ed** se le encogió el corazón

quaint [kweɪnt] ADJ (*compar* **quainter**; *superl* **quaintest**) 1 (= *picturesque*) [*building, street, village*] pintoresco
2 (= *odd*) [*custom, notion*] curioso; [*person*] peculiar, poco corriente; **how ~!** ¡qué curioso!

quaintly ['kweɪntlɪ] ADV 1 (= *charmingly*) [*decorated*] pintorescamente; **the building was ~ old-fashioned** el edificio parecía anticuado y pintoresco
2 (= *oddly*) **the ~ named town of Normal** el pueblo denominado con el curioso nombre de Normal; **this may seem a ~ old-fashioned idea** puede que esta idea parezca extraña y anticuada; **he described it ~ as …** le dio la curiosa calificación de …

quaintness ['kweɪntnɪs] N 1 (= *picturesqueness*) [*of place, object*] lo pintoresco
2 (= *oddness*) [*of custom, word, idea, question*] lo curioso

quake [kweɪk] Ⓐ VI [*person*] (= *shake*) temblar; (*inwardly*) estremecerse; **to ~ with fright** temblar de miedo; **he was quaking at the knees** le temblaban las piernas; **I ~d at the prospect** esa posibilidad me hizo estremecer
Ⓑ N (*) (= *earthquake*) terremoto *m*, temblor *m*

Quaker ['kweɪkəʳ] Ⓐ ADJ cuáquero
Ⓑ N cuáquero/a *m/f*

Quakerism ['kweɪkərɪzəm] N cuaquerismo *m*

qualification [ˌkwɒlɪfɪ'keɪʃən] N 1 (= *diploma*) título *m*; **he left school without any ~s** dejó la escuela sin sacarse ningún título; **what are his ~s?** ¿qué títulos tiene?; **a teaching ~** un título de profesor; **vocational ~s** títulos *mpl* de formación profesional
2 (*for a post*) requisito *m*; **she doesn't have the ~s for the post** no reúne los requisitos para el puesto; **the ~s for membership** lo que se requiere para ser socio
3 (= *description*) calificación *f*
4 (*Sport*) clasificación *f*; **they missed ~ for the finals** no consiguieron clasificarse para la final
5 (= *reservation*) reserva *f*; (= *modification*) salvedad *f*; **without ~** sin reserva; **this is true, with the ~ that …** esto es verdad, con la salvedad de que …; **by way of ~, I should point out that …** quisiera hacer la salvedad de que …

qualified ['kwɒlɪfaɪd] Ⓐ ADJ 1 (*in subject*) (*having exam passes, certificates*) titulado; **a ~ engineer** un ingeniero titulado; **~ ski instructors** instructores *mpl* de esquí titulados; **to be ~ to do sth** (*having passed exams*) estar titulado para hacer algo; (*having right expertise*) estar cualificado para hacer algo; **he was by far the best ~ for the task** era con mucho el mejor cualificado para la tarea; **a group of highly ~ young people** un grupo de jóvenes altamente cualificados; **a newly ~ accountant** un contable recién licenciado; **newly ~ drivers** conductores *mpl* que acaban de sacarse el carné; **to be properly ~** tener los títulos necesarios; **it can be difficult to find suitably ~ staff** a veces es difícil encontrar personal adecuadamente cualificado
2 (= *equipped, capable*) **to be ~ to do sth** estar capacitado para hacer algo; **I don't feel ~ to judge that** no me siento capacitado

para juzgar eso; **no one is better ~ than Maria to do this** nadie está mejor capacitada que María para hacer esto

[3] (= *eligible*) **to be ~ to vote** reunir los requisitos necesarios para votar; **you are not ~ to receive benefit** usted no reúne los requisitos necesarios para recibir ayuda del estado

[4] (= *limited*) **he gave it his ~ approval** lo aprobó con reservas; **the committee gave a ~ endorsement to the plan** el comité aprobó el plan bajo ciertas condiciones; **it was a ~ success** fue un éxito relativo; **to give ~ support to sth** apoyar algo con reservas

Ⓑ CPD ► **qualified majority voting** N votación *f* de mayoría mínima ► **qualified voter** N elector(a) *m/f* habilitado/a

qualifier ['kwɒlɪfaɪəʳ] N [1] (*Sport*) (= *person*) clasificado/a *m/f*; (= *match, heat, round*) eliminatoria *f*

[2] (*Gram*) calificador *m*

qualify ['kwɒlɪfaɪ] Ⓐ VI [1] (= *gain qualification*) (*degree*) terminar la carrera, sacar el título, recibirse (*LAm*); (*professional exams*) obtener la licencia para ejercer (como profesional); **to ~ as an engineer** sacar el título de ingeniero

[2] (= *meet criteria*) [2·1] **to ~ as sth**: **it may ~ as a medical expense** puede que cuente como gastos médicos; **to ~ as disabled, he must ...** para ser declarado minusválido, tiene que ...; **he hardly qualifies as a poet** apenas se le puede calificar de poeta

[2·2] **to ~ for sth** (= *be eligible*) tener derecho a (recibir) algo; **she doesn't ~ for a grant** no tiene derecho a una beca, no puede optar a una beca

[3] (*Sport*) clasificarse (**for** para); **she qualified third** se clasificó en tercer lugar; **the winner qualifies for the second round** el ganador se clasifica para la segunda vuelta

Ⓑ VT [1] (= *give qualifications, knowledge to*) **to ~ sb to do sth** capacitar a algn para hacer algo; **the basic course does not ~ you to practise as a therapist** el curso básico no le capacita para ejercer de terapeuta; **to ~ sb for sth** capacitar a algn para algo

[2] (= *make eligible*) **your age may ~ you for a special discount** puede que tu edad te dé derecho a un descuento especial; **that doesn't ~ him to speak on this** eso no le da derecho a hablar sobre esto

[3] (= *modify*) [+ *statement*] matizar; (= *limit*) [+ *support, conclusion*] condicionar; **I think you should ~ that remark** creo que deberías matizar ese comentario

[4] (= *describe*) [4·1] (*gen*) calificar (**as** de); **some of her statements could be qualified as racist** algunos de sus comentarios se podrían calificar de racistas

[4·2] (*Gram*) calificar a; **the adjective qualifies the noun** el adjetivo califica al sustantivo

qualifying ['kwɒlɪfaɪɪŋ] ADJ [1] (*Univ, Sport*) [*exam, round, game*] eliminatorio; [*team, contestant*] clasificado; **~ heat** prueba *f* clasificatoria; **he failed to achieve the ~ time** (*Sport*) no consiguió el tiempo mínimo requerido para la clasificación; **after a four-month ~ period he will be able to play in the team** después del periodo de cuatro meses estipulado como requisito, podrá formar parte del equipo

[2] (*Gram*) calificativo

qualitative ['kwɒlɪtətɪv] ADJ cualitativo

qualitatively ['kwɒlɪtətɪvlɪ] ADV [*different, new*] cualitativamente, desde un punto de vista cualitativo

quality ['kwɒlɪtɪ] Ⓐ N [1] (= *standard, high standard*) calidad *f*; **of good/high ~** de buena/alta calidad; **of poor/low ~** de mala/baja calidad; **a top-~ hotel** un hotel de primera calidad; **the ~ of life** la calidad de vida; **he has real ~** tiene verdadera calidad; **a product of ~** un producto de calidad; ✦**PROV ~ is more important than quantity** la calidad es más importante que la cantidad, lo que importa es la calidad, no la cantidad

[2] (= *personal attribute*) cualidad *f*; **one of his good qualities** una de sus buenas cualidades; **one of his bad qualities** uno de sus defectos; **leadership qualities** cualidades *fpl* de líder

[3] (= *physical property*) propiedad *f*; **the nutritional qualities of fruit** las propiedades nutritivas de la fruta

[4] (= *nature, character*) cualidad *f*; **a childlike ~** una cualidad infantil

[5] (= *tone*) [*of sound, voice*] timbre *m*, tono *m*

[6] **the qualities** (*Brit Press**) la prensa seria, los periódicos serios

Ⓑ CPD [*product, work*] de calidad; [*newspaper*] serio; **a ~ carpet** una alfombra de calidad ► **quality control** N control *m* de calidad ► **the quality papers** NPL los periódicos serios ► **the quality press** N la prensa seria; → TABLOIDS AND BROADSHEETS ► **quality time** N *tiempo dedicado a la familia y a los amigos*; **I need to spend some ~ time with my children** necesito pasar tiempo disfrutando con mis hijos; **if you don't spend ~ time studying you won't learn very much** si no dedicas tiempo en serio a estudiar no aprenderás mucho

qualm [kwɑːm] N [1] (= *scruple*) escrúpulo *m*; **he had no ~s about throwing them out on the street** no tuvo ningún escrúpulo para echarlos a la calle

[2] (= *misgiving*) duda *f*; **she signed it without a ~** no tuvo ninguna duda al firmarlo; **he had ~s about their trustworthiness** tenía dudas acerca de su honradez; **I would have no ~s about doing the same again** no dudaría en hacer lo mismo otra vez

[3] (*Med*) náusea *f*, mareo *m*

quandary ['kwɒndərɪ] N (= *dilemma*) dilema *m*; (= *difficult situation*) apuro *m*; **to be in a ~** estar en un dilema; **he was in a ~ about whether to accept** estaba en un dilema sobre si aceptar o no; **this put him in a ~** esto lo puso en un dilema; **to get sb out of a ~** sacar a algn de un apuro

quango ['kwæŋgəʊ] N (*Brit*) (= **quasi-autonomous non-governmental organization**) ONG *f*, *organización no gubernamental cuasi autónoma*

> **QUANGO**
>
> *El término* **quango**, *que corresponde a las siglas de* **quasi-autonomous non-governmental organization**, *se empezó a usar en el Reino Unido para referirse a organizaciones tales como la* **Equal Opportunities Commission** *o la* **Race Relations Board**, *que fueron establecidas por el gobierno pero que no dependen de ningún ministerio. Algunos* **quangos** *poseen funciones ejecutivas, mientras que otros son meramente consultivos. La práctica de poner demasiadas responsabilidades en manos de* **quangos** *ha sido criticada debido al hecho de que sus miembros son a menudo nombrados a dedo por el gobierno y no tienen la obligación de responder de sus actividades ante el electorado.*

quanta ['kwɒntə] NPL *of* **quantum**

quantifiable ['kwɒntɪfaɪəbl] ADJ cuantificable

quantifier ['kwɒntɪfaɪəʳ] N cuantificador *m*

quantify ['kwɒntɪfaɪ] VT cuantificar

quantitative ['kwɒntɪtətɪv] ADJ cuantitativo

quantitatively ['kwɒntɪtətɪvlɪ] ADV cuantitativamente

quantity ['kwɒntɪtɪ] Ⓐ N cantidad *f*; **in large quantities** ◊ **in ~** en grandes cantidades; **unknown ~** incógnita *f*

Ⓑ CPD ► **quantity discount** N descuento *m* por cantidad ► **quantity mark** N signo *m* prosódico ► **quantity surveyor** N aparejador(a) *m/f*

quantum ['kwɒntəm] Ⓐ N (*pl* **quanta**) cuanto *m*, quantum *m*

Ⓑ CPD ► **quantum leap** N salto *m* espectacular ► **quantum mechanics** NSING mecánica *f* cuántica ► **quantum number** N número *m* cuántico ► **quantum physics** NSING física *f* cuántica ► **quantum theory** N teoría *f* cuántica

quarantine ['kwɒrəntiːn] Ⓐ N cuarentena *f*; **to be in ~** estar en cuarentena; **to place a dog in ~** poner un perro en cuarentena

Ⓑ VT poner en cuarentena

quark [kwɑːk] N (*Phys*) quark *m*

quarrel ['kwɒrəl] Ⓐ N (= *argument*) riña *f*, pelea *f*; **to have a ~ with sb** reñir *or* pelearse con algn; **I have no ~ with you** no tengo nada en contra de usted, no tengo queja de usted; **to pick a ~** buscar pelea *or* pleito; **to pick a ~ with sb** meterse con algn, buscar pelea *or* pleito con algn; **to take up sb's ~** ponerse de la parte de algn

Ⓑ VI reñir, pelearse; **we ~led and I never saw him again** reñimos y no volví a verlo; **they ~led about** *or* **over money** riñeron por cuestión de dinero; **to ~ with sb** reñir con algn; **I can't ~ with that** eso no lo discuto; **what we ~ with is ...** en lo que discrepamos *or* no estamos de acuerdo es ...

quarrelling, **quarreling** (*US*) ['kwɒrəlɪŋ] N riñas *fpl*, disputas *fpl*, peleas *fpl*; **there was constant ~** había riñas *or* disputas *or* peleas continuas

quarrelsome ['kwɒrəlsəm] ADJ pendenciero, peleón*

quarrelsomeness ['kwɒrəlsəmnɪs] N espíritu *m* pendenciero

quarrier ['kwɒrɪəʳ] N cantero *m*

quarry[1] ['kwɒrɪ] N (*Hunting*) presa *f*; (*fig*) presa *f*, víctima *f*

quarry[2] ['kwɒrɪ] Ⓐ N (= *mine*) cantera *f*

Ⓑ VT sacar, extraer

Ⓒ VI explotar una cantera, extraer piedra de una cantera; **to ~ for marble** abrir una cantera en busca de mármol

Ⓓ CPD ► **quarry tile** N baldosa *f* (no vidriada)

►**quarry out** VT + ADV sacar, extraer

quarryman ['kwɒrɪmən] N (*pl* **quarrymen**) cantero *m*, picapedrero *m*

quart [kwɔːt] N (*gen*) cuarto *m* de galón (*Brit = 1,136 litros; US = 0,946 litros*); ✦**IDIOM you're trying to get a ~ into a pint pot** está claro que no cabe

quarter ['kwɔːtəʳ] Ⓐ N [1] (= *fourth part*) [*of kilo, kilometre, second*] cuarto *m*; [*of price, population*] cuarta parte *f*; **a ~ of a mile** un cuarto de milla; **a ~ (of a pound) of tea** un cuarto de libra de té; **for a ~ of the price** por la cuarta parte del precio; **to divide sth into ~s** dividir algo en cuartos *or* en cuatro; **the tank was only a ~ full** el depósito sólo estaba a un cuarto de su capacidad; **it's a ~ gone already** ya se ha gastado la cuarta parte; **I'm a ~ Spanish** tengo una cuarta parte de sangre española

[2] (*in time*) cuarto *m*; **a ~ of an hour/century** un cuarto de hora/siglo; **an hour and a ~** una hora y cuarto; **three ~s of an hour** tres cuartos de hora; **it's a ~ past** *or* (*US*) **after seven** son las siete y cuarto; **it's a ~ to** *or* (*US*) **of seven** son las siete menos cuarto, es un cuarto para las siete (*LAm*)
[3] (*specific fourth parts*) [3·1] (*US, Canada*) (= *25 cents*) (moneda f de) cuarto *m* de dólar
[3·2] [*of year*] trimestre *m*; **to pay by the ~** pagar trimestralmente *or* al trimestre *or* cada tres meses
[3·3] [*of moon*] cuarto *m*; **when the moon is in its first/last ~** cuando la luna está en cuarto creciente/menguante
[4] (= *part of town*) barrio *m*; **the business ~** el barrio comercial; **the old ~** el casco viejo *or* antiguo
[5] (= *direction, area*) **protest is growing in some ~s** las protestas aumentan en algunos círculos; **from all ~s** de todas partes; **at close ~s** de cerca; **he fired two shots at close ~s** disparó dos tiros a quemarropa; **they are spread over the four ~s of the globe** se extienden por todos los rincones *or* por todas partes del mundo; **help came from an unexpected ~** la ayuda nos llegó de un lugar inesperado
[6] (*Naut, Geog*) [*of compass*] cuarta *f*; **the port/starboard ~** [*of ship*] la aleta de babor/estribor; **the wind was from the port ~** el viento soplaba de babor; **the wind is in the right ~** el viento sopla en dirección favorable
[7] (*Heraldry*) cuartel *m*
[8] (*frm*) (= *mercy*) clemencia *f*; **they knew they could expect no ~** sabían que no podían esperar clemencia; **to give (sb) no ~** no dar cuartel (a algn)
[9] **quarters** (= *accommodation*) [9·1] (*for staff*) (= *building, section*) dependencias *fpl*; (= *rooms*) cuartos *mpl*, habitaciones *fpl*; **the servants' ~s** las dependencias del servicio; **they're living in very cramped ~s** viven hacinados; **the cramped ~s of the space capsule** el reducido espacio de la cápsula espacial; *see also* **living D**
[9·2] (*Mil*) (= *barracks*) cuartel *msing*; (*also* **sleeping ~s**) barracones *mpl*; **the crew's/officers' ~s** (*on ship*) las dependencias de la tripulación/de los oficiales; *see also* **married B**
Ⓑ ADJ cuarto; **he has a ~ share** tiene una cuarta parte; **a ~ pound/century** un cuarto de libra/siglo
Ⓒ VT [1] (= *divide into four*) [+ *apple, potato*] cortar en cuatro (trozos); [+ *carcass, body*] descuartizar; *see also* **hang A3.1**
[2] (*Mil*) acuartelar, alojar; **our soldiers are ~ed in Ramsey** nuestros soldados están acuartelados en Ramsey
[3] (= *range over*) [*person*] recorrer; **to ~ the ground** [*dog*] buscar olfateando; [*bird*] escudriñar el terreno
Ⓓ CPD ► **quarter day** N (*gen*) *primer día del trimestre*; (*Fin*) *el día del vencimiento de un pago trimestral* ► **quarter light** N (*Brit Aut*) ventanilla *f* direccional ► **quarter note** N (*US Mus*) negra *f* ► **quarter tone** N cuarto *m* de tono ► **quarter turn** N cuarto *m* de vuelta

quarterback ['kwɔːtəbæk] N (*US Ftbl*) mariscal *mf* de campo
quarterdeck ['kwɔːtədek] N alcázar *m*
quarter-final ['kwɔːtə,faɪnl] N cuarto *m* de final
quarter-finalist ['kwɔːtə'faɪnəlɪst] N cuartofinalista *mf*
quarter-hour ['kwɔːtə'aʊəʳ] N cuarto *m* de hora
quarter-hourly ['kwɔːtə'aʊəlɪ] Ⓐ ADV cada cuarto de hora
Ⓑ ADJ **at ~ intervals** cada cuarto de hora

quartering ['kwɔːtərɪŋ] N (*Heraldry*) cuartel *m*
quarterly ['kwɔːtəlɪ] Ⓐ ADV trimestralmente, cada tres meses
Ⓑ ADJ trimestral
Ⓒ N publicación *f* trimestral
quartermaster ['kwɔːtə,mɑːstəʳ] Ⓐ N intendente *m*
Ⓑ CPD ► **quartermaster general** N intendente *m* general ► **quartermaster sergeant** N ≈ brigada *m*
quartern ['kwɔːtən] Ⓐ N cuarta *f*
Ⓑ CPD ► **quartern loaf** N pan *m* de cuatro libras
quarterstaff ['kwɔːtəstɑːf] N (*Hist*) barra *f*
quartet, **quartette** [kwɔː'tet] N (*gen, Mus*) cuarteto *m*
quartile ['kwɔːtaɪl] N cuartil *m*
quarto ['kwɔːtəʊ] Ⓐ ADJ [*volume*] en cuarto; [*paper*] tamaño *m* holandesa
Ⓑ N libro *m* en cuarto
quartz ['kwɔːts] Ⓐ N cuarzo *m*
Ⓑ CPD ► **quartz clock** N reloj *m* de cuarzo ► **quartz crystal** N cristal *m* de cuarzo ► **quartz lamp** N lámpara *f* de cuarzo ► **quartz watch** N reloj *m* de cuarzo
quartzite ['kwɔːtsaɪt] N cuarcita *f*
quasar ['kweɪzɑːʳ] N cuasar *m*, quásar *m*
quash ['kwɒʃ] VT [1] [+ *rebellion*] sofocar
[2] [+ *proposal*] rechazar; [+ *verdict*] anular, invalidar
quasi- ['kweɪzaɪ, 'kwɑːzɪ] PREFIX cuasi-; **~religious** cuasi-religioso; **~revolutionary** cuasi-revolucionario
quatercentenary [,kwɒtəsen'tiːnərɪ] N cuarto centenario *m*
quaternary [kwə'tɜːnərɪ] Ⓐ ADJ cuaternario
Ⓑ N cuaternario *m*
quatrain ['kwɒtreɪn] N cuarteto *m*, estrofa *f* de cuatro versos
quaver ['kweɪvəʳ] Ⓐ N (*when speaking*) temblor *m*; (*Mus*) (= *trill*) trémolo *m*; (*Brit*) (= *note*) corchea *f*; **with a ~ in her voice** con voz trémula
Ⓑ VI [*voice*] temblar
Ⓒ VT **"yes," she ~ed** —sí —dijo con voz trémula *or* temblorosa
Ⓓ CPD ► **quaver rest** N (*Brit*) pausa *f* de corchea
quavering ['kweɪvərɪŋ] ADJ trémulo, tembloroso
quavery ['kweɪvərɪ] ADJ = **quavering**
quay [kiː] N muelle *m*; **on the ~** en el muelle
quayside ['kiːsaɪd] N muelle *m*
Que. ABBR (*Canada*) = **Quebec**
queasiness ['kwiːzɪnɪs] N [1] (= *nausea*) náuseas *fpl*, sensación *f* de mareo; **the anaesthetic may cause a little ~** la anestesia puede producirle ligeras náuseas *or* una ligera sensación de mareo; **a feeling of ~** una sensación de mareo
[2] (= *unease*) intranquilidad *f*
queasy ['kwiːzɪ] ADJ (*compar* **queasier**; *superl* **queasiest**) [1] (= *nauseous*) [*stomach*] revuelto; **his stomach was ~** tenía el estómago revuelto; **to be** *or* **feel ~** tener náuseas; **the food made her (feel) ~** la comida le revolvió el estómago; **the slight rocking made her feel ~** el ligero balanceo la mareó; **it made him (feel) ~ to watch it** se mareó al verlo, verlo le revolvió el estómago
[2] (= *uneasy*) intranquilo; **I had a ~ feeling about the whole thing** todo este asunto me inquietaba *or* me hacía sentirme intranquilo
Quebec [kwɪ'bek] N Quebec *m*
queen [kwiːn] Ⓐ N [1] (= *monarch*) reina *f*; (*Chess*) reina *f*; (*Cards*) dama *f*; (*in Spanish pack*) caballo *m*; **she was ~ to Charles II** era la reina de Carlos II
[2] (*Zool*) (*also* **~ bee**) abeja *f* reina; (= *ant*) hormiga *f* reina
[3] (*) marica* *m* (*pej*)
Ⓑ VT (*Chess*) [+ *pawn*] coronar; ✦**IDIOM to ~ it** conducirse como una reina; (*fig*) pavonearse
Ⓒ VI (*Chess*) ser coronado
Ⓓ CPD ► **Queen's Bench** N (*Brit*) *departamento del Tribunal Supremo de Justicia* ► **queen mother** N reina *f* madre ► **Queen's Counsel** N (*Brit*) abogado *mf* (*de categoría superior*); → QC/KC

> **QUEEN'S/KING'S SPEECH**
>
> *En el Reino Unido, el* **Queen's** *o* **King's Speech** *es el discurso que el monarca dirige cada año a las dos cámaras del Estado en la apertura del nuevo curso parlamentario. El discurso se retransmite por radio y televisión y es preparado por el gobierno, ya que en él se indican las directrices del programa de gobierno para el curso que comienza, así como la nueva legislación que se introducirá ese año. Para seguir con la tradición, en este discurso el monarca sigue refiriéndose al gobierno como* **my government**.

queenly ['kwiːnlɪ] ADJ [*manner, bearing*] regio; [*responsibilities*] de reina
queer [kwɪəʳ] Ⓐ ADJ (*compar* **queerer**; *superl* **queerest**) [1] (= *odd*) raro, extraño; **there's something ~ going on** pasa algo raro *or* extraño; **there was a ~ noise coming from the kitchen** había un ruido raro en la cocina; **to be ~ in the head*** andar mal de la cabeza*; ✦**IDIOM to be in Queer Street** (*Brit**) estar en apuros
[2] (*Brit*†) (= *ill*) **to feel ~** no sentirse bien, encontrarse mal; **to come over ~** ponerse malo
[3] (†* *pej*) (= *homosexual*) maricón*, marica*
Ⓑ N (* *pej*) (= *homosexual*) maricón* *m*, marica* *m*
Ⓒ VT ✦**IDIOM to ~ sb's pitch** fastidiar a algn
queer-bashing* ['kwɪə,bæʃɪŋ] N **to go in for ~** atacar a homosexuales
queer-looking ['kwɪə,lʊkɪŋ] ADJ [*animal, plant, insect*] de aspecto extraño
queerly ['kwɪəlɪ] ADV [*behave, laugh, dress*] de modo raro *or* extraño, de forma rara *or* extraña
queerness ['kwɪənɪs] N (= *oddness*) lo raro, lo extraño
queer-sounding ['kwɪə,saʊndɪŋ] ADJ [*name*] raro
quell [kwel] VT [+ *uprising*] sofocar; [+ *opposition*] sobreponerse a, dominar; [+ *fears*] desechar
quench [kwentʃ] VT [+ *flames, thirst*] apagar; [+ *hope*] matar, sofocar; [+ *desire*] satisfacer; [+ *enthusiasm, passion*] enfriar
quenchless ['kwentʃlɪs] ADJ inapagable
quern [kwɜːn] N molinillo *m* de mano
querulous ['kwerʊləs] ADJ quejumbroso
querulously ['kwerʊləslɪ] ADV quejumbrosamente; [*say*] en tono quejumbroso
query ['kwɪərɪ] Ⓐ N [1] (= *question*) pregunta *f*; (*fig*) (= *doubt*) duda *f*, interrogante *m or f*; **if you have any queries, please do not hesitate to call** si tiene alguna pregunta, no dude en llamar; **there are many queries about his suitability for the job** hay muchos interrogantes acerca de su idoneidad para el puesto
[2] (*Gram*) (= *question mark*) signo *m* de inte-

rrogación

Ⓑ VT (= *ask*) preguntar; (= *doubt*) dudar de, expresar dudas acerca de; (= *disagree with, dispute*) cuestionar, poner en duda; (*Comput*) interrogar; **to ~ sb about sth** preguntar a algn sobre algo; **to ~ whether ...** dudar si ...; **I would ~ that** dudo si eso es cierto, tengo mis dudas acerca de eso; **no one queried my decision** nadie cuestionó *or* puso en duda mi decisión; **they queried the bill** pidieron explicaciones sobre la factura; **do you ~ the evidence?** ¿tiene dudas acerca del testimonio?

Ⓒ CPD ► **query language** N lenguaje *m* de interrogación

quest [kwest] Ⓐ N (*lit, fig*) búsqueda *f* (**for** de); **to go in ~ of** ir en busca de

Ⓑ VI **to ~ for sth** buscar algo

▼**question** ['kwestʃən] Ⓐ N [1] (= *query*) (*also in exam*) pregunta *f*; **(are there) any ~s?** ¿(hay) alguna pregunta?; **to ask (sb) a ~** hacer una pregunta (a algn); **ask yourself this ~** hágase esta pregunta; **what a ~ to ask!** ¡vaya preguntita!; **there's a reward for the painting's return, no ~s asked** se ofrece una recompensa sin preguntas por la devolución del cuadro; **ask me no ~s and I'll tell you no lies** más vale que no me preguntes; **"why didn't you appoint him a year ago?" — "good ~"** — ¿por qué no lo nombraste hace un año? —buena pregunta *or* —eso me pregunto yo; **he posed three ~s** hizo *or* planteó tres preguntas; **to put a ~ to sb** (*frm*) hacer una pregunta a algn; **to put down a ~ to** *or* **for sb** (*Parl*) formular una pregunta a algn; **to obey orders without ~** obedecer órdenes sin rechistar; ✦**IDIOM the 64,000 dollar ~** la pregunta del millón; *see also* **leading B, open A10, A11, personal A4, pop C2, trick C**

[2] (= *matter, issue*) cuestión *f*; **the Palestinian ~** la cuestión palestina; **that is the ~** de eso se trata, esa es la cuestión; **that is not the ~** no se trata de eso, no es cuestión de eso; **at the time in ~** a la hora en cuestión; **it is not simply a ~ of money** no se trata simplemente de dinero, no es una simple cuestión de dinero; **this raises the ~ of her suitability** esto plantea la cuestión de si es la persona adecuada; **it's only a ~ of time before he finds out** sólo es cuestión de tiempo que se entere; *see also* **beg A1**

[3] (= *possibility*) posibilidad *f*; **there is no ~ of outside help** no hay posibilidad de ayuda externa; **there can be no ~ of your resigning** su dimisión no se puede admitir; **it's out of the ~!** ¡imposible!, ¡ni hablar!; **an interest rate cut is out of the ~** un recorte de los tipos de interés es imposible

[4] (= *doubt*) duda *f*; **there is no ~ about it** no cabe la menor duda de esto; **as a manager, her ability is beyond ~** como directora, su capacidad está fuera de toda duda; **to bring** *or* **call sth into ~** poner algo en duda; **my integrity has been brought** *or* **called into ~** mi integridad se ha puesto en duda; **to be in ~** estar en duda; **your professional ability is not in ~** no es tu capacidad como profesional lo que se pone en duda; **his findings pose ~s about the future of these drugs** sus descubrimientos hacen que se planteen preguntas sobre el futuro de estas drogas; **this disaster raises ~s about air safety in the region** con el desastre se ha puesto en duda la seguridad aérea en la zona; **the ~ remains (as to) whether he can be trusted** la duda *or* la cuestión sigue siendo si se puede confiar en él; **the ~ remains: how did she escape?** la pregunta sigue ahí: ¿cómo escapó?; **there is some ~ as to whether he will sign** hay *or* existen ciertas dudas sobre si firmará; **without ~** sin duda, indudablemente

[5] (*at meeting*) cuestión *f*, asunto *m*; **to move the previous ~** plantear la cuestión previa; **to put the ~ (to a vote)** someter la moción a votación

Ⓑ VT [1] (= *interrogate*) [+ *exam candidate, interviewee*] hacer preguntas a; [+ *suspect*] interrogar; (*Parl*) [+ *minister, secretary*] interpelar; **you will be ~ed on one of three topics** se te harán preguntas sobre uno de tres temas; **a suspect is being ~ed by police** la policía está interrogando a un sospechoso; **they ~ed him about his past** le hicieron preguntas *or* le preguntaron acerca de su pasado; **the minister was ~ed about his statement to Parliament** se interpeló al ministro sobre su declaración ante el Parlamento

[2] (= *doubt*) [+ *honesty, loyalty, motives*] dudar de, poner en duda; [+ *decision, beliefs*] poner en duda, cuestionar

Ⓒ CPD ► **question mark** N (*lit*) signo *m* de interrogación; (*fig*) interrogante *m or f*; **a big ~ mark hangs over his future** se plantea un enorme interrogante sobre su futuro ► **question master** N interrogador *m* ► **question tag** N coletilla *f* interrogativa ► **question time** N (*Brit Parl*) sesión *f* de interpelaciones a los ministros

▼**questionable** ['kwestʃənəbl] ADJ [1] (= *uncertain, debatable*) [*assumption, significance, value*] discutible, cuestionable; **it is ~ whether ...** es discutible si ...

[2] (= *morally dubious*) [*behaviour, method, practice*] cuestionable; **in ~ taste** de dudoso gusto

questionary ['kwestʃənərɪ] N cuestionario *m*, encuesta *f*

questioner ['kwestʃənəʳ] N interrogador(a) *m/f*; (*at meeting*) interpelante *mf*

questioning ['kwestʃənɪŋ] Ⓐ ADJ [*tone, mind*] inquisitivo, inquisidor; **she gave him a ~ look** le lanzó una mirada inquisitiva *or* inquisidora

Ⓑ N [1] (= *interrogation*) interrogatorio *m*; **he is wanted for ~ by police** la policía requiere su presencia para someterlo a un interrogatorio

[2] (= *doubting*) cuestionamiento *m*, puesta *f* en duda

questioningly ['kwestʃənɪŋlɪ] ADV de manera inquisitiva *or* inquisidora

questionnaire [ˌkwestʃə'nɛəʳ] N cuestionario *m*

questor ['kwiːstəʳ] N (*US*) = **quaestor**

queue [kjuː] (*esp Brit*) Ⓐ N cola *f*; **to form a ~** ◊ **stand in a ~** hacer cola; **to jump the ~** colarse*, saltarse la cola

Ⓑ VI (*also* **~ up**) hacer cola; **to ~ for three hours** pasar tres horas haciendo cola; **we ~d for tickets** hicimos cola para comprar entradas

queue-jump ['kjuːˌdʒʌmp] VI (*Brit*) colarse*

queue-jumper ['kjuːˌdʒʌmpəʳ] N (*Brit*) colón/ona* *m/f*

queue-jumping ['kjuːˌdʒʌmpɪŋ] N (*Brit*) colarse *m*; **~ will not be tolerated** no se permitirá que nadie se cuele

quibble ['kwɪbl] Ⓐ N (= *trivial objection*) objeción *f* de poca monta; **he dismissed their objections as mere ~s** desestimó sus objeciones como si se trataran de simples nimiedades; **the deal was held up by some legal ~** se retrasó el acuerdo a causa de una pequeña objeción de carácter legal

Ⓑ VI hacer objeciones de poca monta; **he always ~s** es un quisquilloso; **to ~ over** *or* **about sth** discutir por algo sin importancia; **I'm not going to ~ over 20 pence** no voy a discutir por 20 peniques; **there's no point in quibbling about who's right and who's wrong** no sirve de nada discutir por quién tiene razón y quién no

quibbler ['kwɪbləʳ] N quisquilloso/a *m/f*

quibbling ['kwɪblɪŋ] Ⓐ ADJ quisquilloso

Ⓑ N objeciones *fpl* de poca monta

quiche [kiːʃ] N quiche *m*

quick [kwɪk] Ⓐ ADJ (*compar* **quicker**, *superl* **quickest**) [1] (= *fast*) [*method, movement*] rápido; **this is the ~est way to do it** ésta es la forma más rápida de hacerlo; **it's ~er by train** es más rápido ir en tren; **be ~!** ¡rápido!, ¡date prisa!, ¡apúrate! (*LAm*); **to be ~ to do sth** hacer algo rápidamente; **he was ~ to see the possibilities** vio rápidamente las posibilidades; **his opponents were ~ to point out that ...** sus adversarios señalaron rápidamente que ...; **to be ~ to act** obrar con prontitud; **to be ~ to anger** enfadarse con facilidad; **to be ~ to take offence** ofenderse por nada; **and be ~ about it!** ¡y date prisa!, ¡y apúrate! (*LAm*); **~ march!** (*Mil*) ¡marchando, ar!; **at a ~ pace** a un paso rápido; **he made a ~ recovery** se recuperó rápidamente; **in ~ succession** en rápida sucesión; **to have a ~ temper** tener un genio vivo; **he's a ~ worker** trabaja rápido, es un trabajador rápido; *see also* **draw A4, mark² A6, uptake 1**

[2] (= *with minimal delay*) [*answer, decision*] rápido; **we must have a ~ answer** necesitamos una respuesta rápida; **we are hoping for a ~ end to the bloodshed** esperamos que el derramamiento de sangre acabe pronto; **a ~ fix** una solución fácil; **the price has been reduced for a ~ sale** han reducido el precio para venderlo pronto

[3] (= *not lengthy*) [*meal*] rápido; **he gave me a ~ kiss on the cheek** me dio un besito en la mejilla; **let's have a ~ look at that*** déjame echarle un vistazo rápido a eso; **to have a ~ one*** (= *drink*) tomarse un trago; **can I have a ~ word (with you)?** ¿puedo hablar un segundo contigo?, ¿podemos hablar un segundo?

[4] (= *sharp*) [*person*] listo; [*wit*] agudo; [*mind, reflexes*] ágil, rápido; **he is very ~ at maths** es muy rápido para las matemáticas; **to have a ~ eye for sth** captar *or* coger algo al vuelo

Ⓑ N [1] (*Anat*) **the ~**: **her nails were bitten down to the ~** se había mordido las uñas hasta dejárselas como muñones; ✦**IDIOM to cut sb to the ~** herir a algn en lo vivo

[2] (†† *liter*) **the ~ and the dead** los vivos y los muertos

Ⓒ ADV deprisa, rápido; **~!** ¡deprisa!, ¡rápido!; **I left as ~ as I could** me fui lo más rápido *or* deprisa que pude; **come as ~ as you can** ven cuanto antes; ✦**IDIOM as ~ as a flash** como un rayo *or* relámpago

quick-acting ['kwɪk'æktɪŋ] ADJ de acción rápida

quick-change ['kwɪk'tʃeɪndʒ] ADJ (*Theat*) **~ artist** transformista *mf*

quick-drying ['kwɪk'draɪɪŋ] ADJ [*paint, varnish*] de secado rápido

quick-eared ['kwɪk'ɪəd] ADJ de oído fino

quicken ['kwɪkən] Ⓐ VT (= *speed up*) acelerar, apresurar; **to ~ one's pace** apretar *or* acelerar el paso

Ⓑ VI [*breathing, pulse*] acelerarse; [*interest*] acrecentarse, avivarse; [*embryo*] empezar a moverse; **the pace ~ed** se aceleró el paso; **men's hearts ~ed whenever she appeared** cuando aparecía ella se les aceleraba el pulso a los hombres

➤ LANGUAGE IN USE: **question A1** 26.1 **A2** 26.1, 26.2, 26.3 **A3** 12.3 **B2** 26.3 **questionable** 26.3

quick-eyed ['kwɪk'aɪd] ADJ de vista aguda

quick-fire ['kwɪkfaɪəʳ] ADJ [*gun*] de tiro rápido; [*question*] rápido, hecho a quemarropa

quick-firing ['kwɪk,faɪərɪŋ] ADJ de tiro rápido

quick-freeze ['kwɪk'fri:z] VT congelar rápidamente

quickie* ['kwɪkɪ] N (= *question*) pregunta *f* cortita*; (= *drink*) copita* *f*; (= *sex*) polvito* *m*; **to have a ~** (= *drink*) tomarse una copita*; (= *sex*) echarse un polvito*

quicklime ['kwɪklaɪm] N cal *f* viva

quickly ['kwɪklɪ] ADV [1] (= *fast*) [*move, work*] deprisa, rápidamente; **I'm working as ~ as I can** estoy trabajando lo más rápido *or* lo mas rápidamente que puedo, no puedo trabajar más deprisa; **he talks too ~ for me to understand** habla demasiado deprisa y no le entiendo
[2] (= *with minimal delay*) [*arrive, answer, react*] en seguida, con prontitud (*more frm*); **the police were ~ on the scene** la policía llegó en seguida; **they answered ~** contestaron pronto; **success ~ followed** el éxito llegó en seguida *or* muy poco después; **come as ~ as you can** ven cuanto antes
[3] (= *not lengthily*) [*embrace, smile*] rápidamente; **he glanced ~ at the note** echó un vistazo rápido a la nota

quickness ['kwɪknɪs] N [1] (= *speed*) rapidez *f*, velocidad *f*; **his ~ on his feet** su velocidad
[2] (= *lack of delay*) prontitud *f*
[3] (= *sharpness*) agudeza *f*; **~ of mind** rapidez *f*, agilidad *f* mental

quicksand ['kwɪksænd] N arenas *fpl* movedizas

quickset ['kwɪkset] Ⓐ ADJ compuesto de plantas vivas (*esp de espinos*)
Ⓑ N (= *slip*) plantón *m*; (= *hawthorn*) espino *m*; (= *hedge*) seto *m* vivo (*esp de espinos*)

quick-setting ['kwɪk,setɪŋ] ADJ **~ glue** pegamento *m* rápido

quick-sighted ['kwɪk'saɪtɪd] ADJ de vista aguda; (*fig*) perspicaz

quicksilver ['kwɪk,sɪlvəʳ] Ⓐ N azogue *m*, mercurio *m*
Ⓑ ADJ (*fig*) [*moods, temperament*] inconstante, caprichoso
Ⓒ VT azogar

quickstep ['kwɪkstep] N (= *dance*) *baile formal a ritmo rápido*

quick-tempered ['kwɪk'tempəd] ADJ de genio vivo, irascible

quick-witted ['kwɪk'wɪtɪd] ADJ agudo, perspicaz; **that was very ~ of you** en eso fuiste muy agudo

quid¹* [kwɪd] N (*Brit*) libra *f* (esterlina); **three ~** tres libras; ✦***IDIOM* to be ~s in** haber ganado bastante

quid² [kwɪd] N [*of tobacco*] mascada *f* (de tabaco)

quiddity ['kwɪdɪtɪ] N (*Philos*) esencia *f*; (= *quibble*) sutileza *f*, sofistería *f*

quid pro quo ['kwɪdprəʊ'kwəʊ] N (*pl* **quid pro quos**) compensación *f* (**for** por)

quiescence [kwaɪ'esns] N (*frm*) inactividad *f*, quietud *f*

quiescent [kwaɪ'esnt] ADJ (*frm*) inactivo, quieto

quiet ['kwaɪət] Ⓐ ADJ (*compar* **quieter**; *superl* **quietest**) [1] (= *not loud*) [*engine*] silencioso; [*music*] tranquilo, suave; [*tone*] bajo, quedo (*liter*); [*laughter*] suave; **he said in a ~ voice** dijo en (un) tono bajo
[2] (= *silent*) [2·1] [*person*] callado; **to be ~** estar callado; **you're very ~ today** hoy estás muy callado; **be ~!** ¡cállate!, ¡silencio!; **to go ~** quedarse callado; **to keep** *or* **stay ~** (= *say nothing*) quedarse callado; (= *not make a noise*) no hacer ruido; **to keep ~ about sth** no decir nada acerca de algo; **to keep sb ~: they paid him £1,000 to keep him ~** le pagaron 1000 libras para que se callara; **that book should keep him ~ for a while** ese libro le tendrá entretenido durante un rato; **I gave him a biscuit to keep him ~** le di una galleta para que estuviese entretenido
[2·2] **to keep sth ~: keep it ~** no se lo digas a nadie; **he managed to keep the whole thing ~** consiguió que nadie se enterara del asunto; **the government has tried to keep the matter ~** el gobierno ha intentado mantener el asunto en secreto
[2·3] [*place*] silencioso; **it was dark and the streets were ~** era de noche y las calles estaban silenciosas; **isn't it ~!** ¡qué silencio!; ✦***IDIOM* it was ~ as the grave** había un silencio sepulcral
[3] (= *peaceful, not busy*) [*life, night, village, area*] tranquilo; **they lead a ~ life** llevan una vida tranquila; **he'll do anything for a ~ life** hará lo que sea para que lo dejen en paz; **the patient has had a ~ night** el paciente ha pasado una noche tranquila; **this town is too ~ for me** esta ciudad es demasiado tranquila para mí; **the shops will be ~er today** las tiendas estarán más tranquilas hoy, hoy habrá menos jaleo en las tiendas; **business is ~ at this time of year** hay poco movimiento en esta época; **everybody needs a ~ time** todo el mundo necesita un rato de tranquilidad; **those were ~ times** aquél fue un tiempo de tranquilidad; ✦***IDIOM* all ~ on the Western front** no hay moros en la costa
[4] (= *calm, placid*) [*person*] callado; [*temperament*] tranquilo, sosegado; [*dog, horse*] manso; **my daughter is a very ~ girl** mi hija es una chica muy callada; **we have very ~ neighbours** tenemos unos vecinos muy tranquilos
[5] (= *discreet*) [*manner, decor, style*] discreto; [*clothes, dress*] discreto, no llamativo; [*colour*] suave, apagado; [*despair*] callado; [*optimism*] comedido; [*ceremony*] íntimo; **the decoration was in ~ good taste** la decoración era de un gusto discreto; **with ~ humour he said ...** con un humor discreto dijo ...; **we had a ~ lunch/supper** comimos/cenamos en la intimidad; **it was a ~ funeral/wedding** el funeral/la boda se celebró en la intimidad; **to have a ~ dig at sb** burlarse discretamente de algn; **we had a ~ laugh over it** nos reímos en privado; **I'll have a ~ word with him** hablaré discretamente con él
Ⓑ N [1] (= *silence*) silencio *m*; **let's have complete ~ for a few minutes** vamos a tener unos minutos de completo silencio; **in the ~ of the night** en el silencio de la noche; **on the ~** a escondidas
[2] (= *peacefulness*) tranquilidad *f*; **there was a period of ~ after the fighting** hubo un periodo de tranquilidad tras los enfrentamientos; *see also* **peace A4**
Ⓒ VT (*US*) = **quieten A**
Ⓓ VI (*US*) = **quieten B**

quieten ['kwaɪətn] Ⓐ VT (*also* **~ down**) (= *calm*) calmar, tranquilizar; (*fig*) (= *silence*) [+ *fears*] acallar; **he managed to ~ the crowd** logró calmar a la multitud
Ⓑ VI (*also* **~ down**) (= *calm down*) calmarse, tranquilizarse; (= *fall silent*) callarse; (*fig*) (*after unruly youth etc*) calmarse, sentar cabeza; (*after rage*) tranquilizarse

quietism ['kwaɪɪtɪzəm] N quietismo *m*

quietist ['kwaɪɪtɪst] N quietista *mf*

quietly ['kwaɪətlɪ] ADV [1] (= *not loudly*) [*say, whisper*] en voz baja; [*sing*] en voz baja, suavemente; [*drink, leave, walk, come in*] silenciosamente, sin hacer ruido; **this part should be played ~** (*Mus*) esta parte hay que tocarla bajo
[2] (= *silently*) en silencio; **she said nothing, but listened ~** no dijo nada, sino que escuchó en silencio
[3] (= *peacefully, calmly*) [*play, read*] tranquilamente; **I was ~ drinking a cup of coffee** estaba tomando café tranquilamente; **he refused to go ~** se negó a irse pacíficamente; **are you coming ~ or are you going to make trouble?** ¿nos acompaña usted pacíficamente o va a causar problemas?; **the house is ~ situated in attractive parkland** la casa está situada en una tranquila zona con jardines; **I'm ~ confident about the future** aunque no lo exteriorice, soy optimista respecto al futuro; **he was ~ content** estaba contento y tranquilo
[4] (= *discreetly*) discretamente; **the president's plan had been ~ shelved** habían dejado de lado discretamente el plan del presidente; **she lives ~ in Suffolk** vive discretamente en Suffolk; **to be ~ dressed** vestirse con discreción; **he slipped off ~** se marchó sin que nadie lo notara; **let's get married ~** casémonos en la intimidad; **we dined ~ at home** cenamos en la intimidad del hogar

quietness ['kwaɪətnɪs] N [1] (= *softness*) [*of voice, music*] suavidad *f*
[2] (= *silence*) silencio *m*
[3] (= *calm*) tranquilidad *f*

quietude ['kwaɪətju:d] N quietud *f*

quietus [kwaɪ'i:təs] N (*pl* **quietuses**) (*liter*) golpe *m* de gracia; (= *death*) muerte *f*; (*Comm*) quitanza *f*, finiquito *m*

quiff [kwɪf] N copete *m*

quill [kwɪl] Ⓐ N (= *feather*) pluma *f* de ave; (= *part of feather*) cañón *m* de pluma; [*of porcupine, hedgehog*] púa *f*; (= *pen*) pluma *f* (de ganso); (= *bobbin*) canilla *f*
Ⓑ CPD ► **quill pen** N pluma *f* (de ganso)

quilt [kwɪlt] Ⓐ N edredón *m*; (*Brit*) (*also* **continental ~**) edredón *m* (nórdico)
Ⓑ VT acolchar

quilted ['kwɪltɪd] ADJ acolchado

quilting ['kwɪltɪŋ] N (= *material*) tela *f* acolchada; (= *act, quilted work*) acolchado *m*

quim** [kwɪm] N coño** *m*

quin* [kwɪn] N (*Brit*) = **quintuplet**

quince [kwɪns] Ⓐ N membrillo *m*
Ⓑ CPD ► **quince cheese**, **quince jelly** N (dulce *m* de) membrillo *m*

quincentenary [,kwɪnsen'ti:nərɪ] N quinto centenario *m*

quinine [kwɪ'ni:n] N quinina *f*

Quinquagesima [,kwɪŋkwə'dʒesɪmə] N Quincuagésima *f*

quinquennial [kwɪŋ'kwenɪəl] ADJ quinquenal

quinquennium [kwɪŋ'kwenɪəm] N (*pl* **quinquennia** [kwɪŋ'kwenɪə]) quinquenio *m*

quinsy ['kwɪnzɪ] N angina *f*

quint* [kwɪnt] N (*US*) quintillizo/a *m/f*

quintessence [kwɪn'tesns] N quintaesencia *f*

quintessential [,kwɪntɪ'senʃəl] ADJ quintaesencial

quintet, **quintette** [kwɪn'tet] N (*gen*) quinteto *m*

quintuple Ⓐ ['kwɪntjʊpl] ADJ quíntuplo
Ⓑ ['kwɪntjʊpl] N quíntuplo *m*
Ⓒ [kwɪn'tju:pl] VT quintuplicar
Ⓓ [kwɪn'tju:pl] VI quintuplicarse

quintuplet [kwɪn'tju:plɪt] N quintillizo/a *m/f*

quip [kwɪp] Ⓐ N ocurrencia *f*, salida *f*
Ⓑ VT **"you'll have to go on a diet!" he ~ped** —¡tendrás que ponerte a dieta! —dijo bromeando
Ⓒ VI bromear

quire ['kwaɪəʳ] N mano *f* (de papel)

quirk [kwɜːk] N [1] (= *oddity*) rareza *f*; **it's just one of his little ~s** es una de sus rarezas; **by some ~ of fate/nature** por algún capricho del destino/de la naturaleza; **a statistical ~** una anomalía estadística
[2] (*Art, Mus*) (= *flourish*) floritura *f*

quirkiness ['kwɜːkɪnɪs] N rareza *f*

quirky ['kwɜːkɪ] ADJ (*compar* **quirkier**; *superl* **quirkiest**) [*humour, behaviour, style*] raro, peculiar; [*person*] raro, estrafalario

quisling ['kwɪzlɪŋ] N colaboracionista *mf*

quit [kwɪt] (*pt, pp* **quit**, **quitted**) Ⓐ VT [1] (= *cease*) **to ~ doing sth** (*esp US*) dejar de hacer algo; **to ~ work** (*during job*) suspender el trabajo, dejar de trabajar; (*at end of day*) salir del trabajo; **~ stalling!** (*esp US**) ¡déjate de evasivas!; **~ fooling!** ¡déjate de tonterías!
[2] (= *leave*) [+ *place*] abandonar, salir de; [+ *premises*] desocupar; (*Comput*) [+ *application*] abandonar; **to ~ one's job** dejar el trabajo, renunciar a su puesto
Ⓑ VI (*esp US*) (= *go away*) irse, marcharse; (= *resign*) dimitir, renunciar; (= *stop work*) suspender el trabajo, dejar de trabajar; (= *give up*) (*in game, task*) abandonar; (*Comput*) terminar, abandonar; **I ~!** ¡lo dejo!; (*from job*) ¡renuncio!; **I've been given notice to ~** he recibido una notificación de desahucio
Ⓒ ADJ **to be ~ of sth/sb** haberse librado de algo/algn

quite [kwaɪt] ADV [1] (= *completely*) totalmente, completamente; **~ new** completamente nuevo; **I'm not ~ sure** no estoy del todo seguro; **I ~ agree with you** estoy totalmente de acuerdo contigo; **it's ~ clear that this plan won't work** está clarísimo que este plan no va a funcionar; **that's ~ enough for me** eso me basta a mí; **that'll be ~ enough of that!** ¡ya está bien!; **I can ~ believe that ...** no me cuesta creer que ...; **I ~ understand** comprendo perfectamente; **I don't ~ understand it** no acabo de entenderlo; **they are ~ simply the best** son simple y llanamente los mejores; **~ frankly, I can't stand him** para ser totalmente sincero, no lo aguanto; **you could ~ easily have killed yourself** podrías haberte matado con toda facilidad; **that's not ~ right** eso no es totalmente cierto; **he has not ~ recovered yet** no se ha repuesto todavía del todo; **it was ~ three months since she had called**† habían pasado por lo menos tres meses desde que llamó; **he's ~ grown up now** ahora está hecho todo un hombre
[2] (= *exactly*) exactamente; **it's not ~ what we wanted** no es exactamente lo que queríamos; **we don't ~ know** no sabemos exactamente; **it's not ~ the same** no es exactamente lo mismo; **~ (so)!** ¡así es!, ¡exacto!; **not ~ as many as last time** no tantos como la última vez
[3] (= *rather*) bastante; **it's ~ good/important** es bastante bueno/importante; **"how was the film?" — "~ good"** —¿qué tal la película? —bastante bien; **it was ~ a surprise** me sorprendió bastante; **it was ~ a shock** fue bastante chocante; **~ a lot** bastante; **I've been there ~ a lot** he ido allí bastante; **~ a lot of money** bastante dinero; **it costs ~ a lot to go abroad** es bastante caro salir al extranjero
[4] (*emphatic use*) **that's ~ a car!** ¡vaya coche!; **~ a hero** todo un héroe (*also iro*); **there were ~ a few people there** había bastante gente allí; **~ suddenly, everything went black** de golpe, todo se volvió oscuro

Quito ['kiːtəʊ] N Quito *m*

quits [kwɪts] ADJ **to be ~ with sb** estar en paz con algn; **now we're ~!** ¡ahora estamos en paz!; **to call it ~** (= *give up*) rendirse; **let's call it ~** (*in argument*) hagamos las paces; (*when settling bill*) digamos que quedamos en paz

quitter* ['kwɪtəʳ] N (*pej*) rajado/a* *m/f*; **he's no ~** no es un rajado*

quiver¹ ['kwɪvəʳ] N [*of arrows*] carcaj *m*, aljaba *f*

quiver² ['kwɪvəʳ] Ⓐ N (= *trembling*) estremecimiento *m*
Ⓑ VI [*person,*] temblar, estremecerse (**with** de); [*voice, eyelids*] temblar

qui vive [kiː'viːv] N ✦**IDIOM to be on the ~** estar alerta

Quixote ['kwɪksət] N Quijote; **Don ~** don Quijote

quixotic [kwɪk'sɒtɪk] ADJ quijotesco

quixotically [kwɪk'sɒtɪkəlɪ] ADV de manera quijotesca; [*behave*] como un quijote

quixotism ['kwɪksətɪzəm] N quijotismo *m*

quiz [kwɪz] Ⓐ N (*pl* **quizzes**) (*TV, Rad*) concurso *m*; (*in magazine*) encuesta *f*; (*US*) test *m*, prueba *f*
Ⓑ VT (= *interrogate*) interrogar (**about** sobre)
Ⓒ CPD ► **quiz master** N moderador *m*
► **quiz programme, quiz show** N programa *m* concurso

quizzical ['kwɪzɪkəl] ADJ [*glance*] burlón, socarrón

quizzically ['kwɪzɪkəlɪ] ADV **he looked at me ~** me miró de manera burlona, me miró socarronamente

quod‡ [kwɒd] N (*Brit*) chirona‡ *f*, cárcel *f*

quoin [kɔɪn] N (= *angle*) esquina *f*, ángulo *m*; (= *stone*) piedra *f* angular; (*Typ*) cuña *f*

quoit [kwɔɪt] N aro *m*, tejo *m*; **quoits** juego *msing* de los aros; **to play ~s** jugar a los aros

quondam†† ['kwɒndæm] ADJ antiguo

quorate ['kwɔːreɪt] ADJ (*esp Brit*) **the meeting was not ~** no había quórum en la reunión

Quorn® [kwɔːn] N *alimento a base de proteínas vegetales*

quorum ['kwɔːrəm] N quórum *m*; **what number constitutes a ~?** ¿cuántos constituyen quórum?

quot. ABBR = **quotation**

quota ['kwəʊtə] Ⓐ N (*gen*) cuota *f*; (*Comm etc*) cupo *m*, contingente *m*; [*of production*] cuota *f*, cupo *m*; **a fixed ~** un cupo fijo; **import ~** cupo *m* de importación; **I've done my ~ of chores** he hecho mi parte de las tareas; **I didn't get my full ~ of sleep last night** anoche no dormí las horas que necesito
Ⓑ CPD ► **quota system** N sistema *m* de cuotas

quotable ['kwəʊtəbl] ADJ citable, digno de citarse; (*Fin*) cotizable

quotation [kwəʊ'teɪʃən] Ⓐ N [1] (= *words, line*) cita *f*; **dictionary of ~s** diccionario *m* de citas famosas
[2] (= *act of quoting*) **he has a fondness for ~** le encanta citar
[3] (*Comm*) (= *estimate*) presupuesto *m*; **shop around for the best insurance ~** pregunte en varias agencias hasta que encuentre la póliza más barata
[4] (*St Ex*) cotización *f*
Ⓑ CPD ► **quotation marks** NPL comillas *fpl*; **in ~ marks** (*lit, fig*) entre comillas; **I use the term "good" in ~ marks** utilizo el término "bueno" entre comillas; **single/double ~ marks** comillas *fpl* simples/dobles

quote [kwəʊt] Ⓐ VT [1] (= *cite*) [+ *writer, line, passage, source*] citar; **to ~ my aunt ...** para citar a mi tía ..., como decía mi tía ...; **you can ~ me** puedes decir que te lo he dicho yo; **don't ~ me on that** no te lo puedo decir a ciencia cierta; **he is ~d as saying that ...** se le atribuye haber dicho que ...
[2] (= *mention*) [+ *example*] dar, citar; [+ *reference number*] indicar; **to ~ sth/sb as an example (of sth)** poner algo/a algn como ejemplo (de algo)
[3] (*Comm*) (= *estimate*) **he ~d/I was ~d a good price** me dio un presupuesto *or* precio muy razonable
[4] (*Fin*) [+ *shares, company, currency*] cotizar (**at** a); **last night, Hunt shares were ~d at 346 pence** anoche las acciones Hunt cotizaron a 346 peniques; **it is not ~d on the Stock Exchange** no se cotiza en la Bolsa; **~d company** empresa *f* que cotiza en Bolsa
Ⓑ VI [1] (= *recite, repeat*) citar; **to ~ from the Bible** citar de la Biblia; **he said, and I ~, ...** dijo, y cito sus propias palabras, ...
[2] (*Comm*) **to ~ for sth** hacer un presupuesto de algo, presupuestar algo; **I got several firms to ~ for the building work** pedí a varias empresas que me hicieran un presupuesto de *or* me presupuestaran la obra
Ⓒ N (*) [1] (= *line, passage*) cita *f*
[2] (*Comm*) (= *estimate*) presupuesto *m*
[3] (*St Ex*) cotización *f*
[4] **quotes** (= *inverted commas*) comillas *fpl*; **in ~s** entre comillas
Ⓓ EXCL **she said, ~, "he was as drunk as a lord", unquote** sus palabras textuales fueron: —estaba como una cuba; **she died in a, ~, "accident", unquote** murió en un accidente, entre comillas *or* por así decirlo; **"quote"** (*in dictation*) "comienza la cita"

quoth†† [kwəʊθ] VI **~ I** dije yo; **~ he** dijo él

quotidian [kwəʊ'tɪdɪən] ADJ (*liter*) cotidiano

quotient ['kwəʊʃənt] N cociente *m*

q.v. ABBR = **quod vide** (= **which see**) véase, q.v.

qwerty keyboard [ˌkwɜːtɪ'kiːbɔːd] N teclado *m* QWERTY

R r

R[1], r[1] [ɑːʳ] N (= *letter*) R, r *f*; **R for Robert** R de Ramón; **the three Rs** (= *reading, writing and arithmetic*) *lectura, escritura y aritmética*; → THREE RS

R[2], r[2] Ⓐ ABBR [1] (*Brit*) (= **Rex**) R
[2] (*Brit*) (= **Regina**) R
[3] (*Geog*) (= **river**) R
[4] (= **right**) dcha, der, derº
[5] = **Réaumur (scale)**
[6] (*US Pol*) = **Republican**
Ⓑ ADJ ABBR (*US Cine*) (= **restricted**) ≈ sólo mayores

® N ABBR (= **registered trade mark**) ®

RA N ABBR [1] (*Brit*) (= **Royal Academy of Arts**) ≈ Real Academia *f* de Bellas Artes
[2] (*Brit*) (= **Royal Academician**) ≈ miembro *mf* de la Real Academia de Bellas Artes
[3] (*Mil*) = **Royal Artillery**
[4] = **Rear Admiral**

> **RA - ROYAL ACADEMY OF ARTS**
>
> *La* **Royal Academy of Arts** *o* **RA** *es la más famosa de las fundaciones de arte británicas. Con sede en Londres, la* **Royal Academy** *presenta exposiciones de artistas modernos y de todas las épocas, y también imparte algunas clases a futuros artistas. Cada verano tiene lugar la* **Summer Exhibition**, *que es la mayor exposición abierta de arte contemporáneo en el mundo. Cualquier artista puede enviar su trabajo y la selección final de obras concentra una amplia gama de estilos, tanto de artistas conocidos como de principiantes. Los artistas miembros de la* **Royal Academy of Arts** *pueden escribir las iniciales* **RA** *después de sus nombres, como si de un título académico se tratase.*

RAAF N ABBR = **Royal Australian Air Force**

Rabat [rəˈbɑːt] N Rabat *m*

rabbi [ˈræbaɪ] N rabino/a *m/f*; (*before name*) rabí *m*; **chief ~** gran rabino

rabbinical [rəˈbɪnɪkəl] ADJ rabínico

rabbit [ˈræbɪt] Ⓐ N (*pl* **rabbit** *or* **rabbits**) conejo *m*; *see also* **Welsh**
Ⓑ VI **to go ~ing** ir a cazar conejos
Ⓒ CPD ► **rabbit burrow** N madriguera *f* ► **rabbit ears*** NPL (*US TV*) antena *f* de cuernos ► **rabbit hole** N madriguera *f* ► **rabbit hutch** N conejera *f* ► **rabbit punch** N golpe *m* de nuca ► **rabbit warren** N conejera *f*, madriguera *f*

► **rabbit on*** VI + ADV enrollarse*

rabble [ˈræbl] N (= *disorderly crowd*) gentío *m*, muchedumbre *f*, mogollón *m* (*Sp**); **the ~** (= *uncultured people*) la chusma; **a ~ of** una multitud turbulenta de

rabble-rouser [ˈræblˌraʊzəʳ] N demagogo/a *m/f*, agitador(a) *m/f*

rabble-rousing [ˈræblˈraʊzɪŋ] Ⓐ N demagogia *f*, agitación *f*
Ⓑ ADJ demagógico

Rabelaisian [ˌræbəˈleɪzɪən] ADJ rabelasiano

rabid [ˈræbɪd] ADJ [*dog*] rabioso; (*fig*) [*person*] fanático

rabies [ˈreɪbiːz] NSING rabia *f*; **a dog with ~** un perro rabioso

RAC N ABBR (*Brit*) [1] (*Aut*) (= **Royal Automobile Club**) ≈ RACE *m* (*Sp*)
[2] (*Mil*) = **Royal Armoured Corps**

raccoon [rəˈkuːn] N (*pl* **raccoon** *or* **raccoons**) mapache *m*

race[1] [reɪs] Ⓐ N [1] (= *contest*) (*lit, fig*) carrera *f*; **it was a ~ to finish it in time** lo hicimos a la carrera para terminarlo a tiempo; **the ~ for the White House** la carrera hacia la Casa Blanca; **the election will be a very close ~** las elecciones van a estar muy reñidas; **a ~ against time/the clock** (*fig*) una carrera contra el tiempo/contra reloj; **the arms ~** la carrera armamentista; **boat ~** regata *f*; **cycle ~** carrera *f* ciclista; **horse ~** carrera *f* de caballos; **the ~ is on to find a donor** ha comenzado la carrera en busca de un donante; **to run (in) a ~** tomar parte en una carrera, participar en una carrera; **you ran a good ~** corriste muy bien; **the ~s** (= *horse races*) las carreras (de caballos); **to go to the ~s** ir a las carreras
[2] (= *swift current*) corriente *f* fuerte
Ⓑ VT [1] (= *enter in race*) [+ *horse*] presentar; [+ *car*] correr con; **they ~ vintage cars** hacen carreras de coches antiguos
[2] (= *run against*) echarle una carrera a; **(I'll) ~ you home!** ¡te echo una carrera hasta casa!
[3] **to ~ an engine** acelerar un motor al máximo
Ⓒ VI [1] (= *compete*) [*driver, athlete, horse*] correr, competir; **to ~ against sb** competir con algn (en una carrera)
[2] (= *go fast*) correr, ir a toda velocidad; **we ~d to get back home for eight o'clock** nos dimos prisa para estar en casa para las ocho; **to ~ against time/the clock (to do sth)** (*fig*) trabajar contra reloj (para hacer algo); **to ~ ahead** ponerse a la cabeza; **he ~d down the street** bajó la calle corriendo *or* a toda velocidad; **we ~d for a taxi** corrimos a coger un taxi; **he ~d past us** nos pasó a toda velocidad *or* a toda carrera; **he ~d through the paperwork as quickly as he could** hizo el papeleo todo lo rápido que pudo
[3] [*pulse, heart*] acelerarse; [*engine*] embalarse; **her heart ~d uncontrollably** el corazón se le aceleró descontrolado, el corazón le latía a un ritmo descontrolado; **my mind was racing** los pensamientos me invadían la mente
Ⓓ CPD ► **race car** N (*US*) coche *m* de carreras ► **race (car) driver** N (*US*) piloto *mf* de carreras, corredor(a) *m/f* de coches ► **race meeting** N (*Brit*) carreras *fpl* (de caballos)

race[2] [reɪs] Ⓐ N (= *racial origin*) raza *f*; **discrimination on the grounds of ~** discriminación *f* por la raza *or* por motivos raciales; **people of mixed ~** (*esp of Indian and white descent*) gente *f* mestiza; (*of black and white descent*) gente *f* mulata; **the human ~** la raza humana, el género humano; **they looked on us as a ~ apart** nos consideraban otra casta
Ⓑ CPD ► **race hatred** N odio *m* racial, racismo *m* ► **race issue** N asunto *m* racial; **a committee was set up to tackle ~ issues** se formó un comité para hacer frente a los asuntos *or* los problemas raciales ► **race relations** NPL relaciones *fpl* interraciales ► **race riot** N disturbio *m* racial

racecard [ˈreɪskɑːd] N programa *m* de carreras

racecourse [ˈreɪskɔːs] N hipódromo *m*

racegoer [ˈreɪsgəʊəʳ] N (*Brit*) aficionado/a *m/f* a las carreras

racehorse [ˈreɪshɔːs] N caballo *m* de carreras

raceme [ˈræsiːm] N racimo *m*

racer [ˈreɪsəʳ] N (= *runner*) corredor(a) *m/f*; (= *horse*) caballo *m* de carreras; (= *car*) coche *m* de carreras; (= *bike*) bicicleta *f* de carreras

racetrack [ˈreɪstræk] N (*for runners*) pista *f*; (*for horses*) hipódromo *m*; (*for cars*) circuito *m* de carreras; (*for cycles*) velódromo *m*

Rachel [ˈreɪtʃəl] N Raquel

rachitic [ræˈkɪtɪk] ADJ raquítico

racial [ˈreɪʃəl] Ⓐ ADJ racial
Ⓑ CPD ► **racial discrimination** N discriminación *f* racial ► **racial integration** N integración *f* racial

racialism [ˈreɪʃəlɪzəm] N (*esp Brit*) racismo *m*

racialist [ˈreɪʃəlɪst] (*esp Brit*) Ⓐ ADJ racista
Ⓑ N racista *mf*

racially [ˈreɪʃəlɪ] ADV racialmente; **children of ~ mixed parents** hijos *mpl* de padres de distintas razas

raciness [ˈreɪsɪnɪs] N lo picante

racing [ˈreɪsɪŋ] Ⓐ N carreras *fpl*; **greyhound/horse ~** carreras *fpl* de galgos/caballos; **motor ~** carreras *fpl* automovilísticas *or* de coches; **the ~ world** el mundo de las carreras (de caballos); *see also* **flat D**
Ⓑ CPD ► **racing bicycle, racing bike** N bicicleta *f* de carreras ► **racing calendar** N calendario *m* de carreras (de caballos) ► **racing car** N coche *m* de carreras ► **racing circuit** N autódromo *m*, pista *f* de carreras ► **racing commentator** N comentarista *mf* hípico/a ► **racing correspondent** N corresponsal *mf* hípico/a ► **racing cyclist** N corredor/a *m/f*

ciclista ► **racing driver** N piloto *mf* de carreras, corredor(a) *m/f* de carreras de coches ► **racing man** N (*horse racing*) aficionado *m* a las carreras (de caballos) ► **racing pigeon** N paloma *f* de carreras ► **racing yacht** N yate *m* de regatas

racism [ˈreɪsɪzəm] N racismo *m*

racist [ˈreɪsɪst] Ⓐ ADJ racista
Ⓑ N racista *mf*

rack[1] [ræk] Ⓐ N 1 (= *dish rack*) escurridor *m*, escurreplatos *m inv*; (= *clothes rack*) perchero *m*, percha *f*; (= *luggage rack*) (*Rail*) portaequipajes *m inv*, rejilla *f*; (= *roof rack*) baca *f*, portaequipajes *m inv*, parrilla *f* (*Andes*); (= *mechanical rack*) cremallera *f*; **to buy clothes off the ~** (*US*) comprar ropa de percha
2 (*for torture*) potro *m*; **to be on the ~** (*fig*) estar en ascuas
3 (*Snooker, Pool*) triángulo *m*
Ⓑ VT 1 [*pain*] atormentar; [*cough*] sacudir; **to be ~ed by remorse** estar atormentado por el remordimiento; **to be ~ed by pains** estar atormentado por el dolor; ✦***IDIOM*** **to ~ one's brains** devanarse los sesos
2 [+ *wine*] (*also* ~ **off**) trasegar
Ⓒ CPD ► **rack railway** N ferrocarril *m* de cremallera ► **rack rent** N alquiler *m* exorbitante

►**rack up** VT + ADV (= *accumulate*) acumular

rack[2] [ræk] N **to go to ~ and ruin** [*building*] echarse a perder, venirse abajo; [*business*] arruinarse, tronar (*LAm*); [*country*] arruinarse; [*person*] dejarse ir

rack-and-pinion [ˌrækəndˈpɪnjən] Ⓐ N (*Tech*) cremallera *f* y piñón
Ⓑ CPD ► **rack-and-pinion steering** N cremallera *f*, piñón *m*

racket[1] [ˈrækɪt] N (*Sport*) raqueta *f*

racket[2] [ˈrækɪt] Ⓐ N 1 (= *din*) [*of machine, engine*] estruendo *m*; (= *loud voices*) follón *m*, bulla *f*; **to kick up** *or* **make a ~** armar follón *or* bulla; **you never heard such a ~!** ¡menudo follón había!, ¡menuda bulla había!
2 (= *organized fraud*) estafa *f*; **the drug ~** el tráfico de drogas; **he was in on the ~** era de los que organizaron la estafa
Ⓑ VI (*make noise*) (*also* ~ **about**) hacer ruido, armar un jaleo

racketeer [ˌrækɪˈtɪəʳ] N (*esp US*) estafador(a) *m/f*

racketeering [ˌrækɪˈtɪərɪŋ] N chantaje *m* sistematizado, crimen *m* organizado

racking [ˈrækɪŋ] ADJ [*pain*] atroz

raconteur [ˌrækɒnˈtɜːʳ] N anecdotista *mf*

racoon [rəˈkuːn] N = **raccoon**

racquet [ˈrækɪt] N = **racket**[1]

racy [ˈreɪsɪ] ADJ (*compar* **racier**, *superl* **raciest**) [*style, speech, humour*] picante

rad⁎ [ræd] ADJ (*esp US*) = **radical**

RADA [ˈrɑːdə] N ABBR (*Brit*) (= **Royal Academy of Dramatic Art**) ≈ C.D.N. *m*

radar [ˈreɪdɑːʳ] Ⓐ N radar *m*
Ⓑ CPD ► **radar scanner** N antena *f* giratoria de radar ► **radar screen** N pantalla *f* de radar ► **radar station** N estación *f* de radar ► **radar trap** N trampa *f* de radar

raddled [ˈrædld] ADJ depravado, decaído

radial [ˈreɪdɪəl] Ⓐ ADJ 1 [*engine, tyre*] radial
2 (*Med*) radial, del radio
Ⓑ N (*also* ~ **tyre**) neumático *m* radial

radiance [ˈreɪdɪəns] N 1 (= *glow*) [*of face, personality, beauty*] lo radiante
2 (*liter*) (= *brightness*) [*of sun, colour, light*] resplandor *m*
3 (*Phys*) radiancia *m*

radiant [ˈreɪdɪənt] Ⓐ ADJ 1 (= *glowing*) [*smile, person, complexion*] radiante; **to look ~** estar radiante; **~ with joy** radiante *or* rebosante de alegría; **~ with health** rebosante de salud
2 (*liter*) (= *bright*) [*sunshine*] resplandeciente; [*colour*] radiante; **bathed in ~ sunshine** bañado en un sol radiante; **~ white robes** batas de un blanco radiante
3 (*Phys*) [*heat, light, energy*] radiante
Ⓑ N (*Astron, Math, Phys*) radiante *m*

radiantly [ˈreɪdɪəntlɪ] ADV 1 (= *glowingly*) **to smile ~ at sb** dirigir una sonrisa radiante a algn; **he smiled ~** sonrió radiante; **she was ~ beautiful** era de una belleza deslumbrante; **she was/looked ~ happy** estaba radiante *or* rebosante de felicidad
2 (*liter*) (= *brightly*) **to shine ~** resplandecer

radiate [ˈreɪdɪeɪt] Ⓐ VT (*lit, fig*) radiar, irradiar
Ⓑ VI **to ~ from** [*lines, streets*] partir de; **light ~d from an opening in the tunnel roof** la luz se difundía por una abertura en el techo del túnel; **lines that ~ from the centre** líneas que parten del centro; **hostility ~d from him** irradiaba hostilidad

radiation [ˌreɪdɪˈeɪʃən] Ⓐ N radiación *f*
Ⓑ CPD ► **radiation sickness** N enfermedad *f* por radiación ► **radiation therapy** N radioterapia *f*, terapia *f* por radiaciones ► **radiation treatment** N tratamiento *m* por radiaciones

radiator [ˈreɪdɪeɪtəʳ] Ⓐ N (*all senses*) radiador *m*
Ⓑ CPD ► **radiator cap** N tapa *f* de radiador ► **radiator grille** N rejilla *f* de radiador

radical [ˈrædɪkəl] Ⓐ ADJ 1 (*Pol*) [*idea, organization*] radical; [*person*] radical, de ideas radicales; **she's very ~** es muy radical, es de *or* tiene ideas muy radicales; **a ~ feminist** una feminista radical
2 (= *extreme, major*) [*change, measures, surgery, reduction*] radical; [*advance*] innovador
Ⓑ N (*Pol*) radical *mf*; (*Bot, Chem, Ling, Math*) radical *m*

radicalism [ˈrædɪkəlɪzəm] N (*Pol*) radicalismo *m*

radicalize [ˈrædɪkəˌlaɪz] VT radicalizar

radically [ˈrædɪkəlɪ] ADV [*differ, change, improve, reduce, affect*] radicalmente, de forma radical; [*different, changed, new*] radicalmente; **to disagree with sb ~** estar en total desacuerdo con algn; **there's something ~ wrong with his knee** hay algo en su rodilla que no marcha bien en absoluto; **his assessment of the situation had been ~ wrong** su valoración de la situación había sido totalmente equivocada

radicle [ˈrædɪkl] N (*Bot*) radícula *f*; (*Chem*) radical *m*

radii [ˈreɪdɪaɪ] NPL *of* **radius**

radio [ˈreɪdɪəʊ] Ⓐ N 1 (= *set*) radio *f*; **over the ~** por radio; **on the ~** en *or* por la radio; **to talk on the ~** hablar por la radio
2 (*Telec*) radio *f*, radiofonía *f*; **by ~** por radio
Ⓑ VI **to ~ to sb** enviar un mensaje a algn por radio; **to ~ for help** pedir socorro por radio
Ⓒ VT [+ *information, news*] radiar, transmitir por radio
Ⓓ CPD ► **radio alarm clock** N radio-reloj *m* despertador ► **radio announcer** N locutor(a) *m/f* de radio ► **radio astronomy** N radioastronomía *f* ► **radio beacon** N radiofaro *m* ► **radio beam** N radiofaro *m* ► **radio broadcast** N emisión *f* de radio ► **radio cab** N = **radio taxi** ► **radio cassette (player)** N (*esp Brit*) radiocasete *m* ► **radio communication, radio contact** N comunicación *f* por radio ► **radio engineer** N radiotécnico *mf* ► **radio engineering** N radiotécnica *f* ► **radio frequency** N frecuencia *f* de radio ► **radio ham** N radioaficionado/a *m/f* ► **radio link** N enlace *m* radiofónico ► **radio mast** N torre *f* de radio ► **radio network** N cadena *f or* red *f* de emisoras ► **radio operator** N radiotelegrafista *mf* ► **radio play** N obra *f* de teatro para la radio ► **radio programme, radio program** (*US*) N programa *m* de radio ► **radio set** N radio *f* ► **radio silence** N silencio *m* radiofónico ► **radio station** N emisora *f* (de radio) ► **radio taxi** N radiotaxi *m* ► **radio telephone** N radioteléfono *m* ► **radio telescope** N radiotelescopio *m* ► **radio tower** N = **radio mast** ► **radio transmitter** N radiotransmisor *m* ► **radio wave** N onda *f* de radio

radio... [ˈreɪdɪəʊ] PREFIX radio...

radioactive [ˈreɪdɪəʊˈæktɪv] Ⓐ ADJ radiactivo, radioactivo
Ⓑ CPD ► **radioactive waste** N residuos *mpl* radiactivos

radioactivity [ˈreɪdɪəʊækˈtɪvɪtɪ] N radiactividad *f*, radioactividad *f*

radiobiology [ˌreɪdɪəʊbaɪˈɒlədʒɪ] N radiobiología *f*

radiocarbon [ˌreɪdɪəʊˈkɑːbən] Ⓐ N radiocarbono *m*
Ⓑ CPD ► **radiocarbon analysis** N análisis *m inv* por radiocarbono ► **radiocarbon dating** N datación *f* por radiocarbono ► **radiocarbon test** N test *m* por radiocarbono

radio-controlled [ˈreɪdɪəʊkənˈtrəʊld] ADJ [*car*] teledirigido

radiogram [ˈreɪdɪəʊgræm] N 1 (*Brit*) (= *combined radio and gramophone*) radiogramola *f*
2 (†) (= *message*) radiograma *m*, radiotelegrama *m*
3 (= *X-ray picture*) radiografía *f*

radiograph [ˈreɪdɪəʊgrɑːf] Ⓐ N radiografía *f*
Ⓑ VT radiografiar

radiographer [ˌreɪdɪˈɒgrəfəʳ] N radiógrafo/a *m/f*

radiography [ˌreɪdɪˈɒgrəfɪ] N radiografía *f*

radioisotope [ˈreɪdɪəʊˈaɪsətəʊp] N radioisótopo *m*

radiolocation [ˌreɪdɪəʊləˈkeɪʃən] N radiolocalización *f*

radiological [ˌreɪdɪəˈlɒdʒɪkəl] ADJ radiológico

radiologist [ˌreɪdɪˈɒlədʒɪst] N radiólogo/a *m/f*

radiology [ˌreɪdɪˈɒlədʒɪ] N radiología *f*

radiopager [ˈreɪdɪəʊˌpeɪdʒəʳ] N localizador *m*

radioscopy [ˌreɪdɪˈɒskəpɪ] N radioscopia *f*

radiotelephony [ˌreɪdɪəʊtəˈlefənɪ] N radiotelefonía *f*

radiotherapist [ˌreɪdɪəʊˈθerəpɪst] N radioterapeuta *mf*

radiotherapy [ˌreɪdɪəʊˈθerəpɪ] N radioterapia *f*

radish [ˈrædɪʃ] N rábano *m*

radium [ˈreɪdɪəm] N radio *m*

radius [ˈreɪdɪəs] N (*pl* **radiuses, radii**) radio *m*; **within a ~ of 50 miles** en un radio de 50 millas

radix [ˈreɪdɪks] N (*pl* **radixes, radices** [ˈreɪdɪsiːz]) (*Bot, Gram*) raíz *f*; (*Math*) base *f*

radon [ˈreɪdɒn] N (*also* ~ **gas**) radón *m*

RAF N ABBR = **Royal Air Force**

raffia [ˈræfɪə] N rafia *f*

raffish [ˈræfɪʃ] ADJ disipado, disoluto

raffle [ˈræfl] Ⓐ N rifa *f*, sorteo *m*
Ⓑ VT [+ *object*] rifar, sortear; **ten bottles will be ~d for charity** se rifarán *or* se sortearán diez botellas con fines benéficos
Ⓒ CPD ► **raffle ticket** N papeleta *f* de rifa

raft [rɑːft] N [1] (*Naut*) balsa *f*
[2] (*) (= *quantity*) cantidad *f*, montón* *m*; (= *set*) serie *f*

rafter [ˈrɑːftəʳ] N viga *f*, cabrio *m*; **the ~s** (*loosely*) el techo

rag[1] [ræg] Ⓐ N [1] (= *piece of cloth*) trapo *m*; **rags** (= *old clothes*) harapos *mpl*, trapos *mpl* viejos; **to be in ~s** andar *or* estar en harapos; **dressed in ~s** cubierto de harapos; **from ~s to riches** de pobre a rico; **to feel like a wet ~*** estar hecho un trapo; **✦IDIOMS to put on one's glad ~s** vestirse de domingo; **to chew the ~** (*US**) (= *chat*) charlar, pasar el rato; (= *argue*) discutir; **it's like a red ~ to a bull** no hay nada que más le enfurezca; **to lose one's ~** (*Brit**) perder los estribos
[2] (*) (= *newspaper*) periodicucho* *m*, periódico *m* de mala muerte*
Ⓑ CPD ► **rag doll** N muñeca *f* de trapo ► **the rag trade*** N la industria de la confección

rag[2] [ræg] Ⓐ N (= *practical joke*) broma *f* pesada; (*Univ*) (= *parade*) fiesta *f* benéfica (de estudiantes)
Ⓑ VT (= *tease*) tomar el pelo a*; **they were ~ging him about his new tie** le estaban tomando el pelo con la corbata nueva*
Ⓒ VI guasearse, bromear; **I was only ~ging** lo dije en broma, era sólo una broma
Ⓓ CPD ► **rag week** N semana *f* de funciones benéficas (estudiantiles)

> **RAG WEEK**
> *Los universitarios británicos suelen organizar cada año lo que llaman* **rag week**. *Es costumbre que, durante esa semana, los estudiantes se disfracen y salgan así vestidos a la calle, pidiendo dinero a los transeúntes con el fin de recaudar fondos para fines benéficos.*

ragamuffin [ˈrægəˌmʌfɪn] N granuja *mf*

rag-and-bone man [ˌrægənˈbəʊnmæn] N (*pl* **rag-and-bone men**) (*Brit*) trapero *m*

ragbag [ˈrægbæg] N (= *mixture*) mezcolanza *f*; (*Sew*) bolsa *f* de recortes; **it's a ~ of a book** es un libro muy farragoso, el libro es todo un fárrago

rage [reɪdʒ] Ⓐ N [1] (= *anger*) furia *f*, cólera *f*, ira *f* (**at** *or* **over sth** ante algo); **he attacked her in a drunken ~** la agredió en un ataque de furia *or* cólera *or* ira causado por la bebida; **in a fit of ~** en un ataque de furia *or* cólera *or* ira; **to fly** *or* **go into a ~** montar en cólera, ponerse hecho una furia; **to be in a ~** estar furioso; **she was trembling with ~** temblaba de furia *or* cólera *or* ira; **he was white with ~** estaba blanco de cólera *or* ira; *see also* **road B**
[2] (= *fashion*) furor *m*; **the ~ for designer jeans** el furor por los vaqueros de diseño exclusivo; **to be all the ~** hacer furor
Ⓑ VI [*person*] estar furioso; [*fire*] propagarse con furia; [*epidemic*] propagarse causando estragos; [*battle*] proseguir con furia; [*wind, storm*] bramar; [*sea*] enfurecerse, embravecerse; **she was raging, but she kept her tone cool** estaba furiosa pero conservaba un tono calmado; **outside the storm still ~d** fuera la tempestad seguía bramando; **the battle ~d for three months** la batalla prosiguió con furia durante tres meses; **the debate ~d the whole day long** el airado debate prosiguió el día entero; **to ~ against sth** protestar furiosamente contra algo; **to ~ against sb** estar furioso con algn; **the sound of the sea raging against the rocks** el sonido del mar chocando enfurecido *or* embravecido contra las rocas; **to ~ at sth** estar furioso ante algo; **my mum ~d at the doctor** mi madre se puso como una fiera con el médico; **controversy is raging over her new economic policy** hay una encendida polémica en torno a su nueva política económica; **an infection was raging through her body** una infección se propagaba por su cuerpo causando estragos
Ⓒ VT **"it's none of your business," he ~d** —no es asunto tuyo —dijo enfurecido

-rage N (*ending in compounds*) **air/parking/trolley-rage** conducta *f* agresiva en los aviones/al estacionar/en el supermercado

ragged [ˈrægɪd] Ⓐ ADJ [1] (= *in tatters*) [*dress, clothes*] andrajoso, hecho jirones; [*person*] andrajoso, harapiento; [*cuff*] deshilachado; **✦IDIOM to run sb ~*** hacer sudar tinta *or* la gota gorda a algn; **they ran themselves ~** sudaron tinta *or* la gota gorda
[2] (= *untidy*) [*beard*] descuidado, desgreñado; [*animal's coat*] desgreñado
[3] (= *uneven*) [*edge*] mellado, irregular; [*rock*] recortado; [*hole, line*] irregular; [*coastline*] accidentado, recortado; **~ clouds** jirones *mpl* de nubes
[4] (= *disorganized*) [*performance*] desigual, irregular; [*queue*] desordenado; [*line, procession*] confuso, desordenado; **a ~ band of men** un grupo desordenado de hombres; **the orchestra sounded rather ~ in places** la orquesta tocaba de forma algo irregular en algunas partes
[5] (*Typ*) **~ left** margen *m* izquierdo irregular; **~ right** margen derecho irregular
Ⓑ CPD ► **ragged robin** N (*Bot*) flor *f* del cuclillo

raggedly [ˈrægɪdlɪ] ADV **he was ~ dressed** iba vestido con andrajos *or* harapos; **they marched ~ up and down** marchaban arriba y abajo de forma desordenada

raging [ˈreɪdʒɪŋ] Ⓐ ADJ [1] (= *fierce*) [*temper*] furioso, rabioso; [*debate*] acalorado; [*nationalist, feminist*] acérrimo, a ultranza; [*nationalism*] enfervorizado; **he was in a ~ temper** estaba muy furioso; **to be ~ mad** estar loco de furia *or* ira
[2] (= *violent*) [*storm, thunder, blizzard*] violento, rugiente; [*wind, torrent*] enfurecido, rugiente; [*sea*] embravecido, enfurecido, rugiente; [*fire*] violento
[3] (= *intense*) [*temperature, fever, inflation*] altísimo; [*illness, headache, toothache*] atroz; [*thirst*] horroroso; **to be a ~ success** tener un éxito tremendo
Ⓑ N [*of person*] furia *f*; **for a few moments he continued his ~** continuó dando rienda suelta a su furia durante un rato; **I couldn't hear her over the ~ of the sea** no podía oírla por el rugir del mar

raglan [ˈræglən] Ⓐ N raglán *m*
Ⓑ CPD ► **raglan sleeve** N manga *f* raglán

ragman [ˈrægmæn] N (*pl* **ragmen**) trapero *m*

ragout [ræˈguː] N guisado *m*

ragpicker [ˈrægpɪkəʳ] N trapero *m*

rag-tag* [ˈræg,tæg] N, **rag-tag and bobtail*** [ˌrægtægənˈbɒbteɪl] N chusma *f*

ragtime [ˈrægtaɪm] N (*Mus*) ragtime *m*; **in ~** sincopado

ragweed [ˈrægwiːd] N ambrosía *f*

ragwort [ˈrægwɜːt] N hierba *f* cana, zuzón *m*, hierba *f* de Santiago

raid [reɪd] Ⓐ N [1] (*into territory, across border*) incursión *f* (**into** en); (*on specific target*) asalto *m* (**on** a); **to carry out** *or* **make a ~ on sth** asaltar algo
[2] (*by air*) ataque *m* (aéreo) (**on** contra), bombardeo *m* (**on** de); **only five aircraft returned from the ~** solamente cinco aviones regresaron después del ataque *or* bombardeo; *see also* **air D**
[3] (*by police*) redada *f*; **a police ~** una redada policial; *see also* **dawn, drug C**
[4] (*Brit*) (*by criminals*) asalto *m* (**on** a); **a bank ~** un asalto a un banco; **there was a ~ on the jeweller's last night** anoche fue asaltada la joyería; *see also* **ram, smash-and-grab raid**
Ⓑ VT [1] (*by land*) [+ *village*] asaltar; [+ *territory*] invadir, hacer una incursión en
[2] (*by air*) atacar, bombardear
[3] [*police*] llevar a cabo una redada en
[4] (*Brit*) [*criminals*] [+ *bank*] asaltar
[5] (*fig*) (*hum*) **shall we ~ the larder?** ¿asaltamos la despensa?; **the boys ~ed the orchard** los muchachos robaron en el huerto
Ⓒ VI hacer incursiones; **they ~ed deep into enemy territory** hicieron incursiones bien adentrados en territorio enemigo

raider [ˈreɪdəʳ] N [1] (*across frontier*) invasor(a) *m/f*
[2] (*in bank etc*) asaltante *mf*
[3] (= *plane*) bombardero *m*
[4] (= *ship*) buque *m* corsario

raiding party [ˈreɪdɪŋˌpɑːtɪ] N grupo *m* de ataque

rail[1] [reɪl] Ⓐ N [1] (= *handrail*) (*on stairs, bridge, balcony*) baranda *f*, barandilla *f*, pasamanos *m inv*; (*for curtains*) riel *m*; (*on ship*) barandilla *f*; (*for feet*) apoyo *m* para los pies; (= *fence*) valla *f*, cerco *m*
[2] (*for train*) carril *m*, riel *m*; **rails** vía *fsing*; **to go off** *or* **come off** *or* **leave the ~s** [*train*] descarrilar; **to send sth by ~** enviar algo por ferrocarril; **to travel by ~** viajar por ferrocarril *or* en tren; **✦IDIOM to go off the ~s*** [*person*] descarrilarse
[3] **rails** (*Fin*) acciones *fpl* de sociedades ferroviarias
Ⓑ CPD ► **rail accident** N accidente *m* de ferrocarril, accidente *m* ferroviario ► **rail journey** N viaje *m* por ferrocarril *or* en tren ► **rail strike** N huelga *f* de ferroviarios ► **rail system** N red *f* ferroviaria, sistema *m* ferroviario ► **rail traffic** N tráfico *m* por ferrocarril ► **rail travel** N viajes *mpl* por ferrocarril *or* en tren ► **rail worker** N (*Brit*) ferroviario/a *m/f*, ferrocarrilero/a *m/f* (*Mex*); *see also* **pass A1**

►**rail off** VT + ADV [+ *land, pond*] cercar con una barandilla, poner barandilla a

rail[2]† [reɪl] VI (*frm*) **to ~ against sth** clamar contra algo; **to ~ at sb** recriminar a algn, recriminarle algo a algn, recriminar a algn por hacer algo

rail[3] [reɪl] N (*Orn*) rascón *m*

railcar [ˈreɪlkɑːʳ] N automotor *m*

railcard [ˈreɪlkɑːd] N carnet *m* para obtener descuento en los ferrocarriles; **family ~** carnet *m* de familia (*para viajes en tren*); **student's ~** carnet *m* de estudiante (*para viajes en tren*)

railhead [ˈreɪlhed] N estación *f* terminal, cabeza *f* de línea

railing [ˈreɪlɪŋ] N baranda *f*, barandilla *f*, pasamanos *m inv*; **~s** verja *fsing*, enrejado *msing*

raillery [ˈreɪlərɪ] N burlas *fpl*, chanzas *fpl*

railroad [ˈreɪlrəʊd] Ⓐ N (*US*) = **railway**
Ⓑ VT (*fig*) **to ~ sb into doing sth** obligar apresuradamente a algn a hacer algo; **to ~ a bill through Parliament** hacer que se apruebe un decreto de ley sin discutirse; **to ~ sth through** llevar algo a cabo muy precipitadamente

railroader [ˈreɪlrəʊdəʳ] N (*US*) = **railwayman**

railway [ˈreɪlweɪ] (*Brit*) Ⓐ N (= *system*) ferrocarril *m*, ferrocarriles *mpl*; (*as track*) vía *f*, vía *f* férrea

Ⓑ CPD ► **railway bridge** N puente *m* de ferrocarril ► **railway carriage** N vagón *m*, coche *m* (de ferrocarril) ► **railway engine** N máquina *f*, locomotora *f* ► **railway line** N (= *route*) línea *f* ferroviaria *or* de ferrocarril; (= *track*) vía *f* (férrea) ► **railway network** N red *f* ferroviaria ► **railway porter** N mozo *m* ► **railway station** N estación *f* (de ferrocarril) ► **railway timetable** N horario *m* de trenes ► **railway track** N vía *f* (férrea) ► **railway yard** N cochera *f*

railwayman ['reɪlweɪmən] N (*pl* **railwaymen**) (*Brit*) ferroviario *m*, ferrocarrilero *m* (*Mex*)

raiment ['reɪmənt] N (= *liter*) vestido *m*, vestimenta *f*

rain [reɪn] Ⓐ N (*Met*) lluvia *f*; **in the ~** bajo la lluvia; **a walk in the ~** un paseo bajo la lluvia; **he left his bike out in the ~** dejó la bicicleta bajo la lluvia; **don't go out in the ~** no salgas, que está lloviendo; **if the ~ keeps off** si no llueve; **it looks like ~** parece que va a llover; **come in out of the ~!** ¡entra, que te vas a mojar!; **the ~s** la época de las lluvias; **come ~ or shine** (*lit*) llueva o haga sol; (*fig*) pase lo que pase; *see also* **right A5**
Ⓑ VI [1] (*Met*) llover; **it's ~ing** está lloviendo; **it ~s a lot here** aquí llueve mucho; ✦***IDIOM*** **to ~ on sb's parade** (*esp US*) aguar la fiesta a algn; ✦***PROVS*** **it never ~s but it pours** las desgracias nunca vienen solas; **it ~s on the just as well as on the unjust** la lluvia cae sobre los buenos como sobre los malos
[2] (*fig*) **ash ~ed from the sky** llovía ceniza
Ⓒ VT llover; **hereabouts it ~s soot** por aquí llueve hollín; **to ~ blows on sb** llover golpes sobre algn; ✦***IDIOM*** **it's ~ing cats and dogs** está lloviendo a cántaros
Ⓓ CPD ► **rain belt** N zona *f* de lluvias ► **rain check** N (*US Sport*) *contraseña para usar otro día en caso de cancelación por lluvia*; **I'll take a ~ check*** (*fig*) de momento, paso ► **rain cloud** N nube *f* de lluvia, nubarrón *m* ► **rain forest** N (*also* **tropical ~ forest**) pluviselva *f*, selva *f* tropical ► **rain gauge** N pluviómetro *m* ► **rain hood** N capucha *f* impermeable

►**rain down** VI + ADV llover; **blows ~ed down on him** llovieron sobre él los golpes

►**rain off, rain out** (*US*) VT + ADV **the match was ~ed off** el partido se canceló por lluvia

rainbow ['reɪnbəʊ] Ⓐ N arco *m* iris
Ⓑ CPD ► **the rainbow coalition** N la coalición multicolor ► **rainbow trout** N trucha *f* arco iris

raincoat ['reɪnkəʊt] N gabardina *f*, impermeable *m*

raindrop ['reɪndrɒp] N gota *f* de lluvia

rainfall ['reɪnfɔːl] N precipitación *f*; (= *quantity*) lluvia *f*, cantidad *f* de lluvia; **the region has three inches of ~ a year** la región recibe tres pulgadas de lluvia al año

raininess ['reɪnɪnɪs] N lo lluvioso, pluviosidad *f*

rainless ['reɪnlɪs] ADJ sin lluvia, seco

rainproof ['reɪnpruːf] ADJ impermeable

rainstorm ['reɪnstɔːm] N aguacero *m*, chaparrón *m*

rainwater ['reɪnwɔːtəʳ] N agua *f* de lluvia

rainwear ['reɪnweəʳ] N ropa *f* para la lluvia, ropa *f* impermeable

rainy ['reɪnɪ] Ⓐ ADJ (*compar* **rainier**; *superl* **rainiest**) [*climate*] lluvioso; [*day*] de lluvia, lluvioso; **it was so ~ yesterday** llovió tanto ayer; ✦***IDIOM*** **to keep or save sth for a ~ day** [+ *object*] guardar algo para una ocasión más propicia; [+ *money*] ahorrar algo para cuando lleguen tiempos peores
Ⓑ CPD ► **rainy season** N época *f* de las lluvias

raise [reɪz] Ⓐ VT [1] (= *lift*) [+ *fallen object, weight, hand*] levantar, alzar; [+ *hat*] levantarse; [+ *blinds, window*] subir; [+ *flag*] izar; [+ *dust*] levantar; [+ *wreck*] sacar a flote; [+ *camp, siege, embargo*] levantar; **to ~ one's eyebrows** (*lit*) arquear las cejas; **her behaviour ~d a lot of eyebrows** (*fig*) su comportamiento escandalizó a mucha gente; **to ~ one's eyes** alzar la vista *or* la mirada, levantar los ojos *or* la vista; **to ~ one's glass to sth/sb** brindar por algo/algn; **he ~d his hands in horror/surrender** levantó *or* alzó las manos horrorizado/rindiéndose; **to ~ o.s.** levantarse, alzarse; **to ~ o.s. into a sitting position** incorporarse; *see also* **curtain, hand A10, hell A1, hope A1, roof, sight A4, spirit A7.1, stake A1**
[2] (= *make higher*) subir; **the rain has ~d the water level in the river** la lluvia ha subido el nivel del agua del río
[3] (= *increase*) [+ *prices, salaries, taxes*] aumentar, subir; [+ *temperature*] subir, aumentar, elevar; [+ *standard, level*] subir; [+ *age limit*] extender; [+ *awareness, consciousness*] aumentar; **to ~ standards in education** subir el nivel de la enseñanza; **to ~ the school leaving age** extender la edad de escolarización mínima obligatoria; **we want to ~ the profile of rugby** queremos realzar la imagen del rugby; **don't you ~ your voice to me!** ¡no me levantes *or* alces la voz!
[4] [+ *person*] (*in rank*) ascender (**to** a); *see also* **peerage**
[5] (= *erect*) [+ *building, statue*] erigir, levantar
[6] (= *bring up*) [+ *child, livestock*] criar; [+ *crop*] cultivar; **the house where she was ~d** la casa donde se crió; **I want to settle down, maybe ~ a family** quiero asentarme, y quizá tener una familia
[7] (= *produce*) [+ *laugh*] provocar; [+ *doubts, fears*] suscitar; [+ *suspicion*] levantar, despertar; [+ *cry*] dar; [+ *bump*] causar; [+ *blister*] levantar; **his speech ~d a cheer from the crowd** su discurso suscitó una ovación del público; **his forlorn attempts to ~ a few laughs** sus intentos desesperados por provocar unas cuantas risas; **she could barely ~ a smile** apenas pudo sonreír; **to ~ suspicion in sb's mind** levantar *or* despertar las sospechas de algn
[8] (= *present, put forward*) [+ *question, point, possibility*] plantear; [+ *subject*] sacar; [+ *complaint*] presentar; **I'll ~ the point with them** se lo mencionaré; **you'll have to ~ that with the director** tendrás que planteárle *or* comentarle eso al director; **to ~ objections to sth** poner objeciones *or* peros a algo; **this ~s the prospect of civil war** esto plantea la posibilidad de una guerra civil; **he gets embarrassed whenever the subject is ~d** se pone violento cada vez que se saca el tema
[9] (= *get together*) [+ *funds, money*] recaudar; [+ *capital*] movilizar; [+ *loan*] conseguir, obtener; [+ *army*] reclutar; **they couldn't ~ his bail** no pudieron reunir el dinero de su fianza; **they ~d a loan against the house** consiguieron un préstamo con la casa como garantía; **to ~ money for charity** recaudar dinero con fines benéficos; *see also* **mortgage**
[10] (*Cards*) **I'll ~ you!** ¡subo la apuesta!; **I'll ~ you £10** te subo 10 libras más; *see also* **bid, stake A1**
[11] (= *contact*) (*by phone*) localizar; (*by radio*) contactar con, localizar; **we tried to ~ him on the radio** intentamos contactar con él *or* localizarlo por radio
[12] (= *conjure*) [+ *spirits*] evocar; **to ~ sb from the dead** resucitar a algn, levantar a algn de entre los muertos
[13] (*Math*) [+ *total*] elevar; **2 ~d to the power 3 is 8** 2 elevado a la tercera potencia es 8
Ⓑ N (*esp US*) (*in salary*) aumento *m*, subida *f*; (*in taxes*) subida *f*

►**raise up** VT + ADV (= *lift*) levantar, alzar; **to ~ o.s. up into a sitting position** incorporarse; **he ~d himself up on one elbow** se apoyó en un codo; **he has ~d himself up from nothing** ha salido de la nada; **to ~ sb up from poverty** sacar a algn de la pobreza, ayudar a algn a salir de la miseria

raised [reɪzd] ADJ [*platform*] elevado; [*temperature, blood pressure, level*] alto, elevado; [*voice*] exaltado; (= *in relief*) en relieve; **I could hear ~ voices in the next room** oía voces exaltadas en la habitación de al lado

raisin ['reɪzən] N pasa *f*, uva *f* pasa

raison d'être ['reɪzɔːn'dɛːtr] N razón *f* de ser

Raj [rɑːdʒ] N **the British ~** el imperio británico (en la India)

rajah ['rɑːdʒə] N rajá *m*

rake¹ [reɪk] Ⓐ N (= *garden rake*) rastrillo *m*
Ⓑ VT [1] (*Agr etc*) [+ *sand, leaves, soil*] rastrillar; [+ *fire*] hurgar
[2] (= *strafe*) [+ *ship, file of men*] barrer

►**rake in** VT + ADV [1] [+ *gambling chips*] recoger
[2] (*) **they ~d in a profit of £100** sacaron 100 libras de ganancia; **he ~s in £50 on every deal** se toma una tajada de 50 libras de cada negocio*; **he must be raking it in** está acuñando dinero

►**rake off** VT + ADV [1] (*lit*) quitar con el rastrillo
[2] (* *pej*) [+ *share of profits, commission*] sacar

►**rake over** VT + ADV [+ *flowerbed*] rastrillar; (*fig*) [+ *memories, past*] remover

►**rake together** VT + ADV reunir *or* recoger con el rastrillo; (*fig*) [+ *money*] reunir; **we managed to ~ a team together** por fin logramos formar un equipo

►**rake up** VT + ADV [+ *subject*] sacar a relucir; [+ *memories, the past*] remover; **why did you have to ~ that up?** ¿para qué has vuelto a mencionar eso?

rake² [reɪk] N (= *dissolute man*) calavera *m*; **old ~** viejo *m* verde

rake³ [reɪk] Ⓐ N (*Archit, Naut*) inclinación *f*
Ⓑ VT inclinar

rake-off* ['reɪkɒf] N comisión *f*, tajada* *f*

rakish ['reɪkɪʃ] ADJ [1] (= *dissolute*) [*person*] libertino, disoluto
[2] **at a ~ angle** echado de lado

rakishly ['reɪkɪʃlɪ] ADV (*of hat etc*) echado al lado

rally¹ ['rælɪ] Ⓐ N [1] (= *mass meeting*) (*gen*) concentración *f*; (*with speeches*) mitin *m*; **there was a ~ in Trafalgar Square** hubo una concentración en Trafalgar Square
[2] (*Aut*) (= *competition*) rally *m*; **the Monte Carlo Rally** el Rally de Montecarlo
[3] (*Tennis*) intercambio *m* de golpes
[4] (*Fin*) (= *revival*) recuperación *f*
[5] (*Med*) (= *recovery*) recuperación *f*; (= *improvement*) mejora *f*
[6] (*Mil*) repliegue *m*
Ⓑ VT [1] (= *gather*) (*Pol*) concentrar; (*Mil*) reunir
[2] (= *exhort, unite in spirit*) levantar el ánimo de, fortalecer el espíritu de; (*fig*) [+ *strength, spirits*] recobrar
Ⓒ VI [1] (= *gather in support*) **to ~ to** *or* **behind sb** ◊ **~ to sb's side** *or* **support** solidarizarse con algn; **to ~ to the call** acudir a la llamada

2 (*in demonstration*) concentrarse, reunirse
3 (*Mil*) reorganizarse
4 (*Fin, Med*) (= *recover*) recuperarse; (= *improve*) mejorar
5 (*Aut*) (= *compete*) competir en rallys
(D) CPD ► **rally car** N coche *m* de rally ► **rally driver** N piloto *m* de rally
►**rally round, rally around** (A) VI + ADV **everyone must ~ round** todos tenemos que cooperar; **we all rallied round to help** todos nos juntamos para ayudar
(B) VI + PREP **to ~ round sb** reunirse en torno a algn, solidarizarse con algn

rally² ['rælɪ] VT (= *tease*) tomar el pelo a

rallying ['rælɪɪŋ] CPD ► **rallying call, rallying cry** N llamamiento *m* (*para reanimar la resistencia etc*) ► **rallying point** N (*Pol, Mil*) punto *m* de reunión

RAM [ræm] (A) N ABBR (*Comput*) (= **random access memory**) RAM *f*
(B) CPD ► **RAM chip** N chip *m* de RAM

ram [ræm] (A) N 1 (*Zool*) carnero *m*
2 (*Astron*) Aries *m*
3 (*Mil*) ariete *m*
(B) VT 1 (= *force*) **to ~ a hat down on one's head** incrustarse el sombrero; **to ~ clothes into a case** meter la ropa a la fuerza en una maleta; **to ~ a nail into a wall** incrustar un clavo en una pared; **to ~ sth into a hole** meter algo a la fuerza en un agujero; **to be ~med up against sth** estar apretado contra algo; **they ~ their ideas down your throat** (*fig*) te hacen tragar sus ideas a la fuerza; **we had Campoamor ~med into us at school** tuvimos que darnos un atracón de Campoamor en el colegio
2 (= *collide with*) (*deliberately*) embestir contra; (*Naut*) embestir con el espolón; (*accidentally*) chocar con *or* contra; **the thieves ~med a police car** los ladrones embistieron contra un coche de la policía; **the car ~med the lamppost as it slid off the road** el coche se metió contra la farola al salirse de la carretera
(C) CPD ► **ram raid*** N robo *m* (*rompiendo el escaparate etc con un coche*) ► **ram raider*** N ladrón/ona *m/f* (*que entra en el establecimiento rompiendo el escaparate etc con un coche*)

Ramadan [,ræmə'dæn] N ramadán *m*

ramble ['ræmbl] (A) N paseo *m*, excursión *f*; **to go for a ~** dar un paseo
(B) VI 1 (= *walk*) pasear; **we spent a week rambling in the hills** pasamos una semana de excursión en la montaña *or* la sierra
2 (*in speech*) divagar, perder el hilo; **he just ~d on and on** siguió divagando
3 [*river*] formar meandros; [*plant*] trepar, enredarse

rambler ['ræmbləʳ] N 1 (*Brit*) (= *hiker*) excursionista *mf* (a pie)
2 (*Bot*) trepadora *f*; (= *rose*) = **rambling rose**

rambling ['ræmblɪŋ] (A) ADJ 1 (= *straggling*) [*plant*] trepador
2 (= *wandering, incoherent*) [*speech, book*] farragoso, inconexo
3 (= *sprawling*) [*house*] laberíntico
(B) N 1 (= *walking*) excursionismo *m* a pie
2 **ramblings** desvaríos *mpl*, divagaciones *fpl*
(C) CPD ► **rambling rose** N rosal *m* trepador

rambunctious* [ræm'bʌŋkʃəs] ADJ (*US*) bullicioso, pendenciero

RAMC N ABBR (*Brit*) = **Royal Army Medical Corps**

ramification [,ræmɪfɪ'keɪʃən] N ramificación *f*; **with numerous ~s** con innumerables ramificaciones; **in all its ~s** en toda su complejidad

ramify ['ræmɪfaɪ] VI ramificarse

ramjet ['ræmdʒet] N estatorreactor *m*

rammer ['ræməʳ] N (*for roadmaking*) pisón *m*; (*for rifle*) baqueta *f*

ramp [ræmp] N (= *incline*) rampa *f*; (*on road*) rampa *f*, desnivel *m*

rampage [ræm'peɪdʒ] (A) N **to go on the ~** desbocarse, desmandarse
(B) VI desmandarse; **the crowd ~d through the market** la multitud corrió alocada por el mercado

rampancy ['ræmpənsɪ] N (= *uncontrolled lust*) desenfreno *m*; (= *aggression*) agresividad *f*; [*of foliage*] exuberancia *f*; [*of disease, inflation, crime*] predominio *m*

rampant ['ræmpənt] ADJ 1 (= *uncontrolled*) [*lust*] desenfrenado; [*inflation*] galopante
2 (= *prevailing*) difundido, de uso común; **anarchism is ~ here** aquí el anarquismo está muy extendido
3 (*Bot*) (= *overgrowing*) [*flower, plant*] exuberante
4 (*Heraldry*) **the lion ~** el león rampante

rampart ['ræmpɑːt] N (= *earthwork*) terraplén *m*; (= *city wall*) muralla *f*; (*fig*) (= *bulwark*) baluarte *m*, defensa *f*; **the ~s of York** la muralla de York

ramrod ['ræmrɒd] N baqueta *f*

ramshackle ['ræm,ʃækl] ADJ (= *tumbledown*) [*house*] destartalado; [*car*] desvencijado

ram's-horn ['ræmzhɔːn] N cuerno *m* de carnero

RAN N ABBR = **Royal Australian Navy**

ran [ræn] PT *of* **run**

ranch [rɑːntʃ] (A) N rancho *m*, hacienda *f* (de ganado) (*LAm*), estancia *f* (*S. Cone*)
(B) CPD ► **ranch hand** N peón *m* ► **ranch house** N casa *f* de rancho

rancher ['rɑːntʃəʳ] N ganadero/a *m/f*, ranchero/a *m/f*

ranching ['rɑːntʃɪŋ] N ganadería *f*

rancid ['rænsɪd] ADJ rancio

rancidity [ræn'sɪdɪtɪ] N, **rancidness** ['rænsɪdnɪs] N rancidez *f*, ranciedad *f*

rancor ['ræŋkəʳ] N (*US*) = **rancour**

rancorous ['ræŋkərəs] ADJ rencoroso

rancour, rancor (*US*) ['ræŋkəʳ] N rencor *m*

rand [rænd] N rand *m*

R & B [,ɑːrən'biː] N ABBR = **Rhythm and Blues**

R & D [,ɑːrən'diː] N ABBR (= **research and development**) I. y D., I + D

randiness* ['rændɪnɪs] N cachondez* *f*

random ['rændəm] (A) ADJ 1 (= *haphazard*) [*arrangement*] hecho al azar; **a ~ selection** una selección hecha al azar; **a wall built of ~ stones** un muro hecho con piedras elegidas al azar
2 (= *capricious, indiscriminate*) caprichoso; **a ~ shot** un disparo hecho sin apuntar, una bala perdida
3 (*Statistics, Maths*) [*sample, distribution*] aleatorio
(B) N **at ~** al azar; **we picked the number at ~** elegimos el número al azar; **to talk at ~** hablar sin pesar las palabras; **to hit out at ~** repartir golpes por todos lados
(C) CPD ► **random access** N (*Comput*) acceso *m* aleatorio ► **random access memory** N (*Comput*) memoria *f* de acceso aleatorio

randomize ['rændəmaɪz] VT aleatorizar

randomly ['rændəmlɪ] ADV **~ chosen** elegido al azar

randomness ['rændəmnɪs] N aleatoriedad *f*

R & R N ABBR (*US Mil*) (= **rest and recreation**) descanso *m*

randy* ['rændɪ] ADJ (*compar* **randier**; *superl* **randiest**) (*Brit*) (= *aroused*) caliente*, cachondo**, arrecho (*esp LAm**); **to feel ~** estar caliente*, estar cachondo**

rang [ræŋ] PT *of* **ring²**

range [reɪndʒ] (A) N 1 [*of mountains*] cadena *f*; **a ~ of hills** una cadena de colinas; **a ~ of mountains** una cadena montañosa *or* de montañas, una cordillera; **the Absaroka Range** la cordillera Absaroka; *see also* **mountain**
2 (= *extent*) **there is a wide ~ of ability in the class** los niveles de aptitud en la clase varían mucho; **your weight is within the normal ~** su peso está dentro de lo normal; **all this was beyond her ~ of experience** todo esto estaba fuera de su campo de experiencia; **the full ~ of his work is on view** se expone su obra en todo su ámbito; *see also* **age, price C**
3 (*Mus*) [*of instrument, voice*] registro *m*
4 (= *selection, variety*) 4·1 (*gen*) variedad *f*; **there was a wide ~ of opinions** había gran variedad de opiniones, las opiniones variaban mucho; **a wide ~ of colours** una amplia gama de colores; **they come in a ~ of sizes** vienen en varios *or* diversos tamaños; **she has a wide ~ of interests** tiene muchos y diversos intereses; **there was a whole ~ of options open to us** frente a nosotros se abría un amplio abanico de posibilidades
4·2 (*Comm*) (= *product line*) línea *f*; (= *selection*) gama *f*, selección *f*; **the new autumn ~** la nueva línea de otoño; **we stock a full ~ of wines** tenemos una selección *or* gama completa de vinos; *see also* **product B**
5 [*of gun, missile*] alcance *m*; [*of plane, ship*] autonomía *f*, radio *m* de acción; [*of car*] autonomía *f*; [*of transmitter*] radio *m* de acción; **a gun with a ~ of three miles** un cañón con un alcance de tres millas; **within ~ (of sth/sb)** a tiro (de algo/algn); **to come within ~ (of sth/sb)** ponerse a tiro (de algo/algn); **out of ~ (of sth/sb)** fuera del alcance (de algo/algn); **~ of vision** campo *m* visual
6 (= *distance from target*) distancia *f*; **at close ~** de cerca, a corta distancia; **at long ~** de lejos, a larga distancia; **to find the/one's ~** determinar la distancia a la que está el objetivo
7 (*Bot, Zool*) [*of species*] (zona *f* de) distribución *f*
8 (*esp US Agr*) pradera *f*, pampa *f* (*S. Cone*), llano *m* (*esp Ven*)
9 (*for shooting*) campo *m* de tiro; *see also* **rifle²**
10 (*also* **kitchen ~**) fogón *m*
(B) VT 1 (= *line up, place*) (*lit*) alinear; **chairs were ~d against one wall** las sillas estaban alineadas frente a una pared; **~d left/right** [*text*] alineado/a a la izquierda/derecha; **most of the party is ~d against him** la mayoría de los miembros del partido se ha alineado en contra suya
2 (*liter*) (= *rove*) [+ *country*] recorrer; **to ~ the seas** surcar los mares
3 **to ~ a gun on sth/sb** apuntar un cañón a algo/algn
(C) VI 1 (= *extend*) extenderse; **the search ~d over the whole country** se llevó a cabo la búsqueda por todo el país; **the conversation ~d over many issues** la conversación abarcó muchos temas; **his eye ~d over the horizon** escudriñó el horizonte; *see also* **wide-ranging**
2 (= *vary within limits*) **prices ~ from £3 to £9** los precios varían de 3 a 9 libras, los precios oscilan entre las 3 y las 9 libras; **the**

women ~d in age from 14 to 40 la edad de las mujeres iba de los 14 a los 40 años *or* oscilaba entre los 14 y los 40 años
[3] (= *wander*) **hyenas ~ widely in search of carrion** las hienas recorren muchos lugares en busca de carroña; **animals ranging through the jungle** animales vagando por *or* merodeando por la jungla
[4] (*Bot*) darse; (*Zool*) distribuirse
[5] [*gun*] **it ~s over 300 miles** tiene un alcance de trescientas millas

-range [reɪndʒ] ADJ (*ending in compounds*) **intermediate-range missile** misil *m* de medio alcance; **short-range missile** misil *m* de corto alcance

rangefinder [ˈreɪndʒˌfaɪndəʳ] N (*Mil, Phot*) telémetro *m*

ranger [ˈreɪndʒəʳ] N [1] (= *Girl Guide*) exploradora *f*
[2] (= *forest ranger*) guardabosques *mf inv*

Rangoon [ræŋˈguːn] N Rangún *m*

rangy [ˈreɪndʒɪ] ADJ alto y delgado

rank¹ [ræŋk] Ⓐ N [1] (= *status*) rango *m*, categoría *f*; (*Mil*) grado *m*, rango *m*; **a writer of the first ~** un escritor de primera categoría; **persons of ~** gente de calidad; **their ~s range from lieutenant to colonel** sus graduaciones van de teniente a coronel; **to attain the ~ of major** ser ascendido a comandante, llegar a(l grado de) comandante; ✦*IDIOM* **to pull ~*** aprovecharse de tener un rango superior
[2] (*Mil*) fila *f*; **the ~s** la tropa; **to break ~(s)** romper filas; **to close ~s** (*Mil*) (*fig*) cerrar filas; **the ~ and file** (*Mil*) los soldados rasos; (*Pol*) la base; **I've joined the ~s of the unemployed** soy un parado más; **to reduce sb to the ~s** degradar a algn a soldado raso; **to rise from the ~s** ascender desde soldado raso
[3] (= *row*) fila *f*, hilera *f*, línea *f*; **the ~s of poplars** las hileras de álamos; **in serried ~s** en filas apretadas
[4] (*also* **taxi ~**) parada *f* de taxis
Ⓑ VT clasificar; **he's ~ed third in the United States** está clasificado tercero en los Estados Unidos; **I ~ him sixth** yo lo pongo en sexto lugar; **where would you ~ him?** ¿qué posición le darías?; **I ~ her among …** yo la pongo entre …; **he was ~ed as (being) …** se le consideraba …; **to ~ A with B** igualar A y B, poner A y B en el mismo nivel
Ⓒ VI **to ~ fourth** ocupar el cuarto lugar; **where does she ~?** ¿qué posición ocupa?; **to ~ above sb** ser superior a *or* sobrepasar a algn; **to ~ among …** figurar entre …; **to ~ as** equivaler a; **to ~ high** ocupar una posición privilegiada; **to ~ second to sb** tener el segundo lugar después de algn; **to ~ with** ser igual a
Ⓓ CPD **as a ~ and file policeman I must say …** como policía de filas, debo decir …

rank² [ræŋk] ADJ [1] (*Bot*) [*plants*] exuberante; [*garden*] muy poblado
[2] (= *smelly*) maloliente, apestoso; **to smell ~** oler mal
[3] (= *utter*) [*hypocrisy, injustice etc*] manifiesto, absoluto; [*beginner, outsider*] completo, puro; **that's ~ nonsense!** ¡puras tonterías!; **he's a ~ liar** es un mentiroso redomado

ranker [ˈræŋkəʳ] N (*Mil*) (= *officer*) oficial *m* patatero*

ranking [ˈræŋkɪŋ] Ⓐ ADJ (*esp US*) superior
Ⓑ N [1] ránking *m*; (*Mil*) graduación *f*
[2] **rankings** (*Sport*) clasificación *fsing*, ránking *msing*

rankle [ˈræŋkl] VI doler; **the fact that he won still ~s with me** todavía me duele *or* me molesta el hecho de que él haya ganado

rankly [ˈræŋklɪ] ADV (*Bot*) con exuberancia

rankness [ˈræŋknɪs] N [1] (*Bot*) exuberancia *f*
[2] (= *bad smell*) mal olor *m*
[3] [*of injustice*] enormidad *f*

ransack [ˈrænsæk] VT [1] (= *search*) registrar de arriba abajo; **they ~ed the house for arms** registraron la casa de arriba abajo buscando armas
[2] (= *pillage*) saquear; [+ *house, shop*] desvalijar; **the place had been ~ed** el lugar había sido saqueado

ransom [ˈrænsəm] Ⓐ N rescate *m*; **to hold sb to ~** pedir un rescate por algn; (*fig*) poner a algn entre la espada y la pared; *see also* **king A1**
Ⓑ VT rescatar; (*Rel*) redimir
Ⓒ CPD ► **ransom demand** N petición *f* de rescate ► **ransom money** N rescate *m*, dinero *m* exigido a cambio del rehén

ransoming [ˈrænsəmɪŋ] N rescate *m*

rant [rænt] Ⓐ VI (= *declaim*) vociferar; **to ~ at sb** (= *be angry*) despotricar contra algn; **to ~ on about sb** (*angrily*) echar pestes de algn; **he ~ed and raved for hours** despotricó durante varias horas
Ⓑ N diatriba *f*

ranting [ˈræntɪŋ] Ⓐ N lenguaje *m* declamatorio; **for all his ~** por mucho que despotrique
Ⓑ ADJ campanudo, declamatorio

ranunculus [rəˈnʌŋkjʊləs] N (*pl* **ranunculuses, ranunculi** [rəˈnʌŋkjʊlaɪ]) ranúnculo *m*

rap [ræp] Ⓐ N [1] golpecito *m*, golpe *m* seco; **there was a ~ at the door** llamaron (suavemente) a la puerta; **to give sb a ~ on** *or* **over the knuckles** (*lit*) dar a algn en los nudillos; (*fig*) echar un rapapolvo a algn
[2] (= *blame*) **to take the ~*** pagar los platos rotos*; **to take the ~ for sth** cargar con la culpa de algo
[3] (*esp US**) (= *charge*) acusación *f*; **murder ~** acusación *f* de homicidio; **to beat the ~** (lograr) ser absuelto
[4] (*Mus*) rap *m*
[5] (*esp US**) **to have a ~ with sb** charlar con algn
Ⓑ VT golpetear, dar un golpecito en; **to ~ sb's knuckles** ◊ **~ sb on the knuckles** (*lit*) dar a algn en los nudillos; (*fig*) echar un rapapolvo a algn
Ⓒ VI [1] (= *knock*) **to ~ at the door** llamar a la puerta
[2] (*US**) (= *chat*) charlar
[3] (*Mus*) hacer rap
►**rap out** VT + ADV [+ *order*] espetar

rapacious [rəˈpeɪʃəs] ADJ rapaz

rapaciously [rəˈpeɪʃəslɪ] ADV con rapacidad

rapacity [rəˈpæsɪtɪ] N rapacidad *f*

rape¹ [reɪp] Ⓐ N [1] [*of woman, man*] violación *f*; [*of minor*] estupro *m* (*frm*); **attempted ~** intento *m* de violación; *see also* **marital**
[2] (*fig*) destrucción *f*; **the ~ of Poland** la destrucción de Polonia
Ⓑ VT [+ *man, woman*] violar; [+ *minor*] estuprar (*frm*)

rape² [reɪp] Ⓐ N (*Bot*) colza *f*
Ⓑ CPD ► **rape oil** N = **rapeseed oil**

rapeseed [ˈreɪpsiːd] Ⓐ N semilla *f* de colza
Ⓑ CPD ► **rapeseed oil** N aceite *m* de colza

Raphael [ˈræfeɪəl] N Rafael

rapid [ˈræpɪd] ADJ rápido

rapidity [rəˈpɪdɪtɪ] N rapidez *f*

rapidly [ˈræpɪdlɪ] ADV rápidamente, rápido

rapids [ˈræpɪdz] NPL (*in river*) rápidos *mpl*

rapier [ˈreɪpɪəʳ] N estoque *m*

rapine [ˈræpaɪn] N rapiña *f*

rapist [ˈreɪpɪst] N violador(a) *m/f*

rapping [ˈræpɪŋ] N [1] (= *knocking*) golpecitos *mpl*, golpes *mpl* secos; (*at door*) llamadas *fpl*, aldabadas *fpl*
[2] (*Mus*) rap *m*

rapport [ræˈpɔːʳ] N [1] (= *relationship*) relación *f*; **I have a good ~ with him** tengo muy buena relación con él, me entiendo muy bien con él; **he has established a good ~ with the customers** ha entablado buenas relaciones con los clientes
[2] (= *understanding*) **there was an instant ~ between them** enseguida congeniaron

rapprochement [ræˈprɒʃmɑ̃ːŋ] N acercamiento *m*

rapscallion†† [ræpˈskælɪən] N (*also hum*) bribón *m*, golfo *m*

rapt [ræpt] ADJ **they were sitting with ~ attention** estaban sentados prestando mucha atención; **he drew ~ audiences** cautivaba al público, dejaba al público embelesado; **with a ~ expression on his face** con cara de embeleso; **Claud was staring at me, ~** Claud me miraba fijamente, absorto *or* embelesado

rapture [ˈræptʃəʳ] N éxtasis *m inv*; **to be in ~s** estar extasiado, extasiarse; **to go into ~s over sth** extasiarse por algo

rapturous [ˈræptʃərəs] ADJ [*applause*] entusiasta; [*look*] extasiado

rapturously [ˈræptʃərəslɪ] ADV [*applaud*] con entusiasmo; [*look*] con embeleso

rare [reəʳ] Ⓐ ADJ (*compar* **rarer**, *superl* **rarest**) [1] (= *uncommon, infrequent*) [*item, book*] raro; [*plant, animal*] poco común; [*ability, opportunity*] excepcional; [*case, occurrence*] poco frecuente; **it is ~ to find that …** es raro encontrarse con que …; **it is ~ for her to come** es raro que venga; **she had a ~ beauty** tenía una belleza singular; **with very ~ exceptions** con muy raras excepciones; **in a moment of ~ generosity** en un momento de inusitada generosidad; **to grow ~(r)** [*animals, plants*] volverse menos común; [*visits*] hacerse más raro; **on the ~ occasions when he spoke** en las poquísimas ocasiones en las que hablaba; **it is a ~ sight** es algo que no se ve frecuentemente; **to have a ~ old time***† pasárselo pipa*; → STRANGE, RARE
[2] (= *rarefied*) [*air, atmosphere*] enrarecido
[3] (*Culin*) [*steak, meat*] vuelta y vuelta, poco hecho (*Sp*)
Ⓑ CPD ► **rare earth** N tierra *f* rara

rarebit [ˈreəbɪt] N **Welsh ~** pan *m* con queso tostado

rarefaction [ˌreərɪˈfækʃən] N rarefacción *f*

rarefied [ˈreərɪfaɪd] ADJ enrarecido

rarefy [ˈreərɪfaɪ] Ⓐ VT enrarecer
Ⓑ VI enrarecerse

rarely [ˈreəlɪ] ADV casi nunca, rara vez, raramente; **that ~ happens** casi nunca *or* rara vez sucede eso; **that method is ~ satisfactory** ese método no es satisfactorio casi nunca; **it is ~ found here** aquí se encuentra con poca frecuencia

rareness [ˈreənɪs] N rareza *f*

raring [ˈreərɪŋ] ADJ **to be ~ to do sth** tener muchas ganas de hacer algo; **to be ~ to go** tener muchas ganas de empezar

rarity [ˈreərɪtɪ] N [1] rareza *f*
[2] (= *rare thing*) rareza *f*, cosa *f* rara; **it's a ~ here** aquí es una rareza *or* una cosa rara

rascal ['rɑːskəl] N (= *scoundrel*) granuja *mf*; (= *child*) granuja *mf*, pillo *m*

rascally ['rɑːskəlɪ] ADJ granuja, bribón; **a ~ trick** una triquiñuela, una artimaña

rash[1] [ræʃ] N [1] (*Med*) sarpullido *m*, erupción *f* (cutánea); **I've got a ~ on my chest** tengo un sarpullido *or* una erupción en el pecho; **she came out in a ~** le salieron ronchas en la piel
[2] (= *spate*) racha *f*, avalancha *f*; **a ~ of complaints** una avalancha *or* una multitud de quejas

rash[2] [ræʃ] ADJ [*act, statement*] temerario, precipitado; [*person*] temerario, imprudente; **that was very ~ of you** en eso has sido muy temerario *or* imprudente

rasher ['ræʃəʳ] N **a ~ of bacon** una loncha de beicon

rashly ['ræʃlɪ] ADV temerariamente

rashness ['ræʃnɪs] N [*of actions*] temeridad *f*, precipitación *f*; [*of person*] temeridad *f*, imprudencia *f*

rasp [rɑːsp] Ⓐ N [1] (= *tool*) escofina *f*, raspador *m*
[2] (= *sound*) chirrido *m*; [*of voice*] tono *m* áspero
Ⓑ VT [1] (*with file*) raspar, escofinar
[2] (= *speak*) (*also* **~ out**) decir con voz áspera; [+ *order*] espetar
Ⓒ VI hacer un sonido desapacible

raspberry ['rɑːzbərɪ] N [1] (= *fruit*) frambuesa *f*
[2] **to blow a ~*** hacer una pedorreta*

rasping ['rɑːspɪŋ] ADJ [*voice*] áspero; [*noise*] chirriante

Rasta* ['ræstə], **Rastafarian** [ˌræstə'fɛərɪən] Ⓐ ADJ rastafario
Ⓑ N rastafario/a *m/f*

rat [ræt] Ⓐ N [1] (*Zool*) rata *f*; ✦*IDIOM* **I smell a ~** aquí hay gato encerrado, aquí se está tramando algo; **he could smell a ~** se olió algo sospechoso, le olió a gato encerrado
[2] (= *person*) **you dirty ~!*** ¡canalla!*
[3] (*as exclamation*) **~s!** (*Brit**) ¡narices!*
Ⓑ VI [1] (*) **to ~ on sb** (= *inform on*) chivarse de algn; (= *desert*) abandonar a algn; **to ~ on a deal** rajarse de un negocio
[2] (= *catch rats*) cazar ratas, matar ratas
Ⓒ CPD ► **rat pack** N (= *journalists*) paparazzi *mpl* ► **rat poison** N matarratas *m inv* ► **the rat race** N la lucha por la supervivencia, la competencia; **it's a ~ race** es un mundo muy competitivo ► **rat run*** N (*Brit Aut*) *calle residencial usada por los conductores para evitar atascos* ► **rat trap** N trampa *f* para ratas, ratonera *f*

ratable ['reɪtəbl] ADJ = **rateable**

rat-a-tat [ˌrætə'tæt], **rat-a-tat-tat** [ˌrætəˌtæt'tæt] N (*at door*) golpecitos *mpl*; (*imitating sound*) ¡toc, toc!; [*of machine-gun*] martilleo *m*

ratcatcher ['rætˌkætʃəʳ] N cazarratas *mf inv*, cazador(a) *m/f* de ratas

ratchet ['rætʃɪt] Ⓐ N (*Tech*) trinquete *m*
Ⓑ CPD ► **ratchet wheel** N rueda *f* de trinquete

►**ratchet up** Ⓐ VT + ADV incrementar
Ⓑ VI + ADV incrementarse, sufrir un incremento

rate[1] [reɪt] Ⓐ N [1] (= *proportion, ratio*) **birth ~** índice *m or* tasa *f* de natalidad, natalidad *f*; **death ~** índice *m or* tasa *f* de mortalidad, mortalidad *f*; **the failure/success ~ for this exam is high** el índice de suspensos/aprobados en este examen es alto; **at a ~ of** a razón de; **it is increasing at a** *or* **the ~ of 5% a year** está aumentando a razón de un 5% al año; **at a** *or* **the ~ of three a minute** a razón de tres por minuto; *see also* **crime**, **divorce D**, **first-rate**, **second-rate**, **third-rate**, **metabolic**, **suicide**
[2] (= *speed*) (*gen*) velocidad *f*; [*of work*] ritmo *m*; **the population is growing at an alarming ~** la población crece a una velocidad alarmante; **at any ~** (= *at least*) al menos, por lo menos; (= *anyway*) en todo caso; **he is the least appealing, to me at any ~** es el menos atractivo, al menos *or* por lo menos para mí; **I don't know what happened, at any ~ she didn't turn up** no sé lo que pasó, el caso es que *or* en todo caso no se presentó; **~ of climb** (*Aer*) velocidad *f* de subida; **~ of flow** [*of electricity, water*] velocidad *f* de flujo; **at a ~ of knots*** [*of person, vehicle*] a toda pastilla*; **at this ~** a este paso; **if things go on at this ~** si las cosas siguen marchando a este paso; **at the ~ you're going, you'll be dead before long** al paso que vas no vas a durar mucho; *see also* **growth B**, **heart B**
[3] (= *price*) (*for tickets*) precio *m*; [*of hotel, telephone service*] tarifa *f*; **there is a reduced ~ for children under 12** a los niños menores de 12 años se les hace un descuento, hay una tarifa reducida para niños menores de 12 años; **calls cost 36p per minute cheap ~** el precio de la llamada es de 36 peniques el minuto, dentro de la tarifa barata; **they were paid a ~ of £5 an hour** les pagaban a razón de 5 libras la hora; **the ~ for the job** el sueldo que corresponde al trabajo; **~s of pay** sueldos *mpl*; *see also* **postage**, **postal**, **peak C**, **standard C**
[4] (*Fin*) [*of stocks*] cotización *f*; **bank ~** tipo *m* de interés bancario; **exchange ~** ◊ **~ of exchange** (tipo *m* de) cambio *m*; **inflation ~** ◊ **~ of inflation** tasa *f* de inflación; **interest ~** ◊ **~ of interest** tipo *m or* tasa *f* de interés; **~ of return** tasa *f* de rentabilidad *or* rendimiento; *see also* **basic**, **fixed-rate**, **mortgage**, **tax**
[5] **rates** (*Brit*) (*formerly*) (= *local tax*) contribución *fsing* municipal, impuesto *msing* municipal; **we pay £900 in ~s** pagamos 900 libras de contribuciones; *see also* **water D**
Ⓑ VT [1] (= *rank*) **how do you ~ her?** ¿qué opinas de ella?; **how do you ~ his performance on a scale of one to ten?** ¿cuántos puntos le darías a su actuación en una escala del uno al diez?; **she is ~d fifth in the world** ocupa el quinto lugar en la clasificación mundial; **to ~ sth/sb highly**: **I ~ the book highly** tengo muy buena opinión del libro; **I ~ him highly** lo tengo en muy alta estima; **the most highly ~d player in English football** el jugador mejor considerado del fútbol inglés; *see also* **X-rated**, **zero-rated**
[2] (= *consider, regard*) considerar; **I ~ him among my friends** le considero un amigo; **I ~ him among my best three pupils** lo tengo por uno de mis tres mejores alumnos; **most ~d it a hit** la mayoría de la gente lo consideraba un éxito; **I ~ myself as fairly fit** considero que estoy bastante en forma
[3] (*) (= *regard as good*) **I don't ~ your chances** creo que tienes pocas posibilidades; **he didn't ~ the movie at all** no concedió ningún mérito a la película; **I don't ~ him (as a composer)** no le valoro (como compositor)
[4] (= *deserve*) merecer(se); **I think he ~s a pass (mark)** creo que (se) merece un aprobado; **it didn't ~ a mention** no lo consideraron digno de mención; **in those crowded streets he wouldn't ~ a second glance** en esas calles llenas de gente pasaría desapercibido
[5] (*Brit*) (*for local tax*) [+ *property*] tasar, valorar (**at** en)
Ⓒ VI [1] (= *perform, measure up*) **how did he ~?** ¿qué tal lo hizo?, ¿qué tal se portó?
[2] **to ~ as**: **it must ~ as one of the most boring films around** debe de estar considerada una de las películas más aburridas del momento
Ⓓ CPD ► **rate rebate** N (*Brit*) (*formerly*) devolución *f* de contribución municipal

rate[2] [reɪt] VT (*liter*) regañar, reñir

-rate [reɪt] ADJ (*ending in compounds*) *see* **first-rate**, **second-rate**, **third-rate**

rateable ['reɪtəbl] Ⓐ ADJ (*Brit*) [*property*] susceptible de pagar contribución
Ⓑ CPD ► **rateable value** N (*Brit*) (*formerly*) valor *m* catastral

rate-capping ['reɪtˌkæpɪŋ] N (*Brit Pol*) (*formerly*) *limitación de la contribución municipal impuesta por el Estado*

ratepayer ['reɪtpeəʳ] N (*Brit*) (*formerly*) contribuyente *mf*

▼**rather** ['rɑːðəʳ] Ⓐ ADV [1] (*preference*) **we decided to camp, ~ than stay at a hotel** decidimos acampar, en lugar de quedarnos en un hotel; **I'll stay ~ than go alone** prefiero quedarme a ir solo; **I'd ~ have this one than that** prefiero éste a aquél; **"would you like a sweet?" — "I'd ~ have an apple"** —¿quieres un caramelo? —preferiría una manzana; **would you ~ stay here?** ¿prefieres quedarte?; **I'd ~ stay in tonight** preferiría no salir esta noche; **I'd ~ he didn't come to the party** preferiría que no viniera a la fiesta; **anything ~ than that!** (*hum*) ¡cualquier cosa menos eso!; **play anything ~ than that** toca cualquier cosa que no sea eso; **I'd ~ not** prefiero no hacerlo; **I'd ~ not say** prefiero no decirlo; **"I'm going to have it out with the boss" — "~ you than me!"** —voy a plantearselo al jefe —¡allá tú!
[2] (= *somewhat*) algo, un poco; **he looks ~ like his mother** se parece un poco a su madre; **I feel ~ more happy today** hoy me siento algo más contento; **I ~ suspected as much** me lo sospechaba; **I ~ think he won't come** me inclino a creer que no vendrá; **that is ~ too dear** es algo caro (para mí *etc*)
[3] (= *quite*) bastante; **it's a ~ difficult task** ◊ **it's ~ a difficult task** es una tarea bastante difícil; **we were ~ tired** estábamos bastante cansados; **I was ~ disappointed** quedé bastante decepcionado; **he did ~ well in the exam** le fue bastante bien en el examen; **"isn't she pretty?" — "yes, she is ~"** —¿es guapa, eh? —sí, bastante; **"are you keen to go?" — "yes, I am ~"** —¿tienes ganas de ir? —sí que quiero; **there's ~ a lot** hay bastante; **£20! that's ~ a lot!** ¡20 libras! ¡es bastante caro!; **I've got ~ a lot of homework to do** tengo muchos deberes que hacer; **it's ~ a pity** es una pena *or* lástima
[4] (= *more accurately*) **~ it is a matter of money** antes es cuestión de dinero, es al contrario *or* más bien cuestión de dinero; **or ~** o mejor dicho, es decir; **a car, or ~ an old banger** un coche, o mejor dicho, un trasto viejo
Ⓑ EXCL (†) ¡ya lo creo!, ¡cómo no! (*LAm*); **"would you like some?" — "rather!"** ¿quieres algo de esto? — ¡ya lo creo! *or* ¡por supuesto!

ratification [ˌrætɪfɪ'keɪʃən] N ratificación *f*

ratify ['rætɪfaɪ] VT [+ *treaty, agreement*] ratificar

rating[1] ['reɪtɪŋ] N [1] (= *ranking*) **Labour's ~s in the polls are high** las encuestas demuestran que el partido laborista goza de un alto nivel de popularidad; **each wine was given a ~ out of ten** cada vino recibió una puntuación del uno al diez; **jobs which have a low ~ on**

➤ LANGUAGE IN USE: **rather A1** 4, 7.4, 26.3 **A4** 26.3

the social scale los trabajos que ocupan una posición baja en la escala social; *see also* **credit C, poll D**

2 **ratings** (*TV, Rad*) índice *msing* de audiencia; **~s war** *guerra por alcanzar el mayor índice de audiencia*

3 (= *act of valuing*) tasación *f*, valuación *f*

4 (*Brit Naut*) (= *sailor*) marinero *m*; (*class*) [*of ship*] clase *f*; **a naval ~** un marinero; *see also* **octane**

rating² ['reɪtɪŋ] N reprensión *f*

ratio ['reɪʃɪəʊ] N razón *f*; **in the ~ of 2 to 1** a razón de 2 a 1; **in inverse ~** en proporción *or* razón inversa; **in direct ~ to** en proporción *or* razón directa con; **the ~ of wages to raw materials** la relación entre los sueldos y las materias primas

ratiocinate [rætɪ'ɒsɪneɪt] VI (*frm*) raciocinar

ratiocination [ˌrætɪɒsɪ'neɪʃən] N (*frm*) raciocinación *f*

ration ['ræʃən] Ⓐ N (= *portion*) ración *f*, porción *f*; **rations** (*Mil etc*) víveres *mpl*, suministro *msing*; **to be on ~** [*bread, milk*] estar racionado; **to be on short ~s** andar escaso de víveres; **when they put bread on the ~** cuando racionaron el pan; **it's off the ~ now** ya no está racionado; **to draw one's ~s** recibir los víveres

Ⓑ VT (*also* **~ out**) racionar; **they are ~ed to one kilo a day** están racionados a un kilo por día

Ⓒ CPD ► **ration book, ration card** N cartilla *f* de racionamiento

rational ['ræʃənl] Ⓐ ADJ 1 (= *logical*) [*argument, explanation*] racional, lógico; **the ~ thing to do would be to ...** lo lógico *or* racional sería ...

2 (= *reasonable*) razonable; **let's be ~ about this** seamos razonables

3 (= *sane*) [*person*] sensato, cuerdo; **he seemed quite ~** parecía estar perfectamente sensato *or* cuerdo

Ⓑ CPD ► **rational number** N (*Math*) número *m* racional

rationale [ræʃə'nɑːl] N base *f*, fundamento *m*; **the ~ of** *or* **behind sth** la razón fundamental de algo

rationalism ['ræʃnəlɪzəm] N racionalismo *m*

rationalist ['ræʃnəlɪst] Ⓐ ADJ racionalista

Ⓑ N racionalista *mf*

rationalistic [ˌræʃnə'lɪstɪk] ADJ racionalista

rationality [ˌræʃə'nælɪtɪ] N racionalidad *f*

rationalization [ˌræʃnəlaɪ'zeɪʃən] N 1 [*of ideas etc*] racionalización *f*

2 (= *reorganization*) reconversión *f*, reorganización *f*; **industrial ~** reconversión *f* industrial, reorganización *f* industrial

rationalize ['ræʃnəlaɪz] VT 1 [+ *ideas etc*] racionalizar

2 (= *reorganize*) [+ *industry etc*] reconvertir, reorganizar

3 (*Math*) quitar los radicales a, racionalizar

rationally ['ræʃnəlɪ] ADV racionalmente

rationing ['ræʃnɪŋ] N racionamiento *m*

rats'-tails [ˌræts'teɪlz] NPL greñas *fpl*

rattan [rə'tæn] N rota *f*, junco *m* *or* caña *f* de Indias

rat-tat-tat [ˌrættæt'tæt] N = **rat-a-tat(-tat)**

rattle ['rætl] Ⓐ N 1 (= *sound*) [*of cart, train, gunfire*] traqueteo *m*; [*of window, chains, stone in tin*] ruido *m*; [*of hail, rain*] tamborileo *m*; (*in throat*) estertor *m*; **there was an ominous ~ coming from the engine** del motor provenía un ruido que no presagiaba nada bueno; **death ~** estertor *m* de la muerte

2 (= *instrument*) (*child's*) sonajero *m*, sonajas *fpl*; [*of football fan etc*] carraca *f*, matraca *f*

Ⓑ VT 1 (= *shake*) **the wind ~d the window** el viento hizo vibrar la ventana; **he ~d the tin** agitó la lata (*haciendo sonar lo que tenía dentro*); **he banged on the table, rattling the cups** golpeó la mesa, haciendo que las tazas tintinearan; **she ~d the door handle** sacudió el picaporte de la puerta; **the monkey was rattling the bars of his cage** el mono estaba sacudiendo los barrotes de la jaula; ✦**IDIOM to ~ sb's cage** hacer la Pascua a algn

2 (*) (= *disconcert*) [+ *person*] desconcertar; **to get ~d** ponerse nervioso, perder la calma; **to get sb ~d** poner nervioso a algn, hacer que algn pierda la calma

Ⓒ VI 1 (= *make sound*) [*cart, train*] traquetear; [*window, chains, stone in tin*] sonar, hacer ruido; [*teeth*] castañetear; [*hail, rain*] tamborilear

2 (*) (= *travel*) **we were rattling along at 50m.p.h.** íbamos traqueteando a 50 millas por hora

►**rattle away*** VI + ADV = **rattle on**

►**rattle off** VT + ADV [+ *names, statistics*] recitar de un tirón *or* de una tirada

►**rattle on*** VI + ADV parlotear (sin parar); **I let him ~ on about the virtues of double glazing** le dejé que parloteara ensalzando las virtudes del doble acristalamiento

►**rattle through*** VI + PREP **she ~d through the translation in about ten minutes** hizo la traducción volando en unos diez minutos, se cepilló la traducción en unos diez minutos*

rattler* ['rætləʳ] N (*esp US*) = **rattlesnake**

rattlesnake ['rætlsneɪk] N serpiente *f* de cascabel, yarará *f* (*Andes*)

rattletrap* ['rætltræp] Ⓐ ADJ desvencijado

Ⓑ N armatoste *m*

rattling ['rætlɪŋ] Ⓐ ADJ **at a ~ pace** muy rápidamente, a gran velocidad

Ⓑ ADV **~ good** (*esp Brit**) realmente estupendo*

ratty* ['rætɪ] ADJ (*compar* **rattier**; *superl* **rattiest**)

1 (*Brit*) (= *bad-tempered*) **to be/get ~** estar/ponerse de malas; **he was pretty ~ about it** se picó mucho por ello

2 (*US*) (= *shabby*) andrajoso

raucous ['rɔːkəs] ADJ (= *harsh*) ronco; (= *loud*) chillón, estridente

raucously ['rɔːkəslɪ] ADV (= *harshly*) roncamente; (= *loudly*) en tono chillón, estridentemente

raucousness ['rɔːkəsnɪs] N (= *harshness*) ronquedad *f*; (= *loudness*) estridencia *f*

raunchy* ['rɔːntʃɪ] ADJ (*compar* **raunchier**, *superl* **raunchiest**) [*story, film, song*] picante, atrevido; [*person*] sexy, provocativo; [*clothing*] atrevido, provocativo

ravage ['rævɪdʒ] Ⓐ N **ravages** estragos *mpl*; **the ~s of time** los estragos del tiempo

Ⓑ VT hacer estragos; **the plague ~d the town** la peste hizo estragos en el pueblo; **the region was ~d by floods** las inundaciones causaron estragos en la región, la región fue asolada por las inundaciones; **a body ~d by disease** un cuerpo desfigurado por la enfermedad; **a picture ~d by time** un cuadro muy deteriorado por el tiempo

rave [reɪv] Ⓐ VI 1 (= *be delirious*) delirar, desvariar; (= *talk wildly*) desvariar

2 (= *talk furiously*) despotricar; **to ~ at sb** despotricar contra algn

3 (= *talk enthusiastically*) **to ~ about sth** entusiasmarse por algo; **they ~d about the film** pusieron la película por las nubes; **to ~ about sb** pirrarse por algn*

Ⓑ N (*Brit**) fiesta *f* acid*

Ⓒ CPD ► **rave review** N reseña *f* entusiasta; **the play got ~ reviews** los críticos pusieron la obra por las nubes

rave-in* ['reɪvɪn] N orgía *f*

ravel ['rævəl] VT enredar, enmarañar (*also fig*)

raven ['reɪvn] Ⓐ N cuervo *m*

Ⓑ ADJ [*hair*] negro

raven-haired [ˌreɪvn'hɛəd] ADJ de pelo negro

ravening ['rævnɪŋ] ADJ rapaz, salvaje

ravenous ['rævənəs] ADJ 1 (= *starving*) hambriento; **I'm ~!** ¡me comería un toro!; **he was ~** tenía un hambre canina

2 (= *voracious*) voraz

ravenously ['rævənəslɪ] ADV vorazmente; **to be ~ hungry** tener un hambre canina

raver* ['reɪvəʳ] N (*Brit*) juerguista* *mf*, marchoso/a* *m/f*

rave-up* ['reɪvʌp] N (*Brit*) juerga* *f*

ravine [rə'viːn] N barranco *m*, quebrada *f* (*esp LAm*)

raving ['reɪvɪŋ] Ⓐ ADJ **he's a ~ lunatic** está loco de remate

Ⓑ ADV **you must be ~ mad!** ¡tú estás loco de atar!

ravings ['reɪvɪŋz] NPL delirio *msing*, desvarío *msing*

ravioli [ˌrævɪ'əʊlɪ] N ravioles *mpl*, ravioli *mpl*

ravish ['rævɪʃ] VT 1 (= *charm*) encantar, embelesar

2 (*liter*) (= *carry off*) raptar, robar; (= *rape*) violar

ravisher†† ['rævɪʃəʳ] N (*liter*) (= *captor*) raptor *m*; (= *rapist*) violador *m*

ravishing ['rævɪʃɪŋ] ADJ [*smile*] encantador; [*woman*] bellísimo; **you look ~** estás deslumbrante

ravishingly ['rævɪʃɪŋlɪ] ADV encantadoramente; **~ beautiful** enormemente bello

ravishment ['rævɪʃmənt] N (*liter*) 1 (= *enchantment*) embeleso *m*, éxtasis *m inv*

2 (*liter*) (= *capture*) rapto *m*, robo *m*; (= *rape*) violación *f*

raw [rɔː] Ⓐ ADJ 1 (= *uncooked*) [*meat, vegetable, egg*] crudo

2 (= *unprocessed*) [*sugar*] sin refinar; [*spirit*] puro; [*silk*] crudo, salvaje; [*cotton*] en rama, sin refinar; [*ore*] bruto; [*rubber*] sin tratar, puro; [*sewage*] sin tratar; **~ data** datos *mpl* sin procesar; **~ materials** materias *fpl* primas

3 (= *sore*) [*wound*] abierto; **to be red and ~** estar en carne viva; **his hands were ~ from the weather** tenía las manos en carne viva a causa del tiempo; **her throat felt ~** se notaba la garganta muy irritada; **~ flesh** carne *f* viva; **his wife's words touched a ~ nerve** las palabras de su mujer le dieron donde más le dolía *or* le dieron en lo más sensible

4 (= *basic*) [*anger, hate, ambition*] puro; **he spoke with ~ emotion** habló con verdadero sentimiento; **the ~ energy of a teenager** la energía en bruto de un adolescente; **he has ~ talent, but it lacks proper direction** tiene el talento en bruto, pero no sabe canalizarlo

5 (= *harsh*) [*wind*] cortante, fuerte; [*weather, night*] crudo

6 (= *inexperienced*) [*person, troops*] novato, inexperto; **they're still very ~** todavía están muy verdes; **a ~ recruit** (*Mil*) quinto *m*, soldado *mf* raso; (*fig*) novato/a *m/f*

7 (*) (= *unfair*) **a ~ deal: he got a ~ deal** le trataron injustamente; **he's got a ~ deal from life** la vida lo ha tratado mal

8 (= *coarse*) [*humour*] crudo

Ⓑ N **it got** *or* **touched him on the ~** (*fig*) lo hirió en lo más vivo, lo hirió donde más le dolía; **life/nature in the ~** la vida/naturaleza tal cual; **in the ~*** (= *naked*) en cueros*, en pelotas‡

rawboned [ˈrɔːˈbəʊnd] ADJ huesudo

rawhide [ˈrɔːhaɪd] Ⓐ N (*US*) cuero *m* de vaca
Ⓑ CPD de cuero crudo

Rawlplug® [ˈrɔːlplʌg] N taco *m*

rawness [ˈrɔːnɪs] N [1] (= *uncooked state*) crudeza *f*
[2] (= *inexperience*) inexperiencia *f*

ray[1] [reɪ] N [1] [*of light, heat, sun*] rayo *m*; *see also* **X-ray**
[2] (*fig*) (= *trace*) **a ~ of hope** un rayo de esperanza

ray[2] [reɪ] N (= *fish*) raya *f*; *see also* **stingray**

ray[3] [reɪ] N (*Mus*) re *m*

Ray [reɪ] N (*familiar form*) *of* **Raymond**

Raymond [ˈreɪmənd] N Raimundo, Ramón

rayon [ˈreɪɒn] N rayón *m*

raze [reɪz] VT (*also* **~ to the ground**) arrasar, asolar

razor [ˈreɪzəʳ] Ⓐ N (*open*) navaja *f*, chaveta *f* (*Peru*); (*safety*) maquinilla *f* de afeitar; **electric ~** máquina *f* de afeitar; **it's on a ~'s edge** está en un brete
Ⓑ CPD ► **razor blade** N hoja *f or* cuchilla *f* de afeitar ► **razor burn** N erosión *f* cutánea ► **razor cut** N (*Hairdressing*) corte *m* a la navaja

razorbill [ˈreɪzəbɪl] N alca *f* común

razor-sharp [ˈreɪzəˈʃɑːp] ADJ [*edge*] muy afilado; [*mind*] agudo, perspicaz

razor-strop [ˈreɪzəstrɒp] N suavizador *m*

razz* [ræz] VT (*US*) tomar el pelo a*

razzle* [ˈræzl] N **to be/go on the ~** estar/ir de juerga*

razzle-dazzle* [ˌræzlˈdæzl] N [1] = **razzle**
[2] = **razzmatazz**

razzmatazz* [ˌræzməˈtæz] N bombo *m* publicitario

RC ABBR = **Roman Catholic**

RCAF N ABBR = **Royal Canadian Air Force**

RCMP N ABBR = **Royal Canadian Mounted Police**

RCN N ABBR = **Royal Canadian Navy**

RD ABBR (*US*) = **rural delivery**

Rd ABBR (= **road**) c/, ctra

R/D ABBR (= **refer to drawer**) *protestar este cheque por falta de fondos*

RDA N ABBR = **recommended daily allowance** *or* **amount**

RDC N ABBR [1] = **Rural District Council**
[2] = **regional distribution centre**

re[1] [riː] PREP (*Comm*) (= *concerning*) relativo a, respecto a; **re my previous account** con referencia a mi cuenta anterior

re[2] [reɪ] N (*Mus*) re *m*

RE N ABBR [1] (*Brit Scol*) (= **religious education**) ed. religiosa
[2] (*Brit Mil*) = **Royal Engineers**

re... [riː] PREFIX re...

reabsorb [ˈriːəbˈzɔːb] VT reabsorber

reabsorption [ˈriːəbˈzɔːpʃən] N reabsorción *f*

reach [riːtʃ] Ⓐ VT [1] (= *get as far as*) [+ *place, person, stage, point, age*] llegar a; [+ *speed, level*] alcanzar, llegar a; **to ~ the terrace you have to cross the garden** para llegar a *or* hasta la terraza tienes que cruzar el jardín; **the door is ~ed by a long staircase** se llega a la puerta por una larga escalera; **your letter ~ed me this morning** su carta me llegó esta mañana; **by the time I ~ed her she was dead** cuando llegué a donde estaba, la encontré muerta; **to ~ 40 (years old)** llegar a los 40; **when you ~ my age** cuando llegues a mi edad; **we hope to ~ a wider audience** esperamos llegar a un público más variado; **not a sound ~ed our ears** ningún sonido llegó a nuestros oídos; **to ~ home** llegar a casa; **I ~ed a point where I was ready to give up** llegué a un punto en el que estaba dispuesto a tirar la toalla; **she ~ed the semi-finals** llegó hasta las semifinales; *see also* **peak A3, point A5**
[2] (= *achieve*) [+ *goal, target*] lograr; [+ *agreement, compromise*] llegar a; [+ *decision*] tomar; **they failed to ~ agreement** no consiguieron llegar a un acuerdo; **have they ~ed a decision yet?** ¿han tomado ya una decisión?; **to ~ perfection** lograr la perfección
[3] (= *extend to*) llegar a; **it doesn't ~ the bottom** no llega al fondo; **her dress ~es the floor** el vestido le llega a *or* hasta el suelo; **the cancer had already ~ed her liver** el cáncer ya le había llegado al hígado; **he ~es her shoulder** le llega al *or* por el hombro; *see also* **far-reaching**
[4] (= *stretch to*) alcanzar; **he is tall enough to ~ the top shelf** es lo suficientemente alto como para alcanzar el estante de arriba del todo
[5] (= *pass*) alcanzar; **can you ~ me (over) the oil?** ¿me alcanzas el aceite por favor?; **can you ~ me (down) that case?** ¿me alcanzas esa maleta por favor?
[6] (= *contact*) [+ *person*] ponerse en contacto con, contactar; **you can ~ me at my hotel** puedes ponerte en contacto conmigo *or* contactarme en el hotel; **you can always ~ me at the office** siempre puedes ponerte en contacto conmigo en la oficina; **to ~ sb by telephone** ponerse en contacto con *or* contactar a algn por teléfono; **the village cannot be ~ed by telephone** no hay comunicación telefónica con el pueblo
[7] (*US Jur*) (= *suborn*) [+ *witness*] sobornar
Ⓑ VI [1] (= *stretch out hand*) alargar la mano (**for sth** para tomar *or* coger algo); **he ~ed across the desk and shook my hand** me tendió la mano por encima del escritorio y estrechó la mía; **she ~ed for the bottle** alargó la mano para tomar *or* coger la botella; **~ for the sky!** (*US**) ¡arriba las manos!; **she ~ed into her bag and pulled out a gun** metió la mano en el bolso y sacó una pistola; **he ~ed up and put the book on the shelf** alargó la mano y puso el libro en el estante; ✦***IDIOM*** **to ~ for the stars** apuntar muy alto
[2] (= *extend*) [*land*] extenderse; [*clothes, curtains, water level*] llegar; (*fig*) (*in time*) remontarse; **their land ~es to the sea** sus tierras se extienden hasta el mar; **her skirt ~ed down to the ground** la falda le llegaba al *or* hasta el suelo; **the water ~ed up to the windows** el agua llegaba a las ventanas; **it ~es back to 1700** se remonta a 1700; **it's a tradition that ~es back (for) centuries** es una tradición que se remonta a varios siglos
[3] (= *stretch far enough*) [*person*] alcanzar; [*cable, hose*] llegar; **can you ~?** ¿alcanzas?; **it won't ~** no va a llegar
Ⓒ N [1] alcance *m*; **beyond (the) ~ of sth/sb: the price is beyond the ~ of ordinary people** el precio está fuera del alcance de la gente corriente; **she was beyond (the) ~ of human help** estaba desahuciada; **this subject is beyond his ~** este tema le viene grande; **beyond the ~ of the law** fuera del alcance de la ley; **to have a long ~** [*boxer, tennis player*] tener brazos largos; **out of ~** fuera del alcance; **the gun lay just out of ~** la pistola estaba justo fuera de su alcance; **keep all medicines out of ~ of children** mantenga todos los medicamentos fuera del alcance de los niños; **within sb's ~** al alcance (de la mano) de algn; **the rope was just within (her) ~** la cuerda estaba justo a su alcance *or* al alcance de su mano; **at last his goal was within ~** por fin el objetivo que tenía estaba a su alcance, por fin tenía su objetivo al alcance de la mano; **cars are within everyone's ~ nowadays** ahora los coches están al alcance (del bolsillo) de cualquiera; **within easy ~** a mano, cerca; **the shops are within easy ~** las tiendas están cerca *or* a mano; **it's within easy ~ by bus** en autobús queda cerca, se puede acceder fácilmente en autobús; **a house within easy ~ of the station** una casa cerca de la estación, una casa bien situada con respecto a la estación; **within ~ of sth** cerca de algo
[2] [*of river, canal*] (= *short stretch*) tramo *m*; **the upper/lower ~es of the Amazon** (= *larger area*) la cuenca alta/baja del Amazonas; **the outer ~es of the solar system** los límites exteriores del sistema solar; **the highest ~es of government** los escalafones más altos del gobierno

►**reach out** Ⓐ VI + ADV [1] (= *stretch out hand*) = **reach B1**
[2] (= *try and get*) **to ~ out for sth: babies will ~ out for brightly coloured objects** los bebés alargan la mano hacia objetos de colores vivos; **it is important that we can ~ out for help when we need it** es importante que podamos tender la mano en busca de ayuda cuando la necesitemos
[3] **to ~ out to sb** (= *communicate with*) llegar a algn; (= *ask for support*) recurrir *or* acudir a algn; **we need to ~ out to new audiences** tenemos que llegar a nuevos públicos
Ⓑ VT + ADV [+ *hand*] alargar, extender

reachable [ˈriːtʃəbl] ADJ [*place*] accesible; [*object*] asequible; [*goal*] alcanzable, accesible; [*person*] accesible; **she is ~ at ...** se la puede localizar en ...

reach-me-down [ˈriːtʃmɪˌdaʊn] Ⓐ ADJ [*ideas*] común y corriente; [*clothes*] usado, de segunda mano
Ⓑ **reach-me-downs** NPL ropa *fsing* usada

react [riːˈækt] VI [1] (*gen*) reaccionar; **to ~ against sth/sb** reaccionar contra algo/algn; **companies have ~ed by increasing their prices** la reacción de las empresas ha sido subir los precios, las empresas han reaccionado subiendo los precios; **to ~ on sth/sb** afectar algo/a algn; **alcohol always ~ed badly on him** el alcohol siempre le afectaba negativamente, siempre tenía una reacción mala con el alcohol; **to ~ to** [+ *news, situation*] reaccionar ante; [+ *foreign substance*] reaccionar a; **to ~ to sb** reaccionar *or* responder ante algn
[2] (*Chem, Phys*) reaccionar (**with** con); **to ~ together** tener una reacción conjunta, reaccionar conjuntamente

reaction [riːˈækʃən] N [1] (= *response*) reacción *f*; **what was his ~ to your suggestion?** ¿cuál fue su reacción a tu sugerencia?, ¿cómo reaccionó frente a tu sugerencia?; **it produced no ~** no surtió efecto; **some foods cause allergic ~s** algunos alimentos provocan reacciones alérgicas
[2] **reactions** (= *reflexes*) reacciones *fpl*; **his ~s were slow because he'd been drinking** tardaba en reaccionar porque había estado bebiendo
[3] (*Pol pej*) reacción *f*; **the forces of ~** las fuerzas de la reacción, las fuerzas reacciona-

rias
4 (*Chem*) reacción *f*

reactionary [riːˈækʃənri] Ⓐ ADJ reaccionario Ⓑ N reaccionario/a *m/f*

reactivate [riːˈæktɪveɪt] VT reactivar

reactivation [riːˌæktɪˈveɪʃən] N reactivación *f*

reactive [riːˈæktɪv] ADJ reactivo

reactor [riːˈæktəʳ] N reactor *m*; **nuclear ~** reactor *m* nuclear

read [riːd] (*pt, pp* **read** [red]) Ⓐ VT 1 [+ *book, poem, story, music, sign*] leer; [+ *author*] leer a; **can you ~ Russian?** ¿sabes leer en ruso?; **she can't ~ music** no sabe leer música; **I can't ~ your writing** no entiendo tu letra, no puedo leer tu letra; **for "boon" ~ "bone"** en lugar de "boon" léase "bone"; **I ~ "good" as "mood"** al leer confundí "good" con "mood"; **to ~ sth to sb** ◊ **to ~ sb sth** leer algo a algn; **to ~ sth to o.s.** leer algo para sí mismo; **to ~ sb's lips** leer los labios a algn; **~ my lips** (*fig*) fíjate bien en lo que digo; **to ~ the news** leer las noticias; **to ~ sb to sleep** leerle a algn hasta que se quede dormido; **to ~ o.s. to sleep** leer hasta quedarse dormido; ✦*IDIOM* **to take sth as ~** dar algo por sentado; **to take the minutes as ~** (*in meeting*) dar las actas por leídas; *see also* **riot**
2 (*esp Brit Univ*) (= *study*) **to ~ chemistry** estudiar química, cursar estudios de química
3 (= *interpret*) [+ *map, meter, thermometer*] leer; [+ *information, remarks, expression, situation*] interpretar; [+ *person*] entender; **the same information can be ~ in different ways** la misma información se puede interpretar de varias formas; **I've never been able to ~ him** nunca he sido capaz de entenderle; **this is how I ~ the situation** así es como yo interpreto *or* veo la situación; **I ~ the disappointment in her face** le noté la decepción en la cara; **to ~ sth as sth** interpretar algo como algo; **to ~ the future** leer *or* adivinar el porvenir; **to ~ sb's hand** *or* **palm** leerle la mano a algn; **to ~ sth into sth**: **you're ~ing too much into it** le estás dando demasiada importancia; **to ~ into a sentence what is not there** ver en una frase un significado que no tiene; **to ~ sb's mind** *or* **thoughts** leerle el pensamiento a algn, adivinar el pensamiento a algn; *see also* **book A1**
4 (*Telec*) **do you ~ me?** ¿me oye?; **I ~ you loud and clear** le oigo perfectamente
5 (= *say, indicate*) [*notice*] decir; [*thermometer, instrument*] indicar, marcar; **it should ~ "friends" not "fiends"** debería decir *or* poner "friends", no "fiends"; **the sign on the bus ~ "private, not in service"** el letrero del autobús decía *or* en el letrero del autobús ponía "privado, fuera de servicio"
6 (*Comput*) leer
Ⓑ VI 1 [*person*] leer; **to ~ about sth/sb** leer sobre *or* acerca de algo/algn; **I ~ about it in the papers** lo leí en los periódicos; **I've ~ about him** he leído sobre *or* acerca de él; **I'm ~ing about Napoleon** me estoy documentando sobre Napoleón, estoy leyendo acerca de Napoleón; **to ~ aloud** leer en voz alta; **the ~ing public** el público que lee; **to ~ silently** leer para sí; **to ~ through sth** leer algo de principio a fin; **I've ~ through your letter very carefully** he leído tu carta minuciosamente de principio a fin; **to ~ to sb**: **he ~ to us from the Bible** nos leyó extractos de la Biblia; **my daughter asked me to ~ to her** mi hija me pidió que le leyera un libro; **I like being ~ to** me gusta que me lean; **to ~ to o.s.** leer para sí; ✦*IDIOM* **to ~ between the lines** leer entre líneas
2 (= *give impression*) **the book ~s well** el libro está bien escrito; **it would ~ better if you put ...** quedaría mejor si pusieras ...; **it ~s very awkwardly** al leerlo suena muy raro; **his article ~s like an official report** su artículo está escrito como un informe oficial
3 (= *say, indicate*) decir; **the text ~s as follows** el texto dice lo siguiente
4 (= *study*) estudiar; **to ~ for the Bar** estudiar Derecho (para hacerse abogado); **to ~ for a degree** hacer una carrera, estudiar la licenciatura
Ⓒ N lectura *f*; **I like a good ~** me gusta leer un buen libro; **it's a good ~** es un libro que se disfruta leyendo; **I was having a quiet ~ in the garden** leía tranquilamente en el jardín; **can I have a ~ of your paper?** ¿puedo echarle un vistazo a tu periódico?
Ⓓ CPD ► **read head** N (*Comput*) cabezal *m* lector

►**read back** Ⓐ VT + ADV volver a leer; **can you ~ it back to me?** ¿puedes volvérmelo a leer?
Ⓑ VI + ADV **I was ~ing back over my notes** estaba releyendo *or* repasando mis apuntes

►**read off** VT + ADV [+ *numbers, items on list*] leer (uno a uno)

►**read on** VI + ADV seguir leyendo

►**read out** VT + ADV (*gen*) leer (en voz alta); (*Comput*) leer; **please ~ it out** por favor, léalo en voz alta; **shall I ~ them out?** ¿los leo (en voz alta)?

►**read over** VT + ADV repasar, volver a leer

►**read through** VT + ADV leer (entero); **tell him to ~ it through first** dile que primero lo lea entero; **I have ~ through your letter** he leído tu carta de cabo a rabo

►**read up** Ⓐ VT + ADV [+ *subject*] estudiar; [+ *notes*] repasar
Ⓑ VI + ADV **to ~ up for an exam** estudiar *or* repasar para un examen; **to ~ up on sth** leer sobre algo, ponerse al tanto de algo

readability [ˌriːdəˈbɪlɪtɪ] N legibilidad *f* (*also Comput*); [*of style*] amenidad *f*, interés *m*

readable [ˈriːdəbl] ADJ [*writing*] legible; [*book etc*] entretenido, que puede leerse

readdress [ˈriːəˈdres] VT [+ *letter*] cambiar la dirección de

reader [ˈriːdəʳ] N 1 (= *person who reads*) lector(a) *m/f*; (*in library*) usuario/a *m/f*; **he's a great ~** lee mucho, es muy aficionado a la lectura; **I'm not much of a ~** leo poco, no me interesan mucho los libros; *see also* **lay**[3]
2 (*also* **publisher's ~**) lector(a) *m/f*; *see also* **proofreader**
3 (*Univ*) profesor(a) *m/f* adjunto/a
4 (= *schoolbook*) (*to teach reading*) libro *m* de lectura; (= *anthology*) antología *f*
5 (= *machine*) máquina *f* lectora, aparato *m* lector; *see also* **microfiche**, **optical**

readership [ˈriːdəʃɪp] N 1 número *m* de lectores
2 (*Brit Univ*) *puesto de profesor adjunto*

readily [ˈredɪlɪ] ADV 1 (= *willingly*) [*accept, admit*] de buena gana; **he had ~ agreed to do the job** había accedido de buena gana a hacer el trabajo
2 (= *easily*) [*accessible*] fácilmente; **they are ~ available** se pueden adquirir fácilmente; **I could ~ understand her anxiety** entendía perfectamente su ansiedad; **her confusion was ~ apparent** (*frm*) se advertía su confusión de inmediato

readiness [ˈredɪnɪs] N 1 (= *willingness*) buena disposición *f*; **his ~ to help us** su buena disposición para ayudarnos
2 (= *preparedness*) **we laid the tables in ~ for the guests** preparamos las mesas para la llegada de los invitados; **equipment that is kept in ~ for an emergency** material que se mantiene listo *or* preparado para una emergencia; **to hold o.s. in ~ (for sth)** mantenerse listo (para algo)
3 (= *sharpness*) **~ of wit** viveza *f* de ingenio

reading [ˈriːdɪŋ] Ⓐ N 1 (= *activity*) lectura *f*; **suggestions for further ~** sugerencias de lecturas suplementarias; **I only know about it from ~** todo lo que sé sobre ello es a través de lo que he leído
2 (*also* **~ matter**) **the book is** *or* **makes interesting ~** el libro es *or* resulta interesante; **I'd prefer some light ~** preferiría algo fácil *or* ameno de leer, preferiría algo que no sea muy pesado de leer
3 (= *interpretation*) interpretación *f*; (*Cine, Theat*) [*of part*] lectura *f*; **my ~ of the situation is this** así es como yo interpreto *or* veo la situación
4 (*on thermometer, instrument*) lectura *f*; **to give a true/false ~** [*instrument*] marcar bien/mal; **~s of more than 40°C are common** es normal que los termómetros marquen más de 40°C; **to take a ~ of sth** hacer una lectura de algo, leer algo
5 (= *passage*) lectura *f*
6 (= *recital*) [*of play, poem*] recital *m*; *see also* **play D**, **poetry**
7 (*Parl*) [*of bill*] lectura *f*; **the bill has had its first ~** el proyecto de ley ha pasado por su primera lectura; **to give a bill a second ~** leer un proyecto de ley por segunda vez
8 (*Jur*) [*of will, banns*] lectura *f*
9 (= *knowledge*) **a person of wide ~** una persona muy leída
Ⓑ ADJ **the ~ public** el público que lee, el público lector; **he's a great ~ man** es un hombre que lee mucho, es hombre muy aficionado a la lectura
Ⓒ CPD ► **reading age** N nivel *m* de lectura; **he has a ~ age of eight** tiene el nivel de lectura de un niño de ocho años ► **reading book** N libro *m* de lectura ► **reading glasses** NPL gafas *fpl* para leer ► **reading knowledge** N **she has a ~ knowledge of Spanish** sabe leer el español ► **reading lamp**, **reading light** N lámpara *f* para leer, lámpara *f* portátil ► **reading list** N lista *f* de lecturas ► **reading matter**, **reading material** N material *m* de lectura ► **reading room** N sala *f* de lectura ► **reading speed** N velocidad *f* de lectura

readjust [ˈriːəˈdʒʌst] Ⓐ VT reajustar
Ⓑ VI reajustarse

readjustment [ˈriːəˈdʒʌstmənt] N reajuste *m*

readmit [ˈriːədˈmɪt] VT readmitir, volver a admitir

read-only memory [ˌriːdəʊnlɪˈmeməri] N (*Comput*) memoria *f* muerta, memoria *f* de sola lectura

read-out [ˈriːdaʊt] N lectura *f* de salida

read-write [ˌriːdˈraɪt] CPD ► **read-write head** N cabeza *f* de lectura-escritura ► **read-write window** N ventana *f* de lectura-escritura

ready [ˈredɪ] Ⓐ ADJ (*compar* **readier**, *superl* **readiest**) 1 (= *prepared*) 1·1 (*physically*) listo; **your glasses will be ~ in a fortnight** sus gafas estarán listas dentro de quince días, tendrá sus gafas listas dentro de quince días; **(are you) ~?** ¿(estás) listo?; **~ when you are!** ¡cuando quieras!; **~, steady, go!** ¡preparados, listos, ya!; **to be ~ to do sth** estar listo para hacer algo; **~ to serve** [*food*] listo para servir; **to be ~ for sth** estar listo para algo; **everything is ~ for the new arrival** todo está listo *or* dispuesto para la llegada del bebé; **~ for use** listo para usar; **the doctor's ~ for you**

now el doctor ya puede verlo; **to get (o.s.) ~** prepararse, arreglarse; **to get ~ for school/bed** prepararse para ir al colegio/a la cama; **to get** *or* **make sth ~** preparar algo; **he was getting the children ~ to go out** estaba arreglando a los niños para salir; **I'll have everything ~** lo tendré todo listo; **I had my camera ~** tenía la cámara preparada; **to hold o.s. ~ (for sth)** mantenerse listo (para algo); **~ and waiting** a punto

1·2 (*mentally, emotionally*) preparado; **I was all ~ with a prepared statement** me había preparado bien con una declaración hecha de antemano; **she wanted a baby but didn't feel ~ yet** quería un bebé, pero todavía no se sentía preparada; **she had her excuses ~** tenía sus excusas preparadas; **to be ~ to do sth** estar preparado para hacer algo; **she's not ~ to take on that kind of responsibility** no está preparada para asumir tanta responsabilidad; **I'm ~ to face him now** ahora me siento con ánimos para enfrentarme a él; **are you ~ to order?** (*in restaurant*) ¿desean pedir ya?; **to be ~ for sth** estar preparado para algo; **to be ~ for anything** estar preparado para lo que sea, estar dispuesto a lo que sea; **I'm ~ for a drink** me muero por beber algo; **I'm ~ for (my) bed** yo ya tengo sueño; **to be ~ with an excuse** tener preparada una excusa; **to be ~ with a joke** tener una broma a punto

2 (= *available*) disponible

3 (= *willing*) dispuesto; **to be ~ to do sth** estar dispuesto a hacer algo; **to be only too ~ to do sth** estar más que dispuesto a hacer algo

4 (= *quick*) [*solution, explanation, smile*] fácil; [*wit*] agudo, vivo; [*market*] muy receptivo; **to have a ~ answer/excuse (for sth)** tener una respuesta/excusa a punto (para algo); **don't be so ~ to criticize** no te des tanta prisa en criticar; **one advantage of this model is the ~ availability of spare parts** una de las ventajas de este modelo es que se pueden obtener recambios fácilmente; **to ensure a ~ supply of fresh herbs, why not try growing your own?** para contar siempre con una provisión de hierbas ¿por qué no cultivarlas tú mismo?

5 (= *on the point of*) **to be ~ to do sth** estar a punto de hacer algo; **we were ~ to give up there and then** estábamos a punto de abandonar sin más

Ⓑ N 1 **at the ~** listo, preparado; **with rifles at the ~** con los fusiles listos *or* preparados para disparar; **pencil at the ~** lápiz en ristre, lápiz en mano; **riot police were at the ~** la policía antidisturbios estaba lista *or* preparada para actuar

2 **the readies*** (= *cash*) la pasta*, la plata (*LAm**), la lana (*LAm**)

Ⓒ VT (*frm*) (= *prepare*) [+ *object*] disponer, preparar (**for** para); **to ~ o.s.** (*for news, an event, a struggle*) disponerse, prepararse; (*for a party etc*) arreglarse (**for** para)

Ⓓ CPD ► **ready cash, ready money** N dinero *m* en efectivo ► **ready meal** N comida *f* precocinada *or* preparada ► **ready reckoner** N tabla *f* de equivalencias

ready-cooked ['redɪ'kʊkt] ADJ precocinado, preparado

ready-made ['redɪ'meɪd] ADJ [*clothes, curtains*] confeccionado, ya hecho; [*meal, sauce*] precocinado, preparado; [*excuses, ideas*] preparado; **we can't expect to find a ~ solution for our problems** no podemos esperar que la solución a nuestros problemas nos llegue como caída del cielo; **a ~ basis for negotiations** una base para las negociaciones muy oportuna; **you can buy your greenhouse ~** puede comprar un invernadero ya prefabricado

ready-mixed [ˌredɪ'mɪkst] ADJ [*concrete*] mezclado de antemano, ya preparado; [*cake*] de sobre

ready-to-serve [ˌredɪtə'sɜːv] ADJ preparado

ready-to-wear [ˌredɪtə'weəʳ] ADJ [*clothes*] confeccionado, listo para llevar

reaffirm ['riːə'fɜːm] VT [+ *loyalty, affection etc*] reafirmar, reiterar

reaffirmation ['riːæfə'meɪʃən] N reafirmación *f*, reiteración *f*

reafforest ['riːə'fɒrɪst] VT (*Brit*) repoblar de árboles

reafforestation ['riːəˌfɒrɪs'teɪʃən] N (*Brit*) repoblación *f* forestal

reagent [riː'eɪdʒənt] N (*Chem*) reactivo *m*

real [rɪəl] Ⓐ ADJ 1 (= *true*) [*reason, surprise, talent, achievement, progress*] verdadero; [*power*] efectivo, verdadero; [*cost, income*] real; [*threat, hardship*] serio, verdadero; **Tina was not their ~ mother** Tina no era su verdadera madre; **you're a ~ friend** eres un verdadero amigo; (*iro*) ¡vaya un amigo estás hecho!; **the only ~ car accident that I've ever had** el único accidente de coche de verdad que he tenido jamás; **we have no ~ reason to suspect him** no tenemos ninguna razón en particular para sospechar de él; **it came as no ~ surprise to him** no le sorprendió en absoluto; **now, that's a ~ paella!** ¡esto sí que es una paella (de verdad)!; **get ~!*** ¡baja de las nubes!; **there was ~ concern that the children were in danger** la gente estaba realmente preocupada por que los niños estuvieran en peligro; **I was never in any ~ danger** nunca estuve realmente en peligro; **the danger was very ~** el peligro era muy real; **there was no ~ evidence that ...** no había pruebas contundentes de que ...; **my ~ home is in London** mi verdadera casa *or* mi casa de verdad está en Londres; **he showed ~ interest in science** se mostraba verdaderamente interesado por la ciencia; **in ~ life** en la vida real, en la realidad; **~ life just isn't like that** lo que pasa es que la vida real no es así; **a ~ live film star** una estrella de cine en carne y hueso; **a ~ man** un hombre de verdad, todo un hombre; **she's in ~ pain** le duele de verdad; **it's a ~ problem** es un verdadero problema; **in ~ terms** en términos reales; **to be in ~ trouble** estar metido en un buen lío*; **the ~ world** el mundo real

2 (= *not fake*) [*gold*] de ley, auténtico; [*leather, diamond*] auténtico; [*flowers*] de verdad; [*silk*] puro; [*cream*] fresco; **~ coffee** café de cafetera, café de verdad; **it was caviar, the ~ McCoy*** era caviar del auténtico; **this diamond's the ~ thing** *or* **the ~ McCoy*** este diamante es auténtico; **this isn't the ~ thing, it's just a copy** esto no es auténtico *or* genuino, es sólo una copia; **this was definitely love, the ~ thing** esto era amor de verdad

3 (= *great*) verdadero; **it's a ~ shame** es una verdadera lástima; **this dessert is a ~ treat** este postre es un verdadero gustazo; **to make ~ money** ganar dinero de verdad

Ⓑ ADV (*US**) (= *really*) muy; **he wrote some ~ good stories** escribió unos relatos muy buenos *or* buenísimos; **we had a ~ good time** lo pasamos realmente bien; **it's ~ heavy** pesa mucho

Ⓒ N **for ~*** de veras, de verdad; **is this guy for ~?** ¿de qué va este tío?*; **are you for ~?** ¿me estás tomando el pelo?*

Ⓓ CPD ► **real ale** N cerveza *f* de barril tradicional ► **real assets** NPL propiedad *fsing* inmueble, bienes *mpl* raíces ► **real estate** N (*US*) bienes *mpl* raíces, bienes *mpl* inmuebles ► **real property** N = **real estate** ► **real time** N (*Comput*) tiempo *m* real

realign [riːə'laɪn] VT [+ *currency*] realinear; **to ~ o.s. with** (*Pol*) realinearse con

realignment [riːə'laɪnmənt] N [*of currency*] (*also Pol*) realineamiento *m*

realism ['rɪəlɪzəm] N realismo *m*

realist ['rɪəlɪst] N realista *mf*

realistic [rɪə'lɪstɪk] ADJ [*person, approach, painting*] realista; [*price*] razonable; **let's be ~** seamos realistas; **we had no ~ chance of winning** no teníamos posibilidades reales de ganar

realistically [rɪə'lɪstɪkəlɪ] ADV [*think, consider, describe*] de manera realista; **~ minded people** la gente que piensa de manera realista; **the best we can ~ expect is ...** lo mejor que podemos esperar, siendo realistas, es ...; **it just isn't ~ possible** siendo realistas, es sencillamente imposible; **her designs are ~ priced** sus diseños tienen un precio razonable; **~, he had little chance of winning** siendo realistas, tenía pocas posibilidades de ganar

reality [riː'ælɪtɪ] N Ⓐ 1 (= *real world*) realidad *f*; **let's get back to ~** volvamos a la realidad

2 (= *fact, truth*) realidad *f*; **the harsh ~ of daily life** la cruda realidad de la vida diaria; **let's stick to realities** atengámonos a la realidad; **to become (a) ~** convertirse en realidad; **in ~** (= *actually*) en realidad

3 (= *trueness to life*) realismo *m*

Ⓑ CPD ► **reality TV** N telerrealidad *f*

realizable ['rɪəlaɪzəbl] ADJ [*goal, ambition*] alcanzable; [*plan*] realizable, factible

realization [ˌrɪəlaɪ'zeɪʃən] N 1 (= *comprehension*) comprensión *f*, entendimiento *m*; **she awoke to the ~ that ...** cayó en la cuenta de que ... 2 (= *completion*) realización *f*

realize ['rɪəlaɪz] VT 1 (= *comprehend, become aware of*) darse cuenta de; **he ~d his mistake and went back** se dio cuenta de su error y volvió; **once I ~d how it was done** una vez que caí en la cuenta de cómo se hacía; **then I ~d what had happened** entonces me di cuenta de lo que había pasado, entonces comprendí lo que había pasado; **to ~ that** darse cuenta de que, comprender que; **I began to ~ that it would be impossible** empecé a darme cuenta de que sería imposible, empecé a comprender que sería imposible

2 (= *know*) darse cuenta de; **without realizing it** sin darse cuenta; **I ~ it's difficult, but ...** (ya) sé que es difícil, pero ..., comprendo *or* entiendo que es difícil, pero ...; **yes, I ~ that!** ¡sí, ya me doy cuenta!, ¡sí, ya me hago cargo!; **do you ~ what you've done?** ¿te das cuenta de lo que has hecho?

3 (= *carry out*) [+ *plan*] llevar a cabo; **my worst fears were ~d** mis mayores temores se hicieron realidad; **to ~ one's hopes/ambitions** hacer realidad sus esperanzas/ambiciones; **to ~ one's potential** desarrollar al máximo su potencial

4 (*Comm*) (= *convert into cash*) [+ *assets*] realizar; (= *produce*) [+ *profit*] producir; [+ *savings*] hacer; **the sale of the house ~d £250,000** la venta de la casa generó 250.000 libras

real-life [ˌrɪəl'laɪf] ADJ de la vida real, auténtico

reallocate [riː'ælәˌkeɪt] VT [+ *resources, land, time*] redistribuir

reallocation [ˌriːælə'keɪʃən] N [*resources, land, time*] redistribución *f*

really ['rɪəlɪ] (A) ADV 1 (*as intensifier*) (= *very*) **it's ~ ugly** es feísimo, es feo de verdad; **a ~ good film** una película buenísima *or* verdaderamente buena; **you ~ must see it** no puedes perdértelo; **I ~ ought to go** de verdad que me tengo que ir; **I'm very sorry, I ~ am** lo siento mucho, de veras; **I ~ don't know** de verdad que no lo sé; **this time we're ~ done for*** esta vez sí que la hemos hecho*, esta vez la hemos hecho de verdad*; *see also* **something A2**
2 (= *genuinely*) **I don't ~ know** en realidad no lo sé; **what ~ happened?** ¿qué fue lo que pasó en realidad *or* realmente?; **has he ~ gone?** ¿de verdad que *or* es cierto que se ha ido?; **she's quite pretty ~** la verdad es que es bastante guapa; **"would you like to go?" — "not ~"** —¿te gustaría ir? —la verdad es que no mucho
(B) EXCL **really?: "he left an hour ago" — "really?"** (*expressing doubt*) —se marchó hace una hora —¿de verdad? *or* —¿de veras?; **"I was in Mexico last month" — "really?"** (*expressing interest*) —estuve en Méjico el mes pasado —¿ah sí?; **"she's getting divorced again" — "really!"** (*in surprise, disbelief*) —se va a divorciar otra vez —¡no me digas!; **I'm fine, ~** (*in assurance*) estoy bien, de verdad; **(well) ~!** (*in disapproval*) ¡de verdad!; **(well) ~! it's too bad of him** ¡pero bueno! *or* ¡de verdad!, vaya una forma de comportarse la suya

realm [relm] N (*lit, Jur*) reino *m*; (*fig*) (= *field*) esfera *f*, campo *m*; **in the ~s of fantasy** en el reino de la fantasía; **in the ~ of the possible** dentro de lo posible; **in the ~ of speculation** en la esfera de la especulación

realtor ['rɪəltɔːʳ] N (*US*) corredor(a) *m/f* de bienes raíces

realty ['rɪəltɪ] N bienes *mpl* raíces

ream1 [riːm] N [*of paper*] resma *f*; **reams*** (*fig*) montones *mpl*

ream2 [riːm] VT (*Tech*) (*also* **~ out**) escariar

reamer ['riːməʳ] N escariador *m*

reanimate ['riː'ænɪmeɪt] VT reanimar

reap [riːp] VT (*Agr*) (= *cut*) segar; (= *harvest*) cosechar, recoger; **to ~ what one has sown** (*fig*) recoger lo que uno ha sembrado; **who ~s the reward?** ¿quién se lleva los beneficios?

reaper ['riːpəʳ] N 1 (= *person*) segador(a) *m/f*
2 (= *machine*) segadora *f*, agavilladora *f*

reaping ['riːpɪŋ] (A) N siega *f*
(B) CPD ► **reaping hook** N hoz *f*

reappear ['riːə'pɪəʳ] VI reaparecer, volver a aparecer

reappearance ['riːə'pɪərəns] N reaparición *f*

reapply ['riːə'plaɪ] (A) VI hacer una nueva solicitud, presentar una nueva solicitud; **he reapplied for a transfer** volvió a solicitar traslado, hizo *or* presentó una nueva solicitud de traslado
(B) VT [+ *paint, varnish*] dar otra capa de

reappoint ['riːə'pɔɪnt] VT volver a nombrar

reappointment ['riːə'pɔɪntmənt] N nuevo nombramiento *m*

reapportion ['riːə'pɔːʃən] VT volver a repartir (**among** entre)

reappraisal ['riːə'preɪzəl] N revaluación *f*

reappraise ['riːə'preɪz] VT reevaluar

rear1 [rɪəʳ] (A) N 1 (= *back part*) parte *f* trasera, parte *f* posterior; (*esp of building*) parte *f* de atrás; **the car behind skidded into his ~** el coche que venía detrás patinó, chocando contra la parte trasera *or* posterior del suyo; **the ~ of the train** la parte trasera *or* posterior del tren, los últimos vagones del tren; **from the ~ he looked just like everybody else** por detrás parecía como todo el mundo
2 [*of procession*] cola *f*, final *m*; [*of battle formation*] retaguardia *f*; **to attack the enemy from the ~** atacar al enemigo por la retaguardia
3 (*) (= *buttocks*) trasero* *m*
4 (*in phrases*) **at** *or* **in the ~** [*of vehicle*] en la parte trasera; [*of building*] en la parte trasera *or* de atrás; [*of procession*] en la cola, al final; **there is a garden at** *or* (*US*) **in the ~ of the house** detrás de la casa hay un jardín; **he sat in the ~ of the taxi** se sentó en el asiento de atrás del taxi; **to bring up the ~** cerrar la marcha; **to the ~** (*gen*) detrás, en la parte trasera *or* de atrás; (*Mil*) en la retaguardia; **a house with a patio to the ~** una casa con un patio detrás, una casa con un patio en la parte trasera *or* de atrás; **to be well to the ~** quedar muy atrás; **to the ~ of** detrás de; **to the ~ of the house was open countryside** detrás de la casa había campo abierto
(B) ADJ (*gen*) de atrás, trasero
(C) CPD ► **rear admiral** N contraalmirante *mf* ► **rear door** N (*in building, of vehicle*) puerta *f* trasera *or* de atrás ► **rear end** N [*of vehicle*] parte *f* trasera *or* posterior; (* *hum*) (= *buttocks*) trasero* *m* ► **rear gunner** N artillero *m* de cola ► **rear light** N piloto *m*, luz *f* trasera, calavera *f* (*Mex*) ► **rear seat** N asiento *m* trasero *or* de atrás ► **rear wheel** N rueda *f* trasera *or* de atrás; **~-wheel drive** tracción *f* trasera ► **rear window** N [*of building*] ventana *f* de atrás; [*of vehicle*] luneta *f* trasera, cristal *m* de atrás

rear2 [rɪəʳ] (A) VT 1 (= *raise, bring up*) [+ *children, animals*] criar; **an audience ~ed on a diet of pop music** un público que ha crecido oyendo música pop; *see also* **hand-rear**
2 (= *raise*) levantar, alzar; **fascism/jealousy ~s its ugly head again** el fascismo/la envidia vuelve a levantar la cabeza
3 (= *build*) erigir
(B) VI (*also* **to ~ up**) 1 (*on hind legs*) [*horse*] empinarse; (*in fright*) encabritarse
2 (= *rise steeply*) [*building, mountain, wave*] alzarse, erguirse; **the mountains ~ed up on each side** las montañas se alzaban *or* se erguían a cada lado

rear-engined ['rɪər,endʒɪnd] ADJ con motor trasero

rearguard ['rɪəgɑːd] (A) N (*Mil*) retaguardia *f*
(B) CPD ► **rearguard action** N combate *m* para cubrir una retirada; **to fight a ~ action** (*fig*) resistir en lo posible

rearm ['riː'ɑːm] (A) VT rearmar
(B) VI rearmarse

rearmament ['riː'ɑːməmənt] N rearme *m*

rearmost ['rɪəməʊst] ADJ trasero, último de todos

rear-mounted ['rɪə'maʊntɪd] ADJ **~ engine** motor *m* trasero *or* posterior

rearrange ['riːə'reɪndʒ] VT [+ *meeting, appointment*] cambiar de fecha/hora; [+ *furniture*] cambiar de sitio

rearrangement ['riːə'reɪndʒmənt] N [*of meeting*] cambio *m* de fecha/hora; [*of furniture*] (= *act*) cambio *m* de sitio; (= *effect*) nueva disposición *f*

rear-view mirror [,rɪəvjuː'mɪrəʳ] N (*Aut*) (espejo *m*) retrovisor *m*

rearward ['rɪəwəd] (A) ADJ trasero, de atrás, posterior
(B) ADV hacia atrás

rearwards ['rɪəwədz] ADV = **rearward B**

reason ['riːzn] (A) N 1 (= *motive*) razón *f*, motivo *m*; **the only ~ (that) I went was because I was told to** la única razón por la que *or* el único motivo por el que fui fue porque me dijeron que lo hiciera; **who would have a ~ to want to kill her?** ¿quién podría tener motivos para matarla?; **we have ~ to believe that …** (*frm*) tenemos motivos para creer que …; **he had every ~ to be upset** estaba disgustado y con razón; **there seems to be no ~ to stay** parece que no hay razón *or* motivo para quedarse; **by ~ of** en virtud de; **the ~ for (doing) sth: the ~ for my going** *or* **my ~ for going** la razón por la que *or* el motivo por el que me marcho; **she is my ~ for living** ella es mi razón de ser; **for ~s best known to himself** por motivos que sólo él sabe; **for no ~** sin motivo, sin razón; **for personal/health ~s** por motivos personales/de salud; **for some ~** por la razón *or* el motivo que sea; **for this ~** por esta razón, por eso; **all the more ~ why you should not sell it** razón de más para que no lo vendas; **if he doesn't come I shall want to know the ~ why** si no viene tendrá que explicarme por qué; **I see no ~ why we shouldn't win** no veo razón por la que *or* motivo por el que no debiéramos ganar; **with good ~** con razón; **without ~** sin razón, sin motivo; **not without ~** no sin razón; *see also* **rhyme**
2 (= *faculty*) razón *f*; **only mankind is capable of ~** sólo el ser humano es capaz de razonar; **to lose one's ~** perder la razón
3 (= *good sense*) sentido *m* común, sensatez *f*; **the Age of Reason** la Edad de la Razón; **beyond (all) ~: I resented his presence beyond all ~** su presencia me molestaba de una forma inexplicable *or* fuera de toda lógica; **to listen to ~** atender a razones; **to see ~** entrar en razón; **he tried to make her see ~** intentó hacerla entrar en razón; **the voice of ~** la voz de la razón; **within ~** dentro de lo razonable; *see also* **appeal, stand C12**
(B) VT razonar; **I called him, ~ing that I had nothing to lose** me dije que no tenía nada que perder así que lo llamé; **ours (is) not to ~ why** no es responsabilidad nuestra saber el porqué
(C) VI razonar, discurrir

►**reason out** VT + ADV [+ *argument, answer*] razonar; [+ *problem*] resolver razonándolo; **she had felt the same as he did, until ~ing it out** opinaba como él hasta que se paró a pensarlo con un poco de lógica

►**reason with** VI + PREP **to ~ with sb** razonar con algn (para convencerle); **she was in no mood to be ~ed with** no estaba de humor como para que razonaran con ella; **there's no ~ing with him** no hay forma de razonar con él

reasonable ['riːznəbl] ADJ 1 (= *sensible, fair*) [*person, decision, explanation, request*] razonable; [*behaviour*] sensato; **I kept my voice calm and ~** mantuve un tono de voz calmado y de persona razonable; **be ~!** ¡sé razonable!; **it is ~ to suppose that …** es razonable suponer que …; **beyond (a** *or* **any) ~ doubt** sin que quede lugar a dudas; **to use ~ force** (*Jur*) hacer uso moderado de la fuerza; **~ grounds** motivos *mpl* fundados; **within a ~ time** dentro de un plazo de tiempo razonable
2 (= *acceptable*) [*amount, distance, price, offer*] razonable; [*standard, results*] aceptable; **there was a ~ chance of finding a peaceful solution** existían bastantes posibilidades de encontrar una solución pacífica; **this suit is very ~** este traje no es nada caro *or* no está nada mal de precio

reasonableness ['riːznəblnɪs] N [*of person, request, offer, behaviour*] lo razonable

➤ LANGUAGE IN USE: **reason A1** 17.1, 26.3 **reasonable 1** 26.3

reasonably [ˈriːznəblɪ] ADV [1] (= *sensibly*) [*discuss, expect, suppose*] razonablemente; [*behave*] de manera razonable; **he acted very ~** obró de manera muy razonable; **he argued, quite ~, that ...** argumentó, con toda la razón, que ...; **~ priced clothes** ropa a precios razonables
[2] (= *fairly*) [*good, happy, sure, safe*] bastante; **a ~ accurate report** un informe bastante exacto, más o menos; **~ well** bastante bien, dentro de lo que cabe

reasoned [ˈriːznd] ADJ [*argument*] razonado; **well-~** bien argumentado

reasoning [ˈriːznɪŋ] Ⓐ N razonamiento *m*, lógica *f*; **I don't see the ~ behind this decision** no veo la lógica *or* el razonamiento que hay detrás de esta decisión; **this line of ~ is supported by recent figures** estos argumentos están respaldados por cifras recientes
Ⓑ ADJ racional

reassemble [ˈriːəˈsembl] Ⓐ VT [1] (*Tech*) montar de nuevo, volver a armar
[2] [+ *people*] volver a reunir
Ⓑ VI [1] [*people*] volver a reunirse, juntarse de nuevo
[2] (*Parl*) volver a celebrar una sesión

reassembly [ˌriːəˈsemblɪ] N [1] (*Tech*) nuevo montaje *m*
[2] (*Parl*) inauguración *f* de la nueva sesión, nueva sesión *f*

reassert [ˈriːəˈsɜːt] VT [+ *authority, influence*] reafirmar

reassertion [ˌriːəˈsɜːʃən] N reafirmación *f*

reassess [ˈriːəˈses] VT [+ *situation*] estudiar de nuevo, reestudiar; [+ *tax*] calcular de nuevo; **we shall have to ~ the situation** tendremos que estudiar de nuevo *or* reestudiar la situación

reassessment [ˌriːəˈsesmənt] N [*of situation*] nuevo estudio *m*; (*Fin*) revaloración *f*

reassurance [ˈriːəˈʃʊərəns] N consuelo *m*, confianza *f*; **sometimes we all need ~** hay veces cuando todos necesitamos que se nos anime nuestra confianza

reassure [ˈriːəˈʃʊəʳ] VT tranquilizar; **we ~d her that everything was OK** le aseguramos que todo iba bien; **she felt ~d in the morning** por la mañana ya se sentía más tranquila, por la mañana ya había recuperado la confianza

reassuring [ˈriːəˈʃʊərɪŋ] ADJ (= *pacifying*) tranquilizador; (= *encouraging*) alentador; **to make ~ noises** (*fig*) hacer comentarios tranquilizadores; **it is ~ to know that ...** (me) tranquiliza saber que ..., es tranquilizador saber que ...

reassuringly [ˈriːəˈʃʊərɪŋlɪ] ADV de modo tranquilizador; **he spoke ~** nos tranquilizó con sus palabras; **a ~ strong performance** una actuación cuya fuerza nos alentó; **he was now in ~ familiar surroundings** el entorno era ahora familiar y le hacía sentirse más tranquilo

reawaken [ˈriːəˈweɪkən] Ⓐ VT volver a despertar
Ⓑ VI volver a despertarse, despertarse

reawakening [ˈriːəˈweɪknɪŋ] N despertar *m*

REB N ABBR (= **Revised English Bible**) *versión revisada de la Biblia*

rebarbative [rɪˈbɑːbətɪv] ADJ (*frm*) repugnante, repelente

rebate [ˈriːbeɪt] N [1] (= *discount*) rebaja *f*, descuento *m*
[2] (= *money back*) reembolso *m*, devolución *f*

Rebecca [rɪˈbekə] N Rebeca

rebel [ˈrebl] Ⓐ N rebelde *mf*; **I was a bit of a ~ at school** era un poco rebelde en el colegio
Ⓑ [rɪˈbel] VI (= *rise up*) rebelarse, sublevarse; (= *refuse to conform*) rebelarse; **to ~ against sth/sb** rebelarse contra algo/algn; **at the sight of all that food, his stomach ~led** su estómago se rebeló al ver tanta comida; **I tried to get up but my legs ~led** intenté levantarme pero mis piernas se negaron *or* no me respondieron las piernas
Ⓒ ADJ [*forces, soldiers, factions*] rebelde
Ⓓ CPD ► **rebel leader** N cabecilla *mf*

rebellion [rɪˈbeljən] N rebelión *f*, sublevación *f*

rebellious [rɪˈbeljəs] ADJ rebelde

rebelliousness [rɪˈbeljəsnɪs] N rebeldía *f*

rebind [ˈriːˈbaɪnd] (*pt, pp* **rebound**) VT [1] (*with string etc*) volver a atar
[2] [+ *book, volume*] reencuadernar

rebirth [ˈriːˈbɜːθ] N (*gen*) renacimiento *m*; (= *re-emergence*) resurgimiento *m*

reboot [ˌriːˈbuːt] VT, VI (*Comput*) reinicializar, reiniciar

rebore [ˈriːˈbɔːʳ] (*Tech*) Ⓐ N rectificado *m*
Ⓑ VT rectificar

reborn [ˈriːˈbɔːn] PP **to be ~** renacer

rebound [ˈriːbaʊnd] Ⓐ N **on the ~** (*Sport*) de rebote; **she hit the ball on the ~** dio al balón de rebote; **she married him on the ~** se casó con él por despecho
Ⓑ [rɪˈbaʊnd] VI rebotar

►**rebound on** VI + PREP estallar en la cara de

rebroadcast [ˈriːˈbrɔːdkɑːst] Ⓐ N retransmisión *f*
Ⓑ VT retransmitir

rebuff [rɪˈbʌf] Ⓐ N desaire *m*, rechazo *m*; **to meet with a ~** sufrir un desaire *or* rechazo
Ⓑ VT rechazar, desairar

rebuild [ˈriːˈbɪld] (*pt, pp* **rebuilt**) VT reconstruir

rebuilding [ˈriːˈbɪldɪŋ] N reconstrucción *f*

rebuilt [ˈriːˈbɪlt] PT, PP *of* **rebuild**

rebuke [rɪˈbjuːk] Ⓐ N reprimenda *f*, reproche *m*
Ⓑ VT reprender, reprochar; **to ~ sb for having done sth** reprender a algn por haber hecho algo, reprochar a algn haber hecho algo

rebus [ˈriːbəs] N (*pl* **rebuses**) jeroglífico *m*

rebut [rɪˈbʌt] VT rebatir, impugnar

rebuttal [rɪˈbʌtl] N refutación *f*, impugnación *f*

recalcitrance [rɪˈkælsɪtrəns] N terquedad *f*, contumacia *f* (*frm*)

recalcitrant [rɪˈkælsɪtrənt] ADJ recalcitrante, contumaz (*frm*)

recall [rɪˈkɔːl] Ⓐ N [1] (= *recollection*) recuerdo *m*; (= *ability to remember*) memoria *f*; **those days are gone beyond ~** aquellos días pasaron al olvido; **he has no ~ of what he did** no recuerda nada de lo que hizo; **to have total ~** tener una memoria infalible
[2] (= *calling back*) [*of Parliament*] convocatoria *f* extraordinaria; (*Mil*) [*of troops*] nueva convocatoria *f*
[3] (= *withdrawal*) [*of ambassador*] retirada *f*; [*of defective product*] retirada *f* (del mercado); (*US*) [*of elected official*] destitución *f*; (*Mil*) [*of troops*] retirada *f*; **to sound the ~** tocar la retirada, tocar retreta
Ⓑ VT [1] (= *call back*) [+ *Parliament*] convocar en sesión extraordinaria; [+ *ambassador, capital*] retirar; [+ *sports player*] volver a llamar; [+ *library book*] reclamar; [+ *defective product*] retirar (*del mercado*); (*Mil*) (= *call up*) llamar; (*US Pol*) (= *dismiss*) destituir
[2] (= *remember*) recordar; **I can't ~ exactly what we agreed** no recuerdo exactamente en qué quedamos; **I don't ~ saying that** no recuerdo haber dicho eso; **I seem to ~ that ...** creo recordar que ...
[3] (= *bring to mind*) recordar a; **it ~s the time when ...** recuerda a aquella ocasión en la que ...
[4] (*Comput*) volver a llamar
Ⓒ VI recordar; **I'm sorry, I don't ~** lo siento, no recuerdo; **as I ~ ...** según recuerdo ..., que yo recuerde ...

recant [rɪˈkænt] Ⓐ VT retractar, desdecir
Ⓑ VI retractarse, desdecirse

recantation [ˈriːkænˈteɪʃən] N retractación *f*

recap* [ˈriːkæp] Ⓐ N recapitulación *f*, resumen *m*
Ⓑ VI (= *sum up*) recapitular, resumir

recapitulate [ˌriːkəˈpɪtjʊleɪt] Ⓐ VT [+ *argument, facts*] recapitular, resumir
Ⓑ VI recapitular, resumir

recapitulation [ˈriːkəˌpɪtjʊˈleɪʃən] N recapitulación *f*, resumen *m*

recapture [ˈriːˈkæptʃəʳ] Ⓐ VT [+ *prisoner*] volver a detener; [+ *town*] reocupar, reconquistar (*Hist*); [+ *memory, scene*] hacer revivir, recordar
Ⓑ N [*of prisoner*] detención *f*; [*of town*] reocupación *f*, reconquista *f* (*Hist*)

recast [ˈriːˈkɑːst] (*pt, pp* **recast**) Ⓐ VT [1] (*Theat*) [+ *play*] hacer un nuevo reparto para
[2] (*Tech*) refundir
Ⓑ N (*Tech*) refundición *f*

recce* [ˈrekɪ] (*Brit*) Ⓐ N ABBR (*Mil*) (= **reconnaissance**) reconocimiento *m*
Ⓑ VT (*Mil*) (= **reconnoitre**) reconocer

recd., rec'd ABBR (*Comm*) (= **received**) rbdo

recede [rɪˈsiːd] VI [*tide, flood*] bajar; [*person etc*] volverse atrás; [*view*] alejarse; [*danger*] disminuir; [*chin*] retroceder; **his hair is receding** tiene entradas

receding [rɪˈsiːdɪŋ] Ⓐ ADJ [*prospect*] que va disminuyendo; [*tide*] que va bajando; [*forehead*] huidizo, achatado; [*chin*] (hundida) hacia atrás
Ⓑ CPD ► **receding hairline** N entradas *fpl*

➤**receipt** [rɪˈsiːt] Ⓐ N [1] (= *act of receiving*) recepción *f*, recibo *m*; **to acknowledge ~ of** acusar recibo de; **on ~ of** al recibo de, al recibir; **on ~ of these goods** al recibo de *or* al recibir estas mercancías; **I am in ~ of your letter** (*frm*) he recibido su carta, obra su carta en mi poder (*more frm*); **pay on ~** pago *m* contra entrega *or* al recibo
[2] (= *document*) recibo *m*; **please give me a ~** haga el favor de darme un recibo
[3] **receipts** (= *money taken*) recaudación *fsing*
Ⓑ VT [+ *goods*] dar recibo por; [+ *bill*] poner el "recibí" en
Ⓒ CPD ► **receipt book** N libro *m* talonario

receivable [rɪˈsiːvəbl] Ⓐ ADJ (*Comm*) por cobrar, a cobrar
Ⓑ **receivables** NPL cuentas *fpl* por cobrar

receive [rɪˈsiːv] Ⓐ VT [1] (= *get*) [+ *letter, gift, money, visit, salary, sacrament*] recibir; [+ *stolen goods*] comerciar con; (*Tennis*) [+ *ball, service*] recibir; **all contributions will be gratefully ~d** todas las contribuciones que nos lleguen serán bien recibidas; **she ~d the Nobel Peace Prize in 1989** le otorgaron el premio Nobel de la Paz en 1989; **I never ~d her message** nunca llegué a recibir su mensaje, nunca me llegó su mensaje; **she ~d no support from her colleagues** sus colegas no la apoyaron; **he ~d a wound in the leg** resultó herido en la pierna, sufrió una herida en la pierna; **he ~d a blow to the head** recibió un golpe en la cabeza; **a bowl to ~ the liquid that drains off** un cuenco para recoger el líquido que se escurra; **"received with thanks"** (*Comm*) "recibí"; **their plans ~d a**

➤ LANGUAGE IN USE: **receipt A1** 20.4, 20.5, 20.6

setback sus planes sufrieron un revés; **she is receiving treatment for eczema** está siendo tratada de eczema; **he ~d hospital treatment for cuts to the face** fue tratado en el hospital de unos cortes que tenía en la cara; **he ~d a life sentence** lo sentenciaron a cadena perpetua; **he ~d a suspended sentence** le suspendieron la condena
2 (= *greet*) [+ *visitors*] recibir; [+ *guests*] recibir, acoger; [+ *publication, idea, performance*] acoger; **to be well ~d** [*book, idea*] tener buena acogida; **his suggestion was not well ~d** su sugerencia no tuvo buena acogida; **her book was well ~d** su libro tuvo buena acogida
3 (= *admit*) [+ *new member*] admitir; **to ~ sb into the Church** acoger a algn en el seno de la Iglesia
4 (*Rad, TV*) [+ *transmission*] recibir; **are you receiving me?** ¿me recibe?
Ⓑ VI 1 (= *get*) recibir; ✦*PROV* **it is better to give than to ~** más vale dar que recibir
2 (*Jur*) (= *buy and sell stolen goods*) comerciar con artículos robados
3 (*Tennis*) recibir
4 (*frm*) (*socially*) recibir; **the Duchess ~s on Thursdays** la duquesa recibe los jueves
5 (*Rad, TV*) recibir; **whisky two receiving!** ¡aquí whisky two, te recibo!

received [rɪˈsiːvd] ADJ [*opinion*] aceptado; [*wisdom*] popular; **the ~ wisdom is that ...** la creencia popular es que ...; **it came to represent ~ wisdom in classical Marxist theory** llegó a ser parte de lo que se daba por sentado en la teoría marxista clásica; → ENGLISH

receiver [rɪˈsiːvəʳ] N 1 (= *recipient*) [*of gift, letter*] destinatario/a *m/f*; [*of stolen goods*] comerciante *mf* (*de artículos robados*); (*Psych*) receptor(a) *m/f*
2 (*Telec*) auricular *m*; **to pick up** *or* **lift the ~** coger *or* levantar el auricular; **to put down** *or* **replace the ~** colgar el auricular
3 (*Rad, TV*) receptor *m*
4 (= *liquidator*) (*also* **official ~**) síndico/a *m/f*; **to call in the ~(s)** entrar en liquidación
5 (*US Ftbl*) receptor(a) *m/f*; **wide ~** receptor(a) *m/f* abierto/a

receivership [rɪˈsiːvəʃɪp] N **to go into ~** entrar en liquidación

receiving [rɪˈsiːvɪŋ] Ⓐ N recepción *f*; [*of stolen goods*] receptación *f*, encubrimiento *m*
Ⓑ ADJ ✦*IDIOM* **to be on** *or* **at the ~ end (of sth)*** ser el blanco *or* la víctima (de algo)
Ⓒ CPD ► **receiving set** N receptor *m*, radiorreceptor *m*

recension [rɪˈsenʃən] N recensión *f*

recent [ˈriːsnt] ADJ [*event, survey, trip, photograph, history*] reciente; **his most ~ book** su libro más reciente; **a ~ acquaintance** un conocido de hace poco tiempo; **a ~ arrival** (= *person*) un recién llegado; **~ developments in Biology** los últimos avances en el campo de la biología; **in the ~ past** en los últimos tiempos, en un pasado reciente; **in ~ years** en los últimos años

recently [ˈriːsntlɪ] ADV 1 (= *not long ago*) recientemente, hace poco, recién (*LAm*); **until ~** hasta hace poco; **it is only very ~ that I started painting** empecé a pintar hace muy poco *or* apenas nada; **as ~ as 1998 he was living in London** aún en 1998, todavía vivía él en Londres; **it was discovered as ~ as 1903** se descubrió hace apenas nada, en 1903
2 (= *lately*) últimamente, recientemente; **I haven't heard from her ~** últimamente *or* recientemente no he sabido nada de ella; **just ~ he's been acting strangely** últimamente se ha estado comportando de un modo extraño
3 (*before pp*) recién; **~ arrived** recién llegado

receptacle [rɪˈseptəkl] N (*frm*) receptáculo *m*, recipiente *m*

reception [rɪˈsepʃən] Ⓐ N 1 (= *act of receiving*) recepción *f*, recibimiento *m*
2 (= *welcome*) acogida *f*; **to get a warm ~** tener buena acogida, ser bien recibido
3 (= *social function*) recepción *f*; **the ~ will be at a big hotel** la recepción tendrá lugar en un gran hotel; *see also* **wedding**
4 (*Rad etc*) recepción *f*
5 (*esp Brit*) (*also* **~ desk**) recepción *f*; **please leave your key at ~** por favor dejen la llave en recepción
6 (*Educ*) clase *f* de primer año
Ⓑ CPD ► **reception centre, reception center** (*US*) N centro *m* de recepción ► **reception class** N (*Educ*) clase *f* de primer año ► **reception desk** N (*esp Brit*) (*in hotel, hospital etc*) mostrador *m* de recepción, recepción *f* ► **reception room** N (*esp Brit*) sala *f* de visitas

receptionist [rɪˈsepʃənɪst] N recepcionista *mf*

receptive [rɪˈseptɪv] ADJ receptivo

receptiveness [rɪˈseptɪvnɪs] N, **receptivity** [rɪsepˈtɪvɪtɪ] N receptividad *f*

recess [rɪˈses] Ⓐ N 1 (*Jur, Pol*) (= *cessation of business*) clausura *f*; (*US Jur*) (= *short break*) descanso *m*; (*esp US Scol*) recreo *m*; **parliament is in ~** la sesión del parlamento está suspendida
2 (*Archit*) hueco *m*, nicho *m*
3 (= *secret place*) escondrijo *m*; (*fig*) la parte más oculta; **in the ~es of his mind** en los recovecos de su mente, en lo más oculto de su mente
Ⓑ VI (*US Jur, Parl*) prorrogarse, suspenderse la sesión

recession [rɪˈseʃən] N 1 (*Econ*) recesión *f*; **to be in ~** estar en recesión *or* retroceso
2 (*frm*) (= *receding*) retroceso *m*

recessional [rɪˈseʃənl] N himno *m* de fin de oficio

recessive [rɪˈsesɪv] ADJ recesivo

recharge [ˈriːˈtʃɑːdʒ] VT [+ *battery*] recargar, volver a cargar; **to ~ one's batteries** (*fig*) ponerse las pilas

rechargeable [rɪˈtʃɑːdʒəbl] ADJ recargable

recherché [rəˈʃeəʃeɪ] ADJ rebuscado

rechristen [ˈriːˈkrɪsn] VT (*Rel*) rebautizar; (= *rename*) poner nuevo nombre a; **they have ~ed the boat "Gloria"** han puesto al barco el nuevo nombre de "Gloria"

recidivism [rɪˈsɪdɪvɪzəm] N reincidencia *f*

recidivist [rɪˈsɪdɪvɪst] N reincidente *mf*

recipe [ˈresɪpɪ] Ⓐ N receta *f* (de cocina); **a ~ for** (*also fig*) una receta para; **it's a ~ for disaster** es una forma segura de buscarse problemas
Ⓑ CPD ► **recipe book** N libro *m* de cocina, recetario *m*

recipient [rɪˈsɪpɪənt] N [*of letter, gift*] destinatario/a *m/f*

reciprocal [rɪˈsɪprəkəl] Ⓐ ADJ recíproco, mutuo
Ⓑ N (*Math*) recíproca *f*

reciprocally [rɪˈsɪprəkəlɪ] ADV recíprocamente, mutuamente

reciprocate [rɪˈsɪprəkeɪt] Ⓐ VT [+ *good wishes*] intercambiar, devolver; **and this feeling is ~d** y compartimos este sentimiento; **her kindness was not ~d** su amabilidad no fue correspondida
Ⓑ VI 1 (*gen*) corresponder; **but they did not ~** pero ellos no correspondieron a esto; **he ~d with a short speech** pronunció un breve discurso a modo de contestación
2 (*Mech*) oscilar, alternar

reciprocation [rɪˌsɪprəˈkeɪʃən] N reciprocidad *f*, correspondencia *f*; **there was no ~ of his generosity** su generosidad no fue correspondida

reciprocity [ˌresɪˈprɒsɪtɪ] N reciprocidad *f*

recital [rɪˈsaɪtl] N (*Mus*) recital *m*; (= *story*) relato *m*

recitation [ˌresɪˈteɪʃən] N [*of poetry*] recitación *f*; [*of facts*] relación *f*

recitative [ˌresɪtəˈtiːv] Ⓐ ADJ recitativo
Ⓑ N recitado *m*

recite [rɪˈsaɪt] Ⓐ VT [+ *poetry*] recitar; [+ *story*] relatar; [+ *list*] enumerar; **she ~d her troubles all over again** volvió a detallar todas sus dificultades
Ⓑ VI recitar

reckless [ˈreklɪs] ADJ [*person*] (= *rash*) temerario; (= *wild*) descabellado; (= *thoughtless*) imprudente; [*speed*] peligroso; [*statement*] inconsiderado; **~ driving** conducción *f* temeraria; **he's a ~ driver** conduce temerariamente

recklessly [ˈreklɪslɪ] ADV (= *rashly*) temerariamente; (= *thoughtlessly*) imprudentemente; **to drive ~** conducir temerariamente; **to spend ~** derrochar dinero

recklessness [ˈreklɪsnɪs] N (= *rashness*) temeridad *f*; (= *thoughtlessness*) imprudencia *f*; **the ~ of youth** la temeridad de la juventud; **the ~ of her driving** su modo imprudente de conducir

reckon [ˈrekən] Ⓐ VT 1 (= *calculate*) calcular; **prices are ~ed to be about 2% up on last year** se calcula que los precios han subido en un 2% comparados con respecto al año pasado
2 (= *consider*) considerar; **he is ~ed to be Spain's top conductor** está considerado como el mejor director de orquesta de España
3 (*) (= *think*) creer; **she'll come, I ~** creo *or* me parece que vendrá, se me hace que vendrá (*Mex*); **you ~?** ¿tú crees?, ¿te parece a ti?; **I ~ so** eso creo, creo *or* me parece que sí; **I ~ he must be about 40** calculo que debe estar rondando los 40; **what do you ~ our chances are?** ¿qué posibilidades crees *or* te parece que tenemos?
4 (= *plan, expect*) **to ~ to do sth** contar con poder hacer algo, esperar poder hacer algo; **they ~ to sell most of them abroad** cuentan con *or* esperan poder vender la mayoría en el extranjero
Ⓑ VI (= *count*) contar; **~ing from today** contando a partir de hoy
► **reckon in** VT + ADV tener en cuenta, incluir
► **reckon on** VI + PREP contar con; **you can ~ on 30 people** puedes contar con 30 personas; **to ~ on (sth/sb) doing sth: I'd ~ed on doing that tomorrow** había contado con (que iba a) hacer eso mañana; **I hadn't ~ed on the police arriving** no había contado con que llegara la policía
► **reckon up** VT + ADV (= *calculate, add up*) calcular
► **reckon with** VI + PREP 1 (= *take into account*) contar con, tener en cuenta; **there were factors we had not ~ed with** había factores con los que no habíamos contado, había factores que no habíamos tenido en cuenta; **we hadn't ~ed with having to walk** no habíamos contado con tener que ir a pie; *see also* **force A3**
2 (= *contend with*) vérselas con; **if you offend him you'll have the whole family to ~**

➤ LANGUAGE IN USE: **reception A3** 25.1, 25.2

with si le ofendes tendrás que vértelas con toda la familia

►**reckon without** VI + PREP no contar con, no tener en cuenta; **I had ~ed without her brother** no había contado con *or* tenido en cuenta a su hermano

reckoning ['reknɪŋ] N **1** (= *calculation*) cálculo *m*; **according to my ~** según mis cálculos; **to be out in one's ~** errar en el cálculo; **to come into the ~** entrar en los cálculos; **by any ~** a todas luces
2 (= *bill*) cuenta *f*; **to pay the ~** pagar la cuenta
3 **day of ~** (*fig*) ajuste *m* de cuentas
4 (*Naut*) *see* **dead D**

reclaim [rɪ'kleɪm] Ⓐ VT **1** [+ *throne, title*] reclamar; [+ *language, culture*] recuperar; [+ *inheritance, rights*] reclamar, reivindicar; [+ *baggage*] recoger, reclamar; **she ~ed her British skating title yesterday** ayer reclamó su título británico de patinaje; **you may be eligible to ~ income tax** puede que tenga derecho a que le devuelvan parte de lo que ha pagado del impuesto sobre la renta; **he intended to ~ the money as expenses** tenía pensado cargarlo a la cuenta de la compañía; **the town is gradually being ~ed by the desert** el desierto está reclamando poco a poco el terreno a la ciudad
2 (= *salvage*) [+ *land*] (*gen*) aprovechar; (*from sea*) ganar al mar; [+ *swamp*] sanear; [+ *materials*] recuperar, reciclar
Ⓑ N *see* **baggage**

reclaimable [rɪ'kleɪməbl] ADJ [*land*] recuperable; [*materials, by-products*] recuperable, reciclable

reclamation [,reklə'meɪʃən] N **1** [*of land*] *acción de ganarle terreno al mar o de recuperar tierras pantanosas*; **land ~ scheme/project** un proyecto para ganarle terreno al mar/ recuperar tierras pantanosas
2 [*of materials*] recuperación *f*, reciclaje *m*

recline [rɪ'klaɪn] Ⓐ VI recostarse, reclinarse
Ⓑ VT [+ *head*] recostar, reclinar

reclining [rɪ'klaɪnɪŋ] Ⓐ ADJ [*seat*] reclinable; [*figure, statue*] yacente
Ⓑ CPD ► **reclining chair** N sillón *m* reclinable; (*Med*) silla *f* de extensión

recluse [rɪ'klu:s] N solitario/a *m/f*

reclusion [rɪ'klu:ʒən] N reclusión *f*, soledad *f*

reclusive [rɪ'klu:zɪv] ADJ dado a recluirse, solitario

recognition [,rekəg'nɪʃən] N **1** (= *identification, recollection*) reconocimiento *m*; **he gazed blankly at her, then ~ dawned** la miró sin comprender, entonces cayó en la cuenta de quién era; **the bodies were mutilated beyond** *or* **out of (all) ~** los cuerpos estaban tan mutilados que resultaba imposible reconocerlos; **she has changed beyond ~** ha cambiado tanto que está irreconocible; *see also* **optical, speech**
2 (= *acknowledgement*) reconocimiento *m*; **she hasn't got the ~ she deserves** no ha recibido el reconocimiento que se merece; **there is a growing ~ that ...** hay cada vez más gente que admite que ...; **in ~ of** en reconocimiento de; **the awards he won in ~ of his work** los premios que ganó en reconocimiento del trabajo realizado

recognizable ['rekəgnaɪzəbl] ADJ reconocible; **it is ~ as ...** se le reconoce *or* identifica como ...

recognizance [rɪ'kɒgnɪzəns] N (*esp US Jur*) obligación *f* contraída; (= *sum*) fianza *f*; **to enter into ~s to** + *infin* comprometerse legalmente a + *infin*

►**recognize** ['rekəgnaɪz] VT **1** (= *know again*) reconocer; **I hardly ~d myself** apenas me reconocía *or* me conocía a mí mismo; **he was ~d by two policemen** lo reconocieron dos policías
2 (= *acknowledge*) reconocer, admitir; **are these qualifications ~d in other European countries?** ¿están estos títulos reconocidos en otros países europeos?; **we do not ~ your claim** no reconocemos su derecho a reclamarlo; **they ~ Bosnia as an independent nation** reconocen a Bosnia como nación independiente
3 (*US*) (= *give right to speak*) **the Chair ~s Mr White** el Sr. White tiene la palabra

recognized ['rekəgnaɪzd] ADJ **1** (= *acknowledged*) (*gen*) reconocido, conocido; [*expert*] reconocido; **it is a ~ fact that ...** es un hecho conocido que ....
2 (= *accredited*) [*institution, qualifications*] acreditado

recoil [rɪ'kɔɪl] Ⓐ VI [*person*] echarse atrás, retroceder; [*gun*] dar un culatazo; **to ~ from sth** retroceder *or* dar marcha atrás ante algo; **to ~ from doing sth** rehuir hacer algo; **to ~ in fear** retroceder espantado
Ⓑ N (*at disgusting sight*) retroceso *m*; [*of gun*] culatazo *m*

recoilless [rɪ'kɔɪllɪs] ADJ [*gun*] sin retroceso

recollect [,rekə'lekt] Ⓐ VT recordar, acordarse de
Ⓑ VI recordar, acordarse

recollection [,rekə'lekʃən] N recuerdo *m*; **to the best of my ~** que yo recuerde

recommence ['ri:kə'mens] Ⓐ VT reanudar, recomenzar, volver a comenzar
Ⓑ VI reanudarse, recomenzar, volver a comenzar

►**recommend** [,rekə'mend] VT **1** (= *advocate, speak well of*) recomendar; **to ~ sb for a job** recomendar a algn para un trabajo; **she comes highly ~ed (by Anne)** viene muy bien recomendada (por Anne); **I don't ~ the pizza** no recomiendo la pizza; **the town has much/little to ~ it** el pueblo tiene mucho/ poco atractivo
2 (= *advise*) recomendar, aconsejar; **what do you ~ for a sore throat?** ¿qué recomienda para el dolor de garganta?; **the ~ed daily intake is ...** el consumo diario recomendado *or* aconsejado es ...; **this method is not to be ~ed** este método no es nada recomendable *or* aconsejable; **to ~ doing sth** recomendar *or* aconsejar hacer algo; **the doctor ~ed that he (should) stay in bed** el médico le recomendó *or* aconsejó que guardara cama; **to ~ sb to do sth** recomendar *or* aconsejar a algn hacer algo *or* que haga algo; **I would ~ against going on your own** le recomendaría *or* aconsejaría no ir solo *or* que no fuera solo; **~ed retail price** precio *m* de venta al público recomendado
3 (*frm*) (= *commit*) [+ *person, soul*] encomendar; **I ~ him to your keeping** se lo encomiendo

recommendable [,rekə'mendəbl] ADJ recomendable

recommendation [,rekəmen'deɪʃən] N **1** (= *endorsement*) recomendación *f*; *see also* **letter**
2 (= *suggestion, proposal*) recomendación *f*, sugerencia *f*; **it is my ~ that it should be destroyed** recomiendo que se destruya; **to make ~s** hacer recomendaciones *or* sugerencias; **to do sth on sb's ~** *or* **on the ~ of sb** hacer algo por recomendación *or* consejo de algn, hacer algo siguiendo la recomendación *or* consejo de algn
3 (= *statement*) recomendación *f*
4 (= *good point*) **his good looks were his only ~** su buena presencia era lo único que le salvaba *or* su único atractivo

recommendatory [,rekə'mendətərɪ] ADJ recomendatorio

recompense ['rekəmpens] Ⓐ N (*gen*) recompensa *f*; (*financial*) indemnización *f*
Ⓑ VT (*gen*) recompensar; (*financially*) indemnizar

reconcilable ['rekənsaɪləbl] ADJ conciliable, reconciliable

reconcile ['rekənsaɪl] VT **1** (= *reunite*) [+ *persons*] reconciliar; **to be ~d (with)** estar reconciliado (con); **the couple are now ~d** la pareja está ahora reconciliada
2 (= *make compatible*) [+ *theories, ideals*] conciliar; **she ~d the conflicting pressures of motherhood and career** concilió las exigencias contrapuestas de la maternidad y de una profesión
3 (= *settle*) [+ *differences*] resolver; **you must try and ~ your differences** tenéis que intentar resolver vuestras diferencias
4 (= *resign*) **what ~d him to it was ...** lo que hizo que lo aceptara fue ...; **to become ~d to sth** aceptar algo, resignarse a algo; **to ~ o.s. to sth** resignarse a algo
5 [+ *accounts*] hacer cuadrar, conciliar (*frm*)

reconciliation [,rekənsɪlɪ'eɪʃən] N **1** (= *reuniting*) reconciliación *f*; **to bring about a ~** lograr una reconciliación
2 (= *making compatible*) [*of theories, ideals*] conciliación *f*
3 [*of accounts*] conciliación *f*

recondite [rɪ'kɒndaɪt] ADJ (*frm*) recóndito

recondition ['ri:kən'dɪʃən] VT reacondicionar

reconnaissance [rɪ'kɒnɪsəns] Ⓐ N reconocimiento *m*; **to make a ~** reconocer *or* explorar el terreno, hacer un reconocimiento del terreno
Ⓑ CPD ► **reconnaissance flight** N vuelo *m* de reconocimiento

reconnoitre, **reconnoiter** (*US*) [,rekə'nɔɪtəʳ] (*Mil*) Ⓐ VT reconocer, explorar
Ⓑ VI hacer un reconocimiento

reconquer ['ri:'kɒŋkəʳ] VT reconquistar

reconquest ['ri:'kɒŋkwest] N reconquista *f*; **the Reconquest** [*of Spain*] la Reconquista

reconsider ['ri:kən'sɪdəʳ] Ⓐ VT reconsiderar, repensar
Ⓑ VI reconsiderar, repensar

reconsideration ['ri:kən,sɪdə'reɪʃən] N reconsideración *f*; **on ~** después de volver sobre ello

reconstitute ['ri:'kɒnstɪtju:t] VT [+ *events*] (= *piece together*) reconstituir; **~d food** alimentos *mpl* reconstituidos

reconstitution ['ri:,kɒnstɪ'tju:ʃən] N reconstitución *f*

reconstruct ['ri:kən'strʌkt] VT [+ *building*] reconstruir; [+ *crime, scene of crime*] reconstituir

reconstruction ['ri:kən'strʌkʃən] N reconstrucción *f*

reconvene [,ri:kən'vi:n] Ⓐ VT reconvocar
Ⓑ VI [*committee, jury etc*] reunirse

reconvert ['ri:kən'vɜ:t] VT volver a convertir (**to** en)

record ['rekɔ:d] Ⓐ N **1** (= *report, account*) (*gen*) documento *m*; (= *note*) nota *f*, apunte *m*; [*of meeting*] acta *f*; [*of attendance*] registro *m*; (*Jur*) [*of case*] acta *f*; **it is the earliest written ~ of this practice** es el documento escrito más antiguo que registra esta costumbre; **there is no ~ of it** no hay constancia de ello, no consta en ningún sitio; **the highest**

➤ LANGUAGE IN USE: **recognize 2** 26.3 **recommend 1, 2** 2.2, 19.4

temperatures since ~s began las temperaturas más altas que se han registrado hasta la fecha; **for the ~**: **for the ~, I disagree** no estoy de acuerdo, que conste; **will you tell us your full name for the ~, please?** ¿podría decirnos su nombre completo para que quede constancia?; **to keep** *or* **make a ~ of sth** apuntar algo, tomar nota de algo; **it is a matter of (public) ~ that ...** hay constancia de que ...; **off the ~** [*statement, comment*] extraoficial; [*speak, say*] extraoficialmente; **this is strictly off the ~** esto es estrictamente extraoficial; **he told me off the ~** me dijo confidencialmente *or* extraoficialmente; **on ~**: **there is no similar example on ~** no existe constancia de nada semejante; **the police had kept his name on ~** la policía lo había fichado; **the highest temperatures on ~** las temperaturas más altas que se han registrado hasta la fecha; **to be/have gone on ~ as saying that ...** haber declarado públicamente que ...; **to place** *or* **put sth on ~** hacer constar algo, dejar constancia de algo; **just to put** *or* **set the ~ straight, let me point out that ...** simplemente para que quede claro, permítanme señalar que ...; *see also* **off-the-record**

2 (= *memorial*) testimonio *m*; **the First World War is a ~ of human folly** la primera Guerra Mundial es un testimonio de la locura humana

3 (*Comput*) registro *m*

4 **records** (= *files*) archivos *mpl*; **according to our ~s, you have not paid** según nuestros datos, usted no ha pagado; **public ~s** archivos *mpl* públicos

5 (= *past performance*) 5·1 (*in work*) **to have a good ~ at school** tener un buen expediente escolar; **the airline has a good safety ~** la compañía aérea tiene un buen historial en materia de seguridad; **his past ~ is against him** su historial obra en perjuicio suyo; **a country's human rights ~** el historial *or* la trayectoria de un país en materia de derechos humanos; **he left behind a splendid ~ of achievements** ha dejado atrás una magnífica hoja de servicios; *see also* **track D**

5·2 (*Med*) historial *m*; **the result will go on your medical ~** el resultado se incluirá en su historial médico

5·3 (*also* **criminal ~**) antecedentes *mpl* (penales); **he's got a clean ~** no tiene antecedentes (penales); **he's got a ~ as long as my arm** tiene un historial más largo que un día sin pan; **~ of previous convictions** antecedentes penales; *see also* **police**

5·4 (*Mil*) hoja *f* de servicios; **war ~** historial *m* de guerra

6 (*Sport etc*) récord *m*; **the long jump ~** el récord del salto de longitud; **to beat** *or* **break the ~** batir el récord; **the film broke box office ~s** la película batió récords de taquilla; **he won a place in the ~ books** se ganó un lugar en el libro de los récords; **to hold the ~ (for sth)** tener *or* ostentar el récord (de algo); **to set a ~ (for sth)** establecer un récord (de algo); *see also* **world B**

7 (= *disc*) disco *m*; **to cut** *or* **make a ~** grabar un disco; **on ~** en disco; *see also* **long-playing**

Ⓑ ADJ récord, sin precedentes; **in ~ time** en un tiempo récord; **share prices closed at a ~ high** la bolsa cerró con los precios más altos jamás registrados

Ⓒ [rɪˈkɔːd] VT 1 (= *set down*) [+ *facts*] registrar; [+ *events*] (*in journal, diary*) tomar nota de; [+ *protest, disapproval*] hacer constar, dejar constancia de; **the fastest speed ever ~ed** la mayor velocidad jamás registrada; **shares ~ed a 16% fall** las acciones registraron una bajada de un 16%; **it is not ~ed anywhere** no consta en ninguna parte; **her letters ~ the details of diplomatic life in China** sus cartas dejan constancia de los detalles de la vida diplomática en China; **history ~s that ...** la historia cuenta que ...

2 (= *show*) [*instrument*] registrar, marcar

3 [+ *sound, images, data*] grabar

4 (*Comput*) grabar

Ⓓ [rɪˈkɔːd] VI (*on tape, film etc*) grabar; **his voice does not ~ well** su voz no sale bien en las grabaciones

Ⓔ [ˈrekɔːd] CPD ► **record breaker** N (= *woman*) plusmarquista *f*; (= *man*) recordman *m*, plusmarquista *m* ► **record card** N ficha *f* ► **record company** N casa *f* discográfica ► **record holder** N (= *woman*) plusmarquista *f*; (= *man*) recordman *m*, plusmarquista *m*; **she is the world 800 metre ~ holder** tiene *or* ostenta el récord mundial de los 800 metros, es la plusmarquista mundial de los 800 metros ► **record keeping** N archivación *f* ► **record library** N discoteca *f* ► **record player** N tocadiscos *m inv* ► **record producer** N productor(a) *m/f* discográfico/a ► **record token** N vale *m* para discos

record-breaking [ˈrekɔːd,breɪkɪŋ] ADJ [*person, team*] batidor del récord; [*effort, run*] récord

recorded [rɪˈkɔːdɪd] ADJ 1 [*music, programme*] grabado

2 [*history*] escrito, documentado; **it is a ~ fact that ...** hay constancia de que ...; **~ delivery** (*Brit Post*) servicio *m* de entrega con acuse de recibo

recorder [rɪˈkɔːdəʳ] N 1 (= *tape recorder*) casete *m* (*Sp*), grabadora *f* (*LAm*); (*reel-to-reel*) magnetófono *m*; (= *video recorder*) vídeo *m*, video *m* (*LAm*)

2 (*Jur*) juez *mf* municipal

3 (*Mus*) (= *instrument*) flauta *f* dulce

4 (= *person*) registrador(a) *m/f*, archivero/a *m/f*; **he was a faithful ~ of the facts** registró puntualmente los hechos

recording [rɪˈkɔːdɪŋ] Ⓐ N 1 (= *tape, disc*) grabación *f*; **to make a ~ (of sth)** realizar una grabación (de algo); *see also* **sound D**, **tape C**, **video C**

2 (= *act*) [*of sound, images*] grabación *f*; [*of facts*] registro *m*

Ⓑ CPD ► **the Recording Angel** N *el ánge que registra las acciones buenas o malas de los hombres* ► **recording artist** N artista *mf* dedicado/a a la grabación ► **recording density** N densidad *f* de grabación ► **recording equipment** N equipo *m* de grabación ► **the recording industry** N la industría discográfica ► **recording session** N sesión *f* de grabación ► **recording studio** N estudio *m* de grabación ► **recording tape** N cinta *f* de grabación, cinta *f* magnetofónica ► **recording van** N camión *m* de grabación

recordist [rɪˈkɔːdɪst] N (*Cine, TV*) sonista *mf*

recount [ˈriːˈkaʊnt] VT contar, relatar

re-count [ˈriːkaʊnt] Ⓐ N [*of votes etc*] recuento *m*; **to have a ~** someter los votos a un segundo escrutinio

Ⓑ [riːˈkaʊnt] VT volver a contar

recoup [rɪˈkuːp] VT recobrar, recuperar

recourse [rɪˈkɔːs] N **to have ~ to** recurrir a

recover [rɪˈkʌvəʳ] Ⓐ VT 1 (= *regain*) [+ *faculty*] recuperar, recobrar (*frm*); **he fought to ~ his balance** luchó por recuperar *or* (*frm*) recobrar el equilibrio; **to ~ consciousness** recobrar el conocimiento; **~ing himself with a masterly effort he resumed his narrative** reponiéndose *or* sobreponiéndose con un esfuerzo sobrehumano, terminó su narración; *see also* **composure**

2 (= *retrieve*) [+ *bodies, wreck*] rescatar; [+ *debt*] cobrar; [+ *stolen property, costs, losses, investment*] recuperar; (*Jur*) [+ *money*] recuperar; [+ *property*] reivindicar, recuperar; (*Comput*) [+ *data*] recobrar, recuperar; **to ~ damages from sb** ser indemnizado por daños y perjuicios por algn

3 (= *reclaim*) [+ *materials*] recuperar

Ⓑ VI 1 (*after accident, illness*) reponerse, recuperarse, restablecerse (**from** de); (*after shock, blow*) sobreponerse, reponerse (**from** de); **he ~ed from being 4-2 down to reach the semi-finals** se recuperó tras ir perdiendo 4-2 y llegó a las semifinales

2 (*Fin*) [*currency*] recuperarse, restablecerse; [*shares, stock market*] volver a subir; [*economy*] reactivarse

re-cover [ˈriːˈkʌvəʳ] VT [+ *chair, sofa*] tapizar de nuevo; [+ *book*] forrar de nuevo

recoverable [rɪˈkʌvərəbl] ADJ recuperable; (*at law*) reivindicable

recovery [rɪˈkʌvərɪ] Ⓐ N 1 (*after accident, illness*) recuperación *f*, restablecimiento *m* (*frm*); (*after shock, blow*) recuperación *f*; (*Fin*) [*of currency*] recuperación *f*; (*Econ*) reactivación *f*; **her chances of ~ are not good** no tiene muchas posibilidades de recuperarse; **to be in ~** (*from addiction*) estar en rehabilitación; **to make a ~** recuperarse, restablecerse; **she has made a full ~** se ha recuperado *or* restablecido completamente; **prices made a slow ~** las cotizaciones tardaron en restablecerse; **to be on the road** *or* **way to ~** (*Med*) estar camino de la recuperación; (*Econ*) estar camino de la reactivación

2 (= *retrieval*) [*of bodies, wreck*] rescate *m*; [*of debt*] cobro *m*; [*of stolen property*] recuperación *f*; (*Jur*) [*of money*] recuperación *f*; [*of property*] reivindicación *f*, recuperación *f*; (*Comput*) [*of data*] recuperación *f*; **an action for ~ of damages** una demanda por daños y perjuicios

3 (= *reclaiming*) [*of materials*] recuperación *f*

Ⓑ CPD ► **recovery room** N (*Med*) sala *f* de posoperatorio ► **recovery service** N (*Aut*) servicio *m* de rescate ► **recovery ship, recovery vessel** N nave *f* de salvamento ► **recovery time** N tiempo *m* de recuperación ► **recovery vehicle** N (*Aut*) grúa *f* ► **recovery ward** N (*Med*) sala *f* de posoperatorio

recreant†† [ˈrekrɪənt] Ⓐ N cobarde *mf*

Ⓑ ADJ cobarde

re-create [ˈriːkrɪˈeɪt] VT (= *create again*) recrear, volver a crear

recreation [,rekrɪˈeɪʃən] Ⓐ N 1 (= *amusement*) (*also Scol*) recreo *m*

2 (= *reconstruction*) reconstrucción *f*; (*Theat*) recreación *f*; (= *representation*) representación *f*

Ⓑ CPD ► **recreation centre, recreation center** (*US*) N centro *m* de recreo ► **recreation ground** N campo *m* de deportes ► **recreation room** N salón *m* de recreo

recreational [,rekrɪˈeɪʃənəl] Ⓐ ADJ [*activity*] recreativo; [*drug*] de placer

Ⓑ CPD ► **recreational facilities** NPL facilidades *fpl* de recreo ► **recreational vehicle** N (*US*) caravana *f or* rulota *f* pequeña

recreative [ˈrekrɪ,eɪtɪv] ADJ recreativo

recriminate [rɪˈkrɪmɪneɪt] VI recriminar

recrimination [rɪ,krɪmɪˈneɪʃən] N recriminación *f*

recross [ˈriːˈkrɒs] VT, VI volver a cruzar

recrudesce [,riːkruːˈdes] VI (*liter*) recrudecer

recrudescence [ˌriːkruːˈdesns] N (*liter*) recrudescencia *f*, recrudecimiento *m*

recrudescent [ˌriːkruːˈdesnt] ADJ (*liter*) recrudescente

recruit [rɪˈkruːt] Ⓐ N (*Mil*) recluta *mf*; (*to organization*) adquisición *f*; **Janet is our latest ~** (*hum*) Janet es nuestra última adquisición *or* nuestro último fichaje*; **new ~** (*Mil*) nuevo recluta; (*to organization*) nuevo/a *m/f*; **raw ~** (*Mil*) quinto *m*, soldado *mf* raso; (*fig*) novato/a *m/f*
Ⓑ VT [1] (= *enlist*) (*Mil*) reclutar; [+ *staff*] contratar; [+ *new members*] buscar; **he was ~ed into the army at 18** lo reclutaron con 18 años; **they ~ed me to help** me reclutaron para que ayudara
[2] (= *obtain, seek out*) [+ *help*] reclutar; [+ *talent*] buscar
Ⓒ VI (*Mil*) alistar reclutas; (*Comm*) reclutar gente; **I am ~ing for staff now** ahora estoy reclutando personal para la plantilla

recruiting [rɪˈkruːtɪŋ] Ⓐ N reclutamiento *m*
Ⓑ CPD ► **recruiting office** N caja *f* de reclutas ► **recruiting officer** N oficial *mf* de reclutamiento

recruitment [rɪˈkruːtmənt] Ⓐ N (*Mil*) reclutamiento *m*; [*of staff*] contratación *f*
Ⓑ CPD ► **recruitment agency** N agencia *f* de colocaciones

rec't ABBR = **receipt**

rectal [ˈrektəl] ADJ rectal

rectangle [ˈrekˌtæŋgl] N rectángulo *m*

rectangular [rekˈtæŋgjʊləʳ] ADJ rectangular

rectifiable [ˈrektɪfaɪəbl] ADJ rectificable

rectification [ˌrektɪfɪˈkeɪʃən] N rectificación *f*

rectifier [ˈrektɪfaɪəʳ] N (*Elec, Chem etc*) rectificador *m*; (*Mech*) rectificadora *f*

rectify [ˈrektɪfaɪ] VT rectificar

rectilinear [ˌrektɪˈlɪnɪəʳ] ADJ rectilíneo

rectitude [ˈrektɪtjuːd] N (*frm*) rectitud *f*

rector [ˈrektəʳ] N (*Rel*) párroco *m*; (*Univ etc*) rector(a) *m/f*

rectory [ˈrektərɪ] N casa *f* del párroco

rectum [ˈrektəm] N (*pl* **rectums, recta**) (*Anat*) recto *m*

recumbent [rɪˈkʌmbənt] ADJ [*figure, statue*] yacente; [*person*] recostado, acostado

recuperate [rɪˈkuːpəreɪt] Ⓐ VI recuperarse, reponerse, restablecerse; **to ~ after an illness** recuperarse *or* reponerse de una enfermedad; **to be recuperating from sth** estar convaleciente de algo
Ⓑ VT [+ *losses*] recuperar

recuperation [rɪˌkuːpəˈreɪʃən] N (*Med*) recuperación *f*, restablecimiento *m*; [*of losses*] recuperación *f*

recuperative [rɪˈkuːpərətɪv] ADJ [*powers, medicine*] recuperativo

recur [rɪˈkɜːʳ] VI (= *happen again*) [*pain, illness*] producirse de nuevo; [*event, mistake, theme*] repetirse; [*difficulty, opportunity*] volver a presentarse; **the idea ~s constantly in his work** la idea se repite constantemente en su obra

recurrence [rɪˈkʌrəns] N [*of event, mistake, theme*] repetición *f*; (*Med*) reaparición *f*, recurrencia *f*

recurrent [rɪˈkʌrənt] ADJ [*problem, feature*] repetido, constante; (*Anat, Med*) recurrente; **it is a ~ theme** es un tema constante *or* que se repite a menudo

recurring [rɪˈkɜːrɪŋ] Ⓐ ADJ (*Math*) **3.3333 ~** 3,3 periódico puro
Ⓑ CPD ► **recurring decimal** N decimal *m* periódico

recusant [ˈrekjʊzənt] Ⓐ ADJ recusante
Ⓑ N recusante *mf*

recyclable [ˌriːˈsaɪkləbl] ADJ reciclable

recycle [ˌriːˈsaɪkl] VT reciclar

recycling [ˌriːˈsaɪklɪŋ] Ⓐ N reciclado *m*, reciclaje *m*
Ⓑ CPD ► **recycling plant** N planta *f* de reciclado *or* reciclaje

red [red] Ⓐ ADJ (*compar* **redder**, *superl* **reddest**)
[1] (*gen*) [*apple, sweater, lips, pen*] rojo, colorado; [*flower, sky*] rojo; [*wine*] tinto; **the traffic lights are ~** el semáforo está en rojo; **his eyes were ~** (*from crying*) tenía los ojos rojos; **the ~ evening sun** el sol rojizo del atardecer; **bright ~** rojo fuerte *or* chillón; **dark ~** rojo oscuro; **deep ~** rojo intenso; **to have ~ hair** ser pelirrojo; ✦***IDIOMS*** **it's like a ~ rag to a bull** es lo que más le saca de quicio; **to roll out the ~ carpet for sb** recibir a algn por todo lo alto *or* a bombo y platillo; **to give sb the ~ carpet treatment** tratar a algn a cuerpo de rey; **not a ~ cent** (*US**) ni una gorda*; ✦***PROV*** **~ sky at night, shepherd's delight, ~ sky in the morning, shepherd's warning** el cielo rojo por la noche es señal de buen tiempo, el cielo rojo por la mañana de mal tiempo; *see also* **paint B2**
[2] (= *flushed*) [*face, cheeks*] (*with shame*) sonrojado; (*with anger*) rojo; (*with embarrassment*) rojo, colorado; **to be ~ in the face** (*from anger, exertion, heat*) estar rojo, tener la cara encendida (*liter*); (*from embarrassment*) estar rojo *or* colorado, tener la cara encendida (*liter*); **to go ~ in the face** (*from anger, exertion, heat*) ponerse rojo *or* colorado; (*with embarrassment*) ponerse colorado; (*with shame*) sonrojarse; ✦***IDIOM*** **to go** *or* **turn as ~ as a beetroot** ponerse como un tomate
[3] (*Pol** *pej*) rojo; ✦***PROV*** **better ~ than dead** más vale el vivir bajo los comunistas que morir luchando contra ellos
Ⓑ N [1] (= *colour*) (color *m*) rojo *m*; **to be dressed in ~** ir vestido de rojo; **it was underlined in ~** estaba subrayado en rojo; ✦***IDIOMS*** **to be in the ~** [*account, firm*] estar en números rojos; **I'm £100 in the ~** tengo un descubierto de 100 libras en el banco; **to go into** *or* **get into the ~** contraer deudas; **to get out of the ~** liquidar las deudas; **to see ~** sulfurarse, salirse de sus casillas; **this makes me see ~** esto me saca de quicio
[2] (*Pol** *pej*) (= *person*) rojo/a *m/f*; ✦***IDIOM*** **~s under the bed*** la amenaza comunista
[3] (= *red wine*) tinto *m*
Ⓒ CPD ► **red admiral** N vanesa *f* roja ► **red alert** N alerta *f* roja; **to be on ~ alert** estar en alerta roja ► **the Red Army** N el Ejército Rojo ► **red blood cell** N glóbulo *m* rojo ► **red cabbage** N col *f* lombarda, lombarda *f* ► **red card** N (*Ftbl*) tarjeta *f* roja; **to show sb the ~ card** sacar a algn la tarjeta roja; (*fig*) (= *reprimand*) llamar al orden a algn, amonestar a algn; (= *force to resign*) destituir a algn ► **red cedar** N cedro *m* rojo ► **red cell** N glóbulo *m* rojo ► **Red China** N China *f* comunista ► **red corpuscle** N corpúsculo *m* rojo ► **Red Cross** N Cruz *f* Roja ► **red deer** N ciervo *m* común ► **red ensign** N (*Naut*) enseña *f* roja ► **red eye** N (*Phot*) ojo *m* rojo; *see also* **redeye** ► **red flag** N (*on beach, etc*) bandera *f* roja ► **red giant** N (*Astron*) gigante *m* rojo ► **red heat** N calor *m* rojo ► **red herring** N (*fig*) pista *f* falsa, despiste *m* ► **Red Indian** N piel roja *mf* ► **red lead** N minio *m* ► **red light** N (*Aut*) luz *f* roja; **to go through a ~ light** saltarse un semáforo en rojo; *see also* **red-light district** ► **red meat** N carne *f* roja ► **red mullet** N salmonete *m* ► **red pepper** N (= *capsicum*) pimiento *m* rojo, pimiento *m* morrón, pimentón *m* rojo (*LAm*); (= *powder*) pimienta *f* de cayena ► **Red Riding Hood** N (*also* **Little Red Riding Hood**) Caperucita *f* Roja ► **red salmon** N salmón *m* rojo ► **Red Sea** N Mar *m* Rojo ► **red sea bream** N besugo *m* (rojo) ► **red setter** N setter *m* irlandés ► **red snapper** N pargo *m* ► **red spider mite** N arador *m* *or* ácaro *m* de la sarna ► **Red Square** N (*in Moscow*) Plaza *f* Roja ► **red squirrel** N ardilla *f* roja ► **red tape** N trámites *mpl*, papeleo *m* ► **red wine** N vino *m* tinto, tinto *m*

redact [rɪˈdækt] VT redactar

redaction [rɪˈdækʃən] N redacción *f*

red-berried [ˈredˈberɪd] ADJ con bayas rojas

red-blooded [ˈredˈblʌdɪd] ADJ (*fig*) viril

redbreast [ˈredbrest] N (= *bird*) petirrojo *m*; **robin ~** petirrojo *m*

redbrick [ˈredbrɪk] ADJ [*university*] *construido en el siglo XIX y fuera de Londres*; [*building*] de ladrillo

REDBRICK UNIVERSITY

El término **redbrick university** *se aplica a las universidades británicas construidas en los grandes centros urbanos industriales como Birmingham, Liverpool o Manchester a finales del siglo XIX o principios del XX. Deben su nombre a que sus edificios son normalmente de ladrillo, a diferencia de las universidades tradicionales de Oxford y Cambridge, cuyos edificios suelen ser de piedra.*

redcap [ˈredkæp] N [1] (*Brit Mil**) policía *mf* militar
[2] (*US Rail*) mozo *m* de estación

red-card [redˈkɑːd] VT (*Sport*) expulsar, mostrar la tarjeta roja a

redcoat [ˈredkəʊt] N (*Hist*) *soldado inglés del siglo XVIII etc*

redcurrant [ˈredˈkʌrənt] N (= *fruit*) grosella *f* roja; (= *bush*) grosellero *m* rojo

redden [ˈredn] Ⓐ VT enrojecer, teñir de rojo
Ⓑ VI [1] [*sky, leaves*] enrojecerse, ponerse rojo
[2] [*person*] (= *blush*) ponerse colorado, ruborizarse; (*with anger*) ponerse rojo *or* colorado

reddish [ˈredɪʃ] ADJ [*colour, hair*] rojizo

redecorate [ˈriːˈdekəreɪt] VT [+ *room, house*] redecorar, renovar el decorado de; (*with paint*) pintar de nuevo; (*with wallpaper*) volver a empapelar

redecoration [riːˌdekəˈreɪʃən] N renovación *f*

redeem [rɪˈdiːm] VT (*Rel*) [+ *sinner*] redimir; (= *buy back*) [+ *pawned goods*] desempeñar; (*Fin*) [+ *debt, mortgage*] amortizar; (= *fulfil*) [+ *promise, obligation*] cumplir; (= *compensate for*) [+ *fault*] expiar; **to ~ o.s.** redimirse

redeemable [rɪˈdiːməbl] ADJ (*Comm*) reembolsable; (*Fin*) amortizable

Redeemer [rɪˈdiːməʳ] N (*Rel*) Redentor *m*

redeeming [rɪˈdiːmɪŋ] ADJ **I see no ~ feature in it** no le encuentro ninguna cosa buena *or* ningún punto favorable; **~ virtue** virtud *f* compensadora

redefine [ˌriːdɪˈfaɪn] VT redefinir

redemption [rɪˈdempʃən] Ⓐ N (*Rel*) redención *f*; (*Fin*) amortización *f*; **to be beyond** *or* **past ~** (*fig*) no tener remedio
Ⓑ CPD ► **redemption price** N precio *m* de retroventa ► **redemption value** N valor *m* de rescate

redemptive [rɪˈdemptɪv] ADJ redentor

redeploy [ˈriːdɪˈplɔɪ] VT [+ *troops, forces*] cambiar de destino; [+ *resources*] disponer de otro modo, reorganizar; [+ *workers, staff*] (*at existing location*) redistribuir, adscribir; (*to new location*) cambiar de oficina/sucursal, *etc*

redeployment [ˈriːdɪˈplɔɪmənt] N (= *rearrangement*) disposición *f* nueva; (= *redistribution*) redistribución *f*; (*Mil*) cambio *m* de destino

redevelop [ˌriːdɪˈveləp] VT [+ *land, site*] reurbanizar; [+ *building, property*] remodelar

redevelopment [ˌriːdɪˈveləpmənt] N [*of land, site*] reurbanización *f*; [*of building, property*] remodelación *f*

redeye* [ˈredˌaɪ] N (*esp US*) (= *night flight*) (*also* ~ **flight**) vuelo *m* de noche

red-eyed [ˈredˈaɪd] ADJ con los ojos enrojecidos

red-faced [ˈredˈfeɪst] ADJ (*lit*) con la cara roja; (*fig*) (= *ashamed*) ruborizado, avergonzado; (*with anger*) con la cara encendida *or* colorada *or* roja (*de ira*)

red-haired [ˈredˈhɛəd] ADJ pelirrojo

red-handed [ˈredˈhændɪd] ADJ ♦*IDIOM* **to catch sb ~** pillar *or* coger *or* (*LAm*) agarrar a algn con las manos en la masa

redhead [ˈredhed] N pelirrojo/a *m/f*

red-headed [ˈredˈhedɪd] ADJ pelirrojo

red-hot [ˈredˈhɒt] ADJ 1 (*lit*) [*iron, poker*] candente
2 (*) (*fig*) 2·1 (= *up to the moment*) [*news, information*] de última hora
2·2 (= *very sharp*) [*cardplayer, tennis player etc*] de primera categoría
2·3 (= *very popular*) muy de moda

redial [riːˈdaɪəl] Ⓐ VT volver a marcar
Ⓑ VI volver a marcar el número
Ⓒ N **automatic ~** marcación *f* automática

redirect [ˈriːdaɪˈrekt] VT [+ *letter*] remitir; [+ *energies*] emplear de otro modo; [+ *traffic*] desviar, dirigir por otra ruta

rediscover [ˈriːdɪsˈkʌvəʳ] VT redescubrir, volver a descubrir

rediscovery [ˈriːdɪsˈkʌvərɪ] N redescubrimiento *m*

redistribute [ˈriːdɪsˈtrɪbjuːt] VT distribuir de nuevo, volver a distribuir

redistribution [ˈriːˌdɪstrɪˈbjuːʃən] N redistribución *f*

red-letter [ˈredˈletəʳ] ADJ **~ day** (*fig*) (= *memorable day*) día *m* señalado; **~ version** (*of Bible*) *edición de la Biblia con la palabra de Jesucristo impresa en rojo*

red-light district [ˌredˈlaɪtdɪstrɪkt] N zona *f* de tolerancia, barrio *m* chino (*Sp*)

redneck [ˈrednek] N (*US*) campesino *m* blanco de los estados del Sur

redness [ˈrednɪs] N [*of skin, hair*] rojez *f*

redo [ˈriːˈduː] (*pt* **redid**; *pp* **redone**) VT rehacer, volver a hacer

redolence [ˈredəʊləns] N fragancia *f*, perfume *m*

redolent [ˈredəʊlənt] ADJ **~ of** oliente *or* con fragancia a; **to be ~ of** (*fig*) recordar, hacer pensar en

redouble [riːˈdʌbl] Ⓐ VT 1 (= *intensify*) [+ *activity, effort*] redoblar, intensificar
2 (*Bridge*) redoblar
Ⓑ VI 1 (= *intensify*) redoblarse, intensificarse
2 (*Bridge*) redoblar

redoubt [rɪˈdaʊt] N reducto *m*; **the last ~ of** el último reducto de

redoubtable [rɪˈdaʊtəbl] ADJ temible

redound [rɪˈdaʊnd] VI **to ~ upon sb** repercutir sobre algn; **to ~ to sb's credit** redundar en beneficio de algn

redraft [ˈriːˈdrɑːft] VT redactar de nuevo

redraw [ˈriːˈdrɔː] (*pt* **redrew**; *pp* **redrawn**) VT [+ *picture*] volver a dibujar; [+ *map, plan*] volver a trazar

redress [rɪˈdres] Ⓐ N (= *compensation*) compensación *f*, indemnización *f*; (*for offence*) reparación *f*; (= *satisfaction*) desagravio *m*; **to seek ~ for** solicitar compensación por; **in such a case you have no ~** en tal caso usted no tiene derecho a compensación
Ⓑ VT (= *compensate for*) reparar, indemnizar; [+ *offence*] reparar; [+ *fault*] remediar; **to ~ the balance** equilibrar la balanza

redshank [ˈredʃæŋk] N archibebe *m*

redskin [ˈredskɪn] N piel roja *m*

redstart [ˈredstɑːt] N colirrojo *m* real

reduce [rɪˈdjuːs] Ⓐ VT 1 (= *decrease*) [+ *number, costs, expenditure, inflation*] reducir; [+ *price*] rebajar; (*Ind*) [+ *output*] reducir, recortar; [+ *speed, heat, visibility*] disminuir; [+ *temperature*] bajar; [+ *stress, tension*] reducir, disminuir; [+ *pain*] aliviar; **it ~s the risk of heart disease (by 20%)** disminuye el riesgo de enfermedades cardíacas (en un 20%); **"reduce speed now"** "disminuya la velocidad"
2 (= *cut price of*) [+ *goods*] rebajar
3 (= *make smaller*) [+ *drawing*] reducir; (*Med*) [+ *swelling*] bajar; (*Culin*) [+ *sauce*] reducir
4 (= *bring to specified state*) **to ~ sb to despair** llevar a algn a la desesperación; **to ~ sb to tears** hacer llorar a algn; **to be ~d to penury** estar sumido en la miseria; **to ~ sth to ashes/rubble** reducir algo a cenizas/escombros; **to ~ sb to silence** hacer callar a algn; **we were ~d to begging on the streets** nos vimos obligados a mendigar por las calles; *see also* **minimum**
5 (= *capture, subjugate*) tomar, conquistar
6 (*Mil*) (= *demote*) degradar; **to ~ sb to the ranks** degradar a algn a soldado raso
7 (= *simplify*) reducir; **to ~ an argument to its simplest form** reducir un argumento a su esencia
8 (*Math*) [+ *equation, expression*] reducir
9 (*Chem*) reducir
Ⓑ VI 1 (= *decrease*) reducirse, disminuir
2 (*Culin*) espesarse
3 (= *slim*) adelgazar

reduced [rɪˈdjuːst] ADJ 1 (= *lower*) [*numbers, cost, expenditure*] reducido; [*price*] reducido, rebajado; **at a ~ rate** con una tarifa reducida *or* rebajada, con rebaja *or* descuento; **non-smokers have a ~ risk of heart disease** los no fumadores tienen menos riesgo de contraer enfermedades cardíacas; **I had to get used to living on a ~ income** me tuve que acostumbrar a vivir con pocos ingresos; **"reduced to clear"** "rebajas por liquidación"
2 (= *smaller*) [*size*] reducido; **French troops will have a ~ role in the area** las tropas francesas desempeñarán un papel poco importante en la zona; **on a ~ scale** a escala reducida
3 (= *straitened*) **to be living in ~ circumstances** (*frm, hum*) pasar necesidades *or* estrecheces

reducible [rɪˈdjuːsəbl] ADJ reducible

reduction [rɪˈdʌkʃən] N 1 (*in size, number, costs, expenditure*) reducción *f*; **a 15% ~ in costs** una reducción del 15% por ciento en los costes; **there has been no ~ in demand** no ha disminuido la demanda; **we have had to make ~s in the budget** hemos tenido que recortar el presupuesto
2 (*in price*) rebaja *f*; **a 50% ~** una rebaja del 50%
3 (*Mil*) (*in rank*) degradación *f*
4 (= *simplification*) reducción *f*
5 (*Phot*) copia *f* reducida
6 (*Math*) reducción *f*
7 (*Chem*) reducción *f*
8 (= *capture, subjugation*) toma *f*, conquista *f*

redundance [rɪˈdʌndəns] N redundancia *f*

redundancy [rɪˈdʌndənsɪ] (*Brit*) Ⓐ N 1 (= *state of being superfluous*) exceso *m*, superfluidad *f*
2 (*Brit*) [*of worker*] despido *m*; (*among workers*) desempleo *m*; *see also* **compulsory, voluntary**
Ⓑ CPD ► **redundancy compensation, redundancy payment** N indemnización *f* por desempleo

redundant [rɪˈdʌndənt] ADJ 1 (= *superfluous*) superfluo; **to be ~** estar de más
2 (*Gram*) redundante
3 (*Brit*) [*worker*] sin trabajo, parado; **to be made ~** ser despedido (*por reducción de plantilla*), quedar sin trabajo; **he was made ~ in 1999** lo despidieron en 1999, quedó sin trabajo en 1999; **automation may make some workers ~** la automatización puede hacer que varios obreros pierdan sus puestos

reduplicate [rɪˈdjuːplɪkeɪt] VT reduplicar

reduplication [rɪˌdjuːplɪˈkeɪʃən] N reduplicación *f*

reduplicative [rɪˈdjuːplɪkətɪv] ADJ reduplicativo

redwing [ˈredwɪŋ] N malvís *m*

redwood [ˈredwʊd] N (= *tree*) secoya *f*

redye [ˈriːˈdaɪ] VT reteñir, volver a teñir

re-echo [ˈriːˈekəʊ] Ⓐ VT repetir, resonar con
Ⓑ VI [*sound*] resonar; (*fig*) repercutirse

reed [riːd] Ⓐ N 1 (*Bot*) junco *m*, caña *f*; **broken ~** (*fig*) persona *f* quemada
2 (*Mus*) (*in mouthpiece*) lengüeta *f*
3 (= *pipe*) caramillo *m*
Ⓑ CPD ► **reed bed** N juncal *m*, cañaveral *m* ► **reed bunting** N verderón *m* común ► **reed instrument** N instrumento *m* de lengüeta ► **reed mace** N anea *f*, espadaña *f* ► **reed stop** N registro *m* de lengüetas ► **reed warbler** N carricero *m* común

re-edit [ˈriːˈedɪt] VT reeditar

re-educate [ˈriːˈedjʊkeɪt] VT reeducar

re-education [ˈriːˌedjʊˈkeɪʃən] N reeducación *f*

reedy [ˈriːdɪ] ADJ (*compar* **reedier**; *superl* **reediest**) 1 [*place*] lleno de cañas, cubierto de juncos
2 [*voice, tone, instrument*] aflautado

reef[1] [riːf] N (*Geog*) arrecife *m*

reef[2] [riːf] Ⓐ N (= *sail*) rizo *m*; **to let out a ~** largar rizos; (*fig*) aflojar el cinturón; **to take in a ~** tomar rizos; (*fig*) apretarse el cinturón
Ⓑ VT arrizar
Ⓒ CPD ► **reef knot** N nudo *m* de rizo

reefer[1] [ˈriːfəʳ] N (= *jacket*) chaquetón *m*

reefer[2]* [ˈriːfəʳ] N (= *joint*) porro* *m*

reek [riːk] Ⓐ N tufo *m*, hedor *m* (**of** a)
Ⓑ VI 1 (= *smell*) **to ~ of sth** apestar a algo; **he comes home simply ~ing** (*of drink*) vuelve a casa que apesta a alcohol; **this ~s of treachery** (*fig*) esto huele a traición; **she ~s with affectation** (*fig*) su afectación es inaguantable
2 (= *smoke*) humear, vahear

reel [riːl] Ⓐ N 1 (*for cable, hose*) rollo *m*; (*for tape recorder, in fishing*) carrete *m*; (*for thread*) carrete *m*, bobina *f*; (*Phot*) (*for small camera*) carrete *m*, rollo *m*; [*of cine film*] cinta *f*; *see also* **cotton, inertia-reel**
2 (*Mus*) (= *dance*) *baile escocés*
Ⓑ VT (= *wind*) [+ *thread, fishing line, film, tape*] enrollar, devanar
Ⓒ VI 1 (= *sway, stagger*) tambalear(se); **he**

was sent ~ing by a blow to the head un golpe en la cabeza hizo que se tambaleara; **he was ~ing about drunkenly** caminaba tambaleándose, caminaba haciendo eses*; **he lost his balance and ~ed backwards** perdió el equilibrio y se fue para atrás
[2] (= *be shaken*) **our troops were ~ing under the enemy bombardment** nuestras tropas sufrían el impacto del bombardeo enemigo; **I'm still ~ing from the shock** todavía no me he recuperado del susto
[3] (= *spin*) [*mind, head, brain*] dar vueltas; **the room ~ed before her eyes** la habitación le daba vueltas
► **reel in** VT + ADV [+ *fish*] sacar del agua (enrollando el sedal); [+ *line*] recoger, ir cobrando
► **reel off** VT + ADV [+ *statistics, list of names*] recitar de un tirón

re-elect [ˈriːɪˈlekt] VT reelegir

re-election [ˈriːɪˈlekʃən] N reelección *f*

re-eligible [ˈriːˈelɪdʒəbl] ADJ reelegible

reel-to-reel [ˈriːltəˈriːl] ADJ **~ tape-recorder** grabadora *f* de carrete

re-emerge [ˈriːɪˈmɜːdʒ] VI volver a salir

re-employ [ˌriːɪmˈplɔɪ] VT volver a emplear

re-enact [ˈriːɪˈnækt] VT [1] (*Parl*) [+ *legislation*] volver a promulgar
[2] (*Theat*) volver a representar; [+ *crime, battle*] reconstruir

re-enactment [ˌriːɪˈnæktmənt] N reconstrucción *f*

re-engage [ˈriːɪnˈgeɪdʒ] VT contratar de nuevo

re-enlist [ˈriːɪnˈlɪst] VI reengancharse, alistarse de nuevo

re-enter [ˈriːˈentəʳ] Ⓐ VI [1] volver a entrar
[2] **to ~ for an exam** volver a presentarse a un examen, presentarse de nuevo a un examen
Ⓑ VT (= *return to*) [+ *room, building, country*] volver a entrar en, entrar de nuevo en; [+ *hospital*] reingresar en, ingresar de nuevo en; [+ *data*] reintroducir en; **to ~ the Earth's atmosphere** volver a penetrar *or* reentrar en la atmósfera terrestre

re-entry [ˈriːˈentrɪ] N (*to hospital*) reingreso *m*; (*into politics etc*) [*of spacecraft*] reentrada *f*; **the house has been bolted to prevent ~** han atrancado la puerta para evitar que se vuelva a entrar en ella

re-equip [ˈriːɪˈkwɪp] VT equipar de nuevo (**with** con)

re-erect [ˌriːɪˈrekt] VT reerigir

re-establish [ˈriːɪsˈtæblɪʃ] VT restablecer

re-establishment [ˈriːɪsˈtæblɪʃmənt] N restablecimiento *m*

reeve[1] [riːv] VT (*Naut*) [+ *rope, cable*] (= *fasten*) asegurar (con cabo); (= *thread*) pasar por un ojal

reeve[2] [riːv] N (*Hist*) juez *mf* local

re-examination [ˈriːɪgˌzæmɪˈneɪʃən] N reexaminación *f*

re-examine [ˈriːɪgˈzæmɪn] VT [+ *facts, evidence*] reexaminar, repasar; (*Jur*) [+ *witness*] volver a interrogar

re-export [ˈriːˈekspɔːt] Ⓐ VT reexportar
Ⓑ N reexportación *f*

ref[1]* [ref] N (*Sport*) árbitro/a *m/f*

ref[2] PREP ABBR [1] (= **with reference to**) respecto de
[2] (*in letter-head*) (= **reference**) ref.

reface [ˈriːˈfeɪs] VT revestir de nuevo (**with** de)

refashion [ˈriːˈfæʃən] VT formar de nuevo, rehacer

refectory [rɪˈfektərɪ] N refectorio *m*

refer [rɪˈfɜːʳ] Ⓐ VT [1] (= *send, direct*) remitir; **to ~ sth to sb** remitir algo a algn; **I have to ~ it to my boss** tengo que remitírselo a mi jefe, tengo que consultarlo con mi jefe; **to ~ a dispute to arbitration** someter *or* remitir una disputa al arbitraje; **the case has been ~red to the Supreme Court** han diferido el caso al Tribunal Supremo; **the decision has been ~red to us** la decisión se ha dejado a nuestro juicio; **to ~ sb to sth/sb**: **I ~red him to the manager** lo envié a que viera al gerente; **the doctor ~red me to a specialist** el médico me mandó a un especialista; **the reader is ~red to page 15** remito al lector a la página 15; **"refer to drawer"** (*on cheque*) "devolver al librador"
[2] (= *ascribe*) atribuir; **he ~s his mistake to tiredness** el error lo achaca a su cansancio, atribuye el error a su cansancio; **he ~s the painting to the 14th century** atribuye el cuadro al siglo XIV
[3] (*Brit Univ*) [+ *student*] suspender
[4] (*Med*) **~red pain** dolor *m* reflejo
Ⓑ VI **to ~ to** [1] (= *relate to*) referirse a; **this ~s to you all** esto se refiere a todos ustedes, esto va para todos ustedes; **the rules do not ~ to special cases** las normas no son aplicables a los casos especiales
[2] (= *allude to*) referirse a; **I am not ~ring to you** no me estoy refiriendo a ti; **I ~ to your letter of 1st May** con relación a su carta con fecha del uno de mayo
[3] (= *mention*) mencionar; **he never ~s to that evening** nunca menciona aquella noche
[4] (= *consult*) consultar; **she had to ~ to her notes** tuvo que consultar sus apuntes; **please ~ to section three** véase la sección tres
[5] (= *describe*) **he ~red to her as his assistant** cuando se refería a ella la llamaba su ayudante; **this kind of art is often ~red to as "minimal art"** este tipo de arte a menudo se denomina "arte minimalista"
► **refer back** Ⓐ VT + ADV [+ *matter, decision*] volver a remitir; [+ *person*] volver a mandar; **the case was ~red back to the Court of Appeal** el caso se volvió a remitir al Tribunal de Apelación; **the pharmacist may ~ you back to your doctor** puede que el farmacéutico te vuelva a mandar al médico de cabecera
Ⓑ VI + ADV **to ~ back to sth**: **you should ~ back to your notes** deberías volver a consultar tus apuntes; **~ back to the table in chapter seven** véase de nuevo el recuadro del capítulo siete

referable [rɪˈfɜːrəbl] ADJ **~ to** (= *related to*) relacionado con; (= *attributable to*) atribuible a; (= *classifiable as*) que se puede clasificar como

referee [ˌrefəˈriː] Ⓐ N [1] (*in dispute, Sport*) árbitro/a *m/f*
[2] (*Brit*) (*for application, post*) avalista *mf*, persona *f* que avala; **Pérez has named you as a ~** Pérez dice que usted está dispuesto a avalarle
[3] [*of learned paper*] evaluador(a) *m/f*
Ⓑ VT [1] [+ *game*] dirigir, arbitrar en
[2] [+ *learned paper*] evaluar
Ⓒ VI arbitrar, hacer de árbitro

▼ **reference** [ˈrefrəns] Ⓐ N [1] (= *act of referring*) consulta *f*; **an index is included for ease of ~** *or* **for easy ~** se incluye un índice para facilitar la consulta; **it was agreed without ~ to me** se acordó sin consultarme; **for future ~, please note that ...** por si importa en el futuro, obsérvese que ...; **I'll keep it for future ~** lo guardo por si hace falta consultarlo en el futuro
[2] (= *allusion*) alusión *f*, referencia *f*; **I can't find any ~ to him in the files** no encuentro nada que haga referencia a él en los archivos; **he does this by ~ to the same principles** hace esto tomando como referencia los mismos principios; **without ~ to any particular case** sin referirse a ningún caso (en) concreto; **with particular ~ to ...** con referencia especial a ...; **he spoke without any ~ to you** habló sin mencionarte para nada; **to make ~ to sth/sb** hacer referencia a algo/algn, hacer alusión a algo/algn; *see also* **passing**
[3] (= *identifying source*) (*in text*) referencia *f*, remisión *f*; (= *citation*) referencia *f*; (*Comm*) (*in letter, catalogue*) (*also* **~ number**) número *m* de referencia; (*on map*) indicación *f*; (*Typ*) (*also* **~ mark**) llamada *f*; **"~ XYZ2"** "número de referencia: XYZ2"; **to look up a ~** (*in book*) buscar una referencia; (*on map*) seguir las coordenadas; *see also* **cross-reference, grid**
[4] (= *testimonial*) (= *document*) referencia *f*, informe *m*; (= *person*) garante *mf*, fiador(a) *m/f*; **she has good ~s** tiene buenas referencias, tiene buenos informes; **the firm offered to give her a ~** la empresa se ofreció a darle referencias *or* informes; **to take up (sb's) ~s** pedir referencias *or* informes (de algn); *see also* **character, credit**
[5] (= *remit*) *see* **frame A4, point D, term A6.1**
Ⓑ VT [1] (= *provide references for*) [+ *book*] dotar de referencias a
[2] (= *refer to*) [+ *source*] citar
Ⓒ CPD [*material, tool, room*] de consulta
► **reference book** N libro *m* de consulta
► **reference group** N (*Sociol*) grupo *m* de estudio ► **reference library** N biblioteca *f* de consulta ► **reference mark** N llamada *f*
► **reference number** N número *m* de referencia ► **reference point** N punto *m* de referencia ► **reference price** N (*Agr*) precio *m* de referencia

referendum [ˌrefəˈrendəm] N (*pl* **referendums, referenda** [ˌrefəˈrendə]) referéndum *m*; **to call a ~** convocar un referéndum; **to hold a ~** celebrar un referéndum; **to hold a ~ on sth** someter algo a referéndum

referral [rɪˈfɜːrəl] N [1] (*Med, Psych*) **ask your GP for a ~ to a clinical psychologist** pídale a su médico que le envíe a un psicólogo clínico; **letter of ~** volante *m* médico
[2] (*to higher authority*) remisión *f*
[3] (*Jur*) [*of case*] remisión *f*

refill [ˈriːfɪl] Ⓐ N recambio *m*; (*for pencil*) mina *f*; **would you like a ~?** ¿te pongo más vino *etc*?, ¿otro vaso?
Ⓑ [ˌriːˈfɪl] VT [+ *lighter, pen*] recargar; [+ *glass*] volver a llenar

refinance [rɪˈfaɪnæns] VT refinanciar

refine [rɪˈfaɪn] Ⓐ VT [1] [+ *sugar, oil*] refinar; [+ *fats*] clarificar; [+ *metal*] refinar, afinar
[2] (= *improve*) [+ *design, technique, machine*] perfeccionar; [+ *methods*] refinar; [+ *style*] limar, purificar; [+ *behaviour, style of writing*] pulir, refinar
Ⓑ VI **to ~ upon sth** (= *improve*) refinar algo, mejorar algo; (= *discuss*) discutir algo con mucha sutileza

refined [rɪˈfaɪnd] ADJ [1] (= *purified*) [*sugar, flour*] refinado
[2] (= *sophisticated*) [*clothes, manners, sense of humour*] fino, refinado
[3] (= *subtle, polished*) [*style of writing*] elegante, pulido

refinement [rɪˈfaɪnmənt] N [1] [*of person, language*] refinamiento *m*; [*of manners*] educación *f*, finura *f*; [*of style*] elegancia *f*, urbani-

➤ LANGUAGE IN USE: reference A2 21.1

dad *f*; **a person of some ~** una persona fina
2 (= *improvement*) mejora *f*; (*in machine*) perfeccionamiento *m*
3 (= *subtle detail*) [*of language*] sutileza *f*; **that is a ~ of cruelty** eso es ser más cruel todavía; **with every possible ~ of cruelty** con las formas más refinadas de la crueldad

refiner [rɪˈfaɪnəʳ] N refinador *m*

refinery [rɪˈfaɪnərɪ] N refinería *f*

refit [ˈriːˈfɪt] Ⓐ N (*gen*) reparación *f*, compostura *f*; (*Naut*) reparación *f*
Ⓑ VT (*gen*) reparar, componer; (*Naut*) reparar
Ⓒ VI (*Naut*) repararse

refitment [ˈriːˈfɪtmənt] N (*gen*) reparación *f*, compostura *f*; (*Naut*) reparación *f*

refitting [ˈriːˈfɪtɪŋ] N = **refitment**

reflate [ˌriːˈfleɪt] VT [+ *economy*] reflacionar

reflation [riːˈfleɪʃən] N reflación *f*

reflationary [riːˈfleɪʃnərɪ] ADJ reflacionario

reflect [rɪˈflekt] Ⓐ VT 1 [+ *light, image*] reflejar; **plants ~ed in the water** plantas reflejadas en el agua; **I saw him/myself ~ed in the mirror** lo vi/me vi reflejado en el espejo
2 [+ *situation, emotion, opinion*] reflejar, hacerse eco de; **the difficulties are ~ed in his report** las dificultades se reflejan en su informe, el informe se hace eco de las dificultades; **the speech ~s credit on him** el discurso le hace honor; **to bask in ~ed glory** disfrutar de la gloria ajena
3 (= *say*) reflexionar; **"the war has educated many of us," he ~ed** —la guerra nos ha concienciado a muchos —reflexionó; **he ~ed that life had not treated him so badly** pensándolo bien, la vida no le había tratado tan mal
Ⓑ VI 1 **to ~ off sth** [*light, heat*] reflejarse en algo; [*sound*] salir rebotado de algo
2 (= *think, meditate*) reflexionar, pensar; **~ before you act** reflexione antes de obrar; **if we but ~ a moment** sí sólo reflexionamos un instante; **to ~ on sth** reflexionar *or* meditar sobre algo
3 **to ~ on** *or* **upon sth/sb: it ~s on all of us** eso tiende a perjudicarnos *or* desprestigiarnos a todos; **it ~s on her reputation** eso pone en tela de juicio su reputación; **to ~ well on** *or* **upon sb** hacer honor a algn; **to ~ badly on** *or* **upon sb** decir poco en favor de algn; **it will ~ badly on the university** eso dará una imagen poco favorable de la universidad

reflection [rɪˈflekʃən] N 1 [*of light*] (= *act*) reflexión *f*; (= *image*) reflejo *m*; **the ~ of the light in the mirror** el reflejo de la luz en el espejo; **a pale ~ of former glories** un ligero reflejo de glorias pasadas; **to see one's ~ in a shop window** verse reflejado en un escaparate
2 (= *thought*) meditación *f*, reflexión *f*; **on ~** pensándolo bien; **without due ~** sin pensarlo lo suficiente; **mature ~ suggests that ...** una meditación más profunda indica que ...
3 (= *aspersion, doubt*) tacha *f*, descrédito *m*; **this is no ~ on your work** esto no significa crítica alguna a su trabajo; **this is no ~ on your honesty** esto no dice nada en contra de su honradez, esto no es ningún reproche a su honradez; **to cast ~s on sb** reprochar a algn
4 (= *idea*) pensamiento *m*, idea *f*; **"Reflections on Ortega"** "Meditaciones sobre Ortega"

reflective [rɪˈflektɪv] ADJ 1 [*surface*] brillante, lustroso
2 (= *meditative*) pensativo, reflexivo
3 **to be ~ of** reflejar

reflectively [rɪˈflektɪvlɪ] ADV pensativamente; **he said ~** dijo pensativo; **she looked at me ~** me miró pensativa

reflector [rɪˈflektəʳ] N 1 (*Aut*) (*also* **rear ~**) reflector *m inv*
2 (= *telescope*) reflector *m*

reflex [ˈriːfleks] Ⓐ ADJ reflejo; (*Math*) [*angle*] de reflexión; **~ camera** (*Phot*) cámara *f* reflex
Ⓑ N reflejo *m*

reflexive [rɪˈfleksɪv] Ⓐ ADJ (*Ling*) [*verb, pronoun*] reflexivo
Ⓑ N (*Ling*) (= *pronoun*) pronombre *m* reflexivo; (= *verb*) verbo *m* reflexivo

reflexively [rɪˈfleksɪvlɪ] ADV reflexivamente

reflexology [ˌriːflekˈsɒlədʒɪ] N reflexología *f*, reflejoterapia *f*

refloat [ˈriːˈfləʊt] VT [+ *ship*] poner a flote

reflux [ˈriːflʌks] N reflujo *m*

reforest [ˈriːˈfɒrɪst] VT repoblar de árboles

reforestation [ˈriːˌfɒrɪsˈteɪʃən] N repoblación *f* forestal

reform [rɪˈfɔːm] Ⓐ N reforma *f*; *see also* **land**
Ⓑ VT [+ *law, institution, person*] reformar; [+ *conduct*] corregir
Ⓒ VI [*person*] reformarse
Ⓓ CPD ► **Reform Jew** N judío/a *m/f* reformista ► **Reform Judaism** N judaísmo *m* reformista ► **reform law** N ley *f* de reforma ► **reform movement** N movimiento *m* de reforma ► **reform school** N (*US*) reformatorio *m*

re-form [ˈriːˈfɔːm] Ⓐ VT volver a formar, reconstituir
Ⓑ VI [*organization, party*] volver a formarse, reconstituirse; (*Mil*) rehacerse

reformat [ˈriːˈfɔːmæt] VT reformatear

reformation [ˌrefəˈmeɪʃən] N reformación *f*; **the Reformation** (*Rel*) la Reforma

reformatory [rɪˈfɔːmətərɪ] N (*Brit*) reformatorio *m*

reformed [rɪˈfɔːmd] ADJ reformado; **he's a ~ character these days** últimamente se ha reformado

reformer [rɪˈfɔːməʳ] N reformista *mf*, reformador(a) *m/f*

reformist [rɪˈfɔːmɪst] Ⓐ ADJ reformista
Ⓑ N reformista *mf*

refract [rɪˈfrækt] VT refractar

refracting [rɪˈfræktɪŋ] ADJ **~ telescope** telescopio *m* de refracción, telescopio *m* refractor

refraction [rɪˈfrækʃən] N refracción *f*

refractive [rɪˈfræktɪv] ADJ refractivo

refractor [rɪˈfræktəʳ] N refractor *m*

refractoriness [rɪˈfræktərɪnɪs] N obstinación *f*

refractory [rɪˈfræktərɪ] ADJ 1 (= *obstinate*) obstinado 2 (*Tech*) refractario

refrain[1] [rɪˈfreɪn] N (*Mus*) estribillo *m*; **his constant ~ is ...** siempre está con la misma canción ...

refrain[2] [rɪˈfreɪn] VI **to ~ from sth/from doing sth** abstenerse de algo/de hacer algo; **I couldn't ~ from laughing** no pude contener la risa

refresh [rɪˈfreʃ] VT 1 [*drink, sleep, bath*] refrescar; **to ~ sb's memory** refrescar la memoria a algn; **to ~ o.s.** refrescarse, tomar un refresco
2 (*Comput*) [+ *screen, page*] actualizar

refresher [rɪˈfreʃəʳ] Ⓐ N 1 (= *drink*) refresco *m*
2 (*Jur*) honorarios *mpl* suplementarios
Ⓑ CPD ► **refresher course** N curso *m* de actualización

refreshing [rɪˈfreʃɪŋ] ADJ 1 (*lit*) [*drink*] refrescante
2 (*fig*) **it's ~ to hear some new ideas** da gusto escuchar nuevas ideas; **it's a ~ change to find this** es alentador encontrar esto

refreshingly [rɪˈfreʃɪŋlɪ] ADV **she's ~ honest** da gusto ver lo honesta que es; **his style of writing is ~ different** tiene un estilo distinto, lo cual resulta muy grato

refreshment [rɪˈfreʃmənt] Ⓐ N (= *food*) piscolabis *m*; (= *drink*) (*non-alcoholic*) refresco *m*; (*alcoholic*) copa *f*; **refreshments** refrigerio *msing*, comida *fsing* liviana; **"~s will be served"** "se servirá un refrigerio"; **to take some ~** tomar algo, comer *or* beber *etc*
Ⓑ CPD ► **refreshment bar** N chiringuito *m* de refrescos ► **refreshment room** N (*Rail*) cantina *f*, comedor *m* ► **refreshment stall**, **refreshment stand** N puesto *m* de refrescos

refrigerant [rɪˈfrɪdʒərənt] N refrigerante *m*

refrigerate [rɪˈfrɪdʒəreɪt] VT refrigerar

refrigeration [rɪˌfrɪdʒəˈreɪʃən] N refrigeración *f*

refrigerator [rɪˈfrɪdʒəreɪtəʳ] Ⓐ N frigorífico *m*, nevera *f*, refrigeradora *f* (*LAm*)
Ⓑ CPD ► **refrigerator lorry** N camión *m* frigorífico ► **refrigerator ship** N buque *m* frigorífico

refuel [ˈriːˈfjʊəl] Ⓐ VI [*tank, plane*] repostar
Ⓑ VT llenar de combustible; [+ *speculation*] renovar, volver a despertar

refuelling, **refueling** (*US*) [ˈriːˈfjʊəlɪŋ] Ⓐ N reabastecimiento *m* de combustible
Ⓑ CPD ► **refuelling stop** N escala *f* para repostar

refuge [ˈrefjuːdʒ] N (= *shelter*) refugio *m*; (= *shelter for climbers*) albergue *m*; (= *hut*) albergue *m*; (*fig*) amparo *m*, abrigo *m*; **God is my ~** Dios es mi amparo; **to seek ~** buscar refugio, buscar dónde guarecerse; **to take ~** ponerse al abrigo, guarecerse; **to take ~ in sth** refugiarse en algo; (*fig*) recurrir a algo

refugee [ˌrefjʊˈdʒiː] Ⓐ N refugiado/a *m/f*; **~ from justice** prófugo/a *m/f* de la justicia
Ⓑ CPD ► **refugee camp** N campamento *m* para refugiados ► **refugee status** N estatus *m inv* de refugiado

refulgence [rɪˈfʌldʒəns] N refulgencia *f*

refulgent [rɪˈfʌldʒənt] ADJ refulgente

refund [ˈriːfʌnd] Ⓐ N (= *act*) devolución *f*; (= *amount*) reembolso *m*
Ⓑ [rɪˈfʌnd] VT devolver, reembolsar

refundable [rɪˈfʌndəbl] ADJ reembolsable

refurbish [ˈriːˈfɜːbɪʃ] VT [+ *building, paintwork*] restaurar; [+ *literary work*] refundir

refurnish [ˈriːˈfɜːnɪʃ] VT amueblar de nuevo

refusal [rɪˈfjuːzəl] N 1 negativa *f*; **she brushed aside my ~s** hizo caso omiso de mis negativas; **he didn't take her ~ seriously** no tomó en serio su negativa; **he was shot for his ~ to obey orders** lo mataron de un tiro por negarse a obedecer órdenes; **I'm giving you/you have first ~ (on the house)** le daré/tendrá prioridad en la compra (de la casa); **a flat ~** una negativa rotunda; **her request met with a flat ~** su solicitud fue rechazada de plano
2 [*of application*] denegación *f*
3 (*by horse*) **the horse had two ~s** el caballo se plantó dos veces

▼**refuse**[1] [rɪˈfjuːz] Ⓐ VT 1 (= *decline*) [+ *offer, chance*] rechazar, rehusar; [+ *applicant*] rechazar; **it was an offer he couldn't ~** era una oferta que no podía rechazar *or* rehusar; **the patient has the right to ~ treatment** el paciente tiene derecho a negarse a someterse a tratamiento; **he was devastated when she ~d him** estaba desolado cuando ella lo rechazó; **she ~d their invitation to stay to dinner** rechazó *or* no aceptó su invitación para

➤ LANGUAGE IN USE: **refuse**[1] **A1, 2** 8.4, 9.5, 12.2, 12.3

quedarse a cenar; **he never ~s a drink** nunca dice que no a una copa; **to ~ to do sth** [*person*] negarse a hacer algo; **he ~d to comment after the trial** se negó a *or* rehusó hacer comentarios después del juicio; **my legs ~d to function** mis piernas se negaban a funcionar

[2] (= *not grant*) [+ *request, permission*] (*gen*) negar; (*officially*) denegar; **the police ~d permission for the march** la policía denegó el permiso *or* les negó el permiso para hacer la marcha; **to ~ sb sth** (*gen*) negar algo a algn; (*officially*) denegar algo a algn; **they were ~d permission to leave** les negaron autorización para salir; **I was ~d entry to Malawi** me denegaron la entrada a Malaui; **they can ~ her nothing** no le pueden negar nada

Ⓑ VI [1] [*person*] negarse; **I don't see how I can ~** no veo cómo puedo negarme

[2] [*horse*] plantarse

refuse[2] ['refju:s] Ⓐ N [1] (= *rubbish*) basura *f*, desperdicios *mpl*; **garden ~** desperdicios *mpl* del jardín; **household ~** basura *f* doméstica, residuos *mpl* domésticos

[2] (= *industrial waste*) desechos *mpl*, residuos *mpl*

Ⓑ CPD ► **refuse bin** N cubo *m or* (*LAm*) bote *m or* tarro *m* de la basura ► **refuse chute** N rampa *f* de desperdicios, rampa *f* de la basura ► **refuse collection** N recogida *f* de basura ► **refuse collector** N basurero *m* ► **refuse disposal** N eliminación *f* de basuras ► **refuse disposal unit** N triturador *m* de basura ► **refuse dump** N = **refuse tip** ► **refuse lorry** N camión *m* de la basura ► **refuse tip** N vertedero *m*, basural *m* (*LAm*)

refutable [rɪ'fju:təbl] ADJ refutable

refutation [ˌrefjʊ'teɪʃən] N refutación *f*

refute [rɪ'fju:t] VT refutar, rebatir

reg. [redʒ] Ⓐ N ABBR (*Brit**) = **registration number**

Ⓑ ADJ ABBR = **registered**

regain [rɪ'geɪn] VT recobrar, recuperar; [+ *breath*] cobrar; **to ~ consciousness** recobrar el conocimiento, volver en sí

regal ['ri:gəl] ADJ regio, real

regale [rɪ'geɪl] VT (= *entertain*) entretener; (= *delight*) divertir; **to ~ sb on oysters** agasajar a algn con ostras; **he ~d the company with a funny story** para entretener a la compañía les contó un chiste; **to ~ o.s. on** *or* **with sth** regalarse con algo, darse el lujo de algo

regalia [rɪ'geɪlɪə] NPL (= *royal trappings*) atributos *mpl*; (*gen*) (= *insignia*) insignias *fpl*

regally ['ri:gəlɪ] ADV regiamente; (*pej*) con pompa regia

▼ **regard** [rɪ'gɑ:d] Ⓐ N [1] (= *relation*) respecto *m*, aspecto *m*; **in** *or* **with ~ to** con respecto a; **with ~ to your letter of 25th June** con respecto a su carta del 25 de junio; **government policy with ~ to immigration** la política del gobierno con respecto a la inmigración *or* en materia de inmigración; **I was right in one ~** tenía razón en un aspecto; **in this/that ~** en este/ese aspecto, a este/ese respecto

[2] (= *esteem*) estima *f*, respeto *m*; **my ~ for him** la estima *or* el respeto que le tengo; **to have a high** *or* **great ~ for sb** ◊ **hold sb in high ~** tener a algn en gran estima, tener un gran concepto de algn; **out of ~ for** por respeto a; *see also* **self-regard**

[3] (= *attention, consideration*) **it should be done with a proper ~ for safety** debería hacerse prestándole la atención debida a la seguridad; **having ~ to** teniendo en cuenta; **he shows little ~ for their feelings** muestra poca consideración por sus sentimientos; **they have no ~ for human life** no tienen *or* muestran ningún respeto a la vida humana; **without ~ to/for sth: without ~ to race, creed or sex** sin considerar *or* sin tener en cuenta la raza, la religión o el sexo; **without ~ for her own safety** sin reparar en *or* tener en cuenta su propia seguridad

[4] **regards** (*in messages*) recuerdos *mpl*, saludos *mpl*; **(give my) ~s to Yvonne** (dele) recuerdos a Yvonne, salude a Yvonne de mi parte; **(with) kind/best ~s** (*as letter ending*) saludos; **he sends his ~s** os manda recuerdos *or* saludos

[5] (*liter*) (= *gaze*) mirada *f*

Ⓑ VT [1] (= *look at*) (*liter*) contemplar, observar; (*fig*) (= *view*) mirar; **to ~ sb with suspicion** mirar a algn con recelo

[2] (= *consider*) considerar; **he is ~ed as Britain's foremost composer** se lo considera *or* está considerado el compositor más importante de Gran Bretaña; **we don't ~ it as necessary** no lo consideramos necesario, no nos parece necesario; **would you ~ yourself as a feminist?** ¿se considera usted feminista?

[3] (= *esteem*) **he was a highly ~ed scholar** era un académico muy respetado *or* de mucha reputación

[4] (= *concern*) tratar, tocar; **the next item ~s the proposed merger** el siguiente punto trata *or* toca la fusión propuesta; **as ~s** en *or* por lo que respecta a, en *or* por lo que se refiere a, en cuanto a

regardful [rɪ'gɑ:dfʊl] ADJ **~ of** atento a

regarding [rɪ'gɑ:dɪŋ] PREP con respecto a, en relación con; (*introducing sentence*) en *or* por lo que respecta a, en *or* por lo que se refiere a; **he refused to divulge any information ~ the man's whereabouts** rehusó facilitar cualquier información con respecto a *or* en relación con el paradero del hombre; **and other things ~ money** y otras cosas relativas al dinero

regardless [rɪ'gɑ:dlɪs] Ⓐ ADJ **~ of** sin reparar en; **buy it ~ of the cost** cómpralo, cueste lo que cueste; **they shot them all ~ of rank** los fusilaron a todos sin miramientos a su graduación; **we did it ~ of the consequences** lo hicimos sin tener en cuenta las consecuencias

Ⓑ ADV a pesar de todo, pase lo que pase; **he went on ~** continuó a pesar de todo; **carry** *or* **press on ~!** ¡a seguir, sin reparar en las consecuencias!

regatta [rɪ'gætə] N regata *f*

regd ADJ ABBR [1] (*Comm*) = **registered**

[2] (*Post*) = **registered**

regency ['ri:dʒənsɪ] Ⓐ N regencia *f*

Ⓑ CPD ► **Regency furniture** N mobiliario *m* Regencia, mobiliario *m* estilo Regencia

regenerate Ⓐ [rɪ'dʒenəreɪt] VT regenerar

Ⓑ [rɪ'dʒenərɪt] ADJ regenerado

regeneration [rɪˌdʒenə'reɪʃən] N regeneración *f*

regenerative [rɪ'dʒenərətɪv] ADJ regenerador

regent ['ri:dʒənt] Ⓐ ADJ **prince ~** príncipe *m* regente

Ⓑ N regente *mf*

reggae ['regeɪ] N (*Mus*) reggae *m*

regicide ['redʒɪsaɪd] N [1] (= *act*) regicidio *m*

[2] (= *person*) regicida *mf*

régime, regime [reɪ'ʒi:m] N [1] (*Pol*) régimen *m*; **the ancien ~** el antiguo régimen; **under the Nazi ~** bajo el régimen de los nazis

[2] (= *system, programme*) régimen *m*

regimen ['redʒɪmən] N régimen *m*

regiment ['redʒɪmənt] Ⓐ N (*Mil*) regimiento *m*; (*fig*) ejército *m*, batallón *m*; **a whole ~ of mice** todo un ejército *or* batallón de ratones

Ⓑ ['redʒɪment] VT (*fig*) [+ *life*] reglamentar; **trees planted in ~ed rows** árboles plantados en hileras perfectamente alineadas

regimental [ˌredʒɪ'mentl] Ⓐ ADJ (*Mil*) de regimiento; (*fig*) militar; **~ sergeant major** ≈ brigada *m* de regimiento; **with ~ precision** con precisión militar

Ⓑ NPL **~s** (*Mil*) uniforme *msing*

regimentation [ˌredʒɪmen'teɪʃən] N reglamentación *f*

Reginald ['redʒɪnld] N Reinaldo, Reginaldo

region ['ri:dʒən] N [1] [*of country, human body*] región *f*, zona *f*; **the densely populated coastal ~** la región *or* zona costera densamente poblada; **Asia and the Pacific ~** Asia y la región del Pacífico; **the pelvic ~** la región *or* la zona pélvica; **a pain in the ~ of my kidneys** un dolor a la altura de los riñones; **the ~s** (= *provinces*) las provincias

[2] (= *field, sphere*) campo *m*; **and here we enter a ~ of moral ambiguity** y aquí entramos en un campo de ambigüedad moral

[3] **in the ~ of** (= *approximately*) aproximadamente, alrededor de; **it will cost in the ~ of £6 million** costará aproximadamente *or* alrededor de 6 millones de libras; **I would say she's in the ~ of 40** yo diría que ronda los 40, yo diría que tiene unos 40 años

regional ['ri:dʒənl] Ⓐ ADJ [*conflicts, autonomy, government, accent*] regional

Ⓑ CPD ► **regional authority** N autoridad *f* regional ► **regional council** N (*Scot*) consejo *m* regional ► **regional development** N (*Brit Admin*) desarrollo *m* regional ► **regional development grant** N subsidio *m* para el desarrollo regional ► **regional planning** N planificación *f* regional

regionalism ['ri:dʒənəlɪzəm] N regionalismo *m*

regionalist ['ri:dʒənəlɪst] Ⓐ ADJ regionalista

Ⓑ N regionalista *mf*

register ['redʒɪstə'] Ⓐ N [1] (= *list*) (*in hotel*) registro *m*; (*in school*) lista *f*; [*of members*] lista *f*, registro *m*; **the ~ of births, marriages and deaths** el registro civil; **to call** *or* **take the ~** pasar lista; *see also* **electoral, parish**

[2] (*Mus*) [*of instrument, voice*] registro *m*

[3] (*Ling*) registro *m*; **there's a difference of** *or* **in ~ between the two terms** existe una diferencia de registro entre los dos términos

[4] (*also* **cash ~**) caja *f* registradora

[5] (*Tech*) (= *gauge of speed, numbers*) indicador *m*

[6] (= *air vent*) rejilla *f* de ventilación

[7] (*Comput*) registro *m*

Ⓑ VT [1] (= *record*) [+ *fact, figure*] registrar, hacer constar; [+ *birth, marriage, death*] registrar, inscribir; [+ *company, property*] registrar; [+ *car, ship*] matricular, registrar; [+ *letter*] certificar; **are you ~ed with a doctor?** ¿está inscrito en la lista de pacientes de algún médico?; **to be ~ed to vote** estar inscrito en el censo electoral; **to be ~ed blind/disabled** estar registrado como ciego/minusválido

[2] (= *show*) [+ *reading*] marcar, indicar; [+ *improvement, reduction*] experimentar; **the petrol gauge was ~ing empty** el indicador de gasolina marcaba *or* indicaba que el depósito estaba vacío; **production has ~ed a big fall** la producción ha experimentado un descenso considerable

[3] (= *express*) [+ *emotion*] manifestar, mostrar; [+ *protest, support*] expresar, manifestar; [+ *complaint*] presentar; **he ~ed no surprise** no manifestó *or* mostró sorpresa alguna

Ⓒ VI [1] (= *sign on*) (*with agency, for course or conference*) inscribirse; (*at hotel*) registrarse; (*Univ*) [*student*] matricularse, inscribirse; **to ~ with a doctor** inscribirse en la lista de un

➤ LANGUAGE IN USE: regard A1 26.2

médico; **to ~ as unemployed** registrarse como parado; **to ~ with the police** dar parte a la policía; **to ~ to vote** inscribirse *or* registrarse en el censo electoral
[2] (*) (= *be understood*) **it doesn't seem to have ~ed with her** no parece haber hecho mella en ella; **when it finally ~ed** cuando por fin cayó en la cuenta
[3] (= *show*) [*reading*] ser detectado; [*emotion*] manifestarse; **surprise ~ed on her face** la sorpresa se manifestó en su cara
Ⓓ CPD ► **register office** N = **registry office**

registered ['redʒɪstəd] Ⓐ ADJ [*letter*] certificado; [*student, car*] matriculado; [*voter*] inscrito; **to be a ~ Democrat/Republican** (*US Pol*) estar inscrito como votante demócrata/ republicano
Ⓑ CPD ► **registered charity** N sociedad *f* benéfica legalmente constituida ► **registered company** N sociedad *f* legalmente constituida ► **registered mail** N = **registered post** ► **registered nurse** N (*US*) enfermero/a *m/f* titulado/a ► **registered office** N domicilio *m* social ► **registered post** N (*Brit*) servicio *m* de entrega con acuse de recibo ► **registered trademark** N marca *f* registrada

registrar [,redʒɪs'trɑːʳ] N [1] [*of births, marriages, deaths*] secretario/a *m/f* del registro civil
[2] (*Univ*) secretario/a *m/f* general
[3] (*Med*) interno/a *m/f*
[4] [*of society*] secretario/a *m/f*

registration [,redʒɪs'treɪʃən] Ⓐ N [1] (*for course, conference, of voter*) inscripción *f*; (*Univ*) [*of student*] matriculación *f*, inscripción *f*; [*of company, property, trademark, dog, gun*] registro *m*; [*of car*] matriculación *f*; [*of ship*] matriculación *f*, abanderamiento *m*
[2] (= *number*) (*Aut, Naut, Univ*) matrícula *f*
Ⓑ CPD ► **registration document** N (*Brit Aut*) documento *m* de matriculación ► **registration fee** N (*Univ*) matrícula *f*; (*for agency*) cuota *f* de inscripción ► **registration form** N formulario *m* de inscripción ► **registration number** N (*Brit Aut*) matrícula *f* ► **registration tag** N (*US Aut*) (placa *f* de) matrícula *f*

registry ['redʒɪstrɪ] Ⓐ N registro *m*, archivo *m*; (*Univ*) secretaría *f* general; **servants' ~** agencia *f* de colocaciones
Ⓑ CPD ► **registry office** N registro *m* civil; **to get married at a ~ office** casarse por lo civil; **it was a ~ office wedding** fue una boda por lo civil

Regius ['riːdʒjəs] ADJ (*Brit Univ*) regio

regress Ⓐ [rɪ'gres] VI retroceder
Ⓑ ['riːgres] N regreso *m*

regression [rɪ'greʃən] N regresión *f*

regressive [rɪ'gresɪv] ADJ regresivo

▼**regret** [rɪ'gret] Ⓐ N [1] (= *sorrow*) pena *f*, pesar *m*; **she accepted his resignation with ~** aceptó su dimisión con pena *or* pesar; **the President expressed his ~ for the deaths of civilians** el presidente expresó su pesar *or* dolor por las muertes de los civiles; **my one** *or* **only ~ is that I didn't see her before she died** lo único que siento *or* lamento es no haberla visto antes de que muriera; **I felt no ~ at giving up my work** no sentí dejar el trabajo; **much to my ~** ◊ **to my great ~** con gran pesar mío
[2] (= *remorse*) remordimiento(s) *m(pl)*; **I felt a pang of ~** me entraron remordimientos; **I have no ~s** no me arrepiento de nada
[3] **regrets** (= *excuses*) excusas *fpl*, disculpas *fpl*; **to send one's ~s** excusarse *or* mandar sus disculpas (por no poder acudir)
Ⓑ VT [1] (= *apologize for, be sorry for*) [+ *death, inconvenience, error*] lamentar; **we ~ any inconvenience caused by the delay** lamentamos cualquier inconveniente que les pueda haber causado el retraso; **it is to be ~ted that he did not act sooner** lo lamentable es que no actuó antes; **the President ~s (that) he cannot see you today** el presidente lamenta *or* siente no poder verle hoy; **we ~ to inform you that ...** lamentamos tener que informarle que ...; **her lack of co-operation is nothing new, I ~ to say** lamento decir que su falta de cooperación no es algo nuevo; **we ~ having to do this, but it is necessary** lamentamos *or* sentimos tener que hacer esto, pero es necesario; **he ~ted what had happened** lamentó lo ocurrido
[2] (= *rue*) [+ *decision*] arrepentirse de, lamentar; **you won't ~ it!** ¡no te arrepentirás!, ¡no lo lamentarás!; **he ~s saying it** se arrepiente de *or* lamenta haberlo dicho; **he was ~ting that he had asked the question** se arrepentía de *or* lamentaba haber hecho la pregunta; **I don't ~ what I did** no me arrepiento de *or* lamento lo que hice; **to live to ~ sth** arrepentirse de *or* lamentar algo más tarde

regretful [rɪ'gretfʊl] ADJ arrepentido, pesaroso; **to be ~ that ...** lamentar que + *subjun*; **he was most ~ about it** lo lamentó profundamente; **we are not ~ about leaving** no nos pesa tener que partir

regretfully [rɪ'gretfəlɪ] ADV (= *sadly*) con pesar; **"I'm sorry that I am unable to go", he said ~** —lamento no poder ir —dijo con pesar; **she spoke ~** habló con sentimiento; **~ I have to tell you that ...** siento tener que decirles que ...

regrettable [rɪ'gretəbl] ADJ lamentable; **it is ~ that** es lamentable que + *subjun*, es de lamentar que + *subjun*

regrettably [rɪ'gretəblɪ] ADV (= *unfortunately*) desgraciadamente, lamentablemente; **there were ~ few replies** fue una lástima que hubiera tan pocas respuestas

regroup ['riː'gruːp] Ⓐ VT reagrupar; (*Mil*) reorganizar
Ⓑ VI reagruparse; (*Mil*) reorganizarse

regrouping ['riː'gruːpɪŋ] N reagrupación *f*

Regt. ABBR (= **Regiment**) regto

regular ['regjʊləʳ] Ⓐ ADJ [1] (= *symmetrical*) [*shape, pattern*] (*also Math*) regular; **he has ~ features** es de facciones regulares
[2] (= *even*) [*surface, teeth*] uniforme, parejo (*esp LAm*)
[3] (= *recurring at even intervals*) [*pulse, flights, breathing, order*] regular; **to take ~ exercise** hacer ejercicio con regularidad; **at ~ intervals** (*in time*) con regularidad; (*in space*) a intervalos regulares; **the doctor examined the baby at ~ intervals** el médico examinaba al bebé con regularidad; **the signs were placed at ~ intervals along the beach** las señales estaban situadas a intervalos regulares a lo largo de la playa; **it's important to eat ~ meals** es importante comer con regularidad; **he placed a ~ order with us** nos hizo un pedido regular; **to make ~ use of sth** usar algo con regularidad; **to be in ~ use** utilizarse de manera regular; ✦***IDIOM*** **as ~ as clockwork** como un cronómetro, como un reloj
[4] (= *habitual, customary*) [*visitor, customer, reader, listener*] habitual, asiduo; [*doctor, partner*] habitual; [*action, procedure*] acostumbrado, normal; **they are ~ churchgoers** van a misa con regularidad *or* con asiduidad; **our ~ waiter** el camarero que nos sirve normalmente; **it's past his ~ bedtime** ya ha pasado su hora normal de acostarse; **on a ~ basis** con regularidad; **to be in ~ employment** tener un trabajo fijo; **the ~ staff** el personal habitual; **to have a ~ time for doing sth** tener hora fija para hacer algo, hacer algo siempre a la misma hora
[5] (= *unvarying*) **a man of ~ habits** un hombre metódico, un hombre ordenado (en sus costumbres); **to keep ~ hours** llevar una vida ordenada
[6] (= *frequent*) frecuente; **I have to make ~ trips to France** tengo que viajar a Francia con frecuencia, tengo que hacer viajes frecuentes a Francia; **to be in** *or* **to have ~ contact with sb** mantener *or* tener un contacto frecuente con algn; **it's a ~ occurrence** pasa con frecuencia, es algo frecuente
[7] (*Mil*) [*soldier, army*] profesional, de carrera
[8] (*Ling*) [*verb etc*] regular
[9] (*) (*as intensifier*) **a ~ bore** un auténtico pesado; **a ~ feast** un verdadero banquete; **he's a ~ fool** es un verdadero idiota; **a ~ nuisance** = **a regular bore**
[10] (*US*) (= *ordinary, normal*) normal; **I'm just a ~ guy** no soy más que un tío normal (y corriente); **~ fries** porción *f* mediana de patatas fritas; **~ gasoline** gasolina *f* normal; **~ size** tamaño *m* normal
[11] (*) (= *not constipated*) **to be ~** hacer de vientre con regularidad
[12] (*) (*in menstruation*) **I'm quite ~** mi periodo es bastante regular
Ⓑ N [1] (= *customer*) (*in pub, bar*) cliente *mf* habitual, parroquiano/a *m/f*; **one of the ~s at the club** un asiduo del club; **he's a ~ on the programme** es un invitado habitual del programa
[2] (*Mil*) militar *mf* de carrera
[3] (*US*) (= *petrol*) gasolina *f* normal

regularity [,regjʊ'lærɪtɪ] N regularidad *f*

regularize ['regjʊləraɪz] VT (= *standardize*) [+ *activities, procedure*] regularizar, estandarizar; (= *make official*) [+ *situation*] formalizar, regularizar

regularly ['regjʊləlɪ] ADV [1] (= *at regular arranged times*) [*exercise, visit*] con regularidad; [*meet, use*] regularmente, con regularidad
[2] (= *frequently*) frecuentemente, con frecuencia, a menudo; **the shop is ~ featured in fashion magazines** la tienda aparece frecuentemente *or* con frecuencia *or* a menudo en revistas de moda; **he's ~ late** llega tarde con frecuencia *or* a menudo
[3] (= *at evenly spaced intervals*) a intervalos regulares; **beeches were planted ~ along the avenue** había hayas plantadas a intervalos regulares *or* cada cierta distancia a lo largo de la avenida
[4] (*Ling*) **a ~ declined noun** un sustantivo de declinación regular

regulate ['regjʊleɪt] VT [1] (= *control*) [+ *expenditure, prices, temperature, level, pressure*] regular; **a well-~d life** una vida ordenada
[2] (= *make rules for*) [+ *industry, products*] regular; **a new body to ~ TV advertising** un nuevo organismo que regula la publicidad que se emite por televisión; *see also* **self-regulating**
[3] (*Tech*) [+ *machine, mechanism*] regular

regulation [,regjʊ'leɪʃən] Ⓐ N [1] (= *rule*) norma *f*; **fire ~s** normas *fpl* de seguridad contraincendios; **safety ~s** normas *fpl* de seguridad; **it's against (the) ~s** va contra las normas *or* el reglamento; *see also* **rule**
[2] (= *control*) (*no pl*) [*of industry, products, prices, temperature, level, pressure*] regulación *f*; **a body responsible for the ~ of independent television** un organismo regulador responsable de las cadenas de televisión independientes; *see also* **self-regulation**

➤ LANGUAGE IN USE: **regret B1** 18.2

3 (*Tech*) [*of machine, mechanism*] regulación *f*, reglaje *m*
Ⓑ CPD (= *statutory*) [*dress, size, haircut*] reglamentario

regulative ['regjʊlətɪv] ADJ reglamentario

regulator ['regjʊleɪtəʳ] N 1 (*Tech*) regulador *m*
2 (= *person, organization*) *persona u organización que regula oficialmente un sector de los negocios o la industria*

regulatory ['regjʊ,leɪtərɪ] ADJ regulador

Regulo® ['regjʊləʊ] N (*Brit*) *número del mando de temperatura de un horno a gas*

regurgitate [rɪ'gɜːdʒɪteɪt] Ⓐ VT regurgitar; (*fig*) repetir maquinalmente Ⓑ VI regurgitar

regurgitation [rɪ'gɜːdʒɪ'teɪʃən] N regurgitación *f*; (*fig*) reproducción *f* maquinal

rehab* ['riːhæb] N = **rehabilitation**

rehabilitate [,riːə'bɪlɪteɪt] VT [+ *offenders, drug addicts*] rehabilitar

rehabilitation ['riːə,bɪlɪ'teɪʃən] Ⓐ N rehabilitación *f*
Ⓑ CPD ► **rehabilitation centre** N centro *m* de rehabilitación

rehash ['riːhæʃ] Ⓐ N (*gen*) refrito *m*
Ⓑ [,riː'hæʃ] VT [+ *book, speech*] hacer un refrito de; [+ *food*] recalentar

rehearsal [rɪ'hɜːsəl] N (*Mus, Theat*) ensayo *m*; (= *enumeration*) enumeración *f*, repetición *f*; **it was just a ~ for bigger things to come** fue como un ensayo para las empresas mayores que vendrían después

rehearse [rɪ'hɜːs] Ⓐ VT (*Mus, Theat*) ensayar; (= *enumerate*) enumerar, repetir
Ⓑ VI (*Mus, Theat*) ensayar

reheat [,riː'hiːt] VT recalentar

rehouse ['riː'haʊz] VT [+ *family*] dar una nueva vivienda a; **200 families have been ~d** 200 familias tienen vivienda nueva ya

reification [,riːɪfɪ'keɪʃən] N cosificación *f*

reify ['riːɪ,faɪ] VT cosificar

reign [reɪn] Ⓐ N [*of king, queen*] reinado *m*; (*fig*) dominio *m*; **in** *or* **under the ~ of Queen Elizabeth II** bajo el reinado de la Reina Isabel II; **~ of terror** régimen *m* de terror; **the ~ of the miniskirt** la moda de la minifalda; **her ~ as champion came to an end** su reino *or* hegemonía como campeona terminó
Ⓑ VI [*king, queen*] reinar; (*fig*) (= *prevail*) predominar; **total silence ~ed** reinaba el silencio más absoluto; ✦**PROV it is better to ~ in hell than serve in heaven** más vale ser cabeza de ratón que cola de león

reigning ['reɪnɪŋ] ADJ [*monarch*] reinante, actual; (*fig*) predominante, que impera; **~ champion** campeón *m* actual

reiki ['reɪkɪ] N reiki *m*

reimburse [,riːɪm'bɜːs] VT **to ~ sb for sth** reembolsar a algn por algo

reimbursement [,riːɪm'bɜːsmənt] N reembolso *m*

reimpose ['riːɪm'pəʊz] VT volver a imponer, reimponer

rein [reɪn] N (*usu pl*) rienda *f*; **the ~s of government** (*fig*) las riendas del gobierno; **to draw ~** detenerse, tirar de la rienda (*also fig*); **to keep a tight ~ on sb** (*fig*) refrenar a algn; **we must keep a tight ~ on expenditure** tenemos que restringir los gastos; **to give sb free ~** (*fig*) dar rienda suelta a algn

►**rein back** VT + ADV refrenar

►**rein in** Ⓐ VT + ADV refrenar
Ⓑ VI + ADV detenerse

reincarnate [,riːɪn'kɑːneɪt] VT reencarnar; **to be ~d** reencarnar, volver a encarnar

reincarnation ['riːɪnkɑː'neɪʃən] N reencarnación *f*

reindeer ['reɪndɪəʳ] N (*pl* **reindeer, reindeers**) reno *m*

reinforce [,riːɪn'fɔːs] VT (*gen, fig*) reforzar; [+ *concrete*] armar

reinforced [,riːɪn'fɔːst] ADJ reforzado; **~ concrete** hormigón *m* armado

reinforcement [,riːɪn'fɔːsmənt] N 1 (= *act*) refuerzo *m*
2 (*Mil*) **reinforcements** refuerzos *mpl*

reinsert ['riːɪn'sɜːt] VT volver a insertar *or* introducir

reinstate ['riːɪn'steɪt] VT [+ *suppressed passage*] reincorporar, incluir de nuevo (**in** a); [+ *dismissed worker*] reincorporar, volver a emplear; [+ *dismissed official*] restituir a su puesto

reinstatement ['riːɪn'steɪtmənt] N [*of suppressed passage*] reincorporación *f*, restitución *f* (**in** a); [*of dismissed worker*] reincorporación *f* al puesto; [*of dismissed official*] restitución *f* en el puesto

reinsurance ['riːɪn'ʃʊərəns] N reaseguro *m*

reinsure ['riːɪn'ʃʊəʳ] VT reasegurar

reintegrate ['riː'ɪntɪgreɪt] VT reintegrar; (*socially*) reinsertar (**into** en)

reintegration ['riːɪntɪ'greɪʃən] N reintegración *f*; (*socially*) reinserción *f*

reinter ['riːɪn'tɜːʳ] VT enterrar de nuevo

reinvent [,riːɪn'vent] VT 1 ✦**IDIOM to ~ the wheel** reinventar la rueda
2 **to ~ o.s.** reinventarse

reinvest ['riːɪn'vest] VT reinvertir, volver a invertir

reinvestment ['riːɪn'vestmənt] N reinversión *f*

reinvigorate ['riːɪn'vɪgəreɪt] VT vigorizar, infundir nuevo vigor a; **to feel ~d** sentirse con nuevas fuerzas, sentirse vigorizado

reissue ['riː'ɪʃjuː] Ⓐ VT [+ *stamp*] volver a emitir; [+ *recording*] reeditar; [+ *film*] reestrenar; [+ *book*] [*publisher*] reimprimir, reeditar; [*library*] renovar
Ⓑ N 1 (= *act*) [*of stamp*] reemisión *f*; [*of recording*] reedición *f*; [*of film*] reestreno *m*; [*of book*] reimpresión *f*, reedición *f*
2 (= *stamp*) nueva emisión *f*; (= *recording*) reedición *f*; (= *film*) reestreno *m*; (= *book*) reimpresión *f*, reedición *f*

reiterate [riː'ɪtəreɪt] VT [+ *statement*] reiterar, repetir; **I must ~ that ...** quiero recalcar que ...

reiteration [riːɪtə'reɪʃən] N reiteración *f*, repetición *f*

reiterative [riː'ɪtərətɪv] ADJ reiterativo

reject [rɪ'dʒekt] Ⓐ VT 1 (= *refuse, turn down*) [+ *application*] (*for job*) rechazar; (*for asylum, citizenship*) denegar, rechazar; [+ *candidate, offer, manuscript, sb's advances*] rechazar; [+ *bad coin, damaged goods*] rechazar, no aceptar; [+ *plea*] ignorar, hacer caso omiso de
2 (= *dismiss*) [+ *suggestion, possibility, solution*] descartar, rechazar; [+ *motion, plan, proposal*] rechazar; [+ *argument*] rechazar, no aceptar; [+ *accusation*] negar; **the proposal was ~ed by a narrow margin** la propuesta fue rechazada por un escaso margen; **she ~ed accusations that ...** negó las acusaciones de que ...
3 (= *disown*) [+ *person*] rechazar; **to feel ~ed** (*emotionally*) sentirse rechazado; (*socially*) sentirse marginado, sentirse rechazado
4 (*Med*) [+ *food, tissue, new organ*] [*body*] rechazar
Ⓑ ['riːdʒekt] N 1 (= *person*) **society's ~s** los marginados de la sociedad
2 (= *unwanted thing*) desecho *m*
3 (*Comm*) (= *product*) artículo *m* defectuoso
Ⓒ ['riːdʒekt] CPD (*Comm, Ind*) [*goods*] defectuoso

rejection [rɪ'dʒekʃən] Ⓐ N (*gen*) rechazo *m*; [*of help*] denegación *f*; **to meet with a ~** sufrir una repulsa; **the novel has already had three ~s** ya han rechazado la novela tres veces
Ⓑ CPD ► **rejection slip** N (*Publishing*) nota *f* de rechazo

rejig [riː'dʒɪg], **rejigger*** [riː'dzɪgəʳ] VT [+ *schedule, programme*] reajustar

rejoice [rɪ'dʒɔɪs] Ⓐ VI 1 (= *be happy*) alegrarse, regocijarse (*liter*) (**at, about** de); **let us not ~ too soon** no echemos las campanas al vuelo demasiado pronto, conviene no alegrarse demasiado pronto
2 (*hum, iro*) **he ~s in the name of Marmaduke** luce el nombre de Marmaduke
Ⓑ VT alegrar, regocijar (*liter*); **to ~ that ...** alegrarse de que + *subjun*

rejoicing [rɪ'dʒɔɪsɪŋ] N 1 (*general, public*) fiestas *fpl*; **the ~ lasted far into the night** continuaron las fiestas hasta una hora avanzada
2 **rejoicings** (= *festivities*) regocijo *msing*, júbilo *msing*

rejoin¹ ['riː'dʒɔɪn] Ⓐ VT (= *join again*) reincorporarse a Ⓑ VI reincorporarse

rejoin² [rɪ'dʒɔɪn] VT (= *retort*) replicar

rejoinder [rɪ'dʒɔɪndəʳ] N (= *retort*) réplica *f*; **as a ~ to ...** como contestación a ...

rejuvenate [rɪ'dʒuːvɪneɪt] VT rejuvenecer

rejuvenating [rɪ'dʒuːvɪneɪtɪŋ] ADJ [*effect*] rejuvenecedor

rejuvenation [rɪ,dʒuːvɪ'neɪʃən] N rejuvenecimiento *m*

rekindle ['riː'kɪndl] VT 1 [+ *fire*] volver a encender 2 (*fig*) [+ *enthusiasm, hatred*] reanimar, reavivar

relapse [rɪ'læps] Ⓐ N (*Med*) recaída *f*; **to have** *or* **suffer a ~** sufrir una recaída
Ⓑ VI 1 (*Med*) recaer
2 (= *revert*) **to ~ into sth**: **he ~d into his old ways** volvió a las andadas; **he ~d into his usual state of depression** volvió a sumirse en su habitual estado de depresión; **she had ~d into silence** había vuelto a sumirse en el silencio; **he ~d into a coma** volvió a entrar en coma

relate [rɪ'leɪt] Ⓐ VT 1 (= *tell*) [+ *story*] contar, relatar; [+ *conversation*] relatar, referir; **she ~d details of the meeting to her boss** le relató *or* refirió a su jefe detalles de la reunión; **history ~s that he landed here in AD 470** la historia cuenta *or* relata que desembarcó aquí en el año 470 AD; **sad to ~** aunque sea triste decirlo; **strange to ~** aunque parezca mentira, por extraño que parezca
2 (= *establish relation between*) **to ~ sth to sth** relacionar algo con algo; **they ~ what they read to their own experiences** relacionan lo que leen con sus propias experiencias
Ⓑ VI 1 (= *communicate*) relacionarse, comunicarse; **how you ~ depends on the kind of person you are** cómo te relacionas *or* te comunicas depende del tipo de persona que eres
2 **to ~ to (sth/sb)** 2·1 (= *form a relationship with*) **to ~ to sb** relacionarse con algn; **he is unable to ~ to other people** no es capaz de relacionarse con otras personas
2·2 (= *understand, identify with*) **to ~ to sth/sb** identificarse con algo/algn; **I can ~ to that*** yo eso lo entiendo*, yo me identifico con eso; **women ~ more to this than men** las muje-

res comprenden esto mejor que los hombres; **it's important for children to have brothers and sisters they can ~ to** es importante que los niños tengan hermanos y hermanas con los que puedan identificarse

2.3 (= *connect with*) **to ~ to sth** relacionarse con algo; **the way that words in a sentence ~ to each other** la manera en la que las palabras de una frase se relacionan las unas con las otras; **relating to** (*as prep*) relativo a, referente a, relacionado con

2.4 (= *appertain to*) **to ~ to sth** referirse a algo, estar relacionado con algo, tener que ver con algo; **most of the enquiries ~ to debt** la mayoría de las preguntas se refieren a deudas *or* tienen que ver con deudas; **this ~s to what I said yesterday** esto se refiere a *or* está relacionado con lo que dije ayer

related [rɪ'leɪtɪd] ADJ 1 (= *connected*) [*subject*] relacionado, afín; [*language*] afín; [*issue, problem, offence*] relacionado; **this murder is not ~ to the other** este asesinato no está relacionado con el otro; **pay rises are ~ to performance** los aumentos de sueldo guardan relación con el rendimiento; **the two events are not ~** los dos sucesos no guardan relación

2 (= *attached by family*) 2.1 [*people*] **they are ~** son parientes, están emparentados; **are you two ~?** ¿sois familia?, ¿sois parientes?; **we are closely/distantly ~** somos parientes cercanos/lejanos; **are you ~ to the prisoner?** ¿es usted pariente del prisionero?; **the two women aren't ~ to each other** las dos mujeres no están emparentadas; **to be ~ to sb by** *or* **through marriage** ser pariente político de algn

2.2 [*animals, plants*] **termites are closely ~ to cockroaches** las termitas son de la misma familia que las cucarachas

-related [rɪ'leɪtɪd] ADJ (*ending in compounds*) **football-related hooliganism** gamberrismo *m* relacionado con el fútbol

relation [rɪ'leɪʃən] N 1 (= *relationship*) relación *f* (**to, with** con); **the ~ between A and B** la relación entre A y B; **to bear little/no ~ to sth** tener poco/no tener nada que ver con algo; **it bears no ~ to the facts** no tiene que ver con los hechos; **to bear a certain ~ to ...** guardar cierta relación con ...; **to have little/no ~ to sth** tener poco/no tener nada que ver con algo; **the story has little ~ to historical fact** la versión tiene poco que ver con los hechos históricos; **in ~ to** (= *compared to*) en relación con, con relación a; (= *in connection with*) en lo que se refiere a; **Proust in ~ to the French novel** Proust en relación con la novela francesa; **doubts that parents may have in ~ to their children's education** dudas que los padres pudieran tener en lo que se refiere a la ecucación de sus hijos

2 (= *relative*) pariente *mf*, familiar *mf*; **friends and ~s** amigos *mpl* y familiares *mpl*; **all my ~s came** vinieron todos mis parientes, vino toda mi familia; **close ~** pariente *mf* cercano/a; **this grape is a close ~ to the Gamay** esta uva es de la misma familia que la uva Gamay; **distant ~** pariente *mf* lejano/a; **she's no ~** no es parienta mía; **what ~ is she to you?** ¿qué parentesco tiene contigo?; *see also* **blood B**, **poor A1**

3 (= *contact*) **relations** relaciones *fpl*; **good ~s** buenas relaciones *fpl*; **~s are rather strained** las relaciones están algo tirantes; **to break off ~s with sb** romper (relaciones) con algn; **we have broken off ~s with Ruritania** hemos roto las relaciones con Ruritania; **we have business ~s with them** tenemos relaciones comerciales con ellos; **diplomatic ~s** relaciones *fpl* diplomáticas; **to enter into ~s with sb** establecer relaciones con algn; **to establish ~s with sb** establecer relaciones con algn; **international ~s** relaciones *fpl* internacionales; **to have sexual ~s with sb** tener relaciones sexuales con algn; *see also* **industrial**, **public C**, **race**²

4 (= *narration*) relato *m*, relación *f*, narración *f*

relational [rɪ'leɪʃənl] ADJ relacional

relationship [rɪ'leɪʃənʃɪp] N 1 (*between persons*) (*gen*) relación *f*; (*sexual*) relación *f*, relaciones *fpl*; **the mother-child ~** la relación madre-hijo; **our ~ lasted five years** nuestras relaciones continuaron durante cinco años; **they have a beautiful ~** (*US*) tienen una relación de amistad muy bonita; **a business ~** una relación comercial; **to have a ~ with sb** (*gen*) tener relación con algn; (*sexual*) tener relaciones *or* una relación con algn; *see also* **love-hate**

2 (*between things*) relación *f*; **the ~ of A to B** ◊ **the ~ between A and B** la relación entre A y B; **to see a ~ between two events** ver una relación entre dos sucesos

3 (*between countries*) relación *f*; **Britain's special ~ with the USA** la especial relación entre Gran Bretaña y EE. UU.

4 (= *kinship*) parentesco *m*; **what is your ~ to the prisoner?** ¿qué parentesco hay entre usted y el acusado?

relative ['relətɪv] Ⓐ ADJ 1 (= *comparative*) [*safety, peace, comfort, ease*] relativo; **her ~ lack of experience** su relativa falta de experiencia; **he is a ~ newcomer** es relativamente nuevo; **it's all ~** todo es relativo; **in ~ terms** relativamente; **petrol consumption is ~ to speed** el consumo de gasolina está en relación con la velocidad; **there is a shortage of labour ~ to demand** hay escasez de trabajadores en relación con la demanda

2 (= *respective*) **the ~ merits of the two systems** los méritos de cada uno de los dos sistemas

3 (= *relevant*) **~ to** relativo a, concerniente a; **the documents ~ to the problem** la documentación relativa *or* concerniente al problema

4 (*Ling*) relativo; **~ clause** oración *f* subordinada relativa, oración *f* (subordinada) de relativo; **~ pronoun** pronombre *m* relativo

5 (*Mus*) relativo

Ⓑ N pariente *mf*, familiar *mf*; **friends and ~s** amigos *mpl* y familiares; **a close/distant ~** un pariente cercano/lejano

relatively ['relətɪvlɪ] ADV [*few, small, slow*] relativamente; **~ speaking** relativamente; **the tests are ~ easy to carry out** las pruebas se pueden llevar a cabo con relativa facilidad

relativism ['relətɪvɪzəm] N relativismo *m*

relativist ['relətɪvɪst] N relativista *mf*

relativistic [,relətɪv'ɪstɪk] ADJ relativista

relativity [,relə'tɪvɪtɪ] N relatividad *f*

relaunch ['riː'lɔːntʃ] VT [+ *plan, career*] relanzar

relaunching ['riː'lɔːntʃɪŋ] N relanzamiento *m*

relax [rɪ'læks] Ⓐ VT [+ *person, body, part of body*] relajar; [+ *discipline, rules, controls*] relajar; [+ *standards*] dejar que bajen; **to ~ one's muscles** relajar los músculos; **to ~ one's grip** *or* **hold on sth** dejar de agarrarse de *or* a algo tan apretadamente, soltar algo; (*fig*) ejercer menor control sobre algo

Ⓑ VI 1 [*person*] (= *rest, lose inhibitions*) relajarse; (= *calm down*) relajarse, tranquilizarse; (= *amuse oneself*) esparcirse, expansionarse; **I like to ~ with a book** me gusta relajarme leyendo; **~! everything's fine** ¡tranquilízate! todo está bien; **we ~ed in the sun of Majorca** nos relajamos bajo el sol de Mallorca; **I find it difficult to ~ with her** me resulta difícil estar relajado cuando estoy con ella

2 [*person, body, muscles*] relajarse; **his face ~ed into a smile** relajó la cara y sonrió; **we must not ~ in our efforts** es preciso no cejar en nuestros esfuerzos (**to** + *infin* por + *infin*)

relaxant [rɪ'læksənt] N (= *drug*) relajante *m*

relaxation [,riːlæk'seɪʃən] N 1 (= *loosening*) [*of discipline*] relajación *f*, relajamiento *m*

2 (= *rest*) descanso *m*, relajación *f*; **to get some ~** esparcirse, expansionarse; **to seek ~ in painting** esparcirse dedicándose a la pintura

3 (= *amusement*) recreo *m*, distracción *f*; **a favourite ~ of the wealthy** un pasatiempo favorito de los ricos

relaxed [rɪ'lækst] ADJ (*gen*) relajado; **in a ~ atmosphere** en un clima de distensión; **he always seems so ~** siempre parece tan sosegado; **try to be more ~** procura ser más tranquilo

relaxing [rɪ'læksɪŋ] ADJ relajante

relay ['riːleɪ] Ⓐ N 1 [*of workmen*] turno *m*; [*of horses*] posta *f*; **to work in ~s** trabajar por turnos, ir relevándose en el trabajo

2 (*Sport*) (*also* **~ race**) carrera *f* de relevos; **the 400 metres ~** los 400 metros relevos

3 (*Tech*) relé *m*

4 (*Rad, TV*) repetidor *m*

Ⓑ VT 1 (*Rad, TV*) [+ *concert, football match*] retransmitir

2 (= *pass on*) transmitir, pasar; **to ~ a message to sb** transmitir *or* pasar un mensaje a algn

Ⓒ CPD ► **relay station** N (*Elec*) estación *f* repetidora

re-lay ['riː'leɪ] VT [+ *carpet*] volver a colocar; [+ *cable, rail*] volver a tender

release [rɪ'liːs] Ⓐ N 1 (= *liberation*) [*of prisoner, hostage*] liberación *f*, puesta *f* en libertad; [*of convict*] excarcelación *f*, puesta *f* en libertad; **his ~ came through on Monday** se aprobó su excarcelación el lunes, la orden de su puesta en libertad llegó el lunes; **on his ~ from prison he ...** al salir de la cárcel ...; **complications have delayed his ~ from hospital** ciertas complicaciones han impedido que se le dé de alta todavía; *see also* **day**

2 (*fig*) (= *relief*) alivio *m*; **death came as a merciful ~** la muerte fue una bendición *or* un gran alivio

3 (= *issue*) [*of film*] estreno *m*; [*of record, video*] puesta *f* en venta; [*of book*] puesta *f* en venta *or* circulación; [*of news*] publicación *f*; **to be on general ~** exhibirse en todos los cines

4 (= *record, book, film, video*) **their new ~ is called ...** su nuevo disco se llama ...; **the pick of this month's video ~s** las mejores novedades en vídeo *or* (*LAm*) video de este mes; **new ~s** (= *records*) novedades *fpl* discográficas; (= *films*) nuevas producciones *fpl*; (= *books*) nuevas publicaciones *fpl*; *see also* **press D**

5 (= *making available*) [*of documents*] publicación *f*; [*of funds*] cesión *f*

6 (= *emission*) [*of gas, smoke*] escape *m*, emisión *f*; [*of hormones*] secreción *f*; **a sudden ~ of creative energy** un estallido de energía creadora

7 (*Tech, Phot*) (= *catch*) disparador *m*; *see also* **shutter**

8 (*Jur*) [*of right, property*] cesión *f*

Ⓑ VT 1 (= *set free*) [+ *prisoner, hostage*] poner en libertad, liberar; [+ *convict*] excarcelar, poner en libertad; [+ *patient*] dar de alta; [+ *victim*] (*from wreckage*) liberar; [+ *animal*] soltar, dejar en libertad; [+ *person*] (*from obligation*) eximir; **she was ~d from hospital after treatment** le dieron de alta del hospital después de un tratamiento; **they ~d him to go to a new post** permitieron que se fuera a ocupar un nuevo puesto; **to ~ sb from a debt** eximir a algn de una deuda, condonar una deuda a algn (*frm*); **she ~d him from all his vows** lo eximió de cumplir todas sus promesas; **the bird was ~d into the wild** el pájaro fue devuelto a su hábitat natural; *see also* **bail**

2 (= *issue*) [+ *film*] estrenar; [+ *record, video*] sacar, poner a la venta; [+ *book*] publicar; [+ *news, report, information, statement*] hacer público, dar a conocer; **the police have ~d the names of the victims** la policía ha hecho públicos *or* dado a conocer los nombres de las víctimas

3 (= *make available*) [+ *documents*] facilitar; [+ *funds*] facilitar, ceder

4 (= *emit*) [+ *gas, smoke, heat, energy*] despedir, emitir; [+ *hormones*] secretar, segregar

5 (= *let go*) [+ *sb's hand, arm*] soltar; (*Tech*) [+ *spring, clasp, catch*] soltar; (*Phot*) [+ *shutter*] disparar; **to ~ one's grip** *or* **hold (on sth/sb): he ~d his grip on my arm** me soltó el brazo; **the state has to ~ its hold on the economy** el estado tiene que soltar las riendas de la economía

6 (= *let out, give vent to*) [+ *anger, frustration*] descargar, dar rienda suelta a; [+ *creativity*] sacar a flote; [+ *memories*] desatar, desencadenar; [+ *tension*] relajar; **your book has ~d a flood of memories** tu libro ha desatado *or* desencadenado una lluvia de recuerdos

7 (*Aut*) [+ *brake*] soltar

8 (*Jur*) [+ *right, property*] ceder

relegate [ˈrelɪgeɪt] VT 1 (= *demote*) [+ *person, old furniture*] relegar; **the news had been ~d to the inside pages** la noticia había sido relegada a las páginas interiores

2 (*Brit Sport*) [+ *team*] **they were ~d to the second division** bajaron *or* descendieron a segunda división

relegation [ˌrelɪˈgeɪʃən] N (= *demotion*) relegación *f*; (*Brit Sport*) descenso *m*

relent [rɪˈlent] VI 1 (= *show compassion*) ablandarse, aplacarse

2 (= *let up*) [*person*] descansar; (*fig*) [*weather*] mejorar

relentless [rɪˈlentlɪs] ADJ 1 (= *heartless*) [*cruelty*] cruel, despiadado

2 (= *persistent*) [*hard work*] incesante; **with ~ severity** con implacable severidad; **he is quite ~ about it** en esto se muestra totalmente implacable

relentlessly [rɪˈlentlɪslɪ] ADV 1 (= *heartlessly*) cruelmente, despiadadamente

2 (= *persistently*) sin descanso; **he presses on ~** avanza implacable

relet [ˈriːˈlet] (*pt, pp* **relet**) VT [+ *flat, house*] realquilar

relevance [ˈreləvəns] N pertinencia *f*, relevancia *f*; **matters of doubtful ~** asuntos de dudosa pertinencia *or* relevancia; **what is the ~ of that?** y eso ¿tiene que ver (con lo que estamos discutiendo)?

relevancy [ˈreləvənsɪ] N = **relevance**

relevant [ˈreləvənt] ADJ [*information, facts, document, page*] pertinente; **they had all the ~ information at their disposal** tenían toda la información pertinente a su disposición; **Shakespeare's plays are still ~ today** las obras de Shakespeare tienen aún trascendencia hoy en día; **he talked to the ~ officials to see what could be done** habló con los oficiales competentes para ver qué se podía hacer; **applicants need a year's ~ experience** los solicitantes necesitan tener un año de experiencia en el campo; **~ to: details ~ to this affair** detalles relacionados con *or* concernientes a este asunto; **information which may be ~ to this case** información que puede ser relevante para este caso; **that's not ~ to the case** eso no viene al caso; **your question is not ~ to the issues we're discussing** tu pregunta no guarda relación con lo que estamos discutiendo

reliability [rɪˌlaɪəˈbɪlɪtɪ] N 1 (= *dependability*) [*of person, firm*] seriedad *f*, formalidad *f*; [*of car, method*] fiabilidad *f*; **they have a reputation for good service and ~** tienen fama de dar un buen servicio y ser formales

2 (= *trustworthiness*) [*of facts*] verosimilitud *f*; [*of information, figures, account*] fiabilidad *f*; **we have doubts about the ~ of the results** dudamos de la fiabilidad de los resultados

reliable [rɪˈlaɪəbl] ADJ 1 (= *dependable*) [*person, firm*] digno de confianza, formal; [*ally*] en el que se puede confiar; [*car*] seguro, fiable; [*method*] de fiar; **she's very ~** puedes confiar completamente en ella, es una persona muy formal; **they provide a cheap and ~ service** proporcionan un servicio barato y fiable

2 (= *trustworthy*) [*information, figures, guide, indicator*] fiable; [*evidence, report, description, account*] fidedigno; [*memory*] de fiar; **~ sources** fuentes *fpl* fidedignas

reliably [rɪˈlaɪəblɪ] ADV **I am ~ informed that …** sé de fuentes fidedignas que …; **equipment that works ~ in most conditions** equipo que funciona sin fallos en la mayoría de las condiciones; **stars whose distances we can ~ measure** estrellas cuyas distancias podemos medir con cierta precisión

reliance [rɪˈlaɪəns] N **~ on sth** (= *trust*) confianza *f* en algo; (= *dependence*) dependencia *f* de algo; **our excessive ~ on him** nuestra excesiva dependencia con respecto de él, el que dependamos tanto de él; **you can place no ~ on that** no hay que fiarse de eso, no hay que tener confianza en eso

reliant [rɪˈlaɪənt] ADJ **to be ~ on sth/sb** depender de algo/algn

relic [ˈrelɪk] N (*Rel*) reliquia *f*; (*fig*) vestigio *m*

relict†† [ˈrelɪkt] N viuda *f*

relief [rɪˈliːf] Ⓐ N 1 (*from pain, anxiety*) alivio *m*; **that's a ~!** ¡qué alivio!; **the news came as a great ~ to her parents** la noticia fue un gran alivio para sus padres; **there was a sense of ~ that the war was finally over** todos sintieron un gran alivio cuando se supo que la guerra había terminado por fin; **the ~ of nasal congestion** el alivio de la congestión nasal; **to bring** *or* **give** *or* **provide ~ from sth** aliviar algo; **drugs provide ~ from the pain** las drogas alivian el dolor; **to heave** *or* **breathe a sigh of ~** dar un suspiro de alivio; **to our (great) ~, she accepted** para (gran) alivio nuestro, aceptó; **she almost wept with** *or* **in ~** casi lloró del alivio que sintió

2 (*from monotony*) **it's a ~ to get out of the office once in a while** es un respiro salir de la oficina de vez en cuando; **by way of light ~** a modo de diversión; *see also* **comic**

3 (= *aid*) auxilio *m*, ayuda *f*; **disaster ~** *auxilio a las víctimas de una catástrofe*; **~ efforts have been hampered by the rains** la lluvia ha dificultado las operaciones de auxilio; *see also* **famine**

4 (= *state welfare*) **to be on** *or* **get ~** (*US*) recibir prestaciones de la seguridad social; **poor ~** (*Brit Hist*) socorro *m*, beneficencia *f*

5 (*Mil*) [*of town*] liberación *f*

6 (*Art, Geog*) relieve *m*; **in ~** en relieve; **in high/low ~** en alto/bajo relieve; **to stand out in (bold** *or* **sharp** *or* **stark) ~ against sth** (*lit, fig*) contrastar dramáticamente con algo; **to throw** *or* **bring sth into (sharp) ~** (*fig*) poner algo de relieve, hacer resaltar algo; *see also* **bas-relief**

7 (= *replacement*) relevo *m*, sustituto *m*

8 (= *exemption*) (*from taxation*) desgravación *f*; *see also* **debt**

9 (*Jur*) desagravio *m*

Ⓑ CPD [*train, bus*] de reemplazo; [*typist, secretary*] suplente; [*work, worker, agency, organization, convoy*] de ayuda, de auxilio ► **relief driver** N conductor(a) *m/f* de relevo ► **relief fund** N fondo *m* de auxilio (a los damnificados) ► **relief map** N mapa *m* físico *or* de relieve; (*3-D*) mapa *m* en relieve ► **relief road** N carretera *f* de descongestión ► **relief supplies** NPL provisiones *fpl* de auxilio ► **relief troops** NPL tropas *fpl* de relevo

relieve [rɪˈliːv] VT 1 (= *alleviate*) [+ *sufferings, pain, headache*] aliviar; [+ *burden*] aligerar; [+ *tension, boredom, anxiety*] disipar, aliviar; **to feel ~d** sentirse aliviado; **to ~ the boredom of the journey** para que el viaje se haga menos aburrido; **the plain is ~d by an occasional hill** de vez en cuando una colina rompe con la monotonía de la llanura

2 (= *ease*) [+ *person's mind*] tranquilizar; **it ~s me to hear it** me tranquiliza saberlo

3 [+ *feelings, anger*] desahogar; **to ~ one's feelings** desahogarse; **I ~d my feelings in a letter** me desahogué escribiendo una carta

4 **to ~ o.s.** (= *go to lavatory*) ir al baño, hacer pis*

5 (= *release*) **to ~ sb of a duty** exonerar a algn de un deber; **to ~ sb of a post** destituir a algn; **he was ~d of his command** fue relevado de su mando; **let me ~ you of your coat** permítame tomarle el abrigo; **to ~ sb of his wallet** (*hum*) quitar la cartera a algn, robar la cartera a algn

6 (*Mil*) [+ *city*] descercar, socorrer; [+ *troops*] relevar; **I'll come and ~ you at six** vengo a las seis a relevarte

7 **to ~ the poor** (= *help*) socorrer a los pobres

religion [rɪˈlɪdʒən] N (= *belief*) religión *f*; **football is like a ~ with him** el fútbol es su religión; **it's against my ~ to do that** hacer eso es contrario a mis creencias religiosas, hacer eso va contra mi religión; **to get ~*** darse a la religión

religiosity [rɪˌlɪdʒɪˈɒsɪtɪ] N religiosidad *f*

religious [rɪˈlɪdʒəs] Ⓐ ADJ 1 [*beliefs, leader, service, life*] religioso; [*practice*] de la religión, religioso; [*war*] de religión, religioso; **for ~ reasons** por razones religiosas; **she's deeply ~** es profundamente religiosa; **~ freedom** libertad *f* de culto

2 (*fig*) (= *meticulous*) **~ attention to detail** una atención minuciosa para los detalles

Ⓑ N **the ~** las personas religiosas, los religiosos

Ⓒ CPD ► **religious education, religious instruction** N enseñanza *f* religiosa

religiously [rɪˈlɪdʒəslɪ] ADV 1 (*Rel*) **a ~ diverse country** un país con diversidad religiosa *or* de religiones; **~ minded people** gente con inclinaciones religiosas; **~ motivated** motivado por la religión

2 (= *meticulously*) religiosamente

religiousness [rɪˈlɪdʒəsnɪs] N religiosidad *f*

reline [ˈriːˈlaɪn] VT reforrar, poner nuevo forro a

relinquish [rɪˈlɪŋkwɪʃ] VT [+ *claim, right*] renunciar a; [+ *control*] ceder; [+ *post*] renunciar a, dimitir de; **to ~ one's grip on sth** (*lit*) soltar algo

relinquishment [rɪˈlɪŋkwɪʃmənt] N [*of claim, right*] renuncia *f*; [*of post*] dimisión *f*

reliquary [ˈrelɪkwərɪ] N relicario *m*

relish [ˈrelɪʃ] Ⓐ N [1] (= *distinctive flavour*) sabor *m*

[2] (= *gusto, enthusiasm*) entusiasmo *m*; **to do sth with ~** hacer algo de buena gana; **to eat sth with ~** comer algo con apetito; **hunting has no ~ for me now** ya no disfruto tanto cazando

[3] (= *sauce*) salsa *f*

Ⓑ VT [1] (= *taste, savour*) [+ *a good meal*] saborear

[2] (= *like*) **I don't ~ the idea of staying up all night** no me hace gracia la idea de estar levantado toda la noche

relive [ˈriːˈlɪv] VT [+ *past*] revivir; **to ~ old memories** rememorar los recuerdos

reload [ˈriːˈləʊd] VT recargar, volver a cargar

relocate [ˈriːləʊˈkeɪt] Ⓐ VT [+ *factory, employees*] trasladar, reubicar (*LAm*)

Ⓑ VI trasladarse

relocation [ˌriːləʊˈkeɪʃən] Ⓐ N traslado *m*, nueva ubicación *f*

Ⓑ CPD ► **relocation package** N prima *f* de traslado

reluctance [rɪˈlʌktəns] N reticencia *f*, renuencia *f* (*frm*); **her ~ to allow it was understandable** era comprensible que se mostrase reacia *or* reticente a permitirlo, su reticencia *or* (*frm*) renuencia a permitirlo era comprensible; **to show ~ (to do sth)** mostrarse reacio *or* reticente *or* (*frm*) renuente (a hacer algo), mostrar reticencia *or* (*frm*) renuencia (a hacer algo); **with ~** con reticencia, a regañadientes; **to make a show of ~** aparentar reticencia, aparentar estar reticente

reluctant [rɪˈlʌktənt] ADJ [*person*] reacio, reticente, renuente (*frm*); [*praise*] a regañadientes; **the case was hampered by ~ witnesses** testigos reacios a colaborar obstaculizaron el caso; **I would make a ~ secretary** yo trabajaría como secretario con desgana *or* a regañadientes; **the ~ dragon** el dragón que no quería; **he indicated his ~ acceptance of the proposals** indicó que aceptaba las propuestas con reservas; **he left with Bernstein's ~ consent** se fue con el consentimiento que Bernstein le había dado a regañadientes *or* muy a su pesar; **he took the ~ decision to stop production** tomó la decisión, muy a su pesar, de parar la producción; **to be ~ to do sth: she was ~ to ask for help** se mostraba reacia a pedir ayuda; **we were ~ to sell the house** éramos reacios a vender la casa, nos resistíamos a vender la casa

reluctantly [rɪˈlʌktəntlɪ] ADV [*agree, accept*] de mala gana, a regañadientes; **he ~ accepted their advice** aceptó sus consejos de mala gana *or* a regañadientes

rely [rɪˈlaɪ] VI **to ~ (up)on sth/sb** (= *depend on*) depender de algo/algn; (= *count on*) contar con algo/algn; (= *trust*) confiar en algo/algn, fiarse de algo/algn; **he had gradually come to ~ on her** había llegado poco a poco a depender de ella; **can we ~ on your help?** ¿podemos contar con tu ayuda?; **she'll come, you can ~ upon it** vendrá, con eso puedes contar, vendrá, cuenta con ello; **you can't ~ on the trains/the weather** no se puede uno fiar de los trenes/del tiempo; **to ~ (up)on sth/sb for sth** depender de algo/algn para algo; **the island relies on tourism for its income** la isla depende del turismo como fuente de ingresos; **to ~ (up)on sth/sb to do sth: we are ~ing on you to do it** contamos con usted para hacerlo; **you can ~ on him to be late** puedes tener por seguro *or* ten por seguro que va a llegar tarde; **can I ~ on you to behave?** ¿puedo confiar en que te vas a comportar?, ¿puedo fiarme de que te vas a comportar?

REM [rem] N ABBR [1] (*Physiol*) (= **rapid eye movement**) movimiento *m* rápido del ojo

[2] (*Phys*) = **roentgen equivalent man**

remain [rɪˈmeɪn] VI [1] (= *be left*) quedar; **little now ~s of the old city** poco queda ya del casco antiguo; **the few pleasures that ~ to me** los pocos placeres que me quedan; **much ~s to be done** queda mucho por hacer; **nothing ~s to be said** no queda nada por decir, no hay nada más que decir; **nothing ~s but to accept** no queda más remedio que aceptar; **it only ~s to thank you** sólo queda darle las gracias; **that ~s to be seen** eso está por ver

[2] (= *continue to be*) seguir, continuar; **the problem ~s unsolved** el problema sigue *or* continúa sin resolverse; **he ~ed a formidable opponent** siguió *or* continuó siendo un rival formidable; **to ~ seated/standing** permanecer sentado/de pie; **to ~ faithful to sb** seguir *or* permanecer fiel a algn; **they ~ed silent** permanecieron en silencio; **the government ~ed in control** el gobierno mantuvo *or* sostuvo el control; **the two men have ~ed friends** los dos hombres han seguido siendo amigos; **if the weather ~s fine** si el tiempo sigue bueno; **the fact ~s that …** (*referring to previous statement*) no es menos cierto que …, sigue siendo un hecho que …

[3] (= *stay*) quedarse; **we ~ed there three weeks** nos quedamos allí tres semanas; **to ~ behind** (*gen*) quedarse; (*after school*) quedarse después de las clases

[4] (*in letters*) **I ~, yours faithfully** le saluda atentamente

remainder [rɪˈmeɪndəʳ] Ⓐ N [1] (= *part left over*) resto *m*; **the ~ of the debt** el resto de la deuda; **during the ~ of the day** durante el resto del día; **the ~ would not come** los otros *or* los demás no quisieron venir

[2] (*Math*) resto *m*

[3] **remainders** (*Comm*) artículos *mpl* no vendidos; (= *books*) restos *mpl* de edición

Ⓑ VT [+ *copies of book*] saldar

remaining [rɪˈmeɪnɪŋ] ADJ **the three ~ hostages** los tres rehenes restantes *or* que quedaban; **he is her only ~ relative** él es el único pariente que le queda; **the ~ passengers** los otros *or* los demás pasajeros

remains [rɪˈmeɪnz] NPL [*of building*] restos *mpl*; [*of food*] sobras *fpl*, restos *mpl*; **the ~ of the picnic** los restos *or* las sobras del picnic; **human ~** restos *mpl* humanos; **Roman ~** ruinas *fpl* romanas

remake Ⓐ [ˌriːˈmeɪk] VT rehacer, volver a hacer

Ⓑ [ˈriːmeɪk] N (*Cine*) nueva versión *f*

remand [rɪˈmɑːnd] (*Jur*) Ⓐ N **to be on ~** estar en prisión preventiva

Ⓑ VT [+ *case*] remitir; **to ~ sb in custody** poner a algn en prisión preventiva; **to ~ sb on bail** libertar a algn bajo fianza

Ⓒ CPD ► **remand centre** N cárcel *f* transitoria ► **remand home** N cárcel *f* transitoria para menores ► **remand wing** N galería *f* de prisión preventiva

remark [rɪˈmɑːk] Ⓐ N [1] (= *comment*) comentario *m*, observación *f*; **to let sth pass without ~** dejar pasar algo sin (hacer) comentario; **after some introductory ~s** tras unos comentarios introductorios; **to make a ~** hacer un comentario *or* una observación; **she made the ~ that** observó que; **to make** *or* **pass ~s about sb** (*usu pej*) hacer comentarios sobre algn; *see also* **personal A4**

[2] (= *notice*) **worthy of ~** digno de mención

Ⓑ VT [1] (= *say*) comentar, observar; **to ~ that** comentar que, observar que, decir que; **"it's a pity," she ~ed** —es una lástima —dijo

[2] (= *notice*) observar, notar

Ⓒ VI (= *comment*) **to ~ on sth** hacer observaciones sobre algo

remarkable [rɪˈmɑːkəbl] ADJ [*person, success, ability, performance*] extraordinario; [*achievement, recovery, progress*] notable, extraordinario; [*results*] excelente, extraordinario; [*story*] singular; **what's ~ about that?** no sé qué tiene eso de extraordinario; **~ for sth** notable por algo; **his statement was ~ for its clarity** su declaración fue notable por su claridad; **a teacher ~ for her patience** un profesor que destaca por su paciencia; **it's ~ how quickly children grow up** es extraordinario lo rápido que crecen los niños; **he's a most ~ man** es un hombre extraordinario; **we have made ~ progress** hemos realizado notables *or* extraordinarios progresos; **it is ~ that** es sorprendente que + *subjun*; **it was ~ to see how quickly she recovered** fue sorprendente *or* extraordinario lo pronto que se recuperó; **what's ~ to me is that so many people came** lo que me parece sorprendente es que viniera tanta gente

remarkably [rɪˈmɑːkəblɪ] ADV [*similar, beautiful, cheap*] extraordinariamente; [*well, quickly*] increíblemente; **the factory had, ~, escaped the bombing** la fábrica, increíblemente, no resultó dañada en el bombardeo; **~ few people** un número increíblemente escaso de personas; **there have been ~ few complaints** sorprendentemente, ha habido muy pocas quejas; **the general standard was ~ high** el nivel general era notablemente alto; **he looked ~ like his father** guardaba un parecido extraordinario con su padre; **it tastes ~ good** tiene un sabor extraordinario

remarriage [ˈriːˈmærɪdʒ] N segundo casamiento *m*

remarry [ˈriːˈmærɪ] VI volver a casarse; **she remarried three years ago** se volvió a casar hace tres años

rematch [ˈriːˌmætʃ] N partido *m* de vuelta, revancha *f*

remediable [rɪˈmiːdɪəbl] ADJ remediable

remedial [rɪˈmiːdɪəl] Ⓐ ADJ (*Med*) reparador; (*fig*) correctivo

Ⓑ CPD ► **remedial course** N curso *m* correctivo ► **remedial education** N educación *f* especial ► **remedial teaching** N enseñanza *f* de los niños *etc* con dificultades

remedy [ˈremədɪ] Ⓐ N (*gen*) remedio *m*; **a good ~ for a sore throat** un buen remedio para el dolor de garganta; **to be past ~** (*Med, fig*) no tener remedio; **there's no ~ for that** eso no tiene remedio; **the best ~ for that is to protest** eso se remedia protestando; **to have no ~ at law** no tener recurso legal

Ⓑ VT (*Med*) [+ *illness*] curar; (*fig*) [+ *situation*] remediar; **that's soon remedied** eso es fácil remediarlo, eso queda arreglado fácilmente

remember [rɪˈmembəʳ] Ⓐ VT [1] (= *recall*) [+ *person, fact, promise*] acordarse de, recordar; **don't you ~ me?** ¿no se acuerda usted de mí?, ¿no me recuerda?; **I can never ~ phone numbers** tengo muy mala memoria para los

► LANGUAGE IN USE: remember A1 26.1

números de teléfono, soy incapaz de recordar números de teléfono; **I don't ~ a thing about it** no recuerdo ni un solo detalle de ello; **I ~ seeing it** ◊ **I ~ having seen it** me acuerdo de *or* recuerdo haberlo visto, me acuerdo de *or* recuerdo que lo vi; **I seem to ~ (that) you used to do the same** si mal no recuerdo, tú hacías lo mismo; **I don't ~ what he looks like** no me acuerdo de *or* no recuerdo cómo es; **I ~ him as tall and slim** lo recuerdo alto y delgado; **give me something to ~ you by** dame algún recuerdo tuyo; **so I gave him sth to ~ me by** (*fig*) así que le di algo para que no me olvidara *or* para que se acordara de mí; **she will be ~ed for her wonderful sense of humour** se la recordará por su maravilloso sentido del humor; **it was a night to ~** fue una noche memorable *or* inolvidable

2 (= *bear in mind*) recordar, tener presente; **~ that he carries a gun** recuerda *or* ten presente que lleva una pistola; **that's worth ~ing** eso merece la pena recordarlo; **it is worth ~ing that ...** merece la pena recordar que ...

3 (= *not forget*) acordarse de; **have you ~ed your passport?** ¿te has acordado del pasaporte *or* de traer el pasaporte?; **she always ~s the children at Christmas** siempre se acuerda de los niños por Navidad; **to ~ sb in one's prayers** rezar por algn; **to ~ sb in one's will** mencionar a algn en el testamento; **she ~ed to do it** se acordó de hacerlo; **~ to turn out the light** no te olvides de apagar la luz; **~ what happened before** no te olvides *or* acuérdate de lo que pasó antes

4 (= *commemorate*) recordar; **today we ~ those who gave their lives in the war** hoy recordamos a aquellos que dieron sus vidas en la guerra

5 (*with wishes*) **she asks to be ~ed to you all** manda recuerdos a todos; **~ me to your family** dale recuerdos a tu familia, saluda a tu familia de mi parte

Ⓑ VI 1 (= *recall*) acordarse, recordar; **do you ~?** ¿te acuerdas?, ¿recuerdas?; **try to ~!** ¡haz memoria!, ¡intenta acordarte!; **I don't** *or* **can't ~** no me acuerdo, no recuerdo; **as I ~, you said you would pay** que yo recuerde *or* si mal no recuerdo, tú dijiste que pagarías; **it was a cold day, as you will ~** era un día de frío, como recordarás; **as far as I (can) ~** que yo recuerde; **not as far as I ~** no que yo recuerde; **as far back as** *or* **for as long as I can ~** desde siempre; **if I ~ right(ly)** si mal no recuerdo, si la memoria no me falla

2 (= *not forget*) acordarse; **I asked you to get some stamps, did you ~?** te pedí que compraras sellos, ¿te acordaste?; **I'll try to ~** intentaré acordarme, intentaré no olvidarme *or* que no se me olvide

remembrance [rɪˈmembrəns] Ⓐ N (= *remembering*) recuerdo *m*; **~s** recuerdos *mpl*; **in ~ of** en conmemoración de; **I have no ~ of it** no lo recuerdo en absoluto

Ⓑ CPD ► **Remembrance Day, Remembrance Sunday** N (*Brit*) *día en el que se recuerda a los caídos en las dos guerras mundiales*; → POPPY DAY

▼ **remind** [rɪˈmaɪnd] VT recordar a; **thank you for ~ing me** gracias por recordármelo; **to ~ sb that** recordar a algn que; **customers are ~ed that ...** se recuerda a los clientes que ...; **to ~ sb to do sth** recordar a algn que haga algo; **~ me to fix an appointment** recuérdame que ponga una cita; **you have to keep ~ing him to do it** hay que recordárselo constantemente; **need I ~ you who he is?** ¿tengo que recordarte quién es?; **to ~ sb about sth** recordar algo a algn; **don't forget to ~ her about the party** no te olvides de recordarle lo de la fiesta; **don't ~ me!*** ¡no me lo recuerdes!; **to ~ sb of sth** recordar algo a algn; **that ~s me of last time** eso me recuerda la última vez; **she ~s me of Anne** me recuerda a Anne; **to ~ o.s.: I have to ~ myself to relax** tengo que recordarme a mí mismo que debo relajarme; **he's only a boy, I ~ed myself** no es más que un niño, me recordé; **that ~s me!** ¡a propósito!; **I saw John today, which ~s me ...** hoy vi a John, a propósito ...; → REMEMBER

> **REMEMBER**
>
> **"acordarse de" or "recordar"?**
>
> • Both **acordarse de** and **recordar** can be used to translate **to remember** (used transitively), provided the object of **remember** is not another verb. **Recordar** is becoming less common, however, in everyday informal contexts:
>
> Do you remember where he lives?
> ***¿Te acuerdas de dónde vive?, ¿Recuerdas dónde vive?***
>
> • Use **acordarse de** + INFINITIVE to translate **to remember to** + VERB:
>
> Did you remember to close the door?
> ***¿Te acordaste de cerrar la puerta?***
>
> ! Don't use **recordar** for **remembering to do sth**.
>
> • Use **recordar** + PERFECT INFINITIVE/CLAUSE or **acordarse de** + CLAUSE to translate **to remember** + -ING:
>
> I remember closing the door
> ***Recuerdo haber cerrado*** *or* ***Recuerdo que cerré*** *or* ***Me acuerdo de que cerré la puerta***
>
> **NOTE: Recordar** also translates **remind**:
>
> I must remind Richard to pay the rent
> ***Tengo que recordarle a Richard que pague el alquiler***
>
> *For further uses and examples, see main entry.*

reminder [rɪˈmaɪndəʳ] Ⓐ N 1 (= *letter etc*) notificación *f*, aviso *m*; **we will send a ~** le enviaremos un recordatorio; **it's a gentle ~** es una advertencia amistosa

2 (= *memento*) recuerdo *m*; **it's a ~ of the good old days** recuerda los buenos tiempos pasados

Ⓑ CPD ► **subscription reminder card** N tarjeta *f* recordatoria de renovación de suscripción

reminisce [ˌremɪˈnɪs] VI recordar, rememorar

reminiscence [ˌremɪˈnɪsəns] N (= *act*) reminiscencia *f*; (= *individual recollection*) recuerdo *m*

reminiscent [ˌremɪˈnɪsənt] ADJ 1 (= *nostalgic*) nostálgico; **to be in a ~ mood** ponerse nostálgico

2 **to be ~ of** recordar; **that bit is ~ of Rossini** ese trozo recuerda a *or* tiene reminiscencia de Rossini; **that's ~ of another old joke** eso suena a otro conocido chiste

reminiscently [ˌremɪˈnɪsəntlɪ] ADV **he spoke ~** habló pensando en el pasado

remiss [rɪˈmɪs] ADJ negligente, descuidado; **I have been very ~ about it** he sido muy negligente *or* descuidado en eso; **it was ~ of me** fue un descuido de mi parte

remission [rɪˈmɪʃən] N 1 (*Rel*) (= *forgiveness*) remisión *f*, perdón *m*; (*gen*) (= *annulment*) exoneración *f*; **~ of sins** remisión *or* perdón de los pecados

2 (*Brit*) (= *shortening of prison sentence*) disminución *f* de pena

3 (*Med*) **to be in ~** [*sick person*] haberse recuperado (temporalmente); [*disease*] remitir, estar en fase de remisión

remissness [rɪˈmɪsnɪs] N negligencia *f*, descuido *m*

remit [ˈriːmɪt] Ⓐ N (*Brit*) (= *area of responsibility*) competencia *f*; (= *terms of reference*) [*of committee etc*] cometido *m*

Ⓑ [rɪˈmɪt] VT 1 (= *pay by sending*) [+ *amount due*] remitir

2 (= *refer*) [+ *decision*] remitir

3 (*Rel*) (= *forgive*) [+ *sins*] perdonar, remitir

4 (= *let off*) [+ *debt*] remitir; **three months of the sentence were ~ted** se le redujo la pena en tres meses

Ⓒ [rɪˈmɪt] VI disminuir, reducirse

remittal [rɪˈmɪtl] N (*Jur*) remisión *f*

remittance [rɪˈmɪtəns] Ⓐ N (= *payment*) pago *m*, giro *m*

Ⓑ CPD ► **remittance advice** N aviso *m* de pago

remittee [rɪmɪˈtiː] N consignatario/a *m/f*

remittent [rɪˈmɪtənt] ADJ [*fever etc*] remitente

remitter [rɪˈmɪtəʳ] N remitente *mf*

remnant [ˈremnənt] Ⓐ N (= *remainder*) resto *m*, remanente *m*; (= *scrap of cloth*) retal *m*

Ⓑ CPD ► **remnant day** N (*Comm*) día *m* de venta de restos de serie ► **remnant sale** N venta *f* de restos de serie, liquidación *f* total

remodel [ˈriːˈmɒdl] VT remodelar

remold [ˈriːˈməʊld] N, VT (*US*) = **remould**

remonstrance [rɪˈmɒnstrəns] N (*frm*) (= *complaint, protest*) protesta *f*, queja *f*

remonstrate [ˈremənstreɪt] VI (= *protest*) protestar, quejarse; (= *argue*) discutir; **to ~ about sth** protestar contra algo, poner reparos a algo; **to ~ with sb** reconvenir a algn

remorse [rɪˈmɔːs] N (= *regret*) remordimiento *m*; **without ~** sin remordimientos; **to feel ~** arrepentirse

remorseful [rɪˈmɔːsfʊl] ADJ (= *regretful*) arrepentido

remorsefully [rɪˈmɔːsfəlɪ] ADV con remordimiento; **he said ~** dijo arrepentido

remorsefulness [rɪˈmɔːsfʊlnɪs] N remordimiento *m*

remorseless [rɪˈmɔːslɪs] ADJ 1 (= *merciless*) despiadado

2 (= *relentless*) [*advance, progress*] implacable, inexorable

remorselessly [rɪˈmɔːslɪslɪ] ADV 1 (= *mercilessly*) [*pursue, tease*] despiadadamente, de forma despiadada

2 (= *relentlessly*) implacablemente, inexorablemente; **the spread of the virus is continuing ~** el virus continúa propagándose implacablemente, la propagación del virus continúa implacable

remorselessness [rɪˈmɔːslɪsnɪs] N 1 (= *mercilessness*) lo despiadado

2 (= *relentlessness*) lo implacable, inexorabilidad *f*

remote [rɪˈməʊt] Ⓐ ADJ (*compar* **remoter**, *superl* **remotest**) 1 (= *distant*) [*village, spot, area*] remoto, apartado; [*star, galaxy*] lejano, remoto; [*relative, ancestor, descendant*] lejano; **in the ~st parts of Africa** en las partes más remotas *or* más apartadas de África; **the ~ past/future** el pasado/futuro remoto; **~ antiquity** la antigüedad remota; **it's ~ from any towns** está muy lejos *or* muy apartado de cualquier ciudad; **events which seem ~ from our daily lives** hechos que parecen muy alejados de nuestras vidas cotidianas; **a village ~ from the world** un pueblo apartado del mundo

2 (= *removed*) lejano, remoto; **villages where the war seemed ~** pueblos donde la guerra parecía algo lejano *or* remoto; **to be ~**

> ➤ LANGUAGE IN USE: **remind** 20.7

from sth estar alejado de algo; **these events seem ~ from contemporary life** estos sucesos parecen estar alejados de la vida contemporánea; **what he said was rather ~ from the subject in hand** lo que dijo no tenía mucha relación con el tema que se trataba
3 (= *aloof*) [*person, manner, voice*] distante
4 (= *slight*) [*possibility, chance, prospect, hope*] remoto; [*risk, resemblance*] ligero; [*connection*] remoto; **I haven't the ~st idea** no tengo ni la más remota idea
5 (= *remote-controlled*) a distancia
Ⓑ N (*also* ~ **control**) mando *m* a distancia, telemando *m*
Ⓒ CPD ► **remote access** N (*Comput*) acceso *m* remoto ► **remote control** N (= *system*) control *m* remoto; (= *device*) mando *m* a distancia, telemando *m* ► **remote learning** N (*Educ*) educación *f* a distancia ► **remote sensing** N detección *f* a distancia

remote-controlled [rɪ'məʊtkən'trəʊld] ADJ [*toy aircraft etc*] teledirigido

remotely [rɪ'məʊtlɪ] ADV 1 (= *distantly*) en un lugar apartado; **they are ~ related** son parientes lejanos; **to be ~ situated** estar situado en un lugar apartado
2 (= *slightly*) [*connected, possible*] remotamente; **it wasn't even ~ amusing** no era ni por asomo divertido; **he isn't even ~ interested in opera** no está ni siquiera remotamente interesado en la ópera; **he failed to say anything ~ interesting** no consiguió decir nada mínimamente interesante; **I've never seen anything ~ like it** nunca he visto nada (ni) remotamente parecido; **it's not even ~ likely** de eso no hay la más remota posibilidad; **he'll eat anything that looks ~ edible** es capaz de comerse cualquier cosa con un mínimo aspecto de comestible; **the struggle to maintain anything ~ resembling decent standards** la lucha por mantener algo que se pareciera aunque fuera de lejos a unos niveles decentes
3 (= *in a detached manner*) [*say, behave*] de forma distante
4 (= *by remote control*) [*control*] a distancia; [*detonate*] por control remoto

remoteness [rɪ'məʊtnɪs] N 1 (*in space*) [*of galaxy, village, house*] lo remoto
2 (*in time*) [*of period, age*] lo lejano
3 (= *aloofness*) **he found her ~ hard to cope with** no llevaba bien que ella fuese tan distante; **her ~ from everyday life** su alejamiento de la vida diaria

remould, remold (*US*) [,riː'məʊld] Ⓐ VT recauchutar
Ⓑ ['riːməʊld] N neumático *m* recauchutado, llanta *f* recauchutada (*LAm*)

remount ['riː'maʊnt] Ⓐ VT (*gen*) montar de nuevo en, volver a montar en
Ⓑ VI montar de nuevo, volver a montar
Ⓒ N (*Mil etc*) remonta *f*

removable [rɪ'muːvəbl] ADJ 1 (= *detachable*) movible; [*collar etc*] de quita y pon
2 (*from job*) amovible

removal [rɪ'muːvəl] Ⓐ N (= *transfer*) traslado *m*; [*of word etc*] supresión *f*; (*esp Brit*) (*to new house*) mudanza *f*; (*fig*) (= *murder*) eliminación *f*; **his ~ to a new post** su traslado a un nuevo puesto; **the ~ of this threat** la eliminación de esta amenaza
Ⓑ CPD ► **removal allowance** N (*Brit*) subvención *f* de mudanza ► **removal expenses** NPL (*Brit*) gastos *mpl* de traslado de efectos personales ► **removal man** N mozo *m* de mudanzas ► **removal van** N (*Brit*) camión *m* de mudanzas

remove [rɪ'muːv] Ⓐ VT 1 (= *take away*) [+ *object*] quitar; [+ *documents, evidence*] llevarse; **~ the pan from the heat** quite la cacerola del fuego; **to ~ a child from school** sacar *or* quitar a un niño de la escuela; **the demonstrators were forcibly ~d by police** (*from building*) la policía echó a los manifestantes a la fuerza; **to ~ o.s.** irse, marcharse; **kindly ~ yourself at once** haga el favor de irse *or* marcharse inmediatamente; **to ~ sth/sb to** trasladar *or* llevar algo/a algn a; **her body had been ~d to the mortuary** habían trasladado *or* llevado su cuerpo al tanatorio
2 (= *take off*) quitar; [+ *one's clothing, make-up*] quitarse; **first ~ the lid** primero quite la tapa; **he ~d his jacket** se quitó la chaqueta; **he ~d his hat** se quitó el sombrero, se descubrió; **she had the tattoo ~d from her arm** se fue a que le quitaran *or* se quitó el tatuaje del brazo
3 (= *take out*) [+ *object*] sacar; (*Med*) [+ *organ, tumour*] extirpar, quitar; [+ *bullet*] extraer, quitar; **~ the cake from the oven** saque la tarta del horno
4 (= *delete*) [+ *word, sentence, paragraph*] suprimir, quitar; [+ *name from list*] quitar, tachar (**from** de)
5 (= *get rid of*) [+ *obstacle, threat, waste, problem*] eliminar; [+ *doubt, suspicion*] disipar; [+ *fear*] acabar con; [+ *stain*] quitar; **an agreement on removing trade barriers** un acuerdo sobre la eliminación de las barreras comerciales; **products that ~ unwanted hair** productos que eliminan *or* quitan el vello superfluo
6 (= *dismiss*) [+ *person*] (*from post*) destituir; **to ~ sb from office** destituir a algn de su cargo; **to ~ sb from power** destituir a algn del poder
Ⓑ VI (*Brit frm*) (= *move house*) mudarse, trasladarse, cambiarse (*Mex*) (**to** a)
Ⓒ N **this is but one ~ from disaster** esto raya en la catástrofe, esto está a un paso de la catástrofe; **this is several ~s from our official policy** esto dista *or* se aparta mucho de nuestra política oficial; **it's a far ~ from …** dista mucho de …; **at a** *or* **one ~** de lejos; **to experience a foreign culture, albeit at a ~** vivir una cultura extranjera, aunque sea de lejos

removed [rɪ'muːvd] ADJ **to be far ~ from sth** distar *or* apartarse mucho de algo; **his political views are far ~ from theirs** sus ideas políticas distan *or* se apartan mucho de las de ellos; **an indifference not far ~ from contempt** una indiferencia rayana con *or* que rayaba en el desprecio; **first cousin once ~** (= *parent's cousin*) tío/a *m/f* segundo/a; (= *cousin's child*) sobrino/a *m/f* segundo/a, hijo/a *m/f* de primo carnal

remover [rɪ'muːvəʳ] N 1 (= *person*) agente *mf* de mudanzas
2 (= *substance*) **make-up ~** desmaquillador *m*, desmaquillante *m*; **nail polish ~** quitaesmalte *m*; **stain ~** quitamanchas *m inv*

remunerate [rɪ'mjuːnəreɪt] VT remunerar

remuneration [rɪ,mjuːnə'reɪʃən] N remuneración *f*

remunerative [rɪ'mjuːnərətɪv] ADJ remunerativo

Renaissance [rə'neɪsɑːns] (*Art, Hist*) Ⓐ N **the ~** el Renacimiento; **the 12th century ~** el renacimiento del siglo XII
Ⓑ CPD renacentista, del Renacimiento

renaissance [rə'neɪsɑːns] N renacimiento *m*; **a spiritual ~** un renacimiento *or* despertar espiritual

renal ['riːnl] Ⓐ ADJ (*Anat*) renal
Ⓑ CPD ► **renal failure** N insuficiencia *f* renal

rename ['riː'neɪm] VT poner nuevo nombre a; **they have ~d it "Mon Repos"** le han puesto el nuevo nombre de "Mon Repos"

renascence [rɪ'næsns] N = **renaissance**

renascent [rɪ'næsnt] ADJ renaciente, que renace

renationalization ['riː,næʃnəlaɪ'zeɪʃən] N renacionalización *f*

renationalize ['riː'næʃnəlaɪz] VT renacionalizar

rend [rend] (*pt, pp* **rent**) VT 1 (*poet*) (= *tear*) rasgar, desgarrar; (= *split*) hender; **to ~ sth in twain** partir algo por medio, hender algo; **to ~ one's clothes** rasgar *or* desgarrar su ropa
2 (*fig*) **a cry rent the air** un grito cortó el aire

render ['rendəʳ] VT 1 (*frm*) (= *give*) [+ *honour*] dar, rendir; [+ *service, assistance*] dar, prestar; **to ~ good for evil** devolver bien por mal; **to ~ thanks to sb** dar las gracias a algn; **~ unto Caesar …** al César lo que es del César (y a Dios lo que es de Dios); **to ~ an account of one's stewardship** dar cuenta de su gobierno, justificar su conducta durante su mando; **to ~ an account to God** dar cuenta de sí ante Dios
2 (*frm*) (= *make*) dejar, volver; **the accident ~ed him blind** el accidente lo dejó ciego; **to ~ sth useless** inutilizar algo
3 (= *interpret*) [+ *sonata etc*] interpretar; [+ *role, play*] representar, interpretar; (= *translate*) [+ *text*] traducir; **no photograph could adequately ~ the scene** ninguna fotografía podría reproducir con justicia la escena
4 (*Culin*) (*also* ~ **down**) derretir
5 (*Constr*) enlucir
6 (*Comm*) **to ~ an account** pasar factura; **to account ~ed** según factura anterior

►**render down** VT + ADV [*fat*] derretir

►**render up** VT + ADV [+ *one's/sb's soul*] entregar; **the earth ~s up its treasures** la tierra rinde sus tesoros

rendering ['rendərɪŋ] N (= *translation*) traducción *f*; [*of song, role*] interpretación *f*; **her ~ of the sonata** su interpretación de la sonata; **an elegant ~ of Machado** una elegante versión de Machado

rendezvous ['rɒndɪvuː] Ⓐ N (*pl* **rendezvous** ['rɒndɪvuːz]) 1 (= *date*) cita *f*; (= *meeting*) reunión *f*; **to have a ~ with sb** tener una cita con algn; **~ in space** ◊ **space ~** cita espacial; **to make a ~ with another ship at sea** efectuar un enlace con otro buque en el mar
2 (= *meeting-place*) lugar *m* de reunión
Ⓑ VI reunirse, encontrarse; [*spaceship*] tener un encuentro en el espacio (**with** con); **we will ~ at eight** nos reuniremos a las ocho; **the ships will ~ off Vigo** los buques efectuarán el enlace a la altura de Vigo

rendition [ren'dɪʃən] N (*Mus*) interpretación *f*

renegade ['renɪgeɪd] Ⓐ ADJ renegado
Ⓑ N renegado/a *m/f*

renege [rɪ'niːg] VI faltar a su palabra; **to ~ on a promise** no cumplir una promesa

renew [rɪ'njuː] VT 1 (= *restore*) renovar; **skin ~s itself every 28 days** la piel se renueva *or* se regenera cada 28 días
2 (= *resume*) [+ *negotiations, relations*] reanudar; **the storm ~ed itself with a vengeance** la tormenta volvió aún peor, se recrudeció la tormenta; **to ~ the attack** (*Mil*) volver al ataque; **he ~ed his attack on government policy** volvió a arremeter contra la política del gobierno; **to ~ one's efforts (to do sth)** volver a esforzarse (por hacer algo), reanudar

sus esfuerzos (por hacer algo) (*frm*); *see also* **acquaintance**
3 (= *extend date of*) [+ *contract, passport, subscription, library book*] renovar; [+ *lease, loan*] renovar, prorrogar
4 (= *reaffirm*) [+ *promise, vow*] renovar
5 (= *replace*) [+ *component*] cambiar; [+ *supplies*] reponer

renewable [rɪˈnjuːəbl] ADJ [*contract*] renovable; [*energy, resources*] no perecedero

renewal [rɪˈnjuːəl] N 1 (= *reinvigoration*) renacimiento *m*; **there was a ~ of faith in the old values** hubo un renacimiento de la fe en viejos valores; **a spiritual ~** un renacimiento espiritual, una renovación espiritual
2 (= *renovation*) renovación *f*; **a housing ~ programme** un programa de renovación de viviendas; **urban ~** renovación *f* urbanística
3 (= *restarting*) [*of negotiations, relations*] reanudación *f*; [*of attack, hostilities*] recrudecimiento *m*
4 (= *revalidation*) [*of contract, passport, subscription, library book*] renovación *f*; [*of lease, loan*] prórroga *f*, renovación *f*; **his contract is up for ~** le toca que le renueven el contrato

renewed [rɪˈnjuːd] ADJ [*enthusiasm*] renovado; [*outbreaks*] nuevo; **with ~ enthusiasm** con renovado entusiasmo; **with ~ strength** con fuerzas renovadas, con nuevas fuerzas; **~ outbreaks of violence** nuevos brotes de violencia; **there have been ~ calls for his resignation** se ha vuelto a pedir su dimisión; **there have been ~ attempts/efforts to reach agreement** se han reanudado los intentos/esfuerzos por llegar a un acuerdo; **there has been a ~ interest in …** se ha renovado el interés por …

rennet [ˈrenɪt] N cuajo *m*

renounce [rɪˈnaʊns] Ⓐ VT [*right, inheritance, offer etc*] renunciar; [*plan, post, the world etc*] renunciar a
Ⓑ VI (*Cards*) renunciar

renouncement [rɪˈnaʊnsmənt] N renuncia *f*

renovate [ˈrenəʊveɪt] VT (= *renew*) renovar; (= *restore*) restaurar

renovation [ˌrenəʊˈveɪʃən] N [*of house, building*] restauración *f*

renown [rɪˈnaʊn] N renombre *m*, fama *f*

renowned [rɪˈnaʊnd] ADJ renombrado, famoso; **it is ~ for …** es famoso por …, es célebre por …

rent[1] [rent] Ⓐ N alquiler *m*, arriendo *m* (*LAm*); **we pay £350 in ~** pagamos 350 libras de alquiler; **to build flats for ~** construir pisos para alquilarlos; **"for rent"** (*US*) "se alquila"
Ⓑ VT [+ *house, TV, car*] alquilar, arrendar (*LAm*); **to ~ a flat from sb** alquilar un piso a algn, arrendar un departamento a algn (*LAm*); **to ~ a house (out) to sb** alquilar una casa a algn; **it is ~ed out at £400 a week** está alquilado a 400 libras por semana
Ⓒ CPD ► **rent book** N (*for accommodation*) librito *m* del alquiler ► **rent boy*** N chapero* *m* ► **rent collector** N recaudador(a) *m/f* de alquileres ► **rent control** N control *m* de alquileres ► **rent rebate** N devolución *f* de alquiler ► **rent roll** N lista *f* de alquileres, total *m* de ingresos por alquileres

rent[2] [rent] Ⓐ PT, PP *of* **rend**
Ⓑ N (= *tear*) rasgón *m*, rasgadura *f*; (= *split*) abertura *f*, raja *f*, hendedura *f*; (*fig*) escisión *f*, cisma *m*

rental [ˈrentl] Ⓐ N [*of car, TV etc*] (= *hire*) alquiler *m*; (*Brit*) (= *cost*) alquiler *m*, arriendo *m* (*LAm*); **car ~ is included in the price** el alquiler del coche está incluido en el precio
Ⓑ CPD ► **rental car** N (*US*) coche *m* de alquiler ► **rental value** N valor *m* de alquiler

rent-a-mob* [ˈrentəmɒb] N (*Brit*) turba *f* alquilada

rent-controlled [ˈrentkən,trəʊld] ADJ **a ~ flat** un piso *or* (*LAm*) un departamento de alquiler controlado

rent-free [ˈrentˈfriː] Ⓐ ADJ [*house etc*] exento de alquiler
Ⓑ ADV **to live ~** ocupar una casa sin pagar alquiler

rentier [ˈrɒntɪeɪ] N rentista *mf*

renting [ˈrentɪŋ] N arrendamiento *m*

renumber [ˈriːˈnʌmbəʳ] VT volver a numerar

renunciation [rɪˌnʌnsɪˈeɪʃən] N renuncia *f*

reoccupy [ˈriːˈɒkjʊpaɪ] VT volver a ocupar

reopen [ˈriːˈəʊpən] Ⓐ VT 1 [+ *shop, theatre, border, route*] volver a abrir, reabrir
2 [+ *negotiations, relations, investigation, debate*] reanudar; **to ~ a case** [*police*] reabrir un caso; [*prosecutor, judge*] revisar un proceso; **to ~ old wounds** reabrir viejas heridas
Ⓑ VI [*shop, theatre*] volverse a abrir; [*negotiations*] reanudarse; **school ~s on the 8th** el nuevo curso comienza el día 8

re-opening [ˈriːˈəʊpnɪŋ] N 1 [*of shop, theatre, border, route*] reapertura *f*
2 [*of negotiations, relations, investigation, debate*] reanudación *f*; (*Jur*) [*of case*] revisión *f*

reorder [ˈriːˈɔːdəʳ] VT 1 (*Comm*) volver a pedir
2 (= *rearrange*) [+ *objects*] ordenar de nuevo, volver a poner en orden

reorganization [ˈriːˌɔːɡənaɪˈzeɪʃən] N reorganización *f*

reorganize [ˈriːˈɔːɡənaɪz] Ⓐ VT reorganizar
Ⓑ VI reorganizarse

rep[1] [rep] N (= *fabric*) reps *m*

rep[2]* [rep] Ⓐ N (*Comm*) (= **representative**) viajante *mf*, agente *mf*; [*of union etc*] representante *mf*
Ⓑ VI **to ~ for** ser agente de

rep[3]* [rep] N (*Theat*) = **repertory**

Rep. ABBR 1 (= **Republic**) Rep.
2 (*US Pol*) = **Republican**
3 (*US Pol*) = **Representative**

repack [ˈriːˈpæk] VT [+ *object*] reembalar, reenvasar, devolver a su caja *etc*; [+ *suitcase*] volver a hacer

repaid [riːˈpeɪd] PT, PP *of* **repay**

repaint [ˈriːˈpeɪnt] VT repintar; **to ~ sth blue** repintar algo de azul

repair[1] [rɪˈpɛəʳ] Ⓐ N 1 (= *act*) reparación *f*, arreglo *m*; **she had taken her car in for ~s** había llevado el coche al taller; **to be beyond ~** (*lit, fig*) no tener arreglo; **the chair is broken beyond ~** la silla no tiene arreglo; **"closed for repairs"** "cerrado por obras", "cerrado por reforma"; **"(shoe) repairs while you wait"** "arreglamos zapatos al momento", "reparaciones de calzado en el acto"; *see also* **road**
2 (= *state*) **to be in bad** *or* **poor ~** ◊ **be in a bad** *or* **poor state of ~** estar en mal estado; **to be in good ~** ◊ **be in a good state of ~** estar en buen estado
Ⓑ VT 1 (= *mend*) [+ *car, machinery, roof*] arreglar, reparar; [+ *clothes, shoes, road*] arreglar
2 (= *heal*) **they wish to ~ relations with the West** quieren cerrar la brecha *or* conciliarse con Occidente
3 (= *rectify*) [+ *wrong*] reparar
Ⓒ CPD ► **repair job** N arreglo *m*, reparación *f*; **they've done a superb ~ job on my car** me han arreglado el coche estupendamente ► **repair shop** N taller *m* de reparaciones; **auto ~ shop** (*US*) taller *m* mecánico; **bicycle ~ shop** taller *m* de reparación de bicicletas ► **repair work** N arreglos *mpl*, reparaciones *fpl*

repair[2] [rɪˈpɛəʳ] VI (*frm*) (= *go*) **to ~ to** dirigirse a; **we all ~ed to a restaurant** todos nos dirigimos a un restaurante

repairable [rɪˈpɛərəbl] ADJ reparable

repairer [rɪˈpɛərəʳ] N reparador(a) *m/f*

repairman [rɪˈpɛəmæn] N (*pl* **repairmen**) (*US*) reparador *m*

repaper [ˈriːˈpeɪpəʳ] VT empapelar de nuevo

reparable [ˈrepərəbl] ADJ = **repairable**

reparation [ˌrepəˈreɪʃən] N reparación *f*; **to make ~ to sb for sth** indemnizar a algn por algo

repartee [ˌrepɑːˈtiː] N réplicas *fpl* agudas

repass [ˈriːˈpɑːs] VT repasar

repast [rɪˈpɑːst] N (*liter*) comida *f*

repatriate Ⓐ [riːˈpætrɪeɪt] VT repatriar
Ⓑ [riːˈpætrɪət] N repatriado/a *m/f*

repatriation [riːˌpætrɪˈeɪʃən] N repatriación *f*

repay [riːˈpeɪ] (*pt, pp* **repaid**) VT [+ *money*] reembolsar, devolver; [+ *debt*] liquidar, pagar; [+ *person*] reembolsar, pagar; [+ *kindness etc*] devolver, corresponder a; [+ *visit*] devolver, pagar; **to ~ sb in full** pagar *or* devolver a algn todo lo que se le debe; **how can I ever ~ you?** ¿podré corresponderle alguna vez?; **I don't know how I can ever ~ you** no sé cómo podré devolverle el favor; **it ~s study** vale la pena estudiarlo; **it ~s a visit** vale la pena visitarlo; **it ~s reading** vale la pena leerlo

repayable [riːˈpeɪəbl] ADJ reembolsable; **~ on demand** reembolsable a petición; **~ in ten instalments** a pagar en diez cuotas; **£5 deposit not ~** desembolso inicial de 5 libras no reembolsable; **the money is ~ on the 5th of June** el dinero ha de ser devuelto el 5 de junio

repayment [riːˈpeɪmənt] Ⓐ N [*of expenses*] reembolso *m*; **now he asks for ~** ahora pide que se le devuelva el dinero; **in six ~s of £8** en seis cuotas de 8 libras cada uno; **mortgage ~s** los pagos de la hipoteca
Ⓑ CPD ► **repayment schedule** N plan *m* de amortización

repeal [rɪˈpiːl] Ⓐ VT revocar, abrogar
Ⓑ N revocación *f*, abrogación *f*

repeat [rɪˈpiːt] Ⓐ VT 1 (= *say or do again*) repetir; [+ *thanks*] reiterar, volver a dar; [+ *demand, request, promise*] reiterar; (*Scol*) [+ *year, subject*] repetir; **could you ~ that, please?** ¿podría repetir (eso), por favor?; **this offer cannot be ~ed** esta oferta no se repetirá; **the pattern is ~ed on the collar and cuffs** el dibujo se repite en el cuello y en los puños; **~ after me, I must not steal** repetid conmigo, no debo robar; **could history ~ itself?** ¿se podría repetir la historia?; **to ~ o.s.** repetirse; **at the risk of ~ing myself** con el peligro de repetirme
2 (= *divulge*) contar; **don't ~ this to anybody** no le cuentes esto a nadie
3 (= *recite*) recitar
4 (*esp Brit TV*) [+ *programme*] repetir; [+ *series*] repetir, reponer; **the programme will be ~ed on Monday** el programa se repetirá el lunes
Ⓑ VI 1 (= *say or do again*) repetir; **we are not, I ~, not going to give up** no vamos, repito, no vamos a ceder; **lather the hair, rinse and ~** aplicar al cabello formando espuma, aclarar y repetir la operación

2 (*) [*food*] repetir*; **radishes ~ on me** me repite el rábano*
3 (*Math*) [*number*] repetirse
Ⓒ N 1 repetición *f*; **in order to prevent a ~ of the tragedy** para evitar la repetición de la tragedia, para evitar que la tragedia se repita
2 (*esp Brit TV*) [*of programme*] repetición *f*; [*of series*] repetición *f*, reposición *f*; **it can be seen tonight at eight, with a ~ on Monday** se podrá ver esta noche a las ocho y será repetido el lunes
3 (*Mus*) repetición *f*
Ⓓ CPD ► **repeat mark(s)** N(PL) (*Mus*) símbolo(s) *m(pl)* de repetición ► **repeat offender** N delincuente *mf* reincidente ► **repeat performance** N (*Theat, fig*) repetición *f*; **he will give a ~ performance on Friday** hará una repetición el viernes, repetirá la función el viernes; **I don't want a ~ performance of your behaviour last time** que no se repita tu comportamiento de la útima vez ► **repeat prescription** N (*Brit*) receta *f* renovada ► **repeat sign** N (*Mus*) = **repeat mark**

repeated [rɪˈpiːtɪd] ADJ [*attacks, warnings, attempts*] repetido; [*requests, demands*] reiterado; [*criticism*] constante; **there have been ~ calls for his resignation** se ha pedido su dimisión reiteradamente *or* repetidas veces

repeatedly [rɪˈpiːtɪdlɪ] ADV repetidamente, reiteradamente, repetidas veces; **he has ~ denied the allegations** ha desmentido repetidamente *or* reiteradamente *or* repetidas veces las acusaciones; **they tried ~ to free her** hubo repetidos intentos de liberarla; **he ~ broke the rules** infringía las reglas constantemente

repeater [rɪˈpiːtəʳ] N 1 (= *watch*) reloj *m* de repetición; (= *rifle*) rifle *m* de repetición
2 (*US Jur*) reincidente *mf*

repeating [rɪˈpiːtɪŋ] ADJ [*clock, rifle*] de repetición; [*pattern*] repetido; (*Math*) periódico

repechage [ˌrepɪˈʃɑːʒ] N repesca *f*

repel [rɪˈpel] Ⓐ VT 1 (= *force back*) repeler, rechazar
2 (= *disgust*) repugnar, dar asco a; **he ~s me** me da asco, me repugna; **it ~s me to have to** + INFIN me repugna tener que + *infin*
Ⓑ VI repelerse mutuamente

repellant [rɪˈpelənt] N = **repellent B**

repellent [rɪˈpelənt] Ⓐ ADJ 1 (= *disgusting*) repugnante, asqueroso
2 **it is ~ to insects** (= *drives away*) ahuyenta los insectos
Ⓑ N (*also* **insect ~**) repelente *m* contra insectos

repent [rɪˈpent] Ⓐ VI arrepentirse (**of** de)
Ⓑ VT arrepentirse de

repentance [rɪˈpentəns] N arrepentimiento *m*

repentant [rɪˈpentənt] ADJ arrepentido

repeople [ˈriːˈpiːpl] VT repoblar

repercussion [ˌriːpəˈkʌʃən] N repercusión *f*; **~s** (*fig*) repercusiones *fpl*; **as for the political ~s** en cuanto a las repercusiones políticas; **it had great ~s in France** tuvo gran resonancia en Francia

repertoire [ˈrepətwɑːʳ] N [*of songs, jokes*] repertorio *m*

repertory [ˈrepətərɪ] Ⓐ N (= *stock*) repertorio *m*
Ⓑ CPD ► **repertory company** N compañía *f* de repertorio ► **repertory theatre**, **repertory theater** (*US*) N teatro *m* de repertorio

repetition [ˌrepɪˈtɪʃən] N repetición *f*

repetitious [ˌrepɪˈtɪʃəs] ADJ = **repetitive**

repetitive [rɪˈpetɪtɪv] Ⓐ ADJ repetitivo, reiterativo; **the book is a bit ~** el libro tiene sus repeticiones
Ⓑ CPD ► **repetitive strain injury**, **repetitive stress injury** N *lesión en las muñecas y los brazos sufrida por teclistas*

rephrase [riːˈfreɪz] VT expresar de otro modo, decir con otras palabras

repine [rɪˈpaɪn] VI (*liter*) quejarse (**at** de), afligirse (**at** por)

replace [rɪˈpleɪs] VT 1 (= *put back*) volver a colocar; **~ the cap after use** vuelva a colocar la tapa después de usarlo; **he ~d the letter in his pocket** se volvió a meter la carta en el bolsillo; **to ~ the receiver** colgar (el auricular)
2 (= *get replacement for*) [+ *object*] reponer; [+ *person*] sustituir, reemplazar; **the body has to ~ lost fluid** el cuerpo tiene que reponer los líquidos perdidos; **we will ~ the broken glasses** repondremos *or* pagaremos los vasos rotos; **they are not going to ~ her when she leaves** cuando se vaya no van sustituirla *or* reemplazarla, no van a poner a nadie en su lugar cuando se vaya
3 (= *put in place of*) **to ~ sth with sth** sustituir algo por algo; **the airline is replacing its DC10s with Boeing 747s** la compañía aérea está sustituyendo los DC10 por Boeings 747; **to ~ sb with sth/sb** sustituir a algn por algo/algn, reemplazar a algn por *or* con algo/algn; **many workers are being ~d by machines** están sustituyendo a muchos trabajadores por máquinas, están reemplazando a muchos trabajadores por *or* con máquinas
4 (= *take the place of*) [+ *thing*] sustituir; [+ *person*] sustituir, reemplazar; **chopped chives can ~ the parsley** el perejil se puede sustituir por cebolletas picadas; **he ~d Evans as managing director** sustituyó *or* reemplazó a Evans en el puesto de director gerente; **nobody could ever ~ him in my heart** nadie podrá jamás ocupar su lugar en mi corazón
5 (= *change*) cambiar; **the battery needs replacing** hay que cambiar la pila

replaceable [rɪˈpleɪsəbl] ADJ reemplazable, sustituible; **it will not easily be ~** no será fácil encontrar uno igual; **he will not easily be ~** no será fácil encontrar un sustituto

replacement [rɪˈpleɪsmənt] Ⓐ N 1 (= *putting back*) reposición *f*; (= *substituting*) sustitución *f* (**by, with** por); *see also* **hormone**
2 (= *substitute*) 2·1 (= *person*) sustituto/a *m/f*, suplente *mf* (**for** de)
2·2 (= *thing*) **it took three days to find a ~** tardaron tres días en encontrar un repuesto; **you can get a ~ if the goods are faulty** le damos uno nuevo si el artículo está defectuoso
Ⓑ CPD ► **replacement cost** N costo *m* de sustitución ► **replacement engine** N motor *m* de repuesto ► **replacement part** N repuesto *m* ► **replacement value** N valor *m* de sustitución

replant [ˈriːˈplɑːnt] VT replantar

replay [ˌriːˈpleɪ] (*esp Brit*) Ⓐ VT (*Sport*) [+ *match*] volver a jugar; (*Mus*) volver a tocar; [+ *tape*] volver a poner
Ⓑ [ˌriːˈpleɪ] VI (*Sport*) volver a jugar
Ⓒ [ˈriːpleɪ] N [*of match*] repetición *f* de un partido; **there will be a ~ on Friday** el partido se volverá a jugar el viernes; *see also* **action C**

replenish [rɪˈplenɪʃ] VT [+ *tank etc*] rellenar, llenar de nuevo; [+ *stocks*] reponer

replenishment [rɪˈplenɪʃmənt] N [*of tank*] rellenado *m*; [*of stocks*] reposición *f*

replete [rɪˈpliːt] ADJ (*liter*) repleto, lleno (**with** de)

repletion [rɪˈpliːʃən] N (*liter*) saciedad *f*, repleción *f*; **to eat to ~** comer realmente bien

replica [ˈreplɪkə] N réplica *f*, reproducción *f*

replicate [ˈreplɪˌkeɪt] VT reproducir exactamente

reply [rɪˈplaɪ] Ⓐ N 1 (*spoken, written*) respuesta *f*, contestación *f*; **he has had 12 replies to his ad** han contestado 12 personas a su anuncio; **I sent a ~ to her letter this morning** contesté *or* respondí a su carta esta mañana; **"reply paid"** "no necesita sello", "a franquear en destino"; **~-paid envelope** sobre *m* a franquear en destino; **in ~** en respuesta; **in ~ to your letter** en respuesta a *or* contestando a su carta; **he had nothing to say in ~** no tenía nada que responder *or* contestar; **there's no ~** (*Telec*) no contestan; **to make no ~ (to sth)** no responder (a algo), no contestar (algo); **she made no ~ except to nod** su única reacción fue asentir con la cabeza
2 (= *reaction, response*) reacción *f*, respuesta *f*; **a loud sob was his only ~** un fuerte sollozo fue su única reacción *or* respuesta
3 (*abrupt*) réplica *f*
4 (*Jur*) réplica *f*
Ⓑ VI 1 responder, contestar; **to ~ to sb** contestar *or* responder a algn; **to ~ to sth** responder *or* contestar a algo; **to ~ to a letter** contestar (a) una carta; **the police replied with tear gas** la policía respondió con gas lacrimógeno
2 (*Jur*) replicar
Ⓒ VT 1 (*gen*) responder, contestar; **he replied that this was impossible** respondió *or* contestó que esto era imposible
2 (*abruptly*) replicar

repoint [riːˈpɔɪnt] VT rejuntar

repointing [riːˈpɔɪntɪŋ] N rejuntamiento *m*

repopulate [ˈriːˈpɒpjʊleɪt] VT repoblar

repopulation [ˈriːˌpɒpjʊˈleɪʃən] N repoblación *f*

report [rɪˈpɔːt] Ⓐ N 1 (= *account*) informe *m*; (*Press, Rad, TV*) reportaje *m*, crónica *f*; (= *piece of news*) noticia *f*; **there were no ~s of casualties** no se anunciaron víctimas; **to give** *or* **make** *or* **present a ~ (on sth)** presentar un informe (sobre algo); *see also* **law**, **progress D**
2 (*Brit*) (*also* **school ~**) boletín *m or* cartilla *f* de notas; (*US*) (= *assignment*) trabajo *m*; **to get a good/bad ~** sacar buenas/malas notas
3 (= *rumour*) rumor *m*; **according to ~(s)** según se dice
4 (*liter*) (= *reputation*) reputación *f*, fama *f*; **a person of good ~** una persona de buena reputación *or* fama
5 (= *bang*) estallido *m*; (= *shot*) disparo *m*
Ⓑ VT 1 (= *state, make known*) **it is ~ed from Berlin that …** comunican *or* se informa desde Berlín que …; **nothing to ~** sin novedad
2 (*Press, TV, Rad*) [+ *event*] informar acerca de, informar sobre
3 (= *allege*) **she is ~ed to be in Italy** se dice que está en Italia; **he is ~ed to have said that …** parece que dijo que …
4 (= *notify*) [+ *crime*] denunciar, dar parte de; [+ *accident*] dar parte de; **13 people were ~ed killed** hubo informes de que murieron 13 personas; **to ~ sb missing** denunciar la desaparición de algn, declarar a algn desaparecido
5 (= *denounce*) [+ *person*] denunciar; **to ~ sb (to sb) (for sth)** denunciar a algn (a algn) (por algo); **he ~ed her to the Inland Revenue for not paying her taxes** la denunció

a Hacienda por no pagar impuestos
[6] **~ed speech** estilo *m* indirecto
Ⓒ VI [1] (= *make report*) presentar un informe
[2] (*Press, TV, Rad*) (*gen*) informar; (*as reporter*) ser reportero/a; **he ~ed for the Daily Echo for 40 years** durante 40 años fue reportero del "Daily Echo"; **this is Jim Dale ~ing from Chicago** aquí Jim Dale (informando) desde Chicago; **to ~ on sth** informar sobre algo
[3] (= *present oneself*) presentarse; **when you arrive, ~ to the receptionist** cuando llegue, preséntese en recepción; **he has to ~ to the police every five days** tiene que personarse *or* presentarse en la comisaría cada cinco días; **to ~ for duty** (*Mil*) presentarse para el servicio; **to ~ sick** darse de baja por enfermedad
[4] **to ~ to sb** (= *be responsible to*) estar bajo las órdenes de algn; **he ~s to the marketing director** está bajo las órdenes del director de márketing; **who do you ~ to?** ¿quién es tu superior *or* tu jefe?
Ⓓ CPD ► **report card** N (*US Scol*) boletín *m* *or* cartilla *f* de notas ► **report stage** N (*Brit Parl*) **the bill has reached** *or* **is at the ~ stage** se están debatiendo los informes de las comisiones sobre el proyecto de ley

►**report back** Ⓐ VI + ADV [1] (= *give report*) (*gen*) informar; (*officially*) presentar un informe
[2] (= *return*) volver (a presentarse); **~ back at six o'clock** vuelva (a presentarse) a las seis
Ⓑ VT + ADV **my every move was ~ed back to my superiors** se informaba a mis superiores de todo lo que hacía

reportage [ˌrepɔːˈtɑːʒ] N (= *news report*) reportaje *m*; (= *technique*) periodismo *m*

reportedly [rɪˈpɔːtɪdlɪ] ADV según se dice; **he is ~ living in Australia** se dice que está viviendo en Australia

reporter [rɪˈpɔːtəʳ] N (*Press*) periodista *mf*, reportero/a *m/f*; (*TV, Rad*) locutor(a) *m/f*

reporting [rɪˈpɔːtɪŋ] Ⓐ N (*Press, TV, Rad*) cobertura *f*, reportajes *mpl*; **her ~ of the war in Bosnia** su cobertura *or* sus reportajes de la guerra en Bosnia
Ⓑ CPD ► **reporting restrictions** NPL (*Press, TV, Rad*) restricciones *fpl* informativas

repose [rɪˈpəʊz] (*frm*) Ⓐ N (= *rest, sleep*) reposo *m*, descanso *m*; (= *calm*) calma *f*, tranquilidad *f*
Ⓑ VI (= *rest, be buried*) reposar, descansar; **to ~ on** descansar sobre
Ⓒ VT [1] (= *lay*) reposar, descansar
[2] (= *put*) **to ~ confidence in sb** depositar confianza en algn

repository [rɪˈpɒzɪtərɪ] N depósito *m*; **furniture ~** guardamuebles *m inv*

repossess [ˈriːpəˈzes] VT recobrar; **to ~ o.s. of sth** recobrar algo, volver a tomar algo

repossession [ˌriːpəˈzeʃən] N recuperación *f* (*de un artículo no pagado*)

repot [riːˈpɒt] VT poner en nueva maceta, cambiar de maceta

reprehend [ˌreprɪˈhend] VT reprender

reprehensible [ˌreprɪˈhensɪbl] ADJ reprensible, censurable

reprehensibly [ˌreprɪˈhensɪblɪ] ADV censurablemente

reprehension [ˌreprɪˈhenʃən] N reprensión *f*

represent [reprɪˈzent] VT [1] (= *stand for, symbolize*) representar
[2] (= *act or speak for*) [+ *client, country*] representar a; [+ *company*] ser agente de; [+ *change, achievement*] representar; **he ~s nobody but himself** no representa a nadie sino a sí mismo; **his early work is well ~ed in the exhibition** sus primeros trabajos están bien representados en la exposición, su primera época está bien representada
[3] (*frm*) (= *convey, explain*) presentar, describir; **you ~ed it falsely to us** usted nos lo describió falsamente; **it has been ~ed to us that …** se ha pretendido que …, se nos ha dicho que …; **the goods are not as ~ed** las mercancías no son como nos las describieron

re-present [ˈriːprɪˈzent] VT volver a presentar

representation [ˌreprɪzenˈteɪʃən] N [1] (*gen, Pol*) representación *f*; **to make false ~s** describir algo falsamente
[2] (= *protest*) **to make ~s to sb** levantar una protesta a algn; **to make ~s about sth** quejarse de algo; *see also* **proportional**

representational [ˌreprɪzenˈteɪʃənəl] ADJ (*Art*) figurativo

representative [ˌreprɪˈzentətɪv] Ⓐ ADJ representativo (**of** de); **these figures are more ~** estas cifras son más representativas; **~ government** gobierno *m* representativo; **a person not fully ~ of the group** una persona que no representa adecuadamente el grupo
Ⓑ N [1] (*gen*) representante *mf*
[2] (*esp Brit Comm*) viajante *mf*
[3] (*US Pol*) **Representative** ≈ diputado/a *m/f*; **the House of Representatives** la cámara de Representantes, ≈ el Senado

repress [rɪˈpres] VT reprimir

repressed [rɪˈprest] ADJ reprimido

repression [rɪˈpreʃən] N (*gen, Psych*) represión *f*

repressive [rɪˈpresɪv] ADJ represivo

reprieve [rɪˈpriːv] Ⓐ N [1] (*Jur*) indulto *m*; [*of sentence*] conmutación *f*; **to win a last-minute ~** ser indultado a última hora
[2] (= *delay*) aplazamiento *m*, alivio *m* temporal; **the building got a ~** se retiró la orden de demoler el edificio
Ⓑ VT [1] (*Jur*) indultar; **to ~ sb from death** suspender la pena de muerte de algn
[2] (*fig*) salvar

reprimand [ˈreprɪmɑːnd] Ⓐ N reprimenda *f*
Ⓑ VT reprender, regañar

reprint [ˈriːprɪnt] Ⓐ N reimpresión *f*, reedición *f*
Ⓑ [ˌriːˈprɪnt] VT reimprimir

reprisal [rɪˈpraɪzəl] N represalia *f*; **to take ~s** tomar represalias; **as a ~ for** como represalia por; **by way of ~** a modo de represalia

reproach [rɪˈprəʊtʃ] Ⓐ N reproche *m*; **above** *or* **beyond ~** intachable, irreprochable; **that is a ~ to us all** es un reproche a todos nosotros; **poverty is a ~ to civilization** la pobreza es una vergüenza para la sociedad; **term of ~** término *m* oprobioso
Ⓑ VT **to ~ sb for sth** reprochar algo a algn; **to ~ o.s. for sth** reprocharse algo; **you have no reason to ~ yourself** no tienes motivos para reprocharte (nada)

reproachful [rɪˈprəʊtʃfʊl] ADJ [*look etc*] de reproche, de acusación

reproachfully [rɪˈprəʊtʃfəlɪ] ADV [*look*] con reproche; [*speak*] en tono acusador

reprobate [ˈreprəʊbeɪt] N réprobo/a *m/f*

reprobation [ˌreprəʊˈbeɪʃən] N reprobación *f*

reprocess [ˌriːˈprəʊses] VT reprocesar

reprocessing [ˌriːˈprəʊsesɪŋ] Ⓐ N reprocesamiento *m*
Ⓑ CPD ► **reprocessing plant** N planta *f* de reprocesamiento

reproduce [ˌriːprəˈdjuːs] Ⓐ VT reproducir
Ⓑ VI (*Bio*) reproducirse

reproduction [ˌriːprəˈdʌkʃən] Ⓐ N [1] (= *act of reproducing*) reproducción *f*; (= *copy*) copia *f*, reproducción *f*
[2] (*Bio*) reproducción *f*
Ⓑ CPD ► **reproduction furniture** N muebles *mpl* antiguos de imitación

reproductive [ˌriːprəˈdʌktɪv] ADJ reproductor

reprography [rɪˈprɒgrəfɪ] N reprografía *f*

reproof [ˌriːˈpruːf] N reprobación *f*, regaño *m*; **to administer a ~ to sb** reprender a algn

re-proof [ˌriːˈpruːf] VT [+ *garment*] impermeabilizar de nuevo

reproval [rɪˈpruːvəl] N reprobación *f*

reprove [rɪˈpruːv] VT **to ~ sb for sth** reprobar a algn por algo

reproving [rɪˈpruːvɪŋ] ADJ reprobador, lleno de reproches

reprovingly [rɪˈpruːvɪŋlɪ] ADV [*speak*] en tono reprobador, con reprobación; **she looked at me ~** me miró severa, me reprendió con la mirada

reptile [ˈreptaɪl] N reptil *m*

reptilian [repˈtɪlɪən] Ⓐ ADJ reptil
Ⓑ N reptil *m*

Repub. ABBR [1] = **Republic**
[2] = **Republican**

republic [rɪˈpʌblɪk] N república *f*

republican [rɪˈpʌblɪkən] Ⓐ ADJ republicano
Ⓑ N republicano/a *m/f*

republicanism [rɪˈpʌblɪkənɪzəm] N republicanismo *m*

republication [ˈriːˌpʌblɪˈkeɪʃən] N reedición *f*

republish [ˈriːˈpʌblɪʃ] VT reeditar

repudiate [rɪˈpjuːdɪeɪt] VT [1] (= *deny*) [+ *charge*] rechazar, negar
[2] (= *refuse to recognize*) [+ *debt, treaty*] negarse a reconocer, desconocer; [+ *attitude, values, wife, violence*] repudiar

repudiation [rɪˌpjuːdɪˈeɪʃən] N [1] (= *denial*) rechazo *m*, negación *f*
[2] (= *refusal to recognize*) [*of debt, treaty*] negativa *f* a reconocer, desconocimiento *m*; [*of attitude, values, wife, violence*] repudio *m*

repugnance [rɪˈpʌgnəns] N repugnancia *f*

repugnant [rɪˈpʌgnənt] ADJ repugnante; **it is ~ to me** me repugna

repulse [rɪˈpʌls] Ⓐ VT (*gen*) rechazar
Ⓑ N rechazo *m*; **to suffer a ~** ser rechazado

repulsion [rɪˈpʌlʃən] N [1] (= *disgust*) repulsión *f*, repugnancia *f*
[2] (= *rejection*) rechazo *m*

repulsive [rɪˈpʌlsɪv] ADJ repulsivo, repugnante

repulsively [rɪˈpʌlsɪvlɪ] ADV de modo repulsivo, de modo repugnante; **~ ugly** tan feo que da/daba *etc* asco

repulsiveness [rɪˈpʌlsɪvnɪs] N lo repulsivo, lo repugnante

repurchase [ˈriːˈpɜːtʃɪs] Ⓐ N readquisición *f*
Ⓑ VT readquirir, volver a comprar

reputable [ˈrepjʊtəbl] ADJ [*firm, brand*] acreditado, de confianza; [*person*] honroso, formal

reputation [ˌrepjʊˈteɪʃən] N reputación *f*, fama *f*; **to have a bad ~** tener mala fama; **of good ~** de buena fama; **he has a ~ for being awkward** tiene fama de difícil; **the hotel has a ~ for good food** el hotel es célebre por su buena comida; **to live up to one's ~** merecer la reputación; **to ruin a girl's ~** acabar con la buena reputación de una joven

repute [rɪˈpjuːt] Ⓐ N reputación *f*, renombre *m*; **a firm of ~** una casa acreditada; **a café of ill ~** un café con mala fama; **a house of ill ~** (*euph*) una casa de mala fama; **to hold sb in (high) ~** tener un alto concepto de algn; **his skill was held in high ~** su destreza era muy estimada; **by ~** según la opinión común, se-

gún se dice; **to know sb by ~ only** conocer a algn sólo por su reputación *or* de oídas nada más
Ⓑ VT **he is ~d to be very fast** se dice que es muy rápido; **she is ~d to be the world's best** tiene fama de ser la mejor del mundo

reputed [rɪ'pju:tɪd] ADJ [1] (= *supposed*) supuesto, presunto
[2] (= *well known*) renombrado

reputedly [rɪ'pju:tɪdlɪ] ADV según dicen

request [rɪ'kwest] Ⓐ N (*gen*) solicitud *f*; (= *plea*) petición *f*; **at the ~ of** a petición de; **by ~** a petición; **to play a record by ~** tocar un disco a petición de un oyente; **by popular ~** por petición popular, a petición del público; **a ~ for help** una petición de socorro; **to grant sb's ~** acceder al ruego de algn; **it is much in ~** tiene mucha demanda, está muy solicitado; **to make a ~ for sth** pedir algo; **on ~** a solicitud
Ⓑ VT pedir, solicitar; **to ~ sb to do sth** pedir a algn hacer algo; **to ~ sth of sb** pedir algo a algn; **"visitors are requested not to talk"** "se ruega a los visitantes respetar el silencio"
Ⓒ CPD ► **request (bus) stop** N parada *f* discrecional ► **request programme** N (*Rad*) programa *m* con peticiones de discos

requiem ['rekwɪem] N réquiem *m*

require [rɪ'kwaɪə^r] VT [1] (= *need*) necesitar; **is there anything you ~?** ¿necesita usted algo?; **this plant ~s watering frequently** esta planta hay que regarla con frecuencia; **we will do all that is ~d** haremos todo lo que haga falta; **as (and when) ~d** cuando haga falta; **I am willing to give evidence if ~d** estoy dispuesto a testificar si se requiere *or* si es necesario
[2] (= *call for, take*) [+ *patience, effort*] requerir; **it ~s a lot of patience** requiere mucha paciencia
[3] (= *ask, demand*) **it's not up to the standard I ~** no tiene el nivel que yo exijo; **your presence is ~d** se requiere su presencia; **what qualifications are ~d?** ¿qué títulos se requieren?; **to ~ that: the law ~s that safety belts be worn** la ley exige que se usen los cinturones de seguridad; **to ~ sb to do sth** exigir que algn haga algo; **the course ~s you to be bilingual** el curso exige que seas bilingüe; **as ~d by law** como *or* según exige la ley; **find out what is ~d of you** averigua qué es lo que te piden

required [rɪ'kwaɪəd] ADJ [1] (= *necessary*) necesario; **cut the wood to the ~ length** corte la madera del largo que se necesite; **he couldn't raise the ~ amount of money** no pudo recaudar los fondos necesarios; **the qualities ~ for the job** las cualidades que se requieren para el puesto
[2] (= *fixed*) establecido; **within the ~ time** dentro del plazo establecido
[3] (= *compulsory*) [*reading*] obligatorio

requirement [rɪ'kwaɪəmənt] N [1] (= *need*) necesidad *f*; **our ~s are few** nuestras necesidades son pocas, necesitamos poco
[2] (= *condition*) requisito *m*; **Latin is a ~ for the course** el latín es un requisito para este curso, para este curso se exige el latín; **it is one of the ~s of the contract** es una de las estipulaciones del contrato; **to meet all the ~s for sth** reunir todos los requisitos para algo

requisite ['rekwɪzɪt] Ⓐ ADJ = **required**
Ⓑ N requisito *m*; **office ~s** material *msing* de oficina; **toilet ~s** artículos *mpl* de tocador

requisition [,rekwɪ'zɪʃən] Ⓐ N (*Mil*) requisa *f*, requisición *f*; (= *formal request*) solicitud *f*
Ⓑ VT (*Mil*) requisar; (= *formally request*) solicitar

requital [rɪ'kwaɪtl] N (*frm*) (= *repayment*) compensación *f*; (= *revenge*) desquite *m*

requite [rɪ'kwaɪt] VT (*frm*) (= *make return for*) compensar, recompensar; **to ~ sb's love** corresponder al amor de algn; **that love was not ~d** ese amor no fue correspondido

reran [,ri:'ræn] PT *of* **rerun**

reread [,ri:'ri:d] (*pt, pp* **reread** [,ri:'red]) VT releer, volver a leer

reredos ['rɪədɒs] N (*pl* **reredoses**) retablo *m*

reroute [,ri:'ru:t] VT desviar; **the train was ~d through Burgos** el tren pasó por Burgos al ser desviado de su ruta habitual

rerun (*vb: pt* **reran**; *pp* **rerun**) Ⓐ ['ri:rʌn] N repetición *f*; (*Theat*) reestreno *m*, reposición *f*
Ⓑ [,ri:'rʌn] VT [+ *race*] correr de nuevo; (*Theat*) reestrenar, reponer

resale [,ri:'seɪl] Ⓐ N reventa *f*; **"not for ~"** "prohibida la venta"
Ⓑ CPD ► **resale price maintenance** N mantenimiento *m* del precio de venta ► **resale value** N valor *m* de reventa

resat [,ri:'sæt] PT, PP *of* **resit**

reschedule [,ri:'ʃedju:l, (*US*) ,ri:'skedju:l] VT [+ *meeting, visit, trip, programme*] cambiar la fecha/hora de; [+ *train service etc*] cambiar el horario de; [+ *repayments, debt*] renegociar; [+ *plans, course*] volver a planificar

rescheduling [,ri:'ʃedju:lɪŋ, (*US*) ,ri:'skedju:lɪŋ] N [*of meeting, visit, trip, programme*] cambio *m* de fecha/hora; [*of debt*] renegociación *f*

rescind [rɪ'sɪnd] VT [+ *contract*] rescindir; [+ *order*] anular; (*Jur*) abrogar

rescission [rɪ'sɪʒən] N [*of contract*] rescisión *f*; [*of order*] anulación *f*; (*Jur*) abrogación *f*

rescue ['reskju:] Ⓐ N rescate *m*, salvamento *m*; **the hero of the ~ was ...** el héroe del rescate *or* salvamento fue ...; **to come/go to sb's ~** acudir en auxilio de algn, socorrer a algn; **to the ~!** ¡al socorro!; **Batman to the ~!** ¡Batman acude a la llamada!
Ⓑ VT salvar, rescatar; **three men were ~d** se salvaron tres hombres; **they waited three days to be ~d** esperaron tres días hasta ser rescatados; **to ~ sb from death** salvar a algn de la muerte; **the ~d man is in hospital** el hombre rescatado está en el hospital
Ⓒ CPD ► **rescue attempt** N tentativa *f* de salvamento, tentativa *f* de rescate ► **rescue dig** N excavación *f* de urgencia ► **rescue operations** NPL operaciones *fpl* de salvamento, operaciones *fpl* de rescate ► **rescue package** N (*Pol, Comm*) paquete *m* de medidas urgentes ► **rescue party** N equipo *m* de salvamento, equipo *m* de rescate ► **rescue services** NPL servicios *mpl* de rescate, servicios *mpl* de salvamento ► **rescue team** N = **rescue party** ► **rescue vessel** N buque *m* de salvamento ► **rescue work** N operación *f* de salvamento, operación *f* de rescate

rescuer ['reskjʊə^r] N salvador(a) *m/f*

research [rɪ'sɜ:tʃ] Ⓐ N investigación *f*, investigaciones *fpl* (**in, into** de); **~ and development** investigación *f* y desarrollo *m*; **atomic ~** investigaciones *fpl* atómicas; **our ~ shows that ...** nuestras investigaciones demuestran que ...; **a piece of ~** una investigación; *see also* **market D**
Ⓑ VI hacer investigaciones; **to ~ into sth** investigar algo
Ⓒ VT investigar; **to ~ an article** preparar el material para un artículo, reunir datos para escribir un artículo; **a well ~ed book** un libro bien documentado; **a well ~ed study** un estudio bien preparado
Ⓓ CPD ► **research establishment** N instituto *m* de investigación ► **research fellow** N investigador(a) *m/f* ► **research grant** N beca *f* de investigación ► **research laboratory** N laboratorio *m* de investigación ► **research staff** N personal *m* investigador ► **research student** N estudiante *mf* investigador(a) ► **research team** N equipo *m* de investigación ► **research work** N trabajo(s) *m(pl)* de investigación ► **research worker** N investigador(a) *m/f*

researcher [rɪ'sɜ:tʃə^r] N investigador(a) *m/f*

reseat [,ri:'si:t] VT [+ *chair*] poner nuevo asiento a

resection [ri:'sekʃən] N [1] (*Survey*) triangulación *f*
[2] (*Med*) resección *f*

resell ['ri:'sel] (*pt, pp* **resold**) VT revender

resemblance [rɪ'zembləns] N semejanza *f*, parecido *m*; **to bear a strong ~ to sb** parecerse mucho a algn, estar clavado a algn; **to bear no ~ to sb** no parecerse en absoluto a algn; **there is no ~ between them** los dos no se parecen en absoluto; **there is hardly any ~ between this version and the one I gave you** apenas existe parecido entre esta versión y la que te di

resemble [rɪ'zembl] VT parecerse a; **he doesn't ~ his father** no se parece a su padre; **they do ~ one another** sí se parecen el uno al otro

resent [rɪ'zent] VT **I ~ that!** ¡me molesta *or* me ofende que digas eso!; **he ~s my being here** le molesta que esté aquí; **I ~ your tone** encuentro tu tono ofensivo; **he ~ed my promotion** le molestaba que me hubiesen ascendido; **he ~s having lost his job** no lleva bien lo de haber perdido el trabajo, le amarga haber perdido el trabajo; **he ~ed the fact that I married her** le molestaba que me hubiese casado con ella; **she ~s having to look after her mother** le amarga tener que cuidar de su madre; **I ~ed him because he was her favourite** tenía celos de él porque era su preferido

resentful [rɪ'zentfʊl] ADJ [*person*] resentido; [*tone*] resentido, de resentimiento; [*look, air*] de resentimiento; **he watched them, envious and ~** los observaba, con envidia y resentimiento; **to be** *or* **feel ~ about/at sth** estar resentido por algo; **he felt ~ about his dismissal** estaba resentido porque lo habían despedido; **he was ~ at the way he had been treated** estaba resentido por la forma en que lo habían tratado; **to be** *or* **feel ~ of sb: she was ~ of her sister, who was cleverer than her** tenía celos de su hermana, que era más inteligente que ella; **to be ~ of sb's success** tener envidia del éxito de algn; **he still felt ~ towards her because she had rejected him** todavía estaba resentido con ella porque lo había rechazado

resentfully [rɪ'zentfəlɪ] ADV [*look, behave*] con resentimiento; **he said ~** dijo resentido *or* con resentimiento

resentment [rɪ'zentmənt] N resentimiento *m*, rencor *m* (**about** por); **I feel no ~ towards him** no le guardo rencor, no estoy resentido con él

reservation [,rezə'veɪʃən] Ⓐ N [1] (= *booking*) reserva *f*; (= *seat*) plaza *f* reservada; (= *table in restaurant*) mesa *f* reservada; **to make a ~ in a hotel** reservar una habitación en un hotel
[2] (= *doubt*) reserva *f*, duda *f*; **I had ~s about it** tenía ciertas dudas sobre ese punto; **with certain ~s** con ciertas reservas; **to accept sth without ~** aceptar algo sin reserva

➤ LANGUAGE IN USE: **request A** 12.3 **B** 20.2 **require 2, 3** 10.1

3 (*in contract*) salvedad *f*; (*in argument*) distingo *m*
4 (= *area of land*) reserva *f*
5 (*on road*) mediana *f*, franja *f* central; *see also* **central C**
Ⓑ CPD ► **reservation desk** N (*Brit*) (*in airport, hotels etc*) mostrador *m* de reservas; (*US*) (= *hotel reception desk*) recepción *f*

reserve [rɪ'zɜːv] Ⓐ N 1 [*of money, fuel, minerals*] reserva *f*; **to have sth in ~** tener algo de reserva; **to have a ~ of strength** tener una reserva de fuerzas; **to keep sth in ~** guardar algo en reserva; **there are untapped ~s of energy** hay fuentes de energía sin explotar todavía; **Spain possesses half the world's ~s of pyrites** España posee la mitad de las reservas mundiales de piritas
2 (*Mil*) **the ~** la reserva
3 (*esp Brit Sport*) reserva *mf*, suplente *mf*; **to play in** *or* **with the ~s** jugar en el segundo equipo
4 (= *land*) reserva *f*; (*also* **game ~**) coto *m* (de caza); (*also* **nature ~**) reserva *f* natural
5 (= *restriction*) **without ~** sin reserva
6 (= *hiding one's feelings*) reserva *f*; **without ~** sin reserva
Ⓑ VT 1 (= *book, set aside*) reservar; **that's being ~d for me** eso está reservado para mí; **did you ~ the tickets?** ¿has reservado los billetes?; **to ~ the right to do sth** reservarse el derecho de hacer algo; **to ~ one's strength** conservar las fuerzas; **I'm reserving myself for later** me reservo para más tarde
2 (*Jur*) aplazar; **I ~ judgment on this** me reservo el juicio en este asunto; **the judge ~d sentence** el juez difirió la sentencia
Ⓒ CPD ► **reserve currency** N divisa *f* de reserva ► **reserve fund** N fondo *m* de reserva ► **reserve petrol tank** (*Brit*), **reserve gas tank** (*US*) N depósito *m* de gasolina de reserva ► **reserve player** N suplente *mf* ► **reserve price** N (*Brit*) precio *m* mínimo (*fijado en una subasta*) ► **reserve team** N (*Brit Sport*) equipo *m* de reserva

reserved [rɪ'zɜːvd] ADJ [*person, behaviour, room, table, seat*] reservado; **to be ~ about sth** ser reservado acerca de algo

reservedly [rɪ'zɜːvɪdlɪ] ADV con reserva

reservist [rɪ'zɜːvɪst] N (*Mil*) reservista *mf*

reservoir ['rezəvwɑːʳ] N 1 (= *lake*) embalse *m*, represa *f* (*LAm*); (= *tank*) depósito *m*; **natural underground ~** depósito *m* subterráneo natural 2 (*fig*) [*of strength, experience*] reserva *f*

reset ['riː'set] (*vb: pt, pp* **reset**) Ⓐ VT [+ *machine*] reajustar; [+ *printing press*] recomponer; [+ *computer*] reinicializar; [+ *bone*] volver a encajar; [+ *jewel*] reengastar
Ⓑ CPD ► **reset switch** N conmutador *m* de reajuste

resettle ['riː'setl] Ⓐ VT [+ *persons*] reasentar; [+ *land*] repoblar Ⓑ VI reasentarse

resettlement ['riː'setlmənt] N [*of people*] reasentamiento *m*; [*of land*] nueva colonización *f*, repoblación *f*

reshape ['riː'ʃeɪp] VT [+ *clay, vase*] remodelar; [+ *policy, constitution*] reformar; [+ *organization*] reorganizar

reshuffle ['riː'ʃʌfl] Ⓐ N (*Pol*) remodelación *f*; **Cabinet ~** remodelación *f* del gabinete
Ⓑ VT 1 [+ *cards*] volver a barajar
2 [+ *cabinet, board of directors*] remodelar

reside [rɪ'zaɪd] VI (*frm*) residir, vivir; **to ~ in** *or* **with** (*fig*) residir en; **the problem ~s there** ahí radica el problema

residence ['rezɪdəns] Ⓐ N 1 (= *stay*) permanencia *f*, estancia *f* (*LAm*); **after six months' ~** después de seis meses de permanencia; **to take up ~** (*in house*) instalarse; (*in country*) establecerse; **in ~** residente; **when the students are in ~** cuando están los estudiantes; **there is a doctor in ~** hay un médico interno; **artist in ~** artista *mf* residente; **writer in ~** escritor(a) *m/f* residente
2 (= *home*) residencia *f*, domicilio *m*; **"town and country ~s for sale"** "se venden fincas urbanas y rurales"; **the minister's official ~** la residencia oficial del ministro
3 (*Univ*) (*also* **hall of ~**) colegio *m* mayor
Ⓑ CPD ► **residence permit** N permiso *m* de residencia

residency ['rezɪdənsɪ] N residencia *f*

resident ['rezɪdənt] Ⓐ ADJ 1 [*person, Comput*] residente; [*population*] permanente; [*doctor, servant*] interno; [*bird*] no migratorio; **to be ~ in a town** tener domicilio fijo en una ciudad; **we were ~ there for some years** residimos allí durante varios años
2 (*Comput*) residente
Ⓑ N [*of hotel, guesthouse*] huésped *mf*; [*of area, in block of flats*] vecino/a *m/f*; (*in country*) residente *mf*; **~s' association** asociación *f* de vecinos; **the ~s got together to protest** los vecinos se reunieron para protestar

residential [ˌrezɪ'denʃəl] Ⓐ ADJ [*area*] residencial; [*work*] interno
Ⓑ CPD ► **residential home** N (*for old people*) residencia *f* (de ancianos), hogar *m*; (*for handicapped people*) hogar *m* para minusválidos

residual [rɪ'zɪdjʊəl] Ⓐ ADJ residual
Ⓑ N **residuals** derechos *mpl* residuales de autor

residuary [rɪ'zɪdjʊərɪ] ADJ residual; **~ legatee** legatario/a *m/f* universal

residue ['rezɪdjuː] N 1 (= *remainder*) resto *m*, residuo *m*; **a ~ of bad feeling** un residuo de rencor, un rencor que queda
2 (*Jur*) bienes *mpl* residuales
3 (*Chem*) residuo *m*

residuum [rɪ'zɪdjʊəm] N (*pl* **residua**) residuo *m*

resign [rɪ'zaɪn] Ⓐ VT [+ *office, post*] dimitir de, renunciar a; [+ *claim, task*] renunciar a; **to ~ a task to others** ceder un cometido a otros; **when he ~ed the leadership** cuando dimitió de *or* renunció a la jefatura; **to ~ o.s. to (doing) sth** resignarse a (hacer) algo; **I ~ed myself to never seeing her again** me resigné a no volverla a ver nunca más
Ⓑ VI 1 dimitir, renunciar; **to ~ in favour of sb** renunciar en favor de algn
2 (*Chess*) abandonar

resignation [ˌrezɪg'neɪʃən] N 1 (= *act*) dimisión *f*, renuncia *f*; **to offer** *or* **send in** *or* **hand in** *or* **submit one's ~** presentar la dimisión 2 (= *state*) resignación *f* (**to** a); **to await sth with ~** esperar algo resignado, esperar algo con resignación

resigned [rɪ'zaɪnd] ADJ resignado (**to** a)

resignedly [rɪ'zaɪnɪdlɪ] ADV con resignación

resilience [rɪ'zɪlɪəns] N (*Tech*) elasticidad *f*; (*fig*) resistencia *f*

resilient [rɪ'zɪlɪənt] ADJ (*Tech*) elástico; (*fig*) resistente

resin ['rezɪn] N resina *f*

resinous ['rezɪnəs] ADJ resinoso

resist [rɪ'zɪst] Ⓐ VT (= *oppose*) resistir(se) a; (= *be unaffected by*) resistir; **to ~ arrest** resistirse a ser detenido, oponer resistencia a la policía; **they ~ed the attack vigorously** resistieron vigorosamente el ataque; **we ~ this change** nos oponemos a este cambio; **to ~ temptation** resistir la tentación; **I couldn't ~ buying it** no me resistí a comprarlo; **I can't ~ saying that ...** no puedo resistir al impulso de decir que ...; **I can't ~ squid** me vuelven loco los calamares; **she can't ~ sweets** no puede resistirse a los dulces
Ⓑ VI resistir

resistance [rɪ'zɪstəns] Ⓐ N (*gen*) resistencia *f*; **the Resistance** (*Pol*) la Resistencia; **to offer ~** oponer resistencia (**to** a); **to have good ~ to disease** tener mucha resistencia a la enfermedad; **to take the line of least ~** seguir la ley del mínimo esfuerzo
Ⓑ CPD ► **resistance fighter** N militante *mf* de la Resistencia ► **resistance movement** N (movimiento *m* de) resistencia *f* ► **resistance worker** N militante *mf* de la Resistencia

resistant [rɪ'zɪstənt] ADJ resistente (**to** a)

resistible [rɪ'zɪstɪbl] ADJ resistible

resistor [rɪ'zɪstəʳ] N resistor *m*

resit (*vb: pt, pp* **resat**) (*Brit*) Ⓐ ['riːsɪt] N reválida *f*
Ⓑ ['riː'sɪt] VT [+ *exam*] presentarse otra vez a; [+ *subject*] recuperar, examinarse otra vez de
Ⓒ [ˌriː'sɪt] VI presentarse otra vez, volver a examinarse

reskill [ˌriː'skɪl] (*Ind*) Ⓐ VI reciclarse (*laboralmente*)
Ⓑ VT reciclar (*laboralmente*)

resold [ˌriː'səʊld] PT, PP *of* **resell**

resole [ˌriː'səʊl] VT sobresolar, remontar

resolute ['rezəluːt] ADJ [*person*] resuelto, decidido; [*opposition, refusal, faith*] firme; **to take ~ action** actuar con resolución *or* firmeza; **I am ~ in my opposition to these proposals** me opongo firmemente a estas propuestas; **the government is ~ in countering terrorism** el gobierno lucha con firmeza contra el terrorismo

resolutely ['rezəluːtlɪ] ADV [*stride*] resueltamente; [*stare*] con resolución; [*refuse, resist*] firmemente, con firmeza; [*act*] con resolución, con determinación; **to be ~ opposed to sth** ◊ **stand ~ against sth** oponerse firmemente *or* con firmeza a algo

resoluteness ['rezəluːtnɪs] N resolución *f*, determinación *f*

resolution [ˌrezə'luːʃən] N 1 (= *determination*) resolución *f*, determinación *f*; **to show ~** mostrarse resuelto *or* determinado
2 (= *solving*) resolución *f*
3 (= *motion*) (*gen*) resolución *f*, proposición *f*; (*Parl*) acuerdo *m*; **to pass a ~** tomar un acuerdo; **to put a ~ to a meeting** someter una moción a votación
4 (= *resolve*) propósito *m*; **good ~s** buenos propósitos *mpl*; **New Year ~s** buenos propósitos *mpl* para el Año Nuevo; **to make a ~ to do sth** resolverse a hacer algo
5 (*Chem*) resolución *f*
6 (*Comput*) definición *f*

resolvable [rɪ'zɒlvəbl] ADJ soluble

resolve [rɪ'zɒlv] Ⓐ N 1 (= *resoluteness*) resolución *f*; **unshakeable ~** resolución *f* inquebrantable
2 (= *decision*) propósito *m*; **to make a ~ to do sth** resolverse a hacer algo
Ⓑ VT 1 (= *find solution to*) resolver, solucionar; **this will ~ your doubts** esto solucionará sus dudas; **the problem is still not ~d** el problema está por resolver
2 (= *decide*) resolver, decidir; **to ~ that ...** acordar que ...; **it was ~d that ...** se acordó que ...
Ⓒ VI 1 (= *separate*) resolverse (**into** en); **the question ~s into four parts** la cuestión se resuelve en cuatro partes
2 (= *decide*) **to ~ on sth** optar por algo, re-

➤ LANGUAGE IN USE: reserve B1 21.4

solverse por algo; **to ~ on doing sth** acordar hacer algo; **to ~ to do sth** resolverse a hacer algo

resolved [rɪ'zɒlvd] ADJ **to be ~ to do sth** estar resuelto a hacer algo

resonance ['rezənəns] N resonancia *f*

resonant ['rezənənt] ADJ [*sound*] resonante

resonate ['rezəneɪt] VI resonar (**with** de)

resonator ['rezəneɪtəʳ] N resonador *m*

resorption [rɪ'zɔːpʃən] N resorción *f*

resort [rɪ'zɔːt] Ⓐ N 1 (= *recourse*) recurso *m*; **as a last ~** ◊ **in the last ~** como último recurso; **without ~ to force** sin recurrir a la fuerza

2 (= *place*) lugar *m* de reunión; **holiday ~** (= *area, town*) lugar *m* turístico; (= *complex, hotel*) complejo *m* turístico; **it is a ~ of thieves** es lugar frecuentado por los ladrones, es donde se reúnen los ladrones; *see also* **seaside**

Ⓑ VI 1 (= *have recourse to*) recurrir (**to** a); **to ~ to violence** recurrir a la violencia; **then they ~ed to throwing stones** pasaron luego a tirar piedras; **then you ~ to me for help** así que acudes a mí a pedir ayuda

2 (= *frequent, visit*) **to ~ to** frecuentar

resound [rɪ'zaʊnd] VI [*sound*] resonar; [*place*] **the valley ~ed with shouts** resonaron los gritos por el valle; **the house ~ed with laughter** resonaron las risas por toda la casa

resounding [rɪ'zaʊndɪŋ] ADJ [*noise*] sonoro; [*victory, success*] resonante; [*failure*] estrepitoso

resoundingly [rɪ'zaʊndɪŋlɪ] ADV **to defeat sb ~** obtener una victoria resonante sobre algn

resource [rɪ'sɔːs] Ⓐ N 1 (= *expedient*) recurso *m*, expediente *m*

2 **resources** (= *wealth, goods*) recursos *mpl*; **financial ~s** recursos *mpl* financieros; **natural ~s** recursos *mpl* naturales; **to be at the end of one's ~s** haber agotado sus recursos; **to leave sb to his own ~s** (*fig*) dejar que algn se apañe como pueda; **those ~s are as yet untapped** esos recursos quedan todavía sin explotar

3 (= *resourcefulness*) inventiva *f*

Ⓑ VT proveer fondos para; **we are ~d by Pentos** nuestra fuente de fondos es Pentos; **they are generously ~d** son tratados generosamente en cuanto a la provisión de fondos; **an inadequately ~d project** un proyecto insuficientemente financiado

resourceful [rɪ'sɔːsfʊl] ADJ ingenioso, con iniciativa

resourcefully [rɪ'sɔːsfəlɪ] ADV ingeniosamente, mostrando tener iniciativa

resourcefulness [rɪ'sɔːsfʊlnɪs] N ingenio *m*, iniciativa *f*

re-sow [ˌriː'səʊ] VT resembrar, volver a sembrar

re-sowing [ˌriː'səʊɪŋ] N resembrado *m*

respect [rɪs'pekt] Ⓐ N 1 (= *consideration*) respeto *m*, consideración *f*; **she has no ~ for other people's feelings** no respeta los sentimientos de los demás; **out of ~ for sth/sb** por respeto a algo/algn, por consideración hacia algo/algn; **I didn't mention it, out of ~ for Alan** no lo mencioné por respeto a *or* por consideración hacia Alan; **to treat sb with ~** tratar a algn respetuosamente *or* con respeto; **the drink is quite strong so treat it with ~** la bebida es bastante fuerte, así que ten cuidado; **without ~ to the consequences** sin tener en cuenta las consecuencias

2 (= *admiration, esteem*) respeto *m*; **to command ~** imponer respeto, hacerse respetar; **to earn** *or* **gain sb's ~** ganarse el respeto de algn; **we have the greatest ~ for him** le respetamos muchísimo; **she is held in great ~ by her employees** sus empleados le tienen mucho respeto, sus empleados la respetan mucho; **show some ~!** ¡un poco de respeto!; **to win sb's ~** ganarse el respeto de algn; **with (all due) ~** con el debido respeto; **with all due ~, you have no experience in this field** con el debido respeto *or* con todo el respeto del mundo, no tienes experiencia en este campo

3 **respects** respetos *mpl* (*frm*), recuerdos *mpl*, saludos *mpl*; **give my ~s to everyone** da recuerdos *or* saludos a todos de mi parte; **to pay one's ~s to sb** (*frm*) presentar sus respetos a algn; **to pay one's last ~s to sb** presentar mis/tus/sus *etc* últimos respetos a algn; **John sends his ~s** John os manda recuerdos *or* saludos

4 (= *point, detail*) aspecto *m*, sentido *m*; **in all ~s** en todos los aspectos *or* sentidos; **in certain ~s** hasta cierto punto, en cierta medida, en cierto modo; **in every ~** en todos los aspectos *or* sentidos; **their policies differ in one ~** sus políticas difieren en un aspecto; **in other ~s** por lo demás; **in some/many ~s** en algunos/muchos aspectos *or* sentidos; **in this ~** en este sentido

5 (= *reference, regard*) respecto *m*; **in ~ of** (*frm*) respecto a *or* de; **with ~ to** (*frm*) en lo que respecta a, con respecto a

Ⓑ VT 1 (= *esteem*) respetar; **I want him to ~ me as a career woman** quiero que me respete como mujer de carrera; **I ~ him as a musician** lo respeto como músico

2 (= *have consideration for*) [+ *wishes, privacy, opinions*] respetar

3 (= *observe*) [+ *law, treaty*] acatar

4 **as ~s** por lo que respecta a, en lo concerniente a

respectability [rɪsˌpektə'bɪlɪtɪ] N respetabilidad *f*

respectable [rɪs'pektəbl] ADJ 1 (= *deserving respect*) respetable; **for perfectly ~ reasons** por motivos perfectamente legítimos

2 (= *of fair social standing, decent*) respetable, decente; **that's not ~** eso no es respetable *or* decente; **that skirt isn't ~** esa falda no es decente; **a ~ family** una familia respetable; **~ people** gente *f* bien; **in ~ society** en la buena sociedad

3 [*amount*] apreciable; **at a ~ distance** a una distancia prudente; **she lost a ~ sum** perdió una cantidad respetable

4 (= *passable*) **we made a ~ showing** lo hicimos más o menos bien; **his work is ~ but not brilliant** su obra es aceptable pero no increíble; **my marks were quite ~** mis notas eran bastante decentes

respectably [rɪs'pektəblɪ] ADV 1 (= *decently*) [*dress, behave*] respetablemente, decentemente

2 (= *quite well*) aceptablemente

respected [rɪs'pektɪd] ADJ respetado; **a much ~ person** una persona muy respetada

respecter [rɪs'pektəʳ] N **to be no ~ of persons** no hacer distinción de personas

respectful [rɪs'pektfʊl] ADJ respetuoso

respectfully [rɪs'pektfəlɪ] ADV respetuosamente

respectfulness [rɪs'pektfʊlnɪs] N respetuosidad *f*, acatamiento *m*

respecting [rɪs'pektɪŋ] PREP en lo que concierne a, con respecto a

respective [rɪs'pektɪv] ADJ respectivo

respectively [rɪs'pektɪvlɪ] ADV respectivamente

respiration [ˌrespɪ'reɪʃən] N respiración *f*

respirator ['respɪreɪtəʳ] N 1 (*Med*) respirador *m*

2 (*Mil*) (= *gas mask*) careta *f* antigás

respiratory [rɪs'pɪrətərɪ] ADJ respiratorio; **~ tract** vías *fpl* respiratorias

respire [rɪs'paɪəʳ] Ⓐ VI respirar

Ⓑ VT respirar

respite ['respaɪt] N (*gen*) respiro *m*, tregua *f*; (*Jur*) prórroga *f*, plazo *m*; **without ~** sin descanso; **to get no ~** no tener alivio, no poder descansar; **we got no ~ from the heat** el calor apenas nos dejó respirar; **they gave us no ~** no nos dejaron respirar

resplendence [rɪs'plendəns] N resplandor *m*, refulgencia *f*

resplendent [rɪs'plendənt] ADJ resplandeciente, refulgente; **to be ~** resplandecer, refulgir; **she looked ~ in that new dress** estaba espléndida con ese vestido nuevo; **the car is ~ in green** el coche estaba resplandeciente pintado de verde

respond [rɪs'pɒnd] VI 1 (= *answer*) contestar, responder

2 (= *be responsive*) responder, reaccionar (**to** a); **it ~s to sunlight** reacciona a la luz solar, es sensible a la luz solar; **to ~ to treatment** responder al tratamiento; **the cat ~s to kindness** el gato es sensible a los buenos tratos

respondent [rɪs'pɒndənt] N (*Jur*) demandado/a *m/f*; (*to questionnaire*) persona *f* que responde al cuestionario *or* que rellena el cuestionario

response [rɪs'pɒns] Ⓐ N 1 (= *answer*) (*gen*) contestación *f*, respuesta *f*; (*to charity appeal*) acogida *f*; **his only ~ was to yawn** por toda respuesta dio un bostezo; **in ~ to** como respuesta a; **in ~ to many requests ...** accediendo a muchos ruegos ...; **we got a 73% ~** respondió el 73 por ciento; **we had hoped for a bigger ~ from the public** habíamos esperado más correspondencia *or* una mayor respuesta del público; **it found no ~** no encontró eco alguno; **it met with a generous ~** tuvo una generosa acogida

2 (*Rel*) responsorio *m*

3 (= *reaction*) reacción *f*; **the ~ was not favourable** la reacción no fue favorable

Ⓑ CPD ► **response time** N tiempo *m* de respuesta

responsibility [rɪsˌpɒnsə'bɪlɪtɪ] N 1 (= *liability*) responsabilidad *f*; **he has accepted** *or* **admitted ~ for the tragedy** ha aceptado ser responsable de la tragedia; **the group which claimed ~ for the attack** el grupo que reivindicó el atentado; **joint ~** responsabilidad *f* conjunta; **to place** *or* **put the ~ for sth on sb** hacer a algn responsable de algo, hacer que la responsabilidad de algo recaiga sobre algn; **shared ~** responsabilidad *f* compartida; **the company takes no ~ for objects left here** la empresa no asume responsabilidad por los objetos que se dejen aquí, la empresa no se responsabiliza de los objetos que se dejen aquí; *see also* **diminished**

2 (= *duty, obligation*) responsabilidad *f*; **that's his ~** eso es responsabilidad suya; **she's not your ~** ella no es responsabilidad tuya, ella no está bajo tu responsabilidad; **it's a big ~ for him** supone una gran responsabilidad para él; **it's my ~ to lock up** cerrar es responsabilidad mía, yo soy el responsable de cerrar; **she didn't want to take on more responsibilities** no quería asumir más responsabilidades; **you have a ~ to your family** tienes una responsabilidad con *or* hacia tu familia

3 (= *authority, accountability*) responsabilidad *f*; **she wants a position with more ~** quiere un puesto de mayor responsabilidad; **to have ~ for sth** ser responsable de algo; **to take**

➤ LANGUAGE IN USE: **responsibility 1** 18.3, 20.5

on/take over (the) ~ for sth asumir la responsabilidad de algo, responsabilizarse de algo, hacerse responsable de algo

4 (= *maturity*) responsabilidad *f*; **try to show some ~** a ver si somos más responsables; **he has no sense of ~** no tiene ningún sentido de la responsabilidad

▼responsible [rɪsˈpɒnsəbl] ADJ 1 (= *accountable*) responsable; **those ~ will be punished** se castigará a los responsables; **who is ~ if anything goes wrong?** ¿quién es el responsable si algo sale mal?; **to be ~ for sth**: **he is not ~ for his actions** no es responsable de sus actos; **who is ~ for this?** ¿quién es el responsable de esto?; **who was ~ for the delay?** ¿quién tiene la culpa del retraso?; **to hold sb ~ for sth** hacer a algn responsable de algo, responsabilizar a algn de algo; **to be ~ to sb (for sth)** ser responsable ante algn (de algo)

2 (= *in charge of*) **to be ~ for sth/sb**: **the children were ~ for tidying their own rooms** los niños tenían la responsabilidad *or* eran responsables de ordenar sus habitaciones; **she is ~ for 40 children** tiene a su cargo 40 niños; **the secretary is ~ for taking the minutes** la secretaria se hace cargo de levantar el acta

3 (= *sensible*) [*person*] serio, responsable; [*behaviour, attitude*] responsable; **to act in a ~ fashion** obrar de forma responsable *or* con responsabilidad; **that wasn't very ~ of you!** ¡eso ha sido una falta de responsabilidad por tu parte!

4 (= *important*) [*post, job*] de responsabilidad

responsibly [rɪsˈpɒnsəblɪ] ADV de forma responsable, responsablemente, con responsabilidad

responsive [rɪsˈpɒnsɪv] ADJ 1 (= *sensitive*) sensible; **to be ~ to sth** ser sensible a algo

2 (= *interested*) (*gen*) interesado; [*audience*] que reacciona con entusiasmo, que reacciona con interés; **he was not very ~** apenas dio muestras de interés

responsiveness [rɪsˈpɒnsɪvnɪs] N 1 (= *sensitivity*) sensibilidad *f* (**to** a)

2 (= *interest*) grado *m* de reacción (**to** a)

rest¹ [rest] Ⓐ N 1 (= *repose*) descanso *m*; **I need a ~** necesito descansar, me hace falta un descanso; **to be at ~** (= *not moving*) estar en reposo; (*euph*) (= *dead*) descansar; **to come to ~** [*ball, vehicle, person*] pararse, detenerse; [*bird, insect, eyes, gaze*] posarse; **her eyes came to ~ on the book** su mirada se posó en el libro; **day of ~** día *m* de descanso; **I need a ~ from gardening** me hace falta descansar de la jardinería; **try to get some ~** intenta descansar; **to give sth a ~** dejar algo (por un tiempo); **I think you ought to give football a ~** creo que deberías dejar el fútbol por un tiempo; **give it a ~!*** ¡déjalo ya!, ¡vale ya!*; **to have a ~** tomarse un descanso; **why don't you have a ~?** (= *take a break*) ¿por qué no te tomas un descanso?; (= *lie down*) ¿por qué no descansas un rato?; **to have a good night's ~** dormir bien; **to lay sb to ~** enterrar a algn; **to lay** *or* **put sth to ~** [+ *theory*] enterrar algo; **his speech should lay those fears to ~** su discurso debería acabar con *or* enterrar esos temores; **to take a ~** = **to have a rest** *see also* **bed C**, **change A1**, **mind A1**, **wicked**

2 (*Mus*) silencio *m*

3 (= *support*) apoyo *m*, soporte *m*; (*Billiards*) soporte *m*; (*Telec*) horquilla *f*

Ⓑ VT 1 (= *give rest to*) descansar; **try to ~ the ankle as much as possible** intente descansar el tobillo lo más que pueda; **the horses have to be ~ed** hay que dejar descansar a los caballos; **I feel very ~ed** me siento muy descansado; **to ~ o.s.** descansar; **God ~ his soul!** ¡Dios le acoja en su seno!

2 (= *support*) apoyar (**on** en, sobre; **against** contra); **~ the ladder against the tree** apoya la escalera contra el árbol; **to ~ one's hand on sb's shoulder** apoyar la mano en el hombro de algn

3 (= *settle*) **to ~ one's eyes/gaze on sth** posar la mirada en algo

4 (*Jur*) **to ~ one's case** concluir su alegato; **I ~ my case** concluyo mi alegato; (*fig*) (*hum*) he dicho

Ⓒ VI 1 (= *repose*) descansar; **go back to bed and ~** vuelve a la cama y descansa; **the waves never ~** las olas no descansan nunca; **he won't ~ until he finds out the truth** no descansará hasta que descubra la verdad; **may he ~ in peace** (*euph*) que en paz descanse; *see also* **laurel**

2 (= *lean, be supported*) [*person*] apoyarse (**on** en); [*roof, structure*] estar sostenido (**on** por); (*fig*) [*responsibility*] pesar (**on** sobre); **he ~ed on his spade for a while** se apoyó en la pala un rato; **his head was ~ing on her shoulder** tenía la cabeza apoyada en su hombro; **her arm ~ed on my chair** su brazo estaba apoyado en mi silla; **her elbows were ~ing on the table** tenía los codos apoyados en la mesa; **the ladder was ~ing against the wall** la escalera estaba apoyada contra la pared; **a heavy responsibility ~s on him** sobre él pesa una grave responsabilidad

3 (= *alight*) [*eyes, gaze*] posarse; **his eyes ~ed on me** su mirada se posó en mí

4 (= *depend, be based*) [*argument, case*] basarse (**on** en); [*sb's future*] depender (**on** de); **the future of the country ~s on how we teach our children** el futuro del país depende de la enseñanza que demos a nuestros hijos

5 (= *be, remain*) quedar; **we cannot let the matter ~ there** no podemos permitir que la cosa quede ahí; **the decision ~s with her** ◊ **it ~s with her to decide** la decisión la tiene que tomar ella, ella es la que tiene que decidir, la decisión es suya; *see also* **assure**, **easy A2**

6 (*Theat euph*) **to be ~ing** no tener trabajo

7 (*Jur*) **the defence/prosecution ~s** la defensa/el fiscal concluye su alegato

Ⓓ CPD ► **rest area** N (*Aut*) área *f* de descanso ► **rest cure** N cura *f* de reposo ► **rest home** N residencia *f* de ancianos, asilo *m* (de ancianos) ► **rest room** N (*US*) servicios *mpl*, baño(s) *m(pl)* (*LAm*) ► **rest stop** N (= *pause*) parada *f* para descansar, parada *f* de descanso; (*Aut*) = **rest area**

►**rest up*** (*esp US*) VI + ADV descansar

rest² [rest] N **the ~** (= *remainder*) [*of money, food, month*] el resto; [*of people, things*] el resto, los/las demás; **I'm taking the ~ of the week off** me tomaré el resto *or* lo que queda de la semana libre; **the dog ate the ~** el perro se comió el resto *or* lo que sobró; **you go home — I'll do the ~** tú vete a casa, yo hago lo demás *or* lo que queda; **I'll take half of the money — you keep the ~** yo me llevo la mitad del dinero, tú te quedas con el resto; **the ~ of the money** el resto del dinero; **all the ~ of the money** todo lo que sobró del dinero; **they left the ~ of the meal untouched** no tocaron el resto de la comida; **the ~ stayed outside** los demás se quedaron fuera; **the ~ of us will wait here** los demás esperaremos aquí; **the ~ of the boys** los otros chicos, los demás chicos; **he was as drunk as the ~ of them** estaba tan borracho como los demás; **the ~ of them couldn't care less** a los demás *or* a los otros les trae sin cuidado; **what shall we give the ~ of them?** ¿qué les daremos a los otros?; **the ~ of the soldiers** los otros soldados, los demás soldados; **I will take this book and you keep the ~** yo me llevo este libro y tú quédate con los demás; **all the ~ of the books** todos los demás libros, todos los otros libros; **it was just another grave like all the ~** no era más que otra tumba, como todas las demás *or* todas las otras; **and all the ~ (of it)*** etcétera, etcétera*; **he was from a wealthy family, went to Eton, Oxford and all the ~ of it** era de familia rica, estudió en Eton, Oxford etcétera, etcétera*; **she was a deb and all the ~ of it*** era debutante y todo lo demás; **(as) for the ~** por lo demás; **only there did his age show, for the ~, he might have been under seventy** sólo en eso se le notaba la edad, por lo demás, podía haber tenido menos de setenta años; *see also* **history**

restart [ˈriːˈstɑːt] Ⓐ VT [+ *book, drawing*] empezar de nuevo, volver a empezar; [+ *negotiations, meeting*] reanudar; [+ *engine*] volver a arrancar

Ⓑ VI [*meeting etc*] empezar de nuevo, reanudarse

restate [ˌriːˈsteɪt] VT 1 (= *repeat*) [+ *argument*] repetir, reafirmar; [+ *case*] volver a exponer; [+ *problem*] volver a plantear

2 (= *change terms of*) [+ *argument*] modificar

restatement [ˌriːˈsteɪtmənt] N [*of argument*] repetición *f*, reafirmación *f*; [*of case*] nueva exposición *f*; [*of problem*] nuevo planteamiento *m*

restaurant [ˈrestərɒŋ] Ⓐ N restaurante *m*

Ⓑ CPD ► **restaurant car** N (*Brit*) coche-comedor *m*

restaurateur [ˌrestərəˈtɜːʳ] N dueño/a *m/f* de un restaurante, restaurador(a) *m/f*

restful [ˈrestfʊl] ADJ descansado, tranquilo

restfully [ˈrestfəlɪ] ADV reposadamente, sosegadamente

resting place [ˈrestɪŋpleɪs] N (*also* **last** *or* **final ~**) última morada *f*

restitution [ˌrestɪˈtjuːʃən] N 1 (= *return*) restitución *f*; **to make ~ of sth to sb** restituir algo a algn, devolver algo a algn

2 (= *compensation*) **to make ~ to sb for sth** indemnizar a algn por algo

restive [ˈrestɪv] ADJ [*person, audience, voters*] inquieto; [*horse*] nervioso, inquieto; **to get ~** [*person*] impacientarse; [*horse*] ponerse nervioso *or* inquieto

restiveness [ˈrestɪvnɪs] N [*of person*] inquietud *f*, malestar *m*; [*of horse*] nerviosismo *m*, inquietud *f*

restless [ˈrestlɪs] ADJ 1 (= *unsettled*) [*person*] inquieto, intranquilo; [*mind*] intranquilo; **he's the ~ sort** es de los inquietos, es de los que no saben quedarse quietos; **to feel ~** sentirse intranquilo; **I had a ~ night** pasé muy mala noche, no dormí bien

2 (= *fidgety*) inquieto; **to become** *or* **get** *or* **grow ~** inquietarse, impacientarse

3 (= *discontented*) [*crowd, mob*] agitado

4 (*liter*) (= *moving*) [*wind, sea, clouds*] agitado

restlessly [ˈrestlɪslɪ] ADV nerviosamente; **he paced ~ around the room** se paseaba nerviosamente de un lado a otro de la habitación; **she moved ~ in her sleep** se movió inquieta mientras dormía

restlessness [ˈrestlɪsnɪs] N 1 (= *unsettled feeling*) agitación *f*, inquietud *f*

2 (= *fidgety feeling*) agitación *f*

3 (= *discontent*) agitación *f*

➤ LANGUAGE IN USE: **responsible 1** 26.3

restock [ˈriːˈstɒk] Ⓐ VT [+ *larder*] reabastecer; [+ *pond*] repoblar (**with** de)
Ⓑ VI **we ~ed with Brand X** renovamos las existencias con la Marca X

restoration [ˌrestəˈreɪʃən] N 1 [*of money, possession*] devolución *f*, restitución *f* (*frm*)
2 [*of relations, links, order*] restablecimiento *m*; [*of confidence*] devolución *f*; [*of monarchy, democracy*] restauración *f*
3 [*of building, painting, antique*] restauración *f*
4 (*Brit Hist*) **the Restoration** la Restauración (*época que comienza con la restauración de Carlos II en el trono británico*)

restorative [rɪsˈtɔːrətɪv] Ⓐ ADJ reconstituyente
Ⓑ N reconstituyente *m*

restore [rɪsˈtɔːʳ] VT 1 (= *give back*) [+ *money, possession*] devolver, restituir (*frm*); **to ~ sth to sb** devolver algo a algn, restituir algo a algn (*frm*)
2 (= *re-establish, reinstate*) [+ *relations, links, order*] restablecer; [+ *monarch, president, democracy*] restaurar; [+ *confidence, strength*] devolver; [+ *tax, law*] reimplantar, volver a implantar; **order was soon ~d** pronto se restableció el orden; **to ~ sb's sight** devolver la vista a algn; **to ~ sb's strength** devolver las fuerzas a algn; **to ~ sb to health/life** devolver la salud a algn/reanimar a algn; **his supporters want to ~ him to power** sus partidarios quieren conseguir que vuelva al poder; **the investment needed to ~ these depressed areas to life** la inversión que se necesita para reactivar estas zonas deprimidas
3 [+ *building, painting, antique*] restaurar; **to ~ sth to its original state** *or* **condition** restituir *or* devolver algo a su estado original

restorer [rɪsˈtɔːrəʳ] N 1 (= *person*) restaurador(a) *m/f*
2 (= *hair restorer*) loción *f* capilar, regenerador *m* del cabello

restrain [rɪsˈtreɪn] VT 1 (= *hold back*) refrenar; (= *repress*) reprimir; (= *dissuade*) disuadir; (= *prevent*) impedir; (= *inhibit*) cohibir; **to ~ sb from doing sth** (= *dissuade*) disuadir a algn de hacer algo; (= *physically prevent*) impedir a algn hacer algo; **kindly ~ your friend** haga el favor de refrenar a su amigo
2 (= *contain*) contener; (= *confine*) encerrar; **I managed to ~ my anger** logré contener mi enojo; **to ~ o.s.** contenerse; **to ~ o.s. from doing sth** dominarse para que no haga algo; **but I ~ed myself** pero me contuve, pero me dominé; **please ~ yourself!** ¡por favor, cálmese!

restrained [rɪsˈtreɪnd] ADJ [*person*] cohibido; [*style*] reservado; **he was very ~ about it** estuvo muy comedido

restraint [rɪsˈtreɪnt] N 1 (= *check*) restricción *f*; (= *control*) control *m*; (= *check on wages*) moderación *f*; **a ~ on trade** una restricción sobre el comercio; **a ~ on free enterprise** una limitación de la libre empresa; **to be under a ~** estar cohibido; **to fret under a ~** impacientarse por una restricción; **to put sb under a ~** refrenar a algn; (*Jur*) imponer una restricción legal a algn; **without ~** sin restricción
2 (= *constraint*) [*of manner*] reserva *f*; [*of character*] moderación *f*, comedimiento *m*
3 (= *self-control*) autodominio *m*, control *m* de sí mismo; **he showed great ~** mostró poseer un gran autodominio

restrict [rɪsˈtrɪkt] VT [+ *visits, price rise*] limitar; [+ *authority, freedom*] restringir, limitar; **the plant is ~ed to Andalusia** la planta está restringida a Andalucía; **his output is ~ed to novels** su producción se limita a las novelas; **to ~ o.s. to sth** limitarse a algo; **I ~ myself to the facts** me limito a exponer los hechos; **nowadays I ~ myself to a litre a day** hoy día me limito a beber un litro diario

restricted [rɪsˈtrɪktɪd] ADJ 1 (= *prohibited*) vedado, prohibido; **~ area** (*Mil*) zona *f* prohibida
2 (= *limited*) limitado; **~ area** (*Brit Aut*) zona *f* de velocidad limitada; **he has rather a ~ outlook** (*fig*) es de miras estrechas
3 (= *kept small*) [*area, circulation*] reducido; [*distribution*] restringido; **~ document** documento *m* de circulación restringida; **~ market** mercado *m* restringido

restriction [rɪsˈtrɪkʃən] N restricción *f*, limitación *f*; **without ~ as to ...** sin restricción de ...; **to place ~s on the sale of a drug** poner limitaciones a la venta de una droga; **to place ~s on sb's liberty** restringir la libertad de algn

restrictive [rɪsˈtrɪktɪv] ADJ restringido, limitado; **~ practices** (*Brit*) prácticas *fpl* restrictivas

restring [ˌriːˈstrɪŋ] (*pt, pp* **restrung** [ˌriːˈstrʌŋ]) VT [+ *pearls, necklace*] ensartar de nuevo; [+ *violin, racket*] poner nuevas cuerdas a; [+ *bow*] poner una nueva cuerda a

restructure [ˌriːˈstrʌktʃəʳ] VT reestructurar

restructuring [ˌriːˈstrʌktʃərɪŋ] N reestructuración *f*

restrung [ˌriːˈstrʌŋ] PT, PP *of* **restring**

restyle [ˌriːˈstaɪl] VT [*car*] remodelar, remozar; **I asked her to ~ my hair** le pedí que me hiciera otro corte de pelo, le pedí que me hiciera un corte de pelo diferente

result [rɪˈzʌlt] Ⓐ N 1 (= *outcome*) resultado *m*; **this oven gives better ~s** este horno da mejores resultados; **he followed his own advice, with disastrous ~s** hizo lo que le pareció, con consecuencias desastrosas *or* resultados desastrosos; **as a ~** por consiguiente; **as a ~ of** como *or* a consecuencia de; **he died as a ~ of his injuries** murió como *or* a consecuencia de las heridas; **to achieve/produce the desired ~** lograr/producir los resultados deseados; **with the ~ that ...** con la consecuencia de que ...; **without ~** sin resultado; ✦***IDIOM*** **to get a ~** (*Brit**) (= *succeed*) obtener resultados*; *see also* **end**
2 [*of election, race, match*] resultado *m*; **the election ~s** los resultados de las elecciones; **her exam ~s were excellent** en los exámenes sacó unas notas excelentes; **the football ~s** los resultados de los partidos de fútbol
3 (*Math*) resultado *f*
4 **results** 4·1 (= *favourable outcome*) resultados *mpl*; **to get ~s: if they don't get ~s, heads will begin to roll** como no obtengan resultados, empezarán a cortar cabezas; **if a child sees that crying gets ~s he will take advantage of that** si un niño ve que llorar le da resultado se aprovechará de ello
4·2 (*St Ex*) resultados *mpl*; **half-year ~s** resultados *mpl* semestrales
Ⓑ VI resultar; **a saving in cost would ~** se obtendría como resultado un ahorro en los costos; **the fire had ~ed from carelessness** el incendio fue resultado de un descuido; **to ~ in sth**: **it ~ed in his death** le acarreó la muerte, tuvo como resultado su muerte; **it ~ed in a large increase** dio como resultado un aumento apreciable; **it didn't ~ in anything useful** no dio ningún resultado útil; **such behaviour may ~ in dismissal** semejante comportamiento puede acarrear el despido

resultant [rɪˈzʌltənt] ADJ resultante

resume [rɪˈzjuːm] Ⓐ VT 1 (= *start again*) [+ *meeting, negotiations, session*] reanudar; [+ *office*] reasumir; **to ~ one's seat** volver al asiento; **to ~ one's work** reanudar el trabajo; **"now then," he ~d** —ahora bien —dijo reanudando la conversación *or* su discurso
2 (= *sum up*) resumir
Ⓑ VI [*class, meeting*] reanudarse

résumé [ˈreɪzjuːmeɪ] N 1 (= *summary*) resumen *m*
2 (*US*) (= *curriculum vitae*) currículum *m* (vitae)

resumption [rɪˈzʌmpʃən] N (*gen*) reanudación *f*; (= *continuation*) continuación *f*; **on the ~ of the sitting** al reanudarse la sesión

resurface [ˈriːˈsɜːfɪs] Ⓐ VT (*gen*) revestir; [+ *road*] rehacer el firme de
Ⓑ VI [*submarine*] volver a la superficie; [*person*] reaparecer

resurgence [rɪˈsɜːdʒəns] N resurgimiento *m*

resurgent [rɪˈsɜːdʒənt] ADJ resurgente, renaciente

resurrect [ˌrezəˈrekt] VT resucitar

resurrection [ˌrezəˈrekʃən] N (*Rel*) Resurrección *f*; (*fig*) resurrección *f*

resuscitate [rɪˈsʌsɪteɪt] VT resucitar

resuscitation [rɪˌsʌsɪˈteɪʃən] N resucitación *f*

resuscitator [rɪˈsʌsɪteɪtəʳ] N resucitador *m*

ret. ABBR = **retired**

retail [ˈriːteɪl] Ⓐ N venta *f* al por menor, venta *f* al detalle
Ⓑ ADV **to buy/sell sth ~** comprar/vender algo al por menor, comprar/vender algo al detalle
Ⓒ VT 1 (*Comm*) vender al por menor, vender al detalle
2 [+ *gossip*] repetir; [+ *story*] contar
Ⓓ VI (*Comm*) **to ~ at** tener precio de venta al público de
Ⓔ CPD ► **retail business** N comercio *m* al por menor, comercio *m* al detalle ► **retail dealer** N comerciante *mf* al por menor, detallista *mf* ► **retail outlet** N punto *m* de venta al por menor, punto *m* de venta al detalle ► **retail park** N *zona de hipermercados* ► **retail price** N precio *m* de venta al público ► **retail price index** N índice *m* de precios al consumo ► **retail sales** NPL ventas *fpl* al detalle ► **retail trade** N comercio *m* al por menor, comercio *m* detallista ► **retail trader** N = **retail dealer**

retailer [ˈriːteɪləʳ] N comerciante *mf* al por menor, detallista *mf*

retain [rɪˈteɪn] VT 1 (= *hold back*) retener; (= *keep in one's possession*) guardar, quedarse con; (= *keep in memory*) recordar, retener
2 (= *sign up*) [+ *lawyer*] contratar

retained [rɪˈteɪnd] ADJ **~ earnings** beneficios *mpl* retenidos; **~ profit** beneficios *mpl* retenidos

retainer [rɪˈteɪnəʳ] N 1 (= *servant*) criado/a *m/f*; **family ~** ◊ **old ~** viejo criado *m* (*que lleva muchos años sirviendo en la misma familia*)
2 (= *fee*) anticipo *m*; (= *payment on flat, room*) depósito *m*, señal *f* (*para que se guarde el piso etc*)

retaining [rɪˈteɪnɪŋ] ADJ **~ wall** muro *m* de contención

retake (*vb: pt* **retook**; *pp* **retaken**) Ⓐ [ˈriːteɪk] N (*Cine*) repetición *f*
Ⓑ [ˌriːˈteɪk] VT 1 (*Mil*) volver a tomar
2 (*Cine*) repetir, volver a tomar
3 [+ *exam*] presentarse segunda vez a; [+ *subject*] examinarse otra vez de

retaliate [rɪˈtæliert] VI (= *respond*) responder; (*Mil*) tomar represalias; **to ~ against sth/sb**

➤ LANGUAGE IN USE: **result A1** 17.1, 26.3 **B** 26.3

tomar represalias contra algo/algn; **they ~d by bombing Israeli ports** tomaron represalias bombardeando los puertos israelíes; **she ~d by switching the television off** su respuesta fue apagar el televisor, respondió apagando el televisor

retaliation [rɪˌtælɪˈeɪʃən] N (*Mil*) represalias *fpl*; (= *revenge*) represalia *f*; **he sulks as a form of ~** su forma de desquitarse es enfurruñarse; **in** *or* **by way of ~ (for sth)**: **he was executed in ~ for a raid on their headquarters** lo ejecutaron como represalia por el asalto de su sede

retaliatory [rɪˈtælɪətərɪ] ADJ de represalia; **~ raid** ataque *m* de represalia; **to take ~ measures** tomar represalias

retard [rɪˈtɑːd] Ⓐ VT retardar, retrasar
Ⓑ [ˈriːtɑːd] N (*US**) atrasado/a *m/f* mental*

retarded [rɪˈtɑːdɪd] Ⓐ ADJ retardado, retrasado
Ⓑ NPL **the ~** los retrasados (mentales)

retch [retʃ] VI tener arcadas

retching [ˈretʃɪŋ] N esfuerzo *m* por vomitar

retd ABBR = **retired**

retell [ˈriːˈtel] (*pt, pp* **retold**) VT volver a contar

retention [rɪˈtenʃən] N retención *f* (*also Med*)

retentive [rɪˈtentɪv] ADJ retentivo; **a ~ memory** una buena memoria

retentiveness [rɪˈtentɪvnɪs] N retentiva *f*, poder *m* de retención

rethink [ˈriːˈθɪŋk] (*vb: pt, pp* **rethought**) Ⓐ N **to have a ~** volver a pensarlo
Ⓑ VT reconsiderar

reticence [ˈretɪsəns] N reticencia *f*, reserva *f*

reticent [ˈretɪsənt] ADJ reticente, reservado; **he has been very ~ about it** ha tratado el asunto con la mayor reserva

reticently [ˈretɪsəntlɪ] ADV con reticencia, con reserva

reticle [ˈretɪkl] N retículo *m*

reticulate [rɪˈtɪkjʊlɪt] ADJ reticular

reticulated [rɪˈtɪkjʊleɪtɪd] ADJ = **reticulate**

reticule [ˈretɪkjuːl] N [1] (*Opt*) retículo *m*
[2] (*Hist*) (= *bag*) ridículo *m*

retina [ˈretɪnə] N (*pl* **retinas** *or* **retinae** [ˈretɪniː]) (*Anat*) retina *f*

retinue [ˈretɪnjuː] N séquito *m*, comitiva *f*

retire [rɪˈtaɪəʳ] Ⓐ VI [1] (= *give up work*) [*worker*] retirarse; (*at age limit*) jubilarse, retirarse; [*professional sportsperson, military officer*] retirarse; **she is retiring from professional tennis this year** se retira del tenis profesional este año; **she ~d on a good pension** se jubiló *or* se retiró con una buena pensión; **he ~d to the South of France** se jubiló *or* se retiró y se fue a vivir al sur de Francia
[2] (*frm*) (= *withdraw*) retirarse; **the jury has ~d to consider its verdict** el jurado se ha retirado a deliberar para dar su veredicto; **to ~ from public life** retirarse de *or* abandonar la vida pública
[3] (*frm*) (= *go to bed*) acostarse, retirarse (*frm*); **to ~ to bed** ◊ **~ for the night** ir a dormir, ir a acostarse
[4] (*Sport*) [*competitor*] abandonar, retirarse; [*horse*] retirarse; **he ~d in the fifth lap with engine trouble** abandonó *or* se retiró en la quinta vuelta debido a problemas con el motor
[5] (*Mil*) [*troops, army*] retirarse
Ⓑ VT [1] (*from work, service*) [+ *worker*] jubilar; (*Mil*) [+ *officer*] retirar; **he was compulsorily ~d** le dieron la jubilación forzosa, le obligaron a jubilarse
[2] (*Horse racing*) [+ *horse*] retirar; (*Baseball*) [+ *batter*] eliminar
[3] (*Fin*) [+ *bond*] redimir
[4] (*Mil*) [+ *troops, army*] retirar

retired [rɪˈtaɪəd] ADJ (*from work*) (*gen*) jubilado, retirado; (*esp Mil*) retirado; **I've been ~ since 1996** me jubilé en 1996; **a ~ person** un jubilado/una jubilada; **a lot of ~ people come here** aquí vienen muchos jubilados

retiree [rɪˈtaɪəˌriː] N (*US*) jubilado/a *m/f*

retirement [rɪˈtaɪəment] Ⓐ N [1] (= *state of being retired*) retiro *m*; **to live in ~** vivir en el retiro; **to spend one's ~ growing roses** dedicarse a cultivar rosas después de la jubilación; **how will you spend your ~?** ¿qué piensa hacer cuando se jubile?
[2] (= *act of retiring*) (*gen*) jubilación *f*; (*esp Mil*) retiro *m*
[3] (*Mil*) (= *withdrawal*) retirada *f*
Ⓑ CPD ► **retirement age** N edad *f* de jubilación; (*Mil*) edad *f* de retiro ► **retirement benefit** N prestaciones *fpl* por jubilación ► **retirement pay, retirement pension** N jubilación *f*; (*Mil*) retiro *m*

retiring [rɪˈtaɪərɪŋ] ADJ [1] [*chairman, president*] saliente; [*age*] de jubilación
[2] (= *shy*) reservado, retraído

retook [ˌriːˈtʊk] PT of **retake**

retort [rɪˈtɔːt] Ⓐ N [1] (= *answer*) réplica *f*
[2] (*Chem*) retorta *f*
Ⓑ VT replicar; **he ~ed that ...** replicó que ...

retouch [ˈriːˈtʌtʃ] VT retocar

retrace [riːˈtreɪs] VT [+ *path*] desandar; [+ *sb's journey etc*] seguir las huellas de; (*in memory*) recordar, ir recordando, rememorar; **to ~ one's steps** (*lit, fig*) desandar lo andado

retract [rɪˈtrækt] Ⓐ VT [1] [+ *statement*] retractar, retirar
[2] (= *draw in*) [+ *claws*] retraer; [+ *head*] meter; (*Tech*) [+ *undercarriage etc*] replegar
Ⓑ VI [1] (= *apologize*) retractarse, desdecirse; **he refuses to ~** se niega a retractarse *or* desdecirse
[2] (= *be drawn in*) retraerse, meterse; (*Tech*) replegarse

retractable [rɪˈtræktəbl] ADJ retractable; (*Tech*) replegable, retráctil

retraction [rɪˈtrækʃən] N retractación *f*, retracción *f*

retrain [ˈriːˈtreɪn] Ⓐ VT [+ *workers*] reciclar, recapacitar, reconvertir
Ⓑ VI reciclarse, reconvertirse

retraining [ˈriːˈtreɪnɪŋ] N reciclaje *m*, recapacitación *f*

retransmit [ˈriːtrænzˈmɪt] VT retransmitir

retread [ˈriːtred] Ⓐ N (= *tyre*) neumático *m* recauchutado, llanta *f* recauchutada, llanta *f* reencauchada (*LAm*)
Ⓑ [ˌriːˈtred] VT [+ *tyre*] recauchutar, reencauchar (*CAm*)

re-tread [ˌriːˈtred] VT [+ *path etc*] volver a pisar

retreat [rɪˈtriːt] Ⓐ N [1] (*Mil*) (= *withdrawal*) retirada *f*; (*fig*) vuelta *f* atrás, marcha *f* atrás; **the ~ from Mons** la retirada de Mons; **to beat the ~** dar el toque de retreta; **to beat a ~** retirarse, batirse en retirada; (*fig*) emprender la retirada; **to beat a hasty ~** (*fig*) retirarse en desorden; **the government is in ~ on this issue** en este asunto el gobierno se está echando atrás; **this represents a ~ from his promise** con esto se está volviendo atrás de su promesa; **to be in full ~** retirarse en masa, retirarse en todo el frente
[2] (= *place*) (*also Rel*) retiro *m*, refugio *m*; (= *state*) retraimiento *m*, apartamiento *m*
Ⓑ VI [1] (*Mil, Rel*) (= *move back*) retirarse; **they ~ed to Dunkirk** se retiraron a Dunquerque
[2] (= *draw back*) retroceder; **the waters are ~ing** las aguas están bajando

retrench [rɪˈtrentʃ] Ⓐ VT reducir, cercenar
Ⓑ VI economizar, hacer economías

retrenchment [rɪˈtrentʃmənt] N [1] (*frm*) (= *cutting back*) racionalización *f* de gastos, recorte *m* de gastos
[2] (*Mil*) empalizada *f* interior

retrial [ˈriːˈtraɪəl] N [*of person*] nuevo juicio *m*; [*of case*] revisión *f*

retribution [ˌretrɪˈbjuːʃən] N justo castigo *m*, pena *f* merecida

retributive [rɪˈtrɪbjʊtɪv] ADJ castigador, de castigo

retrievable [rɪˈtriːvəbl] ADJ recuperable; [*error etc*] reparable

retrieval [rɪˈtriːvəl] N [1] (*Comput*) recuperación *f*; **data ~** recuperación *f* de datos
[2] (= *recovery*) recuperación *f*; **beyond ~** irrecuperable
[3] (*Hunting*) cobra *f*

retrieve [rɪˈtriːv] VT [1] (= *get back*) [+ *object*] recuperar, recobrar; (*Hunting*) cobrar; **to ~ sth from the water** rescatar algo del agua; **she ~d her handkerchief** recogió su pañuelo, volvió a tomar su pañuelo
[2] (= *put right*) [+ *error etc*] reparar, subsanar; [+ *fortunes*] reparar
[3] (*fig*) (= *rescue*) [+ *situation*] salvar; **we shall ~ nothing from this disaster** no salvaremos nada de esta catástrofe
[4] (*Comput, Psych*) [+ *information*] recuperar

retriever [rɪˈtriːvəʳ] N perro *m* cobrador

retro... [ˈretrəʊ] PREFIX retro...

retroactive [ˌretrəʊˈæktɪv] ADJ retroactivo

retrofit [ˈretrəʊfɪt] VT actualizar el diseño de

retroflex [ˈretrəʊfleks] ADJ vuelto hacia atrás

retrograde [ˈretrəʊgreɪd] ADJ (*fig*) [*step, measure*] retrógrado

retrogress [ˌretrəʊˈgres] VI [1] (= *recede*) retroceder
[2] (*fig*) (= *degenerate*) empeorar, degenerar, decaer

retrogression [ˌretrəʊˈgreʃən] N retroceso *m*, retrogradación *f*

retrogressive [ˌretrəʊˈgresɪv] ADJ retrógrado

retrorocket [ˈretrəʊˈrɒkɪt] N retrocohete *m*

retrospect [ˈretrəʊspekt] N retrospección *f*, mirada *f* retrospectiva; **in ~** retrospectivamente; **in ~ it seems a happy time** volviendo la vista atrás parece haber sido un período feliz

retrospection [ˌretrəʊˈspekʃən] N retrospección *f*, consideración *f* del pasado

retrospective [ˌretrəʊˈspektɪv] Ⓐ ADJ retrospectivo; [*law etc*] retroactivo, de efecto retroactivo
Ⓑ N (*Art*) (exposición *f*) retrospectiva *f*

retrospectively [ˌretrəʊˈspektɪvlɪ] ADV (*gen*) retrospectivamente; (*Admin, Jur*) de modo retroactivo, con efecto retroactivo

retroussé [rəˈtuːseɪ] ADJ **~ nose** nariz *f* respingona

retrovirus [ˈretrəʊˌvaɪrəs] N retrovirus *m inv*

retry [ˈriːˈtraɪ] VT (*Jur*) [+ *person*] procesar de nuevo, volver a procesar; [+ *case*] rever

retune [ˌriːˈtjuːn] Ⓐ VT [+ *musical instrument*] afinar de nuevo; [+ *engine*] poner a punto de nuevo; [+ *radio, video recorder*] volver a sintonizar
Ⓑ [ˈriːtjuːn] N [*of engine*] nueva puesta *f* a punto

▼ **return** [rɪˈtɜːn] Ⓐ N [1] (= *going/coming back*) vuelta *f*, regreso *m*; **the ~ home** la vuelta *or* el regreso a casa; **the ~ to school** la vuelta *or* el

➤ LANGUAGE IN USE: **return** A1 20.3, 26.6

regreso al colegio; **he advocates a ~ to Victorian values** aboga por una vuelta *or* un regreso a los valores victorianos; **their ~ to power** su vuelta *or* retorno al poder; **many happy ~s (of the day)!** ¡feliz cumpleaños!, ¡felicidades!; **he has not ruled out the possibility of making a ~ to football** no ha descartado la posibilidad de volver al fútbol; **on my ~** a mi vuelta, a mi regreso; **by ~ (of) post** *or* (*US*) **by ~ mail** a vuelta de correo; *see also* **point A5**

2 (*= reappearance*) [*of symptoms, pain*] reaparición *f*; [*of doubts, fears*] resurgimiento *m*; **there was no ~ of the symptoms** los síntomas no volvieron a aparecer, los síntomas no reaparecieron

3 (*= giving back*) [*of thing taken away*] devolución *f*, restitución *f* (*frm*); [*of thing borrowed*] devolución *f*; (*Comm*) [*of merchandise*] devolución *f*; [*of money*] reembolso *m*, devolución *f*; **they are demanding the ~ of their lands** exigen la devolución *or* (*frm*) la restitución de sus tierras; **he appealed for the ~ of the hostages** hizo un llamamiento pidiendo la liberación de los rehenes; *see also* **sale**

4 (*= thing returned*) (*Comm*) (*= merchandise*) devolución *f*; (*= theatre, concert ticket*) devolución *f*, entrada *f* devuelta; (*= library book*) libro *m* devuelto; **it's sold out but you might get a ~ on the night** se han agotado las localidades, pero puede que consiga una entrada devuelta *or* una devolución la misma noche de la función

5 (*Fin*) (*= profit*) ganancia *f*; (*from investments, shares*) rendimiento *m*; **he is looking for quick ~s** está buscando rendimiento rápido *or* ganancias rápidas; **they want to get some ~ on their investment** quieren obtener cierto rendimiento de su inversión; **~ on capital** rendimiento del capital; *see also* **diminishing, rate A4**

6 (*= reward, exchange*) **in ~** a cambio; **they had nothing to give in ~** no tenían nada que dar a cambio; **in ~ for this service** a cambio de este servicio

7 **returns** (*= figures*) estadísticas *fpl* (**for** de); (*= election results*) resultados *mpl* (del escrutinio); **early ~s show Dos Santos with 52% of the vote** los primeros resultados del escrutinio muestran que Dos Santos tiene un 52% de los votos; *see also* **tax C**

8 (*= answer*) (*in surveys*) respuesta *f*, declaración *f*

9 (*Parl*) [*of member*] (*= election*) elección *f*; (*= reelection*) reelección *f*

10 (*also* **~ ticket**) billete *m* de ida y vuelta, billete *m* redondo (*Mex*); *see also* **day 2**

11 (*Sport*) devolución *f*; **~ of serve** *or* **service** devolución *f* del servicio *or* saque, resto *m*

12 = **return key**

13 = **carriage return**; *see* **carriage**

Ⓑ VT 1 (*= give back*) [*+ item*] devolver, regresar (*LAm*), restituir (*frm*); [*+ favour, sb's visit, telephone call, blow*] devolver; [*+ kindness, love*] corresponder a; [*+ greeting, look, gaze*] devolver, responder a; **they never ~ my calls** nunca me devuelven las llamadas; **to ~ good for evil** devolver bien por mal; **to ~ the compliment** devolver el cumplido; **to ~ fire** (*Mil*) devolver el fuego, responder a los disparos; **"return to sender"** "devuélvase al remitente"

2 (*= put back*) volver a colocar; **we ~ed the books to the shelf** volvimos a colocar los libros en el estante

3 (*Sport*) [*+ ball*] devolver; (*Tennis*) devolver, restar; (*Bridge*) [*+ suit of cards*] devolver

4 (*= declare*) [*+ income, details*] declarar; **to ~ a verdict** emitir *or* pronunciar un veredicto, emitir un fallo; **they ~ed a verdict of guilty/not guilty** lo declararon culpable/inocente

5 (*Pol*) (*= elect*) elegir, votar a; (*= reelect*) reelegir; **to ~ sb to power** reelegir a algn

6 (*Fin*) [*+ profit, income*] reportar, rendir

7 (*= reply*) responder, contestar

Ⓒ VI 1 (*= go/come back*) volver, regresar; **he left home, never to ~** se marchó de casa, para no volver *or* regresar jamás; **to ~ home** volver *or* regresar a casa; **to ~ to** [*+ place*] volver *or* regresar a; [*+ activity, state*] volver a; **I ~ed to my hotel** volví *or* regresé a mi hotel; **things have ~ed to normal** las cosas han vuelto a la normalidad; **to ~ to a task** volver a una tarea; **to ~ to a theme** volver sobre un tema; **to ~ to what we were talking about, ...** volviendo al asunto del que estábamos hablando, ...

2 (*= reappear*) [*symptoms*] volver a aparecer, reaparecer; [*doubts, fears, suspicions*] volver a surgir, resurgir; **his good spirits ~ed** renació su alegría

3 (*Jur*) revertir (**to** a); **on my father's death the farm ~ed to my brother** al morir mi padre, la granja revirtió a mi hermano

Ⓓ CPD [*journey, flight*] de regreso, de vuelta ► **return address** N señas *fpl* del remitente ► **return fare** N billete *m* de ida y vuelta, billete *m* redondo (*Mex*) ► **return game** N = **return match** ► **return key** N (*Comput*) tecla *f* de retorno ► **return match** N (*Brit Sport*) partido *m* de vuelta ► **return ticket** N (*Brit*) billete *m* de ida y vuelta *or* (*Mex*) redondo

returnable [rɪˈtɜːnəbl] ADJ restituible; [*deposit*] reintegrable, reembolsable; [*bottle*] retornable; (*Jur*) devolutivo; (*= on approval*) a prueba; **~ empties** envases *mpl* a devolver; **the book is ~ on the 14th** el libro deberá estar de vuelta el 14; **the deposit is not ~** no se reembolsa el depósito

returnee [rɪtɜːˈniː] N retornado/a *m/f*

returner [rɪˈtɜːnəʳ] N (*Brit Ind*) *persona que regresa al mundo laboral tras un periodo de inactividad*

returning officer [rɪˈtɜːnɪŋˌɒfɪsəʳ] N (*Pol*) escrutador(a) *m/f*

reunification [ˈriːˌjuːnɪfɪˈkeɪʃən] N reunificación *f*

reunify [ˈriːˈjuːnɪfaɪ] VT reunificar

reunion [riːˈjuːnjən] N reencuentro *m*, reunión *f*

reunite [ˈriːjuːˈnaɪt] Ⓐ VT (*often passive*) (volver a) reunir; **eventually the family was ~d** por fin la familia volvió a verse unida; **she was ~d with her husband** volvió a verse al lado de su marido

Ⓑ VI (volver a) reunirse

re-usable [ˌriːˈjuːzəbl] ADJ reutilizable, que se puede volver a emplear

re-use [ˌriːˈjuːz] VT volver a usar, reutilizar

rev* [rev] (*Aut etc*) Ⓐ N revolución *f*

Ⓑ VT (*also* **to ~ up**) [*+ engine*] girar

Ⓒ VI (*also* **to ~ up**) girar (rápidamente); **the plane was ~ving up** se aceleraban los motores del avión

Rev. ABBR (= **Reverend**) R, Rdo, Rvdo; **the ~*** (*Catholic*) el padre, el cura; (*Protestant*) el pastor

revaluation [riːˌvæljʊˈeɪʃən] N revaluación *f*, revalorización *f*

revalue [ˈriːˈvæljuː] VT [*+ property, currency*] revaluar, revalorizar

revamp [ˌriːˈvæmp] Ⓐ VT modernizar, renovar

Ⓑ N [ˈriːvæmp] modernización *f*, renovación *f*

revanchism [rɪˈvæntʃɪzəm] N revanchismo *m*

revanchist [rɪˈvæntʃɪst] Ⓐ ADJ revanchista

Ⓑ N revanchista *mf*

Revd. ABBR (= **Reverend**) R, Rdo, Rvdo; **the ~*** (*Catholic*) el padre, el cura; (*Protestant*) el pastor

reveal [rɪˈviːl] VT 1 (*= uncover*) revelar, dejar al descubierto

2 (*= show*) [*survey, test*] poner de manifiesto; (*= make public*) [*person*] revelar; [*+ feelings*] exteriorizar; **I cannot ~ to you what he said** no puedo revelarte *or* contarte lo que dijo; **on that occasion he ~ed great astuteness** en aquella ocasión desplegó gran astucia; **he ~ed himself to be** *or* **as ...** demostró ser ...

revealing [rɪˈviːlɪŋ] ADJ (*gen*) revelador

revealingly [rɪˈviːlɪŋlɪ] ADV de modo revelador

reveille [rɪˈvælɪ] N (*Mil*) (toque *m* de) diana *f*

revel [ˈrevl] Ⓐ VI 1 (*= make merry*) ir de juerga *or* de parranda

2 (*= delight*) **to ~ in sth/doing sth** gozar de algo/haciendo algo

Ⓑ N **revels** (*liter*) jolgorio *msing*, jarana *fsing*; (*organized*) fiestas *fpl*, festividades *fpl*; **let the ~s begin!** ¡que comience la fiesta!; **the ~s lasted for three days** continuaron las fiestas durante tres días

revelation [ˌrevəˈleɪʃən] N revelación *f*; **(Book of) Revelations** el Apocalipsis; **it was a ~ to me** fue una revelación para mí

reveller, reveler (*US*) [ˈrevləʳ] N juerguista *mf*, parrandero/a *m/f*; (*= drunk*) borracho/a *m/f*

revelry [ˈrevlrɪ] N juerga *f*, parranda *f*, jarana *f*; (*organized*) fiestas *fpl*, festividades *fpl*; **the spirit of ~** el espíritu de festivo

revenge [rɪˈvendʒ] Ⓐ N venganza *f*; **in ~** para vengarse (**for** de); **to get one's ~ (for sth)** vengarse (de algo); **to take ~ on sb for sth** vengarse de algn por algo

Ⓑ VT vengar, vengarse de; **to ~ o.s. on sb** ◊ **be ~d on sb** vengarse de *or* en algn

revengeful [rɪˈvendʒfʊl] ADJ vengativo

revengefully [rɪˈvendʒfəlɪ] ADV vengativamente

revenger [rɪˈvendʒəʳ] N vengador(a) *m/f*

revenue [ˈrevənjuː] Ⓐ N (*= profit, income*) ingresos *mpl*, rentas *fpl*; (*on investments*) rédito *m*; [*of country*] rentas *fpl* públicas; *see also* **inland**

Ⓑ CPD ► **revenue account** N cuenta *f* de ingresos presupuestarios ► **revenue expenditure** N gasto *m* corriente ► **revenue stamp** N timbre *m* fiscal

reverberate [rɪˈvɜːbəreɪt] VI 1 [*sound*] resonar, retumbar; **the sound ~d in the distance** el sonido resonaba *or* retumbaba a lo lejos; **the valley ~d with the sound** el ruido resonaba *or* retumbaba por el valle

2 (*fig*) [*news, protests etc*] tener amplia resonancia, tener una fuerte repercusión

3 (*Tech*) [*light*] reverberar

reverberation [rɪˌvɜːbəˈreɪʃən] N 1 [*of sound*] retumbo *m*, eco *m*

2 **reverberations** (*fig*) [*of news, protests etc*] consecuencias *fpl*

3 [*of light*] reverberación *f*

reverberator [rɪˈvɜːbəreɪtəʳ] N reverberador *m*

revere [rɪˈvɪəʳ] VT venerar; **a ~d figure** una figura venerada

reverence [ˈrevərəns] Ⓐ N 1 (*= respect*) reverencia *f*

2 (*Rel*) **Your Reverence** Reverencia

Ⓑ VT (*frm*) (*= revere*) venerar

reverend [ˈrevərənd] Ⓐ ADJ (*in titles*) reverendo; **right** *or* **very ~** reverendísimo; **Reverend Mother** reverenda madre *f*

Ⓑ N (*) (*Catholic*) padre *m*, cura *m*; (*Protestant*) pastor *m*

reverent ['revərənt] ADJ reverente

reverential [,revə'renʃəl] ADJ reverencial

reverently ['revərəntlɪ] ADV reverentemente, con reverencia

reverie ['revərɪ] N ensueño *m*; **to be lost in ~** estar absorto, estar ensimismado

revers [rɪ'vɪəʳ] N (*pl* **revers** [rɪ'vɪəz]) solapa *f*

reversal [rɪ'vɜːsəl] N [1] (= *change*) [*of order, roles*] inversión *f*; [*of policy*] cambio *m* de rumbo; [*of decision etc*] revocación *f*
[2] (= *setback*) revés *m*, contratiempo *m*

reverse [rɪ'vɜːs] Ⓐ ADJ [1] [*order*] inverso; [*direction*] contrario, opuesto; **the ~ side** (*of coin, medal*) el reverso; (*of sheet of paper*) el dorso; **in ~ order** en orden inverso
[2] (*Aut*) [*gear*] de marcha atrás
Ⓑ N [1] (= *opposite*) **the ~** lo contrario; **no, quite the ~!** no, ¡todo lo contrario!; **but the ~ is true** pero es al contrario; **it was the ~ of what we had expected** fue todo lo contrario de lo que habíamos esperado; **his remarks were the ~ of flattering** sus observaciones eran poco halagüeñas, todo lo contrario; **it's the same process in ~** es el mismo proceso al revés
[2] (= *face*) [*of coin*] reverso *m*; [*of paper etc*] dorso *m*; [*of cloth*] revés *m*
[3] (*Aut*) (*also* **~ gear**) marcha *f* atrás; **to go** *or* **change into ~** dar marcha atrás; **to put a car into ~** dar marcha atrás a un coche; **my luck went into ~** mi suerte dio marcha atrás
[4] (= *setback*) revés *m*, contratiempo *m*; (= *defeat*) derrota *f*
Ⓒ VT [1] (= *invert order of*) invertir, invertir el orden de; (= *turn other way*) volver al revés; [+ *arms*] llevar a la funerala; **to ~ A and B** invertir el orden de A y B, anteponer B a A
[2] (= *change*) [+ *opinion*] cambiar completamente de; [+ *decision*] revocar, anular, cancelar
[3] (*Brit Telec*) **to ~ the charges** cobrar al número llamado, llamar a cobro revertido
[4] (*esp Brit*) [+ *car, train etc*] dar marcha atrás a; **he ~d the car into the garage** dio marcha atrás para entrar en el garaje; **he ~d the car into a pillarbox** al dar marcha atrás chocó con un buzón
Ⓓ VI (*esp Brit Aut*) dar marcha atrás; **I ~d into a van** al dar marcha atrás choqué con una furgoneta
Ⓔ CPD ► **reverse charge call** N (*Brit Telec*) llamada *f* a cobro revertido ► **reverse discrimination** N (*US*) discriminación *f* positiva ► **reverse turn** N (*Aut*) vuelta *f* al revés ► **reverse video** N (*Comput*) vídeo *m* inverso

reverse-engineer [rɪ,vɜːsenʒɪ'nɪəʳ] VT (*Comput*) aplicar un proceso de retroingeniería a

reversible [rɪ'vɜːsəbl] ADJ reversible

reversing [rɪ'vɜːsɪŋ] Ⓐ N marcha *f* atrás
Ⓑ CPD ► **reversing light** N (*Aut*) luz *f* de marcha atrás

reversion [rɪ'vɜːʃən] N (*also Bio, Jur*) reversión *f*; **~ to type** reversión *f* al tipo, salto *m* atrás

reversionary [rɪ'vɜːʃnərɪ] ADJ reversionario, reversible

revert [rɪ'vɜːt] VI [1] (= *return*) volver; **to ~ to a subject** volver a un tema; **~ing to the matter under discussion …** volviendo al tema de la discusión …
[2] (*Jur*) revertir (**to** a)
[3] (*Bio*) saltar atrás; **to ~ to type** (*Bio*) saltar atrás en la cadena natural; (*fig*) volver por donde solía, volver a ser el mismo/la misma de antes

revetment [rɪ'vetmənt] N revestimiento *m*

revictual ['riː'vɪtl] Ⓐ VT reabastecer
Ⓑ VI reabastecerse

review [rɪ'vjuː] Ⓐ N [1] (= *survey, taking stock*) examen *m*, análisis *m inv*; [*of research etc*] evaluación *f*; **the annual ~ of expenditure** el examen anual de los gastos; **salaries are under ~** los sueldos están sujetos a revisión; **we shall keep your case under ~** volveremos a considerar su caso
[2] (*Mil*) [*of troops*] revista *f*; **the Spithead Review** la revista naval de Spithead; **the general passed the troops in ~** el general pasó revista a las tropas; **the troops passed in ~ before the general** las tropas desfilaron en revista ante el general
[3] (*Jur*) (= *revision*) revisión *f*; **when the case comes up for ~** cuando el asunto se someta a revisión; **the sentence is subject to ~ in the high court** la sentencia puede volver a ser vista en el tribunal supremo
[4] (= *critique*) crítica *f*, reseña *f*; **the play got good ~s** la obra fue bien recibida por los críticos
[5] (= *journal*) revista *f*
[6] (*Theat*) revista *f*
Ⓑ VT [1] (= *take stock of*) examinar, analizar; [+ *research etc*] evaluar; **we will ~ the position in a month** volveremos a estudiar la situación dentro de un mes; **we shall have to ~ our policy** tendremos que reconsiderar nuestra política
[2] (*Mil*) [+ *troops*] pasar revista a
[3] (*Jur*) (= *reconsider*) [+ *case*] revisar
[4] (= *write review of*) reseñar, hacer una crítica de
[5] (*US Scol*) repasar
Ⓒ CPD ► **review copy** N ejemplar *m* para reseñar

reviewer [rɪ'vjuːəʳ] N [*of book, concert*] crítico/a *m/f*

revile [rɪ'vaɪl] VT insultar, injuriar

revise [rɪ'vaɪz] Ⓐ VT [1] (= *alter*) [+ *estimate, figures*] corregir; [+ *offer*] reconsiderar; [+ *schedule*] ajustar; **to ~ one's opinion of sb** cambiar de opinión sobre algn; **to ~ sth upward(s)** ajustar *or* revisar algo al alza
[2] (= *amend, update*) [+ *text, dictionary*] revisar; [+ *proofs*] corregir
[3] (*Brit Scol*) [+ *subject, notes*] repasar
Ⓑ VI (*Brit*) (*for exams*) repasar

revised [rɪ'vaɪzd] ADJ [*text, plan, procedure*] revisado; [*version, figure, estimate*] corregido; [*offer*] reconsiderado; [*schedule*] ajustado; **~ edition** edición *f* revisada; **Revised Standard Version** *versión revisada en 1953 de la biblia anglicana*; **Revised Version** (*Brit*) *versión revisada en 1885 de la biblia anglicana*

reviser [rɪ'vaɪzəʳ] N revisor(a) *m/f*, refundidor(a) *m/f*; (*Typ*) corrector(a) *m/f*

revision [rɪ'vɪʒən] N [1] (*for exams*) repaso *m*; **I need two weeks for ~** necesito dos semanas para repasar
[2] (= *amendment, updating*) [*of text, dictionary*] revisión *f*; [*of proofs*] corrección *f*
[3] (= *alteration*) [*of estimate, figures*] corrección *f*; [*of offer*] reconsideración *f*; [*of schedule*] ajuste *m*
[4] (= *revised version*) edición *f* revisada

revisionism [rɪ'vɪʒənɪzəm] N revisionismo *m*

revisionist [rɪ'vɪʒənɪst] Ⓐ ADJ revisionista
Ⓑ N revisionista *mf*

revisit ['riː'vɪzɪt] VT volver a visitar; **"Brideshead Revisited"** "Retorno *m* a Brideshead"

revitalize ['riː'vaɪtəlaɪz] VT revitalizar, revivificar

revival [rɪ'vaɪvəl] N [1] (= *bringing back*) [*of custom, usage*] recuperación *f*; [*of old ideas*] resurgimiento *m*
[2] (= *coming back*) [*of custom, usage*] vuelta *f*; [*of old ideas*] renacimiento *m*; **the Revival of Learning** (*Hist*) el Renacimiento
[3] (*from illness, faint*) reanimación *f*
[4] (*Theat*) [*of play*] reposición *f*

revivalism [rɪ'vaɪvə,lɪzəm] N (*Rel*) evangelismo *m*

revivalist [rɪ'vaɪvəlɪst] Ⓐ N evangelista *mf*; (= *preacher*) predicador(a) *m/f* evangelista
Ⓑ CPD ► **revivalist meeting** N reunión *f* evangelista

revive [rɪ'vaɪv] Ⓐ VT [1] [+ *person*] (*to life, spirits*) reanimar; **this will ~ you** esto te reanimará
[2] [+ *fire*] avivar; [+ *old customs*] restablecer, recuperar; [+ *hopes, suspicions*] despertar; [+ *accusation*] volver a, volver a hacer; **to ~ sb's courage** infundir nuevos ánimos a algn
[3] (*Theat*) [+ *play*] reponer
Ⓑ VI [1] [*person*] (*from faint*) reanimarse, volver en sí; (*from tiredness, shock etc*) reponerse, recuperarse; (*from apparent death*) revivir
[2] [*hope, emotions*] renacer; [*business, trade*] reactivarse; **interest in Gongora has ~d** ha renacido el interés por Góngora; **the pound has ~d** la libra se ha recuperado; **his courage ~d** recobró su fortaleza de ánimo

revivify [riː'vɪvɪfaɪ] VT revivificar

revocation [,revə'keɪʃən] N revocación *f*

revoke [rɪ'vəʊk] Ⓐ N (*Cards*) renuncio *m*
Ⓑ VT (*gen*) revocar; [+ *licence*] suspender
Ⓒ VI (*Cards*) renunciar

revolt [rɪ'vəʊlt] Ⓐ N (= *insurrection*) levantamiento *m*, revuelta *f*, sublevación *f*; (= *rejection of authority*) rebelión *f*; **a popular ~** un levantamiento *or* una revuelta popular; **southern cities are in (open) ~ against the regime** las ciudades del sur se han sublevado contra el régimen; **students are in (open) ~ against the new examination system** los estudiantes se han rebelado contra el nuevo sistema de exámenes; **to rise (up) in ~** sublevarse, rebelarse
Ⓑ VT (= *disgust*) dar asco a, repugnar; **I was ~ed by the sight** la escena me dio asco *or* me repugnó
Ⓒ VI (= *rebel*) sublevarse, rebelarse (**against** contra)

revolting [rɪ'vəʊltɪŋ] ADJ (= *disgusting*) [*smell, taste, sight, habit, person*] repugnante, asqueroso; [*behaviour, story*] repugnante; [*place, weather*] asqueroso; [*colour, dress*] horroroso, repelente; **it smells/tastes ~** tiene un olor/sabor repugnante, huele/sabe que da asco

revoltingly [rɪ'vəʊltɪŋlɪ] ADV [*dirty, fat, greasy*] repugnantemente, asquerosamente; [*ugly*] horrorosamente; [*sentimental*] empalagosamente; **they're ~ rich** son tan ricos que da asco, son asquerosamente ricos

revolution [,revə'luːʃən] N [1] (*Pol, fig*) revolución *f*
[2] (= *turn*) revolución *f*, vuelta *f*; (*Tech*) rotación *f*, giro *m*; **~s per minute** revoluciones por minuto
[3] (*Astron*) (= *orbit*) revolución *f*; (*on axis*) rotación *f*

revolutionary [,revə'luːʃənərɪ] Ⓐ ADJ (*gen*) revolucionario
Ⓑ N (*Pol*) revolucionario/a *m/f*

revolutionize [,revə'luːʃənaɪz] VT revolucionar

revolve [rɪ'vɒlv] Ⓐ VT girar, hacer girar; (*fig*) (*in the mind*) dar vueltas a, meditar
Ⓑ VI girar, dar vueltas; (*Astron*) revolverse; **to ~ around** (*lit*) girar alrededor de; (*fig*) girar en

torno a; **everything ~s round him** todo gira en torno a él; **the discussion ~d around three topics** el debate se centró en tres temas

revolver [rɪ'vɒlvəʳ] N revólver *m*

revolving [rɪ'vɒlvɪŋ] Ⓐ ADJ [*bookcase, stand etc*] giratorio
Ⓑ CPD ► **revolving credit** N crédito *m* rotativo ► **revolving door** N puerta *f* giratoria; **the ~ door of the justice system** (*fig*) el círculo vicioso del sistema judicial; **the ~ door of senior executives** (*fig*) los constantes vaivenes laborales de los altos ejecutivos, el baile de nombres constante entre los altos ejecutivos ► **revolving presidency** N presidencia *f* rotativa ► **revolving stage** N (*Theat*) escena *f* giratoria

revue [rɪ'vjuː] N (*Theat*) (teatro *m* de) revista *f* *or* variedades *fpl*

revulsion [rɪ'vʌlʃən] N 1 (= *disgust*) repugnancia *f*, asco *m*; (*Med*) revulsión *f*
2 (= *sudden change*) reacción *f*, cambio *m* repentino

reward [rɪ'wɔːd] Ⓐ N recompensa *f*, premio *m*; (*for finding sth*) gratificación *f*; **as a ~ for** en recompensa de, como premio a; **"£50 reward"** "50 libras de recompensa"; **a ~ will be paid for information about ...** se recompensará al que dé alguna información acerca de ...
Ⓑ VT recompensar; (*fig*) premiar; **to ~ sb for his services** recompensar a algn por sus servicios; **she ~ed me with a smile** me premió con una sonrisa; **it might ~ your attention** podría valer la pena ir a verlo; **the case would ~ your investigation** le valdría la pena investigar el asunto

rewarding [rɪ'wɔːdɪŋ] ADJ gratificante

rewind ['riː'waɪnd] VT [+ *cassette, videotape*] rebobinar; [+ *watch*] dar cuerda a; [+ *wool etc*] devanar

rewinding ['riː'waɪndɪŋ] N [*of cassette, videotape*] rebobinado *m*

rewire ['riː'waɪəʳ] VT [+ *house*] rehacer la instalación eléctrica de

reword ['riː'wɜːd] VT expresar en otras palabras

rework [riː'wɜːk] VT [+ *novel, piece of writing*] refundir; [+ *idea*] repensar, reelaborar; [+ *song, schedule*] rehacer

rewritable [ˌriː'raɪtəbl] ADJ [*CD, disk*] reescribible

rewrite [ˌriː'raɪt] (*pt* **rewrote** [ˌriː'rəʊt]; *pp* **rewritten** [ˌriː'rɪtn]) Ⓐ VT reescribir; [+ *text*] rehacer, refundir
Ⓑ ['riːraɪt] N nueva versión *f*, refundición *f*

Reykjavik ['reɪkjəviːk] N Reykjavik *m*

RFD N ABBR (*US Post*) = **rural free delivery**

RFU N ABBR (*Brit*) = **Rugby Football Union**; → RUGBY

RGN N ABBR = **Registered General Nurse**

Rgt ABBR (= **Regiment**) regto.

Rh Ⓐ N ABBR (= **Rhesus**) Rh
Ⓑ CPD ► **Rh factor** N factor *m* Rh

r.h. ABBR (= **right hand**) der., der[a]

rhapsodic [ræp'sɒdɪk] ADJ (*Mus*) rapsódico; (*fig*) extático, locamente entusiasmado

rhapsodize ['ræpsədaɪz] VI **to ~ over sth** extasiarse ante algo, entusiasmarse por algo

rhapsody ['ræpsədɪ] N 1 (*Mus*) rapsodia *f*
2 (*fig*) transporte *m* de admiración; **to be in rhapsodies** estar extasiado; **to go into rhapsodies over** extasiarse por

rhea ['riːə] N ñandú *m*

Rhenish ['renɪʃ] Ⓐ ADJ renano
Ⓑ N vino *m* del Rin

rhenium ['riːnɪəm] N renio *m*

rheostat ['riːəʊstæt] N reóstato *m*

rhesus ['riːsəs] Ⓐ N 1 (= *monkey*) macaco *m* de la India
2 (*Med*) **~ negative** Rh negativo, Rhesus negativo; **~ positive** Rh positivo, Rhesus positivo
Ⓑ CPD ► **rhesus baby** N bebé *m* con factor Rhesus ► **rhesus factor** N (*Med*) factor *m* Rhesus ► **rhesus monkey** N macaco *m* de la India

rhetic ['riːtɪk] ADJ rético

rhetoric ['retərɪk] N retórica *f*

rhetorical [rɪ'tɒrɪkəl] ADJ retórico; **~ question** pregunta *f* retórica

rhetorically [rɪ'tɒrɪkəlɪ] ADV retóricamente; **I speak ~** hablo en metáfora

rhetorician [ˌretə'rɪʃən] N retórico/a *m/f*

rheumatic [ruː'mætɪk] Ⓐ ADJ reumático
Ⓑ N (= *person*) reumático/a *m/f*
Ⓒ CPD ► **rheumatic fever** N fiebre *f* reumática

rheumaticky* [ruː'mætɪkɪ] ADJ reumático

rheumatics* [ruː'mætɪks] NSING reúma *m*, reumatismo *m*

rheumatism ['ruːmətɪzəm] N reumatismo *m*

rheumatoid ['ruːmətɔɪd] Ⓐ ADJ reumatoideo
Ⓑ CPD ► **rheumatoid arthritis** N reúma *m* articular

rheumatologist [ˌruːmə'tɒlədʒɪst] N reumatólogo/a *m/f*

rheumatology [ˌruːmə'tɒlədʒɪ] N reumatología *f*

rheumy ['ruːmɪ] ADJ [*eyes*] legañoso, pitañoso

Rhine [raɪn] Ⓐ N **the ~** el Rin
Ⓑ CPD ► **Rhine wine** N vino *m* blanco del Rin

Rhineland ['raɪnlənd] N Renania *f*

rhinestone ['raɪnˌstəʊn] N diamante *m* de imitación

rhino ['raɪnəʊ] N ABBR (*pl* **rhino** *or* **rhinoes**) = **rhinoceros**

rhinoceros [raɪ'nɒsərəs] N (*pl* **rhinoceros** *or* **rhinoceroses**) rinoceronte *m*

rhinoplasty ['raɪnəʊplæstɪ] N rinoplastia *f*

rhizome ['raɪzəʊm] N rizoma *m*

Rhodes [rəʊdz] N Rodas *f*

Rhodesia [rəʊ'diːʒə] N (*Hist*) Rodesia *f*

Rhodesian [rəʊ'diːʒən] (*Hist*) Ⓐ ADJ rodesiano
Ⓑ N rodesiano/a *m/f*

rhodium ['rəʊdɪəm] N rodio *m*

rhododendron [ˌrəʊdə'dendrən] N rododendro *m*

rhomb [rɒm] N = **rhombus**

rhomboid ['rɒmbɔɪd] Ⓐ ADJ romboidal
Ⓑ N romboide *m*

rhombus ['rɒmbəs] N (*pl* **rhombuses** *or* **rhombi**) rombo *m*

Rhone [rəʊn] N **the ~** el Ródano

rhubarb ['ruːbɑːb] Ⓐ N 1 (*Bot, Culin*) ruibarbo *m*
2 (*Theat*) *palabra que se repite para representar la conversación callada en escenas de comparsas*
Ⓑ CPD [*jam, pie, tart*] de ruibarbo

rhyme [raɪm] Ⓐ N 1 (= *identical sound*) rima *f*; ✦**IDIOM without ~ or reason** sin ton ni son
2 (= *poem*) poesía *f*, versos *mpl*; **in ~** en verso
Ⓑ VI rimar; **to ~ with sth** rimar con algo
Ⓒ VT rimar
Ⓓ CPD ► **rhyme scheme** N esquema *m* de la rima, combinación *f* de rimas

rhymed [raɪmd] ADJ rimado

rhymer ['raɪməʳ] N, **rhymester** ['raɪmstəʳ] N rimador(a) *m/f*

rhyming ['raɪmɪŋ] Ⓐ ADJ [*couplet, verse*] rimado
Ⓑ CPD ► **rhyming slang** N argot *m* basado en rimas (*p.ej, "apples and pears" = "stairs"*)

> **RHYMING SLANG**
>
> *El* **rhyming slang** *(***jerga rimada***) es un tipo muy peculiar de jerga que usan los habitantes de un barrio en el este de Londres, los (***cockneys***), en la que una palabra o frase determinada se sustituye por otra que rima con ella; por ejemplo, dicen* **apples and pears** *en vez de* **stairs**. *Puede resultar muy confuso para las personas que no lo conocen bien, sobre todo porque, además, muchas veces se establece un doble juego de palabras en el que la palabra que rima no se dice; por ejemplo,* **butcher's hook** *quiere decir* **look**, *pero a menudo sólo se dice* **butcher's**, *como en la frase* **let's have a butcher's**. *El uso de algunas de estas expresiones se ha extendido al inglés coloquial habitual, como* **use your loaf**, *donde* **loaf**, *que viene de* **loaf of bread**, *quiere decir* **head**.
>
> ⇨ *Ver tb* COCKNEY

rhythm ['rɪðəm] Ⓐ N ritmo *m*; **~ and blues** (*Mus*) rhythm and blues *m*
Ⓑ CPD ► **rhythm guitar** N guitarra *f* rítmica ► **rhythm method** N [*of contraception*] método *m* de Ogino-Knaus ► **rhythm section** N (*Mus*) sección *f* rítmica

rhythmic ['rɪðmɪk], **rhythmical** ['rɪðmɪkəl] ADJ rítmico, acompasado

rhythmically ['rɪðmɪkəlɪ] ADV rítmicamente, de forma rítmica

RI Ⓐ N ABBR (*Scol*) (= **religious instruction**) ed. religiosa Ⓑ ABBR = **Rhode Island**

rib [rɪb] Ⓐ N 1 (*Anat, Culin*) costilla *f*
2 [*of umbrella*] varilla *f*; [*of leaf*] nervio *m*; (*Knitting*) cordoncillo *m*; (*Archit*) nervadura *f*; (*Naut*) costilla *f*, cuaderna *f*
Ⓑ VT (*) (= *tease*) tomar el pelo a, mofarse de
Ⓒ CPD ► **rib cage** N tórax *m*

RIBA N ABBR = **Royal Institute of British Architects**

ribald ['rɪbəld] ADJ [*jokes, laughter*] verde, colorado (*LAm*); [*person*] irreverente, procaz

ribaldry ['rɪbəldrɪ] N 1 [*of jokes*] chocarrería *f*; [*of person*] procacidad *f*
2 (= *jokes etc*) cosas *fpl* verdes, cosas *fpl* obscenas

ribbed [rɪbd] ADJ **~ sweater** jersey *m* de cordoncillo

ribbing ['rɪbɪŋ] N (*in fabric*) cordoncillos *mpl*; (*Archit*) nervaduras *fpl*

ribbon ['rɪbən] Ⓐ N (*gen*) cinta *f*; (*for hair*) moña *f*, cinta *f*; (*Mil*) galón *m*; **to tear sth to ~s** (*lit*) hacer algo trizas; (*fig*) hacer algo pedazos
Ⓑ CPD ► **ribbon development** N urbanización *f* a lo largo de una carretera

riboflavin [ˌraɪbəʊ'fleɪvɪn] N riboflavina *f*

ribonucleic [ˌraɪbəʊnjuː'kleɪɪk] ADJ **~ acid** ácido *m* ribonucleico

rib-tickler* ['rɪb'tɪkləʳ] N (*Brit*) chiste *m* desternillante*

rice [raɪs] Ⓐ N arroz *m* Ⓑ CPD ► **rice paddy** N (*US*) arrozal *m* ► **rice paper** N papel *m* de arroz ► **rice pudding** N arroz *m* con leche ► **rice wine** N vino *m* de arroz

ricefield ['raɪsfiːld] N arrozal *m*

rice-growing ['raɪsˌgrəʊɪŋ] ADJ arrocero

rich [rɪtʃ] Ⓐ ADJ (*compar* **richer**; *superl* **richest**) 1 (= *wealthy*) [*person, country*] rico; **to be-**

come *or* **get** *or* **grow ~(er)** hacerse (más) rico, enriquecerse (más); **to get ~ quick** hacer fortuna *or* enriquecerse rápidamente; ✦*IDIOMS* **to be as ~ as Croesus** nadar en la abundancia; **for ~er, for poorer** en la riqueza y en la pobreza; *see also* **get-rich-quick, strike B6**

2 (= *abundant*) [*variety, source*] grande; [*deposit, harvest*] abundante; [*reward*] generoso; **seaweed is a ~ source of iodine** las algas son una gran fuente de yodo; **to be ~ in** [+ *flora, fauna*] tener abundancia de, tener gran riqueza de; [+ *natural resources, nutrients, protein*] ser rico en; **the island is ~ in history** la isla tiene mucha historia; **to be ~ in detail** ser rico *or* (*frm*) profuso en detalles; **the story is ~ in comic and dramatic detail** la historia es rica en *or* abunda en detalles cómicos y dramáticos; **a style ~ in metaphors** un estilo en el que abundan las metáforas; *see also* **pickings**

3 (= *full*) [*life, experience, history*] rico

4 (= *fertile*) [*soil*] rico, fértil

5 (= *heavy, concentrated*) [*food, sauce*] sustancioso (*que contiene mucha grasa, azúcar, etc*); (*pej*) pesado, fuerte; [*coffee*] con mucho sabor; [*wine*] generoso; **it's too ~ for me** es muy pesado (*or* dulce *or* grasiento *etc*) para mí; **this chocolate gateau is very ~** esta tarta de chocolate llena mucho, esta tarta de chocolate es muy empalagosa *or* pesada (*pej*)

6 (= *intense*) [*colour*] vivo, cálido; [*sound, smell*] intenso

7 (= *mellow*) [*voice*] sonoro

8 (= *luxurious*) [*tapestries*] lujoso; [*velvet*] exquisito

9 (*) (= *laughable*) **that's ~!** ¡mira por dónde!*; **that's ~, coming from her!** ¡ella no es quién para hablar!, ¡tiene gracia que sea ella la que diga eso!

Ⓑ NPL **the ~** los ricos; **the ~ and famous** los ricos y famosos

Ⓒ CPD ► **rich tea biscuit** N galleta *f* (*que se toma con una taza de té*)

Richard [ˈrɪtʃəd] N Ricardo; **~ (the) Lionheart** Ricardo Corazón de León

riches [ˈrɪtʃɪz] NPL riqueza *fsing*

richly [ˈrɪtʃlɪ] ADV 1 (= *generously*) [*rewarded*] generosamente; [*illustrated*] profusamente; **we were ~ rewarded** fuimos generosamente recompensados; **a boy ~ endowed with talent** un chico dotado de un enorme talento; **a ~ endowed library** una biblioteca con abundantes fondos

2 (= *ornately*) [*decorated, furnished*] suntuosamente, lujosamente; **a ~ adorned chair** una silla con exquisitos adornos; **~ patterned fabrics** telas con ricos estampados

3 (= *strongly*) **~ coloured fabrics** telas de colores vivos; **a ~ flavoured sauce** una salsa de sabor fuerte; **the flowers are ~ scented** las flores tienen un perfume intenso

4 (= *intensely*) **the work is ~ rewarding** el trabajo es sumamente *or* enormemente gratificante; **she ~ deserves it** se lo tiene bien merecido; **the success they so ~ deserve** el éxito que tanto merecen

richness [ˈrɪtʃnɪs] N 1 (= *wealth*) [*of person, culture*] riqueza *f*

2 (= *abundance*) [*of variety*] lo enorme; [*of deposits, harvest*] abundancia *f*; **~ in vitamins** riqueza *f* en vitaminas

3 (= *fullness*) [*of life, experience*] riqueza *f*

4 (= *fertility*) [*of soil*] fertilidad *f*

5 (= *heaviness*) [*of food*] lo sustancioso; (*pej*) pesadez *f*

6 (= *intensity*) [*of colour*] viveza *f*; [*of sound, smell*] intensidad *f*

7 (= *mellowness*) [*of voice*] sonoridad *f*

Richter scale [ˈrɪxtəˌskeɪl] N (*Geol*) escala *f* Richter

rick¹ [rɪk] (*Agr*) Ⓐ N almiar *m*

Ⓑ VT almiarar, amontonar

rick² [rɪk] VT = **wrick**

rickets [ˈrɪkɪts] NSING raquitismo *m*

rickety [ˈrɪkɪtɪ] ADJ 1 (= *wobbly*) tambaleante, inseguro; [*old car*] desvencijado

2 (*Med*) raquítico

rickshaw [ˈrɪkʃɔː] N *carrito de estilo oriental tirado por un hombre*

ricochet [ˈrɪkəʃeɪ] Ⓐ N [*of stone, bullet*] rebote *m*

Ⓑ VI rebotar (**off** de)

rictus [ˈrɪktəs] N (*pl* **rictus** *or* **rictuses**) rictus *m*

rid [rɪd] (*pt, pp* **rid, ridded**) VT **to be ~ of sth/sb: she was glad to be ~ of him** estaba contenta de haberse librado de él, estaba contenta de habérselo quitado de encima*; **will I never be ~ of these debts?** ¿me libraré alguna vez de estas deudas?, ¿me quitaré algún día estas deudas de encima?*; **to be well ~ of sb** haber hecho bien en librarse de algn; **to get ~ of** [+ *unwanted item*] deshacerse de; [+ *habit*] quitarse; [+ *rats, smell, waste, corruption*] eliminar; (= *sell*) vender, deshacerse de; **he denied helping him get ~ of evidence** negó haberle ayudado a deshacerse de las pruebas; **I've been trying to get ~ of this headache all day** he estado intentando quitarme esta jaqueca todo el día; **you need to get ~ of that excess weight** tienes que eliminar todos esos kilos de más; **to get ~ of sb** librarse de algn; [+ *tedious person*] quitarse a algn de encima*; (*euph*) (= *kill*) deshacerse de algn, eliminar a algn; **you won't get ~ of me that easily** no te librarás *or* desharás de mí tan fácilmente; **to ~ o.s. of sth/sb: I couldn't ~ myself of the feeling that I was being watched** no me podía librar de la sensación de que alguien me estaba vigilando; **I can't seem to ~ myself of the habit** no me puedo quitar la costumbre; **to ~ sth/sb of sth: I couldn't ~ my mind of these thoughts** no podía quitarme estos pensamientos de la cabeza; **we want to ~ the world of this disease** queremos erradicar esta enfermedad en el mundo, queremos librar a la humanidad de esta enfermedad

riddance [ˈrɪdəns] N **good ~ (to bad rubbish)!*** (*pej*) ¡vete con viento fresco!; **and good ~ to him!** ¡que se pudra!

ridden [ˈrɪdn] PP *of* **ride**; **a horse ~ by ...** un caballo montado por ...

riddle¹ [ˈrɪdl] N (= *word puzzle*) acertijo *m*, adivinanza *f*; (= *mystery*) enigma *m*, misterio *m*; (= *person etc*) enigma *m*; **to ask sb a ~** proponer un acertijo a algn; **to speak in ~s** hablar en clave

riddle² [ˈrɪdl] Ⓐ N (= *sieve*) criba *f*, criba *f* gruesa; (= *potato sorter etc*) escogedor *m*

Ⓑ VT 1 (= *sieve*) cribar; [+ *potatoes etc*] pasar por el escogedor

2 **to ~ with** [+ *bullets etc*] acribillar a; **the house is ~d with damp** la casa tiene humedad por todas partes; **the organization is ~d with communists** el organismo está plagado de comunistas; **the army is ~d with subversion** el ejército está infectado de elementos subversivos

ride [raɪd] (*vb: pt* **rode**; *pp* **ridden**) Ⓐ N 1 (= *journey*) paseo *m*; (= *car ride*) vuelta *f* en coche; (= *bike ride*) paseo en bicicleta; (= *horse ride*) paseo a caballo; (*esp US*) (= *free ride*) viaje *m* gratuito; **the ~ of the Valkyries** la cabalgata de las valquirias; **it's my first ~ in a Rolls** es la primera vez que viajo en un Rolls; **he gave me a ~ into town** (*in car*) me llevó en coche a la ciudad, me dio aventón hasta la ciudad (*Mex*); **to get a ~: I got a ~ all the way to Bordeaux** un automovilista me llevó todo hasta Burdeos; **to go for a ~** (*in car, on bike, on horse*) dar una vuelta, pasear; **it was a rough ~** fue un viaje bastante incómodo; **to give sb a rough ~** (*fig*) hacer pasar un mal rato a algn; **to take a ~ in a helicopter** dar un paseo en helicóptero; **to take sb for a ~** (*in car*) dar una vuelta en coche a algn; (*) (= *make fool of*) tomarle el pelo a algn; (*) (= *swindle*) dar gato por liebre a algn; (*US*‡) (= *kill*) mandar a algn al otro barrio‡; ✦*IDIOMS* **to be taken for a ~*** hacer el primo*; **to come/go along for the ~** apuntarse por gusto

2 (= *distance travelled*) viaje *m*, recorrido *m*; **it's only a short ~** es poco camino; **it's a ten-minute ~ on the bus** son diez minutos en autobús *or* (*Mex*) en camión; **it's a 70p ~ from the station** el viaje desde la estación cuesta 70 peniques

3 (*at fairground*) (= *attraction*) atracción *f*; (= *trip*) viaje *m*; **"50p a ride"** "50 peniques por persona"

4 (= *path*) vereda *f*

Ⓑ VT 1 [+ *horse*] montar; [+ *bicycle*] montar en, ir en, andar en; **to ~ an elephant** ir montado en un elefante; **he rode his horse into town** fue a caballo hasta la ciudad; **he rode his horse into the shop** entró a caballo en la tienda; **to ~ a horse hard** castigar mucho a un caballo; **can you ~ a bike?** ¿sabes montar en bicicleta?; **it has never been ridden** hasta ahora nadie ha montado en él; **he rode it in two races** lo corrió en dos carreras

2 [+ *distance*] **we rode ten km yesterday** recorrimos diez kilómetros ayer

3 **to ~ a good race** hacer bien una carrera, dar buena cuenta de sí (en una carrera)

4 (*esp US**) **to ~ sb** tenerla tomada con algn, no dejar en paz a algn; **to ~ sb hard** exigir mucho a algn, darle duro a algn*; **don't ~ him too hard** no seas demasiado severo con él; **to ~ an idea to death** explotar una idea con demasiado entusiasmo, acabar con una idea a fuerza de repetirla demasiado

5 (*Naut*) [+ *waves*] hender, surcar

Ⓒ VI 1 (*on horse*) montar; **to ~ on an elephant** ir montado en un elefante; **can you ~?** ¿sabes montar a caballo?; **she ~s every day** monta todos los días; **to ~ astride** montar a horcajadas; **to ~ like mad** correr como el demonio; **he ~s for a different stable** monta para otra cuadra

2 (*in car*) ir, viajar; **to ~ on a bus/in a car/in a train** viajar en autobús/en coche/en tren; **some rode but I had to walk** algunos fueron en coche pero yo tuve que ir a pie

3 (*with prep, adv*) **he rode straight at me** arremetió contra mí; **to ~ home on sb's shoulders** ser llevado a casa en los hombros de algn; **to ~ over/through** andar a caballo *etc* por/a través de; **we'll ~ over to see you** vendremos a verte; **to ~ to Jaén** ir (a caballo) a Jaén; **he rode up to me** se me acercó a caballo

4 **to ~ at anchor** (*Naut*) estar fondeado

5 (*fig*) **the moon was riding high in the sky** la luna estaba en lo alto del cielo; ✦*IDIOMS* **to be riding high** [*person*] estar alegre, estar en la cumbre de la felicidad; **he's riding high at the moment** por ahora lo va muy bien; **to let things ~** dejar que las cosas sigan su curso

►**ride about, ride around** VI + ADV pasearse a caballo/en coche/en bicicleta *etc*

►**ride away** VI + ADV alejarse, irse, partir

►**ride back** VI + ADV volver (a caballo, en bicicleta *etc*)

►**ride behind** VI + ADV ir después, caminar a la zaga; (= *in rear seat*) ir en el asiento de atrás; (= *on same horse*) cabalgar a la grupa

►**ride by** VI + ADV pasar (*a caballo, en bicicleta etc*)

►**ride down** VT + ADV 1 (= *trample*) atropellar
2 (= *catch up with*) coger, alcanzar

►**ride off** VI + ADV alejarse, irse, partir; **they rode off in pursuit** se marcharon a caballo en persecución

►**ride on** VI + ADV seguir adelante

►**ride out** VT + ADV (*Naut*) [+ *storm*] capear, aguantar; (*fig*) [+ *crisis*] sobrevivir, sobreponerse a

►**ride up** VI + ADV 1 [*horseman, motorcyclist etc*] llegar, acercarse
2 [*skirt, dress*] subirse

rider [ˈraɪdəʳ] N 1 (= *horserider*) jinete *mf*; **I'm not much of a ~** apenas sé montar; **he's a fine ~** es un jinete destacado
2 (= *cyclist*) ciclista *mf*; (= *motorcyclist*) motociclista *mf*, motorista *mf*; (*US Aut*) pasajero/a *m/f*, viajero/a *m/f*
3 (= *additional clause*) aditamento *m*; **with the ~ that ...** a condición de que ...; **I must add the ~ that ...** debo añadir que ...

ridge [rɪdʒ] Ⓐ N [*of hills, mountains*] cadena *f*; [*of nose*] puente *m*, caballete *m*; [*of roof*] caballete *m*; (*Agr*) caballón *m*; (= *crest of hill*) cumbre *f*, cresta *f*; (*Met*) **~ of high/low pressure** línea *f* de presión alta/baja
Ⓑ CPD ► **ridge pole** N (*on tent*) caballete *m*, cumbrera *f* ► **ridge tent** N tienda *f* canadiense ► **ridge tile** N teja *f* de caballete

ridgeway [ˈrɪdʒweɪ] N ruta *f* de las crestas

ridicule [ˈrɪdɪkjuːl] Ⓐ N irrisión *f*, burla *f*; **to expose sb to public ~** exponer a algn a la mofa pública; **to hold sth/sb up to ~** poner algo/a algn en ridículo; **to lay o.s. open to ~** exponerse al ridículo
Ⓑ VT dejar *or* poner en ridículo, ridiculizar

▼**ridiculous** [rɪˈdɪkjʊləs] ADJ [*idea etc*] ridículo, absurdo; **to look ~** [*person*] estar ridículo; [*thing*] ser ridículo; **to make o.s. (look) ~** ponerse en ridículo; **don't be ~!** ¡no seas ridículo!, no digas tonterías *or* chorradas*; **~!** ◊ **how ~!** ¡qué ridículo!, ¡qué estupidez!

ridiculously [rɪˈdɪkjʊləslɪ] ADV 1 (= *stupidly*) de forma ridícula
2 (*fig*) (= *disproportionately etc*) absurdamente, ridículamente; **it is ~ easy** es absurdamente *or* ridículamente fácil

ridiculousness [rɪˈdɪkjʊləsnɪs] N ridiculez *f*

riding [ˈraɪdɪŋ] Ⓐ N equitación *f*; **I like ~** me gusta montar a caballo
Ⓑ CPD ► **riding boots** NPL botas *fpl* de montar ► **riding breeches** NPL pantalones *mpl* de montar ► **riding crop** N fusta *f* ► **riding habit** N amazona *f*, traje *m* de montar ► **riding jacket** N chaqueta *f* de montar ► **riding master** N profesor *m* de equitación ► **riding school** N escuela *f* de equitación ► **riding stables** NPL cuadras *fpl* ► **riding whip** N = **riding crop**

rife [raɪf] ADJ **to be ~** [*problem*] ser muy común; [*rumours, speculation, fears*] abundar, proliferar; [*disease*] hacer estragos; [*unemployment, crime*] abundar, hacer estragos; [*racism, corruption*] estar muy extendido; **smallpox was still ~** la viruela aún hacía estragos; **(to be) ~ with sth**: **countries ~ with Aids** países plagados de sida, países donde el sida hace estragos; **it is ~ with mistakes** está plagado de errores; **the whole industry is ~ with corruption** la corrupción reina *or* está muy extendida en todo el sector; **the whole town is ~ with rumours** en la ciudad proliferan los rumores; **a region ~ with unemployment** una región donde abunda el paro *or* donde el paro hace estragos; **the media is ~ with speculation about ...** los medios de comunicación no dejan de especular acerca de ..., en los medios de comunicación abundan *or* proliferan las especulaciones acerca de ...

riffle [ˈrɪfəl] VT (*also* **~ through**) hojear; **to ~ (through) a book** hojear (rápidamente) un libro

riff-raff [ˈrɪfræf] N gentuza *f*, chusma *f*; **and all the ~ of the neighbourhood** y todos los sinvergüenzas del barrio

rifle[1] [ˈraɪfl] VT (= *search*) desvalijar; **to ~ a case** desvalijar una maleta; **the house had been ~d** habían saqueado la casa; **they ~d the house in search of money** saquearon la casa en busca de dinero; **to ~ sb's pockets** vaciar los bolsillos a algn

►**rifle through** VI + PREP rebuscar en, revolver

rifle[2] [ˈraɪfl] Ⓐ N 1 (= *gun*) rifle *m*, fusil *m*
2 **the Rifles** (= *regiment*) los fusileros, el regimiento de fusileros
Ⓑ VT (*Tech*) estriar, rayar
Ⓒ CPD ► **rifle butt** N culata *f* de rifle ► **rifle fire** N fuego *m* de fusilería ► **rifle range** N (*Mil*) campo *m* de tiro; (*at fair*) barraca *f* de tiro al blanco ► **rifle shot** N tiro *m* de fusil; **within ~ shot** a tiro de fusil

rifled [ˈraɪfld] ADJ (*Tech*) estriado, rayado

rifleman [ˈraɪflmən] N (*pl* **riflemen**) fusilero *m*

rifling [ˈraɪflɪŋ] N (*Tech*) estría *f*, estriado *m*, rayado *m*

rift [rɪft] N 1 (= *fissure*) grieta *f*, fisura *f*; (*in clouds*) claro *m*
2 (*fig*) ruptura *f*, desavenencia *f*; (*in relations etc*) grieta *f*; (*in political party*) escisión *f*, cisma *m*

rig [rɪg] Ⓐ N 1 (*Naut*) aparejo *m*
2 (*also* **oil ~**) (*on land*) torre *f* de perforación; (*at sea*) plataforma *f* petrolífera
3 (†*) (= *outfit*) (*also* **~ out**) vestimenta *f*, atuendo *m*
Ⓑ VT 1 (*Naut*) [+ *ship*] aparejar, equipar
2 (= *fix dishonestly*) [+ *election, competition*] amañar; [+ *prices*] manipular; **the government had got it all ~ged** el gobierno lo había arreglado todo de modo fraudulento; **to ~ the market** (*Comm*) manipular la lonja *or* la bolsa; **it was ~ged*** hubo tongo*

►**rig out** VT + ADV 1 (*Naut*) proveer (**with** de), equipar (**with** con)
2 (*) (= *dress*) ataviar, vestir; **to ~ sb out in sth** ataviar *or* vestir a algn de algo; **to be ~ged out in a new dress** lucir un vestido nuevo

►**rig up** VT + ADV (= *build*) improvisar; (*fig*) (= *arrange*) organizar, trabar; **we'll see what we can ~ up** veremos si podemos arreglar algo

rigger [ˈrɪgəʳ] N (*Naut*) aparejador *m*; (*Aer*) mecánico *m*

rigging [ˈrɪgɪŋ] N (*Naut*) jarcia *f*, aparejo *m*

▼**right** [raɪt] Ⓐ ADJ 1 (= *morally good, just*) justo; **it is not ~ that he should pay for their mistake** no es justo que él pague por su error; **it is/seems only ~ that she should get the biggest share** es/me parece justo que ella reciba la mayor parte, está/me parece bien que ella reciba la mayor parte; **it doesn't seem ~ that his contribution should not be acknowledged** parece injusto que no se reconozca su aportación; **it's not ~!** ¡no hay derecho!; **I thought it ~ to ask permission first** me pareció conveniente preguntarle antes, pensé que debía preguntarle antes; **would it be ~ for me to ask him?** ¿debería preguntárselo?; **it is only ~ and proper that people should know what is going on** lo suyo es que la gente sepa lo que pasa; **to do the ~ thing** ◊ **do what is ~** hacer lo correcto, actuar correctamente; **to do the ~ thing by sb** portarse como es debido con algn; **doing the ~ thing by a pregnant girlfriend meant marrying her** hacer lo que Dios manda con una novia embarazada significaba casarse con ella
2 (= *suitable*) [*tool, clothes*] apropiado, adecuado; [*time*] oportuno; **to choose the ~ moment for sth/to do sth** elegir el momento oportuno para algo/para hacer algo; **that's the ~ attitude!** ¡haces bien!; **I haven't got the ~ clothes for a formal dinner** no tengo ropa apropiada *or* adecuada para una cena de etiqueta; **you're not using the ~ tool for the job** no estás empleando la herramienta apropiada *or* adecuada para el trabajo; **he's the ~ man for the job** es el hombre más indicado para el cargo; **I don't think he's the ~ sort of person for you** me parece que no es la persona que te conviene; **they holiday in all the ~ places** toman sus vacaciones en todos los sitios que están de moda; **the balance of humour and tragedy is just ~** el equilibrio entre humor y tragedia es perfecto; **she's just ~ for the job** es la persona perfecta para el puesto; **the flat is just ~ for me** el piso es justo lo que necesito; **"is there too much salt in it?" — "no, it's just ~"** — ¿tiene demasiada sal? —no, está en su punto justo; **Mr Right** el novio soñado, el marido ideal; **to know the ~ people** tener enchufes *or* (*LAm*) palanca; **he knows all the ~ people** tiene enchufes *or* (*LAm*) palanca en todas partes; **I just happened to be in the ~ place at the ~ time** dio la casualidad de que estaba en el sitio adecuado en el momento adecuado; **if the price is ~** si el precio es razonable; **he's on the ~ side of 40** tiene menos de 40 años; **to say the ~ thing** decir lo que hay que decir, tener las palabras justas; **we'll do it when the time is ~** lo haremos en el momento oportuno *or* a su debido tiempo; **the ~ word** la palabra exacta *or* apropiada
3 (= *correct*) correcto, exacto; **~ first time!** ¡exactamente!, ¡exacto!; **"she's your sister?" — "that's ~!"** —¿es tu hermana? —¡eso es! *or* ¡así es! *or* ¡exacto!; **that's ~! it has to go through that hole** ¡eso es! tiene que pasar por ese agujero; **she said she'd done it, isn't that ~, mother?** dijo que lo había hecho ¿no es así, madre? *or* ¿a que sí, madre?; **you mean he offered to pay? is that ~, Harry?** ¿dices que se ofreció a pagar? ¿es eso cierto, Harry?; **and quite ~ too!** ¡y con razón!; **am I ~ for the station?** ¿por aquí se va a la estación?, ¿voy bien (por aquí) para la estación?; **the ~ answer** la respuesta correcta; (*Math*) (*to problem*) la solución correcta; **~ you are!*** ¡vale!, ¡muy bien!; **I was beginning to wonder whether I had the ~ day** empezaba a preguntarme si me habría equivocado de día; **to get sth ~** (= *guess correctly*) acertar en algo; (= *do properly*) hacer algo bien; **I got the date ~ but not the time** acerté en la fecha pero me equivoqué de hora; **it's vital that we get the timing ~** es esencial que escojamos bien el momento; **you didn't get it ~, so you lose five points** no acertaste *or* te equivocaste, así que pierdes cinco puntos;

➤ LANGUAGE IN USE: ridiculous 12.2, 14 right A3 26.3

let's get it ~ this time! ¡a ver si esta vez nos sale bien!; **we must get it ~ this time** esta vez tenemos que hacerlo bien *or* nos tiene que salir bien; **is this the ~ house?** ¿es ésta la casa?; **he can't even sing the ~ notes** no sabe ni dar las notas bien; **are you sure you've got the ~ number?** (*Telec*) ¿seguro que es ése el número?; **to put sb ~** sacar a algn de su error; (*unpleasantly*) enmendar la plana a algn; **I'm confused, and I wanted you to put me ~** tengo dudas y quisiera que tú me las aclararas; **if you tell the story wrong the child will soon put you ~** si te equivocas al contar la historia, el niño enseguida te corrige *or* te saca de tu error; **to put a clock ~** poner un reloj en hora; **to put a mistake ~** corregir *or* rectificar un error; **is this the ~ road for Segovia?** ¿es éste el camino de Segovia?, ¿por aquí se va a Segovia?; **are we on the ~ road?** ¿vamos por buen camino?, ¿vamos bien por esta carretera?; **it's not the ~ shade of green** no es el tono de verde que yo busco; **the ~ side of the fabric** el (lado) derecho de la tela; **is the skirt the ~ size?** ¿va bien la falda de talla?; **it's not the ~ size/length** no vale de talla/de largo; **the ~ time** la hora exacta; **is that the ~ time?** ¿es ésa la hora?; **do you have the ~ time?** ¿tienes hora buena?, ¿sabes qué hora es exactamente?; ✦*IDIOM* **to get on the ~ side of sb** (*fig*) congraciarse con algn

4 (= *in the right*) **to be ~ to do sth** hacer bien en hacer algo; **you were ~ to come to me** has hecho bien en venir a verme; **to be ~** [*person*] tener razón, estar en lo cierto; **you're quite ~** ◊ **you're dead ~*** tienes toda la razón; **how ~ you are!** ¡qué razón tienes!; **to be ~ about sth/sb: you were ~ about there being none left** tenías razón cuando decías que no quedaba ninguno; **you were ~ about Peter, he's totally unreliable** tenías razón en lo de Peter *or* con respecto a Peter: no hay quien se fíe de él; **am I ~ in thinking that we've met before?** si no me equivoco ya nos conocemos ¿no?; **you were ~ in calling the doctor, it was appendicitis** hiciste bien en llamar al médico, era apendicitis

5 (= *in order*) **I don't feel quite ~** no me siento del todo bien; **I knew something wasn't ~ when she didn't call as usual** supe que algo no iba bien cuando no llamaba como de costumbre; **his leg hasn't been ~ since the accident** tiene la pierna mal desde el accidente; **my stereo still isn't ~** mi equipo sigue sin ir bien; **it will all come ~ in the end** todo se arreglará al final; **she's not quite ~ in the head** no está en sus cabales; **to be in one's ~ mind** en su sano juicio; **to put sth/sb ~: I hope the garage can put the car ~** espero que me sepan arreglar el coche en el taller; **you've offended her but it's not too late to put things ~** la has ofendido pero aún puedes arreglarlo; **it's nothing a night's sleep won't put ~** no es nada que no se arregle durmiendo toda la noche de un tirón; **a couple of aspirin will put me ~** con un par de aspirinas me pondré bien; **that's soon put ~** eso se arregla fácilmente, eso tiene fácil arreglo; **all's ~ with the world** todo va bien; ✦*IDIOM* **to be/feel as ~ as rain** encontrarse perfectamente; **she'll be as ~ as rain in a few days** en unos pocos días se repondrá completamente de esto

6 (= *not left*) derecho; **I'd give my ~ arm to know** daría cualquier cosa *or* todo el oro del mundo por saberlo; **we are a ~ of centre party** somos un partido de centro derecha; ✦*IDIOM* **it's a case of the ~ hand not knowing what the left hand is doing** es uno de esos casos en que la mano derecha no sabe lo que hace la izquierda

7 (*Math*) [*angle*] recto

8 (*Brit**) (*as intensifier*) (= *complete*) **he's a ~ idiot** es un auténtico idiota; **I felt a ~ twit** me sentí como un verdadero imbécil; **she made a ~ mess of it** lo hizo fatal*, le salió un buen churro (*Sp**); **you're a ~ one to talk** (*iro*) mira quién habla; *see also* **Charlie**

9 *see* **all right**

Ⓑ ADV 1 (= *directly, exactly*) **~ away** en seguida, ahora mismo, ahorita (mismo) (*Mex, Andes*); **it happened ~ before our eyes** ocurrió delante de nuestros propios ojos; **she was standing ~ behind/in front of him** estaba justo detrás/delante de él; **~ here** aquí mismo *or* (*CAm*) mero; **he was standing ~ in the middle of the road** estaba justo en el centro *or* (*CAm*) en el mero centro de la calle; **~ now** (= *immediately*) ahora mismo; (= *at the moment*) (justo) ahora; **I want this done ~ now** quiero que se haga esto ahora mismo; **she's busy ~ now** ahora mismo *or* justo ahora está ocupada; **he could tell ~ off that I was a foreigner** reconoció de inmediato que yo era extranjero; **to go ~ on** seguir todo derecho; **~ on!*†** ¡eso es!, ¡de acuerdo!; **he (just) went ~ on talking** siguió hablando como si nada; **it hit him ~ on the chest** le dio de lleno en el pecho; **she should come ~ out and say so** debería ser clara y decirlo; **it fell ~ on top of me** me cayó justo encima

2 (= *immediately*) justo, inmediatamente; **I'll do it ~ after dinner** lo haré justo *or* inmediatamente después de cenar; **I'll be ~ back** vuelvo en seguida; **come ~ in!** ¡ven aquí dentro!; **I'll be ~ over** voy en seguida; **I had to decide ~ then** tenía que decidirme allí mismo

3 (= *completely*) **we were sat ~ at the back** estábamos sentados atrás del todo; **we'll have to go ~ back to the beginning now** ahora habrá que volver al principio del todo; **he put his hand in ~ to the bottom** introdujo la mano hasta el mismo fondo; **their house is ~ at the end of the street** su casa está justo al final de la calle; **she was a very active old lady, ~ to the end** fue una anciana muy activa hasta el final; **to go ~ to the end of sth** ir hasta el final de algo; **to push sth ~ in** meter algo hasta el fondo; **there is a fence ~ round the house** hay una valla que rodea la casa por completo; **to read a book ~ through** leer un libro hasta el final; **you could see ~ through her blouse** se le transparentaba la blusa; **he filled it ~ up** lo llenó del todo

4 (= *correctly*) bien, correctamente; **you did ~ to/not to invite them** hiciste bien en invitarlos/en no invitarlos; **to understand sb ~** entender bien a algn; **if I remember ~** si mal no recuerdo, si no me falla la memoria; **it's him, ~ enough!** ¡seguro que es él!

5 (= *fairly*) **to do ~ by sb** portarse como es debido con algn; **don't worry about the pay, John will see you ~** no te preocupes por el sueldo, John se encargará de que te paguen lo que te corresponde; **to treat sb ~** tratar bien a algn; *see also* **serve**

6 (= *properly, satisfactorily*) bien; **you're not doing it ~** no lo estás haciendo bien; **I felt nothing was going ~ for me** sentía que nada me iba bien; **nothing goes ~ with them** nada les sale bien

7 (= *not left*) a la derecha; **he looked neither left nor ~** no miró a ningún lado; **eyes ~!** (*Mil*) ¡vista a la derecha!; **to turn ~** torcer a la derecha; **~ (about) turn!** ¡media vuelta a la derecha!; *see also* **left²**

8 (*as linker*) **~, who's next?** a ver, ¿quién va ahora?; **~ then, let's begin!** ¡empecemos, pues!

9 (*in titles*) **the Right Honourable Edmund Burke** el Excelentísimo Señor Edmund Burke; **the Right Honourable member for Huntingdon** Su Señoría el diputado por Huntingdon; **my Right Honourable friend** mi honorable amigo; **Right Reverend** Reverendísimo

Ⓒ N 1 (= *what is morally right, just*) **~ and wrong** el bien y el mal; **I don't know the ~s of the matter** no sé quién tiene razón en el asunto; **to know ~ from wrong** saber distinguir el bien del mal; **by ~s the house should go to me** lo suyo *or* lo propio es que la casa me correspondiera a mí; **to be in the ~** tener razón, estar en lo cierto; **to put** *or* **set sth to ~s** arreglar algo; **this government will put the country to ~s** este gobierno va a arreglar el país; **to set** *or* **put the world to ~s** arreglar el mundo; **to have ~ on one's side** tener la razón de su parte; *see also* **wrong C**

2 (= *prerogative*) derecho *m*; **they have a ~ to privacy** tienen derecho a la *or* su intimidad; **people have the ~ to read any kind of material they wish** la gente tiene derecho a leer lo que desee; **you had no ~ to take it** no tenías (ningún) derecho a llevártelo; **what gives you the ~** *or* **what ~ have you got to criticize me?** ¿qué derecho tienes tú a criticarme?; **who gave you the ~ to come in here?** ¿quién te ha dado permiso para entrar aquí?; **as of ~** por derecho propio; **by ~ of** por *or* en razón de; **by what ~ do you make all the decisions?** ¿con qué derecho tomas tú todas las decisiones?; **to own sth in one's own ~** poseer algo por derecho propio; **she's a celebrity in her own ~ now** ahora es una celebridad por méritos propios; **the baby is a person in his own ~** el bebé es una persona de pleno derecho; **~ to reply** derecho *m* de réplica; **~ of way** derecho *m* de paso; (*Aut etc*) (= *precedence*) prioridad *f*; *see also* **abode, assembly, exercise, reserve B1**

3 **rights** derechos *mpl*; **civil ~s** derechos *mpl* civiles; **film ~s** derechos *mpl* cinematográficos; **human ~s** derechos *mpl* humanos; **insist on your legal ~s** hazte valer tus derechos legales; **they don't have voting ~s** no tienen derecho al voto *or* de voto; **to be (well) within one's ~s** estar en su derecho; **you'd be well within your ~s to refuse to cooperate** estarías en tu derecho a negarte a cooperar; **women's ~s** derechos de la mujer; **"all rights reserved"** "es propiedad", "reservados todos los derechos"

4 (= *not left*) derecha *f*; **reading from ~ to left** leyendo de derecha a izquierda; **to keep to the ~** (*Aut*) circular por la derecha; **"keep to the right"** "manténgase a la derecha"; **our house is the second on the ~** nuestra casa es la segunda a *or* de la derecha; **on** *or* **to my ~** a mi derecha

5 (*Pol*) **the ~** la derecha; **to be on** *or* **to the ~ of sth/sb** (*Pol*) estar a la derecha de algo/algn; **he's further to the ~ than I am** es más de derecha *or* (*Sp*) de derechas que yo

6 (= *right turn*) **it's the next ~ after the lights** es la próxima a la derecha después del semáforo; **to take** *or* **make a ~** girar a la derecha

7 (*Boxing*) (= *punch*) derechazo *m*; (= *right hand*) derecha *f*

Ⓓ VT (= *put straight*) [+ *crooked picture*] enderezar; (= *correct*) [+ *mistake*] corregir; [+ *injustice*] reparar; (= *put right way up*) [+ *vehicle, person*] enderezar; **he tried to ~ himself but the leg was broken** intentó ponerse de pie pero tenía la pierna rota; **to ~ itself** [*vehicle*]

➤ LANGUAGE IN USE: **right** A4 11.1 **C2** 10.4

enderezarse; [*situation*] rectificarse; **to ~ a wrong** deshacer un agravio, reparar un daño
Ⓔ CPD ► **right angle** N ángulo *m* recto; **to be at ~ angles (to sth)** estar en *or* formar ángulo recto (con algo) ► **right back** N (*Sport*) (= *player*) lateral *mf* derecho/a; (= *position*) lateral *m* derecho ► **right half** N (*Sport*) medio *m* (volante) derecho ► **rights issue** N emisión *f* de acciones ► **right turn** N **to take** *or* **make a ~ turn** (*Aut*) girar a la derecha; (*Pol*) dar un giro a la derecha ► **right wing** N (*Pol*) derecha *f*; *see also* **right-wing** (*Sport*) (= *position*) ala *f* derecha

right-angled [ˈraɪtˌæŋgld] ADJ [*bend, turning*] en ángulo recto; (*Math*) [*triangle*] rectángulo

right-click [ˈraɪtklɪk] Ⓐ VI cliquear con la parte derecha del ratón (**on** en)
Ⓑ VT **to ~ an icon** cliquear en un icono con la parte derecha del ratón

righteous [ˈraɪtʃəs] Ⓐ ADJ 1 (= *virtuous*) [*person, conduct*] honrado, recto
2 (= *self-righteous*) [*tone, manner*] de superioridad moral; **her ~ manner irritated him** su aire de superioridad moral lo irritaba
3 (= *justified*) [*indignation, anger*] justificado, justo
Ⓑ N **the ~** (*Bible*) los justos

righteously [ˈraɪtʃəslɪ] ADV 1 (= *virtuously*) honradamente, rectamente 2 (= *self-righteously*) con un aire de superioridad moral; [*say*] con un tono de superioridad moral 3 (= *justifiably*) justamente; **to be ~ indignant/angry** estar justamente indignado/enfadado

righteousness [ˈraɪtʃəsnɪs] N 1 (= *virtuousness*) rectitud *f*; **moral ~** rectitud *f* moral; **to keep to/stray from the path of ~** mantenerse en el/apartarse del camino recto
2 (= *self-righteousness*) aire *m* de superioridad moral

rightful [ˈraɪtfʊl] ADJ [*owner, heir to throne*] legítimo; **~ claimant** derechohabiente *mf*

rightfully [ˈraɪtfəlɪ] ADV legítimamente, por derecho; **she's inherited the money which is ~ hers** ha heredado el dinero que legítimamente *or* por derecho le pertenece; **it's something that's taken very seriously, and ~ so** es algo que se ha tomado muy en serio y con razón

right-hand [ˈraɪthænd] Ⓐ ADJ derecho; **~ side** derecha *f*; **~ turn** (*Aut*) giro *m* a la derecha
Ⓑ CPD ► **right-hand drive** N (*Aut*) conducción *f* por la derecha ► **right-hand man** N (= *personal aide*) brazo *m* derecho

right-handed [ˈraɪtˈhændɪd] ADJ [*person*] que usa la mano derecha, diestro; [*tool*] para la mano derecha

right-hander [ˌraɪtˈhændəʳ] N diestro/a *m/f*

right-ho*, **right-oh*** [ˌraɪtˈhəʊ] EXCL (*Brit*) ¡vale!, ¡bien!

rightism [ˈraɪtɪzəm] N (*Pol*) derechismo *m*

rightist [ˈraɪtɪst] (*Pol*) ADJ, N derechista *mf*

▼ **rightly** [ˈraɪtlɪ] ADV 1 (= *correctly*) [*fear, suspect*] con razón; [*assume*] sin equivocarse; [*act, behave*] correctamente, bien; **they ~ feared that she had caught tuberculosis** se temían, y con razón, que había cogido tuberculosis; **the credit for this achievement ~ belongs to her** el mérito por este logro le pertenece a ella con todas las de la ley *or* en justicia le pertenece a ella; **as she ~ points out, more research is needed** como muy bien ella señala, hace falta una mayor investigación; **he ~ points out that these problems are connected** señala con acierto *or* con razón que estos problemas están relacionados; **quite ~** con toda la razón; **if I remember ~** si mal no recuerdo, si no me falla la memoria; **as he (so) ~ said ...** como bien dijo él ...
2 (= *justifiably*) con (toda la) razón; **they are ~ regarded as the best in the world** se les considera, con (toda la) razón, los mejores del mundo; **and ~ so** y con (toda la) razón; **her colleagues were ~ upset by her dismissal** sus colegas estaban disgustados por su dimisión y con razón, sus colegas estaban, con toda justificación, disgustados por su dimisión; **~ or wrongly** con razón o sin ella, justa o injustamente
3 (= *really*) **I don't ~ know** no sé exactamente; **I can't ~ say** no lo puedo decir con seguridad

right-minded [ˈraɪtˈmaɪndɪd] ADJ (= *decent*) honrado; (= *sensible*) prudente

rightness [ˈraɪtnɪs] N (= *correctness*) exactitud *f*; (= *justice*) justicia *f*

rightsizing [ˈraɪtsaɪzɪŋ] N reestructuración *f* (*que conlleva recortes de plantilla*)

right-thinking [ˈraɪtˈθɪŋkɪŋ] ADJ = **right-minded**

right-to-life [ˌraɪttəˈlaɪf] ADJ [*movement, group*] pro derecho a la vida

rightward [ˈraɪtwəd] Ⓐ ADJ [*movement etc*] a *or* hacia la derecha
Ⓑ ADV [*move etc*] a *or* hacia la derecha

rightwards [ˈraɪtwədz] ADV (*Brit*) = **rightward B**

right-wing [ˈraɪtˈwɪŋ] ADJ (*Pol*) derechista, de derechas; *see also* **right**

right-winger [ˈraɪtˈwɪŋəʳ] N 1 (*Pol*) derechista *mf*
2 (*Sport*) jugador(a) *m/f* de la banda derecha

rigid [ˈrɪdʒɪd] ADJ 1 (= *stiff*) [*material*] rígido, tieso; **to be ~ with fear** estar paralizado de miedo; ✦**IDIOM to be bored ~*** estar aburrido *or* aburrirse como una ostra*
2 (= *strict*) [*rules*] riguroso, estricto
3 (= *inflexible*) [*person, ideas*] inflexible, intransigente; **he is quite ~ about it** es bastante inflexible *or* intransigente sobre ese punto

rigidity [rɪˈdʒɪdɪtɪ] N 1 (= *stiffness*) [*of material*] rigidez *f* 2 (= *strictness*) [*of rules*] rigor *m* 3 (= *inflexibility*) [*of person, ideas*] inflexibilidad *f*, intransigencia *f*

rigidly [ˈrɪdʒɪdlɪ] ADV 1 (= *stiffly*) rígidamente
2 (= *strictly*) estrictamente
3 (= *inflexibly*) con inflexibilidad, con intransigencia; **he is ~ opposed to it** está totalmente en contra de esto

rigmarole [ˈrɪgmərəʊl] N (= *process*) galimatías *m inv*, lío *m*; (= *paperwork etc*) trámites *mpl*, papeleo *m*

rigor [ˈrɪgəʳ] N (*US*) = **rigour**

rigor mortis [ˈrɪgəˈmɔːtɪs] N rigidez *f* cadavérica

rigorous [ˈrɪgərəs] ADJ riguroso

rigorously [ˈrɪgərəslɪ] ADV rigurosamente

rigour, **rigor** (*US*) [ˈrɪgəʳ] N (= *severity*) rigor *m*; [*of climate*] rigores *mpl*; **the full ~ of the law** el máximo rigor de la ley

rig-out* [ˈrɪgaʊt] N atuendo *m*, atavío *m*

rile* [raɪl] VT sulfurar*, reventar*; **there's nothing that ~s me more** no hay nada que me reviente más*; **it ~s me terribly** me irrita muchísimo

Riley [ˈraɪlɪ] N ✦**IDIOM to live the life of ~** (*Brit**) darse buena vida

rill [rɪl] N (= *liter*) arroyo *m*, riachuelo *m*

rim [rɪm] N [*of cup etc*] borde *m*; [*of wheel*] llanta *f*; [*of spectacles*] montura *f*; [*of dirt etc*] cerco *m*; **the ~ of the sun** el borde del sol

rime¹ [raɪm] N (*poet*) rima *f*

rime² [raɪm] N (*liter*) (= *frost*) escarcha *f*

rimless [ˈrɪmlɪs] ADJ [*spectacles*] sin aros

rimmed [rɪmd] ADJ **~ with ...** con un borde de ...; **glasses ~ with gold** gafas *fpl* con montura dorada

rind [raɪnd] N [*of fruit*] cáscara *f*; [*of cheese, bacon*] corteza *f*

ring¹ [rɪŋ] Ⓐ N 1 (*on finger*) (*plain*) anillo *m*; (*jewelled*) anillo *m*, sortija *f*; (*in nose*) arete *m*, aro *m*; (*on bird's leg, for curtain*) anilla *f*; (*for napkin*) servilletero *m*; (*on stove*) quemador *m*, hornillo *m*; (*for swimmer*) flotador *m*; **rings** (*Gymnastics*) anillas *fpl*; **electric ~** quemador *m* eléctrico, hornillo *m* eléctrico; **gas ~** fuego *m* de gas; **onion ~s** aros *mpl* de cebolla rebozados; **pineapple ~s** rodajas *fpl* de piña; *see also* **diamond**, **engagement**, **key**, **nose**, **piston**, **signet**, **wedding**
2 (= *circle*) [*of people*] círculo *m*; (*in game, dance*) corro *m*; [*of objects*] anillo *m*; (*in water*) onda *f*; (*around planet, on tree, of smoke*) anillo *m*; (*around bathtub*) cerco *m*; **to stand/sit in a ~** ponerse/sentarse en círculo; **a ~ of hills** un anillo de colinas; **he always leaves a dirty ~ round the bath** siempre deja un cerco de suciedad en la bañera; **to have ~s round one's eyes** tener ojeras; **the ~s of Saturn** los anillos de Saturno; ✦**IDIOM to run ~s round sb** dar mil vueltas a algn*; *see also* **smoke**
3 (= *group*) [*of criminals, drug dealers*] banda *f*, red *f*; [*of spies*] red *f*; (*Comm*) cartel *m*, cártel *m*; *see also* **drug**, **spy**, **vice**¹
4 (= *arena*) (*Boxing*) cuadrilátero *m*, ring *m*; (*at circus*) pista *f*; (= *bullring*) ruedo *m*, plaza *f*; (*at horse race*) cercado *m*, recinto *m*; (*in livestock market*) corral *m* (de exposiciones); **the ~** (*fig*) el boxeo; ✦**IDIOM to throw** *or* **toss one's hat** *or* **cap into the ~** echarse *or* lanzarse al ruedo; *see also* **show**
Ⓑ VT 1 (= *surround*) rodear, cercar; **the building was ~ed by police** la policía rodeaba *or* cercaba el edificio; **the town is ~ed by hills** la ciudad está rodeada de colinas
2 [+ *bird*] anillar
3 (= *mark with ring*) poner un círculo a
Ⓒ CPD ► **ring binder** N carpeta *f* de anillas *or* (*LAm*) anillos ► **ring finger** N (dedo *m*) anular *m* ► **ring main** N (*Elec*) red *f* de suministro *or* abastecimiento ► **ring road** N (*Brit*) carretera *f* de circunvalación, ronda *f*, periférico *m* (*LAm*) ► **ring spanner** N llave *f* dentada

▼ **ring**² [rɪŋ] (*vb: pt* **rang**; *pp* **rung**) Ⓐ N 1 (= *sound*) [*of bell*] toque *m* de timbre; (*louder, of alarm*) timbrazo *m*; [*of voice*] timbre *m*; (*metallic sound*) sonido *m* metálico; **there was a ~ at the door** llamaron al timbre de la puerta, sonó el timbre de la puerta; **he answered the telephone on the first ~** contestó el teléfono al primer pitido; **the familiar ~ of her voice** el timbre familiar de su voz; **the ~ of sledge runners on the ice** el sonido metálico de los trineos sobre el hielo
2 (*Brit Telec*) **to give sb a ~** llamar a algn (por teléfono), dar un telefonazo *or* un toque a algn*; **I'll give you a ~** te llamo, te doy un telefonazo *or* un toque*
3 (= *nuance*) **the name has a (certain) ~ to it** el nombre tiene algo; **his laugh had a hollow ~ to it** su risa tenía algo de superficial, su risa sonaba (a) superficial; **that has the ~ of truth about it** eso suena a cierto
Ⓑ VT 1 [+ *doorbell, buzzer, handbell, church bell*] tocar; ✦**IDIOMS that ~s a bell (with me)** eso me suena; **it doesn't ~ any bells** no me suena; **to ~ the changes**: **you could ~ the changes by substituting ground almonds** podrías cambiar *or* variar sustituyendo la almendra molida; **he decided to ~ the changes after his side's third consecutive defeat** decidió cambiar de táctica tras la ter-

➤ LANGUAGE IN USE: **rightly** 26.3 **ring**² C1 27

cera derrota consecutiva de su equipo; *see also* **alarm**

2 (*Brit Telec*) [+ *house, office, number*] llamar a; [+ *person*] llamar (por teléfono) a; **you must ~ the hospital** tienes que llamar al hospital

Ⓒ VI 1 (= *make sound*) [*doorbell, alarm, telephone*] sonar; [*church bell*] sonar, repicar, tañer (*liter*); ✦*IDIOM* **to ~ off the hook** (*US*) [*telephone*] sonar constantemente, no parar de sonar

2 (= *use bell*) llamar; **you rang, madam?** ¿me llamó usted, señora?; **to ~ at the door** llamar a la puerta; **to ~ for sth: we'll ~ for some sugar** llamaremos para pedir azúcar; **to ~ for sb** llamar para que venga algn; **"please ring for attention"** "rogamos toque el timbre para que le atiendan"

3 (*Brit*) (= *telephone*) llamar (por teléfono); **could someone ~ for a taxi?** ¿podría alguien llamar a un taxi?

4 (= *echo*) (*gen*) resonar; [*ears*] zumbar; **the valley rang with cries** los gritos resonaron por el valle; **his words were ~ing in my head** sus palabras resonaban en mi cabeza; **the news set the town ~ing** la noticia causó furor en la ciudad; **the town rang with his praises** por toda la ciudad no se oían más que alabanzas suyas; ✦*IDIOM* **to ~ true/false/hollow** sonar a cierto/falso/hueco; **his suddenly friendly tone rang false** su tono amistoso tan repentino sonaba a falso; **her story just didn't ~ true** la historia no parecía verdad

►**ring back** (*Brit Telec*) Ⓐ VT + ADV (= *ring again*) volver a llamar; (= *return sb's call*) llamar; **could you ask him to ~ me back?** ¿le podría decir que me llame?

Ⓑ VI + ADV (= *ring again*) volver a llamar; (= *return call*) llamar; **can you ~ back later?** ¿puede volver a llamar más tarde?

►**ring down** VT + ADV [+ *curtain*] bajar; ✦*IDIOM* **to ~ down the curtain on sth** poner punto final a algo

►**ring in** Ⓐ VT + ADV anunciar; ✦*IDIOM* **to ~ in the New Year** celebrar el año nuevo; *see also* **ring out**

Ⓑ VI + ADV 1 (*Brit Telec*) llamar (por teléfono); **I rang in to say I was ill** llamé (por teléfono) para decir que estaba enfermo

2 (*US Ind*) fichar (al entrar)

►**ring off** VI + ADV (*Brit Telec*) colgar

►**ring out** Ⓐ VI + ADV 1 [*bell*] sonar, repicar; [*shot*] oírse, sonar; [*voice*] oírse

2 (*US Ind*) fichar (al salir)

Ⓑ VT + ADV **to ~ out the old year** (*lit*) tocar las campanas para señalar el fin del año; (*fig*) despedir el ano; **~ out the old, ~ in the new** que suenen las campanas para despedir al año viejo y recibir el nuevo año

►**ring round, ring around** Ⓐ VI + ADV (*Brit Telec*) llamar (por teléfono); **if you ~ round, you can usually get a good deal** si llamas a varios sitios, generalmente se consiguen gangas

Ⓑ VI + PREP (*Brit Telec*) **I'll ~ round my friends** llamaré a mis amigos

►**ring up** Ⓐ VI + ADV (*Brit Telec*) llamar (por teléfono)

Ⓑ VT + ADV 1 (*Brit Telec*) **to ~ sb up** llamar a algn (por teléfono)

2 [+ *curtain*] subir, levantar; ✦*IDIOM* **to ~ up the curtain on sth** dar comienzo a algo, iniciar algo

3 (*on cash-register*) [+ *amount, purchase*] registrar; (*fig*) [+ *sales, profits, losses*] registrar

ring-a-ring-a-roses [ˈrɪŋəˈrɪŋəˈrəʊzɪz] N corro *m*; **to play ~** jugar al corro

ringbolt [ˈrɪŋbəʊlt] N perno *m* con anillo; (*Naut*) cáncamo *m*

ringdove [ˈrɪŋdʌv] N paloma *f* torcaz

ringer [ˈrɪŋəʳ] N 1 (= *bell ringer*) campanero/a *m/f*

2 (*) (*also* **dead ~**) doble *mf*, viva imagen *f*; **he is a (dead) ~ for the President** se le parece en todo al presidente

3 (*US Horse racing*) caballo *m* sustituido

ringing¹ [ˈrɪŋɪŋ] N (*Orn*) anillado *m*, anillamiento *m*

ringing² [ˈrɪŋɪŋ] Ⓐ ADJ 1 (*lit*) [*telephone*] que suena *or* sonaba *etc*; **~ tone** (*Brit Telec*) señal *f* de llamada

2 (= *resounding*) [*voice*] sonoro, resonante; [*declaration*] grandilocuente; [*endorsement, condemnation*] enérgico; **in ~ tones** en tono enérgico

Ⓑ N [*of large bell*] repique *m*, tañido *m* (*liter*); [*of handbell*] campanilleo *m*; [*of electric bell*] toque *m*; [*of telephone*] timbre *m*, pitidos *mpl*; (*in ears*) zumbido *m*

ringleader [ˈrɪŋˌliːdəʳ] N cabecilla *mf*

ringlet [ˈrɪŋlɪt] N rizo *m*, tirabuzón *m*

ringmaster [ˈrɪŋˌmɑːstəʳ] N maestro *m* de ceremonias

ring-pull [ˈrɪŋpʊl] (*Brit*) Ⓐ N anilla *f*

Ⓑ CPD ► **ring-pull can** N lata *f* (*de refrescos, cerveza, etc*)

ringside [ˈrɪŋsaɪd] Ⓐ N **to be at the ~** estar junto al cuadrilátero

Ⓑ CPD ► **ringside seat** N butaca *f* de primera fila; **to have a ~ seat** (*fig*) verlo todo desde muy cerca

ringtone [ˈrɪŋtəun] N (*Telec*) tono *m* de llamada

ringway [ˈrɪŋweɪ] N (*US*) = **ring road**; *see* **ring¹**

ringworm [ˈrɪŋwɜːm] N tiña *f*

rink [rɪŋk] N (*for ice-skating*) pista *f* de hielo; (*for roller-skating*) pista *f* de patinaje

rinse [rɪns] Ⓐ N 1 [*of clothes*] aclarado *m*; [*of dishes etc*] enjuague *m*; **to give one's stockings a ~** aclarar las medias

2 (= *hair colouring*) reflejo *m*; **to give one's hair a blue ~** dar reflejos azules al pelo

Ⓑ VT 1 [+ *dishes, clothes*] aclarar, enjuagar; [+ *mouth*] lavar, enjuagar; **to ~ one's hands** aclararse *or* enjuagarse las manos

2 (= *colour*) [+ *hair*] dar reflejos a

►**rinse out** VT + ADV [+ *dirt*] lavar; [+ *cup*] enjuagar; [+ *one's mouth*] enjuagarse

Rio de Janeiro [ˌriːəʊdədʒəˈnɪərəʊ] N Río *m* de Janeiro

riot [ˈraɪət] Ⓐ N 1 (= *uprising*) disturbio *m*, motín *m*; (*in prison*) amotinamiento *m*, sublevación *f*; **there was nearly a ~** hubo casi un motín; **to put down a ~** controlar un disturbio

2 (*fig*) **a ~ of colour** un derroche de color; ✦*IDIOM* **to run ~** (= *go out of control*) desmandarse; (= *spread*) extenderse por todas partes, cubrirlo todo; **to let one's imagination run ~** dejar volar la imaginación

3 (*) (*fig*) (= *wild success*) exitazo *m*; **it was a ~!** ¡fue divertidísimo!, ¡fue la monda!*; **he's a ~!** ¡es un tipo desternillante!, ¡te mondas de risa con él!

Ⓑ VI amotinarse

Ⓒ CPD ► **riot act** N ✦*IDIOM* **to read sb the ~ act*** leerle la cartilla a algn ► **riot gear** N uniforme *m* antidisturbios ► **riot police** N policía *f* antidisturbios ► **riot shield** N escudo *m* antidisturbios ► **riot squad** N = **riot police**

rioter [ˈraɪətəʳ] N amotinado/a *m/f*

riotous [ˈraɪətəs] ADJ 1 [*person, mob*] amotinado; [*assembly*] desordenado, alborotado

2 (= *wild, exciting*) [*party, living*] desenfrenado, alborotado; (= *very funny*) [*comedy*] divertidísimo; **it was a ~ success** obtuvo un éxito ruidoso; **we had a ~ time** nos divertimos una barbaridad

riotously [ˈraɪətəslɪ] ADV bulliciosamente, ruidosamente; **~ funny** divertidísimo

▼**RIP** ABBR = **requiescat in pace** (= *may he etc rest in peace*) q.e.p.d., D.E.P., E.P.D.

rip [rɪp] Ⓐ N rasgón *m*, desgarrón *m*

Ⓑ VT rasgar, desgarrar; **to ~ open** [+ *envelope, parcel, wound*] abrir desgarrando; **to ~ sth to pieces** hacer algo trizas

Ⓒ VI 1 [*cloth*] rasgarse, desgarrarse

2 (*) (*fig*) **to ~ along** volar, ir a todo gas; **to let ~** desenfrenarse; **to let ~ at sb** arremeter contra algn; **let her ~!** ¡más rápido!, ¡más gas!*

►**rip off** VT + ADV 1 (*lit*) arrancar

2 (‡) (= *overcharge, cheat*) estafar

3 (‡) (= *steal*) [+ *object*] pulir‡, birlar*; (= *copy*) [+ *idea, book, film*] calcar, plagiar

►**rip out** VT + ADV arrancar

►**rip through** VI + PREP **the fire/explosion ~ped through the house** el incendio/la explosión arrasó la casa; **the jet ~ped through the sky** el jet surcaba veloz el cielo

►**rip up** VT + ADV hacer pedazos; **the train ~ped up 100 metres of track** el tren destrozó 100 metros de la vía

riparian [raɪˈpeərɪən] Ⓐ ADJ ribereño

Ⓑ N ribereño/a *m/f*

ripcord [ˈrɪpkɔːd] N (*Aer*) cuerda *f* de apertura

ripe [raɪp] ADJ (*compar* **riper**; *superl* **ripest**) 1 [*fruit etc*] maduro; **to be ~ for picking** estar bastante maduro para poderse coger; **to grow ~** madurar

2 (*fig*) listo; **to be ~ for sth** [*person*] estar dispuesto a algo; [*situation etc*] estar listo para algo; **the country is ~ for revolution** la revolución está a punto de estallar en el país; **the company is ~ for a takeover** la empresa está en su punto para un cambio de dueño; **to live to a ~ old age** llegar a muy viejo; **until/when the time is ~** hasta/en un momento oportuno

3 (*) [*language*] grosero, verde; [*smell*] fuerte, desagradable; **that's pretty ~!** ¡eso no se puede consentir!

ripen [ˈraɪpən] Ⓐ VT [+ *fruit, cheese, corn*] madurar

Ⓑ VI [*fruit, cheese, corn*] madurar

ripeness [ˈraɪpnɪs] N madurez *f*

rip-off‡ [ˈrɪpɒf] N 1 (= *swindle*) **it's a ~!** ¡es una estafa *or* un robo! 2 (= *imitation*) [*of film, song etc*] plagio *m*, copia *f*

riposte [rɪˈpɒst] Ⓐ N 1 (= *retort*) réplica *f*

2 (*Fencing*) estocada *f*

Ⓑ VI replicar (con agudeza)

ripper [ˈrɪpəʳ] N **Jack the Ripper** Juanito el Destripador

ripping*† [ˈrɪpɪŋ] ADJ (*Brit*) estupendo*, bárbaro*

ripple [ˈrɪpl] Ⓐ N (= *small wave*) onda *f*, rizo *m*; (= *sound*) murmullo *m*; **a ~ of excitement** un susurro *or* murmullo de emoción; **a ~ of applause** unos cuantos aplausos

Ⓑ VT ondular, rizar

Ⓒ VI rizarse; **the crowd ~d with excitement** el público se estremeció emocionado

Ⓓ CPD ► **ripple effect** N reacción *f* en cadena, efecto *m* dominó; **to have a ~ effect** pro-

➤ LANGUAGE IN USE: **RIP** 24.5

vocar una reacción en cadena, tener un efecto dominó

rip-roaring* ['rɪp,rɔːrɪŋ] ADJ [*party*] desmadrado*, animadísimo; [*speech*] apasionado, violento; [*success*] clamoroso

riptide ['rɪptaɪd] N aguas *fpl* revueltas

RISC N ABBR (*Comput*) 1 = **reduced instruction set computer**
2 = **reduced instruction set computing**

rise [raɪz] (*vb: pt* **rose**; *pp* **risen**) Ⓐ N 1 (= *upward movement*) subida *f*, ascenso *m*; [*of tide*] subida *f*; [*of river*] crecida *f*; (*in tone, pitch*) subida *f*, elevación *f*; **a rapid ~ in sea level** una rápida subida del nivel del mar; **the gentle ~ and fall of his breathing** el ligero movimiento de su pecho al inspirar y espirar; **✦IDIOMS to get a ~ out of sb*** chinchar a algn*; **to take the ~ out of sb*** tomar el pelo a algn*
2 (= *increase*) (*in number, rate, value*) aumento *m*; (*in price, temperature*) subida *f*, aumento *m*; (*Brit*) (*in salary*) aumento *m* (de sueldo); **to ask for a ~** pedir un aumento (de sueldo); **he was given a 30% pay ~** le dieron un aumento de sueldo del 30%; **they got a ~ of 50 dollars** les aumentaron el sueldo en 50 dólares; **a ~ in interest rates** un aumento de los tipos de interés; **prices are on the ~** los precios están subiendo
3 (*fig*) (= *advancement*) ascenso *m*, subida *f*; (= *emergence*) desarrollo *m*; **his meteoric ~ to fame** su ascenso meteórico *or* su subida meteórica a la fama; **Napoleon's ~ to power** el ascenso *or* la subida de Napoleón al poder; **the ~ of the middle class** el desarrollo de la clase media; **the ~ and fall of** [*of organization*] el auge y (la) decadencia de; [*of person*] el ascenso y (la) caída de; **the ~ and fall of the empire** el auge y (la) decadencia del imperio; **nazism was on the ~ in Europe** el nazismo estaba creciendo en Europa
4 (= *small hill*) colina *f*, loma *f*; (= *upward slope*) cuesta *f* (arriba), pendiente *f*; [*of stairs*] subida *f*
5 (= *origin*) [*of river*] nacimiento *m*; **to give ~ to** [+ *innovation*] dar origen a; [+ *problems, impression*] causar; [+ *interest, ideas*] suscitar; [+ *speculation, doubts, suspicion, fear*] suscitar, dar lugar a
Ⓑ VI 1 (= *get up*) (*from bed*) levantarse; (= *stand up*) ponerse de pie, levantarse; (= *rear up*) [*building, mountain*] elevarse, alzarse; **to ~ early** madrugar, levantarse temprano; **he rose to greet us** se levantó para recibirnos; **the mountains rose up before him** las montañas se elevaban *or* se alzaban frente a él; **the horse rose on its hind legs** el caballo se alzó sobre sus patas traseras; **to ~ from the dead** resucitar; **to ~ to one's feet** ponerse de pie; **~ and shine!** ¡levántate y espabila!; **to ~ from (the) table** levantarse de la mesa; *see also* **ash²**
2 (= *get higher*) [*sun, moon*] salir; [*smoke, mist, balloon*] subir, ascender, elevarse (*liter*); [*dust, spray, theatre curtain*] levantarse; [*water, tide, level, aircraft, lift*] subir; [*dough, cake*] aumentar, subir; [*river*] crecer; [*hair*] ponerse de punta; **the plane rose to 4,000 metres** el avión subió a 4.000 metros; **his eyebrows rose at the sight of her** al verla se le arquearon las cejas; **her actions caused a few eyebrows to ~** sus acciones causaron cierto escándalo; **her eyes rose to meet mine** alzó la mirada y se encontró con la mía; **the fish are rising well** los peces están picando bien; **to ~ above** (*fig*) [+ *differences, poverty*] superar; [+ *prejudice*] estar por encima de; **to ~ to the bait** (*lit, fig*) picar *or* morder el anzuelo; **to ~ to the surface** (*lit*) salir a la superficie; (*fig*) [*tensions, contradictions*] surgir, aflorar; **it is a time when these tensions may ~ to the surface** es un momento en el que puede que surjan *or* afloren estas tensiones; *see also* **challenge**, **occasion**
3 (= *increase*) [*price, temperature, pressure*] subir, aumentar; [*number, amount, tension*] aumentar; [*barometer, stocks, shares*] subir; [*wind*] arreciar, levantarse; [*sound*] hacerse más fuerte; **it has ~n 20% in price** su precio ha subido *or* aumentado en un 20%; **new houses are rising in value** las viviendas nuevas se están revalorizando; **unemployment was rising** el paro aumentaba; **the noise rose to almost unbearable levels** el ruido se hizo tan fuerte que era casi insoportable; **her voice rose in anger** levantó *or* alzó la voz enfadada
4 [*ground*] subir (en pendiente)
5 (*in rank*) ascender; **he rose to colonel** ascendió a coronel; **he rose to be president** llegó a ser presidente; **she rose to the top of her profession** llegó a la cumbre de su profesión; **to ~ in sb's estimation** ganar en la estima de algn; **to ~ from nothing** salir de la nada; **to ~ from** *or* **through the ranks** (*Mil*) ascender de soldado raso; *see also* **prominence**
6 (= *improve*) [*standards*] mejorar; **our spirits rose** nos animamos; **it could cause expectations to ~** podría hacer que las expectativas crecieran
7 (= *come forth*) **a loud gasp rose from the audience** el público soltó un grito ahogado; **laughter rose from the audience** entre el público estallaron las risas; **from the people, a cheer rose up** la gente empezó a vitorear todos a una; **she could feel a blush rising to her cheeks** sentía que se le subía el color a las mejillas, sentía que se le subían los colores; **tears rose to his eyes** se le saltaron las lágrimas; **a feeling of panic was rising in him** empezó a entrarle una sensación de pánico
8 (= *originate*) [*river*] nacer
9 (= *rebel*) (*also* **~ up**) sublevarse, levantarse (**against** contra); **the people rose (up) against their oppressors** el pueblo se sublevó *or* levantó contra sus opresores; **to ~ (up) in arms** alzarse en armas; **to ~ (up) in revolt** sublevarse, rebelarse
10 (= *adjourn*) [*parliament, court*] levantar la sesión; **the House rose at 2a.m.** se levantó la sesión parlamentaria a las 2 de la madrugada

risen ['rɪzn] PT, PP *of* **rise**

riser ['raɪzəʳ] N 1 **to be an early/late ~** ser madrugador(a)/dormilón/ona
2 [*of stair*] contrahuella *f*

risibility [,rɪzɪ'bɪlɪtɪ] N risibilidad *f*

risible ['rɪzɪbl] ADJ risible

rising ['raɪzɪŋ] Ⓐ ADJ 1 (= *increasing*) [*number, quantity*] creciente; [*prices etc*] en aumento, en alza; (*Fin*) [*trend*] alcista; **the ~ number of murders** el creciente número de homicidios; **with ~ alarm** con creciente alarma
2 (= *getting higher*) [*sun, moon*] naciente; [*ground*] en pendiente; [*tide*] creciente; **the house stood on ~ ground** la casa estaba construída sobre una pendiente
3 (*fig*) (= *promising*) prometedor; **~ politician** político *m* en alza; **the ~ generation** las nuevas generaciones
Ⓑ ADV (*) (= *almost*) casi; **he's ~ 12** pronto tendrá 12 años
Ⓒ N 1 (= *uprising*) rebelión *f*, sublevación *f*
2 [*of river*] nacimiento *m*; [*of sun etc*] salida *f*
3 **on the ~ of the House** (*Parl*) al suspenderse la sesión
Ⓓ CPD ► **rising damp** N humedad *f* de paredes ► **rising star** N (*fig*) (= *person*) figura *f* emergente

▼ **risk** [rɪsk] Ⓐ N 1 (*gen*) riesgo *m*; **it's not worth the ~** no merece la pena correr el riesgo; **there is an element of ~** hay un componente de riesgo; **there's too much ~ involved** supone demasiados riesgos; **the benefits outweigh the ~s** los beneficios son mayores que los riesgos; **the building is a fire ~** el edificio es un peligro en caso de un incendio; **a health/security ~** un peligro para la salud/la seguridad; **at ~**: **the children most at ~** los niños que corren más riesgo *or* peligro; **up to 25,000 jobs are at ~** hay hasta 25.000 trabajos que peligran *or* que están en peligro; **to put sth at ~** poner algo en peligro; **at the ~ of** a riesgo de; **at the ~ of seeming stupid** a riesgo de parecer estúpido; **at the ~ of one's life** con peligro de su vida, arriesgando la vida; **there is no ~ of his coming** *or* **that he will come** no hay peligro de que venga; **there is little ~ of infection** el riesgo *or* peligro de infección es pequeño; **at one's own ~** por su cuenta y riesgo; **at (the) owner's ~** bajo la responsabilidad del dueño; **you run the ~ of being dismissed** corres el riesgo de que te despidan; **I can't take the ~** no me puedo exponer *or* arriesgar a eso, no puedo correr ese riesgo; **that's a ~ you'll have to take** ése es un riesgo que vas a tener que correr; **you're taking a big ~** te estás arriesgando mucho; *see also* **calculated**
2 (*Fin, Insurance*) riesgo *m*; **insured against all ~s** asegurado contra *or* a todo riesgo; **a bad/good ~**: **you may be turned down as a bad ~** puede que te rechacen por constituir un riesgo inadmisible; **she is considered a good ~** a sus ojos constituye un riesgo admisible; *see also* **all-risks**, **high-risk**, **low-risk**
Ⓑ VT 1 (= *put at risk*) arriesgar, poner en peligro; **she ~ed her life for me/to save me** arriesgó su vida por mí/por rescatarme, puso en peligro su vida por mí/por rescatarme; **to ~ everything** arriesgarlo todo; **I'm ~ing my job by saying this** estoy arriesgando *or* poniendo en peligro el puesto al decir esto; **he ~ed all his savings on the project** arriesgó todos sus ahorros en el proyecto; *see also* **life**, **neck**
2 (= *run the risk of*) correr el riesgo de, arriesgarse a; **I don't want to ~ another accident** no quiero correr el riesgo de *or* arriesgarme a *or* exponerme a otro accidente; **to ~ losing/being caught** correr el riesgo de perder/ser cogido, arriesgarse a perder/ser cogido
3 (= *venture, take a chance on*) arriesgarse a; **shall we ~ it?** ¿nos arriesgamos?; **I'll ~ it** me arriesgo, me voy a arriesgar; **I can't ~ it** no me puedo arriesgar (a eso); **I ~ed a glance behind me** me arriesgué a mirar hacia atrás; **she won't ~ coming today** no va a arriesgarse a venir hoy
Ⓒ CPD ► **risk capital** N capital *m* riesgo ► **risk factor** N factor *m* de riesgo; **smoking is a ~ factor for** *or* **in heart disease** fumar constituye un factor de riesgo en las enfermedades cardíacas ► **risk management** N gestión *f* de riesgos

riskiness ['rɪskɪnɪs] N peligro *m*, lo arriesgado, lo riesgoso (*LAm*); **in view of the ~ of the plan** visto lo peligroso del plan

risky ['rɪskɪ] ADJ (*compar* **riskier**, *superl* **riskiest**) 1 (= *dangerous*) [*venture, plan, investment*] arriesgado, riesgoso (*LAm*); **investing on the stock market is a ~ business** invertir en

➤ LANGUAGE IN USE: risk A1 2.3

bolsa supone muchos riesgos
2 = **risqué**

risotto [rɪˈzɒtəʊ] N (*Culin*) risotto *m*, arroz *m* a la italiana

risqué [ˈriːskeɪ] ADJ [*humour, joke*] subido de tono

rissole [ˈrɪsəʊl] N (*Brit Culin*) ≈ croqueta *f*

rite [raɪt] Ⓐ N rito *m*; (= *funeral rites*) exequias *fpl*; **"The Rite of Spring"** "La Consagración de la Primavera"; *see also* **last A3**
Ⓑ CPD ► **rite of passage** N rito *m* de paso, rito *m* de tránsito; *see also* **rite(s)-of-passage**

rite(s)-of-passage [ˌraɪt(s)əvˈpæsɪdʒ] ADJ **a ~ novel** una novela iniciática; *see also* **rite**

ritual [ˈrɪtjʊəl] Ⓐ ADJ 1 [*dancing, murder*] ritual
2 (*fig*) (= *conventional*) consabido; **in the ~ phrase** en la expresión consagrada
Ⓑ N 1 (*Rel*) (*Christian*) ritual *m*, ceremonia *f*; (*non-Christian*) rito *m*
2 (*fig*) (= *custom*) rito *m*, ritual *m*

ritualism [ˈrɪtjʊəlɪzəm] N ritualismo *m*

ritualist [ˈrɪtjʊəlɪst] N ritualista *mf*

ritualistic [ˌrɪtjʊəˈlɪstɪk] ADJ ritualista; (*fig*) consagrado, sacramental

ritually [ˈrɪtjʊəlɪ] ADV ritualmente

ritzy* [ˈrɪtsɪ] ADJ (*compar* **ritzier**; *superl* **ritziest**) [*car, house*] de lujo

rival [ˈraɪvəl] Ⓐ ADJ [*team, firm*] rival, contrario; [*claim, attraction*] competidor
Ⓑ N rival *mf*, contrario/a *m/f*; **to be sb's closest ~** ser el rival más cercano de algn
Ⓒ VT competir con, rivalizar con

rivalry [ˈraɪvəlrɪ] N rivalidad *f*, competencia *f*; **to enter into ~ with sb** empezar a competir con algn

riven [ˈrɪvən] ADJ, PT, PP (*liter*) rajado, hendido; **~ by** desgarrado por, dividido por, escindido por

river [ˈrɪvəʳ] Ⓐ N río *m*; **up/down ~** río arriba/abajo; **up ~ from Toledo** aguas arriba de Toledo; ✦***IDIOM*** **to sell sb down the ~*** traicionar a algn
Ⓑ CPD ► **river basin** N cuenca *f* de río ► **river fish** N pez *m* de río ► **river fishing** N pesca *f* de río ► **river mouth** N desembocadura *f* del río ► **river police** N brigada *f* fluvial ► **river traffic** N tráfico *m* fluvial

riverbank [ˈrɪvəbæŋk] Ⓐ N orilla *f*, ribera *f*
Ⓑ ADJ ribereño

riverbed [ˈrɪvəbed] N lecho *m* (del río)

riverine [ˈrɪvəraɪn] ADJ fluvial, ribereño

River Plate [ˌrɪvəˈpleɪt] Ⓐ N Río *m* de la Plata
Ⓑ ADJ rioplatense

riverside [ˈrɪvəsaɪd] Ⓐ N orilla *f*, ribera *f*
Ⓑ ADJ ribereño

rivet [ˈrɪvɪt] Ⓐ N remache *m*
Ⓑ VT 1 (*Tech*) remachar
2 (*fig*) (= *grasp*) [+ *attention*] captar; (= *fasten*) [+ *eyes, attention, gaze*] (*on sth/sb*) fijar; **it ~ed our attention** nos llamó fuertemente la atención, lo miramos fascinados; **to be ~ed to sth** tener los ojos puestos en algo

riveter [ˈrɪvɪtəʳ] N remachador(a) *m/f*

riveting, rivetting [ˈrɪvɪtɪŋ] Ⓐ N (*Tech*) remachado *m*
Ⓑ ADJ (= *fascinating*) fascinante, cautivador

Riviera [ˌrɪvɪˈɛərə] N (*French*) Riviera *f* (francesa), Costa *f* Azul; (*Italian*) Riviera *f* italiana

rivulet [ˈrɪvjʊlɪt] N riachuelo *m*, arroyuelo *m*

Riyadh [rɪˈyɑːd] N Riyadh *m*

RK N ABBR (*Scol*) (= **Religious Knowledge**) ed. religiosa

RL N ABBR = **Rugby League**

Rly ABBR (= **Railway**) ferrocarril, f.c., FC

RM N ABBR (*Brit Mil*) = **Royal Marines**

RMT N ABBR (*Brit*) = **National Union of Rail, Maritime and Transport Workers**

RN N ABBR 1 (*Brit Mil*) = **Royal Navy**
2 (*US*) = **registered nurse**

RNA N ABBR (= **ribonucleic acid**) ARN *m*

RNAS N ABBR (*Brit*) = **Royal Naval Air Services**

RNLI N ABBR (= **Royal National Lifeboat Institution**) *servicio de lanchas de socorro*

RNR N ABBR (*Brit Mil*) = **Royal Naval Reserve**

RNVR N ABBR = **Royal Naval Volunteer Reserve**

RNZAF N ABBR = **Royal New Zealand Air Force**

RNZN N ABBR = **Royal New Zealand Navy**

roach [rəʊtʃ] N (*pl* **roach** *or* **roaches**) 1 (= *fish*) gobio *m*
2 (*US*) (= *cockroach*) cucaracha *f*
3 (*Drugs*‡) cucaracha‡ *f*

road [rəʊd] Ⓐ N 1 (*residential: Road*) calle *f*; (= *main road*) carretera *f*; (= *route*) camino *m*; (= *surface*) firme *m*; (= *roadway, not pavement*) calzada *f*; **at the 23rd kilometre on the Valencia ~** en el kilómetro 23 de la carretera de Valencia; **"road narrows"** "estrechamiento de la calzada"; **"road up"** "cerrado por obras"; **across the ~** al otro lado de la calle; **she lives across the ~ from us** vive en frente de nosotros; **by ~** por carretera; **to hold the ~** [*car*] agarrar, tener buena adherencia; **to be off the ~** [*car*] estar fuera de circulación; **to be on the ~** (= *be travelling*) estar en camino; (*Comm*) ser viajante de comercio; (*Mus, Theat*) estar de gira; **the dog was wandering on the ~** el perro iba andando por mitad de la calzada; **he shouldn't be allowed on the ~** no deberían permitirle conducir; **my car is on the ~ again** he vuelto a poner mi coche en circulación; **to take the ~** ponerse en camino (**to X** para ir a X); **to take to the ~** [*tramp*] ponerse en camino; **the ~ to Teruel** el camino de Teruel
2 (*fig*) **somewhere along the ~** tarde o temprano; **our relationship has reached the end of the ~** nuestras relaciones han llegado al punto final; **to be on the right ~** ir por buen camino; **the ~ to success** el camino del éxito; **he's on the ~ to recovery** se está reponiendo; **we're on the ~ to disaster** vamos camino del desastre; ✦***IDIOM*** **one for the ~*** la penúltima; **to have one for the ~*** tomarse la penúltima (copa); ✦***PROV*** **the ~ to hell is paved with good intentions** con buenas intenciones no basta; *see also* **Rome**
3 (‡) (*fig*) (= *way*) **to get out of the ~** quitarse de en medio
4 **roads** (*Naut*) (= *roadstead*) rada *fsing*
Ⓑ CPD ► **road accident** N accidente *m* de tráfico, accidente *m* de circulación, accidente *m* de tránsito (*LAm*) ► **road book** N libro *m* de mapas e itinerarios ► **road bridge** N puente *m* de carretera ► **road construction** N construcción *f* de carreteras ► **road haulage** N transporte *m* por carretera ► **road haulier** N (= *company*) compañía *f* de transporte por carretera; (= *person*) transportista *mf* ► **road hump** N banda *f* sonora, banda *f* de desaceleración ► **road junction** N empalme *m* ► **road manager** N (*Mus*) encargado/a *m/f* del transporte del equipo ► **road map** N (*lit*) mapa *m* de carreteras; (*for future actions*) hoja *f* de ruta; **~ map to peace** hoja *f* de ruta para la paz ► **road metal** N grava *f*, lastre *m* ► **road movie** N película *f* de carretera, road movie *f* ► **road pricing** N (*Brit*) *sistema electrónico que permite el cobro de peaje a conductores en ciertas carreteras* ► **road race** N carrera *f* en carretera ► **road racer** N (*Cycling*) ciclista *mf* de fondo en carretera ► **road rage*** N *conducta agresiva de los conductores* ► **road repairs** NPL obras *fpl* en la vía ► **road roller** N apisonadora *f* ► **road safety** N seguridad *f* vial ► **road sense** N conocimiento *m* de la carretera ► **road sign** N señal *f* de tráfico ► **road sweeper** N (= *person*) barrendero/a *m/f*; (= *vehicle*) máquina *f* barrendera ► **road tax** N impuesto *m* de rodaje ► **road test** N prueba *f* en carretera ► **road traffic accident** N = **road accident** ► **road transport** N transportes *mpl* por carretera ► **road trial** N = **road test** ► **road user** N usuario/a *m/f* de la vía pública ► **road vehicle** N vehículo *m* de motor, vehículo *m* de carretera

roadbed [ˈrəʊdbed] N (*US*) [*of road*] firme *m*; [*of railroad*] capa *f* de balasto

roadblock [ˈrəʊdblɒk] N control *m*, barricada *f*, retén *m* (*LAm*)

roadhog [ˈrəʊdhɒg] N loco(a) *m/f* del volante

roadhouse [ˈrəʊdhaʊs] N (*pl* **roadhouses** [ˈrəʊdhaʊzɪz]) (*US*) albergue *m* de carretera, motel *m*

roadie* [ˈrəʊdɪ] N (*Mus*) *encargado del transporte y montaje del equipo de un grupo de música*

roadmaking [ˈrəʊdˌmeɪkɪŋ] N construcción *f* de carreteras

roadman [ˈrəʊdmæn] (*pl* **roadmen**) N peón *m* caminero

roadmender [ˈrəʊdmendəʳ] N = **roadman**

roadshow [ˈrəʊdʃəʊ] N (*Theat*) compañía *f* teatral en gira; (*Rad*) programa *m* itinerante

roadside [ˈrəʊdsaɪd] Ⓐ N borde *m* de la carretera, orilla *f* del camino (*LAm*)
Ⓑ CPD de carretera ► **roadside inn** N fonda *f* de carretera ► **roadside repairs** NPL reparaciones *fpl* al borde de la carretera ► **roadside restaurant** N (*US*) café-restaurante *m* (de carretera)

roadstead [ˈrəʊdsted] N (*Naut*) rada *f*

roadster [ˈrəʊdstəʳ] N (= *car*) coche *m* de turismo; (= *bicycle*) bicicleta *f* de turismo

roadway [ˈrəʊdweɪ] N calzada *f*

roadworks [ˈrəʊdwɜːks] NPL obras *fpl* (*en la calzada*)

roadworthy [ˈrəʊdˌwɜːðɪ] ADJ [*car etc*] en buen estado (para circular)

roam [rəʊm] Ⓐ VT [+ *streets etc*] rondar, vagar por Ⓑ VI [*person etc*] vagar, errar; [*thoughts*] divagar

►**roam about, roam around** VI + ADV andar sin rumbo fijo

roamer [ˈrəʊməʳ] N hombre *m* errante, andariego *m*; (= *tramp*) vagabundo *m*

roaming [ˈrəʊmɪŋ] N vagabundeo *m*; (*as tourist etc*) excursiones *fpl*, paseos *mpl*

roan [rəʊn] Ⓐ ADJ ruano
Ⓑ N caballo *m* ruano

roar [rɔːʳ] Ⓐ N 1 [*of animal*] rugido *m*, bramido *m*; [*of person*] rugido *m*; [*of crowd*] clamor *m*; [*of laughter*] carcajada *f*; **with great ~s of laughter** con grandes carcajadas; **he said with a ~** dijo rugiendo
2 (= *loud noise*) estruendo *m*, fragor *m*; [*of fire*] crepitación *f*; [*of river, storm etc*] estruendo *m*
Ⓑ VI 1 [*animal*] rugir, bramar; [*crowd, audience*] clamar; **to ~ (with laughter)** reírse a carcajadas; **this will make you ~** con esto os vais a morir de risa; **to ~ with pain** rugir de dolor
2 [*guns, thunder*] retumbar; **the lorry ~ed past** el camión pasó ruidosamente
Ⓒ VT rugir, decir a gritos; **to ~ one's disap-**

proval manifestar su disconformidad a gritos; **he ~ed out an order** lanzó una orden a voz en grito; **to ~ o.s. hoarse** ponerse ronco gritando, gritar hasta enronquecerse

roaring [ˈrɔːrɪŋ] Ⓐ ADJ **in front of a ~ fire** ante un fuego bien caliente; **it was a ~ success** fue un tremendo éxito; **to do a ~ trade** hacer muy buen negocio
Ⓑ ADV (*Brit**) **he was ~ drunk** estaba borracho y despotricaba
Ⓒ CPD ► **the Roaring Forties** NPL (*Geog*) los cuarenta rugientes

roast [rəʊst] Ⓐ N asado *m*
Ⓑ ADJ asado; [*coffee*] torrefacto, tostado; **~ beef** rosbif *m*
Ⓒ VT [1] [*+ meat*] asar; [*+ coffee*] tostar
[2] (*fig*) **the sun which was ~ing the city** el sol que achicharraba la ciudad; **to ~ one's feet by the fire** asarse los pies junto al fuego; **to ~ o.s. in the sun** tostarse al sol
[3] **to ~ sb*** (*= criticize*) criticar a algn, censurar a algn; (*= scold*) desollar vivo a algn
Ⓓ VI [*meat*] asarse; (*fig*) [*person*] tostarse; **we ~ed there for a whole month** nos asamos allí durante un mes entero

roaster [ˈrəʊstəʳ] N [1] (*= implement*) asador *m*, tostador *m*
[2] (*= bird*) pollo *m* para asar

roasting [ˈrəʊstɪŋ] Ⓐ ADJ [1] [*chicken etc*] para asar
[2] (*) (*= hot*) [*day, heat*] abrasador
Ⓑ N [1] (*Culin*) asado *m*; [*of coffee*] tostadura *f*, tueste *m*
[2] **to give sb a ~*** (*= criticize*) criticar a algn, censurar a algn; (*= scold*) desollar vivo a algn
Ⓒ CPD ► **roasting jack, roasting spit** N asador *m*

rob [rɒb] VT robar; [*+ bank etc*] atracar; **to ~ sb of sth** [*+ money etc*] robar algo a algn; (*fig*) [*+ happiness etc*] quitar algo a algn; **I've been ~bed!** ¡me han robado!; **we were ~bed!** (*Sport**) ¡nos robaron el partido!; *see also* **Peter**

robber [ˈrɒbəʳ] Ⓐ N ladrón/ona *m/f*; (*= bank-robber*) atracador(a) *m/f*; (*= highwayman*) salteador *m* (de caminos); (*= brigand*) bandido *m*
Ⓑ CPD ► **robber baron** N (*pej*) magnate *mf* desaprensivo/a

robbery [ˈrɒbərɪ] N robo *m*; **~ with violence** (*Jur*) robo *m* a mano armada, atraco *m*, asalto *m*; **it's daylight ~!*** ¡es una estafa!, ¡es un robo a mano armada!

robe [rəʊb] Ⓐ N (*= ceremonial garment*) traje *m* de ceremonia, túnica *f*; (*= bathrobe*) bata *f*; (*= christening robe*) traje *m* del bautizo; (*lawyer's, academic's etc*) toga *f*; (*monk's*) hábito *m*; (*priest's*) sotana *f*; **robes** traje *msing* de ceremonia, traje *msing* talar
Ⓑ VT **to ~ sb in black** vestir a algn de negro; **to appear ~d in a long dress** aparecer vestido de un traje largo; **to ~ o.s.** vestirse

Robert [ˈrɒbət] N Roberto

robin [ˈrɒbɪn] N (*= bird*) petirrojo *m*

robot [ˈrəʊbɒt] N robot *m*

robotic [rəʊˈbɒtɪk] ADJ [*equipment, arm etc*] robótico; (*fig*) de robot, robotizado

robotics [rəʊˈbɒtɪks] NSING robótica *f*

robust [rəʊˈbʌst] ADJ [1] (*= solid, hardy*) [*person, constitution*] robusto, fuerte; [*plant*] robusto; [*material, design, object*] resistente, sólido; [*economy*] fuerte; **the chair didn't look very ~** la silla no parecía muy sólida; **to have a ~ appetite** tener buen apetito; **to be in ~ health** tener una salud de hierro
[2] (*= vigorous*) [*defence*] enérgico, vigoroso; [*sense of humour*] saludable; **to make a ~ defence of sth** defender algo enérgicamente *or* vigorosamente
[3] (*= strong*) [*flavour, aroma, wine*] fuerte

robustly [rəʊˈbʌstlɪ] ADV [1] (*= solidly*) **to be ~ built** [*person*] ser de constitución robusta *or* fuerte; **to be ~ built** *or* **made** [*thing*] estar sólidamente construido
[2] (*= vigorously*) [*oppose, attack, defend*] enérgicamente, vigorosamente
[3] (*= strongly*) **a ~ flavoured red wine** un vino tinto con un sabor fuerte

robustness [rəʊˈbʌstnɪs] N [1] (*= strength*) [*of person, plant*] robustez *f*; [*of material, design, object*] solidez *f*
[2] (*= vigour*) [*of defence, attack*] lo enérgico, vigor *m*

rock¹ [rɒk] Ⓐ N [1] (*= substance*) roca *f*; (*= crag, rock face*) peñasco *m*, peñón *m*; (*= large stone, boulder*) roca *f*; (*US*) (*= small stone*) piedra *f*; (*in sea*) escollo *m*, roca *f*; **hewn out of solid ~** tallado en la roca viva; **they were drilling into solid ~** estaban perforando rocas vivas; **porous/volcanic ~** roca porosa/volcánica; **the Rock (of Gibraltar)** el Peñón (de Gibraltar); **an outcrop of ~** un peñasco, un peñón; **"danger: falling rocks"** "desprendimiento de rocas"
[2] (*in phrases*) **to be at ~ bottom** [*person, prices, morale, confidence*] estar por los suelos, haber tocado fondo; **prices are at ~ bottom** los precios están por los suelos *or* han tocado fondo; **morale in the armed forces was at ~ bottom** los ánimos en las fuerzas armadas habían tocado fondo *or* estaban por los suelos; **to hit** *or* **reach ~ bottom** [*person, prices*] tocar fondo; **to go on(to) the ~s = to run on(to) the rocks**; **~ hard** duro como una piedra; **it dries ~ hard in less than an hour** en menos de una hora se seca hasta quedarse duro como una piedra; **he's like a ~, I totally depend on him** es mi pilar *or* puntal, dependo totalmente de él; **whisky on the ~s** whisky con hielo; **to run on(to) the ~s** (*Naut*) chocar contra los escollos, encallar en las rocas; **~ solid** (*lit, fig*) sólido como una roca; **the pound was ~ solid against the mark** la libra permanecía sólida como una roca frente al marco; *see also* **rock-solid**; **he held the gun ~ steady** sujetó la pistola con pulso firme; ✦***IDIOMS*** **to be on the ~s*** (*= be broke*) no tener un céntimo, estar sin blanca (*Sp**); (*= fail*) [*marriage*] andar fatal*; **his business went on the ~s last year** su negocio se fue a pique *or* se hundió el año pasado; **to be between** *or* **be caught between a ~ and a hard place** estar entre la espada y la pared; *see also* **hard, solid**
[3] (*Brit*) (*= sweet*) palo *m* de caramelo; **a stick of ~** un palo de caramelo
[4] (*) (*= diamond*) diamante *m*; **rocks** piedras *fpl*, joyas *fpl*
[5] (*) (*= drug*) crack *m*
[6] (*esp US*) **rocks**‡: ✦***IDIOM*** **to get one's ~s off** echar un polvo‡
Ⓑ CPD ► **rock cake, rock bun** N *bollito con frutos secos* ► **rock candy** N (*US*) palo *m* de caramelo ► **rock carving** N escultura *f* rupestre ► **rock climber** N escalador(a) *m/f* (de rocas) ► **rock climbing** N (*Sport*) escalada *f* en rocas; **to go ~ climbing** ir a escalar en roca ► **rock crystal** N cristal *m* de roca ► **rock face** N vertiente *f* rocosa, pared *f* de roca ► **rock fall** N desprendimiento *m* de rocas ► **rock formation** N formación *f* rocosa ► **rock garden** N jardín *m* de roca *or* de rocalla ► **rock painting** N pintura *f* rupestre ► **rock plant** N planta *f* rupestre *or* de roca ► **rock pool** N charca *f* (de agua de mar) entre rocas ► **rock rose** N jara *f*, heliantemo *m* ► **rock salmon** N (*Brit*) cazón *m* ► **rock salt** N sal *f* gema *or* mineral *or* sin refinar

rock² [rɒk] Ⓐ VT [1] (*= swing to and fro*) [*+ child*] acunar; [*+ cradle*] mecer; **she ~ed the child in her arms** acunó al niño en sus brazos; **to ~ o.s. in a chair** mecerse en una silla; **to ~ a child to sleep** arrullar a un niño
[2] (*= shake*) (*lit, fig*) sacudir; **his death ~ed the fashion business** su muerte sacudió *or* convulsionó al mundo de la moda; *see also* **boat**
Ⓑ VI [1] (*gently*) mecerse, balancearse; **the ship ~ed gently on the waves** el buque se mecía *or* se balanceaba suavemente en las olas; **his body ~ed from side to side with the train** su cuerpo se mecía *or* se balanceaba de un lado a otro con el movimiento del tren; **he ~ed back on his heels** apoyando los talones, se inclinó hacia atrás
[2] (*violently*) [*ground, vehicle, building*] sacudirse; **the theatre ~ed with laughter** las risas estremecieron el teatro; **the audience ~ed with laughter** el público se rió a carcajada limpia
[3] (*= dance*) bailar rock
Ⓒ N (*Mus*) (*also* **~ music**) rock *m*, música *f* rock; **heavy/soft ~** rock *m* duro/blando
Ⓓ CPD ► **rock and roll** N rocanrol *m*, rock and roll *m*; **to do the ~ and roll** bailar el rocanrol *or* el rock and roll; *see also* **rock-and-roll** ► **rock band** N grupo *m* de rock ► **rock concert** N concierto *m* de rock ► **rock festival** N festival *m* de rock ► **rock group** N grupo *m* de rock ► **rock music** N rock *m*, música *f* rock ► **rock musical** N musical *m* de rock ► **rock musician** N músico/a *m/f* de rock ► **rock 'n' roll** N = **rock and roll** ► **rock star** N estrella *f* de rock

rock-and-roll [ˌrɒkənˈrəʊl] ADJ **a ~ band/singer** un grupo/cantante de rocanrol *or* rock and roll; *see also* **rock²**

rock-bottom [ˌrɒkˈbɒtəm] Ⓐ N fondo *m*, parte *f* más profunda
Ⓑ ADJ **~ prices** precios *mpl* mínimos, precios *mpl* tirados

rocker [ˈrɒkəʳ] N [1] [*of cradle etc*] balancín *m*; (*US*) (*= chair*) mecedora *f*, mecedor *m* (*LAm*); ✦***IDIOM*** **to be off one's ~**‡ estar majareta*
[2] (*Mus*) (*= person*) rockero/a *m/f*

rockery [ˈrɒkərɪ] N jardín *m* de roca *or* de rocalla

rocket¹ [ˈrɒkɪt] Ⓐ N [1] (*Mil*) cohete *m*; (*= space rocket*) cohete *m* espacial
[2] (*= firework*) cohete *m*
[3] (*Brit**) (*fig*) **to get a ~ from sb** recibir una peluca de algn; **to give sb a ~ (for the mistake)** echar un rapapolvo a algn (por el error)
Ⓑ VI **to ~ upwards** subir como un cohete; **to ~ to the moon** ir en cohete a la luna; **to ~ to fame** ascender vertiginosamente a la fama; **prices have ~ed** los precios han subido vertiginosamente
Ⓒ VT (*Mil*) atacar con cohetes
Ⓓ CPD ► **rocket attack** N ataque *m* con cohetes ► **rocket launcher** N lanzacohetes *m inv* ► **rocket propulsion** N propulsión *f* a cohete ► **rocket range** N base *f* de lanzamiento de cohetes ► **rocket science** N astronáutica *f* (de cohetes); **this isn't ~ science*** para esto no hay que saber latín ► **rocket scientist** N ingeniero/a *m/f* astronáutico/a; **it doesn't take a ~ scientist to ...*** no hace falta ser una lumbrera para ...

rocket² [ˈrɒkɪt] N (*Bot*) oruga *f*

rocket-propelled [ˈrɒkɪtprəˌpeld] ADJ propulsado por cohete(s)

rocketry ['rɒkɪtrɪ] N cohetería *f*

rockfish ['rɒkfɪʃ] N (*pl* **rockfish** *or* **rockfishes**) pez *m* de roca

rock-hard [ˌrɒk'hɑːd] ADJ [*ground*] duro como la roca; [*chair, bed*] duro como una piedra

Rockies ['rɒkɪz] NPL = **Rocky Mountains**; *see* **rocky**[1]

rocking ['rɒkɪŋ] Ⓐ N balanceo *m*
Ⓑ CPD ► **rocking chair** N mecedora *f*, mecedor *m* (*LAm*) ► **rocking horse** N caballito *m* de balancín

rock 'n' roll [ˌrɒkən'rəʊl] N = **rock and roll**; *see* **rock**[2]

rock-solid [ˌrɒk'sɒlɪd] ADJ sólido

rocky[1] ['rɒkɪ] Ⓐ ADJ (*compar* **rockier**; *superl* **rockiest**) [*substance*] (duro) como la piedra; [*slope etc*] rocoso
Ⓑ CPD ► **Rocky Mountains** NPL Montañas *fpl* Rocosas

rocky[2] ['rɒkɪ] ADJ (*compar* **rockier**; *superl* **rockiest**) (= *shaky, unsteady*) inestable, bamboleante; (*fig*) [*situation*] inseguro, inestable; [*government etc*] débil

rococo [rəʊ'kəʊkəʊ] Ⓐ ADJ rococó
Ⓑ N rococó *m*

Rod [rɒd] N, **Roddy** ['rɒdɪ] N (*familiar forms*) *of* **Roderick, Rodney**

rod [rɒd] N [1] [*of wood*] vara *f*; [*of metal*] barra *f*; (= *fishing rod*) caña *f*; (= *curtain rod*) barra *f*; (= *connecting rod*) biela *f*; (*Survey*) jalón *m*; ✦*IDIOMS* **to rule with a ~ of iron** gobernar con mano de hierro; **to make a ~ for one's own back** hacer algo que después resultará contraproducente; ✦*PROV* **spare the ~ and spoil the child** quien bien te quiere te hará llorar; *see also* **spare C3**
[2] (= *measure*) *medida de longitud = 5,029 metros*
[3] (*US*‡) (= *gun*) pipa‡ *f*, pistola *f*
[4] (*US Aut*‡) = **hotrod**

rode [rəʊd] PT *of* **ride**

rodent ['rəʊdənt] N roedor *m*

rodeo ['rəʊdɪəʊ] N rodeo *m*, charreada *f* (*Mex*)

Roderick ['rɒdərɪk] N Rodrigo; **~, the last of the Goths** Rodrigo el último godo

rodomontade [ˌrɒdəmɒn'teɪd] N fanfarronada *f*

roe[1] [rəʊ] N (*pl* **roe** *or* **roes**) [*of fish*] **hard ~** hueva *f*; **soft ~** lecha *f*

roe[2] [rəʊ] N (*also* **~ deer**) (*male*) corzo *m*; (*female*) corza *f*

roebuck ['rəʊbʌk] N (= *male roe deer*) corzo *m*

rogation [rəʊ'geɪʃən] (*Rel*) Ⓐ N **rogations** rogativas *fpl*
Ⓑ CPD ► **Rogation Days** NPL Rogativas *fpl* de la Ascensión ► **Rogation Sunday** N Domingo *m* de la Ascensión

Roger ['rɒdʒəʳ] N Rogelio; **~!** (*Telec etc*) ¡bien!, ¡de acuerdo!

roger‡ ['rɒdʒəʳ] VT joder**‡

rogue [rəʊg] Ⓐ N [1] (= *thief etc*) pícaro/a *m/f*, pillo/a *m/f*; (*hum*) granuja *mf*; **you ~!** ¡canalla!
[2] (*Zool*) animal *m* solitario, animal *m* apartado de la manada
Ⓑ ADJ [1] (*Zool*) [*lion, male*] solitario, apartado de la manada; **~ elephant** elefante *m* solitario (y peligroso)
[2] (*Bio, Med*) [*gene*] defectuoso
[3] (= *maverick*) [*person*] que va por libre, inconformista; [*company*] sin escrúpulos; **~ cop*** (= *criminal*) policía *mf* corrupto/a
Ⓒ CPD ► **rogue's gallery** N fichero *m* de delincuentes

roguery ['rəʊgərɪ] N picardía *f*, truhanería *f*; (= *mischief*) travesuras *fpl*, diabluras *fpl*; **they're up to some ~** están haciendo alguna diablura

roguish ['rəʊgɪʃ] ADJ [*child*] travieso; [*look, smile etc*] pícaro

roguishly ['rəʊgɪʃlɪ] ADV [*look, smile etc*] con malicia; **she looked at me ~** me miró picaruela

ROI N ABBR [1] (= **return on investments**) rendimiento *m* de las inversiones
[2] = **Republic of Ireland**

roil [rɔɪl] (*esp US*) Ⓐ VI [*water*] enturbiarse
Ⓑ VT (*fig*) agitar; **to ~ the waters** enturbiar *or* agitar las aguas

roister ['rɔɪstəʳ] VI jaranear

roisterer ['rɔɪstərəʳ] N jaranero/a *m/f*, juerguista *mf*

Roland ['rəʊlənd] N Roldán, Rolando

role [rəʊl] Ⓐ N (*Theat, fig*) papel *m*; **to cast sb in the ~ of** (*Theat, fig*) dar a algn el papel de; **to play a ~** (*Theat*) hacer un papel; (*fig*) desempeñar un papel (**in** en); **supporting ~** papel *m* secundario
Ⓑ CPD ► **role model** N modelo *m* a imitar ► **role play(ing)** N juego *m* de roles ► **role reversal** N inversión *f* de papeles

roll [rəʊl] Ⓐ N [1] [*of paper, cloth, wire, tobacco*] rollo *m*; [*of banknotes*] fajo *m*; **a ~ of film** un carrete *or* un rollo de fotos; **a ~ of wallpaper** un rollo de papel pintado; **~s of fat** (*gen*) rollos *mpl or* pliegues *mpl* de grasa; (*on stomach*) michelines *mpl* (*hum*)
[2] [*of bread*] panecillo *m*, bolillo *m* (*Mex*); **a ~ and butter** un panecillo *or* (*Mex*) bolillo con mantequilla; *see also* **sausage, Swiss**
[3] (= *list*) lista *f*; **to have 500 pupils on the ~** tener inscritos a 500 alumnos; **membership ~** ◊ **~ of members** lista *f* de miembros; **to call the ~** pasar lista; **falling ~s** *disminución en el número de alumnos inscritos*; **~ of honour** ◊ **honor ~** (*US*) lista de honor
[4] (= *sound*) [*of thunder, cannon*] retumbo *m*; [*of drum*] redoble *m*; **there was a ~ of drums** se oyó un redoble de tambores
[5] [*of gait*] contoneo *m*, bamboleo *m*; [*of ship, plane*] balanceo *m*
[6] (= *act of rolling*) revolcón *m*; **the horse was having a ~ on the grass** el caballo se estaba revolcando en la hierba; ✦*IDIOM* **a ~ in the hay*** (*euph*) un revolcón*; **to have a ~ in the hay (with sb)*** (*euph*) darse un revolcón *or* revolcarse (con algn)*
[7] [*of dice*] tirada *f*; ✦*IDIOM* **to be on a ~** estar en racha, tener una buena racha
Ⓑ VT [1] (= *send rolling*) [+ *ball*] hacer rodar; **to ~ the dice** tirar los dados
[2] (= *turn over*) **~ the meat in the breadcrumbs** rebozar la carne con el pan rallado; **I ~ed her onto her back** la puse boca arriba
[3] (= *move*) **I ~ed the trolley out of the way** empujé el carro para quitarlo del medio; **to ~ sth between one's fingers** hacer rodar algo entre los dedos; **to ~ one's eyes** poner los ojos en blanco
[4] (= *make into roll*) [+ *cigarette*] liar; **he ~ed himself in a blanket** se enrolló en una manta; **she ~ed her sweater into a pillow** hizo una bola con el jersey para usarlo como almohada; **she is trainer and manager ~ed into one** es entrenadora y representante a la vez; **it's a kitchen and dining room ~ed into one** es una cocina comedor; **to ~ one's r's** pronunciar fuertemente las erres; **to ~ one's tongue** enrollar la lengua; *see also* **ball**[1]
[5] (= *flatten*) [+ *road*] apisonar; [+ *lawn, pitch*] pasar el rodillo por, apisonar; [+ *pastry, dough*] estirar; [+ *metal*] laminar
[6] (*US*‡) (= *rob*) atracar
Ⓒ VI [1] (= *go rolling*) ir rodando; (*on ground, in pain*) revolcarse; **the ball ~ed into the net** el balón entró rodando en la red; **the children were ~ing down the slope** los niños iban rodando cuesta abajo; **it ~ed under the chair** desapareció *or* rodó debajo de la silla; **it went ~ing downhill** fue rodando cuesta abajo; **the horse ~ed in the mud** el caballo se revolcó en el barro; ✦*IDIOMS* **to be ~ing in the aisles*** estar muerto de risa; **they're ~ing in money*** ◊ **they're ~ing in it*** están forrados*; *see also* **ball**[1], **head A1**
[2] (= *move*) **the bus ~ed to a stop** el autobús se paró; **the tanks ~ed into the city** los tanques entraron en la ciudad; **the convoy ~ed slowly along the road** el convoy avanzaba lentamente por la carretera; **newspapers were ~ing off the presses** los periódicos estaban saliendo de las prensas; **tears ~ed down her cheeks** las lágrimas le corrían *or* caían por la cara; **the waves were ~ing onto the beach** las olas batían contra la playa; **his eyes ~ed wildly** los ojos se le ponían en blanco y parpadeaba descontroladamente; *see also* **tongue**
[3] (= *turn over*) [*person, animal*] **he ~ed off the sofa** se dio la vuelta y se cayó del sofá; **she ~ed onto her back** se puso boca arriba
[4] (*fig*) [*land*] ondular; **vast plains ~ed into the distance** las vastas llanuras se perdían en la distancia
[5] (= *operate*) [*camera*] rodar; [*machine*] funcionar, estar en marcha; **the presses are ~ing again** las prensas están funcionando *or* en marcha otra vez; **I couldn't think of anything to say to get the conversation ~ing** no se me ocurría nada para empezar la conversación; **his first priority is to get the economy ~ing again** su mayor prioridad es volver a sacar la economía a flote
[6] (= *sound*) [*thunder*] retumbar; [*drum*] redoblar
[7] (= *sway*) (*in walking*) contonearse, bambolearse; (*Naut*) balancearse
Ⓓ CPD ► **roll bar** N (*Aut*) barra *f* antivuelco ► **roll call** N lista *f*; **to take (a) ~ call** pasar lista

►**roll about, roll around** VI + ADV [*ball, coin*] rodar de un lado a otro; [*person, dog*] revolcarse; [*ship*] balancearse

►**roll around** VI + ADV [1] (*fig*) [*time, event*] llegar; **I was eager for five o'clock to ~ around** tenía muchas ganas de que llegaran las cinco; **by the time the next election ~s around** para cuando sean las próximas elecciones
[2] = **roll about**

►**roll away** Ⓐ VT + ADV [+ *trolley, bed*] apartar, quitar; [+ *carpet*] enrollar, quitar
Ⓑ VI + ADV [1] [*ball*] alejarse (rodando), irse (rodando); [*person*] apartarse (rodando); [*clouds, mist*] disiparse
[2] (*fig*) [*years*] esfumarse; [*landscape*] **grassland ~ing away to the horizon** praderas que se pierden en el horizonte

►**roll back** Ⓐ VT + ADV [1] [+ *carpet*] enrollar; [+ *bedcovers*] echar para atrás
[2] (*fig*) [+ *taxes*] reducir, bajar; [+ *enemy*] hacer retroceder; **the government's attempts to ~ back the welfare state** los intentos por parte del gobierno de reducir el estado del bienestar; **to ~ back the years** retroceder en el tiempo, volver atrás en el tiempo
Ⓑ VI + ADV [*clouds, mist*] disiparse; [*eyes*] ponerse en blanco

►**roll by** VI + ADV [*vehicle, clouds, time, years*] pasar

►**roll down** VT + ADV [+ *sleeve, stockings, car window, shutter*] bajar

►**roll in** Ⓐ VI + ADV [1] (*) [*money, letters*] llover, llegar a raudales; [*person*] aparecer; **offers of help continued to ~ in** seguían lloviendo ofertas de ayuda, seguían llegando ofertas de ayuda a raudales; **he ~ed in at 2a.m.** apareció a las 2 de la mañana

[2] [*waves, cloud, mist*] llegar; **the waves came ~ing in** llegaban grandes olas a la playa

Ⓑ VT + ADV [+ *trolley, barrel*] llevar (rodando)

►**roll off** VI + ADV caerse (*rodando*)

►**roll on** VI + ADV [1] (= *go by*) [*time*] pasar

[2] (= *carry on*) [*event*] continuar; **the bombardment of Iraq could ~ on indefinitely** el bombardeo de Iraq podría continuar indefinidamente

[3] (*Brit**) (= *arrive quickly*) **~ on the summer!** ¡que llegue pronto el verano!; **~ on Friday!** ¡que llegue pronto el viernes!

►**roll out** VT + ADV [1] [+ *barrel, trolley*] sacar (rodando); (*Comm*) [+ *product*] sacar *or* lanzar (al mercado)

[2] [+ *pastry*] extender con el rodillo *or* uslero (*Andes*); [+ *carpet, map*] desenrollar; [+ *metal*] laminar; **to ~ out the red carpet** sacar la alfombra roja

[3] [+ *statistics*] soltar una retahíla de

►**roll over** Ⓐ VI + ADV [*object, vehicle*] (*180°*) volcar, voltearse (*LAm*); (*360°*) (*once*) dar una vuelta de campana; (*several times*) dar vueltas de campana; [*person, animal*] darse la vuelta; **she ~ed over onto her back** se dio la vuelta poniéndose boca arriba; **the dog ~ed over with his paws in the air** el perro se dio la vuelta quedándose patas arriba; **we ~ed over and over down the slope** rodamos cuesta abajo

Ⓑ VT + ADV [1] [+ *object*] volver; [+ *body*] poner boca arriba

[2] [+ *debt*] refinanciar

►**roll past** VI + ADV [*cart, procession*] pasar

►**roll up** Ⓐ VI + ADV [1] [*vehicle*] llegar, acercarse

[2] (*) [*person*] presentarse, aparecer; **you can't ~ up half way through the rehearsal** no puedes presentarte *or* aparecer en mitad del ensayo; **~ up, ~ up!** ¡acérquense!, ¡vengan todos!

[3] **to ~ up in a ball** [*hedgehog*] hacerse un ovillo *or* una bola

Ⓑ VT + ADV [1] (= *close*) [+ *map*] enrollar; [+ *umbrella*] cerrar; [+ *car window*] subir

[2] **to ~ up one's sleeves** remangarse, arremangarse

[3] (= *wrap*) enrollar; **to ~ sth up in paper** enrollar algo en un papel, envolver algo en papel; **to ~ o.s. up in a blanket** envolverse en una manta

[4] (= *form*) **to ~ o.s. up into a ball** hacerse un ovillo

rollaway [ˈrəʊləweɪ] N (*US*) (*also* **~ bed**) cama *f* desmontable *or* abatible (sobre ruedas)

rollback [ˈrəʊlbæk] N (*US*) [1] (= *reduction*) (*in taxes, prices*) reducción *f*; [*of rights*] restricción *f*

[2] (= *reversal*) [*of decision*] revocación *f*

rolled [rəʊld] ADJ [*umbrella*] cerrado; **~ gold** oro *m* chapado; **a ~ gold bracelet** una pulsera chapada en oro; **~ oats** copos *mpl* de avena; **~ r's** (*Ling*) erres *fpl* vibrantes

roller [ˈrəʊləʳ] Ⓐ N [1] (*Agr, Tech*) rodillo *m*; (= *road-roller*) apisonadora *f*; (= *caster*) ruedecilla *f*; (*for hair*) rulo *m*

[2] (= *wave*) ola *f* grande

Ⓑ CPD ► **roller bandage** N venda *f* enrollada ► **roller blind** N (*Brit*) persiana *f* enrollable ► **roller coaster** N montaña *f* rusa ► **roller skate** N patín *m* (de ruedas) ► **roller towel** N toalla *f* de rodillo *or* sin fin; *see also* **roller-skate, roller-skating**

roller-skate [ˈrəʊlə,skeɪt] VI ir en patines de ruedas

roller-skating [ˈrəʊlə,skeɪtɪŋ] N patinaje *m* sobre ruedas

rollick [ˈrɒlɪk] VI (= *play*) jugar; (= *amuse o.s.*) divertirse

rollicking [ˈrɒlɪkɪŋ] Ⓐ ADJ alegre, divertido; **we had a ~ time** nos divertimos una barbaridad; **it was a ~ party** fue una fiesta animadísima; **it's a ~ farce** es una farsa de lo más divertido

Ⓑ N **to give sb a ~** (*Brit**) poner a algn como un trapo*

rolling [ˈrəʊlɪŋ] Ⓐ ADJ [*waves*] fuerte; [*sea*] agitado; [*ship*] que se balancea; [*countryside, hills*] ondulado; **bring the water to a ~ boil** esperar a que el agua alcance su verdadero punto de ebullición; **to walk with a ~ gait** andar bamboleándose; **a ~ programme of privatization** un programa de privatización escalonado; ✦***IDIOM*** **he's a ~ stone** es muy inquieto, es culo de mal asiento*; ✦***PROV*** **a ~ stone gathers no moss** piedra movediza nunca moho la cobija

Ⓑ ADV **he was ~ drunk*** estaba tan borracho que se caía, estaba borracho como una cuba*

Ⓒ N (*Naut*) balanceo *m*

Ⓓ CPD ► **rolling mill** N taller *m* de laminación ► **rolling pin** N rodillo *m* (de cocina), uslero *m* (*Andes*) ► **rolling stock** N material *m* rodante *or* móvil

rollmop [ˈrəʊlmɒp] N arenque *m* adobado

roll-neck [ˈrəʊlnek] N (*Brit*) jersey *m* cuello cisne

roll-on [ˈrəʊlɒn] Ⓐ N [1] (= *girdle*) faja *f* elástica, tubular *m*

[2] (= *deodorant*) = **roll-on deodorant**

Ⓑ CPD ► **roll-on deodorant** N desodorante *m* roll-on, bola *f* desodorante

roll-on-roll-off [,rəʊlɒnrəʊlˈɒf] ADJ **~ facility** facilidad *f* para la carga y descarga autopropulsada; **~ ship** ro-ro *m*

roll-top desk [ˈrəʊltɒpˈdesk] N buró *m*, escritorio *m* de tapa rodadera

roly-poly [ˈrəʊlɪˈpəʊlɪ] Ⓐ N (*Brit*) (*also* **~ pudding**) brazo *m* de gitano

Ⓑ ADJ regordete

ROM [rɒm] N ABBR (= **Read-Only Memory**) ROM *f*

romaine [rəʊˈmeɪn] N (*US, Canada*) (*also* **~ lettuce**) lechuga *f* romana, lechuga *f* cos

Roman [ˈrəʊmən] Ⓐ ADJ romano

Ⓑ N (*person*) romano/a *m/f*

Ⓒ CPD ► **Roman alphabet** N alfabeto *m* romano ► **Roman candle** N candela *f* romana ► **Roman Catholicism** N catolicismo *m* ► **Roman law** N derecho *m* romano ► **Roman nose** N nariz *f* aguileña ► **Roman numeral** N número *m* romano

roman [ˈrəʊmən] N (*Typ*) tipo *m* romano

Roman Catholic [,rəʊmənˈkæθəlɪk] Ⓐ ADJ católico (apostólico y romano)

Ⓑ N católico/a *m/f* (apostólico/a y romano/a)

romance [rəʊˈmæns] Ⓐ N [1] (= *love affair*) romance *m*, idilio *m*, amores *mpl*; **their ~ lasted exactly six months** su romance *or* idilio duró exactamente seis meses, sus amores duraron exactamente seis meses; **a young girl waiting for ~** una joven que espera su primer amor; **I've finished with ~** para mí no más amores

[2] (= *romantic character*) lo romántico, lo poético; (= *picturesqueness*) lo pintoresco; **the ~ of travel** lo romántico del viajar; **the ~ of history** lo atractivo *or* lo poético de la historia; **the ~ of the sea** el encanto del mar

[3] (= *tale*) novela *f* (sentimental), cuento *m* (de amor); (*medieval*) libro *m* de caballerías, poema *m* caballeresco; (*Mus*) romanza *f*

[4] (*Ling*) **Romance** romance *m*

Ⓑ ADJ [*language*] romance

Ⓒ VI soñar, fantasear

Romanesque [,rəʊməˈnesk] ADJ (*Archit*) románico

Romania [rəʊˈmeɪnɪə] N Rumania *f*, Rumanía *f*

Romanian [rəʊˈmeɪnɪən] Ⓐ ADJ rumano

Ⓑ N [1] (= *person*) rumano/a *m/f*

[2] (*Ling*) rumano *m*

Romanic [rəʊˈmænɪk] ADJ = **Romanesque**

romanize [ˈrəʊmənaɪz] VT romanizar

Romansch [rəʊˈmænʃ] Ⓐ ADJ rético

Ⓑ N [1] rético/a *m/f*

[2] (*Ling*) rético *m*

romantic [rəʊˈmæntɪk] Ⓐ ADJ romántico

Ⓑ N romántico/a *m/f*

romantically [rəʊˈmæntɪkəlɪ] ADV románticamente, de modo romántico

romanticism [rəʊˈmæntɪsɪzəm] N romanticismo *m*

romanticist [rəʊˈmæntɪsɪst] N **he's a bit of a ~** es un romántico

romanticize [rəʊˈmæntɪsaɪz] Ⓐ VT sentimentalizar

Ⓑ VI fantasear

Romany [ˈrɒmənɪ] Ⓐ ADJ gitano

Ⓑ N [1] gitano/a *m/f*

[2] (*Ling*) romaní *m*, lengua *f* gitana; (*in Spain*) caló *m*

Rome [rəʊm] N [1] Roma *f*; ✦***PROVS*** **all roads lead to ~** todos los caminos llevan a Roma; **~ was not built in a day** no se ganó Zamora en una hora; **when in ~ (do as the Romans do)** donde fueres, haz lo que vieres

[2] (*Rel*) la Iglesia, el catolicismo; **Manning turned to ~** Manning se convirtió al catolicismo

Romeo [ˈrəʊmɪəʊ] N Romeo

Romish [ˈrəʊmɪʃ] ADJ (*pej*) católico

romp [rɒmp] Ⓐ N retozo *m*; **to have a ~** retozar; **the play was just a ~** la obra era una farsa alegre nada más; ✦***IDIOM*** **to have a ~ in the hay*** darse un revolcón en el pajar *or* en la hierba*

Ⓑ VI retozar; [*lambs etc*] brincar, correr alegremente; **she ~ed through the examination** no tuvo problema alguno para aprobar el examen; **to ~ home** (= *win easily*) ganar fácilmente

rompers [ˈrɒmpəz] NPL mono *msing*, pelele *msing*

Romulus [ˈrɒmjʊləs] N Rómulo

rondeau [ˈrɒndəʊ] N (*pl* **rondeaux** [ˈrɒndəʊz]) (*Literat*) rondó *m*

rondo [ˈrɒndəʊ] N (*Mus*) rondó *m*

Roneo® [ˈrəʊnɪəʊ] VT reproducir con multicopista

rood [ru:d] N cruz *f*, crucifijo *m*

roodscreen [ˈru:dskri:n] N reja *f* entre la nave y el coro

roof [ru:f] Ⓐ N (*pl* **roofs**) [*of building*] tejado *m* (*esp Sp*), techo *m* (*esp LAm*); [*of car etc*] techo *m*; **flat ~** azotea *f*; **to have a ~ over one's head** tener dónde cobijarse; **the ~ of heaven** la bóveda celeste; **the ~ of the mouth** el paladar; **to live under the same ~** vivir bajo el mismo techo; **prices are going through the ~** los precios están por las nubes; ✦***IDIOMS*** **he**

hit the ~* se subió por las paredes*; **to lift the ~** (*Brit*) ◊ **raise the ~** (= *protest*) poner el grito en el cielo; **when the staff arrived the infant was still raising the ~** cuando el personal llegó, el niño todavía estaba llorando a grito pelado; **the cheers and roars of approval lifted the pavilion ~** el pabellón se vino abajo con los vivas y los gritos de aprobación
Ⓑ VT (*also* **~ in, ~ over**) techar, poner techo a; **it is ~ed in wood** tiene techo de madera; **to ~ a hut in** *or* **with wood** poner techo de madera a una caseta
Ⓒ CPD ► **roof garden** N azotea *f* con flores y plantas ► **roof rack** N (*esp Brit Aut*) baca *f*, portamaletas *m inv*, portaequipajes *m inv*, parrilla *f* (*LAm*)

roofing ['ru:fɪŋ] Ⓐ N (= *roof*) techumbre *f*; (= *roofing material*) material *m* para techado
Ⓑ CPD ► **roofing felt** N fieltro *m* para techar

roofless ['ru:flɪs] ADJ sin techo

rooftop ['ru:ftɒp] Ⓐ N techo *m*; (*with flat roof*) azotea *f*; ✦**IDIOM we will proclaim it from the ~s** lo proclamaremos a los cuatro vientos
Ⓑ CPD ► **rooftop restaurant** N restaurante *m* de azotea

rook[1] [rʊk] Ⓐ N (*Orn*) grajo *m*
Ⓑ VT (= *swindle*) estafar, timar; **you've been ~ed** te han estafado *or* timado

rook[2] [rʊk] N (*Chess*) torre *f*

rookery ['rʊkərɪ] N colonia *f* de grajos

rookie ['rʊkɪ] (*US*) N [1] (*Mil**) novato/a *m/f*, bisoño/a *m/f*
[2] (*Sport*) debutante *mf* (*en la temporada*)

▼**room** [rʊm] Ⓐ N [1] (*in house, hotel*) habitación *f*, cuarto *m*, pieza *f* (*esp LAm*), recámara *f* (*Mex*), ambiente *m* (*Arg*); (*large, public*) sala *f*; **in ~ 504** (*hotel*) en la habitación número 504; **double ~** habitación *f etc* doble; **furnished ~** cuarto *m* amueblado; **ladies' ~** servicios *mpl* de señoras; **this is my ~** ésta es mi habitación; **single ~** habitación *f* individual
[2] **rooms** (= *lodging*) alojamiento *msing*; **they've always lived in ~s** siempre han vivido de alquiler; **he has ~s in college** tiene un cuarto en el colegio
[3] (= *space*) sitio *m*, espacio *m*, campo *m* (*Andes*); **is there ~?** ¿hay sitio?; **there's plenty of ~** hay sitio de sobra; **is there ~ for this?** ¿cabe esto?, ¿hay cabida para esto?; **is there ~ for me?** ¿quepo yo?, ¿hay sitio para mí?; **to make ~ for sb** hacer sitio a algn; **make ~!** ¡abran paso!; **there's no ~ for anything else** no cabe más; **standing ~ only!** no queda asiento
[4] (*fig*) **there is no ~ for doubt** no hay lugar a dudas; **to leave ~ for imponderables** dar cabida a un margen de imponderables; **there is ~ for improvement** esto se puede mejorar todavía
Ⓑ VI (*US*) **to ~ with three other students** estar en una pensión con otros tres estudiantes, compartir un piso *or* (*LAm*) un departamento con otros tres estudiantes; **to ~ with a landlady** alojarse en casa de una señora
Ⓒ CPD ► **room clerk** N (*US*) recepcionista *mf* (de hotel) ► **room divider** N (= *screen*) biombo *m*; (= *wall*) tabique *m* ► **room service** N (*in hotel*) servicio *m* de habitaciones ► **room temperature** N temperatura *f* ambiente

-roomed [rʊmd] ADJ (*ending in compounds*) de ... piezas; **seven-roomed** de siete piezas

roomer ['rʊməʳ] N (*US*) inquilino/a *m/f*

roomette [ru:'met] N (*US*) departamento *m* de coche-cama

roomful ['rʊmfʊl] N **a ~ of priests** un cuarto lleno de curas; **they have Picassos by the ~** tienen salas enteras llenas de cuadros de Picasso

roominess ['rʊmɪnɪs] N espaciosidad *f*, amplitud *f*; [*of garment*] holgura *f*

rooming house ['rʊmɪŋhaʊs] N (*pl* **rooming houses** ['rʊmɪŋ,haʊzɪz]) (*US*) pensión *f*

roommate ['rʊmmeɪt] N compañero/a *m/f* de cuarto

roomy ['rʊmɪ] ADJ (*compar* **roomier**; *superl* **roomiest**) (*flat, cupboard etc*) amplio, espacioso; (*garment*) holgado

roost [ru:st] Ⓐ N (*gen*) percha *f*; (= *hen roost*) gallinero *m*; ✦**IDIOM to rule the ~** llevar la batuta
Ⓑ VI [1] (*lit*) dormir posado
[2] (*fig*) **now his policies have come home to ~** ahora su política produce su fruto amargo, ahora se están viendo los malos resultados de su política; **these measures only camouflaged the real problem, now the chickens are coming home to ~** estas medidas no eran más que una manera de camuflar el problema y ahora se vuelven contra nosotros, estas medidas sólo camuflaban el problema y ahora se ve que fueron pan para hoy y hambre para mañana

rooster ['ru:stəʳ] N (*esp US*) gallo *m*

root [ru:t] Ⓐ N [1] (*Bot*) raíz *f*; **the plant's ~ system** las raíces de la planta; **to pull sth up by the ~s** arrancar algo de raíz; **to take ~** echar raíces, arraigar; ✦**IDIOM ~ and branch** completamente, del todo; **they aimed to eliminate Marxism ~ and branch** su objetivo era erradicar el marxismo, su objetivo era acabar con el marxismo de raíz; **a ~ and branch overhaul of the benefits system** una revisión completa *or* de cabo a rabo del sistema de prestaciones
[2] (*Bio*) [*of hair, tooth*] raíz *f*
[3] (= *origin*) [*of problem, word*] raíz *f*; **the ~ of the problem is that ...** la raíz del problema es que ...; **her ~s are in Manchester** tiene sus raíces en Manchester; **she has no ~s** no tiene raíces; **to pull up one's ~s** levantar raíces; **to put down ~s in a country** echar raíces en un país; **to take ~** [*idea*] arraigarse; *see also* **money**
[4] (*Math*) **square ~** raíz *f* cuadrada
[5] (*Ling*) raíz *f*, radical *m*
Ⓑ VT [1] (*Bot*) [+ *plant*] hacer arraigar
[2] (*fig*) **to be ~ed to the spot** quedar paralizado; **a deeply ~ed prejudice** un prejuicio muy arraigado
Ⓒ VI [1] (*Bot*) [*plant*] echar raíces, arraigar
[2] (= *search*) [*animal*] hozar, hocicar; **I was ~ing through some old photos the other day** el otro día estaba husmeando entre viejas fotos
Ⓓ CPD ► **root beer** N (*US*) *bebida refrescante elaborada a base de raíces* ► **root cause** N causa *f* primordial ► **root crops** NPL cultivos *mpl* de tubérculos ► **root ginger** N raíz *f* de jengibre ► **root vegetable** N tubérculo *m* comestible ► **root word** N (*Ling*) palabra *f* que es raíz *or* radical de otras

►**root about, root around** VI + ADV [*pig*] hozar, hocicar; [*person*] (= *search*) andar buscando por todas partes; (= *investigate*) investigar; **to ~ around for sth** andar buscando algo

►**root for*** VI + PREP [+ *team*] animar (*con gritos y pancartas*); [+ *cause*] hacer propaganda por, apoyar a

►**root out** VT + ADV [+ *plant*] arrancar (de raíz), desarraigar; (= *find*) desenterrar, encontrar; (= *do away with*) acabar con, arrancar de raíz, extirpar

►**root through** VI + PREP [1] [*pig*] hocicar
[2] (*fig*) examinar, explorar

►**root up** VT + ADV [+ *plant, tree*] arrancar (de raíz), desarraigar

rootless ['ru:tlɪs] ADJ [*person etc*] desarraigado

rootstock ['ru:tstɒk] N rizoma *m*

rope [rəʊp] Ⓐ N cuerda *f*, soga *f*, mecate *m* (*Mex*); (*Naut*) (= *hawser*) maroma *f*, cable *m*; (*in rigging*) cabo *m*; (*hangman's*) dogal *m*; [*of pearls*] collar *m*; [*of onions etc*] ristra *f*; **the ~s** (*Boxing*) las cuerdas; **to jump** *or* **skip ~** (*US*) saltar a la comba; **there were three of us on the ~** (*Mountaineering*) éramos tres los encordados; ✦**IDIOMS to give sb more ~** dar a algn mayor libertad de acción; **if you give him enough ~ he'll hang himself** déjale actuar y él se condenará a sí mismo; **to know/learn the ~s** estar/ponerse al tanto; **to be on the ~s** estar en las cuerdas; **I'll show you the ~s** te voy a mostrar cómo funciona todo; **to be at the end of one's ~** (*esp US*) no poder soportarlo más, no aguantar más
Ⓑ VT atar *or* (*LAm*) amarrar con (una) cuerda; (*US*) [+ *animal*] coger *or* (*LAm*) agarrar con lazo; **to ~ two things together** atar dos cosas con una cuerda; **they ~d themselves together** (*Mountaineering*) se encordaron; **there were four climbers ~d together** había cuatro escaladores que formaban una cordada *or* iban encordados
Ⓒ CPD ► **rope burn** N quemadura *f* por fricción ► **rope ladder** N escala *f* de cuerda ► **rope trick** N truco *m* de la cuerda

►**rope in*** VT + ADV **they managed to ~ in their friends** consiguieron arrastrar a sus amigos; **to ~ sb in (to do sth)** enganchar a algn (para que haga algo)

►**rope off** VT + ADV acordonar; **to ~ off an area** acordonar un espacio, cercar un espacio con cuerdas

►**rope up** VI + ADV [*climbers*] encordarse, formar una cordada

ropemaker ['rəʊp,meɪkəʳ] N cordelero/a *m/f*

ropewalker ['rəʊp,wɔ:kəʳ] N funámbulo/a *m/f*, volatinero/a *m/f*

ropy*, **ropey*** ['rəʊpɪ] (*Brit*) ADJ (*compar* **ropier**; *superl* **ropiest**) (= *off colour*) pachucho*, chungo*; (= *weak*) [*plan, argument etc*] nada convincente, flojo; (= *sinewy*) [*muscles, arms*] fibroso; **I feel a bit ropey** me siento un poco chungo*, no me siento del todo bien; **this car looks a bit ropey** este coche parece una auténtica tartana*

RORO, RO/RO ['rəʊrəʊ] ABBR = **roll-on-roll-off**

rosary ['rəʊzərɪ] N (*Rel*) rosario *m*; **to say the/one's ~** rezar el rosario

rose[1] [rəʊz] Ⓐ N [1] (*Bot*) (= *flower*) rosa *f*; (= *bush, tree*) rosal *m*; **the Wars of the Roses** (*Brit Hist*) la Guerra de las Dos Rosas; **wild ~** rosal silvestre; ✦**IDIOMS all ~s***: **it's all ~s among them by the end of the film** al final de la película todo es maravilloso entre ellos; **life isn't all ~s** la vida no es un lecho de rosas; **to come up ~s** salir a pedir de boca; **the fresh air will soon put the ~s back in your cheeks** el aire fresco te devolverá rápidamente el color a las mejillas; **an English ~** una belleza típicamente inglesa; **an English ~ complexion** un cutis de porcelana; ✦**PROV there's no ~ without a thorn** no hay rosa sin espina; *see also* **bed, Christmas, damask, tea**
[2] (= *colour*) rosa *m*
[3] (*on shower*) alcachofa *f*; (*on watering can*) alcachofa *f*, roseta *f*
[4] (*Archit*) (*also* **ceiling ~**) roseta *f*, rosetón *m*
Ⓑ ADJ (= *rose-coloured*) (de color de) rosa *inv*,

➤ LANGUAGE IN USE: room A1 21.4

rosado; **~ pink** rosado, rosa; **~ red** rojo de rosa
Ⓒ CPD ► **rose bush** N rosal *m* ► **rose garden** N rosaleda *f* ► **rose grower** N cultivador(a) *m/f* de rosas ► **rose petal** N pétalo *m* de rosa ► **rose quartz** N cuarzo *m* rosa ► **rose tree** N rosal *m* ► **rose window** N (*Archit*) rosetón *m*

rose² [rəʊz] PT of **rise**

Rose [rəʊz] N Rosa

rosé ['rəʊzeɪ] Ⓐ ADJ rosado
Ⓑ N rosado *m*

roseate ['rəʊzɪɪt] ADJ róseo, rosado

rosebay ['rəʊzbeɪ] N adelfa *f*

rosebed ['rəʊzbed] N rosaleda *f*

rosebowl ['rəʊzbəʊl] N jarrón *m* or florero *m* para rosas

rosebud ['rəʊzbʌd] N capullo *m* or botón *m* de rosa

rose-coloured, **rose-colored** (*US*) ['rəʊz,kʌləd] ADJ color de rosa; ✦**IDIOM** **to see everything through ~ spectacles** verlo todo color de rosa

rosehip ['rəʊzhɪp] Ⓐ N escaramujo *m*
Ⓑ CPD ► **rosehip syrup** N jarabe *m* de escaramujo

rosemary ['rəʊzmərɪ] N (= *herb*) romero *m*

rose-pink [,rəʊz'pɪŋk] ADJ rosado, rosa

rose-red [,rəʊz'red] ADJ color rojo de rosa

rosette [rəʊ'zet] N (*Archit*) rosetón *m*; (= *emblem*) escarapela *f*; (= *prize*) premio *m*

rosewater ['rəʊz,wɔːtəʳ] N agua *f* de rosas

rosewood ['rəʊzwʊd] N palo *m* de rosa, palisandro *m*

Rosicrucian [,rəʊzɪ'kruːʃən] Ⓐ N rosacruz *mf*
Ⓑ ADJ rosacruz

rosin ['rɒzɪn] N colofonia *f*

ROSPA ['rɒspə] N ABBR = **Royal Society for the Prevention of Accidents**

roster ['rɒstəʳ] Ⓐ N lista *f*; **duty ~** lista *f* de turnos
Ⓑ VT distribuir tareas entre; **to be ~ed for sth/to do sth** tener asignado algo/hacer algo

rostrum ['rɒstrəm] N (*pl* **rostrums** or **rostra** ['rɒstrə]) Ⓐ N tribuna *f*
Ⓑ CPD ► **rostrum cameraman** N (*TV*) cámara-truca *m*

rosy ['rəʊzɪ] ADJ (*compar* **rosier**; *superl* **rosiest**)
1 [*cheeks*] sonrosado; [*colour*] rosáceo
2 (*fig*) [*future, prospect*] prometedor, halagüeño

rot [rɒt] Ⓐ N 1 (= *process*) putrefacción *f*; (= *substance*) podredumbre *f*; ✦**IDIOMS** **the ~ set in** la decadencia comenzó, todo empezó a decaer; **to stop the ~** cortar el problema de raíz, cortar por lo sano
2 (*esp Brit**) (= *nonsense*) tonterías *fpl*, babosadas *fpl* (*LAm*); **oh ~!** ◊ **what ~!** ¡qué tonterías!; **don't talk ~!** ¡no digas bobadas!
Ⓑ VT pudrir, descomponer
Ⓒ VI pudrirse, descomponerse; **to ~ in jail** pudrirse en la cárcel; **you can ~ for all I care!** ¡que te pudras!

►**rot away** VI + ADV pudrirse, descomponerse; **it had ~ted away with the passage of time** con el tiempo se había pudrido or descompuesto; **it had quite ~ted away** se había pudrido or descompuesto del todo

rota ['rəʊtə] N (*esp Brit*) lista *f* (de tareas)

Rotarian [rəʊ'teərɪən] Ⓐ ADJ rotario
Ⓑ N rotario/a *m/f*

rotary ['rəʊtərɪ] Ⓐ ADJ [*movement*] giratorio; [*blade*] rotativo, giratorio
Ⓑ CPD ► **Rotary Club** N Sociedad *f* Rotaria ► **rotary press** N prensa *f* rotativa

rotate [rəʊ'teɪt] Ⓐ VT hacer girar, dar vueltas a; [+ *crops*] alternar, cultivar en rotación; [+ *staff*] alternar; (*Comput*) [+ *graphics*] rotar, girar; **to ~ A and B** alternar A con B
Ⓑ VI girar, dar vueltas; [*staff*] alternarse

rotating [rəʊ'teɪtɪŋ] ADJ [*blade*] rotativo, giratorio; [*presidency*] rotatorio

rotation [rəʊ'teɪʃən] N rotación *f*; **~ of crops** rotación de cultivos; **in ~** por turnos; **orders are dealt with in strict ~** los pedidos se sirven por riguroso orden

rotational [rəʊ'teɪʃənəl] ADJ rotacional

rotatory [rəʊ'teɪtərɪ] ADJ rotativo

rotavate ['rəʊtəveɪt] VT trabajar con motocultor

Rotavator® ['rəʊtəveɪtəʳ] N (*Brit*) motocultor *m*

rote [rəʊt] Ⓐ N **by ~** de memoria; **to learn sth by ~** aprender algo a fuerza de repetirlo
Ⓑ CPD ► **rote learning** N **~ learning was the fashion** era costumbre aprender las cosas a fuerza de repetirlas

rotgut⁑ ['rɒtgʌt] N (*pej*) matarratas *m inv*

rotisserie [rəʊ'tɪsərɪ] N rotisserie *f*

rotor ['rəʊtəʳ] Ⓐ N rotor *m*
Ⓑ CPD ► **rotor arm** N (*Aut*) rotor *m* ► **rotor blade** N paleta *f* de rotor

Rototiller® ['rəʊtəʊtɪləʳ] N (*US*) motocultor *m*

Rotovator® ['rəʊtəveɪtəʳ] N (*Brit*) motocultor *m*

rotproof ['rɒtpruːf] ADJ a prueba de putrefacción, imputrescible

rotten ['rɒtn] Ⓐ ADJ 1 (*gen*) podrido; [*food*] pasado; [*tooth*] cariado, podrido; [*wood*] carcomido, podrido; **to smell ~** oler a podrido; *see also* **apple**
2 (*fig*) [*system, government*] corrompido; (*) (= *of bad quality*) pésimo, fatal*; **it's a ~ novel** es una novela pésima or malísima; **his English is ~** tiene un inglés fatal*; **how ~ for you!** ¡cuánto te compadezco!, ¡lo que habrás sufrido!; **he's ~ at chess** para el ajedrez es un desastre; **I feel ~** (= *ill*) me encuentro fatal*; (= *mean*) me siento culpable; **they made me suffer something ~*** me hicieron pasarlas negras; **what a ~ thing to do!** ¡qué maldad!; **what a ~ thing to happen!** ¡qué mala suerte!; **to be ~ to sb*** portarse como un canalla con algn; **what ~ weather!** ¡qué tiempo de perros!; **he's ~ with money** está podrido de dinero*
Ⓑ ADV (⁑) malísimamente, fatal*; **they played real ~** jugaron fatal*

rottenly* ['rɒtnlɪ] ADV **to behave ~ to sb** portarse como un canalla con algn

rottenness ['rɒtnnɪs] N podredumbre *f*; (*fig*) corrupción *f*

rotter†* ['rɒtəʳ] N (*Brit*) caradura* *mf*, sinvergüenza *mf*; **you ~!** ¡canalla!

rotting ['rɒtɪŋ] ADJ podrido, que se está pudriendo

rotund [rəʊ'tʌnd] ADJ [*person*] corpulento, rotundo

rotunda [rəʊ'tʌndə] N rotonda *f*

rotundity [rəʊ'tʌndɪtɪ] N corpulencia *f*

rouble, **ruble** (*US*) ['ruːbl] N rublo *m*

roué ['ruːeɪ] N libertino *m*

Rouen ['ruːɑ̃ːŋ] N Ruán *m*

rouge [ruːʒ] Ⓐ N colorete *m*, carmín *m*
Ⓑ VT **to ~ one's cheeks** ponerse colorete

rough [rʌf] Ⓐ ADJ (*compar* **rougher**; *superl* **roughest**) 1 (= *coarse*) [*surface, texture*] áspero, rugoso; [*skin*] áspero; [*cloth*] basto; [*hand*] calloso; ✦**IDIOM** **to give sb the ~ edge** or **side of one's tongue*** echar una buena bronca a algn
2 (= *uneven*) [*terrain*] accidentado, escabroso; [*road*] desigual, lleno de baches; [*track, ground*] desigual; [*edge*] irregular; **he'll be a good salesman once we knock off the ~ edges** será un buen vendedor una vez que lo hayamos pulido un poco
3 (= *harsh, unpleasant*) [*voice, sound*] ronco; [*wine*] áspero; [*life*] difícil, duro; [*climate, winter*] duro, severo
4 (= *not gentle*) [*behaviour, person, voice, manner*] brusco; [*words, tone*] severo, áspero; [*play, sport, game*] violento; [*neighbourhood, area*] malo, peligroso; **you're too ~** eres demasiado bruto; **he's a ~ customer** es un tipo peligroso; **to get ~** [*person*] ponerse bruto; [*game*] volverse violento; **children's toys must be able to withstand a lot of ~ handling** los juguetes de niños tienen que ser resistentes porque con frecuencia los tratan sin ningún cuidado; **he got ~ justice** recibió un castigo duro pero apropiado; **~ stuff*** violencia *f*; **there were complaints of ~ treatment at the hands of the police** hubo quejas de malos tratos a manos de la policía; **he came in for some ~ treatment in the press** fue objeto de duras críticas por parte de la prensa; **to be ~ with sb** ser brusco con algn; **to be ~ with sth** ser brusco con algo
5 (= *stormy*) [*sea*] agitado, encrespado; [*wind*] violento; [*weather*] tormentoso, tempestuoso; **we had a ~ crossing** el barco se movió mucho durante la travesía; **to get ~** [*sea*] embravecerse
6 (= *unpolished, crude*) [*person*] tosco, rudo; [*manners, speech*] tosco; [*shelter, table, tunic*] tosco, basto; [*gemstone*] en bruto; ✦**IDIOM** **he's a ~ diamond** es un diamante en bruto
7 (*) (= *hard, tough*) duro; **things are ~ now, but they will get better** las cosas están un poco difíciles ahora pero mejorarán; **to be ~ on sb** [*situation*] ser duro para algn; [*person*] ser duro con algn; **parents' divorce can be really ~ on children** el divorcio de los padres puede ser muy duro para los niños; **don't be so ~ on him, it's not his fault** no seas tan duro con él, no es culpa suya; **it's a bit ~ on him to have to do all the housework** no es muy justo que él tenga que hacer todo el trabajo de la casa; **to give sb a ~ ride** or **a ~ time** hacérselo pasar mal a algn; **to have a ~ time (of it)** pasarlo mal; ✦**IDIOM** **when the going gets ~** cuando las cosas se ponen feas
8 (*Brit**) (= *ill*) **"how are you?" — "a bit ~"** —¿cómo estás? —no muy bien; **to feel ~** encontrarse mal; **to look ~** tener muy mal aspecto or muy mala cara
9 (= *approximate*) [*calculation, estimate, description, outline*] aproximado; [*translation*] hecho a grandes rasgos, aproximado; **I would say 50 at a ~ guess** diría que 50 aproximadamente; **as a ~ guide, it should take about ten minutes** llevará unos diez minutos más o menos, llevará aproximadamente diez minutos; **can you give me a ~ idea of how long it will take?** ¿puedes darme una idea aproximada or más o menos una idea de cuánto tiempo llevará?
10 (= *preparatory*) [*work*] de preparación, preliminar; **~ book** cuaderno *m* de borrador; **~ copy** ◊ **~ draft** borrador *m*; **~ paper** papel *m* de borrador; **~ plan** ◊ **~ sketch** bosquejo *m*, boceto *m*
Ⓑ ADV **to live ~** vivir sin las comodidades más básicas; **to play ~** jugar duro; **to sleep ~** dormir a la intemperie; ✦**IDIOM** **to cut up ~***: **she cut up ~ when she discovered what had been going on** se puso hecha una furia cuando descubrió lo que había estado pasando

Ⓒ N [1] (= *person*) matón *m*, tipo *m* duro
[2] (= *draft*) borrador *m*; **we'll do it in ~ first** lo haremos primero en borrador
[3] ✦*IDIOM* **to take the ~ with the smooth** tomar las duras con las maduras
[4] (*Golf*) rough *m*, zona *f* de matojos
Ⓓ VT **to ~ it** vivir sin comodidades
Ⓔ CPD ► **rough puff pastry** N hojaldre *m*

►**rough in** VT + ADV [+ *shape, figure, outline*] esbozar, bosquejar

►**rough out** VT + ADV [+ *plan*] esbozar, bosquejar

►**rough up** VT + ADV [1] [+ *hair*] despeinar
[2] (*) **to ~ sb up** dar una paliza a algn

roughage ['rʌfɪdʒ] N (*for animals*) forraje *m*; (*for people*) alimentos *mpl* ricos en fibra

rough-and-ready ['rʌfən'redɪ] ADJ [*person*] tosco, burdo, basto; [*structure*] tosco, basto; [*accommodation*] humilde, sencillo; [*method*] improvisado

rough-and-tumble ['rʌfən'tʌmbl] N **the ~ play of young boys** las peleíllas *or* riñas de los chavales; **the ~ of life** los vaivenes de la vida; **the ~ of politics** los avatares *or* los altibajos de la política

roughcast ['rʌfkɑːst] N mezcla *f* gruesa

roughen ['rʌfn] Ⓐ VT [+ *skin*] poner áspero, dejar áspero; [+ *surface*] raspar; (*Carpentry*) desbastar
Ⓑ VI [*skin*] ponerse áspero; [*sea*] embravecerse; [*voice*] volverse ronco, enronquecer

rough-hewn ['rʌf'hjuːn] ADJ toscamente labrado; (*fig*) tosco, inculto

roughhouse* ['rʌfhaʊs] N (*pl* **roughhouses** ['rʌfhaʊzɪz]) trifulca* *f*, riña *f* general, reyerta *f*

roughly ['rʌflɪ] ADV [1] (= *approximately*) [*equal*] aproximadamente, más o menos; **he was ~ the same age/height as me** tenía aproximadamente *or* más o menos la misma edad/altura que yo; **~ similar** más o menos parecido; **~ translated** traducido a grandes rasgos *or* de forma aproximada
[2] (= *generally*) [*describe, outline*] en líneas generales, más o menos; **they fall ~ into two categories** en términos generales se dividen en dos categorías; **~ speaking, it means an increase of 10%** en líneas generales, supone un incremento del 10%; **~ speaking, it acts as a transformer** viene a actuar más o menos como un transformador; **~ speaking, his job is that of an administrator** su trabajo es, por así decirlo, de administrador
[3] (= *not gently*) [*push*] bruscamente; [*play*] de forma violenta; [*speak, order*] con brusquedad; **to treat sth/sb ~** tratar mal algo/tratar a algn con brusquedad
[4] (= *crudely*) [*constructed, built, carved*] toscamente; **to sketch sth ~** hacer un bosquejo de algo
[5] (*Culin*) [*chop*] en trozos grandes; [*slice*] en rodajas grandes

roughneck* ['rʌfnek] N (*US*) duro *m*, matón *m*

roughness ['rʌfnɪs] N [*of hands, surface*] aspereza *f*; [*of sea*] agitación *f*, encrespamiento *m*; [*of road*] desigualdad *f*; [*of person*] (= *brusqueness*) brusquedad *f*; (= *crudeness*) tosquedad *f*; (= *violence*) violencia *f*

roughrider ['rʌf,raɪdəʳ] N domador(a) *m/f* de caballos

roughshod ['rʌfʃɒd] ADV **to ride ~ over sth/sb** pisotear algo/a algn; **he thinks he can ride ~ over the wishes of the majority** se cree que puede saltarse a la torera *or* pisotear la voluntad de la mayoría

rough-spoken ['rʌf'spəʊkən] ADJ malhablado

roulette [ruː'let] N ruleta *f*

Roumania *etc* [ruː'meɪnɪə] = **Romania** *etc*

round [raʊnd]

> *When* **round** *is an element in a phrasal verb, eg* **ask round, call round, rally round**, *look up the verb.*

Ⓐ ADJ (*compar* **rounder**; *superl* **roundest**) (*gen*) redondo; [*sum, number*] redondo; **a ~ dozen** una docena redonda; **in ~ figures** *or* **numbers** en números redondos
Ⓑ ADV **the park is eight miles ~** el parque tiene un perímetro de ocho millas; **there is a fence all ~** está rodeado por un cercado; **it would be better all ~ if we didn't go** (*in every respect*) sería mejor en todos los sentidos que no fuéramos; (*for all concerned*) sería mejor para todos que no fuéramos; **all year ~** (durante) todo el año; **drinks all ~!** ¡pago la ronda para todos!; **we shook hands all ~** todos nos dimos la mano; **to ask sb ~** invitar a algn a casa *or* a pasar (por casa); **we were ~ at my sister's** estábamos en casa de mi hermana; **we'll be ~ at the pub** estaremos en el bar; **the wheels go ~** las ruedas giran *or* dan vuelta; **it flew round and round** voló dando vueltas; **the long way ~** el camino más largo; **it's a long way ~** es mucho rodeo; **the other/wrong way ~** al revés
Ⓒ PREP [1] (*of place etc*) alrededor de; **we were sitting ~ the table/fire** estábamos sentados alrededor de la mesa/en torno a la chimenea; **the wall ~ the garden** el muro que rodea el jardín; **a walk ~ the town** un paseo por la ciudad; **all the people ~ about** toda la gente alrededor; **all ~ the house** (*inside*) por toda la casa; (*outside*) alrededor de toda la casa; **she's 36 inches ~ the bust** tiene 90 de busto *or* de pecho; **~ the clock** (= *at any time*) a todas horas, a cualquier hora; (= *non-stop*) permanentemente, día y noche, las 24 horas del día; **~ the corner** a la vuelta de la esquina; **are you from ~ here?** ¿eres de por aquí?; **to look ~ the shop** echar una mirada por la tienda; **wear it ~ your neck** llévalo en el cuello; **he sells them ~ the pubs** los vende de bar en bar; **when you're ~ this way** cuando pases por aquí; **a trip ~ the world** un viaje alrededor del mundo
[2] (*esp Brit*) (= *approximately*) (*also* **~ about**) alrededor de, más o menos; **~ four o'clock** a eso de las cuatro; **~ about £50** alrededor de 50 libras, 50 libras más o menos; **somewhere ~ Derby** cerca de Derby; **somewhere ~ that sum** esa cantidad más o menos
[3] (= *using as theme*) **it's written ~ the Suez episode** tiene por tema principal el episodio de Suez
Ⓓ N [1] (= *circle*) círculo *m*; (= *slice*) tajada *f*, rodaja *f*; **a ~ of sandwiches** (*Brit*) un sandwich; **a ~ of toast** una tostada
[2] [*of postman, milkman etc*] recorrido *m*; [*of watchman*] ronda *f*; **the watchman was doing his ~** el vigilante estaba de ronda; **the story is going the ~s that ...** se dice *or* se rumorea que ...; **she did** *or* **went** *or* **made the ~s of the agencies** visitó *or* recorrió todas las agencias; **the story went the ~s of the club** el chiste se contó en todos los corrillos del club; **the doctor's on his ~s** el médico está haciendo sus visitas
[3] (*Boxing*) asalto *m*, round *m*; (*Golf*) partido *m*, recorrido *m*, vuelta *f*; (*Showjumping*) recorrido *m*; (*Cards*) (= *game*) partida *f*; (*in tournament*) vuelta *f*; **to have a clear ~** hacer un recorrido sin penalizaciones; **the first ~ of the elections** la primera vuelta de las elecciones
[4] [*of drinks*] ronda *f*; **whose ~ is it?** ¿a quién le toca (pagar)?; **it's my ~** yo invito, me toca a mí; **~ of ammunition** cartucho *m*, bala *f*, tiro *m*; **~ of applause** salva *f* de aplausos; **let's have a ~ of applause for ...** demos un fuerte aplauso a ...; **~ of shots** descarga *f*
[5] (= *series*) **the first ~ of negotiations** la primera ronda de negociaciones; **life was one long ~ of parties** la vida consistía en una sucesión constante de fiestas
[6] (= *routine*) **the daily ~** la rutina cotidiana
[7] **in the ~** (*Theat*) circular, en redondo
[8] (*Mus*) canon *m*
Ⓔ VT [1] (= *make round*) [+ *lips, edges*] redondear
[2] (= *go round*) [+ *corner*] doblar, dar la vuelta a; (*Naut*) doblar; **the ship ~ed the headland** el buque dobló el promontorio
Ⓕ CPD ► **round arch** N arco *m* de medio punto ► **round dance** N baile *m* en corro ► **round robin** N (= *request*) petición *f* firmada en rueda; (= *protest*) protesta *f* firmada en rueda ► **Round Table** N (*Hist*) Mesa *f* Redonda ► **round trip** N viaje *m* de ida y vuelta; **~ trip ticket** (*US*) billete *m* de ida y vuelta

►**round down** VT + ADV [+ *price etc*] redondear (rebajando)

►**round off** VT + ADV acabar, rematar; **to ~ off the evening** dar el remate a la fiesta

►**round on, round upon** VI + PREP volverse en contra de

►**round up** VT + ADV [+ *cattle*] acorralar, rodear; [+ *friends*] reunir; [+ *criminals*] coger, agarrar (*LAm*); [+ *figures*] redondear por arriba

roundabout ['raʊndəbaʊt] Ⓐ ADJ indirecto; **by a ~ way** dando un rodeo, por una ruta alternativa; **to speak in a ~ way** ir con rodeos, hablar con circunloquios
Ⓑ N [1] (*Brit*) (*at fair*) tiovivo *m*; (*in playground*) carrusel *m*, *plataforma giratoria que se instala en parques infantiles para que los niños la empujen y se monten*
[2] (*Brit Aut*) cruce *m* giratorio, glorieta *f*, rotonda *f* (*S. Cone*), redoma *f* (*Carib*)

rounded ['raʊndɪd] ADJ [1] (= *curved*) [*shape, hills, hips, shoulders*] redondeado; [*face*] redondo, relleno; [*handwriting*] redondo
[2] (= *complete, mature*) [*style, film, book*] pulido, maduro; [*individual*] maduro, equilibrado; [*character*] (*in novel etc*) bien desarrollado; [*education*] completo; [*flavour*] equilibrado
[3] (= *resonant*) [*vowel*] redondeado; **the beautifully ~ tone of the clarinet** el tono profundo y lleno de belleza del clarinete
[4] (*Culin*) [*tablespoon, dessertspoon*] casi colmado

roundelay ['raʊndɪleɪ] N (= *song*) canción *f* que se canta en rueda; (= *dance*) baile *m* en círculo

rounders ['raʊndəz] NSING (*Brit*) *juego similar al béisbol*

round-eyed ['raʊnd'aɪd] ADJ, ADV **to look at sb ~** mirar a algn con los ojos desorbitados

round-faced ['raʊnd'feɪst] ADJ de cara redonda

Roundhead ['raʊndhed] N (*Brit Hist*) cabeza *f* pelada

roundhouse ['raʊndhaʊs] N (*pl* **roundhouses** ['raʊndhaʊzɪz]) [1] (*Rail*) cocherón *m* circular, rotonda *f* para locomotoras
[2] (*Naut††*) chupeta *f*

roundly ['raʊndlɪ] ADV [*condemn, criticize*] duramente; [*reject, deny*] categóricamente, rotundamente; **he was ~ defeated in the election** sufrió una derrota aplastante en las elecciones

round-necked ['raʊnd,nekt] ADJ **~ pullover** jersey *m* de cuello cerrado *or* redondo

roundness ['raʊndnɪs] N redondez *f*, rotundidad *f*

round-shouldered ['raʊnd'ʃəʊldəd] ADJ cargado de espaldas

roundsman ['raʊndzmən] N (*pl* **roundsmen**) (*Brit*) repartidor *m or* proveedor *m* casero

round-the-clock ['raʊndðə'klɒk] ADJ (*surveillance etc*) de veinticuatro horas

round-up ['raʊndʌp] N (*Agr*) rodeo *m*; [*of suspects etc*] detención *f*; (*by police*) redada *f*; **a ~ of the latest news** un resumen de las últimas noticias

roundworm ['raʊndwɜːm] N lombriz *f* intestinal

rouse [raʊz] Ⓐ VT [+ *person*] despertar; [+ *interest*] despertar, suscitar; [+ *anger*] provocar; **to ~ sb from sleep** despertar a algn; **it ~d the whole house** despertó a todo el mundo; **to ~ sb to action** mover a algn a actuar; **to ~ sb to fury** enfurecer a algn; **to ~ o.s.** despertarse; **to ~ o.s. to do sth** animarse a hacer algo; **he ~d himself from his lazy contemplation of the scene** salió del ensimismamiento indiferente con el que contemplaba la escena
Ⓑ VI despertar, despertarse

rousing ['raʊzɪŋ] ADJ [*applause*] caluroso; [*song*] vivo, lleno de vigor; [*speech*] conmovedor; [*welcome*] emocionado, entusiasta

Roussillon ['ruːsɪjɔ̃ŋ] N Rosellón *m*

roustabout* ['raʊstəbaʊt] N (*US*) peón *m*

rout[1] [raʊt] Ⓐ N (= *defeat*) derrota *f* aplastante; (= *flight*) desbandada *f*, fuga *f* desordenada
Ⓑ VT aplastar, derrotar aplastantemente; **the enemy was ~ed** (= *defeated*) el enemigo fue aplastado; (= *put to flight*) el enemigo salió en desbandada

rout[2] [raʊt] VI (*also* **~ about**) (= *search*) hurgar

► **rout out** VT + ADV [1] (= *force out*) **to ~ sb out** hacer salir a algn; **to ~ sb out of bed** sacar a algn de la cama
[2] (= *search for*) buscar; (= *discover*) desenterrar

route [ruːt] Ⓐ N [1] (*gen*) ruta *f*, camino *m*; [*of bus*] recorrido *m*; [*of ship*] rumbo *m*, derrota *f*; (= *itinerary*) itinerario *m*; (= *direction*) rumbo *m*; **Route 31** (*US*) Ruta 31; **the ~ to the coast** el camino de la costa; **to go by a new ~** seguir una ruta nueva; **shipping ~** vía *f* marítima; **air ~** ruta *f* aérea
[2] (*US*) [ruːt, raʊt] (= *delivery round*) recorrido *m*
Ⓑ VT fijar el itinerario de; (*Comput*) encaminar; **the train is now ~d through Derby** ahora el tren pasa por Derby
Ⓒ CPD ► **route map** N mapa *m* de carreteras ► **route march** N marcha *f* de entrenamiento

routine [ruː'tiːn] Ⓐ N [1] (= *normal procedure*) rutina *f*; **the daily ~** la rutina diaria; **the school ~** la rutina escolar; **she went through the ~ of introducing everyone** hizo las presentaciones de rigor; **as a matter of ~** como parte de la rutina; **people entering the country are asked certain questions as a matter of ~** como parte de la rutina a la gente que entra en el país se le hacen ciertas preguntas; **schoolchildren were tested for tuberculosis as a matter of ~** de forma rutinaria *or* rutinariamente se les hacía a los alumnos la prueba de la tuberculosis
[2] (*esp Theat*) número *m*; **dance ~** número *m* de baile; **exercise ~** tabla *f* de ejercicios
[3] (= *spiel*) **he gave me the old ~ about his wife not understanding him*** me vino con la historia de siempre de que su mujer no le entendía; **he went through his sales ~** metió el típico rollo de vendedor
[4] (*Comput*) rutina *f*
Ⓑ ADJ [*test, check-up, maintenance, inspection*] de rutina; [*matter, problem*] rutinario; [*work*] habitual, de rutina; **to make ~ enquiries** hacer averiguaciones rutinarias *or* de rutina; **it's just ~** es cosa de rutina; **reports of thefts had become almost ~** las denuncias de robos se habían convertido en algo casi habitual; **on a ~ basis** de forma rutinaria

routinely [ruː'tiːnlɪ] ADV [*use, check*] de forma rutinaria, rutinariamente; **the drug is ~ used to treat depression** el fármaco es utilizado rutinariamente para el tratamiento de la depresión; **she ~ works a 60-hour week** trabajar 60 horas por semana forma parte de su rutina

routing ['ruːtɪŋ] N (*Comput*) encaminamiento *m*

rove [rəʊv] Ⓐ VT vagar *or* errar por, recorrer
Ⓑ VI vagar, errar; **his eye ~d over the room** recorrió la habitación con la vista

rover ['rəʊvə^r] N vagabundo/a *m/f*

roving ['rəʊvɪŋ] ADJ (= *wandering*) errante; [*salesman*] ambulante; [*ambassador*] itinerante; [*reporter*] volante, sin puesto fijo; [*disposition*] andariego; **to have a ~ commission** (*fig*) tener vía libre para investigar donde sea necesario; **he has a ~ eye** se le van los ojos tras las faldas

row[1] [rəʊ] Ⓐ N (= *line*) fila *f*, hilera *f*; (*Theat etc*) fila *f*; [*of books, houses etc*] hilera *f*, fila *f*; (*in knitting*) pasada *f*, vuelta *f*; **in a ~** en fila; **in the front ~** en primera fila, en la fila uno; **in the fourth ~** en la cuarta fila, en la fila cuatro; **he killed four in a ~** mató cuatro seguidos, mató cuatro uno tras otro; **for five days in a ~** durante cinco días seguidos
Ⓑ CPD ► **row house** N (*US*) casa *f* adosada

row[2] [rəʊ] Ⓐ N (= *trip*) paseo *m* en bote de remos; **to go for a ~** pasearse *or* hacer una excursión en bote; **it was a hard ~ to the shore** nos costó llegar a la playa remando
Ⓑ VT [+ *boat*] remar; [+ *person*] llevar en bote; **you ~ed a good race** habéis remado muy bien; **he ~ed the Atlantic** cruzó el Atlántico a remo; **to ~ sb across a river** llevar a algn en bote al otro lado de un río; **can you ~ me out to the yacht?** ¿me lleva en bote al yate?
Ⓒ VI remar; **to ~ hard** esforzarse remando, hacer fuerza de remos; **he ~ed for Oxford** remó en el bote de Oxford; **to ~ against sb** competir con algn en una regata a remo; **we ~ed for the shore** remamos hacia la playa, nos dirigimos remando hacia la playa; **to ~ across a river** cruzar un río a remo; **to ~ round an island** dar la vuelta a una isla remando *or* a remo

row[3] [raʊ] (*esp Brit*) Ⓐ N [1] (= *noise*) ruido *m*, bulla* *f*; **the ~ from the engine** el ruido del motor; **it makes a devil of a ~** hace un ruido de todos los demonios; **hold your ~!** ◊ **stop your ~!** ¡cállate!
[2] (= *dispute*) bronca *f*, pelea *f*; **to have a ~** reñir, pelearse (*LAm*); **now don't let's start a ~** no riñamos; **the ~ about wages** la disputa acerca de los salarios
[3] (= *fuss, disturbance, incident*) jaleo *m*, escándalo *m*, lío *m*, follón *m* (*Sp*), bronca *f* (*esp LAm*); **what's the ~ about?** ¿a qué se debe el lío?; **to kick up** *or* **make a ~*** armar un lío; (= *protest*) poner el grito en el cielo
[4] (= *scolding*) regaño *m*, regañina *f*; **to get into a ~** ganarse una regañina (**for** por); **you'll get into a ~** te van a regañar
Ⓑ VI reñir, pelear (*LAm*); **they're always ~ing** siempre están riñendo; **to ~ with sb** reñir *or* pelearse con algn

rowan ['raʊən] N (*also* **~ tree**) serbal *m*; (= *berry*) serba *f*

rowboat ['rəʊbəʊt] N (*US*) = **rowing boat**

rowdiness ['raʊdɪnɪs] N escándalo *m*, alboroto *m*

rowdy ['raʊdɪ] Ⓐ ADJ (*compar* **rowdier**; *superl* **rowdiest**) [*person*] (= *loud*) escandaloso; (= *quarrelsome*) pendenciero; [*meeting etc*] alborotado, agitado
Ⓑ N (= *person*) (= *loud*) escandaloso/a *m/f*; (= *quarrelsome*) pendenciero/a *m/f*

rowdyism ['raʊdɪɪzəm] N disturbios *mpl*

rower ['rəʊə^r] N remero/a *m/f*

rowing ['rəʊɪŋ] Ⓐ N remo *m*
Ⓑ CPD ► **rowing boat** N (*Brit*) barca *f* de remos, bote *m* de remos ► **rowing club** N club *m* de remo ► **rowing machine** N máquina *f* de remo

rowlock ['rɒlək] N (*esp Brit*) tolete *m*, escálamo *m*, chumacera *f*

royal ['rɔɪəl] Ⓐ ADJ [1] real; **His/Her Royal Highness** Su Alteza Real; **the ~ "we"** el plural mayestático
[2] (= *splendid*) magnífico, espléndido, regio; **to have a right ~ time** pasarlo en grande
Ⓑ N (*) personaje *m* real, miembro *mf* de la familia real; **the ~s*** la realeza
Ⓒ CPD ► **the Royal Academy (of Arts)** N (*Brit*) la Real Academia (de Bellas Artes); → RA - ROYAL ACADEMY OF ARTS ► **the Royal Air Force** N las Fuerzas Aéreas Británicas ► **royal blue** N azul *m* marino intenso; *see also* **royal-blue** ► **Royal Commission** N (*Brit*) Comisión *f* Real ► **the Royal Engineers** NPL (*Brit*) el Cuerpo de Ingenieros ► **the royal family** N la familia real ► **the royal household** N la casa real ► **royal line** N familia *f* real, casa *f* real ► **the Royal Navy** N la Marina Británica ► **Royal Society** N (*Brit*) ≈ Real Academia *f* de Ciencias

royal-blue [ˌrɔɪəl'bluː] ADJ azul marino intenso; *see also* **royal**

royalism ['rɔɪəlɪzəm] N sentimiento *m* monárquico, monarquismo *m*

royalist ['rɔɪəlɪst] Ⓐ ADJ monárquico
Ⓑ N monárquico/a *m/f*

royally ['rɔɪəlɪ] ADV (*fig*) magníficamente, espléndidamente

royalty ['rɔɪəltɪ] N [1] realeza *f*, familia *f* real; **in the presence of ~** estando presente un miembro de la familia real, en presencia de la realeza; **a shop patronized by ~** una tienda que visita la familia real, una tienda donde la familia real hace compras
[2] (= *payment*) (*also* **royalties**) (*on books*) derechos *mpl* de autor; (*gen*) regalías *fpl*, royalti(e)s *mpl* (*LAm*)

rozzer‡ ['rɒzə^r] N (*Brit*) poli* *mf*, guindilla *mf* (*Sp‡*), cana *mf* (*S. Cone‡*), tira *mf* (*Mex‡*)

RP Ⓐ N ABBR (*Brit Ling*) (= **Received Pronunciation**) *pronunciación estándar del inglés*; → ENGLISH, HOME COUNTIES
Ⓑ ABBR (*Post*) (= **reply paid**) CP

RPI N ABBR (= **Retail Price Index**) IPC *m*

RPM N ABBR = **resale price maintenance**

rpm N ABBR (= **revolutions per minute**) r.p.m.

RR ABBR (*US*) (= **Railroad**) FC, f.c.

RRP N ABBR (= **recommended retail price**) PVP *m*

RSA N ABBR [1] = **Republic of South Africa**
[2] (*Brit*) = **Royal Society of Arts**
[3] = **Royal Scottish Academy**

RSC N ABBR (*Brit*) = **Royal Shakespeare Company**

RSC-ROYAL SHAKESPEARE COMPANY

La **Royal Shakespeare Company** *o* **RSC** *es una compañía de teatro británica fundada en*

1960 en Stratford-Upon-Avon, el lugar de nacimiento de William Shakespeare. Además de esta sede, la compañía cuenta en la actualidad con otro teatro en el complejo Barbican de Londres y, aunque están especializados en la representación de obras de Shakespeare, también ponen en escena obras de otros dramaturgos clásicos y contemporáneos. En los últimos años la **RSC** *ha dedicado la mitad del año a hacer giras por todo el Reino Unido, lo que ha acrecentado aún más su popularidad, con la que ya contaba dada la fama internacional que han alcanzado sus representaciones.*

RSI N ABBR = **repetitive strain injury**

RSM N ABBR = **Regimental Sergeant Major**

RSPB N ABBR (*Brit*) = **Royal Society for the Protection of Birds**

RSPCA N ABBR (*Brit*) = **Royal Society for the Prevention of Cruelty to Animals**

RSV N ABBR = **Revised Standard Version**

▼**RSVP** ABBR = **répondez s'il vous plaît** (= *please reply*) S.R.C.

rt ABBR = **right**

RTA N ABBR = **road traffic accident**

Rt Hon. ABBR (*Brit*) (= **Right Honourable**) *título honorífico de diputado*

Rt Rev. ABBR (= **Right Reverend**) Rmo.

RU N ABBR = **Rugby Union**

rub [rʌb] Ⓐ N [1] (*gen*) **to give sth a ~** frotar algo; **to give one's shoes a ~ (up)** limpiar los zapatos; **to give the silver a ~** sacar brillo a la plata; **to give sb's back a ~** frotar la espalda de algn
[2] (*fig*) **there's the ~** ahí está el problema, ésa es la dificultad; **the ~ is that ...** el problema es que ...
Ⓑ VT (= *apply friction*) frotar; (*hard*) restregar, estregar; (*Med etc*) friccionar; (*to clean*) limpiar frotando; (= *polish*) sacar brillo a; **to ~ one's hands together** frotarse las manos; **to ~ sth dry** secar algo frotándolo; **to ~ a surface bare** alisar una superficie a fuerza de frotarla; **to ~ a cream into the skin** frotar la piel con una crema
Ⓒ VI **to ~ against/on sth** rozar algo

►**rub along*** VI + ADV (*Brit*) ir tirando; **I can ~ along in Arabic** me defiendo en árabe; **to ~ along with sb** llevarse *or* entenderse bastante bien con algn

►**rub away** VT + ADV (= *wipe away*) quitar frotando; (= *wear off*) desgastar

►**rub down** Ⓐ VT + ADV [1] [+ *body*] secar frotando; [+ *horse*] almohazar
[2] [+ *door, wall etc*] lijar
Ⓑ VI + ADV [*person*] secarse frotándose con una toalla

►**rub in** Ⓐ VT + ADV [1] [+ *ointment, cream*] aplicar frotando
[2] (*) **don't ~ it in!** ¡no me lo refriegues por las narices!
Ⓑ VT + PREP ✦*IDIOM* **to ~ sb's nose in it** *or* **in the dirt** restregarle algo a algn por las narices

►**rub off** Ⓐ VI + ADV [*dirt*] quitarse (frotando); [*writing, pattern*] borrarse; [*paint*] quitarse; **to ~ off on sb** (*fig*) pegarse a algn; **some of their ideas have ~bed off on him** se le han pegado algunas de sus ideas, ha hecho suyas algunas de sus ideas
Ⓑ VT + ADV [+ *writing, pattern*] borrar; [+ *dirt etc*] quitar (frotando); [+ *paint*] quitar

►**rub out** Ⓐ VT + ADV [1] (= *erase*) borrar
[2] (‡) (= *kill*) **to ~ sb out** cargarse a algn*
Ⓑ VI + ADV borrarse; **it ~s out easily** es fácil de quitar, se borra fácilmente

►**rub up** VT + ADV pulir, sacar brillo a; ✦*IDIOM* **to ~ sb up the wrong way** buscar las cosquillas a algn

rub-a-dub [ˈrʌbəˈdʌb] N rataplán *m*

rubber¹ [ˈrʌbəʳ] Ⓐ N [1] (= *material*) goma *f*, caucho *m*, hule *m* (*LAm*), jebe *m* (*Col, Peru*)
[2] (*Brit*) (= *eraser*) goma *f* de borrar
[3] (*esp US‡*) (= *condom*) condón *m*, goma *f*
[4] (*Mech etc*) paño *m* de pulir
Ⓑ CPD [*ball, dinghy, gloves, boots*] de goma *etc* ► **rubber band** N goma *f*, gomita *f* ► **rubber boots** NPL (*US*) botas *fpl* de agua, botas *fpl* altas de goma ► **rubber bullet** N bala *f* de goma ► **rubber cement** N adhesivo *m* de goma ► **rubber cheque*** N (*Brit*) cheque *m* sin fondos ► **rubber dinghy** N lancha *f* neumática ► **rubber gloves** NPL guantes *mpl* de goma ► **rubber goods** NPL artículos *mpl* de goma ► **rubber industry** N industria *f* del caucho, industria *f* cauchera ► **rubber plant** N ficus *m inv* ► **rubber plantation** N cauchal *m* ► **rubber raft** N balsa *f* neumática ► **rubber ring** N (*for swimming*) flotador *m* ► **rubber solution** N disolución *f* de goma ► **rubber stamp** N estampilla *f* de goma; *see also* **rubber-stamp** ► **rubber tree** N árbol *m* gomero *or* de caucho

rubber² [ˈrʌbəʳ] N (*Cards*) partida *f*

rubberize [ˈrʌbəraɪz] VT engomar, cauchutar

rubberized [ˈrʌbəraɪzd] ADJ engomado, cauchutado, cubierto de goma

rubberneck* [ˈrʌbənek] (*US*) Ⓐ N mirón/ona *m/f*
Ⓑ VI curiosear

rubber-stamp [ˌrʌbəˈstæmp] VT (*officially*) aprobar con carácter oficial; (*fig*) (= *without questioning*) aprobar maquinalmente; *see also* **rubber**

rubbery [ˈrʌbərɪ] ADJ gomoso, parecido a la goma

rubbing [ˈrʌbɪŋ] Ⓐ N [1] (= *act*) frotamiento *m*
[2] (= *brass rubbing*) calco *m*
Ⓑ CPD ► **rubbing alcohol** N (*US*) alcohol *m*

rubbish [ˈrʌbɪʃ] Ⓐ N [1] basura *f*
[2] (*) (*fig*) (= *goods, film etc*) basura *f*, birria *f*, porquería *f*; (*spoken, written*) tonterías *fpl*, disparates *mpl*; **he talks a lot of ~** no dice más que tonterías; **the book is ~** la novela es una basura
Ⓑ ADJ **to be ~ at sth** (*Brit**) (= *useless*) no tener ni idea de algo*, ser un negado* *or* (*Sp**) un manta en algo
Ⓒ VT (*) poner por los suelos
Ⓓ CPD ► **rubbish bin** N (*Brit*) cubo *m* de la basura, basurero *m* ► **rubbish chute** N rampa *f* de la basura ► **rubbish collection** N recogida *f* de basuras, recolección *f* de la basura ► **rubbish dump, rubbish heap** N basurero *m*, vertedero *m*, basural *m* (*LAm*)

rubbishy* [ˈrʌbɪʃɪ] ADJ (*esp Brit*) [*goods*] de pacotilla; [*film, novel etc*] que no vale para nada, malísimo

rubble [ˈrʌbl] N escombros *mpl*; **the town was reduced to ~** el pueblo quedó reducido a escombros

rub-down [ˈrʌbdaʊn] N (*gen*) masaje *m*, friega *f*; (*drying*) secada *f* con toalla; **to give o.s. a ~** secarse frotándose con una toalla

rube‡ [ru:b] N (*US*) patán *m*, palurdo *m*

rubella [rʊˈbelə] N rubéola *f*

Rubicon [ˈru:bɪkən] N Rubicón *m*; **to cross the ~** pasar el Rubicón

rubicund [ˈru:bɪkənd] ADJ rubicundo

rubidium [ru:ˈbɪdɪəm] N rubidio *m*

ruble [ˈru:bl] N (*US*) = **rouble**

rubric [ˈru:brɪk] N rúbrica *f*

ruby [ˈru:bɪ] Ⓐ N rubí *m*
Ⓑ ADJ (*in colour*) color rubí
Ⓒ CPD [*necklace, ring*] de rubí(es)

RUC N ABBR (= **Royal Ulster Constabulary**) *Policía de Irlanda del Norte*

ruck¹ [rʌk] N (*Racing*) grueso *m* del pelotón; (*Rugby*) melé *f*; (*fig*) gente *f*, común personas *fpl* corrientes; **to get out of the ~** empezar a destacar, adelantarse a los demás

ruck² [rʌk] Ⓐ N (*in clothing etc*) arruga *f*
Ⓑ VT (*also* **to ~ up**) arrugar
Ⓒ VI arrugarse

ruckle [ˈrʌkl] N, VT, VI = **ruck²**

rucksack [ˈrʌksæk] N (*esp Brit*) mochila *f*

ruckus* [ˈrʌkəs] N (*pl* **ruckuses**) (*US*) = **ructions**

ructions [ˈrʌkʃənz] N lío* *m*, follón *m*, jaleo *m*; **there will be ~** se va a armar la gorda

rudder [ˈrʌdəʳ] N (*Naut, Aer*) timón *m*

rudderless [ˈrʌdəlɪs] ADJ sin timón

ruddiness [ˈrʌdɪnɪs] N [*of complexion*] rubicundez *f*; [*of sky*] lo rojizo

ruddy [ˈrʌdɪ] ADJ (*compar* **ruddier**; *superl* **ruddiest**) [1] [*complexion*] rubicundo, coloradote; [*sky*] rojizo
[2] (*Brit†‡ euph*) maldito, condenado*

rude [ru:d] ADJ (*compar* **ruder**; *superl* **rudest**) [1] (= *impolite*) [*person*] grosero, maleducado; [*remark*] grosero; **to be ~ to sb** ser grosero con algn; **it's ~ to stare** mirar fijamente es de mala educación; **it was ~ of you to ignore him** ignorarlo fue una grosería por tu parte; **he was ~ about her new dress** hizo comentarios poco halagüeños respecto a su vestido nuevo; **how ~!** ¡qué poca educación!, ¡qué grosero!
[2] (= *indecent*) [*gesture*] grosero, obsceno; [*joke, song*] verde, colorado (*LAm*); **a ~ word** una grosería, una mala palabra
[3] (*liter*) (= *primitive*) [*shelter, table*] tosco, rudimentario; [*tool, device, implement*] burdo, rudimentario
[4] (*liter*) (= *unexpected and unpleasant*) **a ~ awakening** una sorpresa muy desagradable; **a ~ shock** un golpe inesperado
[5] (*liter*) (= *vigorous*) **to be in ~ health** gozar de muy buena salud, estar más sano que un roble

rudely [ˈru:dlɪ] ADV [1] (= *impolitely*) [*say, interrupt, stare*] groseramente; [*push*] bruscamente; **before I was so ~ interrupted** antes de que me interrumpieran tan groseramente *or* de forma tan grosera
[2] (= *crudely*) [*carved, shaped*] toscamente, de forma rudimentaria
[3] (= *unexpectedly*) bruscamente; **she was ~ awakened** la despertaron bruscamente; (*fig*) le dieron una sorpresa muy desagradable

rudeness [ˈru:dnɪs] N [1] (= *impoliteness*) [*of person, behaviour*] grosería *f*, falta *f* de educación; [*of reply, remark*] falta *f* de educación
[2] (= *obscenity*) grosería *f*
[3] (= *primitiveness*) [*of shelter, table*] tosquedad *f*, lo rudimentario; [*of tool, device, implement*] lo burdo, lo rudimentario

rudiment [ˈru:dɪmənt] N (*Bio*) rudimento *m*; **rudiments** rudimentos *mpl*, primeras nociones *fpl*

rudimentary [ˌru:dɪˈmentərɪ] ADJ (*gen*) rudimentario; (*Bio*) rudimental; **he has ~ Latin** tiene las primeras nociones de latín, sabe un poquito de latín

rue¹ [ru:] VT arrepentirse de, lamentar; **you shall ~ it** te arrepentirás de haberlo hecho; **I ~ the day when I did it** ojalá no lo hubiera hecho nunca; **he lived to ~ it** vivió para arrepentirse

➤ LANGUAGE IN USE: RSVP 25.2

rue² [ruː] N (*Bot*) ruda *f*

rueful ['ruːfʊl] ADJ (= *sorrowful*) triste; (= *repentant*) arrepentido

ruefully ['ruːfəlɪ] ADV (= *sorrowfully*) tristemente; (= *with repentance*) con arrepentimiento

ruefulness ['ruːfʊlnɪs] N (= *sorrowfulness*) tristeza *f*; (= *repentance*) arrepentimiento *m*

ruff¹ [rʌf] N 1 (*Dress*) gorguera *f*, gola *f*
2 (*Orn, Zool*) collarín *m*

ruff² [rʌf] (*Cards*) Ⓐ N 1 (= *game*) *viejo juego de cartas similar al whist*
2 (= *act of trumping*) fallo *m*
Ⓑ VT fallar

ruffian ['rʌfɪən] N rufián *m*

ruffianly ['rʌfɪənlɪ] ADJ brutal

ruffle ['rʌfl] Ⓐ N arruga *f*; (*Sew*) volante *m* fruncido; (= *ripple*) rizo *m*
Ⓑ VT [+ *surface of water*] agitar, rizar; [+ *hair*] despeinar; [+ *feathers*] erizar; [+ *fabric*] fruncir; [+ *bedclothes*] arrugar; **nothing ~s him** no se altera por nada; **she wasn't at all ~d** no se perturbó en lo más mínimo; ✦***IDIOMS*** **to ~ sb's feathers** herir las susceptibilidades de algn; **to smooth sb's ~d feathers** alisar las plumas erizadas de algn

rug [rʌg] N 1 (= *floor-mat*) alfombrilla *f*, tapete *m*; ✦***IDIOM*** **to pull the ~ from under sb** *or* **sb's feet** mover la silla para que algn se caiga
2 (*esp Brit*) (= *wrap*) manta *f*; **travel(ling) ~** manta *f* de viaje
3 (‡ *hum*) (= *wig*) peluquín *m*

rugby ['rʌgbɪ] Ⓐ N (*also* ~ **football**) rugby *m*
Ⓑ CPD [*player, match*] de rugby ► **rugby league** N rugby *m* a trece

> **RUGBY**
>
> *Se cree que el rugby comenzó a jugarse en el colegio* **Rugby** *de Inglaterra en 1823. Sin embargo, cuando la* **Rugby Football Union** *estableció las reglas de este deporte, el juego profesional quedó prohibido, por lo que un grupo decidió formar el* **Rugby League**, *lo que dio origen a dos tipos distintos de rugby. El* **Rugby League** *se juega con 13 jugadores por equipo, tiene sus propias reglas y sistema de tanteo y sus jugadores pueden ser profesionales. Se juega sobre todo en el norte de Inglaterra y Australia.*
> *Por su parte, el* **Rugby Union** *se juega con equipos compuestos por 15 jugadores y es un deporte muy popular en todo el mundo. El carácter amateur de esta versión del rugby se mantuvo hasta 1995, año en que la Federación Internacional de este deporte (***International Rugby Board***) decidió permitir que los jugadores y directivos pudiesen cobrar. Como deporte escolar en el Reino Unido, el rugby es frecuente en los colegios privados, mientras que, en los colegios públicos, el fútbol es el deporte más extendido.*

rugged ['rʌgɪd] ADJ 1 (= *rough*) [*terrain, landscape*] accidentado, escabroso; [*coastline, mountains*] escarpado; **the ~ beauty of the island** la belleza violenta de la isla
2 (= *strongly built, angular*) [*features*] duro; [*man*] de rasgos duros
3 (= *tough*) [*personality, character*] duro, áspero; [*conditions*] duro; [*individualism*] fuerte; [*determination*] inquebrantable; **hill farmers are a ~ breed** los ganaderos de las montañas son una raza dura de pelar
4 (= *unrefined*) [*manners, character*] tosco, rudo
5 (= *durable*) [*machine, clothing*] resistente; [*construction*] fuerte, resistente

ruggedness ['rʌgɪdnɪs] N [*of terrain*] lo accidentado, lo escabroso; [*of coastline*] lo escarpado; [*of features*] dureza *f*; [*of character*] (= *toughness*) aspereza *f*; (= *lack of refinement*) tosquedad *f*, rudeza *f*; [*of conditions*] dureza *f*; [*of machine, clothing, construction*] resistencia *f*

rugger* ['rʌgəʳ] N (*Brit*) = **rugby**

ruin ['ruːɪn] Ⓐ N 1 (= *building*) ruina *f*; **the ~s of a castle** las ruinas *or* los restos de un castillo; **to fall into ~** convertirse en ruinas; **the town lay** *or* **was in ~s** la ciudad estaba en ruinas
2 (*fig*) ruina *f*, perdición *f*; **he faced the prospect of financial ~** se enfrentaba a la posibilidad de la ruina económica *or* de acabar en la bancarrota; **her hopes were in ~s** sus esperanzas estaban destruidas; **my life/career is in ~s** mi vida/carrera está destruida *or* arruinada; **drink will be his ~** *or* **the ~ of him** el alcohol será su ruina *or* su perdición; **the country has gone to ~** el país se ha arruinado; *see also* **rack²**
Ⓑ VT 1 (= *destroy*) [+ *reputation, career, life*] arruinar, destruir; [+ *hopes*] destruir, echar por tierra; [+ *plans*] estropear, echar por tierra; **it ~ed his chances of playing in the final** dio al traste con sus posibilidades de jugar en la final
2 (= *spoil*) [+ *clothes, car*] estropear, destrozar; [+ *meal, event, eyesight*] estropear; **look at my dress, it's ~ed!** mira mi vestido, ¡está destrozado!; **don't eat that now, you'll ~ your appetite** no te comas eso ahora, se te quitarán las ganas de comer; **their chatter ~ed my enjoyment of the concert** su charla no me dejó disfrutar del concierto
3 [+ *person*] (*financially*) arruinar; (*morally*) perder; **what ~ed him was gambling** lo que le perdió fue el juego, el juego fue su ruina

ruination [,ruːɪ'neɪʃən] N ruina *f*, perdición *f*

ruined ['ruːɪnd] ADJ [*building*] en ruinas; [*reputation, career, life*] arruinado; [*hopes*] defraudado; [*plans*] frustrado

ruinous ['ruːɪnəs] ADJ ruinoso

ruinously ['ruːɪnəslɪ] ADV ruinosamente; **~ expensive** carísimo, de lo más caro

rule [ruːl] Ⓐ N 1 (= *regulation*) regla *f*, norma *f*; **rules** [*of competition*] bases *fpl*; **it's the ~s** son las reglas, ésa es la norma; **the ~s of the game** las reglas del juego; **the ~s of chess** las reglas del ajedrez; **school ~s** reglamento *msing* escolar; **it's a ~ that all guests must vacate their rooms by 10a.m.** por norma los clientes tienen que dejar la habitación antes de las 10 de la mañana; **running is against the ~s** ◊ **it's against the ~s to run** está prohibido correr; **to break the ~s** infringir las reglas *or* las normas *or* el reglamento; **to make the ~s** dictar las normas; **in my job I'm allowed to make my own ~s** en mi trabajo se me permite decidir cómo se hacen las cosas; **to play by the ~s** (*fig*) obedecer las reglas *or* las normas; **I couldn't stand a life governed by ~s and regulations** no soportaría una vida llena de reglas y normas; **~s of the road** normas *fpl or* reglamento *m* de tráfico *msing see also* **bend B1**, **golden**, **ground**, **work B1**
2 (= *guiding principle*) regla *f*; **~ of three** (*Math*) regla *f* de tres; **~ of thumb** regla *f* general; **as a ~ of thumb, a bottle of wine holds six glasses** por regla general, una botella de vino da para seis vasos; **I just do it by ~ of thumb** lo hago simplemente siguiendo mi criterio
3 (= *habit, custom*) norma *f*; **short haircuts became the ~** el pelo corto se convirtió en la norma; **as a (general) ~** por regla general, en general, normalmente; **he makes it a ~ to get up early** tiene por norma *or* por sistema levantarse temprano; *see also* **exception**
4 (= *government*) gobierno *m*; (= *reign*) reinado *m*; **military/one-party ~** gobierno *m* militar/unipartidista; **the ~ of law** el imperio de la ley; **under British ~** bajo el dominio británico; **under the ~ of Louis XV** bajo el reinado de Luis XV
5 (*for measuring*) regla *f*
Ⓑ VT 1 (= *govern*) gobernar; ✦***IDIOM*** **to ~ the roost** llevar la batuta
2 (= *dominate, control*) controlar, dominar; **you shouldn't let work ~ your life** no deberías permitir que el trabajo controlara *or* dominara tu vida; **Mars ~s Aries** Aries está bajo la influencia de Marte; *see also* **heart A2**
3 (*esp Jur*) (= *declare*) dictaminar; **the court has ~d the strike to be illegal** el tribunal ha dictaminado que la huelga es ilegal; **the motion was ~d out of order** se decidió que la moción no procedía
4 (= *draw*) [+ *line*] trazar; (= *draw lines on*) [+ *paper*] reglar; *see also* **ruled**
Ⓒ VI 1 (= *govern*) gobernar; [*monarch*] reinar; **to ~ over sth/sb** gobernar algo/a algn; **the king ~d over his subjects wisely** el rey gobernaba a sus súbditos con sabiduría; **the British ~d over a vast empire** los británicos poseyeron un vasto imperio; **the ancient dynasties that ~d over China** las viejas dinastías que reinaban en China; **one god who ~s over all mankind** un dios que tiene poder sobre toda la humanidad; *see also* **rod**
2 (= *prevail*) reinar; **United ~s OK** (*in graffiti*) ¡aúpa United!, ¡arriba United!
3 (= *decide*) [*chairman, president*] decidir, resolver; [*judge, jury*] fallar; **to ~ against sth/sb** fallar *or* resolver en contra de algo/algn; **to ~ in favour of sth/sb** fallar en *or* a favor de algo/algn, resolver en *or* a favor de algo/algn; **to ~ on sth** fallar *or* resolver *or* decidir en algo
Ⓓ CPD ► **rule book** N reglamento *m*; **we'll do it by** *or* **go by the ~ book** lo haremos de acuerdo con las normas

►**rule off** VT + ADV 1 (*with ruler*) separar con una línea
2 (*Comm*) [+ *account*] cerrar

►**rule out** VT + ADV 1 (= *exclude*) [+ *action, possibility*] descartar, excluir; [+ *candidate*] excluir; **military intervention has not been ~d out** no se ha descartado una intervención militar; **a back injury has ~d him out of the match** una lesión en la espalda lo ha excluido del partido; **the age limit ~s him out** el límite de edad lo excluye, queda excluido por el límite de edad
2 (= *make impossible*) hacer imposible, imposibilitar; **the TV was on, effectively ruling out conversation** la televisión estaba puesta, lo que de hecho hacía imposible *or* imposibilitaba toda conversación

> **RULE BRITANNIA**
>
> **Rule Britannia** *es una canción patriótica que data de 1740. La letra, escrita por el poeta escocés James Thomson, celebra el control marítimo del que Gran Bretaña disfrutaba en aquella época. Aunque algunos critican el tono excesivamente chovinista de la canción,* **Rule Britannia** *aún se canta en algunas celebraciones de carácter patriótico, como la* **Last Night of the Proms**. *El estribillo reza así:* **Rule Britannia, Britannia rule the waves, Britons never never never shall be slaves.**
> ⇨ *Ver tb* PROM

ruled [ruːld] ADJ [*paper*] de rayas, pautado

ruler [ˈruːləʳ] N 1 (= *person*) gobernante *mf*; (= *monarch*) soberano/a *m/f*
2 (*for measuring*) regla *f*

ruling [ˈruːlɪŋ] Ⓐ ADJ 1 (= *governing*) [*class, body*] dirigente; [*party*] en el poder; [*monarch*] reinante; **~ planet** (*Astrol*) planeta *m* dominante
2 (= *predominant*) [*passion, factor*] dominante
3 (*Fin*) [*price*] que rige, vigente
Ⓑ N (*Jur*) fallo *m*, resolución *f*; (*Admin, Sport*) decisión *f*; **to give a ~ on a dispute** fallar en una disputa

rum¹ [rʌm] Ⓐ N (= *drink*) ron *m*
Ⓑ CPD ► **rum toddy** N *ron con agua caliente y azúcar*

rum²*† [rʌm] ADJ (*Brit*) raro

Rumania *etc* [ruːˈmeɪnɪə] = **Romania** *etc*

rumba [ˈrʌmbə] N rumba *f*

rumble¹ [ˈrʌmbl] Ⓐ N [*of traffic etc*] ruido *m* sordo, retumbo *m*, rumor *m*; [*of thunder etc*] estruendo *m*; [*of tank, heavy vehicle*] estruendo *m*; **~s of discontent** murmullos *mpl* de descontento
Ⓑ VI [*thunder*] retumbar; [*guns*] hacer un ruido sordo; [*stomach*] sonar, hacer ruidos; **the train ~d past** el tren pasó con estruendo
Ⓒ CPD ► **rumble seat** N (*US Aut*) asiento *m* trasero exterior ► **rumble strip** N banda *f* sonora

►**rumble on** VI + ADV (*Brit*) [*argument, scandal*] colear, seguir coleando; **he ~d on another half-hour*** se enrolló media hora más*

rumble²* [ˈrʌmbl] VT (*Brit*) calar, pillar; **we've been ~d** nos han calado *or* pillado; **I soon ~d what was going on** pronto me olí lo que estaban haciendo

rumbling [ˈrʌmblɪŋ] N = **rumble¹ A**

rumbustious* [rʌmˈbʌstʃəs] ADJ (*Brit*) bullicioso, ruidoso

ruminant [ˈruːmɪnənt] Ⓐ ADJ rumiante
Ⓑ N rumiante *m*

ruminate [ˈruːmɪneɪt] Ⓐ VI (*lit, fig*) rumiar; **to ~ on sth** rumiar algo
Ⓑ VT (*lit, fig*) rumiar

rumination [ˌruːmɪˈneɪʃən] N (= *act*) rumia *f*; (= *thought*) meditación *f*, reflexión *f*

ruminative [ˈruːmɪnətɪv] ADJ 1 (*Bio*) rumiante
2 (*fig*) pensativo, meditabundo

ruminatively [ˈruːmɪnətɪvlɪ] ADV pensativamente; **"I hope so", he said ~** —espero que sí —dijo pensativo

rummage [ˈrʌmɪdʒ] Ⓐ VI hurgar; **he ~d in his pocket and produced a key** hurgando en el bolsillo sacó una llave; **to ~ about** revolverlo todo, buscar revolviéndolo todo; **to ~ about in a drawer** hurgar *or* revolver en un cajón
Ⓑ N (*US*) (= *clothes*) ropa *f* usada; (= *bric-à-brac*) objetos *mpl* usados
Ⓒ CPD ► **rummage sale** N (*US*) venta *f* de objetos usados (*con fines benéficos*)

rummy¹* [ˈrʌmɪ] Ⓐ ADJ (*Brit*) = **rum²**
Ⓑ N (*US**) (= *drunk*) borracho/a *m/f*

rummy² [ˈrʌmɪ] N (*Cards*) rummy *m*

rumour, rumor (*US*) [ˈruːməʳ] Ⓐ N rumor *m*; **~ has it that ...** se rumorea que ..., corre la voz de que ...
Ⓑ VT **it is ~ed that ...** se rumorea que ..., corre la voz de que ...; **he is ~ed to be rich** se rumorea que es rico

rump [rʌmp] Ⓐ N 1 (*Anat*) [*of horse etc*] ancas *fpl*, grupa *f*; [*of bird*] rabadilla *f*; (*) [*of person*] trasero *m*; (*Culin*) cuarto *m* trasero, cadera *f*
2 (*esp Brit*) [*of party etc*] parte *f* que queda; **there's just a ~ left** quedan solamente unos pocos
Ⓑ CPD ► **rump steak** N filete *m* de lomo de vaca *or* (*LAm*) de res

rumple [ˈrʌmpl] VT arrugar; [+ *hair*] despeinar

rumpus* [ˈrʌmpəs] Ⓐ N (*pl* **rumpuses**) lío* *m*, jaleo *m*; **to kick up a ~** armar un lío* *or* un jaleo
Ⓑ CPD ► **rumpus room** N (*US*) cuarto *m* de los niños, cuarto *m* de juegos

run [rʌn] (*vb: pt* **ran**; *pp* **run**) Ⓐ N 1 (= *act of running*) carrera *f*; **at a ~** corriendo, a la carrera; **to go at a steady ~** correr a un paso regular; **to break into a ~** echar a correr, empezar a correr; **to go for/have a ~ before breakfast** (salir a) correr antes del desayuno; **to make a ~ for it** (= *escape*) darse a al fuga, huir; (= *move quickly*) echarse a correr; **we shall have to make a ~ for it** tendremos que correr; **to be on the ~** (*from police*) estar huido de la justicia, ser fugitivo; **a prisoner on the ~** un preso fugado; **he's on the ~ from prison** (se) escapó *or* se fugó de la cárcel; **he's on the ~ from his creditors** se está escapando de sus acreedores; **to keep sb on the ~** mantener a algn en constante actividad; **we've got them on the ~** (*Mil etc*) los hemos puesto en fuga; (*fig*) están casi vencidos; ✦**IDIOM to give sb a ~ for their money** hacer sudar a algn; **he's had a good ~ (for his money)*** (*on sb's death*) ha tenido una vida larga y bien aprovechada
2 (= *outing in car etc*) vuelta *f*, paseo *m*, excursión *f*; **let's go for a ~ down to the coast** vamos a dar una vuelta por la costa
3 (= *journey*) viaje *m*; (*Aer, Rail etc*) (= *route*) ruta *f*, línea *f*; **it's a short ~ in the car** es un breve viaje en coche; **it's a 30-minute ~ by bus** en autobús se tarda 30 minutos; **the Calais ~** la ruta de Calais; **the Plymouth-Santander ~** la línea Plymouth-Santander, el servicio de Plymouth a Santander; **the boat no longer does that ~** el barco ya no hace esa ruta
4 (= *sequence*) serie *f*; **in the long ~** a la larga; **a ~ of luck** una racha de suerte; **a ~ of bad luck** una racha *or* temporada de mala suerte; **in the short ~** a plazo corto; **a ~ of five wins** una racha de cinco victorias
5 (*Theat, TV*) temporada *f*; **the play had a long ~** la obra se mantuvo mucho tiempo en cartelera; **when the London ~ was over** al terminarse la serie de representaciones en Londres
6 (= *generality*) **the common ~** lo común y corriente; **it stands out from the general ~ of books** destaca de la generalidad de los libros
7 (= *trend*) **the ~ of the market** la tendencia del mercado; **they scored against the ~ of play** marcaron un gol cuando menos se podía esperar
8 (*Comm, Fin*) (= *increased demand*) gran demanda *f*; **there was a ~ on sugar** el azúcar tenía mucha demanda; **a ~ on the banks** una gran demanda de fondos en los bancos; **a ~ on sterling** una gran demanda de libras esterlinas
9 (*for animals*) corral *m*; **ski ~** pista *f* de esquí
10 (*Cards*) escalera *f*
11 (*Cricket, Baseball*) carrera *f*; **to make** *or* **score a ~** hacer *or* anotar(se) una carrera; → CRICKET
12 (*Publishing*) **a ~ of 5,000 copies** una tirada de 5.000 ejemplares
13 (*in tights*) carrera *f*
14 (*Mus*) carrerilla *f*
15 (*Aer etc*) (= *raid*) ataque *m*; **a bombing ~** un bombardeo
16 (*US Pol*) (= *bid for leadership*) carrera *f*, campaña *f*
17 (= *access, use*) **they gave us the ~ of their garden** nos dejaron usar su jardín; **to have the ~ of sb's house** tener el libre uso de la casa de algn
18 **to have the ~s*** andar muy suelto*, tener cagalera*
Ⓑ VT 1 (*gen*) correr; **she ran 20km** corrió 20km; **to ~ the 100 metres** participar en *or* correr los 100 metros lisos; **let things ~ their course** (*fig*) deja que las cosas sigan su curso; **to ~ errands** hacer recados; **to ~ a horse** correr un caballo; **to ~ a race** participar en una carrera; **the race is ~ over four km** la carrera se hace sobre una distancia de cuatro km; **you ran a good race** corriste muy bien; ✦**IDIOMS to ~ sb close** casi alcanzar a algn, ir pisando los talones a algn; **to ~ it close** *or* **fine** dejarse muy poco tiempo; **to be ~ off one's feet** estar ocupadísimo; *see also* **mile**
2 (= *take, drive*) **to ~ a boat ashore** varar una embarcación; **this will ~ you into debt** esto te endeudará; **I'll ~ you home** te llevo a casa; **to ~ a car into a lamppost** estrellar un coche contra un farol; **to ~ sb into town** llevar a algn (en coche) a la ciudad; **the sheriff ran him out of town** el sheriff lo echó del pueblo
3 (= *put, move*) **to ~ a comb through one's hair** peinarse rápidamente; **to ~ one's eye over a letter** echar un vistazo a una carta; **to ~ a fence round a field** poner una valla alrededor de un campo; **to ~ one's fingers through sb's hair** pasar los dedos por el pelo de algn; **let me ~ this idea past you** (*US*) a ver qué piensas de esta idea; **to ~ a pipe through a wall** pasar un tubo por una pared; **to ~ water into a bath** hacer correr agua en un baño, llenar un baño de agua; **to ~ one's words together** comerse las palabras, hablar atropelladamente
4 (= *organize etc*) [+ *business, hotel etc*] dirigir, llevar; [+ *country*] gobernar; [+ *campaign, competition*] organizar; **she's the one who really ~s everything** la que en realidad lo dirige todo es ella; **the school ~s courses for foreign students** la escuela organiza cursos para estudiantes extranjeros; **to ~ the house for sb** llevar la casa a algn; **a house which is easy to ~** una casa de fácil manejo; **he wants to ~ my life** quiere organizarme la vida; **they ran a series of tests on the product** llevaron a cabo *or* efectuaron una serie de pruebas con el producto
5 (*esp Brit*) (= *operate, use*) [+ *car*] tener; [+ *machine*] hacer funcionar, hacer andar; [+ *train*] poner; (*Comput*) [+ *programme*] ejecutar; **to ~ a new bus service** poner en funcionamiento un nuevo servicio de autobuses; **we don't ~ a car** no tenemos coche; **he ~s two cars** tiene dos coches; **the car is very cheap to ~** el coche gasta muy poco *or* tiene muy pocos gastos de mantenimiento; **you can ~ this machine on gas** puedes hacer funcionar esta máquina a gas; **you can ~ it on** *or* **off the mains** funciona con corriente de la red; **they ran an extra train** pusieron un tren suplementario
6 (= *enter in contest*) **the liberals are not ~ning anybody this time** esta vez los liberales no tienen candidato; **to ~ a candidate** presentar (un) candidato; **to ~ a horse** correr un caballo
7 (= *publish*) [+ *report, story*] publicar, imprimir

8 (= *smuggle*) [+ *guns, whisky*] pasar de contrabando
9 (= *not stop for*) **to ~ a blockade** saltarse un bloqueo, burlar un bloqueo; **to ~ a stoplight** (*US*) saltarse un semáforo en rojo; *see also* **gauntlet**, **risk**, **temperature**
Ⓒ VI 1 (*gen*) correr; (*in race*) competir, correr, tomar parte; (= *flee*) huir; **to ~ across the road** cruzar la calle corriendo; **to ~ down the garden** correr por el jardín; **to ~ downstairs** bajar la escalera corriendo; **to ~ for a bus** correr tras el autobús; **we shall have to ~ for it** (= *move quickly*) tendremos que correr; (= *escape*) habrá que darse a la fuga; **to ~ for all one is worth** ◊ **~ like the devil** correr a todo correr; **~ for your lives!** ¡sálvese el que pueda!; **to ~ to help sb** correr al auxilio de algn; **to ~ to meet sb** correr al encuentro de algn; **he ran up to me** se me acercó corriendo; **he ran up the stairs** subió la escalera corriendo; ✦*IDIOM* **he's trying to ~ before he can walk** (*Brit*) quiere empezar la casa por el tejado
2 (*of bus service etc*) **the train ~s between Glasgow and Edinburgh** el tren circula entre Glasgow y Edimburgo; **the bus ~s every 20 minutes** hay un autobús cada 20 minutos; **there are no trains ~ning to Toboso** no hay servicio de trenes a Toboso; **steamers ~ daily between the two ports** hay servicio diario de vapores entre los dos puertos; **that train does not ~ on Sundays** ese tren no circula los domingos
3 (*Naut*) **to ~ aground** encallar; **to ~ before the wind** navegar con viento a popa
4 (= *function*) funcionar; **the car is not ~ning well** el coche no funciona bien; **you mustn't leave the engine ~ning** no se debe dejar el motor en marcha; **the lift isn't ~ning** el ascensor no funciona; **it ~s off the mains** funciona con corriente de la red; **it ~s on petrol** funciona con gasolina, tiene motor de gasolina; **things did not ~ smoothly for them** (*fig*) las cosas no les fueron bien
5 (= *extend*) 5·1 (*in time*) **the contract has two years left to ~** al contrato le quedan dos años de duración; **the contract ran for seven years** el contrato duró siete años; **it ~s in the family** [*characteristic*] viene de familia; [*disease*] es algo genético; **the play ran for two years** la obra estuvo dos años en cartelera; **the play ran for 200 performances** la obra tuvo 200 representaciones seguidas; **the programme ran for an extra ten minutes** el programa se prolongó diez minutos, el programa duró diez minutos de más; **the sentences will ~ concurrently** las condenas se cumplirán al mismo tiempo; **it ~s through the whole history of art** afecta toda la historia del arte, se observa en toda la historia del arte
5·2 (*in space*) **he has a scar ~ning across his chest** tiene una cicatriz que le atraviesa el pecho; **the road ~s along the river** la carretera va a lo largo del río; **a fence ~s along that side** hay una cerca por ese lado; **the road ~s by our house** la carretera pasa delante de nuestra casa; **the path ~s from our house to the station** el sendero va de nuestra casa a la estación; **this street ~s into the square** esta calle desemboca en la plaza; **a balcony ~s round the hall** una galería se extiende a lo largo del perímetro de la sala; **the city has walls ~ning right round it** la ciudad está completamente rodeada por una muralla; **the ivy ~s up the wall** la hiedra trepa por la pared
6 (= *flow*) correr; (*Med*) [*sore*] supurar; **your bath is ~ning** tienes el baño llenándose; **blood ran from the wound** la sangre manaba de la herida, la herida manaba sangre; **to ~ dry** [*river, well*] secarse; [*resources*] agotarse; **the milk ran all over the floor** la leche se derramó por todo el suelo; **money simply ~s through his fingers** es un manirroto; **his nose was ~ning** le moqueaba la nariz; **my pen ~s** mi pluma gotea; **the river ~s for 300 miles** el río corre 300 millas; **the river ~s into the sea** el río desemboca en el mar; **you left the tap ~ning** dejaste abierto el grifo *or* (*LAm*) abierta la llave; **the tears ran down her cheeks** las lágrimas le corrían por las mejillas; **when the tide is ~ning strongly** cuando sube la marea rápidamente; **the streets were ~ning with water** el agua corría por las calles; **we were ~ning with sweat** chorreábamos (de) sudor
7 [*colour*] correrse, desteñirse; **the colours have ~** los colores se han corrido *or* desteñido; **colours that will not ~** colores que no (se) destiñen *or* que no se corren
8 (= *melt*) derretirse; **my ice cream is ~ning** mi helado se está derritiendo
9 (= *go*) **a rumour ran through the town** corrió la voz por la ciudad; **a ripple of excitement ran through the crowd** una ola de entusiasmo hizo vibrar *or* estremeció a la multitud; **that tune keeps ~ning through my head** esa melodía la tengo metida en la cabeza; **the thought ran through my head that …** se me ocurrió pensar que …; *see also* **seed A1**, **wild B2**
10 (= *be*) **the train is ~ning late** el tren lleva retraso; **I'm ~ning a bit late** se me está haciendo un poco tarde; **the service usually ~s on time** el servicio generalmente es puntual; *see also* **high B**, **low[1] A4**
11 (*Pol*) (= *stand for election*) presentarse como candidato/a; **are you ~ning?** ¿vas a presentar tu candidatura?; **to ~ against sb** medirse con algn, enfrentarse a algn; **to ~ for office** presentarse como candidato a un cargo
12 (= *say*) **so the story ~s** así dice el cuento; **the text ~s like this** el texto dice así, el texto reza así
13 [*stocking*] hacerse una carrera
14 (*Comput*) ejecutarse

►**run about** VI + ADV = **run around**

►**run across** VI + PREP (= *encounter*) [+ *person*] tropezar con, encontrarse con; [+ *object*] encontrar, topar(se) con

►**run after** VI + PREP (= *to catch up*) correr tras; (= *chase*) perseguir; (*fig*) [+ *women, men*] correr detrás de, perseguir

►**run along** VI + ADV **~ along now!** (*to child*) ¡hala, vete!; (*to children*) ¡idos ya!

►**run around** VI + ADV ir corriendo de aquí para allá; **I've been ~ning around all day trying to get everything ready** llevo todo el día corriendo de aquí para allá para que todo esté listo; **to ~ around with** (*fig*) [+ *person*] salir con; [+ *group*] andar con, juntarse con

►**run at** VI + PREP lanzarse sobre, precipitarse sobre

►**run away** VI + ADV 1 [*prisoner*] escaparse, fugarse; **don't ~ away, I need your advice** no te escapes, que necesito que me des tu opinión; **to ~ away from home** huir de casa; **to ~ away from one's responsibilities** evadir sus responsabilidades
2 [*water*] correr

►**run away with** VI + PREP 1 [+ *money, jewels etc*] llevarse; [+ *person*] fugarse con; **don't ~ away with the idea that …** (*fig*) no te vayas a imaginar que …
2 (= *control*) **he let his imagination ~ away with him** se dejó llevar por su imaginación; **don't let your feelings ~ away with you** no te dejes dominar por las emociones
3 (= *win easily*) **to ~ away with a race** ganar fácilmente una carrera
4 (= *use up*) [+ *funds, resources*] comerse; **it simply ~s away with the money** es que se come todo el dinero

►**run back** Ⓐ VT + ADV 1 [+ *film, tape*] rebobinar
2 (= *drive*) [+ *person*] llevar (a su casa *etc*) en coche
Ⓑ VI + ADV volver corriendo

►**run down** Ⓐ VT + ADV 1 (*Aut*) (= *knock down*) atropellar; (*Naut*) hundir
2 (*esp Brit*) (= *reduce*) [+ *production*] ir reduciendo; [+ *supplies*] agotar
3 (= *find*) localizar, encontrar; (= *catch up with*) alcanzar; (= *capture*) coger, cazar
4 (= *disparage*) menospreciar
Ⓑ VI + ADV [*battery*] acabarse, gastarse, agotarse; [*car battery*] descargarse; [*supplies*] agotarse; **the spring has ~ down** se ha acabado la cuerda

►**run in** VT + ADV 1 (*Brit*) [+ *new machine*] rodar, hacer funcionar; (*Aut*) **"running in"** "en rodaje"
2 (*) (= *arrest*) detener

►**run into** VI + PREP 1 (= *encounter*) [+ *person*] tropezar con, encontrarse con; [+ *problems*] tropezar con; **to ~ into debt** contraer deudas, endeudarse; **the negotiations have ~ into difficulties** ha habido dificultades que han entorpecido *or* obstaculizado las negociaciones
2 (= *collide with*) **the car ran into the lamppost** el coche chocó contra el farol; **the two cars ran into each other** chocaron los dos coches
3 (= *merge*) **the colours have ~ into each other** se han mezclado *or* desteñido los colores
4 (= *amount to*) elevarse a, ascender a; **the cost will ~ into millions** el coste se elevará a *or* ascenderá a varios millones

►**run off** Ⓐ VI + ADV 1 [*prisoner*] escaparse, fugarse; **don't ~ off, I need your advice** no te escapes, que necesito que me des tu opinión
2 (= *drain away*) [*water*] correr
Ⓑ VT + ADV 1 (= *print*) [+ *copies*] tirar; [+ *photocopies*] hacer, sacar; (= *recite*) enumerar rápidamente; **he ran off the opera in six weeks** (*music*) compuso toda la ópera en sólo seis semanas; (*lyrics*) escribió el libreto de la ópera en sólo seis semanas
2 (= *drain away*) [+ *water etc*] vaciar, dejar salir

►**run off with** VI + PREP = **run away with**

►**run on** Ⓐ VI + ADV 1 (= *continue*) prolongarse; **the film ran on too long** la película duraba *or* se prolongaba demasiado; **the list ran on and on** la lista era interminable
2 (*) (= *talk*) seguir hablando
3 (*Typ*) continuar sin dejar espacio
Ⓑ VT + ADV (*Typ*) unir al párrafo anterior
Ⓒ VI + PREP **the conversation ran on wine** el tema de la conversación era el vino; **my thoughts ran on Mary**† mi pensamiento se concentró en Mary

►**run out** Ⓐ VI + ADV 1 [*person etc*] salir corriendo; [*liquid*] irse
2 (= *come to an end*) [*time, food, money*] acabarse; [*contract*] vencer; [*supplies*] agotarse; **when the money ~s out** cuando se acabe el dinero; **my patience is ~ning out** se me está agotando la paciencia, estoy perdiendo la paciencia; **their luck ran out** se les acabó la

suerte
Ⓑ VT + ADV [+ *rope*] soltar, ir dando
►**run out of** VI + PREP [+ *food, money*] quedarse sin; **I've ~ out of petrol** me he quedado sin gasolina, se me acabó la gasolina; **I'm afraid we've ~ out of time** me temo que no nos queda más tiempo *or* que se nos ha acabado el tiempo; **I ran out of patience** se me acabó la paciencia
►**run out on** VI + PREP (= *abandon*) abandonar; **she ran out on her husband** abandonó a su marido; **you're not going to ~ out on us now?** ¿no nos irás a dejar tirados?
►**run over** Ⓐ VI + ADV [1] (= *overflow*) [*liquid*] rebosar, derramarse; [*cup, saucepan etc*] rebosar(se), desbordarse
[2] (*in time*) durar más de la cuenta, pasarse del tiempo; **the show ran over by five minutes** la función duró cinco minutos más de la cuenta; **this text ~s over by 200 words** este texto tiene 200 palabras más de lo permitido
Ⓑ VI + PREP (= *read quickly*) leer (por encima), echar un vistazo a; (= *go through again*) repasar; (= *rehearse*) volver a hacer, volver a ensayar; **I'll ~ over your part with you** repasaremos juntos tu papel
Ⓒ VT + ADV (*Aut*) atropellar
►**run through** Ⓐ VI + PREP [1] (= *use up*) (*gen*) consumir; [+ *money*] gastar
[2] (= *read quickly*) leer (por encima), echar un vistazo a
[3] (= *rehearse*) [+ *play*] ensayar; (= *recapitulate*) repasar; **let's ~ through the chorus bit again** ensayemos otra vez la parte del coro; **let's just ~ through that again** vamos a repasarlo otra vez
Ⓑ VT + ADV (*with sword etc*) traspasar, atravesar
►**run to** VI + PREP [1] (= *extend to*) **the talk ran to two hours** la charla se extendió a dos horas; **the book has ~ to 20 editions** el libro ha alcanzado 20 ediciones; **the book will ~ to 700 pages** el libro tendrá 700 páginas en total
[2] (= *amount to*) elevarse a, ascender a; **the cost ran to hundreds of pounds** el coste se elevó a *or* ascendió a cientos de libras
[3] (= *be enough for*) alcanzar para; **my salary won't ~ to a car** mi sueldo no alcanza para un coche
[4] (= *afford*) permitirse; **I can't ~ to a second holiday** no me puedo permitir (el lujo de) otras vacaciones; **we can't possibly ~ to a grand piano** no podemos permitirnos *or* nos es imposible comprar un piano de cola
►**run up** Ⓐ VT + ADV [1] [+ *debt*] contraer; [+ *account*] crear, hacerse; **she had ~ up a huge bill at the hairdresser's** tenía acumulada una factura enorme de peluquería
[2] [+ *dress etc*] hacer rápidamente
[3] [+ *flag*] izar
Ⓑ VI + ADV *see* **run C1**
Ⓒ VI + PREP *see* **run C6**
►**run up against** VI + PREP [+ *problem etc*] tropezar con; **to ~ up against sb** tener que habérselas con algn
runabout ['rʌnəbaʊt] N [1] (*Aut*) coche *m* pequeño
[2] (*Rail etc*) billete *m* kilométrico
runaround ['rʌnəraʊnd] N ✦*IDIOM* **to give sb the ~*** traer a algn al retortero
runaway ['rʌnəweɪ] Ⓐ ADJ [*prisoner, slave*] fugitivo; [*soldier*] desertor; [*horse*] desbocado; [*lorry*] sin frenos, fuera de control; [*inflation*] galopante, desenfrenado; [*success*] arrollador; [*victory*] aplastante, abrumador; [*marriage*] clandestino, fugitivo
Ⓑ N (= *person*) fugitivo/a *m/f*; (= *horse*) caballo *m* desbocado
rundown ['rʌndaʊn] N [1] (= *slowing down, reduction*) [*of industry etc*] cierre *m* gradual; [*of activity, production*] disminución *f*, reducción *f*
[2] (= *résumé*) resumen *m* (**on** de); **to give sb a ~** poner a algn al tanto
run-down ['rʌn'daʊn] ADJ [*battery*] agotado, gastado; [*car battery*] descargado; [*building*] destartalado, ruinoso; [*organization*] en decadencia; [*health*] debilitado; **to be ~** [*person*] estar pachucho*, no encontrarse bien
rune [ru:n] N runa *f*
rung[1] [rʌŋ] N escalón *m*, peldaño *m*
rung[2] [rʌŋ] PP *of* **ring**[2]
runic ['ru:nɪk] ADJ rúnico
run-in ['rʌnɪn] N [1] (= *approach*) etapa *f* previa
[2] (*) (= *argument*) altercado *m*
[3] (*in contest, election*) desempate *m*
[4] (= *rehearsal*) ensayo *m*
[5] (*Typ*) palabras *fpl* insertadas en un párrafo
runlet ['rʌnlɪt] N, **runnel** ['rʌnl] N arroyuelo *m*
runner ['rʌnə^r] Ⓐ N [1] (= *athlete*) corredor(a) *m/f*; (= *horse*) (*in race*) caballo *m*; (= *messenger*) mensajero/a *m/f*; (*Mil*) ordenanza *mf*; (*Fin*) corredor(a) *m/f*
[2] (= *wheel*) ruedecilla *f*; [*of sledge, aircraft*] patín *m*; [*of skate*] cuchilla *f*
[3] (= *carpet*) alfombra *f* de pasillo; (= *table runner*) tapete *m*
[4] (*Bot*) tallo *m* rastrero, estolón *m*
[5] ✦*IDIOM* **to do a ~*** largarse* (*sin pagar*)
Ⓑ CPD ► **runner bean** N (*Brit*) judía *f* (escarlata), habichuela *f*
runner-up ['rʌnər'ʌp] N (*pl* **runners-up**) subcampeón/ona *m/f*, segundo/a *m/f*
running ['rʌnɪŋ] Ⓐ ADJ [1] (= *flowing*) [*water*] corriente; [*tap*] abierto; [*stream*] de agua corriente; **hot and cold ~ water** agua corriente caliente y fría
[2] (= *continuous*) continuo; **a ~ battle** (*lit*) continuos enfrentamientos *mpl*; (*fig*) una lucha continua; **a ~ commentary (on sth)** (*TV, Rad*) un comentario en directo (sobre algo); **we can do without a ~ commentary on the plot, thank you!** (*iro*) ¡podemos pasar perfectamente sin que nos cuentes el argumento de la película a cada paso!; **a ~ joke** una broma continua; *see also* **long-running**
[3] (*Med*) [*nose*] que moquea; [*sore*] que supura
Ⓑ ADV **for five days ~** durante cinco días seguidos *or* consecutivos; **for the third year ~, the weather was awful** por tercer año consecutivo el tiempo era horroroso
Ⓒ N [1] (= *management*) [*of business, organization, school*] gestión *f*, dirección *f*; [*of country*] gestión *f*
[2] (= *operation*) [*of machine, car*] funcionamiento *m*, marcha *f*; **to be in ~ order** [*vehicle*] estar en buen estado
[3] (= *activity, sport*) **~ is not allowed in the school corridors** no está permitido correr por los pasillos del colegio; **his hobby is ~** le gusta correr; **~ gear** ropa *f* de correr; **he started professional ~ eight years ago** empezó a correr profesionalmente hace ocho años
[4] (*fig*) **to be in the ~ for sth**: **she's in the ~ for promotion** tiene posibilidades de que la asciendan; **to make the ~** (*esp Brit Sport*) ir a la cabeza; (*fig*) tomar la iniciativa; **to be out of the ~** (*lit, fig*) estar fuera de combate; **his illness put him out of the ~ for the presidency** su enfermedad lo ha dejado fuera de combate en lo que respecta a la presidencia, su enfermedad ha acabado con sus posibilidades de conseguir la presidencia; **he's out of the ~ for the job now** ahora no tiene posibilidades de conseguir el trabajo
Ⓓ CPD ► **running board** N (*Aut*) estribo *m* ► **running costs, running expenses** NPL (*esp Brit*) [*of business*] gastos *mpl* corrientes; [*of car*] gastos *mpl* de mantenimiento ► **running head** N (*Typ, Comput*) título *m* de página ► **running in** N (*Aut*) rodaje *m* ► **running jump** N (*Sport*) salto *m* con carrerilla; **to take a ~ jump** (*lit*) saltar tomando carrerilla; ✦*IDIOM* **he can (go) take a ~ jump!*** ¡puede irse a la porra!* ► **running mate** N (*US Pol*) [*of presidential candidate*] candidato/a *m/f* a la vicepresidencia ► **running repairs** NPL reparaciones *fpl* provisionales ► **running shoe** N zapatilla *f* de correr *or* de deporte ► **running stitch** N (*countable*) puntada *f* de bastilla; (*uncountable*) bastilla *f* ► **running total** N suma *f* parcial; **to keep a ~ total (of sth)** llevar la cuenta del total (de algo) ► **running track** N pista *f* (de atletismo)
runny ['rʌnɪ] ADJ (*compar* **runnier**; *superl* **runniest**) [*substance*] líquido; [*eyes*] lloroso; **I don't like my boiled egg to be ~** no me gustan los huevos cocidos poco hechos; **I've got a ~ nose** no paro de moquear
run-off ['rʌnɒf] Ⓐ N [1] (*Sport*) carrera *f* de desempate; (*Pol*) desempate *m*, segunda vuelta *f*
[2] (*Agr*) escorrentía *f*
Ⓑ CPD ► **run-off water** N aguas *fpl* de escorrentía
run-of-the-mill ['rʌnəvðə'mɪl] ADJ (= *ordinary*) común y corriente, corriente y moliente; (= *mediocre*) mediocre
runproof ['rʌnpru:f] ADJ [*mascara*] que no se corre; [*tights*] indesmallable
runt [rʌnt] N (*also fig*) redrojo *m*, enano *m*; **you little ~!** ¡canalla!
run-through ['rʌnθru:] N ensayo *m*
run-up ['rʌnʌp] N [1] (*Brit*) (*to election etc*) período *m* previo (**to** a)
[2] (*Sport*) carrerilla *f*
runway ['rʌnweɪ] Ⓐ N [1] (*Aer*) pista *f* (de aterrizaje)
[2] (*US Theat etc*) pasarela *f*
Ⓑ CPD ► **runway lights** NPL balizas *fpl*
rupee [ru:'pi:] N rupia *f*
rupture ['rʌptʃə^r] Ⓐ N (*Med*) hernia *f*; (*fig*) ruptura *f*
Ⓑ VT [1] causar una hernia en, quebrarse; **to ~ o.s.** causarse una hernia, herniarse; (*fig*) (*hum*) herniarse
[2] (*fig*) romper, destruir
rural ['rʊərəl] ADJ rural; **~ development** desarrollo *m* rural; **~ planning** planificación *f* rural
ruse [ru:z] N ardid *m*, treta *f*, estratagema *f*
rush[1] [rʌʃ] Ⓐ N (*Bot*) junco *m*
Ⓑ CPD ► **rush basket** N cesto *m* de mimbre ► **rush light** N vela *f* de junco ► **rush mat** N estera *f* ► **rush matting** N estera *f*, esterilla *f*
rush[2] [rʌʃ] Ⓐ N [1] (= *act of rushing*) **there was a ~ for the door** se precipitaron todos hacia la puerta; **the gold ~** la fiebre del oro; **two were injured in the ~** hubo dos heridos en el tumulto; **the annual ~ to the beaches** la desbandada de todos los años hacia las playas
[2] (= *hurry*) prisa *f*, apuro *m* (*LAm*); **what's all the ~ about?** ¿por qué tanta prisa?; **we had a ~ to get it ready** tuvimos que darnos prisa *or* (*LAm*) apurarnos para tenerlo listo; **is there any ~ for this?** ¿corre prisa esto?; **it got lost in the ~** con el ajetreo se perdió; **I'm in a ~** tengo prisa *or* (*LAm*) apuro; **I did it in a ~** lo

hice deprisa, lo hice muy apurada (*LAm*); **it all happened in a ~** todo pasó deprisa y corriendo; **he's in no ~** no tiene prisa alguna *or* (*LAm*) apuro ninguno
3 (= *current, torrent*) **a ~ of warm air** una ráfaga de aire caliente; **a ~ of water** un torrente de agua; **a ~ of words** un torrente de palabras; **the words came out in a ~** las palabras salieron a borbotones
4 (*Comm*) demanda *f*; **we've had a ~ of orders** ha habido una enorme demanda de pedidos; **the Christmas ~** la actividad frenética de las Navidades; **a ~ for tickets** una enorme demanda de entradas; **there has been a ~ on suntan lotion** ha habido una enorme demanda de crema bronceadora
5 (*US Ftbl*) carga *f*
6 **rushes** (*Cine*) primeras pruebas *fpl*
Ⓑ VT 1 [+ *person*] meter prisa a, apurar (*LAm*); **don't ~ me!** ¡no me metas prisa!, ¡no me apures! (*LAm*); **I hate being ~ed** no aguanto que me metan prisa, no aguanto que me apuren (*LAm*); **to ~ sb into (doing) sth**: **she knew he was trying to ~ her into a decision** sabía que trataba de meterle prisa *or* (*LAm*) apurarla para que se decidiera; **don't be ~ed into signing anything** no dejes que te hagan firmar deprisa y corriendo, no dejes que te metan prisa *or* (*LAm*) que te apuren para firmar; **we were ~ed off our feet** estábamos hasta arriba de trabajo*
2 [+ *work, job*] hacer con mucha prisa *or* a la carrera; **I ~ed my lunch** comí el almuerzo a toda prisa *or* a todo correr *or* a la carrera; **I'm not going to ~ things** no voy a precipitarme
3 (= *carry, take*) **reinforcements were ~ed to the scene** mandaron rápidamente refuerzos al lugar del incidente; **he was ~ed (off) to hospital** lo llevaron al hospital con la mayor urgencia; **please ~ me my free copy** por favor, mándenme la copia gratuita tan pronto como puedan
4 (= *attack*) [+ *building, enemy positions*] asaltar, atacar; [+ *opponent, barrier, stage*] abalanzarse sobre
5 (*) (= *charge*) soplar*, clavar‡
Ⓒ VI 1 (= *run*) **to ~ by** = **to rush past**; **to ~ downstairs** bajar la escalera corriendo *or* a toda prisa; **to ~ past** pasar a toda velocidad; **everyone ~ed to the windows** todos corrieron *or* se precipitaron hacia las ventanas; **neighbours ~ed to his aid** los vecinos corrieron en su ayuda; **I ~ed to her side** corrí a su lado; **to ~ upstairs** subir la escalera corriendo *or* a toda prisa
2 (= *hurry*) **I must ~** me voy corriendo; **don't ~!** ¡con calma!; **I was ~ing to finish it** me daba prisa *or* (*LAm*) me estaba apurando por terminarlo; **people are ~ing to buy the book** la gente corre a comprar el libro; **the blood ~ed to her cheeks** *or* **face** enrojeció violentamente; **to ~ to conclusions** sacar conclusiones precipitadas; **the train went ~ing into the tunnel** el tren entró en el túnel a toda velocidad; **he will not ~ into any decisions** no tomará ninguna decisión precipitada; **the sound of ~ing water** el sonido de agua corriendo con fuerza; *see also* **headlong**
Ⓓ CPD ► **rush hour** N hora *f* punta, hora *f* pico (*LAm*); **~ hour traffic** tráfico *m* de hora punta *or* (*LAm*) de hora pico ► **rush job** N (= *urgent*) trabajo *m* urgente; (= *too hurried*) trabajo *m* hecho deprisa y corriendo ► **rush order** N pedido *m* urgente
►**rush about, rush around** VI + ADV correr de un lado a otro, correr de acá para allá
►**rush at** VI + PREP 1 (= *run towards*) [+ *door, exit*] precipitarse hacia; [+ *person*] abalanzarse sobre
2 (= *hurry*) **you tend to ~ at things** sueles precipitarte al hacer las cosas
►**rush away** VI + ADV irse corriendo, largarse a toda prisa*; **don't go ~ing away!** ¡no te vayas tan deprisa!
►**rush in** VI + ADV (*lit*) entrar corriendo, entrar a toda prisa; (*fig*) precipitarse; **before you ~ in, get some advice** no te precipites, pide consejo; *see also* **fool**
►**rush off** VI + ADV irse corriendo, largarse a toda prisa*; **don't ~ off!** ¡no te vayas tan deprisa!; **don't ~ off and buy the first one you see** no vayas corriendo y compres el primero que veas
►**rush out** Ⓐ VT + ADV [+ *book*] publicar a toda prisa; [+ *statement*] hacer público a toda prisa
Ⓑ VI + ADV salir corriendo
►**rush over** VI + ADV ir/venir corriendo
►**rush through** Ⓐ VI + PREP [+ *meal*] comer a toda prisa *or* a todo correr; [+ *work, job*] hacer a toda prisa *or* a todo correr *or* a la carrera; [+ *place*] pasar a toda velocidad; **we ~ed through dinner** cenamos a toda prisa *or* a todo correr *or* a la carrera; **the orchestra ~ed through the Mozart** la orquesta impuso un ritmo demasiado rápido a la pieza de Mozart
Ⓑ VT + ADV [+ *legislation*] aprobar a toda prisa; (*Comm*) [+ *order, supplies*] despachar rápidamente
►**rush up** VI + ADV = **rush over**
rushed [rʌʃt] ADJ **I didn't feel ~ or under pressure** no sentí que me estuvieran metiendo prisa *or* presionando, no me sentí presionado *or* (*LAm*) apurado; **breakfast had been a ~ affair** habíamos desayunado a toda prisa *or* a todo correr *or* a la carrera
rushy [ˈrʌʃɪ] ADJ juncoso
rusk [rʌsk] N (*esp Brit*) (*esp for babies*) galleta *f*, bizcocho *m* tostado
russet [ˈrʌsɪt] Ⓐ N (= *colour*) color *m* rojizo *or* bermejo
Ⓑ ADJ (*in colour*) rojizo, bermejo
Russia [ˈrʌʃə] N Rusia *f*
Russian [ˈrʌʃən] Ⓐ ADJ ruso
Ⓑ N 1 (= *person*) ruso/a *m/f*
2 (*Ling*) ruso *m*
Ⓒ CPD ► **Russian roulette** N ruleta *f* rusa ► **Russian salad** N ensaladilla *f* (rusa), ensalada *f* rusa
Russki*, **Russky*** [ˈrʌskɪ] ADJ, N (*esp US pej, hum*) = **Russian**
rust [rʌst] Ⓐ N (= *action*) oxidación *f*; (= *substance*) orín *m*, herrumbre *f*, óxido *m*; (= *colour*) color *m* herrumbre *or* de orín; (*Agr*) roya *f*
Ⓑ VI oxidarse, aherrumbrarse
Ⓒ VT oxidar, aherrumbrar
Ⓓ CPD ► **the Rust Belt** N (*US*) el cinturón industrial; → SUNBELT
rust-coloured, rust-colored (*US*) [ˈrʌstˌkʌləd] ADJ de color herrumbre *or* de orín
rusted [ˈrʌstɪd] ADJ oxidado, aherrumbrado
rustic [ˈrʌstɪk] Ⓐ ADJ [*pursuits*] rústico, del campo; [*restaurant, cottage*] rústico, de campo; [*style*] rústico; [*setting, atmosphere*] rústico, campestre
Ⓑ N aldeano/a *m/f*
rusticate [ˈrʌstɪkeɪt] Ⓐ VT (*Brit Univ*) suspender temporalmente
Ⓑ VI rusticar
rustication [ˌrʌstɪˈkeɪʃən] N (*Brit Univ*) suspensión *f* temporal
rusticity [rʌsˈtɪsɪtɪ] N rusticidad *f*
rustiness [ˈrʌstɪnɪs] N 1 herrumbre *f*, lo aherrumbrado
2 (*fig*) falta *f* de práctica
rustle[1] [ˈrʌsl] Ⓐ N [*of leaves, wind*] susurro *m*; [*of paper*] crujido *m*; [*of silk, dress*] frufrú *m*, crujido *m*
Ⓑ VT [+ *leaves*] hacer susurrar; [+ *paper*] mover ligeramente, hacer crujir
Ⓒ VI [*leaves*] susurrar; [*paper*] crujir; [*silk, dress*] hacer frufrú
rustle[2] [ˈrʌsl] VT (= *steal*) robar, abigear (*Mex*)
►**rustle up*** VT + ADV (= *find*) encontrar, dar con; (= *obtain*) conseguir, (lograr) reunir; (= *make*) [+ *meal*] improvisar, preparar; **I'll see what I can ~ up** veré lo que hay; **can you ~ up some coffee?** ¿podrías hacernos un café?
rustler [ˈrʌsləʳ] N ladrón/ona *m/f* de ganado, abigeo/a *m/f* (*Mex*)
rustless [ˈrʌstlɪs] ADJ inoxidable
rustling[1] [ˈrʌslɪŋ] N = **rustle**[1] **A**
rustling[2] [ˈrʌslɪŋ] N (*US*) (*also* **cattle ~**) robo *m* de ganado, abigeato *m* (*Mex*)
rustproof [ˈrʌstpruːf] Ⓐ ADJ inoxidable
Ⓑ VT tratar contra la corrosión
rustproofing [ˈrʌstˌpruːfɪŋ] N tratamiento *m* anticorrosión
rust-resistant [ˈrʌstrɪˌzɪstənt] ADJ anticorrosivo, antioxidante
rusty [ˈrʌstɪ] ADJ (*compar* **rustier**; *superl* **rustiest**)
1 oxidado, herrumbrado, herrumbroso; [*colour*] de orín
2 (*fig*) **my Greek is pretty ~** me falta práctica en griego, tengo el griego muy olvidado
rut[1] [rʌt] N surco *m*, rodera *f*, rodada *f*; ✦*IDIOMS* **to be in/get into a ~** ser/hacerse esclavo de la rutina; **I need to change jobs, I'm in a ~ here** necesito cambiar de trabajo, aquí me estoy anquilosando *or* estancando; **to get out of the ~** salir de la rutina
rut[2] [rʌt] Ⓐ N (*Bio*) celo *m*; **to be in ~** estar en celo
Ⓑ VI (= *be in rut*) estar en celo; (= *begin to rut*) caer en celo
rutabaga [ˌruːtəˈbeɪgə] N (*US*) nabo *m* sueco, naba *f*
ruthenium [ruːˈθiːnɪəm] N rutenio *m*
ruthless [ˈruːθlɪs] ADJ [*person, act*] despiadado, cruel; [*efficiency, determination*] inquebrantable, implacable; [*opponent, enemy*] implacable
ruthlessly [ˈruːθlɪslɪ] ADV [*exploit, suppress, kill*] despiadadamente; [*hunt down*] implacablemente, inexorablemente
ruthlessness [ˈruːθlɪsnɪs] N crueldad *f*
rutted [ˈrʌtɪd] ADJ lleno de baches
rutting [ˈrʌtɪŋ] Ⓐ ADJ (*Bio*) en celo
Ⓑ CPD ► **rutting season** N época *f* de celo
rutty [ˈrʌtɪ] ADJ lleno de baches
RV N ABBR 1 (*Bible*) (= **Revised Version**) *versión revisada de la Biblia*
2 (*US*) = **recreational vehicle**
Rwanda [rʊˈændə] N Ruanda *f*
Rwandan [rʊˈændən] Ⓐ ADJ ruandés
Ⓑ N ruandés/esa *m/f*
rye [raɪ] Ⓐ N (= *grain, grass*) centeno *m*
Ⓑ CPD ► **rye bread** N pan *m* de centeno ► **rye (whisky)** N whisky *m* de centeno
ryegrass [ˈraɪgrɑːs] N ballico *m*, césped *m* inglés

S s

S[1], **s**[1] [es] N (*letter*) S, s *f*; **S for sugar** S de Soria; **S-bend** curva *f* en S

S[2] ABBR [1] (= **south**) S
[2] (= **Saint**) Sto., Sta., S.
[3] (*US Scol*) (= **satisfactory**) suficiente

s[2] ABBR [1] = **second**
[2] = **son**
[3] (*Brit Fin*†) = **shilling(s)**

SA N ABBR [1] = **South Africa**
[2] = **South America**
[3] = **South Australia**

Saar [zɑːʳ] N Sarre *m*

sab* [sæb] N (*Brit*) *persona que se opone activamente a deportes que, como la caza, impliquen el sacrificio de animales*

sabbatarian [ˌsæbəˈtɛərɪən] Ⓐ ADJ sabatario
Ⓑ N sabatario/a *m/f*, *partidario/a de guardar estrictamente el domingo*

Sabbath [ˈsæbəθ] N (*Jewish*) sábado *m*; (*Christian*) domingo *m*; *see also* **keep A11**

sabbatical [səˈbætɪkəl] Ⓐ ADJ (*Rel*) sabático
Ⓑ N (*also* ~ **year**) año *m* sabático

saber [ˈseɪbəʳ] N (*US*) = **sabre**

saber-rattler [ˈseɪbəˌrætləʳ] N (*US*) = **sabre-rattler**

saber-rattling [ˈseɪbəˌrætlɪŋ] N (*US*) = **sabre-rattling**

sable [ˈseɪbl] Ⓐ N (= *fur*) marta *f* cibelina *or* cebellina; (= *colour*) negro *m*
Ⓑ ADJ negro

sabot [ˈsæbəʊ] N zueco *m*

sabotage [ˈsæbətɑːʒ] Ⓐ N sabotaje *m*; **an act of ~** un acto de sabotaje
Ⓑ VT (*also fig*) sabotear

saboteur [ˌsæbəˈtɜːʳ] N saboteador(a) *m/f*

sabre, **saber** (*US*) [ˈseɪbəʳ] N sable *m*

sabre-rattler, **saber-rattler** (*US*) [ˈseɪbəˌrætləʳ] N *alguien que hace alarde de un poder militar que generalmente no tiene*

sabre-rattling, **saber-rattling** (*US*) [ˈseɪbəˌrætlɪŋ] N *alarde de un poder militar que generalmente no se tiene*

sac [sæk] N (*Anat, Bio*) saco *m*

saccharin, **saccharine** [ˈsækərɪn] Ⓐ N sacarina *f*
Ⓑ ADJ sacarino; (*fig*) (= *sentimental*) azucarado, empalagoso

sacerdotal [ˌsæsəˈdəʊtl] ADJ sacerdotal

sachet [ˈsæʃeɪ] N [*of shampoo, ketchup, sugar, coffee*] sobrecito *m*, bolsita *f*

sack[1] [sæk] Ⓐ N [1] (= *bag*) [1·1] (*Brit*) (*for coal, grain*) saco *m*; **a ~ of potatoes** un saco de patatas; ✦*IDIOM* **to look like a ~ of potatoes** parecer un saco de patatas
[1·2] (*US*) (*for shopping*) bolsa *f* de papel
[2] (*) (*from job*) **to get the ~** ser despedido; **he got the ~** lo despidieron; **to give sb the ~** despedir *or* echar a algn
[3] (*esp US*‡) (= *bed*) **the ~** la cama, el sobre*; **to hit the ~** echarse a dormir
Ⓑ VT [1] (= *put into sacks*) ensacar, meter en sacos
[2] (*) (= *dismiss*) despedir; **he was ~ed** lo despidieron; **to be ~ed for doing sth** ser despedido por hacer algo
Ⓒ CPD ► **sack dress** N vestido *m* tipo saco
► **sack race** N carrera *f* de sacos

sack[2] [sæk] (*liter*) Ⓐ N (= *plundering*) saqueo *m*
Ⓑ VT (= *lay waste*) saquear

sackbut [ˈsækbʌt] N (*Mus*) sacabuche *m*

sackcloth [ˈsækklɒθ] N arpillera *f*; **to wear ~ and ashes** ponerse el hábito de penitencia, ponerse cenizas en la cabeza

sackful [ˈsækfʊl] N saco *m*, contenido *m* de un saco

sacking[1] [ˈsækɪŋ] N [1] (= *cloth*) arpillera *f*
[2] (*) (= *dismissal*) despido *m*

sacking[2] [ˈsækɪŋ] N (*Mil*) (= *plundering*) saqueo *m*

sacra [ˈsækrə] NPL *of* **sacrum**

sacral [ˈseɪkrəl] ADJ sacral

sacrament [ˈsækrəmənt] N (*Rel*) sacramento *m*; **to receive the Holy Sacrament** comulgar

sacramental [ˌsækrəˈmentl] ADJ sacramental

sacred [ˈseɪkrɪd] ADJ (= *holy*) [*shrine, object*] sagrado; **~ places** lugares *mpl* sagrados; **~ music** música *f* sacra; **~ to the memory of …** consagrado a la memoria de …; **a ~ promise** (*fig*) una promesa solemne; **is nothing ~?** ¿ya no se respeta nada?; **~ cow*** (*lit, fig*) vaca *f* sagrada; **the Sacred Heart** el Sagrado Corazón

sacredness [ˈseɪkrɪdnɪs] N lo sagrado

sacrifice [ˈsækrɪfaɪs] Ⓐ N (*lit, fig*) sacrificio *m*; **to offer sth in ~** ofrecer algo como sacrificio; **no ~ was too great** todo sacrificio merecía la pena; **to make ~s (for sb)** hacer sacrificios (por algn), sacrificarse (por algn); **the ~ of the mass** el sacrificio de la misa; **to sell sth at a ~** vender algo con pérdida
Ⓑ VT (*lit, fig*) sacrificar; (*Comm*) vender con pérdida; **she ~d everything for me** lo ha sacrificado todo por mí; **to ~ o.s. (for sb/sth)** sacrificarse (por algn/algo); **accuracy should never be ~d to speed** nunca debería sacrificarse la exactitud por la rapidez

sacrificial [ˌsækrɪˈfɪʃəl] ADJ sacrificatorio; **~ lamb** chivo *m* expiatorio

sacrilege [ˈsækrɪlɪdʒ] N (*lit, fig*) sacrilegio *m*

sacrilegious [ˌsækrɪˈlɪdʒəs] ADJ sacrílego

sacrist [ˈsækrɪst] N = **sacristan**

sacristan [ˈsækrɪstən] N sacristán *m*

sacristy [ˈsækrɪstɪ] N sacristía *f*

sacrosanct [ˈsækrəʊsæŋkt] ADJ (*lit, fig*) sacrosanto

sacrum [ˈsækrəm] N (*pl* **sacra**) (*Anat*) sacro *m*

SAD [sæd] N ABBR = **seasonal affective disorder**

sad [sæd] Ⓐ ADJ (*compar* **sadder**; *superl* **saddest**) [1] (= *unhappy*) [*person, eyes, smile*] triste; **I'm ~ that I won't be able to play football any more** estoy triste porque no voy a poder volver a jugar al fútbol, me entristece no poder volver a jugar al fútbol; **we were ~ about** *or* **at the news of her illness** nos entristeció *or* nos apenó enterarnos de su enfermedad; **to become ~** entristecerse, ponerse triste; **to feel ~** sentirse triste, estar triste; **to grow ~** = **to become sad**; **to be ~ at heart** estar profundamente triste, tener el corazón oprimido; **to make sb ~** entristecer *or* poner triste a algn; **he left a ~der and a wiser man** cuando se marchó era un hombre escarmentado
[2] (= *distressing*) [*story, occasion, loss*] triste; [*news*] malo, triste; **it is my ~ duty to inform you that …** tengo el penoso deber de informarle de que …; **the ~ fact** *or* **truth is that …** la triste realidad es que …; **how ~!** ¡qué triste!, ¡qué pena!; **it is ~ to see such expertise wasted** es lamentable *or* da pena ver tanta pericia echada a perder; **it was a ~ sight** era una triste escena
[3] (= *deplorable*) [*situation, state of affairs*] lamentable, penoso; **it's a ~ business** es un asunto lamentable; **a ~ mistake** un error lamentable; **~ to say** lamentablemente
[4] (*pej*) (= *pathetic*) [*performance, attempt, joke*] penoso; **what ~ people they must be if they have to complain about a little innocent fun** si se quejan de que la gente lo pase bien un rato es realmente como para tenerles pena
Ⓑ CPD ► **sad sack*** N (*US*) inútil* *mf*

> **SAD**
>
> **Position of "triste"**
>
> You should generally put **triste** after the noun when translating **sad** in the sense of "unhappy", and before the noun in the sense of "distressing":
>
> He always seemed a sad little boy
> ***Siempre pareció un niño triste***
> ...the sad reality...
> ***...la triste realidad...***
>
> *For further uses and examples, see main entry.*

sadden [ˈsædn] VT entristecer; **it ~s me** me entristece mucho, me da (mucha) pena

saddle [ˈsædl] Ⓐ N [1] [*of bicycle*] silla *f*; [*of horse*] silla *f* de montar; **Red Rum won with Stack in the ~** ganó Red Rum montado por Stack; **to be in the ~** (*fig*) estar en el poder
[2] (*Culin*) **~ of lamb** cuarto *m* (trasero) de cordero
[3] [*of hill*] collado *m*

Ⓑ VT [1] (*also* ~ **up**) [+ *horse*] ensillar
[2] (*) (= *lumber*) **to ~ sb with sth** cargar a algn con algo; **now we're ~d with it** ahora tenemos que cargar con ello; **to get ~d with sth** tener que cargar con algo; **to ~ o.s. with sth** cargar con algo

saddle-backed ['sædlbækt] ADJ (*Zool*) ensillado

saddlebag ['sædlbæg] N alforja *f*

saddlebow ['sædlbəʊ] N arzón *m* delantero

saddlecloth ['sædlklɒθ] N sudadero *m*

saddler ['sædləʳ] N talabartero/a *m/f*, guarnicionero/a *m/f*

saddlery ['sædlərɪ] N talabartería *f*, guarnicionería *f*

saddle-sore ['sædl,sɔːʳ] ADJ **he was ~** le dolían las posaderas de tanto montar

saddo* ['sædəʊ] (*pl* **saddos** *or* **saddoes**) (*Brit*)
Ⓐ ADJ penoso, patético
Ⓑ N mamarracho/a* *m/f*

sadism ['seɪdɪzəm] N sadismo *m*

sadist ['seɪdɪst] N sadista *mf*

sadistic [sə'dɪstɪk] ADJ sádico

sadly ['sædlɪ] ADV [1] (= *sorrowfully*) [*say, smile*] con tristeza, tristemente
[2] (= *regrettably*) desgraciadamente, lamentablemente; **~, we don't have much chance of winning** desgraciadamente *or* lamentablemente, no tenemos muchas posibilidades de ganar; **his uncle, who ~ died** su tío, que tristemente *or* desgraciadamente falleció; **it is a ~ familiar pattern** es un hecho por desgracia familiar; **~ for him** lamentablemente *or* desgraciadamente para él
[3] (= *severely*) **their education has been ~ neglected** han descuidado su educación de forma lamentable; **to be ~ lacking in sth** ser muy deficiente en algo; **he will be ~ missed** se le echará mucho de menos; **you are ~ mistaken** estás muy equivocado; **to be ~ in need of sth** necesitar imperiosamente algo

sadness ['sædnɪs] N tristeza *f*

sadomasochism [,seɪdəʊ'mæsə,kɪzəm] N sadomasoquismo *m*

sadomasochist [,seɪdəʊ'mæsəkɪst] N sadomasoquista *mf*

sadomasochistic [,seɪdəʊ,mæsə'kɪstɪk] ADJ sadomasoquista

s.a.e. N ABBR [1] (= **stamped addressed envelope**) *sobre con las propias señas de uno y con sello*
[2] = **self-addressed envelope**

safari [sə'fɑːrɪ] Ⓐ N safari *m*; **to be on ~** estar de safari
Ⓑ CPD ► **safari jacket** N chaqueta *f* de safari, sahariana *f* ► **safari park** N (*Brit*) safari park *m*

safe [seɪf] Ⓐ ADJ (*compar* **safer**, *superl* **safest**)
[1] (= *not in danger*) [*person*] a salvo, seguro; [*object*] seguro; **you'll be ~ here** aquí no correrás peligro, aquí estarás a salvo; **your pearls will be quite ~ in the bank** tus perlas estarán totalmente seguras en el banco; **to feel ~** sentirse seguro; **to be ~ from** [+ *attack, predator, sarcasm*] estar a salvo de; [+ *contamination*] estar libre de; **to keep sth ~** guardar algo (en lugar seguro); **I'll keep it ~ for you** yo te lo guardo; **where can I put this to keep it ~?** ¿dónde puedo poner esto para que esté seguro?; **the secret is ~ with me** guardaré el secreto; **the documents are ~ with him** cuidará bien de los documentos, con él los documentos están en buenas manos; ✦*IDIOMS* **~ and sound** sano y salvo; **as ~ as houses** completamente seguro; ✦*PROV* **better ~ than sorry** más vale prevenir que curar
[2] (= *not dangerous*) [*ladder, load, vehicle, option*] seguro; [*method, handling*] seguro, fiable; [*structure, bridge*] sólido; [*investment*] seguro, sin riesgo; [*level*] que no entraña riesgo; **the ~ disposal of hazardous wastes** la eliminación sin riesgos de residuos peligrosos; **is nuclear power ~?** ¿es segura la energía nuclear?; **these stairs are not very ~** esta escalera no es muy segura; **don't walk on the ice, it isn't ~** no andes por el hielo, es peligroso; **keep your alcohol consumption within ~ limits** mantén tu consumo de alcohol dentro de los límites de seguridad; **it's not ~ to go out after dark** es peligroso salir de noche; **it's ~ to eat** se puede comer sin peligro; **it's ~ to say that ...** se puede decir sin miedo a equivocarse que ...; **it's ~ to assume that ...** cabe suponer con bastante seguridad que ...; **it might be ~r to wait** puede que sea mejor esperar; **it is a ~ assumption that she was very disappointed** a buen seguro que estaba muy decepcionada; **it's a ~ bet!** ¡es cosa segura!; **to keep a ~ distance from sth** mantenerse a una distancia prudencial de algo; (*when driving*) mantener la distancia de seguridad con algo; **to follow sb at a ~ distance** seguir a algn manteniendo cierta distancia; **to be a ~ driver** conducir con prudencia *or* con cuidado; **a team of experts made the building ~** un equipo de expertos se ocupó de que el edificio no constituyese un peligro; **a ~ margin** un margen de seguridad; **just to be on the ~ side** para mayor seguridad, por si acaso; **the ~st thing is to ...** lo más seguro es + *infin*; **he's ~ with children** [*man*] es de fiar con los niños; [*dog*] no es un peligro para los niños
[3] (= *secure*) [*environment, neighbourhood, harbour*] seguro; **to be in ~ hands** estar a salvo, estar en buenas manos; **to keep sth in a ~ place** guardar algo en un lugar seguro; ✦*IDIOM* **a ~ pair of hands** (*Brit*) una persona competente
[4] (= *trouble-free*) [*arrival, delivery*] sin problemas; [*landing*] sin riesgo, sin peligro; **~ journey!** ¡buen viaje!; **have a ~ journey home!** ¡que llegues bien (a casa)!; **~ passage** paso *m* franco, libre tránsito *m*; **the ~ return of the hostages** la vuelta de los rehenes sanos y salvos
Ⓑ N (*for valuables*) caja *f* fuerte; (*for meat*) fresquera *f*
Ⓒ ADV **to play (it) ~** ir a lo seguro, no arriesgarse
Ⓓ CPD ► **safe deposit** N (= *vault*) cámara *f* acorazada; (= *box*) (*also* ~ **deposit box**) caja *f* fuerte, caja *f* de seguridad ► **safe haven** N refugio *m* seguro ► **safe house** N piso *m* franco ► **the safe period*** N (*Med*) el periodo de infertilidad ► **safe seat** N (*esp Brit Pol*) **it was a ~ Conservative seat** era un escaño prácticamente seguro para los conservadores, el escaño estaba prácticamente asegurado para los conservadores ► **safe sex** N sexo *m* seguro *or* sin riesgo

safe-blower ['seɪf,bləʊəʳ] N, **safe-breaker** ['seɪf,breɪkəʳ] N ladrón/ona *m/f* de cajas fuertes

safe-conduct ['seɪf'kɒndəkt] N salvoconducto *m*

safe-cracker ['seɪf,krækəʳ] N (*US*) ladrón/ona *m/f* de cajas fuertes

safeguard ['seɪfgɑːd] Ⓐ N resguardo *m*; **as a ~ against ...** como defensa contra ...
Ⓑ VT proteger, resguardar

safe-keeping [,seɪf'kiːpɪŋ] N custodia *f*; **in his ~** bajo su custodia; **to put into ~** poner a buen recaudo *or* bajo custodia

safely ['seɪflɪ] ADV [1] (= *without danger*) **it can ~ be frozen for months** se puede congelar sin ningún problema *or* sin peligro durante varios meses; **you can walk about quite ~ in this town** no se corre peligro andando por esta ciudad, no es peligroso andar por esta ciudad; **drive ~!** conduce con prudencia *or* cuidado; **I can ~ say that ...** puedo afirmar con toda seguridad *or* sin miedo a equivocarme que ...
[2] (= *without incident*) [*land, return*] (*gen*) sin ningún percance; (*in the midst of danger*) sano y salvo; **to arrive ~** llegar bien, llegar sin ningún percance
[3] (= *securely*) **all the doors were ~ shut** todas las puertas estaban bien cerradas; **to put sth away ~** guardar algo en un lugar seguro; **she was ~ tucked up in bed** estaba bien metidita en la cama; **the dogs were ~ locked in the van** los perros estaban encerrados en la furgoneta, donde no podían hacer daño; **he's ~ through to the semi-final** ya se ha asegurado el paso a las semifinales; **now that the exams are ~ out of the way we can relax a bit** ahora que no tenemos la preocupación de los exámenes podemos relajarnos un poco

safeness ['seɪfnɪs] N seguridad *f*

safety ['seɪftɪ] Ⓐ N seguridad *f*; **our primary concern is ~** nuestra principal preocupación es la seguridad; **for his (own) ~** por su seguridad; **people worry about the ~ of nuclear energy** a la gente le preocupa que la energía nuclear no sea segura; **they helped the survivors to ~** ayudaron a los sobrevivientes a ponerse a salvo; **he sought ~ in flight** intentó ponerse a salvo huyendo; **to ensure sb's ~** garantizar la seguridad de algn; **~ first!** ¡lo primero es la seguridad!; **there's ~ in numbers** cuantos más, menos peligro; **in a place of ~** en un lugar seguro; **to reach ~** ponerse a salvo; **for ~'s sake** para mayor seguridad; **with complete ~** con la mayor seguridad; *see also* **road B**
Ⓑ CPD ► **safety belt** N cinturón *m* de seguridad ► **safety catch** N (*on gun*) seguro *m*; (*on bracelet*) cierre *m* de seguridad ► **safety chain** N (*on bracelet*) cadena *f* de seguridad ► **safety curtain** N (*in theatre*) telón *m* de seguridad ► **safety deposit box** N caja *f* fuerte, caja *f* de seguridad ► **safety device** N dispositivo *m* de seguridad ► **safety factor** N factor *m* de seguridad ► **safety glass** N vidrio *m* inastillable *or* de seguridad ► **safety harness** N arnés *m* de seguridad ► **safety helmet** N casco *m* de protección ► **safety inspector** N (*at workplace*) inspector(a) *m/f* de seguridad en el trabajo ► **safety lamp** N [*of miner*] lámpara *f* de seguridad ► **safety lock** N seguro *m*, cerradura *f* de seguridad ► **safety margin** N margen *m* de seguridad ► **safety match** N fósforo *m* *or* (*Sp*) cerilla *f* de seguridad ► **safety measure** N medida *f* de seguridad *or* de precaución ► **safety mechanism** N (*lit, fig*) mecanismo *m* de seguridad ► **safety net** N (*in circus*) red *f* de seguridad; (*fig*) protección *f* ► **safety officer** N encargado/a *m/f* de seguridad ► **safety pin** N imperdible *m* (*Sp*), seguro *m* (*CAm, Mex*) ► **safety precaution** N medida *f* de seguridad *or* de precaución ► **safety rail** N barandilla *f* ► **safety razor** N maquinilla *f* de afeitar ► **safety regulations** NPL normas *fpl* de seguridad ► **safety valve** N válvula *f* de seguridad *or* de escape; (*fig*) válvula *f* de escape, desahogo *m*

saffron ['sæfrən] Ⓐ N (= *powder*) azafrán *m*; (=

colour) color *m* azafrán
Ⓑ ADJ azafranado, color azafrán

sag [sæg] Ⓐ VI [*roof, awning etc*] combarse; [*bed*] hundirse; [*shoulders*] encorvarse; [*rope*] aflojarse; [*prices*] bajar; **his spirits ~ged** le flaquearon los ánimos, se desanimó
Ⓑ N (*in roof, ceiling*) combadura *f*

saga ['sɑːgə] N (*Hist*) saga *f*; (= *novel*) serie *f* (de novelas); (*fig*) epopeya *f*; **he told me the whole ~ of what had happened** me contó toda la odisea *or* historia de lo ocurrido

sagacious [sə'geɪʃəs] ADJ (*frm*) [*person, remark*] sagaz

sagaciously [sə'geɪʃəslɪ] ADV (*frm*) sagazmente

sagacity [sə'gæsɪtɪ] N (*frm*) sagacidad *f*

sage[1] [seɪdʒ] Ⓐ ADJ (= *wise*) sabio; (= *sensible*) cuerdo
Ⓑ N sabio/a *m/f*

sage[2] [seɪdʒ] Ⓐ N (= *herb*) salvia *f*
Ⓑ CPD ► **sage and onion stuffing** N relleno *m* de cebolla con salvia ► **sage green** ADJ verde salvia *inv* N verde *m* salvia

sagebrush ['seɪdʒbrʌʃ] N (*US*) artemisa *f*; **the Sagebrush State** Nevada

sagely ['seɪdʒlɪ] ADV (= *wisely*) sabiamente; (= *sensibly*) con cordura

sagging ['sægɪŋ] ADJ [*ground*] hundido; [*beam*] combado; [*cheek*] fofo; [*rope*] flojo; [*gate, hemline, breasts*] caído; [*shoulders*] encorvado

Sagittarius [ˌsædʒɪ'tɛərɪəs] N 1 (= *sign, constellation*) Sagitario *m*
2 (= *person*) sagitario *mf*; **she's (a) ~** es sagitario

sago ['seɪgəʊ] Ⓐ N sagú *m*
Ⓑ CPD ► **sago palm** N palmera *f* sagú

Sahara [sə'hɑːrə] N Sáhara *m*; **the ~ Desert** el (desierto del) Sáhara

Sahel [sɑː'hel] N Sahel *m*

sahib ['sɑːhɪb] N (*India*) 1 señor *m*; **Smith Sahib** (el) señor Smith
2 (*hum*) caballero *m*; **pukka ~** caballero *m* de verdad

said [sed] Ⓐ PT, PP *of* **say**
Ⓑ ADJ dicho; **the ~ animals** dichos animales; **the ~ general** dicho general

Saigon [saɪ'gɒn] N Saigón *m*

sail [seɪl] Ⓐ N 1 (*Naut*) (= *cloth*) vela *f*; **the age of ~** la época de la navegación a vela; **in** *or* **under full ~** a toda vela, a vela llena; **to lower the ~s** arriar las velas; **to set ~** [*ship, person*] hacerse a la vela, zarpar; **we set ~ from Portsmouth** nos hicimos a la vela en Portsmouth; **to set ~ for Liverpool** zarpar hacia Liverpool, hacerse a la vela con rumbo a Liverpool; **to take in the ~s** amainar las velas; **under ~** a vela; ✦**IDIOM to take the wind out of sb's ~s** bajarle los humos a algn
2 (*Naut*) (= *trip*) paseo *m* en barco; **it's three days' ~ from here** desde aquí se tarda tres días en barco; **to go for a ~** dar una vuelta en barco
3 (*Naut*) (= *boat*) (*pl* **sail**) barco *m* de vela, velero *m*; **20 ~** 20 veleros
4 [*of windmill*] aspa *f*
Ⓑ VT [+ *boat, ship*] gobernar; **to ~ the Atlantic** cruzar el Atlántico; **he ~s his own boat** tiene barco propio; **they ~ed the ship to Cadiz** fueron con el barco a Cádiz; ✦**IDIOM to ~ the (seven) seas** navegar (en alta mar)
Ⓒ VI 1 (*Naut*) [*boat, ship, person*] navegar; **to ~ at 12 knots** navegar a 12 nudos, ir a 12 nudos; **we ~ed into harbour** entramos a puerto; **we ~ed into Lisbon** llegamos a Lisboa; **to ~ round the world** dar la vuelta al mundo en barco; **to ~ round a headland** doblar un cabo; **to ~ up the Tagus** navegar por el Tajo, subir el Tajo; ✦**IDIOM to ~ close to the wind** pisar terreno peligroso
2 (*Naut*) (= *leave*) zarpar, salir; **the boat ~s at eight o'clock** el barco zarpa *or* sale a las ocho; **we ~ for Australia soon** pronto zarpamos *or* salimos hacia Australia; **she ~s on Monday** zarpa *or* sale el lunes
3 (*fig*) **she ~ed into the room** entró majestuosamente en la sala; **the plate ~ed over my head** el plato voló por encima de mi cabeza

► **sail into*** VI + PREP **to ~ into sb** (= *scold*) poner a algn como un trapo*; (= *attack*) arremeter contra algn, atacar a algn

► **sail through** VI + PREP [+ *life, situation*] pasar sin esfuerzo por; [+ *exam, driving test*] no tener problemas para aprobar; **don't worry, you'll ~ through it** no te preocupes, todo te resultará facilísimo

sailboard ['seɪlbɔːd] N plancha *f* de windsurf

sailboarder ['seɪlbɔːdə^r] N windsurfista *mf*

sailboarding ['seɪlbɔːdɪŋ] N windsurf *m*, surf *m* a vela

sailboat ['seɪlbəʊt] N (*US*) = **sailing boat**

sailcloth ['seɪlklɒθ] N lona *f*

sailfish ['seɪlfɪʃ] N aguja *f* de mar, pez *m* vela

sailing ['seɪlɪŋ] Ⓐ N 1 (*Sport*) vela *f*, navegación *f* a vela; **to go ~** hacer vela; ✦**IDIOM to be plain ~**: **now it's all plain ~** ahora es coser y cantar; **it's not exactly plain ~** no es muy sencillo que digamos
2 (*Naut*) (= *departure*) salida *f*
Ⓑ CPD ► **sailing boat** N velero *m*, barco *m* de vela ► **sailing date** N fecha *f* de salida (*de un barco*) ► **sailing orders** NPL últimas instrucciones *fpl* (*dadas al capitán de un buque*) ► **sailing ship** N velero *m*, buque *m* de vela ► **sailing time** N hora *f* de salida (*de un barco*)

sailmaker ['seɪlˌmeɪkə^r] N velero *m*

sailor ['seɪlə^r] Ⓐ N marinero *m*; **to be a bad ~** marearse fácilmente; **to be a good ~** no marearse
Ⓑ CPD ► **sailor hat** N sombrero *m* de marinero ► **sailor suit** N traje *m* de marinero (*de niño*)

sainfoin ['sænfɔɪn] N pipirigallo *m*

▼**saint** [seɪnt] N 1 santo/a *m/f*; **~'s day** fiesta *f* (de santo); **All Saints' Day** día *m* de Todos los Santos (*1 noviembre*); **my mother was a ~** (*fig*) mi madre era una santa; **she's no ~** (*iro*) ella no es una santa, que digamos
2 (*in names*) **Saint John** San Juan; **Saint Bernard** (= *dog*) perro *m* de San Bernardo; **Saint Elmo's fire** fuego *m* de Santelmo; **Saint Kitts** (*in West Indies*) San Cristóbal; **Saint Patrick's Day** el día *or* la fiesta de San Patricio; **Saint Theresa** Santa Teresa; **Saint Vitus' dance** baile *m* de San Vito; *see also* **valentine**
3 (*as name of church*) **they were married at Saint Mark's** se casaron en la iglesia de San Marcos

sainted ['seɪntɪd] ADJ [*martyr*] canonizado; [*wife, mother*] santo, bendito; (*of dead*) que en gloria esté; **my ~ aunt!***† (*hum*) ¡caray!*

sainthood ['seɪnthʊd] N santidad *f*

saint-like ['seɪntlaɪk] ADJ = **saintly**

saintliness ['seɪntlɪnɪs] N santidad *f*

saintly ['seɪntlɪ] ADJ (*compar* **saintlier**; *superl* **saintliest**) (*gen*) santo; (= *pious*) pío; (*pej*) santurrón

sake[1] [seɪk] N **for the ~ of sb/sth** por algn/algo; **for the ~ of the children** por (el bien de) los niños; **(just) for the ~ of it** (sólo) porque sí; **he was talking just for the ~ of it** estaba hablando por hablar; **a film with a lot of violence thrown in just for the ~ of it** una película con mucha violencia añadida que no venía a cuento; **for the ~ of argument** digamos, pongamos por caso; **art for art's ~** el arte por el arte; **for goodness ~!** ¡por el amor de Dios!; **for God's ~!** ◊ **for heaven's ~!** ¡por Dios!; **for my ~** por mí; **for old times' ~** por los viejos tiempos; **for your own ~** por tu propio bien; **she likes this kind of music for its own ~** le gusta este tipo de música por sí misma; **for the ~ of peace** para garantizar la paz; **to talk for the ~ of talking** hablar por hablar; *see also* **Pete**, **safety A**

sake[2] ['sɑːkɪ] N sake *m*, saki *m*

sal [sæl] Ⓐ N sal *f*
Ⓑ CPD ► **sal ammoniac** N sal *f* amoníaca ► **sal volatile** N sal *f* volátil

salaam [sə'lɑːm] Ⓐ N zalema *f*
Ⓑ VI hacer zalemas

salability [ˌseɪlə'bɪlɪtɪ] N (*US*) = **saleability**

salable ['seɪləbl] ADJ (*US*) = **saleable**

salacious [sə'leɪʃəs] ADJ (*frm*) salaz

salaciousness [sə'leɪʃəsnɪs] N, **salacity** [sə'læsɪtɪ] N (*frm*) salacidad *f*

salad ['sæləd] Ⓐ N ensalada *f*; **fruit ~** ensalada *f* de frutas, macedonia *f* de frutas (*Sp*); **Russian ~** ensaladilla *f* (rusa), ensalada *f* rusa
Ⓑ CPD ► **salad bowl** N ensaladera *f* ► **salad cream** N (*Brit*) mayonesa *f* ► **salad days** NPL juventud *fsing* ► **salad dish** N ensaladera *f* ► **salad dressing** N aliño *m* ► **salad oil** N aceite *m* para ensaladas

salamander ['sæləˌmændə^r] N salamandra *f*

salami [sə'lɑːmɪ] N salami *m*, salame *m* (*S. Cone*)

salaried ['sælərɪd] ADJ [*person*] asalariado; [*position*] retribuido, con sueldo

▼**salary** ['sælərɪ] Ⓐ N salario *m*, sueldo *m*; **"~ negotiable"** "salario *or* sueldo a convenir"
Ⓑ CPD ► **salary bracket** N categoría *f* salarial ► **salary earner** N asalariado/a *m/f* ► **salary package** N paquete *m* salarial ► **salary range** N gama *f* de salarios ► **salary review** N revisión *f* de sueldos ► **salary scale** N escala *f* salarial ► **salary structure** N estructuración *f* salarial

sale [seɪl] Ⓐ N 1 [*of item, object, house*] venta *f*; **newspaper ~s have fallen** ha descendido la venta de periódicos; **~ and lease back** venta y arrendamiento al vendedor; **is it for ~?** ¿está en venta?; **the house is for ~** la casa está en venta, esta casa se vende; **it's not for ~** no está en venta; **to put a house up for ~** poner una casa en venta; **"for sale"** "se vende"; **to be on ~** (*Brit*) estar a la venta; (*US*) estar rebajado; **on ~ at all fishmongers** de venta en todas las pescaderías; **it's going cheap for a quick ~** se ofrece a bajo precio porque se tiene prisa en venderlo; **it found a ready ~** se vendió pronto; **on a ~ or return basis** en depósito
2 (= *event*) rebajas *fpl*; **there's a ~ on at Harrods** en Harrods están de rebajas; **"sale"** (*in shop window*) "rebajas"; **clearance ~** liquidación *f* (total); **he bought a leather jacket in a ~** compró una chaqueta de cuero en unas rebajas; **the January ~s** las rebajas de enero; **the ~s are on** hay rebajas
3 (= *auction*) subasta *f*; *see also* **jumble C**
Ⓑ CPD ► **sale goods** NPL artículos *mpl* rebajados ► **sale item** N artículo *m* rebajado ► **sale price** N (= *cost*) precio *m* de venta; (= *reduced cost*) precio *m* rebajado, precio *m* de rebaja ► **sales agent** N agente *mf* de ventas ► **sales assistant** N (*Brit*) dependiente/a *m/f* ► **sales brochure** N folleto *m* publicitario ► **sales budget** N presupuesto *m* de ventas

➤ LANGUAGE IN USE: **saint 1** 23.3 **salary A** 19.2

► **sales campaign** N campaña *f* de promoción y venta ► **sales check** N (*US*) hoja *f* de venta ► **sales clerk** N (*US*) dependiente/a *m/f* ► **sales conference** N conferencia *f* de ventas ► **sales department** N sección *f* de ventas ► **sales drive** N promoción *f* de ventas ► **sales executive** N ejecutivo/a *m/f* de ventas ► **sales figures** NPL cifras *fpl* de ventas ► **sales force** N personal *m* de ventas ► **sales forecast** N previsión *f* de ventas ► **sales invoice** N factura *f* de ventas ► **sales leaflet** N folleto *m* publicitario ► **sales ledger** N libro *m* de ventas ► **sales literature** N folletos *mpl* de venta ► **sales manager** N jefe/a *m/f* de ventas ► **sales meeting** N reunión *f* de ventas ► **sales office** N oficina *f* de ventas ► **sales pitch*** N rollo *m* publicitario* ► **sales promotion** N campaña *f* de promoción de ventas ► **sales rep, sales representative** N representante *mf*, agente *mf* comercial ► **sales resistance** N resistencia *f* a comprar ► **sales slip** N (*US*) (= *receipt*) hoja *f* de venta ► **sales talk** N jerga *f* de vendedor ► **sales tax** N (*US*) impuesto *m* sobre las ventas ► **sale value** N valor *m* comercial, valor *m* en el mercado

saleability [ˌseɪləˈbɪlɪtɪ] N vendibilidad *f*

saleable, salable (*US*) [ˈseɪləbl] ADJ vendible

saleroom [ˈseɪlrʊm] N (*Brit*) sala *f* de subastas

salesgirl [ˈseɪlzgɜːl] N dependienta *f*, vendedora *f*

salesman [ˈseɪlzmən] N (*pl* **salesmen**) (*in shop*) dependiente *m*, vendedor *m*; (= *traveller*) viajante *m*, representante *m*; **a car ~** un vendedor de coches; **an insurance ~** un representante de seguros; **"Death of a Salesman"** "La muerte de un viajante"

salesmanship [ˈseɪlzmənʃɪp] N arte *m* de vender

salesperson [ˈseɪlzˌpɜːsn] N (*esp US*) vendedor(a) *m/f*, dependiente/a *m/f*

salesroom [ˈseɪlzrʊm] N (*US*) = **saleroom**

saleswoman [ˈseɪlzwʊmən] N (*pl* **saleswomen**) (*in shop*) dependienta *f*, vendedora *f*; (= *traveller*) viajante *f*, representante *f*; **an insurance ~** una representante de seguros

salient [ˈseɪlɪənt] Ⓐ ADJ [1] [*angle*] saliente [2] (*fig*) sobresaliente; **the most ~ feature** el aspecto más notable; **~ points** puntos *mpl* principales
Ⓑ N saliente *m*

salina [səˈliːnə] N [1] (= *marsh etc, saltworks*) salina *f*
[2] (= *mine*) mina *f* de sal, salina *f*

saline [ˈseɪlaɪn] ADJ salino; **~ drip** gota-a-gota *m* salino

salinity [səˈlɪnɪtɪ] N salinidad *f*

saliva [səˈlaɪvə] N saliva *f*

salivary gland [ˈsælɪvərɪˌglænd] N glándula *f* salival

salivate [ˈsælɪveɪt] VI salivar

salivation [ˌsælɪˈveɪʃən] N salivación *f*

sallow¹ [ˈsæləʊ] ADJ amarillento, cetrino

sallow² [ˈsæləʊ] N (*Bot*) sauce *m* cabruno

sallowness [ˈsæləʊnɪs] N lo amarillo, lo cetrino

Sallust [ˈsæləst] N Salustio

Sally [ˈsælɪ] N (*familiar form*) *of* **Sarah**

sally [ˈsælɪ] Ⓐ VI **to ~ forth** *or* **out** salir airado
Ⓑ N salida *f*; **to make a ~** hacer una salida

Sally Army* [ˈsælɪˈɑːmɪ] N (*Brit*) = **Salvation Army**

salmon [ˈsæmən] Ⓐ N (*pl* **salmons** *or* **salmon**)
[1] (= *fish*) salmón *m*
[2] (= *colour*) color *m* salmón
Ⓑ ADJ color salmón *inv*, asalmonado
Ⓒ CPD ► **salmon farm** N piscifactoría *f* de salmónidos ► **salmon fishing** N pesca *f* del salmón ► **salmon pink** N color *m* salmón, color *m* asalmonado ► **salmon river** N río *m* salmonero ► **salmon steak** N filete *m* de salmón ► **salmon trout** N trucha *f* asalmonada

salmonella [ˌsælməˈnelə] N (*pl* **salmonellae** [ˌsælməˈneliː]) salmonela *f*; **~ food-poisoning** salmonelosis *f*

salmonellosis [ˌsælmәneˈləʊsɪs] N salmonelosis *f*

Salome [səˈləʊmɪ] N Salomé

salon [ˈsælɒn] N salón *m*; **hair ~** salón *m* de peluquería; **beauty ~** salón *m* de belleza

saloon [səˈluːn] Ⓐ N [1] (*Brit*) (= *car*) turismo *m*
[2] (= *room*) **billiard/dancing ~** sala *f* or salón *m* de billar/de baile
[3] (*US*) (= *bar*) taberna *f*, bar *m*, cantina *f* (*esp Mex*)
[4] (*on ship*) salón *m*
Ⓑ CPD ► **saloon car** N (*Brit*) turismo *m*

salopettes [ˌsæləˈpets] NPL peto *msing* de esquiar

salsify [ˈsælsɪfɪ] N (*Bot*) salsifí *m*

SALT [sɔːlt] N ABBR = **Strategic Arms Limitation Talks**

salt [sɔːlt] Ⓐ N [1] (*Culin*) sal *f*; **✦IDIOMS the ~ of the earth** la sal de la tierra; **to take sth with a pinch** *or* **grain of ~** no tomarse algo al pie de la letra; **to rub ~ into the wound** poner sal en la llaga; **he's worth his ~** es una persona que vale
[2] (*Med*) **salts** sales *fpl*; **✦IDIOM like a dose of ~s*** en un santiamén*, en menos que canta un gallo*
Ⓑ VT (= *flavour*) salar; (= *preserve*) conservar en sal; [+ *road*] poner sal en, tratar con sal
Ⓒ ADJ [*meat, water, taste*] salado; **it's very ~** está muy salado
Ⓓ CPD ► **salt beef** N carne *f* de vaca salada ► **salt fish** N pescado *m* salado, pescado *m* en salazón ► **salt flats** NPL salinas *fpl* ► **salt lake** N lago *m* de agua salada ► **salt marsh** N saladar *m*, salina *f* ► **salt mine** N mina *f* de sal ► **salt pan** N salina *f* ► **salt shaker** N salero *m* ► **salt spoon** N cucharita *f* de sal ► **salt water** N agua *f* salada; *see also* **saltwater**

►**salt away** VT + ADV ahorrar, ocultar para uso futuro

►**salt down** VT + ADV conservar en sal, salar

saltcellar [ˈsɔːltˌseləʳ] N salero *m*

salted [ˈsɔːltɪd] ADJ salado, con sal

salt-free [ˈsɔːltfriː] ADJ sin sal

saltiness [ˈsɔːltɪnɪs] N [1] (= *salty flavour*) sabor *m* a sal, salobridad *f*
[2] (= *salinity*) salinidad *f*

saltings [ˈsɔːltɪŋz] NPL saladar *msing*

saltpetre, saltpeter (*US*) [ˈsɔːltˌpiːtəʳ] N salitre *m*

saltwater [ˈsɔːltˌwɔːtəʳ] ADJ [*fish etc*] de agua salada

saltworks [ˈsɔːltwɜːks] N salinas *fpl*

salty [ˈsɔːltɪ] ADJ [*taste*] salado

salubrious [səˈluːbrɪəs] ADJ (*frm*) (= *healthy*) saludable, salubre; (*fig*) (= *desirable, pleasant*) [*district etc*] salubre

salubrity [səˈluːbrɪtɪ] N salubridad *f*

salutary [ˈsæljʊtərɪ] ADJ (= *healthy*) saludable; (= *beneficial*) conveniente

salutation [ˌsæljʊˈteɪʃən] N salutación *f*, saludo *m*

salute [səˈluːt] Ⓐ N (*Mil*) (*with hand*) saludo *m*; (*with guns*) salva *f*; **to take the ~** responder al saludo (*en un desfile militar*); **to fire a ~ of 21 guns for sb** saludar a algn con una salva de 21 cañonazos
Ⓑ VT [1] (*Mil etc*) saludar, hacer un saludo
[2] (*fig*) (= *acclaim*) aclamar
Ⓒ VI saludar, hacer un saludo

Salvadoran [ˌsælvəˈdɔːrən], **Salvadorean**, **Salvadorian** [ˌsælvəˈdɔːrɪən] Ⓐ ADJ salvadoreño
Ⓑ N salvadoreño/a *m/f*

salvage [ˈsælvɪdʒ] Ⓐ N [1] (= *rescue*) [*of ship etc*] salvamento *m*
[2] (= *things rescued*) objetos *mpl* salvados; (*for re-use*) material *m* reutilizable
[3] (= *fee*) derechos *mpl* de salvamento
Ⓑ VT [1] (= *save*) salvar; **to ~ sth from the wreckage** salvar algo de las ruinas
[2] (*fig*) [+ *sth from theory, policy etc*] rescatar; [+ *pride, reputation*] (= *manage to keep*) conservar; (= *regain*) recuperar, salvar
Ⓒ CPD ► **salvage fee** N derechos *mpl* de salvamento ► **salvage operation** N operación *f* de rescate, operación *f* de salvamento ► **salvage value** N valor *m* de desecho ► **salvage vessel** N buque *m* de salvamento

salvation [sælˈveɪʃən] Ⓐ N salvación *f*
Ⓑ CPD ► **Salvation Army** N Ejército *m* de Salvación

salvationist [sælˈveɪʃnɪst] N miembro *mf* del Ejército de Salvación

salve¹ [sælv] Ⓐ VT (= *soothe*) **to ~ one's conscience** descargar la conciencia
Ⓑ N (*lit*) pomada *f* bálsamica; (*fig*) bálsamo *m*

salve² [sælv] VT (*Naut etc*) (= *salvage*) salvar

salver [ˈsælvəʳ] N bandeja *f*

salvia [ˈsælvɪə] N salvia *f*

salvo¹ [ˈsælvəʊ] N (*pl* **salvos** *or* **salvoes**) (*Mil*) salva *f*; **a ~ of applause** una salva de aplausos

salvo² [ˈsælvəʊ] N (*pl* **salvos**) (*Jur*) salvedad *f*, reserva *f*

Salzburg [ˈsæltsbɜːg] N Salzburgo *m*

SAM [sæm] N ABBR = **surface-to-air missile**

Sam [sæm] N (*familiar form*) *of* **Samuel**; **~ Browne (belt)** correaje *m* de oficial

Samaritan [səˈmærɪtn] Ⓐ N **the Good ~** el buen samaritano; **to call the ~s** (*organization*) llamar al teléfono de la esperanza
Ⓑ ADJ samaritano

samarium [səˈmɛərɪəm] N samario *m*

samba [ˈsæmbə] N samba *f*

sambo‼ [ˈsæmbəʊ] N (*pej*) negro/a *m/f*

▼**same** [seɪm] Ⓐ ADJ mismo; **two different photographs of the ~ man** dos fotografías diferentes del mismo hombre; **he and Tom were exactly the ~ age** Tom y él tenían exactamente la misma edad; **he will never be the ~ again** nunca volverá a ser el mismo; **the two houses are the ~** las dos casas son iguales; **it's always the ~** siempre pasa lo mismo; **it's not the ~ at all** no es en absoluto lo mismo; **for the ~ reason** por la misma razón; **if it's all the ~ to you*** si a ti te da igual *or* lo mismo; **we sat at the ~ table as usual** nos sentamos en la (misma) mesa de siempre; **the carpet was the ~ colour as the wall** la moqueta era del mismo color que la pared; **the price is the ~ as last year** el precio es el mismo que el año pasado; **their house is almost the ~ as ours** su casa es casi igual a *or* que la nuestra; **"how's Derek?" — "~ as usual/ever"** —¿qué tal está Derek? —como siempre; **the ~ day** el mismo día; **~ day delivery** entrega *f* en el mismo día; **~ difference*** lo mismo da*; **they are much the ~** son más o menos iguales; **they ask the ~**

➤ LANGUAGE IN USE: **same** A 5.2 B 5.2, 5.3

old questions siempre hacen las mismas preguntas, hacen las mismas preguntas de siempre; **the ~ one** el mismo; **the ~ ones** los mismos; **one and the ~ person** la misma persona; **it comes to the ~ thing** viene a ser lo mismo; **at the ~ time** (= *at once*) al mismo tiempo, a la vez; (= *on the other hand*) por otro lado; **the very ~ day/person** justo ese mismo día/esa misma persona; **in the ~ way** de la misma manera *or* forma; **do you still feel the ~ way about me?** ¿aún sientes lo mismo por mí?; **do you still feel the ~ way about it?** ¿sigues pensando lo mismo?, ¿lo sigues viendo de la misma forma?; **to go the ~ way as sth/sb** (*fig*) (*pej*) seguir el mismo camino que algo/algn; *see also* **boat A**, **breath A1**, **language A1**, **mind A6**, **story A1**, **tar B**, **token A**, **wavelength**

Ⓑ PRON 1 **the ~** lo mismo; **I'd do the ~ again** volvería a hacer lo mismo, haría lo mismo otra vez; **I don't feel the ~ about it as I did** ya no lo veo de la misma forma; **I still feel the ~ about you** sigo sintiendo lo mismo por ti; **the ~ again!** (*in bar etc*) ¡otra de lo mismo!; **the ~ is true of the arts** lo mismo se puede decir de las artes; **all** *or* **just the ~** (*as adverb*) (= *even so*) de todas formas *or* maneras; **no, but thanks all the ~** no, pero de todas formas, gracias; **I want the best for him, the ~ as you** quiero lo mejor para él, igual que tú; **the ~ goes for you** eso también va por ti; **~ here!*** ¡yo también!; **one and the ~** el mismo/la misma; **(and the) ~ to you!*** (*returning insult*) ¡lo mismo digo!; (*returning good wishes*) ¡igualmente!; **"Mr. Smith?" — "the very ~!"** —¿el Sr. Smith? —¡el mismo!

2 (*Comm*) **for repair of door and repainting of ~** reparación de la puerta y pintar la misma

sameness [ˈseɪmnɪs] N (= *similarity*) igualdad *f*, identidad *f*; (= *monotony*) monotonía *f*, uniformidad *f*

Sammy [ˈsæmɪ] N (*familiar form*) *of* **Samuel**

Samoa [səˈməʊə] N Samoa *f*

Samoan [səˈməʊən] Ⓐ ADJ samoano

Ⓑ N samoano/a *m/f*

samosa [səˈməʊsə] N (*pl* **samosas** *or* **samosa**) samosa *f*

samovar [ˌsæməʊˈvɑːʳ] N samovar *m*

sampan [ˈsæmpæn] N sampán *m*

sample [ˈsɑːmpl] Ⓐ N 1 (= *example*) muestra *f*; **send in a ~ of your artwork** envíe una muestra de sus ilustraciones

2 (*Med, Bot, Zool*) [*of substance*] muestra *f*; **a blood/urine ~** una muestra de sangre/orina; **to take a ~** tomar una muestra

3 (*Comm*) [*of product*] muestra *f*; **free ~** muestra *f* gratuita

Ⓑ VT 1 (= *try out*) [+ *food, drink*] probar; **the chance to ~ a different way of life** la oportunidad de probar un modo de vida distinto

2 (= *take samples*) tomar muestras de

3 (*Statistics*) muestrear

Ⓒ CPD ► **sample book** N muestrario *m* ► **sample pack** N paquete *m* de muestra ► **sample survey** N estudio *m* de muestras

sampler [ˈsɑːmpləʳ] N 1 (= *person*) catador(a) *m/f*

2 (*Sew*) dechado *m*

sampling [ˈsɑːmplɪŋ] N muestreo *m*

Samson [ˈsæmsn] N Sansón

Samuel [ˈsæmjʊəl] N Samuel

San Andreas Fault [ˌsænænˌdreɪəsˈfɔːlt] N falla *f* de San Andrés

sanatorium [ˌsænəˈtɔːrɪəm] N (*pl* **sanatoriums** *or* **sanatoria** [ˌsænəˈtɔːrɪə]) sanatorio *m*

sanctification [ˌsæŋktɪfɪˈkeɪʃən] N santificación *f*

sanctify [ˈsæŋktɪfaɪ] VT santificar

sanctimonious [ˌsæŋktɪˈməʊnɪəs] ADJ mojigato, santurrón

sanctimoniously [ˌsæŋktɪˈməʊnɪəslɪ] ADV con mojigatería, con santurronería; **she said ~** dijo con mojigatería *or* santurronería

sanctimoniousness [ˌsæŋktɪˈməʊnɪəsnɪs] N mojigatería *f*, santurronería *f*

sanction [ˈsæŋkʃən] Ⓐ N 1 (= *approval*) permiso *m*, autorización *f*

2 (= *penalty*) sanción *f*; (*esp Pol*) **sanctions** sanciones *fpl*; **to impose economic ~s on** *or* **against** imponer sanciones económicas a *or* contra

Ⓑ VT 1 (= *approve, authorize*) sancionar, autorizar

2 (= *penalize*) sancionar

Ⓒ CPD ► **sanction busting** N ruptura *f* de sanciones

sanctity [ˈsæŋktɪtɪ] N (= *sacredness*) lo sagrado; (= *inviolability*) inviolabilidad *f*

sanctuary [ˈsæŋktjʊərɪ] N (*Rel*) santuario *m*; (*fig*) (= *refuge*) asilo *m*; (*for wildlife*) reserva *f*; **to seek ~** acogerse a sagrado; **to seek ~ in** refugiarse en; **to seek ~ with** acogerse a

sanctum [ˈsæŋktəm] N (*pl* **sanctums** *or* **sancta**) lugar *m* sagrado; (*fig*) sanctasanctórum *m*; *see also* **inner A1**

sand [sænd] Ⓐ N 1 (= *substance*) arena *f*; **grains of ~** granos *mpl* de arena; ✦*IDIOM* **the ~s are running out** queda poco tiempo

2 **sands** (= *beach*) playa *fsing*; [*of desert*] arenas *fpl*

Ⓑ VT 1 [+ *road*] echar arena a

2 (*also* **~ down**) [+ *wood etc*] lijar; [+ *floor*] pulir

Ⓒ CPD ► **sand bar** N barra *f* de arena, banco *m* de arena ► **sand dune** N duna *f* ► **sand martin** N avión *m* zapador

sandal [ˈsændl] N sandalia *f*, guarache *m* *or* huarache *m* (*Mex*); **a pair of ~s** unas sandalias

sandalwood [ˈsændlwʊd] N sándalo *m*

sandbag [ˈsænd*b*æg] Ⓐ N saco *m* de arena

Ⓑ VT proteger con sacos de arena

sandbank [ˈsænd*b*æŋk] N banco *m* de arena

sandblast [ˈsænd*b*lɑːst] VT [+ *building*] limpiar con chorro de arena

sandbox [ˈsænd*b*ɒks] N (*US*) cajón *m* de arena

sandboy [ˈsænd*b*ɔɪ] N ✦*IDIOM* **to be as happy as a ~** estar como unas pascuas

sandcastle [ˈsænd̩ˌkɑːsl] N castillo *m* de arena

sander [ˈsændəʳ] N (= *tool*) (*gen*) lijadora *f*; (*for floor*) pulidora *f*

sandglass [ˈsænd*g*lɑːs] N reloj *m* de arena

sanding [ˈsændɪŋ] N [*of road*] enarenamiento *m*; [*of floor*] pulimiento *m*; (= *sandpapering*) lijamiento *m*

S & L N ABBR (*US Fin*) = **savings and loan association**

sandlot [ˈsændlɒt] (*US*) Ⓐ N *terreno en una ciudad que se usa para el béisbol etc*

Ⓑ ADJ (*Sport*) de barrio, de vecindad; **~ baseball** béisbol *m* de barrio

S & M Ⓐ N ABBR = **sadomasochism**

Ⓑ ADJ (= **sadomasochistic**) sadomasoca*

sandman [ˈsænd*m*æn] N (*pl* **sandmen**) *ser imaginario que hace que los niños se duerman trayéndoles sueño*

sandpaper [ˈsænd̩ˌpeɪpəʳ] Ⓐ N papel *m* de lija

Ⓑ VT lijar

sandpiper [ˈsænd̩ˌpaɪpəʳ] N andarríos *m*, lavandera *f*

sandpit [ˈsænd*p*ɪt] N (*esp Brit*) *recinto de arena para juegos infantiles*

sandshoes [ˈsænd*ʃ*uːz] NPL playeras *fpl*, tenis *mpl*

sandstone [ˈsænd*s*təʊn] N arenisca *f*

sandstorm [ˈsænd*s*tɔːm] N tempestad *f* de arena

sandwich [ˈsænwɪdʒ] Ⓐ N (*with French bread*) bocadillo *m* (*Sp*), sándwich *m* (*esp LAm*), emparedado *m* (*esp LAm*); (*with sliced bread*) sándwich *m*

Ⓑ VT (*also* **~ in**) [+ *person, appointment etc*] intercalar; **to ~ sth between two things** hacer un hueco para algo entre dos cosas

Ⓒ CPD ► **sandwich bar** N bar *m* de bocadillos, bocadillería *f* ► **sandwich board** N cartelón *m* (*que lleva el hombre-anuncio*) ► **sandwich course** N (*Univ etc*) *programa que intercala periodos de estudio con prácticas profesionales* ► **sandwich man** N (*pl* **sandwich men**) hombre-anuncio *m*

sandworm [ˈsænd*w*ɜːm] N gusano *m* de arena

sandy [ˈsændɪ] ADJ (*compar* **sandier**; *superl* **sandiest**) 1 [*beach*] arenoso

2 (*in colour*) [*hair*] rubio

sane [seɪn] ADJ (*compar* **saner**; *superl* **sanest**) [*person*] cuerdo; [*judgment etc*] sabio, sensato

sanely [ˈseɪnlɪ] ADV sensatamente

Sanforized® [ˈsænfəraɪzd] ADJ sanforizado®

sang [sæŋ] PT *of* **sing**

sangfroid [ˈsɑ̃ːŋˈfrwɑː] N sangre *f* fría

sanguinary [ˈsæŋgwɪnərɪ] ADJ (*frm*) 1 (= *bloodthirsty*) sanguinario

2 (= *bloody*) [*battle*] sangriento

sanguine [ˈsæŋgwɪn] ADJ (*fig*) optimista

sanguineous [sæŋˈgwɪnɪəs] ADJ sanguíneo

sanitarium [ˌsænɪˈtɛərɪəm] N (*pl* **sanitariums** *or* **sanitaria** [ˌsænɪˈtɛərɪə]) (*esp US*) = **sanatorium**

sanitary [ˈsænɪtərɪ] ADJ (= *clean*) higiénico; (= *for health protection*) de sanidad; **~ towel** (*Brit*) ◊ **~ napkin** (*US*) compresa *f*, paño *m* higiénico; **~ engineer** ingeniero/a *m/f* sanitario/a; **~ inspector** inspector(a) *m/f* de sanidad

sanitation [ˌsænɪˈteɪʃən] Ⓐ N (= *science*) higiene *f*; (= *plumbing*) instalación *f* sanitaria

Ⓑ CPD ► **sanitation department** N (*US*) departamento *m* de limpieza y recogida de basuras

sanitize [ˈsænɪtaɪz] VT sanear; **to ~ the image of war** dar una imagen aséptica de la guerra

sanitized [ˈsænɪtaɪzd] ADJ saneado

sanity [ˈsænɪtɪ] N [*of person*] cordura *f*, juicio *m*; [*of judgment*] sensatez *f*; **to lose one's ~** perder el juicio *or* la razón; **to be restored to ~** ◊ **return to ~** recobrar el juicio *or* la razón; **fortunately ~ prevailed** afortunadamente prevaleció el sentido común

sank [sæŋk] PT *of* **sink¹**

San Marino [ˌsænməˈriːnəʊ] N San Marino *m*

Sanskrit [ˈsænskrɪt] Ⓐ ADJ sánscrito

Ⓑ N sánscrito *m*

sans serif [ˌsænˈserɪf] N grotesca *f*

Santa Claus [ˌsæntəˈklɔːz] N Papá Noel *m*, San Nicolás *m*

Santiago [ˌsæntɪˈɑːgəʊ] N (*in Chile*) Santiago *m* (de Chile); (*in Spain*) **~ de Compostela** Santiago *m* (de Compostela)

sap¹ [sæp] N (*Bot*) savia *f*

sap² [sæp] Ⓐ N (*Mil*) (= *trench*) zapa *f*

Ⓑ VT (= *undermine*) minar; (= *weaken*) debilitar; (= *exhaust*) agotar (las fuerzas de)

sap³* [sæp] N (= *fool*) bobo/a *m/f*; **you ~!** ¡bobo!

sapling [ˈsæplɪŋ] N árbol *m* joven

sapper [ˈsæpəʳ] N (*Brit Mil*) zapador *m*

sapphire [ˈsæfaɪəʳ] Ⓐ N zafiro *m*
Ⓑ CPD [*ring, necklace*] de zafiro ► **sapphire blue** N azul *m* zafiro ► **sapphire (blue) sky** N cielo *m* azul zafiro

sappiness [ˈsæpɪnɪs] N jugosidad *f*

sappy[1] [ˈsæpɪ] ADJ (*Bot*) lleno de savia, jugoso

sappy[2]‡ [ˈsæpɪ] ADJ (= *foolish*) bobo

SAR N ABBR = **Search and Rescue**

saraband [ˈsærəbænd] N zarabanda *f*

Saracen [ˈsærəsn] Ⓐ ADJ sarraceno
Ⓑ N sarraceno/a *m/f*

Saragossa [ˌsærəˈgɒsə] N Zaragoza *f*

Sarah [ˈseərə] N Sara

Saranwrap® [səˈræn,ræp] N (*US*) film *m* adherente (*para envolver alimentos*)

sarcasm [ˈsɑːkæzəm] N sarcasmo *m*

sarcastic [sɑːˈkæstɪk] ADJ [*person, remark*] sarcástico

sarcastically [sɑːˈkæstɪkəlɪ] ADV con sarcasmo, sarcásticamente

sarcoma [sɑːˈkəʊmə] N (*pl* **sarcomas** *or* **sarcomata** [sɑːˈkəʊmətə]) sarcoma *m*

sarcophagus [sɑːˈkɒfəgəs] N (*pl* **sarcophaguses** *or* **sarcophagi** [sɑːˈkɒfəgaɪ]) sarcófago *m*

sardine [sɑːˈdiːn] N (*pl* **sardine** *or* **sardines**) sardina *f*; **packed in like ~s** como sardinas en lata

Sardinia [sɑːˈdɪnɪə] N Cerdeña *f*

Sardinian [sɑːˈdɪnɪən] Ⓐ ADJ sardo
Ⓑ N sardo/a *m/f*

sardonic [sɑːˈdɒnɪk] ADJ [*humour, laugh*] sardónico; [*person*] sarcástico, burlón; [*tone*] burlón; **she gave a ~ smile** sonrió con sarcasmo *or* con aire burlón

sardonically [sɑːˈdɒnɪkəlɪ] ADV [*smile*] con sarcasmo, con aire burlón; [*say*] con sarcasmo

sarge* [sɑːdʒ] N = **sergeant**; **yes, ~** sí, mi sargento

sari [ˈsɑːrɪ] N sari *m*

sarky‡ [ˈsɑːkɪ] ADJ = **sarcastic**

sarnie* [ˈsɑːnɪ] N (*Brit*) bocata* *f*

sarong [səˈrɒŋ] N sarong *m*

SARS [sɑːz] N ABBR (= **severe acute respiratory syndrome**) neumonía *f* asiática, SARS *m*

sarsaparilla [ˌsɑːsəpəˈrɪlə] N zarzaparrilla *f*

sartorial [sɑːˈtɔːrɪəl] ADJ relativo al vestido; **~ elegance** elegancia *f* en el vestido; **~ taste** gusto *m* en vestidos

SAS N ABBR (*Brit Mil*) = **Special Air Service**

SASE, s.a.s.e. N ABBR (*US*) (= **self-addressed stamped envelope**) *sobre con las propias señas de uno y con sello*

sash[1] [sæʃ] N [*of dress etc*] faja *f*

sash[2] [sæʃ] Ⓐ N (= *window sash*) bastidor *m* de ventana, marco *m* de ventana Ⓑ CPD ► **sash cord** N cuerda *f* de ventana (de guillotina) ► **sash window** N ventana *f* de guillotina

sashay* [sæˈʃeɪ] VI pasearse; **to ~ off** largarse*

Sask. ABBR (*Canada*) = **Saskatchewan**

sass* [sæs] (*US*) Ⓐ N réplicas *fpl*, descoco *m*
Ⓑ VT **to ~ sb** replicar a algn

sassafras [ˈsæsəfræs] N sasafrás *m*

Sassenach [ˈsæsənæx] N (*Scot sometimes pej*) inglés/esa *m/f*

sassy* [ˈsæsɪ] ADJ (*US*) fresco, descarado

SAT N ABBR (*US Educ*) = **Scholastic Aptitude Test**

sat [sæt] PT, PP *of* **sit**

Sat. N ABBR (= **Saturday**) sáb.

Satan [ˈseɪtn] N Satanás *m*

satanic [səˈtænɪk] ADJ satánico

Satanism [ˈseɪtənɪzəm] N satanismo *m*

Satanist [ˈseɪtənɪst] Ⓐ N satanista *mf*
Ⓑ ADJ = **satanic**

satchel [ˈsætʃəl] N cartera *f*, mochila *f* (*S. Cone*)

sate [seɪt] VT saciar, hartar

sateen [sæˈtiːn] N satén *m*

satellite [ˈsætəlaɪt] Ⓐ N [1] (*artificial*) satélite *m*; **by** *or* **via ~** vía satélite
[2] (*natural*) satélite *m*; **the ~s of Jupiter** los satélites de Júpiter
[3] (*Pol*) (= *country, organisation*) satélite *m*; **Russia and its former ~s** Rusia y sus antiguos estados satélite
Ⓑ CPD ► **satellite broadcast** N retransmisión *f* vía satélite ► **satellite broadcasting** N retransmisión *f* vía satélite ► **satellite channel** N canal *m* de retransmisión por vía satélite ► **satellite country** N país *m* satélite ► **satellite dish** N antena *f* parabólica para TV por satélite ► **satellite link** N conexión *f* vía satélite ► **satellite technology** N tecnología *f* de retransmisiones vía satélite ► **satellite television** N televisión *f* vía satélite ► **satellite town** N ciudad *f* satélite ► **satellite transmission** N retransmisión *f* vía satélite ► **satellite TV** N TV *f* vía satélite

satiate [ˈseɪʃɪeɪt] VT (*with food*) hartar; (*with pleasures*) saciar

satiated [ˈseɪʃɪeɪtɪd] ADJ (*with food*) harto; (*with pleasures*) saciado

satiation [ˌseɪʃɪˈeɪʃən] N, **satiety** [səˈtaɪətɪ] N (*with food*) hartura *f*; (*with pleasures*) saciedad *f*

satin [ˈsætɪn] Ⓐ N satén *m*, raso *m*
Ⓑ ADJ [*dress, blouse etc*] de satén; [*paper, finish*] satinado

satinwood [ˈsætɪnwʊd] N madera *f* satinada de las Indias, doradillo *m*, satín *m*

satiny [ˈsætɪnɪ] ADJ satinado

satire [ˈsætaɪəʳ] N sátira *f* (**on** contra)

satiric [səˈtɪrɪk] ADJ satírico

satirical [səˈtɪrɪkəl] ADJ satírico

satirically [səˈtɪrɪkəlɪ] ADV satíricamente

satirist [ˈsætərɪst] N (= *writer*) escritor(a) *m/f* satírico/a; (= *cartoonist*) caricaturista *mf*

satirize [ˈsætəraɪz] VT satirizar

satisfaction [ˌsætɪsˈfækʃən] N [1] (= *contentment*) satisfacción *f*; **has it been done to your ~?** ¿se ha hecho a su gusto?; **it gives me every ~ ...** es para mí una gran satisfacción ...; **to demand ~** pedir satisfacción; **to express one's ~ at a result** expresar su satisfacción con un resultado, declararse satisfecho con un resultado
[2] [*of debt*] pago *m*, liquidación *f*

satisfactorily [ˌsætɪsˈfæktərɪlɪ] ADV de modo satisfactorio

satisfactory [ˌsætɪsˈfæktərɪ] ADJ (= *pleasing*) satisfactorio; (= *sufficient*) adecuado

▼ **satisfy** [ˈsætɪsfaɪ] VT [1] (= *make content*) satisfacer, dejar satisfecho; **it completely satisfies me** me satisface del todo, me ha dejado totalmente satisfecho; **he's never satisfied** no está nunca contento *or* satisfecho; **we are very satisfied with it** estamos muy satisfechos con ello, nos satisface en grado sumo; **you'll have to be satisfied with that** tendrás que contentarte con eso; **to ~ o.s. with sth** contentarse con algo
[2] (= *convince*) convencer; **to ~ sb that ...** convencer a algn de que ...; **I am not satisfied that ...** no estoy convencido de que ...; **to ~ o.s. that ...** convencerse de que ...
[3] (= *fulfil*) satisfacer, cumplir; **to ~ the examiners** recibir la aprobación del tribunal examinador; **to ~ the requirements** cumplir los requisitos
[4] (= *pay off*) [+ *debt*] pagar, liquidar

satisfying [ˈsætɪsfaɪɪŋ] ADJ [*result etc*] satisfactorio; [*food, meal*] que satisface, que llena

satsuma [ˌsætˈsuːmə] N satsuma *f*

saturate [ˈsætʃəreɪt] VT empapar, saturar (**with** de); **to be ~d with** (*fig*) estar empapado de; **to ~ o.s. in** (*fig*) empaparse en

saturated [ˈsætʃəreɪtɪd] ADJ (= *soaking wet*) empapado; **~ fat** grasa *f* saturada

saturation [ˌsætʃəˈreɪʃən] Ⓐ N saturación *f*
Ⓑ CPD ► **saturation bombing** N bombardeo *m* por saturación ► **saturation diving** N buceo *m* de saturación ► **saturation point** N **to reach ~ point** (*Chem, fig*) alcanzar el punto de saturación

Saturday [ˈsætədɪ] Ⓐ N sábado *m*; *see* **Tuesday** *for usage* Ⓑ CPD ► **Saturday job** N **I've got a ~ job** tengo un trabajo los sábados

Saturn [ˈsætən] N Saturno *m*

Saturnalia [ˌsætəˈneɪlɪə] NPL (*pl* **Saturnalia** *or* **Saturnalias**) saturnales *fpl*

saturnine [ˈsætənaɪn] ADJ saturnino

satyr [ˈsætəʳ] N sátiro *m*

sauce [sɔːs] Ⓐ N [1] (*savoury*) salsa *f*; (*sweet*) crema *f*; **tomato ~** salsa *f* de tomate; (= *ketchup*) salsa *f* de tomate, ketchup *m*; **chocolate ~** crema *f* de chocolate; ✦*PROV* **what's ~ for the goose is ~ for the gander** lo que es bueno para uno es bueno para el otro; *see also* **apple B, cheese C, cranberry B, mint**[2] **B, orange C, soya B, white C**
[2] (†*) (= *impudence*) frescura *f*, descaro *m*; **what ~!** ¡qué frescura!; **none of your ~!** ¡eres un fresco!*
[3] (*US*‡) (= *drink*) **the ~** la bebida, la priva (*Sp*‡); **to hit the ~** ◊ **to be on the ~** empinar el codo*, darle a la bebida, darle a la priva (*Sp*‡)
Ⓑ CPD ► **sauce boat** N salsera *f*

saucepan [ˈsɔːspən] N cacerola *f*, cazo *m*, olla *f* (*esp LAm*)

saucer [ˈsɔːsəʳ] N platillo *m*

saucily [ˈsɔːsɪlɪ] ADV [*reply etc*] con frescura, con descaro

sauciness [ˈsɔːsɪnɪs] N frescura *f*, descaro *m*

saucy* [ˈsɔːsɪ] ADJ (*compar* **saucier**, *superl* **sauciest**) [1] (= *cheeky*) [*person*] fresco, descarado; **don't be ~!** ¡qué fresco! [2] (*esp Brit*) [*joke, humour, postcard, photo*] picante; [*clothes*] provocativo

Saudi [ˈsaʊdɪ] Ⓐ ADJ saudí, saudita
Ⓑ N saudí *mf*, saudita *mf*

Saudi Arabia [ˈsaʊdɪəˈreɪbɪə] N Arabia *f* Saudí, Arabia *f* Saudita

Saudi Arabian [ˈsaʊdɪəˈreɪbɪən] ADJ, N = **Saudi**

sauerkraut [ˈsaʊəkraʊt] N chucrut *m*, chucrú *m*

Saul [sɔːl] N Saúl

sauna [ˈsɔːnə] N sauna *f* (*m in Cono Sur*)

saunter [ˈsɔːntəʳ] Ⓐ N paseo *m* tranquilo; **to go for a ~ around the park** pasearse *or* (*LAm*) caminar por el parque
Ⓑ VI pasearse, deambular (*LAm*); **to ~ in/out** entrar/salir sin prisa; **to ~ up and down** pasearse para arriba y para abajo; **he ~ed up to me** se acercó a mí con mucha calma

saurian [ˈsɔːrɪən] N saurio *m*

sausage [ˈsɒsɪdʒ] Ⓐ N (*to be cooked*) salchicha *f*; (= *salami, mortadella etc*) embutido *m*, fiambre *m*; **not a ~** (*Brit**) ¡ni un botón!*, ¡nada de nada!
Ⓑ CPD ► **sausage dog*** N perro *m* salchicha* ► **sausage machine** N máquina *f* de hacer salchichas ► **sausage meat** N carne *f* de salchicha ► **sausage roll** N (*esp Brit*) *masa de hojaldre con una salchicha en su interior*

sauté [ˈsəʊteɪ] Ⓐ ADJ salteado; **~ potatoes** patatas *fpl* salteadas
Ⓑ VT saltear

savage [ˈsævɪdʒ] Ⓐ ADJ [1] (= *ferocious*) [*animal, attack*] feroz, salvaje; [*person*] salvaje; [*blow*] violento; [*war, criticism, remark*] despiadado; **to have a ~ temper** tener un carácter muy violento
[2] (= *primitive*) [*custom, tribe*] salvaje, primitivo
[3] (= *drastic*) [*cuts, reductions*] drástico, radical
Ⓑ N salvaje *mf*; *see also* **noble C**
Ⓒ VT [1] (= *injure*) atacar salvajemente; **two children have been ~d by an alsatian** dos niños fueron salvajemente atacados por un pastor alemán
[2] (= *criticize*) atacar ferozmente *or* despiadadamente; **she was ~d by the press** la prensa la atacó ferozmente *or* despiadadamente, la prensa se ensañó con ella

savagely [ˈsævɪdʒlɪ] ADV [1] (= *ferociously*) [*beat, attack*] salvajemente, violentamente; [*fight*] violentamente; [*say*] con crueldad, despiadadamente; **a ~ funny film** una película brutalmente divertida; **the ~ beautiful scenery** el paisaje de belleza salvaje
[2] (= *severely*) [*criticise, attack*] despiadadamente
[3] (= *drastically*) [*cut, edit*] drásticamente, radicalmente

savageness [ˈsævɪdʒnɪs] N = **savagery 1, 3**

savagery [ˈsævɪdʒrɪ] N [1] (= *violence*) [*of attack, blow*] ferocidad *f*, violencia *f*; [*of criticism*] saña *f*, ferocidad *f*; **the sheer ~ of war** el puro salvajismo *or* la pura brutalidad de la guerra
[2] (= *primitiveness*) salvajismo *m*, estado *m* salvaje
[3] (= *drastic nature*) [*of cuts, reductions*] radicalidad *f*, carácter *m* drástico

savannah [səˈvænə] N sabana *f*, pampa *f* (*S. Cone*), llanos *mpl* (*Ven*)

savant [ˈsævənt] N (*frm*) sabio/a *m/f*, erudito/a *m/f*

save[1] [seɪv] Ⓐ VT [1] (= *rescue*) [+ *person in danger*] rescatar, salvar; [+ *lives, jobs*] salvar; (*Rel*) [+ *soul*] salvar; **she wants to ~ the world** quiere salvar el mundo; **firefighters were unable to ~ the children** los bomberos no pudieron rescatar *or* salvar a los niños; **they accepted a pay cut to ~ their jobs** han aceptado una reducción de sueldo para salvar sus puestos de trabajo; **to ~ the day: reinforcements sent by the Allies ~d the day** los refuerzos que enviaron los Aliados los sacaron del apuro; **to ~ face** guardar las apariencias; **to ~ sth/sb from sth/doing sth: he ~d the company from bankruptcy** salvó a la empresa de la bancarrota; **he ~d me from falling/drowning** me salvó de caerme/de morir ahogado, impidió que me cayera/que muriera ahogado; **you have to ~ these people from themselves** tienes que salvar a esta gente del daño de sus propias acciones; **to ~ sb's life** salvar la vida a algn; **I can't sing to ~ my life** soy una negada para cantar*; **I put out a hand to ~ myself** estiré el brazo y me agarré con la mano para salvarme de una caída; **to ~ the situation** = **to save the day**; ✦**IDIOMS to ~ one's bacon** *or* **one's (own) skin*** salvar el pellejo*; **all he's bothered about is saving his own skin** lo único que le importa es salvar el pellejo*; **to ~ sb's ass** *or* **butt** (*esp US***) salvar el pellejo a algn*
[2] (= *preserve, conserve*) **to ~ a building for posterity** conservar un edificio para la posteridad; **I'm saving my voice for the concert** estoy reservando la voz para el concierto; **to ~ o.s. for sth** reservarse para algo; **God ~ the Queen!** ¡Dios salve *or* guarde a la Reina!; **to ~ one's strength (for sth)** conservar *or* reservar (las) fuerzas (para algo)
[3] (= *keep, put aside*) (*gen*) guardar; [+ *money*] (*also* **~ up**) ahorrar; **to ~ sb sth** ◊ **to ~ sth for sb** guardar algo a algn; **we've ~d you a piece of cake** te hemos guardado un pedazo de tarta; **to ~ sth till last** guardar algo para el final; **he ~d the best till last, scoring two goals in the final ten minutes** guardó lo mejor para el final, marcando dos goles en los últimos diez minutos; **~ me a seat** guárdame un asiento; **if you ~ six tokens you get a free book** si junta *or* reúne seis vales, recibirá un libro gratis
[4] (= *not spend*) [+ *time*] ahorrar, ganar; [+ *money*] ahorrar; [+ *trouble*] evitar, ahorrar; **we did it to ~ time** lo hicimos para ahorrar *or* ganar tiempo; **it ~d us a lot of trouble** nos evitó *or* ahorró muchas molestias; **it will ~ me an hour** ganaré una hora; **that way you ~ £10** así (te) ahorras 10 libras; **it ~s fuel** economiza *or* ahorra combustible; **to ~ sb (from) sth/doing sth: it ~s me (from) having to make a decision** me ahorra *or* evita tener que tomar una decisión; **I'll take him, it'll ~ you the journey** yo lo llevaré, así te ahorras *or* evitas el viaje; ✦**IDIOM ~ your breath** no gastes saliva (en balde)
[5] (*Sport*) [+ *penalty, shot*] parar; **to ~ a goal** hacer una parada, parar un disparo a gol
[6] (*Comput*) archivar, guardar
Ⓑ VI [1] (*also* **~ up**) ahorrar; **he's saving for a new bike** está ahorrando (dinero) para (comprarse) una bici nueva
[2] (= *economize*) **to ~ on sth: to ~ on petrol** ahorrar gasolina; **the new system ~s on staff time** el nuevo sistema economiza el tiempo del personal; **appliances that ~ on housework** aparatos que aligeran las tareas domésticas
[3] (*US*) (= *keep*) [*food*] conservarse, aguantar*
Ⓒ N (*Sport*) parada *f*; **to make a ~** hacer una parada

> **SAVE THE CHILDREN**
>
> **Save the Children** *es una organización benéfica fundada en el Reino Unido en 1919 para ayudar a los niños que sufrieron las secuelas de la Revolución Rusa y de la Segunda Guerra Mundial. Hoy en día se dedica a ofrecer ayuda de emergencia a los niños de todo el mundo que sufren de inanición o son víctimas de los efectos de guerras y desastres naturales y desarrolla proyectos a largo plazo para mejorar la higiene, la nutrición y la educación, además de luchar para que los gobiernos den prioridad a los derechos de los niños.*

save[2] [seɪv] PREP (*liter*) salvo; **all ~ one** todos excepto *or* menos uno; **~ for** excepto; **~ that ...** excepto que ...

saveloy [ˈsævəlɔɪ] N frankfurt *m*

saver [ˈseɪvəʳ] N [1] (= *person*) (*having account*) ahorrador(a) *m/f*; (*by nature*) persona *f* ahorrativa, persona *f* ahorradora
[2] (= *ticket*) billete-abono *m*

saving [ˈseɪvɪŋ] Ⓐ N [1] (= *putting aside*) ahorro *m*; **a policy to encourage ~ and investment** una política para fomentar el ahorro y la inversión; **regular ~ is the best provision for the future** ahorrar con regularidad es la mejor manera de hacer previsiones para el futuro
[2] (= *economy*) ahorro *m*; **this price represents a ~ of £100** este precio supone un ahorro de 100 libras; **we must make ~s** tenemos que economizar *or* hacer economías; **this ticket enables you to make a ~ on standard rail fares** este billete le supondrá un ahorro con respecto a las tarifas de tren normales
[3] **savings** ahorros *mpl*; **she has ~s of £3,000** sus ahorros suman 3.000 libras, tiene ahorradas 3.000 libras; **life ~s** los ahorros de toda una vida
Ⓑ ADJ **~ grace: his only ~ grace was that ...** lo único que lo salvaba era que ...
Ⓒ PREP (= *apart from*) salvo, excepto
Ⓓ CPD ► **savings account** N cuenta *f* de ahorros ► **savings and loan association** N (*US*) sociedad *f* de ahorro y préstamo ► **savings bank** N caja *f* de ahorros ► **savings bond** N bono *m* de ahorros ► **savings book** N cartilla *f* *or* libreta *f* de ahorros ► **savings certificate** N bono *m* de ahorros ► **savings stamp** N sello *m* de ahorros

saviour, savior (*US*) [ˈseɪvjəʳ] N salvador(a) *m/f*; **Saviour** Salvador *m*

savoir-faire [ˈsævwɑːˈfɛəʳ] N desparpajo *m*

savor *etc* [ˈseɪvəʳ] (*US*) = **savour** *etc*

savory[1] [ˈseɪvərɪ] N (*Bot*) tomillo *m* salsero

savory[2] [ˈseɪvərɪ] (*US*) = **savoury**

savour, savor (*US*) [ˈseɪvəʳ] Ⓐ N sabor *m*, gusto *m*; **to add ~ to sth** dar sabor a algo; **it has lost its ~** ha perdido su sabor
Ⓑ VT saborear

savouriness, savoriness (*US*) [ˈseɪvərɪnɪs] N lo sabroso, buen sabor *m*

savourless, savorless (*US*) [ˈseɪvəlɪs] ADJ soso, insípido

savoury, savory (*US*) [ˈseɪvərɪ] Ⓐ ADJ [1] (= *appetizing*) sabroso
[2] (= *not sweet*) salado
[3] (*fig*) **it's not a very ~ district** no es un barrio muy respetable; **it's not a very ~ subject** no es un tema muy apto
Ⓑ N entremés *m* salado

Savoy [səˈvɔɪ] N Saboya *f*

savoy [səˈvɔɪ] N berza *f* de Saboya

savvy* [ˈsævɪ] Ⓐ N inteligencia *f*
Ⓑ VT comprender; **~?** ¿comprende?

saw[1] [sɔː] (*vb: pt* **sawed**; *pp* **sawed** *or* **sawn**) Ⓐ N (= *tool*) sierra *f*
Ⓑ VT serrar
Ⓒ VI **to ~ through** cortar con (una) sierra
Ⓓ CPD ► **saw edge** N filo *m* dentado *or* de sierra

►**saw away** Ⓐ VT + ADV quitar con la sierra
Ⓑ VI + ADV **she was ~ing away at the violin** iba rascando el violín

►**saw off** VT + ADV cortar con la sierra

►**saw up** VT + ADV cortar con la sierra

saw[2] [sɔː] PT *of* **see**[1]

saw[3] [sɔː] N (= *saying*) refrán *m*, dicho *m*

sawbench [ˈsɔːbentʃ] N (*US*) caballete *m* para serrar

sawbones†* [ˈsɔːbəʊnz] N (*pej*) matasanos *m inv*

sawbuck [ˈsɔːbʌk] N (*US*) caballete *m* para serrar

sawdust [ˈsɔːdʌst] N serrín *m*, aserrín *m*

sawed-off shotgun [ˌsɔːdɒfˈʃɒtgʌn] N (*US*) = **sawn-off shotgun**

sawfish [ˈsɔːfɪʃ] N (*pl* **sawfish** *or* **sawfishes**) pez *m* sierra

sawhorse [ˈsɔːhɔːs] N caballete *m*

sawmill [ˈsɔːmɪl] N aserradero *m*

sawn [sɔːn] PP *of* **saw**[1]

sawn-off shotgun [ˌsɔːnɒfˈʃɒtgʌn] N (*Brit*) escopeta *f* de cañones recortados

sawyer [ˈsɔːjəʳ] N aserrador *m*

sax* [sæks] N saxo* *m*

saxhorn [ˈsækshɔːn] N bombardino *m*

saxifrage [ˈsæksɪfrɪdʒ] N saxífraga *f*

Saxon [ˈsæksn] Ⓐ ADJ sajón
Ⓑ N [1] (= *person*) sajón/ona *m/f*
[2] (*Ling*) sajón *m*

Saxony [ˈsæksənɪ] N Sajonia *f*

saxophone [ˈsæksəfəʊn] N saxofón *m*, saxófono *m*

saxophonist [ˌsækˈsɒfənɪst] N saxofonista *mf*, saxofón *mf*

say [seɪ] (*vb: pt, pp* **said**) Ⓐ VT, VI [1] [*person*] (= *speak, tell*) decir; **"hello," he said** —hola —dijo; **what did you ~?** ¿qué dijiste?; **he said to me that ...** me dijo que ...; **to ~ to o.s.** decir para sí; **he said (that) he'd do it** dijo que él lo haría; **she said (that) I was to give you this** me pidió que te diera esto; **I ~ (that) we should go** yo digo que nos vayamos; **~ after me** repite lo que digo yo; **to ~ sth again** repetir algo; **to ~ goodbye to sb** despedirse de algn; **to ~ good morning/goodnight to sb** dar los buenos días/las buenas noches a algn; **to ~ mass** decir misa; **I've nothing more to ~** se acabó; **let's ~ no more about it** se acabó el asunto; **I must ~ (that) I disapprove of the idea** la verdad es que no me parece bien la idea; **I must ~ she's very pretty** tengo que *or* debo reconocer que es muy guapa; **it's difficult, I must ~** es difícil, lo confieso; **to ~ no** decir que no; **to ~ no to a proposal** rechazar una propuesta; **I wouldn't ~ no** (*Brit**) me encantaría; **to ~ a prayer** rezar; **that's what I ~** eso digo yo, lo mismo digo yo; **I will ~ this about him, he's bright** reconozco (a pesar de todo) que es listo; **to ~ yes** decir que sí; **to ~ yes to a proposal** aceptar una propuesta
[2] (= *show on dial*) marcar; (= *show in print*) poner, decir; **my watch ~s three o'clock** mi reloj marca las tres; **it ~s 30 degrees** marca 30 grados; **it ~s here that it was built in 1066** aquí pone *or* dice que se construyó en 1006; **the rules ~ that ...** según las reglas ..., en las reglas pone ...
[3] (*in phrases*) **when all is said and done** al fin y al cabo, a fin de cuentas; **she has nothing to ~ for herself** no tiene conversación, nunca abre la boca; **what have you got to ~ for yourself?** ¿y tú, qué dices?; **he never has much to ~ for himself** habla poco; **that doesn't ~ much for him** eso no es una gran recomendación para él; **it ~s much for his courage that he stayed** el que permaneciera allí demuestra su valor; **it's not for me to ~** no me toca a mí decir; **to ~ the least** para no decir más; **~ what you like about her hat, she's charming** dígase lo que se quiera acerca de su sombrero, es encantadora; **that's ~ing a lot** y eso es algo; **his suit ~s a lot about him** su traje dice mucho de él; **though I ~ it** *or* **so myself** aunque soy yo el que lo dice; **there's no ~ing what he'll do** quién sabe lo que hará; **I'd rather not ~** prefiero no decir (nada); **it's an original, not to ~ revolutionary, idea** la idea es original y hasta revolucionaria; **to ~ nothing of the rest** sin hablar de lo demás; **would you really ~ so?** ¿lo crees de veras?; **that is to ~** o sea, es decir; **what do** *or* **would you ~ to a walk?** ¿le apetece *or* se le antoja un paseo?; **what would you ~ to that?** ¿qué contestas a eso?; **it goes without ~ing that ...** ni que decir tiene que ..., huelga decir que ...; **that goes without ~ing** eso cae de su peso; ✦**IDIOM what he ~s goes** aquí manda él
[4] (*impersonal use*) **it is said that ...** ◊ **they ~ that ...** se dice que ..., dicen que ...; **he is said to have been the first** dicen que fue el primero; **it's easier said than done** del dicho al hecho hay gran trecho; **there's a lot to be said for it/for doing it** hay mucho que decir a su favor/a favor de hacerlo; **it must be said that ...** hay que decir *or* reconocer que ...; **there's something to be said for it/for doing it** hay algo que decir a su favor/a favor de hacerlo; **there's something to be said on both sides** hay algo que decir en pro y en contra; **no sooner said than done** dicho y hecho
[5] (*in exclamations*) **say!** (*esp US*) ◊ **I'll ~!*** ◊ **I should ~ so!*** ◊ **you can ~ that again!*** ¡ya lo creo!, ¡exacto!; **you don't ~!*** (*often hum*) ¡no me digas!; **enough said!** ¡basta!; **I say!** (*Brit*) (*calling attention*) ¡oiga!; (*in surprise, appreciation*) ¡vaya!, ¡anda!; **~ no more!** ¡basta!, ¡ni una palabra más!; **so you ~!** ¡eso es lo que tú dices!; **well said!** ¡muy bien dicho!; **you've said it!*** ¡exacto!, ¡tú lo dijiste!
[6] (= *suppose*) suponer, decir, poner; **(let's) ~ it's worth £20** supongamos *or* digamos *or* pon que vale 20 libras; **I should ~ it's worth about £100** yo diría que vale unas cien libras; **shall we ~ Tuesday?** ¿quedamos en el martes?; **shall we ~ £5?** ¿convenimos en 5 libras?; **we sell it at ~ £25** pongamos que lo vendemos por 25 libras; **we were going at ~ 80kph** íbamos a 80kph más o menos
Ⓑ N **to have one's ~** dar su opinión; **I've had my ~** yo he dado mi opinión *or* he dicho lo que pensaba; **to have a ~ in the matter** tener voz y voto; **if I had had a ~ in it** si hubieran pedido mi parecer *or* opinión; **to have no ~ in the matter** no tener voz en capítulo; **let him have his ~!** ¡que hable él!

SAYE ABBR = **save as you earn**

▼ **saying** [ˈseɪɪŋ] N dicho *m*, refrán *m*; **it's just a ~** es un refrán, es un dicho; **as the ~ goes** como dice el refrán

say-so* [ˈseɪsəʊ] N (= *authority*) **on whose ~?** ¿autorizado por quién?, ¿con permiso de quién?; **it depends on his ~** tiene que darle el visto bueno

SBA N ABBR (*US*) = **Small Business Administration**

SBU N ABBR = **strategic business unit**

SC ABBR (*US*) [1] = **Supreme Court**
[2] = **South Carolina**

s/c, s.c. ABBR = **self-contained**

scab [skæb] N [1] (*Med*) costra *f*
[2] (*Vet*) roña *f*
[3] (* *pej*) (= *strikebreaker*) esquirol *mf*, rompehuelgas *mf inv*

scabbard [ˈskæbəd] N vaina *f*, funda *f*

scabby [ˈskæbɪ] ADJ [1] [*skin, knee etc*] lleno de costras
[2] (*Vet*) roñoso

scabies [ˈskeɪbiːz] NSING sarna *f*

scabious¹ [ˈskeɪbɪəs] ADJ (*Med*) sarnoso

scabious² [ˈskeɪbɪəs] N (*Bot*) escabiosa *f*

scabrous [ˈskeɪbrəs] ADJ escabroso

scads* [skædz] NPL montones* *mpl*; **we have ~ of it** lo tenemos a montones*, tenemos montones de eso*

scaffold [ˈskæfəld] N [1] (*Constr*) (*also* **~ing**) andamio *m*, andamiaje *m*
[2] (*for execution*) patíbulo *m*, cadalso *m*

scaffolding [ˈskæfəldɪŋ] N andamio *m*, andamiaje *m*

scag‡ [skæg] N (= *heroin*) caballo‡ *m*

scalawag* [ˈskæləwæg] N (*US*) = **scallywag**

scald [skɔːld] Ⓐ N escaldadura *f*
Ⓑ VT (*gen*) escaldar; [+ *milk*] calentar; ✦**IDIOM to run like a ~ed cat** (*Brit**) correr como gato escaldado, correr como alma que lleva el diablo*

scalding [ˈskɔːldɪŋ] ADJ **it's ~ (hot)** está hirviendo *or* (*LAm*) que arde; **the soup is ~** la sopa está muy caliente

scale¹ [skeɪl] Ⓐ N [*of fish, reptile etc*] escama *f*; (= *flake*) [*of rust, chalk*] hojuela *f*; [*of skin*] escama *f*; (*inside kettle, boiler*) costra *f*; (*on teeth*) sarro *m*
Ⓑ VT [+ *fish*] quitar las escamas a, escamar; (*Tech*) raspar; [+ *teeth*] quitar el sarro a
Ⓒ VI (*also* **to ~ off**) [*skin*] descamarse

scale² [skeɪl] N [1] (= *weighing device*) (*often pl*) balanza *f*; (*for heavy weights*) báscula *f*; **bathroom ~(s)** báscula *f* (de baño); **a kitchen ~** ◊ **a pair of kitchen ~s** una balanza de cocina; **he tips the ~s at 70 kilos** pesa 70 kilos; **to turn** *or* **tip the ~s (in sb's favour/against sb)** inclinar la balanza (a favor de algn/en contra de algn)
[2] [*of balance*] platillo *m*

scale³ [skeɪl] Ⓐ N [1] (= *size, extent*) (*gen*) escala *f*; [*of problem, disaster*] magnitud *f*, escala *f*; **he likes to do things on a grand ~** le gusta hacer las cosas a gran escala *or* por todo lo alto *or* a lo grande; **on a large ~** a gran escala; **they were engaged in fraud on a massive ~** estaban realizando un fraude a gran escala *or* de gran envergadura; **on a national ~** a escala nacional; **on a small ~** a pequeña escala; **borrowing on this ~ will bankrupt the country** el país va a caer en la bancarrota si sigue aceptando préstamos de esta magnitud
[2] (= *graduated system*) (*gen, for salaries*) escala *f*; **~ of charges** (lista *f* de) tarifas *fpl*; **the Richter ~** la escala de Richter; **the social ~** la escala *or* jerarquía social; *see also* **pay**, **sliding**
[3] (= *ratio, proportion*) [*of map, model*] escala *f*; **on a ~ of 1cm to 5km** con una escala de 1cm a 5km; **to be out of ~ (with sth)** no guardar proporción (con algo); **the drawing is not to ~** el dibujo no está a escala; **to draw sth to ~** dibujar algo a escala
[4] (*Mus*) escala *f*
Ⓑ VT [+ *wall*] trepar a, escalar; [+ *tree*] trepar a; [+ *mountain*] escalar
Ⓒ CPD ► **scale drawing** N dibujo *m* a escala
► **scale model** N modelo *m* a escala

► **scale back** VT + ADV (= *reduce*) [+ *production, operations, demands, plan*] recortar

► **scale down** VT + ADV [1] (= *make proportionately smaller*) reducir a escala; **it is a ~d down replica of the real building** es una réplica del edificio a escala reducida, es una maqueta del edificio
[2] (= *reduce*) = **scale back**

► **scale up** VT + ADV [1] (= *make proportionately bigger*) aumentar a escala
[2] (= *increase*) [+ *operations*] ampliar

scallion [ˈskæljən] N cebolleta *f* (para ensalada), cebollita *f* (*LAm*)

scallop [ˈskɒləp] Ⓐ N [1] (*Zool*) venera *f*
[2] (*Sew*) festón *m*, onda *f*
Ⓑ VT [1] (*Culin*) guisar en conchas
[2] (*Sew*) festonear
Ⓒ CPD ► **scallop shell** N venera *f*

scallywag* [ˈskælɪwæg] N (= *child*) diablillo *m*, travieso/a *m/f*; (= *rogue*) pillín/ina *m/f*; **you little ~!** ¡ay pillín!

scalp [skælp] Ⓐ N cuero *m* cabelludo; (*as trophy*) cabellera *f*; **to demand sb's ~** (*fig*) exigir la cabeza de algn

➤ LANGUAGE IN USE: saying 26.2

Ⓑ VT [1] (*lit*) arrancar la cabellera de; **he'll ~ you if he finds out!*** ¡si se entera, te arranca la cabellera!
[2] (*US**) [+ *tickets*] revender
Ⓒ VI (*US**) revender

scalpel ['skælpəl] N escalpelo *m*

scalper* ['skælpəʳ] N (*US*) revendedor(a) *m/f*

scalping* ['skælpɪŋ] N (*US*) reventa *f*

scaly ['skeɪlɪ] ADJ (*compar* **scalier**; *superl* **scaliest**) escamoso

scam* [skæm] N estafa *f*, timo *m*

scamp¹* [skæmp] N = **scallywag**

scamp² [skæmp] VT [+ *one's work etc*] chapucear, frangollar

scamper ['skæmpəʳ] VI escabullirse; **to ~ in/out** entrar/salir corriendo; **to ~ along** ir corriendo

►**scamper about** VI + ADV corretear

►**scamper away**, **scamper off** VI + ADV escabullirse

scampi ['skæmpɪ] N gambas *fpl* rebozadas

scan [skæn] Ⓐ VT [1] (= *inspect closely*) escudriñar; [+ *horizon etc*] otear; (*Comput*) examinar, explorar
[2] (= *glance at*) echar un vistazo a
[3] (*Radar*) explorar, registrar
[4] (*Poetry*) [+ *verse*] medir, escandir
Ⓑ VI [*poetry*] estar bien medido; **it does not ~** no está bien medido
Ⓒ N (*Med*) exploración *f* con un escáner; **to go for a ~** ◊ **have a ~** hacerse un escáner

scandal ['skændl] N [1] (= *public furore*) escándalo *m*; **it caused** *or* **created a ~** causó escándalo; **he was involved in a sex/drugs ~** estuvo involucrado en un escándalo sexual/de drogas
[2] (= *disgraceful state of affairs*) vergüenza *f*; **it's a ~!** ◊ **what a ~!** ¡qué vergüenza!
[3] (= *gossip*) chismes *mpl*; **it's just ~** no son más que habladurías *or* chismes; **she reads all the ~ in the tabloid press** se lee todos los chismes de los periódicos sensacionalistas; **there's a lot of ~ going round about her** circulan muchos chismes sobre ella; **the local ~** los chismes del pueblo *or* del barrio *etc*; **the latest ~** lo último en cotilleo; **to talk ~** murmurar, contar chismes

scandalize ['skændəlaɪz] VT escandalizar; **she was ~d** se escandalizó

scandalmonger ['skændl,mʌŋgəʳ] N chismoso/a *m/f*

scandalous ['skændələs] ADJ [*behaviour, story, price*] escandaloso; **to reach ~ proportions** alcanzar proporciones escandalosas; **it's simply ~!** ¡es un escándalo!; **it's ~ that ...** es vergonzoso que ...; **~ talk** habladurías *fpl*, chismes *mpl*

scandalously ['skændələslɪ] ADV escandalosamente

Scandinavia [,skændɪ'neɪvɪə] N Escandinavia *f*

Scandinavian [,skændɪ'neɪvɪən] Ⓐ ADJ escandinavo
Ⓑ N escandinavo/a *m/f*

scandium ['skændɪəm] N escandio *m*

scanner ['skænəʳ] N [1] (*Med*) escáner *m*, scanner *m*; (*also* **ultra-sound ~**) ecógrafo *m*
[2] (*Comput*) (*in airports*) escáner *m*
[3] (*Radar*) antena *f* direccional

scanning ['skænɪŋ] Ⓐ N (*Med*) visualización *f* radiográfica
Ⓑ CPD ► **scanning device** N detector *m*

scansion ['skænʃən] N [*of poetry*] escansión *f*

scant [skænt] ADJ (*compar* **scanter**; *superl* **scantest**) escaso; **it measures a ~ 2cm** mide dos centímetros escasos; **to pay ~ attention to sth** prestar escasa atención a algo; **a ~ tablespoon of sugar** una cucharada rasa de azúcar

scantily ['skæntɪlɪ] ADV insuficientemente; **~ clad** *or* **dressed** ligero de ropa; **~ provided with ...** con escasa cantidad de ...

scantiness ['skæntɪnɪs] N escasez *f*, insuficiencia *f*

scanty ['skæntɪ] ADJ (*compar* **scantier**; *superl* **scantiest**) [*meal etc*] insuficiente; [*clothing*] ligero; [*evidence*] insuficiente; [*information*] insuficiente, escaso

scapegoat ['skeɪpgəʊt] N cabeza *f* de turco, chivo *m* expiatorio; **to be a ~ for** pagar el pato por, pagar los cristales rotos por

scapegrace† ['skeɪpgreɪs] N pícaro *m*, bribón *m*

scapula ['skæpjʊlə] N (*pl* **scapulas** *or* **scapulae** ['skæpjʊli:]) escápula *f*

scar¹ [skɑ:ʳ] Ⓐ N (*Med*) cicatriz *f*; (*fig*) (*on building, landscape etc*) huella *f*; **it left a deep ~ on his mind** dejó una huella profunda en su ánimo
Ⓑ VT dejar una cicatriz en; (*fig*) marcar, rayar; **he was ~red with many wounds** tenía cicatrices de muchas heridas; **he was ~red for life** quedó marcado para toda la vida; **the walls are ~red with bullets** las balas han dejado marca en las paredes
Ⓒ VI (= *leave a scar*) cicatrizar; (*also* **~ over**) (= *heal*) cicatrizarse

scar² [skɑ:ʳ] N (*Geog*) (= *crag*) paraje *m* rocoso, pendiente *f* rocosa

scarab ['skærəb] N escarabajo *m*

scarce ['skɛəs] Ⓐ ADJ (*compar* **scarcer**; *superl* **scarcest**) [*reserves, resources*] escaso; **to be ~** [*doctors, food, resources*] escasear; [*money*] escasear, faltar; **jobs were very ~ in those days** en aquella época escaseaban los puestos de trabajo; **paintings of this quality are ~** no abundan los cuadros de esta calidad; **to grow** *or* **become ~** volverse escaso, escasear; **to make o.s. ~*** largarse*, esfumarse*
Ⓑ ADV (†) = **scarcely**

scarcely ['skɛəslɪ] ADV (= *barely*) apenas; **~ anybody** casi nadie; **I can ~ believe it** apenas puedo creerlo, casi no puedo creerlo; **~ ever** casi nunca; **I ~ know what to say** no sé qué puedo decir; **he was ~ more than a boy** era apenas un niño; **we could ~ refuse** ¿cómo podíamos negarnos?, difícilmente podíamos negarnos; **it is ~ surprising that ...** no es ni mucho menos sorprendente que ...; **he's ~ what you'd call a cordon bleu chef** (*iro*) no es precisamente un maestro de la cocina; **the car had ~ drawn to a halt when ...** apenas se había parado el coche cuando ...

scarceness ['skɛəsnɪs] N *see* **scarcity**

scarcity ['skɛəsɪtɪ] Ⓐ N (= *shortage*) [*of money, food, resources*] escasez *f*, carestía *f*; [*of doctors, teachers*] escasez *f*
Ⓑ CPD ► **scarcity value** N **it has ~ value** tiene valor por lo escaso que es

scare ['skɛəʳ] Ⓐ N [1] (= *fright*) susto *m*; **to cause a ~** sembrar el pánico; **to give sb a ~** dar un susto *or* asustar a algn; **what a ~ you gave me!** ¡qué susto me diste!; **we got a bit of a ~** nos pegamos un susto, tuvimos un sobresalto
[2] (= *panic, threat*) **bomb ~** amenaza *f* de bomba; **the invasion ~** (= *panic*) el pánico de la invasión; (= *rumours*) los rumores alarmistas de una invasión
Ⓑ VT [1] (= *frighten*) asustar; **you ~d me!** ¡me has asustado!; **to ~ sb to death*** darle un susto de muerte a algn; **to ~ the hell** *or* **life out of sb*** darle un susto de muerte a algn; **to ~ sb stiff*** darle un susto de muerte a algn
[2] **to be ~d** (= *frightened*) tener miedo, estar asustado; **don't be ~d** no tengas miedo, no te asustes; **we were really ~d** teníamos mucho miedo, estábamos muy asustados; **to be ~d to do sth** tener miedo de hacer algo; **she was too ~d to talk** estaba demasiado asustada para poder hablar, no podía hablar del susto; **to be ~d to death*** estar muerto de miedo; **to be ~d of sb/sth**: **he's ~d of women** tiene miedo a las mujeres; **are you ~d of him?** ¿le tienes miedo?; **I'm ~d of spiders** les tengo miedo a *or* me dan miedo las arañas; **to be ~d of doing sth** tener miedo de hacer algo; **to be ~d stiff*** estar muerto de miedo; **to be ~d out of one's wits*** estar muerto de miedo
Ⓒ VI **he doesn't ~ easily** no se asusta fácilmente
Ⓓ CPD ► **scare campaign** N campaña *f* alarmista, campaña *f* de intimidación ► **scare story** N **it's only a ~ story** se trata de un reportaje alarmista

►**scare away**, **scare off** VT + ADV espantar, ahuyentar

scarecrow ['skɛəkrəʊ] N espantapájaros *m inv*, espantajo *m*

scared ['skɛəd] ADJ *see* **scare B**

scaredy-cat* ['skɛədɪ,kæt] N miedica* *mf*

scarehead* ['skɛəhed] N (*US Press*) titulares *mpl* sensacionales

scaremonger ['skɛəmʌŋgəʳ] N alarmista *mf*

scaremongering ['skɛə,mʌŋgərɪŋ] N alarmismo *m*

scarf [skɑ:f] N (*pl* **scarfs** *or* **scarves**) (*woollen, for neck*) bufanda *f*; (= *headscarf*) pañuelo *m*

scarface ['skɑ:feɪs] N (*as nickname*) caracortada *mf*

scarify ['skɛərɪfaɪ] VT (*Med, Agr*) escarificar; (*fig*) despellejar, desollar, criticar severamente

scarifying ['skɛərɪfaɪɪŋ] ADJ [*attack etc*] mordaz, severo

scarlatina [,skɑ:lə'ti:nə] N escarlatina *f*

scarlet ['skɑ:lɪt] Ⓐ N escarlata *f*
Ⓑ ADJ color escarlata, colorado (*LAm*); **~ fever** escarlatina *f*; **~ pimpernel** (*Bot*) pimpinela *f*; **~ runner** judía *f* escarlata; **to blush ~** ◊ **turn ~** enrojecer, ponerse colorado; **he was ~ with rage** se puso rojo de furia

scarp [skɑ:p] N escarpa *f*, declive *m*

scarper‡ ['skɑ:pəʳ] VI (*Brit*) largarse*

scarves [skɑ:vz] NPL *of* **scarf**

scary* ['skɛərɪ] ADJ (*compar* **scarier**; *superl* **scariest**) [*face, house, person, monster*] que da miedo; [*moment*] espeluznante; **it was really ~** daba verdadero miedo; **a ~ film** una película de miedo; **that's a ~ thought** ésa es una idea espeluznante

scat¹* [skæt] EXCL ¡zape!, ¡fuera de aquí!

scat² [skæt] N (*Mus*) *modalidad de jazz en la que el cantante emite sonidos inconexos en lugar de palabras enteras*

scathing ['skeɪðɪŋ] ADJ [*criticism, article, remark*] mordaz; [*look*] feroz; **he was ~ about our trains** hizo comentarios mordaces sobre nuestros trenes; **he was pretty ~** dijo cosas bastante duras; **to make a ~ attack on sb/sth** atacar mordazmente a algn/algo

scathingly ['skeɪðɪŋlɪ] ADV mordazmente; **he spoke ~ of ...** habló mordazmente *or* con mordacidad de ...

scatological [,skætə'lɒdʒɪkəl] ADJ escatológico

scatology [skæ'tɒlədʒɪ] N escatología *f*

scatter ['skætəʳ] Ⓐ VT 1 (= *strew around*) [+ *crumbs, papers etc*] esparcir, desparramar; [+ *seeds*] sembrar a voleo, esparcir; **the flowers were ~ed about on the floor** las flores estaban desparramadas por el suelo; **the floor was ~ed with flowers** en el suelo había flores desparramadas
2 (= *disperse*) [+ *clouds*] dispersar; [+ *crowd*] dispersar; **her relatives are ~ed about the world** sus familiares se encuentran dispersos por el mundo
Ⓑ VI [*crowd*] dispersarse; **the family ~ed to distant parts** la familia se dispersó por lugares alejados
Ⓒ N (*Math, Tech*) dispersión *f*; **a ~ of houses** unas casas dispersas; **a ~ of raindrops** unas gotas dispersas de lluvia
Ⓓ CPD ► **scatter cushions** NPL almohadones *mpl*

scatterbrain* ['skætəbreɪn] N cabeza *mf* de chorlito

scatterbrained* ['skætəbreɪnd] ADJ (= *scatty*) atolondrado, ligero de cascos

scattered ['skætəd] ADJ disperso; **the village is very ~** las casas del pueblo son muy dispersas; **~ showers** chubascos *mpl* dispersos

scattering ['skætərɪŋ] N **a ~ of books** unos cuantos libros aquí y allá

scattiness* ['skætɪnɪs] N (*Brit*) ligereza *f* de cascos, atolondramiento *m*

scatty* ['skætɪ] ADJ (*Brit*) ligero de cascos, atolondrado; **to drive sb ~** volver majareta a algn*

scavenge ['skævɪndʒ] Ⓐ VT [+ *streets*] limpiar las calles de, recoger la basura de
Ⓑ VI remover basuras, pepenar (*Mex*); **to ~ for food** andar buscando comida (entre la basura)

scavenger ['skævɪndʒəʳ] N 1 (= *person*) persona *f* que rebusca en las basuras, pepenador(a) *m/f* (*Mex*)
2 (*Zool*) (= *animal*) animal *m* carroñero; (= *bird*) ave *f* de carroña; (= *insect*) insecto *m* de carroña

Sc.D. N ABBR = **Doctor of Science**

SCE N ABBR = **Scottish Certificate of Education**

scenario [sɪ'nɑːrɪəʊ] N 1 (*Theat*) argumento *m*; (*Cine*) guión *m*
2 (*fig*) escenario *m*

scenarist ['siːnərɪst] N guionista *mf*

scene [siːn] Ⓐ N 1 (*Theat, Cine, TV, Literat*) escena *f*; **Act I, Scene 1** acto I, escena 1; **a bedroom ~** una escena de dormitorio; **behind the ~s** (*lit, fig*) entre bastidores; **the big ~ in the film** la principal escena de la película; **indoor ~** interior *m*; **love ~s** escenas *fpl* de amor; **outdoor ~** exterior *m*; **the ~ is set in a castle** la escena tiene lugar en un castillo; **to set the ~ for a love affair** crear el ambiente para una aventura sentimental; **now let our reporter set the ~ for you** ahora permitan que nuestro reportero les describa la escena
2 (= *sight*) escena *f*; **it was an amazing ~** era una escena asombrosa; **it was a ~ of utter destruction** la escena *or* el panorama era de destrucción total; **there were ~s of violence** hubo escenas de violencia
3 (= *view*) vista *f*, panorama *m*; (= *landscape*) paisaje *m*; **the ~ from the top is marvellous** desde la cumbre la vista es maravillosa *or* el panorama es maravilloso; **the ~ spread out before you** el panorama que tienes delante; **it is a lonely ~** es un paisaje solitario
4 (= *place*) escenario *m*, lugar *m*; **the ~s of one's early life** los lugares frecuentados por uno en su juventud; **to appear** *or* **come on the ~** llegar; **when I came on the ~** cuando llegué; **he appeared unexpectedly on the ~** se presentó inesperadamente; **I need a change of ~** necesito un cambio de aires; **the ~ of the crime** el lugar *or* escenario del crimen; **to disappear from the ~** desaparecer (de escena); **the ~ of the disaster** el lugar de la catástrofe; **the police were soon on the ~** la policía no tardó en acudir al lugar de los hechos; (*Mil*) **the ~ of operations** el teatro de operaciones
5 (= *sphere of activity*) **to be part of the Madrid ~** formar parte de la movida madrileña*; **the music ~** la escena musical; **it's not my ~*** no me interesa *or* llama la atención; **the political ~ in Spain** el panorama político español; **to disappear from the political ~** desaparecer de la escena política; **the pop ~** el mundo del pop
6 (= *painting, drawing*) escena *f*; **country ~s** escenas *fpl* campestres
7 (*) (= *fuss*) escena *f*, escándalo *m*, bronca *f* (*esp LAm*); **try to avoid a ~** procura que no se monte una escena *or* el número*; **I hate ~s** detesto las escenas *or* los escándalos; **to make a ~** hacer *or* montar una escena, montar un número*; **she had a ~ with her husband** riñó con su marido
8 (= *display of emotion*) **there were emotional ~s as the hostages appeared** hubo escenas de emoción cuando aparecieron los rehenes; **their argument ended in an ugly ~** su discusión acabó mal; **there were unhappy ~s at the meeting** en la reunión pasaron cosas nada agradables
Ⓑ CPD ► **scene change** N (*Theat*) cambio *m* de escena ► **scene painter** N (= *designer*) escenógrafo/a *m/f*; (= *workman*) pintor(a) *m/f* (de paredes) ► **scene shift** N cambio *m* de escena ► **scene shifter** N tramoyista *mf*

scenery ['siːnərɪ] N 1 (= *landscape*) paisaje *m*
2 (*Theat*) decorado *m*

scenic ['siːnɪk] ADJ 1 (*gen*) pintoresco; **an area of ~ beauty** una región de bellos paisajes; **~ railway** (= *miniature railway*) *tren pequeño que hace recorridos turísticos por un recinto*; (*Brit*) (= *roller coaster*) montaña *f* rusa; **~ road** carretera *f* que recorre lugares pintorescos
2 (*Theat*) escénico, dramático

scenography [siː'nɒgrəfɪ] N escenografía *f*

scent [sent] Ⓐ N 1 (= *smell*) [*of flowers, perfume*] perfume *m*, fragancia *f*; [*of food*] aroma *m*
2 (*esp Brit*) (= *perfume, toilet water*) perfume *m*, fragancia *f*
3 (*Hunting etc*) rastro *m*, pista *f*; **to be on the ~** (*also fig*) seguir el rastro *or* la pista; **to pick up/lose the ~** (*also fig*) encontrar/perder el rastro *or* la pista; **to put** *or* **throw sb off the ~** (*fig*) despistar a algn
Ⓑ VT 1 (= *make sth smell nice*) perfumar (**with** de)
2 (= *smell*) olfatear; (*fig*) [+ *danger, trouble etc*] presentir, sentir; **to ~ sth out** olfatear *or* husmear algo
Ⓒ CPD ► **scent bottle** N (*esp Brit*) frasco *m* de perfume ► **scent spray** N atomizador *m* (de perfume), pulverizador *m* (de perfume)

scented ['sentɪd] ADJ perfumado

scentless ['sentlɪs] ADJ inodoro

scepter ['septəʳ] N (*US*) = **sceptre**

sceptic, skeptic (*US*) ['skeptɪk] N escéptico/a *m/f*

sceptical, skeptical (*US*) ['skeptɪkəl] ADJ escéptico (**of, about** acerca de); **he was ~ about it** se mostró escéptico acerca de ello, tenía dudas sobre ello

sceptically, skeptically (*US*) ['skeptɪkəlɪ] ADV con escepticismo

scepticism, skepticism (*US*) ['skeptɪsɪzəm] N escepticismo *m*

sceptre, scepter (*US*) ['septəʳ] N cetro *m*

schedule ['ʃedjuːl, (*US*) 'skedjuːl] Ⓐ N 1 (= *timetable*) [*of work, visits, events*] programa *m*, calendario *m*; [*of trains, buses*] horario *m*; (*TV, Rad*) (*often pl*) programación *f*; **a busy/punishing ~** un programa *or* calendario apretado/agotador, una agenda apretada/agotadora; **we are working to a very tight ~** tenemos un programa *or* calendario de trabajo muy apretado; **the strike could threaten Christmas ~s** la huelga podría afectar a la programación de Navidad; **everything went according to ~** todo sucedió según se había previsto; **the work is behind/ahead of ~** el trabajo lleva retraso/va adelantado (con respecto al programa *or* calendario); **I was running one hour behind ~** llevaba una hora de retraso con respecto a mi agenda; **the train arrived on/ahead of ~** el tren llegó a la hora prevista/antes de lo previsto
2 (= *list*) [*of contents, goods, charges*] lista *f*
3 (*Jur*) inventario *m*
Ⓑ VT (= *programme, timetable*) [+ *meeting*] programar, fijar; [+ *TV programmes*] programar; [+ *trains, planes*] programar el horario de; **the meeting is ~d for seven o'clock** *or* **to begin at seven o'clock** la reunión está programada *or* fijada para las siete; **the plane is ~d for two o'clock** *or* **to land at two o'clock** la hora de llegada prevista del avión es a las dos; **an election was ~d for last December** se habían programado *or* planeado unas elecciones para el pasado mes de diciembre; **you are ~d to speak for 20 minutes** según el programa hablarás durante 20 minutos; **I have nothing ~d for Friday** no tengo nada programado *or* planeado para el viernes; **I've ~d an appointment with the doctor** he pedido hora con el médico; **a second attempt to ~ a presidential debate has failed** ha fracasado un segundo intento de fijar una fecha para el debate presidencial; **this building is ~d for demolition** se ha previsto la demolición de este edificio; **as ~d** según lo previsto, de acuerdo con lo previsto

scheduled ['ʃedjuːld, (*US*) 'skedjuːld] Ⓐ ADJ [*date, time*] previsto, programado; [*meeting, visit*] programado; **at the ~ time** a la hora prevista *or* programada; **a week before the ~ date** una semana antes de lo previsto *or* programado
Ⓑ CPD ► **scheduled building** N edificio *m* protegido ► **scheduled flight** N vuelo *m* regular ► **scheduled stop** N parada *f* programada; (*Aer*) escala *f* programada

scheduling ['ʃedjuːlɪŋ, (*US*) 'skedjuːlɪŋ] N [*of event, visit, meeting*] organización *f*; [*of TV programmes*] programación *f*; (*Comput*) planificación *f*; **the ~ of classes** la programación del horario de clases

Scheldt [ʃelt] N Escalda *m*

schema ['skiːmə] N (*pl* **schemata** ['skiːmətə]) esquema *m*

schematic [skɪ'mætɪk] ADJ esquemático

schematically [skɪ'mætɪkəlɪ] ADV esquemáticamente

scheme [skiːm] Ⓐ N 1 (= *project*) plan *m*, proyecto *m*; (= *plan*) plan *m*; **a road-widening ~** un plan de ensanchamiento de calzadas
2 (= *idea*) idea *f*; **it's not a bad ~*** no es

mala idea; **it's some crazy ~ of his** es otro de sus proyectos alocados

[3] (= *programme*) programa *m*; **a ~ of work** un programa de trabajo

[4] (= *structure*) esquema *m*; **colour ~** combinación *f* de colores; **pension ~** sistema *m* de pensión; **man's place in the ~ of things** el puesto del hombre en el diseño divino; **in the government's ~ of things there is no place for protest** la política del gobierno no deja espacio para la protesta

[5] (= *conspiracy*) intriga *f*; (*crafty*) ardid *m*; **it's a ~ to get him out of the way** es una jugada para quitarle de en medio

(B) VI intrigar (**to do** para hacer); **they're scheming to get me out** están intrigando para expulsarme; **their opponents were scheming against them** sus adversarios estaban conspirando contra ellos

(C) VT proyectar; (*pej*) tramar, urdir

schemer ['ski:məʳ] N (*pej*) intrigante *mf*

scheming ['ski:mɪŋ] (A) ADJ (*pej*) maquinador, intrigante

(B) N conspiración *f*, maquinación *f*

scherzo ['skɜ:tsəʊ] N (*pl* **scherzos** *or* **scherzi** ['skɜ:tsi:]) scherzo *m*

schism ['sɪzəm, 'skɪzəm] N cisma *m*

schismatic [sɪz'mætɪk, skɪz'mætɪk] (A) ADJ cismático

(B) N cismático/a *m/f*

schismatical [sɪz'mætɪkəl, skɪz'mætɪkəl] ADJ cismático

schist [ʃɪst] N esquisto *m*

schizo‡ ['skɪtsəʊ] N esquizo/a* *m/f*

schizoid ['skɪtsɔɪd] (A) ADJ esquizoide

(B) N esquizoide *mf*

schizophrenia [ˌskɪtsəʊ'fri:nɪə] N esquizofrenia *f*

schizophrenic [ˌskɪtsəʊ'frenɪk] (A) ADJ esquizofrénico

(B) N esquizofrénico/a *m/f*

schlemiel‡, **schlemihl**‡ [ʃlə'mi:l] N (*US*) (= *clumsy person*) persona *f* desmañada; (= *unlucky person*) persona *f* desgraciada

schmaltz* [ʃmɔ:lts] N sentimentalismo *m*, sensiblería *f*

schmaltzy* ['ʃmɔ:ltsɪ] ADJ sentimental, sensiblero

schmuck‡ [ʃmʌk] N (*US*) imbécil *mf*

schnapps [ʃnæps] N schnapps *m*

schnozzle‡ ['ʃnɒzəl] N (*esp US*) napia‡ *f*, nariz *f*

scholar ['skɒləʳ] N [1] (= *learned person*) sabio/a *m/f*; (= *expert*) estudioso/a *m/f*, experto/a *m/f*; **a famous Dickens ~** un conocido especialista en Dickens; **I'm no ~** yo apenas sé nada, yo no soy nada intelectual

[2] † (= *pupil*) alumno/a *m/f*; (= *scholarship holder*) becario/a *m/f*; **he's never been much of a ~** nunca fue muy aficionado a los libros; **~'s list** (*US Univ*) *lista de honor académica*; → DEAN'S LIST

scholarly ['skɒlәlɪ] ADJ (= *studious*) erudito, estudioso; (= *pedantic*) pedante

scholarship ['skɒləʃɪp] (A) N [1] (= *learning*) erudición *f*

[2] (= *money award*) beca *f*

(B) CPD ► **scholarship holder** N becario/a *m/f*

scholastic [skə'læstɪk] (A) ADJ [1] (= *educational*) escolar; **~ books** libros *mpl* escolares; **the ~ year** el año escolar; **the ~ profession** el magisterio; **Scholastic Aptitude Test** (*US*) examen *m* de acceso a la universidad

[2] (= *relative to scholasticism*) escolástico

(B) N escolástico *m*

scholasticism [skə'læstɪsɪzəm] N escolasticismo *m*

school[1] [sku:l] (A) N [1] (*for children*) [1·1] (= *institution*) escuela *f*, colegio *m*; **what did you learn at ~ today?** ¿qué has aprendido hoy en el colegio?; **to be at ~** asistir a la escuela; **which ~ were you at?** ¿a qué colegio fue?; **we have to be at ~ by nine** tenemos que estar en el colegio a las nueve; **you weren't at ~ yesterday** ayer faltaste a la clase; **to go to ~** ir a la escuela; **which ~ did you go to?** ¿a qué colegio fue?; **to leave ~** terminar el colegio; *see also* **primary C**, **secondary B**, **high D**

[1·2] (= *lessons*) clase *f*; **after ~** después de clase; **there's no ~ today** hoy no hay clase; **~ starts again in September** las clases empiezan de nuevo en septiembre

[2] (*Univ*) [2·1] (= *faculty*) facultad *f*; **art ~** Facultad *f* de bellas artes; **School of Languages** departamento *m* de lenguas modernas; **law ~** Facultad *f* de derecho; **medical ~** Facultad *f* de medicina

[2·2] (*US*) (= *university*) universidad *f*; **I went back to ~ at 35** a los 35 años volví a la universidad

[3] (= *group of artists, writers, thinkers*) escuela *f*; **the Dutch ~** la escuela holandesa; **Plato and his ~** Platón y su escuela, Platón y sus discípulos

[4] (*specialist*) escuela *f*; **~ of art** escuela *f* de bellas artes; **~ of dancing** escuela *f* de baile; **~ of motoring** autoescuela *f*, escuela *f* de manejo (*LAm*); **~ of music** academia *f* de música, conservatorio *m*; *see also* **ballet B**, **driving C**, **riding B**

[5] (*in expressions*) **I am not of that ~** yo no soy de esa opinión, yo no pertenezco a esa escuela; **I am not of the ~ that ...** yo no soy de los que ...; **of the old ~** (*fig*) de la vieja escuela; **~ of thought** (*fig*) corriente *f* de opinión

(B) VT [+ *horse*] amaestrar; [+ *person*] educar, instruir; [+ *reaction, voice etc*] dominar; **he has been well ~ed** ha recibido una buena educación; **to ~ sb in sth** educar *or* instruir a algn en algo; **to ~ sb to do sth** preparar a algn para hacer algo; **to ~ o.s.** instruirse; **to ~ o.s. in patience** aprender a tener paciencia

(C) CPD ► **school age** N edad *f* escolar; **~-age child** niño *m* en edad escolar ► **school attendance** N asistencia *f* a la escuela; **~ attendance officer** *inspector de educación encargado de problemas relacionados con la falta de asistencia o el bajo rendimiento de los alumnos* ► **school bus** N autobús *m* escolar ► **school dinner** N comida *f* escolar, comida *f* de colegio ► **school doctor** N médico *mf* de escuela ► **school fees** NPL matrícula *fsing* (escolar) ► **school friend** N amigo/a *m/f* de clase ► **school holidays** NPL vacaciones *fpl* escolares ► **school hours** NPL **during ~ hours** durante las horas de clase ► **school inspector** N inspector(a) *m/f* de enseñanza ► **school leaver** N persona *f* que termina la escuela ► **school life** N vida *f* escolar ► **school lunch** N comida *f* escolar, comida *f* de colegio; **to take ~ lunches** comer *or* almorzar en la escuela ► **school meal** N comida *f* provista por la escuela ► **school outing** N **to go on a ~ outing to the zoo** ir de visita al zoo con el colegio ► **school playground** N (*Brit*) patio *m* (de recreo) ► **school report** N boletín *m* escolar ► **school time** N = **school hours** ► **school trip** N = **school outing** ► **school uniform** N uniforme *m* escolar ► **school yard** N (*US*) = **school playground** ► **school year** N año *m* escolar

school[2] [sku:l] N [*of fish, dolphins, whales*] banco *m*

schoolbag ['sku:lbæg] N bolso *m*, cabás *m*

schoolbook ['sku:lbʊk] N libro *m* de texto (escolar)

schoolboy ['sku:lbɔɪ] (A) N alumno *m* (de escuela), colegial *m*

(B) CPD ► **schoolboy slang** N jerga *f* de colegial

schoolchild ['sku:ltʃaɪld] N (*pl* **schoolchildren**) alumno/a *m/f*, colegial(a) *m/f*

schooldays ['sku:ldeɪz] NPL años *mpl* del colegio

schoolfellow ['sku:lˌfeləʊ] N compañero/a *m/f* de clase

schoolgirl ['sku:lgɜ:l] (A) N colegiala *f*

(B) CPD ► **schoolgirl complexion** N cutis *m* de colegiala ► **schoolgirl crush*** N enamoramiento *m* de colegiala

schoolhouse ['sku:lhaʊs] N (*US*) (*pl* **schoolhouses**) escuela *f*

schooling ['sku:lɪŋ] N (= *education*) instrucción *f*, enseñanza *f*; (= *studies*) estudios *mpl*; **compulsory ~** escolaridad *f* obligatoria; **he had little formal ~** apenas asistió a la escuela

school-leaving age [ˌsku:l'li:vɪŋˌeɪdʒ] N edad *f* en que se termina la escuela; **to raise the ~** aumentar la edad de escolaridad obligatoria

schoolman ['sku:lmən] N (*pl* **schoolmen**) (*Philos*) escolástico *m*

schoolmarm* ['sku:lmɑ:m] N (*pej*) institutriz *f*

schoolmaster ['sku:lˌmɑ:stəʳ] N maestro *m* (de escuela), profesor *m* (de escuela)

schoolmate ['sku:lmeɪt] N compañero/a *m/f* de clase

schoolmistress ['sku:lˌmɪstrɪs] N maestra *f* (de escuela), profesora *f* (de escuela)

schoolroom ['sku:lrʊm] N aula *f*, sala *f* de clase

schoolteacher ['sku:lˌti:tʃəʳ] N (*gen*) maestro/a *m/f* (de escuela), profesor(a) *m/f* (de escuela)

schoolteaching ['sku:lˌti:tʃɪŋ] N enseñanza *f*

schoolwork ['sku:lwɜ:k] N trabajo *m* de clase

schooner ['sku:nəʳ] N [1] (*Naut*) goleta *f*

[2] (*for sherry*) copa *f* grande

schwa, **schwah** [ʃwɑ:] N vocal *f* neutra

sciatic [saɪ'ætɪk] ADJ ciático

sciatica [saɪ'ætɪkə] N (*Med*) ciática *f*

science ['saɪəns] (A) N ciencia *f*; **the natural/social ~s** las ciencias naturales/sociales; **the ~s** las ciencias; **it's a real ~*** es una verdadera ciencia; **to blind sb with ~** impresionar *or* deslumbrar a algn citándole muchos datos científicos

(B) CPD de ciencias ► **science fiction** N ciencia-ficción *f* ► **science park** N zona *f* de ciencias ► **science teacher** N profesor(a) *m/f* de ciencias

scientific [ˌsaɪən'tɪfɪk] ADJ científico

scientifically [ˌsaɪən'tɪfɪkəlɪ] ADV científicamente

scientist ['saɪəntɪst] N científico/a *m/f*

scientologist [ˌsaɪən'tɒlədʒɪst] N cientólogo/a *m/f*

scientology [ˌsaɪən'tɒlədʒɪ] N cienciología *f*, cientología *f*

sci-fi* ['saɪfaɪ] N ABBR = **science-fiction**

Scillies ['sɪlɪz] NPL, **Scilly Isles** ['sɪlɪˌaɪlz] NPL Islas *fpl* Sorlinga

scimitar ['sɪmɪtəʳ] N cimitarra *f*

scintillate ['sɪntɪleɪt] VI centellear, chispear; (*fig*) brillar

scintillating ['sɪntɪleɪtɪŋ] ADJ [*wit, conversation,*

company] chispeante, brillante; [*jewels, chandelier*] relumbrante

scion ['saɪən] N (*Bot, fig*) vástago *m*; **~ of a noble family** vástago *m* de una familia noble

Scipio ['skɪpɪəʊ] N Escipión

scissors ['sɪzəz] Ⓐ NPL tijeras *fpl*; **a pair of ~** unas tijeras
Ⓑ CPD ► **scissors jump** N tijera *f* ► **scissors kick** N chilena *f*, tijereta *f*

sclerosis [sklɪ'rəʊsɪs] N (*pl* **scleroses** [sklɪ'rəʊsiːz]) (*Med*) esclerosis *f*; *see also* **multiple C**

SCM N ABBR (*Brit*) = **State-Certified Midwife**

scoff [skɒf] Ⓐ VI mofarse, burlarse (**at sb/sth** de algn/algo); **my friends ~ed at the idea** mis amigos se mofaron *or* se burlaron de la idea
Ⓑ VT (*) (= *eat*) zamparse*, papearse‡; **she ~ed the lot** se lo zampó todo; **my brother ~ed all the sandwiches** mi hermano se zampó todos los bocadillos

scoffer ['skɒfəʳ] N mofador(a) *m/f*

scoffing ['skɒfɪŋ] N mofas *fpl*, burlas *fpl*

scold [skəʊld] Ⓐ VT reñir, regañar (**for** por)
Ⓑ N (= *woman*) virago *f*

scolding ['skəʊldɪŋ] N reprimenda *f*, regañina *f*

scoliosis [ˌskəʊlɪ'əʊsɪs] N escoliosis *f*

scollop ['skɒləp] = **scallop**

sconce [skɒns] N candelabro *m* de pared

scone [skɒn] N bollo *m* (inglés)

scoop [skuːp] Ⓐ N 1 (*for flour*) pala *f*; (*for ice cream, water*) cucharón *m*; (= *quantity scooped*) palada *f*, cucharada *f*
2 (*by newspaper*) exclusiva *f*; (*Comm**) golpe *m* financiero, pelotazo* *m*; **to make a ~** (*Press*) dar una exclusiva; (*Comm*) ganar un dineral de golpe y porrazo*, dar el pelotazo*; **it was a ~ for the paper** fue un gran éxito para el periódico; **we brought off the ~** logramos un triunfo con la exclusiva
Ⓑ VT 1 (= *pick up*) recoger
2 (*Comm*) [+ *profit*] sacar; (*Comm, Press*) [+ *competitors*] adelantarse a; (*Press*) [+ *exclusive story*] publicar en exclusiva; **we ~ed the other papers** quedamos por encima de los demás periódicos con nuestra exclusiva
3 [+ *prize, award*] hacerse con, obtener

► **scoop out** VT + ADV (*with scoop*) sacar con pala; (*with spoon*) sacar con cuchara; [+ *water*] achicar; [+ *hollow*] excavar, ahuecar

► **scoop up** VT + ADV recoger

scoot* [skuːt] VI (*also* **~ away, ~ off**) largarse*, rajarse (*LAm*); **~!** ¡lárgate!*; **I must ~** tengo que marcharme

scooter ['skuːtəʳ] N (*child's*) patinete *m*; (*adult's*) moto *f*, escúter *m*, motoneta *f* (*LAm*)

scope [skəʊp] N (= *opportunity*) (*for action etc*) libertad *f*, oportunidades *fpl*; (= *range*) [*of law, activity*] ámbito *m*; [*of responsibilities*] ámbito *m*; (= *capacity*) [*of person, mind*] alcance *m*; (= *room*) (*for manoeuvre etc*) esfera *f* de acción, campo *m* de acción; **a programme of considerable ~** un programa de gran alcance; **the ~ of the new measures must be defined** conviene delimitar el campo de aplicación de las nuevas medidas; **it is beyond her ~** está fuera de su alcance; **it is beyond the ~ of this book** está fuera del ámbito del presente libro; **to extend the ~ of one's activities** ampliar su campo de actividades; **there is plenty of ~ for** hay bastante campo para; **this should give you plenty of ~ for your talents** esto ha de darte grandes posibilidades para explotar tus talentos; **to give sb full ~** dar carta blanca a algn; **I'm looking for a job with more ~** busco un puesto que ofrezca más posibilidades; **it is outside my ~** eso está fuera de mi alcance; **it is within her ~** está a su alcance; **it is within the ~ of this book** está dentro del ámbito del presente libro

scorbutic [skɔː'bjuːtɪk] ADJ escorbútico

scorch [skɔːtʃ] Ⓐ N (*also* **~ mark**) quemadura *f*
Ⓑ VT (= *burn*) quemar; [*sun*] abrasar; (= *singe*) chamuscar; [+ *plants, grass*] quemar, secar; **~ed earth policy** política *f* de tierra quemada
Ⓒ VI 1 [*linen*] chamuscarse; [*grass*] agostarse, secarse
2 **to ~ along** (*Brit**) ir volando, correr a gran velocidad

scorcher* ['skɔːtʃəʳ] N (= *hot day*) día *m* abrasador

scorching ['skɔːtʃɪŋ] ADJ (*also* **~ hot**) [*heat, day, sun*] abrasador; [*sand*] que quema; **it's a ~ day** hoy hace un día abrasador; **it's ~ hot** hace un calor tremendo; **a few ~ remarks** algunas observaciones mordaces

score [skɔːʳ] Ⓐ N 1 (*in game, match*) (= *result*) resultado *m*; (= *goal*) gol *m*, tanto *m*; (*at cards, in test, competition*) puntuación *f*, puntaje *m* (*LAm*); **there's no ~ yet** están a cero; (*in commentary*) no se ha abierto el marcador todavía; **there was no ~ at half-time** en el primer tiempo no hubo goles; **what's the ~?** ¿cómo van?, ¿cómo va el marcador?; **the final ~ was 4-1** el resultado final fue 4 a 1; **we give each entry a ~ out of ten** damos una puntuación *or* (*LAm*) un puntaje de uno a diez a cada participante; **he missed a chance to make the ~ 1-1** perdió la oportunidad de empatar a 1 *or* de igualar el marcador a 1; **with the ~ at 40-0 she has three match points** con 40-0 a su favor, tiene tres bolas de partido; **to keep (the) ~** (*Sport*) llevar la cuenta; (*Cards*) sumar los puntos
2 **the ~*** (= *situation*) **what's the ~?** ¿qué pasa?, ¿qué hubo? (*Mex, Chile*); **you know the ~** ya estás al cabo de la calle *or* de lo que pasa*, ya estás al tanto
3 (= *subject*) **you've got no worries on that ~** en ese sentido *or* aspecto no tienes por qué preocuparte
4 (= *dispute*) **to have a ~ to settle with sb** tener cuentas pendientes con algn; **to settle** *or* **pay off old ~s (with sb)** saldar las cuentas pendientes (con algn)
5 (*Mus*) partitura *f*; [*of show, play*] música *f*; [*of film*] banda *f* sonora (original); **film ~** banda *f* sonora (original); **piano ~** partitura para piano; **vocal ~** partitura para voz
6 (= *line*) (*on card*) raya *f*, línea *f*; (= *scratch*) (*on wood*) marca *f*, muesca *f*
7 (= *twenty*) veintena *f*; **three ~ years and ten** (*liter*) 70 años; **~s of people** montones de gente*, muchísima gente; **bombs were falling by the ~** caían bombas a mansalva
Ⓑ VT 1 (*Sport*) [+ *points*] conseguir, anotarse (*LAm*), apuntarse (*LAm*); [+ *runs*] hacer; [+ *goal, try*] marcar; **they went five games without scoring a point** en cinco partidos no consiguieron *or* no se anotaron un solo punto; **to ~ a hit** (*Shooting*) dar en el blanco; **to ~ a run** (*Baseball*) hacer una carrera
2 (*in exam, test, competition*) [+ *marks, points*] sacar; **to ~ 75% in an exam** sacar 75 sobre 100 en un examen; **she ~d well in the test** sacó *or* obtuvo buena nota en el test; **if you answered yes, ~ five points** si contestó "sí", saca *or* suma cinco puntos
3 [+ *success, victory*] conseguir; **he's certainly ~d a hit with the voters/with his latest novel** no cabe la menor duda de que ha impresionado a los votantes/ha tenido mucho éxito con su última novela; **to ~ points off sb** aventajarse con respecto a algn
4 (*Mus*) [+ *piece*] instrumentar, orquestar
5 (= *cut*) [+ *meat*] hacer unos pequeños cortes en; (= *mark*) [+ *line*] marcar; **her face was weathered, ~d with lines** su rostro estaba curtido y surcado de arrugas
6 (‡) [+ *drugs*] conseguir, comprar, pillar (*Sp‡*)
Ⓒ VI 1 (*Sport*) marcar; **no one has ~d yet** aún no ha marcado nadie; (*in commentary*) aún no se ha abierto el marcador; **he has failed to ~ this season** no ha marcado esta temporada; **that's where he ~s (over the others)** (*fig*) en eso es en lo que tiene más ventaja (sobre los demás)
2 (= *keep score*) (*Sport*) llevar la cuenta; (*Cards*) sumar los puntos
3 (‡) (= *buy drugs*) conseguir drogas, pillar (*Sp‡*); **to ~ with sb** (= *have sex*) acostarse con algn; (= *get off with*) ligarse a algn
Ⓓ CPD ► **score draw** N (*Ftbl*) empate *m*; **no-~ draw** empate *m* a cero

► **score off, score out, score through** VT + ADV [+ *text*] tachar

scoreboard ['skɔːbɔːd] N marcador *m*

scorebook ['skɔːbʊk] N cuaderno *m* de tanteo

scorecard ['skɔːkɑːd] N (*Golf*) tarjeta *f* donde se apuntan los resultados

scorekeeper ['skɔːˌkiːpəʳ] N tanteador(a) *m/f*

scoreless ['skɔːlɪs] ADJ **~ draw** empate *m* a cero

scorer ['skɔːrəʳ] N (= *person keeping score*) persona *f* que va apuntando los resultados; (= *player*) (*also* **goal ~**) él/la *m/f* que marca un gol *etc*; **he is top ~ in the league** es el principal goleador en la liga, ha marcado más goles que ningún otro en la liga; **the ~s were Juan and Pablo** marcaron los goles Juan y Pablo

scoresheet ['skɔːʃiːt] N acta *f* de tanteo

scoring ['skɔːrɪŋ] N 1 (*Sport*) (= *keeping score*) tanteo *m*
2 (= *act of scoring*) **Evans opened the ~ in the third minute** Evans abrió el marcador en el tercer minuto; **he has a good ~ record** marca muchos goles *or* tantos
3 (*Mus*) orquestación *f*

scorn ['skɔːn] Ⓐ N desprecio *m*, menosprecio *m*; **to pour ~ on sth** ◊ **laugh sth to ~** ridiculizar algo
Ⓑ VT despreciar, menospreciar; **to ~ to do sth** no dignarse a hacer algo

scornful ['skɔːnfʊl] ADJ desdeñoso, despreciativo; **to be ~ about sth** desdeñar algo

scornfully ['skɔːnfəlɪ] ADV desdeñosamente, con desprecio

Scorpio ['skɔːpɪəʊ] N 1 (= *sign, constellation*) Escorpión *m*
2 (= *person*) escorpión *mf*; **I'm (a) ~** soy escorpión

scorpion ['skɔːpɪən] N alacrán *m*, escorpión *m*

Scot [skɒt] N escocés/esa *m/f*

Scotch [skɒtʃ] Ⓐ ADJ **~ broth** sopa *f* de verduras; **~ egg** (*esp Brit*) huevo *m* cocido rodeado de carne de salchicha y rebozado; **~ mist** llovizna *f*; **~ tape®** (*esp US*) cinta *f* adhesiva, scotch *m* (*LAm*), durex *m* (*Mex*); **~ terrier** terrier *m* escocés; **~ whisky** = **Scotch B**
Ⓑ N (= *whisky*) whisky *m* escocés, scotch *m*

scotch [skɒtʃ] Ⓐ VT [+ *attempt, plan*] frustrar; [+ *rumour, claim*] acallar
Ⓑ N (= *wedge*) calza *f*, cuña *f*

scot-free ['skɒt'friː] ADJ **to get off ~** (= *unpunished*) salir impune; (= *unhurt*) salir ileso

Scotland ['skɒtlənd] Ⓐ N Escocia *f*
Ⓑ CPD ► **Scotland Yard** N *oficina central de la policía de Londres*

Scots [skɒts] Ⓐ ADJ escocés; **a ~ accent** un acento escocés; **~ pine** pino *m* escocés
Ⓑ N (*Ling*) escocés *m*

Scotsman ['skɒtsmən] N (*pl* **Scotsmen**) escocés *m*

Scotswoman ['skɒts,wʊmən] N (*pl* **Scotswomen**) escocesa *f*

Scotticism ['skɒtɪsɪzəm] N giro *m* escocés, escocesismo *m*

Scottie ['skɒtɪ] N (= *dog*) terrier *m* escocés

Scottish ['skɒtɪʃ] ADJ escocés; **a ~ accent** un acento escocés; **~ Office** Ministerio *m* de Asuntos Escoceses; **the ~ Parliament** el Parlamento Escocés

scoundrel ['skaʊndrəl] N sinvergüenza *mf*

scoundrelly† ['skaʊndrəlɪ] ADJ canallesco, vil

scour ['skaʊəʳ] Ⓐ VT 1 [+ *pan, floor*] fregar, restregar (*esp LAm*); [+ *channel*] limpiar
2 (= *search*) registrar; **we ~ed the countryside for him** hicimos una batida por el campo buscándole
Ⓑ VI **to ~ about for sth** buscar algo por todas partes

►**scour out** VT + ADV [+ *pan etc*] fregar, restregar (*esp LAm*); [+ *channel*] limpiar; **the river had ~ed out part of the bank** el río se había llevado una parte de la orilla

scourer ['skaʊərəʳ] N (= *pad*) estropajo *m*; (= *powder*) limpiador *m*, quitagrasas *m inv*

scourge [skɜːdʒ] Ⓐ N (*lit, fig*) azote *m*; **the ~ of malaria** el azote del paludismo; **the ~ of war** el azote de la guerra; **it is the ~ of our times** es la plaga de nuestros tiempos; **God sent it as a ~** Dios lo envió como castigo
Ⓑ VT (*lit*) azotar, flagelar; (*fig*) hostigar

scouring pad ['skaʊrɪŋpæd] N estropajo *m*

scouring powder ['skaʊrɪŋpaʊdəʳ] N limpiador *m* (en polvos), quitagrasas *m inv* (en polvo)

Scouse* [skaʊs] Ⓐ ADJ de Liverpool
Ⓑ N 1 nativo/a *m/f* de Liverpool, habitante *mf* de Liverpool
2 (*Ling*) dialecto *m* de Liverpool

scout [skaʊt] Ⓐ N 1 (= *person*) (*Mil*) explorador(a) *m/f*; (*also* **boy ~**) muchacho *m* explorador; **(talent) ~** (*Sport, Cine, Theat*) cazatalentos *mf inv*
2 (*) (= *reconnaissance*) reconocimiento *m*; (= *search*) búsqueda *f*; **to have a ~ round** reconocer *or* explorar el terreno; **we'll have a ~ (round) for it** (*fig*) lo buscaremos
Ⓑ VI (= *explore*) explorar; (*Mil*) reconocer el terreno; **to ~ for sth** buscar algo
Ⓒ CPD ► **scout car** N (*Mil*) vehículo *m* de reconocimiento

►**scout about, scout around, scout round** VI + ADV (*Mil*) ir de reconocimiento, reconocer el terreno; **to ~ around for sth** (*Mil*) hacer un reconocimiento *or* explorar buscando algo; (*fig*) buscar algo

scouting ['skaʊtɪŋ] N actividades *fpl* de los exploradores

scoutmaster ['skaʊt,mɑːstəʳ] N jefe *m* de exploradores

scow [skaʊ] N gabarra *f*

scowl [skaʊl] Ⓐ N ceño *m* fruncido; **he said with a ~** dijo con el ceño fruncido
Ⓑ VI fruncir el ceño, fruncir el entrecejo; **to ~ at sb** mirar a algn con el ceño fruncido, mirar a algn frunciendo el ceño *or* el entrecejo

scowling ['skaʊlɪŋ] ADJ ceñudo

SCR N ABBR (*Brit Univ*) = **senior common room**

scrabble ['skræbl] Ⓐ VI **to ~ about** *or* **around for sth** revolver todo buscando algo; **she was scrabbling about in the coal** andaba rebuscando por entre el carbón
Ⓑ N **Scrabble**® (*game*) Scrabble® *m*

scrag [skræg] Ⓐ N pescuezo *m*
Ⓑ VT [+ *animal*] torcer el pescuezo a; (*) [+ *person*] dar una paliza a

scragginess ['skrægɪnɪs] N flaqueza *f*

scraggy ['skrægɪ] ADJ (*compar* **scraggier**; *superl* **scraggiest**) flacucho

scram* [skræm] VI largarse*, rajarse (*LAm*); **~!** ¡lárgate!*

scramble ['skræmbl] Ⓐ VI 1 **to ~ up/down** subir gateando/bajar con dificultad; **to ~ out** salir con dificultad; **we ~d through the hedge** nos abrimos paso con dificultad a través del seto; **to ~ for** [+ *coins, seats*] luchar entre sí por, pelearse por; (*fig*) [+ *jobs*] pelearse por
2 (*Sport*) **to go scrambling** hacer motocross
Ⓑ VT 1 (*Culin*) revolver; **~d eggs** huevos *mpl* revueltos
2 (*Telec*) [+ *message*] cifrar; (*TV*) codificar
3 [+ *aircraft*] hacer despegar con urgencia (*por alarma*)
Ⓒ N 1 (= *rush*) lucha *f*, pelea *f* (**for** por)
2 (*Sport*) (= *motorcycle meeting*) carrera *f* de motocross
3 (= *climb*) subida *f*; (= *outing*) excursión *f* de montaña (*por terreno escabroso etc*)

scrambler ['skræmbləʳ] N 1 (*Telec*) emisor *m* de interferencias
2 (= *motorcyclist*) motociclista *mf* de motocross

scrambling ['skræmblɪŋ] N 1 (*Sport*) motocross *m* campo a través
2 (*TV*) codificación *f*

scran‡ [skræn] N (*Brit*) comida *f*

scrap[1] [skræp] Ⓐ N 1 (= *small piece*) pedacito *m*; [*of newspaper*] recorte *m*; [*of material*] retal *m*, retazo *m*; (*fig*) pizca *f*; **it's a ~ of comfort** es una migaja de consolación; **a ~ of conversation** un fragmento de conversación; **a few ~s of news** unos fragmentos de noticias; **there is not a ~ of truth in it** no hay ni un ápice de verdad en eso, no tiene nada de cierto; **not a ~ of proof** ni la más mínima prueba; **not a ~ of use** sin utilidad alguna; **not a ~!** ¡ni pizca!, ¡en absoluto!; **a ~ of paper** un trocito de papel
2 **scraps** (= *leftovers*) restos *mpl*, sobras *fpl*; **the dog feeds on ~s** el perro come de las sobras de la mesa
3 (*also* **~ metal**) chatarra *f*, desecho *m* de hierro; **what is it worth as ~?** ¿cuánto vale como chatarra?; **to sell a ship for ~** vender un barco como chatarra
Ⓑ VT [+ *car, ship etc*] chatarrear, convertir en chatarra; [+ *old equipment etc*] tirar; [+ *idea, plan etc*] desechar, descartar; **we had to ~ that idea** tuvimos que descartar *or* desechar esa idea; **in the end the plan was ~ped** al final se desechó *or* se descartó el plan
Ⓒ CPD ► **scrap dealer** N chatarrero/a *m/f* ► **scrap heap** N montón *m* de desechos; **this is for the ~ heap** esto es para tirar; **to throw sth on the ~ heap** (*fig*) desechar *or* descartar algo; **I was thrown on the ~ heap at the age of 50** me dieron la patada cuando tenía 50 años; **workers are being thrown on the ~ heap** los obreros van al basurero; **to be on the ~ heap** [*person*] no tener nada a que agarrarse; **he ended up on the ~ heap** se quedó sin nada a que agarrarse ► **scrap iron** N chatarra *f*, hierro *m* viejo ► **scrap merchant** N chatarrero/a *m/f* ► **scrap metal** N chatarra *f* ► **scrap paper** N pedazos *mpl* de papel suelto (*que se utilizan para borrador*) ► **scrap value** N valor *m* como chatarra; **its ~ value is £30** como chatarra vale 30 libras ► **scrap yard** N chatarrería *f*; (*for cars*) cementerio *m* de coches

scrap[2]* [skræp] Ⓐ N (= *fight*) riña *f*, pelea *f*; **there was a ~ outside the pub** hubo una riña *or* pelea a la salida del pub; **to get into** *or* **have a ~ with sb** reñir *or* pelearse con algn
Ⓑ VI reñir, pelearse (**with sb** con algn); **they were ~ping in the street** se estaban peleando en la calle

scrapbook ['skræpbʊk] N álbum *m* de recortes

scrape [skreɪp] Ⓐ N 1 (= *act*) raspado *m*, raspadura *f*; (= *sound*) chirrido *m*; (= *mark*) arañazo *m*, rasguño *m*; **to give sth a ~** raspar algo, limpiar algo raspándolo; **to give one's knee a ~** rasguñarse la rodilla
2 (*fig*) lío *m*, aprieto *m*; **to get into/out of a ~** meterse en/salir de un lío *or* aprieto; **to get sb out of a ~** sacar a algn de un lío *or* aprieto
Ⓑ VT [+ *knee, elbow*] arañarse, rasguñarse; (= *clean*) [+ *vegetables*] raspar, limpiar; [+ *walls, woodwork*] raspar; **to ~ on/along/against sth** arrastrar en/a lo largo de/contra algo; **the lorry ~d the wall** el camión rozó el muro; **to ~ one's boots** limpiarse las botas; **to ~ one's plate clean** dejar completamente limpio el plato; **to ~ a living** sacar lo justo para vivir; **the ship ~d the bottom** el barco rozó el fondo; **to ~ one's feet across the floor** arrastrar los pies por el suelo; ✦*IDIOM* **to ~ the bottom of the barrel** tocar fondo
Ⓒ VI (= *make sound*) chirriar; (= *rub*) **to ~ (against)** pasar rozando; **to ~ past** pasar rozando; **we just managed to ~ through the gap** nos costó pasar por la abertura sin tocar las paredes

►**scrape along*** VI + ADV (*financially*) sacar lo justo para vivir; (= *live*) ir tirando; **I can ~ along in Arabic** me defiendo en árabe

►**scrape away** Ⓐ VT + ADV raspar, quitar raspando
Ⓑ VI + ADV **to ~ away at the violin** ir rascando el violín

►**scrape off** Ⓐ VT + ADV raspar, quitar raspando
Ⓑ VT + PREP raspar de

►**scrape out** VT + ADV [+ *contents*] remover raspando

►**scrape through** Ⓐ VI + ADV (= *succeed*) lograr hacer algo por los pelos; **I just ~d through** aprobé por los pelos
Ⓑ VI + PREP [+ *narrow gap*] pasar muy justo por; **to ~ through an exam** aprobar un examen por los pelos

►**scrape together** VT + ADV (*fig*) reunir poco a poco; **we managed to ~ enough money together** logramos reunir suficiente dinero

►**scrape up** VT + ADV (*fig*) reunir poco a poco; **to ~ up an acquaintance with sb** trabar amistad con algn

scraper ['skreɪpəʳ] N (= *tool*) raspador *m*, rascador *m*; (*on doorstep*) limpiabarros *m inv*

scraperboard ['skreɪpəbɔːd] N *cartulina entintada sobre la cual se realiza un dibujo rascando la capa de tinta*

scrapings ['skreɪpɪŋz] NPL raspaduras *fpl*; **~ of the gutter** (*fig*) hez *fsing* de la sociedad

scrappy ['skræpɪ] ADJ (*compar* **scrappier**; *superl* **scrappiest**) [*essay etc*] deshilvanado; [*knowledge, education*] incompleto; [*meal*] hecho con sobras

scratch ['skrætʃ] Ⓐ N 1 (= *mark*) (*on skin*) arañazo *m*, rasguño *m*; (*on surface, record*) raya *f*; **it's just a ~** es sólo un rasguño, nada más; **the cat gave her a ~** el gato la arañó; **he**

hadn't a ~ on him no tenía ni un arañazo; **to have a good ~** rascarse con ganas
[2] (= *noise*) chirrido *m*
[3] **to start from ~** (*fig*) partir de *or* empezar desde cero; **we shall have to start from ~ again** tendremos que partir nuevamente de cero, tendremos que comenzar desde el principio otra vez; **to be** *or* **come up to ~** cumplir con los requisitos; **to bring/keep sth up to ~** poner/mantener algo en buenas condiciones
Ⓑ VT [1] (*with claw, nail etc*) rasguñar, arañar; (*making sound*) rascar, raspar; [+ *surface, record*] rayar; (= *scramble, dig*) escarbar; **you'll ~ the worktop with that knife** vas a rayar la encimera con ese cuchillo; **the glass of this watch cannot be ~ed** el cristal de este reloj no se raya; **he ~ed his hand on a rose bush** se arañó la mano en un rosal; **the lovers ~ed their names on the tree** los amantes grabaron sus nombres en el árbol; *see also* **surface A1**
[2] (*to relieve itch*) rascarse; **he ~ed his head** se rascó la cabeza; **she ~ed the dog's ear** le rascó la oreja al perro; ✦**IDIOM** **you ~ my back and I'll ~ yours** un favor con favor se paga
[3] (= *cancel*) [+ *meeting, game*] cancelar; (= *cross off list*) [+ *horse, competitor*] tachar, borrar; **to ~ sb off a list** tachar a algn de una lista
[4] (*Comput*) borrar
Ⓒ VI [*person, dog etc*] rascarse; [*hens*] escarbar; [*pen*] rascar; [*clothing*] rascar, picar; **stop ~ing!** ¡deja de rascarte!; **the dog ~ed at the door** el perro arañó la puerta
Ⓓ CPD [*competitor*] sin ventaja ► **scratch card** N tarjeta *f* de "rasque y gane" ► **scratch file** N (*Comput*) fichero *m* de trabajo ► **scratch meal** N comida *f* improvisada ► **scratch paper** N (*US*) papel *m* de borrador ► **scratch score** N (*Golf*) puntuación *f* par ► **scratch tape** N cinta *f* reutilizable ► **scratch team** N equipo *m* improvisado

►**scratch out** VT + ADV (*from list*) borrar, tachar; **to ~ sb's eyes out** sacarle los ojos a algn

scratchpad [ˈskrætʃpæd] N (*US*) bloc *m* (*para apuntes o para borrador*)

scratchy [ˈskrætʃɪ] ADJ (*compar* **scratchier**; *superl* **scratchiest**) [*fabric*] que rasca *or* pica; [*pen*] que rasca; [*writing*] flojo, irregular

scrawl [skrɔːl] Ⓐ N garabatos *mpl*; **I can't read her ~** no puedo leer sus garabatos; **the word finished in a ~** la palabra terminaba en un garabato
Ⓑ VT garabatear; **to ~ a note to sb** garabatear una nota a algn; **a wall ~ed all over with rude words** una pared llena de palabrotas
Ⓒ VI garabatear, hacer garabatos

scrawny [ˈskrɔːnɪ] ADJ (*compar* **scrawnier**; *superl* **scrawniest**) [*neck, limb*] flaco; [*animal*] escuálido, descarnado

scream [skriːm] Ⓐ N [1] (= *yell*) grito *m*; (*high-pitched*) chillido *m*; (*stronger*) alarido *m*; **a ~ of agony** un grito *or* alarido de dolor; **a ~ of delight** un grito de alegría; **the ~ of the eagle** el chillido del águila; **to give a ~** pegar un grito, soltar un grito; **a ~ of joy** un grito de alegría; **there were ~s of laughter** hubo sonoras carcajadas; **to let out a ~ = to give a scream**; **his voice rose to a ~** levantó la voz y empezó a gritar; **a ~ of terror** un grito *or* alarido de terror
[2] [*of machinery, brakes*] chirrido *m*
[3] (*) (*fig*) **it was a ~** fue la monda*, fue para morirse de la risa; **he's a ~** es graciosísimo, es de lo más chistoso, es la monda*
Ⓑ VT [1] [+ *abuse, orders*] gritar; **they started ~ing abuse at us** nos empezaron a insultar a voz en grito, nos empezaron a gritar insultos; ✦**IDIOM** **to ~ blue murder** (= *protest*) poner el grito en el cielo
[2] [*headlines*] **"90 dead," ~ed the headlines** 90 muertos rezaban los enormes titulares
Ⓒ VI [*person*] chillar, gritar; [*baby*] berrear; **if I hear one more joke about my hair, I shall ~** una palabra más acerca de mi pelo y me pongo a gritar; **they dragged him ~ing out of the shop** lo tuvieron que sacar de la tienda a rastras; **I was kept awake by a ~ing baby** me tenía despierto un niño que no hacía más que berrear; **to ~ at sb** gritar a algn; **to ~ for help** pedir ayuda a gritos; **to ~ in** *or* **with pain** pegar *or* soltar un grito de dolor, gritar de dolor; **I must have ~ed out in my sleep** debí de chillar *or* gritar entre sueños; **the headline ~ed out from the page** el titular saltaba a la vista; **to ~ with laughter** reírse a carcajada limpia

screamingly* [ˈskriːmɪŋlɪ] ADV **a ~ funny joke** un chiste de lo más divertido; **it was ~ funny** fue para morirse de risa*

scree [ˈskriː] N pedregal *m* (*en una ladera*)

screech [skriːtʃ] Ⓐ N [*of brakes, tyres*] chirrido *m*; [*of person*] grito *m*; [*of animal*] chillido *m*
Ⓑ VI [*brakes, tyres*] chirriar; [*person*] gritar, chillar; [*animal*] chillar

screech-owl [ˈskriːtʃaʊl] N lechuza *f*

screed* [skriːd] NPL rollo *m*; **to write ~s** estar venga a escribir, escribir hojas y hojas

screen [skriːn] Ⓐ N [1] (= *physical barrier*) (*in room*) biombo *m*; (*on window, door*) (*to keep out mosquitos*) mosquitera *f*; (*for fire*) pantalla *f*; (*in front of VDU*) filtro *m*
[2] (*Cine, TV, Radar, Comput*) [*of television, computer, in cinema, for slides*] pantalla *f*; **radar ~** pantalla *f* de radar; **she was the ideal mother, both on and off ~** era la madre ideal, tanto dentro como fuera de la pantalla; **to write for the ~** escribir para el cine; **stars of the ~** estrellas *fpl* de la pantalla, estrellas *fpl* de cine; **the big/small ~** la pantalla grande/pequeña
[3] (*fig*) **a ~ of trees** una pantalla de árboles; **a ~ of smoke** una cortina de humo
[4] (*Mil*) cortina *f*
Ⓑ VT [1] **to ~ (from)** (= *hide*) (*from view, sight*) ocultar *or* tapar (de); (= *protect*) proteger (de); **the house is ~ed (from view) by trees** la casa queda oculta detrás de los árboles; **he ~ed his eyes with his hand** se puso la mano sobre los ojos a modo de pantalla; **in order to ~ our movements from the enemy** para impedir que el enemigo pudiera ver nuestros movimientos
[2] (= *show*) [+ *film*] proyectar; [+ *TV programme*] emitir; (*for the first time*) estrenar; [+ *novel etc*] adaptar para el cine, hacer una versión cinematográfica de
[3] (= *sieve*) [+ *coal*] tamizar
[4] (*for security*) [+ *suspect, applicant*] investigar; **he was ~ed by Security** Seguridad le investigó, estuvo sometido a investigaciones de Seguridad
[5] (*Med*) **to ~ sb for sth** hacer una exploración a algn buscando algo
[6] [+ *telephone calls*] filtrar
Ⓒ CPD ► **screen actor** N actor *m* de cine ► **screen actress** N actriz *f* de cine ► **screen door** N puerta *f* con mosquitera ► **screen editing** N (*Comput*) corrección *f* en pantalla ► **screen memory** N (*Comput*) memoria *f* de la pantalla ► **screen rights** NPL derechos *mpl* cinematográficos ► **screensaver** N salvapantallas *m inv* ► **screen test** N prueba *f* cinematográfica ► **screen writer** N guionista *mf*

►**screen off** VT + ADV tapar

►**screen out** VT + ADV [+ *light, noise*] eliminar, filtrar

screenful [ˈskriːnfʊl] N pantalla *f*

screening [ˈskriːnɪŋ] N [1] [*of film*] proyección *f*; [*of TV programme*] emisión *f*; (*for the first time*) estreno *m* [2] (*for security*) investigación *f* [3] (*Med*) [*of person*] exploración *f*

screenplay [ˈskriːnpleɪ] N guión *m*

screenwriting [skriːnraɪtɪŋ] N escritura *f* de guiones

screw [skruː] Ⓐ N [1] tornillo *m*; ✦**IDIOMS** **he's got a ~ loose*** le falta un tornillo; **to put the ~s on sb*** apretar las clavijas a algn, presionar a algn
[2] (*Aer, Naut*) hélice *f*
[3] (‡) (= *prison officer*) carcelero/a *m/f*
[4] (‡‡) (= *sexual intercourse*) polvo‡‡ *m*
Ⓑ VT [1] [+ *screw*] atornillar; [+ *nut*] apretar; [+ *lid*] dar vueltas a, enroscar; **to ~ sth down** fijar algo con tornillos; **to ~ sth to the wall** fijar algo a la pared con tornillos; **to ~ sth (in) tight** atornillar algo bien fuerte; **to ~ money out of sb*** sacarle dinero a algn; **to ~ the truth out of sb*** arrancarle la verdad a algn
[2] (‡‡) (= *have sex with*) joder‡‡; **~ the cost, it's got to be done!** (*fig*) ¡a la porra el gasto, tiene que hacerse!
[3] (*) (= *defraud*) timar, estafar
Ⓒ VI (‡‡) joder‡‡, echar un polvo‡‡, coger (*LAm*‡‡), chingar (*Mex*‡‡)
Ⓓ CPD ► **screw top** N tapa *f* de tornillo; *see also* **screw-top**

►**screw around**‡‡ VI + ADV ligar*

►**screw off** Ⓐ VT + ADV desenroscar
Ⓑ VI + ADV desenroscarse; **the lid ~s off** la tapadera se desenrosca

►**screw on** Ⓐ VT + ADV [1] (*with screws*) **to ~ sth on to a board** fijar algo en un tablón con tornillos; **he's got his head ~ed on** sabe cuántas son cinco
[2] (*by twisting*) **to ~ on a lid** enroscar una tapa; **~ the lid on tightly** enrosca *or* mete bien la tapa
Ⓑ VI + ADV [1] (*with screws*) **it ~s on here** se fija aquí con tornillos
[2] (*by twisting*) **the lid ~s on** la tapa se cierra a rosca *or* enroscándose

►**screw together** Ⓐ VI + ADV juntarse con tornillos Ⓑ VT + ADV armar (con tornillos)

►**screw up** Ⓐ VT + ADV [1] [+ *paper, material*] arrugar; **to ~ up one's eyes** arrugar el entrecejo; **to ~ up one's face** torcer la cara; **to ~ up one's courage** (*fig*) armarse de valor; **to ~ o.s. up to do sth** armarse de valor para hacer algo
[2] [+ *screw*] atornillar; [+ *nut*] apretar; **to ~ sth up tight** atornillar algo bien fuerte
[3] (*) (= *ruin*) fastidiar, joder‡‡, fregar (*LAm*), chingar (*Mex*‡‡); **the experience really ~ed him up** la experiencia lo dejó completamente hecho polvo
Ⓑ VI + ADV [1] (*by turning*) **it will ~ up tighter than that** se puede apretar todavía más
[2] (*US**) **he really ~ed up this time** esta vez sí que lo fastidió *or* (*LAm*) fregó

screwball* [ˈskruːbɔːl] (*esp US*) Ⓐ ADJ excéntrico, estrafalario Ⓑ N chiflado/a* *m/f*, chalado/a* *m/f*, tarado/a *m/f* (*esp LAm**)

screwdriver [ˈskruːˌdraɪvəʳ] N [1] (= *tool*) destornillador *m*, desarmador *m* (*Mex*)
[2] (= *drink*) destornillador *m*

screw-top [ˈskruːtɒp] ADJ, **screw-topped** [ˈskruːtɒpt] ADJ [*bottle, jar*] de rosca; *see also* **screw**

screw-up‡ ['skru:ʌp] N lío* *m*, embrollo *m*, cacao* *m*

screwy* ['skru:ɪ] ADJ (*compar* **screwier**; *superl* **screwiest**) (= *mad*) chiflado, tarado (*LAm*)

scribble ['skrɪbl] Ⓐ N garabatos *mpl*; **I can't read his ~** no consigo leer sus garabatos; **a wall covered in ~s** una pared llena de garabatos
Ⓑ VT garabatear; **to ~ sth down** garabatear algo; **to ~ one's signature** garabatear la firma, firmar a toda prisa; **a word ~d on a wall** una palabra garabateada en una pared; **a sheet of paper ~d (over) with notes** una hoja de papel emborronada de notas
Ⓒ VI garabatear

scribbler ['skrɪbləʳ] N escritorzuelo/a *m/f*

scribbling ['skrɪblɪŋ] Ⓐ N garabato *m*
Ⓑ CPD ► **scribbling pad** N bloc *m* (*para apuntes o para borrador*)

scribe [skraɪb] N [*of manuscript*] escribiente/a *m/f*; (*Bible*) escriba *m*

scrimmage ['skrɪmɪdʒ] N 1 (= *fight*) escaramuza *f*
2 (*US Sport*) = **scrum**

scrimp [skrɪmp] VI **to ~ and save** hacer economías, apretarse el cinturón

scrimpy ['skrɪmpɪ] ADJ [*person*] tacaño; [*supply etc*] escaso

scrimshank* ['skrɪmʃæŋk] VI (*Brit Mil*) racanear*, hacer el rácano*

scrimshanker* ['skrɪm,ʃæŋkəʳ] N (*Brit Mil*) rácano* *m*

scrip [skrɪp] N (*Fin*) vale *m*, abonaré *m*

script [skrɪpt] Ⓐ N 1 (*Cine*) guión *m*; **film ~** guión *m*; (*Theat, TV, Rad*) argumento *m*
2 (= *system of writing*) escritura *f*; (= *handwriting*) letra *f*; (= *typeface*) fuente *f*, tipo *m* de letra; **Arabic/Gothic ~** escritura *f* árabe/gótica
3 (*in exam*) escrito *m*
Ⓑ VT [+ *film*] escribir el guión de; [+ *play*] escribir el argumento de; **the film was not well ~ed** la película no tenía un buen guión
Ⓒ CPD ► **script editor** N (*Cine, TV*) revisor(a) *m/f* de guión ► **script girl** N (*Cine*) script *f*, anotadora *f*

scripted ['skrɪptɪd] ADJ (*Rad, TV*) escrito

scriptural ['skrɪptʃərəl] ADJ escriturario, bíblico

Scripture ['skrɪptʃəʳ] N 1 (*also* **Holy ~**) Sagrada Escritura *f*
2 (*Scol*) (= *subject, lesson*) Historia *f* Sagrada

scriptwriter ['skrɪpt,raɪtəʳ] N guionista *mf*

scrofula ['skrɒfjʊlə] N escrófula *f*

scrofulous ['skrɒfjʊləs] ADJ escrofuloso

scroll [skrəʊl] Ⓐ N 1 (= *roll of parchment*) rollo *m*; (= *ancient manuscript*) manuscrito *m*; **the Dead Sea ~s** los manuscritos del Mar Muerto; **~ of fame** lista *f* de la fama
2 (*Archit*) voluta *f*
Ⓑ VT (*Comput*) desplazar
Ⓒ CPD ► **scroll key** N (*Comput*) tecla *f* de desplazamiento

►**scroll down** Ⓐ VT + ADV desplazar hacia abajo
Ⓑ VI + ADV desplazarse hacia abajo

►**scroll up** Ⓐ VT + ADV desplazar hacia arriba
Ⓑ VI + ADV desplazarse hacia arriba

scrolling ['skrəʊlɪŋ] N (*Comput*) desplazamiento *m*

Scrooge [skru:dʒ] N el avariento típico (*personaje del "Christmas Carol" de Dickens*)

scrotum ['skrəʊtəm] N (*pl* **scrotums** *or* **scrota** ['skrəʊtə]) escroto *m*

scrounge* [skraʊndʒ] Ⓐ N **to be on the ~ (for sth)** ir sacando (algo) de gorra; **to have a ~ round for sth** ir por ahí pidiendo algo
Ⓑ VT gorronear*, gorrear*; **I ~d a ticket** gorroneé una entrada; **to ~ sth from sb** gorronear algo a algn; **can I ~ a drink from you?** ¿me invitas a un trago?*
Ⓒ VI **to ~ on** *or* **off sb** vivir a costa de algn; **to ~ around for sth** ir por ahí pidiendo algo

scrounger* ['skraʊndʒəʳ] N gorrón/ona *m/f*, sablista *mf*

scrub[1] [skrʌb] Ⓐ N (*Bot*) (= *undergrowth*) monte *m* bajo, maleza *f*; (= *bushes*) matas *fpl*, matorrales *mpl*
Ⓑ CPD ► **scrub fire** N incendio *m* de monte bajo

scrub[2] [skrʌb] Ⓐ N fregado *m*, restregado *m* (*esp LAm*); **to give sth a (good) ~** fregar *or* restregar algo (bien); **it needs a hard ~** hay que fregarlo *or* restregarlo con fuerza
Ⓑ VT 1 (= *clean*) [+ *floor, hands etc*] fregar; **to ~ sth clean** fregar *or* restregar algo hasta que quede limpio
2 (*) (= *cancel*) cancelar, anular; **let's ~ it** bueno, lo borramos
Ⓒ CPD ► **scrub brush** N (*US*) cepillo *m* de fregar

►**scrub away** VT + ADV [+ *dirt*] quitar restregando; [+ *stain*] quitar frotando

►**scrub down** VT + ADV [+ *room, wall*] fregar; **to ~ o.s. down** fregarse

►**scrub off** Ⓐ VT + ADV [+ *mark, stain*] quitar cepillando; [+ *name*] tachar
Ⓑ VT + PREP quitar de

►**scrub out** VT + ADV [+ *stain*] limpiar restregando; [+ *pan*] fregar; [+ *name*] tachar

►**scrub up** VI + ADV [*doctor, surgeon*] lavarse

scrubber[1] ['skrʌbəʳ] N (*also* **pan ~**) estropajo *m*

scrubber[2]‡ ['skrʌbəʳ] N (*Brit*) (= *whore*) putilla‡ *f*

scrubbing brush ['skrʌbɪŋ,brʌʃ] N cepillo *m* de fregar

scrubby ['skrʌbɪ] ADJ 1 [*person*] achaparrado, enano
2 [*land*] cubierto de maleza

scrubland ['skrʌblænd] N monte *m* bajo, maleza *f*

scrubwoman ['skrʌb,wʊmən] N (*pl* **scrubwomen**) (*US*) fregona *f*

scruff [skrʌf] N 1 **by the ~ of the neck** del cogote
2 (*) (= *untidy person*) dejado/a *m/f*

scruffily ['skrʌfɪlɪ] ADV **~ dressed** mal vestido, vestido con desaliño

scruffiness ['skrʌfɪnɪs] N (= *untidiness*) desaliño *m*; (= *dirtiness*) suciedad *f*

scruffy ['skrʌfɪ] ADJ (*compar* **scruffier**; *superl* **scruffiest**) [*person, appearance*] desaliñado, dejado; [*clothes*] desaliñado; [*building*] destartalado; **he looks ~** tiene aspecto descuidado

scrum [skrʌm] Ⓐ N (*Rugby*) melé *f*; **loose ~** melé *f* abierta *or* espontánea; **set ~** melé *f* cerrada *or* ordenada
Ⓑ CPD ► **scrum half** N medio *m* de melé

►**scrum down** VI + ADV formar la melé (cerrada *or* ordenada)

scrummage ['skrʌmɪdʒ] N = **scrum A**

scrumptious* ['skrʌmpʃəs] ADJ delicioso, sabrosísimo

scrunch [skrʌntʃ] VT (*also* **to ~ up**) ronzar

scruple ['skru:pl] Ⓐ N escrúpulo *m*; **a person of no ~s** una persona sin escrúpulos; **he is entirely without ~s** no tiene conciencia; **to have no ~s about ...** no tener escrúpulos acerca de ...; **to make no ~ to do sth** no tener escrúpulos para hacer algo
Ⓑ VI (*frm*) **not to ~ to do sth** no vacilar en hacer algo

scrupulous ['skru:pjʊləs] ADJ escrupuloso (**about** en cuanto a)

scrupulously ['skru:pjʊləslɪ] ADV escrupulosamente; **~ honest/clean** sumamente honrado/limpio

scrupulousness ['skru:pjʊləsnɪs] N escrupulosidad *f*

scrutineer [,skru:tɪ'nɪəʳ] N escrutador(a) *m/f*

scrutinize ['skru:tɪnaɪz] VT [+ *work etc*] escudriñar; [+ *votes*] efectuar el escrutinio de

scrutiny ['skru:tɪnɪ] N (= *examination*) examen *m* detallado; (*Pol*) [*of votes*] escrutinio *m*, recuento *m*; **under the ~ of sb** bajo la mirada de algn; **under his ~ she felt nervous** bajo su mirada se sintió nerviosa; **to keep sb under close ~** vigilar a algn de cerca; **to submit sth to a close ~** someter algo a un detallado *or* cuidadoso examen; **it does not stand up to ~** no resiste un examen

SCSI ['skʌzɪ] N ABBR (*Comput*) (= **small computer systems interface**) SCSI *m or f*, *controlador de dispositivos de entrada y salida de alta velocidad de transferencia*

scuba ['sku:bə] ADJ **~ diving** submarinismo *m*; **~ suit** traje *m* de submarinismo

scud [skʌd] VI **to ~ along** correr (llevado por el viento), deslizarse rápidamente; **the clouds were ~ding across the sky** las nubes pasaban rápidamente a través del cielo; **the ship ~ded before the wind** el barco iba viento en popa

scuff [skʌf] Ⓐ VT [+ *shoes, floor*] rayar, marcar; [+ *feet*] arrastrar
Ⓑ VI andar arrastrando los pies
Ⓒ CPD ► **scuff marks** NPL rozaduras *fpl*

scuffle ['skʌfl] Ⓐ N refriega *f*
Ⓑ VI tener una refriega (**with sb** con algn); **to ~ with the police** tener una refriega con la policía

scull [skʌl] Ⓐ N espadilla *f*
Ⓑ VT remar (*con espadilla*)
Ⓒ VI remar (*con espadilla*)

scullery ['skʌlərɪ] Ⓐ N (*esp Brit*) trascocina *f*, fregadero *m*
Ⓑ CPD ► **scullery maid** N fregona *f*

sculpt [skʌlpt] Ⓐ VT esculpir
Ⓑ VI esculpir

sculptor ['skʌlptəʳ] N escultor(a) *m/f*

sculptress ['skʌlptrɪs] N escultora *f*

sculptural ['skʌlptʃərəl] ADJ escultural

sculpture ['skʌlptʃəʳ] Ⓐ N escultura *f*
Ⓑ VT = **sculpt**
Ⓒ VI = **sculpt**

scum [skʌm] N 1 (*on liquid*) espuma *f*; (*on pond*) verdín *m*
2 (*pej*) (= *people*) escoria *f*; **the ~ of the earth** la escoria de la tierra
3 (** *pej*) = **scumbag**

scumbag** ['skʌm,bæg] N cabronazo* *m*, borde‡ *mf*

scummy ['skʌmɪ] ADJ 1 [*liquid*] lleno de espuma; [*pond*] cubierto de verdín
2 (‡ *pej*) canallesco, vil

scupper ['skʌpəʳ] Ⓐ N (*Naut*) imbornal *m*
Ⓑ VT 1 (*Naut*) abrir los imbornales de, barrenar
2 (*Brit**) [+ *plan*] echar por tierra

scurf [skɜ:f] N caspa *f*

scurfy ['skɜ:fɪ] ADJ casposo

scurrility [skʌ'rɪlɪtɪ] N lo difamatorio, lo calumnioso

scurrilous ['skʌrɪləs] ADJ [*gossip, allegations, article*] difamatorio, calumnioso; [*publication*] calumnioso; **to make a ~ attack on sb** calumniar a algn, difamar a algn

scurrilously ['skʌrɪləslɪ] ADV con calumnias

scurry ['skʌrɪ] VI (= *run*) ir corriendo; (= *hurry*) apresurarse, apurarse (*LAm*); **to ~ along** ir corriendo; **to ~ for shelter** correr para ponerse al abrigo; **to ~ away** *or* **off** escabullirse

scurvy ['skɜːvɪ] Ⓐ ADJ vil, canallesco
Ⓑ N escorbuto *m*

scut [skʌt] N rabito *m* (*esp de conejo*)

scutcheon ['skʌtʃən] N = **escutcheon**

scuttle[1] ['skʌtl] VT [1] [+ *ship*] barrenar
[2] (*fig*) [+ *hopes, plans*] dar al traste con, echar por tierra

scuttle[2] ['skʌtl] VI (= *run*) echar a correr; **to ~ away** *or* **off** escabullirse; **to ~ along** correr, ir a toda prisa; **we must ~** tenemos que marcharnos

scuttle[3] ['skʌtl] N (*for coal*) cubo *m*, carbonera *f*

scuzzy* ['skʌzɪ] ADJ (*esp US*) cutre*

Scylla ['sɪlə] N **~ and Charybdis** Escila y Caribdis

scythe [saɪð] Ⓐ N guadaña *f*
Ⓑ VT guadañar, segar

SD ABBR (*US*) = **South Dakota**

S.Dak. ABBR (*US*) = **South Dakota**

SDI N ABBR (= **Strategic Defense Initiative**) IDE *f*

SDLP N ABBR (*Northern Irl Pol*) = **Social Democratic and Labour Party**

SDP N ABBR (*Brit Pol*) (*formerly*) = **Social Democratic Party**

SDR N ABBR (= **special drawing rights**) DEG *mpl*

SE ABBR (= **southeast**) SE

sea [siː] Ⓐ N [1] (= *not land*) mar *m* (*or f in some phrases*); **(out) at ~** en alta mar; **to spend three years at ~** pasar tres años navegando; **to remain two months at ~** estar navegando durante dos meses, pasar dos meses en el mar; **beside the ~** a la orilla del mar, junto al mar; **beyond the ~s** más allá de los mares; **from beyond the ~s** desde más allá de los mares; **to go by ~** ir por mar; **a house by the ~** una casa junto al mar *or* a la orilla del mar; **heavy ~(s)** mar agitado *or* picado; **to ship a heavy ~** ser inundado por una ola grande; **on the high ~s** en alta mar; **on the ~** (*boat*) en alta mar; **rough ~(s)** mar agitado *or* picado; **to sail the ~s** navegar los mares; **the seven ~s** todos los mares del mundo; **in Spanish ~s** en aguas españolas; **the little boat was swept out to ~** la barquita fue arrastrada mar adentro; **to go to ~** [*person*] hacerse marinero; **to put (out) to ~** [*sailor, boat*] hacerse a la mar, zarpar; **to stand out to ~** apartarse de la costa; ✦***IDIOM*** **to be all at ~ (about** *or* **with sth)** estar en un lío (por algo); ✦***PROV*** **worse things happen at ~** cosas peores ocurren por ahí; *see also* **north**
[2] (*fig*) **a ~ of blood** un río *or* mar de sangre; **a ~ of corn** un mar de espigas; **a ~ of faces** un mar de caras; **a ~ of flame** un mar de llamas; **a ~ of troubles** un mar de penas
Ⓑ CPD ► **sea air** N aire *m* de mar ► **sea anemone** N anémona *f* de mar ► **sea bass** N corvina *f* ► **sea bathing** N baño *m* en el mar ► **sea battle** N batalla *f* naval ► **sea bed** N fondo *m* del mar, lecho *m* marino (*frm*) ► **sea bird** N ave *f* marina ► **sea boot** N bota *f* de marinero ► **sea bream** N besugo *m* ► **sea breeze** N brisa *f* marina ► **sea captain** N capitán *m* de barco ► **sea change** N (*fig*) viraje *m*, cambio *m* radical ► **sea chest**† N cofre *m* ► **sea coast** N litoral *m*, costa *f* marítima ► **sea cow** N manatí *m* ► **sea crossing** N travesía *f* ► **sea dog** N (*lit, fig*) lobo *m* de mar ► **sea fight** N combate *m* naval ► **sea fish** N pez *m* marino ► **sea front** N paseo *m* marítimo ► **sea green** N verde mar *m*; *see also* **sea-green** ► **sea horse** N caballito *m* de mar, hipocampo *m* ► **sea kale** N col *f* marina ► **sea lamprey** N lamprea *f* marina ► **sea lane** N ruta *f* marítima ► **sea legs** NPL **to find one's ~ legs** mantener el equilibrio (en barco) ► **sea level** N nivel *m* del mar; **800 metres above ~ level** 800 metros sobre el nivel del mar ► **sea lion** N león *m* marino ► **sea mist** N bruma *f* marina ► **sea perch** N perca *f* de mar ► **sea power** N potencia *f* naval ► **sea room** N espacio *m* para maniobrar ► **sea route** N ruta *f* marítima ► **sea salt** N sal *f* marina ► **sea serpent** N serpiente *f* de mar ► **sea shanty** N saloma *f* ► **sea transport** N transporte *m* por mar, transporte *m* marítimo ► **sea trip** N viaje *m* por mar ► **sea trout** N trucha *f* marina, reo *m* ► **sea urchin** N erizo *m* de mar ► **sea wall** N malecón *m*, rompeolas *m inv* ► **sea water** N agua *f* de mar ► **sea wrack** N algas *fpl* (en la playa)

seaboard ['siːbɔːd] N (*US*) litoral *m*

seaborne ['siːbɔːn] ADJ transportado por mar

seafarer ['siːˌfɛərər] N marinero *m*

seafaring ['siːˌfɛərɪŋ] Ⓐ ADJ [*community*] marinero; [*life*] de marinero; **~ man** marinero *m*
Ⓑ N (*also* **~ life**) vida *f* de marinero

seafood ['siːfuːd] Ⓐ N marisco *m*, mariscos *mpl*
Ⓑ CPD ► **seafood cocktail** N cóctel *m* de marisco(s) ► **seafood restaurant** N marisquería *f*

seagirt ['siːgɜːt] ADJ (*liter*) rodeado por el mar

seagoing ['siːˌgəʊɪŋ] ADJ marítimo

sea-green ['siːgriːn] ADJ verdemar

seagull ['siːgʌl] N gaviota *f*

seal[1] [siːl] Ⓐ N (*Zool*) foca *f*
Ⓑ CPD ► **seal cull, seal culling** N matanza *f* (selectiva) de focas
Ⓒ VI **to go ~ing** ir a cazar focas

seal[2] [siːl] Ⓐ N [1] (= *official stamp*) sello *m*; **the papal/presidential ~** el sello papal/presidencial; **they have given their ~ of approval to the proposed reforms** han dado el visto bueno a *or* han aprobado las reformas que se planean; **it has the Royal Academy's ~ of approval** cuenta con la aprobación *or* el visto bueno de la Real Academia; **~ of quality** sello *or* marchamo *m* de calidad; **this set the ~ on their friendship/on her humiliation** esto selló su amistad/remató su humillación; **under my hand and ~** (*frm*) firmado y sellado por mí
[2] [*of envelope, parcel, exterior of bottle, jar*] precinto *m*; (*inside lid of jar*) aro *m* de goma; (*on fridge door*) cierre *m* de goma; (*on door, window*) burlete *m*; **the ~ on the windows is not very good** estas ventanas no cierran bien
[3] (*Rel*) **the ~ of the confessional** el secreto de confesión
Ⓑ VT [1] (= *close*) [+ *envelope*] cerrar; [+ *package, coffin*] precintar; [+ *border*] cerrar; **a ~ed envelope** un sobre cerrado; *see also* **lip A1**, **sign B1**
[2] (= *stop up, make airtight*) [+ *container*] tapar *or* cerrar herméticamente; [+ *surface*] sellar; **the wood is ~ed with several coats of varnish** la madera se sella con varias capas de barniz
[3] (= *enclose*) **to ~ sth in sth**: **~ the letter in a blank envelope** mete la carta en un sobre en blanco y ciérralo; **~ in airtight containers** guárdelos en recipientes herméticos
[4] (*fig*) (= *confirm*) [+ *bargain, deal*] sellar; [+ *victory*] decidir; [+ *sb's fate*] decidir, determinar; **that goal ~ed the match** ese gol decidió *or* determinó el resultado del partido
[5] (*Culin*) [+ *meat*] sofreír a fuego vivo (*para que no pierda el jugo*)

► **seal in** VT + ADV conservar; **this ~s in the flavour** esto conserva el sabor

► **seal off** VT + ADV [+ *building, room*] cerrar; [+ *area, road*] acordonar

► **seal up** VT + ADV [+ *letter, parcel, building, tunnel*] precintar; [+ *window, door*] condenar, precintar; [+ *hole*] rellenar, tapar

sealant ['siːlənt] N (= *device*) sellador *m*, tapador *m*; (= *substance*) silicona *f* selladora

sealer ['siːlər] N (= *person*) cazador(a) *m/f* de focas; (= *boat*) barco *m* para la caza de focas

sealing ['siːlɪŋ] N caza *f* de focas

sealing wax ['siːlɪŋwæks] N lacre *m*

sealskin ['siːlskɪn] N piel *f* de foca

seam [siːm] Ⓐ N [1] (*Sew*) costura *f*; **to fall** *or* **come apart at the ~s** descoserse; **to be bursting at the ~s** [*dress etc*] estar a punto de reventar por las costuras; (*fig*) (*) [*room etc*] estar a rebosar
[2] (*Welding*) juntura *f*
[3] (*Geol*) filón *m*, veta *f*
Ⓑ VT (*Sew*) coser; (*Tech*) juntar

seaman ['siːmən] N (*pl* **seamen**) marinero *m*, marino *m*

seamanlike ['siːmənlaɪk] ADJ de buen marinero

seamanship ['siːmənʃɪp] N náutica *f*

seamless ['siːmlɪs] ADJ (*Sew*) sin costura; (*Tech*) sin soldadura

seamstress ['semstrɪs] N costurera *f*

seamy* ['siːmɪ] ADJ (*compar* **seamier**; *superl* **seamiest**) sórdido, insalubre; **the ~ side** (*fig*) el revés de la medalla

seance, séance ['seɪɑːns] N sesión *f* de espiritismo

seapiece ['siːpiːs] N (*Art*) marina *f*

seaplane ['siːpleɪn] N hidroavión *m*

seaport ['siːpɔːt] N puerto *m* de mar

SEAQ ['siːˌæk] N ABBR = **Stock Exchange Automated Quotations**

sear [sɪər] VT (= *wither*) secar, marchitar; (*Med*) cauterizar; [*pain etc*] punzar; (= *scorch*) chamuscar, quemar; **it was ~ed into my memory** me quedó grabado en la memoria

► **sear through** VI + PREP [+ *walls, metal*] penetrar a través de

search [sɜːtʃ] Ⓐ N [1] (= *hunt*) búsqueda *f* (**for** de); **after a long ~ I found the key** después de mucho buscar, encontré la llave; **police launched a massive ~ for the killer** la policía ha emprendido una enorme operación de búsqueda para encontrar al asesino; **the ~ for peace** la búsqueda de la paz; **to conduct a ~** = **to make a search**; **in ~ of** en busca de; **they come to the city in ~ of work** vienen a la ciudad en busca de trabajo; **we went in ~ of a restaurant** fuimos a buscar un restaurante; **to make a ~** llevar a cabo una búsqueda; **~ and rescue** búsqueda y rescate
[2] (= *inspection*) [*of building, place*] registro *m*; [*of records*] inspección *f*; **she had to submit to a body ~** tuvo que dejar que la registraran *or* cachearan; **police made a thorough ~ of the premises** la policía registró todo el local
[3] (*Comput*) búsqueda *f*
[4] (*Brit Jur*) *comprobación de datos de un inmueble en el registro de la propiedad*; **to get a (local authority) ~ done** ≈ sacar una nota simple en el registro de la propiedad (*Sp*)
Ⓑ VT [1] [+ *building, luggage, pockets*] registrar, catear (*Mex*); [+ *person*] registrar, cachear, catear (*Mex*); **to ~ sth/sb (for sth/sb)**: **he ~ed**

his pockets for change se miró los bolsillos en busca de monedas; **she ~ed the kitchen drawers for her keys** buscó las llaves en los cajones de la cocina; **I ~ed the whole house for food** he revuelto toda la casa en busca de comida; **we ~ed the entire office but the file didn't turn up** registramos la oficina de arriba abajo pero no encontramos el archivo; **they were ~ed for weapons as they left** los registraron *or* cachearon *or* (*Mex*) catearon a la salida para ver si llevaban armas; **to ~ high and low (for sth/sb)** remover el cielo y la tierra (en busca de algo/algn); **~ me!*** ¡yo qué sé!, ¡ni idea!

2 (= *scan*) [+ *documents, records*] examinar; **his eyes ~ed the sky for the approaching helicopter** escudriñó el cielo en busca del helicóptero que se acercaba; **his eyes ~ed my face for any sign of guilt** sus ojos escudriñaban mi rostro en busca de algún rastro de culpabilidad; **to ~ one's conscience** examinar (uno) su conciencia; **to ~ one's memory** hacer memoria

3 (*Comput*) buscar en

Ⓒ VI buscar; **to ~ after truth/happiness** buscar la verdad/la felicidad; **to ~ for sth/sb** buscar algo/a algn; **we ~ed everywhere for the missing keys** buscamos las llaves que faltaban en todas partes; **they are ~ing for a solution to the crisis** están buscando una solución a la crisis; **to ~ through sth (for sth)**: **rescuers ~ed through the rubble for survivors** los del equipo de rescate buscaron supervivientes entre los escombros; **he ~ed through our passports** examinó nuestros pasaportes

Ⓓ CPD ► **search engine** N (*Internet*) buscador *m*, motor *m* de búsqueda ► **search party** N pelotón *m* de búsqueda ► **search warrant** N orden *f* de registro

►**search about, search around** VI + ADV buscar por todas partes

►**search out** VT + ADV **I ~ed him out in the coffee break** fui a buscarlo durante la pausa para el café; **if you can ~ out a copy, it is worth reading** si encuentras un ejemplar, merece la pena que lo leas; **~ out the less well-known wines** trate de descubrir los vinos menos conocidos

searcher ['sɜːtʃəʳ] N buscador(a) *m/f*

searching ['sɜːtʃɪŋ] ADJ [*look, glance*] inquisitivo; [*eyes*] penetrante; [*question, mind*] perspicaz; [*examination*] exhaustivo; [*test*] duro; **you need to ask yourself some ~ questions** te hace falta hacerte de verdad ciertas preguntas

searchingly ['sɜːtʃɪŋlɪ] ADV [*look, ask*] inquisitivamente

searchlight ['sɜːtʃlaɪt] N reflector *m*, proyector *m*

searing ['sɪərɪŋ] ADJ [*heat*] ardiente; [*pain*] agudo; [*criticism*] mordaz, acerbo

seascape ['siːskeɪp] N (*Art*) paisaje *m* marino

seashell ['siːʃel] N concha *f* marina

seashore ['siːʃɔːʳ] N (= *beach*) playa *f*; (*gen*) orilla *f* del mar; **by** *or* **on the ~** en la playa, a la orilla del mar

seasick ['siːsɪk] ADJ mareado; **to get** *or* **be ~** marearse (*en barco*)

seasickness ['siːsɪknɪs] N mareo *m* (*al estar en una embarcación*)

seaside ['siːsaɪd] Ⓐ N (= *beach*) playa *f*; (= *shore*) orilla *f* del mar; **we want to go to the ~** queremos ir a la playa; **to take the family to the ~ for a day** llevar a la familia a pasar un día a la playa; **at the ~** en la playa

Ⓑ CPD [*hotel*] de playa, en la playa; [*town*] costero, costeño ► **seaside holidays** NPL **we like ~ holidays** nos gusta pasar las vacaciones en la playa *or* costa, nos gusta veranear junto al mar ► **seaside resort** N *lugar de veraneo en la playa*

season ['siːzn] Ⓐ N 1 (= *period of the year*) estación *f*; **the four ~s** las cuatro estaciones; **what's your favourite ~?** ¿cuál es tu estación preferida?; **at this ~** en esta época del año; **the dry/rainy ~** la temporada de secas/de lluvias

2 (*for specific activity*) temporada *f*; **for a ~** durante una temporada; **we did a ~ at La Scala** (*Theat*) representamos en la Scala durante una temporada; **did you have a good ~?** ¿qué tal la temporada?; **"Season's Greetings"** "Felices Pascuas"; **the busy ~** la temporada alta; **the Christmas ~** las navidades; **the closed ~** (*Hunting*) la veda; **the fishing/football ~** la temporada de pesca/de fútbol; **at the height of the ~** en plena temporada; **during the holiday ~** en la temporada de vacaciones; **to be in ~** [*fruit*] estar en sazón; [*animal*] estar en celo; **the London ~** la temporada social de Londres; **the open ~** (*Hunting*) la temporada de caza *or* de pesca; **to be out of ~** estar fuera de temporada

3 (*liter*) (= *appropriate time*) **for everything there is a ~** todo tiene su momento; **in due ~** a su tiempo; **it was not the ~ for jokes** no era el momento oportuno para chistes; **a word in ~** una palabra a propósito; **in ~ and out of ~** a tiempo y a destiempo

Ⓑ VT 1 (*Culin*) sazonar, condimentar (**with** con); **~ to taste** sazonar a gusto; **a speech ~ed with wit** un discurso salpicado de agudezas

2 [+ *wood, timber*] curar

Ⓒ CPD ► **season ticket** N (*Theat, Rail, Sport*) abono *m* ► **season ticket holder** N abonado/a *m/f*

seasonable ['siːznəbl] ADJ [*weather*] propio de la estación

seasonal ['siːzənl] Ⓐ ADJ [*work, labour, migration*] de temporada, estacional; [*changes, variations*] estacional; [*fruit, vegetable*] del tiempo, de temporada; [*migrant*] temporal; **the tourism business is ~** el negocio del turismo es de temporada

Ⓑ CPD ► **seasonal adjustment** N (*Econ, Pol*) ajuste *m* estacional, desestacionalización *f*; **prices rose 0.2% in July, after ~ adjustments** tras eliminar las fluctuaciones estacionales se vio que los precios subieron un 0,2% en julio, las cifras desestacionalizadas demostraron una subida de los precios del 0,2% en julio ► **seasonal affective disorder** N trastorno *m* afectivo estacional ► **seasonal worker** N temporero/a *m/f*

seasonally ['siːzənəlɪ] ADV **~ adjusted figures** cifras *fpl* desestacionalizadas

seasoned ['siːznd] ADJ 1 (*Culin*) [*food*] sazonado, condimentado

2 (= *matured*) [*wood, timber*] curado; [*wine*] maduro

3 (*fig*) [*soldier*] aguerrido, veterano; [*worker, actor*] experimentado; [*player*] experimentado, curtido; [*traveller*] curtido, con muchos kilómetros a sus espaldas; **she's a ~ campaigner** es una veterana de las campañas, está curtida en mil y una campañas

seasong ['siːsɒŋ] N canción *f* de marineros; (= *shanty*) saloma *f*

seasoning ['siːznɪŋ] N 1 (*for food*) aliño *m*, condimentos *mpl*; **with a ~ of jokes** con un aliño de chistes

2 [*of wood, timber*] cura *f*

seat [siːt] Ⓐ N 1 (= *place to sit*) asiento *m*; (*in cinema, theatre*) butaca *f*, asiento *m*; (*in car, plane, train, bus*) asiento *m*; (*on cycle*) sillín *m*, asiento *m*; **is this ~ free?** ¿está libre este asiento?; **the back ~ of the car** el asiento trasero del coche; **save me a ~** guárdame un sitio *or* asiento; **he used the log as a ~** usaba el tronco de silla; **do have** *or* **take a ~** siéntese por favor, tome asiento por favor (*frm*); **to take one's ~** sentarse, tomar asiento; **please take your ~s for supper** la cena está servida; **✦IDIOM to take a back ~** mantenerse al margen; **his private life takes a back ~ to the problems of the company** su vida privada ocupa un segundo lugar después de los problemas de la compañía; *see also* **driving C, hot D**

2 [*of chair, toilet*] asiento *m*

3 (= *ticket*) (*Theat, Cine, Sport*) localidad *f*, entrada *f*; (*for plane, train, bus*) plaza *f*; **we need two ~s on the first available flight** necesitamos dos plazas en el primer vuelo disponible; **are there any ~s left?** (*Theat, Cine, Sport*) ¿quedan localidades *or* entradas?; (*on plane*) ¿quedan plazas?

4 (*Pol*) (*in parliament*) escaño *m*, curul *f* (*Col*); (= *constituency*) circunscripción *f* electoral; **she kept/lost her ~ in the election** retuvo/perdió su escaño en las elecciones; *see also* **safe D**

5 (*on board, committee*) puesto *m*; **to have a ~ on the board** ser miembro de la junta directiva

6 [*of trousers*] fondillos *mpl*; **✦IDIOM to do sth by the ~ of one's pants** hacer algo guiado por el instinto

7 (= *centre*) [*of government*] sede *f*; [*of family*] residencia *f*, casa *f* solariega; **family ~** casa *f* solariega; **~ of learning** (*liter*) centro *m* de estudios, templo *m* del saber (*liter*)

8 (= *source*) [*of infection, problem*] foco *m*

9 (= *buttocks*) (*euph*) trasero* *m*, posaderas* *fpl*

10 [*of rider*] **to have a good ~** montar bien; **to keep one's ~** mantenerse sobre el caballo; **to lose one's ~** caer del caballo

Ⓑ VT 1 [+ *person, + child, invalid*] sentar; **they ~ guests at a different table every day** todos los días ponen a los invitados en mesas diferentes; **please remain ~ed** por favor permanezcan sentados (*frm*); **please be ~ed** tome asiento por favor (*frm*); **to ~ o.s.** sentarse, tomar asiento (*frm*)

2 (= *hold*) [*hall, vehicle*] tener cabida para; **the bus ~s 53 people** el autobús tiene cabida para 53 personas (sentadas), el autobús tiene 53 plazas *or* asientos; **the car ~s five** caben cinco personas en el coche, el coche tiene cabida para cinco personas; **the theatre ~s 900** el teatro tiene un aforo de 900 localidades, el teatro tiene cabida para 900 personas; **the table can ~ 20 comfortably** en la mesa caben 20 personas cómodamente

3 (*Mech*) [+ *valve, bearing*] asentar, ajustar

4 (*fig*) **deeply ~ed attitudes** actitudes *fpl* muy arraigadas

Ⓒ CPD ► **seat back** N respaldo *m* del asiento ► **seat belt** N cinturón *m* de seguridad; **he wasn't wearing a ~ belt** no llevaba puesto el cinturón de seguridad; **fasten your ~ belts** (*Aer*) abróchense el cinturón de seguridad; **put your ~ belt on** (*Aut*) póngase el cinturón de seguridad

-seater ['siːtəʳ] (*ending in compounds*) Ⓐ N **a two-seater** (= *car etc*) un coche *etc* de dos asientos

Ⓑ ADJ **a ten-seater plane** un avión de diez plazas, un avión con capacidad para diez personas

seating ['si:tɪŋ] Ⓐ N asientos *mpl*
Ⓑ CPD ► **seating accommodation** N plazas *fpl*, asientos *mpl* ► **seating arrangements** NPL = **seating plan** ► **seating capacity** N número *m* de asientos, cabida *f* ► **seating plan** N disposición *f* de los asientos

SEATO ['si:təʊ] N ABBR (= **Southeast Asia Treaty Organization**) OTASE *f*

seaward ['si:wəd] Ⓐ ADJ de hacia el mar, de la parte del mar; **on the ~ side** en el lado del mar
Ⓑ ADV hacia el mar; **to ~** en la dirección del mar

seawards ['si:wədz] ADV (*esp Brit*) = **seaward B**

seaway ['si:weɪ] N vía *f* marítima

seaweed ['si:wi:d] N alga *f*

seaworthiness ['si:ˌwɜ:ðɪnɪs] N navegabilidad *f*

seaworthy ['si:ˌwɜ:ðɪ] ADJ en condiciones de navegar

sebaceous [sɪ'beɪʃəs] ADJ sebáceo

SEC N ABBR (*US*) = **Securities and Exchange Commission**

sec* [sek] N ABBR = **second**

Sec. ABBR (= **Secretary**) Sec., Srio., Sria.

SECAM ['si:kæm] N ABBR (*TV*) (= **séquentiel à mémoire**) SECAM *m*

secant ['si:kənt] N secante *f*

secateurs [ˌsekə'tɜ:z] NPL podadera *fsing*

secede [sɪ'si:d] VI separarse, escindirse (**from** de)

secession [sɪ'seʃən] N secesión *f*, separación *f* (**from** de)

secessionist [sɪ'seʃnɪst] Ⓐ ADJ secesionista, separatista
Ⓑ N secesionista *mf*, separatista *mf*

secluded [sɪ'klu:dɪd] ADJ retirado, apartado

seclusion [sɪ'klu:ʒən] N aislamiento *m*; **to live in ~** vivir aislado

second[1] ['sekənd] Ⓐ ADJ [1] (*gen*) segundo; **they have a ~ home in Oxford** tienen otra casa en Oxford, en Oxford tienen una segunda vivienda; **will you have a ~ cup?** ¿quieres otra taza?; **give him a ~ chance** dale otra oportunidad; **you won't get a ~ chance** no tendrás otra oportunidad; **in ~ gear** (*Aut*) en segunda (velocidad); **it's ~ nature to her** lo hace sin pensar; **for some of us swimming is not ~ nature** para muchos de nosotros nadar no es algo que nos salga hacer de forma natural; **violence was ~ nature to him** la violencia era parte de su naturaleza; **he had practised until it had become ~ nature** había practicado hasta que le salía con naturalidad; **to ask for a ~ opinion** pedir una segunda opinión; **to be/lie in ~ place** estar/encontrarse en segundo lugar *or* segunda posición; **to have ~ sight** tener clarividencia, ser clarividente; **Charles the Second** (*spoken form*) Carlos Segundo; (*written form*) Carlos II; **without a** *or* **with hardly a ~ thought** sin pensarlo dos veces; **I didn't give it a ~ thought** no volví a pensar en ello; **to have ~ thoughts (about sth/about doing sth)** tener sus dudas (sobre algo/si hacer algo); **I'm having ~ thoughts about hiring him** tengo mis dudas sobre si contratarle; **on ~ thoughts ...** pensándolo bien ...; **for the ~ time** por segunda vez; **fatherhood ~ time around has not been easy for him** volver a ser padre no le ha resultado fácil; **to be ~ to none** no tener rival, ser inigualable; **Bath is ~ only to Glasgow as a tourist attraction** Bath es la atracción turística más popular aparte de Glasgow, sólo Glasgow gana en popularidad a Bath como atracción turística; **to get one's ~ wind** conseguir recobrar fuerzas; *see also* **floor A**
[2] (*Mus*) segundo; **I played ~ clarinet** era segundo clarinete; *see also* **fiddle A1**
Ⓑ ADV [1] (*in race, competition, election*) en segundo lugar; **to come/finish ~** quedar/llegar en segundo lugar *or* segunda posición; **in popularity polls he came ~ only to Nelson Mandela** en los sondeos era el segundo más popular por detrás de Nelson Mandela
[2] (= *secondly*) segundo, en segundo lugar
[3] (*before superl adj*) **the ~ tallest building in the world** el segundo edificio más alto del mundo; **the ~ largest fish** el segundo pez en tamaño, el segundo mayor pez; **this is the ~ largest city in Spain** ocupa la segunda posición entre las ciudades más grandes de España
Ⓒ N [1] (*in race, competition*) **he came a good/poor ~** quedó segundo a poca/gran distancia del vencedor; **studying for his exams comes a poor ~ to playing football** prepararse los exámenes no tiene ni de lejos la importancia que tiene jugar al fútbol; **I feel I come a poor ~ in my husband's affections to our baby daughter** tengo la sensación de que mi marido vuelca todo su cariño en la pequeña y a mí me tiene olvidada; *see also* **close B1**
[2] (*Aut*) segunda velocidad *f*; **in ~** en segunda (velocidad)
[3] (= *assistant*) (*in boxing*) segundo *m*, cuidador *m*; (*in duel*) padrino *m*; **~s out!** ¡segundos fuera!
[4] (*Brit Univ*) **Lower/Upper Second** *calificación que ocupa el tercer/segundo lugar en la escala de las que se otorgan con un título universitario*; → DEGREE
[5] **seconds** [5·1] (*Comm*) artículos *mpl* con defecto de fábrica; **these dresses are slight ~s** estos vestidos tienen pequeños defectos de fábrica
[5·2] (*Culin*) **will you have ~s?** ¿quieres más?; **I went back for ~s** volví a repetir
Ⓓ VT [1] [+ *motion, speaker, nomination*] apoyar, secundar; **I'll ~ that*** lo mismo digo yo, estoy completamente de acuerdo
[2] [sɪ'kɒnd] [+ *employee*] trasladar temporalmente; [+ *civil servant*] enviar en comisión de servicios (*Sp*)
Ⓔ CPD ► **second childhood** N segunda infancia *f*; **he's in his ~ childhood** está en su segunda infancia ► **the Second Coming** N (*Rel*) el segundo Advenimiento ► **second generation** N segunda generación *f* ► **second half** N (*Sport*) segundo tiempo *m*, segunda parte *f*; (*Fin*) segundo semestre *m* (*del año económico*) ► **second house** N (*Theat*) segunda función *f* ► **second language** N segunda lengua *f*; **English as a ~ language** inglés como segunda lengua ► **second lieutenant** N (*in army*) alférez *mf*, subteniente *mf* ► **second mate, second officer** N (*in Merchant Navy*) segundo *m* de a bordo ► **second mortgage** N segunda hipoteca *f* ► **second person** N (*Gram*) segunda persona *f*; **the ~ person singular/plural** la segunda persona del singular/plural ► **the Second World War** N la Segunda Guerra Mundial; *see also* **cousin**

second[2] ['sekənd] Ⓐ N (*in time, Geog, Math*) segundo *m*; **just a ~!** ◊ **half a ~!*** ¡un momento!, ¡momentito! (*esp LAm*); **I'll be with you in (just) a ~** un momento y estoy contigo; **in a split ~** en un instante, en un abrir y cerrar de ojos; **the operation is timed to a split ~** la operación está concebida con la mayor precisión en cuanto al tiempo; **it won't take a ~** es cosa de un segundo, es un segundo nada más; **at that very ~** en ese mismo instante
Ⓑ CPD ► **second hand** N [*of clock*] segundero *m*

secondary ['sekəndərɪ] Ⓐ ADJ [1] (= *less important*) [*character, role, effect, source*] secundario; **of ~ importance** de importancia secundaria, de segundo orden; **the cost is a ~ consideration** el coste es un factor secundario *or* de interés secundario; **my desire to have children was always ~ to my career** el deseo de tener hijos siempre se vio supeditado a mi carrera, el deseo de tener hijos siempre ocupó un lugar secundario en relación con mi carrera
[2] (*Educ*) [*education*] secundario; [*schooling, student, teacher*] de enseñanza secundaria; **after five years of ~ education** tras cinco años de educación *or* enseñanza secundaria; **subjects taught at ~ level** materias impartidas en los ciclos de educación *or* enseñanza secundaria
Ⓑ N [1] (*Univ etc*) (= *minor subject*) asignatura *f* menor
[2] (*also* **~ school**) centro *m* or instituto *m* de enseñanza secundaria;
→ COMPREHENSIVE SCHOOLS
[3] (*Med*) (*also* **~ tumour**) tumor *m* secundario
Ⓒ CPD ► **secondary action** N (*Pol*) movilizaciones *fpl* de apoyo ► **secondary cancer** N (*Med*) metástasis *f inv* ► **secondary education** N educación *f or* enseñanza *f* secundaria, segunda enseñanza *f* ► **secondary era** N (*Geol*) era *f* secundaria ► **secondary explosion** N explosión *f* por simpatía ► **secondary infection** N (*Med*) infección *f* secundaria ► **secondary modern (school)** N (*Brit*) (*formerly*) *instituto de enseñanza secundaria que centraba su actividad docente más en conocimientos prácticos y tecnológicos que en la formación académica* ► **secondary picket(ing)** N piquete *m* secundario (*en centros relacionados con el sector o fábrica en huelga*) ► **secondary production** N producción *f* secundaria ► **secondary road** N carretera *f* secundaria ► **secondary school** N centro *m or* instituto *m* de enseñanza secundaria; → COMPREHENSIVE SCHOOLS ► **secondary storage** N almacenamiento *m* secundario ► **secondary tumour** N = **B3**

second-best ['sekənd'best] Ⓐ N segundo *m*
Ⓑ ADV **to come off ~** quedar en segundo lugar
Ⓒ ADJ segundo; **our ~ car** nuestro coche número dos

second-class ['sekənd'klɑ:s] Ⓐ ADJ [*compartment, carriage*] de segunda clase; **~ citizen** ciudadano/a *m/f* de segunda clase; **~ degree** (*Univ*) licenciatura *f* con media de notable; **~ hotel** hotel *m* de segunda; **~ mail** ◊ **~ post** correo *m* de segunda clase; **a ~ return to London** (*Rail*) un billete de ida y vuelta a Londres en segunda; **~ seat** (*Rail*) asiento *m* de *or* en segunda; **~ stamp** sello *m* para correo ordinario; **~ ticket** billete *m* de segunda clase
Ⓑ ADV **to send sth ~** enviar algo por segunda clase; **to travel ~** viajar en segunda

seconder ['sekəndə^r] N *el/la que apoya una moción*

second-hand ['sekənd'hænd] Ⓐ ADJ (*gen*) de segunda mano; [*car*] usado, de segunda mano; **~ bookseller** librero/a *m/f* de viejo; **~ bookshop** librería *f* de viejo; **~ clothes** ropa *f* usada *or* de segunda mano; **~ information**

información *f* de segunda mano; **~ shop** tienda *f* de segunda mano, bazar *m* (*Mex*), cambalache *m* (*S. Cone*)
Ⓑ ADV **to buy sth ~** comprar algo de segunda mano; **I heard it only ~** yo lo supe solamente por otro; **she heard it ~ from her friend** se enteró por su amiga

second-in-command ['sekəndɪnkə'mɑ:nd] N segundo/a *m/f* de a bordo

▼ **secondly** ['sekəndlɪ] ADV en segundo lugar

secondment [sɪ'kɒndmənt] N traslado *m*; **on ~** trasladado, destacado; **she is on ~ to section B** ha sido trasladada temporalmente a la sección B, está destacada en la sección B

second-rate ['sekənd'reɪt] ADJ de segunda fila; **some ~ writer** algún escritor de segunda fila

secrecy ['si:krəsɪ] N secreto *m*; **in ~** en secreto, a escondidas; **in the strictest ~** de manera totalmente confidencial, en el más absoluto secreto; **I was told in the strictest ~** se me dijo de manera totalmente confidencial; **to swear sb to ~** hacer que algn jure no revelar algo; **there's no ~ about it** no es ningún secreto; **there was an air of ~ about her** la rodeaba un halo de misterio; *see also* **shroud B2**, **veil A**

secret ['si:krɪt] Ⓐ ADJ [*plan, ingredient, admirer, mission*] secreto; [*information, document*] secreto, confidencial; [*drinker, drug addict*] a escondidas; **it's all highly ~** todo es de lo más secreto; **to keep sth ~** mantener algo en secreto; **to keep sth ~ from sb** ocultar algo a algn; **they held a ~ meeting** mantuvieron una reunión en secreto
Ⓑ N secreto *m*; **the ~s of nature** los misterios de la naturaleza; **to do sth in ~** hacer algo en secreto *or* a escondidas; **to be in on the ~** estar en el secreto, estar al corriente; **to keep a ~** guardar un secreto; **to keep sth a ~ from sb** ocultar algo a algn; **to let sb into a/the ~** contar *or* revelar a algn un/el secreto; **it's no ~ that ...** no es ningún secreto que ...; **there's no ~ about it** esto no tiene nada de secreto; **to have no ~s from sb** no tener secretos para algn; **to make no ~ of sth** no ocultar algo; **to remain a ~** seguir siendo un secreto; **to tell sb a ~** contar un secreto a algn; **the ~: the ~ is to** (+ *INFIN*) el secreto consiste en + *infin*; **the ~ of success** el secreto del éxito; *see also* **open A9**, **state C**
Ⓒ CPD ► **secret agent** N agente *mf* secreto/a, espía *mf* ► **secret drawer** N cajón *m* secreto *or* oculto ► **secret police** N policía *f* secreta ► **secret service** N servicio *m* secreto ► **secret society** N sociedad *f* secreta ► **secret weapon** N (*lit, fig*) arma *f* secreta

secretarial [,sekrə'tɛərɪəl] ADJ **~ college** colegio *m* de secretariado; **~ course** curso *m* de secretariado; **~ services** servicios *mpl* de secretaría; **~ school** = **secretarial college**; **~ skills** técnicas *fpl* de secretaría; **~ work** trabajo *m* de secretario

secretariat [,sekrə'tɛərɪət] N secretaría *f*, secretariado *m*

secretary ['sekrətrɪ] Ⓐ N [1] (= *profession*) secretario/a *m/f*
[2] (*Pol*) ministro/a *m/f*; **Secretary of State** (*Brit*) Ministro/a *m/f* (**for** de); (*US*) Ministro/a *m/f* de Asuntos Exteriores
Ⓑ CPD ► **secretary pool** N (*US*) servicio *m* de mecanógrafos

secretary-general ['sekrətrɪ'dʒenərəl] N (*pl* **secretaries-general**) secretario-general/secretaria-general *m/f*

secretaryship ['sekrətrɪʃɪp] N secretaría *f*, secretariado *m*

secrete [sɪ'kri:t] VT [1] (*Med*) secretar, segregar
[2] (= *hide*) ocultar, esconder

secretion [sɪ'kri:ʃən] N [1] (*Med*) secreción *f*
[2] (= *hiding*) ocultación *f*

secretive ['si:krətɪv] ADJ [*person*] reservado, callado; [*behaviour*] reservado; [*organization*] hermético; **to be ~ about sth** ser reservado con respecto a algo

secretively ['si:krətɪvlɪ] ADV [1] (= *furtively*) [*behave, smile*] con mucho secreto
[2] (= *in secret*) a escondidas

secretiveness ['si:krətɪvnɪs] N **she knew that something was up because of the children's ~** supo que pasaba algo porque los niños actuaban con mucho secreto

secretly ['si:krɪtlɪ] ADV [*meet, plan, film*] en secreto, a escondidas; [*marry*] en secreto; [*hope, want*] en el fondo; **she was ~ relieved/pleased** en su fuero interno sintió alivio/estaba contenta

sect [sekt] N secta *f*

sectarian [sek'tɛərɪən] Ⓐ ADJ sectario
Ⓑ N sectario/a *m/f*

sectarianism [sek'tɛərɪənɪzəm] N sectarismo *m*

section ['sekʃən] Ⓐ N [1] (= *part*) [*of pipeline, road*] tramo *m*; [*of self-assembly item*] pieza *f*, parte *f*; [*of orange etc*] gajo *m*; [*of book, text*] parte *f*; [*of code, law*] artículo *m*; [*of document, report*] apartado *m*, punto *m*; [*of orchestra*] sección *f*; [*of country*] región *f*; [*of community, opinion*] sector *m*; [*of town*] (*Brit*) sector *m*, zona *f*; (*US*) (= *district*) barrio *m*; **the ship was transported in ~s** el barco fue trasladado por partes; **the bookcase comes in ~s** la estantería viene desmontada (en piezas *or* partes); **the first-class ~ of the train** los vagones de primera clase del tren; **passports ~** sección *f* de pasaportes; **the sports/finance ~** [*of newspaper*] la sección de deportes/economía; **in all ~s of the public** en todos los sectores del público; *see also* **brass C**, **string C**, **percussion B**, **woodwind**
[2] (= *cut*) (*in diagram, dissection*) sección *f*, corte *m*; **cross ~** (*lit*) sección *f* transversal; **the research was compiled using a cross ~ of the British population** el estudió se realizó utilizando un sector representativo de la población británica
[3] (*Med*) (*also* **Caesarean ~**) *see* **Caesarean**
Ⓑ VT [1] (= *divide*) partir, trocear
[2] [+ *mentally ill person*] internar en un psiquiátrico
Ⓒ CPD ► **section mark** N párrafo *m*

► **section off** VT + ADV cortar, seccionar

sectional ['sekʃənl] ADJ [1] [*bookcase etc*] desmontable
[2] [*interests*] particular
[3] [*diagram*] en corte

sectionalism ['sekʃənəlɪzəm] N faccionalismo *m*

sector ['sektəʳ] N [1] (*Econ, Ind*) sector *m*; **the public ~** el sector público; *see also* **voluntary C**
[2] (*Mil*) sector *m*
[3] (*Geom*) sector *m*

secular ['sekjʊləʳ] ADJ [*authority*] laico; [*writings, music*] profano; [*priest*] secular, seglar; **~ school** escuela *f* laica

secularism ['sekjʊlərɪzəm] N laicismo *m*

secularization [,sekjʊləraɪ'zeɪʃən] N secularización *f*

secularize ['sekjʊləraɪz] VT secularizar

secure [sɪ'kjʊəʳ] Ⓐ ADJ [1] (= *firm, solid*) [*knot, rope, hold*] seguro; [*door, window, lock, bolt*] bien cerrado; [*structure, foothold*] firme; [*ladder*] bien sujeto; [*base, foundation*] sólido; **to have a ~ foothold in a market** tener un punto de apoyo firme en un mercado
[2] (= *safe*) [*job, place, building*] seguro; [*position*] garantizado; [*career, future*] asegurado; **to be ~ against sth** = **to be secure from sth**; **to be financially ~** tener seguridad económica; **to be ~ from sth** estar protegido contra algo; **I want to make my home ~ against burglars** quiero proteger mi casa contra los ladrones; **to make an area ~** hacer de una zona un lugar seguro
[3] (*emotionally*) [*person*] seguro; [*relationship, environment*] estable; **children need a ~ home life** los niños necesitan un ambiente estable en el hogar; **to be emotionally ~** tener estabilidad emocional; **to feel ~ (about sth)** sentirse seguro (con respecto a algo); **to make sb feel ~** hacer a algn sentirse seguro; **~ in the knowledge that** seguro de que, confiado de que
Ⓑ VT [1] (= *make fast*) [+ *rope*] sujetar bien; (*to floor etc*) afianzar; [+ *load*] asegurar; [+ *door, window*] cerrar bien; (= *tie up*) [+ *person, animal*] atar, amarrar (*LAm*); **a shawl ~d at the neck by a brooch** un chal sujeto a la altura del cuello con un broche
[2] (= *make safe*) [+ *home, building*] proteger (**against** de, contra; **from** de, contra); [+ *career, future*] asegurar
[3] (*frm*) (= *obtain*) [+ *job, peace, freedom, support*] conseguir, obtener; **they have not got enough evidence to ~ a conviction** no tienen suficientes pruebas para conseguir que lo condenen; **a win that ~d them a place in the final** una victoria que les aseguró un puesto en la final; **to ~ victory** conseguir la victoria
[4] (*Fin*) [+ *loan, debt*] garantizar; **you can ~ the loan against your home** puedes poner la casa como garantía *or* aval del préstamo; **~d creditor** acreedor(a) *m/f* con garantía; **~d debt** deuda *f* garantizada; **~d loan** préstamo *m* con garantía
[5] (*Mil*) (= *capture*) tomar, capturar
Ⓒ CPD ► **secure accommodation** N (*Brit Jur*) *centro de prevención contra la delincuencia* ► **secure unit** N (*Brit*) (*for young offenders, mental patients*) unidad *f* de seguridad

securely [sɪ'kjʊəlɪ] ADV [1] (= *firmly*) [*fasten, lock, fix, tie*] bien; **it is ~ fastened** está bien abrochado
[2] (= *safely*) firmemente; **he remains ~ in power** permanece firmemente afincado en el poder; **~ established** firmemente establecido

security [sɪ'kjʊərɪtɪ] Ⓐ N [1] (= *precautions*) seguridad *f*; **for ~ reasons** ◊ **for reasons of ~** por razones de seguridad; **the Queen's visit has been marked by tight ~** la visita de la reina se ha visto caracterizada por estrechas medidas de seguridad; *see also* **maximum A**
[2] (= *safety*) [2·1] (*from harm or loss*) seguridad *f*; **the ~ of the passengers on the aircraft** la seguridad de los pasajeros a bordo del avión; **~ of tenure** (*in one's job*) seguridad *f* en el cargo; [*of tenant*] derecho *m* de ocupación (*de un inmueble*); *see also* **job C**, **national C**
[2·2] (*from worry*) seguridad *f*, estabilidad *f*; **emotional/financial ~** estabilidad *f* emocional/económica, seguridad *f* en el plano emocional/económico; *see also* **false A1**
[3] (= *guarantee*) garantía *f*, aval *m*; **to lend money on ~** prestar dinero con un aval *or* bajo fianza; **to stand** *or* **go ~ for sb** salir garante *or* avalista de algn, avalar a algn
[4] **securities** valores *mpl*, títulos *mpl*; **government securities** bonos *mpl* del Estado
Ⓑ CPD ► **security agreement** N (*Fin*) acuer-

➤ LANGUAGE IN USE: secondly 26.2

do *m* de garantía ► **securities market** N (*Fin*) mercado *m* bursátil ► **securities portfolio** N cartera *f* de valores ► **security alarm** N alarma *f* de seguridad ► **security blanket** N (*Psych*) manta *f* de seguridad ► **security check** N control *m* de seguridad ► **Security Council** N Consejo *m* de Seguridad; **the Security Council of the United Nations** el Consejo de Seguridad de las Naciones Unidas ► **security firm** N empresa *f* de seguridad ► **security forces** NPL fuerzas *fpl* de seguridad ► **security guard** N guarda *mf* jurado ► **security leak** N filtración *f* de información secreta ► **security measures** NPL medidas *fpl* de seguridad ► **security officer** N (*Mil, Naut*) oficial *mf* de las fuerzas de seguridad; (*Comm, Ind*) encargado/a *m/f* de seguridad ► **security police** N policía *f* de seguridad ► **security precaution** N precaución *f* ► **security risk** N riesgo *m* para la seguridad ► **security system** N sistema *m* de seguridad ► **security vetting** N acreditación *f* por la Seguridad

Secy. ABBR (= **Secretary**) Sec., Srio., Sria.

sedan [sɪ'dæn] N [1] (*also* ~ **chair**) silla *f* de manos
[2] (*US Aut*) sedán *m*

sedate [sɪ'deɪt] Ⓐ ADJ (*compar* **sedater**; *superl* **sedatest**) serio, formal
Ⓑ VT (*Med*) sedar

sedately [sɪ'deɪtlɪ] ADV seriamente, formalmente

sedateness [sɪ'deɪtnɪs] N seriedad *f*

sedation [sɪ'deɪʃən] N sedación *f*; **under ~** bajo sedación

sedative ['sedətɪv] Ⓐ ADJ sedante
Ⓑ N sedante *m*

sedentary ['sedntrɪ] ADJ sedentario

sedge [sedʒ] N junco *m*, juncia *f*

sediment ['sedɪmənt] N (*in liquids, boiler*) sedimento *m*, poso *m*; (*Geol*) sedimento *m*

sedimentary [ˌsedɪ'mentərɪ] ADJ sedimentario

sedimentation [ˌsedɪmen'teɪʃən] N sedimentación *f*

sedition [sə'dɪʃən] N sedición *f*

seditious [sə'dɪʃəs] ADJ sedicioso

seduce [sɪ'djuːs] VT (*sexually*) seducir; **to ~ sb into doing sth** (*fig*) engatusar *or* convencer a algn para que haga algo; **to ~ sb from his duty** apartar a algn de su deber

seducer [sɪ'djuːsəʳ] N seductor(a) *m/f*

seduction [sɪ'dʌkʃən] N (= *act*) seducción *f*; (= *attraction*) tentación *f*

seductive [sɪ'dʌktɪv] ADJ [*person, voice, clothes, perfume*] seductor; [*smile*] seductor, provocativo; [*offer*] tentador, atractivo

seductively [sɪ'dʌktɪvlɪ] ADV [*smile, behave, look at, dress*] de modo seductor, de manera seductora; [*say*] en tono seductor

seductiveness [sɪ'dʌktɪvnɪs] N [*of person, look, clothes, smile*] seducción *f*; [*of offer*] atractivo *m*

seductress [sɪ'dʌktrɪs] N seductora *f*

sedulous ['sedjʊləs] ADJ asiduo, diligente

sedulously ['sedjʊləslɪ] ADV asiduamente, diligentemente

▼**see**[1] [siː] (*pt* **saw**; *pp* **seen**) VT, VI [1] (*gen*) ver; **I saw him yesterday** lo vi ayer; **I can't ~** no veo nada; **to ~ sb do** *or* **doing sth** ver a algn hacer algo; **I saw him coming** lo vi venir; **(go and) ~ who's at the door** ve a ver quién llama (a la puerta); **he was ~n to fall** se le vio caer; **I saw it done in 1988** lo vi hacer en 1988; **"see page eight"** "véase la página ocho"; **did you ~ that Queen Anne is dead?** ¿has oído que ha muerto la reina Ana?; **he's ~n it all** está de vuelta de todo; **there was nobody to be ~n** no se veía ni nadie; **there was not a house to be ~n** no se veía ni una sola casa; **as you can ~** como ves; **as far as the eye can ~** hasta donde alcanza la vista; **from here you can ~ for miles** desde aquí se ve muy lejos; **I'll ~ him damned first** antes le veré colgado; **I never thought I'd ~ the day when ...** nunca pensé ver el día en que ...; **this car has ~n better days** este coche ha conocido mejores tiempos; **this dress isn't fit to be ~n** este vestido no se puede ver; **he's not fit to be ~n in public** no se le puede presentar a los ojos del público; **~ for yourself** velo tú; **I'll go and ~** voy a ver; **now ~ here!** (*in anger*) ¡mira!, ¡oiga!, ¡escuche!; **I ~ nothing wrong in it** no le encuentro nada malo; **I don't know what she ~s in him** no sé lo que encuentra en él; **I ~ in the paper that ...** sale en el periódico que ...; **let me ~** ◊ **let's ~** (= *show me/us*) a ver; (= *let me/us think*) vamos a ver; **she's certainly ~ing life** es seguro que está viendo muchas cosas; **we'll not ~ his like again** no veremos otro como él; **he's ~n a lot of the world** ha visto mucho mundo; **so I ~** ya lo veo; **I must be ~ing things*** estoy viendo visiones; **I can't ~ to read** no veo lo suficiente para leer; **can you ~ your way to helping us?** (*fig*) ¿nos hace el favor de ayudarnos?; **we'll ~** ya veremos, a ver; **I'll ~ what I can do** veré si puedo hacer algo; **she won't ~ 40 again** los 40 ya no los cumple
[2] (= *visit, meet*) ver, visitar; (= *have an interview with*) tener una entrevista con, entrevistarse con; **the minister saw the Queen yesterday** el ministro se entrevistó *or* tuvo una entrevista con la Reina ayer; **I'm afraid I can't ~ you tomorrow** lamento no poder verle mañana; **I want to ~ you about my daughter** quiero hablar con usted acerca de mi hija; **what did he want to ~ you about?** ¿qué asunto quería discutir contigo?, ¿qué motivo tuvo su visita?; **we'll be ~ing them for dinner** vamos a cenar con ellos; **to ~ the doctor** ir a ver al médico, consultar al médico; **you need to ~ a doctor** tienes que ir a ver *or* consultar a un médico; **to go and ~ sb** ir a ver a algn; (*a friend*) visitar a algn; **we don't ~ much of them nowadays** ahora les vemos bastante poco; **~ you!*** chau*; **~ you on Sunday!** ¡hasta el domingo!; **~ you tomorrow!** ¡hasta mañana!; **~ you later!** ¡hasta luego!; **~ you soon!** ¡hasta pronto!
[3] (= *understand, perceive*) entender; **I ~** lo veo; **I ~!** ya entiendo; **this is how I ~ it** éste es mi modo de entenderlo, yo lo entiendo así; **I saw only too clearly that ...** percibí claramente que ...; **it's all over, ~?*** se acabó, ¿entiendes?; **I can't** *or* **don't ~ why/how** *etc* **...** no veo *or* entiendo por qué/cómo *etc* ...; **I don't ~ it, myself** yo no creo que sea posible; **he's dead, don't you ~?** está muerto, ¿me entiendes?; **the Russians ~ it differently** los rusos lo miran desde otro punto de vista, el criterio de los rusos es distinto; **I fail to ~ how** no comprendo *or* entiendo cómo; **as far as I can ~** por lo visto, por lo que yo veo; **the way I ~ it** a mi parecer
[4] (= *accompany*) acompañar; **he was so drunk we had to ~ him to bed** estaba tan borracho que tuvimos que llevarle a la cama; **to ~ sb to the door** acompañar a algn a la puerta; **to ~ sb home** acompañar a algn a casa; **may I ~ you home?** ¿puedo acompañarte a casa?
[5] (= *try*) procurar; **~ if ...** ve a ver si ..., mira a ver si ...
[6] (= *imagine*) imaginarse; **I can just ~ him as a teacher** me lo imagino de profesor; **I don't ~ her as a minister** no la veo *or* no me la imagino de ministra; **I can't ~ myself doing that** no me imagino con capacidad para hacer eso; **I can't really ~ myself being elected** en realidad no creo que me vayan a elegir; **I can't ~ him winning** me parece imposible que gane
[7] (= *ensure*) **to ~ (to it) that** procurar que + *subjun*; **~ that he has all he needs** procura que tenga todo lo que necesita; **to ~ that sth is done** procurar que algo se haga; **~ that you have it ready for Monday** procura tenerlo listo para el lunes; **~ that it does not happen again** y que no vuelva a ocurrir

►**see about** VI + PREP [1] (= *deal with*) ocuparse de; **I'll ~ about it** yo me ocupo *or* me encargo de eso; **he came to ~ about our TV** vino a ver nuestra televisión
[2] (= *consider*) pensar; **I'll ~ about it** lo veré, lo pensaré; **we'll ~ about that!** ¡eso está por ver!; **we must ~ about getting a new car** tenemos que pensar en comprar un nuevo coche

►**see in** Ⓐ VT + ADV [+ *person*] hacer entrar, hacer pasar; **to ~ the New Year in** celebrar *or* festejar el Año Nuevo
Ⓑ VI + ADV **he was trying to ~ in** se esforzaba por ver el interior

►**see into** VI + PREP (= *study, examine*) investigar, examinar

►**see off** VT + ADV [1] (= *say goodbye to*) despedir, despedirse de; **we went to ~ him off at the station** fuimos a despedirnos de él *or* a despedirlo a la estación
[2] (*) (= *defeat*) vencer; (= *destroy*) acabar con
[3] (*) (= *send away*) **the policeman saw them off** el policía les dijo que se fueran

►**see out** Ⓐ VT + ADV [1] (= *survive*) sobrevivir a; **we wondered if he would ~ the month out** nos preguntábamos si viviría hasta el fin del mes; **to ~ a film out** quedarse hasta el final de una película
[2] (= *take to the door*) acompañar hasta la puerta; **I'll ~ myself out*** no hace falta que me acompañe hasta la puerta
Ⓑ VI + ADV **we shan't be able to ~ out** no podremos ver el exterior

►**see over** VI + PREP recorrer

►**see through** Ⓐ VI + PREP [+ *person, behaviour*] calar; **I can ~ right through him** lo tengo calado; **I saw through him at once** lo calé enseguida, enseguida lo vi venir; **to ~ through a mystery** penetrar un misterio
Ⓑ VT + ADV [+ *project, deal*] llevar a cabo; **don't worry, we'll ~ it through** no te preocupes, nosotros lo llevaremos a cabo; **we'll ~ him through** nosotros le ayudaremos; **£100 should ~ you through** tendrás bastante con 100 libras
Ⓒ VT + PREP **this money should ~ you through your stay in Egypt** este dinero te bastará para tu estancia en Egipto

►**see to** VI + PREP (= *deal with*) atender a; (= *take care of*) ocuparse de, encargase de; **the shower isn't working, can you ~ to it please?** la ducha se ha estropeado ¿podrías ocuparte *or* encargarte de eso?; **please ~ to it that ...** por favor procura que ...; **the rats saw to that** las ratas se encargaron de eso

see[2] [siː] N (*Rel*) sede *f*; [*of archbishop*] arzobispado *m*; [*of bishop*] obispado *m*; **the Holy See** la Santa Sede

seed [siːd] Ⓐ N [1] (*Bot*) [*of plant*] semilla *f*, simiente *f*; (*inside fruit*) pepita *f*; [*of grain*] grano *m*; **poppy ~s** semillas *fpl* de amapola; **to go** *or* **run to ~** (*lit*) granar, dar en grana; (*fig*) ir a

➤ LANGUAGE IN USE: see[1] 3 26.2

menos; **he's really gone to ~** se ha echado a perder, ha ido cada vez a peor; *see also* **sesame B, sunflower B**
[2] (*Sport*) (= *player, team*) cabeza *mf* de serie; **she's the number one ~** es cabeza de serie número uno; **she's the first ~** es la primera cabeza de serie
[3] (*fig*) [*of idea etc*] germen *m*; **to sow ~s of doubt in sb's mind** sembrar la duda en la mente de algn
[4] (*euph*) (= *semen*) simiente *f*; (= *offspring*) descendencia *f*
(B) VT [1] (= *plant with seeds*) sembrar (**with** de)
[2] (= *remove seed of*) [+ *fruits*] despepitar
[3] (*Sport*) clasificar como cabeza de serie; **the US are ~ed number one** Estados Unidos parte como cabeza de serie número uno
(C) VI (*Bot*) (= *form seeds*) granar, dar en grana; (= *shed seeds*) dejar caer semillas
(D) CPD ► **seed box** N caja *f* de simientes, semillero *m* ► **seed corn** N (*lit*) trigo *m* de siembra ► **seed drill** N sembradora *f* ► **seed merchant** N vendedor(a) *m/f* de semillas ► **seed pearl** N aljófar *m* ► **seed pod** N vaina *f* ► **seed potato** N patata *f* or (*LAm*) papa *f* de siembra ► **seed time** N siembra *f* ► **seed tray** N = **seed box**

seedbed ['si:dbed] N semillero *m*

seedcake ['si:dkeɪk] N torta *f* de alcaravea

seedily ['si:dɪlɪ] ADV [*dress*] andrajosamente, desastradamente

seediness ['si:dɪnɪs] N (= *shabbiness*) [*of hotel, nightclub*] sordidez *f*, cutrez *f* (*Sp**); [*of clothes*] lo raído, cutrez *f* (*Sp**); [*of person*] pinta *f* desastrada

seedless ['si:dlɪs] ADJ sin semillas

seedling ['si:dlɪŋ] N planta *f* de semillero

seedsman ['si:dzmən] N (*pl* **seedsmen**) = **seed merchant**

seedy ['si:dɪ] ADJ (*compar* **seedier**, *superl* **seediest**) [1] (= *shabby*) [*hotel, nightclub*] sórdido, de mala muerte*, cutre (*Sp**); [*clothes*] raído, cutre (*Sp**); [*person*] de pinta desastrada; **a ~-looking bar** un bar sórdido, un bar de mala muerte*, un bar cutre (*Sp**)
[2] (= *unwell*) **I'm feeling ~** tengo un poco de mal cuerpo; **he looks a bit ~** tiene mala cara

seeing ['si:ɪŋ] (A) CONJ **~ (that)** visto que, en vista de que
(B) N ✦*PROV* **~ is believing** ver para creer

seeing-eye dog [ˌsi:ɪŋ'aɪdɒg] N (*US*) perro *m* guía

seek [si:k] (*pt, pp* **sought**) (A) VT [1] (= *look for*) [+ *work, refuge*] buscar; [+ *candidate*] solicitar; [+ *honour*] ambicionar; **he has been sought in many countries** se le ha buscado en muchos países; **it is much sought after** está muy cotizado; **to ~ death** buscar la muerte; **the reason is not far to ~** no es difícil indicar la causa; **to ~ shelter (from)** buscar abrigo (de)
[2] (= *ask for*) pedir, solicitar; **to ~ advice from sb** pedir consejo a algn; **the couple sought a second opinion** la pareja quiso tener una segunda opinión
[3] (*frm*) (= *attempt*) **to ~ to do sth** tratar de *or* procurar hacer algo
(B) VI (*frm*) **to ~ after** *or* **for** buscar

►**seek out** VT + ADV buscar

seeker ['si:kəʳ] N buscador(a) *m/f*

▼ **seem** [si:m] VI parecer; **he ~s capable** parece capaz; **he ~ed absorbed in ...** parecía estar absorto en ...; **he ~ed to be in difficulty** parecía tener dificultades; **the shop ~ed to be closed** parecía que la tienda estaba cerrada; **she ~s not to want to go** parece que no quiere ir; **what ~s to be the trouble?** ¿qué pasa?; **I ~ to have heard that before** me parece que ya me contaron eso antes; **it ~s that ...** parece que ...; **it ~s you have no alternative** parece que no te queda otra alternativa; **it ~s she's getting married** por lo visto se casa; **I can't ~ to do it** me parece imposible hacerlo; **that ~s like a good idea** parece una buena idea; **it ~s not** parece que no; **it ~s so** parece que sí; **so it ~s** así parece; **there ~s to be a problem** parece que hay un problema; **there ~s to be a mistake** parece que hay un error; **it ~s to me/him that ...** me/le parece que ...; **how did he ~ to you?** ¿qué te pareció?

seeming ['si:mɪŋ] (A) ADJ aparente
(B) N apariencia *f*

seemingly ['si:mɪŋlɪ] ADV según parece, aparentemente; **it is ~ finished** según parece *or* aparentemente está terminado; **there has ~ been a rise in inflation** parece que ha habido un aumento de la inflación; **"he's left then?" — "~"** —¿o sea que se ha ido? —eso parece

seemliness ['si:mlɪnɪs] N (*frm*) decoro *m*, decencia *f*

seemly ['si:mlɪ] ADJ (*compar* **seemlier**, *superl* **seemliest**) (*frm*) [*behaviour, language, dress*] decoroso, decente

seen [si:n] PP *of* **see**[1]

seep [si:p] VI filtrarse; **to ~ through/into/from** filtrarse *or* colarse por/en/de

►**seep away** VI + ADV escurrirse

►**seep in** VI + ADV filtrarse

►**seep out** VI + ADV escurrirse

seepage ['si:pɪdʒ] N filtración *f*

seer [sɪəʳ] N vidente *mf*

seersucker ['sɪəˌsʌkəʳ] N sirsaca *f*

seesaw ['si:sɔ:] (A) N (= *apparatus, game*) subibaja *m*, balancín *m*
(B) ADJ [*movement*] oscilante, de vaivén; **~ motion** movimiento *m* oscilante *or* de vaivén
(C) VI columpiarse; (*fig*) vacilar

seethe [si:ð] VI [1] (*lit*) borbotear, hervir
[2] (*fig*) **he's seething** está furioso; **to ~ with anger** estar furioso

see-through ['si:θru:] ADJ transparente

segment (A) N ['segmənt] (*gen*) segmento *m*; [*of citrus fruit*] gajo *m*; (*Geom*) [*of circle*] segmento *m*
(B) [seg'ment] VT [+ *circle, society, journey, market*] segmentar; [+ *citrus fruit*] desgajar, separar en gajos
(C) [seg'ment] VI segmentarse

segmentation [ˌsegmən'teɪʃən] N segmentación *f*

segregate ['segrɪgeɪt] VT segregar, separar (**from** de); **to be ~d from** estar separado de

segregated ['segrɪgeɪtɪd] ADJ segregado, separado

segregation [ˌsegrɪ'geɪʃən] N segregación *f*, separación *f*; **racial ~** la segregación racial

segregationist [ˌsegrɪ'geɪʃnɪst] N segregacionista *mf*

Seine [seɪn] N Sena *m*

seine [seɪn] N jábega *f*

seismic ['saɪzmɪk] ADJ (*lit*) sísmico; (*fig*) [*shift, change*] radical

seismograph ['saɪzməgrɑ:f] N sismógrafo *m*

seismography [saɪz'mɒgrəfɪ] N sismografía *f*

seismologist [saɪz'mɒlədʒɪst] N sismólogo/a *m/f*

seismology [saɪz'mɒlədʒɪ] N sismología *f*

seize [si:z] (A) VT [1] (= *physically take hold of*) coger, agarrar; **to ~ hold of sth/sb** coger *or* agarrar algo/a algn; **to ~ sb by the arm** coger *or* agarrar a algn por el brazo
[2] (= *capture*) [+ *person*] detener; [+ *territory*] apoderarse de; [+ *power*] tomar, hacerse con
[3] (*Jur*) (= *confiscate*) [+ *property*] incautar, embargar
[4] (= *kidnap*) secuestrar
[5] (*fig*) [+ *opportunity*] aprovechar; **to be ~d with fear/rage** estar sobrecogido por el miedo/la cólera; **he was ~d with a desire to leave** el deseo de marcharse se apoderó de él
(B) VI *see* **seize up**

►**seize on** VI + PREP = **seize upon**

►**seize up** VI + ADV [*machine, limbs*] agarrotarse

►**seize upon** VI + PREP [+ *chance*] aprovechar; [+ *idea*] fijarse en

seizure ['si:ʒəʳ] N [1] [*of goods*] embargo *m*, incautación *f*; [*of person*] secuestro *m*; [*of land, city, ship*] toma *f* [2] (*Med*) ataque *m*; **to have a ~** sufrir un ataque

seldom ['seldəm] ADV rara vez, pocas veces, casi nunca; **it ~ rains here** aquí rara vez llueve, aquí llueve pocas veces, aquí no llueve casi nunca; **~, if ever** rara vez *or* pocas veces, si es que alguna

select [sɪ'lekt] (A) VT [+ *team, candidate*] seleccionar; [+ *book, gift etc*] escoger, elegir; **~ed works** obras *fpl* escogidas
(B) ADJ [*school, restaurant, club*] selecto, exclusivo; [*tobacco, wine, audience*] selecto; **a ~ group of people** un grupo selecto de personas; **a very ~ neighbourhood** un barrio de muy buen tono; **a ~ few** una minoría privilegiada
(C) CPD ► **select committee** N comité *m* de investigación

selection [sɪ'lekʃən] (A) N [1] (= *act of choosing*) elección *f*
[2] (= *person/thing chosen*) elección *f*, selección *f*; **~s from** (*Mus, Literat*) selecciones de
[3] (= *range, assortment*) surtido *m*, selección *f*; **the widest ~ on the market** el más amplio surtido *or* la más amplia selección del mercado
(B) CPD ► **selection committee** N (*esp Pol*) comisión *f* de nombramiento ► **selection procedure, selection process** N proceso *m* de selección ► **selection test** N prueba *f* de selección

selective [sɪ'lektɪv] ADJ selectivo; **one has to be ~** hay que escoger

selectively [sɪ'lektɪvlɪ] ADV selectivamente

selectivity [sɪlek'tɪvɪtɪ] N selectividad *f*

selector [sɪ'lektəʳ] N (= *person*) seleccionador(a) *m/f*; (*Tech*) selector *m*

selenium [sɪ'li:nɪəm] N selenio *m*

self [self] N (*pl* **selves**) uno/a mismo/a *m/f*; **the ~** el yo; **my better ~** mi lado bueno; **my former ~** el que era; **my true ~** mi verdadero yo; **he's quite his old ~ again** vuelve a ser el que era; **if your good ~ could possibly ...**† (*also hum*) si usted tuviera la suprema amabilidad de ...; **he thinks of nothing but ~** no piensa más que en sí mismo

self- [self] PREFIX auto..., ... de sí mismo

self-abasement [ˌselfə'beɪsmənt] N rebajamiento *m* de sí mismo, autodegradación *f*

self-absorbed [ˌselfəb'zɔ:bd] ADJ ensimismado

self-abuse† [ˌselfə'bju:s] N (*euph*) masturbación *f*

self-acting [ˌself'æktɪŋ] ADJ automático

self-addressed [ˌselfə'drest] ADJ **~ envelope** (*Brit*) ◊ **~ stamped envelope** (*US*) sobre *m* con dirección propia

➤ LANGUAGE IN USE: **seem** 15.2, 16.3

self-adhesive [ˌselfəd'hiːzɪv] ADJ [*envelope, label, tape*] autoadhesivo, autoadherente

self-advertisement [ˌselfəd'vɜːtɪsmənt] N autobombo *m*

self-aggrandizement [ˌselfə'grændɪzmənt] N autobombo *m*

self-analysis [ˌselfə'næləsɪs] N autoanálisis *m*

self-apparent [ˌselfə'pærənt] ADJ evidente, patente

self-appointed [ˌselfə'pɔɪntɪd] ADJ que se ha nombrado a sí mismo

self-appraisal [ˌselfə'preɪzl] N autovaloración *f*

self-assembly [selfə'semblɪ] ADJ [*furniture etc*] automontable

self-assertion [ˌselfə'sɜːʃən] N asertividad *f*

self-assertive [ˌselfə'sɜːtɪv] ADJ asertivo

self-assertiveness [ˌselfə'sɜːtɪvnɪs] N asertividad *f*

self-assessment [ˌselfə'sesmənt] N [1] autoevaluación *f* [2] (*Brit Tax*) autoliquidación *f*

self-assurance [ˌselfə'ʃʊərəns] N confianza *f* en sí mismo

self-assured [ˌselfə'ʃʊəd] ADJ seguro de sí mismo

self-awareness [ˌselfə'wɛənɪs] N conocimiento *m or* conciencia *f* de sí mismo

self-catering [ˌself'keɪtərɪŋ] ADJ **~ apartment** apartamento *m* con acceso a cocina (*p.ej. en unas vacaciones organizadas*); **~ holiday** vacaciones *fpl* en piso *or* chalet *or* casita con cocina propia

self-centred, **self-centered** (*US*) [ˌself'sentəd] ADJ egocéntrico

self-cleaning [ˌself'kliːnɪŋ] ADJ [*oven etc*] autolimpiable

self-closing [ˌself'kləʊzɪŋ] ADJ de cierre automático

self-coloured, **self-colored** (*US*) [ˌself'kʌləd] ADJ de color uniforme, unicolor

self-command [ˌselfkə'mɑːnd] N dominio *m* sobre sí mismo, autodominio *m*

self-complacent [ˌselfkəm'pleɪsənt] ADJ satisfecho de sí mismo

self-composed [ˌselfkəm'pəʊzd] ADJ sereno, dueño de sí mismo

self-composure [ˌselfkəm'pəʊʒəʳ] N serenidad *f*, dominio *m* de sí mismo

self-conceit [ˌselfkən'siːt] N presunción *f*, vanidad *f*, engreimiento *m*

self-conceited [ˌselfkən'siːtɪd] ADJ presumido, vanidoso, engreído

self-confessed [ˌselfkən'fest] ADJ confeso

self-confidence [ˌself'kɒnfɪdəns] N confianza *f* en sí mismo; **I lost all my ~** perdí toda la confianza en mí mismo

self-confident [ˌself'kɒnfɪdənt] ADJ seguro de sí mismo, lleno de confianza en sí mismo

self-congratulation [ˌselfkənˌgrætjʊ'leɪʃən] N autofelicitación *f*

self-conscious [ˌself'kɒnʃəs] ADJ cohibido, tímido; **she was really ~ at first** al principio estaba muy cohibida; **she was ~ about her height** estaba acomplejada por su estatura

self-consciously [ˌself'kɒnʃəslɪ] ADV cohibidamente, tímidamente

self-consciousness [ˌself'kɒnʃəsnɪs] N timidez *f*, inseguridad *f*

self-contained [ˌselfkən'teɪnd] ADJ [*flat*] con entrada propia, independiente; [*person*] autónomo, autosuficiente

self-contradiction [ˌselfkɒntrə'dɪkʃən] N contradicción *f* en sí

self-contradictory [ˌselfkɒntrə'dɪktərɪ] ADJ que se contradice a sí mismo, que lleva implícita una contradicción

self-control [ˌselfkən'trəʊl] N dominio *m* de sí mismo, autocontrol *m*; **to exercise one's ~** contenerse, dominarse; **to lose one's ~** no poder contenerse *or* dominarse

self-controlled [ˌselfkən'trəʊld] ADJ sereno; **she's very ~** tiene mucho autocontrol

self-correcting [ˌselfkə'rektɪŋ] ADJ autocorrector

self-critical [ˌself'krɪtɪkl] ADJ autocrítico

self-criticism [ˌself'krɪtɪsɪzəm] N autocrítica *f*

self-deception [ˌselfdɪ'sepʃən] N engaño *m* de sí mismo; **this is mere ~** esto es engañarse a sí mismo

self-defeating [ˌselfdɪ'fiːtɪŋ] ADJ contraproducente

self-defence, **self-defense** (*US*) [ˌselfdɪ'fens] Ⓐ N autodefensa *f*, defensa *f* propia; **she killed him in ~** lo mató en defensa propia; **to act in ~** obrar en defensa propia
Ⓑ CPD ► **self-defence classes** NPL clases *fpl* de defensa personal

self-delusion [ˌselfdɪ'luːʒən] N autoengaño *m*

self-denial [ˌselfdɪ'naɪəl] N abnegación *f*

self-denying [ˌselfdɪ'naɪɪŋ] ADJ abnegado; **~ ordinance** resolución *f* abnegada

self-destruct [ˌselfdɪs'trʌkt] VI autodestruirse

self-destruction [ˌselfdɪs'trʌkʃən] N suicidio *m*; [*of weapon*] autodestrucción *f*

self-destructive [ˌselfdɪs'trʌktɪv] ADJ autodestructivo

self-determination [ˌselfdɪˌtɜːmɪ'neɪʃən] N autodeterminación *f*

self-determined [ˌselfdɪ'tɜːmɪnd] ADJ autodeterminado

self-discipline [ˌself'dɪsɪplɪn] N autodisciplina *f*

self-disciplined [ˌself'dɪsɪplɪnd] ADJ autodisciplinado

self-doubt [ˌself'daʊt] N desconfianza *f* de sí mismo

self-drive hire [ˌselfdraɪv'haɪəʳ] N (*Brit Aut*) alquiler *m* sin chófer

self-educated [ˌself'edjʊkeɪtɪd] ADJ autodidacta

self-effacement [ˌselfɪ'feɪsmənt] N modestia *f*, humildad *f*

self-effacing [ˌselfɪ'feɪsɪŋ] ADJ modesto, humilde

self-employed [ˌselfɪm'plɔɪd] ADJ autónomo, que trabaja por cuenta propia; **to be ~** ser autónomo, trabajar por cuenta propia; **the ~** los trabajadores autónomos, los que trabajan por cuenta propia

self-employment [ˌselfɪm'plɔɪmənt] N trabajo *m* autónomo, trabajo *m* por cuenta propia

self-esteem [ˌselfɪs'tiːm] N amor *m* propio

self-evident [ˌself'evɪdənt] ADJ manifiesto, patente

self-examination [ˌselfɪgˌzæmɪ'neɪʃən] N autoexamen *m*; (*Rel*) examen *m* de conciencia

self-explanatory [ˌselfɪks'plænɪtərɪ] ADJ que se explica por sí mismo *or* solo

self-expression [ˌselfɪks'preʃən] N autoexpresión *f*

self-filling [ˌself'fɪlɪŋ] ADJ de relleno automático

self-financing [ˌselffaɪ'nænsɪŋ] Ⓐ N autofinanciación *f*, autofinanciamiento *m*
Ⓑ ADJ autofinanciado

self-fulfilling [ˌselffʊl'fɪlɪŋ] ADJ **~ prophecy** profecía *f* que por su propia naturaleza contribuye a cumplirse

self-fulfilment, **self-fulfillment** (*US*) [ˌselffʊl'fɪlmənt] N realización *f* de los más íntimos deseos de uno, realización *f* completa de la potencialidad de uno

self-governing [ˌself'gʌvənɪŋ] ADJ autónomo

self-government [ˌself'gʌvəmənt] N autonomía *f*, autogobierno *m*

self-help [ˌself'help] Ⓐ N autosuficiencia *f*
Ⓑ CPD [*book, method*] de autoayuda ► **self-help group** N grupo *m* de apoyo mutuo

self-image [ˌself'ɪmɪdʒ] N autoimagen *f*, imagen *f* de sí mismo

self-importance [ˌselfɪm'pɔːtəns] N prepotencia *f*

self-important [ˌselfɪm'pɔːtənt] ADJ prepotente

self-imposed [ˌselfɪm'pəʊzd] ADJ [*punishment etc*] autoimpuesto, voluntario

self-improvement [ˌselfɪm'pruːvmənt] N autosuperación *f*

self-induced [ˌselfɪn'djuːst] ADJ autoinducido

self-indulgence [ˌselfɪn'dʌldʒəns] N excesos *mpl* (*en el comer etc*), falta *f* de moderación

self-indulgent [ˌselfɪn'dʌldʒənt] ADJ que se permite excesos

self-inflicted [ˌselfɪn'flɪktɪd] ADJ [*wound*] autoinfligido, infligido a sí mismo

self-interest [ˌself'ɪntrɪst] N interés *m* propio

self-interested [ˌself'ɪntrɪstɪd] ADJ que actúa en interés propio, egoísta

selfish ['selfɪʃ] ADJ egoísta

selfishly ['selfɪʃlɪ] ADV con egoísmo, de modo egoísta

selfishness ['selfɪʃnɪs] N egoísmo *m*

self-justification [ˌselfˌdʒʌstɪfɪ'keɪʃən] N autojustificación *f*

self-knowledge [ˌself'nɒlɪdʒ] N conocimiento *m* de sí mismo

selfless ['selflɪs] ADJ desinteresado

selflessly ['selflɪslɪ] ADV desinteresadamente

selflessness ['selflɪsnɪs] N desinterés *m*

self-loading [ˌself'ləʊdɪŋ] ADJ autocargador, de autocarga

self-locking [ˌself'lɒkɪŋ] ADJ de cierre automático

self-love [ˌself'lʌv] N egoísmo *m*, narcisismo *m*

self-made [ˌself'meɪd] ADJ **~ man** hombre *m* que ha llegado a su posición actual por sus propios esfuerzos, hijo *m* de sus propias obras

self-management [ˌself'mænɪdʒmənt] N autogestión *f*

self-mockery [ˌself'mɒkərɪ] N burla *f* de sí mismo

self-neglect [ˌselfnɪ'glekt] N abandono *m* de sí mismo

self-opinionated [ˌselfə'pɪnjəneɪtɪd] ADJ terco

self-perpetuating [ˌselfpə'petjʊeɪtɪŋ] ADJ que se autoperpetúa

self-pity [ˌself'pɪtɪ] N autocompasión *f*

self-pitying [ˌself'pɪtɪɪŋ] Ⓐ ADJ autocompasivo
Ⓑ N autocompasión *f*

self-pollination [ˌselfpɒlɪ'neɪʃən] N autopolinización *f*

self-portrait [ˌself'pɔːtrɪt] N autorretrato *m*

self-possessed [ˌselfpə'zest] ADJ sereno, dueño de sí mismo

self-possession [ˌselfpə'zeʃən] N serenidad *f*, autodominio *m*

self-praise [ˌself'preɪz] N autobombo *m*

self-preservation [ˌselfprezə'veɪʃən] N autopreservación *f*, propia conservación *f*

self-proclaimed [ˌselfprə'kleɪmd] ADJ autoproclamado

self-propelled [ˌselfprə'peld] ADJ autopropulsado, automotor (*fem: automotriz*)

self-raising flour ['self,reɪzɪŋ'flaʊəʳ] N (*Brit*) harina *f* con levadura *or* (*Andes, S. Cone*) leudante

self-regard [,selfrɪ'gɑːd] N amor *m* propio; (*pej*) egoísmo *m*

self-regulating [,self'regjʊleɪtɪŋ] ADJ de regulación automática

self-regulation [,selfregjʊ'leɪʃən] N autorregulación *f*

self-regulatory [,self'regjʊlətərɪ] ADJ autorregulado

self-reliance [,selfrɪ'laɪəns] N independencia *f*, autosuficiencia *f*

self-reliant [,selfrɪ'laɪənt] ADJ independiente, autosuficiente

self-reproach [,selfrɪ'prəʊtʃ] N remordimiento *m*

self-respect [,selfrɪs'pekt] N amor *m* propio

self-respecting [,selfrɪs'pektɪŋ] ADJ que tiene amor propio

self-restraint [,selfrɪs'treɪnt] N = **self-control**

self-righteous [,self'raɪtʃəs] ADJ santurrón, farisaico, creído (*LAm*)

self-righteousness [,self'raɪtʃəsnɪs] N santurronería *f*, farisaísmo *m*

self-rising flour ['self,raɪzɪŋ'flaʊəʳ] N (*US*) = **self-raising flour**

self-rule [,self'ruːl] N autonomía *f*

self-sacrifice [,self'sækrɪfaɪs] N abnegación *f*

self-sacrificing [,self'sækrɪfaɪsɪŋ] ADJ abnegado

self-same ['selfseɪm] ADJ mismo, mismísimo

self-satisfaction [,selfsætɪs'fækʃən] N satisfacción *f* de sí mismo

self-satisfied [,self'sætɪsfaɪd] ADJ satisfecho de sí mismo

self-sealing [,self'siːlɪŋ] ADJ [*envelope*] autoadhesivo, autopegado

self-seeking [,self'siːkɪŋ] Ⓐ ADJ egoísta
Ⓑ N egoísmo *m*

self-service [,self'sɜːvɪs] Ⓐ ADJ de autoservicio
Ⓑ CPD ► **self-service laundry** N lavandería *f* de autoservicio ► **self-service restaurant** N autoservicio *m*, self-service *m*

self-serving [,self'sɜːvɪŋ] ADJ egoísta, interesado

self-starter [,self'stɑːtəʳ] N 1 (*Aut*) arranque *m* automático
2 (*Comm etc*) persona *f* dinámica

self-study [self'stʌdɪ] Ⓐ N autoaprendizaje *m*, autoestudio *m*
Ⓑ CPD ► **self-study course** N curso *m* de autoaprendizaje *or* autoestudio

self-styled [,self'staɪld] ADJ supuesto, sedicente

self-sufficiency [,selfsə'fɪʃənsɪ] N [*of person*] independencia *f*, confianza *f* en sí mismo; (*economic*) autosuficiencia *f*

self-sufficient [,selfsə'fɪʃənt] ADJ [*person*] independiente, seguro de sí mismo; (*economically*) autosuficiente

self-supporting [,selfsə'pɔːtɪŋ] ADJ económicamente independiente

self-taught [,self'tɔːt] ADJ autodidacta

self-test [,self'test] N (*Comput*) Ⓐ N autocomprobación *f* Ⓑ VI autocomprobarse

self-willed [,self'wɪld] ADJ terco, voluntarioso

self-winding watch ['self,waɪndɪŋ'wɒtʃ] N reloj *m* de cuerda automática

sell [sel] (*pt, pp* **sold**) Ⓐ VT vender; **do you ~ flowers?** ¿vende flores?; **to ~ sth to sb** vender algo a algn; **he sold it to me** me lo vendió; **I was sold this in London** me vendieron esto en Londres; **you've been sold*** (*fig*) te han dado gato por liebre; **to ~ sth for £1** vender algo por una libra; **he doesn't ~ himself very well** no es capaz de causar buena impresión, no convence mucho; **to ~ sb an idea** (*fig*) convencer a algn de una idea; **to be sold on sth/sb*** estar cautivado por algo/algn; **I'm not exactly sold on the idea** no me entusiasma la idea, para mí la idea deja mucho que desear; **to ~ sb into slavery** vender a algn como esclavo; ✦**IDIOM to ~ sb down the river** traicionar a algn
Ⓑ VI 1 [*merchandise*] venderse; **these ~ at 15p** éstos se venden a 15 peniques; **this line just isn't ~ing** esta línea no tiene demanda; **it ~s well** se vende bien; **the idea didn't ~** (*fig*) la idea no convenció
2 (= *person*) **the owner seemed a bit reluctant to ~** parecía que el dueño estaba un poco reacio a vender
Ⓒ N (*Comm*) *see* **hard C**, **soft B**

►**sell back** VT + ADV **to ~ sth back to sb** revender algo a algn

►**sell off** VT + ADV [+ *stocks and shares*] vender; [+ *goods*] liquidar

►**sell out** Ⓐ VI + ADV 1 [*tickets, goods*] agotarse; **the tickets sold out in three hours** las entradas se agotaron en tres horas; **football matches often ~ out in advance** en los partidos de fútbol a menudo se venden todas las entradas antes del partido; **"could I buy some sun cream?" — "sorry, we've sold out"** —¿me puede dar bronceador? —lo siento, no nos queda; **to ~ out of sth** vender todas las existencias de algo; **we've sold out of bananas** no nos quedan plátanos, hemos agotado las existencias de plátanos
2 (*fig*) claudicar, venderse, transar (*LAm*)
3 (*US*) = **sell up A**
Ⓑ VT + ADV 1 [+ *goods*] agotar las existencias de, venderlo todo; **the tickets are all sold out** los billetes están agotados; **stocks of umbrellas are sold out** las existencias de paraguas están agotadas; **we are sold out of bread** se terminó el pan, no nos queda pan
2 [+ *person*] traicionar; [+ *compromise*] transigir, transar (*LAm*)

►**sell up** Ⓐ VI + ADV (*esp Brit*) liquidarse, venderlo todo Ⓑ VT + ADV vender

sell-by date ['selbaɪ,deɪt] N fecha *f* de caducidad

seller ['seləʳ] N 1 (= *person who sells*) vendedor(a) *m/f*; (= *dealer*) comerciante *mf* (**of** en); **~'s market** mercado *m* favorable al vendedor
2 (= *item*) **a good ~** un artículo que se vende bien

selling ['selɪŋ] Ⓐ N venta *f*, el vender; **a career in ~** una carrera en ventas
Ⓑ CPD ► **selling point** N punto *m* fuerte ► **selling price** N precio *m* de venta *or* (*LAm*) de menudeo ► **selling rate** N (*Fin*) precio *m* de venta medio

selloff ['selɒf] N (*Econ*) liquidación *f*, venta *f*; [*of public company*] privatización *f*

Sellotape® ['seləʊteɪp] Ⓐ N cinta *f* adhesiva, celo *m*, Scotch® *m* (*esp LAm*), Durex® *m* (*LAm*) Ⓑ VT pegar con cinta adhesiva *etc*

sellout ['selaʊt] N 1 (*Theat*) lleno *m*, éxito *m* de taquilla
2 (= *betrayal*) claudicación *f*, traición *f*

seltzer water ['seltsə,wɔːtəʳ] N agua *f* de seltz

selvage, selvedge ['selvɪdʒ] N (*Sew*) orillo *m*, bordo *m*

selves [selvz] NPL *of* **self**

semantic [sɪ'mæntɪk] ADJ semántico

semantically [sɪ'mæntɪkəlɪ] ADV semánticamente

semanticist [sɪ'mæntɪsɪst] N semasiólogo/a *m/f*, semantista *mf*

semantics [sɪ'mæntɪks] NSING semántica *f*

semaphore ['seməfɔːʳ] Ⓐ N semáforo *m*
Ⓑ VT comunicar por semáforo

semblance ['sembləns] N apariencia *f*; **when they have restored the country to some ~ of order** cuando hayan devuelto al país cierta apariencia de normalidad; **without a ~ of regret** sin mostrar ningún remordimiento; **without a ~ of fear** sin dar señal alguna de miedo; **to put on a ~ of sorrow** procurar mostrarse *or* parecer triste

seme [siːm] N sema *m*

semen ['siːmən] N semen *m*

semester [sɪ'mestəʳ] N (*esp US*) semestre *m*

semi* ['semɪ] N 1 (*Brit*) (*also* **~-detached house**) casa *f* con una pared medianera
2 = **semi-final**
3 (*US*) (*also* **~-trailer**) trailer *m*

semi... ['semɪ] PREFIX semi..., medio...

semi-automatic [,semɪ,ɔːtə'mætɪk] Ⓐ ADJ semiautomático Ⓑ N arma *f* semiautomática

semi-basement ['semɪ'beɪsmənt] N semisótano *m*

semibreve ['semɪbriːv] N (*Brit*) semibreve *f*

semicircle ['semɪ,sɜːkl] N semicírculo *m*

semicircular ['semɪ'sɜːkjʊləʳ] ADJ semicircular

semi-colon ['semɪ'kəʊlən] N punto y coma *m*

semiconductor [,semɪkən'dʌktəʳ] N semiconductor *m*

semi-conscious ['semɪ'kɒnʃəs] ADJ semiconsciente

semi-consonant ['semɪ'kɒnsənənt] N semiconsonante *f*

semi-darkness ['semɪ'dɑːknɪs] N **in the semi-darkness** en la casi oscuridad

semi-detached ['semɪdɪ'tætʃt] Ⓐ ADJ **~ house** (*Brit*) casa *f* con una pared medianera
Ⓑ N = **semi-detached house**

semi-final ['semɪ'faɪnl] N semifinal *f*; **they went out in the ~s** los eliminaron en las semifinales

semi-finalist ['semɪ'faɪnəlɪst] N semifinalista *mf*

semi-finished [,semɪ'fɪnɪʃt] ADJ [*product*] semiacabado, semielaborado

semi-literate [,semɪ'lɪtərɪt] ADJ semialfabetizado

seminal ['semɪnl] ADJ 1 (*Physiol*) [*fluid, liquid*] seminal
2 (*fig*) [*idea, work, event, study*] seminal

seminar ['semɪnɑːʳ] N (*Univ*) (= *class*) clase *f*, seminario *m*; (= *conference*) congreso *m*

seminarian [,semɪ'neərɪən] N, **seminarist** ['semɪnərɪst] N seminarista *m*

seminary ['semɪnərɪ] N seminario *m*

semi-official ['semɪə'fɪʃəl] ADJ semioficial

semiology [,semɪ'ɒlədʒɪ] N semiología *f*

semiotic [,semɪ'ɒtɪk] ADJ semiótico

semiotics [,semɪ'ɒtɪks] NSING semiótica *f*

semi-precious ['semɪ,preʃəs] ADJ semiprecioso; **semiprecious stone** piedra *f* semipreciosa

semi-quaver ['semɪ,kweɪvəʳ] N (*Brit*) semicorchea *f*

semi-skilled ['semɪ'skɪld] ADJ semicalificado, semicualificado (*Sp*); [*work*] para persona semicalificada *or* (*Sp*) semicualificada

semi-skimmed milk [,semɪskɪmd'mɪlk] N leche *f* semidesnatada, leche *f* semidescremada (*LAm*)

Semite ['siːmaɪt] N semita *mf*

Semitic [sɪ'mɪtɪk] ADJ semítico

semitone ['semɪtəʊn] N semitono *m*

semi-trailer ['semɪ'treɪləʳ] N (*US*) trailer *m*

semi-vowel ['semɪ'vaʊəl] N semivocal *f*

semolina [ˌseməˈliːnə] N sémola *f*

sempiternal [ˌsempɪˈtɜːnl] ADJ sempiterno

sempstress [ˈsempstrɪs] N costurera *f*

SEN N ABBR (*Brit*) (*formerly*) = **State-Enrolled Nurse**

Sen. ABBR 1 = **Senior**
2 (*US Pol*) = **Senator**
3 (*US Pol*) = **Senate**

sen. ABBR = **senior**

senate [ˈsenɪt] N 1 (*Pol*) senado *m*; **the Senate** (*US*) el Senado; → CABINET, CONGRESS
2 (*Univ*) consejo *m* universitario

senator [ˈsenɪtəʳ] N (*Pol*) senador(a) *m/f*; → CONGRESS

senatorial [ˌsenəˈtɔːrɪəl] ADJ senatorial

send [send] (*pt, pp* **sent**) Ⓐ VT 1 (= *dispatch*) [+ *letter, parcel, money, telegram*] mandar, enviar; **please ~ me further details** ruego me mande *or* me envíe más detalles; **I wrote the letter but didn't ~ it** escribí la carta pero no la eché al correo; **Jan ~s her apologies** Jan pide que la disculpen *or* excusen; **I had some flowers sent to her** le mandé *or* envié unas flores; **to ~ sb one's love** mandar recuerdos a algn; **he sent word that he wished to discuss peace** avisó *or* (*LAm*) mandó (a) decir que quería hablar de hacer las paces; ✦*PROV* **these things are sent to try us** esto es que Dios *or* el Señor nos pone a prueba
2 (= *cause to go*) [+ *person*] mandar; [+ *troops*] mandar, enviar; **they sent him here to help** lo mandaron para que nos ayudara, lo mandaron a ayudarnos; **to ~ a child to bed/to school** mandar a un niño a la cama/a la escuela; **to ~ sb for sth: I sent her for some bread** la mandé a comprar pan *or* (*Sp*) a por pan; **they sent me for an X-ray** me mandaron a hacerme una radiografía; **to ~ sb home** mandar a algn a casa; (*from abroad*) repatriar a algn; **to ~ sb to prison** mandar a algn a la cárcel; **he was sent to prison for seven years** fue condenado a siete años de cárcel; ✦*IDIOMS* **to ~ sb to Coventry** hacer el vacío a algn; **to ~ sb packing** mandar a algn a freír espárragos*
3 (= *convey*) [+ *signal*] enviar, mandar
4 (= *propel*) **he sent the ball into the back of the net** lanzó *or* mandó el balón al fondo de la red; **the blow sent him sprawling** el golpe lo tumbó; **it has sent prices through the roof** ha hecho que los precios se pongan por las nubes *or* se disparen; **to ~ sth/sb flying** mandar algo/a algn volando por los aires; *see also* **shiver¹ A**
5 (= *drive*) **their music sent the fans wild** su música volvía locos a los fans; **my attempt sent him into fits of laughter** le entró un ataque de risa al ver cómo lo intentaba; **the rain sent us indoors** la lluvia nos obligó a meternos en casa; **the sight sent her running to her mother** lo que vio la hizo ir corriendo a su madre; **his lessons used to ~ me to sleep** me solía quedar dormido en sus clases
6 (*) (= *enthral*) **that tune ~s me** esa melodía me chifla*; **he ~s me** me vuelve loca
Ⓑ VI **she sent to say that …** mandó *or* envió un recado diciendo que …, mandó (a) decir que … (*LAm*); **we shall have to ~ to France for reinforcements** tendremos que pedir *or* (*LAm*) mandar a pedir refuerzos a Francia

►**send away** Ⓐ VI + ADV **to ~ away for sth** escribir pidiendo algo, pedir algo por correo
Ⓑ VT + ADV 1 [+ *person*] (= *dismiss*) despachar; (= *send to another place*) mandar; **I ordered the servants to ~ him away** ordené a los criados que lo despacharan; **I was sent away to boarding school at 13** me mandaron a un internado a los 13 años; **please don't ~ me away again** por favor no me vuelvas a pedir que me vaya; *see also* **flea A**
2 [+ *goods*] mandar, enviar; **it will have to be sent away to be repaired** habrá que mandarlo *or* enviarlo a que lo arreglen

►**send back** VT + ADV [+ *person*] hacer volver, hacer regresar; [+ *goods*] mandar de vuelta, devolver; [+ *ball*] devolver

►**send down** VT + ADV 1 (= *cause to go down*) [+ *prices*] provocar la bajada de, hacer bajar; [+ *diver*] mandar, enviar
2 (*Brit Univ*) (= *expel*) expulsar
3 (*) (= *imprison*) meter en la cárcel; **he was sent down for two years** lo condenaron a dos años de cárcel

►**send for** VI + PREP 1 [+ *person*] mandar a buscar, mandar llamar; **the manager sent for me** el jefe mandó a buscarme *or* me mandó llamar
2 [+ *catalogue, information*] escribir pidiendo, pedir por correo

►**send forth** VT + ADV (*liter*) [+ *smoke etc*] emitir, arrojar; [+ *sparks*] lanzar; **to ~ sb forth into the world** enviar a algn a vivir en el mundo

►**send in** VT + ADV [+ *report, application, competition entry*] mandar, enviar; [+ *resignation*] presentar; [+ *troops, reinforcements*] enviar, mandar; [+ *visitor*] hacer pasar; **~ him in!** ¡que pase!

►**send off** Ⓐ VI + ADV = **send away A**
Ⓑ VT + ADV 1 [+ *letter, parcel*] mandar, enviar; [+ *goods*] despachar, expedir
2 [+ *person*] mandar; (= *say goodbye to*) despedir; **they sent the children off to play** mandaron a los niños a jugar
3 (*Sport*) [+ *player*] expulsar; **he got sent off for swearing** lo expulsaron por decir palabrotas

►**send on** VT + ADV 1 [+ *letter*] remitir, reexpedir; [+ *luggage, document, report*] remitir; [+ *person*] mandar; **an advance guard was sent on ahead with the news** mandaron a una avanzadilla por delante con la noticia
2 (*Sport*) [+ *substitute*] mandar a jugar

►**send out** Ⓐ VI + ADV **to ~ out for sth: we sent out for sandwiches** mandamos a alguien a traer *or* (*Sp*) a por unos sándwiches
Ⓑ VT + ADV 1 (= *dispatch*) [+ *invitations, circulars, scout, envoy*] mandar, enviar; [+ *person*] (*on errand*) mandar; **I sent him out to get a paper** lo mandé a comprar un periódico
2 (= *dismiss*) echar; **she was sent out for talking** la echaron (de clase) por hablar
3 (= *emit*) [+ *smoke*] despedir; [+ *signal*] emitir; (*Bot*) [+ *shoot*] echar

►**send round** VT + ADV (= *dispatch*) [+ *item*] mandar, enviar; [+ *person*] mandar; **can you ~ someone round to fix it?** ¿puede mandar a alguien a arreglarlo *or* para que lo arregle?; **we'll ~ a car round to pick you up** mandaremos un coche a recogerlo; **I'll have it sent round to you** haré que te lo manden *or* envíen

►**send up** VT + ADV 1 (= *cause to rise*) [+ *rocket, balloon,*] lanzar; [+ *smoke, dust, spray*] despedir; [+ *prices*] provocar la subida de, hacer subir
2 (= *dispatch*) **~ him up!** ¡que suba!; **I'll have some coffee sent up** mandaré *or* pediré que me suban café
3 (*Brit**) (= *parody*) burlarse de, parodiar
4 (= *blow up*) volar

➤ LANGUAGE IN USE: **send A1** 20.1, 20.3, 21.1, 21.3

sender [ˈsendəʳ] N 1 (*Post*) remitente *mf*
2 (*Elec*) transmisor *m*

sending-off [ˌsendɪŋˈɒf] N (*Sport*) expulsión *f*

send-off [ˈsendɒf] N despedida *f*; **they gave him a rousing ~** le hicieron una gran despedida

send-up* [ˈsendʌp] N (*Brit*) parodia *f*

Seneca [ˈsenɪkə] N Séneca

Senegal [ˌsenɪˈɡɔːl] N el Senegal

Senegalese [ˈsenɪɡəˈliːz] Ⓐ ADJ senegalés
Ⓑ N senegalés/esa *m/f*

senile [ˈsiːnaɪl] Ⓐ ADJ senil; **to go ~** empezar a chochear; **to have gone ~** padecer debilidad senil
Ⓑ CPD ► **senile dementia** N demencia *f* senil

senility [sɪˈnɪlɪtɪ] N senilidad *f*

senior [ˈsiːnɪəʳ] Ⓐ ADJ 1 (*in age*) mayor; **he is ~ to me by five years** (*frm*) es cinco años mayor que yo, tiene cinco años más que yo; **Douglas Fairbanks Senior** Douglas Fairbanks padre; **~ pupils** los alumnos de los cursos más avanzados
2 (*in rank*) [*position, rank*] superior; [*partner, executive, officer*] mayoritario; (*in length of service*) de más antigüedad; **he is ~ to me in the firm** es mi superior en la compañía; **~ management** los altos directivos
Ⓑ N 1 (*in age*) mayor *mf*; **he is my ~** es mayor que yo; **he's my ~ by two years** es dos años mayor que yo, tiene dos años más que yo
2 (*in rank*) superior *mf*, socio/a *m/f* más antiguo/a; **he's my ~** es mi superior
3 (*Scol*) alumno/a *m/f* de los cursos más avanzados; (*US*) estudiante *mf* del último año; → GRADE
4 (*US*) = **senior citizen**
Ⓒ CPD ► **senior citizen** N jubilado/a *m/f*, persona *f* de la tercera edad ► **senior high school** N (*US*) ≈ instituto *m* de enseñanza superior (*Sp*), ≈ preparatoria *f* (*Mex*) ► **senior partner** N socio/a *m/f* mayoritario/a ► **senior school** N instituto *m* de enseñanza secundaria ► **the Senior Service** N (*Brit*) la marina

seniority [ˌsiːnɪˈɒrɪtɪ] N antigüedad *f*

senna [ˈsenə] N sena *f*

sensation [senˈseɪʃən] N 1 (= *feeling*) sensación *f*; **to have a dizzy ~** tener (una) sensación de mareo; **to lose all ~ in one's arm** perder la sensibilidad en el brazo
2 (= *impression*) sensación *f*; **to have the ~ of doing sth** tener la sensación de estar haciendo algo; **I had the ~ that I was being watched** tenía la sensación de que me estaban observando
3 (= *excitement, success*) sensación *f*; **to be a ~** ser un éxito; **it was a ~ in New York** en Nueva York causó sensación; **to cause** *or* **create a ~** causar sensación

sensational [senˈseɪʃənl] ADJ 1 [*event*] sensacional; [*fashion*] que causa sensación; **~ murder** espectacular asesinato *m*
2 [*film, novel, newspaper*] sensacionalista; **he gave a ~ account of the accident** hizo un relato sensacionalista del accidente
3 (*) (= *marvellous*) sensacional, fantástico

sensationalism [senˈseɪʃnəlɪzəm] N sensacionalismo *m*

sensationalist [senˈseɪʃnəlɪst] Ⓐ ADJ sensacionalista
Ⓑ N sensacionalista *mf*

sensationalize [senˈseɪʃnəlaɪz] VT sensacionalizar, presentar en términos sensacionales

sensationally [senˈseɪʃnəlɪ] ADV [*report, describe*] sensacionalmente; **it was ~ successful**

tuvo un éxito sensacional; **it was ~ popular** era increíblemente popular

sense [sens] Ⓐ N [1] (*bodily*) sentido *m*; **~ of hearing/smell/taste/touch** sentido *m* del oído/olfato/gusto/tacto; **~ of sight** sentido *m* de la vista; **to have a keen ~ of smell** tener un (sentido del) olfato muy agudo; **sixth ~** sexto sentido
[2] (= *feeling*) sensación *f*; **I was overcome by a ~ of failure** me invadió una sensación de fracaso; **I felt a terrible ~ of guilt** me invadió un tremendo sentimiento de culpa *or* culpabilidad; **I felt a terrible ~ of loss** sentí un tremendo vacío; **have you no ~ of shame?** ¿es que no tienes vergüenza?; **there is a ~ of space in his paintings** sus cuadros transmiten una sensación de espacio; **I lost all ~ of time** perdí la noción del tiempo
[3] (= *good judgement*) sentido *m* común; **she has more ~ than to go out on her own** tiene el suficiente sentido común como para no salir sola; **I thought you would have had more ~** pensé que eras más sensato *or* tenías más sentido común; **he has more money than ~** le sobra dinero pero le falta sentido común; **he had the ~ to call the doctor** tuvo bastante sentido común como para llamar al médico; **to make sb see ~** hacer que algn entre en razón; **to talk ~** hablar con sentido común, hablar con juicio
[4] **to make ~** (= *be advisable*) ser conveniente; (= *be comprehensible, logical*) tener sentido; **it makes ~ to eat a balanced diet** es conveniente llevar una dieta equilibrada; **it makes ~ to me** a mí me parece lógico; **it doesn't make ~** *or* **it makes no ~** no tiene sentido; **to make ~ of sth**: **I could make no ~ of what he was saying** no entendía nada de lo que decía, no podía sacar nada en claro de lo que decía
[5] (= *point, use*) sentido *m*; **what's the ~ of having another meeting?** ¿qué sentido tiene celebrar otra reunión?; **there's no ~ in making people unhappy** no tiene sentido disgustar a la gente
[6] **senses** (= *sanity*) **I hope this warning will bring him to his ~s** espero que esta advertencia le haga entrar en razón; **to come to one's ~s** entrar en razón; **no-one in his right ~s would do that** nadie (que esté) en su sano juicio haría eso; **have you taken leave of your ~s?** ¿has perdido el juicio?
[7] (= *meaning*) (*gen*) sentido *m*; (*in dictionary*) acepción *f*, significado *m*; **it has several ~s** tiene varias acepciones *or* varios significados; **in what ~ are you using the word?** ¿qué significado le das a la palabra?; **in a ~** en cierto modo; **in every ~ (of the word)** en todos los sentidos (de la palabra); **in the full ~ of that word** en toda la extensión de la palabra; **in no ~ can it be said that ...** de ninguna manera se puede decir que ...; **in one ~** en cierto modo; **in the strict/true ~ of the word** en el sentido estricto/en el verdadero sentido de la palabra
[8] (= *awareness*) sentido *m*; **she has very good business ~** tiene muy buen ojo para los negocios; **~ of direction** sentido *m* de la orientación; **she has a strong ~ of duty** tiene un arraigado sentido del deber; **~ of humour** sentido *m* del humor; **they have an exaggerated ~ of their own importance** se creen bastante más importantes de lo que son; **where's your ~ of occasion?** tienes que estar a la altura de las circunstancias *or* la ocasión; **we must keep a ~ of proportion about this** no debemos darle a esto más importancia de la que tiene; **one must have some ~ of right and wrong** uno tiene que tener cierta noción de lo que está bien y lo que está mal; **~ of self** (señas *fpl* de) identidad *f*; **he has no ~ of timing** es de lo más inoportuno; **she needs to regain a ~ of her own worth** necesita recuperar la confianza en sí misma
[9] (= *opinion*) opinión *f*; **what is your ~ of the mood of the electorate?** ¿qué opinión le merece el clima que se respira entre el electorado?
Ⓑ VT [1] (= *suspect, intuit*) presentir; **he looked about him, sensing danger** miró a su alrededor, presintiendo peligro; **to ~ that** notar que; **he ~d that he wasn't wanted** notó que estaba de más
[2] (= *be conscious of*) percibir; **the horse can ~ your fear** el caballo percibe si tienes miedo
[3] (= *realize*) darse cuenta de
Ⓒ CPD ► **sense organ** N órgano *m* sensorial

senseless ['senslɪs] ADJ [1] [*waste, violence etc*] sin sentido; **it is ~ to protest** no tiene sentido protestar
[2] (= *unconscious*) sin sentido, inconsciente; **he was lying ~ on the floor** yacía sin sentido *or* inconsciente en el suelo; **to knock sb ~** derribar a algn y dejarle sin sentido; **he fell ~ to the floor** cayó al suelo sin sentido

senselessly ['senslɪslɪ] ADV sin sentido

senselessness ['senslɪsnɪs] N falta *f* de sentido

sensibility [,sensɪ'bɪlɪtɪ] N [1] sensibilidad *f* (**to** a)
[2] **sensibilities** susceptibilidad *fsing*

sensible ['sensəbl] ADJ [1] (= *having good sense*) sensato; **she's a very ~ girl** es una chica muy sensata; **be ~!** ¡sé sensato!; **it would be ~ to check first** lo más sensato sería comprobarlo antes
[2] (= *reasonable*) [*act*] prudente; [*decision, choice*] lógico; [*clothing, shoes*] práctico; **that is very ~ of you** en eso haces muy bien, me parece muy lógico; **try to be ~ about it** procura ser razonable
[3] (†) (= *appreciable*) apreciable, perceptible
[4] (†) (= *aware*) **to be ~ of** ser consciente de, darse cuenta de; **I am ~ of the honour you do me** soy consciente del honor que se me hace

sensibleness ['sensəblnɪs] N [1] (= *good sense*) sensatez *f*
[2] (= *reasonableness*) [*of actions*] prudencia *f*; [*of decision, choice*] lógica *f*; [*of clothing*] lo práctico

sensibly ['sensəblɪ] ADV (= *carefully*) con sensatez; (= *wisely*) prudentemente; **she acted very ~** obró muy prudentemente; **he ~ answered that ...** contestó con tino que ...; **try to behave ~** intenta comportarte como es debido

sensitive ['sensɪtɪv] ADJ [1] (= *emotionally aware, responsive*) [*person*] sensible; [*story, novel, film*] lleno de sensibilidad; **to be ~ to sth** ser sensible a algo, ser consciente de algo
[2] (= *touchy*) [*person*] susceptible; **to be ~ about sth: young people are very ~ about their appearance** a los jóvenes les preocupa mucho su aspecto; **he is deeply ~ to criticism** es muy susceptible a las críticas
[3] (= *delicate*) [*issue, subject*] delicado; [*region, area*] conflictivo; **this is politically very ~** esto es muy conflictivo *or* muy delicado desde el punto de vista político
[4] (= *confidential*) [*document, report, information*] confidencial
[5] (= *easily affected*) [*skin*] delicado, sensible; [*teeth*] sensible
[6] (= *highly responsive*) [*instrument*] sensible; (*Phot*) [*paper, film*] sensible; (*Fin*) [*market*] volátil; **to be ~ to light/heat** ser sensible a la luz/al calor

sensitively ['sensɪtɪvlɪ] ADV (= *sympathetically*) con sensibilidad

sensitiveness ['sensɪtɪvnɪs] N *see* **sensitivity**

sensitivity [,sensɪ'tɪvɪtɪ] N [1] (= *emotional awareness*) sensibilidad *f* (**to** a)
[2] (= *touchiness*) susceptibilidad *f* (**to** a)
[3] (= *delicate nature*) [*of issue, subject*] lo delicado
[4] (= *confidentiality*) [*of document, information*] carácter *m* confidencial, confidencialidad *f*
[5] [*of skin, teeth*] sensibilidad *f* (**to** a)
[6] (= *responsiveness*) [*of instrument, film*] sensibilidad *f*

sensitize ['sensɪtaɪz] VT sensibilizar

sensitized ['sensɪtaɪzd] ADJ sensibilizado

sensor ['sensə^r] N sensor *m*

sensory ['sensərɪ] Ⓐ ADJ sensorial, sensorio
Ⓑ CPD ► **sensory deprivation** N aislamiento *m* sensorial

sensual ['sensjʊəl] ADJ sensual

sensualism ['sensjʊəlɪzəm] N sensualismo *m*

sensualist ['sensjʊəlɪst] N sensualista *mf*

sensuality [,sensjʊ'ælɪtɪ] N sensualidad *f*

sensually ['sensjʊəlɪ] ADV sensualmente

sensuous ['sensjʊəs] ADJ sensual, sensorio

sensuousness ['sensjʊəsnɪs] N sensualidad *f*

sent [sent] PT, PP *of* **send**

sentence ['sentəns] Ⓐ N [1] (*Ling*) frase *f*, oración *f*; **he writes very long ~s** escribe frases *or* oraciones larguísimas; **what does this ~ mean?** ¿qué significa esta frase *or* oración?
[2] (*Jur*) sentencia *f*, fallo *m*; **a ~ of ten years** una condena de diez años; **the judge gave him a six-month ~** el juez le condenó a seis meses de prisión; **the death ~** la pena de muerte; **under ~ of death** condenado a la pena de muerte; **he got a life ~** fue condenado a cadena perpetua; **a long ~** una larga condena; **to pass ~ on sb** (*lit, fig*) condenar a algn (a una pena); **he got a five-year prison ~** se le condenó a cinco años de prisión; **to serve one's ~** cumplir su condena
Ⓑ VT condenar (**to** a); **to ~ sb to life imprisonment** condenar a algn a cadena perpetua; **to ~ sb to death** condenar a muerte a algn
Ⓒ CPD ► **sentence structure** N estructura *f* de la frase

sententious [sen'tenʃəs] ADJ sentencioso

sententiously [sen'tenʃəslɪ] ADV sentenciosamente

sententiousness [sen'tenʃəsnɪs] N sentenciosidad *f*, estilo *m* sentencioso

sentient ['senʃənt] ADJ sensitivo, sensible

sentiment ['sentɪmənt] N [1] (= *feeling*) sentimiento *m*
[2] (= *opinion, thought*) opinión *f*, juicio *m*; **those are my ~s too** ése es mi criterio también, así lo pienso yo también
[3] (= *sentimentality*) sentimentalismo *m*, sensiblería *f*; **to wallow in ~** nadar en el sentimentalismo *or* la sensiblería

sentimental [,sentɪ'mentl] ADJ sentimental; (*pej*) sentimental, sensiblero; **to have ~ value** tener un valor sentimental

sentimentalism [,sentɪ'mentəlɪzəm] N sentimentalismo *m*

sentimentalist [,sentɪ'mentəlɪst] N persona *f* sentimental

sentimentality [,sentɪmen'tælɪtɪ] N sentimentalismo *m*, sensiblería *f*

sentimentalize [,sentɪ'mentəlaɪz] Ⓐ VT senti-

mentalizar, imbuir de sentimiento
Ⓑ VI dejarse llevar por el sentimentalismo

sentimentally [ˌsentɪˈmentəlɪ] ADV de modo sentimental; [*say*] en tono sentimental

sentinel [ˈsentɪnl] N centinela *mf*

sentry [ˈsentrɪ] Ⓐ N centinela *mf*, guardia *mf*
Ⓑ CPD ► **sentry box** N garita *f* de centinela ► **sentry duty** N **to be on ~ duty** estar de guardia ► **sentry go** N turno *m* de centinela; **to be on ~ go** estar de guardia

Seoul [səʊl] N Seúl *m*

Sep. ABBR (= **September**) sep., set.

sepal [ˈsepəl] N sépalo *m*

separable [ˈsepərəbl] ADJ separable

separate [ˈseprɪt] Ⓐ ADJ (= *apart*) separado; (= *different*) distinto, diferente; (= *distant*) apartado, retirado; **"with separate toilet"** "con inodoro separado"; **could we have ~ bills?** queremos cuentas individuales, ¿podemos pagar por separado?; **under ~ cover** por separado; **~ from** (= *apart from*) separado de; (= *different from*) distinto de; **that's a ~ issue** esa es una cuestión aparte; **they live very ~ lives** viven independientes uno de otro; **it was discussed at a ~ meeting** se trató en otra reunión *or* reunión aparte; **on ~ occasions** en diversas ocasiones; **the children have ~ rooms** los niños tienen cada uno su habitación; **they sleep in ~ rooms** duermen en habitaciones distintas; **I wrote it on a ~ sheet** lo escribí en una hoja aparte; **we sat at ~ tables** nos sentamos en mesas distintas; **they went their ~ ways** fueron cada uno por su lado
Ⓑ N **separates** (= *clothes*) coordinados *mpl*
Ⓒ [ˈsepəreɪt] VT (= *keep apart*) separar; (= *set aside*) apartar; (= *divide*) dividir, partir; (= *distinguish*) distinguir; **police moved in to ~ the two groups** la policía intervino para separar a los dos grupos; **to ~ truth from error** separar lo falso de lo verdadero, distinguir entre lo falso y lo verdadero; **he is ~d from his wife** está separado de su mujer
Ⓓ [ˈsepəreɪt] VI separarse; **her parents ~d last year** sus padres se separaron el año pasado

►**separate off** VT + ADV separar

►**separate out** VT + ADV (= *set apart*) apartar

separately [ˈseprɪtlɪ] ADV por separado

separation [ˌsepəˈreɪʃən] N separación *f*

separatism [ˈsepərətɪzəm] N separatismo *m*

separatist [ˈsepərətɪst] Ⓐ ADJ separatista
Ⓑ N separatista *mf*

separator [ˈsepəreɪtəʳ] N separador *m*

Sephardi [seˈfɑːdɪ] N (*pl* **Sephardim** [seˈfɑːdɪm]) sefardí *mf*, sefardita *mf*

Sephardic [seˈfɑːdɪk] ADJ sefardí, sefardita

sepia [ˈsiːpɪə] Ⓐ N (= *colour, ink*) sepia *f*
Ⓑ CPD color sepia

sepoy [ˈsiːpɔɪ] N cipayo *m*

sepsis [ˈsepsɪs] N sepsis *f*

Sept. ABBR (= **September**) sep., set.

September [sepˈtembəʳ] N setiembre *m*, septiembre *m*; *see* **July** *for usage*

septet [sepˈtet] N septeto *m*

septic [ˈseptɪk] Ⓐ ADJ séptico; **to become** *or* **go** *or* **turn ~** infectarse
Ⓑ CPD ► **septic poisoning** N septicemia *f* ► **septic tank** N fosa *f* séptica, pozo *m* séptico

septicaemia, septicemia (*US*) [ˌseptɪˈsiːmɪə] N septicemia *f*

septuagenarian [ˌseptjʊədʒɪˈneərɪən] Ⓐ ADJ septuagenario
Ⓑ N septuagenario/a *m/f*

► LANGUAGE IN USE: **serious 1** 12.1

Septuagesima [ˌseptjʊəˈdʒesɪmə] N Septuagésima *f*

Septuagint [ˈseptjʊədʒɪnt] N versión *f* de los setenta

septuplet [sepˈtjʊplɪt] N septillizo/a *m/f*

sepulchral [sɪˈpʌlkrəl] ADJ sepulcral (*also fig*)

sepulchre, sepulcher (*US*) [ˈsepəlkəʳ] N (*poet*) sepulcro *m*; **whited ~** sepulcro *m* blanqueado

sequel [ˈsiːkwəl] N 1 (= *film, book*) continuación *f*
2 (= *consequence*) consecuencia *f*, resultado *m*; **it had a tragic ~** tuvo un resultado trágico

sequence [ˈsiːkwəns] N 1 (= *order*) orden *m*; **in ~** en orden; **in historical ~** en orden cronológico; **logical ~** secuencia *f* lógica; **to arrange things in ~** ordenar cosas secuencialmente
2 (= *series*) serie *f*; **a ~ of events** una serie de acontecimientos
3 (*Cine*) secuencia *f*; **the best ~ in the film** la mejor secuencia de la película
4 (*Cards*) escalera *f*

sequential [sɪˈkwenʃəl] Ⓐ ADJ secuencial
Ⓑ CPD ► **sequential access** N (*Comput*) acceso *m* en serie

sequester [sɪˈkwestəʳ] VT 1 (= *isolate, shut up*) aislar
2 (*Jur*) [+ *property*] secuestrar, confiscar

sequestered [sɪˈkwestəd] ADJ 1 (= *isolated*) aislado, remoto
2 [*property*] secuestrado, confiscado

sequestrate [sɪˈkwestreɪt] VT secuestrar

sequestration [ˌsiːkwesˈtreɪʃən] N secuestración *f*

sequin [ˈsiːkwɪn] N lentejuela *f*

sequinned, sequined [ˈsiːkwɪnd] ADJ con lentejuelas, cubierto de lentejuelas

sequoia [sɪˈkwɔɪə] N secoya *f*

seraglio [seˈrɑːlɪəʊ] N serallo *m*

seraph [ˈserəf] N (*pl* **seraphs** *or* **seraphim** [ˈserəfɪm]) serafín *m*

seraphic [səˈræfɪk] ADJ seráfico

Serb [sɜːb] N serbio/a *m/f*

Serbia [ˈsɜːbɪə] N Serbia *f*

Serbian [ˈsɜːbɪən] Ⓐ ADJ serbio
Ⓑ N serbio/a *m/f*

Serbo-Croat [ˈsɜːbəʊˈkrəʊæt], **Serbo-Croatian** [ˈsɜːbəʊkrəʊˈeɪʃən] Ⓐ ADJ serbocroata
Ⓑ N 1 (= *person*) serbocroata *mf*
2 (*Ling*) serbocroata *m*

SERC N ABBR (*Brit*) = **Science and Engineering Research Council**

sere [sɪəʳ] ADJ seco, marchito

serenade [ˌserəˈneɪd] Ⓐ N serenata *f*, mañanitas *fpl* (*Mex*)
Ⓑ VT dar una serenata a, cantar las mañanitas a (*Mex*)

serendipity [ˌserənˈdɪpɪtɪ] N serendipia *f*

serene [səˈriːn] ADJ sereno

serenely [səˈriːnlɪ] ADV con serenidad, con calma; **"no," he said ~** —no —dijo con serenidad *or* calma; **~ indifferent to the noise** sin molestarse en lo más mínimo por el ruido

serenity [sɪˈrenɪtɪ] N serenidad *f*

serf [sɜːf] N siervo/a *m/f* (*de la gleba*)

serfdom [ˈsɜːfdəm] N servidumbre *f* (*de la gleba*); (*fig*) servidumbre *f*

serge [sɜːdʒ] N sarga *f*

sergeant [ˈsɑːdʒənt] Ⓐ N 1 (*Mil*) sargento *mf*; **yes, ~** sí, mi sargento
2 (*Pol*) oficial *mf* de policía
Ⓑ CPD ► **sergeant major** N sargento *mf* mayor

serial [ˈsɪərɪəl] Ⓐ N (*in magazine*) novela *f* por entregas; (*on TV, radio*) serial *m* (*f in Cono Sur*), serie *f*; (= *soap opera*) (*on TV*) telenovela *f*; (*on radio*) radio-novela *f*
Ⓑ CPD ► **serial access** N acceso *m* en serie ► **serial interface** N interface *m* (*sometimes f*) en serie ► **serial killer** N asesino/a *m/f* (*que comete crímenes en serie*) ► **serial killing** N asesinatos *mpl* en serie, cadena *f* de asesinatos ► **serial number** N [*of goods, machinery, banknotes etc*] número *m* de serie ► **serial printer** N impresora *f* en serie ► **serial rights** NPL derechos *mpl* de publicación por entregas

serialization [ˌsɪərɪəlaɪˈzeɪʃən] N [*of novel etc*] (*on TV*) serialización *f*; (*in magazine*) publicación *f* por entregas

serialize [ˈsɪərɪəlaɪz] VT (= *publish*) publicar por entregas; (= *show on TV*) televisar por entregas; **it has been ~d in the papers** ha aparecido en una serie de entregas en los periódicos

serially [ˈsɪərɪəlɪ] ADV en serie

seriatim [ˌsɪərɪˈeɪtɪm] ADV (*frm*) en serie

sericulture [ˌserɪˈkʌltʃəʳ] N sericultura *f*

series [ˈsɪərɪz] Ⓐ N (*pl* **series**) 1 (*gen, TV*) serie *f*; [*of lectures, films*] ciclo *m*; **a ~ of events** una serie de acontecimientos
2 (*Math*) serie *f*, progresión *f*
3 (*Elec*) **to connect in ~** conectar en serie
Ⓑ CPD ► **series producer** N (*TV*) productor(a) *m/f* de la serie

series-wound [ˈsɪərɪzˈwaʊnd] ADJ arrollado en serie

▼**serious** [ˈsɪərɪəs] ADJ 1 (= *in earnest, not frivolous*) [*person*] serio, formal; [*expression, discussion, newspaper, music*] serio; **a rather ~ girl** una chica bastante seria *or* formal; **are you ~?** ¿lo dices en serio?; **you can't be ~!** no lo dices en serio, ¿verdad?; **gentlemen, let's be ~** señores, un poco de formalidad; **to be ~ about sth/sb**: **she's ~ about her studies** se toma sus estudios en serio; **are you ~ about giving up the job?** ¿hablas en serio de dejar el trabajo?; **he is ~ about his threat** sus amenazas van en serio; **he's ~ about leaving home** está decidido a irse de casa; **is she ~ about him?** ¿va ella en serio con él?; **they haven't made a ~ attempt to solve the problem** no han intentado realmente resolver el problema; **the ~ business of running the country** la importante tarea de gobernar el país; **eating shellfish is a ~ business in France** comer marisco no es algo que se tome a la ligera en Francia; **to give ~ consideration to sth** considerar algo seriamente; **to take a ~ interest in sth** interesarse seriamente por algo; **don't look so ~!** ¡no te pongas tan serio!; **on a more ~ note** pasando a un tema más serio; **all ~ offers considered** cualquier oferta (que sea) seria se tendrá en cuenta; **to give ~ thought to sth** considerar algo seriamente; *see also* **deadly B**
2 (= *grave*) [*problem, consequences, situation*] grave, serio; [*danger, illness, injury, mistake*] grave; **the patient's condition is ~** el paciente está grave; **to have ~ doubts about sth** tener serias dudas sobre algo; **to get ~** [*shortage, epidemic, drought*] convertirse en un serio *or* grave problema; **things are getting ~** la situación se está poniendo seria; **she is in ~ trouble** está en serios apuros
3 (*) **she's earning ~ money** no está ganando ninguna tontería*

seriously [ˈsɪərɪəslɪ] ADV 1 (= *in earnest*) [*think, consider*] seriamente; [*speak*] seriamente, en serio; **yes, but ~ …** sí, pero en serio …; **we**

are ~ considering emigrating estamos considerando seriamente la posibilidad de emigrar; **do you ~ expect me to believe that?** ¿esperas en serio que me lo crea?, ¿de verdad esperas que me lo crea?; **~?** ¿en serio?, ¿de verdad?; **to take sth/sb ~** tomar algo/a algn en serio; **to take o.s. too ~** tomarse a sí mismo demasiado en serio
2 (= *badly*) [*damage, affect*] seriamente, gravemente; [*injured, wounded*] gravemente; **no-one was ~ hurt** nadie resultó gravemente herido; **he is ~ ill** está grave, está gravemente enfermo; **the pilot realized that something was ~ wrong** el piloto se dio cuenta de que algo iba realmente mal *or* de que pasaba algo muy grave
3 (*) (= *really*) **a hotel like the Grand is ~ expensive** un hotel como el Grand es caro de verdad*; **he's ~ into body-building** está metido a tope en el culturismo*

seriousness [ˈsɪərɪəsnɪs] N 1 (= *earnestness*) [*of suggestion, publication, occasion, voice*] seriedad *f*; [*of report, information, account*] fiabilidad *f*; **in all ~** hablando en serio
2 (= *gravity*) [*of situation, problem, threat, damage*] gravedad *f*, seriedad *f*; [*of illness, injury, mistake*] gravedad *f*

sermon [ˈsɜːmən] N sermón *m*; **the Sermon on the Mount** el Sermón de la Montaña; **to give sb a ~** (*fig*) (*pej*) sermonear a algn, echar un sermón a algn

sermonize [ˈsɜːmənaɪz] Ⓐ VT sermonear
Ⓑ VI sermonear

serology [sɪˈrɒlədʒɪ] N serología *f*

seropositive [ˌsɪərəʊˈpɒzɪtɪv] ADJ seropositivo

serotonin [ˌserəʊˈtəʊnɪn] N serotonina *f*

serous [ˈsɪərəs] ADJ seroso

serpent [ˈsɜːpənt] N (*poet*) serpiente *f*, sierpe *f* (*liter*)

serpentine [ˈsɜːpəntaɪn] Ⓐ ADJ serpentino
Ⓑ N (*Min*) serpentina *f*

SERPS [sɜːps] N ABBR (*Brit*) = **state earnings-related pension scheme**

serrated [seˈreɪtɪd] ADJ serrado, dentellado

serration [seˈreɪʃən] N borde *m* dentado

serried [ˈserɪd] ADJ apretado; **in ~ ranks** en filas apretadas

serum [ˈsɪərəm] N (*pl* **serums** *or* **sera**) suero *m*; **blood ~** suero *m* sanguíneo

servant [ˈsɜːvənt] Ⓐ N 1 (*domestic*) criado/a *m/f*, sirviente/a *m/f*, muchacho/a *m/f*, mucamo/a *m/f* (*S. Cone*); **the ~s** (*collectively*) la servidumbre
2 (*fig*) servidor(a) *m/f*; **your devoted ~** ◊ **your humble ~** un servidor, servidor de usted; **your obedient ~** (*in letters*) suyo afmo., atento y seguro servidor; *see also* **civil B**
Ⓑ CPD ► **servant girl** N criada *f*

serve [sɜːv] Ⓐ VT 1 (= *work for*) [+ *employer, God, country*] servir a; **he ~d his country well** sirvió dignamente a la patria, prestó valiosos servicios a la patria
2 (= *be used for, be useful as*) servir; **that ~s to explain ...** eso sirve para explicar ...; **it ~s its/my purpose** viene al caso; **it ~s you right** te lo mereces, te lo tienes merecido, te está bien empleado; **it ~d him right for being so greedy** se lo mereció por ser tan glotón, le está bien empleado por glotón; **if my memory ~s me right** si la memoria no me falla
3 (*in shop, restaurant*) [+ *customer*] servir, atender; [+ *food, meal*] servir; **to ~ sb with hors d'oeuvres** servir los entremeses a algn; **are you being ~d, madam?** ¿le están atendiendo, señora?; **dinner is ~d** la cena está servida; **they ~d cod as halibut** hicieron pasar bacalao por halibut; **main courses are ~d with vegetables or salad** el plato principal se sirve acompañado de verduras o ensalada
4 (= *complete*) cumplir, hacer; **to ~ an apprenticeship** hacer el aprendizaje; **to ~ ten years in the army** servir diez años en el ejército; **to ~ a prison sentence** ◊ **~ time (in prison)** cumplir una condena *or* una pena de cárcel
5 (*Jur*) [+ *writ, summons*] entregar; **to ~ a summons on sb** entregar una citación a algn
6 (*Travel*) **in towns ~d by this line** en las ciudades por donde pasa esta línea; **these villages used to be ~d by buses** antes en estos pueblos había servicio de autobuses
7 (*Culin*) (= *be enough for*) **this recipe ~s six** esta receta es (suficiente) para seis personas
8 (*Tennis etc*) **to ~ the ball** servir (la bola), sacar; **he ~d 17 double faults** hizo 17 dobles faltas
Ⓑ VI 1 [*servant, soldier*] servir; **he is not willing to ~** no está dispuesto a ofrecer sus servicios; **to ~ on a committee/jury** ser miembro de una comisión/un jurado; **to ~ on the council** ser concejal; **to ~ in parliament** ser diputado
2 (*at mealtime*) servir; **shall I ~?** ¿sirvo?; **to ~ at table** servir en la mesa
3 (*in shop*) atender
4 (= *be useful*) **to ~ for** *or* **as** servir de; **it will ~** servirá para el caso; **it ~s to show that ...** sirve para demostrar que ...
5 (*Tennis*) sacar
Ⓒ N (*Tennis etc*) servicio *m*, saque *m*; **whose ~ is it?** ¿quién saca?, ¿de quién es el servicio?; **he has a strong ~** tiene un servicio *or* saque muy fuerte

►**serve out** VT + ADV 1 (= *complete*) [+ *term of office, sentence*] cumplir
2 (= *dish up*) [+ *food*] servir

►**serve up** VT + ADV 1 [+ *food, drink*] servir
2 (*fig*) **he ~d that up as an excuse*** eso lo ofreció como excusa

server [ˈsɜːvəʳ] N 1 (*Rel*) monaguillo *m*
2 (*Tennis*) jugador(a) *m/f* que tiene el saque *or* servicio
3 [*of food*] camarero/a *m/f*, mesero/a *m/f* (*LAm*), mero/a *m/f* (*Mex*)
4 (*Comput*) servidor *m*
5 (= *cutlery*) cubierto *m* de servir; (= *tray*) bandeja *f*, charola *f* (*Mex*)

service [ˈsɜːvɪs] Ⓐ N 1 (= *work*) 1·1 (= *period of work*) trabajo *m*; **he retired after 50 years' ~** se jubiló después de 50 años de trabajo; **a middle manager with over 20 years ~** un mando medio con más de 20 años de antigüedad (en la empresa); **he saw ~ in Egypt** combatió en Egipto; **he never saw active ~** nunca estuvo en servicio activo
1·2 (= *work provided*) servicio *m*; **the company has a reputation for good ~** la empresa tiene fama de dar un buen servicio (a los clientes); **they offered their ~s free of charge** ofrecieron sus servicios gratuitamente; **they provide a 24-hour ~** proporcionan un servicio de 24 horas
1·3 (*domestic*) **to be in ~** ser criado/a, servir; **she was in ~ at Lord Olton's** era criada *or* servía en casa de Lord Olton; **to go into ~ (with sb)** entrar a servir (en casa de algn)
2 (= *organization, system*) servicio *m*; **the diplomatic ~** el servicio diplomático; **they are attempting to maintain essential ~s** están intentando mantener en funcionamiento los servicios mínimos; **the postal ~** el servicio postal; **rail ~s were disrupted by the strike** el servicio ferroviario se vio afectado por la huelga; **the train ~ to Pamplona** el servicio de trenes a Pamplona; *see also* **secret C, social C**
3 (= *help, use*) servicio *m*; **he was knighted for his ~s to industry** le concedieron el título de Sir por sus servicios a la industria; **he died in the ~ of his country** murió en acto de servicio a su patria; **this machine will give years of ~** esta máquina durará años; **Tristram Shandy, at your ~!** ¡Tristram Shandy, para servirle *or* a sus órdenes!; **I am at your ~** estoy a su disposición; **to be of ~** ayudar, servir; **how can I be of ~?** ¿en qué puedo ayudar *or* servir?; **the new buses were brought into ~ in 1995** los autobuses nuevos entraron en servicio en 1995; **to come into ~** [*vehicle, weapon*] entrar en servicio; **to do sth/sb a ~**: **you have done me a great ~** me ha hecho un gran favor, me ha sido de muchísima ayuda; **they do their country/profession no ~** no hacen ningún favor a su patria/profesión; **to be out of ~** (*Mech*) no funcionar, estar fuera de servicio; *see also* **community B**
4 (*in hotel, restaurant, shop*) servicio *m*; **"service not included"** "servicio no incluido"; *see also* **room C**
5 **services** (*Econ*) (= *tertiary sector*) sector *m* terciario *or* (de) servicios; (*on motorway*) área *f* de servicio
6 (*Mil*) **~ life didn't suit him** la vida militar no le pegaba; **the Services** las fuerzas armadas; *see also* **military C, national C**
7 (*Rel*) (= *mass*) misa *f*; (*other*) oficio *m* (religioso); **I usually go to morning ~** normalmente voy a la misa *or* al oficio matinal; *see also* **funeral B, wedding B**
8 (*Aut, Mech*) revisión *f*; **the car is in for a ~** están revisando el coche, están haciendo una revisión al coche; **to send one's car in for a ~** mandar el coche a revisar
9 (= *set of crockery*) vajilla *f*; **dinner ~** vajilla *f*; **tea ~** juego *m* *or* servicio *m* de té
10 (*Tennis*) servicio *m*, saque *m*; **a break of ~** una ruptura de servicio; **to break sb's ~** romper el servicio a *or* de algn; **to hold/lose one's ~** ganar/perder el servicio
Ⓑ VT 1 [+ *car*] revisar, hacer la revisión a; [+ *appliance*] realizar el mantenimiento de
2 [+ *organization, committee, customers*] dar servicio a, proveer de servicios a
3 [+ *debt*] pagar el interés de
Ⓒ CPD ► **service area** N (*on motorway*) área *f* de servicio ► **service charge** N (*in restaurant*) servicio *m*; [*of flat*] gastos *mpl* de comunidad *or* de escalera (*Sp*), gastos *mpl* comunes (*LAm*) ► **service elevator** N (*US*) = **service lift** ► **service engineer** N técnico/a *m/f* (de mantenimiento) ► **service families** NPL familias *fpl* de miembros de las fuerzas armadas ► **service flat** N (*Brit*) *piso o apartamento con servicio de criada y conserje* ► **service hatch** N ventanilla *f* de servicio ► **service industry** N (= *company*) empresa *f* de servicios; **the ~ industry** *or* **industries** el sector terciario *or* (de) servicios ► **service lift** N montacargas *m inv* ► **service line** N (*Tennis*) línea *f* de servicio *or* saque ► **service provider** N (*Internet*) proveedor *m* de (acceso a) Internet, proveedor *m* de servicios ► **service road** N vía *f* de acceso *or* de servicio ► **service sector** N (*Econ*) sector *m* terciario *or* (de) servicios ► **service station** N gasolinera *f*, estación *f* de servicio, bencinera *f* (*Chile*), grifo *m* (*Peru*) ► **service tree** N serbal *m* ► **service wife** N esposa *f* de un miembro de las fuerzas armadas

serviceable [ˈsɜːvɪsəbl] ADJ (= *practical*) [*clothes*

etc] práctico; (= *lasting*) duradero; (= *usable, working*) utilizable

serviceman ['sɜːvɪsmən] N (*pl* **servicemen**) militar *m*

servicewoman ['sɜːvɪsˌwʊmən] N (*pl* **servicewomen**) (mujer) militar *f*

servicing ['sɜːvɪsɪŋ] N [*of car*] revisión *f*; [*of appliance*] mantenimiento *m*; [*of debt*] pago *m* del interés de

serviette [ˌsɜːvɪ'et] Ⓐ N servilleta *f*
Ⓑ CPD ► **serviette ring** N servilletero *m*

servile ['sɜːvaɪl] ADJ servil

servility [sɜː'vɪlɪtɪ] N servilismo *m*

serving ['sɜːvɪŋ] Ⓐ ADJ [*officer*] en activo
Ⓑ N [*of meal*] servicio *m*
Ⓒ CPD ► **serving cart** N (*US*) ► **serving trolley** N (*Brit*) carrito *m* ► **serving dish** N plato *m* de servir

servitude ['sɜːvɪtjuːd] N servidumbre *f*

servo ['sɜːvəʊ] N servo *m*

servoassisted ['sɜːvəʊə'sɪstɪd] ADJ servoasistido

sesame ['sesəmɪ] Ⓐ N [1] (*Bot*) sésamo *m*
[2] (*Literat*) **open ~!** ¡ábrete sésamo!
Ⓑ CPD ► **sesame oil** N aceite *m* de sésamo ► **sesame seeds** NPL semillas *fpl* de sésamo

sesquipedalian [ˌseskwɪpɪ'deɪlɪən] ADJ sesquipedal, polisilábico; **~ word** palabra *f* kilométrica

sessile ['sesaɪl] ADJ sésil

session ['seʃən] N [1] (= *meeting, sitting, Comput*) sesión *f*; **I had a long ~ with her** tuve una larga entrevista con ella; *see also* **jam D, photo B, recording B**
[2] (*Scol, Univ*) (= *year*) año *m* académico, curso *m*
[3] (*Pol, Jur*) sesión *f*; **to be in ~** estar en sesión, estar reunido; **to go into secret ~** celebrar una sesión secreta

sessional ['seʃənl] ADJ [*exam*] de fin de curso

sestet [ses'tet] N sexteto *m*

set [set] (*vb: pt, pp* **set**) Ⓐ N [1] (= *matching series*) [*of golf clubs, pens, keys*] juego *m*; [*of books, works*] colección *f*; [*of tools*] equipo *m*, estuche *m*; [*of gears*] tren *m*; [*of stamps*] serie *f*; (*Math*) conjunto *m*; **the sofa and chairs are only sold as a ~** el sofá y los sillones no se venden por separado; **a chess ~** un ajedrez; **I need one more to make up the complete ~** me falta uno para completar la serie; **a complete ~ of Jane Austen's novels** una colección completa de las novelas de Jane Austen; **a ~ of crockery** una vajilla; **a ~ of cutlery** una cubertería; **they are sold in ~s** se venden en juegos completos; **a ~ of kitchen utensils** una batería de cocina; **it makes a ~ with those over there** hace juego con los que ves allá; **~ of teeth** dentadura *f*; **a train ~** un tren eléctrico
[2] (*Tennis*) set *m*; **she was leading 5-1 in the first ~** iba ganando 5 a 1 en el primer set
[3] (*Elec*) aparato *m*; (*Rad*) aparato *m* de radio; (*TV*) televisor *m*, televisión *f*
[4] (*Theat*) decorado *m*; (*Cine*) plató *m*; **to be on the ~** estar en plató
[5] (*Hairdressing*) **to have a shampoo and ~** hacerse lavar y marcar el pelo
[6] (*often pej*) (= *group*) grupo *m*, pandilla *f*; (= *clique*) camarilla *f*; **we're not in their ~** no formamos parte de su grupo; **they're a ~ of thieves** son unos ladrones; **they form a ~ by themselves** forman un grupo aparte; **the fast ~** la gente de vida airada; **the literary ~** los literatos, la gente literaria; **the smart ~** el mundo elegante, los elegantes; *see also* **jet[2] D**
[7] (*Brit Scol*) clase *f*; **the mathematics ~** la clase de matemáticas
[8] ✦**IDIOM to make a dead ~ at sb** (= *pick on*) emprenderla resueltamente con algn, escoger a algn como víctima; (*amorously*) proponerse conquistar a algn
[9] (= *disposition*) [*of tide, wind*] dirección *f*; [*of fabric*] caída *f*; [*of dress*] corte *m*, ajuste *m*; [*of head*] porte *m*, manera *f* de llevar; [*of saw*] triscamiento *m*; *see also* **mind-set**
[10] (*Hort*) planta *f* de transplantar; **onion ~s** cebollitas *fpl* de transplantar
Ⓑ ADJ [1] (= *fixed*) [*price, purpose*] fijo; [*smile*] forzado; [*opinions*] inflexible, rígido; [*talk*] preparado de antemano; [*expression*] hecho; [*date, time*] señalado; (*Scol*) [*books, subjects*] obligatorio; [*task*] asignado; **to be ~ in one's ways/opinions** tener costumbres/opiniones profundamente arraigadas; **~ books** (*Scol, Univ*) lecturas *mpl* obligatorias; **with no ~ limits** sin límites determinados; **~ menu** menú *m*, comida *f* corrida (*Mex*); **a ~ phrase** una frase hecha; **~ piece** (*Art*) grupo *m*; (= *fireworks*) cuadro *m*; (*Literat etc*) escena *f* importante; (*Sport*) jugada *f* ensayada, jugada *f* de pizarra; **he gave us a ~ speech** pronunció un discurso preparado de antemano; **he has a ~ speech for these occasions** para estas ocasiones tiene un discurso estereotipado; **at a ~ time** a una hora señalada; **there is no ~ time for it** para eso no hay hora fija; **there's no ~ way to do it** no hay una forma establecida *or* determinada de hacerlo
[2] (= *determined*) resuelto, decidido; **to be (dead) ~ against (doing) sth** estar (completamente) opuesto a (hacer) algo; **to be ~ in one's purpose** tener un propósito firme, mantenerse firme en su propósito; **to be (dead) ~ on (doing) sth** estar (completamente) decidido a *or* empeñado en (hacer) algo; **since you are so ~ on it** puesto que te empeñas en ello, puesto que estás decidido a hacerlo
[3] (= *ready*) listo; **to be all ~ to do sth** estar listo para hacer algo; **to be all ~ for** estar listo para; **all ~?** ¿(estás) listo?; **the scene was ~ for …** (*fig*) todo estaba listo para …
[4] (*Culin*) **the fruit is ~** el fruto está formado; **the jelly is ~** la gelatina está cuajada
[5] (= *disposed*) **the tide is ~ in our favour** la marea fluye para llevarnos adelante; (*fig*) la tendencia actual nos favorece, llevamos el viento en popa; **the wind is ~ strong from the north** el viento sopla recio del norte
Ⓒ VT [1] (= *place, put*) poner; **~ the chairs by the window** pon las sillas junto a la ventana; **she ~ the dish before me** puso el plato delante de mí; **to ~ a plan before a committee** exponer un plan ante una comisión; **the film/scene is ~ in Rome** la película/escena se desarrolla *or* está ambientada en Roma; **to ~ fire to sth** ◊ **~ sth on fire** prender fuego a algo; **a novel ~ in Madrid** una novela ambientada en Madrid; **to ~ places for 14** poner cubiertos para 14 personas; **to ~ a poem to music** poner música a un poema; **what value do you ~ on it?** ¿en cuánto lo valoras?; (*fig*) ¿qué valor tiene para ti?
[2] (= *arrange*) poner, colocar; (= *adjust*) [+ *clock*] poner en hora; [+ *mechanism*] ajustar; [+ *hair*] marcar, fijar; [+ *trap*] armar; **bricks ~ in mortar** ladrillos puestos en argamasa; **the alarm clock is ~ for seven** el despertador está puesto para las siete; **I ~ the alarm for seven o'clock** puse el despertador a las siete; **I'll ~ your room** (*US*) voy a limpiar y arreglar su habitación; **to ~ the table** poner la mesa; **he ~s his watch by Big Ben** pone su reloj en hora por el Big Ben; *see* **sail A1**
[3] (= *mount*) [+ *gem*] engastar, montar
[4] (*Med*) [+ *broken bone*] encajar, reducir
[5] (*Typ*) [+ *type*] componer
[6] (= *fix, establish*) [+ *date, limit*] fijar, señalar; [+ *record*] establecer; [+ *fashion*] imponer; [+ *dye, colour*] fijar; **to ~ a course for** salir rumbo a; **to ~ one's heart on sth** tener algo como máximo deseo; **to ~ limits to sth** señalar límites a algo; **the meeting is ~ for Tuesday** (*US*) la reunión se celebrará el martes; **to ~ a period of three months** señalar un plazo de tres meses; **to ~ a record of ten seconds** establecer un récord de diez segundos; **the world record was ~ last year** el récord mundial se estableció el año pasado; **to ~ a time for a meeting** fijar una hora para una reunión; *see also* **example**
[7] (= *assign*) [+ *task*] dar; **to ~ Lorca for 2001** poner una obra de Lorca en el programa de estudios para 2001; **Cela is not ~ this year** este año Cela no figura en el programa; **to ~ an exam in French** preparar un examen de francés; **to ~ sb a problem** dar a algn un problema que resolver; **to ~ sb a task** dar a algn una tarea que hacer
[8] (= *cause to start*) **the noise ~ the dogs barking** el ruido hizo ladrar a los perros; **to ~ a fire** (*US*) provocar un incendio; **to ~ sth going** poner algo en marcha; **to ~ sb laughing** hacer reír a algn; **to ~ everyone talking** dar que hablar a todos; **it ~ me thinking** me puso a pensar; **to ~ sb to work** poner a algn a trabajar
[9] (= *cause to pursue*) **to ~ a dog on sb** azuzar un perro contra algn; **I was ~ on by three dogs** me atacaron tres perros; **we ~ the police on to him** le denunciamos a la policía; **what ~ the police on the trail?** ¿qué puso a la policía sobre la pista?
[10] (= *make solid*) [+ *cement*] solidificar, endurecer; [+ *jelly*] cuajar
Ⓓ VI [1] (= *go down*) [*sun, moon*] ponerse; **the sun was ~ting** se estaba poniendo el sol
[2] (= *go hard*) [*concrete, glue*] endurecerse; (*fig*) [*face*] congelarse
[3] (*Med*) [*broken bone, limb*] componerse
[4] (*Culin*) [*jelly, jam*] cuajarse
[5] (= *begin*) **to ~ to work** ponerse a trabajar
Ⓔ CPD ► **set designer** N (*Theat*) director(a) *m/f* de arte, decorador(a) *m/f* ► **set point** N (*Tennis*) punto *m* de set ► **set square** N escuadra *f*; (*with 2 equal sides*) cartabón *m*

►**set about** VI + PREP [1] (= *begin*) [+ *task*] empezar; **to ~ about doing sth** ponerse a hacer algo
[2] (= *attack*) atacar, agredir

►**set against** VT + PREP [1] (= *turn against*) **to ~ sb against sb** enemistar a algn contra algn; **to ~ sb against sth** hacer que algn coja aversión por algo; **he is very ~ against it** se opone rotundamente a ello
[2] (= *balance against*) comparar con

►**set apart** VT + ADV (*lit*) separar (**from** de); **his genius ~ him apart from his contemporaries** destacó de entre sus contemporáneos a causa de su genialidad

►**set aside** VT + ADV [1] (= *separate*) [+ *book, work*] poner aparte, apartar
[2] (= *save*) [+ *money, time*] reservar, guardar
[3] (= *put to one side*) [+ *differences, quarrels*] dejar de lado
[4] (= *reject*) [+ *proposal*] rechazar; [+ *petition*] desestimar; [+ *law, sentence, will*] anular
[5] (= *put away*) poner a un lado

►**set back** VT + ADV [1] (= *retard*) [+ *project, process*] retrasar; [+ *clocks*] atrasar; **this has ~ us back some years** esto nos ha retrasado varios años
[2] (= *place apart*) apartar; **a house ~ back**

from the road una casa apartada de la carretera
[3] (*) (= *cost*) costar; **the dinner ~ me back £40** la cena me costó 40 libras
[4] (= *replace*) devolver a su lugar
►**set by** VT + ADV (= *save*) reservar, guardar
►**set down** VT + ADV [1] (= *put down*) [+ *object*] dejar; [+ *passenger*] bajar, dejar; **to ~ sth down on the table** poner algo sobre la mesa
[2] (= *record*) poner por escrito; **to ~ sth down in writing** *or* **on paper** poner algo por escrito
►**set forth** Ⓐ VT + ADV (= *expound*) [+ *theory*] exponer, explicar; (= *display*) mostrar
Ⓑ VI + ADV = **set out A**
►**set in** VI + ADV [*bad weather*] establecerse; [*winter, rain, snow*] empezar; [*night*] caer; **the rain has ~ in for the night** la lluvia continuará toda la noche; **the rain has really ~ in now** ahora está lloviendo de verdad; **the reaction ~ in after the war** la reacción se afianzó después de la guerra
►**set off** Ⓐ VI + ADV (= *leave*) salir, partir (*esp LAm*); **we ~ off for London at nine o'clock** salimos para Londres a las nueve; **to ~ off on a journey** salir de viaje
Ⓑ VT + ADV [1] (= *start*) provocar, desencadenar; **that was what ~ off the riot** eso fue lo que provocó *or* desencadenó el motín; **to ~ sb off** (*laughing*) hacer reír a algn; (*talking*) hacer que algn se ponga a hablar; **that really ~ him off** (*angrily*) aquello le puso furioso; **that ~ him off (all over) again** (*angrily*) eso le provocó de nuevo
[2] (= *trigger off*) [+ *burglar alarm*] hacer sonar; [+ *bomb*] hacer estallar, explotar; [+ *mechanism*] hacer funcionar
[3] (= *enhance*) hacer resaltar; **the black ~s off the red** el negro hace resaltar *or* pone de relieve el rojo; **her dress ~s off her figure** el vestido le realza la figura
[4] (= *balance*) contraponer; **to ~ off profits against losses** contraponer las ganancias a las pérdidas; **these expenses are ~ off against tax** estos gastos son desgravables
►**set on** VI + PREP (= *attack*) (*physically, verbally*) agredir, atacar; **he was ~ on by four of them** fue agredido *or* atacado por cuatro de ellos
►**set out** Ⓐ VI + ADV salir, partir (*esp LAm*) (**for** para; **from** de); **we ~ out for London at nine o'clock** salimos para Londres a las nueve; **to ~ out in search of sth/sb** salir en busca de algo/algn; **to ~ out to do sth** proponerse hacer algo; **what are you ~ting out to do?** ¿qué os proponéis?, ¿cuál es vuestro objetivo?; **we did not ~ out to do that** no teníamos esa intención al principio
Ⓑ VT + ADV [1] (= *display*) [+ *goods*] exponer
[2] (= *present*) [+ *reasons, ideas*] presentar, exponer
►**set to** VI + ADV [1] (= *start*) empezar; (= *start working*) ponerse (resueltamente) a trabajar; (= *start eating*) empezar a comer (con buen apetito); **to ~ to and do sth** ponerse a trabajar para hacer algo; **~ to!** ¡a ello!
[2] **they ~ to with their fists** empezaron a pegarse, se liaron a golpes
►**set up** Ⓐ VI + ADV **to ~ up in business** establecerse en un negocio; **to ~ up (in business) as a baker** establecerse de panadero
Ⓑ VT + ADV [1] (= *place in position*) [+ *chairs, tables etc*] disponer, colocar; [+ *statue, monument*] levantar, erigir; [+ *fence*] construir, poner; **to ~ up camp** acampar
[2] (= *start*) [+ *school, business, company*] establecer, fundar; [+ *committee*] poner en marcha; [+ *inquiry*] constituir; [+ *fund*] crear; [+ *government*] establecer, instaurar; [+ *record*] establecer; [+ *precedent*] sentar; [+ *infection*] causar, producir; **to ~ up house** establecerse, poner casa; **to ~ up shop** (*Comm*) poner (un) negocio; **to ~ sb up in business** poner un negocio a algn, establecer a algn; **he ~ her up in a flat** la instaló en un piso *or* (*LAm*) departamento; **now he's ~ up for life** ahora tiene el porvenir asegurado
[3] (= *pose*) **to ~ o.s. up as sth** presumir de algo, hacérselas de algo
[4] (*) (= *frame*) tender una trampa a
[5] (*) (= *lure into a trap*) engañar, llevar al huerto a*
[6] (*) (= *fix, rig*) [+ *fight*] amañar, apañar
[7] (= *equip*) equipar, proveer (**with** de); **to be well ~ up for** estar bien provisto de, tener buena provisión de
[8] (*Typ*) componer
[9] (= *raise*) [+ *cry*] levantar, lanzar, dar; [+ *protest*] levantar, formular
►**set upon** VI + PREP = **set on**

set-aside ['setəsaɪd] N (*Agr*) retirada *f* de tierras, abandono *m* de tierras; **~ land** tierra *f* en barbecho

setback ['setbæk] N revés *m*; **to suffer a ~** sufrir un revés

setscrew ['setskruː] N tornillo *m* de presión

settee [se'tiː] Ⓐ N sofá *m*
Ⓑ CPD ► **settee bed** N sofá-cama *m*

setter ['setəʳ] N [1] (= *dog*) setter *m*, perro *m* de muestra
[2] [*of puzzle etc*] autor(a) *m/f*
[3] (= *person*) [*of gems*] engastador(a) *m/f*
[4] = **typesetter 1**

setting ['setɪŋ] Ⓐ N [1] [*of novel etc*] escenario *m*; (= *scenery*) marco *m*; [*of jewels*] engaste *m*, montura *f*
[2] (*Mus*) arreglo *m*
[3] [*of controls*] ajuste *m*
[4] [*of sun*] puesta *f*
[5] [*of bone*] encaje *m*, reducción *f*
[6] (*Typ*) composición *f*
Ⓑ CPD ► **setting lotion** N fijador *m* (para el pelo)

setting-up ['setɪŋ'ʌp] N [1] (= *erection*) [*of monument*] erección *f*
[2] (= *foundation*) [*of institution, company*] fundación *f*, establecimiento *m*
[3] (*Typ*) composición *f*

settle[1] ['setl] Ⓐ VT [1] (= *resolve*) [+ *dispute, problem*] resolver; **several points remain to be ~d** quedan varios puntos por resolver; **the result was ~d in the first half** el resultado se decidió en el primer tiempo; **to ~ a case** *or* **claim out of court** llegar a un acuerdo sin recurrir a los tribunales; **the terms were ~d by negotiation** se acordaron las condiciones mediante una negociación; **~ it among yourselves!** ¡arregladlo entre vosotros!; **so that's ~d then** así que ya está decidido; **it's all ~d — we're going in June** ya está decidido — nos vamos en junio; **that ~s it! — you're not going** ¡no hay más que hablar! *or* ¡pues ya está! — tú te quedas; **the couple have ~d their differences** la pareja ha resuelto sus diferencias
[2] (= *make comfortable*) [+ *person*] poner cómodo, acomodar; **to ~ an invalid for the night** poner cómodo *or* acomodar a un enfermo para que duerma (por la noche); **to get (sb) ~d: I'd just got the baby ~d when ...** acababa de acostar al bebé cuando ...; **it took a long time to get ~d in our new home** nos costó mucho instalarnos en la nueva casa; **to ~ o.s.** ponerse cómodo, acomodarse; **she ~d herself at the desk** se puso cómoda *or* se acomodó delante de la mesa
[3] (= *place*) [+ *object*] colocar; [+ *gaze*] posar
[4] (= *colonize*) [+ *land*] colonizar
[5] (= *calm*) [+ *nerves*] calmar, sosegar; [+ *doubts*] disipar, desvanecer; [+ *stomach*] asentar
[6] (= *pay*) [+ *bill*] pagar; [+ *debt*] saldar, liquidar
[7] (= *put in order*) [+ *affairs*] poner en orden; **to ~ one's affairs** poner en orden sus asuntos
[8] (*) (= *deal with*) [+ *person*] **I'll soon ~ him** ya me encargaré de ponerlo en su sitio*; **that ~d him** con eso se le acabó la tontería*
[9] (*Jur*) asignar; **to ~ sth on sb** asignar algo a algn
Ⓑ VI [1] (= *establish o.s.*) (*in a house*) instalarse; (*in a country*) establecerse; [*first settlers*] establecerse; **she visited Paris in 1974 and eventually ~d there** visitó París en 1974 y finalmente decidió establecerse allí
[2] (= *come to rest*) [*bird, insect*] posarse; [*dust*] asentarse; [*snow*] cuajar; **a deep gloom had ~d on the party** un profundo pesimismo se había apoderado del grupo; **my eyes ~d on her immediately** al momento mi mirada se fijó en ella
[3] (= *sink*) [*sediment*] depositarse; [*building*] asentarse; **the boat slowly ~d in the mud** poco a poco el bote se hundió en el barro
[4] (= *separate*) [*liquid*] reposar
[5] (= *get comfortable*) (*in chair*) arrellanarse; (*in new job, routine*) adaptarse, establecerse; **he ~d deeper into the cushions** se arrellanó entre los cojines; **I couldn't ~ to anything** no me podía concentrar en nada, no lograba ponerme a hacer nada
[6] (= *calm down*) [*weather*] estabilizarse, asentarse; [*conditions, situation*] volver a la normalidad, normalizarse; [*nerves*] calmarse; *see also* **dust A1**
[7] (= *reach an agreement*) llegar a un acuerdo *or* arreglo; **they ~d with us for £12,000** lo arreglamos extrajudicialmente y nos pagaron 12.000 libras
[8] (= *pay*) **I'll ~ with you on Friday** te pagaré el viernes, ajustaremos cuentas el viernes
►**settle down** Ⓐ VI + ADV [1] (= *get comfortable*) ponerse cómodo, acomodarse; **I ~d down in my favourite chair** me puse cómodo *or* me acomodé *or* me arrellané en mi silla preferida; **they ~d down to wait** se prepararon para la espera
[2] (= *apply o.s.*) **to ~ down to sth: after dinner, he ~d down to a video** después de cenar se puso a ver un vídeo; **I couldn't get the children to ~ down to work** no conseguía que los niños se pusieran a trabajar
[3] (= *calm down*) calmarse, tranquilizarse
[4] (= *adopt a stable life*) echar raíces; **I'm not ready to ~ down yet** aún no estoy listo para echar raíces; **why don't you ~ down and get married?** ¿por qué no sientas cabeza y te casas?*
[5] (= *get back to normal*) [*situation*] volver a la normalidad, normalizarse; **things are beginning to ~ down** las cosas empiezan a volver a la normalidad
Ⓑ VT + ADV [1] (= *make comfortable*) poner cómodo, acomodar; **he ~d the children down for the night** acostó a los niños; **why don't you help Philippa unpack and ~ her down?** ¿por qué no le ayudas a Philippa a deshacer las maletas e instalarse?
[2] (= *calm down*) calmar, tranquilizar; **I turned on the TV to ~ them down** encendí la tele para calmarlos *or* tranquilizarlos

►**settle for** VI + PREP [1] (= *accept*) conformarse con; **don't ~ for second best** confórmate sólo con lo mejor; **I won't ~ for less** no me conformo con menos; **to ~ for £250** convenir en aceptar 250 libras
[2] (= *choose*) decidirse por, escoger

►**settle in** VI + ADV (*in new home, hotel*) instalarse; (*in new job, school*) adaptarse; **he's settling in well at his new school** se está adaptando bien a la nueva escuela; **are you all ~d in?** ¿ya estás instalado?

►**settle on** VI + PREP (= *choose*) decidirse por, escoger

►**settle up** VI + ADV ajustar cuentas (**with sb** con algn); **I'll pay for everything and we can ~ up later** yo pagaré todo y ya ajustaremos cuentas después

settle² ['setl] N banco *m*, escaño *m* (*a veces con baúl debajo*)

settled ['setld] ADJ [1] (= *fixed, established*) [*ideas, opinions*] fijo; [*order, rhythm*] estable; [*team*] fijo, estable; **a ~ social order** un orden social estable; **the first ~ civilization** la primera civilización estable; **to feel ~** (*in a place, job*) sentirse adaptado; **to get ~** adaptarse, amoldarse
[2] (= *colonized*) **the eastern ~ regions of the country** los poblados *or* asentamientos permanentes de las regiones del este del país
[3] [*weather*] estable, asentado

▼**settlement** ['setlmənt] N [1] (= *payment*) [*of claim, bill, debt*] liquidación *f*; (= *dowry*) dote *f*; **please find enclosed my cheque in full ~ of ...** adjunto le remito el talón a cuenta de la total liquidación de ...
[2] (= *agreement*) acuerdo *m*; **to reach a ~** llegar a un acuerdo; **to secure a peace ~** alcanzar un acuerdo de paz
[3] (= *colony, village*) colonia *f*, poblado *m*; (= *archaeological site*) asentamiento *m*
[4] (= *act of settling persons*) establecimiento *m*; [*of land*] colonización *f*
[5] (*Jur*) (= *sum of money*) **she accepted an out-of-court ~ of £4000** aceptó una compensación de 4000 libras a cambio de no seguir adelante con el juicio

settler ['setləʳ] N colonizador(a) *m/f*

set-to* ['set'tu:] N (= *fight*) pelea *f*; (= *quarrel*) agarrada* *f*, bronca* *f*

setup* ['setʌp] N [1] (= *way sth is organised*) sistema *m*; **it's an odd ~ here** aquí todo es en un plan raro; **you have to know the ~** hay que conocer el tinglado; **what's the ~?** ¿cuál es el sistema?, ¿cómo está organizado?; **he's joining our ~** formará parte de nuestro equipo
[2] (*) (= *trick, trap*) trampa *f*, montaje* *m*

seven ['sevn] Ⓐ ADJ siete; **the ~ wonders of the world** las siete maravillas del mundo; **the ~ deadly sins** los siete pecados capitales; **the ~-year itch*** *sensación de monotonía y aburrimiento a los siete años de estar con la misma pareja*
Ⓑ N siete *m*; *see* **five** *for usage*

sevenfold ['sevnfəʊld] Ⓐ ADJ séptuplo
Ⓑ ADV siete veces

seventeen ['sevn'ti:n] Ⓐ ADJ diecisiete, diez y siete
Ⓑ N diecisiete *m*; *see* **five** *for usage*

seventeenth ['sevn'ti:nθ] Ⓐ ADJ decimoséptimo; **the ~ century** el siglo diecisiete
Ⓑ N (*in series*) decimoséptimo/a *m/f*; (= *fraction*) decimoséptima parte *f*; *see* **fifth** *for usage*

seventh ['sevnθ] Ⓐ ADJ séptimo; **Seventh Cavalry** (*US*) Séptimo *m* de Caballería
Ⓑ N [1] (*in series*) séptimo/a *m/f*; (= *fraction*) séptima parte *f*; *see* **fifth** *for usage*
[2] (*Mus*) (= *interval*) séptima *f*

seventieth ['sevntɪɪθ] Ⓐ ADJ septuagésimo
Ⓑ N (*in series*) septuagésimo/a *m/f*; (= *fraction*) septuagésima parte *f*; *see* **fifth** *for usage*

seventy ['sevntɪ] Ⓐ ADJ setenta
Ⓑ N setenta *m*; *see* **fifty** *for usage*

sever ['sevəʳ] Ⓐ VT cortar; (*fig*) [+ *relations, communications*] romper Ⓑ VI [*rope etc*] cortarse

several ['sevrəl] Ⓐ ADJ [1] (*in number*) varios; **~ times** varias veces; **~ hundred people** varios cientos de personas
[2] (*frm*) (= *separate*) diverso; **their ~ occupations** sus diversas ocupaciones; **they went their ~ ways** tomaron cada uno su camino
Ⓑ PRON varios; **~ of them wore hats** varios (de ellos) llevaban sombrero

severally ['sevrəlɪ] ADV (*frm*) [1] (= *separately, individually*) por separado, individualmente
[2] (= *respectively*) respectivamente

severance ['sevərəns] Ⓐ N ruptura *f*; (*Ind*) despido *m*
Ⓑ CPD ► **severance pay** N indemnización *f* por despido

severe [sɪ'vɪəʳ] ADJ (*compar* **severer**; *superl* **severest**) [1] (= *serious*) [*problem, consequence, damage*] grave, serio; [*injury, illness*] grave; [*defeat, setback, shortage*] serio; [*blow, reprimand*] fuerte, duro; [*pain, headache*] fuerte; **I suffered from ~ bouts of depression** padecía profundas *or* serias depresiones; **many families suffered ~ hardship as a consequence** muchas familias sufrieron enormes penurias a consecuencia de ello; **we have been under ~ pressure to cut costs** nos han presionado mucho para reducir gastos; **to suffer a ~ loss of blood** sufrir gran pérdida de sangre; **~ losses** (*Fin*) enormes *or* cuantiosas pérdidas *fpl*
[2] (= *harsh*) [*weather, conditions, winter*] duro, riguroso; [*cold*] extremo; [*storm, flooding, frost*] fuerte
[3] (= *strict*) [*person, penalty*] severo; [*discipline*] estricto; **I was his ~st critic** yo era su crítico más severo; **to be ~ with sb** ser severo con algn
[4] (= *austere*) [*person, appearance, expression*] severo, adusto; [*clothes, style*] austero; [*hairstyle*] (de corte) serio; [*architecture*] sobrio

severely [sɪ'vɪəlɪ] ADV [1] (= *seriously*) [1·1] (*with verb*) [*damage, disrupt, hamper*] seriamente; [*limit, restrict*] severamente; [*injure, affect*] gravemente; **the competitors were ~ tested by the conditions** las condiciones meteorológicas habían supuesto una dura prueba para los participantes
[1·2] (*with adj*) [*ill, disabled*] gravemente; [*depressed, disturbed*] profundamente
[2] (= *harshly*) [*punish, reprimand, criticize*] duramente, con severidad; [*look*] con severidad
[3] (= *austerely*) [*dress*] austeramente

severity [sɪ'verɪtɪ] N [1] (= *seriousness*) [*of illness*] gravedad *f*, seriedad *f*; [*of pain*] intensidad *f*; [*of attack*] dureza *f*
[2] (= *strictness*) [*of character, criticism*] severidad *f*
[3] (= *harshness*) [*of weather, conditions, winter*] rigor *m*

Seville [sə'vɪl] Ⓐ N Sevilla *f*
Ⓑ CPD ► **Seville orange** N naranja *f* amarga ► **Seville orange tree** N (*Brit*) naranjo *m* amargo

Sevillian [sə'vɪlɪən] Ⓐ ADJ sevillano
Ⓑ N sevillano/a *m/f*

sew [səʊ] (*pt* **sewed**; *pp* **sewn, sewed**) Ⓐ VT **to ~ a button on** *or* **onto sth** coser un botón en algo
Ⓑ VI coser

►**sew up** VT + ADV (*gen*) coser; (*mend*) remendar; **it's all ~n up*** (*fig*) está todo arreglado

sewage ['sju:ɪdʒ] Ⓐ N aguas *fpl* residuales *or* cloacales
Ⓑ CPD ► **sewage disposal** N depuración *f* de aguas residuales *or* cloacales ► **sewage farm**, N **sewage works** NSING estación *f* depuradora ► **sewage system** N alcantarillado *m*

sewer ['sjʊəʳ] N alcantarilla *f*, albañal *m*, cloaca *f*; **to have a mind like a ~** tener la mente podrida

sewerage ['sjʊərɪdʒ] N alcantarillado *m*; (*as service on estate etc*) saneamiento *m*

sewing ['səʊɪŋ] Ⓐ N (*activity, object*) costura *f*
Ⓑ CPD ► **sewing basket** N cesta *f* de costura ► **sewing machine** N máquina *f* de coser ► **sewing silk** N torzal *m*, seda *f* de coser

sewn [səʊn] PP *of* **sew**

sex [seks] Ⓐ N [1] (= *gender*) sexo *m*; **inequalities between the ~es** desigualdades entre los sexos; **the fair** *or* **gentle ~** (*euph*) el sexo débil, el bello sexo; **the opposite ~** el sexo opuesto; **the weaker ~** (*euph, pej*) el sexo débil
[2] (= *sexual activities*) sexo *m*; (= *sexual intercourse*) relaciones *fpl* sexuales; **the film contains no ~ or violence** la película no contiene escenas eróticas *or* de sexo o de violencia; **to have ~** tener relaciones sexuales (**with** con)
[3] (= *sex organ*) sexo *m*, genitales *mpl*
Ⓑ VT [+ *animal, bird*] sexar, determinar el sexo de
Ⓒ CPD ► **the sex act** N el acto sexual, el acto ► **sex appeal** N atractivo *m* sexual, sex-appeal *m* ► **sex change** N cambio *m* de sexo ► **sex change operation** N operación *f* de cambio de sexo ► **sex crime** N (= *criminality*) delitos *mpl* sexuales, delitos *mpl* contra la honestidad (*Jur*), delitos *mpl* contra la libertad sexual (*Jur*); (= *single crime*) delito *m* (de naturaleza) sexual, delito *m* contra la honestidad (*Jur*), delito *m* contra la libertad sexual (*Jur*) ► **sex discrimination** N discriminación *f* por cuestión de sexo ► **sex drive** N libido *f*, líbido *f*, apetito *m* sexual; **to have a high/low ~ drive** tener la libido *or* líbido alta/baja, tener mucho/poco apetito sexual ► **sex education** N educación *f* sexual ► **sex game** N juego *m* erótico ► **sex hormone** N hormona *f* sexual ► **sex life** N vida *f* sexual ► **sex machine** N (*hum*) máquina *f* de hacer el amor, bestia *mf* en la cama ► **sex maniac** N maníaco/a *m/f* sexual ► **sex object** N objeto *m* sexual ► **sex offender** N delincuente *mf* sexual ► **sex organ** N órgano *m* sexual ► **sex partner** N compañero/a *m/f* (de cama), pareja *f* ► **sex scene** N escena *f* erótica, escena *f* de sexo ► **sex shop** N sex-shop *m* ► **sex symbol** N sex-símbol *mf* ► **sex therapist** N sexólogo/a *m/f*, terapeuta *mf* sexual ► **sex therapy** N terapia *f* sexual ► **sex tourism** N turismo *m* sexual

►**sex up*** VT + ADV hacer más atractivo

sexagenarian [,seksədʒɪ'neərɪən] Ⓐ ADJ sexagenario
Ⓑ N sexagenario/a *m/f*

Sexagesima [,seksə'dʒesɪmə] N Sexagésima *f*

sex-crazed ['sekskreɪzd] ADJ obsesionado por el sexo

sexed [sekst] ADJ **to be highly ~** tener un apetito sexual muy alto

sexiness ['seksɪnɪs] N [1] (= *sexual attractiveness*) [*of person, voice, eyes, underwear*] erotismo *m*, atractivo *m* sexual
[2] (= *interest in sex*) excitación *f* sexual, libido

➤ LANGUAGE IN USE: settlement 1 20.6

f alta
[3] (= *eroticism*) [*of film, scene, book*] erotismo *m*
[4] (*) (= *excitement*) gancho* *m*, interés *m*

sexism ['seksɪzəm] N sexismo *m*

sexist ['seksɪst] Ⓐ ADJ sexista
Ⓑ N sexista *mf*

sexless ['sekslɪs] ADJ (= *not interested in sex*) asexuado, desprovisto de instinto sexual; (= *not sexually attractive*) desprovisto de atractivo sexual; (*Bio*) sin sexo, asexual; **a ~ marriage** un matrimonio sin sexo

sex-linked ['seks'lɪŋkt] ADJ (*Bio*) ligado al sexo

sex-mad* [ˌseks'mæd] ADJ obsesionado por el sexo

sexologist [sek'sɒlədʒɪst] N sexólogo/a *m/f*

sexology [sek'sɒlədʒɪ] N sexología *f*

sexpot* ['sekspɒt] N (*hum*) cachonda *f*

sex-starved ['seksstɑːvd] ADJ sexualmente frustrado

sextant ['sekstənt] N sextante *m*

sextet(te) [seks'tet] N (*Mus*) (= *players, composition*) sexteto *m*

sexton ['sekstən] N sacristán *m*

sextuplet ['sekstjʊplɪt] N sextillizo/a *m/f*

sexual ['seksjʊəl] Ⓐ ADJ sexual; **she's very ~** es muy sensual
Ⓑ CPD ► **sexual abuse** N abuso *m* sexual ► **sexual assault** N atentado *m* contra el pudor ► **sexual discrimination** N discriminación *f* a base de sexo ► **sexual harassment** N acoso *m* sexual ► **sexual intercourse** N relaciones *fpl* sexuales; **to have ~ intercourse (with sb)** tener relaciones sexuales (con algn) ► **sexual orientation** N orientación *f* sexual ► **sexual partner** N pareja *f* sexual ► **sexual politics** NPL política *fsing* sexual ► **the sexual revolution** N la revolución sexual

sexuality [ˌseksjʊ'ælɪtɪ] N sexualidad *f*

sexually ['seksjʊəlɪ] ADV sexualmente; **to be ~ abused** ser víctima de abusos sexuales; **to be ~ active** ser sexualmente activo; **to become** *or* **get ~ aroused** excitarse sexualmente; **to be ~ assaulted** ser víctima de una agresión sexual; **to be ~ explicit** contener imágenes de sexo explícito; **to be ~ harrassed** sufrir acoso sexual; **to be ~ involved with sb** mantener relaciones sexuales con algn; **~ mature** sexualmente maduro; **~ transmitted disease** enfermedad *f* de transmisión sexual

sexy ['seksɪ] ADJ (*compar* **sexier**, *superl* **sexiest**)
[1] (= *sexually attractive*) sexy; **you look very ~ in that dress** estás muy sexy con ese vestido
[2] (= *interested in sex*) sensual; **to make sb feel ~** excitar a algn, hacer que algn se excite
[3] (= *erotic*) [*film, scene, book*] erótico
[4] (*) (= *exciting*) [*issue, subject, object*] excitante

Seychelles [seɪ'ʃelz] NPL Seychelles *fpl*

sez‡ [sez] = **says**; **~ you!** ¡lo dices tú!

SF N ABBR [1] = **science fiction**
[2] (*Pol*) = **Sinn Féin**

SFA N ABBR [1] (= **Scottish Football Association**) ≈ AFE *f*
[2] (‡) = **sweet Fanny Adams**

SFO N ABBR (*Brit*) = **Serious Fraud Office**

SG N ABBR (*US*) (= **Surgeon General**) jefe *mf* del servicio federal de sanidad

sgd ABBR = **signed**

Sgt ABBR = **Sergeant**

sh [ʃ] EXCL ¡chitón!, ¡chist!

shabbily ['ʃæbɪlɪ] ADV [1] [*dress*] desaliñadamente, pobremente
[2] [*treat*] fatal, vilmente

shabbiness ['ʃæbɪnɪs] N [1] [*of dress, person*] desaliño *m*, pobreza *f*
[2] [*of treatment*] injusticia *f*, vileza *f*

shabby ['ʃæbɪ] ADJ (*compar* **shabbier**, *superl* **shabbiest**) [1] [*building*] desvencijado; [*clothes*] andrajoso; (*also* **~-looking**) [*person*] andrajoso, desaliñado
[2] [*treatment*] injusto, vil; [*behaviour*] poco honrado; [*excuse*] poco convincente; **a ~ trick** una mala jugada

shabby-looking ['ʃæbɪˌlʊkɪŋ] ADJ [*person*] andrajoso, desaliñado; [*hotel, room*] desvencijado

shack [ʃæk] N choza *f*, jacal *m* (*CAm, Mex*)
►**shack up‡** VI + ADV **to ~ up with sb** arrejuntarse con algn*; **to ~ up together** arrejuntarse*, vivir arrejuntados*

shackle ['ʃækl] Ⓐ VT [+ *prisoner*] poner grilletes a, poner grillos a; (= *obstruct*) echar trabas a
Ⓑ **shackles** NPL (= *chains*) grilletes *mpl*, grillos *mpl*; (*fig*) (= *obstruction*) trabas *fpl*

shad [ʃæd] N (*pl* **shad** *or* **shads**) sábalo *m*

shade [ʃeɪd] Ⓐ N [1] (= *area of darkness*) sombra *f*; **in the ~** a la sombra; **35 degrees in the ~** 35 grados a la sombra; **to put sb in the ~** (*fig*) hacer sombra a algn; **to put sth in the ~** (*fig*) dejar algo en la sombra
[2] [*of colour*] tono *m*, matiz *m*; (*fig*) [*of meaning, opinion*] matiz *m*; **all ~s of opinion are represented** está representada la gama entera de opiniones
[3] (*Art*) sombra *f*
[4] **shades*** (= *sunglasses*) gafas *fpl* de sol
[5] (= *lampshade*) pantalla *f*; (= *eye-shade*) visera *f*; (*US*) (= *blind*) persiana *f*
[6] (= *small quantity*) poquito *m*, tantito *m* (*LAm*); **just a ~ more** un poquito más
[7] (*liter*) (= *ghost*) fantasma *m*
[8] (= *reminder*) **~s of Professor Dodd!** ¡eso recuerda al profesor Dodd!
Ⓑ VT [1] (= *protect from light*) dar sombra a; **the beaches are ~d by palm trees** las palmeras dan sombra a las playas; **she put up her hand to ~ her eyes (from the sun)** levantó la mano para protegerse los ojos (del sol)
[2] (*Art*) (= *shade in*) sombrear
►**shade away** VI + ADV = **shade off B**
►**shade in** VT + ADV sombrear
►**shade off** Ⓐ VT + ADV (*Art*) [+ *colours*] degradar
Ⓑ VI + ADV cambiar poco a poco (**into** hasta hacerse), transformarse gradualmente (**into** en); **blue that ~s off into black** azul que se transforma *or* se funde gradualmente en negro

shadeless ['ʃeɪdlɪs] ADJ sin sombra, privado de sombra

shadiness ['ʃeɪdɪnɪs] N [1] (= *shade*) sombra *f*, lo umbroso
[2] (*) (= *dubiousness*) [*of person*] dudosa honradez *f*; [*of deal*] lo turbio, carácter *m* turbio

shading ['ʃeɪdɪŋ] N [1] [*of colour*] sombreado *m*
[2] (*fig*) [*of meaning*] matiz *m*

shadow ['ʃædəʊ] Ⓐ N [1] (= *dark shape*) sombra *f*; (= *darkness*) oscuridad *f*, tinieblas *fpl*; **in the ~** a la sombra; **five o'clock ~** barba *f* de ocho horas; **doctors have discovered a ~ on his lung** los médicos le han detectado una sombra *or* mancha en el pulmón; **to cast a ~ over sth** (*fig*) ensombrecer algo; **to live in the ~ of sth/sb** vivir eclipsado por algo/algn
[2] (*) (= *tail*) perseguidor(a) *m/f*; **to put a ~ on sb** hacer seguir a algn
[3] (*fig*) (= *faithful companion*) sombra *f*
[4] (*Pol*) *miembro de la oposición con un cargo análogo al de ministro*; **Clarke flung at his ~ the accusation that he was a "tabloid politician"** Clarke lanzó a su homólogo en la oposición la acusación de ser un "político sensacionalista"
[5] (*fig*) (= *small amount*) [*of doubt, suspicion*] atisbo *m*, asomo *m*, sombra *f*; **I never had a** *or* **the ~ of a doubt that he was right** jamás tuve el menor asomo *or* atisbo *or* la menor sombra de duda de que tenía razón; **without a ~ of a doubt** sin (la menor) sombra de duda
[6] (= *vestige*) sombra *f*; **he is a ~ of the man he used to be** no es ni sombra de lo que era; **a ~ of his former self** la sombra de lo que fue
Ⓑ VT [1] (= *follow*) seguir y vigilar; **I was ~ed all the way home** me siguieron hasta mi casa
[2] (= *darken*) ensombrecer, oscurecer; **the hood ~ed her face** la capucha ensombrecía *or* oscurecía su rostro
Ⓒ CPD ► **shadow cabinet** N (*Brit Pol*) consejo *m* de ministros de la oposición; **the ~ Foreign Secretary** el portavoz parlamentario de la oposición en materia de asuntos extranjeros ► **shadow Chancellor** N (*Brit Pol*) responsable *mf* *or* portavoz *mf* de Economía y Hacienda de la oposición

shadow-box ['ʃædəʊbɒks] VI boxear con un adversario imaginario; (*fig*) disputar con un adversario imaginario

shadow-boxing ['ʃædəʊˌbɒksɪŋ] N boxeo *m* con un adversario imaginario; (*fig*) disputa *f* con un adversario imaginario

shadowy ['ʃædəʊɪ] ADJ [1] (= *ill-lit*) oscuro, tenebroso; (= *blurred*) indistinto, vago, indefinido; **a ~ form** un bulto, una sombra
[2] (= *mysterious*) oscuro, misterioso; **the ~ world of espionage** el oscuro *or* misterioso mundo del espionaje

shady ['ʃeɪdɪ] ADJ (*compar* **shadier**, *superl* **shadiest**) [1] (= *shaded*) [*place*] sombreado; **it's ~ here** aquí hay sombra; **under a ~ tree** a la sombra de un árbol frondoso
[2] (*) (= *dubious*) [*person*] dudoso; [*deal*] turbio, chueco (*Mex**)

shaft [ʃɑːft] Ⓐ N [1] (= *stem, handle*) [*of arrow, spear*] astil *m*; [*of tool, golf club etc*] mango *m*; [*of cart etc*] vara *f*; **a ~ of light** un rayo de luz; **drive ~** (*Tech*) árbol *m* motor
[2] [*of mine, lift etc*] pozo *m*
Ⓑ VT (**‡) (= *have sex with*) joder**‡**; **we'll be ~ed if that happens** como pase eso estamos jodidos**‡**

shag[1] [ʃæg] N tabaco *m* picado

shag[2] [ʃæg] N (*Orn*) cormorán *m* moñudo

shag[3]**‡** [ʃæg] (*Brit*) Ⓐ N polvo**‡** *m*; **to have a ~‡** echar un polvo**‡**
Ⓑ VT joder**‡**
Ⓒ VI joder**‡**

shag[4] [ʃæg] N (= *carpet*) tripe *m*

shagged‡ [ʃægd] ADJ (*also* **~ out**) hecho polvo*

shaggy ['ʃægɪ] ADJ (*compar* **shaggier**, *superl* **shaggiest**) [*hair, beard, mane*] greñudo; [*fur, eyebrows, animal*] peludo; [*carpet, rug*] de mucho pelo; [*person*] melenudo, greñudo; **~ dog story** chiste *m* largo y pesado

shagreen [ʃæ'griːn] N chagrín *m*, zapa *f*

Shah [ʃɑː] N cha *m*

shake [ʃeɪk] (*vb: pt* **shook**; *pp* **shaken**) Ⓐ N [1] (= *act of shaking*) sacudida *f*; **to give sth/sb a ~**: **she gave the tin a ~** agitó la lata; **I gave the boy a good ~** zarandeé *or* sacudí bien al chico; **she declined the drink with a ~ of her head** rechazó la copa moviendo la cabeza *or* con un movimiento de la cabeza; **he**

gave a puzzled ~ of his head movió la cabeza confundido; ✦*IDIOMS* **in two ~s*** ◊ **in a brace of ~s*** en un santiamén*, en un abrir y cerrar de ojos*; **no great ~s*: he's no great ~s as a swimmer** *or* **at swimming*** no es nada del otro mundo *or* del otro jueves nadando*
2 **the shakes** el tembleque*, la tembladera*; **to get the ~s: I got a bad case of the ~s** me entró un tembleque* *or* una tembladera* muy fuerte; **to have the ~s** tener el tembleque* *or* la tembladera*
3 (*also* **milkshake**) batido *m*
4 (= *small amount*) [*of liquid*] chorro *m*; [*of salt, sugar*] pizca *f*
Ⓑ VT 1 (= *agitate*) [+ *bottle, tin, dice, cocktail*] agitar; [+ *towel, duster*] sacudir; [+ *head*] mover; [+ *building*] hacer temblar, sacudir; [+ *person*] zarandear, sacudir; **"shake well before use"** "agítese bien antes de usar"; **a fit of coughing that shook his entire body** un ataque de tos que le sacudió *or* le estremeció todo el cuerpo; **high winds shook the trees** fuertes vientos sacudieron los árboles; **to ~ hands** estrecharse la mano; **to ~ hands with sb** estrechar la mano a algn; **to ~ one's head** (*in refusal*) negar con la cabeza; (*in disbelief*) mover la cabeza con gesto incrédulo; (*in dismay*) mover la cabeza con gesto de disgusto; **I shook the snow off my coat** me sacudí la nieve del abrigo; **to ~ o.s.: the dog shook itself** el perro se sacudió; **she tried to hug him but he shook himself free** intentó abrazarlo pero él se la sacudió de encima; **she shook some change out of her purse** sacudió el monedero para sacar calderilla; ✦*IDIOM* **~ a leg!*** ¡ponte las pilas!*, ¡muévete!*
2 (= *wave*) [+ *stick, paper*] blandir, agitar; **to ~ one's finger at sb** señalar a algn agitando el dedo; **to ~ one's fist at sb** amenazar a algn con el puño
3 (*fig*) (= *weaken*) [+ *faith*] debilitar; [+ *resolve*] afectar; (= *impair, upset, shock*) afectar; (= *disconcert*) desconcertar; **the firm's reputation has been badly ~n** la reputación de la empresa se ha visto muy afectada; **he was ~n by the news of her death** la noticia de su muerte lo afectó mucho *or* lo conmocionó; **he needs to be ~n out of his smugness** necesita que se le bajen esos humos; **it shook me rigid** me dejó pasmado *or* helado; **seven days that shook the world** siete días que conmocionaron al mundo
Ⓒ VI 1 (= *tremble*) [*ground, building*] temblar, estremecerse; [*person, animal, voice*] temblar; **I was shaking all over** me temblaba todo el cuerpo; **he was shaking with rage/fear/cold** estaba temblando de rabia/miedo/frío; **her voice shook with rage** la voz le temblaba de rabia; **to ~ with laughter** caerse de risa; ✦*IDIOM* **to ~ like a leaf** temblar como un flan *or* una hoja
2 **to ~ on sth: the two men shook on it** los dos hombres cerraron el trato con un apretón de manos; **let's ~ on it** venga esa mano

►**shake down** Ⓐ VT + ADV 1 [+ *fruit, snow*] hacer caer, sacudir; [+ *thermometer*] agitar (*para bajar la temperatura*)
2 (*US**) **to ~ sb down** (= *rob*) sacar dinero a algn, estafar *or* timar a algn; **they shook him down for 5,000 dollars** le sacaron 5.000 dólares; (= *search*) **to ~ sb down for weapons** cachear a algn en busca de armas
Ⓑ VI + ADV (*) 1 (= *settle for sleep*) acostarse, echarse a dormir
2 (= *settle in*) adaptarse; **I'll give them a few weeks to see how they ~ down** les daré unas semanas para ver cómo se adaptan

►**shake off** VT + ADV 1 (*lit*) [+ *water, snow, dust*] sacudir; **he grabbed my arm, I shook him off** me agarró por el brazo, yo me lo sacudí de encima
2 (*fig*) [+ *pursuer*] zafarse de, dar esquinazo a; [+ *illness*] deshacerse de, librarse de; [+ *cold, habit*] quitarse (de encima); [+ *depression*] salir de

►**shake out** VT + ADV [+ *tablecloth, bedding, rug*] sacudir; **I took off my boot and shook out a stone** me quité la bota y la sacudí para sacar una piedra; **she pulled her hat off and shook out her hair** se quitó el sombrero y se soltó el pelo

►**shake up** VT + ADV 1 [+ *bottle*] agitar; [+ *pillow*] sacudir
2 (= *upset*) conmocionar; **she was badly ~n up** estaba muy conmocionada *or* afectada; **he was ~n up but not hurt** estaba en estado de shock, pero ileso
3 (= *rouse, stir*) [+ *person*] espabilar, despabilar
4 (= *reform*) [+ *company*] reorganizar, reestructurar; [+ *system*] reformar; **you need to ~ up your ideas a bit!** ¡tienes que replantearte las ideas!

shakedown [ˈʃeɪkdaʊn] N 1 (= *shaking*) sacudida *f*
2 (*Brit*) (= *bed*) camastro *m*, cama *f* improvisada
3 (*) (*before noun*) **a ~ cruise/flight** una travesía/un vuelo de prueba
4 (*US**) (= *swindle*) estafa *f*, timo *m*; (= *search*) **to give sth a ~** registrar algo

shaken [ˈʃeɪkən] PP *of* **shake**

shake-out [ˈʃeɪkaʊt] N [*of company*] reorganización *f*, reestructuración *f*; [*of workforce*] reducción *f*

shaker [ˈʃeɪkəʳ] N (= *cocktail shaker*) coctelera *f*

Shakespeare [ˈʃeɪkspɪəʳ] N Shakespeare, Chéspir

Shakespearian [ʃeɪksˈpɪərɪən] ADJ shakespeariano

shake-up [ˈʃeɪkʌp] N [*of company, system*] reorganización *f*, reestructuración *f*; **today a cabinet ~ was announced** hoy se anunció una reestructuración *or* remodelación del gabinete ministerial

shakily [ˈʃeɪkɪlɪ] ADV [*speak*] con voz temblorosa; [*walk*] con paso vacilante; [*write*] con mano temblorosa; **the play started ~** el principio de la obra fue flojo

shakiness [ˈʃeɪkɪnɪs] N 1 (= *trembling*) [*of person, legs*] temblor *m*
2 [*of table, chair, building etc*] (= *wobbliness*) inestabilidad *f*
3 (= *weakness*) [*of person*] debilidad *f*
4 (*fig*) (= *uncertainty*) [*of health, memory*] fragilidad *f*, precariedad *f*; [*of finances*] precariedad *f*; [*of knowledge*] deficiencia *f*

shaking [ˈʃeɪkɪŋ] N 1 (= *trembling*) temblor *m*
2 (= *jolting*) **to give sb a good ~** zarandear bien a algn, sacudir violentamente a algn

shako [ˈʃækəʊ] N (*pl* **shakos** *or* **shakoes**) chacó *m*

shaky [ˈʃeɪkɪ] ADJ (*compar* **shakier**; *superl* **shakiest**) 1 (= *trembling*) [*person, legs*] tembloroso
2 (= *wobbly*) inestable, poco firme
3 (= *weak*) [*person*] débil
4 (*fig*) (= *uncertain*) [*health, memory*] frágil, precario; [*finances*] precario; [*knowledge*] deficiente, flojo; **my Spanish is rather ~** mi español es bastante flojo

shale [ʃeɪl] Ⓐ N esquisto *m*
Ⓑ CPD ► **shale oil** N petróleo *m* de esquisto

▼**shall** [ʃæl] AUX VB 1 (*used to form 1st person in future tense and questions*) **I ~ go** yo iré; **no I ~ not (come)** ◊ **no I shan't (come)** no, yo no (vendré *or* voy a venir); **~ I go now?** ¿me voy ahora?; **let's go in, ~ we?** ¿entramos?; **~ we let him?** ¿se lo permitimos?; **~ we hear from you soon?** ¿te pondrás en contacto pronto?
2 (*in commands, emphatic*) **you ~ pay for this!** ¡me las vas a pagar!; **"but I wanted to see him" — "and so you ~"** —pero quería verle —y le vas a ver

shallot [ʃəˈlɒt] N chalote *m*

shallow [ˈʃæləʊ] Ⓐ ADJ (*compar* **shallower**; *superl* **shallowest**) 1 (*gen*) poco profundo, playo (*S. Cone*); [*dish etc*] llano; **the ~ end** (*of swimming pool*) la parte poco profunda
2 [*breathing*] superficial
3 [*person, mind, character*] superficial; [*argument, novel, film*] superficial, trivial
Ⓑ **shallows** NPL bajío *msing*, bajos *mpl*

shallowness [ˈʃæləʊnɪs] N 1 [*of water, pool*] poca profundidad *f*
2 [*of breathing*] superficialidad *f*
3 [*of person*] superficialidad *f*

shalt†† [ʃælt] VB 2ND PERS SING *of* **shall**

sham [ʃæm] Ⓐ ADJ falso, fingido
Ⓑ N 1 (= *imposture*) farsa *f*; **it was all a ~** fue una farsa, fue pura pantalla (*Mex*)
2 (= *person*) impostor/a *m/f*
Ⓒ VT fingir, simular; **to ~ illness** fingirse enfermo
Ⓓ VI fingir, fingirse; **he's just ~ming** lo está fingiendo

shamateur* [ˈʃæmətəʳ] N amateur *mf* fingido/a

shamble [ˈʃæmbl] VI (*also* **~ along**) andar arrastrando los pies; **he ~d across to the window** fue arrastrando los pies a la ventana

shambles [ˈʃæmblz] NSING (= *scene of confusion*) desorden *m*, confusión *f*; **this room is a ~!** ¡esta habitación está hecha un desastre!; **the place was a ~** el lugar quedó hecho pedazos; **the game was a ~** el partido fue desastroso

shambolic* [ʃæmˈbɒlɪk] ADJ caótico

shame [ʃeɪm] Ⓐ N 1 (= *guilt*) vergüenza *f*, pena *f* (*LAm*); **she has no sense of ~** no tiene vergüenza ninguna; **to put sb to ~** (*fig*) poner a algn en evidencia; **to put sth to ~** (*fig*) dejar algo en la sombra; **the ~ of it!** ¡qué vergüenza!; **~ (on you)!** ¡qué vergüenza!, ¡vergüenza debería darte!
2 (= *loss of respect*) deshonra *f*; **to bring ~ upon sb** deshonrar a algn
3 (= *pity*) lástima *f*, pena *f*; **it's a ~ that ...** es una lástima *or* pena que + *subjun*; **what a ~!** ¡qué lástima!, ¡qué pena!
Ⓑ VT 1 (= *cause to feel shame*) avergonzar; **to ~ sb into/out of doing sth** hacer avergonzarse a algn para que haga/no haga algo
2 (= *cause loss of respect for*) deshonrar

shamefaced [ˈʃeɪmfeɪst] ADJ avergonzado, apenado (*LAm*)

shamefacedly [ˈʃeɪmfeɪsɪdlɪ] ADV con vergüenza, apenadamente (*LAm*)

shamefacedness [ˈʃeɪmfeɪstnɪs] N vergüenza *f*, pena *f* (*LAm*)

shameful [ˈʃeɪmfʊl] ADJ vergonzoso; **how ~!** ¡qué vergüenza!

shamefully [ˈʃeɪmfəlɪ] ADV vergonzosamente; **~ ignorant** tan ignorante que da/daba *etc* vergüenza; **they are ~ underpaid** se les paga terriblemente mal, tienen un sueldo de vergüenza

shamefulness [ˈʃeɪmfʊlnɪs] N vergüenza *f*, lo vergonzoso

shameless [ˈʃeɪmlɪs] ADJ descarado, desvergonzado

➤ LANGUAGE IN USE: shall 1 3

shamelessly ['ʃeɪmlɪslɪ] ADV descaradamente, desvergonzadamente

shamelessness ['ʃeɪmlɪsnɪs] N descaro *m*, desvergüenza *f*

shaming ['ʃeɪmɪŋ] ADJ vergonzoso; **this is too ~!** ¡qué vergüenza!

shammy* ['ʃæmɪ] N gamuza *f*

shampoo [ʃæm'puː] Ⓐ N champú *m*; **a ~ and set** un lavado y marcado Ⓑ VT [+ *carpet*] lavar con champú; **I ~ my hair twice a week** me lavo el pelo dos veces por semana

shamrock ['ʃæmrɒk] N trébol *m*

shandy ['ʃændɪ] N cerveza *f* con gaseosa, clara *f* (*Sp*)

shandygaff ['ʃændɪ,gæf] N (*US*) = **shandy**

Shanghai [,ʃæŋ'haɪ] N Shanghai *m*

shanghai* [ʃæŋ'haɪ] VT **to ~ sb** (*Naut††*) narcotizar *or* emborrachar a algn y llevarle como marinero; (*fig*) secuestrar a algn

Shangri-la ['ʃæŋrɪ'lɑː] N jauja *f*, paraíso *m* terrestre

shank [ʃæŋk] N (= *part of leg*) caña *f*; (= *bird's leg*) zanca *f*; (*Bot*) tallo *m*; (= *handle*) mango *m*; **shanks*** piernas *fpl*; ✦***IDIOM*** **to go on** *or* **by Shanks's pony** (*hum*) ir en el coche de San Francisco, ir a golpe de calcetín

shan't [ʃɑːnt] = **shall not**

shanty[1] ['ʃæntɪ] N (*Brit*) (*also* **sea ~**) saloma *f*

shanty[2] ['ʃæntɪ] N chabola *f*, jacal *m* (*Mex*), bohío *m* (*CAm*), callampa *f* (*Chile*)

shantytown ['ʃæntɪ,taʊn] N chabolas *fpl* (*Sp*), villa *f* miseria (*Mex*), (población *f*) callampa *f* (*Chile*), ciudad *f* perdida (*Mex*), colonia *f* proletaria (*Mex*), pueblo *m* joven (*Peru*), cantegriles *mpl* (*Uru*), ranchitos *mpl* (*Ven*)

SHAPE [ʃeɪp] N ABBR (= **Supreme Headquarters Allied Powers Europe**) *cuartel general de las fuerzas aliadas en Europa*

shape [ʃeɪp] Ⓐ N 1 (= *outline*) forma *f*, figura *f*; (= *figure*) [*of person*] silueta *f*, figura *f*; **what ~ is it?** ¿de qué forma es?; **all ~s and sizes** todas las formas; **universities come in all ~s and sizes** (*fig*) hay universidades de todo tipo; **it is rectangular in ~** es de forma rectangular; **in the ~ of ...** (*fig*) en forma de ...; **to bend** *or* **twist sth into ~** dar forma a algo doblándolo; **to hammer sth into ~** dar forma a algo a martillazos; **to lose its ~** [*sweater etc*] perder la forma; **to bend** *or* **twist sth out of ~** deformar algo doblándolo; **to take ~** cobrar forma; **to take the ~ of sth** cobrar *or* tomar la forma de algo

2 (= *undefined object*) forma *f*, bulto *m*; (= *striking object*) figura *f*; **a ~ loomed up out of the fog/darkness** una forma *or* un bulto surgió de la niebla/la oscuridad; **the great grey ~ of a tank rolled out of the village** la imponente figura gris de un tanque salió del pueblo

3 (= *nature, appearance*) estructura *f*, configuración *f*; **the future ~ of industry** la futura estructura *or* configuración de la industria; **I can't bear gardening in any ~ or form** no aguanto la jardinería bajo ningún concepto; **the ~ of things to come** lo que nos depara el mañana; **to take ~** tomar forma

4 (= *mould*) molde *m*; **use star ~s to cut out the biscuits** utilice moldes en forma de estrella para cortar las galletas

5 (= *condition*) forma *f* (física), estado *m* físico; **to be in bad ~** [*person*] estar en mala forma (física); [*object*] estar en mal estado; **to be in good ~** [*person*] estar en buena forma (física); [*object*] estar en buen estado; **to be in ~** [*person*] estar en buena forma; **to get o.s. into ~** ponerse en forma; **to keep in ~** mantenerse en forma; **to knock** *or* **lick sth/sb into ~** (*fig*) poner algo/a algn a punto; **to be out of ~** [*person*] estar en mala forma; **to whip sth/sb into ~** = **to knock** *or* **lick sth/sb into shape**

Ⓑ VT 1 (*lit*) (= *mould*) dar forma a, formar

2 (*fig*) (= *influence, determine*) conformar, determinar; **the forces that have ~d the 20th century** los elementos que han conformado *or* configurado el siglo XX; **democracy is shaping the future of Western Europe** la democracia está determinando el futuro de Europa Occidental

3 (= *prepare*) [+ *plan*] trazar; **to ~ a plan of action** trazar un plan de acción

►**shape up** VI + ADV 1 (= *progress*) [*person*] ir, marchar; [*campaign, plan*] desarrollarse; **how are the new staff shaping up?** ¿cómo va *or* marcha el personal nuevo?; **to ~ up well** ir bien, marchar bien; **it's shaping up as one of the most intensive sales campaigns ever** se perfila *or* se está desarrollando como una de las campañas de ventas más agresiva de la historia; **it's shaping up to be a terrible winter** (*esp US*) promete ser un invierno muy crudo, ya se perfila como un invierno muy crudo

2 (= *improve*) (*esp US*) espabilarse, enmendarse; **you'd better ~ up or you won't have a job!** ¡más vale que te espabiles o no tendrás trabajo!; ✦***IDIOM*** **~ up or ship out!** (*esp US**) ¡o te pones las pilas o te largas!*

3 (= *get fit*) (*esp US*) ponerse en forma

-shaped ['ʃeɪpt] ADJ (*ending in compounds*) en forma de ...; **heart-shaped** en forma de corazón; *see* **pear-shaped**

shapeless ['ʃeɪplɪs] ADJ sin forma definida, informe (*frm*)

shapelessness ['ʃeɪplɪsnɪs] N falta *f* de forma definida, lo informe (*frm*)

shapeliness ['ʃeɪplɪnɪs] N [*of object*] proporción *f*; [*of woman*] figura *f* bonita, buen cuerpo *m*

shapely ['ʃeɪplɪ] ADJ [*object*] proporcionado, bien formado; [*woman*] con una bonita figura, de buen cuerpo; **~ legs** piernas torneadas

shard [ʃɑːd] N tiesto *m*, casco *m*, fragmento *m*

▼ **share**[1] [ʃɛəʳ] Ⓐ N 1 (= *portion*) parte *f*, porción *f*; **a ~ of** *or* **in the profits** una proporción de las ganancias; **how much will my ~ be?** ¿cuánto me corresponderá a mí?; **your ~ is £5** te tocan 5 libras; **to do one's (fair) ~ (of sth)** hacer lo que a uno le toca *or* corresponde (de algo); **he doesn't do his ~** no hace todo lo que debiera, no hace todo lo que le toca *or* corresponde; **to have a ~ in sth** participar en algo; **we've had our ~ of misfortunes** hemos sufrido bastante infortunio, hemos sufrido lo nuestro; **market ~** cuota *f* del mercado; **to take a ~ in doing sth** hacer su parte en algo; ✦***IDIOM*** **the lion's ~** la parte del león

2 (*Fin*) acción *f*

Ⓑ VT 1 (= *split, divide*) [+ *resource, benefit*] repartir, dividir, partir; **would you like to ~ the bottle with me?** ¿quieres compartir la botella conmigo?; **a ~d room** una habitación compartida

2 (= *accept equally*) [+ *duty, responsibility, task*] compartir, corresponsabilizarse de; **to ~ the blame** [*one person*] aceptar su parte de culpa; [*more than one person*] corresponsabilizarse de la culpa

3 (= *have in common*) [+ *characteristic, quality*] compartir, tener en común; [+ *experience, opinion*] compartir; **two nations who ~ a common language** dos naciones que tienen en común *or* comparten la misma lengua; **I do not ~ that view** no comparto ese criterio

4 (= *tell, relate*) [+ *piece of news, thought*] contar, compartir, hacer partícipe de (*frm*) (**with** a); **it can be beneficial to ~ your feelings with someone you trust** puede resultar beneficioso compartir *or* contar tus sentimientos a alguien de confianza

Ⓒ VI compartir (**with** con); **I ~ with three other women** (*room, flat, etc*) vivo con otras tres mujeres; **to ~ in sth** participar en algo; ✦***IDIOM*** **~ and ~ alike** todos por igual

Ⓓ CPD ► **share capital** N capital *m* social en acciones ► **share certificate** N (certificado *m* *or* título *m* de una) acción *f* ► **share index** N índice *m* de la Bolsa ► **share issue** N emisión *f* de acciones ► **share offer** N oferta *f* de acciones ► **share option** N *plan de compra de acciones de una empresa por sus empleados (a precios ventajosos)* ► **share premium** N prima *f* de emisión ► **share price** N precio *m* de las acciones

►**share out** VT + ADV repartir, distribuir

share[2] [ʃɛəʳ] N (*Agr*) (= *ploughshare*) reja *f*

sharecropper ['ʃɛə,krɒpəʳ] N (*esp US*) aparcero/a *m/f*, mediero/a *m/f* (*Mex*)

sharecropping ['ʃɛə,krɒpɪŋ] N (*esp US*) aparcería *f*

shared [ʃɛəd] ADJ (*gen*) compartido; [*facilities etc*] comunitario

shareholder ['ʃɛə,həʊldəʳ] N accionista *mf*

shareholding ['ʃɛə,həʊldɪŋ] N accionariado *m*

share-out ['ʃɛəraʊt] N reparto *m*

shareware ['ʃɛəwɛəʳ] N (*Comput*) shareware *m*

shark [ʃɑːk] N 1 (= *fish*) tiburón *m*

2 (*) (= *swindler*) estafador(a) *m/f*

sharkskin ['ʃɑːkskɪn] N zapa *f*

sharon ['ʃærən] N (*also* **~ fruit**) sharon *m*

sharp [ʃɑːp] Ⓐ ADJ (*compar* **sharper**, *superl* **sharpest**) 1 (= *not blunt*) [*edge*] afilado; [*needle*] puntiagudo; **to have a ~ point** ser muy puntiagudo; **the stick ended in a ~ point** el palo acababa en una punta afilada; ✦***IDIOM*** **to be at the ~ end*** estar en primera línea de fuego; **they are living at the ~ end of the recession** son los que se llevan la peor parte de la recesión, son los más afectados por la recesión

2 (= *abrupt, acute*) [*bend, angle*] cerrado; [*rise, drop, turn by car*] brusco; **he made a ~ turn to the left** giró bruscamente a la izquierda

3 (*of person*) (= *alert*) avispado, perspicaz; (= *unscrupulous*) listo, vivo; [*mind*] agudo, perspicaz; **you'll have to be ~er than that** tendrás que espabilarte; **he's as ~ as they come** es de lo más listo *or* vivo; **his ~ eyes spotted a free seat** sus ojos de lince vieron un asiento libre; **I have to keep a ~ eye on him** con él tengo que estar ojo avizor; **~ practice** artimañas *fpl*; ✦***IDIOM*** **to be as ~ as a needle** ser más listo que el hambre

4 (= *brusque*) [*retort*] seco, cortante; [*rebuke, tone*] áspero, severo; [*tongue*] afilada, mordaz; **to have a ~ tongue** tener la lengua afilada, tener una lengua viperina; **to be ~ with sb** ser seco *or* cortante con algn

5 (= *strong*) [*taste*] ácido; [*smell, cheese*] fuerte

6 (= *clear, well-defined*) [*outline, image*] nítido; [*contrast*] claro, marcado; [*sound*] claro; [*features*] marcado, anguloso; **these issues have been brought into ~ focus by the economic crisis** la crisis económica ha situado estos temas en primer plano

7 (= *intense*) [*pain*] agudo; [*cold, wind*] cortante; [*frost*] fuerte; **a ~ blow to the head** un fuerte golpe en la cabeza; **with a ~ cry she jumped back** soltando un grito agudo retrocedió de un salto

➤ LANGUAGE IN USE: **share**[1] **B3** 12.1

[8] (*) (= *stylish*) [*suit*] elegante; **he was a ~ dresser** vestía con mucha elegancia
[9] (*Mus*) (= *raised a semitone*) sostenido; (= *too high*) demasiado alto; **C ~** do *m* sostenido
Ⓑ ADV [1] (= *quickly, abruptly*) **and be** *or* **look ~ about it!** ¡y date prisa!; **look ~!** ¡rápido!, ¡apúrate! (*LAm*); **to pull up ~** parar en seco; **you turn ~ left at the lights** al llegar al semáforo se tuerce muy cerrado a la izquierda
[2] (= *precisely*) en punto; **at five o'clock ~** a las cinco en punto
[3] (*Mus*) demasiado alto; **she was singing/playing ~** cantaba/tocaba demasiado alto
Ⓒ N [1] (*Mus*) sostenido *m*
[2] (= *con artist*) estafador(a) *m/f*; (= *cardsharp*) fullero/a *m/f*, tramposo/a *m/f*

sharp-edged ['ʃɑːp'edʒd] ADJ afilado, de filo cortante

sharpen ['ʃɑːpən] Ⓐ VT [1] (= *make sharp*) [+ *tool, blade*] afilar; [+ *pencil*] sacar punta a, afilar; **to ~ sth to a point** afilar algo hasta sacarle punta
[2] (= *intensify, increase*) [+ *reactions*] agudizar; [+ *resolve*] aumentar; [+ *contrast*] marcar; [+ *appetite*] abrir; [+ *skills*] mejorar; **this will ~ awareness of other people's needs** esto hará que se tome más conciencia de las necesidades de los demás; **to ~ one's wits** espabilarse
[3] (= *make clearer*) [+ *image*] definir, hacer más nítido
Ⓑ VI [*voice*] volverse más agudo; [*desire*] avivarse; [*pain*] agudizarse

►**sharpen up** Ⓐ VT + ADV [+ *person*] espabilar; **to ~ up one's act** enmendarse
Ⓑ VI + ADV [*person*] espabilarse

sharpener ['ʃɑːpnəʳ] N (*for pencil*) sacapuntas *m inv*; (*for knife*) afilador *m*

sharper ['ʃɑːpəʳ] N (= *con artist*) estafador(a) *m/f*; (= *card-sharp*) fullero/a *m/f*, tramposo/a *m/f*

sharp-eyed ['ʃɑːp'aɪd] ADJ de vista aguda

sharp-faced ['ʃɑːp'feɪst] ADJ, **sharp-featured** ['ʃɑːp'fiːtʃəd] ADJ de facciones angulosas

sharpish* ['ʃɑːpɪʃ] ADV (= *quickly*) rapidito*; **it needs to be ready ~** hay que hacerlo rapidito

sharply ['ʃɑːplɪ] ADV [1] (= *abruptly*) [*fall, rise, turn, brake*] bruscamente; **the road turned ~ left** la carretera giraba bruscamente hacia la izquierda; **he drew in his breath ~** inspiró bruscamente
[2] (= *clearly*) marcadamente, claramente; **this attitude contrasts ~ with his caring image** esta actitud contrasta marcadamente *or* claramente con su imagen de hombre humanitario; **the party is ~ divided over this issue** el partido está claramente dividido con respecto a este asunto
[3] (= *brusquely*) con aspereza; **he spoke to me quite ~** me habló con bastante aspereza
[4] (= *severely*) [*criticize*] severamente, con dureza
[5] (= *hard*) fuertemente; **the ball struck him ~ on the head** la pelota le golpeó fuertemente en la cabeza

sharpness ['ʃɑːpnɪs] N [1] [*of knife, point*] lo afilado; [*of edge*] lo afilado, lo cortante
[2] (= *abruptness*) [*of bend*] lo cerrado; [*of turn*] brusquedad *f*
[3] (= *clarity*) [*of outline, image*] nitidez *f*, definición *f*; [*of contrast*] lo marcado
[4] (= *keenness*) [*of mind*] perspicacia *f*, agudeza *f*; [*of reflexes*] rapidez *f*; **his eyes hadn't lost any of their ~** sus ojos no habían perdido nada de su agudeza
[5] (= *severity*) [*of pain*] agudeza *f*, intensidad *f*; [*of remark, tone*] aspereza *f*; [*of tongue*] mordacidad *f*; **there was a note of ~ in his voice** se notaba cierta aspereza en su tono; **there is a ~ in the air** empieza a notarse el frío
[6] [*of taste*] acidez *f*

sharpshooter ['ʃɑːpˌʃuːtəʳ] N (*esp US*) tirador(a) *m/f* de primera

sharp-sighted ['ʃɑːp'saɪtɪd] ADJ = **sharp-eyed**

sharp-tempered [ˌʃɑːp'tempəd] ADJ de genio arisco

sharp-tongued ['ʃɑːp'tʌŋd] ADJ de lengua mordaz

sharp-witted ['ʃɑːp'wɪtɪd] ADJ perspicaz, despabilado

shat‡ [ʃæt] PT, PP *of* **shit**

shatter ['ʃætəʳ] Ⓐ VT [1] (= *break*) romper en pedazos *or* añicos, hacer pedazos *or* añicos
[2] (*fig*) **to ~ sb's health/hopes** quebrantar la salud/frustrar las esperanzas de algn; **I was ~ed to hear it** al saberlo quedé estupefacto; **she was ~ed by his death** su muerte la dejó destrozada
Ⓑ VI [1] (= *break*) hacerse pedazos, hacerse añicos
[2] (*fig*) [*health*] quebrantarse; [*hopes*] frustrarse

shattered ['ʃætəd] ADJ [1] (*) (= *exhausted*) hecho polvo*
[2] (= *grief-stricken*) trastornado, destrozado; (= *aghast, overwhelmed*) abrumado, confundido

shattering ['ʃætərɪŋ] ADJ [*attack, defeat*] aplastante; [*experience, news*] pasmoso; **it was a ~ blow to his hopes** deshizo sus esperanzas

shatterproof ['ʃætəpruːf] ADJ inastillable

shave [ʃeɪv] (*vb: pt* **shaved**; *pp* **shaved, shaven**)
Ⓐ N **to have a ~** afeitarse, rasurarse (*esp LAm*); **to have a close** *or* **narrow ~** (*fig*) salvarse de milagro *or* por los pelos; **that was a close ~!** ¡qué poco le ha faltado!, ¡(ha sido) por los pelos!
Ⓑ VT [+ *person, face*] afeitar, rasurar (*esp LAm*); [+ *wood*] cepillar; (*fig*) (= *skim, graze*) pasar rozando; **to ~ (off) one's beard** afeitarse la barba; **to ~ one's legs** afeitarse las piernas
Ⓒ VI [*person*] afeitarse, rasurarse (*esp LAm*)

►**shave off** VT + ADV **to ~ off one's beard** afeitarse la barba

shaven ['ʃeɪvn] Ⓐ PP (††) *of* **shave**
Ⓑ ADJ afeitado

shaver ['ʃeɪvəʳ] N [1] (*electric*) máquina *f* de afeitar, rasuradora *f* eléctrica (*LAm*)
[2] **young ~***† muchachuelo *m*, rapaz *m*, chaval* *m*

Shavian ['ʃeɪvɪən] ADJ shaviano, típico de G. B. Shaw

shaving ['ʃeɪvɪŋ] Ⓐ N [1] (= *act of shaving*) afeitado *m*; **~ is a nuisance** afeitarse es una lata
[2] (= *piece of wood, metal etc*) viruta *f*
Ⓑ CPD ► **shaving brush** N brocha *f* de afeitar ► **shaving cream** N crema *f* de afeitar ► **shaving foam** N espuma *f* de afeitar ► **shaving lotion** N loción *f* para el afeitado ► **shaving mirror** N espejo *m* de tocador (de aumento) ► **shaving soap** N jabón *m* de afeitar ► **shaving stick** N barra *f* de jabón de afeitar

shawl [ʃɔːl] N chal *m*, rebozo *m* (*LAm*)

shawm [ʃɔːm] N chirimía *f*

she [ʃiː] Ⓐ PERS PRON [1] (*emphatic, to avoid ambiguity*) ella; **we went to the cinema but ~ didn't** nosotros fuimos al cine pero ella no; **it's ~ who ...** es ella quien ...; **you've got more money than ~ has** tienes más dinero que ella

Don't translate the subject pronoun when not emphasizing or clarifying:

~'s very nice es muy maja; **~'s a teacher** es profesora
[2] (*frm*) **~ who wishes to ...** quien desee ..., la que desee ...
Ⓑ N **it's a ~** (= *animal*) es hembra; (= *baby*) es una niña
Ⓒ CPD ► **she-bear** N osa *f* ► **she-cat** N gata *f*

sheaf [ʃiːf] N (*pl* **sheaves**) (*Agr*) gavilla *f*; [*of arrows*] haz *m*; [*of papers*] fajo *m*, manojo *m*

shear [ʃɪəʳ] (*pt* **sheared**; *pp* **sheared, shorn**) Ⓐ VT [+ *sheep*] esquilar; **to be shorn of sth** (*fig*) quedar pelado de algo, quedar sin algo
Ⓑ VI (= *give way*) partirse, romperse

►**shear off** Ⓐ VT + ADV cortar; **the machine ~ed off two fingers** la máquina le cortó *or* (*frm*) cercenó dos dedos
Ⓑ VI + ADV (= *break off*) partirse, romperse

►**shear through** VI + PREP cortar

shearer ['ʃɪərəʳ] N esquilador(a) *m/f*

shearing ['ʃɪərɪŋ] Ⓐ N esquileo *m*; **shearings** lana *fsing* esquilada
Ⓑ CPD ► **shearing machine** N esquiladora *f*

shears [ʃɪəz] NPL (*for sheep*) tijeras *fpl* de esquilar; (*for hedges*) tijeras *fpl* de podar; (*for metals*) cizalla *fsing*

shearwater ['ʃɪəˌwɔːtəʳ] N pardela *f*

sheath [ʃiːθ] Ⓐ N (*pl* **sheaths** [ʃiːðz]) [1] (*for sword*) vaina *f*, funda *f*
[2] (*around cable*) cubierta *f*
[3] (*Bio*) vaina *f*
[4] (= *contraceptive*) preservativo *m*
Ⓑ CPD ► **sheath dress** N vestido *m* tubo ► **sheath knife** N cuchillo *m* de monte

sheathe [ʃiːð] VT envainar, enfundar (**in** en)

sheathing ['ʃiːðɪŋ] N revestimiento *m*, cubierta *f*

sheaves [ʃiːvz] NPL *of* **sheaf**

Sheba ['ʃiːbə] N Sabá; **Queen of ~** reina *f* de Sabá

shebang‡ [ʃə'bæŋ] N **the whole ~** (= *the whole thing*) todo el tinglado*

shebeen [ʃɪ'biːn] N (*Irl, South Africa*) bar *m* clandestino

shed¹ [ʃed] (*pt, pp* **shed**) VT [1] (= *get rid of*) [+ *clothes, fur, leaves, skin*] despojarse de; [+ *jobs*] suprimir, recortar; **our dog ~s hair all over the carpet** nuestro perro va soltando pelo por toda la moqueta; **to ~ one's clothes** desvestirse, quitarse la ropa, despojarse de la ropa (*frm*); **the roof is built to ~ water** el techo está construido para que el agua no quede en él; **the lorry ~ its load** la carga cayó del camión; **to ~ one's inhibitions** desinhibirse
[2] [+ *tears, blood*] derramar; **the ~ding of innocent blood** el derramamiento de sangre inocente; **those heroes that ~ their blood in the cause of freedom** aquellos héroes que entregaron sus vidas en pro de la libertad
[3] (= *send out*) [+ *warmth*] dar; [+ *light*] echar; ✦*IDIOM* **to ~ light on sth** (*fig*) arrojar luz sobre algo

shed² [ʃed] N (*in garden*) cobertizo *m*, galpón *m* (*S. Cone*); (*for cattle*) establo *m*; (*Ind, Rail*) nave *f*

she'd [ʃiːd] = **she would, she had**

sheen [ʃiːn] N brillo *m*, lustre *m*

sheeny ['ʃiːnɪ] ADJ brillante, lustroso

sheep [ʃiːp] Ⓐ N (*pl inv*) oveja *f*; ✦*IDIOMS* **to be the black ~ of the family** ser la oveja negra de la familia; **to make ~'s eyes at sb** mirar a algn con ojos de cordero; **we must sort**

out *or* **separate the ~ from the goats** tenemos que apartar *or* separar el grano de la paja
Ⓑ CPD ► **sheep dip** N (baño *m*) desinfectante *m* para ovejas ► **sheep farm** N granja *f* de ovejas, granja *f* ovina, granja *f* de ganado lanar ► **sheep farmer** N criador(a) *m/f* de ganado lanar, ganadero/a *m/f* de ovejas ► **sheep farming** N ganadería *f* ovina *or* lanar, cría *f* de ganado ovino *or* lanar ► **sheep run** N pasto *m* de ovejas, dehesa *f* de ovejas ► **sheep track** N cañada *f* (de pastoreo) ► **sheep worrying** N acoso *m* de ovejas

sheepdog [ˈʃiːpdɒg] N perro *m* pastor

sheepfold [ˈʃiːpfəʊld] N redil *m*, aprisco *m*

sheepish [ˈʃiːpɪʃ] ADJ avergonzado

sheepishly [ˈʃiːpɪʃlɪ] ADV avergonzadamente

sheepishness [ˈʃiːpɪʃnɪs] N vergüenza *f*

sheepmeat [ˈʃiːpmiːt] N carne *f* de oveja

sheepshearer [ˈʃiːpˌʃɪərəʳ] N [1] (= *person*) esquilador(a) *m/f*
[2] (= *machine*) esquiladora *f*

sheepskin [ˈʃiːpskɪn] N piel *f* de carnero

sheepwalk [ˈʃiːpwɔːk] N = **sheep run**

sheer[1] [ʃɪəʳ] Ⓐ ADJ (*compar* **sheerer**; *superl* **sheerest**) [1] (= *absolute*) puro, absoluto; **by ~ accident** ◊ **by ~ chance** de pura casualidad; **in ~ desperation** en último extremo; **by ~ hard work** gracias simplemente al trabajo; **the ~ impossibility of …** la total imposibilidad de …; → PURE
[2] (= *transparent*) transparente, fino
[3] (= *precipitous*) escarpado
Ⓑ ADV **it falls ~ to the sea** baja sin obstáculo alguno hasta el mar; **it rises ~ for 100 metres** se levanta verticalmente unos 100 metros

►**sheer off** VI + ADV (*Naut*) [*ship*] desviarse; (*fig*) largarse

sheer[2] [ʃɪəʳ] VI **to ~ away from a topic** desviarse de un tema, evitar hablar de un tema

sheet [ʃiːt] Ⓐ N [1] (*also* **bedsheet**) sábana *f*
[2] [*of metal, glass, plastic*] lámina *f*
[3] [*of paper*] hoja *f*; [*of labels, stamps, stickers*] pliego *m*, hoja *f*; **an information ~** una hoja informativa; ✦**IDIOM to start again with a clean ~** hacer borrón y cuenta nueva
[4] [*of ice, water*] capa *f*; **a ~ of flame** una cortina de fuego; **the rain was coming down in ~s** estaba cayendo una cortina de agua *or* lluvia, llovía a mares
[5] (*Naut*) escota *f*
[6] (*Press*) periódico *m*
[7] ✦**IDIOM to keep a clean ~** (*Brit Ftbl*) mantener la portería imbatida, no encajar ningún gol
Ⓑ CPD ► **sheet anchor** N (*Naut*) ancla *f* de la esperanza ► **sheet bend** N nudo *m* de escota, vuelta *f* de escota ► **sheet feed** N alimentador *m* de papel ► **sheet ice** N capa *f* de hielo ► **sheet lightning** N fucilazo *m* ► **sheet metal** N metal *m* en lámina ► **sheet music** N hojas *fpl* de partitura

sheeting [ˈʃiːtɪŋ] N (= *cloth*) lencería *f* para sábanas; (= *metal*) laminado *m* metálico, chapa *f* metálica

sheik(h) [ʃeɪk] N jeque *m*

sheik(h)dom [ˈʃeɪkdəm] N reino *m* *or* territorio *m* de un jeque

shekel [ˈʃekl] N (*Hist, Bible etc*) siclo *m*; **shekels*** pasta* *fsing*, parné‡ *msing*

sheldrake [ˈʃeldreɪk] N, **shelduck** [ˈʃeldʌk] N tadorna *f*

shelf [ʃelf] Ⓐ N (*pl* **shelves**) [1] (*fixed to wall, in shop*) estante *m*, balda *f*; (*in cupboard*) tabla *f*, anaquel *m*; (*in oven*) parrilla *f*; **to buy a product off the ~** comprar un producto ya hecho; ✦**IDIOM to be (left) on the ~** [*proposal etc*] quedar arrinconado; (*) [*woman*] quedarse para vestir santos
[2] (= *edge*) (*in rock face*) saliente *m*; (*underwater*) plataforma *f*
Ⓑ CPD ► **shelf life** N (*Comm*) tiempo *m* de durabilidad antes de la venta; ✦**IDIOM most pop stars have a very short ~ life** la mayoría de las estrellas del pop son flor de un día *or* tienen una carrera efímera ► **shelf mark** N (*in library*) código *m* ► **shelf space** N cantidad *f* de estanterías (*para exponer la mercancía*)

she'll [ʃiːl] = **she will, she shall**

shell [ʃel] Ⓐ N [1] [*of egg, nut*] cáscara *f*; [*of tortoise, turtle*] caparazón *m*, carapacho *m*; [*of snail, shellfish*] concha *f*, caracol *m* (*LAm*); [*of pea*] vaina *f*; [*of coconut*] cáscara *f* leñosa; ✦**IDIOMS to come out of one's ~** (*fig*) salir del caparazón *or* (*LAm*) carapacho; **to crawl** *or* **go into one's ~** (*fig*) encerrarse *or* meterse en su concha, encerrarse *or* meterse en su caparazón
[2] [*of building, vehicle, ship*] armazón *m or f*, casco *m*
[3] (= *artillery round*) obús *m*, proyectil *m*; (*US*) [*of shotgun*] cartucho *m*
[4] (*Culin*) [*of pie, flan*] masa *f*
Ⓑ VT [1] [+ *peas*] pelar, desvainar; [+ *nuts*] pelar, descascarar; [+ *mussels, cockles*] quitar la concha a; [+ *prawns*] pelar; [+ *eggs*] quitar la cáscara a; **~ed prawns** gambas *fpl* peladas; ✦**IDIOM it's like** *or* **as easy as ~ing peas** es pan comido, es coser y cantar
[2] (*Mil*) bombardear
Ⓒ CPD ► **shell game** N (*US*) (*lit*) (= *trick*) *juego consistente en adivinar en cuál de tres cubiletes se esconde un objeto*, triles‡ *fpl*; (*fig*) (= *fraud*) artimaña *f* ► **shell hole** N *hoyo que forma un obús al explotar* ► **shell shock** N neurosis *f inv* de guerra ► **shell suit** N *tipo de chandal*

►**shell out*** Ⓐ VI + ADV (= *pay*) soltar el dinero
Ⓑ VT + ADV [+ *money*] desembolsar; **to ~ out for sth** desembolsar para pagar algo

shellac [ʃəˈlæk] N goma *f* (laca *f*)

shelled [ʃeld] ADJ **~ nuts** nueces *fpl* sin cáscara

shellfire [ˈʃelˌfaɪəʳ] N = **shelling**

shellfish [ˈʃelfɪʃ] N (*pl* **shellfish**) (*Zool*) crustáceo *m*; (*as food*) marisco(s) *m(pl)*

shelling [ˈʃelɪŋ] N bombardeo *m*

shellproof [ˈʃelpruːf] ADJ a prueba de bombas

shell-shocked [ˈʃelʃɒkt] ADJ que padece neurosis de guerra

shelter [ˈʃeltəʳ] Ⓐ N [1] (= *protection*) protección *f*, refugio *m*; **there was no ~ from the rain/sun** no había dónde protegerse de la lluvia/del sol; **to seek ~ (from)** (*rain, sun*) buscar dónde protegerse (de); (*persecution*) buscar dónde refugiarse (de); **to take ~** refugiarse, guarecerse; **we took ~ from the storm in a cave** nos refugiamos *or* nos cobijamos de la tormenta en una cueva
[2] (= *accommodation*) alojamiento *m*; **to seek ~ for the night** buscar dónde pasar la noche
[3] (= *construction*) (*on mountain*) refugio *m*, albergue *m*; (*for homeless people, battered women*) refugio *m*, centro *m* de acogida; **bus ~** marquesina *f* de autobús; **air-raid ~** refugio *m* antiaéreo
Ⓑ VT [1] (= *protect*) proteger (**from** de); **a spot ~ed from the wind** un sitio protegido *or* al abrigo del viento
[2] (*fig*) proteger (**from** de); **you can't ~ your children from the outside world forever** no se puede proteger a nuestros hijos del mundo exterior eternamente
[3] (= *hide*) [+ *fugitive, criminal*] esconder, ocultar, dar asilo a
Ⓒ VI refugiarse, guarecerse (**from** de); **to ~ from the rain** refugiarse *or* guarecerse de la lluvia; **to ~ behind sth** (*fig*) escudarse en *or* tras algo, ampararse en algo

sheltered [ˈʃeltəd] ADJ [*harbour, valley, garden*] protegido; [*industry*] protegido (contra la competencia extranjera); **a ~ environment** (*fig*) un ambiente protegido; **~ housing** residencia *f* vigilada (*para ancianos*); **she has led a very ~ life** ha tenido una vida muy protegida

shelve [ʃelv] Ⓐ VT (= *postpone*) dar carpetazo a
Ⓑ VI (= *slope away*) formar declive

shelves [ʃelvz] NPL *of* **shelf**

shelving [ˈʃelvɪŋ] N estantería *f*

shemozzle* [ʃəˈmɒzl] N (*Brit*) (= *confusion*) lío* *m*; (= *dispute*) bronca *f*, follón* *m*

shenanigans* [ʃəˈnænɪgənz] NPL (= *trickery*) chanchullos* *mpl*; (= *mischief*) correrías* *fpl*, travesuras *fpl*; (= *rowdy fun*) bromas *fpl*

shepherd [ˈʃepəd] Ⓐ N [1] pastor *m*; **the Good Shepherd** el Buen Pastor
[2] (*also* **~ dog**) perro *m* pastor
Ⓑ VT **to ~ children across a road** llevar niños a través de una calle, cruzar a los niños la calle; **to ~ sb in/out** acompañar a algn al entrar/salir; **to ~ sb around** hacer de guía para algn
Ⓒ CPD ► **shepherd boy** N zagal *m* ► **shepherd's pie** N pastel *m* de carne con patatas

shepherdess [ˈʃepədɪs] N pastora *f*, zagala *f*

sherbert [ˈʃɜːbɜːt] N = **sherbet**

sherbet [ˈʃɜːbət] N [1] (*Brit*) (= *powder*) polvos *mpl* azucarados
[2] (*US*) (= *water ice*) sorbete *m*

sherd [ʃɜːd] N = **shard**

sheriff [ˈʃerɪf] N (*in US*) alguacil *m*, sheriff *m*; (*in England*) gobernador *m* civil; (*in Scotland*) juez *mf*

Sherpa [ˈʃɜːpə] N (*pl* **Sherpas** *or* **Sherpa**) sherpa *mf*

sherry [ˈʃerɪ] N jerez *m*

she's [ʃiːz] = **she is, she has**

Shetland [ˈʃetlənd] Ⓐ N las Islas Shetland
Ⓑ CPD ► **the Shetland Islands**, **the Shetland Isles**, **the Shetlands** NPL las Islas Shetland ► **Shetland pony** N pony *m* de (las) Shetland ► **Shetland wool** N lana *f* de las Shetland

shew†† [ʃəʊ] VTI = **show**

shewn†† [ʃəʊn] PP *of* **show**

shhh [ʃː] EXCL ¡chitón!

Shia, **Shiah** [ˈʃiːə] Ⓐ N [1] (= *doctrine*) chiísmo *m*
[2] (= *follower*) (*also* **~ Muslim**) chiíta *mf*
Ⓑ ADJ chiíta

shiatsu [ʃiːˈætsuː] N shiatsu *m*, digitopuntura *f*

shibboleth [ˈʃɪbəleθ] N (*Bible*) lema *m*, santo *m* y seña; (*fig*) dogma *m* hoy desacreditado, doctrina *f* que ha quedado anticuada

shield [ʃiːld] Ⓐ N [1] (*armour*) (*also Her*) escudo *m*; (*Tech*) (*on machine etc*) blindaje *m*, capa *f* protectora
[2] (*US*) (= *badge*) [*of policeman*] placa *f*
Ⓑ VT proteger; **to ~ sb from sth** proteger a algn de algo; **to ~ one's eyes** taparse los ojos

shieling [ˈʃiːlɪŋ] N (*Scot*) (= *pasture*) pasto *m*, prado *m*; (= *hut*) choza *f*, cabaña *f*

shift [ʃɪft] Ⓐ N [1] (= *change*) cambio *m*; **there has been a ~ in attitudes on the part of consumers** ha habido un cambio de actitud por parte de los consumidores; **a ~ in weather patterns** un cambio en el comportamiento del tiempo; **there was a ~ in the wind** el viento cambió de dirección, se produjo un cambio de dirección del viento; **the ~ to a market economy** la transición hacia una economía de mercado; **some have problems making the ~ from one culture to another** algunos tienen problemas al hacer el cambio de una cultura a otra; ✦*IDIOM* **to make ~ with/without sth** arreglárselas con/sin algo

[2] (= *period of work*) turno *m*; (= *group of workers*) tanda *f*; **day/night ~** turno *m* de día/noche; **to work (in) ~s** trabajar por turnos; **I work an eight-hour ~** trabajo *or* hago turnos de ocho horas

[3] (*US Aut*) (= *gear shift*) palanca *f* de cambio

[4] (= *dress*) vestido *m* suelto; (= *undergarment*) combinación *f*, viso *m*

[5] (*Geol*) desplazamiento *m*

Ⓑ VT [1] (= *change*) [+ *opinion, tactics, policy*] cambiar; **the result ~ed the balance of power in their favour** el resultado cambió el equilibrio político *or* inclinó la balanza del poder a su favor; **to ~ one's ground** cambiar de opinión *or* parecer; **to ~ one's position** cambiar de postura

[2] (= *transfer*) **she ~ed her weight to the other leg** cambió el peso a la otra pierna, volcó su peso sobre la otra pierna; **voters ~ed their allegiance** los votantes trasladaron su lealtad a otro partido; **to ~ the blame onto sb else** cargar a otro con la culpa, echar la culpa a otro; **they're trying to ~ the blame** intentan cargar a otro con la culpa, intentan echar *or* pasar la culpa a otro; **he ~ed his gaze to me** pasó a fijarse en mí

[3] (= *move*) mover; **he ~ed the chair closer to the bed** movió la silla acercándola a la cama; **to ~ scenery** (*Theat*) cambiar el decorado; **~ yourself!*** ¡quítate del medio *or* de en medio!, ¡muévete!

[4] (= *sell*) [+ *stock*] deshacerse de, vender

[5] (= *get rid of*) [+ *cold*] quitarse (de encima); [+ *stain*] quitar

[6] (*US Aut*) [+ *gear*] cambiar de

Ⓒ VI [1] (= *move*) [*person*] moverse; [*load, cargo*] correrse; **he ~ed uncomfortably in his seat** se removía incómodo en la silla; **she ~ed from one foot to the other** cambiaba de un pie a otro

[2] (= *change, transfer*) [*wind*] cambiar de dirección; [*attitudes, mood*] cambiar; **world attention has ~ed away from China** el foco de atención mundial se ha alejado de China; **the emphasis now has ~ed to preventive medicine** ahora se hace más hincapié en la medicina preventiva; **the scene ~s to Burgos** la escena se traslada a Burgos; **we couldn't get him to ~** no logramos hacerle cambiar de actitud

[3] (*) (= *move quickly*) volar; **that car was really ~ing** ¡ese coche corría que volaba *or* que se las pelaba!*

[4] (*US Aut*) **to ~ into high/low gear** cambiar a una velocidad más alta/baja; **the presidential campaign has ~ed into high gear** la campaña por la presidencia se ha acelerado

[5] **to ~ for o.s.** arreglárselas solo

Ⓓ CPD ► **shift key** N tecla *f* de mayúsculas ► **shift lock** N tecla *f* de bloqueo de mayúsculas (*Sp*), tecla *f* fijamayúsculas (*LAm*) ► **shift system** N [*of work*] sistema *m* de turnos ► **shift register** N registro *m* de desplazamiento ► **shift work** N trabajo *m* por turnos ► **shift worker** N trabajador(a) *m/f* por turnos

► **shift along** VI + ADV = **shift over**

► **shift around, shift about** Ⓐ VI + ADV **his men ~ed around nervously** sus hombres se movían nerviosos de un lado para otro

Ⓑ VT + ADV [+ *objects*] mover, cambiar de sitio

► **shift over*** VI + ADV correrse; **can you ~ over a bit?** ¿puedes correrte un poco a ese lado?

► **shift up** = **shift over**

shiftily [ˈʃɪftɪlɪ] ADV furtivamente, sospechosamente

shiftiness [ˈʃɪftɪnɪs] N [*of person, behaviour*] lo sospechoso; [*of look*] lo furtivo

shifting [ˈʃɪftɪŋ] ADJ [*sand*] movedizo; [*winds*] cambiante; [*values, attitudes*] cambiante; **his constantly ~ moods** sus cambios de humor constantes

shiftless [ˈʃɪftlɪs] ADJ holgazán, perezoso, flojo (*esp LAm*)

shiftlessness [ˈʃɪftlɪsnɪs] N holgazanería *f*, pereza *f*, flojera (*esp LAm*) *f*

shifty [ˈʃɪftɪ] ADJ (*compar* **shiftier**; *superl* **shiftiest**) [*look*] furtivo; [*person, behaviour*] sospechoso

shifty-eyed [ˈʃɪftɪˈaɪd] ADJ de mirada furtiva

Shiite, Shi'ite [ˈʃiːaɪt] Ⓐ N chiíta *mf*

Ⓑ ADJ chiíta

shillelagh [ʃəˈleɪlə, ʃəˈleɪlɪ] N (*Irl*) cachiporra *f*

shilling [ˈʃɪlɪŋ] N (*Brit*) chelín *m*

shilly-shally [ˈʃɪlɪˌʃælɪ] VI vacilar, titubear

shilly-shallying [ˈʃɪlɪˌʃælɪɪŋ] N vacilación *f*, titubeos *mpl*

shimmer [ˈʃɪməʳ] Ⓐ N luz *f* trémula, brillo *m*

Ⓑ VI rielar, relucir

shimmering [ˈʃɪmərɪŋ] ADJ, **shimmery** [ˈʃɪmərɪ] ADJ reluciente

shimmy [ˈʃɪmɪ] N [1] (= *dance*) shimmy *m*

[2] (*Aut*) (= *vibration*) vibraciones *fpl*

[3] (= *chemise*) camisa *f* (*de mujer*)

shin [ʃɪn] Ⓐ N espinilla *f*; (*Brit*) [*of meat*] jarrete *m*

Ⓑ VI **to ~ up/down a tree** trepar a/bajar de un árbol

shinbone [ˈʃɪnbəʊn] N tibia *f*

shindig‡ [ˈʃɪndɪg] N juerga* *f*, guateque *m*

shindy‡ [ˈʃɪndɪ] N (= *noise*) conmoción *f*, escándalo *m*; (= *brawl*) jaleo *m*, bronca *f*; ✦*IDIOM* **to kick up a ~** armar un jaleo *or* una bronca

shine [ʃaɪn] (*vb: pt, pp* **shone**) Ⓐ N (= *brilliance*) brillo *m*, lustre *m*; **to give sth a ~** sacar brillo a algo; **to take the ~ off sth** (*lit*) deslustrar algo; (*fig*) deslucir algo, quitar a algo su encanto; ✦*IDIOM* **come rain or ~** haga el tiempo que haga; **to take a ~ to sb*** tomar simpatía por algn

Ⓑ VT [1] (*pt, pp* **shined**) (= *polish*) sacar brillo a, pulir

[2] **to ~ a light on sth** echar luz sobre algo

Ⓒ VI [1] [*sun, light etc*] brillar; [*metal*] relucir; **the sun is shining** brilla el sol; **the metal shone in the sun** el metal relucía al sol; **her face shone with happiness** su cara irradiaba felicidad

[2] (*fig*) [*student etc*] destacar, sobresalir; **to ~ at English** destacar *or* sobresalir en inglés

► **shine down** VI + ADV [*sun, moon, stars*] brillar

shiner* [ˈʃaɪnəʳ] N (= *black eye*) ojo *m* a la funerala

shingle [ˈʃɪŋgl] N [1] (*on beach*) guijarros *mpl*

[2] (*on roof*) tablilla *f*

[3] (*US*) (= *signboard*) placa *f*; **to hang out one's ~** (*fig*) montar *or* abrir la oficina

[4] (†) (= *hairstyle*) corte *m* a lo garçon

shingles [ˈʃɪŋglz] NPL (*Med*) herpes *msing* (zoster)

shingly [ˈʃɪŋglɪ] ADJ guijarroso

shinguard [ˈʃɪngɑːd] N espinillera *f*

shininess [ˈʃaɪnɪnɪs] N brillo *m*

shining [ˈʃaɪnɪŋ] ADJ [*surface, light*] brillante; [*face*] radiante; [*hair*] brillante, lustroso; [*eyes*] brillante, chispeante; ✦*IDIOM* **a ~ example** un ejemplo perfecto

shinpad [ˈʃɪnpæd] N espinillera *f*

Shintoism [ˈʃɪntəʊɪzəm] N sintoísmo *m*

shinty [ˈʃɪntɪ] N (*Scot*) *especie de hockey*

shiny [ˈʃaɪnɪ] ADJ (*compar* **shinier**; *superl* **shiniest**) brillante

ship [ʃɪp] Ⓐ N [1] (= *sea-going vessel*) (*gen*) barco *m*; (*for carrying cargo*) (*also Mil*) buque *m*, navío *m*; **Her** *or* **His Majesty's Ship Victory** el buque *or* navío Victory de la Marina Real Británica; **to abandon ~** abandonar el barco; **on board ~** a bordo; **by ~** en barco, por barco; **the good ~ Beagle** el buque Beagle, el Beagle; **to jump ~** abandonar el barco, desertar; **to take ~ for** embarcarse para; ✦*IDIOMS* **when my ~ comes in** (*fig*) cuando lleguen las vacas gordas; **~s that pass in the night** personas que pasan por la vida y desaparecen; **the ~ of the desert** (= *the camel*) el camello

[2] (= *aircraft, spacecraft*) nave *f*

Ⓑ VT [1] (= *transport*) enviar, consignar; **to ~ sth/sb in** traer algo/a algn; **to ~ sth/sb off** (*lit*) enviar algo/a algn; **he ~ped all his sons off to boarding school*** (*fig*) mandó a todos sus hijos a un internado; **to ~ sth/sb out** enviar algo/a algn; **a new engine had to be ~ped out to them** hubo que enviarles un nuevo motor

[2] (*Naut*) **we are ~ping water** estamos haciendo agua, nos está entrando agua

[3] [+ *oars*] desarmar

Ⓒ CPD ► **ship broker** N agente *mf* marítimo/a ► **ship canal** N canal *m* de navegación ► **ship chandler, ship's chandler** N proveedor *m* de efectos navales, abastecedor *m* de buques ► **ship's company** N tripulación *f* ► **ship's doctor** N médico *m* de a bordo ► **ship's manifest** N manifiesto *m* del buque ► **ship-to-shore radio** N radio *f* de barco a costa

shipboard [ˈʃɪpbɔːd] N **on ~** a bordo

shipbreaker [ˈʃɪpˌbreɪkəʳ] N desguazador *m*

shipbuilder [ˈʃɪpˌbɪldəʳ] N constructor(a) *m/f* de buques

shipbuilding [ˈʃɪpˌbɪldɪŋ] N construcción *f* marina

shipload [ˈʃɪpləʊd] N cargamento *m*

shipmate [ˈʃɪpmeɪt] N compañero/a *m/f* de tripulación

shipment [ˈʃɪpmənt] N (= *act*) transporte *m*, embarque *m*; (= *load*) consignación *f*; (= *quantity*) cargamento *m*, remesa *f*

shipowner [ˈʃɪpˌəʊnəʳ] N naviero/a *m/f*, armador(a) *m/f*

shipper [ˈʃɪpəʳ] N (= *company*) empresa *f* naviera

shipping [ˈʃɪpɪŋ] Ⓐ N [1] (= *ships*) barcos *mpl*, buques *mpl*; (= *fleet*) flota *f*; **a danger to ~** un peligro para la navegación

[2] (= *transporting*) transporte *m* (en barco), embarque *m*; (= *sending*) envío *m*

Ⓑ CPD ► **shipping agent** N agente *mf* marítimo/a ► **shipping company, shipping line** N compañía *f* naviera ► **shipping instructions** NPL instrucciones *fpl* de embarque ► **shipping lane** N ruta *f* de navegación

shipshape [ˈʃɪpʃeɪp] ADJ en buen orden; **all ~ and Bristol fashion** (*Brit*) todo limpio y en su sitio

shipwreck [ˈʃɪprek] Ⓐ N (= *event*) naufragio *m*; (= *wrecked ship*) buque *m* naufragado, nave *f* or embarcación *f* naufragada

Ⓑ VT **to be ~ed** naufragar; **~ed on a desert island** [*vessel*] naufragado en una isla desierta; [*person*] náufrago en una isla desierta; **a**

~ed person un náufrago; **a ~ed sailor** un marinero náufrago; **a ~ed vessel** un buque naufragado

shipwright ['ʃɪpraɪt] N carpintero *m* de navío

shipyard ['ʃɪpjɑːd] N astillero *m*

shire [ʃaɪəʳ] Ⓐ N (*Brit*) condado *m*
Ⓑ CPD ► **shire horse** N ≈ percherón/ona *m/f*

shirk [ʃɜːk] Ⓐ VT [+ *duty*] esquivar, zafarse de
Ⓑ VI gandulear

shirker ['ʃɜːkəʳ] N gandul(a) *m/f*, flojo/a *m/f* (*LAm*)

shirr [ʃɜːʳ] VT 1 (*Sew*) fruncir
2 (*US*) **~ed eggs** huevos *mpl* al plato

shirring ['ʃɜːrɪŋ] N (*Sew*) frunce *m*

shirt [ʃɜːt] Ⓐ N camisa *f*; ✦***IDIOMS*** **to put one's ~ on a horse** (*fig*) (*Betting*) apostarlo todo a un caballo; **keep your ~ on!*** (*fig*) ¡no te sulfures!*, ¡cálmate!
Ⓑ CPD ► **shirt button** N botón *m* de la camisa ► **shirt collar** N cuello *m* de camisa ► **shirt front** N pechera *f* ► **shirt pocket** N bolsillo *m* de la camisa ► **shirt sleeves** NPL **to be in (one's) ~ sleeves** estar en mangas de camisa ► **shirt tail** N faldón *m* (de camisa)

shirtdress ['ʃɜːtdres] N camisa *f* vestido

shirtless ['ʃɜːtlɪs] ADJ sin camisa, descamisado

shirtwaist ['ʃɜːtweɪst] N (*US*) blusa *f* (de mujer)

shirty ['ʃɜːtɪ] ADJ (*compar* **shirtier**; *superl* **shirtiest**) **he was pretty ~ about it*** no le gustó nada, no le cayó en gracia

shish kebab ['ʃiːʃkə'bæb] N = **kebab**

shit⁑ [ʃɪt] (*vb: pt, pp* **shit** *or* **shat**) Ⓐ N 1 (= *excrement*) mierda⁑ *f*; **to have** *or* **take a ~** cagar⁑; **to have the ~s** tener el vientre descompuesto; **~!** ¡mierda!⁑, ¡joder!⁑, ¡carajo! (*esp LAm*⁑); **tough ~!** ¡mala suerte!; ✦***IDIOM*** **to beat the ~ out of sb** darle hostias a algn*, hostiar a algn*; *see also* **fan A**
2 (= *trouble*) **to be in the ~** estar bien jodido(s)⁑; **he landed us in the ~** nos dejó bien jodidos⁑
3 (= *nonsense*) gilipolleces⁑ *fpl*; ✦***IDIOM*** **no ~?** (= *seriously?*) ¡no (me) jodas!⁑, ¿de verdad?
4 (= *stuff*) mierdas⁑ *fpl*, historias* *fpl*, cosas *fpl*
5 (= *person*) mierda⁑ *mf*
Ⓑ VI cagar⁑
Ⓒ VT cagar⁑; **to ~ o.s.** cagarse⁑; ✦***IDIOM*** **to ~ bricks** (*from fear*) cagarse de miedo⁑

shite⁑ [ʃaɪt] N (*Brit*) = **shit**

shitlist⁑ ['ʃɪtlɪst] N lista *f* negra

shitty⁑ ['ʃɪtɪ] ADJ (*compar* **shittier**; *superl* **shittiest**) 1 (*lit*) lleno de mierda⁑
2 (*fig*) (= *crappy*) de mierda⁑

shiver¹ ['ʃɪvəʳ] Ⓐ N (*with cold*) tiritón *m*; [*of horror etc*] escalofrío *m*; **it sent ~s down my spine** me dio escalofríos; **it gives me the ~s** (*fear*) me da horror; **to get the ~s** (*fear*) aterrorizarse, sentir escalofríos de miedo
Ⓑ VI (*with cold*) tiritar; (*with emotion*) temblar, estremecerse

shiver² ['ʃɪvəʳ] Ⓐ VT (= *break*) romper, hacer añicos
Ⓑ VI romperse, hacerse añicos

shivery ['ʃɪvərɪ] ADJ (= *feverish*) destemplado; (= *shaking*) estremecido; (= *sensitive to cold*) friolero, friolento (*LAm*)

shoal¹ [ʃəʊl] N [*of fish*] banco *m*

shoal² [ʃəʊl] N (= *sandbank etc*) banco *m* de arena, bajío *m*, bajo *m*

shock¹ [ʃɒk] Ⓐ N 1 (*emotional*) conmoción *f*, golpe *m*, impresión *f*; (= *start*) susto *m*; **the ~ killed him** la impresión le mató; **the ~ was too much for him** la impresión fue demasiado para él; **to come as a ~** resultar sorprendente *or* asombroso, causar estupefacción; **it comes as a ~ to hear that ...** resulta sorprendente *or* asombroso saber que ..., causa estupefacción saber que ...; **frankly, this has all come as a bit of a ~** con toda franqueza, para mí esto ha sido un duro golpe; **to get a ~** llevarse *or* pegarse un susto; **to give sb a ~** dar un susto a algn; **what a ~ you gave me!** ¡qué susto me diste!, ¡me has asustado!; **pale with ~** lívido del susto
2 (*lit*) (= *impact*) sacudida *f*; (*fig*) (= *shakeup*) choque *m*, sacudida *f*; **the ~ of the explosion was felt five miles away** la sacudida de la explosión se sintió a una distancia de cinco millas; **~ resistant** antichoque; **it was a ~ to the establishment** sacudió el sistema, fue un serio golpe para el sistema
3 (*Elec*) descarga *f*; **she got a ~ from the refrigerator** la nevera le dio una descarga *or* un calambre
4 (*Med*) shock *m*, postración *f* nerviosa; **to be suffering <u>from</u> ~** ◊ **be <u>in</u> (a state of) ~** estar en estado de shock, padecer una postración nerviosa
5 **shocks*** (*Aut*) (*also* **~ absorbers**) amortiguadores *mpl*
Ⓑ VT 1 (= *startle*) sobresaltar, asustar; **to ~ sb into doing sth** dar una sacudida a algn para animarle a hacer algo
2 (= *affect emotionally*) (= *upset*) conmover, chocar; (= *offend*) escandalizar; **it ~s me that people are so narrow-minded** me choca que la gente sea tan cerrada; **easily ~ed** que se escandaliza por nada
Ⓒ VI causar escándalo, chocar; **this film is not intended to ~** esta película no pretende escandalizar a nadie
Ⓓ CPD ► **shock absorber** N (*Aut*) amortiguador *m* ► **shock tactics** NPL (*lit*) (*Mil*) táctica *fsing* de choque; (*fig*) provocación *f*; **to use ~ tactics** (*fig*) recurrir a la provocación, provocar ► **shock therapy, shock treatment** N (*Med*) (*also* **electric ~ treatment**) tratamiento *m* por electrochoque ► **shock troops** NPL guardias *mpl* de asalto ► **shock wave** N onda *f* de choque

shock² [ʃɒk] N (*also* **~ of hair**) mata *f* de pelo

shock³ [ʃɒk] (*Agr*) Ⓐ N tresnal *m*, garbera *f*
Ⓑ VT poner en tresnales

shockable ['ʃɒkəbl] ADJ **she's very ~** se escandaliza por poca *or* por cualquier cosa

shocked [ʃɒkt] ADJ 1 (= *horrified*) espantado; (= *surprised*) estupefacto; **I was ~ at the verdict** el veredicto me dejó espantado; **don't look so ~!** ¡no pongas esa cara de sorpresa!; **there was a ~ silence** hubo un silencio de estupefacción; **the jury listened to the tape in ~ silence** el jurado escuchaba la cinta enmudecido por el espanto
2 (= *outraged, offended*) escandalizado; **~ listeners/viewers rang up in their thousands** miles de oyentes/espectadores llamaron escandalizados

shocker* ['ʃɒkəʳ] N 1 **it's a ~** es horrible, es un desastre; **he's a ~** es un sinvergüenza
2 (*Literat*) (= *cheap book*) novelucha *f*

shock-headed ['ʃɒk'hedɪd] ADJ melenudo

shocking ['ʃɒkɪŋ] Ⓐ ADJ 1 (= *extremely bad*) [*weather, performance, handwriting*] pésimo, espantoso; **she has ~ taste** tiene un pésimo gusto; **to be in a ~ state** estar en un estado pésimo, estar en un estado penoso
2 (= *appalling*) [*news, sight, murder*] espeluznante, espantoso; **the ~ truth** la sobrecogedora verdad
3 (= *outrageous*) [*book, film, act*] escandaloso; **it was ~ how badly paid these young girls were** era de escándalo *or* era escandaloso lo mal que se pagaba a estas chicas; **it's ~ to think that ...** escandaliza pensar que ...
Ⓑ CPD ► **shocking pink** N rosa *m* estridente, rosa *m* fosforito

shockingly ['ʃɒkɪŋlɪ] ADV 1 (*with adj*) [*bad, expensive*] terriblemente
2 (*with verb*) [*behave*] terriblemente mal, fatal; [*age, change*] de manera espantosa

shockproof ['ʃɒkpruːf] ADJ [*watch*] antichoque; (*) (*fig*) [*person*] que no se escandaliza por nada

shod [ʃɒd] PT, PP *of* **shoe**

shoddily ['ʃɒdɪlɪ] ADV **~ made** chapucero, hecho chapuceramente; **~ built** mal hecho, mal construido; **she was very ~ treated by him** él la trató fatal

shoddiness ['ʃɒdɪnɪs] N [*of merchandise, product*] baja calidad *f*; [*of work, service*] chapucería *f*

shoddy ['ʃɒdɪ] Ⓐ ADJ (*compar* **shoddier**; *superl* **shoddiest**) [*merchandise, product*] de baja calidad, de pacotilla; [*work, service*] chapucero
Ⓑ N (= *cloth*) paño *m* burdo de lana; (= *wool*) lana *f* regenerada; (*as waste, fertilizer*) desechos *mpl* de lana

shoe [ʃuː] (*vb: pt, pp* **shod**) Ⓐ N 1 (= *footwear*) zapato *m*; (*for horse*) herradura *f*; **to put on one's ~s** ponerse los zapatos, calzarse (*frm*); **to take off one's ~s** quitarse los zapatos, descalzarse (*frm*); ✦***IDIOMS*** **I wouldn't like to be in his ~s** no quisiera estar en su lugar *or* pellejo; **if I were in your ~s** si yo estuviese en tu lugar, yo que tú; **to step into sb's ~s** pasar a ocupar el puesto de algn; **to be waiting for dead men's ~s** *esperar a que muera algn (para pasar luego a ocupar su puesto)*
2 (*Aut*) (*also* **brake ~**) zapata *f*
Ⓑ VT [+ *horse*] herrar
Ⓒ CPD ► **shoe box** N caja *f* de zapatos ► **shoe brush** N cepillo *m* para zapatos ► **shoe cream** N crema *f* de zapatos, crema *f* para el calzado ► **shoe leather** N cuero *m* para zapatos; ✦***IDIOM*** **to wear out one's ~ leather** gastarse el calzado; **I wore out a lot of ~ leather** ◊ **it cost me a lot in ~ leather** tuve que andar lo mío, tuve que recorrer mucho camino ► **shoe polish** N betún *m*, lustre *m* (*LAm*) ► **shoe repairer** N zapatero/a *m/f* remendón/ona ► **shoe repairs** NPL reparación *fsing* de zapatos, reparación *fsing* de calzado ► **shoe shop** N zapatería *f*

shoeblack† ['ʃuːblæk] N limpiabotas *mf inv*, lustrabotas *mf inv* (*LAm*)

shoeblacking ['ʃuːˌblækɪŋ] N betún *m*, lustre *m* (*LAm*)

shoehorn ['ʃuːhɔːn] N calzador *m*

shoelace ['ʃuːleɪs] N cordón *m*, pasador *m* (*Andes*)

shoemaker ['ʃuːˌmeɪkəʳ] N zapatero/a *m/f*

shoeshine ['ʃuːʃaɪn] Ⓐ N **to have a ~** hacerse limpiar los zapatos
Ⓑ CPD ► **shoeshine boy, shoeshine man** N limpiabotas *m inv*, lustrabotas *m inv* (*LAm*), bolero *m* (*Mex*), embolador *m* (*Col*)

shoestring ['ʃuːstrɪŋ] Ⓐ N (*US*) cordón *m*, lazo *m*; ✦***IDIOM*** **to do sth on a ~** hacer algo con muy poco dinero; **to live on a ~** vivir muy justo
Ⓑ CPD ► **shoestring budget** N presupuesto *m* muy limitado

shoetree ['ʃuːtriː] N horma *f*

shone [ʃɒn] PT, PP *of* **shine**

shoo [ʃuː] Ⓐ EXCL ¡fuera!, ¡zape!, ¡ándale! (*Mex*)
Ⓑ VT (*also* **~ away, ~ off**) ahuyentar, espantar

shoo-in* [ˈʃuːɪn] N (*US*) **it's a ~** es cosa de coser y cantar; **he's a ~ for the presidency** es el favorito para hacerse con la presidencia, es el más firme candidato a la presidencia

shook [ʃʊk] PT *of* **shake**

shoot [ʃuːt] (*vb: pt, pp* **shot**) Ⓐ N [1] (*Bot*) brote *m*, retoño *m*
[2] (*Cine*) rodaje *m*; (*Phot*) sesión *f* fotográfica
[3] (= *shooting party*) cacería *f*, partida *f* de caza; (= *preserve*) coto *m* de caza, vedado *m* de caza; (= *competition*) concurso *m* de tiro al blanco, certamen *m* de tiro al blanco
Ⓑ VT [1] (= *wound*) pegar un tiro a; (= *kill*) matar de un tiro; (*more brutally*) matar a tiros; (= *execute*) fusilar; (= *hunt*) cazar; **she shot her husband** pegó un tiro a su marido; **you'll get me shot!*** ¡me van a asesinar *or* matar por tu culpa!*; **he was shot as a spy** lo fusilaron por espía; **to ~ sb dead** matar a algn de un tiro *or* a tiros; **we often go ~ing rabbits at the weekend** solemos ir a cazar conejos los fines de semana; **he was shot in the leg** una bala le hirió en la pierna; **he had been shot through the heart** la bala le había atravesado el corazón; **✦IDIOM to ~ o.s. in the foot** cavar su propia fosa sin darse cuenta
[2] (= *launch*) [+ *bullet, gun, arrow*] disparar; [+ *missile*] lanzar
[3] (= *propel*) [+ *object*] lanzar (**at** hacia); **the impact shot them forward** el impacto hizo que salieran despedidos hacia delante; **the volcano shot lava high into the air** el volcán despidió *or* arrojó lava por los aires
[4] (*fig*) [+ *glance, look*] lanzar; [+ *smile*] dedicar; [+ *ray of light*] arrojar, lanzar; **she shot me a sideways glance** me lanzó una mirada de reojo, me miró de reojo; **he began ~ing questions at her** empezó a acribillarla a preguntas; **✦IDIOMS to ~ the breeze** *or* **bull** (*US*‡) darle a la lengua*; **to ~ a line** (*Brit**) marcarse un farol*; **to ~ one's mouth off*** irse de la lengua*, hablar más de la cuenta*; *see also* **bolt A1**
[5] (*Cine*) rodar, filmar; (*Phot*) [+ *subject of picture*] tomar, sacar
[6] (= *speed through*) **to ~ the lights** (*Aut**) saltarse un semáforo en rojo; **to ~ the rapids** sortear *or* salvar los rápidos
[7] (= *close*) [+ *bolt*] correr
[8] (= *play*) **to ~ dice/pool** (*US*) jugar a los dados/al billar
[9] (*) (= *inject*) [+ *drugs*] inyectarse, chutarse*, pincharse*
Ⓒ VI [1] (*with gun*) disparar, tirar; (= *hunt*) cazar; **to ~ at sth/sb** disparar a algo/algn; **to go ~ing** ir de caza; **to ~ to kill** disparar a matar, tirar a matar; **~-to-kill policy** programa *m* de tirar a matar
[2] (*in ball games*) (*gen*) tirar; (*Ftbl*) disparar, chutar; **to ~ at goal** tirar a gol, chutar; **to ~ wide** fallar el tiro, errar el tiro
[3] (= *move rapidly*) **she shot ahead to take first place** se adelantó rápidamente para ponerse en primer puesto; **to ~ by** = **to shoot past**; **the car shot forward** el coche salió disparado hacia delante; **flames shot 100ft into the air** las llamas saltaron por los aires a 100 pies de altura; **he shot out of his chair/out of bed** salió disparado de la silla/de la cama; **to ~ past** pasar como un rayo; **the car shot past us** el coche pasó como un rayo *or* una bala; **to ~ to fame/stardom** lanzarse a la fama/al estrellato; **the pain went ~ing up his arm** un dolor punzante le subía por el brazo
[4] (*Bot*) (= *produce buds*) brotar; (= *germinate*) germinar
[5] (*Cine*) rodar, filmar; (*Phot*) sacar la foto, disparar
[6] (*US**) (*in conversation*) **shoot!** ¡adelante!, ¡dispara!
Ⓓ EXCL (* *euph*) **oh ~!** ¡caracoles!*, ¡mecachis! (*Sp**)

►**shoot away** Ⓐ VT + ADV = **shoot off A2**
Ⓑ VI + ADV [1] (*Mil*) seguir tirando
[2] (= *move*) partir como una bala, salir disparado

►**shoot back** Ⓐ VT + ADV devolver rápidamente, devolver en el acto
Ⓑ VI + ADV [1] (*Mil*) devolver el tiro, responder con disparos
[2] (= *move*) volver como una bala (**to** a)

►**shoot down** VT + ADV [+ *aeroplane*] derribar; [+ *person*] matar a tiros, balear (*LAm*); (*fig*) [+ *argument*] echar por tierra

►**shoot off** Ⓐ VT + ADV [1] [+ *gun*] disparar; *see also* **mouth A**
[2] **he had a leg shot off** un disparo le cercenó una pierna
Ⓑ VI + ADV = **shoot away B2**

►**shoot out** Ⓐ VT + ADV [1] (= *eject*) [+ *sparks*] arrojar, soltar
[2] (= *move rapidly*) [+ *hand*] sacar rápidamente
[3] (*with gun*) [+ *lights*] apagar a tiros; [+ *windows, tyres*] coser a tiros; **to ~ it out** (*lit, fig*) resolverlo a tiros
Ⓑ VI + ADV (= *come out suddenly*) [*person, animal*] salir disparado; **his hand shot out and grabbed a cake** alargó la mano rápidamente y agarró un pastel

►**shoot up** Ⓐ VI + ADV [1] (= *move upwards rapidly*) [*prices, value, temperature*] dispararse; [*hand, head*] alzarse de repente; [*eyebrows*] arquearse de repente; [*smoke, flames, water*] salir disparado; **every hand in the classroom shot up** todas las manos de la clase se alzaron de repente, todo el mundo en la clase alzó la mano de repente
[2] (= *grow quickly*) [*plant*] crecer rápidamente; **your son's shot up over the last few months** tu hijo ha dado un estirón en estos últimos meses*
[3] (*) [*drug user*] chutarse*, pincharse*
Ⓑ VT + ADV [1] [+ *town, district*] barrer a tiros *or* balazos; [+ *vehicle*] coser a tiros *or* balazos; **he's pretty badly shot up, but he'll live** ha recibido bastantes tiros, pero sobrevivirá
[2] (*) [+ *drugs*] chutarse*, pincharse*

shoot-em-up* [ˈʃuːtəmʌp] ADJ [*film*] de tiros; (*Comput*) [*game*] de acción

shooter [ˈʃuːtəʳ] N [1] (‡) (= *gun*) arma *f* (de fuego)
[2] (*also* **target ~**) tirador(a) *m/f*

shooting [ˈʃuːtɪŋ] Ⓐ N [1] (= *shots*) tiros *mpl*, disparos *mpl*; (= *continuous shooting*) tiroteo *m*, balacera *f* (*LAm*)
[2] (= *murder*) asesinato *m*; (= *execution*) fusilamiento *m*
[3] [*of film*] rodaje *m*, filmación *f*
[4] (*esp Brit*) (= *hunting*) caza *f*; **good ~!** (*said as congratulation*) ¡buen tiro!; (*said before hunt*) ¡buena caza!
[5] (*Sport*) tiro *m* al blanco
Ⓑ ADJ [*pain*] punzante
Ⓒ CPD ► **shooting box** N pabellón *m* de caza ► **shooting brake**† N (*Brit Aut*) (= *estate car*) furgoneta *f*, rubia *f*, camioneta *f* ► **shooting gallery** N barraca *f* de tiro al blanco ► **shooting incident** N tiroteo *m*, balacera *f* (*LAm*) ► **shooting iron**† N (*US*) arma *f* (de fuego) ► **shooting jacket** N chaquetón *m* ► **shooting lodge** N = **shooting box** ► **shooting match** N concurso *m* de tiro al blanco, certamen *m* de tiro al blanco; **the whole ~ match*** (= *the whole thing*) todo el tinglado* ► **shooting party** N partida *f* de caza, cacería *f* ► **shooting range** N campo *m* de tiro ► **shooting spree** N **to go on a ~ spree** ir por ahí disparando a la gente ► **shooting star** N estrella *f* fugaz ► **shooting stick** N bastón *m* taburete ► **shooting war** N guerra *f* a tiros

shoot-out [ˈʃuːtaʊt] N [1] tiroteo *m*, balacera *f* (*LAm*)
[2] (*Sport*) *see* **penalty B**

shop [ʃɒp] Ⓐ N [1] (*Comm*) (= *store*) tienda *f*; (= *workshop*) taller *m*; **the ~s** las tiendas, los comercios; **he's just gone (round) to the ~s** acaba de salir a comprar; **it's not available in the ~s** no se encuentra *or* se comercializa en las tiendas; **shop!**† ¿quién despacha?; **butcher's ~** carnicería *f*; **a repair ~** un taller de reparaciones; **to set up ~** montar un negocio, establecerse; **to shut up ~** cerrar; **to talk ~*** hablar de trabajo, hablar de negocios; **✦IDIOM all over the ~**‡ en *or* por todas partes; *see also* **barber, betting B, flower C, sweet C, video C**
[2] (*Brit**) (= *act of shopping*) compra *f*; **the weekly ~** la compra de la semana
Ⓑ VI comprar, hacer las compras; **I hate ~ping in supermarkets** odio hacer (las) compras en los supermercados; **to go ~ping** ir de compras *or* de tiendas
Ⓒ VT (‡) (= *inform on*) delatar
Ⓓ CPD ► **shop assistant** N (*Brit*) dependiente/a *m/f*, empleado/a *m/f* de una tienda ► **shop floor** N (*lit*) taller *m*; (*bigger*) planta *f* de producción; **to work on the ~ floor** trabajar en la producción, ser obrero/a de la producción; **the ~ floor (workers)** los obreros ► **shop front** N fachada *f* de la tienda ► **shop steward** N (*Ind*) enlace *mf* sindical ► **shop talk*** N charla *f* sobre el trabajo ► **shop window** N escaparate *m*, vitrina *f*, vidriera *f* (*S. Cone*)

►**shop around** VI + ADV (*lit*) comparar precios; (*fig*) andar a la caza y captura; **she was ~ping around for the perfect partner** andaba a la caza y captura del novio ideal

shopaholic* [ʃɒpəˈhɒlɪk] N comprador(a) *m/f* obsesivo/a, adicto/a *m/f* a las compras

shopfitter [ˈʃɒpˌfɪtəʳ] N (*esp Brit*) instalador(a) *m/f* comercial

shopgirl [ˈʃɒpgɜːl] N (*Brit*) dependienta *f*, empleada *f* (*de una tienda*) (*LAm*)

shopkeeper [ˈʃɒpˌkiːpəʳ] N tendero/a *m/f*

shoplift [ˈʃɒplɪft] Ⓐ VI hurtar en tiendas
Ⓑ VT robar en una tienda, hurtar en una tienda

shoplifter [ˈʃɒpˌlɪftəʳ] N ratero/a *m/f*, ladrón/a *m/f* (de tiendas)

shoplifting [ˈʃɒpˌlɪftɪŋ] N ratería *f*

shopper [ˈʃɒpəʳ] N [1] (= *person*) comprador(a) *m/f*; (= *customer*) cliente *mf*
[2] (= *bag*) bolsa *f* de compras; (*on wheels*) carrito *m* de la compra

shopping [ˈʃɒpɪŋ] Ⓐ N (= *act of buying*) compra *f*; (= *goods bought*) compras *fpl*; **I like ~** me gusta ir de tiendas; **to do the ~** hacer la compra; **to go ~** ir de tiendas *or* de compras
Ⓑ CPD ► **shopping bag** N bolsa *f* de compras ► **shopping basket** N cesta *f*, canasta *f* (*LAm*) ► **shopping cart** N (*US*) = **shopping trolley** ► **shopping centre, shopping center** (*US*) N (*Brit*) centro *m* comercial

► **shopping channel** N canal *m* de televentas ► **shopping list** N lista *f* de compras ► **shopping mall** N (*esp US*) centro *m* comercial ► **shopping precinct** N (*Brit*) centro *m* comercial ► **shopping spree** N **to go on a ~ spree** salir de compras (*gastando mucho dinero*) ► **shopping trip** N viaje *m* de compras ► **shopping trolley** N (*Brit*) carrito *m* de la compra

shop-soiled [ˈʃɒpsɔɪld] ADJ deteriorado

shopwalker [ˈʃɒpˌwɔːkəʳ] N (*Brit*) vigilante/a *m/f*

shopworn [ˈʃɒpwɔːn] ADJ (*US*) = **shop-soiled**

shore[1] [ʃɔːʳ] Ⓐ N [1] [*of sea, lake*] orilla *f*; **the eastern ~s of Lake Tanganyika** la orilla oriental del lago Tanganika; **we were now a few hundred yards from ~** ahora nos hallábamos a unos cientos de yardas de la orilla *or* de la costa; **on ~** en tierra

[2] **shores** [*of country*] (*liter*) tierras *fpl*; **he will soon be leaving these ~s** pronto abandonará estas tierras

Ⓑ CPD ► **shore bird** N ave *f* zancuda ► **shore leave** N permiso *m* para bajar a tierra ► **shore patrol** N (*US*) patrulla *f* costera

shore[2] [ʃɔːʳ] Ⓐ VT **to ~ up** (*lit*) apuntalar; (*fig*) apoyar, reforzar, sostener

Ⓑ N (= *prop*) puntal *m*

shoreline [ˈʃɔːlaɪn] N línea *f* de la costa

shoreward [ˈʃɔːwəd] ADV hacia la costa, hacia la playa

shorewards [ˈʃɔːwədz] ADV (*esp Brit*) = **shoreward**

shorn [ʃɔːn] PP *of* **shear**

▼**short** [ʃɔːt] Ⓐ ADJ (*compar* **shorter**; *superl* **shortest**) [1] (*in length, distance, duration*) [*message, journey, hair, skirt*] corto; [*person*] bajo, chaparro (*CAm, Mex*); [*vowel, syllable*] breve; [*memory*] malo, flaco; **the ~est route** la ruta más corta; **February is a ~ month** febrero es un mes corto; **it was a great holiday, but too ~** fueron unas vacaciones estupendas, pero demasiado cortas; **she's quite ~** es bastante baja; **the ~ answer is that ...** en pocas palabras la razón es que ...; **to have a ~ back and sides** llevar el pelo corto por detrás y por los lados; **a ~ break** un pequeño descanso; **the days are getting ~er** los días se vuelven más cortos; **time is getting ~er** nos queda poco tiempo; **to win by a ~ head** (*Racing*) ganar por una cabeza escasa; **to be ~ in the leg** [*person*] tener las piernas cortas; **these trousers are a bit ~ in the leg** estos pantalones tienen la pierna algo pequeña; **at ~ notice** con poco tiempo de antelación; **in ~ order** en breve, en seguida; **to take ~ steps** dar pequeños pasos; **in the ~ term** a corto plazo; **a ~ time ago** hace poco; **to work ~ time** ◊ **be on ~ time** (*Ind*) trabajar una jornada reducida; **to take a ~ walk** dar un paseo corto; **a ~ way off** a poca distancia, no muy lejos; **a few ~ words** algunas palabritas; **✦IDIOMS that was ~ and sweet** eso fue corto y bueno; **to make ~ work of sth** despachar algo

[2] (= *insufficient*) escaso; **I'm £3 ~** me faltan 3 libras; **it's two kilos ~** faltan dos kilos; **bananas are very ~** escasean los plátanos, casi no hay plátanos; **I'm a bit ~ at the moment*** en este momento ando un poco corto *or* escaso de dinero; **to be ~ of sth** andar falto *or* escaso de algo; **we're ~ of petrol** andamos escasos de gasolina; **we're not ~ of volunteers** se han ofrecido muchos voluntarios, no andamos escasos de voluntarios; **to be ~ of breath** estar sin aliento; **to give sb ~ change** no darle el cambio completo a algn; **to give ~ measure to sb** dar de menos a algn; **gold is in ~ supply** escasea el oro, hay escasez de oro; **~ ton** (*US*) (= *2,000lb*) tonelada *f* corta; **to give ~ weight to sb** dar de menos a algn; *see* **supply**

[3] **~ of** (= *less than*): **~ of blowing it up** a menos que lo volemos, a no ser que lo volemos; **~ of murder I'll do anything** lo haré todo menos matar; **not far ~ of £100** poco menos de 100 libras; **it's little ~ of madness** dista poco de la locura; **nothing ~ of total surrender** nada menos que la rendición incondicional; **it's nothing ~ of robbery** es nada menos que un robo; **nothing ~ of a bomb would stop him** fuera de una bomba nada le impediría; **nothing ~ of a miracle can save him** sólo un milagro le puede salvar, se necesitaría un milagro para salvarle

[4] (= *concise*) corto, breve; **~ and to the point** corto y bueno; **"Pat" is ~ for "Patricia"** "Patricia" se abrevia en "Pat"; **Rosemary is called "Rose" for ~** a Rosemary le dicen "Rose" para abreviar; **"TV" is ~ for "television"** "TV" es abreviatura de "televisión"; **in ~** en pocas palabras, en resumen; **in ~, the answer is no** en una palabra, la respuesta es no; *see also* **long**[1] **C1**

[5] (= *curt*) [*reply, manner*] brusco, seco; **to have a ~ temper** ser de mal genio, tener mal genio *or* mal carácter *or* corto de genio; **to be ~ with sb** tratar a algn con sequedad

[6] [*pastry*] quebradizo

Ⓑ ADV [1] (= *suddenly, abruptly*) en seco; **to stop ~** ◊ **pull up ~** pararse en seco

[2] (*insufficiency*) **to come ~ of** no alcanzar; **to cut sth ~** suspender algo; **they had to cut ~ their holiday** tuvieron que interrumpir sus vacaciones; **to fall ~ of** no alcanzar; **to fall ~ of the target** no alcanzar el blanco, no llegar al blanco; **to fall ~ of expectations** no cumplir las esperanzas; **it falls far ~ of what we require** dista mucho de satisfacer nuestras exigencias; **production has fallen ~ by 100 tons** la producción arroja un déficit de 100 toneladas; **to go ~ of** pasarse sin; **no one goes ~ in this house** en esta casa nadie padece hambre; **we never went ~ (of anything) as children** no nos faltó nada de niños; **we're running ~ of bread** tenemos poco pan, se nos acaba el pan (*LAm*); **we ran ~ of petrol** se nos acabó la gasolina, quedamos sin gasolina; **to sell ~** vender al descubierto; **to sell sb ~** (*lit*) engañar a algn en un negocio; (*fig*) menospreciar a algn; **to stop ~ of** (*lit*) detenerse antes de llegar a; **I'd stop ~ of murder** (*fig*) menos matar, haría lo que fuera; **to be taken ~** necesitar urgentemente ir al wáter

[3] (= *except*) **~ of apologizing ...** fuera de pedirle perdón ...

Ⓒ N [1] (*Elec*) = **short-circuit A**

[2] (*Brit**) (= *drink*) bebida *f* corta

[3] (*Cine*) cortometraje *m*; *see also* **shorts**

Ⓓ VTI (*Elec*) = **short-circuit B, C**

Ⓔ CPD ► **short cut** N atajo *m* ► **short list** N lista *f* de candidatos preseleccionados ► **short sight** N miopía *f*; **to have ~ sight** ser miope, ser corto de vista ► **short story** N cuento *m*; **~ story writer** escritor(a) *m/f* de cuentos ► **short wave** N (*Rad*) onda *f* corta

shortage [ˈʃɔːtɪdʒ] N [1] (= *lack*) escasez *f*, falta *f*; **a water ~** escasez *or* falta de agua; **~ of staff** escasez *or* falta de personal; **the housing ~** la crisis de la vivienda; **there is no ~ of advice** no es que falten consejos, no faltan los consejos

[2] (= *state of deficiency*) escasez *f*; **in times of ~** en las épocas de escasez

shortbread [ˈʃɔːtbred] N *especie de mantecada*

shortcake [ˈʃɔːtkeɪk] N [1] (*Brit*) *especie de mantecada*

[2] (*US*) torta *f* de frutas

short-change [ˈʃɔːtˈtʃeɪndʒ] VT **to ~ sb** no dar el cambio completo a algn; (*fig*) defraudar a algn; **to do this is to ~ the project** (*esp US*) hacer esto es tratar inadecuadamente el proyecto

short-circuit [ˈʃɔːtˈsɜːkɪt] (*Elec*) Ⓐ N cortocircuito *m*

Ⓑ VT [1] (*Elec*) provocar un cortocircuito en

[2] (*fig*) (= *bypass*) evitar (la necesidad de pasar por)

Ⓒ VI hacer un cortocircuito

shortcomings [ˈʃɔːtkʌmɪŋz] NPL defectos *mpl*

shortcrust pastry [ˈʃɔːtkrʌstˈpeɪstrɪ] N (*Brit*) pasta *f* quebradiza

short-dated [ˈʃɔːtˈdeɪtɪd] ADJ (*Fin*) a corto plazo

shorten [ˈʃɔːtn] Ⓐ VT (*gen*) acortar; [+ *journey etc*] acortar, abreviar; [+ *rations etc*] reducir

Ⓑ VI (*gen*) acortarse, reducirse; **the days are ~ing** los días se están acortando; **the odds have ~ed** los puntos de ventaja se han reducido

shortening [ˈʃɔːtnɪŋ] N [1] (= *making shorter*) (*gen*) acortamiento *m*; [*of rations etc*] reducción *f*

[2] (*esp US Culin*) manteca *f*, grasa *f*

shortfall [ˈʃɔːtfɔːl] N (*in profits*) déficit *m* (**in** en); (*in payments, savings*) disminución *f* (**in** de); (*in numbers*) insuficiencia *f* (**in** de); **~ in earnings** ingresos *mpl* insuficientes; **there is a ~ of £5,000** faltan 5.000 libras; **the ~ of £5,000** las 5.000 libras que faltan; **there is a ~ of 200 in the registrations for this course** hay 200 matriculaciones menos para este curso

short-haired [ˈʃɔːtˈhεəd] ADJ pelicorto

shorthand [ˈʃɔːthænd] Ⓐ N taquigrafía *f*; **to take ~** escribir en taquigrafía; **to take sth down in ~** escribir algo taquigráficamente

Ⓑ CPD ► **shorthand note** N nota *f* taquigráfica ► **shorthand notebook** N cuaderno *m* de taquigrafía ► **shorthand speed** N palabras *fpl* por minuto (en taquigrafía) ► **shorthand typing** N taquimecanografía *f* ► **shorthand typist** N taquimecanógrafo/a *m/f* ► **shorthand writer** N taquígrafo/a *m/f*

short-handed [ˈʃɔːtˈhændɪd] ADJ falto de mano de obra/personal

short-haul [ˈʃɔːthɔːl] ADJ de corto recorrido

shortie* [ˈʃɔːtɪ] N = **shorty**

shortish [ˈʃɔːtɪʃ] ADJ [*person*] más bien bajo, bajito; [*novel, play, film*] más bien corto

short-list [ˈʃɔːtˈlɪst] VT **to ~ sb** preseleccionar a algn, poner a algn en la lista de candidatos a entrevistar

short-lived [ˈʃɔːtˈlɪvd] ADJ (*fig*) [*happiness*] efímero

shortly [ˈʃɔːtlɪ] ADV [1] (= *soon*) dentro de poco, en breve (*frm*), ahorita (*Mex*); **she's going to London ~** irá a Londres dentro de poco; **details will be released ~** los detalles se comunicarán en breve; **we'll be along ~** iremos enseguida; **~ before/after** poco antes/después; **~ before two** poco antes de las dos

[2] (= *curtly*) bruscamente, secamente

shortness [ˈʃɔːtnɪs] N [1] (*in length, distance*) lo corto; [*of message etc*] brevedad *f*; [*of person*] baja estatura *f*; **because of the ~ of my memory** debido a mi mala memoria; **~ of sight** miopía *f*; **~ of breath** falta *f* de aliento, respiración *f* difícil

[2] (= *curtness*) brusquedad *f*, sequedad *f*

➤ LANGUAGE IN USE: **short A4** 26.1

short-range ['ʃɔːt'reɪndʒ] ADJ [*gun*] de corto alcance; [*aircraft*] de autonomía limitada, de corto radio en acción

short-run ['ʃɔːtrʌn] ADJ breve, de alcance limitado

shorts ['ʃɔːts] NPL pantalones *mpl* cortos; **a pair of ~** un pantalón corto, unos pantalones cortos

short-sighted ['ʃɔːt'saɪtɪd] ADJ 1 (*lit*) miope, corto de vista
2 (*fig*) [*person*] miope, con poca visión (de futuro); [*measure etc*] con poca visión (de futuro)

short-sightedly ['ʃɔːt'saɪtɪdlɪ] ADV 1 (*lit*) con ojos de miope
2 (*fig*) con poca visión (de futuro)

short-sightedness ['ʃɔːt'saɪtɪdnɪs] N 1 (*lit*) miopía *f*
2 (*fig*) falta *f* de visión (de futuro)

short-sleeved ['ʃɔːtsliːvd] ADJ de manga corta

short-staffed [ˌʃɔːt'stɑːft] ADJ falto de personal

short-tempered ['ʃɔːt'tempəd] ADJ irritable

short-term ['ʃɔːttɜːm] ADJ a corto plazo; **a ~ loan** un préstamo a plazo corto; **~ car park** zona *f* de estacionamiento limitado

short-time ['ʃɔːt'taɪm] (A) ADJ **~ working** trabajo *m* de horario reducido; **to be on ~ working** trabajar jornadas reducidas *or* de horarios reducidos
(B) ADV **to work ~** trabajar jornadas reducidas *or* de horarios reducidos

short-wave ['ʃɔːtˌweɪv] ADJ (*Rad*) de onda corta

short-winded ['ʃɔːt'wɪndɪd] ADJ corto de resuello

shorty* ['ʃɔːtɪ] N persona *f* bajita

shot [ʃɒt] (A) PT, PP *of* **shoot**
(B) N 1 (= *act of shooting*) tiro *m*; (*causing wound*) balazo *m*; (= *sound*) tiro *m*, disparo *m*; **his ~ missed** erró el tiro; **he received a ~ in the leg** recibió un balazo en la pierna; **two ~s rang out** se oyeron dos tiros *or* disparos; **a ~ across the bows** (*lit, fig*) un cañonazo de advertencia; **there was an exchange of ~s** hubo un tiroteo; **to fire a ~ at sth/sb** disparar a algo/disparar a *or* sobre algn; **he fired two ~s into her head** le disparó dos tiros a la cabeza; **they surrendered without a ~ being fired** se rindieron sin ofrecer resistencia; **he was off like a ~** salió disparado *or* como un rayo; **I'd do it like a ~ if I had the chance** no dudaría en hacerlo si se me presentara la oportunidad; **I was over there like a ~** en un segundo me presenté allí; **to take a ~ at sth/sb** (*lit*) pegar un tiro a algo/algn; (*fig*) atacar algo/a algn; *see also* **long[1] D, parting A**
2 (= *missile*) bala *f*, proyectil *m*; (= *shotgun pellets*) perdigones *mpl*; (*Athletics*) peso *m*; **to put the ~** lanzar el peso
3 (= *person*) tirador(a) *m/f*; **he's a bad/good ~** es un mal/buen tirador; *see also* **big C, hot-shot**
4 (*Ftbl*) tiro *m*; (*Golf, Tennis*) golpe *m*; (*Snooker*) golpe *m*, jugada *f*; (= *throw*) tirada *f*, echada *f*; **he missed two ~s at goal** falló dos tiros a puerta; **good ~!** ¡buen tiro!; ✦***IDIOM*** **to call the ~s** mandar, llevar la voz cantante
5 (= *attempt*) tentativa *f*, intento *m*; **just give it your best ~** limítate a hacerlo lo mejor que puedas; **to have a ~ at sth** intentar algo; **I don't think there's much chance of persuading her but I'll have a ~ at it** no creo que haya muchas posibilidades de convencerla pero probaré *or* lo intentaré; **do you want another ~ at it?** ¿quieres volver a intentarlo?, ¿quieres volver a probar?; ✦***IDIOM*** **a ~ in the dark** un palo de ciego, una tentativa a ciegas
6 (= *turn to play*) **it's your ~** te toca (a ti)
7 (= *injection*) inyección *f*; (= *dose*) dosis *f inv*; [*of alcohol*] trago *m*; (*) [*of drug*] pico* *m*, chute* *m*; **a ~ of rum** un trago de ron; ✦***IDIOM*** **a ~ in the arm***: **it's a ~ in the arm for the peace process** es una importante ayuda para el proceso de paz; **the economy needs a ~ in the arm** la economía necesita estímulo
8 (*Phot*) foto *f*; (*Cine*) toma *f*, plano *m*
(C) ADJ 1 (= *suffused*) **~ silk** seda *f* tornasolada; **his story is ~ through with inconsistencies** su narración está plagada de incongruencias; **black marble ~ through with red veins** mármol negro con vetas rojas
2 (*) (= *rid*) ✦***IDIOM*** **to get ~ of sth/sb** deshacerse *or* librarse de algo/algn
3 (*) (= *exhausted*) [*person, nerves*] deshecho, hecho polvo*; **what little confidence he had is ~ to pieces** la poca seguridad que tenía en sí mismo se ha ido al traste
(D) CPD ► **shot put** N (*Sport*) lanzamiento *m* de pesos ► **shot putter** N lanzador(a) *m/f* de pesos

shotgun ['ʃɒtgʌn] (A) N escopeta *f*
(B) CPD ► **shotgun marriage, shotgun wedding** N casamiento *m* a la fuerza; **to have a ~ wedding** casarse a la fuerza, casarse de penalty*

▼**should** [ʃʊd] AUX VB, MODAL AUX VB 1 (*used to form conditional tense*) **I ~ go if they sent for me** iría si me llamasen; **~ I be out at the time** ◊ **if I ~ be out at the time** si estoy fuera en ese momento; **I ~n't be surprised if …** no me sorprendería si …; **I ~ have liked to …** me hubiera gustado …, quisiera haber …; **thanks, I ~ like to** gracias, me gustaría; **I ~n't like to say** prefiero no decirlo; **I ~ think so** supongo que sí; **I ~ be so lucky!** ¡ojalá!
2 (*duty, advisability, desirability*) deber; **all cars ~ carry a first-aid kit** todos los coches deberían llevar un botiquín; **you ~ take more exercise** deberías hacer más ejercicio; **I ~ have been a doctor** yo debería haber sido médico; **you ~n't do that** no deberías hacerlo, más vale no hacer eso; **I ~n't if I were you** yo que tú no lo haría; **he ~ know that …** debiera *or* debería saber que …; **all is as it ~ be** todo está en regla; **…, which is as it ~ be** …, como es razonable, …, que es como tiene que ser; **why ~ I?** ¿por qué lo voy a hacer?, ¿por qué tengo que hacerlo?; **why ~ he (have done it)?** ¿por qué lo iba a hacer?, ¿por qué tenía que hacerlo?; **why ~ you want to know?** ¿por qué has de saberlo tú?
3 (*statements of probability*) deber de; **he ~ pass his exams** debería de aprobar los exámenes; **they ~ have arrived by now** deben (de) haber llegado ya; **he ~ be there by now** ya debería estar allí; **they ~ arrive tomorrow** deberán *or* deben (de) llegar mañana; **that ~n't be too hard** eso no debería ser muy difícil; **I ~ have told you before** tendría que *or* debería habértelo dicho antes; **this ~ be good** esto promete ser bueno
4 (*subjunctive uses*) **… and who ~ I bump into but Mike?** … ¿y con quién crees que me encuentro? ¡pues con Mike!; **he ordered that it ~ be done** mandó que se hiciera

shoulder ['ʃəʊldəʳ] (A) N 1 (*Anat*) hombro *m*; **to have broad ~s** (*lit*) ser ancho de espaldas; (*fig*) tener mucho aguante; **they carried him ~ high** le llevaron a hombros; **he was carried out on their ~s** le sacaron a hombros; **all the responsibilities fell on his ~s** tuvo que cargar con todas las responsabilidades; **to look over one's ~** mirar por encima del hombro; **to look over sb's ~** (*lit*) mirar por encima del hombro de algn; (*fig*) vigilar a algn; **to carry sth over one's ~** llevar algo en hombros; **to stand ~ to ~** estar hombro con hombro; ✦***IDIOMS*** **to give sb the cold ~** dar de lado a algn; **to cry on sb's ~** desahogarse con algn; **to put one's ~ to the wheel** arrimar el hombro; **to rub ~s with sb** codearse con algn; **to give sb sth straight from the ~** decir algo a algn sin rodeos; *see also* **round-shouldered**
2 [*of coat etc*] hombro *m*; **padded ~s** hombreras *fpl*
3 [*of meat*] lomo *m*
4 [*of hill, mountain*] lomo *m*
5 [*of road*] arcén *m*
(B) VT 1 (= *carry*) llevar al hombro; (*pick up*) poner al hombro; **~ arms!** ¡armas al hombro!
2 (*fig*) [+ *burden, responsibility*] cargar con; **to ~ the blame** cargar con la culpa
3 (= *push*) **to ~ sb aside** apartar a algn a un lado de un empujón; **to ~ one's way through** abrirse paso a empujones
(C) CPD ► **shoulder bag** N bolso *m* de bandolera ► **shoulder blade** N omóplato *m* ► **shoulder flash** N (*Mil*) charretera *f* ► **shoulder holster** N pistolera *f* ► **shoulder joint** N articulación *f* del hombro ► **shoulder pad** N hombrera *f* ► **shoulder patch** N = **shoulder flash** ► **shoulder strap** N tirante *m*; [*of satchel*] bandolera *f*; (*Mil*) dragona *f*

shoulderknot ['ʃəʊldənɒt] N dragona *f*, charretera *f*

shoulder-length ['ʃəʊldəˌleŋθ] ADJ que llega hasta los hombros

shouldn't ['ʃʊdnt] = **should not**

should've ['ʃʊdv] = **should have**

shout [ʃaʊt] (A) N 1 (= *loud cry*) grito *m*; **a ~ of anger** un grito de ira; **there were ~s of applause** hubo grandes aplausos; **to give sb a ~** pegar un grito a algn*, avisar a algn; **give me a ~ when you've finished** pégame un grito* *or* avísame cuando hayas terminado; **a ~ of joy** un grito de alegría; **there were ~s of laughter** hubo grandes carcajadas; **a ~ of pain** un grito de dolor; **a ~ of protest** un grito de protesta; ✦***IDIOM*** **he's still in with a ~*** todavía tiene una posibilidad de ganar
2 (*Brit**) (= *round of drinks*) ronda *f*; **it's my ~ — what are you drinking?** me toca pagar esta ronda — ¿qué tomáis?
(B) VT gritar; **to ~ abuse at sb** insultar a algn a gritos; **to ~ o.s. hoarse** gritar hasta quedarse ronco; **he ~ed a warning** pegó un grito de advertencia
(C) VI (= *cry out*) gritar; **I had to ~ to make myself heard** tenía que gritar para que se me oyese; **his goal gave the fans something to ~ about** su gol les dio motivo a los hinchas para que gritaran; **to ~ at sb** gritar a algn; **his parents were ~ing at each other** sus padres estaban discutiendo a gritos; **to ~ for sth/sb** pedir algo a gritos/llamar a algn a gritos; **I ~ed for help** pedí socorro a gritos; **she ~ed for Jane to come** llamó a Jane a gritos para que viniera; **to ~ with glee/joy** gritar de alegría; **to ~ with laughter** reírse a carcajadas

►**shout down** VT + ADV [+ *person*] abuchear, hacer callar a gritos

►**shout out** (A) VT + ADV gritar, decir a voz en grito; **we ~ed out our thanks** gritamos las gracias, dimos las gracias a gritos; **they ~ed out greetings** gritaron los saludos, nos saludaron a gritos
(B) VI + ADV gritar, dar un grito, pegar un grito*

➤ LANGUAGE IN USE: **should 2** 1.1, 2.2, 10.3, 14

shouting [ˈʃaʊtɪŋ] Ⓐ N gritos *mpl*, vocerío *m*; **within ~ distance (of sth)** a tiro de piedra (de algo); ✦*IDIOM* **it's all over bar the ~** ya es asunto concluido
Ⓑ CPD ► **shouting match** N pelea *f or* riña *f* de gallos; **the TV debate turned into a ~ match** el debate televisado se convirtió en una pelea *or* riña de gallos

shove [ʃʌv] Ⓐ N empujón *m*; **to give sth/sb a ~** dar un empujón a algo/algn; **give it a good ~** dale un buen empujón
Ⓑ VT 1 (= *push*) empujar; **he ~d everyone aside** apartó a un lado a todo el mundo a empujones; **she ~d her plate away** apartó su plato de un empujón; **~ the table back against the wall** empuja la mesa contra la pared; **his friends ~d him forward** sus amigos le empujaron hacia adelante; **to ~ sth/sb in** meter a algo/algn a empujones; **they ~d the car over the cliff** fueron empujando el coche hasta que cayó por el acantilado
2 (*) (= *put*) poner, meter; **~ it here** ponlo aquí; **~ another record on** pon otro disco; **~ it over to me** trae pa'acá*
Ⓒ VI empujar, dar empujones; **stop shoving!*** ¡deja de empujar!

► **shove about, shove around** VT + ADV 1 (*lit*) [+ *object, person*] empujar de un lado a otro
2 (*) (= *bully*) tiranizar

► **shove off** Ⓐ VI + ADV 1 (*Naut*) alejarse del muelle *etc*
2 (*) (= *leave*) largarse, marcharse; **~ off!** ¡lárgate!*
Ⓑ VT + ADV **to ~ a boat off** echar afuera un bote

► **shove out** VT + ADV **to ~ a boat out** echar afuera un bote

► **shove over, shove up** VI + ADV correrse; **~ over!** ¡córrete!

shovel [ˈʃʌvl] Ⓐ N pala *f*; **mechanical ~** pala *f* mecánica, excavadora *f*
Ⓑ VT mover con pala; **to ~ earth into a pile** amontonar tierra con una pala; **to ~ coal on to a fire** añadir carbón a la lumbre con pala; **they were ~ling out the mud** estaban sacando el lodo con palas; **he was ~ling food into his mouth*** se zampaba la comida

► **shovel up** VT + ADV [+ *coal etc*] levantar con una pala; [+ *snow*] quitar con pala

shovelboard [ˈʃʌvlbɔːd] N juego *m* de tejo

shoveler [ˈʃʌvləʳ] N 1 (*Orn*) espátula *f* común, pato *m* cuchareta
2 (= *tool*) paleador *m*

shovelful [ˈʃʌvlfʊl] N paletada *f*

show [ʃəʊ] (*vb: pt* **showed**; *pp* **shown**) Ⓐ N 1 (= *showing*) demostración *f*, manifestación *f*; **~ of hands** votación *f* a mano alzada; **an impressive ~ of power** una impresionante exhibición de poder; **a ~ of strength** una demostración de fuerza
2 (= *exhibition*) exposición *f*; [*of trade*] feria *f*; **agricultural ~** feria *f* agrícola; **fashion ~** pase *m* de modelos; **motor ~** salón *m* del automóvil; **to be on ~** estar expuesto; *see also* **flower C, horse B, Lord Mayor C**
3 (= *sight*) **the garden is a splendid ~** el jardín es un espectáculo; **the dahlias make a fine ~** las dalias están espléndidas
4 (*Theat*) 4·1 (= *performance*) espectáculo *m*, función *f*; **to go to a ~** ir al teatro; **the last ~ starts at 11** la última función empieza a las 11; **there is no ~ on Sundays** el domingo no hay función; **to stage a ~** montar un espectáculo
4·2 (*fig*) **bad ~!** ¡malo!; **good ~!*** ¡muy bien hecho!; **to put up a good ~*** dar buena cuenta de sí, hacer un buen papel; **on with the ~!** ◊ **the ~ must go on!** ¡que siga el espectáculo!; **to put up a poor ~*** no dar buena cuenta de sí, hacer un mal papel; **it's a poor ~*** es una vergüenza; ✦*IDIOMS* **to give the ~ away** (*deliberately*) tirar de la manta; (*involuntarily*) clarearse; **let's get this ~ on the road** echémosnos a la carretera; **to steal the ~** acaparar toda la atención
5 (*Rad, TV*) programa *m*; **a radio ~** un programa de radio
6 (= *outward appearance*) apariencia *f*; **it's all ~ with him** en su caso todo es apariencia, todo lo hace para impresionar; **to do sth for ~** hacer algo para impresionar; **it's just for ~** (*behaviour*) es para impresionar nada más; (*object*) (= *for decoration*) es sólo un adorno; (= *not real*) es de adorno; **the party made a ~ of unity at its conference** el partido presentó una fachada de gran unidad en su congreso; **to make a ~ of resistance** fingir resistencia
7 (= *affected display*) alarde *m*; **to make a great ~ of sympathy** hacer un gran alarde de compasión
8 (*) (= *organization*) **who's in charge of this ~?** ¿quién manda aquí?; **this is my ~** aquí mando yo; **he runs the ~** manda él, él es el amo
Ⓑ VT 1 (*gen*) enseñar, mostrar; **to ~ sb sth** ◊ **~ sth to sb** enseñar *or* mostrar algo a algn; **have I ~n you my hat?** ¿te he enseñado *or* mostrado ya mi sombrero?; **he ~ed me his new car** me enseñó *or* mostró su nuevo coche; **to ~ o.s.: she won't ~ herself here again** no volverá a dejarse ver por aquí; **come on, ~ yourself!** vamos, ¡sal de ahí!; **it ~s itself in his speech** se revela en su forma de hablar, se le nota en el habla; **to ~ one's cards** *or* **one's hand** (*lit*) poner las cartas boca arriba; (*fig*) descubrir el juego; **don't ~ your face here again** no te vuelvas a dejar ver por aquí; **she likes to ~ her legs** le gusta enseñar *or* (*frm*) hacer exhibición de sus piernas; **he had nothing to ~ for his trouble** no vió recompensado su esfuerzo, no le lució nada el esfuerzo; **to ~ one's passport** mostrar *or* presentar su pasaporte
2 (= *exhibit*) [+ *paintings*] exhibir; [+ *goods*] exponer; [+ *film*] proyectar, pasar; [+ *slides*] proyectar; (*Theat*) representar, dar*; **to ~ a picture at the Academy** exhibir un cuadro en la Academia; **to ~ a film at Cannes** proyectar una película en Cannes; **the film was first ~n in 1968** la película se estrenó en 1968
3 (= *indicate*) [*dial, gauge, instrument*] marcar; **the speedometer ~s a speed of ...** el velocímetro marca ...; **it ~s 200 degrees** marca *or* indica 200 grados; **the motorways are ~n in black** las autopistas están marcadas en negro; **the clock ~s two o'clock** el reloj marca las dos; **the figures ~ a rise** las cifras arrojan un aumento; **as ~n in the illustration** como se ve en el grabado; **to ~ a loss/profit** (*Comm*) arrojar un saldo negativo/positivo
4 (= *demonstrate*) demostrar; **to ~ that ...** demostrar que ..., hacer ver que ...; **it just goes to ~ (that) ...** queda demostrado (que) ...; **I ~ed him that this could not be true** le hice ver *or* demostré que esto no podía ser cierto; **this ~s him to be a coward** esto deja manifiesto lo cobarde que es, esto demuestra que es un cobarde; **I'll ~ him!*** ¡ya va a ver!, ¡ese se va a enterar!; **to ~ what one is made of** demostrar de lo que uno es capaz
5 (= *express, manifest*) demostrar; **to ~ one's affection** demostrar su cariño; **she ~ed great courage** demostró gran valentía; **to ~ his disagreement, he ...** para mostrar su disconformidad, él ...; **he ~ed no fear** no demostró tener miedo, no mostró ningún miedo; **her face ~ed her happiness** se le veía la felicidad en la cara; **she ~ed great intelligence** demostró ser muy inteligente, mostró gran inteligencia; **she ~ed no reaction** no acusó reacción alguna; **the choice of dishes ~s excellent taste** la selección de platos demuestra *or* muestra un gusto muy fino
6 (= *reveal*) **she's beginning to ~ her age** ya empieza a aparentar su edad; **white shoes soon ~ the dirt** los zapatos blancos pronto dejan ver la suciedad; **to ~ o.s. incompetent** descubrir su incompetencia, mostrarse incompetente
7 (= *direct, conduct*) **to ~ sb to the door** acompañar a algn a la puerta; **to ~ sb the door** (*fig*) echar a algn con cajas destempladas; **to ~ sb into a room** hacer que pase algn, hacer entrar a algn en un cuarto; **I was ~n into a large hall** me hicieron pasar a un vestíbulo grande; **to ~ sb over** *or* **round a house** enseñar a algn una casa; **they ~ed us round the garden** nos mostraron *or* enseñaron el jardín; **who is going to ~ us round?** ¿quién actuará de guía?, ¿quién será nuestro guía?; **to ~ sb to his seat** acompañar a algn a su asiento; **to ~ sb the way** señalar el camino a algn
Ⓒ VI 1 [*stain, emotion, underskirt*] notarse, verse; **it doesn't ~** no se ve, no se nota; **your slip's ~ing** se te ve la combinación; **fear ~ed on her face** se le notaba *or* (*frm*) manifestaba el miedo en la cara; **don't worry, it won't ~** no te preocupes, no se notará; **"I've never been riding before" — "it ~s"** —nunca había montado a caballo antes —se nota; **the tulips are beginning to ~** empiezan a brotar los tulipanes
2 [*film*] **there's a horror film ~ing at the Odeon** están pasando *or* (*LAm*) dando una película de horror en el Odeón
3 (= *demonstrate*) **it just goes to ~ that ...!** ¡hay que ver que ...!
4 (*esp US*) (*also* **~ up**) (= *arrive*) venir, aparecer
Ⓓ CPD ► **show bill** N cartel *m* ► **show biz***, **show business** N el mundo del espectáculo ► **show home, show house** N (*Brit*) casa *f* modelo ► **show jumper** N participante *mf* en concursos de saltos *or* de hípica ► **show jumping** N concursos *mpl* de saltos *or* de hípica ► **show ring** N pista *f* de exhibición ► **show trial** N proceso *m* organizado con fines propagandísticos ► **show window** N escaparate *m*

► **show in** VT + ADV hacer pasar; **~ him in!** ¡que pase!

► **show off** Ⓐ VI + ADV presumir, darse tono; **to ~ off in front of one's friends** presumir *or* darse tono delante de las amistades; **stop ~ing off!** ¡no presumas!
Ⓑ VT + ADV 1 [+ *beauty etc*] hacer resaltar, destacar
2 (*pej*) (= *display*) hacer alarde de, ostentar

► **show out** VT + ADV acompañar a la puerta

► **show through** VI + ADV verse

► **show up** Ⓐ VI + ADV 1 (= *be visible*) verse, notarse
2 (*) (= *arrive*) venir, aparecer; **he ~ed up late as usual** vino *or* apareció tarde, como de costumbre
Ⓑ VT + ADV 1 [+ *visitor etc*] hacer subir; **~ him up!** ¡hazle subir!
2 (= *reveal*) [+ *defect*] poner de manifiesto; **he was ~n up as an imposter** se demostró que era un impostor; **the bright lighting**

~ed up her scars el alumbrado hizo resaltar sus cicatrices
3 (= *embarrass*) dejar en ridículo, poner en evidencia; **please don't ~ me up!** por favor, no me hagas quedar en ridículo *or* no me pongas en evidencia

showboat ['ʃəʊbəʊt] Ⓐ N barco-teatro *m*
Ⓑ VI (*) alardear, fardar (*Sp**), vacilar (*Sp**)

showcase ['ʃəʊkeɪs] Ⓐ N (*in shop, museum*) vitrina *f*
Ⓑ VT (*fig*) (= *exhibit, display*) exhibir, mostrar; **the festival ~s an impressive line-up of previously banned work** el festival exhibe *or* muestra una impresionante selección de obras anteriormente prohibidas; **an album which also ~s her strong singing voice** un disco que también sirve de escaparate a *or* para su portentosa voz
Ⓒ CPD ► **showcase project** N proyecto *m* modelo

showdown ['ʃəʊdaʊn] N enfrentamiento *m* (final); **to have a ~ with sb** enfrentarse con algn; **if it comes to a ~** si llega a producirse un conflicto; **the Suez ~** la crisis de Suez

shower ['ʃaʊəʳ] Ⓐ N 1 [*of rain*] chubasco *m*, chaparrón *m*; **scattered ~s** chubascos dispersos
2 (*fig*) [*of arrows, stones, blows etc*] lluvia *f*
3 (*in bathroom*) ducha *f*, regadera *f* (*Mex*); **to have** *or* **take a ~** ducharse, tomar una ducha
4 (*Brit* pej*) (= *people*) **what a ~!** ¡que montón de inútiles!
5 (*US*) (= *party*) fiesta *f* de obsequio; *see also* **baby D**
Ⓑ VT (*fig*) **they ~ed gifts (up)on the queen** colmaron a la reina de regalos; **he was ~ed with invitations** le llovieron invitaciones; **to ~ sb with honours** ◊ **~ honours on sb** colmar a algn de honores
Ⓒ VI 1 (= *rain*) caer un chaparrón *or* chubasco
2 (= *take a shower*) ducharse, tomar una ducha
Ⓓ CPD ► **shower cap** N gorro *m* de baño ► **shower curtain** N cortina *f* de ducha ► **shower gel** N gel *m* de baño ► **shower head** N alcachofa *f* de la ducha ► **shower tray** N plato *m* de la ducha ► **shower unit** N ducha *f*

showerbath† ['ʃaʊəbɑːθ] N (*pl* **showerbaths** ['ʃaʊəbɑːðz]) ducha *f*; **to take a ~** ducharse, tomar una ducha

showerproof ['ʃaʊəpruːf] ADJ impermeable

showery ['ʃaʊərɪ] ADJ [*weather*] lluvioso; [*day*] lluvioso, de lluvia; **it will be ~ tomorrow** mañana habrá chubascos *or* chaparrones*

showgirl ['ʃəʊgɜːl] N corista *f*

showground ['ʃəʊgraʊnd] N recinto *m* ferial, real *m* de la feria

showily ['ʃəʊɪlɪ] ADV ostentosamente

showiness ['ʃəʊɪnɪs] N ostentación *f*

showing ['ʃəʊɪŋ] N 1 [*of film*] proyección *f*, pase *m*; [*of paintings etc*] exposición *f*; **a private ~** [*of film*] un pase privado; [*of paintings*] una exposición a puertas cerradas; **a second ~ of "The Blue Angel"** un reestreno de "El Ángel Azul"
2 (= *performance*) actuación *f*; **the poor ~ of the team** la pobre actuación del equipo

showing-off [,ʃəʊɪŋ'ɒf] N 1 (= *displaying*) lucimiento *m*
2 (*pej*) presunción *f*

showman ['ʃəʊmən] N (*pl* **showmen**) (*at fair, circus*) empresario *m*; **he's a real ~!** (*fig*) ¡es todo un número *or* espectáculo!

showmanship ['ʃəʊmənʃɪp] N (*fig*) espectacularidad *f*, teatralidad *f*

shown [ʃəʊn] PP *of* **show**

show-off* ['ʃəʊɒf] N presumido/a *m/f*, fantasmón/ona *m/f* (*Sp**)

showpiece ['ʃəʊpiːs] N (= *centrepiece*) joya *f*, lo mejor; **the ~ of the exhibition is ...** la joya *or* lo mejor de la exposición es ...; **this vase is a real ~** este florero es realmente excepcional

showplace ['ʃəʊpleɪs] N lugar *m* de interés turístico; **Granada is a ~** Granada es un lugar de interés turístico, Granada es ciudad monumental

showroom ['ʃəʊrʊm] N (*Comm*) sala *f* de muestras; (*Art*) sala *f* de exposición, galería *f* de arte; **in ~ condition** en excelentes condiciones, como nuevo

showstopper* ['ʃəʊ,stɒpəʳ] N sensación *f*; **to be a ~** quitar el hipo*, causar sensación

showy ['ʃəʊɪ] ADJ (*compar* **showier**; *superl* **showiest**) ostentoso

shpt ABBR (*Comm*) (= **shipment**) e/

shrank [ʃræŋk] PT *of* **shrink**

shrapnel ['ʃræpnl] N metralla *f*

shred [ʃred] Ⓐ N [*of cloth*] jirón *m*; [*of paper*] tira *f*; **without a ~ of clothing on** sin nada de ropa encima; **if you had a ~ of decency** si usted tuviese un mínimo de honradez; **you haven't got a ~ of evidence** no tienes la más mínima prueba; **in ~s** (*lit, fig*) hecho jirones *or* trizas; **her dress hung in ~s** su vestido estaba hecho jirones *or* trizas; **to tear sth to ~s** (*lit, fig*) hacer algo trizas; **to tear an argument to ~s** hacer pedazos *or* trizas un argumento; **the crowd will tear him to ~s** la gente le hará pedazos; **there isn't a ~ of truth in it** eso no tiene ni pizca *or* chispa de verdad
Ⓑ VT [+ *paper*] hacer trizas, triturar; [+ *food*] despedazar

shredder ['ʃredəʳ] N (*for documents, papers*) trituradora *f*; (*for vegetables*) picadora *f*

shrew [ʃruː] N 1 (*Zool*) musaraña *f*
2 (*fig*) (*pej*) (= *woman*) arpía *f*, fiera *f*; **"The Taming of the Shrew"** "La fierecilla domada"

shrewd [ʃruːd] ADJ (*compar* **shrewder**; *superl* **shrewdest**) [*person, politician, businessperson*] astuto, sagaz; [*observer, glance, look*] perspicaz; [*remark, observation*] sagaz, perspicaz; [*eyes*] perspicaz, inteligente; [*assessment*] muy acertado; [*investment*] inteligente; **it was seen as a ~ political move** se vio como una hábil *or* astuta maniobra política; **I can make a ~ guess at how many people were there** estoy casi seguro de acertar si digo cuánta gente había allí; **she had a ~ idea** *or* **suspicion (that) ...** estaba casi segura de que ...; **I've got a pretty ~ idea of what's going on here** ya me puedo imaginar lo que está pasando aquí; **she's very ~ in matters of money** es un lince para cuestiones de dinero; **to be a ~ judge of character** tener buen ojo para juzgar a la gente; **that was very ~ of you** en eso has sido muy perspicaz

shrewdly ['ʃruːdlɪ] ADV [*say, ask, point out*] sagazmente; [*reason*] con perspicacia, con sagacidad; [*act*] hábilmente, con astucia; [*invest*] inteligentemente; **she had ~ guessed the reason for his absence** había adivinado astutamente la razón de su ausencia, se había dado cuenta hábilmente de la razón de su ausencia

shrewdness ['ʃruːdnɪs] N [*of person*] astucia *f*, sagacidad *f*; [*of assessment, reasoning*] lo acertado; [*of remark, observation*] sagacidad *f*, perspicacia *f*; [*of plan*] lo inteligente

shrewish ['ʃruːɪʃ] ADJ regañón, de mal genio

shriek [ʃriːk] Ⓐ N chillido *m*, grito *m* agudo; **a ~ of pain** un grito de dolor; **with ~s of laughter** con grandes carcajadas
Ⓑ VI chillar; **to ~ with laughter/pain** chillar de risa/dolor; **the colour just ~s at you** es un color de lo más chillón
Ⓒ VT gritar; **"I hate you!" she ~ed** —¡te odio! —gritó; **to ~ abuse at sb** lanzar improperios contra algn

shrieking ['ʃriːkɪŋ] Ⓐ ADJ [*child*] chillón
Ⓑ N chillidos *mpl*, gritos *mpl*

shrift [ʃrɪft] N **to give sb short ~** despachar a algn sin rodeos; **he gave that idea short ~** mostró su completa disconformidad con tal idea; **he got short ~ from the boss** el jefe se mostró poco compasivo con él; **he'll get short ~ from me!** ¡que no venga a mí a pedir compasión!

shrike [ʃraɪk] N alcaudón *m*

shrill [ʃrɪl] Ⓐ ADJ (*compar* **shriller**; *superl* **shrillest**) [*voice*] chillón, agudo; [*sound*] estridente, agudo
Ⓑ VT gritar (con voz estridente)
Ⓒ VI chillar

shrillness ['ʃrɪlnɪs] N [*of voice*] lo chillón, lo agudo; [*of sound*] estridencia *f*, lo agudo

shrilly ['ʃrɪlɪ] ADV de modo estridente

shrimp [ʃrɪmp] Ⓐ N 1 (*Zool*) camarón *m*
2 (*fig*) enano/a *m/f*
Ⓑ VI **to go ~ing** pescar camarones
Ⓒ CPD ► **shrimp cocktail** N cóctel *m* de camarones ► **shrimp sauce** N salsa *f* de camarones

shrine [ʃraɪn] N (*Rel*) (= *tomb*) sepulcro *m*; (= *sacred place*) lugar *m* sagrado

shrink [ʃrɪŋk] (*pt* **shrank**; *pp* **shrunk**) Ⓐ VI 1 (= *get smaller*) encogerse; **to ~ in the wash** encogerse al lavar; **"will not ~"** "no se encoge", "inencogible"; **to ~ away to nothing** reducirse a nada, desaparecer
2 (*also* **~ away, ~ back**) retroceder, echar marcha atrás; **I ~ from doing it** no me atrevo a hacerlo; **he did not ~ from touching it** no vaciló en tocarlo
Ⓑ VT encoger; **to ~ a part on** (*Tech*) montar una pieza en caliente
Ⓒ N (‡) (= *psychiatrist*) psiquiatra *mf*

shrinkage ['ʃrɪŋkɪdʒ] N (*gen*) encogimiento *m*; (*Tech*) (= *contraction*) contracción *f*; (*Comm*) (*in shops*) pérdidas *fpl*

shrinking ['ʃrɪŋkɪŋ] Ⓐ ADJ [*clothes*] que encoge(n); [*resources etc*] que escasea(n)
Ⓑ CPD ► **shrinking violet** N (*fig*) tímido/a *m/f*, vergonzoso/a *m/f*

shrink-wrap ['ʃrɪŋkræp] VT empaquetar *or* envasar al calor

shrink-wrapped ['ʃrɪŋkræpt] ADJ empaquetado *or* envasado al calor

shrink-wrapping ['ʃrɪŋkræpɪŋ] N envasado *m* al calor

shrivel ['ʃrɪvl] (*also* **~ up**) Ⓐ VT [+ *plant etc*] marchitar, secar; [+ *skin*] arrugar
Ⓑ VI [*plant etc*] marchitarse, secarse; [*skin etc*] arrugarse

shrivelled, **shriveled** (*US*) ['ʃrɪvld] ADJ [*plant etc*] marchito, seco; [*skin*] arrugado, apergaminado; **to have a ~ skin** tener la piel arrugada

shroud [ʃraʊd] Ⓐ N 1 (*around corpse*) sudario *m*, mortaja *f*; **the Shroud of Turin** la Sábana Santa de Turín, el Santo Sudario de Turín
2 (*fig*) **a ~ of mystery** un velo *or* halo de misterio
3 **shrouds** (*Naut*) obenques *mpl*
Ⓑ VT 1 [+ *corpse*] amortajar
2 (*fig*) velar, cubrir; **the castle was ~ed in**

mist el castillo estaba envuelto en niebla; **the whole thing is ~ed in mystery** el asunto está envuelto en un halo de misterio; **the whole affair is ~ed in secrecy** el asunto se mantiene en secreto

Shrovetide ['ʃrəʊvtaɪd] N carnestolendas *fpl*

Shrove Tuesday ['ʃrəʊv'tju:zdɪ] N martes *m inv* de Carnaval (*en que en Inglaterra se sirven hojuelas*)

shrub [ʃrʌb] N arbusto *m*

shrubbery ['ʃrʌbərɪ] N arbustos *mpl*

shrug [ʃrʌg] Ⓐ N encogimiento *m* de hombros; **he said with a ~** dijo encogiéndose de hombros
Ⓑ VT **to ~ one's shoulders** encogerse de hombros
Ⓒ VI encogerse de hombros

► **shrug off** VT + ADV no hacer caso de; **he just ~ged it off** se encogió de hombros y no hizo caso; **you can't just ~ that off** no puedes negarle la importancia que tiene

shrunk [ʃrʌŋk] PP *of* **shrink**

shrunken ['ʃrʌŋkən] ADJ encogido

shtoom* [ʃtʊm] ADJ **to keep ~ (about sth)** no decir ni mu (de algo)*, no decir esta boca es mía (sobre algo)*

shuck [ʃʌk] Ⓐ N 1 (= *husk*) vaina *f*, hollejo *m*
2 (*US*) [*of shellfish*] concha *f* (de marisco)
3 **~s!** ¡cáscaras!
Ⓑ VT 1 [+ *peas etc*] desenvainar
2 (*US*) [+ *shellfish*] desbullar

shudder ['ʃʌdəʳ] Ⓐ VI [*person*] estremecerse (**with** de); [*machinery*] vibrar; **the car ~ed to a halt** el coche paró a sacudidas; **I ~ to think** (*fig*) sólo pensarlo me da horror
Ⓑ N [*of person*] estremecimiento *m*, escalofrío *m*; [*of machinery*] vibración *f*, sacudida *f*; **it gave a ~** dio una sacudida; **a ~ ran through her** se estremeció; **she realized with a ~ that …** se estremeció al darse cuenta de que …; **it gives me the ~s** me da escalofríos

shuffle ['ʃʌfl] Ⓐ N 1 **to walk with a ~** caminar arrastrando los pies
2 (*Cards*) **to give the cards a ~** barajar (las cartas); **whose ~ is it?** ¿a quién le toca barajar?
Ⓑ VT 1 [+ *feet*] arrastrar
2 (= *mix up*) [+ *papers*] revolver, traspapelar; [+ *cards*] barajar
3 (= *move*) **to ~ sb aside** apartar a algn, relegar a algn a un puesto menos importante
Ⓒ VI 1 (= *walk*) arrastrar los pies; **to ~ about** moverse de un lado para otro; **to ~ in/out** entrar/salir arrastrando los pies
2 (*Cards*) barajar

► **shuffle off** Ⓐ VI + ADV marcharse arrastrando los pies
Ⓑ VT + ADV [+ *garment*] despojarse de; (*fig*) [+ *responsibility*] rechazar; **to ~ sth off** deshacerse de algo

shuffleboard ['ʃʌflbɔ:d] N juego *m* de tejo

shufti, shufty* ['ʃʊftɪ] N (*Brit*) ojeada *f*; **let's have a ~** a ver, déjame ver; **we went to take a ~** fuimos a echar un vistazo

shun [ʃʌn] VT 1 (= *reject*) [+ *person*] rechazar; **to feel ~ned by the world** sentirse rechazado por la gente
2 (= *avoid*) [+ *work*] evitar; [+ *publicity*] rehuir; **to ~ doing sth** evitar hacer algo

shunt [ʃʌnt] Ⓐ VT 1 (*Rail*) cambiar de vía, shuntar
2 (*fig*) **to ~ sb about** enviar a algn de acá para allá; **the form was ~ed about between different departments** la solicitud fue enviada de departamento a departamento (sin que nadie la atendiese); **we were ~ed about all day** nos tuvieron dando vueltas todo el día; **to ~ sb aside** apartar a algn, relegar a algn a un puesto menos importante; **he was ~ed into retirement** lograron con maña que se jubilase
Ⓑ VI **to ~ to and fro** trajinar de acá para allá

shunter ['ʃʌntəʳ] N (*Brit*) guardagujas *mf inv*

shunting ['ʃʌntɪŋ] Ⓐ N cambio *m* de vía
Ⓑ CPD ► **shunting engine** N locomotora *f* de maniobra ► **shunting yard** N estación *f* de maniobras

shush [ʃʊʃ] Ⓐ EXCL ¡chis!, ¡chitón!
Ⓑ VT (*) callar, hacer callar

shut [ʃʌt] (*pt, pp* **shut**) Ⓐ VT cerrar; **~ the door/window please** cierra la puerta/ventana por favor; **to find the door ~** encontrar que la puerta está cerrada; **they ~ the door in his face** le dieron con la puerta en las narices; **to ~ one's fingers in the door** pillarse los dedos en la puerta
Ⓑ VI cerrarse; **what time do the shops ~?** ¿a qué hora cierran las tiendas?; **we ~ at five** cerramos a las cinco; **the lid doesn't ~** la tapa no cierra (bien)

► **shut away** VT + ADV encerrar; **to ~ o.s. away** encerrarse; **he ~s himself away all day in his room** permanece encerrado todo el día en su habitación

► **shut down** Ⓐ VI + ADV cerrarse; **the cinema ~ down last year** el cine cerró el año pasado
Ⓑ VT + ADV [+ *lid, business, factory*] cerrar; [+ *machine*] apagar; (*by law*) clausurar

► **shut in** VT + ADV (= *enclose*) encerrar; (= *surround*) cercar, rodear; **to feel ~ in** sentirse encerrado; **the runner was ~ in** el atleta se encontró tapado, al atleta se le cerró el paso

► **shut off** VT + ADV 1 (= *stop*) [+ *water, power*] cortar, cerrar; [+ *engine, machine*] apagar
2 (= *isolate*) aislar (**from** de); **to be ~ off from** estar aislado de

► **shut out** VT + ADV (= *leave outside*) dejar fuera; (= *put outside*) sacar; (= *close door on*) cerrar la puerta a; (= *keep out*) excluir; (= *block*) tapar

► **shut to** Ⓐ VT + ADV cerrar
Ⓑ VI + ADV cerrarse

► **shut up** Ⓐ VI + ADV (*) (= *be quiet*) callarse; **~ up!** ¡cállate!; ✦**IDIOM to ~ up like a clam** callarse como un muerto
Ⓑ VT + ADV 1 (= *close*) cerrar
2 (= *enclose*) encerrar
3 (*) (= *silence*) callar, hacer callar

shutdown ['ʃʌtdaʊn] N 1 [*of factory, shop, business*] cierre *m*
2 (*Ftbl*) (*also* **winter ~**) *suspensión temporal de la actividad futbolística durante las semanas más inclementes del invierno*

shut-eye* ['ʃʌtaɪ] N sueño *m*; **to get some ~** echar un sueñecito*

shut-in ['ʃʌtɪn] ADJ encerrado

shutoff ['ʃʌtɒf] N interruptor *m*

shutout ['ʃʌtaʊt] Ⓐ N 1 (*US*) (= *lockout*) cierre *m* patronal
2 (*Brit Sport*) **the goalkeeper had ten successive ~s** el portero salió imbatido en diez partidos sucesivos
Ⓑ CPD ► **shutout bid** N declaración *f* aplastante ► **shutout record** N récord *m* de imbatibilidad

shutter ['ʃʌtəʳ] Ⓐ N 1 (*on window*) contraventana *f*, postigo *m*; **to put up the ~s** [*shop*] cerrar del todo; (*fig*) abandonar; (*Sport**) no arriesgar
2 (*Phot*) obturador *m*
Ⓑ CPD ► **shutter release** N (*Phot*) disparador *m* ► **shutter speed** N velocidad *f* de obturación

shuttered ['ʃʌtəd] ADJ [*house, window*] (= *fitted with shutters*) con contraventanas; (= *with shutters closed*) con las contraventanas cerradas; **the windows were ~** (= *had shutters*) las ventanas tenían contraventana(s); (= *had shutters closed*) las ventanas tenían las contraventanas cerradas

shuttle ['ʃʌtl] Ⓐ N 1 (*for weaving, sewing*) lanzadera *f*
2 (*Aer*) puente *m* aéreo; (= *plane, train etc*) servicio *m* regular de enlace; **air ~** puente *m* aéreo
3 (*Space*) (*also* **space ~**) lanzadera *f or* transbordador *m* espacial
4 (*) (*in badminton*) (= *shuttlecock*) volante *m*
Ⓑ VI [*person*] (= *go regularly*) ir y venir (**between** entre)
Ⓒ VT (= *transport*) transportar, trasladar
Ⓓ CPD ► **shuttle flight** N vuelo *m* de puente aéreo ► **shuttle diplomacy** N viajes *mpl* diplomáticos ► **shuttle service** N servicio *m* regular de enlace

shuttlecock ['ʃʌtlkɒk] N (*Badminton*) volante *m*

shy[1] [ʃaɪ] Ⓐ ADJ (*compar* **shyer**, *superl* **shyest**)
1 (= *nervous*) [*person*] vergonzoso, tímido; [*smile*] tímido; [*animal*] asustadizo, huraño; **he was too ~ to talk to anyone** era demasiado tímido para hablar con nadie; **come on, don't be ~!** ¡venga, no seas tímido *or* no tengas vergüenza!; **she went all ~ when asked to give her opinion** le dio vergüenza cuando le preguntaron su opinión, le dio corte cuando le preguntaron su opinión (*Sp**); **they may feel ~ about talking to her** puede que les dé vergüenza hablar con ella, puede que les dé corte hablar con ella (*Sp**); **she's ~ of cameras** se siente cohibida delante de las cámaras; **don't be ~ of telling them what you think** no tengas miedo decirles lo que piensas; **to be ~ with people** ser tímido con la gente, sentirse cohibido con la gente; *see also* **bite B1, camera-shy, fight C3, gun-shy**
2 **~ of** (*US*): **we're $65,000 ~ of the $1 million that's needed** (= *short of*) nos faltan 65.000 dólares para el millón de dólares que se necesitan; **he's two months ~ of 70** le faltan dos meses para cumplir 70 años; **he passed away two days ~ of his 95th birthday** murió a dos días de cumplir los 95 años
Ⓑ VI [*horse*] asustarse, espantarse (**at** de)

► **shy away** VI + ADV 1 (*lit*) [*horse*] asustarse, espantarse; [*person*] asustarse
2 (*fig*) **to ~ away from sth** huir *or* rehuir de algo; **to ~ away from doing sth** tener miedo a hacer algo

shy[2] [ʃaɪ] (*Brit*) N (= *throw*) tirada *f*; **50 pence a ~** 50 peniques la tirada; **to have a ~ at sth** intentar dar a algo

shyly ['ʃaɪlɪ] ADV tímidamente, con timidez

shyness ['ʃaɪnɪs] N [*of person, smile*] timidez *f*; [*of animal*] lo asustadizo

shyster* ['ʃaɪstəʳ] N (*esp US*) tramposo/a *m/f*, estafador(a) *m/f*; (= *lawyer*) picapleitos *mf inv* sin escrúpulos*

SI N ABBR = **Système Internationale (d'unités)** (= *system of metric units*) sistema *m* métrico internacional

Siam [saɪ'æm] N (*formerly*) Siam *m*

Siamese [,saɪə'mi:z] Ⓐ N 1 (= *person*) siamés/esa *m/f*
2 (*Ling*) siamés *m*
3 (= *cat*) gato *m* siamés
Ⓑ ADJ siamés
Ⓒ CPD ► **Siamese cat** N gato *m* siamés ► **Siamese twins** NPL hermanos/as *mpl/fpl* siameses/esas

SIB N ABBR (*Brit*) = **Securities and Investments Board**

Siberia [saɪˈbɪərɪə] N Siberia *f*

Siberian [saɪˈbɪərɪən] Ⓐ ADJ siberiano
Ⓑ N siberiano/a *m/f*

sibilant [ˈsɪbɪlənt] Ⓐ ADJ sibilante
Ⓑ N sibilante *f*

sibling [ˈsɪblɪŋ] Ⓐ N hermano/a *m/f*
Ⓑ CPD ► **sibling rivalry** N rivalidad *f* entre hermanos

Sibyl [ˈsɪbɪl] N Sibila

sibyl [ˈsɪbɪl] N sibila *f*

sibylline [ˈsɪbɪlaɪn] ADJ sibilino

sic [sɪk] ADV sic

Sicilian [sɪˈsɪlɪən] Ⓐ ADJ siciliano
Ⓑ N [1] (= *person*) siciliano/a *m/f*
[2] (*Ling*) siciliano *m*

Sicily [ˈsɪsɪlɪ] N Sicilia *f*

sick [sɪk] Ⓐ ADJ (*compar* **sicker**; *superl* **sickest**)
[1] (= *ill*) [*person*] enfermo; [*animal*] malo, enfermo; **your uncle is very ~** tu tío está muy enfermo; **to call in ~** = **to phone in sick**; **to fall ~**† enfermar, caer enfermo; **to go ~** faltar por estar enfermo (*al colegio, trabajo, etc*); (*with a medical certificate*) estar de baja; **to make sb look ~** (*US*) (*fig*) (= *appear inferior*) hacer parecer poca cosa a algn; **the Romanians made our team look ~** los rumanos dejaron a nuestro equipo muy atrás, el equipo rumano era como para darle complejo a nuestro equipo*; **to be off ~** faltar por estar enfermo (*al colegio, trabajo, etc*); (*with a medical certificate*) estar de baja; **she phoned in ~** llamó para decir que estaba enferma; ✦**IDIOM to be ~ at heart**† (*also liter*) (= *despondent*) estar angustiado; *see also* **worried 1**, **worry**
[2] **to be ~** (*Brit*) (= *vomit*) devolver, vomitar; **to feel ~** (*Brit*) (= *nauseous*) tener ganas de devolver *or* de vomitar, tener náuseas; **flying makes me feel ~** ir en avión me produce mareo *or* náuseas; **to make sb ~** (*lit*) hacer devolver *or* vomitar a algn; **to make o.s. ~** (*deliberately*) hacerse vomitar *or* devolver; **you'll make yourself ~ if you eat all those sweets** te vas a poner malo si comes todos esos caramelos; ✦**IDIOM to be as ~ as a dog*** echar las tripas**‡**, echar la primera papilla**‡**; *see also* **airsick**, **seasick**, **travel-sick**
[3] (= *fed up*) **to be ~ of (doing) sth** estar harto de (hacer) algo*; **to be ~ and tired** *or* **~ to death of (doing) sth** estar hasta la coronilla de (hacer) algo*, estar más que harto de (hacer) algo*; **to be ~ of the sight of sb** estar más que harto de algn*; ✦**IDIOM to be as ~ as a parrot** (*Brit**) sentirse fatal
[4] (= *disgusted*) **I feel ~ about the way she was treated** me asquea la forma en que la trataron; **it makes me ~ the way they waste our money** me pone enferma ver la manera en que malgastan nuestro dinero; **she's never without a boyfriend, makes you ~, doesn't it?*** siempre tiene algún novio, da rabia ¿no?*; **it's enough to make you ~** es como para sacarle a uno de quicio, es como para desesperarse; **you make me ~!** ¡me das asco!; **it makes me ~ to my stomach** me revienta, me da ganas de vomitar
[5] (*pej*) (= *morbid*) [*joke, act*] de mal gusto; [*person, mind, sense of humour*] morboso
Ⓑ N [1] **the ~** los enfermos
[2] (*Brit*) (= *vomit*) vómito *m*, devuelto *m*
Ⓒ CPD ► **sick bag** N bolsa *f* para el mareo ► **sick building syndrome** N síndrome *m* del edificio enfermo ► **sick leave** N **to be on ~ leave** tener permiso *or* (*Sp*) baja por enfermedad ► **sick list** N lista *f* de enfermos; **to be on the ~ list** estar de permiso *or* (*Sp*) de baja por enfermedad ► **sick note** N justificante *m* por enfermedad ► **sick pay** N *pago que se percibe mientras se está con permiso por enfermedad*, baja *f* (*Sp*)

►**sick up*** VT + ADV (*Brit*) vomitar, devolver

sickbay [ˈsɪkbeɪ] N enfermería *f*

sickbed [ˈsɪkbed] N lecho *m* de enfermo

sicken [ˈsɪkn] Ⓐ VT [1] (= *make ill*) poner enfermo
[2] (*fig*) (= *revolt*) dar asco; **it ~s me** me da asco; **it ~s me to think I missed the party** me enferma pensar que me perdí la fiesta
Ⓑ VI caer enfermo, enfermarse; **to be ~ing for** (= *show signs of*) mostrar síntomas de; (= *miss*) echar de menos, echar a faltar; **I ~ at the sight of blood** (el) ver sangre me da náuseas

sickening [ˈsɪknɪŋ] [1] (= *disgusting*) [*sight, smell*] nauseabundo, asqueroso; [*cruelty, crime*] espeluznante, repugnante; [*waste*] indignante, escandaloso; **a ~ feeling of failure** una asqueante *or* insoportable sensación de fracaso; **a ~ feeling of panic** un sensación de pánico atenazadora
[2] (*) (= *annoying*) [*person, behaviour, situation*] odioso, exasperante
[3] (= *unpleasant*) [*blow, crunch*] tremendo; **with a ~ thud** con un golpetazo tremendo

sickeningly [ˈsɪknɪŋlɪ] ADV [*familiar*] tremendamente; **~ violent/polite** asquerosamente violento/cortés; **it is ~ sweet** es realmente empalagoso; **he made it all look ~ easy** él hacía que todo pareciera tremendamente fácil; **he seems ~ happy** parece tan feliz que da asco; **he stood at the top of a ~ steep gully** estaba subido en la cima de un barranco empinadísimo; **the ship was rolling ~** el barco daba tumbos de acá para allá

sickle [ˈsɪkl] N hoz *f*

sickle-cell anaemia, **sickle-cell anemia** (*US*) [ˈsɪklˌseləˈniːmɪə] N anemia *f* de células falciformes, drepanocitosis *f*

sickliness [ˈsɪklɪnɪs] N [1] (= *ill health, feebleness*) lo enfermizo; (= *paleness*) palidez *f*; (= *weakness*) debilidad *f*
[2] (= *sweetness*) lo empalagoso

sickly [ˈsɪklɪ] ADJ (*compar* **sicklier**; *superl* **sickliest**) [1] [*person*] (= *unwell, feeble*) enfermizo, enclenque; (= *pale*) pálido; [*smile*] forzado; [*plant*] débil
[2] (= *cloying*) [*taste, smell*] empalagoso; **~ sweet** dulzón

sick-making* [ˈsɪkmeɪkɪŋ] ADJ asqueroso

sickness [ˈsɪknɪs] Ⓐ N [1] (= *illness*) enfermedad *f*; **after several months of ~ he was able to return to work** después de varios meses de enfermedad pudo regresar al trabajo; **in ~ and in health** en la salud y en la enfermedad
[2] (= *feeling of nausea*) náuseas *fpl*; (= *vomiting*) vómitos *mpl*; *see also* **altitude B**, **mountain B**, **travel D**
Ⓑ CPD ► **sickness benefit** N subsidio *m* de enfermedad; **to be on ~ benefit** recibir el subsidio de enfermedad

sickroom [ˈsɪkrʊm] N cuarto *m* del enfermo

side [saɪd] Ⓐ N [1] [*of person*] lado *m*, costado *m*; **at** *or* **by sb's ~** (*lit*) al lado de algn; (*fig*) en apoyo a algn; **the assistant was at** *or* **by his ~** el ayudante estaba a su lado; **he had the telephone by his ~** tenía el teléfono a su lado; **by the ~ of** al lado de; **to sit by sb's ~** estar sentado al lado de algn; **~ by ~** uno al lado del otro; **we sat ~ by ~** nos sentamos uno al lado del otro; **to sit ~ by ~ with sb** estar sentado al lado de algn; **to sleep on one's ~** dormir de costado; **to split one's ~s** desternillarse de risa
[2] [*of animal*] ijar *m*, ijada *f*; **~ of bacon/beef** (*Culin*) lonja *f* de tocino/vaca *or* (*LAm*) res
[3] (= *edge*) [*of box, square, building etc*] lado *m*; [*of boat, vehicle*] costado *m*; [*of hill*] ladera *f*, falda *f*; [*of lake*] orilla *f*; [*of road, pond*] borde *m*; **a house on the ~ of a mountain** una casa en la ladera de una montaña; **by the ~ of the lake** a la orilla del lago; **the car was abandoned at the ~ of the road** el coche estaba abandonado al borde de la carretera; **on the other ~ of the road** al otro lado de la calle; **he was driving on the wrong ~ of the road** iba por el lado contrario de la carretera
[4] (= *face, surface*) [*of box, solid figure, paper, record etc*] cara *f*; **please write on both ~s of the paper** escribir en ambas caras del papel; **play ~ A** pon la cara A; **what's on the other ~?** [*of record*] ¿qué hay a la vuelta?; **right ~ up** boca arriba; **wrong ~ up** boca abajo; **to be wrong ~ out** estar al revés; ✦**IDIOMS let's look at the other ~ of the coin** veamos el revés de la medalla; **these are two ~s of the same coin** son dos caras de la misma moneda; **the other ~ of the picture** el reverso de la medalla
[5] (= *aspect*) lado *m*, aspecto *m*; **to see only one ~ of the question** ver sólo un lado *or* aspecto de la cuestión; **to hear both ~s of the question** escuchar los argumentos en pro y en contra; **on one ~ ..., on the other ...** por una parte ..., por otra …
[6] (= *part*) lado *m*; **from all ~s** de todas partes, de todos lados; **on all ~s** por todas partes, por todos lados; **on both ~s** por ambos lados; **to look on the bright ~** ser optimista; **from every ~** de todas partes, de todos lados; **the left-hand ~** el lado izquierdo; **on the mother's ~** por parte de la madre; **to make a bit (of money) on the ~*** ganar algún dinero extra, hacer chapuzas (*Sp*); **to move to one ~** apartarse, ponerse de lado; **to take sb on** *or* **to one ~** apartar a algn; **to put sth to** *or* **on one ~ (for sb)** guardar algo (para algn); **leaving that to one ~ for the moment, …** dejando eso a un lado por ahora, …; **it's the other ~ of Illescas** está más allá de Illescas; **to be on the right ~ of 30** no haber cumplido los 30 años; **to be on the right ~ of sb** caerle bien a algn; **to get on the right ~ of sb** procurar congraciarse con algn; **to keep on the right ~ of sb** congraciarse *or* quedar bien con algn; **the right-hand ~** el lado derecho; **it's on the right-hand ~** está a mano derecha; **to be on the safe ~ ...** para estar seguro …, por si acaso …; **let's be on the safe ~** atengámonos a lo más seguro; **it's this ~ of Segovia** está más acá de Segovia; **it won't happen this ~ of Christmas** no será antes de Navidades; **from ~ to ~** de un lado a otro; **to be on the wrong ~ of 30** haber cumplido los 30 años; ✦**IDIOMS to be on the wrong ~ of sb** caerle mal a algn; **to get on the wrong ~ of sb** ponerse a malas con algn; **to get out of bed on the wrong ~** levantarse con el pie izquierdo
[7] (*fig*) **the weather's on the cold ~** el tiempo es algo frío; **it's a bit on the large ~** es algo *or* (*LAm*) tantito grande; **the results are on the poor ~** los resultados son más bien mediocres
[8] (= *team*) (*Sport*) equipo *m*; **to change ~s** pasar al otro bando; (*opinion*) cambiar de opinión; **to choose ~s** seleccionar el equipo; **to let the ~ down** (*Sport*) dejar caer a los suyos; (*fig*) decepcionar; **he's on our ~** (*fig*) es de los

nuestros; **whose ~ are you on?** ¿a quiénes apoyas?; **I'm on your ~** yo estoy de tu parte; **with a few concessions on the government ~** con algunas concesiones por parte del gobierno; **to be on the ~ of sth/sb** ser partidario de algo/algn; **to have age/justice on one's ~** tener la juventud/la justicia de su lado; **our ~ won** ganaron los nuestros; **to pick ~s** seleccionar el equipo; **to take ~s (with sb)** tomar partido (con algn); **to take sb's ~** ponerse de parte de algn

[9] (*Pol*) (= *party*) partido *m*

[10] (*Brit**) (= *conceit, superiority*) tono *m*, postín* *m*; **there's no ~ about** *or* **to him** ◊ **he's got no ~** no presume, no se da aires de superioridad; **to put on ~** darse tono

Ⓑ VI (*in argument*) **to ~ against sb** tomar el partido contrario a algn, alinearse con los que se oponen a algn; **to ~ with sb** ponerse de parte de algn; **I'm siding with nobody** yo no tomo partido

Ⓒ CPD ► **side arms** NPL armas *fpl* de cinto ► **side dish** N plato *m* adicional (servido con el principal) ► **side door** N puerta *f* de al lado ► **side drum** N tamboril *m* ► **side effect** N efecto *m* secundario ► **side entrance** N entrada *f* lateral ► **side glance** N mirada *f* de soslayo ► **side issue** N cuestión *f* secundaria ► **side plate** N platito *m* (*para el pan, ensalada, etc*) ► **side road** N carretera *f* secundaria ► **side saddle** N silla *f* de amazona; *see also* **side-saddle** ► **side street** N calle *f* lateral ► **side table** N trinchero *m* ► **side view** N perfil *m* ► **side whiskers** NPL patillas *fpl*

sideboard ['saɪdbɔːd] N aparador *m*

sideboards ['saɪdbɔːdz] NPL (*Brit*), **sideburns** ['saɪdbɜːnz] NPL patillas *fpl*

sidecar ['saɪdkɑːʳ] N sidecar *m*

-sided ['saɪdɪd] ADJ (*ending in compounds*) de ... caras, de ... aspectos; **three-sided** de tres caras; **many-sided** de muchos aspectos

side-face ['saɪdfeɪs] ADJ, ADV de perfil

side-foot ['saɪdfʊt] VT [+ *ball, shot*] lanzar con el interior del pie

sidekick* ['saɪdkɪk] N secuaz* *mf*

sidelight ['saɪdlaɪt] N [1] (*Aut*) luz *f* lateral

[2] (*fig*) detalle *m* incidental, información *f* incidental (**on** relativo a)

sideline ['saɪdlaɪn] Ⓐ N [1] (*Ftbl, Tennis etc*) línea *f* de banda; **to be on the ~s** (*Sport*) estar fuera del terreno de juego, estar en la banda; (*fig*) estar al margen

[2] (*Rail*) apartadero *m*, vía *f* secundaria

[3] (*Comm*) actividad *f* suplementaria; **it's just a ~** (*fig*) es un pasatiempo, nada más

Ⓑ VT (*esp US*) marginar; **we won't be ~d** no permitimos que se nos margine; **he was ~d by injury the whole season** quedó fuera del equipo durante toda la temporada debido a una lesión

sidelong ['saɪdlɒŋ] Ⓐ ADV de costado

Ⓑ ADJ [*glance*] de soslayo, de reojo

sidereal [saɪ'dɪːrɪəl] ADJ sidéreo

side-saddle ['saɪd,sædl] ADV **to ride ~** montar a la amazona

sideshow ['saɪdʃəʊ] N (*at fair*) atracción *f* secundaria

sideslip ['saɪdslɪp] N (*Aer*) deslizamiento *m* lateral

side-slipping ['saɪd,slɪpɪŋ] N (*Ski*) derrapaje *m*

sidesman ['saɪdzmən] N (*pl* **sidesmen**) (*Brit Rel*) acólito *m*

side-splitting* ['saɪd,splɪtɪŋ] ADJ para reírse a carcajadas, para morirse de risa

sidestep ['saɪdstep] Ⓐ VT [+ *problem, question*] eludir, esquivar; **he neatly ~ped the question** eludió *or* esquivó hábilmente la pregunta

Ⓑ VI (*Boxing etc*) dar un quiebro, fintar, dar una finta (*LAm*)

Ⓒ N [1] (= *step*) paso *m* hacia un lado

[2] (= *dodge*) esquivada *f*

sidestroke ['saɪdstrəʊk] N natación *f* de costado

sideswipe ['saɪdswaɪp] N (*also fig*) golpe *m* de refilón

sidetrack ['saɪdtræk] Ⓐ VT [+ *person*] despistar; [+ *discussion*] conducir por cuestiones de poca importancia; **I got ~ed** me despisté

Ⓑ N (*Rail*) apartadero *m*, vía *f* muerta; (*fig*) cuestión *f* secundaria

sidewalk ['saɪdwɔːk] N (*US*) (= *pavement*) acera *f*, vereda *f* (*LAm*), andén *m* (*CAm, Col*), banqueta *f* (*Mex*)

sidewards ['saɪdwədz] ADV = **sideways B**

sideways ['saɪd,weɪz] Ⓐ ADJ (*gen*) de lado, lateral; [*look*] de reojo, de soslayo

Ⓑ ADV **to step ~** hacerse a un lado; **to walk/move ~** andar/moverse de lado; **to look ~** mirar de reojo, mirar de soslayo; **it goes** *or* **fits in ~** se mete de lado *or* de costado; **~ on** de perfil

sidewind ['saɪdwɪnd] N viento *m* lateral

siding ['saɪdɪŋ] N (*Rail*) apartadero *m*, vía *f* muerta

sidle ['saɪdl] VI **to ~ up (to sb)** acercarse furtivamente (a algn); **to ~ in/out** entrar/salir furtivamente

Sidon ['saɪdən] N Sidón *m*

SIDS N ABBR (*Med*) = **sudden infant death syndrome**

siege [siːdʒ] Ⓐ N cerco *m*, sitio *m*; **to lay ~ to** cercar, sitiar; **to raise the ~** levantar el cerco

Ⓑ CPD ► **siege economy** N economía *f* de sitio ► **siege mentality** N **to have a ~ mentality** tener manía persecutoria ► **siege warfare** N guerra *f* de sitio *or* asedio

sienna [sɪ'enə] N siena *f*

Sierra Leone [sɪ'ɛərəlɪ'əʊn] N Sierra *f* Leona

Sierra Leonean [sɪ'ɛərəlɪ'əʊnɪən] Ⓐ ADJ sierraleonés

Ⓑ N sierraleonés/esa *m/f*

siesta [sɪ'estə] N siesta *f*; **to have** *or* **take a ~** dormir la siesta

sieve [sɪv] Ⓐ N (*for liquids*) colador *m*; (*for solids*) criba *f*, tamiz *m*

Ⓑ VT [+ *liquid*] colar; [+ *flour, soil*] cribar, tamizar

sift [sɪft] Ⓐ VT [+ *flour, soil*] cerner, tamizar

Ⓑ VI **to ~ through** (*fig*) examinar cuidadosamente

sigh [saɪ] Ⓐ N [*of person*] suspiro *m*; [*of wind*] susurro *m*, gemido *m*; **to give** *or* **heave a ~** dar un suspiro; **to breathe a ~ of relief** suspirar aliviado, dar un suspiro de alivio

Ⓑ VI [*person*] suspirar; [*wind*] susurrar; **to ~ for** suspirar por

sighing ['saɪɪŋ] N [*of person*] suspiros *mpl*; [*of wind*] susurro *m*

sight [saɪt] Ⓐ N [1] (= *eyesight*) vista *f*; **to have good ~** tener buena vista; **I'm losing my ~** estoy perdiendo la vista; **to have poor ~** tener mala vista; **to regain one's ~** recobrar la vista

[2] (= *act of seeing*) vista *f*; **I can't bear the ~ of blood** no aguanto la vista de la sangre; **I can't stand the ~ of him** no le puedo ver; **at ~** a la vista; **at first ~** a primera vista; **it was love at first ~** fue un flechazo; **I know her by ~** la conozco de vista; **it came into ~** apareció; **to catch ~ of sth/sb** divisar algo/a algn; **to be in ~** estar a la vista (**of** de); **to keep sth in ~** no perder de vista algo; **our goal is in ~** ya vemos la meta; **we are in ~ of victory** estamos a las puertas de la victoria; **to find favour in sb's ~** [*plan etc*] ser aceptable a algn; [*person*] merecerse la aprobación de algn; **to lose ~ of sth/sb** perder algo/a algn de vista; **to lose ~ of sb** (*fig*) perder contacto con algn; **to lose ~ of the fact that ...** no tener presente el hecho de que ...; **to be lost to ~** desaparecer, perderse de vista; **to shoot on ~** disparar sin previo aviso; **to be out of ~** no estar a la vista; **keep out of ~!** ¡que no te vean!; **not to let sb out of one's ~** no perder a algn de vista; **to drop out of ~** desaparecer; **out of ~** (*US**) fabuloso*; **to buy sth ~ unseen** comprar algo sin verlo; **to be within ~** estar a la vista (**of** de); **to have sth within ~** tener algo a la vista; **we were within ~ of the coast** teníamos la costa a la vista; ♦**PROV out of ~, out of mind** ojos que no ven, corazón que no siente

[3] (= *spectacle*) espectáculo *m*; **it was an amazing ~** era un espectáculo asombroso; **his face was a ~!** ¡había que ver su cara!; (*after injury etc*) ¡había que ver el estado en que quedaba su cara!; **I must look a ~** debo parecer horroroso, ¿no?; **doesn't she look a ~ in that hat!** ¡con ese sombrero parece un espantajo!; **what a ~ you are!** ¡qué adefesio!; **the ~s** los lugares de interés turístico; **to see** *or* **visit the ~s of Madrid** visitar los lugares de interés turístico de Madrid, hacer turismo por Madrid; **it's not a pretty ~** no es precisamente bonito; **it's a sad ~** es una cosa triste; ♦**IDIOM it's a ~ for sore eyes** da gusto verlo

[4] (*on gun*) (*often pl*) mira *f*, alza *f*; **in one's ~s** en la línea de tiro; ♦**IDIOMS to lower one's ~s** renunciar a algunas de sus aspiraciones; **to raise one's ~s** volverse más ambicioso, apuntar más alto; **to set one's ~s on sth/doing sth** aspirar a *or* ambicionar algo/hacer algo; **to set one's ~s too high** ser demasiado ambicioso

[5] (*) (= *a great deal*) **this is a ~ better than the other one** éste no tiene comparación con el otro; **he's a ~ too clever** es demasiado listo; **it's a ~ dearer** es mucho más caro

Ⓑ VT [1] (*Naut*) [+ *land*] ver, divisar; [+ *bird, rare animal*] observar, ver; [+ *person*] ver

[2] (= *aim*) **to ~ a gun** apuntar un cañón (**at, on** a)

Ⓒ CPD ► **sight draft** N letra *f* a la vista ► **sight translation** N traducción *f* oral *or* a libro abierto

sighted ['saɪtɪd] Ⓐ ADJ vidente

Ⓑ NPL **the ~** los que pueden ver, las personas videntes

-sighted ['saɪtɪd] ADJ (*ending in compounds*) **short-sighted** corto de vista, miope; **long-sighted** hipermétrope

sighting ['saɪtɪŋ] N observación *f*; **further ~s of the missing girl have been reported** se sabe que la chica desaparecida ha sido vista en más ocasiones

sightless ['saɪtlɪs] ADJ ciego, invidente

sightly ['saɪtlɪ] ADJ **not very ~** no muy agradable para la vista

sight-read ['saɪtriːd] (*pt, pp* **sight-read**) (*Mus*)

Ⓐ VT repentizar

Ⓑ VI repentizar

sight-reading ['saɪt,riːdɪŋ] N (*Mus*) repentización *f*, acción *f* de repentizar

sightseeing ['saɪt,siːɪŋ] N turismo *m*; **to go ~** ◊ **do some ~** hacer turismo

sightseer ['saɪt,siːəʳ] N turista *mf*, excursionista *mf*

sight-singing ['saɪt,sɪŋɪŋ] N ejecución *f* a la primera lectura

sign [saɪn] Ⓐ N [1] (*= indication*) señal *f*, indicio *m*; (*Med*) síntoma *m*; **it's a ~ of rain** es señal *or* indicio de lluvia; **he searched for a ~ of recognition on her face** buscó en su rostro una señal *or* muestra de reconocimiento; **there was no ~ of him anywhere** no había ni rastro de él; **there was no ~ of life** no había señales *or* rastro de vida; **it was seen as a ~ of weakness** se interpretaba como una muestra *or* señal de flaqueza; **at the first ~ of a cold, take vitamin C** al primer indicio de un resfriado, tome vitamina C; **it's a good/bad ~** es buena/mala señal; **to show ~s of sth/doing sth** dar muestras *or* señales de algo/de hacer algo; **the economy is beginning to show ~s of recovery** la economía está dando muestras *or* señales de recuperarse; **the storm showed no ~ of abating** la tormenta no daba muestras *or* señales de calmarse; **that's a sure ~ he's feeling better** es una señal inconfundible de que se encuentra mejor; **it's a ~ of the times** es señal de los tiempos que vivimos

[2] (*= gesture*) seña *f*; **to communicate by ~s** hablar *or* comunicarse por señas; **he gave the victory ~** hizo la seña de victoria; **to make a ~ to sb** hacer una seña a algn; **he made a ~ for them to leave** les hizo una seña para que se marcharan; **to make the ~ of the Cross** hacerse la señal de la cruz, santiguarse; **to make the ~ of the Cross over sth** bendecir algo

[3] (*= notice*) letrero *m*; (*= road sign*) señal *f* (de tráfico); (*= direction indicator*) indicador *m*; (*= shop sign*) letrero *m*, rótulo *m*; (*US*) (*carried in demonstration*) pancarta *f*; **exit ~** letrero *m* de salida; **a no-entry ~** una señal de prohibición de entrada; **a give way ~** una señal de ceda el paso

[4] (*= written symbol*) símbolo *m*; (*Math, Mus, Astrol*) signo *m*; **the text was full of strange ~s and symbols** el texto estaba lleno de símbolos extraños; **what ~ are you?** ¿de qué signo eres?; **plus/minus ~** signo de más/menos

Ⓑ VT [1] [*+ contract, agreement, treaty*] firmar; **she ~s herself B. Smith** firma con el nombre B. Smith; **Sue Townsend will be ~ing her new book** Sue Townsend firmará autógrafos en su nuevo libro; **to ~ one's name** firmar; **~ed and sealed** firmado y lacrado, firmado y sellado

[2] (*= recruit*) [*+ player*] fichar, contratar; [*+ actor, band*] contratar

[3] (*= use sign language*) **the programme is ~ed for the hearing-impaired** el programa incluye traducción simultánea al lenguaje de signos para aquellos con discapacidades auditivas

Ⓒ VI [1] (*with signature*) firmar; **~ here please** firme aquí, por favor; *see also* **dotted line**

[2] (*= be recruited*) (*Sport*) firmar un contrato; **he has ~ed for** *or* **with Arsenal** ha firmado un contrato con el Arsenal, ha fichado por el Arsenal (*Sp*)

[3] (*= signal*) hacer señas; **to ~ to sb to do sth** hacer señas a algn para que haga algo; **he ~ed to me to wait** me hizo señas para que esperara

[4] (*= use sign language*) hablar con señas

Ⓓ CPD ► **sign language** N lenguaje *m* por señas; **to talk in ~ language** hablar por señas ► **sign painter, sign writer** N rotulista *mf*

► **sign away** VT + ADV [*+ rights*] ceder; **he ~ed away his soul to the devil** entregó su alma al diablo

► **sign for** VI + PREP [*+ item*] firmar el recibo de

► **sign in** Ⓐ VI + ADV (*at hotel*) firmar el registro (al entrar), registrarse; (*at work*) firmar la entrada

Ⓑ VT + ADV (*at club*) [*+ visitor*] firmar por

► **sign off** VI + ADV [1] (*ending activity*) terminar; (*ending letter*) despedirse; (*Rad, TV*) cerrar el programa, despedirse

[2] (*Brit*) (*as unemployed*) darse de baja en el paro, quitarse del paro

► **sign on** Ⓐ VI + ADV (*Brit*) (*as unemployed*) registrarse como desempleado; (*as employee*) firmar un contrato; (*Mil*) (*= enlist*) alistarse

Ⓑ VT + ADV [*+ employee*] contratar; (*Sport*) [*+ player*] fichar, contratar; (*Mil*) [*+ soldier*] reclutar

► **sign out** Ⓐ VI + ADV [*hotel guest*] firmar el registro (al marcharse); [*employee, visitor*] firmar la salida

Ⓑ VT + ADV [*+ item*] **you must ~ all books out** tiene que firmar al retirar cualquier libro

► **sign over** VT + ADV [*+ property, rights*] ceder; **she ~ed the house over to her son** cedió la casa a su hijo, puso la casa a nombre de su hijo

► **sign up** Ⓐ VI + ADV (*= be recruited*) (*as employee*) firmar un contrato; (*= register*) registrarse; (*Sport*) [*player*] fichar (**with, for** por); (*Mil*) alistarse; **to ~ up for a course** inscribirse en un curso

Ⓑ VT + ADV [*+ employee*] contratar; (*Sport*) [*+ player*] fichar, contratar; (*Mil*) [*+ soldier*] reclutar; **the party desperately needed to ~ up new members** el partido necesitaba conseguir urgentemente nuevos afiliados

signal ['sɪgnl] Ⓐ N señal *f*; (*Telec*) señal *f*, tono *m*; (*TV, Rad*) sintonía *f*; **it was the ~ for revolt** fue la señal para la sublevación; **I can't get a ~** (*Telec*) no hay cobertura; **to give the ~ for** dar la señal de *or* para; **to make a ~ to sb** hacer una señal a algn; **railway ~s** semáforos *mpl* de ferrocarril; **traffic ~s** semáforo *msing*

Ⓑ VT [1] [*+ message*] comunicar por señales; **to ~ sb to do sth** hacer señas a algn para que haga algo; **to ~ that ...** comunicar por señas que ...; **to ~ one's approval** hacer una seña de aprobación; **to ~ sb on/through** dar a algn la señal de pasar; **to ~ a train** anunciar por señales la llegada de un tren; **the train is ~led** la señal indica la llegada del tren; **to ~ a left-/right-hand turn** (*Aut*) indicar un giro a la izquierda/derecha

[2] (*= signify*) señalar

Ⓒ VI (*gen*) dar una señal; (*with hands*) hacer señas; **to ~ to sb to do sth** hacer señas a algn para que haga algo; **to ~ to sb that ...** comunicar a algn por señas que ...; **to ~ before stopping** hacer una señal antes de parar

Ⓓ ADJ (*frm*) notable, señalado, insigne

Ⓔ CPD ► **signal book** N (*Naut*) código *m* de señales ► **signal box** N (*Rail*) garita *f* de señales ► **signal flag** N bandera *f* de señales ► **signal lamp** N reflector *m* or lámpara *f* de señales

signalize ['sɪgnəlaɪz] VT distinguir, señalar

signally ['sɪgnəlɪ] ADV notablemente, señaladamente; **he has ~ failed to do it** ha sufrido un notable fracaso al tratar de hacerlo

signalman ['sɪgnlmən] N (*pl* **signalmen**) (*Rail*) guardavía *mf*

signatory ['sɪgnətərɪ] Ⓐ ADJ firmante, signatario; **the ~ powers to an agreement** las potencias firmantes *or* signatarias de un acuerdo

Ⓑ N firmante *mf*, signatario/a *m/f*

signature ['sɪgnətʃəʳ] Ⓐ N [1] [*of person*] firma *f*; **to put one's ~ to sth** firmar algo

[2] (*Mus*) armadura *f*

Ⓑ CPD ► **signature tune** N (*Brit*) sintonía *f* de apertura (*de un programa*)

signboard ['saɪnbɔːd] N (*small*) letrero *m*; (*large*) cartelera *f*; (*for adverts*) valla *f* publicitaria

signer ['saɪnəʳ] N firmante *mf*

signet ['sɪgnɪt] Ⓐ N sello *m*

Ⓑ CPD ► **signet ring** N sello *m*

significance [sɪg'nɪfɪkəns] N [1] (*= meaning*) **she gave him a look full of ~** le dirigió una mirada muy significativa *or* elocuente

[2] (*= importance*) importancia *f*; **can we attach any ~ to this promise?** ¿podemos darle importancia a esta promesa?; **to be of some ~** ser importante; **to be of no ~** no tener ninguna importancia

significant [sɪg'nɪfɪkənt] ADJ [1] (*= important*) [*number, event, achievement, part, development*] importante; [*effect, amount, improvement, sum of money, victory*] considerable; [*contribution, reduction, increase*] significativo, considerable; [*difference*] significativo; [*change*] importante, considerable; [*factor, impact, step*] significativo, importante; **it is ~ that ...** es significativo que ...; **Japan has made ~ progress in reducing pollution** Japón ha dado un gran paso adelante en la reducción de la contaminación; **~ other** (*= partner*) pareja *f*

[2] (*= meaningful*) [*look, gesture, tone of voice*] significativo, elocuente; **could this be ~ of a change of heart?** ¿podría esto suponer un cambio de idea?

significantly [sɪg'nɪfɪkəntlɪ] ADV [1] (*= considerably*) (*with adj*) [*higher, lower, better, reduced*] considerablemente; (*with verb*) [*change, improve, reduce, increase*] de forma significativa, considerablemente

[2] (*= notably*) **~, most of them are Scottish** es significativo que la mayoría sean escoceses; **they have ~ different ideas** sus ideas son notablemente distintas

[3] (*= meaningfully*) **she looked at me ~** me lanzó una mirada significativa *or* elocuente

signify ['sɪgnɪfaɪ] Ⓐ VT [1] (*= mean*) querer decir, significar; **what does it ~?** ¿qué quiere decir?, ¿qué significa?

[2] (*= make known*) indicar; **to ~ one's approval** indicar su aprobación

Ⓑ VI **it does not ~** no importa; **in the wider context it does not ~** en el contexto más amplio no tiene importancia

signing ['saɪnɪŋ] N [1] [*of letter, contract, treaty etc*] firma *f*

[2] (*Sport*) fichaje *m*

[3] (*= sign language*) lenguaje *m* por señas

signpost ['saɪnpəʊst] Ⓐ N poste *m* indicador

Ⓑ VT indicar; **the road is well ~ed** la carretera tiene buena señalización, la carretera está bien señalizada

signposting ['saɪnpəʊstɪŋ] N señalización *f*

Sikh [siːk] Ⓐ ADJ sij

Ⓑ N sij *mf*

silage ['saɪlɪdʒ] N ensilaje *m*

silence ['saɪləns] Ⓐ N [1] (*= absence of speech*) silencio *m*; **a two minutes' ~** dos minutos de silencio; **~!** ¡silencio!; **they stood in ~** permanecieron en silencio; **in dead** *or* **complete ~** en silencio absoluto; **there was ~ on the matter** no se hizo comentario alguno sobre la cuestión; **to pass over sth in ~** silenciar algo; **to reduce sb to ~** dejar a algn sin argumentos; ✦*PROVS* **~ is golden** en boca cerrada no entran moscas; **~ gives** *or* **means** *or* **lends consent** quien calla otorga

2 (= *absence of sound*) silencio *m*; **a sudden shot broke the ~** un disparo repentino rompió el silencio
3 (= *unwillingness to communicate*) silencio *m*; **he broke his ~ for the first time yesterday** rompió su silencio ayer por primera vez
Ⓑ VT 1 (= *quieten*) [+ *person, crowd*] hacer callar, acallar; [+ *bells, guns, cries*] silenciar, acallar; **to ~ one's conscience** acallar la conciencia
2 (= *put a stop to*) [+ *criticism, fears, doubts*] acallar, silenciar; **he ~d his critics** silenció a sus críticos
3 (= *kill*) eliminar

silencer ['saɪlənsəʳ] N (*Aut, on gun*) silenciador *m*

silent ['saɪlənt] Ⓐ ADJ 1 (= *noiseless, soundless*) **to be ~** [*person*] quedarse callado; [*place, room, street*] estar en silencio; **the law is ~ on this point** la ley no se pronuncia a este respecto; **to fall ~** [*person*] quedarse callado; [*room*] quedar en silencio; **the guns have fallen ~** el tiroteo ha cesado, las armas han quedado en silencio (*liter*); **to lie ~** [*factory, machine*] permanecer parado; **the ~ majority** la mayoría silenciosa; **~ partner** (*US*) socio/a *m/f* comanditario/a; **I've remained ~ for too long on this issue** he guardado silencio sobre este asunto por demasiado tiempo; **you have the right to remain ~** tiene derecho a permanecer callado, no está obligado a responder; **to give sb the ~ treatment** hacer el vacío a algn; **to bear ~ witness to sth** ser mudo testigo de algo; ✦**IDIOM to be as ~ as the grave** *or* **tomb** estar silencioso como una tumba
2 (= *wordless*) [*prayer, march, vigil*] silencioso; [*contempt, protest*] mudo; **she looked at him in ~ contempt** le miró con mudo desprecio; **~ tears ran down her cheeks** las lágrimas le corrían silenciosas por la cara; **to pay ~ tribute to sb** homenajear en silencio a algn
3 (*Cine*) [*film, movie*] mudo; **the ~ screen** el cine mudo
4 (*Ling*) [*letter*] mudo; **the "k" in knee is ~** la "k" en "knee" es muda *or* no se pronuncia
Ⓑ N **the ~s** (*Cine*) las películas mudas; (*as genre*) el cine mudo

silently ['saɪləntlɪ] ADV 1 (= *without speaking*) en silencio; **she ~ cursed her bad luck** maldijo calladamente su mala suerte; **I vowed ~ never to mention it again** juré para mis adentros no volver a mencionarlo
2 (= *without making noise*) silenciosamente

silhouette [ˌsɪluː'et] Ⓐ N silueta *f*; **in ~** en silueta
Ⓑ VT **to be ~d against sth** destacarse *or* perfilarse en *or* contra algo

silica ['sɪlɪkə] N sílice *f*

silicate ['sɪlɪkɪt] N silicato *m*

siliceous [sɪ'lɪʃəs] ADJ silíceo

silicon ['sɪlɪkən] Ⓐ N silicio *m*
Ⓑ CPD ► **silicon carbide** N carburo *m* de silicio ► **silicon chip** N chip *m or* plaqueta *f* de silicio

silicone ['sɪlɪkəʊn] N silicona *f*

silicosis [ˌsɪlɪ'kəʊsɪs] N silicosis *f*

silk [sɪlk] Ⓐ N 1 seda *f*
2 (*Brit Jur*) (= *barrister*) abogado/a *m/f* superior; **to take ~** (*Brit*) ser ascendido a la abogacía superior; → QC/KC
Ⓑ **silks** NPL (*Racing*) colores *mpl*
Ⓒ CPD [*blouse, scarf*] de seda; ✦**IDIOM you can't make a ~ purse out of a sow's ear** aunque la mona se vista de seda, mona se queda ► **silk finish** N **with a ~ finish** (*cloth, paintwork*) satinado ► **silk hat** N sombrero *m* de copa ► **silk industry** N industria *f* sedera ► **silk thread** N hilo *m* de seda

silken ['sɪlkən] ADJ 1 (= *of silk*) de seda; (= *like silk*) sedoso, sedeño
2 (= *suave*) [*manner, voice*] suave, mimoso

silkiness ['sɪlkɪnɪs] N 1 [*of fabric*] sedosidad *f*, lo sedoso
2 [*of manner, voice*] suavidad *f*, lo mimoso

silkmoth ['sɪlkmɒθ] N mariposa *f* de seda

silk-raising ['sɪlkˌreɪzɪŋ] N sericultura *f*

silk-screen printing [ˌsɪlkskriːn'prɪntɪŋ] N serigrafía *f*

silkworm ['sɪlkwɜːm] N gusano *m* de seda

silky ['sɪlkɪ] ADJ (*compar* **silkier**; *superl* **silkiest**) 1 [*material*] sedoso; [*sound, voice*] suave; **a ~ sheen** un brillo sedoso; **~ smooth** *or* **soft** suave como la seda
2 (*fig*) [*skills*] fino, depurado; **a ~ gear change** un suave cambio de marchas

sill [sɪl] N 1 (= *windowsill*) alféizar *m*
2 (*Aut*) umbral *m*

silliness ['sɪlɪnɪs] N (= *quality*) estupidez *f*; (= *act*) tontería *f*

silly ['sɪlɪ] ADJ (*compar* **sillier**; *superl* **silliest**) (= *stupid*) [*person*] tonto, bobo, sonso *or* zonzo (*LAm*); [*act, idea*] absurdo; (= *ridiculous*) ridículo; **how ~ of me!** ◊ **~ me!** ¡qué tonto *or* bobo soy!; **that was ~ of you** ◊ **that was a ~ thing to do** eso que hiciste fue muy tonto *or* bobo, fue una tontería *or* estupidez por tu parte; **don't be ~** no seas tonto *or* bobo; **I feel ~ in this hat** me siento ridículo con este sombrero; **to knock sb ~*** dar una paliza a algn; **the blow knocked him ~** el golpe le dejó tonto *or* sin sentido; **to laugh o.s. ~*** desternillarse de risa*; **you look ~ carrying that fish** pareces tonto llevando ese pez; **to make sb look ~** poner a algn en ridículo; **~ season** temporada *f* boba, canícula *f*; **I've done a ~ thing** he hecho una tontería, he sido un tonto

silo ['saɪləʊ] N (*pl* **silos**) (*gen*) silo *m*

silt [sɪlt] N sedimento *m*, aluvión *m*

►**silt up** Ⓐ VI + ADV obstruirse (con sedimentos) Ⓑ VT + ADV obstruir (con sedimentos)

silting [sɪltɪŋ] N (*also* **~ up**) obstrucción *f* con sedimentos

silver ['sɪlvəʳ] Ⓐ N 1 (= *metal*) plata *f*; (= *silverware, silver cutlery*) plata *f*, vajilla *f* de plata
2 (= *money*) monedas *fpl* de plata, monedas *fpl* plateadas; **"have you got any ~?" — "sorry, only notes and coppers"** —¿tienes monedas de plata? —no, sólo billetes y monedas de cobre; **£2 in ~** 2 libras en monedas de plata
Ⓑ ADJ 1 (= *made of silver*) [*ring, cutlery*] de plata
2 (*in colour*) plateado; [*car*] gris plata *inv*; *see also* **spoon A1**, **cloud A**
Ⓒ VT [+ *metal*] platear; [+ *mirror*] azogar; [+ *hair*] blanquear
Ⓓ VI [*hair*] blanquear
Ⓔ CPD ► **silver beet** N (*US*) acelga *f* ► **silver birch** N abedul *m* plateado ► **silver coin** N moneda *f* de plata ► **silver fir** N abeto *m* blanco, pinabete *m* ► **silver foil** N papel *m* de aluminio *or* plata ► **silver fox** N zorro *m* plateado ► **silver gilt** N plata *f* dorada ► **silver jubilee** N vigésimo quinto aniversario *m* ► **silver lining** N (*fig*) resquicio *m* de esperanza ► **silver medal** N medalla *f* de plata ► **silver medallist** N medallero/a *m/f* de plata ► **silver paper** N papel *m* de plata ► **silver plate** N (= *material*) plateado *m*; (= *objects*) vajilla *f* plateada; *see also* **silver-plate** ► **the silver screen** N la pantalla cinematográfica ► **silver tongue** N **to have a ~ tongue** (*fig*) tener un pico de oro ► **the Silver State** N (*US*) Nevada *f* ► **silver wedding** N bodas *fpl* de plata

silverfish ['sɪlvəfɪʃ] N (*pl* **silverfish**) lepisma *f*

silver-grey ['sɪlvə'greɪ] ADJ gris perla

silver-haired ['sɪlvə'hɛəd] ADJ de pelo entrecano

silver-plate [ˌsɪlvə'pleɪt] VT platear

silver-plated [ˌsɪlvə'pleɪtɪd] ADJ plateado

silversmith ['sɪlvəsmɪθ] N platero/a *m/f*; **~'s (shop)** platería *f*

silver-tongued ['sɪlvə'tʌŋd] ADJ elocuente, con pico de oro

silverware ['sɪlvəwɛəʳ] N plata *f*, vajilla *f* de plata; (* = *trophies*) trofeos *mpl*

silvery ['sɪlvərɪ] ADJ [*colour*] plateado; [*sound, voice*] argentino

silviculture ['sɪlvɪˌkʌltʃəʳ] N silvicultura *f*

SIM card ['sɪmˌkɑːd] N (= **Subscriber Identity Module Card**) tarjeta *f* SIM

simian ['sɪmɪən] ADJ símico

▼**similar** ['sɪmɪləʳ] ADJ 1 parecido, similar, semejante; **they are of a ~ colour** son de un color parecido *or* similar; **they were of a ~ age** eran más o menos de la misma edad; **to be ~ in shape/size** tener una forma parecida *or* similar, tener un tamaño parecido *or* similar, parecerse en la forma *or* el tamaño; **to be ~ to** parecerse a, ser parecido *or* similar *or* semejante a 2 (*Geom*) semejante

similarity [ˌsɪmɪ'lærɪtɪ] N 1 (*uncountable*) (= *resemblance*) parecido *m*, semejanza *f*; **there is no ~ between them** no existe ningún parecido *or* ninguna semejanza entre ellos; **any ~ is purely coincidental** cualquier parecido es pura coincidencia; **the ~ ends there** el parecido no va más allá
2 (*countable*) (= *feature in common*) semejanza *f*, rasgo *m* común, similitud *f*

similarly ['sɪmɪləlɪ] ADV (= *equally*) igualmente; (= *in a like manner*) de modo parecido, de manera parecida, de modo *or* manera similar; **and ~, …** y del mismo modo, …, y asimismo, …

simile ['sɪmɪlɪ] N símil *m*

similitude [sɪ'mɪlɪtjuːd] N similitud *f*, semejanza *f*

simmer ['sɪməʳ] Ⓐ VT cocer a fuego lento
Ⓑ VI hervir a fuego lento; (*fig*) estar a punto de estallar
Ⓒ N **to be/keep on the ~** hervir a fuego lento

►**simmer down*** VI + ADV (*fig*) calmarse, tranquilizarse; **~ down!** ¡cálmate!

Simon ['saɪmən] N Simón

simony ['saɪmənɪ] N simonía *f*

simp* [sɪmp] N (*US*) bobo/a *m/f*

simper ['sɪmpəʳ] Ⓐ N sonrisa *f* afectada
Ⓑ VI sonreír con afectación
Ⓒ VT **"yes," she ~ed** —sí —dijo sonriendo afectada

simpering ['sɪmpərɪŋ] ADJ (= *affected*) afectado; (= *foolish*) atontado

simperingly ['sɪmpərɪŋlɪ] ADV (= *affectedly*) afectadamente; (= *foolishly*) tontamente

simple ['sɪmpl] Ⓐ ADJ (*compar* **simpler**; *superl* **simplest**) 1 (= *uncomplicated*) [*problem, idea, task*] sencillo, simple; **there is no ~ answer** no existe una respuesta sencilla; **nothing could be ~r** no hay nada más simple; **it's as ~ as that** la cosa es así de sencilla; **it's not as ~ as you think** no es tan sencillo como piensas; **it should be a ~ enough job** no debería ser un trabajo difícil; **keep it ~** no lo compliques; **in ~ terms** en lenguaje sencillo; **the ~st**

➤ LANGUAGE IN USE: similar 1 5.2

thing would be to phone lo más sencillo sería llamar por teléfono; **to be ~ to make/use** ser sencillo de hacer/usar
[2] (= *mere*) simple; **a ~ phone call could win you a week's holiday in Florida** con una simple llamada de teléfono podría ganar una semana de vacaciones en Florida; **by the ~ fact that ...** por el simple hecho de que ...; **to be a ~ matter of doing sth** ser simplemente una cuestión de hacer algo
[3] (= *elementary*) simple; **a ~ act of kindness** un simple acto de bondad; **the ~ fact is ...** la pura realidad es ...; **for the ~ reason that ...** por la simple razón de que ...; **the ~ truth** la pura verdad; *see also* **pure A1**
[4] (= *not fussy*) [*dress, style, food*] sencillo
[5] (= *unsophisticated*) [*person, life, pleasures, pursuits*] sencillo; **these are ~ people** son gente sencilla; **the ~ things in** *or* **of life** las cosas sencillas de la vida
[6] (*) (= *mentally retarded*) simple
[7] (*Chem, Bio, Bot, Med*) simple
[8] (*Gram*) [*sentence, tense*] simple
Ⓑ CPD ► **simple division** N división *f* simple ► **simple equation** N ecuación *f* de primer grado ► **simple fraction** N fracción *f* simple ► **simple interest** N interés *m* simple ► **simple majority** N (*Pol*) mayoría *f* simple ► **Simple Simon** N tontorrón *m*, simplón *m*, alma *m* de cántaro (*Sp*) ► **simple tense** N (*Gram*) tiempo *m* simple

simple-hearted [ˈsɪmplˈhɑːtɪd] ADJ candoroso, ingenuo

simple-minded [ˈsɪmplˈmaɪndɪd] ADJ ingenuo, simple; **I'm not so ~** no soy tan ingenuo; **in their ~ way** a su modo ingenuo

simple-mindedness [ˈsɪmplˈmaɪndɪdnɪs] N ingenuidad *f*, simpleza *f*

simpleton [ˈsɪmpltən] N inocentón/ona *m/f*, simplón/ona *m/f*

simplicity [sɪmˈplɪsɪtɪ] N [1] (= *uncomplicated nature*) [*of solution, idea, plan*] sencillez *f*, simplicidad *f*; **it's ~ itself** es la sencillez personificada
[2] (= *unpretentiousness*) [*of dress, style, food*] sencillez *f*
[3] (= *ingenuousness*) [*of person, way of life*] simpleza *f*

simplifiable [ˈsɪmplɪfaɪəbl] ADJ simplificable

simplification [ˌsɪmplɪfɪˈkeɪʃən] N simplificación *f*

simplify [ˈsɪmplɪfaɪ] VT simplificar

simplistic [sɪmˈplɪstɪk] ADJ simplista

simply [ˈsɪmplɪ] ADV [1] (= *in a simple way*) [*dress, furnish*] sencillamente; [*speak, explain*] en términos sencillos; **to put it ~ ...** hablando claro ...
[2] (= *merely, just*) simplemente; **~ add hot water and stir** simplemente, añada agua caliente y remueva; **I ~ said that ...** sólo dije que ...
[3] (*emphatic*) (= *absolutely*) simplemente; **he ~ refused to listen to me** se negó simplemente a escucharme; **it ~ isn't possible** sencillamente no es posible; **that is ~ not true** eso sencillamente, no es verdad; **she's quite ~ the best** sin ninguna duda es la mejor; **I thought her performance was ~ marvellous/awful** su actuación me pareció francamente maravillosa/terrible; **you ~ MUST come!** ¡no dejes de venir!

simulacrum [ˌsɪmjʊˈleɪkrəm] N (*pl* **simulacra** [ˌsɪmjʊˈleɪkrə]) simulacro *m*

simulate [ˈsɪmjʊleɪt] VT simular

simulated [ˈsɪmjʊˌleɪtɪd] ADJ [*surprise, shock*] fingido, simulado; **~ attack** simulacro *m* de ataque; **~ leather** cuero *m* de imitación

simulation [ˌsɪmjʊˈleɪʃən] N simulación *f*

simulator [ˈsɪmjʊleɪtəʳ] N simulador *m*

simulcast [ˈsɪməlˌkɑːst] Ⓐ N emisión *f* simultánea por radio y televisión
Ⓑ VT emitir simultáneamente por radio y televisión

simultaneity [ˌsɪməltəˈniːətɪ] N simultaneidad *f*

simultaneous [ˌsɪməlˈteɪnɪəs] Ⓐ ADJ simultáneo
Ⓑ CPD [*interpreting, translation, processing*] simultáneo ► **simultaneous equation** N ecuación *f* simultánea

simultaneously [ˌsɪməlˈteɪnɪəslɪ] ADV simultáneamente, a la vez

sin [sɪn] Ⓐ N pecado *m*; **~s of omission/commission** pecados *mpl* por omisión/acción; **mortal ~** pecado *m* mortal; **for my ~s** por mis pecados; **it would be a ~ to do that** (*Rel*) sería un pecado hacer eso; (*fig*) sería un crimen hacer eso; **to fall into ~** caer en el pecado; **to live in ~**† (*unmarried*) vivir amancebados, vivir en el pecado; *see also* **ugly A1**
Ⓑ VI pecar; **he was more ~ned against than ~ning** era más bien el ofendido que (no) el ofensor
Ⓒ CPD ► **sin bin*** N (*Sport*) banquillo *m* de los expulsados ► **sin tax*** N (*US*) impuesto *m* sobre el tabaco y/o el alcohol

Sinai [ˈsaɪnaɪ] Ⓐ N Sinaí *m*; **Mount ~** el monte Sinaí
Ⓑ CPD ► **the Sinai Desert** N el desierto del Sinaí

Sinbad [ˈsɪnbæd] N Simbad; **~ the Sailor** Simbad el marino

since [sɪns] Ⓐ ADV desde entonces; **I haven't seen him ~** desde entonces no lo he vuelto a ver; **ever ~** desde entonces; **not long ~** ◊ **a short time ~** hace poco; **a long time ~** hace mucho (tiempo); **her parents have long ~ died** sus padres hace tiempo que fallecieron, sus padres fallecieron tiempo ha (*frm*); **the time for talking has long ~ passed** la hora de hablar ya pasó hace tiempo
Ⓑ PREP desde; **~ Monday** desde el lunes; **~ Christmas** desde Navidad; **~ then** desde entonces; **I've been waiting ~ ten** espero desde las diez; **ever ~ then ...** desde entonces ...; **ever ~ that ...** desde aquello ...; **~ that day he has been a changed man** desde *or* a partir de ese día es un hombre nuevo; **how long is it ~ the accident?** ¿cuánto tiempo ha pasado desde el accidente?; **~ arriving** desde que llegué, desde mi llegada
Ⓒ CONJ [1] (= *from the time that*) desde que; **~ I arrived** desde que llegué; **I haven't seen her ~ she left** no la he visto desde que se fue; **I've been wearing glasses ~ I was three** llevo gafas desde los tres años; **it's a week ~ he left** hace una semana que se fue, se fue hace una semana; **it's a few years ~ I've seen them** hace varios años que no los veo; **ever ~ I've been here** desde que estoy aquí
[2] (= *as, because*) ya que, puesto que, como; **~ you can't come** ya que no puedes venir, como no puedes venir, puesto que no puedes venir; **~ you're tired, let's stay at home** ya que *or* puesto que *or* como estás cansado vamos a quedarnos en casa; **~ he is Spanish** ya que *or* como *or* puesto que es español, siendo él español (*frm*)

sincere [sɪnˈsɪəʳ] ADJ sincero (**about sth** sobre algo, con respecto a algo); **my ~ good wishes** mi más sincera enhorabuena; **it is my ~ belief that ...** creo sinceramente que ...; **to be ~ in one's desire to do sth** *or* **in wanting to do sth** desear *or* querer sinceramente hacer algo

sincerely [sɪnˈsɪəlɪ] ADV [1] (= *genuinely*) [*hope, believe, regret, say*] sinceramente; **his ~ held religious beliefs** sus sinceras creencias religiosas
[2] (*in letters*) **Yours ~** (*Brit*) ◊ **Sincerely yours** (*US*) (le saluda) atentamente

SINCE

Time

• When **since** is followed by a noun or noun phrase, you can usually translate it as **desde**:
Spain has changed a lot since Franco's death
España ha cambiado mucho desde la muerte de Franco
• When **since** is followed by a verb phrase, use **desde que** instead:
Since I saw you a fortnight ago a lot of things have happened
Desde que te vi hace quince días han pasado muchas cosas
! Use the *present tense* in Spanish to describe a situation that started in the past and has continued up to now (present perfect or present perfect continuous in English):
I have been here since this morning
Estoy aquí *or* ***Llevo aquí desde esta mañana***
They've been waiting since nine o'clock
Están esperando *or* ***Llevan esperando desde las nueve***
He has been taking more exercise since he talked to his doctor
Hace más ejercicio desde que habló con el médico
NOTE: But the *perfect tense* is used in Spanish when the verb is in the negative:
I haven't seen her since she left
No la he visto desde que se fue
• Translate **since then** *or* **ever since** using **desde entonces**:
She came home at five and has been studying ever since
Llegó a casa a las cinco y está estudiando desde entonces
• Translate **long since** using **hace tiempo** (+ **que** + **PAST TENSE**) or **hacía tiempo** (+ **que** + **PAST/PAST PERFECT**) as relevant:
His wife has long since died
Hace tiempo que murió su mujer, Su mujer murió hace tiempo

Meaning "as", "because"

• In formal contexts you can usually translate **since** using **ya que** *or* **puesto que**. In more everyday Spanish, use **como**, which must go at the beginning of the sentence:
They could not afford the house since they were not earning enough
No podían pagar la casa puesto que *or* ***ya que no ganaban bastante***
Since I hadn't heard from you, I decided to give you a call
Como no sabía nada de ti, decidí llamarte
For further uses and examples, see main entry.

sincerity [sɪnˈserɪtɪ] N sinceridad *f*; **in all ~** con toda sinceridad

sine [saɪn] N (*Math*) seno *m*

sinecure [ˈsaɪnɪkjʊəʳ] N sinecura *f*

sine qua non [ˈsaɪnɪkweɪˈnɒn] N sine qua non *m*

sinew [ˈsɪnjuː] N [1] (= *tendon*) tendón *m*; (*fig*) (= *strength*) nervio *m*, vigor *m*
[2] **sinews** (= *muscles*) músculos *mpl*

sinewy [ˈsɪnjuːɪ] ADJ [1] (= *muscular*) [*person*]

➤ LANGUAGE IN USE: since C2 17.1, 26.3

musculoso, fibroso; [*body, arms, muscles*] nervudo, fibroso
2 (*Culin*) [*of meat*] fibroso, con mucho nervio
3 (= *vigorous*) [*music, performance, writing, style*] brioso, vigoroso

sinfonietta [ˌsɪnfən'jetə] N sinfonieta *f*

sinful ['sɪnfʊl] ADJ [*act, thought*] pecaminoso; [*person*] pecador; [*town etc*] inmoral, depravado; (*fig*) (= *disgraceful*) escandaloso

sinfully ['sɪnfəlɪ] ADV de modo pecaminoso

sinfulness ['sɪnfʊlnɪs] N [*of behaviour, way of life*] pecaminosidad *f*

sing [sɪŋ] (*pt* **sang**; *pp* **sung**) Ⓐ VT [+ *song, words*] cantar; (*fig*) (= *intone*) entonar; **~ us a song!** ¡cántanos una canción!; **the words are sung to the tune of ...** la letra se canta con la melodía de ...; **she ~s alto** canta contralto; **to ~ a child to sleep** arrullar a un niño, adormecer a un niño cantando; ✦***IDIOMS*** **to ~ sb's praises** cantar las alabanzas de algn; **to ~ a different tune** ver las cosas de otro color; *see also* **heart A2**
Ⓑ VI 1 [*person, bird*] cantar; **"what do you do for a living?" — "I ~"** —¿a qué te dedicas? —canto *or* —soy cantante; **to ~ to/for sb** cantar a algn; **to ~ to o.s.** cantar solo; **they sang to the accompaniment of the piano** cantaban acompañados del piano
2 [*wind, kettle*] silbar; [*ears*] zumbar
3 (*US**) (*fig*) (= *act as informer*) cantar*; (= *confess*) confesar

►**sing along** VI + ADV **he invited the audience to ~ along** invitó al publico a cantar (a coro) con él; **I like records that get people ~ing along** me gustan los discos en que la gente corea las canciones; **to ~ along with** *or* **to a song** corear una canción; **to ~ along with** *or* **to a record/the radio** cantar con un disco/la radio; **the audience was ~ing along to his latest hit** el público cantaba a coro *or* coreaba su último éxito

►**sing out** Ⓐ VI + ADV (*lit*) cantar con voz fuerte; (*fig*) pegar un grito*; **if you want anything, just ~ out** si quieres algo no tienes más que pegarme un grito*
Ⓑ VT + ADV vocear; **"hello! I'm back," he sang out cheerfully** —¡hola! estoy de vuelta —voceó alegre

►**sing up** VI + ADV cantar más fuerte; **~ up!** ¡más fuerte!

sing. ABBR = **singular**

Singapore [ˌsɪŋgə'pɔːʳ] N Singapur *m*

Singaporean [ˌsɪŋgə'pɔːrɪən] Ⓐ ADJ de Singapur
Ⓑ N nativo/a *m/f or* habitante *mf* de Singapur

singe [sɪndʒ] Ⓐ VT (*gen*) chamuscar, quemar; [+ *hair*] quemar las puntas de
Ⓑ N (*also* **~ mark**) quemadura *f*

singer ['sɪŋəʳ] N cantante *mf*

Singhalese [ˌsɪŋgə'liːz] Ⓐ ADJ cingalés
Ⓑ N 1 (= *person*) cingalés/esa *m/f*
2 (*Ling*) cingalés *m*

singing ['sɪŋɪŋ] Ⓐ N 1 (= *act of singing*) canto *m*; **she is studying ~** estudia canto; **the ~ stopped** dejaron de cantar; **his ~ was atrocious** cantaba pésimamente, cantaba fatal*; **they stood for the ~ of the Internationale** se pusieron de pie para cantar la Internacional
2 [*of kettle*] silbido *m*; (*in ears*) zumbido *m*
Ⓑ CPD ► **singing lesson** N lección *f* de canto ► **singing teacher** N profesor(a) *m/f* de canto ► **singing telegram** N telegrama *m* cantado ► **singing voice** N **to have a good ~ voice** tener una buena voz para cantar

single ['sɪŋgl] Ⓐ ADJ 1 (*before noun*) (= *one only*) solo; **in a ~ day** en un solo día; **we heard a ~ shot** oímos un solo disparo; **our team won by a ~ point** nuestro equipo ganó por un solo punto
2 (*before noun*) (*emphatic*) **we didn't see a ~ car that afternoon** no vimos ni un solo coche esa tarde; **not a ~ one was left** no quedó ni uno; **it rained every ~ day** no dejó de llover ni un solo día, llovió todos los días sin excepción; **I did not doubt her sincerity for a ~ moment** no dudé de su sinceridad ni por un momento; **not a** *or* **one ~ person came to her aid** ni una sola persona fue a ayudarla; **the ~ biggest problem** el problema más grande; **the US is the ~ biggest producer of carbon dioxide** los EEUU son los mayores productores de carbón; **I couldn't think of a ~ thing to say** no se me ocurría nada que decir
3 (*before noun*) (= *individual*) **he gave her a ~ rose** le dio una rosa; **a ~ diamond** un solitario
4 (*before noun*) (= *not double*) [*bed, sheet, room*] individual; [*garage*] para un solo coche; [*whisky, gin, etc*] sencillo; [*bloom*] simple; **a ~ knot** un nudo sencillo; *see also* **figure A5**
5 (= *unmarried*) [*person*] soltero; [*mother, father*] sin pareja; [*life*] de soltero; *see also* **single-parent**
6 (*before noun*) (*Brit*) (= *one-way*) [*ticket, fare*] de ida
Ⓑ N 1 (*in hotel*) (*also* **~ room**) habitación *f* individual
2 (*Brit*) (*also* **~ ticket**) billete *m* de ida
3 (= *record*) sencillo *m*, single *m*
4 (*Cricket*) (= *one run*) tanto *m*
5 (*Brit*) (= *pound coin or note*) billete *m or* moneda *f* de una libra; (*US*) (= *dollar note*) billete *m* de un dólar
6 **singles** 6·1 (*Tennis etc*) individuales *mpl*; **the men's ~s** los individuales masculinos
6·2 (= *unmarried people*) solteros *mpl*
Ⓒ CPD ► **single combat** N combate *m* singular; **in ~ combat** en combate singular ► **single cream** N (*Brit*) crema *f* de leche líquida, nata *f* líquida (*Sp*) ► **single density disk** N disco *m* de densidad sencilla ► **single European currency** N moneda *f* europea ► **single file** N **in ~ file** en fila india ► **single honours** N *licenciatura universitaria en la que se estudia una sola especialidad* ► **single lens reflex (camera)** N cámara *f* réflex de una lente ► **single malt (whisky)** N whisky *m* de malta ► **single market** N mercado *m* único ► **single parent** N (= *woman*) madre *f* sin pareja; (= *man*) padre *m* sin pareja; **the rising number of ~ parents** el número cada vez mayor de padres sin pareja ► **singles bar** N bar *m* para solteros ► **single spacing** N (*Typ*) interlineado *m* simple; **in ~ spacing** a espacio sencillo ► **single supplement**, **single person supplement**, **single room supplement** N (*in hotel*) recargo *m* por reserva individual ► **single transferable vote** N (*Pol*) **~ transferable vote system** sistema *m* del voto único transferible

►**single out** VT + ADV (= *choose*) elegir; (= *distinguish*) hacer resaltar; **he was ~d out to lead the team** fue elegido para ser capitán del equipo; **to ~ out plants** entresacar plantas

single-barrelled [ˌsɪŋgl'bærəld] ADJ [*gun*] de cañón único

single-breasted [ˌsɪŋgl'brestɪd] ADJ recto

single-cell [ˌsɪŋgl'sel] ADJ unicelular

single-celled [ˌsɪŋgl'seld] ADJ = **single-cell**

single-chamber [ˌsɪŋgl'tʃeɪmbəʳ] ADJ unicameral

single-decker [ˌsɪŋgl'dekəʳ] N autobús *m* de un solo piso

single-engined [ˌsɪŋgl'endʒɪnd] ADJ monomotor

single-entry [ˌsɪŋgl'entrɪ] Ⓐ N partida *f* simple
Ⓑ CPD ► **single-entry book-keeping** N contabilidad *f* por partida simple

single-family [ˌsɪŋgl'fæmlɪ] ADJ unifamiliar

single-figure [ˌsɪŋgl'fɪgəʳ] ADJ **~ inflation** inflación *f* por debajo del 10%

single-handed [ˌsɪŋgl'hændɪd] ADJ, ADV sin ayuda

single-hearted [ˌsɪŋgl'hɑːtɪd] ADJ 1 (= *loyal*) sincero, leal
2 (= *single-minded*) resuelto, firme

single-masted [ˌsɪŋgl'mɑːstɪd] ADJ de palo único

single-minded [ˌsɪŋgl'maɪndɪd] ADJ resuelto, firme

single-mindedness [ˌsɪŋgl'maɪndɪdnɪs] N resolución *f*, firmeza *f*

singleness ['sɪŋglnɪs] N **~ of purpose** resolución *f*, firmeza *f*

single-parent ['sɪŋglˌpeərənt] ADJ **~ family** familia *f* monoparental; **~ household** hogar *m* sin pareja, familia *f* monoparental

single-party [ˌsɪŋgl'pɑːtɪ] ADJ [*state etc*] de partido único

single-seater [ˌsɪŋgl'siːtəʳ] Ⓐ ADJ **~ aeroplane** monoplaza *m*
Ⓑ N monoplaza *m*

single-sex school [ˌsɪŋgseks'skuːl] N escuela *f* para sólo niños *or* sólo niñas

single-sided disk [ˌsɪŋgsaɪdɪd'dɪsk] N disco *m* de una cara

single-space ['sɪŋgl'speɪs] VT [+ *text*] mecanografiar a espacio sencillo

singlet ['sɪŋglɪt] N camiseta *f* sin mangas, camiseta *f* de tirantes, playera *f* (*LAm*)

singleton ['sɪŋgltən] N (*Bridge*) semifallo *m* (**in** a)

single-track ['sɪŋgl'træk] ADJ de vía única

singly ['sɪŋglɪ] ADV (= *separately*) por separado; (= *one at a time*) uno por uno

singsong ['sɪŋˌsɒŋ] Ⓐ ADJ [*voice, tone*] cantarín
Ⓑ N (*Brit*) (= *songs*) concierto *m* improvisado; (= *sound*) sonsonete *m*; **to get together for a ~** reunirse para cantar (*canciones populares, folklóricas etc*)

singular ['sɪŋgjʊləʳ] Ⓐ ADJ 1 (*Ling*) singular; **a ~ noun** un sustantivo en singular
2 (= *extraordinary*) singular, excepcional; **a most ~ occurrence** un suceso de lo más singular *or* excepcional; **how very ~!** ¡qué raro!
Ⓑ N singular *m*; **in the ~** en singular

singularity [ˌsɪŋgjʊ'lærɪtɪ] N (= *extraordinariness*) singularidad *f*, lo excepcional

singularly ['sɪŋgjʊləlɪ] ADV (= *extraordinarily*) extraordinariamente, singularmente; **he was ~ unhelpful** no se mostró dispuesto a ayudar en absoluto; **a ~ inappropriate remark** una observación de lo más inoportuno

Sinhalese [ˌsɪnə'liːz] = **Singhalese**

sinister ['sɪnɪstəʳ] ADJ siniestro; **a ~-looking man** un hombre de apariencia siniestra

sink[1] [sɪŋk] (*pt* **sank**; *pp* **sunk**) Ⓐ VT 1 (= *submerge*) [+ *ship*] hundir; (*fig*) (= *destroy*) [+ *person*] hundir; [+ *project*] acabar con, dar al traste con; [+ *theory*] destruir, acabar con; **to be sunk*** estar perdido
2 (= *open up*) [+ *mineshaft*] abrir, excavar; [+ *hole*] hacer, excavar; [+ *well*] perforar, abrir
3 (= *bury, lay*) 3·1 [+ *pipe*] enterrar; [+ *foundations*] echar; **to ~ a post two metres into**

the ground fijar un poste dos metros bajo tierra; **she sunk her face into her hands** hundió la cara en las manos; **his eyes were sunk deep into their sockets** tenía los ojos hundidos
[3.2] (*fig*) **to be sunk in thought** estar absorto en mis *etc* pensamientos, estar ensimismado; **to be sunk in depression** estar sumido en la depresión
[4] (= *forget*) [+ *feelings*] ahogar; ✦*IDIOM* **let's ~ our differences** hagamos las paces, olvidemos nuestras diferencias
[5] (= *dig in*) [+ *knife*] hundir, clavar; [+ *teeth*] hincar; **I sank my knife into the cheese** hundí *or* clavé el cuchillo en el queso; **he sank his teeth into my arm** me hincó los dientes en el brazo
[6] (= *invest*) **to ~ money in** *or* **into sth** invertir dinero en algo
[7] (*Brit**) [+ *drink*] tragarse*
[8] (*Sport*) [+ *ball, putt*] embocar
Ⓑ VI [1] [*ship, object*] hundirse; **the body sank to the bottom of the lake** el cadáver se hundió en el fondo del lago; **the yeast ~s to the bottom in beer** la levadura se deposita en el fondo de la cerveza; **to ~ out of sight** desaparecer; **to ~ without trace** (*fig*) desaparecer sin dejar rastro; ✦*IDIOM* **to leave sb to ~ or swim** abandonar a algn a su suerte; **we're all in the same boat and we ~ or swim together** todos estamos en la misma situación, y una de dos: o nos hundimos o salimos a flote juntos
[2] (= *subside*) [*building, land*] hundirse; [*flood waters*] bajar de nivel; [*sun*] ponerse
[3] (= *slump*) [*person*] **to ~ into a chair** arrellanarse en una silla, dejarse caer en una silla; **to ~ to one's knees** caer de rodillas; **I sank into a deep sleep** caí en un sueño profundo; **she would sometimes ~ into depression** a veces se sumía en la depresión; **he sank deeper into debt** se hundió más y más en las deudas; **to ~ into poverty** hundirse *or* caer en la miseria; **my heart sank** se me cayó el alma a los pies; **her spirits sank lower and lower** tenía la moral cada vez más baja
[4] (= *deteriorate*) [*sick person*] **he's ~ing fast** está cada vez peor
[5] (= *fall*) (*in amount, value*) **the shares have sunk to three dollars** las acciones han bajado a tres dólares; **he has sunk in my estimation** ha bajado en mi estima; **his voice sank to a whisper** su voz se redujo a un susurro

►**sink back** VI + ADV (= *slump*) (*into chair*) arrellanarse, ponerse cómodo; **I sank back onto the pillows** me puse cómodo en las almohadas

►**sink down** VI + ADV [*building*] ceder, hundirse; [*post*] hundirse, clavarse; **to ~ down into a chair** apoltronarse *or* arrellanarse en un sillón; **to ~ down on one's knees** caer de rodillas, arrodillarse; **he sank down (out of sight) behind the bush** se agachó detrás del matorral

►**sink in** VI + ADV [1] (= *penetrate*) penetrar; **in time the water ~s in** con el tiempo el agua va penetrando
[2] (*) (*fig*) **she paused to let the news ~ in** hizo una pausa para que pudieran asimilar la noticia; **it hasn't sunk in that he's gone forever** aún no ha asimilado *or* asumido el hecho de que se ha ido para siempre

sink² [sɪŋk] Ⓐ N (*in kitchen*) fregadero *m*, pila *f*; (*in bathroom*) lavabo *m*
Ⓑ ADJ [*estate*] degradado, deprimido; [*school*] con un nivel muy bajo
Ⓒ CPD ► **sink tidy** N *recipiente para lavavajillas, jabón y estropajos* ► **sink unit** N fregadero *m*

sinker [ˈsɪŋkəʳ] N [1] (*Fishing*) (= *lead*) plomo *m*
[2] (*US**) (= *doughnut*) donut *m*

sinking [ˈsɪŋkɪŋ] Ⓐ N (= *shipwreck*) hundimiento *m*
Ⓑ ADJ [1] (= *foundering*) **a ~ ship** (*lit*) un barco que se hunde; (*fig*) (= *cause*) una causa en declive *or* que va a pique; (= *organization*) una organización en declive *or* que va a pique
[2] **with a ~ feeling she picked the phone up** con una sensación de ansiedad contestó el teléfono; **that ~ feeling** esa sensación de ansiedad *or* desazón; **with a ~ heart** entristecido
[3] (*Fin*) **a ~ pound/dollar** una libra/un dólar cayendo en picado
Ⓒ CPD ► **sinking fund** N (*Fin*) fondo *m* de amortización

sinless [ˈsɪnlɪs] ADJ libre de pecado, inmaculado

sinner [ˈsɪnəʳ] N pecador(a) *m/f*

Sino... [ˈsaɪnəʊ] PREFIX sino…, chino…

Sinologist [ˌsaɪˈnɒlədʒɪst] N sinólogo/a *m/f*

Sinology [ˌsaɪˈnɒlədʒɪ] N sinología *f*

sinuosity [ˌsɪnjʊˈɒsɪtɪ] N sinuosidad *f*

sinuous [ˈsɪnjʊəs] ADJ (*gen*) sinuoso; [*road*] serpenteante, con muchos rodeos

sinus [ˈsaɪnəs] N (*pl* **sinuses**) (*Anat*) seno *m*

sinusitis [ˌsaɪnəˈsaɪtɪs] N sinusitis *f*

sip [sɪp] Ⓐ N sorbo *m*
Ⓑ VT sorber, beber a sorbos
Ⓒ VI (*also* **to ~ at**) sorber, beber a sorbitos

siphon [ˈsaɪfən] Ⓐ N sifón *m*
Ⓑ VT (*also* **~ off, ~ out**) sacar con sifón; (*fig*) [+ *traffic, funds*] desviar

sir [sɜːʳ] N señor *m*; **Sirs** (*US*) muy señores nuestros; **yes, ~** sí, señor; **Dear Sir** (*in letter*) muy señor mío, estimado señor; **Sir Winston Churchill** Sir Winston Churchill

sire [ˈsaɪəʳ] Ⓐ N (*Zool*) padre *m*; **Sire**†† (*to monarch*) Señor *m*
Ⓑ VT ser el padre de; **he ~d 49 children** tuvo 49 hijos

siren [ˈsaɪərən] N (*all senses*) sirena *f*

Sirius [ˈsɪrɪəs] N Sirio

sirloin [ˈsɜːlɔɪn] N solomillo *m*

sirocco [sɪˈrɒkəʊ] N siroco *m*

sis* [sɪs] N = **sister**

sisal [ˈsaɪsəl] N (= *material*) sisal *m*, henequén *m* (*LAm*); (= *fibre*) pita *f*, sisal *m*

sissy‡ [ˈsɪsɪ] N [1] (= *effeminate*) marica‡ *m*, mariquita‡ *m*; **the last one's a ~!** ¡maricón el último!‡
[2] (= *coward*) gallina* *f*

sister [ˈsɪstəʳ] Ⓐ N [1] (= *relation*) hermana *f*; **my little ~** mi hermana pequeña; **my brothers and ~s** mis hermanos
[2] (*Brit Med*) (*also* **nursing ~**) enfermera *f* jefe
[3] (*Rel*) hermana *f*; (*before name*) sor *f*; **the Sisters of Charity** las Hermanas de la Caridad
[4] (*US*) **listen ~!**‡ ¡mira, hermana!, ¡mira, tía *or* colega! (*Sp*‡)
Ⓑ CPD ► **sister city** N (*US*) ciudad *f* gemela ► **sister college** N colegio *m* hermano ► **sister company** N empresa *f* hermana, empresa *f* asociada ► **sister nation** N nación *f* hermana ► **sister organization** N organización *f* hermana ► **sister ship** N barco *m* gemelo

sisterhood [ˈsɪstəhʊd] N hermandad *f*

sister-in-law [ˈsɪstərɪnlɔː] N (*pl* **sisters-in-law**) cuñada *f*

sisterly [ˈsɪstəlɪ] ADJ de hermana

Sistine [ˈsɪstiːn] ADJ **the ~ Chapel** la Capilla Sixtina

Sisyphus [ˈsɪsɪfəs] N Sísifo

sit [sɪt] (*pt, pp* **sat**) Ⓐ VI [1] (= *be seated*) [*person*] estar sentado; [*bird*] estar posado; [*hen*] (*on eggs*) empollar; **she was ~ting at her desk** estaba sentada delante de su mesa; **don't just ~ there, do something!** ¡no te quedes ahí sentado, haz algo!; **are you ~ting comfortably?** ¿estás cómodo (en la silla)?; **that's where I ~** ése es mi sitio; **to ~ at home all day** pasar todo el día en casa (sin hacer nada); **they were ~ting in a traffic jam for two hours** estuvieron dos horas metidos en un atasco sin moverse; **we're ~ting on a fortune here** estamos ante una mina de oro; **he sat over his books all night** pasó toda la noche con sus libros; **to ~ still/straight** estarse *or* (*LAm*) quedarse quieto/ponerse derecho (en la silla); **will you ~ still!** ¡te quieres estar *or* quedar quieto (en la silla)!; **to ~ and wait** esperar sentado; ✦*IDIOMS* **to be ~ting pretty*** estar bien colocado *or* situado; **to ~ tight**: **"~ tight, I'll be right back"** —no te muevas, ahora vuelvo; **we'll just have to ~ tight till we hear from him** tendremos que esperar sin hacer nada hasta recibir noticias suyas; *see also* **fence A1**
[2] (= *sit down*) sentarse; (= *alight*) [*bird*] posarse; **~ by me** siéntate a mi lado, siéntate conmigo; **~!** (*to dog*) ¡quieto!
[3] (*Art, Phot*) (= *pose*) **to ~ for a painter/a portrait** posar para un pintor/un retrato
[4] (*Educ*) **to ~ for an examination** presentarse a un examen
[5] (*Brit Pol*) **to ~ for Bury** representar a Bury, ser diputado de *or* por Bury; **to ~ in Parliament** ser diputado, ser miembro del Parlamento; *see also* **sit on 1**
[6] (= *be in session*) [*assembly*] reunirse, celebrar sesión; **the House sat all night** la sesión de la Cámara duró toda la noche; *see also* **judg(e)ment**
[7] (= *be situated*) [*object*] estar colocado; [*building*] estar situado; **the house ~s next to a stream** la casa está situada junto a un arroyo; **the hat sat awkwardly on her head** llevaba el sombrero mal puesto; **the car sat in the garage for over a year** el coche estuvo aparcado en el garaje más de un año
[8] (= *weigh*) **that pie ~s heavy on the stomach** esa empanada es muy indigesta; **it sat heavy on his conscience** le pesaba en la conciencia, le producía remordimientos de conciencia; **her years ~ lightly on her** los años apenas han dejado huella en ella
[9] (= *be compatible*) **his authoritarian style did not ~ well with their progressive educational policies** su estilo autoritario era poco compatible con la política educativa activa de ellos
[10] (= *to fit*) [*clothing*] sentar; **to ~ well/badly (on sb)** sentar bien/mal (a algn)
[11] (= *babysit*) cuidar a los niños
Ⓑ VT [1] [+ *person*] sentar; [+ *object*] colocar; **she sat the vase on the windowsill** colocó el jarrón sobre la repisa de la ventana; **to ~ a child on one's knee** sentar a un niño sobre las rodillas; **he sat himself on the edge of the bed** se sentó en el borde de la cama
[2] (= *have capacity for*) **this table ~s 12 (people)** en esta mesa caben 12 (personas); **the concert hall ~s 2,000 (people)** el auditorio tiene cabida *or* capacidad para 2.000 personas
[3] [+ *exam, test*] presentarse a; **to ~ an examination in French** presentarse a un examen de francés, examinarse de francés

►**sit around** VI + ADV **we can't have you ~ting around wasting your life** no podemos dejar que desperdicies tu vida sin hacer nada; **I'm tired of ~ting around waiting for him** estoy aburrida de esperar sentada a que venga; **we sat around talking** pasamos el tiempo charlando

►**sit back** VI + ADV [1] (*in seat*) recostarse; **just ~ back and enjoy the show** póngase cómodo y disfrute del espectáculo; **she sat back on her heels** se sentó en cuclillas
[2] (*fig*) **we can't just ~ back and do nothing** no podemos quedarnos cruzados de brazos sin hacer nada; **to ~ back and take stock** hacer una pausa y reflexionar

►**sit down** Ⓐ VI + ADV (= *take a seat*) sentarse; **do ~ down!** ¡siéntese por favor!; **we sat down to a huge meal** nos sentamos a darnos un auténtico banquete; **to be ~ting down** estar sentado
Ⓑ VT + ADV [+ *person*] sentar; **I sat him down and gave him a drink** lo senté y le di de beber; **~ yourself down and tell me all about it** siéntate y cuéntamelo todo

►**sit in** VI + ADV [1] (= *observe*) estar presente; **they said I could ~ in on the meeting/the discussions** me dijeron que podía asistir a la reunión/a los debates (como observador)
[2] (= *substitute*) sustituir; **to ~ in for sb** sustituir a algn
[3] [*students, workers*] hacer una sentada, ocupar las aulas/la fábrica *etc*

►**sit on** VI + PREP [1] (= *be member of*) [+ *jury, committee*] ser miembro de, formar parte de
[2] (*) (= *keep secret*) [+ *news, information*] ocultar, callar; (= *delay taking action on*) [+ *document, application, plan*] no dar trámite a, dar carpetazo a*
[3] (*) (= *silence*) [+ *person*] hacer callar; (= *oppress*) [+ *opponents, dissent*] reprimir a, silenciar; **he won't be sat on** no quiere callar, no da su brazo a torcer

►**sit out** VT + ADV [1] (= *not take part in*) [+ *dance*] no bailar; (*Sport*) [+ *game, event*] no participar en; **let's ~ this dance out** no bailemos esta vez
[2] (= *endure*) aguantar; **he decided to ~ the war out in Brussels** decidió aguantar en Bruselas hasta que terminara la guerra; **to ~ it out** aguantarse

►**sit through** VI + PREP **I wouldn't want to have to ~ through that film again** no me gustaría tener que volver a ver esa película otra vez; **it was the most boring speech he'd ever had to ~ through** fue el discurso más aburrido que jamás tuvo que escuchar *or* aguantar

►**sit up** Ⓐ VI + ADV [1] (= *straighten o.s.*) ponerse derecho, enderezarse; (*after lying*) incorporarse; **~ up straight!** ¡ponte derecho!, ¡enderézate!; **when someone was killed they finally began to ~ up and take notice of the situation** tuvo que morir alguien para que finalmente decidieran tomar cartas en la situación; **he knew the offer of money would make them ~ up and take notice** sabía que la oferta de dinero conseguiría hacerles prestar atención; **a defeat like that makes you ~ up and think** una derrota como ésa te da en qué pensar
[2] (= *stay up late*) **they often ~ up late, talking** a menudo trasnochan, hablando; **I sat up all night trying to work it out** me quedé toda la noche levantado intentando descifrarlo; **I'll be late back so don't ~ up for me** volveré tarde así que no me esperes levantado; **to ~ up with a child** pasar la noche en vela con un niño; **I sat up with her for most of the night** estuve con ella casi toda la noche, haciéndole compañía
Ⓑ VT + ADV [+ *doll, baby*] sentar; [+ *patient, invalid*] incorporar

►**sit upon*** VI + PREP = **sit on**

sitar [sɪ'tɑːʳ] N sitar *m*

sitcom* ['sɪtkɒm] N (*Rad, TV*) (*also* **situation comedy**) comedia *f* de situación

sit-down ['sɪtdaʊn] Ⓐ ADJ [*meal*] servido en la mesa; **they gave us a ~ lunch** nos ofrecieron un almuerzo servido en la mesa; **~ protest** sentada *f*; **~ strike** huelga *f* de brazos caídos, sentada *f*
Ⓑ N **I must have a ~*** tengo que sentarme a descansar un rato

site [saɪt] Ⓐ N [1] (= *place*) sitio *m*, lugar *m*; (= *location*) situación *f*; (= *scene*) escenario *m*; (*for building*) solar *m*, terreno *m*; (*archaeological*) yacimiento *m*; **the ~ of the accident** el lugar del accidente; **the ~ of the battle** el escenario de la batalla; **a late Roman ~** un emplazamiento romano tardío; **building ~** obra *f*; **burial ~** necrópolis *f inv*; **camp ~** camping *m*
[2] (*Internet*) = **website**
Ⓑ VT situar, ubicar (*esp LAm*); **a badly ~d building** un edificio mal situado

sit-in ['sɪtɪn] N (= *protest, demonstration*) encierro *m*, ocupación *f*; (= *strike*) huelga *f* de brazos caídos, sentada *f*

siting ['saɪtɪŋ] N (= *position*) situación *f*; (= *placement*) emplazamiento *m*; **the ~ of new industries** la localización de las nuevas industrias

Sits Vac. [ˌsɪts'væk] N ABBR = **Situations Vacant**

sitter ['sɪtəʳ] N [1] (*Art*) modelo *mf*
[2] (= *babysitter*) babysitter *mf*, canguro *mf* (*Sp*)
[3] (*) cosa *f* fácil; **it was a ~** (*Sport**) fue un gol que se canta*; **you missed a ~*** erraste un tiro de lo más fácil

sitting ['sɪtɪŋ] Ⓐ N [1] (= *session*) (*Pol, Art etc*) sesión *f*; (*in canteen*) turno *m*; **second ~ for lunch** segundo turno de comedor; **to eat it all at one ~** comérselo todo de una sentada; **to read a book in one ~** leer un libro de un tirón
[2] (*Zool*) [*of eggs*] nidada *f*
Ⓑ ADJ (*also* **~ down**) sentado; **a ~ bird** una ave que está posada *or* inmóvil; **a ~ hen** una gallina clueca
Ⓒ CPD ► **sitting duck*** N (*fig*) blanco *m* facilísimo ► **sitting member** N miembro *mf* actual *or* en funciones ► **sitting room** N (= *living room*) sala *f*, cuarto *m* de estar, salón *m*, living *m* (*LAm*); (= *space*) **~ and standing room** sitio *m* para sentarse y para estar de pie ► **sitting tenant** N inquilino/a *m/f* en posesión

situate ['sɪtjʊeɪt] VT situar, ubicar (*esp LAm*); **a pleasantly ~d house** una casa bien situada *or* ubicada; **the bank is ~d in the high street** el banco está situado *or* ubicado *or* se encuentra en la calle principal; **how are you ~d for money?** (*fig*) ¿cómo vas *or* andas de dinero?

situation [ˌsɪtjʊ'eɪʃən] Ⓐ N [1] (= *position*) situación *f*, ubicación *f* (*esp LAm*)
[2] (= *circumstances*) situación *f*; **to save the ~** salvar la situación
[3] (= *job*) empleo *m*, vacante *f*; **"situations vacant"** "ofertas de empleo"; **"situations wanted"** "demandas de empleo"
Ⓑ CPD ► **situation comedy** N (*TV, Rad*) comedia *f* de situación

sit-up ['sɪtʌp] N abdominal *m*

six [sɪks] Ⓐ ADJ seis
Ⓑ N [1] seis *m*; ✦**IDIOMS to be (all) at ~es and sevens** [*person*] estar confuso; [*things*] estar en desorden; **it's ~ of one and half a dozen of the other*** ◊ **it's ~ and half a dozen*** da lo mismo, da igual; **~ of the best** (*Brit*) seis azotes *mpl* (*castigo escolar*); **to knock sb for ~*** dejar pasmado a algn
[2] (*Cricket*) seis *m*, *golpe de bate que lanza la bola sin botar fuera del terreno y sirve para anotarse seis carreras*; **to hit a ~** batear un seis, hacer seis carreras de un golpe; **he hit three ~es** bateó tres seises; *see* **five** *for usage*

six-eight time [ˌsɪkseɪt'taɪm] N **in ~** en un compás de seis por ocho

sixfold ['sɪksfəʊld] Ⓐ ADJ séxtuplo
Ⓑ ADV seis veces

six-footer ['sɪks'fʊtəʳ] N hombre *m or* mujer *f* que mide seis pies

six-pack ['sɪkspæk] N paquete *m* de seis

sixpence ['sɪkspəns] N (*Brit*) (*formerly*) seis peniques *mpl*

sixpenny† ['sɪkspənɪ] ADJ (*Brit*) de seis peniques; (*pej*) insignificante, inútil

six-shooter ['sɪks'ʃuːtəʳ] N revólver *m* de seis tiros

sixteen ['sɪks'tiːn] Ⓐ ADJ dieciséis, diez y seis; **she was sweet ~** tenía dieciséis años y estaba en la flor de la vida
Ⓑ N dieciséis *m*, diez y seis *m*; *see* **five** *for usage*

sixteenth ['sɪks'tiːnθ] Ⓐ ADJ decimosexto
Ⓑ N (*in series*) decimosexto/a *m/f*; (= *fraction*) dieciseisavo *m*, decimosexta parte *f*; *see* **fifth** *for usage*

sixth [sɪksθ] Ⓐ ADJ sexto
Ⓑ N (*in series*) sexto/a *m/f*; (= *fraction*) sexto *m*, sexta parte *f*; *see* **fifth** *for usage*
Ⓒ CPD ► **sixth form** N clase *f* de alumnos del sexto año (*de 16 a 18 años de edad*) ► **sixth former** N alumno/a *m/f* de 16 a 18 años

sixth-form college [ˌsɪksθfɔːm'kɒlɪdʒ] N instituto *m* para alumnos de 16 a 18 años

sixtieth ['sɪkstɪɪθ] Ⓐ ADJ sexagésimo
Ⓑ N (*in series*) sexagésimo/a *m/f*; (= *fraction*) sexagésima parte *f*, sesentavo *m*; **the ~ anniversary** el sesenta aniversario; *see* **fifth** *for usage*

sixty ['sɪkstɪ] Ⓐ ADJ sesenta
Ⓑ N sesenta *m*; **to be in one's sixties** tener sesenta y tantos años, ser sesentón; *see* **fifty** *for usage*

sixtyish ['sɪkstɪɪʃ] ADJ de unos sesenta años; **she must be ~** debe andar por los sesenta

size[1] [saɪz] Ⓐ N [*of object, place*] tamaño *m*; [*of person*] talla *f*, estatura *f*; [*of garments*] talla *f*, medida *f*; [*of shoes, gloves*] número *m*; (= *scope*) [*of problem*] magnitud *f*, envergadura *f*; **plates of various ~s** platos de varios tamaños; **it's the ~ of a brick** es del tamaño de un ladrillo; **the skirt is two ~s too big** la falda es dos tallas grande; **a hall of immense ~** una sala de vastas dimensiones; **try this (on) for ~** prueba esto a ver si te conviene; **they're all of a ~** tienen todos el mismo tamaño; **it's quite a ~** es bastante grande; **I take ~ nine** (*shoes*) uso *or* tengo el número nueve; **I take ~ 14** (*blouse etc*) uso *or* tengo la talla 14; **to cut sth to ~** cortar algo al tamaño que se necesita; **what ~ is the room?** ¿de qué tamaño *or* (*LAm*) qué tan grande es el cuarto?; **what ~ are you?** ¿qué talla usas *or* tienes?, ¿de qué talla eres?; **what ~ shoes do you take?** ¿qué número (de zapato) calzas *or* gastas?; **what ~ shirt do you take?** ¿qué talla de camisa tiene *or* es la de usted?; **he's about your**

~ tiene más o menos tu talla; ✦IDIOMS **that's about the ~ of it** eso es lo que puedo decirle acerca del asunto, es más o menos eso; **to cut sb down to ~*** bajar los humos a algn
Ⓑ VT clasificar según el tamaño
►**size up** VT + ADV [+ *problem, situation*] evaluar, apreciar; [+ *person*] **they looked at each other, sizing each other up** se miraban el uno al otro, intentando formarse *or* hacerse un juicio; (*for a fight*) se miraban el uno al otro, tratando de medir sus fuerzas; **I've got her all ~d up** la tengo calada; **I can't quite ~ him up** no consigo hacerme una idea clara de cómo es

size² [saɪz] Ⓐ N (*for plaster, paper*) cola *f*; (*for cloth*) apresto *m*
Ⓑ VT [+ *plaster, paper*] encolar; [+ *cloth*] aprestar

sizeable ['saɪzəbl] ADJ [*sum of money etc*] considerable, importante; [*object*] bastante grande; **it's quite a ~ house** es una casa bastante grande; **a ~ sum** una cantidad importante

sizeably ['saɪzəblɪ] ADV considerablemente

-sized [saɪzd] ADJ (*ending in compounds*) de tamaño …

sizzle ['sɪzl] VI chisporrotear; (*in frying*) crepitar (al freírse)

sizzler* ['sɪzləʳ] N día *f* de calor sofocante

sizzling ['sɪzlɪŋ] Ⓐ ADJ [*heat*] sofocante; [*shot etc*] fulminante
Ⓑ N chisporroteo *m*, crepitación *f*

S.J. ABBR (= **Society of Jesus**) C. de J.

SK ABBR (*Canada*) = **Saskatchewan**

skate¹ [skeɪt] N (= *fish*) raya *f*

skate² [skeɪt] Ⓐ N patín *m*; ✦IDIOM **get your ~s on!*** ¡date prisa!
Ⓑ VI patinar; **it went skating across the floor** se deslizó velozmente sobre el suelo
►**skate around**, **skate over**, **skate round** VI + PREP [+ *problem, issue*] pasar por alto de, pasar por encima de

skateboard ['skeɪtbɔːd] N monopatín *m*

skateboarder ['skeɪtbɔːdəʳ] N monopatinador(a) *m/f*

skateboarding ['skeitbɔːdɪŋ] N monopatinaje *m*; **to go ~** montar en monopatín

skater ['skeɪtəʳ] N patinador(a) *m/f*

skating ['skeɪtɪŋ] Ⓐ N patinaje *m*; **do you like ~?** ¿te gusta patinar?; **to go ~** ir a patinar
Ⓑ CPD ► **skating rink** N (*for ice skating*) pista *f* de hielo; (*for roller skating*) pista *f* de patinaje

skedaddle* [skɪ'dædl] VI escabullirse, salir pitando*; **they ~d in all directions** huyeron por todos lados

skein [skeɪn] N madeja *f*; **a tangled ~** (*fig*) un asunto enmarañado

skeletal ['skelɪtl] ADJ [1] (*Anat*) [*structure, development*] óseo, del esqueleto; [*remains*] de huesos; **~ structure** *or* **system** esqueleto *m*, sistema *m* óseo
[2] (= *emaciated*) [*person, body*] esquelético; [*face*] enjuto
[3] (= *schematic*) [*timetable*] reducido

skeleton ['skelɪtn] Ⓐ N [*of person*] esqueleto *m*; [*of building*] armazón *f*, armadura *f*; (= *structure*) estructura *f*; [*of novel, report*] esquema *m*, bosquejo *m*; ✦IDIOM **~ in the cupboard** secreto *m* de familia
Ⓑ CPD [*service*] mínimo; [*outline*] esquemático ► **skeleton key** N llave *f* maestra ► **skeleton staff** N **with a ~ staff** con un personal mínimo

skeptic *etc* ['skeptɪk] (*US*) = **sceptic** *etc*

sketch [sketʃ] Ⓐ N [1] (= *drawing*) dibujo *m*; (= *preliminary drawing*) esbozo *m*, bosquejo *m*; (= *rough drawing*) croquis *m inv*; (= *plan*) borrador *m*, esquema *m*
[2] (*Theat*) sketch *m*
Ⓑ VT (*gen*) (= *draw*) dibujar; [+ *preliminary drawing, plan etc*] bosquejar, esbozar
Ⓒ VI hacer bosquejos
Ⓓ CPD ► **sketch map** N croquis *m inv* ► **sketch pad** N = **sketching pad**
►**sketch in** VT + ADV [+ *details*] explicar; **he ~ed in the details for me** me explicó los detalles

sketchbook ['sketʃbʊk] N bloc *m* de dibujos

sketchily ['sketʃɪlɪ] ADV incompletamente

sketching ['sketʃɪŋ] Ⓐ N dibujo *m*, arte *m* de dibujar
Ⓑ CPD ► **sketching pad** N bloc *m* de dibujos

sketchy ['sketʃɪ] ADJ (*compar* **sketchier**; *superl* **sketchiest**) incompleto, sin detalles

skew [skjuː] Ⓐ N **to be on the ~** estar desviado, estar sesgado
Ⓑ ADJ sesgado, oblicuo, torcido
Ⓒ VT sesgar, desviar
Ⓓ VI (*also* **to ~ round**) desviarse, ponerse al sesgo, torcerse

skewbald ['skjuːbɔːld] Ⓐ ADJ pintado, con pintas
Ⓑ N pinto *m*

skewed ['skjuːd] ADJ sesgado, torcido (*also fig*)

skewer ['skjʊəʳ] Ⓐ N pincho *m*, broqueta *f*, brocheta *f*
Ⓑ VT ensartar, espetar

skew-whiff* [ˌskjuː'wɪf] ADJ (*Brit*) (= *twisted*) torcido, chueco (*LAm*)

ski [skiː] Ⓐ N (*pl* **skis** *or* **ski**) esquí *m*; **a pair of ~s** unos esquís
Ⓑ VI esquiar; **to go ~ing** practicar el esquí, (ir a) esquiar; **to ~ down** bajar esquiando
Ⓒ CPD ► **ski boot** N bota *f* de esquí ► **ski instructor** N instructor(a) *m/f* de esquí, monitor(a) *m/f* de esquí ► **ski jump** N (= *action*) salto *m* con esquís; (= *course*) pista *f* de salto ► **ski jumper** N saltador(a) *m/f* de esquí ► **ski jumping** N salto *m* de esquí ► **ski lift** N telesquí *m*, telesilla *m or f* ► **ski mask** N (*US*) pasamontaña(s) *m (inv)* ► **ski pants** NPL pantalones *mpl* de esquí ► **ski pole** N bastón *m* ► **ski rack** N baca *f* portaesquís ► **ski resort** N estación *f* de esquí ► **ski run** N pista *f* de esquí ► **ski slope** N pista *f* de esquí ► **ski stick** N bastón *m* ► **ski suit** N traje *m* de esquiar ► **ski trousers** NPL pantalones *mpl* de esquí

skid [skɪd] Ⓐ N [1] (*Aut etc*) patinazo *m*, resbalón *m*
[2] (*Aer*) patín *m*; ✦IDIOMS **to grease the ~s** (*US**) engrasar el mecanismo; **to put the ~s under sb** deshacerse de algn con maña; **her marriage/career is on the ~s** su matrimonio/carrera se está yendo al garete, su matrimonio/carrera está cayendo en picado
Ⓑ VI (*Aut*) patinar; [*person, object*] deslizarse, resbalarse; **it went ~ding across the floor** se deslizó velozmente sobre el suelo; **to ~ into** dar con *or* contra; **I ~ded into a tree** patiné y di contra un árbol, de un patinazo di contra un árbol; **the car ~ded to a halt** el coche patinó y paró
Ⓒ CPD ► **skid row*** N (*US*) *calles donde se refugian los borrachos, drogadictos, etc*

skiddoo* [skɪ'duː] VI (*US*) largarse*

skidlid* ['skɪdlɪd] N casco *m* protector (de motorista)

skidmark ['skɪdmɑːk] N huella *f* de un patinazo

Ski-Doo® [skɪ'duː] N motonieve *f*

skidproof ['skɪdpruːf] ADJ a prueba de patinazos

skier ['skɪːəʳ] N esquiador(a) *m/f*

skiff [skɪf] N esquife *m*

skiing ['skiːɪŋ] Ⓐ N esquí *m*; **do you like ~?** ¿te gusta esquiar?; **to go ~** ir a esquiar
Ⓑ CPD ► **skiing holiday** N vacaciones *fpl* de esquí; **to go on a ~ holiday** irse de vacaciones a esquiar ► **skiing resort** N estación *f* de esquí

skilful, **skillful** (*US*) ['skɪlfʊl] ADJ hábil, diestro (**at, in** en)

skilfully, **skillfully** (*US*) ['skɪlfəlɪ] ADV hábilmente, con destreza

skilfulness, **skillfulness** (*US*) ['skɪlfʊlnɪs] N habilidad *f*, destreza *f*

skill [skɪl] N [1] (= *ability*) (*gen*) habilidad *f*; (*technical*) destreza *f*; **diamond-cutting requires considerable ~** tallar diamantes requiere mucha destreza; **his ~ in battle** su destreza en el campo de la batalla; **his ~ as a fundraiser came in useful** su habilidad para recaudar fondos resultó útil; **a job that matches her ~s** un trabajo que se ajusta a sus aptitudes; **his lack of ~ in dealing with people** su inaptitud *or* falta de capacidad para tratar con la gente; **a game of ~** un juego de habilidad; **we need someone with proven management ~s** necesitamos a alguien con probadas dotes directivas; **technical ~(s)** conocimientos *mpl* técnicos
[2] (= *technique*) técnica *f*; **to learn new ~s** aprender nuevas técnicas; **the basic ~s of reading and writing** los conocimientos básicos de lectura y escritura; **communication ~s** habilidad *f or* aptitud *f* para comunicarse; **language ~s** (*with foreign languages*) habilidad *f* para hablar idiomas; **he seemed to lack the most basic social ~s** carecía totalmente de don de gentes

skilled [skɪld] ADJ [1] [*person*] (= *specialized*) especializado; (= *skilful*) experto, hábil, diestro; **she is a ~ negotiator** es una negociadora muy experta *or* hábil *or* diestra; **~ craftsmen are employed in the restoration work** el trabajo de restauración lo realizan artesanos especializados; **he is ~ at** *or* **in dealing with children** tiene muy buena mano con los niños
[2] [*worker*] cualificado (*esp Sp*), calificado (*esp LAm*), especializado; **~ labour** *or* (*US*) **labor** mano *f* de obra cualificada (*esp Sp*), mano *f* de obra calificada (*esp LAm*), mano *f* de obra especializada
[3] [*job, work*] especializado

skillet ['skɪlɪt] N sartén *f* pequeña, sartén *m* pequeño (*LAm*)

skillful *etc* ['skɪlfʊl] ADJ (*US*) = **skilful** *etc*

skim [skɪm] Ⓐ VT [1] [+ *milk*] desnatar, descremar; [+ *soup, liquid*] espumar; **to ~ the cream off the milk** quitar la nata a la leche, desnatar la leche; **~med milk** leche *f* descremada *or* desnatada
[2] (= *graze*) [+ *surface*] rozar; **to ~ the ground** [*plane, bird etc*] volar a ras de la tierra
[3] [+ *stone*] hacer cabrillas con, hacer el salto de la rana con
[4] (*fig*) [+ *subject*] tratar superficialmente
Ⓑ VI **to ~ across/along the ground** pasar rozando la tierra; **to ~ through a book** (*fig*) echar una ojeada *or* hojear a un libro
►**skim off** VT + ADV [+ *cream, grease*] desnatar; **they ~med off the brightest pupils** separaron a la flor y nata de los alumnos

skimmer ['skɪməʳ] N (*Orn*) picotijera *m*, rayador *m*

skimp [skɪmp] Ⓐ VT [+ *material etc*] escatimar; [+ *work*] chapucear; [+ *praise*] ser tacaño en *or* con

Ⓑ VI economizar; **to ~ on fabric/work/food** escatimar tela/trabajo/alimento

skimpily [ˈskɪmpɪlɪ] ADV [*serve, provide*] escasamente; [*live*] mezquinamente

skimpy [ˈskɪmpɪ] ADJ (*compar* **skimpier**; *superl* **skimpiest**) [*skirt etc*] breve; [*allowance, meal*] escaso, mezquino

skin [skɪn] Ⓐ N 1 [*of person*] piel *f*; [*of face*] cutis *m*; (= *complexion*) tez *f*; **to wear wool next to one's ~** llevar prenda de lana sobre la piel; ✦*IDIOMS* **to be ~ and bone** estar en los huesos; **he's nothing but ~ and bone** está en los huesos; **to jump out of one's ~** llevarse un tremendo susto; **it's no ~ off my nose*** a mí ni me va ni me viene, me da igual *or* lo mismo; **to save one's ~** salvar el pellejo; **by the ~ of one's teeth** por los pelos; **to have a thick/thin ~** ser poco sensible/muy susceptible; **to get under sb's ~** (= *annoy*) irritar *or* molestar a algn; **I've got you under my ~*** no puedo dejar de pensar en ti
2 [*of animal*] piel *f*, pellejo *m*; (*as hide*) piel *f*, cuero *m*
3 [*of fruit, vegetable*] piel *f*, cáscara *f*; (*discarded*) mondaduras *fpl*
4 (= *crust*) (*on paint, milk pudding*) nata *f*
5 (*for wine*) odre *m*
6 (*Aer, Naut*) revestimiento *m*
7 (*) = **skinhead**
8 (*Drugs*‡) (= *cigarette paper*) papelillo* *m*, papel *m* de fumar
Ⓑ VT 1 [+ *animal*] despellejar, desollar; **I'll ~ him alive!** (*fig*) ¡lo voy a matar!*, ¡lo voy a desollar vivo!; ✦*IDIOMS* **to keep one's eyes ~ned for sth*** andar ojo alerta por algo; **there's more than one way to ~ a cat** cada uno tiene su manera de hacer las cosas, cada maestrillo tiene su librillo
2 [+ *fruit*] pelar, quitar la piel a; [+ *tree*] descortezar
3 (= *graze*) **to ~ one's knee/elbow** desollarse la rodilla/el codo
4 (‡) (= *steal from*) despellejar, esquilmar
Ⓒ CPD ► **skin cancer** N cáncer *m* de piel ► **skin colour** N (= *colour of one's skin*) color *m* de la piel; (= *shade*) color *m* natural ► **skin disease** N enfermedad *f* de la piel ► **skin diver** N buceador(a) *m/f*, buzo *mf*, submarinista *mf* ► **skin diving** N buceo *m*, submarinismo *m* ► **skin flick*** N película *f* porno* ► **skin freshener** N tónico *m* para la piel ► **skin game*** N (*US*) estafa *f* ► **skin graft(ing)** N injerto *m* de piel ► **skin trade*** N publicación *f* de revistas porno ► **skin wound** N herida *f* superficial

skin-deep [ˈskɪnˈdiːp] ADJ superficial; *see also* **beauty A1**

skinflick‡ [ˈskɪnflɪk] N película *f* porno*

skinflint [ˈskɪnflɪnt] N tacaño/a *m/f*, roñoso/a *m/f*

skinful* [ˈskɪnfʊl] N **to have had a ~** estar borracho/a *or* (*LAm*) tomado/a

skinhead [ˈskɪnhed] N cabeza *mf* rapada

-skinned [skɪnd] ADJ (*ending in compounds*) de piel ...; **dark-skinned** de piel morena; **rough-skinned** de piel áspera

skinny [ˈskɪnɪ] ADJ (*compar* **skinnier**; *superl* **skinniest**) flaco

skint [skɪnt] ADJ **to be ~*** estar sin cuartos, estar pelado

skin-tight [ˈskɪntaɪt] ADJ muy ajustado

skip¹ [skɪp] Ⓐ N salto *m*, brinco *m*
Ⓑ VI 1 (= *jump*) brincar, saltar; **to ~ with joy** dar brincos *or* saltos de alegría, brincar *or* saltar de alegría; **to ~ in/out** entrar/salir dando brincos; **he ~ped out of the way** se apartó de un salto; **to ~ off** (*fig*) largarse, rajarse (*LAm*)
2 (*with a rope*) saltar a la comba
3 (*fig*) **to ~ over sth** pasar algo por alto, saltarse algo; **to ~ from one thing to another** saltar de un tema a otro; **the book ~s about a lot** el libro da muchos saltos
Ⓒ VT (*fig*) [+ *meal, lesson, page*] saltarse; **to ~ lunch** saltarse el almuerzo, no almorzar; **you should never ~ breakfast** no debes saltarte nunca el desayuno; **to ~ school** hacer novillos, hacer la rabona; **let's ~ it!*** ¡basta de eso!
Ⓓ CPD ► **skip rope** N (*US*) = **skipping rope**

skip² [skɪp] N (*Brit*) (= *container*) contenedor *m* de basuras

skipper [ˈskɪpəʳ] Ⓐ N (*Sport*) capitán/ana *m/f*; (*Naut*) capitán/ana *m/f*, patrón/a *m/f*; **well, you're the ~** bueno, tú eres el jefe
Ⓑ VT [+ *boat*] capitanear, patronear; [+ *team*] capitanear

skipping [ˈskɪpɪŋ] Ⓐ N comba *f*
Ⓑ CPD ► **skipping rope** N (*Brit*) cuerda *f*, comba *f*

skirl [skɜːl] N (*Scot*) **the ~ of the pipes** el son *or* la música de la gaita

skirmish [ˈskɜːmɪʃ] Ⓐ N escaramuza *f*, refriega *f*; (*fig*) roce *m*; **to have a ~ with** (*fig*) tener un roce con
Ⓑ VI pelear

skirmisher [ˈskɜːmɪʃəʳ] N escaramuzador(a) *m/f*

skirt [skɜːt] Ⓐ N falda *f*, pollera *f* (*LAm*); [*of coat etc*] faldón *m*; **flared/split/straight ~** falda *f* acampanada/pantalón/estrecha *or* recta
Ⓑ VT (*also* **~ around**) rodear, dar la vuelta a; (*fig*) (= *avoid*) esquivar; **we ~ed Seville to the north** pasamos al norte de Sevilla
Ⓒ VI **to ~ around** = **B**
Ⓓ CPD ► **skirt length** N tela *f* suficiente para una falda

skirting [ˈskɜːtɪŋ] N, **skirting board** [ˈskɜːtɪŋ,bɔːd] N zócalo *m*, cenefa *f*

skit [skɪt] N (*Theat*) sátira *f* (**on** de)

skitter [ˈskɪtəʳ] VI **to ~ across the water/along the ground** [*bird*] volar rozando el agua/el suelo; [*stone*] saltar por encima del agua/por el suelo

skittish [ˈskɪtɪʃ] ADJ (= *capricious*) caprichoso, delicado; (= *nervous*) [*horse etc*] nervioso, asustadizo; (= *playful*) juguetón

skittishly [ˈskɪtɪʃlɪ] ADV (= *capriciously*) caprichosamente; (= *nervously*) nerviosamente; (= *playfully*) de modo juguetón

skittle [ˈskɪtl] Ⓐ N bolo *m*; **~s** el juego de bolos; **to play ~s** jugar a los bolos
Ⓑ CPD ► **skittle alley** N bolera *f*

skive‡ [skaɪv] (*Brit*) Ⓐ VI (= *not work*) gandulear*, haraganear*; (= *disappear*) escabullirse, escaquearse*, rajarse (*LAm**)
Ⓑ N **to be on the ~** ◊ **have a good ~** gandulear, no hacer nada

►**skive off‡** Ⓐ VI + ADV (*Brit*) (= *not work*) gandulear*, haraganear*; (= *disappear*) escabullirse, escaquearse*, rajarse (*LAm**)
Ⓑ VI + PREP **to ~ off school** hacer novillos, hacer la rabona

skiver‡ [ˈskaɪvəʳ] N (*Brit*) gandul(a) *m/f*

skivvy* [ˈskɪvɪ] N (*pej*) esclava *f* del hogar

skua [ˈskjuːə] N págalo *m*

skulduggery*† [skʌlˈdʌgərɪ] N trampas *fpl*, embustes *mpl*; **a piece of ~** una trampa, un embuste

skulk [skʌlk] VI esconderse; **to ~ about** esconderse

skull [skʌl] N calavera *f*; (*Med*) cráneo *m*; **~ and crossbones** (= *flag*) la bandera pirata; **I can't get it into his (thick) ~ that ...** no hay quien le meta en la cabeza que ...

skullcap [ˈskʌlkæp] N (*gen*) gorro *m*; [*of priest*] solideo *m*

skunk [skʌŋk] N (*pl* **skunk** *or* **skunks**) (*Zool*) mofeta *f*, zorrillo *m* (*LAm**); **you ~!** (*fig*) ¡canalla!

sky [skaɪ] Ⓐ N cielo *m*; **under blue skies** bajo un cielo azul; **the skies over England** el cielo en Inglaterra; **to praise sb to the skies** poner a algn por las nubes; **the ~'s the limit*** (*fig*) no hay límite; **out of a clear blue ~** (*fig*) de repente, inesperadamente
Ⓑ CPD ► **sky marshal** N agente *mf* de seguridad (*en vuelos comerciales*)

sky-blue [ˈskaɪˈbluː] Ⓐ ADJ celeste, azul celeste
Ⓑ N azul *m* celeste

skydive [ˈskaɪdaɪv] Ⓐ N caída *f* libre
Ⓑ VI saltar en caída libre

skydiver [ˈskaɪdaɪvəʳ] N paracaidista *mf* de caída libre, paracaidista *mf* acrobático/a

skydiving [ˈskaɪdaɪvɪŋ] N caída *f* libre, paracaidismo *m* acrobático

sky-high [ˈskaɪˈhaɪ] ADV por las nubes; **prices have gone ~** los precios están por las nubes; **he hit the ball ~** mandó el balón por los aires; *see also* **blow² 3**

skyjack* [ˈskaɪdʒæk] VT [+ *plane*] atracar, piratear

skyjacking* [ˈskaɪdʒækɪŋ] N atraco *m* aéreo, piratería *f* aérea

skylab [ˈskaɪlæb] N skylab *m*, laboratorio *m* espacial

skylark [ˈskaɪlɑːk] Ⓐ N (= *bird*) alondra *f*
Ⓑ VI (*fig*) (*) hacer travesuras

skylight [ˈskaɪlaɪt] N tragaluz *m*, claraboya *f*

skyline [ˈskaɪlaɪn] N (= *horizon*) horizonte *m*; [*of city*] contorno *m*, perfil *m*

skyrocket [ˈskaɪˌrɒkɪt] Ⓐ N cohete *m*
Ⓑ VI subir (como un cohete); (*fig*) [*prices etc*] ponerse por las nubes, dispararse

skyscraper [ˈskaɪˌskreɪpəʳ] N rascacielos *m inv*

skytrain [ˈskaɪtreɪn] N puente *m* aéreo

skyward [ˈskaɪwəd] ADV hacia el cielo

skywards [ˈskaɪwədz] ADV (*esp Brit*) = **skyward**

skyway [ˈskaɪweɪ] N ruta *f* aérea

skywriting [ˈskaɪˌraɪtɪŋ] N publicidad *f* aérea

SL N ABBR = **source language**

slab [slæb] N 1 [*of stone*] losa *f* 2 (*in mortuary*) plancha *f* de mármol, tabla *f* de mármol 3 [*of chocolate*] tableta *f*; [*of cake etc*] trozo *m*, tajada *f*; [*of meat*] tajada *f* (gruesa)

slack [slæk] Ⓐ ADJ (*compar* **slacker**; *superl* **slackest**) 1 (= *not tight or firm*) flojo
2 (= *lax*) descuidado, negligente; (= *lazy*) perezoso, vago, flojo; **to be ~ about one's work** desatender su trabajo, ser negligente en su trabajo; **to be ~ about** *or* **in doing sth** dejar de hacer algo por desidia
3 (*Comm*) [*market*] flojo, encalmado; [*period*] de inactividad; [*season*] muerto; **business is ~** hay poco movimiento *or* poca actividad en el negocio; **demand was ~** hubo poca demanda
Ⓑ N 1 (= *part of rope etc*) comba *f*; **to take up the ~** tensar una cuerda; **to take up the ~ in the economy** utilizar toda la capacidad productiva de la economía
2 (= *coal*) cisco *m*
3 (*Comm*) (= *period*) período *m* de inactividad; (= *season*) estación *f* muerta; *see also* **slacks**
Ⓒ VI (*) gandulear, holgazanear; **he's been ~ing** ha sido muy gandul
Ⓓ VT = **slacken A**

►**slack off** VI + ADV, VT + ADV = **slacken off**

slacken [ˈslækn] Ⓐ VT [+ *reins*] aflojar; (*fig*) [+ *policy*] aflojar; **he ~ed his grip on her wrist** dejó de apretarle tan fuerte la muñeca; **to ~ one's pace** aflojar el paso; **to ~ speed** [*person*] aflojar el paso; [*vehicle*] disminuir la velocidad
Ⓑ VI 1 (= *loosen*) [*rope*] aflojarse; [*muscle*] ponerse flácido
2 (= *reduce*) [*activity, demand*] disminuir, bajar; [*trade*] decaer; [*wind, rain*] amainar; **business tends to ~ in summer** el comercio tiende a decaer en verano
► **slacken off** (*esp Brit*) Ⓐ VI + ADV 1 (= *be less active*) [*person*] aflojar el ritmo (de trabajo, de juego, *etc*); **their game ~ed off in the second half** su juego perdió ímpetu en la segunda mitad
2 (= *reduce*) [*demand, production*] disminuir, bajar
Ⓑ VT + ADV [+ *rope*] aflojar
► **slacken up** VI + ADV = **slacken off A1**

slackening [ˈslæknɪŋ] N 1 (= *loosening*) [*of rope*] aflojamiento *m*; [*of muscles*] pérdida *f* de tensión
2 (= *reduction in amount, intensity*) disminución *f*; **there must be no ~ of vigilance/discipline** no debe bajarse la guardia/relajarse la disciplina

slacker* [ˈslækər] N holgazán/ana *m/f*, vago/a *m/f*, gandul(a) *m/f*

slackly [ˈslæklɪ] ADV 1 (*lit*) [*hang*] flojamente
2 (*fig*) [*work*] sin poner cuidado, negligentemente

slackness [ˈslæknɪs] N 1 [*of rope etc*] flojedad *f*, lo flojo
2 [*of person*] (= *laxity*) descuido *m*, negligencia *f*; (= *laziness*) pereza *f*, vaguedad *f*
3 (*Comm*) flojedad *f*, inactividad *f*

slacks [slæks] NPL pantalones *mpl*

slag[1] [slæg] Ⓐ N (*Min*) escoria *f*
Ⓑ CPD ► **slag heap** N escorial *m*

slag[2]‡ [slæg] N (*Brit pej*) (= *slut*) puta* *f*, ramera *f*
► **slag off‡** VT + ADV (*esp Brit*) (= *criticize*) poner como un trapo*

slain [sleɪn] Ⓐ PP *of* **slay**
Ⓑ NPL **the ~** los caídos *mpl*

slake [sleɪk] VT 1 [+ *one's thirst*] apagar, aplacar
2 (*Chem*) [+ *lime*] apagar; **~d lime** cal *f* muerta

slalom [ˈslɑːləm] N eslálom *m*, slalom *m*

slam [slæm] Ⓐ N 1 [*of door*] portazo *m*; **to close the door with a ~** dar un portazo, cerrar la puerta de un portazo
2 (*Bridge*) slam *m*; **grand ~** gran slam *m*; **small ~** pequeño slam *m*
Ⓑ VT 1 (= *strike*) **to ~ the door** dar un portazo, cerrar (la puerta) de un portazo; **to ~ sth shut** cerrar algo de golpe; **to ~ sth (down) on the table** dejar de golpe algo sobre la mesa, estampar algo sobre la mesa; **to ~ on the brakes** dar un frenazo; **he ~med the ball into the net** disparó la pelota a la red
2 (*) (= *criticize*) vapulear, criticar severamente
3 (*) (= *defeat*) cascar*, dar una paliza a*
4 (‡) **to get ~med** agarrarse una buena curda *or* melopea*
Ⓒ VI 1 [*door*] cerrarse de golpe, cerrarse de un portazo; **the door ~med shut** *or* **to** la puerta se cerró de golpe *or* de un portazo
2 **to ~ into/against sth** estrellarse contra algo
► **slam down** VT + ADV **to ~ sth down on the table** dejar de golpe algo sobre la mesa, estampar algo sobre la mesa

slammer‡ [ˈslæmər] N trena‡ *f*, talego‡ *m*

slander [ˈslɑːndər] Ⓐ N (*gen*) calumnia *f*; (*Jur*) difamación *f*; **they have been spreading ~s about the company** han estado levantando calumnias sobre la empresa; **to sue sb for ~** demandar a algn por difamación
Ⓑ VT (*gen*) calumniar; (*Jur*) difamar; **they have ~ed my name/reputation** han deshonrado mi nombre/han manchado mi reputación

slanderer [ˈslɑːndərər] N calumniador(a) *m/f*, difamador(a) *m/f*

slanderous [ˈslɑːndərəs] ADJ calumnioso, difamatorio

slanderously [ˈslɑːndərəslɪ] ADV calumniosamente

slang [slæŋ] Ⓐ N (*gen*) argot *m*, jerga *f*; [*of a group, trade etc*] jerga *f*; **to talk ~** hablar en argot *or* jerga; **that word is ~** esa palabra es del argot
Ⓑ ADJ argótico, jergal; **~ word** palabra *f* del argot, palabra *f* argótica *or* jergal
Ⓒ VT (*) (= *insult, criticize*) poner verde a, injuriar; **a ~ing match** una disputa a voces

slangily* [ˈslæŋɪlɪ] ADV **to talk ~** hablar con mucho argot *or* mucha jerga

slangy* [ˈslæŋɪ] ADJ (*compar* **slangier**; *superl* **slangiest**) [*person*] que usa mucho argot, que usa mucha jerga; [*style etc*] argótico, jergal

slant [slɑːnt] Ⓐ N 1 (*gen*) inclinación *f*, sesgo *m*; (= *slope*) pendiente *f*, cuesta *f*; **to be on the ~** estar inclinado, estar sesgado
2 (*fig*) (= *point of view*) punto *m* de vista, interpretación *f*; **what is your ~ on this?** ¿cuál es su punto de vista sobre esto?, ¿cómo interpreta usted esto?; **to get a ~ on a topic** pedir pareceres sobre un asunto; **the situation is taking on a new ~** la situación está tomando un nuevo giro
Ⓑ VT inclinar, sesgar; **to ~ a report** (*fig*) enfocar una cuestión de manera parcial
Ⓒ VI inclinarse, sesgarse; **the light ~ed in at the window** la luz entraba oblicuamente por la ventana

slant-eyed [ˈslɑːntˈaɪd] ADJ de ojos almendrados

slanting [ˈslɑːntɪŋ] ADJ inclinado, sesgado

slantwise [ˈslɑːntwaɪz] ADJ oblicuamente, al sesgo

slap [slæp] Ⓐ N palmada *f*, manotada *f*; **a ~ on the back** un espaldarazo; **to give sb a ~ on the back** (*fig*) felicitar a algn; **a ~ in the face** una bofetada, un bofetón; (*fig*) un desaire; **they were having a bit of the old ~ and tickle*** los dos se estaban sobando; **to give sb a ~ on the wrist** (*fig*) dar un tirón de orejas a algn
Ⓑ ADV (*) de lleno; **he ran ~ into a tree** dio de lleno contra un árbol; **it fell ~ in the middle** cayó justo en el medio
Ⓒ VT 1 (= *strike*) dar manotadas a; (*once*) dar una manotada a; (*in the face*) abofetear, dar una bofetada a; **to ~ sb's face** ◊ **~ sb in the face** dar una bofetada a algn, abofetear a algn; **she ~ped the little boy's leg** ◊ **she ~ped the little boy on the leg** le dio al niño un cachete en la pierna; **to ~ sb on the back** dar a algn una palmada en la espalda; **to ~ sb down** (*fig*) bajarle los humos a algn; **to ~ one's knees** palmotearse las rodillas; **to ~ one's thighs** darse palmadas en los muslos; **to ~ sb's wrist** (*fig*) dar un tirón de orejas a algn
2 (= *put*) **he ~ped the book on the table** tiró *or* arrojó el libro sobre la mesa; **the judge ~ped £100 on the fine** el juez aumentó la multa en 100 libras; **they've ~ped another storey on the house** han añadido un piso a la casa (como si tal cosa); **she ~ped on some make-up** se maquilló a la carrera; **to ~ paint on sth** pintar algo a brochazos
Ⓓ EXCL ¡zas!

slap-bang* [ˈslæpˈbæŋ] ADV (*Brit*) justo, exactamente

slapdash [ˈslæpdæʃ] ADJ, **slap-happy** [ˈslæphæpɪ] ADJ descuidado, chapucero

slapper‡ [ˈslæpər] N (*Brit*) putilla‡ *f*

slapstick [ˈslæpstɪk] N (*also* **~ comedy**) bufonada *f*

slap-up* [ˈslæpʌp] ADJ (*Brit*) **~ meal** banquete *m*, comilona *f*

slash [slæʃ] Ⓐ N 1 (*gen*) tajo *m*; (*with knife*) cuchillada *f*; (*with machete*) machetazo *m*; (*with razor*) navajazo *m*
2 (*Typ*) barra *f* oblicua
3 (*esp Brit‡*) **to go for a ~** ◊ **have a ~** cambiar el agua al canario‡
Ⓑ VT 1 (= *cut*) (*with knife etc*) acuchillar; (*with razor*) hacer un tajo a; [+ *tyre*] rajar; **to ~ one's wrists** cortarse las venas (*de la muñeca*)
2 (= *cut down*) [+ *trees*] talar; **~ and burn agriculture** agricultura *f* de rozas y quema
3 (= *reduce*) [+ *price*] reducir, rebajar; [+ *estimate etc*] reducir radicalmente; [+ *text*] cortar; **"prices slashed"** "grandes rebajas"
4 (*) (= *condemn*) atacar, criticar severamente
Ⓒ VI **to ~ at sb** tirar tajos a algn, tratar de acuchillar a algn

slasher film* [ˈslæʃəfɪlm], **slasher movie*** [ˈslæʃəˌmuːvɪ] N película *f* de casquería* (*con muchos degüellos*)

slashing [ˈslæʃɪŋ] ADJ [*attack etc*] fulminante

slat [slæt] N 1 (*wooden*) tablilla *f*, listón *m*
2 [*of blind*] lama *f*

slate [sleɪt] Ⓐ N 1 (= *substance*) pizarra *f*; (= *tile*) teja *f* de pizarra; **put it on the ~** (*Brit**) apúntalo en mi cuenta; **to wipe the ~ clean** (*fig*) hacer borrón y cuenta nueva
2 (*US Pol*) lista *f* de candidatos
Ⓑ ADJ (= *made of slate*) de pizarra; (*in colour*) color pizarra
Ⓒ VT 1 [+ *roof*] empizarrar
2 (*) (= *criticize*) vapulear, criticar duro
3 (*US Pol*) [+ *candidate*] nombrar
4 (*US*) anunciar; **it is ~d to start at nine** según el programa comienza a las nueve, deberá comenzar a las nueve
Ⓓ CPD ► **slate pencil** N pizarrín *m* ► **slate quarry** N pizarral *m* ► **slate roof** N empizarrado *m*

slate-blue [ˈsleɪtˈbluː] ADJ de color azul pizarra

slate-coloured, **slate-colored** (*US*) [ˈsleɪtˌkʌləd] ADJ color pizarra

slate-grey [ˌsleɪtˈgreɪ] Ⓐ ADJ de color gris pizarra
Ⓑ N gris *m* pizarra

slater [ˈsleɪtər] N pizarrero/a *m/f*

slatted [ˈslætɪd] ADJ de tablillas, hecho de listones

slattern [ˈslætən] N mujer *f* dejada, mujer *f* sucia, pazpuerca *f*

slatternly [ˈslætənlɪ] ADJ sucio, puerco, desaseado

slaty [ˈsleɪtɪ] ADJ (*in appearance, texture etc*) parecido a pizarra, pizarroso; (*in colour*) color pizarra

slaughter [ˈslɔːtər] Ⓐ N [*of animals*] matanza *f*, sacrificio *m*; [*of persons*] matanza *f*, carnicería *f*; **the ~ on the roads** el gran número de muertes en las carreteras; **the Slaughter of the Innocents** la Degollación de los Inocentes; **like a lamb to the ~** como borrego al

matadero; **there was great ~** hubo gran mortandad
Ⓑ VT [1] (= *kill*) [+ *animals*] matar, sacrificar; [+ *person, people*] matar brutalmente
[2] (*Sport etc**) (= *beat*) dar una paliza a*
slaughterer ['slɔːtərəʳ] N jifero/a *m/f*, matarife *mf*
slaughterhouse ['slɔːtəhaʊs] N (*pl* **slaughterhouses**) matadero *m*
slaughterman ['slɔːtəmən] N (*pl* **slaughtermen**) jifero *m*, matarife *m*
Slav [slɑːv] Ⓐ ADJ eslavo Ⓑ N eslavo/a *m/f*
slave [sleɪv] Ⓐ N esclavo/a *m/f*; **to be a ~ to sth** (*fig*) ser esclavo de algo; **to be a ~ to tobacco** ser esclavo del tabaco; **to be a ~ to duty** ser esclavo del deber
Ⓑ VI **to ~ (away) at sth/at doing sth** trabajar como un negro en algo/haciendo algo
Ⓒ CPD ► **slave driver** N negrero/a *m/f*; (*fig*) tirano/a *m/f* ► **slave labour** N (= *work*) trabajo *m* de esclavos; (= *persons*) esclavos *mpl* ► **slave trade** N trata *f* de esclavos, comercio *m* de esclavos, tráfico *m* de esclavos ► **slave trader** N traficante *mf* en esclavos
slaver[1] ['slævəʳ] Ⓐ N baba *f* Ⓑ VI babear
slaver[2] ['sleɪvəʳ] N (= *ship*) barco *m* negrero; (= *person*) traficante *mf* en esclavos
slavery ['sleɪvərɪ] N esclavitud *f*
slavey* ['sleɪvɪ] N fregona *f*
Slavic ['slɑːvɪk] Ⓐ ADJ eslavo
Ⓑ N (*Ling*) eslavo *m*
slavish ['sleɪvɪʃ] ADJ servil, de esclavo
slavishly ['sleɪvɪʃlɪ] ADV servilmente
slavishness ['sleɪvɪʃnɪs] N servilismo *m*
Slavonic [slə'vɒnɪk] Ⓐ ADJ eslavo
Ⓑ N eslavo *m*
slaw [slɔː] N (*US*) ensalada *f* de col
slay [sleɪ] (*pt* **slew**; *pp* **slain**) VT [1] (*poet*) (= *kill*) matar [2] (*) hacer morir de risa*; **this will ~ you** esto os hará morir de risa*; **you ~ me!** (*iro*) ¡qué divertido!
slayer ['sleɪəʳ] N asesino/a *m/f*
SLD N ABBR (*Brit Pol*) = **Social and Liberal Democrats**
sleaze* ['sliːz] N, **sleaziness*** ['sliːzɪnɪs] N [1] (= *sordidness*) sordidez *f*, asco *m*; (= *filth*) desaseo *m*, desaliño *m* [2] (*Pol*) (= *corruption*) corrupción *f*
sleazy ['sliːzɪ] ADJ (*compar* **sleazier**; *superl* **sleaziest**) (= *sordid*) [*place*] sórdido, asqueroso; (= *filthy*) [*person*] desaseado, desaliñado; (= *corrupt*) [*deal etc*] poco limpio, sucio
sled [sled] N, VTI = **sledge**[2]
sledge[1] [sledʒ] N = **sledgehammer**
sledge[2] [sledʒ] Ⓐ N trineo *m*
Ⓑ VI ir en trineo
Ⓒ VT transportar por trineo, llevar en trineo
sledgehammer ['sledʒˌhæməʳ] N almádena *f*
sleek [sliːk] Ⓐ ADJ (*compar* **sleeker**; *superl* **sleekest**) [*hair, fur*] lustroso; [*person*] (*of general appearance*) impecable; (*in manner*) zalamero, meloso; [*boat, car*] de líneas puras; [*animal*] gordo y de buen aspecto
Ⓑ VT **to ~ one's hair down** alisarse el pelo
sleekly ['sliːklɪ] ADV [*smile, reply*] zalameramente
sleekness ['sliːknɪs] N [*of hair, fur, animal*] lustre *m*; [*of person's appearance*] pulcritud *f*; [*of car*] pureza *f* de líneas
sleep [sliːp] (*vb: pt, pp* **slept**) Ⓐ N [1] (= *rest*) sueño *m*; **lack of ~** falta *f* de sueño; **I need some ~** necesito dormir; **to drop off to ~** quedarse dormido; **he fell into a deep ~** se quedó profundamente dormido; **I couldn't get to ~** no podía dormirme *or* conciliar el sueño; **to go to ~** [*person*] dormirse, quedarse dormido; (= *limb*) dormirse; **to have a ~** dormir; **to have a good night's ~** dormir bien (durante) toda la noche; **to have a little ~** dormir un rato, descabezar un sueño; **I shan't lose any ~ over it** eso no me va a quitar el sueño; **to put sb to ~** [+ *patient*] dormir a algn; **to put an animal to ~** (*euph*) (= *kill*) sacrificar un animal; **to send sb to ~** (= *bore*) dormir a algn; **to talk in one's ~** hablar en sueños; **to walk in one's ~** pasearse dormido; (*habitually*) ser sonámbulo; **she walked downstairs in her ~** estando dormida bajó la escalera; **I didn't get a wink of ~ all night** no pegué ojo en toda la noche; ✦**IDIOM to ~ the ~ of the just** dormir a pierna suelta
[2] (*) (*in eyes*) legañas *fpl*
Ⓑ VT [1] (= *accommodate*) **we can ~ four** hay cama para cuatro; **can you ~ all of us?** ¿hay cama(s) para todos nosotros?
[2] (= *rest*) dormir; **I only slept a couple of hours** sólo dormí un par de horas; **to ~ the hours away** pasar las horas durmiendo
Ⓒ VI dormir; **I couldn't ~ last night** anoche no pude dormir; **to ~ deeply** dormir profundamente *or* a pierna suelta; **to ~ heavily** (*habitually*) tener el sueño pesado; (*on particular occasion*) dormir profundamente; **to ~ lightly** (*habitually*) tener el sueño ligero; **she was ~ing lightly** no estaba profundamente dormida; **to ~ on sth** (*fig*) consultar algo con la almohada; **to ~ out** (= *not at home*) dormir fuera de casa; (= *in open air*) dormir al aire libre, pasar la noche al raso; **to ~ soundly** dormir profundamente *or* a pierna suelta; **he was ~ing soundly** estaba profundamente dormido; **he slept through the alarm clock** no oyó el despertador; **I slept through till the afternoon** dormí hasta la tarde; **~ tight!** ¡que duermas bien!, ¡que descanses!; **to ~ with sb** (*euph*) (= *have sex*) acostarse con algn; ✦**IDIOM to ~ like a log** *or* **top** *or* **baby** dormir como un tronco; *see also* **rough B**
►**sleep around*** VI + ADV irse a la cama con cualquiera
►**sleep away** VT + ADV **to ~ the morning away** pasarse la mañana durmiendo
►**sleep in** VI + ADV (*deliberately*) dormir hasta tarde; (*accidentally*) quedarse dormido
►**sleep off** VT + ADV **to ~ off a big dinner** dormir hasta que baje una cena grande; **she's ~ing off the effects of the drug** duerme hasta que desaparezcan los efectos de la droga; **to ~ it off*** ◊ **~ off a hangover** dormir la mona*, dormir la curda*
►**sleep over** VI + ADV pasar la noche
►**sleep together** VI + ADV [1] (= *share a room or bed*) dormir juntos
[2] (= *have sex*) acostarse juntos
sleeper ['sliːpəʳ] N [1] (= *person*) durmiente *mf*
[2] (*fig*) (= *spy*) *espía emplazado en un objetivo, pero sin misión concreta o que aún no es operativo*; **to be a heavy/light ~** tener el sueño pesado/ligero; **to be a good/poor ~** dormir bien/mal
[3] (*Brit Rail*) (*on track*) traviesa *f*, durmiente *m*; (= *berth*) litera *f*; (= *compartment*) camarín *m*, alcoba *f*; (= *coach*) coche-cama *m*
[4] (*esp Brit*) (= *earring*) arete *m*
[5] (*US*) (*for baby*) pijama *m* de niño
sleepily ['sliːpɪlɪ] ADV soñolientamente; **"yes," she said ~** —sí —dijo adormilado *or* soñoliento
sleepiness ['sliːpɪnɪs] N [1] [*of person*] somnolencia *f*
[2] [*of town, village*] tranquilidad *f*; (*pej*) sopor *m* (*pej*)
sleeping ['sliːpɪŋ] Ⓐ ADJ dormido; **Sleeping Beauty** la bella durmiente; ✦**PROV let ~ dogs lie** más vale no meneallo
Ⓑ N sueño *m*, el dormir; **between ~ and waking** a duermevela
Ⓒ CPD ► **sleeping bag** N (*camper's*) saco *m* de dormir; (*baby's*) pelele *m* ► **sleeping car** N (*Rail*) coche-cama *m* ► **sleeping draught** N soporífero *m* ► **sleeping partner** N socio/a *m/f* comanditario/a ► **sleeping pill** N somnífero *m* ► **sleeping policeman** N (*Aut*) banda *f* sonora ► **sleeping quarters** NPL dormitorio *msing* ► **sleeping sickness** N encefalitis *f* letárgica ► **sleeping tablet** N = **sleeping pill**
sleepless ['sliːplɪs] ADJ [*person*] insomne; **many ~ nights** muchas noches en blanco *or* sin dormir; **to have a ~ night** pasar la noche en blanco *or* sin dormir
sleeplessness ['sliːplɪsnɪs] N insomnio *m*
sleepover ['sliːpəʊvəʳ] N **we're having a ~ at Fiona's** pasamos la noche en casa de Fiona; **can I have a ~ on Friday?** ¿puedo invitar a mis amigos a pasar la noche el viernes?
sleep-talk ['sliːptɔːk] VI (*US*) hablar estando dormido
sleepwalk ['sliːpˌwɔːk] VI ser sonámbulo, pasearse dormido
sleepwalker ['sliːpˌwɔːkəʳ] N sonámbulo/a *m/f*
sleepwalking ['sliːpˌwɔːkɪŋ] N sonambulismo *m*
sleepwear ['sliːpwɛəʳ] N ropa *f* de dormir
sleepy ['sliːpɪ] ADJ (*compar* **sleepier**; *superl* **sleepiest**) [1] (= *drowsy*) [*person, voice*] soñoliento; **to be** *or* **feel ~** tener sueño; **I began to feel ~** me empezó a entrar sueño, me entró sueño; **she came in looking very ~** entró con cara de sueño
[2] (= *quiet*) [*place*] tranquilo; (*pej*) soporífero; **a ~ little village** un pueblecito tranquilo; **a ~ summer's afternoon** una soporífera tarde de verano
sleepyhead ['sliːpɪhed] N dormilón/ona *m/f*
sleet [sliːt] Ⓐ N aguanieve *f*, cellisca *f*
Ⓑ VI **it was ~ing** caía aguanieve *or* cellisca
sleeve [sliːv] Ⓐ N [1] [*of garment*] manga *f*; **to roll up one's ~s** arremangarse; ✦**IDIOMS to have sth up one's ~** tener algo en reserva; **to laugh up one's ~** reírse para su capote
[2] [*of record*] funda *f*
[3] (*Mech*) manguito *m*, enchufe *m*
Ⓑ CPD ► **sleeve notes** NPL (*Brit Mus*) *texto de la carátula de un disco*
sleeved [sliːvd] ADJ con mangas
-sleeved [sliːvd] ADJ (*ending in compounds*) con mangas …; **long-sleeved** con mangas largas
sleeveless ['sliːvlɪs] ADJ sin mangas
sleigh [sleɪ] Ⓐ N trineo *m*
Ⓑ VI, VT = **sledge**[2]
Ⓒ CPD ► **sleigh bell** N cascabel *m* ► **sleigh ride** N **to go for a ~ ride** ir a pasear en trineo
sleight [slaɪt] N **~ of hand** prestidigitación *f*, juegos *mpl* de manos
slender ['slendəʳ] ADJ [1] [*person*] (= *thin*) delgado, fino; (= *slim and graceful*) esbelto; [*waist, neck, hand*] delgado
[2] (*fig*) [*resources*] escaso; [*hope etc*] lejano, remoto; **by a ~ majority** por escasa mayoría
slenderize ['slendəraɪz] VT (*US*) adelgazar
slenderly ['slendəlɪ] ADV **she is ~ built** es delgada *or* esbelta; **~ made** de construcción delicada
slenderness ['slendənɪs] N [1] [*of person, waist, hand*] delgadez *f*
[2] [*of resources*] escasez *f*; [*of hope etc*] lo lejano, lo remoto

slept [slept] PT, PP of **sleep**

sleuth*† [sluːθ] N (*hum*) detective *mf*, sabueso *mf*

slew¹ [sluː] (*also* **to ~ round**) Ⓐ VT torcer; **to ~ sth to the left** torcer algo a la izquierda; **to be ~ed*** tener una buena curda *or* melopea*
Ⓑ VI torcerse

slew² [sluː] PT of **slay**

slew³ [sluː] N (*esp US*) (= *range*) montón* *m*

slice [slaɪs] Ⓐ N [1] [*of bread*] rebanada *f*; [*of salami, sausage*] loncha *f*, raja *f*; [*of cheese, ham*] loncha *f*; [*of beef, lamb etc*] tajada *f*; [*of lemon, cucumber, pineapple*] rodaja *f*; [*of cake, pie*] trozo *m*
[2] (*fig*) (= *portion*) parte *f*; **it affects a large ~ of the population** afecta a buena parte *or* a un amplio sector de la población; **a ~ of life** un trozo de la vida tal como es; **a ~ of the profits** una participación (en los beneficios)
[3] (= *utensil*) pala *f*
[4] (*Sport*) pelota *f* cortada; (*Golf*) golpe *m* con efecto a la derecha
Ⓑ VT [1] (= *cut into slices*) [+ *bread*] rebanar; [+ *salami, sausage, ham, cheese*] cortar en lonchas; [+ *beef, lamb*] cortar en tajadas; [+ *lemon, cucumber, pineapple*] cortar en rodajas; [+ *cake, pie*] partir en trozos
[2] (= *cut*) cortar; **to ~ sth in two** cortar algo en dos; **to ~ sth open** abrir algo de un tajo
[3] (*Sport*) [+ *ball*] dar efecto a, cortar; (*Golf*) golpear oblicuamente (a derecha)

►**slice off** VT + ADV cortar

►**slice through** VI + PREP cortar, partir

►**slice up** VT + ADV cortar (*en rebanadas etc*)

sliced [slaɪst] ADJ [*bread*] rebanado, en rebanadas; [*lemon*] en rodajas; **it's the best thing since ~ bread*** (*hum*) es la octava maravilla (del mundo)

slicer ['slaɪsəʳ] N máquina *f* de cortar

slick [slɪk] Ⓐ ADJ (*compar* **slicker**, *superl* **slickest**) [1] (*pej*) (= *superficial, glib*) hábil; **he's too ~ for me** es demasiado hábil para mi gusto
[2] (= *polished, skilful*) impecable; **a ~ performance** una actuación impecable; **be ~ about it!** ¡date prisa!
Ⓑ N **oil ~** (*large*) marea *f* negra; (*small*) mancha *f* de petróleo, capa *f* de petróleo (en el agua)
Ⓒ VT alisar; **to ~ down one's hair** alisarse el pelo; **to ~ o.s. up** acicalarse

slicker ['slɪkəʳ] N [1] (= *person*) embaucador(a) *m/f*, tramposo/a *m/f*; **city ~*** capitalino/a* *m/f*
[2] (*US*) (= *coat*) = **oilskins**

slickly ['slɪklɪ] ADV [1] (*pej*) (= *superficially, glibly*) hábilmente
[2] (= *skilfully*) impecablemente

slickness ['slɪknɪs] N [1] (*pej*) (= *superficiality, glibness*) habilidad *f*, maña *f*
[2] (= *skill, efficiency*) habilidad *f*, destreza *f*

slid [slɪd] PT, PP of **slide**

slide [slaɪd] (*vb: pt, pp* **slid**) Ⓐ N [1] (*in playground, swimming pool*) tobogán *m*
[2] (= *act of sliding*) deslizamiento *m*; (*by accident*) resbalón *m*
[3] (= *landslide*) corrimiento *m* de tierras, desprendimiento *m*
[4] (= *fall*) (*in share prices*) baja *f*, bajón* *m*; **the ~ into chaos/debt** la caída en el caos/en la deuda
[5] (*in microscope*) portaobjetos *m inv*, platina *f*
[6] (*Phot*) (= *transparency*) diapositiva *f*, filmina *f*
[7] (*also* **hair ~**) (*Brit*) pasador *m*
[8] (*Mus*) [*of trombone*] vara *f*; (*for guitar*) cuello *m* de botella, slide *m*
Ⓑ VI [1] (= *glide*) deslizarse; (= *slip*) resbalar; **they were sliding across the floor/down the banisters** se deslizaban por el suelo/por la barandilla; **the drawer ~s in and out easily** el cajón se abre y se cierra suavemente; **the lift doors slid open** las puertas del ascensor se abrieron; **I slid into/out of bed** me metí en/me levanté de la cama sigilosamente; **she slid into her seat** se dejó deslizar en su asiento; **a tear slid down his cheek** una lágrima se deslizó por su mejilla; **the book slid off my knee** el libro se me resbaló de la rodilla; ♦**IDIOM to let things ~** dejar que las cosas se vengan abajo; **these last few months he's let everything ~** estos últimos meses se ha desentendido de todo
[2] (= *decline*) **the economy is sliding into recession** la economía está cayendo en la recesión; **the shares slid 12 points** las acciones bajaron 12 puntos
Ⓒ VT **he slid his hands into his pockets** metió las manos en los bolsillos; **she slid a hand along his arm** le deslizó una mano por el brazo; **he slid the plate across the table** hizo deslizar el plato al otro lado de la mesa; **she slid the door open** corrió la puerta para abrirla; **she slid the key into the keyhole** deslizó la llave en el ojo de la cerradura
Ⓓ CPD ► **slide guitar** N guitarra *f* con cuello de botella, guitarra *f* con slide ► **slide-magazine** N (*Phot*) cartucho *m or* guía *f* para diapositivas ► **slide projector** N (*Phot*) proyector *m* de diapositivas ► **slide rule** N regla *f* de cálculo ► **slide show** N (*Phot*) exposición *f* de diapositivas

slideholder ['slaɪd,həʊldəʳ] N portadiapositiva *m*

sliding ['slaɪdɪŋ] ADJ [*part*] corredizo; [*door, seat*] corredero; **~ roof** techo *m* corredizo, techo *m* de corredera; **~ scale** escala *f* móvil

slight [slaɪt] Ⓐ ADJ (*compar* **slighter**, *superl* **slightest**) [1] (= *small, minor*) [1·1] [*difference, change, increase, improvement*] ligero, pequeño; [*injury, problem, exaggeration*] pequeño; [*accent, movement*] ligero; [*breeze*] suave; [*smile, pain*] leve; **after a ~ hesitation, he agreed** después de vacilar ligeramente, accedió; **the chances of him winning are very ~** tiene muy pocas posibilidades de ganar; **the wall is at a ~ angle** la pared está ligeramente inclinada; **to have a ~ cold** tener un pequeño resfriado, estar un poco resfriado; **to walk with a ~ limp** cojear ligeramente; **to have a ~ temperature** tener un poco de fiebre; *see also* **second 5.1**
[1·2] **the ~est: it doesn't make the ~est bit of difference** no importa en lo más mínimo; **without the ~est hesitation** sin dudarlo ni un momento; **I haven't the ~est idea** no tengo ni la más remota idea; **not in the ~est** en absoluto; **nobody showed the ~est interest** nadie mostró el menor interés; **he takes offence at the ~est thing** se ofende por la menor cosa *or* por cualquier nimiedad
[2] (= *slim*) [*figure, person*] delgado, menudo; **to be of ~ build** ser de constitución delgada *or* menuda
[3] (*frm*) (= *insignificant*) [*book, piece of music*] de poca envergadura; **a book of very ~ scholarship** un libro de poca erudición
Ⓑ N (*frm*) desaire *m*; **this is a ~ on all of us** es un desaire para todos nosotros
Ⓒ VT (*frm*) [+ *person*] desairar a, hacer un desaire a; [+ *work, efforts*] menospreciar, despreciar; **he felt that he had been ~ed** sintió que le habían desairado, sintió que le habían hecho un desaire

slighting ['slaɪtɪŋ] ADJ despreciativo, menospreciativo

slightingly ['slaɪtɪŋlɪ] ADV con desprecio

slightly ['slaɪtlɪ] ADV [1] (= *a little*) [*different, uneasy, deaf, damp, damaged*] ligeramente, un poco; [*rise, fall, improve*] ligeramente, levemente, un poco; [*change, cool, rain*] ligeramente, un poco; **~ better** algo mejor, un poco mejor; **he hesitated ever so ~** vaciló apenas un poco; **she was ~ injured** resultó levemente herida; **~ less** un poco menos; **he looks ~ like James Dean** guarda un ligero parecido con James Dean, se parece un poco a James Dean; **~ more** un poco más; **"do you know him?" — "only ~"** —¿lo conoces? —sólo un poco; **it smells ~ of vanilla** huele un poco a vainilla, tiene un ligero olor a vainilla
[2] (= *slenderly*) **~ built** delgado, menudo, de constitución delgada *or* menuda

slightness ['slaɪtnɪs] N [1] [*of difference, change, improvement, increase*] insignificancia *f*; [*of injury, problem*] levedad *f*, poca importancia *f*; [*of accent*] lo poco marcado; [*of movement*] lo leve
[2] (= *slimness*) delgadez *f*, lo menudo

slim [slɪm] Ⓐ ADJ (*compar* **slimmer**, *superl* **slimmest**) [1] [*figure, person*] (= *slender*) delgado, fino; (= *elegant*) esbelto; [*waist, neck, hand*] delgado; **to get ~** adelgazar
[2] (*fig*) [*resources*] escaso; [*evidence*] insuficiente; [*hope etc*] lejano; **his chances are pretty ~** sus posibilidades son bastante limitadas; **by a ~ majority** por escasa mayoría
[3] (= *thin*) [*book, volume, wallet*] fino, delgado
Ⓑ VI adelgazar; **I'm trying to ~** estoy intentando adelgazar; **I'm ~ming** estoy haciendo régimen, estoy a régimen
Ⓒ VT adelgazar

►**slim down** Ⓐ VT + ADV [1] (= *make slender*) adelgazar
[2] (*fig*) **~med down** [+ *business, industry*] reconvertido, saneado
Ⓑ VI + ADV bajar de peso, adelgazar

slime [slaɪm] N (*in pond*) cieno *m*, fango *m*; [*of snail*] baba *f*

sliminess ['slaɪmɪnɪs] N [1] [*of substance*] viscosidad *f*; [*of snail*] lo baboso
[2] [*of person*] zalamería *f*

slimline ['slɪm,laɪn] ADJ [1] [*drink*] light *inv*; [*food*] reductivo, que no engorda
[2] [*body, person*] esbelto, delgadísimo; [*screen, calculator*] extraplano; [*fridge, washing machine*] de diseño estrecho; [*book, diary*] finísimo

slimmer ['slɪməʳ] N persona *f* que está a dieta

slimming ['slɪmɪŋ] Ⓐ ADJ [*dress, skirt etc*] que adelgaza; **~ diet** régimen *m* (para adelgazar); **to be on a ~ diet** seguir un régimen para adelgazar, estar a dieta; **to eat only ~ foods** comer solamente cosas que no engordan
Ⓑ N adelgazamiento *m*
Ⓒ CPD ► **slimming aid** N (= *food*) (producto *m*) adelgazante *m*

slimness ['slɪmnɪs] N delgadez *f*

slimy ['slaɪmɪ] ADJ (*compar* **slimier**, *superl* **slimiest**) limoso [1] [*substance*] viscoso; [*snail*] baboso
[2] (*Brit*) (*fig*) [*person*] adulón, zalamero

sling [slɪŋ] (*vb: pt, pp* **slung**) Ⓐ N [1] (= *weapon*) honda *f*
[2] (*Med*) cabestrillo *m*; **to have one's arm in a ~** llevar el brazo en cabestrillo; ♦**IDIOM to have one's ass in a ~** (*esp US***) estar con el culo a rastras*, tener la soga al cuello*
[3] (*Naut*) eslinga *f*
[4] (*for rifle etc*) portafusil *m*
Ⓑ VT [1] (= *throw*) arrojar, lanzar, echar; **to ~ sth over** *or* **across one's shoulder** lanzar algo al hombro; **with a rifle slung across his**

shoulder con un fusil en bandolera; **to ~ sth over to sb** tirar algo a algn
[2] (= *throw away*) tirar, botar (*LAm*)
[3] (= *hang*) colgar, suspender
[4] (*Naut*) eslingar

►**sling away*** VT + ADV (= *throw away*) echar, tirar, botar (*LAm*)

►**sling out*** VT + ADV [1] (= *throw away*) [+ *rubbish*] echar, tirar, botar (*LAm*)
[2] (= *throw out*) [+ *person*] echar, poner de patitas en la calle*

slingshot [ˈslɪŋʃɒt] N [1] (= *weapon*) honda *f*; (= *shot*) hondazo *m*
[2] (*US*) (= *catapult*) tirador *m*, tirachinas *m inv*

slink [slɪŋk] (*pt, pp* **slunk**) VI **to ~ away** ◊ **~ off** escabullirse, zafarse

slinky* [ˈslɪŋkɪ] ADJ (*compar* **slinkier**; *superl* **slinkiest**) [*clothes*] ajustado, pegado al cuerpo; [*movement*] sensual; [*walk*] sinuoso, ondulante

slip [slɪp] Ⓐ N [1] (= *slide*) resbalón *m*; ✦***IDIOM*** **to give sb the ~** escabullirse *or* zafarse de algn, dar esquinazo a algn
[2] (= *mistake*) error *m*, equivocación *f*; **I must have made a ~ somewhere** debo de haberme equivocado en algo, debo de haber cometido un error en algún sitio; **a ~ of the pen/tongue** un lapsus calami/linguae; ✦***PROV*** **there's many a ~ 'twixt cup and lip** de la mano a la boca desaparece la sopa, del dicho al hecho va mucho trecho; *see also* **Freudian C**
[3] (= *fall*) bajada *f*
[4] (= *undergarment*) combinación *f*, enagua† *f*; (*full length*) viso *m*; (= *pillowcase*) funda *f*
[5] (= *receipt*) (*in filing system*) ficha *f*; **I wrote the number on a ~ of paper** escribí el número en un papelito *or* un trocito de papel; *see also* **betting B**, **deposit C**, **pay D**, **paying-in slip**
[6] (= *landslide*) corrimiento *m* de tierras, desprendimiento *m*
[7] (*Cricket*) (*usu pl*) *la posición posterior derecha del receptor (si el bateador es diestro) ocupada por los defensores de campo en un partido de críquet*
[8] **slips** (*Theat*) **the ~s** la galería
[9] [*of person*] **a ~ of a boy/girl** un chiquillo/una chiquilla
[10] (*in pottery*) *arcilla que se ha mezclado con agua hasta estar cremosa*
[11] (*Bot*) esqueje *m*
[12] (*Naut*) grada *f*
Ⓑ VI [1] (= *slide, shift*) resbalar; **she ~ped and broke her ankle** (se) resbaló y se rompió el tobillo; **my foot ~ped** se me fue el pie; **the knife ~ped and I cut my hand** se me fue el cuchillo y me hice un corte en la mano; **the glass ~ped from her hand** el vaso se le fue *or* se le resbaló de la mano; **the clutch ~s** el embrague patina; **the knot has ~ped** el nudo se ha corrido; **we let the game ~ through our fingers** dejamos que el partido se nos escapara *or* se nos fuera de las manos
[2] (= *move quickly*) **to ~ into bed** meterse en la cama; **he ~ped into his bathrobe** se puso el albornoz; **to ~ out of a dress** quitarse un vestido; **I soon ~ped back into the routine** enseguida volví a adaptarme a la rutina; **I ~ped downstairs to fetch it** bajé a traerlo rápidamente
[3] (= *move imperceptibly*) pasar desapercibido; **he managed to ~ through the enemy lines** consiguió pasar desapercibido por las líneas enemigas; **he ~ped out of the room while my back was turned** salió sigilosamente de la habitación mientras estaba de espaldas; *see also* **net¹ A1**
[4] (= *decline*) [*shares, currency*] bajar; **shares ~ped to 63p** las acciones bajaron a 63 peniques; **to ~ into a coma** caer en coma; **you're ~ping** (*hum*) estás decayendo; **he soon ~ped back into his old ways** al poco tiempo volvió a las andadas
[5] (= *become known*) **he let (it) ~ that he was a Democrat** dejó escapar que era demócrata; **she let ~ the names of the people involved** dejó escapar los nombres de las personas involucradas
Ⓒ VT [1] (= *move quickly and smoothly*) pasar, deslizar; **he ~ped an arm around her waist** le pasó *or* deslizó el brazo por la cintura; **~ a knife round the edges of the tin** pasar un cuchillo por el borde del molde; **I ~ped a note under his door** deslicé *or* le pasé una nota por debajo de la puerta; **to ~ a coin into a slot** introducir una moneda en una ranura
[2] (= *move imperceptibly*) **he ~ped his hand into her bag** le metió disimuladamente la mano en el bolso; **to ~ sth to sb** pasarle disimuladamente algo a algn; **he ~ped the waiter a fiver** le pasó disimuladamente un billete de cinco libras al camarero
[3] (= *escape from*) **the dog ~ped its collar** el perro se soltó del collar; **to ~ anchor** levar anclas; **one or two facts may have ~ped my memory** puede que algún que otro dato se me haya olvidado; **I meant to do it but it ~ped my mind** lo quise hacer pero se me olvidó *or* se me pasó; **the ship could ~ its moorings** al barco podrían soltársele las amarras
[4] (*Med*) **he's ~ped a disc** tiene una hernia de disco
[5] (*Aut*) [+ *clutch*] soltar
[6] (*Knitting*) [+ *stitch*] pasar (sin hacer)
Ⓓ CPD ► **slip road** N (*on motorway*) vía *f* de acceso ► **slip stitch** N (*Knitting*) punto *m* sin hacer

►**slip away** VI + ADV [1] (*also* **~ off**) [*person*] escabullirse, escurrirse
[2] (= *fade*) **he felt his strength ~ping away** sentía que las fuerzas se le iban *or* se le escapaban
[3] (= *pass by*) [*time, opportunity*] = **slip by**

►**slip by** VI + ADV [*time*] pasar; **to let an opportunity ~ by** dejar pasar *or* escapar una oportunidad

►**slip down** VI + ADV [1] [*food, drink*] **this wine ~s down a treat** este vino sienta de maravilla
[2] (= *go quickly*) **I'll just ~ down and get it** bajo un momento y lo traigo
[3] (= *fall*) [*object*] caerse; **she had ~ped down in her chair** se había dejado caer en su silla

►**slip in** Ⓐ VT + ADV [+ *comment, word*] incluir
Ⓑ VI + ADV (= *sneak in*) entrar desapercibido; (= *enter quickly*) entrar deprisa *or* rápidamente

►**slip off** Ⓐ VT + ADV [+ *clothes, shoes, ring*] quitarse
Ⓑ VI + ADV = **slip away**

►**slip on** VT + ADV [+ *clothes, shoes, ring*] ponerse

►**slip out** VI + ADV [*person*] salir un momento; **to ~ out (to the shops)** salir un momento (a las tiendas); [*remark, secret*] **I didn't mean to say it — it just ~ped out** no quería decirlo, pero se me escapó

►**slip past** VI + ADV = **slip by**

►**slip up** VI + ADV (= *make a mistake*) equivocarse; (= *commit a faux pas*) cometer un desliz, meter la pata*

slipcase [ˈslɪpkeɪs] N estuche *m*

slipcovers [ˈslɪpˌkʌvəz] NPL (*US*) fundas *fpl* que se pueden quitar

slipknot [ˈslɪpnɒt] N nudo *m* corredizo

slip-on [ˈslɪpɒn] ADJ **~ shoes** zapatos *mpl* sin cordones

slipover [ˈslɪpəʊvəʳ] N pullover *m* sin mangas

slippage [ˈslɪpɪdʒ] N (= *slip*) deslizamiento *m*; (= *loss*) pérdida *f*; (= *shortage*) déficit *m*; (= *delay*) retraso *m*

slipped [ˈslɪpt] ADJ **~ disc** hernia *f* discal, vértebra *f* dislocada

slipper [ˈslɪpəʳ] N [1] (*for foot*) zapatilla *f*, pantufla *f* (*esp LAm*); **a pair of ~s** unas zapatillas
[2] (*Tech*) zapata *f*, patín *m*

slippery [ˈslɪpərɪ] ADJ [1] (*lit*) [*mud, ground, surface*] resbaladizo, escurridizo; [*hands, skin*] resbaladizo; [*object, fish*] escurridizo; ✦***IDIOM*** **to be on a ~ slope** estar en terreno resbaladizo
[2] (*fig*) (*pej*) [*person*] (= *evasive*) escurridizo; (= *unreliable*) poco de fiar; ✦***IDIOM*** **he's as ~ as they come** *or* **as an eel** tiene más conchas que un galápago

slippy* [ˈslɪpɪ] ADV (*Brit*) **to be ~** ◊ **look ~ about it** darse prisa, menearse; **look ~!** ¡menearse!; **we shall have to look ~** tendremos que darnos prisa

slipshod [ˈslɪpʃɒd] ADJ descuidado, chapucero

slipstream [ˈslɪpstriːm] N estela *f*

slip-up [ˈslɪpʌp] N (= *mistake*) error *m*, desliz *m*, metedura *f* de pata*

slipway [ˈslɪpweɪ] N gradas *fpl*

slit [slɪt] (*vb: pt, pp* **slit**) Ⓐ N [1] (= *opening*) abertura *f*, hendidura *f*; (= *cut*) corte *m*; **to make a ~ in sth** hacer un corte en algo
[2] (*in dress etc*) raja *f*
[3] (**) (= *vagina*) coño** *m*
Ⓑ VT cortar, abrir; **to ~ a sack open** abrir un saco con un cuchillo; **to ~ sb's throat** cortarle el pescuezo a algn

slit-eyed [ˌslɪtˈaɪd] ADJ de ojos rasgados

slither [ˈslɪðəʳ] VI deslizarse; **to ~ down a rope** deslizarse por una cuerda; **to ~ down a slope** ir rodando por una pendiente; **to ~ about on ice** ir resbalando sobre el hielo

sliver [ˈslɪvəʳ] N lonja *f*, tajada *f*; [*of wood*] astilla *f*

Sloane Ranger* [ˌsləʊnˈreɪndʒəʳ] N niño/a *m/f* bien (londinense)*

SLOANE RANGER

El término **Sloane Ranger** *o* **Sloane** *se usa para referirse a los jóvenes de clase alta que viven en las zonas más refinadas de Londres, como por ejemplo Chelsea o Kensington, y que visten ropa muy cara de estilo campero. Los* **Sloane** *hablan con un acento típico de su clase, tienen, en general, ideas conservadoras y le dan mucha importancia al rango social y a la apariencia. Este término fue acuñado por un escritor de moda en los años 70 y se usa en la actualidad con un tono despectivo para referirse a las personas con valores superficiales. La expresión proviene de un juego de palabras hecho con* **Lone Ranger** *(el Llanero Solitario) y el nombre de una zona elegante del centro de Londres,* **Sloane Square**.

slob* [slɒb] N vago/a *m/f*, dejado/a *m/f*

slobber [ˈslɒbəʳ] Ⓐ VI babear; **to ~ over** besuquear; (*fig*) caerse la baba por
Ⓑ N baba *f*

slobbery [ˈslɒbərɪ] ADJ [*kiss*] mojado, baboso; [*person*] sensiblero, tontamente sentimental

sloe [sləʊ] Ⓐ N (= *fruit*) endrina *f*; (= *tree*) endrino *m*
Ⓑ CPD ► **sloe gin** N licor *m* de endrinas

slog [slɒg] Ⓐ N **it was a ~** me costó trabajo; **it's a hard ~ to the top** cuesta trabajo llegar a la cumbre
Ⓑ VI [1] (= *work*) afanarse, sudar tinta; **to ~**

away at sth afanarse por hacer algo
[2] (= *walk etc*) caminar trabajosamente, avanzar trabajosamente; **we ~ged on for eight kilometres** seguimos la marcha otros ocho kilómetros más
Ⓒ VT [+ *ball, opponent*] golpear
►**slog out** VT + ADV **to ~ it out** (*fighting*) luchar hasta el fin, seguir luchando; (*arguing*) discutir sin ceder terreno; (*working*) aguantarlo todo, no cejar

slogan ['sləʊgən] N slogan *m*, lema *m*

slogger ['slɒgəʳ] N trabajador(a) *m/f*

sloop [slu:p] N balandra *f*

slop [slɒp] Ⓐ VI (*also* **~ over**) [*water, tea etc*] derramarse, verterse; **the water was ~ping about in the bucket** el agua se agitaba en el cubo; **to ~ about in the mud** chapotear en el lodo
Ⓑ VT (= *spill*) derramar, verter; (= *tip carelessly*) derramar, tirar; **you've ~ped paint all over the floor** has salpicado todo el suelo de pintura, has puesto el suelo perdido de pintura
Ⓒ **slops** NPL (= *food*) gachas *fpl*; (= *liquid waste*) agua *fsing* sucia, lavazas *fpl*; [*of tea*] posos *mpl* de té; [*of wine*] heces *fpl*
Ⓓ CPD ► **slop basin** N recipiente *m* para agua sucia; (*at table*) taza *f* para los posos del té ► **slop pail** N cubeta *f* para agua sucia

slope [sləʊp] Ⓐ N (*up*) cuesta *f*, pendiente *f*; (*down*) declive *m*, bajada *f*; [*of hill*] falda *f*, ladera *f*; **the street was on a ~** la calle era en cuesta; **the car got stuck on a ~** el coche se atascó en una cuesta; **there is a ~ down to the town** la ciudad está bajando una cuesta *or* ladera; **on the eastern ~** en la vertiente este; **a ~ of ten degrees** una pendiente del diez por ciento
Ⓑ VI inclinarse; **to ~ forwards** estar inclinado hacia delante; **to ~ up/away** *or* **down** subir/bajar en pendiente; **the garden ~s down to the stream** el jardín baja hacia el arroyo
►**slope off*** VI + ADV escabullirse, largarse, rajarse (*LAm*)

sloping ['sləʊpɪŋ] ADJ inclinado, al sesgo

sloppily ['slɒpɪlɪ] ADV [1] (= *carelessly*) en forma descuidada; **to dress ~** vestirse sin atención
[2] (= *sentimentally*) en forma sentimentaloide *or* ñoña

sloppiness ['slɒpɪnɪs] N [1] (= *carelessness*) [*of work*] descuido *m*, lo descuidado; [*of dress, appearance*] desaliño *m*, desaseo *m*
[2] (= *sentimentality*) sentimentalismo *m*, sensiblería *f*

sloppy ['slɒpɪ] ADJ (*compar* **sloppier**, *superl* **sloppiest**) [1] (= *runny*) [*food*] aguado
[2] (= *careless*) [*work etc*] descuidado; [*appearance, dress*] desaliñado, desaseado; [*thinking*] poco riguroso
[3] (= *sentimental*) sentimentaloide, ñoño
[4] (= *wet*) mojado; **a big ~ kiss** un besazo con todas las babas

slops [slɒps] NPL *see* **slop C**

slop shop* ['slɒpʃɒp] N (*US*) bazar *m* de ropa barata, tienda *f* de pacotilla

slosh* [slɒʃ] Ⓐ VT [1] (= *splash*) [+ *liquid*] **to ~ some water over sth** echar agua sobre algo
[2] (= *hit*) [+ *person*] pegar
Ⓑ VI **to ~ about in the puddles** chapotear en los charcos; **the water was ~ing about in the pail** el agua chapoteaba en el cubo

sloshed* [slɒʃt] ADJ **to be ~** tener una buena curda *or* melopea*; **to get ~** agarrarse una buena curda *or* melopea*

slot [slɒt] Ⓐ N [1] (= *hole*) (*in machine etc*) ranura *f*; (= *groove*) muesca *f*; **to put a coin in the ~** meter una moneda en la ranura
[2] (= *space*) (*in timetable, programme etc*) hueco *m*; (= *advertising slot*) cuña *f* (publicitaria); (= *job slot*) vacante *f*
Ⓑ VT **to ~ in(to)** [+ *object*] introducir *or* meter en; (*fig*) [+ *activity, speech*] incluir (en); **to ~ a part into another part** encajar una pieza en (la ranura de) otra pieza; **to ~ sth into place** colocar algo en su lugar; **we can ~ you into the programme** te podemos dar un espacio en el programa, te podemos incluir en el programa
Ⓒ VI introducirse; **it doesn't ~ in with the rest** no encaja con los demás; **it ~s in here** entra en esta ranura, encaja aquí
Ⓓ CPD ► **slot machine** N (*at funfair*) tragaperras *f inv*; (= *vending machine*) máquina *f* expendedora ► **slot meter** N contador *m*

sloth [sləʊθ] N [1] (= *idleness*) pereza *f*, indolencia *f*
[2] (*Zool*) oso *m* perezoso

slothful ['sləʊθfʊl] ADJ perezoso, vago, flojo

slouch [slaʊtʃ] Ⓐ N [1] **to walk with a ~** andar con un aire gacho
[2] (*) **he's no ~** (*in skill*) no es ningún principiante; (*at work*) no es ningún vago; **he's no ~ in the kitchen** tiene buena mano para cocina
Ⓑ VI (*walking*) andar desgarbado; **to ~ in a chair** repantigarse en un sillón; **he was ~ed over his desk** estaba inclinado sobre su mesa de trabajo en postura desgarbada
Ⓒ CPD ► **slouch hat** N sombrero *m* flexible
►**slouch about, slouch around** VI + ADV [1] andar desgarbado; (*aimlessly*) andar de un lado para otro (sin saber qué hacer)
[2] (*fig*) (= *laze around*) gandulear, golfear
►**slouch along** VI + ADV = **slouch about, slouch around 1**
►**slouch off** VI + ADV irse cabizbajo, alejarse con un aire gacho

slough¹ [slʌf] Ⓐ N [1] (*Zool*) camisa *f*, piel *f* vieja (*que muda la serpiente*)
[2] (*Med*) escara *f*
Ⓑ VT mudar, echar de sí; (*fig*) deshacerse de, desechar
Ⓒ VI desprenderse, caerse
►**slough off** Ⓐ VT + ADV mudar, echar de sí; (*fig*) deshacerse de, desechar
Ⓑ VI + ADV desprenderse, caerse

slough² [slaʊ] N (= *swamp*) fangal *m*, cenagal *m*; (*fig*) abismo *m*; **the ~ of despond** el abatimiento más profundo, el abismo de la desesperación

Slovak ['sləʊvæk] Ⓐ ADJ eslovaco
Ⓑ N eslovaco/a *m/f*

Slovakia [sləʊ'vækɪə] N Eslovaquia *f*

Slovakian [sləʊ'vækɪən] ADJ eslovaco

sloven ['slʌvn] N (*in appearance*) persona *f* desgarbada, persona *f* desaseada; (*at work*) vago/a *m/f*

Slovene ['sləʊvi:n] Ⓐ ADJ esloveno
Ⓑ N esloveno/a *m/f*

Slovenia [sləʊ'vi:nɪə] N Eslovenia *f*

slovenliness ['slʌvnlɪnɪs] N [*of appearance*] desaseo *m*; [*of work*] chapucería *f*, descuido *m*

slovenly ['slʌvnlɪ] ADJ [*person*] descuidado; [*appearance*] desaliñado, desaseado; [*work*] chapucero, descuidado

slow [sləʊ] (*compar* **slower**, *superl* **slowest**) Ⓐ ADJ [1] (= *not speedy*) [*vehicle, music, progress, death, pulse*] lento; **putting them all in order is ~ work** es un trabajo lento ponerlos todos en orden; **this car is ~er than my old one** este coche corre menos que el que tenía antes; **he's a ~ eater** come despacio; **to be ~ in doing sth** tardar *or* (*LAm*) demorar en hacer algo; **she wasn't ~ in taking up their offer** no tardó en aceptar su ofrecimiento; **extra lessons for ~ learners** clases extra para alumnos con problemas de aprendizaje; **it has a ~ puncture** está perdiendo aire poco a poco; **he's a ~ reader** lee despacio; **after a ~ start, he managed to end up in third place** después de un comienzo flojo, consiguió llegar en tercer puesto; **to be ~ to do sth** tardar *or* (*LAm*) demorar en hacer algo; **they were ~ to act** tardaron en actuar; **he's ~ to learn** aprende lentamente, tarda mucho en aprender; **to be ~ to anger** tener mucho aguante; *see also* **going A1, mark² A6, uptake 1**
[2] [*clock, watch*] atrasado; **my watch is 20 minutes ~** mi reloj está 20 minutos atrasado
[3] (= *mentally sluggish*) torpe, lento; **he's a bit ~ at maths** es algo torpe para las matemáticas
[4] (= *boring, dull*) [*match, game, film, plot*] lento, pesado; [*party, evening*] pesado, aburrido; **business is ~** hay poco movimiento (en el negocio); **life here is ~** aquí se vive a un ritmo lento *or* pausado
[5] (*Culin*) **cook over a ~ heat** cocinar a fuego lento; **bake for two hours in a ~ oven** cocer dos horas en el horno a fuego lento
[6] (*Sport*) [*pitch, track, surface*] lento
[7] (*Phot*) [*film*] lento
Ⓑ ADV despacio, lentamente, lento; **I began to walk ~er and ~er** empecé a andar cada vez más despacio *or* lentamente *or* lento; **how ~ would you like me to play?** ¿cómo de lento le gustaría que tocara?; **to go ~** [*driver*] conducir despacio; (*in industrial dispute*) trabajar a ritmo lento, hacer huelga de celo (*Sp*)
Ⓒ VT (*also* **~ down, ~ up**) [+ *person*] retrasar; [+ *progress*] retrasar, disminuir el ritmo de; [+ *engine, machine*] reducir la marcha de; [+ *reactions*] entorpecer; [+ *economy*] ralentizar; [+ *development*] retardar; **he ~ed his car before turning in at the gate** redujo la marcha del coche antes de entrar por el portón; **they want to ~ the pace of reform** quieren reducir el ritmo de la reforma; **as she approached, she ~ed her pace** a medida que se acercaba, fue aminorando la marcha *or* fue aflojando el paso; **we ~ed our speed to 30 miles an hour** redujimos la velocidad a 30 millas por hora; **that car is ~ing (up** *or* **down) the traffic** aquel coche está entorpeciendo la circulación
Ⓓ VI [*vehicle, runner*] reducir la marcha; [*driver*] reducir la velocidad *or* la marcha; [*growth*] disminuir; [*breathing*] hacerse más lento; **production has ~ed to almost nothing** la producción ha bajado casi a cero; **he ~ed to a walk** aflojó la marcha y se puso a caminar; **the car ~ed to a stop** el coche redujo la marcha hasta detenerse; **the flow of refugees has ~ed to a trickle** el flujo de refugiados se ha reducido a un goteo
Ⓔ CPD ► **slow burn*** N (*US*) **he did a ~ burn** fue poniéndose cada vez más furioso ► **slow cooker** N olla *f* eléctrica de cocción lenta ► **slow fuse** N espoleta *f* retardada ► **slow handclap** N (*Brit*) (*by audience*) palmadas *fpl* lentas; **he was given a ~ handclap** recibió palmadas lentas ► **slow lane** N (*Brit Aut*) carril *m* de la izquierda; (*most countries*) carril *m* de la derecha ► **slow motion** N (*Cine*) **in ~ motion** a *or* (*LAm*) en cámara lenta; *see also* **slow-motion** ► **slow train** N (*Brit*) *tren que para en todas las estaciones*

►**slow down** Ⓐ VI + ADV [1] (= *go slower*) [*engine, vehicle, runner*] reducir la marcha; [*driver*]

reducir la velocidad *or* la marcha; **~ down, I can't keep up with you** (*to sb running*) no corras tanto, no puedo seguirte; (*to sb speaking*) no hables tan rápido, que no te sigo
[2] (= *work less*) **you must ~ down or you'll make yourself ill** tienes que aflojar el ritmo de vida o te pondrás enfermo
(B) VT + ADV [1] (= *reduce speed of*) [+ *vehicle*] reducir la velocidad de; **his injury ~ed him down** su lesión le restaba rapidez
[2] (= *cause delay to*) retrasar; **all these interruptions have ~ed us down** todas estas interrupciones nos han retrasado
►**slow off** VI + ADV = **slow D**
►**slow up** VI + ADV, VT + ADV = **slow down**

slow-acting [ˈsləʊˌæktɪŋ] ADJ de efecto retardado

slow-burning [ˈsləʊˈbɜːnɪŋ] ADJ que se quema lentamente; **~ fuse** espoleta *f* retardada

slowcoach* [ˈsləʊkəʊtʃ] N (*Brit*) (= *dawdler*) tortuga *f*

slowdown [ˈsləʊdaʊn] N [1] (= *reduction*) [*of productivity, growth*] disminución *f* del ritmo; [*of economy*] ralentización *f*
[2] (*US*) (= *go-slow*) huelga *f* de manos caídas, huelga *f* de celo (*Sp*)

slowing-down [ˈsləʊɪŋˈdaʊn] N [*of productivity, growth*] disminución *f* del ritmo; [*of economy*] ralentización *f*

slowly [ˈsləʊlɪ] ADV [1] (= *not quickly*) [*move*] lentamente, despacio; [*drive*] despacio; [*walk*] lentamente, despacio, con paso lento; [*say*] pausadamente, lentamente; [*nod*] lentamente
[2] (= *gradually*) poco a poco; **~ but surely he was killing himself** lenta pero inexorablemente estaba acabando con su vida; **she is recovering ~ but surely** se está recuperando de manera lenta pero positivamente

slow-mo*, **slomo*** [ˈsləʊməʊ] ADJ, N = **slow-motion**

slow-motion [ˈsləʊˈməʊʃən] (A) ADJ **~ film** película *f* a cámara lenta
(B) N **to show a film in ~** pasar una película a cámara lenta, pasar una película ralentizada

slow-moving [ˌsləʊˈmuːvɪŋ] ADJ [*film, play*] lento, de acción lenta; [*animal, person, vehicle*] lento

slowness [ˈsləʊnɪs] N [1] (= *lack of speed*) lentitud *f*; **he was criticized for his ~ to act** *or* **in acting** le criticaron por la lentitud con la que actuó
[2] (= *mental sluggishness*) torpeza *f*
[3] (= *dullness*) [*of plot, film, book, match*] lentitud *f*, pesadez *f*

slowpoke* [ˈsləʊˌpəʊk] N (*US*) = **slowcoach**

slow-witted [ˈsləʊˈwɪtɪd] ADJ torpe, lento

slowworm [ˈsləʊwɜːm] N lución *m*

SLR N ABBR (*Phot*) = **single lens reflex (camera)**

sludge [slʌdʒ] N (= *mud*) fango *m*, lodo *m*; (= *sediment*) residuos *mpl*; (= *sewage*) aguas *fpl* residuales

slue [sluː] VT, VI (*US*) = **slew**[1]

slug [slʌg] (A) N [1] (*Zool*) babosa *f*
[2] (= *bullet*) posta *f*
[3] (‡) (= *blow*) porrazo *m*; (*with fist*) puñetazo *m*; **a ~ of whisky** un trago de whisk(e)y
(B) VT (‡) pegar, aporrear
►**slug out** VT + ADV **to ~ it out (with sb)** (= *fight*) pegarse (con algn), aporrearse (con algn); (= *end argument*) resolver un asunto con los puños (con algn)

sluggard [ˈslʌgəd] N haragán/ana *m/f*

sluggish [ˈslʌgɪʃ] ADJ [1] (= *indolent*) perezoso, flojo
[2] (= *slow moving*) [*river, engine, car*] lento; [*business, market, sales*] inactivo; [*liver*] perezoso

sluggishly [ˈslʌgɪʃlɪ] ADV [1] (= *indolently*) perezosamente
[2] (= *slowly*) lentamente

sluggishness [ˈslʌgɪʃnɪs] N [1] (= *indolence*) pereza *f*
[2] (= *slowness*) lentitud *f*

sluice [sluːs] (A) N (= *gate*) esclusa *f*, compuerta *f*; (= *waterway*) canal *m*, conducto *m*; (= *barrier*) dique *m* de contención; **to give sth a ~ down** regar algo, echar agua sobre algo (para lavarlo)
(B) VT **to ~ sth down** *or* **out** regar algo, echar agua sobre algo (para lavarlo)

sluicegate [ˈsluːsgeɪt] N esclusa *f*, compuerta *f*

sluiceway [ˈsluːsweɪ] N canal *m*, conducto *m*

slum [slʌm] (A) N (= *area*) barrio *m* bajo, suburbio *m*, colonia *f* proletaria (*Mex*), barriada *f* (*Peru*); (= *house*) casucha *f*, tugurio *m*, chabola *f* (*Sp*); **the ~s** los barrios bajos, los suburbios; **they live in a ~** viven en una casucha *or* en un tugurio; **this house will be a ~ in ten years** dentro de diez años esta casa será una ruina; **they've made their house a ~** su casa es un desastre
(B) VT **to ~ it** (*esp Brit**) vivir como pobres; (= *live cheaply*) vivir muy barato
(C) VI **to ~** ◊ **go ~ming** visitar los barrios bajos
(D) CPD ► **slum area** N barrio *m* bajo ► **slum clearance** N deschabolización *f* ► **slum clearance programme** N programa *m* de deschabolización ► **slum dweller** N barriobajero/a *m/f* ► **slum dwelling** N tugurio *m*

slumber [ˈslʌmbəʳ] (A) N (= *sleep*) sueño *m*; (= *deep sleep*) sopor *m*; **slumbers** sueño *msing*; **my ~s were rudely interrupted** mis sueños fueron bruscamente interrumpidos
(B) VI dormir
(C) CPD ► **slumber wear** N (*Comm*) ropa *f* de dormir

slumberous, **slumbrous** [ˈslʌmbərəs] ADJ soñoliento; (*fig*) inactivo, inerte

slummy* [ˈslʌmɪ] ADJ muy pobre, sórdido

slump [slʌmp] (A) N (*gen*) baja *f* (repentina), bajón *m*; (*in production, sales*) caída *f*, baja *f*; (*economic*) depresión *f*; **the Slump** el crac; **the 1929 ~** la depresión de 1929, la crisis económica de 1929; **~ in prices** hundimiento *m* de los precios; **the ~ in the price of copper** la baja repentina del precio del cobre; **~ in morale** bajón *m* de moral
(B) VI [1] [*price etc*] hundirse; [*production, sales*] bajar, caer; (*fig*) [*morale etc*] desplomarse
[2] **to ~ into a chair** hundirse en una silla; **he ~ed to the floor** se desplomó al suelo; **he was ~ed over the wheel** se había caído encima del volante

slung [slʌŋ] PT, PP *of* **sling**

slunk [slʌŋk] PT, PP *of* **slink**

slur [slɜːʳ] (A) N [1] (= *stigma*) mancha *f*, calumnia *f*; **to cast a ~ on sb** manchar la reputación de algn; **it is no ~ on him to say that …** no es hacer un reparo a él decir que …, no es baldonarle decir que …
[2] (*Mus*) ligado *m*
(B) VT [1] [+ *word etc*] pronunciar mal, tragar
[2] (*Mus*) ligar
►**slur over** VI + PREP pasar por alto de, omitir, suprimir

slurp [slɜːp] (A) VT sorber ruidosamente
(B) VI sorber ruidosamente

slurred [slɜːd] ADJ [*pronunciation*] mal articulado, borroso

slurry [ˈslʌrɪ] N lodo *m* líquido; (*Agr*) estiércol *m* líquido

slush [slʌʃ] (A) N [1] (= *melting snow*) aguanieve *f*, nieve *f* medio derretida
[2] (= *mud*) fango *m*, lodo *m*
[3] (*) (= *bad poetry etc*) sentimentalismo *m*
(B) CPD ► **slush fund** N fondos *mpl* para sobornar

slushy [ˈslʌʃɪ] ADJ (*compar* **slushier**; *superl* **slushiest**) [1] [*snow*] medio derretido
[2] (*) [*poetry etc*] sentimentaloide, sensiblero

slut [slʌt] N (‡) (*immoral*) puta* *f*; (*dirty, untidy*) marrana *f*, guarra *f*

sluttish [ˈslʌtɪʃ] ADJ (= *dirty, untidy*) guarro, puerco

sly [slaɪ] (A) ADJ (*compar* **slyer**; *superl* **slyest**) [1] (= *wily*) [*person*] astuto, taimado; **he's a ~ one!** ¡es un zorro!
[2] (= *mischievous*) [*person*] pícaro, travieso; [*look, smile*] pícaro, malicioso
(B) N **on the ~*** a hurtadillas, a escondidas

slyboots [ˈslaɪˌbuːts] NSING taimado/a *m/f*

slyly [ˈslaɪlɪ] ADV [1] (= *cunningly*) con astucia, astutamente
[2] (= *mischievously*) [*smile, say*] pícaramente

slyness [ˈslaɪnɪs] N [1] (= *wiliness*) astucia *f*, lo taimado
[2] (= *mischievousness*) picardía *f*; (*pej*) malicia *f*

smack[1] [smæk] (A) VI **to ~ of** (= *taste of*) saber a, tener un saborcillo a; (*fig*) oler a; **the whole thing ~s of bribery** todo este asunto huele a corrupción; **it ~s of treachery to me** me huele *or* suena a traición
(B) N (= *taste*) sabor *m*, saborcillo *m*, dejo *m* (**of** a)

smack[2] [smæk] (A) N [1] (= *slap*) bofetada *f*, tortazo *m*; **to give a child a ~** dar una bofetada a *or* abofetear a un niño; **stop it or you'll get a ~** déjalo o te pego; ✦**IDIOM it was a ~ in the eye for them** (*esp Brit**) fue un golpe duro para ellos
[2] (= *sound*) sonido *m* de una bofetada *or* de un tortazo; **it hit the wall with a great ~** chocó contra la pared con un fuerte ruido
[3] (*) (= *kiss*) besazo *m*, besucón *m*
(B) VT (= *slap*) dar una bofetada a, abofetear; **she ~ed the child's bottom** le pegó al niño en el trasero *or* culo; **to ~ one's lips** relamerse, chuparse los labios; **he ~ed it on to the table** lo dejó en la mesa con un fuerte ruido, lo estampó encima de la mesa
(C) ADV **it fell ~ in the middle*** cayó justo en medio; **she ran ~ into the door** chocó contra la puerta, dio de lleno con la puerta
(D) EXCL ¡zas!

smack[3] [smæk] N (*Naut*) barca *f* de pesca

smack[4]‡ [smæk] N heroína *f*

smacker* [ˈsmækəʳ] N [1] (= *kiss*) besazo *m*, besucón *m*
[2] (= *blow*) golpe *m* ruidoso
[3] (*Brit*) (= *pound*) libra *f*; (*US*) (= *dollar*) dólar *m*

smacking [ˈsmækɪŋ] (A) ADJ **at a ~ pace** a gran velocidad, muy rápidamente
(B) N zurra *f*, paliza *f*; **to give sb a ~** dar una paliza a algn

small [smɔːl] (A) ADJ (*compar* **smaller**; *superl* **smallest**) [1] (= *not big*) [*object, building, room, animal, group*] pequeño, chico (*LAm*); (*in height*) bajo, pequeño, chaparro (*LAm*); [*family, population*] pequeño, poco numeroso; [*audience*] reducido, poco numeroso; [*stock, supply*] reducido, escaso; [*waist*] estrecho; [*clothes*] de talla pequeña; [*meal*] ligero; [*coal*] menudo; **the dress is too ~ for her** el vestido le viene pequeño *or* chico; **the ~er of the two** el menor (de los dos); **with a ~ "e"** con "e" minúscula; **to have a ~ appetite** no ser de mucho comer, comer poco; **to become ~er** = **to get** *or* **grow smaller**; **to break/cut sth up ~** romper algo en trozos pequeños/cortar algo en trocitos; **to get** *or* **grow ~er** [*income, difficulties, supply, population, amount*] disminuir, reducirse; [*object*] hacerse más pequeño; **mobile phones are getting ~er** los teléfonos móviles son cada vez más pequeños; **until the ~ hours** hasta altas horas de la noche; **to be ~ in size** [*country*] ser pequeño; [*animal, object*] ser de pequeño tamaño; [*room*] ser de dimensiones reducidas; **in ~ letters** en minúsculas; **this house makes the other one look ~** esta casa hace que la otra se quede pequeña; **to make o.s. ~** achicarse; **to make sth ~er** [+ *income, difficulties, supply, population, amount*] reducir algo; [+ *object, garment*] reducir algo de tamaño, hacer algo más pequeño; **the ~est room** (*euph, hum*) el excusado; ✦***IDIOM*** **to be ~ beer** *or* (*US*) **~ potatoes** ser poca cosa; **it was ~ beer compared to the money he was getting before** no era nada *or* era poca cosa comparado con lo que ganaba antes; *see also* **world A1**, **wee**[1]

[2] (= *minor*) [*problem, mistake, job, task*] pequeño, de poca importancia; [*contribution*] pequeño; [*difference, change, increase, improvement*] pequeño, ligero; **to start in a ~ way** empezar desde abajo

[3] (= *inconsequential*) **to feel ~** sentirse insignificante; **to make sb look ~** rebajar a algn; **she said in a ~ voice** dijo con un hilo de voz

[4] (= *young*) [*child, baby*] pequeño, chico (*esp LAm*); **when we were ~** cuando éramos pequeños *or* chicos

[5] (*frm*) (= *slight, scant*) poco; **to be ~ comfort** *or* **consolation (to sb)** servir de poco consuelo (a algn); **to be of ~ concern (to sb)** importar poco (a algn); **to have ~ hope of success** tener pocas esperanzas de éxito; **a matter of ~ importance** un asunto de poca importancia; *see also* **measure A6**, **wonder A2**

Ⓑ N [1] **the ~ of the back** la región lumbar

[2] **smalls** (*Brit**) (= *underwear*) ropa *fsing* interior *or* (*esp LAm*) íntima

Ⓒ ADV **don't think too ~** piensa más a lo grande; **try not to write so ~** intenta no escribir con una letra tan pequeña

Ⓓ CPD ► **small ad** N (*Brit*) anuncio *m* por palabras ► **small arms** NPL armas *fpl* ligeras de bajo calibre ► **small business** N pequeña empresa *f* ► **the small businessman** N el pequeño empresario ► **small capitals** NPL (*Typ*) (*also* **~ caps**) versalitas *fpl* ► **small change** N suelto *m*, cambio *m*, calderilla *f*, sencillo *m* (*LAm*), feria *f* (*Mex**) ► **small claims court** N tribunal *m* de instancia (*que se ocupa de asuntos menores*) ► **small end** N (*Aut*) pie *m* de biela ► **small fry*** N **to be ~ fry** ser de poca monta ► **small intestine** N intestino *m* delgado ► **small investor** N pequeño/a inversionista *mf* ► **small print** N letra *f* menuda ► **small screen** N pequeña pantalla *f*, pantalla *f* chica (*LAm*) ► **small talk** N charla *f*, charloteo* *m*; **to make ~ talk** charlar, charlotear*

small-boned [ˌsmɔːl'bəʊnd] ADJ de huesos pequeños

smallholder ['smɔːl,həʊldəʳ] N (*Brit*) cultivador(a) *m/f* de una granja pequeña, minifundista *mf*

smallholding ['smɔːl,həʊldɪŋ] N parcela *f*, minifundio *m*, chacra *f* (*S. Cone*)

> **SMALL**
>
> **Position of "pequeño"**
>
> • **Pequeño** usually follows the noun when making implicit or explicit comparison with something bigger:
>
> He picked out a small melon
> ***Escogió un melón pequeño***
> At that time, Madrid was a small city
> ***En aquella época Madrid era una ciudad pequeña***
>
> • When used more subjectively with no attempt at comparison, **pequeño** usually precedes the noun:
>
> But there's one small problem…
> ***Pero existe un pequeño problema…***
> She lives in the little village of La Granada
> ***Vive en el pequeño pueblo de La Granada***
>
> *For further uses and examples, see main entry.*

smallish ['smɔːlɪʃ] ADJ más bien pequeño, más bien chico

small-minded ['smɔːl'maɪndɪd] ADJ mezquino, de miras estrechas

small-mindedness ['smɔːl'maɪndɪdnɪs] N mezquindad *f*, estrechez *f* de miras

smallness ['smɔːlnɪs] N [1] [*of object, animal, room, hand, foot*] pequeñez *f*, lo chico (*LAm*); [*of income, sum, contribution*] lo pequeño; (*in height*) [*of person*] lo bajo, lo chaparro (*LAm*); [*of problem*] insignificancia *f*; [*of waist*] estrechez *f*; [*of group, population*] lo poco numeroso; [*of stock, supply*] lo reducido; [*of print, writing*] pequeñez *f*, lo pequeño, lo menudo

[2] (= *small-mindedness*) estrechez *f* de miras

smallpox ['smɔːlpɒks] N (*Med*) viruela *f*

small-scale ['smɔːl'skeɪl] ADJ (*gen*) en pequeña escala

small-time* ['smɔːl'taɪm] ADJ de poca categoría, de poca monta; **a ~ criminal** un delincuente menor

small-town ['smɔːl'taʊn] ADJ (*esp US*) provinciano, pueblerino

> **SMALL TOWN**
>
> *El término* **small town** *(ciudad pequeña) se usa en Estados Unidos para referirse a las localidades de menos de 10.000 habitantes. La palabra* **village** *(pueblo) no se suele usar por tener connotaciones del Viejo Continente o del Tercer Mundo. Los valores de estas ciudades pequeñas, que se ven como algo positivo, representan sobre todo la amabilidad, la honradez, la ayuda entre vecinos y el patriotismo, aunque a veces la expresión se usa en un sentido negativo, como por ejemplo cuando se habla de* **small-town attitudes** *(actitudes provincianas), haciendo referencia a las mentes estrechas o con prejuicios.*

smarm* [smɑːm] (*Brit*) Ⓐ VT **to ~ one's hair down** alisarse y fijarse el pelo Ⓑ VI dar coba*, hacer la pelota* Ⓒ N coba* *f*, zalamería *f*

smarmy* ['smɑːmɪ] ADJ (*compar* **smarmier**; *superl* **smarmiest**) (*Brit*) zalamero

smart [smɑːt] Ⓐ ADJ (*compar* **smarter**; *superl* **smartest**) [1] (= *elegant*) [*person, appearance, clothes, car, decor*] elegante; [*garden*] bien arreglado; [*house*] bien puesto; **to look ~** [*person*] estar elegante; [*restaurant, hotel*] ser elegante; [*home*] estar muy bien puesto

[2] (= *chic*) [*suburb, party, restaurant*] elegante; [*society*] de buen tono, fino; **the ~ set** la buena sociedad, la gente de buen tono

[3] (= *clever*) [*person*] listo, inteligente; [*idea*] inteligente, bueno; [*computer, bombs, missiles*] inteligente; **that was pretty ~ of you** ¡qué listo *or* astuto!; **that wasn't very ~** no ha sido una idea muy buena; **he was too ~ for me** era muy listo y me ganó la batalla; **~ work by the police led to an arrest** la inteligente labor de la policía condujo a un arresto; **the ~ money is on the French** la gente que entiende de apuesta por los franceses

[4] (*pej*) (= *cocky*) **don't get ~ with me!** ¡no te las des de listo conmigo!; **she's too ~ for her own good** se pasa de lista; **she's got a ~ answer to everything** tiene respuesta para todo

[5] (= *brisk*) [*pace, action*] rápido; **look ~ about it!** ¡date prisa!, ¡apúrate! (*LAm*); **give the nail a ~ tap** dale un golpe seco al clavo

Ⓑ VI [1] (= *sting*) [*wound, eyes*] escocer, picar, arder (*esp LAm*); [*iodine etc*] escocer; **my eyes are ~ing** me escuecen *or* me pican los ojos; **the smoke made his throat ~** el humo le irritó la garganta

[2] (*fig*) dolerse; **she's still ~ing from his remarks** todavía se duele *or* se resiente de sus comentarios; **to ~ under an insult** sentirse dolido por una injuria

Ⓒ N **smarts** (*US**) (= *brains*) cerebro *msing*; **to have the ~s to do sth** ser lo suficientemente inteligente como para hacer algo

Ⓓ CPD ► **smart Alec*** N sabelotodo* *mf*, sabihondo/a* *m/f* ► **smart bomb** N bomba *f* con mecanismo inteligente ► **smart card** N tarjeta *f* electrónica, tarjeta *f* inteligente ► **smart phone** N teléfono *m* inteligente

smart-arse* ['smɑːtɑːs], **smart-ass*** ['smɑːtæs] N sabelotodo* *mf*, sabihondo/a* *m/f*; **~ comments** comentarios *mpl* de sabelotodo

smarten ['smɑːtn] VT = **smarten up**

►**smarten up** Ⓐ VT + ADV arreglar; **to ~ o.s. up** arreglarse, adecentarse; **I must go and ~ myself up** tengo que ir a arreglarme *or* adecentarme un poco; **she has ~ed herself up a lot in the last year** durante el año pasado ha mejorado mucho de aspecto *or* se ha arreglado mucho; **to ~ up one's ideas** espabilarse

Ⓑ VI + ADV [*person*] arreglarse, adecentarse; [*town*] mejorar de aspecto

smartly ['smɑːtlɪ] ADV [1] (= *elegantly*) [*dressed, furnished*] con elegancia, elegantemente; **a ~ tailored suit** un traje de corte elegante [2] (= *cleverly*) inteligentemente [3] (= *briskly*) rápidamente; **we left pretty ~** salimos a toda prisa; **they marched him ~ off to the police station** lo llevaron sin más a la comisaría; **to tap sth ~** dar un golpe seco a algo

smartness ['smɑːtnɪs] N [1] [*of appearance*] (= *elegance*) elegancia *f*; (= *neatness*) lo bien arreglado; **~ is very important when you are going to an interview** la buena presencia es muy importante cuando se va a una entrevista

[2] (= *cleverness*) inteligencia *f*, agudeza *f*

[3] (= *briskness*) rapidez *f*

smarty* ['smɑːtɪ] N (*also* **~-pants**) sabelotodo* *mf*

smash [smæʃ] Ⓐ N [1] (= *breakage*) rotura *f*, quiebra *f* (*LAm*); (= *sound of breaking*) estruendo *m*; **the cup fell with a ~** la taza cayó con gran estruendo

[2] (= *collision*) choque *m*; **he died in a car ~** murió en un accidente de coche; **the 1969 rail ~** el accidente de ferrocarril de 1969

[3] (*Tennis, Badminton etc*) smash *m*, remate *m*, remache *m*

[4] (*Fin*) (= *bankruptcy*) quiebra *f*; (= *crisis*) crisis *f inv* económica; **the 1929 ~** la crisis de 1929

[5] (*) (= *success*) exitazo *m*

Ⓑ VT [1] (= *break*) romper, quebrar (*esp LAm*); (= *shatter*) hacer pedazos, hacer trizas; **they ~ed windows** rompieron ventanas; **I've ~ed my watch** he estropeado mi reloj; **when they ~ed the atom*** cuando desintegraron el átomo; **to ~ sth to pieces** *or* **bits** hacer pedazos *or* añicos algo; **he ~ed it against the wall** lo estrelló contra la pared; **the waves ~ed the boat on the rocks** las olas estrellaron el barco contra las rocas; **he ~ed his way out of the building** se escapó del edificio a base de golpes; **he ~ed his fist into Paul's face** le dio *or* pegó un fuerte puñetazo en la cara a Paul

[2] (= *wreck*) dar al traste con; (= *ruin*) arruinar, minar; **we will ~ this crime ring** acabaremos con esta banda de delincuentes

[3] (= *beat*) [+ *team, enemy, opponent*] aplastar; [+ *record etc*] pulverizar, batir

[4] (*Tennis, Badminton etc*) [+ *ball*] rematar, remachar

Ⓒ VI [1] (= *break*) romperse, hacerse pedazos, quebrarse (*esp LAm*); **the glass ~ed into tiny pieces** el vaso se rompió en pedazos

[2] (= *crash*) **the car ~ed into the wall** el coche se estrelló contra la pared

[3] (*Fin*) quebrar

Ⓓ ADV **to go ~ into sth** dar de lleno contra algo, dar violentamente contra algo

Ⓔ CPD ► **smash hit** N exitazo *m*

►**smash down** VT + ADV [+ *door*] echar abajo

►**smash in** VT + ADV [+ *door, window*] forzar; **to ~ sb's face in*** romperle la cara a algn

►**smash up*** VT + ADV [+ *car, person, place*] pulverizar, hacer pedazos; **he was all ~ed up in the accident** salió destrozado del accidente

smash-and-grab raid [ˈsmæʃənˈgræb,reɪd] N robo *m* relámpago (*con rotura de escaparate*)

smashed‡ [smæʃt] ADJ (= *drunk*) como una cuba*; (= *drugged*) flipado‡, colocado‡

smasher‡ [ˈsmæʃəʳ] N (*esp Brit*) cosa *f* estupenda; (= *esp girl*) bombón* *m*, guayabo* *m*; **she's a ~** está como un tren*; **it's a ~!** ¡es estupendo!

smashing* [ˈsmæʃɪŋ] ADJ estupendo (*Sp*), bárbaro, macanudo (*LAm*); **that's a ~ idea** me parece una idea estupenda; **we had a ~ time** lo pasamos estupendamente *or* de maravilla *or* (*S. Cone*) regio; **isn't it ~?** ¿es estupendo, no?

smash-up [ˈsmæʃʌp] N violenta colisión *f*, grave accidente *m* de tráfico

smattering [ˈsmætərɪŋ] N **to have a ~ of** tener cierta idea *or* algunas nociones de; **I have a ~ of Catalan** tengo cierta idea *or* algunas nociones de catalán

smear [smɪəʳ] Ⓐ N [1] (= *mark*) mancha *f*

[2] (*fig*) (= *libel*) calumnia *f*

[3] (*Med*) frotis *m*

Ⓑ VT [1] untar; **to ~ one's face with blood** untarse la cara de sangre; **to ~ wet paint** manchar la pintura fresca

[2] [+ *print, lettering etc*] borrar

[3] (*fig*) (= *libel*) calumniar, difamar; **to ~ sb as a traitor** tachar a algn de traidor; **to ~ sb because of his past** tachar a algn por su pasado

[4] (*US‡*) (= *defeat*) derrotar sin esfuerzo

Ⓒ VI [*paint, ink etc*] correrse

Ⓓ CPD ► **smear campaign** N campaña *f* de difamación ► **smear tactics** NPL tácticas *fpl* de difamación ► **smear test** N (*Med*) frotis *m*, citología *f*

smell [smel] (*vb: pt, pp* **smelled**, **smelt**) Ⓐ N [1] (= *sense*) olfato *m*; **to have a keen sense of ~** tener buen olfato, tener un buen sentido del olfato

[2] (= *odour*) olor *m*; **it has a nice ~** tiene un olor agradable, huele bien; **there's a ~ of gas/of burning** huele a gas/a quemado; **there was an unpleasant ~** había un olor desagradable; **it eliminates cooking ~s** elimina los olores de la cocina; **the sweet ~ of success** la seducción del éxito

[3] (= *sniff*) **let's have a ~** déjame olerlo, déjame que lo huela; **here, have a ~** huele esto

Ⓑ VT [1] (= *perceive odour*) oler; **I can ~ gas/burning** huele a gas/a quemado, hay olor a gas/a quemado; **I could ~ cigarettes on his breath** el aliento le olía a tabaco; **dogs can ~ fear** los perros pueden olfatear *or* oler el miedo

[2] (= *sniff*) [*person*] oler; [*animal*] olfatear, oler

[3] (*fig*) **he ~ed trouble** se olió problemas; **to ~ danger** olfatear el peligro; **the press ~ed a good story here** la prensa se olió que aquí había noticia; *see also* **rat A1**

Ⓒ VI [1] (= *emit odour*) oler; **it ~s good** huele bien; **that flower doesn't ~** esa flor no tiene olor; **it ~s damp in here** aquí huele a humedad; **to ~ like sth** oler a algo; **what does it ~ like?** ¿a qué huele?; **to ~ of sth** (*lit, fig*) oler a algo; **it ~s of garlic** huele a ajo; **it's beginning to ~ of a cover-up** está empezando a oler a encubrimiento; **if food ~s off, throw it away** si la comida huele mal *or* a pasada, tírela

[2] (= *smell bad*) oler; **that man ~s** ese hombre huele; **your feet ~** te huelen los pies; **her breath ~s** le huele el aliento

[3] (= *have sense of smell*) **since the operation she can't ~** desde que se operó ha perdido el sentido del olfato

[4] (= *sniff*) [*person*] olisquear; [*animal*] olfatear; **the dog ~ed at my shoes** el perro olfateó mis zapatos

►**smell out** VT + ADV [1] (= *find by scent*) [*dog*] olfatear

[2] (= *detect*) **she can always ~ out a bargain** siempre sabe oler *or* olfatear una ganga

[3] (= *cause to smell*) hacer oler mal; (*stronger*) apestar; **it's ~ing the room out** está haciendo oler mal el cuarto, está apestando el cuarto

smelliness [ˈsmelɪnɪs] N peste *f*, hediondez *f*

smelling bottle [ˈsmelɪŋ,bɒtl] N frasco *m* de sales

smelling salts [ˈsmelɪŋsɔːlts] NPL sales *fpl* aromáticas

smelly* [ˈsmelɪ] ADJ (*compar* **smellier**, *superl* **smelliest**) maloliente, apestoso; **the pub was dirty and ~** el pub era sucio y maloliente *or* apestoso; **it's ~ in here** aquí dentro huele mal *or* apesta; **he's got ~ feet** le huelen los pies

smelt¹ [smelt] PT, PP *of* **smell**

smelt² [smelt] VT fundir

smelt³ [smelt] N (= *fish*) eperlano *m*

smelter [ˈsmeltəʳ] N horno *m* de fundición

smelting [ˈsmeltɪŋ] Ⓐ N fundición *f*

Ⓑ CPD ► **smelting furnace** N horno *m* de fundición

smidgen, **smidgin** [ˈsmɪdʒən] N **a ~ of*** un poquito de, un poquitín de

smile [smaɪl] Ⓐ N sonrisa *f*; **... she said with a ~** ... dijo con una sonrisa, ... dijo sonriente *or* sonriendo; **to be all ~s** ser todo sonrisas; **her story brought a ~ to my face** su historia me alegró la cara; **to force a ~** forzar una sonrisa; **to give sb a ~** sonreír a algn; **he gave me a big ~** me sonrió de oreja a oreja; **come on, give me a ~!** ¡vamos, una sonrisa!; **she gave a wry ~** sonrió irónicamente; **with a ~ on one's lips** con una sonrisa en los labios; **he managed a ~** sonrió a duras penas; **his jokes failed to raise a ~** sus chistes no hicieron reír a nadie; **to wipe the ~ off sb's face** quitar a algn las ganas de reír

Ⓑ VI sonreír; **"yes" I said, smiling** —sí , dije sonriente *or* sonriendo; **to ~ at sb** sonreír a algn; **to ~ at sth** reírse de algo; **what are you smiling at?** ¿de qué te ríes?; **to ~ at danger** reírse del peligro; **she's had her problems but she always comes up smiling** ha tenido sus problemas, pero siempre se la ve sonriente; **to keep smiling** seguir con la sonrisa en los labios; **keep smiling!** ¡ánimo!; **fortune ~d on him** le sonrió la fortuna; **to ~ to o.s.** reírse por dentro *or* para sus adentros

Ⓒ VT **"of course!" she ~d** —por supuesto —dijo sonriente *or* sonriendo; **she ~d a faint smile** sonrió débilmente; **he ~d his thanks** dio las gracias sonriente *or* sonriendo

smiling [ˈsmaɪlɪŋ] ADJ sonriente

smilingly [ˈsmaɪlɪŋlɪ] ADV con una sonrisa

smirch [smɜːtʃ] VT (*liter*) mancillar, desdorar

smirk [smɜːk] Ⓐ N sonrisa *f* de satisfacción

Ⓑ VI sonreír de satisfacción

smirkingly [ˈsmɜːkɪŋlɪ] ADV con una sonrisa de satisfacción

smite [smaɪt] (*pt* **smote**; *pp* **smitten**) VT (*†† liter*) (= *strike*) golpear; (= *punish*) castigar; **my conscience smote me** me remordió la conciencia; *see also* **smitten**

smith [smɪθ] N herrero/a *m/f*

smithereens [,smɪðəˈriːnz] NPL **to smash sth to ~** hacer añicos *or* trizas algo; **it was in ~** estaba hecho añicos *or* trizas

> **SMITHSONIAN INSTITUTION**
>
> *La* **Smithsonian Institution**, *en Washington DC, es el complejo de museos más grande del mundo. Fue fundado por el Congreso en 1846 gracias a fondos donados por el científico inglés James Smithson (de ahí su nombre) y en la actualidad está patrocinado por el gobierno estadounidense como centro para la ciencia y el arte. Posee alrededor de cien millones de piezas y catorce museos, que incluyen el* **National Museum of American History**, *la* **National Gallery of Art** *y el* **National Portrait Gallery**. *También cuenta con un zoológico y lleva a cabo labores de investigación. A esta institución se la conoce como* **the nation's attic** *(la buhardilla de la nación).*

smithy [ˈsmɪðɪ] N herrería *f*, fragua *f*

smitten [ˈsmɪtn] Ⓐ PP *of* **smite**

Ⓑ ADJ **to be ~ (with sb)** estar locamente enamorado (de algn); **to be ~ with an idea** entusiasmarse por una idea; **to be ~ with flu** estar aquejado de gripe; **to be ~ with the plague** sufrir el azote de la peste, ser afligido por la peste; **to be ~ with remorse** remorderle a algn la conciencia; **I was ~ by the urge to run out of the house** me daban unas ganas tremendas de salir corriendo de la casa

smock [smɒk] Ⓐ N (*for artist*) bata *f*, guardapolvo *m*; (*for expectant mother*) bata *f* corta, tontón *m*

Ⓑ VT fruncir, adornar con frunces

smocking [ˈsmɒkɪŋ] N adorno *m* de frunces

smog [smɒg] N smog *m*, niebla *f* mezclada con humo

smoke [sməʊk] Ⓐ N [1] humo *m*; **cigarette ~** humo *m* de cigarrillos; **~ blue** azul *m* grisáceo; **~ grey** gris *m* humo; **to go up in ~** [*building*] quemarse (totalmente); [*plans*] quedar en agua de borrajas; [*hopes, money*] esfumarse; [*future*] malograrse; **the (Big) Smoke** (*Brit**) Londres; ♦**IDIOM** **~ and mirrors** (*esp*

US) artificios *mpl*; ✦*PROVS* **there's no ~ without fire** ◊ **where there's ~ there's fire** cuando el río suena, piedras *or* agua lleva
[2] (*) (= *cigarette*) pitillo* *m*, cigarrillo *m*, cigarro *m*; **I'm dying for a ~** tengo unas ganas locas de fumarme un pitillo* *or* un cigarrillo *or* un cigarro; **to have a ~** fumar(se) un pitillo* *or* un cigarrillo *or* un cigarro
[3] (*) (= *drugs*) hierba* *f*, maría* *f*
Ⓑ VT [1] [+ *cigarette, cigar, pipe*] fumar; **she ~d 60 a day** (se) fumaba 60 al día; **she wouldn't let him ~ his pipe** (*in general*) no le dejaba fumar en pipa; (*on one occasion*) no le dejaba fumarse su pipa
[2] (*Culin*) [+ *bacon, fish, cheese*] ahumar
Ⓒ VI [1] (= *emit smoke*) echar humo; **the chimney always ~d** la chimenea siempre estaba echando humo; **the chimney was smoking, so someone was home** salía humo de la chimenea, así que había alguien en casa
[2] [*person*] fumar; **do you ~?** ¿fumas?; **do you mind if I ~?** ¿le importa que fume?; **to ~ like a chimney*** fumar como un carretero *or* como una chimenea*
Ⓓ CPD ► **smoke alarm** N detector *m* de humo, alarma *f* contra incendios ► **smoke bomb** N bomba *f or* granada *f* de humo ► **smoke detector** N detector *m* de humo ► **smoke ring** N anillo *m or* aro *m* de humo; **to blow ~ rings** hacer anillos *or* aros de humo ► **smoke shop** N (*US*) estanco *m* ► **smoke signal** N señal *f* de humo

►**smoke out** VT + ADV (*lit*) [+ *animal, demonstrators*] hacer salir con humo; (*fig*) (= *expose*) poner al descubierto

smoked [sməʊkt] ADJ [*bacon, fish, cheese*] ahumado; **~ glass** cristal *m or* (*LAm*) vidrio *m* ahumado

smoke-dried ['sməʊkdraɪd] ADJ ahumado, curado al humo

smoke-filled ['sməʊkfɪld] ADJ lleno de humo

smokeless ['sməʊklɪs] ADJ **~ fuel** combustible *m* sin humo; **~ zone** zona *f* libre de humos

smoker ['sməʊkəʳ] N [1] (= *person*) fumador(a) *m/f*; **~'s cough** tos *f* de fumador; **I'm not a ~** no fumo; **to be a heavy ~** fumar mucho
[2] (= *railway carriage*) coche *m* de fumar, vagón *m* de fumar

smokescreen ['sməʊkskriːn] N (*lit, fig*) cortina *f* de humo; **to put up a ~** (*fig*) entenebrecer un asunto, enmarañar un asunto (*para despistar a la gente*)

smokestack ['sməʊkstæk] Ⓐ N chimenea *f*
Ⓑ CPD ► **smokestack industries** NPL industrias *fpl* con chimeneas

smoking ['sməʊkɪŋ] Ⓐ N **~ is bad for you** el fumar te perjudica; **~ or non-~?** ¿fumador o no fumador?; **to give up ~** dejar de fumar; **"no smoking"** "prohibido fumar"; **no ~ area** zona *f* de no fumadores
Ⓑ CPD ► **smoking car** N (*US*) coche *m* de fumadores ► **smoking compartment** N compartimento *m* de fumadores ► **smoking jacket** N batín *m* corto ► **smoking room** N sala *f* de fumadores

smoky ['sməʊkɪ] ADJ (*compar* **smokier**, *superl* **smokiest**) [*chimney, fire*] humeante, que humea; [*room, atmosphere*] lleno de humo; [*flavour, surface etc*] ahumado; **it's ~ in here** aquí hay mucho humo

smolder ['sməʊldəʳ] VI (*US*) = **smoulder**

smoldering ['sməʊldərɪŋ] ADJ (*US*) = **smouldering**

smooch* [smuːtʃ] VI besuquearse

smoochy* ['smuːtʃɪ] ADJ [*record, song etc*] sentimental

smooth [smuːð] Ⓐ ADJ (*compar* **smoother**, *superl* **smoothest**) [1] (= *not rough*) [*surface, stone*] liso; [*skin*] suave, terso; [*hair*] suave; [*road*] llano, parejo (*esp LAm*); [*sea, lake*] tranquilo, en calma; **the flagstones had been worn ~ by centuries of use** las losas estaban lisas por siglos de uso; **for a ~er shave, use Gillinson** para un afeitado apurado, use Gillinson; ✦*IDIOMS* **as ~ as a baby's bottom** suave como la piel de un bebé; **to be as ~ as silk** *or* **satin** ser suave como la seda; **the sea was as ~ as glass** la mar estaba lisa como un espejo
[2] (= *not lumpy*) [*paste, sauce*] sin grumos
[3] (= *not jerky*) [*running of engine, take-off, landing, motion*] suave, parejo (*esp LAm*); [*crossing, flight*] bueno; [*breathing*] regular; **extra roads to ensure the ~ flow of traffic** más carreteras para asegurar un tráfico fluido; **he lit his pipe without interrupting the ~ flow of his speech** encendió su pipa sin interrumpir el hilo de su narración; **this car gives a very ~ ride** en este coche se viaja muy cómodo
[4] (= *trouble-free*) [*transition, takeover*] sin problemas, poco conflictivo; [*journey*] sin problemas, sin complicaciones; **the ~ passage of a bill through Parliament** la sosegada discusión de un proyecto de ley en el parlamento; **the ~ running of a company** la fluida gestión de una empresa
[5] (= *mellow*) [*flavour, whisky, cigar, voice, sound*] suave
[6] (= *polished*) [*style*] fluido, suave; [*performance*] fluido
[7] (*pej*) (= *slick*) [*person*] zalamero; [*manner*] experimentado; **beneath the ~ exterior, he's rather insecure** bajo ese aire experimentado, es bastante inseguro; **the ~ talk of the salesman** la labia del vendedor; **to be a ~ talker** tener pico de oro; *see also* **operator 2**
Ⓑ VT [1] (= *flatten*) (*also* **~ down**) [+ *hair, clothes, sheets, piece of paper*] alisar; **she ~ed her skirt** se alisó la falda; **to ~ one's hair back from one's forehead** alisarse el pelo retirándolo de la frente; *see* **flat A2**
[2] (= *polish*) (*also* **~ down**) [+ *wood, surface*] lijar, pulir
[3] (= *soften*) [+ *skin*] suavizar; **to ~ away wrinkles** hacer desaparecer las arrugas, eliminar las arrugas
[4] (= *make easy*) [+ *transition*] facilitar; [+ *process*] suavizar; **to ~ the path or way for sth/sb** allanar el camino para algo/a algn; **to ~ relations** limar asperezas
[5] (= *rub*) **to ~ cream into one's skin** untarse crema en la piel
Ⓒ N *see* **rough C3**

►**smooth down** VT + ADV [1] (= *flatten*) [+ *hair, sheet, covers, clothes*] alisar; [+ *surface, road*] allanar, igualar
[2] (= *polish*) [+ *wood, surface*] lijar, pulir
[3] (= *pacify*) [+ *person*] aplacar

►**smooth out** VT + ADV [1] (= *flatten*) [+ *fabric, creases, dress*] alisar; [+ *road surface*] aplanar, allanar
[2] (*fig*) [+ *problem*] solucionar, resolver; [+ *difficulties*] allanar; [+ *anxieties*] disipar; **to ~ things out** limar las asperezas

►**smooth over** VT + ADV [1] (*lit*) [+ *soil*] allanar; [+ *wood*] lijar, pulir
[2] (*fig*) [+ *difficulties*] allanar; [+ *differences*] resolver; **to ~ things over** limar las asperezas

smooth-faced ['smuːð'feɪst] ADJ [*man*] (*after shaving*) bien afeitado; [*boy*] (*too young to shave*) imberbe, barbilampiño

smoothie‡ ['smuːðɪ] N (*pej*) zalamero/a *m/f*

smoothing-iron ['smuːðɪŋ,aɪən] N plancha *f*

smoothly ['smuːðlɪ] ADV [1] (= *not jerkily*) [*drive, move, land, glide*] suavemente
[2] (= *with no trouble*) **everything went ~** todo fue muy bien, todo fue sobre ruedas; **the move to the new house went off ~** la mudanza a la otra casa transcurrió sin contratiempos, todo fue sobre ruedas cuando nos mudamos a la otra casa; **to run ~** [*engine*] funcionar muy bien; [*event*] transcurrir sin contratiempos *or* complicaciones *or* problemas; [*business, talks*] ir muy bien, marchar sobre ruedas*
[3] (*pej*) (= *slickly*) [*speak, talk*] con mucha labia

smoothness ['smuːðnɪs] N [1] [*of hair*] suavidad *f*; [*of skin*] suavidad *f*, tersura *f*
[2] [*of road, surface*] lo llano; [*of stone*] lisura *f*
[3] [*of sea, lake*] tranquilidad *f*, calma *f*
[4] [*of paste, sauce*] homogeneidad *f*
[5] [*of landing*] la suavidad, lo suave; [*of flight, crossing, journey*] lo poco accidentado
[6] (= *ease*) [*of transition, takeover*] lo poco conflictivo
[7] [*of flavour, whisky, cigar, voice, sound*] suavidad *f*
[8] [*of style, prose*] fluidez *f*
[9] (*pej*) [*of person, manners*] zalamería *f*

smooth-running ['smuːð'rʌnɪŋ] ADJ [*engine etc*] suave, parejo (*esp LAm*)

smooth-shaven ['smuːð'ʃeɪvn] ADJ bien afeitado

smooth-spoken ['smuːð'spəʊkən] ADJ, **smooth-talking** ['smuːð'tɔːkɪŋ] ADJ afable; (*pej*) zalamero, meloso

smooth-tongued ['smuːð'tʌŋd] ADJ zalamero, meloso

smoothy‡ ['smuːðɪ] N = **smoothie**

smorgasbord ['smɔːgəs,bɔːd] N (*Culin*) smorgasbord *m*

smote [sməʊt] PT *of* **smite**

smother ['smʌðəʳ] Ⓐ VT [1] (= *stifle*) [+ *person*] ahogar, asfixiar; [+ *fire*] apagar; [+ *yawn, sob, laughter*] contener [2] (= *cover*) cubrir; **fruit ~ed in cream** fruta *f* cubierta de crema; **a book ~ed in dust** un libro cubierto de polvo; **the child was ~ed in dirt** el niño estaba todo sucio; **they ~ed him with kisses** le colmaron *or* abrumaron de besos
Ⓑ VI (= *asphyxiate*) asfixiarse, ahogarse

smoulder, **smolder** (*US*) ['sməʊldəʳ] VI [*fire*] arder sin llama; (*fig*) [*passion etc*] arder

smouldering, **smoldering** (*US*) ['sməʊldərɪŋ] ADJ que arde lentamente; (*fig*) latente; **she gave me a ~ look** me miró provocativa

SMP [,esem'piː] N ABBR (*Brit*) = **Statutory Maternity Pay**

SMS N ABBR (= **Short Message Service**) SMS *m*

smudge [smʌdʒ] Ⓐ N borrón *m*
Ⓑ VT manchar
Ⓒ VI correrse

smudgy ['smʌdʒɪ] ADJ [*photo*] movido, borroso; [*page*] emborronado, lleno de borrones; [*writing etc*] borroso

smug [smʌg] ADJ (*compar* **smugger**, *superl* **smuggest**) creído, engreído; **he said with ~ satisfaction** dijo muy pagado de sí, dijo con engreimiento; **don't be so ~!** ¡no presumas!

smuggle ['smʌgl] Ⓐ VT (= *bring or take secretly*) pasar de contrabando; **~d goods** mercancías *fpl* de contrabando; **to ~ goods in/out** meter/sacar mercancías de contrabando; **to ~ sth past** *or* **through Customs** pasar algo de contrabando por la aduana; **to ~ sb out in disguise** pasar a algn disfrazado

Ⓑ VI hacer contrabando, dedicarse al contrabando

smuggler ['smʌglə^r] N contrabandista *mf*

smuggling ['smʌglɪŋ] Ⓐ N contrabando *m*
Ⓑ CPD ► **smuggling ring** N red *f* de contrabando, red *f* de contrabandistas

smugly ['smʌglɪ] ADV con engreimiento, con suficiencia

smugness ['smʌgnɪs] N engreimiento *m*, suficiencia *f*

smut [smʌt] N [1] (= *grain of soot*) carbonilla *f*, hollín *m*
[2] (= *crudity*) obscenidades *fpl*; **to talk ~** decir obscenidades
[3] (*Bot*) tizón *m*

smuttiness ['smʌtɪnɪs] N (= *crudity*) obscenidad *f*

smutty ['smʌtɪ] ADJ (*compar* **smuttier**; *superl* **smuttiest**) [1] (= *dirty*) manchado
[2] (= *crude*) obsceno, verde, colorado (*LAm*); **a lot of ~ talk** muchas indecencias; **~ jokes** chistes *mpl* verdes
[3] (*Bot*) atizonado

Smyrna ['smɜ:nə] N Esmirna *f*

snack [snæk] Ⓐ N tentempié *m*; **to have a ~** tomar un tentempié, picar algo
Ⓑ VI = **to have a snack**
Ⓒ CPD ► **snack bar** N cafetería *f*, lonchería *f* (*LAm*)

snaffle¹ ['snæfl] N (*also* ~ **bit**) bridón *m*

snaffle²* ['snæfl] VT (*Brit*) (= *steal*) afanar*, birlar*

snag [snæg] Ⓐ N [1] (= *difficulty*) inconveniente *m*, problema *m*; **there's a ~** hay un inconveniente *or* problema; **what's the ~?** ¿cuál es el problema?, ¿qué pega hay? (*Sp*); **the ~ is that …** la dificultad es que …; **that's the ~** ahí está el problema; **to run into** *or* **hit a ~** encontrar inconvenientes, dar con un obstáculo
[2] [*of tooth*] raigón *m*
[3] [*of tree*] tocón *m*; (*in wood*) nudo *m*
[4] (*in fabric*) enganchón *m*
Ⓑ VT enganchar, coger (**on** en)
Ⓒ VI engancharse, quedar cogido (**on** en)

snail [sneɪl] Ⓐ N caracol *m*; ♦ ***IDIOM*** **at a ~'s pace** a paso de tortuga
Ⓑ CPD ► **snail mail*** N (*hum*) correo *m* normal ► **snail shell** N concha *f* de caracol

snake [sneɪk] Ⓐ N serpiente *f*; (*harmless*) culebra *f*; **a ~ in the grass** (*fig*) un traidor
Ⓑ VI **a hand ~d out of the curtain** una mano apareció por detrás de la cortina; **the road ~d down the mountain** la carretera serpenteaba montaña abajo
Ⓒ CPD ► **snake charmer** N encantador(a) *m/f* de serpientes ► **snakes and ladders** NSING ≈ juego *m* de la oca ► **snake pit** N nido *m* de serpientes

►**snake about, snake along** VI + ADV serpentear

snakebite ['sneɪkbaɪt] N mordedura *f* de serpiente, picadura *f* de serpiente

snakeskin ['sneɪkskɪn] N piel *f* de serpiente

snaky ['sneɪkɪ] ADJ serpentino, tortuoso

snap [snæp] Ⓐ N [1] (= *sound*) golpe *m*, ruido *m* seco; [*of sth breaking, of whip, of fingers*] chasquido *m*; **it shut with a ~** se cerró de golpe, se cerró con un ruido seco
[2] (= *photograph*) foto *f*; **to take a ~ of sb** sacar una foto de algn; **these are our holiday ~s** éstas son las fotos de nuestras vacaciones
[3] (= *short period*) **a cold ~** una ola de frío
[4] (= *attempt to bite*) **the dog made a ~ at the biscuit** el perro se lanzó sobre la galleta
[5] (*) (= *energy*) vigor *m*, energía *f*; **put some ~ into it!** ¡menearse!
[6] **it's a ~** (*US**) (= *easy*) eso está tirado*, es muy fácil
Ⓑ ADJ (= *sudden*) repentino, sin aviso; **~ decision** decisión *f* instantánea; **~ answer** respuesta *f* sin pensar, respuesta *f* instantánea; **~ judgement** juicio *m* instantáneo
Ⓒ VT [1] (= *break*) partir, quebrar (*esp LAm*)
[2] (= *click*) chasquear; **to ~ one's fingers** chasquear los dedos; **to ~ one's fingers at sb/sth** (*fig*) burlarse de algn/algo; **to ~ a box shut** cerrar una caja de golpe; **to ~ sth into place** colocar algo con un golpe seco
[3] **"be quiet!" she ~ped** —¡cállate! —espetó ella enojada
[4] (*Phot*) sacar una foto de
Ⓓ VI [1] (= *break*) [*elastic*] romperse; **the branch ~ped** la rama se partió
[2] (= *make sound*) [*whip*] chasquear; **it ~ped shut** se cerró de golpe; **to ~ into place** meterse de golpe
[3] **to ~ at sb** [*person*] regañarle a algn; [*dog*] intentar morder a algn; **don't ~ at me!** ¡a mí no me hables en ese tono!
[4] (= *move energetically*) **she ~ped into action** echó a trabajar *etc* en seguida
Ⓔ ADV **snap!** ¡crac!; **to go ~** hacer crac
Ⓕ EXCL ¡lo mismo!; (= *me too*) ¡yo también!
Ⓖ CPD ► **snap fastener** N (*US*) cierre *m* (automático)

►**snap back** VI + ADV **to ~ back at sb** contestar *or* hablar *etc* bruscamente a algn

►**snap off** Ⓐ VT + ADV separar, quebrar; **to ~ sb's head off** (*fig*) regañarle a algn, echarle un rapapolvo a algn
Ⓑ VI + ADV **it ~ped off** se desprendió, se partió

►**snap out** Ⓐ VI + ADV (*) **to ~ out of sth** [+ *gloom, lethargy*] sacudirse algo; [+ *self-pity*] dejarse de algo; [+ *bad temper*] quitarse algo de encima; **~ out of it!** [+ *gloom etc*] ¡anímate!; [+ *bad temper*] ¡alegra esa cara!
Ⓑ VT + ADV [+ *question, order etc*] soltar, espetar (*con brusquedad*)

►**snap up** VT + ADV **to ~ up a bargain** (*fig*) agarrar una ganga; **our stock was ~ped up at once** nuestras existencias quedaron agotadas al instante

snapdragon ['snæp,drægən] N (*Bot*) dragón *m*

snapper ['snæpə^r] N (*pl* **snapper** *or* **snappers**) (*Zool, Culin*) pargo *m*

snappish ['snæpɪʃ] ADJ (= *irritable*) [*person*] irritable, gruñón; [*reply, tone*] brusco, seco; [*dog*] con mal genio

snappishness ['snæpɪʃnɪs] N [*of person*] irritabilidad *f*; [*of reply*] brusquedad *f*, sequedad *f*

snappy* ['snæpɪ] ADJ (*compar* **snappier**; *superl* **snappiest**) [1] (= *quick*) rápido; (= *energetic*) enérgico, vigoroso; **make it ~!** ¡date prisa!, ¡apúrate! (*esp LAm*); **to be ~ about sth** hacer algo con toda rapidez; **and be ~ about it!** ¡y date prisa!, ¡y apúrate! (*esp LAm*)
[2] (= *smart*) elegante; **he's a ~ dresser** se viste con elegancia
[3] (= *punchy*) [*slogan*] conciso
[4] = **snappish**

snapshot ['snæpʃɒt] N (*Phot*) foto *f*

snare [snɛə^r] Ⓐ N lazo *m*; (*fig*) trampa *f*
Ⓑ VT coger *or* (*LAm*) agarrar con lazo; (*fig*) atrapar
Ⓒ CPD ► **snare drum** N tambor *m* militar pequeño

snarl¹ [snɑ:l] Ⓐ N (= *noise*) gruñido *m*; **he said with a ~** dijo gruñendo
Ⓑ VI [*dog, lion*] gruñir; **to ~ at sb** [*person, dog*] gruñir a algn
Ⓒ VT gruñir, decir gruñendo; **"no!" he ~ed** —¡no! —gruñó él

snarl² [snɑ:l] Ⓐ N [1] (*in wool etc*) maraña *f*, enredo *m*
[2] (*in traffic*) atasco *m*, embotellamiento *m*
Ⓑ VT (*also* ~ **up**) [+ *wool*] enmarañar; [+ *plans*] confundir, enredar; [+ *traffic*] atascar; **the traffic was all ~ed up** había un gran atasco, el tráfico estaba atascado
Ⓒ VI (*also* ~ **up**) enmarañarse, enredarse

snarl-up ['snɑ:lʌp] N [1] (*Aut etc*) atasco *m*, embotellamiento *m*
[2] (*in plans etc*) enredo *m*, maraña *f*

snatch [snætʃ] Ⓐ N [1] (= *act of snatching*) arrebatamiento *m*; **to make a ~ at sth** intentar arrebatar *or* agarrar algo
[2] (*) (= *theft*) robo *m*, hurto *m*; (= *kidnapping*) secuestro *m*; **jewellery ~** robo *m or* hurto *m* de joyas
[3] (= *snippet*) trocito *m*; **to whistle ~es of Mozart** silbar trocitos de Mozart; **~es of conversation** fragmentos *mpl* de conversación; **to sleep in ~es** dormir a ratos
[4] (**) (= *vagina*) coño** *m*
Ⓑ VT [1] (= *grab*) arrebatar; **to ~ sth from sb** arrebatar algo a algn; **he ~ed the keys from my hand** me arrebató las llaves de la mano; **to ~ a knife out of sb's hand** arrebatarle *or* arrancarle un cuchillo a algn de las manos; **to ~ a meal** comer a la carrera; **to ~ some sleep** buscar tiempo para dormir; **to ~ an opportunity** asir una ocasión; **to ~ an hour of happiness** procurarse (a pesar de todo) una hora de felicidad
[2] (= *steal*) robar; (= *kidnap*) secuestrar; **my bag was ~ed** me robaron el bolso
Ⓒ VI **don't ~!** ¡no me lo quites!; **to ~ at sth** (*lit, fig*) intentar agarrar algo
Ⓓ CPD ► **snatch squad** N unidad *f* de arresto

►**snatch away, snatch off** VT + ADV **to ~ sth away from** *or* **off sb** arrebatar algo a algn

►**snatch up** VT + ADV agarrar (*rápidamente*); **to ~ up a knife** agarrar un cuchillo; **to ~ up a child** agarrar a un niño en brazos

snatchy* ['snætʃɪ] ADJ [*work*] irregular, intermitente; [*conversation*] intermitente, inconexo

snazzy* ['snæzɪ] ADJ (*compar* **snazzier**; *superl* **snazziest**) **a ~ dress** un vestido vistoso

sneak [sni:k] Ⓐ VT **to ~ sth out of a place** sacar algo furtivamente de un lugar; **I managed to ~ one in** logré meter uno sin ser visto; **to ~ a look at sth** mirar algo de reojo *or* soslayo
Ⓑ VI [1] **to ~ about** ir a hurtadillas, moverse furtivamente; **to ~ in/out** entrar/salir a hurtadillas; **to ~ away** *or* **off** escabullirse; **to ~ off with sth** llevarse algo furtivamente; **to ~ up on sb** acercarse sigilosamente a algn
[2] **to ~ on sb*** delatar a algn, dar el soplo sobre algn*, chivarse de algn (*Sp**); **to ~ to the teacher** ir con el cuento *or* (*Sp*) chivarse al profesor*
Ⓒ N (*) (= *tale-teller*) chivato/a *m/f*, soplón/ona *m/f*
Ⓓ CPD ► **sneak preview** N [*of film*] preestreno *m*; (*gen*) anticipo *m* no autorizado ► **sneak thief** N ratero/a *m/f* ► **sneak visit** N visita *f* furtiva

sneakers ['sni:kəz] NPL (*esp US*) zapatos *mpl* de lona, zapatillas *fpl*

sneaking ['sni:kɪŋ] ADJ ligero; **to have a ~ dislike of sb** sentir antipatía hacia algn; **I have a ~ feeling that …** tengo la sensación de que …; **to have a ~ regard for sb** respetar a algn a pesar de todo, respetar a algn sin querer confesarlo abiertamente

sneaky* ['sni:kɪ] ADJ (*compar* **sneakier**; *superl* **sneakiest**) soplón

sneer [snɪəʳ] Ⓐ N (= *expression*) cara *f* de desprecio; (= *remark*) comentario *m* desdeñoso; **he said with a ~** dijo con desprecio; **the book is full of ~s about ...** el libro se mofa constantemente de ...
Ⓑ VI hablar con desprecio, hablar con desdén; **to ~ at sb/sth** (= *laugh*) mofarse de algn/algo; (= *scorn*) despreciar a algn/algo

sneerer ['snɪərəʳ] N mofador(a) *m/f*

sneering ['snɪərɪŋ] ADJ [*tone etc*] burlador y despreciativo, lleno de desprecio

sneeringly ['snɪərɪŋlɪ] ADV [*say*] en tono burlador y despreciativo; [*smile*] con una mueca de desprecio

sneeze [sni:z] Ⓐ N estornudo *m*
Ⓑ VI estornudar; **an offer not to be ~d at** (*fig*) una oferta que no es de despreciar

snick [snɪk] Ⓐ N [1] (= *cut*) corte *m*, tijeretada *f*
[2] (*Sport*) toque *m* ligero
Ⓑ VT [1] (= *cut*) cortar (un poco), tijeretear; **to ~ sth off** cortar algo con un movimiento rápido
[2] (*Sport*) [+ *ball*] desviar ligeramente

snicker ['snɪkəʳ] N, VI = **snigger**

snide* [snaɪd] ADJ bajo, sarcástico

sniff [snɪf] Ⓐ N [1] (= *act*) sorbo *m* (por la nariz); (*by dog*) husmeo *m*; **one ~ of that would kill you** una inhalación de eso te mataría; **to go out for a ~ of air** salir a tomar el fresco; **we never got a ~ of the vodka*** no llegamos siquiera a oler el vodka
[2] (= *faint smell*) olorcito *m*
Ⓑ VT [+ *snuff etc*] sorber (por la nariz), aspirar; [+ *smell*] oler; [*dog etc*] olfatear, husmear; **just ~ these flowers** huele un poco estas flores; **the dog ~ed my hand** el perro me olfateó *or* me husmeó la mano; **you can ~ the sea air here** aquí se huele ese aire de mar; **~ the gas deeply** aspire profundamente el gas; **to ~ glue** esnifar *or* inhalar pegamento
Ⓒ VI [*person*] aspirar por la nariz, sorber, sorberse la nariz; [*dog etc*] oler, husmear, olfatear; **stop ~ing!** ¡deja de sorberte la nariz!; **to ~ at sth** (*lit*) oler algo; (*fig*) despreciar algo, desdeñar algo; **an offer not to be ~ed at** una oferta que no es de despreciar *or* desdeñar; **the dog ~ed at my shoes** el perro olió mis zapatos
►**sniff out** VT + ADV (= *discover*) encontrar husmeando; (= *pry*) fisgar, fisgonear; (*fig*) (= *dig out*) desenterrar

sniffer dog ['snɪfədɒg] N perro *m* rastreador; (*for drugs*) perro *m* antidroga; (*for explosives*) perro *m* antiexplosivos

sniffle ['snɪfl] Ⓐ N **to have the ~s** estar resfriado *or* constipado
Ⓑ VI sorber con ruido

sniffy* ['snɪfɪ] ADJ (= *disdainful*) estirado, desdeñoso; **he was pretty ~ about it** trató el asunto con bastante desdén

snifter* ['snɪftəʳ] N [1] (= *drink*) copa *f*, trago *m*
[2] (*US*) (= *glass*) copita *f* para coñac

snigger ['snɪgəʳ] Ⓐ N risilla *f*, risita *f*
Ⓑ VI reír disimuladamente; **to ~ at sth** reírse tontamente de algo

sniggering ['snɪgərɪŋ] Ⓐ N risillas *fpl*, risitas *fpl*
Ⓑ ADJ que se ríe tontamente

snip [snɪp] Ⓐ N [1] (= *cut*) tijeretada *f*; (= *action, noise*) tijereteo *m*; **to have the ~*** esterilizarse
[2] (= *small piece*) recorte *m*
[3] (*Brit**) (= *bargain*) ganga *f*
Ⓑ VT tijeretear; **to ~ sth off** cortar algo con tijeras

snipe [snaɪp] Ⓐ N (= *bird*) agachadiza *f*
Ⓑ VI **to ~ at sb** (*lit*) disparar a algn desde un escondite; **to ~ at one's critics** responder ante las críticas; **he was really sniping at the Minister** en realidad sus ataques iban dirigidos contra el Ministro

sniper ['snaɪpəʳ] N francotirador(a) *m/f*

snippet ['snɪpɪt] N [*of cloth, paper*] pedacito *m*, recorte *m*; [*of information, conversation etc*] retazo *m*, fragmento *m*; **"Snippets"** (= *heading in press etc*) "Breves", "Noticias Breves"

snitch‡ [snɪtʃ] Ⓐ VI **to ~ on sb** chivarse *or* soplar a algn
Ⓑ VT (= *steal*) birlar*
Ⓒ N [1] (= *nose*) napias‡ *fpl*
[2] (= *informer*) soplón/ona* *m/f*

snivel ['snɪvl] VI lloriquear

sniveller, sniveler (*US*) ['snɪvləʳ] N quejica* *mf*

snivelling, sniveling (*US*) ['snɪvlɪŋ] Ⓐ ADJ llorón
Ⓑ N lloriqueo *m*

snob [snɒb] N snob *mf*, esnob *mf*; **he's an intellectual ~** presume de intelectual

snobbery ['snɒbərɪ] N snobismo *m*, esnobismo *m*

snobbish ['snɒbɪʃ] ADJ snob, esnob

snobbishness ['snɒbɪʃnɪs] N snobismo *m*, esnobismo *m*

snobby* ['snɒbɪ] ADJ snob, esnob

snog‡ [snɒg] Ⓐ N **to have a ~** besuquearse*
Ⓑ VI besuquearse*

snood [snu:d] N (= *band*) cintillo *m*; (= *net*) redecilla *f*

snook* [snu:k] N **to cock a ~ at sb** (*fig*) hacer un palmo de narices a algn, hacer burlas a algn

snooker ['snu:kəʳ] Ⓐ N snooker *m*, billar *m* inglés
Ⓑ VT **to be properly ~ed*** (*fig*) estar en un aprieto serio

snoop [snu:p] Ⓐ N [1] (= *person*) fisgón/ona *m/f*
[2] (= *act*) **to have a ~ round** fisgar, fisgonear; **I had a ~ round the kitchen** estuve fisgando *or* fisgoneando *or* husmeando por la cocina
Ⓑ VI (*also* **~ about, ~ around**) (= *pry*) fisgar, fisgonear; (= *interfere*) entrometerse; **if he comes ~ing around here ...** si viene fisgando *or* fisgoneando por aquí ...

snooper ['snu:pəʳ] N fisgón/ona *m/f*

snooty* ['snu:tɪ] ADJ (*compar* **snootier**; *superl* **snootiest**) presumido; **the people round here are very ~** la gente de por aquí es muy presumida, por aquí la gente se da mucho tono *or* muchos aires; **there's no need to be ~ about it** no hace falta andar presumiendo de ello

snooze [snu:z] Ⓐ N cabezada *f*; (*in the afternoon*) siestecita *f*; **to have a ~** dar *or* echar una cabezada *or* cabezadita; (*in the afternoon*) echar una siestecita
Ⓑ VI dormitar

snore [snɔ:ʳ] Ⓐ N ronquido *m*
Ⓑ VI roncar

snorer ['snɔ:rəʳ] N persona *f* que ronca mucho

snoring ['snɔ:rɪŋ] N ronquidos *mpl*

snorkel ['snɔ:kl] Ⓐ N [*of swimmer*] tubo *m* de respiración; [*of submarine*] snorquel *m*, esnorquel *m*
Ⓑ VI bucear con tubo respiratorio

snort [snɔ:t] Ⓐ N [1] [*of horse, person*] resoplido *m*, bufido *m*; **with a ~ of rage** con un bufido (de enojo)
[2] (‡) [*of whisky etc*] trago *m*; [*of cocaine etc*] esnife* *m*
Ⓑ VI [1] [*horse, person*] resoplar, bufar; **he ~ed with anger** bufó enojado; **he ~ed with impatience** resopló impaciente
[2] (*Drugs**) esnifar*
Ⓒ VT [1] (= *say*) bufar; **"no!" he ~ed** —¡no! —bufó él
[2] (*Drugs**) [+ *cocaine etc*] inhalar, esnifar*

snorter* ['snɔ:təʳ] N [1] **a real ~ of a problem** un problemón; **a ~ of a question** una pregunta dificilísima; **it was a ~ of a game** fue un partido maravilloso
[2] (= *drink*) trago *m*, copa *f*

snot* [snɒt] N [1] (= *mucus*) mocos *mpl*, mocarro *m*
[2] (= *person*) mocoso/a *m/f* insolente*

snotty* ['snɒtɪ] ADJ (*compar* **snottier**; *superl* **snottiest**) [1] [*nose, handkerchief*] lleno de mocos
[2] (*Brit*) (= *snooty*) presumido

snotty-faced* ['snɒtɪ,feɪst] ADJ mocoso

snotty-nosed* ['snɒtɪ,nəʊzd] ADJ [1] (*lit*) mocoso
[2] (*fig*) presumido

snout [snaʊt] N [1] (= *nose*) [*of animal*] hocico *m*, morro *m*; (‡) [*of person*] napias‡ *fpl*
[2] (‡) (= *tobacco*) tabaco *m*, cigarrillos *mpl*

snow [snəʊ] Ⓐ N [1] (*Met*) nieve *f*; ✦**IDIOM white as ~** blanco como la nieve
[2] (*on TV screen*) lluvia *f*, nieve *f*
[3] (‡) (= *cocaine*) nieve‡ *f*, cocaína *f*
Ⓑ VT [1] (*Met*) **to be ~ed in** *or* **up** quedar aislado por la nieve
[2] (*fig*) **to be ~ed under with work** estar agobiado de trabajo
[3] (*US**) (= *charm glibly*) **to ~ sb** camelar a algn*
Ⓒ VI nevar; **it's ~ing** está nevando
Ⓓ CPD ► **snow blindness** N (*Med*) ceguera *f* de nieve ► **snow cap** N casquete *m* de nieve, corona *f* de nieve ► **snow goose** N ánsar *m* nival ► **snow leopard** N onza *f* ► **snow line** N límite *m* de las nieves perpetuas ► **snow machine** N cañón *m* de nieve artificial ► **Snow Queen** N Reina *f* de las nieves ► **snow report** N (*Met*) informe *m* sobre el estado de la nieve ► **snow tyre, snow tire** (*US*) N neumático *m* antideslizante ► **Snow White** N Blancanieves *f*; **"Snow White and the Seven Dwarfs"** "Blancanieves y los siete enanitos"; *see also* **snow-white**

snowball ['snəʊbɔ:l] Ⓐ N bola *f* de nieve
Ⓑ VT lanzar bolas de nieve a
Ⓒ VI (*fig*) aumentar progresivamente, ir aumentándose

snow-blind ['snəʊ,blaɪnd] ADJ cegado por la nieve

snow-bound ['snəʊbaʊnd] ADJ aislado por la nieve, bloqueado por la nieve

snow-capped ['snəʊkæpt] ADJ cubierto de nieve, nevado

snow-covered ['snəʊ'kʌvəd] ADJ cubierto de nieve, nevado

snowdrift ['snəʊdrɪft] N ventisca *f*, ventisquero *m*

snowdrop ['snəʊdrɒp] N campanilla *f* de invierno

snowfall ['snəʊfɔ:l] N nevada *f*

snowfence ['snəʊfens] N valla *f* paranieves

snowfield ['snəʊfi:ld] N campo *m* de nieve

snowflake ['snəʊfleɪk] N copo *m* de nieve

snowman ['snəʊmæn] N (*pl* **snowmen**) muñeco *m* de nieve; **to build a ~** hacer un muñeco de nieve; **the abominable ~** el abominable hombre de las nieves

snowmobile ['snəʊmə,biːl] N motonieve *f*

snowplough, snowplow (*US*) ['snəʊplaʊ] N quitanieves *m inv*

snowshoe ['snəʊʃuː] N raqueta *f* (de nieve)

snowslide ['snəʊslaɪd] N (*US*) alud *m* (de nieve), avalancha *f*

snowstorm ['snəʊstɔːm] N temporal *m* de nieve, ventisca *f*, nevasca *f*

snowsuit ['snəʊsuːt] N mono *m* acolchado de nieve

snow-white ['snəʊ'waɪt] ADJ blanco como la nieve

snowy ['snəʊɪ] ADJ (*compar* **snowier**; *superl* **snowiest**) 1 (*Met*) [*climate, region*] de mucha nieve; [*day etc*] de nieve; [*countryside etc*] cubierto de nieve; **~ season** estación *f* de las nieves; **it was very ~ yesterday** ayer nevó mucho, ayer cayó mucha nieve

2 (= *white as snow*) blanco como la nieve

SNP N ABBR (*Brit Pol*) = **Scottish National Party**

Snr ABBR = **Senior**

snub[1] [snʌb] Ⓐ N desaire *m*

Ⓑ VT [+ *person*] desairar, volver la espalda a; [+ *offer*] rechazar

snub[2] [snʌb] ADJ **~ nose** nariz *f* respingona

snub-nosed ['snʌb'nəʊzd] ADJ chato, ñato (*LAm*)

snuff[1] [snʌf] N rapé *m*; **to take ~** tomar rapé

snuff[2] [snʌf] Ⓐ VT apagar; **to ~ it*** estirar la pata*, liar el petate*

Ⓑ CPD ► **snuff film, snuff movie*** N película *f* porno en que muere realmente uno de los participantes

►**snuff out** VT + ADV [+ *candle*] apagar; (*fig*) extinguir

snuffbox ['snʌfbɒks] N caja *f* de rapé, tabaquera *f*

snuffer ['snʌfəʳ] N matacandelas *m inv*; **snuffers, pair of ~s** (= *scissors*) apagaderas *fpl*

snuffle ['snʌfl] N, VI = **sniffle**

snug [snʌg] Ⓐ ADJ (*compar* **snugger**; *superl* **snuggest**) 1 (= *cosy*) [*house, room*] acogedor; [*bed*] confortable; **it's nice and ~ here** aquí se está bien; **to be/feel ~** estar/sentirse cómodo; **to be ~ in bed** estar calentito y a gusto en la cama, estar arrebujado en la cama; ✦***IDIOM*** **to be as ~ as a bug in a rug*** estar bien tapadito*

2 (= *close-fitting*) ajustado, ceñido, justo (*esp LAm*); (= *too tight*) apretado; **it's a ~ fit** [*garment*] ciñe bien; [*object*] cabe justito

Ⓑ N (*Brit*) (*in pub*) salón *m* pequeño

snuggle ['snʌgl] VI **to ~ down in bed** acurrucarse en la cama; **to ~ up to sb** arrimarse a algn; **I like to ~ up with a book** me gusta ponerme cómodo a leer

snugly ['snʌglɪ] ADV 1 (= *cosily*) **wrap your baby ~ in a blanket** abrigue bien a su bebé con una manta; **the children were ~ tucked up in bed** los niños estaban bien abrigados en la cama, los niños estaban bien tapaditos en la cama*

2 (= *tightly*) **make sure the doors close ~** asegúrate de que las puertas encajan bien al cerrarlas; **it fits ~** [*jacket*] (= *well*) queda bien ajustado *or* ceñido *or* (*esp LAm*) justo; [*one object in another*] encaja perfectamente

so[1] [səʊ] Ⓐ ADV 1 (= *to such an extent*) 1·1 (*with adj/adv*) tan; **I'm so worried** estoy tan preocupado; **it is so big that …** es tan grande que …; **he was talking so fast I couldn't understand** hablaba tan rápido que no lo entendía; **I wish you weren't so clumsy** ¡ojalá no fueras tan patoso!; **it was so heavy!** ¡pesaba tanto!; **"how's your father?" — "not so good"** —¿cómo está tu padre? —no muy bien; **it's about so high/long** es más o menos así de alto/largo; **she's not so clever as him** no es tan lista como él; **he's not so silly as to do that** no es bastante tonto para hacer eso, no es tan tonto como para hacer eso; **so many** tantos/as; **we don't need so many** no necesitamos tantos; **I haven't got so many pairs of shoes as you** no tengo tantos pares de zapatos como tú; **so much** tanto/a; **we spent so much** gastamos tanto; **I haven't got so much energy as you** no tengo tanta energía como tú; **I've got so much to do** tengo tantísimo que hacer; **thank you so much** muchísimas gracias, muy agradecido; **it's not so very difficult** no es tan difícil; *see also* **kind, sure** *etc*

1·2 (*with vb*) tanto; **I love you so** te quiero tanto; **he who so loved Spain** (*liter*) él que amó tanto a España

2 (= *thus, in this way, likewise*) así, de esta manera, de este modo; **so it was that …** así fue que …, de esta manera *or* de este modo fue como …; **it is so** es así; **we so arranged things that …** lo arreglamos de modo que …; **so it is!** ◊ **so it does!** ¡es verdad!, ¡es cierto!, ¡correcto!; **is that so?** ¿de veras?; **isn't that so?** ¿no es así?; **that's so** eso es; **that's not so** no es así; **so be it** así sea; **and he did so** y lo hizo; **do so then!** ¡hazlo, pues!; **by so doing** haciéndolo así; **I expect so** supongo que sí, a lo mejor; **so far** hasta aquí *or* ahora; **and so forth** y así sucesivamente, etcétera; **it so happens that …** resulta que …, el caso es que …; **I hope so** eso espero yo, espero que sí; **how so?** ¿cómo es eso?; **if so** en este caso, en cuyo caso; **just so!** ¡eso!, ¡eso es!; **he likes things just so** le gusta que todo esté en su lugar; **you do it like so*** se hace así, se hace de esta manera; **only more so** pero en mayor grado; **so much so that …** hasta tal punto *or* grado que …, tanto es así que …; **not so!** ¡nada de eso!; **and so on** y así sucesivamente, etcétera; **so saying he walked away** dicho eso, se marchó; **so he says** eso dice él; **so to speak** por decirlo así; **I think so** creo que sí; **I thought so** me lo figuraba *or* suponía; **I told you so** ya te lo dije; **why so?** ¿por qué?, ¿cómo?

3 (= *also*) **he's wrong and so are you** se equivocan tanto usted como él; **so do I** (y) yo también; **"I work a lot" — "so do I"** —trabajo mucho —(y) yo también; **"I love horses" — "so do I"** —me encantan los caballos —a mí también; **"I've been waiting for ages!" — "so have we"** —¡llevo esperando un siglo! —(y) nosotros también; **so would I** yo también

4 (*phrases*) **so long!*** ¡adiós!, ¡hasta luego!; **so much the better/worse** tanto mejor/peor; **she didn't so much as send me a birthday card** no me mandó ni una tarjeta siquiera para mi cumpleaños; **I haven't so much as a penny** no tengo ni un peso; **she gave me back the book without so much as an apology** me devolvió el libro sin pedirme siquiera una disculpa; **so much for her promises!** ¡eso valen sus promesas!; **ten or so** unos diez, diez más o menos; **ten or so people** unas diez personas, diez personas o así *or* más o menos; **at five o'clock or so** a las cinco o así *or* o por ahí *or* más o menos

Ⓑ CONJ 1 (*expressing purpose*) para; **he took her upstairs so they wouldn't be overheard** la subió al piso de arriba para que nadie los oyera; **so as to do sth** para hacer algo, a fin de hacer algo; **we hurried so as not to be late** nos dimos prisa para no llegar tarde *or* a fin de no llegar tarde; **so that** para que + *subjun*, a fin de que + *subjun*; **I bought it so that you should see it** lo compré para que *or* a fin de que lo vieras

2 (*expressing result*) así que, de manera que; **he hadn't studied, so he found the exam difficult** no había estudiado, así que *or* de manera que el examen le resultó difícil; **it rained and so we could not go out** llovió, así que no pudimos salir, llovió y no pudimos salir; **so that** de modo que, de manera que; **he stood so that he faced west** se puso de tal modo que *or* de manera que miraba al oeste, se puso mirando al oeste

3 (= *therefore*) así que; **the shop was closed, so I went home** la tienda estaba cerrada, así que me fui a casa; **so you see …** por lo cual, entenderás …

4 (*in questions, exclamations*) entonces, así que; **so you're Spanish?** entonces *or* así que ¿eres español?; **so?*** ¿y?, ¿y qué?; **so that's the reason!** ¡por eso es!; **so that's why he stayed home** de allí que se quedó en casa; **so there you are!** ¡ahí estás!; **so what?*** ¿y?, ¿y qué?; *see* **there A6**

so[2] [səʊ] N (*Mus*) = **soh**

SO, S/O ABBR = **standing order**

soak [səʊk] Ⓐ VT 1 (= *immerse*) poner en remojo; **~ the beans for two hours** ponga las judías en remojo dos horas; **to ~ sth in a liquid** remojar algo en un líquido

2 (= *make wet*) empapar; **water had ~ed his jacket** el agua le había empapado la chaqueta; **to get ~ed (to the skin)** empaparse *or* quedar empapado, calarse hasta los huesos; **you've ~ed yourself!** ¡te has empapado entero!, ¡te has puesto perdido de agua!

3 (*) **to ~ sb** (= *take money from*) desplumar a algn*, clavar a algn*; **to ~ the rich** clavarles a los ricos; **to ~ sb for a loan** pedir prestado dinero a algn

Ⓑ VI remojarse; **to leave sth to ~** dejar algo en *or* al remojo

Ⓒ N 1 (= *rain*) diluvio *m*; **to have a good ~ in the bath** darse un buen baño; **give your shirt a ~ overnight** deja la camisa en remojo toda la noche

2 (*) (= *drunkard*) borracho/a *m/f*

►**soak in** VI + ADV penetrar

►**soak through** Ⓐ VT + ADV **to be ~ed through** [*person*] estar calado hasta los huesos, estar empapado

Ⓑ VI + PREP calar, penetrar

►**soak up** VT + ADV absorber

soaking ['səʊkɪŋ] Ⓐ ADJ (*also* **~ wet**) [*person*] calado hasta los huesos, empapado; [*object*] empapado, calado; **by the time we got back we were ~** cuando regresamos estábamos calados hasta los huesos *or* empapados; **your shoes are ~ wet** tienes los zapatos empapados *or* calados; **a ~ wet day** un día de muchísima lluvia

Ⓑ N (*in liquid*) remojo *m*; [*of rain*] diluvio *m*; **to get a ~** calarse hasta los huesos, empaparse

so-and-so ['səʊənsəʊ] N (*pl* **so-and-sos**) 1 (= *somebody*) fulano/a *m/f*; **Mr ~** don Fulano (de Tal); **any ~ could steal it** cualquiera podría robarlo

2 (*pej*) **he's a ~** es un tal, es un hijo de su madre*; **you old ~!** (*hum*) ¡sinvergüenza!

soap [səʊp] Ⓐ N 1 (*for washing*) jabón *m*; **soft ~*** coba *f*

2 (*) = **soap opera**

Ⓑ VT jabonar

➤ LANGUAGE IN USE: **so**[1] **A1** 5.1, 17.2 **B2** 17.2

Ⓒ CPD ► **soap dish** N jabonera *f* ► **soap flakes** NPL jabón *msing* en escamas ► **soap opera** N (*TV*) telenovela *f*; (*Rad*) radionovela *f* ► **soap powder** N polvos *mpl* de jabón, detergente *m* en polvo

►**soap up** VT + ADV **to ~ sb up*** dar coba a algn*

soapbox ['səʊpbɒks] Ⓐ N tribuna *f* improvisada

Ⓑ CPD ► **soapbox orator** N orador(a) *m/f* callejero/a

soapstone ['səʊpstəʊn] N esteatita *f*

soapsuds ['səʊpsʌdz] NPL jabonaduras *fpl*, espuma *fsing*

soapy ['səʊpɪ] ADJ (*compar* **soapier**, *superl* **soapiest**) 1 (= *covered in soap*) cubierto de jabón; (= *like soap*) parecido a jabón, jabonoso; **it tastes ~** sabe a jabón

2 (*) (= *flattering*) zalamero, cobista*

soar [sɔːʳ] VI 1 (= *rise*) [*birds etc*] remontar el vuelo

2 (*fig*) [*tower etc*] elevarse; [*price etc*] subir vertiginosamente, ponerse por las nubes; [*ambition, hopes*] aumentar; [*morale, spirits*] renacer, reanimarse; **the new tower ~s over the city** la nueva torre se eleva sobre la ciudad; **our spirits ~ed** renació nuestra esperanza

soaring ['sɔːrɪŋ] ADJ [*flight*] planeador, que vuela; [*building*] altísimo; [*prices*] en alza, en aumento; [*hopes, imagination*] expansivo; [*ambition*] inmenso

sob [sɒb] Ⓐ N sollozo *m*; **she said with a ~** dijo sollozando, dijo entre sollozos

Ⓑ VI sollozar

Ⓒ VT **"no," she ~bed** —no —dijo sollozando, —no —dijo entre sollozos; **to ~ o.s. to sleep** dormirse sollozando; **to ~ one's heart out** llorar a lágrima viva; **she ~bed out her troubles** contó sus penas llorando *or* entre sollozos

Ⓓ CPD ► **sob story*** N tragedia *f* ► **sob stuff*** N sentimentalismo *m*, sensiblería *f*

S.O.B., s.o.b.‡ N ABBR (*US*) (= **son of a bitch**) hijo *m* de puta‡

sobbing ['sɒbɪŋ] N sollozos *mpl*

sober ['səʊbəʳ] Ⓐ ADJ 1 (= *not drunk*) sobrio; **to stay ~** mantenerse sobrio; ✦***IDIOMS*** **to be as ~ as a judge** ◊ **be stone-cold ~*** estar perfectamente sobrio

2 (= *serious, calm*) [*person*] serio, formal; [*expression*] grave; [*attitude, assessment*] serio, sobrio; [*fact*] cruel; [*reality*] crudo, duro; **after ~ reflection** después de una seria reflexión

3 (= *dull, subdued*) [*clothes, suit, style, decor*] sobrio, discreto; [*colour*] discreto

Ⓑ VT 1 (*also* **~ up**) (= *stop being drunk*) despejar, quitar la borrachera a

2 (= *make more serious*) volver más serio

Ⓒ VI 1 (*also* **~ up**) (= *stop being drunk*) despejarse, pasársele la borrachera

2 (= *become more serious*) volverse más serio

►**sober up** Ⓐ VT + ADV 1 (= *stop being drunk*) despejar, quitar la borrachera a

2 (= *make more serious*) volver más serio a

Ⓑ VI + ADV 1 (= *stop being drunk*) **when she had ~ed up** cuando se hubo despejado, cuando se le hubo pasado la borrachera

2 (= *become serious*) volverse más serio

sober-headed ['səʊbə'hedɪd] ADJ [*person*] sensato, sobrio; [*decision*] sensato

sobering ['səʊbərɪŋ] ADJ **it had a ~ effect on me** fue aleccionador; **it's a ~ thought** da que pensar

soberly ['səʊbəlɪ] ADV 1 (= *not drunkenly*) sobriamente

2 (= *seriously*) [*say, look*] con seriedad, sobriamente

3 (= *plainly*) [*decorated, dressed*] sobriamente, discretamente; **he was ~ dressed in a dark suit** vestía un traje oscuro y sobrio *or* discreto

sober-minded ['səʊbə'maɪndɪd] ADJ serio

soberness ['səʊbənɪs] N = **sobriety**

sobersides* ['səʊbəsaɪdz] NSING persona *f* muy reservada

sobriety [səʊ'braɪətɪ] N 1 (= *not being drunk*) **~ test** (*US*) prueba *f* de alcoholemia

2 (= *seriousness, sedateness*) seriedad *f*, sobriedad *f*

3 (= *subdued nature*) sobriedad *f*, discreción *f*

sobriquet ['səʊbrɪkeɪ] N apodo *m*, mote *m*

Soc ABBR 1 = **society**

2 = **Socialist**

soc. ABBR = **society**

so-called ['səʊ'kɔːld] ADJ supuesto, presunto; **all these ~ journalists** todos estos supuestos *or* presuntos *or* así llamados periodistas; **in the ~ rush hours** en las llamadas horas punta

soccer ['sɒkəʳ] Ⓐ N fútbol *m*; **to play ~** jugar al fútbol

Ⓑ CPD ► **soccer player** N futbolista *mf* ► **soccer season** N temporada *f* de fútbol

sociability [,səʊʃə'bɪlɪtɪ] N sociabilidad *f*

sociable ['səʊʃəbl] ADJ [*person*] sociable, tratable; [*occasion*] social; **I don't feel very ~** no estoy para hacer vida social; **I'll have one drink, just to be ~** para hacerles compañía, tomaré una copa

sociably ['səʊʃəblɪ] ADV sociablemente; **to live ~ together** vivir juntos amistosamente

social ['səʊʃəl] Ⓐ ADJ 1 (= *relating to society*) [*customs, problems, reforms*] social; **the ~ order** el orden social; *see also* **conscience A**

2 (= *in society*) [*engagements, life etc*] social; **her ~ acquaintances** sus conocidos; **~ call** = **social visit**; **~ circle** círculo *m* de amistades; **he has little ~ contact with his business colleagues** apenas trata con sus colegas fuera del trabajo; **I'm a ~ drinker only** sólo bebo cuando estoy con gente; **she does not regard me as her ~ equal** no me trata como a alguien de su misma clase; **to have a good ~ life** hacer buena vida social; **clothes for ~ occasions** ropa para la vida social; **this isn't a ~ visit** ésta no es una visita de cortesía

3 (= *interactive*) [*person, animal, behaviour*] social; **man is a ~ animal** el hombre es social por naturaleza; **I don't feel very ~ just now** no me apetece estar con gente ahora mismo; **he has poor ~ skills** no tiene aptitud para el trato social, no tiene mucho don de gentes

Ⓑ N reunión *f* (social)

Ⓒ CPD ► **social anthropologist** N antropólogo/a *m/f* social ► **social anthropology** N antropología *f* social ► **the Social Charter** N [*of EU*] la Carta Social ► **social class** N clase *f* social ► **social climber** N arribista *mf* ► **social climbing** N arribismo *m* (social) ► **social club** N club *m* social ► **social column** N (*Press*) ecos *mpl* de sociedad, notas *fpl* sociales (*LAm*) ► **the social contract** N (*Brit Ind*) el convenio social ► **social democracy** N socialdemocracia *f*, democracia *f* social ► **Social Democrat** N socialdemócrata *mf*; **the Social Democratic Party** el Partido Socialdemócrata ► **social disease** N (*euph*) enfermedad *f* venérea; (*relating to society*) enfermedad *f* social ► **social insurance** N (*US*) seguro *m* social ► **social outcast** N marginado/a *m/f* social ► **social science** N ciencias *fpl* sociales ► **social scientist** N sociólogo/a *m/f* ► **social secretary** N secretario/a *m/f* para asuntos sociales ► **social security** N seguridad *f* social; **to be on ~ security** vivir de la seguridad social ► **the social services** NPL los servicios sociales ► **social studies** NPL estudios *mpl* sociales ► **social welfare** N asistencia *f* social ► **social work** N asistencia *f* social ► **social worker** N asistente/a *m/f* social, trabajador(a) *m/f* social (*Mex*), visitador(a) *m/f* social (*Chile*)

socialism ['səʊʃəlɪzəm] N socialismo *m*

socialist ['səʊʃəlɪst] Ⓐ ADJ socialista

Ⓑ N socialista *mf*

socialistic [,səʊʃə'lɪstɪk] ADJ socialista

socialite ['səʊʃəlaɪt] N famosillo/a* *m/f* (*pej*), vividor(a) *m/f*

socialization [,səʊʃəlaɪ'zeɪʃən] N socialización *f*

socialize ['səʊʃəlaɪz] Ⓐ VT socializar

Ⓑ VI alternar, salir; **you should ~ more** deberías alternar *or* salir más; **we don't ~ much these days** últimamente no alternamos *or* salimos mucho

socially ['səʊʃəlɪ] ADV [*develop, integrate, interact*] socialmente; [*inferior, necessary*] socialmente, desde el punto de vista social; **~ acceptable** aceptado por la sociedad; **~ aware** con conciencia social; **to be ~ aware** tener conciencia social; **the ~ correct way of doing sth** la manera socialmente correcta de hacer algo; **to be ~ inadequate** no tener aptitud para el trato social, no saber tratar con la gente; **I didn't really get to know him ~** apenas tuve trato con él; **I don't really mix with him ~** no suelo alternar con él; **to be ~ unacceptable** ser mal visto

societal [sə'saɪətəl] ADJ societal

society [sə'saɪətɪ] Ⓐ N 1 (= *social community*) sociedad *f*; **he was a danger to ~** era un peligro para la sociedad; **a multi-cultural ~** una sociedad pluricultural

2 (= *company*) compañía *f*; **I enjoyed his ~** me encantó su compañía; **in the ~ of** en compañía de, acompañado por; **in polite ~** entre gente educada

3 (= *high society*) alta sociedad *f*; **to go into ~** [*girl*] ponerse de largo; **to move in ~** frecuentar la alta sociedad

4 (= *club, organization*) asociación *f*, sociedad *f*; **a drama ~** una asociación *or* sociedad de amigos del teatro; **the Glasgow film ~** la sociedad cinematográfica de Glasgow; **learned ~** sociedad *f* científica, academia *f*; **the Society of Friends** los cuáqueros

Ⓑ CPD ► **society column** N ecos *mpl* de sociedad, notas *fpl* sociales (*LAm*) ► **society news** NSING notas *fpl* de sociedad ► **society party** N fiesta *f* de sociedad ► **society wedding** N boda *f* de sociedad ► **society woman** N mujer *f* conocida en la alta sociedad

sociobiology [,səʊsɪəʊbaɪ'ɒlədʒɪ] N sociobiología *f*

socioeconomic ['səʊsɪəʊ,iːkə'nɒmɪk] ADJ socioeconómico

sociolect ['səʊsɪəʊ,lekt] N sociolecto *m*

sociolinguistic [,səʊsɪəʊlɪŋ'gwɪstɪk] ADJ sociolingüístico

sociolinguistics [,səʊsɪəʊlɪŋ'gwɪstɪks] NSING sociolingüística *f*

sociological [,səʊsɪə'lɒdʒɪkəl] ADJ sociológico

sociologist [,səʊsɪ'ɒlədʒɪst] N sociólogo/a *m/f*

sociology [,səʊsɪ'ɒlədʒɪ] N sociología *f*

sociopolitical [,səʊsɪəʊpə'lɪtɪkəl] ADJ sociopolítico

sock[1] [sɒk] N 1 calcetín *m*, media *f* (*LAm*); ✦***IDIOMS*** **to pull one's ~s up** hacer esfuerzos, despabilarse; **put a ~ in it!*** ¡a callar!, ¡cállate!; **this will knock your ~s off*** esto es

para quitarse el sombrero
2 (= *windsock*) manga *f* (de viento)

sock[2]* [sɒk] Ⓐ N (= *blow*) puñetazo *m*; **to give sb a ~ on the jaw** pegar a algn en la cara
Ⓑ VT pegar; **~ him one!** ¡pégale!

socket ['sɒkɪt] Ⓐ N 1 (*Anat*) [*of eye*] cuenca *f*; [*of joint*] glena *f*; [*of tooth*] alvéolo *m*
2 (*Elec*) enchufe *m*, toma *f* de corriente, tomacorriente *m* (*LAm*)
3 (*Mech*) encaje *m*, cubo *m*
Ⓑ CPD ► **socket joint** N (*Carpentry*) machihembrado *m*; (*Anat*) articulación *f* esférica

socko* ['sɒkəʊ] ADJ (*US*) estupendo*, extraordinario

Socrates ['sɒkrəti:z] N Sócrates

Socratic [sɒ'krætɪk] ADJ socrático

sod[1] [sɒd] N [*of earth*] terrón *m*, tepe *m*, césped *m*

sod[2]** [sɒd] (*Brit*) Ⓐ N cabrón/ona** *m/f*; **you ~!** ¡cabrón!**; **he's a real ~** es un auténtico cabrón**; **you lazy ~!** ¡vago!; **some poor ~** algún pobre diablo; **this job is a real ~** este trabajo es la monda*; **the lid is a ~ to get off** quitar la tapa hace sudar la gota gorda; **~'s law** (*Brit*) ley *f* de la indefectible mala voluntad de los objetos inanimados
Ⓑ VT **~ it!** ¡mierda!**; **~ him!** ¡que se joda!**

►**sod off**** VI + ADV **~ off!** ¡vete a la porra!*

soda ['səʊdə] Ⓐ N 1 (*Chem*) sosa *f*; (*Culin*) bicarbonato *m* (sódico)
2 (= *drink*) soda *f*; **whisky and ~** whiskysoda *m*; **do you like ~ with it?** ¿te echo un poco de sifón?, ¿con soda?
3 (*US*) (= *pop*) gaseosa *f*, refresco *m*
Ⓑ CPD ► **soda ash** N sosa *f* comercial, ceniza *f* de soda ► **soda fountain** N café-bar *m* ► **soda siphon** N sifón *m* ► **soda water** N soda *f*

sodality [səʊ'dælɪtɪ] N hermandad *f*, cofradía *f*

sod-all** ['sɒdɔ:l] (*Brit*) = **damn-all**

sodden ['sɒdn] ADJ empapado

sodding** ['sɒdɪŋ] (*Brit*) Ⓐ ADJ jodido**, puñetero*; **her ~ dog** su jodido perro**, su puñetero perro*; **shut the ~ door!** ¡cierra la jodida puerta!**; **it's a ~ disgrace!** ¡no hay derecho, joder!**; **~ hell!** ¡joder!**, ¡me cago en la leche!**
Ⓑ ADV **it's ~ difficult** es muy jodido**, es puñeteramente complicado*; **he's ~ crazy!** ¡está como una puta cabra!**

sodium ['səʊdɪəm] Ⓐ N sodio *m*
Ⓑ CPD ► **sodium bicarbonate** N bicarbonato *m* sódico ► **sodium carbonate** N carbonato *m* sódico ► **sodium chloride** N cloruro *m* sódico, cloruro *m* de sodio ► **sodium lamp** N lámpara *f* de vapor de sodio ► **sodium nitrate** N nitrato *m* sódico ► **sodium sulphate** N sulfato *m* sódico

Sodom ['sɒdəm] N Sodoma *f*

sodomite ['sɒdəmaɪt] N sodomita *mf*

sodomize ['sɒdəmaɪz] VT sodomizar

sodomy ['sɒdəmɪ] N sodomía *f*

sofa ['səʊfə] Ⓐ N sofá *m*
Ⓑ CPD ► **sofa bed** N sofá-cama *m*

Sofia ['səʊfɪə] N Sofía *f*

soft [sɒft] Ⓐ ADJ (*compar* **softer**; *superl* **softest**)
1 (= *not hard*) [*ground, water, cheese, pencil, contact lens*] blando; [*bed, mattress, pillow*] blando, mullido; [*metal*] maleable, dúctil; (*pej*) [*muscles, flesh*] blando; **to go ~** [*biscuits etc*] ablandarse; **his muscles have gone ~** sus músculos han perdido su fuerza, se le han ablandado los músculos
2 (= *smooth*) [*skin, hair, fur, fabric, texture*] suave; **to make ~** [+ *skin, clothes*] suavizar; [+ *leather*] ablandar
3 (= *gentle, not harsh*) [*breeze, landing*] suave; [*accent*] ligero, leve; [*music*] suave; [*light*] tenue; [*colour*] delicado; [*line*] difuminado; **in ~ focus** desenfocado; **~ lighting** luz *f* tenue
4 (= *quiet*) [*whisper, laugh, step*] suave; [*whistle*] flojo; [*voice*] suave, tenue; **his voice was so ~ she scarcely heard it** hablaba tan bajito que apenas le oía; **the music is too ~** esta música está demasiado baja
5 (= *kind*) [*smile, person*] dulce; [*words*] tierno, dulce; **to have a ~ heart** ser todo corazón
6 (= *lenient, weak*) blando; **the ~ left** (*Pol*) la izquierda moderada, el centro-izquierda; **to take a ~ line against sth** adoptar una línea suave en contra de algo; **to be (too) ~ on/with sth/sb** ser (demasiado) blando *or* indulgente con algo/algn
7 (= *easy*) fácil; **~ job** chollo *m* (*Sp**), trabajo *m* fácil; **~ option** camino *m* fácil; **~ target** blanco *m* fácil; *see also* **touch A2**
8 (*) (= *foolish*) bobo*, tonto; **you must be ~!** ¡tú eres tonto!, ¡has perdido el juicio!; **to be ~ in the head** ser un poco bobo*
9 (= *fond*) **to be ~ on sb** sentir afecto por algn; **to have a ~ spot for sb** tener debilidad por algn
10 (*Ling*) débil
11 (*Econ*) [*prices, economy*] débil; [*sales, market, growth*] flojo
Ⓑ CPD [*currency, drug, fruit*] blando ► **soft brown sugar** N azúcar *f* morena blanda, azúcar *m* moreno blando ► **soft centre** N relleno *m* blando ► **soft commodities** NPL (*Fin*) bienes *mpl* perecederos, bienes *mpl* no durables ► **soft copy** N (*Comput*) copia *f* transitoria ► **soft drink** N bebida *f* refrescante, refresco *m* ► **soft furnishings** NPL textiles *mpl* ► **soft goods** NPL (*Comm*) géneros *mpl* textiles, tejidos *mpl* ► **soft money** N (*US*) papel *m* moneda ► **soft palate** N (*Anat*) velo *m* del paladar ► **soft pedal** N (*Mus*) pedal *m* suave; *see also* **soft-pedal** ► **soft porn**, **soft pornography** N pornografía *f* blanda ► **soft sell** N venta *f* por persuasión ► **soft soap*** N coba* *f*; **to give sb ~ soap** dar coba a algn*; *see also* **soft-soap** ► **soft top** N (*esp US*) descapotable *m* ► **soft toy** N juguete *m* de peluche

softback ['sɒftbæk] Ⓐ ADJ = **soft-bound**
Ⓑ N libro *m* en rústica

softball ['sɒftbɔ:l] N (*US*) *especie de béisbol sobre un terreno más pequeño que el normal, con pelota grande y blanda*

soft-boiled ['sɒft,bɔɪld] ADJ [*egg*] pasado (por agua)

soft-bound ['sɒftbaʊnd], **soft-cover** ['sɒftkʌvə^r] ADJ **~ book** libro *m* en rústica

soften ['sɒfn] Ⓐ VT 1 (= *make less hard*) [+ *butter, ground, metal, leather, water*] ablandar
2 (= *make smooth*) [+ *fabric, skin, hair*] suavizar
3 (= *make gentle*) [+ *sound, outline*] suavizar; [+ *lights, lighting*] hacer más tenue; [+ *person*] ablandar
4 (= *mitigate*) [+ *effect, reaction*] mitigar, atenuar; **to ~ the blow** (*fig*) amortiguar el golpe
Ⓑ VI 1 (= *become less hard*) [*butter, ground, metal*] ablandarse
2 (= *become smooth*) [*fabric, skin, hair*] suavizarse
3 (= *become gentle*) [*voice, outline*] suavizarse; [*lighting*] hacerse más tenue; [*person*] ablandarse; **her heart ~ed** se le ablandó el corazón
4 (= *become moderate*) [*effect*] mitigarse, atenuarse; [*attitude*] suavizarse, moderarse

►**soften up** Ⓐ VT + ADV [+ *resistance*] debilitar
Ⓑ VI + ADV **to ~ up on sb** volverse menos severo con algn; **we must not ~ up on communism** debemos seguir tan opuestos como siempre al comunismo

softener ['sɒfnə^r] N (= *water softener*) descalcificador *m*, decalcificador *m*; (= *fabric softener*) suavizante *m*

softening ['sɒfnɪŋ] N [*of ground, metal, leather*] reblandecimiento *m*; (*Fin*) [*of economy, market*] debilitamiento *m*; **~ of the brain** reblandecimiento *m* cerebral; **there has been a ~ of his attitude/position** ha suavizado *or* moderado su actitud/posición

soft-headed ['sɒft'hedɪd] ADJ bobo, tonto

soft-hearted ['sɒft'hɑ:tɪd] ADJ compasivo, bondadoso

soft-heartedness ['sɒft'hɑ:tɪdnɪs] N compasión *f*, bondad *f*

softie* ['sɒftɪ] N = **softy**

soft-liner [,sɒft'laɪnə^r] N blando/a *m/f*

softly ['sɒftlɪ] ADV 1 (= *quietly*) [*walk, move*] silenciosamente, sin hacer ruido; [*say*] bajito, en voz baja; [*whistle*] bajito; **he closed the door ~** cerró la puerta silenciosamente; **he swore ~** dijo una palabrota en voz baja, susurró una palabrota; **the radio was playing ~ in the kitchen** la radio sonaba bajito en la cocina; **a ~ spoken young man** un joven de voz suave
2 (= *gently*) [*touch, tap, kiss*] suavemente; [*smile*] con ternura, dulcemente; [*say*] dulcemente
3 (= *not brightly*) [*glow, gleam, shine*] tenuemente; **~ lit** iluminado con luz tenue

softly-softly [,sɒftlɪ'sɒftlɪ] ADJ **to adopt a ~ approach** adoptar una política cautelosa

softness ['sɒftnɪs] N 1 [*of ground, bread*] blandura *f*, lo blando; [*of pencil, water, butter*] lo blando; [*of bed, pillow*] lo mullido; [*of muscles, flesh*] blandura *f*
2 [*of skin, hair, fabric*] suavidad *f*
3 [*of breeze, touch, voice, light, colour*] suavidad *f*; [*of light*] lo tenue
4 [*of sound, laugh*] suavidad *f*
5 (= *kindness*) ternura *f*
6 (= *leniency*) [*of person, approach*] indulgencia *f*, blandura *f*
7 (= *weakness*) debilidad *f*
8 (= *stupidity*) estupidez *f*

soft-pedal ['sɒft'pedl] VT (*esp US*) (*fig*) minimizar la importancia de

soft-soap* [,sɒft'səʊp] VT dar coba a*

soft-spoken ['sɒft'spəʊkən] ADJ de voz suave

software ['sɒftwɛə^r] Ⓐ N (*Comput*) software *m*
Ⓑ CPD ► **software engineer** N ingeniero/a *m/f* de software ► **software engineering** N ingeniería *f* de software ► **software house** N compañía *f* especializada en programación ► **software package** N paquete *m* de programas

softwood ['sɒftwʊd] N madera *f* blanda

softy* ['sɒftɪ] N blandengue* *mf*; (= *too tender-hearted*) blandengue* *mf*, buenazo/a* *m/f*; (= *no stamina etc*) blandengue* *mf*; (= *coward*) gallina* *mf*, cobardica* *mf*; **you big softie, stop crying!** ¡no seas llorón *or* llorica!*

soggy ['sɒgɪ] ADJ (*compar* **soggier**; *superl* **soggiest**) [*paper*] mojado; [*clothes, ground*] empapado; [*bread, biscuits*] revenido; [*salad, vegetables*] pasado

soh [səʊ] N (*Mus*) sol *m*

soi-disant ['swɑ:'di:zɔ:ŋ] ADJ supuesto, presunto, sedicente

soigné ['swɑ:njeɪ] ADJ pulcro, acicalado

soil[1] [sɔɪl] N (= *earth*) tierra *f*; **his native ~** su tierra natal, su patria; **on British ~** en suelo británico; **the ~** (= *farmland*) la tierra

soil[2] [sɔɪl] Ⓐ VT [1] (= *dirty*) ensuciar; (= *stain*) manchar; **to ~ o.s.** ensuciarse
[2] (*fig*) [+ *reputation, honour etc*] manchar; **I would not ~ myself by contact with ...** no me rebajaría a tener contacto con ...
Ⓑ VI ensuciarse

soiled [sɔɪld] ADJ (= *dirty*) sucio; (= *stained*) manchado

soilpipe ['sɔɪlpaɪp] N tubo *m* de desagüe sanitario

soirée ['swɑːreɪ] N velada *f*

sojourn ['sɒdʒɜːn] Ⓐ N permanencia *f*, estancia *f*
Ⓑ VI permanecer, residir, morar; (*for short time*) pasar una temporada

solace ['sɒlɪs] Ⓐ N consuelo *m*; **to seek ~ with ...** procurar consolarse con ..., buscar consuelo en
Ⓑ VT consolar; **to ~ o.s.** consolarse (**with** con)

solar ['səʊləʳ] Ⓐ ADJ solar
Ⓑ CPD ► **solar battery** N pila *f* solar ► **solar calculator** N calculadora *f* solar ► **solar calendar** N calendario *m* solar ► **solar cell** N célula *f* solar ► **solar eclipse** N eclipse *m* solar ► **solar energy** N energía *f* solar ► **solar flare** N erupción *f* solar ► **solar heat** N calor *m* solar ► **solar heating** N calefacción *f* solar ► **solar panel** N panel *m* solar ► **solar plexus** N (*Anat*) plexo *m* solar ► **solar power** N energía *f* solar ► **solar system** N sistema *m* solar ► **solar wind** N viento *m* solar ► **solar year** N año *m* solar

solarium [səʊ'lɛərɪəm] N (*pl* **solariums** *or* **solaria** [səʊ'lɛərɪə]) solárium *m*, solario *m*

solar-powered ['səʊlə'paʊəd] ADJ de energía solar

sold [səʊld] PT, PP *of* **sell**

solder ['səʊldəʳ] Ⓐ N soldadura *f*
Ⓑ VT soldar

soldering-iron ['səʊldərɪŋ,aɪən] N soldador *m*

soldier ['səʊldʒəʳ] Ⓐ N [1] (*Mil*) soldado *mf*, militar *mf*; **common ~** soldado *mf* raso; **~ of fortune** aventurero/a *m/f* militar; **an old ~** un veterano *or* excombatiente; **to come the old ~ with sb*** tratar de imponerse a algn (por más experimentado); **to play at ~s** jugar a los soldados; **a woman ~** una soldado, una mujer soldado
[2] (*Brit**) (= *strip of bread or toast*) *tira de pan (tostada) para mojar en los huevos pasados por agua*
[3] (*Zool*) (= *ant*) hormiga *f* soldado, soldado *m*
Ⓑ VI ser soldado; **he ~ed for ten years in the East** sirvió durante diez años en el Oriente
Ⓒ CPD ► **soldier ant** N hormiga *f* soldado, soldado *m*

►**soldier on** VI + ADV seguir adelante

soldierly ['səʊldʒəlɪ] ADJ militar

soldiery ['səʊldʒərɪ] N soldadesca *f*; **a brutal and licentious ~** la soldadesca indisciplinada

sole[1] [səʊl] Ⓐ N [1] (*Anat*) planta *f*
[2] [*of shoe*] suela *f*; **half ~** media suela *f*; **inner ~** plantilla *f*
Ⓑ VT poner suela a

sole[2] [səʊl] N (*pl* **sole** *or* **soles**) (= *fish*) lenguado *m*

sole[3] [səʊl] ADJ (= *only*) único; (= *exclusive*) exclusivo, en exclusividad; **the ~ reason is that ...** la única razón es que ...; **to be ~ agent for** tener la representación exclusiva de; **~ owner** propietario/a *m/f* único/a; **~ trader** empresario/a *m/f* individual

solecism ['sɒləsɪzəm] N solecismo *m*

solely ['səʊllɪ] ADV (= *only*) únicamente, solamente, sólo; (= *exclusively*) exclusivamente

solemn ['sɒləm] ADJ [*person, face*] serio, adusto; [*warning*] serio; [*occasion, promise*] solemne; **he looked ~** estaba muy serio, tenía un aspecto adusto

solemnity [sə'lemnɪtɪ] N [*of occasion, promise*] solemnidad *f*; [*of person's expression*] seriedad *f*, adustez *f*; [*of warning*] seriedad *f*

solemnization [,sɒləmnaɪ'zeɪʃən] N solemnización *f*

solemnize ['sɒləmnaɪz] VT solemnizar

solemnly ['sɒləmlɪ] ADV [*nod, look*] seriamente, con gesto adusto; [*say*] con seriedad, con tono solemne; [*promise, declare, swear*] solemnemente

solenoid ['səʊlənɔɪd] N solenoide *m*

sol-fa ['sɒl'fɑː] N (*Mus*) solfeo *m*

solicit [sə'lɪsɪt] Ⓐ VT (= *request*) solicitar; (= *demand*) exigir; (= *beg for*) pedir; **to ~ sb for sth** ◊ **~ sth of sb** solicitar algo a algn
Ⓑ VI [*prostitute*] ejercer la prostitución abordando a clientes

solicitation [sə,lɪsɪ'teɪʃən] N (*esp US*) solicitación *f*

soliciting [sə'lɪsɪtɪŋ] N abordamiento *m*; (*by prostitute*) ejercicio *m* de la prostitución (*abordando a los clientes*)

solicitor [sə'lɪsɪtəʳ] Ⓐ N [1] (*Brit Jur*) (= *lawyer*) procurador(a) *m/f*, abogado/a *m/f*; (*for wills*) notario/a *m/f*; → LAWYERS
[2] (*US*) (= *officer*) representante *mf*, agente *mf*; (*Jur*) abogado/a *m/f* asesor(a) adscrito/a a un municipio
Ⓑ CPD ► **Solicitor General** N (*Brit*) subfiscal *mf* de la corona; (*US*) Procurador(a) *m/f* general del Estado

solicitous [sə'lɪsɪtəs] ADJ **~ (about** *or* **for)** (= *anxious*) atento (a); **~ to please** deseoso de agradar *or* quedar bien

solicitude [sə'lɪsɪtjuːd] N (*frm*) (= *consideration*) solicitud *f*; (= *concern*) preocupación *f*; (= *anxiety*) ansiedad *f*; (= *attention*) atención *f*

solid ['sɒlɪd] Ⓐ ADJ [1] (= *not liquid*) sólido; **to become ~** solidificarse; **~ food** alimentos *mpl* sólidos; **to freeze ~** congelarse por completo; **to be frozen ~** estar completamente congelado; **to go ~** solidificarse
[2] (= *firm*) [*masonry, building, understanding, basis*] sólido; [*argument*] sólido, bien fundamentado; [*relationship*] sólido, firme; **get a good ~ grip on the handle** agarra bien el mango; **~ ground** tierra *f* firme; **to have ~ grounds for thinking that ...** tener bases sólidas para creer que ...; ✦**IDIOM as ~ as a rock** [*structure, relationship*] sólido como una roca; [*substance*] duro como una piedra; [*person*] digno de confianza
[3] (= *not hollow*) [*rock*] sólido; [*wood, steel*] macizo, puro; [*tyre, ball, block*] macizo; **~ gold** oro *m* puro
[4] (= *compact, dense*) [*layer, crowd*] compacto; **flights to Israel are booked ~** los vuelos a Israel están completamente llenos; **a man of ~ build** un hombre fornido *or* de constitución robusta; **a ~ mass of colour** una masa sólida de color; **a ~ mass of people** una masa compacta de gente; **he's six feet of ~ muscle** mide uno ochenta y es todo músculo; **the streets were packed ~ with people** las calles estaban abarrotadas de gente; **the bolts have rusted ~** los tornillos están tan oxidados que es imposible girarlos; **the traffic was ~ going into town** había una caravana tremenda en dirección a la ciudad*
[5] (= *continuous*) [*line, rain*] ininterrumpido; **we waited two ~ hours** esperamos dos horas enteras; **I've been working on this for eight hours ~** he estado trabajando sobre esto durante ocho horas ininterrumpidas, llevo trabajando sobre esto ocho horas sin parar
[6] (= *reliable*) [*person, relationship*] serio; [*evidence, reason, values*] sólido; [*information*] fiable; [*work*] concienzudo; [*citizen*] responsable; [*advice*] útil; **he's a good ~ worker** es un trabajador responsable
[7] (= *substantial*) **a ~ meal** una comida sustanciosa
[8] (= *unanimous*) **~ support** un apoyo unánime
[9] (*Geom*) [*figure*] tridimensional
Ⓑ N [1] (*Phys, Chem*) sólido *m*
[2] (*Geom*) sólido *m*
[3] **solids** (= *solid food*) (alimentos *mpl*) sólidos *mpl*; **is he on ~s yet?** ¿come ya alimentos sólidos?
Ⓒ CPD ► **solid angle** N (*Geom*) ángulo *m* sólido ► **solid compound** N (*Ling*) *compuesto que se escribe como una sola palabra* ► **solid fuel** N combustible *m* sólido ► **solid geometry** N geometría *f* de los cuerpos sólidos

solidarity [,sɒlɪ'dærɪtɪ] Ⓐ N solidaridad *f*; **out of ~ with the workers** por solidaridad con los obreros
Ⓑ CPD ► **solidarity strike** N huelga *f* por solidaridad

solidification [sə,lɪdɪfɪ'keɪʃən] N solidificación *f*

solidify [sə'lɪdɪfaɪ] Ⓐ VI [1] (= *become solid*) solidificarse
[2] (*fig*) (= *become strong, united etc*) unirse
Ⓑ VT solidificar

solidity [sə'lɪdɪtɪ] N solidez *f*

solidly ['sɒlɪdlɪ] ADV [1] (= *firmly*) con firmeza; **he placed his hands ~ on the desk** colocó sus manos con firmeza sobre la mesa; **it was ~ under Communist rule** estaba firmemente sometida a la ley comunista; **a ~ based theory** una teoría bien fundamentada, una teoría de una base sólida
[2] (= *sturdily*) **~ made** sólidamente construido, de construcción sólida; **~ built** *or* **constructed** de construcción sólida; **a ~-built man** un hombre fornido *or* de constitución robusta
[3] (= *without pause*) ininterrumpidamente, sin parar; **we drove/it rained ~ for two days** condujimos/llovió ininterrumpidamente durante dos días, condujimos/llovió dos días sin parar; **to work ~** trabajar sin descanso *or* sin parar
[4] (= *unanimously*) unánimemente; **to vote ~ for sb** votar unánimemente por algn; **to be ~ behind sth/sb** apoyar algo/a algn unánimemente
[5] (= *thoroughly*) **a ~ reasoned argument** un argumento sólidamente razonado; **a ~ middle-class neighbourhood** un barrio totalmente de clase media

solid-state physics [,sɒlɪdsteɪt'fɪzɪks] NSING física *f* del estado sólido

solidus ['sɒlɪdəs] N (*Typ*) barra *f*

soliloquize [sə'lɪləkwaɪz] Ⓐ VI decir un soliloquio, monologar
Ⓑ VT **"perhaps," he ~d** —quizás —dijo para sí

soliloquy [sə'lɪləkwɪ] N soliloquio *m*

solipsism ['səʊlɪpsɪzəm] N solipsismo *m*

solitaire [ˌsɒlɪˈtɛəʳ] N [1] (= *gem*) solitario *m*
[2] (= *board game*) solitario *m*
[3] (*esp US Cards*) solitario *m*; **to play ~** hacer un solitario

solitary [ˈsɒlɪtərɪ] Ⓐ ADJ [1] (= *lonely, lone*) [*person, life, childhood*] solitario; **to take a ~ walk** dar un paseo solo, pasearse sin compañía; **to feel rather ~** sentirse solo, sentirse aislado
[2] (= *secluded*) retirado
[3] (= *sole*) solo, único; **not a ~ one** ni uno (solo); **there has been one ~ case** ha habido un caso único; **there has not been one ~ case** no ha habido ni un solo caso
Ⓑ N [1] (= *person*) solitario/a *m/f*
[2] (*) = **solitary confinement**
Ⓒ CPD ► **solitary confinement** N **to be in ~ confinement** estar incomunicado, estar en pelota‡

solitude [ˈsɒlɪtjuːd] N soledad *f*

solo [ˈsəʊləʊ] Ⓐ N (*pl* **solos**) [1] (*Mus*) solo *m*; **a tenor ~** un solo para tenor; **a guitar ~** un solo de guitarra
[2] (*Cards*) solo *m*
Ⓑ ADJ **~ flight** vuelo *m* a solas; **passage for ~ violin** pasaje *m* para violín solo; **~ trip round the world** vuelta *f* al mundo en solitario
Ⓒ ADV solo, a solas; **to fly ~** volar a solas; **to sing ~** cantar solo

soloist [ˈsəʊləʊɪst] N solista *mf*

Solomon [ˈsɒləmən] Ⓐ N Salomón
Ⓑ CPD ► **Solomon Islands** NPL Islas *fpl* Salomón

solstice [ˈsɒlstɪs] N solsticio *m*; **summer ~** solsticio *m* de verano; **winter ~** solsticio *m* de invierno

solubility [ˌsɒljʊˈbɪlɪtɪ] N solubilidad *f*

soluble [ˈsɒljʊbl] ADJ soluble; **~ in water** soluble en agua

solution [səˈluːʃən] N [1] (= *answer*) solución *f*; **the ~ to a problem** la solución de *or* a un problema
[2] (*Chem*) solución *f*; **in ~** en solución

solvable [ˈsɒlvəbl] ADJ soluble, que se puede resolver

solve [sɒlv] VT [+ *problem, puzzle*] resolver, solucionar; [+ *mystery, crime*] resolver, esclarecer; **to ~ a riddle** resolver una adivinanza, adivinar *or* resolver un acertijo; **that question remains to be ~d** aún queda por resolver esa cuestión

solvency [ˈsɒlvənsɪ] N (*Fin*) solvencia *f*

solvent [ˈsɒlvənt] Ⓐ ADJ (*Chem, Fin*) solvente
Ⓑ N (*Chem*) disolvente *m*
Ⓒ CPD ► **solvent abuse** N abuso *m* de los disolventes

solver [ˈsɒlvəʳ] N solucionista *mf*

Som. ABBR (*Brit*) = **Somerset**

Somali [səʊˈmɑːlɪ] Ⓐ ADJ somalí
Ⓑ N somalí *mf*

Somalia [səʊˈmɑːlɪə] N Somalia *f*

Somalian [səʊˈmɑːlɪən] Ⓐ ADJ somalí
Ⓑ N somalí *mf*

Somaliland [səʊˈmɑːlɪlænd] N Somalia *f*

sombre, somber (*US*) [ˈsɒmbəʳ] ADJ [1] (= *sober*) sombrío; **a ~ prospect** una perspectiva sombría; **in ~ hues** en colores sombríos
[2] (= *pessimistic*) pesimista; **he was ~ about our chances** se mostró pesimista acerca de nuestras posibilidades
[3] (= *melancholy*) melancólico

sombrely, somberly (*US*) [ˈsɒmbəlɪ] ADV [1] (= *soberly*) sombríamente
[2] (= *pessimistically*) con pesimismo, en tono pesimista

sombreness, somberness (*US*) [ˈsɒmbənɪs] N [1] (= *soberness*) lo sombrío
[2] (= *pessimism*) pesimismo *m*

some [sʌm]

[A] ADJECTIVE	[C] ADVERB
[B] PRONOUN	

Ⓐ ADJECTIVE
[1] ***= an amount of***
*When **some** refers to something you can't count, it usually isn't translated:*
will you have ~ tea? ¿quieres té?; **have ~ more cake** toma *or* sírvete más pastel; **you've got ~ money, haven't you?** tienes dinero, ¿no?; **let's have ~ breakfast** vamos a desayunar; [BUT] **we gave them ~ food** les dimos comida *or* algo de comida; **there's ~ great acting in this film** hay algunas actuaciones muy buenas en esta película
[2] ***= a little*** algo de, un poco de; **all I have left is ~ chocolate** solamente me queda algo de *or* un poco de chocolate; **she has ~ experience with children** tiene algo de *or* un poco de experiencia con niños; **the book was ~ help, but not much** el libro ayudó algo *or* un poco, pero no mucho, el libro fue de alguna ayuda, pero no mucha; **I did ~ writing this morning** he escrito un poco esta mañana; **she went out for ~ fresh air** salió para tomar un poco de aire fresco
[3] ***= a number of*** unos; **~ boys were shouting at him** unos chicos le estaban gritando; **I have ~ wonderful memories** tengo unos recuerdos maravillosos; [BUT] **would you like ~ sweets/grapes?** ¿quieres caramelos/uvas?; **we've got ~ biscuits, haven't we?** tenemos galletas, ¿no?; **you need ~ new trousers/glasses** necesitas unos pantalones nuevos/unas gafas nuevas; **surely she has SOME friends?** debe de tener por lo menos algún amigo
[4] ***= certain*** **~ people say that …** algunos dicen que …, algunas personas dicen que …, hay gente que dice que …; **~ people hate fish** algunas personas odian el pescado, hay gente que odia el pescado; **~ people just don't care** hay gente que no se preocupa en lo más mínimo; **~ people have all the luck!** ¡los hay que tienen suerte!, ¡algunos parece que nacen de pie!*; **in ~ ways he's right** en cierto modo *or* sentido, tiene razón; **I paid for mine, unlike ~ people I could mention** yo pagué el mío, no como ciertas personas *or* algunos a los que no quiero nombrar; **~ mushrooms are poisonous** ciertos tipos de setas son venenosas; **I like ~ jazz music** me gusta cierto tipo de jazz
[5] ***indefinite*** algún + *masc noun*, alguna + *fem noun*; **~ day** algún día; **~ day next week** algún día de la semana que viene; **~ idiot of a driver** algún imbécil de conductor; **I read it in ~ book (or other)** lo he leído en algún libro; **for ~ reason (or other)** por alguna razón, por una u otra razón; **there must be SOME solution** alguna solución tiene que haber; [BUT] **~ man was asking for you** un hombre estuvo preguntando por ti; **this will give you ~ idea of …** esto te dará una idea de …; **let's make it ~ other time** hagámoslo otro día
[6] ***= a considerable amount of*** bastante; **it took ~ courage to do that** hacer eso exigió bastante valor; **it's a matter of ~ importance** es un asunto de bastante importancia; **she is ~ few years younger than him** es bastantes años más joven que él; **I haven't seen him for ~ time** hace bastante (tiempo) que no lo veo; *see also* **length A4**
[7] ***= a considerable number of*** **I haven't seen him for ~ years** hace bastantes años que no lo veo; **I posted it ~ days ago (now)** lo mandé por correo hace (ya) varios días
[8] (* *emphatic*) [8·1] (*admiring*) **that's ~ fish!** ¡eso sí que es un pez!, ¡eso es lo que se llama un pez!, ¡vaya pez!; **that's ~ woman** ¡qué mujer!; **it was ~ party** ¡vaya fiesta!, ¡menuda fiesta!
[8·2] (*iro*) **"he says he's my friend" — "~ friend!"** —dice que es mi amigo —¡menudo amigo!; **you're ~ help, you are!** ¡vaya ayuda das!, ¡menuda ayuda eres tú!; **~ expert!** ¡valiente experto!
[8·3] (*in annoyance*) **~ people!** ¡qué gente!
Ⓑ PRONOUN
[1] ***= a certain amount, a little*** un poco; **have ~!** ¡toma un poco!; **could I have ~ of that cheese?** ¿me das un poco de ese queso?; **I only want ~ of it** sólo quiero un poco; [BUT] **thanks, I've got ~** gracias, ya tengo; **"I haven't got any paper" — "I'll give you ~"** —no tengo nada de papel —yo te doy; **it would cost twice that much and then ~*** costaría el doble de eso y algo más de propina*
[2] ***= a part*** una parte; **I've read ~ of the book** he leído (una) parte del libro; **~ of what he said was true** parte de lo que dijo era cierto; **~ (of it) has been eaten** se han comido un poco *or* una parte; **give me ~!** ¡dame un poco!
[3] ***= a number*** algunos/as *mpl/fpl*; **~ (of them) have been sold** algunos (de ellos) se han vendido; **~ of my friends came** vinieron algunos de mis amigos; **I don't want them all, but I'd like ~** no los quiero todos, pero sí unos pocos *or* cuantos, no los quiero todos, pero sí algunos; **would you like ~?** ¿quieres unos pocos *or* cuantos?, ¿quieres algunos?
[4] ***= certain people*** algunos, algunas personas; **~ believe that …** algunos creen que …, algunas personas creen que …, hay gente que cree que …
Ⓒ ADVERB
[1] ***= about*** **~ 20 people** unas 20 personas, una veintena de personas; **~ £30** unas 30 libras
[2] (*esp US**) [2·1] (= *a lot*) mucho; **we laughed ~** nos reímos mucho; **Edinburgh to London in five hours, that's going ~!** de Edimburgo a Londres en cinco horas, ¡eso sí que es rapidez!
[2·2] (= *a little*) **you'll feel better when you've slept ~** te sentirás mejor cuando hayas dormido un poco

somebody [ˈsʌmbədɪ] Ⓐ PRON alguien; **there's ~ coming** viene alguien; **~ knocked at the door** alguien llamó a la puerta; **~ speak to me!** ¡que alguien me diga algo!; **I need ~ to help me** necesito que alguien me ayude, necesito a alguien que me ayude; **~ Italian** un italiano; **~ from the audience** alguien del público; **we need ~ strong for that** necesitamos a alguien fuerte para eso; **you must have seen SOMEBODY!** ¡a alguien tienes que haber visto!; **let ~ else try** deja que otro *or* otra persona *or* alguien más lo intente; **~ or other** alguien; ✦*IDIOM* **~ up there loves/hates me** tengo una buena/mala racha
Ⓑ N **to be ~** ser un personaje, ser alguien; **he really thinks he's ~ doesn't he?** realmente se cree alguien, ¿verdad?

someday [ˈsʌmdeɪ] ADV algún día

somehow [ˈsʌmhaʊ] ADV [1] (= *by some means*) de algún modo, de alguna manera; **I'll do it ~** de algún modo *or* de alguna manera lo haré; **it**

has to be done ~ or other de un modo u otro *or* de una manera u otra tiene que hacerse

[2] (= *for some reason*) por alguna razón; **~ I didn't get on with her** por alguna razón *or* no sé porqué, no me llevaba bien con ella; **~ I don't think he believed me** no sé porqué, pero me parece que no me creyó; **~ or other I never liked him** por alguna razón u otra nunca me cayó bien; **it seems odd, ~ ◊ it seems ~ odd** no sé porqué pero me parece extraño

someone ['sʌmwʌn] PRON = **somebody**

someplace ['sʌmpleɪs] ADV (*US*) = **somewhere**

somersault ['sʌməsɔːlt] Ⓐ N (*by person*) voltereta *f*, salto *m* mortal; (*by car etc*) vuelco *m*, vuelta *f* de campana; **to turn** *or* **do a ~** dar una voltereta, dar un salto mortal

Ⓑ VI [*person*] dar una voltereta, dar un salto mortal; [*car etc*] dar una vuelta de campana

something ['sʌmθɪŋ] Ⓐ PRON [1] algo; **cook ~ nice** haz algo que esté rico; **wear ~ warm** ponte algo que abrigue; **there's ~ about him I don't like** hay algo que no me gusta de él; **let me ask you ~** déjame hacerte una pregunta, deja que te pregunte algo; **it's come to ~ when you get the sack for that** ¡a lo que hemos llegado! ¡que te echen por eso!; **that has ~ to do with accountancy** eso tiene que ver *or* está relacionado con la contabilidad; **he's got ~ to do with it** está metido *or* involucrado en eso; **~ else** otra cosa; **here's ~ for your trouble†** aquí tiene, por la molestia; **I think you may have ~ there** puede que tengas razón, puede que estés en lo cierto; **there's ~ in what you say** hay algo de verdad en lo que dices; **he's ~ in the City** trabaja de algo *or* de no sé qué en la City; **the music spoke to ~ in me** la música inspiró algo en mí; **~ of the kind** algo por el estilo; **do you want to make ~ of it?** ¿quieres hacer un problema de esto?; **there's ~ the matter** pasa algo; **it's not ~ I approve of** no es algo que yo apruebe; **you can't get ~ for nothing** las cosas no las regalan; **there's ~ odd here** aquí hay *or* pasa algo (raro); **it's ~ of a problem** es de algún modo *or* en cierto modo un problema, en cierto sentido representa un problema; **he's ~ of a musician** tiene algo de músico, tiene cierto talento para la música; **he's getting ~ of a reputation around here** se está ganando cierta fama por aquí; **the play proved to be ~ of a letdown** la obra resultó ser un tanto decepcionante; **I hope to see ~ of you** espero que nos seguiremos viendo, nos estaremos viendo, espero (*LAm*); **did you say ~?** ¿dijiste algo?; **well, that's ~** eso ya es algo; **will you have ~ to drink?** ¿quieres tomar algo?; **I need ~ to eat** necesito comer algo; **it gives her ~ to live for** le da un motivo para vivir

[2] (*) (= *something special or unusual*) **he thinks he's ~*** se cree alguien; **their win was quite ~** su victoria fue extraordinaria; **that's really ~!** ¡eso sí que es fenomenal *or* estupendo!

[3] (*in guesses, approximations*) **he's called John ~** se llama John no sé qué, se llama John algo; **there were 30 ~** había 30 y algunos más; **the four ~ train** el tren de las cuatro y pico; **are you mad or ~?** ¿estás loco o qué?, ¿estás loco o algo así?; **her name is Camilla or ~** se llama Camilla o algo así, se llama algo así como Camilla, se llama Camilla o algo por el estilo; **he's got flu or ~** tiene gripe o algo parecido; **~ or other** algo, alguna cosa

Ⓑ ADV [1] (= *a little, somewhat*) [1·1] **there were ~ like 80 people there** había algo así como 80 personas allí, había como unas 80 personas allí; **it's ~ like ten o'clock** son algo así como las diez, son las diez más o menos; **it cost £100, or ~ like that** costó 100 libras, o algo así; **he looks ~ like me** se parece algo *or* un poco a mí; **he talks ~ like his father** tiene algo de su padre cuando habla; **now that's ~ like a rose!** ¡eso es lo que se llama una rosa!; **now that's ~ like it!** ¡así es como debe ser!

[1·2] **~ over 200** algo más de 200, un poco más de 200

[2] (*) **they pull her leg ~ chronic** le toman el pelo una barbaridad*, le toman el pelo que es una cosa mala*; **it hurts ~ awful** duele un montón*; **she loves him ~ awful** le quiere una barbaridad*

Ⓒ N **she has a certain ~** tiene un algo, tiene un no sé qué; **that certain ~ that makes all the difference** ese no sé qué que importa tanto; **it's just a little ~ I picked up in a sale** es una tontería que compré en las rebajas; **would you like a little ~ before dinner?** ¿quieres tomar *or* picar algo antes de la cena?

sometime ['sʌmtaɪm] Ⓐ ADV [1] (*in future*) algún día; **you must come and see us ~** tienes que venir a vernos algún día; **I'll finish it ~** lo voy a terminar un día de estos; **~ soon** un día de estos, antes de que pase mucho tiempo; **~ before tomorrow** antes de mañana; **~ next year** en algún momento el año que viene, el año que viene, no sé cuándo exactamente; **~ or other it will have to be done** tarde o temprano tendrá que hacerse

[2] (*in past*) **~ last month** (en algún momento) el mes pasado, el mes pasado, no sé cuándo exactamente; **the victim died ~ during the last 24 hours** la víctima murió durante las últimas 24 horas, no se sabe el momento preciso; **~ last century** en el siglo pasado, durante el siglo pasado

Ⓑ ADJ [1] (= *former*) ex …, antiguo

[2] (*US*) (= *occasional*) intermitente

sometimes ['sʌmtaɪmz] ADV a veces; **I ~ drink beer** a veces bebo cerveza; **~ I lose interest** hay veces que pierdo el interés

somewhat ['sʌmwɒt] ADV algo, un tanto; **he was ~ puzzled** se quedó algo *or* un tanto perplejo; **we are ~ worried** estamos algo inquietos; **it was done ~ hastily** se hizo con demasiada prisa

somewhere ['sʌmweəʳ] Ⓐ ADV [1] (*location*) en alguna parte, en algún lugar, en algún sitio; (*direction*) a alguna parte, a algún lugar *or* sitio; **I left my keys ~** me he dejado las llaves en alguna parte *or* en algún sitio; **let's go ~ private** vamos a algún sitio *or* lugar donde podamos estar solos; **I'd like to go on holiday ~ exotic** me gustaría irme de vacaciones a algún sitio *or* lugar exótico; **he's ~ around** anda por ahí; **~ else** (*location*) en otra parte; (*direction*) a otra parte, a otro sitio; **the bar was full so we decided to go ~ else** el bar estaba lleno, así es que decidimos ir a otra parte *or* a otro sitio; **she lives ~ in Wales** vive en algún lugar *or* en alguna parte de Gales; **~ in the back of my mind** en algún lugar de mi mente; **~ near Huesca** cerca de Huesca, en algún lugar *or* sitio cerca de Huesca; **I left it ~ or other** lo dejé en alguna parte *or* en algún sitio, lo dejé por ahí; **✦IDIOMS ~ along the line**: **~ along the line they changed the title** en algún momento cambiaron el título; **to get ~*** (= *make progress*) hacer progresos, conseguir algo; **now we're getting ~** ahora sí que estamos haciendo progresos, ahora sí que estamos consiguiendo algo

[2] (= *approximately*) **~ around three o'clock** alrededor de las tres, a eso de las tres; **he's been given ~ between three and six months to live** le han dado entre tres y seis meses de vida; **he's ~ in his fifties** tiene cincuenta y tantos años; **he paid ~ in the region of £1000** pagó alrededor de 1000 libras

Ⓑ PRON algún lugar, algún sitio; **you'll have to find ~ else to live** tendrás que buscarte otro sitio *or* lugar para vivir; **we decided to hire ~ for the party** decidimos alquilar un lugar para la fiesta; **they broadcast from ~ in Europe** emiten desde algún lugar de Europa

Somme [sɒm] N Somme *m*; **the Battle of the ~** la batalla del Somme

somnambulism [sɒm'næmbjʊlɪzəm] N sonambulismo *m*

somnambulist [sɒm'næmbjʊlɪst] N sonámbulo/a *m/f*

somniferous [sɒm'nɪfərəs] ADJ somnífero

somnolence ['sɒmnələns] N somnolencia *f*

somnolent ['sɒmnələnt] ADJ (= *sleepy*) soñoliento

son [sʌn] N hijo *m*; **the youngest/eldest ~** el hijo menor/mayor; **the Son of God** el Hijo de Dios; **the Son of Man** el Hijo del Hombre; **come here, ~*** ven, hijo; **~ of a bitch**‡ hijo *m* de puta‡, hijo *m* de la chingada (*Mex*‡)

sonar ['səʊnɑːʳ] N sonar *m*

sonata [sə'nɑːtə] N sonata *f*

son et lumière [ˌsɔ̃eɪluːm'jeəʳ] N luz *f* y sonido *m*

song [sɒŋ] Ⓐ N [1] (= *ballad etc*) canción *f*; **to sing a ~** cantar una canción; **give us a ~!** ¡cántanos algo!; **festival of Spanish ~** festival *m* de la canción española; **to burst into ~** romper a cantar; **✦IDIOMS to make a ~ and dance about sth** hacer aspavientos por algo; **there's no need to make a ~ and dance about it** no es para tanto; **I got it for a ~** lo compré regalado; **to be on ~** (*Brit*) [*footballer etc*] estar entonado, estar inspirado; **to sing another ~** bajar el tono, desdecirse

[2] [*of birds*] canto *m*

Ⓑ CPD ► **song and dance routine** N número *m* de canción y baile ► **song book** N cancionero *m* ► **song cycle** N ciclo *m* de canciones ► **song hit** N canción *f* de moda, canción *f* popular del momento ► **Song of Solomon**, **Song of Songs** N Cantar *m* de los Cantares ► **song thrush** N tordo *m* cantor, tordo *m* melodioso

songbird ['sɒŋbɜːd] N pájaro *m* cantor

songfest ['sɒŋfest] N festival *m* de canciones

songster ['sɒŋstəʳ] N pájaro *m* cantor

songwriter ['sɒŋˌraɪtəʳ] N compositor(a) *m/f* (de canciones)

sonic ['sɒnɪk] Ⓐ ADJ sónico

Ⓑ CPD ► **sonic boom** N estampido *m* sónico

sonics ['sɒnɪks] NSING sónica *f*

son-in-law ['sʌnɪnlɔː] N (*pl* **sons-in-law**) yerno *m*, hijo *m* político

sonnet ['sɒnɪt] N soneto *m*

sonny* ['sʌnɪ] N hijo *m*

son-of-a-gun‡ [ˌsʌnəvə'gʌn] N hijo *m* de su madre*

sonority [sə'nɒrɪtɪ] N sonoridad *f*

sonorous ['sɒnərəs] ADJ (*gen*) sonoro

sonorousness ['sɒnərəsnɪs] N sonoridad *f*

soon [suːn] ADV [1] (= *before long*) pronto, dentro de poco; **they'll be here ~** pronto llegarán, llegarán dentro de poco; **it will ~ be summer** pronto llegará el verano, falta poco para que llegue el verano; **~ afterwards** poco después; **come back ~** vuelve pronto

[2] (= *early, quickly*) pronto, temprano; **how ~ can you be ready?** ¿cuánto tardas en prepararte?; **how ~ can you come?** ¿cuándo puedes venir?; **Friday is too ~** el viernes es muy pronto; **we got there too ~** llegamos demasiado pronto *or* temprano; **it's too ~ to tell** es demasiado pronto para saber; **we were none too ~** no llegamos antes de tiempo, llegamos justo; **all too ~ it was over** terminó demasiado pronto; **not a minute** *or* **moment too ~** ya era hora

[3] **as ~ as** en cuanto, tan pronto como; **I'll do it as ~ as I can** lo haré en cuanto pueda, lo haré tan pronto como pueda; **as ~ as you see her** en cuanto la veas, tan pronto como la veas; **as ~ as it was finished** en cuanto se terminó; **as ~ as possible** cuanto antes, lo antes posible, lo más pronto posible

[4] (*expressing preference*) **I would (just) as ~ not go** preferiría no ir; **I would (just) as ~ he didn't know** preferiría que él no lo supiera; **she'd marry him as ~ as not** se casaría con él y tan contenta; *see also* **sooner**

AS SOON AS

- As with other time conjunctions, **en cuanto** and **tan pronto como** are used with the *subjunctive* if the action which follows hasn't happened yet or hadn't happened at the time of speaking:

  As soon as *or* The moment we finish, I've got to write an editorial
  En cuanto terminemos *or* ***Tan pronto como terminemos, tengo que escribir un editorial***
  As soon as I know the dates, I'll let you know
  En cuanto sepa *or* ***Tan pronto como sepa las fechas, te lo diré***
- **En cuanto** and **tan pronto como** are used with the *indicative* when the action in the time clause has already taken place:

  He left the podium as soon as *or* the moment he received his prize
  Se bajó del podio en cuanto recibió *or* ***tan pronto como recibió el premio***
- **En cuanto** and **tan pronto como** are also used with the *indicative* when describing habitual actions:

  As soon as any faxes arrive, they're put in a special box
  En cuanto llegan *or* ***Tan pronto como llegan los faxes, se guardan en una caja especial***

For further uses and examples, see main entry.

sooner ['su:nəʳ] ADV [1] (*of time*) antes, más temprano; **can't you come a bit ~?** ¿no puedes venir un poco antes *or* un poco más temprano?; **we got there ~** nosotros llegamos antes; **the ~ we start the ~ we finish** cuanto antes empecemos, antes acabaremos; **the ~ the better** cuanto antes mejor; **~ or later** tarde o temprano; **no ~ had we left than they arrived** apenas nos habíamos marchado cuando llegaron; **no ~ said than done** dicho y hecho

[2] (*of preference*) **I'd** *or* **I would ~ not do it** preferiría no hacerlo; **I'd ~ die!*** ¡antes morir!; **~ you than me!*** ¡allá tú, yo no!

soot [sʊt] N hollín *m*

sooth†† [su:ð] N **in ~** en realidad

soothe [su:ð] Ⓐ VT [+ *person, baby*] calmar, tranquilizar; [+ *nerves*] calmar; [+ *mind*] relajar; [+ *anger*] aplacar; [+ *doubts*] acallar; [+ *pain, cough*] aliviar; **to ~ sb's fears** disipar los temores de algn, tranquilizar a algn; **to ~ sb's vanity** halagar la vanidad a algn

Ⓑ VI aliviar

soothing ['su:ðɪŋ] ADJ [*ointment, lotion*] balsámico, calmante; [*massage, bath, music*] relajante; [*tone, words, voice, manner*] tranquilizador; **it has a ~ effect** [*massage, bath, music*] tiene un efecto relajante; [*ointment*] tiene un efecto balsámico; [*cough mixture, herbal tea*] tiene un efecto calmante; [*words, voice*] tiene un efecto tranquilizador

soothingly ['su:ðɪŋlɪ] ADV [*speak, say, whisper, murmur*] en tono tranquilizador; **the old house was ~ familiar** la familiaridad de la vieja casa tenía un efecto relajante

soothsayer ['su:θ,seɪəʳ] N adivino/a *m/f*

soothsaying ['su:θ,seɪɪŋ] N adivinación *f*

sooty ['sʊtɪ] ADJ (*compar* **sootier**; *superl* **sootiest**) hollinoso; (*fig*) negro como el hollín

SOP N ABBR = **standard operating procedure**

sop [sɒp] N [1] (*fig*) (= *pacifier*) compensación *f*; **as a ~ to his pride** para que su orgullo no quedara/quede herido

[2] **sops** (= *food*) sopa *fsing*

[3] (*) (= *person*) bobo/a *m/f*

►**sop up** VT + ADV absorber

Sophia [səʊ'faɪə] N Sofía

sophism ['sɒfɪzəm] N sofisma *m*

sophist ['sɒfɪst] N sofista *mf*

sophistical [sə'fɪstɪkəl] ADJ sofístico

sophisticated [sə'fɪstɪkeɪtɪd] ADJ [1] (= *refined*) [*person, lifestyle, tastes, clothes*] sofisticado

[2] (= *complex*) [*idea*] sofisticado; [*equipment*] sofisticado, complejo, altamente desarrollado; [*technique*] sofisticado, muy elaborado, complejo; [*play, film, book*] muy elaborado, complejo; **a ~ approach to planning** un modo sofisticado de enfocar la planificación

sophistication [sə,fɪstɪ'keɪʃən] N (= *refinement*) sofisticación *f*; (= *complexity*) complejidad *f*

sophistry ['sɒfɪstrɪ] N sofistería *f*; **a ~** un sofisma

Sophocles ['sɒfəkli:z] N Sófocles

sophomore ['sɒfəmɔ:ʳ] N (*US*) estudiante *mf* de segundo año; → GRADE

soporific [,sɒpə'rɪfɪk] ADJ soporífero

sopping ['sɒpɪŋ] ADJ **it's ~ (wet)** está empapado; **he was ~ wet** estaba hecho una sopa, estaba calado *or* empapado hasta los huesos

soppy* ['sɒpɪ] ADJ [1] (= *mushy*) sentimentaloide

[2] (= *foolish*) bobo, tonto

soprano [sə'prɑ:nəʊ] Ⓐ N (*pl* **sopranos** *or* **soprani** [sə'prɑ:ni:]) (*Mus*) (*female*) soprano *f*; (*male*) tiple *m*; (= *voice, part*) soprano *m*

Ⓑ ADJ [*part*] de soprano, para soprano; [*voice*] de soprano

Ⓒ ADV **to sing ~** cantar soprano

sorb [sɔ:b] N (= *tree*) serbal *m*; (= *fruit*) serba *f*

sorbet ['sɔ:beɪ] N sorbete *m*; **lemon ~** sorbete *m* de limón

sorbitol ['sɔ:bɪtɒl] N sorbitol *m*

sorcerer ['sɔ:sərəʳ] N hechicero *m*, brujo *m*; **the ~'s apprentice** el aprendiz de brujo

sorceress ['sɔ:særes] N hechicera *f*, bruja *f*

sorcery ['sɔ:sərɪ] N hechicería *f*, brujería *f*

sordid ['sɔ:dɪd] ADJ [*place, room etc*] miserable, sórdido; [*deal, motive etc*] mezquino; **it's a pretty ~ business** es un asunto de lo más desagradable

sordidness ['sɔ:dɪdnɪs] N sordidez *f*, lo miserable

sore [sɔ:ʳ] Ⓐ ADJ (*compar* **sorer**; *superl* **sorest**) [1] (*Med*) (= *aching*) [*part of body*] dolorido; (= *painful*) [*cut, graze*] doloroso; **it's ~** me duele; **my eyes are ~** ◊ **I have ~ eyes** me duelen los ojos; **I'm ~ all over** me duele todo el cuerpo; **I have a ~ throat** me duele la garganta; ✦***IDIOM*** **to be ~ at heart** (*liter*): **he was sore at heart** le dolía el corazón

[2] (= *angry, upset*) **to be ~ about sth** estar resentido por algo; **what are you so ~ about?** ¿por qué estás tan resentido?; **to be ~ at sb** estar enfadado *or* (*LAm*) enojado con algn; **don't get ~!*** ¡no te vayas a ofender!, ¡no te enojes! (*LAm*); **it's a ~ point** es un tema delicado *or* espinoso; **to be ~ with sb** estar enfadado *or* (*LAm*) enojado con algn

[3] (*liter*) (= *very great*) **there is a ~ need of ...** hay gran necesidad de ...; **it was a ~ temptation** era una fuerte tentación

Ⓑ N (*Med*) llaga *f*, úlcera *f*; ✦***IDIOM*** **to open up old ~s** abrir viejas heridas

sorehead* ['sɔ:hed] N (*US*) persona *f* resentida

sorely ['sɔ:lɪ] ADV (= *very*) muy; (= *much*) mucho; (= *deeply*) profundamente; (= *seriously*) seriamente; **I am ~ tempted** estoy muy tentado; **I am ~ tempted to dismiss him** casi estoy por despedirlo; **he has been ~ tried** ha tenido que aguantar muchísimo

soreness ['sɔ:nɪs] N (*Med*) dolor *m*

sorghum ['sɔ:gəm] N sorgo *m*

sorority [sə'rɒrɪtɪ] N (*US Univ*) hermandad *f* de mujeres

SORORITY/FRATERNITY

Muchas universidades estadounidenses poseen dentro del campus hermandades conocidas como **fraternities** *o* **frats** *(de hombres) o* **sororities** *(de mujeres). Estas hermandades, a las que sólo se puede ingresar mediante invitación, organizan fiestas, recogen fondos con fines benéficos e intentan hacer que su hermandad sobresalga entre las demás. Suelen tener nombres compuestos de letras del alfabeto griego, como por ejemplo* **Kappa Kappa Gamma**. *Existe división de opiniones en cuanto a los beneficios o ventajas de estas hermandades; para los miembros es una buena manera de hacer amigos, pero la mayoría de los estudiantes piensan que son elitistas y discriminatorias. Durante las ceremonias secretas de iniciación, que incluyen varias pruebas físicas y novatadas que se denominan* **hazing**, *se ha producido la muerte de varios estudiantes, lo cual ha aumentado la polémica.*

sorrel[1] ['sɒrəl] N (*Bot*) acedera *f*

sorrel[2] ['sɒrəl] Ⓐ ADJ alazán

Ⓑ N (= *horse*) alazán *m*, caballo *m* alazán

sorrow ['sɒrəʊ] Ⓐ N (= *grieving*) pena *f*, pesar *m*, dolor *m*; **to my ~** con *or* para gran pesar mío; **her ~ at the death of her son** su pena por la muerte de su hijo; **more in ~ than in anger** con más pesar que enojo; **this was a great ~ to me** esto me causó mucha pena; ✦***IDIOM*** **to drown one's ~s** ahogar las penas (en alcohol)

Ⓑ VI apenarse, afligirse (**at, for, over** de)

sorrowful ['sɒrəfʊl] ADJ afligido, triste, apenado

sorrowfully ['sɒrəflɪ] ADV con pena, tristemente

sorrowing ['sɒrəʊɪŋ] ADJ afligido

▼**sorry** ['sɒrɪ] ADJ (*compar* **sorrier**; *superl* **sorriest**) [1] (= *apologetic*) **I'm so ~!** ¡lo siento mucho!, ¡perdón!; **sorry!** ¡perdón!, ¡perdone!, ¡disculpe! (*esp LAm*); **~ I'm late!** ¡siento llegar tarde!; **I'm ~ to bother you but ...** siento *or* (*frm*) lamento molestarle, pero ...; **to be ~ about/for sth** sentir algo, lamentar algo (*frm*); **I'm ~**

➤ LANGUAGE IN USE: **sorry 1** 18.1

about what I said last night siento lo que dije anoche; **we are ~ for any inconvenience caused** lamentamos cualquier molestia ocasionada; **to say ~ (to sb) (for sth)** pedir perdón *or* (*esp LAm*) disculpas (a algn) (por algo); **go and say ~!** ¡anda ve y pide perdón *or* disculpas!; **I've said I'm ~, what more do you want?** ya he dicho que lo siento, ¿qué más quieres?

2 (= *repentant*) arrepentido; **he wasn't in the least bit ~** no estaba arrepentido en lo más mínimo; **you'll be ~ for this!** ¡me las pagarás!, ¡te arrepentirás (de esto)!

3 (= *regretful, sad*) **I'm ~, she's busy at the moment** lo siento, en este momento está ocupada; **I can't say I'm ~** no puedo decir que lo sienta; **to be ~ about sth/sb**: **I'm ~ about your mother/about what happened** siento *or* (*frm*) lamento lo de tu madre/lo sucedido; **I can't tell you how ~ I am** no te puedes hacer una idea de cuánto lo siento; **to be ~ that ...** sentir *or* (*frm*) lamentar que + *subjun*; **I'm ~ he didn't get the job** siento que no consiguiera el trabajo; **I'm ~ to hear that you're leaving** me da pena saber que te vas; **we are ~ to have to tell you that ...** lamentamos tener que decirle que ...; **I was ~ to hear of your accident** siento *or* lamento lo de tu accidente; **it was a failure, I'm ~ to say** me duele reconocerlo, pero fue un fracaso; **no one seemed very ~ to see him go** nadie parecía sentir *or* lamentar mucho que se fuera

4 (= *pitying*) **to be** *or* **feel ~ for sb**: **I'm ~ for him** lo compadezco; **I feel ~ for the child** el niño me da lástima *or* pena; **it's no good feeling ~ for yourself** no sirve de mucho lamentarte de tu suerte; **to look ~ for o.s.** tener un aspecto triste

5 (= *pitiful*) **the garden was a ~ sight** el jardín estaba en un estado lamentable, el jardín estaba hecho una pena*; **to be in a ~ state** encontrarse en un estado lamentable; **he poured out his ~ tale to his mother** le contó su triste historia a su madre

6 (*when sb has not heard*) **~, I didn't catch what you said** perdón, no entendí lo que dijiste

7 (*when correcting o.s.*) **it's the third, sorry, the fourth on the left** es la tercera, perdón, la cuarta a la izquierda

8 (*when disagreeing*) **I'm ~, I can't agree with you** lo siento *or* perdona, pero no puedo darte la razón

sort [sɔːt] Ⓐ N 1 (= *kind*) clase *f*, tipo *m*; **a new ~ of car** una nueva clase *or* un nuevo tipo de coche; **the ~ you gave me last time** de la misma clase *or* del mismo tipo que me dio la última vez; **books of all ~s** ◊ **all ~s of books** libros de toda clase *or* de todo tipo, toda clase *or* todo tipo de libros; **I know his/her ~** conozco el paño, conozco a esa clase de gente; **he's a painter of a ~** *or* **of ~s** se puede decir que es pintor; **it's tea of a ~** es té, pero de bastante mala calidad; **something of the ~** algo por el estilo; **nothing of the ~!** ¡nada de eso!; **I shall do nothing of the ~** no lo haré bajo ningún concepto, ni se me ocurriría hacerlo; **but not that ~** pero no de ese tipo, pero no así; **he's the ~ who will cheat you** es de esa clase *or* de ese tipo de personas que te engañará, es de esos que *or* de los que te engañan; **what ~ do you want?** (= *make*) ¿qué marca quieres?; (= *type*) ¿de qué tipo lo quieres?; ✦***PROV*** **it takes all ~s (to make a world)** de todo hay en la viña del Señor

2 **~ of** 2·1 (= *type of*) **it's a ~ of dance** es una especie de baile; **he's a ~ of agent** es algo así como un agente; **he's not the ~ of man to say that** no es de los que dicen eso; **an odd ~ of novel** una novela rara, un tipo extraño de novela; **he's some ~ of painter** es pintor de algún tipo; **that's the ~ of person I am** así soy yo; **he's not that ~ of person** no es capaz de hacer eso, no es ese tipo de persona; **I'm not that ~ of girl** yo no soy de ésas; **that's the ~ of thing I need** eso es lo que me hace falta; **that's just the ~ of thing I mean** eso es precisamente lo que quiero decir; **and all that ~ of thing** y otras cosas por el estilo; **this ~ of house** una casa de este estilo; **what ~ of car?** ¿qué tipo de coche?; **what ~ of man is he?** ¿qué clase de hombre es?

2·2 (*) **it's ~ of awkward** es bastante *or* (*LAm*) medio difícil; **it's ~ of blue** es más bien azul; **I'm ~ of lost** estoy como perdido; **it's ~ of finished** está más o menos terminado; **I have a ~ of idea that ...** tengo cierta idea de que ...; **I ~ of thought that ...** quedé con la idea de que ...; **I ~ of feel that ...** en cierto modo creo que ...; **it ~ of made me laugh** no sé por qué pero me hizo reír; **"aren't you pleased?" — "~ of"** —¿no te alegras? —en cierto sentido

3 (= *person*) **he's a good ~** es buena persona *or* (*esp LAm*) buena gente; **he's an odd ~** es un tipo raro; **your ~ never did any good** las personas como usted nunca hicieron nada bueno

4 ✦***IDIOM*** **to be out of ~s** (= *unwell*) estar indispuesto, no estar del todo bien; (= *in bad mood*) estar de mal humor, estar de malas

5 (*Comput*) ordenación *f*

Ⓑ VT 1 (= *classify, arrange*) clasificar; **to ~ the good apples from the bad ones** separar las manzanas malas de las buenas; *see also* **sheep**

2 (*Comput*) ordenar

3 (*) (= *resolve, settle*) arreglar; **we've got it ~ed now** ya se arregló

Ⓒ CPD ► **sort code** N [*of bank*] número *m* de agencia

►**sort out** VT + ADV 1 (= *organize*) ordenar, organizar; **~ out all your books** ordena todos tus libros; **to ~ out the bad ones** separar *or* quitar los malos; *see also* **sheep**

2 (= *resolve*) [+ *problem, situation etc*] arreglar, solucionar; **they've ~ed out their problems** han arreglado *or* solucionado sus problemas

3 **to ~ sb out*** ajustar cuentas con algn; **I'll come down there and ~ you out!*** ¡si bajo, te pego una paliza!

4 (= *explain*) **to ~ sth out for sb** explicar *or* aclarar algo a algn; **can you ~ this out for me?** ¿puede explicarme *or* aclararme esto?

►**sort through** VI + ADV revisar

sorter [ˈsɔːtəʳ] N clasificador(a) *m/f*

sortie [ˈsɔːtɪ] N (*Aer, Mil*) salida *f*; **to make a ~** hacer una salida; **a ~ into town** una escapada a la ciudad

sorting [ˈsɔːtɪŋ] Ⓐ N clasificación *f*; (*Comput*) ordenación *f*

Ⓑ CPD ► **sorting office** N (*Post*) sala *f* de batalla

sort-out* [ˈsɔːtaʊt] N **to have a ~** (= *clean-up*) hacer limpieza; (= *tidy-up*) ordenar las cosas

SOS N (= *signal*) SOS *m*; (*fig*) llamada *f* de socorro

so-so [ˈsəʊˈsəʊ] ADV regular, así así; **"how are you feeling?" — "so-so "** —¿cómo te encuentras? —regular *or* —así así

sot [sɒt] N borrachín/ina* *m/f*

sottish [ˈsɒtɪʃ] ADJ embrutecido (*por el alcohol*)

sotto voce [ˈsɒtəʊˈvəʊtʃɪ] ADV en voz baja

Soudan [suˈdɑːn] = **Sudan**

soufflé [ˈsuːfleɪ] Ⓐ N soufflé *m*, suflé *m*

Ⓑ CPD ► **soufflé dish** N fuente *f* de soufflé

sough [saʊ] Ⓐ N susurro *m*

Ⓑ VI susurrar

sought [sɔːt] PT, PP *of* **seek**

sought-after [ˈsɔːt,ɑːftəʳ] ADJ [*person*] solicitado; [*object*] codiciado; **this much ~ title** este codiciado título

soul [səʊl] Ⓐ N 1 (*Rel*) alma *f*; **with all one's ~** con todo el alma; **All Souls' Day** (el día de) Todos los Santos; **(God) bless my ~!†** ¡que Dios me ampare!; **God rest his ~** que Dios lo acoja en su seno; **upon my ~!†** ¡cielo santo!; ✦***IDIOMS*** **like a lost ~** como alma en pena; **to sell one's ~ to the devil** vender el alma al diablo; *see also* **possess 1**

2 (= *feeling*) **you have no ~!** ¡no tienes sentimientos!; **the music lacks ~** a la música le falta sentimiento; **these places have no ~** estos sitios no tienen vida

3 (= *essence*) [*of people, nation*] espíritu *m*; *see also* **bare B, body A1, heart A2, life A5**

4 (*fig*) (= *person*) alma *f*; **3,000 ~s** 3.000 almas; **there was not a (living) ~ in sight** no se veía (ni) un alma; **a few brave ~s ventured out** unos cuantos valientes se aventuraron a salir; **the poor ~ had nowhere to sleep** el pobre no tenía dónde dormir; **poor ~!** ¡pobrecito!; **I won't tell a ~** no se lo diré a nadie

5 (= *embodiment*) **to be the ~ of discretion** ser la discreción personificada *or* en persona; *see also* **brevity**

6 (*Mus*) (*also* **~ music**) música *f* soul

Ⓑ CPD ► **soul food** N *cocina negra del Sur de EE.UU.* ► **soul music** N música *f* soul ► **soul singer** N cantante *mf* de soul

soul-destroying [ˈsəʊldɪsˈtrɔɪɪŋ] ADJ (*fig*) de lo más aburrido

soulful [ˈsəʊlfʊl] ADJ [*gaze, look, eyes*] conmovedor; [*music*] lleno de sentimiento

soulfully [ˈsəʊlfəlɪ] ADV [*gaze, look*] de forma conmovedora

soulless [ˈsəʊllɪs] ADJ [*person*] sin alma, desalmado; [*work*] mecánico, monótono

soulmate [ˈsəʊlmeɪt] N compañero/a *m/f* del alma, alma *f* gemela

soul-searching [ˈsəʊl,sɜːtʃɪŋ] N **after a lot of ~** después de revolverlo muchas veces

soul-stirring [ˈsəʊl,stɜːrɪŋ] ADJ conmovedor, emocionante, inspirador

sound[1] [saʊnd] Ⓐ N 1 (*Phys*) sonido *m*; **the speed of ~** la velocidad del sonido

2 (= *noise*) ruido *m*; **the ~ of footsteps** el ruido de pasos; **the ~ of breaking glass** el ruido de cristales que se rompen/rompían; **consonant ~s** consonantes *fpl*, sonidos *mpl* consonánticos; **I didn't hear a ~** no oí ni un ruido; **don't make a ~!** ¡no hagas el menor ruido!; **not a ~ was to be heard** no se oía *or* (*esp LAm*) sentía ruido alguno; **to the ~ of the national anthem** al son del himno nacional; **they were within ~ of the camp** el campamento estaba al alcance del oído; **he opened the door without a ~** abrió la puerta sin hacer nada de ruido

3 (= *volume*) volumen *m*; **can I turn the ~ down?** ¿puedo bajar el volumen?

4 (= *musical style*) **the Glenn Miller ~** la música de Glenn Miller

5 (*fig*) (= *impression*) **by the ~ of it** según parece; **I don't like the ~ of it** (*film etc*) por lo que he oído, no me gusta nada; (*situation*) me preocupa, me da mala espina

Ⓑ VT 1 [+ *horn, trumpet*] tocar, hacer sonar; [+ *bell*] tocar; [+ *alarm, warning*] dar; [+

praises] cantar, entonar; **to ~ the charge** (*Mil*) tocar la carga; **~ your horn!** (*Aut*) ¡toca el claxon!; **to ~ a note of warning** (*fig*) dar la señal de alarma; **to ~ the retreat** (*Mil*) tocar la retirada
2 (= *pronounce*) pronunciar; **~ your "r"s more** pronuncia más claro la "r"; **to ~ the "d" in "hablado"** pronunciar la "d" en "hablado"
Ⓒ VI 1 (= *emit sound*) sonar; **the bell ~ed** sonó el timbre; **a cannon ~ed a long way off** se oyó un cañón a lo lejos, sonó *or* resonó un cañón a lo lejos
2 (= *appear to be*) 2·1 (*from aural clues*) sonar; **it ~s hollow** suena a hueco; **he ~s Italian to me** por la voz, diría que es italiano; **he ~ed angry** parecía enfadado; **it ~s like French** suena a francés; **that ~s like them arriving now** parece que llegan ahora
2·2 (*from available information*) sonar, parecer; **it ~s very odd** suena muy raro; **that ~s interesting** eso suena interesante; **it ~s as if** *or* **as though she won't be coming** parece que no va a venir; **how does it ~ to you?** ¿qué te parece?; **that ~s like a good idea** eso parece buena idea; **she ~s like a nice girl** parece una chica simpática
Ⓓ CPD ► **sound archive** N archivo *m* de sonido ► **sound barrier** N barrera *f* del sonido ► **sound bite** N cita *f* jugosa ► **sound card** N (*Comput*) tarjeta *f* de sonido ► **sound effect** N efecto *m* sonoro ► **sound engineer** N ingeniero/a *m/f* de sonido ► **sound file** N (*Comput*) fichero *m* de sonido ► **sound law** N ley *f* fonética ► **sound library** N fonoteca *f* ► **sound recording** N grabación *f* sonora ► **sound recordist** N (*TV*) registrador(a) *m/f* de sonido ► **sound shift** N cambio *m* de pronunciación ► **sound system** N (*Ling*) sistema *m* fonológico; (= *hi-fi*) cadena *f* de sonido ► **sound truck** N (*US*) furgón *m* publicitario ► **sound wave** N (*Phys*) onda *f* sonora

►**sound off*** VI + ADV discursear* (**about** sobre)

sound[2] [saʊnd] VT 1 (*Naut*) sondar
2 (*Med*) [+ *chest*] auscultar; [+ *cavity, passage*] sondar; **to ~ sb's chest** auscultar el pecho a algn

►**sound out** VT + ADV [+ *intentions, person*] sondear, tantear; **to ~ sb out about sth** sondear *or* tantear a algn sobre algo, tratar de averiguar lo que piensa algn sobre algo

sound[3] [saʊnd] Ⓐ ADJ (*compar* **sounder**; *superl* **soundest**) 1 (= *in good condition*) sano; [*constitution*] robusto; [*structure*] sólido, firme; **to be ~ in mind and body** ser sano de cuerpo y de espíritu; **in ~ condition** en buenas condiciones; **to be of ~ mind** estar en su cabal juicio; ✦**IDIOM to be as ~ as a bell** [*person*] gozar de perfecta salud; [*thing*] estar en perfectas condiciones; *see also* **safe A1**
2 (= *well-founded*) [*argument*] bien fundado, sólido; [*ideas, opinions*] válido, razonable; [*investment*] bueno, seguro; [*training*] sólido; [*decision, choice*] acertado; **his reasoning is perfectly ~** su argumentación es perfectamente válida; **she gave me some ~ advice** me dio un buen consejo; **he's ~ enough on the theory** tiene una preparación sólida en cuanto a la teoría
3 (= *dependable*) [*person*] formal, digno de confianza; **he's a very ~ man** es un hombre formal *or* digno de confianza; **he's a ~ worker** es buen trabajador, trabaja con seriedad
4 (= *thorough*) **to give sb a ~ beating** dar a algn una buena paliza
5 (= *deep, untroubled*) [*sleep*] profundo
Ⓑ ADV **to be ~ asleep** estar profundamente dormido; **I shall sleep the ~er for it** por eso dormiré más tranquilamente

sound[4] [saʊnd] N (*Geog*) estrecho *m*, brazo *m* de mar

soundbox ['saʊndbɒks] N (*Mus*) caja *f* de resonancia

sounding[1] ['saʊndɪŋ] Ⓐ N 1 (*Naut*) sondeo *m* 2 **soundings** (*for oil etc*) sondeos *mpl*; **to take ~s** (*lit*) hacer sondeos; (*fig*) sondear la opinión 3 (*Med*) sondeo *m*
Ⓑ CPD ► **sounding board** N (*Mus*) (*fig*) caja *f* de resonancia

sounding[2] ['saʊndɪŋ] N [*of trumpet, bell etc*] sonido *m*, son *m*; **the ~ of the retreat/the alarm** el toque de retirada/de generala

soundless ['saʊndlɪs] ADJ silencioso, mudo

soundlessly ['saʊndlɪslɪ] ADV silenciosamente, sin ruido

soundly ['saʊndlɪ] ADV [*built*] sólidamente; [*argued*] lógicamente; [*invested*] con cordura, con prudencia; **to beat sb ~** dar a algn una buena paliza; **to sleep ~** dormir profundamente

soundness ['saʊndnɪs] N (= *good condition*) [*of structure*] firmeza *f*, solidez *f*; (= *validity*) [*of ideas, opinions*] validez *f*; [*of argument*] solidez *f*; (= *prudence*) [*of investment*] prudencia *f*; (= *solvency*) [*of business*] solvencia *f*

soundproof ['saʊndpru:f] Ⓐ ADJ insonorizado, a prueba de ruidos
Ⓑ VT insonorizar

soundproofing ['saʊndpru:fɪŋ] N insonorización *f*

soundtrack ['saʊndtræk] N banda *f* sonora

soup [su:p] Ⓐ N (*thin*) caldo *m*, consomé *m*; (*thick*) sopa *f*; **vegetable ~** sopa *f* de verduras; ✦**IDIOM to be in the ~*** estar en apuros
Ⓑ CPD ► **soup kitchen** N comedor *m* popular, olla *f* común ► **soup plate** N plato *m* sopero ► **soup spoon** N cuchara *f* sopera ► **soup tureen** N sopera *f*

soupçon ['su:psɔ̃] N (*Culin*) pizca *f*; **with a ~ of ginger** con una pizca de jengibre; **with a ~ of cream** con un chorrito de nata *or* (*LAm*) crema

souped-up* ['su:pt,ʌp] ADJ [*car*] trucado

soupy ['su:pɪ] ADJ [*liquid*] espeso, turbio; [*atmosphere*] pesado, espeso

sour ['saʊəʳ] Ⓐ ADJ (*compar* **sourer**; *superl* **sourest**) 1 (= *not sweet*) [*fruit, flavour*] agrio, ácido; [*smell*] acre; **whisky ~** whisky *m* sour; ✦**IDIOM ~ grapes** envidia *f*; **that's just ~ grapes** eso es simplemente envidia; **it was clearly ~ grapes on his part** estaba claro que tenía envidia
2 (*Agr*) [*soil*] ácido, yermo
3 (= *bad*) [*milk*] cortado, agrio; [*wine*] agrio; **to go** *or* **turn ~** [*milk*] cortarse; [*wine*] agriarse; [*plan*] venirse abajo; **their marriage turned ~** su matrimonio empezó a deteriorarse; **their dream of equality for all turned ~** su sueño de igualdad para todos se tornó amargo; **does this milk taste ~ to you?** ¿te sabe esta leche a cortada?, ¿te sabe esta leche agria?
4 (*fig*) [*person*] avinagrado; [*expression, look, mood, comment*] avinagrado, agrio
Ⓑ VT 1 (*lit*) agriar
2 (*fig*) [+ *person*] agriar, amargar; [+ *relationship*] deteriorar; [+ *atmosphere*] agriar; [+ *outlook, success*] empañar
Ⓒ VI 1 (*lit*) [*wine*] agriarse, volverse agrio; [*milk*] agriarse, cortarse
2 (*fig*) [*mood, attitude*] avinagrarse, agriarse; [*relationship*] deteriorarse; **the atmosphere in the office had ~ed** el ambiente en la oficina se había vuelto rancio; **his financial partners ~ed on the deal** (*US*) sus socios financieros se volvieron en contra del acuerdo
Ⓓ CPD ► **sour cream** N nata *f* or (*LAm*) crema *f* agria

source [sɔ:s] Ⓐ N 1 (= *origin*) fuente *f*; [*of gossip etc*] procedencia *f*; **coal was their only ~ of heat** el carbón era su única fuente de calor; **we have other ~s of supply** tenemos otras fuentes de suministro; **I have it from a reliable ~ that ...** sé de fuente fidedigna que ...; **what is the ~ of this information?** ¿de dónde proceden estos informes?; **his antics were a ~ of much amusement** sus gracias fueron motivo de diversión; **at ~** en su origen
2 [*of river*] nacimiento *m*
Ⓑ CPD ► **source file** N archivo *m* fuente ► **source language** N (*Ling*) lengua *f* de partida; (*Comput*) lenguaje *m* origen ► **source materials** NPL materiales *mpl* de referencia ► **source program** N programa *m* fuente

sourdine [sʊə'di:n] N sordina *f*

sourdough bread [,saʊədəʊ'bred] N (*esp US*) pan *m* de masa fermentada

sour-faced ['saʊəfeɪst] ADJ con cara de pocos amigos, con cara avinagrada

sourish ['saʊərɪʃ] ADJ agrete

sourly ['saʊəlɪ] ADV 1 (= *disagreeably*) [*say, complain, look*] agriamente; [*think*] con amargura
2 **to smell ~ (of sth)** despedir un olor agrio (a algo)

sourness ['saʊənɪs] N 1 (*lit*) [*of fruit, wine, soil*] acidez *f*; [*of milk*] sabor *m* agrio, sabor *m* a cortado
2 (*fig*) [*of person, expression, mood, tone*] amargura *f*

sourpuss* ['saʊəpʊs] N amargado/a *m/f*

souse [saʊs] Ⓐ VT 1 (*Culin*) (= *pickle*) escabechar, adobar (*LAm*)
2 (= *plunge*) zambullir; (= *soak*) mojar; **he ~d himself with water** se empapó de agua
3 ✦**IDIOM to be ~d‡** estar mamado*, estar tomado (*LAm*); **to get ~d** coger una trompa (*Sp**), agarrarse una borrachera (*LAm*)
Ⓑ N (*US‡*) borracho/a *m/f*

south [saʊθ] Ⓐ N (= *direction*) sur *m*; (= *region*) sur *m*, mediodía *m*; **the South of France** el sur de Francia, el mediodía francés, la Francia meridional; **in the ~ of England** al sur *or* en el sur de Inglaterra; **to live in the ~** vivir en el sur; **to the ~ of** al sur de; **the wind is from the** *or* **in the ~** el viento sopla *or* viene del sur; **in the ~ of the country** al sur *or* en el sur del país
Ⓑ ADJ del sur, sureño, meridional
Ⓒ ADV (= *southward*) hacia el sur; (= *in the south*) al sur, en el sur; **to travel ~** viajar hacia el sur; **this house faces ~** esta casa mira al sur *or* tiene vista hacia el sur; **my window faces ~** mi ventana da al sur; **~ of the border** al sur de la frontera; **it's ~ of London** está al sur de Londres; **to sail due ~** (*Naut*) ir proa al sur, navegar rumbo al sur
Ⓓ CPD ► **South Africa** N Suráfrica *f*, Sudáfrica *f*; *see also* **South African** ► **South America** N América *f* del Sur, Sudamérica *f*; *see also* **South American** ► **South Atlantic** N Atlántico *m* Sur ► **South Australia** N Australia *f* del Sur ► **South Carolina** N Carolina *f* del Sur ► **South Dakota** N Dakota *f* del Sur ► **South Georgia** N Georgia *f* del Sur ► **South Korea** N Corea *f* del Sur; *see also* **South Korean** ► **South Pacific** N Pacífico *m* Sur ► **the South Pole** N el Polo sur ► **the South Sea Islands** NPL las Islas de los mares del Sur ► **the South Seas** NPL los mares del

Sur, el mar austral ► **South Vietnam** N Vietnam *m* del Sur; *see also* **South Vietnamese** ► **South Wales** N Gales *m* del Sur ► **South West Africa** N África *f* del Suroeste

South African [saʊθ'æfrɪkən] Ⓐ ADJ sudafricano
Ⓑ N sudafricano/a *m/f*

South American [ˌsaʊθə'merɪkən] Ⓐ ADJ sudamericano
Ⓑ N sudamericano/a *m/f*

southbound ['saʊθbaʊnd] ADJ [*traffic*] en dirección sur; [*carriageway*] de dirección sur, en dirección sur

southeast [saʊθ'iːst] Ⓐ N sudeste *m*, sureste *m*
Ⓑ ADJ [*point, direction*] sudeste, sureste; [*wind*] del sudeste, del sureste
Ⓒ ADV (= *southeastward*) hacia el sudeste *or* sureste; (= *in the southeast*) al sudeste *or* sureste, en el sudeste *or* sureste
Ⓓ CPD ► **Southeast Asia** N el sudeste de Asia, el sudeste asiático

southeasterly [saʊθ'iːstəlɪ] Ⓐ ADJ [*wind*] del sudeste, del sureste; **in a ~ direction** hacia el sudeste *or* sureste, rumbo al sudeste *or* sureste, en dirección sudeste *or* sureste
Ⓑ N viento *m* del sudeste *or* sureste

southeastern [saʊθ'iːstən] ADJ sudeste, sureste; **the ~ part of the island** la parte sudeste *or* sureste de la isla; **in ~ Spain** al sudeste *or* sureste de España; **the ~ coast** la costa sudoriental *or* suroriental

southeastward [saʊθ'iːstwəd] Ⓐ ADJ [*movement, migration*] hacia el sudeste *or* sureste, en dirección sudeste *or* sureste
Ⓑ ADV hacia el sudeste *or* sureste, en dirección sudeste *or* sureste

southeastwards [saʊθ'iːstwədz] ADV (*esp Brit*) = **southeastward B**

southerly ['sʌðəlɪ] Ⓐ ADJ [*wind*] del sur; **we were headed in a ~ direction** íbamos hacia el sur *or* rumbo al sur *or* en dirección sur; **the most ~ point in Europe** el punto más meridional *or* más al sur de Europa
Ⓑ N (= *wind*) viento *m* del sur

southern ['sʌðən] Ⓐ ADJ del sur, sureño, meridional; **in ~ Spain** al sur *or* en el sur de España, en la España meridional; **the ~ part of the island** la parte sur *or* meridional de la isla; **the ~ coast** la costa meridional *or* (del) sur; **~ cuisine** la cocina sureña
Ⓑ CPD ► **Southern Cone** N Cono *m* Sur ► **Southern Cross** N Cruz *f* del Sur ► **Southern Europe** N Europa *f* meridional, Europa del Sur ► **the southern hemisphere** N el hemisferio sur, el hemisferio austral

southerner ['sʌðənəʳ] N habitante *mf* del sur, sureño/a *m/f* (*esp LAm*); **she's a ~** es del sur

southernmost ['sʌðənməʊst] ADJ más meridional, más al sur; **the ~ town in Europe** la ciudad más meridional *or* más al sur de Europa

south-facing ['saʊθˌfeɪsɪŋ] ADJ con cara al sur, orientado hacia el sur; **~ slope** vertiente *f* sur

South Korean ['saʊθkə'rɪən] Ⓐ ADJ surcoreano
Ⓑ N surcoreano/a *m/f*

southpaw ['saʊθpɔː] N (*esp US*) zurdo *m*

south-southeast [ˌsaʊθsaʊθ'iːst] Ⓐ N sudsudeste *m*, sursureste *m*
Ⓑ ADJ sudsudeste, sursureste
Ⓒ ADV (= *toward south-southeast*) hacia el sudsudeste *or* sursureste; [*situated*] al sudsudeste *or* sursureste, en el sudsudeste *or* sursureste

south-southwest [ˌsaʊθsaʊθ'west] Ⓐ N sudsudoeste *m*, sursuroeste *m*
Ⓑ ADJ sudsudoeste, sursuroeste
Ⓒ ADV (= *toward south-southwest*) hacia el sudsudoeste *or* sursuroeste; [*situated*] al sudsudoeste *or* sursuroeste, en el sudsudoeste *or* sursuroeste

South Vietnamese ['saʊθˌvjetnə'miːz] Ⓐ ADJ survietnamita
Ⓑ N survietnamita *mf*

southward ['saʊθwəd] Ⓐ ADJ [*movement, migration*] hacia el sur, en dirección sur
Ⓑ ADV hacia el sur, en dirección sur

southwards ['saʊθwədz] ADV (*esp Brit*) = **southward B**

southwest ['saʊθ'west] Ⓐ N sudoeste *m*, suroeste *m*
Ⓑ ADJ [*point, direction*] sudoeste, suroeste; [*wind*] del sudoeste, del suroeste
Ⓒ ADV (= *toward southwest*) hacia el sudoeste, hacia el suroeste; (= *in the southwest*) al sudoeste, en el sudoeste

southwester [saʊθ'westəʳ] N (= *wind*) sudoeste *m*, suroeste *m*

southwesterly [saʊθ'westəlɪ] Ⓐ ADJ [*wind*] del sudoeste, del suroeste; **in a ~ direction** hacia el sudoeste *or* suroeste, rumbo al sudoeste *or* suroeste, en dirección sudoeste *or* suroeste
Ⓑ N (= *wind*) viento *m* del sudoeste *or* suroeste

southwestern [saʊθ'westən] ADJ sudoeste, suroeste, del sudoeste, del suroeste; **the ~ part of the island** la parte sudoeste *or* suroeste de la isla; **in ~ Spain** en el sudoeste *or* suroeste de España, al sudoeste *or* suroeste de España; **the ~ coast** la costa sudoeste *or* suroeste *or* suroccidental

southwestward [saʊθ'westwəd] Ⓐ ADJ [*movement, migration*] hacia el sudoeste *or* suroeste, en dirección sudoeste *or* suroeste
Ⓑ ADV hacia el sudoeste *or* suroeste, en dirección sudoeste *or* suroeste

southwestwards [saʊθ'westwədz] ADV (*esp Brit*) = **southwestward B**

souvenir [ˌsuːvə'nɪəʳ] Ⓐ N recuerdo *m*, souvenir *m*
Ⓑ CPD ► **souvenir shop** N tienda *f* de recuerdos

sou'wester [saʊ'westəʳ] N sueste *m*

sovereign ['sɒvrɪn] Ⓐ ADJ 1 (= *supreme*) soberano; **with ~ contempt** con soberano desprecio
2 (= *self-governing*) soberano; **~ state** estado *m* soberano
Ⓑ N 1 (= *monarch*) soberano/a *m/f*
2 (*Hist*) (= *coin*) soberano *m*

sovereignty ['sɒvrəntɪ] N soberanía *f*

soviet ['səʊvɪət] Ⓐ (*Pol*) (*formerly*) N soviet *m*; **the Soviets** (= *people*) los soviéticos
Ⓑ ADJ soviético; **Soviet Russia** Rusia *f* Soviética; **the Soviet Union** la Unión Soviética

sow[1] [səʊ] (*pt* **sowed**; *pp* **sown**) VT [+ *seed*] sembrar; **to ~ doubt in sb's mind** sembrar dudas en algn; **to ~ mines in a strait** ◊ **~ a strait with mines** sembrar un estrecho de minas, colocar minas en un estrecho

sow[2] [saʊ] N (*Zool*) puerca *f*, marrana *f*

sower ['səʊəʳ] N sembrador(a) *m/f*

sowing ['səʊɪŋ] Ⓐ N siembra *f*
Ⓑ CPD ► **sowing machine** N sembradora *f* ► **sowing time** N época *f* de la siembra, sementera *f*

sown [səʊn] PP *of* **sow**[1]

sow-thistle ['saʊθɪsl] N cerraja *f*

soy [sɔɪ] (*esp US*) N = **soya**

soya ['sɔɪə] Ⓐ N soja *f*
Ⓑ CPD ► **soya bean** N semilla *f* de soja ► **soya flour** N harina *f* de soja ► **soya milk** N leche *f* de soja ► **soya oil** N aceite *m* de soja ► **soya sauce** N salsa *f* de soja

sozzled* ['sɒzld] ADJ **to be ~** estar mamado*, estar tomado (*LAm*); **to get ~** coger una trompa*, agarrarse una borrachera (*LAm*)

SP N ABBR (*Brit*) = **starting price** 1 (*Racing*) precio *m* de salida
2 (*) (= *information*) **what's the SP on him?** ¿qué sabemos acerca de él?; **to give sb the SP on sb/sth** dar a algn los datos de algn/algo

spa [spɑː] N balneario *m*

space [speɪs] Ⓐ N 1 (*Phys, Astron*) espacio *m*; **in ~** en el espacio; **the rocket vanished into ~** el cohete desapareció en el espacio; **to stare into ~** (*fig*) mirar al vacío; **outer ~** el espacio exterior
2 (= *room*) espacio *m*, sitio *m*; **there isn't enough ~** no hay espacio *or* sitio suficiente; **to buy ~ in a newspaper** comprar espacio en un periódico; **to clear a ~ for sth** ◊ **make ~ for sth** hacer espacio *or* sitio *or* lugar para algo; **to take up a lot of ~** ocupar mucho sitio *or* espacio
3 (= *gap, empty area*) espacio *m*; **blank ~** espacio *m* en blanco; **in a confined ~** en un espacio restringido; **to leave a ~ for sth** dejar sitio *or* lugar para algo; **wide open ~s** campo *m* abierto; **we couldn't find a parking ~** no pudimos encontrar aparcamiento, no pudimos encontrar un sitio para aparcar *or* (*LAm*) estacionar; **answer in the ~ provided** conteste en el espacio indicado
4 [*of time*] espacio *m*, lapso *m*; **after a ~ of two hours** después de un lapso de dos horas; **for a ~** durante cierto tiempo; **for the ~ of a fortnight** durante un período de quince días; **in the ~ of one hour** en el espacio de una hora; **in the ~ of three generations** en el espacio de tres generaciones; **in a short ~ of time** en un corto espacio *or* lapso de tiempo
5 (*fig*) (= *personal space*) espacio *m*
Ⓑ VT 1 (*also* **~ out**) espaciar, separar; **well ~d out** bastante espaciados
2 **to be ~d out*** (= *on drugs*) estar colocado*; (= *drunk*) estar ajumado*
Ⓒ CPD ► **space age** N era *f* espacial ► **space bar** N (*on keyboard*) espaciador *m*, barra *f* espaciadora ► **space capsule** N cápsula *f* espacial ► **space centre, space center** (*US*) N centro *m* espacial ► **space exploration** N exploración *f* espacial ► **space flight** N vuelo *m* espacial ► **space helmet** N casco *m* espacial ► **Space Invaders** NSING (= *game*) Marcianitos *mpl* ► **space lab** N laboratorio *m* espacial ► **space platform** N plataforma *f* espacial ► **space probe** N sonda *f* espacial ► **space programme, space program** (*US*) N programa *m* de investigaciones espaciales ► **space race** N carrera *f* espacial ► **space research** N investigaciones *fpl* espaciales ► **space shot** N (= *vehicle*) vehículo *m* espacial; (= *launch*) lanzamiento *m* de un vehículo espacial ► **space shuttle** N transbordador *m* espacial, lanzadera *f* espacial ► **space sickness** N enfermedad *f* espacial ► **space station** N estación *f* espacial ► **space travel** N viajes *mpl* espaciales ► **space vehicle** N vehículo *m* espacial

spacecraft ['speɪskrɑːft] N (*pl inv*) nave *f* espacial, astronave *f*

spaceman ['speɪsmæn] N (*pl* **spacemen**) astronauta *m*, cosmonauta *m*

space-saving ['speɪsˌseɪvɪŋ] ADJ que economiza espacio, que ahorra espacio

spaceship ['speɪsʃɪp] N nave *f* espacial, astronave *f*

spacesuit ['speɪssuːt] N traje *m* espacial

space-time continuum [ˌspeɪs,taɪmkən'tɪnjʊəm] N continuo *m* espacio-tiempo

spacewalk ['speɪswɔːk] Ⓐ N paseo *m* por el espacio
Ⓑ VI pasear por el espacio

spacewoman ['speɪs,wʊmən] N (*pl* **spacewomen**) astronauta *f*, cosmonauta *f*

spacing ['speɪsɪŋ] Ⓐ N espaciamiento *m*; (*Typ*) espaciado *m*; **in** *or* **with double ~** a doble espacio; **in** *or* **with single ~** a un solo espacio
Ⓑ CPD ► **spacing bar** N espaciador *m*, barra *f* espaciadora

spacious ['speɪʃəs] ADJ espacioso, amplio

spaciousness ['speɪʃəsnɪs] N espaciosidad *f*, amplitud *f*

spade [speɪd] N [1] (= *tool*) pala *f*; ✦*IDIOM* **to call a ~ a ~** llamar al pan pan y al vino vino
[2] **spades** (*Cards*) picas *fpl*, picos *mpl*; (*in Spanish pack*) espadas *fpl*; **the three of ~s** el tres de espadas; **to play ~s** jugar espadas; **to play a ~** jugar una espada
[3] (*pej*, **) negro/a *m/f*

spadeful ['speɪdfʊl] N pala *f*; **by the ~** (*fig*) en grandes cantidades

spadework ['speɪdwɜːk] N (*fig*) trabajo *m* preliminar

spaghetti [spə'getɪ] Ⓐ N (*gen*) espaguetis *mpl*; (*thin*) fideos *mpl*
Ⓑ CPD ► **spaghetti junction*** N scalextric *m* ► **spaghetti western** N película *f* de vaqueros hecha por un director italiano

Spain [speɪn] N España *f*

spake†† [speɪk] PT *of* **speak**

Spam® [spæm] N carne *f* de cerdo en conserva

spam [spæm] (*Internet*) Ⓐ N correo *m* basura (*en Internet*), spam *m* Ⓑ VT enviar spam *or* correo basura por Internet a

spammer ['spæməʳ] N (*Internet*) spammer *mf*

span¹ [spæn] Ⓐ N [1] [*of hand*] palmo *m*; [*of wing*] envergadura *f*
[2] [*of road etc*] tramo *m*; [*of bridge, arch*] luz *f*; [*of roof*] vano *m*; **a ~ of 50 metres** (= *bridge*) una luz de 50 metros; **a bridge with seven ~s** un puente de siete arcadas *or* ojos; **the longest single-span bridge in the world** el puente de una sola arcada más largo del mundo
[3] [*of time*] lapso *m*, espacio *m*; **for a brief ~** durante un breve lapso; **the average ~ of life** la duración promedia de la vida
[4] (*fig*) **the whole ~ of world affairs** toda la extensión de los asuntos mundiales, los asuntos mundiales en toda su amplitud
[5] (†) (= *measure*) palmo *m*
[6] (= *yoke*) [*of oxen*] yunta *f*; [*of horses*] pareja *f*
Ⓑ VT [1] [*bridge*] extenderse sobre, cruzar
[2] (*in time*) abarcar; **his life ~ned four reigns** su vida abarcó cuatro reinados
[3] (= *measure*) medir a palmos

span² [spæn] PT *of* **spin**

spangle ['spæŋgl] Ⓐ N lentejuela *f*
Ⓑ VT adornar con lentejuelas; **~d with** (*fig*) sembrado de; *see also* **star-spangled**

Spanglish ['spæŋglɪʃ] N (*hum*) espanglish *m*

Spaniard ['spænjəd] N español(a) *m/f*

spaniel ['spænjəl] N spaniel *m*

Spanish ['spænɪʃ] Ⓐ ADJ español
Ⓑ N [1] **the ~** (= *people*) los españoles
[2] (*Ling*) español *m*, castellano *m* (*esp LAm*)
Ⓒ CPD ► **Spanish America** N Hispanoamérica *f*; *see also* **Spanish American** ► **the Spanish Armada** N la Armada invencible ► **Spanish chestnut** N castaña *f* dulce ► **Spanish fly** N cantárida *f* ► **Spanish guitar** N guitarra *f* española

Spanish American ['spænɪʃə'merɪkən] Ⓐ ADJ hispanoamericano
Ⓑ N hispanoamericano/a *m/f*

Spanishness ['spænɪʃnɪs] N carácter *m* español, cualidad *f* española

Spanish-speaking ['spænɪʃ'spiːkɪŋ] ADJ hispanohablante, de habla española

spank [spæŋk] Ⓐ N azote *m*, manotazo *m* (en las nalgas); **to give sb a ~** dar un azote a algn (en las nalgas)
Ⓑ VT zurrar*
Ⓒ VI (†) **to be** *or* **go ~ing along** correr, ir volando

spanking ['spæŋkɪŋ] Ⓐ N zurra *f*; **to give sb a ~** zurrar a algn*
Ⓑ ADJ [*pace*] rápido; [*breeze*] fuerte
Ⓒ ADV (†) **in his ~ new uniform/car** con su nuevo y flamante uniforme/coche; **the kitchen was ~ clean** la cocina estaba reluciente

spanner ['spænəʳ] N (*gen*) llave *f* de tuercas, llave *f* de tubo; (*adjustable*) llave *f* inglesa; ✦*IDIOM* **to throw** *or* **put a ~ in the works** meter un palo en la rueda

spar¹ [spɑːʳ] N (*Naut*) palo *m*, verga *f*

spar² [spɑːʳ] VI [1] (*Boxing*) entrenarse en el boxeo; **~ring match** combate *m* con spárring; **~ring partner** sparring *m*
[2] (= *argue*) discutir; **to ~ with sb about sth** discutir algo amistosamente con algn

spar³ [spɑːʳ] N (*Min*) espato *m*

spare [speəʳ] Ⓐ ADJ [1] (= *extra*) de más, de sobra; (= *reserve*) de reserva; (= *free*) libre; **there's a ~ blanket if you're cold** hay una manta de más *or* de sobra si tienes frío; **take a ~ pair of socks** llévate otro par de calcetines; **I keep a ~ pair of glasses** guardo unas gafas de reserva; **I leave a ~ key with the neighbours** dejo una llave de reserva en casa de los vecinos; **I always keep a bit of ~ cash for emergencies** siempre guardo un poco de dinero extra para emergencias; **is there a seat ~?** ¿queda algún asiento libre?; **is there any milk ~?** ¿queda leche?; **have you got a ~ jacket I could borrow?** ¿tienes otra chaqueta para prestarme?; **I do it whenever I get a ~ moment** lo hago cuando tengo un momento libre; **~ time** tiempo *m* libre; **to go ~*** (= *be available*) sobrar, quedar; (*Brit*) (= *get angry*) ponerse como loco*; **there are two tickets going ~** quedan *or* sobran dos entradas; **the boss will go ~ when he finds out** el jefe se pondrá como loco cuando se entere*; **we completed the job with three days to ~** terminamos el trabajo con tres días de antelación; **I arrived at the station with two minutes/time to ~** llegué a la estación con dos minutos de antelación/con tiempo de sobra; **there's enough and to ~** basta y sobra, hay más que suficiente para todos
[2] (= *lean*) [*body, build*] enjuto (*liter*)
[3] (= *sparse*) (*liter*) austero, sobrio
Ⓑ N [1] (*gen*) **always carry a ~ in case you have a puncture** lleve siempre una rueda de recambio *or* repuesto por si tiene un pinchazo; **I've lost my toothbrush and I don't have a ~** he perdido el cepillo de dientes y no tengo otro
[2] (*also* **~ part**) (pieza *f* de) recambio *m*, (pieza *f* de) repuesto *m*, refacción *f* (*Mex*)
Ⓒ VT [1] (= *make available*) **can you ~ the time?** ¿dispones del tiempo?, ¿tienes tiempo?; **it's good of you to ~ the time** es muy amable de su parte dedicarme (este) tiempo; **I can ~ you five minutes** le puedo conceder *or* dedicar cinco minutos; **to ~ a thought for sb** pensar un momento en algn
[2] (= *do without*) **can you ~ this for a moment?** ¿me puedo llevar esto un momento?; **if you can ~ it** si no lo vas a necesitar; **we can't ~ him now** ahora no podemos prescindir de él
[3] (= *be grudging with*) **she ~d no effort in helping me** no escatimó esfuerzos para ayudarme; **they ~d no expense in refurbishing the house** no repararon en *or* escatimaron gastos a la hora de renovar la casa; ✦*PROV* **~ the rod, spoil the child** la letra con sangre entra
[4] (= *show mercy to*) perdonar; **the fire ~d nothing** el incendio no perdonó nada; **to ~ sb's feelings** no herir los sentimientos de algn; **to ~ sb's life** perdonar la vida a algn
[5] (= *save*) ahorrar, evitar; **I'll ~ you the gory details** me ahorraré los detalles escabrosos, te evitaré los detalles escabrosos; **to ~ sb the trouble of doing sth** ahorrar *or* evitar a algn la molestia de hacer algo; **I could have ~d myself the trouble** podía haberme ahorrado *or* evitado la molestia; *see also* **blush A1**
Ⓓ CPD ► **spare part** N (pieza *f* de) repuesto *m*, (pieza *f* de) recambio *m*, refacción *f* (*Mex*) ► **spare room** N cuarto *m* de invitados, cuarto *m* para las visitas ► **spare tyre, spare tire** (*US*) N (*Aut*) neumático *m* de recambio, llanta *f* de recambio (*LAm*); (*Brit hum*) michelín *m* ► **spare wheel** N (*Aut*) rueda *f* de repuesto *or* recambio

spare-part surgery* [ˌspeəpɑːt'sɜːdʒərɪ] N cirugía *f* de trasplantes

sparerib [ˌspeə'rɪb] N (*Culin*) costilla *f* de cerdo

sparing ['speərɪŋ] ADJ [1] (= *economical*) **his ~ use of colour** su parquedad *or* moderación en el uso del color; **to be ~ in one's use of sth** usar algo con moderación; **to be ~ with** *or* (*frm*) **of sth: he was ~ with the wine** no fue muy generoso con el vino; **I've not been ~ with the garlic** he sido generoso con el ajo; **to be ~ of praise** escatimar los elogios, ser parco en elogios
[2] (= *merciful*) piadoso, compasivo

sparingly ['speərɪŋlɪ] ADV [*use, apply*] con moderación, en pequeñas cantidades; [*eat*] frugalmente, con moderación; **he spends his money ~** es cuidadoso con el dinero, mira mucho lo que gasta; **we used water ~** tuvimos cuidado de no gastar mucha agua; **he uses colour ~** es parco en el uso de los colores

spark [spɑːk] Ⓐ N [1] (*from fire, Elec*) chispa *f*; ✦*IDIOMS* **to make the ~s fly** provocar una bronca; **they struck ~s off each other** por efecto mutuo hacían chispear el ingenio; *see also* **bright C**
[2] (= *trace, hint*) pizca *f*; **the book hasn't a ~ of interest** el libro no tiene ni pizca de interés; **there's not a ~ of life about it** no tiene ni un átomo de vida
[3] **sparks*** (*Naut*) telegrafista *mf*; (*Cine, TV*) iluminista *mf*; (*Elec*) electricista *mf*
Ⓑ VT (*also* **~ off**) provocar
Ⓒ VI chispear, echar chispas
Ⓓ CPD ► **spark gap** N entrehierro *m* ► **spark plug** N (*Aut*) bujía *f*

sparking plug ['spɑːkɪŋplʌg] N = **spark plug**

sparkle ['spɑːkl] Ⓐ N centelleo *m*, destello *m*; (*fig*) chispa *f*, viveza *f*; **a person without ~** una persona sin chispa *or* viveza
Ⓑ VI (= *flash*) centellear, echar chispas; (= *shine*) brillar; (= *stand out*) relucir; **the conversation ~d** la conversación fue animadísima;

she doesn't exactly ~ no tiene mucha alegría que digamos

sparkler ['spɑːkləʳ] N 1 (= *firework*) bengala *f*
2 (*) (= *diamond*) diamante *m*
3 (*) (= *sparkling wine*) vino *m* espumoso

sparkling ['spɑːklɪŋ] ADJ 1 (= *bright*) [*glass etc*] centelleante; [*eyes*] chispeante
2 (= *fizzy*) [*wine*] espumoso; **a ~ drink** una bebida espumosa; **~ water** agua con gas
3 (= *scintillating*) [*person, wit, conversation*] chispeante

sparky ['spɑːkɪ] ADJ vivaracho, marchoso*

sparrow ['spærəʊ] N gorrión *m*

sparrowhawk ['spærəʊhɔːk] N gavilán *m*

sparse [spɑːs] ADJ (*compar* **sparser**; *superl* **sparsest**) (= *thin*) escaso; (= *dispersed*) disperso, esparcido; [*hair*] ralo; **~ furnishings** muebles *mpl* escasos; **~ population** poca densidad *f* de población

sparsely ['spɑːslɪ] ADV (= *thinly*) escasamente; (= *in scattered way*) en forma dispersa; **~ populated** escasamente poblado; **a ~ furnished room** un cuarto con pocos muebles

Sparta ['spɑːtə] N Esparta *f*

Spartacus ['spɑːtəkəs] N Espartaco

Spartan ['spɑːtən] Ⓐ ADJ espartano
Ⓑ N espartano/a *m/f*

spartan ['spɑːtən] ADJ (*fig*) espartano

spasm ['spæzəm] N 1 (*Med*) espasmo *m*
2 (= *fit*) ataque *m*, acceso *m*; **a ~ of coughing** un ataque *or* acceso de tos; **in a ~ of fear** en un arrebato de miedo; **a sudden ~ of activity** un arranque *or* arrebato de actividad; **to work in ~s** trabajar a rachas

spasmodic [spæz'mɒdɪk] ADJ 1 (*Med*) espasmódico
2 (= *intermittent*) irregular, intermitente

spasmodically [spæz'mɒdɪkəlɪ] ADV 1 (*Med*) de forma espasmódica
2 (= *intermittently*) de forma irregular, de forma intermitente

spastic ['spæstɪk] Ⓐ ADJ espástico
Ⓑ N espástico/a *m/f*

spasticity [spæs'tɪsɪtɪ] N espasticidad *f*

spat[1] [spæt] PT, PP *of* **spit**[1]

spat[2] [spæt] N (= *overshoe*) polaina *f*

spat[3]* [spæt] (*US*) Ⓐ N riña *f*, disputa *f* (sin trascendencia)
Ⓑ VI reñir

spat[4] [spæt] N (= *oyster*) freza *f*; [*of oysters*] hueva *f* de ostras

spate [speɪt] N 1 (*fig*) torrente *m*, avalancha *f*; [*of burglaries*] serie *f*
2 **to be in (full) ~** [*river*] estar (muy) crecido

spatial ['speɪʃəl] ADJ espacial

spatio-temporal [ˌspeɪʃɪəʊ'tempərəl] ADJ espaciotemporal

spatter ['spætəʳ] VT salpicar (**with** de); **a dress ~ed with mud** un vestido salpicado de lodo; **a wall ~ed with blood** una pared salpicada de sangre

spatula ['spætjʊlə] N espátula *f*

spavin ['spævɪn] N esparaván *m*

spawn [spɔːn] Ⓐ N 1 [*of fish, frogs*] freza *f*, huevas *fpl*; [*of mushrooms*] semillas *fpl*
2 (*pej*) (= *offspring*) prole *f*
Ⓑ VI frezar
Ⓒ VT (*pej*) engendrar, producir

spawning ['spɔːnɪŋ] N desove *m*, freza *f*

spay [speɪ] VT [+ *animal*] sacar los ovarios a

SPCA N ABBR (*US*) = **Society for the Prevention of Cruelty to Animals**

SPCC N ABBR (*US*) = **Society for the Prevention of Cruelty to Children**

speak [spiːk] (*pt* **spoke**; *pp* **spoken**) Ⓐ VI 1 hablar; **to ~ to sb** hablar con algn; **have you spoken to him?** ¿has hablado con él?; **she never spoke to me again** no volvió a dirigirme la palabra; **since they quarrelled they don't ~ to each other** desde que riñeron no se hablan; **I don't know him to ~ to** no lo conozco bastante como para hablar con él; **I know him to ~ to** lo conozco bastante bien para cambiar algunas palabras con él; **did you ~?** ¿dijiste algo?; **technically/biologically ~ing** en términos técnicos/biológicos, desde el punto de vista técnico/biológico; **I'll ~ to him about it** (= *discuss it with him*) lo hablaré con él; (= *point it out to him*) se lo diré; **~ing as a student myself** hablando desde mi experiencia como estudiante; **we're not ~ing** no nos hablamos; **~ now or forever hold your peace** hable ahora o guarde para siempre silencio; **he's very well spoken of** tiene buen nombre *or* buena fama; **~ing of holidays ...** a propósito de las vacaciones ...; **it's nothing to ~ of** no tiene importancia; **he has no money to ~ of** no tiene dinero que digamos; **everything spoke of hatred** en todo había un odio latente; **everything spoke of luxury** todo reflejaba el lujo; **~ing personally ...** en cuanto a mí ..., yo por mi parte ...; **roughly ~ing** en términos generales; **so to ~** por decirlo así, por así decir; **to ~ well of sb** hablar bien de algn; **to ~ in a whisper** hablar bajo
2 (= *make a speech, give one's opinion*) hablar; **he spoke on Greek myths** habló sobre los mitos griegos; **when the minister had spoken ...** cuando terminó de hablar el ministro ...; **the member rose to ~** el diputado se levantó para tomar la palabra; **the chairman asked Mr Wright to ~** el presidente le concedió la palabra al Sr. Wright; **are you ~ing in the debate?** ¿interviene usted en el debate?
3 (*Telec*) **~ing!** ¡al habla!; **"could I ~ to Alison?" — "~ing!"** —¿podría hablar con Alison? —¡al habla! *or* —¡soy yo! *or* (*esp LAm*) —¡con ella!; **this is Peter ~ing** ¡soy Peter!, ¡habla Peter!; **may I ~ to Mr Jones?** ¿me pone con el Sr. Jones, por favor?; **who is that ~ing?** ¿con quién hablo?, ¿quién es?; (*taking message*) ¿de parte (de quién)?
4 (*fig*) [*gun*] oírse, sonar
Ⓑ VT 1 (= *talk*) [+ *language*] hablar; **he ~s Italian** habla italiano; **do you ~ English?** ¿hablas inglés?; **he can ~ seven languages** habla siete idiomas; **"English spoken here"** "se habla inglés"
2 (= *utter*) decir; **to ~ one's mind** hablar claro *or* con franqueza; **to ~ the truth** decir la verdad; **nobody spoke a word** nadie habló, nadie dijo palabra

► **speak for** VI + PREP 1 **to ~ for sb** (*as representative*) hablar por algn, hablar en nombre de algn; (*as defender*) interceder por algn; **he ~s for the miners** habla por los mineros, representa a los mineros; **~ing for myself** en cuanto a mí, yo por mi parte; **~ for yourself!** ¡eso lo dirás tú!; **let her ~ for herself** déjala que hable
2 **it ~s for itself** es evidente, habla por sí mismo; **the facts ~ for themselves** los datos hablan por sí solos
3 **to be spoken for**: **that's already been spoken for** eso ya está reservado *or* apartado; **she's already spoken for*** ya está comprometida

► **speak out** VI + ADV **he's not afraid to ~ out** no tiene miedo a decir lo que piensa; **to ~ out against sth** denunciar algo; **to ~ out for** *or* **on behalf of sb** defender a algn

► **speak up** VI + ADV 1 (= *raise voice*) hablar más fuerte *or* alto; **~ up!** ¡más fuerte!
2 (= *give one's opinion*) decir lo que se piensa; **don't be afraid to ~ up** no tengas miedo de decir lo que piensas; **to ~ up for sb** defender a algn

-speak [spiːk] N (*ending in compounds*) (*pej*) **computer-speak** lenguaje *m* de los ordenadores, jerga *f* informática

speakeasy* ['spiːkˌiːzɪ] N (*US*) taberna *f* clandestina

speaker ['spiːkəʳ] N 1 (*gen*) el/la *m/f* que habla; (*in public*) orador(a) *m/f*; (*at conference*) ponente *mf*, orador(a) *m/f*; (= *lecturer*) conferenciante *mf*; **as the last ~ said ...** como dijo el señor/la señora que acaba de hablar ...; **he's a good ~** es buen orador, habla bien
2 [*of language*] hablante *mf*; **French ~s** los hablantes de francés, los francoparlantes; **he's a French ~** habla francés; **all ~s of Spanish** todos los que hablan español, todos los hispanohablantes; **Catalan has several million ~s** el catalán es hablado por varios millones; **are you a Welsh ~?** ¿habla usted galés?
3 (= *loud-speaker*) altavoz *m*, altoparlante *m* (*LAm*); **speakers** [*of hi-fi system*] bafles *mpl*, parlantes *mpl*
4 (*Pol*) **the Speaker** (*Brit*) el Presidente/la Presidenta de la Cámara de los Comunes; (*US*) el Presidente/la Presidenta de la Cámara de los Representantes; → FRONT BENCH

SPEAKER

En el sistema parlamentario británico el **Speaker** *es la máxima autoridad de la Cámara de los Comunes (***House of Commons***) y su misión es presidirla y hacer que se guarde el orden y que se acaten las normas establecidas. Es elegido al comienzo de la legislatura por parlamentarios (***MPs***) de todos los partidos y puede pertenecer a cualquiera de ellos. Una vez que toma posesión de su cargo, el* **Speaker** *no vota ni toma la palabra (excepto a nivel oficial) y ha de ser totalmente imparcial. Los parlamentarios suelen comenzar sus discursos dirigiéndose al* **Speaker** *en vez de a toda la Cámara, como por ejemplo en:* **Mister/Madam Speaker, I feel very strongly about this.**
En Estados Unidos, el **Speaker** *es el encargado de presidir la Cámara de los Representantes (***House of Representatives***) y es también el dirigente del partido mayoritario, además de miembro de la Cámara. Es elegido por los miembros de su partido y se encarga de las actas de las sesiones de la Cámara y de actuar como portavoz de su partido. Es uno de los puestos más influyentes del gobierno federal, además de ser el que sigue al Vicepresidente (***Vice-President***) en la sucesión a la presidencia.*

speaking ['spiːkɪŋ] Ⓐ ADJ 1 (= *talking*) [*doll, computer*] que habla, parlante
2 (= *eloquent, striking*) **~ likeness** vivo retrato *m*
Ⓑ N (= *skill*) oratoria *f*
Ⓒ CPD ► **speaking clock** N servicio *f* telefónico de información horaria ► **speaking distance** N **to be within ~ distance** estar al alcance de la voz ► **speaking part** N papel *m* hablado ► **speaking terms** NPL **to be on ~ terms with sb** hablarse con algn; **we're not on ~ terms** no nos hablamos ► **speaking trumpet** N bocina *f* ► **speaking tube** N tubo *m* acústico ► **speaking voice** N **a pleasant ~ voice** una voz agradable

-speaking ['spiːkɪŋ] ADJ (*ending in compounds*) **English-speaking** de habla inglesa, anglohablante; **French-speaking** de habla francés, francoparlante; **Spanish-speaking people** los hispanohablantes, los de habla española *or* (*esp LAm*) castellana

spear [spɪəʳ] Ⓐ N (*gen*) lanza *f*; (= *harpoon*) arpón *m*
Ⓑ VT [1] (*with spear*) alancear, herir con lanza; (*with harpoon*) arponear
[2] (*fig*) atravesar, pinchar; **he ~ed a potato with his fork** atravesó *or* pinchó una patata con el tenedor

speargun ['spɪəgʌn] N harpón *m* submarino

spearhead ['spɪəhed] Ⓐ N (*Mil, also fig*) punta *f* de lanza
Ⓑ VT encabezar

spearmint ['spɪəmɪnt] Ⓐ N (*Bot etc*) menta *f* verde, hierbabuena *f*
Ⓑ CPD ► **spearmint chewing gum** N chicle *m* de menta

spec* [spek] N **to buy sth on ~** comprar algo como especulación; **to go along on ~** ir a ver lo que sale; **to turn up on ~** presentarse por si acaso

special ['speʃəl] Ⓐ ADJ [1] (= *important, exceptional*) [*occasion, day, pemission, price, attention, diet*] especial; **my ~ chair** mi silla preferida; **what's so ~ about that?** y eso ¿qué tiene de especial?; **is there anyone ~ in your life?** ¿hay alguien especial en tu vida?; **~ arrangements will be made for disabled people** se tomarán medidas especiales para las personas discapacitadas; **to take ~ care of sth** cuidar especialmente de algo; **in ~ cases** en casos especiales *or* extraordinarios; **to make a ~ effort to do sth** esforzarse especialmente *or* hacer un esfuerzo extra para hacer algo; **you're extra ~** tú eres lo mejor de lo mejor; **to make sb feel ~** hacer que algn se sienta especial; **my ~ friend** mi amigo del alma; **his ~ interest was always music** siempre tuvo especial interés por la música; **there's nothing ~ about being a journalist** ser periodista no tiene nada de especial; **it's nothing ~*** no es nada especial, no es nada del otro mundo; **~ powers** (*Pol*) poderes *mpl* extraordinarios; **I've cooked something ~ for dinner** he preparado algo especial para cenar; **she's very ~ to us** la apreciamos mucho; **~ to that country** exclusivo de ese país; **as a ~ treat** como algo especial; **to expect ~ treatment** esperar un trato especial
[2] (= *specific*) especial; **a ~ tool for working leather** una herramienta especial para trabajar el cuero; **have you any ~ date in mind?** ¿tienes en mente alguna fecha concreta *or* en particular *or* en especial?; **is there anything ~ you would like?** ¿hay algo que quieras en especial?; **I had no ~ reason for suspecting him** no tenía ningún motivo en especial para sospechar de él; **"why do you say that?" — "oh, no ~ reason"** —¿por qué dices eso? —por nada en especial; **I've no-one ~ in mind** no tengo en mente a nadie en concreto *or* en especial; **"what are you doing this weekend?" — "nothing ~"** —¿qué haces este fin de semana? —nada (en) especial *or* nada en particular; **Britain has its own ~ problems** Gran Bretaña tiene sus propios problemas particulares
[3] (*Brit iro*) (= *strange*) **to be a bit ~** [*person*] ser un poco especial
Ⓑ N [1] (= *train*) tren *m* especial; (*TV, Rad*) programa *m* especial; (= *newspaper*) número *m* extraordinario; **the chef's ~** ◊ **today's ~** la especialidad del día
[2] (*US**) (= *special offer*) oferta *f* especial; **to be on ~** estar de oferta
[3] (*Brit**) (= *special constable*) *ciudadano que en determinadas ocasiones realiza funciones de policía*
Ⓒ CPD ► **special adviser** N consejero/a *m/f* de asuntos extraordinarios ► **special agent** N agente *mf* especial ► **Special Air Service** N (*Brit*) *regimiento del ejército británico que se especializa en operaciones clandestinas* ► **Special Branch** N (*Brit*) Servicio *m* de Seguridad del Estado ► **special constable** N (*Brit*) *ciudadano que en ciertas ocasiones realiza funciones de policía* ► **special correspondent** N corresponsal *mf* especial ► **special delivery** N correo *m* exprés ► **special edition** N edición *f* especial ► **special effects** NPL efectos *mpl* especiales ► **special interest group** N grupo *m* de presión que persigue un tema específico ► **special investigator** N investigador(a) *m/f* especial ► **special jury** N jurado *m* especial ► **special licence** N (*Brit Jur*) *permiso especial para contraer matrimonio sin cumplir los requisitos legales normalmente necesarios* ► **special needs** NPL **children with ~ needs** ◊ **~ needs children** niños que requieren una atención diferenciada ► **special offer** N (*Comm*) oferta *f* especial, oferta *f* de ocasión ► **special school** N colegio *m* de educación especial

specialism ['speʃəˌlɪzəm] N especialidad *f*

specialist ['speʃəlɪst] Ⓐ N especialista *mf*; **heart ~** (*Med*) especialista *mf* del corazón
Ⓑ ADJ especializado; **that's ~ work** eso es trabajo especializado; **~ knowledge** conocimientos *mpl* especializados

speciality [ˌspeʃɪ'ælɪtɪ], **specialty** (*US*) ['speʃəltɪ] N especialidad *f*; **to make a ~ of sth** especializarse en algo; **it's a ~ of the house** es una especialidad de la casa, es un plato especial de la casa

specialization [ˌspeʃəlaɪ'zeɪʃən] N (= *act*) especialización *f*; (= *subject*) especialidad *f*

specialize ['speʃəlaɪz] VI especializarse (**in** en); **she ~d in Russian** se especializó en ruso; **we ~ in skiing equipment** estamos especializados en material de esquí

specialized ['speʃəlaɪzd] ADJ **~ knowledge** conocimientos *mpl* especializados

specially ['speʃəlɪ] ADV [1] (= *specifically*) [*designed, made, adapted, trained, selected*] especialmente, expresamente; **a lotion ~ formulated for children** una loción formulada especialmente *or* expresamente para niños; **we asked for it ~** lo pedimos a propósito
[2] (= *particularly*) especialmente, en especial, en particular; **we would ~ like to see the orchard** nos gustaría especialmente *or* en especial ver el huerto, nos gustaría ver el huerto en particular; **~ the yellow ones** especialmente *or* sobre todo los amarillos
[3] (= *exceptionally*) especialmente, particularmente; **her job is not ~ important to her** su trabajo no es especialmente *or* particularmente importante para ella; **the food was ~ good** la comida era excepcional *or* excepcionalmente buena

specialty ['speʃəltɪ] N (*US*) = **speciality**

specie ['spiːʃiː] N metálico *m*, efectivo *m*; **in ~** en metálico

species ['spiːʃiːz] N (*pl inv*) especie *f*

specific [spə'sɪfɪk] Ⓐ ADJ [1] (= *definite, particular*) [*need, plan*] específico; [*issue, area, problem*] específico, concreto; [*question, reason, example*] concreto; **for ~ political ends** con fines políticos concretos; **with the ~ aim of achieving sth** con el propósito expreso de lograr algo; **problems which are ~ to a particular group of people** problemas que son específicos *or* propios de un grupo particular de personas
[2] (= *precise*) [*description, instructions*] preciso; [*meaning*] exacto; **can you be more ~?** ¿puedes ser más concreto?, ¿puedes puntualizar?; **it was a tooth, a shark's tooth, to be more ~** era un diente: un diente de un tiburón para ser más preciso; **you will be asked to be ~ about what the problem is** te pedirán que especifiques con exactitud el problema, te pedirán que seas preciso a la hora de identificar el problema
[3] (*Bio, Phys, Chem, Med*) específico
Ⓑ N [1] (*Med*) (= *drug*) específico *m*
[2] **specifics** (= *particulars*) aspectos *mpl* concretos, detalles *mpl*; **we have yet to work out the ~s of the plan** todavía tenemos que elaborar los aspectos concretos *or* los detalles del plan; **to get down to ~s** ir a los aspectos concretos *or* los detalles
Ⓒ CPD ► **specific gravity** N peso *m* específico

specifically [spə'sɪfɪkəlɪ] ADV [1] (= *especially*) [*design, aim*] específicamente, expresamente; [*relate to*] específicamente; **projects ~ designed to strengthen British industries** proyectos diseñados específicamente *or* expresamente para fortalecer las industrias británicas
[2] (= *more precisely*) en concreto, concretamente; **fear was the main factor, ~ a fear of pregnancy** el temor era el factor principal, en concreto *or* concretamente, el temor a quedarse embarazada
[3] (= *explicitly*) [*mention, refer to*] explícitamente; [*ask, authorize*] expresamente, explícitamente; **he ~ asked us not to mention the fact** nos pidió expresamente *or* explícitamente que no mencionáramos ese hecho; **they will take no further action unless ~ instructed to** no van a tomar más medidas salvo que se les instruya de manera expresa
[4] (= *uniquely*) específicamente; **it isn't a ~ medical problem** no es un problema específicamente médico

specification [ˌspesɪfɪ'keɪʃən] N [1] (= *act of specifying*) especificación *f*
[2] (= *requirement*) especificación *f*; **the computers are customized to your ~(s)** los ordenadores *or* (*LAm*) computadores se diseñan de acuerdo con sus especificaciones
[3] **specifications** (= *plan*) presupuesto *m*, plan *m* detallado

specify ['spesɪfaɪ] Ⓐ VT especificar; **in the order specified** en el orden especificado; **at a specified time** a una hora determinada
Ⓑ VI precisar; **he did not ~** no precisó; **unless otherwise specified** salvo indicaciones en sentido contrario

specimen ['spesɪmɪn] Ⓐ N [1] (= *sample*) [*of blood, urine, tissue, rock*] muestra *f*
[2] (= *example*) [*of species, genus, etc*] ejemplar *m*, espécimen *m*; **that trout is a fine ~** esa trucha es un magnífico ejemplar
[3] (*) (= *person*) **he's an odd ~** es un bicho raro*; **you're a pretty poor ~** no vales para mucho
Ⓑ CPD ► **specimen copy** N ejemplar *m* de muestra ► **specimen page** N página *f* que sirve de muestra ► **specimen signature** N muestra *f* de firma

specious ['spiːʃəs] ADJ especioso

speciousness ['spiːʃəsnɪs] N lo especioso

speck [spek] Ⓐ N [1] (= *small stain*) pequeña mancha *f*
[2] (= *particle*) [*of dust*] mota *f*

➤ LANGUAGE IN USE: **specify** A 20.3

[3] (= *dot, point*) punto *m*; **it's just a ~ on the horizon** es un punto en el horizonte nada más

[4] (= *small portion*) pizca *f*; **there's not a ~ of truth in it** no tiene ni pizca de verdad; **just a ~, thanks** un poquitín, gracias

Ⓑ VT = **speckle**

speckle ['spekl] Ⓐ N punto *m*, mota *f*

Ⓑ VT salpicar, motear (**with** de)

speckled ['spekld] ADJ moteado, con puntos

specs¹* [speks] NPL gafas *fpl*, anteojos *mpl* (*LAm*), lentes *mpl* (*LAm*)

specs²* [speks] NPL ABBR = **specifications**

spectacle ['spektəkl] Ⓐ N [1] espectáculo *m*; **a sad ~** un triste espectáculo; **to make a ~ of o.s.** hacer el ridículo, ponerse en ridículo

[2] **spectacles** gafas *fpl*, lentes *mpl* (*LAm*), anteojos *mpl* (*LAm*); **a pair of ~s** unas gafas; ✦**IDIOM to see everything through rose-coloured** *or* **rose-tinted ~s** verlo todo color de rosa

Ⓑ CPD ► **spectacle case** N estuche *m* de gafas

spectacled ['spektəkld] ADJ con gafas

spectacular [spek'tækjʊlər] Ⓐ ADJ [*results, display, view, scenery, increase, improvement*] espectacular, impresionante; [*success*] impresionante; [*failure, fall, defeat*] espectacular, estrepitoso

Ⓑ N (*TV, Cine*) show *m* espectacular

spectacularly [spek'tækjʊləlɪ] ADV [*increase, grow, improve*] de modo *or* manera espectacular, espectacularmente; [*crash, fail*] de modo espectacular, estrepitosamente; [*good*] verdaderamente, realmente; [*bad*] terriblemente; **~ beautiful** de una belleza impresionante; **the campaign has proved ~ successful** la campaña ha sido todo un éxito *or* ha sido un éxito impresionante; **everything went ~ wrong** todo salió terriblemente mal

spectate [spek'teɪt] VI mirar; **they come to ~** vienen de espectadores

spectator [spek'teɪtər] Ⓐ N espectador(a) *m/f*; **spectators** público *msing*

Ⓑ CPD ► **spectator sport** N deporte *m* espectáculo

specter ['spektər] N (*US*) = **spectre**

spectral ['spektrəl] ADJ espectral

spectre, **specter** (*US*) ['spektər] N espectro *m*, fantasma *m*

spectrogram ['spektrəʊgræm] N espectrograma *m*

spectrograph ['spektrəʊgrɑːf] N espectrógrafo *m*

spectrometer [spek'trɒmɪtər] N espectrómetro *m*

spectrometry [spek'trɒmɪtrɪ] N espectrometría *f*

spectroscope ['spektrəskəʊp] N espectroscopio *m*

spectroscopy [spek'trɒskəpɪ] N espectroscopia *f*

spectrum ['spektrəm] Ⓐ N (*pl* **spectra** ['spektrə]) [1] (= *range*) espectro *m*, gama *f*; **we went through the whole ~ of emotions** experimentamos todo el espectro *or* toda la gama de emociones posibles; **a wide ~ of opinions** un amplio espectro *or* abanico de opiniones, una amplia gama de opiniones; **the political ~** el espectro político

[2] (*Phys*) espectro *m*

Ⓑ CPD ► **spectrum analysis** N análisis *m inv* espectral

speculate ['spekjʊleɪt] VI [1] (= *conjecture*) especular; **to ~ about/on** especular sobre, hacer conjeturas acerca de

[2] (*Fin*) especular (**on** en)

speculation [,spekjʊ'leɪʃən] N [1] (= *conjecture*) especulación *f*; **it is pure ~** es pura especulación; **it is the subject of much ~** se está especulando mucho sobre el tema, es un tema sobre el que se está especulando mucho

[2] (*Fin*) especulación *f*; **to buy sth as a ~** comprar algo con fines especulativas; **it's a good ~** vale como especulación

speculative ['spekjʊlətɪv] ADJ especulativo

speculator ['spekjʊleɪtər] N especulador(a) *m/f*

speculum ['spekjʊləm] N (*pl* **speculums, specula**) espéculo *m*

sped [sped] PT, PP *of* **speed**

speech [spiːtʃ] Ⓐ N [1] (= *faculty*) habla *f*; (= *words*) palabras *fpl*; (= *language*) lenguaje *m*; (= *manner of speaking*) lenguaje *m*, forma *f* de hablar; **to lose the power of ~** perder el habla; **to recover one's ~** recobrar el habla, recobrar la palabra; **his ~ was slurred** arrastraba las palabras, farfullaba al hablar; **he expresses himself better in ~ than in writing** se expresa mejor hablando *or* de palabra que por escrito; **children's ~** el lenguaje de los niños; **freedom of ~** libertad *f* de expresión; **to be slow of ~** hablar lentamente, ser torpe de palabra

[2] (= *address*) discurso *m*; **to make a ~** pronunciar un discurso; **speech, speech!** ¡que hable! ¡que hable!

[3] (*Brit Gram*) **direct/indirect ~** estilo *m* directo/indirecto; *see also* **part A8**

Ⓑ CPD ► **speech act** N acto *m* de habla ► **speech analysis** N análisis *m* de la voz ► **speech command** N comando *m* vocal ► **speech community** N comunidad *f* lingüística ► **speech day** N (*Brit*) reparto *m* de premios ► **speech defect, speech impediment** N defecto *m* del habla ► **speech organ** N órgano *m* del habla ► **speech recognition** N (*Comput*) reconocimiento *m* de voz ► **speech synthesizer** N sintetizador *m* de la voz humana ► **speech therapist** N logopeda *mf* ► **speech therapy** N terapia *f* de la palabra ► **speech training** N lecciones *fpl* de elocución ► **speech writer** N escritor(a) *m/f* de discursos, redactor(a) *m/f* de discursos

speechify ['spiːtʃɪfaɪ] VI (*pej*) disertar prolijamente, perorar

speechifying ['spiːtʃɪfaɪɪŋ] N (*pej*) disertaciones *fpl*, prolijas peroratas *fpl*

speechless ['spiːtʃlɪs] ADJ (= *dumbstruck*) estupefacto, sin habla; **everybody was ~ at this** con esto todos quedaron estupefactos *or* sin habla; **I'm ~!** no sé qué decir, estoy estupefacto; **to be ~ with rage** enmudecer de rabia

speechmaking ['spiːtʃ,meɪkɪŋ] N [1] (= *making of speeches*) pronunciación *f* de discursos

[2] (= *speeches collectively*) discursos *mpl*

[3] (*pej*) = **speechifying**

speed [spiːd] (*vb: pt, pp* **sped** *or* **speeded**) Ⓐ N [1] (= *rate of movement*) velocidad *f*, rapidez *f*; (= *rapidity, haste*) rapidez *f*, prisa *f*; **shorthand/typing ~** velocidad *f* en taquigrafía/mecanografía; **my typing ~ is 60 words per minute** mecanografío 60 palabras por minuto; **at ~** a gran velocidad; **at a ~ of 70km/h** a una velocidad de 70km por hora; **what ~ were you doing?** (*Aut*) ¿a qué velocidad ibas?; **at full ~** a toda velocidad, a máxima velocidad; **full ~ ahead!** ¡avante toda!*; **to gather ~** acelerar, cobrar velocidad; **the ~ of light** la velocidad de la luz; **the maximum ~ is 120km/h** la velocidad máxima es de 120km por hora; **to pick up ~** acelerar, cobrar velocidad; **the ~ of sound** la velocidad del sonido; **at top ~** a toda velocidad, a máxima velocidad; ✦**IDIOMS to be up to ~** (= *well-informed*) estar al día, estar al corriente; (= *functioning properly*) estar a punto, funcionar a pleno rendimiento; **to bring sb up to ~** poner a algn al día *or* al corriente; **to bring sth up to ~** poner algo a punto; *see also* **full A3**

[2] (*Aut, Tech*) (= *gear*) velocidad *f*; **a three-~ bike** una bicicleta de tres marchas *or* velocidades; **a five-~ gearbox** una caja de cambios de cinco velocidades

[3] (*Phot*) velocidad *f*

[4] (*Drugs*‡) speed *m*, anfetamina *f*

Ⓑ VI [1] (*pt, pp* **sped**) (= *go fast*) correr a toda prisa; (= *hurry*) darse prisa, apresurarse; **he sped down the street** corrió a toda prisa por la calle; **to ~ along** ir a gran velocidad; **the years sped by** pasaron los años volando; **to ~ off** marcharse a toda prisa

[2] (*pt, pp* **speeded**) (*Aut*) (= *exceed speed limit*) conducir *or* (*LAm*) manejar por encima del límite de velocidad permitido

Ⓒ VT (*pt, pp* **speeded**) **to ~ sb on his way** despedir a algn, desear un feliz viaje a algn

Ⓓ CPD ► **speed bump** N banda *f* sonora ► **speed cop*** N policía *m* de tráfico, policía *m* de tránsito ► **speed limit** N velocidad *f* máxima, límite *m* de velocidad; **a 50km/h ~ limit** velocidad máxima (permitida) de 50km por hora; **to exceed the ~ limit** exceder la velocidad permitida *or* el límite de velocidad ► **speed merchant*** N corredor(a) *m/f* ► **speed restriction** N limitación *f* de velocidad ► **speed skating** N patinaje *m* de velocidad ► **speed trap** N (*Aut*) *sistema policial para detectar infracciones de velocidad*

►**speed up** (*pt, pp* **speeded up**) Ⓐ VI + ADV [*person*] apresurarse, apurarse (*LAm*); [*process*] acelerarse

Ⓑ VT + ADV [+ *object*] acelerar; [+ *person*] apresurar, apurar (*LAm*)

speedball ['spiːdbɔːl] N [1] (= *game*) speedball *m*

[2] (*Drugs*) chute *m* de cocaína con heroína‡

speedboat ['spiːd,bəʊt] N lancha *f* motora

speeder ['spiːdər] N (= *fast driver*) automovilista *mf* que conduce a gran velocidad; (*convicted*) infractor(a) *m/f* de los límites de velocidad

speedily ['spiːdɪlɪ] ADV (= *quickly*) rápidamente, con la mayor prontitud; (= *promptly*) prontamente, en seguida

speediness ['spiːdɪnɪs] N (= *speed*) velocidad *f*, rapidez *f*; (= *promptness*) prontitud *f*

speeding ['spiːdɪŋ] N (*Aut*) exceso *m* de velocidad; **he was fined for ~** le pusieron una multa por exceso de velocidad

speedo* ['spiːdəʊ] N (*Brit*) = **speedometer**

speedometer [spɪ'dɒmɪtər] N velocímetro *m*, cuentakilómetros *m inv*

speed-up ['spiːdʌp] N aceleración *f*, agilización *f*

speedway ['spiːdweɪ] N [1] (= *sport*) carreras *fpl* de motos

[2] (= *track*) pista *f* de carreras

[3] (*US*) autopista *f*

speedwell ['spiːdwel] N (*Bot*) verónica *f*

speedy ['spiːdɪ] ADJ (*compar* **speedier**; *superl* **speediest**) veloz, rápido; [*answer*] pronto

speleologist [,spiːlɪ'ɒlədʒɪst] N espeleólogo/a *m/f*

speleology [,spiːlɪ'ɒlədʒɪ] N espeleología *f*

spell¹ [spel] N encanto *m*, hechizo *m*; **to be under a ~** estar hechizado; **to be under sb's ~** estar hechizado por algn; **to break the ~** romper el hechizo *or* encanto; **to cast a ~ over** *or* **on sb** ◊ **put sb under a ~** hechizar a algn; **Seville casts its ~ over the tourists** Sevilla embruja a los turistas

spell[2] [spel] (*pt, pp* **spelled** *or* **spelt**) Ⓐ VT [1] (= *write*) escribir; (*letter by letter*) deletrear; **how do you ~ your name?** ¿cómo se escribe tu nombre?; **can you ~ that please?** ¿me lo deletrea, por favor?; **c-a-t ~s "cat"** "cat" se deletrea c-a-t; **what do these letters ~?** ¿qué palabra se forma con estas letras?
[2] (= *denote*) significar, representar; **it ~s ruin** significa *or* representa la ruina; **it ~s disaster for us** significa *or* representa un desastre para nosotros
Ⓑ VI (= *write correctly*) escribir correctamente; **she can't ~** no sabe escribir correctamente, sabe poco de ortografía

►**spell out** VT + ADV [1] (= *read letter by letter*) deletrear [2] (= *explain*) **to ~ sth out for sb** explicar algo a algn en detalle

spell[3] [spel] N [1] (= *period*) racha *f*; **a prolonged ~ of bad weather** una larga racha de mal tiempo; **a cold ~** una racha de frío; **they're going through a bad ~** están pasando por una mala racha
[2] (= *shift, turn*) turno *m*; **we each took a ~ at the wheel** nos turnamos al volante; **a ~ of duty** una temporada; **I did a ~ as a commercial traveller** durante cierto tiempo trabajé como viajante

spellbinder ['spel,baɪndəʳ] N (= *speaker*) orador(a) *m/f* que fascina; (= *book*) obra *f* que fascina

spellbinding ['spel,baɪndɪŋ] ADJ cautivador, fascinante

spellbound ['spelbaʊnd] ADJ embelesado, hechizado; **to hold sb ~** tener a algn embelesado

spellcheck ['spel,tʃek] Ⓐ VT pasar el corrector (ortográfico) a
Ⓑ N **to do a ~ (on sth)** pasar el corrector (ortográfico) (a algo)

spellchecker ['spel,tʃekəʳ] N corrector *m* ortográfico

speller ['speləʳ] N **to be a bad ~** cometer muchas faltas de ortografía, tener mala ortografía

spelling ['spelɪŋ] Ⓐ N ortografía *f*; **the correct ~ is …** la ortografía correcta es …; **my ~ is terrible** cometo muchas faltas de ortografía
Ⓑ CPD ► **spelling bee** N certamen *m* de ortografía ► **spelling checker** N corrector *m* ortográfico ► **spelling mistake** N falta *f* de ortografía ► **spelling pronunciation** N pronunciación *f* ortográfica

spelt[1] [spelt] (*esp Brit*) PT, PP *of* **spell**[2]

spelt[2] [spelt] N (*Bot*) espelta *f*

spelunker [spɪ'lʌŋkəʳ] N (*US*) espeleólogo/a *m/f*

spelunking [spɪ'lʌŋkɪŋ] N (*US*) espeleología *f*

spend [spend] (*pt, pp* **spent**) Ⓐ VT [1] (= *pay out*) [+ *money*] gastar; **to ~ sth on sth/sb** gastar algo en algo/algn; **she ~s too much money on clothes** gasta demasiado dinero en ropa; **they've spent a fortune on the house** (se) han gastado un dineral en la casa; **the buildings need a lot ~ing on them** a los edificios les hace falta una buena inyección de dinero; **it's money well spent** es dinero bien empleado; ✦**IDIOM to ~ a penny** (*Brit euph*) cambiar de agua al canario
[2] (= *devote*) [+ *effort, time*] dedicar; **we ~ time, money and effort training these people** dedicamos tiempo, dinero y trabajo a formar a estas personas
[3] (= *pass*) [+ *period of time*] pasar; **where are you ~ing your holiday?** ¿dónde vas a pasar las vacaciones?; **he spent eight years learning his trade** pasó ocho años aprendiendo los gajes del oficio; **he ~s all his time sleeping** se pasa la vida durmiendo; *see also* **night A1**
[4] (= *use up*) [+ *force, ammunition, provisions*] (*liter*) agotar; **the storm has spent its fury** la tempestad ha agotado *or* perdido su fuerza; **I ~ all my energy just getting to work** nada más que en llegar al trabajo se me van todas las energías; **the bullets spent themselves among the trees** las balas se desperdiciaron en los árboles
Ⓑ VI gastar

spender ['spendəʳ] N gastador(a) *m/f*; **big ~** persona *f* generosa; (*pej*) derrochador(a) *m/f*; **to be a free ~** gastar libremente su dinero; (*pej*) ser derrochador

spending ['spendɪŋ] Ⓐ N gastos *mpl*; **to keep one's ~ down** mantener los gastos bajos; **the latest figures for consumer ~** las últimas cifras correspondientes a los gastos del consumidor; **to reduce government** *or* **public ~** reducir el gasto público; **military/defence ~** gastos *mpl* militares/de defensa; **they pledged to increase ~ on education** prometieron incrementar el presupuesto de educación
Ⓑ CPD ► **spending cuts** NPL recortes *mpl* presupuestarios ► **spending limit** N límite *m* de gastos ► **spending money** N (*for holiday*) dinero *m* para gastar; (= *allowance*) dinero *m* para gastos (personales) ► **spending power** N poder *m* de compra, poder *m* adquisitivo ► **spending spree** N derroche *m* de dinero; **we went on a ~ spree** salimos a gastar dinero

spendthrift ['spendθrɪft] Ⓐ ADJ derrochador, pródigo
Ⓑ N derrochador(a) *m/f*, pródigo/a *m/f*

spent [spent] Ⓐ PT, PP *of* **spend**
Ⓑ ADJ [*match, lightbulb, battery*] gastado; [*bullet, cartridge, ammunition*] usado; **he's a ~ force** ya no es lo que era

sperm [spɜːm] Ⓐ N (*Bio*) esperma *m or f*
Ⓑ CPD ► **sperm bank** N banco *m* de esperma ► **sperm count** N recuento *m* de espermas ► **sperm whale** N cachalote *m*

spermaceti [,spɜːmə'setɪ] N esperma *m or f* de ballena

spermatozoon [,spɜːmətəʊ'zəʊɒn] N (*pl* **spermatozoa** [,spɜːmətəʊ'zəʊə]) espermatozoo *m*

spermicidal [,spɜːmɪ'saɪdl] ADJ espermicida

spermicide ['spɜːmɪsaɪd] N espermicida *m*

spew [spjuː] Ⓐ VT (*also* **~ up**) vomitar; (*fig*) arrojar, vomitar Ⓑ VI vomitar; **it makes me want to ~*** (*fig*) me da asco

SPG N ABBR (*Brit Police*) = **Special Patrol Group**

sphagnum ['sfægnəm] N esfagno *m*

sphere [sfɪəʳ] N [1] (*Astron, Math etc*) esfera *f*
[2] (*fig*) esfera *f*; **in the social ~** en la esfera social; **~ of influence** esfera *f* de influencia; **~ of activity** campo *m* de actividad, esfera *f* de actividad; **his ~ of interest** el ámbito de sus intereses; **in the ~ of politics** en el mundo de la política; **that's outside my ~** eso no es de mi competencia

spherical ['sferɪkəl] ADJ esférico

spheroid ['sfɪərɔɪd] N esferoide *m*

sphincter ['sfɪŋktəʳ] N esfínter *m*

sphinx [sfɪŋks] N (*pl* **sphinxes**) esfinge *f*

spice [spaɪs] Ⓐ N [1] (*Culin*) especia *f*; **mixed ~(s)** especias *fpl* mixtas; ✦**PROV variety is the ~ of life** en la variedad está el gusto
[2] (*fig*) lo picante; **the papers like stories with some ~** a los periódicos les gustan los reportajes con algo de picante; **the details add ~ to the story** los detalles dan sabor a la historia
Ⓑ VT [1] (*Culin*) condimentar, sazonar
[2] (*fig*) **a highly ~d account** un relato de mucho picante; **gossip ~d with scandal** cotilleos con el sabor picante que da el escándalo
Ⓒ CPD ► **spice rack** N especiero *m*

►**spice up** VT + ADV [1] (= *season*) condimentar, dar más sabor a; **use it to ~ up rice dishes and stews** úselo para condimentar *or* dar mas sabor a los platos de arroz y estofados
[2] (= *enliven*) **it could help ~ up your sex life** podría ayudar a estimular su vida sexual

spiciness ['spaɪsɪnɪs] N [1] [*of food*] lo picante
[2] [*of story*] lo picante

Spick‡* [spɪk] N (*US pej*) hispano/a *m/f*

spick-and-span ['spɪkən'spæn] ADJ [*house, room*] impecable, como los chorros del oro*; [*person*] acicalado; **they left the cottage ~** dejaron el chalet impecable, dejaron el chalet como los chorros del oro*; **everything must be kept ~** todo tiene que estar impecable

spicy ['spaɪsɪ] ADJ (*compar* **spicier**, *superl* **spiciest**) [1] (*Culin*) (*gen*) muy condimentado, muy sazonado; (= *hot*) picante, picoso (*LAm*)
[2] (*fig*) [*joke etc*] picante, colorado (*LAm*)

spider ['spaɪdəʳ] Ⓐ N araña *f*; **~'s web** telaraña *f* Ⓑ CPD ► **spider crab** N centollo *m*, centolla *f* ► **spider plant** N cinta *f*

spiderman ['spaɪdəmæn] N (*pl* **spidermen**) (*Constr*) *obrero que trabaja en la construcción de edificios altos*

spidery ['spaɪdərɪ] ADJ delgado; [*writing*] de patas de araña

spiel* [spiːl] N (= *speech*) arenga *f*, discurso *m*; [*of salesman etc*] rollo* *m*, material *m* publicitario; **it's just his usual ~** es el mismo cuento de siempre

spiffing†* ['spɪfɪŋ] ADJ fetén†*, estupendo*, fenomenal*

spigot ['spɪgət] N espita *f*, bitoque *m*

spike [spaɪk] Ⓐ N [1] (= *point*) punta *f*; (= *metal rod*) pincho *m*; (= *stake*) estaca *f*; (= *tool*) escarpia *f*; (*on railing*) barrote *m*; (*on sports shoes*) clavo *m*
[2] (*Zool*) [*of hedgehog etc*] púa *f*
[3] (*Elec*) pico *m* parásito
[4] (*Bot*) espiga *f*
[5] **spikes** (*Sport*) zapatillas *fpl* con clavos
Ⓑ VT [1] (= *fix*) clavar; (= *impale*) atravesar
[2] (= *stop*) [+ *rumour*] acabar con; (= *thwart*) [+ *plan etc*] frustrar; ✦**IDIOM to ~ sb's guns** poner trabas a los planes de algn
[3] **a ~d drink*** (*with added alcohol*) una bebida con alcohol añadido de extranjis; (*drugged*) *una bebida a la que le han echado algo, como un somnífero, droga, etc.*
Ⓒ CPD ► **spike heel** N (*US*) tacón *m* de aguja

spiked [spaɪkt] ADJ [*shoe*] con clavos

spikenard ['spaɪknɑːd] N nardo *m*

spiky ['spaɪkɪ] ADJ (*compar* **spikier**, *superl* **spikiest**) [1] (= *sharp, pointed*) puntiagudo; (= *thorny*) cubierto de púas; (*Zool*) erizado; [*hair*] de punta
[2] (*Brit**) (= *irritable*) [*person*] quisquilloso, susceptible

spill[1] [spɪl] (*pt, pp* **spilled** *or* **spilt**) Ⓐ VT [1] [+ *water, salt*] derramar, verter; **you're ~ing the milk** estás derramando la leche; **you've ~ed** *or* **spilt coffee on your shirt** te ha caído café en la camisa; **she ~ed** *or* **spilt wine all over the table** derramó el vino por toda la mesa; ✦**IDIOM to ~ the beans*** descubrir el pastel*, contarlo todo; *see also* **cry B2**
[2] [+ *rider*] hacer caer, desarzonar
Ⓑ VI derramarse, verterse

Ⓒ N [1] (= *fall*) caída *f*; **to have a ~** sufrir una caída, tener un accidente
[2] (= *spillage*) vertido *m*

►**spill out** Ⓐ VI + ADV [*liquid*] derramarse; [*contents, objects*] desparramarse; [*people*] salir en avalancha; **the crowd ~ed out into the streets** la gente salió a la calle en avalancha; **the audience ~ed out of the cinema** el público salió en masa del cine
Ⓑ VT + ADV volcar; (*fig*) soltar

►**spill over** VI + ADV [*liquid*] derramarse; [*cup, pan*] desbordarse; **these problems ~ed over into his private life** estos problemas llegaron a afectar su vida privada

spill² [spɪl] N (*for lighting fire*) pajuela *f*

spillage [ˈspɪlɪdʒ] N vertido *m*

spillover [ˈspɪləʊvəʳ] N [1] (= *act of spilling*) derrame *m*; (= *quantity spilt*) cantidad *f* derramada [2] (*fig*) (= *excess part*) excedente *m* [3] (*Econ*) (= *effect*) incidencia *f* indirecta en el gasto público

spillway [ˈspɪlweɪ] N (*US*) derramadero *m*, aliviadero *m*

spilt [spɪlt] (*esp Brit*) PT, PP *of* **spill**

spin [spɪn] (*vb: pt, pp* **spun**) Ⓐ N [1] (= *rotating motion*) vuelta *f*, revolución *f*; **to give a wheel a ~** hacer girar una rueda; ✦*IDIOM* **to be in a (flat) ~** (*Brit**) [*person*] andar muy confundido; **the news sent the stock market into a flat ~** la noticia creó un estado de gran confusión en la bolsa
[2] (*in washing machine*) **give the towels another ~** vuelve a centrifugar las toallas (en la lavadora); **long/short ~** centrifugado *m* largo/corto
[3] (*Sport*) (*on ball*) efecto *m*; **to put (a) ~ on a ball** dar efecto a una pelota
[4] (= *loss of control*) (*Aer*) barrena *f*; (*Aut*) trompo *m*; **to go into a ~** (*Aer*) entrar en barrena; (*Aut*) hacer un trompo; **to pull** *or* **come out of a ~** (*Aer*) salir de barrena
[5] (*Brit**) (= *short ride*) vuelta *f*, paseo *m*, garbeo *m* (*Sp**); **to go for a ~** dar una vuelta *or* un paseo (en coche/moto etc), darse un garbeo (en coche/moto etc) (*Sp**)
[6] (*) (= *interpretation*) interpretación *f*; **to put a positive ~ on sth** interpretar positivamente algo, dar un sesgo positivo a algo
Ⓑ VT [1] (= *rotate*) (*gen*) hacer girar; [+ *top*] hacer bailar; **to ~ a coin** hacer girar una moneda; (*to decide sth*) echar una moneda a cara o cruz
[2] (= *spin-dry*) [+ *clothes*] centrifugar
[3] (= *turn suddenly*) girar; **he spun the steering wheel sharply to the right** giró el volante bruscamente hacia la derecha; **to ~ sth/sb round** dar la vuelta a algo/algn
[4] (*Sport*) [+ *ball*] dar efecto a
[5] [+ *thread*] hilar; [+ *web*] tejer; [+ *cocoon*] devanar, hacer; ✦*IDIOMS* **to ~ a web of lies** hilar una sarta de mentiras; **to ~ a yarn*** (*in order to deceive*) inventar una historia
Ⓒ VI [1] (= *rotate*) girar, dar vueltas; **his wheels began to ~ as he tried to get off the grass** las ruedas empezaron a dar vueltas cuando intentó salir de la hierba; **she spun around** *or* **round to face him** se dio la vuelta para tenerlo de frente; **my head is ~ning** me da vueltas la cabeza; **it makes my head ~** me marea
[2] (= *move quickly*) **to ~ along** correr a gran velocidad; **the car spun out of control** el coche se descontroló y empezó a dar vueltas; **to send sth/sb ~ning: the blow sent him ~ning** el golpe le hizo rodar por el suelo; **she sent the plate ~ning through the air** lanzó el plato a rodar por los aires
[3] [*washing machine*] centrifugar
[4] (*with spinning wheel*) hilar
Ⓓ CPD ► **spin® class** N clase *f* de Spinning® ► **spin doctor*** N (*Pol*) asesor(a) *m/f* político(a)

►**spin out*** VT + ADV [+ *process, story*] alargar, prolongar; [+ *money, drink*] estirar

spina bifida [ˌspaɪnəˈbɪfɪdə] N espina *f* bífida

spinach [ˈspɪnɪdʒ] N [1] (*Culin*) espinacas *fpl*
[2] (= *plant*) espinaca *f*

spinal [ˈspaɪnl] Ⓐ ADJ espinal, vertebral
Ⓑ CPD ► **spinal column** N columna *f* vertebral ► **spinal cord** N médula *f* espinal

spindle [ˈspɪndl] N [1] (*for spinning*) huso *m*
[2] (*Tech*) eje *m*

spindleshanks* [ˈspɪndlʃæŋks] N zanquivano/a *m/f*

spindly [ˈspɪndlɪ] ADJ (*compar* **spindlier**; *superl* **spindliest**) [*person*] alto y delgado, larguirucho*; [*legs*] largo y delgado, largo y delgaducho*; [*plant, tree*] alto y delgado, alto y delgaducho*

spin-drier [ˈspɪnˈdraɪəʳ] N = **spin-dryer**

spindrift [ˈspɪndrɪft] N rocío *m* del mar, espuma *f*

spin-dry [ˌspɪnˈdraɪ] VT centrifugar

spin-dryer [ˈspɪnˈdraɪəʳ] N secadora-centrifugadora *f*

spine [spaɪn] N [1] (*Anat*) (= *backbone*) columna *f* (vertebral), espina *f* dorsal
[2] (*Zool*) (= *spike*) púa *f*, pincho *m*; (*Bot*) espina *f*, pincho *m*
[3] [*of book*] lomo *m*
[4] [*of mountain range*] espinazo *m*

spine-chiller [ˈspaɪnˌtʃɪləʳ] N (= *film*) película *f* de terror; (= *book*) libro *m* de terror

spine-chilling [ˈspaɪnˌtʃɪlɪŋ] ADJ escalofriante

spineless [ˈspaɪnlɪs] ADJ (*fig*) débil

spinelessly [ˈspaɪnlɪslɪ] ADV débilmente

spinet [spɪˈnet] N espineta *f*

spinnaker [ˈspɪnəkəʳ] N balón *m*, espinaquer *m*

spinner [ˈspɪnəʳ] N [1] [*of cloth*] hilandero/a *m/f*
[2] (*Cricket, Baseball*) el/la que da efecto a la pelota
[3] (*Fishing*) cebo *m* artificial de cuchara
[4] (*) (= *spin-dryer*) secadora-centrifugadora *f*

spinneret [ˌspɪnəˈret] N pezón *m* hilador

spinney [ˈspɪnɪ] N bosquecillo *m*

spinning [ˈspɪnɪŋ] Ⓐ N (= *act*) hilado *m*; (= *art*) hilandería *f*, arte *m* de hilar
Ⓑ CPD ► **spinning jenny** N máquina *f* de hilar de husos múltiples ► **spinning mill** N hilandería *f* ► **spinning top** N peonza *f*, trompo *m* ► **spinning wheel** N rueca *f* *or* torno *m* de hilar

spin-off [ˈspɪnɒf] N (*Comm*) (= *product*) derivado *m*, producto *m* secundario; (= *secondary effect*) consecuencia *f* indirecta; (= *incidental benefit*) beneficio *m* incidental, beneficio *m* indirecto

spinster [ˈspɪnstəʳ] N soltera *f*; (*pej*) solterona *f*

spiny [ˈspaɪnɪ] ADJ (*compar* **spinier**; *superl* **spiniest**) [1] [*rose*] espinoso; [*animal*] con púas
[2] [*problem*] espinoso

spiracle [ˈspɪrəkl] N espiráculo *m*

spiraea [spaɪˈrɪə] N espirea *f*

spiral [ˈspaɪərəl] Ⓐ ADJ espiral, en espiral; **a ~ staircase** una escalera de caracol
Ⓑ N espiral *f*, hélice *f*; **the inflationary ~** la espiral inflacionista
Ⓒ VI **to ~ up/down** subir/bajar en espiral; **the plane ~led down** el avión bajó en espiral; **the smoke ~led up** ◊ **the smoke went ~ling up** el humo subió formando una espiral; **prices have ~led up** los precios han subido vertiginosamente

spirally [ˈspaɪərəlɪ] ADV en espiral

spire [ˈspaɪəʳ] N aguja *f*

spirea [spaɪˈrɪə] N (*US*) = **spiraea**

spirit [ˈspɪrɪt] Ⓐ N [1] (= *soul, inner force*) espíritu *m*; **I'll be with you in ~** estaré contigo en espíritu; **young in ~** joven de espíritu; **the ~ is willing but the flesh is weak** las intenciones son buenas pero la carne es débil
[2] (= *ghost, supernatural being*) espíritu *m*; **evil ~** espíritu *m* maligno; **the ~ world** el mundo de los espíritus
[3] (= *courage*) espíritu *m*; (= *liveliness*) ímpetu *m*, energía *f*; **to break sb's ~** quebrantar el espíritu a algn; **they lack ~** les falta espíritu; **a woman of ~** una mujer con espíritu *or* brío; **show some ~!** ¡anímate!; **the team soon began to show their ~** el equipo pronto empezó a animarse; **to do sth with ~** hacer algo con energía; **to sing with ~** cantar con brío
[4] (= *attitude, mood*) espíritu *m*; **a ~ of adventure** un espíritu aventurero; **community ~** civismo *m*; **they wish to solve their problems in a ~ of cooperation** quieren resolver sus problemas con espíritu de cooperación; **he refused to enter into the ~ of things** se negó a entrar en ambiente; **festive ~** espíritu *m* festivo; **in a ~ of friendship** con espíritu de amistad; **generosity of ~** bondad *f* de espíritu; **a ~ of optimism** un espíritu optimista; **public ~** civismo *m*; **to take sth in the right/wrong ~** interpretar bien/mal algo; **that's the ~!** ¡así me gusta!, ¡ánimo!; *see also* **fighting D**, **team D**
[5] (= *essence*) [*of agreement, law*] espíritu *m*; **the ~ of the age/the times** el espíritu de la época/de los tiempos; **the ~ of the law** el espíritu de la ley
[6] (= *person*) alma *f*; **the leading** *or* **moving ~ in the party** el alma del partido, la figura más destacada del partido; **she was a free ~** era una persona sin convencionalismos; *see also* **kindred**
[7] **spirits** [7·1] (= *state of mind*) **to be in good ~s** tener la moral alta; **to be in high ~s** estar animadísimo, estar muy alegre; **it was just a case of youthful high ~s** no fue más que una demostración típica del comportamiento impetuoso de la juventud; **I tried to keep his ~s up** intenté animarlo *or* darle ánimos; **we kept our ~s up by singing** mantuvimos la moral alta cantando; **to lift** *or* **raise sb's ~s** levantar el ánimo *or* la moral a algn; **to be in low ~s** tener la moral baja, estar bajo de moral; **my ~s rose somewhat** se me levantó un poco el ánimo *or* la moral
[7·2] (= *alcohol*) licores *mpl*; **I keep off ~s** no bebo licores; **a measure of ~s** un (vasito de) licor; **~s of wine** espíritu *m* de vino
[8] (*Chem*) alcohol *m*
Ⓑ VT (= *take*) **to ~ sth away** llevarse algo como por arte de magia, hacer desaparecer algo; **he was ~ed out of the country** lo sacaron del país clandestinamente *or* de forma clandestina
Ⓒ CPD ► **spirit duplicator** N copiadora *f* al alcohol ► **spirit gum** N cola *f* de maquillaje ► **spirit lamp** N lamparilla *f* de alcohol ► **spirit level** N nivel *m* de burbuja ► **spirit stove** N infernillo *m* de alcohol

spirited [ˈspɪrɪtɪd] ADJ (= *lively*) [*person*] animado, lleno de vida; [*horse*] fogoso; [*debate, discussion*] animado, enérgico; [*attack*] enérgico; **he made a ~ defence of his position** defendió su postura con vehemencia; **he gave a ~ performance** (*Mus*) tocó con brío; **they**

put up a ~ resistance organizaron una enérgica resistencia, resistieron enérgicamente
spiritless ['spɪrɪtlɪs] ADJ apocado, sin ánimo
spiritual ['spɪrɪtjʊəl] Ⓐ ADJ espiritual
Ⓑ N (*Mus*) canción *f* religiosa
spiritualism ['spɪrɪtjʊəlɪzəm] N espiritismo *m*
spiritualist ['spɪrɪtjʊəlɪst] N espiritista *mf*
spirituality [ˌspɪrɪtjʊ'ælɪtɪ] N espiritualidad *f*
spiritually ['spɪrɪtjʊəlɪ] ADV espiritualmente
spirituous ['spɪrɪtjʊəs] ADJ espirituoso
spirt [spɜːt] *see* **spurt**
spit[1] [spɪt] (*vb: pt, pp* **spat**) Ⓐ N saliva *f*, esputo *m*; **a few ~s of rain** unas gotas de lluvia; ✦*IDIOMS* **~ and polish*** limpieza *f*; **that table needs a bit of ~ and polish*** esa mesa hay que limpiarla; **to be the dead ~ of sb*** ser la viva imagen *or* el vivo retrato de algn
Ⓑ VT [1] (*lit*) [+ *blood, crumb*] escupir
[2] (= *exclaim*) espetar, soltar; **"traitor!" he spat** —¡traidor! —espetó *or* soltó él; **he spat the words** escupió las palabras
Ⓒ VI [1] [*person*] escupir (**at** a; **on** en); [*cat*] bufar; **to ~ in sb's face** escupir a la cara a algn; **it's ~ting with rain** (*Brit*) están cayendo algunas gotas
[2] [*fat, fire*] chisporrotear; **the fish is ~ting in the pan** chisporrotea el pescado en la sartén
►**spit forth** VT + ADV = **spit out**
►**spit out** VT + ADV [1] [+ *pip, pill*] escupir; **I spat it out** lo escupí
[2] (*fig*) **~ it out!*** ¡dilo!, ¡habla!; **he spat out the words** escupió las palabras
►**spit up** VT + ADV [+ *blood*] soltar un esputo de
spit[2] [spɪt] Ⓐ N [1] (*Culin*) asador *m*, espetón *m*
[2] (*Geog*) [*of land*] lengua *f*; (= *sandbank*) banco *m* de arena
Ⓑ VT espetar
Ⓒ CPD ► **spit roast** N asado *m*; *see also* **spitroast**
spit[3] [spɪt] N (*Agr*) azadada *f*; **to dig three ~s deep** excavar a una profundidad de tres azadadas
▼ **spite** [spaɪt] Ⓐ N [1] (= *ill will*) rencor *m*, ojeriza *f*; **to do sth out of** *or* **from ~** hacer algo por inquina; **to have a ~ against sb*** tener rencor a *or* hacia algn
[2] **in ~ of** (= *despite*) a pesar de, pese a; **in ~ of the fact that** a pesar de que, pese a que; **in ~ of herself** a pesar de sí misma; **in ~ of all he says** a pesar de todo lo que dice
Ⓑ VT herir, dañar; **she just does it to ~ me** lo hace solamente para causarme pena
spiteful ['spaɪtfʊl] ADJ [*person*] (= *resentful*) rencoroso; (= *malicious*) malicioso; [*action*] malintencionado; **to be ~ to sb** tratar a algn con rencor, ser rencoroso con algn
spitefully ['spaɪtfəlɪ] ADV (= *out of resentment*) por despecho; **she said ~** dijo, con malicia
spitefulness ['spaɪtfʊlnɪs] N (= *resentment*) rencor *m*; (= *malice*) malicia *f*
spitfire ['spɪtˌfaɪə^r] N fierabrás *mf*
spitroast ['spɪtrəʊst] VT rostizar
spitting ['spɪtɪŋ] Ⓐ N **"spitting prohibited"** ◊ **"no spitting"** "se prohíbe escupir"
Ⓑ ADJ **it's within ~ distance*** está muy cerca; ✦*IDIOM* **to be the ~ image of sb** ser la viva imagen *or* el vivo retrato de algn
spittle ['spɪtl] N saliva *f*, baba *f*
spittoon [spɪ'tuːn] N escupidera *f*
spiv* [spɪv] N (*Brit*) chanchullero* *m*, caballero *m* de industria; (= *slacker*) gandul *m*; (= *black marketeer*) estraperlista *mf*
splash [splæʃ] Ⓐ N [1] (= *spray*) salpicadura *f*; (= *splashing noise*) chapoteo *m*; **I heard a ~** oí un chapoteo; **it fell with a great ~ into the water** hizo mucho ruido al caer al agua; **whisky with a ~ of water** whisky *m* con un poquitín de agua
[2] (= *patch, spot*) [*of light*] mancha *f*; **a ~ of colour** una mancha de color
[3] (*fig*) **with a great ~ of publicity*** con mucho bombo publicitario*; ✦*IDIOM* **to make a ~*** causar sensación
Ⓑ VT [1] (*gen*) salpicar; **to ~ sb with water** salpicar a algn de agua; **don't ~ me!** ¡no me salpiques!; **he ~ed water on his face** se echó agua en la cara
[2] (= *stain*) manchar; **to ~ paint on the floor** manchar el suelo de pintura
[3] (*fig*) **the story was ~ed across the front page*** el reportaje apareció con grandes titulares en primera plana
Ⓒ VI [1] [*liquid, mud etc*] **mud ~ed all over his trousers** el barro le salpicó los pantalones
[2] [*person, animal*] (*in water*) chapotear; **to ~ across a stream** cruzar un arroyo chapoteando
►**splash about** Ⓐ VT + ADV **to ~ water about** desparramar (el) agua; **to ~ one's money about** derrochar su dinero por todas partes
Ⓑ VI + ADV chapotear; **to ~ about in the water** chapotear en el agua
►**splash down** VI + ADV amarar, amerizar
►**splash out*** VI + ADV (*Brit*) derrochar dinero; **so we ~ed out and bought it** decidimos echar la casa por la ventana y comprarlo
►**splash up** Ⓐ VT + ADV salpicar
Ⓑ VI + ADV salpicar
splashback ['splæʃbæk] N salpicadero *m*
splashboard ['splæʃbɔːd] N guardabarros *m inv*
splashdown ['splæʃdaʊn] N amaraje *m*, amerizaje *m*
splashy* ['splæʃɪ] ADJ (*US*) (= *showy*) ostentoso
splatter ['splætə^r] = **spatter**
splay [spleɪ] VT [1] [+ *feet, legs*] abrir, extender
[2] (*Tech*) biselar, achaflanar
spleen [spliːn] N [1] (*Anat*) bazo *m*
[2] **to vent one's ~** (*fig*) descargar la bilis
splendid ['splendɪd] ADJ (= *magnificent*) espléndido, magnífico; (= *excellent*) estupendo, magnífico; **he has done ~ work** ha hecho una magnífica labor; **splendid!** ¡magnífico!, ¡estupendo!; **in ~ isolation** en total *or* absoluto aislamiento
splendidly ['splendɪdlɪ] ADV (= *magnificently*) espléndidamente, magníficamente; (= *wonderfully*) estupendamente; **everything went ~** todo fue de maravilla; **we get along ~** nos llevamos muy bien; **you did ~** hiciste muy bien; **a ~ dressed man** un hombre muy bien vestido
splendiferous* [splen'dɪfərəs] ADJ (*hum*) = **splendid**
splendour, **splendor** (*US*) ['splendə^r] N esplendor *m*
splenetic [splɪ'netɪk] ADJ [1] (*Anat*) esplénico
[2] (*frm*) (= *short-tempered*) enojadizo, de genio vivo; (= *bad-tempered*) malhumorado
splice [splaɪs] Ⓐ VT [1] [+ *rope, tape etc*] empalmar, juntar; ✦*IDIOM* **to get ~d*** casarse
[2] (*Naut*) ayustar
Ⓑ N empalme *m*, junta *f*
splicer ['splaɪsə^r] N (*for film*) máquina *f* de montaje
spliff‡ [splɪf] N (*Drugs*) porro *m*, canuto *m*
splint [splɪnt] Ⓐ N (*Med*) tablilla *f*; **to put sb's arm in ~s** entablillar el brazo a algn; **to be in ~s** estar entablillado
Ⓑ VT entablillar
splinter ['splɪntə^r] Ⓐ N [*of wood, metal*] astilla *f*; [*of glass*] fragmento *m*; [*of bone*] esquirla *f*, fragmento *m*; **I've got a ~ in my finger** tengo una astilla en el dedo
Ⓑ VI astillarse, hacerse astillas; (*fig*) [*party*] escindirse; **to ~ off from** escindirse *or* separarse de
Ⓒ VT [1] (*lit*) astillar, hacer astillas
[2] (*fig*) [+ *party*] dividir
Ⓓ CPD ► **splinter group** N grupo *m* disidente, facción *f* ► **splinter party** N partido *m* nuevo (*formado a raíz de la escisión de otro*)
splinterbone ['splɪntəbəʊn] N peroné *m*
splinterless ['splɪntəlɪs] ADJ inastillable
splinterproof ['splɪntəpruːf] ADJ **~ glass** cristal *m* inastillable
split [splɪt] (*vb: pt, pp* **split**) Ⓐ N [1] (= *crack*) (*in wood, rock*) hendidura *f*, grieta *f*
[2] (= *rift*) ruptura *f*, escisión *f*; **there are threats of a ~ in the progressive party** se oyen voces *or* hay amenazas de escisión en el partido progresista
[3] (= *division*) división *f*; **the ~ between the rich and the poor** la división entre ricos y pobres; **a three-way ~** una división en tres partes
[4] **to do the ~s** (*Gymnastics*) hacer el spagat; (*accidentally*) abrirse completamente de piernas, espatarrarse*
[5] (*Culin*) **jam ~** pastel *m* de mermelada; **banana ~** (banana) split *m*
[6] (*Sew*) (*in skirt*) abertura *f*
Ⓑ ADJ [1] (= *cracked*) [*wood, rock*] partido, hendido; **he had a ~ lip** tenía un labio partido
[2] (= *divided*) dividido; **the government is ~ on this question** el gobierno está dividido en este asunto; **it was a ~ decision** la decisión no fue unánime; **the party was ~** el partido estaba escindido *or* dividido; **the votes are ~ 15-13** los votos están repartidos 15 a 13; **the party is ~ three ways** el partido está escindido *or* dividido en tres grupos
Ⓒ VT [1] (= *break*) partir; **the sea had ~ the ship in two** el mar había partido el barco en dos; **he ~ the wood with an axe** partió la madera con un hacha; **to ~ the atom** desintegrar el átomo; **to ~ sth open** abrir algo; **he ~ his head open** se abrió la cabeza de un golpe; ✦*IDIOMS* **to ~ hairs** hilar muy fino *or* delgado, buscarle tres pies al gato, buscarle mangas al chaleco (*LAm*); **to ~ one's sides laughing** partirse de risa, morirse de (la) risa
[2] (= *divide, share*) repartir; **let's ~ the money between us** repartámonos el dinero; **to ~ the difference** repartir la diferencia (a partes iguales); **to ~ sth into three parts** dividir algo en tres partes; **the children were ~ into two groups** dividieron a los niños en dos grupos; **to ~ the vote** (*Pol*) repartirse los votos; **to ~ the profit five ways** repartir las ganancias entre cinco
[3] (*fig*) [+ *government, group*] dividir; [+ *party*] escindir, dividir; **the dispute ~ the party** la disputa escindió *or* dividió el partido
Ⓓ VI [1] (= *come apart*) [*stone etc*] henderse, rajarse; **the jeans ~ the first time she wore them** los vaqueros se le abrieron por las costuras la primera vez que se los puso; **to ~ open** abrirse; **the ship hit a rock and ~ in two** el barco chocó con una roca y se partió en dos; ✦*IDIOM* **my head is ~ting** me va a estallar la cabeza
[2] (*fig*) [*government, group*] dividirse; [*party*] escindirse, dividirse
[3] (*) (= *tell tales*) chivatear‡, soplar*; **to ~ on sb** chivatear contra algn‡, soplar contra algn*; **don't ~ on me** de esto no digas ni pío

➤ LANGUAGE IN USE: spite A2 26.3

4 (*esp US**) (= *leave*) largarse*, irse
Ⓔ CPD ► **split infinitive** N *infinitivo en el que un adverbio o una frase se intercala entre "to" y el verbo* ► **split pea** N guisante *m* majado ► **split personality** N personalidad *f* desdoblada ► **split pin** N (*Brit*) chaveta *f*, pasador *m* ► **split screen** N pantalla *f* partida; *see also* **split-screen** ► **split second** N fracción *f* de segundo; **in a ~ second** en un instante, en un abrir y cerrar de ojos ► **split shift** N jornada *f* partida

►**split off** Ⓐ VI + ADV separarse
Ⓑ VT + ADV separar

►**split up** Ⓐ VI + ADV 1 (= *break up*) estrellarse
2 (= *separate*) [*partners*] separarse; [*meeting, crowd*] dispersarse; **they were married 14 years but then they ~ up** estuvieron casados durante 14 años pero luego se separaron; **let's ~ up for safety** separémonos para mayor seguridad; **we ~ up into two groups** nos dividimos en dos grupos
Ⓑ VT + ADV 1 (= *break up*) partir
2 (= *divide up*) repartir; [+ *estate*] parcelar; **we'll ~ the work up among us** nos repartiremos *or* dividiremos el trabajo
3 (= *separate*) dividir; **~ the children up into small groups** divide a los niños en grupos pequeños

split-level ['splɪt,levl] ADJ [*room*] a desnivel; [*house*] dúplex; [*cooker*] en dos niveles

split-off ['splɪtɒf] N separación *f*; (*Pol*) escisión *f*

split-screen [splɪt'skri:n] CPD ► **split-screen facility** N capacidad *f* de pantalla partida

splitting ['splɪtɪŋ] Ⓐ ADJ [*headache*] terrible
Ⓑ N **~ of the atom** desintegración *f* del átomo

split-up ['splɪtʌp] N ruptura *f*; [*of couple*] separación *f*

splodge [splɒdʒ], **splotch** [splɒtʃ] N mancha *f*, borrón *m*

splurge* [splɜ:dʒ] Ⓐ N (= *excess*) derroche *m*
Ⓑ VI **to ~ on sth** derrochar dinero comprando algo

splutter ['splʌtəʳ] Ⓐ N 1 [*of fat etc*] chisporroteo *m*
2 [*of speech*] farfulla *f*
Ⓑ VI 1 [*person*] (= *spit*) escupir, echar saliva; (= *stutter*) farfullar, balbucear; **to ~ with indignation** farfullar indignado
2 [*fire, fat*] chisporrotear; [*engine*] renquear
Ⓒ VT farfullar, balbucear; **"yes", he ~ed** —sí —farfulló *or* balbuceó

spoil [spɔɪl] (*vb: pt, pp* **spoiled** *or* **spoilt**) Ⓐ VT
1 (= *ruin*) estropear, arruinar; (= *harm*) dañar; (= *invalidate*) [+ *voting paper*] invalidar; **the coast has been ~ed by development** la costa ha sido arruinada por las urbanizaciones; **it ~ed our holiday** nos estropeó las vacaciones; **and there were 20 ~ed papers** y hubo 20 votos nulos; **it will ~ your appetite** te quitará el apetito; **to ~ sb's fun** aguar la fiesta a algn; **to get ~ed** echarse a perder, estropearse
2 (= *pamper*) mimar, consentir (*LAm*); **grandparents like to ~ their grandchildren** a los abuelos les encanta mimar a los nietos
Ⓑ VI 1 [*food*] estropearse, echarse a perder; **if we leave it here it will ~** si lo dejamos aquí se estropeará *or* se echará a perder
2 **to be ~ing for a fight** estar con ganas de luchar *or* (*LAm*) pelear

spoilage ['spɔɪlɪdʒ] N (= *process*) deterioro *m*; (= *thing, amount spoilt*) desperdicio *m*

spoiled [spɔɪld] = **spoilt**

spoiler ['spɔɪləʳ] N 1 (*Aut, Aer*) alerón *m*, spoiler *m*
2 (*Press*) **a rival paper brought out a ~** un periódico rival publicó otra exclusiva para quitarles parte de las ventas
3 (*) (= *person etc*) aguafiestas *mf inv*

spoils [spɔɪlz] NPL botín *msing*; **the ~ of war** el botín de la guerra

spoilsport* ['spɔɪlspɔ:t] N aguafiestas *mf inv*

spoilt [spɔɪlt] Ⓐ PT, PP *of* **spoil**
Ⓑ ADJ 1 (= *ruined*) [*meal etc*] estropeado, echado a perder; [*vote*] nulo
2 (= *pampered*) [*child*] mimado, consentido
3 (*US*) (= *gone off*) [*food*] pasado, malo; [*milk*] cortado

spoke¹ [spəʊk] N [*of wheel*] rayo *m*, radio *m*; ♦**IDIOM to put a ~ in sb's wheel** ponerle trabas a algn

spoke² [spəʊk] PT *of* **speak**

spoken ['spəʊkən] Ⓐ PP *of* **speak**
Ⓑ ADJ hablado; **the ~ language** la lengua hablada; *see also* **well-spoken**

spokeshave ['spəʊkʃeɪv] N raedera *f*

spokesman ['spəʊksmən] N (*pl* **spokesmen**) portavoz *mf*, vocero *mf* (*LAm*); **to act as ~ for** hablar en nombre de; **they made him ~** lo eligieron para hablar en su nombre

spokesperson ['spəʊkspɜ:sn] N (*pl* **spokespeople**) portavoz *mf*, vocero *mf* (*LAm*)

spokeswoman ['spəʊkswʊmən] N (*pl* **spokeswomen**) portavoz *f*, vocero *f* (*LAm*)

spoliation [,spəʊlɪ'eɪʃən] N despojo *m*

spondee ['spɒndi:] N espondeo *m*

sponge [spʌndʒ] Ⓐ N 1 (*for washing*) esponja *f*; ♦**IDIOM to throw in the ~** darse por vencido, tirar la toalla
2 (*Culin*) (*also* **~ cake**) bizcocho *m*, queque *m*, pastel *m* (*LAm*)
3 (*Zool*) esponja *f*
Ⓑ VT 1 (= *wash*) lavar con esponja, limpiar con esponja
2 (*) (= *scrounge*) **he ~d £15 off me** me sacó 15 libras de gorra*
Ⓒ VI (*) (= *scrounge*) dar sablazos*, vivir de gorra*; **to ~ off** *or* **on sb** (= *depend on*) vivir de algn; (*on occasion*) dar sablazos a algn*
Ⓓ CPD ► **sponge bag** N esponjera *f* ► **sponge cake** N bizcocho *m*, queque *m*, pastelito *m* (*LAm*) ► **sponge pudding** N pudín *m* de bizcocho

►**sponge down** VT + ADV limpiar con esponja, lavar con esponja

►**sponge off** Ⓐ VT + ADV quitar con esponja; **to ~ a stain off** quitar una mancha con esponja
Ⓑ VI + ADV quitarse con (una) esponja
Ⓒ VI + PREP *see* **sponge C**

►**sponge up** VT + ADV absorber

sponger* ['spʌndʒəʳ] N gorrón/ona* *m/f*, sablista* *mf*

sponginess ['spʌndʒɪnɪs] N esponjosidad *f*

sponging* ['spʌndʒɪŋ] N gorronería* *f*

spongy ['spʌndʒɪ] ADJ (*compar* **spongier**; *superl* **spongiest**) esponjoso

sponsor ['spɒnsəʳ] Ⓐ N 1 (= *provider of funds*) (*Sport, Rad, TV*) patrocinador(a) *m/f*, sponsor *mf*
2 (*for participant in charity event*) patrocinador(a) *m/f*
3 (*for loan*) fiador(a) *m/f*, avalista *mf*
4 [*of membership*] **your application must be signed by two ~s** su solicitud tiene que estar firmada por dos socios
5 (= *godparent*) (*male*) padrino *m*; (*female*) madrina *f*
6 [*of bill, motion*] proponente *mf*
Ⓑ VT 1 (= *fund*) [+ *event*] patrocinar, auspiciar; [+ *studies, research*] financiar; [+ *participant in charity event*] *respaldar or avalar mediante un donativo a favor de una obra benéfica*; **~ed walk/sim** *marcha/prueba de natación emprendida a cambio de donaciones a una obra benéfica*
2 (= *support*) respaldar, apoyar; **they have been accused of ~ing terrorism** se los ha acusado de respaldar *or* apoyar al terrorismo
3 [+ *bill, motion*] proponer
4 [+ *loan*] fiar, avalar

sponsorship ['spɒnsəʃɪp] N 1 (= *funding*) [*of event*] patrocinio *m*, auspicio *m*; [*of studies, research*] financiación *f*; **corporate ~ of the arts** patrocinio de las artes por parte de empresas; **a £10m ~ deal** un contrato de patrocinio de 10 millones de libras; **under the ~ of** [*event*] bajo los auspicios de, patrocinado por
2 (= *support*) respaldo *m*, apoyo *m*
3 (= *guaranteeing*) fianza *f*, aval *m*

spontaneity [,spɒntə'neɪɪtɪ] N espontaneidad *f*

spontaneous [spɒn'teɪnɪəs] ADJ espontáneo; **~ combustion** combustión *f* espontánea

spontaneously [spɒn'teɪnɪəslɪ] ADV espontáneamente

spoof* [spu:f] Ⓐ N (= *parody*) burla *f*, parodia *f*; (= *hoax*) trampa *f*, truco *m*
Ⓑ ADJ **~ letter** carta *f* paródica
Ⓒ VT (= *parody*) parodiar; (= *trick*) engañar
Ⓓ VI bromear

spook* [spu:k] Ⓐ N 1 (* *hum*) (= *ghost*) espectro *m*, aparición *f*
2 (*US**) (= *secret agent*) espía *mf*, agente *mf* secreto/a
Ⓑ VT (*US*) 1 (= *haunt*) aparecerse en, rondar
2 (= *frighten*) asustar, pegar un susto a

spooky* ['spu:kɪ] ADJ (*compar* **spookier**; *superl* **spookiest**) espeluznante, horripilante; **the house is really ~ at night** la casa te pone los pelos de punta de noche

SPOOL [spu:l] N ABBR = **simultaneous peripheral operation on-line**

spool [spu:l] N (*Phot, for thread*) carrete *m*; (*for film etc*) bobina *f*; (*on fishing line*) cucharilla *f*; (*on sewing machine*) canilla *f*

spoon [spu:n] Ⓐ N 1 (*gen*) cuchara *f*; (= *teaspoon*) cucharita *f*; ♦**IDIOM to be born with a silver ~ in one's mouth** nacer de pie, nacer con un pan debajo del brazo
2 (= *spoonful*) cucharada *f*
Ⓑ VT (*also* **~ out**) **to ~ sth onto a plate** echar cucharadas de algo en un plato
Ⓒ VI (†*) acariciarse amorosamente, besuquearse*

►**spoon off** VT + ADV [+ *fat, cream etc*] quitar con la cuchara

►**spoon out** VT + ADV = **spoon B**

►**spoon up** VT + ADV recoger con cuchara

spoonbill ['spu:nbɪl] N espátula *f*

spoonerism ['spu:nərɪzəm] N trastrueque *m* verbal, trastrueque *m* de palabras

spoon-fed ['spu:nfed] ADJ malacostumbrado, que siempre lo tiene todo hecho

spoon-feed ['spu:nfi:d] (*pt, pp* **spoon-fed**) VT
1 (*lit*) dar de comer con cuchara a
2 (*fig*) dar todo hecho a, poner todo en bandeja a, malacostumbrar; **it isn't good to ~ children** no es bueno dárselo todo hecho *or* ponérselo todo en bandeja *or* malacostumbrar a los niños

spoonful ['spu:nfʊl] N cucharada *f*

spoor [spʊəʳ] N pista *f*, rastro *m*

sporadic [spə'rædɪk] ADJ esporádico; **~ gunfire** tiroteo *m* intermitente *or* esporádico

sporadically [spə'rædɪkəlɪ] ADV esporádicamente

spore [spɔːʳ] N espora *f*

sporran ['spɒrən] N escarcela *f*

sport [spɔːt] Ⓐ N [1] (= *game*) deporte *m*; **he is good at several ~s** se le dan bien varios deportes; **the ~ of kings** el deporte de los reyes, la hípica
[2] (= *games in general*) deporte(s) *m(pl)*; **I love ~** me encantan los deportes *or* el deporte; **to be good at ~** ser buen deportista
[3] **sports** (= *athletics meeting*) juegos *mpl* deportivos
[4] (= *hunting*) caza *f*; **to have some good ~** tener éxito en la caza, lograr unas cuantas piezas hermosas; **the trout here give good ~** aquí las truchas no se rinden fácilmente
[5] (= *fun*) juego *m*, diversión *f*; **to say sth in ~** decir algo en broma; **to make ~ of sb** burlarse de algn
[6] (*) (= *person*) persona *f* amable; **she's a good ~** es buena persona, es buena gente (*esp LAm*); **he's a real ~** es una persona realmente buena; **be a ~!** ¡no seas malo!
[7] (*liter*) (= *plaything*) víctima *f*, juguete *m*
[8] (*Bio*) mutación *f*
Ⓑ VI (*liter*) divertirse
Ⓒ VT lucir, ostentar
Ⓓ CPD ► **sports car** N coche *m* deportivo ► **sports centre, sports complex** N polideportivo *m* ► **sports day** N (*Brit*) día *m* de competiciones deportivas (de un colegio) ► **sports desk** N sección *f* de deportes ► **sports editor** N jefe *mf* de la sección de deportes ► **sports facilities** NPL instalaciones *fpl* deportivas ► **sports ground** N campo *m* deportivo, centro *m* deportivo ► **sports hall** N = **sports centre** ► **sports jacket** N chaqueta *f* sport, saco *m* sport (*LAm*) ► **sports page** N página *f* de deportes ► **sport(s) utility vehicle** N todoterreno *m inv* ► **sports writer** N cronista *mf* deportivo/a

sportiness ['spɔːtɪnɪs] N deportividad *f*

sporting ['spɔːtɪŋ] ADJ [1] [*activity, career*] deportivo
[2] (= *fair*) [*conduct, spirit etc*] deportivo, caballeroso; **that's very ~ of you** eres muy amable, es muy amable de su parte; **there's a ~ chance that ...** existe la posibilidad de que ...

sportingly ['spɔːtɪŋlɪ] ADV [1] (*lit*) de modo deportivo
[2] (*fig*) muy amablemente; **she ~ agreed to help** ella muy amablemente accedió a prestar ayuda

sportive ['spɔːtɪv] ADJ juguetón

sportscast ['spɔːtskɑːst] N (*US*) programa *m* deportivo

sportsman ['spɔːtsmən] N (*pl* **sportsmen**) deportista *m*; **the ~ of the year** el deportista del año

sportsmanlike ['spɔːtsmənlaɪk] ADJ caballeroso

sportsmanship ['spɔːtsmənʃɪp] N espíritu *m* deportivo

sportswear ['spɔːtswɛəʳ] N ropa *f* deportiva

sportswoman ['spɔːtswʊmən] N (*pl* **sportswomen**) deportista *f*

sporty* ['spɔːtɪ] ADJ (*compar* **sportier**, *superl* **sportiest**) deportivo, aficionado a los deportes

spot [spɒt] Ⓐ N [1] (= *dot*) lunar *m*; **a red dress with white ~s** un vestido rojo con lunares blancos; **to have ~s before one's eyes** tener la vista nublada; ✦**IDIOMS to knock ~s off sb*** dar ciento y raya a algn, vencer fácilmente a algn; **this can knock ~s off yours any time*** éste le da ciento y raya al tuyo en cualquier momento
[2] (= *stain, mark*) mancha *f*; **~s of blood/grease** manchas de sangre/grasa; **it made a ~ on the table** hizo una mancha en la mesa; **there's a ~ on your shirt** tienes una mancha en la camisa
[3] (*Med*) (= *pimple*) grano *m*, granito *m*; **she broke out** *or* **came out in ~s** (= *pimples*) le salieron granos en la piel; (= *rash*) le salió un sarpullido, le salieron granos en la piel; **he's covered in ~s** (= *pimples*) está lleno de granos; (= *rash*) le ha salido un sarpullido por todo el cuerpo, está lleno de granos; **measles ~s** manchas *fpl* de sarampión; *see also* **beauty B**
[4] (= *place*) sitio *m*, lugar *m*; (= *scene*) escena *f*, escenario *m*; **it's a lovely ~ for a picnic** es un sitio *or* lugar precioso para un picnic; **a tender ~ on the arm** un punto *or* lugar sensible en el brazo; **an accident black ~** un punto negro para los accidentes; **night ~** centro *m* nocturno; **on the ~** (= *immediately*) en el acto; (= *there*) en el mismo sitio; **they gave her the job on the ~** le dieron el trabajo en el acto; **luckily they were able to mend the car on the ~** afortunadamente consiguieron arreglar el coche allí mismo; **the reporter was on the ~** el reportero estaba presente; **the firemen were on the ~ in three minutes** los bomberos acudieron *or* llegaron en tres minutos; **I always have to be on the ~** estoy de servicio siempre; **our man on the ~** nuestro hombre sobre el terreno; **to run on the ~** correr en parada; **to pay cash on the ~** (*US*) pagar al contado; **his soft ~** su debilidad, su punto flaco, su lado flaco (*LAm*); **to have a soft ~ for sb** tener debilidad por algn; **his weak ~** su debilidad, su punto flaco, su lado flaco (*LAm*); **to know sb's weak ~s** conocer las debilidades de algn, saber de qué pie cojea algn*; ✦**IDIOM to touch a sore ~** tocar la fibra sensible, poner el dedo en la llaga
[5] (*Brit**) (= *small quantity*) poquito *m*, pizca *f*; **just a ~, thanks** un poquitín, gracias; **a ~ of bother** un pequeño disgusto; **he had a ~ of bother with the police** se metió en un lío con la policía*; **we had a ~ of rain yesterday** ayer se sintieron gotas de lluvia; **we're in a ~ of trouble** estamos en un pequeño apuro
[6] (= *difficulty*) apuro *m*, aprieto *m*; **to be in a (tight) ~** estar en un apuro *or* aprieto; **now I'm really on the ~** ahora me veo de verdad entre la espada y la pared; **to put sb on the ~** (= *put in difficulty*) poner a algn en un apuro *or* aprieto; (= *compromise*) comprometer a algn
[7] (*Rad, Theat, TV*) (*in show*) espacio *m*; (*Rad, TV*) (= *advertisement*) espacio *m* publicitario
[8] (*) (= *spotlight*) foco *m*
Ⓑ VT [1] (*with mud etc*) salpicar, manchar (**with** de)
[2] (= *notice*) darse cuenta de, notar; (= *see*) observar, darse cuenta de; (= *recognize*) reconocer; (= *catch out*) coger, pillar; **I ~ted a mistake** descubrí un error; **I ~ted him at once** lo reconocí en seguida; **to ~ the winner** elegir al ganador
Ⓒ VI **to ~ with rain** chispear
Ⓓ CPD ► **spot cash** N dinero *m* contante ► **spot check** N comprobación *f* en el acto, reconocimiento *m* rápido; *see also* **spot-check** ► **spot market** N mercado *m* al contado ► **spot price** N precio *m* de entrega inmediata ► **spot remover** N quitamanchas *m inv* ► **spot survey** N inspección *f* sorpresa

spot-check ['spɒt,tʃek] VT revisar en el acto; *see also* **spot D**

spotless ['spɒtlɪs] ADJ [1] (= *clean*) inmaculado, sin mancha; (= *tidy, neat*) [*appearance*] impecable, pulcro; [*house*] limpísimo
[2] (= *flawless*) [*reputation*] impecable, intachable

spotlessly ['spɒtlɪslɪ] ADV **~ clean** limpísimo

spotlessness ['spɒtlɪsnɪs] N perfecta limpieza *f*

spotlight ['spɒtlaɪt] Ⓐ N (= *beam, lamp*) foco *m*, reflector *m*; (*Theat*) proyector *m*; (*Aut*) faro *m* auxiliar orientable; **he doesn't like being in the ~** no le gusta ser el centro de atención; ✦**IDIOM to turn the ~ on sth/sb** exponer algo/a algn a la luz pública
Ⓑ VT [1] (*lit*) iluminar
[2] (*fig*) destacar, subrayar

spot-on* [,spɒt'ɒn] Ⓐ ADJ **what he said was ~** dio en el claro con lo que dijo
Ⓑ ADV **she guessed ~** lo adivinó exactamente

spotted ['spɒtɪd] ADJ con motas, con puntos; (*with dirt*) salpicado, manchado; **a dress ~ with mud** un vestido salpicado *or* manchado de lodo

spotter ['spɒtəʳ] N (*Aer etc*) observador(a) *m/f*; (*Brit Rail*) (= *trainspotter*) coleccionista *mf* de números de locomotoras

spotting ['spɒtɪŋ] N *see* **trainspotting**

spotty* ['spɒtɪ] ADJ (*compar* **spottier**, *superl* **spottiest**) [1] (= *pimply*) con granos
[2] (*) (= *patterned*) [*dress, material*] de lunares, con motas; [*dog*] con manchas

spouse [spaʊs] N cónyuge *mf*

spout [spaʊt] Ⓐ N [*of jar*] pico *m*; [*of teapot etc*] pitón *m*, pitorro *m*; [*of guttering*] canalón *m*; (= *jet of water*) surtidor *m*, chorro *m*; **to be up the ~** (*Brit**) [*person*] (= *in a jam*) estar en un apuro; (= *pregnant*) estar en estado; **my holiday's up the ~*** mis vacaciones se han ido al garete*
Ⓑ VT [1] [+ *water*] arrojar en chorro
[2] (*) [+ *poetry etc*] declamar
Ⓒ VI [1] [*water*] brotar, salir en chorros
[2] (*) (= *declaim*) hablar incansablemente

sprain [spreɪn] Ⓐ N torcedura *f*
Ⓑ VT torcer; **to ~ one's wrist/ankle** torcerse la muñeca/el tobillo

sprang [spræŋ] PT *of* **spring**

sprat [spræt] N espadín *m*, sardineta *f*

sprawl [sprɔːl] Ⓐ VI [1] [*person*] (= *sit down, lie down*) tumbarse, echarse; (*untidily*) despatarrarse; (= *fall down*) derrumbarse; **the body was ~ed on the floor** el cadáver estaba tumbado en el suelo; **he was ~ed** *or* **~ing in a chair** estaba tumbado de modo poco elegante en un sillón; **to send sb ~ing** (*with a blow*) derribar a algn por el suelo; **the jolt sent him ~ing** la sacudida le hizo ir rodando por el suelo
[2] [*plant, town*] extenderse
Ⓑ N [1] [*of body*] postura *f* desgarbada
[2] [*of town etc*] extensión *f*; **an endless ~ of suburbs** una interminable extensión de barrios exteriores; **urban ~** crecimiento *m* urbano descontrolado

sprawling ['sprɔːlɪŋ] ADJ [*person*] tumbado; [*city, town*] en crecimiento rápido; [*handwriting*] desgarbado

spray[1] [spreɪ] Ⓐ N [1] (= *liquid*) rociada *f*; [*of sea*] espuma *f*; (*from atomizer, aerosol*) pulverización *f*
[2] (= *aerosol, atomizer*) atomizador *m*, spray *m*; (*Med*) rociador *m*; **paint ~** pistola *f* (rociadora) de pintura; **to paint with a ~** pintar con pistola
Ⓑ VT [+ *water etc*] rociar; **she ~ed perfume on my hand** me roció perfume en la mano;

to ~ sth/sb with water/bullets rociar algo/a algn de agua/balas; **to ~ the roses with insecticide** rociar las rosas de insecticida; **to ~ paint on to a car** pintar un coche con una pistola rociadora; **there was graffiti ~ed on the wall** había pintadas de spray en la pared
Ⓒ CPD ► **spray can** N espray *m*, pulverizador *m* ► **spray gun** N pistola *f* rociadora, pulverizador *m* ► **spray paint** N pintura *f* spray
► **spray out** VI + ADV [*liquid etc*] salir a chorro; **water ~ed out all over them** el agua les caló

spray² [spreɪ] N (*Bot*) ramita *f*, ramo *m*

sprayer ['spreɪəʳ] N = **spray¹ A2**

spread [spred] (*vb: pt, pp* **spread**) Ⓐ N 1 (= *propagation*) [*of infection, disease, fire*] propagación *f*; [*of idea, information*] difusión *f*, divulgación *f*; [*of crime*] aumento *m*, proliferación *f*; [*of education*] extensión *f*, generalización *f*; [*of nuclear weapons*] proliferación *f*
2 (= *extent*) (*gen*) extensión *f*; [*of wings, sails*] envergadura *f*; **middle-age ~** gordura *f* de la mediana edad
3 (= *range*) **there is a broad ~ of interest and opinion represented on the committee** hay una gran diversidad de intereses y opiniones representados en el comité
4 (*) (= *meal*) comilona* *f*, banquetazo* *m*; **they laid on a huge ~** ofrecieron una espléndida comilona *or* un banquetazo espléndido*
5 (= *cover*) (*for bed*) cubrecama *m*, sobrecama *m or f*
6 (*Culin*) (*for bread*) pasta *f* para untar; **cheese ~** queso *m* para untar
7 (*Press, Typ*) **a full-page ~** una plana entera; **a two-page** *or* **double-page ~** una página doble, una doble plana
8 (*Fin*) diferencial *m*
9 (*US**) (= *ranch*) finca *f*, hacienda *f* (*LAm*), estancia *f* (*Arg, Uru*), fundo *m* (*Chile*)
Ⓑ VT 1 (*also* **~ out**) (= *lay or open out*) [+ *tablecloth, blanket*] extender, tender; [+ *map*] extender, desplegar; [+ *arms, fingers, legs*] extender; [+ *banner, sails, wings*] desplegar; [+ *net*] tender; **she lay ~ out on the floor** estaba tendida en el suelo; **the peacock ~ its tail** el pavo real hizo la rueda; **he ~ his hands in a gesture of resignation/helplessness** extendió los brazos en ademán de resignación/impotencia; **I like to be able to ~ myself** me gusta tener mucho espacio; **to ~ one's wings** (*lit, fig*) desplegar las alas
2 (= *scatter*) esparcir, desparramar; **her clothes were ~ all over the floor** su ropa estaba esparcida *or* desparramada por todo el suelo
3 (= *apply*) [+ *butter*] untar; **to ~ butter on one's bread** untar mantequilla en el pan, untar el pan con mantequilla; **to ~ cream on one's face** untarse *or* ponerse crema en la cara
4 (= *cover*) **tables ~ with food** mesas llenas *or* repletas de comida; **she ~ her bread with honey** puso miel en el pan, untó el pan con miel; **the floors are ~ with sand** los suelos están cubiertos de arena
5 (= *distribute*) distribuir; **you are advised to ~ the workload** le aconsejamos que se distribuya el trabajo; **repayments will be ~ over 18 months** los pagos se efectuarán a lo largo de 18 meses; ✦**IDIOM don't ~ yourself too thin** no intentes abarcar más de la cuenta
6 (= *disseminate*) [+ *news, information*] divulgar, difundir; [+ *rumour*] hacer correr, difundir; [+ *disease*] propagar; [+ *panic, fear*] sembrar; **he loves ~ing gossip** le encanta difundir *or* divulgar cotilleos; *see also* **word A4**
Ⓒ VI 1 (= *extend, advance*) [*fire*] propagarse, extenderse; [*stain*] extenderse; [*disease*] propagarse; [*panic, fear*] cundir; [*information, news, ideas*] difundirse; **general alarm ~ through the population** cundió la alarma por toda la población; **the cancer had ~ to his lungs** el cáncer se había extendido a los pulmones; **the troops ~ south** las tropas se desplegaron hacia el sur; **a smile ~ over** *or* **across his face** sonrió de oreja a oreja; ✦**IDIOM to ~ like wildfire**: **the rumours ~ like wildfire** los rumores corrieron como la pólvora
2 (= *stretch*) (*in space*) extenderse; **the city ~s several miles to the north** la ciudad se extiende varias millas hacia el norte; **a process ~ing over several months** un proceso que abarca varios meses
3 [*butter*] untarse
Ⓓ CPD ► **spread betting** N ≈ apuesta *f* múltiple, *modalidad de apuesta en la que se juega sobre una variedad de resultados en lugar de uno en concreto*
► **spread out** Ⓐ VI + ADV (= *disperse*) [*people*] dispersarse; (= *extend*) [*city, liquid*] extenderse; (= *widen*) [*river*] ensancharse
Ⓑ VT + ADV *see* **spread B1**

spreadable ['spredəbl] ADJ fácil de untar

spread-eagle [spred'i:gl] VT extender (completamente), despatarrar

spread-eagled [spred'i:gld] ADJ a pata tendida

spreader ['spredəʳ] N 1 (*for butter etc*) cuchillo *m* para esparcir; (*for glue etc*) paleta *f*
2 (*Agr*) esparcidor *m*

spreadsheet ['spredʃi:t] N hoja *f* electrónica, hoja *f* de cálculo

spree* [spri:] N juerga *f*, parranda *f*, farra *f* (*esp S. Cone*); **to go on a ~** ir de juerga *or* parranda *or* (*esp S. Cone*) farra; **to go on a killing ~** matar a una serie de personas; *see also* **spending B**

sprig [sprɪg] N 1 [*of heather etc*] espiga *f*
2 (*Tech*) puntilla *f*

sprightliness ['spraɪtlɪnɪs] N energía *f*

sprightly ['spraɪtlɪ] ADJ (*compar* **sprightlier**; *superl* **sprightliest**) enérgico

spring [sprɪŋ] (*vb: pt* **sprang**; *pp* **sprung**) Ⓐ N 1 (*also* **Spring**) (= *season*) primavera *f*; **in ~** en primavera; **in early/late ~** a principios/a finales de la primavera; **I like to go walking in (the) ~** me gusta salir a pasear en primavera; **in the ~ of 1956** en la primavera de 1956; **one ~ morning** una mañana de primavera; **~ is in the air** se siente la llegada de la primavera
2 (*in watch*) muelle *m*, resorte *m*; (*in mattress, sofa*) muelle *m*; **springs** (*Aut*) ballestas *fpl*
3 [*of water*] fuente *f*, manantial *m*; **a mountain ~** un manantial; **hot ~s** fuentes *fpl* termales
4 (= *leap*) salto *m*, brinco *m*; **in one ~** de un salto *or* brinco; **to walk with a ~ in one's step** caminar con brío
5 (= *elasticity*) elasticidad *f*
6 (*liter*) (*usu pl*) (= *origin, source*) origen *m*
Ⓑ VT 1 (= *present suddenly*) **to ~ sth on sb** soltar algo a algn (de buenas a primeras)*; **the redundancies were sprung on the staff without warning** soltaron la noticia de los despidos a la plantilla sin previo aviso; **to ~ a surprise on sb** dar una sorpresa a algn; **to ~ a leak** [*boat*] empezar a hacer agua; **the fuel tank sprang a leak** el depósito del combustible empezó a perder
2 (= *release*) [+ *trap*] hacer saltar; [+ *lock*] soltar; **to ~ sb from jail*** ayudar a algn a fugarse de la cárcel
3 (= *leap over*) saltar, saltar por encima de
Ⓒ VI 1 (= *leap*) saltar; **to ~ aside** hacerse rápidamente a un lado; **to ~ at sb** abalanzarse sobre algn; **the cat sprang at my face** el gato se me tiró *or* se me abalanzó a la cara; **to ~ back** [*person, animal*] saltar para atrás; **the branch sprang back** la rama volvió hacia atrás como un látigo; **where did you ~ from?*** ¿de dónde diablos has salido?*; **to ~ into action** entrar en acción; **to ~ into the air** dar un salto en el aire; **the engine finally sprang into life** por fin el motor arrancó; **the cat sprang onto the roof** el gato dio un salto y se puso en el tejado; **to ~ open** abrirse de golpe; **her name sprang out at me from the page** al mirar la página su nombre me saltó a la vista; **to ~ out of bed** saltar de la cama; **she sprang over the fence** saltó por encima de la valla; **to ~ shut** cerrarse de golpe; **to ~ to sb's aid** *or* **help** correr a ayudar a algn; **to ~ to attention** ponerse en posición de firme; **to ~ to one's feet** levantarse de un salto; **a number of examples ~ to mind** se me vienen a la mente *or* se me ocurren varios ejemplos
2 (= *originate*) [*stream*] brotar, nacer; [*river*] nacer; [*buds, shoots*] brotar; **to ~ from sth: the idea sprang from a TV programme he saw** la idea surgió de un programa de televisión que vio; **his anger sprang from his suffering** la furia le venía del sufrimiento
3 (*liter*) (= *be born*) [*person*] nacer; **to ~ into existence** surgir de la noche a la mañana, aparecer repentinamente
Ⓓ CPD [*flowers, rain, sunshine, weather*] primaveral, de primavera ► **spring balance** N peso *m* de muelle ► **spring binder** N (= *file*) carpeta *f* de muelles ► **spring bolt** N pestillo *m* de golpe ► **spring break** N (*US Educ*) vacaciones *fpl* de Semana Santa ► **spring chicken** N polluelo *m*; **she's no ~ chicken*** no es ninguna niña ► **spring fever** N fiebre *f* primaveral ► **spring greens** NPL (*Brit*) verduras *fpl* de primavera ► **spring gun** N trampa *f* de alambre y escopeta ► **spring lock** N candado *m* ► **spring mattress** N colchón *m* de muelles, somier *m* ► **spring onion** N cebolleta *f*, cebollino *m* ► **spring roll** N rollito *m* de primavera ► **spring tide** N marea *f* viva ► **spring water** N agua *f* de manantial
► **spring up** VI + ADV 1 [*building, settlement, organization*] surgir; [*plant, weeds*] brotar; [*wind, storm*] levantarse; [*doubt, rumour, friendship*] surgir, nacer
2 [*person*] (*from chair*) levantarse de un salto

springboard ['sprɪŋbɔ:d] Ⓐ N trampolín *m*; (*fig*) plataforma *f* de lanzamiento
Ⓑ CPD ► **springboard dive** N salto *m* de trampolín

springbok ['sprɪŋbɒk] N (*pl* **springbok, springboks**) gacela *f* (*del sur de África*)

spring-clean [,sprɪŋ'kli:n] Ⓐ VT limpiar completamente
Ⓑ VI limpiarlo todo, limpiar toda la casa

spring-cleaning [,sprɪŋ'kli:nɪŋ] N limpieza *f* general; **to do the ~** limpiar toda la casa

springiness ['sprɪŋɪnɪs] N elasticidad *f*; [*of step*] ligereza *f*

spring-like ['sprɪŋlaɪk] ADJ [*day, weather*] primaveral

springtime ['sprɪŋtaɪm] N primavera *f*

springy ['sprɪŋɪ] ADJ (*compar* **springier**; *superl* **springiest**) [*mattress, carpet, turf*] mullido; [*floor, rubber*] elástico; [*step*] ligero

sprinkle ['sprɪŋkl] Ⓐ N rociada *f*, salpicadura *f*; **a ~ of salt** un poquito de sal; **a ~ of rain** unas gotitas de lluvia
Ⓑ VT rociar (**with** de); **to ~ water on a plant** ◊ **~ a plant with water** rociar una planta de

agua; **to ~ sugar over a cake** ◊ **~ a cake with sugar** espolvorear un bizcocho con azúcar; **a rose ~d with dew** una rosa cubierta de rocío; **a lawn ~d with daisies** una extensión de césped salpicada de margaritas; **they are ~d about here and there** están esparcidos aquí y allá
Ⓒ VI (*with rain*) lloviznar

sprinkler ['sprɪŋklə^r] Ⓐ N 1 (*for lawn*) aspersor *m*; (*Agr*) rociadera *f*, aparato *m* de lluvia artificial; [*of watering can etc*] regadera *f*
2 (*for sugar*) espolvoreador *m* de azúcar
3 (= *fire safety device*) aparato *m* de rociadura automática
Ⓑ CPD ► **sprinkler system** N (*Agr*) sistema *m* de regadío por aspersión

sprinkling ['sprɪŋklɪŋ] N 1 (*with water*) rociada *f*; **a ~ of rain** unas gotitas de lluvia
2 (= *small quantity*) **there was a ~ of young people** había unos cuantos jóvenes; **a ~ of knowledge** unos pocos conocimientos

sprint [sprɪnt] Ⓐ N (*in race*) sprint *m*, esprint *m*; (= *dash*) carrera *f* sprint; **the women's 100 metres ~** los 100 metros lisos femeninos
Ⓑ VI (*in race*) sprintar, esprintar; (= *dash*) correr a toda velocidad; (= *rush*) precipitarse; **he ~ed for the bus** corrió tras el autobús; **we'll have to ~** tendremos que correr

sprinter ['sprɪntə^r] N (*Sport*) velocista *mf*, (e)sprínter *mf*

sprit [sprɪt] N botavara *f*, verga *f* de abanico

sprite [spraɪt] N elfo *m*, duende *m*

spritsail ['sprɪtseɪl] (*Naut*) ['sprɪtsl] N cebadera *f*, vela *f* de abanico

sprocket ['sprɒkɪt] Ⓐ N rueda *f* de espigas
Ⓑ CPD ► **sprocket feed** N avance *m* por rueda de espigas ► **sprocket wheel** N rueda *f* de cadena

sprog‡ [sprɒg] N (*Brit pej or hum*) (= *child*) rorro* *m*, bebé *m*

sprout [spraʊt] Ⓐ N 1 (*from bulb, seeds*) brote *m*, retoño *m*
2 (*also* **Brussels ~**) col *f* de Bruselas
Ⓑ VT echar, hacerse; **to ~ new leaves** echar hojas nuevas; **the calf is ~ing horns** le salen los cuernos al ternero; **the town is ~ing new buildings** en la ciudad se levantan edificios nuevos
Ⓒ VI (= *bud*) brotar, retoñar, echar retoños; (= *grow quickly*) crecer rápidamente; **skyscrapers are ~ing up** se están levantando rascacielos por todos lados

spruce[1] [spru:s] N (*Bot*) pícea *f*

spruce[2] [spru:s] ADJ (= *neat*) pulcro

►**spruce up** VT + ADV arreglar; **to ~ o.s. up** arreglarse; **all ~d up** muy acicalado

sprucely ['spru:slɪ] ADV **~ dressed** elegantemente vestido, vestido de punta en blanco

spruceness ['spru:snɪs] N pulcritud *f*

sprung [sprʌŋ] Ⓐ PP *of* **spring**
Ⓑ ADJ **interior ~ mattress** colchón *m* de muelles; **~ bed** cama *f* de muelles; **~ seat** asiento *m* de ballesta

spry [spraɪ] ADJ ágil, activo

SPUC [spʌk] N ABBR = **Society for the Protection of Unborn Children**

spud [spʌd] Ⓐ N 1 (*) (= *potato*) patata *f*, papa *f* (*LAm*)
2 (*Agr*) (= *tool*) escarda *f*
Ⓑ VT (*Agr*) escardar

spume [spju:m] N (*liter*) espuma *f*

spun [spʌn] Ⓐ PT, PP *of* **spin**
Ⓑ ADJ **~ glass** lana *f* de vidrio; **~ silk** seda *f* hilada; **~ yarn** meollar *m*

spunk [spʌŋk] N 1 (*) (= *spirit*) ánimo *m*, valor *m*, agallas* *fpl*
2 (*Brit*‡*) (*sperm*) leche‡* *f*

spunky‡ ['spʌŋkɪ] ADJ (*compar* **spunkier**; *superl* **spunkiest**) 1 (= *spirited*) valiente, arrojado
2 (*esp Australia*) (= *hunky*) guaperas* *inv*

spur [spɜ:^r] Ⓐ N 1 (*for horse riding*) espuela *f*; ✦*IDIOM* **to win one's ~s** pasar pruebas
2 [*of cock*] espolón *m*
3 (*fig*) estímulo *m*, aguijón *m*; **the ~ of hunger** el aguijón del hambre; **it will be a ~ to further progress** servirá de estímulo *or* acicate al progreso; ✦*IDIOM* **on the ~ of the moment** sin pensar; **it was a ~ of the moment decision** fue una decisión tomada al instante
4 (*Geog*) [*of mountain, hill*] espolón *m*
5 (*Rail*) ramal *m* corto
Ⓑ VT (*also* **~ on**) [+ *horse*] espolear, picar con las espuelas; (*fig*) **to ~ sb (on) to do sth** incitar a algn a hacer algo; **this ~red him on to greater efforts** esto lo animó a hacer mayores esfuerzos; **~red on by greed** bajo el aguijón de la codicia
Ⓒ CPD ► **spur gear** N rueda *f* dentada recta ► **spur wheel** N engranaje *m* cilíndrico

spurge [spɜ:dʒ] N euforbio *m*

spurge laurel ['spɜ:dʒ,lɒrəl] N lauréola *f*, torvisco *m*

spurious ['spjʊərɪəs] ADJ falso, espurio

spuriously ['spjʊərɪəslɪ] ADV falsamente

spuriousness ['spjʊərɪəsnɪs] N falsedad *f*

spurn [spɜ:n] VT desdeñar, rechazar

spurt [spɜ:t] Ⓐ N 1 [*of water, blood*] chorro *m*, borbotón *m*
2 [*of energy*] **to put in** *or* **on a ~** hacer un gran esfuerzo; **final ~** esfuerzo *m* final (*para ganar una carrera*)
Ⓑ VI (= *gush*) (*also* **~ out**) salir a chorros, borbotar, chorrear
Ⓒ VT hacer salir a chorros, arrojar un chorro de

sputnik ['spʊtnɪk] N satélite *m* artificial

sputter ['spʌtə^r] = **splutter**

sputum ['spju:təm] N (*pl* **sputa**) esputo *m*

spy [spaɪ] Ⓐ N espía *mf*
Ⓑ VT (= *catch sight of*) divisar; **finally I spied him coming** por fin pude verlo viniendo; **to play I ~** jugar al veo-veo; **I ~, with my little eye, something beginning with A** veo, veo una cosa que empieza con A
Ⓒ VI espiar, ser espía; **to ~ on sb** espiar a algn, observar a algn clandestinamente; **he spied for the USA** fue espía al servicio de los EE.UU.
Ⓓ CPD ► **spy plane** N avión *m* espía ► **spy ring** N red *f* de espionaje ► **spy satellite** N satélite *m* espía ► **spy ship** N buque *m* espía ► **spy story** N novela *f* de espionaje

►**spy out** VT + ADV hacer un reconocimiento de; **to ~ out the land** reconocer el terreno

spycatcher ['spaɪkætʃə^r] N agente *mf* de contraespionaje

spyglass ['spaɪglɑ:s] N catalejo *m*

spyhole ['spaɪhəʊl] N mirilla *f*

spying ['spaɪɪŋ] N espionaje *m*

spy-in-the-sky* [,spaɪɪnðə'skaɪ] N (= *satellite*) satélite *m* espía

Sq ABBR (*in address*) = **square**

sq. ABBR (*Math*) = **square**

sq.ft. ABBR = **square foot/feet**

squab [skwɒb] N (*pl* **squabs, squab**) (*Orn*) (= *young pigeon*) pichón *m*; (= *chick*) pollito *m*, polluelo *m*

squabble ['skwɒbl] Ⓐ N riña *f*, pelea *f*, pleito *m* (*esp LAm*)
Ⓑ VI reñir, pelearse (**over, about** por, sobre); **stop squabbling!** ¡vale ya de pelearse *or* reñir!

squabbler ['skwɒblə^r] N pendenciero/a *m/f*

squabbling ['skwɒblɪŋ] N riñas *fpl*, peleas *fpl*, pleitos *mpl* (*esp LAm*)

squad [skwɒd] Ⓐ N 1 (*Mil*) pelotón *m*
2 [*of police*] brigada *f*; **flying ~** brigada *f* móvil
3 [*of workmen etc*] cuadrilla *f*
4 (*Sport*) [*of players*] equipo *m*
Ⓑ CPD ► **squad car** N (*Police*) coche-patrulla *m*

squaddie* ['skwɒdɪ] N recluta *m*

squadron ['skwɒdrən] Ⓐ N (*Mil*) escuadrón *m*; (*Aer*) escuadrilla *f*, escuadrón *m*; (*Naut*) escuadra *f*
Ⓑ CPD ► **squadron leader** N (*Brit*) comandante *m* (de aviación)

squalid ['skwɒlɪd] ADJ 1 (= *dirty*) miserable, vil
2 (= *base*) [*affair*] asqueroso; [*motive*] vil

squall[1] [skwɔ:l] N 1 (= *wind*) ráfaga *f*; (= *rain*) chubasco *m*
2 (*fig*) tempestad *f*; **there are ~s ahead** el futuro se anuncia no muy tranquilo

squall[2] [skwɔ:l] Ⓐ N (= *cry*) chillido *m*, grito *m*, berrido *m*
Ⓑ VI chillar, gritar, berrear

squalling ['skwɔ:lɪŋ] ADJ [*child*] chillón, berreador

squally ['skwɔ:lɪ] ADJ 1 [*wind*] que viene a ráfagas; [*day*] de chubascos
2 (*fig*) turbulento, lleno de dificultades

squalor ['skwɒlə^r] N miseria *f*, vileza *f*; **to live in ~** vivir en la miseria, vivir en la sordidez

squander ['skwɒndə^r] VT [+ *money*] derrochar, despilfarrar; [+ *opportunity*] desperdiciar; [+ *time, resources*] emplear mal

square [skwɛə^r] Ⓐ N 1 (= *shape*) cuadrado *m*, cuadro *m*; (*on graph paper, chessboard, crossword*) casilla *f*; (= *piece*) [*of material, paper, chocolate etc*] cuadrado *m*; (= *scarf*) pañuelo *m*; **to cut into ~s** cortar en cuadros *or* cuadrados; ✦*IDIOM* **to go back to ~ one*** volver a empezar desde cero
2 (*in town*) plaza *f*; **the town ~** la plaza del pueblo
3 (*US*) (= *block of houses*) manzana *f*, cuadra *f* (*LAm*)
4 (*Math*) cuadrado *m*; **16 is the ~ of 4** 16 es el cuadrado de 4
5 (= *drawing instrument*) escuadra *f*
6 (*) (= *old-fashioned person*) **he's a real ~** es un carca *or* un carroza *or* (*Chile*) un momio*
Ⓑ ADJ 1 (*in shape*) cuadrado; ✦*IDIOM* **to be a ~ peg in a round hole** estar como un pulpo en un garaje
2 (*forming right angle*) en ángulo recto, en escuadra; **to be ~ with sth** estar en ángulo recto *or* en escuadra con algo; **ensure that the frame is ~** asegúrese de que el marco forme ángulos rectos
3 [*face, jaw, shoulder*] cuadrado
4 (*Math*) cuadrado; **a ~ foot/kilometre** un pie/kilómetro cuadrado; **a kilometre ~** un kilómetro por un kilómetro
5 (= *substantial*) [*meal*] decente, como Dios manda; **it's three days since I had a ~ meal** hace tres días que no como decentemente *or* como Dios manda
6 (= *fair, honest*) justo, equitativo; **to give sb a ~ deal** ser justo con algn; **he didn't get a ~ deal** lo trataron injustamente; **I'll be ~ with you** seré justo contigo
7 (= *even*) **now we're all ~** (*Sport*) ahora vamos iguales *or* (*LAm*) parejos, ahora estamos empatados; (*financially*) ahora estamos en paz;

if you pay me a pound we'll call it ~ dame una libra y me quedo conforme; **to get ~ with sb** ajustar las cuentas con algn
8 (*) (= *conventional*) anticuado*, carca*, carroza (*Sp**); **he's so ~** es un carca *or* un carroza *or* (*Chile*) un momio*
Ⓒ ADV **~ in the middle** justo en el centro, justo en el medio; **to look sb ~ in the eye** mirar a algn directamente a los ojos; **the blow caught him ~ on the chin** el golpe le dio en plena barbilla *or* de lleno en la barbilla; **he turned to face me ~ on** se volvió para tenerme de cara; *see also* **fair[1] B1**
Ⓓ VT 1 (= *make square*) cuadrar; **to ~ one's shoulders** ponerse derecho; ✦*IDIOM* **to try to ~ the circle** intentar lograr la cuadratura del círculo
2 (= *settle, reconcile*) [+ *accounts*] ajustar; [+ *debts*] pagar; **can you ~ it with your conscience?** ¿te lo va a permitir tu conciencia?; **I'll ~ it with him*** yo lo arreglo con él
3 (*Math*) elevar al cuadrado; **two ~d is four** dos al cuadrado es cuatro
Ⓔ VI cuadrar (**with** con); **it doesn't ~ with what you said before** esto no cuadra con lo que dijiste antes
Ⓕ CPD ► **square brackets** NPL corchetes *mpl*
► **square dance** N cuadrilla *f* (*baile*)
► **square root** N raíz *f* cuadrada
►**square off** VT + ADV cuadrar
►**square up** VI + ADV 1 [*boxers, fighters*] ponerse en guardia; **to ~ up to sb** enfrentarse con algn
2 (= *settle*) **to ~ up with sb** ajustar cuentas con algn

squarebashing* ['skwɛə,bæʃɪŋ] N (*Brit*) instrucción *f*

squared [skwɛəd] ADJ [*paper*] cuadriculado

square-faced [,skwɛə'feɪst] ADJ de cara cuadrada

squarely ['skwɛəlɪ] ADV 1 (= *directly*) directamente; **responsibility for that failure rests ~ with the President** la responsabilidad de ese fracaso cae directamente sobre el presidente; **to look sb ~ in the eye** mirar a algn directamente a los ojos; **~ in the middle** justo en el centro, justo en el medio; **the blow caught him ~ on the chin** el golpe le dio en plena barbilla *or* de lleno en la barbilla
2 (= *honestly, fairly*) justamente; **to deal ~ with sb** tratar justamente a algn; *see also* **fairly**

square-toed [,skwɛə'təʊd] ADJ [*shoes*] de punta cuadrada

SQUARE DANCE

Se llama **square dance** *a un baile folklórico tradicional de origen francés en el que cuatro parejas de bailarines se colocan formando un cuadrado. Es un baile muy popular en Estados Unidos y Canadá y a veces se enseña en la escuela. En algunas ocasiones alguien se encarga de explicar los pasos que se han de seguir, de modo que los que no los conocen bien puedan participar. El instrumento musical más utilizado en ellos es el violín, aunque también se usan a veces la guitarra, el banjo o el acordeón.*

squarial ['skweərɪəl] N antena *f* cuadrada

squash[1] [skwɒʃ] Ⓐ N (*pl* **squashes, squash**) 1 (= *drink*) **orange ~** naranjada *f* (*sin burbujas*); **lemon ~** limonada *f* (*sin burbujas*)
2 (= *crowd*) apiñamiento *m*, agolpamiento *m*; **there was such a ~ in the doorway** había tantísima gente apiñada en la puerta, se apiñaba tanto la gente en la puerta
Ⓑ VT 1 (= *flatten*) aplastar; **you're ~ing me** me estás aplastando; **to ~ sth in** meter algo a la fuerza; **can you ~ my shoes in?** ¿caben dentro mis zapatos?; **can you ~ two more in the car?** ¿caben dos más en el coche?; **to be ~ed together** ir apretujados
2 (*fig*) [+ *argument*] dar al traste con; [+ *person*] apabullar
Ⓒ VI **to ~ in** entrar con dificultad; **we all ~ed in** entramos todos aunque con dificultad; **to ~ up** arrimarse

squash[2] [skwɒʃ] N (= *vegetable*) calabaza *f*

squash[3] [skwɒʃ] Ⓐ N (= *sport*) (*also* **~ rackets**) squash *m*
Ⓑ CPD ► **squash court** N cancha *f* de squash
► **squash racket** N raqueta *f* de squash

squashy ['skwɒʃɪ] ADJ (*compar* **squashier**; *superl* **squashiest**) blando y algo líquido, muelle y húmedo

squat [skwɒt] Ⓐ ADJ [*person*] rechoncho, achaparrado; [*building, shape etc*] desproporcionadamente bajo
Ⓑ VI 1 (*also* **~ down**) agacharse, sentarse en cuclillas
2 (*on property*) ocupar un inmueble ilegalmente
Ⓒ N *piso etc ocupado ilegalmente*

squatter ['skwɒtə^r] N ocupa *mf*, okupa *mf*

squatting ['skwɒtɪŋ] N *ocupación ilegal de un inmueble*

squaw [skwɔː] N india *f*, piel roja *f*

squawk [skwɔːk] Ⓐ N graznido *m*, chillido *m*
Ⓑ VI graznar, chillar

squeak [skwiːk] Ⓐ N 1 [*of hinge, wheel*] chirrido *m*; [*of mouse, person*] chillido *m*; [*of shoe*] crujido *m*; [*of pen*] raspeo *m*
2 (*fig*) **I don't want to hear another ~ out of you** y no vuelvas a abrir la boca, y sin rechistar; **"have you heard anything from him?" —"not a ~"** (*sleeping child*) —¿le has oído? —ni el menor ruido; (*absent friend*) —¿sabes algo de él? —ni una palabra; ✦*IDIOM* **to have a narrow ~** escaparse por los pelos; **they won, but it was a narrow ~** ganaron, pero por los pelos
Ⓑ VI [*hinge, wheel*] chirriar, rechinar; [*mouse*] chillar; [*shoes*] crujir; [*pen*] raspear; **the door ~ed open** la puerta chirrió *or* rechinó al abrirse, la puerta se abrió con un chirrido
Ⓒ VT chillar
►**squeak by*** VI + ADV 1 (*also* **~ through**) (= *win by a narrow margin*) pasar muy justo, pasar raspando*
2 (= *subsist, manage*) subsistir; **to ~ by on sth** arreglárselas con algo

squeaker ['skwiːkə^r] N (*in toy etc*) chirriador *m*

squeaky ['skwiːkɪ] ADJ (*compar* **squeakier**; *superl* **squeakiest**) [*hinge, door*] chirriante; [*voice*] chillón; [*shoes*] crujiente; **~ clean** (= *clean*) relimpio; (*fig*) perfectamente honrado

squeal [skwiːl] Ⓐ N chillido *m*; **with a ~ of pain** con un chillido de dolor; **a ~ of tyres** un chillido de ruedas
Ⓑ VI 1 (= *make noise*) [*person, animal*] chillar; [*brakes, tyres*] chirriar
2 (‡) (= *inform*) cantar, soplar
3 (*) (= *complain*) quejarse; **don't come ~ing to me** no vengas a quejarte a mí
Ⓒ VT **"yes", he ~ed** —sí —dijo chillando

squeamish ['skwiːmɪʃ] ADJ **it's no good being ~ if you're a surgeon** si eres cirujano no puedes ser aprensivo; **I'm ~ about having needles stuck in me** me da aprensión que me claven agujas; **I felt ~ about touching a live snake** me daba repugnancia tocar una serpiente viva; **I'm not ~** no soy muy delicado; **don't be so ~** no seas tan delicado *or* tiquismiquis

squeamishness ['skwiːmɪʃnɪs] N (= *fear*) aprensión *f*; (= *fussiness*) remilgos *mpl*; **to feel a certain ~** sentir cierta aprensión *or* repugnancia

squeegee ['skwiː'dʒiː] Ⓐ N enjugador *m*
Ⓑ CPD ► **squeegee merchant*** N limpiador(a) *m/f* ambulante de parabrisas

squeeze [skwiːz] Ⓐ N 1 (*act of squeezing*) (= *handclasp*) apretón *m*; (= *hug*) estrujón *m*; **he put his arm round her and gave her a quick ~** le pasó el brazo por encima y le dio un estrujoncito* *or* un apretón; **to give sth a ~** apretar algo; **to give sb's hand a ~** dar a algn un apretón de manos, apretar la mano a algn
2 (= *crush*) **it was a tight ~ in the bus** íbamos muy apretados en el autobús; **it was a tight ~ to get through** había muy poco espacio para pasar
3 (= *restriction*) restricciones *fpl*; **small businesses are feeling the ~** las restricciones están afectando sobre todo a la pequeña empresa; **a ~ on profits** un recorte de beneficios; ✦*IDIOM* **to put the ~ on sb*** apretar las tuercas *or* los tornillos a algn*; *see also* **credit C**
4 (= *small amount*) [*of liquid*] chorrito *m*; [*of toothpaste*] poquito *m*, pizca *f*; **a ~ of lemon (juice)** un chorrito de zumo de limón, unas gotas de limón
5 (*) (= *difficult situation*) aprieto *m*; **to be in a (tight) ~** encontrarse en un aprieto
6 (*Brit**) (= *boyfriend, girlfriend*) noviete/a* *m/f*, novio/a *m/f*
Ⓑ VT 1 (= *press firmly*) [+ *pimple, tube, trigger*] apretar; [+ *citrus fruit*] exprimir; **I ~d her tightly** la estreché entre mis brazos; **to ~ one's eyes shut** cerrar los ojos apretándolos; **to ~ sb's hand** apretar la mano a algn
2 (= *cram, fit*) meter; **to ~ clothes into a suitcase** meter ropa en una maleta a la fuerza; **can you ~ two more in?** ¿puedes hacer hueco para dos más?, ¿puedes meter a dos más?; **I could ~ you in on Thursday** le podría hacer un hueco para el jueves; **she ~d herself into the dress** se enfundó el vestido; **I ~d my way through the crowd** me abrí camino entre la multitud
3 (= *extract*) sacar; **to ~ money/a confession/information out of sb** sacar dinero/una confesión/información a algn; **rich city dwellers are squeezing the locals out** la gente acomodada de la ciudad está echando poco a poco a la población local; **freshly ~d orange juice** zumo *m* de naranjas recién exprimidas
4 (= *reduce*) recortar; **wage increases are squeezing profit margins** los aumentos salariales están recortando los márgenes de beneficios
Ⓒ VI **they all ~d into the car** se metieron todos apretujados en el coche; **could I just ~ past?** ¿me deja pasar?; **he ~d past me** me pasó rozando; **to ~ through a hole** pasar por un agujero con dificultad
Ⓓ CPD ► **squeeze box** N concertina *f*

squeezer ['skwiːzə^r] N exprimidor *m*; **lemon ~** exprimelimones *m inv*, exprimidor *m*

squelch [skweltʃ] Ⓐ VI chapotear; **to ~ through the mud** ir chapoteando por el lodo
Ⓑ VT aplastar, despachurrar

squib [skwɪb] N (= *firework*) buscapiés *m inv*; *see also* **damp**

squid [skwɪd] N (*pl* **squid** *or* **squids**) calamar *m*, sepia *f*

squiffy* ['skwɪfɪ] ADJ (*Brit*) **to be ~** estar achispado*

squiggle ['skwɪgl] N garabato *m*

squint [skwɪnt] Ⓐ N [1] (*Med*) estrabismo *m*; **to have a ~** tener estrabismo, ser bizco; **he has a terrible ~** se le nota mucho que es bizco
[2] (= *sidelong look*) mirada *f* de soslayo, mirada *f* de reojo; **let's have a ~*** déjame ver; **have a ~ at this*** mírame esto
Ⓑ VI [1] (*Med*) bizquear, ser bizco
[2] **to ~ at sth** (*quickly*) echar un vistazo a algo; (*with half-closed eyes*) mirar algo con los ojos entrecerrados; **he ~ed in the sunlight** entrecerró los ojos por el sol

squint-eyed ['skwɪnt'aɪd] ADJ bizco

squire ['skwaɪəʳ] Ⓐ N (†) (= *landowner*) terrateniente *m*, hacendado *m* (*LAm*), estanciero *m* (*LAm*); (*Hist*) (= *knight's attendant*) escudero *m*; (= *lady's escort*) galán *m*, acompañante *m*; **the ~** (*in relation to villagers etc*) el señor; **the ~ of Ambridge** el señor de Ambridge, el mayor terrateniente de Ambridge; **yes, ~!** (*Brit**) ¡sí, jefe!; **which way, ~?*** ¿por dónde, caballero?
Ⓑ VT [+ *lady*] acompañar

squirearchy ['skwaɪərɑːkɪ] N aristocracia *f* rural, terratenientes *mpl*

squirm [skwɜːm] VI retorcerse; **I'll make him ~** yo lo haré sufrir; **to ~ with embarrassment** estar violento, avergonzarse mucho

squirrel ['skwɪrəl] N (*pl* **squirrels** *or* **squirrel**) ardilla *f*

► **squirrel away** VT + ADV [+ *nuts etc*] almacenar

squirt [skwɜːt] Ⓐ N [1] (= *jet, spray*) chorro *m*
[2] (*) (= *child*) mequetrefe *mf*, chiquitajo/a* *m/f*, escuincle *mf* (*Mex*); (= *person*) farolero/a *m/f*, presumido/a *m/f*
Ⓑ VT [+ *liquid*] lanzar; [+ *person, car*] mojar; **to ~ water at sb** lanzar un chorro de agua hacia algn
Ⓒ VI **to ~ out/in** salir/entrar a chorros; **the water ~ed into my eyes** salió un chorro de agua que me dio en los ojos

squirter ['skwɜːtəʳ] N atomizador *m*

Sr ABBR = **Senior**

SRC N ABBR (*Brit*) [1] = **Science Research Council**
[2] = **Students' Representative Council**

Sri Lanka [ˌsriː'læŋkə] N Sri Lanka *m*

Sri Lankan [ˌsriː'læŋkən] Ⓐ ADJ de Sri Lanka
Ⓑ N nativo/a *m/f* de Sri Lanka, habitante *mf* de Sri Lanka

SRN N ABBR (*Brit*) (*formerly*) = **State Registered Nurse**

SRO ABBR (*US*) = **standing room only**

Sr(s). ABBR (= **Sister(s)**) Hna(s).

SS ABBR [1] (*Brit*) = **steamship**
[2] (= **Saints**) SS.

SSA N ABBR (*US*) = **Social Security Administration**

SSE ABBR (= **south-southeast**) SSE

SSI N ABBR = **small-scale integration**

SSSI N ABBR = **Site of Special Scientific Interest**

SST N ABBR (*US*) = **supersonic transport**

SSW ABBR (= **south-southwest**) SSO

St ABBR [1] (*Rel*) (= **Saint**) Sto., Sta., S.
[2] (*Geog*) = **Strait**
[3] (= **Street**) c/
[4] (= **stone**) = *14 libras, = 6,348kg*
[5] = **summer time**

St. ABBR = **Station**

stab [stæb] Ⓐ N [1] (*with knife etc*) puñalada *f*, navajazo *m*; ✦**IDIOM ~ in the back** puñalada *f* por la espalda, puñalada *f* encubierta
[2] [*of pain*] punzada *f*
[3] ✦**IDIOM to have a ~ at sth** intentar hacer algo
Ⓑ VT apuñalar, dar una puñalada a; **to ~ sb with a knife** apuñalar a algn con un cuchillo; **to ~ sb in the back** (*lit*) apuñalar a algn por la espalda; (*fig*) clavar a algn un puñal por la espalda; **to ~ sb to death** matar a algn a puñaladas
Ⓒ VI **to ~ at sb** tratar de apuñalar a algn; **he ~bed at the picture with his finger** señaló el cuadro con un movimiento brusco del dedo
Ⓓ CPD ► **stab wound** N puñalada *f*

stabbing ['stæbɪŋ] Ⓐ N (= *incident*) apuñalamiento *m*
Ⓑ ADJ [*pain, ache*] punzante

stability [stə'bɪlɪtɪ] N estabilidad *f*

stabilization [ˌsteɪbəlaɪ'zeɪʃən] N estabilización *f*

stabilize ['steɪbəlaɪz] Ⓐ VT [+ *boat*] estabilizar
Ⓑ VI [*currency, economy*] estabilizarse

stabilizer ['steɪbəlaɪzəʳ] N [1] (*usu pl*) (*Naut, also on bike*) estabilizador *m*
[2] (*Culin*) estabilizante *m*

stable[1] ['steɪbl] ADJ (*compar* **stabler**, *superl* **stablest**) [*relationship, country, situation, substance*] estable; [*job*] estable, permanente; (*Med*) [*condition*] estacionario; [*blood pressure, weight*] estable, estacionario; (*Psych*) [*person, character*] equilibrado; **sterling has remained ~ against the franc** la libra se ha mantenido estable frente al franco; **the weight of the machine makes it very ~** el peso de la máquina le da estabilidad; **that ladder's not very ~** esa escalera no está muy firme

stable[2] ['steɪbl] Ⓐ N (= *building*) cuadra *f*, caballeriza *f*; (= *establishment*) cuadra *f*
Ⓑ VT (= *keep in stable*) guardar en una cuadra; (= *put in stable*) poner en una cuadra
Ⓒ CPD ► **stable door** N ✦**IDIOM to shut** *or* **close the ~ door after the horse has bolted** a buenas horas, mangas verdes ► **stable lad** N = **stableboy**

stableboy ['steɪblbɔɪ] N mozo *m* de cuadra

stableman ['steɪblmən] N (*pl* **stablemen**) mozo *m* de cuadra

stablemate ['steɪblmeɪt] N (= *horse*) caballo *m* de la misma cuadra; (*fig*) (= *person*) camarada *mf*

staccato [stə'kɑːtəʊ] Ⓐ ADV staccato
Ⓑ ADJ staccato

stack [stæk] Ⓐ N [1] (*) (= *pile*) montón *m*, pila *f*; **there were ~s of books on the table** había montones *or* pilas de libros sobre la mesa
[2] **stacks*** (= *lots*) **I have ~s of work to do** tengo un montón* *or* una gran cantidad de trabajo; **they've got ~s of money** tienen cantidad de dinero; **we have ~s of time** nos sobra tiempo
[3] (= *section in library*) estantería *f*; (= *book stack*) estantería *f* de libros
[4] (*Agr*) almiar *m*, hacina *f*
[5] (*Mil*) pabellón *m* de fusiles
[6] [*of chimney*] cañón *m* de chimenea, fuste *m* de chimenea
Ⓑ VT [1] (= *pile up*) amontonar, apilar; ✦**IDIOM the cards are ~ed against us** todo va en contra nuestra
[2] **(well) ~ed** (*US‡*) [*woman*] bien formada, muy buena*

stacker ['stækəʳ] N (*Comput*) apiladora *f*

stadium ['steɪdɪəm] N (*pl* **stadiums** *or* **stadia** ['steɪdɪə]) estadio *m*

staff[1] [stɑːf] Ⓐ N [1] (= *personnel*) personal *m*, empleados *mpl*; **the administrative ~** (el personal de) la administración; **the teaching ~** el cuerpo docente, el profesorado; **to be on the ~** ser de plantilla; **to join the ~** entrar en la plantilla; **to leave the ~** dimitir
[2] (*Mil*) estado *m* mayor
[3] (†) (= *stick*) bastón *m*, vara *f*; (*pilgrim's*) bordón *m*; (= *symbol of authority*) bastón *m* de mando; (*bishop's*) báculo *m*; [*of flag, lance etc*] asta *f*
Ⓑ VT proveer de personal; **to be well ~ed** (*fully staffed*) tener la plantilla completa; (*with good workers*) tener un buen personal; **the centre is ~ed by qualified lawyers** el centro cuenta con abogados titulados en plantilla
Ⓒ CPD ► **staff association** N asociación *f* del personal ► **staff canteen** N comedor *m* de personal ► **staff college** N escuela *f* militar superior ► **staff meeting** N reunión *f* de personal ► **staff nurse** N enfermero/a *m/f* titulado/a ► **staff officer** N oficial *m* del Estado Mayor ► **staff room** N sala *f* de profesores ► **staff-student ratio** N proporción *f* alumnos-profesor ► **staff training** N formación *f* de personal

staff[2] [stɑːf] N (*pl* **staves, staff**) (*Mus*) pentagrama *m*

staffing ['stɑːfɪŋ] Ⓐ N (= *employment*) empleo *m* de personal; (= *number of employees*) dotación *f* de personal, plantilla *f*; **~ is inadequate** la dotación de personal *or* la plantilla es insuficiente
Ⓑ CPD ► **staffing ratio** N proporción *f* alumnos-profesor

Staffs ABBR (*Brit*) = **Staffordshire**

stag [stæg] Ⓐ N [1] (*Zool*) ciervo *m*, venado *m*
[2] (*Fin*) especulador(a) *m/f* con nuevas emisiones
Ⓑ CPD ► **stag beetle** N ciervo *m* volante ► **stag night** N despedida *f* de soltero ► **stag party** N fiesta *f* de despedida de soltero

stage [steɪdʒ] Ⓐ N [1] (= *platform*) tablado *m*; (*in conference hall*) estrado *m*
[2] (*Theat*) escenario *m*; **I get nervous on ~** me pongo nervioso en el escenario; **to put a play on the ~** poner una obra en escena; **to go on ~** salir a escena *or* al escenario; **you're on ~ in two minutes** sales (a escena) en dos minutos; **~ left/right** *la parte del escenario a la izquierda/derecha del actor (de cara al público)*; **the ~** (*as profession*) el teatro; **he writes for the ~** escribe para el teatro; **to go on the ~** hacerse actor/actriz; ✦**IDIOM to set the ~ for sth** crear el marco idóneo para algo; **the ~ was set for a political showdown** se había creado el marco idóneo para una confrontación política
[3] (*fig*) (= *scene*) escena *f*; **he occupies the centre of the political ~** ocupa el centro de la escena política
[4] (= *step*) (*in process*) etapa *f*, fase *f*; **at this ~ in the negotiations** en esta etapa *or* a estas alturas de las negociaciones; **we can't cancel at this late ~** no podemos cancelarlo a estas alturas; **problems could arise at a later ~** podrían surgir problemas más adelante; **he's bound to find out at some ~** seguro que se entera tarde o temprano; **the project is still in its early ~s** el proyecto se encuentra todavía en su fase *or* etapa inicial; **the war was in its final ~s** la guerra estaba en sus últimas etapas; **to go through a difficult ~** pasar por una etapa difícil; **it's just a ~ he's going through** no es más que una fase que está atravesando; **in ~s** por etapas; **in** *or* **by easy ~s** en etapas *or* fases cortas; *see also* **committee**
[5] [*of rocket*] fase *f*; [*of pipeline*] tramo *m*; **a four-~ rocket** un cohete de cuatro fases
[6] (= *stagecoach*) diligencia *f*
Ⓑ VT [1] (*Theat*) [+ *play*] representar, poner

en escena
2 (= *organize*) [+ *concert, festival*] organizar, montar
3 (= *carry out*) [+ *protest*] organizar; [+ *demonstration, strike*] hacer; [+ *attack*] lanzar; **the sixties rock legend is staging a comeback** la leyenda rockera de los sesenta prepara una vuelta a escena; **sterling has ~d a recovery on foreign exchange markets** la libra esterlina ha experimentado una mejora en los mercados de divisas extranjeros
4 (*pej*) (= *orchestrate*) montar, organizar; **that was no accident, it was ~d** eso no fue ningún accidente, estaba montado *or* organizado
Ⓒ CPD ► **stage adaptation** N adaptación *f* teatral ► **stage designer** N escenógrafo/a *m/f* ► **stage direction** N acotación *f* ► **stage director** N = **stage manager** ► **stage door** N entrada *f* de artistas ► **stage fright** N miedo *m* a las tablas *or* al escenario, miedo *m* escénico; **to get ~ fright** ponerse nervioso al salir a las tablas *or* al escenario ► **stage manager** N director(a) *m/f* de escena ► **stage name** N nombre *m* artístico ► **stage presence** N presencia *f* en el escenario ► **stage set** N decorado *m* ► **stage show** N espectáculo *m* ► **stage whisper** N aparte *m*

stagecoach [ˈsteɪdʒkəʊtʃ] N diligencia *f*

stagecraft [ˈsteɪdʒkrɑːft] N arte *m* teatral, escenotecnia *f*

stagehand [ˈsteɪdʒhænd] N tramoyista *mf*, sacasillas *m*

stage-manage [ˈsteɪdʒˌmænɪdʒ] VT [+ *play, production*] dirigir; (*fig*) [+ *event, confrontation etc*] orquestar

stagestruck [ˈsteɪdʒstrʌk] ADJ enamorado del teatro, fascinado por el teatro

stagey [ˈsteɪdʒɪ] ADJ = **stagy**

stagflation [stægˈfleɪʃən] N (*Econ*) (e)stagflación *f*, estanflación *f*

stagger [ˈstægəʳ] Ⓐ N 1 tambaleo *m*
2 **staggers** (*Vet*) modorra *f*
Ⓑ VI tambalear; **he ~ed to the door** fue tambaleándose hasta la puerta; **he was ~ing about** iba tambaleándose
Ⓒ VT 1 (= *amaze*) dejar anonadado, dejar pasmado; **we were ~ed by the number of letters we received** nos dejó anonadados *or* pasmados la cantidad de cartas que recibimos
2 [+ *hours, holidays, payments, spokes*] escalonar

staggered [ˈstægəd] ADJ 1 (= *amazed*) anonadado, pasmado; **I was ~ to learn I'd won first prize** me quedé anonadado *or* pasmado al enterarme de que había ganado el primer premio; **I was ~ to hear that ...** (= *dismayed*) me consterné al saber que ...
2 [*hours, junction*] escalonado

staggering [ˈstægərɪŋ] ADJ (= *astonishing*) asombroso, pasmoso

staghound [ˈstæghaʊnd] N perro *m* de caza, sabueso *m*

staghunt [ˈstæghʌnt] N cacería *f* de venado

staghunting [ˈstægˌhʌntɪŋ] N caza *f* de venado

staging [ˈsteɪdʒɪŋ] Ⓐ N 1 (= *scaffolding*) andamiaje *m*
2 (*Theat*) escenificación *f*, puesta *f* en escena
3 (*Space*) desprendimiento *m* (de una sección de un cohete)
Ⓑ CPD ► **staging post** N (*Mil, also gen*) escala *f*

stagnancy [ˈstægnənsɪ] N estancamiento *m*

stagnant [ˈstægnənt] ADJ 1 [*water*] estancado
2 (*fig*) [*economy, industry*] estancado, paralizado; [*market*] inactivo, estancado; [*society*] anquilosado

stagnate [stægˈneɪt] VI 1 [*water*] estancarse
2 (*fig*) [*economy, market, industry*] estancarse; [*society, person*] estancarse, anquilosarse

stagnation [stægˈneɪʃən] N 1 [*of water*] estancamiento *m*
2 (*fig*) [*of economy, industry*] estancamiento *m*, paralización *f*; [*of market*] inactividad *f*, estancamiento *m*; [*of society, person*] anquilosamiento *m*, estancamiento *m*

stagy [ˈsteɪdʒɪ] ADJ (*compar* **stagier**; *superl* **stagiest**) (*pej*) teatral, histriónico

staid [steɪd] ADJ [*person*] serio; [*clothes*] sobrio, serio

staidness [ˈsteɪdnɪs] N [*of person*] seriedad *f*; [*of clothes*] sobriedad *f*

stain [steɪn] Ⓐ N 1 (= *mark*) mancha *f*; (= *dye*) tinte *m*, tintura *f*; (= *paint*) pintura *f*
2 (*fig*) mancha *f*; **without a ~ on one's character** sin una sola mancha en la reputación
Ⓑ VT (= *mark*) manchar; (= *dye*) teñir, colorar; (= *paint*) pintar; **her hands were ~ed with blood** sus manos estaban manchadas de sangre, tenía las manos manchadas de sangre
Ⓒ VI manchar
Ⓓ CPD ► **stain remover** N quitamanchas *m inv*

stained glass [ˌsteɪndˈglɑːs] N vidrio *m* de color

stained-glass [ˌsteɪndˈglɑːs] ADJ **~ window** vidriera *f* (de colores)

stainless [ˈsteɪnlɪs] Ⓐ ADJ inmaculado
Ⓑ CPD ► **stainless steel** N acero *m* inoxidable

stair [steəʳ] Ⓐ N 1 (= *single step*) escalón *m*, peldaño *m*; (= *stairway*) escalera *f*
2 **stairs** escalera *f*; **a flight of ~s** un tramo de escalera; **life below ~s** la vida de los criados; **gossip below ~s** habladurías *fpl* de la servidumbre
Ⓑ CPD ► **stair carpet** N alfombra *f* de escalera ► **stair lift** N (plataforma *f*) salvaescaleras *m inv*, elevador *m* de escaleras ► **stair rod** N varilla *f* (para sujetar la alfombra de la escalera)

staircase [ˈsteəkeɪs] N escalera *f*; *see also* **spiral**

stairway [ˈsteəweɪ] N = **staircase**

stairwell [ˈsteəwel] N hueco *m or* caja *f* de la escalera

stake [steɪk] Ⓐ N 1 (= *bet*) apuesta *f*; **the average ~ is just 80p** la apuesta media es de sólo 80 peniques; **to be at ~** estar en juego; **the company's reputation is at ~** la reputación de la empresa está en juego; **there's a lot at ~ in this** es mucho lo que está en juego, hay mucho en juego; **he has got a lot at ~ ◊ there is a lot at ~ for him** es mucho lo que se está jugando; **the issue at ~** el asunto en cuestión, el asunto de que se trata; **the ~s are high** (*lit*) se apuesta fuerte, las apuestas son muy elevadas; (*fig*) es mucho lo que está en juego, hay mucho en juego; **to play for high ~s** (*lit*) apostar fuerte; (*fig*) tener mucho en juego; **to raise the ~s** (*Gambling*) subir la apuesta; **developments that raised the ~s in the elections** acontecimientos que hicieron más aventuradas las elecciones
2 (= *interest*) 2·1 (*Fin*) participación *f*; **he bought a 12 per cent ~ in the company** compró un 12 por ciento de participación en la compañía
2·2 (*fig*) **every employee has a ~ in the success of the firm** a todos los empleados les interesa que la empresa sea un éxito; **through your children you have a ~ in the future** tus hijos son tu participación en el futuro
3 **stakes** 3·1 (= *race*) *carrera de caballos en la que el dinero del premio lo han puesto los propietarios de los caballos*; (= *prize money*) bote *m*
3·2 (*fig*) **he is still in front in the popularity ~s** sigue siendo el más popular de todos; **the President is riding high in the popularity ~s** el presidente goza de mucha popularidad
4 (= *post*) poste *m*; (*for plant*) rodrigón *m*; (*for execution*) hoguera *f*; **to be burned at the ~ ◊ die at the ~** morir en la hoguera
Ⓑ VT 1 (= *bet*) [+ *money, jewels*] jugarse, apostar; (*fig*) [+ *one's reputation, life*] jugarse; **to ~ one's reputation on sth** jugarse la reputación en algo; **I'd ~ my life on it** me jugaría la vida a que es así
2 (*with posts*) 2·1 (= *delimit*) [+ *area, path, line*] marcar con estacas, señalar con estacas; ✦***IDIOM*** **to ~ a** *or* **one's claim to** [+ *piece of land*] reivindicar, reclamar; **with this win he has ~d his claim for a place in the final** con esta victoria se ha asegurado un puesto en la final
2·2 (*also* **~ up**) (= *support with stakes*) [+ *fence*] apuntalar; [+ *plants*] arrodrigar

►**stake off** VT + ADV = **stake out 1**

►**stake out** VT + ADV 1 (*with posts*) [+ *piece of land, path, line*] marcar con estacas, señalar con estacas
2 (= *reserve, lay claim to*) **you have to ~ out your place on the beach early** tienes que asegurarte un lugar en la playa bien temprano; **he has ~d out his position on social policy** ha afianzado su postura en lo referente a política social
3 (= *watch*) [+ *property etc*] [*journalist, criminal*] vigilar; [*police*] poner bajo vigilancia, mantener vigilado

stakeholder [ˈsteɪkˌhəʊldəʳ] Ⓐ N 1 (*in gambling*) *persona que guarda las apuestas*
2 (*Fin*) accionista *mf*
3 (*fig*) interesado/a *m/f*
Ⓑ CPD ► **stakeholder society** N (*Brit Pol*) sociedad *f* participativa

stakeout [ˈsteɪkaʊt] N operación *f* de vigilancia

stalactite [ˈstæləktaɪt] N estalactita *f*

stalagmite [ˈstæləgmaɪt] N estalagmita *f*

stale [steɪl] Ⓐ ADJ (*compar* **staler**; *superl* **stalest**)
1 (= *not fresh*) [*cheese, butter, sweat, cigarette smoke*] rancio; [*breath*] maloliente; [*air*] viciado; [*biscuit, beer*] pasado; [*cake*] seco; [*bread*] correoso; (= *hard*) duro; **to go ~** [*biscuit, beer*] pasarse; [*cake*] secarse; [*bread*] ponerse correoso; (= *become hard*) ponerse duro; **to have gone ~** (*lit*) estar pasado; **to smell ~** oler a viejo
2 (*fig*) [*news, joke*] viejo; [*idea*] marchito; **he felt tired and ~** se sentía cansado y hastiado; **their relationship had become ~** la relación se había estancado *or* anquilosado; **to get** *or* **become ~** [*person*] estancarse, anquilosarse; **I'm getting ~** me estoy estancando *or* anquilosando; **the show's got a little ~** el espectáculo está ya un poco gastado; **if they rehearse too much they'll become ~** si ensayan demasiado se van a quemar
Ⓑ VI (*liter*) [*relationship, author, writing*] quedarse estancado *or* anquilosado; [*pleasures*] perder la frescura (*liter*)

stalemate [ˈsteɪlmeɪt] Ⓐ N 1 (*Chess*) ahogado *m*
2 (*fig*) punto *m* muerto; **there is ~ between the two powers** las relaciones entre las dos potencias están en un punto muerto *or* en un impasse; **the ~ is complete** la paralización es completa; **to reach ~** estancarse

Ⓑ VT (*Chess*) ahogar, dar tablas por ahogado a; (*fig*) paralizar

stalemated ['steɪlmeɪtɪd] ADJ (*fig*) [*discussions*] estancado, en un punto muerto; [*project*] en un punto muerto; [*person*] en tablas

staleness ['steɪlnɪs] N [1] (= *lack of freshness*) [*of cheese, butter, sweat, cigarette smoke*] lo rancio; [*of air*] lo viciado; [*biscuit, beer*] lo pasado; [*of cake*] sequedad *f*, lo seco; [*of bread*] lo correoso; (= *hardness*) dureza *f*

[2] (*fig*) [*of news, joke*] lo viejo; [*of person, relationship*] estancamiento *m*, anquilosamiento *m*

Stalin ['stɑːlɪn] N Stalin

Stalinism ['stɑːlɪnɪzəm] N estalinismo *m*

Stalinist ['stɑːlɪnɪst] Ⓐ ADJ estalinista

Ⓑ N estalinista *mf*

stalk¹ [stɔːk] Ⓐ VT [+ *animal*] [*hunter*] cazar al acecho; [*animal*] acechar; [+ *person*] seguir los pasos de

Ⓑ VI (= *walk*) **to ~ away** *or* **off** irse con paso airado; **she ~ed out of the room** salió airada del cuarto

stalk² [stɔːk] N [1] (*Bot*) tallo *m*, caña *f*; (= *cabbage stalk*) troncho *m*

[2] [*of glass*] pie *m*

[3] (*Aut*) (= *control stalk*) palanca *f*

stalker ['stɔːkəʳ] N *persona que está obsesionada con otra y la acosa constantemente con llamadas telefónicas o siguiéndola a todas partes*

stalk-eyed ['stɔːkaɪd] ADJ (*Zool*) de ojos pedunculares

stalking ['stɔːkɪŋ] Ⓐ N (*Jur*) *acoso cometido por un "stalker" y que constituye un delito*

Ⓑ CPD ► **stalking horse** N pretexto *m*; (*Pol*) *candidato que en unas elecciones desafía a un líder de su propio partido, con el propósito de medir la fuerza de la oposición*

stall [stɔːl] Ⓐ N [1] (*Agr*) (= *stable*) establo *m*; (= *manger*) pesebre *m*; (*for single horse etc*) casilla *f*

[2] (*in market etc*) puesto *m*; (*in fair*) caseta *f*, casilla *f*; (= *newspaper stall*) quiosco *m*, puesto *m* (*esp LAm*); ✦**IDIOM** **to set out one's ~** exponer lo que se ofrece (a la venta)

[3] (*Brit Theat*) **the ~s** el patio de butacas

[4] (*in church*) silla *f* de coro

[5] (*US*) (*in car park*) emplazamiento *m*

Ⓑ VT [1] [+ *car, plane*] parar, calar; **the talks are ~ed** las negociaciones están en un callejón sin salida

[2] [+ *person*] entretener

Ⓒ VI [1] [*car*] pararse; [*plane*] perder velocidad; **we ~ed on a steep hill** quedamos parados en una cuesta abrupta, se nos atascó el motor en una cuesta abrupta; **the talks have ~ed** las negociaciones están en un callejón sin salida

[2] (*fig*) (= *delay*) andar con rodeos, esquivar; **stop ~ing!** ¡déjate de evasivas!; **the minister ~ed for 20 minutes** durante 20 minutos el ministro evitó contestar directamente

stall-fed ['stɔːlfed] ADJ engordado en establo

stallholder ['stɔːl,həʊldəʳ] N dueño/a *m/f* de un puesto, puestero/a *m/f* (*LAm*)

stallion ['stæljən] N semental *m*, padrillo *m* (*LAm*)

stalwart ['stɔːlwət] Ⓐ ADJ [*person*] (*in spirit*) fuerte, robusto; (*in build*) fornido, robusto; [*supporter, opponent*] leal, fiel; [*belief*] empedernido

Ⓑ N partidario/a *m/f* incondicional

stamen ['steɪmen] N (*pl* **stamens** *or* **stamina** ['stæmɪnə]) estambre *m*

stamina ['stæmɪnə] N resistencia *f*, aguante *m*; **has he enough ~ for the job?** ¿tiene bastante resistencia para el puesto?; **you need ~** hace falta tener nervio; **intellectual ~** vigor *m* intelectual

stammer ['stæməʳ] Ⓐ N tartamudeo *m*; **he has a bad ~** tartamudea terriblemente

Ⓑ VI tartamudear

Ⓒ VT (*also* **to ~ out**) decir tartamudeando

stammerer ['stæmərəʳ] N tartamudo/a *m/f*

stammering ['stæmərɪŋ] Ⓐ ADJ tartamudo

Ⓑ N tartamudeo *m*

stammeringly ['stæmərɪŋlɪ] ADV **he said ~** dijo tartamudeando

stamp [stæmp] Ⓐ N [1] (= *postage stamp*) sello *m*, estampilla *f* (*LAm*); (= *fiscal stamp, revenue stamp*) timbre *m*, póliza *f*; (*for free food etc*) bono *m*, vale *m*

[2] (= *rubber stamp*) estampilla *f*; (*for metal*) cuño *m*

[3] (*fig*) (= *mark*) sello *m*; **it bears the ~ of genius** tiene el sello del genio; **to leave** *or* **put one's ~ on sth** poner *or* dejar su sello en algo; **a man of his ~** un hombre de su temple; (*pej*) un hombre de esa calaña

[4] (*with foot*) taconazo *m*; **with a ~ of her foot** dando un taconazo

Ⓑ VT [1] **to ~ one's foot** patear, patalear; (*in dancing*) zapatear; **to ~ the ground** [*person*] dar patadas en el suelo; [*horse*] piafar

[2] [+ *letter*] sellar, poner el sello a; **the letter is insufficiently ~ed** la carta no tiene suficientes sellos

[3] (= *mark with rubber stamp*) marcar con sello; (= *mark with fiscal stamp*) timbrar; (= *emboss*) grabar; [+ *passport*] sellar; **they ~ed my passport at the frontier** sellaron mi pasaporte en la frontera

[4] (= *impress mark etc on*) estampar, imprimir; [+ *coin, design*] estampar; **paper ~ed with one's name** papel *m* con el nombre de uno impreso, papel *m* con membrete

[5] (*fig*) marcar, señalar; **to ~ sth on one's memory** grabar algo en la memoria de uno; **his manners ~ him as a gentleman** sus modales lo señalan como caballero; **to ~ o.s. on sth** poner *or* dejar su sello en algo

Ⓒ VI [1] (*single movement*) patear, patalear; **to ~ on sth** pisotear algo, hollar algo; **ouch, you ~ed on my foot!** ¡ay, me has pisado el pie!

[2] (= *walk*) **to ~ in/out** entrar/salir dando fuertes zancadas; **he ~s about the house** anda por la casa pisando muy fuerte

Ⓓ CPD ► **stamp album** N álbum *m* de sellos ► **stamp book** N (= *collection*) albúm *m* de sellos; (*for posting*) libro *m* de sellos ► **stamp collecting** N filatelia *f* ► **stamp collection** N colección *f* de sellos ► **stamp collector** N filatelista *mf* ► **stamp dealer** N comerciante *mf* en sellos (de correo) ► **stamp duty** N (*Fin*) impuesto *m* *or* derecho *m* del timbre ► **stamp machine** N expendedor *m* automático de sellos (de correo)

►**stamp down** VT + ADV **to ~ sth down** apisonar algo, comprimir algo con los pies

►**stamp out** VT + ADV [1] **they ~ed out the rhythm** marcaron el ritmo con los pies

[2] (= *extinguish*) [+ *fire, cigarette*] apagar con el pie

[3] (= *eliminate*) [+ *crime, corruption, activity*] erradicar, acabar con; [+ *rebellion*] sofocar; **we must ~ out this abuse** tenemos que acabar con esta injusticia; **the doctors ~ed out the epidemic** los médicos erradicaron la epidemia

stamped [stæmpt] ADJ [*envelope*] con sello, que lleva sello; [*paper*] sellado, timbrado; **~ addressed envelope** sobre *m* sellado con las señas propias

stampede [stæm,piːd] Ⓐ N (*lit*) estampida *f*, desbandada *f*; (*fig*) desbandada *f*; **there was a sudden ~ for the door** todo el mundo corrió en estampida hacia la puerta; **the exodus turned into a ~** el éxodo se transformó en una fuga precipitada

Ⓑ VT [+ *cattle*] provocar la desbandada de; **to ~ sb into doing sth** presionar fuerte a algn para que haga algo; **let's not be ~d** no obremos precipitadamente

Ⓒ VI (*lit*) ir en desbandada; (*fig*) precipitarse

stamping-ground* ['stæmpɪŋ,graʊnd] N territorio *m*; **this is his private ~** éste es terreno particular suyo, éste es coto cerrado de su propiedad; **to keep off sb's ~** no invadir el territorio de algn

Stan [stæn] N (*familiar form*) *of* **Stanley**

stance [stæns] N [1] (*lit*) postura *f*

[2] (*fig*) actitud *f*; **to take up a ~** adoptar una actitud

[3] (*Scot*) (= *taxi rank*) parada *f* (de taxis)

stanch [stɑːntʃ] VT [+ *blood*] restañar

stanchion ['stɑːnʃən] N puntal *m*, montante *m*

▼ **stand** [stænd] (*vb: pt, pp* **stood**) Ⓐ N [1] (= *position*) posición *f*, puesto *m*; **to take up a ~ near the door** colocarse cerca de la puerta

[2] (*fig*) (= *stance*) actitud *f*, postura *f*; **to take a ~ on an issue** adoptar una actitud hacia una cuestión; **to take a firm ~** adoptar una actitud firme

[3] (*Mil*) **the ~ of the Australians at Tobruk** la resistencia de los australianos en Tobruk; **Custer's last ~** la última batalla del General Custer; ✦**IDIOM** **to make a ~** hacer parada, plantarse; **to make** *or* **take a ~ against sth** oponer resistencia a algo; *see also* **one-night stand**

[4] (*for taxis*) parada *f* (de taxis)

[5] (= *lamp stand*) pie *m*; (= *music stand*) atril *m*; (= *hallstand*) perchero *m*

[6] (= *newspaper stand*) quiosco *m*, puesto *m* (*esp LAm*); (= *market stall*) puesto *m*; (*in shop*) estante *m*, puesto *m*; (*at exhibition*) caseta *f*, stand *m*; (= *bandstand*) quiosco *m*

[7] (*Sport*) (= *grandstand*) tribuna *f*

[8] (*Jur*) estrado *m*; **to take the ~** (*esp US*) (= *go into witness box*) subir a la tribuna de los testigos; (= *give evidence*) prestar declaración

[9] [*of trees*] hilera *f*, grupo *m*

[10] (**) (= *erection*) empalme** *m*

[11] = **standstill**

Ⓑ VT [1] (= *place*) poner, colocar; **to ~ sth against the wall** apoyar algo en la pared; **to ~ a vase on a table** poner un florero sobre una mesa

[2] (= *withstand*) resistir; **it won't ~ serious examination** no resistirá un examen detallado; **it won't ~ the cold** no resiste el *or* al frío; **his heart couldn't ~ the shock** su corazón no resistió el *or* al choque; ✦**IDIOMS** **to ~ one's ground** mantenerse firme, plantarse; **if you can't ~ the heat, get out of the kitchen** si no puedes lidiar el toro, quítate de en medio

[3] (= *tolerate*) aguantar; **I can ~ anything but that** lo aguanto todo menos eso; **I can't ~ it any longer!** ¡no aguanto más!; **I can't ~ Debussy** no aguanto a Debussy; **I can't ~ (the sight of) him** no lo aguanto, no lo puedo tragar; **I can't ~ waiting for people** no aguanto *or* soporto que me hagan esperar; *see also* **chance A3**

[4] (*) (= *pay for*) **to ~ sb a drink/meal** invitar a algn a una copa/a comer; **he stood me lunch** me pagó la comida; **the company will have to ~ the loss** la compañía tendrá que encargarse de las pérdidas

Ⓒ VI [1] (= *be upright*) estar de pie *or* derecho,

➤ LANGUAGE IN USE: **stand B3** 7.3

estar parado (*LAm*); **he could hardly ~** hasta tenía problemas para ponerse de pie; **the house is still ~ing** la casa sigue en pie; **we must ~ together** (*fig*) debemos unirnos *or* ser solidarios; ✦***IDIOMS*** **to ~ on one's own two feet** valerse por sí mismo, defenderse solo (*LAm*); **to ~ tall** pisar fuerte; *see also* **ease A4**

[2] (= *get up*) levantarse, pararse (*LAm*); **all ~!** ¡levántense!

[3] (= *stay, stand still*) **they were ~ing at the bar** estaban juntos al bar; **to ~ in the doorway** estar en la puerta; **don't just ~ there, do something!** ¡no te quedes ahí parado, haz algo!; **they stood patiently in the rain** se quedaron esperando pacientemente bajo la lluvia; **to ~ talking** seguir hablando, quedarse a hablar; **we stood chatting for half an hour** charlamos durante media hora, pasamos media hora charlando; **~ and deliver!** ¡la bolsa o la vida!; ✦***IDIOM*** **he left the others ~ing** dejó a todos atrás *or* (*LAm*) parados

[4] (= *tread*) **to ~ on sth** pisar algo; **you're ~ing on my foot** me estás pisando; **he stood on the beetle** pisó el escarabajo; **he stood on the brakes** (*Aut**) pisó el freno a fondo

[5] (= *measure*) medir; **he ~s a good six feet** mide seis pies largos; **the tower ~s 50m high** la torre tiene 50m de alta; **the mountain ~s 3,000m high** la montaña tiene una altura de 3.000m

[6] (= *have reached*) **the thermometer ~s at 40°** el termómetro marca 40 grados; **the record ~s at ten minutes** el record está en diez minutos, el tiempo récord sigue siendo de diez minutos; **sales are currently ~ing at two million** las ventas ya han alcanzado los dos millones; **sales ~ at five per cent more than last year** las ventas han aumentado en un cinco por cien en relación con el año pasado

[7] (= *be situated*) encontrarse, ubicarse (*LAm*); **it ~s beside the town hall** está junto al ayuntamiento

[8] (= *be mounted, based*) apoyarse

[9] (= *remain valid*) [*offer, argument, decision*] seguir en pie *or* vigente; **my objection still ~s** mis reservas siguen en pie; **the contract ~s** el contrato sigue en vigor; **the theory ~s or falls on this** de allí depende la teoría entera; **it has stood for 200 years** ha durado 200 años ya, lleva ya 200 años de vida

[10] (*fig*) (= *be placed*) estar, encontrarse; **as things ~** ◊ **as it ~s** tal como están las cosas; **I'd like to know where I ~** quisiera saber a qué atenerme; **how do we ~?** ¿cómo estamos?; **where do you ~ with him?** ¿cuáles son tus relaciones con él?; **nothing ~s between us** nada nos separa; **nothing ~s between you and success** no tienes ningún obstáculo en el camino al éxito

[11] (= *be in a position*) **to ~ to do sth** arriesgar hacer algo; **he ~s to gain a great deal** tiene la posibilidad de ganar mucho; **what do we ~ to gain by it?** ¿qué posibilidades hay para nosotros de ganar algo?, ¿qué ventaja nos daría esto?; **we ~ to lose a lot** para nosotros supondría una pérdida importante, estamos en peligro de perder bastante

[12] (= *be*) **she ~s in need of a friend** lo que necesita es un amigo; **to ~ accused of murder** estar acusado de asesinato; **he ~s alone in this matter** no tiene ningún apoyo en este caso; **to ~ (as) security for sb** (*Fin*) salir fiador de algn; (*fig*) salir por algn; **it ~s to reason that …** es evidente que …, no cabe duda de que …; *see also* **clear B3**, **correct B1**

[13] (= *remain undisturbed*) estar; **to allow a liquid to ~** dejar estar un líquido; **let it ~ for three days** déjelo reposar durante tres días; **don't let the tea ~** no dejes que se pase el té; **to let sth ~ in the sun** poner algo al sol, dejar algo al sol; **the car has been ~ing in the sun** el coche ha estado expuesto al sol

[14] (*Brit Pol*) presentarse (como candidato); **to ~ <u>against</u> sb in an election** presentarse como oponente a algn en unas elecciones; **to ~ <u>as</u> a candidate** presentarse como candidato; **to ~ <u>for</u> Parliament** presentarse como candidato a diputado; **to ~ for president** presentarse como candidato a la presidencia; **he stood for Castroforte** fue uno de los candidatos en Castroforte; **he stood for Labour** fue candidato laborista

[15] (*Fin*) **there is £50 ~ing to your credit** usted tiene 50 libras en el haber

►**stand about, stand around** VI + ADV estar, esperar, seguir en un sitio sin propósito fijo; **they just ~ about all day** pasan todo el día por ahí sin hacer nada; **they kept us ~ing about for ages** nos hicieron esperar mucho tiempo

►**stand aside** VI + ADV apartarse, mantenerse al margen; **~ aside, please!** ¡apártense, por favor!; **we cannot ~ aside and do nothing** no podemos quedarnos sin hacer nada; **he stood aside when he could have helped** se mantuvo al margen en vez de ayudar; **to ~ aside from sth** (*fig*) mantenerse al margen de algo

►**stand back** VI + ADV [1] [*person*] retirarse; (*fig*) tomar una posición más objetiva; **~ back, please!** ¡más atrás, por favor!

[2] [*building*] (= *be placed further back*) estar apartado (**from** de)

►**stand by** Ⓐ VI + ADV [1] (= *do nothing*) mantenerse aparte

[2] (= *be ready*) estar preparado *or* listo; **~ by for further news** seguirán más noticias; **~ by for take-off!** ¡listos para despegar!; **the Navy is ~ing by to help** unidades de la Flota están listas para prestar ayuda

Ⓑ VI + PREP [+ *person*] apoyar *or* respaldar a; [+ *promise*] cumplir con; **we ~ by what we said** nos atenemos a lo dicho; **the Minister stood by his decision** el Ministro mantuvo su decisión

►**stand down** VI + ADV [1] (= *resign*) [*official, chairman*] dimitir; (= *withdraw*) [*candidate*] retirarse; **the candidate is ~ing down in favour of a younger person** el candidato se retira a favor de una persona más joven

[2] (*Jur*) [*witness*] retirarse; **you may ~ down** usted puede retirarse

[3] (*Mil*) **the troops have stood down** ha terminado el estado de alerta (militar)

►**stand for** VI + PREP [1] (= *represent*) [*abbreviation*] significar; **MP ~s for Member of Parliament** MP significa Miembro del Parlamento; **A ~s for apple** M es de manzana; **here a dash ~s for a word** aquí una raya representa una palabra

[2] (= *support*) [+ *principle, honesty*] representar

[3] (= *permit*) permitir; (= *tolerate*) admitir; **I won't ~ for that** eso no lo admito; **I'll not ~ for your whims any longer** no aguanto tus caprichos un momento más

[4] *see* **stand C14**

►**stand in** VI + ADV sustituir; **to ~ in for sb** sustituir a algn

►**stand off** Ⓐ VT + ADV (*Brit*) [+ *workers*] despedir (*temporalmente, por falta de trabajo*), suspender

Ⓑ VI + ADV apartarse, guardar las distancias; (*Naut*) apartarse

►**stand out** VI + ADV [1] (= *project*) [*ledge, buttress, vein*] sobresalir, salir

[2] (= *be conspicuous, clear*) destacar (**against** contra); **to ~ out in relief** resaltar; ✦***IDIOM*** **it ~s out a mile*** se ve a la legua

[3] (= *be outstanding*) destacarse

[4] (= *be firm, hold out*) mantenerse firme, aferrarse; **to ~ out against sth** oponerse a algo; **to ~ out for sth** insistir en algo

►**stand over** Ⓐ VI + PREP **he stood over me while I did it** me vigiló mientras lo hacía

Ⓑ VI + ADV [*items for discussion*] quedar en suspenso; **to let an item ~ over** dejar un asunto para la próxima vez

►**stand to** VI + ADV (*Mil*) estar alerta, estar sobre las armas

►**stand up** Ⓐ VI + ADV [1] (= *rise*) levantarse, ponerse de pie; (= *be standing*) estar de pie; **she had nothing but the clothes she was ~ing up in** no tenía más que lo que llevaba puesto; ✦***IDIOM*** **we must ~ up and be counted** tenemos que declararnos abiertamente

[2] [*argument etc*] ser sólido, ser lógico, convencer; **the case did not ~ up in court** la acusación no se mantuvo en el tribunal

[3] **to ~ up for sb** (*fig*) respaldar a algn; **to ~ up for sth** defender algo; **to ~ up for o.s.** defenderse solo

[4] **to ~ up to sb** hacer frente a algn; **it ~s up to hard wear** es muy resistente; **to ~ up to a test** salir bien de una prueba; **it won't ~ up to close examination** no resistirá un examen minucioso

Ⓑ VT + ADV [1] (= *place upright*) colocar de pie; ✦***IDIOM*** **a soup so thick that you could ~ a spoon up in it** una sopa tan espesa que una cuchara se quedaría de pie en él

[2] (*) [+ *girlfriend, boyfriend*] dejar plantado*, dar plantón a*

stand-alone ['stændələʊn] ADJ [*computer system etc*] autónomo

standard ['stændəd] Ⓐ N [1] (= *measure*) estándar *m*; **his ~s are high/low** sus estándares son altos/bajos, los niveles que requiere son altos/bajos; **by any ~ the work was good** el trabajo era bueno desde cualquier punto de vista; **the food was awful even by my (undemanding) ~s** la comida era espantosa incluso para mí (que soy poco exigente); *see also* **double F**

[2] (= *norm*) **to be <u>below</u> ~** no tener la suficiente calidad; **~s of <u>conduct</u>** normas *fpl* de conducta; **the <u>gold</u> ~** (*Fin*) el patrón oro; **to <u>set</u> a ~**: **the society sets ~s for judging different breeds of dog** la asociación establece ciertos patrones *or* ciertas normas para juzgar las distintas razas de perros; **society sets impossible ~s for feminine beauty** la sociedad impone unos patrones de belleza femenina imposibles; **to set a good ~** imponer un nivel alto; **her work has set a ~ for excellence which it will be hard to equal** su labor ha establecido unos niveles de excelencia que serán muy difíciles de igualar; **this film sets a new ~** esta película establece nuevos niveles de calidad cinematográfica, esta película supera los niveles cinematográficos anteriores; **her work/performance was not <u>up to</u> ~** su trabajo/actuación no estaba a la altura (requerida); **the product is not up to ~** el producto no tiene la calidad requerida

[3] (= *level*) nivel *m*; (= *quality*) calidad *f*; **she has French to first-year university ~** su francés es de un nivel de primer año de carrera; **the ~ of service** el nivel de servicio; **their ~ of hygiene leaves much to be desired** los niveles de higiene que tienen dejan mucho que desear; **the ~ of medical care** la calidad de atención médica; **of (a) <u>high/low</u> ~** de

alto/bajo nivel; **high ~s of conduct are expected of students** a los alumnos se les exige un nivel de comportamiento muy elevado
4 **standards** valores *mpl* morales; **she has no ~s** carece de valores morales *or* principios; **there has been a corruption of moral ~s** han decaído los valores morales
5 (= *flag*) estandarte *m*, bandera *f*
6 (= *pole*) (*for flag*) poste *m*; (*for lamp*) pie *m*
7 (*Bot*) *árbol o arbusto de tronco erecto y desprovisto de ramas*
8 (= *song*) tema *m* clásico, clásico *m*
Ⓑ ADJ 1 (= *normal*) [*design, length*] estándar *adj inv*; [*amount, size*] normal; [*feature*] normal, corriente; [*charge*] fijo; [*procedure*] habitual; **electric windows come as ~ on this car** las ventanillas eléctricas son de serie en este coche; **the ~ treatment is an injection of glucose** el tratamiento habitual es una inyección de glucosa; **to become ~** [*practice, procedure*] imponerse como norma; **it has become ~ practice for many surgeons** se ha convertido en una norma entre muchos cirujanos
2 (= *officially approved*) [*spelling, pronunciation*] estándar *adj inv*; [*grammar*] normativa; [*measure*] legal
3 (= *classic, recommended*) **it's a ~ text** es un texto clásico
Ⓒ CPD ► **standard bearer** N (*lit*) abanderado/a *m/f*; (*fig*) abanderado/a *m/f*, adalid *mf* ► **standard class** N clase *f* turista ► **standard deviation** N (*Statistics*) desviación *f* estándar *or* típica ► **standard English** N inglés *m* estándar *or* normativo ► **standard error** N (*Statistics*) error *m* estándar *or* típico ► **standard gauge** N (*Rail*) vía *f* normal ► **Standard Grade** N (*Scot Scol*) *certificado obtenido tras aprobar los exámenes al final de la educación secundaria obligatoria*; → GCSE ► **standard lamp** N lámpara *f* de pie ► **standard model** N modelo *m* estándar ► **standard of living** N nivel *m* de vida ► **standard price** N precio *m* oficial ► **standard quality** N calidad *f* normal ► **standard rate** N (*Fin*) tipo *m* de interés vigente ► **standard time** N hora *f* oficial ► **standard unit** N (*Elec, Gas*) paso *m* (de contador) ► **standard weight** N peso *m* legal

standard-issue [ˌstændədˈɪʃuː] ADJ **a ~ shirt** una camisa de uniforme

standardization [ˌstændədaɪˈzeɪʃən] N normalización *f*, estandar(d)ización *f*

standardize [ˈstændədaɪz] VT normalizar, estandar(d)izar

stand-by [ˈstændbaɪ] Ⓐ N 1 (*in case of need*) (= *person*) suplente *mf*; (= *spare*) repuesto *m*; (= *loan*) crédito *m* contingente, stand-by *m*
2 (= *alert, readiness*) **to be on ~** [*troops*] (= *ready for attack*) estar preparado para el ataque; [*doctor*] estar listo para acudir; [*passenger*] estar en lista de espera; **to be on 24-hour ~** (= *ready to leave*) estar listo para partir dentro de 24 horas
3 (= *stand-by ticket*) billete *m* de lista de espera, billete *m* de stand-by
Ⓑ CPD ► **stand-by aircraft** N avión *m* de reserva ► **stand-by arrangements** NPL (*Fin*) acuerdo *m* de reserva ► **stand-by credit** N crédito *m* disponible, crédito *m* stand-by ► **stand-by facility** N stand-by *m*, lista *f* de reserva ► **stand-by generator** N generador *m* de reserva ► **stand-by passenger** N (*Aer*) pasajero/a *m/f* de la lista de espera ► **stand-by ticket** N billete *m* de lista de espera, billete *m* stand-by

standee* [stænˈdiː] N (*US*) espectador(a) *m/f* que asiste de pie

stand-in [ˈstændɪn] N sustituto/a *m/f* (**for** por); (*Cine*) doble *mf*

standing [ˈstændɪŋ] Ⓐ ADJ 1 (= *not sitting*) de pie, parado (*LAm*); (= *upright*) [*stone, corn*] derecho, recto; [*water*] estancado, encharcado
2 (= *permanent*) [*army, committee, rule etc*] permanente; [*custom*] arraigado; [*grievance, joke*] constante, eterno
Ⓑ N 1 (= *social position*) rango *m*, estatus *m inv*; (= *reputation*) reputación *f*, fama *f*; **what is his ~ locally?** ¿cómo se le considera en círculos locales?; **financial ~** solvencia *f*; **to be in good ~** tener buena reputación; (*Fin*) gozar de buen crédito; **of high ~** de categoría; **the restaurant has a high ~** el restaurante tiene una buena reputación; **he has no ~ in this matter** no tiene voz ni voto en este asunto; **the relative ~ of these problems** la importancia relativa de estos problemas; **social ~** posición *f* social; **a man of some ~** un hombre de cierta categoría
2 (= *duration*) duración *f*; (= *seniority*) antigüedad *f*; **of six months' ~** que lleva seis meses; **a captain of only a month's ~** un capitán que lleva solamente un mes en el puesto *or* en tal graduación; **of long ~** de mucho tiempo (acá), viejo
3 (*US Aut*) **"no standing"** "prohibido estacionar"
Ⓒ CPD ► **standing order** N (*Fin*) giro *m or* pedido *m* regular; (*Comm*) pedido *m* permanente, pedido *m* regular ► **standing orders** NPL [*of meeting*] reglamento *m*, estatuto *m* ► **standing ovation** N ovación *f* en pie; **he got a ~ ovation** todos se pusieron en pie para ovacionarlo ► **standing room** N sitio *m* para estar de pie; **~ room only** ya no quedan asientos ► **standing start** N (*Sport*) salida *f* desde posición de paro

stand-off [ˈstændɒf] Ⓐ N (= *deadlock*) punto *m* muerto, callejón *m* sin salida; (*Sport*) (= *stalemate*) empate *m*
Ⓑ CPD ► **stand-off half** N (*Rugby*) medio *m* de apertura

stand-offish [ˌstændˈɒfɪʃ] ADJ distante, reservado

stand-offishly [ˌstændˈɒfɪʃlɪ] ADV fríamente

stand-offishness [ˌstændˈɒfɪʃnɪs] N frialdad *f*, reserva *f*

stand-pat* [ˈstændpæt] ADJ (*US*) inmovilista

standpipe [ˈstændpaɪp] N 1 (*Tech*) columna *f* de alimentación
2 (*in street*) fuente *f* provisional

standpoint [ˈstændpɔɪnt] N punto *m* de vista; **from the ~ of ...** desde el punto de vista de ...

standstill [ˈstændstɪl] N parada *f*; **to be at a ~** [*vehicle*] estar parado; [*industry etc*] estar paralizado; **negotiations are at a ~** las negociaciones están paralizadas; **to bring a car to a ~** parar un coche; **to bring an industry to a ~** paralizar una industria; **to bring traffic to a ~** paralizar el tráfico, parar totalmente el tráfico; **to come to a ~** [*person*] pararse, hacer un alto; [*vehicle*] pararse; [*industry etc*] estancarse

stand-to [ˌstændˈtuː] N alerta *f*

stand-up [ˈstændʌp] Ⓐ ADJ **~ buffet** comida *f* tomada de pie; **~ collar** cuello *m* alto; **~ fight** (*lit*) pelea *f* violenta; (*fig*) altercado *m* violento
Ⓑ N (*also* **~ comedian, ~ comic**) cómico/a *m/f*; (*also* **~ comedy**) comedia *f*

stank [stæŋk] PT *of* **stink**

Stanley knife® [ˈstænlɪˌnaɪf] N cuchilla *f* para moqueta

stannic [ˈstænɪk] ADJ estánnico

stanza [ˈstænzə] N estrofa *f*, estancia *f*

stapes [ˈsteɪpiːz] N (*pl* **stapes** *or* **stapedes** [stæˈpiːdiːz]) (*Anat*) estribo *m*

staphylococcus [ˌstæfɪləˈkɒkəs] N (*pl* **staphylococci** [ˌstæfɪləˈkɒkaɪ]) estafilococo *m*

staple[1] [ˈsteɪpl] Ⓐ N (= *fastener*) grapa *f*, corchete *m* (*S. Cone*)
Ⓑ VT sujetar con grapa
Ⓒ CPD ► **staple gun** N grapadora *f*

staple[2] [ˈsteɪpl] Ⓐ ADJ [*product*] de primera necesidad; [*topic of conversation*] clásico; **their ~ food** *or* **diet** su comida cotidiana, su alimento de primera necesidad
Ⓑ N (= *chief product*) artículo *m* de primera necesidad; (= *food*) alimento *m* de primera necesidad; (= *raw material*) materia *f* prima; [*of wool*] fibra *f* (textil); [*of conversation*] asunto *m* principal, elemento *m* esencial

stapler [ˈsteɪplə^r], **stapling machine** [ˈsteɪplɪŋməˌʃiːn] N grapadora *f*

star [stɑː^r] Ⓐ N 1 (*Astron*) estrella *f*, astro *m*; **the Stars and Stripes** (*US*) las barras y las estrellas; **the Stars and Bars** (*US Hist*) la bandera de los estados confederados; ✦*IDIOMS* **to have ~s in one's eyes** estar ilusionado; **to see ~s** ver (las) estrellas; **it's written in the ~s** está escrito (en las estrellas); **to be born under a lucky ~** nacer con estrella; **to believe in one's lucky ~** creer en su buena estrella; **you can thank your lucky ~s that ...** da gracias que ...
2 (= *film star, sports star, etc*) estrella *f*; **the ~ of the team was Green** la figura más destacada del equipo fue Green
3 (*Typ*) asterisco *m*
4 **stars** (= *horoscope*) horóscopo *m*
Ⓑ VT 1 (= *adorn with stars*) estrellar, adornar con estrellas, sembrar de estrellas; (= *mark with star*) señalar con asterisco
2 (*Cine etc*) presentar como estrella; **a film ~ring Greta Garbo** una película con Greta Garbo en el papel principal
Ⓒ VI (*Cine etc*) tener el papel principal; **the three films in which James Dean ~red** las tres películas que protagonizó James Dean
Ⓓ CPD estrella, estelar ► **star attraction** N atracción *f* principal ► **star grass** N azucena *f* ► **Star of David** N estrella *f* de David ► **star of Bethlehem** N (*Bot*) leche *f* de gallina, matacandiles *m* ► **star player** N estrella *f* ► **star prize** N gran premio *m*, primer premio *m* ► **star role** N papel *m* estelar ► **star screwdriver** N destornillador *m* de estrella ► **star shell** N cohete *m* luminoso, bengala *f* ► **star sign** N signo *m* del Zodíaco ► **star turn** N = **star attraction** ► **"Star Wars"** N (*Cine*) "Guerra *f* de las Galaxias"

-star [stɑː^r] ADJ (*ending in compounds*) **four-star hotel** hotel *m* de cuatro estrellas; **4-star (petrol)** gasolina *f* extra, súper *f*

starboard [ˈstɑːbɔːd] Ⓐ N estribor *m*; **the sea to ~** la mar a estribor; **land to ~!** ¡tierra a estribor!
Ⓑ ADJ [*lights*] de estribor; **on the ~ side** a estribor
Ⓒ VT **to ~ the helm** poner el timón a estribor, virar a estribor

starch [stɑːtʃ] Ⓐ N (*for clothes etc*) almidón *m*; (*in food*) fécula *f*
Ⓑ VT almidonar

star-chamber [ˈstɑːˌtʃeɪmbə^r] ADJ (*fig*) secreto y arbitrario

starched [stɑːtʃt] ADJ almidonado

starch-reduced [ˈstɑːtʃrɪˌdjuːst] ADJ [*bread etc*] de régimen, con menos fécula

starchy [ˈstɑːtʃɪ] ADJ (*compar* **starchier**, *superl*

starchiest) 1 [*food*] con fécula
2 (*fig*) [*person*] rígido, estirado

star-crossed ['stɑːˌkrɒst] ADJ malhadado, desventurado

stardom ['stɑːdəm] N estrellato *m*; **to rise to** *or* **achieve ~** alcanzar el estrellato

stardust ['stɑːdʌst] N (*fig*) encanto *m*, embeleso *m*

stare [steəʳ] Ⓐ N mirada *f* fija; **to give sb a ~** mirar fijamente a algn
Ⓑ VT **to ~ sb out** *or* **down** mirar a algn fijamente hasta que aparte la vista; ✦*IDIOM* **it's staring you in the face** salta a la vista
Ⓒ VI mirar fijamente; **he wouldn't stop staring** no paraba de mirar fijamente; **don't ~!** ¡no mires tan fijo!; **to ~ at sth/sb** mirar algo/a algn fijamente, mirar algo/a algn de hito en hito; **it's rude to ~ at people** está mal visto fijar la mirada en la gente; **to ~ into the distance** ◊ **~ into space** estar con la mirada perdida *or* mirando a las nubes

starfish ['stɑːfɪʃ] N (*pl* **starfish, starfishes**) estrella *f* de mar

stargaze ['stɑːgeɪz] VI mirar las estrellas; (*fig*) distraerse, mirar las telarañas

stargazer ['stɑːˌgeɪzəʳ] N astrónomo/a *m/f*

stargazing ['stɑːˌgeɪzɪŋ] N 1 (= *astronomy*) astronomía *f*
2 (= *astrology*) astrología *f*
3 (*fig*) distracción *f*

staring ['steərɪŋ] ADJ que mira fijamente, curioso; [*eyes*] saltón; (*in fear*) lleno de espanto

stark [stɑːk] Ⓐ ADJ (*compar* **starker**; *superl* **starkest**) 1 (= *austere*) [*simplicity, colour, beauty, décor, outline*] austero; [*conditions*] severo, duro; [*landscape*] inhóspito; [*description*] escueto, sucinto
2 (= *harsh*) [*reality, poverty*] crudo, sin adornos; [*choice, warning, reminder*] duro; **those are the ~ facts of the matter** ésa es la cruda realidad del asunto
3 (= *absolute*) [*terror, folly*] absoluto; **to be in ~ contrast to sth** contrastar brutalmente con algo
Ⓑ ADV **~ staring** *or* **raving mad*** loco de remate*; **~ naked*** en cueros*, en pelotas‡, encuerado (*LAm**), pilucho (*Chile**), calato (*Peru, Bol**)

starkers‡ ['stɑːkəz] ADJ **to be ~** (*Brit*) estar en cueros*, estar en pelotas‡, estar encuerado (*LAm**), estar pilucho (*Chile**), estar calato (*Peru, Bol**)

starkly ['stɑːklɪ] ADV 1 (= *austerely*) [*furnished*] austeramente; [*describe*] escuetamente, sucintamente; **~ beautiful** de una belleza austera
2 (= *clearly*) [*illustrate*] crudamente; [*outline*] claramente; [*stand out*] con claridad; [*different, apparent, evident*] completamente; **to contrast ~ with sth** contrastar brutalmente con algo; **to be ~ exposed** quedar completamente al descubierto; **he put the choice ~** expuso la alternativa sin ambages, nos ofreció la alternativa y nada más

starkness ['stɑːknɪs] N 1 (= *austerity*) [*of landscape, desert*] lo inhóspito; [*of conditions*] severidad *f*; [*of simplicity, contrast, décor, outline*] austeridad *f*; [*of colour, beauty*] sobriedad *f*; [*of description*] lo escueto, lo sucinto
2 (= *harshness*) [*of reality, poverty*] crudeza *f*; [*of choice, warning, reminder*] lo duro

starless ['stɑːlɪs] ADJ sin estrellas

starlet ['stɑːlɪt] N (*Cine*) joven aspirante *f* a estrella

starlight ['stɑːlaɪt] N luz *f* de las estrellas; **by ~** a la luz de las estrellas

starling ['stɑːlɪŋ] N estornino *m*

➤ LANGUAGE IN USE: **start** C1 26.1, 26.3

starlit ['stɑːlɪt] ADJ iluminado por las estrellas

starry ['stɑːrɪ] ADJ (*compar* **starrier**; *superl* **starriest**) sembrado de estrellas

starry-eyed ['stɑːrɪ'aɪd] ADJ (= *idealistic*) idealista, ingenuo; (= *in love*) sentimentaloide

star-spangled ['stɑːˌspæŋgld] ADJ estrellado; **the Star-spangled Banner** (*US*) la Bandera Estrellada

star-studded ['stɑːˌstʌdɪd] ADJ [*sky*] estrellado; **a ~ cast** (*Cine, Theat*) un elenco *m* estelar

START [stɑːt] N ABBR = **Strategic Arms Reduction Talks**

start [stɑːt] Ⓐ N 1 (= *beginning*) principio *m*, comienzo *m*; **at the ~** al principio, en un principio; **at the very ~** muy al principio, en los mismos comienzos; **at the ~ of the century** a principios del siglo; **we are at the ~ of something big** estamos en los comienzos de algo grandioso; **for a ~** en primer lugar, para empezar; **from the ~** desde el principio; **from ~ to finish** desde el principio hasta el fin; **to get a good ~ in life** disfrutar de una infancia privilegiada; **to get off to a good/bad/slow ~** empezar bien/mal/lentamente; **to give sb a (good) ~ in life** ayudar a algn a situarse en la vida; **to make a ~** empezar; **to make a ~ on the painting** empezar a pintar; **to make an early ~** (*on journey*) ponerse en camino temprano; (*with job*) empezar temprano; **to make a fresh** *or* **new ~ in life** hacer vida nueva
2 (= *departure*) salida *f* (*also Sport*); (= *starting line*) línea *f* de salida
3 (= *advantage*) ventaja *f*; **to give sb five minutes'** *or* **a five-minute ~** dar a algn cinco minutos de ventaja; **to have a ~ on sb** tener ventaja sobre algn
4 (= *fright etc*) susto *m*, sobresalto *m*; **to give sb a ~** asustar *or* dar un susto a algn; **to give a sudden ~** sobresaltarse; **what a ~ you gave me!** ¡qué susto me diste!; **to wake with a ~** despertarse sobresaltado
Ⓑ VT 1 (= *begin*) empezar, comenzar; [+ *discussion etc*] abrir, iniciar; [+ *bottle*] abrir; [+ *quarrel, argument*] empezar; [+ *journey*] iniciar; **to ~ a new cheque book/page** comenzar or empezar un talonario nuevo/una página nueva; **don't ~ that again!** ¡no vuelvas a eso!; **to ~ doing sth** *or* **to do sth** empezar a hacer algo; **~ moving!** ¡menearse!; **~ talking!** ¡desembucha!; **to ~ sth again** *or* **afresh** comenzar *or* empezar algo de nuevo; **to ~ the day right** empezar bien el día; **he always ~s the day with a glass of milk** lo primero que toma cada mañana es un vaso de leche; **he ~ed life as a labourer** empezó de *or* como peón; **to ~ a new life** comenzar una vida nueva; **to ~ negotiations** iniciar *or* entablar las pláticas; **to ~ a novel** empezar a escribir (*or* leer) una novela; **to ~ school** empezar a ir al colegio; **he ~ed work yesterday** entró a trabajar ayer
2 (= *cause to begin or happen*) [+ *fire*] provocar; [+ *war*] [*person, country*] empezar, iniciar; [*incident, act*] desencadenar; [+ *fashion*] empezar, iniciar; [+ *rumour, tradition*] iniciar, dar comienzo a; **it ~ed the collapse of the empire** provocó el derrumbamiento del imperio; **you ~ed it!** ¡tú diste el primer golpe!; **to ~ a family** (empezar a) tener hijos; **to ~ a race** (= *give signal for*) dar la señal de salida para una carrera
3 **to get ~ed** empezar, ponerse en marcha; **let's get ~ed** empecemos; **to get sth ~ed** [+ *engine, car*] poner algo en marcha, arrancar algo; [+ *project*] poner algo en marcha; **to get sb ~ed** (*on activity*) poner a algn en marcha; (*in career*) iniciar a algn en su carrera; **to get ~ed on (doing) sth** empezar a hacer algo; **to get sb ~ed on (doing) sth** poner a algn a hacer algo
4 (= *found*) (*also* **~ up**) [+ *business*] montar, poner; [+ *newspaper*] fundar, establecer
5 (*also* **~ up**) [+ *car, engine*] arrancar, poner en marcha; [+ *clock*] poner en marcha
6 (*with personal object*) **don't ~ him (off) on that!** ¡no le des cuerda!; **to ~ sb (off) reminiscing** hacer que algn empiece a contar sus recuerdos; **that ~ed him (off) sneezing** eso le hizo empezar a estornudar; **to ~ sb (off) on a career** ayudar a algn a emprender una carrera; **they ~ed her (off) in the sales department** la emplearon primero en la sección de ventas
7 (= *disturb*) **to ~ (up) a partridge** levantar una perdiz
Ⓒ VI 1 (= *begin*) empezar, comenzar; [*conversation, discussion*] iniciarse; [*quarrel, argument*] producirse; [*fashion*] empezar, iniciar; [*war*] estallar, empezar; [*rumour, tradition*] originarse; [*fire*] empezar, iniciarse; [*music*] empezar; **classes ~ on Monday** las clases comienzan *or* empiezan el lunes; **that's when the trouble ~ed** entonces fue cuando empezaron los problemas; **it all ~ed when he refused to pay** todo empezó cuando se negó a pagar; **it ~ed (off) rather well/badly** [*film, match*] empezó bastante bien/mal; **to ~ again** *or* **afresh** volver a empezar, comenzar de nuevo; **he ~ed (off** *or* **out) as a postman** empezó como *or* de cartero; **he ~ed (off** *or* **out) as a Marxist** empezó como marxista; **to ~ at the beginning** empezar desde el principio; **he ~ed (off) by saying …** empezó por decir *or* diciendo …; **the route ~s from here** la ruta sale de aquí; **~ing from Tuesday** a partir del martes; **to ~ (out** *or* **up) in business** montar *or* poner un negocio; **to ~ (off) with …** (= *firstly*) en primer lugar …, para empezar …; (= *at the beginning*) al principio …, en un principio …; **what shall we ~ (off) with?** ¿con qué empezamos?; **to ~ (off) with a prayer** empezar con una oración; **he ~ed (off** *or* **out) with the intention of writing a thesis** empezó con la intención de escribir una tesis
2 (= *embark*) **to ~ on a task** emprender una tarea; **to ~ on something new** emprender algo nuevo; **to ~ on a book** (= *begin reading*) empezar a leer un libro; (= *begin writing*) empezar a escribir un libro; **to ~ on a course of study** empezar un curso; **they ~ed on another bottle** abrieron *or* empezaron otra botella
3 (*also* **~ off, ~ out**) (*on journey*) [*person*] partir, ponerse en camino; [*bus, train, runner*] salir; **to ~ (off** *or* **out) from London/for Madrid** salir de Londres/partir con rumbo a *or* para Madrid; **he ~ed (off) down the street** empezó a caminar calle abajo
4 (*also* **~ up**) [*car, engine*] arrancar, ponerse en marcha; [*washing machine*] ponerse en marcha
5 (= *jump nervously*) asustarse, sobresaltarse (**at** a); **to ~ from one's chair** levantarse asustado de su silla; **tears ~ed to her eyes** se le llenaron los ojos de lágrimas; ✦*IDIOM* **his eyes were ~ing out of his head** se le saltaban los ojos de la cara
6 [*timber etc*] combarse, torcerse; [*rivets etc*] soltarse

►**start after** VI + PREP **to ~ after sb** salir en busca de algn

►**start back** VI + ADV 1 (= *return*) emprender el viaje de regreso (**for** a); **it's time we ~ed back** es hora de volvernos

[2] (= *recoil*) retroceder; **to ~ back in horror** retroceder horrorizado

►**start in** VI + ADV empezar, poner manos a la obra, empezar a trabajar (etc); **then she ~ed in** luego ella metió su cuchara*

►**start off** Ⓐ VI + ADV *see* **start C1, C3**
Ⓑ VT + ADV *see* **start B6**

►**start on*** VI + PREP (= *scold*) regañar; *see also* **start C2**

►**start out** VI + ADV *see* **start C1, C3**

►**start over** (*esp US*) Ⓐ VI + ADV volver a empezar
Ⓑ VT + ADV comenzar *or* empezar de nuevo

►**start up** Ⓐ VI + ADV *see* **start C1, C4**
Ⓑ VT + ADV *see* **start B4, B5, B7**

starter ['stɑːtəʳ] Ⓐ N [1] (*Sport*) (= *judge*) juez *mf* de salida; (= *competitor*) corredor(a) *m/f*; **to be under ~'s orders** (*Horse racing*) estar listos para la salida
[2] (= *button*) botón *m* de arranque; (*Aut*) (= *motor*) motor *m* de arranque
[3] (*Brit Culin*) (= *first course*) entrada *f*; **for ~s*** (*fig*) en primer lugar
Ⓑ CPD ► **starter home** N primera vivienda *f* ► **starter motor** N (*Aut*) motor *m* de arranque

starting ['stɑːtɪŋ] CPD ► **starting block** N (*Athletics*) taco *m* de salida ► **starting gate** N (*US Horse racing*) cajón *m* de salida, parrilla *f* de salida ► **starting grid** N (*Motor racing*) parrilla *f* de arranque ► **starting handle** N (*Brit Aut*) manivela *f* de arranque ► **starting line** N (*Athletics*) línea *f* de salida ► **starting point** N (*fig*) punto *m* de partida ► **starting post** N (*Sport*) poste *m* de salida ► **starting price** N (*St Ex*) cotización *f* ► **starting salary** N sueldo *m* inicial ► **starting stalls** NPL (*Brit Horse racing*) cajones *mpl* de salida

startle ['stɑːtl] VT asustar, sobresaltar; **you quite ~d me!** ¡vaya susto que me has dado!; **it ~d him out of his serenity** le hizo perder su serenidad

startled ['stɑːtld] ADJ [*animal*] asustado, espantado; [*person*] sorprendido; [*expression, voice*] de sobresalto, sobresaltado

startling ['stɑːtlɪŋ] ADJ [*news*] alarmante; [*discovery*] inesperado; [*appearance*] llamativo

start-up ['stɑːtʌp] ADJ [*costs, loan*] de puesta en marcha

starvation [stɑː'veɪʃən] Ⓐ N hambre *f*, inanición *f*, hambruna *f* (*LAm*); (*fig*) privación *f*; **to die of ~** morir de hambre; **they are threatened with ~** les amenaza el hambre; **fuel ~** (*Tech*) agotamiento *m* del combustible
Ⓑ CPD ► **starvation diet** N régimen *m* de hambre ► **starvation wages** NPL sueldo *m* de hambre

starve [stɑːv] Ⓐ VT [1] (= *deprive of food*) privar de comida; **to ~ sb to death** hacer que algn muera de hambre; **to ~ a town into surrender** impedir la entrada de alimentos a una ciudad hasta que se rinda
[2] (= *deprive*) **to ~ sb of sth** privar a algn de algo; **to be ~d of affection** estar privado de afecto
Ⓑ VI (= *lack food*) pasar hambre, padecer hambre; (= *die*) morir(se) de hambre; **to ~ to death** morirse de hambre; **I'm starving!*** estoy muerto de hambre

►**starve out** VT + ADV **to ~ a garrison out** hacer que una guarnición se rinda por hambre

starving ['stɑːvɪŋ] ADJ hambriento

stash* [stæʃ] Ⓐ N escondite *m*, alijo *m*
Ⓑ VT (*also* **~ away**) (= *hide*) esconder; (= *save up, store away*) guardar

stasis ['steɪsɪs] N estasis *f*

state [steɪt] Ⓐ N [1] (= *condition*) estado *m*; **the current ~ of the housing market** el estado actual del mercado inmobiliario; **if this ~ of affairs continues** si las cosas siguen así; **it is a sorry ~ of affairs when ...** es una situación lamentable cuando ...; **~ of alert** estado *m* de alerta; **~ of grace** estado *m* de gracia; **~ of health** (estado *m* de) salud *f*; **to be in a bad** *or* **poor ~** estar en mal estado; **to be in a good ~** estar en buenas condiciones; **it wasn't in a fit ~ to be used** no estaba en condiciones de ser usado; **he's not in a fit ~ to do it** no está en condiciones para hacerlo; **he arrived home in a shocking ~** llegó a casa hecho una pena; **she was in no ~ to talk** no estaba en condiciones para hablar; **~ of mind** estado *m* de ánimo; **he was in an odd ~ of mind** estaba raro; **the ~ of the nation** el estado de la nación; **~ of play** (*Sport*) situación *f* del juego; **what's the ~ of play?** (*fig*) ¿cuál es la situación?; **~ of repair** estado *m*; **~ of siege** estado *m* de sitio; **~ of war** estado *m* de guerra; **~ of weightlessness** estado *m* de ingravidez
[2] (*) (= *poor condition*) **you should have seen the ~ the car was in** tenías que haber visto cómo estaba el coche; **just look at the ~ of this room!** ¡mira cómo está esta habitación!; **the flat was in a right ~ after the party** el piso estaba hecho un asco después de la fiesta*
[3] (*) (= *agitated condition*) **to be in a ~** estar nervioso; **his wife is in a terrible ~** su mujer está nerviosísima; **to get into a ~** ponerse nervioso; **now don't get into a ~ about it** no te pongas nervioso
[4] (= *region, country*) estado *m*; **the State of Washington** el estado de Washington; **the State of Israel** el estado de Israel; **the States*** (= *USA*) los Estados Unidos; **a ~ within a ~** un estado dentro de un estado
[5] (= *government*) **the State** el Estado; **affairs of ~** asuntos *mpl* de estado; **Secretary of State** (*US*) Secretario/a *m/f* de Asuntos Exteriores; **Secretary of State for Education** (*Brit*) Secretario/a *m/f* de Educación
[6] (= *rank*) rango *m*; (= *office*) cargo *m*; **the ~ of bishop** la dignidad de obispo
[7] (= *pomp*) **to dine in ~** cenar con mucha ceremonia; **to lie in ~** estar de cuerpo presente; **to live in ~** vivir lujosamente; **robes of ~** ropas *fpl* de investidura
Ⓑ VT [1] (*frm*) (= *say, show*) **~ your address and telephone number** (*on form*) escriba su dirección y número de teléfono; (*orally*) diga su dirección y número de teléfono; **as ~d above** como se indica más arriba; **to ~ that ...** [*rules, law*] estipular que ...; **it is nowhere ~d that ...** no se dice en ninguna parte que ...; **the article ~d that she had been interviewed by the police** el artículo afirmaba que la policía la había interrogado; **it must be ~d in the records that ...** tiene que hacerse constar en los archivos que ...
[2] (= *declare, affirm*) declarar; **he has ~d his intention to run for President** ha declarado su intención de presentarse como candidato a la presidencia; **he has publicly ~d that ...** ha declarado públicamente que ...
[3] (= *expound on, set out*) [+ *views*] dar, expresar; [+ *facts, case, problem*] exponer; **he was asked to ~ his views on the subject** se le pidió que diera *or* expresara su opinión sobre el asunto; **I'm simply stating the facts** simplemente estoy exponiendo los hechos; **to ~ the case for the prosecution** exponer los argumentos de la acusación
Ⓒ CPD (*Pol*) [*policy, documents, security*] del estado; [*capitalism, socialism, visit, funeral, business*] de estado ► **state aid** N ayuda *f* estatal ► **state apartments** NPL *apartamentos destinados a visitas de mandatarios* ► **state bank** (*US*) N banco *m* estatal *or* del estado ► **state banquet** N banquete *m* de gala ► **state benefit** N subsidios *mpl* del estado, subsidios *mpl* estatales; **those receiving** *or* **on ~ benefit** aquéllos que cobran subsidios del estado *or* estatales ► **State Capitol** N (*US*) *edificio donde tiene su sede el poder legislativo de un estado* ► **state control** N control *m* público *or* estatal; **to be/come under ~ control** pasar a manos del estado ► **State Department** N (*US*) Ministerio *m* de Asuntos Exteriores ► **state education** N enseñanza *f* pública ► **State Enrolled Nurse** N (*Brit*) (*formerly*) enfermero/a *m/f* diplomado/a (*con dos años de estudios*) ► **state fair** N (*US*) feria *f* estatal ► **state funding** N financiación *f* pública ► **state highway** N (*US*) carretera *f* nacional ► **state legislature** N (*US*) poder *m* legislativo del estado ► **state line** N (*US*) frontera *f* de estado ► **state militia** N (*US*) [*of specific state*] milicia *f* del estado ► **state occasion** N acontecimiento *m* solemne ► **state ownership** N **they believe in state ownership of the means of production** creen que los medios de producción deberían estar en manos del estado, son partidarios de que los medios de producción estén en manos del estado ► **state pension** N pensión *f* del estado, pensión *f* estatal ► **state police** N [*of country*] policía *f* nacional; (*US*) [*of specific state*] policía *f* del estado ► **state prison** N (*US*) cárcel *f* estatal, prisión *f* estatal ► **State Registered Nurse** N (*Brit*) (*formerly*) enfermero/a *m/f* diplomado/a (*con tres años de estudios*) ► **State Representative** N (*US Pol*) representante *mf* del estado ► **state school** N (*Brit*) colegio *m* público, escuela *f* pública ► **state secret** N (*lit, fig*) secreto *m* de estado ► **state sector** N sector *m* estatal ► **State Senator** N (*US*) senador(a) *m/f* del estado ► **state subsidy** N subvención *f* estatal ► **state tax** N (*US*) [*of specific state*] impuesto *m* del estado ► **state trooper** N (*US*) [*of specific state*] policía *mf* del estado ► **state university** N (*US*) universidad *f* pública

STATE OF THE UNION ADDRESS

Se denomina **State of the Union Address** *al discurso que el Presidente de Estados Unidos dirige cada mes de enero al Congreso y al pueblo estadounidense, en que muestra su visión de la nación y la economía y explica sus planes para el futuro. Como el discurso recibe una amplia cobertura informativa, el mensaje del Presidente va dirigido no sólo a los parlamentarios sino a todo el país. Esta tradición de dirigirse al Congreso poco después de la vuelta de éste de las vacaciones de Navidad el día 3 de enero se debe a que es un requisito de la Constitución que el Presidente informe al Congreso de vez en cuando sobre* **the State of the Union**.

STATES' RIGHTS

Al hablar de **State's Rights** *los estadounidenses se refieren a los derechos que tienen los estados en relación al gobierno federal, como por ejemplo la capacidad de recaudar impuestos, aprobar leyes o controlar la educación pública. En la Décima Enmienda de la Constitución estadounidense se dice que los poderes que la Constitución no delega a los Estados Unidos "se reservan a cada estado particular o al pueblo", aunque ha habido mucha*

➤ LANGUAGE IN USE: starting 26.1

polémica a la hora de interpretar esta enmienda. Este principio se usó para justificar la secesión de los estados sureños antes de la Guerra Civil y se convirtió en una consigna sureña contra la integración racial durante los años 50. Recientemente esta idea se ha ido extendiendo por todo el país debido a la falta de confianza de la gente en el gobierno federal, que está acaparando cada vez más poderes pero cuyos gastos son también mayores.

state-controlled ['steɪtkən'trəʊld] ADJ controlado por el Estado, estatal

statecraft ['steɪtkrɑːft] N arte *m* de gobernar

stated ['steɪtɪd] ADJ [1] (= *indicated*) indicado, señalado; **on the ~ date** en la fecha indicada *or* señalada; **do not exceed the ~ dose** no exceda la dosis indicada *or* señalada; **the sum ~** la cantidad establecida
[2] (= *declared*) [*aim, purpose*] expresado; **the organization's ~ aim is to improve communications** la intención expresada por la organización es la de mejorar las comunicaciones
[3] (= *fixed*) [*limit*] establecido; **within ~ limits** dentro de límites establecidos; **at the ~ time** a la hora señalada; **within the ~ time** dentro del plazo fijado *or* señalado

statehood ['steɪthʊd] N (= *independence*) independencia *f*; (*as federal state*) categoría *f* de estado

stateless ['steɪtlɪs] ADJ desnacionalizado, apátrida

stateliness ['steɪtlɪnɪs] N majestad *f*, majestuosidad *f*

stately ['steɪtlɪ] Ⓐ ADJ (*compar* **statelier**; *superl* **stateliest**) [*person, manner*] imponente; [*pace, music*] majestuoso
Ⓑ CPD ► **stately home** N casa *f* solariega

statement ['steɪtmənt] N [1] (= *declaration*) (*also Jur*) declaración *f*; **a written ~ of terms and conditions** una declaración escrita de los términos y las condiciones; **to make a ~** (*Jur*) prestar declaración; **he made a ~ to the press** hizo una declaración a la prensa; **in an official ~, the government said ...** en un comunicado oficial, el gobierno dijo ...; **to issue a press ~** emitir un comunicado de prensa; **a signed and sworn ~** una declaración firmada bajo juramento; *see also* **policy B**
[2] (= *exposition*) [*of views, facts, problem, theory*] exposición *f*; **a ~ of fact** una exposición de los hechos; **he gave a detailed ~ of his party's position** hizo una exposición detallada de la postura de su partido
[3] (*fig*) (= *critique*) alegato *m*, proclama *f*; **the film is a powerful anti-war ~** la película es un poderoso alegato contra la guerra; **the paintings are intended to make a ~ about contemporary society** lo que se pretende con los cuadros es expresar una opinión acerca de la sociedad contemporánea
[4] (*Fin*) (*also* **~ of account**) estado *m* de cuenta; (*also* **bank ~**) extracto *m* de cuenta; *see also* **financial**
[5] (*Ling*) afirmación *f*
[6] (*Comput*) instrucción *f*, sentencia *f*

state-of-the-art [ˌsteɪtəvðɪ'ɑːt] ADJ [*equipment*] de lo más moderno *or* reciente; [*technology*] de vanguardia

state-owned [ˌsteɪt'əʊnd] ADJ nacional, estatal

stateroom ['steɪtrʊm] N (*Naut*) camarote *m*; (*esp Brit*) (*in palace etc*) salón *m* de gala

stateside* ['steɪtsaɪd] ADV (*esp US*) [*be*] en Estados Unidos; [*go*] a Estados Unidos, hacia Estados Unidos

statesman ['steɪtsmən] N (*pl* **statesmen**) estadista *m*, hombre *m* de estado

statesmanlike ['steɪtsmənlaɪk] ADJ (digno) de estadista

statesmanship ['steɪtsmənʃɪp] N habilidad *f* política, capacidad *f* para gobernar; **that showed true ~** eso demostró su verdadera capacidad de estadista; **~ alone will not solve the problem** la habilidad de los estadistas no resolverá el problema por sí sola

state-subsidized [ˌsteɪt'sʌbsɪdaɪzd] ADJ subvencionado por el Estado

stateswoman ['steɪtsˌwʊmən] N (*pl* **stateswomen**) mujer *f* de estado

state-trading countries ['steɪtˌtreɪdɪŋ'kʌntrɪz] NPL países *mpl* de comercio estatal

static ['stætɪk] Ⓐ ADJ (*gen*) estático, inmóvil; (*Phys*) estático
Ⓑ N [1] (*Rad etc*) (= *noise*) parásitos *mpl*
[2] (*Phys*) (*also* **~s**) estática *f*
Ⓒ CPD ► **static electricity** N estática *f*

station ['steɪʃən] Ⓐ N [1] (*Rail*) estación *f* (de ferrocarril); (= *police station*) comisaría *f*; (*US*) (= *gas station*) gasolinera *f*, fuente *f*, grifo *m* (*Peru*); *see also* **bus, fire D**
[2] (*esp Mil*) (= *post*) puesto *m*; **to take up one's ~** colocarse, ir a su puesto; **from my ~ by the window** desde el sitio donde estaba junto a la ventana; **Roman ~** sitio *m* ocupado por los romanos; **Stations of the Cross** (*Rel*) Vía *f* Crucis
[3] (*Rad*) emisora *f*
[4] (= *social position*) rango *m*; **to have ideas above one's ~** darse aires de superioridad; **to marry below one's ~** casarse con un hombre/una mujer de posición social inferior; **of humble ~** de baja posición social, de condición humilde; **a man of exalted ~** un hombre de rango elevado
Ⓑ VT [1] (*Mil*) estacionar, apostar; [+ *missile etc*] emplazar
[2] (*fig*) colocar, situar; **to ~ o.s.** colocarse, situarse
Ⓒ CPD ► **station house** N (*US Rail*) estación *f* de ferrocarril; (*US Police*) comisaría *f* ► **station master** N (*Rail*) jefe *m* de estación ► **station wag(g)on** N (*esp US Aut*) furgoneta *f*, camioneta *f*

stationary ['steɪʃənərɪ] ADJ inmóvil; (= *not movable*) parado, estacionario; **to remain ~** quedarse inmóvil

stationer ['steɪʃənə^r] N papelero/a *m/f*; **~'s (shop)** papelería *f*

stationery ['steɪʃənərɪ] Ⓐ N artículos *mpl* de escritorio *or* de papelería
Ⓑ CPD ► **Stationery Office** N (*Brit*) Imprenta *f* Nacional

statistic [stə'tɪstɪk] N estadística *f*, número *m*; *see also* **statistics**

statistical [stə'tɪstɪkəl] ADJ estadístico; **~ package** paquete *m* estadístico

statistically [stə'tɪstɪkəlɪ] ADV según las estadísticas; **to prove sth ~** probar algo por medios estadísticos; **~, that may be true** según las estadísticas *or* estadísticamente, puede ser cierto

statistician [ˌstætɪs'tɪʃən] N estadístico/a *m/f*

statistics [stə'tɪstɪks] Ⓐ NSING (= *subject*) estadística *f*
Ⓑ NPL (= *numbers*) estadísticas *fpl*; *see* **vital C**

stative ['steɪtɪv] ADJ (*Gram*) **~ verb** verbo *m* de estado

stator ['steɪtə^r] N estator *m*

stats* [stæts] NPL ABBR = **statistics**

statuary ['stætjʊərɪ] Ⓐ ADJ estatuario
Ⓑ N (= *art*) estatuaria *f*; (= *statues*) estatuas *fpl*

statue ['stætjuː] N estatua *f*; **the Statue of Liberty** la estatua de la libertad

statuesque [ˌstætjʊ'esk] ADJ escultural

statuette [ˌstætjʊ'et] N figurilla *f*, estatuilla *f*

stature ['stætʃə^r] N [1] (= *size*) estatura *f*, talla *f*; **to be of short ~** ser de baja estatura
[2] (*fig*) rango *m*, estatus *m inv*; **to have sufficient ~ for a post** estar a la altura de un cargo; **he lacks moral ~** le falta carácter

status ['steɪtəs] Ⓐ N (*pl* **statuses**) [1] [*of person*] (*legal*) estado *m*; [*of agreement*] situación *f*; **marital ~** estado *m* civil; **social ~** posición *f* social, estatus *m inv*; **the ~ of the Black population** la posición social de la población negra
[2] (= *rank, prestige*) **what is his ~ in the profession?** ¿qué rango ocupa en la profesión?, ¿cómo se le considera en la profesión?
Ⓑ CPD ► **status inquiry** N comprobación *f* de valoración crediticia ► **status line** N (*Comput*) línea *f* de situación ► **status quo** N (e)statu quo *m* ► **status report** N informe *m* situacional ► **status symbol** N símbolo *m* de rango

statute ['stætjuːt] Ⓐ N ley *f*, estatuto *m*; **by ~** según la ley, de acuerdo con la ley
Ⓑ CPD ► **statute book** N (*esp Brit*) código *m* de leyes; **in** *or* **on the ~ book** en el código de leyes ► **statute law** N derecho *m* escrito

statutory ['stætjʊtərɪ] Ⓐ ADJ [1] reglamentario, estatutario; [*holiday, right etc*] legal; **~ meeting** junta *f* ordinaria
[2] (*pej*) (= *token*) **I was the ~ woman on the committee** yo tan sólo estaba en el comité porque la ley exigía que hubiese una mujer
[3] (= *expected, predictable*) consabido
Ⓑ CPD ► **statutory rape** N (*US Jur*) *relaciones sexuales con un(a) menor*

staunch[1] [stɔːntʃ] ADJ (*compar* **stauncher**; *superl* **staunchest**) leal, firme

staunch[2] [stɔːntʃ] VT [+ *bleeding*] restañar

staunchly ['stɔːntʃlɪ] ADV lealmente, firmemente

staunchness ['stɔːntʃnɪs] N lealtad *f*, firmeza *f*

stave [steɪv] N [1] [*of barrel*] duela *f*; [*of ladder*] peldaño *m*
[2] (*Mus*) pentagrama *m*
[3] (*Literat*) estrofa *f*

► **stave in** VT + ADV (*pt, pp* **stove in**) desfondar

► **stave off** VT + ADV (*pt, pp* **staved off**) [+ *attack, crisis, illness*] evitar; [+ *threat etc*] evitar, conjurar; (*temporarily*) aplazar, posponer

staves [steɪvz] NPL *of* **staff**[1]

stay[1] [steɪ] Ⓐ VI [1] (*in place*) [1·1] (= *remain*) quedarse, permanecer (*more frm*); **she came for a weekend and ~ed three years** vino a pasar el fin de semana y se quedó tres años; **you ~ right there** no te muevas de ahí, quédate ahí; **to ~ at home** quedarse en casa; **video recorders are here to ~** los vídeos no son una simple moda pasajera; **to ~ in bed** guardar cama; **to ~ put** (*on spot*) no moverse; (*in same house, city, job*) quedarse; **did you ~ till the end of the speeches?** ¿te quedaste hasta el final de los discursos?; **can you ~ to dinner?** ¿puedes quedarte a cenar?
[1·2] (*as guest*) (*with friends, relatives*) quedarse, alojarse; (*in hotel*) alojarse, hospedarse; **to ~ with friends** quedarse *or* hospedarse *or* alojarse en casa de unos amigos; **I'm ~ing with my aunt for a few days** estoy pasando unos días en casa de mi tía; **he's ~ing at my house** está *or* se aloja en mi casa; **where are you ~ing?** ¿dónde te alojas *or* hospedas?; **I'm**

~ing at the Europa Hotel estoy *or* me alojo *or* me hospedo en el Hotel Europa; **where do you ~ when you go to London?** ¿dónde te sueles alojar *or* hospedar cuando vas a Londres?; **did he ~ the night?** ¿se quedó a pasar la noche?, ¿se quedó a dormir?
1·3 (*Scot*) (= *live*) vivir; **where do you ~?** ¿dónde vives?
2 (*in current state*) seguir, quedarse; **it ~s motionless for hours** se queda *or* se mantiene inmóvil durante horas; **I just hope the public ~ loyal to us** sólo espero que el público siga (siendo) fiel *or* se mantenga fiel a nosotros; **if only we could ~ this young for ever** ojalá pudiéramos quedarnos así de jóvenes para siempre; **she didn't ~ a teacher for long** no siguió mucho tiempo de profesora; **she didn't ~ a spinster for long** no se quedó soltera mucho tiempo; **to ~ ahead of the competition** mantenerse a la cabeza de la competencia; **to ~ awake** quedarse despierto; **the unemployment rate ~ed below four per cent** el índice de paro continuó *or* siguió por debajo de un cuatro por ciento; **I tried to ~ calm** intenté mantener la calma; **he ~ed faithful to his wife** se mantuvo fiel a su mujer; **if it ~s fine** si continúa el buen tiempo, si el tiempo sigue siendo bueno; **I hope we can ~ friends** espero que podamos seguir siendo amigos; **to ~ healthy** mantenerse en buen estado de salud; **things can't be allowed to ~ like this** no podemos permitir que las cosas sigan así; **pubs should be allowed to ~ open until one a.m.** debería permitirse que los bares estuvieran abiertos hasta la una de la mañana; **while prices rise, our pensions ~ the same** aunque los precios suben, nuestras pensiones siguen igual; **to ~ together** seguir juntos; **they are unbeaten and look likely to ~ that way** nadie los ha vencido y parece que nadie va a hacerlo; **~ with it!*** ¡sigue adelante!, ¡no te desanimes!
Ⓑ VT 1 (*Jur*) (= *delay*) [+ *execution, proceedings*] suspender
2 (= *last out*) [+ *distance*] aguantar, resistir; [+ *race*] terminar; **to ~ the course** terminar la carrera; (*fig*) aguantar hasta el final; **to ~ the pace** (*lit, fig*) aguantar el ritmo
3 (= *check*) [+ *epidemic*] tener a raya; [+ *hunger*] matar, engañar; ✦***IDIOM*** **to ~ one's hand** contenerse
Ⓒ N 1 (= *short period*) estancia *f*, estadía *f* (*LAm*); **this will involve a short ~ in hospital** esto supondrá una corta estancia en el hospital; **during our ~ in London** durante nuestra estancia en Londres; **he is in Rome for a short ~** está en Roma para una estancia corta; **our second ~ in Murcia** nuestra segunda visita a Murcia; **come for a longer ~ next year** el año que viene vente más tiempo
2 (*Jur*) suspensión *f*, prórroga *f*; **~ of execution** aplazamiento *m* de la sentencia

►**stay away** VI + ADV 1 (= *keep at a distance*) (*from person, building*) no acercarse (**from** a); **~ away from my daughter!** ¡no te acerques a mi hija!; **~ away from that machine** no te acerques a esa máquina; **~ away from here** no vuelvas por aquí; **tourists were warned to ~ away from the beaches** se aconsejó a los turistas que no fueran a las playas; **~ away from chocolate** el chocolate ni lo pruebes
2 (= *not attend, be absent*) (*from event*) no acudir (**from** a); **they decided to ~ away from the Olympics** decidieron no acudir a las Olimpiadas; **not all employees ~ed away from work during the strike** durante la huelga, no todos los empleados se abstuvieron de ir a trabajar

►**stay behind** VI + ADV (*after work, school*) quedarse; **they made him ~ behind after school** le hicieron quedarse en la escuela después de las clases; **he usually ~s behind until the last lap** (*Sport*) generalmente se queda atrás hasta la última vuelta

►**stay down** VI + ADV 1 (= *not increase*) mantenerse al mismo nivel, no subir; **we have to ensure inflation ~s down** tenemos que asegurarnos de que la inflación se mantiene al mismo nivel *or* no sube
2 (= *not get up*) no levantarse; (= *remain lying*) permanecer tendido; **~ down!** ¡no te levantes!; **when he ~ed down and didn't move we realized there was a problem** cuando vimos que permanecía tendido sin moverse nos dimos cuenta que le pasaba algo
3 (= *remain under water*) permanecer bajo el agua
4 (*Scol*) (*in lower class*) repetir el curso
5 (*Sport*) (*in lower division*) **the team will have to ~ down again next year** el año que viene el equipo tendrá que seguir en la división a la que había descendido
6 [*food*] **nothing he eats will ~ down** no retiene nada de lo que come, vomita todo lo que come; **rice was the only thing that would ~ down** el arroz era lo único que no vomitaba *or* que retenía

►**stay in** VI + ADV 1 (*at home*) quedarse en casa, no salir
2 (*after school*) quedarse (depués de las clases); **I was made to ~ in (after school)** me hicieron quedarme después de las clases
3 (*in place*) **the filling only ~ed in for a week** el empaste duró sólo una semana; **the nail doesn't seem to want to ~ in** parece que el clavo no quiere quedarse en su sitio; **this paragraph must ~ in** hay que dejar este párrafo

►**stay on** VI + ADV 1 [*person*] (*in job, at school*) seguir, quedarse; (*after party*) quedarse; **he ~ed on as manager** siguió *or* se quedó en la empresa de gerente; **fewer teenagers are ~ing on at school** cada vez menos adolescentes siguen *or* se quedan en la escuela
2 [*lid, top*] quedarse en su sitio; **her wig wouldn't ~ on** no había forma de que la peluca se quedara en su sitio

►**stay out** VI + ADV 1 (= *not come home*) **she ~ed out all night** pasó *or* estuvo toda la noche fuera, no volvió a casa en toda la noche; **get out and ~ out!** ¡vete y no vuelvas!
2 (= *remain outside*) quedarse fuera; **let's ~ out in the sun** quedémosnos fuera al sol
3 (*on strike*) seguir en huelga
4 **to ~ out of** [+ *trouble, discussion*] no meterse en; **she warned her son to ~ out of trouble** advirtió a su hijo que no se metiera en líos*; **~ out of this!** ¡no te metas!; **try to ~ out of sight while he's around** procura pasar desapercibido mientras él está por aquí; **~ out of my sight!** ¡no te quiero ni ver!; **to ~ out of the sun** quedarse a la sombra

►**stay over** VI + ADV pasar la noche, quedarse a dormir

►**stay up** VI + ADV 1 (= *not fall*) [*tent*] mantenerse de pie; [*trousers*] no caerse; **my trousers won't ~ up** los pantalones se me caen; **my zip won't ~ up** la cremallera se me cae; **the tent wouldn't ~ up** no había forma de que la tienda se mantuviera de pie
2 (= *not go to bed*) quedarse levantado; **I'd rather not ~ up too late** preferiría no quedarme levantado hasta muy tarde; **we ~ed up late to see a film** nos quedamos levantados hasta tarde para ver una película; **he ~ed up all night working** se quedó toda la noche trabajando; **don't ~ up for me** no te quedes levantado esperándome
3 (*Sport*) (*in higher division*) **the team ~s up** el equipo no desciende, el equipo mantiene la categoría

stay² [steɪ] Ⓐ N 1 (*Mech*) sostén *m*, soporte *m*, puntal *m*
2 (*Naut*) estay *m*
3 (= *guy rope*) viento *m*
4 **stays** (= *corset*) corsé *m*
5 (*fig*) sostén *m*, apoyo *m*; **the ~ of one's old age** el sostén de su vejez
Ⓑ VT (*frm*) sostener, apoyar, apuntalar; **this will ~ you till lunchtime** con esto te mantendrás hasta la comida, esto engañará el hambre hasta la comida

stay-at-home [ˈsteɪəthəʊm] Ⓐ ADJ casero, hogareño
Ⓑ N persona *f* hogareña, persona *f* casera

stayer [ˈsteɪəʳ] Ⓐ N (*Horse racing*) *caballo de mucha resistencia, apto para carreras de distancia*; (*fig*) persona *f* de mucho aguante *or* resistencia
Ⓑ CPD ► **staying power** N aguante *m*, resistencia *f*

staysail [ˈsteɪseɪl, (*Naut*) ˈsteɪsl] N vela *f* de estay

STD Ⓐ N ABBR 1 (*Brit Telec*) = **Subscriber Trunk Dialling**
2 (*Med*) (= **sexually transmitted disease**) ETS *f*
Ⓑ CPD ► **STD code** N prefijo *m* para conferencias interurbanas (automáticas)

stead [sted] N **in sb's ~** en lugar de algn; **to stand sb in good ~** ser muy útil a algn

steadfast [ˈstedfəst] ADJ [*person*] firme, resuelto; [*gaze*] fijo; **~ in adversity** firme en el infortunio; **~ in danger** impertérrito; **~ in love** constante en el amor

steadfastly [ˈstedfəstlɪ] ADV firmemente, resueltamente

steadfastness [ˈstedfəstnɪs] N (= *determination*) firmeza *f*, resolución *f*; (= *loyalty*) constancia *f*; (= *tenacity*) [*of resistance*] tenacidad *f*

steadily [ˈstedɪlɪ] ADV 1 (= *continuously*) [*improve, grow, move, advance*] a un ritmo constante, de manera *or* forma continuada, de manera *or* forma constante; [*increase, rise*] a un ritmo constante; [*work*] a un ritmo constante; (*without stopping*) sin parar; [*rain*] ininterrumpidamente; **it gets ~ worse** se pone cada vez peor; **a ~ increasing number of people** un número cada vez mayor de gente
2 (= *regularly*) [*breathe, beat*] regularmente
3 (= *calmly*) [*speak*] con firmeza; [*gaze, look*] fijamente, sin pestañear
4 (= *firmly*) [*walk*] con paso seguro; [*hold, grasp*] firmemente

steadiness [ˈstedɪnɪs] N 1 (= *regularity*) [*of demand, supply, rain, temperature*] lo constante; [*of decline, increase, improvement, flow*] lo continuo; [*of pace, breathing*] regularidad *f*; [*of currency, prices, economy*] estabilidad *f*
2 (= *calmness*) [*of voice*] firmeza *f*; [*of gaze*] lo fijo; [*of nerves*] lo templado
3 (= *firmness*) [*of chair, table, ladder*] lo firme; [*of boat*] lo estable; **it requires ~ of hand** se necesita buen pulso
4 (= *reliability*) [*of person*] formalidad *f*, seriedad *f*

steady [ˈstedɪ] Ⓐ ADJ (*compar* **steadier**; *superl* **steadiest**) 1 (= *continuous*) [*decline, increase, improvement, flow*] continuo; [*demand, wind, supply*] constante; [*rain*] constante, ininterrumpido; [*breathing, beat*] regular; [*temperature*] constante, uniforme; **we were going at a ~ 70kph** íbamos a una velocidad constante de 70kph; **there was a ~ downpour for**

three hours llovió durante tres horas ininterrumpidamente *or* sin parar; **he plays a very ~ game** juega sin altibajos; **to hold** *or* **keep sth ~** [+ *prices, demand*] mantener algo estable; **he doesn't have a ~ income** no tiene ingresos regulares *or* estables; **a ~ job** un empleo fijo; **at a ~ pace** a paso regular *or* constante; **we have been making ~ progress** hemos ido mejorando de forma continuada *or* constante; **we have a ~ stream of visitors** tenemos un flujo constante de visitantes
[2] (= *calm*) [*voice*] firme; [*gaze*] fijo; [*nerves*] templado
[3] (= *firm*) [*chair, table*] firme, seguro; [*boat*] estable; **a ~ hand** un pulso firme; **hold the camera ~** no muevas la cámara; **the unemployment rate is holding ~ at 7.3%** el índice de paro se mantiene estable a un 7,3%; **to be ~ on one's feet** caminar con paso seguro; **the car is not very ~ on corners** el coche no es muy estable en las curvas
[4] (= *reliable*) [*person*] formal, serio
[5] (= *regular*) [*boyfriend, girlfriend*] formal; [*relationship*] estable
Ⓑ ADV [1] (*in exclamations*) **~! you're rocking the boat** ¡quieto! estás haciendo que se balancee la barca; **~ as she goes!** (*Naut*) ¡mantenga el rumbo!; **~ on! there's no need to lose your temper** ¡tranquilo! no hay necesidad de perder los estribos
[2] (*) **to go ~ with sb** ser novio formal de algn; **they're going ~** son novios formales
Ⓒ N (†*) novio/a *m/f*
Ⓓ VT [1] (= *stabilize*) [+ *wobbling object*] estabilizar; [+ *chair, table*] (*with hands*) sujetar para que no se mueva; (*with wedge*) poner un calzo a (para que no cojee); **two men steadied the ladder** dos hombres sujetaron la escalera para que no se moviese; **to ~ o.s.** equilibrarse; **to ~ o.s. against** *or* **on sth** recobrar el equilibrio apoyándose en algo
[2] (= *compose*) [+ *nervous person*] calmar, tranquilizar; [+ *wild person*] apaciguar; [+ *horse*] tranquilizar; **to ~ o.s.** calmarse, tranquilizarse; **she smokes to ~ her nerves** fuma para calmar los nervios; **she breathed in to ~ her voice** aspiró para hacer que su voz sonase tranquila
Ⓔ VI [1] (= *stop moving*) dejar de moverse; **the shadows from the lamp steadied** las sombras que hacía la lámpara dejaron de moverse
[2] (= *grow calm*) [*voice*] calmarse; [*prices, market*] estabilizarse, hacerse más estable; **to have a ~ing influence on sb** ejercer una buena influencia sobre algn

steak [steɪk] Ⓐ N (= *one piece*) filete *m* *or* bistec *m* de vaca, filete *m* *or* bistec *m* de res (*LAm*), bife *m* (*Andes, S. Cone*); (*for stewing etc*) carne *f* de vaca *or* res; (= *barbecued steak*) churrasco *m* (*And, S. Cone*)
Ⓑ CPD ► **steak and kidney pie** N pastel *m* de carne y riñones ► **steak house** N asador *m* ► **steak knife** N cuchillo *m* para la carne

steal [stiːl] (*pt* **stole**; *pp* **stolen**) Ⓐ VT [1] (= *take*) [+ *object*] robar, hurtar (*frm*); [+ *idea*] robar; **to ~ sth from sb** robar algo a algn; **he stole it from school** lo robó del colegio; **she used to ~ money from her parents** solía robar dinero a sus padres; **she stole her best friend's boyfriend (from her)** (le) robó el novio a su mejor amiga; ✦**IDIOMS to ~ sb's heart** robar el corazón a algn; **to ~ a march on sb*** adelantarse a algn; **to ~ the show** llevarse todos los aplausos, acaparar la atención de todos; **to ~ sb's thunder** eclipsar a algn
[2] (*liter*) (= *sneak*) **to ~ a glance at sb** mirar a algn de soslayo, echar una mirada de soslayo a algn; **to ~ a kiss from sb** robar un beso a algn
Ⓑ VI [1] (= *take things*) robar; **to ~ from sb** robar a algn
[2] (= *creep*) [2·1] **to ~ into a room** entrar sigilosamente en una habitación, entrar en una habitación a hurtadillas; **to ~ out of a room** salir sigilosamente de una habitación, salir de una habitación a hurtadillas; **to ~ up/down the stairs** subir/bajar sigilosamente las escaleras, subir/bajar las escaleras a hurtadillas; **to ~ up on sb** acercarse a algn sigilosamente
[2·2] (*fig*) **a smile stole across her lips** una sonrisa se escapó de sus labios; **a tear stole down her cheek** una lágrima se deslizó por su mejilla; **the light was ~ing through the shutters** la luz se filtraba por las contraventanas
Ⓒ N (*) (= *bargain*) **it's a ~** es una ganga* *or* un regalo*
►**steal away** VI + ADV escabullirse, irse furtivamente; **the intruders stole away into the night** los intrusos se escabulleron en la noche

stealing ['stiːlɪŋ] N robo *m*, hurto *m* (*frm*); **there have been cases of ~** ha habido casos de robo *or* (*frm*) hurto; **~ is wrong** robar *or* (*frm*) hurtar está mal

stealth [stelθ] N sigilo *m*; **by ~** a hurtadillas, sigilosamente

stealthily ['stelθɪlɪ] ADV a hurtadillas, sigilosamente

stealthiness ['stelθɪnɪs] N sigilo *m*

stealthy ['stelθɪ] ADJ (*compar* **stealthier**; *superl* **stealthiest**) cauteloso, sigiloso

steam [stiːm] Ⓐ N vapor *m*; **to get up** *or* **pick up ~** dar presión; **full ~ ahead!** (*Naut*) ¡a todo vapor!; **the ship went on under its own ~** el buque siguió adelante con sus propios motores; ✦**IDIOMS to go full ~ ahead with sth** avanzar a toda marcha con algo; **to let off ~** desahogarse; **under one's own ~** por sus propios medios *or* propias fuerzas; **to run out of ~** quedar sin fuerza
Ⓑ VT [1] (*Culin*) cocer al vapor
[2] **to ~ open an envelope** abrir un sobre con vapor; **to ~ a stamp off** despegar un sello con vapor
Ⓒ VI [1] (= *give off steam*) echar vapor; **the bowl was ~ing on the table** la cacerola humeaba encima de la mesa
[2] (= *move*) **we were ~ing at 12 knots** íbamos a 12 nudos, navegábamos a 12 nudos; **to ~ ahead** (*lit*) avanzar; (*fig*) adelantarse mucho; **to ~ along** avanzar (echando vapor); **the ship ~ed into harbour** el buque entró al puerto echando vapor; **the train ~ed out** salió el tren
Ⓓ CPD ► **steam bath** N baño *m* de vapor ► **steam engine** N máquina *f* de vapor ► **steam hammer** N martillo *m* pilón ► **steam heat** N calor *m* por vapor ► **steam iron** N plancha *f* de vapor ► **steam organ** N órgano *m* de vapor ► **steam shovel** N (*US*) pala *f* mecánica de vapor, excavadora *f* ► **steam turbine** N turbina *f* de vapor
►**steam up** Ⓐ VI + ADV [*window*] empañarse
Ⓑ VT + ADV [+ *window*] empañar; **the windows quickly get ~ed up** las ventanas se empañan enseguida; ✦**IDIOM to get ~ed up about sth*** (= *angry*) ponerse negro por algo; (= *worried*) preocuparse por algo; **don't get ~ed up!*** ¡no te exaltes!, ¡cálmate!

steamboat ['stiːmbəʊt] N vapor *m*, buque *m* de vapor

steam-driven ['stiːm,drɪvn] ADJ impulsado por vapor, a vapor

steamer ['stiːməʳ] N [1] (*Culin*) olla *f* de estofar
[2] (*Naut*) vapor *m*, buque *m* de vapor

steaming ['stiːmɪŋ] ADJ [1] [*kettle, plate*] humeante
[2] (*) (= *angry*) negro*, furioso
[3] (*Scot**) (= *drunk*) mamado*

steamroller ['stiːm,rəʊləʳ] Ⓐ N apisonadora *f*
Ⓑ VT [1] (*lit*) allanar con apisonadora
[2] (*fig*) aplastar, arrollar; **to ~ a bill through Parliament** hacer aprobar un proyecto de ley por mayoría aplastante *or* arrolladora

steamship ['stiːmʃɪp] Ⓐ N vapor *m*, buque *m* de vapor
Ⓑ CPD ► **steamship company, steamship line** N compañía *f* naviera

steamy ['stiːmɪ] ADJ (*compar* **steamier**; *superl* **steamiest**) [1] [*room etc*] lleno de vapor; [*atmosphere*] húmedo y caluroso; [*window*] empañado
[2] (*) [*film, novel*] erótico; [*relationship*] apasionado

steed [stiːd] N (*liter*) corcel *m*

steel [stiːl] Ⓐ N [1] (= *metal*) acero *m*; **nerves of ~** nervios *mpl* de acero; ✦**IDIOM to fight with cold ~** luchar con armas blancas
[2] (= *sharpener*) chaira *f*, eslabón *m*; (*for striking spark*) eslabón *m*
Ⓑ VT **to ~ one's heart** endurecer el corazón; **to ~ o.s.** fortalecerse (**against** contra); **to ~ o.s. for sth** cobrar ánimo para algo; **to ~ o.s. to do sth** cobrar ánimo para hacer algo
Ⓒ CPD de acero ► **steel band** N (*Mus*) *banda de percusión del Caribe* ► **steel guitar** N guitarra *f* de cordaje metálico ► **steel helmet** N casco *m* (de acero) ► **steel industry** N industria *f* siderúrgica ► **steel maker, steel manufacturer** N fabricante *mf* de acero ► **steel mill** N fundición *f*, fundidora *f* (*LAm*) ► **steel tape** N cinta *f* métrica de acero ► **steel wool** N estropajo *m* de aluminio

steel-clad ['stiːlklæd] ADJ revestido de acero, acorazado

steel-grey [,stiːl'greɪ] ADJ gris metálico

steel-plated [,stiːl'pleɪtɪd] ADJ chapado en acero

steelworker ['stiːl,wɜːkəʳ] N trabajador(a) *m/f* siderúrgico/a

steelworks ['stiːlwɜːks] NSING fundición *f*, fundidora *f* (*LAm*)

steely ['stiːlɪ] ADJ (*compar* **steelier**; *superl* **steeliest**) acerado; (*fig*) [*determination*] inflexible; [*gaze*] duro, de acero; **~ blue** azul metálico

steelyard ['stiːljɑːd] N romana *f*

steely-eyed [,stiːlɪ'aɪd] ADJ de mirada penetrante

steep[1] [stiːp] ADJ (*compar* **steeper**; *superl* **steepest**) [1] [*hill, cliff*] empinado, escarpado; [*stairs, slope, climb*] empinado; **it's too ~ for the tractor** está demasiado pendiente para el tractor, la pendiente es demasiado empinada para el tractor; **it's a ~ climb to the top** hay una subida empinada hasta la cumbre
[2] (= *sharp*) [*drop*] abrupto, brusco; [*increase*] pronunciado
[3] (*) [*price, demands*] excesivo
[4] (*Brit**) (= *unreasonable*) **that's pretty ~!** ¡eso es demasiado!, ¡no hay derecho!; **it's a bit ~ that you've got to do it yourself** no es justo que lo tengas que hacer tú solo

steep[2] [stiːp] Ⓐ VT [1] [+ *washing*] remojar, poner a *or* en remojo (**in** en)
[2] **~ed in** (*fig*) impregnado de; **a town ~ed in history** una ciudad cargada *or* impregnada de historia; **she is ~ed in the Celtic tradition** ella está empapada de la tradición celta; **a ceremony which is ~ed in ancient tradition** una ceremonia que hunde sus raíces en la más antigua tradición; **he was ~ed in the**

religion and laws of Judaism estaba imbuido de la religión y las leyes judaicas
Ⓑ VI **to leave sth to ~** dejar algo a *or* en remojo

steeple ['sti:pl] N aguja *f*, chapitel *m*

steeplechase ['sti:pl,tʃeɪs] N carrera *f* de obstáculos

steeplechasing ['sti:pl,tʃeɪsɪŋ] N deporte *m* de las carreras de obstáculos

steeplejack ['sti:pldʒæk] N *reparador de chimeneas, torres etc*

steeply ['sti:plɪ] ADV **the mountain rises ~** la montaña está cortada a pico; **the road climbs ~** la carretera sube muy empinada; **prices have risen ~** los precios han subido muchísimo

steepness ['sti:pnɪs] N [*of hill, cliff*] lo empinado, lo escarpado; [*of stairs, climb*] lo empinado; [*of drop*] lo abrupto, brusquedad *f*; [*of increase*] lo pronunciado

steer¹ [stɪəʳ] Ⓐ VT 1 [+ *car, van*] conducir, manejar (*LAm*); [+ *trolley*] llevar, conducir; [+ *ship*] gobernar; **he ~ed the wheelbarrow along the garden path** llevó la carretilla por la senda del jardín; **to ~ one's way through a crowd** abrirse paso por entre una multitud; **you nearly ~ed us into that rock** por poco nos llevas contra aquella roca
2 (= *lead*) [+ *person*] dirigir, llevar; [+ *conversation etc*] llevar; **I ~ed her across to the bar** la dirigí hacia el bar; **he ~ed me into a good job*** me enchufó para un buen trabajo*
Ⓑ VI [*car*] conducir, manejar (*LAm*); [*ship*] gobernar; **who's going to ~?** (*in car*) ¿quién manejará el volante?; (*in boat*) ¿quién manejará el timón?; **you ~ and I'll push** tú ponte al volante y yo empujo; **can you ~?** ¿sabes gobernar el barco *etc*?; **to ~ for sth** dirigirse hacia algo; ✦***IDIOM*** **to ~ clear of sb/sth** esquivar a algn/evadir algo
Ⓒ N (*US**) (= *tip, advice*) **to sell sb a bum ~** dar información falsa a algn

steer² [stɪəʳ] N (= *bull*) novillo *m*

steerage ['stɪərɪdʒ] N (*Naut*) entrepuente *m*; **to go ~** viajar en tercera clase

steering ['stɪərɪŋ] Ⓐ N (*Aut etc*) dirección *f*, conducción *f*; (*Naut*) gobierno *m*
Ⓑ CPD ► **steering arm** N brazo *m* de dirección ► **steering column** N columna *f* de dirección ► **steering committee** N comité *m* de dirección ► **steering lock** N (*Aut*) (= *anti-theft device*) dispositivo *m* antirrobo; (= *turning circle*) capacidad *f* de giro ► **steering wheel** N volante *m*, manubrio *m* (*LAm*)

steersman ['stɪəzmən] N (*pl* **steersmen**) (*Naut*) timonero *m*

stellar ['steləʳ] ADJ estelar

stem¹ [stem] Ⓐ N 1 [*of plant*] tallo *m*; [*of tree*] tronco *m*; [*of leaf*] pedúnculo *m*; [*of glass*] pie *m*; [*of pipe*] tubo *m*, cañón *m*; (*Mech*) vástago *m*; [*of word*] tema *m*
2 (*Naut*) roda *f*, tajamar *m*; **from ~ to stern** de proa a popa
Ⓑ VI **to ~ from sth** ser el resultado de algo
Ⓒ CPD ► **stem cell** N célula *f* madre ► **stem cell research** N investigación *f* con células madre

stem² [stem] VT (= *check, stop*) [+ *blood*] restañar; [+ *attack, flood*] detener; **to ~ the tide of events** detener el curso de los acontecimientos

stench [stentʃ] N hedor *m*

stencil ['stensl] Ⓐ N (*for lettering etc*) plantilla *f*; (*for typing*) cliché *m*, clisé *m*
Ⓑ VT estarcir; (*in typing*) hacer un cliché de

stenographer [ste'nɒgrəfəʳ] N (*US*) taquígrafo/a *m/f*, estenógrafo/a *m/f*

stenography [ste'nɒgrəfɪ] N (*US*) taquigrafía *f*, estenografía *f*

stentorian [sten'tɔ:rɪən] ADJ (*liter*) estentóreo

STEP [step] N ABBR = **Science and Technology for Environmental Protection**

step [step] Ⓐ N 1 (= *movement*) (*lit, fig*) paso *m*; (= *sound*) paso *m*, pisada *f*; **with slow ~s** con pasos lentos; **he heard ~s outside** oyó pasos *or* pisadas fuera; **to take a ~ back** dar un paso atrás; **it's a big ~ for him** es un gran paso *or* salto para él; **~ by ~** (*lit, fig*) poco a poco; **to be a ~ closer to doing sth** estar más cerca de hacer algo; **at every ~** (*lit, fig*) a cada paso; **we'll keep you informed every ~ of the way** le mantendremos informado en todo momento; **I'll fight this decision every ~ of the way** voy a oponerme a esta decisión hasta el final; **the first ~ is to decide ...** el primer paso es decidir ...; **to follow in sb's ~s** seguir los pasos de algn; **it's a great ~ forward** es un gran paso *or* salto adelante; **to take a ~ forward** dar un paso adelante; **I would go one ~ further and make all guns illegal** yo iría aún más lejos y prohibiría todo tipo de armas de fuego; **what's the next ~?** ¿cuál es el siguiente paso?; **it's a ~ in the right direction** es un paso adelante; **a ~ towards peace** un paso hacia la paz; **to turn one's ~s towards sth** dirigir los pasos hacia algo; **it's a ~ up in his career** es un ascenso en su carrera profesional; **it's a bit of a ~ up from the house where I was born** es mucho mejor que la casa en la que nací; **to watch one's ~** (*lit, fig*) ir con cuidado; ✦***IDIOMS*** **to be one ~ ahead of sb** llevar ventaja a *or* sobre algn; **to keep one ~ ahead (of)** mantenerse en una posición de ventaja (con respecto a); **it's a case of one ~ forward, two ~s back** es un caso típico de un paso adelante y dos hacia atrás; *see also* **false A1, spring A4**
2 (*in dancing, marching*) paso *m*; **to break ~** romper el paso; **he quickly fell into ~ beside me** no tardó en ajustar su paso al mío; **to be in ~ with sb** (*lit*) llevar el paso de algn; **the party is in ~ with the country** el partido está en sintonía con el país; **to be in ~ with public opinion** sintonizar con la opinión pública; **the bright colours are perfectly in ~ with the current mood** los colores vivos reflejan perfectamente el clima actual; **to be/keep in ~ (with)** (*in marching*) llevar el paso (de); (*in dance*) llevar el compás *or* ritmo (de); **to be out of ~** (*in marching*) no llevar el paso; (*in dance*) no llevar el compás *or* el ritmo; **to get out of ~** (*in march*) perder el paso; (*in dance*) perder el ritmo *or* compás; ✦***IDIOM*** **to be out of ~ with sth/sb** no estar sintonizado con algo/algn; **to fall** *or* **get out of ~ with sth/sb** desconectarse de algo/algn
3 (= *distance*) paso *m*; **I'm just a ~ away if you need me** si me necesitas, sólo estoy a un paso; **the beach is just a ~ away (from the hotel)** la playa está a un paso (del hotel); **it's a good ~** *or* **quite a ~ to the village*** el pueblo queda bastante lejos
4 (= *footprint*) huella *f*
5 (= *measure*) medida *f*; **to take ~s** tomar medidas; **we must take ~s to improve things** tenemos que tomar medidas para mejorar la situación
6 (= *stair*) peldaño *m*, escalón *m*; (*on bus*) peldaño *m*, estribo *m*; (*also* **doorstep**) escalón *m* de la puerta; **"mind the step"** "cuidado con el escalón"; **I'll meet you on the library ~s** quedamos en los escalones *or* la escalinata de la biblioteca; **a flight of stone ~s** un tramo de escalera *or* de escalones de piedra
7 **steps** (= *stepladder*) escalera *f* (de mano/de tijera)
8 (*in scale*) peldaño *m*, grado *m*; **to get onto the next ~ in the salary scale** ascender un peldaño *or* subir de grado en la escala salarial
9 (*also* **~ aerobics**) step *m*
10 (*US Mus*) tono *m*
Ⓑ VI 1 (= *walk*) **to ~ on board** subir a bordo; **won't you ~ inside?** ¿no quiere pasar?; **he ~ped into the room** entró en la habitación; **he ~ped into his slippers/trousers** se puso las zapatillas/los pantalones; **to ~ off a bus/plane/train** bajarse de un autobús/avión/tren; **as he ~ped onto the pavement ...** al poner el pie en la acera ...; **as she ~ped out of the car** al bajar del coche; **she looked as if she had ~ped out of a fairytale** parecía recién salida de un cuento de hadas; **she ~ped out of her dress** se quitó el vestido (por abajo); **I had to ~ outside for a breath of fresh air** tuve que salir fuera a tomar el aire; **to ~ over sth** pasar por encima de algo; **~ this way** haga el favor de pasar por aquí; ✦***IDIOM*** **to ~ out of line** desobedecer, romper las reglas; *see also* **shoe**
2 (= *tread*) **to ~ in/on sth** pisar algo; **don't ~ in that puddle** no te metas en ese charco; **~ on it!*** (= *hurry up*) ¡date prisa!, ¡ponte las pilas!*, ¡apúrate! (*LAm*); (*Aut*) ¡acelera!; **to ~ on the accelerator** (*Brit*) ◊ **~ on the gas** (*US*) pisar el acelerador; *see also* **toe**
Ⓒ CPD ► **step aerobics** N step *m*

►**step aside** VI + ADV (*lit*) hacerse a un lado, apartarse; **many would prefer to see him ~ aside in favour of a younger man** muchos preferirían que renunciase *or* dimitiese en favor de alguien más joven

►**step back** VI + ADV 1 (*lit*) dar un paso hacia atrás, retroceder; **it's like ~ping back in time** es como viajar hacia atrás *or* retroceder en el tiempo
2 (= *detach o.s.*) distanciarse un poco; **I needed to ~ back from the situation** necesitaba distanciarme un poco de la situación

►**step down** VI + ADV 1 (*lit*) bajar (**from** de)
2 (*fig*) (= *resign*) renunciar, dimitir; **to ~ down in favour of sb** renunciar *or* dimitir en favor de algn

►**step forward** VI + ADV 1 (*lit*) dar un paso hacia adelante 2 (*fig*) (= *volunteer*) ofrecerse

►**step in** VI + ADV 1 (*lit*) entrar 2 (*fig*) (= *intervene*) intervenir; (= *volunteer*) ofrecerse; **the government must ~ in and sort out this situation** el gobierno debe intervenir para solucionar esta situación; **Mrs White has kindly ~ped in to help us out** la Sra. White se ha ofrecido amablemente a ayudarnos

►**step out** Ⓐ VI + ADV 1 (= *go outside*) salir
2 (= *present o.s.*) presentarse, aparecer; **she likes to ~ out in designer clothes** le gusta presentarse *or* aparecer llevando ropa exclusiva
3 (†) (*romantically*) salir; **Jake is ~ping out with my niece** Jake sale con mi sobrina
4 (= *walk briskly*) apretar el paso
5 (*US**) **to ~ out on sb** ser infiel a algn
Ⓑ VT + ADV (= *measure*) [+ *distance*] medir a pasos

►**step up** Ⓐ VI + ADV **to ~ up to sth/sb** acercarse a algo/algn
Ⓑ VT + ADV 1 (= *increase*) [+ *production, sales*] aumentar; [+ *campaign*] intensificar; [+ *attacks, attempts, efforts*] intensificar, redoblar
2 (*Elec*) [+ *current*] aumentar

stepbrother ['step,brʌðəʳ] N hermanastro *m*

step-by-step [ˌstepbaɪˈstep] ADJ **~ instructions** instrucciones *fpl* paso a paso

stepchild [ˈsteptʃaɪld] N (*pl* **stepchildren**) hijastro/a *m/f*

stepdaughter [ˈstepˌdɔːtəʳ] N hijastra *f*

stepfather [ˈstepˌfɑːðəʳ] N padrastro *m*

Stephen [ˈstiːvn] N Esteban

stepladder [ˈstepˌlædəʳ] N escalera *f* de mano, escalera *f* de tijera

stepmother [ˈstepˌmʌðəʳ] N madrastra *f*

step-parent [ˈstepˌpeərənt] N (= *father*) padrastro *m*; (= *mother*) madrastra *f*

steppe [step] N (*also* **~s**) estepa *f*

stepping stone [ˈstepɪŋstəʊn] N 1 (*lit*) pasadera *f*
2 (*fig*) trampolín *m* (**to** para llegar a)

stepsister [ˈstepˌsɪstəʳ] N hermanastra *f*

stepson [ˈstepsʌn] N hijastro *m*

step-up [ˈstepʌp] N (= *increase*) (*in production, sales*) aumento *m*; (*in campaign, attempts, efforts*) intensificación *f*

ster. ABBR = **sterling**

stereo [ˈsterɪəʊ] (A) N (= *hi-fi equipment*) equipo *m* estereofónico; (= *sound*) estéreo *m*; **in ~** en estéreo
(B) ADJ estereofónico

stereo... [ˈsterɪəʊ] PREFIX estereo...

stereogram [ˈsterɪəgræm] N, **stereograph** [ˈsterɪəgræf] N estereografía *f*

stereophonic [ˌsterɪəˈfɒnɪk] ADJ estereofónico

stereophony [sterɪˈɒfənɪ] N estereofonía *f*

stereoscope [ˈsterɪəskəʊp] N estereoscopio *m*

stereoscopic [ˌsterɪəsˈkɒpɪk] ADJ estereoscópico; [*film*] tridimensional, en relieve

stereotype [ˈsterɪətaɪp] (A) N estereotipo *m*
(B) VT (*Typ*) clisar, estereotipar; (*fig*) estereotipar

stereotypical [ˌstɪərɪəˈtɪpɪkl] ADJ estereotípico

sterile [ˈsteraɪl] ADJ 1 (= *germ-free*) esterilizado
2 (= *infertile*) estéril

sterility [steˈrɪlɪtɪ] N esterilidad *f*

sterilization [ˌsterɪlaɪˈzeɪʃən] N esterilización *f*

sterilize [ˈsterɪlaɪz] VT (*gen*) esterilizar

sterling [ˈstɜːlɪŋ] (A) ADJ 1 (*Econ*) **pound ~** libra *f* esterlina; **~ traveller's cheques** cheques *mpl* de viaje en libras esterlinas
2 [*quality etc*] destacado; **a ~ character** una persona de toda confianza; **a person of ~ worth** una persona de grandes méritos
(B) N (= *currency*) (libras *fpl*) esterlinas *fpl*
(C) CPD ► **sterling area** N zona *f* de la libra esterlina ► **sterling balances** NPL balances *mpl* de libras esterlinas ► **sterling silver** N plata *f* de ley

stern[1] [stɜːn] ADJ (*compar* **sterner**; *superl* **sternest**) [*person, look*] severo; [*reprimand*] duro; **a ~ glance** una mirada severa; **a ~ warning** un serio aviso; **he was very ~ with me** fue muy duro conmigo; **but he was made of ~er stuff** pero él tenía más carácter

stern[2] [stɜːn] N (*Naut*) popa *f*

sternly [ˈstɜːnlɪ] ADV [*look*] severamente; [*reprimand*] severamente, con dureza; [*warn*] con seriedad

sternness [ˈstɜːnnɪs] N [*of person, look*] severidad *f*; [*of reprimand*] severidad *f*, dureza *f*

sternum [ˈstɜːnəm] N (*pl* **sternums** *or* **sterna**) esternón *m*

steroid [ˈstɪərɔɪd] N esteroide *m*

stertorous [ˈstɜːtərəs] ADJ (*frm*) estertoroso

stet [stet] VI (*Typ*) vale, deje como está

stethoscope [ˈsteθəskəʊp] N estetoscopio *m*

Stetson® [ˈstetsən] N sombrero *m* tejano

Steve [stiːv] N (*familiar form*) of **Stephen, Steven**

stevedore [ˈstiːvɪdɔːʳ] N estibador *m*

Steven [ˈstiːvn] N Esteban

stew [stjuː] (A) N 1 (*Culin*) estofado *m*, guisado *m* (*esp LAm*)
2 (*) ✦**IDIOM to be in a ~** sudar la gota gorda*
(B) VT [+ *meat*] estofar, guisar (*esp LAm*); [+ *fruit*] cocer, hacer una compota de; [+ *tea*] dejar que se repose; **~ed apples** compota *f* de manzanas
(C) VI [*tea*] quedarse reposando demasiado; ✦**IDIOM to let sb ~ in his/her own juice** dejar a algn que cueza en su propia salsa
(D) CPD ► **stew meat** N (*US*) carne *f* de vaca ► **stew pan, stew pot** N cazuela *f*, cacerola *f*, puchero *m*

steward [ˈstjuːəd] N (*on estate*) administrador(a) *m/f*, mayordomo *m*; (= *butler*) mayordomo *m*; (*Aer*) auxiliar *m* de vuelo, auxiliar *m* de cabina, aeromozo *m* (*LAm*), sobrecargo *m* (*Mex*), cabinero *m* (*Col*); (*Naut*) camarero *m*; (= *bouncer*) portero *m*, encargado/a *m/f* del servicio de orden y entrada; *see also* **shop D**

stewardess [ˈstjʊədes] N (*Aer*) azafata *f*, auxiliar *f* de vuelo *or* de cabina, aeromoza *f* (*LAm*), sobrecargo *f* (*Mex*), cabinera *f* (*Col*); (*Naut*) camarera *f*

stewardship [ˈstjʊədʃɪp] N administración *f*, gobierno *m*

stewing steak [ˈstjuːɪŋˌsteɪk] N (*Brit*) carne *f* de vaca *or* (*LAm*) res para estofar

St. Ex., St. Exch. ABBR = **Stock Exchange**

Stg, stg ABBR (= **sterling**) ester.

stick[1] [stɪk] (A) N 1 (= *length of wood*) (trozo *m* de) madera *f*; (*shaped*) palo *m*, vara *f*; (*as weapon*) palo *m*, porra *f*; (= *walking stick*) bastón *m*; (*Aer*) (= *joystick*) palanca *f* de mando; (*Hockey, Ice Hockey etc*) palo *m*; (= *drumstick*) palillo *m*; (*Mus**) (= *baton*) batuta *f*; **~ of furniture** mueble *m*; **to give sb the ~** ◊ **take the ~ to sb** dar palo a algn; ✦**IDIOMS to use** *or* **wield the big ~** amenazar con el garrote; **policy of the big ~** política *f* de la mano dura; **policy of the ~ and carrot** política *f* de incentivos y amenazas; **a ~ to beat sb with** un arma con la que atacar a algn; *see also* **cleft B, end A1**
2 [*of wax, gum, shaving soap*] barra *f*; [*of celery*] rama *f*; [*of dynamite*] cartucho *m*; [*of bombs*] grupo *m*
3 (*esp Brit**) (= *criticism*) **the critics gave him a lot of ~** los críticos le dieron una buena paliza*; **to get** *or* **take a lot of ~** recibir una buena paliza*, tener que aguantar mucho
4 **old ~** (*Brit*†*) tío* *m*; **he's a funny old ~** es un tío raro *or* divertido*
5 **sticks** 5·1 (*for the fire*) astillas *fpl*, leña *f*
5·2 (*Horse racing**) (= *hurdles*) obstáculos *mpl*
5·3 ✦**IDIOMS to live in the ~s*** vivir en el quinto pino *or* infierno; **to up ~s*** recoger los bártulos*
(B) CPD ► **stick insect** N insecto *m* palo ► **stick shift** N (*US Aut*) palanca *f* de marchas

stick[2] [stɪk] (*vb: pt, pp* **stuck**) (A) VT 1 (*with glue etc*) pegar, encolar; **he was ~ing stamps into his album** pegaba sellos en su álbum; **to ~ a poster on the wall** pegar un póster a la pared; **"stick no bills"** "prohibido fijar carteles"; **he tried to ~ the crime on his brother*** trató de colgar el crimen a su hermano*
2 (= *thrust, poke*) meter; (= *stab*) [+ *sth pointed*] clavar, hincar; **he stuck his hand in his pocket** metió la mano en el bolsillo; **to ~ a knife into a table** clavar un cuchillo en una mesa; **I've stuck the needle into my finger** me he clavado la aguja en el dedo; *see also* **nose A1**
3 (= *pierce*) picar; **to ~ sb with a bayonet** herir a algn con bayoneta, clavar la bayoneta a algn; ✦**IDIOM to squeal like a stuck pig** chillar como un cerdo
4 (*) (= *place, put*) poner; (= *insert*) meter; **~ it on the shelf** ponlo en el estante; **~ it in your case** mételo en la maleta; **we'll ~ an advert in the paper** pondremos un anuncio en el periódico; **they stuck him on the committee** lo metieron en el comité; ✦**IDIOM you know where you can ~ that!‡** ¡que te jodas!**; **she told him he could ~ his job‡** le dijo que se metiera el trabajo donde le cupiera‡
5 (*esp Brit**) (= *tolerate*) aguantar; **I can't ~ him** no lo aguanto; **I can't ~ it any longer** no aguanto más
6 **to be stuck** 6·1 (= *jammed*) estar atascado, estar atorado (*esp LAm*); (*in mud etc*) estar atascado; [*sth pointed*] estar clavado; **the mechanism was stuck** el mecanismo estaba atascado *or* bloqueado; **the window is stuck** se ha atrancado la ventana; **the lift is stuck at the ninth floor** el ascensor se ha quedado parado *or* colgado *or* atrancado en el piso nueve; **to be stuck fast** (= *jammed*) estar totalmente atascado *or* atorado; (*in mud etc*) estar totalmente atascado; [*sth pointed*] estar bien clavado
6·2 (= *trapped*) **to be stuck in the lift** quedarse atrapado en el ascensor; **the car was stuck between two trucks** el coche estaba atrapado entre dos camiones; **the train was stuck at the station** el tren se quedó parado en la estación; **I'm stuck at home all day** estoy metida en casa todo el día; **we're stuck here for the night** tendremos que pasar aquí la noche; **he's stuck in France** sigue en Francia sin poder moverse; **he's stuck in a boring job** tiene un trabajo muy aburrido (y no puede buscarse otro)
6·3 (*) (= *have a problem*) estar en un apuro *or* aprieto; **I'm stuck** (*in crossword puzzle, guessing game, essay etc*) estoy atascado; **he's never stuck for an answer** no le falta nunca una respuesta; **the problem had them all stuck** el problema los tenía a todos perplejos
6·4 **to be stuck with sth/sb*** tener que aguantar algo/a algn; **I was stuck with him for two hours*** tuve que soportar su compañía durante dos horas; **and now we're stuck with it*** y ahora no lo podemos quitar de encima, y ahora no hay manera de deshacernos de eso
6·5 **to be stuck on sb*** estar enamorado de algn
7 **to get stuck** 7·1 **to get stuck in the snow** quedar sin poderse mover en la nieve; **a bone got stuck in my throat** se me había clavado una espina en la garganta; **to get stuck fast** (= *jammed*) atascarse totalmente, atorarse totalmente (*esp LAm*); (*in mud etc*) atascarse totalmente; [*sth pointed*] clavarse bien
7·2 **we got stuck with this problem*** nos quedamos con este problema
(B) VI 1 (= *adhere*) [*glue, sticky object etc*] pegarse; **this stamp won't ~** este sello no se pega; **it stuck to the wall** quedó pegado a la pared; **the name seems to have stuck** el apodo se le pegó; **the charge seems to have stuck** la acusación no ha sido olvidada nunca; **to make a charge ~** hacer que una acusación tenga efecto
2 (= *get jammed*) atascarse, atorarse (*esp LAm*); (*in mud etc*) atascarse; [*sth pointed*] quedar clavado, clavarse; **to ~ fast in the mud**

quedar clavado en el barro; **the door ~s in wet weather** en tiempo de lluvia la puerta se pega; **the bidding stuck at £100** la puja no subió de las 100 libras; ✦*IDIOM* **that really ~s in my throat** eso me indigna; **the word "thanks" seems to ~ in her throat** la palabra "gracias" no le sale de la boca

[3] (= *extend, protrude*) **the nail was ~ing through the plank** el clavo sobresalía del tablón

[4] (= *be embedded*) **he had a knife ~ing into his back** tenía una navaja clavada en la espalda

[5] (*fig*) (*with prep or adv*) **just ~ at it and I'm sure you'll manage it** no te amedrentes y al fin llegarás; **we'll all ~ by you** (= *support you*) te apoyaremos todos; (= *stay with you*) no te abandonaremos; **to ~ close to sb** pegarse a algn, no separarse de algn; **it stuck in my mind** se me quedó grabado; **to ~ to one's principles** seguir fiel a sus principios, aferrarse a sus principios; **to ~ to a promise** cumplir una promesa; **she stuck to her decision** se plantó en su decisión; **decide what you're going to do, then ~ to it** ¡decídete y no te dejes desviar!; **he stuck to his story** se mantuvo firme en su versión de los hechos; **let's ~ to the matter in hand** ciñámonos al asunto, no perdamos de vista el tema principal; **I'd better ~ to fruit juice** creo que seguiré con el zumo de frutas; **if I ~ to a saltless diet, I'm fine** mientras siga una dieta sin sal voy bien; **let's ~ to the main roads** vamos a seguir por carreteras principales; **~ with us and you'll be all right** quédate con nosotros y todo saldrá bien; **I'll ~ with the job for another few months** seguiré con el trabajo unos meses más; **you'll have to ~ with it** tendrás que seguir del mismo modo; ✦*IDIOM* **to ~ to sb like a limpet** *or* **leech** pegarse a algn como una lapa; *see also* **gun A1**

[6] (= *balk*) **she will ~ at nothing to get what she wants** no se para en barras para conseguir lo que quiere; **he wouldn't ~ at murder** hasta cometería un asesinato, no se arredraría ante el homicidio; **that's where I ~** yo de ahí no paso

[7] (*Cards*) **I ~** ◊ **I'm ~ing** me planto

► **stick around*** VI + ADV quedarse

► **stick back** VT + ADV [1] (*) (= *replace*) volver a su lugar
[2] (*with glue etc*) volver a pegar

► **stick down** VT + ADV [1] (*with glue etc*) pegar; **she stuck the envelope down** pegó el sobre
[2] (*) (= *put down*) poner, dejar
[3] (*) (= *write down*) apuntar (rápidamente)

► **stick in** VT + ADV [1] (= *thrust in*) [+ *knife, fork etc*] clavar, hincar; [+ *one's hand*] meter, introducir; (*) (= *add, insert*) introducir, añadir
[2] (*) **get stuck in!** (= *work*) ¡manos a la obra!; (= *eat*) ¡atacar!; **let's get stuck in!** (= *work*) ¡(pongamos) manos a la obra!; (= *eat*) ¡atacar!; **to get stuck into sth** meterse de lleno en algo

► **stick on** Ⓐ VT + ADV [1] [+ *stamp, label*] pegar
[2] (*) [+ *hat*] ponerse, calarse; [+ *coat etc*] ponerse; [+ *tape, CD*] meter, poner
[3] (*) [+ *extra cost*] añadir; **they've stuck ten pence on a litre** han subido el precio del litro diez peniques
Ⓑ VI + ADV [*label, stamp*] adherirse, pegarse

► **stick out** Ⓐ VI + ADV [1] (= *protrude*) [*balcony*] sobresalir; [*nail*] sobresalir; **her feet stuck out over the end of the bed** sus pies asomaban por la punta de la cama; **his teeth ~ out** tiene los dientes salidos; **his ears ~ out** tiene las orejas de soplillo

[2] (= *be noticeable*) destacarse, resaltar; ✦*IDIOMS* **it ~s out a mile** salta a la vista; **to ~ out like a sore thumb** llamar la atención
[3] (= *insist, persevere*) **to ~ out for sth** empeñarse en conseguir algo; **they're ~ing out for more money** porfían en reclamar más dinero, se empeñan en pedir más dinero
Ⓑ VT + ADV [1] (= *extend*) [+ *tongue*] asomar, sacar; [+ *leg*] extender; [+ *chest*] sacar; [+ *head*] asomar
[2] (*) (= *tolerate, endure*) aguantar; **to ~ it out** aguantar

► **stick to** VI + PREP *see* **stick² B1, B5**

► **stick together** Ⓐ VT + ADV (*with glue etc*) pegar, unir con cola *etc*; **to ~ two things together** pegar dos cosas
Ⓑ VI + ADV [1] (= *adhere*) pegarse, quedar pegados
[2] [*people*] mantenerse unidos, no separarse; (*fig*) cerrar las filas

► **stick up** Ⓐ VT + ADV [1] (= *raise*) [+ *notice etc*] fijar, pegar; [+ *hand etc*] levantar; **~ 'em up!*** ¡arriba las manos!
[2] (‡) (= *rob*) [+ *person*] atracar, encañonar‡; [+ *bank*] asaltar
Ⓑ VI + ADV [1] (= *protrude*) sobresalir; [*hair*] ponerse de punta, pararse (*LAm*)
[2] (*) **to ~ up for sb** defender a algn; **to ~ up for o.s.** hacerse valer; **to ~ up for one's rights** hacer valer sus derechos, defender sus derechos

sticker [ˈstɪkəʳ] N [1] (= *label*) etiqueta *f*; (*with slogan*) pegatina *f*
[2] (*) (= *person*) persona *f* aplicada, persona *f* perseverante

stickiness [ˈstɪkɪnɪs] N [1] (= *gooiness*) [*of substance, object*] lo pegajoso; **to remove ~ from your hands, use a damp cloth** para que los dedos dejen de estar pegajosos, usar un trapo húmedo
[2] (= *adhesiveness*) adherencia *f*; **the tape has lost its ~** la cinta ya no pega
[3] (= *mugginess*) [*of weather, day*] lo bochornoso; [*of climate, heat*] lo húmedo
[4] (= *sweatiness*) [*of person, palms*] lo húmedo
[5] (*) (= *awkwardness*) [*of situation*] lo difícil, lo delicado; [*of problem, moment*] lo difícil

sticking plaster [ˈstɪkɪŋˌplɑːstəʳ] N (*Brit*) esparadrapo *m*, tirita *f*, curita *f* (*LAm*)

sticking point [ˈstɪkɪŋpɔɪnt] N (*fig*) punto *m* de fricción

stick-in-the-mud* [ˈstɪkɪnðəmʌd] N (*Brit*) *persona rutinaria y poco aventurera*

stickleback [ˈstɪklbæk] N espinoso *m*

stickler [ˈstɪkləʳ] N **to be a ~ for** insistir mucho en; **he's a real ~ for correct spelling** insiste mucho en la correcta ortografía

stick-on [ˈstɪkɒn] ADJ adhesivo; **~ label** etiqueta *f* adhesiva

stickpin [ˈstɪkpɪn] N (*US*) alfiler *m* de corbata

stick-up‡ [ˈstɪkʌp] N atraco *m*, asalto *m*

sticky [ˈstɪkɪ] Ⓐ ADJ (*compar* **stickier**, *superl* **stickiest**) [1] (= *gooey*) [*substance, object*] pegajoso; [*fingers*] pegajoso, pringoso; **to have ~ eyes** tener los ojos legañosos; (*Med*) tener los ojos pegados por la conjuntivitis; ✦*IDIOMS* **to have ~ fingers*** tener la mano larga*; **to be** *or* **bat on a ~ wicket*** estar en un aprieto
[2] (= *adhesive*) [*label*] engomado, adhesivo
[3] (= *muggy*) [*weather, day*] bochornoso; [*climate*] húmedo (y caluroso); [*heat*] húmedo
[4] (= *sweaty*) sudado; **to feel hot and ~** sudar y pasar calor
[5] (*) (= *awkward*) [*situation*] difícil, delicado; [*problem, moment, start*] difícil; **to be ~ about doing sth** ser reticente a hacer algo, poner muchas pegas para hacer algo; **to go through a ~ patch** pasar por una mala racha; ✦*IDIOM* **to come to a ~ end** acabar mal
Ⓑ CPD ► **sticky bun** N *bollo, a menudo de frutas o especias, cubierto con una capa de azúcar*
► **sticky tape** N cinta *f* adhesiva

stiff [stɪf] Ⓐ ADJ (*compar* **stiffer**, *superl* **stiffest**)
[1] (= *rigid*) [*card, paper, chair*] rígido, duro; [*collar, fabric*] duro, tieso; [*brush, boots*] duro; [*corpse*] rígido
[2] (= *firm*) [*paste, mixture*] compacto, consistente; **beat the egg whites until ~** bata las claras de huevo a punto de nieve
[3] (*Physiol*) [*joints, limbs, muscles*] entumecido, agarrotado; [*fingers*] rígido, agarrotado; [*movement*] rígido; **inactivity can make your joints ~** sus articulaciones se pueden entumecer *or* agarrotar por la inactividad; **to become** *or* **get ~** [*joints, limbs, muscles*] entumecerse, agarrotarse; **to feel ~** (*because of cold, injury etc*) sentirse agarrotado; (*after exercise*) tener agujetas; **I feel ~ all over** (*after exercise*) tengo agujetas por todo el cuerpo; **to have a ~ neck** tener tortícolis; **to be ~ with cold** estar aterido, estar entumecido de frío; ✦*IDIOMS* **to be (as) ~ as a board** *or* **poker** estar más tieso que un palo*; **to keep a ~ upper lip** mantener el tipo, poner a mal tiempo buena cara
[4] (= *unresponsive*) [*door, drawer, lock*] duro, que no abre bien, atorado (*esp LAm*); **the lock was ~** costaba abrir el cerrojo, el cerrojo no abría bien
[5] (= *cold, formal*) [*smile, bow*] frío; [*person, manner*] estirado, frío; [*atmosphere*] estirado, frío; **he gave a ~ bow** se inclinó con frialdad *or* con formalidad; **~ and formal** [*person, manner, atmosphere*] estirado y formal
[6] (= *tough*) [*climb, test*] difícil, duro; [*penalty, sentence, fine*] severo; [*resistance*] tenaz; [*challenge*] difícil; [*opposition, competition*] duro
[7] (= *high*) [*price*] excesivo, exorbitante; [*price rise*] fuerte
[8] (= *strong*) [*breeze*] fuerte; [*drink*] cargado; **she poured herself a ~ whisky** se sirvió un vaso grande de whisky; **that's a bit ~!*** ¡eso es mucho *or* demasiado!, ¡se han pasado!*
Ⓑ ADV **to be bored ~** aburrirse como una ostra; **to be frozen ~** estar muerto de frío; **to be scared ~** estar muerto de miedo; **to be worried ~** estar muy preocupado, estar preocupadísimo
Ⓒ N (‡) [1] (= *corpse*) cadáver *m*, fiambre* *m* (*hum*)
[2] (*US*) (= *tramp*) vagabundo/a *m/f*; (= *drunk*) borracho/a *m/f*

stiffen [ˈstɪfn] Ⓐ VT [1] [+ *card, fabric etc*] reforzar; (*with starch*) almidonar
[2] (*also* **~ up**) [+ *limb, muscle*] contraer, poner tieso; [+ *joint*] agarrotar
[3] (*fig*) [+ *morale, resistance etc*] fortalecer
Ⓑ VI [1] [*card, fabric*] hacerse más rígido, atiesarse
[2] (*also* **~ up**) [*limb, muscle*] contraerse, ponerse tieso; [*joint*] agarrotarse
[3] (*fig*) [*person, manner*] endurecerse; **the breeze ~ed** refrescó el viento; **resistance to the idea seems to have ~ed** la oposición a esta idea parece haberse hecho más tenaz aún

stiffener [ˈstɪfənəʳ] N [1] (= *starch etc*) apresto *m*
[2] (= *plastic strip*) lengüeta *f*
[3] (*) (= *drink*) trago* *m*

stiffly [ˈstɪflɪ] ADV [1] (= *firmly*) **the napkins were ~ starched** las servilletas estaban almidonadas y tiesas
[2] (= *uncomfortably*) [*walk, move, bend*] con rigidez; **she stood up ~** se levantó tieso

[3] (*= coldly, formally*) [*smile, greet*] con formalidad; [*say*] con frialdad, fríamente; [*nod, bow*] fríamente, con formalidad; **they sat ~ on the edges of their chairs** estaban sentados tiesos en el borde de las sillas

stiff-necked [ˈstɪfˈnekt] ADJ (*fig*) porfiado, terco

stiffness [ˈstɪfnɪs] N [1] (*= rigidness*) [*of card, paper, chair, collar, fabric*] rigidez *f*, dureza *f*; [*of boots, brush*] dureza *f*
[2] (*= firmness*) [*of paste, mixture*] lo compacto, consistencia *f*
[3] (*Physiol*) [*of joints, muscles, limbs*] entumecimiento *m*, agarrotamiento *m*; [*of fingers*] agarrotamiento *m*; **~ in** *or* **of the neck** tortícolis *f (sometimes m)*; **the ~ you feel after exercise** las agujetas que sientes después de hacer ejercicio
[4] (*= unresponsiveness*) [*of door, drawer, lock*] dificultad *f* en abrirse
[5] (*= coldness, formality*) [*of smile, bow, atmosphere, person, manner*] frialdad *f*
[6] (*= toughness*) [*of climb, test*] dificultad *f*; [*of penalty, sentence, fine*] severidad *f*; [*of resistance*] tenacidad *f*; [*of opposition, competition*] dureza *f*
[7] (*= strength*) [*of breeze*] fuerza *f*

stifle [ˈstaɪfl] Ⓐ VT [1] [*+ person*] ahogar, sofocar
[2] (*fig*) suprimir; **to ~ a yawn** contener un bostezo; **to ~ opposition** reprimir a la oposición
Ⓑ VI ahogarse, sofocarse

stifling [ˈstaɪflɪŋ] ADJ (*lit, fig*) agobiante; **it's ~ in here** ¡hace un calor agobiante *or* sofocante aquí dentro!; **the atmosphere in the company is ~** en la compañía hay una atmósfera agobiante

stigma [ˈstɪgmə] N (*pl* **stigmas** *or* **stigmata** [stɪgˈmɑːtə]) (*Rel*) estigma *m*; (*= moral stain*) estigma *m*, tacha *f*, baldón *m*

stigmatic [stɪgˈmætɪk] (*Rel*) Ⓐ ADJ estigmatizado
Ⓑ N estigmatizado/a *m/f*

stigmatize [ˈstɪgmətaɪz] VT estigmatizar; **to ~ sb as** calificar a algn de, tachar a algn de

stile [staɪl] N escalones *mpl* para saltar una cerca

stiletto [stɪˈletəʊ] Ⓐ N (*pl* **stilettos** *or* **stilettoes**) [1] (*= knife*) estilete *m*; (*= tool*) pinzón *m*
[2] (*Brit*) (*= shoe*) zapato *m* con tacón de aguja
Ⓑ CPD ► **stiletto heel** N (*Brit*) tacón *m* de aguja

still[1] [stɪl] Ⓐ ADJ (*compar* **stiller**; *superl* **stillest**)
[1] (*= motionless*) [*person, hands*] inmóvil, quieto; [*air*] en calma, manso; [*water*] quieto, manso; **try to hold it ~** intenta que no se te mueva; **to keep ~** quedarse quieto; **keep ~!** ¡no te muevas!, ¡quédate quieto!; **to lie ~**: **she lay ~** estaba tendida sin moverse; **to sit/stand ~** (*lit*) estarse quieto; **sit/stand ~!** ¡estáte quieto!, ¡quieto!; **time stood ~** el tiempo se detuvo; **her heart stood ~** se le paró el corazón; ✦*PROV* **~ waters run deep** las apariencias engañan, es más inteligente de lo que parece
[2] (*= quiet, calm*) [*place, night*] tranquilo, silencioso; **all was ~** todo estaba en calma; **a ~, small voice** una voz queda
[3] (*= not fizzy*) [*orange drink, mineral water*] sin gas
Ⓑ N [1] (*= quiet*) **in the ~ of the night** en el silencio de la noche
[2] (*Cine*) fotograma *m*
Ⓒ VT [1] (*liter*) (*= silence*) [*+ protest, voice*] acallar; (*= calm*) [*+ waves*] calmar; [*+ storm*] calmar, apaciguar; **he wanted to ~ the gossiping tongues** quería acallar los rumores
[2] (*= allay*) [*+ doubt, fear*] disipar; [*+ anger*] aplacar
Ⓓ VI apagarse; **the roar of the crowd ~ed to an expectant murmur** el rugido de la multitud se apagó hasta convertirse en un murmullo de expectación
Ⓔ CPD ► **still life** N (*Art*) naturaleza *f* muerta, bodegón *m*; *see also* **still-life**

> **STILL**
>
> • Translate **still** relating to time using **todavía** or **aún** (with an accent):
>
> They are still working for the same company
> ***Todavía*** *or* ***Aún están trabajando en la misma empresa***
>
> **NOTE:** Both **todavía** and **aún** normally come before the verb group in this meaning.
>
> • Alternatively, use **seguir** + **GERUND** (with or without **todavía/aún**):
>
> ***Siguen*** *or* ***Todavía siguen*** *or* ***Aún siguen trabajando en la misma empresa***
>
> • **Still** with **more**, **less** and other comparatives is normally translated by **todavía** or **aún** (with an accent):
>
> More important still are the peace talks
> ***Todavía*** *or* ***Aún más importantes son las negociaciones de paz***
> He lowered his voice still further
> ***Bajó la voz todavía*** *or* ***aún más***
> Within a couple of weeks matters got still worse
> ***Al cabo de dos semanas los problemas empeoraron todavía*** *or* ***aún más***
>
> **!** Whenever it is synonymous with **todavía**, **aún** carries an accent.
>
> *For further uses and examples, see main entry.*

still[2] [stɪl] ADV [1] (*= up to this/that time*) todavía, aún; **she ~ lives in London** todavía *or* aún vive en Londres, sigue viviendo en Londres; **I ~ don't understand** sigo sin entender, todavía *or* aún no lo entiendo; **you could ~ change your mind** todavía *or* aún puedes cambiar de idea; **I was very angry, I ~ am** estaba muy enfadado, todavía *or* aún lo estoy; **I've ~ got three left** todavía *or* aún me quedan tres; **there are ~ two more** quedan dos más, todavía *or* aún quedan dos
[2] (*= nevertheless, all the same*) aun así, de todas formas; **I didn't win, still, it's been a good experience** no he ganado, pero aun así *or* de todas formas *or* con todo, ha sido una buena experiencia; **I'm ~ going, even if it rains** iré de todas formas, incluso si llueve; **his mother was Canadian, Irish-Canadian, but ~ Canadian** su madre era canadiense, irlandesa y canadiense, pero con todo *or* aun así canadiense; **~, it was worth it** pero en fin, valió la pena; **whatever they have done, they are ~ your parents** a pesar de todo lo que han hecho, siguen siendo tus padres
[3] (*= besides, in addition*) todavía, aún; **the next day there were ~ more problems** al día siguiente había todavía *or* aún más problemas; **the hall was full and there were ~ more people waiting outside** el vestíbulo estaba lleno y había todavía *or* aún más gente esperando fuera; **~ another possibility would be to …** e incluso otra posibilidad sería …
[4] (*with compar*) (*= even*) todavía, aún; **more serious ~** ◊ **~ more serious** aún *or* todavía más grave, más grave aún *or* todavía; **you need a rest, better ~, have a holiday** necesitas un descanso, mejor todavía *or* aún, tómate unas vacaciones; **worse ~, the disease seems to be spreading** (lo que es) peor todavía *or* aún, la enfermedad parece propagarse

still[3] [stɪl] N (*for alcohol*) alambique *m*

stillbirth [ˈstɪl,bɜːθ] N mortinato *m*

stillborn [ˈstɪl,bɔːn] ADJ [1] (*Med*) nacido muerto; **the child was ~** el niño nació muerto
[2] (*fig*) fracasado, malogrado

still-life [,stɪlˈlaɪf] CPD ► **still-life painter** N pintor(a) *m/f* de bodegones ► **still-life painting** N bodegón *m*

stillness [ˈstɪlnɪs] N [1] (*= motionlessness*) [*of person, hands, air, water*] quietud *f*
[2] (*= quiet, calm*) tranquilidad *f*, calma *f*

stilt [stɪlt] N zanco *m*; (*Archit*) pilar *m*, soporte *m*

stilted [ˈstɪltɪd] ADJ [*person*] afectado; [*conversation, style, manner*] forzado, poco natural; **her English is rather ~** (*non-native speaker*) su inglés no suena muy natural; (*native speaker*) tiene un inglés bastante rebuscado *or* afectado

stimulant [ˈstɪmjʊlənt] Ⓐ ADJ estimulante
Ⓑ N (*= drug, coffee, cigarettes*) estimulante *m*, excitante *m*; (*fig*) acicate *m* (**to** para)

stimulate [ˈstɪmjʊleɪt] VT estimular; [*+ growth etc*] favorecer; [*+ demand*] estimular; **to ~ sb to do sth** alentar a algn a que haga algo

stimulating [ˈstɪmjʊleɪtɪŋ] ADJ (*Med etc*) estimulador, estimulante; [*experience, book etc*] estimulante, inspirador

stimulation [,stɪmjʊˈleɪʃən] N (*= stimulus*) estímulo *m*; (*= act*) estimulación *f*; (*= state*) excitación *f*

stimulus [ˈstɪmjʊləs] N (*pl* **stimuli** [ˈstɪmjʊlaɪ]) estímulo *m*, incentivo *m*

sting [stɪŋ] (*vb: pt, pp* **stung**) Ⓐ N [1] (*Zool, Bot*) (*= organ*) aguijón *m*; ✦*IDIOM* **but there's a ~ in the tail** pero viene algo no tan agradable al final
[2] (*= act, wound*) [*of insect, nettle*] picadura *f*; (*= sharp pain*) punzada *f*; **a ~ of remorse** el gusanillo de la conciencia; **the ~ of the rain in one's face** el azote de la lluvia en la cara; **I felt the ~ of his irony** su ironía me hirió en lo vivo; ✦*IDIOM* **to take the ~ out of sth** restar fuerza a algo
[3] (*esp US**) (*= confidence trick*) timo *m*
Ⓑ VT [1] [*insect, nettle*] picar; (*= make smart*) escocer, picar, arder (*esp LAm*); [*hail*] azotar
[2] (*fig*) [*conscience*] remorder; [*remark, criticism*] herir; **my conscience stung me** me remordió la conciencia; **the reply stung him to the quick** la respuesta lo hirió en lo vivo; **he was clearly stung by this remark** era evidente que este comentario hizo mella en él
[3] (*= provoke*) **he was stung into action** lo provocaron a actuar
[4] (✱) **they stung me for four pounds** me clavaron cuatro libras*; **how much did they ~ you for?** ¿cuánto te clavaron?*
Ⓒ VI [1] [*insect etc*] picar; **moths don't ~** las mariposas no pican
[2] **my eyes ~** me pican los ojos; **that blow really stung** ese golpe me dolió de verdad

stingily [ˈstɪndʒɪlɪ] ADV con tacañería

stinginess [ˈstɪndʒɪnɪs] N tacañería *f*

stinging [ˈstɪŋɪŋ] Ⓐ ADJ [1] [*insect etc*] que pica, que tiene aguijón; [*pain*] punzante
[2] [*remark etc*] mordaz
Ⓑ N (*= sensation*) escozor *m*
Ⓒ CPD ► **stinging nettle** N ortiga *f*

stingray [ˈstɪŋreɪ] N pastinaca *f*

stingy [ˈstɪndʒɪ] ADJ (*compar* **stingier**; *superl* **stingiest**) [*person*] tacaño; [*meal*] parco, escaso; **to be ~ with sth** ser tacaño con algo

stink [stɪŋk] (*vb: pt* **stank**; *pp* **stunk**) Ⓐ N [1] (*= smell*) peste *f*, hedor *m*; **a ~ of …** un hedor a

…; **the ~ of corruption** el olor a corrupción
2 (*) (*fig*) (= *row, trouble*) lío* *m*, follón *m* (*Sp**); **there was a tremendous ~ about it** se armó un tremendo lío*; **to kick up** *or* **raise** *or* **make a ~** armar un escándalo
Ⓑ VI 1 **to ~ (of)** apestar (a), heder (a); **it ~s in here** aquí apesta
2 (‡) (= *be very bad*) **the idea ~s** es una pésima idea; **I think the plan ~s** creo que es un proyecto abominable; **as a headmaster he ~s** como director es fatal*
Ⓒ VT **to ~ the place out*** infestar el lugar de olor
Ⓓ CPD ► **stink bomb** N bomba *f* fétida

stinker‡ ['stɪŋkəʳ] N (= *person*) mal bicho* *m*, canalla* *mf*; **you ~!** ¡bestia!*; **this problem is a ~** es un problema peliagudo

stinking ['stɪŋkɪŋ] Ⓐ ADJ 1 (*lit*) hediondo, fétido
2 (*) horrible, bestial, asqueroso
Ⓑ ADV **they are ~ rich*** son unos ricachos*

stint [stɪnt] Ⓐ N 1 (= *amount of work*) **to do a** *or* **one's ~ (at)** hacer su parte (de); **I've done my ~** he hecho lo que me corresponde
2 (= *period*) periodo *m*, período *m*; **she did a two-year ~ on the committee** fue miembro del comité durante un periodo *or* período de dos años; **after a brief ~ in a law firm he went to Hong Kong** tras una breve temporada trabajando en un bufete de abogados, se fue a Hong-Kong
3 **without ~** libremente, generosamente
Ⓑ VT limitar, restringir; **he did not ~ his praises** no escatimó elogios; **to ~ sb of sth** privar a algn de algo, dar a algn menor cantidad de algo de la que pide *or* necesita; **to ~ o.s.** estrecharse, privarse de cosas; **don't ~ yourself!** ¡no te prives de nada!; **to ~ o.s. of sth** privarse de algo, negarse algo, no permitirse algo
Ⓒ VI **he did not ~ on praise** no escatimó elogios

stipend ['staɪpend] N salario *m*, estipendio *m*

stipendiary [staɪ'pendɪərɪ] Ⓐ ADJ estipendiario
Ⓑ N estipendiario *m*

stipple ['stɪpl] VT puntear

▼**stipulate** ['stɪpjʊleɪt] Ⓐ VT estipular, poner como condición, especificar
Ⓑ VI **to ~ for sth** estipular algo, poner algo como condición

stipulation [,stɪpjʊ'leɪʃən] N estipulación *f*, condición *f*

stir¹ [stɜːʳ] Ⓐ N 1 **to give sth a ~** remover algo
2 (= *disturbance, ado*) conmoción *f*; **to cause a ~** causar conmoción; **there was a great ~ in parliament** hubo una gran conmoción en el parlamento; **it didn't make much of a ~** apenas despertó interés alguno
Ⓑ VT 1 [+ *liquid etc*] remover, revolver; [+ *fire*] atizar, hurgar; **to ~ sugar into coffee** añadir azúcar al café removiéndolo; **"stir before using"** "agítese antes de usar"
2 (= *move*) mover; **a breeze ~red the leaves** una brisa agitó las hojas; **nothing could ~ him from his chair** no había nada que lo levantara de la silla; **come on, ~ yourself** *or* **your stumps*** ¡venga, muévete!, ¡anda, muévete!
3 (*fig*) [+ *interest*] despertar; [+ *emotions*] provocar, excitar; [+ *imagination*] estimular, avivar; **to ~ sb to pity** causar compasión a algn; **to feel deeply ~red** conmoverse profundamente, estar muy emocionado; **we were all ~red by the speech** el discurso nos conmovió a todos; **to ~ sb to do sth** incitar a algn a hacer algo
Ⓒ VI 1 (= *move*) moverse; **she hasn't ~red all day** no se ha movido en todo el día; **don't you ~ from here** no te muevas de aquí; **he never ~red from the spot** no se apartó del lugar ni un momento; **nobody is ~ring yet** están todavía en la cama
2 (*) (= *make trouble*) acizañar, meter cizaña

►**stir up** VT + ADV 1 [+ *liquid etc*] remover, agitar, revolver; [+ *dust*] levantar
2 (*fig*) [+ *memories*] traer a la memoria; [+ *passions*] provocar, despertar; [+ *revolt*] fomentar; [+ *trouble*] provocar; **to ~ up the past** remover el pasado; **he's always trying to ~ things up** siempre anda provocando

stir²‡ [stɜːʳ] N (*esp US*) (= *prison*) chirona‡ *f*

stir-fry ['stɜːfraɪ] Ⓐ VT sofreír
Ⓑ N sofrito *m* (chino)

stirring ['stɜːrɪŋ] Ⓐ ADJ [*speech, music*] emocionante, conmovedor
Ⓑ N **I sense no ~ of interest** no creo que esté despertando ningún interés; **there were ~s of protest** la gente empezó a protestar

stirrup ['stɪrəp] Ⓐ N (*on saddle*) estribo *m*
Ⓑ CPD ► **stirrup cup** N copa *f* del estribo
► **stirrup pump** N bomba *f* de mano

stitch [stɪtʃ] Ⓐ N 1 (*Sew*) puntada *f*, punto *m*; ✦*IDIOM* **she hadn't a ~ on** andaba en cueros *or* (*LAm*) encuerada*; ✦*PROV* **a ~ in time saves nine** más vale prevenir que lamentar, una puntada a tiempo ahorra ciento
2 (*Med*) punto *m* de sutura; **to put ~es in a wound** suturar una herida
3 (= *pain*) punto *m*, punzada *f*; **to have a ~** tener flato; ✦*IDIOMS* **we were in ~es*** nos moríamos *or* (*LAm*) partíamos de (la) risa; **she had us all in ~es*** nos hizo partirnos de risa
Ⓑ VT 1 (*Sew*) coser; **to ~ (up) a hem** coser un dobladillo
2 (*Med*) suturar; **to ~ (up) a wound** suturar una herida
Ⓒ VI (*Sew*) coser

►**stitch up** VT + ADV 1 (*lit*) *see* **stitch B**
2 (*) (= *arrange, finalize*) [+ *agreement, deal*] concertar
3 (‡) (= *frame*) vender*, incriminar dolosamente

stitching ['stɪtʃɪŋ] N (*Sew*) puntadas *fpl*; (*Med*) puntos *mpl*

stoat [stəʊt] N armiño *m*

stock [stɒk] Ⓐ N 1 (*Comm*) existencias *fpl*; **"offer valid while stocks last"** "oferta válida hasta que se agoten las existencias"; **he sold his father's entire ~ of cloth** vendió todas las existencias de telas que tenía su padre; **to have sth in ~** tener algo en existencia; **check that your size is in ~** compruebe que tengan su talla; **to be out of ~** estar agotado; **camping-gas stoves are out of ~** se han agotado las cocinillas de gas; **to take ~** (= *make inventory*) hacer el inventario; (*fig*) evaluar la situación; **to take ~ of** [+ *situation, prospects*] evaluar; [+ *person*] formarse una opinión sobre
2 (= *supply*) reserva *f*; **~s of ammunition** reservas de municiones; **fish/coal ~s are low** las reservas de peces/carbón escasean; **~s of food were running low** se estaban agotando las provisiones de comida; **to get in** *or* **lay in a ~ of sth** abastecerse de algo; **I always keep a ~ of tinned food** siempre estoy bien abastecido de latas de comida; *see also* **housing**
3 (= *selection*) surtido *m*; **luckily he had a good ~ of books** por suerte tenía un buen surtido de libros; **we have a large ~ of sportswear** tenemos un amplio surtido de ropa deportiva
4 (*Theat*) **~ of plays** repertorio *m* de obras
5 (*Fin*) (= *capital*) capital *m* social, capital *m* en acciones; (= *shares*) acciones *fpl*; (= *government securities*) bonos *mpl* del estado; **~s and shares** acciones *fpl*
6 (= *status*) prestigio *m*; **his ~ has gone up** *or* **risen (with the public)** ha ganado prestigio (entre el público); *see also* **laughing**
7 (*Agr*) (= *livestock*) ganado *m*; **breeding ~** ganado de cría
8 (= *descent*) **people of Mediterranean ~** gentes *fpl* de ascendencia mediterránea; **to be of peasant ~** ser de ascendencia campesina; **to be** *or* **come of good ~** ser de buena cepa
9 (*Culin*) caldo *m*; **beef/chicken ~** caldo de vaca/pollo
10 (*Rail*) (*also* **rolling ~**) material *m* rodante
11 (= *handle*) (*gen*) mango *m*; [*of gun, rifle*] culata *f*
12 (*Bot*) 12·1 (= *flower*) alhelí *m*
12·2 (= *stem, trunk*) [*of tree*] tronco *m*; [*of vine*] cepa *f*; (= *source of cuttings*) planta *f* madre; (= *plant grafted onto*) patrón *m*
13 **stocks** 13·1 **the ~s** (*Hist*) el cepo
13·2 (*Naut*) astillero *m*, grada *f* de construcción; **to be on the ~s** [*ship*] estar en vías de construcción; (*fig*) [*piece of work*] estar en preparación; **he has three plays on the ~s** tiene tres obras entre manos
14 (= *tie*) fular *m*
Ⓑ VT 1 (= *sell*) [+ *goods*] vender; **do you ~ lightbulbs?** ¿vende usted bombillas?; **we don't ~ that brand** no vendemos esa marca; **we ~ a wide range of bicycles** tenemos un gran surtido de bicicletas
2 (= *fill*) [+ *shop*] surtir, abastecer (**with** de); [+ *shelves*] reponer; [+ *library*] surtir, abastecer (**with** de); [+ *farm*] abastecer (**with** con); [+ *freezer, cupboard*] llenar (**with** de); [+ *lake, river*] poblar (**with** de); **a well ~ed shop/library** una tienda/biblioteca bien surtida; **the lake is ~ed with trout** han poblado el lago de truchas
Ⓒ ADJ 1 (*Comm*) [*goods, model*] de serie, estándar; **~ line** línea *f* estándar; **~ size** tamaño *m* estándar
2 (= *standard, hackneyed*) [*argument, joke, response*] típico; **"mind your own business" is her ~ response to such questions** —no es asunto tuyo, es la respuesta típica que da a esas preguntas; **a ~ phrase** una frase hecha
3 (*Theat*) [*play*] de repertorio
4 (*Agr*) (*for breeding*) de cría; **~ mare** yegua *f* de cría
Ⓓ CPD ► **stock book** N libro *m* de almacén, libro *m* existencias ► **stock car** N (*US Rail*) vagón *m* para el ganado; (*Aut, Sport*) stock-car *m*; *see also* **stock-car racing** ► **stock certificate** N certificado *m* *or* título *m* de acciones ► **stock company** N sociedad *f* anónima, sociedad *f* de acciones ► **stock control** N control *m* de existencias ► **stock cube** N (*Culin*) pastilla *f* *or* cubito *m* de caldo ► **stock dividend** N dividendo *m* en acciones ► **Stock Exchange** N (*Fin*) Bolsa *f*; **to be on the Stock Exchange** [*listed company*] ser cotizado en bolsa; **prices on the Stock Exchange** ◊ **Stock Exchange prices** cotizaciones *fpl* en bolsa ► **stock farm** N granja *f* para la cría de ganado ► **stock farmer** N ganadero/a *m/f* ► **stock index** N índice *m* bursátil ► **stock list** N (*Fin*) lista *f* de valores y acciones; (*Comm*) lista *f* *or* inventario *m* de existencias ► **stock management** N gestión *f* de existencias ► **stock market** N (*Fin*) bolsa *f*, mercado *m* bursátil; **~ market activity** actividad *f* bursátil ► **stock option plan** N *plan que permite que los ejecutivos de una empresa compren acciones de la misma a un precio especial*

➤ LANGUAGE IN USE: **stipulate A** 10.1

► **stock raising** N ganadería *f*; *see also* **joint D**

►**stock up** Ⓐ VI + ADV [*shopkeeper*] proveerse de existencias; [*private individual*] abastecerse; **to ~ up on** *or* **with sth** [*shopkeeper*] proveerse de algo; [*private individual*] abastecerse de algo
Ⓑ VT + ADV (= *fill*) [+ *larder, cupboard, freezer*] llenar (**with** de); [+ *shelves*] reponer (**with** con)

stockade [stɒ'keɪd] N 1 (= *fencing*) estacada *f*
2 (*US Mil*) prisión *f* militar

stockbreeder ['stɒk,briːdəʳ] N ganadero/a *m/f*

stockbreeding ['stɒk,briːdɪŋ] N ganadería *f*

stockbroker ['stɒk,brəʊkəʳ] Ⓐ N corredor(a) *m/f* de Bolsa, bolsista *mf*
Ⓑ CPD ► **stockbroker belt** N (*Brit*) zona *f* residencial de los bolsistas

stockbroking ['stɒk,brəʊkɪŋ] N correduría *f* de bolsa

stock-car racing ['stɒkkɑː,reɪsɪŋ] N carreras *fpl* de stock-car, carreras *fpl* de choque

stockfish ['stɒkfɪʃ] N pescado *m* de seco

stockholder ['stɒk,həʊldəʳ] N (*US*) accionista *mf*

Stockholm ['stɒkhəʊm] N Estocolmo *m*

stockily ['stɒkɪlɪ] ADV **~ built** de complexión robusta

stockiness ['stɒkɪnɪs] N robustez *f*

stockinet [,stɒkɪ'net] N tela *f* de punto

stocking ['stɒkɪŋ] Ⓐ N media *f*; (*knee-length*) calceta *f*; **a pair of ~s** unas medias, un par de medias
Ⓑ CPD ► **stocking(ed) feet** NPL **in one's ~(ed) feet** sin zapatos ► **stocking filler** N pequeño regalo *m* de Navidad

stock-in-trade ['stɒkɪn'treɪd] N (= *tools etc*) existencias *fpl*; (*fig*) repertorio *m*; **that joke is part of his ~** es un chiste de su repertorio

stockist ['stɒkɪst] N (*Brit*) distribuidor(a) *m/f*, proveedor(a) *m/f*

stockjobber ['stɒk,dʒɒbəʳ] N (*Brit*) agiotista *mf*

stockjobbing ['stɒk,dʒɒbɪŋ] N (*Brit*) agiotaje *m*

stockkeeper ['stɒk,kiːpəʳ] N almacenero/a *m/f*

stockman ['stɒkmən] N (*pl* **stockmen**) (*Agr*) ganadero *m*

stockpile ['stɒkpaɪl] Ⓐ N reservas *fpl*
Ⓑ VT (= *accumulate*) acumular; (= *store*) almacenar

stockroom ['stɒkrʊm] N almacén *m*, depósito *m*

stock-still ['stɒk'stɪl] ADV **to be** *or* **stand ~** mantenerse *or* quedarse inmóvil

stocktaking ['stɒk,teɪkɪŋ] Ⓐ N (*Brit*) inventario *m*, balance *m*; **to do the ~** hacer el inventario
Ⓑ CPD ► **stocktaking sale** N venta *f* postbalance

stocky ['stɒkɪ] ADJ (*compar* **stockier**; *superl* **stockiest**) fornido

stockyard ['stɒkjɑːd] N (= *pens etc*) corral *m* de ganado; (*US*) (= *abattoir*) matadero *m*

stodge* [stɒdʒ] N (*Brit*) comida *f* indigesta

stodgy ['stɒdʒɪ] ADJ (*compar* **stodgier**; *superl* **stodgiest**) 1 [*food*] indigesto
2 (*fig*) [*book, style, person*] pesado

stogie*, **stogy*** ['stəʊgɪ] N (*US*) cigarro *m*, puro *m*

stoic ['stəʊɪk] Ⓐ ADJ estoico
Ⓑ N estoico *m*

stoical ['stəʊɪkəl] ADJ estoico

stoically ['stəʊɪklɪ] ADV estoicamente, impasiblemente

stoicism ['stəʊɪsɪzəm] N estoicismo *m*

stoke [stəʊk] VT (*also* **~ up**) 1 [+ *fire, furnace*] atizar
2 (*fig*) [+ *fears, hopes*] cebar

►**stoke up** Ⓐ VI + ADV (*lit*) cebar el hogar, echar carbón a la lumbre; (* *hum*) (= *eat*) atiborrarse
Ⓑ VT + ADV = **stoke**

stokehold ['stəʊkhəʊld] N cuarto *m* de calderas

stokehole ['stəʊkhəʊl] N boca *f* del horno

stoker ['stəʊkəʳ] N fogonero *m*

STOL [stɒl] N ABBR = **short take-off and landing**

stole¹ [stəʊl] N (= *garment*) estola *f*

stole² [stəʊl] PT *of* **steal**

stolen ['stəʊlən] Ⓐ PP *of* **steal**
Ⓑ ADJ 1 (*lit*) robado; **~ goods** artículos *mpl* robados; **~ property** bienes *mpl* robados; *see also* **dealer**
2 (*fig*) [*moment, pleasures, kisses*] robado

stolid ['stɒlɪd] ADJ impasible, imperturbable; (*pej*) terco

stolidity [stɒ'lɪdɪtɪ] N impasibilidad *f*, imperturbabilidad *f*; (*pej*) terquedad *f*

stolidly ['stɒlɪdlɪ] ADV impasiblemente, imperturbablemente

stomach ['stʌmək] Ⓐ N 1 (= *organ*) estómago *m*; **I've got a pain in my ~** me duele el estómago, tengo dolor de estómago; **it turns my ~** (*lit, fig*) me revuelve el estómago; **he had an upset ~** tenía el estómago revuelto; ✦***IDIOM*** **to have no ~ for sth**: **he had no ~ for another argument with them** no se sentía con ánimos para tener otra discusión con ellos; **they have no ~ for the fight** no tienen agallas para luchar; ✦***PROV*** **an army marches on its ~** la marcha de un ejército depende del contenido de los estómagos de sus soldados; *see also* **empty A1**, **full A7**, **sick A4**
2 (= *belly*) barriga *f*; **to hold one's ~ in** meter estómago; **to lie on one's ~** estar tumbado boca abajo; **I always sleep on my ~** siempre duermo boca abajo
Ⓑ VT 1 (*lit*) [+ *food*] tolerar
2 (*) (*fig*) aguantar, soportar; **I can't ~ the thought of him cheating on her** no aguanto *or* soporto la idea de que la esté engañando; **it was more than I could ~** era inaguantable *or* insoportable
Ⓒ CPD ► **stomach ache** N dolor *m* de estómago, dolor *m* de barriga ► **stomach cramps** NPL retortijones *mpl* de barriga ► **stomach disorder** N trastorno *m* estomacal ► **stomach lining** N membrana *f* que recubre las paredes del estómago ► **stomach muscle** N músculo *m* del abdomen ► **stomach pump** N bomba *f* gástrica ► **stomach ulcer** N úlcera *f* gástrica ► **stomach upset** N trastorno *m* estomacal; **to have a ~ upset** tener un trastorno estomacal ► **stomach wall** N pared *f* del estómago ► **stomach wound** N herida *f* estomacal

stomp [stɒmp] Ⓐ VI dar patadas; **to ~ in/out** entrar/salir dando fuertes pisotones
Ⓑ VT (*US*) = **stamp B1**

stone [stəʊn] Ⓐ N 1 (*gen*) piedra *f*; (= *gravestone*) lápida *f*; (= *gemstone*) piedra *f*, gema *f*; ✦***IDIOMS*** **a ~'s throw away** ◊ **within a ~'s throw** a un tiro de piedra; **to cast the first ~** lanzar la primera piedra; **which of you shall cast the first ~?** ¿cuál de vosotros se atreve a lanzar la primera piedra?; **to leave no ~ unturned** no dejar piedra por mover; **it isn't cast** *or* **set in ~** no es inamovible, no es para toda la vida
2 (*Brit*) [*of fruit*] hueso *m*
3 (*Med*) cálculo *m*, piedra *f*; (*as complaint*) mal *m* de piedra
4 (*Brit*) (= *weight*) 6.350kg; **he weighs 12 ~(s)** pesa 76 kilos; → IMPERIAL SYSTEM
Ⓑ VT 1 [+ *person*] apedrear, lapidar; ✦***IDIOMS*** **~ me!**‡ ◊ **~ the crows!**‡ ¡caray!*
2 [+ *fruit*] deshuesar
Ⓒ CPD de piedra ► **the Stone Age** N la Edad de Piedra ► **stone pit**, **stone quarry** N cantera *f*

stone-blind ['stəʊn'blaɪnd] ADJ completamente ciego

stone-broke* ['stəʊn'brəʊk] ADJ (*US*) = **stony-broke**

stonechat ['stəʊntʃæt] N culiblanco *m*

stone-cold [,stəʊn'kəʊld] ADJ como un témpano; **to be ~ sober*** estar completamente sobrio

stonecrop ['stəʊnkrɒp] N uva *f* de gato

stonecutter ['stəʊn,kʌtəʳ] N = **stonemason**

stoned‡ [stəʊnd] ADJ (*on drugs*) colocado*; (= *drunk*) borracho

stone-dead ['stəʊn'ded] ADJ tieso; **it killed the idea ~** dio completamente al traste con la idea

stone-deaf ['stəʊn'def] ADJ sordo como una tapia, sordo del todo

stoneground ['stəʊn,graʊnd] ADJ [*flour*] molido por piedras

stonemason ['stəʊn,meɪsn] N albañil *mf*; (*in quarry*) cantero *m*

stonewall ['stəʊn'wɔːl] VI 1 (*Sport*) jugar a la defensiva
2 (*in answering questions*) negarse a contestar

stonewalling ['stəʊn'wɔːlɪŋ] N táctica *f* de cerrojo

stoneware ['stəʊnwɛəʳ] Ⓐ N gres *m*
Ⓑ ADJ de gres

stonewashed ['stəʊn,wɒʃt] ADJ [*jeans*] lavado a la piedra

stonework ['stəʊnwɜːk] N cantería *f*

stonily ['stəʊnɪlɪ] ADV (*fig*) glacialmente, fríamente

stony ['stəʊnɪ] ADJ (*compar* **stonier**; *superl* **stoniest**) 1 [*ground, beach*] pedregoso; [*material*] pétreo
2 (*fig*) [*glance, silence*] glacial, frío; [*heart*] empedernido; [*stare*] duro

stony-broke* ['stəʊnɪ'brəʊk] ADJ **to be ~** (*Brit*) estar sin un duro*, estar pelado*, estar sin un peso (*LAm**)

stony-faced [,stəʊnɪ'feɪst] ADJ de expresión pétrea

stony-hearted ['stəʊnɪ'hɑːtɪd] ADJ de corazón empedernido

stood [stʊd] PT, PP *of* **stand**

stooge [stuːdʒ] Ⓐ N [*of comedian*] compañero/a *m/f*; (*) (= *lackey*) secuaz *mf*, siervo/a *m/f*
Ⓑ VI **to ~ for sb*** servir humildemente a algn

►**stooge about***, **stooge around*** VI + ADV estar por ahí

stook [stuːk] Ⓐ N tresnal *m*, garbera *f*
Ⓑ VT poner en tresnales

stool [stuːl] Ⓐ N 1 (= *seat*) taburete *m*, escabel *m*; (*folding*) silla *f* de tijera; ✦***IDIOM*** **to fall between two ~s** quedarse sin lo uno y sin lo otro, quedarse nadando entre dos aguas y no llegar a ningún lado
2 (*Med*) (= *faeces*) deposición *f*
3 (*Bot*) planta *f* madre
Ⓑ CPD ► **stool pigeon*** N (= *informer*) chivato/a* *m/f*, soplón/ona* *m/f*; (= *decoy*) señuelo *m*

stoop[1] [stu:p] (A) N **to have a ~** ser un poco encorvado; **to walk with a ~** andar encorvado
(B) VI 1 (= *bend*) (*also* **~ down**) inclinarse, agacharse; (*permanently, as defect*) andar encorvado; **to ~ to pick sth up** inclinarse para recoger algo
2 (*fig*) **to ~ to sth/doing sth** rebajarse a algo/hacer algo; **I wouldn't ~ so low!** ¡a eso no llegaría!, ¡no me rebajaría tanto!

stoop[2] [stu:p] N (*US*) (= *verandah*) pórtico *m*, pequeña veranda *f*

stooping ['stu:pɪŋ] ADJ encorvado

stop [stɒp] (A) N 1 (= *halt*) parada *f*, alto *m*; **to be at a ~** [+ *vehicle*] estar parado; [+ *production, process*] quedar paralizado; **to bring to a ~** [+ *vehicle*] parar, detener; [+ *production, process*] paralizar, interrumpir; **to come to a ~** [*vehicle*] parar(se), detenerse; [*production, progress*] interrumpirse; **to come to a dead** *or* **sudden ~** pararse en seco, detenerse repentinamente; **to come to a full ~** [*negotiations, discussions*] paralizarse, quedar detenido en un punto muerto; **to put a ~ to sth** poner fin *or* término a algo, acabar con algo
2 (= *break, pause*) descanso *m*, pausa *f*; (*overnight*) estancia *f*, estadía *f* (*LAm*), estada *f* (*LAm*); (*for refuelling*) escala *f*; **a ~ for coffee** un descanso para tomar café; **to make a ~ at Bordeaux** hacer escala en Burdeos; **a ~ of a few days** una estancia de unos días; **without a ~** sin parar
3 (= *stopping place*) (*for bus etc*) parada *f*; (*Aer, Naut*) escala *f*
4 (*Typ*) (*also* **full ~**) punto *m*
5 (*Mus*) (*on organ*) registro *m*; [*of guitar*] traste *m*; [*of other instrument*] llave *f*; ✦***IDIOM*** **to pull out all the ~s** tocar todos los registros
6 (*Mech*) tope *m*, retén *m*
7 (*Phon*) (*also* **~ consonant**) (consonante *f*) oclusiva *f*
(B) VT 1 (= *block*) [+ *hole*] tapar; [+ *leak, flow of blood*] restañar; [+ *tooth*] empastar; **to ~ one's ears** taparse los oídos; **to ~ a gap** tapar un agujero; (*fig*) llenar un vacío; **the curtains ~ the light** las cortinas impiden la entrada de la luz; **the walls ~ some of the noise** las paredes absorben parte del ruido
2 (= *arrest movement of*) [+ *runaway engine, car*] detener, parar; [+ *blow, punch*] parar; ✦***IDIOM*** **to ~ a bullet*** (= *be shot*) ser disparado *or* (*LAm*) baleado
3 (= *put an end to*) [+ *rumour, abuse, activity, injustice*] poner fin a, poner término a, acabar con; [+ *conversation*] interrumpir, suspender; [+ *aggression*] rechazar, contener; [+ *production*] (*permanently*) terminar; (*temporarily*) interrumpir
4 (= *prevent*) evitar; (= *forbid*) prohibir, poner fin a; **this should ~ any further trouble** esto debería evitar cualquier dificultad en el futuro; **to ~ sth (from) happening** evitar que algo ocurra; **to ~ sb (from) doing sth** (= *prevent*) impedir a algn hacer algo, impedir que algn haga algo; (= *forbid*) prohibir a algn hacer algo, prohibir a algn que haga algo; **can't you ~ him?** ¿no le puedes impedir que lo haga?; **there is nothing to ~ him** y no hay nada que se lo impida; **to ~ o.s. (from doing sth)** abstenerse (de hacer algo); **I can't seem to ~ myself doing it** parece que no puedo dejar de hacerlo; **I ~ped myself in time** me detuve a tiempo
5 (= *cease*) **to ~ doing sth** dejar de hacer algo; **~ it!** ¡basta ya!; **I just can't ~ it** (= *help it*) ¡qué remedio!, ¡qué le vamos a hacer!; **~ that noise!** ¡basta ya de ruido!; **~ that nonsense!** ¡déjate de tonterías!; **it has ~ped raining** ha dejado de llover, ya no llueve; **I'm trying to ~ smoking** estoy intentando dejar de fumar; **she never ~s talking** habla sin parar; **to ~ work** dejar de trabajar
6 (= *suspend*) [+ *payments, wages, subscription*] suspender; [+ *cheque*] invalidar; [+ *supply*] cortar, interrumpir; **to ~ sb's electricity** cortar la electricidad a algn; **all leave is ~ped** han sido cancelados todos los permisos; **to ~ the milk for a fortnight** (*Brit*) pedir al lechero que no traiga leche durante quince días; **to ~ sb's wages** suspender el pago del sueldo de algn; **to ~ ten pounds from sb's wages** retener diez libras del sueldo de algn
(C) VI 1 (= *stop moving*) [*person, vehicle*] pararse, detenerse; [*clock, watch*] pararse; **the car ~ped** se paró el coche; **where does the bus ~?** ¿dónde para el autobús?; **the clock has ~ped** el reloj se ha parado; **stop!** ¡pare!; **~, thief!** ¡al ladrón!
2 (= *pause, take a break*) parar, hacer alto; **to ~ to do sth** detenerse a hacer algo; **without ~ping** sin parar
3 (= *cease, come to an end*) terminar, acabar(se); [*supply etc*] cortarse, interrumpirse; [*process, rain etc*] terminar, cesar; **payments have ~ped** (*temporarily*) se han suspendido los pagos; (*permanently*) han terminado los pagos; **when the programme ~s** cuando termine el programa; **the rain has ~ped** ha dejado de llover; **he seems not to know when to ~** parece no saber cuándo conviene hacer alto; ✦***IDIOM*** **to ~ at nothing (to do sth)** no detenerse ante nada (para hacer algo)
4 (*) (= *stay*) **to ~ (at/with)** hospedarse *or* alojarse (con); **she's ~ping with her aunt** se hospeda en casa de su tía; **I'm not ~ping** no me quedo; **did you ~ till the end?** ¿te quedaste hasta el final?
(D) CPD ► **stop press** N noticias *fpl* de última hora; **"stop press"** (*as heading*) "al cierre de la edición" ► **stop sign** N (*Aut*) stop *m*, señal *f* de stop

► **stop away*** VI + ADV ausentarse (**from** de), no asistir (**from** a)

► **stop behind*** VI + ADV quedarse; **they made him ~ behind after school** le hicieron quedar en la escuela después de las clases

► **stop by*** (A) VI + ADV detenerse brevemente; **I'll ~ by on the way to school** me asomaré de paso al colegio
(B) VI + PREP **I'll ~ by your place later** pasaré por tu casa más tarde

► **stop in*** VI + ADV quedarse en casa, no salir; **don't ~ in for me** no te quedes esperándome en casa

► **stop off** VI + ADV interrumpir el viaje; **to ~ off at** (= *drop by*) pasar por; (= *stop at*) parar en

► **stop out*** VI + ADV (= *remain outside*) quedarse fuera; (= *not come home*) no volver a casa

► **stop over** VI + ADV (= *stay the night*) pasar la noche; (*Aer*) (*for refuelling etc*) hacer escala

► **stop up** (A) VT + ADV [+ *hole*] tapar
(B) VI + ADV (*Brit**) velar, no acostarse, seguir sin acostarse; **don't ~ up for me** no os quedéis esperándome hasta muy tarde

stop-and-go ['stɒpən'gəʊ] N (*US*) = **stop-go**

stopcock ['stɒpkɒk] N llave *f* de paso

stopgap ['stɒpgæp] (A) N (= *thing*) recurso *m* provisional, expediente *m*; (= *person*) sustituto/a *m/f*
(B) CPD ► **stopgap measure** N medida *f* provisional

stop-go ['stɒp'gəʊ] N (*Brit*) **period of ~** periodo *m* cuando una política de expansión económica alterna con otra de restricción

stoplights ['stɒplaɪts] NPL 1 (= *brake lights*) luces *fpl* de freno
2 (*US*) (= *traffic lights*) luces *fpl* de tráfico, semáforo *m*

stop-off ['stɒpɒf] N = **stopover**

stopover ['stɒpəʊvəʳ] N (*Aer*) escala *f*

stoppage ['stɒpɪdʒ] (A) N 1 [*of work*] paro *m*, suspensión *f*; (= *strike*) huelga *f*
2 [*of pay*] suspensión *f*; (*from wages*) deducción *f*
3 (*Sport*) detención *f*
4 (*in pipe etc*) obstrucción *f*
(B) CPD ► **stoppage time** N (*Sport*) tiempo *m* de descuento

stopper ['stɒpəʳ] (A) N tapón *m*; (*Tech*) taco *m*, tarugo *m*
(B) VT tapar, taponar

stopping ['stɒpɪŋ] (A) N 1 (= *halting*) [*of activity, progress, process*] suspensión *f*, interrupción *f*; [*of vehicle*] detención *f*, parada *f*; [*of cheque, wages*] bloqueo *m*, retención *f*; [*of match, game, payment*] suspensión *f*; [*of allowance, leave, privileges*] retirada *f*
2 (= *filling*) [*of tooth*] empaste *m*
3 (= *blocking*) [*of hole, pipe, leak*] relleno *m*, sellado *m*
(B) CPD ► **stopping place** N paradero *m*; [*of bus*] parada *f* ► **stopping train** N tren *m* correo, tren *m* ómnibus

stopwatch ['stɒpwɒtʃ] N cronómetro *m*

storage ['stɔ:rɪdʒ] (A) N almacenaje *m*, almacenamiento *m*; (*Comput*) almacenamiento *m*; **to put sth into ~** (*in a warehouse*) almacenar algo; (*in a furniture store*) llevar algo a un guardamuebles
(B) CPD ► **storage battery** N acumulador *m* ► **storage capacity** N capacidad *f* de almacenaje ► **storage charges** NPL derechos *mpl* de almacenaje ► **storage heater** N acumulador *m* ► **storage room** N (*US*) trastero *m* ► **storage space** N lugar *m* para los trastos ► **storage tank** N (*for oil etc*) tanque *m* de almacenamiento; (*for rainwater*) tanque *m* de reserva ► **storage unit** N (= *furniture*) armario *m*

store [stɔ:ʳ] (A) N 1 (= *supply, stock*) 1·1 [*of food, candles, paper*] reserva *f*; **to have** *or* **keep sth in ~** tener algo en reserva; **to keep a ~ of sth** tener una reserva de algo; **to lay in a ~ of sth** hacer una reserva de algo, proveerse de algo
1·2 (*fig*) [*of jokes, stories*] repertorio *m*; [*of information*] cúmulo *m*; **he has a vast ~ of dirty jokes** tiene un repertorio enorme de chistes verdes; **he possessed a vast ~ of knowledge** tenía una cultura muy amplia; **the company has a great ~ of expertise** la compañía cuenta con una multitud de gente competente; **to be in ~ for sb** (*fig*) aguardar a algn; **you never know what's in ~ (for you)** nunca se sabe lo que le aguarda a uno; **little did I know what the future had in ~** qué poco sabía lo que nos deparaba el futuro; **there's a surprise in ~ for you!** ¡te espera una sorpresa!; **to set great/little ~ by sth** tener algo en mucho/poco, dar mucho/poco valor a algo; **I wouldn't set much ~ by that** yo no le daría mucho valor
2 (= *depository*) almacén *m*, depósito *m*; **to put sth in(to) ~** (*in a warehouse*) almacenar algo; (*in a furniture store*) llevar algo a un guardamuebles; **to be in ~** (*in a warehouse*) estar en un almacén; (*in a furniture store*) estar en un guardamuebles; **furniture ~** guardamuebles *m inv*
3 **stores** (= *provisions*) provisiones *fpl*, existencias *fpl*; (*esp Mil*) (= *equipment*) pertrechos *mpl*

4 (= *shop*) 4·1 (*esp US*) [*of any size*] tienda *f*; **record ~** tienda *f* de discos; **book ~** librería *f*; **hardware ~** ferretería *f*; ✦**IDIOM to mind the ~** (*US**) cuidar de los asuntos; *see also* **grocery**, **village**
4·2 (*also* **department ~**) grandes almacenes *mpl*; **he owns a ~ in Oxford Street** es propietario de unos grandes almacenes en Oxford Street; *see also* **chain**, **department**
Ⓑ VT 1 (= *keep, collect*) 1·1 (*gen*) [+ *food*] conservar, guardar; [+ *water, fuel, electricity*] almacenar; [+ *heat*] acumular; [+ *documents*] archivar; **~ in an airtight tin** consérvense en un frasco hermético; **avoid storing food for too long** evite tener la comida guardada durante mucho tiempo
1·2 (*Comput*) [+ *information*] almacenar, guardar; (*Physiol*) [+ *fat, energy*] almacenar, acumular; **where in the brain do we ~ information about colours?** ¿en qué parte del cerebro almacenamos *or* guardamos información sobre los colores?
2 (= *put away*) guardar; **I've got the camping things ~d (away) till we need them** tengo las cosas de acampar guardadas hasta que las necesitemos
3 (= *put in depository*) [+ *furniture*] depositar en un guardamuebles; [+ *goods, crop, waste*] almacenar
Ⓒ VI conservarse; **fruits which won't ~ (well)** fruta que no se conserva (bien)
Ⓓ CPD ► **store card** N tarjeta *f* de compra ► **store clerk** N (*US*) dependiente/a *m/f* ► **store cupboard** N despensa *f* ► **store detective** N vigilante *mf* jurado (*de paisano en grandes almacenes*) ► **store manager** N gerente *mf* de tienda (*de grandes almacenes*)

►**store away** VT + ADV (*in bulk*) almacenar; [+ *individual items*] guardar

►**store up** VT + ADV [+ *fat, energy*] almacenar, acumular; [+ *feelings, bitterness, memories*] acumular, ir acumulando; **a hatred ~d up over centuries** un odio acumulado durante siglos; **to ~ up trouble** *or* **problems for the future** ir acumulando problemas para el futuro

store-bought [ˈstɔːbɔːt] ADJ (*US*) de confección, de serie

storefront [ˈstɔːfrʌnt] N (*US*) escaparate *m*

storehouse [ˈstɔːhaʊs] N (*pl* **storehouses** [ˈstɔːhaʊzɪz]) almacén *m*, depósito *m*; (*fig*) mina *f*, tesoro *m*

storekeeper [ˈstɔːˌkiːpəʳ] N 1 (= *warehouseman*) almacenero *m*
2 (*US*) (= *shopkeeper*) tendero/a *m/f*
3 (*Naut*) pañolero *m*

storeroom [ˈstɔːrʊm] N despensa *f*; (*Naut*) pañol *m*

storey, **story** (*US*) [ˈstɔːrɪ] N piso *m*

-storey, **-story** (*US*) [ˈstɔːrɪ] ADJ (*ending in compounds*) **a nine-storey building** un edificio de nueve pisos *or* plantas

-storeyed, **-storied** (*US*) [ˈstɔːrɪd] ADJ (*ending in compounds*) **an eight-storeyed building** un edificio de ocho pisos

stork [stɔːk] N cigüeña *f*

storm [stɔːm] Ⓐ N 1 (*gen*) tormenta *f*, tempestad *f*; (= *gale*) vendaval *m*; (= *hurricane*) huracán *m*; (*Naut*) borrasca *f*, tormenta *f*; ✦**IDIOMS to brave the ~** aguantar la tempestad; **to ride out a ~** capear un temporal, hacer frente a un temporal
2 (= *uproar*) escándalo *m*, bronca *f*; **there was a political ~** hubo un gran revuelo político; **it caused an international ~** levantó una polvareda internacional; **a ~ of abuse** un torrente de injurias; **a ~ of applause** una salva de aplausos; **a ~ of criticism** un aluvión *or* vendaval de críticas; ✦**IDIOM a ~ in a teacup** (*Brit*) una tormenta *or* tempestad en un vaso de agua
3 **to take by ~: to take a town by ~** (*Mil*) tomar una ciudad por asalto; **the play took Paris by ~** la obra cautivó a todo París
Ⓑ VT (*Mil*) asaltar, tomar por asalto; **angry ratepayers ~ed the town hall** los contribuyentes enfurecidos asaltaron *or* invadieron el ayuntamiento
Ⓒ VI 1 (= *move angrily*) **he came ~ing into my office** entró en mi despacho echando pestes; **he ~ed out of the meeting** salió de la reunión como un huracán
2 (= *speak angrily*) bramar, vociferar; **"you're fired!" he ~ed** —¡quedá despedido! —bramó *or* vociferó; **to ~ at sb** tronar contra algn, enfurecerse con algn; **he ~ed on for an hour about the government** pasó una hora lanzando improperios contra el gobierno
Ⓓ CPD ► **storm centre**, **storm center** (*US*) N centro *m* de la tempestad; (*fig*) foco *m* de los disturbios, centro *m* de la agitación ► **storm cloud** N nubarrón *m* ► **storm door** N contrapuerta *f* ► **storm signal** N señal *f* de temporal ► **storm trooper** N (*Mil*) guardia *mf* de asalto ► **storm troops** NPL (*Mil*) tropas *fpl* de asalto, guardia *fsing* de asalto

stormbound [ˈstɔːmbaʊnd] ADJ inmovilizado por el mal tiempo

storming [ˈstɔːmɪŋ] Ⓐ (= *impressive*) arrollador, arrasador
Ⓑ N (*Mil etc*) asalto *m* (**of** a)

stormproof [ˈstɔːmpruːf] ADJ a prueba de tormentas

storm-tossed [ˈstɔːmtɒst] ADJ sacudido por la tempestad

stormwater [ˈstɔːmˌwɔːtəʳ] N agua *f* de lluvia

stormy [ˈstɔːmɪ] Ⓐ ADJ (*compar* **stormier**; *superl* **stormiest**) 1 (*lit*) [*weather, night, skies*] tormentoso; **it's ~** hay tormenta
2 (*fig*) (= *turbulent*) [*meeting, scene*] tumultuoso, turbulento; [*relationship*] tormentoso
Ⓑ CPD ► **stormy petrel** N (*Orn*) petrel *m* de la tempestad; (*fig*) persona *f* pendenciera, persona *f* de vida borrascosa

story¹ [ˈstɔːrɪ] Ⓐ N 1 (= *account*) historia *f*; (= *tale*) cuento *m*, relato *m*; (= *joke*) chiste *m*; **his ~ is that ...** según él dice ..., según lo que él cuenta ...; **but that's another ~** pero eso es otro cantar; **a children's ~** un cuento infantil; **the ~ goes that ...** se dice *or* se cuenta que ...; **the ~ of her life** la historia de su vida; **that's the ~ of my life!*** ¡siempre me pasa lo mismo!; **it's a long ~** es/sería largo de contar; **to cut a long ~ short** en resumidas cuentas, en pocas palabras; **it's the same old ~** es la historia de siempre; **to tell a ~** (*fictional*) contar un cuento; (= *recount what happened*) contar *or* narrar una historia; **the marks tell their own ~** las señales hablan por sí solas, las señales no necesitan interpretación; **the full ~ has still to be told** todavía no se ha hecho pública toda la historia; **what a ~ this house could tell!** ¡cuántas cosas nos diría esta casa!; **the ~ of their travels** la relación de sus viajes; **that's not the whole ~** eso no es todo
2 (= *plot*) argumento *m*, trama *f*
3 (*Press*) artículo *m*, reportaje *m*
4 (*euph*) (= *lie*) mentira *f*, cuento *m*; **a likely ~!** ¡puro cuento!; **to tell stories** (*lies*) contar embustes
Ⓑ CPD ► **story writer** N narrador(a) *m/f*

story² [ˈstɔːrɪ] N (*US*) = **storey**

storyboard [ˈstɔːrɪˌbɔːd] (*Cine*) Ⓐ N story board *m*, desarrollo *m* secuencial en viñetas
Ⓑ VT hacer el story board de, hacer el desarrollo secuencial en viñetas de

storybook [ˈstɔːrɪbʊk] Ⓐ N libro *m* de cuentos
Ⓑ ADJ **a ~ ending** un final como el de una novela

storyline [ˈstɔːrɪlaɪn] N argumento *m*

storyteller [ˈstɔːrɪˌteləʳ] N 1 (*gen*) cuentista *mf*
2 (*) (= *liar*) cuentista *mf*, embustero/a *m/f*

stoup [stuːp] N copa *f*, frasco *m*; (*Rel*) pila *f*

stout [staʊt] Ⓐ ADJ (*compar* **stouter**; *superl* **stoutest**) 1 (= *sturdy*) [*stick, shoes etc*] fuerte, sólido
2 (= *fat*) [*person*] gordo, robusto
3 (= *determined*) [*supporter, resistance*] resuelto, empedernido; **~ fellow!**† ¡muy bien!; **he's a ~ fellow**† es un buen chico; **with ~ hearts** resueltamente
Ⓑ N (*Brit*) (= *beer*) cerveza *f* negra

stout-hearted [ˈstaʊtˈhɑːtɪd] ADJ valiente, resuelto

stoutly [ˈstaʊtlɪ] ADV 1 **~ built** de construcción sólida, fuerte
2 [*deny*] categóricamente, rotundamente; [*resist*] tenazmente; **he ~ maintains that ...** sostiene resueltamente que ...

stoutness [ˈstaʊtnɪs] N gordura *f*, corpulencia *f*

stove¹ [stəʊv] N (*for heating*) estufa *f*; (*for cooking*) cocina *f*, horno *m* (*LAm*)

stove² [stəʊv] PT, PP *of* **stave** *see* **stave in**

stovepipe [ˈstəʊvpaɪp] Ⓐ N tubo *m* de estufa
Ⓑ CPD ► **stovepipe hat** N chistera *f*

stow [stəʊ] VT 1 (*Naut*) [+ *cargo*] estibar, arrumar
2 (= *put away*) guardar; **where can I ~ this?** ¿esto dónde lo pongo?; **~ it!‡** ¡déjate de eso!, ¡cállate!, ¡basta ya!

►**stow away** Ⓐ VT + ADV (= *put away*) guardar; (= *hide*) esconder; **to ~ food away*** (*fig*) despachar rápidamente una comida, zamparse una comida
Ⓑ VI + ADV (*on ship, plane*) viajar de polizón

stowage [ˈstəʊɪdʒ] N (= *act*) estiba *f*, arrumaje *m*; (= *place*) bodega *f*

stowaway [ˈstəʊəweɪ] N polizón *m*, llovido *m*

strabismus [strəˈbɪzməs] N estrabismo *m*

Strabo [ˈstreɪbəʊ] N Estrabón

straddle [ˈstrædl] VT [+ *horse*] montar a horcajadas, ponerse a horcajadas sobre; [+ *target*] horquillar; [*town*] [+ *river etc*] hacer puente sobre

strafe [strɑːf] VT ametrallar, abalear (*LAm*)

strafing [ˈstrɑːfɪŋ] N ametrallamiento *m*

straggle [ˈstrægl] VI 1 (= *lag behind*) rezagarse; **the guests ~d out into the night** los invitados salieron poco a poco y desaparecieron en la noche; **as the last runners ~d over the finishing line ...** a medida que iban cruzando la meta los últimos corredores ...
2 (= *spread untidily*) (*Bot*) lozanear; [*hair*] caer lacio; **the village ~s on for miles** el pueblo se extiende varios kilómetros (sin tener un plano fijo); **her hair ~s over her face** el pelo le cae lacio delante de la cara

►**straggle away**, **straggle off** VI + ADV dispersarse

straggler [ˈstræglәʳ] N rezagado/a *m/f*

straggling [ˈstræglɪŋ], **straggly** [ˈstræglɪ] ADJ [*town*] disperso; [*plants*] extendido; [*hair*] despeinado, desordenado

straight [streɪt] Ⓐ ADJ (*compar* **straighter**; *superl* **straightest**) 1 (= *not bent or curved*) [*line, road, nose, skirt*] recto; [*trousers*] de perneras estrechas, de pata estrecha*; [*hair*] lacio, liso; [*shoulders*] erguido, recto; **he couldn't even walk in a ~ line** ni siquiera podía caminar en línea recta; **she was keeping the boat on a ~ course** mantenía el barco navegando en línea recta; **to have a ~ back** tener la espalda erguida *or* recta; **I couldn't keep a ~ face** ◊ **I couldn't keep my face ~** no podía mantener la cara seria; **she said it with a completely ~ face** lo dijo con la cara totalmente seria

2 (= *not askew*) [*picture, rug, hat, hem*] derecho; **the picture isn't ~** el cuadro está torcido *or* (*LAm*) chueco; **your tie isn't ~** tienes la corbata torcida, tu corbata no está bien; **to put** *or* **set ~** [+ *picture, hat, tie, rug*] poner derecho

3 (= *honest, direct*) [*answer*] franco, directo; [*question*] directo; [*refusal, denial*] categórico, rotundo; **all I want is a ~ answer to a ~ question** lo único que pido es que respondas con franqueza a una pregunta directa; **it's time for some ~ talking** es hora de hablar con franqueza *or* claramente; **to be ~ with sb** ser franco con algn, hablar a algn con toda franqueza; ✦*IDIOM* **as ~ as a die** honrado a carta cabal

4 (= *unambiguous*) claro; **is that ~?** ¿está claro?; **to get sth ~**: **let's get that ~ right from the start** vamos a dejar eso claro desde el principio; **there are a couple of things we'd better get ~** hay un par de cosas que debemos dejar claras; **have you got that ~?** ¿lo has entendido?, ¿está claro?; **he had to get things ~ in his mind** tenía que aclararse las ideas; **he hasn't got his facts ~** no tiene la información correcta; **to put** *or* **set sth ~** aclarar algo; **to put** *or* **set things** *or* **matters ~** aclarar las cosas; **to put** *or* **set the record ~** aclarar las cosas; **he soon put** *or* **set me ~** enseguida me aclaró las cosas

5 (= *tidy, in order*) [*house, room*] arreglado, ordenado; [*books, affairs, accounts*] en orden; **I like to keep my house ~** me gusta tener la casa arreglada *or* ordenada; **the paperwork still isn't ~** los papeles no están todavía en orden; **to get** *or* **put sth ~** arreglar algo

6 (= *clear-cut, simple*) [*choice, swap*] simple; **her latest novel is ~ autobiography** su última novela es una simple autobiografía; **we made £50 ~ profit on the deal** sacamos 50 libras limpias del negocio; **a ~ cash offer** una oferta de dinero en mano

7 (= *consecutive*) [*victories, defeats, games*] consecutivo; **this is the fifth ~ year that she has won** este es el quinto año consecutivo en el que ha ganado; **to get ~ As** sacar sobresaliente en todo; **a ~ flush** (*in poker*) una escalera real; **she lost in ~ sets to Pat Hay** (*in tennis*) perdió contra Pat Hay sin ganar ningún set; **we had ten ~ wins** ganamos diez veces seguidas, tuvimos diez victorias consecutivas

8 (= *neat*) [*whisky, vodka*] solo

9 (*Theat*) (= *not comic*) [*part, play, theatre, actor*] dramático, serio

10 (*) (= *conventional*) [*person*] de cabeza cuadrada*; **she's a nice person, but very ~** es maja pero tiene la cabeza demasiado cuadrada*

11 (*) (= *not owed or owing money*) **if I give you a fiver, then we'll be ~** si te doy cinco libras, estamos en paz

12 (*) (= *heterosexual*) heterosexual, hetero*

13 (*) (= *not criminal*) [*person*] **he's been ~ for two years** ha llevado una vida honrada durante dos años

14 (‡) (= *not using drugs*) **I've been ~ for 13 years** hace 13 años que dejé las drogas, llevo 13 años desenganchado de las drogas

Ⓑ ADV 1 (= *in a straight line*) [*walk, shoot, fly*] en línea recta; [*grow*] recto; **they can't even shoot ~** ni siquiera saben disparar en línea recta; **he was sitting up very ~** estaba sentado muy derecho *or* erguido; **stand up ~!** ¡ponte derecho *or* erguido!; **~ above us** directamente encima de nosotros; **it's ~ across the road from us** está justo al otro lado de la calle; **to go ~ ahead** ir todo recto, ir todo derecho; **to look ~ ahead** mirar al frente, mirar hacia adelante; **~ ahead of us** justo en frente de nosotros; **to look ~ at sb** mirar derecho hacia algn; **he came ~ at me** vino derecho hacia mí; **to hold o.s. ~** mantenerse derecho; **to look sb ~ in the eye** mirar directamente a los ojos de algn; **to look sb ~ in the face** mirar a algn directamente a la cara; **to go ~ on** ir todo recto, ir todo derecho; **the bullet went ~ through his chest** la bala le atravesó limpiamente el pecho; **I saw a car coming ~ towards me** vi un coche que venía derecho hacia mi; **to look ~ up** mirar hacia arriba; **the cork shot ~ up in the air** el corcho salió disparado hacia arriba

2 (= *level*) **to hang ~** [*picture*] estar derecho; **the picture isn't hanging ~** el cuadro está torcido *or* (*LAm*) chueco

3 (= *directly*) directamente; (= *immediately*) inmediatamente; **youngsters who move ~ from school onto the dole queue** jóvenes que pasan directamente del colegio a la cola del paro; **I went ~ home/to bed** fui derecho a casa/a la cama; **come ~ back** vuelve directamente aquí; **to come ~ to the point** ir al grano; **to drink ~ from the bottle** beber de la botella; **~ after this** inmediatamente después de esto; **~ away** inmediatamente, en seguida, al tiro (*Chile*); **~ off** (= *without hesitation*) sin vacilar; (= *immediately*) inmediatamente; (= *directly*) directamente, sin rodeos; **she just went ~ off** se marchó sin detenerse; ✦*IDIOM* **I heard it ~ from the horse's mouth** se lo oí decir a él mismo (*or* a ella misma)

4 (= *frankly*) francamente, con franqueza; **just give it to me** *or* **tell me ~** dímelo francamente *or* con franqueza; **to tell sb sth ~ out** decir algo a algn sin rodeos *or* directamente; **~ up** (*Brit**) en serio; ✦*IDIOM* **~ from the shoulder**: **I let him have it ~ from the shoulder** se lo dije sin rodeos

5 (= *neat*) [*drink*] solo; **I prefer to drink whisky ~** prefiero tomar el whisky solo

6 (= *clearly*) [*think*] con claridad; **he was so frightened that he couldn't think ~** tenía tanto miedo que no podía pensar con claridad; **I was so drunk I couldn't see ~** estaba tan borracho que no veía

7 (*) **to go ~** (= *reform*) [*criminal*] enmendarse; [*drug addict*] dejar de tomar drogas, desengancharse; **he's been going ~ for a year now** [*ex-criminal*] hace ahora un año que lleva una vida honrada; [*ex-addict*] hace un año que dejó las drogas, lleva un año desenganchado de las drogas

8 (*Theat*) **he played the role ~** interpretó el papel de manera clásica

9 (= *consecutively*) **we worked on the harvest for three days ~** hicimos la cosecha durante tres días seguidos

Ⓒ N 1 (= *straight line*) **to cut sth on the ~** cortar algo derecho; ✦*IDIOM* **the ~ and narrow** el buen camino; **to keep to the ~ and narrow** ir por buen camino; **to keep sb on the ~ and narrow** mantener a algn por el buen camino; **to depart from the ~ and narrow** apartarse del buen camino

2 (*Brit*) (*on racecourse*) **the ~** la recta; **as the cars entered the final ~ Hill was in the lead** cuando los coches entraron en la recta final Hill iba a la cabeza

3 (*Cards*) runfla *f*, escalera *f*

4 (*) (= *heterosexual*) heterosexual *mf*

Ⓓ CPD ► **straight angle** N ángulo *m* llano ► **straight arrow*** N (*US*) estrecho/a *m/f* de miras ► **straight man** N actor *m* que da pie al cómico; **I was the ~ man and he was the comic** yo era el actor que daba pie a sus chistes y él era el cómico ► **straight razor** N (*US*) navaja *f* de barbero ► **straight sex** N (= *not homosexual*) sexo *m* entre heterosexuales; (= *conventional*) relaciones *fpl* sexuales convencionales, sexo *m* sin florituras* ► **straight ticket** N (*US Pol*) **to vote a ~ ticket** votar a candidatos del mismo partido para todos los cargos

straightaway [ˈstreɪtəˈweɪ] ADV inmediatamente, en seguida, al tiro (*Chile*)

straightedge [ˈstreɪtedʒ] N regla *f* de borde recto

straighten [ˈstreɪtn] Ⓐ VT [+ *wire, nail*] (*also* **~ out**) enderezar; [+ *picture, tie, hat*] poner derecho, enderezar; [+ *tablecloth*] (= *arrange*) poner bien; (= *smooth out*) alisar; [+ *hair*] alisar; [+ *hem*] igualar; (*also* **~ up**) [+ *room, house*] ordenar, arreglar; [+ *papers*] ordenar; **to have one's teeth ~ed** ponerse bien los dientes; **to ~ one's shoulders** poner la espalda erguida *or* recta *or* derecha; **to ~ one's back** ponerse derecho *or* erguido; **to ~ o.s. (up)** arreglarse

Ⓑ VI = **straighten out B**

► **straighten out** Ⓐ VT + ADV 1 [+ *wire, nail*] enderezar

2 (= *resolve*) [+ *problem*] resolver

3 (*) [+ *person*] **I soon ~ed him out on that point** enseguida le aclaré las cosas a ese respecto; **they sent me to a psychoanalyst to try and ~ me out** me mandaron a un psicoanalista para ver si resolvía mis problemas; **if you don't behave I'll send your father in to ~ you out** si no te comportas llamaré a tu padre para que te ajuste las cuentas

Ⓑ VI + ADV 1 [*road*] **after the crossroads the road ~s out** tras el cruce ya no hay más curvas; **the road hardly ~s out at all from here to Bangor** son todo curvas de aquí a Bangor

2 (‡) (= *give up drugs*) desengancharse*

straight-faced [ˈstreɪtˈfeɪst] Ⓐ ADJ serio; **a ~ newsreader** un locutor de expresión seria

Ⓑ ADV con cara seria; **"whatever gives you that idea?" she asked ~** —¿qué te hace pensar eso? —preguntó con cara seria

straightforward [ˌstreɪtˈfɔːwəd] ADJ 1 (= *honest*) honrado; (= *sincere*) sincero

2 (= *simple*) sencillo; [*answer*] claro, franco

straightforwardly [ˌstreɪtˈfɔːwədlɪ] ADV (= *honestly*) honradamente; (= *frankly*) francamente; (= *simply*) sencillamente

straightforwardness [ˌstreɪtˈfɔːwədnɪs] N (= *honesty*) honradez *f*; (= *frankness*) franqueza *f*; (= *simplicity*) sencillez *f*; [*of answer*] claridad *f*

straightness [ˈstreɪtnɪs] N 1 (*lit*) [*of road, arm leg*] lo recto; [*of hair*] lo liso; [*of back*] lo recto, lo erguido

2 (*fig*) (= *honesty*) honestidad *f*; (= *frankness*) franqueza *f*

straight-out* [ˈstreɪtaʊt] ADJ [*answer*] sincero, franco; [*refusal*] tajante, rotundo; [*supporter, enthusiast, thief*] cien por cien; *see also* **straight B4**

strain[1] [streɪn] Ⓐ N 1 (= *physical pressure*) (*on rope, cable*) tensión *f*; (*on beam, bridge, structure*) presión *f*; **the ~ on a rope** la tensión de una cuerda; **this puts a ~ on the cable** esto tensa el cable; **that puts a great ~ on the beam** esto pone mucha presión sobre la viga; **to take the ~** (*lit*) aguantar el peso; **to take the ~ off** [+ *rope, cable*] disminuir la tensión de; [+ *beam, bridge, structure*] disminuir la presión sobre; **to break under the ~** [*rope, cable*] romperse debido a la tensión; **to collapse under the ~** [*bridge, ceiling*] venirse abajo debido a la presión

2 (*fig*) (= *burden*) carga *f*; (= *pressure*) presión *f*; (= *stress*) tensión *f*; **I found it a ~ being totally responsible for the child** me suponía una carga llevar toda la responsabilidad del niño yo solo; **it was a ~ on the economy/his purse** suponía una carga para la economía/su bolsillo; **the ~s on the economy** las presiones sobre la economía; **the ~s of modern life** las tensiones de la vida moderna; **mental ~** cansancio *m* mental; **to put a ~ on** [+ *resources*] suponer una carga para; [+ *system*] forzar al límite; [+ *relationship*] crear tirantez *or* tensiones en; **it put a great ~ on their friendship** creó mucha tirantez en su amistad; **his illness has put a terrible ~ on the family** su enfermedad ha creado mucha tensión *or* estrés para la familia; **he has been under a great deal of ~** ha estado sometido a mucha presión; *see also* **stress**

3 (= *effort*) esfuerzo *m*; **the ~ of climbing the stairs** el esfuerzo de subir las escaleras

4 (*Physiol*) 4·1 (= *injury*) (*from pull*) esguince *m*; (*involving twist*) esguince *m*, torcedura *f*; **back ~** torcedura de espalda; **muscle ~** esguince muscular

4·2 (= *wear*) (*on eyes, heart*) esfuerzo *m*; **he knew tennis put a ~ on his heart** sabía que el tenis le sometía el corazón a un esfuerzo *or* le forzaba el corazón; *see also* **eyestrain, repetitive**

5 **strains** (*liter*) (= *sound*) compases *mpl*; **we could hear the gentle ~s of a Haydn quartet** oíamos los suaves compases de un cuarteto de Haydn; **the bride came in to the ~s of the wedding march** la novia entró al son *or* a los compases de la marcha nupcial

Ⓑ VT 1 (= *stretch*) (*beyond reasonable limits*) [+ *system*] forzar al límite; [+ *friendship, relationship, marriage*] crear tensiones en, crear tirantez en; [+ *resources, budget*] suponer una carga para; [+ *patience*] poner a prueba; **the demands of the welfare state are ~ing public finances to the limit** las exigencias del estado de bienestar están resultando una carga excesiva para las arcas públicas; **to ~ relations with sb** tensar las relaciones con algn

2 (= *damage, tire*) [+ *back*] dañar(se), hacerse daño en; [+ *eyes*] cansar; **to ~ a muscle** hacerse un esguince; **to ~ o.s.: you shouldn't ~ yourself** no deberías hacer mucha fuerza; **he ~ed himself lifting something** se hizo daño levantando algo; **don't ~ yourself!** (*iro*) ¡no te vayas a quebrar *or* herniar!

3 (= *make an effort with*) [+ *voice, eyes*] forzar; **to ~ one's ears to hear sth** aguzar el oído para oír algo; **to ~ every nerve *or* sinew to do sth** esforzarse mucho por hacer algo, hacer grandes esfuerzos por hacer algo

4 (= *filter*) (*Chem*) filtrar; (*Culin*) [+ *gravy, soup, custard*] colar; [+ *vegetables*] escurrir; **to ~ sth into a bowl** colar algo en un cuenco; **~ the mixture through a sieve** pase la mezcla por un tamiz

Ⓒ VI (= *make an effort*) **to ~ to do sth** esforzarse por hacer algo; **he ~ed to hear what she was saying** se esforzaba por oír lo que decía; **he ~ed against the bonds that held him** (*liter*) hacía esfuerzos para soltarse de las cadenas que lo retenían; **to ~ at sth** tirar de algo; **to ~ at the leash** [*dog*] tirar de la correa; (*fig*) saltar de impaciencia; **to ~ under a weight** ir agobiado por un peso

►**strain off** Ⓐ VT + ADV [+ *liquid*] escurrir

Ⓑ VT + PREP **to ~ the water off sth** escurrir el agua a algo

strain² [streɪn] N 1 (= *breed*) (*of animal*) raza *f*; (*of plant*) variedad *f*; (*of virus*) tipo *m*; **every year new ~s of flu develop** cada año aparecen nuevos tipos de gripe

2 (= *streak, element*) vena *f*; **there is a ~ of madness in the family** tienen vena de locos en la familia; **there is a ~ of cynicism in her writing** hay cierta vena de cinismo en sus escritos

strained [streɪnd] ADJ 1 (= *tense*) [*person*] tenso; [*face*] crispado; [*voice, laugh, jollity, politeness*] forzado; [*atmosphere, relations, silence*] tirante, tenso; **she gave a ~ laugh** forzó una risa, se rió con una risa forzada

2 [*wrist, ankle*] torcido; [*eyes*] cansado; [*voice*] cansado; **a ~ muscle** un esguince; **he has a ~ shoulder/back** tiene una lesión en un hombro/en la espalda

3 (= *overtaxed*) [*economy*] debilitado

4 (*Culin*) [*baby food*] pasado por el pasapurés *or* el tamiz; [*soup, gravy*] colado; [*yoghurt*] espeso

strainer [ˈstreɪnəʳ] N (*Culin*) colador *m*; (*Tech*) filtro *m*, coladero *m*

strait [streɪt] N 1 (*Geog*) (*also* **~s**) estrecho *m*; **the Straits of Dover** el estrecho de Dover

2 **straits** (*fig*) situación *f* apurada, apuro *m*; **to be in dire ~s** estar en un gran apuro; **the economic ~s we are in** el apuro económico en que nos encontramos

straitened [ˈstreɪtnd] ADJ (*frm*) **in ~ circumstances** en condiciones difíciles, en condiciones de apuro

straitjacket [ˈstreɪt,dʒækɪt] N camisa *f* de fuerza; (*fig*) corsé *m*

strait-laced [ˈstreɪtˈleɪst] ADJ puritano

strand¹ [strænd] N 1 [*of thread*] hebra *f*, hilo *m*; [*of hair*] pelo *m*; [*of rope*] ramal *m*; [*of plant*] brizna *f*

2 (*fig*) [*of plan, theory*] aspecto *m*, faceta *f*; [*of story*] hilo *m* argumental

strand² [strænd] Ⓐ N (= *liter*) (= *beach, shore*) playa *f*

Ⓑ VT [+ *ship*] varar, encallar; **to be (left) ~ed** [*ship, fish*] quedar varado; (*fig*) [*person*] (*without money*) quedar desamparado; (*without transport*) quedar tirado; ✦***IDIOM* to leave sb ~ed** (*in the lurch*) dejar a algn plantado

strange [streɪndʒ] ADJ (*compar* **stranger**, *superl* **strangest**) 1 (= *odd*) [*person, event, behaviour, feeling*] extraño, raro; [*experience, place, noise*] extraño; [*coincidence, story*] extraño, curioso; **it is ~ that …** es extraño *or* raro que + *subjun*; **it's ~ that he should come today of all days** es extraño *or* raro que venga precisamente hoy; **there's something ~ about him** hay algo extraño *or* raro en él; **what's so ~ about that?** ¿qué tiene eso de extraño *or* raro?; **I felt rather ~ at first** al principio me sentía bastante raro; **I find her attitude rather ~** encuentro su actitud un tanto extraña *or* rara; **I find it ~ that we never heard anything about this** me parece raro *or* me extraña que nunca hayamos oído hablar de esto; **how ~!** ¡qué raro!, ¡qué extraño!; **for some ~ reason** por alguna razón inexplicable; **~ as it may seem** ◊ **~ to say** por extraño que parezca, aunque parezca mentira; **the ~ thing is that he didn't even know us** lo extraño *or* lo curioso es que ni nos conocía; **children come out with the ~st things** a los niños se les ocurren las cosas más extrañas; **the family would think it ~ if we didn't go** la familia se extrañaría si no fuésemos; *see also* **bedfellow, truth**

2 (= *unknown, unfamiliar*) [*person, house, car, country*] desconocido; [*language*] desconocido, extranjero; **I never sleep well in a ~ bed** nunca duermo bien en una cama que no sea la mía; **don't talk to any ~ men** no hables con ningún desconocido; **I was ~ to this part of town** esta parte de la ciudad me era desconocida; **this man I loved was suddenly ~ to me** este hombre al que amaba era de pronto un desconocido para mí *or* un extraño

> **STRANGE, RARE**
>
> **Position of "raro"**
>
> You should generally put **raro** after the noun when you mean **strange** or **odd** and before the noun when you mean **rare**:
>
> He has a strange name
>
> ***Tiene un nombre raro***
>
> ...a rare congenital syndrome...
>
> ***... un raro síndrome congénito...***
>
> *For further uses and examples, see main entry.*

strangely [ˈstreɪndʒlɪ] ADV [*act, behave*] de una forma extraña *or* rara; **the room was ~ quiet** en la habitación había un silencio extraño; **her voice sounded ~ familiar** su voz me resultaba extrañamente familiar; **the ~ named death's head moth** la extrañamente denominada mariposa de calavera; **~ (enough), …** por extraño que parezca, …, aunque resulte extraño, …

strangeness [ˈstreɪndʒnɪs] N 1 (= *oddness*) lo extraño, rareza *f*

2 (= *unfamiliarity*) novedad *f*

stranger [ˈstreɪndʒəʳ] N (= *unknown person*) desconocido/a *m/f*, extraño/a *m/f*; (*from another area etc*) forastero/a *m/f*; **he's a ~ to me** es un desconocido para mí; **I'm a ~ here** yo soy nuevo aquí; **hello, ~!** ¡cuánto tiempo sin vernos!; **you're quite a ~!** ¡apenas te dejas ver!; **he is no ~ to vice** conoce bien los vicios

strangle [ˈstræŋgl] VT estrangular; (*fig*) [+ *sob*] ahogar; **a ~d cry** un grito entrecortado

stranglehold [ˈstræŋglhəʊld] N 1 (*Sport*) collar *m* de fuerza

2 (*fig*) dominio *m* completo; **to have a ~ on sb/sth** tener dominio completo sobre algn/monopolizar algo

strangler [ˈstræŋgləʳ] N estrangulador(a) *m/f*

strangling [ˈstræŋglɪŋ] N estrangulación *f*, estrangulamiento *m*

strangulated [ˈstræŋgjʊleɪtɪd] ADJ estrangulado; **~ hernia** hernia *f* estrangulada

strangulation [,stræŋgjʊˈleɪʃən] N estrangulación *f*

strap [stræp] Ⓐ N correa *f*, tira *f*; (= *shoulder strap*) tirante *m*, bretel *m* (*LAm*); (= *safety strap*) cinturón *m*; **to give sb the ~** (= *punish*) azotar a algn con la correa, dar a algn con la correa

Ⓑ VT 1 (= *fasten*) atar con correa; **to ~ sth on/down** sujetar algo con correa; **to ~ sb/o.s. in** (*with seatbelt*) poner a algn/ponerse el cinturón de seguridad; **he isn't properly ~ped in** no está bien atado

2 (*Med*) (*also* **~ up**) vendar

3 **to ~ sb** (*as punishment*) azotar a algn con la correa, dar a algn con la correa

strap-hang* [ˈstræphæŋ] VI viajar de pie (*agarrado a la correa*)

strap-hanger* [ˈstræphæŋəʳ] N pasajero/a *m/f* que va de pie (*agarrado a la correa*)

strap-hanging* [ˈstræp,hæŋɪŋ] N viajar *m* de pie

strapless ['stræplɪs] ADJ [*dress, bra*] sin tirantes

strapped* [stræpt] ADJ **to be ~ for cash** andar escaso de dinero

strapping ['stræpɪŋ] ADJ [*person*] fornido, robusto

Strasbourg ['stræzbɜ:g] N Estrasburgo *m*

strata ['strɑ:tə] NPL *of* **stratum**

stratagem ['strætɪdʒəm] N estratagema *f*

strategic [strə'ti:dʒɪk] ADJ estratégico

strategical [strə'ti:dʒɪkəl] ADJ = **strategic**

strategically [strə'ti:dʒɪkəlɪ] ADV [*act, think*] con una estrategia, estratégicamente; [*important, positioned*] estratégicamente

strategist ['strætɪdʒɪst] N estratega *mf*

strategy ['strætɪdʒɪ] N estrategia *f*

stratification [ˌstrætɪfɪ'keɪʃən] N estratificación *f*

stratified ['strætɪfaɪd] ADJ estratificado

stratify ['strætɪfaɪ] Ⓐ VT estratificar
Ⓑ VI estratificarse

stratigraphic [ˌstrætɪ'græfɪk] ADJ estratigráfico

stratigraphy [strə'tɪgrəfɪ] N estratigrafía *f*

stratocumulus [ˌstreɪtəʊ'kju:mjʊləs] N (*pl* **stratocumuli** [ˌstreɪtəʊ'kju:mjʊlaɪ]) estratocúmulo *m*

stratosphere ['strætəʊsfɪəʳ] N estratosfera *f*

stratospheric [ˌstrætəʊs'ferɪk] ADJ estratosférico

stratum ['strɑ:təm] N (*pl* **stratums** *or* **strata**) 1 (*lit*) estrato *m*
2 (*fig*) estrato *m*, capa *f*

stratus ['streɪtəs] N (*pl* **strati** ['streɪtaɪ]) estrato *m*

straw [strɔ:] Ⓐ N 1 (*Agr*) paja *f*; ✦***IDIOMS*** **the ~ that breaks the camel's back** la gota que colma el vaso; **to clutch** *or* **grasp at ~s** agarrarse a un clavo ardiendo; **to draw** *or* **get the short ~** ser elegido para hacer algo desagradable; **I always draw the short ~** siempre me toca a mí la china*; **it's the last ~!** ¡es el colmo!, ¡sólo faltaba eso!; **it's a ~ in the wind** sirve de indicio
2 (= *drinking straw*) pajita *f*, caña *f*, popote *m* (*Mex*); **to drink through a ~** beber con pajita
Ⓑ ADJ (= *made of straw*) de paja; (= *colour*) pajizo, color paja
Ⓒ CPD ► **straw hat** N sombrero *m* de paja ► **straw man** N hombre *m* de paja ► **straw poll**, **straw vote** N votación *f* de tanteo

strawberry ['strɔ:bərɪ] Ⓐ N (= *fruit, plant*) fresa *f*, frutilla *f* (*LAm*); (*large, cultivated*) fresón *m*
Ⓑ CPD [*jam, ice cream, tart*] de fresa ► **strawberry bed** N fresal *m* ► **strawberry blonde** N rubia *f* fresa; *see also* **strawberry-blonde** ► **strawberry mark** N (*on skin*) mancha *f* de nacimiento

strawberry-blonde [ˌstrɔ:bərɪ'blɒnd] ADJ bermejo

straw-coloured, **straw-colored** (*US*) ['strɔ:kʌləd] ADJ pajizo, (de) color de paja

strawloft ['strɔ:lɒft] N pajar *m*, pajera *f*

stray [streɪ] Ⓐ ADJ 1 (= *errant*) [*bullet*] perdido; [*sheep*] descarriado; [*cow, dog*] extraviado; **a ~ cat** (= *lost*) un gato extraviado; (= *alley cat*) un gato callejero
2 (= *isolated, occasional*) aislado; **in a few ~ cases** en algunos casos aislados; **a few ~ cars** algún que otro coche; **a few ~ thoughts** unos cuantos pensamientos inconexos
Ⓑ N 1 (= *animal*) animal *m* extraviado; (= *child*) niño/a *m/f* sin hogar, niño/a *m/f* desamparado/a
2 **strays** (*Rad*) parásitos *mpl*
Ⓒ VI 1 [*animal*] (= *roam*) extraviarse; (= *get lost*) perderse, extraviarse; **if the gate is left open the cattle ~** si se deja abierta la puerta las vacas se escapan
2 (= *wander*) [*person*] vagar, ir sin rumbo fijo; [*speaker, thoughts*] desvariar; **to ~ from** (*also fig*) apartarse de; **we had ~ed two kilometres from the path** nos habíamos desviado dos kilómetros del camino; **they ~ed into the enemy camp** erraron el camino y se encontraron en el campamento enemigo; **my thoughts ~ed to the holidays** empecé a pensar en las vacaciones

streak [stri:k] Ⓐ N 1 (*line*) raya *f*; [*of mineral*] veta *f*, vena *f*; **to have ~s in one's hair** tener mechas en el pelo; ✦***IDIOM*** **like a ~ of lightning** como un rayo
2 (*fig*) [*of madness etc*] vena *f*; [*of luck*] racha *f*; **he had a cruel ~ (in him)** tenía un rasgo cruel; **there is a ~ of Spanish blood in her** tiene una pequeña parte de sangre española; **he had a yellow ~** era un tanto cobarde
Ⓑ VT rayar (**with** de)
Ⓒ VI 1 (= *rush*) **to ~ along** correr a gran velocidad; **to ~ in/out/past** entrar/salir/pasar como un rayo
2 (*) (= *run naked*) correr desnudo

streaker* ['stri:kəʳ] N corredor(a) *m/f* desnudo/a

streaking* ['stri:kɪŋ] N carrera *f* desnudista

streaky ['stri:kɪ] Ⓐ ADJ rayado, listado; [*rock etc*] veteado
Ⓑ CPD ► **streaky bacon** N (*Brit*) tocino *m* con grasa, bacon *m*, beicon *m*

stream [stri:m] Ⓐ N 1 (= *brook*) arroyo *m*, riachuelo *m*
2 (= *current*) corriente *f*; **to go with/against the ~** (*lit, fig*) ir con/contra la corriente
3 (= *jet, gush*) [*of liquid*] chorro *m*; [*of light*] raudal *m*; [*of air*] chorro *m*, corriente *f*; [*of lava*] río *m*; [*of insults, abuse*] sarta *f*; [*of letters, questions, complaints*] lluvia *f*; **a thin ~ of water** un chorrito de agua; **she exhaled a thin ~ of smoke** lanzó *or* exhaló un chorrillo de humo; **a steady ~ of cars** un flujo constante *or* ininterrumpido de coches; **people were coming out of the cinema in a steady ~** había una continua hilera de gente que iba saliendo del cine; **we had a constant ~ of visitors** recibíamos visitas continuamente *or* sin parar; **he let out a ~ of insults** soltó una sarta de insultos; **~ of consciousness** monólogo *m* interior
4 (*Brit Scol*) *grupo de alumnos de la misma edad y aptitud académica*; **the top/middle/bottom ~** la clase de nivel superior/medio/inferior
5 (*Ind*) **to be on/off ~** [*machinery, production line*] estar/no estar en funcionamiento; [*oil well*] estar/no estar en producción; **to come on ~** [*machinery, production line*] entrar en funcionamiento; [*oil well*] entrar en producción
Ⓑ VI 1 (= *pour*) 1·1 (*lit*) **tears were ~ing down her face** le corrían las lágrimas por la cara; **rain ~ed down the windows** la lluvia chorreaba por las ventanas; **blood ~ed from a cut on his knee** le chorreaba sangre de un corte en la rodilla; **water ~ed from a cracked pipe** salía agua a chorros de una cañería rota; **his head was ~ing with blood** la cabeza le chorreaba sangre
1·2 (*fig*) **people ~ed into the hall** la gente entró en tropel a la sala; **bright sunlight ~ed in through the window/into the room** la fuerte luz del sol entraba a raudales por la ventana/en la habitación; **people came ~ing out** la gente salía en tropel; **as holiday traffic ~s out of the cities ...** a medida que las caravanas de las vacaciones van saliendo de las ciudades ...; **the cars kept ~ing past** los coches pasaban ininterrumpidamente *or* sin parar
2 (= *water, run*) **her eyes were ~ing** le lloraban los ojos; **my nose was ~ing** me moqueaba la nariz
3 (= *flutter*) [*flag, hair, scarf*] ondear; **flags ~ed in the wind** las banderas ondeaban al viento
Ⓒ VT 1 **his face ~ed blood** la sangre le corría *or* chorreaba por la cara
2 (*Brit Scol*) [+ *pupils*] agrupar, clasificar (*según su aptitud académica*)

streamer ['stri:məʳ] N 1 [*of paper, at parties etc*] serpentina *f*
2 (*Naut*) gallardete *m*

streaming ['stri:mɪŋ] Ⓐ ADJ **to have a ~ cold** tener un resfriado muy fuerte; **I had a ~ nose** me moqueaba la nariz; **to have ~ eyes** tener los ojos llorosos
Ⓑ N (*Scol*) división *f* de alumnos por grupos (*según su aptitud académica*)

streamline ['stri:mlaɪn] VT (*lit*) aerodinamizar; (*fig*) racionalizar

streamlined ['stri:mlaɪnd] ADJ [*air*] aerodinámico; (*fig*) racionalizado

street [stri:t] Ⓐ N calle *f*, jirón *m* (*Peru*); **he lives in** *or* **on the High Street** vive en la Calle Mayor; **to be on the ~s** (= *homeless*) estar sin vivienda; (*euph*) (*as prostitute*) hacer la calle; ✦***IDIOMS*** **to be ~s ahead of sb** (*Brit**) adelantarle por mucho a algn; **we are ~s ahead of them in design** les damos ciento y raya en el diseño; **they're ~s apart** (*Brit**) los separa un abismo; **they're not in the same ~ as us** (*Brit**) no están a nuestra altura, no admiten comparación con nosotros; **it's right up my ~** (*Brit**) esto es lo que me va, esto es lo mío
Ⓑ CPD ► **street arab**† N golfo *m*, chicuelo *m* de la calle ► **street cleaner** N barrendero/a *m/f* ► **street corner** N esquina *f* (de la calle) ► **street cred***, **street credibility** N dominio *m* de la contracultura urbana ► **street door** N puerta *f* principal, puerta *f* de la calle ► **street fight** N pelea *f* callejera ► **street fighting** N peleas *fpl* callejeras ► **street lamp** N farola *f*, faro *m* (*LAm*) ► **street level** N **at ~ level** en el nivel de la calle ► **street light** N = **street lamp** ► **street lighting** N alumbrado *m* público ► **street map** N plano *m* (de la ciudad) ► **street market** N mercado *m* callejero, tianguis *m* (*Mex*), feria *f* (*LAm*) ► **street musician** N músico *m* ambulante ► **street photographer** N fotógrafo *m* callejero ► **street plan** N plano *m*, callejero *m* ► **street sweeper** N barrendero/a *m/f* ► **street theatre** N teatro *m* en la calle, teatro *m* de calle ► **street urchin** N golfo *m*, chicuelo *m* de la calle ► **street value** N valor *m* en la calle ► **street vendor** N (*US*) vendedor/a *mf* callejero/a

streetcar ['stri:tkɑ:ʳ] N (*US*) tranvía *m*, tren *m*

streetsmart ['stri:tsmɑ:t] ADJ (*US*) = **streetwise**

streetwalker ['stri:tˌwɔ:kəʳ] N (= *prostitute*) mujer *f* de la vida

streetwise ['stri:twaɪz] ADJ despabilado

strength [streŋθ] N 1 (= *might, energy*) (*for particular task*) fuerzas *fpl*; (= *general attribute*) fuerza *f*; **he hadn't the ~ to lift it** no tenía fuerzas para levantarlo; **his ~ failed him** le fallaron las fuerzas; **she swims to build up the ~ in her muscles** nada para fortalecer los músculos *or* coger fuerza en los músculos; **you don't know your own ~** no controlas tu propia fuerza; **you'll soon get your ~ back** pronto recobrarás las fuerzas *or* te repondrás;

to save one's ~ ahorrar las energías; **with all my ~** con todas mis fuerzas
2 (= *fortitude*) fortaleza *f*, fuerzas *fpl*; (= *firmness*) [*of belief, conviction*] firmeza *f*; **his help gives me the ~ to carry on** su ayuda me da fortaleza *or* fuerzas para seguir adelante; **~ of character** fortaleza *f or* firmeza *f* de carácter; **to draw ~ from sth** sacar fuerzas de algo; **the independence movement is gathering ~** el movimiento independiente está cobrando fuerza; **give me ~!*** ¡Dios dame paciencia!*; **inner ~** fuerza interior; **~ of purpose** determinación *f*; *see also* **gather, tower**
3 (= *sturdiness*) [*of material, structure, frame*] resistencia *f*
4 (= *power*) [*of argument*] lo convincente, solidez *f*; [*of claim, case, evidence*] peso *m*; [*of protests*] lo enérgico; [*of magnet, lens, drug*] potencia *f*; [*of wind*] fuerza *f*; [*of alcohol*] graduación *f*; **on the ~ of that success she applied for promotion** en base a ese éxito, solicitó un ascenso; **he was recruited on the ~ of his communication skills** lo contrataron en virtud de *or* debido a su aptitud para comunicarse
5 (= *intensity*) [*of emotion*] intensidad *f*, fuerza *f*; [*of sound*] potencia *f*; [*of colour*] intensidad *f*; **he warned the government not to underestimate the ~ of feeling among voters** advirtió al gobierno que no subestimara la intensidad *or* fuerza de los sentimientos de los votantes
6 [*of currency*] (= *value*) valor *m*; (= *high value*) solidez *f*, fuerza *f*; **our decision will depend on the ~ of the pound** nuestra decisión dependerá del valor de la libra; **exports fell owing to the ~ of the pound** las exportaciones bajaron debido a la solidez *or* la fuerza de la libra
7 (= *good point, asset*) punto *m* fuerte; **their chief ~ is technology** su punto fuerte es la tecnología; ***✦IDIOM*** **to go from ~ to ~: his movie career is going from ~ to ~** su carrera cinematográfica marcha viento en popa; **the company has gone from ~ to ~** la empresa ha ido teniendo un éxito tras otro
8 (*in number*) número *m*; (*Mil, Police*) efectivos *mpl*; **he has promised to increase the ~ of the police force** ha prometido incrementar los efectivos de la policía; **to be below ~ = to be under strength**; **to be at full ~** [*army*] disponer de todos sus efectivos; (*Sport*) [*team*] contar con todos sus jugadores; [*office*] contar con todo el personal; **his supporters were there in ~** *or* **had come in ~** sus partidarios habían acudido en masa; **to be on the ~** (*gen*) formar parte de la plantilla; (*Mil*) formar parte del regimiento; **to take sb on to the ~** admitir a algn en la plantilla; (*Mil*) admitir a algn en el regimiento; **to be under ~: the team was under ~ due to injuries** el equipo contaba con pocos jugadores debido a las lesiones; **two people are off sick so we're a bit under ~** dos de los empleados se encuentran enfermos y estamos un poco cortos de personal; **his army was seriously under ~** su ejército contaba con poquísimos efectivos

strengthen ['streŋθən] Ⓐ VT 1 (*lit*) [+ *wall, roof, building*] reforzar; [+ *back, muscle*] fortalecer; **he does exercises to ~ his legs** hace ejercicios para fortalecer las piernas
2 (*fig*) [+ *currency, economy, bond, relationship, character*] fortalecer, consolidar; [+ *government*] consolidar; [+ *case, argument, law*] reforzar; [+ *power*] consolidar, afianzar; [+ *resolve, belief, impression*] reafirmar; [+ *person*] (*morally*) fortalecer; **this served to ~ opposition to the strike** esto sirvió para afianzar la oposición a la huelga; **her rejection only ~ed his resolve** el rechazo de ella sólo sirvió para hacer más firme su propósito de conquistarla; **to ~ sb's position** ◊ **~ sb's hand** afianzar la posición de algn
Ⓑ VI 1 (*lit*) [*muscle, arm, back*] fortalecerse; [*wind, storm*] hacerse más fuerte
2 (*fig*) [*currency, economy*] fortalecerse, consolidarse; [*prices*] afianzarse; [*desire, determination*] redoblarse, intensificarse

strengthening ['streŋθənɪŋ] Ⓐ ADJ (*physically*) fortificante, tonificante; **~ exercises** ejercicios *mpl* fortificantes *or* tonificantes; **this may have a ~ effect on the economy** puede que esto tenga un efecto fortificante en la economía
Ⓑ N 1 [*of arm, back, muscles*] fortalecimiento *m*
2 (*fig*) [*of currency, stock market*] fortalecimiento *m*, consolidación *f*; [*of prices*] afianzamiento *m*

strenuous ['strenjʊəs] ADJ 1 (= *physically demanding*) [*efforts*] intenso, arduo; [*work*] agotador, arduo; [*exercise, walk*] agotador, fatigoso
2 (= *vigorous*) [*objections, protest, opposition*] enérgico; [*denial*] enérgico, rotundo; **to make ~ efforts to do sth** esforzarse afanosamente *or* hacer intensos esfuerzos por hacer algo

strenuously ['strenjʊəslɪ] ADV [*deny*] enérgicamente, rotundamente; [*object, protest, oppose*] enérgicamente; [*resist*] tenazmente, con tenacidad; [*exercise*] con intensidad; **he has ~ denied the allegations** ha rechazado enérgicamente *or* rotundamente las acusaciones; **to try ~ to do sth** esforzarse afanosamente por hacer algo, procurar por todos los medios hacer algo

streptococcus [ˌstreptəʊ'kɒkəs] N (*pl* **streptococci** [ˌstreptəʊ'kɒkaɪ]) estreptococo *m*

streptomycin [ˌstreptəʊ'maɪsɪn] N estreptomicina *f*

stress [stres] Ⓐ N 1 (*Tech*) tensión *f*, carga *f*
2 (*psychological etc*) (= *strain*) estrés *m*, tensión *f* (nerviosa); **in times of ~** en épocas de estrés *or* tensión; **to subject sb to great ~** someter a algn a grandes tensiones; **the ~es and strains of modern life** las presiones de la vida moderna; **to be under ~** estar estresado, tener estrés
3 (= *emphasis*) hincapié *m*, énfasis *m*; **to lay great ~ on sth** recalcar algo
4 (*Ling, Poetry*) acento *m*; **the ~ is on the second syllable** el acento tónico cae en la segunda sílaba
Ⓑ VT 1 (= *emphasize*) subrayar, insistir en; **I must ~ that ...** tengo que subrayar que ...
2 (*Ling, Poetry*) acentuar
Ⓒ CPD ► **stress mark** N (*Ling*) tilde *f*
► **stress system** N (*Ling*) sistema *m* de acentos, acentuación *f*

►**stress out*** VT + ADV estresar, agobiar; **to be ~ed out** estar estresado *or* agobiado

stressed [strest] ADJ 1 (= *tense*) [*person*] estresado, agobiado
2 (*Ling, Poetry*) [*syllable*] acentuado

stressful ['stresfʊl] ADJ [*job*] estresante, que produce tensión nerviosa

stretch [stretʃ] Ⓐ N 1 (= *elasticity*) elasticidad *f*
2 (= *act of stretching*) **to have a ~** [*person*] estirarse; **to be at full ~** [*person*] (*physically*) estirarse al máximo; (*at work*) estar trabajando a toda mecha*; **with arms at full ~** con los brazos completamente extendidos; **when the engine is at full ~** cuando el motor está a la máxima potencia, cuando el motor rinde su potencia máxima; **by a ~ of the imagination** con un esfuerzo de imaginación; **by no ~ of the imagination** bajo ningún concepto
3 (= *distance*) trecho *m*; **for a long ~ it runs between mountains** corre entre montañas durante un buen trecho
4 (= *expanse*) extensión *f*; [*of road etc*] tramo *m*; [*of rope*] trozo *m*; [*of time*] periodo *m*, tiempo *m*; **in that ~ of the river** en aquella parte del río; **a splendid ~ of countryside** un magnífico paisaje; **for a long ~ of time** durante mucho tiempo; **for hours at a ~** durante horas enteras; **for three days at a ~** tres días de un tirón *or* (*LAm*) jalón; **he read the lot at one ~** se los leyó todos de un tirón *or* (*LAm*) jalón
5 (‡) (*in prison*) **a five-year ~** una condena de cinco años; **he's doing a ~** está en chirona‡
Ⓑ VT 1 (= *pull out*) [+ *elastic*] estirar; [+ *rope etc*] tender (**between** entre)
2 (= *make larger*) [+ *pullover, shoes*] ensanchar; (= *make longer*) alargar; (= *spread on ground etc*) extender; **the blow ~ed him (out) cold on the floor** el golpe lo tumbó sin sentido en el suelo
3 (= *exercise*) **to ~ one's legs** estirar las piernas; (*after stiffness*) desentumecerse las piernas; (*fig*) (= *go for a walk*) dar un paseíto; **to ~ o.s.** (*after sleep etc*) desperezarse
4 [+ *money, resources, meal*] hacer que llegue *or* alcance; **our resources are fully ~ed** nuestros recursos están aprovechados al máximo
5 [+ *meaning, law, truth*] forzar, violentar; **that's ~ing it too far** eso va demasiado lejos; **to ~ a point** hacer una excepción; **to ~ the rules for sb** ajustar las reglas a beneficio de algn
6 [+ *athlete, student etc*] exigir el máximo esfuerzo a; **the course does not ~ the students enough** el curso no exige bastante esfuerzo a los estudiantes; **to be fully ~ed** llegar a sus límites; **to ~ o.s.** esforzarse; **he doesn't ~ himself** no se esfuerza bastante, puede dar más de sí; **to ~ sb to the limits** sacar el máximo provecho de algn
Ⓒ VI 1 (= *be elastic*) estirar(se), dar (de sí); **this cloth won't ~** esta tela no se estira, esta tela no da de sí
2 (= *become larger*) [*clothes, shoes*] ensancharse
3 (= *stretch one's limbs, reach out*) estirarse; (*after sleep etc*) desperezarse
4 (= *reach, extend*) [*rope, area of land*] llegar (**to** a); [*power, influence*] permitir (**to** que); **will it ~?** ¿llega?; **it ~es for miles along the river** se extiende varios kilómetros a lo largo del río
5 (= *be enough*) [*money, food*] alcanzar (**to** para)
Ⓓ CPD ► **stretch fabric** N tela *f* elástica
► **stretch limo*** N limusina *f* extralarga
► **stretch marks** NPL (*Med*) estrías *fpl*

►**stretch out** Ⓐ VT + ADV 1 [+ *arm*] extender; [+ *hand*] tender, alargar; [+ *leg*] estirar
2 (= *lengthen*) [+ *essay, discussion*] alargar
Ⓑ VI + ADV 1 [*person*] estirarse; (= *lie down*) tumbarse, tenderse; **he ~ed out on the ground** se tumbó *or* se tendió en el suelo; **to ~ out to take sth** alargar el brazo para tomar algo
2 [*space, time*] extenderse

►**stretch up** VI + ADV **to ~ up to take sth** alargar el brazo para tomar algo

stretcher ['stretʃəʳ] Ⓐ N 1 (*Med*) camilla *f*
2 (*Tech*) (*for gloves etc*) ensanchador *m*; (*for canvas*) bastidor *m*

[3] (*Archit*) soga *f*
Ⓑ VT (*Med*) llevar en camilla
Ⓒ CPD ► **stretcher bearer** N camillero/a *m/f* ► **stretcher case** N *enfermo o herido que tiene que ser llevado en camilla* ► **stretcher party** N equipo *m* de camilleros

►**stretcher away** VT + ADV retirar en camilla, llevarse en camilla

►**stretcher off** VT + ADV retirar en camilla

stretchy ['stretʃɪ] ADJ elástico

strew [struː] (*pt* **strewed**; *pp* **strewed**, **strewn** [struːn]) VT [1] (= *scatter*) regar, esparcir; **there were fragments ~n about everywhere** había fragmentos esparcidos por todas partes; **to ~ sand on the floor** cubrir el suelo de arena, esparcir arena sobre el suelo; **to ~ one's belongings about the room** desparramar las cosas por el cuarto
[2] (= *cover*) cubrir, tapizar (**with** de); **the floors are ~n with rushes** los suelos están cubiertos de juncos

striated [straɪ'eɪtɪd] ADJ estriado

stricken ['strɪkən] Ⓐ (†) PP *of* **strike**
Ⓑ ADJ [1] (= *distressed, upset*) afligido, acongojado; **to be ~ with** estar afligido por; **to be ~ with grief** estar agobiado por el dolor; **she was ~ with remorse** le remordía la conciencia
[2] (= *damaged*) [*ship etc*] destrozado, dañado; (= *wounded*) herido; (= *ill*) enfermo; (= *suffering*) afligido; (= *doomed*) condenado; **the ~ families** las familias afligidas; **the ~ city** la ciudad condenada, la ciudad destrozada

-stricken ['strɪkən] ADJ (*ending in compounds*) **drought-stricken** aquejado de sequía, afectado por la sequía

strict [strɪkt] ADJ (*compar* **stricter**; *superl* **strictest**) [1] (= *stern, severe*) [*person, discipline*] estricto, severo; **her ~ upbringing** la educación estricta *or* rigurosa que recibió; **to be ~ with sb** ser estricto *or* severo con algn
[2] (= *stringent*) [*rules*] estricto; [*control*] estricto, riguroso; [*limit*] riguroso; [*security measures*] riguroso, estricto; [*orders*] tajante, terminante, estricto; **to be under ~ orders (not) to do sth** tener órdenes estrictas de (no) hacer algo
[3] (= *precise*) [*meaning*] estricto; **in ~ order of precedence** por riguroso *or* estricto orden de precedencia; **in the ~ sense of the word** en el sentido estricto de la palabra
[4] (= *absolute*) [*secrecy*] absoluto; **I told you that in ~ confidence** te lo dije con la más absoluta reserva; **all your replies will be treated in the ~est confidence** todas las respuestas serán tratadas con la reserva más absoluta; **~ liability** (*Jur*) responsabilidad *f* absoluta
[5] (= *rigorous*) [*Methodist*] estricto; [*vegetarian, diet*] estricto, riguroso; [*hygiene*] absoluto; **I'm a ~ teetotaller** soy estrictamente *or* rigurosamente abstemio

strictly ['strɪktlɪ] ADV [1] (= *sternly, severely*) severamente; **she was ~ brought up** recibió una educación muy estricta *or* rigurosa
[2] (= *stringently*) [*control, adhere to*] estrictamente, rigurosamente; [*limit*] rigurosamente
[3] (= *absolutely*) [*forbidden*] terminantemente; [*necessary*] absolutamente; [*confidential*] estrictamente; **it is not ~ accurate to say that ...** no es del todo preciso decir que ...; **"strictly private"** (*on fence, gate*) "prohibido el paso", "propiedad privada"; (*on letter*) "estrictamente confidencial"; **~ speaking** en (el) sentido estricto (de la palabra); **that's not ~ true** eso no es del todo cierto, eso no es rigurosamente cierto
[4] (= *exclusively*) exclusivamente; **this is ~ business** esto es exclusivamente una cuestión de trabajo; **the car park is ~ for the use of residents** el aparcamiento es para uso exclusivo de los residentes; **everything he said was ~ to the point** todo lo que decía iba directamente al grano

strictness ['strɪktnɪs] N [1] (= *severity*) [*of person*] severidad *f*; [*of discipline*] lo estricto, severidad *f*
[2] (= *stringency*) [*of rules, control, security*] lo riguroso

stricture ['strɪktʃəʳ] N [1] (*usu pl*) (= *criticism*) censura *f*, crítica *f*; **to pass ~s on sb** censurar a algn, poner reparos a algn
[2] (*Med*) constricción *f*

stridden ['strɪdn] PP *of* **stride**

stride [straɪd] (*vb: pt* **strode**; *pp* **stridden**) Ⓐ N zancada *f*, tranco *m*; (*in measuring*) paso *m*; **to make great ~s** (*fig*) hacer grandes progresos; ✦*IDIOMS* **to get into** *or* **hit one's ~** coger *or* (*LAm*) agarrar el ritmo; **to take things in one's ~** *or* (*US*) **in ~** tomar las cosas con calma; **to put sb off their ~** (*Brit*) hacer perder los papeles a algn
Ⓑ VI (*also* **~ along**) andar a zancadas
Ⓒ VT [1] (†) [+ *horse*] montar a horcajadas sobre
[2] (= *cross*) [+ *deck, yard etc*] cruzar de un tranco

►**stride away**, **stride off** VI + ADV alejarse a grandes zancadas

►**stride up** VI + ADV **to ~ up to sb** acercarse resueltamente a algn; **to ~ up and down** andar de aquí para allá a pasos largos

stridency ['straɪdənsɪ] N [*of voice, colour, person*] estridencia *f*; [*of protests*] fuerza *f*, lo ruidoso

strident ['straɪdənt] ADJ [*voice, sound*] estridente; [*colour, person*] chillón, estridente; [*protest*] fuerte, ruidoso

stridently ['straɪdəntlɪ] ADV [*hoot, sound, whistle*] con estridencia, de modo estridente; [*demand, declare*] con estridencia, con grandes alharacas; [*protest*] ruidosamente

strife [straɪf] N conflictos *mpl*; **domestic ~** riñas *fpl* domésticas; **internal ~** conflictos *mpl* internos; **to cease from ~** (*frm*) deponer las armas

strife-ridden ['straɪf,rɪdn] ADJ conflictivo

strike [straɪk] (*vb: pt, pp* **struck**) Ⓐ N [1] (*by workers*) huelga *f*, paro *m*; **to be on ~** estar en huelga; **to come out** *or* **go on ~** declarar la huelga; *see* **hunger C**
[2] (= *discovery*) [*of oil, gold*] descubrimiento *m*; **a big oil ~** un descubrimiento de petróleo en gran cantidad; **to make a ~** hacer un descubrimiento
[3] (*Baseball*) golpe *m*; (*Bowling*) strike *m*; **you have two ~s against you** (*esp US*) (*fig*) tienes dos cosas en contra; **three ~s and you're out** (*US Jur*) *pena de cadena perpetua tras el tercer delito*
[4] (*Mil*) ataque *m*; (= *air strike*) ataque *m* aéreo, bombardeo *m*
Ⓑ VT [1] (= *hit*) golpear; (*with fist etc*) pegar, dar una bofetada a; (*with bullet etc*) alcanzar; [+ *ball*] golpear; [+ *chord, note*] tocar; [+ *instrument*] herir, pulsar; **never ~ a woman** no pegar nunca a una mujer; **the president was struck by two bullets** dos balas alcanzaron al presidente; **to ~ sb a blow** ◊ **~ a blow at sb** pegar *or* dar un golpe a algn, pegar a algn; **to ~ one's fist on the table** ◊ **~ the table with one's fist** golpear la mesa con el puño; **the clock struck the hour** el reloj dio la hora; **to be struck by lightning** ser alcanzado por un rayo; **the tower was struck by lightning** la torre fue alcanzada por un rayo, cayó un rayo en la torre; ✦*IDIOMS* **to ~ a blow for sth** romper una lanza a favor de algo; **to ~ a blow against sth** socavar algo; **that ~s a chord!** ¡eso me suena!
[2] (= *collide with*) [+ *rocks, landmine etc*] chocar con, chocar contra; [+ *difficulty, obstacle*] encontrar, dar con, tropezar con; **the ship struck an iceberg** el buque chocó con *or* contra un iceberg; **his head struck the beam** ◊ **he struck his head on the beam** dio con la cabeza contra *or* en la viga; **the light ~s the window** la luz hiere la ventana; **disaster struck us** el desastre nos vino encima; **a sound struck my ear** (*liter*) un ruido hirió mi oído; **what ~s the eye is the poverty** lo que más llama la atención es la pobreza; **a ghastly sight struck our eyes** se nos presentó un panorama horroroso
[3] (= *produce, make*) [+ *coin, medal*] acuñar; [+ *a light, match*] encender, prender (*LAm*); **to ~ root** (*Bot*) echar raíces, arraigar; **to ~ sparks from sth** hacer que algo eche chispas; **to ~ terror into sb's heart** infundir terror a algn
[4] (= *appear to, occur to*) **it ~s me as being most unlikely** me parece poco factible, se me hace poco probable (*LAm*); **how did it ~ you?** ¿qué te pareció?, ¿qué impresión te causó?; **at least that's how it ~s me** por lo menos eso es lo que pienso yo; **it ~s me that ...** ◊ **the thought ~s me that ...** se me ocurre que ...; **has it ever struck you that ...?** ¿has pensado alguna vez que ...?
[5] (= *impress*) **I was much struck by his sincerity** su sinceridad me impresionó mucho; **I'm not much struck (with him)** no me llama la atención, no me impresiona mucho
[6] (= *find*) [+ *gold, oil*] descubrir; ✦*IDIOMS* **to ~ gold** triunfar; **to ~ it lucky** tener suerte; **he struck it rich** le salió el gordo
[7] (= *arrive at, achieve*) [+ *agreement*] alcanzar, llegar a; **to ~ an average** sacar el promedio; **to ~ a balance** encontrar el equilibrio; **to ~ a bargain** cerrar un trato; **to ~ a deal** alcanzar un acuerdo, llegar a un acuerdo; (*Comm*) cerrar un trato
[8] (= *assume, adopt*) **to ~ an attitude** adoptar una actitud
[9] (= *cause to become*) **to ~ sb blind** cegar a algn; **to ~ sb dead** matar a algn; **may I be struck dead if ...** que me maten si ...; **to be struck dumb** quedarse sin habla
[10] (= *take down*) **to ~ camp** levantar el campamento; **to ~ the flag** arriar la bandera
[11] (= *remove, cross out*) suprimir (**from** de)
Ⓒ VI [1] (*Mil etc*) (= *attack*) atacar; [*disaster*] sobrevenir; [*disease*] golpear; [*snake etc*] morder, atacar; **now is the time to ~** éste es el momento en que conviene atacar; **when panic ~s** cuando cunde el pánico, cuando se extiende el pánico; **to ~ against sth** dar con algo, dar contra algo, chocar contra algo; **to ~ at sb** (*with fist*) tratar de golpear a algn; (*Mil*) atacar a algn; **we must ~ at the root of this evil** debemos atacar la raíz de este mal, debemos cortar este mal de raíz; **this ~s at our very existence** esto amenaza nuestra existencia misma; **to be within striking distance of** [+ *of place*] estar a poca distancia *or* a un paso de; **he had come within striking distance of the presidency** estuvo muy cerca de ocupar la presidencia; *see* **home A2**, **iron A1**
[2] [*workers*] declarar la huelga, declararse en huelga; **to ~ for higher wages** hacer una huelga para conseguir un aumento de los sueldos
[3] [*clock*] dar la hora; **the clock has struck** ha dado la hora ya

4 [*match*] encenderse
5 ✦*IDIOM* **to ~ lucky** tener suerte
6 (= *move, go*) **to ~ across country** ir a campo traviesa; **to ~ into the woods** ir por el bosque, penetrar en el bosque
7 (*Naut*) (= *run aground*) encallar, embarrancar
8 (*esp Naut*) (= *surrender*) arriar la bandera
9 (*Bot*) echar raíces, arraigar
Ⓓ CPD ► **strike ballot** N votación *f* a huelga ► **strike committee** N comité *m* de huelga ► **strike force** N fuerza *f* de asalto, fuerza *f* de choque ► **strike fund** N fondo *m* de huelga ► **strike pay** N subsidio *m* de huelga ► **strike vote** N = **strike ballot**

►**strike back** VI + ADV (*gen*) devolver el golpe (**at** a); (*Mil*) contraatacar

►**strike down** VT + ADV [*illness*] (= *incapacitate*) fulminar; (= *kill*) matar; **he was struck down by paralysis** tuvo una parálisis; **he was struck down in his prime** se lo llevó la muerte en la flor de la vida

►**strike off** Ⓐ VT + ADV 1 (= *cut off*) [+ *branch*] cortar; **to ~ off sb's head** decapitar a algn, cortar la cabeza a algn, cercenar la cabeza a algn
2 [+ *name from list*] tachar; [+ *doctor*] suspender
3 (*Typ*) tirar, imprimir
Ⓑ VI + ADV (= *change direction*) **the road ~s off to the right** el camino se desvía para la derecha

►**strike on** VI + PREP **to ~ on an idea: he struck on an idea** se le ocurrió una idea

►**strike out** Ⓐ VT + ADV (= *cross out*) tachar
Ⓑ VI + ADV 1 (= *hit out*) arremeter (**at** contra); **to ~ out wildly** dar golpes sin mirar a quien
2 (= *set out*) dirigirse; **to ~ out for the shore** (empezar a) nadar (resueltamente) hacia la playa; **to ~ out on one's own** (*in business*) volar con sus propias alas

►**strike through** VI + PREP 1 (= *delete*) [+ *word, name*] tachar
2 **the sun ~s through the mist** el sol penetra por entre la niebla

►**strike up** Ⓐ VT + ADV 1 [+ *friendship, conversation*] entablar, empezar
2 [+ *tune*] atacar
Ⓑ VI + ADV [*band*] empezar a tocar

►**strike upon** VI + PREP = **strike on**

strike-bound [ˈstraɪkbaʊnd] ADJ paralizado por la huelga

strikebreaker [ˈstraɪkˌbreɪkəʳ] N esquirol(a) *m/f*, rompehuelgas *mf inv*

striker [ˈstraɪkəʳ] N 1 (*in industry*) huelguista *mf*
2 (*Sport*) delantero/a *m/f*, ariete *m*

striking [ˈstraɪkɪŋ] ADJ 1 (= *remarkable, arresting*) [*picture, clothes, colour*] llamativo; [*contrast*] notable; [*similarity, difference*] sorprendente; [*beauty*] imponente, impresionante; [*woman*] imponente; **her ~ good looks** su imponente *or* impresionante belleza; **to bear a ~ resemblance to sb** parecerse muchísimo a algn; **the most ~ feature of the house** el detalle que más llama la atención de la casa; **her thesis has several ~ features** su tesis contiene varios aspectos sobresalientes; **it is ~ that ...** es impresionante que ...
2 **a ~ clock** un reloj que marca las horas
3 (*Ind*) **the ~ workers** los obreros en huelga

strikingly [ˈstraɪkɪŋlɪ] ADV [*similar, different, bold*] sorprendentemente; [*attractive*] extraordinariamente; **a ~ attractive woman** una mujer extraordinariamente atractiva, una mujer imponente; **to contrast ~ with sth** contrastar notablemente con algo

string [strɪŋ] (*vb: pt, pp* **strung**) Ⓐ N 1 (= *cord*) cuerda *f*, cordel *m*, cabuya *f* (*LAm*), mecate *m* (*Mex*); (= *lace etc*) cordón *m*; ✦*IDIOMS* **to have sb on a ~** dominar a algn completamente, tener a algn en un puño; **to pull ~s** mover palancas; **to have two ~s to one's bow** tener dos cuerdas en su arco
2 (= *row*) [*of onions, garlic*] ristra *f*; [*of beads*] hilo *m*, sarta *f*; [*of vehicles*] caravana *f*, fila *f*; [*of people*] hilera *f*, desfile *m*; [*of horses etc*] reata *f*; [*of excuses, lies*] sarta *f*, serie *f*; [*of curses*] retahíla *f*; **a whole ~ of errors** toda una serie de errores
3 (*on musical instrument, racket*) cuerda *f*; **the ~s** (= *instruments*) los instrumentos de cuerda
4 (*fig*) condición *f*; **without ~s** sin condiciones; **there are no ~s attached** esto es sin compromiso alguno; **with no ~s attached** sin compromiso
5 (*Comput*) cadena *f*
6 (*Bot*) fibra *f*, nervio *m*
Ⓑ VT 1 [+ *pearls etc*] ensartar; **he can't even ~ two sentences together** ni sabe conectar dos frases seguidas; **they are just stray thoughts strung together** son pensamientos aislados que se han ensartado sin propósito
2 [+ *violin, tennis racket, bow*] encordar
3 [+ *beans etc*] desfibrar
Ⓒ CPD ► **string bag** N bolsa *f* de red ► **string bean** N (*US*) judía *f* verde, ejote *m* (*Mex*), poroto *m* verde (*S. Cone*) ► **string instrument** N instrumento *m* de cuerda ► **string orchestra** N orquesta *f* de cuerdas ► **string quartet** N cuarteto *m* de cuerda(s) ► **string section** N (*Mus*) sección *f* de cuerda(s), cuerda(s) *f(pl)* ► **string vest** N camiseta *f* de malla

►**string along*** Ⓐ VT + ADV (= *give false hope to*) dar falsas esperanzas a; (= *con*) embaucar
Ⓑ VI + ADV ir también, venir también; **to ~ along with sb** acompañar a algn, pegarse a algn (*pej*)

►**string out** VT + ADV 1 (= *space out*) **to be strung out behind sb** seguir a algn en fila; **to be strung out along sth** hacer fila a lo largo de algo; **the posts are strung out across the desert** hay una serie de puestos aislados a través del desierto; **his plays were strung out over 40 years** aparecieron sus obras cada cierto tiempo durante 40 años
2 (*Drugs*‡) **to be strung out** (= *addicted*) estar enganchado (**on** a); (= *under influence*) estar colgado* *or* flipado‡ *or* colocado‡ (**on** de); (= *suffering withdrawal symptoms*) estar con el mono*

►**string up** VT + ADV 1 [+ *onions etc*] colgar (con cuerda); [+ *nets*] extender
2 (*) (= *hang*) ahorcar; (= *lynch*) linchar
3 (*Brit**) **to be all strung up** estar muy tenso, estar muy nervioso
4 **to ~ o.s. up to do sth** resolverse a hacer algo, cobrar ánimo para hacer algo

stringed [strɪŋd] ADJ [*instrument*] de cuerdas; **four-~** de cuatro cuerdas

stringency [ˈstrɪndʒənsɪ] N 1 [*of regulations, controls, standards*] rigor *m*, severidad *f*
2 (*Fin*) tirantez *f*, dificultad *f*; **economic ~** situación *f* económica apurada, estrechez *f*

stringent [ˈstrɪndʒənt] ADJ 1 [*controls, standards*] riguroso, severo, estricto; **~ rules** reglas *fpl* estrictas
2 (*Fin*) tirante, difícil

stringently [ˈstrɪndʒəntlɪ] ADV severamente, rigurosamente

stringer [ˈstrɪŋəʳ] N (= *journalist*) corresponsal *mf* local (*a tiempo parcial*)

string-pulling* [ˈstrɪŋˌpʊlɪŋ] N enchufismo* *m*

stringy [ˈstrɪŋɪ] ADJ fibroso, lleno de fibras

strip [strɪp] Ⓐ N 1 [*of paper etc*] tira *f*; [*of metal*] fleje *m*; ✦*IDIOMS* **to tear sb off a ~*** ◊ **tear a ~ off sb*** echar una bronca a algn*
2 [*of land*] franja *f*, faja *f*; (*Aer*) (= *landing strip*) pista *f*
3 (*Brit Ftbl etc*) (= *clothes*) uniforme *m*; (= *colours*) colores *mpl*
4 (*) (= *striptease*) striptease *m*, despelote* *m*; **to do a ~** desnudarse, hacer un striptease, despelotarse*
5 (= *strip cartoon*) tira *f*
Ⓑ VT 1 [+ *person*] desnudar; **to ~ sb naked** desnudar a algn completamente, dejar a algn en cueros*; **to ~ sb to the skin** dejar a algn en cueros*
2 [+ *bed*] quitar la ropa de; [+ *wall*] desempapelar; [+ *wallpaper*] quitar; **to ~ the bark off sth** descortezar algo
3 (= *deprive*) **to ~ sb of sth** despojar a algn de algo; **to ~ a house of its furniture** dejar una casa sin muebles; **to ~ a company of its assets** despojar a una empresa de su activo; **~ped of all the verbiage, this means ...** sin toda la palabrería, esto quiere decir ...
4 (*Tech*) 4·1 (*also* **~ down**) [+ *engine*] desmontar
4·2 (= *damage*) [+ *gears*] estropear
Ⓒ VI 1 (= *undress*) desnudarse; **to ~ naked** *or* **to the skin** quitarse toda la ropa; **to ~ to the waist** desnudarse hasta la cintura
2 (= *do striptease*) hacer striptease
Ⓓ CPD ► **strip cartoon** N (*Brit*) tira *f* cómica, historieta *f*, caricatura *f* (*LAm*) ► **strip club** N club *m* de striptease ► **strip joint*** N (*esp US*) = **strip club** ► **strip light** N lámpara *f* fluorescente ► **strip lighting** N (*Brit*) alumbrado *m* fluorescente, alumbrado *m* de tubos ► **strip mine** N (*US*) mina *f* a cielo abierto ► **strip mining** N (*US*) minería *f* a cielo abierto ► **strip poker** N strip póker *m* ► **strip search** N registro *m* integral; *see also* **strip-search** ► **strip show** N espectáculo *m* de striptease ► **strip wash** N lavado *m* por completo; *see also* **strip-wash**

►**strip down** VT + ADV = **strip B4.1**

►**strip off** Ⓐ VT + ADV 1 [+ *paint etc*] quitar; (*violently*) arrancar; **the wind ~ped the leaves off the trees** el viento arrancó las hojas de los árboles
2 **to ~ off one's clothes** quitarse (rápidamente) la ropa
Ⓑ VI + ADV 1 [*person*] desnudarse
2 [*paint etc*] desprenderse

stripe [straɪp] Ⓐ N 1 (= *line*) raya *f*, lista *f*; (*on flag etc*) franja *f*
2 (*Mil*) galón *m*
3 (†) (= *lash*) azote *m*; (= *weal*) cardenal *m*
4 (*esp US*) (= *kind, sort*) **of the worst ~** de la peor calaña
Ⓑ VT rayar, listar (**with** de)

striped [straɪpt] ADJ [*clothes, trousers*] de rayas, a rayas; [*pattern, wallpaper*] rayado, listado, de rayas

stripling [ˈstrɪplɪŋ] N mozuelo *m*, joven *m* imberbe

stripped pine [ˌstrɪptˈpaɪn] N pino *m* natural, pino *m* desnudo

stripper [ˈstrɪpəʳ] N stripper *mf*, *persona que hace striptease*

strip-search [ˈstrɪpsɜːtʃ] VT **he was ~ed at the airport** lo desnudaron para registrarlo en el aeropuerto

striptease [ˈstrɪptiːz] N striptease *m*

strip-wash [ˈstrɪpwɒʃ] VT lavar por completo

stripy ['straɪpɪ] ADJ [*clothes, trousers*] de rayas, a rayas; [*pattern, wallpaper*] rayado, listado, de rayas

strive [straɪv] (*pt* **strove**; *pp* **striven**) VI esforzarse, procurar; **to ~ after** *or* **for sth** esforzarse por conseguir algo; **to ~ against sth** luchar contra algo; **to ~ to do sth** esforzarse por hacer algo

striven ['strɪvn] PP *of* **strive**

striving ['straɪvɪŋ] N esfuerzos *mpl*, el esforzarse

strobe [strəʊb] Ⓐ ADJ [*lights*] estroboscópico
Ⓑ N 1 (*also* **~ light**) luz *f* estroboscópica; (*also* **~ lighting**) luces *fpl* estroboscópicas
2 = **stroboscope**

stroboscope ['strəʊbəskəʊp] N estroboscopio *m*

strode [strəʊd] PT *of* **stride**

stroke [strəʊk] Ⓐ N 1 (= *blow*) golpe *m*; **ten ~s of the lash** diez azotes; **with one ~ of his knife** de un solo navajazo; **at a** *or* **one ~** de un solo golpe; **~ of lightning** rayo *m*
2 (*fig*) **his greatest ~ was to …** su golpe maestro fue …; **a ~ of diplomacy** un éxito diplomático; **he hasn't done a ~ (of work)** no ha dado golpe; **a ~ of genius** una ocurrencia genial; **the idea was a ~ of genius** la idea ha sido genial; **a ~ of luck** un golpe de suerte; **by a ~ of luck** por suerte; **then we had a ~ of luck** luego nos favoreció la suerte
3 (= *caress*) caricia *f*; **she gave the cat a ~** acarició el gato; **with a light ~ of the hand** con un suave movimiento de la mano
4 [*of pen*] trazo *m*, plumada *f*; [*of brush*] pincelada *f*; (*Typ*) barra *f* oblicua; **with a thick ~ of the pen** con un trazo grueso de la pluma; **at a ~ of the pen** ◊ **with one ~ of the pen** de un plumazo
5 (*Cricket, Golf*) golpe *m*, jugada *f*; (*Billiards*) tacada *f*; **good ~!** ¡buen golpe!, ¡muy bien!; **to put sb off his/her ~** (= *distract*) hacer perder la concentración a algn, distraer a algn; **he tried to put me off my ~** (*Sport*) trató de hacerme errar el golpe; **✦IDIOM different ~s for different folks** (*esp US*) cada cual tiene sus gustos, hay gustos como colores
6 (*Swimming*) (= *single movement*) brazada *f*; (= *type of stroke*) estilo *m*; **he went ahead at every ~** se adelantaba con cada brazada
7 (*Rowing*) remada *f*; (= *person*) primer(a) remero/a *m/f*; **they are rowing a fast ~** reman a ritmo rápido; **to row ~** ser el primer remero, remar en el primer puesto
8 [*of bell, clock*] campanada *f*; **on the ~ of 12** al dar las 12
9 [*of piston*] carrera *f*
10 (*Med*) derrame *m* cerebral, apoplejía *f*; **to have a ~** tener un derrame cerebral, tener un ataque de apoplejía
Ⓑ VT 1 [+ *cat, sb's hair*] acariciar; [+ *chin*] pasar la mano sobre, pasar la mano por
2 (*Rowing*) **to ~ a boat** ser el primero remero; **to ~ a boat to victory** ser el primero remero del bote vencedor

stroll [strəʊl] Ⓐ N paseo *m*, vuelta *f*; **to go for a ~** ◊ **have** *or* **take a ~** dar un paseo, dar una vuelta
Ⓑ VI dar un paseo, pasear, dar una vuelta; **to ~ up and down** pasearse de acá para allá; **to ~ up to sb** acercarse tranquilamente a algn

stroller ['strəʊləʳ] N 1 (= *person*) paseante *mf*
2 (*esp US*) (= *pushchair*) cochecito *m*, sillita *f* de paseo

strong [strɒŋ] Ⓐ ADJ (*compar* **stronger**; *superl* **strongest**) 1 (= *physically tough*) fuerte; **I'm not ~ enough to carry him** no soy lo suficientemente fuerte para cargar con él; **to have ~ nerves** tener nervios de acero; **to have a ~ stomach** (*lit, fig*) tener un buen estómago; **✦IDIOM to be as ~ as an ox** ser fuerte como un toro; *see also* **arm[1] 1**
2 (= *healthy*) [*teeth, bones*] sano; [*heart*] fuerte, sano; **she has never been very ~** nunca ha tenido una constitución fuerte; **he's getting ~er every day** (*after operation*) se va reponiendo poco a poco
3 (= *sturdy*) [*material, structure, frame*] fuerte
4 (= *powerful*) [*drug, wine, cheese, wind, voice*] fuerte; [*coffee*] fuerte, cargado; [*argument, evidence*] sólido, de peso; [*currency*] fuerte; [*magnet, lens*] potente; [*impression, influence*] grande; **music with a ~ beat** música *f* con mucho ritmo; **we have a ~ case (against them)** las razones que nosotros exponemos son muy sólidas (en contraposición a las de ellos)
5 (= *firm*) [*opinion, belief, supporter*] firme; **a man of ~ principles** un hombre de principios firmes; **Delhi developed ~ ties with Moscow** Delhi desarrolló vínculos muy estrechos con Moscú; **I am a ~ believer in tolerance** creo firmemente en *or* soy gran partidario de la tolerancia
6 (= *mentally*) fuerte; **he has a ~ personality** tiene un carácter *or* una personalidad fuerte; **he tries to be ~ for the sake of his children** intenta mostrarse fuerte por el bien de sus hijos; **he is a ~ leader** es un líder fuerte *or* sólido; **he's the ~ silent type** es de los muy reservados
7 (= *intense*) [*emotion, colour, smell*] fuerte, intenso; [*light*] potente, intenso; **there was a ~ smell of petrol** había un fuerte *or* intenso olor a gasolina
8 (= *good*) [*team*] fuerte; [*candidate*] bueno, firme; [*marriage, relationship*] sólido; **he is a ~ swimmer/runner** es un buen nadador/corredor; **the show has a ~ cast** el espectáculo tiene un buen reparto *or* un reparto muy sólido; **a ~ performance from Philippa Lilly in the title role** una actuación sólida *or* convincente por parte de Philippa Lilly en el papel de protagonista; **she is ~ in maths** las matemáticas se le dan muy bien; **he's not very ~ on grammar** no está muy fuerte en gramática; **discretion is not Jane's ~ point** la discreción no es el fuerte de Jane; **geography was never my ~ point** la geografía nunca fue mi fuerte; **to be in a ~ position** encontrarse en una buena posición; **there is a ~ possibility that …** hay muchas posibilidades de que …; *see also* **suit A3**
9 (= *severe, vehement*) [*words*] subido de tono, fuerte; [*denial*] tajante; **there has been ~ criticism of the military regime** se ha criticado duramente el régimen militar; **he has written a very ~ letter of protest to his MP** ha escrito una carta de protesta muy enérgica a su diputado; **~ language** (= *swearing*) lenguaje *m* fuerte; (= *frank*) lenguaje *m* muy directo; **in the ~est possible terms** enérgicamente
10 (= *noticeable*) [*resemblance*] marcado; [*presence*] fuerte; **he had a ~ German accent** tenía un fuerte *or* marcado acento alemán; **there is a ~ element of truth in this** hay gran parte de verdad en esto
11 [*features*] pronunciado, marcado
12 (*in number*) **they are 20 ~** son 20 en total; **a group 20 ~** un grupo de 20 (miembros *etc*); **a 1000-~ crowd** una multitud de 1000 personas
13 (*Ling*) [*verb*] irregular
Ⓑ ADV (*) 1 **to come on ~** (= *be harsh*) ser duro, mostrarse demasiado severo; **don't you think you came on a bit ~ there?** ¿no crees que fuiste un poco duro?, ¿no crees que te mostraste un poco severo?; **she was coming on ~** (= *showing attraction*) se veía que él le gustaba
2 **to be going ~**: **the firm is still going ~** la empresa se mantiene próspera; **their marriage is still going ~ after 50 years** después de 50 años su matrimonio sigue viento en popa; **he was still going ~ at 90** a sus 90 años todavía se conservaba en forma

strong-arm ['strɒŋɑːm] ADJ [*tactics, methods*] represivo

strong-armed ['strɒŋ'ɑːmd] ADJ de brazos fuertes

strongbox ['strɒŋbɒks] N caja *f* fuerte

stronghold ['strɒŋhəʊld] N fortaleza *f*, plaza *f* fuerte; (*fig*) baluarte *m*, centro *m*; **the last ~ of …** el último baluarte de …

strongly ['strɒŋlɪ] ADV 1 (= *sturdily*) **~ built** [*person*] de constitución fuerte *or* robusta; **~ constructed** *or* **made** *or* **built** [*furniture, structure*] de construcción sólida
2 (= *firmly*) [*recommend, advise*] encarecidamente; [*believe, suspect*] firmemente; **I would ~ urge you to reconsider** le ruego encarecidamente que recapacite; **I feel very ~ that …** creo firmemente que …; **I ~ disagree with the decision** estoy totalmente en desacuerdo con la decisión; **he is a man with ~ held views** es un hombre de convicciones firmes; **~ recommended** [*book, film*] muy recomendado
3 (= *vehemently*) 3·1 (*with verb*) [*criticize*] duramente; [*oppose, support, protest, react*] enérgicamente; [*deny*] tajantemente, rotundamente; [*defend, argue*] firmemente; **a ~ worded letter** una carta subida de tono
3·2 (*with adj, prep*) **the mood here is still very ~ anti-British** el clima aquí continúa siendo profundamente antibritánico; **to be ~ against** *or* **opposed to sth** estar totalmente en contra de algo, oponerse enérgicamente a algo; **to be ~ critical of sth/sb** criticar duramente algo/a algn; **to be ~ in favour of sth** estar totalmente a favor de algo
4 (= *powerfully*) [*indicate*] claramente; **she was ~ attracted to him** sentía una fuerte atracción hacia él, se sentía fuertemente atraída hacia él; **if you feel ~ about this issue …** si este tema te parece que es importante …; **his early works were ~ influenced by jazz** sus primeras obras estaban muy influenciadas por el jazz; **he reminds me ~ of his uncle** me recuerda mucho a su tío; **to smell/taste ~ of sth** tener un fuerte olor/sabor a algo, oler/saber mucho a algo; **I'm ~ tempted to accompany you** me siento muy tentado a acompañarte; **she is ~ tipped to become party leader** es una de las favoritas para convertirse en líder del partido
5 (= *prominently*) **to feature** *or* **figure ~ in sth** ocupar un lugar destacado *or* prominente en algo; **two stories feature ~ in today's papers** hay dos noticias que ocupan un lugar destacado *or* prominente en los periódicos de hoy; **fish features ~ in the Japanese diet** el pescado ocupa un lugar destacado *or* prominente en la dieta japonesa

strongman ['strɒŋmæn] N (*pl* **strongmen**) (*Circus*) forzudo *m*, hércules *m*; (*Pol etc*) hombre *m* fuerte

strong-minded ['strɒŋ'maɪndɪd] ADJ resuelto, decidido

strong-mindedly [ˌstrɒŋ'maɪndɪdlɪ] ADV resueltamente

strong-mindedness ['strɒŋ'maɪndɪdnɪs] N resolución *f*

strongpoint ['strɒŋpɔɪnt] N fuerte *m*, puesto *m* fortificado

strongroom ['strɒŋrʊm] N cámara *f* acorazada

strong-willed [ˈstrɒŋˈwɪld] ADJ resuelto, decidido; (*pej*) obstinado

strontium [ˈstrɒntɪəm] N estroncio *m*; **~ 90** estroncio *m* 90

strop [strɒp] Ⓐ N suavizador *m*
Ⓑ VT suavizar

strophe [ˈstrəʊfɪ] N estrofa *f*

stroppy* [ˈstrɒpɪ] ADJ (*Brit*) borde‡; **to get ~** ponerse borde‡

strove [strəʊv] PT *of* **strive**

struck [strʌk] PT, PP *of* **strike**

structural [ˈstrʌktʃərəl] ADJ estructural

structuralism [ˈstrʌktʃərəlɪzəm] N estructuralismo *m*

structuralist [ˈstrʌktʃərəlɪst] Ⓐ ADJ estructuralista
Ⓑ N estructuralista *mf*

structurally [ˈstrʌktʃərəlɪ] ADV estructuralmente, desde el punto de vista de la estructura; **~ sound** de estructura sólida

structure [ˈstrʌktʃəʳ] Ⓐ N [1] (= *organization, make-up*) estructura *f*
[2] (= *thing constructed*) construcción *f*
Ⓑ VT [+ *essay, argument*] estructurar

structured [ˈstrʌktʃəd] ADJ estructurado; **~ activity** actividad *f* estructurada

struggle [ˈstrʌgl] Ⓐ N [1] (*lit*) pelea *f*, forcejeo *m*; **there were signs of a ~** había señales de haberse producido una pelea *or* un forcejeo; **two men went up to him and a ~ broke out** dos hombres se acercaron a él y se desencadenó una pelea; **he lost his glasses in the ~** perdió las gafas en la pelea *or* refriega; **to put up a ~** oponer resistencia, forcejear; **he handed over his wallet without a ~** entregó su billetera sin oponer resistencia
[2] (*fig*) lucha *f* (**for** por); **her ~ to feed her children** su lucha por poder dar de comer a sus hijos; **I had a ~ to persuade her** me costó trabajo persuadirla; **he finally lost his ~ against cancer** finalmente perdió su lucha contra el cáncer; **the ~ for survival** la lucha por la supervivencia; **there is a fierce power ~ going on behind the scenes** hay una intensa lucha por el poder entre bastidores; **local shopkeepers are not giving up without a ~** los tenderos del barrio no van a rendirse sin luchar; *see also* **class D, uphill**
Ⓑ VI [1] (= *scuffle*) forcejear; **stop struggling!** ¡deja de forcejear!; **he ~d to get free from the ropes** forcejeó para soltarse de las cuerdas; **we were struggling for the gun when it went off** forcejeábamos para hacernos con la pistola cuando se disparó; **to ~ with sb** forcejear con algn
[2] (= *move with difficulty*) **to ~ free** lograr soltarse con dificultad; **I ~d into my costume** logré ponerme el disfraz como pude; **we ~d through the crowd** nos abrimos paso a duras penas entre la multitud; **she ~d to her feet** logró ponerse de pie; **the bus was struggling up the hill** el autobús subía con dificultad la cuesta; **he was struggling with his luggage** cargaba con su equipaje con gran esfuerzo
[3] (= *fight against odds*) luchar; **to ~ to do sth** luchar por hacer algo, esforzarse por hacer algo; **to ~ against sth** luchar contra algo; **he ~d against the disease for 20 years** luchó contra la enfermedad durante 20 años; **we could see she was struggling for breath** veíamos como respiraba con dificultad; **to ~ in vain** luchar en vano
[4] (= *have difficulties*) tener problemas; **they were struggling to pay their bills** tenían problemas *or* iban apurados para pagar las facturas; **the economy is struggling** la economía está en apuros; **he's struggling in his present class** se ve apurado en la clase en la que está ahora; **I ~d through the book** me costó terminar de leer el libro, tuve problemas para terminar de leer el libro; **she has ~d with her weight for years** ha tenido problemas con su peso durante años

►**struggle along** VI + ADV [1] (*lit*) avanzar con dificultad *or* penosamente
[2] (*fig*) (*financially*) ir apurado

►**struggle on** VI + ADV [1] (= *keep moving*) **we ~d on for another kilometre** conseguimos avanzar otro kilómetro a duras penas
[2] (*fig*) seguir bregando; **many old people choose to ~ on alone** muchas personas mayores prefieren seguir bregando solas

►**struggle through** VI + ADV **we'll ~ through somehow** saldremos adelante de algún modo

struggling [ˈstrʌglɪŋ] ADJ [*artist, writer, actor*] que lucha por abrirse camino; [*business, team*] en apuros

strum [strʌm] Ⓐ VT [+ *guitar etc*] rasguear
Ⓑ VI cencerrear

strumpet† [ˈstrʌmpɪt] N ramera *f*

strung [strʌŋ] PT, PP *of* **string** *see also* **highly 1**

strut¹ [strʌt] Ⓐ VI (*also* **~ about, ~ along**) pavonearse, contonearse; **to ~ into a room** entrar dándose aires *or* pavoneándose en una habitación; **to ~ past sb** pasar delante de algn pavoneándose
Ⓑ VT ✦**IDIOM to ~ one's stuff*** pavonearse, darse pisto*

strut² [strʌt] N (= *beam*) puntal *m*, riostra *f*

strychnine [ˈstrɪkniːn] N estricnina *f*

Stuart [ˈstjuːət] N Estuardo

stub [stʌb] Ⓐ N [*of cigarette*] colilla *f*, pitillo *m*; [*of candle, pencil etc*] cabo *m*; [*of cheque, receipt*] talón *m*; [*of tree*] tocón *m*
Ⓑ VT **to ~ one's toe (on sth)** dar con el dedo del pie (contra algo)

►**stub out** VT + ADV [+ *cigarette*] apagar

►**stub up** VT + ADV [+ *tree trunks*] desarraigar, quitar, arrancar

stubble [ˈstʌbl] N [1] (*Agr*) rastrojo *m*
[2] (*on chin*) barba *f* (incipiente)

stubblefield [ˈstʌblfiːld] N rastrojera *f*

stubbly [ˈstʌblɪ] ADJ [*chin*] sin afeitar; [*beard*] de tres días; [*person*] con barba de tres días

stubborn [ˈstʌbən] ADJ [1] (= *obstinate*) [*person*] testarudo, terco, tozudo; [*animal*] terco; [*nature, attitude, silence, refusal*] obstinado; [*resistance, insistence, determination*] obstinado, pertinaz; **she has a very ~ streak** puede ser muy testaruda *or* terca *or* tozuda; ✦**IDIOM as ~ as a mule** terco como una mula
[2] (= *hard to deal with*) [*problem*] pertinaz; [*stain, lock*] difícil, resistente; **he had a ~ cold** tenía un resfriado persistente

stubbornly [ˈstʌbənlɪ] ADV [*insist, say*] obstinadamente, tercamente; [*refuse, continue, oppose*] obstinadamente; [*resist, cling*] (= *steadfastly*) tenazmente; (= *pig-headedly*) obstinadamente; **he was ~ determined/persistent** su resolución era obstinada/su insistencia era tenaz; **interest rates have remained ~ high** perduran los tipos altos de interés

stubbornness [ˈstʌbənnɪs] N [*of person*] testarudez *f*, terquedad *f*, tozudez *f*; [*of animal*] terquedad *f*; [*of cough, cold*] lo persistente

stubby [ˈstʌbɪ] ADJ (*compar* **stubbier**; *superl* **stubbiest**) achaparrado

STUC N ABBR = **Scottish Trades Union Congress**

stucco [ˈstʌkəʊ] Ⓐ N (*pl* **stuccoes** *or* **stuccos**) estuco *m*
Ⓑ ADJ de estuco
Ⓒ VT estucar

stuck [stʌk] PT, PP *of* **stick**

stuck-up* [ˈstʌkˈʌp] ADJ presumido, engreído; **to be very ~ about sth** presumir mucho a causa de algo

stud¹ [stʌd] Ⓐ N (*in road*) clavo *m*, tope *m* (*Mex*); (*decorative*) tachón *m*, clavo *m* (de adorno); (*on boots*) taco *m*; (= *collar stud, shirt stud*) corchete *m*
Ⓑ VT [+ *boots, jacket, shield, door*] tachonar; **~ded with** (*fig*) salpicado de

stud² [stʌd] Ⓐ N [1] (*also* **~ farm**) caballeriza *f*, cuadra *f*; (*also* **~ horse**) caballo *m* semental
[2] (‡) (= *man*) semental* *m*
Ⓑ CPD ► **stud book** N registro *m* genealógico de caballos ► **stud mare** N yegua *f* de cría

student [ˈstjuːdənt] Ⓐ N (*Scol*) alumno/a *m/f*; (*Univ*) estudiante *mf*, universitario/a *m/f*; (= *researcher*) investigador(a) *m/f*; **a law/medical ~** un(a) estudiante de derecho/medicina; **French ~** (*by nationality*) estudiante *mf* francés/esa; (*by subject*) estudiante *mf* de francés; **he is a ~ of bird life** es un estudioso de las aves
Ⓑ CPD [*life, unrest, attitude*] estudiantil ► **student body** N [*of school*] alumnado *m*; [*of university*] estudiantado *m* ► **student driver** N (*US*) *persona que está sacando el carnet de conducir* ► **student grant** N beca *f* ► **student loan** N crédito *m* personal para estudiantes ► **student nurse** N estudiante *mf* de enfermería ► **student teacher** N (*studying*) (*at college*) estudiante *mf* de magisterio; (*doing teaching practice*) (*in secondary school*) profesor(a) *m/f* en prácticas; (*in primary school*) maestro/a *m/f* en prácticas ► **student(s') union** N (= *building*) centro *m* estudiantil; (*Brit*) (= *association*) federación *f* de estudiantes

studentship [ˈstjuːdəntʃɪp] N beca *f*

studied [ˈstʌdɪd] ADJ (*gen*) estudiado, pensado; [*calm, insult*] calculado, premeditado; [*pose, style*] estudiado, afectado

studio [ˈstjuːdɪəʊ] Ⓐ N (*TV, Mus*) estudio *m*; [*of artist*] estudio *m*, taller *m*
Ⓑ CPD ► **studio apartment** N estudio *m* ► **studio audience** N público *m* de estudio ► **studio couch** N sofá-cama *m* ► **studio director** N director(a) *m/f* de interiores ► **studio flat** N (*Brit*) estudio *m*

studious [ˈstjuːdɪəs] ADJ [1] (= *devoted to study*) estudioso
[2] (= *thoughtful*) atento; [*effort*] asiduo; [*politeness*] calculado, esmerado

studiously [ˈstjuːdɪəslɪ] ADV con aplicación; **he ~ avoided mentioning the matter** evitó cuidadosamente aludir al asunto, se guardó muy bien de aludir al asunto

studiousness [ˈstjuːdɪəsnɪs] N aplicación *f*

study [ˈstʌdɪ] Ⓐ N [1] (*gen*) estudio *m*; [*of text, evidence etc*] investigación *f*, estudio *m*; **my studies show that ...** mis estudios demuestran que ...; **to make a ~ of sth** realizar una investigación de algo; ✦**IDIOM his face was a ~** (*hum*) ¡si le hubieras visto la cara!; *see also* **brown E**
[2] (= *room*) biblioteca *f*, despacho *m*
Ⓑ VT [1] (*gen*) estudiar; (*as student*) estudiar, cursar
[2] (= *examine*) [+ *evidence, painting*] examinar, investigar
Ⓒ VI estudiar; **to ~ to be an agronomist** estudiar para agrónomo; **to ~ under sb** estudiar con algn, trabajar bajo la dirección de algn; **to ~ for an exam** estudiar *or* preparar un examen

Ⓓ CPD ► **study group** N grupo *m* de estudio ► **study tour** N viaje *m* de estudios

stuff [stʌf] Ⓐ N [1] (*) (= *substance, material*) [1·1] (*lit*) **what's that ~ in the bucket?** ¿qué es eso que hay en el cubo?; **"do you want some beetroot?" — "no, I hate the ~"** —¿quieres remolacha? —no, la detesto; **"would you like some wine?" — " no, thanks, I never touch the ~"** —¿quieres un poco de vino? —no gracias, nunca lo pruebo; **have you got any more of that varnish ~?** ¿tienes más barniz de ése?; **do you call this ~ beer?** ¿a esto lo llamas cerveza?; **radioactive waste is dangerous ~** los residuos radiactivos son cosa peligrosa
[1·2] (*fig*) **there is some good ~ in that book** ese libro tiene cosas buenas; **I can't read his ~** no puedo con sus libros; **he was made of less heroic ~** no tenía tanta madera de héroe; **to be made of sterner ~** no ser tan blandengue*; **show him what kind of ~ you are made of** demuéstrale que tienes madera; **that's the ~!** ¡muy bien!, ¡así se hace!
[2] (*) (= *belongings*) cosas *fpl*, bártulos* *mpl*, chismes *mpl* (*Sp**); **where have you put my ~?** ¿dónde has puesto mis cosas?, ¿dónde has puesto mis bártulos *or* (*Sp*) chismes?*; **quite a lot of ~ had been stolen** habían robado bastantes cosas; **can I put my ~ in your room?** ¿puedo poner mis cosas en tu cuarto?; **he brought back a lot of ~ from China** trajo muchas cosas de China
[3] (*) (= *nonsense*) historias *fpl*; **all that ~ about how he wants to help us** todas esas historias *or* todo el cuento ese de que quiere ayudarnos; **don't give me that ~! I know what you're been up to!** ¡no me vengas con esas historias *or* ese cuento! ¡sé lo que pretendes!; **~ and nonsense!**†* ¡tonterías!, ¡puro cuento!
[4] (*) ✦**IDIOMS to do one's ~: go on, Jim, do your ~! let's see a goal!** ¡venga Jim! ¡muéstranos lo que vales, mete ese gol!; **we'll have to wait for the lawyers to do their ~** tendremos que esperar a que los abogados hagan su parte; **to know one's ~** ser un experto; *see also* **strut**[1] **B**
[5] (*) **and ~** y tal*; **he was busy writing letters and ~** estaba ocupado escribiendo cartas y tal*; **I haven't got time for boyfriends, the cinema and ~ like that** *or* **and all that ~** no tengo tiempo para novios, el cine y rollos por el estilo*
[6] (= *essence*) **the (very) ~ of sth: the pleasures and pains that are the ~ of human relationships** las alegrías y las penas que constituyen la esencia de las relaciones humanas; **he's hardly the ~ of romantic dreams** no es precisamente el ideal de los sueños románticos; **his feats on the tennis court are the ~ of legend** sus proezas en la cancha de tenis son legendarias
[7] (‡) **I couldn't give a ~ what he thinks** me importa un comino lo que piense*
[8] (*Brit*‡) (= *girl, woman*) **she's a nice bit of ~** está bien buena‡; *see also* **hot C**
[9] (*Drugs*‡) mercancía‡ *f*
[10] (††) (= *fabric*) género *m*, tela *f*
Ⓑ VT [1] (= *fill, pack*) [+ *chicken, peppers, cushion, toy*] rellenar (**with** con); [+ *sack, box, pockets*] llenar (**with** de); [+ *hole, leak*] tapar; (*in taxidermy*) [+ *animal*] disecar, embalsamar; **he had to ~ his ears with cotton wool** tuvo que llenarse las orejas de algodón; **they ~ed him with morphine*** lo atiborraron de morfina*; **to ~ one's head with useless facts*** llenarse la cabeza de información que no vale para nada; **her head is ~ed with formulae*** tiene la cabeza llena de fórmulas; **to ~ a ballot box** (*US Pol*) *llenar una urna de votos fraudulentos*; **to ~ one's face*** ◊ **~ o.s. (with food)*** atracarse *or* atiborrarse de comida*, darse un atracón*
[2] (*) (= *put*) **to ~ sth in** *or* **into sth** meter algo en algo; **he ~ed his hands in his pockets** se metió las manos en los bolsillos; **he ~ed it into his pocket** se lo metió de prisa en el bolsillo; **can we ~ any more in?** ¿caben más?; **~ your books on the table** pon tus libros en la mesa; ✦**IDIOM to ~ sth down sb's throat** meter a algn algo por la fuerza*; **I'm sick of having ideology ~ed down my throat** estoy harto de que me metan la ideología a la fuerza*
[3] (*Brit*‡) (*in exclamations*) **~ you!** ¡vete a tomar por culo! (*Sp*‡‡), ¡vete al carajo! (*LAm*‡‡); **oh, ~ it! I've had enough for today** ¡a la mierda! ¡por hoy ya vale!‡; **if you don't like it, you can ~ it** si no te gusta te jodes‡‡; **(you know where) you can ~ that!** ¡ya sabes por dónde te lo puedes meter!‡; **~ the government!** ¡que se joda el gobierno!‡‡; **get ~ed!** ¡vete a tomar por culo! (*Sp*‡‡), ¡vete al carajo! (*LAm*‡‡)
[4] (‡) (= *defeat*) dar un palizón a*, machacar*
Ⓒ VI (*) (= *guzzle*) atracarse de comida*, atiborrarse de comida*, darse un atracón*

►**stuff up** VT + ADV **to be ~ed up** [*person*] estar constipado; **my nose is ~ed up** tengo la nariz taponada *or* atascada; **to get ~ed up** [*pipe*] atascarse

stuffed [stʌft] Ⓐ ADJ [1] (*in taxidermy*) [*animal*] disecado, embalsamado
[2] (*Culin*) **~ peppers/tomatoes** pimientos *mpl*/tomates *mpl* rellenos
[3] (*) (= *full*) **I'm ~** estoy hasta arriba*
Ⓑ CPD ► **stuffed shirt*** N (*fig*) **he's a bit of a ~ shirt** es un poco estirado* ► **stuffed toy** N (*US*) muñeco *m* de peluche

stuffily ['stʌfɪlɪ] ADV [*say*] en tono de desaprobación, con desaprobación

stuffiness ['stʌfɪnɪs] N [1] (*in room*) mala ventilación *f*, falta *f* de aire
[2] (*fig*) (= *narrow-mindedness*) estrechez *f* de miras, remilgos *mpl*; (= *starchiness*) lo estirado; (= *prudishness*) remilgos *mpl*; (= *dullness*) pesadez *f*

stuffing ['stʌfɪŋ] N [*of furniture, stuffed animal*] relleno *m*, borra *f*; (*Culin*) relleno *m*; ✦**IDIOMS he's got no ~*** no tiene carácter, no tiene agallas; **to knock the ~ out of sb*** dejar a algn para el arrastre; **he had the ~ knocked out of him by the blow*** el golpe lo dejó sin fuerzas ni ánimo

stuffy ['stʌfɪ] ADJ (*compar* **stuffier**; *superl* **stuffiest**) [1] [*room*] mal ventilado; [*atmosphere*] cargado, sofocante; **it's ~ in here** aquí huele a cerrado, el ambiente está un poco cargado aquí
[2] [*person*] (= *narrow-minded*) remilgado, de miras estrechas; (= *prudish*) remilgado; (= *stiff, starchy*) tieso; (= *dull, boring*) pesado, poco interesante
[3] (= *congested*) [*nose*] taponado, atascado; **I've got a ~ nose** tengo la nariz taponada *or* atascada

stultify ['stʌltɪfaɪ] VT anular, aniquilar

stultifying ['stʌltɪfaɪɪŋ] ADJ [*work, regime, routine*] embrutecedor; [*atmosphere*] sofocante, agobiante

stumble ['stʌmbl] Ⓐ N tropezón *m*, traspié *m*
Ⓑ VI tropezar, dar un traspié; **to ~ against sth** tropezar contra algo; **to ~ on** ◊ **to go stumbling on** (= *keep walking*) avanzar dando traspiés; **to ~ over sth** tropezar en algo; **to ~ through a speech** pronunciar un discurso de cualquier manera, pronunciar un discurso atracándose; **to ~ (up)on** *or* **across sth** (*fig*) tropezar con algo

stumbling block ['stʌmblɪŋblɒk] N (*fig*) tropiezo *m*, escollo *m*

stump [stʌmp] Ⓐ N [1] (*gen*) cabo *m*; [*of limb*] muñón *m*; [*of tree*] tocón *m*; [*of tooth*] raigón *m*; ✦**IDIOM to find o.s. up a ~** (*US**) quedarse de piedra, estar perplejo
[2] (*Cricket*) palo *m*
[3] (*Art*) difumino *m*, esfumino *m*
[4] **to be** *or* **go on the ~** (*US Pol*) hacer campaña electoral
[5] (‡) (= *leg*) pierna *f*; *see also* **stir B2**
Ⓑ VT [1] (*) (= *perplex*) dejar perplejo *or* confuso; **I'm completely ~ed** estoy totalmente perplejo; **to be ~ed for an answer** no tener respuesta
[2] (*Cricket*) eliminar
[3] **to ~ the country** (*US Pol*) *recorrer el país pronunciando discursos*
Ⓒ VI (= *hobble, limp*) renquear, cojear

►**stump up*** (*Brit*) Ⓐ VT + ADV **to ~ up five pounds** apoquinar cinco libras, desembolsar cinco libras (**for sth** para comprar algo *or* por algo)
Ⓑ VI + ADV apoquinar, soltar la guita* (**for sth** para pagar algo)

stumpy ['stʌmpɪ] ADJ [*person etc*] achaparrado; [*pencil etc*] corto, reducido a casi nada, muy gastado

stun [stʌn] Ⓐ VT [1] (= *render unconscious*) dejar sin sentido
[2] (= *daze*) aturdir, atontar; **he was ~ned by the blow** el golpe lo aturdió *or* atontó, el golpe lo dejó aturdido *or* atontado
[3] (= *amaze*) dejar pasmado
[4] (= *shock*) dejar anonadado; **the news ~ned everybody** la noticia dejó anonadados a todos; **the family were ~ned by his death** la familia quedó anonadada a raíz de su muerte
Ⓑ CPD ► **stun grenade** N granada *f* detonadora, granada *f* de estampida ► **stun gun** N *arma para inmovilizar a animales o a personas temporalmente*

stung [stʌŋ] PT, PP *of* **sting**

stunk [stʌŋk] PP *of* **stink**

stunned [stʌnd] ADJ [1] (= *unconscious*) sin sentido
[2] (= *dazed*) aturdido, atontado
[3] (= *amazed*) pasmado; **I was absolutely ~ when I realized I had won** me quedé pasmado cuando me di cuenta de que había ganado, me quedé alucinado cuando me di cuenta de que había ganado*; **~ passers-by could not believe what was happening** los transeúntes, estupefactos, no podían creer lo que estaba sucediendo
[4] (= *shocked*) anonadado; **I was too ~ to reply** me quedé tan anonadado que no pude contestar; **he had a ~ expression on his face** tenía una expresión de asombro en el rostro; **I sat in ~ silence** me senté en silencio, anonadado; **people reacted to the news with ~ disbelief** al enterarse de la noticia la gente se quedó anonadada, sin dar crédito a lo que oía

stunner* ['stʌnəʳ] N (= *person*) persona *f* maravillosa; (= *thing*) cosa *f* estupenda*; **she's a real ~** está buenísima *or* como un tren*, es una mujer despampanante*; **the picture is a ~** el cuadro es maravilloso

stunning ['stʌnɪŋ] ADJ [1] (= *fabulous*) [*dress, girl*] imponente, deslumbrante, despampanante*; [*film, performance*] impresionante, sensacional; **a ~ blonde** una rubia imponente, una rubia despampanante*; **you look absolutely ~** estás deslumbrante; **the effect is ~** el efecto es impresionante

2 (= *startling*) [*news*] asombroso; [*success*] increíble; [*defeat*] aplastante; **his death came as a ~ blow** su muerte fue un golpe tremendo

3 (= *violent*) **he dealt me a ~ blow on the jaw** me dio un golpe en la mandíbula que me dejó aturdido *or* atontado

stunningly [ˈstʌnɪŋlɪ] ADV [*dressed, painted*] maravillosamente; [*original*] increíblemente; **she was ~ beautiful** tenía una belleza deslumbrante, era de una belleza imponente; **she looked ~ beautiful** estaba deslumbrante *or* imponente; **~ beautiful scenery** paisajes de una belleza impresionante; **a ~ simple design** un diseño de una sencillez asombrosa

stunt[1] [stʌnt] VT [+ *tree, growth*] impedir (el crecimiento de), atrofiar

stunt[2] [stʌnt] Ⓐ N 1 (= *feat*) proeza *f*, hazaña *f*; (*for film*) escena *f* peligrosa, toma *f* peligrosa; (*Aer*) vuelo *m* acrobático, ejercicio *m* acrobático; **to pull a ~** hacer algo peligroso (y tonto)

2 (= *publicity stunt*) truco *m* publicitario; **it's just a ~ to get your money** es sólo un truco para sacarte dinero

Ⓑ VI (*Aer*) hacer vuelos acrobáticos

Ⓒ CPD ► **stunt flier** N aviador(a) *m/f* acrobático/a

stunted [ˈstʌntɪd] ADJ enano, mal desarrollado

stuntman [ˈstʌntmæn] N (*pl* **stuntmen**) doble *m* (*especializado en escenas peligrosas*)

stuntwoman [ˈstʌntwʊmən] N (*pl* **stuntwomen**) doble *f* (*especializada en escenas peligrosas*)

stupefaction [ˌstjuːpɪˈfækʃən] N estupefacción *f*

stupefy [ˈstjuːpɪfaɪ] VT 1 (*through tiredness, alcohol*) atontar; **stupefied by drink** en estado de estupor después de haber bebido; (*permanently*) embrutecido por el alcohol

2 (= *astound*) dejar estupefacto *or* pasmado

stupefying [ˈstjuːpɪfaɪɪŋ] ADJ (*fig*) pasmoso

stupendous* [stjuːˈpendəs] ADJ (= *wonderful*) estupendo; (= *extraordinary*) extraordinario

stupendously* [stjuːˈpendəslɪ] ADV (= *wonderfully*) estupendamente; (= *extraordinarily*) extraordinariamente

stupid [ˈstjuːpɪd] Ⓐ ADJ 1 (= *unintelligent*) [*person*] estúpido, tonto, imbécil; [*question, remark, idea*] estúpido, tonto; [*mistake, game*] tonto, bobo; **don't be (so) ~** no seas tonto; **I'll never do anything so ~ again** nunca volveré a cometer semejante estupidez; **don't do anything ~, will you?** no vayas a hacer alguna tontería ¿eh?; **it's ~ to leave money lying around** es una estupidez *or* es de tontos dejar el dinero a la vista de todos; **to act ~*** (= *pretend to be stupid*) hacerse el tonto; (= *behave stupidly*) hacer el tonto; **she looks ~ in that hat** ◊ **that hat looks ~ on her** está ridícula con ese sombrero; **it looks ~** se ve ridículo, queda ridículo; **to make sb look ~** dejar a algn en ridículo; **it was ~ of you** fue una tontería por tu parte, ¡qué tonto *or* imbécil fuiste!; **it was ~ of me to say that** fui tonto al decir eso, cometí una estupidez al decir eso; **it was a ~ thing to do** fue una tontería *or* una estupidez; **that's the ~est thing I ever heard** jamás he oído semejante tontería *or* estupidez; *see also* **plain B1**

2 (*) (= *insensible, dazed*) atontado; **to bore sb ~** matar a algn de aburrimiento; **to drink o.s. ~** pillarse una trompa de miedo*; **to knock sb ~** dejar a algn atontado *or* aturdido de un golpe, dejar a algn tonto *or* lelo de un golpe*; **to laugh o.s. ~** partirse de risa*

3 (*) (= *pesky*) maldito*, condenado*; **I hate these ~ shoes** odio estos malditos *or* condenados zapatos*; **you ~ idiot!** ¡idiota!, ¡imbécil!; **she gets annoyed by ~ little things** se molesta por cualquier tontería, se molesta por cualquier chorrada (*Sp**)

Ⓑ N (*) (*as excl*) **don't do that, ~!** ¡no hagas eso, imbécil!*; **come on, ~!** (*said affectionately*) ¡venga bobo!*

Ⓒ ADV (*) **don't talk ~!** ¡no digas tonterías *or* estupideces!*

stupidity [stjuːˈpɪdɪtɪ] N 1 (= *quality*) estupidez *f*; **he laughed at their ~** se reía de su estupidez; **an act of ~** una acción estúpida

2 (= *stupid thing*) estupidez *f*, tontería *f*

stupidly [ˈstjuːpɪdlɪ] ADV [*behave, act*] como un idiota; [*stare, grin*] como un bobo, como un tonto; **~, I said I would help her** como un tonto, dije que la ayudaría, cometí la estupidez de decir que la ayudaría; **~, he'd not anticipated that this might happen** había sido una estupidez por su parte, pero no había previsto que esto pudiera ocurrir; **somebody had ~ left the door open** alguien había cometido la estupidez de dejar la puerta abierta

stupidness [ˈstjuːpɪdnɪs] N = **stupidity**

stupor [ˈstjuːpəʳ] N estupor *m*

sturdily [ˈstɜːdɪlɪ] ADV 1 **~ built** [*house*] de construcción sólida; [*person*] robusto; [*furniture*] sólido

2 (= *stoically*) [*say*] firmemente, enérgicamente; [*oppose*] enérgicamente, tenazmente

sturdiness [ˈstɜːdɪnɪs] N 1 [*of person, tree*] robustez *f*, fuerza *f*; [*of boats, material*] fuerza *f*; [*of furniture*] solidez *f* 2 (*fig*) [*of supporter, refusal*] energía *f*, firmeza *f*

sturdy [ˈstɜːdɪ] ADJ (*compar* **sturdier**; *superl* **sturdiest**) 1 [*person, tree*] robusto, fuerte; [*boat, material*] fuerte; [*table, furniture*] sólido

2 (*fig*) [*supporter, refusal*] enérgico, firme; [*resistance*] tenaz; **~ independence** espíritu *m* fuerte de independencia

sturgeon [ˈstɜːdʒən] N esturión *m*

stutter [ˈstʌtəʳ] Ⓐ N tartamudeo *m*; **he has a bad ~** tartamudea terriblemente; **to say sth with a ~** decir algo tartamudeando

Ⓑ VI tartamudear

Ⓒ VT (*also* **~ out**) decir tartamudeando

stutterer [ˈstʌtərəʳ] N tartamudo/a *m/f*

stuttering [ˈstʌtərɪŋ] Ⓐ ADJ tartamudo

Ⓑ N tartamudeo *m*

stutteringly [ˈstʌtərɪŋlɪ] ADV **he said ~** dijo tartamudeando

STV N ABBR 1 (*Pol*) = **Single Transferable Vote** 2 = **Scottish Television**

sty[1] [staɪ] N 1 [*of pigs*] pocilga *f*, chiquero *m* (*S. Cone*)

2 (*‡*) (*fig*) pocilga* *f*, leonera* *f*

sty[2], **stye** [staɪ] N (*Med*) orzuelo *m*

Stygian [ˈstɪdʒɪən] ADJ estigio

style [staɪl] Ⓐ N 1 (*Mus, Art, Literat*) estilo *m*; **in the ~ of Mozart** al estilo de Mozart; **a building in the neoclassical ~** un edificio de estilo neoclásico

2 (= *design, model*) estilo *m*; **I want something in that ~** quiero algo de ese estilo

3 (= *mode*) estilo *m*; **we must change our ~ of play** debemos cambiar nuestro estilo de juego; **the present ~ of leadership** el estilo actual de liderazgo; **management ~** estilo *m* administrativo; **~ of living** estilo *m* de vida; **in the Italian ~** al estilo italiano, a la italiana; **that's the ~!** ¡así se hace!, ¡muy bien!; **this is a lesson in economics, nineties ~** ésta es una lección de economía al estilo de los noventa; **March 6th, old/new ~** 6 de marzo, según el calendario juliano/gregoriano; *see also* **house C**

4 (= *elegance*) estilo *m*; **there's no ~ about him** no tiene nada de estilo; **to have ~** tener estilo; **to do sth in ~** hacer algo por todo lo alto *or* a lo grande; **they celebrated in ~** lo celebraron por todo lo alto *or* a lo grande; **to live in ~** vivir por todo lo alto *or* rodeado de lujo; **to travel in ~** viajar por todo lo alto; **he won in fine ~** ganó de manera impecable

5 (= *fashion*) moda *f*; **to go out of ~** [*mode of dress*] pasar de moda; **they spent money like it was going out of ~*** (*hum*) gastaban dinero a troche y moche *or* como si fuera agua; **she was drinking vodka like it was going out of ~** bebía vodka como si se estuviera acabando el mundo

6 (*) (= *way of behaving*) estilo *m*; **I like your ~** me gusta tu estilo; **that's not her ~** eso no es su estilo; *see also* **cramp**[1]

7 (*also* **hairstyle**) peinado *m*

8 (= *form of address*) título *m*

Ⓑ VT 1 (*frm*) (= *call, designate*) **the headmaster is ~d "rector"** al director se le llama "rector"; **he ~s himself "Doctor"** se hace llamar "Doctor"; *see also* **self-styled**

2 (= *design*) [+ *clothes, car, model*] diseñar; **to ~ sb's hair** peinar a algn; **Jackie's hair was ~d by ...** Jackie ha sido peinada por ...; **her hair is ~d in a bob** lleva una melena corta

3 (*Typ*) [+ *manuscript*] editar (*siguiendo el estilo de la editorial*)

Ⓒ CPD ► **style book** N (*Typ*) libro *m* de estilo ► **style guru*** N gurú *mf* de la moda ► **style sheet** N (*Comput*) hoja *f* de estilo

style-conscious [ˈstaɪlkɒnʃəs] ADJ **the ~ teenager** el/la adolescente que se preocupa por la moda

styli [ˈstaɪlaɪ] NPL *of* **stylus**

styling [ˈstaɪlɪŋ] N estilización *f*

stylish [ˈstaɪlɪʃ] ADJ [*performance*] elegante; [*clothes, car, décor, area*] (= *elegant*) elegante; (= *modern*) moderno; **she's a ~ dresser** (= *elegant*) viste con elegancia *or* con estilo; (= *fashionable*) siempre va vestida muy a la moda

stylishly [ˈstaɪlɪʃlɪ] ADV [*perform*] con estilo, con elegancia; [*dress*] (= *elegantly*) con estilo, con elegancia; (= *fashionably*) a la moda; [*write*] con elegancia

stylishness [ˈstaɪlɪʃnɪs] N [*of area, resort, performance*] elegancia *f*; [*of clothes, car, décor, person*] estilo *m*, elegancia *f*

stylist [ˈstaɪlɪst] N 1 (*also* **hair ~**) peluquero/a *m/f* 2 (*Literat*) estilista *mf*

stylistic [staɪˈlɪstɪk] ADJ [*device*] estilístico; [*improvement*] del estilo

stylistically [staɪˈlɪstɪklɪ] ADV estilísticamente

stylistics [staɪˈlɪstɪks] NSING estilística *f*

stylized [ˈstaɪlaɪzd] ADJ estilizado

stylus [ˈstaɪləs] N (*pl* **styluses** *or* **styli**) (= *pen*) estilo *m*; [*of record-player*] aguja *f*

stymie* [ˈstaɪmɪ] VT **to ~ sb** bloquear a algn, poner obstáculos infranqueables delante de algn; **now we're really ~d!** ¡la hemos pringado de verdad!*, ¡la hemos liado!*

styptic [ˈstɪptɪk] Ⓐ ADJ astringente

Ⓑ N estíptico *m*

Ⓒ CPD ► **styptic pencil** N lapicero *m* hemostático

Styrofoam® [ˈstaɪrəˌfəʊm] Ⓐ N (*US*) poliestireno *m*

Ⓑ CPD [*cup*] de poliestireno

Styx [stɪks] N Estigio *m*, Laguna *f* Estigia

suasion ['sweɪʒən] N (= *liter*) persuasión *f*
suave [swɑːv] ADJ fino; (*pej*) hábil
suavely ['swɑːvlɪ] ADV (*pej*) [*say, smile*] hábilmente
suavity ['swɑːvɪtɪ] N finura *f*; (*pej*) habilidad *f*
sub[1] [sʌb] Ⓐ N ABBR 1 = **subaltern**
2 = **subeditor**
3 = **submarine**
4 = **subscription**
5 = **substitute**
Ⓑ VT ABBR = **sub-edit**
sub[2] [sʌb] VI **to ~ for sb** hacer las veces de algn
sub[3]* [sʌb] Ⓐ N (= *advance on wages*) avance *m*, anticipo *m*
Ⓑ VT anticipar dinero a
sub... [sʌb] PREFIX sub...
subalpine ['sʌb'ælpaɪn] ADJ subalpino
subaltern ['sʌbltən] N (*Brit Mil*) alférez *mf*
subarctic ['sʌb'ɑːktɪk] ADJ subártico
subatomic [ˌsʌbə'tɒmɪk] ADJ subatómico
sub-branch ['sʌbbrɑːntʃ] N subdelegación *f*
subcommittee ['sʌbkəˌmɪtɪ] N subcomisión *f*, subcomité *m*
subconscious ['sʌb'kɒnʃəs] Ⓐ ADJ subconsciente
Ⓑ N **the ~** el subconsciente; **in one's ~** en el subconsciente
subconsciously ['sʌb'kɒnʃəslɪ] ADV subconscientemente
subcontinent ['sʌb'kɒntɪnənt] N **the (Indian) ~** el subcontinente (de la India)
subcontract Ⓐ [ˌsʌb'kɒntrækt] N subcontrato *m*
Ⓑ [ˌsʌbkən'trækt] VT subcontratar
subcontractor [ˌsʌbkən'træktəʳ] N subcontratista *mf*
subculture ['sʌbˌkʌltʃəʳ] N subcultura *f*
subcutaneous ['sʌbkjʊ'teɪnɪəs] ADJ subcutáneo
subdivide ['sʌbdɪ'vaɪd] Ⓐ VT subdividir
Ⓑ VI subdividirse
subdivision ['sʌbdɪˌvɪʒən] N subdivisión *f*
subdue [səb'djuː] VT [+ *enemy*] someter, sojuzgar; [+ *children, revellers*] calmar, tranquilizar; [+ *animal*] amansar, domar; [+ *noise*] bajar; [+ *passions*] dominar
subdued [səb'djuːd] ADJ [*colours, light, lighting*] tenue, suave; [*voice*] suave; [*mood*] apagado; [*person*] (= *quiet*) apagado; (= *passive*) sumiso, manso; (= *depressed*) deprimido; **you were very ~ last night** anoche se te veía muy apagado
sub-edit ['sʌb'edɪt] VT (*Brit*) [+ *article*] corregir, preparar para la prensa
sub-editor ['sʌb'edɪtəʳ] N redactor(a) *m/f*
sub-entry ['sʌbentrɪ] N (*Book-keeping*) subasiento *m*, subapunte *m*
subgroup ['sʌbgruːp] N subgrupo *m*
subhead(ing) ['sʌbˌhed(ɪŋ)] N subtítulo *m*
subhuman ['sʌb'hjuːmən] ADJ infrahumano
subject Ⓐ ['sʌbdʒɪkt] N 1 (= *topic, theme*) tema *m*; (= *plot*) argumento *m*, asunto *m*; **to change the ~** cambiar de tema; **let's change the ~** cambiemos de tema; **changing the ~ ...** hablando de otra cosa ..., cambiando de tema ...; **it's a delicate ~** es un asunto delicado; **on the ~ of ...** a propósito de ...; **(while we're) on the ~ of money ...** ya que de dinero se trata ...; **this raises the whole ~ of money** esto plantea el problema general del dinero
2 (*Scol, Univ*) asignatura *f*
3 (*Gram*) sujeto *m*
4 (*Med*) caso *m*; **he's a nervous ~** es un caso nervioso
5 (*Sci*) **guinea pigs make excellent ~s** los conejillos son materia excelente (*para los experimentos etc*)
6 (*esp Brit Pol*) súbdito/a *m/f*; **British ~** súbdito/a *m/f* británico/a; **liberty of the ~** libertad *f* del ciudadano
Ⓑ ['sʌbdʒɪkt] ADJ 1 [*people, nation*] dominado, subyugado
2 **subject to** (= *liable to*) [+ *law, tax, delays*] sujeto a; [+ *disease*] propenso a; [+ *flooding*] expuesto a; (= *conditional on*) [+ *approval etc*] sujeto a; **these prices are ~ to change without notice** estos precios están sujetos a cambio sin previo aviso; **~ to correction** bajo corrección; **~ to confirmation in writing** sujeto a confirmación por escrito
Ⓒ [səb'dʒekt] VT **to ~ sb to sth** someter a algn a algo; **to ~ a book to criticism** someter un libro a la crítica; **to be ~ed to inquiry** ser sometido a una investigación; **I will not be ~ed to this questioning** no tolero este interrogatorio *or* esta interrogación; **she was ~ed to much indignity** tuvo que aguantar muchas afrentas
Ⓓ ['sʌbdʒɪkt] CPD ► **subject heading** N título *m* de materia ► **subject index** N (*in book*) índice *m* de materias; (*in library*) catálogo *m* de materias ► **subject matter** N (= *topic*) tema *m*, asunto *m*; [*of letter*] contenido *m* ► **subject pronoun** N pronombre *m* (de) sujeto
subjection [səb'dʒekʃən] N sometimiento *m* (**to** a); **to be in ~ to sb** estar sometido a algn; **to bring a people into ~** subyugar a un pueblo; **to hold a people in ~** tener subyugado a un pueblo
subjective [səb'dʒektɪv] ADJ subjetivo
subjectively [səb'dʒektɪvlɪ] ADV subjetivamente
subjectivism [səb'dʒektɪvɪzəm] N subjetivismo *m*
subjectivity [ˌsʌbdʒek'tɪvɪtɪ] N subjetividad *f*
subjoin ['sʌb'dʒɔɪn] VT adjuntar
sub judice [sʌb'djuːdɪsɪ] ADJ (*Jur*) **the matter is ~** el asunto está en manos del tribunal
subjugate ['sʌbdʒʊgeɪt] VT subyugar, sojuzgar
subjugation [ˌsʌbdʒʊ'geɪʃən] N subyugación *f*; **to live in ~** vivir subyugado
subjunctive [səb'dʒʌŋktɪv] Ⓐ ADJ subjuntivo; **~ mood** modo *m* subjuntivo
Ⓑ N subjuntivo *m*; **the verb is in the ~** el verbo está en subjuntivo
sublease Ⓐ ['sʌb'liːs] VT subarrendar
Ⓑ ['sʌbˌliːs] N subarriendo *m*
sublessee [ˌsʌble'siː] N subarrendatario/a *m/f*
sublessor [ˌsʌble'sɔːʳ] N subarrendador(a) *m/f*
sublet ['sʌb'let] (*pt, pp* **sublet**) Ⓐ VT subarrendar
Ⓑ VI **they were considering ~ting** estaban pensando en subarrendar el piso (*or* la casa *etc*)
sub-librarian ['sʌblaɪ'breərɪən] N subdirector(a) *m/f* de biblioteca
sub-lieutenant ['sʌblef'tenənt] N (*Naut*) alférez *mf* de fragata; (*Mil*) subteniente *mf*, alférez *mf*
sublimate Ⓐ ['sʌblɪmeɪt] VT (*all senses*) sublimar
Ⓑ ['sʌblɪmɪt] N sublimado *m*
sublimation [ˌsʌblɪ'meɪʃən] N sublimación *f*
sublime [sə'blaɪm] Ⓐ ADJ sublime; (*iro*) [*indifference, contempt*] supremo, total
Ⓑ N **the ~** lo sublime; **to go from the ~ to the ridiculous** pasar de lo sublime a lo ridículo
sublimely [sə'blaɪmlɪ] ADV maravillosamente; **he played ~** tocó maravillosamente; **~ funny** terriblemente graciosa; **~ beautiful** de una belleza sublime; **~ unaware of ...** completamente *or* absolutamente inconsciente de ...
subliminal [sʌb'lɪmɪnl] ADJ subliminal; **~ advertising** publicidad *f* subliminal
subliminally [sʌb'lɪmɪnəlɪ] ADV subliminalmente
sublimity [sə'blɪmɪtɪ] N sublimidad *f*
submachine gun ['sʌbmə'ʃiːngʌn] N ametralladora *f*, pistola *f* ametralladora, metralleta *f*
submarine [ˌsʌbmə'riːn] Ⓐ N 1 (= *vessel*) submarino *m*
2 (*US**) *sándwich mixto de tamaño grande*
Ⓑ ADJ submarino
Ⓒ CPD ► **submarine chaser** N cazasubmarinos *m inv*
submariner [sʌb'mærɪnəʳ] N submarinista *mf*
sub-menu ['sʌbˌmenjuː] N submenú *m*
submerge [səb'mɜːdʒ] Ⓐ VT 1 (= *plunge*) hundir (**in** en)
2 (= *flood*) inundar
Ⓑ VI [*submarine, person*] sumergirse
submerged [səb'mɜːdʒd] ADJ sumergido
submergence [səb'mɜːdʒəns] N sumersión *f*, sumergimiento *m*, hundimiento *m*
submersible [səb'mɜːsəbl] ADJ sumergible
submersion [səb'mɜːʃən] N sumersión *f*
submicroscopic ['sʌbˌmaɪkrəs'kɒpɪk] ADJ submicroscópico
submission [səb'mɪʃən] N 1 (= *submissiveness*) sumisión *f*; **to beat sb into ~** (*lit*) someter a algn a base de golpes; (*fig*) someter a algn, subyugar a algn
2 (= *handing in*) [*of evidence, plan*] presentación *f*; [*of proposal, application*] presentación *f*, entrega *f*
3 (*Jur etc*) alegato *m*
4 (*to committee etc*) (= *plan, proposal*) propuesta *f*; **a written ~ is required** se requiere una propuesta por escrito; **~s are judged by a panel of authors** un panel de autores juzga las obras
submissive [səb'mɪsɪv] ADJ sumiso
submissively [səb'mɪsɪvlɪ] ADV sumisamente
submissiveness [səb'mɪsɪvnɪs] N sumisión *f*
submit [səb'mɪt] Ⓐ VT 1 (= *put forward*) [+ *proposal, claim, report*] presentar; [+ *evidence*] presentar, aducir; [+ *account*] rendir; **to ~ that ...** proponer que ..., sugerir que ...; **I ~ that ...** me permito sugerir que ...; **to ~ a play to the censor** someter una obra a la censura; **to ~ a dispute to arbitration** someter una disputa a arbitraje
2 (= *subject*) someter; **to ~ o.s. to sth** someterse a algo; **to ~ o.s. to sb** someterse a algn
Ⓑ VI (= *give in*) rendirse, someterse; **to ~ to sth** someterse a algo; **he refused to ~ to drugs tests** se negó a someterse a la prueba del doping; **to ~ to authority** someterse a la autoridad; **to ~ to pressure** ceder ante la presión; **he had to ~ to this indignity** tuvo que aguantar esta afrenta
subnormal ['sʌb'nɔːməl] Ⓐ ADJ subnormal
Ⓑ NPL **the ~** los subnormales
suborbital ['sʌb'ɔːbɪtəl] ADJ suborbital
subordinate Ⓐ [sə'bɔːdnɪt] N subordinado/a *m/f*
Ⓑ [sə'bɔːdnɪt] ADJ [*officer, member of staff, group*] subordinado; [*role*] subordinado, secundario; **to be ~ to sb** (*in rank*) ser subordinado de algn; **to be ~ to sth** (= *secondary*) estar subordinado a algo; **~ clause** oración *f* subordinada
Ⓒ [sə'bɔːdɪneɪt] VT subordinar; **to ~ sth to**

sth subordinar algo a algo; **subordinating conjunction** conjunción *f* de subordinación

subordination [sə,bɔːdɪ'neɪʃən] N subordinación *f*

suborn [sʌ'bɔːn] VT (*frm*) sobornar

subparagraph [sʌb'pærə,grɑːf] N subpárrafo *m*

subplot ['sʌb,plɒt] N intriga *f* secundaria

subpoena [səb'piːnə] (*Jur*) (A) N citación *f*; **to serve sb with a ~** ◊ **serve a ~ on sb** enviar una citación a algn
(B) VT [+ *witness*] citar; [+ *document*] reclamar como pruebas; **to ~ sb to do sth** citar a algn para hacer algo

subpopulation ['sʌb,pɒpjʊ'leɪʃən] N subgrupo *m* de población

sub post-office [,sʌb'pəʊst,ɒfɪs] N subdelegación *f* de correos

subrogate ['sʌbrəgɪt] ADJ subrogado, sustituido; **~ language** lenguaje *m* subrogado

sub rosa ['sʌb'rəʊzə] (A) ADJ secreto, de confianza
(B) ADV en secreto, en confianza

subroutine [,sʌbruː'tiːn] N subrutina *f*

sub-Saharan ['sʌbsə'hɑːrən] ADJ subsahariano

subscribe [səb'skraɪb] (A) VI 1 **to ~ to** 1·1 (= *buy, pay for*) [+ *magazine, newspaper*] su(b)scribirse *or* abonarse a; [+ *e-mail list*] su(b)scribirse a; **he ~s to a pay TV channel** está abonado a un canal de televisión de pago
1·2 (= *contribute to*) [+ *charity, good cause*] contribuir con
1·3 (= *share*) **I've personally never ~d to that view** yo personalmente nunca he sido de esa opinión; **I don't ~ to the idea that money should be given to people like that** yo no soy partidario de que se dé dinero a gente como esa
2 **to ~ for** [+ *stocks, shares*] su(b)scribir; **~d capital** (*Comm*) capital *m* su(b)scrito
(B) VT 1 (= *contribute*) [+ *money*] donar
2 (= *apply for*) **the share issue was heavily ~d** la oferta de venta de acciones ha tenido mucha demanda; **the language courses are all fully ~d** la matrícula de los cursos de idiomas está completa
3 (*frm*) [+ *signature*] poner; [+ *document*] su(b)scribir

subscriber [səb'skraɪbəʳ] N 1 (*to magazine, newspaper*) su(b)scriptor(a) *m/f*, abonado/a *m/f*; (*to pay TV, telephone, concert series*) abonado/a *m/f*; (*to e-mail*) su(b)scriptor(a) *m/f*; (*to charity*) donante *mf*; (*to campaign*) partidario/a *m/f*, seguidor(a) *m/f*
2 (*St Ex*) su(b)scriptor(a) *m/f*

subscript ['sʌbskrɪpt] N subíndice *m*

subscription [səb'skrɪpʃən] (A) N 1 (= *act of subscribing*) (*to magazine, newspaper*) su(b)scripción *f*; (*to club, telephone service, pay TV*) abono *m*; (*to e-mail provider*) conexión *f*
2 (= *fee*) (*to magazine, newspaper, pay TV, e-mail provider*) su(b)scripción *f*, tarifa *f* de su(b)scripción; (*to club*) cuota *f*; **to pay one's ~** (*monthly, annually etc*) (*to magazine, newspaper*) pagar la su(b)scripción; (*to pay TV*) pagar el abono *or* la cuota de abono; (*to club*) pagar la cuota; **annual** *or* **yearly ~** (*to magazine, journal*) su(b)scripción *f* anual; (*to club*) cuota *f* anual; **by public ~** con donativos (de particulares); **to take out a ~ to sth** (*to club, pay TV, telephone service*) abonarse a algo; (*to magazine, newspaper*) su(b)scribirse a algo
(B) CPD ► **subscription fee** N (*for magazine, e-mail, pay TV*) tarifa *f* de su(b)scripción; (*for club membership, telephone service*) cuota *f* ► **subscription form** N hoja *f* de su(b)scripción ► **subscription rate** N tarifa *f* de su(b)scripción

subsection ['sʌb,sekʃən] N subsección *f*, subdivisión *f*

subsequent ['sʌbsɪkwənt] ADJ posterior, subsiguiente (*more frm*); **on a ~ visit** en una visita posterior; **in ~ years** en años posteriores; **all ~ studies confirmed that finding** todos los estudios subsiguientes *or* posteriores confirmaron esa conclusión; **~ to** con posterioridad a; **~ to that** posteriormente

subsequently ['sʌbsɪkwəntlɪ] ADV posteriormente

subserve [səb'sɜːv] VT ayudar, favorecer

subservience [səb'sɜːvɪəns] N 1 [*of person*] (= *submissiveness*) sumisión *f*; (= *servility*) servilismo *m*; **a life of ~ and drudgery** una vida de sumisión y monotonía; **~ to sb** sumisión a algn
2 (= *secondary position*) subordinación *f* (**to** a)

subservient [səb'sɜːvɪənt] ADJ 1 [*person*] (= *submissive*) sumiso; (*pej*) (= *servile*) servil; **to be ~ to sb** someterse a algn
2 (= *secondary*) subordinado (**to** a)

subset ['sʌb,set] N subconjunto *m*

subside [səb'saɪd] VI [*floods*] bajar, descender; [*road, land, house*] hundirse; [*wind*] amainar; [*anger, laughter, excitement*] apagarse; [*threat*] disminuir, alejarse; [*violence, pain*] disminuir; **to ~ into a chair** dejarse caer en una silla

subsidence [səb'saɪdəns] N [*of road, land, house*] hundimiento *m*; [*of floods*] bajada *f*, descenso *m*; **"road liable to subsidence"** "firme en mal estado"

subsidiary [səb'sɪdɪərɪ] (A) ADJ 1 (= *secondary*) [*interest, importance, role, question*] secundario
2 (*Comm*) [*company, bank*] filial
3 (*Univ*) [*subject, course*] complementario; **I want to do ~ Spanish** quiero hacer español como asignatura complementaria
(B) N 1 (*Comm*) (= *company*) filial *f*; (= *bank*) sucursal *f*, filial *f*
2 (*Univ*) asignatura *f* complementaria

subsidize ['sʌbsɪdaɪz] VT subvencionar; **rice is imported at ~d prices** el arroz se importa subvencionado

subsidy ['sʌbsɪdɪ] N subvención *f*; **government ~** subvención *f* estatal, subvención *f* del gobierno; **state ~** subvención *f* estatal

subsist [səb'sɪst] VI subsistir; **to ~ on sth** subsistir a base de algo

subsistence [səb'sɪstəns] (A) N (= *nourishment*) sustento *m*, subsistencia *f*; (= *existence*) existencia *f*; **means of ~** medios *mpl* de subsistencia
(B) CPD ► **subsistence allowance** N dietas *fpl* ► **subsistence economy** N economía *f* de subsistencia ► **subsistence farmer** N *campesino que se dedica a la agricultura de subsistencia* ► **subsistence farming** N agricultura *f* de subsistencia ► **subsistence level** N nivel *m* mínimo de subsistencia; **to live at ~ level** vivir muy justo, poderse sustentar apenas ► **subsistence wage** N salario *m* de subsistencia

subsoil ['sʌbsɔɪl] N subsuelo *m*

subsonic ['sʌb'sɒnɪk] ADJ subsónico

subspecies ['sʌb'spiːʃiːz] N (*pl inv*) subespecie *f*

substance ['sʌbstəns] (A) N 1 (*physical*) 1·1 (= *solution, chemical*) sustancia *f*; **a sticky ~** una sustancia pegajosa; *see also* **illegal**
1·2 (= *solidity*) corporeidad *f*; [*of fabric*] cuerpo *m*; **line the fabric to give it more ~** ponle un forro a la tela para darle más cuerpo
2 (*fig*) 2·1 (= *basis*) (*to allegation*) base *f*, fundamento *m*; **the rumours are completely without ~** los rumores no tienen ninguna base *or* ningún fundamento
2·2 (= *profundity*) (*to book, plot, argument*) enjundia *f*, sustancia *f*; **there wasn't much ~ in** *or* **to his lectures** sus conferencias no tenían mucha enjundia *or* sustancia; **issues of ~** asuntos fundamentales *or* de importancia
2·3 (= *gist, essence*) [*of speech, writing*] esencia *f*; **the ~ of his talk** la esencia de su charla; **I agree with the ~ of his proposals** estoy de acuerdo en lo esencial de sus propuestas; **the dispute was about style not ~** la discusión fue sobre forma, no sobre fondo; **what he is saying in ~ is that ...** en esencia, lo que está diciendo es que ...; **the Court agreed in ~ with this argument** el tribunal estuvo de acuerdo con este argumento en lo esencial
2·4 **a man/woman of ~** (= *wealthy person*) un hombre/una mujer de fortuna
(B) CPD ► **substance abuse** N abuso *m* de estupefacientes, toxicomanía *f* ► **substance abuser** N toxicómano/a *m/f*

substandard ['sʌb'stændəd] ADJ 1 (= *inferior*) [*products, material*] de calidad inferior; [*service, work, performance*] poco satisfactorio; **~ housing** viviendas que no reúnen condiciones de habitabilidad
2 (*Ling*) (= *nonstandard*) no estándar

substantial [səb'stænʃəl] ADJ 1 (= *significant*) [*amount, progress, improvement, damage*] considerable, importante; [*difference*] importante, sustancial; **there has been ~ agreement on this question** ha habido un alto *or* considerable grado de acuerdo sobre esta cuestión; **to win by a ~ majority** ganar por una mayoría considerable; **a ~ majority of families** una mayoría considerable de familias
2 (= *weighty*) [*evidence*] sustancial, de peso; [*document, book*] sustancioso
3 (= *solid*) [*building*] sólido
4 (= *filling*) [*meal, dish*] sustancioso

substantially [səb'stænʃəlɪ] ADV 1 (= *significantly*) [*increase, change, contribute*] sustancialmente, considerablemente; **a ~ different approach** un enfoque sustancialmente *or* considerablemente distinto; **~ higher/lower** bastante más alto/bajo
2 (= *largely*) [*correct, true*] básicamente; **Webster's thesis is ~ correct** la tesis de Webster es básicamente correcta

substantiate [səb'stænʃɪeɪt] VT [+ *claims, allegations, evidence*] confirmar, corroborar

substantiation [səb,stænʃɪ'eɪʃən] N comprobación *f*, justificación *f*

substantival [,sʌbstən'taɪvəl] ADJ (*Ling*) sustantivo

substantive ['sʌbstəntɪv] (A) ADJ 1 (= *significant*) [*role*] fundamental; [*talks, progress, difference*] sustancial; [*reason*] de peso; **the two sides remain divided on several ~ issues** las dos partes permanecen divididas en varios puntos fundamentales *or* de importancia
2 (*Mil*) [*captain, lieutenant*] sustantivo
(B) N (*Gram*) sustantivo *m*
(C) CPD ► **substantive law** N derecho *m* sustantivo ► **substantive motion** N moción *f* de fondo

substation ['sʌb,steɪʃən] N (*Elec*) subestación *f*

substitute ['sʌbstɪtjuːt] (A) N 1 (= *thing, artificial product*) sucedáneo *m*; **it may replace saccharin as a sugar ~** puede reemplazar a la sacarina como sucedáneo del azúcar; **he uses honey as a ~ for sugar** usa miel como sustituto del azúcar; **a correspondence course is a poor** *or* **no ~ for personal tuition** un curso por correspondencia no puede sustituir a

la enseñanza cara a cara; **there's no ~ for being informed** no hay nada como estar informado
2 (= *person*) sustituto/a *m/f*, suplente *mf*; (*Sport*) suplente *mf*; **to be a poor** *or* **no ~ for sb** no poder sustituir a algn; **friends are no ~ for parents** los amigos no pueden sustituir a los padres; **he seems to be looking for a mother ~** parece que está buscando a alguien que reemplace a su madre; **to come on as (a) ~** (*Sport*) entrar como suplente
Ⓑ VT (*gen, Sport*) sustituir; **the striker was ~d by Johnston** Johnston sustituyó al delantero; **to ~ margarine for butter** ◊ **~ butter with margarine** sustituir la mantequilla por margarina
Ⓒ VI **to ~ for sth/sb** (*gen, Sport*) sustituir a algo/algn
Ⓓ CPD ► **substitute goalkeeper** N portero/a *m/f* suplente ► **substitute teacher** N (*US*) profesor(a) *m/f* suplente

substitution [ˌsʌbstɪˈtjuːʃən] N **1** sustitución *f*; **a simple ~ of cocoa for chocolate** una simple sustitución de chocolate por cacao
2 (*Sport*) (= *action*) suplencia *f*, sustitución *f*; (= *person*) suplente *mf*; **to make a ~** hacer una suplencia *or* sustitución

substratum [ˈsʌbˈstrɑːtəm] N (*pl* **substrata** [ˈsʌbˈstrɑːtə]) sustrato *m*

substructure [ˈsʌbˌstrʌktʃəʳ] N infraestructura *f*

subsume [sʌbˈsjuːm] VT (*frm*) subsumir

subsystem [ˈsʌbˌsɪstəm] N subsistema *m*

subteen* [ˌsʌbˈtiːn] N preadolescente *mf*, menor *mf* de 13 años

subtenancy [ˈsʌbˈtenənsɪ] N subarriendo *m*

subtenant [ˈsʌbˈtenənt] N subarrendatario/a *m/f*

subterfuge [ˈsʌbtəfjuːdʒ] N subterfugio *m*

subterranean [ˌsʌbtəˈreɪnɪən] ADJ (*lit, fig*) subterráneo

subtext [ˈsʌbtekst] N subtexto *m*

subtilize [ˈsʌtɪlaɪz] Ⓐ VT sutilizar
Ⓑ VI sutilizar

subtitle [ˈsʌbˌtaɪtl] Ⓐ N [*of book, play etc*] subtítulo *m*; **~s** (*Cine, TV*) subtítulos *mpl*
Ⓑ VT **1** (*Cine, TV*) subtitular
2 [+ *book, play*] subtitular

subtle [ˈsʌtl] ADJ (*compar* **subtler**; *superl* **subtlest**) **1** (= *delicate, fine*) [*perfume, flavour*] suave, sutil; [*colour*] tenue; [*charm, beauty, nuance, reminder, person*] sutil; [*humour, irony*] sutil, fino; **the ~ fragrance of the violet** la suave fragancia *or* la fragancia sutil de la violeta; **a ~ hint of pink** un ligero toque de rosa; **there's a ~ difference between these two words** hay una diferencia sutil entre estas dos palabras; **she was never very ~** nunca fue muy sutil; **it was a ~ form of racism** era una forma sutil de racismo
2 (= *perceptive*) [*person*] perspicaz, agudo; [*mind*] sutil, agudo; [*analysis*] ingenioso

subtlety [ˈsʌtltɪ] N **1** (= *delicacy, refinement*) [*of colour, book, humour, person*] sutileza *f*; **his performance lacked ~** su actuación carecía de matices; **he has all the ~ of a herd of rhinoceroses** es más bruto que un arao; **the subtleties of English** los matices del inglés
2 (= *perceptiveness*) perspicacia *f*, agudeza *f*; **he analyses the situation with great ~** analiza la situación con gran perspicacia *or* agudeza

subtly [ˈsʌtlɪ] ADV **1** (= *delicately*) [*imply, remind, suggest*] sutilmente, de manera sutil; **~ flavoured dishes** platos ligeramente sazonados; **~ coloured garments** prendas de colores tenues; **~ erotic images** imágenes de un sutil erotismo
2 (= *slightly*) [*change*] ligeramente, levemente; [*enhance*] sutilmente, de manera sutil; **~ different** ligeramente distinto

subtopia [ˌsʌbˈtəʊpɪə] N (*hum*) (vida *f* de los) barrios *mpl* exteriores

subtotal [ˈsʌbˌtəʊtl] Ⓐ N subtotal *m*; **to do a ~ (of)** calcular el subtotal (de)
Ⓑ VT calcular el subtotal de

subtract [səbˈtrækt] Ⓐ VT (*gen*) restar; (*fig*) sustraer; **to ~ five from nine** restar cinco de nueve
Ⓑ VI restar; **it doesn't ~ from her beauty** no le resta belleza

subtraction [səbˈtrækʃən] N resta *f*

subtropical [ˈsʌbˈtrɒpɪkəl] ADJ subtropical

suburb [ˈsʌbɜːb] N **1** (*affluent*) **a London ~** una zona residencial de las afueras de Londres; **I live in the ~s** vivo en una zona residencial de las afueras (de la ciudad); **new ~** barrio *m* nuevo, ensanche *m*
2 (*poor*) suburbio *m*; **one of the city's poorer ~s** uno de los suburbios más pobres de la ciudad

suburban [səˈbɜːbən] ADJ **1** (*lit*) **people who live in ~ areas** la gente que vive en las zonas residenciales de las afueras de una ciudad; **he was born in ~ London** nació en una zona residencial de las afueras de Londres; **~ train** tren *m* de cercanías
2 (= *middle-class*) [*lifestyle, values, housewife, family*] de clase media

suburbanite [səˈbɜːbənaɪt] N *habitante de una zona residencial de las afueras de una ciudad*

suburbia [səˈbɜːbɪə] N *zonas residenciales de las afueras de las ciudades*

subvention [səbˈvenʃən] N (*frm*) subvención *f*

subversion [səbˈvɜːʃən] N subversión *f*; **she was arrested on charges of ~** fue arrestada y acusada de subversión

subversive [səbˈvɜːsɪv] Ⓐ ADJ [*activity, literature, idea, group*] subversivo; **the court found him guilty of ~ activities** el tribunal lo declaró culpable de llevar a cabo actividades subversivas
Ⓑ N elemento *m* subversivo

subvert [sʌbˈvɜːt] VT (*frm*) subvertir, trastornar

subway [ˈsʌbweɪ] Ⓐ N **1** (= *underpass*) paso *m* subterráneo
2 (*US Rail*) metro *m*, subterráneo *m* (*Arg*), subte *m* (*Arg**); **to go by ~** ir en metro; **to ride** *or* **take the ~** coger *or* tomar el metro
Ⓑ CPD ► **subway station** N (*US*) estación *f* de metro

sub-zero [ˈsʌbˈzɪərəʊ] ADJ **~ temperatures** temperaturas *fpl* por debajo del cero

succeed [səkˈsiːd] Ⓐ VI **1** [*person*] **1·1** (*in business, career*) tener éxito, triunfar (**in** en); **he ~ed in business** tuvo éxito *or* triunfó en los negocios; **a burning desire to ~** un deseo ardiente de triunfar; **to ~ in life** triunfar en la vida
1·2 (*in task, aim*) **she tried to smile but did not ~** intentó sonreír pero no lo consiguió *or* no lo logró; **to ~ in doing sth** conseguir hacer algo, lograr hacer algo; **they ~ed in finishing the job** consiguieron *or* lograron terminar el trabajo; **he only ~ed in making it worse** lo único que consiguió *or* logró fue empeorar las cosas; **I finally ~ed in getting him out of the room** por fin conseguí *or* logré que saliera de la habitación; **I ~ed in getting the job** conseguí el empleo; ✦*PROV* **if at first you don't ~, try, try again** si no lo consigues a la primera, sigue intentándolo
1·3 (= *take over*) **if she dies, who will ~?** si muere, ¿quién la sucederá?; **to ~ to the throne** subir al trono; **to ~ to a title** heredar un título
2 [*thing*] **2·1** (= *work*) [*plan, strategy, experiment*] dar resultado, salir bien; **had the plan ~ed, our lives might have been very different** si el plan hubiera dado resultado *or* salido bien, nuestras vidas podrían haber sido muy distintas
2·2 (= *do well*) [*business*] prosperar; [*film*] tener éxito; **to ~ at the box office** ser un éxito de taquilla; ✦*IDIOM* **nothing ~s like success** el éxito llama al éxito
Ⓑ VT (= *follow*) suceder a; **the dry weather was ~ed by a month of rain** un mes de lluvia sucedió al tiempo seco; **on his death, his eldest son ~ed him** a su muerte, su hijo mayor lo sucedió; **he ~ed Lewis as Olympic champion** sucedió a Lewis como campeón olímpico

succeeding [səkˈsiːdɪŋ] ADJ sucesivo; **each ~ year brought further tribulations** cada año sucesivo trajo más tribulaciones; **in ~ chapters** en capítulos sucesivos; **on two/three ~ Saturdays** dos/tres sábados seguidos; **~ generations** generaciones sucesivas

success [səkˈses] Ⓐ N **1** (*at task*) éxito *m* (**at, in** en); **the ~ or failure of the strategy** el éxito o el fracaso de la estrategia; **~ never went to his head** el éxito nunca se le subió a la cabeza; **congratulations on your ~!** ¡enhorabuena, lo has conseguido!; **the key to ~ at school** la clave del éxito escolar; **his ~ at the Olympics** sus logros en las Olimpiadas; **we have had some ~ in reducing the national debt** hemos conseguido *or* logrado reducir en parte la deuda pública; **to make a ~ of sth**: **would you say he's made a ~ of his life?** ¿dirías que ha triunfado en la vida?; **we have made a ~ of the venture** hemos conseguido *or* logrado que la operación sea un éxito; **to meet with ~** tener éxito; **to wish sb every ~** desear a algn todo lo mejor; **she tried without ~ to get a loan from the bank** intentó, sin éxito, obtener un préstamo del banco; **I tried to distract him but without ~** intenté distraerlo pero no lo conseguí *or* logré
2 (= *sensation, hit*) éxito *m*; **to be a ~** [*product, event*] ser un éxito; [*person*] tener éxito; **he was a great ~** tuvo un gran éxito; **he was a ~ at last** por fin consiguió el éxito; **a commercial ~** un éxito comercial
Ⓑ CPD ► **success rate** N **the ~ rate of organ transplants** el índice de transplantes de órganos que salen bien, el número de transplantes de órganos realizados con éxito (*frm*); **the police ~ rate in tracking down murderers** el número de asesinos que la policía logra atrapar ► **success story** N éxito *m*

successful [səkˈsesfʊl] ADJ **1 to be ~ 1·1** [*campaign, scheme, attempt, book*] tener éxito; [*plan, strategy, experiment*] salir bien; **the campaign was very ~** la campaña tuvo mucho éxito; **their mission was ~** llevaron la misión a buen término; **the company has been very ~ over the past five years** a la empresa le ha ido muy bien en los últimos cinco años; **the film was very ~ at the box office** la película fue muy taquillera *or* fue todo un éxito de taquilla; **the film is ~ at capturing the atmosphere of the time** la película consigue *or* logra captar el ambiente de la época
1·2 [*person*] (= *do well*) tener éxito; (= *reach the top*) triunfar; **the secret of being ~ with men** el secreto para tener éxito *or* triunfar con los hombres; **they are ambitious and want to be ~** son ambiciosos y quieren triunfar; **we have been ~ at achieving our objec-**

tives hemos conseguido *or* logrado alcanzar nuestros objetivos; **we have not been very ~ at** *or* **in attracting new contracts** no hemos tenido mucho éxito a la hora de atraer nuevos contratos
[2] (*before noun*) [2·1] (= *winning*) [*product, film, novelist*] de éxito; **one of the most ~ movies of all time** una de las películas de más éxito de todos los tiempos; **a ~ range of giftware** una gama de artículos de regalo que ha tenido mucho éxito; **a commercially ~ work** una obra de éxito comercial
[2·2] (= *prosperous*) [*company, businessperson*] próspero
[2·3] (= *effective*) [*treatment, remedy*] eficaz; **a generally ~ attempt to adapt this novel** una adaptación, en general lograda, de esta novela; **he had a ~ operation for an eye problem** lo operaron con éxito de un problema en el ojo
[2·4] (= *satisfactory*) [*conclusion*] satisfactorio; [*deal*] favorable; **it was a ~ end to an excellent campaign** fue un final satisfactorio para una campaña excelente; **to bring sth to a ~ conclusion** llevar algo a buen término; **there is little hope of a ~ outcome to the meeting** hay pocas esperanzas de que la reunión dé resultados satisfactorios; **we've had a very ~ day** nos han salido muy bien las cosas hoy
[2·5] [*applicant*] **the ~ candidate will be notified by post** se notificará al candidato elegido por correo

successfully [səkˈsesfəlɪ] ADV [1] (= *effectively*) con éxito; **he ~ defended his title** defendió con éxito su título; **our main objective has been ~ accomplished** hemos conseguido *or* logrado nuestro objetivo principal; **Pattie ~ evaded the police** Pattie consiguió *or* logró evadir a la policía
[2] (= *satisfactorily*) satisfactoriamente; **the problem has been ~ resolved** el problema se ha resuelto satisfactoriamente

succession [səkˈseʃən] Ⓐ N [1] (= *series*) sucesión *f*, serie *f*; **after a ~ of disasters** después de una sucesión *or* serie de catástrofes; **they each went in ~ to the headmaster** fueron todos a ver al director uno detrás de otro; **she has won three games in ~** ha ganado tres partidos seguidos *or* sucesivos *or* consecutivos; **he was my tutor two years in ~** fue mi tutor dos años seguidos *or* consecutivos; **for the third day/year in ~** por tercer día/año consecutivo; **in close** *or* **quick** *or* **rapid ~** uno tras de otro, en rápida sucesión; **four times in ~** cuatro veces seguidas
[2] (*to a post*) sucesión *f*; **in ~ to sb** sucediendo a algn; **Princess Rebecca is seventh in (line of) ~ to the throne** la princesa Rebeca ocupa el séptimo puesto en la línea de sucesión a la corona
[3] (= *descendants*) descendencia *f*
Ⓑ CPD ► **succession duty** N derechos *mpl* de sucesión

successive [səkˈsesɪv] ADJ [*governments, generations, owners*] sucesivo; [*nights, days*] seguido, consecutivo; **~ governments have failed to resolve the problem** sucesivos gobiernos no han logrado resolver el problema; **on four/five ~ nights** cuatro/cinco noches seguidas *or* consecutivas; **for the third/fourth ~ time** por tercera/cuarta vez consecutiva; **the percentage of female students increased with each ~ year** el porcentaje de estudiantes del sexo femenino aumentaba año tras año

successively [səkˈsesɪvlɪ] ADV sucesivamente; **they lived ~ in Denmark, Sweden and Finland** vivieron en Dinamarca, Suecia y Finlandia sucesivamente; **~ higher levels of unemployment** niveles de desempleo cada vez más altos

successor [səkˈsesəʳ] N (*in office*) sucesor(a) *m/f*

succinct [səkˈsɪŋkt] ADJ [*comment, account, person*] sucinto, conciso

succinctly [səkˈsɪŋktlɪ] ADV [*express, reply, sum up*] sucintamente, de manera sucinta, concisamente; **to put sth ~** decir algo en pocas palabras; **or, to put it ~, …** o, en pocas palabras, …

succinctness [səkˈsɪŋktnɪs] N concisión *f*

succour, **succor** (*US*) [ˈsʌkəʳ] (*frm*) Ⓐ N socorro *m*
Ⓑ VT socorrer

succulence [ˈsʌkjʊləns] N suculencia *f*

succulent [ˈsʌkjʊlənt] Ⓐ ADJ [1] [*meat, fruit, vegetable*] suculento
[2] (*Bot*) [*plant, leaves*] carnoso
Ⓑ N (*Bot*) planta *f* carnosa

succumb [səˈkʌm] VI sucumbir (**to** a)

such [sʌtʃ] Ⓐ ADJ (= *of that kind*) tal; (= *so much*) tanto; **~ a book** tal libro; **~ books** tales libros; **books ~ as these** semejantes libros; **did you ever see ~ a thing?** ¿has visto alguna vez cosa semejante?, ¿se vio jamás tal cosa?; **I was in ~ a hurry** tenía tanta prisa; **it caused ~ trouble that …** dio lugar a tantos disgustos que …; **~ an honour!** ¡tanto honor!; **it made ~ a stir as had not been known before** tuvo una repercusión como no se había conocido hasta entonces; **in ~ cases** en tales casos, en semejantes casos; **we had ~ a case last year** tuvimos un caso parecido el año pasado; **~ is not the case** (*frm*) la cosa no es así; **on just ~ a day in June** justo en un día parecido de junio; **~ a plan is most unwise** un proyecto así es poco aconsejable, un proyecto de ese tipo no es aconsejable; **writers ~ as Updike** ◊ **~ writers as Updike** autores como Updike; **~ a man as Ganivet** un hombre tal como Ganivet; **~ a man as you** un hombre como tú; **~ money as I have** el dinero que tengo; **~ stories as I know** las historias que conozco; **this is my car ~ as it is** aunque valga poco, es mi coche; **he read the documents ~ as they were** leyó los documentos que había; **~ as?** ¿por ejemplo?; **~ is life** así es la vida; **there's no ~ thing** no existe tal cosa; **there's no ~ thing as a unicorn** el unicornio no existe; **the Gautier case was ~ a one** el caso Gautier era de ese tipo; **some ~ idea** algo por el estilo
Ⓑ ADV tan; **~ good food** comida tan buena; **~ a clever girl** una muchacha tan inteligente; **it's ~ a long time now** hace tanto tiempo
Ⓒ PRON los que, las que; **we took ~ as we wanted** tomamos los que queríamos; **I will send you ~ as I receive** te mandaré los que reciba; **may all ~ perish!** ¡mueran cuantos hay como él!; **rabbits and hares and ~** conejos y liebres y tal; **as ~: and as ~ he was promoted** y así fue ascendido; **there are no trees as ~** no hay árboles propiamente dichos, no hay árboles que digamos; **we know of none ~** no tenemos noticias de ninguno así

such-and-such [ˈsʌtʃənsʌtʃ] ADJ tal o cual; **she lives in ~ a street** vive en tal o cual calle; **on ~ a day in May** a tantos de mayo; **he wanted the report completed by ~ a date** quería el informe terminado en tal o cual fecha

suchlike [ˈsʌtʃlaɪk] Ⓐ ADJ semejante; **pots, pans and ~ things** cazuelas, sartenes y cosas semejantes *or* cosas por el estilo
Ⓑ PRON **media people and ~** gente de los medios de comunicación y personas por el estilo; **buses, lorries and ~** autobuses, camiones y vehículos por el estilo

suck [sʌk] Ⓐ VT [*person*] sorber; [*machine*] aspirar; **to ~ one's thumb/fingers** chuparse el dedo/los dedos; **we were ~ed into the controversy** nos vimos envueltos en la polémica; ✦*IDIOMS* **to ~ sb dry (of sth)** exprimir (algo) a algn; **to ~ it and see** (*Brit*) probar a ver
Ⓑ VI [1] (*gen*) chupar; [*baby*] (*at breast*) mamar; **to ~ on/at sth** chupar algo; **to ~ at one's mother's breast** mamar del pecho de su madre
[2] (*esp US*) **this ~s**‡ es una mierda‡
► **suck down** VT + ADV [*current, mud*] tragar
► **suck in** VT + ADV [1] (*lit*) [1·1] [*machine*] [+ *dust, air*] aspirar
[1·2] [*black hole*] [+ *matter*] tragar, aspirar
[1·3] [*person*] [+ *air*] tomar; **he heard her ~ in her breath sharply** le oyó aspirar sobresaltada; **to ~ one's cheeks in** hundir los carrillos; **to ~ one's stomach in** meter el estómago
[2] (*fig*) **to get ~ed in** (*to war, argument*) verse envuelto
► **suck off**‡ VT + ADV (*sexually*) mamar‡
► **suck up** Ⓐ VT + ADV [+ *dust, liquid*] aspirar
Ⓑ VI + ADV **to ~ up to sb*** dar coba a algn

sucker [ˈsʌkəʳ] Ⓐ N [1] (*Zool, Tech*) ventosa *f*; (*Bot*) serpollo *m*, mamón *m*
[2] (*US*) (= *lollipop*) pirulí *m*, chupete *m* (*LAm*)
[3] (*) (= *gullible person*) primo/a *m/f*, bobo/a *m/f*; **there's a ~ born every minute** nace un primo *or* un bobo cada minuto; **he's a ~ for a pretty girl*** no puede resistirse a una chica guapa
Ⓑ VT (*US*‡) **to ~ sb into doing sth** embaucar a algn para que haga algo; **they ~ed him out of six grand** le estafaron *or* timaron 6.000 dólares
Ⓒ CPD ► **sucker pad** N ventosa *f* ► **sucker punch** N (*Boxing, also fig*) golpe *m* a traición

sucking pig [ˈsʌkɪŋpɪg] N lechón *m*, lechoncillo *m*, cochinillo *m*

suckle [ˈsʌkl] Ⓐ VT amamantar, dar de mamar
Ⓑ VI mamar; **to ~ at one's mother's breast** mamar del pecho de su madre

suckling [ˈsʌklɪŋ] N mamón/ona *m/f*; **~ pig** lechón *m*, lechoncillo *m*, cochinillo *m*

sucks-boo* [ˈsʌksˈbuː] EXCL ¡narices!*

sucrose [ˈsuːkrəʊz] N sucrosa *f*

suction [ˈsʌkʃən] Ⓐ N succión *f*, aspiración *f*; **by ~** por succión *or* aspiración
Ⓑ CPD ► **suction cup** N ventosa *f* ► **suction disc** N ventosa *f* ► **suction pump** N bomba *f* de aspiración, bomba *f* de succión ► **suction valve** N válvula *f* de aspiración

Sudan [sʊˈdɑːn] N Sudán *m*

Sudanese [ˌsuːdəˈniːz] Ⓐ ADJ sudanés
Ⓑ N (*pl inv*) sudanés(esa) *m/f*

sudden [ˈsʌdn] Ⓐ ADJ [1] (= *hasty, swift*) repentino; (= *unexpected*) inesperado; **a ~ drop in temperature** un descenso repentino de la temperatura; **a ~ increase in unemployment** un aumento repentino del número de parados; **with ~ enthusiasm** con un entusiasmo repentino; **this is all so ~!** ¡todo esto es tan repentino!; **his death was ~** su muerte ocurrió de repente, su muerte fue inesperada; **she looked startled by his ~ appearance** parecía asustada cuando él apareció de repente; **when the soldiers came it was very ~** la llegada de los soldados ocurrió de improviso; **all of a ~** de pronto, de repente
[2] (= *abrupt*) [*movement*] brusco
Ⓑ CPD ► **sudden death** N (*Tennis*) muerte *f* súbita; **they had to go to ~ death** (*Tennis*)

tuvieron que recurrir a la muerte súbita; (*Ftbl*) (*penalty shoot-out*) tuvieron que recurrir a los goles; (*extra time*) tuvieron que recurrir a la prórroga de desempate ► **sudden death extra time** N prórroga *f* de desempate ► **sudden death goal** N gol *m* de desempate ► **sudden death play-off** N desempate *m* instantáneo ► **sudden infant death syndrome** N (*Med*) síndrome *m* de la muerte súbita infantil

suddenly ['sʌdnlɪ] ADV [1] (= *all at once*) de repente, de pronto; **I ~ felt faint** de repente *or* de pronto sentí que me mareaba; **he resigned ~ in June** de repente en junio dimitió; **~, the door opened** de repente *or* de pronto se abrió la puerta
[2] (= *abruptly*) [*cease, die*] repentinamente, de repente; [*move*] bruscamente; **the rain stopped as ~ as it had begun** la lluvia paró tan repentinamente *or* de repente como había empezado; **the taxi stopped ~ in front of the hotel** el taxi paró bruscamente delante del hotel

suddenness ['sʌdnnɪs] N [1] (= *speed*) lo repentino; **I do wonder at the ~ of his decision** me sorprende lo repentino *or* lo súbito de su decisión; **it had all happened with terrifying ~** todo había ocurrido con una rapidez espantosa; **having started suddenly, the pain stops with equal ~** habiendo empezado repentinamente, el dolor cesa con la misma rapidez
[2] (= *unexpectedness*) lo inesperado; **the ~ of his resignation** lo inesperado *or* imprevisto de su dimisión
[3] (= *abruptness*) brusquedad *f*; **the car came to a halt with a ~ that sent her jerking forward** el coche se paró con tal brusquedad que la lanzó hacia adelante

suds [sʌdz] NPL [1] espuma *fsing* de jabón
[2] (*US‡*) cerveza *fsing*

Sue [suː] N (*familiar form*) *of* **Susan**

sue [suː] (A) VT demandar (**for** por); **to ~ sb for damages** demandar *or* poner pleito a algn por daños y perjuicios; **he was ~d for libel** lo demandaron por difamación
(B) VI (*Jur*) presentar una demanda; **to ~ for divorce** solicitar el divorcio; **to ~ for peace** pedir la paz

suede, suède [sweɪd] (A) N ante *m*
(B) CPD de ante ► **suede gloves** NPL guantes *mpl* de ante ► **suede shoes** NPL zapatos *mpl* de ante

suet [sʊɪt] N sebo *m*; **~ pudding** pudín *m* a base de sebo

Suetonius [swiː'təʊnɪəs] N Suetonio

suety ['sʊɪtɪ] ADJ seboso

Suez ['suːɪz] CPD ► **Suez Canal** N Canal *m* de Suez

Suff ABBR (*Brit*) = **Suffolk**

suffer ['sʌfəʳ] (A) VT [1] (= *experience*) [+ *pain, hardship*] sufrir, padecer; [+ *loss, decline, setback*] sufrir, experimentar; **to ~ a heart attack** sufrir un infarto; **the peace process has ~ed a serious blow** el proceso de paz ha sufrido *or* experimentado un serio contratiempo; **to ~ the same fate as** sufrir la misma suerte que; **to ~ the consequences** sufrir las consecuencias
[2] (= *tolerate*) [+ *opposition, rudeness*] soportar, aguantar; **I can't ~ it a moment longer** no lo soporto *or* aguanto un minuto más; **to ~ sb to do sth** (*Literat*) permitir que algn haga algo; ✦*IDIOM* **he/she doesn't ~ fools gladly** no soporta a los imbéciles
(B) VI [1] (= *experience pain*) sufrir; **to ~ for sth** sufrir las consecuencias de algo; **you'll ~ for this!** ¡me las pagarás!; **I'll make him ~ for it!** ¡me las pagará!; **to ~ for one's sins** expiar sus pecados; **to make sb ~** hacer sufrir a algn; **to ~ in silence** sufrir en silencio
[2] **to ~ from sth** (= *experience*): **the house is ~ing from neglect** la casa está en un cierto estado de abandono; **Madrid ~s from overcrowding** Madrid adolece de superpoblación; **to ~ from an illness** padecer una enfermedad; **they were ~ing from shock** se encontraban en estado de shock; **to ~ from the effects of alcohol** sufrir los efectos del alcohol; **to ~ from the effects of a fall** resentirse de una caída
[3] (= *worsen*) [*studies, business, eyesight, health*] verse afectado, resentirse; **sales have ~ed badly** las ventas se han visto afectadas seriamente

sufferance ['sʌfərəns] N **on ~** a disgusto, a regañadientes; **she made it clear that he was only here on ~** dejó claro que él sólo estaba aquí a disgusto *or* a regañadientes; **the civilian authorities are only there on ~ of the military** las autoridades civiles están allí sólo porque los militares las toleran

sufferer ['sʌfərəʳ] N (*Med*) enfermo/a *m/f* (**from** de); **~s from diabetes** los enfermos de diabetes, los diabéticos; **asthma ~s** las personas que sufren de asma, los asmáticos

suffering ['sʌfərɪŋ] (A) ADJ que sufre; (*Med*) doliente, enfermo
(B) N sufrimiento *m*, padecimiento *m*; **the ~s of the soldiers** los sufrimientos *or* padecimientos de los soldados; **after months of ~** después de sufrir durante meses, después de meses de sufrimiento

suffice [sə'faɪs] (*frm*) (A) VI ser suficiente, bastar; **a short letter will ~** una carta breve será suficiente *or* bastará; **military initiatives alone will not ~** por sí solas las iniciativas militares no serán suficientes *or* bastarán
(B) VT **~ it to say** basta con decir

sufficiency [sə'fɪʃənsɪ] N (*pl* **sufficiencies**) (= *state*) suficiencia *f*; (= *quantity*) cantidad *f* suficiente

sufficient [sə'fɪʃənt] ADJ [1] (*before noun*) suficiente; **given ~ time** con suficiente tiempo; **if the matter is of ~ importance** si el asunto es lo bastante importante *or* lo suficientemente importante
[2] **to be ~** bastar, ser suficiente; **ten minutes is quite ~** con diez minutos basta *or* es suficiente; **it is ~ to say that ...** basta decir *or* es suficiente decir que ...; ✦*PROV* **~ unto the day (is the evil thereof)** ya nos preocuparemos de eso cuando llegue el momento

sufficiently [sə'fɪʃəntlɪ] ADV [1] (*before adjective, adverb*) (lo) suficientemente, (lo) bastante; **~ large/high to do sth** (lo) suficientemente *or* (lo) bastante grande/alto (como) para hacer algo
[2] (*after verb*) lo suficiente; **I think he has been punished ~** creo que ya lo han castigado lo suficiente; **he had recovered ~ to get out of bed** se había recuperado lo suficiente como para levantarse de la cama

suffix ['sʌfɪks] (A) N sufijo *m*
(B) VT añadir como sufijo (**to** a)

suffocate ['sʌfəkeɪt] (A) VT asfixiar, ahogar
(B) VI asfixiarse, ahogarse

suffocating ['sʌfəkeɪtɪŋ] ADJ [1] (= *choking*) [*heat*] sofocante, agobiante; [*fumes, smell*] asfixiante; **the ~ heat of the day** el calor sofocante *or* agobiante del día; **it's ~ in here** hace un calor sofocante *or* agobiante aquí dentro
[2] (= *oppressive*) [*atmosphere, life, relationship*] agobiante; [*regime*] opresivo; **the ~ atmosphere of life in the country** el ambiente agobiante de la vida en el campo

suffocation [ˌsʌfə'keɪʃən] N asfixia *f*, ahogo *m*

suffragan ['sʌfrəgən] (A) ADJ sufragáneo
(B) N obispo *m* sufragáneo

suffrage ['sʌfrɪdʒ] N [1] (= *franchise*) sufragio *m*; **universal ~** sufragio *m* universal
[2] (*frm*) (= *vote*) sufragio *m*, voto *m*

suffragette [ˌsʌfrə'dʒet] (A) N sufragista *f*
(B) CPD ► **suffragette movement** N movimiento *m* sufragista

suffuse [sə'fjuːz] VT [*light*] bañar; [*colour, flush*] teñir; [*delight, relief*] inundar; **~d with light** bañado de luz; **eyes ~d with tears** ojos bañados de lágrimas; **this book is ~d with the author's Irish humour** este libro está impregnado del humor irlandés del autor

suffusion [sə'fjuːʒən] N difusión *f*

sugar ['ʃʊgəʳ] (A) N [1] azúcar *m or f*; **to put ~ in sth** echar azúcar en algo; **how many ~s do you take?** (*in general*) ¿cuánta *or* cuánto azúcar tomas?; (*offering tea, coffee*) ¿cuánta *or* cuánto azúcar quieres?, ¿cuántos terrones quieres?
[2] (*US**) **hi, ~!** ¡oye, preciosidad!*
[3] (* *euph*) **oh ~!** ¡mecachis!*
(B) VT [+ *tea etc*] azucarar, echar azúcar a; *see also* **pill**
(C) CPD ► **sugar basin** N (*Brit*) azucarero *m* ► **sugar beet** N remolacha *f* azucarera ► **sugar bowl** N azucarero *m* ► **sugar candy** N azúcar *m* candi ► **sugar cane** N caña *f* de azúcar ► **sugar cube** N terrón *m* de azúcar ► **sugar daddy*** N *viejo adinerado amante o protector de una joven* ► **sugar loaf** N pan *m* de azúcar ► **sugar lump** N terrón *m* de azúcar ► **sugar mill** N ingenio *m* azucarero ► **sugar plantation** N plantación *f* azucarera ► **sugar refinery** N ingenio *m* azucarero ► **sugar tongs** NPL tenacillas *fpl* para azúcar

sugar-coated ['ʃʊgə'kəʊtɪd] ADJ azucarado

sugared ['ʃʊgəd] ADJ **~ almonds** almendras *fpl* garrapiñadas

sugar-free [ˌʃʊgə'fri], **sugarless** ['ʃʊgəlɪs] ADJ sin azúcar

sugarplum ['ʃʊgəplʌm] N confite *m*

sugary ['ʃʊgərɪ] ADJ [1] (= *sweet*) [*food*] dulce; (*more technical*) con alto contenido en azúcar; [*drink*] azucarado, dulce; [*taste*] dulce
[2] (*pej*) (= *sentimental*) [*film, smile, words*] empalagoso; [*voice*] meloso

▼**suggest** [sə'dʒest] VT [1] (= *propose, put forward*) [+ *plan, candidate, idea etc*] sugerir, proponer; **to ~ sth to sb** sugerir algo a algn, proponer algo a algn; **I ~ed to him that we go out for a drink** le sugerí *or* propuse ir a tomar algo; **I ~ed taking her out to dinner** propuse llevarla a cenar; **could you ~ someone to advise me?** ¿se te ocurre alguien que me pueda aconsejar?; **an idea ~ed itself (to me)** se me ocurrió una idea; **nothing ~s itself** no se me ocurre nada
[2] (= *advise*) aconsejar; **we ~ you contact him** le aconsejamos que contacte con él; **he ~ed that they (should) go** *or* **that they went to London** les aconsejó que fueran a Londres; **to ~ doing sth** aconsejar que se haga algo
[3] (= *imply*) insinuar; **what are you trying to ~?** ¿qué insinúas?; **I'm not ~ing that the accident was your fault** no estoy insinuando que el accidente fuera culpa tuya; **it has been ~ed that ...** se ha insinuado que ...
[4] (= *evoke*) sugerir, hacer pensar en; **what does that smell ~ to you?** ¿qué te sugiere ese olor?, ¿en qué te hace pensar ese olor?
[5] (= *indicate*) parecer indicar; **this ~s that**

➤ LANGUAGE IN USE: **suggest** 1.1, 2.2, 26.3

... esto hace pensar que ...; **the coins ~ a Roman settlement** las monedas parecen indicar *or* nos hacen pensar que era una colonia romana; **it doesn't exactly ~ a careful man** no parece indicar que sea un hombre cauteloso

suggestibility [sə,dʒestɪ'bɪlɪtɪ] N sugestionabilidad *f*

suggestible [sə'dʒestɪbl] ADJ sugestionable

suggestion [sə'dʒestʃən] N 1 (= *proposal, recommendation*) sugerencia *f*; **have you any ~s?** ¿tienes alguna sugerencia?, ¿se te ocurre algo?; **if I may make** *or* **offer a ~** si se me permite proponer algo; **to be open to ~s** estar abierto a cualquier sugerencia; **my ~ is that we ignore her** yo propongo que no la hagamos caso; **my ~ to you would be to take the job** yo te aconsejaría que aceptaras el trabajo; **I am writing at the ~ of Hugh Smith** le escribo siguiendo la indicación de Hugh Smith
2 (= *implication*) insinuación *f*; **we reject any ~ that the law needs amending** rechazamos cualquier insinuación de que la ley necesite una modificación
3 (= *indication*) indicio *m*; **there is no ~ that the two sides are any closer** no hay indicios de que ambas partes se hayan acercado; **there are ~s that he might be supported by the socialists** hay indicios de que le puedan apoyar los socialistas, se comenta que quizá le apoyen los socialistas
4 (= *trace*) [*of doubt*] sombra *f*; **he replied with the ~ of a smile** contestó esbozando una sonrisa; **with just a ~ of garlic** con una pizca de ajo
5 (*Psych*) sugestión *f*; **the power of ~** el poder de la sugestión

suggestive [sə'dʒestɪv] ADJ 1 (= *improper*) [*remark, look, clothing*] provocativo, insinuante; **sexually ~** provocativo
2 (= *indicative*) **to be ~ of sth: symptoms which were ~ of heart failure** síntomas que sugerían que pod(r)ía tratarse de un fallo cardíaco, síntomas que parecían indicar que se trataba de un fallo cardíaco; **his behaviour was ~ of a cultured man** su comportamiento parecía indicar que era un hombre culto; **the atmosphere was ~ of a jazz session** (= *evocative of*) el ambiente evocaba el de una sesión de jazz
3 (= *thought-provoking*) sugerente

suggestively [sə'dʒestɪvlɪ] ADV [*dance, move, leer*] de manera provocativa, de manera insinuante; **"like to see my etchings?" he asked ~** —¿quieres ver mi colección de sellos? —preguntó de manera insinuante *or* provocativa

suggestiveness [sə'dʒestɪvnɪs] N **~ and titillation are the main ingredients of these films** la insinuación y la excitación son los principales ingredientes de estas películas; **the ~ of the phrase** lo insinuante de la frase

suicidal [,sʊɪ'saɪdl] ADJ 1 (= *depressed*) [*feeling, tendency*] suicida; **~ prisoners** prisioneros suicidas; **to be ~** estar al borde del suicidio; **he has often felt ~** a menudo ha tenido ganas de suicidarse
2 (*fig*) **such a policy is ~** una política semejante es suicida; **an act of ~ bravery** un acto de valentía suicida; **it would be ~ to do that** sería suicida hacer eso

suicide ['sʊɪsaɪd] Ⓐ N 1 (= *act*) suicidio *m*; **to commit ~** suicidarse; **it would be ~ to do that** (*lit, fig*) sería suicida hacer eso; **it would be political ~ to agree to this** consentir esto supondría el suicidio político; **a case of attempted ~** un caso de intento de suicidio
2 (= *person*) suicida *mf*
Ⓑ CPD ► **suicide attempt** N intento *m* de suicidio ► **suicide bomber** N terrorista *mf* suicida ► **suicide bombing** N bombardeo *m* suicida ► **suicide mission** N misión *f* suicida ► **suicide note** N *carta en que se explica el motivo del suicidio* ► **suicide pact** N pacto *m* suicida ► **suicide rate** N índice *m* de suicidios ► **suicide squad** N comando *m* suicida

suit [su:t] Ⓐ N 1 (= *clothing*) (*for man*) traje *m*, terno *m* (*LAm*); (*for woman*) traje *m* (de chaqueta); **three-piece/two-piece ~** traje *or* (*LAm*) terno de tres/dos piezas; **a rubber ~** un traje de goma; **~ of armour** armadura *f*; **~ of clothes** conjunto *m*; *see also* **bathing, birthday**
2 (*also* **lawsuit**) pleito *m*; **to bring** *or* **file a ~ (against sb)** entablar un pleito (contra algn); **civil ~** pleito *m* civil
3 (*Cards*) palo *m*; **to follow ~** (*in cards*) jugar una carta del mismo palo; (*fig*) seguir el ejemplo; ✦*IDIOM* **modesty is not his strong** *or* (*esp US*) **long ~** la modestia no es su fuerte
4 (*frm*) (= *petition*) petición *f*; (*liter*) (*for marriage*) petición *f* de mano; **her parents gave me permission to plead** *or* **press my ~** sus padres me dieron permiso para pedir su mano
5 (*) (= *business executive*) ejecutivo/a *m/f*
Ⓑ VT 1 (= *look good on*) [*clothes, shoes, hairstyle*] quedar bien a, sentar bien a; **the coat ~s you** el abrigo te queda *or* te sienta bien; **choose earrings which ~ the shape of your face** elige pendientes que vayan bien con la forma de tu cara
2 (= *be acceptable to, please*) 2·1 [*date, time, arrangement*] venir bien a, convenir; **when would ~ you?** ¿cuándo te viene bien *or* te conviene?; **I'll do it when it ~s me** lo haré cuando me venga bien *or* cuando me convenga; **I don't think a sedentary life would ~ me** no creo que la vida sedentaria sea para mí; **it ~s him to work nights** le viene *or* le va bien trabajar de noche; **choose the method which ~s you best** elige el método que te vaya mejor *or* que más te convenga; **it would ~ us better to come back tomorrow** nos vendría mejor *or* nos convendría más volver mañana; **he found a life that ~ed him better** encontró una forma de vida más apropiada para él; **that ~s me fine** eso me va bien *or* me conviene; **the climate ~s me fine** el clima me sienta bien; **to ~ sth to sth/sb** (*frm*) adaptar algo a algo/algn; ✦*IDIOM* **to ~ sb down to the ground** [*plan, situation*] venir de perlas a algn; [*house, job*] ser perfecto para algn; *see also* **book A1**
2·2 (*reflexive*) **I can come and go to ~ myself** puedo ir y venir como me convenga *or* plazca; **he has already arranged his life to ~ himself** ya ha organizado su vida como le conviene *or* place; **~ yourself!** ¡como quieras!; **~ yourself whether you do it or not** hazlo o no según te parezca
Ⓒ VI (= *be convenient*) **will tomorrow ~?** ¿te viene bien mañana?; **come whenever it ~s** ven cuando más te convenga

suitability [,su:tə'bɪlɪtɪ] N 1 (= *adequacy*) [*of person, tool*] idoneidad *f*; **criteria for judging an applicant's ~ for a job** criterios para juzgar la idoneidad de un candidato para un trabajo; **there is some doubt about the ~ of this house for disabled occupants** existen dudas de que esta casa sea adecuada para personas discapacitadas, existen dudas sobre la idoneidad de esta casa para personas discapacitadas
2 (= *fitness*) [*of clothes*] lo apropiado; **I'd question the ~ of wearing low-cut blouses to work** pondría en duda lo apropiado de llevar blusas escotadas al trabajo

suitable ['su:təbl] ADJ 1 (= *satisfactory*) adecuado, apropiado; **the shortage of ~ housing** la escasez de viviendas adecuadas *or* apropiadas; **his qualifications weren't considered ~** consideraron que no tenía la formación adecuada *or* apropiada
2 (= *valid, apt*) apropiado; **both courses are ~ for beginners** ambos cursos son apropiados para principiantes; **the products are ~ for all skin types** los productos son apropiados para todo tipo de pieles; **the garden is not ~ for wheelchairs** el jardín no está adaptado para sillas de ruedas; **dishes that are ~ for freezing** platos preparados que se pueden congelar; **"suitable for children"** "apto para niños"; **eminently ~** idóneo; **to make sth ~ for sth** (= *adapt*) adaptar algo para algo
3 (= *fitting*) apropiado; **a ~ reply** una respuesta apropiada; **a ~ dress for the occasion** un vestido apropiado para la ocasión; **the committee met to consider ~ action** el comité se reunió para considerar las medidas oportunas *or* convenientes *or* apropiadas; **choose a ~ moment to talk** escoja un momento oportuno *or* apropiado para hablar
4 (= *recommendable*) adecuado; **a more ~ diet** una dieta más adecuada; **the most ~ man for the job** el hombre más indicado *or* adecuado para el puesto

suitably ['su:təblɪ] ADV [*dressed*] apropiadamente, adecuadamente; [*equipped*] adecuadamente; **~ qualified staff** personal con la formación adecuada *or* apropiada; **I heard their album, and was ~ impressed** escuché su disco y como era de esperar me causó muy buena impresión; **Andy tried to look ~ impressed** Andy intentó parecer todo lo impresionado que la ocasión requería; **he tried to adopt a ~ grave tone** intentó adoptar un tono serio acorde con *or* apropiado para la ocasión

suitcase ['su:tkeɪs] N maleta *f*, valija *f* (*LAm*), veliz *m* (*Mex*)

suite [swi:t] N 1 (*Mus*) suite *f*
2 (= *rooms*) suite *f*; **a ~ of rooms** habitaciones *fpl*; **bridal ~** suite *f* nupcial; **honeymoon ~** suite *f* nupcial; **a ~ of offices** un grupo de oficinas
3 [*of furniture*] juego *m*; **we're going to buy a new ~ this year** vamos a comprar un nuevo juego de sofá y sillones este año; **bathroom ~** conjunto *m or* muebles *mpl* de baño; **bedroom ~** (juego *m* de) dormitorio *m*; **dining-room ~** comedor *m*; **a ~ of furniture** un juego de muebles; **three-piece ~** tresillo *m*
4 (= *entourage*) séquito *m*
5 (*Comput*) **a ~ of programs** una serie *f* de programas

suited ['su:tɪd] ADJ 1 **to be ~ to** 1·1 [+ *environment, user*] [*thing*] ser apropiado para; **these crops are more ~ to monsoon lands than to deserts** estos cultivos son más apropiados para las tierras de monzón que para el desierto; **goats are well ~ to the terrain** las cabras están bien adaptadas al terreno
1·2 [+ *task*] [*person, thing*] servir para, estar hecho para; **many people are not ~ to this work** mucha gente no sirve para *or* no está hecha para este trabajo; **some people are not ~ to parenthood** algunas personas no están hechas para ser padres; **women are better ~ to computing than men** las mujeres están

➤ LANGUAGE IN USE: suggestion 1 1.1, 1.2

más capacitadas para la informática que los hombres; **a camera which is well ~ to all types of photography** una cámara que sirve para *or* que se adapta bien a todo tipo de fotografía

2 **to be well ~** [*couple*] hacer buena pareja

suiting ['su:tɪŋ] N (*Textiles*) tela *f* para trajes

suitor ['su:tər] N 1 (= *lover*) pretendiente *m*

2 (*Jur*) demandante *mf*

sulfate ['sʌlfeɪt] N (*US*) = **sulphate**

sulfide ['sʌlfaɪd] N (*US*) = **sulphide**

sulfonamide [sʌl'fɒnəmaɪd] N (*US*) = **sulphonamide**

sulfur ['sʌlfər] N (*US*) = **sulphur**

sulfureous [sʌl'fjʊərɪəs] ADJ (*US*) = **sulphureous**

sulfuric [sʌl'fjʊərɪk] ADJ (*US*) = **sulphuric**

sulfurous ['sʌlfərəs] ADJ (*US*) = **sulphurous**

sulk [sʌlk] Ⓐ VI (= *get sulky*) enfurruñarse; (= *be sulky*) estar enfurruñado

Ⓑ N **to get the ~s** enfurruñarse; **to have (a fit of) the ~s** enfurruñarse; **to go off in a ~** irse enfurruñado

sulkily ['sʌlkɪlɪ] ADV de mal humor; **"I don't like it," he said ~** —no me gusta —dijo enfurruñado *or* de mal humor

sulkiness ['sʌlkɪnɪs] N mal humor *m*, enfurruñamiento *m*

sulky ['sʌlkɪ] ADJ (*compar* **sulkier**; *superl* **sulkiest**) [*person, voice*] malhumorado, enfurruñado; [*expression*] ceñudo, malhumorado; **to be ~ about sth** estar malhumorado *or* enfurruñado por algo, estar de mal humor por algo

sullen ['sʌlən] ADJ 1 (= *moody*) [*person, expression, voice*] hosco, huraño; **the men lapsed into a ~ silence** los hombres se sumieron en un hosco silencio

2 (= *leaden*) [*sky, landscape*] plomizo, triste

sullenly ['sʌlənlɪ] ADV hoscamente; **they stared ~ at him** le miraron hoscamente, con fijeza; **the ~ resentful expression on her face** la expresión huraña y de resentimiento de su rostro

sullenness ['sʌlənnɪs] N hosquedad *f*

sully ['sʌlɪ] VT (*poet*) [+ *name, reputation*] manchar, mancillar

sulphate ['sʌlfeɪt] N sulfato *m*; **copper ~** sulfato *m* de cobre

sulphide ['sʌlfaɪd] N sulfuro *m*

sulphonamide [sʌl'fɒnəmaɪd] N sulfamida *f*

sulphur ['sʌlfər] Ⓐ N azufre *m*

Ⓑ CPD ► **sulphur dioxide** N dióxido *m* de azufre

sulphureous [sʌl'fjʊərɪəs] ADJ sulfúrico

sulphuric [sʌl'fjʊərɪk] ADJ **~ acid** ácido *m* sulfúrico

sulphurous ['sʌlfərəs] ADJ sulfuroso, sulfúreo

sultan ['sʌltən] N sultán *m*

sultana [sʌl'tɑ:nə] N 1 (*esp Brit*) pasa *f* sultana

2 (= *person*) sultana *f*

sultanate ['sʌltənɪt] N sultanato *m*

sultriness ['sʌltrɪnɪs] N 1 (= *mugginess*) bochorno *m*, calor *m* sofocante

2 (= *seductiveness*) sensualidad *f*

sultry ['sʌltrɪ] ADJ 1 (= *muggy*) [*day, weather*] bochornoso, sofocante; [*heat, air*] sofocante, agobiante; **it was hot and ~** hacía bochorno, hacía un calor sofocante

2 (= *seductive*) [*woman*] seductor, sensual; **she gave him a ~ look** lo miró seductora, lo miró de forma sensual

▼**sum** [sʌm] N 1 (= *piece of arithmetic*) suma *f*, adición *f*; **I was very bad at ~s** era muy malo en aritmética; **to do one's ~s** hacer cuentas; **to do ~s in one's head** hacer un cálculo mental

2 (= *total*) suma *f*, total *m*; (= *amount of money*) suma *f*, importe *m*; **in ~** en suma, en resumen; **more/greater than the ~ of its parts** más que la suma de las partes; **~ total** total *m* (completo); **the ~ total of my ambitions is ...** la meta de mis ambiciones es ..., lo único que ambiciono es ...; **that was the ~ (total) of his achievements** y de allí no pasó; *see also* **lump**

►**sum up** Ⓐ VI + ADV (= *summarize*) resumir; [*judge*] recapitular; **to ~ up, I would say** en resumidas cuentas, yo diría

Ⓑ VT + ADV 1 (= *summarize*) [+ *speech, facts, argument*] resumir; **you could ~ up what he said in a couple of words** se podría resumir lo que dijo en dos palabras; **to ~ up an argument** resumir un argumento

2 (= *encapsulate*) resumir; **that picture ~med up the situation for me** esa fotografía resumió la situación para mí *or* captaba la situación en un solo trazo

3 (= *assess*) [+ *person*] calar; [+ *situation*] evaluar; **they had ~med him up and liked what they found** lo habían calado y les había agradado lo que descubrieron; **he ~med up the situation quickly** se dio cuenta rápidamente de la situación

sumac(h) ['su:mæk] N zumaque *m*

Sumatra [sʊ'mɑ:trə] N Sumatra *f*

summarily ['sʌmərɪlɪ] ADV [*execute, dismiss, shoot*] sumariamente

summarize ['sʌməraɪz] Ⓐ VT resumir

Ⓑ VI resumir; **to ~, ...** en resumen, ...

summary ['sʌmərɪ] Ⓐ N resumen *m*; **in ~** en resumen

Ⓑ ADJ [*trial, execution, justice*] sumario

summation [sʌ'meɪʃən] N (= *act*) adición *f*; (= *summary*) recapitulación *f*, resumen *m*; (= *total*) suma *f*, total *m*

summer ['sʌmər] Ⓐ N verano *m*, estío *m* (*liter, poet*); **to go away for the ~** irse fuera todo el verano; **a ~'s day** un día de verano; **in ~** en verano; **I like to go walking in (the) ~** me gusta ir a la playa en verano; **in the ~ of 1987** en el verano de 1987; **to spend the ~ in Spain** veranear en España, pasar el verano en España; ✦*IDIOM* **a girl of 17 ~s** (*liter*) una chica de 17 primaveras *or* abriles

Ⓑ CPD [*clothing, residence, holiday*] de verano; [*weather, heat*] veraniego ► **summer camp** N colonia *f* *or* campamento *m* de vacaciones ► **summer holidays** NPL vacaciones *fpl* de verano, veraneo *msing* ► **summer school** N escuela *f* de verano ► **summer season** N temporada *f* veraniega, temporada *f* estival, temporada *f* de verano ► **summer time** N (*Brit*) (*daylight saving*) hora *f* de verano; *see also* **summertime**

Ⓒ VI [*birds*] pasar el verano; **we ~ed in Maine** veraneamos *or* pasamos el verano en Maine

summerhouse ['sʌməhaʊs] N (*pl* **summerhouses** ['sʌməhaʊzɪz]) cenador *m*, glorieta *f*

summertime ['sʌmətaɪm] N (= *season*) verano *m*

summery ['sʌmərɪ] ADJ [*day*] veraniego; [*clothes, colour*] veraniego, de verano; [*weather*] estival

summing-up ['sʌmɪŋ'ʌp] N (*Jur*) resumen *m*

summit ['sʌmɪt] Ⓐ N 1 [*of mountain*] cima *f*, cumbre *f*; **did anyone reach the ~?** ¿alcanzó alguien la cima *or* la cumbre?

2 (*fig*) cima *f*, cumbre *f*; **a man at the ~ of his career** un hombre en la cima *or* la cumbre de su trayectoria profesional

3 (*Pol*) (*also* **~ conference**) cumbre *f*, conferencia *f* al más alto nivel

Ⓑ CPD ► **summit conference** N cumbre *f*, conferencia *f* al más alto nivel ► **summit meeting** N cumbre *f*

summitry ['sʌmɪtrɪ] N (*esp US hum*) práctica *f* de celebrar conferencias cumbre

summon ['sʌmən] VT [+ *servant, doctor etc*] llamar; [+ *meeting*] convocar; [+ *aid*] pedir; (*Jur*) citar, emplazar; **to be ~ed to sb's presence** ser llamado a la presencia de algn; **they ~ed me to advise them** me llamaron para que les aconsejara; **to ~ a town to surrender** hacer una llamada a una ciudad para que se rinda

►**summon up** VT + ADV [+ *courage*] armarse de, cobrar; [+ *memory*] evocar

summons ['sʌmənz] Ⓐ N (*pl* **summonses**) (*Jur*) citación *f* judicial, emplazamiento *m*; (*fig*) llamada *f*; **he got a ~ for drink driving** recibió una citación por conducir borracho; **she received a ~ to appear in court** recibió una citación para presentarse en el juzgado; **to serve a ~ on sb** entregar una citación a algn; **to take out a ~ against sb** entablar demanda contra algn, citar a algn (para estrados)

Ⓑ VT citar, emplazar; **she has been ~ed to appear in court** ha sido citada *or* emplazada a presentarse en el juzgado

sumo ['su:məʊ] N 1 (*Sport*) (*also* **~ wrestling**) sumo *m*

2 (*also* **~ wrestler**) luchador *m* de sumo

sump [sʌmp] N (*Aut*) cárter *m*; (*Min*) sumidero *m*; (= *cesspool*) letrina *f*

sumptuary ['sʌmptjʊərɪ] ADJ suntuario

sumptuous ['sʌmptjʊəs] ADJ [*feast, fabrics, silk*] suntuoso

sumptuously ['sʌmptjʊəslɪ] ADV suntuosamente

sumptuousness ['sʌmptjʊəsnɪs] N suntuosidad *f*

sun [sʌn] Ⓐ N sol *m*; **the ~ is shining** brilla el sol, hace sol; **the ~ is in my eyes** me da el sol en los ojos; **he rises with the ~** se levanta con el sol; **to catch the ~: you've caught the ~** te ha cogido el sol; **to be (out) in the ~** estar al sol; ✦*IDIOM* **under the ~: they have everything under the ~** no les falta de nada; **they would do anything under the ~ to stay in power** serían capaces de hacer cualquier cosa para seguir en el poder; **he called me all the names under the ~** me llamó de todo; ✦*PROV* **there is nothing new under the ~** no hay nada nuevo bajo el sol

Ⓑ VT **to ~ o.s.** tomar el sol, asolearse (*LAm*), tomar sol (*S. Cone*)

Ⓒ CPD ► **sun dress** N vestido *m* de playa ► **sun god** N dios *m* del sol, divinidad *f* solar ► **sun hat** N pamela *f*, sombrero *m* de ala ancha ► **sun lamp** N lámpara *f* solar ultravioleta ► **sun lotion** N bronceador *m* ► **sun lounge** N solana *f* ► **sun lounger** N tumbona *f* ► **sun parlour, sun parlor** (*US*) N solana *f* ► **sun umbrella** N sombrilla *f*

Sun. ABBR (= **Sunday**) dom.º

sunbaked ['sʌnbeɪkt] ADJ endurecido al sol

sunbathe VI tomar el sol, asolearse (*LAm*), tomar sol (*S. Cone*)

sunbather ['sʌnbeɪðər] N persona *f* que toma el sol

sunbathing ['sʌnbeɪðɪŋ] N baños *mpl* de sol; **I like ~ in the garden** me gusta tomar el sol *or* (*LAm*) asolearme *or* (*S. Cone*) tomar sol en el jardín

sunbeam ['sʌnbi:m] N rayo *m* de sol

sunbed ['sʌnbed] N cama *f* solar

➤ LANGUAGE IN USE: sum 2 20.6

sunbelt ['sʌnbelt] N (*US*) *franja del sur de Estados Unidos caracterizada por su clima cálido*

SUNBELT

A los estados del sur de EE.UU. que van desde Carolina del Norte hasta California se les denomina **sunbelt** *(cinturón del sol) por su clima cálido. Este nombre también se asocia con el reciente desarrollo económico de la zona, lo cual ha dado lugar a un aumento de población (por el movimiento demográfico de norte a sur) y a un mayor poder político. Por oposición a este término, a los estados del norte se les llama a veces* **frostbelt** *(cinturón de escarcha) o* **rustbelt** *(cinturón de óxido), por el número de fábricas ya en declive que hay en la zona.*

sunblind ['sʌnblaɪnd] N toldo *m*
sunblock ['sʌnblɒk] N filtro *m* solar
sunbonnet ['sʌn,bɒnɪt] N gorro *m* de sol
sunburn ['sʌnbɜːn] N quemaduras *fpl* del sol
sunburned ['sʌnbɜːnd], **sunburnt** ['sʌnbɜːnt] ADJ (*painfully*) quemado por el sol; (= *tanned*) bronceado; **a badly ~ back** una espalda muy quemada por el sol; **to get ~** (*painfully*) quemarse
sundae ['sʌndeɪ] N helado *m* con frutas y nueces
Sunday ['sʌndɪ] Ⓐ N domingo *m*; *see* **Tuesday** *for usage*
Ⓑ CPD ► **Sunday best** N **in one's ~ best** en traje de domingo, endomingado ► **Sunday opening** N = **Sunday trading** ► **Sunday paper** N periódico *m* del domingo ► **Sunday school** N escuela *f* dominical, catequesis *f* ► **Sunday school teacher** N profesor(a) *m/f* de escuela dominical ► **Sunday supplement** N suplemento *m* dominical ► **Sunday trading** N apertura *f* en domingo ► **Sunday trading laws** NPL leyes *fpl* reguladoras de la apertura en domingo

SUNDAY PAPERS

*Los periódicos dominicales (***Sunday Papers***) juegan un papel importante en el Reino Unido. Algunos de ellos, como* **The Observer** *o* **News of the World** *sólo se publican ese día, mientras que otros, como* **The Sunday Times, The Sunday Telegraph, The Independent on Sunday, The Sunday Express** *o* **The Sunday Mirror***, son ediciones especiales de periódicos diarios. Los dominicales suelen tener distintas secciones, con espacios para cultura, viajes, deportes o negocios, además de incluir muchos de ellos una revista en color.*
En Estados Unidos se suelen comprar más los periódicos locales que los de tirada nacional. De éstos, el principal es el **New York Times***. Al igual que en el Reino Unido, los periódicos dominicales tienen más secciones de lo habitual, con artículos más extensos y venden más ejemplares. Pero a diferencia de los británicos, los estadounidenses suelen comprar un solo periódico los domingos.*

sundeck ['sʌndek] N cubierta *f* superior
sunder ['sʌndəʳ] VT (*liter*) romper, dividir, hender
sundew ['sʌndjuː] N rocío *m* de sol
sundial ['sʌndaɪəl] N reloj *m* de sol
sundown ['sʌndaʊn] N (*US*) anochecer *m*; **at ~** al anochecer; **before ~** antes del anochecer
sundowner* ['sʌndaʊnəʳ] N trago *m* de licor que se toma al anochecer
sun-drenched ['sʌndrentʃt] ADJ bañado de sol
sun-dried ['sʌndraɪd] ADJ secado al sol
sundry ['sʌndrɪ] Ⓐ ADJ diversos, varios; **all and ~** todos sin excepción
Ⓑ N **sundries** (*Comm*) artículos *mpl* diversos; (= *expenses*) gastos *mpl* diversos
sun-filled ['sʌnfɪld] ADJ soleado
sunfish ['sʌnfɪʃ] N peje-sol *m*
sunflower ['sʌn,flaʊəʳ] Ⓐ N girasol *m*
Ⓑ CPD ► **sunflower oil** N aceite *m* de girasol ► **sunflower seeds** NPL pipas *fpl*
sung [sʌŋ] PP *of* **sing**
sunglasses ['sʌn,glɑːsɪz] NPL gafas *fpl* de sol, anteojos *mpl* de sol (*LAm*)
sunk [sʌŋk] PP *of* **sink**
sunken ['sʌŋkən] ADJ 1 (*liter*) (= *submerged*) [*ship, treasure*] hundido
2 (= *hollow*) [*cheeks, eyes*] hundido
3 (= *low*) [*garden, road, bath*] que está a un nivel inferior *or* más bajo
sunless ['sʌnlɪs] ADJ sin sol
sunlight ['sʌnlaɪt] N sol *m*, luz *f* del sol; **those plants must be kept out of direct ~** a esas plantas no las debe dar el sol directamente; **hours of ~** (*Met*) horas *fpl* de sol; **in the ~** al sol
sunlit ['sʌnlɪt] ADJ iluminado por el sol
Sunni ['sʌnɪ] Ⓐ ADJ sunita, suní
Ⓑ N sunita *mf*, suní *mf*
sunny ['sʌnɪ] ADJ (*compar* **sunnier**, *superl* **sunniest**) 1 (= *bright*) [*weather, climate, morning, place*] soleado; **it was a ~ spring morning** era una soleada mañana de primavera; **on ~ days** los días soleados *or* en que hace sol; **it's a lovely ~ day** hace un día de sol precioso; **the sunniest place in Alaska** el lugar de Alaska donde hace más sol, el lugar más soleado de Alaska; **~ intervals** (*Met*) intervalos *mpl* soleados; **it's ~** hace sol; **the outlook is ~** el pronóstico es soleado; ✦*IDIOM* **I'd like my egg ~ side up** (*Culin*) quiero que mi huevo esté frito sólo por un lado
2 (= *cheery*) [*person*] risueño, alegre; [*smile, disposition*] alegre; **to have a ~ disposition** *or* **temperament** ser de temperamento alegre
sunray ['sʌnreɪ] ADJ **~ lamp** lámpara *f* ultravioleta; **~ treatment** helioterapia *f*, tratamiento *m* con lámpara ultravioleta
sunrise ['sʌnraɪz] Ⓐ N salida *f* del sol; **at ~** al amanecer; **from ~ to sunset** de sol a sol
Ⓑ CPD ► **sunrise industries** NPL industrias *fpl* del porvenir, industrias *fpl* de alta tecnología
sunroof ['sʌnruːf] N (*on building*) azotea *f*, terraza *f*; (*Aut*) techo *m* solar
sunset ['sʌnset] N puesta *f* del sol; **at ~** al atardecer, al ponerse el sol
sunshade ['sʌnʃeɪd] N (*portable*) sombrilla *f*; (= *awning*) toldo *m*
sunshine ['sʌnʃaɪn] Ⓐ N 1 sol *m*, luz *f* del sol; **in the ~** al sol; **hours of ~** (*Met*) horas *fpl* de sol; **daily average ~** media *f* de horas de sol diarias
2 (*) **hello, ~!** (*to little girl*) ¡hola, nena!*; **now look here, ~** (*iro*) mira, macho*
Ⓑ CPD ► **sunshine law** N (*US*) *ley que obliga a mantener informado al público* ► **sunshine roof** N (*Aut*) techo *m* solar
sunspot ['sʌnspɒt] N 1 (= *resort*) *centro turístico muy soleado*
2 (*Astron*) mancha *f* solar
sunstroke ['sʌnstrəʊk] N insolación *f*; **to get** *or* **catch ~** coger *or* agarrar una insolación; **to have ~** tener una insolación
sunsuit ['sʌnsuːt] N traje *m* de playa
suntan ['sʌntæn] Ⓐ N bronceado *m*, moreno *m* (*Sp*); **to get a ~** broncearse, ponerse moreno (*Sp*)
Ⓑ CPD ► **suntan lotion** N bronceador *m*
suntanned ['sʌntænd] ADJ bronceado, moreno (*Sp*)
suntrap ['sʌntræp] N *lugar muy soleado y protegido*
sunup ['sʌnʌp] N (*US*) salida *f* del sol
sup [sʌp] Ⓐ VI cenar; **to ~ off sth** ◊ **~ on sth** cenar algo
Ⓑ VT (*also* **to ~ up**) sorber, beber a sorbos
super* ['suːpəʳ] ADJ (*esp Brit*) bárbaro, estupendo (*Sp*), tremendo, macanudo (*LAm*), regio (*S. Cone**), chévere (*Ven*); **we had a ~ time** lo pasamos la mar de bien *or* (*S. Cone*) regio*; **that's a ~ idea** es una idea estupenda; **that would be ~** sería estupendo
super... ['suːpəʳ] PREFIX (= *more than the norm*) super…, sobre…
superabound [,suːpərə'baʊnd] VI sobreabundar (**in, with** en)
superabundance [,suːpərə'bʌndəns] N superabundancia *f*, sobreabundancia *f*
superabundant [,suːpərə'bʌndənt] ADJ sobreabundante, superabundante
superannuate [,suːpə'rænjʊeɪt] VT jubilar
superannuated [,suːpə'rænjʊeɪtɪd] ADJ jubilado; (*fig*) anticuado
superannuation [,suːpə,rænjʊ'eɪʃən] (*Brit*) Ⓐ N (= *pension*) jubilación *f*, pensión *f*
Ⓑ CPD ► **superannuation contribution** N cuota *f* de jubilación ► **superannuation scheme** N plan *m* de jubilación
superb [suː'pɜːb] ADJ estupendo, magnífico
superbly [suː'pɜːblɪ] ADV [*play, perform*] estupendamente; [*crafted, decorated, equipped*] magníficamente; **the strategy worked ~** la estrategia funcionó estupendamente; **a ~ fit man** un hombre en estupendo estado físico; **some ~ elegant curtains** unas cortinas sumamente elegantes
supercargo ['suːpə,kɑːgəʊ] N sobrecargo *m*
supercharged ['suːpətʃɑːdʒd] ADJ 1 (*Aut*) sobrealimentado
2 [*atmosphere, environment*] sobrecargado
supercharger ['suːpətʃɑːdʒəʳ] N compresor *m* de sobrealimentación
supercilious [,suːpə'sɪlɪəs] ADJ desdeñoso, altanero
superciliously [,suːpə'sɪlɪəslɪ] ADV (*pej*) con desdén, desdeñosamente
superciliousness [,suːpə'sɪlɪəsnɪs] N desdén *m*, altanería *f*
superconductivity [,suːpə,kɒndʌk'tɪvɪtɪ] N superconductividad *f*
superconductor [,suːpəkən'dʌktəʳ] N superconductor *m*
super-duper* ['suːpə'duːpəʳ] ADJ estupendo, magnífico
superego ['suːpər,iːgəʊ] N superego *m*
supererogation [,suːpər,erə'geɪʃən] N supererogación *f*
superficial [,suːpə'fɪʃəl] ADJ 1 (= *not deep*) superficial; **she was treated for ~ cuts and bruises** le curaron algunos cortes superficiales y moratones; **most of the buildings had sustained only ~ damage** la mayoría de los edificios sólo habían sufrido daños superficiales; **I suddenly realized how ~ she was** de repente me di cuenta de lo superficial que era
2 (*in measurements*) [*area*] de superficie
superficiality [,suːpə,fɪʃɪ'ælɪtɪ] N superficialidad *f*

superficially [ˌsu:pəˈfɪʃəlɪ] ADV 1 (*= in a shallow way*) [*deal with, treat, know, discuss*] superficialmente, de manera superficial, por encima
2 (*= at first glance*) **~, the plane looked more or less conventional, but actually ...** en apariencia era un avión convencional pero de hecho ...; **although this explanation seems ~ attractive ...** aunque superficialmente *or* a primera vista esta explicación parece interesante ...
3 (*Tech, Med*) **the incision is made ~** la incisión se hace en la superficie

superfine [ˈsu:pəfaɪn] ADJ extrafino

superfluity [ˌsu:pəˈflʊɪtɪ] N superfluidad *f*; **there is a ~ of** hay exceso de

superfluous [sʊˈpɜ:flʊəs] ADJ superfluo; **~ details** detalles superfluos; **to be ~** [*comment, detail, explanation*] ser superfluo, sobrar; [*object, person*] sobrar; **further comment was ~** todo otro comentario era superfluo, sobraba decir nada más; **maps were ~ with Eddie around** cuando estaba Eddie, sobraban los mapas; **my presence was ~** mi presencia estaba de más; **he felt rather ~** se sentía bastante de más

superfluously [sʊˈpɜ:flʊəslɪ] ADV innecesariamente; **... he added ~** ... añadió sin necesidad

superglue [ˈsu:pəˌglu:] N supercola *f*

supergrass* [ˈsu:pəgrɑ:s] N (*Brit*) soplón/ona *m/f*

superheat [ˌsu:pəˈhi:t] VT sobrecalentar

superhighway [ˈsu:pəˈhaɪweɪ] N (*US*) autopista *f* (de varios carriles); *see also* **information**

superhuman [ˌsu:pəˈhju:mən] ADJ [*strength, efforts, powers*] sobrehumano

superimpose [ˈsu:pərɪmˈpəʊz] VT sobreponer (**on** en)

superinduce [ˈsu:pərɪnˈdju:s] VT sobreañadir, inducir por añadidura

superintend [ˌsu:pərɪnˈtend] VT supervisar

superintendence [ˌsu:pərɪnˈtendəns] N supervisión *f*; **under the ~ of** bajo la supervisión *or* dirección de

superintendent [ˌsu:pərɪnˈtendənt] N [*of institution, orphanage*] director(a) *m/f*; (*in swimming pool*) vigilante *mf*; (*US*) (*= porter*) conserje *mf*; **police ~** (*Brit*) subjefe *mf* de policía; (*US*) superintendente *mf*

▼**superior** [sʊˈpɪərɪəʳ] Ⓐ ADJ 1 (*= better*) superior; **to be ~ to sth/sb** ser superior a algo/algn; **to be ~ to sth/sb in sth** superar *or* ser superior a algo/algn en algo
2 (*= good*) [*product*] de primera calidad; **it's a very ~ model** es un modelo de primerísima calidad, es un modelo muy superior; **thanks to its ~ design** gracias a la supremacía del diseño; **a ~ being** un ser superior
3 (*= senior*) (*in hierarchy, rank*) superior; **to be ~ to sb** ser superior a algn; **his ~ officer** (*Mil*) su superior
4 (*numerically*) **the enemy's ~ numbers** la superioridad numérica del enemigo; **the enemy were ~ to them in number** el enemigo los superaba *or* era superior a ellos en número
5 (*= smug*) [*person*] altanero, desdeñoso; [*tone, expression, smile*] de superioridad, de suficiencia; **"you don't understand," Clarissa said in a ~ way** —tú no lo entiendes —dijo Clarissa con aire de superioridad *or* de suficiencia
6 (*Tech*) (*= upper*) superior
Ⓑ N 1 (*in rank, organization*) superior *m*; **people he perceives as his social ~s** personas que él considera de un nivel social superior
2 (*in ability*) **to be sb's ~ in sth** superar a algn en algo
3 (*Rel*) superior *m*; **Mother Superior** madre *f* superiora
Ⓒ CPD ► **superior court** N tribunal *m* superior

superiority [sʊˌpɪərɪˈɒrɪtɪ] N 1 (*in quality, amount*) superioridad *f*
2 (*= smugness*) superioridad *f*, altanería *f*

superlative [sʊˈpɜ:lətɪv] Ⓐ ADJ 1 (*= outstanding*) excepcional; **~ wines** vinos de excepcional calidad
2 (*Gram*) superlativo *m*
Ⓑ N 1 (*Gram*) superlativo *m*; **in the ~** en el superlativo
2 (*fig*) **the critics were reaching for ~s** los críticos se deshacían en elogios; **he tends to talk in ~s** tiende a hablar en términos muy elogiosos de todo

superlatively [sʊˈpɜ:lətɪvlɪ] ADV [*perform, sing*] excepcionalmente, de manera excepcional; **a ~ nice man** un hombre extremadamente *or* excepcionalmente agradable; **~ fit** en una forma física excepcional; **his ability to get things ~ right** su habilidad para hacer las cosas excepcionalmente *or* extraordinariamente bien; **he knew his job ~ well** conocía su trabajo a la perfección, conocía su trabajo excepcionalmente *or* extraordinariamente bien

superman [ˈsu:pəmæn] N (*pl* **supermen**) superhombre *m*

supermarket [ˈsu:pəˌmɑ:kɪt] N supermercado *m*

supernatural [ˌsu:pəˈnætʃərəl] Ⓐ ADJ sobrenatural
Ⓑ N **the ~** lo sobrenatural

supernormal [ˌsu:pəˈnɔ:məl] ADJ superior a lo normal

supernova [ˌsu:pəˈnəʊvə] N (*pl* **supernovae** [ˌsu:pəˈnəʊvi:]) (*Astron*) supernova *f*

supernumerary [ˌsu:pəˈnju:mərərɪ] Ⓐ ADJ (*Admin, Bio etc*) supernumerario
Ⓑ N (*Admin etc*) supernumerario/a *m/f*; (*Theat, Cine*) figurante/a *m/f*, comparsa *mf*

superphosphate [ˌsu:pəˈfɒsfeɪt] N superfosfato *m*

superpose [ˈsu:pəpəʊz] VT sobreponer, superponer

superposition [ˈsu:pəpəzɪʃən] N superposición *f*

superpower [ˈsu:pəˌpaʊəʳ] N superpotencia *f*

superscript [ˌsu:pəˈskrɪpt] N superíndice *m*

superscription [ˌsu:pəˈskrɪpʃən] N sobrescrito *m*

supersede [ˌsu:pəˈsi:d] VT desbancar, suplantar

supersensitive [ˈsu:pəˈsensɪtɪv] ADJ extremadamente sensible (**to** a)

supersonic [ˈsu:pəˈsɒnɪk] ADJ [*aircraft, speed, flight*] supersónico

supersonically [ˈsu:pəˈsɒnɪkəlɪ] ADV [*fly*] a velocidad supersónica

superstar [ˈsu:pəstɑ:ʳ] N superestrella *f*

superstition [ˌsu:pəˈstɪʃən] N superstición *f*

superstitious [ˌsu:pəˈstɪʃəs] ADJ supersticioso; **to be ~ about sth** ser supersticioso con respecto a algo

superstitiously [ˌsu:pəˈstɪʃəslɪ] ADV supersticiosamente

superstore [ˈsu:pəstɔ:ʳ] N (*Brit*) hipermercado *m*

superstratum [ˌsu:pəˈstrɑ:təm] N (*pl* **superstratums** *or* **superstrata** [ˌsu:pəˈstrɑ:tə]) superstrato *m*

superstructure [ˈsu:pəˌstrʌktʃəʳ] N superestructura *f*

supertanker [ˈsu:pəˌtæŋkəʳ] N superpetrolero *m*

supertax [ˈsu:pətæks] N sobretasa *f*, sobreimpuesto *m*

supervene [ˌsu:pəˈvi:n] VI sobrevenir

supervise [ˈsu:pəvaɪz] VT 1 [+ *work, people*] supervisar
2 (*Univ*) [+ *thesis*] dirigir

supervision [ˌsu:pəˈvɪʒən] N supervisión *f*; **to work under the ~ of** trabajar bajo la supervisión de

supervisor [ˈsu:pəvaɪzəʳ] N 1 (*gen*) supervisor(a) *m/f*
2 (*Univ*) [*of thesis*] director(a) *m/f*

supervisory [ˈsu:pəvaɪzərɪ] ADJ [*body, staff, powers*] de supervisión; [*role*] de supervisor; **he stayed on in a ~ capacity** se quedó en calidad de supervisor; **~ board** (*Comm, Ind*) junta *f* de supervisión

superwoman [ˈsu:pəˌwʊmən] N (*pl* **superwomen**) supermujer *f*

supine [ˈsu:paɪn] Ⓐ ADJ (*frm*) 1 (*= prostrate*) [*person, position*] de espaldas, sobre el dorso, supino (*more frm*); **he lay ~ on the couch** estaba tendido sobre el dorso *or* (*more frm*) en posición supina en el sofá
2 (*fig*) (*= passive*) abúlico; **the government's ~ response to the rise in petrol prices** la reacción abúlica del gobierno ante la subida de los precios de la gasolina
Ⓑ N supino *m*

supper [ˈsʌpəʳ] N (*= evening meal*) cena *f*; **what's for ~ tonight?** ¿qué hay de cena hoy?; **to stay to ~** quedarse a cenar; **to have ~** cenar; **the Last Supper** (*Rel*) La Ultima Cena; ✦***IDIOM*** **to sing for one's ~** trabajárselo

suppertime [ˈsʌpətaɪm] N hora *f* de cenar

supplant [səˈplɑ:nt] VT suplantar, reemplazar

supple [ˈsʌpl] ADJ [*body, leather*] flexible; [*joint, limb*] ágil; [*skin*] suave; **this will keep your skin ~** esto mantendrá tu piel suave; **to keep o.s. ~** mantenerse flexible

supplement Ⓐ [ˈsʌplɪmənt] N (*gen*) suplemento *m*
Ⓑ [ˌsʌplɪˈment] VT complementar; **to ~ sth with sth** complementar algo con algo; **I ~ my diet with vitamin pills** complemento mi dieta con vitaminas; **to ~ one's income by writing** aumentar sus ingresos escribiendo

supplemental [ˌsʌplɪˈmentəl] ADJ (*esp US*) suplementario

supplementary [ˌsʌplɪˈmentərɪ] ADJ suplementario

suppleness [ˈsʌplnɪs] N [*of body, leather*] flexibilidad *f*; [*of joint, limb*] agilidad *f*; [*of skin*] suavidad *f*

suppliant [ˈsʌplɪənt] (*frm*) Ⓐ ADJ suplicante
Ⓑ N suplicante *mf*

supplicant [ˈsʌplɪkənt] N suplicante *mf*

supplicate [ˈsʌplɪkeɪt] VT, VI suplicar

supplication [ˌsʌplɪˈkeɪʃən] N súplica *f*

supplier [səˈplaɪəʳ] N (*Comm*) (*= distributor*) distribuidor(a) *m/f*; (*= provider*) abastecedor(a) *m/f*, proveedor(a) *m/f*; **from your usual ~** de su proveedor habitual

supply [səˈplaɪ] Ⓐ N 1 (*= stock, amount*) [*of oil, coal, water*] reservas *fpl*, existencias *fpl*; [*of goods, merchandise*] existencias *fpl*; **America has a 300-year ~ of coal** América tiene reservas *or* existencias de carbón para 300 años; **oil supplies are running low** las reservas de petróleo se están agotando; **he must have used up his ~ of drugs by now** ahora ya debe haber agotado todas sus reservas *or* exis-

➤ LANGUAGE IN USE: superior A1 5.4

tencias de medicamentos; **he had only a small ~ of gin left** sólo le quedaba una pequeña cantidad de ginebra; **a three-month ~ of drugs** medicinas suficientes para tres meses; **an adequate ~ of food** suficientes víveres *or* provisiones; **we need a fresh ~ of coffee** nos hace falta proveernos de café; **they seem to have an inexhaustible ~ of ammunition** parece que tengan una reserva inagotable de municiones; **to lay in a ~ of sth** proveerse de algo, hacer provisión de algo; **a limited ~ of fine wines** existencias limitadas de buenos vinos; **there is a plentiful ~ of fish in the river** en el río hay peces en abundancia; **to be in short ~** escasear; **vegetables are in short ~** hay escasez de verduras, escasean las verduras

2 **supplies** (= *provisions*) provisiones *fpl*, víveres *mpl*; (*Mil*) pertrechos *mpl*; **supplies are still being flown into the capital** aún se están llevando provisiones *or* víveres a la capital por aire; **emergency supplies** provisiones *fpl* de emergencia; **food supplies** víveres *mpl*, provisiones *fpl*; **medical supplies** suministros *mpl* médicos; **office supplies** materiales *mpl or* artículos *mpl* de oficina

3 (= *provision*) suministro *m*; **the ~ of fuel to the engine** el suministro de combustible al motor; **electricity/gas ~** suministro de electricidad/gas; **blood ~** (*Physiol*) riego *m* sanguíneo

4 (*Econ*) oferta *f*; **~ and demand** la oferta y la demanda

5 (*Parl*) provisión *f* financiera; **to vote supplies** votar créditos

Ⓑ VT 1 (= *provide*) 1·1 [+ *merchandise, goods, materials, food*] suministrar, proporcionar; [+ *information*] facilitar, proporcionar; **Japan will ~ the materials** Japón suministrará *or* proporcionará los materiales; **he accused the company of ~ing arms to terrorists** acusó a la empresa de suministrar *or* proporcionar armas a grupos terroristas; **~ the missing word and win a prize** adivine la palabra que falta y gane un premio; **she supplied the vital clue** ella nos dio la pista esencial; **I supplied the feminine intuition** yo aportaba la intuición femenina; **the arteries that ~ blood to the heart** las arterias que llevan la sangre al corazón, las arterias que irrigan el corazón

1·2 **to ~ sb with** [+ *merchandise, equipment*] suministrar algo a algn, proporcionar algo a algn; [+ *services*] proveer a algn de algo; [+ *information*] facilitar algo a algn; **they kept us supplied with milk/vegetables** nos fueron abasteciendo de leche/verduras

2 (*frm*) (= *satisfy*) [+ *need*] satisfacer; [+ *want*] suplir

Ⓒ CPD ► **supply dump** N (*Mil*) intendencia *f* ► **supply line** N línea *f* de abastecimiento ► **supply route** N ruta *f* de abastecimiento ► **supply ship** N buque *m* de abastecimiento ► **supply teacher** N (*Brit*) profesor(a) *m/f* suplente, profesor(a) *m/f* sustituto/a ► **supply teaching** N (*Brit*) suplencias *fpl* ► **supply truck** N camión *m* de abastecimiento

supply-side [sə'plaɪ,saɪd] ADJ **~ economics** economía *f* de oferta

▼**support** [sə'pɔ:t] Ⓐ N 1 (*for weight*) 1·1 (= *object*) soporte *m*; **use the stool as a ~ for your feet** usa el taburete como soporte para los pies; **steel ~s** soportes *mpl* de acero

1·2 (= *capacity to support*) soporte *m*; **a good bed should provide adequate ~ for your back** una buena cama debe ofrecerle un soporte adecuado para su espalda; **to lean on sb for ~** apoyarse en algn

1·3 (*Med*) soporte *m*; **back ~** espaldera *f*

2 (*fig*) 2·1 (= *help*) apoyo *m*; **I've had a lot of ~ from my family** mi familia me ha apoyado mucho *or* me ha dado mucho apoyo; **she was a real ~ to her mother** fue un verdadero apoyo para su madre; **to give sb ~** dar apoyo a algn, apoyar a algn; **moral ~** apoyo moral

2·2 (= *backing*) apoyo *m*; **he has given his ~ to the reform programme** ha apoyado *or* respaldado el programa de reforma, ha dado su apoyo *or* respaldo al programa de reforma; **do I have I your ~ in this?** ¿puedo contar con tu apoyo para esto?; **our ~ comes from the workers** los que nos apoyan son los obreros; **their capacity to act in ~ of their political objectives** su capacidad de actuar en pos de sus objetivos políticos; **a campaign in ~ of these aims** una campaña en apoyo de estos objetivos; **he spoke in ~ of the motion** habló en apoyo de la moción; **popular ~** apoyo *m* popular

2·3 (*financial*) ayuda *f*, respaldo *m*; **financial ~** ayuda *f* económica, respaldo *m* económico; **they depend on him for financial ~** económicamente dependen de él; **with Government ~** con la ayuda del Gobierno, respaldado por el Gobierno; **a man with no visible means of ~** un hombre sin una fuente de ingresos aparente

2·4 (*esp Comm*) (= *backup*) servicio *m* de asistencia (al cliente); **after-sales ~** servicio *m* posventa, asistencia *f* posventa; **technical ~** servicio *m* de asistencia técnica

2·5 (*Mil*) apoyo *m*; **military ~** apoyo militar

2·6 (= *evidence*) **history offers some ~ for this view** la historia respalda en cierta medida esta opinión; **scholars have found little ~ for this interpretation** los académicos han encontrado pocas pruebas que apoyen *or* respalden esta interpretación; **in ~ of this argument he states that ...** para apoyar *or* respaldar este argumento aduce que ...; **evidence in ~ of a particular theory** pruebas que confirman una determinada teoría

Ⓑ VT 1 (= *hold up*) sostener; **his knees wouldn't ~ him any more** sus rodillas ya no lo sostenían; **that chair won't ~ your weight** esa silla no resistirá *or* aguantará tu peso; **raise your upper body off the ground, ~ing your weight on your arms** apoyándose en los brazos levante el tronco del suelo; **to ~ o.s.** (*physically*) apoyarse (**on** en)

2 (= *help*) 2·1 (*emotionally*) apoyar

2·2 (*financially*) [+ *person*] mantener; [+ *organization, project*] financiar; **he has a wife and three children to ~** tiene una mujer y tres hijos que mantener; **to ~ o.s.** (*financially*) ganarse la vida

3 (= *back*) [+ *proposal, project, person*] apoyar; **his colleagues refused to ~ him** sus colegas se negaron a apoyarlo

4 (*Sport*) [+ *team*] **who do you ~?** ¿de qué equipo eres (hincha)?; **Tim ~s Manchester United** Tim es hincha de Manchester United; **come and ~ your team!** ¡ven a animar a tu equipo!

5 (= *corroborate*) [+ *theory, view*] respaldar, confirmar

6 (= *sustain*) **an environment capable of ~ing human life** un medio en que existen las condiciones necesarias para que se desarrolle la vida humana; **land so poor that it cannot ~ a small family** un terreno tan poco fértil que no puede sustentar a una familia pequeña

7 (*frm*) (= *tolerate*) tolerar

8 (*Mus*) [+ *band*] actuar de telonero/ teloneros de; **a good band ~ed by an exciting new group** un buen grupo con unos teloneros nuevos muy interesantes

9 (*Cine, Theat*) [+ *principal actor*] secundar; **he is ~ed by a wonderful cast** está secundado por un estupendo reparto

Ⓒ CPD ► **support band** N (*Mus*) teloneros *mpl* ► **support group** N grupo *m* de apoyo; **a ~ group for victims of crime** un grupo de apoyo *or* una asociación de ayuda a las víctimas de la delincuencia ► **support hose** N medias *fpl* de compresión graduada ► **support network** N red *f* de apoyo ► **support ship** N barco *m* de apoyo ► **support stocking** N media *f* de compresión graduada ► **support tights** NPL medias *fpl* de compresión (graduada) ► **support troops** NPL tropas *fpl* de apoyo

supportable [sə'pɔ:təbl] ADJ soportable

supporter [sə'pɔ:təʳ] N 1 [*of proposal, party etc*] partidario/a *m/f*; (*Sport*) hincha *mf*; **I'm a United ~** soy del United, soy hincha del United; **supporters** la afición; **the ~s really got behind the team last night** la afición apoyó totalmente al equipo ayer; **~s' club** peña *f* deportiva; **football ~s** hinchas *mpl* de fútbol

2 (*Tech*) soporte *m*, sostén *m*; (*Heraldry*) tenante *m*, soporte *m*

supporting [sə'pɔ:tɪŋ] Ⓐ ADJ 1 [*documents*] acreditativo; **there is no ~ evidence for this theory** no hay pruebas que confirmen esta teoría

2 (*Theat*) [*role, cast*] secundario; [*actor*] secundario, de reparto

Ⓑ CPD ► **supporting feature** N (*Cine*) cortometraje *m* ► **supporting wall** N pared *f* maestra

supportive [sə'pɔ:tɪv] ADJ [*role*] de apoyo; **a ~ role** un papel de apoyo; **I have a very ~ family** tengo una familia que me apoya mucho; **to be ~: her boss was very ~ and gave her time off work** su jefe la apoyó mucho y le dio unos días libres; **to be ~ of sb** apoyar a algn

supportiveness [sə'pɔ:tɪvnɪs] N sustentación *f*

▼**suppose** [sə'pəʊz] VT 1 (= *assume*) suponer; **let us ~ that** supongamos que, pongamos por caso que; **but just ~ he's right** y ¿si tiene razón?; **supposing it rains, what shall we do?** pongamos que llueve, entonces ¿qué hacemos?; **always supposing he comes** siempre y cuando venga; **even supposing that were true** aun en el caso de que fuera verdad

2 (= *assume, believe*) suponer, creer; **I ~ she'll come** supongo que vendrá; **I don't ~ she'll come** no creo que venga; **you'll accept, I ~?** aceptarás, supongo, ¿no?; **who do you ~ was there?** ¿quién crees tú que estaba allí?; **you don't ~ they'd start without us, do you?** no empezarán sin nosotros, ¿verdad?; **I ~ so/not** supongo que sí/no

3 **to be ~d to do sth**: **you're ~d to be in bed by ten** tendrías que estar acostado a las diez; **you're not ~d to do that** no deberías hacer eso; **you're ~d to be my friend!** ¡yo creía que eras mi amigo!; **what am I ~d to have done wrong now?** ¿qué se supone que he hecho mal ahora?; **what's that ~d to mean?** ¿qué quieres decir con eso?; **he's ~d to be an expert** se le supone un experto

4 (*in requests, suggestions*) **do you ~ we could take a lunch break now?** ¿podríamos hacer un descanso para almorzar ahora?; **do you ~ you could wrap this up for me?** ¿podrías envolverme esto?; **I don't ~ you could lend me ten pounds** ¿no podrías prestarme diez libras?; **~ we talk about something else now** ¿y si hablamos sobre algo distinto ahora?

5 (= *presuppose*) suponer, presuponer

supposed [sə'pəʊzd] ADJ [*ally, benefit, threat*] supuesto

➤ LANGUAGE IN USE: support B3 12.2 suppose 1 6.2 2 26.2

supposedly [sə'pəʊzɪdlɪ] ADV supuestamente; **he had ~ gone to Scotland** según se suponía había ido a Escocia, supuestamente había ido a Escocia; **the ~ brave James Bond** el James Bond que se suponía tan valiente

supposing [sə'pəʊzɪŋ] CONJ si, en el caso de que; *see also* **suppose A1**

supposition [ˌsʌpə'zɪʃən] N suposición *f*; **that is pure ~** eso es una suposición *or* hipótesis nada más; **the report was based on ~** el informe estaba basado en suposiciones; **it's based on the ~ that …** se basa en la hipótesis de que …

suppositious [ˌsʌpə'zɪʃəs] ADJ, **supposititious** [səˌpɒzɪ'tɪʃəs] ADJ espurio, supositicio

suppository [sə'pɒzɪtərɪ] N supositorio *m*

suppress [sə'pres] VT [+ *symptoms, dissent, opposition, publication*] suprimir; [+ *feelings*] reprimir; [+ *emotion*] contener, dominar; [+ *yawn, smile*] contener; [+ *news, the truth*] callar, ocultar; [+ *scandal*] acallar, ocultar; [+ *revolt, uprising*] sofocar, reprimir; **with ~ed emotion** con emoción contenida; **a half ~ed laugh** una risa mal disimulada

suppressant [sə'presnt] N inhibidor *m*; **appetite ~** inhibidor *m* del apetito

suppression [sə'preʃən] N [*of symptoms, dissent, opposition, publication*] supresión *f*; [*of feelings*] represión *f*; [*of news, scandal, the truth*] ocultación *f*; [*of revolt*] represión *f*

suppressor [sə'presəʳ] N supresor *m*

suppurate ['sʌpjʊəreɪt] VI supurar

suppuration [ˌsʌpjʊə'reɪʃən] N supuración *f*

supra… ['su:prə] PREFIX supra …; **supranormal** supranormal; **suprarenal** suprarrenal

supranational ['su:prə'næʃənl] ADJ supranacional

suprasegmental [ˌsu:prəseg'mentl] ADJ suprasegmental

supremacist [sʊ'preməsɪst] N *partidario o defensor de la supremacía de un grupo, raza etc*; **male ~** machista *mf*; **white ~** racista *mf* (blanco/a)

supremacy [sʊ'preməsɪ] N supremacía *f*; **naval/political ~** supremacía *f* naval/política; **the struggle for ~** la lucha por la supremacía

supreme [sʊ'pri:m] Ⓐ ADJ [*effort*] supremo; [*heroism, confidence*] sumo; [*achievement*] mayor; **it is of ~ importance** es de suma importancia; **with ~ indifference** con suma indiferencia; **it was a ~ irony that …** la mayor ironía fue que …; **the ~ sacrifice** el sacrificio supremo; **to reign ~** (*fig*) [*team, individual, city*] no tener rival, gozar del dominio absoluto; [*ideology, tradition*] predominar por encima de todo

Ⓑ CPD ► **the Supreme Being** N el Ser Supremo ► **supreme champion** N campeón/ona *m/f* absoluto/a ► **Supreme Commander** N comandante *mf* en jefe, comandante *mf* supremo/a ► **Supreme Court** N Tribunal *m* Supremo, Corte *f* Suprema (*LAm*)

supremely [sʊ'pri:mlɪ] ADV [*confident, important, elegant*] sumamente; **she does her job ~ well** hace su trabajo a la perfección *or* sumamente bien; **he is a ~ gifted musician** es un músico de extraordinario talento

supremo [sʊ'pri:məʊ] N jefe *m*

Supt ABBR (*Brit*) = **Superintendent**

sura ['sʊərə] N sura *m*

surcharge ['sɜ:tʃɑ:dʒ] Ⓐ N recargo *m*; **to introduce/impose a ~ on sth** introducir/imponer un recargo en algo; **import ~** sobretasa *f* de importación

Ⓑ VT [+ *person*] cobrar un recargo a

surd [sɜ:d] N número *m* sordo

▼**sure** [ʃʊəʳ] ADJ (*compar* **surer**; *superl* **surest**) Ⓐ ADJ 1 (= *certain*) 1·1 seguro; **"do you want to see that film?" — "I'm not ~"** — ¿quieres ver esa película? —no sé *or* no estoy seguro; **she seemed honest enough but I had to be ~** parecía bastante sincera, pero tenía que asegurarme *or* estar seguro; **"I know my duty" — "I'm ~ you do"** —sé cuál es mi deber —de eso estoy seguro; **to be ~ that** estar seguro de que; **I'm ~ that she's right** estoy seguro de que tiene razón; **I'm not ~ that I can help you** no estoy seguro de que te pueda ayudar, no estoy seguro de poder ayudarte; **are you ~ you won't have another drink?** ¿seguro que no quieres tomarte otra copa?; **I'm quite ~ her decision was right** estoy convencido de que *or* estoy completamente seguro de que su decisión fue correcta; **to be ~ about sth** estar seguro de algo; **I'm not ~ about the date yet** todavía no estoy seguro de la fecha; **I like the colour but I'm not ~ about the shape** me gusta el color pero la forma no acaba de convencerme; **to be ~ what/who** estar seguro de qué/quién; **Jane wasn't ~ (in her mind) what she thought about abortion** Jane no tenía muy claras las ideas sobre el aborto; **I'm not ~ whether …** no estoy seguro (de) si …

1·2 **to be ~ of sth** estar seguro de algo; **you can be ~ of our support** puedes estar seguro de nuestro apoyo; **Cameroon is ~ of a place in the second round** Camerún tiene una plaza asegurada *or* segura en la segunda ronda; **book now to be ~ of a place on the course** haga la reserva ahora para tener la plaza en el curso asegurada *or* segura; **we can't be ~ of winning** no podemos estar seguros de que vayamos a ganar; **to be ~ of one's facts** estar seguro de lo que se dice

1·3 **to be ~ of sb: I've always felt very ~ of John** siempre he confiado mucho en John; **he was not quite ~ of Flora** tenía sus dudas acerca de Flora; **to be ~ of o.s.** estar seguro de sí mismo; **to be ~ of sb** confiar en algn

1·4 (+ *INFIN*) **it is ~ to rain** seguro que llueve, seguramente lloverá; **she is ~ to agree** seguro que está de acuerdo, seguramente estará de acuerdo; **be ~ to** *or* **be ~ and close the window** asegúrate de que cierras la ventana; **be ~ to** *or* **be ~ and tell me** que no se te olvide contármelo; **be ~ not to take any weapons** no se te ocurra ir armado

1·5 **to make ~ (that)** asegurarse (de que); **I knocked on his door to make ~ that he was all right** llamé a su puerta para asegurarme de que estaba bien; **make ~ it doesn't happen again** asegúrate de que no vuelva a ocurrir; **her friends made ~ that she was never alone** sus amigos se encargaron de que no estuviera nunca sola; **please make ~ that your children get to school on time** consiga de la forma que sea que sus hijos lleguen a la escuela a tiempo; **better get a ticket beforehand, just to make ~** mejor compre el billete de antemano, más que nada para ir sobre seguro *or* para tener esa seguridad; **to make ~ to do sth** asegurarse de hacer algo

2 (= *reliable*) [*sign*] claro; [*way*] seguro; **one ~ way to lose is …** una forma segura de perder es …; **she had a ~ grasp of the subject** tenía un gran dominio del tema; **to do sth in the ~ knowledge that** hacer algo sabiendo bien que *or* con la seguridad de que

3 (*in phrases*) **it's a ~ bet that he'll come** segurísimo que viene; **for ~*** seguro*; **you'll get it tomorrow for ~** lo recibirás mañana seguro; **nobody** *or* **no one knows for ~** nadie lo sabe con seguridad; **I can't say for ~** no puedo decirlo con seguridad; **that's for ~** ◊ **one thing's for ~** una cosa está clara; **~ thing: a month ago, a yes-vote seemed a ~ thing** hace un mes, el voto a favor parecía algo seguro; **he's a ~ thing for president** no cabe la menor duda de que llegará a presidente; (*esp US*) **"I'd like to hire a car" — "~ thing"** —quiero alquilar un coche —sí, claro; **"can I go with you?" — "~ thing"** —¿puedo ir contigo? —claro que sí *or* por supuesto; **"did you like it?" — "~ thing"** —¿te ha gustado? —ya lo creo; **this is a plausible interpretation, to be sure, but …** desde luego que *or* claro que ésta es una interpretación muy verosímil pero …; **well, that's bad luck to be ~!** vaya, ¡eso sí que es tener mala suerte!

Ⓑ ADV 1 (*US**) (= *certainly*) (*emphatic*) **he ~ is cute** no veas si es guapo*; **I ~ am bored** no veas si estoy aburrido*; **"know what I mean?" — "~ do"** —sabes, ¿no? —claro que sí *or* claro que lo sé; **(as) ~ as: I'm ~ as hell not going to help him** yo sí que no le voy a ayudar; **✦IDIOM as ~ as eggs is eggs, he did it*** lo hizo él, como que me llamo Elena/Juan *etc*

2 (*esp US*) (= *of course*) claro; **"did you tell your uncle about her?" — "oh, sure"** —¿le hablaste a tu tío de ella? —¡claro! *or* (*LAm*) —¡cómo no!; **"can I go with you?" — "sure"** —¿puedo ir contigo? —¡por supuesto! *or* —¡claro que sí!; **"is that OK?" — "sure!"** —¿está bien así? —¡claro que sí! *or* (*LAm*) —¡cómo no!

3 (= *true*) claro; **~, it's never been done before** claro que no se ha hecho antes

4 **~ enough** efectivamente, en efecto; **he said he'd be here, and ~ enough, there he is** dijo que estaría aquí y efectivamente *or* en efecto, aquí está

sure-fire* ['ʃʊəfaɪəʳ] ADJ [*way*] seguro; [*method*] infalible; **a ~ success** un éxito seguro; **he's a ~ winner** tiene el éxito asegurado

sure-footed ['ʃʊə'fʊtɪd] ADJ (*lit*) de pie firme; (*fig*) [*leadership*] firme; **to be ~** (*lit, fig*) conocer el terreno que se pisa

surely ['ʃʊəlɪ] ADV 1 (*emphatic*) 1·1 (*in questions*) **~ there must be something we can do?** algo habrá que podemos hacer, ¿no?

1·2 (*expressing opinion*) **there must ~ be a more effective way of punishing such people** tiene que haber una forma más eficaz de castigar a esa clase de gente, digo *or* creo yo; **~ it is better to steal than to starve** mejor será robar que pasar hambre, digo *or* creo yo; **it is ~ no coincidence that …** digo *or* creo yo que no es una coincidencia que …

1·3 (*expressing surprise*) **~ you are not suggesting she did it on purpose?** no estarás insinuando que lo hizo a propósito ¿verdad?; **~ it's obvious?** pero si es obvio, ¿no?; **~ the logical thing would have been to change banks?** lo más lógico habría sido cambiar de banco, ¿no?; **you ~ don't think it was me!** ¡no pensarás que fui yo!; **~ not** no puede ser; **~ to God‡** ◊ **~ to goodness*: ~ to God that's what everyone wants‡** está claro que es eso lo que quiere todo el mundo ¿no?; **~ to goodness that itself is reason enough to call the police*** seguro que eso en sí mismo es motivo suficiente para llamar a la policía, ¿no?

2 (= *undoubtedly*) sin duda; **she was ~ one of the greatest sopranos of all time** sin duda fue una de las sopranos más destacadas de todos los tiempos; **justice will ~ prevail** sin duda la justicia prevalecerá; **he is an artist, just as ~ as Rembrandt** es pintor, tan se-

➤ LANGUAGE IN USE: **sure A1** 6.2, 12.2, 15.1, 16.1

guro como que lo era Rembrandt; **his time will ~ come** no cabe duda de que le llegará su momento

[3] (*US*) (= *of course*) por supuesto, ¡cómo no! (*LAm*); **"will you excuse me just a second?" — "surely"** —¿me permite un momento? —¡por supuesto! *or* (*LAm*) —¡cómo no!

[4] (= *safely, confidently*) con seguridad; **he handles the issue ~ but with sensitivity** maneja el asunto con seguridad y sensibilidad a la vez; **slowly but ~** lento pero seguro

sureness [ˈʃʊənɪs] N [*of aim, footing*] firmeza *f*; (= *certainty*) seguridad *f*; **the ~ of his touch** su pulso firme

surety [ˈʃʊərətɪ] N (= *sum*) garantía *f*, fianza *f*, caución *f*; (= *person*) fiador(a) *m/f*, garante *mf*; **on his own ~ of £500** bajo su propia fianza de 500 libras; **to go** *or* **stand ~ for sb** ser fiador de algn, salir garante de algn; **to take sth as ~** usar algo como fianza

surf [sɜːf] Ⓐ N (= *waves*) olas *fpl*, rompientes *mpl*; (= *foam*) espuma *f*; (= *swell*) oleaje *m*; (= *current*) resaca *f*

Ⓑ VI hacer surf

Ⓒ VT [1] (*lit*) hacer surf en

[2] (*Internet*) **to ~ the Net** navegar por Internet

surface [ˈsɜːfɪs] Ⓐ N [1] [*of table, skin, lake, sun*] superficie *f*; [*of road*] firme *m*; **beneath** *or* **below the ~: the box was buried two metres beneath** *or* **below the ~** la caja estaba enterrada a dos metros por debajo de la superficie; **the tensions that simmer beneath** *or* **below the ~ in our society** las tensiones que bullen por debajo de la superficie en nuestra sociedad; **she appeared calm, but beneath** *or* **below the ~ she was seething with rage** parecía estar tranquila pero en el fondo *or* por dentro hervía de rabia; **to break the ~** romper la superficie; **to be close to the ~** (*lit*) estar cerca de la superficie; **her grief was still close to the ~** su dolor estaba todavía a flor de piel; **ethnic tensions are never far from the ~** las tensiones étnicas siempre parece que están a punto de estallar; **on the ~ it seems that …** a primera vista parece que …; **outer ~** capa *f* exterior *or* externa; **to come** *or* **rise to the ~** (*lit*) salir a la superficie; (*fig*) aflorar (a la superficie); **these feelings may come** *or* **rise to the ~** estos sentimientos pueden aflorar (a la superficie); **under the ~ = beneath the surface**; **upper ~** superficie *f* de la parte superior; ✦**IDIOM to scratch or touch the ~ (of sth)** arañar la superficie (de algo); **this book only scratches the ~ of philosophical thought** este libro aborda el pensamiento filosófico sólo por encima, este libro sólo araña la superficie del pensamiento filosófico; *see also* **work**

[2] (*Math, Geom*) [2·1] (*also* **~ area**) superficie *f*

[2·2] (= *side*) [*of solid*] cara *f*

Ⓑ VT [+ *road*] revestir, asfaltar

Ⓒ VI [1] (*lit*) [*swimmer, diver, whale*] salir a la superficie; [*submarine*] emerger

[2] (*fig*) [*information, news*] salir a la luz; [*feeling*] salir, aflorar; [*issue*] salir a relucir; [*problem*] presentarse, surgir; [*person*] (*in place*) dejarse ver; (*hum*) (= *get up*) salir de la cama; **what time did you ~?** ¿a qué hora saliste de la cama?

Ⓓ CPD ► **surface area** N área *f* (de la superficie) ► **surface fleet** N flota *f* de superficie ► **surface force** N (*Mil*) fuerza *f* de superficie ► **surface mail** N **by ~ mail** por vía terrestre ► **surface temperature** N temperatura *f* en la superficie ► **surface tension** N (*Phys*) tensión *f* superficial ► **surface water** N agua *f* de la superficie

surface-(to-)air [ˈsɜːfɪs(tuː)ˈɛəʳ] ADJ **~ missile** misil *m* tierra-aire

surfboard [ˈsɜːfbɔːd] N plancha *f* de surf, tabla *f* de surf

surfboarder [ˈsɜːfˌbɔːdəʳ] N surfista *mf*, tablista *mf* de surf

surfboarding [ˈsɜːfˌbɔːdɪŋ] N surf *m*

surfeit [ˈsɜːfɪt] Ⓐ N exceso *m*; **there is a ~ of** hay exceso de

Ⓑ VT hartar, saciar (**on, with** de); **to ~ o.s.** hartarse, saciarse (**on, with** de)

surfer [ˈsɜːfəʳ] N surfista *mf*, tablista *mf* de surf

surfing [ˈsɜːfɪŋ], **surfriding** [ˈsɜːfˌraɪdɪŋ] N surf *m*

surge [sɜːdʒ] Ⓐ N [*of sea*] oleaje *m*, oleada *f*; **a ~ of people** una oleada de gente; **a ~ of sympathy** una oleada de compasión; **a power ~** (*Elec*) una subida de tensión

Ⓑ VI [*water*] levantarse, hincharse; [*people*] **to ~ in/out** entrar/salir en tropel; **the crowd ~d into the building** la multitud entró en tropel en el edificio; **people ~d down the street** una oleada de gente avanzó por la calle; **they ~d round him** se apiñaban en torno suyo; **the blood ~d to her cheeks** se le subió la sangre a las mejillas

surgeon [ˈsɜːdʒən] Ⓐ N cirujano/a *m/f*; (*Mil, Naut*) médico *m*, oficial *m* médico; *see also* **veterinary**

Ⓑ CPD ► **Surgeon General** N (*US*) *jefe del servicio federal de sanidad*

surgery [ˈsɜːdʒərɪ] Ⓐ N [1] (*Med*) (= *branch of medicine, operation*) cirugía *f*; **brain ~** neurocirugía *f*; **heart ~** cardiocirugía *f*; **he was admitted for ~ on his knee** lo ingresaron para operarlo de la rodilla; **to have ~** ser operado, someterse a una operación (quirúrgica); *see also* **plastic**

[2] (*Brit*) (= *consulting room*) (*doctor's, vet's*) consultorio *m*

[3] (*Brit*) (= *consultation*) [3·1] (*with doctor, vet*) consulta *f*; **she has a Wednesday afternoon ~** tiene *or* pasa consulta los miércoles por la tarde

[3·2] (*with MP*) *sesión de consulta y atención de reclamaciones de un diputado con los electores de su circunscripción*; **he holds a ~ for his constituents every Saturday** todos los sábados atiende las reclamaciones de los electores de su circunscripción

[4] (*US*) (= *operating theatre*) quirófano *m*, sala *f* de operaciones

Ⓑ CPD ► **surgery hours** NPL (*Med*) horas *fpl* de consulta

surgical [ˈsɜːdʒɪkəl] Ⓐ ADJ quirúrgico

Ⓑ CPD ► **surgical dressing** N vendaje *m* quirúrgico ► **surgical spirit** N alcohol *m* de 90º

surgically [ˈsɜːdʒɪklɪ] ADV quirúrgicamente

Surinam [ˌsʊərɪˈnæm] N Surinam *m*

Surinamese [ˌsʊərɪnæˈmiːz] Ⓐ ADJ surinamés

Ⓑ N surinamés/esa *m/f*

surliness [ˈsɜːlɪnɪs] N hosquedad *f*, mal humor *m*

surly [ˈsɜːlɪ] ADJ (*compar* **surlier**, *superl* **surliest**) hosco, malhumorado; **he gave me a ~ answer** contestó malhumorado

surmise [sɜːˈmaɪz] Ⓐ N conjetura *f*, suposición *f*

Ⓑ VT conjeturar, suponer; **I ~d as much** ya me lo suponía *or* imaginaba

surmount [sɜːˈmaʊnt] VT [1] [+ *difficulty*] superar, vencer

[2] **~ed by** (*Archit*) coronado de

surmountable [sɜːˈmaʊntəbl] ADJ superable

surname [ˈsɜːneɪm] Ⓐ N apellido *m*

Ⓑ VT apellidar

surpass [sɜːˈpɑːs] VT (= *go above*) [+ *amount, level, record*] superar, sobrepasar; (= *go beyond*) [+ *expectations*] rebasar, superar; **he has never been ~ed in his mastery of the violin** su maestría al violín nunca ha sido superada; **to ~ o.s.** (*lit*) superarse a sí mismo; (*iro*) pasarse (de la raya); **I know you're tactless, but this time you've ~ed yourself!** sabía que no eras muy discreto, pero esta vez sí que te has pasado

surpassing [sɜːˈpɑːsɪŋ] ADJ (*liter*) incomparable, sin par; **of ~ beauty** de hermosura sin par

surplice [ˈsɜːpləs] N sobrepelliz *f*

surplus [ˈsɜːpləs] Ⓐ N (*pl* **surpluses**) [1] (= *excess*) exceso *m*; (*Comm, Agr*) (*from overproduction*) excedente *m*; **a ~ of teachers** un exceso de profesores; **the 1995 wheat ~** el excedente *or* los excedentes de trigo de 1995; **a pair of army ~ boots** un par de botas provenientes de excedentes militares

[2] (*Fin, Econ*) superávit *m*; **budget ~** superávit *m* presupuestario; **trade ~** balanza *f* comercial favorable, superávit *m* (en balanza) comercial

Ⓑ ADJ sobrante; (*Comm, Agr*) (*from overproduction*) excedentario, excedente; **~ energy** energía *f* sobrante; **to be ~ to requirements** no ser ya necesario, sobrar; **stocks ~ to requirements** existencias *fpl* que exceden de las necesidades; **I was made to feel ~ to requirements** (*iro*) hicieron que me sintiera (como que estaba) de más

Ⓒ CPD ► **surplus stock** N saldos *mpl*; **sale of ~ stock** liquidación *f* de saldos ► **surplus store** N tienda *f* de excedentes

✓ **surprise** [səˈpraɪz] Ⓐ N [1] (= *astonishment*) sorpresa *f*; **imagine my ~ when I found a cheque for £5,000** puedes imaginarte la sorpresa que me llevé al encontrar *or* cuando encontré un cheque de 5.000 libras; **"what?" George asked in ~** —¿qué? —preguntó George sorprendido; **he saw my look of ~** me vio la cara de sorpresa; **there was a look of ~ on his face** tenía cara de sorpresa; **surprise, surprise!** (*iro*) ¡menuda sorpresa!; **to my/his ~** para mi/su sorpresa; **much to my ~, he agreed** para gran sorpresa mía, accedió

[2] (*as tactic*) sorpresa *f*; **the element of ~** el elemento sorpresa; **to catch** *or* **take sb by ~** coger *or* (*LAm*) tomar a algn por sorpresa

[3] (= *unexpected thing*) sorpresa *f*; **I have a ~ for you** tengo una sorpresa para ti; **what a lovely ~!** ¡qué sorpresa más *or* tan agradable!; **all this comes as something of a ~** todo esto es en cierto modo una sorpresa; **it may come as a ~ to some people** puede que algunos se lleven una sorpresa; **it came as a ~ to me to learn that …** me llevé una sorpresa al enterarme de que …; **life is full of ~s** la vida está llena de sorpresas; **to give sb a ~** dar una sorpresa a algn

Ⓑ ADJ [*party, present*] sorpresa *inv*; [*announcement, defeat, decision*] inesperado; **a ~ visit** una visita sorpresa *or* inesperada; **a ~ attack** un ataque por sorpresa

Ⓒ VT [1] (= *astonish*) sorprender; **he may ~ us all one day** puede que algún día nos sorprenda a todos; **go on, ~ me!** (*iro*) ¡venga, sorpréndeme! (*iro*); **you ~ me** (*also iro*) me sorprende usted; **it ~d her to hear John sounding so angry** le sorprendió oír a John hablar tan enfadado; **no one will be ~d by her appointment** a nadie le extrañará *or* sorprenderá su nombramiento; **it wouldn't ~ me if he ended up in jail** no me extrañaría *or* sorprendería que terminara en la cárcel; **it ~s**

➤ LANGUAGE IN USE: **surprise C1** 15.2, 16.7

me that … me sorprende que + *subjun*; **to ~ o.s.** sorprenderse (a sí mismo)
2 (= *catch unawares*) coger por sorpresa, tomar por sorpresa (*LAm*); **to ~ sb in the act** sorprender a algn in fraganti, coger a algn in fraganti

surprised [sə'praɪzd] ADJ [*look, expression, smile*] de sorpresa; **he was ~ to hear that …** se sorprendió *or* quedó sorprendido al enterarse de que …; **I was rather ~ to see Martin there** me sorprendió bastante ver a Martin allí, me quedé bastante sorprendido al ver a Martin allí; **they were ~ that she hadn't told them about her new job** se sorprendieron de que no les hubiera dicho nada de su nuevo trabajo; **I was ~ at his ignorance** me sorprendió su ignorancia, me quedé sorprendido de lo ignorante que era; **I'm ~ at you!** ¡me sorprendes!; **he was ~ how good the food tasted** se sorprendió de lo buena que estaba la comida, se quedó sorprendido de lo buena que estaba la comida; **you'd be ~ how many people have difficulty reading** te sorprenderías de la cantidad de gente que tiene problemas para leer, te quedarías sorprendido si supieras la cantidad de gente que tiene problemas para leer; **don't be ~ if he doesn't recognize you** no te sorprendas si no te reconoce; **I wouldn't be ~ if he won** no me sorprendería que ganara; *see also* **surprise**

➤**surprising** [sə'praɪzɪŋ] ADJ sorprendente; **he won the match with ~ ease** ganó el partido con una facilidad sorprendente; **it is ~ how many people eat chips every day** es sorprendente la cantidad de gente que come patatas fritas todos los días; **it is ~ that no one has thought of it before** es sorprendente que no se le haya ocurrido a nadie antes; **it is not** *or* **hardly ~ that some teachers are leaving the profession** no es de extrañar que algunos profesores estén dejando la profesión; **it would be ~ if errors did not occur from time to time** sería extraño que no se cometieran errores de vez en cuando

surprisingly [sə'praɪzɪŋlɪ] ADV [*good, large, easy*] sorprendentemente; **~, it's been a great success** lo sorprendente es que ha sido todo un éxito; **~ enough this is her first film** esta es su primera película, lo cual es bastante sorprendente; **~ few people are interested** lo sorprendente es que muy poca gente está interesada, muy poca gente está interesada, lo cual es sorprendente; **~ little information is available** es sorprendente la poca información que existe; **not ~ he didn't come** como era de esperar, no vino; **the referee, rather ~, awarded a penalty** el árbitro, para sorpresa de todos, señaló penalty; **they are coping ~ well** es sorprendente lo bien que se las están arreglando, se las están arreglando sorprendentemente bien

surreal [sə'rɪəl] ADJ surreal, surrealista

surrealism [sə'rɪəlɪzəm] N surrealismo *m*

surrealist [sə'rɪəlɪst] Ⓐ ADJ surrealista
Ⓑ N surrealista *mf*

surrealistic [sə,rɪə'lɪstɪk] ADJ surrealista

surrender [sə'rendəʳ] Ⓐ N 1 (= *capitulation*) (*Mil*) rendición *f*; (*fig*) claudicación *f*; **no ~!** ¡no nos rendimos nunca!
2 (= *handover*) [*of weapons*] entrega *f*
3 (*Jur*) [*of lease, property*] cesión *f*
4 (*Insurance*) [*of policy*] rescate *m* (previo al vencimiento)
Ⓑ VI (*Mil*) rendirse; **I ~!** ¡me rindo!; **to ~ to the police** entregarse a la policía; **to ~ to despair** abandonarse *or* entregarse a la desesperación
Ⓒ VT 1 (*Mil*) [+ *weapons*] rendir, entregar; [+ *territory, city*] entregar; **to ~ o.s.** (*Mil*) rendirse; (*to police*) entregarse; **to ~ o.s. to despair** abandonarse *or* entregarse a la desesperación; **I ~ed myself to his charms** me rendí a *or* ante sus encantos
2 (= *renounce, give up*) [+ *claim, right*] renunciar a; [+ *lease, ownership*] ceder; (*liter*) [+ *hope*] abandonar
3 (= *hand over*) [+ *passport, ticket*] entregar, hacer entrega de (*more frm*)
4 (= *redeem*) [+ *insurance policy*] rescatar (antes del vencimiento)
Ⓓ CPD ► **surrender value** N valor *m* de rescate

surreptitious [,sʌrəp'tɪʃəs] ADJ subrepticio; **she took a ~ look at her watch** miró furtivamente su reloj

surreptitiously [,sʌrəp'tɪʃəslɪ] ADV [*glance, signal*] subrepticiamente; **he was ~ stuffing himself with chocolate** se estaba atiborrando de chocolate a escondidas

surrogacy ['sʌrəgəsɪ] N (*in child-bearing*) alquiler *m* de úteros

surrogate ['sʌrəgeɪt] Ⓐ N sustituto *m*; (= *substance, material*) sucedáneo *m*; (*Brit Rel*) vicario *m*
Ⓑ ADJ [*substance, material*] sucedáneo; **the army became his ~ family** el ejército se convirtió en su segunda familia
Ⓒ CPD ► **surrogate mother** N madre *f* de alquiler ► **surrogate motherhood** N alquiler *m* de úteros

surround [sə'raʊnd] Ⓐ VT 1 (= *encircle*) rodear; **a town ~ed by hills** una ciudad rodeada de montes; **the house was ~ed by a high wall** la casa estaba rodeada por un muro muy alto; **she was ~ed by children** estaba rodeada de niños; **the uncertainty ~ing the future of the project** la incertidumbre que envuelve *or* rodea al proyecto
2 (*Mil, Pol*) [*troops, police*] [+ *enemy, town, building*] rodear, cercar; **you are ~ed!** ¡estáis rodeados!
Ⓑ N (= *border*) marco *m*, borde *m*; [*of fireplace*] marco *m*; **the bath/swimming pool had a tiled ~** el baño/la piscina tenía un borde de alicatado
Ⓒ CPD ► **surround sound** N sonido *m* (de efecto) surround

surrounding [sə'raʊndɪŋ] ADJ [*countryside*] circundante; [*hills*] circundante, de alrededor; **they disappeared into the ~ darkness** desaparecieron en la oscuridad (que los envolvía)

surroundings [sə'raʊndɪŋz] NPL [*of town, city*] alrededores *mpl*, cercanías *fpl*; (= *environment*) ambiente *msing*; (= *setting*) entorno *msing*; **he'll soon get used to his new ~** pronto se acostumbrará al nuevo ambiente *or* entorno que le rodea; **a hotel set in peaceful ~** un hotel situado en un apacible entorno; **he looked around at his ~** miró a su alrededor, miró en torno suyo

surtax ['sɜːtæks] N sobreimpuesto *m*; (= *rate*) sobretasa *f*

surtitle ['sɜːtaɪtl] N sobretítulo *m*

surveil [sə'veɪl] VT (*US*) vigilar

surveillance [sɜː'veɪləns] N **to be under ~** estar vigilado, estar bajo vigilancia; **to keep sb under ~** vigilar a algn, tener vigilado a algn

survey ['sɜːveɪ] Ⓐ N 1 (= *study*) estudio *m*; **to make a ~ of housing in a town** estudiar la situación de la vivienda en una ciudad
2 (= *poll*) encuesta *f*; **to carry out** *or* **conduct a ~** realizar una encuesta; **they did a ~ of a thousand students** hicieron una encuesta a mil estudiantes
3 (*esp Brit*) [*of land*] inspección *f*, reconocimiento *m*; (*in topography*) medición *f*; [*of building, property*] tasación *f*, peritaje *m*; (= *report to purchaser*) informe *m* de tasación, informe *m* de peritaje; **to have a ~ done** (*of property*) mandar hacer una tasación
4 (= *general view*) visión *f* global, vista *f* de conjunto; **he gave a general ~ of the situation** dio una visión global *or* de conjunto de la situación
Ⓑ [sɜː'veɪ] VT 1 (= *contemplate*) contemplar, mirar; **he ~ed the desolate scene** miró detenidamente la triste escena; **he was master of all he ~ed** era dueño de todo cuanto alcanzaba a dominar con la vista
2 (= *study*) estudiar, hacer un estudio de; **the report ~s housing in Glasgow** el informe estudia la situación de la vivienda en Glasgow
3 (= *poll*) [+ *person, group*] encuestar; [+ *town*] hacer una encuesta en, pulsar la opinión de; [+ *reactions*] sondear; **95% of those ~ed believed that …** el 95% de los encuestados creía que …
4 (= *inspect*) [+ *building*] inspeccionar; [+ *land*] hacer un reconocimiento de; (*in topography*) medir; (= *map*) [+ *town*] levantar el plano de
5 (= *take general view of*) pasar revista a; **the book ~s events up to 1972** el libro pasa revista a los sucesos acaecidos hasta 1972

surveying [sɜː'veɪɪŋ] N agrimensura *f*, topografía *f*

surveyor [sə'veɪəʳ] N (*Brit*) [*of land*] agrimensor(a) *m/f*, topógrafo/a *m/f*; [*of property*] tasador(a) *m/f* (de la propiedad), perito *mf* tasador(a)

survival [sə'vaɪvəl] Ⓐ N 1 (= *act*) supervivencia *f*; **the ~ of the fittest** la ley del más fuerte
2 (= *relic*) vestigio *m*, reliquia *f*; **this practice is a ~ from Victorian times** esta costumbre es un vestigio *or* una reliquia de la época victoriana
Ⓑ CPD ► **survival bag** N saco *m* de supervivencia ► **survival course** N curso *m* de supervivencia ► **survival kit** N equipo *m* de emergencia ► **survival rate** N tasa *f* de supervivencia ► **survival skills** NPL técnicas *fpl* de supervivencia

survive [sə'vaɪv] Ⓐ VI 1 (= *remain alive, in existence*) [*person, species*] sobrevivir; [*painting, building, manuscript*] conservarse; [*custom*] pervivir; **not one of the passengers ~d** no sobrevivió ninguno de los pasajeros; **he ~d on nuts for several weeks** logró sobrevivir durante varias semanas comiendo nueces; **he ~d to the age of 83** vivió hasta los 83 años; **only two of his paintings ~** sólo se conservan dos de sus cuadros
2 (= *cope*) sobrevivir; **people struggling to ~ without jobs** gente luchando para sobrevivir sin trabajo; **I'll ~!** ¡de ésta no me muero!, ¡sobreviviré!; **Jim ~s on £65 a fortnight** Jim se las arregla para vivir con 65 libras a la quincena
Ⓑ VT 1 (= *outlive*) [+ *person*] sobrevivir a; **she will probably ~ me by many years** probablemente me sobreviva por muchos años, probablemente viva muchos más años que yo; **he is ~d by a wife and two sons** deja una mujer y dos hijos
2 (= *not die in*) [+ *accident, illness, war*] sobrevivir a; **he ~d a heart attack** sobrevivió a un ataque al corazón; **he ~d being struck by lightning** sobrevivió tras haberle caído un rayo
3 (= *cope with*) aguantar, sobrellevar; **I couldn't ~ the day without breakfast** no

➤ LANGUAGE IN USE: surprising 15.2

podría aguantar *or* sobrellevar el día sin desayunar

surviving [sə'vaɪvɪŋ] ADJ (= *living*) vivo; (*after catastrophe, also Jur*) sobreviviente; **the last ~ member of the band** el último miembro vivo del grupo; **he had no ~ siblings** no dejó hermanos vivos; **the ~ wife is entitled to a widow's pension** la esposa sobreviviente tiene derecho a una pensión de viudedad; **~ company** (*after merger*) compañía *f* resultante, empresa *f* resultante

survivor [sə'vaɪvə^r] Ⓐ N (*lit, fig*) superviviente *mf*, sobreviviente *mf*; **the sole ~ of the 1979 cabinet** el único superviviente *or* sobreviviente del consejo de ministros de 1979; **I'm a ~, I'll get by** soy de los que no se hunden, me las arreglaré

Ⓑ CPD ► **survivor benefits** NPL (*US*) *ayuda que el Estado presta a la familia de una persona fallecida*

sus⁑ [sʌs] N (= *suspicion*) **he was picked up on ~** la policía le detuvo por sospechoso

Susan ['suːzn] N Susana

susceptibility [səˌseptə'bɪlɪtɪ] N (*to attack*) susceptibilidad *f*; (*Med*) (*to illness, infection*) propensión *f* (**to** a); (*to persuasion, flattery*) sensibilidad *f* (**to** a); **to offend sb's susceptibilities** herir la sensibilidad de algn

susceptible [sə'septəbl] ADJ (*to attack*) susceptible (**to** a); (*Med*) (*to illness, infection*) propenso (**to** a); (*to persuasion, flattery*) sensible (**to** a); (= *easily moved*) impresionable; **to be ~ of** admitir, ser susceptible de; **it is ~ of several interpretations** admite diversas interpretaciones, es susceptible de (recibir) diversas interpretaciones

sushi ['suːʃɪ] Ⓐ N sushi *m*

Ⓑ CPD ► **sushi bar** N bar *m* de sushi ► **sushi restaurant** N restaurante *m* de sushi

Susie ['suːzɪ] N (*familiar form*) *of* **Susan**

▼ **suspect** ['sʌspekt] Ⓐ ADJ [*person, package*] sospechoso; [*motives*] dudoso, sospechoso; [*testimony*] dudoso; **his credentials are ~** su historial deja lugar a muchas dudas

Ⓑ N sospechoso/a *m/f*; **the prime** *or* **chief ~ is the butler** el principal sospechoso es el mayordomo; **is she a ~?** ¿está ella bajo sospecha?; **the usual ~s** (*fig*) los de siempre, los habituales

Ⓒ [səs'pekt] VT [1] (= *have suspicions about*) [+ *person*] sospechar de; [+ *plot*] sospechar la existencia de; **he never ~ed her** él nunca sospechó de ella; **to ~ sb of a crime** sospechar que algn ha cometido un crimen; **I ~ her of having stolen it** sospecho que ella lo ha robado; **he ~s nothing** no sospecha nada

[2] (= *believe*) **I ~ it's not paid for** sospecho que *or* me temo que no está remunerado; **I ~ it may be true** tengo la sospecha de que puede ser verdad, sospecho que *or* me temo que puede ser verdad; **foul play is not ~ed** no se advierten indicios de juego sucio; **I ~ed you weren't listening** me figuraba *or* me imaginaba que no estabas escuchando; **I ~ed as much** ya me lo figuraba *or* imaginaba

suspected [səs'pektɪd] ADJ [*thief, murderer, crime*] presunto; **she was taken to hospital with ~ appendicitis** la llevaron al hospital pensando que podía tener apendicitis; **she collapsed yesterday with a ~ heart attack** ayer sufrió un colapso y se sospecha que la causa fue un ataque al corazón

suspend [səs'pend] VT [1] (= *hang*) suspender, colgar

[2] (= *remove*) (*from job*) suspender (**from** de); (*from school*) expulsar temporalmente (**from** de); (*from team*) excluir (**from** de); **to ~ sb from office** relevar a algn de su cargo (provisionalmente)

[3] (= *discontinue*) [+ *hostilities, aid, flights*] suspender; [+ *licence*] retirar; **his licence was ~ed for six months** (*Aut*) le retiraron el carnet durante seis meses

[4] (= *withold, defer*) [+ *judgement, decision*] aplazar, posponer; (*Jur*) [+ *sentence*] suspender provisionalmente, dejar en suspenso; **he was given a two-year ~ed sentence** fue condenado a dos años en libertad condicional; **to ~ disbelief** creer lo inverosímil

[5] **~ed animation** constantes *fpl* vitales mínimas; **in a state of ~ed animation** (*lit*) con las constantes vitales al mínimo; **the audience was in a state of ~ed animation** el público tenía el alma en vilo *or* el corazón en un puño

suspender [səs'pendə^r] Ⓐ N (*for stocking, sock*) liga *f*; **~s** (*US*) (= *braces*) tirantes *mpl*, tiradores *mpl* (*S. Cone*) Ⓑ CPD ► **suspender belt** N portaligas *m inv*, liguero *m*

suspense [səs'pens] Ⓐ N incertidumbre *f*; (*Theat, Cine*) intriga *f*, suspense *m*; **to keep sb in ~** mantener a algn en vilo; **don't keep me in ~!** ¡no me tengas en vilo!; **the ~ became unbearable** la tensión se hizo inaguantable; **the ~ is killing me!** ¡no puedo con tanta emoción!

Ⓑ CPD ► **suspense account** N cuenta *f* en suspenso, cuenta *f* transitoria

suspension [səs'penʃən] Ⓐ N [1] (*from job*) suspensión *f*; (*from school*) expulsión *f* temporal; (*from team*) exclusión *f*; **~ of payments** suspensión *f* de pagos

[2] (*Aut, Chem*) suspensión *f*

Ⓑ CPD ► **suspension bridge** N puente *m* colgante ► **suspension file** N archivador *m* colgante ► **suspension points** NPL puntos *mpl* suspensivos

suspensory [səs'pensərɪ] Ⓐ ADJ suspensorio

Ⓑ N (*also* **~ bandage**) suspensorio *m*

suspicion [səs'pɪʃən] N [1] (= *belief*) sospecha *f*; **my ~ is that …** tengo la sospecha de que …; **my ~ is that they are acting on their own** tengo la sospecha de que actúan solos; **there is a ~ that …** se sospecha que …; **to be <u>above</u> ~** estar por encima de toda sospecha; **to <u>have</u> one's ~s (about sth)** tener sus sospechas (acerca de algo); **she had her ~s** ella tenía sus sospechas; **I have a sneaking ~ that …** tengo la leve sospecha de que …; **I had <u>no</u> ~ that …** no sospechaba que …; **he was arrested <u>on</u> ~ of spying** fue arrestado bajo sospecha de espionaje, fue arrestado como sospechoso de espionaje; **to lay o.s. <u>open</u> to ~** hacerse sospechoso; **to be <u>shielded</u> from ~** estar a salvo de sospechas; **to be <u>under</u> ~** estar bajo sospecha

[2] (= *mistrust*) desconfianza *f*, recelo *m*; **to <u>arouse</u> sb's ~s** despertar los recelos de algn; **to <u>regard</u> sb/sth with ~** desconfiar de algn/algo

[3] (= *trace*) rastro *m*; **with just a ~ of lemon/garlic** con apenas un ligero sabor a limón/ajo, con apenas un rastro de sabor a limón/ajo; **"good morning," he said without a ~ of a smile** —buenos días —dijo sin la más leve insinuación de una sonrisa

suspicious [səs'pɪʃəs] ADJ [1] (= *mistrustful*) [*person, nature*] desconfiado; [*glance*] receloso; **Paul was a ~ man** Paul era un hombre desconfiado; **many people are ~ that the government will reduce benefits further** mucha gente tiene la sospecha de que el gobierno va a reducir aún más los subsidios; **to be ~ <u>about</u> sth** desconfiar de algo; **to <u>become</u>** *or* **<u>grow</u> ~ (of sth/sb)** empezar a desconfiar (de algo/algn); **that <u>made</u> him ~** eso le hizo sospechar; **to have a ~ <u>mind</u>** tener una mente desconfiada *or* recelosa; **he is ~ <u>of</u> visitors** se muestra receloso ante las visitas

[2] (= *causing suspicion*) [*person, behaviour, package*] sospechoso; **did you see anything ~?** ¿viste algo sospechoso?; **it looks very ~ to me** me parece muy sospechoso; **is there anything ~ <u>about</u> the crash?** ¿hay algo sospechoso acerca del choque?; **in ~ <u>circumstances</u>** en circunstancias sospechosas

suspiciously [səs'pɪʃəslɪ] ADV [1] (= *mistrustfully*) [*look, ask*] con recelo, con desconfianza

[2] (= *causing suspicion*) [*behave, act*] de modo sospechoso; **their essays were ~ similar** sus trabajos se parecían sospechosamente; **he arrived ~ early** llegó sospechosamente pronto; **to look ~ like sth** tener todo el aspecto de ser algo; **the stain looked ~ like blood** la mancha tenía todo el aspecto de ser de sangre; **the man looked ~ like her husband** el hombre se parecía sospechosamente a su marido; **it looks ~ like measles to me** para mí que *or* (*LAm*) se me hace que es sarampión

suspiciousness [səs'pɪʃəsnɪs] N [1] (= *mistrust*) desconfianza *f*, recelo *m* [2] (= *questionable nature*) [*of circumstances etc*] lo sospechoso

suss* [sʌs] VT (*Brit*) (*also* **~ out**) [1] (= *realize*) percatarse de, coscarse de*; **they never ~ed what was going on** no llegaron a percatarse *or* coscarse* de lo que pasaba

[2] (= *understand*) [+ *person*] calar*; **I ~ed him out at once** lo calé en seguida*; **she's got you ~ed** te tiene calado*; **we couldn't ~ it out at all** no logramos sacar nada en claro

[3] (= *investigate*) investigar, echar un ojo a; **I'll have to ~ out the job market** tendré que ver cómo está la cosa de trabajo

[4] (= *find out*) averiguar; **I've ~ed out the best restaurants** he averiguado cuáles son los mejores restaurantes

sustain [səs'teɪn] VT [1] (= *keep going*) [+ *interest, relationship, marriage*] mantener; [+ *effort*] sostener, continuar; [+ *life*] sustentar; (*Mus*) [+ *note*] sostener; **the economy was not able to ~ a long war** la economía no podía soportar una guerra larga

[2] (*frm*) (= *suffer*) [+ *attack*] sufrir (y rechazar); [+ *damage, loss*] sufrir; [+ *injury*] recibir, sufrir; [+ *defeat*] padecer; **both ships ~ed minor damage** ambos buques sufrieron daños de menor consideración

[3] (= *support*) (*lit*) [+ *weight*] sostener, apoyar; (*fig*) [+ *theory*] confirmar, corroborar; **it is his belief in God that ~s him** su fe en Dios es lo que lo sostiene *or* mantiene

[4] (*Jur*) (= *uphold*) [+ *objection*] admitir; [+ *claim*] corroborar, respaldar; [+ *charge*] confirmar, corroborar; **objection ~ed** la objeción está admitida

sustainable [səs'teɪnəbl] ADJ [*growth, development etc*] sostenible; [*charge*] sustentable

sustained [səs'teɪnd] ADJ [*effort*] constante, ininterrumpido; [*note*] sostenido; [*applause*] prolongado; **a period of ~ economic growth** un periodo de crecimiento económico sostenido

sustaining [səs'teɪnɪŋ] Ⓐ ADJ [*food*] nutritivo

Ⓑ CPD ► **sustaining pedal** N pedal *m* de apoyo, pedal *m* derecho

sustenance ['sʌstɪnəns] N sustento *m*; **they depend for their ~ on** ◊ **they get their ~ from** se sustentan *or* alimentan de

suture ['suːtʃə^r] Ⓐ N sutura *f*

Ⓑ VT suturar, coser

SUV N ABBR (= **sport(s) utility vehicle**) todoterreno *m inv*

➤ LANGUAGE IN USE: suspect C2 6.2

suzerain ['su:zəreɪn] N (= *state*) estado *m* protector; (= *sovereign*) monarca *mf* protector(a)

suzerainty ['su:zəreɪntɪ] N protectorado *m*

svelte [svelt] ADJ esbelto

SVGA N ABBR (*Comput*) = **super video graphics array**

SVQ N ABBR = **Scottish Vocational Qualification**; → NVQ

SW ABBR [1] (= **southwest**) SO
[2] (*Rad*) (= **short wave**) OC *f*

swab [swɒb] Ⓐ N [1] (= *cloth, mop*) estropajo *m*, trapo *m*
[2] (*Naut*) lampazo *m*
[3] (*Med*) (*for cleaning wound*) algodón *m*, tampón *m*; (*for specimen*) frotis *m*
Ⓑ VT [1] (*Naut*) (*also* **~ down**) limpiar, fregar
[2] (*Med*) [+ *wound*] limpiar (con algodón)

swaddle ['swɒdl] VT envolver (**in** en)

swaddling clothes ['swɒdlɪŋkləʊðz] NPL (*Literat*) pañales *mpl*

swag* [swæg] N botín *m*

swagger ['swægəʳ] Ⓐ N [1] (*in walk*) paso *m* decidido y arrogante, pavoneo *m* al caminar; **to walk with a ~** andar con paso decidido y arrogante, pavonearse al caminar
[2] (= *bravado*) fanfarronería *f*, pavoneo *m*
Ⓑ VI (*also* **to ~ about, ~ along**) pavonearse, andar pavoneándose; **he ~ed over to our table** se acercó a nuestra mesa dándoselas de algo, se acercó a nuestra mesa con aire fanfarrón; **with that he ~ed out** dijo eso y salió con paso firme y arrogante
Ⓒ CPD ► **swagger stick** N bastón *m* de mando

swaggering ['swægərɪŋ] ADJ [*person*] fanfarrón, jactancioso; [*gait*] importante, jactancioso

swain [sweɪn] N (†† *or hum*) (= *lad*) zagal *m*; (= *suitor*) pretendiente *m*, amante *m*

swallow¹ ['swɒləʊ] Ⓐ N trago *m*; **in** *or* **with one ~** de un trago
Ⓑ VT [1] [+ *food, drink*] tragar; [+ *pill*] tomar; ✦***IDIOM*** **to ~ the bait** (*fig*) tragar el anzuelo
[2] (*fig*) [+ *insult*] tragarse; **he ~ed the story** se tragó el cuento; **he ~ed the lot** se lo tragó todo; **to ~ one's words** desdecirse, retractarse; ✦***IDIOM*** **to ~ one's pride** tragarse el orgullo
Ⓒ VI tragar; **to ~ hard** (*fig*) tragar saliva

►**swallow down** VT + ADV tragar

►**swallow up** VT + ADV [+ *savings*] agotar, consumir; [*sea*] tragar; **the mist ~ed them up** la niebla los envolvió; **they were soon ~ed up in the darkness** al poco desaparecieron en la oscuridad *or* se los tragó la oscuridad; **I wish the ground would open and ~ me up!** ¡trágame tierra!

swallow² ['swɒləʊ] Ⓐ N (= *bird*) golondrina *f*; ✦***PROV*** **one ~ doesn't make a summer** una golondrina no hace primavera
Ⓑ CPD ► **swallow dive** N salto *m* del ángel

swallowtail ['swɒləʊteɪl] N (= *butterfly*) macaón *m*

swam [swæm] PT *of* **swim**

swamp [swɒmp] Ⓐ N pantano *m*, ciénaga *f*, marisma *f*
Ⓑ VT [1] [+ *land*] inundar; [+ *boat*] hundir
[2] (*fig*) abrumar (**with** con), agobiar (**with** de); **they have been ~ed with applications** se han visto abrumados *or* desbordados por las solicitudes; **we're ~ed with work** estamos agobiados de trabajo
Ⓒ CPD ► **swamp fever** N paludismo *m*

swampland ['swɒmplænd] N ciénaga *f*, pantano *m*, marisma *f*

swampy ['swɒmpɪ] ADJ pantanoso, cenagoso

swan [swɒn] Ⓐ N cisne *m*; **Swan Lake** El Lago de los Cisnes
Ⓑ VI (*) **to ~ around** pavonearse; **to ~ off to New York** escaparse a Nueva York
Ⓒ CPD ► **swan dive** N (*US*) = **swallow dive**
► **swan song** N canto *m* del cisne

swank* [swæŋk] Ⓐ N [1] (= *vanity, boastfulness*) fanfarronada* *f*; **he does it for ~** lo hace para darse tono *or* lucirse
[2] (= *person*) fanfarrón/ona *m/f*
Ⓑ VI fanfarronear*; **to ~ around** pavonearse

swanky* ['swæŋkɪ] ADJ (*compar* **swankier**; *superl* **swankiest**) [*person*] fanfarrón*, presumido; [*car*] despampanante; [*restaurant, hotel*] de postín

swannery ['swɒnərɪ] N colonia *f* de cisnes

swansdown ['swɒnzdaʊn] N (= *feathers*) plumón *m* de cisne; (*Textiles*) fustán *m*, muletón *m*

swap [swɒp] Ⓐ N (= *exchange*) trueque *m*, canje *m*; **~s** (*when collecting*) duplicados *mpl*; **it's a fair ~** es un trato equitativo
Ⓑ VT [+ *cars, stamps*] trocar, canjear, intercambiar; **will you ~ your hat for my jacket?** ¿quieres cambiar tu sombrero por mi chaqueta?; **we sat ~ping reminiscences** estábamos contando nuestros recuerdos; **to ~ stories (with sb)** contarse chascarrillos *or* historietas (con algn); **to ~ places (with sb)** (*lit*) cambiar(se) de sitio con algn; **I wouldn't mind ~ping places with him!** (*fig*) ¡ya me gustaría a mí estar en su pellejo!
Ⓒ VI hacer un intercambio; **I asked her but she wouldn't ~** se lo pedí pero no quería cambiarse; **I wouldn't ~ with anyone** no me cambiaría por nadie; **do you want to ~?** ¿quieres que cambiemos?

►**swap around, swap over, swap round** Ⓐ VT + ADV cambiar de sitio; **I like to ~ the furniture around** me gusta cambiar los muebles de sitio
Ⓑ VI + ADV cambiar de sitio

SWAPO ['swɑ:pəʊ] N ABBR = **South-West Africa People's Organization**

sward [swɔ:d] N (*liter*) césped *m*

swarm¹ [swɔ:m] Ⓐ N [*of bees, mosquitoes*] enjambre *m*; [*of people*] multitud *f*; **there were ~s of people** había (una) multitud de gente; **they came in ~s** vinieron en tropel
Ⓑ VI [*bees*] enjambrar; **Stratford is ~ing with tourists** Stratford está plagado de turistas; **journalists ~ed around her** los periodistas se arremolinaban alrededor de ella; **children ~ed all over the car** había niños pululando alrededor del coche

swarm² [swɔ:m] VI **to ~ up a tree/rope** trepar rápidamente por un árbol/una cuerda

swarthiness ['swɔ:ðɪnɪs] N tez *f* morena, color *m* moreno

swarthy ['swɔ:ðɪ] ADJ (*compar* **swarthier**; *superl* **swarthiest**) moreno

swashbuckler ['swɒʃˌbʌkləʳ] N (*Hist*) espadachín *m*; (= *adventurer*) intrépido *m*

swashbuckling ['swɒʃˌbʌklɪŋ] ADJ [*hero*] de historia de aventuras, bravucón; [*film*] de aventuras, de capa y espada

swastika ['swɒstɪkə] N esvástica *f*, cruz *f* gamada

SWAT [swɒt] ABBR (*esp US*) = **Special Weapons and Tactics**; **~ team** *un cuerpo especial de intervención de la policía*

swat [swɒt] Ⓐ VT [+ *fly*] aplastar, matar
Ⓑ VI **to ~ at a fly** tratar de aplastar *or* matar una mosca
Ⓒ N **to give sth/sb a ~** dar un zurriagazo a algo/algn; **to take a ~ at sth/sb** intentar darle un zurriagazo a algo/algn

swatch [swɒtʃ] N (*Textiles*) muestra *f*

swath [swɔ:θ] N (*pl* **swaths**), **swathe**¹ [sweɪð] N [*of hay*] ringlera *f*; **to cut corn in ~s** segar el trigo y dejarlo en ringleras; **to cut a ~ through sth** avanzar por algo a guadañadas

swathe² [sweɪð] VT (= *wrap*) envolver; (= *bandage*) vendar; **~d in sheets** envuelto en sábanas

swatter ['swɒtəʳ] N palmeta *f* matamoscas

sway [sweɪ] Ⓐ N [1] (*also* **~ing**) (= *movement*) balanceo *m*, oscilación *f*; [*of train, bus, boat*] vaivén *m*, balanceo *m*; (= *violent swaying*) bamboleo *m*; (= *violent jerk*) sacudimiento *m*; (= *totter*) tambaleo *m*
[2] (= *rule*) dominio *m*; (= *influence*) influencia *f*; (= *power*) poder *m*; **his ~ over the party** su influencia en el partido, su dominio del partido; **to bring a people under one's ~** sojuzgar un pueblo; **to hold ~ over a nation** gobernar *or* dominar una nación; **to hold ~ over sb** mantener el dominio sobre algn; **this theory held ~ during the 1970s** esta teoría se impuso durante la década de los setenta
Ⓑ VI (= *swing*) balancearse, oscilar; (*gently*) mecerse; (*violently*) bambolearse; (= *totter*) tambalearse; **the train ~ed from side to side** el tren se balanceaba *or* bamboleaba de un lado para otro; **she ~s as she walks** se cimbrea al andar
Ⓒ VT [1] (= *move*) balancear; (*gently*) mecer; [+ *hips*] menear, cimbrear
[2] (= *influence*) mover, influir en; **he is not ~ed by any such considerations** tales cosas no influyen en él en absoluto; **I allowed myself to be ~ed** me dejé influir; **these factors finally ~ed me** estos factores terminaron de *or* por convencerme

Swazi ['swɑ:zɪ] Ⓐ ADJ swazilandés, suazilandés
Ⓑ N swazilandés/esa *m/f*, suazilandés/esa *m/f*

Swaziland ['swɑ:zɪlænd] N Swazilandia *f*, Suazilandia *f*

swear [sweəʳ] (*pt* **swore**; *pp* **sworn**) Ⓐ VT jurar; **I ~ it!** ¡lo juro!; **I ~ (that) I did not steal it** juro que no lo robé; **to ~ to do sth** jurar hacer algo; **I could have sworn that it was Janet** juraría que fue Janet; **to ~ sb to secrecy** hacer que algn jure guardar el secreto; **to ~ allegiance to** jurar lealtad a; **they swore an oath of allegiance to him** le prestaron juramento de fidelidad; **they swore an oath not to fight again** juraron no volver a pelear
Ⓑ VI [1] (*solemnly*) jurar; **to ~ on the Bible** jurar sobre la Biblia; **I could ~ to it** juraría que fue así; **I can't ~ to it** no lo juraría
[2] (= *use swearwords*) decir palabrotas, soltar tacos; (*blasphemously*) blasfemar; **don't ~ in front of the children** no digas palabrotas estando los niños delante; **to ~ at sb** insultar a algn, mentar la madre a algn (*Mex*); ✦***IDIOM*** **to ~ like a trooper** jurar como un carretero

►**swear by*** VI + PREP tener plena confianza en, creer ciegamente en

►**swear in** VT + ADV [+ *witness, president*] tomar juramento a, juramentar a; **to be sworn in** prestar juramento

►**swear off** VI + PREP **to ~ off alcohol** (jurar) renunciar al alcohol

swearword ['sweəwɜ:d] N palabrota *f*, taco *m*

sweat [swet] Ⓐ N [1] sudor *m*; **to be in a ~** estar sudando, estar todo sudoroso; (*) (*fig*) estar en un apuro; **to be in a ~ about sth*** estar muy preocupado por algo; **to get into a ~** empezar a sudar; **to get into a ~ about**

sth* apurarse por algo; ✦*IDIOM* **by the ~ of one's brow** con el sudor de su frente; *see also* **cold**

2 (*) (= *piece of work*) trabajo *m* difícil, trabajo *m* pesado; **what a ~ that was!** eso ¡cómo nos hizo sudar!; **we had such a ~ to do it** nos costó hacerlo; **no ~!** ¡ningún problema!

3 **old ~*** veterano *m*

4 **sweats** (*US**) = **sweatsuit, sweatpants**

Ⓑ VI sudar, transpirar; (*) (= *work hard*) sudar la gota gorda (**over sth** por algo); **they will lose everything they have ~ed for** van a perder todo lo que tanto sudor les ha costado conseguir; ✦*IDIOM* **he was ~ing buckets** *or* **like a pig*** estaba sudando tinta *or* como un pollo

Ⓒ VT 1 (*Anat*) sudar; ✦*IDIOM* **to ~ blood** sudar tinta

2 (*Culin*) [+ *vegetables*] rehogar

Ⓓ CPD ► **sweat gland** N glándula *f* sudorípara

►**sweat off** VT + ADV **I ~ed off half a kilo** me quité medio kilo sudando

►**sweat out** VT + ADV **to ~ a cold/fever out** quitarse un resfriado/la fiebre sudando; ✦*IDIOM* **to ~ it out*** aguantar, aguantarse; **we'll let him ~ it out for a couple of weeks** lo vamos a dejar que sufra un par de semanas, vamos a dejarlo sufrir un par de semanas; **they left him to ~ it out** no hicieron nada para ayudarlo

sweatband ['swetbænd] N 1 (*Sport*) (*round forehead*) banda *f* elástica; (*round wrist*) muñequera *f*

2 (*on hat*) badana *f*

sweated ['swetɪd] ADJ **~ labour** trabajo *m* muy mal pagado

sweater ['swetəʳ] N suéter *m*, jersey *m*, chompa *f* (*Peru*)

sweating ['swetɪŋ] Ⓐ ADJ sudoroso

Ⓑ N transpiración *f*

sweatpants ['swetpænts] NPL (*US*) pantalón *m* de chándal

sweatshirt ['swetʃɜːt] N sudadera *f*

sweatshop ['swetʃɒp] N *fábrica donde se explota al obrero*

sweatsuit ['swetsuːt] N (*US*) chandal *m*, buzo *m* (*Chile, Bol, Peru*)

sweaty ['swetɪ] ADJ (*compar* **sweatier**, *superl* **sweatiest**) [*face, hands, person, horse*] sudoroso; [*clothes*] sudado; **to be all ~** estar todo sudoroso

Swede [swiːd] N sueco/a *m/f*

swede [swiːd] N (= *vegetable*) nabo *m* sueco

Sweden ['swiːdn] N Suecia *f*

Swedish ['swiːdɪʃ] Ⓐ ADJ sueco

Ⓑ N 1 (= *people*) **the ~** los suecos

2 (*Ling*) sueco *m*

sweep [swiːp] (*vb: pt, pp* **swept**) Ⓐ VT 1 [+ *place, area*] 1·1 (= *clean*) [+ *floor, room, street*] barrer; [+ *chimney*] deshollinar; **have you had your chimney swept lately?** ¿te han deshollinado la chimenea recientemente?; **the floor had been swept clean** el suelo estaba limpio porque lo habían barrido

1·2 (= *touch*) rozar; **her long dress swept the ground as she walked** su vestido largo rozaba el suelo al caminar

1·3 (= *spread through*) [*disease, idea, craze*] arrasar; [*rumours*] correr por, extenderse por; **the cycling craze ~ing the nation** la locura del ciclismo que está arrasando el país

1·4 (= *lash*) [*storm, rain, waves*] azotar, barrer; **torrential storms swept the country** tormentas torrenciales azotaron *or* barrieron el país; **the beach was swept by great waves** olas gigantescas azotaron *or* barrieron la playa

1·5 (= *scan*) [*searchlight, eyes*] recorrer; **he swept the horizon with his binoculars** recorrió el horizonte con sus prismáticos

1·6 (= *search*) peinar; **to ~ the sea for mines** dragar el mar en busca de minas

2 (= *move*) 2·1 (*with brush*) **she was ~ing crumbs into a dustpan** estaba recogiendo las migas con una escoba y un recogedor; **she swept the snow into a heap** barrió la nieve y la amontonó; **he swept the leaves off the path** barrió las hojas del camino; ✦*IDIOMS* **to ~ sth under the carpet** (*Brit*) ◊ **~ sth under the rug** (*US*) ocultar algo

2·2 (*with hand, arm*) **she swept her hair back with a flick of her wrist** se echó el pelo hacia atrás con un movimiento rápido de muñeca; **her hair was swept back in a ponytail** tenía el pelo peinado hacia atrás con una cola de caballo; **the curtains were swept back in an elegant fashion** las cortinas estaban recogidas con elegancia; **he swept the stamps into a box** recogió los sellos en una caja; **to ~ sb into one's arms** coger *or* tomar a algn en brazos; **I swept the rainwater off the bench with my hand** quité el agua de la lluvia del banco con la mano

2·3 (*forcefully*) **she was swept along by the crowd** ◊ **the crowd swept her along** la multitud la arrastró; **to be swept along by** *or* **on a wave of sth** (*fig*) dejarse llevar por una ola de algo; **landslides that swept cars into the sea** corrimientos de tierra que arrastraron coches hasta el mar; **the election which swept Labour into office** *or* **power** las elecciones en la que los laboristas arrasaron haciéndose con el poder; **the water swept him off his feet** la fuerza del agua lo derribó; **he swept her off her feet** la conquistó totalmente; **they swept him off to lunch** se lo llevaron a comer apresuradamente; **a wave swept him overboard** una ola lo arrastró por encima de la borda; ✦*IDIOM* **to ~ all before one** arrasar con todo

3 (= *win decisively*) [+ *election*] arrasar en; ✦*IDIOM* **to ~ the board** (= *win prizes*) arrasar con todo; **the socialists swept the board at the election** los socialistas arrasaron en las elecciones

Ⓑ VI 1 (= *clean*) barrer

2 (= *spread*) 2·1 [*violence, disease, storm*] **the violence which swept across Punjab** la violencia que arrasó el Punjab; **the storm which swept over the country** la tormenta que arrasó el país; **plague swept through the country** la peste arrasó el país

2·2 [*fire, smoke*] **the fire swept rapidly through the forest** el fuego se propagó *or* extendió rápidamente por el bosque; **thick smoke swept through their home** una densa humareda se propagó *or* extendió por la casa

2·3 [*emotion*] **a great wave of anger swept over me** me invadió una gran oleada de ira; **panic swept through the city** en la ciudad cundió el pánico

3 (= *move*) 3·1 [*crowd, procession*] **an angry crowd swept along the main thoroughfare** una multitud airada avanzaba por la calle principal

3·2 (*majestically*) [*person, car*] **to ~ past/in/out** pasar/entrar/salir majestuosamente; **to ~ into** *or* **out of a place** entrar/salir de un sitio majestuosamente

3·3 (*quickly*) [*vehicle, convoy*] **the convoy swept along the road** la caravana pasó por la carretera a toda velocidad; ✦*IDIOM* **to ~ into power** arrasar haciéndose con el poder

4 (= *stretch*) [*land, water*] **the bay ~s away to the south** la bahía se extiende (majestuosamente) hacia el sur; **the hills/woods ~ down to the sea** las colinas/los bosques bajan (majestuosamente) hacia el mar; *see also* **sweep up**

Ⓒ N 1 (*with broom, brush*) barrido *m*, barrida *f*; **the floor/the kitchen could do with a ~** al suelo/a la cocina le hace falta un barrido *or* una barrida; **to give sth a ~** darle un barrido *or* una barrida a algo

2 (*Brit*) (*also* **chimney ~**) deshollinador(a) *m/f*

3 (= *movement*) [*of pendulum*] movimiento *m*; [*of scythe*] golpe *m*; [*of beam*] trayectoria *f*; (*fig*) [*of events, progress, history*] marcha *f*; **with a ~ of his arm** con un amplio movimiento del brazo; **with one ~ of his scythe, he cleared all the nettles** con un golpe de guadaña hizo desaparecer todas las ortigas; **with a ~ of her hand she indicated the desk** extendió la mano indicando el pupitre con un gesto amplio

4 (= *search*) (*for criminals, drugs*) batida *f*, rastreo *m*; **to make a ~: they made a ~ for hidden arms** dieron una batida *or* hicieron un rastreo buscando armas ocultas; **to make a ~ of sth** (*with binoculars, torch*) hacer una pasada por algo; (*with team of people*) rastrear algo; **the police began making a ~ of the premises** la policía comenzó a rastrear el lugar; **his eyes made a ~ of the audience** paseó la mirada por el público

5 **clean ~** 5·1 (= *change*) **to make a clean ~** hacer tabla rasa; **there will be a clean ~ of all those involved in this cover-up** se hará tabla rasa con todos los que estén involucrados en esta tapadera

5·2 (*in competition, series of competitions*) **to make a clean ~** arrasar ganándolo todo; (*Cards*) ganar todas las bazas; **it was the first club to make a clean ~ of all three trophies** fue el primer club que arrasó llevándose *or* ganando el total de los tres trofeos

6 (= *curve, line*) [*of coastline, river*] curva *f*; [*of land*] extensión *f*; [*of staircase*] trazado *m*; [*of long skirt, curtains*] vuelo *m*; [*of wings*] envergadura *f*; **a wide ~ of meadowland** una gran extensión de pradera

7 (= *range*) 7·1 (*lit*) [*of telescope, gun, lighthouse, radar*] alcance *m*; **with a ~ of 180°** con un alcance de 180°

7·2 (*fig*) [*of views, ideas*] espectro *m*; **representatives from a broad ~ of left-wing opinion** representantes de un amplio espectro de la izquierda

8 (= *wave*) [*of emotion*] ola *f*

9 = **sweepstake**

►**sweep aside** VT + ADV 1 (*lit*) [+ *object*] apartar bruscamente

2 (*fig*) [+ *objections protest, suggestion*] desechar, descartar; [+ *obstacle*] pasar por alto; [+ *difficulty*] sortear; **accusations that customers' interests were being swept aside** acusaciones de que se estaban pasando por alto los intereses de los clientes

►**sweep away** Ⓐ VI + ADV *see* **sweep B4**

Ⓑ VT + ADV 1 (= *remove with brush*) barrer

2 (= *wash away*) [*river, storm*] [+ *building, car, person*] llevarse por delante; **he was swept away by strong currents** fuertes corrientes se lo llevaron por delante

3 (= *rush away*) llevar a (toda) prisa (**to** a); **his aides swept him away** sus ayudantes se lo llevaron a (toda) prisa

4 (*fig*) (= *throw out*) eliminar; (= *put an end to*) barrer, poner fin a; **scripture and traditional values were swept away in our determination to accept the feminist chal-**

lenge la religión y los valores tradicionales fueron barridos cuando resolvimos aceptar el reto feminista, pusimos fin a la religión y los valores tradicionales al resolvernos a aceptar el reto feminista

5 (= *overwhelm*) **she was swept away by his charm** su encanto la conquistó, se dejó llevar por su encanto; **he let himself be swept away by emotion** se dejó llevar por la emoción

► **sweep up** Ⓐ VI + ADV 1 (*with broom, brush*) barrer

2 **to ~ up to sth**: **the car swept up to the house** (*majestically*) el coche subió majestuosamente hasta la casa; (*fast*) el coche subió a toda velocidad hasta la casa; **the lawn swept up to the woods** el césped llegaba *or* se extendía hasta el bosque; **the drive ~s up to the house** el camino de entrada se alza majestuoso hasta la casa

Ⓑ VT + ADV 1 (= *clean up*) [+ *glass*] recoger con un cepillo, recoger con una escoba; [+ *leaves*] recoger con un rastrillo

2 (= *seize, pick up*) [*person*] coger, agarrar (*LAm*); [*storm*] arrastrar; **I swept her up in my arms** la levanté en mis brazos

3 (= *arrange*) recoger; **her hair was swept up in a bun** tenía el pelo recogido en un moño

4 (*fig*) (= *carry along*) **she had been swept up in an exciting relationship** se había dejado arrastrar por una relación apasionante; **they became so swept up with excitement that ...** se dejaron llevar tanto por el entusiasmo que ...

sweepback ['swi:pbæk] N [*of aircraft wing*] ángulo *m* de flecha

sweeper ['swi:pəʳ] N 1 (= *cleaner*) barrendero/a *m/f*; (= *machine*) (*for streets*) barredora *f*; (*also* **carpet** ~) cepillo *m* mecánico

2 (*Ftbl*) líbero *m*

sweeping ['swi:pɪŋ] Ⓐ ADJ [*gesture, movement*] amplio; [*generalization*] excesivo; [*curve*] abierto; [*view*] magnífico; [*skirt*] de vuelo amplio; [*change*] radical; [*victory*] arrollador, aplastante; **a large house with ~ lawns** una gran casa con amplias extensiones de césped; **that's rather a ~ statement** eso es generalizar demasiado

Ⓑ N 1 (= *action*) barrido *m*, barrida *f*; **we gave it a ~** le dimos un barrido *or* una barrida, lo barrimos

2 **sweepings** basura *f* (*tras un barrido*); (*fig, of society etc*) desechos *mpl*, escoria *f*

sweepstake ['swi:psteɪk] N, **sweepstakes** (*US*) N (= *lottery*) lotería *f* (*esp de carreras de caballos*); (= *race*) *carrera de caballos en que el ganador recibe el dinero de las apuestas del resto de los participantes*

sweet [swi:t] Ⓐ ADJ (*compar* **sweeter**; *superl* **sweetest**) 1 (= *sugary*) [*taste, drink, food*] dulce; **this coffee is too ~** este café está demasiado dulce; **a glass of ~ white wine** una copa de vino blanco dulce; **I love ~ things** me encanta lo dulce, me encantan las cosas dulces; **are those pies ~ or savoury?** esos pasteles, ¿son dulces o salados?; **~ and sour** agridulce; **to taste ~** tener un sabor dulce; **the beer was ~ to the taste** la cerveza tenía un gusto dulce

2 (= *agreeable*) [*smell, perfume*] agradable; [*sound*] melodioso, dulce; **~ dreams!** (*Brit*) (*gen*) que duermas bien; (*to child*) ¡que sueñes con los angelitos!; **to smell ~** tener un olor fragante *or* aromático; **the ~ smell of success** las mieles del éxito; **the ~ taste of victory** el dulce sabor de la victoria; ✦**IDIOMS the news was ~ music to my ears** la noticia fue música celestial para mis oídos; **to whisper ~ nothings in sb's ear/to sb** decirle cariñitos a algn al oído; ✦**PROV revenge is ~!** ¡la dulce venganza!

3 (= *gentle, kind*) [*nature, smile*] dulce; [*face*] dulce, lindo (*esp LAm*); **she is a very ~ person** es un verdadero encanto, es una persona muy linda (*LAm*); **that's very ~ of you** es muy amable de tu parte, ¡qué amable!; **how ~ of you to think of me!** ¡qué detalle acordarte de mí!; **to keep sb ~*** tener a algn contento; **~ Jesus!*̣*** ¡Dios Bendito!*̣*; **to be ~ to sb** ser bueno con algn; ✦**IDIOM to do ~ Fanny Adams** *or* **~ F.A.**: **politicians do ~ Fanny Adams** *or* **~ F.A.** (*Brit*̣*) los políticos no hacen más que tocarse las narices*̣*

4 (= *enchanting*) [*child, animal, house, hat*] mono, lindo (*esp LAm*); **he was a ~ little boy** ¡era un niñito tan mono!; **what a ~ little puppy!** ¡qué perrito más *or* tan mono!; **the cottage was really ~** la casita era monísima *or* una monada *or* (*esp LAm*) lindísima

5 (= *fresh*) [*water*] dulce; [*air*] fresco; [*breath*] sano; **~ milk** leche fresca

6 (*iro*) **to do sth in one's own ~ time** hacer algo a su aire, hacer algo cuando le parece a uno; **to go one's own ~ way** ir a su aire; **he carried on in his own ~ way** siguió a su aire

7 ✦**IDIOM to be ~ on sb**†* estar colado por algn*

Ⓑ N 1 (*esp Brit*) (= *piece of confectionery*) [*of any sort*] golosina *f*; (= *boiled sweet, toffee*) caramelo *m*

2 (*Brit*) (= *dessert*) postre *m*

3 **my ~**†* mi cielo*

4 (*fig*) **the ~s of success** las mieles del éxito; **the ~s of solitude** el encanto de la soledad

Ⓒ CPD ► **sweet basil** N albahaca *f* ► **sweet bay** N laurel *m* ► **sweet cherry** N cereza *f* dulce ► **sweet chestnut** N castaño *m* dulce ► **sweet pea** N guisante *m* de olor, clarín *m* (*Chile*) ► **sweet pepper** N pimiento *m* (dulce) ► **sweet potato** N batata *f*, boniato *m*, camote *m* (*LAm*) ► **sweet shop** N (*Brit*) tienda *f* de chucherías, dulcería *f* (*esp LAm*) ► **sweet talk*** N zalamerías *fpl*; *see also* **sweet-talk** ► **sweet tooth** N **to have a ~ tooth** ser goloso ► **sweet trolley** N carrito *m* de los postres ► **sweet william** N minutisa *f*

sweet-and-sour [,swi:tən'saʊəʳ] Ⓐ ADJ agridulce

Ⓑ N plato *m* agridulce (*especialmente en la comida china*); **is ~ all right for you?** ¿te parece bien un plato agridulce?

sweetbreads ['swi:tbredz] NPL mollejas *fpl*, lechecillas *fpl* (*Sp*)

sweetbriar, **sweetbrier** ['swi:tbraɪəʳ] N eglantina *f*, escaramujo *m* oloroso

sweetcorn ['swi:tkɔ:n] N maíz *m* dulce (*Sp*), maíz *m* tierno (*esp LAm*), elote *m* (*Mex*), choclo *m* (*Andes, S. Cone*)

sweeten ['swi:tn] Ⓐ VT 1 [+ *tea, coffee, dish*] endulzar; **~ to taste** endulzar al gusto; **~ with honey if desired** endulzar con miel si se desea

2 (= *freshen*) [+ *breath*] refrescar; [+ *room*] ambientar

3 (*fig*) 3·1 (= *placate, soften*) [+ *temper*] aplacar, calmar; [+ *process, reforms*] suavizar, facilitar; (*also* **~ up**) [+ *person*] ablandar; *see also* **pill**

3·2 (*with financial incentives*) [+ *deal*] hacer más atractivo; [+ *person*] (= *bribe*) sobornar; (= *win over*) ganarse a

Ⓑ VI [*person*] volverse (más) dulce

sweetener ['swi:tnəʳ] N 1 (*Culin*) dulcificante *m*; (*artificial*) edulcorante *m*

2 (*) (= *incentive*) incentivo *m*

sweetening ['swi:tnɪŋ] N (*Culin*) dulcificante *m*

sweetheart ['swi:thɑ:t] N novio/a *m/f*, amor *mf*; **he was her childhood ~** era su amor de infancia; **yes, ~** sí, mi amor

sweetie* ['swi:tɪ] N 1 (*also* **~-pie**) **he's/she's a ~** es un cielo*; **yes, ~** sí, cielo*

2 (*esp Scot*) (= *sweet*) [*of any sort*] golosina *f*; (= *boiled sweet, toffee*) caramelo *m*

sweetish ['swi:tɪʃ] ADJ algo dulce

sweetly ['swi:tlɪ] ADV [*sing*] dulcemente; [*smile, answer, act*] con dulzura; (= *kindly*) (muy) amablemente; **she ~ offered to bring some refreshments** se ofreció (muy) amablemente a traer algo para comer y beber

sweetmeats ['swi:tmi:ts] NPL dulces *mpl*, confites *mpl*

sweet-natured [,swi:t'neɪtʃəd] ADJ dulce, amable

sweetness ['swi:tnɪs] N 1 [*of food*] sabor *m* dulce, dulzor *m*

2 (*fig*) [*of smell*] fragancia *f*, buen olor *m*; [*of sound*] suavidad *f*; [*of person, character*] dulzura *f*; [*of appearance*] encanto *m*; (= *kindness*) simpatía *f*; ✦**IDIOM now all is ~ and light** reina ahora la más perfecta armonía; **he was all ~ and light yesterday** ayer estuvo la mar de amable

sweet-scented ['swi:t,sentɪd] ADJ fragante, de aroma agradable

sweet-smelling ['swi:t,smelɪŋ] ADJ fragante, de olor agradable

sweet-talk* ['swi:ttɔ:k] VT engatusar*, camelar*; **to ~ sb into doing sth** engatusar *or* camelar a algn para que haga algo*

sweet-talking* ['swi:ttɔ:kɪŋ] ADJ zalamero

sweet-tempered [,swi:t'tempəd] ADJ de carácter dulce, amable; **she's always ~** es siempre amable, no se altera nunca

sweet-toothed [,swi:t'tu:θt] ADJ goloso

swell [swel] (*vb: pt* **swelled**; *pp* **swollen**) Ⓐ N 1 (*Naut*) (= *movement*) oleaje *m*; (= *large wave*) marejada *f*

2 (= *bulge*) **the gentle ~ of her hips** la suave turgencia de sus caderas

3 (= *surge*) [*of anger*] arrebato *m*, arranque *m*; [*of sympathy, emotion*] oleada *f*

4 (*Mus*) crescendo *m*; (*on organ*) regulador *m* de volumen

5 (†*) (= *stylish man*) majo *m*; (= *important man*) encopetado *m*; **the ~s** la gente bien, la gente de buen tono

Ⓑ ADJ (*US**) (= *fine, good*) fenomenal*, bárbaro*; **we had a ~ time** lo pasamos en grande*; **it's a ~ place** es un sitio estupendo*

Ⓒ VI 1 (*physically*) [*ankle, eye etc*] (*also* **~ up**) hincharse; [*sails*] (*also* **~ out**) inflarse, hincharse; [*river*] crecer; **her arm ~ed up** se le hinchó el brazo; **to ~ with pride** hincharse de orgullo

2 (*in size, number*) aumentar, crecer; **numbers have swollen greatly** el número ha aumentado muchísimo; **the little group soon ~ed into a crowd** el pequeño grupo se transformó pronto en multitud; **the cheers ~ed to a roar** los vítores fueron creciendo hasta convertirse en un estruendo

Ⓓ VT 1 (*physically*) hinchar; **to have a swollen hand** tener la mano hinchada; **my ankle is very swollen** tengo el tobillo muy hinchado; **her eyes were swollen with tears** tenía los ojos hinchados de lágrimas; **the rains had swollen the river** las lluvias habían hecho crecer el río; **the river is swollen** el río está crecido; ✦*IDIOM* **you'll give him a swollen head** le vas a hacer que se lo crea

[2] [+ *numbers, sales*] aumentar; **all they are doing is ~ing the ranks of the unemployed** lo único que hacen es engrosar las cifras de desempleados

swellhead* ['swelhed] N (*US*) engreído/a *m/f*

swell-headed* ['swel'hedɪd] ADJ engreído, presumido, presuntuoso

swelling ['swelɪŋ] N (*Med*) hinchazón *f*

swelter ['sweltəʳ] VI abrasarse, sofocarse de calor; **we ~ed in 40°** nos sofocábamos a una temperatura de 40 grados

sweltering ['sweltərɪŋ] ADJ [*day*] de calor sofocante, de muchísimo calor; [*heat*] sofocante, abrasador; **it's ~ in here** hace un calor sofocante aquí; **I'm ~** me ahogo de calor

swept [swept] PT, PP *of* **sweep**

sweptback ['swept'bæk] ADJ [*wing*] en flecha; [*aircraft*] con alas en flecha

swerve [swɜːv] Ⓐ N (*by car, driver*) viraje *m* brusco; (*by boxer, runner*) finta *f*, regate *m*; **to put a ~ on a ball** darle con efecto a la pelota

Ⓑ VI [1] (*lit*) [*boxer, fighter*] hurtar el cuerpo; [*ball*] ir con efecto; (*on hitting obstacle*) desviarse; [*vehicle, driver*] virar bruscamente; **I was forced to ~ violently to avoid him** me vi obligado a virar bruscamente para esquivarlo; **the car ~d away from the lorry** el coche viró bruscamente para esquivar el camión; **the car ~d in and out of traffic** el coche zigzagueaba bruscamente por entre el tráfico; **to ~ to the right** [*vehicle, driver*] virar bruscamente a *or* hacia la derecha

[2] (*frm*) (*fig*) desviarse, apartarse (**from** de); **we shall not ~ from our duty** no nos apartaremos del cumplimiento de nuestro deber

Ⓒ VT [+ *boat, horse, car*] hacer virar bruscamente; [+ *ball*] dar efecto a, sesgar

swift [swɪft] Ⓐ ADJ (*compar* **swifter**, *superl* **swiftest**) [*runner, animal, vehicle, current*] rápido, veloz; [*reaction*] pronto, rápido; [*decision, response, journey, victory*] rápido; [*river*] de corriente rápida; **we must be ~ to act** tenemos que obrar con prontitud; **to wish sb a ~ recovery** desear a algn una pronta mejoría; **~ of foot** de pies ligeros; **to be ~ to anger** ser propenso a enfadarse

Ⓑ N (= *bird*) vencejo *m*

swift-flowing ['swɪft'fləʊɪŋ] ADJ [*current*] rápido; [*river*] de corriente rápida

swift-footed ['swɪft'fʊtɪd] ADJ veloz, de pies ligeros

swiftly ['swɪftlɪ] ADV [*run*] rápidamente, velozmente; [*react, act*] con prontitud, rápidamente; [*become, walk*] rápidamente; [*spread, rise, flow*] con rapidez; **events have moved ~** los acontecimientos se han desencadenado con rapidez; **the company has moved** *or* **acted ~ to deny the rumours** la empresa ha actuado con prontitud para desmentir los rumores; **for most of them, death came ~** para casi todos, la muerte llegó repentinamente; **a ~ flowing river** un río de corriente rápida

swiftness ['swɪftnɪs] N [*of runner*] rapidez *f*, velocidad *f*; [*of reaction*] prontitud *f*, rapidez *f*

swig* [swɪg] Ⓐ VT beber (a tragos)

Ⓑ N trago *m*; **have a ~ of this** bébete un poco de esto; **he took a ~ from his flask** se echó un trago de la botella

swill [swɪl] Ⓐ N [1] (= *food for pigs*) comida *f* para los cerdos; (= *revolting food, drink*) bazofia *f*, basura *f*; **how can you drink this ~?** ¿cómo te es posible beber esta basura?

[2] (= *wash*) **to give sth a ~ (out)** limpiar algo con agua

[3] (= *swallow, draught*) **he took a ~ from the bottle** echó *or* dio un trago de la botella

Ⓑ VT [1] (= *clean*) (*also* **~ out**) lavar, limpiar con agua

[2] (= *drink*) [+ *beer*] beber a tragos

swim [swɪm] (*vb: pt* **swam**; *pp* **swum**) Ⓐ N **to have a ~** darse un baño, nadar; **I had a lovely ~ this morning** me di un baño estupendo esta mañana; **after a two-kilometre ~** después de nadar dos kilómetros; **it's a long ~ back to the shore** hay un buen trecho a nado hasta la playa; **that was a long ~ for a child** eso fue mucho nadar para un niño; **to go for a ~** ir a nadar *or* a bañarse; ✦*IDIOMS* **to be in the ~†** estar al corriente *or* al tanto; **to keep in the ~†** mantenerse al día

Ⓑ VT [1] [+ *stretch of water*] pasar a nado, cruzar a nado; **he was the first man to ~ the English channel** fue el primer hombre que cruzó a nado el Canal de la Mancha

[2] [+ *length, race*] nadar; **he can ~ two lengths** puede nadar dos largos; **she swam ten lengths of the pool** se hizo diez largos en la piscina; **to ~ (the) crawl** nadar a crol; **before I had swum ten strokes** antes de haber dado diez brazadas; **she can't ~ a stroke** no sabe nadar en absoluto; **she swam the 400 metres medley** nadó los 400 metros a cuatro estilos

Ⓒ VI [1] [*person, fish*] nadar; **I can't ~** no sé nadar; **to ~ across a river** pasar *or* cruzar un río a nado; **we managed to ~ ashore** logramos llegar nadando hasta la orilla; **then we swam back** luego volvimos (nadando); **we shall have to ~ for it*** tendremos que echarnos al agua, tendremos que salvarnos nadando; **to go ~ming** ir a nadar *or* bañarse; **to learn to ~** aprender a nadar; **to ~ out to sea** alejarse nadando de la playa; **to ~ under water** nadar debajo del agua, bucear; ✦*IDIOMS* **to ~ against the stream** *or* **tide** nadar contra corriente; **to ~ with the stream** *or* **tide** dejarse llevar por la corriente

[2] (= *float*) flotar; **the meat was ~ming in gravy** la carne flotaba *or* nadaba en la salsa; **her eyes were ~ming with tears** tenía los ojos inundados de lágrimas; ✦*IDIOM* **to be ~ming in money** nadar en la abundancia

[3] (*dizzily*) (= *reel*) [*room, head*] dar vueltas; **my head is ~ming** me estoy mareando, me da vueltas la cabeza; **everything swam before my eyes** todo parecía que daba vueltas ante mis ojos

swimmer ['swɪməʳ] N nadador(a) *m/f*

swimming ['swɪmɪŋ] Ⓐ N natación *f*; **do you like ~?** ¿te gusta nadar?

Ⓑ CPD ► **swimming bath(s)** N(PL) = **swimming pool** ► **swimming cap** N gorro *m* de baño ► **swimming costume** N traje *m* de baño, bañador *m* (*Sp*) ► **swimming gala** N festival *m* de natación ► **swimming lesson** N clase *f* de natación ► **swimming pool** N piscina *fsing*, alberca *fsing* (*Mex*), pileta *fsing* (de natación) (*S. Cone*) ► **swimming trunks** NPL bañador *msing* (*Sp*)

swimmingly ['swɪmɪŋlɪ] ADV **to go ~** ir a las mil maravillas

swimsuit ['swɪmsuːt] N traje *m* de baño, bañador *m* (*Sp*)

swimwear ['swɪmwɛəʳ] N trajes *mpl* de baño

swindle ['swɪndl] Ⓐ N estafa *f*, timo *m*; **it's a ~!** ¡nos han estafado *or* timado!

Ⓑ VT estafar, timar; **to ~ sb out of sth** estafar algo a algn, quitar algo a algn estafándolo

swindler ['swɪndləʳ] N estafador(a) *m/f*, timador(a) *m/f*

swine [swaɪn] Ⓐ N [1] (*Zool*) (*pl inv*) cerdo *m*, puerco *m*

[2] (*fig*) (*) (= *person*) canalla *mf*, cochino/a *m/f*, marrano/a *m/f*; **you ~!** ¡canalla!; **what a ~ he is!** ¡es un canalla!

Ⓑ CPD ► **swine fever** N fiebre *f* porcina

swineherd†† ['swaɪnhɜːd] N porquero *m*

swing [swɪŋ] (*vb: pt, pp* **swung**) Ⓐ N [1] (= *movement*) [*of needle, pointer, boom*] movimiento *m*; [*of pick, axe*] movimiento *m* (amplio); [*of pendulum*] oscilación *f*, movimiento *m*; (*Boxing, Cricket, Golf*) (= *technique*) swing *m*; **with a quick ~ of his axe he felled the young tree** con un amplio y rápido movimiento del hacha taló el arbolito; **he was out on the course practising his ~** estaba en el campo de golf practicando su swing; **to take a ~ at sb*** (*with fist*) intentar darle un puñetazo a algn; (*with weapon*) intentar darle un golpe a algn; **the golfer took a ~ at the ball** el golfista intentó darle a la pelota

[2] (= *change*) (*in opinion*) cambio *m*; (*in vote*) desplazamiento *m*; **a sudden ~ in opinion** un cambio repentino de opinión; **they need a ~ of 5% to win** necesitan un desplazamiento de los votos de un 5% para ganar; **the ~s of the market** las fluctuaciones del mercado; **a ~ to the left** un viraje *or* desplazamiento hacia la izquierda

[3] (= *rhythm*) (*in dance, etc*) ritmo *m*; **to walk with a ~ (in one's step)** andar rítmicamente; **music/poetry with a ~ to it** *or* **that goes with a ~** música/poesía con ritmo *or* que tiene ritmo; ✦*IDIOMS* **to go with a ~** [*evening, party*] estar muy animado; [*business*] ir a las mil maravillas; **to be in full ~** [*party, election, campaign*] estar en pleno apogeo; [*business*] estar en pleno desarrollo; **to get into the ~ of things** coger el tranquillo a algo, captar el ritmo de las cosas (*LAm*)

[4] (*also* **~ music**) swing *m*, música *f* swing

[5] (= *scope, freedom*) **he was given full ~ to make decisions** le dieron carta blanca para que tomara decisiones; **he gave his imagination full ~** dio rienda suelta a su imaginación

[6] (= *garden swing*) columpio *m*; **to have a ~** columpiarse; ✦*IDIOMS* **it's ~s and roundabouts** ◊ **what you lose on the ~s you gain on the roundabouts** lo que se pierde aquí, se gana allá

Ⓑ VI [1] (= *move to and fro*) [*hanging object, hammock*] balancearse; [*pendulum, pointer*] oscilar; [*person*] (*on swing, hammock*) columpiarse; **it ~s in the wind** se balancea al viento; **he was sitting on the end of the table, his legs ~ing** estaba sentado en el borde de la mesa, columpiando las piernas; **her handbag swung back and forth** *or* **to and fro as she walked** su bolso se balanceaba (de un lado al otro) al andar; **the pendulum swung back and forth** *or* **to and fro** el péndulo oscilaba *or* se movía de un lado para otro; **a revolver swung from his belt** un revólver colgaba de su cinturón; **he was ~ing from a trapeze** se columpiaba colgado de un trapecio

[2] (= *pivot*) girar; **the door ~s on its hinges** la puerta gira sobre sus goznes; **he was hit by the car door as it swung back** la puerta del coche le golpeó al volver a cerrarse; **to ~ open/shut** abrirse/cerrarse; **the bar swung round and hit him in the jaw** la barra giró y le dio en la mandíbula; ✦*IDIOM* **now the pendulum has swung back the other way** ahora se ha dado la vuelta la tortilla

[3] **to ~ at sb (with one's fist)** intentar dar un puñetazo a algn; **he swung at me with an axe** intentó darme (un golpe) con un hacha; **he swung at the ball** intentó dar a la pelota

4 (= *turn*) **the car swung into the square** el coche viró *or* dio un viraje y entró en la plaza; **he swung out to overtake** viró *or* dio un viraje para adelantar; *see also* **swing round**
5 (= *jump*) **he swung across the river on a rope** cruzó el río colgado de una cuerda; **I swung down from my bunk** salté de mi litera; **the orang-utang swung from tree to tree** el orangután se columpiaba de árbol en árbol; ✦*IDIOM* **to ~ into action** ponerse en marcha
6 (= *move rhythmically*) **a group of schoolchildren were ~ing along up the road** un grupo de colegiales subían por la calle, andando al compás; **as the military band went ~ing along up the road ...** a medida que la banda militar marchaba siguiendo el compás calle arriba ...; **music that really ~s** música que tiene mucho ritmo
7 (*) (= *be hanged*) **he'll ~ for it** le colgarán por eso
8 (= *change*) **local opinion could ~ against the company** la opinión local podría cambiar y ponerse en contra de la empresa; **the balance of power is ~ing away from him** la balanza del poder se está inclinando hacia el lado contrario al suyo; **the currency should ~ back to its previous level** es de esperar que las divisas vuelvan a su nivel anterior; **to ~ to the left/right** dar un viraje hacia la izquierda *or* derecha
9 (*Psych*) [*mood*] cambiar; **his mood ~s wildly** le cambia el humor de forma descontrolada
10 (*) (= *be lively*) [*entertainment, party*] ambientarse; [*place*] tener ambiente; **the party's beginning to ~** la fiesta está empezando a ambientarse
11 (⁑) (*sexually*) **everyone seemed to be ~ing in those days** en aquellos tiempos parecía que a todo el mundo le iba la marcha⁑; ✦*IDIOM* **to ~ both ways** ser bisexual
Ⓒ VT 1 (= *move to and fro*) [+ *bag, arms, legs*] columpiar, balancear; **he was ~ing his bag back and forth** *or* **to and fro** columpiaba *or* balanceaba la bolsa de un lado al otro; **to ~ one's hips** andar contoneándose; ✦*IDIOMS* **there isn't enough room in here to ~ a cat*** aquí no caben ni cuatro gatos; **to ~ the lead†*** hacerse el remolón*
2 (= *pivot*) [+ *door*] **he swung the door open/closed** abrió/cerró la puerta de un golpe
3 (= *move*) 3·1 [+ *weapon*] blandir; **he swung his sword above his head** blandió la espada por encima de la cabeza; **he swung his axe at the tree** blandió el hacha con intención de darle al árbol; **he swung his racket at the ball** intentó darle a la pelota con la raqueta; **he swung his case down from the rack** bajó su maleta de la rejilla portaequipajes con un rápido movimiento del brazo; **Roy swung his legs off the couch** Roy quitó rápidamente las piernas del sofá; **he swung the box up onto the roof of the car** con un amplio movimiento de brazos, puso la caja en el techo del coche; **he swung the case up onto his shoulder** se echó la maleta a los hombros
3·2 (*reflexive*) **he swung himself across the stream** cruzó el arroyo de un salto; **to ~ o.s. (up) into the saddle** subirse a la silla de montar de un salto; **he swung himself over the wall** saltó la tapia apoyándose en un brazo
4 (= *turn*) **he swung the car off the road** viró con el coche y se salió de la carretera
5 (= *influence*) [+ *opinion, decision, vote, voters*] decidir; [+ *outcome*] determinar, decidir; **his speech swung the decision against us** su discurso dio un giro a la decisión desfavorable para nosotros; **the promised tax cuts could ~ the vote in our favour** los recortes prometidos en los impuestos podrían hacer cambiar el voto a nuestro favor; **she managed to ~ it so that we could all go** consiguió arreglarlo para que todos pudiéramos ir; **what swung it for me was ...** lo que me decidió fue ...; **it could ~ the election his way** podría decidir el resultado de las elecciones a su favor
6 (*Mus*) [+ *tune*] tocar con swing
Ⓓ CPD ► **swing band** N (*Mus*) banda *f* de música swing ► **swing bin** N cubo *m* de la basura (con tapa oscilante) ► **swing bridge** N puente *m* giratorio ► **swing door** N puerta *f* de batiente, puerta *f* de vaivén ► **swing music** N música *f* swing

►**swing round, swing around** Ⓐ VI + ADV 1 (*lit*) [*person*] girar sobre sus talones, girar en redondo; [*car, plane, procession*] girar en redondo
2 (*fig*) [*voters*] cambiar de opinión; [*opinion*] cambiar
Ⓑ VT + ADV [+ *object on rope etc*] hacer girar; [+ *sword, axe*] blandir; [+ *car, ship, procession, horse*] hacer girar en redondo

►**swing to** VI + ADV [*door*] cerrarse

swingeing ['swɪndʒɪŋ] ADJ (*Brit*) [*increase*] vertiginoso; [*cut*] fulminante, drástico; [*fine*] severísimo; [*majority*] abrumador

swinger ['swɪŋəʳ] N **he's a ~†*** (*gen*) es muy marchoso, le va la marcha; (*sexually*) le va la marcha

swinging ['swɪŋɪŋ] Ⓐ ADJ 1 (*lit*) **the rhythmic ~ motion of his axe against the wood** el rítmico vaivén *or* balanceo de su hacha al golpear la madera; **she walked along with a ~ gait** andaba con garbo
2 (†*) (= *lively*) [*city, party*] con mucha marcha*; **~ London** el Londres marchoso *or* de la marcha*; **the Swinging Sixties** los marchosos años sesenta*
3 [*music, rhythm*] con swing
Ⓑ N vaivén *m*, oscilación *f*
Ⓒ CPD ► **swinging door** N (*US*) puerta *f* de vaivén, puerta *f* de batiente

swing-wing ['swɪŋwɪŋ] ADJ [*aircraft*] con alas de geometría variable

swinish* ['swaɪnɪʃ] ADJ (*fig*) cochino, canallesco

swipe [swaɪp] Ⓐ N **to take a ~ at sb** asestar un golpe a algn
Ⓑ VT 1 (= *hit*) golpear, pegar
2 (*) (= *steal*) birlar*, afanar*
3 (*Comput*) [+ *card*] pasar (*por un lector de tarjetas*)
Ⓒ VI **to ~ at sth/sb** asestar un golpe a algo/algn
Ⓓ CPD ► **swipe card** N tarjeta *f* de banda magnética

swirl [swɜːl] Ⓐ N (= *movement*) remolino *m*, torbellino *m*; **it disappeared in a ~ of water** desapareció en un remolino de agua; **the ~ of the dancers' skirts** el girar *or* el movimiento de las faldas de las bailadoras
Ⓑ VI [*water, dust, mist*] arremolinarse; [*person*] dar vueltas, girar

swish [swɪʃ] Ⓐ N [*of cane*] silbido *m*; [*of skirt*] frufrú *m*; [*of water*] susurro *m*
Ⓑ ADJ (*) (= *smart*) muy elegante
Ⓒ VT [+ *cane*] agitar, blandir (*produciendo un silbido*); [+ *skirt*] hacer frufrú con; [+ *tail*] agitar, menear
Ⓓ VI [*skirts*] hacer frufrú; [*long grass*] silbar; [*water*] susurrar; **a car ~ed past** pasó un coche deslizándose por el asfalto mojado

Swiss [swɪs] Ⓐ ADJ suizo Ⓑ N suizo/a *m/f*
Ⓒ CPD ► **Swiss army knife** N navaja *f* multiuso(s), navaja *f* suiza ► **Swiss cheese plant** N costilla *f* de Adán ► **Swiss Guard** N (= *corps*) Guardia *f* Suiza; (= *person*) guardia *m* suizo ► **Swiss roll** N (*Brit Culin*) brazo *m* de gitano

Swiss-French [swɪs'frentʃ] N (*Ling*) el francés de Suiza

Swiss-German [swɪs'dʒɜːmən] N **~** (*Ling*) el alemán de Suiza

switch [swɪtʃ] Ⓐ N 1 (*Elec*) interruptor *m*, suich(e) *m* (*LAm*), switch *m* (*LAm*); **the ~ was on/off** el interruptor estaba encendido/apagado; **at the flick of a ~** con sólo darle a un interruptor; **to flick a ~ on/off** encender/apagar un interruptor; **light ~** interruptor *m* de la luz; **the on-off ~** el interruptor de encendido y apagado; **he threw the ~ on the tape recorder** dio al interruptor del magnetofón
2 (= *change*) cambio *m* (**from** de; **to** a); **this represents a dramatic ~ in US policy** esto representa un cambio dramático en la política estadounidense; **to make the ~ from X to Y** pasar de X a Y; **he had made the ~ from writing screenplays to novels** había pasado de escribir guiones a escribir novelas; **they have made the ~ from dictatorship to democracy** han hecho la transición de la dictadura a la democracia
3 (= *swap, substitution*) cambio *m*; **to make a ~** hacer un cambio; **that's not my necklace, there has been a ~** ésa no es mi gargantilla, me la han cambiado *or* me han hecho un cambio, ésa no es mi gargantilla, me han dado un cambiazo*
4 (†) (= *stick*) vara *f*; (*for riding*) fusta *f*
5 [*of hair*] postizo *m*
6 (*US Rail*) (= *points*) agujas *fpl*; (= *siding*) vía *f* muerta
Ⓑ VT 1 (= *change*) [+ *tactics*] cambiar de; **if you ~ allegiance from one party to another ...** si cambias de bando y vas de un partido a otro ...; **how quickly people ~ allegiances!** ¡hay que ver con qué rapidez se cambia de chaqueta la gente!; **50 per cent of car buyers are prepared to ~ brands** un 50 por ciento de los compradores de coche están dispuestos a pasarse a una nueva marca
2 (= *move*) [+ *production*] trasladar (**from** de; **to** a); **she quickly ~ed the conversation to another topic** rápidamente desvió la conversación hacia otro tema
3 (= *swap, exchange*) (*honestly*) cambiar; (*dishonestly*) cambiar, dar el cambiazo a*; **we had to ~ taxis when the first broke down** tuvimos que cambiar de taxi cuando el primero tuvo una avería; **the ballot boxes have been ~ed** han cambiado las urnas, han dado el cambiazo a las urnas*; **to ~ sth for sth** cambiar algo por algo; **he ~ed the real painting with the fake one** cambió el cuadro verdadero por el falso
4 (*Elec*) **he ~ed the heater to "low"** puso el calentador en "bajo"
5 (*esp US Rail*) **to ~ a train to another line** cambiar un tren a otra vía
6 (= *lash*) [+ *tail*] mover, agitar; **to ~ the grass with one's cane** agitar la hierba con la vara
Ⓒ VI 1 (= *change*) cambiar (**from** de; **to** a); **he ~ed to another topic** cambió de tema; **I've ~ed to a cheaper brand of washing powder** (me) he cambiado a una marca de detergente más barata
2 (= *swap round*) hacer un cambio, cambiarse (**with** con); **he had ~ed with another driver** había hecho un cambio con otro con-

ductor, se había cambiado con otro conductor

[3] (= *move*) [*production*] trasladarse (**to** a); **production will ~ to the Glasgow plant next week** la producción se trasladará a la planta de Glasgow la semana que viene; **you can ~ between windows using the mouse** puedes cambiar de una ventana a otra utilizando el ratón

►**switch back** Ⓐ VI + ADV (*to original plan, product, allegiance*) volver a cambiarse; **to ~ back to sth** volver a (cambiar a) algo; **let's ~ back to the other programme** volvamos (a cambiar) al otro programa

Ⓑ VT + ADV **she ~ed the heater back to high/low** volvió a cambiar el calentador a la posición alta/baja; **to ~ the light back on** volver a encender la luz; **to ~ the heater/oven back on** volver a poner *or* encender el calentador/horno

►**switch off** Ⓐ VT + ADV [+ *light, television, gas*] apagar; (*Aut*) [+ *ignition, engine*] parar; **he ~ed the radio off** apagó la radio; **the oven ~es itself off** el horno se apaga solo; **to ~ off the electricity** apagar la corriente *or* la luz

Ⓑ VI + ADV [1] (*Elec*) [*washing-machine, light, heating*] apagarse; **the dryer ~es on and off automatically** la secadora se enciende y apaga automáticamente

[2] (*) (= *stop listening*) desconectar(se)

►**switch on** Ⓐ VT + ADV [1] (*Elec, Aut*) [+ *light, television, gas, electricity*] encender, prender (*LAm*); [+ *alarm clock, burglar alarm*] poner; **he ~ed on the light** encendió la luz; **to leave the television ~ed on** dejar la televisión puesta *or* encendida; *see also* **ignition**

[2] (*fig*) [2·1] (= *use*) **to ~ on the charm** ponerse encantador

[2·2] (= *excite*) **his music ~es me on**‡ su música me pone a tono‡

Ⓑ VI + ADV (*Elec*) [*washing-machine, light, heating*] encenderse; [*viewer*] encender la televisión, poner la televisión, prender la televisión (*LAm*); [*listener*] encender la radio, poner la radio, prender la radio (*LAm*); [*driver*] arrancar; **the light ~es on automatically** las luces se encienden automáticamente

►**switch over** Ⓐ VT + ADV **to ~ over A and B** cambiar A por B; **to ~ the programme over** cambiar de cadena

Ⓑ VI + PREP **to ~ over** (*TV, Rad*) cambiar de canal; **to ~ over to another station** cambiar a otra emisora; **we've ~ed over to gas** (nos) hemos cambiado *or* pasado a gas

►**switch round, switch around** Ⓐ VT + ADV

[1] (= *swap round*) cambiar

[2] (= *move*) [+ *furniture*] cambiar de sitio

Ⓑ VI + ADV cambiarse

switchback [ˈswɪtʃbæk] N (*Brit*) (*at fair*) montaña *f* rusa; (= *road*) camino *m* de fuertes altibajos

switchblade [ˈswɪtʃˌbleɪd] N (*US*) navaja *f* de muelle *or* de resorte

switchboard [ˈswɪtʃbɔːd] Ⓐ N (*Telec*) (*at exchange*) central *f*; (*in offices*) centralita *f*, conmutador *m* (*LAm*)

Ⓑ CPD ► **switchboard operator** N telefonista *mf*

switch-hit [ˌswɪtʃˈhɪt] (*US*) VI ser ambidextro en el bateo

switch-hitter [ˌswɪtʃˈhɪtəʳ] N [1] (*Baseball*) bateador *m* ambidextro

[2] (*US*‡) (= *bisexual*) bisexual *mf*

switchman [ˈswɪtʃmən] N (*pl* **switchmen**) (*US*) guardagujas *m inv*

switch-over [ˈswɪtʃəʊvəʳ] N cambio *m* (**from** de; **to** a)

switchtower [ˈswɪtʃˌtaʊəʳ] N (*US Rail*) garita *f* de señales

switchyard [ˈswɪtʃjɑːd] N (*US Rail*) patio *m* de maniobras, estación *f* clasificadora

Switzerland [ˈswɪtsələnd] N Suiza *f*

swivel [ˈswɪvl] Ⓐ N eslabón *m* giratorio

Ⓑ VI (*also* **~ round**) girar; [*person*] volverse, girar sobre los talones

Ⓒ VT (*also* **~ round**) girar

Ⓓ CPD ► **swivel chair** N silla *f* giratoria

swizz* [swɪz] N, **swizzle** [ˈswɪzl] N (*Brit*) camelo* *m*

swizzle-stick [ˈswɪzlstɪk] N paletilla *f* para cóctel

swollen [ˈswəʊlən] PP *of* **swell**

swollen-headed [ˈswəʊlənˈhedɪd] ADJ engreído, presumido, presuntuoso

swoon [swuːn] Ⓐ N desmayo *m*, desvanecimiento *m*; **to fall in a ~** desmayarse, desvanecerse

Ⓑ VI desmayarse, desvanecerse

swoop [swuːp] Ⓐ N [*of bird*] descenso *m* súbito; (*by police*) redada *f* (**on** de); ✦***IDIOM* at one fell ~** de un solo golpe

Ⓑ VI [*bird*] (*also* **~ down**) abatirse, lanzarse en picado (**on** sobre); [*police*] hacer una redada (**on** en); **the plane ~ed low over the village** el avión se lanzó en picado y pasó en vuelo rasante sobre el pueblo; **the police ~ed on the club and arrested eight suspects** la policía hizo una redada en el club y detuvo a ocho sospechosos; **he ~ed on this mistake** se lanzó sobre este error

swoosh [swʊ(ː)ʃ] = **swish**

swop [swɒp] = **swap**

sword [sɔːd] Ⓐ N espada *f*; **to put sb to the ~** pasar a algn a cuchillo; ✦***IDIOMS* to cross ~s with sb** habérselas con algn; **to be a double-edged ~** ser un arma de doble filo; ✦***PROV* those that live by the ~ die by the ~** el que a hierro mata a hierro muere

Ⓑ CPD ► **sword dance** N danza *f* de espadas

swordfish [ˈsɔːdfɪʃ] (*pl* **swordfish, swordfishes**) N pez *m* espada

swordplay [ˈsɔːdpleɪ] N manejo *m* de la espada

swordsman [ˈsɔːdzmən] N (*pl* **swordsmen**) espada *f*, espadachín *m*; **a good ~** una buena espada

swordsmanship [ˈsɔːdzmənʃɪp] N manejo *m* de la espada

swordstick [ˈsɔːdstɪk] N bastón *m* de estoque

sword-swallower [ˈsɔːdˌswɒləʊəʳ] N tragasables *mf inv*

sword-thrust [ˈsɔːdθrʌst] N estocada *f*

swore [swɔːʳ] PT *of* **swear**

sworn [swɔːn] Ⓐ PP *of* **swear**

Ⓑ ADJ [*enemy*] declarado; [*testimony*] dado bajo juramento, jurado

swot* [swɒt] Ⓐ N empollón/ona *m/f*

Ⓑ VT, VI **to ~ up (on) sth** empollar algo*; **to ~ for an exam** empollar para un examen*

swotting* [ˈswɒtɪŋ] N **to do some ~** empollar*

swum [swʌm] PP *of* **swim**

swung [swʌŋ] PT, PP *of* **swing**

sybarite [ˈsɪbəraɪt] N sibarita *mf*

sybaritic [ˌsɪbəˈrɪtɪk] ADJ sibarita, sibarítico

sycamore [ˈsɪkəmɔːʳ] N (*also* **~ tree**) sicomoro *m*, sicómoro *m*

sycophancy [ˈsɪkəfənsɪ] N adulación *f*, servilismo *m*

sycophant [ˈsɪkəfənt] N adulador(a) *m/f*

sycophantic [ˌsɪkəˈfæntɪk] ADJ [*person*] servil, sobón; [*speech*] adulatorio; [*manner*] servil

Sydney [ˈsɪdnɪ] N Sidney *m*

syllabi [ˈsɪləˌbaɪ] NPL *of* **syllabus**

syllabic [sɪˈlæbɪk] ADJ silábico

syllabication [sɪˌlæbɪˈkeɪʃən] N, **syllabification** [sɪˌlæbɪfɪˈkeɪʃən] N silabeo *m*, división *f* en sílabas

syllable [ˈsɪləbl] N sílaba *f*; **I will explain it in words of one ~** te lo explico como a un niño

syllabub [ˈsɪləbʌb] N *dulce frío hecho con nata o leche, licor y zumo de limón*

syllabus [ˈsɪləbəs] N (*pl* **syllabuses** *or* **syllabi**) (*Scol, Univ*) (*gen*) plan *m* de estudios; (*specific*) programa *m* (de estudios)

syllogism [ˈsɪlədʒɪzəm] N silogismo *m*

syllogistic [ˌsɪləˈdʒɪstɪk] ADJ silogístico

syllogize [ˈsɪlədʒaɪz] VI silogizar

sylph [sɪlf] N (*Myth*) (*male*) silfo *m*, sílfide *f*; (*female*) sílfide *f*

sylphlike [ˈsɪlflaɪk] ADJ de sílfide

sylvan [ˈsɪlvən] ADJ silvestre

Sylvia [ˈsɪlvɪə] N Silvia

symbiosis [ˌsɪmbɪˈəʊsɪs] N simbiosis *f*

symbiotic [ˌsɪmbɪˈɒtɪk] ADJ simbiótico

symbol [ˈsɪmbəl] N [1] (= *representation*) símbolo *m*; **she became a ~ of hope to the downtrodden** se convirtió en un símbolo de esperanza para los oprimidos

[2] (*Chem*) símbolo *m*; (*Math*) signo *m*; **the chemical ~ for mercury** el símbolo químico del mercurio

symbolic [sɪmˈbɒlɪk] Ⓐ ADJ simbólico (**of** de)

Ⓑ CPD ► **symbolic logic** N lógica *f* simbólica

symbolical [sɪmˈbɒlɪkəl] ADJ simbólico

symbolically [sɪmˈbɒlɪkəlɪ] ADV simbólicamente

symbolism [ˈsɪmbəlɪzəm] N simbolismo *m*

symbolist [ˈsɪmbəlɪst] Ⓐ ADJ simbolista

Ⓑ N simbolista *mf*

symbolize [ˈsɪmbəlaɪz] VT simbolizar

symmetrical [sɪˈmetrɪkəl] ADJ simétrico

symmetrically [sɪˈmetrɪkəlɪ] ADV simétricamente

symmetry [ˈsɪmɪtrɪ] N simetría *f*

sympathetic [ˌsɪmpəˈθetɪk] ADJ [1] (= *showing pity*) compasivo (**to** con); (= *kind, understanding*) comprensivo; **they were ~ but could not help** estaban de nuestra parte pero no podían ayudarnos; **we found a ~ policeman who helped us** encontramos a un policía que amablemente nos ayudó; **he wasn't in the least ~** no mostró compasión alguna; **they are ~ to actors** están dispuestos a escuchar a los actores; **to be ~ to a cause** (= *well-disposed*) solidarizarse con *or* apoyar una causa

[2] [*ink, nerve, pain etc*] simpático

sympathetically [ˌsɪmpəˈθetɪkəlɪ] ADV (= *showing pity*) con compasión; (= *with understanding*) con comprensión; **she looked at me ~** me miró compasiva; **the book has been ~ adapted for the screen** el libro ha sido llevado a la pantalla con gran esmero

sympathize [ˈsɪmpəθaɪz] VI (= *feel pity*) compadecerse; (= *understand*) comprender; **to ~ with sb** compadecerse de algn, compadecer a algn; **I ~ with what you say, but …** comprendo tu punto de vista, pero …; **those who ~ with our demands** los que apoyan nuestras reclamaciones; **to ~ with sb in his bereavement** acompañar a algn en el sentimiento; **they wrote to ~** escribieron para dar el pésame

sympathizer [ˈsɪmpəθaɪzəʳ] N simpatizante *mf*, partidario/a *m/f* (**with** de)

sympathy ['sɪmpəθɪ] Ⓐ N [1] (= *compassion*) compasión *f*; **have you no ~?** ¿no tiene compasión?; **his ~ for the underdog** su compasión por los desvalidos; **you have my deepest ~** te compadezco; **you won't get any ~ from me!** ¡no me das ninguna pena!; **a letter of ~** un pésame; **I have no ~ for him** no siento ninguna compasión *or* pena por él; **to express one's ~ (on the death of)** dar el pésame (por la muerte de)
[2] (= *agreement*) solidaridad *f*; **they came out in ~ with their colleagues** se declararon en huelga por solidaridad con sus colegas; **I have some ~ with this point of view** comparto en parte este punto de vista; **the sympathies of the crowd were with him** la multitud estaba de su lado *or* lo apoyaba; **the sky clouded over, in ~ with her mood** el cielo se nubló, poniéndose así a tono con su estado de ánimo
[3] **sympathies** (*Pol*) simpatías *fpl*; **she has expressed Republican sympathies** ha expresado sus simpatías por los republicanos
[4] (= *affinity*) comprensión *f*, afinidad *f* (**between** entre)
Ⓑ CPD ► **sympathy strike** N huelga *f* de solidaridad ► **sympathy vote** N voto *m* de solidaridad

symphonic [sɪm'fɒnɪk] ADJ sinfónico

symphony ['sɪmfənɪ] Ⓐ N sinfonía *f*
Ⓑ CPD ► **symphony orchestra** N orquesta *f* sinfónica

symposium [sɪm'pəʊzɪəm] N (*pl* **symposiums** *or* **symposia** [sɪm'pəʊzɪə]) simposio *m*

symptom ['sɪmptəm] N [1] (*Med*) síntoma *m*
[2] (*fig*) (= *indication*) síntoma *m*, indicio *m*

symptomatic [ˌsɪmptə'mætɪk] ADJ sintomático (**of** de)

synaesthesia, **synesthesia** (*US*) [ˌsɪnəs'θiːzɪə] N sinestesia *f*

synagogue ['sɪnəgɒg] N sinagoga *f*

sync* [sɪŋk] N ABBR = **synchronization**; **in ~** en sincronización; **they are in ~** (*fig*) están sincronizados; **out of ~** (*fig*) desincronizado

synchro* ['sɪŋkrəʊ] (*Aut*) = **synchromesh** Ⓐ N ABBR = **synchromesh**
Ⓑ CPD ► **synchro gearbox** N caja *f* de cambios sincronizada

synchromesh ['sɪŋkrəʊ'meʃ] N (*also* **~ gear**) cambio *m* sincronizado de velocidades

synchronic [sɪŋ'krɒnɪk] ADJ sincrónico

synchronism ['sɪŋkrənɪzəm] N sincronismo *m*

synchronization [ˌsɪŋkrənaɪ'zeɪʃən] N sincronización *f*

synchronize ['sɪŋkrənaɪz] Ⓐ VT sincronizar (**with** con); **~d swimming** natación *f* sincronizada
Ⓑ VI sincronizarse, ser sincrónico (**with** con)

synchronous ['sɪŋkrənəs] ADJ sincrónico, síncrono

synchrotron ['sɪŋkrəˌtrɒn] N sincrotrón *m*

syncopate ['sɪŋkəpeɪt] VT sincopar

syncopation [ˌsɪŋkə'peɪʃən] N síncopa *f*

syncope ['sɪŋkəpɪ] N [1] (*Med*) síncope *m*
[2] (*Ling, Mus*) síncopa *f*

syncretism ['sɪŋkrətɪzəm] N sincretismo *m*

syndic ['sɪndɪk] N síndico *m*

syndicalism ['sɪndɪkəlɪzəm] N sindicalismo *m*

syndicalist ['sɪndɪkəlɪst] Ⓐ ADJ sindicalista
Ⓑ N sindicalista *mf*

syndicate Ⓐ ['sɪndɪkɪt] N [1] (*Comm*) sindicato *m*, corporación *f*
[2] (*esp US*) (= *news agency*) agencia *f* de prensa; (= *chain of papers*) cadena *f* de periódicos
[3] (*) (= *criminals*) **crime ~** banda *f* de malhechores, cuadrilla *f* de bandidos
Ⓑ ['sɪndɪkeɪt] VT [1] (*esp US Press*) [+ *article, interview etc*] sindicar
[2] (*Fin*) **~d loan** préstamo *m* sindicado

syndrome ['sɪndrəʊm] N síndrome *m*

synecdoche [sɪ'nekdəkɪ] N sinécdoque *f*

synergy ['sɪnədʒɪ] N sinergia *f*

synesthesia [ˌsɪnəs'θiːzɪə] N (*US*) = **synaesthesia**

synod ['sɪnəd] N sínodo *m*

synonym ['sɪnənɪm] N sinónimo *m*

synonymous [sɪ'nɒnɪməs] ADJ sinónimo (**with** con)

synonymy [sɪ'nɒnəmɪ] N sinonimia *f*

synopsis [sɪ'nɒpsɪs] N (*pl* **synopses** [sɪ'nɒpsiːz]) sinopsis *f inv*

synoptic [sɪ'nɒptɪk] ADJ sinóptico

synoptical [sɪ'nɒptɪkəl] ADJ = **synoptic**

synovial [saɪ'nəʊvɪəl] ADJ sinovial

syntactic [sɪn'tæktɪk], **syntactical** [sɪn'tæktɪkəl] ADJ sintáctico

syntagm ['sɪntæm] N (*pl* **syntagms**), **syntagma** [sɪn'tægmə] N (*pl* **syntagmata** [sɪn'tægmətə]) sintagma *m*

syntagmatic [ˌsɪntæg'mætɪk] ADJ sintagmático

syntax ['sɪntæks] Ⓐ N sintaxis *f*
Ⓑ CPD ► **syntax error** N error *m* sintáctico

synth* ['sɪnθ] ADJ, N (*Mus*) = **synthesizer**

synthesis ['sɪnθəsɪs] N (*pl* **syntheses** ['sɪnθəsiːz]) síntesis *f inv*

synthesize ['sɪnθəsaɪz] VT sintetizar

synthesizer ['sɪnθəsaɪzəʳ] N sintetizador *m*

synthetic [sɪn'θetɪk] Ⓐ ADJ [1] (= *man-made*) [*material, chemical, drug*] sintético
[2] (*pej*) (= *false*) [*person, behaviour, emotion, taste*] artificial
Ⓑ N fibra *f* sintética; **~s** fibras *fpl* sintéticas
Ⓒ CPD ► **synthetic fibre, synthetic fiber** (*US*) N fibra *f* sintética ► **synthetic rubber** N caucho *m* artificial

synthetically [sɪn'θetɪkəlɪ] ADV sintéticamente

syphilis ['sɪfɪlɪs] N sífilis *f*

syphilitic [ˌsɪfɪ'lɪtɪk] Ⓐ ADJ sifilítico
Ⓑ N sifilítico/a *m/f*

syphon ['saɪfən] = **siphon**

Syracuse ['saɪərəkjuːz] N Siracusa *f*

Syria ['sɪrɪə] N Siria *f*

Syrian ['sɪrɪən] Ⓐ ADJ sirio
Ⓑ N sirio/a *m/f*

syringe [sɪ'rɪndʒ] Ⓐ N jeringa *f*, jeringuilla *f*
Ⓑ VT jeringar

syrup ['sɪrəp] N (*Culin*) almíbar *m*, jarabe *m*; (*Med*) jarabe *m*

syrupy ['sɪrəpɪ] ADJ [1] parecido a jarabe, espeso como jarabe
[2] (*fig*) sensiblero, almibarado

system ['sɪstəm] Ⓐ N [1] (= *method*) sistema *m*; **new teaching ~s** nuevos sistemas *or* métodos de enseñanza
[2] (*Pol, Sociol*) (= *organization*) sistema *m*; **a political/economic/social ~** un sistema político/económico/social
[3] (*Math, Sci*) (= *principles*) sistema *m*; **binary/decimal/metric ~** sistema *m* binario/decimal/métrico
[4] (*Elec, Comput, Mech*) sistema *m*; **the ~'s down again** el sistema no funciona otra vez
[5] (= *network*) sistema *m*, red *f*; **transport ~** sistema *m or* red *f* de transportes
[6] (= *order*) método *m*; **he lacks ~** carece de método
[7] (*Med*) (= *organism*) organismo *m*, cuerpo *m*; **the nervous/immune ~** el sistema nervioso/inmunitario; **the digestive ~** el aparato digestivo; **it was quite a shock to the ~** (*fig*) fue un buen golpe para el organismo; ✦**IDIOM to get sth out of one's ~** quitarse algo de encima
[8] **the ~** (= *the establishment*) el sistema; **to beat the ~** burlar el sistema
[9] (= *classification*) sistema *m*; **a chronological ~** un sistema cronológico
[10] (*Astron*) sistema *m*; **solar ~** sistema *m* solar
Ⓑ CPD ► **system disk** N disco *m* del sistema ► **systems analysis** N análisis *m inv* de sistemas ► **systems analyst** N (*Comput*) analista *mf* de sistemas ► **systems engineer** N (*Comput*) ingeniero/a *m/f* de sistemas ► **systems engineering** N ingeniería *f* de sistemas ► **systems programmer** N programador(a) *m/f* de sistemas ► **systems software** N software *m* del sistema

systematic [ˌsɪstə'mætɪk] ADJ sistemático, metódico

systematically [ˌsɪstə'mætɪkəlɪ] ADV sistemáticamente, metódicamente

systematization ['sɪstəmətaɪ'zeɪʃən] N sistematización *f*

systematize ['sɪstəmətaɪz] VT sistematizar

systemic [sɪ'stemɪk] ADJ [1] sistémico
[2] [*chemicals, drugs*] sistémico

systole ['sɪstəlɪ] N (*Med*) sístole *f*

systolic [sɪ'stɒlɪk] ADJ **~ pressure** presión *f* sistólica

➤ LANGUAGE IN USE: sympathy A1 24.5

T t

T, t [tiː] N (= *letter*) T, t *f*; **T for Tommy** T de Tommy; **the buildings were arranged in a T** los edificios estaban situados en forma de T; **✦IDIOM to a T**: **it fits you to a T** te sienta que ni pintado; **it suits you to a T** te viene de perlas; **he described the house to a T** describió la casa hasta el último detalle; **that's it to a T** es eso exactamente

TA N ABBR [1] (*Brit Mil*) = **Territorial Army**; → TERRITORIAL ARMY

[2] (*US Univ*) ABBR = **teaching assistant**

ta* [tɑː] EXCL (*Brit*) gracias; **ta very much!** ¡muchas gracias!

tab [tæb] Ⓐ N [1] (*on garment*) (= *flap*) oreja *f*, lengüeta *f*; (= *loop*) presilla *f*; (= *label*) etiqueta *f*; (= *marker*) (*on file*) ceja *f*; [*of cheque*] resguardo *m*; **✦IDIOMS to keep ~s on sb*** vigilar a algn; **to keep ~s on** [+ *situation*] seguir de cerca

[2] (*US*) cuenta *f*; **✦IDIOM to pick up the ~*** pagar la cuenta; (*fig*) asumir la responsabilidad

[3] (*also* **tabulator**) tabulador *m*

Ⓑ CPD ► **tab key** N tecla *f* de tabulación

tabard [ˈtæbəd] N tabardo *m*

Tabasco® [təˈbæskəʊ] N salsa *f* tabasco, tabasco *m*

tabby [ˈtæbɪ] Ⓐ ADJ atigrado

Ⓑ N (*also* ~ **cat**) gato/a *m/f* atigrado/a

tabernacle [ˈtæbənækl] N (*in Judaism*) tabernáculo *m*; (= *church*) templo *m*, santuario *m*; (*in church*) sagrario *m*

table [ˈteɪbl] Ⓐ N [1] (= *piece of furniture*) mesa *f*; **I'd like a ~ for two, please** (quiero) una mesa para dos, por favor; **kitchen ~** mesa *f* de cocina; **they were at ~ when we arrived** (*frm*) estaban sentados a la mesa cuando llegamos; **don't read at the ~** no leas en la mesa; **you will join us at our ~, won't you?** se sentará (a la mesa) con nosotros ¿verdad?; **to clear the ~** quitar *or* recoger *or* levantar la mesa; **to lay the ~** poner la mesa; **why isn't dinner on the ~?** ¿por qué no está servida la cena?; **to set the ~** poner la mesa; **to sit down to ~** sentarse a la mesa; **✦IDIOMS under the ~**: **I'll be under the ~ if I have any more wine** si bebo más vino me voy a caer redondo *or* no voy a tenerme en pie; **he was accepting money under the ~*** aceptaba dinero bajo cuerda *or* bajo mano; **to get one's feet under the ~*** hacerse un hueco*; **to turn the ~s** dar la vuelta a la tortilla; **to turn the ~s on sb** volver las tornas a *or* contra algn; *see also* **card**[1], **drink B**, **high D**, **wait**

[2] (= *people at table*) mesa *f*

[3] (*frm*) (= *food*) mesa *f*; **to keep a good ~** tener buena mesa

[4] (*for discussion*) mesa *f* de negociaciones; **he managed to get all the parties around the ~** consiguió que todos los interesados se sentaran a la mesa de negociaciones; **to put sth on the ~** (*Brit*) poner algo sobre el tapete; **there are two proposals on the ~** hay dos propuestas sobre el tapete; **they're willing to put 12 million dollars on the ~ to get this company** están dispuestos a pagar 12 millones de dólares para conseguir esta empresa; **round ~** mesa *f* redonda

[5] (= *chart*) tabla *f*, cuadro *m*; **a ~ of the top 12 best and worst performers** una tabla *or* un cuadro de los 12 mejores y los 12 peores; **~ of contents** índice *m* de materias; *see also* **periodic**

[6] (*Math*) (*also* **multiplication ~**) tabla *f* de multiplicar; **the eleven-times ~** la tabla (de multiplicar) del once

[7] (*Sport*) (*also* **league ~**) liga *f*, clasificación *f*

[8] (*Geog*) (*also* **water ~**) capa *f* freática; (*also* **~land**) meseta *f*, altiplano *m* (*LAm*)

Ⓑ VT [1] (*Brit frm*) (= *propose*) [+ *motion, amendment*] presentar

[2] (*US*) (= *postpone*) aplazar, posponer

Ⓒ CPD ► **table dancing** N striptease *m* en pasarela *or* en barra ► **table football** N futbolín *m* ► **table lamp** N lámpara *f* de mesa ► **table leg** N pata *f* de mesa ► **table linen** N mantelería *f* ► **table manners** NPL comportamiento *msing* en la mesa, modales *mpl* en la mesa ► **Table Mountain** N Montaña *f* de la Tabla ► **table napkin** N servilleta *f* ► **table runner** N tapete *m* ► **table salt** N sal *f* de mesa ► **table setting** N cubierto *m*, servicio *m* ► **table talk** N sobremesa *f*, conversación *f* de sobremesa ► **table tennis** N ping-pong *m*, pimpón *m*, tenis *m* de mesa ► **table wine** N vino *m* de mesa

tableau [ˈtæbləʊ] N (*pl* **tableaux** *or* **tableaus** [ˈtæbləʊz]) (*Art, Theat*) cuadro *m* (vivo)

tablecloth [ˈteɪblklɒθ] N mantel *m*

table d'hôte [ˈtɑːblˈdəʊt] N menú *m*, comida *f* (corrida) (*Mex*)

tableland [ˈteɪbllænd] N meseta *f*, altiplano *m* (*LAm*)

tablemat [ˈteɪblmæt] N salvamanteles *m inv*

tablespoon [ˈteɪblspuːn] N (= *spoon*) cuchara *f* grande, cuchara *f* de servir; (= *quantity*) cucharada *f* grande

tablespoonful [ˈteɪbl,spuːnfʊl] N cucharada *f* grande

tablet [ˈtæblɪt] N [1] (*Med*) (*gen*) pastilla *f*; (= *round pill*) comprimido *m*

[2] [*of soap, chocolate*] pastilla *f*

[3] (= *writing tablet*) bloc *m*, taco *m* (de papel)

[4] (= *inscribed stone*) lápida *f*

tabletop [ˈteɪbltɒp] Ⓐ N tablero *m* de la mesa

Ⓑ CPD ► **tabletop games** NPL juegos *mpl* de mesa

tableware [ˈteɪblwɛəʳ] N vajilla *f*, servicio *m* de mesa

tabloid [ˈtæblɔɪd] N (= *newspaper*) tabloide *m*, periódico *m* popular; **the ~s** (*pej*) la prensa amarilla

> **TABLOIDS AND BROADSHEETS**
>
> *En el Reino Unido hay dos tipos de periódicos, llamados, según su tamaño,* **tabloids** *o* **broadsheets**. *Éstos son más grandes y suelen centrarse en noticias serias, artículos de contenido cultural y un análisis en profundidad de la actualidad, por lo que también se les denomina* **quality press**. *Algunos nombres muy conocidos son* **The Daily Telegraph**, **The Times**, **The Guardian** *y* **The Independent**. *Los llamados* **tabloids** *suelen tener grandes titulares, artículos cortos, muchas fotografías, opiniones espontáneas y muestran una clara preferencia por las historias escandalosas o sentimentales. Por sus contenidos sensacionalistas también reciben el nombre de* **gutter press**. *Los más conocidos de éstos son* **The Sun**, **The Daily Mirror**, **The Daily Express**, **The Daily Mail** *y* **The Daily Star**.
>
> *En Estados Unidos, el término* **standard-sized newspapers** *es el equivalente de* **broadsheet**. *El principal periódico de este tipo es la edición nacional del* **New York Times**. *Entre los* **tabloids** *más conocidos están el* **New York Daily News** *y el* **Chicago Sun-Times**.

taboo [təˈbuː] Ⓐ ADJ (*socially*) tabú; (*religiously*) sagrado; **the subject is ~** el asunto es tema tabú

Ⓑ N (*social*) tabú *m*

Ⓒ VT declarar tabú, prohibir

tabular [ˈtæbjʊləʳ] ADJ tabular

tabulate [ˈtæbjʊleɪt] VT exponer en forma de tabla; (*Comput*) tabular

tabulation [,tæbjʊˈleɪʃən] N [*of information, results*] exposición *f* en forma de tabla; (= *table*) tabla *f*

tabulator [ˈtæbjʊleɪtəʳ] N tabulador *m*

tachograph [ˈtækəgrɑːf] N (*Brit*) tacógrafo *m*

tachometer [tæˈkɒmɪtəʳ] N taquímetro *m*

tachycardia [,tækɪˈkɑːdɪə] N taquicardia *f*

tachymeter [tæˈkɪmɪtəʳ] N taquímetro *m*

tacit [ˈtæsɪt] ADJ tácito

tacitly [ˈtæsɪtlɪ] ADV tácitamente

taciturn [ˈtæsɪtɜːn] ADJ taciturno

taciturnity [,tæsɪˈtɜːnɪtɪ] N taciturnidad *f*

Tacitus [ˈtæsɪtəs] N Tácito

tack [tæk] Ⓐ N [1] (= *nail*) tachuela *f*; (*US*) (*also* **thumb~**) chincheta *f*, chinche *m or f*; *see also* **brass**

2 (*Naut*) (= *course*) bordada *f*; (= *turn*) virada *f*
3 (*fig*) rumbo *m*, dirección *f*; ♦*IDIOMS* **to change ~** cambiar de rumbo *or* sentido; **to try a different ~** abordar un problema desde otro punto de partida; **to be on the right ~** ir por buen camino; **to be on the wrong ~** estar equivocado
4 (*Sew*) hilván *m*
5 (*for horse*) arreos *mpl*
6 (*) (= *cheap shoddy objects*) baratijas *fpl*, chucherías *fpl*, horteradas *fpl* (*Sp**)
Ⓑ VT 1 (= *nail*) clavar con tachuelas
2 (*Sew*) (*also* ~ **up**) hilvanar
Ⓒ VI (*Naut*) dar bordadas; (= *change course*) virar, cambiar de bordada
►**tack down** VT + ADV (*Carpentry, etc*) **to ~ sth down** afirmar algo con tachuelas, sujetar algo con tachuelas
►**tack on** VT + ADV **to ~ sth on to a letter** añadir algo a una carta; **somehow it got ~ed on** de algún modo u otro llegó a ser añadido a la parte principal

tackle ['tækl] Ⓐ N 1 (= *lifting gear*) aparejo *m*, polea *f*; (= *ropes*) jarcia *f*, cordaje *m*
2 (= *equipment*) equipo *m*, avíos *mpl*; (*fig*) (= *bits and pieces*) cosas *fpl*, trastos *mpl*; (*also* **fishing** ~) equipo *m* de pesca
3 (*Ftbl*) entrada *f*; (*Rugby*) placaje *m*; **flying ~** placaje *m* en el aire
Ⓑ VT 1 (= *attempt to deal with*) [+ *problem*] abordar, enfrentar; [+ *task*] enfrentar, emprender; **firemen ~d the blaze** los bomberos lucharon contra las llamas; **can you ~ another helping?** ¿quieres comerte otra porción?; **he ~d Greek on his own** emprendió el estudio del griego sin ayuda de nadie
2 (= *grapple with*) [+ *thief, intruder*] enfrentarse con; (*fig*) (= *confront*) encararse con; **I'll have to ~ him about that money he owes me** voy a tener que encararme con él y plantearle lo del dinero que me debe
3 (*Ftbl*) entrar a; (*Rugby*) placar, taclear
Ⓒ VI (*Sport*) placar, taclear

tacky ['tækɪ] ADJ (*compar* **tackier**, *superl* **tackiest**) 1 (*) (= *cheap-looking*) [*furniture*] chabacano, hortera (*Sp**); [*restaurant, hotel*] destartalado; (= *tasteless*) [*behaviour, remark*] de mal gusto, vulgar
2 (= *sticky*) pegajoso

taco ['tɑːkəʊ] N *tortilla rellena hecha con harina de maíz*

tact [tækt] N tacto *m*

tactful ['tæktfʊl] ADJ [*person, behaviour, remark, question*] diplomático, discreto; **she's very ~** ◊ **she's a very ~ person** tiene mucho tacto, es muy diplomática *or* discreta; **the ~ thing would have been to say nothing** lo diplomático hubiese sido no decir nada; **that wasn't a very ~ question** no fue una pregunta muy diplomática *or* discreta; **he maintained a ~ silence** mantuvo un discreto silencio

tactfully ['tæktfəlɪ] ADV [*suggest, point out*] con mucho tacto, discretamente; **as ~ as possible** con el mayor tacto posible, lo más diplomáticamente posible

tactfulness ['tæktfʊlnɪs] N tacto *m*, discreción *f*

tactic ['tæktɪk] N táctica *f*

tactical ['tæktɪkəl] ADJ táctico; **~ voting** votación *f* táctica

tactically ['tæktɪkəlɪ] ADV tácticamente

tactician [tæk'tɪʃən] N táctico/a *m/f*

tactics ['tæktɪks] NPL (*gen, Mil*) táctica *fsing*; **to change ~** cambiar de táctica; **delaying ~** tácticas *fpl* dilatorias; **scare ~** tácticas *fpl* para infundir miedo

tactile ['tæktaɪl] ADJ táctil

tactless ['tæktlɪs] ADJ [*person*] falto de tacto, poco diplomático; [*comment, behaviour*] indiscreto, poco diplomático; **it was a ~ remark** fue un comentario poco diplomático *or* bastante indiscreto; **how could you be so ~?** ¿cómo puedes haber tenido tan poco tacto?, ¿cómo puedes haber sido tan poco diplomático?

tactlessly ['tæktlɪslɪ] ADV con poco tacto

tactlessness ['tæktlɪsnɪs] N falta *f* de tacto

Tadjikistan [tɑ,dʒɪkɪ'stɑːn] = **Tadzhikistan**

tadpole ['tædpəʊl] N renacuajo *m*

Tadzhikistan [tɑ,dʒɪkɪ'stɑːn] N Tayikistán *m*

taffeta ['tæfɪtə] N tafetán *m*

taffrail ['tæfreɪl] N (*Naut*) (= *part of stern*) coronamiento *m*; (= *rail*) pasamano *m* de la borda

Taffy* ['tæfɪ] N (*pej*) galés *m*

taffy ['tæfɪ] N (*US*) (= *toffee*) melcocha *f*

tag [tæg] Ⓐ N 1 (= *label*) etiqueta *f*, marbete *m*; (*on shoelace*) herrete *m*; (*for identification*) chapa *f*; (= *surveillance device*) etiqueta *f* personal de control; **name ~** etiqueta *f* de identificación; *see also* **price C**
2 (= *game*) **to play ~** jugar al cogecoge *or* (*LAm*) a la pega
3 (= *cliché*) tópico *m*, dicho *m*, lugar *m* común; (= *catchword*) muletilla *f*; (= *quotation*) cita *f* trillada; (= *proverb*) refrán *m*
4 (*Ling*) (*also* ~ **question**) cláusula *f* final interrogativa
Ⓑ VT 1 (= *follow*) seguirle la pista a
2 (= *describe*) [+ *person*] poner una etiqueta a
3 [+ *criminal*] controlar electrónicamente
Ⓒ VI **to ~ after sb** seguir a algn
►**tag along** VI + ADV **we don't want your brother ~ging along** no queremos que tu hermano se nos pegue; **there was another boat ~ging along behind us** había otro barco que nos seguía
►**tag on** Ⓐ VT + ADV añadir
Ⓑ VI + ADV **to ~ on to sb** pegarse a algn

tagmeme ['tægmiːm] N tagmema *m*

tagmemics [tæg'miːmɪks] N tagmética *f*

Tagus ['teɪgəs] N Tajo *m*

Tahiti [tɑː'hiːtɪ] N Tahití *m*

tail [teɪl] Ⓐ N 1 [*of bird, horse, fish, plane*] cola *f*; [*of dog, bull, ox*] cola *f*, rabo *m*; [*of comet*] cabellera *f*, cola *f*; [*of shirt*] faldón *m*; [*of procession*] cola *f*, tramo *m* final; (= *loose end*) cabo *m*; [*of hair*] mechón *m*; ♦*IDIOMS* **to turn ~ (and flee)** huir; **he went off with his ~ between his legs** se fue con el rabo entre las piernas; **it's a case of the ~ wagging the dog** es el mundo al revés
2 **tails** (= *coat*) frac *msing*; [*of coin*] cruz *fsing*; **heads or ~s** cara o cruz; **~s you lose** si sale cruz pierdes
3 (‡) (= *buttocks*) trasero *m*; **to work one's ~ off** sudar tinta*
4 (= *person following*) sombra *f*; **to put a ~ on sb** hacer seguir a algn
5 (*US***) (= *girls*) tipas* *fpl*, tías *fpl* (*Sp**); **a piece of ~** una tipa*, una tía (*Sp**)
Ⓑ VT (= *follow*) seguirle la pista a; *see also* **top[1] D4**
Ⓒ CPD ► **tail end** N [*of procession, queue*] cola *f*, tramo *m* final; (*fig*) [*of party, storm*] final *m*; **at the ~ end of the summer** en los últimos días del verano
►**tail away** VI + ADV [*sound*] ir apagándose; **his voice ~ed away** su voz se fue desvaneciendo *or* apagando; **after that the book ~s away** después de eso el libro pierde interés
►**tail back** VI + ADV **the traffic ~ed back to the bridge** la cola de coches se extendía atrás hasta el puente
►**tail off** VI + ADV 1 [*production, demand*] disminuir; **business has ~ed off lately** el negocio ha decaído *or* empeorado últimamente; *see also* **tail-off**
2 [*voice, sound*] ir apagándose; **his voice ~ed off** su voz se fue desvaneciendo *or* apagando

tailback ['teɪlbæk] N caravana *f*, cola *f*

tailboard ['teɪlbɔːd] = **tailgate**

tailcoat ['teɪlkəʊt] N frac *m*

-tailed [teɪld] ADJ (*ending in compounds*) con rabo ...; **long-tailed** con rabo largo, rabilargo

tailgate ['teɪlgeɪt] Ⓐ N (*Aut*) puerta *f* trasera
Ⓑ VT ir a rebufo de
Ⓒ VI ir a rebufo

tail-gunner ['teɪl,gʌnəʳ] N artillero *m* de cola

tail-lamp ['teɪllæmp] = **tail-light**

tailless ['teɪllɪs] ADJ sin rabo

tail-light ['teɪllaɪt] N (*US*) piloto *m*, luz *f* trasera, calavera *f* (*Mex*)

tail-off ['teɪlɒf] N disminución *f* (paulatina)

tailor ['teɪləʳ] Ⓐ N sastre *m*; **~'s (shop)** sastrería *f*
Ⓑ VT [+ *suit*] confeccionar, hacer; (*fig*) adaptar; **a well-~ed suit** un traje bien hecho, un traje que entalla bien
Ⓒ CPD ► **tailor's chalk** N jabón *m* de sastre
► **tailor's dummy** N maniquí *m*

tailored ['teɪləd] ADJ (= *fitted*) [*shirt, jacket*] entallado; (= *tailor-made*) [*suit*] hecho a (la) medida

tailoring ['teɪlərɪŋ] N (= *craft*) sastrería *f*; (= *cut*) corte *m*, hechura *f*

tailor-made ['teɪləmeɪd] ADJ 1 [*suit*] hecho a (la) medida
2 (*fig*) (= *customized*) [*computer program*] hecho según los requisitos del usuario; **it's ~ for you** te viene al pelo; **the part could have been ~ for her** (*Theat*) parece que el papel se ha escrito para ella

tailpiece ['teɪlpiːs] N [*of violin*] cordal *m*; (= *addition*) apéndice *m*, añadidura *f*

tailpipe ['teɪlpaɪp] N (*US*) tubo *m* de escape

tailplane ['teɪlpleɪn] N (*Aer*) plano *m* de cola

tailskid ['teɪlskɪd] N patín *m* de cola

tailspin ['teɪlspɪn] N (*Aer*) barrena *f*; **the market went into a ~** (*St Ex*) el mercado cayó en picado *or* (*LAm*) picada

tailwheel ['teɪl'wiːl] N rueda *f* de cola

tailwind ['teɪlwɪnd] N viento *m* de cola

taint [teɪnt] Ⓐ N (*liter*) mancha *f*, mácula *f* (*liter*); **the ~ of sin** la mancha del pecado
Ⓑ VT 1 (= *spoil*) [+ *food, medicine*] contaminar
2 (*fig*) [+ *reputation*] mancillar; **the elections have been ~ed by corruption** las elecciones se han visto empañadas *or* salpicadas por la corrupción

tainted ['teɪntɪd] ADJ 1 (= *contaminated*) [*food, air, blood, medicine*] contaminado; **her breath was ~ with alcohol** su aliento estaba corrompido por el alcohol
2 (= *tarnished*) [*reputation*] mancillado; **the issue is ~ with racism** el tema está contaminado de racismo

Taiwan [,taɪ'wɑːn] N Taiwán *m*

Taiwanese [,taɪwə'niːz] Ⓐ ADJ taiwanés
Ⓑ N taiwanés/esa *m/f*

take [teɪk] (*vb: pt* **took**, *pp* **taken**) Ⓐ VT 1 (= *remove*) llevarse; (= *steal*) robar, llevarse; **who took my beer?** ¿quién se ha llevado mi cerveza?; **someone's ~n my handbag** alguien se ha llevado mi bolso, alguien me ha robado el bolso; **I picked up the letter but he took it from me** cogí la carta pero él me la quitó; **to ~ a book from a shelf** sacar un libro de un estante; **to ~ a passage from an author** tomar un pasaje de un autor; **~ 37 from 121** resta 37 de 121

2 (= *take hold of, seize*) tomar, coger, agarrar (*LAm*); **she took the spade and started digging** cogió la pala y empezó a excavar; **I took him by the scruff of the neck** le cogí por el pescuezo; **let me ~ your case/coat** permíteme tu maleta/abrigo; **I'll ~ the blue one, please** me llevaré el azul; **to ~ sb's arm** tomar del brazo a algn; **to ~ sb in one's arms** abrazar a algn; **the devil ~ it!** ¡maldición!†; **~ five!*** ¡hagan una pausa!, ¡descansen un rato!; **~ your partners for a waltz** saquen a su pareja a bailar un vals; **to ~ sb into partnership** tomar a algn como socio; **please ~ a seat** tome asiento, por favor; **is this seat ~n?** ¿está ocupado este asiento?; **it took me by surprise** me cogió desprevenido, me pilló *or* agarró desprevenido (*LAm*); **~ ten!** (*US**) ¡hagan una pausa!, ¡descansen un rato!; **to ~ a wife**† casarse, contraer matrimonio

3 (= *lead, transport*) llevar; **to ~ sth to sb** llevar algo a algn; **I took her some flowers** le llevé unas flores; **her work took her to Bonn** su trabajó la destinó *or* llevó a Bonn; **we took her to the doctor** la llevamos al médico; **he took me home in his car** me llevó a casa en su coche; **they took me over the factory** me mostraron la fábrica, me acompañaron en una visita a la fábrica; **he took his suitcase upstairs** subió su maleta; **to ~ sb for a walk** llevar a algn de paseo; **it took us out of our way** nos hizo desviarnos

4 [+ *bus, taxi*] (= *travel by*) ir en; (*at specified time*) coger, tomar (*esp LAm*); [+ *road, short cut*] ir por; **I took a taxi because I was late** fui en taxi porque llegaba tarde; **we decided to ~ the train** decidimos ir en tren; **we took the five o'clock train** cogimos *or* tomamos el tren de las cinco; **~ the first on the right** vaya por *or* tome la primera calle a la derecha; **we took the wrong road** nos equivocamos de camino

5 (= *capture*) [+ *person*] coger, agarrar (*LAm*); [+ *town, city*] tomar; (*Chess*) comer; **to ~ sb hostage** tomar *or* (*LAm*) agarrar a algn como rehén; **to ~ sb prisoner** tomar preso a algn

6 (= *obtain, win*) [+ *prize*] ganar, llevarse; [+ *1st place*] conseguir, obtener; [+ *trick*] ganar, hacer; **we took £500 today** (*Brit Comm*) hoy hemos ganado 500 libras

7 (= *accept, receive*) [+ *money*] aceptar; [+ *advice*] seguir; [+ *news, blow*] tomar, recibir; [+ *responsibility*] asumir; [+ *bet*] aceptar, hacer; **~ my advice, tell her the truth** sigue mi consejo *or* hazme caso y dile la verdad; **he took the ball full in the chest** el balón le dio de lleno en el pecho; **what will you ~ for it?** ¿cuál es tu mejor precio?; **he took it badly** le afectó mucho; **London took a battering in 1941** Londres recibió una paliza en 1941, Londres sufrió terriblemente en 1941; **will you ~ a cheque?** ¿aceptaría un cheque?; **he can certainly ~ his drink** tiene buen aguante para la bebida; **you must ~ us as you find us** nos vas a tener que aceptar tal cual; **~ it from me!** ¡escucha lo que te digo!; **you can ~ it from me that ...** puedes tener la seguridad de que ...; **losing is hard to ~** es difícil aceptar la derrota; **it's £50, ~ it or leave it!** son 50 libras, lo toma o lo deja; **whisky? I can ~ it or leave it** ¿el whisky? ni me va ni me viene; **I won't ~ no for an answer** no hay pero que valga; **I ~ your point** entiendo lo que dices; **he took a lot of punishment** (*fig*) le dieron muy duro; **~ that!** ¡toma!

8 (= *rent*) alquilar, tomar; (= *buy regularly*) [+ *newspaper*] comprar, leer; **we shall ~ a house for the summer** alquilaremos una casa para el verano

9 (= *have room or capacity for*) tener cabida para; (= *support weight of*) aguantar; **a car that ~s five passengers** un coche con cabida para *or* donde caben cinco personas; **can you ~ two more?** ¿puedes llevar dos más?, ¿caben otros dos?; **it won't ~ any more** no cabe(n) más; **it ~s weights up to eight tons** soporta pesos hasta de ocho toneladas

10 (= *wear*) [+ *clothes size*] gastar, usar (*LAm*); [+ *shoe size*] calzar; **what size do you ~?** (*clothes*) ¿qué talla usas?; (*shoes*) ¿qué número calzas?

11 (= *call for, require*) necesitar, requerir; **it took three policemen to hold him down** se necesitaron tres policías para sujetarlo; **it ~s a lot of courage** exige *or* requiere gran valor; **it ~s a brave man to do that** hace falta que un hombre tenga mucho valor para hacer eso; **that will ~ some explaining** a ver cómo explicas eso; **it ~s two to make a quarrel** uno solo no puede reñir; **she's got what it ~s** tiene lo que hace falta

12 (*of time*) **it ~s an hour to get there** se tarda una hora en llegar; **a letter ~s four days to get there** una carta tarda cuatro días en llegar allá; **it will only ~ me five minutes** sólo tardo cinco minutos; **the job will ~ a week** el trabajo llevará una semana; **I'll just iron this, it won't ~ long** voy a planchar esto, no tardaré *or* no me llevará mucho tiempo; **however long it ~s** el tiempo que sea; **it ~s time** lleva tiempo; **~ your time!** ¡despacio!

13 (= *conduct*) [+ *meeting, church service*] presidir; (= *teach*) [+ *course, class*] enseñar; [+ *pupils*] tomar; (= *study*) [+ *course*] hacer; [+ *subject*] dar, estudiar; (= *undergo*) [+ *exam, test*] presentarse a, pasar; **what are you taking next year?** ¿qué vas a hacer *or* estudiar el año que viene?; **the teacher who took us for economics** el profesor que nos daba clase de económicas; **he is not taking any more pupils at the moment** en este momento no está cogiendo a más estudiantes; **to ~ a degree in** licenciarse en; **to ~ (holy) orders** ordenarse de sacerdote

14 (= *record*) [+ *sb's name, address*] anotar, apuntar; [+ *measurements*] tomar; **to ~ notes** tomar apuntes

15 (= *understand, assume*) **I ~ it that ...** supongo que ..., me imagino que ...; **am I to ~ it that you refused?** ¿he de suponer que te negaste?; **I ~ her to be about 30** supongo que tiene unos 30 años; **how old do you ~ him to be?** ¿cuántos años le das?; **I took him for a doctor** lo tenía por médico, creí que era médico; **what do you ~ me for?** ¿por quién me has tomado?; **I don't quite know how to ~ that** no sé muy bien cómo tomarme eso

16 (= *consider*) [+ *case, example*] tomar; **now ~ Ireland, for example** tomemos, por ejemplo, el caso de Irlanda, pongamos como ejemplo Irlanda; **let us ~ the example of a family with three children** tomemos el ejemplo de una familia con tres hijos; **~ John, he never complains** por ejemplo John, él nunca se queja; **taking one thing with another ...** considerándolo todo junto ..., considerándolo en conjunto ...

17 (= *put up with, endure*) [+ *treatment, climate*] aguantar, soportar; **we can ~ it** lo aguantamos *or* soportamos todo; **I can't ~ any more!** ¡no aguanto más!, ¡no soporto más!; **I won't ~ any nonsense!** ¡no quiero oír más tonterías!

18 (= *eat*) comer; (= *drink*) tomar; **will you ~ sth before you go?** ¿quieres tomar algo antes de irte?; **"to be taken three times a day"** "a tomar tres veces al día"; **"not to be taken (internally)"** "para uso externo"; **to ~ drugs** (*narcotics*) tomar drogas; **he took no food for four days** estuvo cuatro días sin comer; **don't forget to ~ your medicine** no te olvides de tomar la medicina; **he ~s sugar in his tea** toma *or* pone azúcar en el té; **to ~ a tablet** tomar una pastilla; **to ~ tea (with sb)**† tomar té (con algn)

19 (= *negotiate*) [+ *bend*] tomar; [+ *fence*] saltar, saltar por encima de

20 (= *acquire*) **to ~ against sb** ◊ **~ a dislike to sb** tomar antipatía a algn; **to ~ fright** asustarse (**at** de); **to be ~n ill** ponerse enfermo, enfermar; **he took great pleasure in teasing her** se regodeaba tomándole el pelo; **I do not ~ any satisfaction in knowing that ...** no experimento satisfacción alguna sabiendo que ...

21 (*Ling*) [+ *case*] regir; **that verb ~s the dative** ese verbo rige el dativo

22 **to be ~n with sth/sb** (= *attracted*): **he's very ~n with her** le gusta mucho; **I'm not at all ~n with the idea** la idea no me gusta nada *or* no me hace gracia

23 († *liter*) (= *have sexual intercourse with*) tener relaciones sexuales con

24 (*as function verb*) [+ *decision, holiday*] tomar; [+ *step, walk*] dar; [+ *trip*] hacer; [+ *opportunity*] aprovechar; **to ~ a bath** bañarse; **to ~ a photograph** sacar una fotografía

Ⓑ VI 1 (= *be effective*) [*dye*] coger, agarrar (*LAm*); [*vaccination, fire*] prender; [*glue*] pegar

2 (*Bot*) [*cutting*] arraigar

3 (= *receive*) **she's all ~, ~, ~** ella mucho dame, dame, pero luego no da nada; *see also* **give**

Ⓒ N 1 (*Cine*) toma *f*

2 (= *takings*) ingresos *mpl*; (= *proceeds*) recaudación *f*; (*US Comm*) caja *f*, ventas *fpl* del día

3 ✦**IDIOM** **to be on the ~** (*US**) estar dispuesto a dejarse sobornar

4 (= *share*) parte *f*; (= *commission*) comisión *f*, tajada* *f*

5 (*) (= *opinion*) opinión *f*; **what's your ~ on the new government?** ¿qué piensas de *or* qué opinión te merece el nuevo gobierno?

►**take aback** VT + ADV *see* **aback**

►**take after** VI + PREP (*in looks*) parecerse a, salir a

►**take along** VT + ADV [+ *person, thing*] llevar (consigo)

►**take apart** Ⓐ VT + ADV 1 (= *dismantle*) [+ *clock, machine*] desmontar, desarmar

2 (*) (= *destroy*) [+ *room, premises*] destrozar; (= *defeat*) [+ *opponent, team*] dar una paliza a*; **I'll ~ him apart!*** ¡le rompo la cara!

3 (= *search*) **the police took the place apart** la policía registró el local de arriba abajo

Ⓑ VI + ADV **it ~s apart easily** se desmonta fácilmente

►**take aside** VT + ADV llevar aparte, llevar a un lado

►**take away** Ⓐ VT + ADV 1 (= *remove*) [+ *person, thing*] llevarse; [+ *privilege*] quitar; (= *carry away, transport*) llevar; **she took her children away from the school** sacó a los niños del colegio; **"not to be taken away"** (*on book*) "para consulta en sala"

2 (= *subtract*) restar; **~ 9 away from 12** reste 9 de 12; **7 ~ away 4 is 3** 7 menos 4 son 3

Ⓑ VI + ADV **to ~ away from sth: this does not ~ away from their achievement** esto no quita mérito *or* resta valor a su éxito; **the argument took away from the joy of the occasion** la discusión aguó la ocasión; **putting butter on it ~s away from the taste of the bread itself** añadiendo mantequilla se estropea lo que es el sabor del pan

►**take back** VT + ADV [1] (= *return*) [+ *book, goods*] devolver; [+ *person*] llevar (de vuelta); **can you ~ him back home?** ¿le puedes acompañar a su casa?
[2] (= *accept back*) [+ *purchase, gift*] aceptar la devolución de; [+ *one's wife, husband*] aceptar que vuelva; **the company took him back** la compañía volvió a emplearlo *or* lo restituyó a su puesto
[3] (= *retract*) [+ *statement, words*] retirar; **she took back everything she had said about him** retiró todo lo que había dicho de él; **I ~ it all back!** ¡retiro lo dicho!; **to ~ back one's promise** retirar su promesa
[4] (= *get back, reclaim*) [+ *territory*] retomar
[5] (*fig*) (= *transport*) **it ~s me back to my childhood** me recuerda a mi niñez; **it ~s you back, doesn't it?** ¡cuántos recuerdos (de los buenos tiempos)!

►**take down** VT + ADV [1] (*off shelf etc*) bajar; [+ *decorations, curtains*] quitar; [+ *picture*] descolgar, bajar; [+ *poster*] despegar; [+ *trousers*] bajar; *see also* **peg A1**
[2] (= *dismantle*) [+ *scaffolding*] desmantelar, desmontar; [+ *building*] derribar
[3] (= *write down*) apuntar

►**take from** VT + PREP = **take away from**; *see* **take away**

►**take in** VT + ADV [1] (= *bring in*) [+ *person*] hacer entrar; [+ *chairs, toys*] recoger, meter para dentro; [+ *harvest*] recoger; [+ *sail*] desmontar
[2] (= *give home to*) [+ *orphan, stray dog*] acoger, recoger; **to ~ in lodgers** alquilar habitaciones
[3] (= *receive*) [+ *laundry, sewing*] coger para hacer en casa
[4] [+ *skirt, dress, waistband*] achicar
[5] (= *include, cover*) [+ *possibilities, cases*] abarcar, incluir; **we took in Florence on the way** pasamos por Florencia en el camino; **to ~ in a movie*** ir al cine
[6] (= *grasp, understand*) [+ *situation*] comprender; [+ *impressions*] asimilar; (*visually*) [+ *surroundings*] captar; **that child ~s everything in** a esa criatura no se le escapa nada; **it's so incredible you can't quite ~ it in** es tan increíble que es difícil de asimilar; **he took the situation in at a glance** comprendió la situación con una sola mirada
[7] (= *deceive, cheat*) engañar; **to be ~n in by appearances** dejarse engañar por las apariencias

►**take off** Ⓐ VT + ADV [1] (= *remove*) [+ *lid, wrapping, label, stain*] quitar; [+ *clothes*] quitarse, sacarse (*LAm*); [+ *limb*] amputar; [+ *train*] cancelar; [+ *item from menu*] quitar; **the five o'clock train has been ~n off** han cancelado el tren de las cinco
[2] (= *deduct*) (*from bill, price*) descontar; **she took 50p off** descontó *or* hizo un descuento de 50 peniques
[3] (= *lead away*) [+ *person, object*] llevarse; **they took him off to lunch** se lo llevaron a comer; **she was ~n off to hospital** la llevaron al hospital; **to ~ o.s. off** irse, largarse*
[4] (= *not work*) **he took the day off work** se tomó el día libre; **I'm going to ~ two weeks off at Christmas** me voy a tomar dos semanas de vacaciones en Navidad; **he has to work weekends but ~s time off in lieu** tiene que trabajar los fines de semana pero le dan días libres a cambio
[5] (= *imitate*) imitar
Ⓑ VI + ADV [1] [*plane, passengers*] despegar, decolar (*LAm*) (**for** con rumbo a); [*high jumper*] saltar
[2] (= *succeed*) empezar a tener éxito; **the idea never really took off** la idea no llegó a cuajar; **the style really took off among young people** el estilo se puso muy de moda entre los jóvenes
Ⓒ VT + PREP [1] (= *remove*) quitar, sacar (*LAm*); **they took two names off the list** quitaron *or* tacharon dos nombres de la lista; **she's been ~n off the case** le han hecho dejar el caso; **to ~ sth off sb*** quitar algo a algn; **~ your hands off me!** ¡no me toques!; **her new hairstyle ~s ten years off her** ese peinado nuevo le quita diez años de encima
[2] (= *deduct*) (*from bill, price*) descontar; **he took £5 off the price** descontó 5 libras del precio

►**take on** Ⓐ VT + ADV [1] [+ *work*] aceptar, encargarse de; [+ *responsibility, risk*] asumir; [+ *bet, challenge*] aceptar; [+ *challenger*] enfrentarse a, aceptar el reto de; **when she invited Hayley to come and stay for a week she took on more than she bargained for** cuando invitó a Hayley a quedarse una semana, no sabía lo que le esperaba; **I felt I could ~ on the whole world** sentía que me podía comer el mundo
[2] [+ *worker*] contratar; [+ *passengers*] recoger; [+ *cargo*] cargar
[3] (= *assume*) [+ *form, qualities*] asumir; **her face took on a wistful expression** quedó cariacontecida
Ⓑ VI + ADV [1] (†*) (= *become upset*) **don't ~ on so!** ¡no te pongas así!, ¡no te agites!
[2] (= *become popular*) [*fashion*] hacerse muy popular; [*song*] hacerse muy popular, ponerse de moda

►**take out** VT + ADV [1] (= *bring, carry out*) sacar; **he took the dog out for a walk** sacó el perro a pasear; **can I ~ you out to lunch/the cinema?** ¿le puedo invitar a almorzar/al cine?
[2] (= *remove*) (*gen*) sacar; [+ *tooth*] extraer, sacar; [+ *stain*] quitar, limpiar; (*Mil*) [+ *target, enemy position*] eliminar
[3] (= *procure*) [+ *patent, licence*] obtener; [+ *insurance policy*] sacar; **to ~ out insurance** hacerse un seguro
[4] **to ~ it out on sb: when he got the sack he took it out on his wife** cuando le despidieron del trabajo, se desquitó con su mujer; **don't ~ it out on me!** ¡no te desquites conmigo!
[5] **to ~ out of: seeing that film took me out of myself** esa película me hizo olvidar mis propios problemas; **it ~s it out of you** te deja hecho pedazos*

►**take over** Ⓐ VT + ADV [1] (= *assume*) [+ *responsibility*] asumir; (= *become responsible for*) [+ *job*] encargarse de; **he took over the business from his father** se hizo cargo del negocio cuando lo dejó su padre; **to ~ over sb's job** sustituir a algn
[2] (= *take control of*) [+ *building, country*] tomar; (*Fin*) [+ *company*] adquirir; **the tourists have ~n over the beaches** los turistas han invadido *or* acaparado las playas
Ⓑ VI + ADV [1] (= *take charge*) [*new president, official*] entrar en funciones; (*Aut*) [*driver*] tomar el volante; (*Aer*) [*pilot*] tomar los mandos; **when the new government ~s over** cuando el nuevo gobierno entre en poder; **to ~ over from sb** (*in job*) (*temporarily*) hacer de suplente para algn; (*permanently*) reemplazar a algn; **they want me to ~ over as editor when Evans leaves** quieren que reemplace a Evans como editor cuando éste marche; **can you ~ over for a few minutes, while I go to the Post Office?** ¿puedes cubrirme unos minutos mientras voy a Correos?
[2] (= *seize control*) [*dictator, political party*] tomar el poder
[3] (= *become more important*) **then panic took over** luego cundió el pánico; **cars gradually took over from horses** poco a poco el automóvil fue sustituyendo al caballo

►**take to** VI + PREP [1] (= *form liking for*) [+ *person*] tomar cariño a algn, encariñarse con algn; [+ *sport*] aficionarse a; [+ *surroundings, idea*] hacerse a; **she didn't ~ kindly to the idea** no le gustó *or* no le hizo gracia la idea; **they took to one another on the spot** se congeniaron al instante; **I didn't much ~ to him** no me resultó simpático
[2] (= *form habit of*) **to ~ to doing sth: she took to inviting them round every Sunday** empezó a invitarles a casa todos los domingos; **she took to telling everyone that ...** le dio por contar a todos que ...
[3] (= *escape to*) **to ~ to one's bed** guardar cama; **to ~ to drink** darse a la bebida; *see also* **heel[1]**, **hill**, **wood**

►**take up** Ⓐ VT + ADV [1] (= *raise, lift*) [+ *object from ground*] levantar, recoger; [+ *carpet, floorboards*] quitar; [+ *road*] levantar; [+ *dress, hem*] acortar; *see also* **arm[2]**, **slack**
[2] (= *lead, carry upstairs*) subir
[3] (= *pick up*) [+ *pen, one's work*] coger, agarrar (*LAm*); [+ *passengers*] recoger
[4] (= *continue*) [+ *story*] continuar con
[5] (= *occupy*) [+ *time, attention*] ocupar; [+ *space*] llenar, ocupar; **it ~s up a lot of his time** le dedica mucho tiempo; **he's very ~n up with his work** está absorto en el trabajo; **he's very ~n up with her** está ocupado con ella; *see also* **post[3]**, **residence**
[6] (= *absorb*) [+ *liquid*] absorber
[7] (= *raise question of*) [+ *matter, point*] retomar, volver sobre; **I shall ~ the matter up with the manager** hablaré del asunto con el gerente
[8] (= *take issue with*) **I feel I must ~ you up on that** siento que debo contestar a lo que has dicho
[9] (= *start*) [+ *hobby, sport*] dedicarse a; [+ *career*] emprender
[10] (= *accept*) [+ *offer, challenge*] aceptar; **I'll ~ you up on your offer** te acepto la oferta; **I'll ~ you up on that some day** algún día recordaré lo que has dicho
[11] (= *adopt*) [+ *cause*] apoyar; [+ *case*] ocuparse de; [+ *person*] adoptar
Ⓑ VI + ADV **to ~ up with sb** (*as friend*) hacerse amigo de algn; (*romantically*) juntarse con algn; **he took up with a woman half his wife's age** se juntó con una mujer que tenía la mitad de la edad de su mujer

►**take upon** VT + PREP **to ~ sth upon o.s.** tomar algo sobre sí; **to ~ it upon o.s. to do sth** atreverse a hacer algo

takeaway ['teɪkəweɪ] Ⓐ N (= *restaurant*) tienda *f* de comida para llevar; (= *meal*) comida *f* para llevar; **a Chinese ~** una comida china para llevar
Ⓑ CPD [*food*] para llevar

take-home pay [ˌteɪkhəʊm'peɪ] N sueldo *m* neto, sueldo *m* líquido

taken ['teɪkən] PP *of* **take**

takeoff ['teɪkɒf] N [1] (*Aer, Econ*) despegue *m*

[2] (= *imitation*) imitación *f*, parodia *f*
[3] (*Mech*) **power ~** toma *f* de fuerza

TAKE

Both **tardar** and **llevar** can be used to translate **take** with *time*.

• Use **tardar** (**en** + **INFINITIVE**) to describe how long someone or something will take to do something. The subject of **tardar** is the person or thing that has to complete the activity or undergo the process:

How long do letters take to get to Spain?
¿Cuánto (tiempo) tardan las cartas en llegar a España?
How much longer will it take you to do it?
¿Cuánto más vas a tardar en hacerlo?
It'll take us three hours to get to Douglas if we walk
Tardaremos tres horas en llegar a Douglas si vamos andando

• Use **llevar** to describe how long an activity, task or process takes to complete. The subject of **llevar** is the activity or task:

The tests will take at least a month
Las pruebas llevarán por lo menos un mes
How long will it take?
¿Cuánto tiempo llevará?

• Compare the different focus in the alternative translations of the following example:

It'll take me two more days to finish this job
Me llevará dos días más terminar este trabajo, Tardaré dos días más en terminar este trabajo

For further uses and examples, see main entry.

takeover ['teɪk,əʊvə^r] Ⓐ N [1] (*Comm*) [*of company*] adquisición *f*, compra *f*
[2] (*Pol*) [*of new government*] toma *f* de posesión; [*of new premier*] entrada *f* en funciones
[3] (*Mil*) (= *coup*) toma *f* del poder; **military ~** golpe *m* de estado
Ⓑ CPD ► **takeover bid** N oferta *f* pública de adquisición (de acciones), OPA *f*

taker ['teɪkə^r] N **at £5 there were no ~s** a un precio de 5 libras nadie se ofreció a comprarlo; **the challenge found no ~s** no hubo nadie que quisiera aceptar el desafío

take-up ['teɪkʌp] N (*Brit*) **this benefit has a low ~ rate** muy poca gente reclama esta prestación; **there was an enthusiastic public ~ of shares in privatized companies** hubo muchísima demanda para comprar acciones en las empresas privatizadas

taking ['teɪkɪŋ] Ⓐ ADJ (= *attractive*) atractivo
Ⓑ N (*Mil*) [*of town*] toma *f*, conquista *f*; [*of hostages*] toma *f*; **the job's yours for the ~** el trabajo es tuyo si lo quieres; **the match was theirs for the ~** tenían el partido prácticamente ganado

takings ['teɪkɪŋz] (*Brit*) NPL (*Comm*) recaudación *fsing*; (*at show*) taquilla *fsing*, entrada *fsing*; **this year's ~ were only half last year's** la recaudación de este año ha sido sólo la mitad que la del año pasado

talc [tælk] N talco *m*

talcum powder ['tælkəm,paʊdə^r] N polvos *mpl* de talco, talco *m*

tale [teɪl] N [1] (= *story*) cuento *m*, historia *f*; **he told us the ~ of his adventures** nos contó sus aventuras; **he had quite a ~ to tell** vaya historia que tenía para contar; **it tells its own ~** habla por sí solo; **"Tales of King Arthur"** "Leyendas *fpl* del Rey Arturo"; **sound the alarm, or we shan't live to tell the ~** toca el timbre, o no salimos vivos de esto, toca el timbre, o no lo contamos; **few people get caught in an avalanche and live to tell the ~** muy poca gente sobrevive una avalancha; *see also* **fairy**, **hang B1**, **woe**
[2] (= *fabrication*) cuento *m*, patraña *f*; ✦**IDIOM to tell ~s (out of school)** (= *inform*) chivarse, chismear; (= *fib*) contar cuentos; *see also* **old C**

talebearer ['teɪl,beərə^r] N soplón/ona *m/f*, chismoso/a *m/f*

talent ['tælənt] Ⓐ N [1] (= *natural ability*) talento *m* (**for** para); **a writer of great ~** un escritor de muchísimo talento; **to have a ~ for sth: he's got a real ~ for languages** tiene verdadera facilidad para los idiomas; **she had a ~ for making people laugh** tenía el don de saber hacer reír a la gente
[2] (= *talented people*) gente *f* capaz, gente *f* de talento; (= *talented person*) talento *m*; **he encourages young ~** promociona a los jovenes talentos; **he watches for ~ at away matches** busca jugadores de talento en los partidos fuera de casa
[3] (*) (= *opposite sex*) tíos/as *mpl/fpl* buenos/as*, material*; **there's not much ~ here tonight** aquí no hay mucho donde escoger esta noche, aquí no hay material*; **to eye up the ~** pasar revista a lo que se ofrece*, comprobar el material*
[4] (*Hist*) (= *coin, weight*) talento *m*
Ⓑ CPD ► **talent contest** N concurso *m* de talentos ► **talent scout**, **talent spotter** N cazatalentos *mf inv*

talented ['tæləntɪd] ADJ talentoso, de talento

taletelling ['teɪl,telɪŋ] N chismorreo *m*

Taliban ['tælɪbæn] Ⓐ NPL **the ~** los talibanes
Ⓑ ADJ talibán/ana

talisman ['tælɪzmən] N (*pl* **talismans**) talismán *m*

talk [tɔːk] Ⓐ N [1] (= *conversation*) conversación *f*, charla *f*, plática *f* (*Mex*); **I enjoyed our (little) ~** disfruté de nuestra (pequeña) conversación *or* charla; **to have a ~ (with sb)** hablar (con algn), tener una conversación (con algn); **I think it's time we had a ~** creo que es hora de que hablemos (seriamente); **we had a long ~ over supper** hablamos largo y tendido durante la cena
[2] (= *lecture*) charla *f*; **to give a ~ (on sth)** dar una charla (sobre algo)
[3] **talks** (= *negotiations*) (*gen*) conversaciones *fpl*, pláticas *fpl* (*Mex*); (*with defined aim*) negociaciones *fpl*; **the foreign secretary will be holding ~s with his French counterpart** el ministro de asuntos exteriores mantendrá conversaciones con su homólogo francés
[4] (= *rumours*) rumores *mpl*; **there is some ~ of his resigning** se habla de *or* corren rumores sobre su posible dimisión; **there's been a lot of ~ about you two** se ha hablado mucho de vosotros dos, están circulando muchos rumores acerca de vosotros dos; **any ~ of divorce is just wild speculation** cualquier rumor acerca de un divorcio no es más que pura especulación; ✦**IDIOM to be the ~ of the town** ser la comidilla de la ciudad, estar en boca de todos
[5] (= *remarks*) **that's the kind of ~ we could do without** esos comentarios sobran; **careless ~ costs lives** las palabras dichas a la ligera cuestan vidas; *see also* **small D**
[6] (= *speech, language*) lenguaje *m*; **children's ~** lenguaje *m* infantil *or* de niños
[7] (= *hot air*) (*pej*) palabrería *f*, cuento *m*; **it's just ~** es pura palabrería, es todo cuento; **he'll never give up smoking, he's all ~** nunca va a dejar de fumar, mucho hablar pero luego nada *or* no es más que un cuentista; **he's all ~ and no action** ¿ése? ¡mucho ruido y pocas nueces!, habla mucho pero no hace nada

Ⓑ VI [1] (= *speak*) hablar; **she can't ~ yet** aún no sabe hablar; **can you ~ a little more slowly?** ¿podría hablar un poquito más despacio?; **a doll that can ~** una muñeca que habla; **it's easy for you to ~** para ti es fácil hablar; **he ~s too much** habla demasiado; **she never stops ~ing** no deja *or* para de hablar; **I wasn't ~ing about you** no hablaba de ti; **he doesn't know what he's ~ing about** no sabe de qué habla; **everyone's ~ing about him** anda en boca de todos; **it's the most ~ed-about film this year** es la película más comentada del año; **we're ~ing about a potentially enormous loss here** estamos hablando de una pérdida potencialmente enorme; **~ about rich! he's absolutely loaded*** ¡vaya que si es rico! ¡está forrado!*; **~ about a stroke of luck!*** ¡qué suerte!; **to ~ big** (*fig*) darse importancia, fanfarronear; **"and she's so untidy around the house" — "you can ~! *or* look who's ~ing!"** —y además, es tan desordenada en casa —¡mira quién habla! *or* —¡mira quién fue a hablar!; **now you're ~ing!** ¡así se habla!; **~ing of films, have you seen ...?** hablando de películas, ¿has visto ...?; **don't ~ to your mother like that!** ¡no le hables así a tu madre!; **I'm not ~ing to him any more** ya no me hablo con él; **the way you ~ you'd think this was all my fault!** ¡oyéndote hablar cualquiera diría que toda la culpa es mía!; ✦**IDIOMS money ~s** poderoso caballero es don dinero, el dinero todo lo puede; **~ of the devil!** ¡hablando del rey de Roma...!; **to ~ through one's hat** decir tonterías; *see also* **dirty B2**
[2] (= *converse*) hablar, platicar (*Mex*) (**to** con); **we ~ed all night** nos pasamos toda la noche hablando; **I was only ~ing to her last week** si justo estuve hablando con ella la semana pasada; **stop ~ing!** ¡callaos!, ¡dejad de hablar!; **she had no one to ~ to** no tenía con quién hablar; **who were you ~ing to on the phone just now?** ¿con quién hablabas (por teléfono) ahora mismo?; **were you ~ing to me?** ¿me hablas a mí?; **to ~ to o.s.** hablar solo; **to ~ about sth/sb** hablar de algo/algn; **they ~ed about old times** hablaron de los viejos tiempos; **I don't want to ~ about it** no quiero hablar de ello; **the sort of person who ~s at you rather than to you** el tipo de persona que habla mucho pero no escucha nada; **to get ~ing** ponerse a hablar, entablar conversación; **to keep sb ~ing** dar charla a algn para entretenerlo, entretener a algn hablando; **it was easy to ~ with her** era fácil hablar con ella
[3] (= *have discussion*) hablar, hablar seriamente; **we really need to ~** tenemos que hablar (seriamente); **the two sides need to sit down and ~** las dos partes necesitan reunirse para hablar (seriamente); **GA and Fox Ltd might be ~ing** puede que GA y Fox Ltd estén manteniendo negociaciones; **to ~ (to sb) about sth** discutir algo (con algn); **the two companies are ~ing about a possible merger** las dos empresas están discutiendo *or* negociando una posible fusión
[4] (= *gossip*) hablar (**about** de); **people will ~** la gente hablará *or* murmurará
[5] (= *lecture*) dar una charla, hablar (**about, on** de, sobre); **he'll be ~ing on his life in India** dará una charla sobre su vida en la India, hablará de *or* sobre su vida en la India
[6] (= *reveal information*) hablar; **we have ways of making you ~** sabemos cómo hacerle hablar

Ⓒ VT [1] (= *speak*) hablar; **they were ~ing Arabic** hablaban (en) árabe; **we're ~ing big money here*** estamos hablando de mucho dinero; **she ~ed herself hoarse** habló tanto que se quedó afónica; **to ~ nonsense** ◊ **~ rubbish** decir tonterías; **to ~ sense** hablar con juicio *or* sensatez; ✦*IDIOM* **to ~ the hind legs off a donkey** hablar por los codos*

[2] (= *discuss*) hablar de; **we were ~ing politics/business** hablábamos de política/negocios; ✦*IDIOM* **to ~ shop** hablar del trabajo

[3] (= *persuade*) **to ~ sb into doing sth** convencer a algn de que haga algo; **I was a fool to have let her ~ me into it** fui idiota por dejarle convencerme; **ok! you've ~ed me into it** ¡vale! me has convencido; **I ~ed myself into believing it** yo solo me terminé convenciendo de que era cierto; **to ~ sb out of doing sth** convencer a algn de que no haga algo, disuadir a algn de que haga algo; **we managed to ~ him out of it** conseguimos convencerle de que no lo hiciera, conseguimos disuadirle de que lo hiciera; **he performed so badly in the interview he ~ed himself out of the job** habló tan mal en la entrevista que consiguió que no le dieran el puesto; **he managed to ~ his way out of a prison sentence** habló de tal manera que no le condenaron a pena de cárcel

Ⓓ CPD ► **talk show** N (*Rad, TV*) programa *m* de entrevistas

►**talk back** VI + ADV (*gen*) replicar; **this is where voters get the chance to ~ back** ahora es cuando los votantes tienen la oportunidad de replicar; (*rudely*) **how dare you ~ back to me?** ¿cómo te atreves a replicarme *or* llevarme la contraria?; **he's very good — he never ~s back** es muy bueno — no es nada respondón

►**talk down** Ⓐ VI + ADV **to ~ down to sb** hablar con aires de superioridad a algn

Ⓑ VT + ADV [1] (= *help to land*) [+ *pilot*] dirigir por radio el aterrizaje a

[2] (= *dissuade from jumping*) [+ *suicidal person*] disuadir (*para que no salte*)

[3] (*esp Brit Fin*) [+ *currency, shares*] hacer bajar; (*in deal*) **I ~ed him down another thousand** hice que rebajara el precio otras mil libras

[4] (= *denigrate*) menospreciar

[5] (= *interrupt remorselessly*) hacer callar

►**talk on** VI + ADV no parar de hablar

►**talk out** VT + ADV [1] (= *discuss thoroughly*) **to ~ it/things out** hablar detenidamente de ello/la situación

[2] (*Parl*) **to ~ out a bill** *alargar el debate para que no dé tiempo a votar un proyecto de ley*

►**talk over** VT + ADV (= *discuss*) hablar, discutir; **let's ~ it/things over** vamos a hablarlo *or* discutirlo; **to ~ sth over with sb** consultar algo con algn

►**talk round** VT + ADV **to ~ sb round** (*esp Brit*) llegar a convencer a algn

►**talk through** Ⓐ VT + ADV (= *discuss*) [+ *plan, problem*] discutir detenidamente

Ⓑ VT + PREP (= *explain*) **to ~ sb through sth** explicar algo a algn

►**talk up** Ⓐ VI + ADV (*US*) (= *speak frankly*) hablar claro *or* sin rodeos

Ⓑ VT + ADV [1] (= *exaggerate*) exagerar

[2] (*Fin*) [+ *economy*] inflar; [+ *shares*] inflar la cotización de, inflar el valor de

[3] (*esp Brit*) (*in deal*) **to ~ sb up** hacer que algn mejore la oferta; **try to ~ him up to 50,000** intenta que mejore su oferta a 50.000

talkative [ˈtɔːkətɪv] ADJ hablador, platicón (*Mex*); **he became quite ~** habló mucho; **she wasn't very ~ at breakfast** estuvo bastante callada durante el desayuno

talkativeness [ˈtɔːkətɪvnɪs] N locuacidad *f*

talked-of [ˈtɔːktɒv] ADJ **a much ~ event** un suceso muy comentado

talker [ˈtɔːkəʳ] N hablador(a) *m/f*; **to be a good ~** hablar con soltura, tener una conversación amena; **I'm not much of a ~** no soy buen conversador; **he's just a ~** se le va la fuerza por la boca

talkie [ˈtɔːkɪ] N película *f* sonora; **the ~s** el cine sonoro

talking [ˈtɔːkɪŋ] Ⓐ ADJ [*bird, doll*] que habla

Ⓑ N **we could hear ~ downstairs** oíamos a algn hablando abajo; **she does all the ~** ella es quien habla siempre; **I'll do the ~** yo seré el que hable; **no ~, please!** ¡silencio, por favor!

Ⓒ CPD ► **talking book** N audiolibro *m* ► **talking head** N (*TV*) busto *m* parlante* ► **talking newspaper** N periódico *m* grabado (en cinta) ► **talking picture** N película *f* sonora ► **talking point** N tema *m* de conversación ► **talking shop** N (*esp Brit*) reunión *f* donde se habla mucho pero no se hace nada

talking-to [ˈtɔːkɪŋtuː] N **I gave him a good ~** le llamé al orden, le leí la cartilla; **that boy needs a good ~** a ese chico le hace falta que le lean la cartilla

tall [tɔːl] Ⓐ ADJ (*compar* **taller**, *superl* **tallest**) alto; **he's very ~ for his age** es *or* está muy alto para su edad; **a six-foot ~ man** ≈ un hombre de uno ochenta; **how ~ are you?** ¿cuánto mides?, ¿qué altura tienes?; **I'm 1.6 metres ~** mido 1,60m (de alto); **he's not as ~ as me** no es tan alto como yo; **she's ~er than me** es más alta que yo, mide más que yo; **she's 5cm ~er than me** ◊ **she's ~er than me by 5cm** es cinco centímetros más alta que yo, mide cinco centímetros más que yo, me saca cinco centímetros; **it's the ~est building in Europe** es el edificio más alto *or* de más altura de Europa; **to get** *or* **grow ~er** crecer, ponerse más alto; *see also* **stand C1**, **walk C1**

Ⓑ CPD ► **tall order*** N **it's a bit of a ~ order, but we'll try** no es fácil, pero lo intentaremos; **it was a ~ order to expect us to finish in three days** esperar que terminásemos en tres días era mucho pedir* ► **tall story*** N cuento *m* chino*

tallboy [ˈtɔːlbɔɪ] N (*Brit*) cómoda *f* alta

tallness [ˈtɔːlnɪs] N altura *f*

tallow [ˈtæləʊ] N sebo *m*

tallowy [ˈtæləʊɪ] ADJ seboso

tally [ˈtælɪ] Ⓐ N [1] (= *running total, score*) cuenta *f*, total *m*; **to keep a ~ of** llevar la cuenta de

[2] (= *stick*) tarja *f*

Ⓑ VI [*stories, accounts*] concordar, coincidir (**with** con)

Ⓒ VT (*also* **~ up**) contar, hacer recuento de

Ⓓ CPD ► **tally clerk** N medidor(a) *m/f*

tallyho [ˈtælɪˈhəʊ] EXCL ¡hala! (*grito del cazador de zorras*)

Talmud [ˈtælmʊd] N Talmud *m*

Talmudic [tælˈmʊdɪk] ADJ talmúdico

talon [ˈtælən] N garra *f*

tamable [ˈteɪməbl] ADJ domable, domesticable

tamale [təˈmɑːlɪ] N tamal *m*

tamarind [ˈtæmərɪnd] N tamarindo *m*

tamarisk [ˈtæmərɪsk] N tamarisco *m*

tambour [ˈtæmbʊəʳ] N tambor *m*

tambourine [ˌtæmbəˈriːn] N pandereta *f*

Tamburlaine [ˈtæmbəˌleɪn] N Tamerlán

tame [teɪm] Ⓐ ADJ (*compar* **tamer**, *superl* **tamest**) [1] (= *no longer wild*) [*lion, tiger*] domesticado, manso; [*hedgehog, fox*] dócil, manso; **do you know of a ~ plumber who can fix it?** (*hum*) ¿sabes de un fontanero fiable que lo pueda arreglar?

[2] (= *boring*) [*book, film, match, performance*] soso, insulso; **the report was pretty ~ stuff** el informe era bastante anodino; **these films are ~ by today's standards** estas películas resultan poco atrevidas para los tiempos que corren

Ⓑ VT [+ *lion, tiger*] domar, amansar; [+ *passion*] dominar; **no man could ~ her** no había hombre que pudiese domarla

tamely [ˈteɪmlɪ] ADV dócilmente

tameness [ˈteɪmnɪs] N [1] [*of lion, tiger*] mansedumbre *f*; [*of hedgehog, fox*] docilidad *f*, mansedumbre *f*

[2] [*of person*] sosería *f*; [*of book, film*] (= *lacking excitement*) sosería *f*; (= *lacking sex, violence*) falta *f* de atrevimiento

tamer [ˈteɪməʳ] N domador(a) *m/f*

Tamil [ˈtæmɪl] Ⓐ ADJ tamil

Ⓑ N tamil *mf*

taming [ˈteɪmɪŋ] N domadura *f*; **"the Taming of the Shrew"** "la fierecilla domada"

tam o' shanter [ˌtæməˈʃæntəʳ] N boina *f* escocesa

tamp [tæmp] VT (*also* **~ down, ~ in**) apisonar; (*Min*) (*in blasting*) atacar

Tampax® [ˈtæmpæks] N tampax® *m*, támpax *m*

tamper [ˈtæmpəʳ] VI **to ~ with** (= *interfere with*) [+ *machinery, brakes etc*] manipular; [+ *lock*] tratar de forzar; (= *alter*) [+ *papers, evidence*] falsificar; (= *attempt to influence*) [+ *witness, jury*] sobornar; (= *handle*) manosear; **my car had been ~ed with** algo se había hecho a mi coche

tampon [ˈtæmpən] N tampón *m*

tan [tæn] Ⓐ N [1] (= *suntan*) bronceado *m*; **to get a ~** broncearse

[2] (= *colour*) canela *f*, café *m* claro (*esp LAm*)

[3] (= *bark*) (*also* **~bark**) casca *f*

Ⓑ ADJ color canela, color café claro (*esp LAm*); [*shoes*] marrón

Ⓒ VI [*person*] broncearse, ponerse moreno, tostarse

Ⓓ VT [1] [+ *person, skin*] broncear, poner moreno (*esp Sp*), quemar (*LAm*)

[2] [+ *leather*] curtir; ✦*IDIOM* **to ~ sb's hide*** curtir a algn a palos*, zurrarle la badana a algn (*Sp**)

tandem [ˈtændəm] Ⓐ N (= *bicycle*) tándem *m*

Ⓑ ADV **in ~** [*work, function*] conjuntamente; **the two systems will run in ~** los dos sistemas funcionarán conjuntamente *or* en tándem; **the two plays were written in ~** las dos obras fueron escritas simultáneamente; **in ~ with** conjuntamente con; **to ride ~** montar en un tándem

tang [tæŋ] N [1] (= *taste*) sabor *m* fuerte y picante; (= *smell*) olor *m* acre; **the salt ~ of the sea air** el olor salobre de la brisa marina

[2] [*of knife*] espiga *f*

tangent [ˈtændʒənt] N (*Geom*) tangente *f*; ✦*IDIOM* **to go** *or* **fly off at a ~** salirse por la tangente

tangential [tænˈdʒenʃəl] ADJ tangencial

tangerine [ˌtændʒəˈriːn] N mandarina *f*, tangerina *f*

tangibility [ˌtændʒɪˈbɪlɪtɪ] N tangibilidad *f*

tangible [ˈtændʒəbl] ADJ [*object*] tangible; [*difference, proof, evidence*] tangible, palpable; **~ assets** bienes *mpl* tangibles, inmovilizado *msing* material

tangibly [ˈtændʒəblɪ] ADV [*demonstrate, show*] de modo palpable; **it is ~ different** la diferencia es tangible *or* palpable

Tangier(s) [tænˈdʒɪə(z)] N Tánger *m*

tangle ['tæŋgl] Ⓐ N (*in hair*) enredo *m*, maraña *f*; [*of streets*] laberinto *m*; (*fig*) (= *muddle*) enredo *m*, lío *m*; **a ~ of weeds** una maraña de malas hierbas; **a ~ of wool** una maraña de lana; **to be in a ~** [*hair, thread*] estar enredado; **the sheets were in a ~** las sábanas estaban hechas una maraña; **I'm in a ~ with the accounts** me he hecho un lío con las cuentas*; **to get into a ~** [*hair, thread*] enredarse; **I got into a ~ with the police** me metí en un lío con la policía
Ⓑ VT (*also* **~ up**) enredar, enmarañar
Ⓒ VI (*also* **~ up**) enredarse, enmarañarse; **to ~ with sth/sb*** (*fig*) meterse en algo/con algn

tangled ['tæŋgld] ADJ [*hair, wool*] enredado, enmarañado; (*fig*) enmarañado, complicado

tango ['tæŋgəʊ] Ⓐ N (*pl* **tangos**) tango *m*
Ⓑ VI bailar el tango; ✦*IDIOM* **it takes two to ~*** es cosa de dos

tangy ['tæŋɪ] ADJ fuerte y picante

tank [tæŋk] Ⓐ N 1 (= *container*) (*for liquid*) tanque *m*, depósito *m*; (*large*) cisterna *f*; (*Aut*) depósito *m* (*Sp*), tanque *m* (*esp LAm*); **fuel ~** depósito *m* (de combustible); **fish ~** acuario *m*; **petrol** *or* (*US*) **gas ~** depósito *m* (de gasolina); **water ~** (*for village, in house*) depósito *m* de agua; (*on lorry*) cisterna *f*; *see also* **septic, think D**
2 (*also* **~ful**) (= *quantity*) depósito *m*
3 (*Mil*) tanque *m*, carro *m* (de combate)
4 (*Phot*) (*also* **developing ~**) cubeta *f* de revelado
5 (*also* **swimming ~**) (*US*) piscina *f*, alberca *f* (*Mex*), pileta *f* (de natación) (*S. Cone*)
6 (*US‡*) (= *jail*) cárcel *f*, chirona *f* (*Sp**)
Ⓑ CPD ► **tank car** N (*US*) vagón *m* cisterna ► **tank engine** N locomotora *f* ténder ► **tank wagon** N (*Rail*) vagón *m* cisterna; (*Aut*) camión *m* cisterna

►**tank along*** VI + ADV ir a toda pastilla*

►**tank up** VI + ADV (*with fuel*) llenar el tanque (**with** de); (*) (*with alcohol*) emborracharse (**on** bebiendo)

tankard ['tæŋkəd] N bock *m*, pichel *m*

tanked up* [ˌtæŋkt'ʌp] ADJ (*Brit*) **to be ~ (on sth)** estar borracho (de algo); **to get ~ (on sth)** emborracharse (de algo)

tanker ['tæŋkəʳ] N (= *ship*) buque-cisterna *m*; (*carrying oil*) petrolero *m*; (= *lorry*) camión *m* cisterna; **an oil ~** un petrolero; **a petrol ~** un camión cisterna

tankful ['tæŋkfʊl] N tanque *m*; **to get a ~ of petrol** llenar el depósito de gasolina; **a ~ is 25 litres** la capacidad del depósito es de 25 litros

tanned [tænd] ADJ moreno, bronceado

tanner¹ ['tænəʳ] N curtidor(a) *m/f*

tanner²* ['tænəʳ] N (*Brit*) (*formerly*) *moneda de seis peniques (antiguos)*

tannery ['tænərɪ] N curtiduría *f*, tenería *f*

tannic ['tænɪk] Ⓐ ADJ [*wine*] con mucho tanino
Ⓑ CPD ► **tannic acid** N ácido *m* tánico

tannin ['tænɪn] N tanino *m*

tanning ['tænɪŋ] Ⓐ N 1 [*of leather*] curtido *m*
2 (*) zurra* *f*; **to give sb a ~*** zurrar a algn*
Ⓑ CPD ► **tanning cream**, **tanning lotion** N bronceador *m*

tannoy® ['tænɔɪ] N sistema *m* de anuncios por altavoces; **on** *or* **over the ~** por los altavoces

tansy ['tænzɪ] N tanaceto *m*, atanasia *f*

tantalize ['tæntəlaɪz] VT 1 (= *excite*) tentar; **he was ~d by her perfume** su perfume le resultaba incitante
2 (= *torment*) **to ~ sb (with sth)** atormentar a algn (con algo)

tantalizing ['tæntəlaɪzɪŋ] ADJ [*aroma, sight, offer*] tentador; [*perfume*] incitante

tantalizingly ['tæntəlaɪzɪŋlɪ] ADV **the chocolate biscuits beckoned ~** las galletas de chocolate se ofrecían tentadoras, las galletas de chocolate estaban diciendo "cómeme"; **we came ~ close to victory** tuvimos la victoria casi en nuestras manos

tantamount ['tæntəmaʊnt] ADJ **~ to** equivalente a; **this is ~ to a refusal** esto equivale a una negativa

tantrum ['tæntrəm] N rabieta* *f*, berrinche* *m*; **she had** *or* **threw a ~** le dio una rabieta *or* un berrinche*

Tanzania [ˌtænzə'niːə] N Tanzania *f*

Tanzanian [ˌtænzə'nɪən] Ⓐ ADJ tanzano
Ⓑ N tanzano/a *m/f*

Taoist ['tɑːəʊɪst] Ⓐ ADJ taoísta
Ⓑ N taoísta *mf*

tap¹ [tæp] Ⓐ N 1 (*Brit*) (= *water tap*) grifo *m*, canilla *f* (*S. Cone*); (= *gas tap*) llave *f*; **cold/hot water ~** grifo *m* de agua fría/caliente; **you've left the ~ running** has dejado el grifo abierto; **to turn the ~ on/off** abrir/cerrar el grifo
2 (= *stopper*) [*of barrel*] espita *f*, canilla *f*; **on ~: beer on ~** cerveza *f* de barril; **to have sth on ~** disponer de algo; **he seems to have unlimited money on ~** parece disponer de un caudal de dinero ilimitado
3 (*Telec*) micrófono *m*; **to put a ~ on sb's phone** intervenir *or* pinchar* el teléfono de algn
4 (*Med*) punción *f*; **spinal ~** punción *f* lumbar
Ⓑ VT 1 (= *use*) [+ *resource, situation*] explotar; **to ~ sb for information*** tratar de (son)sacar información a algn; **he tried to ~ me for £5** intentó sonsacarme cinco libras
2 [+ *barrel*] espitar
3 (*Telec*) [+ *telephone*] intervenir, pinchar*; [+ *conversation*] interceptar; **my phone is ~ped** mi teléfono está intervenido *or* pinchado*
4 (= *cut into*) [+ *tree*] sangrar; **to ~ the rubber from a tree** sangrar un árbol para extraer el caucho
5 (*Elec*) [+ *electricity, current*] derivar; [+ *wire*] hacer una derivación en
6 (*Med*) [+ *spine*] hacer una punción en
Ⓒ VI *see* **tap into**
Ⓓ CPD ► **tap water** N agua *f* corriente, agua *f* del grifo (*Sp*)

tap² [tæp] Ⓐ N 1 (= *knock*) (*on door*) toque *m*; (*on back, shoulder*) golpecito *m*, toque *m*; **I felt a ~ on my shoulder** sentí un golpecito *or* toque en el hombro; **there was a ~ at** *or* **on the door** llamaron *or* tocaron suavemente a la puerta; **I gave him a gentle ~ on the back** le di un golpecito en la espalda
2 (*also* **~ dancing**) claqué *m*
3 (*on dancing shoe*) lámina *f* de metal, tapa *f* de metal
Ⓑ VT (= *hit lightly*) [+ *table, surface*] golpear suavemente; [+ *typewriter keys*] pulsar; **he was ~ping his fingers on the steering wheel** estaba repiqueteando *or* tamborileando sobre el volante con los dedos; **to ~ one's foot** (*impatiently*) taconear (impacientemente); **they were ~ping their feet in time to the music** seguían el compás de la música con el pie; **to ~ sb on the back/shoulder** dar un golpecito *or* toque a algn en la espalda/el hombro; **she ~ped a rhythm on the table** golpeó la mesa marcando un ritmo, repiqueteó un ritmo en la mesa
Ⓒ VI dar golpecitos; **please, stop ~ping!** ¡haz el favor de dejar de dar golpecitos!; **she ~ped at the door** llamó suavemente a la puerta; **she ~ped at the window** dio unos golpecitos en la ventana; **he was ~ping away at his word processor** estaba (tecleando) dale que te pego en su procesador de textos; **I could hear sth ~ping on the window** oía que algo daba golpecitos en la ventana
Ⓓ CPD ► **tap dance** N claqué *m*; *see also* **tap-dance** ► **tap dancer** N bailarín/ina *m/f* de claqué ► **tap dancing** N claqué *m*

►**tap in** VT + ADV 1 (*on computer*) [+ *number, code*] teclear
2 **to ~ in a nail** hacer que entre un clavo golpeándolo suavemente

►**tap into** VI + PREP **to ~ into a computer** acceder ilegalmente a un ordenador (*Sp*) *or* (*LAm*) una computadora; **they are trying to ~ into the youth market** están intentando introducirse en el mercado juvenil; **to ~ into sb's ideas** aprovechar las ideas de algn; **to ~ into one's potential** aprovechar al máximo su capacidad

►**tap out** VT + ADV 1 **to ~ out a message in morse** enviar un mensaje en Morse
2 **to ~ out one's pipe** vaciar la pipa golpeándola suavemente

tap-dance ['tæpdɑːns] VI bailar claqué; *see also* **tap D**

tape [teɪp] Ⓐ N 1 (*made of cloth*) cinta *f*; (= *adhesive tape*) cinta *f* adhesiva, Scotch® *m*; (*Sport*) meta *f*; (*ceremonial*) cinta *f* simbólica; (*also* **~ measure**) cinta *f* métrica, metro *m*; *see also* **name**
2 (*for recording*) (= *magnetic strip*) cinta *f* (magnetofónica); (= *cassette, recording*) cinta *f*; **I'll do you a ~ of it** te lo grabaré (en cinta); **a blank ~** una cinta virgen; **on ~** grabado (en cinta); *see also* **cassette**
Ⓑ VT 1 (= *record*) grabar (en cinta)
2 (= *seal*) (*also* **~ up**) cerrar con cinta, poner una cinta a
3 (= *fasten*) **to ~ sth to sth** pegar algo a algo con cinta adhesiva
4 ✦*IDIOM* **to have sth/sb ~d***: **I've got him ~d** ya le tengo calado*; **I've got it ~d** ya le he cogido el tranquillo*; **we've got it all ~d** lo tenemos todo organizado, todo funciona perfectamente
Ⓒ CPD ► **tape deck** N pletina *f*, unidad *f* de cinta ► **tape drive** N (*Comput*) accionador *m* de cinta ► **tape machine** N casete *m*, magnetofón *m* ► **tape measure** N cinta *f* métrica, metro *m* ► **tape recorder** N casete *m* (*Sp*), grabadora *f* (*esp LAm*); (*reel-to-reel*) magnetofón *m*, magnetófono *m* ► **tape recording** N grabación *f* (en cinta) ► **tape streamer** N (*Comput*) dispositivo *m* de copia de seguridad

taper ['teɪpəʳ] Ⓐ N (= *spill*) astilla *f*; (= *candle*) vela *f*
Ⓑ VI afilarse, estrecharse; **to ~ to a point** rematar en punta
Ⓒ VT afilar, estrechar

tape-record ['teɪprɪˌkɔːd] VT grabar (en cinta)

tapered ['teɪpəd], **tapering** ['teɪpərɪŋ] ADJ [*shape*] ahusado, que termina en punta; [*finger*] afilado; [*table leg*] que se va estrechando; (*Mech*) cónico

►**taper off**, **taper away** VI + ADV 1 (= *narrow*) *see* **taper B**
2 (= *reduce*) [*spending, fighting, violence*] ir disminuyendo; [*storm, snowfall*] ir amainando; **his popularity is tapering off** su popularidad está decayendo

tapestry ['tæpɪstrɪ] N (= *object*) tapiz *m*; (= *art*) tapicería *f*

tapeworm ['teɪpwɜːm] N tenia *f*, solitaria *f*

tapioca [ˌtæpɪˈəʊkə] Ⓐ N tapioca *f*
Ⓑ CPD ► **tapioca pudding** N postre *m* de tapioca

tapir [ˈteɪpəʳ] N tapir *m*

tapper [ˈtæpəʳ] N (*Elec, Telec*) manipulador *m*

tappet [ˈtæpɪt] N empujador *m*, empujaválvula *m*

taproom [ˈtæprʊm] N (*Brit*) bar *m*

taproot [ˈtæpruːt] N raíz *f* central

tar [tɑːʳ] Ⓐ N 1 (= *substance*) alquitrán *m*, brea *f*, chapopote *m* (*Mex*); **low/middle ~ cigarettes** cigarrillos con contenido bajo/medio de alquitrán
2 (*also* **Jack Tar**) (†) marinero *m*
Ⓑ VT [+ *road, surface*] alquitranar; **to ~ and feather sb** emplumar a algn; ✦**IDIOM to be ~red with the same brush** (*fig*) estar cortado por el mismo patrón

tarantella [ˌtærənˈtelə] N tarantela *f*

tarantula [təˈræntjʊlə] N (*pl* **tarantulas** *or* **tarantulae** [təˈræntjʊliː]) tarántula *f*

tardily [ˈtɑːdɪlɪ] ADV (*frm*) (= *belatedly*) tardíamente; (= *slowly*) lentamente

tardiness [ˈtɑːdɪnɪs] N (*frm*) (= *lateness*) tardanza *f*; (= *slowness*) lentitud *f*

tardy [ˈtɑːdɪ] ADJ (*compar* **tardier**; *superl* **tardiest**) (*frm*) (= *late*) tardío; (= *slow*) lento

tare [tɛəʳ] N (*Bot*) (*also* **~s**) arveja *f*; (*Bible*) cizaña *f*; (*Comm*) tara *f*

target [ˈtɑːgɪt] Ⓐ N 1 (*Sport*) blanco *m*, diana *f*; (*Mil*) objetivo *m*; **he missed the ~** no dio en el blanco *or* la diana; **they deliberately attacked civilian ~s** atacaron objetivos civiles deliberadamente; **an easy ~** (*lit, fig*) un blanco fácil; **a fixed ~** un blanco fijo; **a moving ~** un blanco móvil; **the shot was off ~** (*Ftbl, Hockey, etc*) el tiro iba desviado a gol; **the bombs were way off ~** las bombas cayeron muy lejos del objetivo; **the shot was on ~** (*Ftbl, Hockey, etc*) el tiro iba directo a gol; **a soft ~** (*lit, fig*) un blanco fácil
2 (= *person on receiving end*) [*of criticism, remark*] blanco *m*; [*of advertising*] objetivo *m*; **he has been the ~ of criticism over his handling of the affair** ha sido el blanco de las críticas por su manejo del asunto; **this made him a prime ~ for blackmail** esto le convirtió en un blanco perfecto para el chantaje
3 (= *objective*) objetivo *m*, meta *f*; **production ~s for 1980** los objetivos *or* las metas de producción para 1980; **the project is on ~ for completion** el proyecto lleva camino de terminarse dentro del plazo previsto; **to set a ~ for sth** fijar un objetivo para algo; **to set o.s. a ~** fijarse un objetivo
Ⓑ VT 1 (*Mil*) [+ *positions, installations*] fijar como objetivo
2 (= *select, single out*) **cigarette companies seem to be ~ing children intentionally** las tabacaleras parecen estar dirigiendo su publicidad a los niños deliberadamente; **a mugger who ~ed elderly women** un atracador que asaltaba en particular a ancianas; **to ~ sth/sb for sth: the government will ~ high earners for tax increases** el gobierno hará recaer la subida de los impuestos particularmente sobre aquellos con sueldos elevados; **the factory is ~ed for closure** se propone cerrar la fábrica
3 (*fig*) (= *aim*) **to ~ sth at sb/sth: products ~ed at children** productos dirigidos a los niños; **programs ~ed at reducing infant deaths** programas que tienen como objetivo reducir el número de muertes infantiles; **to ~ aid at the people who need it** concentrar la ayuda en las personas que la necesitan
Ⓒ CPD ► **target area** N (*Mil*) zona *f* objetivo ► **target audience** N público *m* objetivo ► **target date** N fecha *f* límite ► **target group** N grupo *m* objetivo, grupo *m* destinatario ► **target language** N lengua *f* de destino ► **target market** N mercado *m* objetivo ► **target practice** N tiro *m* al blanco, prácticas *fpl* de tiro ► **target price** N precio *m* indicativo ► **target weight** N peso *m* ideal

targetable [ˈtɑːgɪtəbl] ADJ dirigible

tariff [ˈtærɪf] Ⓐ N 1 (= *tax*) tarifa *f*, arancel *m*
2 (= *schedule of prices*) tarifa *f*
Ⓑ CPD ► **tariff barrier** N barrera *f* arancelaria ► **tariff reform** N reforma *f* arancelaria ► **tariff wall** N = **tariff barrier**

Tarmac®, **tarmac** [ˈtɑːmæk] (*vb: pt, pp* **tarmacked**) (*esp Brit*) Ⓐ N (= *substance*) asfalto *m*, alquitranado *m*; **the ~** (*Aer*) (= *runway*) la pista de despegue; (*Aut*) (= *road*) el asfalto
Ⓑ VT asfaltar, alquitranar

tarn [tɑːn] N lago *m* pequeño de montaña

tarnation†* [tɑːˈneɪʃən] N (*US dial*) ¡diablos!

tarnish [ˈtɑːnɪʃ] Ⓐ VT (*lit*) deslustrar, quitar el brillo a; (*fig*) manchar, empañar
Ⓑ VI [*metal*] deslustrarse, perder el brillo

tarnished [ˈtɑːnɪʃt] ADJ [*metal*] deslustrado, sin brillo; [*reputation*] manchado, empañado

tarot [ˈtærəʊ] Ⓐ N tarot *m*
Ⓑ CPD ► **tarot card** N carta *f* de tarot

tarp* [tɑːp] N (*US*) = **tarpaulin**

tarpaulin [tɑːˈpɔːlɪn] N lona *f* alquitranada

tarpon [ˈtɑːpɒn] N tarpón *m*

tarragon [ˈtærəgən] N (*Bot*) estragón *m*

tarry[1] [ˈtærɪ] VI († *or liter*) (= *stay*) quedarse; (= *dally*) entretenerse, quedarse atrás; (= *be late*) tardar (en venir), demorarse

tarry[2] [ˈtɑːrɪ] ADJ [*substance*] alquitranado, embreado; (= *covered with tar*) cubierto de alquitrán; (= *stained with tar*) manchado de alquitrán; **to taste ~** saber a alquitrán

tarsus [ˈtɑːsəs] N (*pl* **tarsi** [ˈtɑːsaɪ]) tarso *m*

tart[1] [tɑːt] ADJ 1 (= *sour*) [*flavour, fruit*] ácido, agrio
2 (*fig*) [*expression, remark*] áspero

tart[2] [tɑːt] N 1 (*Culin*) (*large*) tarta *f*; (*small*) pastelillo *m*; **jam ~** tarta *f* de mermelada
2 (‡) (= *prostitute*) puta** *f*, furcia *f* (*Sp*‡); (*pej*) (= *promiscuous woman*) fulana* *f*

►**tart up*** VT + ADV (*Brit*) [+ *house*] pintar, remodelar, renovar; **to ~ o.s. up** vestirse y pintarse

tartan [ˈtɑːtən] N tartán *m*, tela *f* a cuadros escoceses; **a ~ scarf** una bufanda escocesa

Tartar [ˈtɑːtəʳ] Ⓐ ADJ tártaro
Ⓑ N tártaro/a *m/f*

tartar [ˈtɑːtəʳ] N 1 (*on teeth*) sarro *m*, tártaro *m*
2 (*Chem*) tártaro *m*
3 (*Culin*) (*also* **cream of ~**) crémor *m* tártarico
4 (= *woman*) (*fig*) fiera *f*

tartar(e) [ˈtɑːtəʳ] CPD ► **tartar(e) sauce** N salsa *f* tártara ► **tartar(e) steak** N *biftec crudo, picado y condimentado con sal, pimiento, cebolla etc*

tartaric acid [tɑːˌtærɪkˈæsɪd] N ácido *m* tartárico

Tartary [ˈtɑːtərɪ] N Tartaria *f*

tartly [ˈtɑːtlɪ] ADV (*fig*) ásperamente

tartness [ˈtɑːtnɪs] N 1 [*of flavour, fruit*] acidez *f*
2 (*fig*) aspereza *f*

tarty* [ˈtɑːtɪ] ADJ putesco*

Tarzan [ˈtɑːzən] N Tarzán

task [tɑːsk] Ⓐ N 1 (= *job*) tarea *f*; **I had to keep the children amused, which was no easy ~** tenía que entretener a los niños, lo cual no era tarea fácil; **to give** *or* **set sb the ~ of doing sth** pedir a algn que haga algo; ✦**IDIOM to take sb to ~ (for sth)** reprender *or* regañar a algn (por algo), llamar a algn a capítulo (por algo) (*frm*)
2 (= *function, stated aim*) cometido *m*; **it was the ~ of the army to maintain order** mantener el orden era el cometido del ejército
3 (*Comput*) tarea *f*
Ⓑ VT **to ~ sb with sth** hacer que algn se encargue de algo
Ⓒ CPD ► **task force** N (*Mil*) destacamento *m* especial; (*Naut*) fuerza *f* expedicionaria; (= *working group*) grupo *m* de trabajo

taskmaster [ˈtɑːskˌmɑːstəʳ] N **he's a hard ~** es muy exigente, es un tirano

Tasmania [tæzˈmeɪnɪə] N Tasmania *f*

Tasmanian [tæzˈmeɪnɪən] Ⓐ ADJ tasmanio
Ⓑ N tasmanio/a *m/f*

tassel [ˈtæsəl] N borla *f*

taste [teɪst] Ⓐ N 1 (= *sense*) gusto *m*; **a keen sense of ~** un agudo sentido del gusto; **it's quite sweet to the ~** tiene un gusto bastante dulce al paladar
2 (= *flavour*) sabor *m*, gusto *m*; **it has an odd ~** tiene un sabor *or* gusto raro; **to leave a bad** *or* **nasty ~ in the mouth** (*fig*) dejar mal sabor de boca; **his jokes leave a bad** *or* **nasty ~ in the mouth** sus chistes te dejan mal sabor de boca; **it has no ~** no sabe a nada, no tiene sabor
3 (= *small amount*) **"more wine?" — "just a ~"** —¿más vino? —sólo un poco *or* un poquito; **would you like a ~?** ¿quieres probarlo?; **may I have a ~?** ¿puedo probarlo?; ✦**IDIOMS to give sb a ~ of their own medicine** pagar a algn con la misma moneda; **to get a ~ of one's own medicine** recibir el mismo (mal) trato que uno da a los demás
4 (= *experience*) experiencia *f*; (= *sample*) muestra *f*; **it was her first ~ of freedom** fue su primera experiencia de la libertad *or* su primer contacto con la libertad; **we got a ~ of his anger** nos ofreció una muestra de su enfado; **now that she has had a ~ of stardom, she won't ever be content with ordinariness again** ahora que ha probado las mieles del estrellato *or* saboreado el estrellato, nunca más se conformará con lo normal y corriente; **he's had a ~ of prison** ha conocido *or* probado la cárcel; **to give sb a ~ of sth** dar una idea de algo a algn; **it gave him a ~ of military life** le dio una idea de lo que era la vida militar; **it was a ~ of things to come** era una muestra de lo que estaba por venir
5 (= *liking*) gusto *m*; **~s differ** los gustos cambian; **he was a man of catholic ~s** era un hombre de gustos variados; **a ~ for sth**: **to acquire** *or* **develop a ~ for sth** tomarle gusto a algo; **it gave him a ~ for reading** esto hizo que le tomara gusto a la lectura; **she has a ~ for adventure** le gusta la aventura; **we have the same ~s in music** tenemos el mismo gusto para la música; **he has expensive ~s in cars** en cuanto a coches, tiene gustos caros; **season to ~** (*Culin*) sazonar al gusto; **it's not to my ~** no es de mi gusto; **is it to your ~?** ¿le gusta?, ¿es de su gusto?; ✦**IDIOM there's no accounting for ~** sobre gustos no hay nada escrito; *see also* **acquired**
6 (= *discernment*) gusto *m*; **people of ~** la gente con gusto; **to be in bad ~** ser de mal gusto; **it would be in bad ~ to meet without him** sería de mal gusto reunirnos sin él, reunirnos sin él sería hacerle un desprecio *or* un feo; **she has very good ~** tiene muy buen gusto; **his ~ in clothes is extremely good** viste con muchísimo gusto; **I don't think**

that remark was in very good ~ no me pareció un comentario de muy buen gusto; **to have ~** [*person*] tener gusto; **to have no ~** [*person*] no tener gusto; **the house is furnished in impeccable ~** la casa está amueblada con muchísimo gusto *or* con un gusto exquisito; **to be in poor ~** ser de mal gusto

Ⓑ VT [1] (= *sample*) [+ *food, drink*] probar; (*at tasting*) degustar, catar; **just ~ this** pruebe esto; *see also* **wine**

[2] (= *perceive flavour of*) **I can't ~ the rum in this** no noto el sabor del ron en esto, esto apenas me sabe a ron; **I can't ~ anything when I have a cold** la comida no me sabe a nada cuando estoy resfriado

[3] (= *eat*) comer, probar; **I haven't ~d salmon for years** hace años que no como salmón *or* pruebo el salmón; **he had not ~d food for a week** llevaba una semana sin probar bocado

[4] (= *experience*) [+ *success, power*] saborear; [+ *poverty, loneliness*] conocer

Ⓒ VI (= *have flavour*) saber; **the brandy ~d bitter** el brandy sabía amargo, el brandy tenía un sabor *or* un gusto amargo; **it ~s good** está rico *or* bueno; **it ~s all right to me** a mí me sabe bien; **it ~s horrible** tiene un sabor horrible, sabe horrible *or* a rayos*; **to ~ like sth** saber a algo; **the meat ~d like chicken** la carne sabía a pollo; **to ~ of sth** saber a algo; **what does it ~ of?** ¿a qué sabe?

Ⓓ CPD ► **taste bud** N papila *f* gustativa

tasteful [ˈteɪstfʊl] ADJ de buen gusto

tastefully [ˈteɪstfəlɪ] ADV con buen gusto; **the sex scenes are very ~ done** las escenas sexuales están hechas con buen gusto

tastefulness [ˈteɪstfʊlnɪs] N buen gusto *m*

tasteless [ˈteɪstlɪs] ADJ [1] (= *without flavour*) [1·1] (*by nature*) [*substance*] insípido; **sodium is ~** el sodio es insípido *or* no tiene sabor

[1·2] (*pej*) (*through cooking*) [*food, meal*] soso, insípido; **the fish was ~** el pescado estaba soso *or* no sabía a nada

[2] (= *vulgar*) [*ornament, decor*] de mal gusto, ordinario

[3] (= *offensive*) [*remark, joke*] de mal gusto

tastelessly [ˈteɪstlɪslɪ] ADV con mal gusto

tastelessness [ˈteɪstlɪsnɪs] N [1] (= *lack of flavour*) [*of food, substance*] insipidez *f*

[2] (= *bad taste*) [*of ornament, joke, remark*] mal gusto *m*

taster [ˈteɪstəʳ] N [1] (= *person*) catador(a) *m/f*, degustador(a) *m/f*

[2] (*Brit*) (*fig*) muestra *f*; **that is just a ~ of things to come** esto es un anticipo de lo que nos espera

tastiness [ˈteɪstɪnɪs] N lo sabroso, lo apetitoso

tasty [ˈteɪstɪ] ADJ (*compar* **tastier**; *superl* **tastiest**) [1] (= *well-flavoured*) [*food, dish*] sabroso, apetitoso; **this is very ~** esto sabe muy rico

[2] (*) (= *salacious*) **a ~ piece of gossip** un cotilleo sustancioso; **a ~ piece of news** una noticia jugosa

[3] (‡) (= *sexy*) **he/she's very ~!** ¡está buenísimo/buenísima!*, ¡está más bueno/buena que el pan!‡

tat¹ [tæt] VI (*Sew*) hacer encaje

tat²* [tæt] N (*Brit*) basura* *f*

ta-ta* [ˈtæˈtɑː] EXCL (*Brit*) adiós, adiosito*

Tatar [ˈtɑːtəʳ] = **Tartar**

tattered [ˈtætəd] ADJ [*clothes, flag*] en jirones; [*book*] destrozado; [*person*] andrajoso, harapiento; (*fig*) [*reputation*] hecho trizas

tatters [ˈtætəz] NPL (= *rags*) andrajos *mpl*, harapos *mpl*; (= *shreds*) jirones *mpl*; **to be in ~** [*clothes*] estar hecho jirones; (*fig*) [*reputation*] estar hecho trizas; [*marriage*] andar muy mal; **the coalition is in ~** la coalición anda muy mal

tatting [ˈtætɪŋ] N trabajo *m* de encaje, encaje *m*

tattle [ˈtætl] Ⓐ N (= *chat*) charla *f*; (= *gossip*) chismes *mpl*, habladurías *fpl*

Ⓑ VI (= *chat*) charlar, parlotear; (= *gossip*) chismear, contar chismes

tattler [ˈtætləʳ] N (= *chatterbox*) charlatán/ana *m/f*; (= *gossip*) chismoso/a *m/f*

tattletale* [ˈtætlteɪl] N (*US*) (= *person*) soplón/ona *m/f*, acusica *mf* (*Sp**); (= *talk*) cotilleo *m*, chismes *mpl* y cuentos *mpl*

tattoo¹ [təˈtuː] Ⓐ N (*on body*) tatuaje *m*

Ⓑ VT (*pt, pp* **tattooed**) tatuar

tattoo² [təˈtuː] N (*Mil*) (= *signal*) retreta *f*; (*Brit*) (= *pageant*) gran espectáculo *m* militar, exhibición *f* del arte militar; **the Edinburgh ~** el espectáculo militar de Edimburgo; **to beat a ~ with one's fingers** tamborilear con los dedos; → EDINBURGH FESTIVAL

tattooist [təˈtuːɪst] N tatuador(a) *m/f*

tatty* [ˈtætɪ] ADJ (*compar* **tattier**; *superl* **tattiest**) (= *shabby*) [*clothes*] raído, deshilachado; [*furniture*] estropeado

taught [tɔːt] PT, PP *of* **teach**

taunt [tɔːnt] Ⓐ N (= *jeer*) pulla *f*, mofa *f*; (= *insult*) insulto *m*

Ⓑ VT (= *jeer at*) mofarse de; (= *insult*) insultar; **to ~ sb (with sth)** mofarse de algn (por algo)

taunting [ˈtɔːntɪŋ] ADJ (= *jeering*) mofador, burlón; (= *insulting*) insultante

tauntingly [ˈtɔːntɪŋlɪ] ADV burlonamente, en son de burla

Taurean [ˌtɔːˈriːən] N **to be a ~** ser Tauro

tauromachy [ˈtɔːrəmækɪ] N tauromaquia *f*

Taurus [ˈtɔːrəs] N [1] (= *sign, constellation*) Tauro *m*

[2] (= *person*) tauro *mf*; **she's (a) ~** es tauro

taut [tɔːt] ADJ [1] (= *tight*) [*rope*] tirante, tenso; [*skin*] tirante; **the rope is held ~ by weights** la cuerda se mantiene tirante *or* tensa mediante unos pesos; **to pull sth ~** tensar algo; **to stretch sth ~** estirar algo hasta que quede tirante

[2] (= *tense*) [*person, face, voice*] tenso; **their faces were ~ with fear** tenían el rostro tenso por el miedo

[3] (= *firm*) [*body, legs*] firme, de carnes prietas; [*muscles*] firme

[4] (= *tightly written*) [*novel, film*] compacto

tauten [ˈtɔːtn] Ⓐ VT [+ *muscles, body, rope, cable*] tensar; [+ *skin*] estirar; (*Naut*) tesar

Ⓑ VI [*muscles, body, rope, cable*] tensarse; [*skin*] ponerse tirante

tautness [ˈtɔːtnɪs] N [1] [*of rope*] tensión *f*; [*of skin*] tirantez *f*

[2] [*of face, expression*] tensión *f*

[3] [*of body, muscles*] firmeza *f*

[4] [*of writing*] lo compacto

tautological [ˌtɔːtəˈlɒdʒɪkəl] ADJ tautológico

tautology [tɔːˈtɒlədʒɪ] N tautología *f*

tavern†† [ˈtævən] N taberna *f*

tawdriness [ˈtɔːdrɪnɪs] N [*of place, town*] chabacanería *f*

tawdry [ˈtɔːdrɪ] ADJ (*compar* **tawdrier**; *superl* **tawdriest**) [*jewellery*] de oropel, de relumbrón; [*clothes*] chabacano, hortera (*Sp**); [*decor*] charro, hortera (*Sp**); [*place, town*] chabacano; (= *sordid*) [*affair, business*] sórdido

tawny [ˈtɔːnɪ] (*compar* **tawnier**; *superl* **tawniest**) Ⓐ ADJ leonado; (*wine parlance*) ámbar oscuro, tostado

Ⓑ CPD ► **tawny owl** N cárabo *m* ► **tawny port** N puerto *m* seco

tax [tæks] Ⓐ N [1] (*Fin*) (= *contribution*) impuesto *m*, tributo *m* (*frm*); **half of it goes in ~** la mitad se me va en impuestos; **petrol ~** ◊ **~ on petrol** impuesto *m* sobre la gasolina; **profits after ~** beneficios después de impuestos; **profits before ~** beneficios antes de impuestos; **free of ~** exento *or* libre de impuestos; **to impose** *or* **levy** *or* **put a ~ on sth** gravar algo con un impuesto; **to pay ~ on sth** pagar impuestos por algo; **to pay one's ~es** pagar los impuestos; **how much ~ do you pay?** ¿cuánto paga de impuestos?; **I paid £3,000 in ~ last year** el año pasado pagué 3.000 libras de impuestos; **for ~ purposes** a efectos fiscales; *see also* **capital C**, **council B**, **income B**, **value-added tax**

[2] (= *strain*) **the extra administrative work was a ~ on the resources of schools** el trabajo adicional de administración supuso una carga pesada para los recursos de las escuelas; **it was a ~ on his strength/patience** puso a prueba sus fuerzas/su paciencia

Ⓑ VT [1] (*Fin*) [+ *income, profit*] gravar; [+ *person*] cobrar impuestos a, imponer cargas fiscales a; **household goods are ~ed at the rate of 15%** los artículos del hogar se gravan con el 15% *or* llevan un impuesto del 15%; **the wife is separately ~ed** la esposa paga impuestos por separado

[2] (*Brit Aut*) **I haven't got my car ~ed yet** aún no he pagado el impuesto de circulación

[3] (= *place a burden on*) poner a prueba; **these dilemmas would ~ the best of statesmen** estos dilemas pondrían a prueba al mejor de los estadistas

[4] (*frm*) (= *accuse*) **to ~ sb with sth** acusar a algn de algo

[5] (*Jur*) [+ *costs*] tasar

Ⓒ CPD ► **tax allowance** N desgravación *f* fiscal ► **tax avoidance** N evasión *f* legal de impuestos ► **tax base** N base *f* imponible ► **tax bracket** N grupo *m* impositivo ► **tax code, tax coding** N código *m* impositivo ► **tax collecting** N recaudación *f* de impuestos ► **tax collector** N recaudador(a) *m/f* de impuestos ► **tax cuts** NPL reducciones *fpl* en los impuestos ► **tax disc** N (*Brit*) pegatina *f* del impuesto de circulación ► **tax dodge*** N evasión *f* de impuestos ► **tax evasion** N evasión *f* fiscal ► **tax exemption** N exención *f* de impuestos, exención *f* tributaria ► **tax exile** N (= *person*) *persona autoexiliada para evitar los impuestos*; (= *state*) exilio *m* voluntario para evitar los impuestos ► **tax haven** N paraíso *m* fiscal ► **tax incentive** N aliciente *m* fiscal ► **tax inspector** N inspector(a) *m/f* fiscal, inspector(a) *m/f* de Hacienda ► **tax law** N derecho *m* tributario ► **tax liability** N obligación *f* fiscal, obligación *f* tributaria ► **tax rate** N tasa *f* impositiva ► **tax rebate** N devolución *f* de impuestos ► **tax relief** N desgravación *f* fiscal ► **tax return** N declaración *f* fiscal *or* de la renta; **to fill in** *or* **out one's ~ return** hacer la declaración fiscal *or* de la renta ► **tax revenue** N ingresos *mpl* tributarios ► **tax shelter** N refugio *m* fiscal ► **tax system** N sistema *m* tributario, sistema *m* fiscal ► **tax year** N año *m* fiscal, ejercicio *m* fiscal

taxable [ˈtæksəbl] Ⓐ ADJ gravable, imponible

Ⓑ CPD ► **taxable income** N renta *f* gravable, renta *f* imponible

taxation [tækˈseɪʃən] Ⓐ N (= *taxes*) impuestos *mpl*, contribuciones *fpl*; (= *system*) sistema *m* tributario

Ⓑ CPD ► **taxation system** N sistema *m* tributario, tributación *f*

tax-deductible ['tæksdɪ'dʌktəbl] ADJ desgravable

taxeme ['tæksi:m] N taxema *m*

tax-exempt [,tæksɪg'zempt] ADJ (*US*) exento de impuestos, libre de impuestos

tax-free ['tæks'fri:] (*Brit*) Ⓐ ADJ exento de impuestos, libre de impuestos
Ⓑ ADV **to live ~** vivir sin pagar impuestos

taxi ['tæksɪ] Ⓐ N (*pl* **taxis** *or* **taxies**) (= *cab*) taxi *m*; (= *collective taxi*) colectivo *m* (*LAm*), pesero *m* (*Mex*)
Ⓑ VI [1] (*Aer*) rodar por la pista
[2] (= *go by taxi*) ir en taxi
Ⓒ CPD ► **taxi driver** N taxista *mf* ► **taxi fare** N tarifa *f* de taxi; **I'll pay the ~ fare** yo pagaré el taxi ► **taxi rank** (*Brit*), **taxi stance** (*Scot*), **taxi stand** (*US*) N parada *f* de taxis

taxicab ['tæksɪkæb] N (*esp US*) taxi *m*

taxidermist ['tæksɪdɜ:mɪst] N taxidermista *mf*

taxidermy ['tæksɪdɜ:mɪ] N taxidermia *f*

taxi-man ['tæksɪmæn] N (*pl* **taxi-men**) taxista *m*

taximeter ['tæksɪ,mi:təʳ] N taxímetro *m*

taxing ['tæksɪŋ] ADJ [1] (*mentally*) [*problem, task*] dificilísimo; [*period, time*] muy duro; **his job was mentally ~** su trabajo requería muchísima concentración mental
[2] (*physically*) [*task, journey*] agotador, duro; **physically ~** agotador

taxiway ['tæksɪweɪ] N (*Aer*) pista *f* de rodaje

taxman* ['tæksmæn] N (*pl* **taxmen**) recaudador *m* de impuestos; (*euph*) (= *tax authorities*) **the ~** Hacienda *f*

taxonomist [tæk'sɒnəmɪst] N taxonomista *mf*

taxonomy [tæk'sɒnəmɪ] N taxonomía *f*

taxpayer ['tæks,peɪəʳ] N contribuyente *mf*

TB N ABBR = **tuberculosis**

tba ABBR = **to be arranged** *or* **to be announced**

T-bar ['ti:bɑ:ʳ] N hierro *m* en T; (*also* **~ lift**) (*Ski*) telesquí *m*

tbc ABBR = **to be confirmed**

T-bone (steak) ['ti:bəʊn,(steɪk)] N chuleta *f* en forma de T

tbs (*pl* **tbs**), **tbsp** (*pl* **tbsp** *or* **tbsps**), **tblsp** (*pl* **tblsp** *or* **tblsps**) ABBR = **tablespoonful**

TD N ABBR [1] (*American Ftbl*) = **touchdown**
[2] (*US*) = **Treasury Department**
[3] (*Irl*) (= **Teachta Dála**) *miembro del parlamento irlandés*
[4] (*Brit*) = **Territorial Decoration**

te [ti:] N (*Mus*) si *m*

tea [ti:] Ⓐ N [1] (= *drink, plant*) té *m*; **would you like some ~?** ¿te apetece un té?; **a cup of ~** una taza de té; **I'm making another pot of ~** voy a hacer otra tetera; **~ with lemon** ◊ **lemon ~** té con limón; **camomile ~** manzanilla *f*; **herbal/mint ~** té *m* de hierbas/menta; **iced ~** te *m* helado; ✦*IDIOMS* **not for all the ~ in China** por nada del mundo; **~ and sympathy** (*euph*) té y sonrisas; *see also* **cup**
[2] (= *cup of tea*) té *m*; **three ~s and a coffee please** tres tés y un café por favor
[3] (= *meal*) (*afternoon*) té *m*, merienda *f*; (*evening*) (*Brit*) cena *f*; **an invitation to ~** una invitación a tomar el té *or* merendar; **high ~** merienda-cena *f* (*que se toma con té*); **to have ~** tomar el té, merendar
Ⓑ CPD ► **tea bag** N bolsita *f* de té ► **tea boy** N *chico que prepara y sirve el té en una fábrica u oficina* ► **tea break** N descanso *m* para el té ► **tea caddy** N bote *m* para té ► **tea cart** N (*US*) = **tea trolley** ► **tea chest** N caja *f* grande de madera ► **tea cloth** N (*for trolley, tray*) mantelito *m*, pañito *m*; (*for dishes*) = **tea towel** ► **tea cosy**, **tea cozy** (*US*) N cubretetera *m* ► **tea dance** N té *m* bailable, té-baile *m* ► **tea garden** N (= *café*) café *m* al aire libre; (*Agr*) plantación *f* de té ► **tea lady** N (*Brit*) *señora que prepara y sirve el té en una fábrica u oficina* ► **tea leaf** N hoja *f* de té ► **tea party** N té *m*, merienda *f* ► **tea rose** N rosa *f* de té ► **tea service**, **tea set** N servicio *m* de té, juego *m* de té ► **tea strainer** N colador *m* de té ► **tea table** N mesita *f* de té ► **tea things** NPL servicio *m* del té ► **tea towel** N paño *m* de cocina, trapo *m* de cocina (*LAm*) ► **tea tray** N bandeja *f* del té ► **tea trolley** N (*Brit*) carrito *m* del té ► **tea urn** N tetera *f* grande ► **tea wagon** N (*US*) carrito *m* del té

teacake ['ti:keɪk] N *bollo con pasas que generalmente se come tostado y untado con mantequilla*

teach [ti:tʃ] (*pt, pp* **taught**) Ⓐ VT [1] (*in class*) [+ *subject*] dar clases de, enseñar; [+ *group*] dar clases a; **Miss Hardy taught us needlework** la Srta. Hardy nos daba clases de *or* nos enseñaba costura; **he ~es primary-school children** es maestro de escuela (primaria), da clases a niños de primaria; **to ~ school** (*US*) (*primary*) dar clases en un colegio de enseñanza primaria; (*secondary*) dar clases en un colegio de enseñanza secundaria; **she taught English to Japanese businessmen** enseñaba inglés *or* daba clases de inglés a ejecutivos japoneses
[2] (*not in class*) enseñar; **to ~ sb to do sth** enseñar a algn a hacer algo; **his parents taught him never to lie** sus padres le enseñaron a no mentir nunca; **he taught himself Arabic** aprendió árabe por su cuenta; **I'll ~ you to speak to me like that!** ¡ya te enseñaré yo a hablarme así!; **you can't ~ him anything about cars** no le puedes enseñar nada sobre coches; **my mother taught me how to cook** mi madre me enseñó a cocinar; **history ~es us a valuable lesson** la historia nos enseña una valiosa lección; **that'll ~ you!** ¡eso te servirá de lección!, ¡te está bien empleado!; **that will ~ you to mind your own business!** ¡eso te enseñará a no meterte en lo que no te importa!; ✦*IDIOMS* **don't ~ your grandmother to suck eggs** a tu padre no le puedes enseñar a ser hijo; **to ~ sb a lesson*** darle una lección a algn; **you can't ~ an old dog new tricks** perro viejo no aprende gracias
Ⓑ VI (= *give classes*) dar clases; **his wife ~es at our school** su esposa da clases *or* es profesora en nuestro colegio; **he has always wanted to ~** siempre ha querido ser profesor *or* dedicarse a la enseñanza

teachability [,ti:tʃə'bɪlɪtɪ] N (*esp US*) educabilidad *f*

teachable ['ti:tʃəbl] ADJ (*esp US*) educable

teacher ['ti:tʃəʳ] Ⓐ N (*in secondary school*) profesor(a) *m/f*; (*in primary school*) maestro/a *m/f*; **French ~** profesor(a) *m/f* de francés
Ⓑ CPD ► **teacher training** N (*Brit*) formación *f* pedagógica ► **teacher training college** N (*for primary schools*) escuela *f* normal; (*for secondary schools*) ≈ Instituto *m* de Ciencias de la Educación, ICE *m*; *see also* **pet A2**

teacher-pupil ratio [,ti:tʃə,pju:pl'reɪʃɪəʊ] N proporción *f* profesor-alumnos

teach-in ['ti:tʃ,ɪn] N reunión *f* de autoenseñanza colectiva

teaching ['ti:tʃɪŋ] Ⓐ N [1] (= *profession*) enseñanza *f*, docencia *f* (*more frm*); **have you considered a career in ~?** ¿has pensado en dedicarte a la enseñanza?; **her son's gone into ~** su hijo se ha metido a profesor
[2] (= *activity*) enseñanza *f*; **our aim is to improve the ~ in our schools** nuestra meta es mejorar (el nivel de) la enseñanza en los colegios; **he's got 16 hours ~ a week** da 16 horas de clase a la semana; **I like ~** me gusta dar clases *or* enseñar; **the Teaching of English as a Foreign Language** la enseñanza del inglés como lengua extranjera; → TEFL/EFL, TESL/ESL, ELT, TESOL/ESOL
[3] (*esp pl*) [*of philosopher, prophet*] enseñanzas *fpl*; **according to the ~(s) of Socrates** según las enseñanzas de Sócrates; **the church's ~ on birth control** las enseñanzas *or* la doctrina de la Iglesia con respecto al control de la natalidad
Ⓑ CPD ► **teaching aid** N artículo *m* didáctico, artículo *m* de enseñanza ► **teaching aids** NPL material *m* didáctico, material *m* de enseñanza ► **teaching hospital** N (*Brit*) hospital *m* clínico ► **teaching material** N material *m* didáctico, material *m* de enseñanza ► **teaching post** N puesto *m* de profesor, puesto *m* docente ► **teaching practice** N (*Brit*) prácticas *fpl* de enseñanza ► **the teaching profession** N la profesión docente, la docencia ► **the teaching staff** N el profesorado, el cuerpo docente

teacup ['ti:kʌp] N taza *f* para el té

teahouse ['ti:haʊs] N (*pl* **teahouses** ['ti:haʊzɪz]) salón *m* de té

teak [ti:k] N teca *f*, madera *f* de teca

teakettle ['ti:ketl] N (*US*) tetera *f*

teal [ti:l] N (*pl* **teal** *or* **teals**) cerceta *f*

team [ti:m] Ⓐ N (*gen*) equipo *m*; (= *group*) grupo *m*, equipo *m*; [*of horses*] tiro *m*; [*of oxen*] yunta *f*; **the national ~** la selección nacional; **home/away ~** equipo *m* de casa/visitante
Ⓑ VT **to ~ sth with sth** [+ *clothes*] combinar algo con algo; **to ~ sb with sb** asociar a algn con algn
Ⓒ VI **to ~ with sth** [*items of clothing*] combinar con algo
Ⓓ CPD ► **team championship** N campeonato *m* por equipos ► **team game** N juego *m* de equipo ► **team member** N miembro *mf* del equipo ► **team spirit** N espíritu *m* de equipo, compañerismo *m*

►**team up** VI + ADV juntarse, asociarse (**with** con); (*Sport*) formar un equipo (**with** con)

team-mate ['ti:mmeɪt] N compañero/a *m/f* de equipo

teamster ['ti:mstəʳ] N (*US*) camionero *m*, camionista *m*

teamwork ['ti:mwɜ:k] N labor *f* de equipo, trabajo *m* en *or* de equipo

teapot ['ti:pɒt] N tetera *f*

tear¹ [teəʳ] (*vb: pt* **tore**; *pp* **torn**) Ⓐ N [1] (= *rip*) (*in fabric, paper*) roto *m*, rasgón *m*, desgarrón *m*; **your shirt has a ~ in it** llevas la camisa rota, tu camisa está rota, tienes un roto *or* rasgón *or* desgarrón en la camisa; *see also* **wear A2**
[2] (*Med*) (= *injury*) (*in muscle*) desgarro *m*; (*in ligament*) rotura *f*; [*of tissue*] (*in childbirth*) desgarro *m*
Ⓑ VT [1] (= *rip*) [+ *fabric, paper*] romper, rasgar; **you've torn your trousers** te has roto *or* rasgado el pantalón; **Jane tore my dress** Jane me rompió *or* rasgó el vestido; **~ along the dotted line** rasgar por la línea de puntos; **to ~ a hole in sth** hacer un agujero en algo; **she tore open the envelope** abrió el sobre rápidamente; **to ~ sth to pieces** *or* **bits** (*lit*) [+ *letter, photograph*] hacer pedazos algo, destrozar algo; [+ *animal*] descuartizar algo; (*fig*) [+ *argument, essay, idea*] echar algo por tierra; **the antelope was torn to pieces by the lions** los leones descuartizaron el antílope; **to ~ sb to pieces** *or* **bits** (*lit*) descuartizar a algn; (*fig*) poner a algn por los suelos; ✦*IDIOM*

that's torn it!* ¡ya la hemos fastidiado!*, ¡buena la hemos hecho!*; *see also* **hair A1**, **limb**
[2] (= *injure*) [+ *muscle*] desgarrarse; [+ *ligament*] romperse; **he tore a muscle in his thigh** se desgarró un músculo del muslo; **torn ligaments** rotura *f* de ligamentos
[3] (= *pull, remove*) **he tore the shelf away from the wall with his bare hands** arrancó el estante de la pared con sus propias manos; **to ~ o.s. free** *or* **loose** soltarse; **to ~ sth from/off sth** arrancar algo de algo; **he tore a page from** *or* **out of his notebook** arrancó una hoja del bloc de notas; **she tried to ~ the book from my hands** intentó arrancarme el libro de las manos; **the wind tore the roof off a building** el viento arrancó (de cuajo) el tejado de un edificio; ✦*IDIOM* **to ~ sb off a strip** (*Brit**) poner a algn de vuelta y media*
[4] (*fig*) **having to make a decision like that can ~ you in two** tomar una decisión así puede ser una experiencia desgarradora; **he was torn by his emotions** estaba desgarrado por las emociones; **a country torn by war** un país desgarrado por la guerra; **she is torn between her job and her family** se debate entre su trabajo y su familia; **she was torn between the two men in her life** no se decidía entre los dos hombres que formaban parte de su vida; *see also* **tear apart 3**
Ⓒ VI [1] (= *get torn*) [*fabric, paper*] rasgarse, romperse; (*Med*) [*muscle, tissue*] desgarrarse; [*ligament*] romperse
[2] (= *pull*) **to ~ at sth**: **he tore at the wrapping paper** tiró del papel de regalo; **the eagles tore at its flesh with their beaks** las águilas le arrancaban la carne con los picos; **the brambles tore at his face** las zarzas le arañaron la cara; **she managed to ~ free** *or* **loose** logró soltarse
[3] (= *rush*) **to ~ along/out/down** *etc* ir/salir/bajar *etc* embalado, ir/salir/bajar *etc* a toda velocidad; **she tore out of the room/up the stairs** salió de la habitación/subió las escaleras embalada, salió de la habitación/subió las escaleras a toda velocidad; **we were ~ing along the motorway** íbamos embalados por la autopista, íbamos por la autopista a toda velocidad *or* a toda pastilla*; **to ~ past** pasar como un rayo; **an explosion tore through the building** una explosión sacudió el edificio
Ⓓ CPD ► **tear sheet** N hoja *f* separable, página *f* recortable

► **tear along** Ⓐ VI + ADV (= *run*) correr precipitadamente, precipitarse, ir a máxima velocidad
Ⓑ VI + PREP *see* **tear¹ C2, C3**

► **tear apart** VT + ADV [1] (= *rip to pieces*) [+ *object*] hacer pedazos, hacer trizas; [+ *prey*] descuartizar
[2] (*in search*) [+ *room, house*] destrozar; **they tore the room apart, searching for drugs** destrozaron la habitación en busca de drogas
[3] (= *damage*) [+ *family, organization, person*] desgarrar; **the family had been torn apart by the divorce** el divorcio había desgarrado a la familia; **it ~s me apart to know you're unhappy** me desgarra el corazón saber que no eres feliz
[4] (= *criticize*) [+ *idea, theory*] echar por tierra

► **tear away** Ⓐ VT + ADV (*fig*) **the exhibition was so interesting I could hardly ~ myself away** era una exposición tan interesante que me costaba horrores marcharme; **eventually we tore him away from the party** por fin conseguimos arrancarlo de la fiesta, por fin conseguimos que se marchara de la fiesta; **I couldn't ~ my eyes away from him** no le podía quitar los ojos de encima; **if you can ~ yourself away from that book/the television** si puedes dejar ese libro/despegarte del televisor un momento
Ⓑ VI + ADV (*at speed*) salir embalado, salir a toda velocidad

► **tear down** VT + ADV [+ *building, statue*] derribar; [+ *poster, flag*] arrancar

► **tear off** Ⓐ VT + ADV [1] (= *remove*) [+ *sheet of paper, label, wrapping*] arrancar; **he tore off his clothes and fell into bed** se quitó la ropa a tirones y cayó sobre la cama; **he tried to ~ off her burning dress** intentó quitarle a tirones el vestido en llamas; **the hurricane/explosion tore off the roof** el huracán/la explosión arrancó el techo de cuajo
[2] (*) (= *write hurriedly*) [+ *letter*] escribir deprisa y corriendo, garrapatear
Ⓑ VI + ADV [1] (*at speed*) salir embalado, salir a toda velocidad; **she tore off on her motorbike** salió embalada *or* a toda velocidad en la moto
[2] (= *be removable*) **the label ~s off** la etiqueta se puede arrancar
Ⓒ VT + PREP *see* **tear¹ B3**

► **tear out** Ⓐ VT + ADV [+ *cheque, page*] arrancar; [+ *plant, stake, tree*] arrancar, arrancar de cuajo; **to ~ sb's eyes out** sacar los ojos a algn; **to ~ one's hair (out)** (*lit*) arrancarse el pelo a manojos; (*in exasperation, worry*) tirarse de los pelos
Ⓑ VI + ADV (= *rush*) *see* **tear¹ C3**

► **tear up** VT + ADV [1] (= *rip to pieces*) (*lit*) [+ *letter, photo*] romper, hacer pedazos; (*fig*) [+ *contract, agreement*] romper, anular
[2] (= *pull up*) [+ *plant, stake, tree*] arrancar, arrancar de cuajo; [+ *forest, woodland*] talar, despoblar; [+ *road*] levantar
[3] (= *damage*) [+ *pitch, surface*] destrozar

tear² [tɪəʳ] Ⓐ N lágrima *f*; **to burst into ~s** echarse a llorar; **she was close to ~s** estaba a punto de llorar; **to dissolve into ~s** deshacerse en lágrimas; **to be in ~s** estar llorando; **to end in ~s: it'll end in ~s!** (*lit*) ¡luego vendrán los llantos!, ¡al final acabaráis llorando!; (*fig*) acabará mal; **it was a marriage destined to end in ~s** era un matrimonio que estaba condenado a acabar mal; **to be moved to ~s** llorar de la emoción; **I was moved to ~s by their generosity** lloré de la emoción por la generosidad que mostraron; **to reduce sb to ~s** hacerle llorar a algn; **she didn't shed a single ~** no derramó ni una sola lágrima; **nobody is going to shed a ~ over that** nadie se va a disgustar por eso; **to wipe away one's ~s** secarse las lágrimas; ✦*IDIOM* **to bore sb to ~s** aburrir soberanamente a algn; **I was bored to ~s** me aburrí soberanamente *or* como una ostra*
Ⓑ CPD ► **tear duct** N conducto *m* lacrimal ► **tear gas** N gas *m* lacrimógeno ► **tear gas bomb** N bomba *f* lacrimógena ► **tear gas canister** N bote *m* de gas lacrimógeno ► **tear gas grenade** N granada *f* lacrimógena

tearaway* ['tɛərəweɪ] N (*Brit*) gamberro/a *m/f*, alborotador(a) *m/f*

teardrop ['tɪədrɒp] N lágrima *f*

tearful ['tɪəfʊl] ADJ [*eyes, voice*] lloroso; [*farewell, reunion*] emotivo; **she was surrounded by ~ children** estaba rodeada de niños que lloraban; **she felt a bit ~** se le saltaron las lágrimas; **to become** *or* **get ~** ponerse a llorar

tearfully ['tɪəfəlɪ] ADV [*say, reply, smile*] con lágrimas en los ojos, llorando

tearing ['tɛərɪŋ] ADJ [1] **with a ~ noise** con un ruido de tela que se rasga
[2] (*fig*) **at a ~ pace** a un paso vertiginoso; **to be in a ~ hurry** estar muy de prisa

tear-jerker* ['tɪə,dʒɜːkəʳ] N (= *film*) película *f* lacrimógena; (= *play*) dramón *m* muy sentimental*, obra *f* lacrimógena

tear-jerking* ['tɪə,dʒɜːkɪŋ] ADJ lacrimógeno, muy sentimental

tear-off ['tɛərɒf] Ⓐ ADJ [*tab, ticket*] con trepado, con taladrado
Ⓑ CPD ► **tear-off calendar** N calendario *m* de taco ► **tear-off notebook** N bloc *m* de notas

tearoom ['tiːrʊm] N salón *m* de té

tear-stained ['tɪəsteɪnd] ADJ manchado de lágrimas

tease [tiːz] Ⓐ N [1] (= *person*) (= *leg-puller*) bromista *mf*, guasón/ona* *m/f*; **he's a dreadful ~** es muy bromista, es muy guasón*
[2] (= *flirt*) **he's a dreadful ~** le gusta mucho flirtear
[3] (= *joke*) **to do sth for a ~** hacer algo para divertirse
Ⓑ VT [1] [+ *person*] (= *make fun of*) tomar el pelo a, mofarse de; (= *annoy*) fastidiar, molestar; (*cruelly*) atormentar; (*sexually*) coquetear con; **they ~ her about her hair** la molestan con chistes acerca de su pelo; **I don't like being ~d** no me gusta que se me tome el pelo
[2] [+ *animal*] provocar
[3] (*Tech*) [+ *fibres*] cardar

► **tease out** VT + ADV [+ *tangles*] desenredar, separar; (*fig*) [+ *information*] sonsacar, ir sacando

teasel ['tiːzl] N [1] (*Bot*) cardencha *f*
[2] (*Tech*) carda *f*

teaser ['tiːzəʳ] N [1] (= *person*) = **tease A**
[2] (*) (= *problem*) rompecabezas *m inv*

teashop ['tiːʃɒp] N (*Brit*) café *m*, cafetería *f*; (*strictly*) salón *m* de té

teasing ['tiːzɪŋ] Ⓐ ADJ burlón, guasón*
Ⓑ N burlas *fpl*, guasa* *f*

teasingly ['tiːzɪŋlɪ] ADV [1] (= *jokingly*) [*say*] de manera burlona, de cachondeo (*Sp**)
[2] (= *flirtatiously*) [*smile*] coquetamente

teaspoon ['tiːspuːn] N (= *spoon*) cucharilla *f*, cucharita *f* (de postre); (= *quantity*) cucharadita *f*

teaspoonful ['tiːspʊnfʊl] N cucharadita *f*

teat [tiːt] N [*of bottle*] tetina *f*; [*of animal*] teta *f*

teatime ['tiːtaɪm] N (*esp Brit*) [1] (= *time for drinking tea*) hora *f* del té; **at ~** a la hora del té
[2] (= *time of evening meal*) hora *f* de cenar

TEC N ABBR (*Brit*) = **Training and Enterprise Council**

'tec* [tek] N = **detective**

tech [tek] N ABBR [1] = **technology**
[2] = **technical college**

technetium [tek'niːʃɪəm] N tecnetio *m*

technical ['teknɪkəl] Ⓐ ADJ técnico; **this is getting too ~** esto se está poniendo muy técnico; **a ~ hitch** un fallo técnico; **a ~ offence** (*Jur*) un delito de carácter técnico, un cuasidelito; **a ~ point** un detalle técnico; **for ~ reasons** por motivos técnicos; **the government has scored a ~ victory** teóricamente, el gobierno ha logrado una victoria
Ⓑ CPD ► **technical college** N (*Brit Scol*) ≈ escuela *f* politécnica, ≈ instituto *m* de formación profesional (*Sp*) ► **technical drawing** N dibujo *m* técnico ► **technical knockout** N (*Boxing*) K.O. *m* técnico ► **technical support** N (*Comput*) (servicio *m* de) asistencia *f* técnica

technicality [ˌteknɪˈkælɪtɪ] N 1 (= *technical detail*) detalle *m* (técnico); (= *word*) tecnicismo *m*; **I don't understand all the technicalities** no entiendo todos los detalles (técnicos); **it failed because of a ~** fracasó debido a una dificultad técnica
2 (= *nature*) tecnicidad *f*, carácter *m* técnico

technically [ˈteknɪkəlɪ] ADV 1 (= *technologically*) [*advanced*] técnicamente; [*superior, feasible*] técnicamente, desde el punto de vista técnico
2 (= *strictly*) [*illegal, correct*] técnicamente; **~, they aren't eligible for a grant** técnicamente *or* en teoría, no tienen derecho a una ayuda; **~ speaking** hablando en sentido estricto, en puridad (*frm*)
3 (= *regarding technique*) [*proficient, demanding*] desde el punto de vista técnico, técnicamente

technician [tekˈnɪʃən] N técnico/a *m/f*; *see also* **dental, laboratory**

Technicolor® [ˈteknɪˌkʌləʳ] Ⓐ N tecnicolor® *m*; **in ~** en tecnicolor
Ⓑ ADJ en tecnicolor, de tecnicolor

technique [tekˈniːk] N (*gen*) técnica *f*

techno... [ˈteknəʊ] PREFIX tecno...

technocracy [tekˈnɒkrəsɪ] N tecnocracia *f*

technocrat [ˈteknəʊkræt] N tecnócrata *mf*

technocratic [ˌteknəˈkrætɪk] ADJ tecnocrático

technological [ˌteknəˈlɒdʒɪkəl] ADJ tecnológico

technologically [ˌteknəˈlɒdʒɪkəlɪ] ADV tecnológicamente

technologist [tekˈnɒlədʒɪst] N tecnólogo/a *m/f*

technology [tekˈnɒlədʒɪ] N tecnología *f*

techy [ˈtetʃɪ] ADJ = **tetchy**

tectonic [tekˈtɒnɪk] ADJ tectónico; **~ movement** movimiento *m* tectónico; **~ plate** placa *f* tectónica

tectonics [tekˈtɒnɪks] N tectónica *f*

Ted [ted] N (*familiar form*) *of* **Edward**

tedder [ˈtedəʳ] N heneador *m*

Teddy [ˈtedɪ] N (*familiar form*) *of* **Edward**

teddy [ˈtedɪ] Ⓐ N (*also* **~ bear**) osito *m* (de peluche)
Ⓑ CPD ► **teddy boy** N (*Brit*) *hombre vestido a la moda de los rockeros de los años 50 y considerado a menudo una persona violenta*

tedious [ˈtiːdɪəs] ADJ pesado, aburrido

tediously [ˈtiːdɪəslɪ] ADV **~ dull** mortalmente aburrido; **his speech was ~ long** su discurso fue largo y pesado *or* aburrido

tediousness [ˈtiːdɪəsnɪs], **tedium** [ˈtiːdɪəm] N pesadez *f*, lo aburrido

tee [tiː] N 1 (*Golf*) (= *object*) tee *m*; (= *area*) punto *m* de salida; **the third ~** el punto de salida del tercer hoyo
2 *see* **T**

►**tee off** VI + ADV dar el primer golpe

►**tee up** Ⓐ VT + ADV (*Golf*) [+ *ball*] colocar en el tee; (*Ftbl*) preparar
Ⓑ VI + ADV colocar la pelota en el tee

tee-hee [ˈtiːˈhiː] Ⓐ N risita *f* (tonta)
Ⓑ EXCL ¡ji!, ¡ji!, ¡je!, ¡je!
Ⓒ VI reírse con una risita tonta, reírse un poquito

teem [tiːm] VI 1 **to ~ (with)** [+ *insects, fish*] abundar (en); **a lake ~ing with fish** un lago que abunda en peces, un lago repleto de peces; **through streets ~ing with people** por calles atestadas de gente
2 **it's ~ing (with rain)** está lloviendo a mares *or* a cántaros

teeming [ˈtiːmɪŋ] ADJ numerosísimo; [*rain*] torrencial; **the ~ millions** los muchos millones

teen* [tiːn] ADJ = **teenage**

teenage [ˈtiːneɪdʒ] ADJ [*fashion*] para adolescentes, juvenil; **a ~ boy/girl** un/una adolescente; **memories of her ~ years** recuerdos *mpl* de sus años de adolescencia; **to reduce the number of ~ pregnancies** reducir el número de embarazos entre las jóvenes adolescentes

teenager [ˈtiːnˌeɪdʒəʳ] N adolescente *mf*; **a club for ~s** un club para jóvenes

teens [tiːnz] NPL adolescencia *fsing*; **to be in one's ~** ser adolescente; **he is still in his ~** es adolescente todavía, no ha cumplido aún los 20

teensy(-weensy)* [ˈtiːnzɪ(ˈwiːnzɪ)] ADJ = **teeny(-weeny)**

teenybopper [ˈtiːnɪˈbɒpəʳ] N quinceañero/a *m/f*

teeny(-weeny)* [ˈtiːnɪ(ˈwiːnɪ)] ADJ chiquito, chiquitín

tee-shirt [ˈtiːʃɜːt] N = **T-shirt**

teeter [ˈtiːtəʳ] VI bambolearse, tambalearse; (*fig*) vacilar, titubear; **to ~ on the edge of a nervous breakdown** estar al borde de un ataque nervioso

teeth [tiːθ] NPL *of* **tooth**

teethe [tiːð] VI echar los dientes; **he's teething** le están saliendo los dientes, está echando los dientes

teething [ˈtiːðɪŋ] Ⓐ N dentición *f*
Ⓑ CPD ► **teething ring** N chupador *m*, mordedor *m* ► **teething troubles, teething problems** NPL (*Brit*) (*fig*) problemas *mpl* iniciales

teetotal [ˈtiːˈtəʊtl] ADJ [*person*] abstemio; **the Methodist church used to be ~** los metodistas eran abstemios

teetotalism [ˈtiːˈtəʊtəlɪzəm] N abstinencia *f* (de bebidas alcohólicas)

teetotaller, teetotaler (*US*) [ˈtiːˈtəʊtləʳ] N (= *person*) abstemio/a *m/f*

TEFL [ˈtefl] N ABBR = **Teaching of English as a Foreign Language**

TEFL/EFL, TESL/ESL, ELT, TESOL/ESOL

Los términos **TEFL (Teaching (of) English as a Foreign Language**: *enseñanza del inglés como lengua extranjera) y* **EFL (English as a Foreign Language**: *inglés para extranjeros) se usan para hablar de la enseñanza del inglés a personas que no viven en un país de habla inglesa.*

TESL (Teaching (of) English as a Second Language: *enseñanza del inglés como segunda lengua) y* **ESL (English as a Second Language**: *inglés como segunda lengua) se refieren a la enseñanza del inglés a personas que viven en un país de habla inglesa pero tienen otra lengua materna, por ejemplo, los miembros de las minorías étnicas. Este tipo de enseñanza intenta integrar el entorno cultural del alumno y aprovechar el conocimiento de su lengua materna en el proceso de aprendizaje.*

ELT (English Language Teaching: *enseñanza del inglés) es el término que se aplica a la enseñanza del inglés en general y, por tanto, engloba a los ya mencionados.*

TESOL (Teaching (of) English to Speakers of Other Languages) *es el término de inglés americano que equivale a* **TEFL** *y a* **TESL. ESOL (English for Speakers of Other Languages)** *es el equivalente a* **EFL** *y* **ESL.**

Teflon® [ˈteflɒn] N teflón® *m*

tegument [ˈtegjʊmənt] N tegumento *m*

Teheran, Tehran [teəˈrɑːn] N Teherán *m*

tel. ABBR (= **telephone**) tel, tfno, Tfno

tele... [ˈtelɪ] PREFIX tele...

telebanking [ˈtelɪˌbæŋkɪŋ] N telebanco *m*, telebanca *f*

telecast [ˈtelɪkɑːst] (*US*) Ⓐ N programa *m* de televisión
Ⓑ VT, VI transmitir (por televisión)

telecommunications [ˈtelɪkəˌmjuːnɪˈkeɪʃənz] Ⓐ N (= *area of study*) telecomunicaciones *fpl*
Ⓑ CPD [*company, equipment*] de telecomunicaciones ► **the telecommunications industry** N el sector de telecomunicaciones, la industria de telecomunicaciones

telecommute [ˈtelɪkəmˌjuːt] VI teletrabajar, trabajar a distancia

telecommuter [ˈtelɪkəmˌjuːtəʳ] N teletrabajador(a) *m/f*, trabajador(a) *m/f* a distancia

telecommuting [ˈtelɪkəmˌjuːtɪŋ] N teletrabajo *m*, trabajo *m* a distancia

teleconference [ˈtelɪkɒnfərəns] N teleconferencia *f*

teleconferencing [ˈtelɪkɒnfərənsɪŋ] N teleconferencias *fpl*

telefilm [ˈtelɪfɪlm] N telefilm(e) *m*

telegenic [ˌtelɪˈdʒenɪk] ADJ televisivo, telegénico

telegram [ˈtelɪgræm] N telegrama *m*

telegraph [ˈtelɪgrɑːf] Ⓐ N (= *message*) telegrama *m*; (= *apparatus*) aparato *m* telegráfico
Ⓑ VT, VI telegrafiar
Ⓒ CPD ► **telegraph pole, telegraph post** N poste *m* telegráfico ► **telegraph wire** N hilo *m* telegráfico

telegraphese [ˈtelɪgrɑːˈfiːz] N estilo *m* telegráfico

telegraphic [ˌtelɪˈgræfɪk] ADJ telegráfico

telegraphist [tɪˈlegrəfɪst] N telegrafista *mf*

telegraphy [tɪˈlegrəfɪ] N telegrafía *f*

telekinesis [ˌtelɪkɪˈniːsɪs] N telequinesia *f*

telemarketing [ˈtelɪmɑːkɪtɪŋ] N (*Comm*) telemárketing *m*

telematic [ˌtelɪˈmætɪk] ADJ telemático

telemessage [ˈtelɪmesɪdʒ] N (*Brit*) telegrama *m*

telemetry [tɪˈlemɪtrɪ] N telemetría *f*

teleology [ˌtelɪˈɒlədʒɪ] N teleología *f*

teleordering [ˈtelɪˌɔːdərɪŋ] N pedido *m* telefónico

telepath [ˈtelɪpæθ] N telépata *mf*

telepathic [ˌtelɪˈpæθɪk] ADJ telepático

telepathically [ˌtelɪˈpæθɪklɪ] ADV telepáticamente, por telepatía

telepathist [tɪˈlepəθɪst] N telepatista *mf*

telepathy [tɪˈlepəθɪ] N telepatía *f*

telephone [ˈtelɪfəʊn] Ⓐ N teléfono *m*; **to be on the ~** (= *be connected*) tener teléfono; (= *be speaking*) estar hablando por teléfono; **you're wanted on the ~** le llaman al teléfono
Ⓑ VI telefonear; **I'll ~ for an ambulance** llamaré a una ambulancia
Ⓒ VT llamar por teléfono, telefonear
Ⓓ CPD ► **telephone answering machine** N contestador *m* automático ► **telephone book** N = **telephone directory** ► **telephone booth** (*US*), **telephone box** (*Brit*) N cabina *f* telefónica ► **telephone call** N llamada *f* (telefónica) ► **telephone directory** N guía *f* telefónica ► **telephone exchange** N central *f* (telefónica); (*private*) centralita *f* (*Sp*), conmutador *m* (*LAm*) ► **telephone kiosk** N = **telephone box**

► **telephone number** N número *m* de teléfono, fono *m* (*Chile*); **he's paid in ~ numbers*** le pagan un dineral* ► **telephone operator** N telefonista *mf* ► **telephone sex** N teléfono *m* erótico ► **telephone subscriber** N abonado/a *m/f* telefónico/a ► **telephone tapping** N intervención *f* telefónica ► **telephone warning** N aviso *m* telefónico

telephonic [ˌtelɪˈfɒnɪk] ADJ telefónico

telephonist [tɪˈlefənɪst] N telefonista *mf*

telephony [tɪˈlefənɪ] N telefonía *f*

telephoto lens [ˈtelɪˌfəʊtəʊˈlenz] N teleobjetivo *m*

teleprinter [ˈtelɪˌprɪntəʳ] N teletipo *m*

teleprocessing [ˌtelɪˈprəʊsesɪŋ] N teleproceso *m*

teleprompter® [ˈtelɪˌprɒmptəʳ] N teleprompter *m*

telesales [ˈtelɪˌseɪlz] Ⓐ NPL televenta(s) *f(pl)*
Ⓑ CPD ► **telesales person** N televendedor(a) *m/f*

telescope [ˈtelɪskəʊp] Ⓐ N telescopio *m*
Ⓑ VI [*aerial, umbrella*] plegarse
Ⓒ VT abatir, plegar; **to ~ A into B** meter A dentro de B

telescopic [ˌtelɪsˈkɒpɪk] Ⓐ ADJ telescópico
Ⓑ CPD ► **telescopic lens** N teleobjetivo *m* ► **telescopic sight** N mira *f* telescópica, visor *m* telescópico ► **telescopic umbrella** N paraguas *m* plegable

teleshopping [ˈtelɪˌʃɒpɪŋ] N (*US*) telecompra(s) *f(pl)*

teletext [ˈtelɪtekst] N teletex(to) *m*

telethon [ˈteləθɒn] N (*TV*) telemaratón *m* (con fines benéficos)

Teletype® [ˈtelɪˌtaɪp] N teletipo *m*

teletypewriter [ˌtelɪˈtaɪpraɪtəʳ] (*US*) N = **teleprinter**

televangelist [ˌtelɪˈvændʒəlɪst] N evangelista *mf* de la tele

televiewer [ˈtelɪˌvjuːəʳ] N televidente *mf*, telespectador(a) *m/f*

televise [ˈtelɪvaɪz] VT transmitir (por televisión), televisar

television [ˈtelɪˌvɪʒən] Ⓐ N (= *broadcast, broadcasting industry*) televisión *f*; (*also* ~ **set**) televisor *m*, aparato *m* de televisión; **to be on ~** [*person*] salir por la televisión; **to watch ~** ver *or* mirar la televisión; **to speak on ~** hablar por televisión
Ⓑ CPD [*broadcast, play, report, serial*] televisivo; [*camera*] de televisión; [*personality*] de la televisión ► **television aerial** N antena *f* de televisión ► **television announcer** N locutor(a) *m/f* de televisión ► **television broadcast** N emisión *f* televisiva ► **television licence** N *licencia que se paga por el uso del televisor, destinada a financiar la BBC* ► **television lounge** N sala *f* de televisión ► **television network** N cadena *f* de televisión, red *f* de televisión ► **television programme** N programa *m* de televisión ► **television room** N sala *f* de televisión ► **television screen** N pantalla *f* de televisión ► **television set** N televisor *m*, aparato *m* de televisión ► **television studio** N estudio *m* de televisión ► **television tube** N tubo *m* de rayos catódicos, cinescopio *m*

televisual [telɪˈvɪzjʊəl] ADJ (*Brit*) televisivo

telework [ˈtelɪwɜːk] VI teletrabajar

teleworker [ˈtelɪwɜːkəʳ] N teletrabajador(a) *m/f*

teleworking [ˈtelɪwɜːkɪŋ] N teletrabajo *m*

telex [ˈteleks] Ⓐ N (*gen*) télex *m inv*
Ⓑ VT, VI enviar un télex (a)

tell [tel] (*pt, pp* **told**) Ⓐ VT [1] [+ *story, experiences*] contar; [+ *truth*] decir; [+ *secret*] contar, divulgar (*frm*); (*formally*) comunicar, informar; **to ~ sb sth** decir algo a algn; **to ~ sb whether/how/why** *etc* decir a algn si/cómo/por qué *etc*; **to ~ sb that ...** decir a algn que ...; **I have been told that ...** me han dicho que ..., se me ha dicho que ... (*frm*); **I am pleased to ~ you that ...** (*frm*) me complace comunicarle que ..., me es grato comunicarle que ...; **I ~ you it isn't!** ¡te digo que no!; **let me ~ you, I didn't enjoy it** si te digo la verdad, no me gustó nada; **there were three, I ~ you, three** había tres, ¿me oyes?, tres; **I ~ myself it can't be true** digo para mí que no puede ser verdad; **I told him about the missing money** le dije lo del dinero que faltaba, le informé acerca del dinero que faltaba (*frm*); **~ me all about it** cuéntame todo; **I'll ~ you all about it** te (lo) diré todo; **~ me another!*** ¡cuéntaselo a tu abuela!*; **he's no saint, I can ~ you!** ¡no es ningún santo, te lo aseguro!; **so much happened that I can't begin to ~ you** pasaron tantas cosas no sé por dónde empezar a contarte; **I cannot ~ you how pleased I am** no encuentro palabras para expresarle lo contento que estoy; **I could ~ you a thing or two about him** hay cosas de él que yo me sé; **don't ~ me you can't do it!** ¡no me vayas a decir *or* no me digas que no lo puedes hacer!; **to ~ sb's fortune** ◊ **~ sb the future** decir a algn la buenaventura; **to ~ a lie** mentir; **you're ~ing me!*** ¡a quién se lo cuentas!, ¡a mí no me lo vas a contar!; **I told you so!** ¡ya lo decía yo!; **didn't I ~ you so?** ¿no te lo dije ya?; **(I) ~ you what, let's go now** sabes qué, vámonos ya; **I ~ you what!** ¡se me ocurre una idea!; *see also* **marine**
[2] (= *order*) **to ~ sb to do sth** decir a algn que haga algo, mandar a algn a hacer algo; **do as you are told!** ¡haz lo que te digo!; **he won't be told** no acepta consejos de nadie, no quiere hacer caso de nadie; **I told you not to** te dije que no lo hicieras
[3] (= *indicate*) [*sign, dial, clock*] indicar; **to ~ sb sth** indicar algo a algn; **there was a sign ~ing us which way to go** una señal nos indicaba el camino; **the clock ~s the quarter hours** el reloj da los cuartos de hora
[4] (= *distinguish*) distinguir; **I couldn't ~ them apart** no sabía distinguirlos; **to ~ the difference between A and B** distinguir entre A y B; **I can't ~ the difference** no veo la diferencia; **to ~ right from wrong** distinguir el bien del mal; *see also* **time A5**
[5] (= *know, be certain*) saber; **you can ~ he's a German** se (le) nota que es alemán; **you can ~ a horse's age by its teeth** la edad de un caballo se sabe por los dientes; **how can I ~ what she will do?** ¿cómo voy a saber lo que ella hará?; **you can't ~ much from his letter** su carta nos dice bien poco; **I couldn't ~ how it was done** no sabía cómo se hizo; **there is no ~ing what he will do** es imposible saber qué va a hacer
[6] (= *count*) **to ~ one's beads** rezar el rosario; **400 all told** 400 en total
Ⓑ VI [1] (= *speak*) **to ~ (of)** hablar de; **the ruins told of a sad history** las ruinas hablaban de una triste historia; **"did you love her?" — "more than words can ~"** —¿la amabas? —más de lo que pueda expresar con palabras; **it hurt more than words can ~** dolió una barbaridad, dolió lo indecible; **I hear ~ that ...** dicen que ...; **I hear ~ of a disaster** he oído que ha ocurrido una catástrofe; **I have never heard ~ of it** no he oído nunca hablar de eso
[2] (*) (= *sneak, tell secrets*) **please don't ~!** ¡no vayas contándolo *or* soplándolo* por ahí!; **he told on me to my parents** se chivó de mí a mis padres (*Sp**); **that would be ~ing!** ¡es un secreto!
[3] (= *know, be certain*) saber; **how can I ~?** ¿cómo lo voy a saber?, ¿yo qué sé?; **I can't ~** (me) es imposible saberlo, no le puedo decir, no sabría decirle; **who can ~?** ¿quién sabe?; **there is no ~ing** no se puede saber; **you never can ~** nunca se sabe; *see also* **time A1**
[4] (= *have an effect*) **every blow told** cada golpe tuvo su efecto; **stamina ~s in the long run** a la larga importa *or* vale más la resistencia; **blood will ~** la sangre cuenta; **to ~ against sb** obrar en contra de algn; **the strain is beginning to ~ on him** la tensión está empezando a afectarle

►**tell off** VT + ADV [1] (= *order*) ordenar, mandar
[2] (*) **to ~ sb off (for sth/for doing sth)** regañar a algn (por algo/por haber hecho algo)

teller [ˈteləʳ] N [1] [*of story*] narrador(a) *m/f*
[2] (*US, Scot*) (*in bank*) cajero/a *m/f*; (*at election*) escrutador(a) *m/f*

telling [ˈtelɪŋ] Ⓐ ADJ (= *effective*) [*blow*] certero; [*argument*] contundente, eficaz; (= *significant*) [*figures, remark*] revelador
Ⓑ N narración *f*; **the story did not lose in the ~** la historia no perdió nada al ser narrada

telling-off [ˌtelɪŋˈɒf] N bronca *f*, reprimenda *f*; **to give sb a ~** echar una bronca *or* regañar a algn

telltale [ˈtelteɪl] Ⓐ ADJ [*sign*] revelador, indicador
Ⓑ N [1] (= *person*) soplón/ona *m/f*
[2] (*Naut*) catavientos *m inv*

tellurium [teˈlʊərɪəm] N telurio *m*

telly* [ˈtelɪ] N (*Brit*) tele* *f*

temblor [ˈtembləʳ] N (*US*) temblor *m* de tierra

temerity [tɪˈmerɪtɪ] N temeridad *f*; **to have the ~ to** + *infin* atreverse a + *infin*; **and you have the ~ to say that ...!** ¡y usted se atreve a decir que ...!, ¡y usted me dice tan fresco que ...!

temp* [temp] Ⓐ N ABBR (= **temporary**) empleado/a *m/f* eventual, temporero/a *m/f*
Ⓑ VI trabajar como empleado/a eventual, trabajar de temporero

temp. ABBR = **temperature**

temper [ˈtempəʳ] Ⓐ N [1] (= *nature*) carácter *m*, genio *m*; (= *mood*) humor *m*; **to be in a ~** estar furioso; **to be in a good/bad ~** estar de buen/mal humor; **to keep one's ~** no perder la calma, contenerse; **to lose one's ~** perder los estribos; **to have a quick ~** tener genio; **in a fit of ~** en un acceso de furia *or* ira; **to fly into a ~** ponerse furioso, montar en cólera; **mind your ~!** ◊ **temper, temper!** ¡contrólate *or* controla ese genio!
[2] [*of metal*] temple *m*
Ⓑ VT [1] (= *moderate*) [+ *remarks*] suavizar, atenuar; [+ *energy, enthusiasm*] atemperar; **to ~ justice with mercy** templar la justicia con la compasión
[2] (= *soften*) [+ *metal*] templar

tempera [ˈtempərə] N pintura *f* al temple

temperament [ˈtempərəmənt] N [1] (= *disposition*) temperamento *m*, disposición *f*
[2] (= *moodiness, difficult temperament*) genio *m*; **he has a ~** tiene genio

temperamental [ˌtempərəˈmentl] ADJ [1] (= *moody*) [*person, machine*] caprichoso
[2] (= *caused by one's nature*) temperamental, por temperamento

temperance [ˈtempərəns] Ⓐ N [1] (= *moderation*) templanza *f* (*frm*), moderación *f*

2 (= *teetotalism*) abstinencia *f* de bebidas alcohólicas
Ⓑ CPD ► **temperance hotel** N hotel *m* donde no se sirven bebidas alcohólicas
► **temperance movement** N campaña *f* antialcohólica

temperate ['tempərɪt] ADJ [*climate, zone*] templado; [*person*] moderado; (*in drinking*) abstemio; **to be ~ in one's demands** ser moderado en sus exigencias

temperature ['tempritʃəʳ] Ⓐ N 1 (*Met*) temperatura *f*
2 (*Med*) (= *high temperature*) calentura *f*, fiebre *f*; **to have** *or* **run a ~** tener fiebre *or* calentura; **she has a ~ of 103°** ≈ tiene 39° de fiebre; **to take sb's ~** tomar la temperatura a algn
Ⓑ CPD ► **temperature chart** N gráfico *m* de temperaturas

tempered ['tempəd] ADJ templado

-tempered ['tempəd] ADJ (*ending in compounds*) de ... humor

tempest ['tempɪst] N (*poet*) tempestad *f*; ✦***IDIOM*** **a ~ in a teapot** (*US*) una tormenta *or* tempestad en un vaso de agua

tempestuous [tem'pestjʊəs] ADJ [*relationship, meeting*] tempestuoso

Templar ['templəʳ] N templario *m*

template, templet (*US*) ['templɪt] N plantilla *f*

temple ['templ] N 1 (*Rel*) templo *m*
2 (*Anat*) sien *f*
3 **the Temple** (*in London*) el Colegio de Abogados

templet ['templɪt] N (*US*) = **template**

tempo ['tempəʊ] N (*pl* **tempos,** (*Mus*) **tempi** ['tempi:]) (*Mus*) tempo *m*; (*fig*) ritmo *m*

temporal ['tempərəl] ADJ (*Ling*) [*conjunction, clause*] temporal

temporarily ['tempərərɪlɪ] ADV temporalmente

temporary ['tempərərɪ] ADJ [*accommodation, solution, licence*] temporal, provisional; [*secretary, job, staff*] temporal, eventual; [*problem*] pasajero, temporal; **this is just a ~ measure** esto es sólo una medida temporal *or* provisional; **orthodox treatment gave only ~ relief** el tratamiento ortodoxo proporcionó sólo un alivio temporal *or* pasajero; **~ workers** trabajadores *mpl* temporales; (*agricultural*) temporeros *mpl*; **"temporary road surface"** "asfalto provisional"

temporize ['tempəraɪz] VI tratar de ganar tiempo

tempt [tempt] VT 1 (*gen*) tentar; **to ~ sb to do sth** tentar a algn a hacer algo; **I'm ~ed to do it** estoy tentado de hacerlo; **they've offered me a job in France and I must say I'm ~ed** me han ofrecido un trabajo en Francia y la verdad es que me tienta mucho; **can I ~ you to another cake?** ¿le apetece otro pastelito?
2 (*Rel*) tentar, poner a prueba; **you shouldn't ~ fate** *or* **providence** no hay que tentar a la suerte

temptation [temp'teɪʃən] N tentación *f*; **there is always a ~ to ...** existe siempre la tentación de ...; **to resist ~** resistir (a) la tentación; **I couldn't resist the ~ to tell him** *or* **of telling him** no pude resistir la tentación de decírselo; **to give way** *or* **yield to ~** ceder a la tentación; **to put ~ in sb's way** exponer a algn a la tentación; **lead us not into ~** (*Bible*) no nos dejes caer en la tentación

tempter ['temptəʳ] N tentador *m*

tempting ['temptɪŋ] ADJ [*food*] apetitoso; [*offer, idea*] tentador; **it would be ~ to agree** uno se siente tentado a pensar lo mismo

temptingly ['temptɪŋlɪ] ADV [*displayed, arrayed*] de modo tentador; **their strawberry gateau is ~ fruity** su pastel de fresa lleno de fruta resulta de lo más apetitoso; **it is ~ easy to ...** lo más fácil sería ..., uno se siente tentado a ...

temptress ['temptrɪs] N tentadora *f*

ten [ten] Ⓐ ADJ diez
Ⓑ N diez *m*; **~s of thousands** decenas de miles; **~ to one he'll be late*** te apuesto que llega tarde; ✦***IDIOM*** **they're ~ a penny*** se encuentran en todas partes; *see* **five** *for usage*

tenable ['tenəbl] ADJ [*argument*] sostenible, defendible; [*proposal*] válido

tenacious [tɪ'neɪʃəs] ADJ [*person*] tenaz; [*belief, idea*] firme

tenaciously [tɪ'neɪʃəslɪ] ADV tenazmente, con tenacidad

tenacity [tɪ'næsɪtɪ] N tenacidad *f*

tenancy ['tenənsɪ] N (= *possession, period*) tenencia *f*, inquilinato *m*; (= *lease*) arriendo *m*, alquiler *m*; **joint/multiple ~** arriendo *m or* alquiler *m* conjunto/múltiple

tenant ['tenənt] Ⓐ N inquilino/a *m/f*, arrendatario/a *m/f*
Ⓑ CPD ► **tenant farmer** N agricultor(a) *m/f* arrendatario/a

tenantry ['tenəntrɪ] N inquilinos *mpl*; (*Agr*) agricultores *mpl* arrendatarios

tench [tentʃ] N (*pl inv*) tenca *f*

tend¹ [tend] VI 1 **to ~ to do sth** tender a hacer algo, soler hacer algo; **men ~ to die younger than women** los hombres tienden a *or* suelen morir más jóvenes que las mujeres; **this type of material ~s to shrink** este tipo de tela tiene tendencia a *or* tiende a *or* suele encoger; **that ~s to be the case** tiende a ser así, suele ser así; **I ~ to agree** me inclino a pensar lo mismo
2 **to ~ towards** tender a; **her stories ~ towards the melodramatic** sus historias tienden a ser melodramáticas; **he ~s towards conservatism** es de tendencias conservadoras

tend² [tend] Ⓐ VT 1 (= *care for*) [+ *patient, invalid*] cuidar, atender; [+ *sheep, cattle, horses*] cuidar, ocuparse de; [+ *garden*] ocuparse de; [+ *grave*] cuidar de; [+ *fire*] atender, ocuparse de
2 **to ~ bar** (*US*) servir en el bar
Ⓑ VI **to ~ to** [+ *patient, invalid*] atender a, cuidar; [+ *sheep, cattle, horses*] cuidar, ocuparse de; [+ *fire*] atender, ocuparse de; [+ *housework, wounds, needs*] ocuparse de

tendency ['tendənsɪ] N 1 (*gen*) tendencia *f*; **to have a ~ to do sth** [*person*] tener tendencia a hacer algo; (*Med*) tener propensión *or* ser propenso a hacer algo; **he has a ~ to exaggerate** tiene tendencia a exagerar; **there is a ~ for companies to recruit fewer staff** existe tendencia por parte de las empresas a emplear a menos trabajadores; **there is a ~ for prices to rise** los precios tienen tendencia a subir; **she has a ~ to** *or* **towards depression** tiene propensión *or* es propensa a la depresión
2 (= *leaning*) **left-wing/right-wing tendencies** tendencias *fpl* izquierdistas/derechistas; **suicidal tendencies** tendencias *fpl or* inclinaciones *fpl* suicidas

tendentious [ten'denʃəs] ADJ tendencioso

tendentiously [ten'denʃəslɪ] ADV de modo tendencioso

tendentiousness [ten'denʃəsnɪs] N tendenciosidad *f*

tender¹ ['tendəʳ] Ⓐ N 1 (*Comm*) oferta *f*; **call for ~** propuesta *f* para licitación de obras; **to put in** *or* **make a ~ (for)** presentarse a concurso *or* a una licitación (para); **to put sth out to ~** sacar algo a concurso *or* a licitación
2 [*of currency*] **legal ~** moneda *f* corriente *or* de curso legal
Ⓑ VT (*frm*) (= *proffer*) [+ *money*] ofrecer; [+ *thanks*] dar; **he ~ed his resignation** presentó su dimisión
Ⓒ VI (*Comm*) **to ~ (for)** presentarse a concurso *or* a una licitación (para)
Ⓓ CPD ► **tender documents** NPL pliegos *mpl* de propuesta

tender² ['tendəʳ] N 1 (*Rail*) ténder *m*
2 (*Naut*) gabarra *f*, embarcación *f* auxiliar

tender³ ['tendəʳ] ADJ 1 (= *gentle, affectionate*) [*person, expression, kiss, word*] tierno; [*voice*] lleno de ternura; **he gave her a ~ smile** le sonrió tiernamente *or* con ternura; **a child needs ~ loving care** un niño necesita que le den cariño y que lo cuiden; **to bid sb a ~ farewell** (*liter*) despedirse de algn con ternura, dar a algn una cariñosa despedida
2 (*esp hum*) (= *young*) tierno; **at the ~ age of seven** a la tierna edad de siete años; **in spite of his ~ years** a pesar de su tierna edad
3 (= *sensitive, sore*) sensible, dolorido; **the skin will be ~ for a while** la piel te dolerá durante algún tiempo; **~ to the touch** sensible al tacto
4 (*Culin*) [*meat, vegetables*] tierno; **cook the vegetables until ~** cocer las verduras hasta que estén *or* se pongan tiernas
5 (*Bot*) [*plant*] delicado; [*shoot*] tierno

tenderfoot ['tendəfʊt] N (*pl* **tenderfoots**) (*esp US*) principiante *m*, novato *m*

tender-hearted ['tendə'hɑ:tɪd] ADJ compasivo, bondadoso, tierno de corazón

tender-heartedness ['tendə'hɑ:tɪdnɪs] N compasión *f*, bondad *f*, ternura *f*

tenderize ['tendəraɪz] VT ablandar

tenderizer ['tendəraɪzəʳ] N ablandador *m*

tenderloin ['tendəlɔɪn] N 1 (= *meat*) lomo *m*, filete *m*
2 (*US**) *barrio de vicio y corrupción reconocidos*

tenderly ['tendəlɪ] ADV (= *affectionately*) [*kiss, say, smile*] tiernamente, con ternura

tenderness ['tendənɪs] N 1 (= *gentleness*) [*of person, kiss, smile*] ternura *f*
2 (= *sensitivity, soreness*) dolor *m*; **breast ~** dolor *m* en el pecho; **some ~ around the area is to be expected** es de esperar que la zona duela un poco
3 (*Culin*) [*of meat, vegetables*] lo tierno
4 (*Bot*) fragilidad *f*

tendon ['tendən] N tendón *m*

tendril ['tendrɪl] N zarcillo *m*

tenement ['tenɪmənt] Ⓐ N vivienda *f*; (*Scot*) (= *flat*) piso *m* (*Sp*), departamento *m* (*LAm*)
Ⓑ CPD ► **tenement block** N bloque *m* de pisos (*Sp*), bloque *m* de departamentos (*LAm*)
► **tenement house** N casa *f* de vecinos, casa *f* de vecindad

Tenerife [,tenə'ri:f] N Tenerife *m*

tenet ['tenət] N principio *m*

tenfold ['tenfəʊld] Ⓐ ADJ **there has been a ~ increase in accidents** se ha multiplicado por diez el número de accidentes, el número de accidentes es diez veces mayor
Ⓑ ADV diez veces

ten-gallon hat [,tengælən'hæt] N sombrero *m* tejano

Tenn. ABBR (*US*) = **Tennessee**

tenner* ['tenəʳ] N (*Brit*) (= *£10*) diez libras; (= *£10 note*) billete *m* de diez libras; (*US*) (= *$10*) diez dólares; (= *$10 note*) billete *m* de diez dólares

tennis ['tenɪs] Ⓐ N tenis *m*
Ⓑ CPD ► **tennis ball** N pelota *f* de tenis ► **tennis court** N pista *f* de tenis (*Sp*), cancha *f* de tenis (*LAm*) ► **tennis elbow** N (*Med*) sinovitis *f* del codo, codo *m* de tenista ► **tennis match** N partido *m* de tenis ► **tennis player** N tenista *mf* ► **tennis racquet** N raqueta *f* de tenis ► **tennis shoe** N zapatilla *f* de tenis

tenon ['tenən] N espaldón *m*

tenor ['tenəʳ] Ⓐ ADJ [*instrument, part, voice*] de tenor; [*aria*] para tenor
Ⓑ N 1 (*Mus*) tenor *m*
2 (= *purport*) [*of speech*] tenor *m*

tenpin bowling [ˌtenpɪn'bəʊlɪŋ] N, **tenpins** ['tenpɪnz] NPL bolos *mpl*, bolera *f*

tense[1] [tens] N (*Ling*) tiempo *m*; **in the present ~** en presente

tense[2] [tens] Ⓐ ADJ (*compar* **tenser**; *superl* **tensest**) 1 (= *nervous*) [*person, expression*] tenso; **her voice was ~** se le notaba la tensión en la voz; **to feel ~** sentirse tenso; **to get** *or* **grow ~** ponerse tenso
2 (= *stiff*) [*body, muscles, neck*] tenso, en tensión; **my shoulders are ~** tengo los hombros tensos *or* en tensión
3 (= *strained*) [*atmosphere, silence*] tenso; [*relations*] tenso, tirante; [*period, moment*] de tensión; **the ~ situation in the Persian Gulf** la situación de tensión en el Golfo Pérsico
4 (= *taut*) [*rope, wire*] tenso, tirante
Ⓑ VI (*also* ~ **up**) [*person*] ponerse tenso; [*muscle, body*] ponerse tenso, ponerse en tensión
Ⓒ VT (*also* ~ **up**) tensar, poner tenso; **she ~d her muscles** tensó *or* puso tensos los músculos

► **tense up** Ⓐ VI + ADV *see* **tense**[2] **B**
Ⓑ VT + ADV *see* **tense**[2] **C**

tensely ['tenslɪ] ADV [*say, wait*] tensamente

tenseness ['tensnɪs] N tensión *f*

tensile ['tensaɪl] ADJ (= *relating to tension*) de tensión, relativo a la tensión; (= *stretchable*) extensible; **~ strength** resistencia *f* a la tensión

tension ['tenʃən] N 1 (= *unease*) (*in atmosphere, situation*) tensión *f*; (*in relations*) tensión *f*, tirantez *f*; **there is a lot of ~ between them** entre ellos existe mucha tirantez
2 (= *stiffness*) [*of person, in shoulders*] tensión *f*
3 (= *tightness*) [*of rope, wire*] tensión *f*, tirantez *f*

tent [tent] Ⓐ N tienda *f* de campaña, carpa *f* (*LAm*)
Ⓑ CPD ► **tent peg** N (*Brit*) estaca *f* de tienda, estaquilla *f* ► **tent pole**, **tent stake** N palo *m*

tentacle ['tentəkl] N tentáculo *m*

tentative ['tentətɪv] ADJ 1 (= *provisional*) [*agreement, plan, arrangement*] provisional, provisorio (*LAm*); [*conclusion*] provisional, no definitiva
2 (= *hesitant*) [*gesture*] vacilante, tímido; [*smile, attempt*] tímido; **the first ~ steps toward democracy** los primeros pasos vacilantes hacia la democracia; **he made a ~ suggestion that ...** sugirió tímidamente que ...

tentatively ['tentətɪvlɪ] ADV 1 (= *provisionally*) [*agree, arrange, plan*] provisionalmente, provisoriamente (*LAm*)
2 (= *hesitantly*) [*smile*] tímidamente; [*say*] tímidamente, con vacilación; **he touched one of the boxes ~** tocó una de las cajas con cuidado

tenterhooks ['tentəhʊks] NPL ♦**IDIOMS** **to be on ~** estar sobre ascuas, tener el alma en vilo; **to keep sb on ~** tener a algn sobre ascuas

tenth [tenθ] Ⓐ ADJ décimo
Ⓑ N (*in series*) décimo *m*; (= *fraction*) décimo *m*, décima parte *f*; *see* **fifth** *for usage*

tenuity [te'njʊɪtɪ] N tenuidad *f*

tenuous ['tenjʊəs] ADJ [*connection, link*] vago, ligero; [*argument*] flojo, endeble; [*evidence*] poco sólido; [*alliance, peace*] frágil, endeble; **he has only a ~ grasp of reality** sólo tiene una escasa conciencia de la realidad; **to have a ~ hold on sth** tener (un) escaso control sobre algo

tenuously ['tenjʊəslɪ] ADV [*linked, connected*] vagamente

tenuousness ['tenjʊəsnɪs] N [*of link, connection*] lo vago; [*of argument*] endeblez *f*, falta *f* de fundamento; [*of evidence*] falta *f* de solidez

tenure ['tenjʊəʳ] Ⓐ N 1 [*of land*] posesión *f*, tenencia *f*, ocupación *f*; [*of office*] ocupación *f*, ejercicio *m*
2 (= *guaranteed employment*) puesto *m* asegurado, permanencia *f*; **teacher with ~** profesor(a) *m/f* de número, profesor(a) *m/f* numerario/a; **teacher without ~** profesor(a) *m/f* no numerario/a
Ⓑ CPD **~ track position** (*US*) puesto *m* con posibilidad de obtener la permanencia

tepee ['ti:pi:] N (*US*) tipi *m*

tepid ['tepɪd] ADJ (*lit*) tibio; (*fig*) [*reception, welcome*] poco entusiasta, poco caluroso

tepidity [te'pɪdɪtɪ], **tepidness** ['tepɪdnɪs] N tibieza *f*

tequila [tɪ'ki:lə] N tequila *m*

Ter. ABBR = **Terrace**

terbium ['tɜ:bɪəm] N terbio *m*

tercentenary [ˌtɜ:sen'ti:nərɪ] N tricentenario *m*

tercet ['tɜ:sɪt] N terceto *m*

Terence ['terəns] N Terencio

term [tɜ:m] Ⓐ N 1 (= *period*) periodo *m*, período *m*; (*as President, governor, mayor*) mandato *m*; **in the long ~** a largo plazo; **in the longer ~** a un plazo más largo; **in the medium ~** a medio plazo; **during his ~ of office** bajo su mandato; **we have been elected for a three-year ~ (of office)** hemos sido elegidos para un periodo legislativo de tres años; **he will not seek a third ~ (of office) as mayor** no irá a por un tercer mandato de alcalde, no renovará por tercera vez su candidatura como alcalde; **he is currently serving a seven-year prison ~** actualmente está cumpliendo una condena de siete años; **he served two ~s as governor** ocupó el cargo de gobernador durante dos periodos de mandato; **in the short ~** a corto plazo; **despite problems, she carried the baby to ~** a pesar de los problemas llevó el embarazo a término
2 (*Educ*) trimestre *m*; **in the autumn** *or* (*US*) **fall/spring/summer ~** en el primer/segundo/tercer trimestre; **they don't like you to take holidays during ~** no les gusta que se tomen vacaciones durante el trimestre *or* en época de clases
3 (*Comm, Jur, Fin*) (= *period of validity*) plazo *m*; **the policy is near the end of its ~** el plazo de la póliza está a punto de vencer; **interest rates change over the ~ of the loan** los tipos de interés cambian a lo largo del plazo del préstamo
4 (= *word*) término *m*; **what do you understand by the ~ "radical"?** ¿qué entiende usted por (el término) "radical"?; **explain it in ~s a child might understand** explícalo de manera que un niño lo pueda entender; **legal/medical ~s** términos *mpl* legales/médicos; **a ~ of abuse** un término ofensivo, un insulto; **a ~ of endearment** un apelativo cariñoso; **he spoke of it only in general ~s** sólo habló de ello en términos generales; **he spoke of her in glowing ~s** habló de ella en términos muy elogiosos; **in simple ~s** de forma sencilla; **she condemned the attacks in the strongest ~s** condenó los ataques de la forma más enérgica; **technical ~** tecnicismo *m*, término *m* técnico; *see also* **contradiction**, **uncertain**
5 (*Math, Logic*) término *m*
6 **terms** 6·1 (= *conditions*) condiciones *fpl*, términos *mpl*; **according to the ~s of the contract** según las condiciones *or* los términos del contrato; **to dictate ~s (to sb)** poner condiciones (a algn); **we offer easy ~s** ofrecemos facilidades de pago; **~s of employment** condiciones *fpl* de empleo; **to compete on equal ~s** competir en igualdad de condiciones *or* en pie de igualdad; **they accepted him on his own ~s** lo aceptaron con las condiciones que él había puesto; **~s of reference** (= *brief*) [*of committee, inquiry*] cometido *m*, instrucciones *fpl*; [*of study*] ámbito *m*; (= *area of responsibility*) responsabilidades *fpl*, competencia *f*; (= *common understanding*) puntos *mpl* de referencia; **~s of sale** condiciones *fpl* de venta; **~s of trade** condiciones *fpl* de transacción; ♦**IDIOM** **to come to ~s with sth** asumir *or* asimilar algo
6·2 (= *relations*) **to be on bad ~s with sb** llevarse mal con algn, no tener buenas relaciones con algn; **we're on first name ~s with all the staff** nos tuteamos con todos los empleados; **she is still on friendly ~s with him** todavía mantiene una relación amistosa con él; **to be on good ~s with sb** llevarse bien con algn, tener buenas relaciones con algn; **they have managed to remain on good ~s** se las arreglaron para quedar bien; **we're not on speaking ~s at the moment** actualmente no nos hablamos
6·3 (= *sense*) **in ~s of: in ~s of production we are doing well** en cuanto a la producción vamos bien, por lo que se refiere *or* por lo que respecta a la producción vamos bien; **he never describes women in ~s of their personalities** nunca describe a las mujeres refiriéndose a su personalidad; **he was talking in ~s of buying it** hablaba como si fuera a comprarlo; **in economic/political ~s** desde el punto de vista económico/político, en términos económicos/políticos; **in practical ~s this means that ...** en la práctica esto significa que ...; **in real ~s incomes have fallen** en términos reales los ingresos han bajado; **seen in ~s of its environmental impact, the project is a disaster** desde el punto de vista de su impacto en el medio ambiente, el proyecto es un desastre; **we were thinking more in ~s of an au pair** nuestra idea era más una au pair, teníamos en mente a una au pair
Ⓑ VT (= *designate*) calificar de; **he was ~ed a thief** lo calificaron de ladrón; **he ~ed the war a humanitarian nightmare** calificó la guerra de pesadilla humanitaria; **I was what you might ~ a gangster** yo era lo que se podría llamar un gángster; **the problems of what is now ~ed "the mixed economy"** los problemas de lo que ahora se da en llamar "la economía mixta"
Ⓒ CPD ► **term insurance** N seguro *m* temporal ► **term loan** N préstamo *m* a plazo fijo ► **term paper** N (*US*) trabajo *m* escrito trimestral

➤ LANGUAGE IN USE: term A6 20.1

termagant ['tɜːməgənt] N arpía *f*, fiera *f*

terminal ['tɜːmɪnl] Ⓐ ADJ **1** (= *incurable*) [*cancer, patient, case*] terminal, en fase terminal; **the government's problems may be ~** los problemas del gobierno pueden no tener solución; **to be in (a state of) ~ decline** estar en un estado de declive irreversible
2 (*) (= *utter*) [*boredom*] mortal*; [*adolescent*] incorregible, impenitente; **an act of ~ stupidity** un acto de una estupidez supina*
Ⓑ N **1** (*Elec*) borne *m*, polo *m*; (*Comput*) terminal *m*
2 [*of bus, train*] terminal *f*; **~ building** edificio *m* de la terminal

terminally ['tɜːmɪnəlɪ] ADV **1** (= *incurably*) **to be ~ ill** estar en fase terminal; **he was ~ ill with lung cancer** sufría un cáncer de pulmón en fase terminal **2** (*) (= *utterly*) [*boring, dull*] mortalmente*; [*stupid*] irremediablemente

terminate ['tɜːmɪneɪt] Ⓐ VT [+ *meeting*] concluir; [+ *conversation, relationship*] poner fin a; [+ *contract*] finalizar; [+ *pregnancy*] interrumpir
Ⓑ VI [*contract*] finalizarse, concluir; [*train, bus*] terminar; **this train ~s here** este tren termina aquí su recorrido, este tren muere aquí

termination [,tɜːmɪ'neɪʃən] N [*of contract*] terminación *f*; [*of pregnancy*] interrupción *f*; **~ of employment** baja *f*, cese *m*

termini ['tɜːmɪnaɪ] NPL *of* **terminus**

terminological [,tɜːmɪnə'lɒdʒɪkəl] ADJ terminológico

terminologist [,tɜːmɪ'nɒlədʒɪst] N terminólogo/a *m/f*

terminology [,tɜːmɪ'nɒlədʒɪ] N terminología *f*

terminus ['tɜːmɪnəs] N (*pl* **terminuses, termini**)
1 (*Rail*) estación *f* terminal
2 [*of buses*] (= *last stop*) última parada *f*, final *f* del recorrido; (= *building*) terminal *f*

termite ['tɜːmaɪt] N termita *f*, comején *m*

termtime ['tɜːmtaɪm] N **in ~** durante el trimestre; **they don't like you to take holidays during ~** no les gusta que se tomen vacaciones durante el trimestre *or* en época de clases

tern [tɜːn] N golondrina *f* de mar; **common ~** charrán *m* común

ternary ['tɜːnərɪ] ADJ ternario

Terr. ABBR = **Terrace**

terrace ['terəs] Ⓐ N **1** (= *patio, verandah*) terraza *f*; (= *roof*) azotea *f*
2 (= *raised bank*) terraplén *m*
3 [*of houses*] hilera *f* de casas (adosadas); (= *name of street*) calle *f*
4 (*Agr*) terraza *f*
5 (*Sport*) **the ~s** las gradas *fpl*, el graderío
Ⓑ VT [+ *hillside, garden*] construir terrazas en, terraplenar

terraced ['terəst] ADJ (= *layered*) [*hillside, garden*] en terrazas, terraplenado; (= *in a row*) [*house, cottage*] adosado; **~ gardens** jardines *mpl* formando terrazas, jardines *mpl* colgantes

terracotta ['terə'kɒtə] Ⓐ N terracota *f*
Ⓑ ADJ terracota

terra firma [,terə'fɜːmə] N tierra *f* firme

terrain [te'reɪn] N terreno *m*

terrapin ['terəpɪn] N tortuga *f* de agua dulce

terrarium [te'reərɪəm] N terrario *m*

terrazzo [te'rætsəʊ] N terrazo *m*

terrestrial [tɪ'restrɪəl] ADJ **1** [*life, animal, plant*] terrestre **2** (*esp Brit TV*) [*broadcasting, channel*] de transmisión (por) vía terrestre

terrible ['terəbl] ADJ **1** (= *very unpleasant*) [*experience, accident, disease*] terrible, espantoso; **it was a ~ thing to have happened** era terrible que hubiese sucedido algo así; **it was a ~ thing to see** era horrible verlo; **the ~ thing is that I've lost it** lo peor de todo es que lo he perdido
2 (*) (= *very bad*) [*weather, food*] horrible, espantoso; **her French is ~** habla fatal el francés, habla un francés espantoso; **"what was it like?" — "terrible!"** —¿qué tal fue? —¡espantoso!; **I'm ~ at cooking** se me da fatal la cocina*; **I'm ~ at remembering names** se me da fatal recordar (los) nombres, soy malísimo para recordar (los) nombres; **I've got a ~ cold** tengo un resfriado espantoso; **I've had a ~ day at the office** he tenido un día malísimo *or* horrible en la oficina; **to feel ~** (= *guilty, ill*) sentirse fatal *or* muy mal; **to look ~** (= *ill*) tener muy mal aspecto; **she looked ~ in that trouser suit** ese traje pantalón le quedaba fatal; **I've got a ~ memory** tengo una memoria malísima; **I've made a ~ mistake** he cometido un terrible error; **you sound ~, is something wrong?** ¡vaya tono!, ¿pasa algo?; **we had a ~ time** lo pasamos fatal
3 (*) (*as intensifier*) (= *great*) [*pity, shame*] verdadero; **I've been a ~ fool** he sido un verdadero imbécil; **the garden is in a ~ mess** el jardín está hecho un verdadero desastre; **it was** *or* **it came as a ~ shock** fue un golpe terrible; **he's having ~ trouble with his homework** le está costando horrores *or* un montón hacer los deberes*

terribly ['terəblɪ] ADV **1** (= *extremely*) [*worried, difficult, important*] terriblemente, tremendamente; **it's ~ good/bad** es buenísimo/malísimo; **it's ~ hard for me to make a decision** me resulta dificilísimo *or* terriblemente difícil tomar una decisión; **he's been ~ ill** ha estado terriblemente enfermo, ha estado fatal; **I'm ~ sorry** lo siento muchísimo; **we aren't doing ~ well at the moment** ahora no nos va muy bien que digamos; **he plays the piano a little, not ~ well** toca un poco el piano, no excesivamente bien; **there's something ~ wrong here** aquí hay algo que va realmente mal; **a practical joke which had gone ~ wrong** una broma que había tenido unos resultados terribles
2 (*) (= *very much*) **I miss him ~** le echo muchísimo de menos; **to suffer ~** sufrir horrores*, pasarlo fatal*
3 (= *very poorly*) [*play, perform, behave*] muy mal, fatal

terrier ['terɪəʳ] N terrier *m*

terrific [tə'rɪfɪk] ADJ **1** (= *very great*) [*explosion, problem, disappointment*] tremendo, enorme; [*pain, noise, heat*] terrible, tremendo; **a ~ amount of money** una enorme cantidad de dinero
2 (*) (= *excellent*) [*idea, news, person*] genial*, estupendo; **terrific!** ¡genial!, ¡estupendo!; **we had ~ fun** nos lo pasamos estupendamente *or* fenomenal*; **to do a ~ job** hacer un trabajo estupendo *or* fantástico*; **you look ~!** ¡estás guapísimo/a!; **she looked ~ in a leotard** estaba sensacional en mallas; **~ stuff!** ¡estupendo!, ¡fenomenal!; **to have a ~ time** pasárselo estupendamente *or* fenomenal*

terrifically [tə'rɪfɪkəlɪ] ADV **1** (= *extremely*) terriblemente; **it's a ~ funny book** es un libro graciosísimo *or* terriblemente gracioso; **it was ~ hot** hacía un calor terrible *or* tremendo; **house prices have gone up ~** las casas han subido terriblemente de precio; **we get on ~ well** nos llevamos estupendamente bien; **they did ~ well to reach the final** fue un tremendo logro que llegasen a la final
2 (*) (= *very well*) [*play, perform*] fenomenal*, genial*

terrified [terɪfaɪd] ADJ **to be ~** estar aterrorizado, estar aterrado; **to be ~ of sth/sb** tener terror *or* pavor a algo/algn; **he was ~ of catching AIDS** le aterrorizaba *or* le daba terror (la idea de) coger el sida; **I was ~ that he might follow me** tenía terror de que pudiera seguirme

terrify ['terɪfaɪ] VT (= *terrorize*) [*animal, violent person etc*] aterrorizar; (= *horrify*) aterrar; **it terrifies me to think that I might lose her** me aterra pensar que podría perderla; **to ~ sb out of his wits** dar un susto mortal a algn

terrifying ['terɪfaɪɪŋ] ADJ [*experience, sound, sight*] espantoso, aterrador; [*person*] aterrador; **it was ~!** ¡fue espantoso *or* aterrador!; **what a ~ thought!** ¡qué idea más aterradora!, ¡qué espanto!; **I still find it ~ to walk along that street** todavía me da muchísimo miedo caminar por esa calle

terrifyingly ['terɪfaɪɪŋlɪ] ADV espantosamente, aterradoramente

terrine [te'riːn] N terrina *f*

territorial [,terɪ'tɔːrɪəl] Ⓐ ADJ territorial; **Territorial Army** ejército *m* de reserva; **~ waters** aguas *fpl* jurisdiccionales *or* territoriales
Ⓑ N (*Brit*) reservista *m*

> **TERRITORIAL ARMY**
>
> *La organización británica* **Territorial Army** *o* **TA** *es un ejército de reserva formado exclusivamente por voluntarios civiles que reciben entrenamiento militar en su tiempo libre y están disponibles para ayudar al ejército profesional en tiempos de guerra o crisis. Como compensación por sus servicios, los voluntarios reciben una paga. En Estados Unidos el equivalente es la llamada* **National Guard**.

territoriality [,terɪ,tɔːrɪ'ælɪtɪ] N territorialidad *f*

territory ['terɪtərɪ] N territorio *m*; [*of salesman*] zona *f*, sector *m*; (*Sport*) campo *m*, terreno *m*; **mandated ~** territorio *m* bajo mandato; ✦*IDIOM* **it comes** *or* **goes with the ~** es parte del juego, es un gaje del oficio

terror ['terəʳ] Ⓐ N **1** (= *fear*) terror *m*; **to live in ~** vivir en el terror; **to live in ~ of sth** vivir aterrorizado por algo; **he went** *or* **was in ~ of his life** temía por su vida, temía ser asesinado; **I have a ~ of bats** tengo horror a los murciélagos; **he had a ~ of flying** le daba miedo volar; **the headmistress holds no ~s for me** la directora no me infunde miedo a mí; **to sow ~ everywhere** sembrar el terror por todas partes; **~ campaign** campaña *f* de terror **2** (*) (= *person, child*) **she's a ~ on the roads** es un peligro conduciendo; **you little ~!** ¡eres un diablillo!*
Ⓑ CPD ► **terror attack** N atentado *m* (terrorista)

terrorism ['terərɪzəm] N terrorismo *m*

terrorist ['terərɪst] ADJ, N terrorista *mf*

terrorize ['terəraɪz] VT (= *terrify*) aterrorizar; (= *threaten, coerce*) atemorizar; **they ~d the population into submission** hicieron que la población se sometiera a base de atemorizarlos

terror-stricken ['terə,strɪkən], **terror-struck** ['terə,strʌk] ADJ aterrorizado

Terry ['terɪ] N (*familiar form*) *of* **Terence, Theresa**

terry ['terɪ] N (*US*) (*also* **~ towelling, ~ cloth**) (*Brit*) felpa *f*, toalla *f*

terse [tɜːs] ADJ (*compar* **terser**, *superl* **tersest**) [*reply, tone, person*] lacónico, seco; [*statement*] escueto

tersely ['tɜːslɪ] ADV lacónicamente, secamente

terseness ['tɜːsnɪs] N laconismo *m*, sequedad *f*

tertiary ['tɜːʃərɪ] ADJ 1 (*Econ*) [*sector*] terciario 2 (*Educ*) **~ education** enseñanza *f* superior 3 (*Geol*) [*rocks, deposits*] terciario; **the Tertiary period** la época terciaria

Tertullian [tɜː'tʌlɪən] N Tertuliano

Terylene® ['terəliːn] N (*Brit*) terylene® *m*

TESL ['tes(ə)l] N ABBR = **Teaching (of) English as a Second Language**; → TEFL/EFL

TESOL ['tesɒl] N ABBR = **Teaching of English to Speakers of Other Languages**; → TEFL/EFL

Tess [tes], **Tessa** ['tesə] N (*familiar forms*) *of* **Teresa**

tessel(l)ated ['tesɪleɪtɪd] ADJ de mosaico, formado con teselas; **~ pavement** mosaico *m*

tessel(l)ation [ˌtesɪ'leɪʃən] N mosaico *m*

test [test] Ⓐ N 1 (*Scol, Univ*) examen *m*; (*multiple-choice*) test *m*; (*esp for job*) prueba *f*; **we've got a maths ~ tomorrow** mañana tenemos (un) examen de matemáticas; **to do a ~** (*Scol, Univ*) hacer un examen; (*multiple choice*) hacer un test; (*for job*) hacer una prueba; **to fail a ~** (*Scol, Univ*) suspender un examen; (*multiple choice*) suspender un test; (*for job*) no pasar una prueba; **to give sb a ~ (in sth)** examinar a algn (de algo), poner a algn un examen (de algo); **an oral ~** un examen oral; **to pass a ~** (*Scol, Univ*) aprobar un examen; (*multiple choice*) aprobar un test; (*for job*) pasar una prueba; **to take a ~** (*Scol, Univ*) hacer un examen; (*multiple choice*) hacer un test; (*for job*) hacer una prueba; **a written ~** un examen oral/escrito; *see also* **aptitude, intelligence**

2 (*Aut*) (*also* **driving ~**) examen *m* de conducir; **to fail one's ~** suspender el examen de conducir; **to pass one's ~** aprobar el examen de conducir; **to take one's ~** hacer el examen de conducir

3 (*Med*) [*of organs, functioning*] prueba *f*; [*of sample, substance*] análisis *m inv*; **AIDS ~** prueba *f* del sida; **blood ~** análisis *m inv* de sangre; **eye ~** revisión *f* de la vista; **it was sent to the laboratory for ~s** lo mandaron al laboratorio para que lo analizaran; **hearing ~** revisión *f* del oído; **medical ~** examen *m* médico; **pregnancy ~** prueba *f* del embarazo; **urine ~** análisis *m inv* de orina; *see also* **breath, fitness, litmus, smear**

4 (= *trial*) [*of aircraft, new product, drug*] prueba *f*; **nuclear ~** prueba *f* nuclear; **they want to ban cosmetics ~s on animals** quieren prohibir las pruebas de cosméticos en animales; *see also* **flight**[1], **screen C**

5 (*fig*) prueba *f*; **he now faces the toughest ~ of his leadership** ahora se enfrenta a la prueba más difícil durante su periodo como líder; **holidays are a major ~ of any relationship** irse de vacaciones es una de las pruebas más difíciles a la que se somete cualquier relación; **to put sth to the ~** poner *or* someter algo a prueba; **to stand the ~ of time** resistir el paso del tiempo; *see also* **acid, endurance**

6 (*Cricket, Rugby*) (*also* **~ match**) partido *m* internacional

Ⓑ VT 1 [+ *student, pupil*] examinar; [+ *candidate*] (*for job*) hacer una prueba a; [+ *knowledge*] evaluar; [+ *understanding*] poner a prueba; **to ~ sb on sth** (*Scol, Univ*) examinar a algn de algo; (*esp for job*) hacer una prueba de algo a algn; (*for revision*) hacer preguntas de algo a algn (para repasar); **she was ~ed on her computer skills** le hicieron una prueba de informática; **can you ~ me on my French/spelling?** ¿me haces preguntas de francés/ortografía?

2 (*Med*) [+ *blood, urine, sample*] analizar; **to have one's eyes ~ed** hacerse una revisión de la vista; **to ~ sb/sth for sth**: **to ~ sb for AIDS** hacer la prueba del SIDA a algn; **to ~ sb for drugs** (*gen*) realizar pruebas a algn para comprobar si ha consumido drogas; [+ *athlete, sportsperson*] realizar el control antidoping a algn; **my doctor wants me to be ~ed for diabetes** mi médico quiere que me haga un análisis para ver *or* (*frm*) determinar si tengo diabetes; **the urine is ~ed for protein** se hace un análisis de orina para determinar el contenido de proteínas

3 (= *conduct trials on*) [+ *aircraft, weapon, new product, drug*] probar; **the drug was ~ed in clinical trials** se sometió el medicamento a pruebas clínicas; **all our products are ~ed for quality** probamos la calidad de todos nuestros productos; **to ~ sth on sth/sb** probar algo con *or* en algo/algn; **none of our products are ~ed on animals** ninguno de nuestros productos se prueba con *or* en animales; **~ the cream on an unaffected area of skin** pruebe la crema sobre una zona cutánea no afectada

4 (= *check*) probar; **~ the water temperature with your elbow** pruebe la temperatura del agua con el codo; **he ~ed the ice with a stick** usó un palo para comprobar la solidez del hielo; ✦**IDIOM to ~ the water(s)** tantear el terreno

5 (*fig*) (= *put to the test*) [+ *person, courage*] poner a prueba; **his resolve will be ~ed to the limits this week** su resolución se pondrá a prueba al máximo esta semana; **to ~ sb's patience** poner a prueba la paciencia de algn

Ⓒ VI (= *conduct a test*) **testing, testing ...** (*Telec*) probando, probando ...; **it is a method used to ~ for allergies** es un método utilizado en pruebas de alergia; **just ~ing!** (*hum*) ¡por si acaso pregunto!; **to ~ negative/positive (for sth)** dar negativo/positivo (en la prueba de algo)

Ⓓ CPD ► **(nuclear) test ban** N prohibición *f* de pruebas nucleares ► **test bed** N banco *m* de pruebas ► **test card** N (*TV*) carta *f* de ajuste ► **test case** N (*Jur*) juicio *m* que sienta jurisprudencia ► **test cricket** N críquet *m* a nivel internacional ► **test data** NPL resultados *mpl* de prueba ► **test drive** N (*by potential buyer*) prueba *f* en carretera; (*by mechanic, technician*) prueba *f* de rodaje; **to take sth for a ~ drive** probar algo en carretera; *see also* **test-drive** ► **test flight** N vuelo *m* de prueba, vuelo *m* de ensayo ► **test marketing** N *pruebas de un producto nuevo en el mercado*; **~ marketing has already shown the product to be a great success** las pruebas realizadas en el mercado ya han mostrado que el producto tiene un éxito tremendo ► **test match** N (*Cricket, Rugby*) partido *m* internacional ► **test paper** N (*Scol, Univ*) examen *m*; (*multiple-choice*) test *m*; (*Chem*) papel *m* reactivo ► **test pattern** N (*US TV*) = **test card** ► **test piece** N (*Mus*) pieza *f* elegida para un certamen de piano ► **test pilot** N piloto *mf* de pruebas ► **test run** N (*lit*) vuelta *f* de prueba, prueba *f*; (*fig*) puesta *f* a prueba ► **test tube** N probeta *f*, tubo *m* de ensayo ► **test tube baby** N bebé *mf* probeta

►**test out** VT + ADV probar

testament ['testəmənt] N 1 (= *will*) testamento *m*; *see also* **will**[2] **A2** 2 (*Bible*) **the Old/New Testament** el Antiguo/Nuevo Testamento 3 (= *proof*) testimonio *m*; **the building is a ~ to his skills as an architect** el edificio es testimonio de su competencia como arquitecto

testamentary [ˌtestə'mentərɪ] ADJ testamentario

testator [tes'teɪtəʳ] N testador *m*

testatrix [tes'teɪtrɪks] N testadora *f*

test-drill ['testˌdrɪl] VI sondear

test-drive ['testˌdraɪv] (*vb: pt* **test-drove**; *pp* **test-driven**) VT [+ *car*] [*prospective buyer*] probar en carretera; [*mechanic, technician*] hacer la prueba de rodaje a; *see also* **test D**

tester[1] ['testəʳ] N (= *person*) ensayador(a) *m/f*; (= *sample, trial product*) muestra *f*, artículo *m* de muestra

tester[2]† ['testəʳ] N baldaquín *m*

testes ['testiːz] NPL testes *mpl*

testicle ['testɪkl] N testículo *m*

testify ['testɪfaɪ] Ⓐ VI 1 (*Jur*) prestar declaración, declarar 2 **to ~ to sth** (*Jur*) declarar algo, testificar algo; (= *be sign of*) atestiguar algo, dar fe de algo Ⓑ VT declarar, testificar; **to ~ that ...** declarar *or* testificar que ...

testily ['testɪlɪ] ADV con irritación, malhumoradamente

testimonial [ˌtestɪ'məʊnɪəl] N 1 (= *certificate*) certificado *m*; (= *reference about person*) carta *f* de recomendación, recomendación *f* 2 (= *gift*) obsequio *m* 3 (*Sport*) (*also* **~ match**) partido *m* homenaje

testimony ['testɪmənɪ] N (*Jur*) (= *statement in court*) testimonio *m*, declaración *f*; (*fig*) (= *indication of sth*) muestra *f*, señal *f*; **in ~ whereof ...** (*frm*) en fe de lo cual ...; **to bear ~ to sth** atestiguar algo, dar fe de algo

testing ['testɪŋ] Ⓐ ADJ (= *difficult*) duro; **it was a ~ experience for her** fue una experiencia muy dura para ella; **it was a ~ time** fue un período difícil Ⓑ N pruebas *fpl* Ⓒ CPD ► **testing ground** N zona *f* de pruebas, terreno *m* de pruebas

testis ['testɪs] N (*pl* **testes** ['testiːz]) testículo *m*, teste *m*

testosterone [te'stɒstərəʊn] N testosterona *f*

testy ['testɪ] ADJ (*compar* **testier**; *superl* **testiest**) [*person*] irritable; [*reply*] irritado

tetanus ['tetənəs] Ⓐ N tétanos *m* Ⓑ CPD [*injection*] del tétanos, contra el tétanos; [*vaccine*] contra el tétanos, antitetánica

tetchily ['tetʃɪlɪ] ADV con irritación, malhumoradamente

tetchiness ['tetʃɪnɪs] N irritabilidad *f*

tetchy ['tetʃɪ] ADJ (*compar* **tetchier**; *superl* **tetchiest**) [*person*] irritable, picajoso*; [*mood*] irritable

tête-à-tête ['teɪtɑː'teɪt] N (*pl* **tête-à-tête, tête-à-têtes**) conversación *f* íntima

tether ['teðəʳ] Ⓐ N ronzal *m*, soga *f*; ✦**IDIOM to be at the end of one's ~** no aguantar más, no poder más Ⓑ VT [+ *animal*] atar (con una cuerda) (**to** a)

tetragon ['tetrəgən] N tetrágono *m*

tetrahedron ['tetrə'hiːdrən] N (*pl* **tetrahedrons, tetrahedra** [ˌtetrə'hiːdrə]) tetraedro *m*

tetrameter [te'træmɪtəʳ] N tetrámetro *m*

tetrathlon [te'træθlən] N tetratlón *m*

Teuton ['tjuːtən] N teutón/ona *m/f*

Teutonic [tjʊ'tɒnɪk] ADJ teutónico

Tex. ABBR (*US*) = **Texas**

Texan ['teksən] Ⓐ ADJ tejano Ⓑ N tejano/a *m/f*

Texas ['teksəs] N Tejas *m*

Texican ['teksɪkən] (*hum*), **Tex-Mex** [ˌteks-

'meks] N *lengua mixta angloespañola de los estados del suroeste de EE.UU.*

text [tekst] Ⓐ N 1 (= *written or printed matter*) texto *m*; (= *book*) libro *m* de texto; (= *subject*) tema *m*; (*Rel*) pasaje *m*; **to stick to one's ~** no apartarse de su tema
2(*) (*also* **~ message**) mensaje *m* (de texto)
Ⓑ VT **to ~ sb*** enviar un mensaje a algn
Ⓒ CPD ► **text editor** N (*Comput*) editor *m* de texto ► **text message** N mensaje *m* de texto ► **text messaging** N (envío *m* de) mensajes *mpl* de texto ► **text processing** N proceso *m* de textos, tratamiento *m* de textos ► **text processor** N procesador *m* de textos

textbook ['tekstbʊk] N libro *m* de texto; **a ~ case of ...** un caso clásico de ...

textile ['tekstaɪl] Ⓐ ADJ textil
Ⓑ N textil *m*, tejido *m*
Ⓒ CPD ► **textile industry** N industria *f* textil ► **textile worker** N obrero/a *m/f* (del ramo) textil

texting ['tekstɪŋ] N = **text messaging**

textual ['tekstjʊəl] ADJ 1 (= *of, relating to text*) [*criticism*] de textos; [*alterations*] textual; **~ notes** notas *fpl* al pie de página
2 (= *literal*) textual

textually ['tekstjʊəlɪ] ADV textualmente

texture ['tekstʃəʳ] N textura *f*

TGIF* ABBR (*hum*) = **Thank God it's Friday**

TGWU N ABBR (*Brit*) = **Transport and General Workers' Union**

Thai [taɪ] Ⓐ ADJ tailandés Ⓑ N 1 (= *person*) tailandés/esa *m/f* 2 (*Ling*) tailandés *m*

Thailand ['taɪlænd] N Tailandia *f*

thalassaemia [ˌθælə'siːmɪə] N anemia *f* de Cooley

thalidomide® [θə'lɪdəʊmaɪd] N talidomida *f*

thallium ['θælɪəm] N talio *m*

Thames [temz] N **the ~** el Támesis

▼ **than** [ðæn] CONJ 1 (*in comparisons*) que; **I have more ~ you** tengo más que usted; **nobody is more sorry ~ I (am)** nadie lo siente más que yo; **more often ~ not** en la mayoría de los casos; **they have more money ~ we have** tienen más dinero que nosotros; **the car went faster ~ we had expected** el coche alcanzó una velocidad mayor de lo que habíamos esperado; **it is better to phone ~ to write** más vale llamar por teléfono que escribir
2 (*with numerals*) de; **more/less ~ 90** más/menos de 90; **more ~ once** más de una vez
3 (*stating preference*) antes que; **rather you ~ me** tú antes que yo

▼ **thank** [θæŋk] Ⓐ VT 1 **to ~ sb** dar las gracias *or* agradecer a algn; **I cannot ~ you enough!** ¡cuánto te lo agradezco!; **to ~ sb for sth** agradecer algo a algn, dar las gracias a algn por algo; **did you ~ him for the flowers?** ¿le diste las gracias por las flores?; **he has only himself to ~ for that** él mismo tiene la culpa de eso; **I have John to ~ for that** eso se lo tengo que agradecer a Juan; (*iro*) Juan tiene la culpa de eso; **he won't ~ you for telling her** no te agradecerá de que se lo hayas dicho; **I'll ~ you not to interfere!** ¡agradecería que no te metieras!; **~ heavens/goodness/God (for that)!** ¡gracias a Dios!, ¡menos mal!
2 **~ you** (*as excl*) ¡gracias!; **~ you very much** muchas gracias; **~ you for the present** muchas gracias por el regalo; **no ~ you** no, gracias; **¡no ~ you!** (*iro*) ¡ni hablar!, ¡no faltaba más!; **did you say ~ you?** ¿has dado las gracias?; *see also* **thanks, thank-you**
Ⓑ CPD ► **thank offering** N prueba *f* de gratitud

thankful ['θæŋkfʊl] ADJ agradecido; **to be ~ for sth** estar agradecido por algo; **I've got so much to be ~ for** tengo tantas cosas por las que estar agradecido; **let's be ~ that it's over** demos gracias que haya terminado; **she was ~ to be alive** daba gracias por estar viva; ✦**IDIOM to be ~ for small mercies** dar gracias por que la cosa no sea peor

thankfully ['θæŋkfəlɪ] ADV 1 (= *fortunately*) gracias a Dios, afortunadamente; **~, someone had called the police** menos mal que alguien había llamado a la policía, gracias a Dios *or* afortunadamente, alguien había llamado a la policía; **~ for my family, I wasn't hurt** afortunadamente *or* por suerte para mi familia, no resulté herido
2 (= *gratefully*) **he accepted the drink ~** aceptó la bebida agradecido

thankfulness ['θæŋkfʊlnɪs] N gratitud *f*, agradecimiento *m*

thankless ['θæŋklɪs] ADJ (= *unrewarding, ungrateful*) ingrato

▼ **thanks** ['θæŋks] Ⓐ NPL 1 (= *gratitude*) agradecimiento *msing*, gratitud *fsing*; **they deserve our ~** merecen nuestro agradecimiento *or* nuestra gratitud; **in his speech of ~** en su discurso de agradecimiento; **that's all the ~ I get!** ¡y así se me agradece!; **she murmured her ~** dio las gracias murmurando; **to give ~** dar las gracias (**for** por); **~ be to God** (*Rel*) alabado sea Dios
2 **~ to: ~ to you ...** gracias a ti ...; (*iro*) por culpa tuya ...; **small/no ~ to you** no fue gracias a ti; **I got the job ~ to him** conseguí el trabajo a *or* por mediación suya; **~ to the rain the game was abandoned** debido a la lluvia el partido fue anulado
Ⓑ EXCL (*) **thanks!** ¡gracias!; **many ~!** ◊ **~ very much!** ◊ **~ a lot!** ¡muchas gracias!, ¡muchísimas gracias!; **you went and told her? ~ a lot!** (*iro*) ¡y se lo dijiste!, ¡gracias, hombre! (*iro*); *see also* **bunch**
Ⓒ CPD ► **thanks offering** N prueba *f* de gratitud

thanksgiving ['θæŋksˌgɪvɪŋ] Ⓐ N acción *f* de gracias, voto *m* de gracias
Ⓑ CPD ► **Thanksgiving Day** N (*US*) día *m* de Acción de Gracias

> **THANKSGIVING**
>
> *El Día de Acción de Gracias, en inglés* **Thanksgiving** *o* **Thanksgiving Day** *es un día de fiesta en Estados Unidos que se celebra el cuarto jueves de noviembre y que data de 1621. En esta fecha los primeros colonos norteamericanos (***Pilgrim Fathers***) celebraron un acto de acción de gracias por el éxito de su primera cosecha en suelo americano. La comida típica del Día de Acción de Gracias (***Thanksgiving meal***) consiste en pavo asado y pastel de calabaza. Muchas personas recorren largas distancias para estar junto a sus familias en este día.*
> *En Canadá se celebra una fiesta semejante el segundo lunes de octubre, aunque no está relacionada con dicha fecha histórica.*
> ⇨ *Ver tb* PILGRIM FATHERS, MACY'S THANKSGIVING PARADE

thank-you, thankyou ['θæŋkjʊ] N **to say a special ~ to sb** agradecer a algn especialmente; **she said her ~s and goodbyes and left** dio las gracias, se despidió y se marchó; **now a big ~ to John** ahora, nuestras gracias más sinceras para John; **without so much as a ~** sin la menor señal de agradecimiento

that [(*strong form*) ðæt, (*weak form*) ðət], (*pl* **those**)

> A DEMONSTRATIVE ADJECTIVE
> B DEMONSTRATIVE PRONOUN
> C RELATIVE PRONOUN
> D ADVERB
> E CONJUNCTION
>
> ***Those*** *is treated as a separate entry.*

Ⓐ DEMONSTRATIVE ADJECTIVE
1 ***+ objects/people***

You can generally use **ese** *etc when pointing to something near the person you are speaking to. Use* **aquel** *etc for something which is distant from both of you:*

(*nearer*) ese *m*, esa *f*; (*more remote*) aquel *m*, aquella *f*; **~ book** ese libro; **~ hill over there** aquella colina de allí; **~ car is much better value than ~ sports model at the end** ese coche está mejor de precio que aquel modelo deportivo que hay al final; **~ lad of yours** ese chico tuyo; **~ wretched dog!** ¡ese maldito perro!; **what about ~ cheque?** ¿y el cheque ese?; **I only met her ~ once** la vi solamente aquella vez; **~ one** ése *m*, ésa *f*; (*more remote*) aquél *m*, aquélla *f*; **there's little to choose between this model and ~ one** no hay mucho que elegir entre este modelo y aquél
2 ***+ event, year, month***

Aquel *is used to refer to a time in the distant past. Use* **ese** *if you mention a concrete date, month, year, etc:*

do you remember ~ holiday we had in Holland? ¿te acuerdas de aquellas vacaciones que pasamos en Holanda?; **1992? I can't remember where we holidayed ~ year** ¿1992? no recuerdo dónde pasamos las vacaciones ese año; **May? we can't come ~ month because we'll be moving house** ¿en mayo? no podemos venir ese mes porque nos estaremos mudando de casa
Ⓑ DEMONSTRATIVE PRONOUN

The pronoun **that** *(***one***) is translated by* **ése** *and* **aquél** *(masc),* **ésa** *and* **aquélla** *(fem) and* **eso** *and* **aquello** *(neuter). You can generally use* **ése** *etc when pointing to something near the person you are speaking to. Use* **aquél** *etc for something which is distant from both of you. Note that the masculine and feminine pronouns carry accents to distinguish them from the masculine and feminine adjectives, though these can be omitted if there is no ambiguity. Neuter pronouns never carry an accent:*

who's ~? ¿quién es ése?; **what is ~?** ¿qué es eso?, ¿eso qué es?; **~'s my French teacher over there** aquél es mi profesor de francés; **~'s my sister over by the window** aquélla de la ventana es mi hermana; **~'s Joe** es Joe; **is ~ you, Paul?** ¿eres tú, Paul?; **£5? it must have cost more than ~** ¿5 libras? debe haber costado más (que eso); **~'s true** eso es verdad, es cierto (*esp LAm*); **~'s odd!** ¡qué raro!, ¡qué cosa más rara!; **1988? ~ was the year you graduated, wasn't it?** ¿1988? ése fue el año en que acabaste la carrera, ¿no es así?; **"will he come?" — "~ he will!"**† — ¿vendrá? —¡ya lo creo!; **after ~** después de eso; **bees and wasps and all ~** abejas, avispas y cosas así; **~'s all I can tell you** eso es todo lo que puedo decirte; **is ~ all?** ¿eso es todo?, ¿nada más?; **she's not as stupid as (all) ~** no es tan estúpida como para eso; **and it was broken at ~** y además estaba roto; **I realized he meant to speak to me and at ~ I panicked** me di cuenta de que quería hablar conmigo y entonces me entró el pánico; **what do you mean by ~?** ¿qué quieres decir con eso?; **if it comes to ~** en tal caso, si llegamos a eso; **it will cost $20, if that** costará

➤ LANGUAGE IN USE: **than 1** 5.3, 5.5 **thank A1** 22 **thanks A1, 2** 17.1, 22, 26.3

20 dólares, si es que llega; **~ is** (= *ie*) es decir …; **~'s it, we've finished** ya está, hemos terminado; **they get their wages and ~'s it** tienen un sueldo y eso es todo; **~'s it! she can find her own gardener!** ¡se acabó! ¡que se busque un jardinero por su cuenta!; **~ of** el/la de; **a hurricane like ~ of 1987** un huracán como el de 1987; **a recession like ~ of 1973-74** una recesión como la de 1973-1974; **~ is to say** es decir …; **why worry about ~ which may never happen?** (*frm*) ¿por qué preocuparse por aquello que *or* por lo que puede que nunca vaya a pasar?; **with ~** con eso; *✦IDIOMS* **that's that**: **you can't go and that's that** no puedes irte sin más, no puedes ir y no hay más qué decir, no puedes ir y sanseacabó; **so ~ was ~** y no había más que hacer, y ahí terminó la cosa

Ⓒ RELATIVE PRONOUN

Unlike **that**, *the Spanish relative cannot be omitted.*

1 que; **the man ~ came in** el hombre que entró; **the book ~ I read** el libro que leí; **the houses ~ I painted** las casas que pinté; **the girl ~ he met on holiday and later married** la chica que conoció durante las vacaciones y con la que después se casó; **all ~ I have** todo lo que tengo; **fool ~ I am!** ¡tonto que soy!

2 ***with preposition***

If the **that** *clause ends in a preposition, you can either translate* **that** *as* **que** *(usually preceded by the definite article) or as* ARTICLE + **cual/cuales**. *Use the second option particularly in formal language or after long prepositions or prepositional phrases:*

the actor ~ I was telling you about el actor del que te hablaba; **the car ~ she got into** el coche al que se subió; **the film ~ I read about in the papers** la película sobre la que leí en el periódico; **the box ~ I put it in** la caja donde lo puse, la caja en la que *or* en la cual lo puse; **a planet ~ satellites go round** un planeta alrededor del cual giran satélites

3 ***in expressions of time*** **the evening ~ we went to the theatre** la tarde (en) que fuimos al teatro; **the summer ~ it was so hot** el verano que hizo tanto calor

Ⓓ ADVERB

1 ***= so*** tan; **~ far** tan lejos; **he can't be ~ clever** no puede ser tan inteligente; **I didn't know he was ~ ill** no sabía que estuviera tan enfermo; **it's about ~ big** (*with gesture*) es más o menos así de grande; **cheer up! it isn't ~ bad** ¡ánimo! ¡no es para tanto!; **~ many frogs** tantas ranas; **~ much money** tanto dinero

2 **** = so very*** tan; **he was ~ wild** estaba tan furioso; **it was ~ cold!** ¡hacía tanto frío!

Ⓔ CONJUNCTION

Unlike **that**, **que** *cannot be omitted.*

1 (*after verb*) que; **he said ~ …** dijo que …; **he said ~ he was going to London and would be back in the evening** dijo que se iba a Londres y (que) volvería por la tarde; **I believe ~ he exists** creo que existe

2 (*after noun*)

Translate as **de que** *in phrases like* **the idea/belief/hope that**:

any hope ~ they might have survived was fading toda esperanza de que hubiesen sobrevivido se estaba desvaneciendo; **the idea ~ we can profit from their labour** la idea de que podemos aprovecharnos de su trabajo; **…, not ~ I want to, of course** …, no es que yo quiera, por supuesto; **oh ~ we could!** ¡ojalá pudiéramos!, ¡ojalá!

3 (*that clause as subject*)

If the **that** CLAUSE *is the subject of another verb it is usual to translate* **that** *as* **el que** *rather than* **que** *especially if it starts the sentence:*

~ he did not know surprised me (el) que no lo supiera me extrañó, me extrañó (el) que no lo supiera

In these cases the verb which follows will be in the subjunctive:

~ he refuses is natural (el) que rehúse es natural; **~ he should behave like this is incredible** (el) que se comporte así es increíble, es increíble que se comporte así; *see also* **would 7**

4 ***= in order that*** para que + *subjun*; **it was done (so) ~ he might sleep** se hizo para que pudiera dormir; **those who fought and died ~ we might live** los que lucharon y murieron para que nosotros pudiésemos vivir

5 **in ~** en el sentido de que; **it's an attractive investment in ~ it is tax-free** es una inversión atractiva en el sentido de que está exenta de impuestos

thatch [θætʃ] Ⓐ N (= *straw*) paja *f*; (= *roof*) techo *m* de paja

Ⓑ VT cubrir con paja, poner techo de paja a

thatched [θætʃt] ADJ **~ cottage** casita *f* con techo de paja **~ roof** techo *m* de paja

thatcher [ˈθætʃəʳ] N empajador(a) *m/f* de tejados

Thatcherism [ˈθætʃərɪzəm] N thatcherismo *m*

Thatcherite [ˈθætʃəraɪt] Ⓐ ADJ thatcheriano

Ⓑ N thatcheriano/a *m/f*

thatching [ˈθætʃɪŋ] N (= *material*) paja *f* (para techar); (= *activity*) empajado *m* de tejados

thaw [θɔː] Ⓐ N 1 (*gen*) deshielo *m*; [*of snow*] derretimiento *m*; **a ~ had set in** había empezado el deshielo

2 (*fig*) (= *easing up*) descongelación *f*; **the ~ in East-West relations** la distensión en las relaciones Este-Oeste

Ⓑ VT (*also* **~ out**) [+ *frozen food*] descongelar

Ⓒ VI 1 (*Met*) [*snow*] derretirse; [*ice*] deshelarse; **it is ~ing** está deshelando

2 (*also* **~ out**) [*frozen food, cold toes*] descongelarse; (*fig*) [*relations*] distenderse; **I sat by the fire to ~ out** me senté junto al fuego para entrar en calor; **after a couple of glasses of wine he soon began to ~** tras tomar un par de vasos de vino empezó a relajarse *or* perder su reserva inicial

the [(*strong form*) ðiː, (*weak form*) ðə] Ⓐ DEF ART 1 (*singular*) el/la; (*plural*) los/las; **~ boy** el niño; **~ woman** la mujer; **~ cars** los coches; **~ chairs** las sillas; **do you know ~ Smiths?** ¿conoce a los Smith?; **how's ~ leg?** ¿cómo va la pierna?; **all ~ …** todo el …/toda la …, todos los …/todas las …; **I'll meet you at ~ bank/station** quedamos en el banco/la estación; **~ cheek of it!** ¡qué frescura!; **he's ~ man for ~ job** es el más indicado para el puesto; **from ~** del/de la, de los/las; **it's ten miles from ~ house/village** está a diez millas de la casa/del pueblo; **I haven't ~ money** no tengo dinero; **of ~** del/de la, de los/las; **~ soup of ~ day** la sopa del día; **it was ~ year of ~ student riots** fue el año de los disturbios estudiantiles; **oh, ~ pain!** ¡ay qué dolor!; **he hasn't ~ sense to understand** no tiene bastante inteligencia para comprender; **I haven't ~ time** no tengo tiempo; **to ~** al/a la, a los/las; **we went to ~ theatre** fuimos al teatro

2 (+ *adjective*) 2·1 (*denoting plural*) los/las; **~ rich and ~ poor** los ricos y los pobres

2·2 (*denoting sing*) lo; **within ~ realms of ~ possible** dentro de lo posible; **~ good and ~ beautiful** lo bueno y lo bello

3 (+ *noun*) (*denoting whole class*) el/la; **to play ~ piano/flute** tocar el piano/la flauta; **in this age of ~ computer …** en esta época del ordenador …

4 (+ *comparative*) el/la; **she was ~ elder** era la mayor

5 (*distributive*) **50 pence ~ pound** 50 peniques la libra; **eggs are usually sold by ~ dozen** los huevos se venden normalmente por docena; **paid by ~ hour** pagado por hora; **25 miles to ~ gallon** 25 millas por galón; **700 lire to ~ dollar** 700 liras por dólar

6 (*emphatic*) **you don't mean THE professor Bloggs?** ¿quieres decir el profesor Bloggs del que tanto se habla?; **it was THE colour of 1995** fue el color que estaba tan de moda en 1995

7 (*in titles*) **Richard ~ Second** Ricardo Segundo; **Ivan ~ Terrible** Iván el Terrible

Ⓑ ADV **she looks all ~ better for it** se la ve mucho mejor por eso; **it will be all ~ better** será tanto mejor; **~ more he works ~ more he earns** cuanto más trabaja más gana; **(all) ~ more so because …** tanto más cuanto que …; **~ more … ~ less** mientras más ... menos …; **~ sooner ~ better** cuanto antes mejor

theatre, **theater** (*US*) [ˈθɪətəʳ] N 1 (= *building*) teatro *m*; **to go to the ~** ir al teatro; **lecture ~** aula *f*; **operating ~** sala *f* de operaciones

2 (= *profession*) teatro *m*; **she's been working in the ~ for 20 years** lleva trabajando el teatro 20 años

3 (= *drama*) teatro *m*; **~ of the absurd** teatro *m* del absurdo

4 (*fig*) teatro *m*, escenario *m*

theatre-goer, **theater-goer** (*US*) [ˈθɪətəˌgəʊəʳ] N aficionado/a *m/f* al teatro; **I'm not a keen ~** no soy un gran aficionado al teatro

theatre-in-the-round [ˈθɪətərɪnðəˈraʊnd] N (*pl* **theatres-in-the-round**) teatro *m* de escenario central

theatreland [ˈθɪətəlænd] N teatrolandia *f*

theatrical [θɪˈætrɪkəl] Ⓐ ADJ 1 (= *of the theatre*) [*production, performance, tradition*] teatral; **the ~ world** el mundo del teatro *or* de las tablas; **she comes from a ~ background** viene de un ambiente de teatro

2 (*fig*) [*person, gesture, manner*] teatral, histriónico, teatrero*; **there was something very ~ about him** tenía un aire muy teatral; **don't be so ~!** ¡no seas tan teatral *or* teatrero*!, ¡no hagas tanto teatro!

Ⓑ **theatricals** NPL funciones *fpl* teatrales

theatricality [θɪˌætrɪˈkælɪtɪ] N teatralidad *f*

theatrically [θɪˈætrɪkəlɪ] ADV 1 (*Theat*) [*accomplished, effective*] desde el punto de vista teatral

2 (= *exaggeratedly*) de manera teatral; **he groaned ~** soltó un gemido teatral, gimió de manera teatral

Thebes [θiːbz] N Tebas *f*

thee [ðiː] PRON (†, *poet*) te; (*after prep*) ti; **with ~** contigo

theft [θeft] N (*gen*) robo *m*

their [ðɛəʳ] POSS ADJ (*with singular noun*) su; (*with plural noun*) sus; **~ father** su padre; **~ house** su casa; **~ parents** sus padres; **~ sisters** sus hermanas; **they took off ~ coats** se quitaron los abrigos; **after washing ~ hands** después de lavarse las manos; **someone stole ~ car** alguien les robó el coche

theirs [ðɛəz] POSS PRON (*referring to singular possession*) (el/la) suyo/a; (*referring to plural possession*) (los/las) suyos/as; **it's not our car, it's ~** no es nuestro coche, es suyo *or* es de ellos;

the suitcase is ~ la maleta es suya *or* es de ellos; **"whose is this?" — "it's ~"** —¿de quién es esto? —es suyo *or* de ellos; **~ is a happy home** el suyo es un hogar feliz; **Isobel is a friend of ~** Isobel es amiga suya; **"is this their house?" — "no, ~ is white"** —¿es ésta su casa? —no, la suya *or* la de ellos es blanca; **my parents and ~** mis padres y los suyos

theism [ˈθiːɪzəm] N teísmo *m*

theist [ˈθiːɪst] N teísta *mf*

theistic [θiːˈɪstɪk] ADJ teísta

them [ðem, ðəm] PRON [1] (*direct object*) los/las; **I didn't know ~** no los conocía; **look at ~!** ¡míralos!; **I had to give ~ to her** tuve que dárselos
[2] (*indirect object*) les; (*combined with direct object pron*) se; **I gave ~ some brochures** les di unos folletos; **you must tell ~ the truth** tienes que decirles la verdad; **yes, of course I gave ~ the book** sí, claro que les di el libro; **yes, of course I gave it to ~** sí, claro que se lo di; **I gave the money to THEM, not their parents** les di el dinero a ellos, no a sus padres; **I'm giving it to THEM not you** se lo doy a ellos, no a ti; **give it to ~ when you go to Liverpool** dáselo cuando vayas a Liverpool; **give it to THEM, not me** dáselo a ellos, no a mí
[3] (*after prepositions, in comparisons, with verb "to be"*) ellos/ellas; **it's for ~** es para ellos; **my sisters didn't go, my mother stayed with ~** mis hermanas no fueron, mi madre se quedó con ellas; **we are older than ~** somos mayores que ellos; **it must be ~** deben de ser ellos; **that's ~, they're coming now** son ellos, ya vienen; **they were carrying them on ~** los llevaban consigo
[4] (*referring back to "someone", "anyone" etc: direct object*) lo *or* (*Sp*) le/la; (*indirect object*) le; **if anyone tries to talk to you, ignore ~** si alguien trata de hablar contigo, no le hagas caso

thematic [θɪˈmætɪk] ADJ temático

theme [θiːm] Ⓐ N (*gen*) tema *m*
Ⓑ CPD ► **theme park** N parque *m* de atracciones temático ► **theme song** N tema *m* musical ► **theme tune** N **he was humming the ~ tune of James Bond** tarareaba la música de James Bond

themselves [ðəmˈselvz] PRON [1] (*reflexive*) se; **did they hurt ~?** ¿se hicieron daño?
[2] (*for emphasis*) ellos mismos/ellas mismas; (*after prep*) sí (mismos/as); **they built it ~** lo construyeron ellos mismos; **they talked mainly about ~** hablaron principalmente de sí mismos
[3] (*phrases*) **by ~** solos/as; **she left the children at home by ~** dejó a los niños solos en casa; **don't leave the two of them alone by ~** no se te ocurra dejar a estos dos solos; **the girls did it all by ~** las chicas lo hicieron todo por sí mismas

then [ðen] Ⓐ ADV [1] (= *at that time*) entonces; (= *on that occasion*) en aquel momento, en aquella ocasión; (= *at that period in time*) en aquel entonces, en aquella época, a la sazón (*frm*); **it was ~ that ...** fue entonces cuando ...; **it was ~ eight o'clock** eran las ocho; **~ he used to go out, but now he never does** entonces *or* en aquella época salía, pero ahora no sale nunca; **before ~: she couldn't remember anything that had happened before ~** no podía recordar nada de lo que había ocurrido hasta entonces *or* hasta ese momento; **you should have told me before ~** me lo tenías que haber dicho antes; **by ~** para entonces; **even ~: they existed even ~, in 1953** existían incluso entonces, en 1953; **even ~ it didn't work** aún así, no funcionaba; **from ~ on** desde aquel momento, desde entonces, a partir de entonces; **just ~: just ~ he came in** entró justo entonces; **I wasn't doing anything just ~** justo en ese momento no estaba haciendo nada; **(every) now and ~** de vez en cuando; **since ~** desde entonces; **he wanted it done ~ and there** quería que lo hicieran en el acto *or* en ese mismo momento; **until ~** hasta entonces
[2] (= *afterwards, next*) después, luego; **~ we went to Jaca** después *or* luego fuimos a Jaca; **what happened ~?** ¿qué pasó después *or* luego?; **I chop the onions and ~ what?** pico las cebollas, ¿y luego qué?; *see also* **now A6**
[3] (= *in that case*) entonces; **what do you want me to do ~?** ¿entonces, qué quieres que haga?; **"but I don't want a new one" — "what DO you want ~?"** —pero yo no quiero uno nuevo —¿pues, qué es lo que quieres entonces?; **~ you don't want it?** ¿así que no lo quieres?; **can't you hear me ~?** ¿es que no me oyes?, ¿pues *or* entonces no me oyes?; **but ~ we shall lose money** pero en ese caso perderemos dinero; **that's settled ~** entonces quedamos en eso; **"it doesn't work" — "well ~, we'll buy another one"** —no funciona —bueno, pues entonces compraremos otro
[4] (= *furthermore*) además; **it would be awkward at work, and ~ there's the family** en el trabajo habría problemas, y además tengo que pensar en la familia
[5] (*in summarizing*) **this, ~, was the situation at the beginning of his reign** esta era, pues, *or* esta era, por (lo) tanto, la situación al principio de su reinado
[6] (= *having said that*) **and** *or* **but ~ again** por otra parte; **I like it, but ~ I'm biased** a mí sí me gusta, pero yo no soy objetivo; **but ~, you never can tell** pero vamos, nunca se sabe
Ⓑ ADJ entonces, de entonces; **the ~ Labour government** el gobierno laborista de entonces, el entonces gobierno, que era laborista; **the ~ king** el entonces rey

thence [ðens] ADV (*frm, liter*) [1] (= *from that place*) de allí, desde allí
[2] (= *consequently*) por lo tanto, por eso, por consiguiente; **~ the fact that** de ahí que
[3] (= *from that time*) = **thenceforth**

thenceforth [ˌðensˈfɔːθ], **thenceforward** [ˌðensˈfɔːwəd] ADV (*frm, liter*) desde entonces, de allí en adelante, a partir de entonces

theocracy [θɪˈɒkrəsɪ] N teocracia *f*

theocratic [θɪəˈkrætɪk] ADJ teocrático

theodolite [θɪˈɒdəlaɪt] N teodolito *m*

theologian [θɪəˈləʊdʒən] N teólogo/a *m/f*

theological [θɪəˈlɒdʒɪkəl] Ⓐ ADJ teológico
Ⓑ CPD ► **theological college** N seminario *m*

theologist [θɪˈɒlədʒɪst] N teólogo/a *m/f*

theology [θɪˈɒlədʒɪ] N teología *f*

theorem [ˈθɪərəm] N (*Math*) teorema *m*

theoretic [θɪəˈretɪk] ADJ = **theoretical**

theoretical [θɪəˈretɪkəl] ADJ (*gen*) teórico

theoretically [θɪəˈretɪkəlɪ] ADV (*gen*) teóricamente, en teoría

theoretician [ˌθɪərəˈtɪʃən], **theorist** [ˈθɪərɪst] N teórico/a *m/f*

theorize [ˈθɪəraɪz] VI **to ~ (about/on)** teorizar (acerca de/sobre)

theorizer [ˈθɪəraɪzəʳ] N teorizante *mf*

THEN

Time

- When **then** means "at that time", translate using **entonces**:

It was then that she heard Gwen cry out
Fue entonces cuando oyó gritar a Gwen
I hadn't heard about it till then
Hasta entonces no había oído hablar de ello

- Alternatively, use expressions like **en aquella época** to refer to a particular period or **en ese momento** to refer to a particular moment:

...my sister, who was then about 17...
...mi hermana, que en aquella época tenía unos 17 años... *or* ***que tenía entonces unos 17 años...***

- When **then** is used in the sense of "next", translate using **luego** or **después**:

At first he refused but then he changed his mind
Primero se negó, pero luego *or* ***después cambió de opinión***
He went to Julián's house and then to the chemist's
Fue a casa de Julián y luego *or* ***después a la farmacia***

Reason

- When **then** means "so" or "in that case", translate using **entonces** (placed at the beginning of the sentence):

"I have a headache" — "So you won't be coming to the theatre, then?"
"Me duele la cabeza" — "¿Entonces no vienes al teatro?"
Then you'll already know about the bomb
Entonces ya sabrás lo de la bomba

- Alternatively, use **pues entonces**:

Pues entonces ya sabrás lo de la bomba

- In more formal and written language, use **por (lo) tanto** or alternatively, **pues**, particularly when you are introducing a summary or a conclusion. These often appear between commas:

Their decision, then, was based on a detailed analysis of the situation
Su decisión, pues, *or* ***Su decisión, por (lo) tanto, estaba basada en un análisis detallado de la situación***

For further uses and examples, see main entry.

▼ **theory** [ˈθɪərɪ] N (= *statement, hypothesis*) teoría *f*; **in ~** en teoría, teóricamente; **it's my ~** *or* **my ~ is that ...** tengo la teoría de que ..., mi teoría es que ...

theosophical [θɪəˈsɒfɪkəl] ADJ teosófico

theosophy [θɪˈɒsəfɪ] N teosofía *f*

therapeutic [ˌθerəˈpjuːtɪk] ADJ terapéutico

therapeutical [ˌθerəˈpjuːtɪkl] ADJ terapéutico

therapeutics [ˌθerəˈpjuːtɪks] N terapéutica *f*

therapist [ˈθerəpɪst] N terapeuta *mf*

therapy [ˈθerəpɪ] N terapia *f*

there Ⓐ [ðɛəʳ] ADV [1] (*place*) (= *there near you*) ahí; (*less precisely*) allí; (*further away*) allá; **put it ~, on the table** ponlo ahí, en la mesa; **when we left ~** cuando partimos de allí; **I don't know how to get ~** no sé cómo llegar allí; **~ he is!** ¡allí está!; **~'s the bus** ahí viene el autobús, ya viene el autobús; **~ we were, stuck** así que nos encontramos allí sin podernos mover; **to go ~ and back** ir y volver; **12 kilometres ~ and back** 12 kilómetros ida y vuelta; **we left him back ~ at the crossroads** lo dejamos allí atrás, en el cruce; **to be ~ for sb** (= *supportive*) estar al lado de algn, apoyar a algn; **down ~ on the floor** ahí en el suelo; **let's go down ~ by the river** vamos

➤ LANGUAGE IN USE: **theory** 26.2

allí por el río; **I'm going to London, my sister's already down ~** voy a Londres, mi hermana ya está allí; **it's in ~** está ahí dentro; **it's on ~** está ahí encima; **it's over ~ by the TV** está allí, junto al televisor; **~ and then** en el acto, en seguida; **they're through ~ in the dining room** están por esa puerta *or* por ahí, en el comedor; **what's the cat doing up ~?** ¿qué hace el gato ahí arriba?; ✦*IDIOM* **he's not all ~*** le falta un tornillo*

2 (*as addition to phrase*) **hurry up ~!** ¡menearse!; **mind out ~!** ¡cuidado ahí!; **move along ~!** (*on street*) ¡retírense!; (*in bus, train*) ¡muévanse!, ¡no se paren, sigan para atrás!; **you ~!** ¡oye, tú!, ¡eh, usted! (*more frm*)

3 (= *in existence, available*) **if the demand is ~, the product will appear** si existe la demanda, aparecerá el producto; **it's no good asking because the money just isn't ~** no sirve de nada pedir dinero, sencillamente porque no hay; **the old church is still ~ today** la vieja iglesia todavía está en pie *or* existe hoy; **is John ~, please?** (*on phone*) ¿está John?

4 (= *on that point*) en eso; **~ we differ** en eso discrepamos *or* no estamos de acuerdo; **you're right ~** en eso tienes razón; **I agree with you ~** en eso estoy de acuerdo contigo; **~ you are wrong** ahí se equivoca, en eso te equivocas

5 (= *at that point*) **we'll leave it ~ for today** lo dejaremos aquí por hoy; **could I just stop you ~ and say something?** ¿puedo interrumpirte para decir algo al respecto?

6 (*emphasizing, pointing out*) **~, now look what you've done!** desde luego, ¡mira lo que has hecho!; **~ again** por otra parte; **~ you are, what did I tell you!** ¿ves? es lo que te dije; **"~ you are," he said, handing the book over** —ahí lo tienes —dijo, entregando el libro; **~ you go again, upsetting the children** ¿vuelta a las andadas, molestando a los niños?, ¿ya estamos otra vez molestando a los niños?; **it wasn't what I wanted, but ~ you go*** no era lo que buscaba, pero ¿qué le vamos a hacer?; **I'm not going, so ~!*** pues no voy, y fastídiate*

Ⓑ PRON **~ is** ◊ **~ are** hay; **~ will be** habrá; **~ were ten bottles** había *or* (*esp LAm*) habían diez botellas; **how many are ~?** ¿cuántos hay?; **~ will be eight people for dinner tonight** seremos ocho para cenar esta noche; **~ was laughter at this** en esto hubo risas; **~ was singing and dancing** se cantó y se bailó; **~ has been an accident** ha habido un accidente; **are ~ any bananas?** ¿hay plátanos?; **is ~ any coffee?** ¿hay café?; **~ is no wine left** no queda vino; **~ might be time/room** puede que haya tiempo/sitio; **~ is a pound missing** falta una libra

Ⓒ [ðɛəʳ] EXCL **~, drink this** bebe esto; **there, there** (*comforting*) no te preocupes, no pasa nada; **but ~, what's the use?** pero ¡vamos!, es inútil

thereabouts [ˈðɛərəbaʊts] ADV 1 (*place*) por ahí, allí cerca

2 (*number*) **12 or ~** 12 más o menos, alrededor de 12; **£5 or ~** cinco libras o así

thereafter [ðɛərˈɑːftəʳ] ADV (*frm*) después de eso, de allí en adelante, a partir de entonces

thereat [ðɛərˈæt] ADV (*frm*) (= *thereupon*) con eso, acto seguido; (= *for that reason*) por eso, por esa razón

thereby [ˈðɛəˈbaɪ] ADV así, de ese modo; **~ hangs a tale** eso tiene su cuento

therefore [ˈðɛəfɔːʳ] ADV por tanto, por lo tanto; **he wanted to become the richest, and ~ the happiest, man in the world** quería convertirse en el hombre más rico, y por (lo) tanto más feliz, del mundo; **I think, ~ I am** pienso, luego existo; **therefore X = 4** luego X es igual a 4 (*Math*)

➤ LANGUAGE IN USE: **therefore** 17.2, 26.1

THERE IS, THERE ARE

• Unlike **there is/are** *etc*, **hay**, **hubo**, **había**, **ha habido** *etc* do not change to reflect number:

There were two kidnappings and a murder
Hubo dos secuestros y un asesinato
Will there be many students at the party?
¿Habrá muchos estudiantes en la fiesta?

• To translate **there must be**, **there may be**, *etc*, you can use **tiene que haber**, **debe (de) haber**, **puede haber**, *etc* although other constructions will also be possible:

There may be a strike
Puede haber *or* ***Puede que haya huelga***
There must be all sorts of things we could do
Tiene que haber muchas cosas que podamos hacer

• If **there is/there are** is followed by **the**, you should normally not use **hay** *etc*. Use **estar** instead:

And then there are the neighbours to consider
Están también los vecinos, a los que hay que tener en cuenta
There is also the question of the money transfer
Está también la cuestión de la transferencia del dinero

• **Hay** *etc* should only be used to talk about existence and occurrence. Don't use it to talk about location. Use **estar** instead to say where things are:

After the shop there's the bus station
Después de la tienda está la estación de autobuses

• Don't use **hay** *etc* to translate phrases like **there are four of us**, **there will be six of them**. Instead, use **ser** in the relevant person:

There are four of us
Somos cuatro
There will be six of them
Serán seis

• Remember to use **que** in the construction **hay algo que hacer** (**there is sth to do**):

There is a lot to do
Hay mucho que hacer
What is there to do?
¿Qué hay que hacer?

For further uses and examples, see main entry at ***there****.*

therefrom [ðɛəˈfrɒm] ADV (*frm*) de ahí, de allí

therein [ðɛərˈɪn] ADV (*frm*) 1 (= *inside*) allí dentro

2 (= *in this regard*) en eso, en esto; **~ lies the danger** ahí está el peligro, en eso consiste el peligro

thereof [ðɛərˈɒv] ADV (*frm*) de eso, de esto, de lo mismo

thereon [ðɛərˈɒn] ADV (*frm*) **the land and the buildings ~** la tierra y los edificios que se asientan sobre ella; **the symbol of the Lion is embroidered ~** el símbolo del león aparece bordado sobre ello

there's [ðɛəz] = **there is, there has**

Theresa [tɪˈriːzə] N Teresa

thereto [ðɛəˈtuː] ADV (*frm*) a eso, a ello

thereunder [ˌðɛərˈʌndəʳ] ADV (*frm*) allí expuesto

thereupon [ˈðɛərəˈpɒn] ADV (*frm*) 1 (= *at that point*) acto seguido, en eso, con eso

2 (= *on that subject*) sobre eso

therewith [ðɛəˈwɪθ] ADV (*frm*) con eso, con lo mismo

therm [θɜːm] N termia *f*

thermal [ˈθɜːməl] Ⓐ ADJ [*current*] termal; [*underwear, blanket*] térmico

Ⓑ N 1 (*Met*) térmica *f*, corriente *f* térmica

2 **thermals** (= *underwear*) ropa *f* interior térmica

Ⓒ CPD ► **thermal baths** NPL = **thermal springs** ► **thermal printer** N termoimpresora *f* ► **thermal reactor** N reactor *m* térmico ► **thermal springs** NPL termas *fpl*, fuentes *fpl* termales

thermic [ˈθɜːmɪk] ADJ térmico

thermionic [ˌθɜːmɪˈɒnɪk] Ⓐ ADJ termiónico

Ⓑ CPD ► **thermionic valve** N lámpara *f* termiónica

thermo… [ˈθɜːməʊ] PREFIX termo…

thermocouple [ˈθɜːməʊˌkʌpl] N termopar *m*, par *m* térmico

thermodynamic [ˈθɜːməʊdaɪˈnæmɪk] ADJ termodinámico

thermodynamics [ˈθɜːməʊdaɪˈnæmɪks] NSING termodinámica *f*

thermoelectric [ˈθɜːməʊɪˈlektrɪk] Ⓐ ADJ termoeléctrico

Ⓑ CPD ► **thermoelectric couple** N par *m* termoeléctrico

thermometer [θəˈmɒmɪtəʳ] N termómetro *m*

thermonuclear [ˈθɜːməʊˈnjuːklɪəʳ] ADJ termonuclear

thermopile [ˈθɜːməʊpaɪl] N termopila *f*

thermoplastic [ˌθɜːməʊˈplæstɪk] N termoplástico *m*

Thermopylae [θɜːˈmɒpɪliː] N Termópilas *fpl*

Thermos® [ˈθɜːməs] N (*also* **~ flask** *or* **bottle**) termo *m*

thermosetting [ˌθɜːməʊˈsetɪŋ] ADJ **~ plastics** plásticos *mpl* termoestables

thermostat [ˈθɜːməstæt] N termostato *m*

thermostatic [ˌθɜːməsˈtætɪk] ADJ termostático

thesaurus [θɪˈsɔːrəs] N (*pl* **thesauruses, thesauri** [θɪˈsɔːraɪ]) tesauro *m*

these [ðiːz] Ⓐ DEM ADJ éstos/éstas; **it's not ~ chocolates but those ones I like** no son estos bombones los que me gustan sino aquéllos; **~ ones over here** éstos/éstas de aquí, éstos/éstas que están aquí; **how are you getting on ~ days?** ¿cómo le va últimamente?

Ⓑ DEM PRON éstos/éstas; **I'm looking for some sandals. can I try ~?** quiero unas sandalias. ¿puedo probarme éstas?; **what are ~?** ¿qué son éstos?; **~ are my friends/my books** éstos son mis amigos/mis libros; **I prefer ~ to those** prefiero éstos a aquéllos

Theseus [ˈθiːsjuːs] N Teseo

thesis [ˈθiːsɪs] N (*pl* **theses** [ˈθiːsiːz]) tesis *f inv*

Thespian [ˈθespɪən] Ⓐ ADJ 1 (= *of Thespis*) de Tespis

2 (*fig*) dramático, trágico

Ⓑ N actor *m*, actriz *f*

Thespis [ˈθespɪs] N Tespis

Thessalonians [ˌθesəˈləʊnɪənz] NPL tesalonios *mpl*

Thessaly [ˈθesəlɪ] N Tesalia *f*

Thetis [ˈθiːtɪs] N Tetis

they [ðeɪ] PRON 1 (*referring to particular people, things*) 1·1 (*emphatic, to avoid ambiguity*) ellos/ellas; **we went to the cinema but ~ didn't** nosotros fuimos al cine pero ellos no; **I spoke to my sisters and THEY agreed with me** hablé con mis hermanas y ellas estaban de acuerdo conmigo; **it's ~ who …** son ellos quienes …; **we work harder than ~ do** trabajamos más que ellos

1·2

Don't translate the subject pronoun when not emphasizing or clarifying:

they're fine, thanks están bien, gracias; **they're yellow** son amarillos

1·3 (*frm*) **~ who …** los que …, quienes …

2 (*referring to "someone", "anyone"*) **if anyone tells you otherwise, ~ are wrong** si alguien te dice lo contrario, no tiene razón

3 (*generalizing*) **~ say that …** se dice que …, dicen que …; **as ~ say** como dicen, según dicen; **~ are making it illegal** lo van a hacer ilegal

they'd [ðeɪd] = **they would, they had**

they'll [ðeɪl] = **they will, they shall**

they're [ðeəʳ] = **they are**

they've [ðeɪv] = **they have**

thiamine ['θaɪəmiːn] N tiamina *f*

thick [θɪk] Ⓐ ADJ (*compar* **thicker**; *superl* **thickest**) 1 (*= not thin*) [*wall, line, slice, neck*] grueso; [*lips*] grueso, carnoso; [*waist*] ancho; [*sweater*] gordo; [*spectacles*] de lente gruesa; **a ~ layer of snow/dust** una espesa capa de nieve/polvo; **a ~ layer of potatoes/butter** una capa gruesa de patatas/mantequilla; **a tree root as ~ as a man's arm** una raíz de árbol tan gruesa *or* gorda como el brazo de un hombre; **it's 2m ~** tiene 2 metros de grosor; **a 5cm ~ door** una puerta de 5 centímetros de grosor; **to give sb a ~ ear*** dar un sopapo a algn*; **how ~ is it?** ¿qué grosor tiene?, ¿cómo es de grueso?; **it's** *or* **that's a bit ~*** (*= unreasonable*) eso ya pasa de castaño oscuro*

2 (*= dense*) [*beard, eyebrows*] poblado; [*carpet, fur*] tupido; [*forest*] tupido, poblado; [*vegetation, dust*] espeso; [*air, atmosphere*] cargado, denso; [*smoke, clouds, night*] denso; [*fog*] espeso, denso; **to have ~ hair** tener mucho pelo, tener una melena tupida; **to be ~ with** (*gen*) estar lleno de; **the pavements were ~ with people** las aceras estaban abarrotadas *or* llenas de gente; **the air was ~ with smoke** el aire estaba cargado *or* lleno de humo; **the air was ~ with rumours** (*fig*) corrían *or* circulaban muchos rumores; ✦*IDIOM* **to be ~ on the ground***: **cameramen and interviewers were ~ on the ground** había cámaras y entrevistadores a patadas*

3 (*= not runny*) [*yoghurt, sauce*] espeso; **if the soup becomes too ~, add more water** si la sopa se pone muy espesa, añada más agua; **whisk until ~** bátase hasta que se ponga espeso

4 (*) (*= stupid*) corto*, burro*; **he's a bit ~** es un poco corto *or* burro*; **I finally got it into** *or* **through his ~ head** por fin conseguí que le entrase en esa cabeza hueca*; ✦*IDIOMS* **to be as ~ as a brick** *or* **two short planks** ser más burro *or* bruto que un arado*; **as ~ as (pig)shit**** más burro *or* bruto que la hostia**

5 (*= strong*) [*accent*] fuerte, marcado

6 (*from drink, illness, tiredness*) [*voice*] pastoso; **his voice was ~ with emotion** su voz estaba empañada por la emoción *or* cargada de emoción; **his voice was ~ with sarcasm** su tono iba cargado de sarcasmo

7 (*) (*= very friendly*) **to be ~ (with sb)** ser uña y carne (con algn)*; ✦*IDIOM* **to be (as) ~ as thieves** ser uña y carne*

8 (*= groggy*) **I woke up with a ~ head** me desperté con la cabeza embotada

Ⓑ ADV (*= in a thick layer*) **the fog hung ~ over the city** una capa espesa de niebla pendía sobre la ciudad; **the dust/snow lay ~** había una capa espesa de polvo/nieve; **slice the bread nice and ~** corte el pan en rebanadas bien gruesas; **he spread the butter on ~** untó una capa gruesa de mantequilla; ✦*IDIOMS* **to come/follow ~ and fast** llegar/sucederse con rapidez; **the jokes came ~ and fast** los chistes iban surgiendo uno detrás de otro con rapidez; **distress calls were coming in ~ and fast** llovían las llamadas de auxilio; **the snow was falling ~ and fast** nevaba copiosamente *or* sin parar; **to lay it on ~*** (*= exaggerate*) cargar *or* recargar las tintas*

Ⓒ N **to be in the ~ of sth: he likes to be in the ~ of it** *or* **things** *or* **the action** le gusta estar metido en el meollo del asunto *or* en el ajo; **he was in the ~ of the fighting** estaba en lo más intenso de la lucha; ✦*IDIOM* **through ~ and thin** en las duras y en las maduras

thicken ['θɪkən] Ⓐ VT espesar, hacer más espeso

Ⓑ VI 1 (*Culin*) [*mixture, sauce*] espesarse

2 [*darkness*] aumentar; [*clouds, wood, jungle*] hacerse más denso; **her voice ~ed with emotion** se le empañó la voz de emoción *or* por la emoción; ✦*IDIOM* **the plot ~s** la cosa se complica

thickener ['θɪkənəʳ] N espesador *m*

thicket ['θɪkɪt] N matorral *m*

thickhead* ['θɪkhed] N bruto/a *m/f*

thickheaded* [ˌθɪk'hedɪd] ADJ 1 (*= stupid*) bruto, estúpido

2 (*= obstinate*) terco, cabezón

3 (*= groggy*) grogui

thickheadedness* [ˌθɪk'hedɪdnɪs] N 1 (*= stupidness*) estupidez *f*

2 (*= obstinacy*) terquedad *f*

thickie** ['θɪkɪ] N bobo/a *m/f*

thick-lipped [ˌθɪk'lɪpt] ADJ de labios gruesos, bezudo

thickly ['θɪklɪ] ADV 1 (*= densely*) **a ~ populated area** una zona densamente poblada; **the snow was falling ~** la nieve caía con fuerza *or* copiosamente; **the trees grew ~ along the river** los árboles crecían en abundancia a orillas del río; **~ wooded** densamente poblado de árboles

2 (*= in a thick layer*) **she spread the butter ~ on the toast** untó una gruesa capa de mantequilla en la tostada; **dust/snow lay ~** había una espesa capa de polvo/nieve; **the ~ carpeted dining room** el comedor con el suelo cubierto por una tupida moqueta; **the ground was ~ carpeted with pine needles** el suelo estaba cubierto de una gruesa capa de agujas de pino

3 (*= in thick pieces*) **to cut/slice sth ~** cortar algo en rodajas gruesas

4 (*= unclearly*) [*say, reply*] (*from drink, tiredness*) con voz pastosa; (*with emotion*) con voz emocionada

thickness ['θɪknɪs] N 1 (*= denseness*) [*of wall, door, layer*] grosor *m*, espesor *m*; [*of line, slice, fabric, lens*] grosor *m*; [*of hair*] abundancia *f*; [*of fur, carpet*] lo tupido; [*of smoke*] densidad *f*; [*of cream, sauce*] lo espeso; **it is 4mm in ~** tiene 4 milímetros de grosor

2 (*= layer*) capa *f*; **three ~es of material** tres capas de tela

thicko** ['θɪkəʊ] N = **thickie**

thickset [ˌθɪk'set] ADJ [*person*] robusto, fornido; [*features*] grueso, gordo

thick-skinned [ˌθɪk'skɪnd] ADJ 1 [*orange*] de piel gruesa

2 (*= insensitive*) [*person*] insensible, duro

thief [θiːf] N (*pl* **thieves** [θiːvz]) ladrón/ona *m/f*; **stop ~!** ¡al ladrón!; ✦*IDIOM* **you have to set a ~ to catch a ~** no hay como un ladrón para atrapar a otro; *see also* **thick A7**

thieve [θiːv] VT, VI robar, hurtar

thievery ['θiːvərɪ] N robo *m*, hurto *m*

thieving ['θiːvɪŋ] Ⓐ ADJ ladrón

Ⓑ N robo *m*, hurto *m*

thievish ['θiːvɪʃ] ADJ ladrón; **to have ~ tendencies** ser largo de uñas

thievishness ['θiːvɪʃnɪs] N propensión *f* a robar

thigh [θaɪ] Ⓐ N muslo *m*

Ⓑ CPD ► **thigh bone** N fémur *m*

thimble ['θɪmbl] N 1 (*Sew*) dedal *m*

2 (*Naut*) guardacabo *m*

thimbleful ['θɪmblfʊl] N dedada *f*; **just a ~** unas gotas nada más

thin [θɪn] Ⓐ ADJ (*compar* **thinner**; *superl* **thinnest**) 1 (*= not fat*) [*person, legs, arms*] delgado, flaco (*pej*); [*waist*] delgado, estrecho; [*face*] delgado; [*nose*] delgado, afilado; [*lips*] fino; [*animal*] flaco; **to get** *or* **grow ~** adelgazar; **I want to get nice and ~ for the holidays** quiero adelgazar bien para estas vacaciones; **you're getting ~ — aren't you eating enough?** te estás quedando muy delgado, ¿comes lo suficiente?; **she was painfully ~** estaba tan flaca que daba pena verla; ✦*IDIOM* **to be as ~ as a rake*** estar en los huesos*

2 (*= not thick*) [*layer, sheet*] fino, delgado; [*wall*] delgado; [*slice, line, fabric*] fino; **a ~ layer of paint** una capa fina de pintura; **a ~ volume of poetry** un delgado tomo de poesía; **to wear ~** [*fabric, clothing*] desgastarse; **his trousers had worn ~ at the knee** el pantalón se le había desgastado por las rodillas; **the joke had begun to wear very ~** (*fig*) la broma ya empezaba a resultar muy pesada; **my patience is wearing ~** (*fig*) se me está agotando *or* acabando la paciencia; ✦*IDIOMS* **it's the ~ end of the wedge** es el principio de algo que puede tener terribles consecuencias; **to be** *or* **skate** *or* **walk on ~ ice** estar pisando terreno resbaladizo *or* peligroso; **to have a ~ skin** ofenderse por nada, tomárselo todo a mal; *see also* **line A1**

3 (*= watery*) [*custard, sauce, paint*] poco espeso

4 (*= not dense*) [*smoke, fog, rain*] fino

5 (*= sparse*) [*beard, hair*] ralo, escaso; [*eyebrows*] fino, delgado; [*crowd*] escaso, poco numeroso; ✦*IDIOMS* **to be ~ on the ground** (*esp Brit*) escasear; **to be ~ on top** estar casi calvo, tener poco pelo (en la cabeza)

6 (*= unconvincing*) [*excuse*] pobre, poco convincente; [*evidence*] poco concluyente; [*argument, essay, script*] pobre, flojo; **a ~ majority** una mayoría escasa; **a ~ smile** una débil sonrisa

7 (*= weak*) [*voice*] aflautado

8 (*Fin*) [*profit*] escaso; **trading was ~ on the stock market** hubo poca actividad en la bolsa

9 (*= lacking oxygen*) [*air, atmosphere*] enrarecido, rarificado; ✦*IDIOM* **out of/into ~ air**: **to appear out of ~ air** aparecer como por arte de magia; **to produce sth out of ~ air** sacar algo de la nada; **I can't conjure up the money out of ~ air** no puedo sacar el dinero de la nada; **he disappeared** *or* **vanished into ~ air** desapareció como por arte de magia, se lo tragó la tierra

Ⓑ ADV (*= thinly*) **slice the potatoes very ~** corta las patatas en rodajas muy finas; **don't slice the bread too ~** no cortes el pan demasiado fino; **spread the butter very ~** untar una capa muy fina de mantequilla; *see also* **spread B5**

Ⓒ VT 1 (*also* **~ out**) (*= reduce in number*) [+ *population, group*] mermar; [+ *seedlings*] entresacar

2 (*also* ~ **down**) (= *dilute*) [+ *sauce, soup*] aclarar; [+ *paint*] diluir; **aspirin ~s the blood** la aspirina hace que la sangre sea menos espesa; **greenhouse gases are ~ning the ozone layer** los gases que causan el efecto invernadero están haciendo que la capa de ozono sea cada vez menos espesa

Ⓓ VI (*also* ~ **out**) (= *lessen*) [*fog*] aclararse; [*ozone layer*] hacerse menos espeso; [*crowd*] disminuir; [*population*] mermar, reducirse; **his hair is ~ning slightly** está empezando a perder pelo

►**thin down** Ⓐ VT + ADV (= *dilute*) [+ *sauce, gravy, custard*] aclarar; [+ *paint*] diluir

Ⓑ VI + ADV (= *become slim*) adelgazar

►**thin out** Ⓐ VT + ADV (= *reduce in number*) [+ *population, group*] mermar; [+ *seedlings*] entresacar

Ⓑ VI + ADV (= *lessen*) [*fog*] aclararse; [*ozone layer*] hacerse menos denso; [*crowd*] disminuir; [*population*] mermar, reducirse; **his hair is ~ning out** está empezando a perder pelo

thine [ðaɪn] Ⓐ POSS PRON (†, *poet*) (*sing*) (el) tuyo, (la) tuya; (*pl*) (los) tuyos, (las) tuyas; **for thee and ~** para ti y los tuyos; **what is mine is ~** lo que es mío es tuyo

Ⓑ ADJ (*sing*) tu; (*pl*) tus

thing [θɪŋ] N 1 (*concrete*) (= *object*) cosa *f*; **they were selling all sorts of ~s** vendían todo tipo de cosas; **what's that ~ called?** ¿cómo se llama eso?; **get that ~ off the sofa!** ¡quita esa cosa del sofá!; **dogs? I can't stand the ~s** ¿perros? no puedo con ellos; **a ~ of beauty** una belleza, un objeto bello; **~s of value** objetos *mpl* de valor; ✦*IDIOM* **you must be seeing ~s** estás viendo visiones

2 (*non-concrete*) (= *matter, circumstance, action*) cosa *f*, asunto *m*, cuestión *f*; **as ~s are** ◊ **with ~s as they are** tal como están las cosas; **that's how ~s are** así están las cosas; **how are ~s?** ¿qué tal?; **how are ~s with you?** ¿qué tal te va?, ¿cómo andas?; **~s are going badly** las cosas van *or* marchan mal; **~s aren't what they used to be** las cosas ya no son como antes *or* ya no son lo que eran; **the ~ is ...** lo que pasa es que ..., el caso es que ...; **the ~ is to sell your car first** conviene vender primero tu coche; **what a ~ to say!** ¡qué dices!, ¡cómo se te ocurre!; **I haven't done a ~ about it** no he hecho nada de nada al respecto; **I don't know a ~ about cars** no sé nada en absoluto de coches; **I didn't know a ~ for that exam** para ese examen no sabía nada de nada, para ese examen yo estaba pez (*Sp**); **above all ~s** ante todo, sobre todo; **all ~s considered** bien mirado; **all ~s being equal** si las cosas siguen como ahora; **the system cannot be all ~s to all people** el sistema no puede contentar a todo el mundo; **a gentleman in all ~s** un caballero en todos los aspectos; **and for another ~ ...** y además ..., y por otra parte ...; **the best ~ would be to wait** lo mejor sería esperar; **the next best ~** lo mejor después de eso; **we had hoped for better ~s** habíamos esperado algo mejor; **it was a close ~** [*race*] fue una carrera muy reñida; [*accident*] por poco chocamos, casi chocamos; [*escape*] escapamos por un pelo; **it's not the done ~** eso no se hace; **the first ~ to do is ...** lo primero que hay que hacer es ...; **first ~ (in the morning)** a primera hora (de la mañana); **you don't know the first ~ about it** no sabes nada en absoluto de esto; **first ~s first!** ¡lo primero es lo primero!; **it's a good ~ he didn't see you** menos mal que no te vio; **the good ~ about it is that ...** lo bueno es que ...; **it's finished and a good ~ too** se acabó y me alegro de ello; **she knows a good ~ when she sees it** sabe obrar de acuerdo con su propio interés; **this is too much of a good ~** esto es demasiado; **it's just the ~!** ¡es justo lo que me faltaba!; **that's the last ~ we want** eso es lo último que queremos; **last ~ (at night)** antes de acostarse; **the main ~** lo más importante, lo principal; **to make a mess of ~s** estropearlo todo; **it was a near ~ = it was a close thing**; **(the) next ~ I knew, he'd gone** cuando me di cuenta, ya se había ido; **not a ~** nada; **for one ~** en primer lugar; **what with one ~ and another** entre una(s) cosa(s) y otra(s); **it's one ~ to buy it, quite another to make it work** es fácil comprarlo, pero no es tan fácil hacerlo funcionar; **if it's not one ~ it's the other** si no es una cosa es otra; **neither one ~ nor the other** ni lo uno ni lo otro; **the only ~ is to paint it** la única cosa que se puede hacer es pintarlo; **I showed him the copy and he thought it was the real ~** le enseñé la copia y pensó que era el auténtico; **this time I'm in love, it's the real ~** esta vez estoy enamorada de verdad; **to do the right ~** obrar bien, obrar honradamente; **you did the right ~** hiciste bien; **I've done a silly ~** he hecho algo tonto; **did you ever see such a ~?** ¿se vio jamás tal cosa?; **there's no such ~!** ¡no hay tal!; **the play's the ~** lo que importa es la representación; **it's just one of those ~s** son cosas que pasan, son cosas de la vida; **he knows a ~ or two** sabe de qué va; **I could tell you a ~ or two about her** podría decirte unas cuantas cosas sobre ella; **it's the very ~!** ¡es justo lo que me faltaba!; ✦*IDIOMS* **to try to be all ~s to all men** tratar de serlo todo para todos; **to be on to a good ~**: **he knew he was on to a good ~ when the orders started flowing in** supo que había dado con chollo cuando empezaron a llover los pedidos*; **to make a (big) ~ (out) of sth***: **he made a big ~ out of the accident** exageró mucho el accidente; **she made a big ~ of introducing him to me** me lo presentó con mucho aparato; **don't make a ~ of it!** ¡no es para tanto!

3 **things** (= *belongings*) cosas *fpl*; (= *clothes*) ropa *fsing*; (= *luggage*) equipaje *msing*; **where shall I put my ~s?** ¿dónde pongo mis cosas?; **to pack up one's ~s** hacer las maletas; **she had brought her painting ~s with her** se había traído sus utensilios de pintura; **to wash up/clear away the supper ~s** lavar los platos/quitar la mesa de la cena; **to take off one's ~s** quitarse la ropa, desnudarse

4 (*) (= *person*) **you mean ~!** ¡mira que eres tacaño!; **you nasty ~!** ¡mira que eres desagradable!; **you poor (old) ~!** ◊ **poor ~!** ¡pobrecito!; **the stupid ~ went and sold it** el muy estúpido fue y lo vendió; **she's a sweet little ~, isn't she?** es monísima, ¿verdad?

5 (= *fashion*) **the latest ~ in hats** lo último en sombreros; **it's quite the ~** está muy de moda

6 (*) (= *activity, preference*) **his ~ is fast cars** lo suyo son los coches rápidos; **it's not my ~** no es lo mío; ✦*IDIOM* **to do one's own ~*** ir a su aire; **you know her, she likes to do her own ~** ya la conoces, le gusta ir a su aire

7 (*) (= *obsession*) obsesión *f*; **he has a ~ about cleanliness** está obsesionado con la limpieza, tiene obsesión *or* manía con la limpieza; **he has a ~ about steam engines** está obsesionado por las locomotoras a vapor, le obsesionan las locomotoras a vapor; **I have a ~ about punctuality** soy un maniático de la puntualidad; **he's got a ~ for her*** está colado por ella*

8 (*) (= *phobia*) fobia *f*; **she has a ~ about snakes** le tiene fobia a las serpientes

9 (*) (= *relationship, affair*) **he's got a ~ going with her** se entiende con ella; **he had a ~ with her two years ago** se lió con ella hace dos años*

thingumabob* ['θɪŋəmɪbɒb], **thingamajig** ['θɪŋəmɪdʒɪg], **thingummy** ['θɪŋəmɪ], **thingy** ['θɪŋɪ] N (= *object*) chisme *m*, cosa *f*; (= *person*) fulano/a *m/f*; **old ~ with the specs** fulano el de las gafas

▼**think** [θɪŋk] (*vb: pt, pp* **thought**) Ⓐ VI 1 (= *exercise mind*) pensar; (= *ponder*) reflexionar; **I ~, therefore I am** pienso, luego existo; **give me time to ~** dame tiempo para reflexionar; **to act without ~ing** actuar sin pensar; **~ before you reply** piénselo antes de contestar; **I'm sorry, I wasn't ~ing** lo siento, estaba distraído; **now let me ~, where did I last see it?** a ver, déjame pensar, ¿cuándo lo vi por última vez?; **to ~ about sth** (= *occupy one's thoughts with*) pensar en algo; (= *consider*) pensar algo; **what are you ~ing about?** ¿en qué estás pensando?; **you've given us a lot to ~ about** nos ha dado mucho en que pensar; **I'll ~ about it** lo voy a pensar; **it's worth ~ing about** vale la pena de pensarlo; **you ~ too much about money** le das demasiada importancia al dinero; **what he said made me ~ again** lo que dijo hizo que me lo volviera a pensar; **did you ~ I was going to give you the money? well, ~ again!** ¿creíste que iba a darte el dinero? ¡vamos, piensa un poco!; **to ~ aloud** pensar en voz alta; **~ carefully before you reply** piénsalo bien antes de responder; **to ~ for o.s.** pensar por sí mismo; **to ~ (long and) hard** pensar mucho; **I ~ of you always** ◊ **I am always ~ing of you** pienso constantemente en ti; **I'll be ~ing of you** me acordaré de ti; **~ of me tomorrow in the exam** acuérdate de mí mañana, haciendo el examen; **to ~ straight** concentrarse; **to ~ twice before doing sth** pensar algo dos veces antes de hacerlo; **we didn't ~ twice about it** no vacilamos un instante

2 (= *imagine*) imaginarse; **just ~!** ¡fíjate!, ¡imagínate!, ¡te das cuenta!; **~ of the expense** imagínate lo que costaría; **~ of what might have happened!** ¡piensa en lo que podía haber ocurrido!; **and to ~ of her going there alone!** ¡y pensar que ella fue allí sola!

3 (= *remember*) **you can't ~ of everything** no se puede estar en todo; **now I come to ~ of it ...** ahora que lo pienso ...; **I couldn't ~ of the right word** no pude acordarme de la palabra exacta

4 (= *have opinion*) **see what you ~ about it and let me know** piénsalo y dime luego tu opinión; **I didn't ~ much of the play** la obra no me convenció, la obra no me gustó mucho; **we don't ~ much of him** tenemos un concepto más bien bajo de él; **what do you ~ of it?** ¿qué te parece?; **what do you ~ of him?** ¿qué opinas de él?, ¿qué te parece (él)?; **to ~ highly of sb** tener muy buena opinión de algn, tener a algn en muy buen concepto; **I told him what I thought of him** le dije lo que pensaba de él; *see also* **well² A1**

5 (= *consider, take into account*) **to ~ of other people's feelings** pensar en *or* tener en cuenta los sentimientos de los demás; **one has to ~ of the expense** hay que pensar en lo que se gasta; **there are the children to ~ about** hay que pensar en los niños; **he ~s of nobody but himself** no piensa más que en sí mismo

6 **to ~ of** (= *wonder about, dream up*): **I thought of going to Spain** pensé en ir a España; **have you ever thought of going to**

➤ LANGUAGE IN USE: **think A4** 1.2, 6.1 **B2** 1.2, 6.2, 26.3

Cuba? ¿has pensado alguna vez en ir a Cuba?; **don't you ever ~ of washing?** ¿no se te ocurre alguna vez lavarte?; **whatever were you ~ing of?** ¿cómo se te ocurrió hacer eso?; **I was the one who thought of it first** fui yo quien tuve la idea primero; **whatever will he ~ of next?** ¡a ver qué es lo que se le ocurre ahora!

7 (= *choose*) **~ of a number** piensa en un número

Ⓑ VT 1 (= *cogitate*) pensar; **to ~ great thoughts** pensar cosas profundas, tener pensamientos profundos; **to ~ evil thoughts** tener malos pensamientos; **~ what you've done** piense en lo que hizo

2 (= *believe*) creer; **I ~ (that) it is true** creo que es verdad; **I don't ~ it can be done** no creo que se pueda hacer; **you must ~ me very rude** va a creer que soy muy descortés; **we all thought him a fool** lo teníamos todos por idiota; **he ~s himself very clever** se cree muy listo; **I don't ~ it likely** lo creo *or* me parece muy poco probable; **I ~ (that) you're wrong** me parece que estás equivocado; **she's very pretty, don't you ~?** es muy guapa, ¿no crees?; **he'll be back, I don't ~!*** ¿que volverá? ¡no creo!; **I ~ not** creo que no; **I ~ so** creo que sí, me parece que sí; **I don't ~ so** creo que no; **now I don't know what to ~** ahora estoy en duda; **what do you ~ I should do?** ¿qué crees que debo hacer?; **what do you ~ you're doing?** ¿se puede saber lo que estás haciendo?; **who do you ~ you are?** ¿quién te crees que eres?; **who do you ~ you are to come marching in here?** y tú ¿qué derecho crees tener para entrar aquí tan fresco?; **anyone would ~ she was dying** cualquiera diría que se estaba muriendo; **I would have thought that …** hubiera creído que …; **that's what you ~!** ¡(que) te crees tú eso!

3 (= *imagine*) imaginar(se); **~ what we could do with that house!** ¡imagina lo que podríamos hacer con esa casa!; **to ~ she once slept here!** ¡pensar que ella durmió aquí una vez!; **I can't ~ what he can want** no me puedo imaginar qué quiere; **I can't ~ what you mean** no llego a entender lo que quieres decir; **I thought as much** ya me lo figuraba, ya lo sabía; **I never thought that …** nunca pensé *or* imaginé que …; **who'd have thought it?** ¿quién lo diría?; **who'd have thought it possible?** ¿quién se lo hubiera imaginado?

4 (= *remember*) recordar; **try to ~ where you last saw it** intenta recordar dónde lo viste por última vez

5 (= *be of opinion*) opinar; **this is my new dress, what do you ~?** éste es mi vestido nuevo, ¿qué te parece? *or* ¿qué opinas?; **I ~ we should wait, what do you ~?** creo que deberíamos esperar, ¿qué opinas?

6 (= *envisage, have idea*) **I was ~ing that …** estaba pensando que …; **did you ~ to bring a corkscrew?** ¿te acordaste de traer un sacacorchos?; **I didn't ~ to tell him** no se me ocurrió decírselo; **I thought/I'd thought I might go swimming** pensé/había pensado en ir a nadar

7 (= *expect*) pensar, esperar; **I didn't ~ to see you here** no pensaba *or* esperaba verte aquí; **I came here ~ing to get some answers** vine aquí pensando que obtendría *or* esperando recibir algunas respuestas; **I never thought to hear that from you** nunca pensé que te oiría decir eso, nunca esperé oírte decir eso; **we little thought that …** estábamos lejos de pensar que …; **"is she going?" — "I should/shouldn't ~ so"** —¿va a ir? —yo diría que sí/no; **"I paid him for it" — "I should ~ so too!"** —se lo he pagado —¡faltaría más!

Ⓒ N **to have a ~**: **I'll have a ~ about it** lo pensaré; **I was just having a quiet ~** meditaba tranquilamente; ✦**IDIOM if you ~ that, you've got another ~ coming*** si crees eso, te equivocas

Ⓓ CPD ► **think tank** N grupo *m* de expertos; (*in government*) gabinete *m* de estrategia

►**think back** VI + ADV recordar; **try to ~ back** trata de recordar; **I ~ back to that moment when …** recuerdo ese momento cuando …; **when I ~ back over my life** cuando hago un repaso de mi vida

►**think out** VT + ADV [+ *plan*] elaborar; [+ *problem*] meditar a fondo; [+ *solution, response*] encontrar; **I need to ~ out what I'm going to do** tengo que planear bien lo que voy a hacer; **his ideas are well thought out** tiene ideas muy elaboradas; **a well thought out answer** una respuesta muy elaborada; **he ~s things out for himself** razona por sí mismo

►**think over** VT + ADV [+ *offer, suggestion*] pensar, considerar; **I'll ~ it over** lo pensaré; **~ it over!** ¡piénsatelo!, ¡piénsalo!; **I've thought it over very carefully** lo he pensado muy bien

►**think through** VT + ADV [+ *plan*] planear detenidamente, planear cuidadosamente; [+ *objectives*] pensar detenidamente en, pensar cuidadosamente en; **this plan has not been properly thought through** este proyecto no ha sido planeado con el debido cuidado; **we need to ~ through the implications of this proposal** tenemos que considerar *or* examinar detenidamente las implicaciones de esta propuesta

►**think up** VT + ADV [+ *plan*] idear; [+ *idea*] tener; [+ *solution*] idear, inventar; **who thought this one up?** ¿quién ideó esto?, ¿a quién se le ocurrió esto?

thinkable [ˈθɪŋkəbl] ADJ concebible; **it isn't ~ that …** es inconcebible *or* impensable que …

thinker [ˈθɪŋkəʳ] N pensador(a) *m/f*

thinking [ˈθɪŋkɪŋ] Ⓐ N 1 (= *ideas, opinions*) pensamiento *m*, ideas *fpl*; **the new direction of Tyler's ~** el nuevo enfoque en el pensamiento *or* las ideas de Tyler; **we are so alike in our ~** pensamos de una forma tan parecida; **he hoped we would come round to his way of ~** esperaba que al final terminaríamos pensando como él; **to my way of ~** en mi opinión, bajo mi punto de vista; **good ~!** ¡buena idea!; **the ~ behind the campaign** la línea de pensamiento en la que se basa la campaña

2 (= *activity*) **I've done some ~** he estado pensando; **I'll have to do some serious ~** voy a tener que pensar *or* reflexionar seriamente; *see also* **lateral**, **wishful**

3 (= *ability to think*) pensamiento *m*

Ⓑ ADJ [*person, machine*] inteligente; **it is obvious to any ~ person** resulta obvio para cualquier persona inteligente; **the ~ mind** la mente racional; ✦**IDIOM to put on one's ~ cap** estrujarse el cerebro*

Ⓒ CPD ► **thinking patterns** NPL (*Psych*) modelos *mpl* de pensamiento ► **thinking process** N proceso *m* mental ► **thinking time** N tiempo *m* para pensar

thin-lipped [ˈθɪnˈlɪpt] ADJ de labios apretados

thinly [ˈθɪnlɪ] ADV 1 (= *in thin pieces*) **~ cut/sliced** [*vegetable, fruit*] cortado en rodajas finas; [*bread*] cortado en rebanadas finas; [*ham, bacon*] cortado en lonchas finas

2 (= *in a thin layer*) **roll out the pastry very ~** estirar la masa hasta que quede muy fina; **~ clad** ligero de ropa; **~ disguised** poco *or* apenas disimulado; **spread the butter ~** untar una capa fina de mantequilla; **the troops were ~ spread** las tropas se hallaban muy diseminadas *or* dispersas; **our resources are too ~ spread** nuestros recursos están distribuidos por un área demasiado grande; **a ~ veiled threat/warning** una amenaza/advertencia mal disimulada

3 (= *sparsely*) **the island is ~ populated** la isla tiene poca densidad de población *or* está escasamente poblada; **there were a few ~ scattered houses** había unas cuantas casas dispersas; **the seed is ~ sown** las semillas se siembran bien esparcidas; **a ~ wooded area** un área con pocos árboles

4 (= *without humour*) [*smile*] fríamente

thinner [ˈθɪnəʳ] N disolvente *m*

thinness [ˈθɪnnɪs] N 1 [*of person, arms, face*] delgadez *f*; [*of animal*] flacura *f*

2 [*of layer, sheet, wall*] delgadez *f*; [*of slice, line*] lo fino; [*of fabric*] finura *f*

3 [*of liquid, sauce, paint*] poco espesor *m*

4 [*of excuse, argument*] pobreza *f*

5 [*of air, atmosphere*] lo enrarecido

thin-skinned [ˈθɪnˈskɪnd] ADJ (*fig*) [*person*] sensible, susceptible

third [θɜːd] Ⓐ ADJ tercero; (*before m sing noun*) tercer; **~ time lucky!** ¡a la tercera va la vencida!

Ⓑ N 1 (*in series*) tercero/a *m/f*

2 (= *fraction*) tercio *m*, tercera parte *f*; **two ~s of the votes** dos tercios de los votos; **two ~s of those present** las dos terceras partes de los asistentes

3 (*Mus*) tercera *f*

4 (*Brit Univ*) tercera clase *f*

5 (*Aut*) tercera *f* velocidad, tercera *f*; **in ~** en tercera; *see* **fifth** *for usage*

Ⓒ ADV en tercer lugar; **to finish ~** (*in race*) llegar en tercer lugar; **to travel ~** viajar en tercera clase

Ⓓ CPD ► **third degree** N *see* **degree A3**; *see also* **third-degree** ► **third estate** N estado *m* llano ► **third party** N tercero *m*, tercera persona *f* ► **third party insurance** N seguro *m* contra terceros, seguro *m* de responsabilidad social (*Sp*); **an insurance policy with ~-party liability** una póliza de seguros con responsabilidad contra terceros ► **third person** N (*Ling*) tercera persona *f* ► **third way** N (*Pol*) tercera vía *f* ► **Third World** N Tercer Mundo *m*; *see also* **third-world**

third-class [ˌθɜːdˈklɑːs] Ⓐ ADJ de tercera clase; (*pej*) de tercera

Ⓑ ADV **to travel ~** viajar en tercera

Ⓒ N (*US Post*) tarifa *f* de impreso

third-degree [ˌθɜːdɪˈgriː] ADJ [*burns*] de tercer grado

thirdly [ˈθɜːdlɪ] ADV en tercer lugar

third-rate [ˌθɜːdˈreɪt] ADJ (*pej*) de tercera

third-world [ˈθɜːdwɜːld] ADJ tercermundista

thirst [θɜːst] Ⓐ N sed *f*; **to have a ~ for sth** (*fig*) tener sed *or* ansias de algo; **the ~ for knowledge** la sed *or* el afán de saber; **I've got a real ~ (on me)*** ¡me muero de sed!*

Ⓑ VI **to ~ after** *or* **for sth** (*fig*) tener sed *or* ansias de algo, estar sediento de algo (*liter*)

thirstily [ˈθɜːstɪlɪ] ADV **he drank it ~** lo bebió con avidez; **young Emlyn read ~ anything he could get hold of** el joven Emlyn leía con avidez todo lo que caía en sus manos

thirsty [ˈθɜːstɪ] ADJ (*compar* **thirstier**, *superl* **thirstiest**) 1 (*lit*) [*person, animal*] que tiene sed, sediento (*liter*); **to be ~** tener sed; **I suddenly felt very ~** de pronto me entró mucha sed; **to be ~ for sth** (*fig*) tener sed *or* ansias

de algo, estar sediento de algo (*liter*); **I'm getting ~** me está entrando *or* dando sed; **all this work is making me ~** todo este trabajo me está dando sed; **gardening is ~ work** (*hum*) trabajar en el jardín da sed
[2] (*fig*) [*land, fields*] sediento; [*car*] que consume mucha gasolina

thirteen ['θɜː'tiːn] Ⓐ ADJ trece
Ⓑ N trece *m*; *see* **five** *for usage*

thirteenth ['θɜː'tiːnθ] Ⓐ ADJ decimotercero
Ⓑ N (*in series*) decimotercero/a *m/f*; (= *fraction*) decimotercio *m*; *see* **fifth** *for usage*

thirtieth ['θɜːtɪɪθ] Ⓐ ADJ trigésimo; **the ~ anniversary** el treinta aniversario
Ⓑ N (*in series*) trigésimo/a *m/f*; (= *fraction*) treintavo *m*; *see* **fifth** *for usage*

thirty ['θɜːtɪ] Ⓐ ADJ treinta
Ⓑ N treinta *m*; **the thirties** (*1930s*) los años treinta; **to be in one's thirties** tener treinta y tantos años; *see* **fifty** *for usage*

thirtyish ['θɜːtɪɪʃ] ADJ treintañero, de unos treinta años; **he must be ~** debe andar por los treinta

thirty-second ['θɜːtɪ'sekənd] ADJ **~ note** (*US*) fusa *f*

this [ðɪs] Ⓐ DEM ADJ (*pl* **these**) este/a; **~ man/book** este hombre/libro; **~ woman** esta mujer; **~ evening** esta tarde; **~ one here** éste/ésta que está aquí, éste/ésta de aquí; **it's not that picture but ~ one I like** no es ese cuadro el que me gusta sino éste; **~ time** esta vez; **~ time next week** de hoy en una semana; **~ time last year** hoy hace un año; **~ way** por aquí; **~ week** esta semana; **~ coming week** esta semana que viene; *see also* **these**
Ⓑ DEM PRON (*pl* **these**) éste/a; (*neuter*) esto; **who is ~?** ¿quién es?; **what is ~?** ¿qué es esto?; **~ is new** esto es nuevo; **~ is Mr Brown** (*in introductions*) le presento al señor Brown; (*in photo*) éste es el señor Brown; (*on phone*) soy *or* habla el señor Brown; **I prefer ~ to that** prefiero esto a aquello; **but ~ is April** pero estamos en abril; **~ is Friday** hoy es viernes; **where did you find ~?** ¿dónde encontraste esto?; **~ is where I live** aquí vivo; **"but he's nearly bald" — "~ is it"** —pero está casi calvo —ahí está la dificultad; **what's all ~?** ¿qué pasa?; **what's all ~ I hear about you leaving?** ¿qué es eso de que te vas?; **do it like ~** hágalo así; **it was like ~ …** te diré lo que pasó …; **what with ~, that and the other I was busy all week** entre una cosa y otra estuve ocupado toda la semana; **they sat talking of ~ and that** sentados, hablaban de esto y lo otro; *see also* **these**
Ⓒ DEM ADV **I didn't know it was ~ far** no sabía que estaba tan lejos; **I've never been ~ far before** nunca había llegado hasta aquí; **the wall is ~ high** la pared es así de alta; **he is ~ high** es así de alto; **I've never seen ~ much money** nunca había visto tanto dinero junto; **I can tell you ~ much …** lo que sí te puedo decir es …

THIS

The masculine and feminine *pronouns* **éste** and **ésta** usually carry accents. In theory, this is to distinguish them from the masculine and feminine *adjectives*, "**este**" and "**esta**". When there is no ambiguity, the accent can be omitted. The neuter pronoun **esto** does not have an accent as there is no neuter adjective with which to confuse it.

thistle ['θɪsl] N cardo *m*

thistledown ['θɪsldaʊn] N vilano *m* (de cardo)

thistly ['θɪslɪ] ADJ [1] (= *prickly*) espinoso; (= *full of thistles*) lleno de cardos
[2] [*problem*] espinoso, erizado de dificultades

thither† ['ðɪðəʳ] ADV allá

tho'* [ðəʊ] CONJ = **though**

thole [θəʊl] N escálamo *m*

Thomas ['tɒməs] N Tomás; **Saint ~** Santo Tomás; **~ More** Tomás Moro

Thomism ['tɒmɪzəm] N tomismo *m*

Thomist ['tɒmɪst] Ⓐ ADJ tomista
Ⓑ N tomista *mf*

thong [θɒŋ] N [1] (= *strap*) correa *f*
[2] (= *sandal*) chancleta *f*

Thor [θɔːʳ] N Tor *m*

thoracic [θɔː'ræsɪk] ADJ torácico

thorax ['θɔːræks] N (*pl* **thoraxes, thoraces**) tórax *m*

thorium ['θɔːrɪəm] N torio *m*

thorn [θɔːn] Ⓐ N [1] (= *prickle*) espina *f*; ✦***IDIOM*** **to be a ~ in sb's side** *or* **flesh** ser una espina para algn
[2] (= *bush, tree*) espino *m*
Ⓑ CPD ► **thorn bush**, **thorn tree** N espino *m*

thornless ['θɔːnlɪs] ADJ sin espinas

thorny ['θɔːnɪ] ADJ (*compar* **thornier**; *superl* **thorniest**) (*lit, fig*) espinoso

thorough ['θʌrə] ADJ [1] (= *complete*) [*examination, search, investigation*] riguroso, minucioso; [*training*] riguroso, a fondo; [*knowledge, understanding*] profundo, sólido; **to give sth a ~ clean/wash** limpiar/lavar algo bien *or* a fondo; **the room needed a ~ clean** la habitación necesitaba una buena limpieza *or* una limpieza a fondo; **to have a ~ grounding in sth** tener una base sólida en algo
[2] (= *meticulous*) [*person, teacher*] concienzudo, meticuloso; **to be ~ in doing sth** hacer algo a conciencia, ser meticuloso a la hora de hacer algo
[3] (*as intensifier*) (= *complete, total*) **it was a ~ waste of time** era una pérdida de tiempo absoluta *or* total; **to make a ~ nuisance of o.s.** dar la lata a base de bien*; **he made a ~ fool of himself** hizo un ridículo espantoso; **he gave them a ~ walloping** les dio una buena zurra*; **it's a ~ disgrace** es un verdadero escándalo

thoroughbred ['θʌrəbred] Ⓐ ADJ [*horse*] de pura sangre
Ⓑ N pura sangre *mf*

thoroughfare ['θʌrəfɛəʳ] N (= *public highway*) vía *f* pública, carretera *f*; (= *street*) calle *f*; **"no thoroughfare"** "callejón sin salida"; (= *no entry*) "prohibido el paso"

thoroughgoing ['θʌrə,gəʊɪŋ] ADJ [*analysis*] minucioso; [*restructuring*] concienzudo, a fondo; [*conservative, revolutionary*] convencido, auténtico

thoroughly ['θʌrəlɪ] ADV [1] (= *meticulously*) [*clean, rinse*] a fondo, a conciencia; [*search, check*] a fondo; [*research*] minuciosamente, meticulosamente; [*mix*] bien; **they examined me ~** (*Med*) me hicieron un reconocimiento a fondo *or* a conciencia; **to know sth ~** conocer algo a fondo
[2] (= *utterly*) [2·1] (*with verb*) [*understand*] plenamente, a la perfección; [*deserve*] totalmente; [*discredit*] totalmente, por completo; **he ~ enjoyed himself** se divirtió muchísimo, se lo pasó en grande*
[2·2] (*with adj*) [*enjoyable, unpleasant, miserable*] realmente, verdaderamente; [*modern*] totalmente; **a ~ bad influence** una influencia realmente mala; **that was a ~ stupid thing to do** hacer eso fue una completa estupidez

thoroughness ['θʌrənɪs] N [*of examination, search, research*] rigurosidad *f*, minuciosidad *f*; [*of person*] meticulosidad *f*

those [ðəʊz] Ⓐ DEM ADJ esos/esas; (*further away*) aquellos/aquellas; **ask ~ children** pregúntales a esos niños; **~ ones over there** aquéllos de allí, aquéllos que están allí; **it's not these chocolates but ~ ones I like** no son estos bombones los que me gustan sino aquéllos
Ⓑ DEM PRON ésos/ésas; (*further away*) aquéllos/aquéllas; **~ which** los que, las que; **~ who** los que, las que, quienes; **~ of you/us who …** los/las que …; **I prefer these to ~** prefiero éstos a aquéllos; *see also* **that**

thou¹ [ðaʊ] PRON (†, *poet*) tú, vos††

thou²* [θaʊ] N ABBR (*pl* **thou** *or* **thous**) = **thousand, thousandth**

though [ðəʊ] Ⓐ CONJ aunque; **~ it was raining** aunque llovía; **~ small, it's good** aunque (es) pequeño, es bueno, si bien es pequeño, es bueno; **as ~** como si + *subjun*; **even ~ he doesn't want to** aunque no quiera; **strange ~ it may appear** aunque parezca extraño, por muy extraño que parezca; **young ~ she is** aunque es joven, por muy joven que sea; *see also* **as A5**
Ⓑ ADV sin embargo, aun así; **it's not so easy, ~** sin embargo *or* pero no es tan fácil; **it's difficult, ~, to put into practice** pero es difícil llevarlo a la práctica; **did he ~?** ¿de veras?

thought [θɔːt] Ⓐ PT, PP *of* **think**
Ⓑ N [1] (= *mental activity*) pensamiento *m*; *see also* **line A11**, **train A3**
[2] (= *philosophy*) pensamiento *m*; **Western ~** el pensamiento occidental; *see also* **school¹ A5**
[3] (= *cogitation*) pensamiento *m*; **you need to free your mind of negative ~s** tienes que despejar los malos pensamientos de tu mente; **to collect one's ~s** ordenar sus pensamientos *or* ideas; **to be deep in ~** estar ensimismado, estar absorto en sus pensamientos; **my ~s were elsewhere** estaba pensando en otra cosa; **to gather one's ~s** ordenar sus pensamientos *or* ideas; **he was always in her ~s** lo tenía *or* llevaba siempre en el pensamiento; **to be lost in ~** estar ensimismado, estar absorto en sus pensamientos; **he pushed the ~ from his mind** se obligó a dejar de pensar en ello, borró la idea de su mente; *see also* **penny, read A3**
[4] (= *consideration*) **after much ~** después de mucho pensarlo *or* pensarlo mucho; **a lot of ~ went into the work** se dedicó mucho tiempo a pensar en el trabajo; **I'll give it some ~ over the next few days** lo pensaré durante los próximos días; **I've given it a lot of ~** lo he pensado mucho; **I didn't give it another ~** no volví a pensar en ello; **don't give it another ~** no te preocupes, no lo pienses más; **spare a ~ for the homeless at Christmas** acuérdese de la gente sin hogar en Navidad; *see also* **food, pause, second A1**
[5] (= *concern*) **his first ~ was always for other people** siempre pensaba primero en los demás; **with no ~ for o.s.** sin pensar en sí mismo; **with no ~ of reward** sin pensar en una recompensa
[6] (= *intention*) intención *f*; **they had no ~ of surrender** no tenían ninguna intención de rendirse; **he gave up all ~(s) of marrying her** renunció a la idea de casarse con ella; ✦***IDIOM*** **it's the ~ that counts** la intención es lo que cuenta
[7] (= *idea*) idea *f*; **what a frightening ~!** ¡qué idea más aterradora!; **what a lovely ~!** ¡qué

detalle!; **the ~ crossed my mind that …** se me ocurrió que …; **the ~ HAD crossed my mind** la idea se me llegó a pasar por la cabeza; **to have a ~**: **I've just had a ~** se me acaba de ocurrir una idea; **he hasn't a ~ in his head** no tiene ni idea de nada; **never mind, it was just a ~** no importa, no era más que una idea; **that's a ~!** ¡no es mala idea!, ¡qué buena idea!; **"she might still be there" — "that's a ~"** —puede que todavía esté allí —es una posibilidad; **the very** *or* **mere ~ of him made her nervous** se ponía nerviosa sólo de pensar en él

[8] **thoughts** (= *opinion*) **do you have any ~s on that?** ¿tiene alguna opinión al respecto?; **he keeps his ~s to himself** se reserva su opinión

[9] (= *little*) **it is a ~ too large** es un poquito grande; **that was a ~ unwise, wasn't it?** eso fue un tanto imprudente, ¿no?

Ⓒ CPD ► **thought process** N proceso *m* mental ► **thought reader** N adivino/a *m/f*; **I'm not a ~ reader** no soy adivino, no leo el pensamiento ► **thought reading** N adivinación *f* de pensamientos ► **thought transference** N transmisión *f* de pensamientos

thoughtful ['θɔːtfʊl] ADJ [1] (= *pensive*) [*expression, look*] pensativo, meditabundo; **he looked ~** estaba pensativo *or* meditabundo

[2] (= *considerate*) [*person*] atento, considerado; [*gesture*] amable, atento; **these items make ~ gifts** como regalos, estos artículos son un detalle; **to be ~ of others** pensar en los demás, tener en cuenta a los demás; **it was very ~ of you** fue muy amable de tu parte; **how ~ of him to invite me!** ¡qué detalle tuvo al invitarme!, ¡qué detalle por su parte el invitarme!

[3] (= *mindful*) **he was very ~ of the family reputation** siempre tenía muy en cuenta la reputación de la familia

[4] (= *serious*) [*book, film, person*] serio, sesudo

thoughtfully ['θɔːtfəlɪ] ADV [1] (= *pensively*) [*look, nod, smile*] pensativamente, con aire pensativo; **"I see," said Holmes ~** —ya veo —dijo Holmes (con aire) pensativo

[2] (= *considerately*) **she very ~ left out some food for us** tuvo el detalle de dejarnos algo de comida; **land mines which the enemy had ~ left behind** (*iro*) minas terrestres que el enemigo había ido plantando con todo el cariño a su paso (*iro*)

[3] (= *intelligently*) [*designed, constructed, produced*] cuidadosamente, con esmero

thoughtfulness ['θɔːtfʊlnɪs] N [1] (= *pensiveness*) **her face was a picture of ~** su rostro tenía un aire muy pensativo

[2] (= *consideration*) amabilidad *f*; **I appreciate your ~** te agradezco la amabilidad *or* que seas tan amable

[3] (= *serious thought*) seriedad *f*; **it is a work of great ~** es un trabajo muy serio *or* meditado, es un trabajo de mucha seriedad

thoughtless ['θɔːtlɪs] ADJ [1] (= *inconsiderate*) [*person*] poco considerado, desconsiderado; [*remark*] desconsiderado; **how ~ of you!** ¡qué desconsiderado *or* poco considerado por tu parte!, ¡qué falta de consideración por tu parte!; **it was ~ of him to say that** fue una falta de consideración por su parte decir eso

[2] (= *unthinking*) irreflexivo, inconsciente

thoughtlessly ['θɔːtlɪslɪ] ADV [1] (= *inconsiderately*) desconsideradamente

[2] (= *unthinkingly*) sin pensar, inconscientemente

thoughtlessness ['θɔːtlɪsnɪs] N [1] (= *lack of consideration*) falta *f* de consideración, descon[redacted] irreflexión *f*, inconsciencia *f*

thought-provoking ['θɔːtprəˌvəʊkɪŋ] ADJ que hace reflexionar

thousand ['θaʊzənd] Ⓐ ADJ mil

Ⓑ N mil *m*; **a ~** ◊ **one ~** mil; **two/five ~** dos/cinco mil; **a ~ and one/two** mil uno/dos; **I've got a ~ and one things to do** tengo la mar de cosas que hacer*; **they sell them by the ~** los venden a millares; **in their ~s** a millares; **~s of …** miles de …; **I've told you a ~ times** *or* **~s of times** te lo he dicho mil veces

thousandfold ['θaʊzəndfəʊld] Ⓐ ADJ multiplicado por mil, de mil veces

Ⓑ ADV mil veces

thousandth ['θaʊzəntθ] Ⓐ ADJ milésimo

Ⓑ N (*in classification*) número mil *m*; (= *fraction*) milésimo *m*

thraldom ['θrɔːldəm] N (*liter*) esclavitud *f*

thrall [θrɔːl] N (*liter*) (= *person*) esclavo/a *m/f*; (= *state*) esclavitud *f*; **to be in ~ to** ser esclavo de; **to hold sb in ~** retener a algn en la esclavitud

thrash [θræʃ] Ⓐ VT [1] (= *beat*) golpear; [+ *person*] apalear, dar una paliza a; (*as punishment*) azotar

[2] (*) (= *defeat*) dar una paliza a*, cascar*

[3] (*also* **~ about, ~ around**) [+ *legs, arms*] agitar mucho

Ⓑ VI (*also* **~ about, ~ around**) revolverse; (*in water*) revolcarse; **he ~ed about with his stick** daba golpes por todos lados con su bastón; **they were ~ing about in the water** se estaban revolcando en el agua

Ⓒ N (*Brit**) juerga *f*, fiesta *f*

► **thrash out** VT + ADV [+ *problem, difficulty*] discutir a fondo; [+ *plan*] idear; [+ *deal*] alcanzar; **to ~ out an agreement** llegar a un acuerdo

thrashing ['θræʃɪŋ] N zurra *f*, paliza *f*; **to give sb a ~** (*lit*) (= *beat*) zurrar a algn, dar una paliza a algn; (*Sport*) (= *defeat*) dar una paliza a algn*, cascar a algn*

thread [θred] Ⓐ N [1] (*Sew*) hilo *m*; **a needle and ~** una aguja e hilo; **cotton/nylon ~** hilo *m* de algodón/nylon; ✦**IDIOM to hang by a ~** pender de un hilo

[2] [*of silkworm, spider*] hebra *f*

[3] (= *drift, theme*) hilo *m*; **to lose the ~ (of what sb is saying)** perder el hilo (de lo que algn está diciendo); **to pick up the ~(s) again** [*of conversation, thought*] retomar el hilo; [*of process, problem*] volver a tomar las riendas; **she picked up the ~s of her life/career again** tomó de nuevo las riendas de su vida/carrera

[4] [*of screw*] rosca *f*, filete *m*

Ⓑ VT [+ *needle*] enhebrar; [+ *beads*] ensartar; **he ~ed the string through the hole** ensartó la cuerda por el agujero; **to ~ one's way through a crowd** colarse entre *or* abrirse paso por una multitud; **the river ~s its way through the valley** el río se abre paso a través del valle

threadbare ['θredbɛəʳ] ADJ [*coat, blanket, carpet*] raído, gastado; (*fig*) [*argument*] trillado

threadworm ['θredwɜːm] N lombriz *f* intestinal

threat [θret] N amenaza *f*; **to be a ~ to sth/sb** ser una amenaza para algo/algn; **their lives are constantly under ~** sus vidas se ven constantemente amenazadas; **agricultural land is under ~ from urban development** las tierras de cultivo se ven amenazadas por el crecimiento de las ciudades; **the factory is under ~ of closure** existe el peligro de que cierren la fábrica

threaten ['θretn] Ⓐ VT [1] (= *menace verbally*) amenazar; **to ~ to do sth** amenazar con hacer algo; **she ~ed to kill him** amenazó con matarlo; **to ~ sb with sth** amenazar a algn con algo; **they were ~ed with the sack** los amenazaron con el despido, amenazaron con despedirlos

[2] (= *pose a threat to*) [+ *environment, community, way of life*] amenazar; **some schools have been ~ed with closure** la amenaza de cierre se cierne sobre algunos colegios; **to be ~ed with extinction** estar amenazado de extinción

[3] (= *promise*) [+ *rain, bad weather*] amenazar; **it's ~ing to rain** amenaza lluvia, amenaza (con) llover; **it's ~ing to turn into a full-scale war** amenaza (con) convertirse en una guerra declarada

Ⓑ VI [*sky, clouds*] amenazar

threatened ['θretnd] ADJ **to feel ~** sentirse amenazado

threatening ['θretnɪŋ] ADJ [1] (= *menacing*) [*letter, gesture, phone call*] amenazador, de amenaza; [*manner, voice*] amenazador; **some men find her ~** algunos hombres se sienten intimidados por ella; **~ behaviour** comportamiento *m* intimidatorio, conducta *f* intimidatoria *or* amenazadora

[2] (= *unpromising*) [*clouds, sky*] amenazador; **the weather looked ~** amenazaba temporal

threateningly ['θretnɪŋlɪ] ADV [*behave*] de modo amenazador; [*say*] en tono amenazador

three [θriː] Ⓐ ADJ tres

Ⓑ N tres *m*; **the best of ~** (*Sport*) hasta tres sets *or* partidos; **~ cheers!** ¡tres hurras!; *see* **five** *for usage*; *see also* **two**

THREE RS

La expresión **the three Rs** *hace referencia a los tres aspectos que se consideran fundamentales en educación:* **reading, writing, and arithmetic** *(lectura, escritura y aritmética). La expresión, que tiene su origen en la forma humorística en la que se escribe a veces la frase:* **reading, 'riting, and 'rithmetic**, *se menciona a menudo cuando se habla de la necesidad de mejorar la calidad de la enseñanza.*

three-act ['θriː'ækt] ADJ [*play*] de *or* en tres actos

three-colour(ed), **three-color(ed)** (*US*) ['θriː'kʌləd] ADJ de tres colores, tricolor

three-cornered ['θriː'kɔːnəd] ADJ triangular; **~ hat** tricornio *m*, sombrero *m* de tres picos

three-D, 3-D ['θriː'diː] (*also* **three-dimensional**) Ⓐ ADJ tridimensional

Ⓑ N **in ~** en tres dimensiones

three-day eventing [ˌθriːdeɪ'ventɪŋ] N *concurso hípico que dura tres días y consta de tres pruebas distintas*

three-decker ['θriː'dekəʳ] N [1] (*Naut*) barco *m* de tres cubiertas

[2] (*Literat*) novela *f* de tres tomos

[3] (*Culin*) sándwich *m* de tres pisos

three-dimensional ['θriːdɪ'menʃənl] ADJ tridimensional

threefold ['θriːfəʊld] Ⓐ ADJ triple

Ⓑ ADV tres veces

three-legged ['θriː'legɪd] ADJ de tres patas, de tres pies

threepence ['θrepəns] N (*Brit*) tres peniques *mpl*

threepenny ['θrepənɪ] ADJ (*Brit*) de tres peniques; (*fig*) de poca monta, despreciable; **~ bit**

◊ ~ **piece** moneda *f* de tres peniques; **Threepenny Opera** Ópera *f* de perra gorda

three-phase ['θri:feɪz] ADJ (*Elec*) trifásico

three-piece ['θri:pi:s] ADJ ~ **band** trío *m*; ~ **suit** terno *m*, traje *m* de tres piezas; ~ **suite** tresillo *m*, juego *m* de living (*LAm*)

three-ply ['θri:plaɪ] ADJ [*wool*] triple, de tres hebras, de tres cabos; [*wood, tissue paper*] de tres capas

three-point turn [ˌθri:pɔɪnt'tɜ:n] N (*Aut*) cambio *m* de sentido haciendo tres maniobras

three-quarter [ˌθri:'kwɔ:tər] ADJ **~-length sleeves** mangas *fpl* tres cuartos

three-quarters [ˌθri:'kwɔ:təz] Ⓐ N tres cuartos *mpl*, tres cuartas partes *fpl*; **~ of the people** las tres cuartas partes de la gente; **in ~ of an hour** en tres cuartos de hora
Ⓑ ADV **the tank is ~ full** el depósito está lleno en sus tres cuartas partes

threescore ['θri:skɔ:r] N (†, *liter*) sesenta; ~ **years and ten** setenta años

three-sided ['θri:'saɪdɪd] ADJ trilátero

threesome ['θri:səm] N (= *group of 3 people*) grupo *m* de tres, trío *m*

three-way ['θri:weɪ] ADJ [*conversation*] entre tres personas; [*race, competition, debate*] *entre tres personas, grupos etc*; (*Comm*) entre tres compañías; [*mirror*] de tres lunas; **~ split** división *f* en tercios

three-wheeler ['θri:'wi:lər] N (= *car*) coche *m* de tres ruedas; (= *tricycle*) triciclo *m*

threnody ['θrenədɪ] N lamento *m*; (*for the dead*) canto *m* fúnebre

thresh [θreʃ] Ⓐ VT [+ *corn*] trillar
Ⓑ VI trillar

thresher ['θreʃər] N (= *person*) trillador(a) *m/f*; (= *machine*) trilladora *f*

threshing ['θreʃɪŋ] Ⓐ N trilla *f*
Ⓑ CPD ► **threshing floor** N era *f* ► **threshing machine** N trilladora *f*

threshold ['θreʃhəʊld] Ⓐ N [1] (= *doorway*) umbral *m*
[2] (*fig*) umbral *m*, puertas *fpl*; **to be on the ~ of** estar en el umbral *or* a las puertas de; **pain ~** umbral *m* de dolor; **sound ~** umbral *m* sonoro; **to have a low pain ~** tener poca tolerancia del dolor
Ⓑ CPD ► **threshold agreement** N convenio *m* de nivel crítico ► **threshold price** N precio *m* umbral, precio *m* mínimo

threw [θru:] PT *of* **throw**

thrice†† [θraɪs] ADV tres veces

thrift [θrɪft], **thriftiness** ['θrɪftɪnɪs] Ⓐ N economía *f*, frugalidad *f*
Ⓑ CPD ► **thrift store** (*US*) N *tienda de artículos de segunda mano que dedica su recaudación a causas benéficas*

thriftless ['θrɪftlɪs] ADJ malgastador, pródigo

thriftlessness ['θrɪftlɪsnɪs] N prodigalidad *f*

thrifty ['θrɪftɪ] ADJ (*compar* **thriftier**; *superl* **thriftiest**) económico, frugal, ahorrativo

thrill [θrɪl] Ⓐ N emoción *f*; **all the ~s of the circus** todas las emociones del circo; **she felt a ~ (of joy)** se estremeció (de alegría); **it gives him a cheap ~ to spy on her in the bathroom** le da morbo espiarla en el baño; **it was a great ~ to meet her** me hizo muchísima ilusión conocerla; **he gets a real ~ out of parachuting** hacer paracaidismo le resulta muy emocionante *or* excitante; **the film is full of ~s and spills** la película está llena de emoción; **what a ~!** ¡qué emoción!
Ⓑ VT [+ *person, audience*] emocionar, excitar; **I'm not exactly ~ed by the idea** la idea no es que me entusiasme precisamente
Ⓒ VI ... ció cua...

thrilled [θrɪ... ...es) — estar content... **"oh, he was** ... ó? —¡huy! se puso c... muchísima ilusión; **to** ... estar contentísimo con algo, ... **him** me hizo mucha ilusión co...

thriller ['θrɪlər] N (= *novel*) no... ...spense *or* (*LAm*) de suspenso, novela *f* de misterio; (= *film*) película *f* de suspense *or* (*LAm*) de suspenso, thriller *m*

thrilling ['θrɪlɪŋ] ADJ [*experience, match, climax*] emocionante; [*performance*] apasionante; **it was one of the most ~ moments of my life** fue uno de los momentos más emocionantes de mi vida; **you've actually met her? how ~!** ¿llegaste a conocerla? ¡qué emoción!

thrive [θraɪv] (*pt* **throve** *or* **thrived**; *pp* **thrived** *or* **thriven**) VI (= *do well*) [*company, economy*] prosperar; (= *grow*) [*plant*] crecer muy bien, prosperar; [*animal, child*] desarrollarse; (*fig*) prosperar, medrar; **the plant ~s here** la planta crece muy bien *or* prospera aquí; **business is thriving** el negocio prospera; **to ~ on sth: children ~ on milk** la leche contribuye al desarrollo de los niños; **she seems to ~ on adversity** parece que se crece en la adversidad

thriven ['θrɪvn] PP *of* **thrive**

thriving ['θraɪvɪŋ] ADJ [*industry, business*] próspero, floreciente

throat [θrəʊt] N [1] (*interior*) garganta *f*; **to clear one's ~** aclararse la voz, carraspear; **to have a sore ~** tener dolor de garganta; ♦**IDIOMS to jump down sb's ~** arremeter contra algn sin más (*fig*); **to ram sth down sb's ~** meter algo a algn por las narices; **there's no need to ram it down my ~** no hace falta que me lo metas por las narices
[2] (*from exterior*) cuello *m*; **they are at each other's ~s all the time** se atacan uno a otro todo el tiempo; **to cut** *or* **slit sb's ~** cortar el cuello a algn; **to cut** *or* **slit one's ~** cortarse la garganta, cortarse el cuello; **he's cutting his own ~** (*fig*) está actuando en perjuicio propio, se está haciendo daño a sí mismo

throaty ['θrəʊtɪ] ADJ (*compar* **throatier**; *superl* **throatiest**) [*person, voice*] ronco, afónico; [*laugh*] gutural; [*roar of engine*] ronco

throb [θrɒb] Ⓐ N [*of heart etc*] latido *m*, pulso *m*; [*of engine*] vibración *f*
Ⓑ VI [*heart*] latir, palpitar; [*engine*] vibrar; [*wound, sore finger*] dar punzadas; **my head was ~bing** la cabeza estaba a punto de estallarme de dolor; **Berlin is ~bing with life** Berlín está rebosante de vida

throbbing ['θrɒbɪŋ] Ⓐ ADJ [*heart*] palpitante; [*engine*] vibrante; [*pain*] punzante; [*rhythm*] palpitante, vibrante
Ⓑ N [*of heart*] latido *m*; [*of sore finger, head*] punzadas *fpl*; [*of engine, music*] vibración *f*

throes [θrəʊz] NPL [*of death*] agonía *f*; **to be in the ~ of sth/doing sth: she was in the ~ of an unpleasant divorce** estaba en medio de los trámites de un divorcio nada agradable; **I was still in the first ~ of grief** eran sólo los primeros ramalazos de una profunda pena; **we're in the ~ of a major restructuring at work** en el trabajo estamos en plena reestructuración; **to be in the ~ of childbirth** estar en medio de los dolores del parto; **while he was in the ~ of writing his book** mientras estaba inmerso en la redacción de su libro; **while we were in the ~ of deciding what to do** mientras nos debatíamos sobre qué decisión tomar; *see also* **death**

thrombosis [θrɒm'bəʊsɪs] N (*pl* **thromboses** [θrɒm'bəʊsi:z]) trombosis *f*; **coronary ~** trombosis *f* coronaria

throne [θrəʊn] Ⓐ N trono *m*; **to ascend the ~** ◊ **come to the ~** subir al trono; **to succeed to the ~** suceder en el trono; **the heir to the ~** el/la heredero/a del trono; **the ~ of France** ◊ **the French ~** el trono de Francia, el trono francés
Ⓑ CPD ► **throne room** N sala *f* del trono

throng [θrɒŋ] Ⓐ N multitud *f*, muchedumbre *f*; **great ~s of tourists** multitudes *fpl* de turistas
Ⓑ VT atestar; **the streets are ~ed with tourists** las calles están atestadas de turistas
Ⓒ VI **the schoolchildren came ~ing in** los escolares entraron en tropel; **to ~ round sb** apiñarse en torno a algn; **to ~ to hear sb** venir en tropel *or* en masa a escuchar a algn

thronging ['θrɒŋɪŋ] ADJ [*crowd etc*] grande, apretado, nutrido

throttle ['θrɒtl] Ⓐ N (*Mech*) regulador *m*, válvula *f* reguladora, estrangulador *m*; (*Aut*) (= *accelerator*) acelerador *m*; **the engine was at full ~** el motor estaba funcionando a toda marcha; **to give an engine full ~** acelerar un motor al máximo
Ⓑ VT (= *strangle*) ahogar, estrangular

►**throttle back, throttle down** (*Mech*) Ⓐ VT + ADV **to ~ back** *or* **~ down the engine** moderar la marcha
Ⓑ VI + ADV moderar la marcha

through [θru:]

> *When* **through** *is an element in a phrasal verb, eg* **break through, fall through**, *look up the verb.*

Ⓐ PREP [1] (*place*) por; **to look ~ a telescope** mirar por un telescopio; **to walk ~ the woods** pasear por el bosque; **he shot her ~ the head** le pegó un tiro en la cabeza; **I saw him ~ the crowd** lo vi entre la multitud; **to go ~ sth: to go ~ a tunnel** atravesar un túnel; **the bullet went ~ three layers** la bala penetró tres capas; **it went right ~ the wall** atravesó por toda la pared; **to go ~ sb's pockets/belongings/papers** hurgar en los bolsillos/entre las cosas/entre los papeles de algn; **to post a letter ~ the letterbox** echar una carta al buzón
[2] (*time, process*) **we're staying ~ till Tuesday** nos quedamos hasta el martes; **(from) Monday ~ Friday** (*US*) de lunes a viernes; **to go ~ a bad/good period** pasar una mala/buena racha; **we've been ~ a lot together** hemos pasado mucho juntos; **to be halfway ~ a book** ir por la mitad de un libro; **halfway ~ the film** a la mitad de la película; **all** *or* **right ~ the night** durante toda la noche; **right ~ the year** durante el año entero *or* todo el año
[3] (*means*) por; **~ lack of resources** por falta de recursos; **~ him I found out that …** por *or* a través de él supe que …; **it was ~ you that we were late** fue por tu culpa que llegamos tarde; **to act ~ fear** obrar movido por el miedo; **he got the job ~ friends** consiguió el trabajo por mediación de *or* a través de unos amigos
[4] (*having completed*) **he's ~ the exam** ha aprobado el examen
Ⓑ ADV [1] (*place*) **it's frozen (right) ~** está completamente helado; **does this train go ~ to London?** ¿este tren va directamente a Londres?; **he went straight ~ to the dining room** pasó directamente al comedor; **the nail**

went right ~ el clavo penetró de parte a parte; **can you put me ~ to sales, please?** (*Telec*) ¿puede ponerme *or* pasarme con el departamento de ventas, por favor?; **the wood has rotted ~** la madera se ha podrido completamente; **the window was dirty and I couldn't see ~** la ventana estaba sucia y no podía ver nada; **wet ~** [*person*] mojado hasta los huesos, empapado; [*object*] empapado

2 (*time, process*) **I read the book right ~** leí el libro entero; **to sleep the whole night ~** dormir la noche entera; **did you stay right ~ to the end?** ¿te quedaste hasta el final?; **we're staying ~ till Tuesday** nos quedamos hasta el martes; **he is ~ to the finals of the competition** pasó a la final del concurso

3 **~ and ~** [*be something*] hasta la médula, completamente; [*know something*] de pe a pa

(C) ADJ 1 [*road, train*] directo; [*traffic*] de paso; **"no through road"** "calle sin salida"

2 (= *finished*) terminado; **we'll be ~ at seven** terminaremos a las siete; **you're ~!** ¡se acabó (para ti)!; **are you ~ criticizing?** ¿has terminado *or* acabado de criticarme?; **she told him they were ~** ella le dijo que todo había acabado entre ellos; **I'm ~ with my girlfriend** he roto *or* terminado con mi novia; **are you ~ with that book?** ¿has terminado de leer ese libro?; **I'm ~ with bridge** renuncio al bridge, ya no vuelvo a jugar al bridge; **I'm not ~ with you yet** todavía no he terminado contigo; **when I'm ~ with him** cuando haya terminado con él

3 (*Telec*) **you're ~!** ¡ya puede hablar!, ¡hable!

throughout [θrʊ'aʊt] (A) PREP 1 (*place*) por todo; **we have branches ~ the country** tenemos sucursales por todo el país; **there were flowers ~ the house** había flores por toda la casa; **the company is known ~ the world** la compañía es conocida en todo el mundo

2 (*time, process*) durante todo; **~ last winter** durante todo el invierno pasado; **he was a socialist ~ his life** fue un socialista durante toda su vida

(B) ADV 1 (= *fully*) completamente; (= *everywhere*) en todas partes, por todas partes; **the house is carpeted ~** la casa está completamente alfombrada

2 (*time, process*) de principio a fin; **on this project, the emphasis has been on teamwork ~** en este proyecto, se ha hecho hincapié en el trabajo en equipo de principio a fin; **the film was boring ~** la película fue aburrida de principio a fin; **the weather was good ~** hizo buen tiempo todos los días

throughput ['θruːpʊt] N (= *production*) producción *f*; (= *total quantity*) [*of applicants, patients*] movimiento *m*, número *m*; (*Comput*) capacidad *f* de procesamiento; **to increase the volume of ~** incrementar el volumen de producción; **patient ~ has not been affected by hospital closures** el movimiento de pacientes *or* el número de pacientes tratados no se ha visto afectado por el cierre de hospitales

throughway ['θruːweɪ] N (*US*) autopista *f* (*de peaje*)

throve [θrəʊv] PT *of* **thrive**

throw [θrəʊ] (*vb: pt* **threw**, *pp* **thrown**) (A) VT 1 (= *toss*) [+ *ball, stone*] tirar, echar; (*violently*) tirar, arrojar, lanzar; [+ *dice*] echar, tirar; [+ *javelin, discus, grenade*] lanzar; **the crowd began ~ing stones** la multitud empezó a tirar *or* arrojar *or* lanzar piedras; **he threw a double six** sacó dos seises; **to ~ sb sth** ◊ **~ sth to sb** tirar *or* echar algo a algn; **he threw Brian a rope** le tiró *or* echó una cuerda a Brian; **to ~ sth at sb** tirar *or* arrojar algo a algn; **on one occasion he threw a radio at his mother** en una ocasión le tiró *or* arrojó una radio a su madre; **they think they can solve problems by ~ing money at them** (*fig*) piensan que metiendo dinero pueden solucionar cualquier problema; **she threw the letters in the bin** tiró *or* echó las cartas a la basura; **he threw a glass of water over her head** le echó *or* vació un vaso de agua en la cabeza; ♦ *IDIOM* **to ~ one's hat** *or* **cap into the ring** echarse *or* lanzarse al ruedo; *see also* **book A1**, **caution**, **cold A1**, **glass**, **spanner**

2 (= *hurl to the ground*) [+ *person*] (*in fight, wrestling*) derribar; [*horse*] desmontar

3 (= *send, hurl*) **the blast threw her across the room** la explosión la lanzó *or* arrojó al otro lado de la sala; **to ~ o.s. at sb** (*lit*) abalanzarse sobre algn, echarse encima de algn; (*fig*) (= *flirt*) insinuarse descaradamente a algn, tirar los tejos a algn*; **to ~ o.s. at sb's feet** echarse a los pies de algn; **he was ~n clear of the car** salió despedido del coche; **she threw herself into the river** se tiró al rió; **the kidnap threw the family into panic** el secuestro infundió pánico *or* hizo que cundiera el pánico en la familia; **the country was ~n into turmoil** el país se sumió en el caos; **to ~ sb into jail** *or* **prison** meter a algn en la cárcel; **he threw himself into his work** se metió de lleno en el trabajo; **to ~ o.s. on sb's mercy** ponerse a merced de algn; **she threw herself onto the bed** se tiró en la cama; **she was ~n out of her seat** salió despedida de su asiento; **the recession has ~n millions out of work** la recesión ha dejado a millones de personas sin trabajo; **he threw me to the ground** me arrojó al suelo; *see also* **scent**, **track A1**

4 (= *direct*) [+ *light, shadow*] proyectar; [+ *look, smile*] lanzar; **this new information ~s doubt on their choice** esta nueva información pone en duda su elección; **this question has been ~n at me many times** me han hecho esta pregunta *or* me han preguntado esto muchas veces; **he was ~ing random suggestions at her** le estaba sugiriendo cosas al azar; **she didn't attempt to ~ any suspicion on you** no intentó hacer que las sospechas recayeran sobre ti; **to ~ one's voice** [*actor, public speaker*] proyectar la voz; *see also* **light[1] A1**, **punch[1] A2**

5 (= *disconcert*) desconcertar; **this answer seemed to ~ him** esta respuesta pareció desconcertarle; **he was ~n by her question** su pregunta lo desconcertó *or* lo dejó desconcertado

6 (= *put*) **she threw her arms around his neck** le echó los brazos al cuello, le abrazó por el cuello; **to ~ a coat round one's shoulders** echarse un abrigo por los hombros; **a police cordon was ~n around the area** la policía acordonó la zona, se cercó la zona con un cordón policial; **to ~ open** [+ *doors, windows*] abrir de par en par; [+ *house, gardens*] abrir al público; [+ *competition, race*] abrir a todos

7 (= *have*) **she threw a fit (of hysterics)** le dio un ataque (de histeria); **to ~ a party** dar *or* hacer una fiesta; **she threw a tantrum** le dio una rabieta *or* un berrinche*

8 (= *move*) [+ *lever, switch*] dar a

9 (*Pottery*) **to ~ a pot** tornear un tiesto, hacer un tiesto con el torno

10 (*) (= *lose on purpose*) [+ *contest, game*] perder a posta

11 (*Zool*) (= *give birth to*) parir

(B) N 1 (*lit*) [*of ball, stone*] tiro *m*; [*of javelin, discus*] lanzamiento *m*; [*of dice*] tirada *f*; (*in judo, wrestling*) derribo *m*; **it's your ~** te toca tirar (a ti); **I needed a ~ of four to win** necesitaba sacar un cuatro para ganar; *see also* **stone**

2 (*) (= *each one*) **"how much are they?" — "50 quid a ~"** —¿cuánto cuestan? —50 libras cada uno

3 (= *cover*) (*for sofa*) cubresofá *m*; (*for bed*) cubrecama *m*, colcha *f*

►**throw about**, **throw around** VT + ADV 1 (*lit*) **they were throwing a ball about** jugaban con una pelota; **don't throw it about or it might break** no lo manosees para arriba y para abajo, que se puede romper; **they were thrown about in the back of the lorry** se zarandeaban de un lado para otro en la parte trasera del camión

2 (*fig*) [+ *ideas*] intercambiar; **let's have a meeting and throw a few ideas about** vamos a reunirnos para intercambiar ideas; **occasionally he throws fancy words about** de vez en cuando se deja caer con alguna palabreja *or* suelta alguna palabreja; **his name is thrown about a lot** su nombre no para de sonar por ahí; **to throw one's arms about** agitar mucho los brazos; **to throw (one's) money about** derrochar *or* despilfarrar el dinero, tirar el dinero; *see also* **weight A3**

►**throw aside** VT + ADV (*lit*) [+ *object*] echar a un lado; (*fig*) dejar; **I've been ~n aside for a younger woman** me han dejado por una mujer más joven

►**throw away** VT + ADV 1 (= *discard*) [+ *rubbish*] tirar, botar (*LAm*); (*Cards*) echar

2 (= *waste*) [+ *chance, opportunity*] desperdiciar; [+ *one's life, health, happiness*] echar a perder; [+ *money*] tirar, derrochar, despilfarrar; **don't ~ your money away on that** no malgastes el dinero en eso; **we should have won — we just threw it away** deberíamos haber ganado, y no hicimos más que echarlo (todo) a perder

3 (= *say casually*) [+ *line, remark*] soltar

►**throw back** VT + ADV 1 (*lit*) (= *return*) [+ *ball*] devolver; [+ *fish*] devolver al agua; (= *move backwards*) [+ *head, shoulders, hair*] echar para atrás, echar hacia atrás

2 (*fig*) (= *reject*) [+ *offer, suggestion*] rechazar (*con desprecio*); (= *drive back*) [+ *enemy*] rechazar, repeler; **they threw his generosity back in his face** le devolvieron su generosidad con una patada; **I should never have told you that, I knew you'd ~ it back at me** nunca debería habértelo dicho, sabía que me lo echarías en cara; **he was ~n back on his own resources** tuvo que depender de sus propios recursos

►**throw down** VT + ADV [+ *object*] tirar; [+ *challenge*] lanzar

►**throw in** VT + ADV 1 (*Sport*) [+ *ball*] sacar; ♦ *IDIOM* **to ~ in the towel** (*lit, fig*) tirar la toalla; *see also* **deep A1**, **lot 6**

2 (= *include*) incluir; **a cruise round the Caribbean with Cuba ~n in for good measure** un crucero por el Caribe en el que además se incluye Cuba para que no falte de nada; **pay for extra prints and they ~ in a photo album** pague copias extra y le regalan un álbum de fotos

3 (= *interpose*) [+ *remark, question*] soltar; **"she's done this before," Joan threw in** —esto ya lo ha hecho antes —añadió Joan

►**throw off** VT + ADV 1 (= *remove*) [+ *clothes, shoes, disguise*] quitarse a toda prisa

2 (= *get rid of*) [+ *depression*] salir de; [+ *cold, infection, habit*] quitarse; [+ *burden, yoke*] librarse de, quitarse de encima; **I can't seem to ~ off this cold** no consigo quitarme este

resfriado

[3] (= *escape*) [+ *pursuers*] zafarse de, dar esquinazo a

[4] (= *make wrong*) [+ *calculations, timing*] desbaratar, dar al traste con

[5] (= *emit*) [+ *heat*] despedir, emitir; [+ *sparks*] echar

[6] (*) (= *write quickly*) [+ *poem, composition*] improvisar

► **throw on** VT + ADV [1] (*lit*) [+ *coal, fuel*] echar

[2] (*fig*) (= *put on quickly*) [+ *clothes, make-up*] ponerse a toda prisa; **he threw his clothes on** se puso la ropa a toda prisa

► **throw out** VT + ADV [1] (= *throw away*) [+ *rubbish, old clothes*] tirar, botar (*LAm*); *see also* **baby**

[2] (= *expel*) [+ *person*] (*from organization, team*) echar; (*from country*) expulsar, echar; **he was ~n out of the team** lo echaron del equipo

[3] (= *reject*) [+ *proposal*] rechazar; (*Jur*) [+ *case, claim*] desestimar, rechazar; (*Parl*) [+ *bill*] rechazar

[4] (= *make*) [+ *idea, suggestion, remark*] soltar

[5] (= *emit*) [+ *heat*] despedir, emitir; [+ *smoke, lava*] arrojar

[6] (= *disconcert*) [+ *person*] desconcertar, dejar totalmente confundido

[7] (= *make wrong*) [+ *calculation, prediction*] desbaratar, dar al traste con

[8] **to ~ out one's chest** sacar pecho

► **throw over** VT + ADV [+ *friend, lover*] dejar, abandonar

► **throw together** VT + ADV [1] (= *make hastily*) [+ *costume, plan, essay*] hacer a la carrera, pergeñar; [+ *meal*] preparar a la carrera, improvisar

[2] (= *gather together*) [+ *clothes*] juntar rápidamente; [+ *people*] juntar; **he threw a few things together and dashed out of the house** juntó rápidamente unas cuantas cosas y salió disparado de la casa; **fate had ~n them together** el destino les había juntado; **people whom circumstances have ~n together** personas a las que han juntado *or* unido las circunstancias; **we were ~n together a good deal, working in the same office** como trabajábamos en la misma oficina nos veíamos mucho

► **throw up** Ⓐ VI + ADV (*) (= *vomit*) devolver*, vomitar; **it makes me want to ~ up** (*lit*) me da ganas de devolver*; (*fig*) me da asco

Ⓑ VT + ADV [1] (*lit*) [+ *object*] lanzar *or* echar al aire; [+ *dust*] levantar; [+ *sparks*] echar; **to ~ up one's hands in horror** llevarse las manos a la cabeza horrorizado

[2] (*esp Brit*) (= *produce, bring to light*) [+ *result*] dar, producir; [+ *idea, dilemma*] producir; [+ *problem*] crear

[3] (*) (= *give up*) [+ *job, task, studies*] dejar

[4] (= *make quickly*) [+ *building*] construir rápidamente

[5] (*) (= *vomit*) devolver*, vomitar

throwaway [ˈθrəʊəweɪ] ADJ [1] (= *disposable*) [*bottle, container*] desechable, para tirar

[2] (= *casual*) [*remark*] hecho de paso

throwback [ˈθrəʊbæk] N (*gen*) salto *m* atrás; **it's like a ~ to the old days** es como un salto atrás a los viejos tiempos; **the film is a ~ to early Minelli movies** la película supone una vuelta a las primeras películas de Minelli

thrower [ˈθrəʊəʳ] N lanzador(a) *m/f*

throw-in [ˈθrəʊɪn] N (*Ftbl*) saque *m* (de banda)

throwing [ˈθrəʊɪŋ] N (*Sport*) lanzamiento *m*

thrown [θrəʊn] PP *of* **throw**

throw-out [ˈθrəʊaʊt] N cosa *f* desechada; **his flat is furnished with other people's ~s** tiene amueblado el piso con lo que otra gente no quería

thru [θruː] (*US*) = **through**

thrum [θrʌm] Ⓐ VT [+ *guitar*] rasguear, rasguear las cuerdas de

Ⓑ VI [*wings of bird*] producir un aleteo vibrante; [*machine, engine*] producir un sonido vibrante

thrush[1] [θrʌʃ] N (= *bird*) zorzal *m*, tordo *m*

thrush[2] [θrʌʃ] N (*Med*) afta *f*

thrust [θrʌst] (*vb: pt, pp* **thrust**) Ⓐ N [1] (= *push*) empujón *m*; [*of dagger*] puñalada *f*; [*of knife*] cuchillada *f*; [*of sword*] estocada *f*; (*Mil*) (= *offensive*) ofensiva *f*; (= *advance*) avance *m*

[2] (*Mech*) empuje *m*; (*Aer, Naut*) propulsión *f*; **forward/reverse ~** empuje *m* de avance/de marcha atrás

[3] (= *basic meaning*) [*of speech*] idea *f* clave

[4] (= *dynamism*) empuje *m*, dinamismo *m*

Ⓑ VT (= *push*) empujar; (= *insert*) introducir, meter (**into** en); (= *insert piercingly*) clavar, hincar (**into** en); **to ~ one's hands into one's pockets** meter las manos en los bolsillos; **he ~ a book into my hands** me metió un libro entre las manos; **to ~ a dagger into sb's back** clavar un puñal a algn en la espalda; **to ~ a stick into the ground** clavar *or* hincar un palo en el suelo; **she ~ her head out of the window** asomó *or* sacó la cabeza por la ventana; **she found herself suddenly ~ into the limelight** de pronto, sin comerlo ni beberlo, se vio convertida en el centro de atención; **he ~ out his lower lip** sacó hacia fuera el labio inferior; **to ~ sth on** *or* **upon sb** imponer algo a algn, obligar a algn a aceptar algo; **they ~ the job on me** me cargaron el trabajo; **Spain had greatness ~ upon her** España recibió su grandeza sin buscarla, se le impuso la grandeza a España sin quererlo ella; **to ~ o.s. (up)on sb** (*fig*) pegarse a algn; **to ~ sb through with a sword** atravesar a algn (de parte a parte) con una espada; **I ~ my way through the crowd/to the front** me abrí paso entre la multitud/hacia adelante

Ⓒ VI **to ~ at sb**: **he ~ at me with a sword/knife** me asestó una estocada/cuchillada; **to ~ past sb** apartar de un empujón a algn para pasar; **he ~ past me into the room** me apartó bruscamente para entrar en la habitación; **to ~ through** abrirse paso a la fuerza

► **thrust aside** VT + ADV [+ *person*] apartar bruscamente; (*fig*) dar de lado; [+ *objections*] ignorar; [+ *plan, proposal*] rechazar

► **thrust forward** Ⓐ VT + ADV [+ *head, chin*] sacar hacia adelante

Ⓑ VI + ADV (*Mil*) avanzar

thrustful [ˈθrʌstfʊl], **thrusting** [ˈθrʌstɪŋ] ADJ emprendedor, vigoroso, dinámico; (*pej*) agresivo

thrustfulness [ˈθrʌstfʊlnɪs] N empuje *m*, pujanza *f*, dinamismo *m*; (*pej*) agresividad *f*

thruway [ˈθruːweɪ] N (*US*) autopista *f* de peaje

Thu ABBR = **Thursday**

Thucydides [θjuːˈsɪdɪdiːz] N Tucídides

thud [θʌd] Ⓐ N ruido *m* sordo, golpe *m* sordo; **he landed on the floor with a dull ~** cayó al suelo con un ruido sordo

Ⓑ VI hacer un ruido sordo; **to ~ to the ground** caer al suelo con un ruido sordo; **a shell ~ded into the hillside** una granada estalló en el monte; **he was ~ding about upstairs all night** pasó la noche andando con pasos pesados por el piso de arriba

thug [θʌg] N matón/ona *m/f*; (*fig, as term of abuse*) bruto *m*, bestia *f*

thuggery [ˈθʌgərɪ] N matonismo *m*, brutalidad *f*

thulium [ˈθjuːlɪəm] N tulio *m*

thumb [θʌm] Ⓐ N pulgar *m*; **he gave me a ~s-up sign** me indicó con el pulgar que todo iba bien; ✦***IDIOMS*** **to be all ~s**: **I'm all ~s today** hoy soy un manazas; **to twiddle one's ~s** estar mano sobre mano, estar sin hacer nada; **to be under sb's ~** estar dominado por algn; **she's got him under her ~** le tiene metido en un puño; **they gave it the ~s down** lo rechazaron, lo desaprobaron; **they gave it the ~s up** lo aprobaron; **the voters have given him the ~s up/down** el electorado votó a favor de/en contra de él; *see also* **rule A2**

Ⓑ VT [1] [+ *book*] manosear; **a well-~ed book** un libro muy manoseado

[2] **to ~ a lift** *or* **a ride** hacer autostop, hacer dedo, pedir aventón (*LAm*); **to ~ a lift to London** viajar en autostop a Londres

[3] **to ~ one's nose at sth/sb** (*lit*) hacer burla a algo/algn (*agitando la mano con el pulgar sobre la nariz*); (*fig*) burlarse de algo/algn

Ⓒ VI **to ~ through a book/magazine** hojear un libro/una revista

Ⓓ CPD ► **thumb index** N índice *m* recortado

thumbnail [ˈθʌmneɪl] Ⓐ N uña *f* del pulgar

Ⓑ CPD ► **thumbnail sketch** N pequeño *m* esbozo

thumbprint [ˈθʌmprɪnt] N impresión *f* del pulgar

thumbscrew [ˈθʌmskruː] N empulgueras *fpl*

thumbstall [ˈθʌmstɔːl] N dedil *m*

thumbtack [ˈθʌmtæk] N (*US*) chincheta *f*, chinche *m or f* (*LAm*)

thump [θʌmp] Ⓐ N (= *blow*) golpetazo *m*, porrazo *m*; (= *noise of fall etc*) golpetazo *m*; **it came down with a ~** cayó dando un golpetazo

Ⓑ VT (= *hit hard*) golpear; (*accidentally*) [+ *head etc*] dar *or* topar con; (= *put down heavily*) poner *or* (*frm*) deponer violentamente; **to ~ sb** pegar un puñetazo a algn; **to ~ the table** golpear la mesa, dar golpes en la mesa; **he ~ed me on the back** me dio un golpetazo en la espalda; **to ~ out a tune on the piano** tocar una melodía aporreando el piano

Ⓒ VI [1] [*person*] (*on door, table*) dar golpes, aporrear; [*heart*] (= *pound*) latir con fuerza; [*machine*] vibrar con violencia; **someone was ~ing on the door** había alguien dando golpes a *or* aporreando la puerta

[2] (= *move heavily*) **he ~ed upstairs** subió pesadamente las escaleras

thumping* [ˈθʌmpɪŋ] (*Brit*) Ⓐ ADJ enorme, descomunal; **the company has suffered a ~ loss this year** este año la compañía ha sufrido unas pérdidas enormes *or* descomunales; **a ~ headache** una jaqueca terrible

Ⓑ ADV **a ~ great book** un tocho de libro*

thunder [ˈθʌndəʳ] Ⓐ N (*Met*) truenos *mpl*; [*of traffic, applause*] estruendo *m*; [*of hooves*] estampido *m*; **a clap of ~** un trueno; **there is ~ in the air** amenaza tronar; **with a face like** *or* **as black as ~** con cara de furia, con cara de pocos amigos; ✦***IDIOM*** **to steal sb's ~** robar el éxito a algn

Ⓑ VI (*Met*) tronar; [*waterfall, waves*] bramar; **the guns ~ed in the distance** los cañones tronaban a lo lejos; **the train ~ed by** el tren pasó con gran estruendo; **to ~ at sb** (= *shout*) gritar muy fuerte a algn

Ⓒ VT **to ~ out an order** dar una orden a gritos; **"yes!", he ~ed** —¡sí! —rugió

thunderbolt [ˈθʌndəbəʊlt] N rayo *m*; (*fig*) rayo *m*, bomba *f*

thunderclap ['θʌndəklæp] N trueno *m*

thundercloud ['θʌndəklaʊd] N nube *f* tormentosa, nubarrón *m*

thunderflash ['θʌndəflæʃ] N petardo *m*

thundering* ['θʌndərɪŋ] Ⓐ ADJ **it's a ~ disgrace** es un escándalo; **it was a ~ success** obtuvo un tremendo éxito
Ⓑ ADV **a ~ great row** un ruido de todos los demonios; **it's a ~ good film** es una película la mar de buena*

thunderous ['θʌndərəs] ADJ [*applause*] estruendoso, atronador

thunderstorm ['θʌndəstɔːm] N tormenta *f*

thunderstruck ['θʌndəstrʌk] ADJ (*fig*) atónito, pasmado, estupefacto; **he was ~ by what he discovered** lo que descubrió lo dejó atónito *or* pasmado *or* estupefacto

thundery ['θʌndərɪ] ADJ [*weather, shower, sky*] tormentoso

Thur. ABBR (= **Thursday**) juev.

Thuringia [θjʊə'rɪndʒɪə] N Turingia *f*

Thurs. ABBR (= **Thursday**) juev.

Thursday ['θɜːzdɪ] N jueves *m inv*; *see* **Tuesday** *for usage*

thus [ðʌs] ADV (= *in this way*) así, de este modo; (= *as a result*) por eso, así que, de modo que; **he withdrew from the competition, ~ allowing his rival to win** se retiró de la competición, así que *or* de modo que ganó su rival; **~ it is that ...** así es que ..., es por eso que ...; **~, when he got home ...** así que, cuando llegó a casa ...; **~ far** hasta ahora *or* aquí

thwack [θwæk] = **whack**

thwart¹ [θwɔːt] VT [+ *plan*] frustrar, desbaratar; [+ *attempt, efforts*] frustrar; **to be ~ed at every turn** verse frustrado en todo; **there's no knowing what she'll do if she's ~ed** quién sabe qué hará si alguien se interpone en su camino; **he was trying to commit suicide but had been ~ed** intentaba suicidarse pero alguien interrumpió su propósito; **their takeover bid was ~ed** su intento de adquirir la compañía fue frustrada

thwart² [θwɔːt] N (*Naut*) bancada *f*

thy†† [ðaɪ] POSS ADJ (*sing*) tu; (*pl*) tus

thyme [taɪm] N tomillo *m*

thymus ['θaɪməs] N (*pl* **thymuses, thymi** ['θaɪmaɪ]) timo *m*

thyroid ['θaɪrɔɪd] Ⓐ N (*also* **~ gland**) tiroides *m or f inv*
Ⓑ ADJ tiroideo

thyself†† [ðaɪ'self] PRON (*acc, dative*) te; (*after prep*) ti (mismo/a); **know ~** conócete a ti mismo

ti [tiː] N (*Mus*) si *m*

tiara [tɪ'ɑːrə] N (*royal*) diadema *f*; (*pope's*) tiara *f*

Tiber ['taɪbəʳ] N Tíber *m*

Tiberius [taɪ'bɪərɪəs] N Tiberio

Tibet [tɪ'bet] N el Tibet

Tibetan [tɪ'betən] Ⓐ ADJ tibetano
Ⓑ N [1] (= *person*) tibetano/a *m/f*
[2] (*Ling*) tibetano *m*

tibia ['tɪbɪə] N (*pl* **tibias, tibiae** ['tɪbɪiː]) tibia *f*

tic [tɪk] N (*Med*) tic *m*; **a nervous ~** un tic nervioso

tich* [tɪtʃ] N = **titch**

tichy* ['tɪtʃɪ] ADJ = **titchy**

tick¹ [tɪk] Ⓐ N [1] [*of clock*] tictac *m*
[2] (*Brit**) (= *moment*) momentito *m*, segundito *m*; **half a ~!** ◊ **just a ~!** ¡un momentito or segundito!; **I shan't be a ~** en seguida voy, no tardo, ahorita voy (*LAm*); **it won't take two ~s** será sólo un momentito *or* segundito
[3] (*esp Brit*) (= *mark*) señal *f*, visto *m*; **to put a ~ against sth** poner una señal *or* un visto a algo; **place a ~ in the appropriate box** marque la casilla correspondiente
Ⓑ VT (*esp Brit*) [+ *right answer*] marcar, poner una señal *or* un visto; (*also* **~ off**) [+ *name, item on list*] marcar, poner una señal contra
Ⓒ VI [*clock*] hacer tictac; **I can't understand what makes him ~** no comprendo su forma de ser

►**tick away, tick by** VI + ADV **time is ~ing away** *or* **by** el tiempo pasa

►**tick off** VT + ADV [1] (= *mark with tick*) [+ *name, item on list*] marcar, poner una señal contra
[2] (= *count*) contar en los dedos
[3] (*Brit**) (= *reprimand*) **to ~ sb off** echar una bronca a algn, regañar *or* reñir a algn; **he was ~ed off for being late** le regañaron *or* riñeron por llegar tarde
[4] (*US**) (= *annoy*) fastidiar, dar la lata a*

►**tick over** VI + ADV (*Brit Aut, Mech*) marchar al ralentí; (*fig*) [*business*] ir tirando; **she's keeping things ~ing over until the new boss arrives** hace que las cosas sigan funcionando hasta que llegue el nuevo jefe

tick² [tɪk] N (*Zool*) garrapata *f*

tick³ [tɪk] N (= *cover*) funda *f*

tick⁴* [tɪk] N (= *credit*) ✦*IDIOM* **to buy sth on ~** comprar algo de fiado

ticker ['tɪkəʳ] Ⓐ N (*) (= *watch*) reloj *m*; (= *heart*) corazón *m*
Ⓑ CPD ► **ticker tape** N cinta *f* de teletipo

ticket ['tɪkɪt] Ⓐ N [1] (*for bus, train*) billete *m*, boleto *m* (*LAm*); (*for plane*) pasaje *m*, billete *m* (*esp Sp*); (*for concert, film, play*) entrada *f*, boleto *m* (*LAm*), boleta *f* (*LAm*); (*for library membership*) carné *m*, carnet *m*; (*Comm*) (= *label*) etiqueta *f*; (= *counterfoil*) talón *m*; (*at dry-cleaner's etc*) resguardo *m*; (*in lottery*) boleto *m*; **return ~** ◊ **round-trip ~** (*US*) billete *m* de ida y vuelta, billete *m* redondo (*Mex*); **hold it there, that's the ~!** ¡sujételo ahí! ¡eso es!; **that holiday was just the ~** esas vacaciones eran justo lo que necesitaba
[2] (*for parking offence*) multa *f* (por estacionamiento indebido); **to get a (parking) ~** ser multado por aparcar mal* *or* por estacionamiento indebido
[3] (*US Pol*) (= *candidates*) lista *f* (de candidatos), candidatura *f*, planilla *f* (*LAm*); (= *programme*) programa *m* político, programa *m* electoral; **to run on a republican ~** presentarse como candidato republicano
Ⓑ VT [1] (*Aut*) (= *fine*) [+ *person*] multar; [+ *vehicle*] dejar la papeleta de una multa en
[2] (*US*) [+ *passenger*] expedir un billete a
Ⓒ CPD ► **ticket agency** N (*Rail etc*) agencia *f* de viajes; (*Theat*) agencia *f* de localidades, boletería *f* (*LAm*) ► **ticket barrier** N (*Brit Rail*) *barrera más allá de la cual se necesita billete* ► **ticket collector, ticket inspector** N revisor(a) *m/f*, controlador(a) *m/f* de boletos (*LAm*) ► **ticket holder** N poseedor(a) *m/f* de billete; (= *season-ticket holder*) (*Theat*) abonado/a *m/f*; (*Ftbl*) socio/a *m/f*; (*of travelcard etc*) titular *mf* ► **ticket machine** N máquina *f* de billetes ► **ticket office** N (*Rail*) despacho *m* de billetes, despacho *m* de boletos (*LAm*); (*Theat, Cine*) taquilla *f*, boletería *f* (*LAm*) ► **ticket of leave†** N (*Brit*) cédula *f* de libertad condicional ► **ticket tout** N revendedor *m* (de entradas) ► **ticket window** N ventanilla *f*; (*Rail etc*) despacho *m* de billetes; (*Theat etc*) taquilla *f*

ticking ['tɪkɪŋ] N [1] [*of clock*] tictac *m*
[2] (= *material*) cutí *m*, terliz *m*

ticking-off* ['tɪkɪŋ'ɒf] N bronca *f*; **to give sb a ~** echar una bronca a algn, regañar *or* reñir a algn

tickle ['tɪkl] Ⓐ VT [1] [+ *person*] hacer cosquillas a; [+ *cat, dog*] acariciar; **she enjoyed tickling the baby** le gustaba hacer cosquillas al niño
[2] (*) (= *amuse*) divertir, hacer gracia a; **it ~d us no end** nos divirtió mucho, nos hizo mucha gracia
[3] (*) (= *please*) **we were ~d to death at being invited** fue una sorpresa maravillosa que nos invitaran; **it ~d his fancy** se le antojó; ✦*IDIOM* **to be ~d pink*** estar encantado *or* como unas castañuelas
Ⓑ VI **my ear ~s** siento cosquillas *or* hormiguillo en la oreja; **it ~s** [*material*] pica; **don't, it ~s!** ¡no, que me hace cosquillas!
Ⓒ N **to give sb a ~** hacer cosquillas a algn; **to have a ~ in one's throat** tener picor de garganta; **he never got a ~ all day** (*Fishing*) no picó ni un pez en todo el día; **at £5 he never got a ~*** a cinco libras nadie le echó un tiento*

tickler* ['tɪkləʳ] N (*Brit*) problema *m* difícil

tickling ['tɪklɪŋ] N cosquillas *fpl*

ticklish ['tɪklɪʃ], **tickly** ['tɪklɪ] ADJ [1] (*lit*) (= *sensitive to tickling*) [*person*] cosquilloso; (= *which tickles*) [*blanket*] que pica; [*cough*] irritante; **to be ~** [*person*] tener cosquillas, ser cosquilloso
[2] (*fig*) (= *touchy*) [*person*] picajoso, delicado; (= *delicate*) [*situation, problem*] peliagudo, delicado; **it's a ~ business** es un asunto delicado

ticktack ['tɪktæk] N (*Racing*) *lenguaje de signos utilizado por los corredores de apuestas en las carreras de caballos*

tick-tock ['tɪk'tɒk] N tictac *m*

tic-tac-toe [ˌtɪktæk'təʊ] N (*US*) tres *m* en raya

tidal ['taɪdl] Ⓐ ADJ de (la) marea; **the river is ~ up to here** la marea sube hasta aquí; **the Mediterranean is not ~** en el Mediterráneo no hay mareas
Ⓑ CPD ► **tidal basin** N dique *m* de marea ► **tidal energy** N energía *f* de las mareas, energía *f* mareomotriz ► **tidal wave** N maremoto *m*; (*fig*) ola *f* gigantesca

tidbit ['tɪdbɪt] N (*US*) = **titbit**

tiddler ['tɪdləʳ] N [1] (= *small fish*) pececillo *m*; (= *stickleback*) espinoso *m*
[2] (*) (= *child*) nene/a *m/f*, renacuajo* *m*

tiddly* ['tɪdlɪ] ADJ (*compar* **tiddlier**; *superl* **tiddliest**) (*Brit*) [1] (= *drunk*) alegre, achispado, tomado (*LAm**)
[2] (= *tiny*) pequeñito, pequeñín

tiddlywink ['tɪdlɪwɪŋk] N pulga *f*; **tiddlywinks** (= *game*) juego *m* de las pulgas

tide [taɪd] N [1] [*of sea*] marea *f*; **high ~** marea *f* alta, pleamar *f*; **we sailed at high ~** *or* **with the high ~** zarpamos cuando la marea estaba alta; **low ~** marea *f* baja, bajamar *f*; **it is possible to walk across at low ~** es posible cruzar cuando la marea está baja; **the ~ has turned** ha cambiado la marea
[2] (*fig*) corriente *f*; [*of emotion*] ola *f*; **the rising ~ of public indignation** la creciente indignación pública; **the ~ of events** la marcha de los sucesos; **the ~ has turned** han cambiado las cosas; **the ~ of battle turned** cambió la suerte de la batalla; ✦*IDIOMS* **to go against the ~** ir contra la corriente; **to go with the ~** seguir la corriente

►**tide over** Ⓐ VT + ADV **can you lend me some money to ~ me over till the end of the month?** ¿puedes dejarme algo de dinero para que pueda llegar a final de mes *or* para sacarme de apuros hasta final de mes?

Ⓑ VT + PREP **he got a loan to ~ him over the first three months** consiguió un préstamo para salir adelante los tres primeros meses; **to ~ sb over a difficult period** ayudar a algn a salir de un apuro

tideless ['taɪdlɪs] ADJ sin mareas

tideline ['taɪdlaɪn] N línea *f* de la marea alta

tidemark ['taɪdmɑːk] N [1] (= *tideline*) línea *f* de la marea alta
[2] (*hum*) (*in bath, on neck*) cerco *m* (de suciedad)

tiderace ['taɪdreɪs] N aguaje *m*, marejada *f*

tidewater ['taɪd,wɔːtəʳ] (*Brit*) Ⓐ N agua *f* de marea
Ⓑ CPD [*land, area*] drenado por las mareas, costero

tideway ['taɪdweɪ] N canal *m* de marea

tidily ['taɪdɪlɪ] ADV [*arranged, piled, stacked*] ordenadamente; [*dressed*] bien, perfectamente

tidiness ['taɪdɪnɪs] N [*of room, house, desk*] orden *m*; [*of person's appearance*] pulcritud *f*

tidings ['taɪdɪŋz] NPL († *or liter*) noticias *fpl*

tidy ['taɪdɪ] Ⓐ ADJ (*compar* **tidier**, *superl* **tidiest**)
[1] (= *neat, orderly*) [1·1] (*in appearance*) [*house, room*] ordenado, arreglado; [*garden*] cuidado; [*cupboard, desk, pile*] ordenado; [*appearance*] aseado, pulcro; [*hair*] arreglado; [*schoolwork*] limpio; **he likes to keep the house ~** le gusta tener la casa ordenada *or* arreglada; **to look ~** [*person*] tener un aspecto aseado *or* pulcro; [*room*] tener un aspecto ordenado
[1·2] (*in character*) [*person, child*] ordenado; **she's not very ~** no es muy ordenada; **I'm an obsessively ~ person** soy un obseso del orden
[2] (*) (= *sizeable*) [*sum*] bonito*; [*income, profit*] bueno; **he'll make a ~ sum out of it** sacará de ello un buen dinero *or* una bonita cantidad*
Ⓑ VT (*also* **~ up**) [+ *room, house*] ordenar, arreglar; [+ *drawer, cupboard, desk*] ordenar
Ⓒ N [1] (= *container for desk, kitchen, etc*) *recipiente para poner utensilios de escritorio, cubiertos etc*
[2] (= *act*) **I gave the lounge a quick ~ (up)** arreglé un poco el salón

► **tidy away** VT + ADV (*Brit*) [+ *toys, books, papers*] guardar, poner en su sitio; **to ~ the dishes away** guardar los platos, poner los platos en su sitio

► **tidy out** VT + ADV limpiar, ordenar

► **tidy up** Ⓐ VI + ADV ordenar
Ⓑ VT + ADV [1] = **tidy B**
[2] **to ~ o.s. up** arreglarse

tidy-out ['taɪdɪ'aʊt] N, **tidy-up** ['taɪdɪ'ʌp] N **to have a ~** ordenar (la casa, la habitación *etc*)

tie [taɪ] Ⓐ N [1] (= *necktie*) corbata *f*; *see also* **black, bow, white**
[2] (= *fastening*) (*for plastic bags*) atadura *f*; (*on garment*) lazo *m*
[3] (= *bond*) lazo *m*, vínculo *m*; **the ~s of friendship** los lazos *or* vínculos de la amistad; **the ~s that bind us** los lazos que nos unen; **he wants to maintain close ~s with the US** quiere mantener unos vínculos *or* lazos estrechos con Estados Unidos; **diplomatic ~s** relaciones *fpl* diplomáticas; **family ~s** lazos *mpl* familiares
[4] (= *hindrance, obligation*) atadura *f*; **pets are as much of a ~ as children** las mascotas te atan tanto como los niños, las mascotas son una atadura tan grande como los niños; **I have no ~s here** no tengo nada que me retenga aquí *or* que me impida irme de aquí; **I can't go because of family ~s** no puedo ir debido a obligaciones familiares
[5] (*esp Sport*) (= *draw*) empate *m*; **the match ended in a ~** el partido terminó en empate *or* con (un) empate
[6] (*Brit Sport*) (*also* **cup ~**) partido *m* (de copa), eliminatoria *f* (de copa)
[7] (*Archit*) (= *support*) tirante *m*
[8] (*Mus*) ligadura *f*
[9] (*US Rail*) traviesa *f*
Ⓑ VT [1] (= *fasten*) [+ *one's shoelaces*] atarse, amarrarse (*LAm*); [+ *sb's shoelaces*] atar, amarrar (*LAm*); [+ *one's necktie*] hacerse el nudo de; [+ *sb's necktie*] hacer el nudo de; [+ *parcel*] atar, amarrar (*LAm*); **she ~d a ribbon around the kitten's neck** ató un lazo al cuello del gatito; **he ~d the rope around his waist** se ató la cuerda a la cintura; **her hands were ~d behind her back** tenía las manos atadas a la espalda; **to ~ sth in a bow** hacer un lazo con algo; **to ~ a knot in sth** hacer un nudo en *or* con algo; **he ~d the dog to a lamppost** ató el perro a una farola; **he ~d the ends of the cord together** ató los extremos de la cuerda; **he ~d her hands together** le ató las manos; ✦*IDIOM* **we'd like to help, but our hands are ~d** nos gustaría ayudar pero tenemos atadas las manos; *see also* **knot**
[2] (= *link*) relacionar (**to** con); **rates are ~d to property values** las contribuciones urbanas están relacionadas con el valor *or* van ligadas al valor del inmueble
[3] (= *restrict*) atar; **I'm ~d to the house/my desk all day** me paso todo el día atada a la casa/la mesa de trabajo; **are we ~d to this plan?** ¿estamos atados *or* restringidos a este plan?; **she didn't want to be ~d to a long-term contract** no quería atarse a un contrato a largo plazo
[4] (*Sport*) [+ *game, match*] empatar
Ⓒ VI [1] (= *fasten*) atarse; **the overall ~s at the back** el delantal se ata a la espalda
[2] (= *draw*) (*in match, competition, election*) empatar
Ⓓ CPD ► **tie clip, tie clasp** N pinza *f* de corbata ► **tie rack** N corbatero *m* ► **tie tack** N (*US*) = **tiepin**

► **tie back** VT + ADV [+ *curtains*] recoger; **to ~ one's hair back** recogerse el pelo; **her hair was ~d back with a ribbon** llevaba el pelo recogido con un lazo

► **tie down** VT + ADV [1] (*with rope*) [+ *object, person, animal*] sujetar, amarrar (*LAm*)
[2] (= *restrict*) atar; **having a pet ~s you down** tener una mascota te ata; **he felt ~d down by the relationship** se sentía atado por la relación; **we didn't want to ~ ourselves down to a mortgage** no queríamos atarnos a una hipoteca
[3] (= *commit*) **to ~ sb down** hacer que algn se comprometa; **we can't ~ him down to a date** no conseguimos que se comprometa a una fecha concreta

► **tie in** Ⓐ VI + ADV **to ~ in with sth** (= *tally*) (*with facts*) concordar *or* cuadrar con algo; (= *fit in*) (*with arrangements*) coincidir con algo; **it doesn't ~ in with what he told us** no concuerda *or* cuadra con lo que nos dijo; **the wedding was arranged to ~ in with David's leave** la boda se planeó de modo que coincidiera con el permiso de David
Ⓑ VT + ADV **to ~ sth in with sth** (= *link*) relacionar algo con algo; (= *fit in*) [+ *meeting, visit*] hacer coincidir algo con algo; **you can't ~ me in with any of the killings** no puedes relacionarme con *or* vincularme a ninguno de los asesinatos

► **tie on** VT + ADV atar

► **tie up** Ⓐ VT + ADV [1] (= *fasten, secure*) [+ *parcel, person, horse, sb's shoelaces*] atar, amarrar (*LAm*); [+ *one's shoelaces*] atarse, amarrarse (*LAm*); [+ *boat*] amarrar; *see also* **loose**
[2] (= *make inaccessible*) [+ *money, capital*] inmovilizar; **he has a fortune ~d up in property** tiene una fortuna inmovilizada *or* invertida en bienes inmuebles; **how much money have you got ~d up in the product?** ¿cuánto dinero tienes invertido *or* metido en el producto?
[3] (= *conclude*) [+ *business deal*] concluir, cerrar
[4] (= *link*) **to be ~d up with sth** estar relacionado con algo, estar vinculado a algo; **I'm sure her disappearance is ~d up with the robbery** estoy seguro de que su desaparición está relacionada con el robo *or* vinculada al robo; **don't get ~d up with people like him** no te mezcles con gente como él
[5] (= *occupy*) **to be ~d up (with sth/sb)** estar ocupado (con algo/algn); **he's ~d up with the manager just now** ahora está ocupado *or* tratando un asunto con el jefe; **I'm ~d up tomorrow** mañana estoy ocupado; **sorry I'm late, I got ~d up** siento llegar tarde, me entretuvieron
[6] (*esp US*) (= *obstruct, hinder*) [+ *traffic*] paralizar, inmovilizar; [+ *production*] paralizar; [+ *programme*] interrumpir
Ⓑ VI + ADV [1] (= *be linked*) **to ~ up with sth** estar relacionado con algo, estar vinculado a algo
[2] (*Naut*) atracar, amarrar

tie-break(er) ['taɪbreɪk(əʳ)] N (*Sport*) muerte *f* rápida, desempate *m*

tied [taɪd] ADJ [1] (*Sport*) empatado; **the match was ~ at 2-2** el partido estaba empatado a dos
[2] (*Mus*) [*note*] ligado
[3] (*Brit*) **~ cottage** *casa de campo cedida o alquilada a un empleado, generalmente a un trabajador del campo*; **~ house** (= *pub*) *bar que está obligado a vender una marca de cerveza en exclusiva*

tie-in ['taɪɪn] N (= *link*) vinculación *f*, relación *f*; **police are looking for a ~ to connect the two cases** la policía busca una vinculación *or* relación entre ambos casos; **guides on cooking and gardening with a TV ~** libros de cocina y jardinería relacionados *or* vinculados con un programa de TV

tieless ['taɪlɪs] ADJ sin corbata

tie-on ['taɪɒn] ADJ [*label*] para atar

tiepin ['taɪpɪn] N alfiler *m* de corbata

tier [tɪəʳ] N [1] (*in stadium, amphitheatre*) (= *row of seats*) grada *f*; [*of cake*] piso *m*; **to arrange in ~s** disponer en gradas *or* pisos
[2] (*fig*) (*in management, system*) nivel *m*; **a two-~ health service** un sistema sanitario que hace distinciones entre dos grupos

tiered ['tɪəd] ADJ con gradas, en una serie de gradas; **steeply ~** con gradas en fuerte pendiente; **a three-~ cake** un pastel de tres pisos

tie-up ['taɪʌp] N [1] (= *connection*) enlace *m*, vínculo *m*; (*Comm*) (*between companies*) acuerdo *m* (*para llevar a cabo un proyecto*)
[2] (*US*) [*of traffic*] embotellamiento *m*

tiff* [tɪf] N pelea *f*, riña *f* (sin trascendencia); **a lover's ~** una pelea de amantes

tiffin† ['tɪfɪn] N almuerzo *m*

tig [tɪg] N **to play ~** jugar al marro

tiger ['taɪgəʳ] Ⓐ N tigre *m*
Ⓑ CPD ► **tiger economy** N economía *f* emergente ► **tiger lily** N tigridia *f* ► **tiger moth** N mariposa *f* tigre ► **tiger's eye** N (*Min*) ojo *m* de gato

tigerish ['taɪgərɪʃ] ADJ (*fig*) salvaje, feroz

tight [taɪt] Ⓐ ADJ (*compar* **tighter**; *superl* **tightest**) [1] [*clothes, jeans*] (= *close-fitting*) ajustado, ceñido; (= *uncomfortably tight*) apretado, estrecho; **my shoes are too ~** me aprietan los zapatos; **the hat was a ~ fit** el sombrero quedaba muy apretado *or* muy justo
[2] (= *stretched out*) [*rope, skin*] tirante; **my skin feels ~** tengo la piel tirante, me tira la piel; **to pull sth ~** tensar algo; ✦**IDIOMS as ~ as a drum** [*surface, material*] tenso como la piel de un tambor; **she has a body as ~ as a drum** tiene el cuerpo firme como una piedra; **to keep a ~ rein on sth/sb** mantener un control estricto sobre algo/algn; *see also* **skin-tight**
[3] (= *not loose*) [*screw, knot, curl*] apretado; [*seal*] hermético; [*embrace, grip*] fuerte; **his fingers were ~ on Thomas's arm** le apretaba el brazo a Thomas fuertemente con los dedos; **the insect curled up in a ~ ball** el insecto se enroscó formando una pequeña bola; **to have a ~ grip on sth** (*on power, economy*) ejercer un firme control sobre algo; **to keep a ~ grip on sth** (*on finances, discipline*) mantener un firme control de algo; **to have a ~ hold of sth** tener algo bien agarrado; **to keep a ~ hold of sth** agarrar algo con fuerza; **it was a ~ squeeze in the lift** íbamos muy apretados *or* apiñados en el ascensor; ✦**IDIOM to keep a ~ lid on sth** (*fig*) controlar bien algo, mantener algo bajo control; *see also* **airtight**, **watertight**
[4] (= *tense*) [*voice, throat, smile*] tenso; [*muscle*] tenso, tirante; **my chest feels ~** siento una opresión en el pecho
[5] (= *strict*) [*schedule*] apretado; [*budget*] ajustado, limitado; [*control*] estricto; **security will be ~** habrá fuertes medidas de seguridad
[6] (= *close-knit*) [*group, community*] muy unido
[7] (= *sharp*) [*bend*] cerrado; **to make a ~ turn** girar bruscamente, dar un giro brusco
[8] (*) (= *scarce*) [*space, resources*] limitado, escaso; **things were ~ during the war** el dinero era escaso durante la guerra; **when we first got married money was ~** al principio de casarnos estábamos bastante escasos de dinero
[9] (*) (= *difficult*) [*situation*] apurado, difícil; ✦**IDIOM to be in a ~ corner** *or* **spot*** estar en una situación apurada *or* comprometida
[10] (= *close*) [*competition, match*] reñido
[11] (*) (= *drunk*) mamado*, tomado (*LAm**); **to get ~** agarrarse una moña*, cogérsela*
[12] (*) (= *tight-fisted*) agarrado*
Ⓑ ADV [*hold, grip*] bien, con fuerza; [*squeeze*] con fuerza; [*shut, seal, tie*] bien; **hold (on) ~!** ¡agárrate *or* sujétate bien!, ¡agárrate *or* sujétate fuerte!; **to be packed ~ (with sth)** estar lleno hasta arriba (de algo)*, estar abarrotado (de algo)*; ✦**IDIOMS to sit ~: do we just sit ~ while thousands of people are dying?** ¿vamos a quedarnos cruzados de brazos *or* sin hacer nada mientras mueren miles de personas?; **sleep ~!** ¡que duermas bien!, ¡que descanses!

tighten ['taɪtn] Ⓐ VT (*also* **~ up**) [+ *rope*] estirar, tensar; [+ *nut, belt, shoes*] apretar; [+ *regulations*] hacer más severo; [+ *restrictions, discipline, security*] reforzar
Ⓑ VI (*also* **~ up**) [*rope, knot*] estirarse; [*skin*] ponerse tirante; [*grasp*] apretarse

► **tighten up** Ⓐ VT + ADV [1] = **tighten A**
[2] **to ~ up on sth** ser más estricto con algo; **they have decided to ~ up on this type of import** han decidido controlar más este tipo de importaciones
Ⓑ VI + ADV = **tighten B**

tightening ['taɪtnɪŋ] N [*of rope*] tensamiento m; [*of controls, security*] refuerzo *m*; [*of skin*] tirantez *f*

tight-fisted ['taɪt'fɪstɪd] ADJ (= *mean*) [*person*] tacaño, agarrado*

tight-fitting ['taɪt'fɪtɪŋ] ADJ muy ajustado, muy ceñido

tight-knit ['taɪt'nɪt] ADJ [*family, group, community*] muy unido

tight-lipped ['taɪt'lɪpt] ADJ [1] (= *secretive*) hermético; **to be/remain ~ about sth** mantener la boca cerrada respecto a algo; **~ silence** silencio *m* hermético
[2] (= *angry*) [*person*] mudo de rabia; [*expression*] de rabia contenida

tightly ['taɪtlɪ] ADV [1] (= *firmly*) [*hold*] bien, con fuerza; [*close, tie, wrap*] bien; [*bind*] firmemente; **the prisoners were ~ bound** los prisioneros estaban firmemente atados; **the bandages need to be ~ bound** hay que apretar bien los vendajes; **they hold on ~ to their religious traditions** se aferran firmemente a sus tradiciones religiosas
[2] (= *closely*) **the shelves were packed ~ with books** las estanterías estaban abarrotadas de libros; **~ fitting clothes** ropa ceñida *or* ajustada
[3] (= *strictly*) [*controlled, enforced*] estrictamente

tightness ['taɪtnɪs] N [1] [*of clothes*] (*comfortable*) lo ceñido, lo ajustado; (*uncomfortable*) estrechez *f*; [*of shoes*] estrechez *f*; [*of lid, screw*] lo apretado
[2] [*of muscle, throat*] tensión *f*; **I can feel a ~ in my chest** siento una opresión en el pecho
[3] [*of budget, schedule*] lo ajustado, lo limitado; [*of discipline, regulations*] severidad *f*
[4] [*of bend, corner*] lo cerrado

tightrope ['taɪtrəʊp] Ⓐ N cuerda *f* floja; ✦**IDIOMS to be on a ~** ◊ **be walking a ~** andar en la cuerda floja
Ⓑ CPD ► **tightrope walker** N equilibrista *mf*, funámbulo/a *m/f*

tights [taɪts] (*Brit*) NPL (= *clothes*) pantis *mpl*, medias *fpl*; (*for sport, ballet*) leotardos *mpl*

tightwad* ['taɪtwɒd] N (*US*) cicatero/a* *m/f*, agarrado/a* *m/f*

tigress ['taɪgrɪs] N tigresa *f*

Tigris ['taɪgrɪs] N Tigris *m*

tilde ['tɪldɪ] N tilde *f*

tile [taɪl] Ⓐ N (= *roof tile*) teja *f*; (= *floor tile*) baldosa *f*; (= *wall tile, decorative tile*) azulejo *m*; ✦**IDIOM a night on the ~s*** una noche de juerga *or* parranda*
Ⓑ VT [+ *floor*] embaldosar; [+ *wall*] revestir de azulejos, alicatar (*Sp*); [+ *ceiling*] tejar

tiled [taɪld] ADJ [*floor*] embaldosado; [*wall*] revestido de azulejos, alicatado (*Sp*); [*ceiling*] tejado de tejas; **~ roof** tejado *m*

tiling ['taɪlɪŋ] N (*on roof*) tejas *fpl*, tejado *m*; (*on floor*) baldosas *fpl*, embaldosado *m*; (*on wall*) azulejos *mpl*

till[1] [tɪl] VT (*Agr*) [+ *land, soil*] cultivar, labrar

till[2] [tɪl] PREP, CONJ = **until**

till[3] [tɪl] N (*for money*) (= *drawer*) cajón *m*; (= *machine*) caja *f*, caja *f* registradora; **they caught him with his hand** *or* **fingers in the ~** lo cogieron robando (dentro de la empresa *etc*)

tillage ['tɪlɪdʒ] N cultivo *m*, labranza *f*

tiller ['tɪləʳ] N (*Naut*) caña *f* del timón, timón *m*

tilt [tɪlt] Ⓐ N [1] (= *slant*) inclinación *f*; **the ~ of the earth's axis** la inclinación del eje de la Tierra; **the ~ of his head when he listened** la inclinación *or* el ladeo de su cabeza cuando escuchaba; **a ~ in the balance of power** un cambio en el equilibrio del poder; **to give sth a ~** inclinar algo, ladear algo; **on/at a ~** inclinado, ladeado
[2] (*Hist*) torneo *m*, justa *f*; **(at) full ~** a toda velocidad *or* carrera; **to run full ~ into a wall** dar de lleno contra una pared; **to have a ~ at** arremeter contra
Ⓑ VT inclinar, ladear; **~ it this way/the other way** inclínalo hacia este/el otro lado; **he ~ed his chair back** inclinó la silla hacia atrás
Ⓒ VI [1] (= *lean*) inclinarse, ladearse; **to ~ to one side** inclinarse hacia un lado; **he ~ed back in his chair** se recostó en la silla; **to ~ over** (= *lean*) inclinarse; (= *fall*) volcarse, caer; **a lorry that ~s up** un camión basculante *or* que bascula
[2] (*Hist*) justar; **to ~ against** arremeter contra

tilth [tɪlθ] N (= *act*) cultivo *m*, labranza *f*; (= *state*) condición *f* (cultivable) de la tierra

Tim [tɪm] N (*familiar form*) *of* **Timothy**

timber ['tɪmbəʳ] Ⓐ N (= *wood*) madera *f*; (= *growing trees*) árboles *mpl* (productores de madera); (= *beam*) viga *f*, madero *m*; (*Naut*) cuaderna *f*; **timber!** ¡tronco va!
Ⓑ CPD ► **timber merchant** N (*Brit*) maderero *m* ► **timber wolf** N lobo *m* gris norteamericano ► **timber yard** N (*Brit*) almacén *m* de madera

timbered ['tɪmbəd] ADJ [*house*] (= *made of wood*) de madera; (= *with individual timbers*) con vigas de madera; [*land*] arbolado; **the land is well ~** el terreno tiene mucho bosque

timbering ['tɪmbərɪŋ] N maderamen *m*

timberland ['tɪmbəlænd] N (*US*) tierras *fpl* maderables

timberline ['tɪmbəlaɪn] N límite *m* forestal

timbre ['tæmbrə] N (*Mus*) [*of instrument, voice*] timbre *m*

timbrel ['tɪmbrəl] N pandereta *f*

Timbuktu [,tɪmbʌk'tuː] N Timbuktú *m*; **he could be in ~ for all I know** podría estar en la conchinchina

time [taɪm] Ⓐ N [1] (*gen*) tiempo *m*; **as ~ goes on** *or* **by** con el (paso del) tiempo, a medida que pasa/pasaba el tiempo; **race against ~** carrera *f* contra (el) reloj; **for all ~** para siempre; **one of the best of all ~** uno de los mejores de todos los tiempos; **Father Time** el Tiempo; **to find (the) ~ for sth** encontrar tiempo para algo; **I can't find the ~ for reading** no encuentro tiempo para leer; **~ flies** el tiempo vuela; **how ~ flies!** ¡cómo pasa el tiempo!; **to gain ~** ganar tiempo; **half the ~ he's drunk** la mayor parte del tiempo está borracho; **to have (the) ~ (to do sth)** tener tiempo (para hacer algo); **we have plenty of ~** tenemos tiempo de sobra; **to make ~** (*US**) ganar tiempo, apresurarse; **to make up for lost ~** recuperar el tiempo perdido; **it's only a matter** *or* **question of ~ before it falls** sólo es cuestión de tiempo antes de que caiga; **I've no ~ for him** (*too busy*) no tengo tiempo para él; (*contemptuous*) no le aguanto; **I've no ~ for sport** odio los deportes; **there is no ~ to lose** no hay tiempo que perder; **he lost no ~ in doing it** no tardó en hacerlo; **my ~ is my own** yo dispongo de mi tiempo; **~ presses** el tiempo apremia; **~ is on our side** el tiempo obra a nuestro favor; **~ and space** el tiempo y el espacio; **to take ~: it takes ~** requiere tiempo, lleva su tiempo; **it'll take ~ to get over the loss of her family** le llevará tiempo superar la pérdida de su familia; **it took him all his ~ to find it** sólo encontrarlo le ocupó bastante tiempo; **to take one's ~** hacer las cosas con calma; **take your ~!** tómate el tiempo que necesites, ¡no hay prisa!; **you certainly took your ~!** (*iro*) ¡no es precisamente que te mataras corriendo!; **(only) ~ will tell** el tiempo lo dirá; ✦*IDIOMS* **to have ~ on one's hands**: **she has too much ~ on her hands** dispone de demasiado tiempo libre; **once you retire you'll have ~ on your hands** cuando te hayas jubilado, tendrás todo el tiempo del mundo; **to kill ~** entretener el tiempo, pasar el rato, matar el tiempo; **to pass the ~ of day with sb** detenerse a charlar un rato con algn; **to play for ~** tratar de ganar tiempo; **to be pressed for ~** andar escaso de tiempo; ✦*PROV* **~ is money** el tiempo es oro; *see also* **spare**, **waste**

[2] (= *period of time*) tiempo *m*, período *m*; (*relatively short*) rato *m*; **have you been here all this ~?** ¿has estado aquí todo este tiempo?; **for the ~ being** por ahora, de momento; **for a ~** durante un rato; (*longer*) durante una temporada; **a long ~** mucho tiempo; **to take a long ~ to do sth** tardar mucho en hacer algo; **a long ~ ago** hace mucho (tiempo), hace tiempo; **he hasn't been seen for a long ~** hace mucho tiempo que no se le ve; **she'll be in a wheelchair for a long ~ to come** le queda mucho tiempo de estar en silla de ruedas por delante; **in no ~ at all** en un abrir y cerrar de ojos; **it will last our ~** durará lo que nosotros; **a short ~** poco tiempo, un rato; **a short ~ ago** hace poco; **a short ~ after** poco (tiempo) después, al poco tiempo; **in a short ~ they were all gone** muy pronto habían desaparecido todos; **for some ~ past** de algún tiempo a esta parte; **after some ~ she looked up at me/wrote to me** después de cierto tiempo levantó la vista hacia mí/me escribió, pasado algún tiempo levantó la vista hacia mí/me escribió; **in a week's ~** dentro de una semana; **in two weeks' ~** en dos semanas, al cabo de dos semanas; ✦*IDIOM* **to do ~*** cumplir una condena; *see also* **serve**

[3] (*at work*) **on Saturdays they pay ~ and a half** los sábados pagan lo normal más la mitad; **he did it in his own ~** lo hizo en su tiempo libre *or* fuera de (las) horas de trabajo; **to be on short ~** ◊ **work short ~** trabajar en jornadas reducidas; *see also* **full-time**, **part-time**, **short-time**

[4] (= *moment, point of time*) momento *m*; **I was watching TV at the ~** en ese momento estaba viendo la televisión; **from ~ to ~** de vez en cuando; **about ~ too!** ¡ya era hora!; **it's about ~ you had a haircut** ya es hora de que te cortes el pelo; **come (at) any ~ (you like)** ven cuando quieras; **it might happen (at) any ~** podría ocurrir de un momento a otro *or* en cualquier momento; **any ~ now** de un momento a otro; **at ~s** a veces, a ratos; **at all ~s** siempre, en todo momento; **to die before one's ~** morir temprano; **not before ~!** ¡ya era hora!; **between ~s** en los intervalos; **by the ~ he arrived** para cuando él llegó; **by the ~ we got there he'd left** cuando llegamos allí ya se había ido; **by this ~** ya, antes de esto; **(by) this ~ next year** el año que viene por estas fechas; **to choose one's ~ carefully** elegir con cuidado el momento más propicio; **the ~ has come to leave** ha llegado el momento de irse; **when the ~ comes** cuando llegue el momento; **at a convenient ~** en un momento oportuno; **at any given ~** en cualquier momento dado; **her ~ was drawing near** (*to give birth*) se acercaba el momento de dar a luz; (*to die*) estaba llegando al final de su vida; **it's high ~ you got a job** ya va siendo hora de que consigas un trabajo; **at my ~ of life** a mi edad, con los años que yo tengo; **at no ~ did I mention it** no lo mencioné en ningún momento; **this is no ~ for jokes** éste no es momento para bromas; **now is the ~ to go** ahora es el momento de irse; **now is the ~ to plant roses** ésta es la época para plantar las rosas; **at odd ~s** (= *occasionally*) de vez en cuando; **he calls at some odd ~s** llama a las horas más intempestivas; **from that ~ on** a partir de entonces, desde entonces; **at one ~** en cierto momento, en cierta época; **this is neither the ~ nor the place to discuss it** éste no es ni el momento ni el lugar oportuno para hablar de eso; **there's a ~ and a place for everything** todo tiene su momento y su lugar; **at the present ~** actualmente, en la actualidad; **at the proper ~** en el momento oportuno; **at the same ~** (= *simultaneously*) al mismo tiempo, a la vez; (= *even so*) al mismo tiempo, por otro lado; **until such ~ as he agrees** hasta que consienta; **at that ~** por entonces, en aquel entonces, en aquella época; **at this particular ~** en este preciso momento; **at this ~ of the year** en esta época del año; **it's a lovely ~ of year** es una estación encantadora; *see also* **bide**

[5] (*by clock*) hora *f*; **what's the ~?** ¿qué hora es?; **the ~ is 2.30** son las dos y media; **it's ~ to go** es hora de irse; **~ gentlemen please!** ¡se cierra!; **to arrive ahead of ~** llegar temprano; **to be 30 minutes ahead of ~** llevar 30 minutos de adelanto; **at any ~ of the day or night** en cualquier momento *or* a cualquier hora del día o de la noche; **to be 30 minutes behind ~** llevar 30 minutos de retraso; **it's coffee ~** es la hora del café; **at this ~ of day** a esta hora; **it's ~ for the news** es (la) hora de las noticias; **it's ~ for lunch** es (la) hora de comer; **let me know in good ~** avíseme con anticipación; **make sure you get there in good ~** asegúrate de que llegas allí con tiempo; **he'll come in his own good ~** vendrá cuando le parezca conveniente; **all in good ~** todo a su (debido) tiempo; **to start in good ~** partir a tiempo, partir pronto; **have you got the (right) ~?** ¿tiene la hora (exacta)?; **Greenwich mean ~** hora *f* de Greenwich; **we were just in ~ to see it** llegamos justo a tiempo para verlo; **a watch that keeps good ~** un reloj muy exacto; **just look at the ~!** ¡fíjate qué hora es ya!, ¡mira qué tarde es!; **what ~ do you make it?** ◊ **what do you make the ~?** ¿qué hora es *or* tiene?; **we made good ~ on the journey** el viaje ha sido rápido; **to be on ~** [*person*] ser puntual, llegar puntualmente; [*train, plane*] llegar puntual; **to tell the ~** [*clock*] dar la hora; [*child*] saber decir la hora; ✦*IDIOM* **I wouldn't give him the ~ of day** a mi él me tiene sin cuidado; *see* **closing**, **opening**

[6] (= *era, period*) tiempo *m*, época *f*; **in Elizabethan ~s** en tiempos isabelinos, en la época isabelina; **in our own ~(s)** en nuestra época; **in my ~(s)** en mis tiempos; **what ~s they were!** ◊ **what ~s we had!** ¡qué tiempos aquellos!; **one of the greatest footballers of our ~** uno de los mejores futbolistas de nuestros tiempos; **to be ahead of one's ~** adelantarse a su época; **that was all before my ~** todo eso fue antes de mis tiempos; **to be behind the ~s** [*person*] estar atrasado de noticias; [*thing, idea*] estar fuera de moda, haber quedado anticuado; **how ~s change!** ¡cómo cambian las cosas!; **in ~s to come** en tiempos venideros; **~s were hard** fueron tiempos duros; **~s are hard** atravesamos un período bastante difícil; **they fell on hard ~s** entraron en un periodo de vacas flacas; **to keep abreast of** *or* **up with the ~s** ir con los tiempos, mantenerse al día; **the ~s we live in** los tiempos en que vivimos; **in modern ~s** en tiempos modernos; **to move with the ~s** ir con los tiempos, mantenerse al día; **in olden ~s** ◊ **in ~s past** en otro tiempo, antiguamente; **~ was when ...** hubo un tiempo en que ...; *see also* **sign**

[7] (= *experience*) **to have a bad** *or* **rough** *or* **thin ~ (of it)** pasarlo mal, pasarlas negras; **to have a good ~** pasarlo bien, divertirse; **all they want to do is have a good ~** no quieren más que divertirse; **to give sb a good ~** hacer que algn lo pase bien; **she's out for a good ~** se propone divertirse; **we had a high old ~*** lo hemos pasado en grande*; **we have a lovely ~** lo pasamos la mar de bien*; **have a nice ~!** ¡que lo pases/paséis *etc* bien!; ✦*IDIOM* **the big ~*** el estrellato, el éxito; **to make the big ~** alcanzar el éxito, triunfar; *see also* **big-time**

[8] (= *occasion*) vez *f*; **three ~s** tres veces; **I remember the ~ he came here** recuerdo la ocasión en que vino por aquí, me acuerdo de cuando vino por aquí; **~ after ~** ◊ **~ and again** repetidas veces, una y otra vez; **to carry three boxes at a ~** llevar tres cajas a la vez; **he ran upstairs three at a ~** subió la escalera de tres en tres escalones; **for weeks at a ~** durante semanas enteras *or* seguidas; **each ~** ◊ **every ~** cada vez; **he won every ~** ganó todas las veces; **it's the best, every ~!** ¡es el mejor, no hay duda!; **give me beer every ~!** ¡para mí, siempre cerveza!; **the first ~ I did it** la primera vez que lo hice; **for the first ~** por primera vez; **last ~** la última vez; **the last ~ I did it** la última vez que lo hice; **for the last ~** por última vez; **many ~s** muchas veces; **many's the ~ ...** no una vez, sino muchas ...; **next ~** la próxima vez, a la próxima (*esp LAm*); **the second ~ round** (= *second marriage*) la segunda intentona de matrimonio; **several ~s** varias veces; **this ~** esta vez; **at various ~s in the past** en determinados momentos del pasado; ✦*IDIOMS* **nine ~s out of ten** ◊ **ninety-nine ~s out of a hundred** casi siempre; **third ~ lucky!** ¡a la tercera va la vencida!

[9] (*Mus*) compás *m*; **in 3/4 ~** al compás de 3 por 4; **to beat ~** marcar el compás; **in ~ to the music** al compás de la música; **to keep ~** llevar el compás; **to get out of ~** perder el compás; *see also* **beat B4**, **mark² B7**

[10] (*Math*) **4 ~s 3 is 12** 4 por 3 son 12; **it's five ~s faster than** *or* **as fast as yours** es cinco veces más rápido que el tuyo

[11] (*Mech*) **the ignition is out of ~** el encendido está fuera de fase

Ⓑ VT [1] (= *schedule*) planear, calcular; (= *choose time of*) [+ *remark, request*] elegir el momento para; **the race is ~d for 8.30** el comienzo de la carrera está previsto para las 8.30; **you ~d that perfectly** elegiste a la perfección el momento para hacerlo; **the bomb was ~d to explode five minutes later** la bomba estaba sincronizada para explotar cinco minutos más tarde; **the strike was carefully ~d to cause maximum disruption** se había escogido el momento de la huelga para ocasionar el mayor trastorno posible; **the decision to sell was badly ~d** se decidió vender en un mal momento; *see also* **ill-timed**, **well-timed**

[2] (= *reckon time of*) [+ *call, journey*] calcular la duración de; (*with stopwatch*) cronometrar; **to ~ o.s.** cronometrarse; **I ~d him doing the washing-up** le cronometré mientras lavaba los platos

Ⓒ CPD ► **time and motion study** N estudio *m* de tiempos y movimientos ► **time bomb** N bomba *f* de relojería ► **time capsule** N cápsula *f* del tiempo ► **time card** N tarjeta *f* de registro horario ► **time clock** N reloj *m* registrador, reloj *m* de control de asistencia ► **time deposit** N (*US*) depósito *m* a plazo ► **time exposure** N (*Phot*) exposición *f* ► **time fuse** N temporizador *m*, espoleta *f* graduada, espoleta *f* de tiempo ► **time lag** N (= *delay*) retraso *m*; (= *lack of synchronization*) desfase *m* ► **time limit** N plazo *m*, límite *m* de tiempo; (= *closing date*) fecha *f* tope; **to set a ~ limit (for sth)** fijar un plazo (para algo) ► **time loan** N (*US*) préstamo *m* a plazo fijo ► **time lock** N cerradura *f* de tiempo ► **time machine** N máquina *f* de transporte a través del tiempo ► **time out** N (*esp US Sport, also fig*) tiempo *m* muerto; **to take ~ out (from sth/from doing sth)** descansar (de algo/de hacer algo) ► **time payment** N (*US*) pago *m* a plazos ► **time saver** N **it is a great ~ saver** ahorra mucho tiempo ► **time sheet** N = **time card** ► **time signal** N señal *f* horaria ► **time signature** N (*Mus*) compás *m*, signatura *f* de compás ► **time slice** N fracción *f* de tiempo ► **time switch** N interruptor *m* horario ► **time trial** N (*Cycling*) prueba *f* contra reloj, contrarreloj *f* ► **time warp** N salto *m* en el tiempo, túnel *m* del tiempo ► **time zone** N huso *m* horario

time-consuming ['taɪmkən,sjuːmɪŋ] ADJ que requiere mucho tiempo

time-honoured, **time-honored** (*US*) ['taɪm,ɒnəd] ADJ consagrado

timekeeper ['taɪm,kiːpəʳ] N [1] (= *watch*) reloj *m*, cronómetro *m*
[2] (= *official*) cronometrador/a *m/f*
[3] **to be a good ~** (= *punctual*) ser puntual; **to be a poor ~** (= *not punctual*) no ser nada puntual

timekeeping ['taɪm,kiːpɪŋ] N (*gen*) cronometraje *m*; (*in factory etc*) control *m*; **her ~ has always been very good** siempre ha sido muy puntual

time-lapse photography ['taɪmlæpsfə'tɒgrəfɪ] N fotografía *f* de lapso de tiempo

timeless ['taɪmlɪs] ADJ [*book, experience*] intemporal

timelessness ['taɪmlɪsnɪs] N intemporalidad *f*, atemporalidad *f*

timeliness ['taɪmlɪnɪs] N oportunidad *f*

timely ['taɪmlɪ] ADJ oportuno

timepiece ['taɪmpiːs] N reloj *m*

timer ['taɪməʳ] N [1] (= *egg timer*) reloj *m* de arena
[2] (*Aut*) distribuidor *m*; (*Tech*) reloj *m* automático; (= *regulator*) temporizador *m*

time-saving ['taɪm,seɪvɪŋ] ADJ que ahorra tiempo

timescale ['taɪmskeɪl] N escala *f* de tiempo

time-server ['taɪm,sɜːvəʳ] N (*pej*) contemporizador *m*

time-share ['taɪmʃɛəʳ] Ⓐ N [1] (*for holiday*) multipropiedad *f*
[2] (*Comput*) tiempo *m* compartido
Ⓑ VT (*Comput*) utilizar colectivamente, utilizar en sistema de tiempo compartido
Ⓒ CPD ► **time-share apartment** N piso *m* en multipropiedad

time-sharing ['taɪm,ʃɛərɪŋ] N [1] (*for holiday*) multipropiedad *f*
[2] (*Comput*) tiempo *m* compartido

timetable ['taɪm,teɪbl] Ⓐ N (*for trains, buses*) horario *m*; (= *programme of events etc*) programa *m*, agenda *f*; [*of negotiations*] calendario *m*; (*Scol*) horario *m*; (*as booklet*) guía *f*, horario *m*
Ⓑ VT (*Brit*) programar

timetabling ['taɪmteɪblɪŋ] N programación *f*

time-waster ['taɪm,weɪstəʳ] N (= *activity*) pérdida *f* de tiempo; **to be a ~** (= *person*) ser de los que pierden el tiempo

time-wasting ['taɪmweɪstɪŋ] ADJ que hace perder tiempo

time-worn ['taɪmwɔːn] ADJ [*building*] deteriorado por el tiempo; [*custom, method*] añejo; [*anecdote, phrase*] gastado

timid ['tɪmɪd] ADJ [*person*] tímido; [*animal*] huraño, asustadizo

timidity [tɪ'mɪdɪtɪ] N timidez *f*

timidly ['tɪmɪdlɪ] ADV tímidamente

timidness ['tɪmɪdnɪs] N timidez *f*

timing ['taɪmɪŋ] Ⓐ N [1] (= *time chosen*) **the ~ of the meeting was inconvenient** la hora fijada para la reunión no era muy conveniente; **the ~ of this is important** es importante hacer esto en el momento exacto; **it's all a matter of ~** todo es cuestión de elegir el momento oportuno; **that was good/bad ~** (= *opportunity*) lo hiciste en buen/mal momento; (= *on time*) lo hiciste a tiempo/destiempo
[2] (*Sport*) cronometraje *m*
[3] (= *rhythm*) ritmo *m*, cadencia *f*, compás *m*
Ⓑ CPD (*Mech, Aut*) de distribución, de encendido ► **timing device** N [*of bomb*] temporizador *m* ► **timing gear** N engranaje *m* de distribución ► **timing mechanism** N dispositivo *m* para medir el tiempo

timorous ['tɪmərəs] ADJ (*liter*) [*person*] temeroso, tímido; [*animal*] huraño, asustadizo

Timothy ['tɪməθɪ] N Timoteo

timpani ['tɪmpənɪ] NPL (*Mus*) tímpanos *mpl*, timbales *mpl*

timpanist ['tɪmpənɪst] N timbalero/a *m/f*

tin [tɪn] Ⓐ N [1] (= *ore*) estaño *m*; (= *metal*) hojalata *f*
[2] (*Brit*) (= *container*) lata *f*, bote *m*; **meat in ~s** carne *f* en lata *or* enlatada
Ⓑ VT [1] (*Brit*) [+ *food*] enlatar
[2] (= *coat with tin*) estañar
Ⓒ CPD [*roof, tray, trunk*] de hojalata ► **tin can** N lata *f*, bote *m* ► **tin ear** N (*Mus*) **he has a ~ ear** tiene mal oído ► **tin god** N (*fig*) héroe *m* de cartón ► **tin hat** N casco *m* de acero ► **tin lizzie*** N (*Aut*) genoveva *f*, viejo trasto *m* ► **tin mine** N mina *f* de estaño ► **tin miner** N minero/a *m/f* de estaño ► **tin opener** N (*Brit*) abrelatas *m inv* ► **Tin Pan Alley** N (*Mus*) industria *f* de la música pop ► **tin plate** N hojalata *f* ► **tin soldier** N soldadito *m* de plomo ► **tin tack** N (*Brit*) tachuela *f* ► **tin whistle** N (*Mus*) pito *m*

tincture ['tɪŋktʃəʳ] Ⓐ N tintura *f*
Ⓑ VT tinturar, teñir (**with** de)

tinder ['tɪndəʳ] N (*lit, fig*) yesca *f*; ✦***IDIOM*** **to burn like ~** arder como la yesca

tinderbox ['tɪndəbɒks] N yescas *fpl*; (*fig*) polvorín *m*

tinder-dry [,tɪndə'draɪ] ADJ muy seco, reseco

tine [taɪn] N [*of fork*] diente *m*; [*of pitchfork*] púa *f*

tinfoil ['tɪnfɔɪl] N papel *m* de estaño

ting [tɪŋ] = **tinkle**

ting-a-ling ['tɪŋə'lɪŋ] N tilín *m*; **to go ~** hacer tilín

tinge [tɪndʒ] Ⓐ N [1] [*of colour*] tinte *m*, matiz *m*
[2] (*fig*) [*of irony, sadness*] deje *m*, matiz *m*; **a ~ of nostalgia** cierta nostalgia; **not without a ~ of regret** no sin cierto arrepentimiento
Ⓑ VT [1] (*lit*) teñir, matizar (**with** de)
[2] (*fig*) matizar (**with** de); **pleasure ~d with sadness** placer *m* matizado *or* no exento de tristeza

tingle ['tɪŋgl] Ⓐ N [*of skin*] hormigueo *m*; (= *thrill*) estremecimiento *m*
Ⓑ VI [*ears*] zumbar; **her cheeks were tingling after a walk in the snow** después de pasear por la nieve le ardían las mejillas; **your skin will ~ a bit when you apply the cream** te escocerá un poco la piel al aplicar la crema; **to ~ with excitement** estremecerse de emoción

tingling ['tɪŋglɪŋ] Ⓐ N hormigueo *m*
Ⓑ ADJ **a ~ sensation** una sensación de hormigueo

tingly ['tɪŋglɪ] ADJ **a ~ feeling** una sensación de hormigueo; **my arm feels ~** siento hormigueo en el brazo; **I feel ~ all over** se me estremece todo el cuerpo

tinker ['tɪŋkəʳ] Ⓐ N (*esp Brit*) [1] (= *mender*) calderero *m*; (*pej*) (= *gipsy*) gitano *m*
[2] (*Brit*†*) (= *child*) pícaro/a *m/f*, tunante/a *m/f*; **you little ~!** ¡tunante!
Ⓑ VI (*also* **~ about**) **to ~ with** toquetear, jugar con; **he's been ~ing with the car all day** ha pasado todo el día tratando de reparar el coche; **they're only ~ing with the problem** no se esfuerzan seriamente por resolver el problema

tinkle ['tɪŋkl] Ⓐ N [1] [*of bell etc*] tintín *m*, tintineo *m*
[2] (*Brit Telec**) llamada *f*; **give me a ~ some time** llámame *or* pégame un telefonazo algún día
Ⓑ VI tintinear
Ⓒ VT hacer tintinear

tinkling ['tɪŋklɪŋ] Ⓐ ADJ que hace tilín; **a ~ sound** un tilín; **a ~ stream** un arroyo cantarín
Ⓑ N tintineo *m*, tilín *m*

tinned [tɪnd] ADJ (*Brit*) en *or* de lata, enlatado; **~ peaches** melocotones *mpl* en lata *or* en conserva

tinnitus [tɪ'naɪtəs] N tinnitus *m*, zumbido *m*

tinny ['tɪnɪ] ADJ (*compar* **tinnier**; *superl* **tinniest**)
[1] (= *metallic*) [*sound*] metálico; [*taste*] que sabe a lata
[2] (*pej*) [*car, machine*] poco sólido, de pacotilla

tinpot* ['tɪnpɒt] ADJ de pacotilla, de poca monta

tinsel ['tɪnsəl] Ⓐ N (*lit, fig*) oropel *m*; (= *cloth*) lama *f* de oro/plata
Ⓑ ADJ de oropel; (*fig*) de oropel, de relumbrón

tinsmith ['tɪnsmɪθ] N hojalatero/a *m/f*

tint [tɪnt] Ⓐ N (*gen*) tono *m*, matiz *m*; (*for hair*) tinte *m*
Ⓑ VT teñir, matizar; **to ~ sth blue** teñir *or* matizar algo de azul; **it's yellow ~ed with red** es amarillo matizado de rojo; **to ~ one's hair** teñirse el pelo

tinted ['tɪntɪd] ADJ [*glass, windscreen*] tintado; [*spectacles*] ahumado; [*hair*] teñido

tintinnabulation ['tɪntɪ,næbjʊ'leɪʃən] N (*liter*) campanilleo *m*

tiny ['taɪnɪ] ADJ (*compar* **tinier**; *superl* **tiniest**) diminuto, minúsculo

tip¹ [tɪp] N [1] (= *end*) [*of knife, paintbrush, finger, nose*] punta *f*; [*of shoe, boot*] puntera *f*; **he stood on the ~s of his toes** se puso de puntillas; **he touched it with the ~ of his toe** lo tocó con la punta del pie; **from ~ to toe** de pies a cabeza; **the southern ~ of Florida** el extremo sur de Florida; ✦***IDIOMS*** **it's only the ~ of the iceberg** no es más que la punta del iceberg; **I had it** *or* **it was on the ~ of my tongue** lo tenía en la punta de la lengua; *see also* **asparagus**

[2] (= *protective piece*) [*of umbrella*] contera *f*
[3] (= *filter*) [*of cigarette*] filtro *m*

tip² [tɪp] Ⓐ N [1] (= *gratuity*) propina *f*; **to give sb a ~** dar una propina a algn; **to leave (sb) a ~** dejar propina (a algn)
[2] (= *hint*) consejo *m*; (*Racing, Gambling*) pronóstico *m*; **to give sb a ~** dar un consejo a algn; **let me give you a ~** déjame que te dé un consejo; **take a ~ from an old friend and leave well alone** acepta un consejo de un viejo amigo y mantente bien alejado; **a hot ~*** (*Racing, Gambling*) un pronóstico fiable
Ⓑ VT [1] [+ *driver, waiter*] dar una propina a; **she ~ped the barman ten dollars** le dio diez dólares de propina *or* una propina de diez dólares al barman; **I never know how much to ~** nunca sé cuánto dar de propina
[2] (*Racing, Gambling*) **to ~ the winner** pronosticar quién va a ganar; **her horse was ~ped to win** se pronosticaba que su caballo sería el ganador; **they are ~ped to win the next election** son los favoritos para ganar las próximas elecciones; **he is already being ~ped as a future prime minister** ya se habla de él como de un futuro primer ministro
Ⓒ VI (= *give gratuity*) dar propina

►**tip off** VT + ADV (= *forewarn*) (*gen*) avisar; [+ *police*] dar el soplo a*, dar el chivatazo a (*Sp**); **the police had been ~ped off** a la policía le habían dado el soplo *or* el chivatazo*, la policía había recibido un soplo*

tip³ [tɪp] Ⓐ N [1] (= *rubbish dump*) vertedero *m*, basurero *m*, basural *m* (*LAm*), tiradero(s) *m(pl)* (*Mex*)
[2] (*Brit**) (= *mess*) **this room is a ~** este cuarto es una pocilga*
Ⓑ VT [1] (= *tilt*) inclinar; **he ~ped the soup bowl towards him** inclinó el cuenco de sopa hacia sí; **to ~ sb off their seat** quitar a algn de su asiento (inclinándolo); **~ the cat off the chair** inclina un poco la silla para que se baje el gato; **to ~ one's hat to sb** saludar a algn con el sombrero *or* ladeando el sombrero; ✦***IDIOMS* to ~ the balance** *or* **scales (in sb's favour/against sb)** inclinar la balanza (a favor de algn/en contra de algn); **to ~ sb over the edge** (*into insanity*) sumir algn en la locura; *see also* **scales²**
[2] (= *pour*) **to ~ sth into sth: ~ the vegetables into a bowl** eche las verduras en un cuenco; **they ~ the rubbish into the river** vierten *or* tiran la basura en el río; **he ~ped some sweets into her hand** le echó unos caramelos en la mano; **she ~ped her things out of the suitcase** volcó la maleta y sacó sus cosas
Ⓒ VI [1] (= *incline*) inclinarse, ladearse; (= *topple*) (*also* **~ over**) volcarse, voltearse (*LAm*)
[2] (= *dump rubbish*) tirar *or* (*LAm*) botar basura; **"no tipping"** "prohibido arrojar basura"
[3] ✦***IDIOM* it's ~ping (down)*** está diluviando*

►**tip away** VT + ADV tirar, botar (*LAm*)
►**tip back** Ⓐ VT + ADV [+ *chair*] inclinar hacia atrás; [+ *one's head*] echar hacia atrás
Ⓑ VI + ADV [*chair*] inclinarse hacia atrás
►**tip forward, tip forwards** (*esp Brit*) Ⓐ VT + ADV inclinar hacia delante
Ⓑ VI + ADV [*seat*] inclinarse hacia delante
►**tip out** VT + ADV [+ *contents*] verter; [+ *container*] vaciar
►**tip over** Ⓐ VI + ADV [*chair, vehicle*] volcar, volcarse, voltearse (*LAm*)
Ⓑ VT + ADV volcar
►**tip up** Ⓐ VI + ADV [*seat*] levantarse; [*lorry*] bascular
Ⓑ VT + ADV [+ *chair*] levantar, alzar; [+ *container*] volcar; **she ~ped up her chin defiantly** alzó la barbilla con gesto desafiante

tip⁴ [tɪp] Ⓐ N (= *tap*) golpecito *m*
Ⓑ VT (= *tap, touch*) tocar ligeramente

tip-off [ˈtɪpɒf] N (= *warning*) información *f*, advertencia *f*; (*to police*) soplo* *m*, chivatazo *m* (*Sp**)

tipped [tɪpt] ADJ [*cigarette*] con filtro; **the end of the walking stick was ~ with metal** la contera del bastón era de metal; **they use arrows which are ~ with poison** utilizan flechas con las puntas envenenadas; **the parrots' wings were ~ with red** los loros tenían los extremos de las alas de color rojo

-tipped [tɪpt] ADJ (*ending in compounds*) **a gold-tipped cane** un bastón con la contera de oro; **the black-tipped wings of the albatross** las alas de puntas negras *or* negras en los extremos de los albatros

tipper [ˈtɪpəʳ] Ⓐ N [1] (= *vehicle*) volquete *m*
[2] (= *person*) **he is a good** *or* **big ~** es de los que dejan buenas propinas
Ⓑ CPD ► **tipper truck** N volquete *m*

tippet [ˈtɪpɪt] N esclavina *f*

Tipp-Ex® [ˈtɪpeks] Ⓐ N Tippex® *m*, corrector *m*
Ⓑ VT (*also* **~ out, ~ over**) corregir con Tippex

tipple* [ˈtɪpl] (*Brit*) Ⓐ N **his ~ is Cointreau** él bebe Cointreau; **what's your ~?** ¿qué quieres tomar?
Ⓑ VI empinar el codo

tippler* [ˈtɪpləʳ] N (*Brit*) amante *mf* de la bebida; **he's a bit of a ~** le gusta tomar un trago de vez en cuando

tippy-toe [ˈtɪpɪtəʊ] (*US*) = **tiptoe**

tipsily [ˈtɪpsɪlɪ] ADV como borracho; **to walk ~** andar con pasos de borracho

tipster [ˈtɪpstəʳ] N pronosticador(a) *m/f*

tipsy [ˈtɪpsɪ] ADJ (*compar* **tipsier**, *superl* **tipsiest**) achispado, piripi (*Sp**), tomado (*LAm**)

tiptoe [ˈtɪptəʊ] Ⓐ N **to walk on ~** andar *or* (*LAm*) caminar de puntillas; **to stand on ~** ponerse de puntillas
Ⓑ VI ir de puntillas; **to ~ to the window** ir de puntillas a la ventana; **to ~ across the floor** cruzar el cuarto de puntillas; **to ~ in/out** entrar/salir de puntillas

tiptop [ˈtɪpˈtɒp] ADJ de primera, excelente; **in ~ condition** [*car*] en excelentes condiciones; [*person*] en plena forma; **a ~ show** un espectáculo de primerísima calidad

tip-truck [ˈtɪptrʌk] N volquete *m*

tip-up [ˈtɪpʌp] ADJ [*truck*] con volquete; [*seat*] abatible

tirade [taɪˈreɪd] N diatriba *f*

tire¹ [ˈtaɪəʳ] Ⓐ VT cansar
Ⓑ VI cansarse; **he ~s easily** se cansa fácilmente; **to ~ of sb/sth** cansarse *or* aburrirse de algn/algo

►**tire out** VT + ADV agotar, dejar rendido

tire² [ˈtaɪəʳ] N (*US*) = **tyre**

tired [ˈtaɪəd] ADJ [1] [*person, eyes*] cansado; [*voice*] cansino; **to be/feel ~** estar/sentirse cansado; **my legs/eyes are ~** tengo las piernas cansadas/los ojos cansados; **to get ~** cansarse; **to look ~** tener cara de cansancio; **to be ~ of sb/sth** estar cansado *or* aburrido de algn/algo; **to get** *or* **grow ~ of (doing) sth** cansarse *or* aburrirse de (hacer) algo; **to be ~ out** estar agotado *or* rendido; *see also* **sick A3**
[2] (*fig*) (= *worn-out*) [*coat*] raído, gastado; [*car, chair*] cascado; [*cliché, ritual, excuse*] manido, trillado; **a ~ lettuce leaf** una hoja de lechuga mustia; **it's a ~ old cliché** es un tópico muy manido *or* trillado

tiredly [ˈtaɪədlɪ] ADV [*smile, get up*] con aire cansado; [*say, reply*] con voz cansina

tiredness [ˈtaɪədnɪs] N cansancio *m*

tireless [ˈtaɪəlɪs] ADJ [*person, work*] incansable, infatigable

tirelessly [ˈtaɪəlɪslɪ] ADV incansablemente, infatigablemente

tiresome [ˈtaɪəsəm] ADJ [*job, situation, person*] pesado, aburrido

tiring [ˈtaɪərɪŋ] ADJ cansado, cansador (*S. Cone*); **it's very ~** es muy cansado

tiro [ˈtaɪərəʊ] N = **tyro**

tisane [tɪˈzæn] N tisana *f*

tissue [ˈtɪʃuː] Ⓐ N [1] (= *thin paper*) (*for wrapping, decoration*) papel *m* de seda; (= *paper handkerchief*) pañuelo *m* de papel, klínex *m inv*
[2] (*Anat*) tejido *m*
[3] (*fig*) **a ~ of lies** una sarta de mentiras
Ⓑ CPD ► **tissue paper** N (*for wrapping, decoration*) papel *m* de seda; (= *paper handkerchief*) pañuelo *m* de papel, klínex® *m inv*

tit¹ [tɪt] N (= *bird*) paro *m*, herrerillo *m*; **blue ~** herrerillo *m* común, alionín *m*; **coal ~** carbonero *m* garrapinos; **long-tailed ~** mito *m*

tit² [tɪt] N ✦***IDIOM* ~ for tat** ojo por ojo; **so that was ~ for tat** así que ajustamos cuentas, así que le pagué en la misma moneda; **~-for-tat killing** asesinato *m* en represalia, (asesinato *m* por) ajuste *m* de cuentas

tit³** [tɪt] N [1] (= *breast*) teta* *f*; ✦***IDIOM* to get on sb's ~s**** sacar de quicio a algn, cabrear a algn*
[2] (= *person*) gilipollas** *m*

Titan [ˈtaɪtən] N titán *m*

titanic [taɪˈtænɪk] ADJ [*struggle*] titánico; [*scale, proportions*] inmenso, gigantesco

titanium [tɪˈteɪnɪəm] N titanio *m*

titbit [ˈtɪtbɪt], **tidbit** [ˈtɪdbɪt] (*US*) N [*of food*] golosina *f*; [*of gossip*] cotilleo *m*

titch* [tɪtʃ] N enano/a* *m/f*, renacuajo* *m*

titchy* [ˈtɪtʃɪ] ADJ pequeñito*, chiquitito*

titfer†** [ˈtɪtfəʳ] N (*Brit*) sombrero *m*

tithe [taɪð] N diezmo *m*

Titian [ˈtɪʃɪən] N Ticiano

titillate [ˈtɪtɪleɪt] VT [+ *audience, reader*] despertar el interés de; (*sexually*) excitar

titillation [ˌtɪtɪˈleɪʃən] N [*of audience, reader*] estimulación *f*; (*sexual*) excitación *f*

titivate [ˈtɪtɪveɪt] Ⓐ VT emperejilar, arreglar; **to ~ o.s.** emperejilarse, arreglarse
Ⓑ VI emperejilarse, arreglarse

title [ˈtaɪtl] Ⓐ N [1] [*of book, chapter*] título *m*; (= *headline*) titular *m*, cabecera *f*; **what ~ are you giving the book?** ¿qué título vas a dar al libro?, ¿cómo vas a titular el libro?
[2] (= *form of address*) fórmula *f* de tratamiento, tratamiento *m*; [*of nobility etc*] título *m*; **what ~ should I give him?** ¿qué tratamiento debo darle?; **noble ~** ◊ **~ of nobility** título *m* de nobleza; **George V gave him a ~** Jorge V le dio un título de nobleza *or* le ennobleció; **what's your job ~?** ¿cómo se llama *or* qué nombre recibe tu puesto?
[3] (*Sport*) título *m*; **to hold a ~** ser campeón/ona *m/f*, tener un título
[4] (*Publishing*) (= *book, periodical*) título *m*, publicación *f*
[5] (*Jur*) (= *right*) derecho *m*; **his ~ to the property** su derecho a la propiedad
[6] **titles** (*Cine, TV*) créditos *mpl*; **the opening/closing ~s** créditos *mpl* iniciales/finales

Ⓑ VT titular, intitular (*frm*)
Ⓒ CPD ► **title deed** N (*Jur*) título *m* de propiedad ► **title fight** N combate *m* por el título ► **title holder** N (*Sport*) campeón/ona *m/f* ► **title page** N portada *f* ► **title role** N (*Theat, Cine*) papel *m* principal ► **title track** N (*Mus*) corte *m* que da nombre al álbum

titled ['taɪtld] ADJ [*person*] con título de nobleza

titmouse ['tɪtmaʊs] N (*pl* **titmice** ['tɪtmaɪs]) paro *m*

titrate ['taɪtreɪt] VT valorar

titration [taɪ'treɪʃən] N valoración *f*

titter ['tɪtəʳ] Ⓐ N (= *snigger*) risa *f* tonta
Ⓑ VI reírse tontamente

tittle ['tɪtl] N pizca *f*, ápice *m*; **there's not a ~ of truth in it** eso no tiene ni pizca de verdad

tittle-tattle* ['tɪtl,tætl] Ⓐ N chismes *mpl*
Ⓑ VI chismear

titty* ['tɪtɪ] N teta* *f*; ✦**IDIOM that's tough ~!** ¡mala suerte!

titular ['tɪtjʊləʳ] ADJ titular; (= *in name only*) nominal

tiz* [tɪz] N = **tizzy**

tizzy* ['tɪzɪ] N **to be in/get into a ~ (about sth)** (= *nervous*) estar/ponerse nervioso (por algo); (= *hassled*) estar hecho/hacerse un lío (por algo)

T-junction ['tiː,dʒʌŋkʃən] N (*Aut*) cruce *m* en T

TLC N ABBR = **tender loving care**

TLS N ABBR (*Brit*) (= **Times Literary Supplement**) *revista literaria*

TM N ABBR [1] = **transcendental meditation**
[2] (*Comm*) = **trademark**

TN ABBR (*US*) = **Tennessee**

TNT N ABBR (= **trinitrotoluene**) TNT *m*

---

to [tʊ, tuː, tə]

[A] PREPOSITION	[C] ADVERB
[B] INFINITIVE PARTICLE	

Ⓐ PREPOSITION

When **to** *is the second element in a phrasal verb, eg* **set to, heave to**, *look up the phrasal verb. When* **to** *is part of a set combination, eg* **nice to, to my mind, to all appearances, appeal to**, *look up the other word.*

[1] *destination* a

Note: **a** + **el** = **al**

it's 90 kilometres to Lima de aquí a Lima hay 90 kilómetros, hay 90 kilómetros a Lima; **a letter to his wife** una carta a su mujer; **he fell to the floor** cayó al suelo; **to go to Paris/Spain** ir a París/España; **to go to Peru** ir al Perú; **to go to school/university** ir al colegio/a la Universidad; **to go to the doctor's** ir al médico; **I liked the exhibition, I went to it twice** me gustó la exposición, fui a verla dos veces; [BUT] **we're going to John's/my parents' for Christmas** vamos a casa de John/mis padres por Navidad; **have you ever been to India?** ¿has estado alguna vez en la India?; **flights to Heathrow** vuelos a *or* con destino a Heathrow; **the road to Edinburgh** la carretera de Edimburgo; *see also* **church A2**

[2] *= towards* hacia; **he walked slowly to the door** caminó despacio hacia la puerta; **he turned to me** se giró hacia mí; **move it to the left/right** muévelo hacia la izquierda/derecha

[3] *= as far as* hasta; **from here to London** de aquí a *or* hasta Londres; **I'll see you to the door** te acompaño hasta la puerta

[4] *= up to* hasta; **to count to ten** contar hasta diez; **it's accurate to (within) a millimetre** es exacto hasta el milímetro; [BUT] **to some extent** hasta cierto punto, en cierta medida; **we are expecting 40 to 50 people** esperamos entre 40 y 50 personas; **to this day I still don't know what he meant** aún hoy no sé lo que quiso decir; **eight years ago to the day** hoy hace exactamente ocho años; **he didn't stay to the end** no se quedó hasta el final; **from Monday to Friday** de lunes a viernes; **from morning to night** de la mañana a la noche, desde la mañana hasta la noche; **funds to the value of ...** fondos por valor de ...; *see also* **decimal A**

[5] *= located at* a; **the door is to the left (of the window)** la puerta está a la izquierda (de la ventana); **the airport is to the west of the city** el aeropuerto está al oeste de la ciudad

[6] *= against* contra; **he stood with his back to the wall** estaba con la espalda contra la pared; **he clasped her to him** la estrechó contra sí; [BUT] **to turn a picture to the wall** volver un cuadro mirando a la pared

[7] *when telling time* **it's a quarter to three** son las tres menos cuarto, es *or* (*LAm*) falta un cuarto para las tres; **at eight minutes to ten** a las diez menos ocho

[8] *introducing indirect object* a; **to give sth to sb** dar algo a algn; **I gave it to my friend** se lo di a mi amigo; **the man I sold it to** *or* (*frm*) **to whom I sold it** el hombre a quien se lo vendí; [BUT] **it belongs to me** me pertenece (a mí), es mío; **they were kind to me** fueron amables conmigo; **it's new to me** es nuevo para mí; **what is that to me?** ¿y a mí qué me importa eso?; **"that's strange," I said to myself** —es raro —me dije para mis adentros

[9] *in dedications, greetings* **greetings to all our friends!** ¡saludos a todos los amigos!; **welcome to you all!** ¡bienvenidos todos!; **"to P.R. Lilly"** (*in book*) "para P.R. Lilly"; **here's to you!** ¡va por ti!, ¡por ti!; **a monument to the fallen** un monumento a los caídos, un monumento en honor a los caídos

[10] *in ratios, proportions* por; **there were three men to a cell** había tres hombres por celda; **it does 30 miles to the gallon** hace 30 millas por galón; **eight apples to the kilo** ocho manzanas por kilo; **there are about five pesos to the dollar** son unos cinco pesos por dólar; **a scale of 1 centimetre to 1 kilometre** una escala de 1 centímetro por kilómetro; **200 people to the square mile** 200 personas por milla cuadrada; [BUT] **the odds are 8 to 1** las probabilidades son de 8 a 1; **the odds against it happening are a million to one** las probabilidades de que eso ocurra son una entre un millón; **by a majority of 12 to 10** por una mayoría de 12 a 10; **they won by four goals to two** ganaron por cuatro goles a dos; **three to the fourth** ◊ **three to the power of four** (*Math*) tres a la cuarta potencia

[11] *in comparisons* a; **superior to the others** superior a los demás; **A is to B as C is to D** A es a B como C es a D; [BUT] **that's nothing to what is to come** eso no es nada en comparación con lo que está por venir

[12] *= about, concerning* **what do you say to that?** ¿qué te parece (eso)?; **what would you say to a beer?** ¿te parece que tomemos una cerveza?; **"to repairing pipes: ..."** (*on bill*) "reparación de las cañerías: ..."

[13] *= according to* según; **to my way of thinking** a mi modo de ver, según mi modo de pensar

[14] *= to the accompaniment of* **we danced to the music of the band** bailamos con la música de la orquesta; **they came out to the strains of the national anthem** salieron a los compases del himno nacional; **it is sung to the tune of "Tipperary"** se canta con la melodía de "Tipperary"

[15] *= of, for* de; **the key to the front door** la llave de la puerta principal; **assistant to the manager** asistente del gerente; [BUT] **he was a good father to the children** fue un buen padre para sus hijos; **it offers a solution to your problem** te ofrece una solución para el problema; **we've found the solution to the problem** hemos encontrado solución al problema; **the British ambassador to Moscow** el embajador británico en Moscú; **he has been a good friend to us** ha sido un buen amigo para nosotros

[16] *with gerund/noun* **to look forward to doing sth** tener muchas ganas de hacer algo; **I'm really looking forward to the holidays** estoy deseando que lleguen las vacaciones; **to prefer painting to drawing** preferir pintar a dibujar; **to be used to (doing) sth** estar acostumbrado a (hacer) algo

[17] *in set expressions* **to this end** a *or* con este fin; **to my enormous shame I did nothing** para gran vergüenza mía, no hice nada; **to my great surprise** con gran sorpresa por mi parte, para gran sorpresa mía

Ⓑ INFINITIVE PARTICLE

[1] *infinitive* **to come** venir; **to sing** cantar; **to work** trabajar

[2] *following another verb* [2·1]

A preposition may be required with the Spanish infinitive, depending on what precedes it: look up the verb.

she refused to listen se negó a escuchar; **to start to cry** empezar *or* ponerse a llorar; **to try to do sth** tratar de hacer algo, intentar hacer algo; **to want to do sth** querer hacer algo

[2·2] (*object as subject of following infinitive*) **I'd advise you to think this over** te aconsejaría que te pensaras bien esto; **he'd like me to give up work** le gustaría que dejase de trabajar; **we'd prefer him to go to university** preferiríamos que fuese a la universidad; **I want you to do it** quiero que lo hagas

[2·3] **I have things to do** tengo cosas que hacer; **he has a lot to lose** tiene mucho que perder; **there was no one for me to ask** ◊ **there wasn't anyone for me to ask** no había nadie a quien yo pudiese preguntar; **he's not the sort** *or* **type to do that** no es de los que hacen eso; **that book is still to be written** ese libro está todavía por escribir; **now is the time to do it** ahora es el momento de hacerlo; **and who is he to criticize?** ¿y quién es él para criticar?

[3] *purpose, result* para; **he did it to help you** lo hizo para ayudarte; **I have done nothing to deserve this** no he hecho nada para merecer esto; **it disappeared, never to be seen again** desapareció para siempre; [BUT] **I arrived to find she had gone** cuando llegué me encontré con que se había ido; **he came to see you** vino a verte; **he's gone to get the paper** ha ido a por el periódico

[4] *standing in for verb*

to *is not translated when it stands for the infinitive:*

we didn't want to sell it but we had to no queríamos venderlo pero tuvimos que hacerlo *or* no hubo más remedio; **"would you like to come to dinner?" — "I'd love to!"** —¿te gustaría venir a cenar? —¡me encantaría!; **you may not want to do it but you ought to for the sake of your education** tal vez no quieres hacerlo pero deberías en aras de tu educación; **I don't want to** no quiero; **I for-**

got to se me olvidó

5 *after adjective*

For combinations like **difficult/easy/foolish/ready/slow to** *etc, look up the adjective.*

it is very expensive to live in London resulta muy caro vivir en Londres; **it's hard to describe the feeling** es difícil describir la sensación; **these dogs are hard to control** estos perros son difíciles de controlar; **the first/last to go** el primero/último en irse; **he's young to be a grandfather** es joven para ser abuelo; → EASY, DIFFICULT, IMPOSSIBLE

6 *in exclamations* **and then to be let down like that!** ¡y para que luego te decepcionen así!; **and to think he didn't mean a word of it!** ¡y pensar que nada de lo que dijo era de verdad!

7 **to see him now one would never think that …** al verlo *or* viéndolo ahora nadie creería que …

Ⓒ ADVERB

to pull the door to tirar de la puerta para cerrarla, cerrar la puerta tirando; **to push the door to** empujar la puerta para cerrarla, cerrar la puerta empujando

toad [təʊd] N sapo *m*

toadflax ['təʊdflæks] N linaria *f*

toad-in-the-hole [ˌtəʊdɪnðə'həʊl] N (*Brit Culin*) salchichas *fpl* en pasta

toadstool ['təʊdstuːl] N hongo *m* venenoso

toady ['təʊdɪ] (*pej*) Ⓐ N adulador(a) *m/f*, pelotilla* *mf inv*, pelota* *mf*

Ⓑ VI **to ~ to sb** adular *or* hacer la pelotilla a algn*, dar coba a algn*

toadying ['təʊdɪɪŋ], **toadyism** ['təʊdɪɪzəm] N adulación *f* servil, coba* *f*

toast [təʊst] Ⓐ N 1 (= *bread*) pan *m* tostado, tostada *f*; **a piece of ~** una tostada

2 (= *drink*) brindis *m inv* (**to** por); **to drink a ~ to sb** brindar por algn; **here's a ~ to all who …** brindemos por todos los que …; **to propose a ~ to sb** proponer un brindis por algn; ✦*IDIOM* **to be the ~ of the town** ser el niño bonito/la niña bonita de la ciudad

Ⓑ VT 1 [+ *bread*] tostar; **~ed sandwich** sándwich *m* tostado; **to ~ one's toes by the fire** calentar los pies cerca del fuego

2 (= *drink to*) brindar por; **we ~ed the newlyweds** brindamos por los recién casados; **we ~ed the victory in champagne** celebramos la victoria con champán

Ⓒ CPD ► **toast list** N lista *f* de brindis ► **toast rack** N rejilla *f* para tostadas

toaster ['təʊstəʳ] N tostadora *f*

toasting fork ['təʊstɪŋfɔːk] N tostadera *f*

toastmaster ['təʊstˌmɑːstəʳ] N *persona que propone los brindis y presenta a los oradores*

toasty ['təʊstɪ] Ⓐ N sándwich *m* tostado

Ⓑ ADJ (*) (= *warm*) calentito

tobacco [tə'bækəʊ] Ⓐ N (*pl* **tobaccos, tobaccoes**) tabaco *m*; *see also* **pipe**

Ⓑ CPD ► **tobacco industry** N industria *f* tabacalera ► **tobacco jar** N tabaquera *f* ► **tobacco plant** N planta *f* de tabaco ► **tobacco plantation** N tabacal *m* ► **tobacco pouch** N petaca *f*

tobacconist [tə'bækənɪst] N (*Brit*) estanquero/a *m/f*, tabaquero/a *m/f*; **~'s (shop)** estanco *m*, tabaquería *f*

Tobago [tə'beɪgəʊ] N Tobago *f*

-to-be [tə'biː] ADJ (*ending in compounds*) futuro; **mothers-to-be** futuras madres

toboggan [tə'bɒgən] Ⓐ N tobogán *m*

Ⓑ VI ir en tobogán, deslizarse en tobogán

Ⓒ CPD ► **toboggan run** N pista *f* de tobogán

toby jug ['təʊbɪdʒʌg] N *bock de cerveza en forma de hombre*

toccata [tə'kɑːtə] N tocata *f*

tocsin ['tɒksɪn] N 1 (= *alarm*) campana *f* de alarma, rebato *m*

2 (*fig*) voz *f* de alarma; **to sound the ~** dar la voz de alarma, tocar a rebato

tod* [tɒd] N (*Brit*) **on one's ~** a solas

today [tə'deɪ] Ⓐ ADV 1 (= *the present day*) hoy; **from ~** desde hoy, a partir de hoy; **early ~** hoy temprano; **all day ~** todo el día de hoy; **what day is it ~?** ¿qué día es hoy?, ¿a cuántos estamos?; **what date is it ~?** ¿a qué fecha estamos?; **~ week** ◊ **a week ~** de hoy en ocho días, dentro de una semana; **a fortnight ~** de hoy en quince días, dentro de dos semanas; **a year ago ~** hoy hace un año; ✦*IDIOM* **here ~ and gone tomorrow** se cambia constantemente

2 (= *these days*) hoy (en) día; **young people ~ have it easy** la gente joven lo tiene muy fácil hoy en día

Ⓑ N 1 (= *the present day*) hoy *m*; **~ is Monday** hoy es lunes; **~ is the 4th of March** hoy es el cuatro de marzo; **~'s paper** el periódico de hoy

2 (= *these days*) hoy *m*, el presente; **the writers of ~** los escritores de hoy

toddle ['tɒdl] VI 1 (= *begin to walk*) empezar a andar, dar los primeros pasos; (= *walk unsteadily*) caminar sin seguridad

2 (*) (= *go*) marcharse; (= *stroll*) dar un paseo; (= *depart*) (*also* **~ off**) irse, marcharse; **he ~d off** se marchó; **we must be toddling** es hora de irnos; **so I ~d round to see him** así que fui a visitarle

toddler ['tɒdləʳ] N (= *small child*) niño/a *m/f* pequeño/a (que empieza a caminar *or* en edad de aprender a andar)

toddy ['tɒdɪ] N **hot ~** ponche *m*

to-do* [tə'duː] N (*pl* **to-dos**) (= *fuss*) lío *m*, follón *m* (*Sp**); **there was a great ~** hubo un tremendo lío; **what's all the ~ about?** ¿a qué tanto jaleo?; **she made a great ~** armó un lío imponente*

toe [təʊ] Ⓐ N (*Anat*) dedo *m* del pie; [*of shoe*] puntera *f*; [*of sock*] punta *f*; **big/little ~** dedo *m* gordo/pequeño del pie; **to tread** *or* **step on sb's ~s** (*lit*) pisar el pie a algn; (*fig*) meterse con algn; ✦*IDIOMS* **to keep sb on his ~s** mantener a algn sobre ascuas; **to keep on one's ~s** estar alerta, mantenerse bien despierto; **you have to keep on your ~s** hay que estar alerta, hay que mantenerse bien despierto; **to turn up one's ~s*** estirar la pata*

Ⓑ VT tocar con la punta del pie; ✦*IDIOM* **to ~ the line** (= *conform*) conformarse

Ⓒ CPD ► **toe clip** N (*for cycling*) rastral *m*, calapiés *m* ► **toe piece** N espátula *f*, punta *f*

toecap ['təʊkæp] N puntera *f*

toe-curling* ['təʊˌkɜːlɪŋ] ADJ sonrojante, bochornoso

-toed [təʊd] ADJ (*ending in compounds*) de … dedos del pie; **four-toed** de cuatro dedos del pie

TOEFL ['təʊfəl] N ABBR = **Test of English as a Foreign Language**

toehold ['təʊhəʊld] N punto *m* de apoyo (para el pie); (*fig*) espacio *m*

toenail ['təʊneɪl] N uña *f* del dedo del pie

toerag* ['təʊræg] N (*Brit*) mequetrefe* *m*

toff* [tɒf] N (*Brit*) encopetado/a *m/f*

toffee ['tɒfɪ] Ⓐ N caramelo *m*, dulce *m* de leche; ✦*IDIOM* **he/she can't do it for ~*** no tiene ni idea de cómo hacerlo

Ⓑ CPD ► **toffee apple** N manzana *f* de caramelo

toffee-nosed* ['tɒfɪ'nəʊzd] ADJ presumido, engreído

tofu ['təʊˌfuː] N tofu *m*, tofú *m*

tog [tɒg] Ⓐ VT (*) **to ~ sb up** ataviar a algn (**in** de); **to ~ o.s. up** ataviarse, vestirse (**in** de), emperejilarse; **to get ~ged up** ataviarse, vestirse

Ⓑ N 1 (*Brit*) (= *measure*) tog *m* calorífico, *unidad que sirve para medir lo que abrigan los tejidos, prendas de ropa, edredones, etc.*

2 **togs*** (= *clothes*) ropa *fsing*

toga ['təʊgə] N toga *f*

together [tə'geðəʳ]

When **together** *is an element in a phrasal verb, eg* **bring together, get together, sleep together**, *look up the verb.*

Ⓐ ADV 1 (= *in company*) [*live, work, be*] juntos/as; **now we're ~** ahora estamos juntos; **they work ~** trabajan juntos; **~ they managed it** entre los dos lo lograron; **all ~** todos/as juntos/as, todos/as en conjunto; **they were all ~ in the bar** todos estaban reunidos en el bar; **they belong ~** [*couple*] están hechos el uno para el otro; [*socks*] esos van juntos; **let's get it ~*** (*fig*) organicémonos, pongamos manos a la obra; **we're in this ~** estamos metidos todos por igual; **they were all in it ~** (*pej*) todos estaban metidos en el asunto; **to put a meal ~** preparar una comida; **to put a show ~** montar un show; **~ with** junto con; **~ with his colleagues, he accepted responsibility** él, junto con sus colegas, admitió ser responsable

2 (= *simultaneously*) a la vez; **you can't all get in ~** no podéis entrar todos a la vez; **don't all talk ~** no habléis todos a la vez; **all ~ now!** (*singing*) ¡todos en coro!; (*pulling*) ¡todos a la vez!; **we'll do parts A and B ~** haremos juntamente las partes A y B

3 (= *continuously*) seguidos/as; **for weeks ~** durante semanas seguidas

Ⓑ ADJ (*) (= *well-adjusted*) equilibrado, cabal

togetherness [tə'geðənɪs] N compañerismo *m*

toggle ['tɒgl] Ⓐ N (*on coat*) botón *m* alargado de madera

Ⓑ CPD ► **toggle key** N (*Comput*) tecla *f* de conmutación binaria ► **toggle switch** N (*Elec*) conmutador *m* de palanca

Togo ['təʊgəʊ] N Togo *m*

Togolese [ˌtəʊgəʊ'liːz] Ⓐ ADJ togolés

Ⓑ N togolés/esa *m/f*

toil [tɔɪl] (*liter*) Ⓐ N trabajo *m*, esfuerzo *m*; **after months of ~** después de meses de trabajo (agotador)

Ⓑ VI 1 (= *work hard*) trabajar duro; **to ~ away at sth** darle duro a algo; **to ~ to do sth** esforzarse *or* afanarse por hacer algo; **they ~ed on into the night** siguieron trabajando hasta muy entrada la noche

2 (= *move with difficulty*) **to ~ along** caminar con dificultad, avanzar penosamente; **to ~ up a hill** subir trabajosamente una cuesta; **the engine is beginning to ~** el motor empieza a funcionar con dificultad

toilet ['tɔɪlɪt] Ⓐ N 1 (= *lavatory*) 1·1 (= *room*) servicio *m*, wáter *m*, lavabo *m*, baño *m* (*esp LAm*); **"Toilets"** "Servicios", "Baño"; **to go to the ~** ir al servicio *or* al baño; **she's in the ~** está en el servicio *or* el baño

1·2 (= *installation*) wáter *m*, retrete *m*, inodoro *m* (*euph, frm*); **the ~ is blocked** se ha atascado el wáter *or* retrete; **to throw sth down the ~** tirar algo al wáter *or* retrete

2 (= *dressing, washing etc*) aseo *m*

Ⓑ CPD ► **toilet articles** NPL artículos *mpl* de

tocador ► **toilet bag** N neceser *m* ► **toilet bowl** N taza *f* (de retrete) ► **toilet case** N = **toilet bag** ► **toilet pan** N = **toilet bowl** ► **toilet paper** N papel *m* higiénico ► **toilet requisites** NPL = **toilet articles** ► **toilet roll** N rollo *m* de papel higiénico ► **toilet seat** N asiento *m* de retrete ► **toilet set** N juego *m* de tocador ► **toilet soap** N jabón *m* de tocador ► **toilet tissue** N = **toilet paper** ► **toilet training** N **~ training can be difficult** acostumbrar a un niño a ir solo al baño puede resultar difícil ► **toilet water** N agua *f* de colonia, colonia *f*

toiletries [ˈtɔɪlɪtrɪz] NPL artículos *mpl* de tocador

toilette [twɑːˈlet] N = **toilet A2**

toilet-train [ˈtɔɪlɪttreɪn] VT **to ~ a child** acostumbrar a un niño a ir solo al baño

toils [tɔɪlz] NPL (*liter*) (= *snares, nets*) redes *fpl*, lazos *mpl*

toilsome [ˈtɔɪlsəm] ADJ (*liter*) penoso, laborioso, arduo

toilworn [ˈtɔɪlwɔːn] ADJ (*liter*) completamente cansado

toing [ˈtuːɪŋ] N **~ and froing** ir y venir *m*, idas y vueltas *fpl*

toke‡ [təʊk] (*Drugs*) Ⓐ N calada* *f*
Ⓑ VI dar una calada*

token [ˈtəʊkən] Ⓐ N [1] (= *voucher*) vale *m*; (= *metal disc*) ficha *f*
[2] (= *sign, symbol*) muestra *f*, señal *f*; (= *remembrance*) prenda *f*, recuerdo *m*; [*of one's appreciation etc*] detalle *m*; **love ~** prenda *f* de amor; **as a ~ of friendship** como prueba de amistad; **this is just a small ~ of our appreciation** esto no es más que un detalle en señal de (nuestro) agradecimiento; **by the same ~** por la misma razón
Ⓑ ADJ [*payment, resistance, gesture*] simbólico; [*strike*] nominal, simbólico; **the ~ black** el negro simbólico; **~ woman** mujer-muestra *f*, representación *f* femenina

tokenism [ˈtəʊkənɪzəm] N programa *m* político de fachada

Tokyo [ˈtəʊkjəʊ] N Tokio *m*, Tokío *m*

told [təʊld] PT, PP *of* **tell**

tolerable [ˈtɒlərəbl] ADJ [1] (= *bearable*) [*pain, heat*] soportable, tolerable
[2] (= *not too bad*) [*film, food*] pasable

tolerably [ˈtɒlərəblɪ] ADV (= *moderately*) [*good, comfortable*] medianamente; **a ~ good player** un jugador pasable; **it is ~ certain that …** es casi seguro que …

tolerance [ˈtɒlərəns] N tolerancia *f*; **she had shown great ~** había mostrado una gran tolerancia; **he had built up a ~ to his medication** (= *receptiveness*) cada vez toleraba mejor la medicación; (= *resistance*) la medicación ya no le surtía efecto

tolerant [ˈtɒlərənt] ADJ [1] (= *open-minded*) [*person, society, attitude*] tolerante; **to be ~ of sb/sth** ser tolerante con algn/algo
[2] (*Med*) **to be ~ to sth** tolerar algo; **his body is becoming ~ to the drugs** (= *receptive*) su cuerpo tolera cada vez mejor los medicamentos; (= *resistant*) los medicamentos ya no le surten efecto

tolerantly [ˈtɒlərəntlɪ] ADV con tolerancia

▼**tolerate** [ˈtɒləreɪt] VT [+ *heat, pain*] aguantar, soportar; [+ *person*] tolerar, soportar; **I can't ~ any more** no aguanto más; **are we to ~ this?** ¿hemos de soportar esto?; **it is not to be ~d** es intolerable, es insoportable

toleration [ˌtɒləˈreɪʃən] N tolerancia *f*; **religious ~** tolerancia *f* religiosa

toll¹ [təʊl] Ⓐ N [1] (*on road, bridge*) peaje *m*, cuota *f* (*Mex*); **to pay ~** pagar el peaje
[2] (= *losses, casualties*) número *m* de víctimas, mortandad *f*; **the death ~ on the roads** el número de víctimas de accidentes de tráfico; **there is a heavy ~** hay muchas víctimas, son muchos los muertos; **the disease takes a heavy ~ each year** cada año la enfermedad se lleva a muchas víctimas *or* causa gran número de muertes; **the effort took its ~ on all of us** el esfuerzo tuvo un grave efecto en todos nosotros; **the severe weather has taken its ~ on the crops** el mal tiempo ha ocasionado pérdidas en la cosecha
Ⓑ CPD ► **toll bar** N barrera *f* de peaje ► **toll booth** N cabina *f* de peaje ► **toll bridge** N puente *m* de peaje *or* (*Mex*) de cuota ► **toll call** N (*US Telec*) conferencia *f* ► **toll gate** N barrera *f* de peaje ► **toll motorway** N (*Brit*) autopista *f* de peaje ► **toll road** N carretera *f* de peaje

toll² [təʊl] Ⓐ VT [+ *bell*] tañer, tocar; **to ~ the hour** dar la hora
Ⓑ VI [*bell*] tañer, doblar; **the bells were ~ing in mourning for …** doblaron las campanas en señal de duelo por …; **"for whom the bell ~s"** "por quién doblan las campanas"
Ⓒ N [*of bell*] tañido *m*, doblar *m*

toll-free [ˌtəʊlˈfriː] ADV (*US Telec*) **to call ~** llamar gratuitamente

tolling [ˈtəʊlɪŋ] N tañido *m*, doblar *m*

tollkeeper [ˈtəʊlˌkiːpəʳ] N peajero *m*, portazguero *m*

tollway [ˈtəʊlweɪ] N (*US*) autopista *f* de peaje *or* (*Mex*) cuota

Tom [tɒm] Ⓐ N (*familiar form*) *of* **Thomas**; ✦*IDIOM* **any ~, Dick or Harry** un fulano cualquiera
Ⓑ CPD ► **Tom Thumb** N Pulgarcito

tom [tɒm] N (*also* **~ cat**) gato *m* (macho)

tomahawk [ˈtɒməhɔːk] N tomahawk *m*; ✦*IDIOM* **to bury the ~** (*US*) echar pelillos a la mar, envainar la espada

tomato [təˈmɑːtəʊ, (*US*) təˈmeɪtəʊ] Ⓐ N (*pl* **tomatoes**) (= *fruit*) tomate *m*, jitomate *m* (*Mex*); (= *plant*) tomatera *f*
Ⓑ CPD ► **tomato juice** N jugo *m* de tomate ► **tomato ketchup** N salsa *f* de tomate, ketchup *m* ► **tomato paste** N = **tomato purée** ► **tomato plant** N tomatera *f* ► **tomato purée** N puré *m* de tomate, concentrado *m* de tomate ► **tomato sauce** N salsa *f* de tomate; (*Brit*) (*in bottle, sachet*) = **tomato ketchup**

tomb [tuːm] N tumba *f*, sepulcro *m*

tombola [tɒmˈbəʊlə] N (*Brit*) tómbola *f*

tomboy [ˈtɒmbɔɪ] N marimacho *m*

tomboyish [ˈtɒmbɔɪɪʃ] ADJ marimacho

tombstone [ˈtuːmstəʊn] N lápida *f* (sepulcral)

tomcat [ˈtɒmkæt] N [1] (= *cat*) gato *m* (macho)
[2] (*US‡*) (= *womanizer*) mujeriego *m*, calavera *m*

tome [təʊm] N (*hum*) mamotreto* *m*; **a weighty ~** un pesado mamotreto*

tomfool [ˈtɒmˈfuːl] Ⓐ ADJ tonto, estúpido
Ⓑ N tonto/a *m/f*, imbécil *mf*

tomfoolery [tɒmˈfuːlərɪ] N payasadas *fpl*, tonterías *fpl*

Tommy [ˈtɒmɪ] Ⓐ N [1] (*familiar form*) *of* **Thomas**
[2] (*Brit Mil**) (*also* **tommy**) soldado *m* raso inglés
Ⓑ CPD ► **Tommy gun** N pistola *f* ametralladora, ametralladora *f*, metralleta *f*

tommyrot* [ˈtɒmɪrɒt] N tonterías *fpl*

tomorrow [təˈmɒrəʊ] Ⓐ ADV [1] mañana; **~ evening** mañana por la tarde; **~ morning** mañana por la mañana; **a week ~** de mañana en ocho días
[2] (= *in the future*) en el mañana, en el futuro
Ⓑ N [1] mañana *f*; **~ is Sunday** mañana es domingo; **the day after ~** pasado mañana; **will ~ do?** (*for piece of work*) ¿lo puedo dejar para mañana?; (*for appointment*) ¿te conviene mañana?; **~'s paper** el periódico de mañana; ✦*IDIOMS* **~ is another day** mañana sera otro día; **like there's no ~**: **he drank like there was no ~*** bebió como si le fuera la vida en ello
[2] (= *the future*) mañana *m*, porvenir *m*; **the writers of ~** los escritores del mañana

tom-tit [ˈtɒmtɪt] N paro *m*, carbonero *m* común

tom-tom [ˈtɒmtɒm] N (= *drum*) tantán *m*

ton [tʌn] N [1] (= *weight*) tonelada *f* (*Brit* = *1016.06kg; Can, US etc.* = *907.20kg*); **metric ~** tonelada *f* métrica (= *1.000kg*); **this cargo weighs 1,000 ~s** esta carga pesa 1.000 toneladas; **a three-~ lorry** un camión de tres toneladas; ✦*IDIOMS* **to weigh a ~*** pesar un quintal*; **this suitcase weighs a ~*** esta maleta pesa un quintal*; **to come down on sb like a ~ of bricks** echar una bronca descomunal a algn
[2] (*) **~s of sth** montones *mpl* de algo*; **we have ~s of it at home** en casa lo tenemos a montones*; **we have ~s of time** nos sobra tiempo, tenemos tiempo de sobra
[3] (*Aut‡*) (= *100mph*) velocidad *f* de 100 millas por hora; **to do a ~** ir a 100 millas por hora
[4] (*Cricket**) (= *100 runs*) cien carreras *fpl*

tonal [ˈtəʊnl] ADJ tonal

tonality [təʊˈnælɪtɪ] N tonalidad *f*

tone [təʊn] Ⓐ N [1] (*Mus*) tono *m*
[2] [*of voice*] tono *m*; **in an angry ~** en tono de enojo; **in low ~s** en tono bajo; **they were whispering in low ~s** cuchicheaban; **~ of voice** tono *m* de voz; ✦*IDIOM* **to praise sb in ringing ~s** poner a algn por las nubes
[3] (*Telec*) señal *f*; **dialling ~** señal *f* para marcar; **please speak after the ~** (*Telec*) por favor, hable después de oír la señal
[4] (= *shade of colour*) tono *m*, matiz *m*; **two-~ colour scheme** combinación *f* de dos tonalidades
[5] (= *tendency*) tono *m*, nota *f*; [*of speech, article*] tono *m*, cariz *m*; **the ~ of the market** (*Fin*) la nota dominante del mercado, el tono del mercado
[6] (= *character, dignity*) buen tono *m*, elegancia *f*; **the place has ~** el sitio tiene buen tono, es un sitio elegante; **the clientèle gives the restaurant ~** la clientela da distinción al restaurante; **to raise/lower the ~ of sth** levantar/bajar el nivel de algo
[7] [*of muscles etc*] **muscle ~** tono *m* muscular
Ⓑ VI (*Brit*) (*also* **~ in**) [*colours*] armonizar, combinar
Ⓒ VT [1] (*Mus*) entonar
[2] (*Phot*) virar
[3] [+ *body, muscles*] (*also* **~ up**) tonificar, fortalecer
Ⓓ CPD ► **tone colour, tone color** (*US*) N (*Mus*) timbre *m* ► **tone control** N control *m* de tonalidad ► **tone language** N lengua *f* tonal ► **tone poem** N poema *m* sinfónico

►**tone down** VT + ADV (= *moderate*) [+ *colour*] atenuar, suavizar; [+ *noise*] reducir, disminuir; (*fig*) [+ *language, criticism etc*] moderar

►**tone up** VT + ADV [+ *muscles*] tonificar, fortalecer

➤ LANGUAGE IN USE: **tolerate** 9.3, 10.4, 14

tone-deaf ['təʊn'def] ADJ que no tiene oído musical

toneless ['təʊnlɪs] ADJ [*voice*] monótono, apagado, inexpresivo; [*muscle tissue*] flojo

tonelessly ['təʊnlɪslɪ] ADV monótonamente

toner ['təʊnəʳ] N (*for photocopier*) tóner *m*; (*Phot*) virador *m*; (*for skin*) tonificante *m*

toney* ['təʊnɪ] ADJ (*US*) = **tony**

Tonga ['tɒŋə] N Tonga *f*

tongs [tɒŋz] NPL (*for coal etc*) tenazas *fpl*; (= *curling tongs*) tenacillas *fpl*; **a pair of ~** unas tenazas, unas tenacillas

tongue [tʌŋ] Ⓐ N [1] (*Anat, Culin*) lengua *f*; **to put** *or* **stick one's ~ out (at sb)** sacar la lengua (a algn); **she has a quick/nasty ~** (*fig*) tiene mucha labia/una lengua viperina; ✦*IDIOMS* **with (one's) ~ in (one's) cheek** irónicamente, burla burlando; **to say sth ~ in cheek** decir algo en tono de burla; **to keep a civil ~ in one's head** moderar las palabras *or* el lenguaje; **to get one's ~ around sth**: **I can't get my ~ round these Latin names** estos nombres latinos resultan impronunciables; **to find one's ~**: **so you've found your ~?** ¿así que estás dispuesto por fin a hablar?; **to give ~** [*hounds*] empezar a ladrar; **to hold one's ~** callarse; **hold your ~!** ¡cállate la boca!; **to loosen sb's ~** hacer hablar a algn; **wine loosens the ~** el vino suelta la lengua; **to lose one's ~**: **have you lost your ~?** ¿te has tragado la lengua?; **to trip or roll off the ~**: **the formula came tripping** *or* **rolling off his/her ~** pronunció la fórmula con la mayor facilidad; **it doesn't exactly trip off the ~** no se puede decir que sea fácil de pronunciar
[2] [*of shoe*] lengüeta *f*; [*of bell*] badajo *m*; (*fig*) [*of flame, land*] lengua *f*
[3] (= *language*) lengua *f*, idioma *m*; **in the German ~** en alemán, en la lengua alemana; **to speak in ~s** (*Rel*) hablar en lenguas desconocidas
Ⓑ CPD ► **tongue twister** N trabalenguas *m inv*

tongue-and-groove [ˌtʌŋən'gruːv] N machihembrado *m*

tongue-in-cheek ['tʌŋɪn'tʃiːk] ADJ [*remark*] irónico

tongue-lashing* ['tʌŋˌlæʃɪŋ] N latigazo *m*, reprensión *f*; **to give sb a ~** poner a algn como un trapo

tongue-tied ['tʌŋtaɪd] ADJ con la lengua trabada; (*fig*) tímido, cortado, premioso (*frm*)

tonic ['tɒnɪk] Ⓐ N [1] (*Med*) (*also fig*) tónico *m*; **this news will be a ~ for the market** esta noticia será un tónico para la bolsa
[2] (*also* **~ water**) agua *f* tónica, tónica *f*
[3] (*Mus*) tónica *f*
Ⓑ ADJ (*all senses*) tónico
Ⓒ CPD ► **tonic accent** N (*Mus*) acento *m* tónico

tonicity [tɒ'nɪsɪtɪ] N tonicidad *f*

tonight [tə'naɪt] Ⓐ ADV esta noche; **I'll see you ~** nos vemos esta noche
Ⓑ N **~'s TV programmes** los programas de TV de esta noche

tonnage ['tʌnɪdʒ] N (= *weight*) tonelaje *m*

tonne [tʌn] N tonelada *f* (métrica) (*1.000kg*)

-tonner ['tʌnəʳ] N (*ending in compounds*) de ... toneladas; **a 1,000-tonner** un barco de 1.000 toneladas

tonometer [təʊ'nɒmɪtəʳ] N tonómetro *m*

tonsil ['tɒnsl] N amígdala *f*, angina *f* (*Mex*); **to have one's ~s out** quitarse las amígdalas

tonsillectomy [ˌtɒnsɪ'lektəmɪ] N tonsilectomía *f*, amigdalotomía *f*

tonsillitis [ˌtɒnsɪ'laɪtɪs] N amigdalitis *f*; **to have ~** tener amigdalitis

tonsorial [tɒn'sɔːrɪəl] ADJ (*esp hum*) [*look, style*] barberil; [*matters*] relativo a la barba

tonsure ['tɒnʃəʳ] (*frm*) Ⓐ N tonsura *f*
Ⓑ VT tonsurar

Tony ['təʊnɪ] N (*familiar form*) *of* **Anthony**

tony* ['təʊnɪ] ADJ (*US*) de buen tono, elegante

too [tuː] ADV [1] (= *excessively*) demasiado; **it's ~ easy** es demasiado fácil; **it's ~ sweet** está demasiado *or* muy dulce; **it's ~ heavy for me to lift** es demasiado pesado para que yo lo levante; **it's ~ hot to drink** está demasiado caliente para beberlo; **it's not ~ difficult** no es muy difícil; **~ bad!** ¡mala suerte!, ¡qué le vamos a hacer!, ¡ni modo! (*Mex*); **it's ~ early for that** es (muy) temprano para eso; **it's ~ good to be true** no puede ser; **I'm not ~ keen on the idea** la idea no me hace gracia que digamos; **~ many** demasiados; **~ many difficulties** demasiadas dificultades; **~ much** demasiado; **~ much jam** demasiada mermelada *f*; **he talks ~ much** habla demasiado; **you gave me a dollar ~ much** me dio un dólar de más; **that's ~ much by half** de eso sobra la mitad; **don't make ~ much of it** no le des mucha importancia; **it was all ~ much for her** [*emotion*] era demasiado para ella, era más de lo que pudo soportar; [*work*] estaba agobiada por tanto trabajo; **it's ~ much for me to cope with** yo no puedo con tanto; **his rudeness is ~ much** su descortesía es intolerable; **it's ~ much!*** (= *fantastic*) ¡qué demasiado!*, ¡esto es demasiado!; (= *excessive*) esto pasa de la raya, esto pasa de castaño oscuro; **~ often** con demasiada frecuencia, muy a menudo; **~ right!*** ◊ **~ true!** ¡muy bien dicho!, ¡y cómo!
[2] (= *also*) también; (= *moreover*) además; **I went ~** yo fui también; **I speak French and Japanese ~** hablo francés y también japonés; **not only that, he's blind ~!** no sólo eso, ¡además es ciego!; **she is, ~!** ¡y tanto que lo es!

took [tʊk] PT *of* **take**

tool [tuːl] Ⓐ N [1] (*carpenter's, mechanic's etc*) herramienta *f*; (*gardener's*) útil *m*, utensilio *m*; **a set of ~s** un juego de herramientas; **the ~s of his trade** las herramientas de su trabajo; **give us the ~s and we will finish the job** (*fig*) dadnos las herramientas y nosotros terminaremos la obra; *see* **down[1] D2**
[2] (*fig*) (= *person, book etc*) instrumento *m*; **he was a mere ~ in their hands** fue instrumento en sus manos, nada más; **the book is an essential ~** el libro es indispensable, el libro es instrumento imprescindible
Ⓑ VT [+ *wood, metal*] labrar con herramienta; [+ *book, leather*] estampar en seco
Ⓒ CPD ► **tool bag** N estuche *m* de herramientas ► **tool box**, **tool chest** N caja *f* de herramientas ► **tool kit** N juego *m* de herramientas, estuche *m* de herramientas ► **tool room** N departamento *m* de herramientas ► **tool shed** N cobertizo *m* para herramientas

toolbar ['tuːlbɑːʳ] N barra *f* de herramientas

tooled-up‡ ['tuːld'ʌp] ADJ armado

tooling ['tuːlɪŋ] N (*on book*) estampación *f* en seco

toolmaker ['tuːlˌmeɪkəʳ] N tallador *m* de herramientas

toolmaking ['tuːlˌmeɪkɪŋ] N talladura *f* de herramientas

toot [tuːt] Ⓐ N toque *m*, bocinazo *m*; **he went off with a ~ on the horn** partió con un breve toque de bocina
Ⓑ VT [+ *horn*] tocar, hacer sonar
Ⓒ VI [*person*] tocar la bocina, dar un bocinazo

tooth [tuːθ] Ⓐ N (*pl* **teeth**) [1] (*Anat*) diente *m*; (*esp molar*) muela *f*; **to clean one's teeth** lavarse los dientes; **to cut a ~** echar un diente; **she's cutting her first ~** le está saliendo el primer diente, está echando el primer diente; **to have a ~ out** sacarse una muela; **to show one's teeth** (*smiling or aggressive*) enseñar los dientes; ✦*IDIOMS* **to cut one's teeth on sth** foguearse con *or* en algo, dar los primeros pasos con algo; **to be fed up to the (back) teeth with sth/sb*** estar hasta la coronilla de algo/algn; **to get one's teeth into sth** hincarle el diente a algo, meterse de lleno en algo; **in the teeth of the wind** contra un viento violento; **in the teeth of great opposition** haciendo frente a una gran resistencia; **to lie through one's teeth** mentir descaradamente; **long in the ~*** con muchos años a cuestas; **to fight ~ and nail** luchar a brazo partido; **it sets my/his teeth on edge** me/le da dentera; **by the skin of one's teeth** por un pelo; **to have a sweet ~** ser goloso; *see also* **armed**, **false**, **grit**, **wisdom**
[2] [*of saw, wheel*] diente *m*; [*of comb*] púa *f*
[3] (*fig*) **the Commission must be given more teeth** hay que dar poderes efectivos a la Comisión
Ⓑ CPD ► **tooth fairy** N ≈ ratoncito *m* Pérez ► **tooth powder** N polvos *mpl* dentífricos

toothache ['tuːθeɪk] N dolor *m* de muelas; **to have ~** tener dolor de muelas

toothbrush ['tuːθbrʌʃ] Ⓐ N cepillo *m* de dientes Ⓑ CPD ► **toothbrush moustache** N bigote *m* de cepillo

toothed [tuːθt] ADJ [*wheel*] dentado; **big-~** de dientes grandes

toothless ['tuːθlɪs] ADJ desdentado, sin dientes; (*fig*) sin poder efectivo, ineficaz

toothpaste ['tuːθpeɪst] N pasta *f* de dientes, dentífrico *m*

toothpick ['tuːθpɪk] N palillo *m* (de dientes)

toothsome ['tuːθsəm] ADJ (*liter*) sabroso

toothy* ['tʊθɪ] ADJ (*compar* **toothier**; *superl* **toothiest**) dentudo; **to give sb a ~ smile** sonreír a algn enseñando mucho los dientes

tootle ['tuːtl] Ⓐ N (*Mus*) sonido *m* breve (de flauta, trompeta *etc*)
Ⓑ VT [+ *flute etc*] tocar
Ⓒ VI [1] (*Mus*) tocar la flauta *etc*
[2] (*Aut**) **we ~d down to Brighton** hicimos una escapada a Brighton, fuimos de excursión a Brighton; **we were tootling along at 60** íbamos a 60

tootsie‡, **tootsy**‡ ['tʊtsɪ] N [1] (= *toe*) dedo *m* del pie; (= *foot*) pie *m*
[2] (*US*) (= *girl*) chica *f*, gachí‡ *f*; **hey ~!** ¡oye, guapa!

top[1] [tɒp] Ⓐ N [1] (= *highest point, peak*) cumbre *f*, cima *f*; [*of hill*] cumbre *f*; [*of tree*] copa *f*; [*of head*] coronilla *f*; [*of building*] remate *m*; [*of wall*] coronamiento *m*; [*of wave*] cresta *f*; [*of stairs, ladder*] lo alto; [*of page*] cabeza *f*; [*of list, table, classification*] cabeza *f*, primer puesto *m*, primera posición *f*; **at the ~ of the hill** en la cumbre de la colina; **to reach the ~** ◊ **make it to the ~** [*of career etc*] alcanzar la cumbre (del éxito); **the men at the ~** (*fig*) los que mandan; **executives who are at the ~ of their careers** ejecutivos que están en la cumbre de sus carreras; **~ of the charts** (*Mus*) el número uno; **to be at the ~ of the class** (*Scol*) ser el/la mejor de la clase; **Liverpool are at the ~ of the league** Liverpool encabeza la liga; **at the ~ of the page** a la cabeza de la página; **~ of the range** (*Comm*) lo mejor de la gama; **at the ~ of the stairs** en lo alto de la escalera; **at the ~ of the tree** (*lit*) en lo alto del árbol; (*Brit*) (*fig*) en la cima, en lo más alto; ✦*IDIOM* **at the ~ of the pile** *or* **heap*** en la cima, en lo más alto; *see also* **blow² A3**

2 (= *upper part*) parte *f* superior, parte *f* de arriba; [*of bus*] piso *m* superior; [*of turnip, carrot, radish*] rabillo *m*, hojas *fpl*; **he lives at the ~ of the house** ocupa el piso más alto de la casa; **the ~ of the milk** la nata; **at the ~ of the street** al final de la calle; **he sits at the ~ of the table** se sienta a la cabecera de la mesa

3 (= *surface*) superficie *f*; **oil comes** *or* **floats** *or* **rises to the ~** el aceite sube a la superficie; **the ~ of the table needs wiping** hay que pasar una bayeta por la mesa

4 (= *lid*) [*of pen, bottle, jar*] tapa *f*, cubierta *f*, tapón *m*

5 (= *blouse*) blusa *f*; **pyjama ~** parte *f* de arriba del pijama; **I want a ~ to go with this skirt** quiero algo para arriba que me vaya con esta falda

6 (*Brit Aut*) = **top gear**

7 (*US Aut*) capota *f*

8 (*Naut*) cofa *f*

9 **on ~** encima, arriba; **to be on ~** estar encima; (*fig*) (= *winning etc*) llevar ventaja, estar ganando; **seats on ~!** (*on bus*) ¡hay sitio arriba!; **let's go up on ~** (*Naut*) vamos a (subir a) cubierta; **thin on ~*** con poco pelo, medio calvo; **on ~ of** sobre, encima de; **it floats on ~ of the water** flota sobre el agua; **the next second the lorry was on ~ of us** al instante el camión se nos echó encima; **the flat is so small we live on ~ of each other** el piso es tan pequeño que vivimos amontonados; **on ~ of (all) that** (= *in addition to that*) y encima *or* además de (todo) eso; **on ~ of which** y para colmo, más encima; **it's just one thing on ~ of another** es una cosa tras otra; **to be/get on ~ of things** estar/ponerse a la altura de las cosas; **I'm on ~ of my work now** ahora puedo con el trabajo; **things are getting on ~ of me** ya no puedo más; ✦*IDIOMS* **to come out on ~** salir ganando *or* con éxito; **to be/feel on ~ of the world** estar/sentirse en el paraíso *or* en el séptimo cielo

10 **~s: it's (the) ~s*** es tremendo*, es fabuloso*; **she's (the) ~s** es la reoca*

11 (*in phrases*) **from ~ to bottom** de arriba abajo; **the system is rotten from ~ to bottom** el sistema entero está podrido; **to be at the ~ of one's form** estar en plena forma; **the ~ of the morning to you!** (*Irl*) ¡buenos días!; **over the ~** (*Brit**) (= *excessive*) excesivo, desmesurado; **this proposal is really over the ~** (*Brit*) esta propuesta pasa de la raya; **to go over the ~** (*Mil*) lanzarse al ataque (saliendo de las trincheras); (*Brit**) (*fig*) pasarse (de lo razonable), desbordarse; **he doesn't have much up ~*** (= *stupid*) no es muy listo que digamos; (= *balding*) tiene poco pelo, se le ven las ideas*; **she doesn't have much up ~*** (= *flat-chested*) está lisa (basilisa)*; **at the ~ of one's voice** a voz en grito; ✦*IDIOM* **he said it off the ~ of his head*** lo dijo sin pensar; **speaking off the ~ of my head, I would say ...** hablando así sin pensarlo, yo diría que ...

Ⓑ ADJ **1** (= *highest*) [*drawer, shelf*] de arriba, más alto; [*edge, side, corner*] superior, de arriba; [*floor, step, storey*] último; **at the ~ end of the scale** en el extremo superior de la escala; **at the ~ end of the range** (*Comm*) en el escalón más alto de la gama; **~ note** (*Mus*) nota *f* más alta

2 (= *maximum*) [*price*] máximo; **~ priority** principal prioridad *f*, asunto *m* primordial; **at ~ speed** a máxima velocidad, a toda carrera

3 (*in rank etc*) más importante; **the ~ class at school** (= *final year*) el último año en la escuela; **a ~ executive** un(a) alto/a ejecutivo/a; **a ~ job** un puesto de importancia; **~ management** alta gerencia *f*; **~ people** gente *f* bien; **the ~ people in the party** la dirección del partido; **~ stream** (*Scol*) clase *f* del nivel más avanzado

4 (= *best, leading*) mejor; **a ~ surgeon** uno de los mejores cirujanos; **the ~ 10/20/30** (*Mus*) los 10/20/30 mejores éxitos, el hit parade de los 10/20/30 mejores; **to come ~** ganar, ganar el primer puesto; **to come ~ of the class** ser el primero de la clase; **he came ~ in maths** sacó la mejor nota de la clase en matemáticas; **to be on ~ form** estar en plena forma; **to get ~ marks** sacar la mejor nota; **~ scorer** máximo/a goleador(a) *m/f*, pichichi *mf* (*Sp**); **~ team** equipo *m* líder

5 (= *final*) [*coat of paint*] último; **the ~ layer of skin** la epidermis

6 (= *farthest*) superior; **the ~ right-hand corner** la esquina superior derecha; **the ~ end of the field** el extremo superior del campo

Ⓒ ADV **~s*** (= *maximum, at most*) como mucho

Ⓓ VT **1** (= *form top of*) [+ *building*] coronar; [+ *cake*] cubrir, recubrir; **a cake ~ped with whipped cream** una tarta cubierta *or* recubierta de nata *or* (*LAm*) crema; **a church ~ped by a steeple** una iglesia coronada por un campanario; **the wall is ~ped with stone** el muro tiene un coronamiento de piedras

2 (= *be at top of*) [+ *class, list*] encabezar, estar a la cabeza de; **to ~ the bill** (*Theat*) encabezar el reparto; **to ~ the charts** (*Mus*) ser el número uno de las listas de éxitos *or* de los superventas; **the team ~ped the league all season** el equipo iba en cabeza de la liga toda la temporada

3 (= *exceed, surpass*) exceder, superar; **profits ~ped £50,000 last year** las ganancias excedieron (las) 50.000 libras el año pasado; **sales ~ped the million mark** las ventas rebasaron el millón; **we have ~ped last year's takings by £200** hemos recaudado 200 libras más que el año pasado, los ingresos exceden a los del año pasado en 200 libras; **and to ~ it all ...** y para colmo ..., como remate ..., y para rematar las cosas ...; **how are you going to ~ that?** (*joke, story etc*) ¿cómo vas a superar eso?, te han puesto el listón muy alto

4 [+ *vegetables, fruit, plant*] descabezar; [+ *tree*] desmochar; **to ~ and tail fruit** (*Brit*) quitar los extremos de la fruta

5 (= *reach summit of*) llegar a la cumbre de

6 (‡) (= *kill*) colgar; **to ~ o.s.** suicidarse

Ⓔ CPD ► **top banana*** N (*US*) pez *m* gordo* ► **top boots** NPL botas *fpl* de campaña ► **top brass*** N jefazos* *mpl* ► **top copy** N original *m* ► **top dog*** N **she's ~ dog at work** ella es mandamás en el trabajo ► **top dollar*** N (*esp US*) **to pay ~ dollar for sth** pagar algo a precio de oro ► **the top drawer** N (*fig*) la alta sociedad, la crema; *see also* **top-drawer** ► **top dressing** N (*Hort, Agr*) abono *m* (aplicado a la superficie) ► **top gear** N (*Brit Aut*) directa *f*; **in ~ gear** (*four-speed box*) en cuarta, en la directa; (*five-speed box*) en quinta, en la directa ► **top hat** N sombrero *m* de copa, chistera *f* ► **top spin** N (*Tennis*) efecto *m* alto, efecto *m* liftado

►**top off** VT + ADV (= *complete*) coronar, rematar; **he ~ped this off by saying that ...** esto lo remató diciendo que ...; **he ~ped off the fourth course with a cup of coffee** para completar el cuarto plato se bebió una taza de café

►**top up** (*Brit*) Ⓐ VT + ADV llenar; **to ~ sb's glass up** rellenar el vaso de algn; **shall I ~ you up?** ¿te doy más?; **to ~ up a battery** (= *refill it*) llenar a nivel una batería; **her parents ~ped up her grant** sus padres le añadieron un complemento *or* suplemento a la beca

Ⓑ VI + ADV **to ~ up with oil** poner aceite; **we ~ped up with a couple of beers*** como remate nos bebimos un par de cervezas

top² [tɒp] N **1** (= *spinning top*) peonza *f*, peón *m*; (= *humming top, musical top*) trompa *f*; *see also* **sleep**

2 (*Circus*) *see* **big**

topaz [ˈtəʊpæz] N topacio *m*

topcoat [ˈtɒpkəʊt] N (= *overcoat*) abrigo *m*, sobretodo *m*

top-drawer [ˌtɒpˈdrɔːʳ] ADJ (*fig*) de alta sociedad; *see also* **top**

tope† [təʊp] VI beber (más de la cuenta), emborracharse

topee [ˈtəʊpiː] N salacot *m*

toper† [ˈtəʊpəʳ] N borrachín/ina *m/f*

top-flight [ˈtɒpflaɪt] ADJ de primera (categoría)

topgallant [tɒpˈgælənt, (*Naut*) təˈgælənt] N (*also* **~ sail**) juanete *m*

top-hatted [ˈtɒpˈhætɪd] ADJ en chistera, enchisterado

top-heaviness [ˈtɒpˈhevɪnɪs] N (*fig*) (*in organization*) exceso *m* de altos cargos

top-heavy [ˌtɒpˈhevɪ] ADJ (*lit*) demasiado pesado en la parte superior; (*fig*) **the army was ~ with officers** el ejército tenía demasiados oficiales

topiary [ˈtəʊpɪərɪ] N arte *m* de recortar los arbustos en formas de animales *etc*

topic [ˈtɒpɪk] N tema *m*, asunto *m*

topical [ˈtɒpɪkəl] ADJ **1** (= *of current interest*) de interés actual, de actualidad; **a highly ~ question** un tema de gran actualidad; **~ talk** charla *f* sobre cuestiones del día

2 (*US*) local

topicality [ˌtɒpɪˈkælɪtɪ] N **1** (= *current interest, importance*) actualidad *f*, interés *m* actual, importancia *f* actual

2 (*US*) localidad *f*

topknot [ˈtɒpnɒt] N **1** (*on head*) moño *m*

2 (*Orn*) moño *m*

topless [ˈtɒplɪs] Ⓐ ADJ topless

Ⓑ ADV **to go ~** ir en topless

Ⓒ CPD ► **topless bar** N bar *m* topless ► **topless swimsuit** N monoquini *m*

top-level [ˌtɒpˈlevl] ADJ del más alto nivel; **~ conference** conferencia *f* de alto nivel

top-loader [ˌtɒpˈləʊdəʳ] N (= *washing machine*) lavadora *f* de carga superior

topmast [ˈtɒpmɑːst] N mastelero *m*

topmost [ˈtɒpməʊst] ADJ más alto

top-notch* [ˌtɒpˈnɒtʃ] ADJ de primerísima categoría

topographer [təˈpɒgrəfəʳ] N topógrafo/a *m/f*

topographic [ˌtɒpəˈgræfɪk] ADJ = **topographical**

topographical [ˌtɒpəˈgræfɪkl] ADJ topográfico

topography [təˈpɒgrəfɪ] N topografía *f*

topper* [ˈtɒpəʳ] N **1** (= *hat*) sombrero *m* de copa, chistera *f*

2 (*US*) **the ~ was that ...** para colmo ..., para acabar de rematar ...*

topping [ˈtɒpɪŋ] Ⓐ N (*Culin*) cubierta *f*

Ⓑ ADJ (*Brit*†) bárbaro*, pistonudo*

topple ['tɒpl] Ⓐ VT [1] (*also* ~ **over**) (= *knock over*) volcar; (= *cause to fall*) hacer caer
[2] (= *overthrow*) derribar, derrocar
Ⓑ VI [1] (*also* ~ **down**) caerse, venirse abajo; (*also* ~ **over**) volcarse; (= *lose balance*) perder el equilibrio; **he ~d over a cliff** cayó por un precipicio; **after the crash the bus ~d over** después del choque el autobús se volcó
[2] (*fig*) [*government etc*] venirse abajo, caer

top-ranking [,tɒp'ræŋkɪŋ] ADJ de alto rango; [*officer*] de alta graduación

topsail ['tɒpsl] N gavia *f*

top-secret [,tɒp'siːkrɪt] ADJ de alto secreto

top-security [,tɒpsɪ'kjʊərɪtɪ] ADJ [*prison, hospital*] de alta seguridad, de máxima seguridad

top-selling [,tɒp'selɪŋ] ADJ = **best-selling**

topside ['tɒpsaɪd] N [1] (= *uppermost side*) lado *m* superior, superficie *f* superior
[2] (*Culin*) tapa *f* y tajo redondo

topsoil ['tɒpsɔɪl] N capa *f* superficial del suelo

topsy-turvy [,tɒpsɪ'tɜːvɪ] Ⓐ ADJ en desorden, revuelto
Ⓑ ADV patas arriba, al revés; **everything is ~** todo está patas arriba

top-up ['tɒpʌp] Ⓐ N (*Brit**) (= *refill*) **can I give you a ~?** ¿te sirvo un poco más?
Ⓑ CPD ► **top-up loan** N (*Brit*) préstamo *m* gubernamental a estudiantes

tor [tɔːʳ] N colina *f* abrupta y rocosa, pico *m* pequeño (*esp en el suroeste de Inglaterra*)

torc [tɔːk] N = **torque A 1**

torch [tɔːtʃ] Ⓐ N [1] (*flaming*) antorcha *f*, tea *f*; **to carry the ~ of democracy/progress** (*fig*) mantener viva la llama de la democracia/del progreso; ✦**IDIOM to carry a ~ for sb** estar enamorado de algn
[2] (*Brit*) (*electric*) linterna *f*
[3] (*Tech*) (*also* **blow** ~) soplete *m*
Ⓑ VT (= *set fire to*) [+ *building, vehicle*] prender fuego a, incendiar

torchbearer ['tɔːtʃ,beərəʳ] N persona *f* que lleva una antorcha

torchlight ['tɔːtʃlaɪt] Ⓐ N (*flaming*) luz *f* de antorcha; (*electric*) luz *f* de linterna
Ⓑ CPD ► **torchlight procession** N desfile *m* con antorchas

tore [tɔːʳ] PT *of* **tear**

toreador ['tɒrɪədɔːʳ] N torero *m*

torment Ⓐ ['tɔːment] N tormento *m*; **the ~s of jealousy** los tormentos de los celos; **to be in ~** estar atormentado
Ⓑ [tɔː'ment] VT (= *hurt*) atormentar, torturar; (= *annoy*) fastidiar, molestar; (= *torture*) (*fig*) atormentar; **she was ~ed by doubts** la atormentaban las dudas; **we were ~ed by thirst** nos moríamos de sed; **don't ~ the cat** no le des guerra al gato

tormentor [tɔː'mentəʳ] N atormentador(a) *m/f*

torn [tɔːn] PP *of* **tear**

tornado [tɔː'neɪdəʊ] N (*pl* **tornados, tornadoes**) tornado *m*

torpedo [tɔː'piːdəʊ] Ⓐ N (*pl* **torpedoes**) torpedo *m*
Ⓑ VT (*lit, fig*) torpedear
Ⓒ CPD ► **torpedo boat** N torpedero *m*, lancha *f* torpedera ► **torpedo tube** N tubo *m* lanzatorpedos, lanzatorpedos *m inv*

torpid ['tɔːpɪd] ADJ aletargado

torpidity [tɔː'pɪdɪtɪ] N letargo *m*

torpor ['tɔːpəʳ] N letargo *m*

torque [tɔːk] Ⓐ N [1] (*also* **torc**) (= *jewellery*) torques *f inv*
[2] (*Mech*) par *m* de torsión
Ⓑ CPD ► **torque wrench** N llave *f* dinamométrica

torrent ['tɒrənt] N (*lit, fig*) torrente *m*; **it rained in ~s** llovía a cántaros; **a ~ of abuse** un torrente de insultos, una sarta de injurias

torrential [tɒ'renʃəl] ADJ torrencial

torrid ['tɒrɪd] ADJ [1] (= *hot and dry*) [*climate, heat, sun*] tórrido
[2] (= *passionate*) [*love affair, romance*] tórrido, apasionado
[3] (= *very difficult*) **to have a ~ time** (*Brit*) pasar las de Caín, sufrir lo indecible

torsion ['tɔːʃən] N torsión *f*

torso ['tɔːsəʊ] N (*pl* **torsos,** (*rare*) **torsi**) [1] (*Anat*) torso *m*
[2] (= *sculpture*) torso *m*

tort [tɔːt] N (*Jur*) agravio *m*, tuerto *m*

tortilla [tɔː'tiːə] N tortilla *f*

tortoise ['tɔːtəs] N tortuga *f*

tortoiseshell ['tɔːtəsʃel] Ⓐ N [1] (= *shell*) carey *m*, concha *f*
[2] (= *cat*) gato *m* pardo
[3] (= *butterfly*) ortiguera *f*
Ⓑ CPD [*box, ornament*] de carey, de concha ► **tortoiseshell glasses** NPL gafas *fpl* de carey

tortuous ['tɔːtjʊəs] ADJ [1] (= *winding*) [*path, road, process*] tortuoso
[2] (= *convoluted*) [*sentence, essay, logic*] enrevesado

torture ['tɔːtʃəʳ] Ⓐ N [1] (*lit*) tortura *f*; **to put sb to (the) ~** torturar a algn
[2] (*fig*) tormento *m*; **it was sheer ~!** ¡era una verdadera tortura!
Ⓑ VT [1] (*lit*) torturar
[2] (= *torment*) atormentar; **to be ~d by doubts** ser atormentado por las dudas
Ⓒ CPD ► **torture chamber** N cámara *f* de tortura

torturer ['tɔːtʃərəʳ] N torturador(a) *m/f*

torturing ['tɔːtʃərɪŋ] ADJ torturador, atormentador

Tory ['tɔːrɪ] (*Brit*) Ⓐ ADJ conservador; **the ~ Party** el Partido Conservador
Ⓑ N conservador(a) *m/f*

Toryism ['tɔːrɪɪzəm] N (*Brit*) conservatismo *m*, conservadurismo *m*

tosh* [tɒʃ] N tonterías *fpl*

toss [tɒs] Ⓐ N [1] (= *shake*) [*of head*] sacudida *f*; **a ~ of the head** una sacudida de cabeza; ✦**IDIOM I don't give a ~** (*Brit*⁑) me importa un bledo*
[2] (= *throw*) echada *f*, tirada *f*; (*by bull*) cogida *f*; **the ball came to him full ~** la pelota llegó a sus manos sin tocar la tierra; **to take a ~** (*from horse*) caerse del caballo
[3] [*of coin*] tirada *f*, echada *f* (*esp LAm*); **to win/lose the ~** ganar/perder (a cara o cruz); ✦**IDIOM to argue the ~*** machacar el asunto*
Ⓑ VT [1] (= *shake*) sacudir; **the boat was ~ed by the waves** las olas sacudían el barco; **the horse ~ed its head** el caballo sacudió la cabeza
[2] (= *throw*) tirar, lanzar, echar, aventar (*Mex*); [*bull*] coger (y lanzar al aire); **to ~ sth to sb** tirar *or* lanzar algo a algn; **to ~ sb in a blanket** mantear a algn; **to ~ the caber** (*Scot*) lanzar troncos; **to ~ a coin** echar a cara o cruz; **I'll ~ you for it** lo echamos a cara o cruz; **to ~ a pancake** dar la vuelta a *or* voltear una tortita; **to ~ a salad** mezclar una ensalada; → HIGHLAND GAMES
Ⓒ VI [1] (*also* ~ **about,** ~ **around**) sacudirse, agitarse; [*boat*] (*gently*) balancearse sobre las ondas; (*violently*) ser sacudido por las ondas; **to ~ (in one's sleep)** ◊ **~ and turn** dar vueltas *or* revolverse (en la cama)
[2] (*also* ~ **up**) echar a cara o cruz; (*Sport*) sortear (**for sth** algo); **we ~ed (up) for the last piece of cake** nos jugamos *or* echamos a cara o cruz el último trozo de pastel; **we'll ~ (up) to see who does it** echaremos a cara o cruz quién lo hace

►**toss about, toss around** Ⓐ VT + ADV lanzar acá y allá; **the currents ~ed the boat about** las corrientes zarandeaban el barco
Ⓑ VI + ADV = **toss C1**

►**toss aside** VT + ADV [+ *object*] echar a un lado, apartar bruscamente; [+ *person*] abandonar; [+ *objection*] desechar, desestimar

►**toss away** VT + ADV echar, tirar

►**toss off** Ⓐ VT + ADV [1] (*) [+ *poem etc*] escribir rapidísimamente; **to ~ off a drink** beberse algo de un trago
[2] (⁑) (= *masturbate*) hacer una paja a⁑
Ⓑ VI + ADV (⁑) (= *masturbate*) hacerse una paja⁑

►**toss over** VT + ADV **to ~ a book over to sb** tirar un libro a algn; **~ it over!** ¡dámelo!

►**toss up** Ⓐ VT + ADV [+ *coin*] echar a cara o cruz
Ⓑ VI + ADV = **toss C2**

tosser⁑ ['tɒsəʳ], **tosspot**⁑ ['tɒspɒt] N (*Brit*) mamón⁑ *m*, gilipollas⁑ *m*

toss-up ['tɒsʌp] N **we'll settle it by a ~** nos lo jugaremos *or* lo echaremos a cara o cruz; **it was a ~ between me and him** la cosa estaba entre él y yo (al cincuenta por ciento); **it's a ~ whether I go or stay** no me decido si irme o quedarme

tot[1] [tɒt] N [1] (= *child*) nene/a *m/f*, chiquillo/a *m/f*, niñito/a *m/f*
[2] (*esp Brit*) (= *drink*) trago *m*, traguito *m*; **a ~ of rum** un dedo de ron

tot[2] [tɒt] (*esp Brit*) Ⓐ VT **to ~ up** sumar, hacer la cuenta de
Ⓑ VI **it ~s up to £5** suma cinco libras, viene a ser cinco libras; **what does it ~ up to?** ¿cuánto suma?

▼ **total** ['təʊtl] Ⓐ ADJ [1] (= *complete, utter*) [*lack, commitment*] total, absoluto; [*ban*] total; [*failure*] rotundo, absoluto; **his attempt to try to resolve the dispute was a ~ failure** su intento de resolver la disputa fue un fracaso rotundo *or* absoluto; **he felt like a ~ failure** se sentía un completo fracasado; **a ~ stranger** un completo desconocido; **the car was a ~ write-off** el coche quedó totalmente destrozado; *see also* **eclipse, recall**
[2] (= *overall*) [*amount, number, cost*] total; [*effect, policy*] global; **a ~ population of 650,000** una población total de 650.000 habitantes; **~ sales/assets** el total de ventas/activo; **~ losses amount to £100,000** las pérdidas ascienden a (un total de) 100.000 libras, el total de pérdidas asciende a 100.000 libras
Ⓑ N total *m*; **the jobless ~ was three million** el total de parados fue de tres millones; **in ~** en total; **a ~ of** un total de; *see also* **grand, sum**
Ⓒ VT [1] (= *add up*) [+ *figures*] sacar el total de, sumar el total de
[2] (= *amount to*) ascender a; **that ~s £20** el total asciende a 20 libras; **the class now ~s 20 students** en la clase hay ahora un total de 20 alumnos; **prizes ~ling £300** premios por un (valor) total de 300 libras
[3] (*esp US**) (= *wreck*) destrozar, hacer fosfatina*; **the car was completely ~led** el coche quedó hecho fosfatina*, el coche quedó para el arrastre*

totalitarian [,təʊtælɪ'teərɪən] ADJ totalitario

totalitarianism [,təʊtælɪ'teərɪənɪzəm] N totalitarismo *m*

➤ LANGUAGE IN USE: **total B 20.6**

totality [təʊˈtælɪtɪ] N totalidad *f*; **in its ~** en su totalidad

totalizator [ˈtəʊtəlaɪzeɪtəʳ] N totalizador *m*

totalize [ˈtəʊtəlaɪz] VT totalizar

totally [ˈtəʊtəlɪ] ADV totalmente; **such a compromise would be ~ unacceptable** un compromiso así sería totalmente *or* completamente *or* del todo inaceptable; **he's not ~ without principle** no carece totalmente de principios; **I'm still not ~ convinced** aún no estoy del todo convencido; **a view which has been almost ~ ignored** una postura que ha sido ignorada casi por completo

tote¹ [təʊt] N (*Racing*) totalizador *m*

tote² [təʊt] Ⓐ VT (*) (= *carry*) cargar con; **I ~d it around all day** cargué con él todo el día; **to ~ a gun** llevar pistola; **gun-toting policemen** policías *mpl* pistoleros
Ⓑ CPD ► **tote bag** N bolsa *f*, bolso *m*

totem [ˈtəʊtəm] Ⓐ N tótem *m*
Ⓑ CPD ► **totem pole** N tótem *m*

totemic [təʊˈtemɪk] ADJ totémico

totemism [ˈtəʊtəmɪzəm] N totemismo *m*

totter [ˈtɒtəʳ] VI (= *stagger*) bambolearse, tambalearse; (= *be about to fall*) tambalearse, estar para desplomarse

tottering [ˈtɒtərɪŋ] ADJ [*step*] tambaleante, inseguro, vacilante; [*economy, government*] inestable

tottery [ˈtɒtərɪ] ADJ [*elderly person*] de paso tambaleante, de paso nada seguro; **he's getting ~** empieza a andar con poca seguridad

totty‡ [ˈtɒtɪ] N (*Brit*) nenas* *fpl*, tías‡ *fpl*, titis‡ *fpl*; **a nice piece of ~** una tía buenísima‡

toucan [ˈtuːkən] N tucán *m*

touch [tʌtʃ] Ⓐ N 1 (= *sense, feel*) tacto *m*; **sense of ~** sentido *m* del tacto, tacto *m*
2 (= *pressure*) **he felt the ~ of a hand on his shoulder** sintió el tacto *or* el roce de una mano en su hombro; **the merest ~ might break it** el más mínimo roce podría romperlo; **at the ~ of a button** con sólo dar a un botón; **it's soft to the ~** es blando al tacto; **she responded to his ~** reaccionaba a sus caricias; ✦*IDIOM* **to be an easy** *or* **a soft ~*** ser fácil de convencer
3 (= *technique, manner*) **to have the common ~** saber tratar *or* sintonizar con el pueblo; **to have a light ~** [*pianist*] tocar con delicadeza *or* suavidad; **you need a light ~ to make good pastry** necesitas manos de seda para conseguir una buena masa; **to lose one's ~** perder facultades; **he had lost his scoring ~** había perdido habilidad *or* eficacia de cara al gol; **the director handles these scenes with a sure ~** el director trata estas escenas con mucha seguridad *or* gran pericia; *see also* **common**
4 (= *stamp, mark*) toque *m*; **the final ~** ◊ **the finishing ~** el último toque, el toque final; **to put the finishing ~es to sth** dar los últimos toques *or* los toques finales a algo; **it has a ~ of genius** tiene un toque de genialidad; **the human ~** el calor humano; **the personal ~** el toque personal; **the house needs a woman's ~** la casa necesita un toque femenino
5 (= *detail*) detalle *m*; **that was a nice ~** eso fue un bonito detalle
6 (= *small quantity*) 6·1 **a ~ of** [*of milk, water*] un chorrito de; [*of salt, pepper*] una pizca de; [*of irony, sarcasm*] un toque *or* un dejo de; **to have a ~ of flu** estar algo griposo; **there was a ~ of frost this morning** había algo de *or* un poco de escarcha esta mañana; **it needs a ~ of paint** le hace falta un poquito de pintura; **he got a ~ of the sun** le dio el sol un poquito
6·2 (*with adjective, adverb*) **it's a ~ (too) expensive** es algo *or* un poquito caro; **move it just a ~ to the left** muévelo un poquito a *or* hacia la izquierda
7 (= *contact*) **to be in ~ (with sb)** estar en contacto (con algn); **we are still in ~** todavía estamos en contacto; **I'll be in ~** (*writing*) te escribiré; (*phoning*) te llamaré; **to get in ~ (with sb)** ponerse en contacto (con algn); **get in ~ with your emotions** conecte con sus emociones; **to keep in ~ (with sb)** mantener el contacto (con algn); **well, keep in ~!** ¡bueno, no pierdas contacto!, ¡bueno, no dejes de llamar o escribir!; **to lose ~ (with sth/sb)** perder el contacto (con algo/algn); **I lost ~ with her after she moved to London** perdí el contacto con ella después de que se mudara a Londres; **the party has lost ~ with the voters** el partido está desconectado de los votantes; **to be out of ~** no estar al corriente; **the Prime Minister was completely out of ~** el Primer Ministro no estaba al corriente de nada; **I'm out of ~ with the latest political developments** no estoy al corriente de los últimos acontecimientos políticos; **to put sb in ~ with sb** poner a algn en contacto con algn
8 (*Rugby*) **to kick the ball into ~** poner el balón fuera de juego; **he had a foot in ~** tenía un pie fuera del terreno de juego *or* más allá de la línea de banda
Ⓑ VT 1 (*with hand*) tocar; **she ~ed his arm** le tocó el brazo; **they can't ~ you** (*fig*) no te pueden hacer nada; **to ~ one's toes** tocarse los dedos de los pies; **~ wood!** ¡toca madera!; *see also* **raw A3**
2 (= *come into contact with*) tocar; (= *brush against*) rozar; **I just ~ed the car in front** no hice más que rozar el coche que tenía delante; **I can ~ the bottom** (*in swimming pool*) puedo tocar el fondo; (*in sea*) hago pie; **my feet haven't ~ed the ground since I started this job** desde que empecé en este trabajo no he parado; *see also* **barge D**, **base A4**
3 (= *harm, disturb*) tocar; **don't ~ anything!** ¡no toques nada!; **I never ~ed him!** ¡ni le toqué!; **if you ~ him I'll kill you!** ¡como le pongas la mano encima *or* si le tocas te mato!
4 (= *try*) [+ *food, drink*] probar; **I never ~ gin** no pruebo la ginebra; **you haven't ~ed your dinner** no has probado bocado, no has tocado la cena; **I haven't ~ed a typewriter in ages** hace siglos que no toco una máquina de escribir
5 (= *affect*) afectar; **it ~es all our lives** nos afecta a todos
6 (= *move*) **her faith ~ed me** su fe me conmovió *or* me llegó al alma; **she was ~ed by his gift** el regalo la emocionó mucho
7 (= *compare with*) igualar; **no artist in the country can ~ him** no hay artista en todo el país que (se) le iguale; **nobody can ~ him as a pianist** como pianista es inigualable
8 (*esp Brit*) (= *reach*) **he was ~ing 290mph** alcanzaba las 290 millas por hora; **his hair ~es his shoulders** tiene una melena que le llega por los hombros
9 (*Brit**) **to ~ sb for money** dar un sablazo a algn*, pedir dinero prestado a algn
10 **to be ~ed with sth: clouds ~ed with pink** nubes con un toque rosa; **his hair was ~ed with grey** tenía algunas canas en el pelo
Ⓒ VI 1 (*with hand*) **don't ~!** (*to child*) ¡no se toca!; **"please do not touch"** "se ruega no tocar"
2 (= *come into contact*) [*hands*] encontrarse; [*lips*] rozarse; [*wires*] hacer contacto; **our hands ~ed** nuestras manos se encontraron
Ⓓ CPD ► **touch judge** N (*Rugby*) juez *mf* de línea, juez *mf* de banda

►**touch at** VI + PREP tocar en, hacer escala en

►**touch down** Ⓐ VI + ADV 1 (*Aer, Space*) (*on land*) aterrizar; (*on sea*) amerizar; (*on water*) acuatizar; (*on moon*) alunizar; *see also* **touchdown**
2 (*Rugby*) marcar un ensayo; (*American Ftbl*) (= *score*) hacer un touchdown; (*behind one's own goal line*) poner balón en tierra; *see also* **touchdown**
Ⓑ VT + ADV (*Rugby*) **he ~ed the ball down** (= *scored a try*) marcó un ensayo; (*behind his own goal line*) puso el balón en tierra

►**touch off** VT + ADV [+ *argument, violence, riot, fire*] provocar; [+ *explosive*] hacer estallar

►**touch on, touch upon** VI + PREP [+ *subject*] [*speaker, film, book*] tocar; [+ *fact*] [*speaker*] mencionar (de pasada)

►**touch up** VT + ADV 1 (= *improve*) [+ *photograph, painting, make-up*] retocar
2 (*) (*sexually*) meter mano a*, sobar*

touch-and-go [ˈtʌtʃənˈgəʊ] Ⓐ N **it's ~ whether he'll survive** no se sabe si sobrevivirá; **it was ~ whether we'd arrive before we ran out of petrol** no estaba nada seguro de que la gasolina nos fuera a dar para llegar; **we made it, but it was ~** lo conseguimos, pero por los pelos*
Ⓑ ADJ [*decision*] difícil, dudoso

touchdown [ˈtʌtʃdaʊn] N 1 (*Aer, Space*) (*on land*) aterrizaje *m*; (*on sea*) amerizaje *m*; (*on water*) acuatizaje *m*; (*on moon*) alunizaje *m*
2 (*Rugby*) ensayo *m*; (*American Ftbl*) touchdown *m*

touché [tuːˈʃeɪ] EXCL ¡dices bien!

touched* [tʌtʃt] ADJ (= *crazy*) tocado*, majara*; **he must be ~ in the head!** ¡tiene que estar tocado del ala!*

touchiness [ˈtʌtʃɪnɪs] N susceptibilidad *f*

touching [ˈtʌtʃɪŋ] Ⓐ ADJ conmovedor, patético
Ⓑ PREP tocante a

touchingly [ˈtʌtʃɪŋlɪ] ADV de modo conmovedor, patéticamente

touchline [ˈtʌtʃlaɪn] N (*Brit Sport*) línea *f* de banda

touchpaper [ˈtʌtʃpeɪpəʳ] N mecha *f*

touch-sensitive [ˈtʌtʃˈsensɪtɪv] ADJ sensible al tacto

touchstone [ˈtʌtʃstəʊn] N (*lit, fig*) piedra *f* de toque

touch-tone [ˈtʌtʃtəʊn] ADJ (*Telec*) digital, por tonos

touch-type [ˈtʌtʃtaɪp] VI mecanografiar al tacto

touch-typing [ˈtʌtʃˌtaɪpɪŋ] N mecanografía *f* al tacto

touch-typist [ˈtʌtʃˌtaɪpɪst] N mecanógrafo/a *m/f* al tacto

touchy [ˈtʌtʃɪ] ADJ (*compar* **touchier**; *superl* **touchiest**) 1 (= *sensitive*) [*person*] susceptible; [*subject*] delicado; **to be ~** ofenderse por poca cosa, ser (muy) susceptible; **he's ~ about his weight** su peso es un tema delicado; **that's a ~ subject with him** es delicado mencionarle ese asunto
2 (*) (= *tactile*) [*person*] sobón

touchy-feely* [ˈtʌtʃɪfiːlɪ] ADJ [*person*] sobón; [*talk, session*] íntimo

tough [tʌf] Ⓐ ADJ (*compar* **tougher**; *superl* **toughest**) 1 (= *robust*) fuerte; **granny may be old, but she's ~** puede que la abuela sea vieja, pero es fuerte; ✦*IDIOM* **to be (as) ~ as old boots*** (*hum*) [*person*] ser fuerte como un roble*

2 (= *hard, uncompromising*) [*person*] duro; [*neighbourhood, school*] peligroso; **~ customer*** tío/a *m/f* duro/a*; **~ guy*** tipo *m* duro; **~ nut*** tío/a *m/f* duro/a*; **to do some ~ talking** hablar sin rodeos
3 (= *resistant*) [*substance, material*] fuerte, resistente; [*skin*] duro
4 (= *not tender*) [*meat*] duro; **the steak was as ~ as old boots*** el filete estaba duro como la suela de un zapato*
5 (= *harsh*) [*policies*] duro, de mano dura; [*measures*] duro; [*teacher, parent*] severo; **to take a ~ line on sth** adoptar una línea dura con respecto a algo; **to take a ~ line with sb** ponerse duro con algn; **to be ~ on sb** ser duro con algn
6 (= *difficult*) [*way of life, situation, day*] duro, difícil; [*choice, question*] difícil; [*competition*] fuerte; **it's a ~ job being Prime Minister** es duro ser primer ministro; **it's a ~ job, but somebody has to do it** es un trabajo duro, pero alguien tiene que hacerlo; **it's ~ when you have kids** es difícil cuando tienes niños; **it will be ~ to finish it in time** va a ser difícil acabarlo a tiempo; **his team will be ~ to beat** su equipo será difícil de vencer, va a ser difícil vencer a su equipo; **it was ~ trying to raise the cash** fue difícil conseguir el dinero; **he has found it ~ going this year** este año se le ha hecho muy cuesta arriba, este año le ha resultado muy difícil; **when the going gets ~** cuando las cosas se ponen difíciles; **to have a ~ time (of it)** pasarlo mal *or* fatal*, pasar las de Caín*; ✦*IDIOM* **when the going gets ~, the ~ get going** la gente con arrestos se crece ante las adversidades
7 (*set expressions*) **tough!** ◊ **~ luck!*** ¡mala suerte!; **that's your ~ luck!** ¡te fastidias!; **~ shit**** te jodes**
Ⓑ N (*) (= *thug*) matón *m*, macarra* *m*
Ⓒ VT (*) **to ~ it out** aguantar el tipo*
Ⓓ ADV (*) 1 **to act/talk ~** hacerse el duro*
2 (*US*) **to hang ~** mantenerse firme

toughen ['tʌfn] (*also* **~ up**) Ⓐ VT [+ *material*] endurecer; [+ *person*] fortalecer, hacer más fuerte; (*fig*) [+ *position*] endurecer
Ⓑ VI endurecerse

toughened ['tʌfnd] ADJ [*material*] endurecido

tough-minded ['tʌf'maɪndɪd] ADJ duro, nada sentimental

toughness ['tʌfnɪs] N 1 [*of person*] dureza *f*; **she has a reputation for ~** tiene fama de dura
2 [*of substance, material*] dureza *f*, resistencia *f*
3 [*of meat*] dureza *f*
4 [*of policy, measure*] dureza *f*

Toulon ['tuː'lɔ̃ːŋ] N Tolón *m*

Toulouse ['tuː'luːz] N Tolosa *f* (*de Francia*)

toupée ['tuːpeɪ] N peluca *f*, postizo *m*

tour ['tʊər] Ⓐ N 1 (*by tourist*) [*of country*] gira *f*, viaje *m*; [*of city*] recorrido *m*; [*of building, exhibition*] visita *f*; **a ~ around Europe** una gira *or* un viaje por Europa; **to go on a ~ of sth: they went on a ~ of the Lake District** hicieron una excursión *or* un viaje por la Región de los Lagos; **to go on a walking/cycling ~** hacer una excursión a pie/en bicicleta; **we went on a ~ around London** hicimos un recorrido por Londres; **guided ~** [*of famous building*] visita *f* guiada *or* con guía; [*of city*] recorrido *m* turístico (con guía); *see also* **coach, conducted B1, grand, mystery**
2 (*by musician, team, statesman*) gira *f*; **concert ~** gira *f* de conciertos; **he is currently on a lecture ~ in the States** actualmente está dando una serie de conferencias por Estados Unidos; **they gave us a ~ of the factory** nos enseñaron la fábrica; **~ of inspection** recorrido *m or* ronda *f* de inspección; **he made a ~ of the villages threatened by the volcano** visitó *or* recorrió los pueblos amenazados por el volcán; **to be/go on ~** estar/ir de gira; **to take a play on ~** hacer una gira con una obra de teatro; **world ~** gira *f* mundial; *see also* **whistle-stop**
3 (*Mil*) **~ of duty** periodo *m* de servicio
4 (*US Golf*) **the ~** la temporada
Ⓑ VT 1 (*as tourist*) [+ *country, region*] recorrer, viajar por; [+ *town*] recorrer; **they are ~ing France** están recorriendo Francia, están viajando por Francia
2 (*officially*) ir de gira por; **the band ~ed Europe last year** el año pasado el grupo se fue de gira por Europa; **the Royal Opera is currently ~ing Japan** actualmente la Royal Opera está de gira por Japón; **the play is ~ing the provinces** están de gira con la obra por provincias; **the England team will be ~ing South Africa this winter** el equipo inglés hará una gira por Sudáfrica este invierno; **the Prince ~ed the factory** el Príncipe visitó la fábrica
Ⓒ VI 1 [*tourist*] viajar; **they went ~ing in Italy** se fueron de viaje por Italia
2 (*officially*) [*musician, team*] ir de gira; **he's currently ~ing in the States** actualmente está de gira por Estados Unidos
Ⓓ CPD ► **tour director** N (*US*) guía *mf* turístico/a ► **tour guide** N guía *mf* turístico/a ► **tour manager** N (*Sport, Mus*) encargado/a *m/f* de gira ► **tour operator** N touroperador(a) *m/f*

Touraine [tʊ'reɪn] N Turena *f*

tour de force ['tʊədə'fɔːs] N (*pl* **tours de force**) proeza *f*, hazaña *f*

tourer ['tʊərər] N coche *m* de turismo, turismo *m*

touring ['tʊərɪŋ] Ⓐ N 1 (*by tourist*) turismo *m*; **I'd like to do some ~ in a camper van** me gustaría hacer un poco de turismo en una autocaravana
2 (*by band, statesman etc*) giras *fpl*; **the company has done more ~ this year** la compañía ha realizado más giras este año
Ⓑ CPD ► **touring bicycle** N bicicleta *f* de paseo ► **touring company** N (*Theat*) compañía *f* (de teatro) ambulante ► **touring exhibition** N exposición *f* itinerante ► **touring holiday** N viaje *m* turístico ► **touring map** N mapa *m* turístico ► **touring production** N montaje *m* itinerante ► **touring team** N equipo *m* en gira

tourism ['tʊərɪzəm] N turismo *m*

tourist ['tʊərɪst] Ⓐ N 1 (*on holiday*) turista *mf*
2 (*Sport*) (= *visiting team*) **the ~s** el equipo visitante
Ⓑ CPD [*attraction, season*] turístico ► **tourist agency** N agencia *f* de turismo ► **tourist bureau** N = **tourist information centre** ► **tourist class** N clase *f* turista ► **tourist industry** N industria *f* del turismo ► **tourist information centre, tourist office** N oficina *f* de turismo, oficina *f* de información turística ► **tourist season** N temporada *f* del turismo ► **the tourist trade** N el turismo ► **tourist trap** N sitio *m* para turistas ► **tourist visa** N visado *m* turístico, visa *f* turística (*LAm*)

touristy* ['tʊərɪstɪ] ADJ (demasiado) turístico, turistizado

tournament ['tʊənəmənt] N torneo *m*; **tennis ~** torneo *m* de tenis

tourney ['tʊənɪ] N (*Hist*) torneo *m*

tourniquet ['tʊənɪkeɪ] N (*Med*) torniquete *m*

touse* [taʊz] VT (*lit, fig*) dar una paliza a

tousing* ['taʊzɪŋ] N (*lit, fig*) paliza *f*

tousle ['taʊzl] VT ajar, desarreglar; [+ *hair*] despeinar

tousled ['taʊzld] ADJ [*appearance, style*] desaliñado, desarreglado; [*hair*] despeinado

tout [taʊt] Ⓐ N (*for hotels etc*) gancho/a *m/f*; (*Racing*) pronosticador(a) *m/f*; (*Brit*) (= *ticket tout*) revendedor(a) *m/f*
Ⓑ VI (*Brit*) **to ~ for business** *or* **custom** tratar de captar clientes
Ⓒ VT [+ *wares*] ofrecer, pregonar; (*Brit*) [+ *tickets*] revender

tout court ['tuː'kʊər] ADV **his name is Rodríguez ~** se llama Rodríguez a secas

tow[1] [təʊ] Ⓐ N 1 (*Aut*) (= *act*) remolque *m*; (= *rope*) remolque *m*, cable *m* de remolque; (= *thing towed*) vehículo *m* remolcado; **to give sb a ~** dar remolque *or* remolcar a algn; **on ~** (*Brit*) ◊ **in ~** (*US*) a remolque; **to have a car in ~** llevar un coche de remolque; **to take in ~** dar remolque a
2 (*fig*) (*) **he arrived with a friend in ~** llegó acompañado de un amigo; (*unwillingly*) llegó con un amigo a rastras *or* a remolque
Ⓑ VT 1 [+ *car, caravan, boat*] remolcar; [+ *barge*] (*on canal*) sirgar
2 (*fig*) **to ~ sth about** llevar algo consigo
Ⓒ CPD ► **tow bar** N barra *f* de remolque ► **tow car** N (*US*) grúa *f*, coche *m* de remolque ► **tow line** N (*Naut*) (*at sea*) maroma *f* de remolque; (*on canal*) sirga *f*; (*Aut*) remolque *m*, cable *m* de remolque ► **tow truck** N (*esp US*) camión *m* grúa, grúa *f*, coche *m* de remolque
► **tow away** VT + ADV remolcar, quitar remolcando; **to ~ a car away** llevar un coche a la comisaría

tow[2] [təʊ] N (*Textiles*) estopa *f*

towage ['təʊɪdʒ] N (= *act*) remolque *m*; (= *fee*) derechos *mpl* de remolque

toward [tə'wɔːd] PREP 1 (*direction*) hacia; **we walked ~ the sea** caminamos hacia el mar *or* rumbo al mar; **the government is moving ~ disaster** el gobierno se encamina hacia el desastre
2 (*time*) alrededor de, a eso de; **~ noon** alrededor de mediodía; **~ six o'clock** hacia las seis, a eso de las seis
3 (*attitude*) para con, con respecto a, hacia; **his attitude ~ the church** su actitud para con *or* con respecto a *or* hacia la iglesia; **to feel friendly ~ sb** sentir simpatía hacia *or* por algn
4 (*purpose*) para; **we're saving ~ our holiday** ahorramos dinero para nuestras vacaciones; **it helps ~ a solution** contribuye a la solución, ayuda en el esfuerzo por encontrar una solución; **half my salary goes ~ paying the rent** la mitad de mi sueldo se va en el alquiler

towards [tə'wɔːdz] PREP (*esp Brit*) = **toward**

towaway zone ['təʊəweɪˌzəʊn] N (*US Aut*) *zona de aparcamiento prohibido donde la grúa procede a retirar los vehículos*

towboat ['təʊbəʊt] N (*US*) remolcador *m*

towel ['taʊəl] Ⓐ N (*for body*) toalla *f*; (*for hands*) paño *m*, toalla *f*; ✦*IDIOM* **to throw in the ~** darse por vencido
Ⓑ VT frotar con toalla; **to ~ sth/sb dry** secar algo/a algn con toalla
Ⓒ CPD ► **towel rack, towel rail** N toallero *m*

towelling, toweling (*US*) ['taʊəlɪŋ] N felpa *f*

tower ['taʊər] Ⓐ N 1 [*of castle*] torre *f*; **the Tower of London** la Torre de Londres; **a ~ of strength** (*fig*) una gran ayuda

2 (*also* **bell ~**) campanario *m*

B VI elevarse; **it ~s to over 300 metres** se eleva a más de 300 metros; **to ~ above** *or* **over sth** dominar algo; **to ~ above** *or* **over sb** destacar *or* descollar sobre algn; **he ~s above** *or* **over his contemporaries** (*fig*) destaca *or* descuella claramente entre sus coetáneos

C CPD ► **tower block** N (*Brit*) bloque *m* de pisos, torre *f* de pisos

towering ['taʊərɪŋ] ADJ [*peak, mountain*] elevado, imponente; [*building*] muy alto, imponente por su altura; [*figure*] (*in stature*) imponente, altísimo; (*in literature, arts etc*) destacado, sobresaliente; **in a ~ rage** con una rabia terrible

tow-headed [,təʊ'hedɪd] ADJ rubio, rubiacho

town [taʊn] A N ciudad *f*; (*smaller*) pueblo *m*, población *f*; **~ and gown** (*Univ*) ciudadanos *mpl* y universitarios, ciudad *f* y universidad; **to live in a ~** vivir en una ciudad; **Jake's back in ~!** ¡ha vuelto Jake!; **to be out of ~** [*place*] estar fuera de la ciudad; [*person*] estar de viaje; **he's from out of ~** (*US*) es forastero, no es de aquí; **to go into ~** ir al centro; ✦*IDIOMS* **to go out on the ~*** salir de juerga *or* de parranda*; **to go to ~ (on sth)*** dedicarse con entusiasmo (a algo), no cortarse nada (con algo); (*spending*) no reparar en gastos (con algo); *see also* **paint B2**

B CPD ► **town centre, town center** (*US*) N centro *m* urbano ► **town clerk** N secretario/a *m/f* del ayuntamiento ► **town council** N ayuntamiento *m* ► **town councillor** N concejal(a) *m/f* ► **town crier** N pregonero *m* público ► **town dweller** N habitante *mf* de la ciudad ► **town hall** N ayuntamiento *m*, municipalidad *f* ► **town house** N casa *f* adosada; (= *not country*) residencia *f* urbana ► **town meeting** N (*US*) pleno *m* municipal ► **town plan** N plan *m* de desarrollo urbano ► **town planner** N (*Brit*) urbanista *mf* ► **town planning** N (*Brit*) urbanismo *m*

townee [taʊ'niː], **townie** ['taʊnɪ] N habitante *mf* de la ciudad

townscape ['taʊnskeɪp] N paisaje *m* urbano

townsfolk ['taʊnzfəʊk] NPL ciudadanos *mpl*

township ['taʊnʃɪp] N (= *small town*) pueblo *m*; (*US*) municipio *m*; (*South Africa*) *asentamiento urbano creado en tiempos del apartheid para gente de raza negra en Sudáfrica*

townsman ['taʊnzmən] N (*pl* **townsmen**) ciudadano *m*; (*as opposed to country-dweller*) hombre *m* de la ciudad, habitante *m* de la ciudad

townspeople ['taʊnz,piːpl] NPL ciudadanos *mpl*

townswoman ['taʊnzwʊmən] N (*pl* **townswomen**) ciudadana *f*; (*as opposed to country-woman*) habitante *f* de la ciudad

towpath ['təʊpɑːθ] N camino *m* de sirga

towrope ['təʊrəʊp] N remolque *m*, cable *m* de remolque; (*on canal*) sirga *f*

toxaemia, **toxemia** (*US*) [tɒk'siːmɪə] N toxemia *f*

toxic ['tɒksɪk] A ADJ [*substance, alga*] tóxico

B N tóxico *m*

C CPD ► **toxic waste** N desechos *mpl* tóxicos

toxicity [,tɒk'sɪsɪtɪ] N toxicidad *f*

toxicological [,tɒksɪkə'lɒdʒɪkəl] ADJ toxicológico

toxicologist [,tɒksɪ'kɒlədʒɪst] N toxicólogo/a *m/f*

toxicology [,tɒksɪ'kɒlədʒɪ] N toxicología *f*

toxin ['tɒksɪn] N toxina *f*

toy [tɔɪ] A N juguete *m*

B VI **to ~ with** [+ *object, sb's affections*] jugar con, juguetear con; [+ *food*] comiscar; [+ *idea*] acariciar

C CPD ► **toy car** N coche *m* de juguete ► **toy dog** N (= *small breed of dog*) perrito *m*, perro *m* faldero ► **the toy industry** N la industria juguetera ► **toy maker** N (= *person*) fabricante *mf* de juguetes; (= *company*) empresa *f* de juguetes ► **toy poodle** N (= *small breed of poodle*) caniche *mf* enano/a ► **toy soldier** N soldadito *m* de juguete ► **toy theatre** N teatro *m* de títeres ► **toy train** N tren *m* de juguete

toybox ['tɔɪbɒks] N caja *f* de juguetes

toyboy ['tɔɪbɔɪ] N (*Brit*) amante *m* (de una mujer mayor)

toyshop ['tɔɪʃɒp] N juguetería *f*

toytown ['tɔɪtaʊn] ADJ 1 = **Mickey Mouse**

2 **he's a ~ revolutionary** es un aspirante a revolucionario

tpi N ABBR (*Comput*) = **tracks per inch**

trace [treɪs] A N 1 (= *sign*) rastro *m*, señal *f*; **the search for ~s of life on Mars** la búsqueda de señales *or* indicios de vida en Marte; **she wanted to remove all ~ of him from the flat** quería deshacerse de todo rastro de él en el piso; **I've lost all ~ of my relations** perdí todo contacto con mis familiares, les perdí la pista *or* el rastro a mis familiares; **there was no ~ of him having been there** no había ningún indicio *or* rastro de que hubiera estado allí; **she had no ~ of an accent** no tenía ni pizca de acento; **he showed no ~ of shyness** no dio muestras de timidez, no mostró señales de timidez; **to disappear** *or* **vanish without (a) ~** desaparecer sin dejar huella *or* rastro; **the group had a few hits then sank without ~** el grupo tuvo unos cuantos éxitos y luego desapareció sin dejar huella *or* rastro

2 (= *remains*) vestigio *m*; **they found ~s of an ancient settlement** encontraron vestigios de un antiguo poblado

3 (= *small amount*) rastro *m*; **the blood test revealed ~s of poison** el análisis de sangre reveló rastros de veneno; **there was a ~ of a smile on her face** tenía el esbozo de una sonrisa en la cara; **rinse well and remove all ~s of soap** enjuague bien y elimine cualquier rastro *or* resto de jabón; **she said it without a ~ of irony** lo dijo sin (ningún) asomo de ironía

4 (*Tech*) (= *line*) traza *f*

5 (= *strap on harness*) tirante *m*, correa *f*; ✦*IDIOM* **to kick over the ~s** rebelarse, sacar los pies del plato *or* tiesto*

B VT 1 (= *find*) [+ *missing document, fault*] localizar, encontrar; [+ *missing person, suspect*] averiguar el paradero de, localizar, ubicar (*LAm*); **we have been unable to ~ your letter** no hemos podido localizar *or* encontrar su carta; **I cannot ~ any reference to it** no encuentro ninguna referencia a eso

2 (= *follow trail of*) [+ *person*] seguir la pista a; **she was finally ~d to a house in Soho** le siguieron la pista hasta dar con ella en una casa del Soho; **they ~d the van to a car rental agency** averiguaron que la furgoneta era de una agencia de alquiler de automóviles

3 (= *find source of*) [+ *phone call*] averiguar el origen de; **I can ~ my family back to Elizabethan times** las raíces de mi familia se remontan a la época isabelina; **to ~ a rumour back to its source** averiguar dónde se originó un rumor, seguir la pista de un rumor hasta llegar a su punto de partida

C CPD ► **trace element** N oligoelemento *m*

traceable ['treɪsəbl] ADJ **a person not now ~** una persona cuyo paradero actual es imposible de encontrar; **an easily ~ reference** una referencia fácil de encontrar

tracer ['treɪsəʳ] A N (*Chem, Med*) indicador *m*, trazador *m*

B CPD ► **tracer bullet** N bala *f* trazadora ► **tracer element** N elemento *m* trazador

tracery ['treɪsərɪ] N tracería *f*

trachea [trə'kɪə] N (*pl* **tracheas, tracheae** [trə'kiːiː]) (*Anat*) tráquea *f*

tracheotomy [,trækɪ'ɒtəmɪ] N traqueotomía *f*

trachoma [træ'kəʊmə] N tracoma *m*

tracing ['treɪsɪŋ] A N 1 (*with tracing paper*) calco *m*

2 (*electronically*) traza *f*

3 [*of phone call*] seguimiento *m*

B CPD ► **tracing paper** N papel *m* de calco

track [træk] A N 1 (= *trail*) [*of animal, person*] rastro *m*, pista *f*; [*of vehicle*] rastro *m*; [*of wheel*] huellas *fpl*, rodada *f*; **to cover one's ~s** borrar las huellas; **to keep ~ of sth/sb**: **they prefer him to live at home where they can keep ~ of him** prefieren que viva en casa donde le pueden seguir la pista; **do you find it hard to keep ~ of all your bills?** ¿le resulta difícil mantenerse al corriente de todas sus facturas?; **start keeping ~ of how much you spend** empiece a tomar nota de cuánto gasta; **to lose ~ of sth/sb**: **I lost all ~ of time** perdí la noción del tiempo por completo; **to lose ~ of what sb is saying** perder el hilo de lo que está diciendo algn; **to make ~s*** (*fig*) irse marchando, empezar a irse; **it's time we were making ~s** es hora de irse marchando *or* de que empecemos a irnos; **to be on sb's ~** seguirle la pista *or* el rastro a algn; **to stop (dead) in one's ~s** pararse en seco; **the sound stopped him in his ~s** el sonido le hizo pararse en seco; **to throw sb off the ~** (*fig*) despistar a algn

2 (= *course*) [*of missile, bullet, satellite*] trayectoria *f*; [*of storm*] curso *m*; **it will take time to get the economy back on ~** se tardará un tiempo en volver a encarrilar la economía; **to be on the right ~** ir por buen camino; **to be on the wrong ~** ir por mal camino; *see also* **one-track**

3 (= *path*) camino *m*, sendero *m*

4 (*Sport*) pista *f*; **~ and field** atletismo *m*; **~ and field events** pruebas *fpl* de atletismo; **race ~** (*for horses*) hipódromo *m*; (*for bicycles*) velódromo *m*; (*for cars*) autódromo *m*, pista *f* *or* circuito *m* de automovilismo; **running ~** pista *f* de atletismo; ✦*IDIOMS* **to be on a fast ~ to sth** ir rápidamente camino de algo; **to have the inside ~** (*esp US*) estar en una posición de ventaja

5 (*Rail*) vía *f*; **double ~** vía *f* doble; **to jump the ~s** descarrilar; **single ~** vía *f* única; ✦*IDIOM* **the wrong side of the ~s** (*esp US**) los barrios bajos; **she was born on the wrong side of the ~s** nació en los barrios bajos; **she's from the wrong side of the ~s** proviene de los barrios bajos

6 (*Aut*) (*on tank, tractor*) oruga *f*; (*between wheels*) ancho *m* de vía (*Tech*) (*distancia entre los puntos de contacto con el suelo de dos ruedas paralelas*)

7 (*Audio*) pista *f*; **four/eight ~ recording system** equipo *m* de grabación de cuatro/ocho pistas

8 (*Comput*) pista *f*

9 (= *song, piece*) tema *m*; **title ~** tema *m* que da título *or* nombre al álbum

10 (*for curtains*) riel *m*

11 (*US Educ*) (= *stream*) *agrupamiento de alum-*

nos según su capacidad

Ⓑ VT 1 (= *follow*) [+ *animal*] seguir las huellas de, seguir el rastro de; [+ *person, vehicle*] seguir la pista a; [+ *satellite, missile*] seguir la trayectoria de, rastrear; **the camera was ~ing his movements** la cámara seguía sus movimientos

2 (= *deposit*) ir dejando; **she was ~ing dirt all over the carpet** iba dejando suciedad por toda la moqueta

Ⓒ VI [*stylus*] seguir el surco

Ⓓ CPD ► **track events** NPL (*Sport*) pruebas *fpl* en pista ► **track meet** N (*US*) concurso *m* de atletismo ► **track race** N carrera *f* en pista ► **track racing** N carreras *fpl* en pista, ciclismo *m* en pista ► **track record** N historial *m*; **he had a good ~ record** su historial era bueno; **it's a company with a poor ~ record** es una empresa con un historial no muy bueno (en materia de ganancias) ► **track shoes** NPL zapatillas *fpl* para pista de atletismo (claveteadas)

►**track down** VT + ADV (= *locate*) [+ *suspect, document, information*] localizar, ubicar (*LAm*); [+ *missing person*] averiguar el paradero de, localizar; **we eventually ~ed him down in the library** finalmente lo localizamos *or* dimos con él en la biblioteca; **scientists have ~ed down the bacteria that causes the infection** los científicos han localizado la bacteria que causa la infección; **eventually I ~ed down a copy of the novel** finalmente localicé un ejemplar de la novela

trackball [ˈtrækbɔːl] N (*Comput*) bola *f* rastreadora, trackball *m*

tracked [trækt] ADJ **~ vehicle** vehículo *m* de oruga

tracker [ˈtrækəʳ] Ⓐ N rastreador *m*

Ⓑ CPD ► **tracker dog** N perro *m* rastreador ► **tracker fund** N = **index-tracking fund**

tracking [ˈtrækɪŋ] Ⓐ N rastreo *m*

Ⓑ CPD ► **tracking device** N dispositivo *m* de localización ► **tracking shot** N (*Cine, TV*) travelling *m* ► **tracking station** N estación *f* de seguimiento

trackless [ˈtræklɪs] ADJ sin caminos, impenetrable

trackman [ˈtrækmən] N (*pl* **trackmen**) (*US*) obrero *m* de ferrocarril

tracksuit [ˈtræksuːt] N (*Brit*) chándal *m*

tract¹ [trækt] N 1 (= *area of land, sea*) extensión *f*

2 (*Anat*) tracto *m*; **respiratory ~** vías *fpl* respiratorias, aparato *m* respiratorio

tract² [trækt] N (= *pamphlet*) folleto *m*, panfleto *m*; (= *treatise*) tratado *m*

tractable [ˈtræktəbl] ADJ [*person*] tratable; [*problem*] soluble; [*material*] dúctil, maleable

traction [ˈtrækʃən] Ⓐ N tracción *f*

Ⓑ CPD ► **traction engine** N locomotora *f* de tracción

tractive [ˈtræktɪv] ADJ tractivo

tractor [ˈtræktəʳ] Ⓐ N tractor *m*

Ⓑ CPD ► **tractor drive** N tractor *m* ► **tractor driver** N tractorista *mf* ► **tractor feed** N arrastre *m* de papel por tracción

tractor-drawn [ˈtræktədrɔːn] ADJ arrastrado por tractor

trad* [træd] ADJ ABBR (*esp Brit Mus*) = **traditional**

trade [treɪd] Ⓐ N 1 (= *buying and selling*) comercio *m*; **domestic/foreign/world ~** comercio *m* interior/exterior/internacional; **to do ~ with sb** comerciar con algn; **to do a good** *or* **brisk** *or* **roaring ~ (in sth)** (*Brit*) hacer (un) buen negocio (con algo); **all ~ in ivory is banned** el comercio de todo tipo de *or* con marfil está prohibido; **to be in ~**† ser comerciante

2 (= *industry*) industria *f*; **the building ~** la industria de la construcción; **the antiques ~** la compraventa de antigüedades; **the arms ~** el tráfico de armas; **the tourist ~** el turismo, el sector turístico

3 (= *profession, occupation*) oficio *m*; **he's a butcher by ~** es carnicero de oficio; **known in the ~ as ...** conocido en el gremio como ...; **as we/they say in the ~** como decimos/dicen en el oficio; *see also* **tool, trick**

4 (= *people in trade*) **to sell to the ~** vender al por mayor *or* (*LAm*) al mayoreo; **"no trade"** "sólo particulares"; **"trade only"** "sólo mayoristas"

5 (= *clientele*) clientela *f*; **passing ~** clientela *f* de paso; **he hires boats out for the tourist ~** alquila barcas a los turistas

6 (*esp US*) (= *exchange*) cambio *m*; **it was fair ~** fue un cambio justo; **I'm willing to do** *or* **make a ~ with you** estoy dispuesto a hacerte un cambio *or* a hacer un cambio contigo

Ⓑ VT (*esp US*) (= *exchange*) [+ *goods*] cambiar; [+ *blows, insults, jokes*] intercambiar; **to ~ sth for sth** cambiar algo por algo; **to ~ sth with sb** intercambiar algo con algn; **I wouldn't ~ places with her for anything** no quisiera estar en su lugar por nada del mundo; **managers ~d places with cleaners for a day** los gerentes y el personal de limpieza se cambiaron los trabajos por un día

Ⓒ VI 1 (= *do business*) comerciar; **we are trading at a loss** estamos comerciando con pérdida; **to cease trading** cerrar; **to ~ in sth** comerciar con algo; **to ~ in ivory/hardware** comerciar con marfil/artículos de ferretería; **he ~s in antique dolls** se dedica a la compraventa de muñecas antiguas; **he ~s under a business name** opera con un nombre comercial; **to ~ with sb** comerciar con algn

2 (= *exchange*) (*esp US*) hacer un cambio

3 (= *sell*) [*currency, shares*] cotizarse (**at** a)

Ⓓ CPD ► **trade agreement** N acuerdo *m* comercial, convenio *m* comercial ► **trade association** N asociación *f* gremial, asociación *f* mercantil ► **trade barriers** NPL barreras *fpl* arancelarias ► **trade deficit** N déficit *m* comercial ► **Trade Descriptions Act** N (*Brit*) ley *f* de protección al consumidor ► **trade discount** N descuento *m* comercial ► **trade embargo** N embargo *m* comercial ► **trade fair** N feria *f* de muestras, feria *f* comercial ► **trade figures** NPL estadísticas *fpl* comerciales ► **trade gap** N déficit *m* comercial ► **trade journal** N revista *f* especializada ► **trade magazine** N = **trade journal** ► **trade name** N nombre *m* comercial ► **trade price** N precio *m* al por mayor, precio *m* de mayoreo (*LAm*) ► **trade restrictions** NPL restricciones *fpl* comerciales ► **trade route** N ruta *f* comercial ► **trade sanctions** NPL sanciones *fpl* comerciales ► **trade secret** N secreto *m* comercial; (*fig*) secreto *m* profesional ► **trades union** N = **trade union** ► **Trades Union Congress** N (*Brit*) Federación *f* de los Sindicatos ► **trade surplus** N balanza *f* comercial favorable, superávit *m* (en balanza) comercial ► **trade union** N sindicato *m* ► **trade unionism** N sindicalismo *m* ► **trade unionist** N sindicalista *mf*, miembro *mf* de un sindicato ► **trade union leader** N líder *mf* sindicalista ► **trade union movement** N movimiento *m* sindical, movimiento *m* sindicalista ► **trade union official** N representante *mf* sindical ► **trade war** N guerra *f* comercial ► **trade winds** NPL vientos *mpl* alisios

►**trade in** VT + ADV (= *exchange*) cambiar; (= *give as deposit*) [+ *car, appliance*] ofrecer como parte del pago

►**trade off** VT + ADV **to ~ off manpower costs against computer costs** compensar los costes de personal con los costes de informatización; **he ~d off information for a reduced sentence** pasó información a cambio de una reducción de la condena

►**trade on** VI + PREP explotar, aprovecharse de; **he ~s shamelessly on his good looks** explota su atractivo sin vergüenza ninguna, se aprovecha de su atractivo sin avergonzarse en absoluto

►**trade up** VI + ADV **they buy a house and then ~ up as their income rises** compran una casa y luego, cuando aumentan sus ingresos, la venden para comprar otra mejor

trade-in [ˈtreɪdɪn] Ⓐ N *sistema de devolver un artículo usado al comprar uno nuevo*; **it proved difficult to negotiate a ~ on a new property** resultó difícil negociar un cambio como parte del pago de una propiedad nueva; **the company operates a ~ policy** la empresa acepta la entrega de artículos usados como parte del pago

Ⓑ CPD ► **trade-in price, trade-in value** N *valor de un artículo usado que se descuenta del precio de otro nuevo*

trademark [ˈtreɪdmɑːk] N (*Comm*) marca *f* de fábrica, marca *f* comercial; (*fig*) marca *f* personal; *see also* **registered**

trade-off [ˈtreɪdɒf] N **there is always a ~ between risk and return** siempre existe un elemento de compensación entre el riesgo y las ganancias

trader [ˈtreɪdəʳ] N comerciante *mf*, negociante *mf*; (= *street trader*) vendedor(a) *m/f* ambulante; (*Hist*) mercader *m*

tradescantia [ˌtrædəsˈkæntɪə] N tradescantia *f*

tradesman [ˈtreɪdzmən] N (*pl* **tradesmen**) (= *shopkeeper*) tendero *m*; (= *roundsman*) repartidor *m*, proveedor *m*; (= *artisan*) artesano *m*; **~'s entrance** entrada *f* de servicio

tradespeople [ˈtreɪdzˌpiːpl] NPL tenderos *mpl*

tradeswoman [ˈtreɪdzˌwʊmən] N (*pl* **tradeswomen**) (= *shopkeeper*) tendera *f*; (= *roundswoman*) repartidora *f*, proveedora *f*; (= *artisan*) artesana *f*

trading [ˈtreɪdɪŋ] Ⓐ N 1 (*Comm*) comercio *m*, actividad *f* comercial; **the laws on Sunday ~** las leyes con respecto al comercio los domingos

2 (*St Ex*) operaciones *fpl* bursátiles; **to stop** *or* **suspend ~** suspender las operaciones bursátiles

Ⓑ CPD ► **trading account** N (*St Ex*) cuenta *f* de explotación ► **trading centre** N centro *m* de comercio ► **trading estate** N (*Brit*) zona *f* industrial, polígono *m* industrial (*Sp*) ► **trading floor** N parqué *m*, patio *m* de operaciones ► **trading links** NPL vínculos *mpl* comerciales ► **trading loss** N pérdidas *fpl* comerciales, pérdidas *fpl* de explotación ► **trading partner** N socio/a *m/f* comercial ► **trading post** N factoría *f* ► **trading profits** N beneficios *mpl* comerciales, beneficios *mpl* de explotación ► **trading stamp** N cupón *m*

tradition [trəˈdɪʃən] N tradición *f*; **according to ~** de acuerdo con la tradición; **~ has it that ...** según la tradición ...; **in the (best) ~ of** a la mejor usanza de; **it is a ~ that ...** es tradición que ...

traditional [trəˈdɪʃənl] ADJ tradicional; **the**

clothes which are ~ to his country la ropa tradicional de su país

traditionalism [trəˈdɪʃnəlɪzəm] N tradicionalismo *m*

traditionalist [trəˈdɪʃnəlɪst] Ⓐ ADJ tradicionalista

Ⓑ N tradicionalista *mf*

traditionality [trəˌdɪʃəˈnælətɪ] N tradicionalidad *f*

traditionally [trəˈdɪʃnəlɪ] ADV [1] (= *according to custom*) tradicionalmente; **~, election campaigns start on Labor Day** tradicionalmente *or* por tradición, las campañas electorales comienzan el Día del Trabajo

[2] (= *in the traditional way*) [*produced, made*] de forma tradicional, a la manera tradicional

traduce [trəˈdjuːs] VT (*frm*) calumniar, denigrar

traffic [ˈtræfɪk] (*vb: pt, pp* **trafficked**) Ⓐ N [1] (*Aut, Aer, Naut, Rail*) tráfico *m*, circulación *f*, tránsito *m* (*esp LAm*); **the ~ is heavy during the rush hour** hay mucho tráfico durante las horas punta; **~ was quite light** había poco tráfico; **~ was blocked for some hours** la circulación quedó interrumpida durante varias horas; **closed to heavy ~** cerrado a los vehículos pesados; **air ~** tráfico *m* aéreo

[2] (= *trade*) tráfico *m*, comercio *m* (**in** en); **drug ~** narcotráfico *m*, tráfico *m* de drogas

Ⓑ VI **to ~ (in)** traficar (en)

Ⓒ CPD (*Aut*) [*regulations*] de circulación, de tránsito (*esp LAm*) ► **traffic accident** N accidente *m* de tráfico, accidente *m* de circulación, accidente *m* de tránsito (*LAm*) ► **traffic circle** N (*US*) rotunda *f*, glorieta *f* ► **traffic cone** N cono *m* señalizador ► **traffic control** N (= *act*) control *m* del tráfico; (= *lights*) semáforo *m* ► **traffic duty** N **to be on ~ duty** estar en tráfico ► **traffic flow** N flujo *m* de tráfico ► **traffic island** N refugio *m* ► **traffic jam** N embotellamiento *m*, atasco *m*; **a five-mile ~ jam** un atasco de cinco millas ► **traffic lights** NPL semáforo *msing* ► **traffic offence** N (*Brit*) infracción *f* de tráfico ► **traffic police** N policía *f* de tráfico, policía *f* de tránsito ► **traffic sign** N señal *f* de tráfico ► **traffic violation** N (*US*) = **traffic offence** ► **traffic warden** N guardia *mf* de tráfico *or* tránsito; *see also* **road**

trafficator [ˈtræfɪkeɪtəʳ] N (*Brit*) indicador *m* de dirección, flecha *f* de dirección

trafficker [ˈtræfɪkəʳ] N traficante *mf* (**in** en)

tragedian [trəˈdʒiːdɪən] N trágico *m*

tragedienne [trədʒiːdɪˈen] N trágica *f*, actriz *f* trágica

tragedy [ˈtrædʒɪdɪ] N (*gen, Theat*) tragedia *f*; **it is a ~ that …** es una tragedia que …; **the ~ of it is that …** lo trágico del asunto es que …; **a personal ~** una tragedia personal

tragic [ˈtrædʒɪk] ADJ (*gen, Theat*) trágico

tragically [ˈtrædʒɪkəlɪ] ADV trágicamente; **her career ended ~ at the age of 19** su carrera se vio truncada trágicamente a la edad de 19 años; **~, she never lived to see her grandson** desgraciadamente, jamás llegó a ver a su nieto; **he died ~ young** murió terriblemente joven; **the operation went ~ wrong** la operación tuvo consecuencias trágicas

tragicomedy [ˈtrædʒɪˈkɒmɪdɪ] N tragicomedia *f*

tragicomic [ˈtrædʒɪˈkɒmɪk] ADJ tragicómico

trail [treɪl] Ⓐ N [1] (= *wake*) [*of dust, smoke*] estela *f*; [*of blood*] reguero *m*; [*of comet, meteor*] cola *f*; **the hurricane left a ~ of destruction** el huracán dejó una estela de estragos; **the murderer left a ~ of clues** el asesino dejó un reguero de pistas; **he left a ~ of wet footprints all through the house** dejó pisadas húmedas por toda la casa

[2] (= *track*) (*left by animal, person*) rastro *m*, pista *f*; **to be on sb's ~** seguir la pista a algn; **the police are hard** *or* **hot on his ~** la policía le sigue de cerca *or* está sobre su pista; **to pick up sb's ~** dar con algn; **we managed to throw** *or* **put them off our ~** conseguimos despistarlos

[3] (= *path*) camino *m*, sendero *m*; **tourist ~** ruta *f* turística; (*fig*) *see also* **blaze²**, **nature**

Ⓑ VT [1] (= *drag*) arrastrar; **he was ~ing his schoolbag behind him** iba arrastrando la cartera (de la escuela); **the jeep ~ed clouds of dust behind it** el jeep iba dejando nubes de polvo a su paso; **to ~ one's fingers in** *or* **through the water** hacer surcos en el agua con los dedos

[2] (= *deposit*) **the children ~ed dirt all over the carpet** los niños iban dejando suciedad por toda la moqueta

[3] (= *track*) [+ *animal, person*] seguir la pista a, seguir el rastro a; [+ *suspect*] seguir de cerca; **two detectives were ~ing him** dos detectives le seguían de cerca

[4] (= *lag behind*) ir rezagado con respecto a, ir a la zaga de; **the President ~s his opponent in opinion polls** el Presidente va rezagado con respecto a *or* va a la zaga de su adversario en las encuestas de opinión; **they are ~ing the leaders by just two points** los líderes sólo les llevan *or* sacan dos puntos de ventaja

Ⓒ VI [1] (= *drag*) arrastrarse; **your coat is ~ing in the mud** se te está arrastrando *or* vas arrastrando el abrigo por el barro; **she walked with her skirt ~ing on the ground** andaba arrastrando la falda por el suelo

[2] (= *dangle, spread*) **plants ~ from balconies** las plantas cuelgan de los balcones; **wires ~ing across the floor are dangerous** los cables sueltos por el suelo son peligrosos

[3] (= *trudge*) **I spent the afternoon ~ing around the shops** pasé la tarde pateándome las tiendas; **we ~ed home again in the rain** a duras penas y lloviendo nos hicimos el camino de vuelta a casa; **her husband ~ed along behind** su marido iba detrás arrastrando los pies

[4] (= *lag behind*) ir rezagado, ir a la zaga; **to ~ (far) behind sb** quedar (muy) a la zaga de algn, ir (muy) rezagado con respecto a algn; **he's ~ing in the polls** va por detrás *or* a la zaga en las encuestas; **they were ~ing 2-0 at half-time** en el descanso iban perdiendo dos a cero

► **trail away, trail off** VI + ADV [*sound*] irse apagando; **the last note ~s away to nothing** la última nota se va apagando hasta dejar de oírse; **her voice ~ed off** *or* **away** se le fue la voz; **he let the sentence ~ off meaningfully** dejó la frase en puntos suspensivos de forma significativa

trailblazer [ˈtreɪlbleɪzəʳ] N pionero/a *m/f*

trailblazing [ˈtreɪlbleɪzɪŋ] Ⓐ ADJ pionero

Ⓑ N *trabajo o viaje etc pionero*

trailer [ˈtreɪləʳ] Ⓐ N [1] (*Aut*) remolque *m*; (*of truck*) tráiler *m*, remolque *m*; (*US*) (= *caravan*) caravana *f*, rulot *f*

[2] (*Cine*) tráiler *m*, avance *m*

Ⓑ CPD ► **trailer park** N (*US*) (*for caravans*) camping *m* para caravanas *or* rulots; (*for trailers*) camping *m* para remolques

trailing [ˈtreɪlɪŋ] ADJ [*plant*] trepador; [*branches*] colgante; **she wore a long ~ scarf** llevaba un pañuelo largo que le colgaba; **~ edge** (*Aer*) borde *m* de salida, borde *m* posterior

train [treɪn] Ⓐ N [1] (*Rail*) tren *m*; **diesel/electric ~** tren *m* diesel/eléctrico; **express/fast/slow ~** tren *m* expreso/rápido/ordinario; **high-speed ~** tren *m* de alta velocidad; **steam ~** tren *m* de vapor; **connecting ~** tren *m* de enlace; **through ~** (tren *m*) directo *m*; **to catch a ~ (to)** coger *or* (*LAm*) tomar un tren (a); **I've got a ~ to catch** tengo que coger *or* (*LAm*) tomar un tren; **to change ~s** cambiar de tren, hacer tra(n)sbordo; **to go by ~** ir en tren; **to send sth by ~** mandar algo por ferrocarril; **to take the ~** coger *or* (*LAm*) tomar el tren; **to travel by ~** viajar en tren; *see also* **gravy**

[2] (= *line*) [*of people, vehicles*] fila *f*; [*of mules, camels*] recua *f*, reata *f*; **a ~ of reporters followed her everywhere** una cohorte de reporteros la seguía a todos sitios

[3] (= *sequence*) serie *f*; **a ~ of disasters/events** una serie de catástrofes/acontecimientos; **the earthquake brought great suffering in its ~** el terremoto trajo consigo gran sufrimiento; **the next stage of the operation was well in ~** la siguiente fase de la operación ya estaba en marcha; **to put sth in ~** ◊ **set sth in ~** poner algo en marcha; **~ of thought**: **to lose one's ~ of thought** perder el hilo; **you're interrupting my ~ of thought** me cortas el hilo de mis pensamientos; **they were both silent, each following her own ~ of thought** estaban las dos calladas, cada una pensando en lo suyo

[4] (= *entourage*) séquito *m*, comitiva *f*

[5] [*of dress*] cola *f*; **to carry sb's ~** llevar la cola del vestido de algn

[6] (*Mech*) [*of gears*] tren *m*

Ⓑ VT [1] (= *instruct*) [+ *staff*] formar; [+ *worker*] (*in new technique*) capacitar; [+ *soldier, pilot*] adiestrar; [+ *athlete, team*] entrenar; [+ *animal*] (*for task*) adiestrar; (*to do tricks*) amaestrar; [+ *racehorse*] entrenar, preparar; **our staff are ~ed to the highest standards** el nivel de formación de nuestros empleados es del más alto nivel; **you've got him well ~ed!** (*hum*) ¡le tienes bien enseñado! (*hum*); **he was ~ed in Salamanca** (*for qualification*) estudió en Salamanca; (*for job*) recibió su formación profesional en Salamanca; **to ~ sb to do sth: his troops are ~ed to kill** a sus tropas se les enseña a matar; **professional counsellors are ~ed to be objective** los consejeros profesionales están capacitados *or* adiestrados para ser objetivos; **he had ~ed himself to write left-handed** aprendió por su cuenta a escribir con la izquierda; **~ yourself to think positively** habitúate a pensar de manera positiva; **the dogs were ~ed to attack intruders** se adiestraba a los perros para que atacaran a los intrusos; **to ~ sb for sth**: **the programme ~s young people for jobs in computing** el programa forma a la gente joven para realizar trabajos en informática; **nobody ~s you for the job of being a parent** nadie te enseña a ser padre; **to ~ sb in sth**: **officers ~ed in the use of firearms** oficiales entrenados *or* adiestrados en el uso de armas de fuego; **they are ~ing women in non-traditional female jobs** están formando a mujeres en trabajos que tradicionalmente no realizan las mujeres

[2] (= *develop*) [+ *voice, mind*] educar

[3] (= *direct*) [+ *gun*] apuntar (**on** a); [+ *camera, telescope*] enfocar (**on** a); **his gun was ~ed on Jo** apuntaba a Jo con la pistola; **the camera was ~ed on me** la cámara me estaba enfocando

[4] (= *guide*) [+ *plant*] guiar (**up, along** por)

Ⓒ VI [1] (= *learn a skill*) estudiar; **where did you ~?** (*for qualification*) ¿dónde estudió?; (*for job*) ¿dónde se formó?; **he ~ed to be a lawyer** estudió derecho; **she was ~ing to be a teacher** estudiaba para (ser) maestra, estudiaba magisterio; **she ~ed as a hairdresser** estudió peluquería, aprendió el oficio de peluquera; **he's ~ing for the priesthood** estudia para meterse en el sacerdocio

[2] (*Sport*) entrenar, entrenarse; **I ~ for six hours a day** (me) entreno seis horas diarias; **to ~ for sth** entrenar(se) para algo

Ⓓ CPD ► **train crash** N accidente *m* ferroviario ► **train driver** N maquinista *mf* ► **train fare** N **I gave him the money for the ~ fare** le di dinero para el billete de tren ► **train journey** N viaje *m* en tren ► **train service** N servicio *m* de trenes ► **train set** N tren *m* de juguete (*con vías, estaciones, etc*) ► **train station** N estación *f* de ferrocarril, estación *f* de tren

►**train up*** VT + ADV (*Brit*) [+ *new staff*] empezar a formar a partir de cero

trained [treɪnd] ADJ [1] [*teacher, nurse*] titulado; [*worker, staff*] cualificado; [*animal*] (*for task*) adiestrado; (*to do tricks*) amaestrado; **there was a lack of ~ men and equipment** faltaban hombres entrenados y equipo; **she is a ~ singer** ha recibido formación de cantante, ha estudiado canto; **we have counsellors ~ to deal with these sorts of problems** tenemos asesores capacitados para llevar este tipo de problemas; **they have a highly-~ workforce** tienen una mano de obra altamente cualificada; **a well-~ army** un ejército disciplinado, un ejército bien entrenado

[2] [*eye, ear, voice*] educado

trainee [treɪ'niː] Ⓐ N aprendiz(a) *m/f*; (*US Mil*) recluta *mf* en período de aprendizaje; **management ~ = trainee manager**

Ⓑ CPD ► **trainee manager** N aprendiz(a) *m/f* de administración ► **trainee teacher** N estudiante *mf* de magisterio

trainer ['treɪnəʳ] N [1] (*Sport*) [*of athletes, gymnasts, footballers*] entrenador(a) *m/f*; [*of horses*] preparador(a) *m/f*; [*of circus animals*] domador(a) *m/f*

[2] (= *plane*) entrenador *m*

[3] **trainers** (= *shoes*) zapatillas *fpl* de deporte

training ['treɪnɪŋ] Ⓐ N [1] (*for job*) formación *f*; (*Mil*) instrucción *f*; [*of animals*] (*for task*) adiestramiento *m*; (*to do tricks*) amaestramiento *m*; (= *teaching*) enseñanza *f*, instrucción *f*; (= *period of training*) aprendizaje *m*, periodo *m* de formación; **~ will be provided** se ofrece formación; **she has no ~ or experience with children** no tiene formación o experiencia con niños; **she has no ~ as a nurse** no tiene (el) título de enfermera; **staff ~** formación *f* de empleados; *see also* **assertiveness, teacher**

[2] (*Sport*) entrenamiento *m*; **he injured a knee during** *or* **in ~** se lesionó una rodilla durante el entrenamiento; **to be in ~ for sth** estar entrenando *or* entrenándose para algo; **to be out of ~** estar desentrenado *or* bajo de forma; *see also* **weight**

Ⓑ CPD ► **training camp** N (*Mil*) campo *m* de instrucción, campo *m* de entrenamiento; (*Sport*) lugar *m* de concentración ► **training centre, training center** (*US*) N centro *m* de formación, centro *m* de capacitación ► **training college** N escuela *f* de formación profesional; (*for teachers*) escuela *f* normal ► **training course** N curso *m* de formación, curso *m* de capacitación ► **training flight** N vuelo *m* de instrucción ► **training ground** N (*Mil*) campo *m* de pruebas; (*Sport*) campo *m* de entrenamiento; (*fig*) **the band was a ~ ground for future jazz giants** la banda era como una especie de escuela para las futuras estrellas del jazz ► **training manual** N manual *m* de instrucción ► **training scheme** N plan *m* de formación profesional ► **training ship** N buque *m* escuela ► **training shoes** NPL zapatillas *fpl* de deporte

trainman ['treɪnmæn] N (*pl* **trainmen**) (*US Rail*) ferroviario *m*

trainspotter ['treɪnspɒtəʳ] N (*Brit*) [1] *persona cuyo hobby es apuntar los números de serie de los trenes que pasan*

[2] (*Brit* pej*) pelmazo/a* *m/f*, petardo/a* *m/f*

trainspotting ['treɪnspɒtɪŋ] N (*Brit*) **to go train-spotting** *ir a apuntar el número de serie de los trenes que pasan*

traipse [treɪps] Ⓐ VI (*) andar penosamente; **to ~ in/out** entrar/salir penosamente; **we ~d about all morning** pasamos toda la mañana yendo de acá para allá; **I had to ~ over to see him** tuve que tomarme la molestia de ir a verle

Ⓑ N caminata *f*

trait [treɪt] N rasgo *m*

traitor ['treɪtəʳ] N traidor(a) *m/f*; **to be a ~ to one's country** traicionar a la patria; **to turn ~** volverse traidor

traitorous ['treɪtərəs] ADJ [*person*] traidor; [*attempt, intention*] traicionero

traitorously ['treɪtərəslɪ] ADV traidoramente, a traición

traitress ['treɪtrɪs] N traidora *f*

Trajan ['treɪdʒən] N Trajano

trajectory [trə'dʒektərɪ] N trayectoria *f*, curso *m*

tram [træm] N [1] (*Brit*) tranvía *m*

[2] (*in mine*) vagoneta *f*

tramcar ['træmkɑːʳ] N = **tram**

tramlines ['træmlaɪnz] NPL (*Brit*) [1] (*for tram*) rieles *mpl* de tranvía

[2] (*Tennis*) líneas *f* laterales

trammel ['træməl] Ⓐ VT poner trabas a

Ⓑ NPL **trammels** trabas *fpl*

tramp [træmp] Ⓐ N [1] (= *sound of feet*) ruido *m* de pasos

[2] (= *long walk*) caminata *f*; **to go for a ~ in the hills** ir de paseo por la montaña; **it's a long ~** es mucho camino

[3] (= *homeless person*) vagabundo/a *m/f*

[4] (*esp US* pej*) (= *loose woman*) **she's a ~** es una zorra*, es una golfa*

[5] (*Naut*) (*also* **~ steamer**) vapor *m* volandero

Ⓑ VT [1] (= *stamp on*) pisar con fuerza

[2] (= *walk across*) recorrer a pie, hacer una excursión por; **to ~ the streets** andar por las calles, callejear

Ⓒ VI **to ~ (along)** caminar (con pasos pesados); **the soldiers ~ed past** los soldados pasaron marchando; **to ~ up and down** andar de acá para allá; **he ~ed up to the door** se acercó con pasos pesados a la puerta

trample ['træmpl] Ⓐ VT (*also* **to ~ underfoot**) pisar, pisotear

Ⓑ VI (*also* **to ~ about, to ~ along**) pisar fuerte, andar con pasos pesados; **to ~ on sth** pisar algo, pisotear algo; **to ~ on sb** (*fig*) tratar a algn sin miramientos; **to ~ on sb's feelings** herir los sentimientos de algn

trampoline ['træmpəlɪn] N cama *f* elástica

tramway ['træmweɪ] N (*Brit*) tranvía *m*

trance [trɑːns] N trance *m*; **to go into a ~** (*lit, fig*) entrar en trance

tranche [trɑːnʃ] N parte *f*, tajada *f*

trannie, tranny ['trænɪ] N (*pl* **trannies**) [1] (*) = **transistor (radio)**

[2] (*Phot**) = **transparency 3**

[3] (‡) (= *transvestite*) travesti‡ *mf*

tranquil ['træŋkwɪl] ADJ tranquilo, calmo

tranquillity, tranquility (*US*) [træŋ'kwɪlɪtɪ] N tranquilidad *f*, calma *f*

tranquillize, tranquilize (*US*) ['træŋkwɪlaɪz] VT tranquilizar

tranquillizer, tranquilizer (*US*) ['træŋkwɪlaɪzəʳ] N (*Med*) tranquilizante *m*

trans ABBR [1] = **translation**

[2] (= **translated**) trad.

[3] = **translator**

[4] = **transitive**

[5] = **transport(ation)**

[6] = **transferred**

trans... [trænz] PREFIX trans...

transact [træn'zækt] VT negociar, tramitar

transaction [træn'zækʃən] N [1] (= *deal*) operación *f*, transacción *f*; **cash ~s** operaciones *fpl* al contado

[2] (= *paperwork*) tramitación *f*

[3] **transactions** (= *records*) [*of society*] actas *fpl*, memorias *fpl*

transatlantic ['trænzət'læntɪk] ADJ [1] [*flight, crossing, phone call, liner*] transatlántico

[2] (*Brit*) (= *American*) norteamericano

transceiver [træn'siːvəʳ] N transceptor *m*, transmisor-receptor *m*

transcend [træn'send] VT sobrepasar, rebasar

transcendence [træn'sendəns] N [1] (= *superiority*) lo sobresaliente

[2] (*Philos*) trascendencia *f*

transcendency [træn'sendənsɪ] N = **transcendence**

transcendent [træn'sendənt] ADJ [1] (= *outstanding*) sobresaliente

[2] (*Philos*) transcendente

transcendental [ˌtrænsen'dentl] Ⓐ ADJ (*Philos*) trascendental

Ⓑ CPD ► **transcendental meditation** N meditación *f* trascendental

transcontinental ['trænzˌkɒntɪ'nentl] ADJ transcontinental

transcribe [træn'skraɪb] VT transcribir, copiar

transcript ['trænskrɪpt] N [1] (= *copy*) transcripción *f*

[2] (*US Scol*) expediente *m*

transcription [træn'skrɪpʃən] N (*gen*) transcripción *f*; **phonetic ~** pronunciación *f* fonética

transculturation [ˌtrænzkʌltʃʊ'reɪʃən] N transculturación *f*

transducer [trænz'djuːsəʳ] N transductor *m*

transect [træn'sekt] N transecto *m*

transept ['trænsept] N crucero *m*

transfer ['trænsfəʳ] Ⓐ N [1] (= *conveyance*) traslado *m*; **we will arrange the ~ of your medical records** nos encargaremos del traslado de su historial médico; **technology ~** transferencia *f* de tecnología

[2] (= *change*) [*of job*] traslado *m*; [*of power*] traspaso *m*; [*of vehicle*] transbordo *m*; **I've applied for a ~ to head office** he solicitado el traslado a la oficina central

[3] (*Jur, Fin*) [*of property*] transmisión *f*, traspaso *m*; [*of funds*] transferencia *f*; **bank ~** transferencia *f* bancaria; **direct ~** abono *m* en cuenta; **~ of ownership** traspaso *m* de propiedad

[4] (*Sport*) traspaso *m*; **to ask for a ~** pedir el traspaso

[5] (= *picture*) calcomanía *f*

Ⓑ VT [1] (= *convey*) [+ *object, person*] trasladar (**from** de; **to** a); **~ the chops to a serving dish** pase las chuletas a una fuente; **the train broke down and passengers were ~red to a bus** el tren se averió y los pasajeros tuvieron que pasarse a un autobús; **the disease can be ~red to humans** la enfermedad puede transmitirse *or* contagiarse a seres humanos

2 (= *relocate*) [+ *person*] trasladar (**from** de; **to** a); [+ *power*] traspasar; [+ *allegiance*] mudar; **the company ~red her to another department** la empresa la trasladó a otro departamento; **to ~ one's affections to another** dar su amor a otro

3 (*Jur, Fin*) [+ *property*] traspasar, transmitir; [+ *funds*] transferir; **she ~red the house to her son's name** puso la casa a nombre de su hijo; **to ~ money from one account to another** transferir dinero de una cuenta a otra

4 (*Sport*) [+ *player*] traspasar

5 (= *copy*) [+ *design*] pasar, trasladar; **the documents were ~red to microfilm** los documentos se pasaron *or* se trasladaron a microfilm

6 (*Telec*) [+ *call*] pasar; **please hold while I ~ you** no cuelgue, que ahora mismo le paso; **can you ~ me back to the switchboard?** ¿puede volverme a pasar con la centralita?

Ⓒ VI 1 (= *change*) (*from course, job*) trasladarse; (*from vehicle*) hacer transbordo; **he has ~red to another department** se ha trasladado a otro departamento; **I've ~red to a new pension scheme/course/school** me he pasado a otro plan de pensiones/curso/colegio; **she ~red from French to Spanish** se cambió *or* se trasladó del curso de francés al de español; **passengers ~red from a train to a bus** los pasajeros hicieron transbordo del tren al autobús; **we had to ~ to another coach** tuvimos que pasarnos a otro autobús

2 (*Sport*) [*player*] ser traspasado, traspasarse

Ⓓ CPD ► **transfer fee** N traspaso *m* ► **transfer list** N lista *f* de posibles traspasos

transferable [træns'fɜːrəbl] ADJ transferible; **not ~** no transferible

transference ['trænsfərəns] N 1 (= *relocation*) [*of information*] transferencia *f*, transmisión *f*; [*of affection*] cambio *m*; [*of power*] traspaso *m*; **the ~ of the papal seat to Avignon** el traslado de la sede pontificia a Avignon

2 (*Psych*) transferencia *f*; **thought ~** transmisión *f* de pensamientos

transfiguration [ˌtrænsfɪgə'reɪʃən] N transfiguración *f*

transfigure [træns'fɪgəʳ] VT transfigurar, transformar (**into** en)

transfix [træns'fɪks] VT traspasar, paralizar; **he stood ~ed with fear** se quedó paralizado por el miedo

transform [træns'fɔːm] VT transformar (**into** en)

transformation [ˌtrænsfə'meɪʃən] N transformación *f*

transformational [ˌtrænsfə'meɪʃənl] ADJ transformacional

transformer [træns'fɔːməʳ] Ⓐ N (*Elec*) transformador *m*

Ⓑ CPD ► **transformer station** N estación *f* transformadora

transfuse [træns'fjuːz] VT transfundir; [+ *blood*] hacer una transfusión de

transfusion [træns'fjuːʒən] N transfusión *f*; **to give sb a blood ~** hacer a algn una transfusión de sangre

transgenic [trænz'dʒenɪk] ADJ transgénico

transgress [træns'gres] Ⓐ VT 1 (= *go beyond*) traspasar

2 (= *violate*) violar, infringir

3 (= *sin against*) pecar contra

Ⓑ VI pecar, cometer una transgresión

transgression [træns'greʃən] N transgresión *f*, infracción *f*; (*Rel*) pecado *m*

transgressor [træns'gresəʳ] N transgresor(a) *m/f*, infractor(a) *m/f*; (*Rel*) pecador(a) *m/f*

tranship [træn'ʃɪp] VT = **transship**

transhipment [træn'ʃɪpmənt] N = **transshipment**

transience ['trænzɪəns] N lo pasajero, transitoriedad *f*

transient ['trænzɪənt] Ⓐ ADJ transitorio, pasajero

Ⓑ N (*US*) transeúnte *mf*

transistor [træn'zɪstəʳ] Ⓐ N (*Elec*) transistor *m*; (*also* ~ **set**) transistor *m*

Ⓑ CPD ► **transistor radio** N radio *f* de transistores

transistorized [træn'zɪstəraɪzd] ADJ [*circuit*] transistorizado

▼**transit** ['trænzɪt] Ⓐ N tránsito *m*; **in ~** en tránsito

Ⓑ CPD ► **transit camp** N campo *m* de tránsito ► **transit lounge** N (*Brit*) sala *f* de tránsito ► **transit visa** N visado *m or* (*LAm*) visa *f* de tránsito

transition [træn'zɪʃən] Ⓐ N transición *f*

Ⓑ CPD ► **transition period** N período *m* de transición

transitional [træn'zɪʃənəl] ADJ transicional, de transición

transitive ['trænzɪtɪv] ADJ transitivo; **~ verb** verbo *m* transitivo

transitively ['trænzɪtɪvlɪ] ADV transitivamente

transitory ['trænzɪtərɪ] ADJ transitorio

translatable [trænz'leɪtəbl] ADJ traducible

translate [trænz'leɪt] Ⓐ VT 1 (*Ling*) traducir (**from** de; **into** a); **~ this text into Spanish** traduzca este texto al español; **how do you ~ "posh"?** ¿cómo se traduce "posh"?

2 (= *convert*) **to ~ centigrade into Fahrenheit** convertir grados centígrados en Fahrenheit; **to ~ words into deeds** convertir palabras en acción

3 (= *transfer*) (*esp Rel*) trasladar (**from** de; **to** a)

Ⓑ VI [*person*] traducir; [*word, expression*] traducirse; **poetry does not ~ easily** la poesía no es fácil de traducir

translation [trænz'leɪʃən] N 1 (*Ling*) traducción *f*

2 (= *transfer*) (*esp Rel*) traslado *m*

translator [trænz'leɪtəʳ] N traductor(a) *m/f*

transliterate [trænz'lɪtəreɪt] VT transcribir

transliteration [ˌtrænzlɪtə'reɪʃən] N transliteración *f*, transcripción *f*

translucence [trænz'luːsns] N translucidez *f*

translucent [trænz'luːsnt] ADJ translúcido

transmigrate ['trænzmaɪ'greɪt] VI transmigrar

transmigration [ˌtrænzmaɪ'greɪʃən] N transmigración *f*

transmissible [trænz'mɪsəbl] ADJ transmisible

transmission [trænz'mɪʃən] Ⓐ N (*Rad, TV, Aut*) transmisión *f*

Ⓑ CPD ► **transmission shaft** N (*Aut*) eje *m* de transmisión

transmit [trænz'mɪt] VT [+ *illness, programme, message*] transmitir (**to** a)

transmitter [trænz'mɪtəʳ] N (*Rad, TV, Telec*) emisora *f*

transmogrify [trænz'mɒgrɪfaɪ] VT transformar (como por encanto) (**into** en), metamorfosear (extrañamente) (**into** en)

transmutable [trænz'mjuːtəbl] ADJ transmutable

transmutation [ˌtrænzmjuː'teɪʃən] N transmutación *f*

transmute [trænz'mjuːt] VT **to ~ (into)** transmutar (en)

transnational [trænz'næʃənəl] Ⓐ ADJ transnacional

Ⓑ N transnacional *f*

transom ['trænsəm] N (*Archit*) (*across window*) travesaño *m*; (*US*) (= *window*) montante *m* de abanico, abanico *m*

transparency [træns'pærənsɪ] N 1 [*of object, material, substance*] transparencia *f*

2 [*of statement*] claridad *f*

3 (*Phot*) (*for overhead projector*) transparencia *f*; (= *slide*) diapositiva *f*

transparent [træns'pærənt] ADJ 1 (= *see-through*) [*object, material, substance*] transparente

2 (= *easy to understand*) [*situation, system, operation*] claro, transparente; **I like his ~ honesty** me gusta el que sea de una honestidad tan clara; **he's so ~** se le ve venir, es una persona sin tapujos*; **it is ~ that …** está claro que …, se ve claramente que …

3 (= *blatant*) [*lie*] obvio; [*attempt, device*] claro

transparently [træns'pærəntlɪ] ADV claramente; **a ~ one-sided examination of the pros and cons of nuclear power** un examen claramente sesgado de los pros y los contras de la energía nuclear; **it is ~ clear** *or* **obvious that …** está meridianamente claro que …; **the reason is ~ obvious** la razón está clarísima, la razón está más clara que el agua; **he had been ~ honest with her** había sido claro y sincero con ella

transpiration [ˌtrænspɪ'reɪʃən] N transpiración *f*

transpire [træns'paɪəʳ] Ⓐ VI 1 (*Bot, Anat*) transpirar

2 (= *become known*) **it finally ~d that …** al final se supo que …

3 (= *happen*) ocurrir, suceder; **his report on what ~d** su informe acerca de lo que pasó

Ⓑ VT transpirar

transplant Ⓐ [træns'plɑːnt] VT (*Bot, Med*) trasplantar

Ⓑ ['trænsplɑːnt] N (*Med*) trasplante *m*; **she had a heart ~** le hicieron un trasplante de corazón

transplantation [ˌtrænsplɑːn'teɪʃən] N (*Bot, Med*) trasplante *m*

transponder [træn'spɒndəʳ] N transpondedor *m*

transport ['trænspɔːt] Ⓐ N 1 (= *conveying, movement*) transporte *m*; **air ~** transporte *m* aéreo; **Department of Transport** (*Brit*) Ministerio *m* de Transporte(s); **means of ~** medio *m* de transporte; **I was stranded with no means of ~** me quedé colgado sin medio de transporte; **rail ~** transporte *m* ferroviario; **road ~** transporte *m* por carretera; **sea ~** transporte *m* marítimo; *see also* **public C**

2 (= *vehicle*) transporte *m*; **I haven't got any ~** no tengo transporte; **own ~ required** se requiere vehículo propio

3 (= *ship*) buque *m* de transporte

4 (= *plane*) avión *m* de transporte

5 (*fig*) (*liter*) **it sent her into ~s of delight** la dejó extasiada; **to be in a ~ of rage** estar fuera de sí (de rabia)

Ⓑ VT 1 (= *move*) [+ *goods, people*] transportar

2 (*Hist*) (= *deport*) [+ *criminal*] deportar

3 (*fig*) transportar; **the musical ~s the audience to the days of 1950s America** el musical transporta *or* traslada al público a la América de los años 50; **I felt as though I'd been ~ed back in time** me sentí como si me

➤ LANGUAGE IN USE: **transit A** 20.5

hubiera remontado en el tiempo; **to be ~ed with joy** (*liter*) quedarse embelesado *or* (*liter*) arrobado, estar extasiado

Ⓒ CPD ► **transport café** N cafetería *f* de carretera ► **transport costs** NPL gastos *mpl* de transporte ► **transport plane** N avión *m* de transporte ► **transport police** N policía *f* de tráfico ► **transport policy** N política *f* de transportes ► **transport ship** N buque *m* de transporte ► **transport system** N sistema *m* de transportes, red *f* de transportes

transportable [træns'pɔːtəbl] ADJ transportable

transportation [ˌtrænspɔː'teɪʃən] N [1] (*esp US*) (= *transport*) transporte *m*; **mass ~** (*US*) transporte *m* público

[2] (*Hist*) [*of criminal*] deportación *f*

transporter [træns'pɔːtəʳ] N transportador *m*

transpose [træns'pəʊz] VT [1] [+ *words*] transponer

[2] (*Mus*) transportar

[3] (= *transfer*) trasladar

transposition [ˌtrænspə'zɪʃən] N [1] [*of words*] transposición *f*

[2] (*Mus*) transporte *m*

[3] (= *transfer*) traslado *m*

trans-Pyrenean [trænzˌpɪrə'niːən] ADJ transpirenaico

transsexual [trænz'seksjʊəl] Ⓐ ADJ transexual

Ⓑ N transexual *mf*

transship [træns'ʃɪp] VT transbordar

transshipment [træns'ʃɪpmənt] N transbordo *m*

trans-Siberian [trænzsaɪ'bɪərɪən] ADJ transiberiano

transubstantiate [ˌtrænsəb'stænʃɪeɪt] VT transubstanciar

transubstantiation ['trænsəbˌstænʃɪ'eɪʃən] N transubstanciación *f*

transversal [trænz'vɜːsəl] ADJ transversal

transverse ['trænzvɜːs] ADJ transverso, transversal

transversely [trænz'vɜːslɪ] ADV transversalmente

transvestism ['trænzˌvestɪzəm] N travestismo *m*

transvestite [trænz'vestaɪt] Ⓐ ADJ travestido, travesti

Ⓑ N travesti *mf*, travestido/a *m/f*

trap [træp] Ⓐ N [1] (*lit, fig*) trampa *f*; **it's a ~!** ¡es una trampa!; **he was caught in his own ~** cayó en su propia trampa; **we were caught like rats in a ~** estábamos atrapados como en una ratonera; **that car is a death ~** ese coche es una bomba *or* tiene mucho peligro; **curtains are a natural dust ~** en las cortinas se suele acumular mucho el polvo; **to fall into a ~** caer en una trampa; **to lay a ~ (for sb)** tender una trampa (a algn); **to lure sb into a ~** hacer que algn caiga en una trampa; **to set a ~ (for sb)** tender una trampa (a algn); **they walked straight into our ~** cayeron de lleno en nuestra trampa; *see also* **poverty, speed, tourist**

[2] (‡) (= *mouth*) boca *f*; **shut your ~!** ¡cierra el pico!*, ¡cállate la boca!*; **to keep one's ~ shut** cerrar el pico*, callar la boca*; **you keep your ~ shut about this** de esto no digas ni pío*

[3] (= *carriage*) *coche ligero de dos ruedas*

[4] (*in greyhound racing*) caseta *f* de salida

[5] (*for clay pigeon shooting*) lanzaplatos *m inv*

[6] (*Golf*) búnker *m*

[7] (*Tech*) sifón *m*, bombillo *m*

[8] (*also* **~door**) trampilla *f*; (*Theat*) escotillón *m*

Ⓑ VT [1] (= *snare*) [+ *animal*] atrapar, cazar con trampa; [+ *criminal*] atrapar, coger, agarrar (*LAm*)

[2] (= *dupe*) hacer caer en la trampa, engañar; **you're not going to ~ me like that** con esas no me vas a hacer caer en la trampa, con esas no me vas a engañar; **to ~ sb into sth** tender una trampa a algn para que haga algo; **he felt he had been ~ped into marriage** le parecía que le habían cazado al casarse, le parecía que le habían tendido una trampa para que se casara; **they ~ped her into confessing** le tendieron una trampa y confesó

[3] (= *hold fast, confine*) atrapar; **survivors are ~ped in the rubble** los supervivientes están enterrados *or* atrapados bajo los escombros; **the miners are ~ped underground** los mineros están atrapados bajo tierra; **heavy snowfalls had ~ped us in the village** las fuertes nevadas nos habían dejado incomunicados *or* aislados en el pueblo; **they tied a rope around his body, ~ping his arms** le ataron una cuerda alrededor del cuerpo, inmovilizándole los brazos; **to ~ one's finger in sth** pillarse *or* cogerse *or* (*LAm*) atraparse el dedo con algo; **to ~ a nerve** pillar *or* (*Sp*) coger un nervio

[4] (= *retain*) [+ *heat, gas, water*] retener

[5] (*Sport*) [+ *ball*] parar (con el pie)

Ⓒ CPD ► **trap door** N trampilla *f*; (*Theat*) escotillón *m*

trapes [treɪps] VI = **traipse**

trapeze [trə'piːz] Ⓐ N trapecio *m*

Ⓑ CPD ► **trapeze artist** N trapecista *mf*

trapezium [trə'piːzɪəm] N (*pl* **trapeziums, trapezia** [trə'piːzɪə]) (*Math*) trapecio *m*

trapezoid ['træpɪzɔɪd] N (*Math*) trapezoide *m*

trapper ['træpəʳ] N trampero *m*, cazador *m*

trappings ['træpɪŋz] NPL [1] [*of horse*] arreos *mpl*, jaeces *mpl*

[2] (*fig*) adornos *mpl*; **shorn of all its ~** sin ninguno de sus adornos, desprovisto de adorno; **that statement, shorn of its ~ …** esa declaración, en términos escuetos …; **with all the ~ of kingship** con todo el boato de la monarquía

Trappist ['træpɪst] Ⓐ ADJ trapense

Ⓑ N trapense *m*

Ⓒ CPD ► **Trappist monk** N monje *m* trapense

trash [træʃ] (*US*) Ⓐ N [1] (= *rubbish*) basura *f*, desperdicios *mpl*

[2] (*fig*) tonterías *fpl*, babosadas *fpl* (*LAm*); **the book is ~** el libro es una basura; **he talks a lot of ~** no dice más que tonterías; **trash!** ¡tonterías!

[3] (*pej*) (= *people*) **(human) ~** gente *f* inútil, gentuza *f*; *see also* **white**

Ⓑ VT (*) [1] (= *wreck*) hacer polvo*, destrozar

[2] (= *criticize*) [+ *person*] poner verde*; [+ *ideas*] poner por los suelos

Ⓒ CPD ► **trash can** N cubo *m* de la basura, bote *m* de la basura, tarro *m* de la basura (*LAm*) ► **trash heap** N basurero *m*

trashy ['træʃɪ] ADJ malo, barato

trauma ['trɔːmə] Ⓐ N (*pl* **traumas, traumata** ['trɔːmətə]) [1] (*Psych*) trauma *m*

[2] (*Med*) traumatismo *m*, trauma *m*

Ⓑ CPD ► **trauma centre, trauma center** (*US*) N departamento *m* (hospitalario) de urgencias

traumatic [trɔː'mætɪk] ADJ traumatizante, traumático

traumatism ['trɔːmætɪzəm] N traumatismo *m*

traumatize ['trɔːmətaɪz] VT traumatizar

travail ['træveɪl] N (†† *or hum*) esfuerzo *m* penoso; (*Med*) dolores *mpl* del parto; **to be in ~** afanarse, azacanarse††; (*Med*) estar de parto

travel ['trævl] Ⓐ N [1] (= *travelling*) viajes *mpl*; **the job involves frequent ~** el trabajo requiere viajes frecuentes; **she is returning after two years' ~ in Africa** vuelve tras dos años de viajes por África, vuelve después de viajar dos años por África; **students can get cheap ~** los estudiantes pueden viajar a precios reducidos; **~ broadens the mind** viajar te abre más la mente *or* te da más amplitud de miras; **air ~** viajes *mpl* en avión; **I have made my own ~ arrangements** he hecho mis propios planes para el viaje; **foreign ~** viajes *mpl* por el extranjero

[2] **travels** viajes *mpl*; **she told us about her ~s in Africa** nos habló de sus viajes por Africa; **to set off on one's ~s** emprender el viaje; **you'll never guess who I met on my ~s today!** ¡no te vas a imaginar *or* a que no sabes con quién me he topado en la calle hoy!

[3] (= *movement*) **direction/line of ~** dirección *f*/línea *f* de desplazamiento

[4] (*Tech*) [*of lever, pedal*] desplazamiento *m*

Ⓑ VI [1] (= *make a journey*) viajar; **she'd always wanted to ~** siempre había querido viajar; **she ~s into the centre to work** se desplaza *or* va al centro a trabajar; **to ~ abroad**: **she spent six months ~ling abroad** pasó seis meses viajando por el extranjero; **he was forbidden to ~ abroad** le prohibieron que viajara al extranjero; **to ~ by sth**: **to ~ by air/plane** viajar en avión; **to ~ by car/train/bus** (*short journeys*) ir en coche/tren/autobús; (*longer journeys*) viajar en coche/tren/autobús; **I ~ to work by train** voy al trabajo en tren; **to ~ light** viajar con poco equipaje; **we'll be ~ling round Italy** recorreremos Italia; **we'll be ~ling through France** viajaremos *or* pasaremos por Francia; **he's ~ling to Helsinki tomorrow** mañana viaja a Helsinki; **he has ~led widely** ha viajado mucho

[2] (= *move*) ir; **we were ~ling at 30mph** íbamos a 30 millas por hora; **light/sound ~s at a speed of …** la luz/el sonido viaja *or* se desplaza a una velocidad de …; **the current ~s along this wire** la corriente va *or* pasa por este alambre; **news ~s fast** las noticias vuelan; **his eyes ~led swiftly around the room** recorrió rápidamente la habitación con la mirada

[3] (*) (= *move quickly*) **he was really ~ling!** ¡iba a toda pastilla *or* a toda mecha!*; **that car certainly ~s** ese coche sí que corre

[4] (= *react to travelling*) **this wine ~s well** este vino no se estropea con los viajes; **British dance music does not ~ well** la música de baile británica no se recibe bien en otros países

[5] (*Comm*) ser viajante (de comercio); **he ~s in soap** es representante de jabones

[6] (*Basketball*) dar pasos, hacer pasos

Ⓒ VT [+ *country*] viajar por, recorrer; [+ *road*] recorrer; [+ *distance*] recorrer, hacer; **he has ~led the world** ha viajado por *or* ha recorrido todo el mundo

Ⓓ CPD ► **travel agency** N agencia *f* de viajes ► **travel agent** N agente *mf* de viajes ► **travel alarm** N despertador *m* de viaje ► **travel bag** N bolso *m* de viaje ► **travel brochure** N folleto *m* turístico ► **travel bureau** N agencia *f* de viajes ► **travel company** N empresa *f* de viajes ► **travel documents** NPL documentos *mpl* de viaje ► **travel expenses** NPL gastos *mpl* de viaje, gastos *mpl* de desplazamiento ► **travel insurance** N seguro *m* de viaje ▸ **travel news** N información *f* sobre viajes y transporte ▸ **travel sickness** N mareo *m* (*por el viaje*) ▸ **travel writer** N *escritor o periodista que escribe libros o artículos sobre viajes*

travelator [ˈtrævəleɪtəʳ] N (*US*) cinta *f* transbordadora, pasillo *m* móvil

traveler [ˈtrævləʳ] N (*US*) *see* **traveller**

travelled, traveled (*US*) [ˈtrævld] ADJ **it is a little-~ route** es una ruta (que ha sido) poco transitada; **she is much** *or* **well** *or* **widely ~** ha viajado mucho, ha visto mucho mundo; **he was carrying a much-~ suitcase** llevaba una maleta muy usada

traveller, traveler (*US*) [ˈtrævləʳ] Ⓐ N (*gen*) viajero/a *m/f*; (*Comm*) (*also* **commercial ~**) viajante *mf*; **a ~ in soap** un viajante en jabones

Ⓑ CPD ▸ **traveller's cheque, traveler's check** (*US*) N cheque *m* de viajero ▸ **traveller's joy** N (*Bot*) clemátide *f*

travelling, traveling (*US*) [ˈtrævlɪŋ] Ⓐ ADJ [*circus*] ambulante; [*exhibition*] itinerante

Ⓑ N **I've always loved ~** siempre me ha encantado viajar, siempre me han encantado los viajes; **he had done a bit of ~ in Europe** había viajado un poco por Europa

Ⓒ CPD ▸ **travelling bag** N bolso *m* de viaje ▸ **travelling companion** N compañero/a *m/f* de viaje ▸ **travelling expenses** NPL gastos *mpl* de viaje, gastos *mpl* de desplazamiento ▸ **travelling salesman** N viajante *mf* (de comercio), representante *mf*

travelogue, travelog (*US*) [ˈtrævəlɒg] N (= *brochure*) folleto *m* de viajes; (= *lecture*) charla *f* sobre viajes; (= *film*) película *f* de viajes; (= *documentary*) documental *m* de viajes

travel-sick [ˈtrævəlsɪk] ADJ mareado (*por el viaje*); **to get ~** marearse al viajar

travel-weary [ˈtrævlwɪərɪ] ADJ fatigado por el viaje

travel-worn [ˈtrævlwɔːn] ADJ fatigado por el viaje, rendido después de tanto viajar

traverse [ˈtrævəs] Ⓐ N ① (*Tech*) travesaño *m*

② (*Mil*) través *m*

③ (*Mountaineering*) escalada *f* oblicua, camino *m* oblicuo

Ⓑ VT (*frm*) atravesar; **we are traversing a difficult period** atravesamos un período difícil

Ⓒ VI (*Mountaineering*) hacer una escalada oblicua

travesty [ˈtrævɪstɪ] Ⓐ N parodia *f*, farsa *f*

Ⓑ VT parodiar

trawl [trɔːl] Ⓐ N ① (= *net*) red *f* barredera, red *f* de arrastre

② (= *act*) rastreo *m*; **a ~ through police files** un rastreo de los archivos policiales

Ⓑ VT [+ *area*] rastrear; [+ *river, lake*] dragar; **to ~ up** pescar, sacar a la superficie

Ⓒ VI ① (= *fish*) pescar al arrastre, rastrear; **to ~ (for sth)** rastrear (algo)

② (= *search*) **to ~ through the files** rastrear los archivos; **to ~ for evidence** rastrear buscando pruebas

trawler [ˈtrɔːləʳ] N trainera *f*, barco *m* pesquero de arrastre

trawling [ˈtrɔːlɪŋ] N pesca *f* a la rastra

tray [treɪ] Ⓐ N (*for food, dishes*) bandeja *f*, charola *f* (*Mex*); (= *tea tray*) bandeja *f* del té; (= *filing tray*) cesta *f*; [*of balance*] platillo *m*; (= *drawer*) cajón *m*, batea *f*; (*Phot, Tech*) cubeta *f*

Ⓑ CPD ▸ **tray cloth** N cubrebandeja *m*

treacherous [ˈtretʃərəs] ADJ ① (= *disloyal*) [*person*] traidor; [*attempt, intention*] traicionero; **a ~ act** *or* **action** una traición

② (= *dangerous*) [*road, bend*] peligroso; [*tide, current*] traicionero; **~ road** *or* **driving conditions** condiciones peligrosas para la conducción

treacherously [ˈtretʃərəslɪ] ADV ① (= *disloyally*) traidoramente, a traición

② (= *dangerously*) **the roads are ~ icy** el hielo que cubre las carreteras hace peligrosa la conducción

treachery [ˈtretʃərɪ] N traición *f*; **an act of ~** una traición

treacle [ˈtriːkl] Ⓐ N melaza *f*

Ⓑ CPD ▸ **treacle tart** N tarta *f* de melaza

treacly [ˈtriːklɪ] ADJ (= *like treacle*) parecido a melaza; (= *covered in treacle*) cubierto de melaza

tread [tred] (*vb: pt* **trod**; *pp* **trodden**) Ⓐ N ① (= *footsteps*) paso *m*; (= *gait*) andar *m*, modo *m* de andar; **with (a) heavy ~** con paso pesado; **with measured ~** con pasos rítmicos

② [*of stair*] huella *f*; [*of shoe*] suela *f*; [*of tyre*] rodadura *f*, banda *f* rodante (*LAm*)

Ⓑ VT [+ *ground, grapes*] pisar; [+ *path*] (= *make*) marcar; (= *follow*) seguir; **to ~ water** flotar en el agua en posición vertical; **a place never trodden by human feet** un sitio no hollado por pie humano; **he trod his cigarette end into the mud** apagó la colilla pisándola en el barro

Ⓒ VI (= *walk*) andar, caminar (*LAm*); (= *put foot down*) **to ~ (on)** pisar; **to ~ on sb's heels** pisar los talones a algn; **careful you don't ~ on it!** ¡ojo, que lo vas a pisar!, cuidado, no vas a pisarlo; **to ~ softly** pisar dulcemente, no hacer ruido al andar; ✦***IDIOMS*** **to ~ carefully** *or* **warily** andar con pies de plomo; **we must ~ very carefully in this matter** debemos andarnos con pies de plomo en este asunto; **to ~ on sb's toes** meterse con algn

▸**tread down** VT + ADV pisar

▸**tread in** VT + ADV [+ *root, seedling*] asegurar pisando la tierra alrededor

treadle [ˈtredl] N pedal *m*

treadmill [ˈtredmɪl] N rueda *f* de andar; (*fig*) rutina *f*; **back to the ~!** ¡volvamos al trabajo!

Treas. ABBR = **Treasurer**

treason [ˈtriːzn] N traición *f*; **high ~** alta traición *f*

treasonable [ˈtriːzənəbl] ADJ traidor, desleal

treasure [ˈtreʒəʳ] Ⓐ N (= *gold, jewels*) tesoro *m*; **buried ~** tesoro *m* enterrado *or* escondido; (= *valuable object, person*) joya *f*; **our charlady is a real ~** nuestra asistenta es una verdadera joya; **~s of Spanish art** joyas del arte español; **yes, my ~** sí, mi tesoro

Ⓑ VT ① (= *value*) valorar

② (*also* **~ up**) (= *keep*) [+ *memories, mementos*] guardar, atesorar

Ⓒ CPD ▸ **treasure house** N (*fig*) mina *f* ▸ **treasure hunt** N caza *f* del tesoro ▸ **treasure trove** N tesoro *m* hallado

treasured [ˈtreʒəd] ADJ [*memory*] entrañable; [*possession*] preciado

treasurer [ˈtreʒərəʳ] N tesorero/a *m/f*

treasury [ˈtreʒərɪ] Ⓐ N ① (*Pol*) **the Treasury** la Secretaría de Hacienda

② (*fig*) (= *anthology*) antología *f*

Ⓑ CPD ▸ **Treasury Bench** N (*Brit Pol*) banco *m* azul, banco *m* del gobierno ▸ **treasury bill, treasury bond** N (*US*) pagaré *m* del Tesoro, bono *m* del Tesoro ▸ **the Treasury Department** N (*US Pol*) la Secretaría de Hacienda ▸ **Treasury promissory note** N pagaré *m* del Tesoro ▸ **Treasury stock** N (*Brit*) bonos *mpl* del Tesoro; (*US*) acciones *fpl* rescatadas ▸ **treasury warrant** N autorización *f* para pago de fondos públicos

treat [triːt] Ⓐ N ① (= *something special*) **I've bought a few little ~s for the children** les he comprado unas cosillas *or* unas chucherías a los niños; **a birthday/Christmas ~** un regalo de cumpleaños/Navidad; **as** *or* **for a (special) ~** como algo (muy) especial; **to give sb a ~** obsequiar a algn con algo especial; **you should give her a ~ as a reward for her good grades** deberías obsequiarla con algo especial en premio a sus buenas notas; **I wanted to give myself a ~** quería darme un gusto *or* permitirme un lujo; **viewers are in for a ~ this weekend** los televidentes se llevarán una agradable sorpresa este fin de semana; **the trip to the cinema was an unexpected ~** fue una agradable sorpresa que me llevara al cine

② (= *offer to pay*) **"I'll pay" — "no, this is my ~"** —yo pago —no, invito yo; **to stand sb a ~** invitar a algn; *see also* **Dutch D**

③ (= *pleasure*) placer *m*, gusto *m*; **it was a ~ to see him happy again** era un placer *or* daba gusto volver a verle feliz

④ **a ~*** (*as adv*) (*Brit*) **the garden is coming on a ~** el jardín va de maravilla*; **this wine goes down a ~** este vino sienta de maravilla*; **take this powder for a headache, it works a ~** tómate estos polvos para el dolor de cabeza, hacen milagros *or* son mano de santo*

Ⓑ VT ① (= *behave towards*) [+ *person, animal*] tratar; (= *handle*) [+ *object*] manejar; **we were ~ed with respect/contempt** nos trataron con respeto/desprecio; **to ~ sb well/badly** tratar bien/mal a algn; **the chemical should be ~ed with caution** este producto químico debería manejarse con cuidado; **to ~ sb like a child** tratar a algn como a un niño; **how's life ~ing you these days?** ¿cómo te va la vida últimamente?; ✦***IDIOM*** **to ~ sb like dirt*** tratar a algn a patadas*, tratar a algn como a un perro*

② (= *consider, view*) tratar; **his statements should be ~ed with caution** hay que tomar sus declaraciones con cautela; **to ~ sth as a joke** tomarse algo a risa; **this is not a subject that should be ~ed lightly** este no es un asunto para ser tratado a la ligera; **police are ~ing the threats seriously** la policía está tratando las amenazas como un asunto serio

③ (= *deal with*) [+ *subject*] tratar; **the issues should be ~ed separately** los asuntos se deberían tratar por separado

④ (= *invite*) invitar; **I'm ~ing you** yo te invito; **to ~ sb to sth** invitar *or* convidar a algn a algo; **she was always ~ing him to ice cream** siempre le invitaba *or* convidaba a un helado, siempre le estaba comprando helados; **he ~ed us to a monologue on the virtues of abstinence** (*iro*) nos soltó un monólogo sobre las virtudes de la abstinencia; **to ~ o.s to sth** darse el gusto *or* permitirse el lujo de (hacer) algo; **we ~ed ourselves to a meal out** nos dimos el gusto *or* nos permitimos el lujo de comer fuera; **he ~ed himself to another drink** se permitió otra copa; **go on — ~ yourself!** ¡venga, date el gusto *or* el lujo!

⑤ (*Med*) [+ *patient*] tratar, atender; [+ *illness*] tratar; **which doctor is ~ing you?** ¿qué médico te atiende *or* trata?; **the condition can be ~ed successfully with antibiotics** la enfermedad se puede curar con antibióticos; **they were ~ed for shock** recibieron tratamiento por shock; **do not try and ~ yourself** no intente automedicarse

6 (= *process*) [+ *wood, crops, sewage*] tratar
Ⓒ VI (*frm*) 1 (= *negotiate*) **to ~ with sb** negociar con algn
2 (= *deal with*) **to ~ of sth** [*author*] tratar algo; [*book, article*] versar sobre algo

treatise ['triːtɪz] N tratado *m*

treatment ['triːtmənt] Ⓐ N 1 (= *handling*) [*of people*] trato *m*; [*of object*] trato *m*, manejo *m*; [*of subject, idea*] tratamiento *m*; **our ~ of foreigners** el trato que damos a los extranjeros; **I wouldn't put up with such ~** yo no permitiría que me trataran así *or* que me dieran ese trato; **the judge was criticized for his harsh ~ of offenders** el juez fue criticado por su trato duro hacia los delincuentes; **his ~ of the subject is superficial** el tratamiento que da al tema es superficial; **for a more extensive ~ of this subject I refer the reader to ...** para ver este tema en más profundidad remito al lector a ...; **at that restaurant you get the full ~** en ese restaurante te tratan a cuerpo de rey*; **to give sb preferential ~** dar a algn un trato preferente; **to get preferential ~** recibir un trato preferente; **he has come in for some rough ~ from the press** ha recibido un trato duro por parte de la prensa; ✦**IDIOM to give sb the ~*** (= *beat up*) dar caña a algn*; (= *entertain well*) tratar a algn a cuerpo de rey*
2 (*Med*) tratamiento *m*; **she has** *or* **receives** *or* **undergoes ~ twice a month** la someten a tratamiento dos veces al mes; **a course of ~** un tratamiento; **he needs medical ~** le hace falta atención médica *or* tratamiento médico; **I am still receiving ~ for the injury** todavía estoy en tratamiento por la lesión; **to respond to ~** responder al tratamiento
3 (= *processing*) [*of sewage, waste*] tratamiento *m*
Ⓑ CPD ► **treatment room** N (*Med*) sala *f* de curas

treaty ['triːtɪ] N tratado *m*; **Treaty of Accession** (*to EC*) Tratado *m* de Adhesión; **Treaty of Rome** Tratado *m* de Roma; **Treaty of Utrecht** Tratado *m* de Utrecht

treble ['trebl] Ⓐ N 1 (*Mus*) (= *voice*) voz *f* de tiple
2 (= *drink*) triple *m*
Ⓑ ADJ 1 (= *triple*) triple
2 (*Mus*) [*voice, note, instrument*] de tiple
Ⓒ VT triplicar
Ⓓ VI triplicarse
Ⓔ ADV (= *3 times*) tres veces
Ⓕ CPD ► **treble clef** N clave *f* de sol

trebly ['treblɪ] ADV tres veces; **it is ~ dangerous to ...** es tres veces más peligroso ...

tree [triː] Ⓐ N 1 (*Bot*) árbol *m*; **~ of knowledge** árbol *m* de la ciencia; ✦**IDIOMS to be at the top of the ~** (*Brit*) estar en la cumbre de su carrera profesional; **to be out of one's ~*** (= *crazy*) estar como una cabra*, estar como una moto‡; (*on drugs, alcohol*) estar colocadísimo‡, haberse puesto como una moto‡; **to be up a ~*** (= *in a fix*) estar en un aprieto; (= *mad*) estar chalado*, estar como una cabra *or* regadera*; **to be barking up the wrong ~** tomar el rábano por las hojas; **we can't see the wood** *or* (*US*) **the forest for the ~s** los árboles no dejan ver el bosque; *see also* **family**
2 (*for shoes*) horma *f*
3 [*of saddle*] arzón *m*
Ⓑ VT [+ *animal*] hacer refugiarse en un árbol
Ⓒ CPD ► **tree creeper** N trepatroncos *mf inv* ► **tree frog** N rana *f* de San Antonio, rana *f* arbórea ► **tree house** N casita *f* en un árbol ► **tree planting** N plantación *f* de árboles ► **tree surgeon** N arboricultor(a) *m/f* ► **tree trunk** N tronco *m* (de árbol)

tree-covered ['triː,kʌvəd] ADJ arbolado

treeless ['triːlɪs] ADJ sin árboles, pelado

tree line ['triːlaɪn] N límite *m* forestal

tree-lined ['triːlaɪnd] ADJ bordeado de árboles

treetop ['triːtɒp] N copa *f* (de árbol)

trefoil ['trefɔɪl] N trébol *m*

trek [trek] Ⓐ N 1 (= *hike*) expedición *f*
2 (*) (= *long, tiring walk*) caminata *f*; **it's quite a ~ to the shops*** las tiendas quedan muy lejos
Ⓑ VI 1 (= *hike*) (*also Mil*) caminar; **we ~ked for days on end** caminamos día tras día
2 (*) (= *traipse*) ir (penosamente); **I had to ~ up to the top floor*** tuve que subir hasta el último piso

trekking ['trekɪŋ] N trekking *m*

trellis ['trelɪs] N espaldera *f*, enrejado *m*; (*Bot*) espaldera *f*, espaldar *m*

trelliswork ['trelɪswɜːk] N enrejado *m*

tremble ['trembl] Ⓐ N temblor *m*; **to be all of a ~** estar tembloroso; **she said with a ~ in her voice** dijo con voz temblorosa
Ⓑ VI **to ~ (with)** temblar (de); **to ~ with fear** temblar de miedo; **to ~ at the thought of sth** temblar ante la idea de algo; **to ~ all over** estar todo tembloroso; **to ~ like a leaf** estar como un flan

trembling ['tremblɪŋ] Ⓐ ADJ tembloroso
Ⓑ N temblor *m*, estremecimiento *m*

tremendous [trə'mendəs] ADJ 1 (= *huge*) [*pressure, success, explosion, problem*] tremendo, enorme; **it cost a ~ amount of money** costó muchísimo dinero, costó una enorme *or* tremenda cantidad de dinero; **you've been a ~ help** me has ayudado enormemente *or* muchísimo; **~ progress has been made** se ha progresado enormemente *or* muchísimo; **at (a) ~ speed** a una velocidad increíble *or* tremenda
2 (= *wonderful*) [*person, goal, performance, achievement*] formidable, extraordinario; [*opportunity*] tremendo, estupendo; **the food is ~** la comida está estupenda *or* riquísima; **she has done a ~ job** ha hecho un trabajo formidable *or* magnífico *or* estupendo

tremendously [trə'mendəslɪ] ADV [*exciting, important, useful, satisfying*] tremendamente, enormemente; [*improve, vary, help*] enormemente, muchísimo; **he was ~ helpful** nos ayudó enormemente *or* muchísimo

tremolo ['treməlәʊ] N trémolo *m*

tremor ['tremər] N 1 (= *earthquake*) temblor *m*; **earth ~** temblor *m* de tierra
2 (= *tremble*) estremecimiento *m*; **he said without a ~** dijo sin inmutarse; **it sent ~s through the system** sacudió el sistema

tremulous ['tremjʊləs] ADJ trémulo (*liter*), tembloroso

tremulously ['tremjʊləslɪ] ADV trémulamente (*liter*), temblorosamente

trench [trentʃ] Ⓐ N (*gen*) zanja *f*; (*Mil*) trinchera *f*
Ⓑ VT (*gen*) hacer zanjas en; (*Mil*) hacer trincheras en, atrincherar; (*Agr*) excavar
Ⓒ CPD ► **trench coat** N trinchera *f* ► **trench warfare** N guerra *f* de trincheras

trenchant ['trentʃənt] ADJ mordaz

trenchantly ['trentʃəntlɪ] ADV mordazmente

trencher ['trentʃər] N tajadero *m*

trencherman ['trentʃəmæn] N (*pl* **trenchermen**) **to be a good ~** comer bien, tener siempre buen apetito

trend [trend] Ⓐ N (= *tendency*) tendencia *f*; (= *fashion*) moda *f*; **to set the ~** marcar la pauta; **a ~ towards (doing) sth** una tendencia hacia (hacer) algo; **a ~ away from (doing) sth** una tendencia en contra de (hacer) algo; **~s in popular music** tendencias *fpl* de la música popular
Ⓑ VI tender

trendiness ['trendɪnɪs] N 1 (= *fashionableness*) lo moderno, modernidad *f*
2 (*pej*) (= *desire to be in fashion*) afán *m* de estar al día

trendsetter ['trend,setər] N iniciador(a) *m/f* de una moda

trendy* ['trendɪ] Ⓐ ADJ (*compar* **trendier**, *superl* **trendiest**) a la moda, moderno
Ⓑ N persona *f* de tendencias ultramodernas; **~ leftie*** progre* *mf*

Trent [trent] N Trento *m*

trepan [trɪ'pæn] VT trepanar

trephine [tre'fiːn] Ⓐ N trépano *m*
Ⓑ VT trepanar

trepidation [,trepɪ'deɪʃən] N (= *fear*) temor *m*; (= *anxiety*) inquietud *f*, agitación *f*; **in some ~** algo turbado, agitado

trespass ['trespəs] Ⓐ VI 1 (*on land*) entrar ilegalmente (**on** en); **"no ~ing"** "prohibida la entrada"; **to ~ upon** (*fig*) abusar de; **may I ~ upon your kindness to ask that ...** (*frm*) permítame abusar de su amabilidad pidiendo que ...; **to ~ upon sb's privacy** invadir la vida íntima de algn
2 (= *do wrong*) (*Rel*) pecar (**against** contra); **to ~ against** (*Jur*) infringir, violar
Ⓑ N 1 (*on land*) entrada *f* ilegal, invasión *f* (de propiedad ajena)
2 (= *transgression*) infracción *f*, violación *f*; (*Rel*) pecado *m*; **forgive us our ~es** perdónanos nuestras deudas

trespasser ['trespəsər] N intruso/a *m/f*; **"~s will be prosecuted"** "entrada terminantemente prohibida"

tress [tres] N 1 (= *lock of hair*) trenza *f*
2 **tresses** (= *head of hair*) cabellera *f*, pelo *m*

trestle ['tresl] Ⓐ N caballete *m*
Ⓑ CPD ► **trestle bridge** N puente *m* de caballetes ► **trestle table** N mesa *f* de caballete

trews [truːz] NPL (*Scot*) pantalón *m* de tartán

tri... [traɪ] PREFIX tri...

triad ['traɪəd] N tríada *f*

trial ['traɪəl] Ⓐ N 1 (*Jur*) juicio *m*, proceso *m*; **the ~ continues today** el juicio *or* proceso se reanuda hoy; **to be awaiting ~** estar a la espera de juicio *or* de ser procesado; **to bring sb to ~** llevar a algn a juicio, procesar a algn; **the case never came to ~** el caso nunca se llevó a juicio; **~ by jury** proceso *m or m* juicio ante jurado; **murder ~** proceso *m or* juicio *m* por asesinato; **new ~** revisión *f* (de juicio); **on ~: he is on ~ for murder** se lo está procesando por acusado de asesinato; **to be on ~ for one's life** ser acusado de un crimen capital; **to go on ~** ser procesado; **to stand ~** ser procesado; **detention without ~** detención *f* sin procesamiento; *see also* **commit A2**; → GRAND JURY
2 (= *test*) [*of drug, machine*] prueba *f*; [*of person, for job*] periodo *m* de prueba, prueba *f*; **clinical ~s** ensayos *mpl* clínicos; **by** *or* **through ~ and error** a base de probar y cometer errores; **finding the right skin cream is a question of ~ and error** encontrar la crema apropiada para la piel es cuestión de probar *or* ir probando; **flight ~s** vuelos *mpl* de prueba, vuelos *mpl* experimentales; **to give sb a ~** (*for job*) ofrecer a algn un periodo de prueba; **to be on ~** (*lit, fig*) estar a prueba; **the fullback has been on ~ at the club for ten days** el defensa lleva diez días a prueba

en el club; **I felt as if I was continually on ~** me sentía como si estuviera a prueba continuamente; **her reputation is on ~** su reputación está a prueba; **a ~ of strength** una prueba de fuerza

[3] (= *hardship*) **the ~s of old age** los padecimientos de la vejez; **a movie about the ~s of family life** una película sobre las dificultades de la vida familiar; **the interview was a great ~** la entrevista fue todo un suplicio; **the child is a great ~ to them** el niño les hace sufrir mucho; **~s and tribulations** tribulaciones *fpl*; **the ~s and tribulations of parenthood** las tribulaciones de ser padre

[4] **trials** (*Sport*) pruebas *fpl* de selección; **the Olympic ~s** las pruebas de selección para los Juegos Olímpicos; **horse ~s** concurso *m* hípico; **sheepdog ~s** concurso *m* de perros pastores; **time ~s** pruebas *fpl* contrarreloj

Ⓑ VT (*Comm*) [+ *product*] poner a prueba; **products are ~led for six months before they go on the market** los productos se ponen a prueba durante seis meses antes de lanzarlos al mercado

Ⓒ CPD ► **trial balance** N balance *m* de comprobación ► **trial balloon** N (*US*) globo *m* sonda ► **trial basis** N **on a ~ basis** (en periodo) de prueba ► **trial flight** N vuelo *m* de prueba ► **trial jury** N (*US*) jurado *m* de juicio ► **trial offer** N oferta *f* de prueba ► **trial period** N periodo *m* de prueba ► **trial run** N prueba *f*; **I took the car out for a ~ run** saqué el coche para probarlo *or* ponerlo a prueba ► **trial separation** N periodo *m* de separación como prueba; **they are having a ~ separation** se han separado temporalmente como prueba

triangle ['traɪæŋgl] N (*also Mus*) triángulo *m*

triangular [traɪ'æŋgjʊlə^r] ADJ triangular

triangulate [traɪ'æŋgjʊleɪt] VT triangular

triangulation [traɪ,æŋgjʊ'leɪʃən] N triangulación *f*

triathlon [traɪ'æθlən] N triatlón *m*

tribal ['traɪbəl] ADJ tribal, de tribu

tribalism ['traɪbəlɪzəm] N tribalismo *m*

tribe [traɪb] N (*Anthropology, Zool*) tribu *f*; (*fig*) (= *family*) familia *f*; (*pej*) (= *group*) tribu *f*, pandilla *f*, horda *f*

tribesman ['traɪbzmən] N (*pl* **tribesmen**) miembro *m* de una tribu

tribeswoman ['traɪbz,wʊmən] N (*pl* **tribeswomen**) miembro *f* de una tribu

tribulation [,trɪbjʊ'leɪʃən] N [1] (*frm*) tribulación *f*

[2] **tribulations** aflicciones *fpl*

tribunal [traɪ'bjuːnl] N tribunal *m*

tribune ['trɪbjuːn] N [1] (= *stand*) tribuna *f*

[2] (= *person*) tribuno *m*

tributary ['trɪbjʊtərɪ] Ⓐ ADJ tributario

Ⓑ N [1] (*Geog*) afluente *m*

[2] (= *state, ruler*) tributario *m*

tribute ['trɪbjuːt] N [1] (= *payment, tax*) tributo *m*

[2] (*fig*) homenaje *m*, tributo *m*; **to pay ~ to sth/sb** rendir homenaje a algo/algn; **that is a ~ to his loyalty** eso acredita su lealtad, eso hace honor a su lealtad; *see also* **floral**

trice [traɪs] N **in a ~** en un santiamén

tricentenary [,traɪsen'tiːnərɪ] Ⓐ ADJ (de) tricentenario

Ⓑ N tricentenario *m*

Ⓒ CPD ► **tricentenary celebrations** NPL celebraciones *fpl* de(l) tricentenario

triceps ['traɪseps] N (*pl* **triceps** *or* **tricepses**) tríceps *m*

trick [trɪk] Ⓐ N [1] (= *joke, hoax*) broma *f*; (= *mischief*) travesura *f*; (= *ruse*) truco *m*, ardid *m*; **dirty** *or* **mean ~** mala pasada *f*, jugada *f* sucia; **the ~s of the trade** los trucos del oficio; **to play a ~ on sb** gastar una broma a algn; **unless my eyes are playing ~s on me** si los ojos no me engañan; **his memory played a ~ on him** le falló la memoria; **~ or treat!** *frase amenazante que pronuncian en tono jocoso los niños que rondan las casas en la noche de Halloween; quiere decir: —¡danos algo o te hacemos una trastada!*; → HALLOWE'EN

✦*IDIOMS* **he's up to his old ~s again** ha vuelto a hacer de las suyas; **how's ~s?*** ¿cómo te va?

[2] (= *card trick*) baza *f*; (= *conjuring trick*) truco *m*; (*in circus*) número *m*; **to take all the ~s** ganar *or* hacer todas las bazas; ✦*IDIOMS* **he/she knows a ~ or two** se lo sabe todo; **I know a ~ worth two of that** yo me sé algo mucho mejor; **that should do the ~** esto servirá; **he/she doesn't miss a ~** no se pierde nada; **to try every ~ in the book** emplear todos los trucos; **that's the oldest ~ in the book** eso es un viejo truco; **the whole bag of ~s*** todo el rollo*

[3] (= *special knack*) truco *m*; **there's a ~ to opening this door** esta puerta tiene truco para abrirla; **to get the ~ of it** coger el truco, aprender el modo de hacerlo

[4] (= *peculiarity, strange habit*) manía *f*, peculiaridad *f*; **certain ~s of style** ciertas peculiaridades estilísticas, ciertos rasgos del estilo; **it's just a ~ he has** es una manía suya; **to have a ~ of doing sth** tener la manía de hacer algo; **history has a ~ of repeating itself** la historia tiene tendencia a repetirse; **it's a ~ of the light** es una ilusión óptica

[5] (= *catch*) trampa *f*; **there must be a ~ in it** aquí seguro que hay trampa

[6] (‡) [*of prostitute*] cliente *m*; **to turn ~s** ligarse clientes*

Ⓑ VT (= *deceive*) engañar; (= *swindle*) estafar, timar; **I've been ~ed!** ¡me han engañado!; **to ~ sb into doing sth** engañar a algn para que haga algo, conseguir con engaños que algn haga algo; **to ~ sb out of sth** quitar algo a algn con engaños

Ⓒ CPD ► **trick cyclist** N ciclista *mf* acróbata ► **trick photography** N trucaje *m* ► **trick question** N pregunta *f* de pega ► **trick riding** N acrobacia *f* ecuestre

►**trick out, trick up** VT + ADV (= *decorate*) ataviar (**with** de)

trickery ['trɪkərɪ] N engaño *m*, superchería *f* (*frm*); **to obtain sth by ~** obtener algo fraudulentamente

trickle ['trɪkl] Ⓐ N [1] (*gen*) chorrito *m*; [*of blood*] hilo *m*

[2] (*fig*) **a ~ of people** un goteo de personas; **we received a ~ of news** nos llegaba alguna que otra noticia; **what was a ~ is now a flood** lo que era un goteo es ya un torrente

Ⓑ VI [1] [*liquid*] escurrir; **blood ~d down his cheek** la sangre le caía a gotas por la mejilla

[2] (*fig*) (*slowly*) ir despacio; (*gradually*) poco a poco; **people kept trickling in** la gente seguía entrando poco a poco

Ⓒ VT (*lit*) gotear; **you're trickling blood** estás sangrando un poco

Ⓓ CPD ► **trickle charger** N (*Elec*) cargador *m* de batería

►**trickle away** VI + ADV **our money is trickling away** nuestro dinero se consume poco a poco

trickle-down economics [,trɪkldaʊn-iːkə'nɒmɪks] N *efecto de filtración de la riqueza desde las capas sociales más altas hasta las más bajas*

trick-or-treat [,trɪkɔː'triːt] VI **to go ~ing** *rondar de casa en casa disfrazados (los niños) en la noche de Halloween (víspera del día de Todos los Santos) pidiendo una propina o golosinas a cambio de no gastar una broma o hacer una trastada*

trickster ['trɪkstə^r] N estafador(a) *m/f*, embustero/a *m/f*

tricksy ['trɪksɪ] ADJ [1] (= *playful*) juguetón

[2] (= *crafty*) astuto, mañoso

tricky ['trɪkɪ] ADJ (*compar* **trickier**; *superl* **trickiest**) [1] [*situation*] complicado, difícil; [*problem*] delicado; **it's all rather ~** es un poco complicado, es un tanto difícil

[2] [*person*] (= *sly*) tramposo, ladino; (= *difficult*) difícil

tricolour, tricolor (*US*) ['trɪkələ^r] N (= *flag*) bandera *f* tricolor, tricolor *f*

tricorn ['traɪkɔːn] Ⓐ ADJ tricornio

Ⓑ N tricornio *m*

tricycle ['traɪsɪkl] N triciclo *m*

trident ['traɪdənt] N tridente *m*

Tridentine [traɪ'dentaɪn] ADJ tridentino

tried [traɪd] Ⓐ PT, PP *of* **try**

Ⓑ ADJ **~ and tested** ◊ **~ and trusted** probado

triennial [traɪ'enɪəl] ADJ trienal

triennially [traɪ'enɪəlɪ] ADV trienalmente, cada tres años

trier ['traɪə^r] N persona *f* aplicada

trifle ['traɪfl] N [1] (= *cheap object*) baratija *f*, fruslería *f* (*frm*)

[2] (= *unimportant issue*) pequeñez *f*, nimiedad *f* (*frm*); **he worries about ~s** se preocupa por nimiedades; **any ~ can distract her** le distrae cualquier tontería

[3] (= *small amount*) insignificancia *f*; **£5 is a mere ~** cinco libras son una insignificancia; **you could have bought it for a ~** hubieras podido comprarlo por una insignificancia *or* por nada

[4] **a ~** (*as adv*) (= *somewhat*) algo, un poquito; **it's a ~ difficult** es un poco *or* poquito difícil; **we were a ~ put out** quedamos algo desconcertados, nos quedamos un poquito desconcertados

[5] (*Culin*) dulce *m* de bizcocho borracho

►**trifle away** VT + ADV malgastar, desperdiciar

►**trifle with** VI + PREP jugar con; **to ~ with sb** jugar con algn, tratar a algn con poca seriedad; **he's not a person to be ~d with** con ése (es) mejor no meterse; **to ~ with sb's affections** jugar con los sentimientos de algn; **to ~ with one's food** hacer melindres *or* remilgos a la comida

trifler ['traɪflə^r] N persona *f* frívola, persona *f* informal

trifling ['traɪflɪŋ] ADJ (= *insignificant*) sin importancia, frívolo

triforium [traɪ'fɔːrɪəm] N (*pl* **triforia** [traɪ'fɔːrɪə]) triforio *m*

trigger ['trɪgə^r] Ⓐ N [*of gun*] gatillo *m*; [*of bomb, machine*] disparador *m*; **to pull the ~** apretar el gatillo, disparar

Ⓑ VT (*also* **~ off**) [+ *bomb*] hacer estallar; [+ *fight, explosion*] provocar; [+ *mechanism*] hacer funcionar, poner en movimiento; [+ *chain of events*] desencadenar

Ⓒ CPD ► **trigger finger** N índice *m* de la mano derecha (empleado para apretar el gatillo)

trigger-happy* ['trɪgə,hæpɪ] ADJ pronto a disparar, que dispara a la mínima

trigonometric [,trɪgɒnə'metrɪk] ADJ trigonométrico

trigonometrical [ˌtrɪɡɒnəˈmetrɪkəl] ADJ = **trigonometric**

trigonometry [ˌtrɪɡəˈnɒmɪtrɪ] N trigonometría *f*

trijet [ˈtraɪdʒet] N trirreactor *m*

trike* [traɪk] N triciclo *m*

trilateral [ˈtraɪˈlætərəl] ADJ trilátero

trilby [ˈtrɪlbɪ] N (*Brit*) (*also* ~ **hat**) sombrero *m* flexible, sombrero *m* tirolés

trilingual [ˈtraɪˈlɪŋɡwəl] ADJ trilingüe

trill [trɪl] Ⓐ N [*of bird*] gorjeo *m*, trino *m*; [*of phone*] sonido *m*, ring-ring* *m*; (*Mus*) trino *m*; (*Phon*) [*of "R"*] vibración *f*
Ⓑ VI [*bird*] gorjear, trinar; [*phone*] sonar
Ⓒ VT [1] (*Phon*) hacer vibrar; **to ~ one's Rs** hacer vibrar las erres; **~ed R** erre vibrada
[2] (= *say*) **"how adorable!," she ~ed** —¡qué encantador! —gorjeó

trillion [ˈtrɪlɪən] N trillón *m*; (*US*) billón *m*; **there are ~s of places I want to visit*** hay millones *or* montones de sitios a los que quiero ir

trilogy [ˈtrɪlədʒɪ] N trilogía *f*

trim [trɪm] Ⓐ ADJ (*compar* **trimmer**, *superl* **trimmest**) [1] (= *neat*) [*garden*] bien cuidado, arreglado; [*person*] arreglado; [*clothes*] de corte elegante; [*moustache, beard*] bien cuidado; **a ~ little house** una casita bien cuidada
[2] (= *slim*) [*person, figure*] esbelto; [*waist*] delgado; **to stay ~** conservar una figura esbelta
Ⓑ N [1] (= *cut*) **to get** *or* **have a ~** cortarse un poco el pelo; (*on long hair*) cortarse sólo las puntas; **to give one's beard a ~** recortarse la barba; **to give the lawn/hedge a ~** recortar el césped/el seto
[2] (= *good physical condition*) **to be in (good) ~** [*person*] estar en buena forma *or* en buen estado físico; [*car, house*] estar en buen estado *or* en buenas condiciones; **to get in** *or* **into ~** ponerse en forma; **to keep (o.s.) in (good) ~** mantenerse en buena forma *or* en buen estado físico; **to keep sth in (good) ~** mantener algo en buen estado *or* en buenas condiciones
[3] (= *decoration*) [3·1] (*Sew*) adorno *m*; (*on edge*) ribete *m*, reborde *m*; **a coat with a fur ~** un abrigo con ribetes *or* rebordes de piel
[3·2] (*Aut*) (*on outside of car*) embellecedor *m* (*Sp*); **leather ~** tapizado *m* de cuero; **wheel ~** tapacubos *m inv*, embellecedor *m* de la rueda (*Sp*)
Ⓒ VT [1] (= *clip*) [+ *hair, beard, moustache*] recortar; [+ *hedge*] cortar, podar; [+ *lamp, wick*] despabilar; **to ~ back** [+ *plant, shoot*] podar; **~ excess fat from** *or* **off the chops** quitar el exceso de grasa de las chuletas
[2] (= *reduce*) [+ *costs, prices*] recortar, reducir; [+ *profits*] recortar; [+ *programme, policy*] hacer recortes en; (*also* ~ **back**) [+ *workforce*] recortar, reducir
[3] (= *slim*) [+ *hips, thighs*] adelgazar
[4] (= *decorate*) [+ *dress, hat*] adornar; [+ *Christmas tree*] decorar; **a dress ~med with feathers/lace** un vestido adornado con plumas/con adornos de encaje
[5] (*Naut*) [+ *sails*] orientar; [+ *boat*] equilibrar; ✦*IDIOM* **to ~ one's sails** (*fig*) apretarse el cinturón
[6] (*Aer*) equilibrar
[7] (*Orn*) orientar

►**trim away** VT + ADV cortar, quitar

►**trim down** Ⓐ VT + ADV [+ *wick*] despabilar; [+ *workforce*] recortar, reducir; [+ *hips, thighs*] adelgazar
Ⓑ VI + ADV (= *get slimmer*) adelgazar

►**trim off** VT + ADV = **trim away**

trimaran [ˈtraɪməræn] N trimarán *m*

trimester [trɪˈmestər] N trimestre *m*

trimming [ˈtrɪmɪŋ] N [1] (= *edging*) adorno *m*, guarnición *f*
[2] **trimmings** [2·1] (= *cuttings*) recortes *mpl*
[2·2] (= *extras, embellishments*) **turkey with all the ~s** pavo con su guarnición; **without all the ~s** sin los adornos

trimness [ˈtrɪmnɪs] N (= *elegance*) elegancia *f*; (= *good condition*) buen estado *m*

trimphone® [ˈtrɪmfəʊn] N ≈ teléfono *m* góndola

Trinidad [ˈtrɪnɪdæd] N Trinidad *f*

Trinidadian [ˌtrɪnɪˈdædɪən] Ⓐ ADJ de Trinidad
Ⓑ N nativo/a *m/f* de Trinidad, habitante *mf* de Trinidad

trinitrotoluene [traɪˈnaɪtrəʊˈtɒljuːiːn] N trinitrotolueno *m*

Trinity [ˈtrɪnɪtɪ] Ⓐ N (*Rel*) Trinidad *f*
Ⓑ CPD ► **Trinity Sunday** N Domingo *m* de la Santísima Trinidad ► **Trinity term** N (*Univ*) trimestre *m* de verano

trinket [ˈtrɪŋkɪt] N chuchería *f*, baratija *f*

trinomial [traɪˈnəʊmɪəl] Ⓐ ADJ trinomio
Ⓑ N trinomio *m*

trio [ˈtriəʊ] N trío *m*

trip [trɪp] Ⓐ N [1] (= *journey*) viaje *m*; (= *excursion*) excursión *f*; (= *visit*) visita *f*; (= *outing*) salida *f*; **it's her first ~ abroad** es su primer viaje al extranjero; **it's a 100-mile ~** es un recorrido *or* un viaje de 100 millas; **she's planning a ~ round the world** está planeando hacer un viaje por todo el mundo; **a ~ to the park/seaside** una excursión *or* una salida al parque/a la playa; **a ~ to the cinema** una visita *or* una salida al cine; **a ~ to the doctor** una visita al médico; **boat ~** paseo *m or* excursión *f* en barco; **fishing ~** excursión *f* de pesca; **to make a ~**: **we made a ~ into town** fuimos a la ciudad; **he made several ~s to the toilet** fue varias veces al servicio; **she went on a ~ to Tasmania** (se) fue de viaje a Tasmania; **he's away on a ~** está de viaje; **school ~** excursión *f* del colegio; **shopping ~** visita *f* a las tiendas; **to take a ~**: **they took a ~ to York** fueron de excursión a York; **they took a ~ to Canada** (se) fueron de viaje a Canadá; **take a ~ to your local library** hágale una visita a la biblioteca de su barrio, visite la biblioteca de su barrio; **weekend ~** viaje *m* de fin de semana; ✦*IDIOM* **to take a ~ down memory lane** revivir el pasado; *see also* **business, coach, day, field, round**
[2] (*) (*on drugs*) viaje *m*; **acid ~** viaje *m* de ácido; **she had a bad ~** tuvo un mal viaje*; *see also* **ego, guilt**
[3] (= *stumble*) tropezón *m*; (= *move to make sb trip*) zancadilla *f*; **he brought the other player down with a ~** hizo caer al otro jugador con una zancadilla
[4] (*Elec*) (*also* ~ **switch**) interruptor *m* de desconexión
Ⓑ VI [1] (= *stumble*) tropezar; **he ~ped and fell** tropezó y se cayó al suelo; **to ~ on/over sth** tropezar con algo; *see also* **trip over**
[2] (*liter*) (= *step lightly*) **she ~ped gracefully round the dance floor** se movía con paso ligero y grácil por la pista de baile; **to ~ along** ◊ **go ~ping along** ir con paso ligero; ✦*IDIOM* **to ~ off the tongue**: **it doesn't exactly ~ off the tongue** no se puede decir que sea fácil de pronunciar; **the formula came ~ping off his tongue** pronunció la fórmula con la mayor facilidad; *see also* **tongue A1**
[3] (*) (*on drugs*) **to be ~ping** estar colocado*; **they were all ~ping out on acid** todos estaban colocados con ácido*
Ⓒ VT [1] (*also* ~ **up**) (= *cause to stumble*) (*intentionally*) poner *or* echar la zancadilla a; (*accidentally*) hacer tropezar; **he tried to ~ me** intentó ponerme *or* echarme la zancadilla; **don't leave things on the stairs where they may ~ you** no deje cosas en las escaleras donde se pueda tropezar
[2] (*also* ~ **up**) (= *catch out*) **he was trying to ~ her into contradicting herself** estaba intentando tenderle una trampa para que se contradijera; *see also* **trip up B2**
[3] (= *set off*) [+ *mechanism, switch*] activar
[4] (= *dance*) ✦*IDIOM* **to ~ the light fantastic**†* mover el esqueleto*
Ⓓ CPD ► **trip switch** N interruptor *m* de desconexión

►**trip over** Ⓐ VI + ADV (= *fall*) tropezar y caerse; **he ~ped over and fell flat on his face** tropezó y cayó de bruces
Ⓑ VI + PREP [1] (*lit*) tropezarse con, tropezar con; **he ~ped over a wire** tropezó *or* se tropezó con un cable; **she ~ped over her own feet** se tropezó con sus propios pies; **to ~ over one another to do sth** (*fig*) darse de tortas por hacer algo*
[2] (*fig*) **occasionally he would ~ over a word in his impatience to tell his story** a veces se le trababa la lengua en su impaciencia por contar su historia

►**trip up** Ⓐ VI + ADV [1] (= *stumble*) tropezar
[2] (= *make a mistake*) equivocarse
Ⓑ VT + ADV [1] (= *cause to stumble*) (*intentionally*) poner *or* echar la zancadilla a; (*accidentally*) hacer tropezar
[2] (= *cause to make a mistake*) **she tried to ~ him up** intentó que se equivocase *or* que se confundiese; **the fourth question ~ped him up** la cuarta pregunta le hizo equivocarse *or* le confundió

tripartite [ˈtraɪˈpɑːtaɪt] ADJ tripartito

tripe [traɪp] N [1] (*Culin*) callos *mpl*
[2] (*esp Brit**) tonterías *fpl*, babosadas *fpl* (*LAm**), pendejadas *fpl* (*LAm**); **what utter ~!** ¡tonterías!; **he talks a lot of ~** no habla más que bobadas
[3] **tripes*** (*hum*) (= *guts*) tripas *fpl*

triphase [ˈtraɪfeɪz] ADJ trifásico

triphthong [ˈtrɪfθɒŋ] N triptongo *m*

triple [ˈtrɪpl] Ⓐ ADJ triple
Ⓑ ADV el triple, tres veces; **~ the sum** el triple
Ⓒ N (= *jump*) triple *m*
Ⓓ VT triplicar
Ⓔ VI triplicarse
Ⓕ CPD ► **Triple Alliance** N (*Hist*) Triple Alianza *f* ► **triple glazing** N triple acristalamiento *m* ► **triple jump** N triple salto *m*

triplet [ˈtrɪplɪt] N [1] (= *person*) trillizo/a *m/f*, triate *mf* (*Mex*)
[2] (*Mus*) tresillo *m*
[3] (*Poetry*) terceto *m*

triplicate Ⓐ [ˈtrɪplɪkɪt] ADJ triplicado
Ⓑ [ˈtrɪplɪkɪt] N **in ~** por triplicado
Ⓒ [ˈtrɪplɪkeɪt] VT triplicar

triply [ˈtrɪplɪ] ADV tres veces; **~ dangerous** tres veces más peligroso

tripod [ˈtraɪpɒd] N trípode *m*

Tripoli [ˈtrɪpəlɪ] N Trípoli *m*

tripper [ˈtrɪpər] N (*Brit*) turista *mf*, excursionista *mf*

tripping [ˈtrɪpɪŋ] ADJ [*step*] ligero, airoso

triptych [ˈtrɪptɪk] N tríptico *m*

tripwire [ˈtrɪpwaɪər] N cuerda *f* de trampa

trireme [ˈtraɪriːm] N trirreme *m*

trisect [traɪˈsekt] VT trisecar

Tristan [ˈtrɪstən], **Tristram** [ˈtrɪstrəm] N Tristán

trisyllabic [ˈtraɪsɪˈlæbɪk] ADJ trisilábico

trisyllable ['traɪ'sɪləbl] N trisílabo *m*

trite [traɪt] ADJ trillado, manido

tritely ['traɪtlɪ] ADV con falta de originalidad

triteness ['traɪtnɪs] N lo trillado, lo manido, falta *f* de originalidad

Triton ['traɪtn] N Tritón

tritone ['traɪtəʊn] N tritono *m*

triturate ['trɪtʃəreɪt] VT triturar

trituration [,trɪtʃə'reɪʃən] N trituración *f*

triumph ['traɪʌmf] Ⓐ N [1] (= *victory*) triunfo *m* (**over** sobre); **it is a ~ of man over nature** es un triunfo del hombre sobre la naturaleza; **to achieve a great ~** obtener un gran éxito; **a new ~ for industry** otro éxito para la industria

[2] (= *emotion*) júbilo *m*; **in ~** con júbilo

Ⓑ VI triunfar; **to ~ over the enemy** triunfar sobre el enemigo; **to ~ over a difficulty** triunfar de una dificultad

triumphal [traɪ'ʌmfəl] Ⓐ ADJ triunfal, de triunfo

Ⓑ CPD ► **triumphal arch** N arco *m* triunfal

triumphalism [traɪ'ʌmfəlɪzəm] N triunfalismo *m*

triumphant [traɪ'ʌmfənt] ADJ (= *jubilant*) jubiloso, triunfante; (= *victorious*) victorioso, vencedor

triumphantly [traɪ'ʌmfəntlɪ] ADV triunfalmente, de modo triunfal; **he said ~** dijo en tono triunfal

triumvirate [traɪ'ʌmvɪrɪt] N triunvirato *m*

triune ['traɪju:n] ADJ trino

trivet ['trɪvɪt] N (*US*) salvamanteles *m inv*

trivia ['trɪvɪə] NPL trivialidades *fpl*, nimiedades *fpl*, banalidades *fpl*

trivial ['trɪvɪəl] ADJ [*details, matter*] trivial, banal; [*person*] frívolo; [*sum*] insignificante, nimio; **I found it all rather ~** me parecía todo muy trivial

triviality [,trɪvɪ'ælɪtɪ] N [1] (= *unimportance*) trivialidad *f*, banalidad *f*

[2] (= *trivial detail*) trivialidad *f*

trivialization [,trɪvɪəlaɪ'zeɪʃən] N trivialización *f*, banalización *f*

trivialize ['trɪvɪəlaɪz] VT minimizar, trivializar

trivially ['trɪvɪəlɪ] ADV trivialmente, banalmente

trochaic [trɒ'keɪɪk] ADJ trocaico

trochee ['trɒki:] N troqueo *m*

trod [trɒd] PT *of* **tread**

trodden ['trɒdn] PP *of* **tread**

troglodyte ['trɒglədaɪt] N troglodita *mf*

troika ['trɔɪkə] N troica *f*

Trojan ['trəʊdʒən] Ⓐ ADJ troyano

Ⓑ N troyano/a *m/f*; ✦**IDIOM to work like a ~** trabajar como un mulo/una mula

Ⓒ CPD ► **Trojan horse** N (*lit*) caballo *m* de Troya; (*fig*) (*concealing devious purposes*) tapadera *f*; (*Comput*) troyano *m* ► **Trojan War** N Guerra *f* de Troya

troll [trəʊl] N gnomo *m*, duende *m*

trolley ['trɒlɪ] Ⓐ N [1] (*esp Brit*) (*in station, supermarket*) carrito *m*; (*in hospital*) camilla *f*; (*in mine*) vagoneta *f*; (= *tea trolley*) carrito *m*; (= *drinks trolley*) mesita *f* de ruedas; ✦**IDIOM to be off one's ~** (*Brit**) estar chiflado*

[2] (*US*) (= *tram*) tranvía *m*

[3] (*Tech*) corredera *f* elevada

[4] (*Elec*) trole *m*, arco *m* de trole

Ⓑ CPD ► **trolley bus** N trolebús *m* ► **trolley car** N (*US*) tranvía *m* ► **trolley pole** N trole *m*

trollop ['trɒləp] N (= *slut*) marrana *f*; (= *prostitute*) puta *f*

trombone [trɒm'bəʊn] N trombón *m*

trombonist [trɒm'bəʊnɪst] N (*orchestral*) trombón *mf*; (*jazz etc*) trombonista *mf*

troop [tru:p] Ⓐ N [1] (*Mil*) tropa *f*; [*of cavalry*] escuadrón *m*; **troops** tropas *fpl*

[2] (*gen*) banda *f*, grupo *m*; (= *gang*) cuadrilla *f*; (*Theat*) = **troupe**; **to come in a ~** venir en tropel *or* en masa

[3] (= *sound*) **the steady ~ of feet** el ruido rítmico de pasos

Ⓑ VI (= *walk*) **to ~ in/past/off/out** entrar/pasar/marcharse/salir en tropel, entrar/pasar/marcharse/salir atropelladamente

Ⓒ VT **to ~ the colour** (*Brit*) presentar la bandera

Ⓓ CPD ► **troop carrier** N (= *plane, ship*) transporte *m* (militar) ► **troop ship** N (buque *m* de) transporte *m* ► **troop train** N tren *m* militar

trooper ['tru:pəʳ] N [1] (*Mil*) soldado *mf* (de caballería); ✦**IDIOM to swear like a ~** jurar *or* hablar como un carretero

[2] (*US*) (= *policeman*) policía *mf* montado/a

trope [trəʊp] N tropo *m*

trophy ['trəʊfɪ] Ⓐ N (*gen*) trofeo *m*

Ⓑ CPD ► **trophy wife*** N *joven esposa de un hombre de éxito que éste gusta de exhibir*

tropic ['trɒpɪk] N trópico *m*; **the ~s** el trópico; **the Tropic of Cancer/Capricorn** el Trópico de Cáncer/Capricornio

tropical ['trɒpɪkəl] ADJ [*fruit, climate, disease*] tropical

troposphere ['trɒpəsfɪəʳ] N troposfera *f*

Trot* [trɒt] N ABBR = **Trotskyist**

trot [trɒt] Ⓐ N [1] (= *step*) trote *m*; **at an easy ~** ◊ **at a slow ~** a trote corto; **to break into a ~** [*horse, rider*] echar a trotar; [*person*] echar a correr; **to go for a ~** (*on horse*) ir a montar a caballo; ✦**IDIOMS to be always on the ~** no parar nunca, tener una vida ajetreada; **to keep sb on the ~** no dejar a algn descansar

[2] **on the ~*** seguidos, uno tras otro, uno detrás de otro; **for five days on the ~*** durante cinco días seguidos; **Barcelona won five times on the ~*** Barcelona ganó cinco veces seguidas

[3] **the ~s**‡ (= *diarrhoea*) diarrea *f*; **to have the ~s** tener diarrea

Ⓑ VI [*horse, rider*] trotar, ir al trote; [*person*] ir trotando

Ⓒ VT [+ *horse*] hacer trotar

►**trot along, trot off*** VI + ADV marcharse; **I must be ~ting along now** es hora de que me marche

►**trot out*** VT + ADV [+ *excuse, reason*] ensartar, recitar; [+ *names, facts*] echar mano de; [+ *arguments*] sacar a relucir, presentar otra vez

►**trot over***, **trot round*** VI + ADV **he ~ted round to the shop** fue y volvió de la tienda en un santiamén

troth [trəʊθ] N (†† *or hum*) *see* **plight**²

Trotskyism ['trɒtskɪɪzəm] N trotskismo *m*

Trotskyist ['trɒtskɪɪst] Ⓐ ADJ trotskista

Ⓑ N trotskista *mf*

trotter ['trɒtəʳ] N [1] (= *horse*) trotón *m*, caballo *m* trotón [2] **pig's ~s** manitas *fpl* (de cerdo *or* (*LAm*) chancho)

trotting ['trɒtɪŋ] N (*Sport*) trote *m*

troubadour ['tru:bədɔ:ʳ] N trovador *m*

▼**trouble** ['trʌbl] Ⓐ N [1] (= *problem*) problema *m*, dificultad *f*; (*for doing wrong*) problemas *mpl*, lío *m*; (= *difficult situation*) apuro *m*, aprieto *m*; **life is full of ~s** la vida está llena de problemas *or* aflicciones; **now your ~s are over** ya no tendrás de que preocuparte, se acabaron las preocupaciones; **what's the ~?** ¿cuál es el problema?, ¿qué pasa?; **the ~ is ...** el problema es ..., lo que pasa es ...; **that's just the ~** ahí está (la madre del cordero); **it's just asking for ~** eso es buscarse problemas; **there'll be ~ if she finds out** se armará una buena si se entera; **there's ~ brewing** se va a armar lío*; **to get into ~**: **he got into ~ with the police** se metió en un lío con la policía; **he got into ~ for saying that** se mereció una bronca diciendo eso; **to get sb into ~** meter a algn en un lío *or* problemas; (*euph*) (= *make pregnant*) dejar embarazada a algn; **to get out of ~** salir del apuro; **to get sb out of ~** ayudar a algn a salir del apuro, echar un cable a algn; **to give ~**: **she never gave us any ~** nunca nos causó problemas; **to have ~ doing sth**: **I had no ~ finding the house** encontré la casa sin problemas; **did you have any ~?** ¿tuviste algún problema *or* alguna dificultad?; **we had ~ getting here in time** nos costó trabajo llegar aquí a tiempo; **to be in ~** (= *having problems*) estar en un apuro *or* aprieto; (*for doing wrong*) tener problemas; **to be in great ~** estar muy apurado; **to lay up ~ for o.s.** crearse problemas; **don't go looking for ~** no busques camorra *or* problemas; **to make ~ for sb** crear un lío a algn; **money ~s** dificultades *fpl* económicas; **to stir up ~** meter cizaña, revolver el ajo; **to tell sb one's ~s** contar sus desventuras a algn; ✦**IDIOM my/his ~ and strife** (*Brit*‡) la parienta

[2] (= *effort, bother*) molestia *f*; **to go to (all) the ~ of doing sth** tomarse la molestia de hacer algo; **I went to a lot of ~ to get it for her** me tomé muchas molestias para conseguírselo; **we had all our ~ for nothing** todo aquello fue trabajo perdido; **it's no ~** no es molestia; **to put sb to the ~ of doing sth** molestar a algn pidiéndole que haga algo; **I fear I am putting you to a lot of ~** me temo que esto te vaya a molestar bastante; **to save o.s. the ~** ahorrarse el trabajo; **to spare no ~ in order to** + INFIN no regatear medio para + *infin*; **to take the ~ to do sth** tomarse la molestia de hacer algo; **he didn't even take the ~ to say thank you** ni se dignó siquiera darme las gracias; **to take a lot of ~ over sth** esmerarse en algo, hacer algo con el mayor cuidado; **nothing is too much ~ for her** para ella todo es poco; **it's more ~ than it's worth** ◊ **it's not worth the ~** no vale la pena

[3] (*Med*) **heart/back ~** problemas *mpl* de corazón/espalda; **it's my old ~** ha vuelto lo de antes

[4] (*Mech*) **a mechanic put the ~ right** un mecánico reparó las piezas averiadas; **engine ~** problemas *mpl* con el motor

[5] (= *unrest, fighting*) conflicto *m*, disturbio *m*; **the (Irish) ~s** los conflictos de los irlandeses; **there is constant ~ between them** riñen constantemente; **labour ~s** conflictos laborales; ✦**IDIOM there's ~ at t'mill** (*Brit hum*, *) hay un disturbio en la fábrica; *see also* **brew C2**

Ⓑ VT [1] (= *worry*) preocupar; **the thought ~d him** le preocupaba la idea; **it's not that that ~s me** no me preocupo por eso, eso me trae sin cuidado

[2] (= *cause pain*) **his eyes ~ him** tiene problemas con la vista *or* los ojos; **if the tooth ~s you again call the dentist** si vuelves a tener molestias en el diente llama al dentista

[3] (= *bother*) molestar; **I'm sorry to ~ you** disculpe la molestia; **maths never ~d me at all** las matemáticas no me costaron trabajo en absoluto; **to ~ o.s. about sth** preocuparse por algo; **to ~ o.s. to do sth** molestarse en *or* tomarse la molestia de hacer algo; **don't ~ yourself!** ¡no te molestes!, ¡no te preocupes!;

➤ LANGUAGE IN USE: **trouble A2** 4, 18.5

may I ~ you to hold this? ¿te molestaría tener esto?; **may I ~ you for a light?** ¿le molestaría darme fuego, por favor?; **does it ~ you if I smoke?** ¿le molesta que fume?; **I won't ~ you with all the details** no le voy a aburrir con exceso de detalles

Ⓒ VI (*= make the effort*) preocuparse, molestarse; **please don't ~!** ¡no te molestes!, ¡no te preocupes!; **don't ~ to write** no te molestes en escribir; **he didn't ~ to shut the door** no se tomó la molestia de cerrar la puerta; **if you had ~d to find out** si te hubieras tomado la molestia de averiguarlo

Ⓓ CPD ► **trouble spot** N (*esp Pol*) (*= area, country*) zona *f* conflictiva

troubled ['trʌbld] ADJ 1 (*= worried*) [*person*] preocupado, desazonado; [*mind*] preocupado, agitado; [*conscience*] intranquilo; [*expression, face, look*] de preocupación; **he was deeply ~** estaba profundamente preocupado *or* desazonado; **he was a lonely, ~ man** era un hombre que estaba solo y sin sosiego; **she fell into a ~ sleep** cayó en un sueño inquieto *or* agitado

2 (*= beset by problems*) [*life, marriage, relationship*] lleno de problemas, aquejado de problemas; [*period of time*] turbulento; [*area, country, region*] conflictivo; [*company, bank, industry*] aquejado de problemas; **these are ~ times** estos son tiempos difíciles; *see also* **oil**

trouble-free ['trʌblfriː] ADJ [*life*] sin problemas, tranquilo; [*demonstration, factory*] sin disturbios, pacífico; [*motoring*] sin problemas

troublemaker ['trʌbl,meɪkə(r)] N agitador(a) *m/f*

troublemaking ['trʌbl,meɪkɪŋ] ADJ alborotador, perturbador

troubleshooter ['trʌblʃuːtə(r)] N apagafuegos *mf inv* (*profesional o consultor experto en la detección de problemas y el desarrollo de soluciones empresariales o administrativas*)

troubleshooting ['trʌblʃuːtɪŋ] N *detección de problemas y desarrollo de soluciones empresariales o administrativas*

troublesome ['trʌblsəm] ADJ [*person*] fastidioso, molesto, latoso; [*headache, toothache etc*] molesto; [*dispute, problem*] difícil, penoso; **now don't be ~** no seas difícil

troublous ['trʌbləs] ADJ (*liter*) [*times*] turbulento, difícil

trough [trɒf] N 1 (*= depression*) depresión *f*, hoyo *m*; (*between waves, on graph*) seno *m*; (*= channel*) canal *m*; (*fig*) parte *f* baja, punto *m* más bajo; *see also* **peak A3**

2 (*Met*) zona *f* de bajas presiones

3 (*for animals*) (*= feeding trough*) comedero *m*, pesebre *m*; (*= drinking trough*) abrevadero *m*, bebedero *m*; (*= kneading trough*) artesa *f*

trounce [traʊns] VT 1 (*= defeat*) dar una paliza a*, derrotar

2 (*= thrash*) zurrar, dar una paliza a

troupe [truːp] N (*Theat*) compañía *f* de teatro; (*Circus*) troupe *f*

trouper ['truːpə(r)] N (*Theat*) miembro *mf* de una compañía de actores; **old ~** actor *m* veterano, actriz *f* veterana

trouser ['traʊzə(r)] (*esp Brit*) Ⓐ N **trousers** pantalón *m*, pantalones *mpl*; **short/long ~s** pantalones *mpl* cortos/largos; **a pair of ~s** un pantalón, unos pantalones; ✦*IDIOM* **to wear the ~s** llevar los pantalones

Ⓑ CPD ► **trouser leg** N pierna *f* de pantalón ► **trouser pocket** N bolsillo *m* del pantalón ► **trouser press** N prensa *f* para pantalones ► **trouser suit** N traje-pantalón *m*

trousseau ['truːsəʊ] N (*pl* **trousseaus, trousseaux** ['truːsəʊz]) ajuar *m*

trout [traʊt] (*pl* **trout** *or* **trouts**) Ⓐ N 1 (*= fish*) trucha *f*

2 **old ~*** (*= woman*) arpía *f*, bruja* *f*

Ⓑ CPD ► **trout fishing** N pesca *f* de trucha

trove [trəʊv] N *see* **treasure**

trowel ['traʊəl] N 1 (*Agr*) desplantador *m*

2 (*builder's*) paleta *f*, llana *f*

Troy [trɔɪ] N Troya *f*

troy ['trɔɪ] N (*also* **~ weight**) peso *m* troy

truancy ['trʊənsɪ] N ausencia *f* sin permiso

truant ['trʊənt] Ⓐ N (*Scol*) ausente *mf*; **to play ~** (*Scol*) hacer novillos, hacer la rabona*; (*fig*) ausentarse

Ⓑ VI (*Scol*) hacer novillos, hacer la rabona*; (*fig*) ausentarse (**from** de)

truce [truːs] N (*Mil*) tregua *f*; **to call a ~** (*Mil*) (*fig*) acordar una tregua

truck[1] [trʌk] Ⓐ N 1 (*esp US*) (*= lorry*) camión *m*

2 (*Rail*) (*= wagon*) vagón *m*

3 (*= hand trolley*) carretilla *f*

Ⓑ VT (*US*) llevar, transportar

Ⓒ CPD ► **truck driver** N (*esp US*) camionero/a *m/f* ► **truck stop** N (*US*) restaurante *m* de carretera

truck[2] [trʌk] Ⓐ N (*= dealings*) ✦*IDIOM* **to have no ~ with sb** no tener nada que ver con algn; **we want no ~ with that** no queremos tener nada que ver con eso

Ⓑ CPD ► **truck farm** N (*US*) huerto *m* de hortalizas ► **truck farmer** N (*US*) hortelano/a *m/f* ► **truck farming** N (*US*) horticultura *f* ► **truck garden** N = **truck farm** ► **truck system** N (*Hist*) el trueque

truckage ['trʌkɪdʒ] N (*US*) acarreo *m*

trucker ['trʌkə(r)] N (*US*) camionero/a *m/f*, transportista *mf*

trucking ['trʌkɪŋ] Ⓐ N (*esp US*) acarreo *m*, transporte *m* (en camión)

Ⓑ CPD ► **trucking company** N compañía *f* de transporte por carretera

truckle ['trʌkl] Ⓐ VI **to ~ to sb** someterse servilmente a algn

Ⓑ CPD ► **truckle bed** N carriola *f*

truckload ['trʌkləʊd] N carga *f* de camión; **by the ~** (*fig*) a carretadas

truckman ['trʌkmən] N (*pl* **truckmen**) (*US*) camionero *m*, transportista *m*

truculence ['trʌkjʊləns] N agresividad *f*, mal humor *m*

truculent ['trʌkjʊlənt] ADJ agresivo, malhumorado

truculently ['trʌkjʊləntlɪ] ADV [*behave*] de modo agresivo; [*answer*] ásperamente

trudge [trʌdʒ] Ⓐ N caminata *f* (difícil, larga, penosa)

Ⓑ VT recorrer a pie (penosamente); **we ~d the streets looking for him** nos cansamos buscándole por las calles

Ⓒ VI **to ~ up/down/along** *etc* subir/bajar/caminar *etc* penosamente

▼ **true** [truː] Ⓐ ADJ (*compar* **truer**; *superl* **truest**)

1 (*= not false*) [*story*] real, verídico; [*account*] verídico; [*statement*] cierto, verídico; [*rumour*] cierto, verdadero; **it is ~ that …** es verdad *or* cierto que …; **is it ~?** ¿es (eso) verdad?; **it can't be ~!** ¡no me lo creo!; **I'm quite tired, it's ~** es verdad *or* cierto que estoy bastante cansado; **he's so jealous it's not ~*** es tan celoso que resulta difícil creerlo; **is it ~ about Harry?** ¿es verdad *or* cierto lo de Harry?; **~, but …** cierto, pero …; **to come ~** [*dream*] hacerse realidad; [*wish, prediction*] cumplirse, hacerse realidad; **it's a dream come ~** es un sueño hecho realidad; **~ or false?** ¿verdadero o falso?; **the reverse is ~** ocurre lo contrario; **it is ~ to say that …** puede afirmarse que …; **the film is based on a ~ story** la película está basada en un hecho real *or* verídico; **it's ~r than you know** es más verdad de lo que te imaginas; **that's ~** es cierto, es verdad; **too ~** eso es totalmente cierto; **it is only too ~ that …** es lamentablemente *or* desgraciadamente cierto que …; *see also* **good A1, ring[2] C4**

2 (*= genuine*) [*gentleman, romantic, genius*] verdadero, auténtico; [*friend, courage, happiness*] verdadero, de verdad, auténtico; **music is her ~ love** su verdadero amor es la música; **her ~ love**† (*= sweetheart*) su gran amor *m*; **then he was able to demonstrate his ~ worth** entonces pudo demostrar lo que valía realmente *or* su verdadera valía

3 (*= real, actual*) [*feelings, motives, meaning*] verdadero; [*value, cost*] verdadero, real; **the ~ meaning of love** el verdadero significado del amor; **this helps us to discover our ~ selves** esto nos ayuda a descubrir nuestra verdadera identidad; **in the ~ sense (of the word)** en el sentido estricto (de la palabra), propiamente dicho

4 (*Rel*) verdadero; **the one ~ God** el Dios único y verdadero

5 (*= relevant, applicable*) cierto; **to be ~ for sb/sth** ser cierto en el caso de algn/algo; **this is particularly ~ for single women** esto es cierto particularmente en el caso de las mujeres solteras; **this is ~ for nine out of ten cases** esto es cierto en nueve de cada diez casos; **to hold ~ (for sb/sth)** ser válido (para algn/algo); **this is ~ of any new business venture** este es el caso con cualquier empresa nueva; **the same is ~ of nuclear power stations** el caso es el mismo con las centrales nucleares

6 (*frm*) (*= faithful*) **I am a ~ believer in American values** creo firmemente en los valores americanos; **to be ~ to sb/sth** ser fiel a algn/algo; **to be ~ to o.s.** ser fiel a sí mismo; **~ to form** como es/era de esperar; **to be ~ to life** ser como la vida real; **to be ~ to one's promise** *or* **word** ser fiel a su palabra *or* promesa, cumplir con su palabra *or* promesa; **~ to type** como es/era de esperar

7 (*= accurate*) **his aim was ~** dio en el blanco; **the portrait was a ~ likeness of her grandmother** el cuadro era un fiel retrato de su abuela

8 (*= straight*) derecho; **the window frame isn't quite ~** el marco de la ventana no está del todo derecho

9 (*Mus*) afinado; **his top notes were pure and ~** sus notas más altas eran puras y afinadas

Ⓑ N **to be out of ~: the doorframe is out of ~** el marco de la puerta no cae a plomo; **the top of the window was out of ~** la parte superior de la ventana no estaba nivelada

Ⓒ ADV **to breed ~** (*Bio*) reproducirse conforme con la raza

Ⓓ CPD ► **true colours, true colors** (*US*) NPL **to show one's ~ colours** ◊ **show o.s. in one's ~ colours** mostrarse tal y como se es en realidad; **to see sb in their ~ colours** ver a algn tal y como es en realidad; *see also* **colour A6** ► **true north** N (*Geog*) norte *m* geográfico

true-blue ['truː'bluː] Ⓐ ADJ rancio, de lo más rancio

Ⓑ N partidario/a *m/f* de lo más leal, partidario/a *m/f* acérrimo/a

true-born ['truː'bɔːn] ADJ auténtico, verdadero

true-bred ['truː'bred] ADJ de casta legítima, de pura sangre

➤ LANGUAGE IN USE: **true A1** 11.1, 26.3

true-life ['tru:laɪf] ADJ verdadero, conforme con la realidad

truffle ['trʌfl] N trufa *f*

trug [trʌg] N (*Brit*) *cesto para hortalizas o flores*

truism ['tru:ɪzəm] N (= *well-known truth*) perogrullada *f*; (*pej*) (= *cliché*) tópico *m*

truly ['tru:lɪ] ADV 1 (= *genuinely*) [*happy, democratic, international*] verdaderamente, realmente; [*understand, love*] de verdad; **the only man she ~ loved** el único hombre al que quería de verdad; **really and ~** de verdad
2 (*frm*) (= *sincerely*) [*grateful, worried*] verdaderamente, realmente, de verdad; [*believe, think, feel*] de verdad, realmente; **I ~ believe this** me lo creo de verdad, realmente me lo creo; **I was ~ hurt by what she said** lo que dijo me hizo realmente *or* verdadero daño; **it can ~ be said that …** verdaderamente se puede decir que …, realmente se puede decir que …; **I am ~ sorry for what happened** siento de veras *or* muchísimo lo ocurrido; **it was ~ wrong of him to do that** lo que hizo estuvo verdaderamente *or* realmente mal; **yours ~** (*in letter*) le saluda atentamente; **nobody knows it better than yours ~*** nadie lo sabe mejor que un servidor*
3 (*as intensifier*) (= *absolutely*) [*amazing, remarkable*] verdaderamente, realmente; *see also* **well A2**

trump [trʌmp] Ⓐ N (*Cards*) triunfo *m*; **hearts are ~s** triunfan corazones, pintan corazones; **what's ~s?** ¿a qué pinta?; ✦*IDIOM* **to turn up ~s** (*Brit*) salir *or* resultar bien; **he always turns up ~s** no nos falla nunca
Ⓑ VT (*Cards*) fallar; (*fig*) superar
Ⓒ VI (*Cards*) triunfar, poner un triunfo
Ⓓ CPD ► **trump card** N triunfo *m*; ✦*IDIOM* **to play one's ~ card** jugar su mejor carta

►**trump up** VT + ADV [+ *charge, excuse*] fabricar, inventar

trumped-up ['trʌmpt'ʌp] ADJ [*charge, excuse*] fabricado, inventado

trumpery ['trʌmpərɪ] Ⓐ ADJ (= *frivolous*) frívolo; (= *valueless*) inútil, sin valor; (= *insignificant*) sin importancia; (= *trashy*) de relumbrón
Ⓑ N oropel *m*

trumpet ['trʌmpɪt] Ⓐ N trompeta *f*; ✦*IDIOM* **to blow one's own ~** darse bombo
Ⓑ VI [*elephant*] bramar
Ⓒ VT (*fig*) (*also* **~ forth**) pregonar, anunciar (a son de trompeta)
Ⓓ CPD ► **trumpet blast, trumpet call** N trompetazo *m*; (*fig*) clarinazo *m*

trumpeter ['trʌmpɪtə^r] N (*orchestral*) trompetero *m*, trompeta *mf*; (*jazz*) trompetista *mf*

trumpeting ['trʌmpɪtɪŋ] N [*of elephant*] bramido *m*

truncate [trʌŋ'keɪt] VT [+ *report, speech*] truncar

truncated [trʌŋ'keɪtɪd] ADJ (= *shortened*) [*report*] truncado

truncating [trʌŋ'keɪtɪŋ] N (*Comput*) truncamiento *m*

truncation [trʌŋ'keɪʃən] N truncamiento *m*

truncheon ['trʌntʃən] N porra *f*

trundle ['trʌndl] Ⓐ VT (= *push*) empujar; (= *pull*) tirar, jalar (*LAm*)
Ⓑ VI [*cart etc*] rodar

►**trundle on** VI + ADV avanzar (con mucho ruido, pesadamente)

trunk [trʌŋk] Ⓐ N 1 [*of tree*] tronco *m*
2 (*Anat*) (= *human torso*) tronco *m*
3 [*of elephant*] trompa *f*
4 (= *big suitcase*) baúl *m*
5 (*US*) (= *boot of car*) maletero *m*, baúl *m* (*LAm*), cajuela *f* (*Mex*), maletera *f* (*S. Cone*)
Ⓑ CPD ► **trunk call** N (*Brit Telec*) conferencia *f* (interurbana); **to make a ~ call** llamar a larga distancia ► **trunk line** N (*Rail*) línea *f* troncal; (*Telec*) línea *f* principal ► **trunk road** N (*Brit*) carretera *f* principal

trunks [trʌŋks] NPL (*also* **swimming** *or* **bathing ~**) bañador *m*, slip *m*

trunnion ['trʌnɪən] N muñón *m*

truss [trʌs] Ⓐ VT 1 (= *tie*) liar, atar; [+ *fowl*] espetar
2 (*Archit*) [+ *supporting wall*] apuntalar; [+ *supporting floor*] apoyar con entramado
Ⓑ N 1 (*Med*) braguero *m*
2 (*Archit*) entramado *m*, soporte *m* de puntales
3 (= *bundle*) lío *m*, paquete *m*; [*of hay etc*] haz *m*, lío *m*; [*of fruit*] racimo *m*

►**truss up** VT + ADV **to ~ sb up** atar a algn (*con cuerdas etc*)

trust [trʌst] Ⓐ N 1 (= *faith, confidence*) confianza *f* (**in** en); **you've betrayed their ~** has traicionado la confianza que tenían puesta en ti; **I have complete ~ in you** confío plenamente en ti, tengo absoluta confianza en ti; **to take sth/sb on ~** fiarse de algo/algn; **I'm not going to take what he says on ~** no me voy a fiar de lo que dice *or* de su palabra; **to put one's ~ in sth/sb** depositar su confianza en algo/algn
2 (= *responsibility*) **to give sth into sb's ~** confiar algo a algn; **to be in a position of ~** tener un puesto de confianza *or* responsabilidad; **a sacred ~** un deber sagrado
3 (*Jur*) (= *money*) (*for third party*) fondo *m* fiduciario, fondo *m* de fideicomiso; (*Fin*) (= *investment*) fondo *m* de inversiones; (= *institution*) fundación *f*; **charitable ~** fundación *f* benéfica; **in ~** en fideicomiso; **the money will be held in ~ until she is 18** el dinero se mantendrá en fideicomiso hasta que cumpla los dieciocho años; **to put** *or* **place sth in ~** dejar algo en fideicomiso; **to set up a ~** crear un fondo fiduciario *or* de fideicomiso; *see also* **charitable, investment, unit**
4 (*Comm, Fin*) (*also* **~ company**) trust *m*, compañía *f* fiduciaria, compañía *f* de fideicomiso
5 (*also* **~ hospital**) fundación *f* hospitalaria
Ⓑ VT 1 (= *consider honest, reliable*) [+ *person, judgment, instincts*] fiarse de; **don't you ~ me?** ¿no te fías de mí?; **she is not to be ~ed** ella no es de fiar; **the government can't be ~ed** no se puede uno fiar del gobierno; **do you think we can ~ him?** ¿crees que nos podemos fiar de él?, ¿crees que podemos confiar *or* tener confianza en él?; **~ your own instincts** fíate de tus instintos; **to ~ sb to do sth: I ~ you to keep this secret** confío en que guardes este secreto; **her parents ~ her to make her own decisions** sus padres confían en ella y la dejan que tome sus propias decisiones; **do you think we can ~ him to give us our share?** ¿crees que podemos fiarnos de que nos va a dar nuestra parte?; **he did not ~ himself to speak** no se atrevió a hablar; **you can't ~ a word he says** es imposible creer ninguna palabra suya, no se puede uno fiar de nada de lo que dice; ✦*IDIOM* **I wouldn't ~ him an inch** *or* **as far as I could throw him** no me fío de él ni un pelo
2 (= *have confidence in*) confiar en, tener confianza en; **~ me, I know what I'm doing** confía en mí, sé lo que estoy haciendo; **I ~ you completely** tengo plena confianza en ti; **"I forgot" — "~ you!"** —se me olvidó —¡mira por dónde! *or* —¡cómo no!; **~ you to break it!** ¡era de esperar que lo rompieses!
3 (= *entrust*) **to ~ sth to sb** confiar algo a algn; **to ~ sb with sth**: **he's not the sort of person to be ~ed with a gun** no es la clase de persona de la que se puede uno fiar con una pistola, no es la clase de persona a la que se puede confiar una pistola; **I'd ~ him with my life** pondría mi vida en sus manos
4 (*frm*) (= *hope*) esperar; **I ~ you are all well** espero que estéis todos bien; **I ~ you enjoyed your walk?** espero que haya disfrutado del paseo; **I ~ not** espero que no
Ⓒ VI **to ~ in sth/sb** confiar en algo/algn; **to ~ to luck/fate** encomendarse a la suerte/al destino
Ⓓ CPD ► **trust account** N cuenta *f* fiduciaria, cuenta *f* de fideicomiso ► **trust company** N compañía *f* fiduciaria, compañía *f* de fideicomiso ► **trust fund** N fondo *m* fiduciario, fondo *m* de fideicomiso ► **trust hospital** N fundación *f* hospitalaria

trusted ['trʌstɪd] ADJ [*friend, adviser, servant*] de confianza; [*formula*] probado; *see also* **tried**

trustee [trʌs'ti:] N (*in bankruptcy*) síndico *m*; (= *holder of property for another*) fideicomisario/a *m/f*, depositario/a *m/f*, administrador(a) *m/f*; [*of college*] regente/a *m/f*

trusteeship [trʌs'ti:ʃɪp] N (*in bankruptcy*) cargo *m* de síndico; [*of property*] cargo *m* de fideicomisario, administración *f* fiduciaria

trustful ['trʌstfʊl] ADJ confiado

trusting ['trʌstɪŋ] ADJ [*person, nature*] confiado; [*relationship*] de confianza; **he has learned not to be too ~ of people** ha aprendido a no ser demasiado confiado con la gente

trustingly ['trʌstɪŋlɪ] ADV confiadamente

trustworthiness ['trʌst,wɜ:ðɪnɪs] N [*of person*] formalidad *f*; [*of source, news*] carácter *m* fidedigno, fiabilidad *f*; [*of statistics etc*] fiabilidad *f*, exactitud *f*

trustworthy ['trʌst,wɜ:ðɪ] ADJ [*person*] formal, de confianza; [*source of news*] fidedigno, fiable; [*statistics*] fiable, exacto

trusty ['trʌstɪ] Ⓐ ADJ (*compar* **trustier**; *superl* **trustiest**) [*servant*] fiel, leal; [*weapon*] seguro, bueno
Ⓑ N (*in prison*) recluso/a *m/f* de confianza

truth [tru:θ] (*pl* **truths** [tru:ðz]) Ⓐ N verdad *f*; **there is some ~ in this** hay una parte de verdad en esto; **in ~** en verdad, a la verdad; **the plain ~** la pura verdad, la verdad lisa y llana; **the whole ~** toda la verdad; **to tell the ~** decir la verdad; **to tell (you) the ~ ◊ ~ to tell** a decir verdad; **the ~ of the matter is that …** si te digo la verdad *or* la verdad es que …; **the ~ hurts** las verdades duelen; ✦*PROVS* **~ will out** no hay mentira que no salga; **~ is stranger than fiction** la realidad sobrepasa a la ficción; *see also* **home**
Ⓑ CPD ► **truth drug** N suero *m* de la verdad

truthful ['tru:θfʊl] ADJ [*account*] verídico, veraz; [*person*] veraz; **are you being ~?** ¿es esto la verdad?

truthfully ['tru:θfəlɪ] ADV sinceramente; **now tell me ~** ahora (bien), dime la verdad; **~, I don't know** de veras, no sé nada

truthfulness ['tru:θfʊlnɪs] N veracidad *f*

try [traɪ] Ⓐ N 1 (= *attempt*) intento *m*, tentativa *f*; **after several tries they gave up** tras varios intentos *or* varias tentativas, se dieron por vencidos; **it was a good ~ — better luck next time** no lo conseguiste pero no estuvo mal — otra vez será; **nice ~ Dave, but I know you're lying** no cuela, Dave, sé que estás mintiendo; **to give sth a ~** intentar (hacer) algo; **she's out at the moment — give her a ~ in half an hour** en este momento ha salido, pero llámela dentro de media hora; **let me have a ~** déjame intentarlo; **they're go-**

ing to have another ~ at the summit when the weather improves van a volver a intentar llegar a la cumbre cuando el tiempo mejore; **it's worth a ~** vale *or* merece la pena intentarlo

2 (= *trial*) **to give sth a ~** [+ *product, food, experience*] probar algo; **you'll never know what snake is like if you don't give it a ~** nunca sabrás a qué sabe la serpiente si no la pruebas; **to give sb a ~** darle una oportunidad a algn, poner a algn a prueba; **we'll give her a ~ for a week** le daremos una semana de prueba; **these new burgers are worth a ~** vale *or* merece la pena probar estas nuevas hamburguesas

3 (*Rugby*) ensayo *m*; **to score a ~** marcar un ensayo

Ⓑ VT 1 (= *attempt*) intentar; **you've only tried three questions** sólo has intentado hacer tres preguntas; **to ~ to do sth** intentar hacer algo, tratar de hacer algo; **he was shot while ~ing to escape** lo dispararon mientras intentaba escapar *or* trataba de escapar; **I tried not to think about it** intenté no pensar en ello, traté de no pensar en ello; **~ not to cough** procura no toser, procura contener la tos; **he was ~ing his best not to laugh** estaba haciendo todo lo posible por no reírse; **it's ~ing to rain** tiene ganas como de llover

2 (= *try out, sample*) probar; **have you tried these olives?** ¿has probado estas aceitunas?; **to ~ doing sth** probar a hacer algo; **have you tried soaking the curtains in vinegar?** ¿has probado a poner las cortinas en remojo con vinagre?; **~ turning the key** da vuelta a la llave y a ver qué pasa, prueba a *or* intenta darle la vuelta a la llave; **you ~ bringing up four children on your own!** ¡prueba tú a criar cuatro niños solo!; **I'll ~ anything once** siempre estoy dispuesto a probarlo todo, al menos una vez; **we've tried everything but the car still won't start** lo hemos intentado *or* probado todo, pero el coche todavía no arranca; *see also* **hand A10, size**[1]

3 (= *attempt to work*) [+ *door handle*] tirar de; [+ *telephone number*] intentar llamar a; **he tried the phone but the line was dead** intentó usar el teléfono pero no había línea; **he tried the door — to his surprise it opened** intentó abrir la puerta — para su sorpresa se abrió

4 (= *inquire at*) **we tried three hotels but they had no room** preguntamos en tres hoteles pero no tenían habitación; **have you tried the local music shops?** ¿lo has buscado en las tiendas de música del barrio?

5 (= *put to the test*) [+ *person, strength, patience*] poner a prueba; **why not ~ him for the job?** ¿por qué no ponerle a prueba en el puesto?; **he was tried and found wanting** fue sometido a prueba y resultó ser deficiente; **it would ~ the patience of a saint** pondría a prueba la paciencia de un santo; **to ~ one's luck** probar suerte; **to ~ sth on sb** probar algo con algn; **they haven't tried the drug on humans yet** todavía no han probado la droga con personas; **I tried the idea on a couple of people** le comenté la idea a un par de personas; **they have been sorely tried** (*liter*) han sufrido mucho; ✦*PROV* **these things are sent to ~ us** estas cosas nos las manda el Señor para ponernos a prueba

6 (*Jur*) **to ~ sb (for sth)** procesar *or* enjuiciar a algn (por algo); **to ~ a case** ver una demanda

Ⓒ VI **he didn't even ~** ni siquiera lo intentó; **you're not ~ing!** ¡no estás poniendo todo tu empeño!; **~ again!** ¡vuelve a intentarlo!; **~ as I might I couldn't persuade her** por más que intenté persuadirla no lo conseguí; **I couldn't have done that (even) if I'd tried** no podría haber hecho eso ni (siquiera) queriendo; **you could do it if you tried** podrías hacerlo si lo intentaras; **(just) you ~!** ¡hazlo y verás!, ¡atrévete (y verás)!; **to ~ and do sth*** intentar hacer algo, tratar de hacer algo; **I ought to ~ and get some sleep** debería tratar de *or* intentar dormir un rato; **to ~ one's (very) best** ◊ **~ one's (very) hardest** poner todo su empeño, hacer todo lo posible; **it is not for lack** *or* **want of ~ing** no será porque no se ha intentado; *see also* **succeed A1**

►**try for** VI + PREP intentar conseguir, tratar de conseguir; **he's going to ~ for a place at university** va a tratar de *or* va a intentar conseguir una plaza en la universidad; **they're ~ing for a baby** van a por un bebé

►**try on** VT + ADV 1 [+ *clothes, shoes*] probarse; **would you like to ~ it on?** ¿quiere probárselo?; *see also* **size**[1]

2 (*Brit**) (*fig*) **to ~ it on: she's ~ing it on to see how far she can push you** lo está haciendo para ver hasta cuánto aguantas; **take no notice, he's just ~ing it on** no le hagas caso, sólo está intentando quedarse contigo*; **don't ~ anything on with me!** ¡no intentes quedarte conmigo!*

►**try out** Ⓐ VT + ADV [+ *machine, new product, method*] probar; [+ *new employee*] poner a prueba; **~ it out on yourself first** pruébelo con usted mismo primero

Ⓑ VI + ADV **to ~ out for sth** [*actor, singer, sportsperson*] intentar pasar las pruebas de algo

trying ['traɪɪŋ] ADJ [*time, situation, circumstances*] difícil; [*experience, day*] duro; [*person*] latoso, pesado

try-on* ['traɪɒn] N camelo* *m*

tryout ['traɪaʊt] N prueba *f*; **to give sb a ~** poner a algn a prueba; **to give sth a ~** probar algo

tryst [trɪst] N (*liter, hum*) 1 (= *meeting*) cita *f*

2 (*also* **~ing-place**) lugar *m* de encuentro

tsar [zɑːʳ] N zar *m*

tsarina [zɑː'riːnə] N zarina *f*

tsetse fly ['tsetsɪflaɪ] N mosca *f* tsetsé

T-shaped ['tiːʃeɪpt] ADJ en forma de T

T-shirt ['tiːʃɜːt] N camiseta *f* de manga corta, playera *f*, remera *f* (*Arg*), polera *f* (*Chile, Bol*)

tsp. ABBR (*pl* **tsp.** *or* **tsps.**) = **teaspoon(ful)**

T-square ['tiːskweəʳ] N regla *f* en T

TSS N ABBR = **toxic shock syndrome**

tsunami [tsu'namɪ] N (*pl* **tsunamis** *or* **tsunami**) tsunami *m*

TT Ⓐ ADJ ABBR 1 = **teetotal, teetotaller**

2 (*Agr*) (= **tuberculin-tested**) a prueba de tuberculinas

Ⓑ N ABBR 1 (*Motorcycling*) = **Tourist Trophy**

2 (*Fin*) (= **telegraphic transfer**) transferencia *f* telegráfica

Ⓒ ABBR (*US*) = **Trust Territory**

TU N ABBR = **Trade(s) Union**

tub [tʌb] N 1 (= *large vessel*) cubo *m*, cuba *f*; (*for margarine etc*) tarrina *f*; (= *washtub*) tina *f*; [*of washing-machine*] tambor *m*

2 (*esp US*) (= *bathtub*) bañera *f*, tina *f* (*esp LAm*)

3 (*Naut**) carcamán *m*

tuba ['tjuːbə] N (*pl* **tubas,** (*frm*) **tubae** ['tjuːbiː]) tuba *f*

tubby* ['tʌbɪ] ADJ (*compar* **tubbier**, *superl* **tubbiest**) (= *fat*) gordito, rechoncho

tube [tjuːb] Ⓐ N 1 [*of toothpaste, paint etc*] tubo *m*; (*Anat*) trompa *f*; [*of tyre*] cámara *f* de aire; [*of television*] tubo *m*; (*US*) [*of radio*] lámpara *f*; ✦*IDIOM* **to go down the ~**: **it's all gone down the ~*** todo se ha perdido

2 **the ~** (*US**) (= *television*) la tele*

3 (= *London underground*) metro *m*; **to go by ~** ir en el metro; **to travel by ~** viajar en metro

Ⓑ CPD ► **tube station** N (*Brit*) estación *f* de metro

tubeless ['tjuːblɪs] ADJ [*tyre*] sin cámara

tuber ['tjuːbəʳ] N (*Bot*) tubérculo *m*

tubercle ['tjuːbəkl] N (*all senses*) tubérculo *m*

tubercular [tjʊ'bɜːkjʊləʳ] ADJ tubercular; (*Med*) tuberculoso

tuberculin [tjʊ'bɜːkjʊlɪn] N tuberculina *f*

tuberculosis [tjʊˌbɜːkjʊ'ləʊsɪs] N tuberculosis *f*, tisis *f*

tuberculous [tjʊ'bɜːkjʊləs] ADJ tuberculoso

tubing ['tjuːbɪŋ] N tubería *f*, cañería *f*; **a piece of ~** un trozo de tubo

tub-thumper ['tʌbˌθʌmpəʳ] N (*Brit*) (*fig*) orador *m* demagógico

tub-thumping ['tʌbˌθʌmpɪŋ] (*Brit*) (*fig*) Ⓐ ADJ demagógico

Ⓑ N oratoria *f* demagógica

tubular ['tjuːbjʊləʳ] Ⓐ ADJ (*gen*) tubular, en forma de tubo; [*furniture*] de tubo Ⓑ CPD ► **tubular bells** NPL (*Mus*) campanas *fpl* tubulares

TUC N ABBR (*Brit*) = **Trades Union Congress**

tuck [tʌk] Ⓐ N 1 (*Sew*) (= *fold*) pinza *f*, pliegue *m*; **to make** *or* **put a ~ in sth** poner una pinza en algo

2 (*Brit**) (= *food*) comida *f*; (= *sweets*) dulces *fpl*, golosinas *fpl*

3 (*plastic surgery*) reducción *f* mediante cirugía plástica; *see also* **tummy**

Ⓑ VT 1 (= *put*) meter

2 (*Sew*) plegar

Ⓒ CPD ► **tuck shop** N (*Brit Scol*) tienda *f* de golosinas

►**tuck away** VT + ADV 1 (= *hide*) esconder, ocultar; **~ it away out of sight** ocúltalo para que no se vea; **the village is ~ed away among the woods** la aldea se esconde en el bosque; **he ~ed it away in his pocket** se lo guardó en el bolsillo; **she has her money safely ~ed away** tiene su dinero bien guardado

2 (*Brit**) (= *eat*) devorar, zampar*; **he can certainly ~ it away** ése sí sabe comer; **I can't think where he ~s it all away** no entiendo dónde lo almacena *or* lo echa

►**tuck in** Ⓐ VI + ADV (*Brit**) (= *eat*) comer con apetito; **~ in!** ¡a comer!, ¡a ello!

Ⓑ VT + ADV 1 [+ *shirt, blouse*] remeter, meter dentro; **to ~ in a flap** meter una solapa para dentro; **to ~ the bedclothes in** remeter la ropa de la cama

2 [+ *child*] (*in bed*) arropar

►**tuck into*** VI + PREP (*Brit*) [+ *meal*] comer con buen apetito

►**tuck under** VT + PREP **to ~ one thing under another** remeter una cosa debajo de otra

►**tuck up** VT + ADV 1 (*Sew*) [+ *skirt, sleeves*] remangar 2 (*Brit*) [+ *child*] (*in bed*) arropar; **you'll soon be nicely ~ed up** pronto estarás a gustito en la cama

tucker* ['tʌkəʳ] VT (*US*) **to be ~ed (out)** estar molido *or* rendido*

tuck-in* ['tʌk'ɪn] N (*Brit*) banquetazo* *m*, comilona* *f*; **to have a good ~** darse un atracón*

Tudor ['tjuːdəʳ] ADJ [*monarch, house*] Tudor; **the ~ period** la época de los Tudor

Tue(s). ABBR (= **Tuesday**) mart.

Tuesday ['tju:zdɪ] N martes *m inv*; **the date today is ~ 23rd March** hoy es martes, 23 de marzo; **on ~** (*past or future*) el martes; **on ~s** los martes; **every ~** todos los martes; **every other ~** cada otro martes, un martes sí y otro no; **last ~** el martes pasado; **next ~** ◊ **~ next** el martes próximo, el martes que viene; **this ~** este martes; **the following ~** el martes siguiente; **the ~ before last** el martes antepasado; **the ~ after next** el martes próximo no, el siguiente, el martes que viene no, el siguiente; **a week on ~** ◊ **~ week** del martes en una semana; **a fortnight on ~** ◊ **~ fortnight** del martes en una quincena; **~ morning/night** el martes por la mañana/por la noche; **~ afternoon/evening** el martes por la tarde; **~ lunchtime** el martes a mediodía; **the ~ film** (*TV*) la película del martes; **~'s newspaper** el periódico del martes; *see also* **Shrove Tuesday**

tufa ['tju:fə] N toba *f*

tuft [tʌft] N [*of hair*] copete *m*, mechón *m*; [*of grass*] mata *f*; [*of feathers*] cresta *f*; (*on top of head*) copete *m*; (*on helmet*) penacho *m*

tufted ['tʌftɪd] ADJ copetudo

tug [tʌg] Ⓐ N [1] (= *pull*) tirón *m*, jalón *m* (*LAm*); **to give sth a (good) ~** dar a algo un tirón (fuerte)
[2] (*Naut*) (= *boat*) remolcador *m*
Ⓑ VT [1] (= *pull*) tirar de, jalar (*LAm*); **to ~ sth along** arrastrar algo, llevar algo arrastrándolo
[2] (*Naut*) remolcar; **eventually they ~ged the boat clear** por fin sacaron el barco a flote
Ⓒ VI tirar, jalar (*LAm*); **to ~ at sth** tirar de algo; **they ~ged their hardest** se esforzaron muchísimo tirando de él; **somebody was ~ging at my sleeve** alguien me tiraba de la manga

tugboat ['tʌgbəʊt] N remolcador *m*

tug-of-love* [,tʌgəv'lʌv] N litigio *m* entre padres por la custodia de los hijos (*después de un divorcio etc*)

tug-of-war ['tʌgə(v)'wɔ:ʳ] N (*Sport*) juego *m* de tiro de cuerda; (*fig*) lucha *f*, tira y afloja *m*

tuition [tjʊ'ɪʃən] Ⓐ N enseñanza *f*, instrucción *f*; (*US*) matrícula *f*; **private ~** clases *fpl* particulares (**in** de)
Ⓑ CPD ► **tuition fees** NPL matrícula *fsing*, tasas *fpl* de matriculación

tulip ['tju:lɪp] Ⓐ N tulipán *m*
Ⓑ CPD ► **tulip tree** N tulipanero *m*, tulipero *m*

tulle [tju:l] N tul *m*

tumble ['tʌmbl] Ⓐ N (= *fall*) caída *f*; (= *somersault*) voltereta *f*, rodada *f* (*LAm*); **to have** *or* **take a ~** caerse; **to have a ~ in the hay*** (*euph*) retozar, hacer el amor (en el pajar); **to take a ~** (*fig*) bajar de golpe, dar un bajón; *see also* **rough-and-tumble**
Ⓑ VI [1] (= *fall*) caerse; (= *stumble*) tropezar; **to ~ downstairs/down a hill** rodar por la escalera/por una colina, rodar escaleras abajo/cuesta abajo; **to go tumbling over and over** ir rodando
[2] [*water*] correr con fuerza; (*fig*) [*prices*] caer en picado, desplomarse
[3] (= *rush*) **to ~ into/out of bed** tirarse en/saltar de la cama; **the children ~d out of the room/car** los niños salieron de la habitación/del coche en tropel
[4] (*Brit**) (= *suddenly understand*) **to ~ to sth** caer en la cuenta de algo
Ⓒ VT (= *knock down*) derribar, abatir, tumbar; (*fig*) derrocar; (= *upset*) hacer caer; (= *disarrange*) desarreglar
Ⓓ CPD ► **tumble dryer** N secadora *f*

► **tumble down** VI + ADV desplomarse, venirse abajo

tumbledown ['tʌmbldaʊn] ADJ [*building, shack*] ruinoso, desvencijado

tumbler ['tʌmbləʳ] Ⓐ N [1] (= *glass*) vaso *m*
[2] [*of lock*] seguro *m*, fiador *m*
[3] (= *acrobat*) volteador(a) *m/f*, volatinero/a *mf*
[4] (= *pigeon*) pichón *m* volteador
Ⓑ CPD ► **tumbler switch** N interruptor *m* de resorte

tumbleweed ['tʌmblwi:d] N (*US*) planta *f* rodadora

tumbrel ['tʌmbrəl], **tumbril** ['tʌmbrɪl] N chirrión *m*, carreta *f*

tumefaction [,tju:mɪ'fækʃən] N tumefacción *f*

tumescent [tju:'mesnt] ADJ tumescente

tumid ['tju:mɪd] ADJ túmido

tummy* ['tʌmɪ] Ⓐ N (= *stomach*) barriga* *f*, tripa* *f*
Ⓑ CPD ► **tummy ache** N dolor *m* de barriga*, dolor *m* de tripa* ► **tummy tuck** N cirugía *f* plástica anti-michelines*

tumour, **tumor** (*US*) ['tju:məʳ] N tumor *m*

tumult ['tju:mʌlt] N (= *uproar*) tumulto *m*; **to be in a ~** [*person*] estar agitado *or* alborotado; **her emotions were in a ~** tenía un conflicto emocional

tumultuous [tju:'mʌltjʊəs] ADJ [*applause*] tumultuoso

tumultuously [tju:'mʌltjʊəslɪ] ADV tumultuosamente

tumulus ['tju:mjʊləs] N (*pl* **tumuli** ['tju:mjʊlaɪ]) túmulo *m*

tun [tʌn] N tonel *m*

tuna ['tju:nə] N (*pl* **tuna, tunas**) (*also* **~ fish**) atún *m*

tundra ['tʌndrə] N tundra *f*

tune [tju:n] Ⓐ N [1] (= *melody*) melodía *f*; (= *piece*) tema *m*; (= *song*) canción *f*; **can you remember the ~?** ¿te acuerdas de la melodía *or* la música?; **the cello has the ~ at that point** el chelo lleva la melodía en esa parte; **it hasn't got much ~** no es muy melódico, no tiene mucha melodía; **dance ~** canción *f* bailable; **come on, give us a ~!** (= *sing*) ¡vamos, cántanos algo!; **he gave us a ~ on the piano** nos tocó un tema al piano; **to hum a ~** tararear una melodía/canción; **to the ~ of sth** (*lit*) **(sung) to the ~ of Rule Britannia** con la música de Rule Britannia; (*fig*) **repairs to the ~ of £300** arreglos por la bonita suma de 300 libras; **he was in debt to the ~ of £4,000** tenía deudas que llegaban a 4.000 libras; ✦***IDIOMS*** **to call the ~** llevar la voz cantante; **to change one's ~** cambiar de parecer; **to sing another** *or* **a different ~** bailar a un son distinto; **the same old ~**: **I'm bored with politicians singing the same old ~** estoy harto de oír a los políticos siempre hablar de lo mismo; *see also* **dance C**, **piper**, **signature**
[2] (= *accurate pitch*) **to be in ~** [*instrument*] estar afinado; **he can't sing in ~** no sabe cantar sin desafinar, no sabe cantar afinado; **to be out of ~** [*instrument*] estar desafinado; **to go out of ~** desafinar; **to sing out of ~** cantar desafinado, desafinar; **to be in/out of ~ with sth/sb**: **he is in/out of ~ with the people** sintoniza con/está desconectado con el pueblo; **his ideas were in/out of ~ with the spirit of his age** sus ideas estaban a tono/desentonaban con el espíritu de su época
Ⓑ VT [1] (*Mus*) [+ *piano, guitar*] afinar
[2] (*Mech*) [+ *engine, machine*] poner a punto, afinar
[3] (*TV, Rad*) sintonizar; **you are ~d (in) to ...** está usted sintonizando (la cadena) ...; **stay ~d to this station for a further announcement** sigan en sintonía con esta emisora para escuchar otro anuncio
Ⓒ VI (*TV, Rad*) **to ~ to sth** (*to programme, channel*) sintonizar algo

► **tune in** Ⓐ VI + ADV (*Rad, TV*) sintonizar; **~ in again tomorrow** sintonice con nosotros mañana; **to ~ in to sth** (*Rad, TV*) sintonizar (con) algo; (*fig*) (*to needs, feelings*) conectar con algo
Ⓑ VT + ADV [1] (*Rad, TV*) **you are ~d in to ...** está usted sintonizando (la cadena) ...
[2] (*fig*) **to be ~d in to sth** (*to new developments*) estar al corriente de algo; (*to sb's feelings*) estar conectado con algo

► **tune out** Ⓐ VI + ADV (*US*) [1] (*lit*) desconectar la televisión/radio
[2] (*fig*) desconectar, desconectarse; **he ~d out of the conversation** (se) desconectó de la conversación
Ⓑ VT + ADV [1] (*Rad, TV*) dejar de sintonizar
[2] (*fig*) [+ *distractions, noises*] desconectar de, desconectarse de; **she yelled constantly so I learned to ~ her out** gritaba constantemente, así es que aprendí a desconectar

► **tune up** Ⓐ VT + ADV [1] (*Mus*) afinar
[2] (*Aut*) poner a punto, afinar
Ⓑ VI + ADV (*Mus*) afinar

tuneful ['tju:nfʊl] ADJ [*voice, song*] melodioso, armonioso

tunefully ['tju:nfəlɪ] ADV melodiosamente, armoniosamente

tunefulness ['tju:nfʊlnɪs] N lo melodioso, lo armonioso

tuneless ['tju:nlɪs] ADJ [*voice, song*] poco melodioso

tunelessly ['tju:nlɪslɪ] ADV de forma poco melodiosa

tuner ['tju:nəʳ] N [1] (*Rad*) (= *knob, equipment*) sintonizador *m*
[2] (= *person*) afinador/a *m/f*; *see also* **piano**

tune-up ['tju:nʌp] N [1] (*Mus*) afinación *f*
[2] (*Aut*) puesta *f* a punto, afinado *m*

tungsten ['tʌŋstən] N tungsteno *m*

tunic ['tju:nɪk] N túnica *f*; (*Brit Mil*) guerrera *f*, blusa *f*

tuning ['tju:nɪŋ] Ⓐ N [1] (*Mus*) afinación *f*
[2] (*Rad*) sintonización *f*
[3] (*Aut*) afinado *m*
Ⓑ CPD ► **tuning coil** N bobina *f* sintonizadora ► **tuning fork** N diapasón *m* ► **tuning knob** N sintonizador *m*

Tunis ['tju:nɪs] N Túnez *m*

Tunisia [tju:'nɪzɪə] N Túnez *m*

Tunisian [tju:'nɪzɪən] Ⓐ ADJ tunecino
Ⓑ N tunecino/a *m/f*

tunnel ['tʌnl] Ⓐ N (*gen*) túnel *m*; (*Min*) galería *f*; (= *underpass*) paso *m* subterráneo
Ⓑ VT [+ *one's way, a passage*] cavar; **they ~led their way out** escaparon excavando un túnel; **a mound ~led by rabbits** un montículo lleno de madrigueras de conejo; **shelters ~led out in the hillsides** refugios *mpl* horadados en las colinas
Ⓒ VI construir un túnel; [*animal*] excavar una madriguera; **they ~ into the hill** construyen un túnel bajo la colina; **to ~ down into the earth** perforar un túnel en la tierra; **the rabbits ~ under the fence** los conejos hacen madrigueras que pasan debajo de la valla
Ⓓ CPD ► **tunnel vision** N visión *f* periférica restringida; (*fig*) estrechez *f* de miras

tunny ['tʌnɪ] N (*pl* **tunny, tunnies**) atún *m*; **striped ~** bonito *m*

tuppence* ['tʌpəns] N = **twopence**

tuppenny* ['tʌpənɪ] ADJ (*Brit*) = **twopenny**

turban ['tɜːbən] N turbante *m*

turbid ['tɜːbɪd] ADJ túrbido

turbine ['tɜːbaɪn] N turbina *f*

turbo ['tɜːbəʊ] N (= *fan*) turboventilador *m*; (*in cars*) turbo(compresor) *m*

turbo... ['tɜːbəʊ] PREFIX turbo...

turbocharged ['tɜːbəʊtʃɑːdʒd] ADJ turbocargado, turboalimentado

turbocharger ['tɜːbəʊ,tʃɑːdʒəʳ] N turbocompresor *m*, turbo *m*

turbofan ['tɜːbəʊfæn] N turboventilador *m*

turbogenerator ['tɜːbəʊ'dʒenəreɪtəʳ] N turbogenerador *m*

turbojet ['tɜːbəʊ'dʒet] Ⓐ N turborreactor *m*
Ⓑ CPD turborreactor

turboprop ['tɜːbəʊ'prɒp] Ⓐ N turbohélice *m*
Ⓑ CPD turbohélice

turbot ['tɜːbət] N (*pl* **turbot, turbots**) (= *fish*) rodaballo *m*

turbulence ['tɜːbjʊləns] N 1 [*of air, water*] turbulencia *f*; **the plane ran into some ~** el avión entró en un área de turbulencias
2 (= *unrest*) (*social, political*) turbulencia *f*, agitación *f*

turbulent ['tɜːbjʊlənt] ADJ 1 (= *confused, changing*) [*place, relationship*] turbulento; **these are ~ times** esta es una época turbulenta
2 (= *unruly*) [*person, character*] problemático; [*crowd*] alborotado, soliviantado
3 (= *unsettled*) [*water, sea, air*] turbulento

turd** [tɜːd] N 1 (= *excrement*) cagada** *f*, zurullo** *m*
2 (= *person*) mierda** *mf*

tureen [tə'riːn] N sopera *f*

turf [tɜːf] Ⓐ N (*pl* **turfs** *or* **turves** [tɜːvz]) 1 (= *grass*) césped *m*; (= *clod*) tepe *m*; (*in turfing*) pan *m* de hierba; (= *peat*) turba *f*
2 (*Horse racing*) **the Turf** el turf, el hipódromo
3 (*) [*of gang etc*] territorio *m*, zona *f* de influencia
Ⓑ VT (*also* **~ over**) cubrir con césped
Ⓒ CPD ► **turf accountant** N (*Brit*) corredor(a) *m/f* de apuestas

► **turf out*** VT + ADV (*Brit*) echar (de la casa), plantar en la calle

turgid ['tɜːdʒɪd] ADJ [*prose etc*] inflado, rimbombante

turgidity [tɜː'dʒɪdɪtɪ] N [*of prose etc*] rimbombancia *f*

Turin [tjʊ'rɪn] N Turín *m*

Turk [tɜːk] N 1 (*from Turkey*) turco/a *m/f*
2 (*fig*) (*esp Pol*) elemento *m* alborotador; **young ~** joven reformista *mf*

Turkey ['tɜːkɪ] N Turquía *f*

turkey ['tɜːkɪ] Ⓐ N (*pl* **turkey, turkeys**) 1 (= *bird*) pavo *m*, guajolote *m* (*Mex*), jolote *m* (*CAm*), chompipe *m* (*CAm*); ✦**IDIOM to talk ~** (*US**) hablar en serio; *see also* **cold**
2 (*esp US Cine, Theat**) (= *flop*) fiasco* *m*, fracaso *m*
3 (*US**) (= *person*) patoso/a *m/f*, pato *m* mareado*
Ⓑ CPD ► **turkey buzzard** N (*US*) buitre *m*, zopilote *m* (*CAm, Mex*), aura *f* (*Carib*), gallinazo *m* (*Col, Andes*), zamuro *m* (*Ven*) ► **turkey cock** N (*lit, fig*) pavo *m* ► **turkey shoot*** N (*US*) **to be (like) a ~ shoot** (*fig*) ser coser y cantar*, ser pan comido*

Turkish ['tɜːkɪʃ] Ⓐ ADJ turco
Ⓑ N (= *language*) turco *m*
Ⓒ CPD ► **Turkish bath** N baño *m* turco ► **Turkish coffee** N café *m* turco ► **Turkish delight** N lokum *m*, capricho *m* de reina ► **Turkish towel** N (*US*) toalla *f*

Turkish-Cypriot ['tɜːkɪʃ'sɪprɪət] Ⓐ ADJ turcochipriota
Ⓑ N turcochipriota *mf*

Turkmenistan [tɜːk,menɪs'tɑːn] N Turkmenistán *m*

turmeric ['tɜːmərɪk] N cúrcuma *f*

turmoil ['tɜːmɔɪl] N confusión *f*, desorden *m*; (*mental*) trastorno *m*; **we had complete ~ for a week** durante una semana reinó la confusión; **to be in ~** [*person*] estar totalmente confuso; [*house*] estar alborotado

turn [tɜːn] Ⓐ N 1 (= *rotation*) vuelta *f*, revolución *f*; [*of spiral*] espira *f*; **with a quick ~ of the hand** con un movimiento rápido de la mano; **he gave the handle a ~** dio vuelta a la palanca; **to give a screw another ~** apretar un tornillo una vuelta más; ✦**IDIOM he never does a hand's ~** no da golpe
2 (*Aut*) (*in road*) vuelta *f*, curva *f*; **a road full of twists and ~s** una carretera llena de curvas; **"no left turn"** "prohibido girar a la izquierda"; **to do a left ~** (*Aut*) doblar *or* girar a la izquierda
3 (*Aut*) (= *turn-off*) salida *f*; **I think we missed our ~ back there** creo que allí atrás nos hemos pasado de la salida
4 (*Naut*) viraje *m*; **to make a ~ to port** virar a babor
5 (*Swimming*) vuelta *f*
6 (= *change of direction*) **at the ~ of the century** a finales del siglo; **this was a surprising ~ of events** esto suponía un giro inesperado de los acontecimientos; **at every ~** (*fig*) a cada paso; **to be on the ~: the tide is on the ~** la marea está cambiando; **the milk is on the ~** la leche está a punto de cortarse; **the economy may at last be on the ~** puede que por fin la economía dé un giro importante *or* cambie de signo; **~ of the tide** (*lit, fig*) cambio *m or* vuelta *f* de la marea; **things took a new ~** las cosas tomaron otro cariz *or* aspecto; **events took a tragic ~** los acontecimientos tomaron un cariz trágico; **events are taking a sensational ~** los acontecimientos vienen tomando un rumbo sensacional; **then things took a ~ for the better** entonces las cosas empezaron a mejorar; **the patient took a ~ for the worse** el paciente empeoró; **at the ~ of the year** a fin de año
7 (*in series, etc*) turno *m*, vez *f*; **whose ~ is it?** ¿a quién le toca?; **it's your ~** te toca a ti; **it's her ~ next** le toca a ella después, ella es la primera en turno; **then it was my ~ to protest** luego protesté a mi vez; **your ~ will come** ya te tocará; **~ and ~ about** cada uno por turno, ahora esto y luego aquello; **by ~s** por turnos, sucesivamente; **I felt hot and cold by ~s** tuve calor y luego frío en momentos sucesivos; **to give up one's ~** ceder la vez; **in ~** por turnos, sucesivamente; **they spoke in ~** hablaron por turnos; **and they, in ~, said ...** y ellos a su vez dijeron ...; **to miss one's ~** perder la vez *or* el turno; **the player shall miss two ~s** el jugador deberá perder dos jugadas; **to go out of ~** (*in game*) jugar fuera de orden; **to speak out of ~** (*fig*) hablar fuera de lugar; **to take one's ~** llegarle (a algn) su turno; **to take ~s at doing sth** alternar *or* turnarse para hacer algo; **to take it in ~(s) to do sth** turnarse para hacer algo; **to take ~s at the wheel** conducir por turnos; **to take a ~ at the wheel** turnarse para conducir; **to wait one's ~** esperar (algn) su turno
8 (= *short walk*) vuelta *f*; **to take a ~ in the park** dar una vuelta por el parque
9 (*Med*) (= *fainting fit etc*) vahído *m*, desmayo *m*; (= *crisis*) crisis *f inv*, ataque *m*; **he had a bad ~ last night** anoche tuvo un ataque
10 (*) (= *fright*) susto *m*; **the news gave me quite a ~** la noticia me asustó *or* dejó de piedra
11 (*esp Brit Theat*) número *m*, turno *m*; **he came on and did a funny ~** salió a escena y presentó un número cómico
12 (= *deed*) **to do sb a bad ~** hacer una mala pasada a algn; **to do sb a good ~** hacerle un favor a algn; **his good ~ for the day** su buena acción del día; ✦**PROV one good ~ deserves another** amor con amor se paga
13 (*Culin*) **it's done to a ~** está en su punto
14 (= *inclination*) **an odd ~ of mind** una manera retorcida *or* (*LAm*) chueca de pensar; **to be of** *or* **have a scientific ~ of mind** ser más dado a las ciencias
15 (= *expression*) **~ of phrase** forma *f* de hablar, giro *m*; **that's a French ~ of phrase** eso es un modismo francés
Ⓑ VT 1 (= *rotate*) [+ *wheel, handle*] girar, dar vueltas a; [+ *screw*] atornillar, destornillar; **to ~ the key in the lock** dar vuelta a la llave en la cerradura; **the engine ~s the wheel** el motor hace girar la rueda; **you can ~ it through 90°** se puede girarlo hasta 90 grados; **~ it to the left** dale una vuelta hacia la izquierda
2 (*also* **~ over**) [+ *record, mattress, steak*] dar la vuelta a, voltear (*LAm*); [+ *page*] pasar; [+ *soil*] revolver; [+ *hay*] volver al revés; **the plough ~s the soil** el arado revuelve la tierra; **to ~ one's ankle** torcerse el tobillo; **to ~ a dress inside out** volver un vestido del revés; **it ~s my stomach** me revuelve el estómago; ✦**IDIOM to ~ the page (on sth)** pasar la página (de algo), dar carpetazo (a algo)
3 (= *direct*) dirigir, volver; **they ~ed him against us** le pusieron en contra nuestra; **we managed to ~ his argument against him** pudimos volver su argumento contra él mismo; **to ~ one's attention to sth** concentrar su atención en algo; **to ~ one's back on sb/sth** (*also fig*) volver *or* dar la espalda a algn/algo; **as soon as his back is ~ed** en cuanto mira para otro lado; **to ~ one's eyes in sb's direction** volver la mirada hacia donde está algn; **to ~ a gun on sb** apuntar una pistola a algn; **to ~ one's head** volver la cabeza; **the fireman ~ed the hose on the building** el bombero dirigió la manguera hacia el edificio; **to ~ the lights (down) low** poner la luz más baja; **to ~ one's steps homeward** dirigirse a casa, volver los pasos hacia casa; **to ~ one's thoughts to sth** concentrarse en algo; ✦**IDIOMS to ~ the other cheek** ofrecer la otra mejilla; **without ~ing a hair** sin inmutarse; **to ~ one's hand to sth: he ~ed his hand to cookery** se dedicó a la cocina; **to ~ sb's head: earning all that money has ~ed his/her head** se le han subido los humos con lo de ganar tanto dinero; **already in her first film she ~ed a few heads** ya en su primera película la gente se fijó en ella; **to ~ the tables** dar la vuelta a la tortilla
4 (= *pass*) doblar, dar la vuelta a; **the car ~ed the corner** el coche dobló la esquina; **he's ~ed 50** ha pasado los 50 años; **it's ~ed four o'clock** son las cuatro y pico *or* (*esp LAm*) las cuatro pasadas; ✦**IDIOM to have ~ed the corner** haber salido del apuro, haber pasado lo peor
5 (= *change*) **the heat ~ed the walls black** el calor volvió negras las paredes, el calor ennegreció las paredes; **the shock ~ed her hair white** del susto, el pelo se le puso blanco; **his goal ~ed the game** (*Brit*) su gol le dio un

vuelco al partido; **an actor ~ed writer** un actor metido a escritor; **to ~ sth into sth** convertir algo en algo; **they ~ed the land into a park** convirtieron el terreno en un parque; **to ~ iron into gold** convertir el hierro en oro; **to ~ a play into a film** pasar una obra al cine; **to ~ verse into prose** verter verso en prosa; **to ~ English into Spanish** traducir el inglés al español; **it ~ed him into a bitter man** le volvió un resentido; **she ~ed her dreams to reality** hizo sus sueños realidad, realizó sus sueños

6 (= *deflect*) [+ *blow*] desviar; **nothing will ~ him from his purpose** nada le hará cambiar su intención

7 (= *shape*) [+ *wood, metal*] tornear; **to ~ wood on a lathe** labrar la madera en un torno; *see also* **well-turned**

8 (*Culin*) **the heat has ~ed the milk** el calor ha cortado la leche

9 **to ~ a profit** (*esp US*) sacar un beneficio, tener ganancias

Ⓒ VI 1 (= *rotate*) [*wheel etc*] girar, dar vueltas; **the object ~ed on a stand** el objeto giraba en un pedestal; **the earth ~s on its axis** la Tierra gira sobre su propio eje; **his stomach ~ed at the sight** al verlo se le revolvió el estómago, al verlo se le revolvieron las tripas*; ✦*IDIOMS* **my head is ~ing** la cabeza me está dando vueltas; **to ~ in one's grave**: **she would ~ in her grave if she knew** le daría un síncope si supiera; *see also* **toss C1**

2 (= *change direction*) [*person*] dar la vuelta, voltearse (*LAm*); [*tide*] repuntar; **to ~ and go back** volverse *or* dar la vuelta y regresar; **right ~!** (*Mil*) derecha ... ¡ar!; **the game ~ed after half-time** (*Brit*) el partido dio un vuelco tras el descanso; **to ~ against sb** volverse contra algn; **to ~ against sth** coger aversión a algo; **to ~ for home** volver hacia casa; **farmers are ~ing from cows to pigs** los granjeros cambian de vacas a cerdos; **then our luck ~ed** luego mejoramos de suerte; **to ~ to sb/sth**: **he ~ed to me and smiled** se volvió hacia mí y sonrió; **to ~ to sb for help** acudir a algn en busca de ayuda; **she has no-one to ~ to** no tiene a quién recurrir; **our thoughts ~ to those who ...** pensamos ahora en los que ...; **please ~ to page 34** vamos a la página 34; **he ~ed to politics** se dedicó a la política; **he ~ed to drink** se dio a la bebida, le dio por el alcohol; **the conversation ~ed to religion** la conversación viró hacia la religión; **I don't know which way to ~** (*fig*) no sé qué hacer; **I don't know where to ~ for money** no sé en qué parte ir a buscar dinero; **the wind has ~ed** el viento ha cambiado de dirección; ✦*IDIOM* **the tide is ~ing** (*lit*) está cambiando la marea; (*fig*) las cosas están cambiando

3 (*Aut*) torcer, girar; (*Aer, Naut*) virar; **to ~ left** (*Aut*) torcer *or* girar *or* doblar a la izquierda; **the car ~ed into a lane** el coche se metió en una bocacalle; **to ~ to port** (*Naut*) virar a babor

4 (= *change*) **to ~ into sth** convertirse *or* transformarse en algo; **the whole thing has ~ed into a nightmare** todo el asunto se ha convertido en una pesadilla; **he ~ed into a cynic** se volvió cínico; **the princess ~ed into a toad** la princesa se transformó en sapo, la princesa quedó transformada en sapo; **the leaves were ~ing** se estaban descolorando *or* dorando las hojas; **the milk has ~ed** la leche se ha cortado; **it ~ed to stone** se convirtió en piedra; **his admiration ~ed to scorn** su admiración se tornó *or* se transformó en desprecio; **to wait for the weather to ~** esperar a que cambie el tiempo

5 (= *become*) **then he began to ~ awkward** luego empezó a ponerse difícil; **he ~ed Catholic** se hizo católico; **the weather** *or* **it has ~ed cold** el tiempo se ha puesto frío, se ha echado el frío; **to ~ nasty** [*person*] ponerse *or* volverse antipático; **to ~ professional** hacerse profesional; **to ~ red** ponerse rojo; **matters are ~ing serious** las cosas se ponen graves

6 (= *depend*) **everything ~s on his decision** todo depende de su decisión; **everything ~s on whether ...** todo depende de si ...

Ⓓ CPD ► **turn signal** N (*US Aut*) indicador *m* (de dirección)

►**turn about, turn around** Ⓐ VT + ADV = **turn round**

Ⓑ VI + ADV 1 [*person, vehicle*] dar una vuelta completa; [*wind*] cambiar de dirección, soplar en la dirección contraria; **about ~!** (*Mil*) media vuelta ... ¡ar!

2 (= *improve*) [*business, economy*] recuperarse

►**turn aside** Ⓐ VI + ADV desviarse, apartarse (**from** de)

Ⓑ VT + ADV desviar, apartar

►**turn away** Ⓐ VI + ADV apartarse (**from** de); **I ~ed away in disgust** me aparté lleno de asco

Ⓑ VT + ADV 1 (= *move*) [+ *eyes, head, gun*] desviar, apartar

2 (= *reject*) [+ *person, offer, business, customer*] rechazar

►**turn back** Ⓐ VI + ADV 1 (*in journey etc*) volverse (atrás), desandar el camino; **there can be no ~ing back now** (*fig*) ahora no vale volverse atrás

2 (*in book*) volver

Ⓑ VT + ADV 1 (= *fold*) [+ *bedclothes*] doblar

2 (= *send back*) [+ *person*] hacer volver, hacer regresar, devolver; [+ *vehicle*] volver, dar la vuelta a; **they were ~ed back at the frontier** en la frontera les hicieron volver *or* regresar

3 [+ *clock*] retrasar; ✦*IDIOMS* **to ~ the clock back**: **we can't ~ the clock back** no podemos dar marcha atrás *or* volver al pasado; **to ~ the clock back 20 years** volver 20 años atrás

►**turn down** VT + ADV 1 (= *fold down*) [+ *bedclothes, collar, page*] doblar

2 (= *turn upside down*) [+ *playing card*] poner boca abajo

3 (= *reduce*) [+ *gas, heat, volume*] bajar

4 (= *refuse*) [+ *offer, suitor, candidate*] rechazar; **he was ~ed down for the job** no le dieron el puesto

►**turn in** Ⓐ VI + ADV 1 [*car, person*] entrar

2 (*) (= *go to bed*) acostarse

Ⓑ VT + ADV 1 (= *hand over*) entregar; **to ~ sb in** entregar a algn a la policía; **to ~ o.s. in** entregarse

2 (= *submit*) [+ *essay, report*] entregar, presentar; **to ~ in a good performance** (*Sport*) tener una buena actuación

3 (= *fold*) doblarse hacia adentro, apuntar hacia adentro

►**turn off** Ⓐ VI + ADV 1 (*Aut*) [*person, vehicle*] doblar; **~ off at the next exit** toma la próxima (salida de la autopista)

2 [*appliance etc*] apagarse

Ⓑ VT + ADV 1 [+ *light*] apagar; [+ *appliance*] (= *switch off*) apagar; (= *plug out*) desenchufar; [+ *tap*] cerrar; [+ *engine*] parar; [+ *gas*] cerrar la llave de; [+ *central heating*] apagar; (*Elec*) (*at mains*) desconectar, cortar; [+ *TV programme, radio programme*] quitar; **the oven ~s itself off** el horno se apaga solo

2 (*) [+ *person*] repugnar, repugnar; (= *fail to interest*) dejar frío; (*sexually*) matar el deseo a; **it ~s me right off** me repugna, me deja frío

►**turn on** Ⓐ VI + ADV 1 [*appliance*] encenderse, prender (*LAm*)

2 (*TV, Rad*) [*viewer, listener*] encender *or* (*LAm*) prender el receptor

Ⓑ VT + ADV 1 [+ *appliance, electricity*] encender, prender (*LAm*); [+ *tap*] abrir; [+ *light*] encender; [+ *central heating*] encender; **to leave the radio ~ed on** dejar la radio encendida; **to ~ on the charm*** (*fig*) desplegar todos sus encantos

2 (*) (= *excite*) interesar, despertar; (*sexually*) excitar; **he doesn't ~ me on** no me chifla*; **whatever ~s you on** lo que te guste, lo que quieras

Ⓒ VI + PREP **to ~ on sb** volverse contra algn

►**turn out** Ⓐ VI + ADV 1 (= *appear*) aparecer

2 (= *attend*) [*troops*] presentarse; [*doctor*] atender; **to ~ out for a meeting** asistir a una reunión

3 (= *prove*) resultar; **it ~ed out that ...** resultó (ser) que ...; **it ~s out to be harder than we thought** resulta más difícil de lo que pensábamos

4 (= *transpire*) salir; **how are things ~ing out?** ¿cómo van las cosas?; **it ~ed out well/badly** salió bien/mal; **as it ~s out I already have one** da la casualidad de que ya tengo uno; **as it ~ed out, nobody went** al final no fue nadie; **it's ~ed out nice again** [*weather*] vuelve a hacer bueno

5 (= *point outwards*) **his toes ~ out** tiene los dedos de los pies levantados

Ⓑ VT + ADV 1 [+ *appliance, light*] apagar; [+ *gas*] cortar

2 (= *produce*) [+ *goods*] producir; **the college ~s out good secretaries** el colegio produce buenas secretarias

3 (= *empty*) [+ *pockets*] vaciar; (= *tip out*) [+ *cake*] sacar

4 (= *clean out*) [+ *room*] limpiar

5 (= *expel*) [+ *person*] expulsar, echar; **they ~ed him out of the house** lo expulsaron *or* echaron de la casa

6 [+ *guard, police*] llamar

7 **to be well ~ed out** [*person*] ir elegante *or* bien vestido

8 **to ~ one's toes out** caminar con los dedos de los pies levantados

►**turn over** Ⓐ VI + ADV 1 [*person, car etc*] volverse, voltearse (*LAm*); [*boat*] volcar(se); **it ~ed over and over** fue dando tumbos; **my stomach ~ed over** se me revolvió el estómago

2 (*Aut*) [*engine*] girar

3 (*in reading*) pasar a la siguiente página; (*in letter*) volver la página; **please ~ over** véase al dorso, sigue ...

4 (*TV*) (= *change channel*) cambiar de canal

Ⓑ VT + ADV 1 [+ *page*] volver; [+ *container, vehicle*] volcar; [+ *patient, mattress, card*] dar la vuelta a; [+ *tape, record*] dar la vuelta a, poner la otra cara de; **to ~ over an idea in one's mind** darle vueltas a una idea en la cabeza; **the thieves ~ed the place over*** los ladrones saquearon el local

2 [+ *engine*] hacer girar

3 (= *hand over*) [+ *object, business etc*] ceder, entregar (**to** a); [+ *person*] entregar (**to** a)

4 (*Comm*) [+ *sum*] mover, facturar; **they ~ over a million a year** su volumen de ventas *or* producción *etc* es de un millón al año

5 (= *destine, allocate*) **the land has been ~ed over to sugar production** ahora la tierra está dedicada a la producción de azúcar

►**turn round** Ⓐ VI + ADV 1 (*back to front*) volverse, dar la espalda; **as soon as I ~ed round**

they were quarrelling again en cuanto les volví la espalda se pusieron otra vez a reñir; **the government has ~ed right round** el gobierno ha cambiado completamente de rumbo; **he ~ed round and said ...*** (*fig*) fue y me dijo *or* me soltó ...*
2 (= *rotate*) girar, dar vueltas; **I could hardly ~ round** apenas podía volverme; **to ~ round and round** dar vueltas y más vueltas
3 (= *improve*) [*business, economy*] recuperarse
Ⓑ VT + ADV 1 [+ *person, object*] dar la vuelta a, voltear (*LAm*); [+ *vehicle, ship etc*] dar la vuelta a, girar
2 (*Comm*) **to ~ an order round** tramitar un pedido
3 (= *make successful*) [+ *business, economy*] sacar a flote, hacer despegar; (= *make profitable*) [+ *company, school*] rentabilizar, sanear (las finanzas de); [+ *the economy*] sanear
4 (= *rework*) [+ *sentence, idea*] modificar, alterar

►**turn to** VI + ADV (= *assist, lend a hand*) **everyone had to ~ to and help** todos tuvieron que ayudar; **we must all ~ to** todos tenemos que poner manos a la obra; *see also* **turn C2**

►**turn up** Ⓐ VI + ADV 1 (= *be found*) aparecer
2 (= *arrive, show up*) [*person*] llegar, aparecer; [*playing card etc*] salir; **we waited but she didn't ~ up** esperamos pero no apareció; **we'll see if anyone ~s up** veremos si viene alguien; **he ~ed up two hours late** llegó con dos horas de retraso; **he never ~s up at class** no asiste nunca a la clase; **something will ~ up** algo saldrá
3 (= *point upwards*) volverse hacia arriba; **his nose ~s up** tiene la nariz respingona
Ⓑ VT + ADV 1 [+ *collar, sleeve, hem*] subir; *see also* **nose A1**
2 [+ *heat, gas, sound*] subir; [+ *radio etc*] poner más fuerte, subir; ✦**IDIOM to ~ up the heat (on sth/sb)*** meter más presión (a algo/algn)
3 (= *find*) descubrir, desenterrar; [+ *reference*] buscar, consultar; [+ *evidence, information*] sacar a la luz, revelar
4 (= *dig up*) [+ *earth*] revolver; [+ *buried object*] desenterrar, hacer salir a la superficie
5 (*) (= *disgust*) **it really ~s me up** me revuelve el estómago *or* las tripas*
6 (*Brit**) (= *desist*) **~ it up!** ¡por favor!

turnabout ['tɜːnəbaʊt] N (= *change*) cambio *m* de rumbo, giro *m* radical

turnaround ['tɜːnəraʊnd] N 1 (= *change*) cambio *m* de rumbo, giro *m* radical
2 (= *improvement*) despegue *m*
3 (*also* **~ time**) (*Naut*) tiempo *m* de descarga y carga; (*Comm*) [*of goods*] plazo *m*

turncoat ['tɜːnkəʊt] N renegado/a *m/f*, chaquetero/a *m/f*; **to become a ~** cambiarse de chaqueta

turned-down ['tɜːnd'daʊn] ADJ doblado hacia abajo

turned-up ['tɜːnd'ʌp] ADJ doblado hacia arriba; **a ~ nose** una nariz respingona

turner ['tɜːnəʳ] N tornero *m*

turnery ['tɜːnərɪ] N tornería *f*

turning ['tɜːnɪŋ] Ⓐ N (= *side road*) bocacalle *f*; (= *fork*) cruce *m*, esquina *f*; (= *bend*) curva *f*; **the first ~ on the right** la primera bocacalle a la derecha; **we parked in a side ~** aparcamos el coche en una calle que salía de la carretera
Ⓑ CPD ► **turning circle** N (*Aut*) círculo *m* de viraje, diámetro *m* de giro ► **turning lathe** N torno *m* ► **turning point** N (*fig*) momento *m* decisivo, punto *m* de inflexión

turnip ['tɜːnɪp] N nabo *m*

turnkey ['tɜːnkiː] Ⓐ N 1 (*Hist*) llavero *m* (de una cárcel), carcelero *m*
2 (*Comput*) llave *f* de seguridad
Ⓑ CPD ► **turnkey system** N (*Comput*) sistema *m* de seguridad

turn-off ['tɜːnɒf] N 1 (*in road*) desvío *m*, empalme *m*
2 (*) **he's a real ~** ese me cae gordo*; **the film was a complete ~** la película fue un rollo*; **his breath is a big ~** su aliento me repugna

turn-on* ['tɜːnɒn] N (= *girl*) tía *f* buena*; (= *guy*) tío *m* bueno*; **I don't find those sorts of film a ~ at all** a mí esas películas no me ponen (cachondo) para nada

turnout ['tɜːnaʊt] N 1 (= *attendance*) concurrencia *f*, asistencia *f*; (= *paying spectators*) entrada *f*, público *m*; (*at election*) número *m* de votantes; **there was a poor ~** asistió poca gente; **we hope for a good ~ at the dance** esperamos que el baile sea muy concurrido
2 (= *clean*) limpieza *f*; **she gave the room a good ~** le hizo una buena limpieza al cuarto
3 (*Ind*) (= *output*) producción *f*
4 (= *dress*) atuendo *m*

turnover ['tɜːn,əʊvəʳ] N 1 (*Comm*) [*of stock, goods*] renovación *f* de existencias; (= *total business*) movimiento *m* de mercancías; **he sold the goods cheaply, hoping for a quick ~** vendió barato las existencias, con la idea de renovarlas rápido; **a ~ of £6,000 a week** una facturación de 6000 libras a la semana; **there is a rapid ~ in staff** el personal cambia muy a menudo
2 (*Culin*) empanada *f*

turnpike ['tɜːnpaɪk] N 1 (*Hist*) barrera *f* de portazgo
2 (*US Aut*) autopista *f* de peaje

turnround ['tɜːnraʊnd] N = **turnaround**

turnspit ['tɜːnspɪt] N mecanismo *m* que da vueltas al asador

turnstile ['tɜːnstaɪl] N torniquete *m*

turntable ['tɜːn,teɪbl] Ⓐ N (*for record player*) plato *m* (giratorio), giradiscos *m inv*; (*for trains, car etc*) placa *f* giratoria
Ⓑ CPD ► **turntable ladder** N escalera *f* sobre plataforma giratoria

turn-up ['tɜːnʌp] (*Brit*) N 1 [*of trousers*] vuelta *f*
2 (*) (= *piece of luck*) **that was a ~ for him** en eso tuvo mucha suerte; ✦**IDIOM that was a ~ for the books** eso sí que no se esperaba

turpentine ['tɜːpəntaɪn] Ⓐ N trementina *f*
Ⓑ CPD ► **turpentine substitute** N aguarrás *m*

turpitude ['tɜːpɪtjuːd] N (= *liter*) infamia *f*, vileza *f*; **to be dismissed for gross moral ~** ser despedido por inmoralidad manifiesta, ser expulsado por conducta infame

turps* [tɜːps] N ABBR = **turpentine**

turquoise ['tɜːkwɔɪz] Ⓐ N 1 (= *stone*) turquesa *f*
2 (= *colour*) azul *m* turquesa
Ⓑ ADJ azul turquesa

turret ['tʌrɪt] N [*of castle*] torreón *m*; [*of tank, warship, aircraft*] torreta *f*; (*Mil, Hist*) torre *f*, torrecilla *f*; (*US Tech*) cabrestante *m*

turtle ['tɜːtl] Ⓐ N tortuga *f* (marina); ✦**IDIOM to turn ~*** volverse patas arriba; (*Naut*) volcar(se); (*Aut*) volcarse, dar una vuelta de campana
Ⓑ CPD ► **turtle soup** N sopa *f* de tortuga

turtledove ['tɜːtldʌv] N tórtola *f*

turtleneck ['tɜːtlnek] N (*also* **~ sweater**) jersey *m* de cuello alto *or* vuelto *or* de cisne

Tuscan ['tʌskən] Ⓐ ADJ toscano
Ⓑ N 1 (= *person*) toscano/a *m/f*
2 (*Ling*) toscano *m*

Tuscany ['tʌskənɪ] N la Toscana

tush† [tʌʃ] EXCL ¡bah!

tusk [tʌsk] N colmillo *m*

tussle ['tʌsl] Ⓐ N (= *struggle*) lucha *f* (**for** por); (= *scuffle*) pelea *f*, agarrada *f*; **to have a ~ with** pelearse con
Ⓑ VI pelearse (**with** con; **about, over** por); **they ~d with the police** se pelearon con la policía

tussock ['tʌsək] N mata *f* (de hierba)

tut [tʌt] (*also* **tut-tut**) Ⓐ EXCL ¡vaya!
Ⓑ VI chasquear la lengua en señal de desaprobación

tutelage ['tjuːtɪlɪdʒ] N tutela *f*; **under the ~ of** bajo la tutela de

tutelary ['tjuːtɪlərɪ] ADJ tutelar

tutor ['tjuːtəʳ] Ⓐ N (= *private teacher*) profesor(a) *m/f* particular; (*Brit Univ*) tutor(a) *m/f*; (= *teaching assistant*) profesor(a) *m/f* auxiliar; (= *counsellor, supervisor*) profesor *m* consejero, profesora *f* consejera; (*eg for OU, also Jur*) tutor(a) *m/f*
Ⓑ VT **to ~ sb in Latin** dar clases particulares de latín a algn
Ⓒ CPD ► **tutor group** N (*Brit Scol*) grupo *m* de tutoría

tutorial [tjuː'tɔːrɪəl] Ⓐ ADJ (*Jur*) tutelar
Ⓑ N (*Univ*) seminario *m*; (*eg for OU, UNED*) tutoría *f*

tutti-frutti [,tʊtɪ'frʊtɪ] N (*pl* **tutti-fruttis**) tutti-frutti *m*

tutu ['tuːtuː] N tutú *m*

tuwhit-tuwhoo [tʊ'wɪttə'wuː] N ulular *m*

tuxedo [tʌk'siːdəʊ], **tux*** ['tʌks] N (*esp US*) smoking *m*, esmoquin *m*

TV Ⓐ N ABBR (= **television**) tele *f*, TV *f*
Ⓑ CPD ► **TV dinner** N *cena precocinada que se vende en el recipiente del que se come* ► **TV licence** N = **television licence**

TVA N ABBR (*US*) = **Tennessee Valley Authority**

TVEI N ABBR (*Brit*) = **technical and vocational educational initiative**

TVP N ABBR (= **textured vegetable protein**) *sustituto de carne*

twaddle* ['twɒdl] N tonterías *fpl*, chorradas* *fpl*, babosadas *fpl* (*LAm**), pendejadas *fpl* (*LAm**)

twain†† [tweɪn] N **the ~** los dos; **to split sth in ~** partir algo en dos; ✦**PROV and ne'er the ~ shall meet** sin que el uno se acerque al otro jamás

twang [twæŋ] Ⓐ N [*of wire, bow etc*] tañido *m*; [*of voice*] deje *m*; **to speak with a ~** ganguear
Ⓑ VT (*Mus*) tañer; [+ *bowstring*] estirar y soltar repentinamente
Ⓒ VI producir un sonido agudo; (*in speaking*) hablar con timbre nasal

twangy ['twæŋɪ] ADJ [*string etc*] elástico, muy estirado; [*accent*] nasal, gangoso

'twas†† [twɒz] = **it was**

twat** [twæt] N 1 (*Anat*) coño** *m*
2 (= *person*) gilipollas* *mf*

tweak [twiːk] Ⓐ N 1 (= *pull*) pellizco *m*; **to give sb's nose/ear a ~** pellizcar a algn la nariz/la oreja
2 (*) (= *small alteration*) pequeño retoque *m*
Ⓑ VT 1 (= *pull*) pellizcar
2 (*) (= *alter slightly*) retocar ligeramente

twee* [twiː] ADJ (*Brit pej*) cursi, afectado

tweed [twiːd] N 1 (= *cloth*) tweed *m*
2 **tweeds** (= *suit*) traje *msing* de tweed

tweedy ['twi:dɪ] ADJ con traje de tweed, vestido de tweed; (*fig*) aristocrático (y rural)

'tween (*liter*) [twi:n] PREP = **between**

tweet [twi:t] Ⓐ N [*of bird*] pío pío *m*
Ⓑ VI piar

tweeter ['twi:təʳ] N altavoz *m* para frecuencias altas

tweezers ['twi:zəz] NPL pinzas *fpl*; **a pair of ~** unas pinzas

twelfth [twelfθ] Ⓐ ADJ duodécimo
Ⓑ N (*in series*) duodécimo/a *m/f*; (= *fraction*) doceavo *m*; *see* **fifth** *for usage*
Ⓒ CPD ► **Twelfth Night** N Día *m* de Reyes, Reyes *mpl*

twelve [twelv] Ⓐ ADJ doce
Ⓑ N doce *m*; *see* **five** *for usage*
Ⓒ CPD ► **twelve inch** N (*Mus*) maxisingle *m*

twelvemonth†† ['twelvmʌnθ] N año *m*; **this day ~** de hoy en un año; **we've not seen him for a ~** hace un año que no le vemos

twelve-tone ['twelvtəʊn] ADJ dodecafónico

twentieth ['twentɪɪθ] Ⓐ ADJ vigésimo
Ⓑ N (*in series*) vigésimo/a *m/f*; (= *fraction*) veintésimo *m*; *see* **fifth** *for usage*

twenty ['twentɪ] Ⓐ ADJ veinte; **~-two metre line** (*Rugby*) línea *f* de veintidós metros; **twenty-twenty vision** visión *f* normal
Ⓑ N veinte *m*; **the twenties** (*eg 1920s*) los años veinte; **to be in one's twenties** tener veintitantos (años), ser un veinteañero; *see* **fifty** *for usage*

twenty-first ['twentɪfɜ:st] N (= *birthday*) veintiún cumpleaños *m inv*; (= *party*) fiesta *f* del veintiún cumpleaños

twentyfold ['twentɪfəʊld] Ⓐ ADV veinte veces
Ⓑ ADJ veinte veces mayor

twenty-four ['twentɪ'fɔ:ʳ] ADJ **"twenty-four hour service"** "abierto 24 horas"

twenty-four-seven* [ˌtwentɪˌfɔ:'sevn] ADV (*esp US*) **to do sth ~** hacer algo a todas horas, hacer algo las 24 horas del día

twentyish ['twentɪɪʃ] ADJ de unos veinte años

twerp* [twɜ:p] N idiota *mf*, bruto/a *m/f*; **you ~!** ¡imbécil!

twice [twaɪs] ADV dos veces; **to do sth ~** hacer algo dos veces; **~ as much/many** dos veces más; **~ a week** dos veces a la *or* por semana; **she is ~ your age** ella tiene dos veces tu edad, es dos veces mayor que tú; **~ the sum** ◊ **~ the quantity** el doble; **at a speed ~ that of sound** a una velocidad dos veces superior a la del sonido; **A is ~ as big as B** A es el doble de B, A es dos veces más grande que B; **she's ~ the woman you are** como mujer ella vale dos veces lo que tú; **since the operation he is ~ the man he was** después de la operación vale dos veces lo de antes; **to go to a meeting ~ weekly** ir a una reunión dos veces por semana; **he didn't have to be asked ~** no se hizo de rogar, no se lo tuve que pedir dos veces

twiddle ['twɪdl] Ⓐ N vuelta *f* (ligera); **to give a knob a ~** girar un botón
Ⓑ VT dar vueltas a; ✦***IDIOM*** **to ~ one's thumbs** estar de brazos cruzados, estar mano sobre mano
Ⓒ VI dar vueltas; **to ~ with sth** jugar con algo (entre los dedos)

twig¹ [twɪg] N [1] [*of wood*] ramita *f*
[2] **twigs** (*for fire*) leña *f* menuda

twig²* [twɪg] (*Brit*) Ⓐ VT (= *understand*) caer en la cuenta de
Ⓑ VI caer en la cuenta

twilight ['twaɪlaɪt] Ⓐ N [1] (= *evening*) anochecer *m*, crepúsculo *m*; (= *morning*) madrugada *f*; **at ~** al anochecer; **in the ~** a media luz
[2] (*fig*) crepúsculo *m*, ocaso *m*
Ⓑ CPD ► **twilight area** N = **twilight zone** ► **twilight sleep** N sueño *m* crepuscular ► **a twilight world** N un mundo crepuscular ► **twilight zone** N zona *f* gris

twilit ['twaɪlɪt] ADJ **in the ~ woods** en el bosque con luz crepuscular; **in some ~ area of the mind** en alguna zona crepuscular de la mente

twill [twɪl] N (= *fabric*) tela *f* cruzada

'twill [twɪl] = **it will**

twin [twɪn] Ⓐ N (*identical*) gemelo/a *m/f*; (*non-identical*) mellizo/a *m/f*; **they are ~s** son gemelos, son mellizos; **a pair of ~s** un par de gemelos, un par de mellizos; *see also* **identical, Siamese**
Ⓑ ADJ [1] [*brother, sister*] (*identical*) gemelo; (*non-identical*) mellizo; **she has ~ daughters** tiene dos hijas gemelas, tiene dos hijas mellizas
[2] (= *linked*) [*town, city*] hermano; **Newlyn's ~ town is Concarneau** la ciudad hermana de Newlyn es Concarneau, Newlyn está hermanada con Concarneau
[3] (= *double*) [*towers, peaks, engines*] gemelo; [*propellers*] doble; [*concepts*] hermano; **the ~ aims** *or* **goals of sth** el doble objetivo de algo; **the ~ evils of malnutrition and disease** la malnutrición y la enfermedad, dos males que siempre van juntos; **the ~ pillars of** (*fig*) el doble pilar de; **~ souls** almas *fpl* gemelas
Ⓒ VT [1] (= *link*) [+ *towns, cities, institutions*] hermanar (**with** con); **Manchester is ~ned with St Petersburg** Manchester está hermanada con San Petersburgo
[2] (= *combine*) [+ *clothes*] combinar
Ⓓ CPD ► **twin beds** NPL camas *fpl* gemelas ► **twin cylinder** N bicilindro *m*; *see also* **twin-cylinder** ► **twin jet** N birreactor *m*; *see also* **twin-jet**

twin-bedded ['twɪn'bedɪd] ADJ [*room*] con camas gemelas

twin-cylinder ['twɪn'sɪlɪndəʳ] Ⓐ ADJ de dos cilindros, bicilíndrico
Ⓑ N bicilindro *m*

twine [twaɪn] Ⓐ N bramante *m*
Ⓑ VT [+ *fingers*] entrelazar; [+ *several strings, strands etc together*] trenzar; [+ *one string, strand etc around sth*] enroscar, enrollar; **she ~d the string round her finger** enroscó *or* enrolló la cuerda en el dedo; **to ~ one's arms round sb** abrazar a algn
Ⓒ VI [*spiral, plant*] enroscarse; [*fingers*] entrelazarse; [*road*] serpentear

twin-engined ['twɪn'endʒɪnd] ADJ bimotor

twinge [twɪndʒ] N (= *pain*) dolor *m* agudo; **a ~ of pain** una punzada de dolor, un dolor agudo; **I've been having ~s of conscience** he tenido remordimientos de conciencia

twining ['twaɪnɪŋ] ADJ [*plant*] sarmentoso, trepador

twin-jet ['twɪn'dʒet] ADJ birreactor

twinkle ['twɪŋkl] Ⓐ N centelleo *m*, parpadeo *m*; **in a ~*** en un instante; **"no," he said with a ~** —no, dijo maliciosamente *or* medio riendo; **he had a ~ in his eye** tenía un brillo en sus ojos; ✦***IDIOM*** **when you were only a ~ in your father's eye** cuando tú no eras más que una vida en potencia
Ⓑ VI [*light*] centellear, parpadear; [*eyes*] brillar; (*fig*) [*feet*] moverse rápidamente

twinkling ['twɪŋklɪŋ] Ⓐ ADJ [*light*] centelleante, titilante; [*eye*] brillante, risueño; (*fig*) [*feet*] rápido, ligero
Ⓑ N centelleo *m*, parpadeo *m*; **in the ~ of an eye*** en un abrir y cerrar de ojos

twinning ['twɪnɪŋ] N **the ~ of Edinburgh and Kiev** el hacer a Edimburgo y Kiev ciudades hermanas

twinset ['twɪnset] N (*Brit*) conjunto *m*, juego *m*

twin-tub ['twɪn'tʌb] N lavadora *f* de dos tambores

twirl [twɜ:l] Ⓐ N [1] [*of body*] vuelta *f*, pirueta *f*
[2] (*in writing*) rasgo *m*
Ⓑ VT dar vueltas rápidas a; [+ *baton, lasso*] dar vueltas a; [+ *knob*] girar; [+ *moustache*] atusarse
Ⓒ VI dar vueltas, piruetear

twirp* [twɜ:p] N = **twerp**

twist [twɪst] Ⓐ N [1] (= *coil*) [*of thread, yarn*] torzal *m*; [*of paper*] cucurucho *m*; [*of smoke*] voluta *f*; [*of tobacco*] rollo *m*; **a ~ of lemon** un pedacito *or* un rizo de limón
[2] (= *loaf of bread*) trenza *f*
[3] (= *kink*) (*in wire, cord, hose*) vuelta *f*; ✦***IDIOMS*** **to get (o.s.) into a ~*** ◊ **get one's knickers in a ~**‡ armarse *or* hacerse un lío*
[4] (= *bend*) (*in road*) recodo *m*, curva *f*; (*in river*) recodo *m*; ✦***IDIOMS*** **to be round the ~*** estar chiflado*; **to go round the ~*** volverse loco*; **to drive sb round the ~*** volver loco a algn*
[5] (= *turning action*) **with a quick ~ of the wrist** torciendo *or* girando rápidamente la muñeca; **she smiled with a wry ~ of her mouth** sonrió torciendo la boca; **to give sth a ~** [+ *lid, top*] girar algo
[6] (= *unexpected turn*) [*in plot, story*] giro *m*; **the plot has an unexpected ~** el argumento tiene un giro inesperado; **to put a new ~ on an old argument** darle un nuevo enfoque a un viejo argumento; **by a strange ~ of fate** por una de esas extrañas vueltas que da la vida; **the story has a ~ in the tail** la historia tiene un final inesperado
[7] (= *dance*) twist *m*; **to do the ~** bailar el twist
Ⓑ VT [1] (= *coil*) enroscar, enrollar; **she ~ed her hair into a bun** se enrolló *or* enroscó el pelo en un moño; **the rope got ~ed round the pole** la cuerda se enroscó alrededor del palo; **the strands are ~ed together** las hebras están enrolladas unas a otras; ✦***IDIOM*** **to ~ sb round one's little finger** tener a algn en el bolsillo, hacer con algn lo que le da la gana
[2] (= *turn*) [+ *knob, handle, top, lid*] girar; (= *turn round and round*) [+ *ring*] dar vueltas a; ✦***IDIOMS*** **to ~ sb's arm** (*lit*) retorcerle el brazo a algn; (*fig*) apretarle las tuercas a algn; **to ~ the knife** hurgar en la herida
[3] (*Med*) (= *injure*) torcerse; **he ~ed his ankle** se torció el tobillo
[4] (= *wrench*) **she ~ed herself free** se retorció hasta soltarse
[5] (= *distort, contort*) (*lit*) [+ *girder, metal*] retorcer; (*fig*) [+ *sense, words, argument*] tergiversar; **his face was ~ed with pain** tenía el rostro crispado por el dolor; **his limbs were ~ed by arthritis** sus miembros estaban torcidos por la artritis
Ⓒ VI [1] (= *coil*) enroscarse
[2] (= *bend*) [*road, river*] serpentear
[3] (= *turn*) [*person*] (*also* **~ round**) girar
[4] (= *contort*) retorcerse; **his mouth ~ed into a sardonic smile** se le retorció la boca y soltó una sonrisa socarrona
[5] (= *dance*) bailar el twist

► **twist off** Ⓐ VI + ADV [*top, lid*] desenroscarse
Ⓑ VT + ADV [+ *top, lid*] desenroscar; **you ~ the**

top off like this la tapa se desenrosca así; **to ~ a piece off** separar un trozo torciéndolo

►**twist round** Ⓐ VT + ADV (*lit*) dar vueltas a, girar; (*fig*) [+ *words*] tergiversar
Ⓑ VI + ADV girar

twisted ['twɪstɪd] ADJ 1 (= *distorted*) [*metal, roots, cables, smile*] retorcido; [*face, features*] torcido
2 (= *injured*) [*ankle, wrist*] torcido
3 (= *warped*) [*person, mind, logic*] retorcido

twister* ['twɪstəʳ] N 1 (*US*) (= *tornado*) huracán *m* 2 (*Brit*) (= *crook*) estafador(a) *m/f*

twisting ['twɪstɪŋ] Ⓐ N (*gen*) retorcimiento *m*; [*of meaning, words*] tergiversación *f*
Ⓑ ADJ [*lane, street*] con recodos *or* revueltas; [*staircase*] de caracol

twit¹* [twɪt] N (*esp Brit*) (= *fool*) imbécil *mf*

twit² [twɪt] VT (= *tease*) embromar, tomar el pelo a, guasearse con; **to ~ sb about sth** tomar el pelo a algn con motivo de algo

twitch [twɪtʃ] Ⓐ N 1 (= *slight pull*) tirón *m*; **to give sth a ~** dar un tirón a algo
2 (= *nervous tic*) tic *m*, contracción *f* nerviosa
Ⓑ VI [*hands, face, muscles*] crisparse; [*nose, ears, tail*] moverse nerviosamente
Ⓒ VT [+ *curtains, rope*] pegar un tirón de; [+ *hands*] crispar, retorcer; [+ *nose, ears etc*] mover nerviosamente; **to ~ sth away from sb** quitar algo a algn con un movimiento rápido

twitchy* ['twɪtʃɪ] ADJ (= *nervous*) nervioso, inquieto; **to get ~** ponerse nervioso, inquietarse

twitter ['twɪtəʳ] Ⓐ N [*of bird*] pío *m*; **to be all of a ~*** ◊ **be in a ~*** estar *or* andar agitado *or* nervioso
Ⓑ VI [*bird*] piar; [*person*] hablar nerviosamente

'twixt [twɪkst] (*poet*) PREP = **betwixt**

two [tu:] Ⓐ ADJ dos
Ⓑ N dos *m*; **to break sth in ~** romper algo en dos, partir algo por la mitad; **~ by ~** ◊ **in ~s** de dos en dos; **to arrive in ~s and threes** llegar dos o tres a la vez; **that makes ~ of us** ya somos dos; ✦*IDIOMS* **they're/you're ~ of a kind** son/sois tal para cual; **to put ~ and ~ together** atar cabos; ✦*PROV* **~'s company, three's a crowd** dos son compañía, tres son multitud; *see* **five** *for usage*

two-bit* ['tu:bɪt] ADJ (*US*) de poca monta, de tres al cuarto

two-chamber ['tu:'tʃeɪmbəʳ] ADJ [*parliament*] bicameral, de dos cámaras

two-colour ['tu:'kʌləʳ] ADJ bicolor, de dos colores

two-cycle ['tu:'saɪkl] ADJ [*engine*] de dos tiempos

two-cylinder ['tu:'sɪlɪndəʳ] ADJ bicilíndrico, de dos cilindros

two-dimensional ['tudaɪ'menʃənl] ADJ bidimensional

two-door ['tu:'dɔ:ʳ] ADJ [*car*] de dos puertas

two-edged ['tu:'edʒd] ADJ de doble filo

two-engined ['tu:'endʒɪnd] ADJ bimotor

two-faced ['tu:'feɪst] ADJ (*fig*) [*person*] falso, hipócrita

two-fisted* [ˌtu:'fɪstɪd] ADJ (*US*) fortachón*, chicarrón

twofold ['tu:fəʊld] Ⓐ ADV dos veces
Ⓑ ADJ doble

two-handed ['tu:'hændɪd] ADJ de dos manos; [*tool etc*] para dos manos

two-legged ['tu:'legɪd] ADJ bípedo, de dos piernas

two-masted ['tu:'mɑ:stɪd] ADJ de dos palos

two-party ['tu:'pɑ:tɪ] ADJ [*state, country*] bipartidista

twopence ['tʌpəns] N dos peniques; (= *coin*) moneda *f* de dos peniques; ✦*IDIOM* **it's not worth ~*** no vale una perra gorda; *see also* **care C1**

twopenny ['tʌpənɪ] ADJ 1 (*Brit*) de dos peniques, que vale dos peniques
2 (*fig*) (*) insignificante, de poca monta

twopenny-halfpenny* ['tʌpnɪ'heɪpnɪ] ADJ (*Brit*) (*fig*) insignificante, de poca monta

two-percent milk ['tu:pəˌsent'mɪlk] N (*US*) leche *f* semidesnatada

two-phase ['tu:'feɪz] ADJ (*Elec*) bifásico

two-piece ['tu:'pi:s] Ⓐ ADJ [*suit*] de dos piezas
Ⓑ N (= *suit*) conjunto *m* de dos piezas

two-ply ['tu:'plaɪ] ADJ [*wool*] de dos hebras, doble; [*wood, tissue paper*] de dos capas

two-seater ['tu:'si:təʳ] Ⓐ ADJ biplaza, de dos plazas
Ⓑ N (= *car, plane*) biplaza *m*

twosome ['tu:səm] N (= *people*) pareja *f*

two-star (petrol) ['tu:stɑ:('petrəl)] N (*Brit*) gasolina *f* normal

two-step ['tu:ˌstep] N (= *dance*) paso *m* doble

two-storey, **two-story** (*US*) ['tu:'stɔ:rɪ] ADJ de dos pisos

two-stroke ['tu:'strəʊk] Ⓐ N (= *engine*) motor *m* de dos tiempos
Ⓑ ADJ [*engine*] de dos tiempos; **~ oil** aceite *m* para motores de dos tiempos

two-time* ['tu:'taɪm] VT engañar con otro/a a, ser infiel con otro/a a

two-timer* [ˌtu:'taɪməʳ] N 1 (*gen*) (= *traitor*) traidor(a) *m/f* 2 (*in marriage*) (= *husband*) marido *m* infiel; (= *wife*) mujer *f* infiel

two-tone ['tu:'təʊn] ADJ (*in colour*) de dos tonos, bicolor

'twould†† [twʊd] = **it would**

two-way ['tu:'weɪ] Ⓐ ADJ [*radio*] emisor y receptor; [*street*] de doble sentido
Ⓑ CPD ► **two-way mirror** N luna *f* de efecto espejo ► **two-way switch** N conmutador *m* de dos direcciones ► **two-way traffic** N circulación *f* en dos sentidos

two-wheeler ['tu:'wi:ləʳ] N bicicleta *f*

TX ABBR (*US*) = **Texas**

Tx ABBR = **telex**

tycoon [taɪ'ku:n] N magnate *m*; **an oil ~** un magnate del petróleo

tyke* [taɪk] N 1 (= *child*) chiquillo *m*; (= *dog*) perro *m* de la calle; **you little ~!** ¡tunante!
2 (*Brit pej*) (*also* **Yorkshire ~**) hombre *m* de Yorkshire

tympani ['tɪmpənɪ] NPL (*Mus*) = **timpani**

tympanum ['tɪmpənəm] N (*pl* **tympanums, tympana**) (*Anat, Archit*) tímpano *m*

type [taɪp] Ⓐ N 1 (= *class, kind*) tipo *m*, clase *f*; **what ~ of desk did you want?** ¿qué tipo *or* clase de escritorio quería?; **what ~ of person is he?** ¿qué tipo *or* clase de persona es?; **I'm not the ~ to get carried away** no soy de la clase *or* del tipo de personas que se dejan llevar; **I know the ~ of thing you mean** tengo una idea de a qué te refieres; **nightclubs are not my ~ of thing** los clubes nocturnos no son lo mío; **she's/he's not my ~** no es mi tipo; **it's my ~ of film** es una película de las que a mí me gustan; **she's the motherly ~** es una madraza; **he's an outdoor ~** es el tipo *or* la clase de persona a la que le gusta la vida al aire; **a moisturizer suitable for all skin ~s** una crema hidratante apropiada para todo tipo de pieles
2 (= *character, essence*) tipo *m*; **she was the very ~ of Spanish beauty** era el tipo exacto de la belleza española; **to cast sb against ~** (*Theat, Cine*) darle a algn un papel atípico; **to revert to ~** (*Bio*) volver a su estado primitivo; (*fig*) volver a ser el mismo de siempre; **the government, true to ~, tried to make us believe nothing was wrong** el gobierno, como es característico en él *or* como siempre, intentó hacernos creer que no ocurría nada malo
3 (*) (= *individual*) tipo/a* *m/f*; **she's a strange ~** es un bicho raro*, es una tipa rara*
4 (*Typ*) (= *typeface*) tipo *m*; (= *printed characters*) letra *f*; (= *blocks of characters*) tipos *mpl*; **in bold ~** en negrita; **in italic ~** en cursiva; **in large/small ~** en letra grande/pequeña
Ⓑ VT 1 (*also* **~ out, ~ up**) escribir a máquina, pasar a máquina; **six closely ~d pages** seis hojas escritas a máquina *or* mecanografiadas con letra muy pequeña
2 (= *classify*) [+ *disease, blood*] clasificar
Ⓒ VI escribir a máquina

►**type out** VT + ADV escribir a máquina, pasar a máquina

►**type up** VT + ADV escribir a máquina, pasar a máquina

typecast ['taɪpkɑ:st] (*pt, pp* **typecast**) Ⓐ VT **to ~ an actor** encasillar a un actor
Ⓑ ADJ [*actor*] encasillado

typeface ['taɪpfeɪs] N tipo *m*, tipo *m* de letra, letra *f*

typescript ['taɪpskrɪpt] Ⓐ ADJ mecanografiado
Ⓑ N texto *m* mecanografiado

typeset ['taɪpset] VT componer

typesetter ['taɪpˌsetəʳ] N 1 (= *person*) cajista *mf*, compositor(a) *m/f*
2 (= *machine*) máquina *f* de componer

typesetting ['taɪpˌsetɪŋ] N composición *f* (tipográfica)

typewrite ['taɪpraɪt] (*pt* **typewrote**; *pp* **typewritten**) VT = **type B1**

typewriter ['taɪpˌraɪtəʳ] Ⓐ N máquina *f* de escribir
Ⓑ CPD ► **typewriter ribbon** N cinta *f* para máquina de escribir

typewriting ['taɪpˌraɪtɪŋ] N mecanografía *f*

typewritten ['taɪpˌrɪtn] ADJ escrito a máquina, mecanografiado

typhoid ['taɪfɔɪd] N tifoidea *f*, fiebre *f* tifoidea

typhoon [taɪ'fu:n] N tifón *m*

typhus ['taɪfəs] N tifus *m*

typical ['tɪpɪkəl] ADJ 1 (= *archetypal*) típico; **a ~ Canadian winter** un típico invierno canadiense; **the ~ Englishman** el inglés típico; **he is ~ of many people who …** es un ejemplo típico de mucha gente que …
2 (= *usual, characteristic*) [*behaviour, reaction, style*] típico; **with ~ modesty he said …** con la modestia que le caracterizaba dijo …, con una modestia típica en él dijo …; **it was ~ of her to offer to pay** era típico en ella ofrecerse a pagar
3 (*expressing annoyance*) **"typical!" she shouted** —¡cómo no! —gritó, —¡típico! —gritó; **that's ~ of him!** ¡eso es típico de él!; **it was ~ of our luck that it rained** con la mala suerte que nos caracteriza, llovió, con nuestra mala suerte de siempre, llovió

typically ['tɪpɪkəlɪ] ADV 1 (= *characteristically*) [*defiant, flamboyant, Spanish*] típicamente; **a spell of ~ British weather** un periodo de tiempo típicamente británico; **his letter was ~ humorous, but brief** su carta, como de costumbre, era graciosa pero breve
2 (= *usually*) por regla general, generalmente; **women ~ have lower cholesterol levels than men** por regla general *or* generalmente

las mujeres tienen el colesterol más bajo que los hombres
3 (= *predictably*) (*iro*) como era de esperar, como suele ocurrir

typify ['tɪpɪfaɪ] VT [+ *thing*] representar, tipificar; [+ *person*] ser ejemplo de

typing ['taɪpɪŋ] Ⓐ N mecanografía *f*
Ⓑ CPD ► **typing agency** N agencia *f* mecanográfica ► **typing error** N error *m* mecanográfico ► **typing paper** N papel *m* para máquina de escribir ► **typing pool** N servicio *m* de mecanografía ► **typing speed** N palabras *fpl* por minuto (mecanografiadas)

typist ['taɪpɪst] N mecanógrafo/a *m/f*

typo* ['taɪpəʊ] N errata *f*

typographer [taɪ'pɒgrəfə^r] N tipógrafo/a *m/f*

typographic [ˌtaɪpə'græfɪk] ADJ = **typographical**

typographical [ˌtaɪpə'græfɪkəl] ADJ tipográfico

typography [taɪ'pɒgrəfɪ] N tipografía *f*

typology [taɪ'pɒlədʒɪ] N tipología *f*

tyrannic [tɪ'rænɪk] ADJ = **tyrannical**

tyrannical [tɪ'rænɪkəl] ADJ tiránico, tirano

tyrannically [tɪ'rænɪkəlɪ] ADV tiránicamente

tyrannicide [tɪ'rænɪsaɪd] N (= *act*) tiranicidio *m*; (= *person*) tiranicida *mf*

tyrannize ['tɪrənaɪz] Ⓐ VT tiranizar
Ⓑ VI **to ~ over a people** tiranizar un pueblo

tyranny ['tɪrənɪ] N (*lit, fig*) tiranía *f*

tyrant ['taɪrənt] N tirano/a *m/f*

Tyre ['taɪə^r] N Tiro *m*

tyre, **tire** (*US*) ['taɪə^r] Ⓐ N [*of car, bus, bicycle etc*] neumático *m* (*Sp*), llanta *f* (*LAm*), caucho *m* (*S. Cone*); (= *outer cover*) cubierta *f*; (= *inner tube*) cámara *f* (de aire); [*of cart*] llanta *f*, calce *m*; [*of pram*] rueda *f* de goma; **to have a burst/flat ~** tener una rueda pinchada *or* (*Mex*) ponchada
Ⓑ CPD ► **tyre burst** N pinchazo *m*, reventón *m* ► **tyre gauge** N medidor *m* de presión ► **tyre lever** N palanca *f* para desmontar neumáticos ► **tyre pressure** N presión *f* de los neumáticos ► **tyre valve** N válvula *f* de neumático

tyro ['taɪərəʊ] N novicio/a *m/f*, principiante *mf*

Tyrol [tɪ'rəʊl] N el Tirol

Tyrolean [ˌtɪrə'lɪən], **Tyrolese** [ˌtɪrə'liːz] Ⓐ ADJ tirolés
Ⓑ N tirolés/esa *m/f*

Tyrrhenian [tɪ'riːnɪən] Ⓐ ADJ tirrénico
Ⓑ N **the ~ (Sea)** El Mar Tirreno

tzar [zɑː^r] N zar *m*

tzarina [zɑː'riːnə] N zarina *f*

U u

U, u [ju:] Ⓐ N (= *letter*) U, u *f*; **U for Uncle** U de Uruguay; **U-shaped** en forma de U; *see also* **U-turn**
Ⓑ ADJ ABBR (*Brit*) [1] = **upper-class**
[2] (*Cine*) (= **universal**) todos los públicos
Ⓒ ABBR (= **University**) U.

UAE N ABBR (= **United Arab Emirates**) EAU *mpl*

UB40 [ˌju:bi:ˈfɔ:tɪ] N ABBR (*Brit*) (*formerly*) (= **Unemployment Benefit 40**) tarjeta *f* de desempleo, carné *m* del paro; **UB40s*** (= *unemployed people*) los parados

U-bend [ˈju:bend] N (*Brit*) codo *m*, curva *f* en U

ubiquitous [ju:ˈbɪkwɪtəs] ADJ ubicuo, omnipresente; **it is ~ in Spain** se encuentra en toda España; **the secretary has to be ~** el secretario tiene que estar constantemente en todas partes

ubiquity [ju:ˈbɪkwɪtɪ] N (*frm*) ubicuidad *f*, omnipresencia *f*

U-boat [ˈju:bəʊt] N submarino *m* alemán

UCAS [ˈju:kæs] N ABBR (*Brit*) = **Universities and Colleges Admissions Service**

UCCA [ˈʌkə] N ABBR (*Brit*) (*formerly*) = **Universities Central Council on Admissions**

UDA N ABBR (*Brit*) (= **Ulster Defence Association**) *organización paramilitar protestante en Irlanda del Norte*

UDC N ABBR (*Brit*) = **Urban District Council**

udder [ˈʌdəʳ] N ubre *f*

UDI N ABBR (*Brit*) = **Unilateral Declaration of Independence**

UDP N ABBR (*Brit*) = **Ulster Democratic Party**

UDR N ABBR (= **Ulster Defence Regiment**) *fuerza de seguridad de Irlanda del Norte*

UEFA [jʊˈeɪfə] N ABBR (= **Union of European Football Associations**) UEFA *f*

UFC N ABBR (*Brit*) (= **Universities' Funding Council**) *entidad que controla las finanzas de las universidades*

UFF N ABBR (*Brit*) (= **Ulster Freedom Fighters**) *organización paramilitar protestante en Irlanda del Norte*

UFO N ABBR (= **unidentified flying object**) OVNI *m*

ufologist [ˌju:ˈfɒlədʒɪst] N ufólogo/a *m/f*

ufology [ˌju:ˈfɒlədʒɪ] N ufología *f*

Uganda [ju:ˈgændə] N Uganda *f*

Ugandan [ju:ˈgændən] Ⓐ ADJ ugandés
Ⓑ N ugandés/esa *m/f*

UGC N ABBR (*Brit*) (*formerly*) = **University Grants Committee**

ugh [ɜ:h] EXCL ¡uf!, ¡puf!

ugli fruit [ˈʌglɪˈfru:t] N *fruto parecido a un pomelo, híbrido de tres cítricos*

uglify* [ˈʌglɪfaɪ] VT afear

ugliness [ˈʌglɪnɪs] N fealdad *f*

ugly [ˈʌglɪ] Ⓐ ADJ (*compar* **uglier**; *superl* **ugliest**)
[1] (= *not pretty*) [*appearance, person*] feo; ✦*IDIOM* **to be as ~ as sin** ser feísimo, ser más feo que Picio*
[2] (*fig*) (= *unpleasant*) desagradable; [*mood*] peligroso, violento; [*situation, wound*] peligroso; [*rumour etc*] nada grato, inquietante; [*custom, vice etc*] feo, repugnante; **an ~ customer*** un tipo de cuidado*; **to grow** *or* **turn ~** ponerse violento, amenazar violencia
Ⓑ CPD ► **ugly duckling** N (*fig*) patito *m* feo

UHF N ABBR (= **ultra high frequency**) UHF *f*

uh-huh [ˈʌˌhʌ] EXCL (*agreeing*) ajá

UHT ADJ ABBR (= **ultra heat-treated**) uperizado

UK N ABBR (= **United Kingdom**) Reino *m* Unido, RU; **in the UK** en el Reino Unido; **the UK government** el gobierno del Reino Unido; **a UK citizen** un ciudadano del Reino Unido

Ukraine [ju:ˈkreɪn] N Ucrania *f*

Ukrainian [ju:ˈkreɪnɪən] Ⓐ ADJ ucranio
Ⓑ N ucranio/a *m/f*

ukulele [ˌju:kəˈleɪlɪ] N ukelele *m*

ULC N ABBR (*US*) (= **ultra-large carrier**) superpetrolero *m*

ulcer [ˈʌlsəʳ] N [1] (*Med*) (*internal*) úlcera *f*; (*external*) llaga *f*; **a mouth ~** una llaga en la boca
[2] (*fig*) llaga *f*

ulcerate [ˈʌlsəreɪt] Ⓐ VT ulcerar
Ⓑ VI ulcerarse

ulcerated [ˈʌlsəreɪtɪd] ADJ ulcerado

ulceration [ˌʌlsəˈreɪʃən] N ulceración *f*

ulcerous [ˈʌlsərəs] ADJ ulceroso

ullage [ˈʌlɪdʒ] N (*Customs*) (= *loss*) merma *f*; (= *amount remaining*) atestadura *f*

'ullo* [əˈləʊ] EXCL (*Brit*) = **hello**

ulna [ˈʌlnə] N (*pl* **ulnas** *or* **ulnae** [ˈʌlni:]) cúbito *m*

ULSI N ABBR = **ultra-large-scale integration**

Ulster [ˈʌlstəʳ] N Ulster *m*

Ulsterman [ˈʌlstəmən] N (*pl* **Ulstermen**) nativo *m* de Ulster, habitante *m* de Ulster

Ulsterwoman [ˈʌlstəwʊmən] N (*pl* **Ulsterwomen**) nativa *f* de Ulster, habitante *f* de Ulster

ult. [ʌlt] ADV ABBR (*Comm*) (= **ultimo**) pdo.; **the 5th ~** el 5 del mes pdo., el 5 del mes pasado

ulterior [ʌlˈtɪərɪəʳ] ADJ **~ motive** segunda intención *f*, motivo *m* oculto

ultimata [ˌʌltɪˈmeɪtə] NPL *of* **ultimatum**

ultimate [ˈʌltɪmɪt] Ⓐ ADJ [1] (= *final*) [*aim, decision, destination*] final; **she will retain ~ responsibility for budgets** ella será la responsable en última instancia de los presupuestos, ella tendrá la máxima responsabilidad sobre presupuestos
[2] (= *greatest*) [*power, sacrifice*] máximo; [*control*] total; [*insult*] peor; **the ~ deterrent** (*Mil*) el mayor disuasivo; **it will be the ~ test of his abilities** supondrá la mayor prueba de su capacidad
[3] (= *best*) **the ~ sports car** lo último en coches deportivos
[4] (= *basic*) [*purpose, truth, cause, source*] fundamental, principal
[5] (= *furthest*) más remoto, extremo
Ⓑ N **the ~ in luxury** lo último en lujos; **it's the ~ in hairstyling** es el último grito en estilos de peinado

ultimately [ˈʌltɪmɪtlɪ] ADV (= *eventually*) al final, finalmente; (= *in the end*) en última instancia; (= *in the long run*) a la larga; (= *fundamentally*) en el fondo; **they were ~ responsible for his death** eran responsables en última instancia de su muerte; **the more difficult, but ~ more satisfying, solution** la solución más difícil, pero a la larga la más satisfactoria; **we provide this sort of service because, ~, that's what people want** facilitamos esta clase de servicio porque, en el fondo, eso es lo que la gente quiere

ultimatum [ˌʌltɪˈmeɪtəm] N (*pl* **ultimatums** *or* **ultimata**) (*Mil*) (*fig*) ultimátum *m*; **to deliver** *or* **issue an ~** dar un ultimátum

ultimo [ˈʌltɪməʊ] ADV = **ult.**

ultra... [ˈʌltrə] PREFIX ultra...

ultra-fashionable [ˈʌltrəˈfæʃnəbl] ADJ muy de moda, elegantísimo

ultrafine [ˌʌltrəˈfaɪn] ADJ ultrafino

ultralight [ˈʌltrəˈlaɪt] Ⓐ ADJ ultraligero
Ⓑ N (*Aer*) ultraligero *m*

ultramarine [ˌʌltrəməˈri:n] Ⓐ ADJ ultramarino
Ⓑ N azul *m* ultramarino *or* de ultramar

ultramodern [ˈʌltrəˈmɒdən] ADJ ultramoderno

ultra-red [ˌʌltrəˈred] ADJ ultrarrojo, infrarrojo

ultrasensitive [ˈʌltrəˈsensɪtɪv] ADJ ultrasensitivo

ultra-short wave [ˈʌltrəˌʃɔ:tˈweɪv] Ⓐ N onda *f* ultracorta
Ⓑ CPD de onda ultracorta

ultrasonic [ˈʌltrəˈsɒnɪk] ADJ ultrasónico

ultrasound [ˈʌltrəsaʊnd] Ⓐ N ultrasonido *m*
Ⓑ CPD ► **ultrasound scan** N ecografía *f*

ultraviolet [ˈʌltrəˈvaɪəlɪt] Ⓐ ADJ ultravioleta *inv*
Ⓑ CPD ► **ultraviolet light** N luz *f* ultravioleta ► **ultraviolet radiation** N radiación *f* ultravioleta ► **ultraviolet rays** NPL rayos *mpl* ultravioleta ► **ultraviolet treatment** N tratamiento *m* de onda ultravioleta

ululate [ˈju:ljʊleɪt] VI ulular

ululation [ˌju:ljʊˈleɪʃən] N ululato *m*

Ulysses [ju:ˈlɪsi:z] N Ulises

um [ʌm] EXCL (*in hesitation*) esto (*Sp*), este (*LAm*); **to um and err** vacilar

umber [ˈʌmbəʳ] Ⓐ N (= *colour*) ocre *m or* pardo

m oscuro; (= *earth*) tierra *f* de sombra
Ⓑ ADJ color ocre oscuro, pardo oscuro

umbilical [ˌʌmbɪˈlaɪkəl] Ⓐ ADJ umbilical
Ⓑ CPD ► **umbilical cord** N cordón *m* umbilical

umbilicus [ˌʌmbɪˈlaɪkəs] N (*pl* **umbilici** [ˌʌmbəˈlaɪsaɪ]) ombligo *m*

umbrage [ˈʌmbrɪdʒ] N resentimiento *m*; **to take ~ (at sth)** ofenderse *or* quedarse resentido (por algo)

umbrella [ʌmˈbrelə] Ⓐ N 1 paraguas *m inv*; **beach/sun ~** sombrilla *f*; **under the ~ of** (*fig*) (= *protected*) al abrigo de; (= *incorporating*) comprendido en
2 (*Mil*) [*of fire*] cortina *f* de fuego antiaéreo; [*of aircraft*] sombrilla *f* protectora
Ⓑ CPD ► **umbrella organization** N organización *f* paraguas ► **umbrella stand** N paragüero *m*

umlaut [ˈʊmlaʊt] N 1 (= *vowel change*) metafonía *f*, inflexión *f* vocálica
2 (= *symbol*) diéresis *f*

umpire [ˈʌmpaɪəʳ] Ⓐ N árbitro/a *m/f*
Ⓑ VT arbitrar
Ⓒ VI arbitrar, hacer de árbitro

umpteen* [ˈʌmptiːn] ADJ tropecientos*; **I've told you ~ times** te lo he dicho tropecientas veces*, te lo he dicho miles de veces

umpteenth* [ˈʌmptiːnθ] ADJ enésimo; **for the ~ time** por enésima vez

UMW N ABBR (*US*) = **United Mineworkers of America**

UN N ABBR (= **United Nations**) ONU *f*

'un* [ʌn] PRON **that's a good ~!** (*joke etc*) ¡qué bueno!; **he did well, for an old ~** lo hizo bien, para ser un viejo; **she's got two little ~s** tiene dos críos

un... [ʌn] PREFIX in..., des..., no ..., poco ..., sin ..., anti...

unabashed [ˈʌnəˈbæʃt] ADJ (= *shameless*) descarado, desvergonzado; (= *unperturbed*) impertérrito; **"yes," he said quite ~** —sí —dijo sin alterarse

unabated [ˈʌnəˈbeɪtɪd] ADJ sin disminución, no disminuido; **the storm continued ~** la tormenta siguió sin amainar

unabbreviated [ˈʌnəˈbriːvɪeɪtɪd] ADJ íntegro, completo

▼ **unable** [ˈʌnˈeɪbl] ADJ **to be ~ to do sth** (*gen*) no poder hacer algo; (= *be incapable of*) ser incapaz de hacer algo; (= *be prevented from*) verse imposibilitado de hacer algo; **unfortunately, he was ~ to come** desafortunadamente, no ha podido venir; **I am ~ to see why ...** no veo por qué ..., no comprendo por qué ...; **those ~ to go** los que no pueden ir

unabridged [ˈʌnəˈbrɪdʒd] ADJ íntegro; **~ edition/version** edición *f*/versión *f* íntegra

unaccented [ˈʌnækˈsentɪd] ADJ inacentuado, átono

▼ **unacceptable** [ˈʌnəkˈseptəbl] ADJ inaceptable

unacceptably [ˈʌnəkˈseptəblɪ] ADV inaceptablemente

unaccommodating [ˈʌnəˈkɒmədeɪtɪŋ] ADJ poco amable, poco servicial

unaccompanied [ˈʌnəˈkʌmpənɪd] ADJ 1 solo, no acompañado; **to go somewhere ~** ir a un sitio sin compañía, ir solo a un sitio
2 (*Mus*) sin acompañamiento

unaccomplished [ˈʌnəˈkʌmplɪʃt] ADJ 1 [*task*] incompleto, sin acabar
2 [*person*] sin talento

unaccountable [ˈʌnəˈkaʊntəbl] ADJ 1 (= *inexplicable*) [*fear, pain*] inexplicable; **for some ~ reason** por alguna razón inexplicable *or* incomprensible
2 (= *not answerable*) [*institution, person*] no responsable (**to** ante)

unaccountably [ˈʌnəˈkaʊntəblɪ] ADV (= *inexplicably*) inexplicablemente; (= *strangely, incomprehensibly*) extrañamente; **she was ~ late** llegó inexplicablemente tarde; **he felt ~ depressed/cheerful** se sentía extrañamente deprimido/animado

unaccounted [ˈʌnəˈkaʊntɪd] ADJ **two passengers are still ~ for** aún (nos) faltan dos pasajeros; **two books are ~ for** faltan dos libros

unaccustomed [ˈʌnəˈkʌstəmd] ADJ 1 **to be ~ to sth** no estar acostumbrado a algo, no tener costumbre de algo; **to be ~ to doing sth** no tener costumbre de hacer algo, no acostumbrar hacer algo; **~ as I am to public speaking** aunque no tengo experiencia de hablar en público
2 (= *unusual*) **with ~ zeal** con un entusiasmo insólito

unacknowledged [ˈʌnəkˈnɒlɪdʒd] ADJ no reconocido; [*letter etc*] no contestado, sin contestar

unacquainted [ˈʌnəˈkweɪntɪd] ADJ **to be ~ with** desconocer, ignorar

unadaptable [ˈʌnəˈdæptəbl] ADJ inadaptable

unadapted [ˈʌnəˈdæptɪd] ADJ inadaptado

unaddressed [ˈʌnəˈdrest] ADJ [*letter*] sin señas

unadjusted [ˌʌnəˈdʒʌstɪd] ADJ no corregido; **seasonally ~ employment figures** estadísticas *fpl* de desempleo no desestacionalizadas

unadopted [ˈʌnəˈdɒptɪd] ADJ (*Brit*) [*road*] no oficial (*siendo de los vecinos la responsabilidad de su mantenimiento*)

unadorned [ˈʌnəˈdɔːnd] ADJ sin adorno, sencillo; **beauty ~** la hermosura sin adorno; **the ~ truth** la verdad lisa y llana

unadulterated [ˈʌnəˈdʌltəreɪtɪd] ADJ sin mezcla, puro

unadventurous [ˈʌnədˈventʃərəs] ADJ poco atrevido

unadvisable [ˈʌnədˈvaɪzəbl] ADJ poco aconsejable; **it is ~ to** (+ *INFIN*) es poco aconsejable + *infin*

unaesthetic, unesthetic (*US*) [ˌʌniːsˈθetɪk] ADJ antiestético

unaffected [ˈʌnəˈfektɪd] ADJ 1 (= *sincere*) sin afectación, sencillo
2 (*emotionally*) no afectado, inmutable; **to be ~ by ...** no verse afectado por ...

unaffectedly [ˈʌnəˈfektɪdlɪ] ADV sin afectación, sencillamente

unaffiliated [ˌʌnəˈfɪlɪˌeɪtɪd] ADJ no afiliado

unafraid [ˈʌnəˈfreɪd] ADJ sin temor *or* miedo, impertérrito; **to be ~ of (doing) sth** no temer (hacer) algo, no tener miedo de (hacer) algo

unaided [ˈʌnˈeɪdɪd] Ⓐ ADV sin ayuda, por sí solo
Ⓑ ADJ **by his own ~ efforts** sin ayuda de nadie, por sí solo

unalike [ˌʌnəˈlaɪk] ADJ no parecido; **to be ~** no parecerse (en nada); **the two children are so ~** los dos niños no se parecen en nada

unalloyed [ˈʌnəˈlɔɪd] ADJ [*metal*] sin mezcla, puro; [*pleasure*] en estado puro

unalterable [ʌnˈɒltərəbl] ADJ inalterable

unalterably [ʌnˈɒltərəblɪ] ADV de modo inalterable; **we are ~ opposed to it** nos oponemos rotundamente a ello

unaltered [ˈʌnˈɒltəd] ADJ inalterado, sin cambiar; **his appearance was ~** no había cambiado

unambiguous [ˈʌnæmˈbɪgjʊəs] ADJ inequívoco

unambiguously [ˈʌnæmˈbɪgjʊəslɪ] ADV de modo inequívoco

unambitious [ˈʌnæmˈbɪʃəs] ADJ [*person*] sin ambición, poco ambicioso; [*plan*] poco ambicioso, modesto

un-American [ˈʌnəˈmerɪkən] ADJ 1 (*pej*) (= *anti-American*) antiamericano
2 (= *not typical*) poco americano

unamiable [ˈʌnˈeɪmɪəbl] ADJ poco simpático

unanimity [ˌjuːnəˈnɪmɪtɪ] N unanimidad *f*

unanimous [juːˈnænɪməs] ADJ [*group, decision, vote*] unánime; **the committee was ~ in its condemnation of** *or* **in condemning this** el comité condenó esto unánimemente; **it was accepted by a ~ vote** fue aprobado por unanimidad

unanimously [juːˈnænɪməslɪ] ADV unánimemente, por unanimidad; **the motion was passed ~** la moción fue aprobada por unanimidad

unannounced [ˈʌnəˈnaʊnst] Ⓐ ADJ [*visitor, visit*] inesperado
Ⓑ ADV **to arrive ~** llegar sin dar aviso

unanswerable [ʌnˈɑːnsərəbl] ADJ [*question*] incontestable; [*attack etc*] irrebatible, irrefutable

unanswered [ˈʌnˈɑːnsəd] ADJ [*question*] incontestado, sin contestar; [*letter*] sin contestar

unappealable [ˈʌnəˈpiːləbl] ADJ inapelable

unappealing [ˈʌnəˈpiːlɪŋ] ADJ poco atractivo

unappetizing [ˈʌnˈæpɪtaɪzɪŋ] ADJ poco apetitoso, poco apetecible; (*fig*) poco apetecible, nada atractivo

unappreciative [ˈʌnəˈpriːʃɪətɪv] ADJ desagradecido; **to be ~ of sth** no apreciar algo

unapproachable [ˈʌnəˈprəʊtʃəbl] ADJ 1 (= *inaccessible*) inaccesible
2 (= *aloof*) [*person*] intratable, inasequible

unappropriated [ˌʌnəˈprəʊprɪeɪtɪd] ADJ [*balance etc*] no asignado, sin asignar

unarguable [ʌnˈɑːgjʊəbəl] ADJ indiscutible, incuestionable

unarguably [ʌnˈɑːgjʊəblɪ] ADV indiscutiblemente; **it is ~ true that ...** es una verdad incuestionable que ...

unarmed [ˈʌnˈɑːmd] Ⓐ ADJ desarmado; (= *defenceless*) inerme
Ⓑ CPD ► **unarmed combat** N combate *m* sin armas

unashamed [ˈʌnəˈʃeɪmd] ADJ desvergonzado, descarado; **she was quite ~ about it** no se avergonzó en lo más mínimo

unashamedly [ˈʌnəˈʃeɪmɪdlɪ] ADV desvergonzadamente; **to be ~ proud of sth** enorgullecerse desvergonzadamente de algo

unasked [ˈʌnˈɑːskt] Ⓐ ADJ [*guest*] no invitado; [*advice*] no solicitado
Ⓑ ADV **to do sth ~** hacer algo motu proprio; **they came to the party ~** vinieron a la fiesta sin ser invitados

unassailable [ˌʌnəˈseɪləbl] ADJ [*proof*] incontestable; [*position, influence*] inatacable; [*argument*] irrefutable, irrebatible; [*fortress*] inexpugnable; **he is quite ~ on that score** no se le puede atacar por ese lado

unassisted [ˈʌnəˈsɪstɪd] ADJ, ADV sin ayuda, por sí solo

unassuming [ˈʌnəˈsjuːmɪŋ] ADJ modesto, sin pretensiones

unassumingly [ˈʌnəˈsjuːmɪŋlɪ] ADV modestamente

unattached [ˈʌnəˈtætʃt] ADJ 1 (= *loose*) suelto; (*fig*) (*gen*) libre; [*employee*] disponible
2 (= *unmarried*) soltero, libre
3 (*Mil*) de reemplazo
4 (*Jur*) no embargado

► LANGUAGE IN USE: **unable** 16.4, 25.3 **unacceptable** 26.3

unattainable [ˈʌnəˈteɪnəbl] ADJ inaccesible; [*record, objective*] inalcanzable

unattended [ˈʌnəˈtendɪd] ADJ [1] (= *not looked after*) [*shop, machine, luggage*] desatendido, sin atender; [*child*] solo; **to leave sth ~** dejar algo desatendido; **please do not leave your luggage ~** por favor, no abandonen su equipaje
[2] (= *unaccompanied*) [*king etc*] sin escolta

unattractive [ˈʌnəˈtræktɪv] ADJ poco atractivo

unattractiveness [ˈʌnəˈtræktɪvnɪs] N falta *f* de atractivo

unattributable [ˈʌnəˈtrɪbjʊtəbl] ADJ de fuente que no se puede confirmar

unattributed [ˌʌnəˈtrɪbjʊtɪd] ADJ [*quote, remarks*] de fuente desconocida, anónimo; [*source*] anónimo, no confirmado

unauthenticated [ˈʌnɔːˈθentɪkeɪtɪd] ADJ no autentificado, no autenticado

unauthorized [ˈʌnˈɔːθəraɪzd] ADJ (*gen*) no autorizado; **this was ~** esto no estaba autorizado

unavailable [ˈʌnəˈveɪləbl] ADJ [1] (*gen*) no disponible; (= *busy*) ocupado; **the Minister was ~ for comment** el ministro no se prestó a hacer comentarios
[2] (*Comm*) (= *out of stock*) [*article*] agotado

unavailing [ˈʌnəˈveɪlɪŋ] ADJ inútil, vano

unavailingly [ˈʌnəˈveɪlɪŋlɪ] ADV inútilmente, en vano

unavoidable [ˌʌnəˈvɔɪdəbl] ADJ inevitable, ineludible

unavoidably [ˌʌnəˈvɔɪdəblɪ] ADV inevitablemente; **he was ~ detained** no pudo evitar retrasarse, se retrasó por causas ajenas a su voluntad

unaware [ˈʌnəˈwɛəʳ] ADJ **to be ~ that …** ignorar que …; **she was ~ that she was being filmed** no se había dado cuenta de que la estaban filmando; **I am not ~ that …** no ignoro que …; **to be ~ of sth** ignorar algo, no darse cuenta de algo; **I was ~ of the regulations** ignoraba el reglamento

unawareness [ˈʌnəˈwɛənɪs] N inconsciencia *f* (**of** de)

unawares [ˈʌnəˈwɛəz] ADV sin saberlo, sin darse cuenta; **to catch** *or* **take sb ~** pillar a algn desprevenido

unbacked [ˈʌnˈbækt] ADJ sin respaldo; (*Fin*) al descubierto

unbalance [ˈʌnˈbæləns] Ⓐ N desequilibrio *m*
Ⓑ VT desequilibrar

unbalanced [ˈʌnˈbælənst] ADJ [1] (*physically*) desequilibrado; (*mentally*) trastornado, desequilibrado
[2] (*Fin*) no conciliado

unban [ˈʌnˈbæn] VT levantar la prohibición de

unbandage [ˈʌnˈbændɪdʒ] VT desvendar, quitar las vendas a

unbaptized [ˈʌnbæpˈtaɪzd] ADJ sin bautizar

unbar [ˈʌnˈbɑːʳ] VT [+ *door etc*] desatrancar; (*fig*) abrir, franquear

unbearable [ʌnˈbɛərəbl] ADJ inaguantable, insoportable

unbearably [ʌnˈbɛərəblɪ] ADV insoportablemente; **it is ~ hot** hace un calor insoportable; **she is ~ vain** es vanidosa hasta lo inaguantable

unbeatable [ˈʌnˈbiːtəbl] ADJ [*team, opponent, army*] invencible; [*price, offer*] inmejorable

unbeaten [ˈʌnˈbiːtn] ADJ [*team, opponent*] imbatido, invicto; [*army*] invicto; [*price*] insuperable

unbecoming [ˈʌnbɪˈkʌmɪŋ] ADJ [1] (= *unseemly*) [*behaviour etc*] indecoroso, impropio
[2] (= *unflattering*) [*dress etc*] poco favorecedor

➤ LANGUAGE IN USE: **unbelievable** 14

unbeknown [ˌʌnbɪˈnəʊn], **unbeknownst** [ˌʌnbɪˈnəʊnst] ADJ **~ to me** sin yo saberlo

unbelief [ˈʌnbɪˈliːf] N [1] (*Rel*) (*in general*) descreimiento *m*; [*of person*] falta *f* de fe
[2] (= *astonishment*) incredulidad *f*

▼**unbelievable** [ˌʌnbɪˈliːvəbl] ADJ [1] (= *incredible*) increíble; **it is ~ that** es increíble que + *subjun*
[2] (*) (= *fantastic*) increíble

unbelievably [ˌʌnbɪˈliːvəblɪ] ADV increíblemente; **they're ~ lucky** tienen una suerte increíble

unbeliever [ˈʌnbɪˈliːvəʳ] N no creyente *mf*

unbelieving [ˈʌnbɪˈliːvɪŋ] ADJ incrédulo

unbelievingly [ˌʌnbɪˈliːvɪŋlɪ] ADV [*watch, stare*] sin dar crédito a sus ojos

unbend [ˈʌnˈbend] (*pt, pp* **unbent**) Ⓐ VT enderezar
Ⓑ VI (*fig*) [*person*] relajarse

unbending [ˈʌnˈbendɪŋ] ADJ inflexible, rígido; (*fig*) [*person, attitude*] inflexible; (= *strict*) estricto, severo

unbent [ˈʌnˈbent] PT, PP *of* **unbend**

unbias(s)ed [ˈʌnˈbaɪəst] ADJ imparcial

unbidden [ˈʌnˈbɪdn] ADV (*liter*) **to do sth ~** hacer algo espontáneamente

unbind [ˈʌnˈbaɪnd] (*pt, pp* **unbound**) VT desatar; (= *unbandage*) desvendar

unbleached [ˈʌnˈbliːtʃt] ADJ sin blanquear

unblemished [ʌnˈblemɪʃt] ADJ sin tacha, sin mancha

unblinking [ʌnˈblɪŋkɪŋ] ADJ imperturbable; (*pej*) desvergonzado

unblock [ˈʌnˈblɒk] VT [+ *sink, pipe*] desatascar; [+ *road etc*] despejar

unblushing [ʌnˈblʌʃɪŋ] ADJ desvergonzado, fresco

unblushingly [ʌnˈblʌʃɪŋlɪ] ADV desvergonzadamente; **he said ~** dijo tan fresco

unbolt [ˈʌnˈbəʊlt] VT desatrancar, quitar el cerrojo de

unborn [ˈʌnˈbɔːn] ADJ no nacido aún, nonato; **the ~ child** el feto; **generations yet ~** generaciones *fpl* que están todavía por nacer *or* que están por venir

unbosom [ʌnˈbʊzəm] VT (*liter*) **to ~ o.s. of sth** desahogarse de algo; **to ~ o.s. to sb** abrir su pecho a algn, desahogarse con algn

unbound [ˈʌnˈbaʊnd] ADJ [*book*] sin encuadernar, en rústica

unbounded [ʌnˈbaʊndɪd] ADJ ilimitado, sin límites

unbowed [ˈʌnˈbaʊd] ADJ **with head ~** con la cabeza erguida

unbreakable [ˈʌnˈbreɪkəbl] ADJ irrompible

unbribable [ˈʌnˈbraɪbəbl] ADJ insobornable

unbridgeable [ˌʌnˈbrɪdʒəbl] ADJ insalvable, infranqueable

unbridled [ʌnˈbraɪdld] ADJ (*fig*) desenfrenado

unbroken [ˌʌnˈbrəʊkən] ADJ [1] (= *intact*) entero, intacto
[2] (= *continuous*) ininterrumpido, continuo
[3] (= *unbeaten*) no batido; [*spirit*] indómito; **his spirit remained ~** no se hundió
[4] [*animal*] indomado

unbuckle [ˈʌnˈbʌkl] VT desabrochar

unbudgeted [ʌnˈbʌdʒɪtɪd] ADJ no presupuestado

unburden [ʌnˈbɜːdn] VT [1] (*lit*) [+ *person*] aliviar; **to ~ sb of a load** aliviar a algn quitándole un peso
[2] (*fig*) **to ~ one's heart to sb** abrir su pecho a algn; **to ~ o.s.** *or* **one's conscience to sb** desahogarse con algn; **to ~ o.s. of sth** desahogarse de algo

unburied [ˈʌnˈberɪd] ADJ insepulto

unbusinesslike [ʌnˈbɪznɪslaɪk] ADJ (= *without method*) poco profesional; (*in appearance etc*) poco formal

unbutton [ˈʌnˈbʌtn] Ⓐ VT desabrochar, desabotonar
Ⓑ VI (*) hacerse más afable

uncalled-for [ʌnˈkɔːldfɔːʳ] ADJ gratuito, impropio; **that was quite ~** eso fue totalmente gratuito *or* impropio

uncannily [ʌnˈkænɪlɪ] ADV misteriosamente; **it is ~ like the other one** tiene un asombroso parecido con el otro, se parece extraordinariamente al otro

uncanny [ʌnˈkænɪ] ADJ (*compar* **uncannier**; *superl* **uncanniest**) (= *peculiar*) raro, extraño; (= *ghostly*) misterioso; **it's quite ~** es extraordinario; **it's ~ how he does it** no llego a comprender cómo lo hace; **an ~ resemblance** un asombroso parecido

uncap [ˈʌnˈkæp] VT destapar

uncapped [ˌʌnˈkæpt] ADJ (*Sport*) debutante; **~ player** debutante *mf* (*en la selección nacional*)

uncared-for [ˈʌnˈkɛədfɔːʳ] ADJ [*person*] abandonado, desamparado; [*appearance*] desaseado, de abandono; [*building etc*] abandonado

uncaring [ˈʌnkɛərɪŋ] ADJ poco compasivo; **he went on all ~** (*liter*) siguió sin hacer caso

uncarpeted [ˈʌnˈkɑːpɪtɪd] ADJ no enmoquetado (*Sp*), no alfombrado (*LAm*)

uncashed [ˈʌnˈkæʃt] ADJ [*cheque*] no cobrado, sin cobrar

uncatalogued [ˈʌnˈkætəlɒgd] ADJ no catalogado

unceasing [ʌnˈsiːsɪŋ] ADJ incesante

unceasingly [ʌnˈsiːsɪŋlɪ] ADV incesantemente, sin cesar

uncensored [ˈʌnˈsensəd] ADJ no censurado

unceremonious [ˈʌnˌserɪˈməʊnɪəs] ADJ (= *abrupt, rude*) brusco, hosco

unceremoniously [ˈʌnˌserɪˈməʊnɪəslɪ] ADV bruscamente, sin cortesías

uncertain [ʌnˈsɜːtn] ADJ [1] (= *unsure*) **for a moment he looked ~** por un momento pareció no estar seguro; **to be ~ about/of sth** no estar seguro de algo; **she is ~ about the future/what to do next/how to proceed** no está segura sobre el futuro/de qué hacer ahora/de cómo proceder; **I am ~ as to whether she was involved in the accident** no estoy seguro si ella estuvo implicada en el accidente; **I am ~ whether to accept** no estoy seguro si aceptar
[2] (= *doubtful*) [*future, outcome, destiny*] incierto; **the fate of the refugees remains ~** la suerte de los refugiados sigue siendo incierta *or* sigue sin conocerse; **in no ~ terms** sin dejar lugar a dudas, claramente
[3] (= *changeable*) [*conditions*] inestable; [*weather, temper*] variable; **we live in ~ times** vivimos en unos tiempos muy inestables
[4] (= *indecisive*) [*voice*] indeciso; [*smile*] tímido, indeciso; [*step*] vacilante
[5] (= *indeterminate*) indeterminado; **a smartly-dressed man of ~ age** un hombre elegantemente vestido de edad indeterminada

uncertainly [ʌnˈsɜːtnlɪ] ADV **he stood there ~ for a moment** por un momento se quedó allí de pie con aire indeciso *or* vacilante; **she smiled ~** sonrió con timidez, esbozó una sonrisa tímida *or* indecisa; **he said ~** dijo indeciso

uncertainty [ʌn'sɜːtntɪ] N [1] (= *doubt*) duda *f*, incertidumbre *f*; **in view of this ~** *or* **these uncertainties** teniendo en cuenta estas dudas *or* este grado de incertidumbre; **there is ~ about the number of wounded** no se sabe con seguridad el número de heridos; **stress is caused by ~ about the future** el estrés está causado por la incertidumbre *or* inseguridad sobre el futuro
[2] (= *indecision*) indecisión *f*; **he heard the ~ in her voice** notó la indecisión en su voz

uncertificated ['ʌnsə'tɪfɪkeɪtɪd] ADJ [*teacher etc*] sin título

unchain ['ʌn'tʃeɪn] VT desencadenar

unchallengeable ['ʌn'tʃælɪndʒəbl] ADJ incontestable, incuestionable

unchallenged ['ʌn'tʃælɪndʒd] ADJ (= *unnoticed*) inadvertido; (= *undeniable*) incontrovertible; (*Jur*) incontestado; **his ideas went ~** sus ideas no fueron cuestionadas; **we cannot let that go ~** eso no lo podemos dejar pasar sin protesta

unchangeable [ʌn'tʃeɪndʒəbl] ADJ inalterable, inmutable

unchanged ['ʌn'tʃeɪndʒd] ADJ igual, sin cambiar; **everything is still ~** todo sigue igual

unchanging [ʌn'tʃeɪndʒɪŋ] ADJ inalterable, inmutable

uncharacteristic [ˌʌnkæræktə'rɪstɪk] ADJ [*hostility, politeness etc*] inusitado, nada típico; **to be ~ of sth** ser inusitado en algo; **to be ~ of sb** no ser propio de algn; **it's very ~ of her** no es nada propio de ella

uncharacteristically [ˌʌnkærɪktə'rɪstɪklɪ] ADV **~ rude/generous** de una grosería/generosidad inusitada; **to behave ~** comportarse de manera inusual

uncharitable [ʌn'tʃærɪtəbl] ADJ poco caritativo

uncharitably [ʌn'tʃærɪtəblɪ] ADV poco caritativamente

uncharted ['ʌn'tʃɑːtɪd] ADJ inexplorado, desconocido

unchaste ['ʌn'tʃeɪst] ADJ impúdico; [*spouse*] infiel

unchecked ['ʌn'tʃekt] (A) ADV [*continue etc*] libremente, sin estorbo *or* restricción; **the weeds had been allowed to grow ~** habían dejado que las malas hierbas crecieran descontroladamente; **left ~, the virus could spread throughout Africa** si no se controla, el virus podría extenderse por toda África
(B) ADJ [1] (= *unrestrained*) [*growth, power, emotion, anger*] desenfrenado
[2] (= *not verified*) [*data, statement*] no comprobado; (= *not examined*) [*text, manuscript*] sin revisar

unchivalrous ['ʌn'ʃɪvəlrəs] ADJ poco caballeroso, poco caballeresco

unchristian ['ʌn'krɪstɪən] ADJ poco cristiano, impropio de un cristiano

uncial ['ʌnsɪəl] (A) ADJ uncial
(B) N uncial *f*

uncircumcised ['ʌn'sɜːkəmsaɪzd] ADJ incircunciso

uncivil ['ʌn'sɪvɪl] ADJ descortés; **to be ~ to sb** ser descortés con algn

uncivilized ['ʌn'sɪvɪlaɪzd] ADJ [1] (= *primitive*) [*people, country*] poco civilizado; (*fig*) bárbaro
[2] (= *socially unacceptable*) [*conditions, activity*] inaceptable; [*person, behaviour*] grosero
[3] (*) (= *early*) **at this ~ hour** a estas horas tan intempestivas

uncivilly [ˌʌn'sɪvɪlɪ] ADV descortésmente

unclad ['ʌn'klæd] ADJ desnudo

unclaimed ['ʌn'kleɪmd] ADJ sin reclamar

unclasp ['ʌn'klɑːsp] VT [+ *dress etc*] desabrochar; [+ *hands*] soltar, separar

unclassifiable [ˌʌn'klæsɪfaɪəbl] ADJ inclasificable

unclassified ['ʌn'klæsɪfaɪd] ADJ [1] (= *not arranged*) [*items, papers, waste, football results*] sin clasificar
[2] (= *not secret*) [*information, document*] no confidencial

uncle ['ʌŋkl] N [1] tío *m*; **my ~ and aunt** mis tíos; **Uncle Sam*** el tío Sam (*personificación de EE.UU.*); **Uncle Tom** (*US* pej*) *negro que trata de congraciarse con los blancos*; ✦**IDIOM to cry** *or* **say ~** (*US**) rendirse, darse por vencido
[2] (‡) (= *fence*) perista* *m*

unclean ['ʌn'kliːn] ADJ [1] (= *dirty*) [*person, hands, room*] sucio
[2] (= *impure*) [*person, animal, activity, thoughts*] impuro

uncleanliness ['ʌn'klenlɪnɪs] N suciedad *f*

unclear [ˌʌn'klɪəʳ] ADJ [1] (= *not obvious*) **the reasons for this behaviour are ~** las razones de este comportamiento no están claras; **it is ~ what effect this will have** no se sabe muy bien qué efectos tendrá esto; **the impact of these changes remains ~** el impacto de estos cambios sigue sin conocerse con seguridad
[2] (= *not specific*) **he was ~ about the details of what had happened** no fue muy claro respecto a los detalles de lo que había sucedido
[3] (= *confusing*) poco claro; **the wording of the contract is ~** los términos del contrato son poco claros
[4] (= *unsure*) **to be ~ about sth** no tener algo muy claro; **I'm still ~ about it** todavía no lo tengo muy claro

unclench ['ʌn'klentʃ] VT aflojar

unclimbed ['ʌn'klaɪmd] ADJ no escalado

unclog ['ʌn'klɒg] VT desatascar

unclothe ['ʌn'kləʊð] VT desnudar

unclothed ['ʌn'kləʊðd] ADJ desnudo

unclouded ['ʌn'klaʊdɪd] ADJ [1] [*sky etc*] despejado, sin nubes
[2] (*fig*) (= *calm*) tranquilo

uncoil ['ʌn'kɔɪl] (A) VT desenrollar
(B) VI desenrollarse; [*snake*] desenroscarse

uncollected [ˌʌnkə'lektɪd] ADJ [*goods, luggage*] sin recoger; [*tax*] no recaudado, sin cobrar

uncoloured, uncolored (*US*) ['ʌn'kʌləd] ADJ [1] (= *colourless*) [*glass, plastic, liquid*] sin color, incoloro
[2] (= *unbiased*) [*account, description, judgement*] objetivo

uncombed ['ʌn'kəʊmd] ADJ despeinado, sin peinar

uncomely ['ʌn'kʌmlɪ] ADJ desgarbado

uncomfortable [ʌn'kʌmfətəbl] ADJ [1] (*physically*) incómodo; **to be/feel ~** [*chair, shoes, position*] ser *or* resultar incómodo; [*person*] estar/sentirse incómodo
[2] (= *uneasy*) incómodo; **I had an ~ feeling that someone was watching me** tenía la incómoda sensación de que alguien me observaba; **to be ~ about sth** estar incómodo *or* a disgusto con algo; **he's always felt ~ with women** siempre se ha sentido incómodo *or* a disgusto con las mujeres; **to make sb ~** hacer a algn sentirse incómodo, hacer que algn se sienta incómodo; **to make life ~ for sb** ponérselo difícil a algn; **there was an ~ silence** se produjo un silencio muy incómodo
[3] (= *worrying*) molesto; **it was an ~ dilemma** era una molesta disyuntiva
[4] (= *disagreeable*) [*truth, fact*] desagradable

uncomfortably [ʌn'kʌmfətəblɪ] ADV [1] (*lit*) **she felt ~ hot** se encontraba incómoda del calor que tenía; **I'm feeling ~ full** estoy tan lleno que me siento incómodo; **he fidgeted ~** se movió incómodo; **the children were ~ dressed** los niños no llevaban ropa cómoda
[2] (= *uneasily*) **he shifted ~ in his chair** se removía incómodo *or* inquieto en su silla; **I was ~ aware that everyone was watching me** me daba cuenta de que todo el mundo me miraba, lo cual me hacía sentirme incómodo
[3] (= *worryingly*) inquietantemente; **the shell fell ~ close** cayó el proyectil inquietantemente cerca

uncommitted ['ʌnkə'mɪtɪd] ADJ no comprometido; [*nation*] no alineado

uncommon [ʌn'kɒmən] (A) ADJ [1] (= *unusual*) poco común, nada frecuente
[2] (= *outstanding*) insólito, extraordinario
(B) ADV (†) sumamente, extraordinariamente

uncommonly [ʌn'kɒmənlɪ] ADV [1] (†) (= *exceptionally*) [*gifted, pretty, hot*] extraordinariamente; **that's ~ kind of you** ha sido usted amabilísimo
[2] (= *rarely*) [*encountered*] raramente, rara vez; **not ~** con cierta frecuencia

uncommunicative ['ʌnkə'mjuːnɪkətɪv] ADJ poco comunicativo, reservado

uncomplaining ['ʌnkəm'pleɪnɪŋ] ADJ resignado, sumiso

uncomplainingly ['ʌnkəm'pleɪnɪŋlɪ] ADV sin protesta, sumisamente

uncompleted ['ʌnkəm'pliːtɪd] ADJ incompleto, inacabado

uncomplicated [ʌn'kɒmplɪkeɪtɪd] ADJ sin complicaciones, sencillo

uncomplimentary ['ʌnˌkɒmplɪ'mentərɪ] ADJ poco halagüeño *or* halagador, nada lisonjero

uncomprehending ['ʌnˌkɒmprɪ'hendɪŋ] ADJ incomprensivo

uncompromising [ʌn'kɒmprəmaɪzɪŋ] ADJ intransigente, inflexible; **~ loyalty** lealtad *f* absoluta

uncompromisingly [ʌn'kɒmprəmaɪzɪŋlɪ] ADV intransigentemente, inflexiblemente

unconcealed ['ʌnkən'siːld] ADJ evidente, no disimulado; **with ~ glee** con abierta satisfacción

unconcern ['ʌnkən'sɜːn] N (= *calm*) calma *f*, tranquilidad *f*; (*in face of danger*) sangre *f* fría; (= *lack of interest*) indiferencia *f*, despreocupación *f*

unconcerned ['ʌnkən'sɜːnd] ADJ (= *unworried*) despreocupado; (= *indifferent*) indiferente, despreocupado; **to be ~ about sth** no inquietarse *or* preocuparse por algo, mostrarse indiferente a algo

unconcernedly ['ʌnkən'sɜːnɪdlɪ] ADV sin preocuparse, sin inquietarse

unconditional ['ʌnkən'dɪʃənl] ADJ incondicional, sin condiciones; **~ surrender** rendición *f* sin condiciones

unconditionally ['ʌnkən'dɪʃnəlɪ] ADV incondicionalmente

unconfessed ['ʌnkən'fest] ADJ [*sin*] no confesado; [*die*] sin confesar

unconfined ['ʌnkən'faɪnd] ADJ ilimitado, no restringido, libre; **let joy be ~** (*liter*) que se regocijen todos, que la alegría no tenga límite

unconfirmed ['ʌnkən'fɜːmd] ADJ no confirmado, inconfirmado

uncongenial ['ʌnkən'dʒiːnɪəl] ADJ [*person*] antipático, poco amigable; [*company, work, surroundings*] desagradable, poco agradable; **to**

be ~ to sb ser antipático *or* desagradable con algn

unconnected [ˈʌnkəˈnektɪd] ADJ [1] (= *unrelated*) no relacionado
[2] (= *incoherent*) inconexo

unconquerable [ʌnˈkɒŋkərəbl] ADJ inconquistable, invencible

unconquered [ʌnˈkɒŋkəd] ADJ invicto

unconscionable [ʌnˈkɒnʃnəbl] ADJ (*frm*) [1] (= *disgraceful*) [*liar*] desvergonzado; [*behaviour, crime*] inadmisible
[2] (= *excessive*) desmedido, desrazonable

unconscionably [ʌnˈkɒnʃnəblɪ] ADV (*frm*) desmesuradamente

unconscious [ʌnˈkɒnʃəs] Ⓐ ADJ [1] (*Med*) sin sentido, inconsciente; **to be ~** estar sin sentido *or* inconsciente; **to be ~ for three hours** pasar tres horas sin sentido; **to become ~** perder el sentido *or* conocimiento, desmayarse; **to fall ~** caer sin sentido; **they found him ~** lo encontraron inconsciente
[2] (= *unaware*) inconsciente, insensible; **to be ~ of sth** no ser consciente de algo; **he remained blissfully ~ of the danger** continuó tan tranquilo, sin darse cuenta del peligro
[3] (= *unintentional*) inconsciente
Ⓑ N **the ~** (*Psych*) el inconsciente

unconsciously [ʌnˈkɒnʃəslɪ] ADV inconscientemente; **~ funny** cómico sin querer

unconsciousness [ʌnˈkɒnʃəsnɪs] N (*Med*) inconsciencia *f*

unconsidered [ˈʌnkənˈsɪdəd] ADJ (= *hasty*) [*comment, decision, action*] irreflexivo, precipitado; **~ trifles** pequeñeces *fpl* sin ninguna importancia

unconstitutional [ˈʌnˌkɒnstɪˈtjuːʃənl] ADJ inconstitucional, anticonstitucional

unconstitutionally [ʌnˌkɒnstɪˈtjuːʃnəlɪ] ADV inconstitucionalmente, anticonstitucionalmente

unconstrained [ˈʌnkənˈstreɪnd] ADJ libre, espontáneo

unconsummated [ʌnˈkɒnsəmeɪtɪd] ADJ [*marriage*] no consumado

uncontested [ˈʌnkənˈtestɪd] ADJ (*Parl*) [*seat*] ganado sin oposición, no disputado

uncontrollable [ˈʌnkənˈtrəʊləbl] ADJ [1] (= *irrepressible*) [*rage, desire*] incontenible, incontrolable; [*urge*] irrefrenable, incontenible; [*laughter*] incontenible
[2] (= *involuntary*) [*movement, spasm*] incontrolable
[3] (= *unmanageable*) [*person, animal, situation*] incontrolable; [*car, boat, aeroplane*] fuera de control

uncontrollably [ˈʌnkənˈtrəʊləblɪ] ADV [*spread, increase*] incontrolablemente; [*laugh, cry, shake*] sin poder controlarse, inconteniblemente

uncontrolled [ˈʌnkənˈtrəʊld] ADJ (= *out of control*) descontrolado; [*passion*] desenfrenado; [*freedom etc*] irrestricto

uncontroversial [ˈʌnˌkɒntrəˈvɜːʃəl] ADJ no controvertido, nada conflictivo

unconventional [ˈʌnkənˈvenʃənl] ADJ poco convencional; [*person*] original, poco convencional

unconventionality [ˈʌnkənˌvenʃəˈnælɪtɪ] N originalidad *f*

unconversant [ˈʌnkənˈvɜːsənt] ADJ **to be ~ with** no estar al tanto de, estar poco versado en

unconverted [ˈʌnkənˈvɜːtɪd] ADJ no convertido (*also Fin*)

➤ LANGUAGE IN USE: **undeniable** 15.1

unconvertible [ˌʌnkənˈvɜːtɪbl] ADJ [*currency*] inconvertible

unconvinced [ˈʌnkənˈvɪnst] ADJ poco convencido; **I am** *or* **remain ~ by what she said** lo que dijo sigue sin convencerme

unconvincing [ˈʌnkənˈvɪnsɪŋ] ADJ poco convincente

unconvincingly [ˈʌnkənˈvɪnsɪŋlɪ] ADV [*argue etc*] de manera poco convincente

uncooked [ˈʌnˈkʊkt] ADJ (= *raw*) crudo, sin cocer; (= *not properly cooked*) a medio cocer

uncool* [ʌnˈkuːl] ADJ [1] (= *unsophisticated*) nada sofisticado; (= *unfashionable*) pasado de moda, anticuado
[2] (= *excitable*) excitable; (= *tense*) nervioso

uncooperative [ˈʌnkəʊˈɒpərətɪv] ADJ poco dispuesto a cooperar, nada colaborador

uncoordinated [ˈʌnkəʊˈɔːdɪneɪtɪd] ADJ no coordinado, incoordinado

uncork [ˈʌnˈkɔːk] VT descorchar, destapar

uncorrected [ˈʌnkəˈrektɪd] ADJ sin corregir

uncorroborated [ˈʌnkəˈrɒbəreɪtɪd] ADJ no confirmado, sin corroborar

uncorrupted [ˈʌnkəˈrʌptɪd] ADJ incorrupto; **~ by** no corrompido por

uncount [ˈʌnˈkaʊnt] Ⓐ ADJ no contable
Ⓑ CPD ► **uncount noun** N sustantivo *m* no contable

uncountable [ˈʌnˈkaʊntəbl] ADJ incontable

uncounted [ˈʌnˈkaʊntɪd] ADJ sin cuenta

uncouple [ˈʌnˈkʌpl] VT desenganchar, desacoplar

uncouth [ʌnˈkuːθ] ADJ (= *unrefined*) grosero, inculto; (= *clumsy*) torpe, desmañado

uncover [ʌnˈkʌvəʳ] VT [1] (= *find out*) descubrir
[2] (= *remove coverings of*) destapar; (= *disclose*) descubrir, dejar al descubierto

uncovered [ʌnˈkʌvəd] ADJ [1] (= *without a cover*) destapado, descubierto
[2] (*Fin*) [*loan*] en descubierto; [*person*] sin seguro, no asegurado

uncritical [ˈʌnˈkrɪtɪkəl] ADJ falto de sentido crítico

uncritically [ˈʌnˈkrɪtɪkəlɪ] ADV sin sentido crítico

uncross [ˈʌnˈkrɒs] VT [+ *legs*] descruzar

uncrossed [ˈʌnˈkrɒst] ADJ [*cheque*] sin cruzar

uncrowned [ˈʌnˈkraʊnd] ADJ sin corona; **the ~ king of Scotland** el rey sin corona de Escocia

UNCTAD [ˈʌŋktæd] N ABBR = **United Nations Conference on Trade and Development**

unction [ˈʌŋkʃən] N [1] (= *ointment*) unción *f*; **extreme ~** (*Rel*) extremaunción *f*
[2] (*fig*) (= *suaveness*) unción *f*; (*pej*) (= *affected charm*) celo *m* fingido, afectación *f*; **he said with ~** dijo con afectación

unctuous [ˈʌŋktjʊəs] ADJ empalagoso, afectado; **in an ~ voice** en tono meloso, empalagosamente

unctuously [ˈʌŋktjʊəslɪ] ADV con afectación

unctuousness [ˈʌŋktjʊəsnɪs] N celo *m* fingido, afectación *f*

uncultivable [ˈʌnˈkʌltɪvəbl] ADJ incultivable

uncultivated [ˈʌnˈkʌltɪveɪtɪd] ADJ [1] (*Agr*) [*land*] sin cultivar, inculto (*frm*)
[2] (= *uncultured*) [*person, mind*] sin cultivar; [*voice, accent*] no cultivado

uncultured [ˈʌnˈkʌltʃəd] ADJ [*person*] inculto, sin cultura; [*voice*] no cultivado; [*accent*] poco culto

uncurl [ˈʌnˈkɜːl] Ⓐ VT desenroscar
Ⓑ VI [*snake etc*] desenroscarse; (= *straighten out*) estirarse

uncut [ˈʌnˈkʌt] ADJ [1] [*grass, tree, hair, nails*] sin cortar; [*stone*] sin labrar
[2] (= *not faceted*) [*diamond*] en bruto, sin tallar
[3] (= *unabridged*) [*film, text*] integral, sin cortes
[4] (= *pure*) [*heroin, cocaine*] puro

undamaged [ʌnˈdæmɪdʒd] ADJ (*gen*) en buen estado; (= *intact*) intacto

undamped [ˈʌnˈdæmpt] ADJ [*enthusiasm, courage*] no disminuido

undated [ˈʌnˈdeɪtɪd] ADJ sin fecha

undaunted [ˈʌnˈdɔːntɪd] ADJ impávido, impertérrito; **he carried on quite ~** siguió sin inmutarse; **with ~ bravery** con valor indomable; **to be ~ by** no dejarse desanimar por

undeceive [ˈʌndɪˈsiːv] VT desengañar, desilusionar

undecided [ˈʌndɪˈsaɪdɪd] ADJ [*person*] indeciso; [*question*] pendiente, no resuelto; **we are still ~ whether to go** aún no sabemos si ir o no; **that is still ~** eso queda por resolver

undecipherable [ˌʌndɪˈsaɪfərəbl] ADJ indescifrable

undeclared [ˈʌndɪˈkleəd] ADJ no declarado

undeclinable [ˈʌndɪˈklaɪnəbl] ADJ indeclinable

undefeated [ˈʌndɪˈfiːtɪd] ADJ invicto, imbatido; **he was ~ at the end** al final siguió invicto *or* imbatido

undefended [ˈʌndɪˈfendɪd] ADJ [1] (*Mil etc*) indefenso
[2] (*Jur*) [*suit*] ganado por incomparecencia del demandado

undefiled [ˈʌndɪˈfaɪld] ADJ puro, inmaculado; **~ by any contact with …** no corrompido por contacto alguno con …

undefinable [ˌʌndɪˈfaɪnəbl] ADJ indefinible

undefined [ˌʌndɪˈfaɪnd] ADJ indefinido, indeterminado

undelete [ˈʌndɪˈliːt] VT (*Comput*) restaurar

undelivered [ˌʌndɪˈlɪvəd] ADJ no entregado al destinatario

undemanding [ˌʌndɪˈmɑːndɪŋ] ADJ [*person*] poco exigente; [*job*] que exige poco esfuerzo

undemocratic [ˌʌndeməˈkrætɪk] ADJ antidemocrático

undemonstrative [ˈʌndɪˈmɒnstrətɪv] ADJ poco expresivo

▼**undeniable** [ˌʌndɪˈnaɪəbl] ADJ innegable, indudable; **it is ~ that …** es innegable *or* indudable que …

undeniably [ˌʌndɪˈnaɪəblɪ] ADV innegablemente, indudablemente; **it is ~ true that …** es innegable *or* indudable que …; **an ~ successful trip** un viaje de éxito innegable *or* indudable

undenominational [ˈʌndɪˌnɒmɪˈneɪʃənl] ADJ no sectario

undependable [ˈʌndɪˈpendəbl] ADJ poco formal, poco confiable

under [ˈʌndəʳ] Ⓐ ADV [1] (= *beneath*) (*position*) debajo; (*direction*) abajo; **he stayed ~ for three minutes** (= *underwater*) estuvo sumergido durante tres minutos; **he lifted the rope and crawled ~** levantó la cuerda y se deslizó por debajo
[2] (*) (= *under anaesthetic*) **he's been ~ for three hours** lleva tres horas bajo los efectos de la anestesia
[3] (= *less*) menos; **children of 15 and ~** niños *mpl* de 15 años y menores; **ten degrees ~** diez grados bajo cero
Ⓑ PREP [1] (= *beneath*) debajo de; **~ the bed** debajo de la cama; **~ the microscope** bajo el microscopio; **~ the sky** bajo el cielo; **~ the**

water bajo el agua; **the train passed ~ the bridge** el tren pasó por debajo del puente; **the tunnel goes ~ the Channel** el túnel pasa por debajo del Canal; **~ there** ahí debajo; **what's ~ there?** ¿qué hay ahí debajo?
[2] (= *less than*) menos de; **~ 20 people** menos de 20 personas; **in ~ a minute** en menos de un minuto; **any number ~ 90** cualquier número inferior a 90; **aged ~ 21** que tiene menos de 21 años; **children ~ ten** niños menores de diez años; **it sells at ~ £20** se vende a menos de 20 libras
[3] (= *subject to*) bajo; **~ this government/the Romans** bajo este gobierno/los romanos; **~ Ferdinand VII** bajo Fernando VII, durante el reinado de Fernando VII; **he has 30 workers ~ him** tiene 30 obreros a su cargo; **to study ~ sb** estudiar con algn, tener a algn por profesor; **~ the command of** bajo el mando de; **~ construction** bajo construcción, en obras; **~ lock and key** bajo llave; **~ oath** bajo juramento; **~ pain/the pretext of** so pena/pretexto de; **~ full sail** a todo trapo, a vela llena
[4] (*with names*) **~ a false name** con nombre falso; **you'll find him ~ "plumbers" in the phone book** lo encontrarás en la sección de "fontaneros" en el listín
[5] (= *according to, by*) de acuerdo con, según; **~ Article 25 of the Code** conforme al Artículo 25 del Código; **his rights ~ the contract** sus derechos según el contrato
[6] (*Agr*) **the field is ~ wheat** el campo está sembrado de trigo

under- [ˈʌndəʳ] PREFIX [1] (= *insufficiently*) poco, insuficientemente; **~prepared** poco *or* insuficientemente preparado
[2] (= *less than*) **an ~15** (= *child*) un menor de 15 años; **the Spanish ~21 team** la selección española sub-21
[3] [*part etc*] bajo, inferior; [*clothing*] interior; (*in rank*) subalterno, segundo; **the ~cook** el/la cocinero/a ayudante *or* auxiliar

under-achieve [ˌʌndərəˈtʃiːv] VI no desarrollar su potencial, no rendir (como se debe)

under-achievement [ˌʌndərəˈtʃiːvmənt] N bajo rendimiento *m*

under-achiever [ˌʌndərəˈtʃiːvəʳ] N (*Brit*) persona *f* que no desarrolla su potencial, persona *f* que no rinde (como podría)

underact [ˈʌndərˈækt] VI no dar de sí, hacer un papel sin el debido brío

underage [ˌʌndərˈeɪdʒ] ADJ menor de edad; **he's ~** es menor de edad

underarm [ˈʌndərɑːm] Ⓐ N axila *f*, sobaco *m*
Ⓑ CPD (*Anat*) sobacal, del sobaco; [*service etc*] realizado sin levantar el brazo por encima ► **underarm deodorant** N desodorante *m*
Ⓒ ADV **to serve ~** sacar sin levantar el brazo por encima

underbelly [ˈʌndəˌbelɪ] N (*Anat*) panza *f*; **the (soft) ~** (*fig*) la parte indefensa

underbid [ˈʌndəˈbɪd] (*pt* **underbade** *or* **underbid**; *pp* **underbidden** *or* **underbid**) Ⓐ VT ofrecer un precio más bajo que
Ⓑ VI (*Bridge*) declarar por debajo de lo que se tiene

underbody [ˈʌndəbɒdɪ] N (*Aut*) bajos *mpl* (del chasis)

underbrush [ˈʌndəbrʌʃ] N (*US*) maleza *f*, monte *m* bajo

undercapitalized [ˈʌndəˈkæpɪtəlaɪzd] ADJ descapitalizado, subcapitalizado

undercarriage [ˈʌndəˌkærɪdʒ] N (*Aer*) tren *m* de aterrizaje

undercharge [ˈʌndəˈtʃɑːdʒ] VT cobrar de menos a; **he ~d me by £2** me cobró 2 libras de menos

underclass [ˈʌndəklɑːs] N clase *f* inferior

underclothes [ˈʌndəkləʊðz] NPL, **underclothing** [ˈʌndəˌkləʊðɪŋ] N ropa *fsing* interior *or* (*esp LAm*) íntima; **to be in one's ~** estar en ropa interior, estar en paños menores*

undercoat [ˈʌndəkəʊt] Ⓐ N [*of paint*] primera capa *f*, primera mano *f*; (= *paint*) pintura *f* preparatoria
Ⓑ VT dar una primera capa a; (*US Aut*) proteger contra la corrosión

undercooked [ˈʌndəˈkʊkt] ADJ medio crudo, a medio cocer

undercover [ˈʌndəˌkʌvəʳ] Ⓐ ADJ [*operation, activity*] clandestino; [*agent*] secreto
Ⓑ ADV **she was working ~ for the FBI** trabajaba como agente secreto para el FBI

undercurrent [ˈʌndəˌkʌrənt] N (*in sea*) corriente *f* submarina, contracorriente *f*; (*fig*) (*feeling etc*) trasfondo *m*; **an ~ of criticism** un trasfondo de críticas calladas

undercut [ˈʌndəkʌt] (*pt, pp* **undercut**) VT (*Comm*) (= *sell cheaper than*) [+ *competitor*] vender más barato que

underdeveloped [ˈʌndədɪˈveləpt] ADJ [1] (*Econ*) [*country, society, economy*] subdesarrollado
[2] (*Anat*) poco desarrollado
[3] (*Phot*) insuficientemente revelado; **the image looks slightly ~** a la imagen le falta tiempo de revelación

underdevelopment [ˈʌndədɪˈveləpmənt] N subdesarrollo *m*

underdog [ˈʌndədɒg] N **the ~** [1] (*in game, fight*) el/la más débil
[2] (*economically, socially*) el/la desvalido/a, el/la desamparado/a

underdone [ˈʌndəˈdʌn] ADJ [*food*] a medio cocer; (*deliberately*) [*steak*] poco hecho

underdrawers [ˈʌndəˈdrɔːəz] NPL (*US*) calzoncillos *mpl*

underdressed [ˌʌndəˈdrest] ADJ **to be ~** vestirse sin la debida elegancia, no vestirse de forma apropiada

underemphasize [ˌʌndərˈemfəsaɪz] VT subenfatizar

underemployed [ˈʌndərɪmˈplɔɪd] ADJ subempleado

underemployment [ˌʌndərɪmˈplɔɪmənt] N subempleo *m*

underestimate Ⓐ [ˈʌndərˈestɪmɪt] N estimación *f* demasiado baja, cálculo *m* demasiado bajo
Ⓑ [ˈʌndərˈestɪmeɪt] VT [+ *strength, importance, value, person*] subestimar, menospreciar; **you shouldn't ~ her** no deberías subestimarla; **I ~d the size of the sofa** al calcular las dimensiones del sofá me quedé corta; **they had ~d the size of the problem** no le habían dado al problema la importancia que merecía

underexpose [ˈʌndərɪksˈpəʊz] VT (*Phot*) subexponer

underexposed [ˈʌndərɪksˈpəʊzd] ADJ (*Phot*) subexpuesto

underexposure [ˈʌnderɪksˈpəʊʒəʳ] N (*Phot*) subexposición *f*

underfed [ˈʌndəˈfed] ADJ subalimentado

underfeed [ˈʌndəˈfiːd] (*pt, pp* **underfed**) VT alimentar insuficientemente

underfeeding [ˈʌndəˈfiːdɪŋ] N subalimentación *f*

underfelt [ˈʌndəfelt] N arpillera *f*

underfinanced [ˌʌndəfaɪˈnænst] ADJ insuficientemente financiado

underfloor [ˈʌndəflɔːʳ] Ⓐ ADJ de debajo del suelo
Ⓑ CPD ► **underfloor heating** N calefacción *f* bajo el suelo

underfoot [ˈʌndəˈfʊt] ADV debajo de los pies; **it's wet ~** el suelo está mojado

underfund [ˌʌndəˈfʌnd] VT infradotar

underfunded [ˌʌndəˈfʌndɪd] ADJ infradotado

underfunding [ˌʌndəˈfʌndɪŋ] N infradotación *f*

undergarment [ˈʌndəˌgɑːmənt] N (*frm*) prenda *f* de ropa interior *or* (*LAm*) íntima; **undergarments** ropa *fsing* interior, ropa *fsing* íntima (*LAm*)

undergo [ˈʌndəˈgəʊ] (*pt* **underwent**; *pp* **undergone** [ˈʌndəˈgɒn]) VT sufrir, experimentar; [+ *treatment*] recibir; [+ *operation*] someterse a; **to ~ repairs** ser reparado

undergrad* [ˌʌndəˈgræd] ADJ, N = **undergraduate**

undergraduate [ˈʌndəˈgrædjʊɪt] Ⓐ N estudiante *mf* universitario/a
Ⓑ CPD [*student*] no licenciado; [*course*] para universitarios (no licenciados) ► **undergraduate humour** N humor *m* estudiantil

underground [ˈʌndəgraʊnd] Ⓐ ADJ [1] [*building, cave, mine*] subterráneo; **an ~ car park** un parking subterráneo
[2] (*fig*) [*newspaper, movement*] clandestino
[3] (= *alternative*) [*film, magazine, artist, culture*] underground *inv*
Ⓑ ADV [1] (= *under the ground*) bajo tierra; **moles live ~** los topos viven bajo tierra; **it's six feet ~** está a seis pies bajo tierra
[2] (*fig*) (= *into hiding*) **to go ~** (= *hide*) esconderse; (*Pol*) pasar a la clandestinidad
Ⓒ N [1] (*Brit*) (= *railway*) metro *m*, subterráneo *m* (*Arg*), subte *m* (*Arg**)
[2] (*Mil*) resistencia *f* clandestina; (*Pol*) movimiento *m* clandestino; (*Art*) arte *m* marginal *or* underground

undergrowth [ˈʌndəgrəʊθ] N maleza *f*, matorrales *mpl*

underhand [ˈʌndəhænd] Ⓐ ADJ [1] (= *dishonest*) [*person*] solapado; [*behaviour, deals, tactics*] turbio, poco limpio; **critics accuse the President of being ~** los críticos del presidente lo acusan de solapado
[2] (*Sport*) [*throw*] por debajo del hombro
Ⓑ ADV **to serve ~** sacar sin levantar el brazo por encima

underhanded ADJ [ˌʌndəˈhændɪd] = **underhand**

underhandedly [ˌʌndəˈhændɪdlɪ] ADV solapadamente

underinsure [ˌʌndərɪnˈʃʊəʳ] VT asegurar por debajo del valor real; **to be ~d** estar infraasegurado

underinvestment [ˌʌndərɪnˈvestmənt] N infrainversión *f*

underlay [ˈʌndəleɪ] N (*for carpet*) refuerzo *m*

underlie [ˌʌndəˈlaɪ] (*pt* **underlay** [ˌʌndəˈleɪ]; *pp* **underlain** [ˌʌndəˈleɪn]) VT [1] (= *lie under*) estar debajo de, extenderse debajo de
[2] (*fig*) sustentar

underline [ˌʌndəˈlaɪn] VT (*lit, fig*) subrayar

underling [ˈʌndəlɪŋ] N (*pej*) subordinado/a *m/f*, subalterno/a *m/f*

underlining [ˈʌndəˈlaɪnɪŋ] N subrayado *m*

underlip [ˈʌndəlɪp] N labio *m* inferior

underlying [ˈʌndəˈlaɪɪŋ] ADJ [1] (= *fundamental*) [*cause, theme*] subyacente; **the ~ problem is that …** el problema subyacente *or* de fondo es que …

2 [*rock, soil, bone*] subyacente
3 (*Econ*) [*rate, inflation, trend*] subyacente

undermanned [ˈʌndəˈmænd] ADJ **to be ~** no tener (el) personal suficiente

undermanning [ˌʌndəˈmænɪŋ] N falta *f* de personal *or* mano de obra suficiente

undermentioned [ˈʌndəˈmenʃənd] ADJ abajo citado

undermine [ˌʌndəˈmaɪn] VT (*fig*) minar, socavar; **his health is being ~d by overwork** el exceso de trabajo le está minando la salud

undermost [ˈʌndəməʊst] ADJ (el) más bajo

underneath [ˈʌndəˈniːθ] Ⓐ PREP (*position*) bajo, debajo de; **the noise came from ~ the table** el ruido salía de debajo de la mesa; **~ the carpet** debajo de la moqueta; **I walked ~ a ladder** pasé por debajo de una escalera
Ⓑ ADV debajo, por debajo; **I got out of the car and looked ~** bajé del coche y miré (por) debajo
Ⓒ N parte *f* de abajo, fondo *m*
Ⓓ ADJ inferior, de abajo

undernourish [ˌʌndəˈnʌrɪʃ] VT subalimentar, desnutrir

undernourished [ˈʌndəˈnʌrɪʃt] ADJ subalimentado, desnutrido

undernourishment [ˈʌndəˈnʌrɪʃmənt] N subalimentación *f*, desnutrición *f*

underpaid [ˈʌndəˈpeɪd] ADJ mal pagado; **teachers are ~** los profesores están mal pagados

underpants [ˈʌndəpænts] NPL calzoncillos *mpl*, calzones *mpl* (*LAm*); **a pair of ~** unos calzoncillos

underpart [ˈʌndəpɑːt] N parte *f* inferior

underpass [ˈʌndəpɑːs] N (*for cars*) paso *m* a desnivel; (*for pedestrians*) paso *m* subterráneo

underpay [ˈʌndəˈpeɪ] (*pt, pp* **underpaid**) VT pagar mal

underperform [ˌʌndəpəˈfɔːm] VI 1 (*St Ex*) comportarse mal, tener un mal comportamiento; **the stock has ~ed on the Brussels stock market** las acciones han tenido un mal comportamiento en la bolsa de Bruselas
2 (*at work, in school*) rendir poco

underpin [ˌʌndəˈpɪn] VT 1 (*Archit*) apuntalar
2 (*fig*) [+ *argument, case*] sustentar, respaldar

underpinning [ˌʌndəˈpɪnɪŋ] N (*Archit*) apuntalamiento *m*

underplay [ˈʌndəˈpleɪ] Ⓐ VT 1 (= *play down*) [+ *importance*] minimizar; [+ *issue*] quitar *or* restar importancia a
2 (*Theat*) **to ~ a part** hacer flojamente un papel
Ⓑ VI (*Theat*) hacer flojamente su papel, estar muy flojo en su papel

underpopulated [ˈʌndəˈpɒpjʊleɪtɪd] ADJ poco poblado, con baja densidad de población

underprice [ˈʌndəˈpraɪs] VT poner un precio demasiado bajo a; **at £10 this book is ~d** el precio de 10 libras es demasiado bajo para este libro

underpriced [ˈʌndəˈpraɪst] ADJ [*goods*] con un precio demasiado bajo

underpricing [ˈʌndəˈpraɪsɪŋ] N asignación *f* de precios demasiado bajos

underprivileged [ˈʌndəˈprɪvɪlɪdʒd] Ⓐ ADJ menos privilegiado, desfavorecido
Ⓑ NPL **the ~** los menos privilegiados, los desfavorecidos

underproduction [ˈʌndəprəˈdʌkʃən] N producción *f* insuficiente

underqualified [ˈʌndəˈkwɒlɪˌfaɪd] ADJ **to be ~** no estar suficientemente cualificado (**for** para)

➤ LANGUAGE IN USE: **understand A1** 12.1

underrate [ˌʌndəˈreɪt] VT [+ *strength, difficulty, person*] subestimar, menospreciar

underrated [ˌʌndəˈreɪtɪd] ADJ [*play, book, actor*] no debidamente valorado, infravalorado; **he's very ~** no se lo valora debidamente

underripe [ˈʌndəˈraɪp] ADJ poco maduro, verde

underscore [ˌʌndəˈskɔːʳ] VT subrayar, recalcar

undersea [ˈʌndəsiː] Ⓐ ADJ submarino
Ⓑ ADV bajo la superficie del mar

underseal [ˈʌndəsiːl] VT (*Brit*) impermeabilizar (*por debajo*), proteger contra la corrosión

undersealing [ˈʌndəsiːlɪŋ] N (*Brit*) impermeabilización *f* (*de los bajos*)

under-secretary [ˈʌndəˈsekrətərɪ] N subsecretario/a *m/f*

under-secretaryship [ˈʌndəˈsekrətərɪʃɪp] N subsecretaría *f*

undersell [ˈʌndəˈsel] (*pt, pp* **undersold**) VT 1 (= *undercut*) [+ *competitor*] vender a precio más bajo que
2 (*fig*) **to ~ o.s.** subestimarse, infravalorarse; **Burnley has been undersold as a tourist centre** no se ha hecho la debida publicidad de Burnley como centro turístico

undersexed [ˌʌndəˈsekst] ADJ de libido floja

undershirt [ˈʌndəʃɜːt] N (*US*) camiseta *f*

undershoot [ˌʌndəˈʃuːt] (*pt, pp* **undershot**) Ⓐ VT [+ *target*] no alcanzar, no llegar a; **to ~ the runway** (*Aer*) aterrizar antes de llegar a la pista
Ⓑ VI no alcanzar el blanco; **we have undershot by £80** nos faltan 80 libras para alcanzar el objetivo

undershorts [ˈʌndəˌʃɔːts] NPL (*US*) calzoncillos *mpl*, calzones *mpl* (*LAm*)

underside [ˈʌndəsaɪd] N parte *f* inferior

undersigned [ˈʌndəsaɪnd] ADJ (*Jur frm*) **the ~** el/la abajofirmante; **we, the ~** nosotros, los abajofirmantes

undersized [ˈʌndəˈsaɪzd] ADJ (= *too small*) demasiado pequeño

underskirt [ˈʌndəskɜːt] N (*Brit*) enaguas *fpl*

underslung [ˈʌndəslʌŋ] ADJ (*Aut*) colgante

undersoil [ˈʌndəˌsɔɪl] Ⓐ N subsuelo *m*
Ⓑ CPD ► **undersoil heating** N calefacción *f* subterránea

undersold [ˈʌndəˈsəʊld] PT, PP *of* **undersell**

underspend [ˌʌndəˈspend] VI gastar menos de lo previsto

understaffed [ˈʌndəˈstɑːft] ADJ **to be ~** no tener (el) personal suficiente, estar falto de personal

understaffing [ˈʌndəˈstɑːfɪŋ] N falta *f* de personal suficiente

▼**understand** [ˌʌndəˈstænd] (*pt, pp* **understood**) Ⓐ VT 1 (= *comprehend*) (*gen*) entender; (*more formal, esp complex issues*) comprender; **I can't ~ it!** ¡no lo entiendo!; **I can't ~ your writing** no entiendo tu letra; **that's what I can't ~** eso es lo que no logro entender *or* comprender; **that is easily understood** eso se entiende fácilmente; **I don't want to hear another word about it, (is that) understood?** no quiero que se hable más del tema, ¿entendido *or* comprendido?; **the process is still not fully understood** el proceso todavía no se comprende *or* entiende del todo; **doctors are still trying to ~ the disease** los médicos siguen intentando comprender la enfermedad; **it must be understood that ...** debe entenderse que ...; **you must ~ that we're very busy** debes entender *or* comprender que estamos muy ocupados; **to ~ how/why** entender *or* comprender cómo/por qué
2 (= *follow, interpret*) entender; **did I ~ you correctly?** ¿te entendí bien?; **to make o.s. understood** hacerse entender; **he was trying to make himself understood** estaba intentando hacerse entender; **do I make myself understood?** ¿queda claro?
3 (= *empathize with*) [+ *person, point of view, attitude*] comprender, entender; **his wife doesn't ~ him** su mujer no le comprende *or* entiende; **she ~s children** comprende *or* entiende a los niños; **we ~ one another** nos comprendemos *or* entendemos; **I (fully) ~ your position** comprendo *or* entiendo (totalmente) su posición; **I quite ~ that you don't want to come** me hago cargo de que no quieres venir
4 (= *know*) [+ *language*] entender; **he can't ~ a word of Spanish** no entiende ni una palabra de español
5 (= *believe*) tener entendido; **I ~ you have been absent** tengo entendido que usted ha estado ausente; **as I ~ it, he's trying to set up a meeting** según tengo entendido *or* según creo está intentando convocar una reunión; **it's understood that he had a heart attack** se piensa *or* cree que sufrió un infarto; **am I to ~ that ...?** ¿debo entender que ...?; **we confirm our reservation and we ~ (that) the rental will be 500 euros** confirmamos nuestra reserva y entendemos que el alquiler será de 500 euros; **to give sb to ~ that** dar a algn a entender que; **we were given to ~ that ...** se nos dio a entender que ...; **it was understood that he would pay for it** se dio por sentado que él lo pagaría; **he let it be understood that ...** dio a entender que ...
Ⓑ VI 1 (= *comprehend*) entender; (*more emphatic*) comprender; **do you ~?** ¿entiendes *or* comprendes?; **now I ~!** ¡ahora entiendo!, ¡ahora comprendo!; **there's to be no noise, (do you) ~?** que no haya ruido, ¿entiendes *or* comprendes?
2 (= *believe*) **she was, I ~, a Catholic** según tengo entendido era católica
3 (= *accept sb's position*) entender; (*esp in more complex situation*) comprender; **he'll ~** lo entenderá *or* comprenderá; **don't worry, I quite ~** no te preocupes, lo entiendo *or* comprendo perfectamente

understandable [ˌʌndəˈstændəbl] ADJ 1 (= *comprehensible*) [*theory, statement*] comprensible; **he writes in a simple and ~ way** escribe de una forma simple y comprensible
2 (= *natural*) [*reaction, feeling*] comprensible; **an ~ desire to do sth** un deseo comprensible de hacer algo; **"his car broke down and he was late for work" — "well, that's ~"** —se le averió el coche y llegó tarde al trabajo —bueno, eso es comprensible; **it is ~ that ...** se comprende que ...; **it is very ~ that ...** se comprende perfectamente que ...

understandably [ˌʌndəˈstændəblɪ] ADV 1 (= *intelligibly*) [*speak, explain*] de manera clara *or* comprensible
2 (= *naturally*) **~, he was very upset** tenía un disgusto muy grande, y era comprensible; **he's ~ reluctant to talk about the affair** se muestra reacio a hablar del asunto, y es comprensible

understanding [ˌʌndəˈstændɪŋ] Ⓐ ADJ [*person*] comprensivo; [*smile*] de comprensión; **to be ~ about sth** ser comprensivo (respecto a algo); **she was very ~ about it** fue muy comprensiva
Ⓑ N 1 (= *faculty*) entendimiento *m*; **it was beyond my ~** iba más allá de mi entendimiento; **the peace that passeth all ~** (*Bible*) la paz que sobrepasa a todo entendimiento

2 [*of sth*] (= *comprehension*) comprensión *f*; (= *awareness*) conciencia *f*; **we need to test children's ~ of facts** hay que poner a prueba la comprensión que los niños tienen de los hechos; **our ~ of these processes is still poor** todavía no comprendemos muy bien estos procesos; **a basic ~ of computers is essential** se necesitan unos conocimientos básicos de informática; **to have a better** *or* **greater ~ of sth** (= *comprehend better*) entender *or* comprender mejor algo; (= *be more aware of*) tener mayor *or* más conciencia de algo; **to have little/no ~ of sth** saber muy poco/nada de algo; **a shift in public ~ of the issues of crime and punishment** un cambio de la conciencia pública con respecto a la cuestión de los crímenes y los castigos

3 (= *interpretation*) interpretación *f*; **what's your ~ of the Prime Minister's statement?** ¿cómo interpreta usted la declaración del Primer Ministro?, ¿cuál es su interpretación de la declaración del Primer Ministro?; **that's my ~ of the situation** esa es mi interpretación de la situación, así es como veo *or* interpreto la situación

4 (= *sympathy*) comprensión *f*; **thank you for your kindness and ~** le agradezco su amabilidad y comprensión; **to show no/little ~ of sth** no mostrar comprensión/mostrar muy poca comprensión hacia algo

5 (= *belief*) **it was my ~ that ...** ◊ **my ~ was that ...** tenía entendido que ..., según yo creía ...

6 (= *agreement*) acuerdo *m*; **to come to an ~ (with sb)** llegar a un acuerdo (con algn); **to have an ~ (with sb)** tener un acuerdo (con algn); **on the ~ that** a condición de que + *subjun*; **on the ~ that he pays** a condición de que pague; **to reach an ~ (with sb)** llegar a un acuerdo (con algn)

understandingly [ˌʌndəˈstændɪŋlɪ] ADV con comprensión, de manera comprensiva

understate [ˈʌndəˈsteɪt] VT 1 (= *underestimate*) [+ *rate, level, growth*] subestimar; **these estimates ~ the size of the problem** estos pronósticos subestiman las dimensiones del problema

2 (= *underplay*) quitar importancia a; **the authorities originally ~d the disaster** las autoridades inicialmente quitaron importancia al desastre; **to describe it as a triumph is to ~ the orchestra's achievement** describirlo como un triunfo es no dar su merecida importancia a lo que ha logrado la orquesta

understated [ˌʌndəˈsteɪtɪd] ADJ [*style, clothes, elegance*] sencillo, discreto; [*writing, manner*] sencillo; [*performance, acting*] comedido

understatement [ˈʌndəˌsteɪtmənt] N 1 (= *underestimate*) [*of rate, level, growth*] subestimación *f*; **these figures are an ~** estas cifras son una subestimación

2 (= *not exaggeration*) **I think that's something of an ~** creo que eso es quedarse corto; **to say I'm disappointed is an ~** decir que estoy desilusionado es quedarse corto; **interesting? that's the ~ of the year!** ¿interesante? ¡eso es quedarse corto!

3 (= *restraint*) moderación *f*; **typical British ~** la típica moderación británica, el típico comedimiento británico (*frm*)

understood [ˌʌndəˈstʊd] PT, PP *of* **understand**

understorey [ˈʌndəˌstɔːrɪ] N monte *m* bajo

understudy [ˈʌndəˌstʌdɪ] Ⓐ N suplente *mf*
Ⓑ VT prepararse para suplir a

undersubscribed [ˈʌndəsəbˈskraɪbd] ADJ 1 [*course*] que tiene plazas libres *or* vacantes

2 (*St Ex*) **there is the possibility that the share issue will be ~** existe la posibilidad de que no se coloquen todas las acciones de la emisión

undertake [ˌʌndəˈteɪk] (*pt* **undertook**; *pp* **undertaken** [ˌʌndəˈteɪkən]) Ⓐ VT [+ *task*] emprender; [+ *responsibility*] asumir; **to ~ to do sth** comprometerse a hacer algo; **to ~ that ...** comprometerse a que ...
Ⓑ VT (*Brit Aut**) adelantar por el lado contrario *or* el carril indebido
Ⓒ VI (*Brit Aut**) adelantar por el lado contrario *or* el carril indebido

undertaker [ˈʌndəˌteɪkəʳ] N (= *director*) director(a) *m/f* de funeraria *or* pompas fúnebres; (= *employee*) empleado/a *m/f* de una funeraria; **the ~'s** la funeraria

undertaking [ˌʌndəˈteɪkɪŋ] N 1 (= *enterprise*) empresa *f*; (= *task*) tarea *f*

2 (= *pledge*) garantía *f*; **to give an ~ that ...** garantizar que ...; **I can give no such ~** no puedo garantizar tal cosa, no puedo prometer eso

3 [ˈʌndəˌteɪkɪŋ] (*Brit Aut**) adelantamiento *m* por el lado contrario *or* el carril indebido

4 [ˈʌndəˌteɪkɪŋ] (*Brit*) (= *arranging funerals*) pompas *fpl* fúnebres

under-the-counter* [ˌʌndəðəˈkaʊntəʳ] ADJ [*goods etc*] adquirido por la trastienda*; [*deal*] turbio, poco limpio

underthings* [ˈʌndəθɪŋz] NPL paños *mpl* menores; **to be in one's ~** estar en paños menores

undertone [ˈʌndətəʊn] N 1 (= *low voice*) voz *f* baja

2 (= *suggestion, hint*) matiz *m*; [*of criticism*] trasfondo *m*

3 [*of perfume, taste, colour*] matiz *m*

undertook [ˌʌndəˈtʊk] PT *of* **undertake**

undertow [ˈʌndətəʊ] N resaca *f*

underuse Ⓐ [ˌʌndəˈjuːs] N infrautilización *f*
Ⓑ [ˌʌndəˈjuːz] VT infrautilizar

underused [ˌʌndəˈjuːzd] ADJ infrautilizado

underutilization [ˌʌndəˈjuːtəlaɪzeɪʃən] N infrautilización *f*

underutilize [ˌʌndəˈjuːtɪlaɪz] VT infrautilizar

underutilized [ˌʌndəˈjuːtəlaɪzd] ADJ infrautilizado

undervalue [ˈʌndəˈvæljuː] VT 1 (*Comm*) [+ *goods*] valorizar por debajo de su precio

2 (*fig*) subestimar; **he has been ~d as a writer** como escritor no se lo ha valorado debidamente

underwater [ˈʌndəˈwɔːtəʳ] Ⓐ ADJ submarino
Ⓑ ADV debajo del agua; **he swam ~ for several strokes before he surfaced** nadó varias brazas debajo del agua *or* bajo el agua antes de salir a la superficie; **this sequence was filmed ~** esta secuencia se filmó bajo el agua; **to stay ~** permanecer sumergido, permanecer bajo el agua
Ⓒ CPD [*exploration, fishing*] submarino; [*archaeology, photography*] submarino, subacuático ► **underwater camera** N cámara *f* subacuática ► **underwater fisherman** N submarinista *mf*

underway [ˌʌndəˈweɪ] ADJ *see* **way A14**

underwear [ˈʌndəweəʳ] N ropa *f* interior, ropa *f* íntima (*LAm*)

underweight [ˌʌndəˈweɪt] ADJ de peso insuficiente; **to be ~** [*person*] pesar menos de lo debido; **she's 20lb ~** pesa 20 libras menos de lo que debiera

underwent [ˌʌndəˈwent] PT *of* **undergo**

underwhelm* [ˌʌndəˈwelm] VT (*hum*) impresionar muy poco; **this left us somewhat ~ed** eso apenas nos impresionó

underwhelming* [ˌʌndəˈwelmɪŋ] ADJ (*hum*) [*response, applause*] poco entusiasta; [*results, performance*] poco satisfactorio

underworld [ˈʌndəwɜːld] Ⓐ N 1 (= *hell*) **the ~** el infierno

2 (*criminal*) **the ~** el hampa
Ⓑ ADJ 1 (= *Hadian*) infernal

2 (= *criminal*) [*organization*] delictivo; [*personality*] del mundo del hampa; [*connections*] con el hampa

underwrite [ˈʌndəraɪt] (*pt* **underwrote**; *pp* **underwritten**) VT 1 (*Insurance*) asegurar (contra riesgos); (*on 2nd insurance*) reasegurar; (*Fin*) subscribir

2 (= *support*) aprobar, respaldar

underwriter [ˈʌndəˌraɪtəʳ] N (*Insurance*) asegurador(a) *m/f*, reasegurador(a) *m/f*

underwritten [ˈʌndəˌrɪtn] PP *of* **underwrite**

underwrote [ˈʌndərəʊt] PT *of* **underwrite**

undeserved [ˈʌndɪˈzɜːvd] ADJ inmerecido

undeservedly [ˈʌndɪˈzɜːvɪdlɪ] ADV inmerecidamente

undeserving [ˈʌndɪˈzɜːvɪŋ] ADJ [*person*] de poco mérito; [*cause*] poco meritorio; **to be ~ of sth** no ser digno de algo, no merecer algo

undesirable [ˈʌndɪˈzaɪərəbl] Ⓐ ADJ indeseable; **it is ~ that** no es recomendable que + *subjun*, es poco aconsejable que + *subjun*
Ⓑ N indeseable *mf*

undetected [ˈʌndɪˈtektɪd] ADJ no descubierto; **to go ~** pasar inadvertido

undetermined [ˈʌndɪˈtɜːmɪnd] ADJ (= *unknown*) indeterminado; (= *uncertain*) incierto

undeterred [ˈʌndɪˈtɜːd] ADJ **he was ~ by ...** no se dejó intimidar por ...; **he carried on ~** siguió sin inmutarse

undeveloped [ˈʌndɪˈveləpt] ADJ 1 [*country, nation*] no desarrollado; [*land, area, resources*] sin explotar

2 (= *immature*) [*person*] sin desarrollar

3 [*film*] sin revelar

undeviating [ʌnˈdiːvɪeɪtɪŋ] ADJ directo, constante; **to follow an ~ path** seguir un curso recto

undeviatingly [ʌnˈdiːvɪeɪtɪŋlɪ] ADV directamente, constantemente; **to hold ~ to one's course** seguir su curso sin apartarse en absoluto de él

undiagnosed [ʌnˈdaɪəgˌnəʊzd] ADJ sin diagnosticar

undid [ˌʌnˈdɪd] PT *of* **undo**

undies* [ˈʌndɪz] NPL ropa *fsing* interior, ropa *fsing* íntima (*LAm*)

undigested [ˈʌndaɪˈdʒestɪd] ADJ indigesto

undignified [ʌnˈdɪgnɪfaɪd] ADJ [*behaviour*] indecoroso, poco digno; [*posture, position*] indecoroso; [*person*] poco digno

undiluted [ˈʌndaɪˈluːtɪd] ADJ 1 (*lit*) [*fruit juice, chemical*] sin diluir, puro

2 (*fig*) [*pleasure, accent*] puro

undiminished [ˈʌndɪˈmɪnɪʃt] ADJ no disminuido

undimmed [ˈʌnˈdɪmd] ADJ (*fig*) no empañado

undiplomatic [ˈʌnˌdɪpləˈmætɪk] ADJ poco diplomático

undiscernible [ˈʌndɪˈsɜːnəbl] ADJ imperceptible

undiscerning [ˈʌndɪˈsɜːnɪŋ] ADJ sin criterio, sin discernimiento

undischarged [ˈʌndɪsˈtʃɑːdʒd] Ⓐ ADJ [*debt*] impagado, por pagar; [*promise*] no cumplido
Ⓑ CPD ► **undischarged bankrupt** N (*Brit*) quebrado/a *m/f* no rehabilitado/a, persona *f* que sigue en estado de quiebra

undisciplined [ʌnˈdɪsɪplɪnd] ADJ indisciplinado

undisclosed [ˈʌndɪsˈkləʊzd] ADJ no revelado, sin revelar

undiscovered [ˈʌndɪsˈkʌvəd] ADJ 1 (= *undetected*) [*treasure, country*] sin descubrir, no descubierto; [*planet*] no descubierto; **to lie ~** estar sin descubrir; **to remain ~** estar *or* permanecer sin ser descubierto; **he remained ~ for three days** estuvo *or* permaneció tres días sin ser descubierto
2 (= *unknown*) desconocido

undiscriminating [ˈʌndɪsˈkrɪmɪneɪtɪŋ] ADJ sin discernimiento

undisguised [ˈʌndɪsˈgaɪzd] ADJ 1 (= *with no disguise*) sin disfraz
2 (*fig*) [*pleasure, relief, hostility*] manifiesto, indisimulado; **an ~ attempt to do sth** un intento manifiesto de hacer algo

undismayed [ˈʌndɪsˈmeɪd] ADJ impávido; **he was ~ by this** no se dejó desanimar por esto; **... he said ~** ... dijo sin inmutarse

undisposed-of [ˈʌndɪsˈpəʊzdɒv] ADJ (*Comm*) no vendido

undisputed [ˈʌndɪsˈpjuːtɪd] ADJ 1 (= *irrefutable*) [*fact, authority*] innegable; **to have the ~ right to do sth** tener el derecho innegable de hacer algo
2 (= *unchallenged*) [*champion, leader*] indiscutible; **the ~ queen of fashion** la reina indiscutible de la moda

undistinguished [ˈʌndɪsˈtɪŋgwɪʃt] ADJ mediocre

undistributed [ˌʌndɪsˈtrɪbjʊtɪd] Ⓐ ADJ [*mail*] sin repartir
Ⓑ CPD ► **undistributed profit** N beneficios *mpl* no distribuidos

undisturbed [ˈʌndɪsˈtɜːbd] Ⓐ ADJ 1 (= *untouched*) tranquilo; **to leave sth ~** dejar algo como está
2 (= *uninterrupted*) [*sleep*] ininterrumpido; [*person*] **you need a quiet place where you will be ~** necesitas un lugar tranquilo donde no se te moleste; **he likes to be left ~** no le gusta que se le interrumpa, no quiere que le interrumpan las visitas *or* llamadas
3 (= *unconcerned*) **to be ~** no dejarse perturbar *or* (*LAm*) alterar; **he was ~ by this** no se dejó perturbar *or* (*LAm*) alterar por ello
Ⓑ ADV [*work, play, sleep*] sin ser molestado; **he went on with his work ~** continuó su trabajo sin interrupciones

undivided [ˈʌndɪˈvaɪdɪd] ADJ 1 (= *wholehearted*) [*admiration*] sin reservas; **I want your ~ attention** quiero que me prestes toda tu atención
2 (= *not split*) [*country, institution*] íntegro, entero

undo [ˈʌnˈduː] (*pt* **undid**; *pp* **undone**) VT 1 (= *unfasten*) [+ *button, blouse*] desabrochar; [+ *knot, parcel, shoe laces*] desatar; [+ *zipper*] abrir; (= *take to pieces*) desarmar
2 (= *reverse*) deshacer; [+ *damage etc*] reparar; [+ *arrangement etc*] anular
3 (*Comput*) [+ *command*] cancelar

undocumented [ʌnˈdɒkjʊmentɪd] ADJ 1 [*event*] indocumentado
2 (*US*) [*person*] indocumentado

undoing [ˈʌnˈduːɪŋ] N ruina *f*, perdición *f*; **that was his ~** aquello fue su ruina *or* perdición

undomesticated [ˈʌndəˈmestɪkeɪtɪd] ADJ indomado, no domesticado

undone [ˈʌnˈdʌn] Ⓐ PP of **undo**
Ⓑ ADJ 1 (= *unfastened*) [*clasp, blouse*] desabrochado; [*zip, flies*] abierto; [*tie, shoelace, knot*] desatado; [*hair*] despeinado; **to come ~** [*button*] desabrocharse; [*parcel*] desatarse
2 (= *not yet done*) por hacer; **his desk was piled with work as yet ~** su escritorio estaba amontonado de trabajo por hacer; **to leave sth ~** dejar algo sin hacer
3 (= *cancelled out*) deshecho; **she has seen her life's work ~** ha visto el trabajo de toda su vida deshecho; **~ by ambition** destrozado por la ambición
4 († *liter*) (= *ruined*) **I am ~!** ¡estoy perdido!, ¡es mi ruina!

undoubted [ʌnˈdaʊtɪd] ADJ indudable

undoubtedly [ʌnˈdaʊtɪdlɪ] ADV indudablemente, sin duda; **he is ~ the best man for the job** es sin duda alguna el mejor para el trabajo

undreamed-of [ʌnˈdriːmdɒv] ADJ, **undreamt-of** [ʌnˈdremtɒv] (*Brit*) ADJ inimaginable, nunca soñado

undress [ˈʌnˈdres] Ⓐ VT desnudar, desvestir (*LAm*); **to get ~ed** desnudarse, desvestirse (*LAm*)
Ⓑ VI desnudarse, desvestirse (*LAm*); **the doctor told me to ~** el médico me dijo que me desnudase
Ⓒ N 1 **in a state of ~** desnudo
2 (*Mil*) uniforme *m* (de diario)

undressed [ʌnˈdrest] ADJ 1 (= *naked*) [*person*] desnudo
2 [*hide*] sin adobar, sin curtir
3 [*salad etc*] sin salsa
4 [*wound*] sin vendar

undrinkable [ˈʌnˈdrɪŋkəbl] ADJ (= *unpalatable*) imbebible; (= *poisonous*) no potable

undue [ˈʌnˈdjuː] ADJ indebido, excesivo

undulate [ˈʌndjʊleɪt] VI ondular, ondear

undulating [ˈʌndjʊleɪtɪŋ] ADJ ondulante, ondeante; [*land*] ondulado

undulation [ˌʌndjʊˈleɪʃən] N ondulación *f*

undulatory [ˈʌndjʊlətərɪ] ADJ ondulatorio

unduly [ˈʌnˈdjuːlɪ] ADV (= *excessively*) excesivamente; **we are not ~ worried** no estamos demasiado preocupados

undying [ʌnˈdaɪɪŋ] ADJ (*fig*) imperecedero, inmarcesible

unearned [ˈʌnˈɜːnd] Ⓐ ADJ no ganado
Ⓑ CPD ► **unearned income** N renta *f* (no salarial) ► **unearned increment** N plusvalía *f*

unearth [ˈʌnˈɜːθ] VT 1 (= *dig up*) desenterrar
2 (= *uncover*) (*fig*) desenterrar, descubrir

unearthly [ʌnˈɜːθlɪ] ADJ 1 (= *otherworldly*) [*light, sound*] sobrenatural; [*beauty*] sobrenatural, de otro mundo
2 (*) (= *ungodly*) [*noise*] tremendo*; **at some ~ hour** a unas horas intempestivas; **do you still get up at that ~ hour?** ¿todavía te levantas a esas horas (tan intempestivas)?

unease [ʌnˈiːz] N (= *tension*) malestar *m*; (= *apprehension*) inquietud *f*, desasosiego *m*

uneasily [ʌnˈiːzɪlɪ] ADV [*look, say*] con inquietud, inquietamente; **I noted ~ that ...** noté con inquietud que ...; **he shifted ~ in his chair** se removió inquieto en su silla; **she laughed ~** se rió nerviosa

uneasiness [ʌnˈiːzɪnɪs] N inquietud *f*, desasosiego *m*

uneasy [ʌnˈiːzɪ] ADJ 1 (= *worried*) inquieto; (= *ill at ease*) incómodo, molesto; **people are ~ about their future** la gente está preocupada por el futuro; **I felt ~ about doing it on my own** me inquietaba la idea de hacerlo solo; **to become ~ (about sth)** empezar a inquietarse (por algo); **to make sb ~** dejar a algn intranquilo, inquietar a algn
2 (= *uncomfortable*) [*conscience*] intranquilo; [*silence*] incómodo
3 (= *fragile*) [*peace, truce, alliance*] frágil, precario
4 (= *restless*) [*sleep*] agitado; [*night*] intranquilo

uneatable [ˈʌnˈiːtəbl] ADJ incomible, que no se puede comer

uneaten [ˈʌnˈiːtn] ADJ sin comer, sin probar

uneconomic [ˈʌnˌiːkəˈnɒmɪk] ADJ [*business, factory*] poco rentable, no económico; **it's ~ to put on courses for so few students** no es rentable organizar cursos para tan pocos alumnos

uneconomical [ˈʌnˌiːkəˈnɒmɪkəl] ADJ antieconómico, poco económico

unedifying [ˈʌnˈedɪfaɪɪŋ] ADJ indecoroso, poco edificante

unedited [ʌnˈedɪtɪd] ADJ inédito

uneducated [ˈʌnˈedjʊkeɪtɪd] ADJ inculto, ignorante

unemotional [ˈʌnɪˈməʊʃənl] ADJ (*gen*) impasible, insensible; [*account*] objetivo

unemotionally [ˈʌnɪˈməʊʃnəlɪ] ADV **to look on ~** mirar impasible, mirar sin dejarse afectar

unemployable [ˈʌnɪmˈplɔɪəbl] ADJ inútil para el trabajo

unemployed [ˈʌnɪmˈplɔɪd] Ⓐ ADJ 1 [*person*] parado, en paro, desempleado (*LAm*), cesante (*Chile*); **he's been ~ for a year** lleva parado un año
2 [*capital etc*] sin utilizar, no utilizado
Ⓑ NPL **the ~** los parados, los desempleados (*LAm*)

unemployment [ˈʌnɪmˈplɔɪmənt] Ⓐ N paro *m*, desempleo *m*, cesantía *f* (*Chile*)
Ⓑ CPD ► **unemployment benefit** N (*Brit*) subsidio *m* de paro *or* desempleo ► **unemployment figures** NPL cifras *fpl* del paro ► **unemployment line** N (*US*) fila *f* de parados, cola *f* del paro

unencumbered [ˈʌnɪnˈkʌmbəd] ADJ suelto, sin trabas; [*estate etc*] libre de gravamen; **~ by** sin el estorbo de

unending [ʌnˈendɪŋ] ADJ interminable, sin fin

unendurable [ˈʌnɪnˈdjʊərəbl] ADJ inaguantable, insoportable

unengaged [ˈʌnɪnˈgeɪdʒd] ADJ libre

un-English [ˈʌnˈɪŋglɪʃ] ADJ poco inglés

unenlightened [ˈʌnɪnˈlaɪtnd] ADJ [*person, age*] poco instruido; [*policy etc*] poco ilustrado

unenterprising [ˈʌnˈentəpraɪzɪŋ] ADJ [*person*] poco emprendedor, falto de iniciativa; [*character, policy, act*] tímido

unenthusiastic [ˈʌnɪnˌθuːzɪˈæstɪk] ADJ poco entusiasta; **everybody seemed rather ~ about it** nadie se mostró mayormente entusiasmado con la idea

unenthusiastically [ˈʌnɪnˌθuːzɪˈæstɪkəlɪ] ADV sin entusiasmo

unenviable [ˈʌnˈenvɪəbl] ADJ poco envidiable

unequal [ˈʌnˈiːkwəl] ADJ 1 (= *unfair*) desigual; **the ~ distribution of wealth** la distribución desigual de la riqueza
2 (= *differing*) [*size, length*] distinto; **her feet are of ~ sizes** tiene los pies de distinto tamaño
3 (= *inadequate*) **to be ~ to a task** no estar a la altura de una tarea

unequalled, unequaled (*US*) [ˈʌnˈiːkwəld] ADJ inigualado, sin par; **a record ~ by anybody** un historial inigualado *or* sin par

unequally [ˈʌnˈiːkwəlɪ] ADV desigualmente

unequivocal [ˈʌnɪˈkwɪvəkəl] ADJ (= *unmistakeable*) [*response, message, proof*] inequívoco, claro; [*support*] incondicional; [*opposition*] rotundo; **to be ~ in one's support of sth** apoyar algo incondicionalmente

unequivocally ['ʌnɪ'kwɪvəkəlɪ] ADV inequívocamente, de manera inequívoca; **they stated ~ that his heart disease began in childhood** manifestaron inequívocamente *or* de manera inequívoca que ha venido padeciendo del corazón desde la infancia; **the Minister has ~ rejected the idea** el ministro ha rechazado rotundamente la idea; **let's make it ~ clear that we support the president** dejemos bien claro que apoyamos al presidente

unerring ['ʌn'ɜːrɪŋ] ADJ infalible

UNESCO [juː'neskəʊ] N ABBR (= **United Nations Educational, Scientific and Cultural Organization**) UNESCO *f*

unescorted [,ʌnɪs'kɔːtɪd] ADJ [1] (*Mil, Naut*) sin escolta
[2] (= *unaccompanied by a partner*) sin compañía, sin compañero/a

unessential ['ʌnɪ'senʃəl] Ⓐ ADJ no esencial
Ⓑ NPL **the ~s** las cosas *or* los aspectos no esenciales

unesthetic [,ʌniːs'θetɪk] ADJ (*US*) antiestético

unethical ['ʌn'eθɪkəl] ADJ poco ético

uneven ['ʌn'iːvən] ADJ [1] (= *not flat or straight*) [*surface, wall, road*] desigual, irregular; [*teeth*] desigual
[2] (= *irregular*) [*breathing, rate*] irregular; **it was an ~ performance** fue una actuación irregular
[3] (= *unfair*) [*distribution*] desigual, poco equitativo; [*contest*] desigual; **the ~ distribution of aid** la distribución desigual *or* poco equitativa de las ayudas

unevenly ['ʌn'iːvənlɪ] ADV [1] (*lit*) desigualmente, irregularmente; **she had cut his hair ~** se le había cortado el pelo de forma desigual; **apply the paint ~ in broad strokes** aplique la pintura a brochazos desiguales *or* irregulares; **microwaves heat food ~** las microondas no calientan todo el alimento por igual
[2] (= *unfairly*) de manera poco equitativa; **the country's new wealth was ~ distributed** la nueva riqueza del país estaba distribuida de manera poco equitativa

unevenness ['ʌn'iːvənnɪs] N [*of surface*] desigualdad *f*, irregularidad *f*; [*of breathing*] irregularidad *f*; (= *unfairness*) [*of distribution*] desigualdad *f*; [*of contest*] lo desigual

uneventful ['ʌnɪ'ventfʊl] ADJ sin incidentes

uneventfully ['ʌnɪ'ventfʊlɪ] ADV **the days passed ~** los días pasaban sin pena ni gloria; **the race progressed ~ until the fifth lap** la carrera transcurrió sin incidentes hasta la quinta vuelta

unexampled ['ʌnɪg'zɑːmpld] ADJ sin igual, sin precedente

unexceptionable [,ʌnɪk'sepʃnəbl] ADJ intachable, irreprochable

unexceptional [,ʌnɪk'sepʃənl] ADJ sin nada de extraordinario, común y corriente

unexciting ['ʌnɪk'saɪtɪŋ] ADJ sin interés

unexpected ['ʌnɪks'pektɪd] ADJ [*death, arrival, appearance, visit*] inesperado, repentino; [*victory, success*] inesperado; [*problem, expense*] inesperado, imprevisto; **they turn up in the most ~ places** aparecen en los lugares más insospechados; **his arrival was an ~ bonus for the fans** su llegada fue un regalo inesperado para los fans; **it was all very ~** fue todo muy inesperado

unexpectedly ['ʌnɪks'pektɪdlɪ] ADV [*arrive*] de improviso, sin avisar; [*happen*] inesperadamente, de repente; [*die*] repentinamente, inesperadamente; **there was an ~ high turnout of voters** se produjo una asistencia de votantes inesperadamente alta; **not ~, he failed** como era de esperar, suspendió

unexpended ['ʌnɪks'pendɪd] ADJ no gastado

unexpired ['ʌnɪks'paɪəd] ADJ [*bill*] no vencido; [*lease, ticket*] no caducado

unexplained ['ʌnɪks'pleɪnd] ADJ inexplicado

unexploded ['ʌnɪks'pləʊdɪd] ADJ sin explotar

unexploited ['ʌnɪks'plɔɪtɪd] ADJ inexplotado, sin explotar

unexplored ['ʌnɪks'plɔːd] ADJ inexplorado

unexposed ['ʌnɪks'pəʊzd] ADJ no descubierto; (*Phot*) inexpuesto

unexpressed ['ʌnɪks'prest] ADJ no expresado, tácito

unexpressive ['ʌnɪks'presɪv] ADJ inexpresivo

unexpurgated ['ʌn'ekspɜːgeɪtɪd] ADJ sin expurgar, íntegro

unfading [ʌn'feɪdɪŋ] ADJ (*fig*) inmarcesible, imperecedero

unfailing [ʌn'feɪlɪŋ] ADJ (*gen*) indefectible, infalible; [*supply*] inagotable

unfailingly [ʌn'feɪlɪŋlɪ] ADV **to be ~ courteous** ser siempre cortés, no faltar en ningún momento a la cortesía

▼ **unfair** ['ʌn'fɛəʳ] Ⓐ ADJ (*compar* **unfairer**; *superl* **unfairest**) [*system, treatment, decision*] injusto; [*comment, criticism*] injusto, improcedente; [*play*] sucio; [*tactics, practice, methods*] antirreglamentario; [*competition*] desleal; **you're being ~** estás siendo injusto; **how ~!** ¡no hay derecho!; **it's ~ to expect her to do that** no es justo *or* es injusto esperar que ella haga eso; **it's ~ on those who have paid** es injusto para los que han pagado; **to be ~ to sb** ser injusto con algn, no ser justo con algn
Ⓑ CPD ► **unfair dismissal** N despido *m* improcedente, despido *m* injustificado

unfairly ['ʌn'fɛəlɪ] ADV [*treat, dismiss, judge, penalize*] injustamente; [*compete*] deslealmente

unfairness ['ʌn'fɛənɪs] N injusticia *f*

unfaithful ['ʌn'feɪθfʊl] ADJ infiel (**to** a)

unfaithfulness ['ʌn'feɪθfʊlnɪs] N infidelidad *f*

unfaltering [ʌn'fɔːltərɪŋ] ADJ resuelto, firme

unfalteringly [ʌn'fɔːltərɪŋlɪ] ADV resueltamente, firmemente

unfamiliar ['ʌnfə'mɪlɪəʳ] ADJ desconocido, extraño; **I heard an ~ voice** oí una voz desconocida *or* extraña; **to be ~ with sth** no estar familiarizado con algo

unfamiliarity ['ʌnfə,mɪlɪ'ærɪtɪ] N falta *f* de familiaridad

unfashionable ['ʌn'fæʃnəbl] ADJ pasado de moda; **it is now ~ to talk of …** no está de moda ahora hablar de …

unfasten ['ʌn'fɑːsn] VT [+ *button etc*] desabrochar; [+ *rope etc*] desatar, aflojar (*LAm*); [+ *door*] abrir

unfathomable [ʌn'fæðəməbl] ADJ insondable

unfathomed ['ʌn'fæðəmd] ADJ no sondado

unfavourable, **unfavorable** (*US*) ['ʌn'feɪvərəbl] ADJ [1] (= *adverse*) [*situation*] adverso; [*conditions*] poco propicio, desfavorable; [*outlook, weather*] poco propicio; [*wind*] desfavorable; **to be ~ for sth** ser poco propicio para algo, no ser propicio para algo; **to be ~ to sb** no favorecer a algn, ser desfavorable para algn
[2] (= *negative*) [*impression, opinion*] negativo, malo; [*comparison*] poco favorable; **to show sth/sb in an ~ light** presentar algo/a algn de forma negativa *or* poco favorable, dar una imagen negativa *or* poco favorable de algo/algn

unfavourably, **unfavorably** (*US*) ['ʌn'feɪvərəblɪ] ADV [*react, impress*] de forma negativa; **he reviewed your book very ~** hizo una crítica muy negativa de tu libro; **she commented ~ on the way he was dressed** hizo comentarios desfavorables sobre la forma en que iba vestido; **he was compared ~ with his predecessors** se lo comparó desfavorablemente con sus predecesores; **to regard sth ~** no tener una opinión muy favorable *or* buena de algo

unfazed* ['ʌn'feɪzd] ADJ (*esp US*) **her criticism left him quite ~** sus críticas le dejaban tan pancho*; **she was completely ~ by the extraordinary events** se quedó como si nada ante unos sucesos tan extraordinarios

unfeasible [ʌn'fiːzɪbl] ADJ no factible, inviable

unfeeling [ʌn'fiːlɪŋ] ADJ insensible

unfeelingly [ʌn'fiːlɪŋlɪ] ADV insensiblemente

unfeigned [ʌn'feɪnd] ADJ no fingido, verdadero

unfeignedly [ʌn'feɪnɪdlɪ] ADV sin fingimiento, verdaderamente

unfeminine [ʌn'femɪnɪn] ADJ poco femenino

unfermented ['ʌnfə'mentɪd] ADJ no fermentado

unfettered ['ʌn'fetəd] ADJ sin trabas

unfilled ['ʌn'fɪld] ADJ **~ orders** pedidos *mpl* pendientes

unfinished ['ʌn'fɪnɪʃt] ADJ inacabado, sin terminar; **I have three ~ letters** tengo tres cartas por terminar; **we have ~ business** tenemos asuntos pendientes

unfit ['ʌn'fɪt] Ⓐ ADJ [1] (= *unsuitable*) no apto (**for** para); (= *incompetent*) incapaz; (= *unworthy*) indigno (**to** de); **he was considered an ~ parent** se le consideró un padre inepto *or* incompetente; **he is quite ~ to hold office** no está capacitado en absoluto para ejercer ningún cargo; **to be ~ for sth: the road is ~ for lorries** el camino no es apto para el tránsito de camiones; **to be ~ for human consumption** no ser apto para el consumo; **to be ~ for habitation** ser inhabitable; **complaints that he was ~ for the job** quejas *fpl* de que no estaba capacitado para el trabajo; **to be ~ for publication** no ser apto para la publicación
[2] (= *not physically fit*) en mala forma (física), bajo de forma; (= *ill*) indispuesto; **he is very ~** está en muy mala forma (física), está muy bajo de forma; **two of their players are ~** dos de sus jugadores no se encuentran en condiciones de jugar; **~ for military service** no apto para el servicio militar; **she is ~ to drive** no está en condiciones de conducir *or* (*LAm*) manejar
Ⓑ VT (*frm*) **to ~ sb for sth/to do sth** inhabilitar *or* incapacitar a algn para algo/para hacer algo

unfitness ['ʌn'fɪtnɪs] N [1] (= *unsuitability*) (*for job*) incapacidad *f*, ineptitud *f*; (*for use, purpose*) lo poco apropiado
[2] (*physical*) baja forma *f* (física)

unfitting [ʌn'fɪtɪŋ] ADJ impropio

unflagging [ʌn'flægɪŋ] ADJ incansable

unflaggingly [ʌn'flægɪŋlɪ] ADV incansablemente

unflappability* [,ʌnflæpə'bɪlɪtɪ] N imperturbabilidad *f*

unflappable* ['ʌn'flæpəbl] ADJ imperturbable

unflattering ['ʌn'flætərɪŋ] ADJ [*person*] poco lisonjero; [*description*] poco halagüeño; [*clothes, haircut*] poco favorecedor

unflatteringly [ʌn'flætərɪŋlɪ] ADV [*speak*] de modo poco lisonjero; [*describe*] de manera poco halagüeña

➤ LANGUAGE IN USE: **unfair A** 26.3

unfledged ['ʌn'fledʒd] ADJ implume

unflinching ['ʌn'flɪntʃɪŋ] ADJ impávido, resuelto

unflinchingly ['ʌn'flɪntʃɪŋlɪ] ADV impávidamente, resueltamente

unfocused, unfocussed ['ʌn'fəʊkəst] ADJ [*eyes*] desenfocado; [*desires*] sin objetivo concreto, nada concreto; [*energies*] que carece de dirección

unfold [ʌn'fəʊld] Ⓐ VT 1 desplegar, desdoblar; **she ~ed the map** desplegó *or* desdobló el mapa
2 (*fig*) [+ *idea, plan*] exponer; [+ *secret*] revelar
Ⓑ VI desplegarse, desdoblarse; (*fig*) [*view etc*] revelarse

unforced [ʌn'fɔːst] ADJ [*style etc*] natural, sin artificialidad; [*error*] no forzado

unforeseeable ['ʌnfɔː'siːəbl] ADJ imprevisible

unforeseen ['ʌnfɔː'siːn] ADJ imprevisto

unforgettable ['ʌnfə'getəbl] ADJ inolvidable

unforgettably ['ʌnfə'getəblɪ] ADV de manera inolvidable; **~ beautiful** tan hermoso que resulta inolvidable

➤**unforgivable** ['ʌnfə'gɪvəbl] ADJ imperdonable

unforgiven ['ʌnfə'gɪvən] ADJ no perdonado

unforgiving ['ʌnfə'gɪvɪŋ] ADJ implacable

unforgotten ['ʌnfə'gɒtn] ADJ no olvidado

unformatted ['ʌn'fɔːmætɪd] ADJ (*Comput*) [*disk, text*] sin formatear, no formateado

unformed ['ʌn'fɔːmd] ADJ (= *shapeless*) informe; (= *immature*) inmaduro, sin formar aún

unforthcoming ['ʌnfɔː'θʌmɪŋ] ADJ poco comunicativo

unfortified ['ʌn'fɔːtɪfaɪd] ADJ no fortificado; [*town*] abierto

➤**unfortunate** [ʌn'fɔːtʃnɪt] Ⓐ ADJ 1 (= *deserving of pity, unlucky*) **how very ~!** ¡qué mala suerte!, ¡qué desgracia!; **you have been most ~** ha tenido usted muy mala suerte; **we must help these ~ people** debemos ayudar a estas personas tan desafortunadas; **he was ~ enough to be caught** tuvo la desgracia *or* mala suerte de que lo cogieran *or* pillaran; **it is most ~ that he left** es una lástima *or* muy de lamentar que se haya ido
2 (= *unsuitable, regrettable*) [*remark*] poco acertado, inoportuno; [*incident, consequences, tendency*] lamentable; **it was an ~ choice of words** las palabras que se eligieron fueron poco acertadas
Ⓑ N desgraciado/a *m/f*

➤**unfortunately** [ʌn'fɔːtʃnɪtlɪ] ADV 1 (= *unluckily*) desgraciadamente, por desgracia; **~ for you** desgraciadamente para ti, por desgracia para ti
2 (= *regrettably*) lamentablemente
3 (= *inappropriately*) **the statement was rather ~ phrased** la declaración estaba formulada con muy poco acierto

unfounded ['ʌn'faʊndɪd] ADJ infundado, sin fundamento

unframed ['ʌn'freɪmd] ADJ sin marco

unfreeze ['ʌn'friːz] Ⓐ VT descongelar
Ⓑ VI descongelarse

unfrequented ['ʌnfrɪ'kwentɪd] ADJ poco frecuentado

unfriendliness ['ʌn'frendlɪnɪs] N hostilidad *f*

unfriendly ['ʌn'frendlɪ] ADJ (*compar* **unfriendlier**; *superl* **unfriendliest**) [*person*] poco amistoso; (*stronger*) antipático; [*voice*] poco amistoso; [*act, gesture*] poco amistoso; (*stronger*) hostil; [*place, atmosphere*] poco acogedor; [*country, territory*] hostil; **to be ~ to** *or* **towards sb** ser *or* mostrarse antipático *or* poco amistoso con algn

unfrock ['ʌn'frɒk] VT [+ *priest*] secularizar, exclaustrar

unfruitful ['ʌn'fruːtfʊl] ADJ infructuoso

unfulfilled ['ʌnfʊl'fɪld] ADJ 1 (= *unrealized*) [*ambition, hope*] frustrado; [*desire*] no hecho realidad; [*promise*] no cumplido; [*need*] insatisfecho; [*potential*] sin desarrollar
2 (= *dissatisfied*) [*person*] insatisfecho; **to feel ~** sentirse insatisfecho, no sentirse realizado

unfulfilling ['ʌnfʊl'fɪlɪŋ] ADJ **he finds his job ~** su trabajo no le llena (lo suficiente), no se siente realizado en su trabajo

unfunny* ['ʌn'fʌnɪ] ADJ nada divertido

unfurl [ʌn'fɜːl] VT desplegar

unfurnished ['ʌn'fɜːnɪʃt] ADJ sin amueblar

ungainliness [ʌn'geɪnlɪnɪs] N desgarbo *m*, torpeza *f*

ungainly [ʌn'geɪnlɪ] ADJ [*person*] desgarbado; [*animal*] torpe; [*gait*] torpe, desgarbado

ungallant ['ʌn'gælənt] ADJ falto de cortesía, descortés

ungenerous ['ʌn'dʒenərəs] ADJ 1 (= *miserly*) poco generoso
2 (= *uncharitable*) mezquino; **I should not be ~ in my thoughts** no debería tener pensamientos mezquinos

ungentlemanly [ʌn'dʒentlmənlɪ] ADJ poco caballeroso, indigno de un caballero

un-get-at-able* ['ʌnget'ætəbl] ADJ inaccesible

ungird ['ʌn'gɜːd] (*pt, pp* **ungirt**) VT (*liter*) desceñir

unglazed ['ʌn'gleɪzd] ADJ no vidriado; [*window*] sin cristales

ungodliness [ʌn'gɒdlɪnɪs] N impiedad *f*

ungodly [ʌn'gɒdlɪ] ADJ 1 (†) (= *sinful*) [*person, action, life*] impío, irreligioso
2 (*) (= *unreasonable*) [*noise*] tremendo*; **at this ~ hour** a estas horas tan intempestivas

ungovernable [ʌn'gʌvənəbl] ADJ ingobernable; [*temper*] incontrolable, irrefrenable

ungracious ['ʌn'greɪʃəs] ADJ descortés; **it would be ~ to refuse** sería descortés no aceptar

ungraciously ['ʌn'greɪʃəslɪ] ADV descortésmente

ungrammatical ['ʌngrə'mætɪkəl] ADJ incorrecto desde el punto de vista gramatical

ungrammatically ['ʌngrə'mætɪkəlɪ] ADV incorrectamente; **to talk Spanish ~** hablar español con poca corrección

ungrateful [ʌn'greɪtfʊl] ADJ desagradecido, ingrato

ungratefully [ʌn'greɪtfəlɪ] ADV desagradecidamente, con ingratitud

ungrudging ['ʌn'grʌdʒɪŋ] ADJ liberal, generoso; [*support etc*] generoso

ungrudgingly [ʌn'grʌdʒɪŋlɪ] ADV liberalmente, generosamente; [*support etc*] desinteresadamente

unguarded ['ʌn'gɑːdɪd] ADJ 1 (*Mil etc*) indefenso, sin protección
2 (*fig*) (= *open, careless*) descuidado; (= *thoughtless*) imprudente; **in an ~ moment** en un momento de descuido; **I caught him in an ~ moment** lo pillé *or* (*LAm*) agarré (en un momento en que estaba) desprevenido

unguent ['ʌŋgwənt] N ungüento *m*

ungulate ['ʌŋgjʊleɪt] Ⓐ ADJ ungulado
Ⓑ N ungulado *m*

unhallowed [ʌn'hæləʊd] ADJ (*liter*) no consagrado

unhampered ['ʌn'hæmpəd] ADJ libre, sin estorbos; **~ by** no estorbado por

unhand [ʌn'hænd] VT († *or liter*) soltar; **~ me, sir!** ¡suélteme, señor!

unhandy [ʌn'hændɪ] ADJ [*person*] desmañado; [*thing*] incómodo; **to be ~ with sth** ser desmañado en el manejo de algo

unhappily [ʌn'hæpɪlɪ] ADV 1 (= *miserably*) tristemente, con tristeza; **he stared ~ out of the window** miró tristemente *or* con tristeza por la ventana; **he was ~ married** no fue feliz *or* fue infeliz en su matrimonio
2 (= *unfortunately*) lamentablemente; (*stronger*) desgraciadamente, por desgracia; **~, his plans didn't work out as he had wished** desgraciadamente *or* por desgracia, los planes no salieron como había deseado

unhappiness [ʌn'hæpɪnɪs] N 1 (= *sadness*) desdicha *f*, tristeza *f*; (= *absence of happiness*) infelicidad *f*; **he sensed her pain and ~** notó su dolor y su desdicha *or* tristeza; **I don't want to cause more ~ to you both** no quiero causarles más desdicha a los dos, no quiero ser más motivo de infelicidad para los dos; **the ~ of their marriage was public knowledge** la infelicidad de su matrimonio era del dominio público
2 (= *dissatisfaction*) descontento *m*; **they expressed their ~ with** *or* **over the decision** expresaron su descontento con respecto a la decisión

➤**unhappy** [ʌn'hæpɪ] ADJ (*compar* **unhappier**; *superl* **unhappiest**) 1 (= *sad*) [*person*] infeliz; (*stronger*) desdichado; [*childhood*] infeliz; (*stronger*) desgraciado, desdichado; [*marriage*] infeliz; [*memory*] desagradable; **that ~ time** aquella triste época; **I had an ~ time at school** lo pasé muy mal en la escuela; **she was ~ in her marriage** no fue feliz *or* fue infeliz en su matrimonio; **she looked so ~** se la veía tan triste; **don't look so ~!** ¡no pongas esa cara tan triste!; **to make sb ~**: **other children at school were making him ~** otros niños en el colegio le estaban haciendo sufrir; **it makes me ~ to see you upset** me entristece *or* pone triste verte disgustada
2 (= *not pleased*) descontento; **to be ~ about sth** no estar contento con algo, estar descontento con algo; **to be ~ with sth/sb** no estar contento con algo/algn, estar descontento con algo/algn
3 (= *uneasy, worried*) **I'm ~ about leaving him on his own** no estoy a gusto dejándolo solo, me preocupa dejarlo solo
4 (= *unfortunate*) [*remark*] poco acertado, inoportuno; [*experience, situation*] lamentable
5 (= *ill-fated*) [*day*] desafortunado

unharmed ['ʌn'hɑːmd] ADJ [*person, animal*] ileso; [*thing*] intacto; **the baby was found ~ in a bedroom** encontraron al bebé ileso en un dormitorio; **to escape/be released ~** escapar/ser liberado ileso

unharness ['ʌn'hɑːnɪs] VT desguarnecer

UNHCR N ABBR (= **United Nations High Commission for Refugees**) ACNUR *m*

unhealthy [ʌn'helθɪ] ADJ (*compar* **unhealthier**; *superl* **unhealthiest**) 1 (= *unwell*) [*person*] poco sano, enfermizo; [*complexion*] poco saludable; **he was an ~-looking fellow** era un tipo de aspecto poco sano *or* de aspecto enfermizo; **my finances are a bit ~ at the moment** no estoy lo que se dice muy boyante de dinero en estos momentos
2 (= *harmful*) [*climate, place, environment*] malsano, insalubre; [*diet, lifestyle, food*] poco sano; [*working conditions*] poco saludable, insalubre

➤ LANGUAGE IN USE: **unforgivable** 18.3 **unfortunate A2** 18.1 **unfortunately 1, 2** 18.2 **unhappy 2** 14

3 (= *unwholesome*) [*interest, fascination, curiosity*] malsano, morboso; [*obsession*] enfermizo, malsano

unheard ['ʌn'hɜːd] ADJ 1 (= *ignored*) **she condemned him ~** lo condenó sin escucharlo; **his pleas went ~** hicieron caso omiso de sus ruegos
2 (= *not heard*) **his cries went ~** nadie oyó sus gritos; **a previously ~ opera** una ópera inédita

unheard-of [ʌn'hɜːdɒv] ADJ (= *unprecedented*) inaudito; (= *outrageous*) escandaloso

unheated ['ʌn'hiːtɪd] ADJ sin calefacción

unheeded ['ʌn'hiːdɪd] ADJ [*plea, warning*] desatendido; **the warning went ~** la advertencia fue desatendida, no se hizo caso de la advertencia

unheeding ['ʌn'hiːdɪŋ] ADJ desatento, sordo; **they passed by ~** pasaron sin prestar atención

unhelpful ['ʌn'helpfʊl] ADJ [*person*] poco servicial, poco dispuesto a ayudar; [*remark*] inútil; [*advice*] poco útil; **he didn't want to seem ~** no quería parecer poco servicial *or* poco dispuesto a ayudar; **it is ~ to pretend the problem does not exist** no se consigue nada pretendiendo que el problema no existe; **to be ~ to sth/sb** no ayudar a algo/algn

unhelpfully ['ʌn'helpfʊlɪ] ADV [*behave*] con poco espíritu de servicio; [*say, suggest*] con poco ánimo de ayudar

unhelpfulness ['ʌn'helpfʊlnɪs] N [*of person*] falta *f* de espíritu de servicio; [*of remark, advice, book, computer*] inutilidad *f*

unheralded ['ʌn'herəldɪd] ADJ (= *unannounced*) **to arrive ~** llegar sin dar aviso

unhesitating [ʌn'hezɪteɪtɪŋ] ADJ (= *steadfast, unwavering*) resuelto, decidido; (= *prompt, immediate*) inmediato, pronto

unhesitatingly [ʌn'hezɪteɪtɪŋlɪ] ADV sin vacilar; **"yes," she answered ~** —sí —respondió sin vacilar

unhindered ['ʌn'hɪndəd] ADJ libre, sin estorbos; **~ by** no estorbado por

unhinge [ʌn'hɪndʒ] VT desquiciar; (*fig*) [+ *mind*] trastornar; [+ *person*] trastornar el juicio de

unhinged ['ʌn'hɪndʒd] ADJ (= *mad*) trastornado

unhip* [ˌʌn'hɪp] ADJ fuera de onda*, que no está en la onda*

unhistorical ['ʌnhɪs'tɒrɪkəl] ADJ antihistórico, que no tiene nada de histórico

unhitch ['ʌn'hɪtʃ] VT desenganchar

unholy [ʌn'həʊlɪ] ADJ 1 (= *sinful*) [*activity*] impío
2 (*) (= *terrible*) [*mess, row*] tremendo*; [*noise*] tremendo, de mil demonios*

unhook ['ʌn'hʊk] VT 1 (= *remove*) desenganchar, descolgar
2 (= *undo*) [+ *garment*] desabrochar

unhoped-for [ʌn'həʊptfɔːʳ] ADJ inesperado

unhopeful [ʌn'həʊpfʊl] ADJ [*prospect*] poco alentador, poco prometedor; [*person*] pesimista

unhorse ['ʌn'hɔːs] VT desarzonar

unhurried ['ʌn'hʌrɪd] ADJ [*pace*] pausado, lento; [*atmosphere, person*] tranquilo; [*activity*] tranquilo, pausado; **in an ~ way** de forma pausada

unhurriedly ['ʌn'hʌrɪdlɪ] ADV [*walk, speak*] lentamente, pausadamente

unhurt ['ʌn'hɜːt] ADJ ileso; **to escape ~** salir ileso

unhygienic ['ʌnhaɪ'dʒiːnɪk] ADJ antihigiénico

uni... ['juːnɪ] PREFIX uni...

unicameral ['juːnɪ'kæmərəl] ADJ unicameral

UNICEF ['juːnɪsef] N ABBR (= **United Nations International Children's Emergency Fund**) UNICEF *m*

unicellular ['juːnɪ'seljʊləʳ] ADJ unicelular

unicorn ['juːnɪkɔːn] N unicornio *m*

unicycle ['juːnɪˌsaɪkl] N monociclo *m*

unidentifiable ['ʌnaɪˌdentɪ'faɪəbl] ADJ no identificable

unidentified ['ʌnaɪ'dentɪfaɪd] Ⓐ ADJ sin identificar, no identificado
Ⓑ CPD ► **unidentified flying object** N objeto *m* volante no identificado

unidirectional [ˌjuːnɪdɪ'rekʃənl] ADJ unidireccional

UNIDO [juːniːdəʊ] N ABBR (= **United Nations Industrial Development Organization**) ONUDI *f*

unification [ˌjuːnɪfɪ'keɪʃən] N unificación *f*

uniform ['juːnɪfɔːm] Ⓐ ADJ [*shape, size, colour*] uniforme; [*speed*] constante; [*rate, tariff*] fijo, invariable; **a ~ system of payments will be introduced** se introducirá un sistema uniforme de pagos; **to make sth ~** hacer algo uniforme, uniformar algo
Ⓑ N uniforme *m*; **school ~** uniforme *m* escolar *or* de colegio; **he was in full ~** llevaba el uniforme completo; **to be in/out of ~** ir con/sin uniforme; **to wear (a) ~** llevar uniforme, ir de uniforme; *see also* **dress D**

uniformed ['juːnɪfɔːmd] ADJ uniformado, de uniforme

uniformity [ˌjuːnɪ'fɔːmɪtɪ] N [*of appearance, colour, standards*] uniformidad *f*; [*of attitudes, beliefs*] homogeneidad *f*

uniformly ['juːnɪfɔːmlɪ] ADV [*spread, distributed, applied*] uniformemente; **the book has had ~ bad reviews** el libro obtuvo malas críticas en general

unify ['juːnɪfaɪ] VT unificar, unir

unifying ['juːnɪfaɪɪŋ] ADJ [*factor etc*] unificador

unilateral ['juːnɪ'lætərəl] Ⓐ ADJ unilateral
Ⓑ CPD ► **unilateral disarmament** N desarme *m* unilateral; **~ nuclear disarmament** desarme *m* nuclear unilateral

unilateralism ['juːnɪ'lætərəlɪzəm] N unilateralismo *m*

unilateralist ['juːnɪ'lætərəlɪst] N persona *f* que está a favor del desarme unilateral, unilateralista *mf*

unilaterally ['juːnɪ'lætərəlɪ] ADV unilateralmente

unilingual [ˌjuːnɪ'lɪŋgwəl] ADJ monolingüe

unimaginable [ˌʌnɪ'mædʒməbl] ADJ inimaginable, inconcebible

unimaginably [ˌʌnɪ'mædʒməblɪ] ADV inimaginablemente, inconcebiblemente

unimaginative ['ʌnɪ'mædʒmətɪv] ADJ falto de imaginación, poco imaginativo

unimaginatively ['ʌnɪ'mædʒmətɪvlɪ] ADV de manera poco imaginativa

unimaginativeness ['ʌnɪ'mædʒnətɪvnɪs] N falta *f* de imaginación

unimpaired ['ʌnɪm'pɛəd] ADJ [*health, eyesight*] en perfectas condiciones; [*relationship*] intacto; **their faith remains ~** su fe no se ha visto afectada

unimpeachable [ˌʌnɪm'piːtʃəbl] ADJ irreprochable, intachable; **from an ~ source** de fuente fidedigna

unimpeded ['ʌnɪm'piːdɪd] Ⓐ ADJ [*access*] sin impedimentos, sin obstáculos; [*view*] perfecto
Ⓑ ADV sin impedimentos, libremente

unimportant ['ʌnɪm'pɔːtənt] ADJ sin importancia; **they talked of ~ things** hablaron de cosas sin importancia; **the problem itself is relatively ~** el problema en sí tiene relativamente poca importancia

unimposing ['ʌnɪm'pəʊzɪŋ] ADJ (= *not big*) poco impresionante; (= *drab, boring*) con poca gracia

unimpressed ['ʌnɪm'prest] ADJ **I am ~ by the new building** el nuevo edificio no me impresiona; **she was ~ by Palm Beach** Palm Beach no le impresionó demasiado, Palm Beach la dejó igual*; **they were ~ by such arguments** tales argumentos les resultaron muy poco convincentes; **he remained ~** siguió sin convencerse

unimpressive ['ʌnɪm'presɪv] ADJ poco impresionante, poco convincente; [*person*] soso, insignificante

unimproved [ˌʌnɪm'pruːvd] ADJ [*land*] (= *not drained*) sin drenar; (= *not treated*) sin abonar; [*property, house*] sin reformar

uninfluenced ['ʌn'ɪnflʊənst] ADJ **~ by any argument** no afectado por ningún argumento; **a style ~ by any other** un estilo no influido por ningún otro

uninformative ['ʌnɪn'fɔːmətɪv] ADJ poco informativo

uninformed ['ʌnɪn'fɔːmd] ADJ [*comment, rumour, criticism*] infundado; [*attitudes, prejudice*] ignorante; **I did not want to appear ~** no quería parecer ignorante; **well-meaning but ~ people** personas *fpl* de buenas intenciones pero sin conocimientos; **to be ~ about sth** no estar informado sobre algo, no estar al corriente *or* al tanto de algo; **he could not claim that he was ~ about the law** no podía afirmar que no estaba informado sobre la ley, no podía afirmar que no estaba al corriente *or* al tanto de la ley; **people are generally very ~ about the disease** la gente en general está muy poco informada sobre la enfermedad; **the ~ observer** el observador profano

uninhabitable ['ʌnɪn'hæbɪtəbl] ADJ inhabitable

uninhabited ['ʌnɪn'hæbɪtɪd] ADJ (= *deserted*) desierto, despoblado; [*house*] desocupado

uninhibited ['ʌnɪn'hɪbɪtɪd] ADJ [*person*] desinhibido, sin inhibiciones; [*behaviour*] desinhibido, desenfadado; [*emotion*] desbordante; **to be ~ by sth** no estar inhibido por algo, no tener inhibiciones con respecto a algo; **to be ~ in one's questions** hacer preguntas sin inhibiciones; **to be ~ in doing sth** no tener inhibiciones para hacer algo; **to be ~ about doing sth** no tener inhibiciones a la hora de hacer algo

uninitiated ['ʌnɪ'nɪʃɪeɪtɪd] Ⓐ ADJ no iniciado
Ⓑ NPL **the ~** los no iniciados

uninjured ['ʌn'ɪndʒəd] ADJ ileso; **to escape ~** salir ileso

uninspired ['ʌnɪn'spaɪəd] ADJ [*person*] poco inspirado, sin inspiración; [*book, film, performance*] sin inspiración, falto de inspiración; [*food*] poco original

uninspiring ['ʌnɪn'spaɪərɪŋ] ADJ [*person, film, book, play*] poco estimulante, aburrido; [*view*] monótono

uninsured ['ʌnɪn'ʃʊəd] ADJ no asegurado

unintelligent ['ʌnɪn'telɪdʒənt] ADJ poco inteligente

unintelligibility ['ʌnɪnˌtelɪdʒə'bɪlɪtɪ] N ininteligibilidad *f*, incomprensibilidad *f*

unintelligible ['ʌnɪn'telɪdʒəbl] ADJ ininteligible, incomprensible; **she mumbled some-**

thing ~ balbuceó algo ininteligible *or* incomprensible

unintelligibly [ˈʌnɪnˈtelɪdʒəblɪ] ADV de modo ininteligible, de modo incomprensible

unintended [ˈʌnɪnˈtendɪd], **unintentional** [ˈʌnɪnˈtenʃənl] ADJ involuntario, no intencionado; **it was quite ~** fue totalmente involuntario

unintentionally [ˈʌnɪnˈtenʃnəlɪ] ADV sin querer, involuntariamente

uninterested [ʌnˈɪntrɪstɪd] ADJ (= *indifferent*) indiferente, desinteresado; **I am quite ~ in what he thinks** me es igual *or* indiferente lo que piensa; **to be ~ in a subject** no tener interés en un tema

uninteresting [ˈʌnˈɪntrɪstɪŋ] ADJ [*person, book, film, speech*] poco interesante; [*city, building*] sin interés

uninterrupted [ˈʌnˌɪntəˈrʌptɪd] ADJ ininterrumpido

uninterruptedly [ˈʌnˌɪntəˈrʌptɪdlɪ] ADV ininterrumpidamente

uninvited [ˈʌnɪnˈvaɪtɪd] ADJ [*guest etc*] sin invitación; [*criticism, comment*] gratuito; **to do sth ~** hacer algo sin que nadie se lo pida; **they came to the party ~** vinieron a la fiesta sin haber sido invitados; **she helped herself ~ to cake** se sirvió pastel sin esperar que le ofreciesen

uninviting [ˈʌnɪnˈvaɪtɪŋ] ADJ [*appearance, offer*] poco atractivo; [*food*] poco apetitoso

union [ˈjuːnjən] Ⓐ N [1] unión *f*; (= *marriage*) enlace *m*; **the Union** (*US*) la Unión
[2] (= *trade union*) sindicato *m*, gremio *m*
[3] (= *club, society*) club *m*, sociedad *f*
[4] (*Mech*) (*for pipes etc*) unión *f*, manguito *m* de unión
Ⓑ CPD (*Ind*) [*leader, movement, headquarters*] sindical ► **union card** N carnet *m* de afiliado ► **union catalog(ue)** N catálogo *m* colectivo *or* conjunto ► **Union Jack** N bandera *f* del Reino Unido ► **union member** N miembro *mf* del sindicato, sindicalista *mf* ► **union membership** N (= *numbers*) afiliados *mpl* al sindicato; **~ membership has declined** el número de afiliados a los sindicatos ha disminuido; (= *being a member*) afiliación *f* a un/al sindicato; **~ membership is compulsory** es obligatorio afiliarse a *or* hacerse miembro del sindicato ► **Union of Soviet Socialist Republics** N (*formerly*) Unión *f* de Repúblicas Socialistas Soviéticas ► **Union of South Africa** N (*formerly*) Unión *f* Sudafricana ► **union shop** N (*US*) taller *m* de afiliación (sindical) obligatoria ► **union suit** N (*US*) prenda *f* interior de cuerpo entero

unionism [ˈjuːnjənɪzəm] N [1] (*Ind*) sindicalismo *m*
[2] **Unionism** (*Brit Pol*) unionismo *m*

unionist [ˈjuːnjənɪst] Ⓐ ADJ (*Brit Pol*) unionista
Ⓑ N [1] (*Ind*) (*also* **trade ~**) sindicalista *mf*, miembro *mf* de un sindicato
[2] **Unionist** (*Brit Pol*) unionista *mf*

unionize [ˈjuːnjənaɪz] Ⓐ VT sindicar, sindicalizar
Ⓑ VI sindicarse, sindicalizarse

unique [juːˈniːk] ADJ [1] (= *exclusive*) [*style, collection, combination*] único; **to be ~ to sth/sb**: **it is a species ~ to these islands** es una especie que se da únicamente en estas islas; **the experience is ~ to each individual** la experiencia es única (e irrepetible) en cada individuo; **this behaviour is not ~ to men** este comportamiento no se da únicamente en los hombres
[2] (= *exceptional*) [*opportunity*] único; [*ability, talent*] sin igual, excepcional; [*insight*] único, de excepción; [*relationship*] especial

uniquely [juːˈniːklɪ] ADV **she is ~ qualified for the job** está excepcionalmente capacitada para el puesto; **to be ~ placed to do sth** encontrarse en una posición de excepción para hacer algo; **a ~ British characteristic** una característica exclusivamente británica

uniqueness [juːˈniːknɪs] N singularidad *f*

unisex [ˈjuːnɪseks] ADJ unisex *inv*

UNISON [ˈjuːnɪsn] N ABBR (*Brit*) *gran sindicato de funcionarios*

unison [ˈjuːnɪzn] N armonía *f*; (*Mus*) unisonancia *f*; **in ~** (*Mus*) al unísono; **to sing in ~** cantar al unísono; **to act in ~ with sb** obrar al unísono con algn; **"yes," they said in ~** —sí —dijeron al unísono

unissued [ˈʌnˈɪʃuːd] ADJ **~ capital** capital *m* no emitido

unit [ˈjuːnɪt] Ⓐ N [1] (*Admin, Elec, Mech, Math, Mil*) unidad *f*; (*Univ*) (*for marking purposes*) unidad *f* de valor; (*Tech*) (= *mechanism*) conjunto *m*; **administrative/linguistic/monetary ~** unidad *f* administrativa/lingüística/monetaria; **~ of account** unidad *f* de cuenta; **a ~ of measurement** una unidad de medida
[2] (= *complete section, part*) [*of textbook*] módulo *m*, unidad *f*; (= *device*) aparato *m*; **a kitchen ~** un módulo de cocina
[3] (= *building*) **intensive care ~** unidad *f* de cuidados intensivos; **sports ~** polideportivo *m*; **the shop ~s remain unlet** los locales comerciales siguen sin traspasarse; **the staff accommodation ~** las viviendas de los empleados
[4] (= *group of people*) unidad *f*; (*in firm*) centro *m*; **army ~** unidad *f* militar; **research/information ~** centro *m* de investigación/información; **family ~** núcleo *m* familiar, familia *f*
Ⓑ CPD ► **unit charge, unit cost** N (*Brit Fin*) costo *m* unitario *or* por unidad ► **unit furniture** N muebles *mpl* de elementos adicionables, muebles *mpl* combinados ► **unit price** N precio *m* unitario *or* por unidad ► **unit trust** N (*Brit Fin*) (= *fund*) fondo *m* de inversión mobiliaria; (= *company*) sociedad *f* de inversiones

UNITA [juːˈniːtə] N ABBR (= **União Nacional para a Independencia Total de Angola**) UNITA *f*, Unita *f*

Unitarian [ˌjuːnɪˈtɛərɪən] Ⓐ ADJ unitario
Ⓑ N unitario/a *m/f*

Unitarianism [ˌjuːnɪˈtɛərɪənɪzəm] N unitarismo *m*

unitary [ˈjuːnɪtərɪ] Ⓐ ADJ unitario
Ⓑ CPD ► **unitary labour costs** NPL costes *mpl* laborales unitarios

unite [juːˈnaɪt] Ⓐ VT (= *join*) [+ *people, organizations*] unir; [+ *parts of country*] unificar, unir
Ⓑ VI unirse; **to ~ against sb** unirse para hacer frente a algn; **we must ~ in defence of our rights** debemos unirnos para defender nuestros derechos

united [juːˈnaɪtɪd] Ⓐ ADJ [*country, group*] unido; [*effort*] conjunto; **they were ~ by a common enemy** los unía un enemigo común; **to present a ~ front (to sb)** presentar un frente unido (ante algn); **to be ~ in sth**: **the family was ~ in grief** la familia estaba unida por el dolor; **they are ~ in their belief that ...** comparten la creencia de que ...; **they are ~ in their opposition to the plan** los une su oposición al plan; **we are ~ on the need to solve the problem** compartimos la necesidad de resolver el problema; ✦**PROV ~ we stand, divided we fall** unidos venceremos
Ⓑ CPD ► **United Arab Emirates** NPL Emiratos *mpl* Árabes Unidos ► **United Arab Republic** N República *f* Árabe Unida ► **United Kingdom** N Reino *m* Unido (*Inglaterra, Gales, Escocia, Irlanda del Norte*) ► **United Nations (Organization)** N (Organización *f* de las) Naciones *fpl* Unidas ► **United States (of America)** NPL Estados *mpl* Unidos (de América)

unity [ˈjuːnɪtɪ] N (= *oneness*) unidad *f*; (= *harmony*) armonía *f*, acuerdo *m*; **~ of place** unidad *f* de lugar; **~ of time** unidad *f* de tiempo; ✦**PROV ~ is strength** la unión hace la fuerza

Univ. ABBR (= **University**) U

univalent [ˈjuːnɪˈveɪlənt] ADJ univalente

univalve [ˈjuːnɪvælv] Ⓐ ADJ univalvo
Ⓑ N molusco *m* univalvo

universal [ˌjuːnɪˈvɜːsəl] Ⓐ ADJ [1] (= *general*) [*agreement, acceptance*] general, global; **the closures met with ~ condemnation** los cierres provocaron la condena general *or* unánime; **its use has been ~ since 1900** se usa en todas partes *or* globalmente desde 1900; **her writing has ~ appeal** su forma de escribir atrae a todo el mundo; **a ~ truth** una verdad universal, una verdad aceptada por todos *or* por todo el mundo; **to become ~** generalizarse
[2] (= *worldwide*) [*law, language*] universal; **the threat of ~ destruction** la amenaza de la destrucción mundial
Ⓑ CPD ► **universal donor** N donante *mf* universal ► **universal joint** N (*Tech*) junta *f* cardán *or* universal ► **universal product code** N (*US*) código *m* de barras ► **universal suffrage** N sufragio *m* universal

universality [ˌjuːnɪvɜːˈsælɪtɪ] N universalidad *f*

universalize [ˌjuːnɪˈvɜːsəlaɪz] VT universalizar

universally [ˌjuːnɪˈvɜːsəlɪ] ADV [*accepted, acknowledged*] universalmente, generalmente; [*popular, available*] en todas partes; [*known*] mundialmente; [*applicable*] para todo; [*condemned*] unánimemente; **there is no ~ accepted definition** no existe una definición aceptada universalmente *or* generalmente aceptada; **he was ~ liked** caía bien a todo el mundo, todo el mundo lo apreciaba

universe [ˈjuːnɪvɜːs] N universo *m*; **he's the funniest writer in the ~*** es el escritor más divertido del mundo

university [ˌjuːnɪˈvɜːsɪtɪ] Ⓐ N universidad *f*; **to be at ~** estar en la universidad; **to go to ~** ir a la universidad; **to study at ~** estudiar en la universidad; **a ~ place** una plaza universitaria; **he has a ~ education** ha cursado estudios universitarios; **Lancaster University** la Universidad de Lancaster
Ⓑ CPD [*degree, year, professor, student*] universitario; [*library*] de la universidad ► **university entrance** N acceso *m* a la universidad; **~ entrance examination** examen *m* de ingreso a la universidad ► **university hospital** N hospital *m* universitario ► **university town** N ciudad *f* que tiene universidad

unjust [ˈʌnˈdʒʌst] ADJ injusto; **she had been so ~** había sido muy injusta; **to be ~ to sb** ser injusto con algn

unjustifiable [ʌnˈdʒʌstɪfaɪəbl] ADJ injustificable

unjustifiably [ʌnˈdʒʌstɪfaɪəblɪ] ADV injustificadamente; **they have been ~ treated by the media** los medios de comunicación los han tratado injustificadamente *or* de forma injustificada

unjustified [ˈʌnˈdʒʌstɪfaɪd] ADJ [1] (= *unfair*) [*action, attack, reputation*] injustificado; **he described their action as inappropriate and**

~ calificó su acción de impropia e injustificada

2 (*Typ*) [*text*] no alineado, no justificado

unjustly ['ʌn'dʒʌstlɪ] ADV injustamente; **they had ~ accused him of lying** lo habían acusado injustamente de mentir

unkempt ['ʌn'kempt] ADJ [*clothes, appearance*] descuidado, desaliñado; [*hair*] despeinado, descuidado; [*beard, garden, park*] descuidado

unkind [ʌn'kaɪnd] ADJ (*compar* **unkinder**, *superl* **unkindest**) 1 (= *cruel, nasty*) [*person*] poco amable; (*stronger*) cruel; [*criticism*] duro; [*remark*] cruel; [*words*] desagradable; **that was very ~ of him** eso fue muy poco amable de su parte; **I've never known him to be ~** nunca ha sido desagradable, que yo sepa; **she never has an ~ word to say about anyone** nunca dice nada malo de nadie; **it would be ~ to say that ...** sería cruel decir que ...; **to be ~ to sb** portarse mal con algn

2 [*climate*] riguroso; **the weather was ~ to us** el tiempo nos jugó una mala pasada

unkindly [ʌn'kaɪndlɪ] ADV [*say, behave*] cruelmente, con crueldad; **it wasn't meant ~** no iba con malas intenciones; **to speak ~ of sb** hablar mal de algn; **don't take it ~ if ...** no lo tome a mal si ...; **to treat sb ~** tratar con poca amabilidad a algn; (*stronger*) tratar mal a algn

unkindness [ʌn'kaɪndnɪs] N 1 (= *quality*) falta *f* de amabilidad; (= *cruelty*) crueldad *f*

2 (= *act*) acto *m* de crueldad; **to do sb an ~** portarse mal con algn

unknowable ['ʌn'nəʊəbl] ADJ (*esp liter*) inconocible; **the ~** lo inconocible

unknowing ['ʌn'nəʊɪŋ] ADJ inconsciente; **she was the ~ cause** ella fue la causa, inconscientemente

unknowingly ['ʌn'nəʊɪŋlɪ] ADV (= *involuntarily*) inconscientemente, sin querer; (= *in ignorance*) sin darse cuenta, sin saberlo; **he did it all ~** lo hizo sin darse cuenta

unknown ['ʌn'nəʊn] Ⓐ ADJ [*identity, destination, territory, writer*] desconocido; **the Cazorla Sierra is almost ~ outside Spain** la Sierra de Cazorla casi no se conoce fuera de España; **it's ~ for him to refuse a sweet** nunca ha dicho que no a un caramelo que se sepa; **it's not ~ for him to be wrong** (*iro*) no es precisamente que no se haya equivocado nunca (*iro*); **she's a bit of an ~ quantity** ella es una incógnita; **for some ~ reason** por alguna razón desconocida; **the Unknown Soldier** el soldado desconocido; **to be ~ to sb**: **the name is ~ to me** el nombre no me resulta conocido; **a substance ~ to science** una sustancia no conocida por la ciencia, una sustancia que la ciencia desconoce; *see also* **person**

Ⓑ ADV **~ to me** si yo saberlo

Ⓒ N (= *person*) desconocido/a *m/f*; (*Math, fig*) incógnita *f*; **the ~** lo desconocido; **a journey into the ~** un viaje a lo desconocido

unlace ['ʌn'leɪs] VT desenlazar; [+ *shoes*] desatar los cordones de

unladen ['ʌn'leɪdn] ADJ vacío, sin cargamento

unladylike ['ʌn'leɪdɪlaɪk] ADJ impropio de una dama

unlamented ['ʌnlə'mentɪd] ADJ no llorado, no lamentado

unlatch ['ʌn'lætʃ] VT [+ *door*] alzar el pestillo de, abrir levantando el picaporte de

unlawful ['ʌn'lɔːfʊl] ADJ ilegal, ilícito

unlawfully ['ʌn'lɔːfəlɪ] ADV ilegalmente, ilícitamente

unleaded [ˌʌn'ledɪd] Ⓐ ADJ [*petrol*] sin plomo

Ⓑ N gasolina *f* sin plomo

unlearn ['ʌn'lɜːn] (*pt, pp* **unlearned** *or* **unlearnt**) VT desaprender, olvidar

unlearned ['ʌn'lɜːnɪd] ADJ indocto, ignorante

unleash ['ʌn'liːʃ] VT [+ *dog*] desatar, soltar; (*fig*) [+ *anger, imagination etc*] desencadenar, desatar

unleavened ['ʌn'levnd] Ⓐ ADJ ázimo, sin levadura

Ⓑ CPD ► **unleavened bread** N pan *m* ázimo *or* sin levadura

unless [ən'les] CONJ a menos que + *subjun*, a no ser que + *subjun*; **~ he comes tomorrow** a menos que venga mañana, a no ser que venga mañana; **~ I hear to the contrary** a menos que me digan lo contrario, a no ser que me digan lo contrario; **I won't come ~ you phone me** no vendré a menos que me llames, no vendré a no ser que me llames; **~ I am mistaken, we're lost** si no me equivoco, estamos perdidos; **~ otherwise stated** de no especificarse lo contrario

unlettered ['ʌn'letəd] ADJ indocto

unlicensed ['ʌn'laɪsənst] ADJ sin permiso, sin licencia

unlike ['ʌn'laɪk] Ⓐ PREP a diferencia de; **~ him, I really enjoy flying** a diferencia de él, a mí me encanta viajar en avión; **I, ~ others ...** yo, a diferencia de otros ...; **it's quite ~ him** no es nada característico de él; **the photo is quite ~ him** la foto no se le parece en absoluto

Ⓑ ADJ distinto; (*Math*) de signo contrario; **they are quite ~** son muy distintos, no se parecen en nada

unlikeable ['ʌn'laɪkəbl] ADJ antipático

unlikelihood [ʌn'laɪklɪhʊd], **unlikeliness** [ʌn'laɪklɪnɪs] N improbabilidad *f*

unlikely [ʌn'laɪklɪ] ADJ (*compar* **unlikelier**, *superl* **unlikeliest**) 1 (= *improbable*) poco probable, improbable; **it is most ~** es muy poco probable; **he is an ~ candidate for promotion** no tiene muchas probabilidades de que lo asciendan; **it is ~ that he will come** ◊ **he is ~ to come** es poco probable que venga, no es probable que venga; **he's ~ to survive** tiene pocas posibilidades de sobrevivir, es poco probable que sobreviva; **in the ~ event that we win** en el caso improbable de que ganáramos, en el caso de que ganáramos, lo cual es poco probable

2 (= *implausible*) [*explanation, excuse*] inverosímil, increíble; **that sounds an ~ story** me parece una historia inverosímil

3 (= *odd*) insólito, extraño; **he and Paula made an ~ couple** *or* **pair** él y Paula hacían una pareja insólita *or* extraña; **they turn up in the most ~ places** aparecen en los lugares más insospechados *or* extraños

unlimited [ʌn'lɪmɪtɪd] Ⓐ ADJ [*travel, amount, access, use*] ilimitado; [*patience*] inagotable; **we have not got ~ funds** no tenemos fondos ilimitados; **they had ~ time** no tenían límite de tiempo

Ⓑ CPD ► **unlimited company** N (*Comm, Jur*) compañía *f* ilimitada ► **unlimited liability** N (*Comm, Jur*) responsabilidad *f* ilimitada ► **unlimited mileage** N ≈ kilometraje *m* ilimitado

unlined ['ʌn'laɪnd] ADJ 1 (= *without lines*) [*paper*] sin pautar; [*face*] sin arrugas

2 (= *without lining*) [*garment, curtain*] sin forro

unlisted ['ʌn'lɪstɪd] ADJ 1 (*St Ex*) **~ company** sociedad *f* sin cotización oficial, compañía *f* no cotizable; **~ securities** valores *mpl* no inscritos en bolsa

2 (*US Telec*) **~ number** número *m* que no figura en la guía telefónica

3 **~ building** (*Brit*) *edificio no catalogado como de interés histórico o arquitectónico*

unlit ['ʌn'lɪt] ADJ 1 (= *not burning*) [*fire, cigarette, pipe*] sin encender, apagado

2 (= *dark*) [*place*] no iluminado, oscuro

unload ['ʌn'ləʊd] Ⓐ VT 1 descargar; **we ~ed the furniture** descargamos los muebles

2 (*) (= *get rid of*) deshacerse de

Ⓑ VI descargar

unloaded ['ʌn'ləʊdɪd] ADJ [*gun*] descargado; [*truck, ship*] descargado, sin carga

unloading ['ʌn'ləʊdɪŋ] N descarga *f*

unlock ['ʌn'lɒk] Ⓐ VT 1 [+ *door, box*] abrir (con llave); **the door is ~ed** la puerta no está cerrada con llave; **he ~ed the door of the car** abrió la puerta del coche

2 (*fig*) [+ *heart*] ganarse; [+ *mystery*] resolver; [+ *secret*] descubrir; [+ *potential*] liberar

Ⓑ VI [*lock, box, door*] abrirse

unlooked-for [ʌn'lʊktfɔːʳ] ADJ inesperado, inopinado

unloose ['ʌn'luːs], **unloosen** ['ʌn'luːsn] VT aflojar, soltar

unlovable ['ʌn'lʌvəbl] ADJ antipático

unloved ['ʌn'lʌvd] ADJ no amado; **to feel ~** sentirse rechazado

unlovely ['ʌn'lʌvlɪ] ADJ feo, sin atractivo

unloving ['ʌn'lʌvɪŋ] ADJ nada cariñoso

unluckily [ʌn'lʌkɪlɪ] ADV lamentablemente, desgraciadamente; **~, she herself had no creative talent** lamentablemente *or* desgraciadamente, ella no tenía talento creativo; **~ for her** lamentablemente *or* desgraciadamente para ella; **the day started ~** el día empezó sin suerte

unluckiness [ʌn'lʌkɪnɪs] N mala suerte *f*

unlucky [ʌn'lʌkɪ] ADJ (*compar* **unluckier**, *superl* **unluckiest**) 1 (= *luckless*) [*person*] desafortunado; [*day*] de mala suerte; **the ~ ones had to wait another hour** los menos afortunados tuvieron que esperar otra hora; **how very ~!** ¡qué mala suerte!; **to be ~** [*person*] tener mala suerte; **he was ~ enough to meet him** tuvo la mala suerte *or* la desgracia de encontrarse con él; **to be ~ in love** no tener suerte en el amor; **he was ~ not to score a second goal** no tuvo la suerte de marcar un segundo gol

2 (= *causing bad luck*) [*number, object*] que trae mala suerte; **that dress is ~ for me** ese vestido me trae mala suerte; **it's ~ to break a mirror** romper un espejo trae mala suerte

3 (= *ill-omened*) [*day, omen*] funesto, nefasto; **1990 was an ~ year for me** 1990 fue un año de mala suerte para mí

unmade ['ʌn'meɪd] ADJ [*bed*] sin hacer; (*Brit*) (= *unsurfaced*) [*road*] sin pavimentar, sin asfaltar

unmake ['ʌn'meɪk] (*pt, pp* **unmade**) VT deshacer

unman ['ʌn'mæn] VT 1 (*liter*) amedrentar (*liter*), acobardar

2 [+ *post etc*] desguarnecer

unmanageable [ʌn'mænɪdʒəbl] ADJ 1 (= *overwhelming*) [*problem, system, situation, size, number*] imposible de controlar; [*hair*] difícil de peinar, rebelde

2 (= *unruly*) [*person*] rebelde; [*animal*] difícil de controlar, rebelde

unmanly ['ʌn'mænlɪ] ADJ impropio de un hombre; **it is ~ to cry** los hombres no lloran, llorar no es propio de un hombre

unmanned ['ʌn'mænd] ADJ no tripulado

unmannerly [ʌn'mænəlɪ] ADJ (*frm*) descortés

unmarked ['ʌn'mɑːkt] ADJ 1 (= *unscratched*) [*person*] sin ningún rasguño; [*face*] sin señales

2 (= *anonymous*) [*grave*] sin nombre; [*police car*] particular, camuflado (*Sp*); [*container, en-*

► LANGUAGE IN USE: **unlike A** 26.3 **unlikely 1** 16.2, 26.3

velope] sin marcar
3 (*Educ*) (= *uncorrected*) [*essay, exam etc*] sin corregir
4 (*Sport*) [*player*] desmarcado
5 (*Ling*) no marcado

unmarketable ['ʌn'mɑːkɪtəbl] ADJ invendible

unmarriageable ['ʌn'mærɪdʒəbl] ADJ incasable

unmarried ['ʌn'mærɪd] ADJ soltero; **an ~ mother** una madre soltera; **an ~ couple** una pareja no casada; **the ~ state** el estado de soltero, la soltería

unmask ['ʌn'mɑːsk] Ⓐ VT (*lit, fig*) desenmascarar
Ⓑ VI quitarse la máscara, descubrirse

unmast ['ʌn'mɑːst] VT desarbolar

unmatched ['ʌn'mætʃt] ADJ incomparable, sin par

unmemorable ['ʌn'memərəbəl] ADJ nada memorable, indigno de ser recordado

unmentionable [ʌn'menʃnəbl] Ⓐ ADJ que no se puede *or* quiere mencionar *or* nombrar
Ⓑ NPL **unmentionables†** (*hum*) prendas *fpl* íntimas

unmerciful [ʌn'mɜːsɪfʊl] ADJ despiadado

unmercifully [ʌn'mɜːsɪfəlɪ] ADV despiadadamente

unmerited ['ʌn'merɪtɪd] ADJ inmerecido

unmet [ʌn'met] ADJ [*needs, demands*] insatisfecho; **basic needs that are going ~** necesidades *fpl* básicas que no están siendo satisfechas

unmethodical ['ʌnmɪ'θɒdɪkəl] ADJ poco metódico, desordenado

unmindful [ʌn'maɪndfʊl] ADJ **to be ~ of sth** no hacer caso de algo, hacer caso omiso de algo; **~ of the danger, he …** él, haciendo caso omiso del peligro …

unmissable* [,ʌn'mɪsəbəl] ADJ (*Brit*) [*event, film*] que no se puede perder, que hay que ver/coger *etc*; **it was an ~ chance/opportunity** era una oportunidad que no podía/podíamos perder, era una oportunidad que había que coger

unmistakable ['ʌnmɪs'teɪkəbl] ADJ inconfundible, inequívoco

unmistakably ['ʌnmɪs'teɪkəblɪ] ADV de modo inconfundible; **it is ~ mine** sin duda alguna es mío

unmitigated [ʌn'mɪtɪgeɪtɪd] ADJ [*disaster, failure*] auténtico, verdadero; [*success*] rotundo; [*delight*] puro, verdadero; [*nonsense*] puro; [*liar, rogue*] redomado, rematado; **it was an ~ disaster** fue un auténtico *or* verdadero desastre

unmixed ['ʌn'mɪkst] ADJ sin mezcla, puro

unmolested ['ʌnmə'lestɪd] ADJ tranquilo, seguro; **to do sth ~** hacer algo sin ser molestado por otros

unmotivated ['ʌn'məʊtɪveɪtɪd] ADJ sin motivo, inmotivado

unmounted ['ʌn'maʊntɪd] ADJ 1 (= *without horse*) [*rider*] desmontado
2 (= *without mounting*) [*gem*] sin engastar; [*photo, stamp*] sin pegar; [*picture*] sin enmarcar

unmourned ['ʌn'mɔːnd] ADJ no llorado

unmoved ['ʌn'muːvd] ADJ impasible; **to remain ~ by** seguir indiferente ante, permanecer impasible frente a; **it leaves me ~** no me conmueve, me deja frío

unmoving ['ʌn'muːvɪŋ] ADJ inmóvil

unmusical ['ʌn'mjuːzɪkəl] ADJ [*sound, rendition*] inarmónico; [*person*] poco musical, sin oído para la música

unmuzzle [,ʌn'mʌzl] VT [+ *dog*] quitar el bozal a; (*fig*) [+ *press etc*] quitar la mordaza a; **~d** sin bozal; (*fig*) libre, sin mordaza

➤ LANGUAGE IN USE: **unpleasant** 7.3

unnamed ['ʌn'neɪmd] ADJ (= *nameless*) sin nombre; (= *anonymous*) anónimo

unnatural [ʌn'nætʃrəl] ADJ 1 (= *unusual, abnormal*) poco normal, poco natural; **her arm was twisted into an ~ position** tenía el brazo torcido en una postura poco normal *or* natural; **it was ~ for her to be so talkative** era extraño *or* raro en ella hablar tanto; **it's ~ to eat so much** no es normal comer tanto; **~ death** muerte *f* por causas no naturales; **it is not ~ to think that …** es normal pensar que …; **there was an ~ silence** se hizo un silencio irreal
2 (= *affected*) [*smile, voice, manner*] poco natural, forzado
3 (= *perverted*) [*habit, vice, practice*] antinatural

unnaturally [ʌn'nætʃrəlɪ] ADV 1 (= *unusually, abnormally*) extrañamente; **she was ~ subdued that day** estaba extrañamente apagada aquel día; **not ~, he was cross** como es natural *or* lógico se enfadó
2 (= *affectedly*) [*speak, act*] de manera poco natural, afectadamente

unnavigable ['ʌn'nævɪgəbl] ADJ innavegable

unnecessarily [ʌn'nesɪsərɪlɪ] ADV innecesariamente, sin necesidad; **I don't want him to suffer ~** no quiero que sufra innecesariamente *or* sin necesidad

unnecessary [ʌn'nesɪsərɪ] ADJ innecesario; **it is ~ to add that …** no hace falta añadir que …, no es necesario añadir que …

unneighbourly, **unneighborly** (*US*) ['ʌn'neɪbəlɪ] ADJ [*person*] poco amistoso; [*attitude, behaviour*] impropio de un buen vecino

unnerve ['ʌn'nɜːv] VT desconcertar

unnerving ['ʌn'nɜːvɪŋ] ADJ desconcertante

unnervingly ['ʌn'nɜːvɪŋlɪ] ADV **~ quiet/calm** de una frialdad/calma desconcertante

unnoticed ['ʌn'nəʊtɪst] ADJ inadvertido, desapercibido; **to go** *or* **pass ~** pasar inadvertido *or* desapercibido

unnumbered ['ʌn'nʌmbəd] ADJ sin numerar; (= *countless*) innumerable

UNO N ABBR (= **United Nations Organization**) ONU *f*

unobjectionable ['ʌnəb'dʒekʃnəbl] ADJ inofensivo

unobservant ['ʌnəb'zɜːvənt] ADJ [*person etc*] distraído, poco atento

unobserved ['ʌnəb'zɜːvd] ADJ 1 (= *not seen*) inadvertido, desapercibido; **to get away ~** lograr pasar inadvertido *or* desapercibido
2 (= *not celebrated*) sin celebrar *or* (*LAm*) festejar

unobstructed ['ʌnəb'strʌktɪd] ADJ [*pipe etc*] despejado; [*view etc*] perfecto

unobtainable ['ʌnəb'teɪnəbl] ADJ 1 (= *unavailable*) [*goods*] imposible de conseguir
2 (= *unrealizable*) [*goal, objective*] inalcanzable, imposible de conseguir *or* realizar
3 (*Telec*) [*number*] desconectado; **his number was ~** su número estaba desconectado
4 (*sexually*) [*person*] imposible de conseguir

unobtrusive ['ʌnəb'truːsɪv] ADJ discreto, modesto

unobtrusively ['ʌnəb'truːsɪvlɪ] ADV discretamente, modestamente

unoccupied ['ʌn'ɒkjʊpaɪd] ADJ 1 (= *empty*) [*building*] desocupado, vacío; [*room*] vacío; [*seat, table*] libre; [*post*] vacante
2 (*Mil*) [*country, zone*] no ocupado
3 (= *not busy*) [*person*] desocupado

unofficial ['ʌnə'fɪʃəl] ADJ 1 (= *informal*) [*visit, tour*] no oficial, extraoficial; **in an ~ capacity** de forma *or* manera extraoficial *or* no oficial; **from an ~ source** de fuente oficiosa; **~ strike** huelga *f* no oficial
2 (= *de facto*) [*leader, spokesperson*] no oficial
3 (= *unconfirmed*) [*report, results*] no oficial

unofficially ['ʌnə'fɪʃəlɪ] ADV extraoficialmente; **I have already asked him ~** ya le he preguntado extraoficialmente

unopened ['ʌn'əʊpənd] ADJ sin abrir

unopposed ['ʌnə'pəʊzd] ADJ sin oposición; (*Mil*) sin encontrar resistencia; **to be returned ~** (*Parl*) ganar un escaño sin oposición

unorganized ['ʌn'ɔːgənaɪzd] ADJ (= *spontaneous*) no organizado; (= *untidy*) desorganizado

unoriginal ['ʌnə'rɪdʒɪnəl] ADJ poco original

unorthodox ['ʌn'ɔːθədɒks] ADJ 1 (= *unconventional*) poco ortodoxo, poco convencional
2 (*Rel*) heterodoxo

unostentatious ['ʌn,ɒsten'teɪʃəs] ADJ modesto, sin ostentación

unpack ['ʌn'pæk] Ⓐ VT deshacer, desempacar (*LAm*); **I ~ed my suitcase** deshice la maleta; **I haven't ~ed my clothes yet** todavía no he sacado la ropa de la maleta
Ⓑ VI deshacer las maletas, desempacar (*LAm*); **I went to my room to ~** fui a mi habitación a deshacer la(s) maleta(s)

unpacking ['ʌn'pækɪŋ] N **to do one's ~** deshacer las maletas, desempacar (*LAm*)

unpaid ['ʌn'peɪd] ADJ [*staff, worker, overtime*] no remunerado, no retribuido; [*leave*] sin paga, sin sueldo; [*debts, bills*] sin pagar, pendiente; [*taxes, rent*] sin pagar

unpalatable [ʌn'pælɪtəbl] ADJ 1 (*in taste*) [*food*] de mal sabor
2 (*fig*) (= *difficult*) [*truth, fact*] difícil de aceptar

unparalleled [ʌn'pærəleld] ADJ [*opportunity, prosperity, event*] sin precedentes, sin paralelo; [*beauty, wit*] sin par, incomparable; **this is ~ in our history** esto no tiene precedentes en nuestra historia

unpardonable [ʌn'pɑːdnəbl] ADJ imperdonable, indisculpable

unpardonably [ʌn'pɑːdnəblɪ] ADV imperdonablemente

unparliamentary ['ʌn,pɑːlə'mentərɪ] ADJ antiparlamentario

unpatented ['ʌn,peɪtntɪd] ADJ sin patentar

unpatriotic ['ʌn,pætrɪ'ɒtɪk] ADJ antipatriótico, poco patriótico

unpatriotically ['ʌn,pætrɪ'ɒtɪkəlɪ] ADV de modo antipatriótico

unpaved ['ʌn'peɪvd] ADJ sin pavimentar, sin asfaltar

unperceived ['ʌnpə'siːvd] ADJ inadvertido, desapercibido

unperturbed ['ʌnpɜː'tɜːbd] ADJ impertérrito; **he carried on ~** siguió sin inmutarse *or* (*LAm*) alterarse; **~ by this disaster …** sin dejarse desanimar por esta catástrofe …

unpick ['ʌn'pɪk] VT descoser

unpin ['ʌn'pɪn] VT desprender, quitar los alfileres a

unplaced ['ʌn'pleɪst] ADJ (*Sport*) no colocado

unplanned ['ʌn'plænd] ADJ [*pregnancy*] sin planear; [*visit*] imprevisto

unplayable ['ʌn'pleɪəbl] ADJ [*pitch*] en condiciones tan malas que está inservible

➤**unpleasant** [ʌn'pleznt] ADJ (*gen*) desagradable; [*person*] desagradable, antipático; **to be ~ to sb** ser desagradable *or* antipático con algn

unpleasantly [ʌn'plezntlɪ] ADV de manera poco agradable; **"no," he said ~** —no —dijo en tono nada amistoso; **the bomb fell ~ close** la bomba cayó lo bastante cerca como para inquietarnos

unpleasantness [ʌn'plezntnɪs] N (*gen*) lo desagradable; [*of person*] lo antipático, lo desagradable; (= *bad feeling, quarrel*) desavenencia *f*, disgusto *m*; **there has been a lot of ~** ha habido muchos disgustos *or* muchas desavenencias

unpleasing [ʌn'pli:zɪŋ] ADJ poco atractivo, antiestético; **~ to the ear** poco grato al oído

unplug ['ʌn'plʌg] VT desenchufar, desconectar

unplugged [,ʌn'plʌgd] ADJ (*Mus*) unplugged, *sin efectos acústicos ni elementos electrónicos*

unplumbed ['ʌn'plʌmd] ADJ no sondado, insondable

unpoetic ['ʌnpəʊ'etɪk] ADJ poco poético

unpoetical ['ʌnpəʊ'etɪkəl] ADJ = **unpoetic**

unpolished ['ʌn'pɒlɪʃt] ADJ 1 sin pulir; [*diamond*] en bruto
2 (*fig*) tosco, inculto

unpolluted ['ʌnpə'lu:tɪd] ADJ no contaminado, impoluto

unpopular ['ʌn'pɒpjʊləʳ] ADJ (*gen*) impopular, poco popular; (= *unacceptable*) inaceptable, mal visto; **it was an ~ decision** fue una decisión impopular; **she's an ~ child** tiene muy pocos amigos; **it is ~ with the miners** los mineros no lo aceptan, los mineros lo ven mal; **to make o.s. ~** hacerse impopular; **you will be very ~ with me** no te lo agradeceré

unpopularity ['ʌn,pɒpjʊ'lærɪtɪ] N impopularidad *f*

unpopulated ['ʌn'pɒpjʊleɪtɪd] ADJ deshabitado, desierto

unpractical ['ʌn'præktɪkəl] ADJ [*plan, scheme, idea*] poco práctico; [*person*] falto de sentido práctico

unpractised, **unpracticed** (*US*) [ʌn'præktɪst] ADJ inexperto

unprecedented [ʌn'presɪdəntɪd] ADJ sin precedentes, inaudito

unpredictability ['ʌnprɪ,dɪktə'bɪlɪtɪ] N [*of situation*] lo imprevisible, imprevisibilidad *f*; [*of person*] carácter *m* caprichoso, volubilidad *f*

unpredictable ['ʌnprɪ'dɪktəbl] ADJ [*event*] imprevisible; [*situation*] impredecible, incierto; [*weather*] variable; [*person*] caprichoso, de reacción imprevisible

unpredictably ['ʌnprɪ'dɪktəblɪ] ADV de manera imprevisible, imprevisiblemente; [*behave*] caprichosamente, de manera voluble

unprejudiced [ʌn'predʒʊdɪst] ADJ (= *not biased*) imparcial; (= *having no prejudices*) sin prejuicios

unpremeditated ['ʌnprɪ'medɪteɪtɪd] ADJ impremeditado

unprepared ['ʌnprɪ'pɛəd] ADJ 1 (= *unready*) **the student who comes to an exam ~** el estudiante que viene al examen sin estar preparado *or* sin preparación; **to catch sb ~** pillar a algn desprevenido; **to be ~ for sth** (= *not expect*) no contar con algo, no esperar algo; (= *be unequipped*) no estar preparado para algo; **she was totally ~ for motherhood** no estaba preparada para ser madre en absoluto
2 (= *improvised*) [*speech, lecture*] improvisado
3 (= *unwilling*) **to be ~ to do sth** no estar dispuesto a hacer algo

unpreparedness ['ʌnprɪ'pɛərɪdnɪs] N falta *f* de preparación

unprepossessing ['ʌn,pri:pə'zesɪŋ] ADJ poco atractivo

unpresentable ['ʌnprɪ'zentəbl] ADJ mal apersonado

unpretentious ['ʌnprɪ'tenʃəs] ADJ sin pretensiones, modesto

unpriced ['ʌn'praɪst] ADJ sin precio

unprincipled [ʌn'prɪnsɪpld] ADJ sin escrúpulos, cínico

unprintable ['ʌn'prɪntəbl] ADJ 1 (= *unpublishable*) [*article*] impublicable
2 (*hum*) (= *shocking*) [*story*] impublicable; [*remark, comment*] irrepetible

unproductive ['ʌnprə'dʌktɪv] ADJ [*capital, soil etc*] improductivo; [*meeting etc*] infructuoso

unprofessional ['ʌnprə'feʃənl] ADJ [*person, behaviour, attitude*] poco profesional; **it was ~ of her** fue poco profesional de su parte; **~ conduct** comportamiento *m* contrario a la ética profesional

unprofitable [ʌn'prɒfɪtəbl] ADJ 1 (= *uneconomic*) [*business, industry, route*] poco rentable
2 (= *fruitless*) [*argument, activity, day*] inútil

UNPROFOR, Unprofor ['ʌnprəʊfɔ:ʳ] N ABBR (= **United Nations Protection Force**) FORPRONU *f*, Unprofor *f*

unpromising ['ʌn'prɒmɪsɪŋ] ADJ poco prometedor; **it looks ~** no promete mucho

unprompted ['ʌn'prɒmptɪd] ADJ espontáneo

unpronounceable ['ʌnprə'naʊnsəbl] ADJ impronunciable

unpropitious ['ʌnprə'pɪʃəs] ADJ impropicio, poco propicio

unprotected ['ʌnprə'tektɪd] ADJ 1 (= *defenceless*) [*person*] indefenso; **to leave sth ~** dejar algo sin protección; **to be ~ by the law** no estar protegido por la ley
2 (= *uncovered*) [*skin, eyes, plants*] sin protección; **to be ~ from the sun** no estar protegido del sol
3 **~ sex** ◊ **~ intercourse** relaciones *fpl* sexuales sin protección

unproved ['ʌn'pru:vd], **unproven** [ʌn'pru:vən] ADJ no probado

unprovided-for [ʌnprə'vaɪdɪd,fɔ:ʳ] ADJ [*person*] desamparado, desvalido

unprovoked ['ʌnprə'vəʊkt] ADJ no provocado, sin provocación

unpublished ['ʌn'pʌblɪʃt] ADJ inédito, no publicado

unpunctual ['ʌn'pʌŋktjʊəl] ADJ poco puntual; **this train is always ~** este tren siempre llega con retraso

unpunctuality ['ʌn,pʌŋktjʊ'ælɪtɪ] N falta *f* de puntualidad, atraso *m*

unpunished ['ʌn'pʌnɪʃt] ADJ **to go ~** [*crime*] quedar sin castigo, quedar impune; [*person*] escapar sin castigo, salir impune

unputdownable* ['ʌnpʊt'daʊnəbl] ADJ absorbente, que no se puede dejar de la mano

unqualified ['ʌn'kwɒlɪfaɪd] ADJ 1 (= *without qualifications*) [*person, staff, pilot*] no calificado, no cualificado; [*teacher*] sin título, no titulado; **to be ~ to do sth** no estar capacitado para hacer algo
2 (= *unmitigated*) [*success, disaster*] rotundo, total y absoluto; [*acceptance, support, approval*] incondicional

unquenchable [ʌn'kwentʃəbl] ADJ (*fig*) inextinguible; [*thirst*] inapagable; [*desire etc*] insaciable

unquestionable [ʌn'kwestʃənəbl] ADJ indiscutible, incuestionable

➤ **unquestionably** [ʌn'kwestʃənəblɪ] ADV indiscutiblemente, incuestionablemente

unquestioned [ʌn'kwestʃənd] ADJ (= *unchallenged*) indiscutido, incontestable

unquestioning [ʌn'kwestʃənɪŋ] ADJ [*acceptance*] incondicional, ciego; [*loyalty*] incondicional; [*faith etc*] ciego

unquestioningly [ʌn'kwestʃənɪŋlɪ] ADV incondicionalmente; [*accept, obey*] ciegamente

unquiet ['ʌn'kwaɪət] ADJ inquieto

unquote ['ʌn'kwəʊt] N *see* **quote D**

unquoted ['ʌn'kwəʊtɪd] ADJ [*share etc*] no cotizado, sin cotización oficial

unravel [ʌn'rævəl] Ⓐ VT desenredar, desenmarañar
Ⓑ VI desenredarse, desenmarañarse

unread ['ʌn'red] ADJ no leído; **to leave sth ~** dejar algo sin leer

unreadable ['ʌn'ri:dəbl] ADJ 1 (= *turgid*) [*book*] imposible de leer; **I found the book ~** el libro me resultó pesadísimo
2 (= *illegible*) [*handwriting etc*] ilegible
3 (*Comput*) [*data*] ilegible
4 (*liter*) (= *impenetrable*) [*face, eyes*] impenetrable

unreadiness ['ʌn'redɪnɪs] N desprevención *f*

unready ['ʌn'redɪ] ADJ desprevenido

unreal ['ʌn'rɪəl] ADJ 1 (= *not real*) [*situation, world*] irreal
2 (*) (= *excellent*) increíble*; (= *unbelievable*) increíble

unrealistic ['ʌnrɪə'lɪstɪk] ADJ poco realista; **it is ~ to expect that ...** no es realista esperar que ...

unrealistically ['ʌnrɪə'lɪstɪkəlɪ] ADV **the prices are ~ high** los precios son tan altos que no son realistas

unreality ['ʌnrɪ'ælɪtɪ] N irrealidad *f*

unrealizable ['ʌnrɪə'laɪzəbl] ADJ irrealizable

unrealized ['ʌn'ri:əlaɪzd] ADJ [*ambition*] no realizado, que ha quedado sin realizar; [*objective*] no logrado

unreason ['ʌn'ri:zn] N insensatez *f*

unreasonable [ʌn'ri:znəbl] ADJ [*person, behaviour*] irrazonable, poco razonable; [*price, amount*] excesivo; **he was most ~ about it** reaccionó en forma irracional; **I think her attitude is ~** creo que su actitud es poco razonable

unreasonableness [ʌn'ri:znəblnɪs] N irracionalidad *f*, lo irrazonable

unreasonably [ʌn'ri:znəblɪ] ADV **to be ~ difficult about sth** porfiar estúpidamente en algo

unreasoning [ʌn'ri:znɪŋ] ADJ irracional

unreceptive ['ʌnrɪ'septɪv] ADJ poco receptivo

unreclaimed ['ʌnrɪ'kleɪmd] ADJ [*land*] no rescatado, no utilizado

unrecognizable ['ʌn'rekəgnaɪzəbl] ADJ irreconocible

unrecognized ['ʌn'rekəgnaɪzd] ADJ 1 (= *unnoticed*) [*talent, genius*] desapercibido, no reconocido; **to go ~** pasar desapercibido; **he walked along the road ~ by passers-by** fue por la calle sin que los transeúntes le reconocieran
2 (*Pol*) [*government, party, country*] no reconocido

unreconstructed [,ʌnri:kən'strʌktɪd] ADJ [*system, idea, policy*] no reformado, inamovible; [*person*] recalcitrante

unrecorded ['ʌnrɪ'kɔ:dɪd] ADJ no registrado, ignorado

unredeemed ['ʌnrɪ'di:md] ADJ no redimido; [*promise*] sin cumplir, incumplido; [*pledge*] no desempeñado; [*bill*] sin redimir; [*debt*] sin amortizar

➤ LANGUAGE IN USE: **unquestionably** 26.3

unreel [ʌn'rɪəl] VT desenrollar

unrefined ['ʌnrɪ'faɪnd] ADJ [1] (= *not processed*) [*oil, sugar etc*] crudo, sin refinar
[2] (= *coarse*) [*person, manners*] poco refinado

unreflecting ['ʌnrɪ'flektɪŋ] ADJ irreflexivo

unreformed ['ʌnrɪ'fɔ:md] ADJ no reformado

unregarded ['ʌnrɪ'gɑ:dɪd] ADJ desatendido, no estimado; **those ~ aspects** aquellos aspectos de los que nadie hace caso

unregenerate ['ʌnrɪ'dʒenərɪt] ADJ empedernido

unregistered ['ʌn'redʒɪstəd] ADJ no registrado; [*letter*] sin certificar

unregretted ['ʌnrɪ'gretɪd] ADJ no llorado, no lamentado

unrehearsed ['ʌnrɪ'hɜ:st] ADJ (*Theat etc*) no ensayado; (= *spontaneous*) improvisado

unrelated ['ʌnrɪ'leɪtɪd] ADJ [1] (= *unconnected*) inconexo
[2] (*by family*) no emparentado; **they are ~ to each other** no están emparentados

unrelenting ['ʌnrɪ'lentɪŋ] ADJ [*rain, heat, attack*] implacable; [*person*] despiadado

unreliability ['ʌnrɪ,laɪə'bɪlɪtɪ] N falta *f* de fiabilidad

unreliable ['ʌnrɪ'laɪəbl] ADJ [*person*] informal, poco de fiar; [*machine, service*] poco fiable, que no es de fiar; [*information, statistics*] poco fiable; [*weather, climate*] variable, inestable; **they thought British workers were ~** opinaban que a los trabajadores británicos les faltaba formalidad, opinaban que los trabajadores británicos eran muy informales *or* no eran muy de fiar; **the phones here are ~** los teléfonos aquí son poco fiables *or* no son de fiar; **my memory is so ~ these days** mi memoria no es muy de fiar últimamente

unrelieved ['ʌnrɪ'li:vd] ADJ [*work etc*] continuo; **~ by** no aliviado por, no mitigado por; **sadness ~ by hope** tristeza *f* sin alivio de esperanza; **three hours of ~ boredom** tres horas de aburrimiento total

unremarkable ['ʌnrɪ'mɑ:kəbl] ADJ ordinario, corriente

unremarked ['ʌnrɪ'mɑ:kt] ADJ inadvertido

unremitting ['ʌnrɪ'mɪtɪŋ] ADJ incansable; (= *continuous*) continuo

unremittingly ['ʌnrɪ'mɪtɪŋlɪ] ADV incansablemente

unremunerative ['ʌnrɪ'mju:nərətɪv] ADJ poco remunerador, poco lucrativo

unrepealed ['ʌnrɪ'pi:ld] ADJ no revocado

unrepeatable ['ʌnrɪ'pi:təbl] ADJ irrepetible, que no puede repetirse; **what he said is quite ~** no me atrevo a repetir lo que dijo; **an ~ bargain** una ganga única

unrepentant ['ʌnrɪ'pentənt] ADJ impenitente

unreported [,ʌnrɪ'pɔ:tɪd] ADJ [*crime*] no denunciado, sin denunciar; **the news went ~** la noticia no fue comunicada

unrepresentative ['ʌn,reprɪ'zentətɪv] ADJ (= *untypical*) poco representativo; **to be ~ of sth** no ser representativo de algo; **he holds an ~ view** mantiene una opinión poco representativa

unrepresented ['ʌn,reprɪ'zentɪd] ADJ sin representación; **they are ~ in the House** no tienen representación en la Cámara

unrequited ['ʌnrɪ'kwaɪtɪd] ADJ no correspondido

unreserved ['ʌnrɪ'zɜ:vd] ADJ [1] (= *not booked*) no reservado
[2] (= *frank*) franco, directo
[3] (= *complete*) total, completo

unreservedly ['ʌnrɪ'zɜ:vɪdlɪ] ADV sin reserva, incondicionalmente

unresisting ['ʌnrɪ'zɪstɪŋ] ADJ sumiso

unresolved ['ʌnrɪ'zɒlvd] ADJ [*problem*] no resuelto, pendiente

unresponsive ['ʌnrɪs'pɒnsɪv] ADJ insensible, sordo (**to** a)

unrest [ʌn'rest] N [1] (*Pol*) malestar *m*; (= *riots*) disturbios *mpl*; **the ~ in the Congo** los disturbios del Congo
[2] (= *unease*) malestar *m*, inquietud *f*

unrestrained ['ʌnrɪ'streɪnd] ADJ [1] (= *uncontrolled*) [*joy, laughter, violence*] desenfrenado, incontrolado; [*enthusiasm*] desbordante; **to be ~ by morality** no estar frenado por la moralidad; **to be ~ in one's views** expresar su opinión sin reservas
[2] (= *not held physically*) [*car passenger*] sin cinturón; [*patient, prisoner*] sin maniatar

unrestrainedly ['ʌnrɪ'streɪnɪdlɪ] ADV desenfrenadamente, incontroladamente

unrestricted ['ʌnrɪ'strɪktɪd] ADJ [1] (= *unlimited*) [*use, right*] ilimitado; **~ access** libre acceso *m*
[2] (= *unobstructed*) [*view*] perfecto

unrevealed ['ʌnrɪ'vi:ld] ADJ no revelado

unrewarded ['ʌnrɪ'wɔ:dɪd] ADJ sin recompensa; **to go ~** quedar sin recompensa

unrewarding ['ʌnrɪ'wɔ:dɪŋ] ADJ ingrato; (*financially*) improductivo

unrighteous [ʌn'raɪtʃəs] Ⓐ ADJ malo, perverso
Ⓑ NPL **the ~** los malos, los perversos

unripe ['ʌn'raɪp] ADJ verde

unrivalled, unrivaled (*US*) [ʌn'raɪvəld] ADJ sin par, incomparable; **Bilbao is ~ for food** la cocina bilbaína es incomparable

unroadworthy ['ʌn'rəʊd,wɜ:ðɪ] ADJ no apto para circular

unrobe ['ʌn'rəʊb] (*frm*) Ⓐ VI desvestirse, desnudarse
Ⓑ VT desvestir, desnudar

unroll ['ʌn'rəʊl] Ⓐ VT desenrollar
Ⓑ VI desenrollarse

unromantic ['ʌnrə'mæntɪk] ADJ poco romántico

unroof ['ʌn'ru:f] VT destechar, quitar el techo de

unrope ['ʌn'rəʊp] Ⓐ VT desatar
Ⓑ VI desatarse

UNRRA N ABBR (*formerly*) = **United Nations Relief and Rehabilitation Administration**

unruffled ['ʌn'rʌfld] ADJ [1] [*person*] sereno, imperturbable; **he carried on quite ~** siguió sin inmutarse
[2] [*hair, surface*] liso

unruled ['ʌn'ru:ld] ADJ [*paper*] sin rayar, sin pautar

unruly [ʌn'ru:lɪ] ADJ (*compar* **unrulier**; *superl* **unruliest**) [1] [*behaviour*] rebelde; [*child*] revoltoso; [*mob*] alterado
[2] (*liter*) [*hair*] rebelde

UNRWA N ABBR = **United Nations Relief and Works Agency**

unsaddle ['ʌn'sædl] VT [+ *rider*] desarzonar; [+ *horse*] desensillar, quitar la silla a

unsafe ['ʌn'seɪf] ADJ [1] (= *dangerous*) [*building, neighbourhood*] peligroso, poco seguro; [*machine, vehicle, wiring*] poco seguro, peligroso; [*working conditions*] peligroso; **the car is ~ to drive** el coche no está en condiciones de conducirlo; **it is ~ to walk there at night** es peligroso caminar por ahí de noche; **to declare a building ~** declarar un edificio un peligro
[2] (= *in danger*) **to be ~** [*person*] estar en peligro; **to feel ~** no sentirse seguro
[3] (*Jur*) (= *dubious*) [*evidence, conviction, verdict*] abierto a revisión judicial
[4] (= *unprotected*) **~ sex** relaciones *fpl* sexuales sin protección

unsaid ['ʌn'sed] ADJ sin decir; **to leave sth ~** callar algo, dejar de decir algo; **to leave nothing ~** no dejar nada en el tintero; **much was left ~** muchas cosas se quedaron por decir

unsalable ['ʌn'seɪləbl] ADJ (*US*) = **unsaleable**

unsalaried ['ʌn'sælərɪd] ADJ sin sueldo, no remunerado

unsaleable, unsalable (*US*) ['ʌn'seɪləbl] ADJ invendible

unsalted [,ʌn'sɒltɪd] ADJ sin sal

unsanitary [,ʌn'sænɪtərɪ] ADJ insalubre, antihigiénico

unsatisfactory ['ʌn,sætɪs'fæktərɪ] ADJ poco satisfactorio; [*work*] insatisfactorio

unsatisfied ['ʌn'sætɪsfaɪd] ADJ insatisfecho

unsatisfying ['ʌn'sætɪsfaɪɪŋ] ADJ poco satisfactorio; (= *insufficient*) insuficiente

unsaturated ['ʌn'sætʃəreɪtɪd] ADJ no saturado, insaturado

unsavoury, unsavory (*US*) ['ʌn'seɪvərɪ] ADJ [*person*] indeseable; [*remark etc*] desagradable, repugnante

unsay ['ʌn'seɪ] (*pt, pp* **unsaid**) VT desdecirse de

unscathed ['ʌn'skeɪðd] ADJ ileso; **to escape/get out ~** salir ileso

unscheduled ['ʌn'ʃedju:ld] ADJ no programado

unscholarly ['ʌn'skɒləlɪ] ADJ [*person*] nada erudito; [*work*] indigno de un erudito

unschooled ['ʌn'sku:ld] ADJ indocto; **to be ~ in a technique** no haber aprendido nada de una técnica

unscientific ['ʌn,saɪən'tɪfɪk] ADJ poco científico

unscramble ['ʌn'skræmbl] VT (*Telec*) [+ *message*] descifrar; (*TV*) descodificar

unscrew ['ʌn'skru:] Ⓐ VT destornillar; [+ *lid*] desenroscar
Ⓑ VI destornillarse; [*lid*] desenroscar

unscripted ['ʌn'skrɪptɪd] ADJ [*speech, remark*] improvisado; (*Rad, TV*) [*programme*] sin guión

unscrupulous [ʌn'skru:pjʊləs] ADJ sin escrúpulos, poco escrupuloso

unscrupulously [ʌn'skru:pjʊləslɪ] ADV de modo poco escrupuloso

unscrupulousness [ʌn'skru:pjʊləsnɪs] N falta *f* de escrúpulos

unseal ['ʌn'si:l] VT desellar, abrir

unseasonable [ʌn'si:znəbl] ADJ [*weather*] impropio de la estación; [*clothes, food*] fuera de estación

unseasonably [ʌn'si:znəblɪ] ADV **we had an ~ warm spring** tuvimos una primavera calurosa para esa época del año; **it was ~ mild for late January** hacía un tiempo muy moderado para estar a últimos de enero

unseasoned ['ʌn'si:znd] ADJ no sazonado

unseat ['ʌn'si:t] VT [1] [+ *rider*] derribar, desarzonar; [+ *passenger etc*] echar de su asiento
[2] (*Parl*) [+ *MP*] hacer perder su escaño

unseaworthy ['ʌn'si:,wɜ:ðɪ] ADJ innavegable

unsecured ['ʌnsɪ'kjʊəd] Ⓐ ADJ (*Fin*) no respaldado, sin aval
Ⓑ CPD ► **unsecured creditor** N acreedor(a) *m/f* común ► **unsecured debt** N deuda *f* sin respaldo

unseeded ['ʌn'si:dɪd] ADJ [*player, team*] que no es cabeza de serie

unseeing ['ʌn'si:ɪŋ] ADJ (*fig*) ciego; **he stared, ~, out of the window** miraba por la ventana, con la mirada perdida; **to gaze at sth with ~ eyes** mirar algo sin verlo

unseemliness [ʌn'siːmlɪnɪs] N lo indecoroso, falta *f* de decoro, impropiedad *f*

unseemly [ʌn'siːmlɪ] ADJ (*gen*) mal visto; [*behaviour*] impropio, indecoroso

unseen ['ʌn'siːn] Ⓐ ADJ (= *hidden*) oculto; (= *unknown*) desconocido; [*translation*] hecho a primera vista; **he managed to get through ~** logró pasar inadvertido
Ⓑ N [1] (*Scol*) traducción *f* (al idioma materno) hecha a primera vista
[2] **the ~** lo invisible, lo oculto

unsegregated ['ʌn'segrɪgeɪtɪd] ADJ no segregado, sin segregación (racial *etc*)

unselfconscious ['ʌn,self'kɒnʃəs] ADJ natural

unselfconsciously ['ʌn,self'kɒnʃəslɪ] ADV de manera desenfadada

unselfish ['ʌn'selfɪʃ] ADJ desinteresado

unselfishly ['ʌn'selfɪʃlɪ] ADV desinteresadamente

unselfishness ['ʌn'selfɪʃnɪs] N desinterés *m*

unsentimental ['ʌnsentɪ'mentəl] ADJ nada sentimental

unserviceable ['ʌn'sɜːvɪsəbl] ADJ inservible, inútil

unsettle ['ʌn'setl] VT [+ *opponent*] desconcertar; [+ *relationship*] desestabilizar; **if this gets into the papers it will only ~ people** si esto se publica en los periódicos lo único que hará es poner nerviosa *or* inquietar a la gente; **don't let her comments ~ you** no dejes que sus comentarios te pongan nervioso

unsettled ['ʌn'setld] ADJ [1] (= *uneasy, restless*) [*person*] intranquilo; [*sleep, night*] agitado; **he's feeling ~ in his job** no está del todo contento *or* a gusto en su trabajo
[2] (= *undecided*) [*matter, question*] pendiente, sin resolver
[3] (= *changeable*) [*weather*] inestable, variable; [*situation, market*] inestable
[4] (= *not populated*) [*land*] sin colonizar
[5] (= *unpaid*) [*account, bill*] pendiente, sin saldar

unsettling ['ʌn'setlɪŋ] ADJ [*influence, effect*] desestabilizador; [*experience, dream*] perturbador; [*thought*] inquietante; **this is an ~ time for us all** esta época es preocupante para todos nosotros; **it is ~ to know he could be watching me** me inquieta saber que podría estar vigilándome

unsex ['ʌn'seks] VT (*liter*) privar de la sexualidad, suprimir el instinto sexual de

unshackle ['ʌn'ʃækl] VT desencadenar, quitar los grillos a

unshaded ['ʌn'ʃeɪdɪd] ADJ [*place*] sin sombra; [*bulb*] sin pantalla

unshak(e)able [ʌn'ʃeɪkəbl] ADJ [*belief*] inquebrantable; **he was ~ in his resolve** se mostró totalmente resuelto; **after three hours he was still ~** después de tres horas seguía tan resuelto como antes

unshaken ['ʌn'ʃeɪkən] ADJ impertérrito; **he was ~ by what had happened** no se dejó amedrentar por lo que había pasado

unshaven ['ʌn'ʃeɪvn] ADJ sin afeitar

unsheathe ['ʌn'ʃiːð] VT desenvainar

unship ['ʌn'ʃɪp] VT [+ *goods*] desembarcar; [+ *rudder, mast etc*] desmontar

unshockable ['ʌn'ʃɒkəbl] ADJ **she's ~** no se escandaliza por nada

unshod ['ʌn'ʃɒd] ADJ descalzo; [*horse*] desherrado

unshrinkable ['ʌn'ʃrɪŋkəbl] ADJ que no encoge, inencogible

unshrinking [ʌn'ʃrɪŋkɪŋ] ADJ impávido

unsighted ['ʌn'saɪtɪd] Ⓐ ADJ (= *blind*) invidente; (= *with no view*) **I was ~ for a moment** por un momento no pude ver
Ⓑ CPD ► **unsighted person** N invidente *mf*

unsightliness [ʌn'saɪtlɪnɪs] N fealdad *f*

unsightly [ʌn'saɪtlɪ] ADJ feo

unsigned ['ʌn'saɪnd] ADJ (= *without signature*) [*letter, article, contract*] sin firmar

unsinkable ['ʌn'sɪŋkəbl] ADJ insumergible

unskilful, **unskillful** (*US*) ['ʌn'skɪlfʊl] ADJ inexperto, desmañado

unskilled ['ʌn'skɪld] Ⓐ ADJ [*work*] no especializado
Ⓑ CPD ► **unskilled worker** N trabajador(a) *m/f* no cualificado/a, trabajador(a) *m/f* no calificado/a (*LAm*)

unskimmed ['ʌn'skɪmd] ADJ sin desnatar, sin descremar (*LAm*)

unsmiling ['ʌn'smaɪlɪŋ] ADJ adusto

unsmilingly ['ʌn'smaɪlɪŋlɪ] ADV sin sonreír

unsociability ['ʌn,səʊʃə'bɪlɪtɪ] N insociabilidad *f*

unsociable [ʌn'səʊʃəbl] ADJ insociable; [*person*] poco sociable, huraño

unsocial [ʌn'səʊʃəl] ADJ antisocial; **to work ~ hours** trabajar fuera de las horas normales

unsold ['ʌn'səʊld] ADJ por vender, sin venderse; **to remain ~** quedar por vender *or* sin venderse

unsoldierly ['ʌn'səʊldʒəlɪ] ADJ indigno de un militar, impropio de un militar

unsolicited ['ʌnsə'lɪsɪtɪd] ADJ no solicitado

unsolvable ['ʌn'sɒlvəbl] ADJ irresoluble, insoluble

unsolved ['ʌn'sɒlvd] ADJ no resuelto, sin resolver; **~ crime** crimen *m* que sigue sin resolver

unsophisticated ['ʌnsə'fɪstɪkeɪtɪd] ADJ sencillo, cándido; (*pej*) burdo

unsought ['ʌn'sɔːt] ADJ no solicitado; **the offer came quite ~** se hizo la oferta sin que se hubiera pedido nada

unsound ['ʌn'saʊnd] ADJ (*in health*) malo; (*in construction*) defectuoso; (= *unstable*) poco sólido *or* estable; [*argument*] poco sólido; **of ~ mind** (*Jur*) mentalmente incapacitado; **the book is ~ on some points** el libro yerra en algunos puntos, no hay que fiarse del libro en ciertos aspectos

unsoundness ['ʌn'saʊndnɪs] N lo defectuoso; [*of argument*] falta *f* de solidez

unsparing [ʌn'speərɪŋ] ADJ (= *generous*) pródigo, generoso; (= *untiring*) incansable; (= *unmerciful*) despiadado; **to be ~ in one's praise** no escatimar las alabanzas; **to be ~ in one's efforts to** + INFIN no regatear esfuerzo por + *infin*

unsparingly [ʌn'speərɪŋlɪ] ADV (= *generously*) generosamente, pródigamente; (= *untiringly*) incansablemente

unspeakable [ʌn'spiːkəbl] ADJ (= *terrible*) [*pain etc*] horrible; (= *dreadful*) incalificable

unspeakably [ʌn'spiːkəblɪ] ADV **to suffer ~** sufrir lo indecible; **it was ~ bad** fue horroroso

unspecified ['ʌn'spesɪfaɪd] ADJ no especificado

unspectacular [,ʌnspek'tækjʊləʳ] ADJ poco espectacular

unspent ['ʌn'spent] ADJ no gastado

unsplinterable [ʌn'splɪntərəbl] ADJ inastillable

unspoiled ['ʌn'spɔɪld], **unspoilt** ['ʌn'spɔɪlt] ADJ [*place*] que no ha perdido su belleza natural; [*child*] nada mimado; **~ by tourism** no echado a perder por el turismo; **to remain ~** conservar la belleza natural

unspoken ['ʌn'spəʊkən] ADJ tácito, sobreentendido; **to leave sth ~** no expresar algo, dejar de decir algo; **to remain ~** dejarse sin decir

unsporting ['ʌn'spɔːtɪŋ], **unsportsmanlike** ['ʌn'spɔːtsmənlaɪk] ADJ antideportivo

unstable ['ʌn'steɪbl] ADJ [1] (= *unsafe*) [*building, construction*] inestable, poco firme, poco sólido
[2] (= *unpredictable*) [*condition, economy, prices*] inestable; **the country is politically ~** el país es inestable desde el punto de vista político
[3] [*weather*] inestable, variable
[4] (*Psych*) [*person, character*] inestable; **mentally/emotionally ~** mentalmente/emocionalmente inestable
[5] (*Phys*) [*matter, molecule*] inestable

unstamped ['ʌn'stæmpt] ADJ sin sello, sin franquear

unstated [ʌn'steɪtɪd] ADJ [*wish etc*] no expresado; [*understanding*] tácito

unstatesmanlike ['ʌn'steɪtsmənlaɪk] ADJ indigno *or* impropio de un estadista

unsteadily ['ʌn'stedɪlɪ] ADV de manera insegura; [*walk*] con paso vacilante

unsteadiness ['ʌn'stedɪnɪs] N [*of chair, ladder, structure*] inestabilidad *f*, inseguridad *f*; [*of sb's steps, walk*] lo vacilante, inseguridad *f*; [*of voice, hand*] temblor *m*

unsteady ['ʌn'stedɪ] ADJ [*chair, ladder structure*] inestable, inseguro; [*walk*] vacilante; [*voice, hand*] tembloroso; **to be ~ on one's feet** caminar con paso vacilante

unstick ['ʌn'stɪk] VT despegar

unstinted [ʌn'stɪntɪd] ADJ [*effort*] incansable

unstinting [ʌn'stɪntɪŋ] ADJ pródigo; **to be ~ in one's praise** no escatimar las alabanzas, prodigar las alabanzas; **to be ~ in one's efforts to** (+ INFIN) no regatear esfuerzo por + *infin*

unstintingly [,ʌn'stɪntɪŋlɪ] ADV sin escatimar esfuerzos, de manera infatigable y generosa

unstitch ['ʌn'stɪtʃ] VT descoser; **to come ~ed** descoserse

unstop ['ʌn'stɒp] VT desobstruir, desatascar

unstoppable ['ʌn'stɒpəbl] ADJ incontenible, irrefrenable; (*Sport*) [*shot etc*] imparable

unstrap [ʌn'stræp] VT quitar la correa de

unstressed ['ʌn'strest] ADJ (*Ling*) átono, inacentuado

unstring ['ʌn'strɪŋ] (*pt, pp* **unstrung**) VT (*Mus*) desencordar; [+ *pearls*] desensartar; (*fig*) [+ *nerves*] trastornar

unstructured ['ʌn'strʌktʃəd] ADJ sin estructura, no estructurado

unstuck ['ʌn'stʌk] ADJ **to come ~** [*label etc*] despegarse, desprenderse; (*) (*fig*) fracasar, sufrir un revés; **where he comes ~ is ...** a él lo que le pierde es ...

unstudied ['ʌn'stʌdɪd] ADJ natural, sin afectación

unsubdued ['ʌnsəb'djuːd] ADJ indomado

unsubmissive ['ʌnsəb'mɪsɪv] ADJ insumiso

unsubscribe ['ʌnsəb'skraɪb] VI (*Internet*) borrarse

unsubstantial ['ʌnsəb'stænʃəl] ADJ insustancial

unsubstantiated ['ʌnsəb'stænʃɪeɪtɪd] ADJ no comprobado, no demostrado

unsuccessful ['ʌnsək'sesfʊl] ADJ [*attempt, effort*] inútil, infructuoso; [*appeal, search, job application*] infructuoso; **he embarked on an ~ business venture** se embarcó en un negocio que no tuvo éxito *or* que fracasó; **an ~ writer**

un escritor que no consiguió el éxito, un escritor fracasado; **to be ~** no tener éxito, fracasar; **their marriage was ~** el matrimonio fracasó; **we regret to inform you that your application for the post has been ~** lamentamos informarle que no ha sido seleccionado para el puesto de trabajo solicitado; **they were ~ in their efforts to reach an agreement** fracasaron en sus esfuerzos por llegar a un acuerdo; **to be ~ in (doing) sth: he was ~ in getting a job** no consiguió *or* logró encontrar trabajo; **a search for the weapon proved ~** la búsqueda del arma resultó ser infructuosa

unsuccessfully [ˈʌnsəkˈsesfəlɪ] ADV [*try, argue*] sin éxito, en vano; [*compete*] sin éxito

unsuitability [ˈʌn,suːtəˈbɪlɪtɪ] N [*of clothes, shoes*] lo inadecuado, lo inapropiado; [*of moment*] lo inoportuno; [*of behaviour, answer, book, reading*] impropiedad *f*

unsuitable [ˈʌnˈsuːtəbl] ADJ [*clothes, shoes*] inadecuado, inapropiado; [*accommodation, job, site*] inadecuado; [*candidate*] poco idóneo; [*moment*] inoportuno, inconveniente; **the building was ~ as an office** el edificio no reunía las condiciones necesarias para hacer de oficina; **these shoes are ~ for walking** estos zapatos no son los adecuados *or* apropiados para caminar; **the film is ~ for children** la película no es apta para menores; **this book is ~ for children** este libro no es apropiado para niños *or* es impropio para niños; **he is ~ for the post** no es la persona indicada para el puesto; **she always went for ~ men** siempre escogía a hombres que no le convenían; **he married a most ~ girl** se casó con una chica que no le convenía nada

unsuitably [ˈʌnˈsuːtəblɪ] ADV [*dressed*] de manera inapropiada

unsuited [ˈʌnˈsuːtɪd] ADJ **to be ~ for/to sth** no estar hecho para algo, no servir para algo; **he is ~ to be king** no está hecho *or* no sirve para ser rey; **it was a job to which I was totally ~** era un trabajo para el que no estaba hecha *or* no servía en absoluto; **they are ~ to each other** son incompatibles (el uno con el otro); **the vehicles are ~ for use in the desert** los vehículos no son adecuados para su utilización en el desierto

unsullied [ˈʌnˈsʌlɪd] ADJ (*liter*) inmaculado, no corrompido; **~ by** no corrompido por

unsung [ˈʌnˈsʌŋ] ADJ [*person, achievement*] no reconocido; [*hero, heroine*] olvidado

unsupported [ˈʌnsəˈpɔːtɪd] ADJ [1] (= *unsubstantiated*) [*allegation*] sin pruebas que lo respalden; [*claim, statement*] sin base
[2] (= *without backup*) [*troops*] sin refuerzos, sin apoyo; [*expedition*] sin apoyo; (*Pol*) [*candidate*] sin apoyo, no respaldado por nadie; (*financially*) [*mother*] sin ayuda económica
[3] (*physically*) [*person*] sin ayuda; **he was too weak to walk ~** estaba demasiado débil para andar sin ayuda
[4] (*Archit, Constr*) [*structure, wall*] sin sujeción

unsure [ˈʌnˈʃʊəʳ] ADJ [1] (= *doubtful, undecided*) **to be ~ about/of sth** no estar seguro de algo; **he seemed very ~ about it** no parecía estar muy seguro de ello; **she looked at him, ~ of his reaction** lo miró, sin estar segura de su reacción; **he was ~ of his welcome** no estaba seguro de la bienvenida que recibiría; **I was ~ what to expect** no estaba segura de qué esperar; **he was ~ whether he would be able to do it** no estaba seguro de si sería capaz de hacerlo
[2] (= *lacking confidence*) inseguro, poco seguro; **she seemed nervous and ~** parecía nerviosa e insegura, parecía nerviosa y poco segura; **to be ~ of o.s.** no estar seguro de uno mismo, no tener confianza en sí mismo
[3] (= *unreliable*) [*situation, economic climate*] poco seguro; [*loyalty, commitment*] poco fiable

unsurmountable [ˈʌnsəˈmaʊntəbl] ADJ insuperable

unsurpassable [ˈʌnsəˈpɑːsəbl] ADJ inmejorable, insuperable

unsurpassed [ˈʌnsəˈpɑːst] ADJ no superado, sin par; **~ in quality** de calidad inmejorable; **~ by anybody** no superado por nadie

unsurprising [ˈʌnsəˈpraɪzɪŋ] ADJ nada sorprendente

unsurprisingly [ˈʌnsəˈpraɪzɪŋlɪ] ADV como era de esperar; **~, they decided not to pursue the deal** como era de esperar, decidieron no seguir con el trato

unsuspected [ˈʌnsəsˈpektɪd] ADJ insospechado

unsuspecting [ˈʌnsəsˈpektɪŋ] ADJ confiado

unsweetened [ˈʌnˈswiːtnd] ADJ sin azúcar

unswerving [ʌnˈswɜːvɪŋ] ADJ [*resolve*] inquebrantable; [*loyalty*] inquebrantable, firme

unswervingly [ʌnˈswɜːvɪŋlɪ] ADV **to be ~ loyal to sb** ser totalmente leal a algn; **to hold ~ to one's course** no apartarse ni un ápice de su rumbo

unsympathetic [ˈʌn,sɪmpəˈθetɪk] ADJ poco comprensivo; **he was totally ~** no mostró la más mínima comprensión; **they were ~ to my plea** no hicieron caso de mi ruego; **I am not ~ to your request** me parece totalmente comprensible su petición

unsystematic [ˈʌn,sɪstɪˈmætɪk] ADJ poco sistemático, poco metódico

unsystematically [ˈʌn,sɪstɪˈmætɪkəlɪ] ADV de modo poco metódico

untainted [ˈʌnˈteɪntɪd] ADJ inmaculado, no corrompido; [*food*] no contaminado; **~ by** no corrompido por

untam(e)able [ˈʌnˈteɪməbl] ADJ indomable

untamed [ˈʌnˈteɪmd] ADJ indomado

untangle [ˈʌnˈtæŋgl] VT desenredar, desenmarañar

untanned [ˈʌnˈtænd] ADJ sin curtir

untapped [ˈʌnˈtæpt] ADJ sin explotar

untarnished [ˈʌnˈtɑːnɪʃt] ADJ [*reputation etc*] sin tacha

untasted [ˈʌnˈteɪstɪd] ADJ sin probar

untaught [ˈʌnˈtɔːt] ADJ no enseñado; (= *ignorant*) sin instrucción

untaxed [ˈʌnˈtækst] ADJ libre de impuestos, no sujeto a contribuciones

unteachable [ˈʌnˈtiːtʃəbl] ADJ [*subject, syllabus*] imposible de enseñar

untempered [ˈʌnˈtempəd] ADJ [*steel etc*] sin templar

untenable [ˈʌnˈtenəbl] ADJ insostenible

untenanted [ˈʌnˈtenəntɪd] ADJ desocupado, vacío

untended [ʌnˈtendɪd] ADJ desatendido, no vigilado; **he left the car ~** dejó el coche sin vigilar

untested [ˈʌnˈtestɪd] ADJ no probado

unthinkable [ʌnˈθɪŋkəbl] Ⓐ ADJ [1] (= *inconceivable*) inconcebible, impensable; **it is ~ that** es inconcebible *or* impensable que + *subjun*
[2] (= *unbearable*) insoportable
Ⓑ N **the ~** lo inconcebible

unthinking [ˈʌnˈθɪŋkɪŋ] ADJ irreflexivo

unthinkingly [ˈʌnˈθɪŋkɪŋlɪ] ADV irreflexivamente, sin pensar

unthought-of [ʌnˈθɔːtɒv] ADJ inimaginable, inconcebible

unthread [ˈʌnˈθred] VT [+ *cloth*] deshebrar, descoser; [+ *needle*] desenhebrar; [+ *pearls*] desensartar

unthrifty [ˈʌnˈθrɪftɪ] ADJ manirroto*

untidily [ʌnˈtaɪdɪlɪ] ADV [*piled, stacked*] sin orden, de manera desordenada; [*dressed*] de forma desaliñada; **the boxes were piled ~ around the room** las cajas estaban amontonadas sin orden *or* de manera desordenada por la habitación

untidiness [ʌnˈtaɪdɪnɪs] N [1] [*of room, person's habits*] desorden *m*; [*of person's dress*] desaliño *m*
[2] (*fig*) [*of ideas*] falta *f* de método

untidy [ʌnˈtaɪdɪ] ADJ (*compar* **untidier**; *superl* **untidiest**) [1] (*lit*) [*room, desk, heap, person*] desordenado; [*garden*] descuidado; [*appearance*] desaliñado, descuidado; [*clothes*] desarreglado; [*hair*] despeinado; [*work, writing*] poco metódico, descuidado
[2] (*fig*) **the film has an ~ ending** la película tiene un final poco coherente; **an ~ mind** una mente poco metódica

untie [ˈʌnˈtaɪ] VT [+ *shoelace, shoe, animal*] desatar; [+ *knot, parcel*] deshacer

until [ənˈtɪl] Ⓐ PREP hasta; **~ ten** hasta las diez; **~ his arrival** hasta su llegada; **he won't be back ~ tomorrow** no volverá hasta mañana; **from morning ~ night** desde la mañana hasta la noche; **~ now** hasta ahora; **it's never been a problem ~ now** hasta ahora nunca ha sido un problema; **~ then** hasta entonces; **~ then I'd never been to Italy** hasta entonces no había estado nunca en Italia
Ⓑ CONJ [1] (*in future*) hasta que + *subjun*; **wait ~ I get back** espera hasta que yo vuelva; **~ they build the new road** hasta que construyan la nueva carretera; **~ they come/sleep** hasta que vengan/se duerman; **he won't come ~ you invite him** no vendrá hasta que (no) lo invites; **they did nothing ~ we came** no hicieron nada hasta que (no) vinimos nosotros; **I don't get up ~ eight o'clock** no me levanto antes de las ocho
[2] (*in past*) hasta que + *indic*; **he did nothing ~ I told him to** no hizo nada hasta que yo se lo dije, no hizo nada hasta que no se lo dije; **~ they built the new road** hasta que construyeron la nueva carretera; **we stayed there ~ the doctor came** nos quedamos allí hasta que vino el médico; **we didn't stop ~ we reached York** no paramos hasta llegar a York

untilled [ˈʌnˈtɪld] ADJ sin cultivar

untimely [ʌnˈtaɪmlɪ] ADJ (= *premature*) prematuro; (= *inopportune*) inoportuno

untiring [ʌnˈtaɪərɪŋ] ADJ incansable

untiringly [ʌnˈtaɪərɪŋlɪ] ADV incansablemente

unto†† [ˈʌntʊ] PREP (*liter*) = **to, toward**

untold [ˈʌnˈtəʊld] ADJ [1] (= *not recounted*) [*story*] nunca contado; [*secret*] nunca revelado
[2] (= *indescribable, incalculable*) [*suffering*] indecible; [*loss, wealth etc*] incalculable, fabuloso

untouchable [ʌnˈtʌtʃəbl] Ⓐ ADJ intocable
Ⓑ N intocable *mf*

untouched [ˈʌnˈtʌtʃt] ADJ [1] (= *not used etc*) intacto, sin tocar; **to leave one's food ~** dejar su comida sin probar; **she left her breakfast ~** no tocó el desayuno; **a product ~ by human hand** un producto no manipulado, un producto que no ha sido tocado por la mano del hombre
[2] (= *safe*) indemne, incólume
[3] (= *unaffected*) insensible, indiferente; **he is**

~ by any plea es insensible a cualquier súplica; **those peoples ~ by civilization** esos pueblos no alcanzados por la civilización

UNTIL

- As with other time conjunctions, **hasta que** is used with the *subjunctive* if the action which follows hasn't happened yet or hadn't happened at the time of speaking:
  Go on stirring until the sauce is cold
  Sigue removiendo hasta que se enfríe la salsa
  I shan't be happy until you come
  No estaré contenta hasta que (no) vengas
  NOTE: When the main clause is negative, **no** can optionally be given in the **hasta que** clause without changing the meaning.
- **Hasta que** is used with the *indicative* when the action in the **hasta que** clause has already taken place:
  He lived in this house until he died
  Vivió en esta casa hasta que murió
  I didn't see her again until she returned to London
  No volví a verla hasta que (no) regresó a Londres
- **Hasta que** is also used with the *indicative* when describing habitual actions:
  I never wake up until the alarm goes off
  Nunca me despierto hasta que (no) suena el despertador
- Instead of **hasta que** + **VERB**, you can use **hasta** with an *infinitive* when the subject of both clauses is the same:
  Go on stirring until you get a thick creamy mixture
  Sigue removiendo hasta obtener una crema espesa

For further uses and examples, see main entry.

untoward [ˌʌntəˈwɔːd] ADJ (= *adverse*) adverso; (= *inapt*) impropio; (= *unfortunate*) desafortunado

untrained [ˈʌnˈtreɪnd] ADJ [*person*] sin formación, no capacitado; [*teacher etc*] sin título; (*Sport*) no entrenado; [*animal*] sin amaestrar; **to the ~ ear/eye** para el oído/ojo de alguien que no es experto

untrammelled, **untrameled** (*US*) [ʌnˈtræməld] ADJ (*liter*) ilimitado

untransferable [ˈʌntrænsˈfɜːrəbl] ADJ intransferible

untranslatable [ˈʌntrænzˈleɪtəbl] ADJ intraducible

untravelled, **untraveled** (*US*) [ˈʌnˈtrævld] ADJ 1 [*road etc*] no trillado, poco frecuentado; [*place*] inexplorado
2 [*person*] que no ha viajado

untreated [ʌnˈtriːtɪd] ADJ 1 (*Med*) [*patient, injury, illness*] sin tratar
2 (= *unprocessed*) [*sewage, wood, cotton*] no tratado, sin tratar

untried [ˈʌnˈtraɪd] ADJ 1 (= *untested*) [*product, method*] no probado
2 (= *inexperienced*) [*person*] no puesto a prueba; [*soldier*] bisoño
3 (*Jur*) [*person*] no procesado, sin procesar; [*case*] no visto, no juzgado

untrimmed [ˈʌnˈtrɪmd] ADJ [*hedge*] sin recortar, sin podar; [*wood*] sin desbastar; [*dress*] sin guarnición

untrodden [ˈʌnˈtrɒdn] ADJ no trillado, sin pisar

untroubled [ˈʌnˈtrʌbld] ADJ tranquilo; **she was ~ by the news** la noticia no pareció preocuparle; **~ by thoughts of her** sin preocuparse en absoluto por ella

untrue [ˈʌnˈtruː] ADJ 1 (= *inaccurate*) falso; **it is ~ that** no es cierto *or* verdad que, es falso que; **that is wholly ~** eso es completamente falso
2 (*liter*) (= *unfaithful*) infiel; **to be ~ to sb** ser infiel a algn; **to be ~ to one's principles** no ser fiel a sus principios

untrustworthy [ˈʌnˈtrʌstˌwɜːðɪ] ADJ [*person*] de poca confianza, no muy de fiar; [*leadership, results, information, evidence*] poco fiable; [*book etc*] de dudosa autoridad; [*machine, car*] inseguro, no muy de fiar

untruth [ˈʌnˈtruːθ] N (*pl* **untruths** [ˈʌnˈtruːðz]) mentira *f*

untruthful [ˈʌnˈtruːθfʊl] ADJ [*person*] mentiroso, falso; [*account*] falso

untruthfully [ˈʌnˈtruːθfəlɪ] ADV falsamente

untruthfulness [ˈʌnˈtruːθfʊlnɪs] N falsedad *f*

untutored [ˈʌnˈtjuːtəd] ADJ indocto, poco instruido; [*mind, taste*] no formado

untwine [ˈʌnˈtwaɪn], **untwist** [ˈʌnˈtwɪst] VT destorcer

untypical [ˈʌnˈtɪpɪkəl] ADJ atípico

unusable [ˈʌnˈjuːzəbl] ADJ inservible, inútil

unused[1] [ˈʌnˈjuːzd] ADJ (= *new*) nuevo, sin estrenar; (= *not made use of*) sin usar *or* utilizar

unused[2] [ˈʌnˈjuːst] ADJ (= *unaccustomed*) **to be ~ to sth** no estar acostumbrado a algo; **to be ~ to doing sth** no estar acostumbrado a hacer algo

unusual [ʌnˈjuːʒʊəl] ADJ 1 (= *uncommon*) [*sight, circumstances, name*] poco común, poco corriente; [*amount, number*] fuera de lo normal, fuera de lo corriente; **the case has received an ~ amount of publicity** el caso ha recibido una cantidad de publicidad fuera de lo normal *or* lo corriente; **here are some ~ gift ideas** aquí tiene unas ideas para regalos poco corrientes *or* que salen de lo corriente; **I didn't feel hungry, which was ~ for me** no me sentía con hambre, lo cual era raro en mí; **it's ~ for him to be late** no suele llegar tarde; **it's not ~ to see snow in June here** no es raro ver nieve aquí en junio; **there's nothing ~ in that** no hay nada de raro *or* extraordinario en ello
2 (= *odd*) raro, extraño; **don't you find it ~ that he never tells you where he's been?** ¿no te parece raro *or* extraño que nunca te diga dónde ha estado?
3 (= *exceptional*) excepcional, poco común *or* corriente; **a man of ~ intelligence** un hombre de inteligencia excepcional, un hombre de una inteligencia poco común *or* corriente

unusually [ʌnˈjuːʒʊəlɪ] ADV 1 (= *unaccustomedly*) **he arrived ~ late** llegó más tarde que de costumbre; **the streets were ~ quiet** las calles estaban extrañamente silenciosas; **~ for her, she didn't say goodbye** no se despidió, lo cual es raro en ella
2 (= *exceptionally*) excepcionalmente, extraordinariamente; **this year's ~ harsh winter** el invierno excepcionalmente *or* extraordinariamente riguroso de este año; **an ~ gifted man** un hombre de excepcional talento, un hombre de un talento poco común *or* corriente

unutterable [ʌnˈʌtərəbl] ADJ indecible

unutterably [ʌnˈʌtərəblɪ] ADV indeciblemente

unvaried [ʌnˈvɛərɪd] ADJ (*gen*) invariable; (= *unchanged*) sin cambiar, constante; (= *monotonous*) monótono

unvarnished [ˈʌnˈvɑːnɪʃt] ADJ 1 (= *not varnished*) sin barnizar
2 (*fig*) (= *plain*) [*account, description*] llano; **the ~ truth** la verdad lisa y llana, la verdad sin adornos

unvarying [ʌnˈvɛərɪɪŋ] ADJ invariable, constante

unveil [ʌnˈveɪl] VT quitar el velo a; [+ *statue, painting etc*] descubrir

unveiling [ʌnˈveɪlɪŋ] N descubrimiento *m*; (= *ceremony*) inauguración *f*

unventilated [ˈʌnˈventɪleɪtɪd] ADJ sin ventilación, sin aire

unverifiable [ˈʌnˈverɪfaɪəbl] ADJ no comprobable, que no puede verificarse

unverified [ˈʌnˈverɪfaɪd] ADJ sin verificar

unversed [ˈʌnˈvɜːst] ADJ **~ in** no versado en, poco ducho en*

unvisited [ˈʌnˈvɪzɪtɪd] ADJ no visitado, no frecuentado

unvoiced [ˈʌnˈvɔɪst] ADJ 1 [*opinion, sentiment*] no expresado
2 (*Ling*) [*consonant*] sordo

unwaged [ʌnˈweɪdʒd] Ⓐ ADJ sin sueldo
Ⓑ N **the ~** (= *the unemployed*) los no asalariados

unwanted [ˈʌnˈwɒntɪd] ADJ [*item*] superfluo; [*visitor, guest*] poco grato, inoportuno; [*child, pregnancy, advances, attention*] no deseado; **to feel ~** sentirse de más; **an ~ gift** un regalo sin estrenar; **to remove ~ hair** quitar el vello superfluo

unwarily [ʌnˈwɛərɪlɪ] ADV imprudentemente, incautamente

unwariness [ʌnˈwɛərɪnɪs] N imprudencia *f*

unwarlike [ˈʌnˈwɔːlaɪk] ADJ pacífico, poco belicoso

unwarranted [ʌnˈwɒrəntɪd] ADJ injustificado

unwary [ʌnˈwɛərɪ] ADJ imprudente, incauto

unwashed [ˈʌnˈwɒʃt] Ⓐ ADJ sin lavar, sucio
Ⓑ NPL **the Great Unwashed*** (*hum*) la plebe

unwavering [ʌnˈweɪvərɪŋ] ADJ [*loyalty, resolve*] inquebrantable, firme; [*course*] firme; [*gaze*] fijo

unwaveringly [ʌnˈweɪvərɪŋlɪ] ADV firmemente; **to hold ~ to one's course** no apartarse ni un ápice de su rumbo

unweaned [ˈʌnˈwiːnd] ADJ no destetado

unwearable [ˈʌnˈwɛərəbl] ADJ [*clothes, colour*] imposible de llevar

unwearying [ʌnˈwɪərɪŋ] ADJ incansable

unwed† [ʌnˈwed] ADJ soltero

unwedded [ʌnˈwedɪd] ADJ **to live in ~ bliss** vivir felizmente sin estar legítimamente casado(s)

unwelcome [ʌnˈwelkəm] ADJ [*news, surprise*] desagradable, poco grato; [*visitor, guest, intruder*] poco grato, inoportuno; [*visit*] inoportuno; [*reminder, advances, attention*] poco grato; **the change is not ~** el cambio no nos resulta del todo molesto; **I felt ~** sentí que allí sobraba; **to make sb feel ~** hacer que algn sienta que sobra

unwelcoming [ʌnˈwelkəmɪŋ] ADJ [*person*] nada simpático, poco cordial; [*place*] poco acogedor

unwell [ˈʌnˈwel] ADJ **to be ~** estar indispuesto; **to feel ~** sentirse mal; **I felt ~ on the ship** me mareé en el barco

unwholesome [ˈʌnˈhəʊlsəm] ADJ 1 (= *unhealthy*) [*food*] poco sano, poco saludable; [*air*] malsano, poco saludable; [*smell*] desagradable
2 (*morally*) [*lifestyle, desire, habit*] malsano, pernicioso; [*thoughts*] malsano; **to have an ~ interest in sth** tener un interés malsano en algo

unwieldy [ʌn'wiːldɪ] ADJ 1 (= *difficult to handle*) [*object*] difícil de manejar
2 (= *difficult to manage*) [*system, structure, bureaucracy*] rígido

unwilling ['ʌn'wɪlɪŋ] ADJ poco dispuesto; **to be ~ to do sth** estar poco dispuesto a hacer algo, no estar dispuesto a hacer algo; **he was ~ to help me** no estaba dispuesto a ayudarme; **to be ~ for sb to do sth** no estar dispuesto a permitir que algn haga algo

unwillingly ['ʌn'wɪlɪŋlɪ] ADV de mala gana, a regañadientes

unwillingness ['ʌn'wɪlɪŋnɪs] N falta *f* de inclinación, desgana *f*; **his ~ to help us** lo poco dispuesto que está/estaba a ayudarnos, su desgana para ayudarnos

unwind ['ʌn'waɪnd] (*pt, pp* **unwound**) Ⓐ VT desenrollar; [+ *wool, thread*] desovillar Ⓑ VI
1 desenrollarse; [*wool, thread*] desovillarse
2 (*) (*fig*) (= *relax*) relajarse

unwisdom ['ʌn'wɪzdəm] N imprudencia *f*

unwise ['ʌn'waɪz] ADJ (= *careless*) imprudente; (= *inadvisable*) poco aconsejable; **it would be ~ to** (+ *INFIN*) sería poco aconsejable + *infin*; **that was ~ of you** lo que hiciste fue imprudente; **that was most ~ of you** en eso has sido muy imprudente

unwisely ['ʌn'waɪzlɪ] ADV imprudentemente

unwitting [ʌn'wɪtɪŋ] ADJ involuntario; **I was the ~ cause** sin querer, yo fui la causa; **an ~ instrument of sth/sb** un instrumento involuntario de algo/algn

unwittingly [ʌn'wɪtɪŋlɪ] ADV inconscientemente, sin darse cuenta

unwomanly [ʌn'wʊmənlɪ] ADJ poco femenino

unwonted [ʌn'wəʊntɪd] ADJ insólito, inusitado

unworkable ['ʌn'wɜːkəbl] ADJ 1 [*plan, suggestion*] impracticable, no viable
2 [*mine*] inexplotable

unworldly ['ʌn'wɜːldlɪ] ADJ 1 (= *unmaterialistic*) [*person*] nada materialista
2 (= *naïve*) [*person, attitude*] ingenuo, poco realista
3 (= *not of this world*) [*beauty, silence*] de otro mundo

unworn ['ʌn'wɔːn] ADJ nuevo, sin estrenar

unworthiness [ʌn'wɜːðɪnɪs] N falta *f* de valía, indignidad *f*

unworthy [ʌn'wɜːðɪ] ADJ 1 (= *undeserving*) [*person*] indigno, poco digno; **to be ~ to do sth** no ser digno de hacer algo, no merecer hacer algo; **I feel she is ~ to judge them** me parece que no es digna de juzgarlos; **to be ~ of sth/sb** no ser digno de algo/algn, no merecerse algo/a algn; **he felt himself ~ of her** sentía que no era digno de ella, sentía que no se la merecía; **it is ~ of attention/comment** no merece atención/comentario alguno
2 (= *ignoble*) [*activity, thought*] impropio; **his accusations are ~ of a gentleman** sus acusaciones no son dignas *or* son impropias de un caballero

unwound [ˌʌn'waʊnd] PT, PP *of* **unwind**

unwounded ['ʌn'wuːndɪd] ADJ ileso

unwrap ['ʌn'ræp] VT abrir; **after the meal we ~ped the presents** después de comer abrimos los regalos

unwritten ['ʌn'rɪtn] ADJ no escrito; **~ law** ley *f* consuetudinaria

unyielding [ʌn'jiːldɪŋ] ADJ inflexible

unyoke ['ʌn'jəʊk] VT desuncir

unzip ['ʌn'zɪp] VT 1 (= *open zip of*) abrir la cremallera *or* (*LAm*) el cierre de; **can you ~ me?** ¿me puedes bajar la cremallera?
2 (*Comput*) [+ *file*] descomprimir

up [ʌp]

Ⓐ ADVERB	Ⓓ ADJECTIVE
Ⓑ PREPOSITION	Ⓔ INTRANSITIVE VERB
Ⓒ NOUN	Ⓕ TRANSITIVE VERB

When **up** *is the second element in a phrasal verb, eg* **come up, throw up, walk up,** *look up the verb. When it is part of a set combination, eg* **the way up, close up,** *look up the other word.*

Ⓐ ADVERB

1 *direction* hacia arriba, para arriba; **he looked up** (*towards sky*) miró hacia *or* para arriba; **to walk up and down** pasearse de un lado para otro *or* de arriba abajo; **he's been up and down all evening** no ha parado quieto en toda la tarde; **she's still a bit up and down** todavía tiene sus altibajos; **to stop halfway up** pararse a mitad de la subida; **to throw sth up in the air** lanzar algo al aire; **he walked/ran up to the house** caminó/corrió hasta la casa; **a blond boy went up to her** un chico rubio le acercó

2 *position* **the people three floors up (from me)** los que viven tres pisos más arriba; **up above (us) we could see a ledge** por encima (de nosotros) *or* sobre nuestras cabezas podíamos ver una cornisa; **from up above** desde arriba; **my office is five floors up** mi oficina está en el quinto piso; **higher up** más arriba; **up in the mountains** montaña arriba; **up in the sky** en lo alto del cielo; **the jug's up there, on the freezer** la jarra está ahí arriba, en el congelador; **the castle's up there, on top of the hill** el castillo está allí arriba, en la cima del monte

3 *in northern place, capital, etc* **we're up for the day** hemos venido a pasar el día; **when you're next up this way** la próxima vez que pases por aquí; **how long have you lived up here?** ¿cuánto tiempo llevas viviendo aquí?; **when you're next up here** la próxima vez que pases por aquí; **he lives up in Scotland** vive en Escocia; **up in London** (allá) en Londres; **up north** en el norte; **how long did you live up there?** ¿cuánto tiempo estuviste viviendo allí *or* allá?; **the next time you're up there** la próxima vez que pases por allí *or* allá; **to go up to London/to university** ir a Londres/a la universidad

4 *= standing* de pie; **while you're up, can you get me a glass of water?** ya que estás de pie, ¿me puedes traer un vaso de agua?; **the ladder was up against the wall** la escalera estaba apoyada en *or* contra la pared

5 *= out of bed* **to be up** (= *get up*) levantarse; (= *be active*) estar levantado; **we were up at 7** nos levantamos a las 7; **what time will you be up** ¿a qué hora te levantarás?; **is Peter up yet?** ¿está levantado Peter?; **I'm usually up by 7 o'clock** normalmente a las siete estoy levantado; **we were still up at midnight** a medianoche seguíamos sin acostarnos, a medianoche todavía estábamos levantados; **she was up and about at 6 a.m.** lleva en pie desde las 6 de la mañana; **to be up and about again** [*sick person*] estar repuesto; **to be up all night** no acostarse en toda la noche; **get up!** ¡levántate!

6 *= raised* **with his head up (high)** con la cabeza bien levantada *or* erguida; **several children had their hands up** varios niños habían levantado la mano; **the blinds were up** las persianas estaban subidas *or* levantadas; **he sat in the car with the windows up** se sentó en el coche con las ventanillas subidas; **"this side up"** "este lado hacia arriba"; **look, the flag is up!** mira, la bandera está izada

7 *in price, value* **potatoes are up** han subido las patatas; **the thermometer is up 2 degrees** el termómetro ha subido 2 grados; **the interest rate has risen sharply, up from 3% to 5%** los tipos de interés han subido bruscamente del 3% al 5%; **the temperature was up in the forties** la temperatura estaba por encima de los cuarenta; **prices are up on last year** los precios han subido desde el año pasado, del año pasado a éste los precios han subido

8 *in score* **we're a goal up** llevamos un tanto de ventaja; **we were 20 points up on them** les llevábamos una ventaja de 20 puntos

9 *in terms of excellence* **to be up among** *or* **with the leaders** estar a la altura de los líderes; **she's right up there with the jazz greats** está en la cumbre con los grandes del jazz

10 *= built, installed* **the new building isn't up yet** el nuevo edificio no está construido todavía, no han levantado el nuevo edificio todavía; **the tent isn't up yet** la tienda todavía no está puesta; **the scaffolding is now up** el andamio está puesto ahora; **the notice about the outing is up** el cartel de la excursión está puesto; **we've got the pictures up at last** por fin hemos puesto *or* colgado los cuadros; **the curtains are up** las cortinas están colocadas

11 *= finished* [*contract etc*] vencido, caducado; **when the period is up** cuando termine el plazo, cuando venza el plazo; **his holiday is up** han terminado ya sus vacaciones; **time is up** se ha acabado el tiempo; **time is up, put down your pens** se ha acabado el tiempo, dejen los bolígrafos sobre la mesa; **time is up for the people living here, their homes are to be demolished** a la gente que vive aquí le toca marcharse, están derribando sus casas; **our time here is up** no podemos quedarnos más tiempo aquí

12 *= and over* **from £2 up** de 2 libras para arriba; **from the age of 13 up** a partir de los 13 años

13 *= knowledgeable* **he's well up in** *or* **on British politics** está muy al corriente *or* al día en lo referente a la política británica; **how are you up on your military history?** ¿cómo andan tus conocimientos de historia militar?

14 ** = wrong* **there's something up with him** algo le pasa; **there's something up with the TV** le pasa algo a la tele; **what's up?** ¿qué pasa?; **what's up with him?** ¿que le pasa?

15 *in running order* **first up** el primero (de la lista); **next up** el siguiente (de la lista)

16 *Jur* **her case isn't due up until next week** su caso no se verá hasta la próxima semana; **to be up before the judge/board** [*person*] (tener que) comparecer ante el juez/el consejo; [*case, matter*] verse ante el juez/en el consejo

17 *= risen* **the river is up** el río ha subido; **the sun is up** ha salido el sol; **the tide is up** la marea está alta; ✦*IDIOM* **his blood is up** le hierve la sangre

18 *Brit = under repair* **the road is up** la calle está en obras

19 *US Culin** **two fried eggs, up** un par de huevos fritos boca arriba; **a bourbon (straight) up** un bourbon sin hielo

20 *= mounted* **a horse with Dettori up** un caballo montado por Dettori

21 *in exclamations* **up (with) Celtic!** ¡arriba el Celtic!

22 *in set expressions*

◆ **up against**: **he's really up against it** ahora sí que está en un aprieto; **to be up against**

sb tener que habérselas con algn, tener que enfrentarse a algn

◆ **up and running**: **to be up and running** estar en funcionamiento; **to get sth up and running** poner algo en funcionamiento

◆ **up for sth**: **three seats are up for election** tres escaños salen a elecciones; **most politicians up for reelection know this** (= *seeking*) la mayoría de los políticos que se presentan a la reelección lo saben; **every two years, a third of the Senate comes up for election** cada dos años se renueva una tercera parte del Senado; **to be up for sth*** (= *ready, willing*) tener ganas de algo; **are you up for it?** ¿estás dispuesto?

◆ **up to** (= *till, as far as*) hasta; **up to now** hasta ahora, hasta la fecha; **up to this week** hasta esta semana; **up to here** hasta aquí; **up to £10** hasta 10 libras nada más; **to count up to 100** contar hasta 100; **we were up to our knees/waist in water** el agua nos llegaba por *or* hasta las rodillas/la cintura; **what page are you up to?** ¿por qué página vas?; **to be up to a task** (= *capable of*) estar a la altura de una tarea, estar en condiciones de realizar una tarea; **to be up to doing sth** estar en condiciones de hacer algo; **they weren't up to running a company** no estaban en condiciones de gestionar una empresa, no estaban a la altura necesaria para gestionar una empresa

◆ **to be** *or* **feel up to sth**: **are you (feeling) up to going for a walk?** ¿te sientes con ganas de dar un paseo?; **I don't feel up to going out** no tengo ánimos para salir; *see also* **including**

◆ **to be up to sth** (*) (= *doing*) **what are you up to?** ¿qué andas haciendo?; **what are you up to with that knife?** ¿qué haces con ese cuchillo?; **he's up to something** está tramando algo; **what does he think he's up to?** ¿qué diablos piensa hacer?; **I see what you're up to** te veo venir; **what have you been up to lately?** ¿qué has estado haciendo últimamente?

◆ **to be up to a standard/to much** (= *equal to*) **it isn't up to his usual standard** no está a su nivel de siempre; **the book isn't up to much** (*Brit**) el libro no vale mucho

◆ **to be up to sb** (= *depend on*) **it's up to you to decide** te toca (a ti) decidir; **I feel it is up to me to tell him** creo que me corresponde a mí decírselo; **I wouldn't do it but it's up to you** yo (que tú) no lo haría, pero allá tú *or* tú verás; **I'd go, but it's up to you** por mí iría, pero depende de ti; **if it were** *or* **was up to me** si dependiera de mí

Ⓑ PREPOSITION

[1] [= *on top of*] en lo alto de, arriba de (*LAm*); **he was up a ladder pruning the apple trees** estaba subido a una escalera *or* en lo alto de una escalera podando los manzanos; **to be up a tree** estar en lo alto de *or* (*LAm*) arriba de un árbol

[2] [= *along, towards the top*] **he went off up the road** se fue calle arriba; **put your handkerchief up your sleeve** guárdate el pañuelo dentro de la manga; **the heat disappears straight up the chimney** el calor se escapa chimenea arriba, el calor se escapa por lo alto de la chimenea; **to travel up and down the country** viajar por todo el país; **people up and down the country are saying ...** la gente por todo el país dice ...; **they live further up the road** viven en esta calle pero más arriba; **further up the page** en la misma página, más arriba; **halfway up the stairs** a mitad de la escalera; **halfway up the mountain** a mitad de la subida de la montaña; **up north** en el norte; **up river** río arriba

[3] **up yours!**** ¡vete a hacer puñetas!**

Ⓒ NOUN

[1] **ups and downs** altibajos *mpl*, vicisitudes *fpl*; **the ups and downs that every politician is faced with** los altibajos a que se enfrenta todo político, las vicisitudes a que está sometido todo político; **after many ups and downs** después de mil peripecias

[2] **it's on the up and up** (*Brit*) (= *improving*) va cada vez mejor; (*US*) (= *above board*) está en regla

Ⓓ ADJECTIVE

[1] [*Rail*] [*train, line*] ascendente

[2] [= *elated*] **to be up*** estar en plena forma

Ⓔ INTRANSITIVE VERB (*)

[1] [= *jump up*] **he upped and hit him** se levantó (de un salto) y le pegó

[2] (*emphatic*) **she upped and left** (= *stood up*) se levantó y se marchó, se levantó y se largó*; (= *went*) fue y se marchó, fue y se largó*; **he upped and offed** se largó sin más*

Ⓕ TRANSITIVE VERB

[= *raise*] [+ *price, offer*] subir, aumentar; **to up anchor** levar el ancla

---

up-and-coming [ˈʌpəndˈkʌmɪŋ] ADJ prometedor, con futuro

up-and-down [ˈʌpənˈdaʊn] ADJ [*movement*] de arriba a abajo, vertical; (*fig*) [*career, business, progress, relationship*] inestable

up-and-under [ˌʌpənˈʌndəʳ] N (*Rugby*) patada *f* a seguir

upbeat [ˈʌpˈbiːt] Ⓐ ADJ (*) (= *positive*) optimista

Ⓑ N (*Mus*) tiempo *m* débil, tiempo *m* no acentuado; (*fig*) (*in prosperity*) aumento *m*

up-bow [ˈʌpbəʊ] N (*Mus*) movimiento *m* ascendente del arco

upbraid [ʌpˈbreɪd] VT censurar, reprender; **to ~ sb with sth** censurar algo a algn

upbringing [ˈʌpˌbrɪŋɪŋ] N educación *f*

upcast [ˈʌpkɑːst] N (*Min*) (*also* **~ shaft**) pozo *m* de ventilación

upchuck‡ [ˈuptʃʌk] VI (*US*) echar los hígados por la boca*

upcoming [ˈʌpkʌmɪŋ] ADJ [*elections, holidays*] próximo

upcountry [ˈʌpˈkʌntrɪ] Ⓐ ADV **to go ~** ir hacia el interior, ir tierra adentro; **to be ~** estar tierra adentro, estar en el interior

Ⓑ ADJ [*town, school, accent*] del interior; [*trip, tour*] hacia el interior, al interior

up-current [ˈʌpˈkʌrənt] N (*Aer*) corriente *f* ascendente

update Ⓐ [ʌpˈdeɪt] VT poner al día; **to ~ sb on sth** poner a algn al corriente *or* al tanto de algo

Ⓑ [ˈʌpdeɪt] N puesta *f* al día; (*updated version*) versión *f* actualizada; **news ~** últimas noticias *fpl*; **he gave me an ~ on ...** me puso al día con respecto a ..., me puso al corriente *or* al tanto de ...

updating [ʌpˈdeɪtɪŋ] N puesta *f* al día

updraught, **updraft** (*US*) [ˈʌpdræft] N corriente *f* ascendente

upend [ʌpˈend] VT [1] (= *stand on its end*) poner vertical

[2] (*) (= *knock over*) [+ *person*] volcar

upfront [ʌpˈfrʌnt] Ⓐ ADJ [1] (*) (= *frank*) abierto, franco

[2] [*payment*] inicial

Ⓑ ADV [1] (= *in advance*) por adelantado; **to pay ~ for sth** pagar algo por adelantado

[2] (*esp US**) (= *frankly*) sinceramente, francamente

upgrade Ⓐ [ˈʌpgreɪd] N [1] (= *slope*) cuesta *f*, pendiente *f*; **to be on the ~** (*fig*) ir cuesta arriba, prosperar, estar en auge; (*Med*) estar mejor, estar reponiéndose

[2] [*of system etc*] mejoramiento *m*, reforma *f*; (*Comput*) modernización *f*, potenciamiento *m*

Ⓑ [ʌpˈgreɪd] VT [1] (= *promote*) [+ *person*] ascender; [+ *job*] asignar a un grado más alto

[2] [+ *system etc*] mejorar, reformar; (*Comput*) modernizar, mejorar las prestaciones de

upgradeable [ʌpˈgreɪdəbl] ADJ [*computer*] modernizable; [*system*] mejorable

upheaval [ʌpˈhiːvəl] N [1] (*emotional*) trastorno *m*

[2] (*in home, office etc*) trastorno *m*

[3] (*Pol*) agitación *f*

[4] (*Geol*) levantamiento *m*

upheld [ʌpˈheld] PT, PP *of* **uphold**

uphill [ˈʌpˈhɪl] Ⓐ ADV **to go ~** ir cuesta arriba; **the road goes ~ for two miles** la carretera sube durante dos millas

Ⓑ ADJ en cuesta, en pendiente; (*fig*) arduo, penoso; **it's ~ all the way** (*lit*) el camino es todo cuesta arriba; (*fig*) es una tarea laboriosa; **it was an ~ struggle** fue muy difícil; **it's an ~ task** es una tarea laboriosa

uphold [ʌpˈhəʊld] (*pt, pp* **upheld**) VT [1] (= *sustain*) mantener, sostener; (= *support*) apoyar, defender

[2] (*Jur*) confirmar

upholder [ʌpˈhəʊldəʳ] N defensor(a) *m/f*

upholster [ʌpˈhəʊlstəʳ] VT tapizar, entapizar (**with** de); **well ~ed*** (*euph*) rellenito*

upholsterer [ʌpˈhəʊlstərəʳ] N tapicero/a *m/f*

upholstery [ʌpˈhəʊlstərɪ] N [1] (*cushioning etc*) tapizado *m*, almohadillado *m*; (*in car*) tapizado *m*

[2] (= *trade*) tapicería *f*

UPI N ABBR (*US*) = **United Press International**

upkeep [ˈʌpkiːp] N [1] (= *care*) mantenimiento *m*

[2] (= *cost*) gastos *mpl* de mantenimiento

upland [ˈʌplənd] Ⓐ N tierra *f* alta, meseta *f*; **uplands** tierras *fpl* altas

Ⓑ ADJ de la meseta

uplift Ⓐ [ˈʌplɪft] N (= *edification*) inspiración *f*, edificación *f*; **moral ~** edificación *f*

Ⓑ [ʌpˈlɪft] VT (*fig*) (= *encourage*) animar; (= *raise*) mejorar, elevar

uplifted [ʌpˈlɪftɪd] ADJ [1] (= *raised*) [*hand, arm*] levantado, en alto; [*face*] vuelto hacia arriba, mirando hacia arriba

[2] (= *edified*) **to feel ~ (by sth)** sentirse animado (por algo)

uplifting [ʌpˈlɪftɪŋ] ADJ inspirador, edificante

upload [ʌpˈləʊd] VT (*Comput*) subir, poner

up-market [ʌpˈmɑːkɪt] (*Brit*) Ⓐ ADJ [*image, shop, hotel, person*] de categoría; [*product*] de primera calidad, de calidad superior; [*magazine*] para un público de categoría

Ⓑ ADV **to go/move ~** [*company*] (*for clients*) subir de categoría, buscar una clientela más selecta

upmost [ˈʌpməʊst] = **uppermost**

upon [əˈpɒn] PREP [1] (*with place, position*) sobre; **he placed the tray ~ the table** puso la bandeja sobre la mesa; **I saw pictures of him walking ~ the moon** vi fotos de él caminando sobre la luna; **he had a suspicious look ~ his face** en su rostro había una mirada sospechosa; **he recalled the attacks ~ him** recordó los ataques que recibió; **~ my word!**† ¡caramba!

[2] (*with time*) **he emigrated ~ the death of his son** emigró tras la muerte de su hijo; **~ hearing this she wept** al oir esto, lloró; **~**

entering the church, take the door on the left al entrar en la iglesia, siga por la puerta de la izquierda; **Christmas is almost ~ us again** las Navidades ya están otra vez encima
3 (*with large numbers*) **row ~ row of women surged forwards** hilera tras hilera de mujeres iban avanzando; **thousands ~ thousands of people were arriving** iban llegando miles y miles de personas; *see also* **on, once A2**

upper ['ʌpəʳ] Ⓐ ADJ 1 (*in level*) [*deck, floor*] de arriba; (*more frm*) superior; **the ~ atmosphere** la atmósfera superior; **the ~ slopes of Illimani** las pendientes más altas del Illimani; *see also* **hand A11, reach C2, stiff A3**
2 (*in importance, rank*) [*echelons, ranks, caste*] superior; **~ management** los altos cargos de la administración
3 (*on scale*) [*limit*] máximo; **properties at the ~ end of the market** inmuebles de la sección más cara del mercado; **people in the ~ income bracket** las personas con un nivel de ingresos superior
4 (*in Geog names*) alto; **the Upper Nile** el alto Nilo
Ⓑ N 1 **uppers** [*of shoe*] pala *fsing*; ✦**IDIOM to be (down) on one's ~s** estar en las últimas *or* (*Sp*) sin un duro
2 (*) (= *drug*) anfeta* *f*
3 (*Dentistry*) dentadura *f* postiza (*superior*)
4 (*US Rail*) litera *f* de arriba
Ⓒ CPD ► **upper arm** N brazo *m* superior ► **upper case** N (*Typ*) mayúsculas *fpl*; **in ~ case** en mayúsculas ► **upper chamber** N (*Pol*) cámara *f* alta ► **the upper circle** N (*Theat*) la galería superior ► **upper class** N **the ~ classes** la(s) clase(s) alta(s) ► **the upper crust*** N la flor y nata ► **Upper Egypt** N alto Egipto *m* ► **upper house** N (*Pol*) cámara *f* alta ► **upper lip** N labio *m* superior ► **upper school** N cursos *mpl* superiores; (*in names*) instituto *m* de enseñanza media ► **Upper Volta** N alto Volta *m*

upper-case ['ʌpə'keɪs] ADJ mayúsculo, de letra mayúscula

upper-class ['ʌpə'klɑːs] ADJ de clase alta; **an ~ twit** un señorito de clase alta

upper-crust* ['ʌpə'krʌst] ADJ de categoría (social) superior, de buen tono; *see also* **upper C**

uppercut ['ʌpəkʌt] N uppercut *m*, gancho *m* a la cara

upper-division [ˌʌpədɪ'vɪʒən] ADJ **~ student** (*US*) estudiante *mf* de tercer *or* cuarto año

uppermost ['ʌpəməʊst] Ⓐ ADJ 1 el/la más alto/a; **to put sth face ~** poner algo cara arriba
2 (*fig*) principal, predominante; **what is ~ in sb's mind** lo que más le preocupa a algn; **it was ~ in my mind** me preocupaba más que cualquier otra cosa
Ⓑ ADV encima

uppish* ['ʌpɪʃ], **uppity*** ['ʌpɪtɪ] ADJ (*Brit*) presumido, engreído; **to get ~** presumir, darse aires de importancia

upraise [ʌp'reɪz] VT levantar; **with arm ~d** con el brazo levantado

upright ['ʌpraɪt] Ⓐ ADJ 1 (*lit*) derecho, recto
2 (*fig*) honrado, íntegro
Ⓑ ADV erguido, derecho, recto; **to hold o.s. ~** mantenerse erguido; **to sit bolt ~** sentarse muy derecho, sentarse muy erguido
Ⓒ N 1 (= *post*) montante *m*, poste *m*; (= *goalpost*) poste *m*
2 (= *piano*) piano *m* vertical *or* recto
Ⓓ CPD ► **upright piano** N piano *m* vertical *or* recto

uprightly ['ʌpˌraɪtlɪ] ADV (*fig*) honradamente, rectamente

uprightness ['ʌpˌraɪtnɪs] N (*fig*) honradez *f*, rectitud *f*

uprising ['ʌpraɪzɪŋ] N alzamiento *m*, sublevación *f*

up-river ['ʌp'rɪvəʳ] ADV = **upstream**

uproar ['ʌprɔːʳ] N alboroto *m*, jaleo *m*; **this caused an ~** ◊ **at this there was (an) ~** (= *shouting*) en esto se armó un alboroto; (= *protesting*) en esto estallaron ruidosas las protestas; **the hall was in (an) ~** (= *shouting, disturbance*) había alboroto en la sala; (= *protesting*) se oían protestas airadas en la sala

uproarious [ʌp'rɔːrɪəs] ADJ 1 (= *noisy*) [*laughter*] escandaloso; [*meeting*] alborotado, ruidoso; [*success*] clamoroso
2 (= *hilarious*) [*occasion*] divertidísimo; [*comedy*] desternillante; [*personality*] divertidísimo

uproariously [ʌp'rɔːrɪəslɪ] ADV **to laugh ~** reírse a carcajadas; **he told me an ~ funny story** me contó una historia para desternillarse *or* troncharse de risa

uproot [ʌp'ruːt] VT desarraigar, arrancar (de raíz); (= *destroy*) eliminar, extirpar; **whole families have been ~ed** familias enteras se han visto desarraigadas

upsa-daisy* ['ʌpsəˌdeɪzɪ] EXCL ¡aúpa!

upset [ʌp'set] (*vb: pt, pp* **upset**) Ⓐ VT 1 (= *knock over*) [+ *object*] volcar, tirar; [+ *liquid*] derramar, tirar; [+ *boat*] volcar; ✦**IDIOM to ~ the applecart** desbaratar los planes, desbaratar el tinglado*
2 (= *distress*) afectar; (= *hurt, make sad*) disgustar; (= *offend*) ofender, disgustar; **the news ~ her a lot** la noticia la afectó mucho; **it ~ me that he forgot my birthday** me disgustó que se olvidara de mi cumpleaños; **I didn't mean to ~ her** no quería ofenderla *or* disgustarla; **people who are easily ~ may prefer not to watch** puede que las personas que se impresionen fácilmente prefieran no mirar; **to ~ o.s.: you'll only ~ yourself if you see him** no harás más que cogerte un disgusto si te ves con él; **there now, don't ~ yourself** venga, no te disgustes
3 (= *disrupt*) [+ *plans, calculations*] dar al traste con, desbaratar; **this could ~ the balance of power in the region** esto podría alterar el equilibrio de poderes en la región
4 (= *make ill*) sentar mal a, enfermar (*LAm*); **garlic ~s me/my stomach** el ajo no me sienta bien
Ⓑ ADJ 1 (= *distressed*) alterado; (= *hurt, sad*) disgustado; (= *offended*) ofendido, disgustado; (= *annoyed*) molesto; **he's ~ that you didn't tell him** se disgustó *or* se molestó porque no se lo dijiste; **she's ~ about failing** está disgustada por haber suspendido; **what are you so ~ about?** ¿qué es lo que te ha disgustado tanto?; **to get ~** (= *distressed*) alterarse; (= *hurt*) disgustarse; (= *offended*) ofenderse; (= *annoyed*) enfadarse; **don't get ~, they didn't take anything** no te alteres, no se llevaron nada; **she gets ~ when she sees anyone suffering** la afecta mucho ver a alguien sufriendo, lo pasa muy mal *or* sufre mucho si ve a alguien sufriendo; **he gets very ~ if I don't ring him every day** se pone fatal *or* lo pasa fatal si no lo llamo todos los días*
2 ['ʌpset] (= *sick*) **I have an ~ stomach** tengo el estómago revuelto
Ⓒ ['ʌpset] N 1 (= *disturbance*) contratiempo *m*; **she has had to deal with many ~s in her personal life** su vida ha estado llena de contratiempos *or* reveses; **she has had her fair share of ~s in the past few weeks** ya ha tenido bastantes disgustos en las últimas semanas; **people who are prone to emotional ~s** las personas propensas a trastornos emocionales
2 (*Sport, Pol*) (= *unexpected result*) derrota *f* sorpresa
3 (= *illness*) malestar *m*; **stomach ~** malestar *m* de estómago; **to have a stomach ~** tener el estómago revuelto
Ⓓ ['ʌpset] CPD ► **upset price** N (*esp Scot, US*) precio *m* mínimo, precio *m* de reserva

upsetting [ʌp'setɪŋ] ADJ (= *distressing*) [*experience, incident*] terrible; [*image*] sobrecogedor; (= *saddening*) triste; (= *offending*) [*language, remark*] ofensivo; (= *annoying*) fastidioso, molesto; **the whole incident was very ~ for me** todo el incidente me afectó *or* disgustó mucho; **it is ~ for him to talk about it** lo pasa mal *or* se pone mal al hablar de ello; **parts of the film may be ~ to some viewers** algunas partes de la película pueden resultarles sobrecogedoras a algunos espectadores

upshot ['ʌpʃɒt] N resultado *m*; **the ~ of it all was ...** el resultado fue que ...; **in the ~** al fin y al cabo

upside-down ['ʌpsaɪd'daʊn] Ⓐ ADV al revés; (= *untidily*) patas arriba; **to turn sth ~** volver algo al revés; (*fig*) revolverlo todo; **we turned everything ~ looking for it** al buscarlo lo revolvimos todo, en la búsqueda lo registramos todo de arriba abajo
Ⓑ ADJ al revés; **to be ~** estar al revés; **the room was ~** reinaba el desorden en el cuarto, en el cuarto todo estaba patas arriba*

upstage ['ʌp'steɪdʒ] Ⓐ ADV (*Theat*) **to be ~** estar en el fondo del escenario; **to go ~** ir hacia el fondo del escenario
Ⓑ VT **to ~ sb** (*fig*) eclipsar a algn

upstairs ['ʌp'stɛəz] Ⓐ ADV arriba; **"where's your coat?" — "it's ~"** —¿dónde está tu abrigo? —está arriba; **the people ~** los de arriba; **to go ~** subir (al piso superior); **he went ~ to bed** subió para irse a la cama; **to walk slowly ~** subir lentamente la escalera
Ⓑ ADJ de arriba; **we looked out of an ~ window** nos asomamos a una ventana del piso superior *or* de arriba
Ⓒ N piso *m* superior *or* de arriba

upstanding [ʌp'stændɪŋ] ADJ 1 (= *respectable*) honrado; **a fine ~ young man** un joven distinguido y honrado
2 (*frm*) (= *erect*) [*person*] recto
3 (*Jur frm*) **be ~!** ¡pónganse de pie!

upstart ['ʌpstɑːt] (*pej*) Ⓐ ADJ 1 (= *socially ambitious*) arribista, advenedizo
2 (= *arrogant*) presuntuoso; **some ~ youth** un joven presuntuoso
Ⓑ N 1 (= *social climber*) arribista *mf*, advenedizo/a *m/f*
2 (= *arrogant person*) presuntuoso/a *m/f*

upstate ['ʌp'steɪt] (*US*) Ⓐ N interior *m*
Ⓑ ADJ interior, septentrional
Ⓒ ADV [*be*] en el interior; [*go*] al interior

upstream ['ʌp'striːm] ADV río arriba; **to go ~** ir río arriba; **to swim ~** nadar contra la corriente; **a town ~ from Windsor** una ciudad más arriba de Windsor; **about three miles ~ from Windsor** unas tres millas más arriba de Windsor

upstretched ['ʌpstretʃt] ADJ extendido hacia arriba

upstroke ['ʌpstrəʊk] N 1 (*with pen*) trazo *m* ascendente
2 (*Mech*) [*of piston*] carrera *f* ascendente

upsurge ['ʌpsɜːdʒ] N (*in violence, fighting*) recrudecimiento *m*; (*in demand*) fuerte aumento *m*; **a great ~ of interest in Góngora** un gran renacimiento del interés por Góngora; **there has been an ~ of feeling about this ques-**

tion ha aumentado de pronto la preocupación por esta cuestión

upswept ['ʌpswept] ADJ [*wing*] elevado, inclinado hacia arriba; **with ~ hair** con peinado alto

upswing ['ʌpswɪŋ] N (*lit*) movimiento *m* hacia arriba; (*fig*) alza *f*, mejora *f* notable (**in** en); **an ~ in sales** una alza/mejora notable en las ventas; **an ~ in the economy** una notable mejora en la economía; **to be on the ~** estar en alza

uptake ['ʌpteɪk] N [1] (= *understanding*) **to be quick on the ~*** ser muy listo, agarrar las cosas al vuelo*; **to be slow on the ~*** ser corto (de entendederas)*
[2] (= *intake*) consumo *m*
[3] (= *acceptance*) aceptación *f*; (= *number accepted*) cantidad *f* admitida

up-tempo [ˌʌp'tempəʊ] ADJ [*tune*] con ritmo rápido

upthrust ['ʌp'θrʌst] Ⓐ ADJ [1] (*gen*) (*Tech*) empujado hacia arriba, dirigido hacia arriba
[2] (*Geol*) solevantado
Ⓑ N [1] (*gen*) (*Tech*) empuje *m* hacia arriba
[2] (*Geol*) solevantamiento *m*

uptight* [ʌp'taɪt] ADJ nervioso, tenso; **she's very ~ today** está muy nerviosa *or* tensa hoy; **to get (all) ~ about sth** ponerse nervioso por algo; **don't get so ~!** ¡no te pongas tan nervioso!, ¡no te pongas tan neura!*

uptime ['ʌptaɪm] N tiempo *m* de operación

up-to-date ['ʌptə'deɪt] ADJ [*information, edition, report*] al día, actualizado; [*clothes, equipment, technology*] moderno; **to be ~ with one's payments** llevar sus pagos al día; **to bring/keep sth/sb ~** poner/mantener algo/a algn al día *or* al corriente; **we'll keep you ~ with any news** le mantendremos al día *or* al corriente de las noticias; **I like to keep ~ with all the latest fashions** me gusta mantenerme al día *or* al corriente de la última moda

up-to-the-minute ['ʌptəðə'mɪnɪt] ADJ de última hora

uptown ['ʌp'taʊn] (*US*) Ⓐ ADV hacia las afueras, hacia los barrios exteriores
Ⓑ ADJ exterior, de las afueras

uptrend ['ʌptrend] N (*Econ*) tendencia *f* al alza; **in** *or* **on an ~** en alza

upturn Ⓐ ['ʌptɜːn] N (= *improvement*) mejora *f*, aumento *m* (**in** de); (*Econ etc*) repunte *m*
Ⓑ [ʌp'tɜːn] VT (= *turn over*) volver hacia arriba; (= *overturn*) volcar

upturned ['ʌptɜːnd] ADJ [*box etc*] vuelto hacia arriba; [*nose*] respingón

UPU N ABBR (= **Universal Post Union**) UPU *f*

UPVC ABBR = **unplasticized polyvinyl chloride**

upward ['ʌpwəd] Ⓐ ADJ [*slope*] ascendente, hacia arriba; [*tendency*] al alza; **~ mobility** ascenso *m* social, movilidad *f* social ascendente
Ⓑ ADV (*also* **~s**) [1] (*gen*) hacia arriba; **face ~** boca arriba; **to lay sth face ~** poner algo boca arriba; **to look ~** mirar hacia arriba
[2] (*with numbers*) **£50 and ~** de 50 libras para arriba; **from the age of 13 ~** desde los 13 años; **~ of 500** más de 500

upwardly ['ʌpwədlɪ] ADV **~ mobile** [*person*] ambicioso

upwards ['ʌpwədz] ADV (*esp Brit*) = **upward B**

upwind ['ʌp'wɪnd] ADV **to stay ~** quedarse en la parte de donde sopla el viento

URA N ABBR (*US*) = **Urban Renewal Administration**

uraemia [jʊ'riːmɪə] N uremia *f*

uraemic [jʊ'riːmɪk] ADJ urémico

Urals ['jʊərəlz] N (*also* **Ural Mountains**) (Montes *mpl*) Urales *mpl*

uranalysis [jʊərə'nælɪsɪs] N (*pl* **uranalyses** [ˌjʊərə'nælɪsiːz]) = **urinalysis**

uranium [jʊə'reɪnɪəm] N uranio *m*

Uranus [jʊə'reɪnəs] N Urano *m*

urban ['ɜːbən] Ⓐ ADJ urbano
Ⓑ CPD ► **urban guerrilla** N guerrillero/a *m/f* urbano/a ► **urban myth** N leyenda *f* urbana ► **urban renewal** N renovación *f* urbana ► **urban sprawl** N extensión *f* urbana ► **urban warfare** N guerrilla *f* urbana

urbane [ɜː'beɪn] ADJ urbano, cortés

urbanity [ɜː'bænɪtɪ] N urbanidad *f*, cortesía *f*

urbanization ['ɜːbənaɪ'zeɪʃən] N urbanización *f*

urbanize ['ɜːbənaɪz] VT urbanizar

urchin ['ɜːtʃɪn] N pilluelo/a *m/f*, golfillo/a *m/f*; **sea ~** erizo *m* de mar

Urdu ['ʊəduː] N (*Ling*) urdu *m*

urea ['jʊərɪə] N urea *f*

uremia [jʊə'riːmɪə] N (*US*) = **uraemia**

uremic [jʊə'riːmɪk] (*US*) = **uraemic**

ureter [jʊə'riːtə^r^] N uréter *m*

urethra [jʊə'riːθrə] N (*pl* **urethras** *or* **urethrae** [jʊ'riːθriː]) uretra *f*

urge [ɜːdʒ] Ⓐ N impulso *m*; (*sexual etc*) deseo *m*; **the ~ to write** el deseo apremiante de escribir, la ambición de hacerse escritor; **to feel an ~ to do sth** sentir fuertes deseos *or* ganas de hacer algo; **to get** *or* **have the ~ (to do sth)**: **when you get** *or* **have the ~ to eat something exotic ...** cuando te entren ganas de comer algo exótico; **he had the sudden ~ to take all his clothes off** de repente le entraron ganas de desnudarse
Ⓑ VT [1] (= *try to persuade*) animar, alentar; **to ~ sb to do sth** animar *or* instar a algn a hacer algo; **to ~ that sth should be done** recomendar encarecidamente que se haga algo
[2] (= *advocate*) recomendar, abogar por; **to ~ sth on** *or* **upon sb** insistir en algo con algn; **to ~ a policy on the government** hacer presión en el gobierno para que adopte una política

►**urge on** VT + ADV animar, alentar; (*fig*) animar, instar

urgency ['ɜːdʒənsɪ] N [1] (= *haste*) urgencia *f*; **not everyone had the same sense of ~** no todo el mundo tenía el mismo sentido de la urgencia; **it is a matter of ~** es un asunto urgente; **the problem must be tackled as a matter of ~** el problema debe tratarse con la máxima urgencia
[2] [*of tone of voice, pleas*] urgencia *f*; **with a note of ~ in his voice** con un tono de urgencia

urgent ['ɜːdʒənt] ADJ [1] (= *imperative*) [*matter, business, case, message*] urgente; **he needs ~ medical treatment** necesita tratamiento médico urgente *or* urgentemente; **is this ~?** ¿es urgente?, ¿corre prisa esto?; **it is ~ that I see him** tengo que verlo urgentemente; **there is an ~ need for water** se necesita urgentemente agua, hay una necesidad apremiante de agua; **to be in ~ need of sth** necesitar algo urgentemente
[2] (= *earnest, persistent*) [*tone*] de urgencia, insistente; [*voice*] insistente; [*plea, appeal*] urgente

urgently ['ɜːdʒəntlɪ] ADV [1] (= *immediately*) [*need, seek*] urgentemente, con urgencia; **he ~ needs help** necesita ayuda urgentemente *or* con urgencia
[2] (= *earnestly, persistently*) (*gen*) con insistencia; [*speak*] con tono de urgencia

uric ['jʊərɪk] ADJ úrico; **~ acid** ácido *m* úrico

urinal [jʊə'raɪnl] N (= *building*) urinario *m*; (= *vessel*) orinal *m*

urinalysis [jʊərə'nælɪsɪs] N (*pl* **urinalyses** [ˌjʊərɪ'nælɪsiːz]) análisis *m inv* de orina

urinary ['jʊərɪnərɪ] ADJ urinario

urinate ['jʊərɪneɪt] Ⓐ VT orinar
Ⓑ VI orinar(se)

urine ['jʊərɪn] N orina *f*, orines *mpl*

URL N ABBR (*Internet*) (= **uniform resource locator**) URL *m*

urn [ɜːn] N [1] (= *vase*) urna *f*
[2] (= *tea urn*) tetera *f*; (= *coffee urn*) cafetera *f*

urogenital [ˌjʊərəʊ'dʒenɪtl] ADJ urogenital

urological [ˌjʊərəʊ'lɒdʒɪkl] ADJ urológico

urologist [jʊə'rɒlədʒɪst] N urólogo/a *m/f*

urology [jʊə'rɒlədʒɪ] N urología *f*

Ursa Major ['ɜːsə'meɪdʒə^r^] N Osa *f* Mayor

Ursa Minor ['ɜːsə'maɪnə^r^] N Osa *f* Menor

urticaria [ˌɜːtɪ'keərɪə] N urticaria *f*

Uruguay ['jʊərəgwaɪ] N Uruguay *m*

Uruguayan [ˌjʊərə'gwaɪən] Ⓐ ADJ uruguayo
Ⓑ N uruguayo/a *m/f*

US N ABBR = **United States**; **the US** EE.UU., Estados Unidos; **in the US** en Estados Unidos; **the US Army/government** el Ejército/gobierno estadounidense

us [ʌs] PRON [1] (*direct/indirect object*) nos; **they helped us** nos ayudaron; **look at us!** ¡míranos!; **give it to us** dánoslo; **they gave us some brochures** nos dieron unos folletos; **see if you can find us some food** mira a ver si nos encuentras algo de comer
[2] (*after prepositions, in comparisons, with the verb to be*) nosotros/as; **why don't you come with us?** ¿por qué no vienes con nosotros?; **several of us** varios de nosotros; **he is one of us** es uno de nosotros; **both of us** los dos; **they are older than us** son mayores que nosotros; **as for us English, we ...** en cuanto a nosotros los ingleses, ...; **it's us** somos nosotros
[3] (*Brit**) (= *me*) me; **give us a bit!** ¡dame un poco!; **give us a look!** ¡déjame ver!

USA N ABBR [1] = **United States of America**; **the ~** Estados Unidos, EE.UU.; **in the ~** en Estados Unidos
[2] = **United States Army**

usable ['juːzəbl] ADJ utilizable; **~ space** espacio *m* útil; **it is no longer ~** ya no sirve

USAF N ABBR = **United States Air Force**

usage ['juːzɪdʒ] N [1] (= *custom*) costumbre *f*, usanza *f*; **an ancient ~ of the Celts** una antigua usanza de los celtas
[2] (*Ling*) (= *use, way of using*) uso *m*; **in the ~ of railwaymen** en el lenguaje de los ferroviarios, en el uso ferroviario
[3] (= *handling*) manejo *m*; (= *treatment*) tratos *mpl*; **ill ~** mal tratamiento *m*; **it's had some rough ~** ha sido manejado con bastante dureza

USCG N ABBR (*US*) = **United States Coast Guard**

USD ABBR = **US Dollars**

USDA N ABBR (= **United States Department of Agriculture**) ≈ MAPA *m*

USDAW ['ʌzdɔː] N ABBR (*Brit*) = **Union of Shop, Distributive and Allied Workers**

USDI N ABBR = **United States Department of the Interior**

use [juːs] Ⓐ N [1] (= *act of using*) uso *m*, empleo *m*, utilización *f*; (= *handling*) manejo *m*; **the ~ of steel in industry** el empleo *or* la utilización *or* el uso del acero en la industria; **for**

the ~ of the blind para (uso de) los ciegos; **for ~ in case of emergency** para uso en caso de emergencia; **care in the ~ of guns** cuidado *m* en el manejo de las armas de fuego; **a new ~ for old tyres** un nuevo método para utilizar los neumáticos viejos; **"directions for use"** "modo de empleo"; **fit for ~** servible, en buen estado; **in ~**: **word in ~** palabra *f* en uso *or* que se usa; **to be in daily ~** ser de uso diario; **to be no longer in ~** estar fuera de uso; **it is not now in ~** ya no se usa; **it has not been in ~ for five years** hace cinco años que no se usa; **an article in everyday ~** un artículo de uso diario; **to make ~ of** hacer uso de, usar; [+ *right etc*] valerse de, ejercer; **to make good ~ of** sacar partido *or* provecho de; **out of ~** en desuso; **it is now out of ~** ya no se usa, está en desuso; **to go** *or* **fall out of ~** caer en desuso; **to put sth to good ~** hacer buen uso de algo, sacar partido *or* provecho de algo; **to put sth into ~** poner algo en servicio; **ready for ~** listo (para ser usado); **it improves with ~** mejora con el uso

2 (= *way of using*) modo *m* de empleo; (= *handling*) manejo *m*; **we were instructed in the ~ of firearms** se nos instruyó en el manejo de armas de fuego

3 (= *function*) uso *m*; **it has many ~s** tiene muchos usos; **can you find a ~ for this?** ¿te sirve esto?

4 (= *usefulness*) utilidad *f*; **it has its ~s** tiene su utilidad; **to be of ~** servir, tener utilidad; **can I be of any ~?** ¿puedo ayudar?; **to be no ~**: **he's no ~ as a teacher** no vale para profesor, no sirve como profesor; **it's (of) no ~** es inútil, no sirve para nada; **it's no ~ discussing it further** es inútil *or* no vale la pena seguir discutiendo; **I have no further ~ for it** ya no lo necesito, ya no me sirve para nada; **to have no ~ for sb*** no aguantar a algn; **I've no ~ for those who ...** no aguanto a los que ...; **what's the ~ of all this?** ¿de qué sirve todo esto?

5 (= *ability to use, access*) **he gave me the ~ of his car** me dejó que usara su coche; **to have the ~ of**: **to have the ~ of a garage** tener acceso a un garaje; **I have the ~ of it on Sundays** me permiten usarlo los domingos, lo puedo usar los domingos; **I have the ~ of the kitchen until 6p.m.** puedo *or* tengo permitido usar la cocina hasta las seis; **he lost the ~ of his arm** se le quedó inútil el brazo

6 (*Ling*) (= *sense*) uso *m*, sentido *m*

7 (*frm*) (= *custom*) uso *m*, costumbre *f*

Ⓑ [ju:z] VT 1 (*gen*) usar, emplear, utilizar; **he ~d a knife** empleó *or* usó *or* utilizó un cuchillo; **are you using this book?** ¿te hace falta este libro?; **which book did you ~?** ¿qué libro consultaste?; **it isn't ~d any more** ya no se usa; **have you ~d a gun before?** ¿has manejado alguna vez una escopeta?; **"use only in emergencies"** "usar sólo en caso de emergencia"; **to ~ sth as a hammer** emplear *or* usar algo como martillo; **to be ~d**: **what's this ~d for?** ¿para qué sirve esto?, ¿para qué se utiliza esto?; **the money is ~d for the poor** el dinero se dedica a los pobres; **the word is no longer ~d** la palabra ya no se usa; **this room could ~ some paint*** a este cuarto no le vendría mal una mano de pintura; **I could ~ a drink!*** ¡no me vendría mal un trago!; **to ~ sth for**: **to ~ sth for a purpose** servirse de algo con un propósito; **to ~ force** emplear la fuerza; **careful how you ~ that razor!** ¡cuidado con la navaja esa!; **to ~ every means** emplear todos los medios a su alcance (**to do sth** para hacer algo)

2 (= *make use of, exploit*) usar, utilizar; **he said I could ~ his car** dijo que podía usar *or* utilizar su coche; **I don't ~ my Spanish much** no uso mucho el español; **you can ~ the leftovers in a soup** puedes usar las sobras para una sopa; **he wants to ~ the bathroom** quiere usar el cuarto de baño; (= *go to the toilet*) quiere ir al lavabo *or* (*LAm*) al baño; **someone is using the bathroom** el lavabo *or* (*LAm*) el baño está ocupado; **~ your head** *or* **brains!*** ¡usa el coco!*

3 (= *consume*) [+ *fuel*] consumir; **have you ~d all the milk?** ¿has terminado toda la leche?

4 (†) (= *treat*) tratar; **she had been cruelly ~d by ...** había sido tratada con crueldad por ...; **to ~ sb roughly** maltratar a algn; **to ~ sb well** tratar bien a algn

Ⓒ VI (*Drugs**) drogarse

Ⓓ [ju:s] AUX VB (*gen*) soler, acostumbrar (a); **I ~d to go camping as a child** de pequeño solía *or* acostumbraba ir de acampada; **I ~d to live in London** (antes) vivía en Londres; **I didn't ~ to like maths, but now I love it** antes no me gustaban las matemáticas, pero ahora me encantan; **but I ~d not to** pero antes no; **things aren't what they ~d to be** las cosas ya no son lo que eran

► **use up** VT + ADV [+ *supplies*] agotar; [+ *money*] gastar; **we've ~d up all the paint** hemos acabado toda la pintura; **when we've ~d up all our money** cuando hayamos gastado todo el dinero; **please ~ up all the coffee** termínaos el café

> **USED TO**
>
> • To describe what someone **used to do** or what **used to happen**, you should generally just use the imperfect tense of the main verb:
>
> We used to buy our food at the corner shop
> ***Comprábamos la comida en la tienda de la esquina***
> ...as my mother used to say...
> ***...como decía mi madre...***
>
> • Alternatively, to describe someone's habits you can use **solía** + INFINITIVE or **acostumbraba (a)** + INFINITIVE:
>
> He used to go for a walk every day
> ***Solía** or **Acostumbraba (a) dar un paseo todos los días***
>
> • To emphasize the contrast between what **used to** happen previously and what happens now, use **antes** + IMPERFECT:
>
> He used to be a journalist
> ***Antes era periodista***
> She didn't use to or She used not to drink alcohol
> ***Antes no tomaba alcohol***
>
> *For further uses and examples, see main entry at* ***use.***

useable ['ju:zəbl] ADJ = **usable**

used[1] [ju:zd] ADJ 1 (= *finished with*) [*stamp, syringe*] usado; [*battery, tyre*] gastado, usado

2 (= *second-hand*) [*clothing, car*] usado; **a ~ car** un coche de segunda mano

used[2] [ju:st] ADJ **to be ~ to sth** estar acostumbrado a algo; **he wasn't ~ to driving on the right** no estaba acostumbrado a conducir por la derecha; **don't worry, I'm ~ to it** no te preocupes, estoy acostumbrado; **to be ~ to doing sth** estar acostumbrado a hacer algo; **to get ~ to** acostumbrarse a; **I still haven't got ~ to the lifts** todavía no me he acostumbrado a los ascensores

useful ['ju:sfʊl] ADJ 1 (= *valuable*) [*information, advice, tool*] útil; [*discussion, meeting*] fructífero; [*experience*] provechoso, útil; **beans are a ~ source of protein** las judías son una buena fuente de proteína; **a ~ player** un buen jugador, un jugador que vale; **the time we spent in Spain was very ~** nuestra estancia en España fue muy provechosa; **he's a ~ person to know** es una persona que conviene conocer; **it is very ~ to be able to drive** es muy útil saber conducir; **~ capacity** capacidad *f* útil; **to come in ~** ser útil, venir bien; **the machine has reached the end of its ~ life** la máquina ha llegado al final de su periodo de funcionamiento; **he lived a ~ life** tuvo una vida provechosa; **to make o.s. ~** ayudar, echar una mano*; **come on, make yourself ~!** ¡venga, haz algo!, ¡vamos, echa una mano!*; **this discussion is not serving any ~ purpose** esta discusión no está sirviendo para nada útil *or* provechoso; **I feel I am ~ to the company** me parece que le soy de utilidad a *or* útil a la empresa

2 (*) (= *capable*) **he's ~ with his fists** sabe defenderse con los puños; **he's ~ with a gun** sabe manejar un fusil

usefully ['ju:sfəlɪ] ADV de manera provechosa, provechosamente; **you could spend your time more ~ in the library** podrías emplear el tiempo de manera más provechosa *or* más provechosamente en la biblioteca; **the staff are not being ~ employed** la plantilla no se está empleando de manera provechosa *or* provechosamente; **there was nothing that could ~ be said** nada de lo que podía decirse servía de nada

usefulness ['ju:sfʊlnɪs] N utilidad *f*; **it has outlived its ~** ha dejado de tener utilidad

useless ['ju:slɪs] ADJ 1 (= *ineffective*) [*object*] que no sirve para nada; [*person*] inútil; **this can opener's ~** este abrelatas no sirve para nada; **compasses are ~ in the jungle** las brújulas no sirven para *or* de nada en la selva; **she's ~** es una inútil; **he's ~ as a forward** no vale para delantero, no sirve como delantero; **I was always ~ at maths** siempre fui (un) negado *or* un inútil para las matemáticas

2 (= *unusable*) [*object, vehicle*] inservible; [*limb*] inutilizado, inútil; **he's a mine of ~ information!** (*hum*) se sabe todo tipo de datos y chorraditas que no sirven de nada*; **to render** *or* **make sth ~** inutilizar algo

3 (= *pointless*) inútil; **it's ~ to shout** de nada sirve gritar, es inútil gritar

uselessly ['ju:slɪslɪ] ADV (= *ineffectually*) inútilmente; (= *in vain, pointlessly*) inútilmente, en vano

uselessness ['ju:slɪsnɪs] N (= *ineffectualness*) inutilidad *f*; (= *pointlessness*) lo inútil

Usenet ['ju:znet] N Usenet *f or m*

user ['ju:zə^r] Ⓐ N 1 usuario/a *m/f*; **computer ~s** usuarios *mpl* de ordenadores

2 (*Drugs*) **drug ~** drogadicto/a *m/f*; **heroin ~** heroinómano/a *m/f*

Ⓑ CPD ► **user identification** N identificación *f* del usuario ► **user language** N lenguaje *m* del usuario ► **user software** N software *m* del usuario

user-definable [ˌju:zədɪ'faɪnəbl], **user-defined** [ˌju:zədɪ'faɪnd] ADJ definido por el usuario

user-friendliness [ˌju:zə'frendlɪnɪs] N facilidad *f* de uso, facilidad *f* de manejo

user-friendly [ˌju:zə'frendlɪ] ADJ [*computer, software, system, dictionary*] fácil de utilizar *or* usar *or* manejar; **to make sth more ~** hacer algo más fácil de manejar, hacer algo más accesible para el usuario

USES N ABBR = **United States Employment Service**

USGS N ABBR = **United States Geological Survey**

usher [ˈʌʃəʳ] Ⓐ N (*in court etc*) ujier *mf*; (*in theatre, cinema etc*) acomodador(a) *m/f*; (*at public meeting etc*) guardia *mf* de sala, encargado/a *m/f* del orden
Ⓑ VT **to ~ sb into a room** hacer pasar a algn a un cuarto; **to ~ sb to the door** ◊ **~ sb out** acompañar a algn a la puerta; **to ~ sb out** [+ *unwanted individual*] hacer salir a algn

►**usher in** VT + ADV [+ *person*] hacer pasar a; (*Theat etc*) acomodar a, conducir su sitio; **I was ~ed in by the butler** el mayordomo me hizo pasar; **it ~ed in a new reign** anunció un nuevo reinado, marcó el comienzo de un nuevo reinado; **summer was ~ed in by storms** el verano empezó con tormentas

usherette [ˌʌʃəˈret] N acomodadora *f*

USIA N ABBR = **United States Information Agency**

USM N ABBR [1] = **United States Mail**
[2] (*Fin*) (= **unlisted securities market**) mercado *m* de valores no cotizados en la Bolsa
[3] = **United States Mint**

USMC N ABBR = **United States Marine Corps**

USN N ABBR = **United States Navy**

USO N ABBR (*US*) = **United Service Organization**

USP N ABBR [1] = **unique sales** *or* **selling proposition**
[2] = **unique selling point**

USPHS N ABBR = **United States Public Health Service**

USPS N ABBR = **United States Postal Service**

USS N ABBR = **United States Ship** *or* **Steamer**

USSR N ABBR (= **Union of Soviet Socialist Republics**) URSS *f*; **in the ~** en la URSS, en la Unión Soviética

usu. ABBR = **usual(ly)**

usual [ˈjuːʒʊəl] Ⓐ ADJ (= *customary*) [*method, answer*] acostumbrado, habitual, usual; [*place, time, excuse*] de siempre; **more than ~** más que de costumbre; **to come earlier than ~** venir más temprano que de costumbre, venir antes de la hora acostumbrada; **it's ~ to give a tip** es costumbre *or* (*esp LAm*) se acostumbra dar una propina; **as (per) ~** como de costumbre, como siempre; **it's not ~ for her to be late** no suele llegar tarde; **it is not our ~ practice to allow this** no acostumbramos *or* solemos permitir esto; **it's not contagious in the ~ sense of the word** no es contagioso en el sentido normal de la palabra; **he came home late, drunk, the ~ thing** llegó a casa tarde y borracho, lo de siempre; **boil the potatoes in the ~ way** cueza las patatas como de costumbre *or* como siempre
Ⓑ N **the ~ please!*** (= *drink*) lo de siempre, por favor

usually [ˈjuːʒʊəlɪ] ADV normalmente, por lo general; **we ~ go on a Friday** normalmente *or* por lo general vamos un viernes; **what do you ~ do?** ¿qué hacen ustedes normalmente?; **we have to be more than ~ careful** tenemos que tomar más cuidado que de costumbre; **not ~** por lo general *or* normalmente no; **the ~ crowded streets were deserted** las calles normalmente atiborradas de gente estaban desiertas

usufruct [ˈjuːzjʊfrʌkt] N usufructo *m*

usufructuary [ˌjuːzjʊˈfrʌktərɪ] N usufructuario/a *m/f*

usurer [ˈjuːʒərəʳ] N usurero/a *m/f*

usurious [juːˈzjʊərɪəs] ADJ usurario

usurp [juːˈzɜːp] VT usurpar

usurpation [ˌjuːzɜːˈpeɪʃən] N usurpación *f*

usurper [juːˈzɜːpəʳ] N usurpador(a) *m/f*

usurping [juːˈzɜːpɪŋ] ADJ usurpador

usury [ˈjuːʒʊrɪ] N usura *f*

UT ABBR (*US*) = **Utah**

UTC ABBR = **Universal Time Coordinated**

utensil [juːˈtensl] N utensilio *m*; **kitchen ~s** utensilios *mpl* de cocina; (= *set*) batería *f* de cocina

uterine [ˈjuːtəraɪn] ADJ uterino

uterus [ˈjuːtərəs] N (*pl* **uteri** [ˈjuːtəraɪ]) útero *m*

utilitarian [ˌjuːtɪlɪˈtɛərɪən] Ⓐ ADJ utilitario
Ⓑ N utilitarista *mf*

utilitarianism [ˌjuːtɪlɪˈtɛərɪənɪzəm] N utilitarismo *m*

utility [juːˈtɪlɪtɪ] Ⓐ N [1] (= *usefulness*) utilidad *f*
[2] (*also* **public ~**) servicio *m* público
Ⓑ CPD utilitario ► **utility player** N (*Sport*) jugador(a) *m/f* polivalente ► **utility room** N trascocina *f* ► **utility vehicle** N furgoneta *f*, camioneta *f*

utilizable [ˈjuːtɪˌlaɪzəbl] ADJ utilizable

utilization [ˌjuːtɪlaɪˈzeɪʃən] N utilización *f*

utilize [ˈjuːtɪlaɪz] VT utilizar, aprovecharse de

utmost [ˈʌtməʊst] Ⓐ ADJ [1] (= *greatest*) sumo; **of the ~ importance** de la mayor importancia, de suma importancia; **with the ~ ease** con suma facilidad
[2] (= *furthest*) más lejano
Ⓑ N **the ~ that one can do** todo lo que puede hacer uno; **200 at the ~** 200 a lo más, 200 a lo sumo; **to do one's ~ (to do sth)** hacer todo lo posible (por hacer algo); **to the ~** al máximo, hasta más no poder; **to the ~ of one's ability** lo mejor que pueda *or* sepa uno

Utopia [juːˈtəʊpɪə] N Utopía *f*

Utopian [juːˈtəʊpɪən] Ⓐ ADJ [*dream etc*] utópico; [*person*] utopista
Ⓑ N utopista *mf*

Utopianism [juːˈtəʊpɪənɪzəm] N utopismo *m*

utricle [ˈjuːtrɪkl] N utrículo *m*

utter[1] [ˈʌtəʳ] ADJ completo, total; [*madness*] puro; [*fool*] perfecto; **~ nonsense!** ¡tonterías!; **it was an ~ disaster** fue un desastre total; **he was in a state of ~ depression** estaba completamente deprimido

utter[2] [ˈʌtəʳ] VT [1] [+ *words*] pronunciar; [+ *cry*] dar, soltar; [+ *threat, insult etc*] proferir; [+ *libel*] publicar; **she never ~ed a word** no dijo nada *or* (ni una) palabra; **don't ~ a word about it** no le digas nada a nadie
[2] (*Jur*) [+ *counterfeit money*] poner en circulación, expender

utterance [ˈʌtərəns] N [1] (= *remark*) palabras *fpl*, declaración *f*
[2] (= *expression*) expresión *f*; **to give ~ to** expresar, manifestar, declarar
[3] (= *style*) pronunciación *f*, articulación *f*

utterly [ˈʌtəlɪ] ADV totalmente, completamente

uttermost [ˈʌtəməʊst] ADJ = **utmost A**

U-turn [ˈjuːtɜːn] N (*lit, fig*) cambio *m* de sentido, giro *m* de 180 grados; **to do a ~** cambiar de sentido; **"no U-turns"** "prohibido cambiar de sentido"

UV ADJ ABBR (= **ultraviolet**) UV, UVA

UVA, **UV-A** ADJ ABBR **~ rays** rayos *mpl* UVA

UVB, **UV-B** ADJ ABBR **~ rays** rayos *mpl* UVB

UVF N ABBR (*Brit*) (= **Ulster Volunteer Force**) *organización paramilitar protestante en Irlanda del Norte*

uvula [ˈjuːvjələ] N (*pl* **uvulas** *or* **uvulae** [ˈjuːvjəliː]) úvula *f*

uvular [ˈjuːvjələʳ] ADJ uvular

uxorious [ʌkˈsɔːrɪəs] ADJ muy enamorado de su mujer, enamorado con exceso *or* con ostentación de su mujer

Uzbek [ˈʊzbek] Ⓐ ADJ uzbeko
Ⓑ N [1] (= *person*) uzbeko/a *m/f*
[2] (*Ling*) uzbeko

Uzbekistan [ˌʊzbekɪsˈtɑːn] N Uzbekistán *m*

V v

V, v[1] [viː] N (= *letter*) V, v *f*; **V for victory** V de la victoria; **V1** (= *flying bomb*) bomba *f* volante (*1944-45*); **V2** (= *rocket*) cohete *m* (*1944-45*); *see also* **V-sign, V-neck**

v[2] ABBR [1] (*Literat*) (= **verse**) v.
[2] (*Bible*) (= **verse**) vers.º
[3] (*Sport, Jur*) = **versus** (= *against*) v., vs.
[4] (*Elec*) = **volt(s)**
[5] = **vide** (= *see*) vid., v.
[6] = **very**
[7] = **volume**

VA (*US*) Ⓐ ABBR = **Virginia**
Ⓑ N ABBR = **Veterans Administration**

Va. ABBR = **Virginia**

vac* [væk] N [1] (*Brit Univ*) = **vacation**
[2] (*esp Brit*) = **vacuum cleaner**

vacancy [ˈveɪkənsɪ] N [1] (= *job*) vacante *f*; **"vacancies"** "ofertas de trabajo"; **"vacancy for keen young man"** "se busca joven enérgico"; **to fill a ~** proveer una vacante
[2] (*in boarding house etc*) habitación *f* libre, cuarto *m* libre; **have you any vacancies?** ¿tiene *or* hay alguna habitación *or* algún cuarto libre?; **we have no vacancies for August** para agosto no hay nada disponible, en agosto todo está lleno; **"no vacancies"** "completo"; **"vacancies"** "hay habitaciones"
[3] (= *emptiness*) lo vacío; [*of mind*] vaciedad *f*, vacuidad *f*

vacant [ˈveɪkənt] ADJ [1] (= *unoccupied*) [*seat*] libre, desocupado; [*room*] libre, disponible; [*house*] desocupado, vacío; [*space*] vacío; **is this seat ~?** ¿está libre (este asiento)?; **~ lot** (*US*) solar *m*; **~ post** vacante *f*; **to become** *or* **fall ~** [*post*] quedar(se) vacante; *see also* **situation**
[2] (= *expressionless*) [*look*] ausente, vacío
[3] (= *stupid*) [*person*] alelado

vacantly [ˈveɪkəntlɪ] ADV [1] [*look*] con gesto ausente, distraídamente
[2] (= *stupidly*) sin comprender, boquiabierto

vacate [vəˈkeɪt] VT (*frm*) [+ *seat, room*] dejar libre; [+ *premises*] desocupar, desalojar; [+ *post*] dejar; [+ *throne*] renunciar a

vacation [vəˈkeɪʃən] N Ⓐ N [1] (*esp Brit Jur*) receso *m* vacacional (*frm*), periodo *m* vacacional
[2] (*Univ*) **the long ~** las vacaciones de verano
[3] (*US*) (= *holiday*) vacaciones *fpl*; **to be on ~** estar de vacaciones; **to take a ~** tomarse unas vacaciones
[4] (= *vacating*) [*of premises*] desalojo *m*
Ⓑ VI (*US*) pasar las vacaciones
Ⓒ CPD ► **vacation course** N curso *m* extracurricular (*durante las vacaciones*); (*in summer*) curso *m* de verano ► **vacation job** N empleo *m* de verano ► **vacation pay** N paga *f* de las vacaciones ► **vacation resort** N centro *m* turístico ► **vacation season** N temporada *f* de las vacaciones

vacationer [vəˈkeɪʃənəʳ], **vacationist** [vəˈkeɪʃənɪst] N (*US*) (*gen*) turista *mf*; (*in summer*) veraneante *mf*

vaccinate [ˈvæksɪneɪt] VT vacunar

vaccination [ˌvæksɪˈneɪʃən] N vacunación *f*; **you must have the ~ a month before you travel** debes vacunarte un mes antes de viajar

vaccine [ˈvæksiːn] N vacuna *f*

vacillate [ˈvæsɪleɪt] VI (= *hesitate*) vacilar, dudar; (= *waver*) oscilar (**between** entre)

vacillating [ˈvæsɪleɪtɪŋ] ADJ vacilante, irresoluto

vacillation [ˌvæsɪˈleɪʃən] N vacilación *f*

vacua [ˈvækjʊə] NPL *of* **vacuum**

vacuity [væˈkjuːɪtɪ] N (*frm*) [1] (= *vapidity*) vacuidad *f*
[2] **vacuities** (= *silly remarks*) vaciedades *fpl*

vacuous [ˈvækjʊəs] ADJ (*frm*) [*expression*] vacío, ausente; [*face*] alelado, de pasmo; [*comment*] vacuo, vacío; [*person*] alelado, bobo

vacuum [ˈvækjʊm] Ⓐ N (*pl* **vacuums** *or* (*frm*) **vacua**) [1] (*gen*) vacío *m*; **it can't exist in a ~** no puede existir en el vacío
[2] (= *hoover*) **to give a room a ~** limpiar un cuarto con aspiradora
Ⓑ VT pasar la aspiradora por
Ⓒ VI pasar la aspiradora
Ⓓ CPD ► **vacuum bottle** N (*US*) = **vacuum flask** ► **vacuum cleaner** N aspiradora *f* ► **vacuum flask** N termo *m* ► **vacuum pump** N bomba *f* de vacío

vacuum-packed [ˈvækjʊmˈpækt] ADJ envasado al vacío

vade mecum [ˈvɑːdɪˈmeɪkʊm] N vademécum *m*

vagabond [ˈvægəbɒnd] Ⓐ ADJ vagabundo
Ⓑ N vagabundo/a *m/f*

vagary [ˈveɪgərɪ] N (= *whim*) capricho *m*, antojo *m*; (= *strange idea*) manía *f*, capricho *m*; **the vagaries of love** los caprichos del amor; **the vagaries of the weather** los caprichos del tiempo; **it can't be left to the vagaries of chance** no se puede dejar al azar *or* en manos del azar

vagina [vəˈdʒaɪnə] N (*pl* **vaginas** *or* **vaginae** [vəˈdʒaɪniː]) vagina *f*

vaginal [vəˈdʒaɪnəl] ADJ vaginal; **~ smear** frotis *m* vaginal

vagrancy [ˈveɪgrənsɪ] N vagancia *f*, vagabundeo *m*

vagrant [ˈveɪgrənt] Ⓐ N vagabundo/a *m/f*
Ⓑ ADJ vagabundo, vagante; (*fig*) errante

vague [veɪg] ADJ (*compar* **vaguer**; *superl* **vaguest**)
[1] (= *imprecise*) [*concept*] impreciso, vago; [*description*] impreciso; [*outline*] borroso; [*feeling*] indefinido, indeterminado; [*person*] (*in giving details etc*) impreciso; (*by nature*) de ideas poco precisas; **the outlook is somewhat ~** el futuro es algo incierto; **there have been ~ hints of a reconciliation** ha habido ligeros atisbos de reconciliación; **my memories of that time are very ~** mis recuerdos de aquella época son muy vagos, aquella época la recuerdo muy vagamente; **the ~ outline of a ship** el perfil borroso de un buque; **he made some ~ promises** hacía promesas, pero sin concretar; **I haven't the ~st idea** no tengo la más remota idea; **he was ~ about the date** no quiso precisar la fecha; **you mustn't be so ~** hay que decir las cosas con claridad, hay que concretar; **I'm a bit ~ on that subject** sé poco en concreto sobre ese tema; **then he went all ~** luego comenzó a decir vaguedades
[2] (= *absent-minded*) [*person*] despistado, distraído; [*expression, look*] ausente; **he's terribly ~** tiene un tremendo despiste, es un despistado; **to look ~** tener aire distraído

vaguely [ˈveɪglɪ] ADV [1] (= *imprecisely*) [*define, remember*] vagamente; [*embarrassed, guilty*] ligeramente, levemente; **a ~ worded agreement** un acuerdo expresado de forma imprecisa *or* en términos poco claros; **he talks very ~** habla en términos muy vagos; **she was ~ aware of someone else in the room** tenía la ligera *or* vaga impresión de que había alguien más en la habitación; **he gestured ~ towards the hills** señaló con gesto impreciso hacia las colinas; **his face looked ~ familiar** su rostro me resultaba ligeramente familiar; **her style is ~ reminiscent of Jane Austen** su estilo recuerda vagamente a *or* tiene un cierto parecido con Jane Austen
[2] (= *absent-mindedly*) distraídamente; **she looked at me ~** me miró distraída; **I thought ~ of ringing him up** se me pasó por la cabeza la idea de llamarle

vagueness [ˈveɪgnɪs] N [1] (= *imprecision*) vaguedad *f*, imprecisión *f*
[2] (= *absent-mindedness*) distracción *f*

vain [veɪn] ADJ [1] (= *useless*) vano, inútil; **in ~** [*try, struggle*] en vano, inútilmente; [*search*] sin éxito, en vano; **all our efforts were in ~** todos nuestros esfuerzos fueron en vano *or* resultaron inútiles; **I stayed, in the ~ hope that ...** me quedé con la vana esperanza de que ...; ✦***IDIOM*** **to take sb's name in ~** hablar con poco respeto de algn; **to take the Lord's name in ~** tomar el nombre de Dios en vano
[2] (*compar* **vainer**; *superl* **vainest**) (= *conceited*) vanidoso, presumido; **she is very ~ about her hair** siempre está arreglándose el pelo

vainglorious [veɪnˈglɔːrɪəs] ADJ vanaglorioso

vainglory [veɪnˈglɔːrɪ] N vanagloria *f*

vainly [ˈveɪnlɪ] ADV [1] (= *to no effect*) [*try, struggle*] en vano, inútilmente; [*search*] sin éxito, en

vano
2 (= *conceitedly*) vanidosamente

valance ['væləns] N (*on bed*) cenefa *f*; (*on curtains*) [*of wood*] galería *f*; [*of fabric*] cenefa *f*

vale [veɪl] N (*poet*) valle *m*; **~ of tears** valle *m* de lágrimas

valediction [,vælɪ'dɪkʃən] N despedida *f*

valedictory [,vælɪ'dɪktərɪ] Ⓐ ADJ [*address*] de despedida
Ⓑ N (*US*) oración *f* de despedida

valence ['veɪləns] N valencia *f*

Valencian [və'lensɪən] Ⓐ ADJ valenciano
Ⓑ N 1 (= *person*) valenciano/a *m/f*
2 (*Ling*) valenciano *m*

valency ['veɪlənsɪ] N valencia *f*

valentine ['væləntaɪn] N 1 **(St) Valentine's Day** día *m* de San Valentín, día *m* de los enamorados (*14 febrero*)
2 (*also* **~ card**) tarjeta *f* del día de San Valentín, tarjeta *f* de los enamorados (*enviada por jóvenes, sin firmar, de tono amoroso o jocoso*)
3 (= *person*) novio/a *m/f* (*escogido el día de San Valentín*)

valerian [və'lɪərɪən] N valeriana *f*

valet ['væleɪ] Ⓐ N 1 (= *person*) (*in hotel or household*) ayuda *m* de cámara
2 (*for car*) lavado *m* y limpieza *f*, limpieza *f* completa
Ⓑ VT [+ *car*] lavar y limpiar, hacer una limpieza completa de
Ⓒ CPD ► **valet parking** N (*US*) servicio *m* de aparcamiento a cargo del hotel

valeting service ['vælɪtɪŋ,sɜːvɪs] N (*in hotel*) servicio *m* de planchado; (*for car*) servicio *m* de limpieza

valetudinarian ['vælɪ,tjuːdɪ'nɛərɪən] Ⓐ ADJ valetudinario
Ⓑ N valetudinario/a *m/f*

Valhalla [væl'hælə] N Valhala *m*

valiant ['væljənt] ADJ (*poet*) [*person*] valiente, valeroso; [*effort*] valeroso

valiantly ['væljəntlɪ] ADV valientemente, con valor

valid ['vælɪd] ADJ 1 [*argument, point, question*] válido; [*excuse, claim, objection*] válido, legítimo; **that argument is not ~** ese argumento no es válido *or* no vale
2 [*ticket, passport, licence, contract*] válido, valedero; **a ticket ~ for three months** un billete válido *or* valedero para tres meses; **that ticket is no longer ~** ese billete ya no vale *or* ha caducado ya

validate ['vælɪdeɪt] VT (*gen*) validar, dar validez a; [+ *document*] convalidar

validation [,vælɪ'deɪʃən] N convalidación *f*

validity [və'lɪdɪtɪ] N (*all senses*) validez *f*

valise [və'liːz] N valija *f*, maleta *f*

Valium® ['vælɪəm] N valium® *m*

Valkyrie ['vælkɪrɪ] N Valquiria *f*

valley ['vælɪ] N valle *m*

valor ['vælər] N (*US*) = **valour**

valorous ['vælərəs] ADJ (*liter*) valiente, valeroso

valour, **valor** (*US*) ['vælər] N (*frm*) valor *m*, valentía *f*

valuable ['væljʊəbl] Ⓐ ADJ 1 (*in monetary terms*) valioso; **is it ~?** ¿vale mucho?
2 (= *extremely useful*) [*information, assistance, advice*] valioso; **a ~ contribution** una valiosa aportación; **the experience taught me a ~ lesson** aquella experiencia me enseñó una valiosa lección; **we are wasting your ~ time** le estamos haciendo perder su valioso *or* precioso tiempo
Ⓑ N **valuables** objetos *mpl* de valor

valuation [,væljʊ'eɪʃən] N 1 (= *evaluation*) [*of property, house, assets, antique*] tasación *f*, valoración *f*; **to make a ~ of sth** tasar *or* valorar algo
2 (*fig*) [*of person's character*] valoración *f*; **to take sb at his own ~** aceptar todo lo que dice algn acerca de sí mismo

valuator ['væljʊ,eɪtər] N valuador(a) *m/f*, tasador(a) *m/f*

value ['væljuː] Ⓐ N 1 (*monetary*) valor *m*; **property/land ~s** valores *mpl* de propiedad/tierras; **it's good ~** sale a cuenta, está bien de precio; **Spanish wines are still the best ~** los vinos españoles todavía son los que más salen a cuenta *or* los que mejor están de precio; **to go down** *or* **decrease in ~** bajar de valor, depreciarse; **to go up** *or* **increase in ~** subir de valor, revalorizarse; **a rise/drop in the ~ of the pound** una subida/bajada del valor de la libra; **market ~** valor *m* en el mercado; **the company offers good service and ~ for money** la compañía ofrece un buen servicio a buen precio; **it might contain something of ~** puede que contenga algo de valor; **you can't put** *or* **set a ~ on it** (*lit, fig*) no se le puede poner precio; **surplus ~** plusvalía *f*; **goods to the ~ of £100** bienes por valor de 100 libras; *see also* **book D**, **cash C**, **face D**
2 (= *merit*) valor *m*; **literary/artistic/scientific ~** valor *m* literario/artístico/científico; **his visit to the country will have huge symbolic ~** su visita al país tendrá un gran valor simbólico; **to attach a great deal of ~ to sth** conceder gran valor *or* importancia a algo, valorar mucho algo; **to attach no ~ to sth** no dar importancia a algo, no valorar algo; **something of ~** algo valioso *or* de valor; **to be of ~ (to sb)** ser útil *or* de utilidad para algn, servir a algn; **strategically, the city was of little ~ to the British** desde el punto de vista estratégico, la ciudad era de poca utilidad *or* tenía poco valor para los británicos; **her education has been of no ~ to her** su educación no le ha servido de *or* para nada; **to put** *or* **place** *or* **set a high ~ on sth** valorar mucho algo; **sentimental ~** valor *m* sentimental; *see also* **novelty**
3 (*moral*) **values** valores *mpl* (morales); **family ~s** valores *mpl* de familia
4 (*Math, Mus, Gram*) valor *m*; **what is the ~ of x when y is 5?** ¿qué valor tiene x cuando y es igual a 5?
Ⓑ VT 1 (= *estimate worth of*) [+ *property, jewellery, painting*] valorar, tasar; **to ~ sth at £200** valorar *or* tasar algo en 200 libras; **I had to have my jewellery ~d for insurance purposes** tuve que valorar *or* tasar mis joyas para poder asegurarlas
2 (= *appreciate*) [+ *health, life, independence,*] valorar; [+ *sb's work, opinion, friendship*] valorar, apreciar
Ⓒ CPD ► **value judgment** N juicio *m* de valor ► **value system** N sistema *m* de valores, escala *f* de valores

value-added tax ['væljuː'ædɪd'tæks] N (*Brit*) impuesto *m* sobre el valor agregado, impuesto *m* sobre el valor añadido (*Sp*)

valued ['væljuːd] ADJ [*friend, customer*] estimado, apreciado; [*contribution*] valioso

valueless ['væljʊlɪs] ADJ sin valor

valuer ['valjʊər] N (*Brit*) tasador(a) *m/f*

valve [vælv] Ⓐ N (*Anat, Mech*) válvula *f*; (*Rad, TV*) lámpara *f*, válvula *f*; (*Bot, Zool*) valva *f*; [*of musical instrument*] llave *f*
Ⓑ CPD ► **valve tester** N comprobador *m* de válvulas

vamoose* [və'muːs] VI largarse*

vamp [væmp] Ⓐ N 1 (= *woman*) vampiresa *f*, vampi* *f*
2 [*of shoe*] empeine *m*
3 (= *patch*) remiendo *m*
4 (*Mus*) (= *improvised accompaniment*) acompañamiento *m* improvisado
Ⓑ VT 1 (= *flirt with*) coquetear con, flirtear con; **to ~ sb into doing sth** engatusar a algn para que haga algo
2 [+ *shoe*] poner empella a
3 (*Mus*) improvisar, improvisar un acompañamiento para
Ⓒ VI (*Mus*) improvisar (un acompañamiento)

►**vamp up** VT + ADV (= *make more attractive*) [+ *dress, room*] arreglar; **to ~ up an engine** (= *repair*) componer un motor; (= *supercharge*) sobrealimentar un motor

vampire ['væmpaɪər] Ⓐ N 1 (*Zool*) vampiro *m*
2 (*fig*) vampiro *m*; (= *woman*) vampiresa *f*
Ⓑ CPD ► **vampire bat** N vampiro *m*

van[1] [væn] Ⓐ N (*Brit Aut*) camioneta *f*, furgoneta *f*; (*for removals*) camión *m* de mudanzas; (*Brit Rail*) furgón *m*
Ⓑ CPD ► **van driver** N conductor(a) *m/f* de camioneta ► **van pool** N (*US*) parque *m* (móvil) de furgonetas

van[2] [væn] N (*Mil, fig*) vanguardia *f*; **to be in the ~** ir a la vanguardia; **to be in the ~ of progress** estar en la vanguardia del progreso

vanadium [və'neɪdɪəm] N vanadio *m*

V & A N ABBR (*Brit*) = **Victoria and Albert Museum**

Vandal ['vændəl] (*Hist*) Ⓐ ADJ vándalo, vandálico
Ⓑ N vándalo/a *m/f*

vandal ['vændəl] N vándalo/a *m/f*, gamberro/a *m/f*

Vandalic [væn'dælɪk] ADJ vándalo, vandálico

vandalism ['vændəlɪzəm] N vandalismo *m*

vandalize ['vændəlaɪz] VT destrozar

vane [veɪn] N (= *weather vane*) veleta *f*; [*of mill*] aspa *f*; [*of propeller*] paleta *f*; [*of feather*] barbas *fpl*

vanguard ['vængɑːd] N vanguardia *f*; **to be in the ~** ir a la vanguardia, estar en la vanguardia; **to be in the ~ of progress** ir a *or* estar en la vanguardia del progreso

vanilla [və'nɪlə] Ⓐ N vainilla *f*
Ⓑ ADJ de vainilla

vanish ['vænɪʃ] VI desaparecer; **to ~ without trace** desaparecer sin dejar rastro; **to ~ into thin air** esfumarse

vanishing ['vænɪʃɪŋ] CPD ► **vanishing cream** N crema *f* de día ► **vanishing point** N (*fig*) punto *m* de fuga ► **vanishing trick** N truco *m* de desaparecer

vanity ['vænɪtɪ] Ⓐ N 1 (= *conceit*) vanidad *f*; **to do sth out of ~** hacer algo por vanidad
2 (= *pride*) orgullo *m*
3 (= *emptiness*) vanidad *f*; **all is ~** todo es vanidad
Ⓑ CPD ► **vanity case** N neceser *m* ► **vanity (license) plate** N (*esp US Aut*) matrícula *f* personalizada ► **vanity unit** N lavabo *m* empotrado

vanquish ['væŋkwɪʃ] VT (*poet*) vencer, derrotar

vantage ['vɑːntɪdʒ] Ⓐ N 1 ventaja *f*
2 = **vantage point**
Ⓑ CPD ► **vantage point** N posición *f* ventajosa, lugar *m* estratégico; (*for views*) punto *m* panorámico; **from our modern ~ point we can see that ...** desde nuestra atalaya moderna vemos que ..., desde la perspectiva del tiempo presente se ve que ...

vapid [ˈvæpɪd] ADJ insípido, soso

vapidity [væˈpɪdɪtɪ] N insipidez *f*, sosería *f*

vapor [ˈveɪpəʳ] N (*US*) = **vapour**

vaporization [ˌveɪpəraɪˈzeɪʃən] N vaporización *f*

vaporize [ˈveɪpəraɪz] Ⓐ VT vaporizar, volatilizar
Ⓑ VI vaporizarse, volatilizarse

vaporizer [ˈveɪpəraɪzəʳ] N vaporizador *m*; (*for inhalation*) inhalador *m*; (*for perfume*) atomizador *m*

vaporous [ˈveɪpərəs] ADJ vaporoso

vapour, **vapor** (*US*) [ˈveɪpəʳ] Ⓐ N (= *steam*) vapor *m*; (*on breath, window*) vaho *m*; **the ~s** (*Med*†) los vapores
Ⓑ CPD ► **vapour trail** N (*Aer*) estela *f* (de humo)

variability [ˌvɛərɪəˈbɪlɪtɪ] N variabilidad *f*

variable [ˈvɛərɪəbl] Ⓐ ADJ (*gen*) variable; [*person*] variable, voluble; **~ costs** costes *mpl* variables
Ⓑ N variable *f*

variance [ˈvɛərɪəns] N **to be at ~ (with sb over sth)** estar en desacuerdo *or* discrepar (con algn en algo); **his statement is at ~ with the facts** sus afirmaciones no concuerdan con los hechos

variant [ˈvɛərɪənt] Ⓐ ADJ variante; **there are several ~ spellings of this word** esta palabra se escribe de varias formas, hay distintas variantes ortográficas de esta palabra
Ⓑ N variante *f*

variation [ˌvɛərɪˈeɪʃən] N (*gen*) variación *f* (*also Mus*); (= *variant form*) variedad *f*

varicoloured, **varicolored** (*US*) [ˈværɪˈkʌləd] ADJ abigarrado, multicolor

varicose veins [ˈværɪkəʊsˈveɪnz] NPL varices *fpl*

varied [ˈvɛərɪd] ADJ variado

variegated [ˈvɛərɪgeɪtɪd] ADJ [*plant, plumage, markings*] multicolor; [*colour*] abigarrado; [*leaf*] jaspeado, abigarrado (*Bot*)

variegation [ˌvɛərɪˈgeɪʃən] N [*of plants, plumage, markings*] multiplicidad *f* de colores, variedad *f* de colores; [*of colour*] abigarramiento *m*; [*of leaves*] jaspeado *m*, abigarramiento *m* (*Bot*)

variety [vəˈraɪətɪ] Ⓐ N (*gen*) variedad *f*; (= *range, diversity*) diversidad *f*; (*Comm*) [*of stock*] surtido *m*; **he likes a ~ of food** le gustan diversas comidas; **a ~ of opinions was expressed** se expresaron diversas opiniones; **it comes in a ~ of colours** lo hay en varios colores *or* de diversos colores; **for a ~ of reasons** por varias *or* diversas razones; **in a ~ of ways** de diversas maneras; **for ~** por variar; **to lend ~ to sth** dar variedad a algo; ✦**PROV ~ is the spice of life** en la variedad está el gusto
Ⓑ CPD ► **variety artist** N artista *mf* de variedades ► **variety show** N espectáculo *m* de variedades ► **variety store** N (*US*) bazar *m* (*tienda barata que vende de todo*) ► **variety theatre** N teatro *m* de variedades

varifocal [vɛərɪˈfəʊkl] Ⓐ ADJ progresivo
Ⓑ N **varifocals** gafas *fpl* progresivas, lentes *fpl* progresivas

variola [vəˈraɪələ] N viruela *f*

various [ˈvɛərɪəs] ADJ (*gen*) varios, diversos; (= *different*) distintos; **for ~ reasons** por diversas razones; **in ~ ways** de diversos modos; **at ~ times** a distintas horas; **on ~ occasions in the past** en varias ocasiones antes

variously [ˈvɛərɪəslɪ] ADV **the phrase has been ~ interpreted** la frase se ha interpretado de varias *or* diversas maneras; **a pile of ~ coloured socks** un montón de calcetines de distintos *or* diversos colores; **the caravan served ~ as an office, bedroom and changing room** según los casos la caravana hacía de oficina, dormitorio o vestuario

varmint [ˈvɑːmɪnt] N [1] (*Hunting*) bicho *m*
[2] (*) golfo *m*, bribón *m*

varnish [ˈvɑːnɪʃ] Ⓐ N (*for wood*) barniz *m*; (*for nails*) esmalte *m* (para las uñas), laca *f* (para las uñas); (*fig*) barniz *m*, apariencia *f*
Ⓑ VT [+ *wood*] barnizar; [+ *nails*] pintar, laquear

varnishing [ˈvɑːnɪʃɪŋ] N barnizado *m*

varsity [ˈvɑːsɪtɪ] Ⓐ N (*Brit**) universidad *f*
Ⓑ CPD ► **Varsity Match** N partido *m* entre las Universidades de Oxford y Cambridge

vary [ˈvɛərɪ] Ⓐ VT [1] (= *make variable*) [+ *routine, diet*] variar
[2] (= *change*) [+ *temperature, speed*] cambiar, modificar
Ⓑ VI [1] (= *differ*) [*amounts, sizes, conditions*] variar; **prices ~ from area to area** los precios varían con la zona; **to ~ according to sth** variar según *or* dependiendo de algo; **they ~ enormously in quality** la calidad varía enormemente; **they ~ in price** los hay de diversos precios; **it varies** depende, según
[2] (= *be at odds*) **designs may ~ from the illustration on the box** los diseños pueden diferir de la ilustración del paquete; **authors ~ about the date** los autores discrepan con respecto a la fecha; **opinions ~ on this point** las opiniones varían en este punto
[3] (= *change, fluctuate*) [*weight, temperature, number*] oscilar; **my weight varies between 70 and 73 kilos** mi peso oscila entre los 70 y los 73 kilos

varying [ˈvɛərɪɪŋ] ADJ [*amounts*] distinto; [*periods of time*] variado; [*ages, shades, sizes*] diverso; **with ~ degrees of success** con más o menos éxito; **in** *or* **to ~ degrees** en mayor o menor grado

vascular [ˈvæskjʊləʳ] ADJ vascular

vase [vɑːz] N florero *m*, jarrón *m*

vasectomy [væˈsektəmɪ] N vasectomía *f*

Vaseline® [ˈvæsɪliːn] N vaselina® *f*

vasoconstrictor [ˌveɪzəʊkənˈstrɪktəʳ] N vasoconstrictor *m*

vasodilator [ˌveɪzəʊdaɪˈleɪtəʳ] N vasodilatador *m*

vassal [ˈvæsəl] N vasallo *m*

vassalage [ˈvæsəlɪdʒ] N vasallaje *m*

vast [vɑːst] ADJ (*compar* **vaster**; *superl* **vastest**) [*building, quantity, organization*] enorme, inmenso; [*area*] vasto, extenso; [*range, selection*] enorme, amplísimo; [*knowledge, experience*] vasto; **at ~ expense** gastando enormes cantidades de dinero; **it's a ~ improvement on his previous work** es muchísimo mejor que su trabajo anterior; **the ~ majority (of people)** la inmensa mayoría (de la gente)

vastly [ˈvɑːstlɪ] ADV inmensamente, enormemente; **two women from ~ different backgrounds** dos mujeres de orígenes enormemente diferentes; **a ~ improved quality of life** una calidad de vida muchísimo *or* infinitamente mejor; **I think he's ~ overrated** creo que está enormemente sobreestimado; **~ superior to** infinitamente superior a

vastness [ˈvɑːstnɪs] N inmensidad *f*

VAT [viːeɪˈtiː, væt] Ⓐ N ABBR (*Brit*) (= **value-added tax**) IVA *m*, impuesto *m* sobre el valor añadido
Ⓑ CPD ► **VAT man** N recaudador *m* del IVA ► **VAT return** N declaración *f* del IVA

vat [væt] N tina *f*, tinaja *f*; [*of cider*] cuba *f*

Vatican [ˈvætɪkən] Ⓐ N **the ~** el Vaticano
Ⓑ ADJ vaticano, del Vaticano ► **Vatican City** N Ciudad *f* del Vaticano

VAT-registered [ˈvætˌredʒɪstəd] N **~ company** compañía *f* declarante del IVA

vaudeville [ˈvəʊdəvɪl] N vodevil *m*

vault[1] [vɔːlt] N (*Archit*) bóveda *f*; (= *cellar*) sótano *m*; (*for wine*) bodega *f*; [*of bank*] cámara *f* acorazada; (= *tomb*) panteón *m*; [*of church*] cripta *f*; **family ~** panteón *m* familiar; **~ of heaven** bóveda *f* celeste

vault[2] [vɔːlt] Ⓐ N salto *m*; **at one ~** ◊ **with one ~** de un solo salto
Ⓑ VI saltar; **to ~ over a stream** cruzar un arroyo de un salto, saltar un arroyo; **to ~ into the saddle** colocarse de un salto en la silla
Ⓒ VT saltar

vaulted [ˈvɔːltɪd] ADJ abovedado

vaulting [ˈvɔːltɪŋ] Ⓐ N [1] (*Archit*) abovedado *m*
[2] (*Sport*) salto *m* con pértiga
Ⓑ CPD ► **vaulting horse** N potro *m* (de madera)

vaunt [vɔːnt] Ⓐ VT (= *boast of*) jactarse de, hacer alarde de; (= *display*) lucir, ostentar
Ⓑ VI jactarse

vaunted [ˈvɔːntɪd] ADJ cacareado; **much ~** tan cacareado

vaunting [ˈvɔːntɪŋ] Ⓐ ADJ jactancioso
Ⓑ N jactancia *f*

VC N ABBR [1] (*Brit Mil*) (= **Victoria Cross**) *condecoración británica*
[2] (*Univ*) = **Vice-Chancellor**
[3] = **vice-chairman**
[4] (*US*) (*in Vietnam*) = **Vietcong**

VCR N ABBR = **video cassette recorder**

VD N ABBR (= **venereal disease**) enfermedad *f* venérea

VDT N ABBR (*esp US*) = **visual display terminal**

VDU Ⓐ N ABBR (*Comput*) (= **visual display unit**) UDV *f*
Ⓑ CPD ► **VDU operator** N operador(a) *m/f* de UDV

veal [viːl] N ternera *f*

vector [ˈvektəʳ] N vector *m*

Veda [ˈveɪdə] N Veda *m*

V-E Day [ˌviːˈiːdeɪ] N ABBR (= **Victory in Europe Day**) día *m* de la victoria en Europa

> **V-E DAY**
>
> *El 8 de mayo se celebra en el Reino Unido y Estados Unidos el Día de la Victoria Europea o* **V-E Day**: **Victory in Europe Day**. *En este día se conmemora la victoria del ejército aliado en Europa en la Segunda Guerra Mundial en 1945. El 15 de agosto se conmemora el Día de la Victoria sobre Japón o* **V-J Day**: **Victory over Japan Day**, *que ocurrió también en 1945.*

Vedic [ˈveɪdɪk] ADJ védico

veep* [viːp] N (*US*) vicepresidente/a *m/f*

veer [vɪəʳ] VI (*also* **to ~ round**) [*ship*] virar; [*car*] girar, torcer; [*wind*] cambiar de dirección, rolar (*Met, Naut*); (*fig*) cambiar (de rumbo); **the car ~ed off the road** el coche se salió de la carretera; **the wind ~ed to the east** el viento cambió hacia el este, el viento roló al este; **the country has ~ed to the left** el país ha dado un giro hacia *or* a la izquierda; **it ~s from one extreme to the other** oscila desde un extremo al otro; **people are ~ing round to our point of view** la gente está empezando a aceptar nuestro criterio

veg* [vedʒ] N ABBR (= **vegetable(s)**) verdura *f*, vegetales *mpl*

►**veg out*** VI + ADV relajarse

vegan ['vi:gən] N vegeteriano/a *m/f* estricto/a

veganism ['vi:gənɪzəm] N vegetarianismo *m* estricto

vegeburger ['vedʒɪˌbɜ:gəʳ] N hamburguesa *f* vegetariana

vegetable ['vedʒɪtəbl] Ⓐ N [1] (*Bot*) vegetal *m*, planta *f*; (*Culin*) (= *food*) hortaliza *f*, verdura *f*; **we grow a few ~s in our garden** tenemos plantadas algunas verduras *or* hortalizas en el jardín; **green ~s** verdura(s) *f(pl)*; **diced ~s** menestra *f* de verduras; **~s are an important part of the diet** la verdura es *or* las hortalizas son una parte importante de la dieta; **come along, eat up your ~s!** ¡vamos, cómete la verdura!; *see also* **root D**
[2] (= *human vegetable*) vegetal *m*
Ⓑ CPD ► **vegetable dish** N (= *food*) plato *m* de verdura(s); (= *vessel*) fuente *f* de verdura(s) ► **vegetable fat** N grasa *f* vegetal ► **vegetable garden** N (*big*) huerta *f*; (*small*) huerto *m* ► **the vegetable kingdom** N el reino vegetal ► **vegetable marrow** N (*esp Brit*) calabacín *m* ► **vegetable matter** N materia *f* vegetal ► **vegetable oil** N aceite *m* vegetal ► **vegetable patch** N huerto *m*, huertecito *m* ► **vegetable salad** N ensalada *f* verde, macedonia *f* de verduras con mayonesa, ≈ ensaladilla *f* rusa ► **vegetable soup** N sopa *f* de verduras

vegetarian [ˌvedʒɪ'tɛəriən] Ⓐ ADJ vegetariano
Ⓑ N vegetariano/a *m/f*

vegetarianism [ˌvedʒɪ'tɛərɪənɪzəm] N vegetarianismo *m*

vegetate ['vedʒɪteɪt] VI (*lit, fig*) vegetar

vegetated ['vedʒɪteɪtɪd] ADJ **the land is sparsely ~** la tierra tiene escasa vegetación

vegetation [ˌvedʒɪ'teɪʃən] N vegetación *f*

vegetative ['vedʒɪtətɪv] ADJ vegetativo

veggie* ['vedʒɪ] Ⓐ ADJ vegetariano; **~ burger** hamburguesa *f* vegetal, hamburguesa *f* vegetariana
Ⓑ N vegetariano/a *m/f*

vehemence ['vi:ɪməns] N [*of words, person, criticism, protest*] vehemencia *f*; [*of attack*] violencia *f*; [*of opposition*] fuerza *f*, radicalidad *f*; [*of denial*] rotundidad *f*; [*of dislike*] intensidad *f*

vehement ['vi:ɪmənt] ADJ [*person, tone, criticism, protest*] vehemente; [*denial*] rotundo, categórico; [*dislike*] intenso; [*attack*] violento; **there was ~ opposition** hubo una fuerte *or* radical oposición

vehemently ['vi:ɪməntlɪ] ADV [*say, curse*] vehementemente, con vehemencia; [*deny*] rotundamente, categóricamente; [*reject, shake one's head*] ostensiblemente; [*oppose*] radicalmente; [*attack*] violentamente; **to be ~ opposed to sth** oponerse radicalmente a algo, estar radicalmente en contra de algo

vehicle ['vi:ɪkl] N [1] (= *form of transport*) vehículo *m*
[2] (*fig*) (= *means*) vehículo *m*, medio *m*, instrumento *m* (**for** para); **the programme was a ~ for promoting himself** el programa era un vehículo *or* medio *or* instrumento para promocionarse; **they see the new constitution as a ~ for change** ven la nueva constitución como un instrumento de cambio

vehicular [vɪ'hɪkjʊləʳ] ADJ [*road*] de vehículos, para coches; **the roadworks made ~ access difficult** las obras en la calzada complicaban el acceso de los vehículos; **~ traffic** circulación *f* rodada

veil [veɪl] Ⓐ N (*lit, fig*) velo *m*; **a ~ of secrecy surrounded the project** un halo de misterio rodeaba el proyecto; **under a ~ of secrecy** en el mayor secreto; **to draw a ~ over sth** (*fig*) correr un (tupido) velo sobre algo; ✦***IDIOM*** **to take the ~** (*Rel*) tomar el hábito, meterse monja
Ⓑ VT (*lit*) cubrir con un velo; (*fig*) (= *disguise*) [+ *truth, facts*] velar, encubrir; [+ *dislike, hatred*] disimular; **eyes ~ed by tears** ojos *mpl* empañados por lágrimas; **the town was ~ed in mist** la ciudad estaba cubierta por un velo de niebla

veiled [veɪld] ADJ [*threat, hint, criticism, insult*] velado; [*reference*] encubierto; **thinly-~ dislike** antipatía *f* apenas disimulada; **with ~ irony** con velada ironía

veiling ['veɪlɪŋ] N (*Phot*) velo *m*

vein [veɪn] N [1] (*Anat, Bot*) vena *f*
[2] (*Min*) [*of ore*] filón *m*, veta *f*; (*in stone*) vena *f*
[3] (*fig*) (= *streak*) vena *f*; **there is a ~ of anti-semitism running through his writing** hay una vena antisemita en todos sus escritos
[4] (= *mood, tone*) vena *f*; **she went on in this ~ for some time** continuó de esta guisa *or* en este tono durante un rato; **the next two speakers continued in the same ~** los dos siguientes conferenciantes se expresaron en la misma línea

veined [veɪnd] ADJ [*hands, eyes*] venoso; [*leaves*] nervado; **blue-~ cheese** queso *m* azul

veining ['veɪnɪŋ] N [1] (*Anat, Bot*) venas *fpl*
[2] (*Min*) vetas *fpl*, veteado *m*

velar ['vi:ləʳ] ADJ velar

Velasquez, **Velazquez** [vɪ'læskwɪz] N Velázquez

Velcro® ['velkrəʊ] N velcro® *m*

veld(t) [velt] N veld *m* (*meseta esteparia sudafricana*)

vellum ['veləm] N (= *writing paper*) papel *m* vitela

velocipede†† [və'lɒsɪpi:d] N velocípedo *m*

velocity [vɪ'lɒsɪtɪ] N velocidad *f*

velodrome ['vi:ləˌdrəʊm] N velódromo *m*

velour(s) [və'lʊəʳ] N velvetón *m*

velum ['vi:ləm] N (*pl* **vela** ['vi:lə]) velo *m* del paladar

velvet ['velvɪt] Ⓐ N terciopelo *m*; (*on antlers*) piel *f* velluda, vello *m*; **she had skin like ~** tenía una piel aterciopelada
Ⓑ ADJ (= *of velvet*) de terciopelo; (= *velvety*) aterciopelado; **the Velvet Revolution** la revolución de terciopelo

velveteen ['velvɪti:n] N pana *f*

velvety ['velvɪtɪ] ADJ aterciopelado

venal ['vi:nl] ADJ [*person*] venal, sobornable; [*action*] corrupto, corrompido

venality [vi:'nælɪtɪ] N venalidad *f*

vend [vend] VT vender

vendee [ven'di:] N comprador(a) *m/f*

vendetta [ven'detə] N vendetta *f*; **to carry on** *or* **pursue a ~ against sb** (*public*) hacer una campaña contra algn; (*personal*) hostigar *or* perseguir a algn

vending ['vendɪŋ] Ⓐ N venta *f*, distribución *f*
Ⓑ CPD ► **vending machine** N máquina *f* expendedora, vendedora *f* automática

vendor ['vendɔ:ʳ] N vendedor(a) *m/f*; (= *pedlar*) vendedor(a) *m/f* ambulante

veneer [və'nɪəʳ] Ⓐ N chapa *f*, enchapado *m*; (*fig*) barniz *m*, apariencia *f*; **to give** *or* **lend sth a ~ of respectability** dar a algo un barniz *or* una apariencia de respetabilidad
Ⓑ VT chapear

venerable ['venərəbl] ADJ venerable

venerate ['venəreɪt] VT venerar, reverenciar

veneration [ˌvenə'reɪʃən] N veneración *f*; **his ~ for …** la veneración que sentía por …; **to hold sb in ~** reverenciar a algn

venereal [vɪ'nɪərɪəl] ADJ venéreo; **~ disease** enfermedad *f* venérea

Venetian [vɪ'ni:ʃən] Ⓐ ADJ veneciano
Ⓑ N veneciano/a *m/f*
Ⓒ CPD ► **Venetian blind** N persiana *f*

Venezuela [ˌvene'zweɪlə] N Venezuela *f*

Venezuelan [ˌvene'zweɪlən] Ⓐ ADJ venezolano
Ⓑ N venezolano/a *m/f*

vengeance ['vendʒəns] N venganza *f*; **to take ~ on sb** vengarse de algn; **it started raining with a ~*** empezó a llover de verdad, empezó a llover de lo lindo*

vengeful ['vendʒfʊl] ADJ vengativo

venial ['vi:nɪəl] ADJ venial; [*error, fault*] leve

veniality [ˌvi:nɪ'ælɪtɪ] N venialidad *f*

Venice ['venɪs] N Venecia *f*

venison ['venɪzn] N carne *f* de venado

venom ['venəm] N (*lit*) veneno *m*; (*fig*) veneno *m*, malicia *f*; **he spoke with real ~** habló con veneno *or* malicia, habló con palabras envenenadas

venomous ['venəməs] ADJ (*lit*) venenoso; (*fig*) [*look*] maligno; [*tongue*] viperino

venomously ['venəməslɪ] ADV (*fig*) con malignidad

venous ['vi:nəs] ADJ (*Med*) venoso

vent [vent] Ⓐ N [1] (*Mech*) agujero *m*; (= *valve*) válvula *f*; (= *airhole*) respiradero *m*; (= *grille*) rejilla *f* de ventilación; (= *pipe*) ventosa *f*, conducto *m* de ventilación
[2] (= *opening*) (*in jacket, skirt*) abertura *f*
[3] (*Zool*) cloaca *f*
[4] (= *expression*) **to give ~ to one's feelings** desahogarse; **to give ~ to one's anger** dar rienda suelta a su ira, desahogar su ira
Ⓑ VT [1] (*Mech*) purgar; (= *discharge*) descargar, emitir, dejar escapar
[2] (= *release*) [+ *feelings*] desahogar, descargar; **to ~ one's anger on sth/sb** desahogar la ira con algo/algn; **to ~ one's spleen (on)** descargar la bilis (contra)

ventilate ['ventɪleɪt] VT [+ *room*] ventilar, airear; (*fig*) [+ *grievance, question*] ventilar

ventilation [ˌventɪ'leɪʃən] Ⓐ N ventilación *f*
Ⓑ CPD ► **ventilation shaft** N pozo *m* de ventilación

ventilator ['ventɪleɪtəʳ] N [1] (*Constr*) ventilador *m*
[2] (*Med*) respirador *m*

ventral ['ventrəl] ADJ ventral

ventricle ['ventrɪkl] N ventrículo *m*

ventriloquism [ven'trɪləkwɪzəm] N ventriloquia *f*

ventriloquist [ven'trɪləkwɪst] N ventrílocuo/a *m/f*

▼**venture** ['ventʃəʳ] Ⓐ N (= *enterprise*) empresa *f*; (= *exploit, adventure*) aventura *f*; **a business ~** una empresa comercial; **his ~ into business** su aventura en el mundo de los negocios; **a new ~ in publishing** (= *new direction*) un nuevo rumbo en la edición de libros; (= *new company*) una nueva empresa editorial; *see also* **joint D**
Ⓑ VT [+ *money, reputation, life*] arriesgar, jugar(se); [+ *opinion, guess*] aventurar; **they ~d everything** arriesgaron *or* se lo jugaron todo; **if I may ~ an opinion** si se me permite expresar *or* si puedo aventurar una opinión; **may I ~ a guess?** ¿puedo hacer *or* aventurar una conjetura?; **to ~ to do sth** osar *or* atreverse a hacer algo; **he ~d to remark that …** se per-

➤ LANGUAGE IN USE: **venture B** 26.3

mitió observar que …; **but he did not ~ to speak** pero no osó hablar; ♦*PROV* **nothing ~d, nothing gained** quien no se arriesga no pasa la mar
Ⓒ VI **to ~ into a wood** (osar) penetrar en un bosque; **they did not ~ onto the streets after dark** no se aventuraban a salir a la calle de noche; **to ~ out (of doors)** aventurarse a salir (fuera)
Ⓓ CPD ► **venture capital** N capital-riesgo *m*
►**venture forth** VI + ADV (*liter*) aventurarse a salir
venturesome ['ventʃəsəm] ADJ [*person*] atrevido, audaz; [*enterprise*] arriesgado, azaroso
venue ['venju:] N [1] (*for concert*) local *m*; **the ~ for the next match** el escenario del próximo partido; **there has been a change of ~ for the rehearsal** se ha cambiado de lugar para el ensayo
[2] (= *meeting place*) lugar *m* de reunión, punto *m* de reunión
[3] (*Jur*) **change of ~** cambio *m* de jurisdicción
Venus ['vi:nəs] N (*Myth*) Venus *f*; (*Astron*) Venus *m*
veracious [və'reɪʃəs] ADJ (*frm*) veraz
veracity [və'ræsɪtɪ] N (*frm*) veracidad *f*
veranda(h) [və'rændə] N galería *f*, veranda *f*, terraza *f*
verb [vɜ:b] N verbo *m*
verbal ['vɜ:bəl] ADJ verbal; **a ~ agreement** un acuerdo verbal; **~ diarrhoea*** verborrea *f*
verbalize ['vɜ:bəlaɪz] Ⓐ VT expresar verbalmente, expresar en palabras
Ⓑ VI expresarse en palabras
verbally ['vɜ:bəlɪ] ADV [*communicate, abuse*] verbalmente; [*agree*] de palabra
verbatim [vɜ:'beɪtɪm] Ⓐ ADJ textual, literal
Ⓑ ADV textualmente, palabra por palabra
verbena [vɜ:'bi:nə] N verbena *f*
verbiage ['vɜ:bɪɪdʒ] N verborrea *f*, palabrería *f*
verbose [vɜ:'bəʊs] ADJ [*person*] verboso, hablador; [*writing, style*] prolijo, verboso
verbosely [vɜ:'bəʊslɪ] ADV con verbosidad, prolijamente
verbosity [vɜ:'bɒsɪtɪ] N verbosidad *f*, prolijidad *f*
verdant ['vɜ:dənt] ADJ verde
verdict ['vɜ:dɪkt] N (*Jur*) (= *judgment*) veredicto *m*, fallo *m*; [*of judge*] sentencia *f*; (*fig*) opinión *f*, juicio *m*; **~ of guilty/not guilty** veredicto *m* de culpabilidad/inocencia; **to bring in** *or* **return a ~** (*Jur*) emitir *or* pronunciar un veredicto, emitir un fallo; **the inquest recorded an open ~** las pesquisas judiciales no determinaban las causas del fallecimiento; **to give one's ~ (on sb/sth)** dar un veredicto (sobre algn/algo), dar su juicio *or* opinión (sobre algn/algo); **what's your ~?** ¿qué opinas de esto?; **his ~ on the wine was unfavourable** dio un juicio desfavorable sobre el vino
verdigris ['vɜ:dɪgri:s] N verdete *m*, cardenillo *m*
verdure ['vɜ:djʊəʳ] N verdor *m*
verge [vɜ:dʒ] N [1] [*of road*] borde *m*; [*of motorway*] arcén *m*
[2] (*fig*) borde *m*, margen *m*; **to be on the ~ of disaster/a nervous breakdown** estar al borde de la catástrofe/de una crisis nerviosa; **we are on the ~ of war** estamos al borde de la guerra; **to be on the ~ of a great discovery** estar en la antesala de un gran descubrimiento; **she was on the ~ of tears** estaba a punto de llorar; **to be on the ~ of doing sth** estar a punto *or* al borde de hacer algo
►**verge on, verge upon** VI + PREP rayar en; [*colour*] tirar a; **a state verging on madness** un estado que raya en la locura
verger ['vɜ:dʒəʳ] N (*in church*) sacristán *m*
Vergil ['vɜ:dʒɪl] N Virgilio
Vergilian [və'dʒɪlɪən] ADJ virgiliano
verifiability [,verɪfaɪə'bɪlɪtɪ] N verificabilidad *f*
verifiable ['verɪfaɪəbl] ADJ verificable, comprobable
verification [,verɪfɪ'keɪʃən] N (*gen*) verificación *f*, comprobación *f*; [*of result*] confirmación *f*; (= *document*) comprobante *m*
verifier ['verɪfaɪəʳ] N (*Comput*) verificador *m*
verify ['verɪfaɪ] VT verificar, comprobar; [+ *result*] confirmar; (*Comput*) verificar
verily† ['verɪlɪ] ADV en verdad; **~ I say unto you …** en verdad os digo …
verisimilitude [,verɪsɪ'mɪlɪtju:d] N verosimilitud *f*
veritable ['verɪtəbl] ADJ verdadero, auténtico; **a ~ monster** un verdadero monstruo
veritably ['verɪtəblɪ] ADV verdaderamente
verity ['verɪtɪ] N verdad *f*; **the eternal verities** las verdades eternas
vermicelli [,vɜ:mɪ'selɪ] N fideos *mpl* de cabello de ángel
vermicide ['vɜ:mɪsaɪd] N vermicida *m*
vermifuge ['vɜ:mɪfju:dʒ] N vermífugo *m*
vermilion [və'mɪlɪən] Ⓐ N bermellón *m*
Ⓑ ADJ bermejo
vermin ['vɜ:mɪn] N [1] (*lit*) (= *insects*) bichos *mpl*, sabandijas *fpl*; (= *mammals*) alimañas *fpl*
[2] (*fig*) (*pej*) (= *people*) chusma *f*
verminous ['vɜ:mɪnəs] ADJ verminoso, piojoso; (*fig*) vil
vermouth ['vɜ:məθ] N vermut *m*, vermú *m*
vernacular [və'nækjʊləʳ] Ⓐ ADJ [1] (*Ling*) vernáculo, vulgar; **in ~ Persian** en persa vulgar, en la lengua vernácula de Persia
[2] [*architecture*] típico, local, regional
Ⓑ N (*Ling*) lengua *f* vernácula; (*fig*) lenguaje *m* corriente, lenguaje *m* vulgar
vernal ['vɜ:nl] ADJ [*equinox*] de primavera; (*liter*) [*flowers*] de primavera, primaveral
Veronica [və'rɒnɪkə] N Verónica
veronica [və'rɒnɪkə] N (*Bot*) verónica *f*
verruca [və'ru:kə] N (*pl* **verrucae** *or* **verrucas** [ve'ru:si:]) (*esp Brit*) verruga *f*
Versailles [vɛə'saɪ] N Versalles *m*
versatile ['vɜ:sətaɪl] ADJ [*person*] polifacético, versátil; [*material*] versátil, que se presta a usos distintos; **eggs are very ~** los huevos dan mucho juego
versatility [,vɜ:sə'tɪlɪtɪ] N [*of person*] carácter *m* polifacético, versatilidad *f*; [*of tool, machine, material*] versatilidad *f*, múltiple funcionalidad *f*
verse [vɜ:s] Ⓐ N [1] (= *stanza*) estrofa *f*; [*of Bible*] versículo *m*
[2] (= *genre*) verso *m*; (= *poetry*) verso *m*, poesía *f*; **in ~** en verso; **a ~ version of the "Celestina"** una versión en verso de la "Celestina"
Ⓑ CPD ► **verse drama** N teatro *m* en verso, drama *m* poético
versed [vɜ:st] ADJ **to be well ~ in** ser *or* estar versado en, ser experto en
versification [,vɜ:sɪfɪ'keɪʃən] N versificación *f*
versifier ['vɜ:sɪfaɪəʳ] N versificador(a) *m/f*, versista *mf*
versify ['vɜ:sɪfaɪ] Ⓐ VT versificar
Ⓑ VI versificar, escribir versos
version ['vɜ:ʃən] N (*gen*) versión *f*; (= *translation*) traducción *f*; [*of car etc*] modelo *m*; **in Lope's ~ of the story** en la versión que hizo Lope de la historia; **my ~ of events is as follows …** esta es mi versión de los hechos …; **according to his ~** según su versión, según lo que él cuenta
verso ['vɜ:səʊ] N [*of page*] dorso *m*; (*Tech*) verso *m*; [*of coin*] reverso *m*
versus ['vɜ:səs] PREP (*Jur, Sport*) contra
vertebra ['vɜ:tɪbrə] N (*pl* **vertebras** *or* **vertebrae** ['vɜ:tɪbri:]) vértebra *f*
vertebral [vɜ:tɪbrəl] ADJ vertebral
vertebrate ['vɜ:tɪbrɪt] Ⓐ ADJ vertebrado
Ⓑ N vertebrado *m*
vertex [vɜ:teks] N (*pl* **vertexes** *or* **vertices** [vɜ:tɪsi:z]) (*Math, Archit*) vértice *m*
vertical ['vɜ:tɪkəl] Ⓐ ADJ vertical
Ⓑ N vertical *f*
Ⓒ CPD ► **vertical integration** N integración *f* vertical ► **vertical section** N sección *f* vertical, corte *m* vertical
vertically ['vɜ:tɪkəlɪ] ADV verticalmente; **~ challenged** (*hum*) de estatura menuda
vertiginous [vɜ:'tɪdʒɪnəs] ADJ vertiginoso
vertigo ['vɜ:tɪgəʊ] N (*pl* **vertigoes** *or* **vertigines** [vɜ:'tɪdʒɪni:z]) vértigo *m*
verve [vɜ:v] N (= *drive*) energía *f*, empuje *m*; (= *vitality*) brío *m*; (= *enthusiasm*) entusiasmo *m*
very ['verɪ] Ⓐ ADV [1] (= *extremely*) muy; **it is ~ cold** [*object*] está muy frío; [*weather*] hace mucho frío; **the food was ~ good** la comida estuvo muy buena; **"that will be all" — "~ good, sir"** —nada más —muy bien, señor; **you're not being ~ helpful** me ayudas bien poco, no me estás siendo de gran ayuda; **~ high frequency** (*Rad*) (*abbr VHF*) frecuencia *f* muy alta; **that's ~ kind of you** eres muy amable; **~ much** mucho; **"did you enjoy it?" — "~ much (so)"** —¿te ha gustado? —sí, mucho; **she feels ~ much better** se encuentra muchísimo mejor; **I was ~ (much) surprised** me sorprendió mucho, para mí fue una gran sorpresa; **I didn't like it ~ much** no me gustó mucho; **he ~ nearly missed the bus** por muy poco pierde el autobús; **we don't see each other ~ often** nos vemos poco, no nos vemos mucho; **he's so ~ poor** es tan pobre; **it's not so ~ difficult** no es tan difícil; **~ well, I'll do what I can** muy bien *or* bueno, haré lo que pueda; **he couldn't ~ well refuse** no pudo negarse a hacerlo
[2] (= *absolutely*) **the ~ best**; **she eats nothing but the ~ best** sólo come lo mejor de lo mejor; **we did our ~ best** hicimos todo lo que pudimos; **at the ~ earliest** como muy pronto; **the ~ first** el primero de todos; **try your ~ hardest** esfuérzate al máximo; **the ~ last** el último de todos; **at the ~ latest** a más tardar, como muy tarde; **at the ~ least** como mínimo; **at the ~ most** a lo sumo, como mucho, como máximo; **that is the ~ most we can offer** eso es todo lo más que podemos ofrecer; **the ~ next day** precisamente el día siguiente; **she was given her ~ own TV show** le dieron su propio programa de televisión; **it's my ~ own** es el mío; **the ~ same hat** el mismísimo sombrero
[3] (*alone, in reply to question*) mucho; **"are you tired?" — "(yes,) ~"** —¿estás cansado? —(sí,) mucho
Ⓑ ADJ [1] (= *precise*) mismo; **the ~ bishop himself was there** el mismísimo obispo estaba allí; **from the ~ beginning** desde el comienzo mismo; **that ~ day** ese mismo día; **in this ~ house** en esta misma casa; **he's the ~ man we want** es justo el hombre que buscamos; **at that ~ moment** en ese mismo momento; **it's the ~ thing!** ¡es justo lo que nece-

sitamos!; **those were his ~ words** eso fue exactamente lo que dijo
2 (= *mere*) **the ~ idea!** ¡qué cosas dices!, ¡cómo se te ocurre!; **the ~ thought (of it) makes me feel sick** con sólo pensarlo me da náuseas
3 (= *extreme*) **at the ~ bottom** abajo del todo; **at the ~ end** justo al final, al final de todo; **at the ~ top** arriba del todo
4 (*liter*) **the veriest rascal** el mayor bribón; **the veriest simpleton** el más bobo

vesicle ['vesɪkl] N vesícula *f*

vespers ['vespəz] NPL vísperas *fpl*

vessel ['vesl] N 1 (= *ship*) barco *m*, buque *m*, embarcación *f*
2 (= *receptacle*) vasija *f*, recipiente *m*
3 (*Anat, Bot*) vaso *m*; *see also* **blood B**

vest[1] [vest] Ⓐ N 1 (*Brit*) (= *undergarment*) camiseta *f*
2 (*US*) (= *waistcoat*) chaleco *m*
Ⓑ CPD ► **vest pocket** N (*US*) bolsillo *m* del chaleco

vest[2] [vest] VT **to ~ sb with sth** investir a algn de algo; **to ~ rights/authority in sb** conferir *or* conceder derechos/autoridad a algn; **by the authority ~ed in me** en virtud de la autoridad que se me ha concedido; **to ~ property in sb** ceder una propiedad a algn, hacer a algn titular de una propiedad

vesta ['vestə] N cerilla *f*

vestal ['vestl] Ⓐ ADJ vestal; **~ virgin** vestal *f*
Ⓑ N vestal *f*

vested ['vestɪd] ADJ [*right*] inalienable; **~ interest** interés *m* personal; **to have a ~ interest in sth** tener un interés personal en algo; **~ interests** intereses *mpl* creados

vestibule ['vestɪbjuːl] N (*frm*) vestíbulo *m*

vestige ['vestɪdʒ] N 1 (= *trace*) vestigio *m*, rastro *m*; **not a ~ of it remains** no queda rastro de ello, de ello no queda ni el menor vestigio; **without a ~ of decency** sin la menor decencia; **if there is a ~ of doubt** si hay una sombra de duda; **a ~ of truth** un elemento *or* un tanto de verdad
2 (*Bio*) rudimento *m*

vestigial [ves'tɪdʒɪəl] ADJ vestigial; (*Bio*) rudimentario

vestment ['vestmənt] N vestiduras *fpl*; **vestments** (*esp Rel*) vestiduras *fpl*

vestry ['vestrɪ] N sacristía *f*

vesture ['vestʃəʳ] N (*liter*) vestidura *f*

Vesuvius [vɪ'suːvɪəs] N Vesubio *m*

vet[1] [vet] N ABBR 1 (= **veterinary surgeon, veterinarian**) veterinario/a *m/f*
2 (*US**) (= **veteran**) excombatiente *mf*

vet[2] [vet] (*esp Brit*) VT 1 [+ *article, speech*] repasar, revisar
2 (= *examine*) [+ *application*] examinar, investigar; **he was ~ted by Security** fue sometido a una investigación por los servicios de seguridad

vetch [vetʃ] N arveja *f* (*planta*)

veteran ['vetərən] Ⓐ ADJ (*gen*) veterano; (= *battleworn*) aguerrido
Ⓑ N (= *war veteran*) veterano/a *m/f*; (= *ex-serviceman*) excombatiente *mf*; (= *experienced person*) veterano/a *m/f*; **she is a ~ of the anti-nuclear movement** es una veterana del movimiento antinuclear; **a ~ UN diplomat** un veterano diplomático de la ONU
Ⓒ CPD ► **veteran car** N (*Brit*) *coche fabricado antes de 1919, especialmente antes de 1905*

veterinarian [,vetərɪ'nɛərɪən] N (*US*) veterinario/a *m/f*

veterinary ['vetərɪnərɪ] Ⓐ ADJ veterinario
Ⓑ CPD ► **veterinary medicine** N medicina *f* veterinaria, veterinaria *f* ► **veterinary school** N escuela *f* de veterinaria ► **veterinary science** N = **veterinary medicine** ► **veterinary surgeon** N veterinario/a *m/f*

veto ['viːtəʊ] Ⓐ N (*pl* **vetoes**) veto *m*; **to have a ~** tener veto; **to put a ~ on sth** vetar algo, poner veto a algo; **to use** *or* **exercise one's ~** ejercer el (derecho a) veto
Ⓑ VT [+ *bill, application*] vetar, prohibir; **the president ~ed it** el presidente lo vetó *or* le puso su veto; **I suggested it but he ~ed the idea** yo lo sugerí pero el rechazó la idea

vetting ['vetɪŋ] N (= *check*) examen *m* previo; (= *investigation*) investigación *f*; *see also* **positive A2**

vex [veks] VT 1 (= *anger*) fastidiar, irritar; (= *make impatient*) impacientar, sacar de quicio
2 (= *afflict*) afligir; **the problems that are ~ing the country** los problemas que afligen el país

vexation [vek'seɪʃən] N 1 (= *anger*) irritación *f*
2 (= *trouble*) aflicción *f*, disgusto *m*; **he had to put up with numerous ~s** tuvo que soportar muchos disgustos

vexatious [vek'seɪʃəs], **vexing** ['veksɪŋ] ADJ fastidioso, molesto, enojoso (*LAm*)

vexed [vekst] ADJ 1 (= *angry*) enfadado, enojado (*LAm*); **to be ~ (with sb) (about sth)** estar enfadado *or* (*LAm*) enojado (con algn) (por algo); **to get ~ (with sb) (about sth)** enfadarse *or* (*LAm*) enojarse (con algn) (por algo); **in a ~ tone** en tono ofendido, en tono de enojo
2 [*question*] reñido, controvertido
3 (= *puzzled*) perplejo, confuso

vexing ['veksɪŋ] ADJ fastidioso, molesto, enojoso (*LAm*); **it's very ~** da mucha rabia

VFD N ABBR (*US*) = **voluntary fire department**

VG ABBR (*Scol etc*) (= **very good**) S

v.g. ABBR = **very good**

VGA N ABBR = **video graphics array**

vgc ABBR = **very good condition**

VHF N ABBR (= **very high frequency**) VHF

VHS N ABBR = **video home system**

VI ABBR (*US*) = **Virgin Islands**

via ['vaɪə] PREP por; (*esp by plane*) vía; **we drove to Lisbon ~ Salamanca** fuimos a Lisboa por Salamanca; **a flight ~ Brussels** un vuelo vía Bruselas

viability [,vaɪə'bɪlɪtɪ] N viabilidad *f*

viable ['vaɪəbl] ADJ viable

viaduct ['vaɪədʌkt] N viaducto *m*

vial ['vaɪəl] N frasquito *m*

viands ['vaɪəndz] NPL (*liter*) viandas *fpl*

viaticum [vaɪ'ætɪkəm] N (*pl* **viaticums** *or* **viatica** [vaɪ'ætɪkə]) viático *m*

vibes [vaɪbz] NPL ABBR 1 (*) = **vibrations** (*from band, singer*) vibraciones *fpl*, ambiente *m*; **I got good ~ from her** me cayó muy bien
2 (*) (= **vibraphone**) vibráfono *m*

vibrancy ['vaɪbrənsɪ] N [*of colour*] viveza *f*; [*of person*] dinamismo *m*, vitalidad *f*; [*of voice*] sonoridad *f*

vibrant ['vaɪbrənt] Ⓐ ADJ [*colour*] vivo; [*person*] animado; [*personality*] vibrante; [*voice*] vibrante, sonoro
Ⓑ N (*Phon*) vibrante *f*

vibraphone ['vaɪbrə,fəʊn] N vibráfono *m*

vibrate [vaɪ'breɪt] Ⓐ VI vibrar; **the room ~d with tension** se palpaba la tensión en la sala; **her voice ~d with sorrow** la voz le temblaba de pena
Ⓑ VT hacer vibrar

vibration [vaɪ'breɪʃən] N 1 (= *movement*) vibración *f*
2 (*) **vibrations** vibraciones* *fpl*

vibrato [vɪ'brɑːtəʊ] N vibrato *m*

vibrator [vaɪ'breɪtəʳ] N vibrador *m*

vibratory ['vaɪbrətərɪ] ADJ vibratorio

viburnum [vaɪ'bɜːnəm] N viburno *m*

Vic [vɪk] N (*familiar form*) *of* **Victor, Victoria**

vicar ['vɪkəʳ] N (*gen*) vicario *m*; (*Anglican*) cura *m*, párroco *m*

vicarage ['vɪkərɪdʒ] N casa *f* del párroco

vicar-general ['vɪkə'dʒenərəl] N (*pl* **vicars-general**) vicario *m* general

vicarious [vɪ'kɛərɪəs] ADJ (= *indirect*) indirecto; [*substitute*] por referencias; **to get ~ pleasure out of sth** disfrutar indirectamente de algo; **I got a ~ thrill** me emocioné mucho sin tener nada que ver con lo que pasaba

vicariously [vɪ'kɛərɪəslɪ] ADV indirectamente; **he filled his emotional needs ~, through those around him** satisfacía sus necesidades emocionales indirectamente, a través de los que lo rodeaban; **she brought glamour into my life, but only ~** le dio sofisticación a mi vida, aunque sólo de forma indirecta

vice[1] [vaɪs] Ⓐ N vicio *m*; **a life of ~** una vida de vicio y desenfreno; **smoking is his only ~** el tabaco es su único vicio
Ⓑ CPD ► **vice ring** N asociación *f* criminal ► **vice squad** N brigada *f* antivicio

vice[2], **vise** (*US*) [vaɪs] N (*esp Brit Mech*) torno *m* de banco, tornillo *m* de banco

vice[3] ['vaɪsɪ] PREP en lugar de, sustituyendo a

vice- [vaɪs] PREFIX vice-

vice-admiral ['vaɪs'ædmərəl] N vicealmirante *mf*

vice-chairman ['vaɪs'tʃɛəmən] N (*pl* **vice-chairmen**) vicepresidente/a *m/f*

vice-chairmanship ['vaɪs,tʃɛəmənʃɪp] N vicepresidencia *f*

vice-chancellor ['vaɪs'tʃɑːnsələʳ] N (*Univ*) rector(a) *m/f*

vice-consul ['vaɪs'kɒnsəl] N vicecónsul *mf*

vice-presidency ['vaɪs'prezɪdənsɪ] N vicepresidencia *f*

vice-president ['vaɪs'prezɪdənt] N vicepresidente/a *m/f*

vice-principal ['vaɪs'prɪnsɪpəl] N (*US Scol*) subdirector(a) *m/f*

viceroy ['vaɪsrɔɪ] N virrey *m*

viceroyalty ['vaɪs'rɔɪəltɪ] N virreinato *m*

vice versa ['vaɪsɪ'vɜːsə] ADV viceversa, al revés

vicinity [vɪ'sɪnɪtɪ] N 1 (= *neighbourhood*) cercanías *fpl*, alrededores *mpl*, inmediaciones *fpl*; **there has been heavy fighting in the ~ of Tel Aviv** ha habido fuertes enfrentamientos en las cercanías *or* en los alrededores *or* en las inmediaciones de Tel Aviv; **houses in the immediate ~ of the blast were damaged** las viviendas más cercanas a la explosión sufrieron daños; **and other towns in the ~** y otras ciudades de las inmediaciones *or* de la zona *or* cercanas; **he denied being anywhere in the ~** negó encontrarse cerca del lugar; **in the ~ of 20** alrededor de 20, unos 20
2 (= *nearness*) proximidad *f* (**to** a)

vicious ['vɪʃəs] Ⓐ ADJ 1 (= *brutal*) [*person, gang*] despiadado; [*attack, assault, crime*] atroz, brutal; [*animal*] agresivo, fiero; **a ~-looking knife** un cuchillo de aspecto horrorífico
2 (= *malicious*) [*criticism, campaign*] despiadado, cruel; [*remark*] malicioso; **to have a ~ temper** tener muy mal genio; **to have a ~ tongue** tener una lengua viperina

Ⓑ CPD ► **vicious circle** N círculo *m* vicioso; **to be caught in a ~ circle** estar atrapado en un círculo vicioso

viciously [ˈvɪʃəslɪ] ADV [1] (= *brutally*) [*attack, beat, stab*] brutalmente, con saña
[2] (= *maliciously*) [*say, speak*] con malicia

viciousness [ˈvɪʃəsnɪs] N [1] (= *brutality, fierceness*) [*of person, attack, assault*] brutalidad *f*; [*of animal*] fiereza *f*, agresividad *f*
[2] (= *maliciousness*) [*of words*] malicia *f*, malevolencia *f*; [*of criticism, campaign*] lo despiadado, crueldad *f*

vicissitudes [vɪˈsɪsɪtjuːdz] NPL vicisitudes *fpl*, peripecias *fpl*

vicissitudinous [vɪˌsɪsɪˈtjuːdɪnəs] ADJ agitado, accidentado

Vicky [ˈvɪkɪ] N (*familiar form*) *of* **Victoria**

victim [ˈvɪktɪm] Ⓐ N (= *subject of attack*) víctima *f*; **the ~s** (= *survivors of disaster*) los damnificados; **to be the ~ of** [+ *attack, hoax*] ser víctima de; **to fall ~ to** [+ *desire, sb's charms*] sucumbir a, dejarse llevar por
Ⓑ CPD ► **Victim Support** N (*Brit*) *organización de ayuda a las víctimas de actos delictivos*

victimization [ˌvɪktɪmaɪˈzeɪʃən] N persecución *f*; (= *retaliation, punishment*) castigo *m*, represalias *fpl*

victimize [ˈvɪktɪmaɪz] VT (= *pursue*) perseguir; (= *punish*) escoger y castigar, tomar represalias contra; **to be ~d** ser víctima de una persecución; **the strikers should not be ~d** no hay por qué castigar a los huelguistas; **she feels she has been ~d** ella cree que ha sido escogida como víctima

victimless [ˈvɪktɪmlɪs] ADJ sin víctimas

Victor [ˈvɪktəʳ] N Víctor

victor [ˈvɪktəʳ] N (*in match, battle*) vencedor(a) *m/f*

Victoria [vɪkˈtɔːrɪə] N Victoria

Victoria Cross [vɪkˈtɔːrɪəˈkrɒs] N (*Brit*) *la condecoración más alta de las fuerzas armadas británicas y de la Commonwealth*

Victoria Falls [vɪkˈtɔːrɪəˈfɔːlz] NPL Cataratas *fpl* de Victoria

Victorian [vɪkˈtɔːrɪən] Ⓐ ADJ victoriano
Ⓑ N victoriano/a *m/f*

> **VICTORIAN**
>
> *El adjetivo* **Victorian** *se usa para referirse a la época del reinado de la reina Victoria (1837-1901), así como a la cultura y a las personas de dicha época, en frases como, por ejemplo,* **they live in a Victorian house** *o* **the Victorian Prime Minister, Gladstone**. *Las actitudes o cualidades llamadas victorianas son las que se consideran características de la época, tales como el interés por la respetabilidad social, una estricta moralidad represiva, la falta de sentido del humor, la intolerancia y la hipocresía. El término* **Victorian values** *(valores victorianos) se usa en política para abogar por cualidades positivas como la decencia, la superación personal, el respeto a la autoridad y la importancia de la familia, cualidades que muchos opinan que faltan en la sociedad actual. En Estados Unidos también se utiliza el adjetivo* **Victorian** *para describir la arquitectura, muebles, actitudes etc., contemporáneas de la época victoriana en el Reino Unido.*

Victoriana [vɪkˌtɔːrɪˈɑːnə] NPL objetos *mpl* victorianos, antigüedades *fpl* victorianas

victorious [vɪkˈtɔːrɪəs] ADJ [*army*] victorioso, triunfante; [*person, team*] vencedor, triunfador; [*campaign*] triunfal, victorioso; **the ~ team** el equipo vencedor *or* triunfador, los vencedores; **he gave a ~ shout** lanzó un grito triunfal *or* de triunfo; **to be ~** triunfar, salir victorioso, vencer; **he was ~ over his enemies** triunfó sobre sus enemigos, venció a sus enemigos

victoriously [vɪkˈtɔːrɪəslɪ] ADV victoriosamente, triunfalmente

victory [ˈvɪktərɪ] N victoria *f*, triunfo *m* (**over** sobre); **they celebrated their ~ over Arsenal/the Labour Party** celebraron su victoria *or* triunfo sobre el Arsenal/el Partido Laborista; **~ V** la V de la victoria; **to win a famous ~** obtener un triunfo señalado

victual [ˈvɪtl] Ⓐ VT avituallar, abastecer
Ⓑ VI avituallarse, abastecerse
Ⓒ NPL **victuals** víveres *mpl*, vituallas *fpl*

victualler [ˈvɪtləʳ] N *see* **licensed**

vicuña [vɪˈkjuːnə] N vicuña *f*

vid* [vɪd] N ABBR (= **video**) vídeo *f*, video *m* (*LAm*)

vide [ˈvɪdeɪ] VT vea, véase

videlicet [vɪˈdiːlɪset] ADV a saber

video [ˈvɪdɪəʊ] Ⓐ N [1] (*also* **~ recorder**) aparato *m* de vídeo, vídeo *m*, video *m* (*LAm*)
[2] (*also* **~ cassette**) videocinta *f*, cinta *f* de vídeo *or* (*LAm*) video, vídeo *m*, video *m* (*LAm*); **it's out on ~** ha salido en vídeo
Ⓑ VT grabar en vídeo *or* (*LAm*) video
Ⓒ CPD ► **video arcade** N salón *m* recreativo de videojuegos ► **video call** N videollamada *f* ► **video camera** N videocámara *f* ► **video cassette** N = **video A2** ► **video cassette recorder** N = **video A1** ► **video club** N videoclub *m* ► **video conference** N videoconferencia *f* ► **video conferencing** N videoconferencia *f* ► **video diary** N (*TV*) diario *m* en vídeo ► **video disk** N videodisco *m* ► **video film** N película *f* de vídeo, videofilm *m* ► **video frequency** N videofrecuencia *f* ► **video game** N videojuego *m* ► **video library** N videoteca *f* ► **video nasty*** N (= *horror film*) videofilm *m* de horror; (= *pornography*) videofilm *m* porno* ► **video piracy** N videopiratería *f* ► **video recorder** N = **video A1** ► **video recording** N (= *act*) videograbación *f*; (= *object*) grabación *f* de vídeo ► **video shop** N videoclub *m* ► **video wall** N vídeo-panel *m* (*Sp*), panel *m* de vídeo

videophone [ˈvɪdɪəʊˌfəʊn] N videoteléfono *m*

videotape [ˈvɪdɪəʊˌteɪp] Ⓐ N (= *tape*) cinta *f* de vídeo *or* (*LAm*) video; (= *recording*) vídeo *m*, video *m* (*LAm*)
Ⓑ VT grabar en vídeo *or* (*LAm*) video
Ⓒ CPD ► **videotape library** N videoteca *f*

videotaping [ˈvɪdɪəʊˌteɪpɪŋ] N videograbación *f*

Videotex® [ˈvɪdɪəʊˌteks] N vídeotex® *m*

videotext [ˈvɪdɪəʊˌtekst] N videotexto *m*

vie [vaɪ] VI **to ~ for sth** disputarse algo; **to ~ with sb** competir con algn, rivalizar con algn; **to ~ with sb for sth** disputar algo a algn, competir con algn por algo

Vienna [vɪˈenə] N Viena *f*

Viennese [ˌvɪəˈniːz] Ⓐ ADJ vienés
Ⓑ N vienés/esa *m/f*

Vietcong [ˌvjetˈkɒŋ] Ⓐ ADJ del Vietcong
Ⓑ N vietcong *mf*

Vietnam, Viet Nam [ˈvjetˈnæm] N Vietnam *m*

Vietnamese [ˌvjetnəˈmiːz] Ⓐ ADJ vietnamita
Ⓑ N [1] (= *person*) vietnamita *mf*
[2] (*Ling*) vietnamita *m*

vieux jeu [ˈvɪɜːˈʒɜː] ADJ anticuado, fuera de moda

➤**view** [vjuː] Ⓐ N [1] (= *prospect*) vista *f*; **most rooms have ~s over the gardens** la mayoría de las habitaciones tienen vistas a los jardines; **he stood up to get a better ~** se puso de pie para ver mejor; **to have/get a good ~ of sth/sb** ver algo/a algn bien; *see also* **back F**, **front E**, **side C**
[2] (= *line of vision*) **he stopped in the doorway, blocking her ~** se paró en la entrada, tapándole la vista; **am I blocking your ~?** ¿te estoy tapando?; **a cyclist came into ~** apareció un ciclista; **as we rounded the bend the hospital came into ~** al salir de la curva apareció el hospital; **to disappear from ~** perderse de vista; **to be hidden from ~** estar oculto, estar escondido; **to keep sth/sb in ~** no perder de vista algo/a algn; **in full ~ of the crowd** bien a la vista de la multitud; **to be on ~** estar expuesto al público; **the paintings will go on ~ next month** los cuadros se expondrán al público el mes próximo; **the pond was within ~ of my bedroom window** el estanque se veía desde la ventana de mi habitación
[3] (= *picture*) vista *f*; **50 ~s of Venice** 50 vistas de Venecia
[4] (= *mind*) **to have sth in ~** tener algo en mente *or* en perspectiva; **he has only one objective in ~** tiene sólo un objetivo en mente, sólo persigue un objetivo; **with this in ~** con este propósito *or* fin; **with a ~ to doing sth** con miras *or* vistas a hacer algo
[5] (= *opinion*) opinión *f*; **you should make your ~s known to your local MP** debería hacerle saber sus opiniones *or* ideas al diputado de su zona; **my (personal) ~ is that ...** mi opinión (personal) es que ...; **an opportunity for people to express their ~s** una oportunidad para que la gente exprese su opinión; **to express the ~ that ...** opinar que ...; **to hold the ~ that** = **to take the view that**; **in my ~** a mi parecer, en mi opinión; **to take the ~ that** opinar que; **I take a similar/different ~** opino de forma parecida/de distinta forma; **to take the long(-term) ~** adoptar una perspectiva a largo plazo; *see also* **dim A3**, **point A10**
[6] (= *understanding*) visión *f*; **an overall ~ of the situation** una visión de conjunto de la situación; **an idealistic ~ of the world** una visión idealista del mundo
[7] **in ~ of (the fact that)** en vista de (que); **in ~ of this** en vista de esto
Ⓑ VT [1] (= *regard*) ver; **how does the government ~ it?** ¿cómo lo ve el gobierno?; **they ~ the United States as a land of golden opportunity** consideran a los Estados Unidos un país lleno de oportunidades, ven a los Estados Unidos como un país lleno de oportunidades; **we would ~ favourably any sensible suggestion** cualquier sugerencia razonable sería bien acogida; **he is ~ed with suspicion by many MPs** muchos parlamentarios lo miran *or* tratan con recelo
[2] (= *look at, observe*) ver; **mourners were allowed to ~ the body** a los dolientes se les permitió ver el cadáver; **London ~ed from the air** Londres vista desde arriba
[3] (= *inspect, see*) [+ *property, sights, goods, slides*] ver; [+ *accounts*] examinar; **when can we ~ the house?** ¿cuándo podemos ver la casa?
[4] (*frm*) [+ *television*] ver
Ⓒ VI (*TV frm*) ver la televisión; **the ~ing public** los telespectadores, la audiencia televisiva

Viewdata® [ˈvjuːˌdeɪtə] N vídeodatos *mpl*, videodatos *mpl* (*LAm*)

➤ LANGUAGE IN USE: **view A5** 6.2, 11.1, 26.1, 26.2

viewer ['vju:əʳ] N [1] (= *onlooker*) espectador(a) *m/f*; (*TV*) televidente *mf*, telespectador(a) *m/f*
[2] (*for viewing slides*) visor *m*

viewfinder ['vju:ˌfaɪndəʳ] N (*Phot*) visor *m* (de imagen), objetivo *m*

viewing ['vju:ɪŋ] (A) N [1] [*of property, gallery*] visita *f*; (*prior to auction*) exposición *f*, inspección *f*; **"viewing by appointment only"** "estrictamente visitas concertadas"; **the gallery will be open for a private ~ this evening** la galería estará abierta esta noche para una visita privada
[2] (*TV*) [2·1] (= *act*) **"unsuitable for family ~"** "no apto para ver en familia"; **films sold for home ~** películas que se venden para ver en casa; **we strictly limit our children's TV ~** limitamos el tiempo que nuestros hijos ven la televisión de manera estricta
[2·2] (= *programmes*) programas *mpl*, programación *f*; **your weekend ~** sus programas *or* su programación para el fin de semana; **the series has become compulsive ~** la serie se ha convertido en un programa que no debe perderse
(B) CPD ► **TV viewing figures** NPL cifras *fpl* de audiencia televisiva ► **viewing gallery** N (*gen*) galería *f* para observadores; (*balcony-shaped*) palco *m* para observadores ► **viewing habits** NPL hábitos *mpl* de los telespectadores *or* televidentes ► **viewing platform** N plataforma *f* de observación; *see also* **peak C**

viewpoint ['vju:pɔɪnt] N [1] (*on hill etc*) mirador *m*, punto *m* panorámico
[2] (*fig*) punto *m* de vista; **from the ~ of the economy** desde el punto de vista de la economía

vigil ['vɪdʒɪl] N vigilia *f*, vela *f*; **to keep ~ (over sth/sb)** velar (algo/a algn)

vigilance ['vɪdʒɪləns] (A) N vigilancia *f*; **to escape sb's ~** burlar la vigilancia de algn; **to relax one's ~** disminuir la vigilancia, bajar la guardia
(B) CPD ► **vigilance committee** N (*US*) comité *m* de autodefensa

vigilant ['vɪdʒɪlənt] ADJ vigilante, alerta; **staff have been instructed to be extra ~** se ha ordenado a todo el personal que extreme la vigilancia; **under his ~ eye** bajo su atenta mirada; **to be ~ against** [+ *danger, threat*] mantenerse alerta *or* vigilante frente a

vigilante [ˌvɪdʒɪ'læntɪ] N vigilante *mf*

vigilantism [ˌvɪdʒɪ'læntɪzəm] N vigilancia *f* callejera

vigilantly ['vɪdʒɪləntlɪ] ADV vigilantemente

vignette [vɪ'njet] N (*Phot, Typ*) viñeta *f*; (= *character sketch*) esbozo *m* en miniatura, esbocito *m*, estampa *f*

vigor ['vɪgəʳ] N (*US*) = **vigour**

vigorous ['vɪgərəs] ADJ [1] (= *energetic*) [*exercise, activity, training*] enérgico; (= *lively*) [*debate*] enérgico; **she is a ~ 75 year-old** es una mujer de 75 años llena de vigor *or* energía
[2] (= *strong*) [*opponent, campaign, defence*] enérgico; [*denial*] categórico, rotundo; [*growth*] (*Bot, Econ*) vigoroso; [*economy*] pujante

vigorously ['vɪgərəslɪ] ADV [1] (= *energetically*) [*nod, shake*] enérgicamente, vigorosamente; [*exercise*] enérgicamente
[2] (= *strongly*) [*deny*] categóricamente, rotundamente; [*defend, oppose, protest*] enérgicamente; **to campaign ~** realizar una enérgica campaña; **to grow ~** [*plant*] crecer con vigor; [*economy, company*] crecer con vigor *or* vigorosamente

vigour, **vigor** (*US*) ['vɪgəʳ] N vigor *m*, energía *f*; **with great ~** con mucho vigor, con mucha energía; **with renewed ~** con renovado vigor, con renovada energía

Viking ['vaɪkɪŋ] (A) N vikingo/a *m/f*
(B) ADJ vikingo

vile [vaɪl] ADJ [1] (= *base, evil*) [*person, behaviour, attack, regime*] vil, infame; [*language*] abominable; **he was ~ to her** se portó de un modo infame con ella
[2] (*) (= *disgusting*) [*conditions*] miserable, infame; [*weather*] pésimo, infame; [*smell, taste*] repugnante; **it smelled/tasted ~** tenía un olor/sabor repugnante; **to be in a ~ mood** estar de pésimo humor, estar de un humor de mil demonios*; **he has a ~ temper** tiene un genio muy violento, tiene un genio de mil demonios*

vilely ['vaɪllɪ] ADV [*behave*] vilmente, de modo infame

vileness ['vaɪlnɪs] N [*of person, behaviour, action*] vileza *f*

vilification [ˌvɪlɪfɪ'keɪʃən] N vilipendio *m*

vilify ['vɪlɪfaɪ] VT vilipendiar

villa ['vɪlə] N (*Roman*) villa *f*; (= *country house*) casa *f* de campo, quinta *f*; (*for holiday*) chalet *m*

village ['vɪlɪdʒ] (A) N pueblo *m*; (= *small*) aldea *f*, pueblito *m* (*LAm*)
(B) CPD ► **village church** N iglesia *f* del pueblo ► **village cricket** N críquet *m* pueblerino ► **village green** N prado *m* comunal, campo *m* comunal ► **village hall** N sala *f* del pueblo ► **village idiot** N tonto *m* del lugar ► **village life** N la vida rural, la vida de pueblo ► **village shop, village store** N tienda *f* del pueblo

villager ['vɪlɪdʒəʳ] N (= *inhabitant*) vecino/a *m/f* del pueblo; [*of small village*] aldeano/a *m/f*

villain ['vɪlən] N [1] (*) (= *wrongdoer*) maleante *mf*, delincuente *mf*
[2] (*hum*) (= *rascal*) bribón/ona *m/f*, tunante/a *m/f*
[3] (*in novel, film*) malo/a *m/f*; **the ~ of the piece is Malone** (*hum*) el malo de la historia es Malone

villainous ['vɪlənəs] ADJ (= *evil*) malvado, vil; (= *very bad*) malísimo, horrible; **he was a ~-looking character** era un tipo de mala catadura (*frm*), era un tipo de aspecto malvado

villainously ['vɪlənəslɪ] ADV vilmente; **~ ugly** feísimo

villainy ['vɪlənɪ] N (*esp poet*) maldad *f*, vileza *f*

villein ['vɪlɪn] N (*Hist*) villano/a *m/f*

vim [vɪm] N energía *f*, empuje *m*

VIN N ABBR = **vehicle identification number**

vinaigrette [ˌvɪneɪ'gret] N vinagreta *f*

Vincent ['vɪnsənt] N Vicente

vindaloo [ˌvɪndə'lu:] N *plato indio muy picante*

vindicate ['vɪndɪkeɪt] VT [+ *decision, action*] justificar; [+ *claim, right*] reivindicar, hacer valer; **I feel totally ~d by this decision** me siento totalmente resarcido por esta decisión, siento que con esta decisión se me hace justicia; **to ~ o.s.** justificarse

vindication [ˌvɪndɪ'keɪʃən] N justificación *f*; [*of claim, right*] reivindicación *f*, defensa *f*; (= *means of exoneration*) vindicación *f* (*frm*); **it was a ~ of all she had fought for** suponía una justificación de todo aquello por lo que había luchado

vindictive [vɪn'dɪktɪv] ADJ vengativo; (= *spiteful*) rencoroso; **to be ~ towards sb** ser vengativo con algn

vindictively [vɪn'dɪktɪvlɪ] ADV (= *vengefully*) vengativamente, con afán de venganza; (= *unforgivingly*) con rencor, rencorosamente

vindictiveness [vɪn'dɪktɪvnɪs] N (= *desire for revenge*) afán *m* de venganza, revanchismo *m*; (= *spitefulness*) rencor *m*

vine [vaɪn] (A) N vid *f*; (= *climbing, trained*) parra *f*; (= *climber*) enredadera *f*
(B) CPD ► **vine grower** N viticultor(a) *m/f*, viñador(a) *m/f* ► **vine growing** N viticultura *f*; *see also* **vine-growing** ► **vine leaf** N (*pl* **vine-leaves**) hoja *f* de parra, hoja *f* de vid, pámpana *f*

vinegar ['vɪnɪgəʳ] N vinagre *m*

vinegary ['vɪnɪgərɪ] ADJ vinagroso

vine-growing ['vaɪnˌgrəʊɪŋ] ADJ [*region*] viticultor; *see also* **vine**

vineyard ['vɪnjəd] N viña *f*, viñedo *m*

viniculture ['vɪnɪkʌltʃəʳ] N vinicultura *f*

vino* ['vi:nəʊ] N vinacho* *m*, morapio *m* (*Sp**)

vinous ['vaɪnəs] ADJ vinoso

vintage ['vɪntɪdʒ] (A) N (= *season, harvest*) vendimia *f*; (= *year*) cosecha *f*, añada *f*; **the 1970 ~** la cosecha de 1970; **it will be a good ~** la cosecha será buena; **it was a ~ performance** fue una actuación memorable; **this film is ~ Chaplin** ésta es una película clásica de Chaplin, esta película es un clásico de Chaplin; **it has been a ~ year for plays** ha sido un año destacado en lo que a teatro se refiere
(B) CPD ► **vintage car** N coche *m* de época, coche *m* antiguo (*fabricado entre 1919 y 1930*) ► **vintage wine** N vino *m* añejo

vintner ['vɪntnəʳ] N (= *merchant*) vinatero/a *m/f*; (= *wine-maker*) vinicultor(a) *m/f*

vinyl ['vaɪnl] (A) N vinilo *m*
(B) ADJ de vinilo, vinílico
(C) CPD ► **vinyl acetate** N acetato *m* de vinilo

viol ['vaɪəl] N viola *f*

viola[1] [vɪ'əʊlə] (A) N (*Mus*) viola *f*; **~ da gamba** viola *f* de gamba; **~ d'amore** viola *f* de amor
(B) CPD ► **viola player** N viola *mf*

viola[2] ['vaɪələ] N (*Bot*) viola *f*, violeta *f*

violate ['vaɪəleɪt] VT [1] (= *breach*) [+ *law*] violar, infringir, quebrantar; [+ *constitution, agreement, treaty*] violar, infringir, vulnerar; (*Comm, Pol*) [+ *sanctions*] incumplir, desobedecer; [+ *contract*] no cumplir, incumplir; [+ *rights*] violar, vulnerar; [+ *privacy*] invadir; **to ~ sb's trust** abusar de la confianza de algn
[2] (= *defile*) [+ *grave*] profanar
[3] († *or liter*) (= *rape*) violar

violation [ˌvaɪə'leɪʃən] N [1] [*of law*] violación *f*, infracción *f*; [*of rights*] violación *f*; **~ of privacy** entrometimiento *m*, intromisión *f*; **it was in ~ of the law/agreement** violaba la ley/el acuerdo; **it was in ~ of sanctions** incumplía *or* desobedecía las sanciones
[2] (*US*) (= *minor offence*) infracción *f*, falta *f* leve; **a minor traffic ~** una infracción de tráfico
[3] († *or liter*) (= *rape*) violación *f*

violator ['vaɪəleɪtəʳ] N [*of law*] infractor(a) *m/f*, violador(a) *m/f*; [*of agreement, rights*] violador(a) *m/f*

violence ['vaɪələns] N (*gen*) violencia *f*; **an act of ~** un acto de violencia; **crimes of ~** delitos *mpl* violentos; **to do ~ to sb** agredir a algn; **to do ~ to sth** estropear algo; **to resort to ~** recurrir a la violencia *or* a la fuerza; **robbery with ~** robo *m* con violencia

violent ['vaɪələnt] ADJ [*person, quarrel, storm, language*] violento; [*kick*] violento, fuerte; [*pain*] intenso, agudo; [*colour*] chillón; **to become** *or* **turn ~** mostrarse violento; **to die a ~ death** morir de muerte violenta; **~ crimes** delitos *mpl* violentos; **to come to a ~ halt** detenerse *or* (*LAm*) parar bruscamente; **he has a ~ temper** tiene un genio terrible; **to take a ~ dislike to sb** coger *or* (*LAm*) agarrar una profunda antipatía a algn; **to take a ~ dislike to sth** tomar una tremenda *or* profunda aversión a algo; **by ~ means** por la fuerza, por la violencia

violently [ˈvaɪələntlɪ] ADV [*act*] con violencia, de manera violenta; [*tremble*] violentamente; [*brake*] bruscamente; **she shook the child ~** sacudió al niño con violencia; **to die ~** morir violentamente; **to react ~ to sth** reaccionar violentamente *or* con violencia ante algo; **to fall ~ in love with sb** enamorarse perdidamente de algn; **to be ~ opposed to sth** oponerse radicalmente a algo; **he is ~ anti-Communist** es un anticomunista furibundo; **to be ~ sick** vomitar mucho

violet [ˈvaɪəlɪt] Ⓐ N 1 (*Bot*) violeta *f*
2 (= *colour*) violado *m*, violeta *f*
Ⓑ ADJ violado, violeta; **~ colour, ~ color** (*US*) color *m* violeta

violin [ˌvaɪəˈlɪn] Ⓐ N violín *m*
Ⓑ CPD ► **violin case** N estuche *m* de violín ► **violin concerto** N concierto *m* para violín ► **violin player** N violinista *mf* ► **violin section** N sección *f* de violines

violinist [ˌvaɪəˈlɪnɪst] N violinista *mf*

violist [vɪˈəʊlɪst] N (*US*) viola *mf*

violoncellist [ˌvaɪələnˈtʃelɪst] N violonchelista *mf*

violoncello [ˌvaɪələnˈtʃeləʊ] N violonchelo *m*

VIP Ⓐ N ABBR (= **very important person**) VIP *mf*, persona *f* de categoría
Ⓑ CPD ► **VIP lounge** N (*in airport*) sala *f* de VIPs ► **VIP treatment** N **to give sb the ~ treatment** tratar a algn como a un VIP; **to get the ~ treatment** ser tratado como un VIP

viper [ˈvaɪpəʳ] N (*lit, fig*) víbora *f*

viperish [ˈvaɪpərɪʃ] ADJ (*fig*) viperino

virago [vɪˈrɑːgəʊ] N (*pl* **viragoes** *or* **viragos**) fiera *f*, arpía *f*

viral [ˈvaɪərəl] ADJ vírico; **a ~ infection** una infección vírica

Virgil [ˈvɜːdʒɪl] N Virgilio

Virgilian [vɜːˈdʒɪlɪən] ADJ virgiliano

virgin [ˈvɜːdʒɪn] Ⓐ N (*lit*) virgen *mf*; **to be a ~** ser virgen; **the Blessed Virgin** la Santísima Virgen
Ⓑ ADJ (*fig*) [*forest, soil etc*] virgen
Ⓒ CPD ► **virgin birth** N partenogénesis *f inv* ► **the Virgin Isles** NPL las Islas Vírgenes ► **virgin oil** N aceite *m* virgen

virginal [ˈvɜːdʒɪnl] Ⓐ ADJ virginal
Ⓑ N **the ~** (*also* **the ~s**) (*Mus*) la espineta

Virginian [vəˈdʒɪnɪən] Ⓐ ADJ virginiano
Ⓑ N 1 (= *person*) virginiano/a *m/f*
2 (*also* **~ tobacco**) tabaco *m* rubio

virginity [vɜːˈdʒɪnɪtɪ] N virginidad *f*

Virgo [ˈvɜːgəʊ] N 1 (= *sign, constellation*) Virgo *m*
2 (= *person*) virgo *mf*; **she's (a) ~** es virgo

virgule [ˈvɜːgjuːl] N (*US Typ*) barra *f* oblicua

virile [ˈvɪraɪl] ADJ [*man*] viril; [*looks*] varonil

virility [vɪˈrɪlɪtɪ] N virilidad *f*

virologist [ˌvaɪəˈrɒlədʒɪst] N virólogo/a *m/f*

virology [ˌvaɪəˈrɒlədʒɪ] N virología *f*

virtual [ˈvɜːtjʊəl] Ⓐ ADJ real, verdadero; **he's the ~ star of the show** en realidad *or* en la práctica, la estrella del espectáculo es él; **it was a ~ defeat/failure** en realidad fue una derrota/un fracaso
Ⓑ CPD ► **virtual memory** N memoria *f* virtual ► **virtual memory storage** N memoria *f* virtual ► **virtual reality** N realidad *f* virtual

virtuality [vɜːtjʊˈælɪtɪ] N realidad *f* virtual, virtualidad *f*

virtually [ˈveːtjʊəlɪ] ADV prácticamente; **it is ~ impossible to do anything** es prácticamente imposible hacer nada; **it ~ destroyed the building** destruyó prácticamente el edificio; **I've ~ finished the work** casi he terminado el trabajo; **he started with ~ nothing** empezó prácticamente *or* casi sin nada

virtue [ˈvɜːtjuː] N 1 (= *good quality*) virtud *f*; **to extol sb's ~s** alabar *or* ensalzar las virtudes de algn; ✦*IDIOM* **to make a ~ of necessity** hacer de la necesidad virtud
2 (= *advantage*) virtud *f*, ventaja *f*; **it has the ~ of simplicity** *or* **of being simple** tiene la virtud *or* ventaja de ser sencillo; **I see no ~ in (doing) that** no veo ninguna ventaja en (hacer) eso
3 (= *chastity*) castidad *f*, honra *f*; **her ~ was in no danger** su castidad *or* honra no corría peligro; **he had designs on her ~** iba a tratar de seducirla; **a woman of easy ~** una mujer de vida alegre, una mujer de moralidad laxa
4 **by ~ of** ◊ **in ~ of** en virtud de, debido a

virtuosity [ˌvɜːtjʊˈɒsɪtɪ] N virtuosismo *m*

virtuoso [ˌvɜːtjʊˈəʊzəʊ] Ⓐ N (*pl* **virtuosos** *or* **virtuosi** [ˌvɜːtjʊˈəʊziː]) virtuoso/a *m/f*
Ⓑ ADJ de virtuoso/a; **a ~ performance** una interpretación de auténtico virtuoso *or* llena de virtuosismo

virtuous [ˈvɜːtjʊəs] ADJ virtuoso

virtuously [ˈvɜːtjʊəslɪ] ADV virtuosamente

virulence [ˈvɪrʊləns] N virulencia *f*

virulent [ˈvɪrʊlənt] ADJ (*Med*) (*also fig*) virulento

virulently [ˈvɪrʊləntlɪ] ADJ con virulencia

virus [ˈvaɪərəs] Ⓐ N (*pl* **viruses**) (*Med, Comput*) virus *m inv*; **rabies ~** virus *m inv* de la rabia; **the AIDS ~** el virus del SIDA; **a computer ~** un virus informático
Ⓑ CPD ► **virus disease** N enfermedad *f* vírica

visa [ˈviːzə] Ⓐ N (*pl* **visas**) visado *m*, visa *f* (*LAm*)
Ⓑ VT visar

visage [ˈvɪzɪdʒ] N (*liter*) semblante *m*

vis-à-vis [ˈviːzɑːviː] PREP (= *with regard to*) con respecto a, en relación con, con relación a; **Switzerland's position ~ the EC** la posición de Suiza con respecto a *or* en relación con *or* con relación a la CE; **the government's policy ~ the unions** la política del gobierno frente a los sindicatos

viscera [ˈvɪsərə] NPL vísceras *fpl*

visceral [ˈvɪsərəl] ADJ (*liter*) visceral

viscid [ˈvɪsɪd] ADJ viscoso

viscose [ˈvɪskəʊs] Ⓐ ADJ viscoso
Ⓑ N viscosa *f*

viscosity [vɪsˈkɒsɪtɪ] N viscosidad *f*

viscount [ˈvaɪkaʊnt] N vizconde *m*

viscountcy [ˈvaɪkaʊntsɪ] N vizcondado *m*

viscountess [ˈvaɪkaʊntɪs] N vizcondesa *f*

viscous [ˈvɪskəs] ADJ viscoso

vise [vaɪs] N (*US*) = **vice²**

visibility [ˌvɪzɪˈbɪlɪtɪ] N 1 (*Met*) visibilidad *f*; **good/poor ~** buena/poca visibilidad *f*
2 (= *level of recognition*) **the company needs to improve its ~** la compañía necesita darse más a conocer

visible [ˈvɪzəbl] Ⓐ ADJ 1 (= *able to be seen*) **~ to the human eye** perceptible a simple vista, visible al ojo humano; **to be ~: your identity card must be ~ at all times** su carné de identidad tiene que estar siempre a la vista; **the house is ~ from the road** la casa puede verse desde la carretera
2 (= *obvious*) [*effect, sign, result*] evidente; **there was no ~ damage** no se veía ningún daño aparente; **the effects were clearly ~** los efectos saltaban a la vista, eran muy evidentes; **he was showing ~ signs of distress** mostraba evidentes *or* claras señales de agitación; **with a ~ effort** con un esfuerzo evidente; **with no ~ means of support** (*Jur*) sin ninguna fuente de ingresos aparente
3 (= *prominent*) [*person*] destacado, prominente; **at management level women are becoming increasingly ~** a niveles directivos, las mujeres ocupan lugares cada vez más destacados *or* prominentes
Ⓑ CPD ► **visible exports** NPL (*Econ*) exportaciones *fpl* visibles

visibly [ˈvɪzəblɪ] ADV visiblemente; **many were ~ moved by what they saw** muchos estaban visiblemente emocionados por lo que habían visto; **he was ~ shaken by his ordeal** estaba visiblemente afectado por la terrible experiencia vivida; **she was ~ thinner** estaba visiblemente más delgada

Visigoth [ˈvɪzɪgɒθ] N visigodo/a *m/f*

Visigothic [ˌvɪzɪˈgɒθɪk] ADJ visigodo, visigótico

vision [ˈvɪʒən] N 1 (= *eyesight*) vista *f*; **to have normal ~** tener la vista normal; **field of ~** campo *m* visual; *see also* **double F**, **tunnel D**
2 (= *farsightedness*) clarividencia *f*, visión *f* de futuro; (= *imagination*) imaginación *f*; **we need ~ to make this idea work** nos hace falta clarividencia *or* visión de futuro para hacer que esta idea funcione; **he had the ~ to see that ...** tenía la suficiente visión de futuro como para ver que ...; **a man of (broad) ~** un hombre de miras amplias
3 (= *dream, hope*) visión *f*; **he outlined his ~ of the company over the next decade** esbozó su visión de la empresa para la siguiente década; **a ~ of the future** una visión del futuro
4 (= *image*) **I had ~s of having to walk home** ya me veía volviendo a casa a pie
5 (*Rel*) visión *f*; **to have a ~** tener una visión; **Christ appeared to her in a ~** tuvo una visión de Cristo, se le apareció Cristo

visionary [ˈvɪʒənərɪ] Ⓐ N 1 (= *original thinker*) visionario/a *m/f*
2 (= *dreamer*) soñador(a) *m/f*
Ⓑ ADJ 1 (= *farsighted*) [*person, plan*] con visión de futuro, visionario
2 (= *impractical*) [*idea, plan*] utópico, quimérico
3 (= *idealistic*) [*person*] idealista
4 (= *religious, supernatural*) [*experience*] sobrenatural

vision-mixer [ˈvɪʒənˌmɪksəʳ] N (*TV*) mezclador(a) *m/f* de imágenes

visit [ˈvɪzɪt] Ⓐ N (*gen*) visita *f*; **to go on** *or* **make a ~ to** [+ *person, place*] ir de visita a, visitar a; **to pay sb a ~** ◊ **pay a ~ to sb** hacer una visita *or* visitar a algn, pasar a ver a algn (*esp LAm*); **on a private/an official ~** de *or* en visita privada/oficial; **he was taken ill on** *or* **during a ~ to Amsterdam** cayó enfermo durante una visita a Amsterdam; **to return a ~** devolver una visita; **a ~ to the lavatory** *or* **toilet** una visita al servicio, una visita al señor Roca*
Ⓑ VT 1 (= *go and see*) [+ *person*] visitar, hacer una visita a; [+ *place*] ir a, visitar; **to ~ the sick** visitar a los enfermos; **to ~ a patient** ir a ver a un paciente, visitar a un paciente; **he never ~s the doctor** nunca va al médico; **we're hoping to ~ Tarragona** esperamos poder ir a *or* visitar Tarragona; **when we first**

~ed the town la primera vez que fuimos a *or* visitamos la ciudad
[2] (= *stay with*) [+ *person*] visitar, pasar un tiempo con; (= *stay in*) [+ *town, area*] visitar, pasar un tiempo en
[3] (*frm*) (= *inflict, afflict*) **to ~ a punishment on sb** castigar a algn con algo, mandar un castigo a algn; **they were ~ed with the plague††** sufrieron el azote de la peste; **the sins of the fathers are ~ed on the children** los hijos sufren los pecados de los padres
Ⓒ VI [1] (= *make a visit*) hacer una visita; (= *make visits*) hacer visitas; **they always ~ when they're in town** siempre nos hacen una visita cuando vienen a la ciudad; **she has promised to ~ next year** ha prometido venir de visita el año que viene; **to go ~ing** hacer visitas
[2] (*US*) **to ~ with sb** (= *go and see*) visitar a algn; (= *chat with*) charlar con algn

visitation [ˌvɪzɪˈteɪʃən] Ⓐ N [1] (= *visit*) (*by official*) inspección *f*; (*by bishop, cardinal*) visita *f* pastoral; **we had a ~ from her** (*hum*) nos cayó encima una de sus visitas
[2] (*Rel*) visitación *f*; **the Visitation of the Blessed Virgin Mary** la Visitación de la Santísima Virgen María
[3] (= *punishment*) castigo *m*
Ⓑ CPD ► **visitation rights** NPL derecho *msing* de visita

visiting [ˈvɪzɪtɪŋ] Ⓐ ADJ [*speaker, professor*] invitado; [*team*] visitante, de fuera; **we're on ~ terms** nos visitamos
Ⓑ CPD ► **visiting card** N tarjeta *f* de visita ► **visiting hours** NPL horas *fpl* de visita ► **visiting nurse** N (*US*) enfermera *f* que visita a domicilio ► **visiting rights** NPL derecho *msing* de visita ► **visiting time** N horas *fpl* de visita

visitor [ˈvɪzɪtəʳ] Ⓐ N [1] (*to one's home*) visita *f*; **she had a ~ earlier** tuvo una visita antes; **we had a constant stream of ~s** no paraba de visitarnos gente; **to have ~s** tener visita; **we can't invite you because we've got ~s** no podemos invitarte porque tenemos visita
[2] (*in hotel*) huésped(a) *m/f*
[3] (*to place*) (= *tourist*) turista *mf*, visitante *mf*; (= *tripper*) excursionista *mf*; (*to zoo, exhibition*) visitante *mf*; (*to hospital, prison*) visita *f*; **~s to this country must be made to feel welcome** los que visitan este país deben sentirse bien recibidos; **the museum had 900 ~s** el museo recibió a 900 visitantes; **sorry, we're just ~s here** lo siento, estamos aquí de visita nada más; **the summer ~s bring a lot of money** los veraneantes aportan mucho dinero; **he's only allowed two ~s** [*patient, prisoner*] sólo puede recibir dos visitas
Ⓑ CPD ► **visitor centre, visitor center** (*US*) N centro *m* de información ► **visitors' book** N libro *m* de visitas

visor [ˈvaɪzəʳ] N visera *f*

VISTA [ˈvɪstə] N ABBR (*US*) (= **Volunteers in Service to America**) *programa de ayuda voluntaria a los necesitados*

vista [ˈvɪstə] N (*lit*) vista *f*, panorama *m*; (*fig*) perspectiva *f*, horizonte *m*; **to open up new ~s** abrir nuevas perspectivas *or* nuevos horizontes

visual [ˈvɪzjʊəl] Ⓐ ADJ visual
Ⓑ CPD ► **visual aids** N (*in teaching*) medios *mpl* visuales ► **the visual arts** NPL las artes plásticas ► **visual display unit** N unidad *f* de despliegue visual, monitor *m* ► **visual effects** NPL efectos *mpl* visuales ► **visual proof** NPL pruebas *fpl* oculares

visualization [ˌvɪzjʊəlaɪˈzeɪʃən] N visualización *f*

visualize [ˈvɪzjʊəlaɪz] VT [1] (= *imagine*) imaginarse; **he tried to ~ the scene** intentó imaginarse la escena; **he could not ~ her as old** no podía hacerse una idea de ella *or* no podía imaginársela de mayor; **she ~d him working at his desk** se lo imaginó trabajando en su mesa; **try to ~ yourself sitting calmly on a plane** imagínate que vas tranquilamente sentado en un avión
[2] (= *call to mind*) [+ *person, sb's face*] recordar; **he found it difficult to ~ her now** ahora le resultaba difícil recordarla
[3] (= *foresee*) prever; **we do not ~ any great change** no prevemos ningún cambio de importancia; **that is not how we ~d it** eso no corresponde a lo que nosotros preveíamos

visually [ˈvɪzjʊəlɪ] ADV visualmente; **~ handicapped person** invidente *mf*

▼**vital** [ˈvaɪtl] Ⓐ ADJ [1] (= *crucial*) [*part, component, element*] vital, indispensable; [*ingredient*] esencial, indispensable, imprescindible; [*factor*] decisivo; [*link, role*] fundamental; [*question*] vital; [*information*] vital, esencial; **it is ~ to keep accurate records** es imprescindible *or* esencial llevar un registro detallado; **is it really ~ for her to have a new dress?** ¿es realmente imprescindible que se compre un vestido nuevo?; **it is ~ that this be kept secret** es esencial que se mantenga en secreto; **to be of ~ importance (to sth/sb)** ser de suma *or* vital importancia (para algo/algn); **at the ~ moment** en el momento crítico *or* clave; **these meetings are ~ to a successful outcome** estas reuniones son esenciales para un resultado positivo
[2] (= *dynamic*) [*person, organization*] vital, lleno de vitalidad; **~ spark** chispa *f* vital
[3] (*Physiol*) [*organ, function*] vital
Ⓑ N **vitals** (*Anat usu hum*) (= *internal organs*) órganos *mpl* vitales; (= *male genitals*) órganos *mpl* sexuales, partes *fpl* (*hum*)
Ⓒ CPD ► **vital signs** NPL (*Med*) signos *mpl* vitales ► **vital statistics** NPL (*Sociol*) estadísticas *fpl* demográficas; (*) [*of woman's body*] medidas *fpl*

vitality [vaɪˈtælɪtɪ] N vitalidad *f*

vitalize [ˈvaɪtəlaɪz] VT [1] (*lit*) vitalizar, vivificar
[2] (*fig*) [+ *person*] animar; [+ *economy, organization*] vitalizar

vitally [ˈvaɪtəlɪ] ADV [1] (= *extremely*) [*interested, concerned*] sumamente; [*affect*] de forma vital; **it is ~ important that …** es de vital *or* suma importancia que … + *subjun*; **it is ~ necessary that …** es indispensable que … + *subjun*; **~ needed** [*food, tents, money*] indispensable; **this statement ~ ignores a number of issues** estas manifestaciones ignoran de forma fundamental una serie de cuestiones
[2] (= *intensely*) **music which remains ~ fresh today** música que sigue fresca y llena de vitalidad

vitamin [ˈvɪtəmɪn] Ⓐ N vitamina *f*; **with added ~s** vitaminado, reforzado con vitaminas
Ⓑ CPD ► **vitamin content** N contenido *m* vitamínico ► **vitamin deficiency** N avitaminosis *f*, déficit *m* vitamínico ► **vitamin pill** N pastilla *f* de vitaminas ► **vitamin supplement** N suplemento *m* vitamínico ► **vitamin tablet** N pastilla *f* de vitaminas

vitamin-enriched [ˌvɪtəmɪnɪnˈrɪtʃt] ADJ enriquecido con vitaminas

vitaminize [ˈvɪtəmɪnaɪz] VT vitaminar

vitaminized [ˈvɪtəmɪnaɪzd] ADJ vitamin(iz)ado, reforzado con vitaminas

vitiate [ˈvɪʃɪeɪt] VT (*frm*) (= *weaken*) afectar negativamente; (= *spoil*) estropear, arruinar; (= *devalue*) quitar valor a; (*Jur*) [+ *contract, deed*] invalidar

viticulture [ˈvɪtɪkʌltʃəʳ] N viticultura *f*

vitreous [ˈvɪtrɪəs] ADJ vítreo

vitrifaction [ˌvɪtrɪˈfækʃən], **vitrification** [ˌvɪtrɪfɪˈkeɪʃən] N vitrificación *f*

vitrify [ˈvɪtrɪfaɪ] Ⓐ VT vitrificar
Ⓑ VI vitrificarse

vitriol [ˈvɪtrɪəl] N vitriolo *m*

vitriolic [ˌvɪtrɪˈɒlɪk] ADJ [*attack, speech, criticism*] corrosivo, mordaz; [*abuse, outburst*] virulento

vitro [ˈvɪtrəʊ] *see* **in vitro**

vituperate [vɪˈtjuːpəreɪt] (*frm*) Ⓐ VT vituperar, llenar de injurias
Ⓑ VI **to ~ against sth/sb** vituperar algo/a algn

vituperation [vɪˌtjuːpəˈreɪʃən] (*frm*) N vituperio *m*, injurias *fpl*

vituperative [vɪˈtjuːpərətɪv] ADJ (*frm*) injurioso

viva¹ [ˈvaɪvə] N (*also* **~ voce**) examen *m* oral

viva² [ˈviːvə] EXCL **~ Caroline!** ¡viva Caroline!

vivacious [vɪˈveɪʃəs] ADJ vivaz, animado

vivaciously [vɪˈveɪʃəslɪ] ADJ con vivacidad, animadamente

vivacity [vɪˈvæsɪtɪ] N vivacidad *f*, animación *f*

vivarium [vɪˈvɛərɪəm] N (*pl* **vivariums** *or* **vivaria** [vɪˈvɛərɪə]) vivero *m*

viva voce [ˈvaɪvəˈvəʊsɪ] Ⓐ ADV de viva voz
Ⓑ ADJ [*exam*] oral
Ⓒ N (*Brit*) examen *m* oral

vivid [ˈvɪvɪd] ADJ [*colour*] vivo, intenso; [*impression, recollection, memory*] vivo, fuerte; [*dream*] clarísimo; [*description*] gráfico, realista; **to have a ~ imagination** tener una imaginación muy viva *or* despierta

vividly [ˈvɪvɪdlɪ] ADV (*gen*) vivamente; [*describe*] gráficamente

vividness [ˈvɪvɪdnɪs] N [*of colours*] intensidad *f*, viveza *f*; [*of description*] lo gráfico; [*of impression, recollection, memory*] fuerza *f*

vivify [ˈvɪvɪfaɪ] VT vivificar

viviparous [vɪˈvɪpərəs] ADJ vivíparo

vivisection [ˌvɪvɪˈsekʃən] N vivisección *f*

vivisectionist [ˌvɪvɪˈsekʃənɪst] N vivisector(a) *m/f*

vixen [ˈvɪksn] N [1] (= *female fox*) zorra *f*, raposa *f*
[2] (*pej*) (= *bad-tempered woman*) arpía *f*, bruja *f*

viz. [vɪz] ADV ABBR = **videlicet** (= *namely*) v.g., v.gr.

vizier [vɪˈzɪəʳ] N visir *m*; **grand ~** gran visir *m*

V-J Day [ˌviːˈdʒeɪˌdeɪ] N ABBR (= **Victory over Japan Day**) *Brit: 15 agosto 1945; US: 2 setiembre 1945*; → V-E DAY

VLF N ABBR = **very low frequency**

VLSI N ABBR (= **very large-scale integration**) integración *f* a muy gran escala

V-neck [ˈviːnek] Ⓐ N (= *neckline*) cuello *m* en pico; (= *sweater*) jersey *m* de cuello de pico
Ⓑ ADJ (*also* **~ed**) de cuello de pico

V-necked [ˈviːnekt] ADJ = **V-neck B**

VOA N ABBR (= **Voice of America**) Voz *f* de América

vocab* [ˈvəʊkæb] N ABBR = **vocabulary**

vocable [ˈvəʊkəbl] N (*Phon*) vocablo *m*

vocabulary [vəʊˈkæbjʊlərɪ] N [1] [*of person, language, subject*] vocabulario *m*, léxico *m*; **a new word in the German ~** una palabra nueva en el vocabulario *or* léxico alemán
[2] (= *glossary*) glosario *m*

➤ LANGUAGE IN USE: **vital A1** 2.3

vocal ['vəʊkəl] Ⓐ ADJ 1 (*Anat, Mus*) vocal
2 (= *vociferous*) ruidoso; **a small but ~ minority** una minoría pequeña pero ruidosa; **there was some ~ opposition** se dejaron oír voces fuertemente discrepantes; **they are getting rather ~ about it** están empezando a protestar
Ⓑ N *see* **vocals**
Ⓒ CPD ► **vocal cords** NPL cuerdas *fpl* vocales ► **vocal music** N música *f* vocal ► **vocal organs** NPL órganos *mpl* vocales ► **vocal score** N partitura *f* vocal

vocalic [vəʊ'kælɪk] ADJ vocálico

vocalisation [,vəʊkəlaɪ'zeɪʃən] N = **vocalization**

vocalist ['vəʊkəlɪst] N (*in cabaret*) vocalista *mf*; (*in pop group*) cantante *mf*

vocalization [,vəʊkəlaɪ'zeɪʃən] N vocalización *f*

vocalize ['vəʊkəlaɪz] Ⓐ VT vocalizar
Ⓑ VI vocalizarse

vocally ['vəʊkəlɪ] ADV 1 (*Mus*) vocalmente
2 (= *vociferously*) ruidosamente

vocals ['vəʊkəlz] NPL voz *fsing*, canto *msing*; **backing ~** coros *mpl*; **lead ~** voz *f* principal

vocation [vəʊ'keɪʃən] N (= *calling*) vocación *f*; (= *profession*) profesión *f*, carrera *f*; **to have a ~ for art** tener vocación por el arte; **he has missed his ~** se ha equivocado de carrera

vocational [vəʊ'keɪʃənl] ADJ [*subject, course*] de formación profesional; [*qualification, skill*] profesional; **~ guidance** orientación *f* profesional; **~ training** formación *f* *or* capacitación *f* profesional

vocative ['vɒkətɪv] Ⓐ ADJ **~ case** vocativo *m*
Ⓑ N vocativo *m*

vociferate [vəʊ'sɪfəreɪt] Ⓐ VI vociferar, gritar
Ⓑ VT vociferar, gritar

vociferation [vəʊ,sɪfə'reɪʃən] N vociferación *f*

vociferous [vəʊ'sɪfərəs] ADJ 1 (= *forceful, energetic*) ruidoso; **there were ~ protests** hubo ruidosas protestas, se protestó ruidosamente
2 (= *noisy*) vociferante

vociferously [vəʊ'sɪfərəslɪ] ADV 1 (= *forcefully, energetically*) [*protest, campaign*] ruidosamente; [*oppose, deny*] terminantemente, categóricamente
2 (= *noisily*) [*cheer*] a gritos

vodka ['vɒdkə] N vodka *m*

vogue [vəʊg] Ⓐ N moda *f*; **to be in ~** ◊ **be the ~** estar en boga *or* de moda; **the ~ for short skirts** la moda de la falda corta
Ⓑ CPD ► **vogue word** N palabra *f* que está de moda

voice [vɔɪs] Ⓐ N 1 (= *sound, faculty of speech*) voz *f*; **I didn't recognize your ~** no he reconocido tu voz; **her ~ sounded cold** se notaba un dejo de frialdad en su voz; **man's/woman's ~** voz de hombre/mujer; **if you carry on shouting, you won't have any ~ left** si sigues gritando te vas a quedar afónica *or* sin voz; **he is a ~ (crying) in the wilderness** está predicando en el desierto; **he added his ~ to opposition critics** unió su voz a las críticas de la oposición; **to find one's ~** (*lit*) recuperar el habla; (*fig*) encontrar su medio de expresión; **to give ~ to sth** (*frm*) dar expresión a algo; **to hear ~s** oír voces; **human ~** voz *f* humana; **in a deep ~** en tono grave; **in a loud/low ~** en voz alta/baja; **in a small ~** con voz queda; **inner ~** voz *f* interior; **a ~ inside me** una voz en mi interior; **if you don't keep your ~s down, you'll have to leave** si no hablan más bajo tendrán que irse; **keep your ~ down!** ¡no levantes la voz!; **to lose one's ~** quedarse afónico *or* sin voz; **to lower one's ~** bajar la voz; **to raise one's ~** alzar *or* levantar la voz; **the ~ of reason** la voz de la razón; **at the top of one's ~** a voz en grito, a voz en cuello; **he yelled at the top of his ~** gritó con todas sus fuerzas *or* a voz en cuello; ✦**IDIOMS to speak with one ~ (about sth)** expresar una opinión unánime (con respecto a algo); **to like the sound of one's own ~**: **he does like the sound of his own ~** cómo le gusta oírse hablar; *see also* **throw, tone**
2 (*Mus*) voz *f*; **she has a beautiful (singing) ~** tiene una voz preciosa (para el canto), canta muy bien; **a piece for ~ and piano** una pieza para voz y piano; **bass/contralto/soprano/tenor ~** voz *f* de bajo/contralto/soprano/tenor; **to be in good ~** estar bien de voz
3 (= *opinion*) voz *f*; **the ~ of the people/nation** la voz del pueblo/de la nación; **to have a/no ~ in the matter** tener/no tener voz en el asunto; **there were no dissenting ~s** no hubo opiniones en contra; **she is a respected ~ in the women's movement** es una voz respetada dentro del movimiento feminista
4 (= *spokesperson*) portavoz *mf*
5 (*Phon*) sonoridad *f*
6 (*Gram*) **active/passive ~** voz *f* activa/pasiva; **in the active/passive ~** en (voz) activa/pasiva
Ⓑ VT 1 [+ *opinion, feelings, concern, support*] expresar; **he felt obliged to ~ his opposition to the war** se sintió obligado a expresar su oposición a la guerra
2 (*Phon*) [+ *consonant*] sonorizar
3 (*Mus*) [+ *wind instrument*] templar
Ⓒ CPD ► **voice box** N laringe *f* ► **voice mail** N (*Telec*) buzón *m* de voz ► **voice part** N (*Mus*) parte *f* cantable ► **voice production** N producción *f* de voz ► **voice range** N registro *m* de voz ► **voice recognition** N reconocimiento *m* de la voz ► **voice synthesis** N síntesis *f* de voz ► **voice synthesizer** N sintetizador *m* de voz ► **voice training** N educación *f* de la voz ► **voice vote** N (*US Pol*) voto *m* oral

voice-activated ['vɔɪs'æktɪveɪtəd] ADJ activado por voz

voiced [vɔɪst] ADJ (*Phon*) [*consonant*] sonoro

voiceless ['vɔɪslɪs] ADJ (*Ling*) [*consonant*] sordo

voice-over ['vɔɪs,əʊvəʳ] N voz *f* en off

voiceprint ['vɔɪs,prɪnt] N impresión *f* vocal

voicing ['vɔɪsɪŋ] N sonorización *f*

void [vɔɪd] Ⓐ ADJ 1 (*Jur*) (= *invalid*) nulo, inválido; **to make** *or* **render a contract ~** anular *or* invalidar un contrato; *see also* **null**
2 (*frm*) (= *empty*) vacío; **~ of interest** carente *or* desprovisto de interés; **to make sb's efforts ~** hacer inútiles los esfuerzos de algn
Ⓑ N 1 (= *emptiness*) (*lit*) vacío *m*; (*fig*) (= *sense of emptiness*) vacío *m*; **the ~** la nada; **to fill the ~** llenar el hueco *or* vacío
2 (= *hole*) hueco *m*
3 (*Cards*) fallo *m*; **to have a ~ in hearts** tener fallo a corazones
Ⓒ VT 1 (*Med*) evacuar, vaciar
2 (*Jur*) anular, invalidar

voile [vɔɪl] N gasa *f*

vol. ABBR (= **volume**) t.

volatile ['vɒlətaɪl] ADJ 1 (*Chem*) volátil
2 (= *unstable*) [*person*] voluble; [*situation, atmosphere, market*] inestable, volátil
3 (*Comput*) **~ memory** memoria *f* no permanente

volatility [,vɒlə'tɪlɪtɪ] N 1 (*Chem*) volatilidad *f*
2 (= *instability*) [*of person*] volubilidad *f*; [*of situation, atmosphere, market*] inestabilidad *f*, volatilidad *f*

volatilize [vɒ'lætəlaɪz] (*Chem*) Ⓐ VT volatilizar
Ⓑ VI volatilizarse

vol-au-vent ['vɒləʊvɑ̃] N volován *m*

volcanic [vɒl'kænɪk] ADJ volcánico

volcano [vɒl'keɪnəʊ] N (*pl* **volcanoes** *or* **volcanos**) volcán *m*

vole [vəʊl] N campañol *m*, ratón *m* de campo

volition [və'lɪʃən] N **of one's own ~** (*frm*) por voluntad (propia), de libre albedrío

volley ['vɒlɪ] Ⓐ N 1 [*of shots*] descarga *f* (cerrada); [*of applause*] salva *f*; [*of stones, objects*] lluvia *f*; [*of insults*] torrente *m*
2 (*Tennis*) volea *f*
Ⓑ VT 1 [+ *abuse, insults*] dirigir (**at** a)
2 (*Tennis*) volear
Ⓒ VI (*Mil*) lanzar una descarga

volleyball ['vɒlɪbɔːl] N balonvolea *m*, voleibol *m*, volibol *m* (*LAm*), balón volea *m*

volleyer ['vɒlɪəʳ] N especialista *mf* en voleas

vols. ABBR (= **volumes**) t.

volt [vəʊlt] N voltio *m*

voltage ['vəʊltɪdʒ] N voltaje *m*, tensión *f*

voltaic [vɒl'teɪɪk] ADJ voltaico

volte-face ['vɒlt'fɑːs] N viraje *m*, cambio *m* súbito de opinión

voltmeter ['vəʊlt,miːtəʳ] N voltímetro *m*

volubility [,vɒljʊ'bɪlɪtɪ] N locuacidad *f*

voluble ['vɒljʊbl] ADJ [*person*] locuaz; [*speech*] prolijo

volubly ['vɒljʊblɪ] ADV [*speak, talk*] locuazmente; [*write*] prolijamente

volume ['vɒljuːm] Ⓐ N 1 (= *book*) libro *m*, volumen *m*; (= *one of series*) volumen *m*, tomo *m*; **a 125-page ~** un libro *or* volumen de 125 páginas; **in the third ~** en el tercer tomo *or* volumen; **an edition in four ~s** una edición en cuatro tomos *or* volúmenes
2 (= *sound*) volumen *m*; **to turn the ~ up** subir el volumen *or* sonido
3 (*Phys, Math*) volumen *m*; (*when measuring liquids*) capacidad *f*
4 (= *size, bulk*) volumen *m*; [*of water*] cantidad *f*, volumen *m*
5 (= *amount*) [*of work, sales*] volumen *m*; **production ~** volumen *m* de producción
6 **volumes (of)** (= *great quantities*) gran cantidad (de); **~s of smoke** gran cantidad de humo; **to write ~s** escribir mucho; **his expression spoke ~s** su expresión lo decía todo; **it speaks ~s for him** eso lo dice todo de él
Ⓑ CPD ► **volume business** N empresa *f* que comercia sólo en grandes cantidades ► **volume control** N control *m* de volumen ► **volume discount** N descuento *m* por volumen de compras ► **volume sales** NPL ventas *fpl* a granel

volumetric [,vɒljʊ'metrɪk] ADJ volumétrico

voluminous [və'luːmɪnəs] ADJ (= *large, capacious*) voluminoso; (= *prolific*) prolífico; (= *overlong*) prolijo

voluntarily ['vɒləntərɪlɪ] ADV 1 (= *freely*) voluntariamente, por voluntad propia
2 (= *for no payment*) [*work*] como voluntario

voluntarism ['vɒləntərɪzəm] N voluntariado *m*

voluntary ['vɒləntərɪ] Ⓐ ADJ 1 (= *not compulsory*) [*contribution, attendance, scheme*] voluntario; **attendance is on a ~ basis** la asistencia es voluntaria
2 (= *unpaid*) [*work, helper*] voluntario; **he does ~ work in his spare time** trabaja de voluntario en su tiempo libre; **he works at the school on a ~ basis** trabaja en el colegio como voluntario
3 (= *charitable*) [*organization*] benéfico

Ⓑ N (*Mus*) solo *m* musical; **an organ/trumpet ~** un solo de órgano/trompeta
Ⓒ CPD ► **voluntary euthanasia** N eutanasia *f* voluntaria ► **voluntary hospital** N (*US*) hospital *m* benéfico ► **voluntary liquidation** N (*Comm, Fin*) liquidación *f* voluntaria, disolución *f*; **to go into ~ liquidation** entrar en liquidación voluntaria, disolverse voluntariamente ► **voluntary manslaughter** N (*US Jur*) homicidio *m* con circunstancias atenuantes ► **voluntary redundancy** N retiro *m* voluntario, baja *f* voluntaria (*Sp*); **to take ~ redundancy** tomar el retiro voluntario, coger la baja voluntaria (*Sp*) ► **voluntary repatriation** N repatriación *f* voluntaria ► **the voluntary sector** N el voluntariado ► **Voluntary Service Overseas** N (*Brit*) Servicio *m* de Voluntarios en el Extranjero ► **voluntary worker** N voluntario/a *m/f*

volunteer [ˌvɒlənˈtɪəʳ] Ⓐ N (*gen*) voluntario/a *m/f*
Ⓑ ADJ [*forces*] voluntario, de voluntarios; [*helper*] voluntario
Ⓒ VT [1] (= *offer*) [+ *one's help, services*] ofrecer; [+ *remark, suggestion*] hacer; [+ *information*] dar
[2] (= *put forward*) (*) **they ~ed him for the job** le señalaron contra su voluntad para la tarea
Ⓓ VI (*for a task*) ofrecerse; (*for the army*) alistarse como voluntario; **to ~ for service overseas** ofrecerse para servir en ultramar; **to ~ to do sth** ofrecerse (voluntario) para hacer algo; **he wasn't forced to, he ~ed** nadie le obligó a ello, se ofreció libremente

voluptuary [vəˈlʌptjʊərɪ] N voluptuoso/a *m/f*

voluptuous [vəˈlʌptjʊəs] ADJ voluptuoso

voluptuously [vəˈlʌptjʊəslɪ] ADJ voluptuosamente

voluptuousness [vəˈlʌptjʊəsnɪs] N voluptuosidad *f*

vomit [ˈvɒmɪt] Ⓐ N vómito *m*
Ⓑ VI devolver, vomitar
Ⓒ VT [1] (*lit*) (*also* **~ up**) vomitar
[2] (*fig*) (= *pour out*) arrojar, echar

vomiting [ˈvɒmɪtɪŋ] N vómito *m*

voodoo [ˈvuːduː] N vudú *m*

voracious [vəˈreɪʃəs] ADJ [*appetite, person, animal*] voraz; (*fig*) [*reader*] insaciable, ávido

voraciously [vəˈreɪʃəslɪ] ADV (*lit*) [*eat*] vorazmente; (*fig*) [*read*] con avidez

voracity [vɒˈræsɪtɪ] N (*lit*) voracidad *f*; (*fig*) avidez *f* (**for** de)

vortex [ˈvɔːteks] N (*pl* **vortexes** *or* **vortices** [ˈvɔːtɪsiːz]) [1] (*lit*) vórtice *m*, torbellino *m*
[2] (*fig*) [*of activity*] torbellino, remolino *m*

Vosges [vəʊʒ] NPL Vosgos *mpl*

votary [ˈvəʊtərɪ] N [1] (*Rel*) devoto/a *m/f*
[2] (*fig*) partidario/a *m/f*

vote [vəʊt] Ⓐ N [1] (= *single vote*) voto *m* (**for** a favor; **against** en contra de); **he was elected by 102 ~s to 60** salió elegido con 102 votos a favor y 60 en contra; **he gets my ~ any day!** ¡cuenta con mi voto incondicional!; **to count the ~s** escrutar *or* computar los votos; **one person, one ~** una persona, un voto; *see also* **cast B2**
[2] (= *votes cast*) votos *mpl*; **they captured 13 per cent of the ~** se hicieron con un 13 por ciento de los votos; **the middle class ~** los votos de la clase media; **as the 1931 ~ showed** según demostraron las elecciones de 1931; **the ~ was overwhelmingly in favour of the Democratic Party** el partido demócrata obtuvo una aplastante mayoría; **the protest was rejected by a majority ~** la protesta fue rechazada por voto mayoritario
[3] (= *right to vote*) derecho *m* al voto *or* a votar, sufragio *m*; **to give sb the ~** dar a algn el derecho al voto; **to have the ~** tener (el) derecho al voto; **~s for women!** ¡el sufragio para las mujeres!
[4] (= *act*) votación *f*; **to have** *or* **take a ~ on sth** decidir algo por votación, someter algo a votación (*more frm*); **a ~ of confidence** un voto de confianza; **to pass a ~ of confidence (in sb)** dar un voto de confianza (a algn); **to allow a free ~** dejar libertad de voto; **a ~ of no confidence** un voto de censura; **by popular ~** (*lit*) por votación popular; (*fig*) en la opinión de muchos; **to put sth to the ~** someter algo a votación; **a ~ of thanks** un voto de gracias
Ⓑ VT [1] (= *cast one's vote for*) votar; **to ~ Labour/Conservative** votar por *or* a los laboristas/conservadores; **~ Ross at the next election!** ¡vote por *or* a Ross en las próximas elecciones!; **to ~ no** votar no; **to ~ sb into office** votar por *or* a algn para un cargo; **to ~ sb out of office** votar para reemplazar a algn (en un cargo); **to ~ a bill/measure through parliament** aprobar una ley/una medida en el parlamento; **to ~ yes** votar sí
[2] (= *elect*) elegir (por votación); **she was ~d Miss Granada 1995** fue elegida (por votación) Miss Granada 1995
[3] (= *approve*) aprobar (por votación); **MPs have today ~d themselves a pay increase** hoy, los diputados parlamentarios se han aprobado (por votación) un aumento de sueldo
[4] (= *suggest*) **I ~ we turn back** sugiero *or* propongo que regresemos
[5] (= *judge*) **we ~d it a failure** opinamos que fue un fracaso
Ⓒ VI votar; **how did you ~?** ¿a *or* por quién votaste?; **which way will you be voting?** ¿a quién votarás?; **the country ~s in three weeks** el país acudirá a las urnas dentro de tres semanas; **to ~ to do sth** votar por hacer algo; **to ~ against sth** votar en contra de algo; **to ~ in favour of sth** votar a favor de algo; **to ~ for sb** votar por *or* a algn; **to ~ on sth** someter algo a votación; ✦**IDIOM** **to ~ with one's feet**: **if the bank goes on like this, customers may start voting with their feet** si el banco sigue así, es posible que los clientes empiecen a prescindir de sus servicios

►**vote down** VT + ADV (= *reject*) [+ *proposal, motion, amendment*] rechazar por mayoría de votos; **I often get ~d down in my house** en casa a menudo tengo que ceder y hacer lo que deciden los demás

►**vote in** VT + ADV [+ *candidate, party*] elegir (por votación); [+ *law*] aprobar (por votación)

►**vote out** VT + ADV [+ *person, party*] no reelegir

►**vote through** VT + ADV [+ *bill, motion*] aprobar

vote-catching [ˈvəʊtkætʃɪŋ] Ⓐ ADJ electoralista
Ⓑ N electoralismo *m*

voter [ˈvəʊtəʳ] N (*gen*) votante *mf*; (*in election*) elector(a) *m/f*

voting [ˈvəʊtɪŋ] Ⓐ N votación *f*
Ⓑ CPD ► **voting booth** N cabina *f* electoral ► **voting machine** N (*US*) máquina *f* de votar ► **voting paper** N papeleta *f* de votación ► **voting pattern** N tendencia *f* de la votación ► **voting power** N potencia *f* electoral ► **voting right** N derecho *m* a voto ► **voting share** N acción *f* con derecho a voto ► **voting slip** N = **voting paper**

votive [ˈvəʊtɪv] ADJ votivo; **~ offering** ofrenda *f* votiva, exvoto *m*

vouch [vaʊtʃ] Ⓐ VI **to ~ for sth** responder de algo, garantizar algo; **I cannot ~ for its authenticity** no puedo responder de *or* garantizar su autenticidad; **to ~ for sb** responder por *or* salir como fiador de algn
Ⓑ VT **to ~ that …** afirmar que …, asegurar que …

voucher [ˈvaʊtʃəʳ] N vale *m*; (*Comm*) bono *m*; **luncheon/travel ~** vale *m* de comida/viaje

vouchsafe [vaʊtʃˈseɪf] VT [+ *privilege, favour*] conceder; [+ *reply*] servirse hacer, dignarse hacer; **to ~ to** (+ *INFIN*) dignarse + *infin*

vow [vaʊ] Ⓐ N (*Rel*) voto *m*; (= *promise*) promesa *f*, compromiso *m*; **lovers' ~s** promesas *fpl* solemnes de los amantes; **to take** *or* **make a ~ that …** jurar *or* prometer que …; **to take** *or* **make a ~ to do sth** jurar hacer algo, comprometerse a hacer algo; **to break one's ~** faltar a un compromiso; **to take one's ~s** (*Rel*) hacer sus votos (monásticos); **to take a ~ of poverty/chastity** hacer voto de pobreza/castidad
Ⓑ VT [+ *obedience, allegiance*] jurar, prometer; **to ~ to do sth** jurar hacer algo, comprometerse a hacer algo; **to ~ that …** jurar *or* prometer que …

vowel [vaʊəl] Ⓐ N vocal *f*
Ⓑ CPD ► **vowel shift** N cambio *m* vocálico ► **vowel sound** N sonido *m* vocálico ► **vowel system** N sistema *m* vocálico

vox pop* [ˈvɒksˈpɒp] N (*Brit*) voz *f* de la calle

voyage [ˈvɔɪɪdʒ] Ⓐ N viaje *m* (*por mar, por el espacio*); (= *crossing*) travesía *f*; **the ~ out** el viaje de ida; **the ~ home** el viaje de regreso *or* de vuelta
Ⓑ VI viajar (*por mar, por el espacio*); **to ~ across unknown seas** viajar por mares desconocidos

voyager [ˈvɔɪədʒəʳ] N viajero/a *m/f* (*por mar*)

voyeur [vwɑːˈjɜːʳ] N voyeur *mf*, voyer *mf*, mirón/ona *m/f*

voyeurism [vwɑːˈjɜːrɪzəm] N voyeurismo *m*, voyerismo *m*, mironismo *m*

voyeuristic [vwɑːjɜːˈrɪstɪk] ADJ voyeurista, de voyeur

V.P. N ABBR (= **Vice-President**) V.P. *mf*

VPL* N ABBR = **visible panty line**

VR N ABBR (= **virtual reality**) realidad *f* virtual

vs ABBR (= **versus**) vs.

V-sign [ˈviːsaɪn] N V *f* de la victoria; (*obscene*) corte *m* de mangas; **to give sb the ~** hacer un corte de mangas a algn

VSO N ABBR (*Brit*) = **Voluntary Service Overseas**

VSOP N ABBR (*sherry*) = **very special** *or* **superior old pale**

VT ABBR (*US*) = **Vermont**

Vt. ABBR (*US*) = **Vermont**

VTOL [ˈviːtɒl] N ABBR (= **vertical take-off and landing**) ADAC *m*

VTR N ABBR = **videotape recorder**

Vulcan [ˈvʌlkən] N Vulcano

vulcanite [ˈvʌlkənaɪt] N vulcanita *f*, ebonita *f*

vulcanization [ˌvʌlkənaɪˈzeɪʃən] N vulcanización *f*

vulcanize [ˈvʌlkənaɪz] VT vulcanizar

vulcanologist [ˌvʌlkənˈɒlədʒɪst] N vulcanólogo/a *m/f*

vulcanology [ˌvʌlkəˈnɒlədʒɪ] N vulcanología *f*

vulgar [ˈvʌlgəʳ] ADJ [1] (= *unrefined, coarse*) [*person, taste*] ordinario, vulgar; **it is ~ to talk about money** hablar de dinero es una ordinariz *or* vulgaridad, hablar de dinero es de mala educación

[2] (= *tasteless*) de mal gusto, vulgar

[3] (= *indecent*) [*joke*] verde, colorado (*LAm*); [*song*] grosero; [*person, comedian*] grosero, ordinario

[4] (*of the people*) vulgar; **Vulgar Latin** latín *m* vulgar; **in the ~ tongue** en la lengua vulgar *or* vernácula

[5] (*Math*) **~ fraction** fracción *f* común

vulgarian [vʌlˈgɛərɪən] N (= *unrefined*) ordinario/a *m/f*; (= *wealthy*) ricacho/a *m/f*

vulgarism [ˈvʌlgərɪzəm] N vulgarismo *m*

vulgarity [vʌlˈgærɪtɪ] N [1] (= *lack of refinement*) ordinariez *f*, vulgaridad *f*

[2] (= *tastelessness*) mal gusto *m*, vulgaridad *f*

[3] (= *indecency*) grosería *f*, obscenidad *f*; (= *crude remark*) grosería *f*

vulgarize [ˈvʌlgəraɪz] VT vulgarizar

vulgarly [ˈvʌlgəlɪ] ADV [1] (= *in an unrefined way*) de un modo ordinario, vulgarmente

[2] (= *tastelessly*) con mal gusto

[3] (= *indecently*) groseramente

[4] (= *in ordinary parlance*) **sodium chloride, ~ known as salt** cloruro de sodio, vulgarmente conocido como sal

Vulgate [ˈvʌlgɪt] N Vulgata *f*

vulnerability [ˌvʌlnərəˈbɪlɪtɪ] N vulnerabilidad *f*

vulnerable [ˈvʌlnərəbl] ADJ vulnerable

vulpine [ˈvʌlpaɪn] ADJ (*lit, fig*) vulpino

vulture [ˈvʌltʃəʳ] N [1] (*Orn*) buitre *m*, zopilote *m* (*CAm, Mex*), aura *f* (*Carib*), carancho *m* (*S. Cone*), gallinazo *m* (*Col, Andes*), urubú *m* (*Peru, Uruguay*), zamuro *m* (*Ven*); **black ~** buitre *m* negro

[2] (*fig*) buitre *m*; **as the ~s from the press descended** cuando los buitres de la prensa se acercaron; **they're like a lot of ~s** son una panda de buitres; *see also* **culture**

vulva [ˈvʌlvə] N (*pl* **vulvas** *or* **vulvae** [ˈvʌlviː]) vulva *f*

vv. ABBR = **verses**

v.v. ABBR = **vice versa**

vying [ˈvaɪɪŋ] *see* **vie**

W w

W[1], **w**[1] [ˈdʌbljuː] N (= *letter*) W, w *f*; **W for William** W de Washington

W[2] ABBR (= **west**) O

W ABBR[2] (= **watt(s)**) w

W. ABBR = **Wales, Welsh**

WA ABBR (*US*) = **Washington**

WAAF [wæf] N ABBR = **Women's Auxiliary Air Force**

wacko* [ˈwækəʊ] ADJ colgado*, excéntrico

wacky* [ˈwækɪ] ADJ (*compar* **wackier**; *superl* **wackiest**) [*person*] chiflado*; [*idea*] disparatado; **~ baccy** (*Brit hum*, ‡) chocolate* *m*, costo‡ *m*

wad [wɒd] Ⓐ N (= *stuffing*) taco *m*, tapón *m*; (*in gun, cartridge*) taco *m*; [*of cotton wool*] bolita *f*; [*of papers*] fajo *m*, lío *m*; [*of banknotes*] fajo *m*; **~s of money** un dineral
Ⓑ VT (*stuff*) rellenar; (*Sew*) acolchar

wadding [ˈwɒdɪŋ] N (*for packing*) relleno *m*; (*for quilting*) entretela *f*, forro *m*; (*Med*) algodón *m* hidrófilo

waddle [ˈwɒdl] Ⓐ N andares *mpl* de pato; **to walk with a ~** andar como un pato
Ⓑ VI andar como un pato; **she ~d over to the window** fue andando como un pato a la ventana; **to ~ in/out** entrar/salir andando como un pato

wade [weɪd] Ⓐ VI 1 (*also* **~ along**) caminar (por el agua/la nieve/el barro *etc*); **to ~ across a river** vadear un río; **to ~ ashore** llegar a tierra vadeando; **to ~ through the water/snow** caminar por el agua/la nieve; **to ~ through the mud** caminar por el barro; **to ~ through a book** leer(se) un libro con dificultad (*por lo aburrido/lo difícil que es*); **it took me an hour to ~ through your essay** tardé una hora en leer tu ensayo
2 **to ~ into sb** (*physically*) abalanzarse sobre algn; (*fig*) emprenderla con algn, arremeter contra algn; **to ~ into a meal** ponerse a comer
Ⓑ VT [+ *river*] vadear

►**wade in** VI + ADV (*lit*) entrar en el agua; **he ~d in and helped us** (*fig*) se puso a ayudarnos

wader [ˈweɪdəʳ] N 1 (= *bird*) ave *f* zancuda
2 **waders** (= *boots*) botas *fpl* altas de goma

wadge [wɒdʒ] N = **wodge**

wadi [ˈwɒdɪ] N (*pl* **wadies**) *cauce de río en el norte de África*

wading [ˈweɪdɪŋ] CPD ► **wading bird** N ave *f* zancuda ► **wading pool** N (*US*) estanque *m* *or* piscina *f* para niños

wafer [ˈweɪfəʳ] N 1 (= *biscuit*) galleta *f*; (*Rel*) hostia *f*; (*eaten with ice cream*) barquillo *m*
2 (*Comput*) oblea *f*
3 (*for sealing*) oblea *f*

wafer-thin [ˈweɪfəˈθɪn] ADJ 1 (*lit*) finísimo
2 (*fig*) [*majority*] muy estrecho

wafery [ˈweɪfərɪ] ADJ delgado, ligero

waffle [ˈwɒfl] Ⓐ N 1 (*Culin*) gofre *m*
2 (*) (= *talk*) palabrería *f*; (*in essay*) paja *f*
Ⓑ VI (*) (also **~ on**) enrollarse; (*in essay*) poner mucha paja; **he ~s on endlessly about the state of the economy** se enrolla como una persiana cuando habla sobre el estado de la economía*
Ⓒ CPD ► **waffle iron** N molde *m* para hacer gofres

waffler* [ˈwɒfləʳ] N (*Brit*) charlatán/ana *m/f*, pico *m* de oro*

waft [wɑːft] Ⓐ N soplo *m*, ráfaga *f*
Ⓑ VT llevar por el aire
Ⓒ VI flotar, moverse

wag[1] [wæg] Ⓐ N [*of tail*] sacudida *f*, meneo *m*; [*of finger*] movimiento *m*; **the dog gave a ~ of its tail** el perro sacudió *or* meneó la cola
Ⓑ VT [+ *tail*] sacudir, menear; **the dog ~ged its tail** el perro sacudió *or* meneó la cola; **he ~ged a finger at me, "naughty, naughty!" he said** me apuntó agitando el dedo —¡pillín, pillín! —dijo
Ⓒ VI [*tail*] sacudirse, menearse; ✦*IDIOM* **tongues will ~** se dará que hablar; **tongues were ~ging about their relationship** las malas lenguas hablaban de sus relaciones

wag[2]† [wæg] N (= *joker*) bromista *mf*

wage [weɪdʒ] Ⓐ N 1 (= *rate per week, year, etc*) sueldo *m*, salario *m* (*more frm*); **a basic ~ of £55 a week** un sueldo *or* (*more frm*) salario base de 55 libras semanales; **he gets a good ~** gana un buen sueldo; **those on high/low ~s** las personas que ganan sueldos *or* (*more frm*) salarios altos/bajos; **minimum ~** salario mínimo; *see also* **living D**
2 **wages** (= *money received*) paga *f*, sueldo *m*; **a day's ~s** la paga *or* el sueldo de un día; (*Agr*) un jornal; **I get my ~s on Fridays** me pagan los viernes; ✦*PROV* **the ~s of sin is death** el pecado se paga con la muerte
Ⓑ VT [+ *war*] hacer; [+ *campaign*] llevar a cabo, hacer; **to ~ war against** *or* **on sb** hacer la guerra a algn; **to ~ war against** *or* **on inflation** luchar contra la inflación, hacer la guerra a la inflación
Ⓒ CPD ► **wage agreement** N convenio *m* salarial ► **wage bill** N gastos *mpl* de nómina, gastos *mpl* salariales ► **wage claim** N (*Brit*) reivindicación *f* salarial ► **wage clerk** N = **wages clerk** ► **wage contract** N = **wage agreement** ► **wage costs** NPL costes *mpl* del factor trabajo ► **wage demand** N reivindicación *f* salarial ► **wage differential** N diferencia *f* salarial ► **wage earner** N asalariado/a *m/f*; **we are both ~ earners** los dos somos asalariados; **she is the family ~ earner** ella es la que mantiene a la familia ► **wage freeze** N congelación *f* salarial ► **wage increase** N aumento *m* salarial ► **wage levels** NPL salarios *mpl*, niveles *mpl* salariales ► **wage negotiations** NPL negociaciones *fpl* salariales ► **wage packet** N (*esp Brit*) (= *envelope with pay*) sobre *m* de la paga; (*fig*) paga *f* ► **wage restraint** N moderación *f* salarial ► **wage rise** N aumento *m* salarial ► **wages bill** N = **wage bill** ► **wage scale** N escala *f* salarial ► **wages clerk** N habilitado/a *m/f* ► **wage settlement** N acuerdo *m* salarial ► **wage slave*** N currante* *mf* ► **wage slip** N nómina *f*, hoja *f* salarial ► **wages snatch** N robo *m* de nóminas ► **wage talks** NPL negociaciones *fpl* salariales ► **wage worker** N (*US*) asalariado/a *m/f*

waged [weɪdʒd] ADJ [*person*] asalariado; [*employment*] remunerado

wager [ˈweɪdʒəʳ] Ⓐ N apuesta *f* (**on** a); **to lay a ~ on sth** apostar por algo
Ⓑ VT [+ *sum of money*] apostar; **to ~ £20 on a horse** apostar 20 libras por un caballo; **I'll ~ that he already knew** apostaría a que ya lo sabía; **he won't do it, I ~ !** ¡a que no lo hace!, ¡apuesto a que no lo hace!

waggish† [ˈwægɪʃ] ADJ bromista, zumbón

waggishly† [ˈwægɪʃlɪ] ADV **he said ~** dijo zumbón

waggle [ˈwægl] Ⓐ N [*of finger*] movimiento *m*; [*of hips*] contoneo *m*, meneo *m*
Ⓑ VT [+ *finger*] agitar; [+ *hips*] contonear, menear; [+ *tail*] sacudir, menear; **he can ~ his ears** puede mover las orejas

waggon *etc* [ˈwægən] N (*esp Brit*) = **wagon**

Wagnerian [vɑːgˈnɪərɪən] ADJ wagneriano

wagon [ˈwægən] N 1 (*horse-drawn*) carro *m*; (= *truck*) camión *m*; (*Brit Rail*) vagón *m*; (*US*) (*also* **station ~**) furgoneta *f*, camioneta *f*; (*US*) (= *police van*) furgón *m* policial; ✦*IDIOMS* **to be on the ~*** no beber; **he decided to go on the ~** se resolvió a no beber; **to hitch one's ~ to a star** picar muy alto
2 (*also* **tea ~**) carrito *m*

wagonload [ˈwægənləʊd] N carretada *f*, carga *f* de un carro; **50 ~s of coal** 50 vagones de carbón

wagtail [ˈwægteɪl] N lavandera *f*

waif [weɪf] N (= *child*) niño/a *m/f* abandonado/a, niño/a *m/f* desamparado/a; (= *animal*) animal *m* abandonado; **~s and strays** (= *children*) niños *mpl* abandonados *or* desamparados; (= *animals*) animales *mpl* abandonados

waif-like [ˈweɪflaɪk] ADJ [*girl, model*] esquelético

wail [weɪl] Ⓐ N 1 (= *moan*) lamento *m*, gemido *m*; [*of new-born*] vagido *m*; (= *complaint*) queja *f*, protesta *f*; **a great ~ went up** pusieron el grito en el cielo
2 [*of siren, wind*] gemido *m*
Ⓑ VI 1 (= *moan*) lamentarse, gemir; [*child*] llorar; (= *complain*) quejarse, protestar
2 [*siren, wind, bagpipes*] gemir

wailing ['weɪlɪŋ] Ⓐ N [1] (= *moaning*) lamentaciones *fpl*, gemidos *mpl*; [*of child*] llanto *m*; (= *complaints*) quejas *fpl*, protestas *fpl*
[2] [*of siren, wind, bagpipes*] gemido *m*
Ⓑ CPD ► **the Wailing Wall** N el Muro de las Lamentaciones

wain [weɪn] N (*liter*) carro *m*; **the Wain** (*Astron*) el Carro

wainscot ['weɪnskət], **wainscotting** ['weɪnskətɪŋ] N revestimiento *m* (de la pared)

waist [weɪst] N [*of person*] cintura *f*, talle *m*; [*of dress, skirt*] talle *m*; (*Naut*) combés *m*; (*fig*) (= *narrow part*) cuello *m*

waistband ['weɪstbænd] N pretina *f*, cinturilla *f*

waistcoat ['weɪskəʊt] N (*Brit*) chaleco *m*

waist-deep ['weɪst'diːp] ADJ hasta la cintura

-waisted ['weɪstɪd] ADJ (*ending in compounds*) **slim-waisted** de cintura delgada, de talle delgado; **high-/low-waisted** de talle alto/bajo

waist-high ['weɪst'haɪ] Ⓐ ADJ hasta la cintura; **the water was ~** el agua cubría *or* llegaba hasta la cintura
Ⓑ ADV **the ball bounced ~** la pelota dio un bote al nivel de la cintura

waistline ['weɪstlaɪn] N [*of person*] cintura *f*, talle *m*; [*of dress, skirt*] talle *m*

wait [weɪt] Ⓐ VI [1] (= *hold on*) [1·1] [*person*] esperar; **just ~ a moment while I fetch you a chair** espere un momento que voy a traerle una silla; **"repairs while you wait"** "reparaciones en el acto"; **reporters were ~ing to interview her** los reporteros estaban esperando para entrevistarla; **I can't ~ to see his face** estoy deseando ver su cara; **they can't ~ for us to go** están deseando que nos vayamos; **to ~ for sth/sb** esperar algo/a algn; **I'll ~ for you outside** te espero fuera; **what are you ~ing for?** (= *hurry up*) ¡a qué esperas!, ¡venga ya!; **the best things in life are worth ~ing for** en esta vida las cosas buenas merecen la espera; **to ~ for sb to do sth** esperar (a) que algn haga algo; **they ~ed for him to finish** esperaron (a) que terminara; **I'm ~ing for them to make a decision** estoy esperando (a) que tomen una decisión, estoy pendiente de que tomen una decisión; **I can hardly ~!** ¡me muero de impaciencia!; **to keep sb ~ing** hacer esperar a algn; **sorry to keep you ~ing** ◊ **sorry to have kept you ~ing** siento haberle hecho esperar; **~ a minute!** ¡un momento!, ¡momentito! (*esp LAm*), ¡aguarde! (*LAm*); **now ~ a minute, Dave, you never told me that** eh, un momento, Dave, tú nunca me dijiste eso; **~ and see!** ¡espera, ya verás!; **I ~ed till two o'clock** esperé hasta las dos; **~ till you're asked** espera a que te inviten; **just you ~ till your father finds out!** ¡ya verás cuando se entere tu padre!; ✦***IDIOM*** **to be ~ing in the wings** esperar entre bastidores
[1·2] [*thing*] **the dishes can ~** los platos pueden esperar; **there's a parcel ~ing to be collected** hay un paquete que hay que recoger; **there is a big market just ~ing to be opened up** hay un mercado grande para abrir; **the ferry tragedy was a disaster ~ing to happen** la tragedia del ferry se veía venir
[2] (*as servant*) **to ~ at table** servir a *or* atender la mesa
Ⓑ VT [1] (= *await*) **to ~ one's chance** esperar la oportunidad; **can't you ~ your turn like everyone else?** ¿no puedes esperar a que llegue tu turno como los demás?
[2] (*) (= *delay*) [+ *dinner, lunch, etc*] **don't ~ dinner for me** no me esperen para cenar
[3] (= *serve*) **to ~ table** (*US*) servir a la mesa, atender la mesa
Ⓒ N espera *f*; **it was a long ~ for the train** fue una larga espera hasta la llegada del tren; **patients face a 28-week ~ for operations** los pacientes tienen que esperar 28 semanas a que les operen; **to lie in ~ (for sb)** andar *or* estar al acecho (de algn); **you may have quite a ~** puede que tengas que esperar bastante; **dinner was worth the ~** la cena mereció la espera

►**wait around, wait about** VI + ADV quedarse esperando; **to ~ around for sb** quedarse esperando a algn; **to ~ around for sth to happen** quedarse esperando a que pase algo

►**wait behind** VI + ADV esperarse; **to ~ behind for sb** quedarse para esperar a algn

►**wait in** (*esp Brit*) VI + ADV quedarse en casa (esperando); **to ~ in for sb** quedarse en casa esperando a algn

►**wait on** VI + PREP [*waiter, servant*] servir, atender (*esp LAm*); ✦***IDIOM*** **to ~ on sb hand and foot** atender el menor deseo de algn

►**wait out** VT + ADV [1] (= *wait till end of*) [+ *storm*] esperar a que pase; **we have enough capital to ~ it out until the economy improves** tenemos suficiente capital para aguantar hasta que mejore la economía
[2] (*US*) [2·1] (= *wait longer than*) **we can ~ you out indefinitely, why don't you surrender?** podemos esperar indefinidamente *or* tenemos todo el tiempo del mundo, ¿por qué no te rindes?
[2·2] (= *wait for*) **we have to ~ out the results of the vote** tenemos que esperar a que se conozcan los resultados de la votación

►**wait up** VI + ADV [1] (= *stay up*) **to ~ up for sb** quedarse despierto esperando a algn; **don't ~ up for me** no te quedes despierto esperándome
[2] (*US**) (= *wait*) esperar

►**wait upon** VI + PREP **to ~ upon sb** [1] (*frm*) [*ambassador, envoy*] presentar sus respetos a algn, cumplimentar a algn
[2] = **wait on**

waiter ['weɪtəʳ] N camarero *m*, mesero *m* (*Mex*), garzón *m* (*S. Cone*), mesonero *m* (*Ven*)

waiting ['weɪtɪŋ] Ⓐ N [1] espera *f*; **the ~ seemed endless** la espera parecía interminable; **he decided that the ~ had gone on long enough** decidió que ya se había esperado bastante; **"no waiting"** "prohibido aparcar", "prohibido estacionarse (*esp LAm*)"; **a prime minister/government in ~** un primer ministro/gobierno en potencia
[2] (*frm*) (= *service*) servicio *m*; **to be in ~ on sb** estar de servicio con algn
Ⓑ CPD ► **waiting game** N **to play a ~ game** esperar la ocasión apropiada ► **waiting list** N lista *f* de espera ► **waiting room** N sala *f* de espera

waitress ['weɪtrɪs] N camarera *f*, mesera *f* (*Mex*), mesonera *f* (*Ven*)

waitressing ['weɪtrɪsɪŋ] N **to do ~** trabajar de camarera; **to get a job ~** obtener un trabajo de camarera

waive [weɪv] VT [1] (= *not claim*) [+ *right, claim, fee*] renunciar a
[2] (= *exonerate from*) [+ *payment of loan, interest*] exonerar de
[3] (= *suspend*) [+ *regulation*] no aplicar; [+ *condition, restriction*] no exigir

waiver ['weɪvəʳ] N [1] (= *renouncement*) [*of right, claim, fee*] renuncia *f*
[2] (= *exoneration*) (*from payment*) exoneración *f*
[3] (= *suspension*) [*of regulation, condition, restriction*] exención *f*
[4] (= *disclaimer*) [*of responsibility*] descargo *m*

wake¹ [weɪk] N [1] (*Naut*) estela *f*
[2] (*fig*) **the tornado brought/left a trail of destruction in its ~** el tornado dejó una estela de destrucción a su paso; **in the ~ of the storm/riots** tras la tormenta/los disturbios; **to come** *or* **follow in the ~ of sth** producirse a raíz de algo

wake² [weɪk] N (*over corpse*) velatorio *m*, vela *f*, velorio *m* (*esp LAm*)

wake³ [weɪk] (*vb: pt* **woke, waked**; *pp* **woken, waked**) Ⓐ VI (*also* **~ up**) despertar, despertarse; **to ~ from a dream/deep sleep/coma** despertar(se) de un sueño/sueño profundo/coma; **on waking** al despertar
Ⓑ VT (*also* **~ up**) despertar; **they were making enough noise to ~ the dead** hacían un ruido que despertaría a los muertos

►**wake up** Ⓐ VI + ADV [1] (*lit*) despertar, despertarse; **~ up!** ¡despierta!, ¡depiértate!; **to ~ up from a nightmare** despertar(se) de una pesadilla; **to ~ up with a hangover/a headache** despertar(se) con resaca/dolor de cabeza; **he woke up (to find himself) in prison** amaneció en la cárcel; **she woke up to find them gone** cuando (se) despertó se encontró con que se habían ido; ✦***IDIOM*** **~ up and smell the coffee!** (*esp US*) ¡abre los ojos!, ¡pon los pies en la tierra!
[2] (*fig*) despertar(se), despabilar(se); **companies had better ~ up** a las empresas les convendría despertar(se); **~ up, Ian! we've already discussed point 12** ¡despierta *or* despabila Ian! ya hemos discutido el punto 12, ¡despiértate *or* despabílate Ian! ya hemos discutido el punto; **to ~ up to the truth** darse cuenta de la verdad; **to ~ up to reality** darse cuenta de la realidad, despertar a la realidad
Ⓑ VT + ADV [1] (*lit*) despertar; **I was woken up by the phone** el teléfono me despertó, me desperté con el teléfono; **you need a coffee to ~ you up** te hace falta una taza de café para despertarte
[2] (*fig*) despertar; **to ~ one's ideas up*** despabilarse; **to ~ sb up to sth** hacer ver algo a algn, hacer que algn se dé cuenta de algo; **someone needs to ~ him up to the risks involved** alguien tiene que hacerle ver los riesgos que implica

wakeful ['weɪkfʊl] ADJ [1] (= *unable to sleep*) [*person*] desvelado
[2] (= *sleepless*) **to have a ~ night** pasar la noche en vela
[3] (*frm*) (= *vigilant*) alerta, vigilante (**to** a)

wakefulness ['weɪkfʊlnɪs] N [1] (= *sleeplessness*) insomnia *f*, desvelo *m*
[2] (*frm*) (= *watchfulness*) vigilancia *f*

waken ['weɪkən] (*liter*) Ⓐ VT despertar
Ⓑ VI despertar, despertarse

wake-up call ['weɪkʌpˌkɔːl] N [1] (*lit*) **ask the hotel staff for an early ~** pídele al personal del hotel que te despierten temprano
[2] (*fig*) aviso *m*

wakey-wakey* ['weɪkɪ'weɪkɪ] EXCL ¡despierta!; **~, rise and shine!** ¡levanta levanta, que los pajarillos cantan!

waking ['weɪkɪŋ] ADJ **I spent my early childhood in a kind of ~ dream** pasé los primeros años de mi infancia como soñando despierto; **one's ~ hours** las horas en que se está despierto; **he spent every ~ moment in the kitchen** pasaba cada minuto del día en la cocina; **this experience has been a ~ nightmare** esta experiencia ha sido como vivir una pesadilla

Waldorf salad [ˌwɔːldɔːfˈsæləd] N ensalada *f* Waldorf (*ensalada de manzanas, nueces y apio con mayonesa*)

Wales [weɪlz] N (el país de) Gales *m*

walk [wɔːk] Ⓐ N 1 (= *stroll, ramble*) paseo *m*; (= *hike*) caminata *f*, excursión *f* a pie; (= *race*) marcha *f* atlética; **there's a nice ~ by the river** hay un paseo agradable por el río; **this is my favourite ~** éste es mi paseo favorito; **it's only a ten-minute ~ from here** está a sólo diez minutos de aquí a pie; **from there it's a short ~ to his house** desde allí a su casa se va a pie en muy poco tiempo; **to go for** *or* **take a ~** ir de paseo; **we went for a ~ around** fuimos a dar una vuelta; **take a ~!*** ¡lárgate*!; **to take sb for a ~** llevar a algn de paseo; ✦*IDIOM* **it was a ~ in the park** (*esp US*) fue coser y cantar, fue pan comido
2 (= *avenue*) paseo *m*
3 (= *pace*) paso *m*; **he went at a quick ~** caminó a (un) paso rápido; **the cavalry advanced at a ~** la caballería avanzaba al paso
4 (= *gait*) paso *m*, andar *m*; **he has an odd sort of ~** tiene un modo de andar algo raro; **to know sb by his ~** conocer a algn por su modo de andar
5 **~ of life: I meet people from all ~s of life** me encuentro con gente de todas las profesiones y condiciones sociales
Ⓑ VT 1 [+ *distance*] andar, caminar (*esp LAm*); **we ~ed 40 kilometres yesterday** ayer anduvimos 40 kilómetros; **to ~ the streets** andar por las calles; (*aimlessly*) vagar por las calles; (= *be homeless*) no tener hogar, estar sin techo; [*prostitute*] hacer la calle *or* la carrera; **to ~ the wards** (*Med*) hacer prácticas de clínica; **you can ~ it in five minutes** está a cinco minutos andando *or* a pie de aquí; **I had to ~ it** tuve que ir a pie *or* ir andando; **don't worry, you'll ~ it*** (*fig*) no te preocupes, será facilísimo
2 (= *lead*) [+ *dog*] pasear, sacar a pasear; [+ *horse*] llevar al paso; **she ~s the dog every day** pasea *or* saca a pasear al perro todos los días; **I'll ~ you to the station** te acompaño a la estación; ✦*IDIOM* **to ~ sb into the ground** *or* **off his feet** dejar a algn rendido de tanto caminar
Ⓒ VI 1 andar, caminar (*esp LAm*); (*as opposed to riding etc*) ir a pie, ir andando, ir caminando (*esp LAm*); (*Sport*) marchar; **can your little boy ~ yet?** ¿ya anda tu niño?; **to ~ slowly** andar despacio; **don't ~ so fast!** ¡no andes tan deprisa!; **you can ~ there in five minutes** está a cinco minutos andando de aquí; **are you ~ing or going by bus?** ¿vas a ir a pie o en autobús?; **"walk"** (*US*) (*on traffic signal*) "cruzar"; **"don't walk"** (*US*) (*on traffic signal*) "no cruzar"; **~ a little with me** acompáñame un rato; **to ~ in one's sleep** ser sonámbulo, andar dormido; **to ~ downstairs/upstairs** bajar/subir la escalera; **we had to ~** tuvimos que ir a pie *or* andando; **to ~ home** ir andando a casa, volver andando a casa; **we were out ~ing in the hills/in the park** estábamos paseando por la montaña/el parque; **to ~ across sth** cruzar algo; **to ~ slowly up/down the stairs** subir/bajar lentamente la escalera; **to ~ up and down** pasearse (de acá para allá); ✦*IDIOM* **to ~ tall** andar con la cabeza alta
2 [*ghost*] andar, aparecer
3 (*) (= *disappear*) volar*; **my camera's ~ed** mi cámara ha volado *or* desaparecido
4 (*) (= *be acquitted*) salir sin cargos

► **walk about, walk around** VI + ADV pasearse (de acá para allá)

► **walk away** VI + ADV irse, marcharse; **he just got up and ~ed away** simplemente se levantó y se fue *or* se marchó; **she watched him ~ away** lo vio alejarse; **to ~ away unhurt** salir ileso; **to ~ away from a problem** huir de un problema; **you can't just ~ away from it!** ¡no puedes desentenderte!; **to ~ away with** [+ *prize*] llevarse; (= *steal*) robar

► **walk back** VI + ADV volver a pie, regresar andando

► **walk in** VI + ADV entrar; **who should ~ in but Joe** ¿a que no te imaginas quién entró? ¡Joe!; **to ~ in on sb** interrumpir a algn

► **walk into** VI + PREP 1 (= *enter*) [+ *room*] entrar en
2 (= *fall into*) [+ *trap*] caer en; **you really ~ed into that one!*** ¡te has dejado embaucar por las buenas!
3 (= *collide with*) chocar con, dar con, dar contra
4 (*) (= *meet*) topar, tropezar con
5 (*) **to ~ into a job** conseguir fácilmente un puesto

► **walk off** Ⓐ VI + ADV irse, marcharse; **he ~ed off angrily** se fue enfadado
Ⓑ VT + ADV **we ~ed off our lunch** dimos un paseo para bajar la comida

► **walk off with** VI + PREP (= *take, win*) **to ~ off with sth** llevarse algo

► **walk on** VI + ADV (= *go on walking*) seguir andando *or* (*esp LAm*) caminando; (*Theat*) (= *come on stage*) salir a escena; (= *have a walk-on part*) hacer de figurante *or* comparsa

► **walk out** VI + ADV (= *go out*) salir; (*from meeting*) salir, retirarse (**of** de); (*on strike*) abandonar el trabajo; **you can't ~ out now!** ¡no puedes marcharte ahora!

► **walk out on** VI + PREP [+ *spouse, family*] abandonar, dejar; **she ~ed out on her husband** abandonó *or* dejó a su marido; [+ *business partner*] dejar; (= *leave in the lurch*) dejar plantado a*

► **walk out with**† VI + PREP **to ~ out with sb** (*Brit*) (= *court*) salir con algn

► **walk over** VI + PREP (= *defeat*) derrotar; **to ~ all over sb** (= *dominate*) tratar a algn a patadas*, atropellar a algn; **they ~ed all over us in the second half** nos dieron una paliza en el segundo tiempo

► **walk up** VI + ADV (= *ascend*) subir (a pie); (= *approach*) acercarse (**to** a); **~ up, ~ up!** ¡vengan!, ¡acérquense!; **to ~ up to sb** acercarse a algn

walkabout [ˈwɔːkəbaʊt] N (*Brit*) (= *walk*) paseo *m*; (*Australia*) *excursión de un aborigen al bosque interior australiano*; **to go on a ~** [*monarch, politician*] pasearse entre el público; **to go ~** (*Australia*) irse de excursión al bosque; (*) (= *disappear*) desaparecer

walkaway* [ˈwɔːkəweɪ] N (*US*) victoria *f* fácil, paseo *m*, pan *m* comido*

walker [ˈwɔːkəʳ] N 1 (= *person*) (*gen*) paseante *mf*, transeúnte *mf*; (= *pedestrian*) peatón *m*; (*Sport*) marchador(a) *m/f*; (= *hiker*) excursionista *mf*; **to be a great ~** ser gran andarín, ser aficionado a las excursiones a pie
2 (*also* **baby ~**) andador *m*, tacatá *m* (*Sp**)

walker-on [ˈwɔːkərˈɒn] N (*Theat*) figurante/a *m/f*, comparsa *mf*; (*Cine*) extra *mf*

walkies* [ˈwɔːkɪz] NSING paseo *m*; **to go ~** dar un paseo; **to take the dog ~** llevar al perro de paseo

walkie-talkie [ˈwɔːkɪˈtɔːkɪ] N transmisor-receptor *m* portátil, walkie-talkie *m*

walk-in [ˈwɔːkɪn] CPD ► **walk-in closet** N (*US*) alacena *f* ropera ► **walk-in customer** N **a lot of our business is from ~ customers** hacemos mucho negocio con los clientes que entran de la calle ► **walk-in clinic** N *clínica donde no hay que pedir hora para ver al médico* ► **walk-in condition** N **in ~ condition** en condiciones de habitabilidad, habitable ► **walk-in pantry** N despensa *f* ► **walk-in wardrobe** N (*US*) alacena *f* ropera

walking [ˈwɔːkɪŋ] Ⓐ N (= *act*) andar *m*, caminar *m*; (*as pastime*) excursionismo *m*; (= *hill walking*) senderismo *m*; (*Sport*) marcha *f* (atlética); **~ is very good for you** andar *or* caminar es muy sano; **she found ~ painful** le resultaba doloroso andar; **I did some ~ in the Alps last summer** el verano pasado hice senderismo por los Alpes
Ⓑ ADJ ambulante; **he's a ~ encyclopaedia** es una enciclopedia ambulante; **the ~ wounded** los heridos que pueden/podían ir a pie *or* andar
Ⓒ CPD ► **walking distance** N **it's within ~ distance** se puede ir andando ► **walking frame** N andador *m* ► **walking holiday** N **they went on a ~ holiday to Wales** fueron a Gales de vacaciones para caminar; **a hotel which offers ~ holidays** un hotel que ofrece vacaciones con excursiones a pie ► **walking pace** N **at a ~ pace** a paso de peatón, a paso normal; **to slow to a ~ pace** aminorar la marcha a paso normal ► **walking papers*** NPL (*US*) pasaporte* *m*, aviso *m* de despido ► **walking race** N carrera *f* pedestre ► **walking shoes** NPL zapatos *mpl* para andar *or* (*esp LAm*) caminar ► **walking stick** N bastón *m* ► **walking tour** N viaje *m* a pie, excursión *f* a pie

walking-on [ˌwɔːkɪŋˈɒn] ADJ = **walk-on**

Walkman® [ˈwɔːkmən] N Walkman® *m*

walk-on [ˈwɔːkɒn] ADJ (*Theat*) **~ part** papel *m* de figurante *or* de comparsa; (*Cine*) papel *m* de extra

walkout [ˈwɔːkaʊt] N (*from conference*) retirada *f*, abandono *m* (de la sala); (= *strike*) abandono *m* del trabajo

walkover [ˈwɔːkˌəʊvəʳ] N 1 (*Horse racing*) walkover *m*
2 (*fig*) victoria *f* fácil, paseo *m*, pan *m* comido*

walk-through [ˈwɔːkθruː] N ensayo *m*

walk-up [ˈwɔːkʌp] N (*US*) (= *building*) edificio *m* sin ascensor; (= *flat*) piso *m or* (*LAm*) departamento *m* en un edificio sin ascensor

walkway [ˈwɔːkweɪ] N (*raised*) pasarela *f*; (= *passageway*) pasaje *m* (entre edificios)

wall [wɔːl] Ⓐ N 1 (*interior, Anat*) pared *f*; (*outside*) muro *m*; [*of city*] muralla *f*; (= *garden wall*) tapia *f*; **the Great Wall of China** la Gran Muralla China; **the north ~ of the Eiger** la pared norte del Eiger; ✦*IDIOMS* **to come up against a brick ~** tener por delante una barrera infranqueable; **talking to him is like talking to a brick ~** hablar con él es como hablar a la pared; **to do sth off the ~** (*esp US**) hacer algo espontáneamente *or* de improviso; **to climb** *or* **crawl up the ~s*** (*from boredom, frustration*) subirse por las paredes*; **it drives me up the ~*** me saca de quicio; **to go up the ~*** (= *get angry*) ponerse furioso; **to go to the ~** [*firm*] ir a la bancarrota, quebrar; ✦*PROV* **~s have ears** las paredes oyen
2 (*Sport*) [*of players*] barrera *f*
3 (*fig*) barrera *f*; ✦*IDIOM* **to break the ~ of silence** romper el muro *or* la barrera del silencio
Ⓑ CPD [*cupboard, light, clock*] de pared; [*map,

painting] mural ► **wall bars** NPL (*Sport*) espalderas *fpl* ► **wall hanging** N tapiz *m* ► **wall socket** N enchufe *m* de pared

►**wall in** VT + ADV [+ *area of land*] cerrar con muro; [+ *garden*] tapiar, cercar con tapia

►**wall off** VT + ADV separar con un muro

►**wall up** VT + ADV [+ *person*] emparedar; [+ *opening, entrance*] tapiar, cerrar con muro, tabicar; [+ *window*] condenar

wallaby ['wɒləbɪ] N (*pl* **wallabies** *or* **wallaby**) ualabi *m*

wallah* ['wɒlə] N hombre *m*; (*pej*) tío* *m*, sujeto* *m*; **the ice-cream ~** el hombre de los helados; **the ~ with the beard** él de la barba

wallboard ['wɔːlbɔːd] N fibra *f* prensada (para paredes)

wall-covering ['wɔːl,kʌvərɪŋ] N material *m* de decoración de paredes

walled [wɔːld] ADJ [*city*] amurallado; [*garden*] tapiado

wallet ['wɒlɪt] N cartera *f*, billetera *f* (*esp LAm*)

wall-eyed ['wɔːl'aɪd] ADJ (= *with white iris*) de ojos incoloros; (= *with squint*) estrábico

wallflower ['wɔːl,flaʊəʳ] N alhelí *m*; ✦**IDIOM to be a ~** comer pavo, ser la fea del baile

wall-mounted ['wɔːl,maʊntɪd] ADJ fijado a la pared

Walloon [wɒ'luːn] Ⓐ ADJ valón
Ⓑ N [1] (= *person*) valón/ona *m/f*
[2] (*Ling*) valón *m*

wallop* ['wɒləp] Ⓐ N [1] (= *blow*) golpe *m* fuerte, golpazo* *m*; **~!** (= *sound*) ¡zas!; **to give sb a ~** pegar fuerte a algn; **it packs a ~*** es muy fuerte, tiene mucho efecto
[2] (*Brit*‡) (= *beer*) cerveza *f*
Ⓑ VT (= *strike*) golpear fuertemente; (= *punish*) dar una paliza a, zurrar*

walloping* ['wɒləpɪŋ] Ⓐ N **to give sb a ~** dar una paliza a algn, zurrar a algn*
Ⓑ ADJ enorme, colosal
Ⓒ ADV **a ~ great portion of ice-cream** una porción enorme de helado

wallow ['wɒləʊ] Ⓐ N **I had a good ~ in the bath** descansé bañándome largamente
Ⓑ VI (*in water, mud*) revolcarse (**in** en); [*boat*] bambolearse; **to ~ in guilt** regodearse *or* deleitarse en el remordimiento; **to ~ in luxury/money** nadar en la opulencia/abundancia

wallpaper ['wɔːl,peɪpəʳ] Ⓐ N [1] (*for walls*) papel *m* pintado
[2] (*Comput*) fondo *m* de escritorio
Ⓑ VT empapelar

Wall Street ['wɔːlstriːt] N (*US*) *calle de la Bolsa y de muchos bancos en Nueva York*; (*fig*) mundo *m* bursátil; **shares rose sharply on ~** las acciones subieron bruscamente en la Bolsa de Nueva York

wall-to-wall ['wɔːltə'wɔːl] Ⓐ ADJ [1] **~ carpeting** moqueta *f*, alfombra *f* de pared a pared
[2] (*fig*) [*football, music etc*] a todas horas; **there were ~ people** había gente a rebosar, estaba abarrotado de gente
Ⓑ ADV **the room was filled ~ with people** la sala estaba atestada *or* repleta de gente

wally* ['wɒlɪ] (*Brit*) N gili* *mf*

walnut ['wɔːlnʌt] Ⓐ N (= *nut*) nuez *f*; (= *tree, wood*) nogal *m*
Ⓑ ADJ (= *wooden*) de nogal
Ⓒ CPD ► **walnut tree** N nogal *m*

walrus ['wɔːlrəs] Ⓐ N (*pl* **walruses** *or* **walrus**) morsa *f*
Ⓑ CPD ► **walrus moustache** N bigotes *mpl* de foca

Walter ['wɔːltəʳ] N Gualterio

waltz [wɔːlts] Ⓐ N vals *m*
Ⓑ VI bailar el vals; **to ~ in/out*** entrar/salir tan fresco*

►**waltz off with*** VI + PREP [1] (*also* **~ away with**) [+ *title, championship, prize*] hacerse fácilmente con
[2] [+ *object, person*] largarse con*; **she ~ed off with my boyfriend** se largó con mi novio*

►**waltz through*** VT + PREP [+ *match, game*] ganar sin mover un dedo

waltzer ['wɔːltsəʳ] N bailarín/ina *m/f* de vals

WAN [wæn] N ABBR (*Comput*) = **wide area network**

wan [wɒn] ADJ [*complexion, face*] pálido; [*light*] tenue, pálido; [*smile*] lánguido; **she was feeling rather ~** se sentía un poco indispuesto

wand [wɒnd] N (= *magic wand*) varita *f* mágica; [*of office*] bastón *m* de mando; *see also* **wave B1**

wander ['wɒndəʳ] Ⓐ N paseo *m*; **to go for** *or* **have a ~** pasearse, dar un paseo, dar una vuelta
Ⓑ VI [1] (*for pleasure*) pasear; [*aimlessly*] deambular, vagar, errar; **we spent the morning ~ing round the old town** pasamos la mañana paseando por el casco antiguo; **they ~ed aimlessly through the streets** iban deambulando *or* vagando por las calles; **to ~ round the shops** curiosear *or* pasearse por las tiendas
[2] (= *stray*) **to ~ from the path** desviarse *or* alejarse del camino; **the sheep had ~ed into the next field** las ovejas se habían metido en el prado de al lado
[3] (*fig*) [*person*] (*in speech*) divagar; **to ~ from** *or* **off the point** salirse del tema; **to let one's mind ~** dejar vagar la imaginación; **his eyes ~ed round the room** paseó la mirada por la habitación; **his attention ~ed for a moment and the milk boiled over** se distrajo *or* despistó un momento y se le salió la leche; **my attention ~ed a bit in the second half of the film** perdí un poco la concentración *or* me distraje *or* me despisté en la segunda mitad de la película
Ⓒ VT [+ *streets, hills*] recorrer, vagar por; **to ~ the world** recorrer el mundo entero; **he had ~ed the seven seas in search of it** (*liter*) había surcado los siete mares en su busca (*liter*)

►**wander about, wander around** VI + ADV deambular

►**wander off** Ⓐ VI + ADV **the children ~ed off into the woods** los niños se alejaron sin rumbo y entraron en el bosque; **don't go ~ing off** no te alejes demasiado
Ⓑ VI + PREP *see* **wander B3**

wanderer ['wɒndərəʳ] N (= *traveller*) viajero/a *m/f*; (*pej*) vagabundo/a *m/f*; (= *tribesman, nomad*) nómada *mf*; **the ~ returns!** (*hum*) ¡ha vuelto el viajero!; **I've always been a ~** nunca he querido establecerme de fijo en un sitio

wandering ['wɒndərɪŋ] ADJ [*person*] errante; [*tribe*] nómada, errante; [*minstrel*] itinerante; [*path, river*] sinuoso; [*eyes, mind*] distraído; **he suffers from ~ hands** (*hum*) es un sobón*

wanderings ['wɒndərɪŋz] NPL (= *travels*) viajes *mpl*, andanzas *fpl*; [*of mind, speech*] divagaciones *fpl*; **let me know if you see one on your ~** avísame si encuentras uno por ahí

wanderlust ['wɒndəlʌst] N pasión *f* de viajar, ansia *f* de ver mundo

wane [weɪn] Ⓐ VI [*moon*] menguar; (*fig*) [*strength*] decaer; [*popularity, power, enthusiasm, interest, support*] disminuir
Ⓑ N **to be on the ~** [*moon*] estar menguando; [*strength*] estar decayendo; [*popularity, support, power, interest*] estar disminuyendo

wangle* ['wæŋgl] Ⓐ VT [+ *job, ticket*] agenciarse; **I've ~d an invitation to the reception** me he agenciado una invitación para la recepción; **he ~d his way in** se las arregló para entrar; **can you ~ me a free ticket?** ¿puedes conseguirme una entrada gratis?
Ⓑ N chanchullo* *m*, truco *m*

wangler* ['wæŋgləʳ] N chanchullero* *m*, trapisondista* *mf*

wangling* ['wæŋglɪŋ] N chanchullos* *mpl*, trucos *mpl*

waning ['weɪnɪŋ] Ⓐ ADJ [*moon*] menguante; (*fig*) [*popularity, power, enthusiasm, interest, support*] decreciente
Ⓑ N [*of moon*] menguante *f*; (*fig*) [*of popularity, power*] disminución *f*, mengua *f*; [*of enthusiasm, interest, support*] disminución *f*

wank** [wæŋk] (*Brit*) Ⓐ N [1] **to have a ~** hacerse una paja** [2] (= *person*) = **wanker**
Ⓑ VI hacerse una paja**

wanker** ['wæŋkəʳ] N (*Brit*) gilipollas** *mf*

wanly ['wɒnlɪ] ADV [*shine*] tenuemente, pálidamente; [*look, smile, say*] lánguidamente

wanna* ['wɒnə] = **want to**

wannabe* ['wɒnəbiː] Ⓐ N **an Elvis ~** un imitador barato de Elvis
Ⓑ ADJ amateur, aspirante

wanness ['wɒnnɪs] N palidez *f*

▼**want** [wɒnt] Ⓐ VT [1] (= *desire, wish for*) [1·1] querer; **I don't ~ anything more to do with him** no quiero tener nada más que ver con él; **I ~ my mummy!** ¡quiero que venga mi mamá!; **he ~s a lot of attention** quiere que le presten mucha atención; **I don't ~ you interfering!** ¡no quiero que te entrometas!; **I've always ~ed a car like this** siempre he querido un coche como éste; **we only ~ the best/what's best for you** sólo queremos lo mejor para ti; **what do you ~ for your birthday?** ¿qué quieres por tu cumpleaños?; **what I ~ from a computer is ...** lo que quiero de un ordenador es ...; **I ~ an explanation from you** quiero que me des una explicación; **she was everything he ~ed in a woman** era todo lo que él quería en una mujer; **food was the last thing I ~ed** comida era lo último que quería; **I know when I'm not ~ed** sé muy bien cuando sobro *or* estoy de más; **where do you ~ the table?** ¿dónde quieres que pongamos la mesa?; **what does he ~ with/of me?** ¿qué quiere de mí?; ✦**IDIOM you've got him where you ~ him** lo tienes donde tú quieres
[1·2] (*with complement*) **I ~ my son alive** quiero a mi hijo vivo; **you ~ her back, don't you?** quieres que vuelva, ¿no?; **I ~ him dead!** ¡lo quiero muerto!; **I ~ her sacked!** ¡quiero que se la despida!, ¡quiero que la despidan!
[1·3] (*with infinitive*) **to ~ to do sth** querer hacer algo; **I was ~ing to leave anyway** de todas formas yo ya quería marcharme; **if you really ~ to know** si de verdad lo quieres saber; **I don't ~ to** no quiero; **to ~ sb to do sth** querer que algn haga algo; **the last thing we ~ is for them to feel obliged to help** lo último que queremos es que se sientan obligados a ayudar; **without ~ing to sound big-headed, I think I'll succeed** no quiero parecer engreído pero pienso que voy a tener éxito; **I wouldn't ~ to hurt their feelings/cause them any problems** no quisiera herir sus sentimientos/causarles ningún problema
[1·4] (*sexually*) **to ~ sb** desear a algn
[2] (= *ask for*) [+ *money*] querer, pedir; **she ~s £500 for the car** quiere *or* pide 500 libras por el coche; **how much do you ~ for it?** ¿cuánto quiere *or* pide?; **you don't ~ much!** (*iro*)

➤ LANGUAGE IN USE: **want A1** 8.3, 8.4

¡anda que no pides nada! (*iro*)

[3] (= *seek*) [*police*] buscar; **"wanted (dead or alive)"** "se busca (vivo o muerto)"; **"wanted: general maid"** "se necesita asistenta"; **he is ~ed for robbery** se le busca por robo; **you're ~ed in the kitchen** te buscan en la cocina; **the boss ~s you in his office** el jefe quiere verte en su oficina; **you're ~ed on the phone** te llaman al teléfono

[4] (= *need, require*) [*person*] necesitar; **children ~ lots of sleep** los niños necesitan *or* requieren muchas horas de sueño; **this car ~s cleaning** a este coche le hace falta una limpieza, a este coche hay que limpiarlo; **he ~s locking up!** está loco de atar*; **that's the last thing I ~!*** ¡sólo me faltaba eso!*; **you ~ to be more careful when you're driving** tienes que tener más cuidado al conducir; **you ~ to see his new boat!** ¡tienes que ver su nuevo barco!; **what you ~ is a good hiding** lo que necesitas *or* te hace falta es una buena paliza*; **what do you ~ with a house that size?** ¿para qué quieres una casa tan grande?

[5] (= *lack*) **the contract ~s only her signature** al contrato sólo le falta su firma; **it only ~ed the parents to come in** sólo faltaba que llegaran los padres

Ⓑ VI [1] (= *wish, desire*) querer; **you're welcome to stay if you ~** te puedes quedar si quieres; **I ~ for you to be happy** (*US*) quiero que seas feliz

[2] (= *lack*) **they will not ~ for money or food** no les faltará ni dinero ni comida; **they ~ for nothing** no les falta de nada; *see also* **waste C1**

Ⓒ N [1] (= *lack*) falta *f*; **it showed a ~ of good manners** demostró una falta de educación; **for ~ of sth** (*at beginning of clause*) a falta de algo; (*at end of clause*) por falta de algo; **for ~ of anything better to do, I decided to go home** a falta de algo mejor que hacer, decidí irme a casa; **I decided to go home for ~ of anything better to do** decidí irme a casa por falta de algo mejor que hacer; **for ~ of a better word** a/por falta de una palabra más apropiada; **he never did become a minister, but it was not for ~ of trying** nunca llegó a ministro, pero no fue por falta de intentarlo

[2] (= *need*) necesidad *f*; **she had servants to attend to her every ~** tenía sirvientes que atendían todas y cada una de sus necesidades; **my ~s are few** necesito poco; **to be in ~ of sth** necesitar algo

[3] (= *poverty*) necesidad *f*, penuria *f*; **to be in ~** estar necesitado; **to live in ~** pasar necesidades, vivir en la penuria

Ⓓ CPD ► **want ad*** N (*US*) anuncio *m* clasificado

►**want in*** VI + ADV [1] (*to house, building, room*) querer entrar (**to** en)

[2] (*on scheme, project*) querer meterse*; **we're playing cards tonight, do you ~ in?** esta noche jugamos a las cartas, ¿te quieres apuntar?; **it's a huge market and every company ~s in** es un mercado enorme y todas las empresas quieren meterse*; **to ~ in on sth** querer participar en algo

►**want out*** VI + ADV [1] (*of house, room*) querer salir [2] **he ~s out** (*of scheme, project, job*) quiere dejarlo; **to ~ out of** [+ *scheme, project, job*] querer dejar; [+ *relationship*] querer dejar, querer terminar con

wanting ['wɒntɪŋ] ADJ **all the applicants proved ~ in some respect** todos los aspirantes resultaron deficientes en algún aspecto; **he was tried and found ~** fue puesto a prueba y le encontraron carencias *or* deficiencias; **he looked at his life and found it ~** examinó su vida y se dio cuenta de que faltaba algo; **to be ~ in sth** carecer de algo

wanton ['wɒntən] ADJ [1] (= *wilful, gratuitous*) [*neglect*] displicente; [*destruction*] sin sentido, gratuito; [*violence*] gratuito

[2] († *pej*) (= *dissolute*) [*woman*] lascivo, libertino; [*behaviour*] disipado, inmoral

[3] (= *unrestrained*) [*spending*] desenfrenado

wantonly ['wɒntənlɪ] ADV [1] (= *wilfully, gratuitously*) [*neglect*] con displicencia; [*destroy*] gratuitamente, sin sentido; [*cruel*] gratuitamente

[2] (= *dissolutely*) lascivamente

wantonness ['wɒntənnɪs] N [1] (= *gratuitousness*) lo gratuito; (= *senselessness*) falta *f* de sentido [2] (= *dissoluteness*) [*of person*] lascivia *f*; [*of behaviour*] disipación *f*, inmoralidad *f*

WAP [wæp] Ⓐ N ABBR (= **Wireless Application Protocol**) WAP *f*

Ⓑ CPD ► **WAP phone** N teléfono *m* WAP

war [wɔːʳ] Ⓐ N guerra *f*; (*fig*) lucha *f*; **the ~ against inflation** la lucha contra la inflación; **to be at ~ (with)** estar en guerra (con); **the period between the ~s** el período de entreguerras; **to declare ~ (on)** declarar la guerra (a); **to go to ~ (with sb) (over sth)** entrar en guerra (con algn) (por algo); **they went off to ~ singing** fueron a la guerra cantando; **the Great War** la Primera Guerra Mundial; **~ to the knife** guerra *f* a muerte; **to make ~ (on)** hacer la guerra (a); **~ of nerves** guerra *f* de nervios; **to wage ~ with sb** hacer la guerra a algn; **~ of words** guerra de palabras; **the First/Second World War** la Primera/Segunda Guerra Mundial; ✦***IDIOM*** **you've been in the ~s!** (*hum*) ¡parece que vienes de la guerra!

Ⓑ VI (*lit*) combatir, luchar (**with** con); **revulsion and guilt ~red within him** (*liter*) la repugnancia y el sentimiento de culpabilidad luchaban en su interior

Ⓒ CPD de guerra ► **war chest** N (*esp US*) *dinero destinado a apoyar una causa* ► **war clouds** NPL nubes *fpl* de guerra ► **war correspondent** N corresponsal *mf* de guerra ► **war crime** N crimen *m* de guerra ► **war criminal** N criminal *mf* de guerra ► **war cry** N grito *m* de guerra ► **war dance** N danza *f* guerrera ► **the war dead** NPL los muertos en campaña ► **war debt** N deuda *f* de guerra ► **war effort** N esfuerzo *m* bélico ► **war fever** N psicosis *f inv* de guerra ► **war footing** N **on a ~ footing** en pie de guerra ► **war game** N (*Mil*) simulacro *m* de guerra; (= *game*) juego *m* de guerra ► **war hero** N héroe *m* de guerra ► **war loan** N empréstito *m* de guerra ► **war material** N material *m* bélico ► **war memorial** N monumento *m* a los caídos ► **War Office** N (*Hist*) Ministerio *m* de Guerra ► **war paint** N pintura *f* de guerra; (*hum*) (= *make-up*) maquillaje *m* ► **war widow** N viuda *f* de guerra ► **the war wounded** NPL los heridos de guerra ► **war zone** N zona *f* de guerra; *see also* **record A5.4**

warble ['wɔːbl] Ⓐ N [*of bird*] trino *m*, gorjeo *m*

Ⓑ VT cantar trinando, cantar gorjeando

Ⓒ VI gorjear, trinar

warbler ['wɔːbləʳ] N (= *bird*) curruca *f*

warbling ['wɔːblɪŋ] N gorjeo *m*

ward [wɔːd] Ⓐ N [1] (*Jur*) (= *person*) pupilo/a *m/f*; **he is her ~** (él) está bajo su tutela; **to make sb a ~ of court** poner a algn bajo la protección *or* el amparo del tribunal

[2] (*Pol*) distrito *m* electoral

[3] (*in hospital*) sala *f*, pabellón *m*

[4] [*of key*] guarda *f*

Ⓑ CPD ► **ward heeler** N (*US Pol*) muñidor *m* ► **ward round** N (*Med*) visita *f* de salas ► **ward sister** N (*Med*) enfermera *f* jefe de sala

►**ward off** VT + ADV [+ *attack*] rechazar; [+ *blow*] parar, desviar; [+ *infection*] protegerse de; [+ *danger*] protegerse contra, conjurar; [+ *evil spirits*] conjurar; **to ~ off the cold** protegerse del frío

...ward [wəd] SUFFIX hacia; **they looked seaward** miraron hacia el mar; **the homeward journey** el viaje de vuelta a casa *or* de regreso

warden ['wɔːdn] N [*of castle*] guardián/ana *m/f*, alcaide† *m*; (*in institution*) encargado/a *m/f*; (*Univ*) rector(a) *m/f*; (*Aut*) (*also* **traffic ~**) controlador(a) *m/f* de estacionamiento; (*also* **church ~**) coadjutor(a) *m/f*; (*US*) [*of prison*] celador(a) *m/f*

warder ['wɔːdəʳ] N (*esp Brit*) celador(a) *m/f*

wardress ['wɔːdrɪs] N celadora *f*

wardrobe ['wɔːdrəʊb] Ⓐ N [1] (= *cupboard*) guardarropa *m*, armario *m* (ropero), ropero *m* (*LAm*) [2] (= *clothes*) vestuario *m*

Ⓑ CPD ► **wardrobe mistress** N (*Theat*) encargada *f* del vestuario ► **wardrobe trunk** N baúl *m* ropero

wardroom ['wɔːdrʊm] N (*Naut*) cámara *f* de oficiales

...wards [wədz] SUFFIX (*esp Brit*) hacia; **they looked seawards** miraron hacia el mar

wardship ['wɔːdʃɪp] N tutela *f*

warehouse ['weəhaʊs] Ⓐ N (*pl* **warehouses** ['weəhaʊzɪz]) almacén *m*, depósito *m*

Ⓑ ['weəhaʊz] VT almacenar

Ⓒ CPD ► **warehouse club** N (*esp US Comm*) economato *m* ► **warehouse manager** N gerente *mf* de almacén ► **warehouse price** N **at ~ prices** a precios de mayorista

warehouseman ['weəhaʊsmən] N (*pl* **warehousemen**) almacenista *m*

warehousing ['weəhaʊzɪŋ] N almacenamiento *m*

wares [weəz] NPL mercancías *fpl*; **to cry one's ~** pregonar sus mercancías

warfare ['wɔːfeəʳ] N (= *fighting*) guerra *f*; (= *techniques*) artes *mpl* militares; **chemical/germ ~** guerra *f* química/bacteriológica; **trench ~** guerra *f* de trincheras

warfarin ['wɔːfərɪn] N warfarina *f*

warhead ['wɔːhed] N [*of torpedo*] cabeza *f* explosiva; [*of rocket*] cabeza *f* de guerra; **nuclear ~** cabeza *f* nuclear

warhorse ['wɔːhɔːs] N caballo *m* de guerra; (*fig*) veterano *m*

warily ['weərɪlɪ] ADV con cautela, cautelosamente; **she answered his questions ~** contestó con cautela *or* cautelosamente a sus preguntas; **she looked at him ~** lo miró con recelo; ✦***IDIOM*** **to tread ~** (*fig*) andar con cuidado *or* cautela

wariness ['weərɪnɪs] N cautela *f*, recelo *m*

Warks ABBR (*Brit*) = **Warwickshire**

warlike ['wɔːlaɪk] ADJ [*activity*] bélico; [*people, tribe*] guerrero, belicoso

warlock ['wɔːlɒk] N brujo *m*, hechicero *m*

warlord ['wɔːlɔːd] N caudillo *m*

warm [wɔːm] Ⓐ ADJ (*compar* **warmer**; *superl* **warmest**) [1] (= *hot*) [*bath, hands, feet*] caliente; [*water*] templado, tibio; [*air*] templado, cálido; [*room, place, weather*] cálido; **to be ~** [*person*] tener calor; **it's very ~ today** hace calor hoy; **to get ~** [*person*] entrar en calor; [*object, surface*] calentarse; **he started jumping to get ~** empezó a saltar para entrar en calor; **come and get ~** ven a calentarte; **it's getting ~er** [*weather*] ya empieza a hacer más calor; **to be getting ~** (*in guessing game*) ir

acercándose a la respuesta; **you're getting ~(er)!** ¡caliente, caliente!; **to keep sb ~** mantener caliente a algn, mantener a algn abrigado; **to keep (o.s.) ~** mantenerse abrigado; **wear thick gloves to keep your hands ~** usa guantes gruesos para mantener las manos calientes; **keep the sauce ~** mantén la salsa caliente; ✦*IDIOM* **to be as ~ as toast** estar bien calentito*
2 (= *thick*) [*clothes*] de abrigo, abrigado (*S. Cone*); **take something ~ to put on** llévate algo de abrigo *or* abrigado para ponerte; **this blanket's nice and ~** esta manta es muy calentita
3 (= *cosy, homely*) [*colour, shade, sound*] cálido
4 (= *kindly*) [*person, smile, face*] simpático, afable, cálido; **the two leaders exchanged ~ greetings** los dos líderes intercambiaron cordiales saludos; **her speech was received with ~ applause** su discurso fue recibido con un caluroso aplauso; **~est congratulations to ...** la más cordial *or* sincera enhorabuena a ...; **~est thanks to ...** mi/nuestro más sincero agradecimiento a ...; **to give sb a ~ welcome** dar a algn una cordial *or* calurosa bienvenida; **with ~est wishes** (*in letter*) con mis/nuestros mejores deseos
Ⓑ VT 1 (= *heat*) [+ *one's hands, feet*] calentarse; **I ~ed my hands on the radiator** me calenté las manos en el radiador; **to ~ o.s.** calentarse; *see also* **cockle**
2 = **warm up B1**
Ⓒ VI = **warm up**
Ⓓ N **the ~: come into the ~!** ¡entra aquí que hace calorcito!*
Ⓔ ADV (*) **to wrap up ~** abrigarse bien
Ⓕ CPD ► **warm front** N (*Met*) frente *m* cálido
► **warm down** VI + ADV (*after exercise*) hacer ejercicios suaves de recuperación (*tras un esfuerzo*)
► **warm over** VT + ADV (*US*) 1 [+ *food*] (re)calentar
2 (*) (*fig*) **it's just a ~ed over version of the measures he suggested last year** simplemente es un refrito de las medidas que sugirió el año pasado*
► **warm through** VT + ADV [+ *food*] (re)calentar
► **warm to** VI + PREP **I began to ~ to him** empecé a encontrarle agradable; **she was beginning to ~ to the idea** estaba empezando a gustarle la idea; **he began to ~ to his subject** *or* **theme** empezó a entusiasmarse con su tema
► **warm up** Ⓐ VI + ADV 1 (= *get warm*) [*person*] entrar en calor; [*room, engine*] calentarse
2 (*fig*) 2·1 [*athlete, singer*] calentarse
2·2 [*party, game*] animarse
Ⓑ VT + ADV 1 [+ *food*] (re)calentar; [+ *engine*] calentar
2 (*fig*) [+ *party, audience*] animar

warm-blooded ['wɔːm'blʌdɪd] ADJ de sangre caliente

warm-down ['wɔːmdaʊn] N ejercicios *mpl* suaves de recuperación (*tras un esfuerzo*)

warmed-up ['wɔːmd'ʌp] ADJ recalentado

warm-hearted ['wɔːm'hɑːtɪd] ADJ cariñoso, afectuoso

warming ['wɔːmɪŋ] Ⓐ ADJ [*drink*] que hace entrar en calor
Ⓑ N 1 recalentamiento *m*; *see also* **global B**
2 (†*) (= *hiding*) zurra* *f*
Ⓒ CPD ► **warming pan** N calentador *m* (de cama)

warmly ['wɔːmlɪ] ADV 1 (= *cosily*) **to be ~ dressed** ir *or* estar bien abrigado; **remember to wrap up ~** acuérdate de abrigarte bien
2 (= *affectionately*) [*greet, smile*] calurosamente, afectuosamente; [*say, speak*] cariñosamente; [*thank*] cordialmente; **he embraced her ~** la abrazó con ternura
3 (= *enthusiastically*) [*congratulate*] efusivamente; [*welcome*] calurosamente; [*endorse, recommend*] sin reservas; **to be ~ applauded** recibir un caluroso aplauso; **the plan was ~ received** el plan fue recibido con entusiasmo
4 [*shine*] con fuerza; **the sun was shining ~** el sol brillaba con fuerza

warmonger ['wɔːˌmʌŋgəʳ] N belicista *mf*

warmongering ['wɔːˌmʌŋgərɪŋ] Ⓐ ADJ belicista
Ⓑ N belicismo *m*

warmth [wɔːmθ] N 1 [*of sun, fire*] calor *m*
2 [*of clothing, blanket*] **a blanket will provide extra ~** una manta proporcionará más abrigo; **wear a jacket for ~** ponte una chaqueta para ir bien abrigado
3 [*of greeting, welcome*] cordialidad *f*; [*of smile*] simpatía *f*, afabilidad *f*

warm-up ['wɔːmʌp] Ⓐ N 1 (*Sport*) precalentamiento *m*, ejercicios *mpl* de calentamiento
2 (= *preparatory activity*) actividad *f* preliminar, preparativos *mpl*
Ⓑ CPD ► **warm-up suit** N (*US*) chandal *m*

➤**warn** [wɔːn] Ⓐ VT 1 (= *put on guard, urge caution to*) advertir; (= *notify, tell*) avisar, advertir; **children must be ~ed about** *or* **of the dangers of smoking** debe advertirse a los niños de los peligros que conlleva fumar; **I did ~ you that this would happen** ya te avisé *or* advertí que esto pasaría; **I must ~ you that my men are armed** debo avisarle *or* advertirle que mis hombres van armados; **we must ~ them that the police are on their way** debemos avisarles *or* advertirles que la policía está de camino; **you have been ~ed!** ¡ya estás avisado!, ¡quedas advertido!; **but, be ~ed, this is not a cheap option** pero, quedas avisado *or* advertido, ésta no es una opción barata
2 (= *counsel*) advertir; **"don't do anything yet," he ~ed** —no hagas nada todavía —advirtió; **to ~ sb to do sth** advertir *or* aconsejar a algn que haga algo; **people have been ~ed to stay indoors** se ha advertido *or* aconsejado a la gente que no salga; **she ~ed me not to go out alone at night** me advirtió *or* me aconsejó que no saliera sola por la noche; **I ~ed you not to interfere** te advertí que no te entrometieras; **to ~ sb against sth** prevenir a algn contra algo; **he ~ed us against complacency** nos previno contra la autocomplacencia; **to ~ sb against doing sth** aconsejar a algn que no haga algo
3 (= *admonish*) **to ~ sb about sth** llamar la atención a algn por algo; **I've ~ed you about your behaviour before** ya te he llamado la atención por tu comportamiento antes
Ⓑ VI **to ~ about** *or* **of sth** advertir de algo; **he ~ed against complacency** advirtió de las consecuencias de la autocomplacencia; **some doctors ~ against vitamin supplements during pregnancy** algunos médicos desaconsejan el consumo de suplementos vitamínicos durante el embarazo
► **warn away** VT + ADV **a lighthouse was built to ~ sailors away from the area** se construyó un faro para advertir a los marineros que se mantuvieran alejados de la zona; **analysts ~ us away from drawing any conclusions** los analistas nos advierten que no intentemos sacar conclusiones
► **warn off** Ⓐ VT + ADV **he pressed for an investigation but was ~ed off** presionó para que se llevara a cabo una investigación, pero le advirtieron que no lo hiciera *or* se lo desaconsejaron; **the dogs ~ed the intruder off** los perros ahuyentaron al intruso
Ⓑ VT + PREP **he ~ed the children off the grass** advirtió a los niños que no pisaran el césped; **to ~ sb off doing sth** advertir a algn que no haga algo; **I was ~ed off trying to help her** me advirtieron que no intentara ayudarla

warning ['wɔːnɪŋ] Ⓐ N (= *caution*) advertencia *f*; (= *advance notice*) aviso *m*, advertencia *f*; **this is a final ~** esta es la última advertencia; **let me just add a note of ~** quisiera añadir una nota de advertencia; **to be a ~ to sb** ser una advertencia para algn; **let this be a ~ to you** que te sirva de advertencia; **his employer gave him a ~ about lateness** el patrón le advirtió que no debía seguir llegando tarde; **his heart attack was a ~** su ataque al corazón fue un aviso *or* una advertencia; **they only had five minutes' ~ before the bomb went off** les dieron un aviso sólo cinco minutos antes de que la bomba hiciese explosión, sólo les avisaron *or* advirtieron cinco minutos antes de que la bomba hiciese explosión; **you could have given me a bit more ~** me podrías haber avisado *or* advertido con más tiempo; **without (any) ~** sin previo aviso; *see also* **gale B**, **word A1**, **advance D**, **early C**, **fair[1] A2**
Ⓑ ADJ [*sign, signal*] de aviso, de advertencia; [*look, label*] de advertencia; **to sound a ~ note** (*fig*) dar una señal de advertencia; **the ~ signs of depression** los indicios de la depresión
Ⓒ CPD ► **warning bell** N ✦*IDIOM* **to set off ~ bells** enviar señales de alarma ► **warning device** N dispositivo *m* de alarma ► **warning light** N señal *f* luminosa ► **warning shot** N (*lit*) disparo *m* de advertencia; **to deliver** *or* **fire a ~ shot** (*fig*) hacer una advertencia ► **warning triangle** N (*Aut*) triángulo *m* de advertencia

warp [wɔːp] Ⓐ N 1 (*in weaving*) urdimbre *f*
2 [*in wood*] alabeo *m*, comba *f*
Ⓑ VT 1 [+ *wood*] alabear, combar
2 (*fig*) [+ *mind*] pervertir
Ⓒ VI [*wood*] alabearse, combarse

warpath ['wɔːpɑːθ] N **to be on the ~** (*lit*) estar en pie de guerra; (*) (*fig*) estar dispuesto a armar un lío*

warped [wɔːpt] ADJ 1 [*wood*] alabeado, combado
2 (*fig*) [*mind, sense of humour*] pervertido

warping ['wɔːpɪŋ] N [*of wood*] deformación *f*, alabeo *m*; (*Aer*) torsión *f*

warplane ['wɔːpleɪn] N avión *m* de combate

warrant ['wɒrənt] Ⓐ N 1 (= *justification*) justificación *f*
2 (*Comm, Fin*) (= *certificate, bond*) cédula *f*, certificado *m*; (= *guarantee*) garantía *f*
3 (*for travel*) (= *permission*) autorización *f*; (= *permit*) permiso *m*
4 (*Jur*) (*for seizure of goods*) mandamiento *m* judicial; (*also* **search ~**) orden *f* de registro; (*also* **arrest ~**) orden *f* de detención; **there is a ~ out for his arrest** se ha ordenado su detención; *see also* **death B**
Ⓑ VT 1 (= *justify, merit*) merecer; **his complaint ~s further investigation** su queja merece una investigación más a fondo; **her condition did not ~ calling the doctor** su condición no justificaba llamar al médico; **the facts do not ~ it** los hechos no lo justifican
2 (*Comm*) (= *guarantee*) garantizar
3 (= *assure*) asegurar, garantizar; **he didn't do it legally, I'll ~ (you)** no lo hizo por la

➤ LANGUAGE IN USE: **warn A** 2.3

vía legal, te lo aseguro *or* garantizo

Ⓒ CPD ► **warrant officer** N (*Mil*) suboficial *mf*; (*Naut*) contramaestre *mf*

warrantable ['wɒrəntəbl] ADJ justificable

warranted ['wɒrəntɪd] ADJ [1] (= *justified*) [*action, remark*] justificado; **that wasn't ~!** ¡ese comentario está de sobra!

[2] (*Comm*) [*goods*] garantizado; **"warranted 18 carat gold"** "certificado de oro de 18 quilates"

warrantor ['wɒrəntɔːʳ] N garante *mf*

warranty ['wɒrəntɪ] N (*Comm*) garantía *f*

warren ['wɒrən] N [1] (*also* **rabbit ~**) madriguera *f* (de conejos)

[2] (*fig*) (= *place, area*) laberinto *m*; (= *house*) conejera *f*; **it is a ~ of little streets** es un laberinto de callejuelas

warring ['wɔːrɪŋ] ADJ [*interests*] opuesto; [*nations, armies*] en guerra; [*factions, parties*] enfrentado; [*parents, families*] enfrentado; [*emotions*] contradictorio, encontrado

warrior ['wɒrɪəʳ] N guerrero/a *m/f*

Warsaw ['wɔːsɔː] Ⓐ N Varsovia *f*

Ⓑ CPD ► **Warsaw Pact** N Pacto *m* de Varsovia

warship [wɔːʃɪp] N buque *m or* barco *m* de guerra

wart [wɔːt] N (*Med*) verruga *f*; ✦*IDIOM* **~s and all** con todas sus imperfecciones

warthog ['wɔːthɒg] N jabalí *m* verrugoso, facochero *m*

wartime ['wɔːtaɪm] Ⓐ N tiempo *m* de guerra; **in ~** en tiempos de guerra

Ⓑ CPD [*regulations, rationing*] de guerra

war-torn ['wɔː,tɔːn] ADJ destrozado por la guerra, devastado por la guerra

warty ['wɔːtɪ] ADJ verrugoso

war-weary ['wɔː,wɪərɪ] ADJ cansado de la guerra

wary ['weərɪ] ADJ (*compar* **warier**, *superl* **wariest**) [*person*] receloso; [*manner*] cauteloso, precavido; **she seems very ~** parece estar muy recelosa; **banks are becoming increasingly ~** los bancos están volviéndose cada vez más precavidos; **to keep a ~ eye on sth/sb**: **I kept a ~ eye on the gathering stormclouds** observaba con cierta preocupación los nubarrones que se acercaban; **the president had to keep a ~ eye on the radical faction of his party** el presidente tenía que vigilar de cerca al sector más radical de su partido; **he gave her a ~ look** la miró con recelo; **the question made her ~** la pregunta la puso en guardia; **to be ~ of sth/sb** desconfiar de algo/algn, no fiarse de algo/algn; **to be ~ of strangers** desconfiar *or* no fiarse de los desconocidos; **they were very ~ of his violent temper** se mostraban muy cautelosos debido a su temperamento violento

was [wɒz, wəz] PT *of* **be**

wash [wɒʃ] Ⓐ N [1] (= *act of washing*) **that jacket could do with a ~** a esa chaqueta no le vendría mal un lavado; **to give sth a ~** (*gen*) lavar algo; **to give one's hands/face a ~** lavarse las manos/la cara; **to have a ~** lavarse; *see also* **brush-up**

[2] (*in washing-machine*) lavado *m*; **this setting gives you a cool ~** en esta posición la máquina hace un lavado en frío

[3] (= *laundry*) colada *f*; **I do a big ~ on Mondays** los lunes hago una colada grande; **I had two ~es on the line** tenía dos coladas en el tendedero; **your jeans are in the ~** (= *being washed*) tus vaqueros se están lavando; (= *with dirty clothes*) tus vaqueros están con la ropa sucia; **the colours run in the ~** los colores destiñen con el lavado; ✦*IDIOM* **it'll all come out in the ~** al final, todo se arreglará

[4] [*of ship, plane*] estela *f*

[5] [*of paint, distemper*] capa *f*; (*Art*) aguada *f*

Ⓑ VT [1] (= *clean*) [+ *clothes, car*] lavar; [+ *floor*] fregar; **to ~ the dishes** fregar (los platos), lavar los platos; **the rain had ~ed the verandah clean** la lluvia había limpiado la terraza; **to get ~ed** lavarse; **to ~ one's hands/hair** lavarse las manos/el pelo; ✦*IDIOMS* **to ~ one's hands of sth** lavarse las manos de algo, desentenderse de algo; **to ~ one's hands of sb** despreocuparse de algn; *see also* **linen A2**

[2] (= *paint*) **to ~ the walls with distemper** dar una mano de pintura (al temple) a las paredes

[3] (*liter*) (= *lap*) [*sea, waves*] bañar; **an island ~ed by a blue sea** una isla bañada por el mar azul

[4] (= *sweep, carry*) arrastrar; **the sea ~ed it ashore** el mar lo arrastró hasta la playa; **the house was ~ed downstream** la casa fue arrastrada río abajo; **he was ~ed overboard** cayó del barco arrastrado por las olas

Ⓒ VI [1] (= *have a wash*) lavarse; (= *wash the dishes*) fregar; (= *do the washing*) lavar (la) ropa; **I'll ~ and you dry** yo friego y tú secas

[2] (= *be washable*) [*fabric*] **will it ~?** ¿se puede lavar?; **man-made fabrics usually ~ well** los tejidos sintéticos suelen lavarse bien; ✦*IDIOM* **that excuse won't ~!*** ¡esa excusa no cuela!*

[3] [*sea, waves*] **the sea ~ed against the cliffs** el mar batía contra los acantilados; **small waves gently ~ed over the coral reef** las pequeñas olas bañaban suavemente el arrecife de coral; **the oil ~ed ashore quite near here** el petróleo fue arrastrado a la orilla bastante cerca de aquí

Ⓓ CPD ► **wash bag** N (*US*) neceser *m* ► **wash cycle** N ciclo *m* de lavado ► **wash house** N lavadero *m* ► **wash leather** N gamuza *f* ► **wash sale** N (*US*) venta *f* ficticia

►**wash away** Ⓐ VT + ADV [1] [+ *bridge, house, vehicle*] llevarse por delante, arrastrar; [+ *dirt*] quitar (lavando); [+ *taste*] quitar; **several cars were ~ed away in the flood** durante la inundación las aguas se llevaron varios coches por delante, durante la inundación varios coches fueron arrastrados por las aguas

[2] (*fig*) **Christ who ~es away the sins of the world** Cristo que quita los pecados del mundo

Ⓑ VI + ADV **terraces prevent the soil from ~ing away** los bancales evitan que el agua se lleve la tierra

►**wash down** VT + ADV [1] (= *clean*) [+ *walls, car*] lavar

[2] (= *take with*) **he ~ed the tablets down with a glass of water** se tragó las pastillas con ayuda de un vaso de agua; **a cheese sandwich ~ed down with a bottle of beer** un bocadillo de queso acompañado con una botella de cerveza

►**wash off** Ⓐ VT + ADV [+ *stain, dirt*] quitar (lavando)

Ⓑ VI + ADV (= *disappear*) quitarse, limpiarse; **it ~es off easily** se quita *or* se limpia fácilmente; **it won't ~ off** no se quita *or* no sale al lavarlo

►**wash out** Ⓐ VT + ADV [1] [+ *stain*] quitar (lavando); [+ *container*] lavar; [+ *paintbrush*] lavar, enjuagar; **you ought to ~ your mouth out with soap!** ¡con jabón tendrían que lavarte a ti la boca!

[2] (*Sport*) **the game was ~ed out** el partido fue cancelado debido a la lluvia; **rain ~ed out the last four games** los últimos cuatro partidos tuvieron que cancelarse debido a la lluvia

[3] **to feel ~ed out** sentirse rendido *or* agotado; **to look ~ed out** tener aspecto de estar rendido *or* agotado

Ⓑ VI + ADV [1] (= *disappear*) [*stain, mark*] quitarse, limpiarse; **the paint will ~ out** la pintura saldrá *or* se limpiará al lavarlo

[2] (= *fade*) [*dye, colour*] descolorarse, desteñirse; **the colours won't ~ out** los colores no se descolorán *or* desteñirán (con el lavado)

►**wash over** VI + PREP [1] (= *take hold of*) invadir; **a feeling of relief ~ed over her** la invadió una sensación de alivio; **waves of panic ~ed over her** se sentía invadida por oleadas de pánico

[2] (= *pass by*) **I just let all this criticism ~ over me** todas estas críticas simplemente me resbalan

[3] (= *envelop*) **relax and let the music ~ over you** relájese y déjese llevar por la música; *see also* **wash C3**

►**wash through** VT + ADV [+ *clothes*] lavar rápidamente

►**wash up** Ⓐ VI + ADV [1] (*Brit*) (= *wash dishes*) fregar (los platos), lavar los platos

[2] (*US*) (= *have a wash*) lavarse

[3] (= *come ashore*) **it ~ed up with the tide** lo trajo la marea, la marea lo arrastró a la playa

Ⓑ VT + ADV [1] (*Brit*) [+ *dishes*] fregar, lavar

[2] (*onto beach*) arrastrar; **the sea ~ed it up** el mar lo arrastró a la playa; **a body had been ~ed up on the beach** un cuerpo había aparecido en la playa, arrastrado por el mar

[3] (*) ✦*IDIOM* **to be all ~ed up** [*person, marriage*] estar acabado

Wash. ABBR (*US*) = **Washington**

washable ['wɒʃəbl] ADJ lavable

wash-and-wear ['wɒʃən'weəʳ] ADJ que no necesita planchado, de lava y pon

washbasin ['wɒʃbeɪsn] N lavabo *m*, lavamanos *m inv*, lavatorio *m* (*S. Cone*); (= *bowl*) palangana *f*, jofaina *f*

washboard ['wɒʃbɔːd] N tabla *f* de lavar; (*US*) rodapié *m*, zócalo *m*

washbowl ['wɒʃbəʊl] N (*esp US*) = **washbasin**

washcloth ['wɒʃklɒθ] N (*US*) paño *m* para lavarse, manopla *f*

washday ['wɒʃdeɪ] N día *m* de lavado *or* de colada

washed-out* ['wɒʃtaʊt] ADJ (= *faded, pale*) [*fabric*] decolorado, desteñido; [*colour*] pálido; **his ~ blue eyes** sus pálidos ojos azules

washed-up* [,wɒʃt'ʌp] ADJ *see* **wash up B3**

washer ['wɒʃəʳ] N [1] (*Tech*) arandela *f*

[2] (= *washing machine*) lavadora *f*; (= *dishwasher*) lavavajillas *m inv*

washer-dryer ['wɔːʃə'draɪəʳ], **washer-drier** N lavadora-secadora *f*

washerwoman ['wɒʃə,wʊmən] N (*pl* **washerwomen**) lavandera *f*

wash-hand basin ['wɒʃ,hænd,beɪsn] N lavabo *m*, lavamanos *m inv*, lavatorio *m* (*S. Cone*)

washing ['wɒʃɪŋ] Ⓐ N [1] (= *act*) lavado *m*; **some fabrics don't stand up to repeated ~s** algunos tejidos no aguantan constantes lavados

[2] (= *clothes*) (*dirty*) ropa *f* sucia; (*hung to dry*) colada *f*; **to take in ~** [*woman*] ser lavandera

Ⓑ CPD ► **washing day** N día *m* de lavado, día *m* de colada ► **washing line** N tendedero *m* ► **washing machine** N lavadora *f* ► **washing powder** N jabón *m* en polvo, detergente *m* ► **washing soda** N sosa *f*, carbonato *m* sódico

Washington ['wɒʃɪŋtən] N Washington *m*

washing-up ['wɒʃɪŋ'ʌp] Ⓐ N (= *act*) fregado *m*; (= *dishes*) platos *mpl* (para fregar); **to do the ~** fregar (los platos), lavar los platos
Ⓑ CPD ► **washing-up bowl** N barreño *m*, palangana *f* ► **washing-up liquid** N lavavajillas *m inv*

washout* ['wɒʃaʊt] N **it was a ~** [*match*] se suspendió debido a la lluvia; [*plan, party etc*] fue un fracaso *or* desastre; **you're a ~ as a father!** ¡como padre eres un desastre!

washrag ['wɒʃræg] N (*US*) [1] (= *dishcloth*) paño *m* de cocina
[2] (= *flannel*) = **washcloth**

washroom ['wɒʃrʊm] N servicios *mpl*, aseos *mpl*, baño *m*

washstand ['wɒʃstænd] N lavabo *m*, lavamanos *m inv*

washtub ['wɒʃtʌb] N (= *container*) tina *f* de lavar; (= *bath*) bañera *f*

washy ['wɒʃɪ] ADJ (*of food, drink*) aguado

wasn't ['wɒznt] = **was not**

WASP [wɒsp] N ABBR (*US**) = **White Anglo-Saxon Protestant**

> **WASP**
>
> *La expresión* **WASP** *o* **White Anglo-Saxon Protestant** *se usa para referirse a los norteamericanos originarios del norte de Europa. Esta expresión fue acuñada en los años sesenta por E. Digby Baltzell, un escritor de Philadelphia. Es un término peyorativo para los miembros de este grupo étnico y religioso, a los que se considera como los más poderosos, privilegiados e influyentes en Estados Unidos. Este término también se utiliza por extensión para hacer referencia a toda persona blanca de clase media descendiente de los primeros colonos y que cree en los valores tradicionales estadounidenses.*

wasp [wɒsp] Ⓐ N avispa *f*; **~s' nest** (*also fig*) avispero *m*
Ⓑ CPD ► **wasp waist** N (*fig*) talle *m* de avispa

waspish ['wɒspɪʃ] ADJ [*character, person*] irritable, irascible; [*remark*] mordaz, punzante

waspishly ['wɒspɪʃlɪ] ADV [*remark*] mordazmente

wasp-waisted ['wɒsp'weɪstɪd] ADJ (*fig*) con talle de avispa

wassail†† ['wɒseɪl] Ⓐ N (= *drink*) cerveza *f* especiada; (= *festivity*) juerga *f*, fiesta *f* de borrachos
Ⓑ VI beber mucho

wast†† [wɒst] PT (*thou form*) *of* **be**

wastage ['weɪstɪdʒ] N (= *loss*) desperdicio *m*; (= *amount wasted*) pérdidas *fpl*; (*from container*) merma *f*; (= *wear and tear*) desgaste *m*; **the country cannot afford this ~ of human resources** el país no puede permitirse este desperdicio de los recursos humanos; **there is a very high ~ rate among students** existe un porcentaje muy elevado de estudiantes que no terminan sus estudios; **the ~ rate among entrants to the profession** el porcentaje de los que abandonan la profesión poco tiempo después de ingresar en ella; *see also* **natural C**

waste [weɪst] Ⓐ N [1] (= *misuse*) desperdicio *m*, derroche *m*; **I hate ~** odio el desperdicio *or* el derroche; **what a ~!** ¡qué desperdicio *or* derroche!; **her death is a terrible ~** su muerte es una terrible pérdida; **there was no ~ on that meat** esa carne no tenía desperdicio; **an effort to locate and eliminate government ~** una campaña para identificar y eliminar las áreas de ineficacia en el gobierno; **to go to ~** echarse a perder, desperdiciarse; **it's a ~ of money** es dinero perdido, es tirar *or* derrochar el dinero; **it's a ~ of time** es una pérdida de tiempo; **it's a ~ of effort** es un esfuerzo inútil; **that man's a ~ of space!*** ¡ese hombre es un inútil!*
[2] (= *rubbish*) basura *f*, desperdicios *mpl*; (= *waste material, substance*) desechos *mpl*, residuos *mpl*; **household ~** basura *f* doméstica; **human ~** excrementos *mpl*; **nuclear ~** desechos *mpl or* residuos *mpl* nucleares; **toxic ~** desechos *mpl or* residuos *mpl* tóxicos
[3] (= *leftover material*) material *m* sobrante
[4] **wastes**, **the barren ~s of the Sahara** las áridas y baldías inmensidades del Sáhara
Ⓑ VT [1] (= *use inefficiently, squander*) [+ *water, electricity, gas*] derrochar; [+ *money*] malgastar, derrochar; [+ *time*] perder; [+ *life*] echar a perder; [+ *space, opportunity*] desaprovechar, desperdiciar; [+ *food*] desperdiciar, echar a perder; [+ *talent*] desaprovechar; **I ~d a whole day on that journey** perdí un día entero haciendo ese viaje; **don't ~ your time trying to persuade her** no pierdas el tiempo intentando persuadirla; **to ~ no time in doing sth** no tardar en hacer algo; **don't ~ your efforts on him** no derroches tus esfuerzos *or* energías con él; **all my efforts were ~d** todos mis esfuerzos fueron inútiles; **sarcasm is ~d on him** con él el sarcasmo es inútil; **caviar is ~d on him** no sabe apreciar el caviar; **nothing is ~d** no se desperdicia nada, no se echa a perder nada; ✦*IDIOM* **you're wasting your breath!** ¡estás gastando saliva!
[2] (= *weaken*) [+ *muscles*] atrofiar; **cancer was wasting his body** el cáncer lo estaba consumiendo *or* debilitando
[3] (*US**) (= *kill*) cargarse*, liquidar*
Ⓒ VI [1] ✦*PROV* **~ not, want not** quien no malgasta no pasa necesidades
[2] = **waste away**
Ⓓ ADJ [1] (= *for disposal*) [*material*] de desecho; [*gas, oil*] residual
[2] (= *leftover*) [*paper, fabric*] sobrante; [*heat*] residual
[3] (= *unused*) [*ground*] baldío, yermo
[4] **to lay ~** [+ *country, area, town*] devastar, asolar; **to lay ~ to sth** devastar algo, asolar algo
Ⓔ CPD ► **waste disposal** N (*industrial*) eliminación *f* de los desechos *or* residuos; [*of household waste*] eliminación *f* de la basura doméstica; (= *device*) = **waste disposal unit** ► **waste disposal unit** N triturador *m* de basura ► **waste heat** N calor *m* residual ► **waste management** N tratamiento *m* de desechos, tratamiento *m* de residuos ► **waste material** N material *m* de desecho ► **waste matter** N (*industrial*) residuos *mpl*; (*from body*) excrementos *mpl* ► **waste paper** N papel *m* de desecho ► **waste pipe** N tubería *f* de desagüe ► **waste products** NPL (*industrial*) residuos *mpl*; (*from body*) excrementos *mpl* ► **waste water** N aguas *fpl* residuales

►**waste away** VI + ADV [*person*] consumirse; [*muscles*] atrofiarse; **you're not exactly wasting away** (*iro*) no es que te hayas consumido precisamente

wastebasket ['weɪstbɑːskɪt] N (*US*) cesto *m* de los papeles, papelera *f*

waste-bin ['weɪstbɪn] N (*Brit*) cubo *m* de la basura

wasted ['weɪstɪd] ADJ [1] (= *lost, useless*) [*opportunity*] desaprovechado, desperdiciado; [*effort*] inútil; [*years*] perdido; **at least it hadn't been an entirely ~ day** por lo menos no había sido un día completamente perdido; **I'm afraid you've had a ~ journey** me temo que has hecho un viaje inútil *or* en vano; **a vote for them is a ~ vote** votar por ellos es desaprovechar el voto
[2] (= *thin*) [*person*] consumido; [*muscle*] atrofiado; [*arm, leg, hand*] atrofiado, inútil
[3] (*) [3·1] (*from drugs*) destrozado
[3·2] (*from drink*) borracho; **to get ~** emborracharse

wasteful ['weɪstfʊl] ADJ [*person*] despilfarrador, derrochador; [*process, method*] antieconómico; [*expenditure*] pródigo, excesivo; **to be ~ with sth** despilfarrar algo, desperdiciar algo; **the government is ~ of taxpayers' money** el gobierno despilfarra *or* derrocha los impuestos de los contribuyentes; **war is ~ of human lives** la guerra supone un desperdicio de vidas humanas

wastefully ['weɪstfəlɪ] ADV [*use*] antieconómicamente, excesivamente

wastefulness ['weɪstfʊlnɪs] N [*of war*] desperdicio *m*; [*of system*] derroche *m*, despilfarro *m*; [*of person*] falta *f* de economía, prodigalidad *f*

wasteland ['weɪstlænd] N [1] (*undeveloped*) terreno *m* baldío *or* yermo, tierra *f* baldía *or* yerma; (*uncultivated*) erial *m*; **industrial ~** terreno *m* industrial baldío
[2] (*fig*) desierto *m*; **a cultural ~** un desierto cultural

wastepaper basket [,weɪst'peɪpə,bɑːskɪt], **wastepaper bin** [,weɪst'peɪpəbɪn] N cesto *m* de los papeles, papelera *f*

waster ['weɪstəʳ] N [1] (= *good-for-nothing*) gandul *mf*
[2] (= *spendthrift*) derrochador(a) *m/f*

wasting ['weɪstɪŋ] ADJ [*disease*] debilitante; [*asset*] amortizable

wastrel† ['weɪstrəl] N gandul *mf*, derrochador(a) *m/f*

watch¹ [wɒtʃ] N (= *wristwatch*) reloj (de pulsera) *m*; (= *pocket watch*) reloj de bolsillo, leontina *f* (*frm*); **what does your ~ say?** ¿qué hora tienes?

watch² [wɒtʃ] Ⓐ N [1] (= *vigilance*) vigilancia *f*; **to keep ~** hacer guardia, vigilar; **to keep ~ for sth/sb** estar al acecho de algo/algn; **to keep a (close) ~ on sth/sb** (*lit*) vigilar algo/a algn (de cerca); **our task was to keep a ~ on the suspect** nuestra tarea consistía en vigilar al sospechoso *or* mantener al sospechoso bajo vigilancia; **US officials have been keeping a close ~ on the situation** los representantes del gobierno estadounidense han estado siguiendo la situación de cerca; **I keep a close ~ on my expenditure** controlo mucho los gastos; **to be on the ~ for danger** estar atento *or* alerta por si hay peligro; **can you keep a ~ out for Daphne?** ¿puedes estar al tanto para ver cuándo viene Daphne?; **to keep ~ over sth/sb** (= *keep a check on*) vigilar algo/a algn; (= *look after*) cuidar algo/a algn
[2] (= *period of duty*) guardia *f*; **you take the first ~** monta *or* haz tú la primera guardia; **the long ~es of the night** (*liter*) las largas vigilias; **officer of the ~** oficial *mf* de guardia; **to be on ~** estar de guardia, hacer guardia; *see also* **night B**
[3] (= *guard*) [3·1] (*Mil*) (= *individual*) centinela *mf*, guardia *mf*; (= *pair, group*) guardia *f*
[3·2] (*Naut*) (= *individual*) vigía *mf*; (= *pair, group*) guardia *f*, vigía *f*
[3·3] (†) (= *watchman*) **the night ~** (*in streets, flats*) el sereno; (*in factory*) el vigilante nocturno
Ⓑ VT [1] (= *view, spectate at*) [+ *television, programme, game, play*] ver; **some children ~**

too much television algunos niños ven demasiada televisión

2 (= *observe, look at*) (*gen*) mirar; (*more attentively*) observar; **Sue was ~ing me curiously** Sue me miraba/observaba con curiosidad; **now ~ this closely** ahora observen esto detenidamente; **~ what I do** mira/observa lo que hago; **~ how I do it** mira/observa cómo lo hago; **to ~ sth/sb do sth: we ~ed the car turn the corner and disappear from view** vimos cómo el coche torcía la esquina y desaparecía de nuestra vista, vimos al coche torcer la esquina y desaparecer de nuestra vista; **she ~ed me clean the gun** miraba/observaba cómo limpiaba yo la pistola; **just ~ him run!** ¡mira cómo corre!; **"you can't do that" — "just you ~ (me)!"** —no puedes hacer eso —¿que no? ¡ya verás (como puedo)!; **to ~ sth/sb doing sth: I ~ed the gulls hovering overhead** miraba/observaba las gaviotas cerniéndose en lo alto; ✦*IDIOMS* **to ~ the clock** estar pendiente del reloj; **to ~ sb like a hawk** no quitar el ojo *or* la vista de encima a algn; **it's about as exciting as ~ing paint dry** *or* **grass grow** es para morirse de aburrimiento; ✦*PROV* **a ~ed pot** *or* **kettle never boils** quien espera desespera

3 (= *mind*) [+ *children, luggage, shop*] cuidar; [+ *soup, frying pan*] echar un ojo a; **~ that knife/your head/your language!** ¡(ten) cuidado con ese cuchillo/la cabeza/esas palabrotas!; **~ your speed** ten cuidado con la velocidad, atención a la velocidad; **~ you don't burn yourself** ten cuidado de no quemarte; **~ he does his homework** mira de que haga los deberes; **~ how you go!** ¡ve con cuidado!; **~ what you're doing!** ¡cuidado con lo que haces!; **he wasn't ~ing where he was going** no miraba por donde iba; **~ it!** (= *careful!*) ¡ojo!*, ¡cuidado!, ¡abusado! (*Mex**); (*threatening*) ¡cuidadito!*; **to ~ one's step** (*lit, fig*) ir con cuidado

4 (= *be mindful of*) [+ *weight, health*] cuidar; [+ *time*] estar pendiente de; **I have to ~ what I eat** tengo que tener cuidado con lo que como; **we shall have to ~ our spending** tendremos que vigilar *or* tener cuidado con los gastos

5 (= *monitor*) [+ *situation, developments*] seguir; [+ *case*] seguir, vigilar; [+ *suspect, house, sb's movements*] vigilar; **we are being ~ed** nos están vigilando; **Big Brother is ~ing you** el Gran Hermano te vigila; **he needs ~ing** hay que vigilarlo; **a new actor to be ~ed** un nuevo actor muy prometedor; **~ this space** (*lit*) estén pendientes, les mantendremos informados; **"so is the row over?" — "~ this space"** —¿se ha terminado la pelea? —eso habrá que verlo

Ⓒ VI **1** (= *observe*) mirar; (*attentively*) observar; **somebody was ~ing at the window** alguien estaba mirando/observando desde la ventana; **he could only sit and ~ as his team lost 2-0** no pudo hacer más que sentarse y ver como su equipo perdía 2 a 0

2 (= *wait, be alert*) **I was ~ing for the plumber** estaba atento esperando a que llegara el fontanero; **he's ~ing to see what you're going to do** está pendiente de lo que vas a hacer

3 (= *keep watch*) **to ~ by sb's bedside** velar a algn

Ⓓ CPD ► **Watch Night** N (*in Protestant church*) Nochevieja *f* ► **watch night service** N misa *f* de fin de año

►**watch out** VI + ADV tener cuidado, ir con cuidado; **you'll get fat if you don't ~ out** te pondrás gordo como no tengas cuidado; **~ out!** (= *be careful*) ¡(ten) cuidado!, ¡abusado! (*Mex**); (*threatening*) ¡cuidadito!; **~ out for thieves** cuidado con los ladrones; **to ~ out for trouble** estar alerta *or* al acecho por si hay problemas

►**watch over** VI + PREP **1** (= *look after*) [+ *person*] velar por; [+ *sb's rights, safety*] velar por, mirar por; **God is ~ing over me** Dios vela por mí; **to ~ over sb's interests** velar *or* mirar por los intereses de algn

2 (= *monitor*) supervisar

3 (= *guard*) vigilar

watchable [ˈwɒtʃəbl] ADJ [*programme*] que se deja ver; **the film is eminently ~** la película es sumamente entretenida

watchband [ˈwɒtʃbænd] N (*esp US*) pulsera *f* de reloj, correa *f* de reloj

watchcase [ˈwɒtʃkeɪs] N caja *f* de reloj

watchdog [ˈwɒtʃdɒg] Ⓐ N **1** (= *guard dog*) perro *m* guardián

2 (*fig*) (= *person*) guardián/ana *m/f*; (= *organization*) organismo *m* protector; **a consumer ~** un organismo que protege los intereses del consumidor

Ⓑ CPD ► **watchdog committee** N comisión *f* protectora

watcher [ˈwɒtʃəʳ] N [*of situation*] observador(a) *m/f*; [*of event*] espectador(a) *m/f*; (*pej*) mirón/ona *m/f*; **China ~** especialista *mf* en asuntos chinos, sinólogo/a *m/f*; **royal ~** *periodista que escribe sobre la familia real*; *see also* **birdwatcher, weight watcher**

watchful [ˈwɒtʃfʊl] ADJ [*eyes, face*] atento; (*stronger*) vigilante; **to be ~ (for sth)** estar atento (a algo); (*stronger*) mantener una actitud vigilante (ante algo); **to keep a ~ eye on sth/sb** vigilar algo/a algn de cerca; **under the ~ eye of** bajo la atenta mirada de, bajo la mirada vigilante de

watchfully [ˈwɒtʃfəlɪ] ADV vigilantemente

watchfulness [ˈwɒtʃfʊlnɪs] N vigilancia *f*

watchglass [ˈwɒtʃglɑːs] N cristal *m* de reloj

watchmaker [ˈwɒtʃˌmeɪkəʳ] N relojero/a *m/f*; **~'s (shop)** relojería *f*

watchman [ˈwɒtʃmən] N (*pl* **watchmen**) (= *security guard*) guardián *m*, vigilante *m*; (*also* **night ~**) (*in factory*) vigilante *m* nocturno; (*in street*) sereno *m*

watchstem [ˈwɒtʃstəm] N (*US*) cuerda *f*

watchstrap [ˈwɒtʃstræp] N correa *f* de reloj

watchtower [ˈwɒtʃˌtaʊəʳ] N atalaya *f*, torre *f* de vigilancia

watchword [ˈwɒtʃwɜːd] N (*Mil, Pol*) contraseña *f*; (= *motto*) lema *m*, consigna *f*

water [ˈwɔːtəʳ] Ⓐ N **1** agua *f*; **to back ~** ciar; **bottled ~** agua *f* mineral; **by ~** por mar; **fresh ~** agua *f* dulce; **hard ~** agua *f* dura; **high ~** marea *f* alta; **on land and ~** por tierra y por mar; **low ~** marea *f* baja; **salt ~** agua *f* salada; **soft ~** agua *f* blanda; **to turn on the ~** ◊ **turn the ~ on** (*at main*) hacer correr el agua; (*at tap*) abrir el grifo; **under ~: the High Street is under ~** la Calle Mayor está inundada; **to swim under ~** nadar bajo el agua, bucear; ✦*IDIOMS* **a lot of ~ has flowed under the bridge since then** ha llovido mucho desde entonces; **that's all ~ under the bridge now** todo eso ya ha pasado a la historia; **to pour cold ~ on an idea** echar un jarro de agua fría a una idea; **like ~ off a duck's back** como si nada, como quien oye llover; **that theory doesn't hold ~** esa teoría carece de fundamento; **to be in hot ~*** estar metido en un lío*; **to get into hot ~*** meterse en un lío*; **to spend money like ~** despilfarrar *or* tirar el dinero; **to test the ~(s)** probar la temperatura del agua; *see also* **drinking B, running A1, still A1**

2 **waters** (*at spa, of sea, river*) aguas *fpl*; **to drink** *or* **take the ~s at Harrogate** tomar las aguas en Harrogate; **the ~s of the Amazon** las aguas del Amazonas; **British ~s** aguas británicas

3 (= *urine*) aguas *fpl* menores, orina *f*; **to make** *or* **pass ~** orinar, hacer aguas (menores)

4 (*Med*) **~ on the brain** hidrocefalia *f*; **her ~s broke** rompió aguas; **~ on the knee** derrame *m* sinovial

5 (= *essence*) **lavender/rose ~** agua *f* de lavanda/rosa

6 ✦*IDIOM* **of the first ~** de lo mejor, de primerísima calidad

Ⓑ VT [+ *garden, plant*] regar; [+ *horses, cattle*] abrevar, dar de beber a; [+ *wine*] aguar, diluir, bautizar (* *hum*); **the river ~s the provinces of ...** el río riega las provincias de ...; **to ~ capital** emitir un número excesivo de acciones

Ⓒ VI (*Physiol*) **her eyes started ~ing** empezaron a llorarle los ojos; **her mouth ~ed** se le hizo agua la boca; **it's enough to make your mouth ~** se hace la boca agua

Ⓓ CPD ► **water bed** N cama *f* de agua ► **water bird** N ave *f* acuática ► **water biscuit** N galleta *f* de agua ► **water blister** N ampolla *f* ► **water bottle** N (*for drinking*) cantimplora *f*; (*also* **hot-~ bottle**) bolsa *f* de agua caliente, guatona *f* (*Chile*) ► **water buffalo** N búfalo *m* de agua, carabao *m* ► **water butt** N (*Brit*) tina *f* para recoger el agua de la lluvia ► **water cannon** N cañón *m* de agua ► **water carrier** N aguador *m* ► **water cart** N cuba *f* de riego, carro *m* aljibe; (*motorized*) camión *m* de agua ► **water chestnut** N castaña *f* de agua ► **water closet** N (*frm*) wáter *m*, baño *m* ► **water cooler** N enfriadora *f* de agua ► **water cooling** N refrigeración *f* por agua ► **water diviner** N zahorí *mf* ► **water divining** N arte *m* del zahorí ► **water heater** N calentador *m* de agua ► **water ice** N (*Brit*) sorbete *m*, helado *m* de agua (*LAm*) ► **water jacket** N camisa *f* de agua ► **water jump** N foso *m* (de agua) ► **water level** N nivel *m* del agua; (*Naut*) línea *f* de agua ► **water lily** N nenúfar *m* ► **water line** N línea *f* de flotación ► **water main** N cañería *f* principal ► **water meadow** N (*esp Brit*) vega *f*, ribera *f* ► **water meter** N contador *m* de agua ► **water metering** N *control del agua mediante instalación de un contador de agua* ► **water mill** N molino *m* de agua ► **water park** N parque *m* acuático ► **water pipe** N caño *m* de agua ► **water pistol** N pistola *f* de agua ► **water plant** N planta *f* acuática ► **water polo** N waterpolo *m*, polo *m* acuático ► **water power** N energía *f* hidraúlica ► **water pressure** N presión *f* del agua ► **water pump** N bomba *f* de agua ► **water purification plant** N estación *f* depuradora de aguas residuales ► **water rat** N rata *f* de agua ► **water rate** N (*Brit*) tarifa *f* de agua ► **water snake** N culebra *f* de agua ► **water softener** N ablandador *m* de agua ► **water sports** NPL deportes *mpl* acuáticos ► **water supply** N abastecimiento *m* de agua ► **water table** N capa *f* freática, nivel *m* freático ► **water tank** N (*for village, in house*) depósito *m* de agua; (*on lorry*) cisterna *f* ► **water tower** N depósito *f* de agua ► **water vapour, water vapor** (*US*) N vapor *m* de agua ► **water vole** N rata *f* de agua ► **water wagon** N (*US*) vagón-cisterna *m* ► **water wheel** N rueda *f* hidráulica; (*Agr*) noria *f* ► **water wings** NPL manguitos *mpl*, flotadores *mpl* para los brazos

►**water down** VT + ADV [1] (*lit*) [+ *wine*] aguar, bautizar*; [+ *juice, milk, paint*] diluir
[2] (*fig*) [+ *reform, proposal, report*] suavizar

waterage ['wɔːtərɪdʒ] N transporte *m* por barco

waterborne ['wɜːtəbɔːn] ADJ [*disease*] transmitido a través del agua; [*traffic, trade*] (*by river*) fluvial; (*by sea*) marítimo

watercolour, **watercolor** (*US*) ['wɔːtə,kʌləʳ] N acuarela *f*; **to paint in ~s** pintar a la acuarela

watercolourist, **watercolorist** (*US*) ['wɔːtə,kʌlərɪst] N acuarelista *mf*

water-cooled ['wɔːtəkuːld] ADJ refrigerado (por agua)

watercourse ['wɔːtəkɔːs] N (= *river bed*) lecho *m*, cauce *m*; (= *canal*) canal *m*, conducto *m*

watercress ['wɔːtəkres] N berro *m*

watered ['wɔːtəd] Ⓐ ADJ aguado
Ⓑ CPD ► **watered silk** N muaré *m* ► **watered stock** N acciones *fpl* diluidas

watered-down ['wɔːtəd'daʊn] ADJ [1] [*wine*] aguado, bautizado*; [*juice, milk, paint*] diluido
[2] (*fig*) [*account, version*] suavizado; [*bill, reform, compromise*] suavizado

waterfall ['wɔːtəfɔːl] N cascada *f*, salto *m* de agua; (*larger*) catarata *f*

waterfowl ['wɔːtəfaʊl] (*pl* **waterfowl**) N ave *f* acuática

waterfront ['wɔːtəfrʌnt] N (= *harbour area*) puerto *m*, muelle *m*; **a ~ restaurant** *un restaurante situado a orillas de un río/lago etc*

waterhole ['wɔːtəhəʊl] N charco *m*; (*for animals*) abrevadero *m*

watering ['wɔːtərɪŋ] Ⓐ N riego *m*; **frequent ~ is needed** hay que regar con frecuencia
Ⓑ CPD ► **watering can** N regadera *f* ► **watering hole** N (*for animals*) abrevadero *m*; (*) pub *m* ► **watering place** N (= *spa*) balneario *m*; (= *seaside resort*) playa *f*, ciudad *f* marítima, ciudad *f* de veraneo; (*for animals*) abrevadero *m*

waterless ['wɔːtəlɪs] ADJ sin agua, árido

waterlogged ['wɔːtəlɒgd] ADJ [*ground*] anegado, inundado; [*pitch*] encharcado, inundado; [*boat, ship*] inundado; [*wood, paper*] empapado; **to get ~** [*ground*] anegarse, inundarse; [*wood, paper*] empaparse

Waterloo [,wɔːtə'luː] N Waterloo *m*; ✦**IDIOM he met his ~** se le llegó su San Martín

waterman ['wɔːtəmən] N (*pl* **watermen**) barquero *m*

watermark ['wɔːtəmɑːk] N (*on paper*) filigrana *f*; (*left by tide*) marca *f* del nivel del agua

watermelon ['wɔːtə,melən] N sandía *f*

waterproof ['wɔːtəpruːf] Ⓐ ADJ [*material*] impermeable; [*watch, torch*] sumergible; [*mascara, sunscreen, glue*] resistente al agua
Ⓑ N (*Brit*) impermeable *m*
Ⓒ VT impermeabilizar

waterproofing ['wɔːtə'pruːfɪŋ] N (= *process*) impermeabilización *f*; (= *material*) impermeabilizante *m*

water-repellent ['wɔːtərɪ'pelənt] Ⓐ ADJ [*material, clothing*] hidrófugo
Ⓑ N hidrófugo *m*

water-resistant ['wɔːtərɪ'zɪstənt] ADJ [*material*] impermeable; [*sunscreen*] a prueba de agua

watershed ['wɔːtəʃed] N [1] (*Geog*) línea *f* divisoria de las aguas; (= *basin*) cuenca *f*; **the ~ of the Duero** la cuenca del Duero
[2] (*fig*) (= *decisive moment*) momento *m* clave, momento *m* decisivo; (= *landmark*) hito *m*; **she had reached a ~ in her career** había llegado a un momento clave *or* decisivo en su carrera profesional; **the talks marked a ~ in the peace process** las negociaciones marcaron un hito en el proceso de paz
[3] (*Brit TV*) **the nine o'clock ~** *comienzo de la programación televisiva para adultos a las nueve de la noche*

waterside ['wɔːtəsaɪd] Ⓐ N (= *river, lake*) orilla *f*, ribera *f*; (= *harbour*) muelle *m*
Ⓑ ADJ ribereño

water-ski ['wɔːtəskiː] VI esquiar en el agua

water-skier ['wɔːtə,skiːəʳ] N esquiador(a) *m/f* acuático/a

water-skiing ['wɔːtə,skiːɪŋ] N esquí *m* acuático

water-soluble ['wɔːtə'sɒljʊbl] ADJ soluble en agua

waterspout ['wɔːtəspaʊt] N [1] (= *tornado*) tromba *f* marina
[2] (= *drainage pipe*) tubo *m* de desagüe

watertight ['wɔːtətaɪt] ADJ [1] [*bottle, container, seal*] hermético; [*compartment, boat, ship*] estanco; [*door*] de cierre hermético
[2] (*fig*) [*alibi*] perfecto; [*agreement*] sin lagunas; [*guarantee, embargo*] sólido; [*argument, theory*] irrefutable

waterway ['wɔːtəweɪ] N vía *f* fluvial *or* navegable; (= *inland waterway*) canal *m* (navegable)

waterweed ['wɔːtə'wiːd] N alga *f*

waterworks ['wɔːtəwɜːks] N [1] (*for water purification*) central *f* depuradora
[2] (*) (= *tears*) ✦**IDIOM to turn on the ~** echarse a llorar
[3] (‡) (= *urinary tract*) vías *fpl* urinarias; **to have trouble with one's ~** tener problemas de orina

watery ['wɔːtərɪ] ADJ [1] (= *like or containing water*) [*fluid, discharge, solution*] acuoso; [*blood*] líquido; [*paint, ink*] aguado
[2] (*pej*) (= *containing excessive water*) [*tea, soup*] aguado
[3] (= *producing water*) [*eyes*] lloroso
[4] (= *insipid*) [*smile*] tímido; [*sun*] débil; [*light*] desvaído, tenue
[5] (= *pale*) [*colour*] pálido, desvaído
[6] (= *relating to water*) acuático; **to go to a ~ grave** (*liter*) encontrar su lecho de muerte en el fondo del mar (*liter*)

WATS ['wɒts] N ABBR (*US*) = **Wide Area Telecommunications Service**

watt [wɒt] N vatio *m*

wattage ['wɒtɪdʒ] N vatiaje *m*

wattle[1] ['wɒtl] N (*Constr*) zarzo *m*; **~ and daub** zarzos *mpl* y barro

wattle[2] ['wɒtl] N (*Orn*) barba *f*

wave [weɪv] Ⓐ N [1] (*in sea, lake*) ola *f*; **life on the ocean ~** la vida en el *or* la mar; ✦**IDIOM to make ~s** (= *make an impression*) causar sensación; (= *stir up trouble*) crear problemas; *see also* **tidal B**
[2] (*in hair*) onda *f*; **her hair has a natural ~ (in it)** tiene el pelo ondulado por naturaleza; *see also* **permanent C**
[3] (*on surface*) ondulación *f*; *see also* **shock**
[4] (*Phys, Rad*) onda *f*; **long/medium/short ~** onda larga/media/corta; *see also* **light**, **radio**, **sound**
[5] (*in brain*) onda *f*
[6] (= *surge*) [*of strikes, refugees, enthusiasm*] oleada *f*; **the recent ~ of bombings** la reciente oleada de bombardeos; **a ~ of panic swept over me** me invadió el pánico; **in the first ~ of the attack** en la primera oleada del ataque; **the pain comes in ~s** el dolor va y viene; *see also* **crime**, **Mexican**, **new**
[7] (= *wave of hand*) gesto *m* de la mano; **he dismissed me with a ~ of the hand** me echó con un gesto de la mano; **with a ~ he was gone** hizo un gesto con la mano para despedirse y se fue; **to give sb a ~** (*in greeting*) saludar a algn con la mano; (*saying goodbye*) decir adiós a algn con la mano
[8] (*US*) = **Mexican wave**
Ⓑ VT [1] (= *shake, brandish*) [+ *flag, handkerchief, placard*] agitar; [+ *weapon, spear, stick*] blandir, agitar; **he was waving his arms in the air** agitaba los brazos en el aire; **he saw Jarvis, and ~d a hand** (*to catch attention*) vio a Jarvis y le hizo señas con la mano; **she ~d her hand for silence** hizo un gesto con la mano para que se callaran; **he ~d a piece of paper at her** le hizo señas agitando un papel que llevaba en la mano; **he ~d the ticket under my nose** agitó el billete delante de mis narices; **to ~ one's/a magic wand** agitar su varita mágica
[2] (= *gesture*) **to ~ sb goodbye** ◊ **~ goodbye to sb** decir adiós a algn con la mano; **he ~d the car through the gates** le indicó al coche que entrara por el portón
[3] (*Hairdressing*) **it's used for waving hair** se utiliza para hacer ondas (en el pelo); **to have one's hair ~d** hacerse ondas (en el pelo)
Ⓒ VI [1] [*person*] **I saw her and ~d** la vi y la saludé con la mano; **we ~d as the train drew out** cuando partió el tren nos dijimos adiós con la mano; **Ralph ~d for silence** Ralph hizo un gesto con la mano para que se callaran; **to ~ to** *or* **at sb** (= *sign to*) hacer señas a algn con la mano; (= *greet*) saludar a algn con la mano; (= *say goodbye to*) decir adiós a algn con la mano
[2] (= *sway*) [*flag*] ondear; [*branches, grass*] mecerse
Ⓓ CPD ► **wave energy** N energía *f* mareomotriz ► **wave frequency** N frecuencia *f* de las ondas ► **wave mechanics** N mecánica *f* ondulatoria ► **wave power** N energía *f* mareomotriz ► **wave range** N (*Rad*) gama *f* de ondas

►**wave about**, **wave around** VT + ADV [+ *object, arms*] agitar

►**wave aside** VT + ADV (= *dismiss*) [+ *suggestion, objection*] (*verbally*) rechazar, desechar; (*with gesture*) rechazar con (un gesto de) la mano; **I told her how much I appreciated her help but she ~d aside my thanks** le dije cuánto apreciaba su ayuda, pero ella le quitó importancia (con un gesto de la mano)

►**wave away** VT + ADV [+ *sth offered*] rechazar con (un gesto de) la mano; **he ~d the waiter away** con un gesto de la mano le indicó al camarero que se fuera

►**wave down** VT + ADV **to ~ a car down** (= *sign to stop*) hacer señales a un coche para que pare; **we ~d down a passing car** paramos a un coche que pasaba haciéndole señas con las manos

►**wave off** VT + ADV **to ~ sb off** decir adiós a algn con la mano; **she came to the pier to ~ us off** vino al muelle para decirnos adiós

►**wave on** VT + ADV **to ~ sb on** indicar a algn que siga adelante, hacer señas a algn para que siga adelante

waveband ['weɪvbænd] N banda *f* de frecuencia; **long ~** onda *f* larga

wavelength ['weɪvleŋθ] N longitud *f* de onda; ✦**IDIOM we're not on the same ~** no estamos en la misma onda

wavelet ['weɪvlɪt] N pequeña ola *f*, olita *f*

waver ['weɪvəʳ] VI [1] (= *oscillate*) [*needle*] oscilar; [*flame*] temblar
[2] (*fig*) (= *hesitate*) vacilar, dudar (**between** entre); (= *weaken*) [*courage, support*] flaquear; (= *falter*) [*voice*] temblar; **he's beginning to ~** está empezando a vacilar *or* dudar; **his gaze**

never ~ed no apartó la mirada ni por un momento; **she never ~ed in her belief** siempre se mantuvo firme en sus creencias

waverer ['weɪvərəʳ] N indeciso/a *m/f*, irresoluto/a *m/f*

wavering ['weɪvərɪŋ] Ⓐ ADJ indeciso, irresoluto, vacilante
Ⓑ N (= *flickering*) temblor *m*; (= *indecisiveness*) vacilación *f*, indecisión *f*, irresolución *f*

wavy ['weɪvɪ] ADJ (*compar* **wavier**, *superl* **waviest**) [*hair, surface, line*] ondulado

wavy-haired ['weɪvɪ'hɛəd] ADJ de pelo ondulado

wax[1] [wæks] Ⓐ N cera *f*; (*in ear*) cera *f* (de los oídos), cerumen *m*, cerilla *f*
Ⓑ ADJ de cera
Ⓒ VT [+ *furniture, car*] encerar
Ⓓ CPD ► **wax paper** N papel *m* encerado
► **wax seal** N sello *m* de lacre

wax[2] [wæks] VI [*moon*] crecer; **to ~ and wane** crecer y decrecer; **to ~ enthusiastic** († *or hum*) entusiasmarse; **to ~ eloquent about sth** ponerse elocuente acerca de algo; *see also* **lyrical**

waxed [wækst] ADJ [*paper*] encerado; [*jacket*] impermeabilizado

waxen ['wæksən] ADJ 1 (†) (= *made of wax*) de cera, céreo
2 (*liter*) (= *pale*) ceroso

waxing ['wæksɪŋ] Ⓐ ADJ [*moon*] creciente
Ⓑ N crecimiento *m*

waxwork ['wækswɜːk] N figura *f* de cera

waxworks ['wækswɜːks] N (*pl* **waxworks**) museo *m* de cera

waxy ['wæksɪ] ADJ (*compar* **waxier**, *superl* **waxiest**) ceroso

way [weɪ] Ⓐ N 1 (= *road, lane*) camino *m*; (*in street names*) calle *f*, avenida *f*; **Way of the Cross** Vía *f* Crucis, viacrucis *m*; **across** *or* **over the ~ (from)** enfrente (de), frente (a); **permanent ~** vía *f*; **the public ~** la vía pública
2 (= *route*) camino *m* (**to** de); **the ~ to the station** el camino de la estación; **which is the ~ to the station?** ¿cómo se va *or* cómo se llega a la estación?; **this isn't the ~ to Lugo!** ¡por aquí no se va a Lugo!; **he walked all the ~ here** vino todo el camino andando; **it rained all the ~ there** llovió durante todo el viaje; **he ran all the ~ home** hizo todo el camino a casa corriendo; **to ask one's ~ to the station** preguntar el camino *or* cómo se va a la estación; **we came a back ~** vinimos por los caminos vecinales; **she went by ~ of Birmingham** fue por *or* vía Birmingham; **if the chance comes my ~** si se me presenta la oportunidad; **~ down** bajada *f*, ruta *f* para bajar; **to take the easy ~ out** optar por la solución más fácil; **to feel one's ~** (*lit*) andar a tientas; **he's still feeling his ~ in the new job** todavía se está familiarizando con el nuevo trabajo; **to find one's ~** orientarse, ubicarse (*esp LAm*); **to find one's ~ into a building** encontrar la entrada de un edificio, descubrir cómo entrar en un edificio; **the cat found the ~ into the pantry** el gato logró introducirse en la despensa; **I had to find my own ~ home** me las tuve que arreglar para volver a casa; **the ~ is hard** el camino es duro; **the ~ in** (= *entrance*) la entrada; **I don't know the ~ to his house** no sé el camino a su casa, no sé cómo se va *or* llega a su casa; **do you know the ~ to the hotel?** ¿sabes el camino del *or* al hotel?, ¿sabes cómo llegar al hotel?; **I know my ~ about town** conozco la ciudad; **she knows her ~ around** (*fig*) tiene bastante experiencia, no es que sea una inocente; **to lead the ~** (*lit*) ir primero; (*fig*) marcar la pauta, abrir el camino; **to go the long ~ round** ir por el camino más largo; **to lose one's ~** extraviarse; **to make one's ~ to** dirigirse a; **to make one's ~ home** volver a casa; **to make one's ~ in the world** abrirse camino en la vida; **the middle ~** el camino de en medio; **on the ~ here** de camino hacia aquí, mientras veníamos aquí; **on the ~ to London** rumbo a Londres, camino de Londres; **it's on the ~ to Murcia** está en la carretera de Murcia; **we're on our ~!** ¡vamos para allá!; **he's on his ~** está de camino; **they have another child on the ~** tienen otro niño en camino; **you pass it on your ~ home** te pilla de camino a casa; **your house is on my ~** tu casa me viene de camino; **he is well on the ~ to finishing it** lo tiene casi terminado; **he's on the ~ to becoming an alcoholic** va camino de hacerse un alcohólico; **the ~ out** la salida; **you'll find it on the ~ out** lo encontrarás cerca de la salida; **I'll find my own ~ out** no hace falta que me acompañen a la puerta; **to find a ~ out of a problem** encontrar una solución a un problema; **there's no ~ out** (*fig*) no hay salida *or* solución, esto no tiene solución; **there's no other ~ out** (*fig*) no hay más remedio; **it's on its ~ out** está en camino de desaparecer, ya está pasando de moda; **to go out of one's ~** (*lit*) desviarse del camino; **to go out of one's ~ to help sb** desvivirse por ayudar a algn; **I don't want to take you out of your ~** no quiero apartarle del camino; **the village I live in is rather out of the ~** mi pueblo está un poco retirado; **that's nothing out of the ~ these days** eso no es nada extraordinario hoy día; **to pay one's ~** (*in restaurant*) pagar su parte; **the company isn't paying its ~** la compañía no rinde *or* no da provecho; **he put me in the ~ of some good contracts** me conectó *or* enchufó para que consiguiera buenos contratos; **to see one's ~ (clear) to helping sb** ver la forma de ayudar a algn; **could you possibly see your ~ clear to lending him some money?** ¿tendrías la amabilidad de prestarle algo de dinero?; **to go the shortest ~** ir por el camino más corto; **to start on one's ~** ponerse en camino; **~ up** subida *f*, ruta *f* para subir; **the ~ of virtue** el camino de la virtud; ✦**IDIOMS** **to go the ~ of all flesh** fenecer como todo ser humano; **I'm with you all the ~** te apoyo en todo; **to go one's own ~** seguir su propio camino; **she always goes her own sweet ~** hace lo que le da la gana; *see also* **prepare A**
3 (= *space sb wants to go through*) camino *m*; **to bar the ~** ponerse en medio del camino; **to clear a ~ for** abrir camino para; **to clear the ~** despejar el camino; **he crawled his ~ to the gate** llegó arrastrándose hasta la puerta; **to elbow one's ~ through the crowd** abrirse paso por la multitud a codazos; **to fight one's ~ out** lograr salir luchando; **to force one's ~ in** introducirse a la fuerza; **to hack one's ~ through sth** abrirse paso por algo a fuerza de tajos; **to be/get in sb's ~** estorbar a algn; **to get in the ~** estorbar; **am I in the ~?** ¿estorbo?; **you can watch, but don't get in the ~** puedes mirar, pero no estorbes; **to put difficulties in sb's ~** crear dificultades a algn; **to stand in sb's ~** (*lit*) cerrar el paso a algn; (*fig*) ser un obstáculo para algn; **now nothing stands in our ~** ahora no hay obstáculo alguno; **to stand in the ~ of progress** impedir *or* entorpecer el progreso; **to make ~ (for sth/sb)** (*lit, fig*) dejar paso (a algo/algn); **make ~!** ¡abran paso!; **to leave the ~ open for further talks** dejar la puerta abierta a posteriores conversaciones; **this law leaves the ~ open to abuse** esta ley deja vía libre a toda clase de desafueros; **to get out of the ~** quitarse de en medio; **out of my ~!** ¡quítate de en medio!; **I should keep out of his ~ if I were you** yo que tú evitaría el trato con él; **I try to keep out of his ~** procuro evitar cualquier contacto con él; **I kept well out of the ~** me mantuve muy lejos; **to get** *or* **move sth out of the ~** quitar algo de en medio *or* del camino; **put it somewhere out of the ~** ponlo donde no estorbe; **it's out of the ~ of the wind** está al abrigo del viento; **as soon as I've got this essay out of the ~** en cuanto termine este ensayo; **keep those matches out of his ~** no dejes esas cerillas a su alcance; **to push one's ~ through the crowd** abrirse paso por la multitud a empujones; **to work one's ~ to the front** abrirse camino hacia la primera fila; **he worked his ~ up in the company** ascendió en la compañía a fuerza de trabajo; **he worked his ~ up from nothing** empezó sin nada y fue muy lejos a fuerza de trabajo; *see also* **give A18**
4 (= *direction*) **down our ~** por nuestra zona, en nuestro barrio; **are you going my ~?** ¿vas por dónde voy yo?; **everything is going my ~** (*fig*) todo me está saliendo a pedir de boca; **to look the other ~** (*lit*) mirar para otro lado; (*fig*) mirar para otro lado, hacer la vista gorda; **turn it the other ~ round** vuélvelo al revés; **it was you who invited her, not the other ~ round** eres tú quien la invitaste, no al revés; **it's out Windsor ~** está cerca de Windsor; **turn the map the right ~ up** pon el mapa mirando hacia arriba; **the car landed the right ~ up** el coche cayó sobre las ruedas; **to split sth three ~s** dividir algo en tres partes iguales; **come this ~** pase por aquí; **"this way for the lions"** "a los leones"; **this ~ and that** por aquí y por allá; **which ~ did it go?** ¿hacia dónde fue?, ¿por dónde se fue?; **which ~ do we go from here?** (*lit, fig*) ¿desde aquí adónde vamos ahora?; **which ~ is the wind blowing?** ¿de dónde sopla el viento?; **she didn't know which ~ to look** no sabía dónde mirar, no sabía dónde poner los ojos
5 (= *distance*) **a little ~ off** no muy lejos, a poca distancia; **a little ~ down the road** bajando la calle, no muy lejos; **it's a long** *or* **good ~ away** *or* **off** está muy lejos; **spring is a long ~ off** la primavera queda muy lejos; **it's a long** *or* **good ~** es mucho camino; **we have a long ~ to go** tenemos mucho camino por delante; **he'll go a long ~** (*fig*) llegará lejos; **a little of that flavouring goes a long ~** un poco de ese condimento cunde mucho; **a little of her company goes a long ~** (*iro*) sólo se le puede aguantar en pequeñas dosis; **we've come a long ~ since those days** hemos avanzado mucho desde entonces; **it should go a long ~ towards convincing him** (esto) seguramente contribuirá mucho a convencerlo; **that's a long ~ from the truth** eso queda muy lejos de la verdad; **better by a long ~** mucho mejor, mejor pero con mucho; **not by a long ~** ni con mucho; **I can swim quite a ~ now** ahora puedo nadar bastante distancia; **a short ~ off** no muy lejos, a poca distancia
6 (= *means*) manera *f*, forma *f*, modo *m*; **we'll find a ~ of doing it** encontraremos la manera *or* forma *or* modo de hacerlo; **love will find a ~** el amor encontrará el camino; **it's the only ~ of doing it** es la única manera *or* forma *or* modo de hacerlo; **my ~ is to** + INFIN mi sistema consiste en + *infin*; **that's the ~!** ¡así!, ¡eso es!; **that ~ it won't disturb anybody** así no molestará a nadie; **every**

which ~ (*esp US*) (= *in every manner*) de muchísimas maneras; (= *in every direction*) por todas partes; **he re-ran the experiment every which ~ he could** reprodujo el experimento de todas las maneras habidas y por haber; **~s and means** medios *mpl*; **that's not the right ~** así no se hace; **✦IDIOM there are no two ~s about it** no hay vuelta de hoja

7 (= *manner*) manera *f*, forma *f*, modo *m*; **the ~ things are going we shall have nothing left** si esto continúa así nos vamos a quedar sin nada; **she looked at me in a strange ~** me miró de manera *or* forma *or* modo extraña; **it's a strange ~ to thank someone** ¡vaya manera *or* forma *or* modo de mostrar gratitud *or* darle las gracias a alguien!; **without in any ~ wishing to** + INFIN sin querer en lo más mínimo + *infin*, sin tener intención alguna de + *infin*; **in a big ~*** en grande*; **they like to celebrate their birthdays in a big ~** les gusta celebrar sus cumpleaños en grande; **we lost in a really big ~*** perdimos de manera *or* forma *or* modo realmente espectacular; **you can't have it both ~s** tienes que optar por lo uno o lo otro; **each ~** (*Racing*) (a) ganador y colocado; **either ~ I can't help you** de todas formas no puedo ayudarle; **I will help you in every ~ possible** haré todo lo posible por ayudarte; **he insulted us in every possible ~** nos ha insultado en todos los sentidos; **the British ~ of life** el estilo de vida británico; **no ~!*** ¡ni pensarlo!, ¡ni hablar!; **no ~ was that a goal*** ¡imposible que fuera eso un gol!; **there is no ~ I am going to agree*** de ninguna manera *or* forma *or* de ningún modo lo voy a consentir; **(in) one ~ or another** de una u otra manera *or* forma *or* modo; **it doesn't matter to me one ~ or the other** me es igual, me da lo mismo; **a week one ~ or the other won't matter** no importa que sea una semana más o una semana menos; **in the ordinary ~ (of things)** por lo general, en general; **he has his own ~ of doing it** tiene su manera *or* forma *or* modo de hacerlo; **I'll do it (in) my own ~** lo haré a mi manera *or* forma *or* modo; **he's a good sort in his own ~** tiene sus rarezas pero es buena persona; **in the same ~** de la misma manera *or* forma, del mismo modo; **to go on in the same old ~** seguir como siempre; **we help in a small ~** ayudamos un poco; **she's clever that ~** para esas cosas es muy lista; **to my ~ of thinking** a mi parecer, a mi manera *or* forma *or* modo de ver; **do it this ~** hazlo así; **in this ~** así, de esta manera *or* forma *or* modo; **it was this ~ ...** pasó lo siguiente ...; **that's always the ~ with him** siempre le pasa igual

8 [*of will*] **to get one's own ~** salirse con la suya; **have it your own ~!** ¡como quieras!; **they've had it all their own ~ too long** hace tiempo que hacen lo que les da la gana; **they didn't have things all their own ~** (*in football match*) no dominaron el partido completamente; **he had his wicked** *or* **evil ~ with her** (*hum*) se la llevó al huerto*, la sedujo

9 (= *custom*) costumbre *f*; **the ~s of the Spaniards** las costumbres de los españoles; **that is our ~ with traitors** así tratamos a los traidores; **he has his little ~s** tiene sus manías *or* rarezas; **to get into the ~ of doing sth** adquirir la costumbre de hacer algo; **to be/get out of the ~ of doing sth** haber perdido/perder la costumbre de hacer algo; **✦IDIOM to mend one's ~s** enmendarse, reformarse

10 (= *gift, special quality*) **he has a ~ with people** tiene don de gentes; **he has a ~ with children** sabe manejar a los niños; **he has a ~ with him** tiene su encanto

11 (= *respect, aspect*) sentido *m*; **in a ~** en cierto sentido; **in many ~s** en muchos sentidos; **he's like his father in more ~s than one** se parece a su padre en muchos sentidos; **in no ~** ◊ **not in any ~** de ninguna manera, de manera alguna; **in some ~s** en algunos sentidos

12 (= *state*) estado *m*; **the ~ things are** tal como están *or* van las cosas; **to leave things the ~ they are** dejar las cosas como están; **things are in a bad ~** las cosas van *or* marchan mal; **the car is in a bad ~** el coche está en mal estado; **he's in a bad ~** (= *sick*) está grave; (= *troubled*) está muy mal; **he's in a fair ~ to succeed** tiene buenas posibilidades de lograrlo; **it looks that ~** así parece; **✦IDIOM to be in the family ~*** estar embarazada

13 (= *speed*) **to gather ~** [*ship*] empezar a moverse; (*fig*) [*enthusiasm*] encenderse

14 (*in set expressions with preposition*) **by the ~** a propósito, por cierto; **how was your holiday, by the ~?** a próposito *or* por cierto, ¿qué tal tus vacaciones?; **Jones, which by the ~, is not his real name** Jones que, a propósito *or* por cierto, no es su verdadero nombre; **oh, and by the ~** antes que se me olvide; **all this is by the ~** todo esto no viene al caso; **by ~ of a warning** a modo de advertencia; **that was all I got by ~ of an answer** eso es todo lo que conseguí por respuesta; **she's by ~ of being an artist** tiene sus ribetes de artista; **he had little in the ~ of formal education** tuvo poca educación formal; **to be under ~** estar en marcha; **the job is now well under ~** el trabajo ya está muy avanzado; **to get under ~** [*ship*] zarpar; [*person, group*] partir, ponerse en camino; [*work, project*] ponerse en marcha, empezar a moverse; **things are getting under ~ at last** por fin las cosas están empezando a moverse

Ⓑ ADV (*) **that was ~ back** eso fue hace mucho tiempo ya; **~ back in 1900** allá en 1900; **~ down (below)** muy abajo; **it's ~ out in Nevada** está allá en Nevada; **~ out to sea** mar afuera; **he was ~ out in his estimate** se equivocó (en) mucho en su presupuesto; **it's ~ past your bedtime** hace rato que deberías estar en la cama; **it's ~ too big** es demasiado grande; **~ up high** muy alto; **~ up in the sky** muy alto en el cielo

Ⓒ CPD ► **way station** N (*US*) apeadero *m*; (*fig*) paso *m* intermedio

-way [weɪ] ADJ (*ending in compounds*) **a five-way split** una división en cinco partes; **a two-way street** una calle de doble sentido

waybill ['weɪbɪl] N hoja *f* de ruta

wayfarer ['weɪˌfɛərəʳ] N (†) caminante *mf*, viajero/a *m/f*

wayfaring tree ['weɪfɛərɪŋˌtriː] N viburno *m*

waylay [weɪ'leɪ] (*pt, pp* **waylaid** [weɪ'leɪd]) VT abordar, detener; **I was waylaid by the manager** me detuvo el gerente; **they were waylaid by thieves** les atacaron unos ladrones

waymarked ['weɪmɑːkt] ADJ [*path, trail*] señalizado

way-out* ['weɪ'aʊt] ADJ ultramoderno

wayside ['weɪsaɪd] Ⓐ N borde *m* del camino; **by the ~** al borde del camino; **✦IDIOM to fall by the ~** [*project*] quedarse en aguas de borraja; [*person*] quedarse a mitad de camino

Ⓑ CPD [*inn*] de carretera; [*flowers*] al borde del camino

wayward ['weɪwəd] ADJ 1 (= *wilful*) [*person*] rebelde; [*behaviour*] díscolo, rebelde; [*horse*] caprichoso, rebelde; **she separated from her ~ husband** se separó del rebelde de su marido

2 (*gen hum*) (= *unmanageable*) [*hair*] rebelde; [*satellite, missile*] rebelde, incontrolable

waywardness ['weɪwədnɪs] N (= *wilfulness*) rebeldía *f*; (= *capriciousness*) lo caprichoso

WB N ABBR (= **World Bank**) BM

W/B ABBR = **waybill**

WBA N ABBR = **World Boxing Association**

WC N ABBR (*Brit*) (= **water closet**) wáter *m*, WC *m*

WCC N ABBR = **World Council of Churches**

wdv ABBR (= **written-down value**) valor *m* amortizado

we [wiː] PRON (*for emphasis, to avoid ambiguity*) nosotros/as; **you've got kids but we haven't** vosotros tenéis hijos pero nosotros no; **we English** nosotros los ingleses; **it's we who ...** somos nosotros quienes ...; **they work harder than we do** trabajan más que nosotros

Don't translate the subject pronoun when not emphasizing or clarifying:

we were in a hurry teníamos prisa; **we were dissatisfied with the service** estábamos insatisfechos con el servicio

w/e ABBR = **week ending**; **~ 28 Oct** semana que termina el día 28 de octubre

WEA N ABBR (*Brit*) = **Workers' Educational Association**

weak [wiːk] Ⓐ ADJ (*compar* **weaker**; *superl* **weakest**) 1 (*physically*) [*person, limb, constitution*] débil; **he was too ~ to stand up** estaba demasiado débil para levantarse, no tenía fuerzas para levantarse; **to have ~ eyesight** tener mala vista; **to feel ~** sentirse débil; **my legs/arms felt ~** no tenía fuerza en las piernas/los brazos; **to be ~ from hunger** estar debilitado por el hambre; **to grow** *or* **get ~(er)** debilitarse; **to have a ~ heart** padecer del corazón; **the ~er sex**† el sexo débil; **to have a ~ stomach** marearse con facilidad; **to be ~ with hunger** estar debilitado por el hambre; **to be ~ with fear** estar débil por el miedo; **✦IDIOMS to be ~ in the head*** ser cortito de arriba*; **to go ~ at the knees**: **I went ~ at the knees** se me flaquearon las piernas

2 (= *fragile*) [*bone, fingernail, bond*] frágil; [*structure*] endeble, frágil; [*material*] endeble; **that chair's got a ~ leg** a esa silla le falla una pata, esa silla tiene una pata floja; **the ~ link (in the chain)** (*fig*) el eslabón flojo (de la cadena)

3 (= *ineffectual*) [*person, voice, smile, currency, government*] débil; [*economy*] débil, flojo; [*market*] flojo; **they believe it is ~ to cry** creen que llorar es signo de debilidad, creen que llorar es de débiles; **the dollar is ~ against the pound** el dólar está débil en comparación con la libra; **to have a ~ chin** tener una barbilla poco pronunciada

4 (= *poor*) [*subject, student, team*] flojo; **geography is my ~ subject** estoy flojo en geografía, la geografía es mi asignatura floja; **to be ~ at** *or* **in sth** flojear en algo, estar flojo en algo; **the course was very ~ on grammar** el curso era muy flojo en lo referente a gramática; **~ point** punto *m* débil; *see also* **spot A4**

5 (= *unconvincing*) [*argument, evidence*] poco sólido, poco convincente; [*case*] poco sólido; [*excuse, answer*] poco convincente; **the film had a ~ plot** el argumento de la película era muy flojo

6 (= *faint*) [*light*] débil, tenue; [*sun, signal, electric current*] débil; [*tide, current*] flojo; [*pulse*] débil, flojo

7 (= *watery*) [*coffee, tea, alcoholic drink*] poco cargado; [*solution*] diluido

Ⓑ NPL **the ~** los débiles

weaken ['wi:kən] Ⓐ VT [+ *person, heart, structure, economy*] debilitar; [+ *power, influence, resolve*] menguar, debilitar; [+ *case, argument*] quitar fuerza a; [+ *solution, mixture*] diluir; **he ~ed his grip on her arm** dejó de apretarle el brazo con tanta fuerza; **he doesn't want to do anything that might ~ his grip on power** no quiere hacer nada que pueda menguar el control que tiene sobre el país
Ⓑ VI 1 (= *grow weaker*) [*person, muscle, structure, economy*] debilitarse; [*power, influence, resolve*] menguarse, debilitarse; **the pound ~ed against the dollar today** hoy la libra ha bajado frente al dólar
2 (= *give way*) flaquear; **we must not ~ now** no debemos flaquear, ahora menos que nunca

weakening ['wi:kənɪŋ] Ⓐ N [*of muscles, structure, currency, economy, power*] debilitamiento *m*; **we have seen a ~ of government resolve** hemos observado un debilitamiento en la resolución del gobierno
Ⓑ ADJ [*effect*] debilitante

weak-kneed ['wi:k'ni:d] ADJ (*fig*) [*person*] sin carácter, débil

weakling ['wi:klɪŋ] N (*physically*) debilucho/a *m/f*; (*morally*) pelele *m*

weakly ['wi:klɪ] Ⓐ ADV 1 (= *without physical strength*) [*move, lean*] sin fuerzas; **his heart was beating ~** su corazón latía con poca fuerza *or* débilmente; **she struggled ~** forcejeó con pocas fuerzas
2 (= *ineffectually*) [*act, respond*] sin firmeza; [*say, smile*] débilmente, tímidamente; [*laugh*] tímidamente; [*give in*] sin oponer resistencia
Ⓑ ADJ († *or liter*) [*person, child*] enfermizo, enclenque

weak-minded ['wi:k'maɪndɪd] ADJ (= *irresolute*) sin carácter; (= *not sane*) mentecato

weakness ['wi:knɪs] N 1 (*in body*) debilidad *f*; [*of bone, fingernail*] fragilidad *f*; [*of structure*] falta *f* de solidez, lo endeble
2 (= *ineffectuality*) [*of person*] falta *f* de carácter; [*of government, management*] flaqueza *f*, debilidad *f*
3 (= *weak point*) punto *m* débil
4 (= *soft spot*) debilidad *f*; **I'm afraid doughnuts are my ~** me temo que los donuts son mi debilidad; **to have a ~ for sth** tener debilidad por algo

weak-willed ['wi:k'wɪld] ADJ sin voluntad, indeciso

weal[1] [wi:l] N (*esp Brit*) (= *wound*) verdugón *m*

weal[2]†† [wi:l] N (= *well-being*) bienestar *m*; **the common ~** el bien común

wealth [welθ] Ⓐ N 1 (*lit*) riqueza *f*; **for all his ~** a pesar de su riqueza; **the country's mineral ~** las riquezas minerales del país
2 (*fig*) (= *abundance*) abundancia *f* (**of** de); **the report provides a ~ of detail/new information** el informe contiene una abundancia de detalles/de información nueva
Ⓑ CPD ► **wealth tax** N impuesto *m* sobre el patrimonio

wealthy ['welθɪ] ADJ (*compar* **wealthier**, *superl* **wealthiest**) Ⓐ ADJ rico, acaudalado
Ⓑ NPL **the ~** los ricos

wean [wi:n] VT [+ *child*] destetar; **to ~ sb (away) from sth** (*fig*) alejar a algn de algo

weaning ['wi:nɪŋ] N destete *m*, ablactación *f*

weapon ['wepən] Ⓐ N arma *f*
Ⓑ CPD ► **weapons of mass destruction** NPL armas *fpl* de destrucción masiva ► **weapons testing** N pruebas *fpl* con armas

weaponry ['wepənrɪ] N armas *fpl*

wear [wɛəʳ] (*vb: pt* **wore**; *pp* **worn**) Ⓐ N 1 (= *use*) uso *m*; **this material will stand up to a lot of ~** este tejido resistirá mucho uso; **I've had a lot of ~ out of this jacket** le he dado mucho uso a esta chaqueta, esta chaqueta ha aguantado mucho trote*; **there is still some ~ left in it** todavía le queda vida; **clothes for evening ~** ropa *f* para la noche; **clothes for everyday ~** ropa *f* para todos los días, ropa *f* para uso diario
2 (= *deterioration through use*) desgaste *m*; **the ~ on the engine** el desgaste del motor; **to show signs of ~** [*clothes, furniture, tyres*] dar muestras de desgaste, mostrar señales de desgaste; **~ and tear** desgaste natural; **one has to allow for ~ and tear** hay que tener en cuenta el desgaste natural; ✦*IDIOM* **the worse for ~***: **his suit looked decidedly the worse for ~*** el traje se le veía muy deslucido; **she looks the worse for ~** se la ve algo desmejorada; **he returned from the pub rather the worse for ~** volvió del bar algo ajumado*
3 (= *dress, clothing*) ropa *f*; **what is the correct ~ for these occasions?** ¿qué es lo que se debe poner uno en tal ocasión?, ¿qué ropa es la apropiada para tal ocasión?; **casual ~** ropa *f* informal; **children's ~** ropa *f* de niños; **evening ~** ropa *f* para la noche; **ladies'** *or* **womens' ~** ropa *f* de señora; **summer ~** ropa *f* de verano
Ⓑ VT 1 (= *have on*) [+ *clothing, jewellery*] llevar, llevar puesto; [+ *spectacles, hairstyle, perfume*] llevar; [+ *beard*] tener; [+ *smile*] lucir; (= *put on*) [+ *clothes, shoes, perfume*] ponerse; **she was ~ing high-heeled shoes** llevaba (puestos) zapatos de tacón alto; **can you describe what he was ~ing?** ¿puede describir lo que llevaba (puesto)?; **were you ~ing a watch?** ¿llevabas reloj?, ¿llevabas un reloj puesto?; **what the well-dressed woman is ~ing this year** lo que lleva *or* se pone este año la mujer bien vestida; **she wore blue** iba de azul; **what shall I ~?** ¿qué me pongo?; **I have nothing to ~ to the dinner** no tengo qué ponerme para ir a la cena; **I haven't worn that for ages** hace siglos que no me pongo eso; **why don't you ~ your black dress?** ¿por qué no te pones el vestido negro?; **hats are rarely worn nowadays** hoy día apenas se llevan los sombreros; **I never ~ perfume/make-up** nunca llevo *or* me pongo perfume/maquillaje; **what size do you ~?** (*clothes*) ¿qué talla usa?; **what size shoes do you ~?** ¿qué número calza?; **does she ~ glasses/a wig?** ¿usa gafas/peluca?; **to ~ the crown** ceñir la corona; **to ~ one's hair long/short** llevar el pelo largo/corto; ✦*IDIOMS* **she ~s her age** *or* **her years well** se conserva muy bien; **she's the one who ~s the trousers** *or* (*US*) **pants in that house*** en esa casa los pantalones los lleva ella*; *see also* **heart A2**
2 (= *make worn*) **to ~ a path across the lawn** hacer un camino pisando la hierba; **the carpet had been worn threadbare** la alfombra estaba muy desgastada del uso; **to ~ o.s. to death** matarse (trabajando etc); **to ~ a hole in sth** hacer un agujero en algo; **he had worn holes in his socks** les había hecho agujeros a los calcetines; **the flagstones had been worn smooth by centuries of use** tantos siglos de uso habían alisado las losas
3 (*) (= *tolerate*) permitir, consentir; **your father won't ~ it** tu padre no lo va a permitir *or* consentir
Ⓒ VI 1 (= *last*) durar, aguantar; **that dress/carpet has worn well** ese vestido/esa alfombra ha durado *or* aguantado mucho; **it's a friendship that has worn very well** es una amistad que ha resistido *or* aguantado muy bien el paso del tiempo; **she's worn well*** se ha conservado muy bien
2 (= *become worn*) desgastarse; **the trousers have worn at the knees** los pantalones se han desgastado por la rodillas; **the rock has worn smooth** la roca se ha alisado por el desgaste; **to ~ thin** [*material*] desgastarse; **that excuse is ~ing a bit thin** esa excusa está ya muy pasada; **my patience is ~ing thin** se me está agotando la paciencia, estoy perdiendo la paciencia
3 [*day, year, sb's life*] **to ~ to its end** *or* **a close** acercarse a su fin

► **wear away** Ⓐ VT + ADV [+ *rock*] erosionar; [+ *pattern*] desgastar, borrar
Ⓑ VI + ADV [*wood, metal*] desgastarse, gastarse; [*cliffs*] erosionarse; [*inscription, design*] borrarse

► **wear down** Ⓐ VT + ADV 1 (*lit*) [+ *heels, tyre tread, pencil*] gastar, desgastar 2 (*fig*) [+ *opposition, resistance, patience*] agotar; [+ *person*] (*physically*) agotar, cansar; (*mentally*) cansar
Ⓑ VI + ADV [*heels, tyre tread*] desgastarse, gastarse

► **wear off** Ⓐ VI + ADV [*excitement, novelty*] pasar; [*anaesthetic, effects, pain*] pasarse; [*colour, design, inscription*] borrarse; **when the novelty ~s off** cuando pase la novedad; **the pain is ~ing off** se me está pasando el dolor
Ⓑ VT + ADV [+ *design, inscription*] quitar, borrar

► **wear on** VI + ADV [*year, war*] transcurrir, pasar; **the years wore on** transcurrían *or* pasaban los años; **as the evening wore on** a medida que transcurría la noche

► **wear out** Ⓐ VT + ADV 1 (= *ruin*) [+ *clothes, battery, engine, clutch*] gastar, desgastar; **you'll ~ your eyes out doing that** como hagas eso te vas a cansar la vista
2 (= *exhaust*) agotar; **you'll ~ me out!** ¡me vas a agotar!, ¡me vas a matar!*; **I'm worn out** estoy agotado *or* rendido; **to ~ o.s. out** agotarse, matarse*
Ⓑ VI + ADV [*clothes, shoes, battery, engine, clutch*] gastarse, desgastarse; [*knee, elbow of garment*] gastarse

► **wear through** Ⓐ VT + ADV **the sole of his boot was completely worn through** con el uso la suela de la bota se le había agujereado
Ⓑ VI + ADV [*clothing*] romperse *or* agujerearse con el uso; **it has worn through at the elbows** con el uso se ha roto *or* agujereado por los codos

WEAR

- Don't translate the **a** in sentences like **was she wearing a hat?, he wasn't wearing a coat** if the number of such items is not significant since people normally only wear one at a time:

  Was he wearing a hat?
  ¿Llevaba sombrero?
  He wasn't wearing a coat
  No llevaba abrigo

- Do translate the **a** if the garment, item of jewellery etc is qualified:

  Queen Sofía is wearing a long dress
  Doña Sofía lleva un vestido largo

For further uses and examples, see main entry.

wearable ['wɛərəbl] ADJ que se puede llevar, ponible; **it's still ~** todavía está ponible; **I haven't got anything ~ for the wedding** no tengo nada apropiado que ponerme para la boda

wearer ['wɛərəʳ] N **contact lens/denture ~s** personas que usan lentillas/dentadura postiza; **spectacle ~s** personas que llevan gafas; **this device can improve the ~'s hearing considerably** este dispositivo puede mejorar considerablemente la audición del usuario; **~s**

of bowler hats los que llevan sombrero de hongo; **a mask grants the ~ anonymity** una máscara da anonimato a quien la lleva

wearily ['wɪərɪlɪ] ADV (= *with tiredness*) con cansancio; (= *dispiritedly*) con desaliento; **she smiled/sighed ~** sonrió/suspiró cansada

weariness ['wɪərɪnɪs] N (*physical, mental*) cansancio *m*, fatiga *f*; (*emotional*) hastío *m*

wearing ['wɛərɪŋ] ADJ (= *exhausting*) [*journey*] cansado, pesado; [*activity*] pesado; **it was a ~ time for us** fue una época muy pesada para nosotros; **the loud music was ~ on the ear** la música tan alta estaba resultando pesada *or* cansina

wearisome ['wɪərɪsəm] ADJ (*frm*) (= *tiring*) fatigoso, pesado; (= *boring*) aburrido

weary ['wɪərɪ] Ⓐ ADJ (*compar* **wearier**; *superl* **weariest**) [1] [*person*] cansado; [*sigh, smile, voice*] de cansancio; **to be ~ of sth/sb** estar cansado *or* harto de algo/algn; **to be ~ of doing sth** estar cansado *or* harto de hacer algo; **to grow ~** [*person*] cansarse; **he had grown ~ of travelling** se había cansado de viajar
[2] (*liter*) (= *tiring*) [*wait, day*] pesado; **five ~ hours** cinco agotadoras horas
Ⓑ VT (*frm*) cansar, agotar
Ⓒ VI (*frm*) **to ~ of sth/sb** cansarse *or* hartarse de algo/algn

weasel ['wi:zl] Ⓐ N (*pl* **weasel** *or* **weasels**) [1] (*Zool*) comadreja *f* [2] (*) (= *person*) zorro/a* *m/f* Ⓑ VI **to ~ out of sth** (= *extricate o.s.*) escabullirse de algo Ⓒ CPD ► **weasel words** NPL ambages *mpl*, palabras *fpl* equívocas

weather ['weðəʳ] Ⓐ N tiempo *m*; **~ permitting** si el tiempo lo permite, si el tiempo no lo impide; **in this ~** con el tiempo que hace, con este tiempo; **it's very comfortable to wear in hot ~** es muy cómodo de llevar (puesto) cuando hace calor; **what's the ~ like?** ¿qué tiempo hace?; **he has to go out in all ~s** tiene que salir haga el tiempo que haga; **it gets left outside in all ~s** se deja siempre a la intemperie; ✦*IDIOMS* **to keep a ~ eye on sth** observar algo con atención; **to make heavy ~ of sth** complicar algo, hacer algo más difícil de lo que es; **he only needed to change the bulb but he made such heavy ~ of it** ¡sólo tenía que cambiar la bombilla pero lo complicó de una manera!; **to be under the ~** (= *ill*) estar indispuesto, estar pachucho*
Ⓑ VT [1] [+ *storm*] (*also* **~ out**) aguantar; **we've ~ed worse criticism than this** hemos superado peores críticas que éstas, hemos hecho frente a peores críticas que éstas; ✦*IDIOM* **to ~ the storm** capear el temporal
[2] (*Geol*) [+ *rock*] erosionar; [+ *wood*] curar; [+ *skin, face*] curtir; **the rocks had been ~ed into fantastic shapes** las rocas tenían formas fantásticas debido a la erosión
[3] (*Naut*) [+ *cape*] doblar
Ⓒ VI [*rocks*] erosionarse; [*wood*] curarse; [*skin, face*] curtirse
Ⓓ CPD [*bureau, map, station, balloon*] meteorológico ► **weather conditions** NPL estado *m* del tiempo ► **weather forecast** N pronóstico *m* del tiempo, boletín *m* meteorológico ► **weather forecaster** N meteorólogo/a *m/f* ► **weather girl** N mujer *f* del tiempo, meteoróloga *f* ► **weather report** N boletín *m* meteorológico ► **weather ship** N barco *m* del servicio meteorológico ► **weather side** N (*Naut*) costado *m* de barlovento ► **weather strip** N burlete *m* ► **weather vane** N veleta *f*

weather-beaten ['weðə,bi:tn] ADJ [*skin, face*] curtido; [*wood*] deteriorado; [*stone*] erosionado; **the houses have a ~ look** en las casas se nota el efecto de los elementos

weatherboard ['weðəbɔ:d] N tabla *f* de chilla; **~ house** (*US*) casa *f* de madera

weather-bound ['weðəbaʊnd] ADJ bloqueado por el mal tiempo

weathercock ['weðəkɒk] N veleta *f*

weathered ['weðəd] ADJ [*rocks*] erosionado; [*skin, face*] curtido; [*wood*] curado, maduro

weatherman ['weðəmæn] N (*pl* **weathermen**) hombre *m* del tiempo

weatherproof ['weðəpru:f] Ⓐ ADJ [*building*] impermeabilizado; [*clothing*] impermeable, impermeabilizado Ⓑ VT impermeabilizar

weatherwoman ['weðə,wʊmən] (*pl* **weatherwomen**) N mujer *f* del tiempo

weave [wi:v] (*vb: pt* **wove**; *pp* **woven**) Ⓐ N tejido *m*
Ⓑ VT [1] (*lit*) [+ *fabric, basket*] tejer
[2] (*fig*) [+ *story*] urdir; **he wove a story round these experiences** urdió una historia con estas experiencias; **he wove these details into the story** entretejó *or* intercaló estos detalles en el cuento
[3] (*pt* **weaved** *or* **wove**; *pp* **weaved** *or* **woven**) (= *zigzag*) **to ~ one's way through the crowd** abrirse paso entre la multitud; **he ~d** *or* **wove his way to the bathroom** fue hasta el baño haciendo eses
Ⓒ VI [1] (*lit*) tejer
[2] (*pt, pp* **weaved**) (*fig*) (= *move in and out*) zigzaguear; **he ~s from side to side, trying to dodge his opponent** va zigzagueando *or* se mueve de lado a lado intentando esquivar a su rival; **the motorbike was weaving in and out of the traffic** la motocicleta zigzagueaba *or* se abría paso entre los coches; **the road ~s about a lot** el camino tiene muchas curvas, el camino serpentea mucho (*liter*); ✦*IDIOM* **to get weaving**† poner manos a la obra; **let's get weaving!** ¡pongamos manos a la obra!

weaver ['wi:vəʳ] N tejedor(a) *m/f*

weaving ['wi:vɪŋ] Ⓐ N tejido *m*; **basket ~** cestería *f* Ⓑ CPD ► **weaving machine** N telar *m* ► **weaving mill** N tejeduría *f*

Web [web], **web[1]*** (*Internet*) Ⓐ N **the ~** el Web Ⓑ CPD ► **web browser** N navegador *m* de Internet ► **web page** N página *f* web ► **web surfer** N internauta *mf*, cibernauta *mf*

web[2] [web] N [*of spider*] telaraña *f*; (= *fabric*) tela *f*, tejido *m*; (*between toes*) membrana *f*; (*fig*) red *f*; **a complex ~ of relationships** una complicada maraña *or* red de relaciones; **a ~ of intrigue** una red *or* un tejido de intrigas; **a ~ of deceit/lies** una maraña de engaños/mentiras

webbed [webd] ADJ palmeado

webbing ['webɪŋ] Ⓐ N (= *material*) cincha *f*; [*of chair*] cinchas *fpl*
Ⓑ CPD ► **webbing belt** N pretina *f* de reps

webcam ['webkæm] N webcam *f*

webcast ['webkɑ:st] N transmisión *f* por Internet

web-footed [,web'fʊtɪd] ADJ palmípedo

weblog ['weblɒg] N (*Internet*) weblog *f*

webmail ['web,meɪl] N correo *m* web

webmaster ['webmɑ:stəʳ] N (*Internet*) administrador(a) *m/f* de web

website ['websaɪt] N web site *m*, sitio *m* web

webspace ['webspeɪs] N espacio *m* disponible en la Red *or* el Web

webzine ['webzi:n] N (*Internet*) revista *f* electrónica, revista *f* digital

we'd [wi:d] = **we would, we had**

wed [wed] (*frm*) Ⓐ VT **to ~ sb** [*bride, bridegroom*] desposarse con algn, casarse con algn; [*priest*] desposar a algn, casar a algn
Ⓑ VI (†) desposarse, casarse

wedded ['wedɪd] ADJ [1] (*frm*) [*wife, husband*] desposado, casado; [*bliss, life*] conyugal; **his lawful ~ wife** su legítima esposa
[2] (*fig*) **to be ~ to** (= *linked to*) estar ligado *or* unido a; **to be ~ to an idea** [*person*] aferrarse *or* estar aferrado a una idea; **she's ~ to her work** está casada con su trabajo

wedding ['wedɪŋ] Ⓐ N boda *f*, casamiento *m*; **silver/ruby ~** bodas de plata/de rubí; **to have a church ~** casarse por la iglesia; **civil ~** boda *f* civil; **to have a civil ~** casarse por lo civil; **to have a quiet ~** casarse en la intimidad
Ⓑ CPD ► **wedding anniversary** N aniversario *m* de boda ► **wedding band** N = **wedding ring** ► **wedding breakfast** N (*frm*) banquete *m* de bodas ► **wedding cake** N tarta *f* or pastel *m* de boda ► **wedding day** N día *m* de la boda; **on her ~ day** el día de su boda ► **wedding dress** N traje *m* de novia ► **wedding invitation** N invitación *f* de boda ► **wedding march** N marcha *f* nupcial ► **wedding night** N noche *f* de bodas ► **wedding present** N regalo *m* de boda ► **wedding reception** N banquete *m* de bodas ► **wedding ring** N alianza *f*, anillo *m* de boda ► **wedding service** N boda *f*, ceremonia *f* nupcial; → BEST MAN

wedge [wedʒ] Ⓐ N [1] (*for keeping in position*) cuña *f*, calza *f*; **to drive a ~ between two people** abrir una brecha entre dos personas; ✦*IDIOM* **this is the thin end of the ~** esto puede ser el principio de muchos males
[2] (= *piece*) [*of cheese, cake*] porción *f*, pedazo *m* (grande)
[3] (*Golf*) wedge *m*, cucharilla *f*
Ⓑ VT **to ~ sth in place** asegurar algo; **to ~ a door open** mantener abierta una puerta con una cuña *or* una calza; **I was ~d between two other passengers** me estuve apretado *or* inmovilizado entre otros dos pasajeros; **it's ~d** no se puede mover
Ⓒ CPD ► **wedge heel** N tacón *m* de cuña

►**wedge in** VT + ADV **the car was ~d in between two lorries** el coche quedó encajado entre dos camiones; **a short documentary ~d in between sports programmes** un documental corto encasillado entre programas deportivos

wedge-shaped ['wedʒʃeɪpt] ADJ en forma de cuña

wedlock ['wedlɒk] N (*frm*) matrimonio *m*; **to be born out of ~** nacer fuera del matrimonio

Wednesday ['wenzdeɪ] N miércoles *m inv*; *see* **Tuesday** *for usage*

Wed(s). ABBR (= **Wednesday**) miérc.

wee[1]* [wi:] ADJ (*compar* **weer**; *superl* **weest**) (*Scot*) pequeñito, chiquito (*LAm*); **I was a ~ boy when it happened** era pequeñito cuando ocurrió; **a ~ bit** (= *small amount*) un poquitín, un poquito; **I'm a ~ bit worried** estoy un poco inquieto; **poor ~ thing!** ¡pobrecito!; **we were up till the ~ hours (of the morning)** *or* **the ~ small hours** no nos acostamos hasta las altas horas de la madrugada

wee[2]* [wi:] Ⓐ N pipí* *m*; **to have a ~** hacer pipí*; **I need a ~** tengo que hacer pipí*
Ⓑ VI hacer pipí*

weed [wi:d] Ⓐ N [1] mala hierba *f*, hierbajo *m*; (= *waterweed*) alga *f*; **the garden was full of ~s** el jardín estaba lleno de malas hierbas *or* hierbajos
[2] (*) (= *person*) pelele* *m*
[3] **the ~*** (*hum*) (= *tobacco*) el tabaco
[4] (*) (= *marihuana*) hierba* *f*
[5] **(widow's) ~s** ropa *f* de luto

Ⓑ VT [+ *flowerbed*] desherbar
Ⓒ VI desherbar
►**weed out** VT + ADV [+ *plant*] arrancar; (*fig*) eliminar
weeding [ˈwiːdɪŋ] N **to do the ~** desherbar
weedkiller [ˈwiːd,kɪləʳ] N herbicida *m*
weedy [ˈwiːdɪ] ADJ (*compar* **weedier**; *superl* **weediest**) 1 [*ground*] lleno de malas hierbas *or* hierbajos
2 (*Brit* pej*) (= *scrawny*) [*person*] debilucho*, desmirriado*, enclenque
week [wiːk] N semana *f*; **allow four ~s for delivery** la entrega se realiza dentro de cuatro semanas; **twice a ~** dos veces a la semana; **this day ~** ◊ **a ~ today** de hoy en ocho días, dentro de ocho días; **tomorrow ~** de mañana en ocho días; **Tuesday ~** ◊ **a ~ on Tuesday** del martes en ocho días, este martes no, el otro; **in a ~ or so** dentro de una semana; **in the middle of the ~** a mitad de semana; **I don't have time during the ~** entre semana no tengo tiempo; **it changes from ~ to ~** esto cambia cada semana; **~ in, ~ out** semana tras semana; **I haven't seen her for** *or* **in ~s** hace tiempo que no la veo; ✦***IDIOM*** **to knock sb into the middle of next ~*** dar a algn un golpe que le pone en órbita; *see also* **working A2**
weekday [ˈwiːkdeɪ] N día *m* laborable; **on a ~** ◊ **on ~s** entre semana; **I go every ~ morning** entre semana voy todas las mañanas
weekend [ˈwiːkˈend] Ⓐ N 1 fin *m* de semana; **to stay over the ~** pasar el fin de semana; **a long ~** un puente; **to take a long ~** ◊ **make a long ~ of it** hacer puente
2 (*as adv*) **they are away ~s** los fines de semana se van fuera
Ⓑ VI pasar el fin de semana
Ⓒ CPD [*cottage, trip, visit*] de fin de semana ► **weekend case** N maletín *m* de viaje ► **weekend return** N *billete de ida y vuelta para el fin de semana*
weekender [,wiːkˈendəʳ] N *persona que va a pasar solamente el fin de semana*
weekly [ˈwiːklɪ] Ⓐ ADJ semanal
Ⓑ ADV semanalmente, cada semana; **they meet ~** se reúnen semanalmente *or* cada semana; **I am paid ~** me pagan semanalmente *or* por semana; **£15 ~** 15 libras por semana; **twice/three times ~** dos/tres veces por semana *or* a la semana; **the novel was published ~ in instalments** la novela se publicó en fascículos semanales
Ⓒ N (= *magazine*) semanario *m*
weeknight [ˈwiːknaɪt] N noche *f* de entresemana
weenie* [ˈwiːnɪ] N (*US*) = **wienie**
weeny* [ˈwiːnɪ] ADJ chiquitito*, minúsculo
weeny-bopper* [ˈwiːnɪˈbɒpəʳ] N doceañera *f* (aficionada de la música pop)
weep [wiːp] (*vb: pt, pp* **wept**) Ⓐ VI 1 (= *cry*) llorar; **to ~ for joy** llorar de alegría; **to ~ for sb** llorar a algn; **to ~ for one's sins** llorar sus pecados; **to ~ to see sth** llorar al ver algo; **I could have wept** era para desesperarse
2 (*Med*) [*wound*] supurar
Ⓑ VT [+ *tears*] llorar
Ⓒ N **to have a good ~** llorar a lágrima viva
weeping [ˈwiːpɪŋ] Ⓐ N (= *crying*) llanto *m*
Ⓑ ADJ lloroso
Ⓒ CPD ► **weeping willow** N sauce *m* llorón
weepy [ˈwiːpɪ] Ⓐ ADJ 1 (= *tearful*) [*person*] llorón; [*eyes*] lloroso; **to feel ~** sentir *or* tener ganas de llorar; **to get** *or* **become ~ (about sth)** ponerse a llorar (por algo)
2 (*) (= *sentimental*) [*film, novel, song*] lacrimógeno
Ⓑ N (*) (= *film*) película *f* lacrimógena, melodrama *m*; (= *novel*) novela *f* lacrimógena
weever [ˈwiːvəʳ] N peje *m* araña
weevil [ˈwiːvl] N gorgojo *m*
wee-wee* [ˈwiːwiː] Ⓐ N pipí* *m*
Ⓑ VI hacer pipí*
w.e.f. ABBR = **with effect from**
weft [weft] N 1 (*lit*) trama *f*
2 (*fig*) red *f*
weigh [weɪ] Ⓐ VT 1 (= *measure weight of*) pesar; **to ~ o.s.** pesarse
2 (= *consider*) [+ *evidence, options, risks*] sopesar, considerar; **the advantages of surgery have to be ~ed against possible risks** las ventajas de la cirugía se tienen que contraponer a los posibles riesgos; **to ~ the pros and cons (of sth)** sopesar *or* considerar los pros y los contras (de algo); *see also* **word A1**
3 **to ~ anchor** levar anclas
Ⓑ VI 1 (= *tip the scales at*) pesar; **it ~s four kilos** pesa cuatro kilos; **how much** *or* **what do you ~?** ¿cuánto pesas?; **this ~s a ton!*** ¡esto pesa un quintal!*
2 (*fig*) 2·1 (= *be influential*) influir; **to ~ against sth/sb** ser un factor en contra de algo/algn; **there are many factors ~ing against the meeting happening** hay muchos factores en contra de que tenga lugar la reunión; **to ~ in favour of sth/sb** ser un factor a favor de algo/algn, inclinar la balanza a favor de algo/algn; **all these factors will ~ heavily with voters** todos estos factores influirán mucho en los votantes
2·2 (= *be a burden*) **to ~ on sb** agobiar a algn; **her absence began to ~ on me** su ausencia comenzó a agobiarme; **to ~ on sb's conscience** pesar sobre la conciencia de algn; **it ~s (heavily) on her mind** le preocupa (mucho); **eat something that won't ~ on your stomach** come algo que no te resulte pesado al estómago
►**weigh down** Ⓐ VT + ADV 1 (*lit*) 1·1 (= *hold down*) sujetar (con un peso/una piedra *etc*)
1·2 (= *encumber*) **don't take anything with you that will ~ you down** no te lleves nada que te suponga demasiado peso; **she was ~ed down with parcels** iba muy cargada de paquetes; **a branch ~ed down with fruit** una rama muy cargada de fruta
2 (*fig*) agobiar, abrumar (*more liter*); **to be ~ed down with** *or* **by sorrow** estar abrumado por la pena; **he felt ~ed down with** *or* **by responsibilities** se sentía agobiado por las responsabilidades; **I was ~ed down by guilt** me pesaba el sentimiento de culpabilidad; **the government is ~ed down with** *or* **by debt** el gobierno está cargado de deudas
Ⓑ VI + ADV **to ~ down on sb** agobiar a algn, abrumar a algn (*more liter*); **sorrow ~ed down on her** la pena la abrumaba
►**weigh in** Ⓐ VI + ADV 1 [*boxer, jockey*] pesarse; **to ~ in at 65 kilos** pesar 65 kilos
2 (*at airport desk*) facturar el equipaje
3 (= *contribute*) intervenir; **he ~ed in with his opinion** intervino con *or* expresando su opinión; **he ~ed in with the argument that …** intervino afirmando que …
Ⓑ VT + ADV 1 [+ *boxer, jockey*] pesar
2 [+ *luggage*] pesar, facturar
►**weigh out** VT + ADV [+ *goods, ingredients, kilo*] pesar
►**weigh up** (*esp Brit*) VT + ADV [+ *situation, risks, alternatives, evidence*] sopesar, considerar; [+ *person*] sondear, tantear; **we looked at each other, ~ing each other up** nos miramos, sondeándonos *or* tanteándonos el uno al otro; **I'm ~ing up whether to go or not** estoy considerando si ir o no
weighbridge [ˈweɪbrɪdʒ] N báscula-puente *f*, báscula *f* de puente
weigh-in [ˈweɪɪn] N pesaje *m*
weighing machine [ˈweɪɪŋmə,ʃiːn] N báscula *f*
weight [weɪt] Ⓐ N 1 (= *heaviness*) peso *m*; **sold by ~** vendido a peso; **to gain ~** engordar, ganar peso; **a package three kilos in ~** un paquete que pesa tres kilos, un paquete de tres kilos; **to lose ~** adelgazar, perder peso; **to put on ~** engordar, ganar peso; **the fence couldn't take his ~ and collapsed** la valla no aguantó su peso y se vino abajo; **to take the ~ off one's feet** sentarse a descansar; ✦***IDIOMS*** **to chuck** *or* **throw one's ~ about*** ir de sargento*; **to throw one's ~ behind sb** apoyar a algn con toda su fuerza; **the government is throwing its ~ behind the reforms** el gobierno está apoyando con toda su fuerza las reformas; **it is worth its ~ in gold** vale su peso en oro; **that's a ~ off my mind** eso me quita un peso de encima; **he doesn't pull his ~** no hace su parte *or* lo que le corresponde
2 (*in clock, for scales*) pesa *f*; (= *heavy object*) peso *m*; **~s and measures** pesas *fpl* y medidas; **the doctor has forbidden me to lift heavy ~s** el médico me ha prohibido levantar peso
3 (*fig*) (= *importance*) peso *m*; **these are arguments of some ~** son argumentos de cierto peso; **those arguments carry great ~ with the minister** esos argumentos influyen poderosamente en el ministro; **those arguments carry no ~ with the minister** esos argumentos no influyen en el ministro; **they won by sheer ~ of numbers** ganaron simplemente porque eran más; **to give due ~ to sth** dar la debida importancia a algo; **to lend ~ to sth** darle más peso a algo
Ⓑ VT (= *add weight to*) cargar, dar peso a; (= *hold down*) sujetar con un peso
Ⓒ CPD ► **weight gain** N aumento *m* de peso ► **weight limit** N límite *m* de peso ► **weight loss** N pérdida *f* de peso ► **weight problem** N **to have a ~ problem** tener problemas de peso ► **weight training** N entrenamiento *m* con pesas ► **weight watcher** N persona *f* que vigila el peso *or* cuida la línea
►**weight down** VT + ADV sujetar con un peso/una piedra *etc*
weighted [weɪtɪd] ADJ [*clothing, object*] con peso; **~ average** media *f* ponderada; **~ index** índice *m* compensado; **to be ~ in favour of sb** favorecer a algn; **to be ~ against sb** perjudicar a algn
weightiness [ˈweɪtɪnɪs] N 1 (*lit*) peso *m*
2 (*fig*) [*of matter, problem*] gravedad *f*; [*of argument, reason*] peso *m*, importancia *f*
weighting [ˈweɪtɪŋ] N 1 (*on salary*) plus *m* (salarial) por coste de vida; **London ~** plus *m* (salarial) por residir en Londres
2 (*Scol*) factor *m* de valoración
3 (*Statistics*) ponderación *f*
weightless [ˈweɪtlɪs] ADJ ingrávido
weightlessness [ˈweɪtlɪsnɪs] N ingravidez *f*
weightlifter [ˈweɪt,lɪftəʳ] N levantador(a) *m/f* de pesas, halterófilo/a *m/f*
weightlifting [ˈweɪt,lɪftɪŋ] N levantamiento *m* de pesas, halterofilia *f*
weight-train [ˈweɪt,treɪn] VI entrenar con pesas
weighty [ˈweɪtɪ] ADJ (*compar* **weightier**; *superl* **weightiest**) 1 (*lit*) [*load*] pesado; **a ~ tome** *or* **volume** un tomo de peso
2 (*fig*) [*matter, problem*] grave; [*argument, rea-*

son] importante, de peso; [*burden*] pesado; [*responsibility*] grande

weir [wɪəʳ] N 1 (= *dam*) presa *f*
2 (= *fish trap*) encañizada *f*, cañal *m*

weird [wɪəd] ADJ (*compar* **weirder**; *superl* **weirdest**) raro, extraño; **the ~ thing is that ...** lo raro es que ...; **all sorts of ~ and wonderful things** todo tipo de cosas extraordinarias

weirdly ['wɪədlɪ] ADV (= *strange as it may seem*) extrañamente; **it was ~ quiet** reinaba una extraña calma; **he grunted ~** gruñó de una manera rara *or* extraña; **~ enough ...** por raro *or* extraño que parezca ...

weirdo* ['wɪədəʊ] N persona *f* rara

welch [welʃ] VI = **welsh**

welcome ['welkəm] Ⓐ VT (= *receive gladly*) [+ *person*] dar la bienvenida a; [+ *news*] alegrarse de; **he ~d me in** me dio la bienvenida al entrar; **her marriage was not ~d by the family** su matrimonio no fue bien recibido en la familia; **we'd ~ your suggestions** nos alegraría recibir sus sugerencias; ✦*IDIOM* **to ~ sb with open arms** recibir a algn con los brazos abiertos
Ⓑ N bienvenida *f*, recibimiento *m*; **to give sb a warm/frosty ~** dar a algn una calurosa/fría bienvenida, dar a algn un caluroso/frío recibimiento; **let's give a warm ~ to Ed Lilly!** ¡demos una calurosa bienvenida a Ed Lilly!; **to bid sb ~** (*frm*) dar la bienvenida a algn; *see also* **outstay, overstay**
Ⓒ ADJ 1 [*person, guest, visitor*] bienvenido, bien recibido; **everyone is ~** todo el mundo es bienvenido *or* bien recibido; **he's not ~ here any more** aquí ya no es bienvenido; **you're ~** (*esp US*) (*in reply to thanks*) de nada, no hay de qué; **you're ~ to it!** (*iro*) ¡te lo puedes quedar!; **I didn't feel very ~** no me sentí muy bien recibido; **to make sb ~** hacer que algn se sienta acogido; **you're ~ to visit any time** puedes venir cuando quieras; **you're ~ to try** puedes probar si quieres; **you're ~ to use my car** puedes usar mi coche con toda libertad, el coche está a tu disposición; ✦*IDIOM* **to roll** *or* **put out the ~ mat for sb** dar un recibimiento de reyes a algn
2 (= *acceptable*) [*decision*] bienvenido; **the recent changes are very ~** los recientes cambios son muy bienvenidos; **a cup of tea is always ~** una taza de té siempre se agradece; **to be ~ news** ser una noticia grata; **shelters provide ~ relief from the sun and flies** los refugios proporcionan un grato alivio del sol y de las moscas; **the bags of flour were a ~ sight to the refugees** los refugiados recibieron con alegría las bolsas de harina
Ⓓ EXCL **~!** ¡bienvenido!; **~ back!** ¡bienvenido!; **~ home!** ¡bienvenido a casa!; **~ to Scotland!** ¡bienvenido a Escocia!
► **welcome back** VT + ADV **to ~ sb back** dar una buena acogida a algn cuando regresa; *see also* **welcoming D**

welcoming ['welkəmɪŋ] ADJ 1 [*smile*] amable, cordial; [*place, atmosphere*] acogedor; **to be ~ to sb** ser acogedor *or* cordial con algn
2 [*ceremony, banquet, speech*] de bienvenida; **~ party** *or* **committee** comité *m* de bienvenida

weld [weld] Ⓐ N soldadura *f*
Ⓑ VT (*Tech*) soldar; **the hull is ~ed throughout** el casco es totalmente soldado; **to ~ together** (*lit*) soldar; (*fig*) unir, unificar; **to ~ parts together** soldar unas piezas; **we must ~ them together into a new body** hemos de unirlos *or* unificarlos para formar un nuevo organismo
Ⓒ VI soldarse

➤ LANGUAGE IN USE: **welcome A** 13

welder ['weldəʳ] N soldador(a) *m/f*

welding ['weldɪŋ] Ⓐ N soldadura *f*
Ⓑ CPD [*process*] de soldar, soldador
► **welding torch** N soplete *m* soldador

welfare ['welfeəʳ] Ⓐ N 1 (= *well-being*) bienestar *m*; **physical/spiritual ~** bienestar físico/espiritual; **you've got to think about the ~ of the children** tienes que pensar en el bienestar de los niños; **animal ~** la protección de los animales; **child ~** la protección a *or* de la infancia
2 (= *social aid*) asistencia *f* social; **to be on ~** recibir asistencia social; **to live on ~** vivir a cargo de la asistencia social
Ⓑ CPD [*programme, provision*] de asistencia social ► **welfare centre, welfare center** (*US*) N centro *m* de asistencia social ► **welfare mother** N *madre que recibe asistencia social* ► **welfare organization** N organización *f* de asistencia social; **animal ~ organization** una organización para la protección de los animales ► **welfare services** NPL asistencia *fsing* social ► **welfare state** N estado *m* de bienestar social ► **welfare work** N trabajos *mpl* de asistencia social ► **welfare worker** N asistente *mf* social

Welfarism ['welfeərɪzəm] N (*US*) *teoría y práctica de la protección de la salud y del bienestar públicos*

well[1] [wel] Ⓐ N 1 (= *bore*) (*for water*) pozo *m*, fuente *f*; (*for oil*) pozo *m*; **to sink a ~** perforar un pozo
2 [*of stairs*] hueco *m*, caja *f*
3 (*in auditorium*) estrado *m*
Ⓑ VI (*also* **~ out, ~ up**) brotar, manar

well[2] [wel] (*compar* **better**; *superl* **best**) Ⓐ ADV
1 (= *in a good manner*) bien; **I remember it ~** lo recuerdo bien; **I know the place ~** conozco bien el lugar; **(and) ~ I know it!** ¡(y) bien que lo sé!; **to eat/live ~** comer/vivir bien; **he sings as ~ as she does** canta tan bien como ella; **as ~ as he could** lo mejor que pudo; **to do ~ at school** sacar buenas notas en el colegio; **to do ~ in an exam** sacar buena nota en un examen; **the patient is doing ~** el paciente evoluciona bien; **you would do ~ to think seriously about our offer** le convendría considerar seriamente nuestra oferta; **you did ~ to come at once** hizo bien en venir enseguida; **~ done!** ¡bien hecho!; **to go ~** ir bien; **everything is going ~** todo va bien; **~ and good** muy bien; **~ played!** (*Sport*) ¡bien hecho!; **to speak ~ of sb** hablar bien de algn; **to think ~ of sb** tener una buena opinión de algn; **he is ~ thought of here** aquí se le estima mucho
2 (= *thoroughly, considerably*) 2·1 bien; **it was ~ deserved** estuvo bien merecido; **he's ~ away*** (= *drunk*) está borracho perdido; **to be ~ in with sb** llevarse muy bien con algn; **it continued ~ into 1996** siguió hasta bien entrado 1996; **he is ~ over** *or* **past fifty** tiene cincuenta y muchos años; **~ over a thousand** muchos más de mil, los mil bien pasados; **it's ~ past ten o'clock** son las diez y mucho; **she knows you too ~ to think that** te conoce demasiado bien para pensar eso de ti; **she loved him too ~** lo quería demasiado; **as we know all** *or* **only too ~** como sabemos perfectamente; **~ and truly** (*esp Brit*) de verdad, realmente; **we got ~ and truly wet** nos mojamos de verdad; **to wish sb ~** desear todo lo mejor a algn; **it was ~ worth the trouble** realmente valió la pena
2·2 **~ dodgy/annoyed‡** bien chungo*/enfadado
3 (= *probably, reasonably*) **you may ~ be surprised to learn that ...** puede que te sorprenda mucho saber que ...; **it may ~ be that ...** es muy posible que + *subjun*; **they may ~ be lying** es muy posible que mientan; **we may as ~ begin now** ya podemos empezar, ¿no?; **you might as ~ tell me the truth** más valdría decirme la verdad; **"shall I go?" — "you may** *or* **might as ~"** "¿voy?" — "por qué no"; **we might (just) as ~ have stayed at home** para lo que hemos hecho, nos podíamos haber quedado en casa; **she cried, as ~ she might** lloró, y con razón; **you may ~ ask!** ¡buena pregunta!; **I couldn't very ~ leave** me resultaba imposible marcharme
4 (*in set expressions*) 4·1 **as ~** (= *in addition*) también; **I'll take those as ~** me llevo esos también; **and it rained as ~!** ¡y además llovió!; **by night as ~ as by day** tanto de noche como de día; **as ~ as his dog he has two rabbits** además de un perro tiene dos conejos; **I had Paul with me as ~ as Lucy** Paul estaba conmigo, así como Lucy *or* además de Lucy; **could you manage to eat mine as ~ as yours?** ¿podrías comerte el mío y el tuyo?; **all sorts of people, rich as ~ as poor** gente de toda clase, tanto rica como pobre
4·2 **to leave ~ alone: my advice is to leave ~ alone** te aconsejo que no te metas; **this sort of wound is best left ~ alone** lo mejor es ni tocar este tipo de herida
Ⓑ ADJ 1 (= *healthy*) bien; **I'm very ~ thank you** estoy muy bien, gracias; **I hope you're ~** espero que te encuentres bien; **are you ~?** ¿qué tal estás?; **she's not been ~ lately** recientemente ha estado algo indispuesta; **to get ~** mejorarse; **get ~ soon!** ¡que te mejores!
2 (= *acceptable, satisfactory*) bien; **that's all very ~, but ...** todo eso está muy bien, pero ...; **it** *or* **we would be ~ to start early** mejor si salimos temprano; **it would be as ~ to ask** más vale *or* valdría preguntar; **it's as ~ not to offend her** más te vale no ofenderla; **it would be just as ~ for you to stay** mejor si te quedas; **it's ~ for you that nobody saw you** menos mal que nadie te vio; **it's just as ~ we asked** menos mal que preguntamos; ✦*PROV* **all's ~ that ends ~** bien está lo que bien acaba
Ⓒ EXCL 1 (*introducing topic, resuming*) bueno; **~, it was like this** bueno, pues así ocurrió; **~, as I was saying ...** bueno, como iba diciendo; **~, that's that!** ¡bueno, asunto concluido!
2 (*expressing resignation*) **~, if we must go, let's get going** bueno, si nos tenemos que ir, vayámonos; **~ then?** ¿y qué?
3 (*concessive, dismissive*) pues; **~, if you're worried, why don't you call her?** pues si estás tan preocupada ¿por qué no la llamas?; **~, I think she's a fool** pues yo pienso que es tonta
4 (*expressing relief*) **~, thank goodness for that!** (pues) ¡gracias a Dios!
5 (*expressing surprise*) ¡vaya!; **~, what do you know!*** ¡anda, quién lo diría!; **~, who would have thought it!** ¡anda, quién lo diría!; **~, ~!** ¡vaya, vaya!

we'll [wiːl] = **we will, we shall**

well- [wel] PREFIX bien-

well-adjusted [ˌweləˈdʒʌstɪd] ADJ equilibrado

well-aimed [ˌwelˈeɪmd] ADJ certero

well-appointed [ˌweləˈpɔɪntɪd] ADJ bien amueblado

well-argued [ˌwelˈɑːgjuːd] ADJ razonado

well-attended [ˌweləˈtendɪd] ADJ muy concurrido

well-baby clinic [welˈbeɪbɪklɪnɪk] N clínica *f* de revisión pediátrica

well-balanced [ˌwelˈbælənsd] ADJ bien equilibrado
well-behaved [ˌwelbɪˈheɪvd] ADJ que se porta bien
well-being [ˈwelˌbiːɪŋ] N bienestar *m*
well-born [ˌwelˈbɔːn] ADJ bien nacido
well-bred [ˌwelˈbred] ADJ [*person*] educado, cortés; [*accent*] culto; [*animal*] de raza, pura sangre
well-brought-up [ˌwelˈbrɔːtʌp] ADJ [*child*] educado
well-built [ˌwelˈbɪlt] ADJ [*house*] de construcción sólida; [*person*] fornido
well-chosen [ˌwelˈtʃəʊzn] ADJ [*remark, words*] acertado
well-cooked [ˌwelˈkʊkt] ADJ (= *tasty*) bien preparado; (= *well-done*) muy hecho
well-defined [ˌweldɪˈfaɪnd] ADJ bien definido
well-deserved [ˌweldɪˈzɜːvd] ADJ merecido
well-developed [ˌweldɪˈveləpt] ADJ [*arm, muscle*] bien desarrollado; [*sense*] agudo, fino
well-disciplined [ˌwelˈdɪsɪplɪnd] ADJ bien disciplinado
well-disposed [ˌweldɪsˈpəʊzd] ADJ bien dispuesto (**to, towards** hacia)
well-documented [ˌwelˈdɒkjʊˌmentɪd] ADJ documentado
well-dressed [ˌwelˈdrest] ADJ bien vestido
well-earned [ˌwelˈɜːnd] ADJ merecido
well-educated [ˌwelˈedjʊkeɪtɪd] ADJ instruido, culto
well-endowed [ˌwelɪnˈdaʊd] ADJ 1 [*institution*] bien dotado de fondos, con buena dotación monetaria
2 (* *euph*) [*man, woman*] bien dotado, bien despachado*
well-equipped [ˌwelɪˈkwɪpt] ADJ bien equipado
well-established [ˌwelɪˈstæblɪʃt] ADJ (*gen*) sólidamente establecido; [*custom*] muy arraigado; [*firm*] (= *of long standing*) sólido; (= *with good reputation*) de buena reputación
well-favoured, **well-favored** (*US*) [ˌwelˈfeɪvəd] ADJ bien parecido
well-fed [ˌwelˈfed] ADJ (*lit*) bien alimentado; (*in appearance*) regordete
well-fixed* [ˌwelˈfɪkst] ADJ (*US*) **to be ~** nadar en la abundancia, estar boyante; **we're ~ for food** tenemos comida de sobra
well-formed [ˌwelˈfɔːmd] ADJ (*Ling*) gramatical
well-formedness [ˌwelˈfɔːmdnɪs] N gramaticalidad *f*
well-founded [ˌwelˈfaʊndɪd] ADJ fundamentado
well-groomed [ˌwelˈgruːmd] ADJ acicalado
well-grown [ˈwelˈgrəʊn] ADJ grande, maduro, adulto
wellhead [ˈwelhed] N fuente *f*, manantial *m*
well-heeled* [ˌwelˈhiːld] ADJ ricacho*
well-hung [ˌwelˈhʌŋ] ADJ 1 (‡) [*man*] bien dotado, bien despachado*, con un buen paquete‡
2 (*Culin*) [*game*] bien manido
well-informed [ˌwelɪnˈfɔːmd] ADJ bien informado, al corriente
Wellington [ˈwelɪŋtən] N Wellington *m*
wellington [ˈwelɪŋtən] N (*Brit*) (*also* **~ boot**) bota *f* de goma
well-intentioned [ˌwelɪnˈtenʃnd] ADJ [*person*] con buenas intenciones; [*act*] bienintencionado; [*lie*] piadoso
well-judged [ˌwelˈdʒʌdʒd] ADJ bien calculado
well-kept [ˌwelˈkept] ADJ [*secret,*] bien guardado; [*garden*] bien cuidado; [*house*] bien conservado
well-knit [ˌwelˈnɪt] ADJ [*body*] robusto, fornido; [*scheme*] lógico, bien razonado; [*speech*] bien pensado, de estructura lógica
well-known [ˌwelˈnəʊn] ADJ [*name, brand, person*] muy conocido, famoso; **it's a ~ fact that ...** ◊ **it's ~ that ...** es bien sabido que ...
well-liked [ˌwelˈlaɪkt] ADJ querido
well-loved [ˌwelˈlʌvd] ADJ muy querido, amado
well-made [ˌwelˈmeɪd] ADJ bien hecho, fuerte
well-managed [ˌwelˈmænɪdʒd] ADJ bien administrado
well-man clinic [welˈmænklɪnɪk] N clínica *f* de salud (*para hombres*)
well-mannered [ˌwelˈmænəd] ADJ educado, cortés
well-marked [ˌwelˈmɑːkt] ADJ bien marcado
well-matched [ˌwelˈmætʃt] ADJ muy iguales
well-meaning [ˌwelˈmiːnɪŋ] ADJ bienintencionado
well-meant [ˌwelˈment] ADJ bienintencionado
well-nigh [ˈwelnaɪ] ADV **~ impossible** casi imposible
well-nourished [ˌwelˈnʌrɪʃt] ADJ bien alimentado
well-off [ˌwelˈɒf] Ⓐ ADJ 1 (*financially*) acomodado, pudiente; **the less ~** las gentes menos pudientes
2 (*in circumstances*) **she's ~ without him** está mejor sin él; **you don't know when you're ~** no sabes los muchos beneficios que tienes
Ⓑ NPL **the ~** las clases acomodadas
well-oiled* [ˌwelˈɔɪld] ADJ hecho una cuba*
well-padded* [ˌwelˈpædɪd] ADJ bien rellenito
well-paid [ˌwelˈpeɪd] ADJ bien pagado, bien retribuido
well-preserved [ˌwelprɪˈzɜːvd] ADJ [*person*] bien conservado
well-proportioned [ˌwelprəˈpɔːʃnd] ADJ bien proporcionado, de forma elegante; [*person*] de talle elegante
well-read [ˌwelˈred] ADJ culto, instruido; **to be ~ in history** haber leído mucha historia, estar muy documentado en historia
well-respected [ˌwelrɪˈspektɪd] ADJ respetado, estimado
well-rounded [ˌwelˈraʊndɪd] ADJ [*person*] polifacético; [*education*] equilibrado
well-spent [ˌwelˈspent] ADJ bien empleado, fructuoso
well-spoken [ˌwelˈspəʊkən] ADJ bienhablado, con acento culto
wellspring [ˈwelˌsprɪŋ] N (*fig*) fuente *f*
well-stacked* [ˌwelˈstækt] ADJ de buen tipo, curvilínea
well-stocked [ˌwelˈstɒkt] ADJ bien surtido, bien provisto; **~ shelves** estantes *mpl* llenos
well-thought-of [ˌwelˈθɔːtəv] ADJ bien reputado, de buena reputación
well-thought-out [ˌwelθɔːtˈaʊt] ADJ bien planeado
well-thumbed [ˌwelˈθʌmd] ADJ [*book*] muy usado, manoseado; [*pages*] manoseado
well-timed [ˌwelˈtaɪmd] ADJ oportuno
well-to-do [ˌweltəˈduː] Ⓐ ADJ acomodado
Ⓑ NPL **the ~** las clases acomodadas
well-travelled, **well-traveled** (*US*) [ˌwelˈtrævld] ADJ [*person*] que ha viajado mucho, que ha visto mucho mundo; **a ~ path** un camino muy trillado
well-tried [ˌwelˈtraɪd] ADJ [*method*] comprobado
well-trodden [ˌwelˈtrɒdn] ADJ trillado; **a ~ path** un camino muy trillado
well-turned [ˌwelˈtɜːnd] ADJ elegante; **a ~ phrase** una frase elegante; **a ~ ankle** un tobillo bien formado
well-wisher [ˈwelˌwɪʃəʳ] N admirador(a) *m/f*
well-woman clinic [ˈwelwʊmənˌklɪnɪk] N clínica *f* de salud (*para mujeres*)
well-worn [ˌwelˈwɔːn] ADJ [*garment*] raído; [*path, cliché*] trillado
well-written [ˌwelˈrɪtn] ADJ bien escrito
welly* [ˈwelɪ] N (*Brit*) **~ boots** ◊ **wellies** botas *fpl* de goma
Welsh [welʃ] Ⓐ ADJ galés
Ⓑ N 1 (= *language*) galés *m*
2 **the ~** (= *people*) los galeses
Ⓒ CPD ► **the Welsh Assembly** N el parlamento galés ► **Welsh dresser** N *aparador con estantes en la mitad de arriba* ► **Welsh rabbit**, **Welsh rarebit** N pan *m* con queso tostado
welsh [welʃ] VI [*bookmaker*] largarse sin pagar*; **to ~ on a promise** no cumplir una promesa; **they ~ed on the agreement** no respetaron el acuerdo
Welshman [ˈwelʃmən] N (*pl* **Welshmen**) galés *m*
Welshwoman [ˈwelʃˌwʊmən] N (*pl* **Welshwomen**) galesa *f*
welt [welt] Ⓐ N 1 (= *weal*) verdugón *m*
2 [*of garment*] ribete *m*
3 [*of shoe*] vira *f*
Ⓑ VT 1 [+ *shoe*] poner vira a
2 (= *beat*) pegar, zurrar
welter [ˈweltəʳ] Ⓐ N confusión *f*, mezcla *f* confusa, mescolanza *f*, revoltijo *m*; **in a ~ of blood** en un mar de sangre
Ⓑ VI revolcarse; **to ~ in** estar bañado en, bañarse en
welterweight [ˈweltəweɪt] N wélter *m*; **light ~** wélter *m* ligero
wen [wen] N lobanillo *m*, quiste *m* sebáceo; **the Great Wen** el gran tumor (*Londres*)
wench [wentʃ] (††† *or liter*) Ⓐ N moza *f*; (= *whore*) puta *f*
Ⓑ VI (*also* **to go ~ing**) putañear††, ir de fulanas
wend [wend] VT (*liter*) **to ~ one's way to** enderezar sus pasos a; **to ~ one's way home** (*hum*) encaminarse a casa
Wendy house [ˈwendɪhaʊs] N (*pl* **Wendy houses** [ˈwendɪhaʊzɪz]) (*Brit*) casa *f* de juguete (*suficientemente grande para jugar dentro*)
went [went] PT *of* **go**
wept [wept] PT, PP *of* **weep**
we're [wɪəʳ] = **we are**
were [wɜːʳ] PT *of* **be**
weren't [wɜːnt] = **were not**
werewolf [ˈwɪəwʊlf] N (*pl* **werewolves**) hombre *m* lobo
wert†† [wɜːt] PT (*thou form*) *of* **be**
Wesleyan [ˈwezlɪən] Ⓐ ADJ metodista
Ⓑ N metodista *mf*
Wesleyanism [ˈwezlɪənɪzəm] N metodismo *m*
west [west] Ⓐ N oeste *m*, occidente *m*; **the West** (*Pol*) el Oeste, (el) Occidente; **tales of the American West** cuentos *mpl* del Oeste americano; **in the ~ of the country** al oeste *or* en el oeste del país; **the wind is from the ~** *or* **in the ~** el viento sopla *or* viene del oeste; **to the ~ of** al oeste de
Ⓑ ADJ [*part, coast*] oeste, del oeste, occidental; [*wind*] del oeste
Ⓒ ADV (= *westward*) hacia el oeste; (= *in the*

west) al oeste, en el oeste; **we were travelling ~** viajábamos hacia el oeste; **~ of the border** al oeste de la frontera; **it's ~ of London** está al oeste *or* en el oeste de Londres; ✦*IDIOM* **to go ~*** [*object, machine*] cascarse*, estropearse; [*plan*] irse al garete; [*person*] estirar la pata*
Ⓓ CPD ► **West Africa** N África *f* Occidental ► **the West Bank** N Cisjordania *f* ► **West Berlin** N (*Hist*) Berlín *m* Oeste ► **the West Country** N (*Brit*) el West Country (*el sudoeste de Inglaterra, esp. los condados de Cornualles, Devon y Somerset*) ► **the West End** N (*of London*) el West End (de Londres) (*zona del centro de Londres donde hay muchas tiendas y locales de ocio*) ► **West Germany** N (*formerly*) Alemania *f* Occidental; *see also* **West German**, **West Indian** ► **West Indies** NPL Antillas *fpl*

westbound ['westbaʊnd] ADJ [*traffic, carriageway*] con rumbo al oeste

westerly ['westəlɪ] Ⓐ ADJ [*wind*] del oeste; **in a ~ direction** hacia el oeste, rumbo al oeste, en dirección oeste; **the most ~ point in Europe** el punto más occidental *or* más al oeste de Europa
Ⓑ N (= *wind*) viento *m* del oeste

western ['westən] Ⓐ ADJ occidental; **Western** (*Pol*) occidental, del Oeste; **the ~ part of the island** la parte occidental *or* oeste de la isla; **in ~ Spain** en la España occidental; **the ~ coast** la costa occidental *or* oeste
Ⓑ N (= *film*) western *m*, película *f* del oeste
Ⓒ CPD ► **Western Isles** N (*Brit*) las Hébridas

westerner ['westənəʳ] N habitante *mf* del Oeste; (*Pol etc*) occidental *mf*

westernization ['westənaɪ'zeɪʃən] N occidentalización *f*

westernize ['westənaɪz] VT occidentalizar

westernized ['westənaɪzd] ADJ occidentalizado; **to become ~** occidentalizarse

westernmost ['westənməʊst] ADJ más occidental, más al oeste; **the ~ point of Spain** el punto más occidental *or* más al oeste de España

west-facing ['west'feɪsɪŋ] ADJ con cara al oeste, orientado hacia el oeste; **~ slope** vertiente *f* oeste

West German [ˌwest'dʒɜːmən] (*formerly*) Ⓐ ADJ de Alemania Occidental
Ⓑ N alemán/ana *m/f* (de Alemania Occidental)

West Indian [ˌwest'ɪndɪən] Ⓐ ADJ antillano
Ⓑ N antillano/a *m/f*

Westminster ['westˌmɪnstəʳ] N (*Brit*) Westminster *m*

> **WESTMINSTER**
>
> **Westminster**, *también llamado* **City of Westminster**, *es el distrito del centro de Londres que comprende el Parlamento* (**Houses of Parliament**), *la Abadía de Westminster* (**Westminster Abbey**) *y el Palacio de Buckingham* (**Buckingham Palace**). *Este nombre se usa también normalmente en los medios de comunicación para referirse al Parlamento o a los parlamentarios británicos.*

west-northwest [ˌwestnɔːθ'west] Ⓐ N oesnoroeste *m*, oesnorueste *m*
Ⓑ ADJ oesnoroeste, oesnorueste
Ⓒ ADV (= *toward west-northwest*) hacia el oesnoroeste *or* oesnorueste; [*situated*] al oesnoroeste *or* oesnorueste, en el oesnoroeste *or* oesnorueste

west-southwest [ˌwestsaʊθ'west] Ⓐ N oesuroeste *m*, oesurueste *m*
Ⓑ ADJ oesuroeste, oesurueste
Ⓒ ADV (= *toward west-southwest*) hacia el oesuroeste *or* oesurueste; [*situated*] al oesuroeste *or* oesurueste, en el oesuroeste *or* oesurueste

westward ['westwəd] Ⓐ ADJ [*movement, migration*] hacia el oeste, en dirección oeste
Ⓑ ADV hacia el oeste, en dirección oeste

westwards ['westwədz] ADV (*esp Brit*) = **westward B**

wet [wet] Ⓐ ADJ (*compar* **wetter**; *superl* **wettest**)
[1] [*person, clothes, nappy, bed*] mojado; (= *sopping*) calado; [*paint, ink, plaster*] fresco; **the baby was ~** el niño se había hecho pis*; **"wet paint"** "recién pintado"; **to get ~** mojarse; **to get one's feet/shoes ~** mojarse los pies/zapatos; **to be soaking** *or* **wringing ~** estar chorreando; **to be ~ through** estar empapado, estar calado; **the grass was ~ with dew** la hierba estaba mojada de rocío; ✦*IDIOM* **to be ~ behind the ears*** estar verde*
[2] (*from crying*) [*eyes*] lloroso, lleno de lágrimas; [*cheeks, face*] lleno de lágrimas; **her cheeks were ~ with tears** las lágrimas le corrían por las mejillas
[3] (= *rainy*) [*day, month, winter, climate*] lluvioso; **take a raincoat if it's ~** llévate un impermeable si llueve; **we've had a lot of ~ weather** hemos tenido un tiempo muy lluvioso; **it's been very ~** ha llovido mucho; **the ~ season** la estación lluviosa *or* de las lluvias
[4] (* *pej*) (= *feeble*) soso, blandengue; (*Brit Pol*) *término aplicado a los políticos conservadores de tendencias centristas, desdeñados por la parte más radicalmente conservadora del partido*
[5] (*US*) (= *against prohibition*) antiprohibicionista
Ⓑ N [1] **the ~** (= *rain, wet weather*) la lluvia; **the bike had been left out in the ~** habían dejado la bicicleta bajo la lluvia
[2] (*Brit Pol**) *político conservador de tendencias centristas, desdeñado por la parte más radicalmente conservadora del partido*
Ⓒ VT [1] (= *make wet*) mojar; **to ~ one's lips** humedecerse los labios; ✦*IDIOM* **to ~ one's whistle**† mojar el gaznate
[2] (= *urinate on*) **he's ~ his trousers** se ha orinado en los pantalones, se ha hecho pis en los pantalones*, se ha meado en los pantalones‡; **to ~ the bed** orinarse en la cama, hacerse pis en la cama*, mearse en la cama‡; **to ~ o.s.** orinarse encima, hacerse pis encima*, mearse encima‡; ✦*IDIOM* **to ~ o.s.*** (*with amusement*) mearse de risa‡; (*with terror*) mearse de miedo‡
Ⓓ CPD ► **wet blanket*** N aguafiestas* *mf inv* ► **wet dream** N polución *f* nocturna; **to have a ~ dream** tener una polución nocturna, correrse dormido*‡ ► **wet fish** N (*Culin*) pescado *m* fresco; **he's a bit of a ~ fish** (*fig*) es un poco soso ► **wet nurse** N nodriza *f*, ama *f* de cría ► **wet suit** N traje *m* isotérmico

wetback* ['wetbæk] N (*US*) inmigrante *mf* (mejicano) ilegal, espalda *mf* mojada

wether ['weðəʳ] N carnero *m* castrado

wetland ['wetlənd] N pantano *m*, zona *f* húmeda *or* acuosa; **~s** pantanos *mpl*, tierras *fpl* pantanosas

wet-look ['wetlʊk] ADJ [*material, jeans, boots*] con un acabado abrillantado

wetness ['wetnɪs] N [*of surface, road*] estado *m* mojado; [*of substance*] lo mojado; [*of weather*] lo lluvioso

wetting ['wetɪŋ] N **to get a ~** mojarse, empaparse; **to give sb a ~** mojar *or* empapar a algn

WEU ABBR = **Western European Union**

WEU N ABBR (= **Western European Union**) UEO *f*

we've [wiːv] = **we have**

WFP N ABBR (= **World Food Programme**) PMA *m*

WFTU N ABBR (= **World Federation of Trade Unions**) FSM *f*

whack [wæk] Ⓐ N [1] (= *blow*) golpe *m* fuerte, porrazo *m*; **to give sb a ~** dar un golpe fuerte *or* un porrazo a algn; **to give sth a ~** golpear algo ruidosamente
[2] (*) (= *attempt*) **to have a ~ at sth** intentar algo, probar algo; **let's have a ~ (at it)** probemos, intentemos
[3] (*) (= *share*) parte *f*, porción *f*; **you'll get your ~** recibirás tu parte
[4] (*) **the car does 200kph top ~** a toda máquina, el coche alcanza una velocidad de 200km/h
[5] **out of ~** (*US**) fastidiado
Ⓑ EXCL **~!** ¡zas!
Ⓒ VT [1] (= *beat*) golpear, aporrear; (= *defeat*) dar una paliza a*; **he ~ed me with a cane** me dio con una palmeta
[2] (*fig*) **the problem has me ~ed** el problema me trae perplejo; **we've got the problem ~ed at last** por fin hemos resuelto el problema

whacked* ['wækt] ADJ (*Brit*) **to be ~** estar agotado, estar hecho polvo*

whacking ['wækɪŋ] Ⓐ ADJ (*esp Brit**) (also **~ great**) grandote*, enorme; **a ~ (great) book** un tocho de libro*
Ⓑ N zurra *f*; **to give sb a ~** zurrar a algn, pegar a algn

whacky* ['wækɪ] ADJ (*US*) = **wacky**

whale [weɪl] Ⓐ N (*pl* **whales** *or* **whale**) ballena *f*; ✦*IDIOMS* **a ~ of a difference*** una enorme diferencia; **to have a ~ of a time*** pasarlo bomba *or* (*S. Cone*) regio
Ⓑ CPD ► **whale oil** N aceite *m* de ballena

whalebone ['weɪlbəʊn] N barba *f* de ballena; (*in haberdashery*) ballena *f*

whaler ['weɪləʳ] N (= *person, ship*) ballenero *m*

whaling ['weɪlɪŋ] Ⓐ N pesca *f* de ballenas; **to go ~** ir a pescar ballenas
Ⓑ CPD ► **whaling ship** N ballenero *m* ► **whaling station** N estación *f* ballenera

wham [wæm] Ⓐ EXCL **~!** ¡zas!
Ⓑ N golpe *m* resonante
Ⓒ VT golpear de modo resonante
Ⓓ VI **to ~ against/into sth** chocar ruidosamente con algo

whammy* ['wæmɪ] N (*US*) mala sombra *f*, mala suerte *f*, mala pata *f*; *see also* **double F**

whang [wæŋ] Ⓐ N golpe *m* resonante
Ⓑ VT golpear de modo resonante
Ⓒ VI **to ~ against/into sth** chocar ruidosamente con algo

wharf [wɔːf] N (*pl* **wharfs** *or* **wharves** [wɔːvz]) muelle *m*, embarcadero *m*; **ex ~** franco en el muelle; **price ex ~** precio *m* franco de muelle

wharfage ['wɔːfɪdʒ] N muellaje *m*

what [wɒt]

[A] PRONOUN	[C] EXCLAMATION
[B] ADJECTIVE	

Ⓐ PRONOUN
[1] ***in direct questions*** [1·1]
In direct questions, **what** *can generally be translated by* **qué** *with an accent:*
qué; **~ do you want now?** ¿qué quieres ahora?; **~'s in here?** ¿qué hay aquí dentro?; **~ is it now?** y ahora ¿qué?; **~ does he owe his success to?** ◊ **to ~ does he owe his success?** (*frm*) ¿a qué debe su éxito?; **~'s a trac-**

tor, Daddy? ¿qué es un tractor, papá?; **~ are capers?** ¿qué son las alcaparras?

Only use **¿qué es...?/¿qué son...?** *to translate* **what is/are** *when asking for a* **definition**. *In other contexts use* **¿cuál es?/¿cuáles son?**:

~'s the capital of Finland? ¿cuál es la capital de Finlandia?; **~'s her telephone number?** ¿cuál es su número de teléfono?; **~ were the greatest problems?** ¿cuáles eran los mayores problemas?

However, not all expressions with **what** *should be translated literally. Some require* **qué** *used adjectivally:*

~ is the difference? ¿qué diferencia hay?; **~ are your plans?** ¿qué planes tienes?; BUT **~'s the Spanish for "pen"?** ¿cómo se dice "pen" en español?; **~'s your name?** ¿cómo te llamas?

1·2 (= *how much*) cuánto; **~ will it cost?** ¿cuánto va a costar?; **~ does it weigh?** ¿cuánto pesa?; **~'s nine times five?** ¿cuánto es nueve por cinco?

1·3 (= *what did you say*) cómo, qué; **~? I didn't catch that** ¿cómo? *or* ¿qué?, no he entendido eso; **~ did you say?** ¿cómo *or* qué dices?, ¿qué has dicho?, ¿qué dijiste? (*LAm*)

1·4 (*Brit†*) (*as question tag*) verdad; **it's getting late, ~?** se está haciendo tarde ¿no? *or* ¿verdad?

2 *in indirect questions* 2·1

In most cases, translate the pronoun **what** *using either* **qué** *with an accent or* **lo que** *without an accent:*

qué, lo que; **he asked her ~ she thought of it** le preguntó qué *or* lo que pensaba de ello; **I asked him ~ DNA was** le pregunté qué *or* lo que era el ADN

Use **cuál era/cuáles son** *etc instead of* **lo que era/lo que son** *etc if* **what was/are** *etc does not relate to a definition:*

she asked me ~ my hobbies were me preguntó cuáles eran mis hobbys; **please explain ~ you saw** por favor, explique qué *or* lo que vio; **can you explain ~'s happening?** ¿me puedes explicar (qué es) lo que está pasando?; **he explained ~ it was** explicó qué era *or* lo que era; **do you know ~'s happening?** ¿sabes qué *or* lo que está pasando?; **I don't know ~'s happening** no sé qué está pasando, no sé (qué es) lo que está pasando; **tell me ~ happened** cuéntame qué *or* lo que ocurrió

2·2 (= *how much*) cuánto; **he asked her ~ she had paid for it** le preguntó cuánto había pagado por ello

3 *before an infinitive* qué; **I don't know ~ to do** no sé qué hacer

4 *relative use* lo que; **~ I want is a cup of tea** lo que quiero es una taza de té; **it wasn't ~ I was expecting** no era lo que yo me esperaba; **do ~ you like** haz lo que quieras; **business isn't ~ it was** los negocios ya no son lo que eran; **I've no clothes except ~ I'm wearing** no tengo ropa, aparte de lo que llevo puesto; **I saw ~ happened** vi lo que pasó; **she told him ~ she thought of it** le dijo lo que pensaba de ello

5 *in exclamations* **~ it is to be rich and famous!** ¡lo que es ser rico y famoso!; ✦*PROV* **~'s done is done** lo hecho hecho está

6 *in set expressions*

- **and what have you** ◊ **and what not*** y qué sé yo qué más, y qué sé yo cuántas cosas más
- **to give sb what for*** regañar a algn
- **know what**: **it was full of cream, jam, chocolate and I don't know ~** estaba lleno de nata, mermelada, chocolate y no sé cuántas cosas más; **you know ~? I think, he's drunk** creo que está borracho, ¿sabes?; **I know ~, let's ring her up** se me ocurre una idea, vamos a llamarla por teléfono
- **to know what's what*** saber cuántas son cinco*
- **or what?*** **do you want it or ~?** ¿lo quieres o qué?; **are you coming or ~?** entonces ¿vienes o no?; **I mean, is this sick, or ~?** vamos, que es de verdadero mal gusto, ¿o no?; **is this luxury or ~?** esto sí que es lujo, ¿eh?
- **say what you like, ...** digas lo que digas, ..., se diga lo que se diga, ...
- **so what?*** ¿y qué?; **so ~ if it does rain?** ¿y qué, si llueve?; **so ~ if he is gay?** ¿y qué (pasa) si es gay?, ¿y qué importa que sea gay?
- **(I'll) tell you what** se me ocurre una idea, tengo una idea
- **what about**: **~ about me?** y yo ¿qué?; **~ about next week?** ¿qué te parece la semana que viene?; **"your car ..." — "~ about it?"*** —tu coche ... —¿qué pasa con mi coche?; **~ about going to the cinema?** ¿qué tal si vamos al cine?, ¿y si vamos al cine?; **~ about lunch, shall we go out?** ¿y para comer? ¿salimos fuera? *or* ¿qué tal si salimos fuera?; **~ about people who haven't got cars?** ¿y la gente que no tiene coche?
- **what for?** (= *why*) ¿por qué?; (= *to what purpose*) ¿para qué?; **~ are you doing that for?** ¿por *or* para qué haces eso?; **~'s that button for?** ¿para qué es ese botón?
- **what if ...?** ¿y si ...?; **~ if this doesn't work out?** ¿y si esto no funciona?; **~ if he says no?** ¿y si dice que no?
- **what of**: **but ~ of the political leaders?** pero, ¿y qué hay de los líderes políticos?; **~ of it?*** y eso ¿qué importa?
- **what's ...**: **~'s surprising is that we hadn't heard of this before** lo sorprendente es que no nos habíamos enterado antes
- **¿what's it like?** (*asking for description*) ¿cómo es?; (*asking for evaluation*) ¿qué tal es?; **~'s their new house like?** ¿cómo es su nueva casa?; **~'s his first novel like?** ¿qué tal es su primera novela?; **~ will the weather be like tomorrow?** ¿qué tal tiempo va a hacer mañana?
- **and what's more ...** y, además, ...
- **what's that?** (*asking about sth*) ¿qué es eso?; (= *what did you say?*) ¿qué has dicho?; **~'s that to you?*** ¿eso qué tiene que ver contigo?, ¿a ti qué te importa?*
- **what's worse**: **and ~'s worse ...** y lo que es peor ...
- **what with**: **~ with one thing and another** entre una cosa y otra; **~ with the stress and lack of sleep, I was in a terrible state** entre la tensión y la falta de sueño me encontraba fatal

Ⓑ ADJECTIVE

1 *in direct and indirect questions* qué; **~ dress shall I wear?** ¿qué vestido me pongo?; **~ colour is it?** ¿de qué color es?; **she asked me ~ day she should come** me preguntó qué día tenía que venir; **he explained ~ ingredients are used** explicó qué ingredientes se usan; **~ good would that do?** ¿de qué serviría eso?; **do you know ~ music they're going to play?** ¿sabes qué música van a tocar?; **did they tell you ~ time they'd be arriving?** ¿te dijeron a qué hora llegarían?

2 *relative* **~ savings we had are now gone** los ahorros que teníamos ya han desaparecido; **I will give you ~ information we have** te daré la información que tenemos; **I gave him ~ money/coins I had** le di todo el dinero/todas las monedas que tenía; **I gave her ~ comfort I could** la consolé en lo que pude; **they packed ~ few belongings they had** hicieron la maleta con las pocas pertenencias que tenían; **~ little I had** lo poco que tenía

3 *in exclamations*

Remember to put an accent on **qué** *in exclamations as well as in direct and indirect questions:*

~ a nuisance! ¡qué lata!; **~ a fool I was!** ¡qué tonto fui!; **~ an ugly dog!** ¡qué perro más *or* tan feo!; **~ a lot of people!** ¡qué cantidad de gente!; **~ an excuse!** (*iro*) ¡buen pretexto!, ¡vaya excusa!

Ⓒ EXCLAMATION

¡qué!; **~! you sold it!** ¿qué? ¡lo has vendido!; **~! you expect me to believe that!** ¿qué? ¿esperas que me crea eso?; **~! he can't be a spy!** ¿qué? ¿cómo va a ser un espía?; **you told him WHAT?** ¿que le has dicho QUÉ?; **"he's getting married" — "what!"** se casa — ¿cómo dices?

- **you what?**: **"I'm going to be an actress" — "you what?"*** —voy a hacerme actriz —¿cómo *or* qué dices?; **I'm going to have a baby — you WHAT?** —voy a tener un niño —¡¿que vas a tener un QUÉ?!

what-d'you-call-her* [ˈwɒtdʒʊˌkɔːləʳ] PRON fulana *f*, cómo-se-llame *f*; **I bumped into ~ from next door at the party** en la fiesta me encontré con esa chica de al lado, ¿cómo se llame?

what-d'you-call-him* [ˈwɒtdʒʊˌkɔːlɪm] PRON fulano *m*, cómo-se-llame *m*; **I bumped into ~ from next door at the party** en la fiesta me encontré con ese chico de al lado, ¿cómo se llame?; **old ~ with the red nose** ése que tiene la nariz tan coloradota

what-d'you-call-it* [ˈwɒtdʒʊˌkɔːlɪt] PRON cosa *f*, chisme *m*; **he does it with the ~** lo hace con el chisme ese; **that green ~ on the front** esa cosa verde en la parte delantera

whatever [wɒtˈevəʳ] Ⓐ PRON 1 (= *no matter what*) **~ it may be** sea lo que sea; **~ he says** diga lo que diga; **~ happens** pase lo que pase; **get it, ~ it costs** cómpralo, cueste lo que cueste; **~ the weather** haga el tiempo que haga

2 (= *anything that*) lo que; (= *everything that*) todo lo que; **~ you like** lo que quieras; **do ~ you want** haz lo que quieras; **we'll do ~'s necessary** haremos lo que haga falta; **~ you say** (*acquiescing*) lo que quieras; **"I tell you I'm ill" — "~ you say"** (*iro*) —te digo que estoy enfermo —sí, sí *or* —sí, lo que tú quieras; **~ I have is yours** todo lo que tengo es tuyo; **~ you find** todo lo que *or* cualquier cosa que encuentres; **or ~ they're called** o como quiera que se llamen

3 (*in questions*) qué; **~ do you mean?** ¿qué quieres decir?; **~ did you do?** ¿pero qué hiciste?; **~ did you say that for?** ¿a santo de qué dijiste eso?

4 (= *other similar things*) **you can put your pyjamas, sponge bag and ~ in here** aquí puedes guardar el pijama, el neceser y todas esas cosas

Ⓑ ADJ 1 (= *any*) cualquier; (= *all*) todo; **~ book you choose** cualquier libro que elijas; **~ books you choose** cualquier libro de los que elijas; **give me ~ change you've got**

dame todo el cambio que tengas
[2] (= *no matter what*) **~ problems you've got, we'll help** nosotros te ayudaremos, tengas el problema que tengas
[3] (*in questions*) qué; **~ time is it?** ¿qué hora podrá ser?; **~ help will that be?** ¿para qué servirá eso?
Ⓒ ADV (*with negative*) en absoluto; **nothing ~** nada en absoluto; **it's no use ~** no sirve para nada; **he said nothing ~ of interest** no dijo nada en absoluto que tuviera interés

what-ho†* ['wɒt'həʊ] EXCL (*surprise*) ¡caramba!, ¡vaya!; (*greeting*) ¡hola!, ¡oye!

whatnot ['wɒtnɒt] Ⓐ N [1] (*) (*whatsit*) chisme *m*
[2] (= *furniture*) estantería *f* portátil
Ⓑ PRON **and ~*** y qué sé yo, y todas esas cosas

what's-her-name* ['wɒtsəneɪm] PRON fulana *f*, cómo-se-llame *f*; **I ran into ~ from the hairdresser's** me encontré con fulana, la de la peluquería

what's-his-name* ['wɒtsɪzneɪm] PRON fulano *m*, cómo-se-llame *m*; **I ran into ~ from the hairdresser's** me encontré con fulano, el de la peluquería; **old ~ with the limp** fulano el cojo

whatsit* ['wɒtsɪt] N chisme *m*

whatsoever [,wɒtsəʊ'evəʳ] Ⓐ ADV = **whatever C**
Ⓑ PRON (††) = **whatever A**
Ⓒ ADJ (††) = **whatever B**

wheat [wiːt] Ⓐ N trigo *m*; **✦IDIOM to separate the ~ from the chaff** separar la cizaña *or* la paja del buen grano
Ⓑ CPD de trigo, trigueño ► **wheat loaf** N pan *m* de trigo

wheatear ['wiːtɪəʳ] N (*Orn*) collalba *f*

wheaten ['wiːtn] ADJ de trigo

wheatfield ['wiːtfiːld] N trigal *m*

wheatgerm ['wiːtdʒɜːm] N germen *m* de trigo

wheatmeal ['wiːtmiːl] N harina *f* negra

wheatsheaf ['wiːtʃiːf] N gavilla *f* de trigo

wheedle ['wiːdl] VT **to ~ sb into doing sth** engatusar a algn para que haga algo; **to ~ sth out of sb** sonsacar algo a algn

wheedling ['wiːdlɪŋ] Ⓐ ADJ mimoso
Ⓑ N mimos *mpl*, halagos *mpl*

wheel [wiːl] Ⓐ N [1] (*lit*) rueda *f*; (= *steering wheel*) volante *m*; (*Naut*) timón *m*; (*potter's*) torno *m*; **a basket on ~s** una cesta con ruedas; **to be at** *or* **behind the ~** estar al volante; **to take the ~** tomar el volante; *see also* **big C**
[2] (*Mil*) vuelta *f*, conversión *f*; **a ~ to the right** una vuelta hacia la derecha
[3] **wheels** coche *msing*; **do you have ~s?*** ¿tienes coche?
[4] (*in fig phrases*) **the ~ of fortune** la rueda de fortuna; **the ~s of government** el mecanismo del gobierno; **✦IDIOM there are ~s within ~s** esto es más complicado de lo que parece, esto tiene su miga
Ⓑ VT (= *push*) [+ *bicycle, pram*] empujar; [+ *child*] pasear en cochecito; **we ~ed it over to the window** lo empujamos hasta la ventana; **when it broke down I had to ~ it** cuando se averió tuve que empujarlo
Ⓒ VI [1] (= *roll*) rodar
[2] (= *turn*) girar; [*bird*] revolotear; **to ~ left** (*Mil*) dar una vuelta hacia la izquierda; **to ~ round** [+ *person*] girar sobre los talones
[3] **✦IDIOM to ~ and deal*** andar en trapicheos*, hacer chanchullos*
Ⓓ CPD ► **wheel horse*** N (*US*) trabajador(a) *m/f* infatigable, mula *f* de carga

►**wheel out*** VT + ADV [+ *supporter, expert*] traer; [+ *idea, cliché*] desempolvar

wheelbarrow ['wiːl,bærəʊ] N carretilla *f*

wheelbase ['wiːlbeɪs] N batalla *f*, distancia *f* entre ejes

wheelbrace ['wiːlbreɪs] N llave *f* de ruedas en cruz

wheelchair ['wiːltʃɛəʳ] N silla *f* de ruedas

wheel-clamp ['wiːlklæmp] Ⓐ N cepo *m*
Ⓑ VT poner cepo a, inmovilizar con el cepo; **I found I'd been ~ed** me encontré inmovilizado con el cepo

wheeled [wiːld] ADJ [*traffic, transport*] rodado

-wheeled [wiːld] ADJ (*ending in compounds*) **three-wheeled** de tres ruedas

wheeler-dealer ['wiːlə,diːləʳ] N chanchullero/a *m/f*

wheelhouse ['wiːlhaʊs] N timonera *f*, cámara *f* del timonel

wheeling ['wiːlɪŋ] N **~ and dealing** trapicheos* *mpl*, chanchullos* *mpl*

wheelwright ['wiːlraɪt] N ruedero *m*, carretero *m*

wheeze [wiːz] Ⓐ VI resollar, respirar con silbido
Ⓑ VT **"yes," he ~d** —sí —dijo casi sin voz
Ⓒ N [1] (*lit*) resuello *m* (asmático), respiración *f* sibilante
[2] (*Brit**) (= *trick*) truco *m*, treta *f*; (= *idea*) idea *f*; **that's a good ~** es buena idea; **to think up a ~** idear una treta

wheezing ['wiːzɪŋ] ADJ, **wheezy** ['wiːzɪ] ADJ [*breath*] ruidoso, difícil; [*pronunciation*] sibilante

whelk [welk] N buccino *m*

whelp [welp] Ⓐ N cachorro *m*
Ⓑ VI [*bitch*] parir

when [wen]

[A] ADVERB [B] CONJUNCTION

Ⓐ ADVERB
[1] ***in direct and indirect questions, reported speech***

> **When** *in direct and indirect questions as well as after expressions of (un)certainty and doubt (e.g.* **no sé***) translates as* **cuándo** *(with an accent) and is used with the indicative:*

cuándo; **~ did it happen?** ¿cuándo ocurrió?; **he asked me ~ I had seen it** me preguntó cuándo lo había visto; **do you know ~ he died?** ¿sabes cuándo murió?; **I know ~ it happened** yo sé cuándo ocurrió; **he told me ~ the wedding would be** me dijo cuándo sería la boda; **he told me ~ to come in** me indicó cuándo entrar
◆ **say when!** (*when serving food, drink*) ¡dime cuánto!
◆ **since when**: **since ~ do you like** *or* **have you liked Indian food?** ¿desde cuándo te gusta la comida india?
◆ **till when?** ¿hasta cuándo?
[2] ***in exclamations*** cuándo; **~ will we learn to keep our mouths shut!** ¡cuándo aprenderemos a callar la boca!
[3] ***in other statements*** [3·1] (= *the time, day, moment, etc*) cuando; **that was ~ the trouble started** entonces fue cuando empezaron los problemas; **Monday? that's ~ Ted gets back** ¿el lunes? ese día es cuando vuelve Ted; **that's ~ the programme starts** a esa hora es cuando empieza el programa; **1958: that's ~ I was born** 1958: (en) ese año nací yo; **she told me about ~ she was in London** me contó lo que le pasó cuando estuvo en Londres
[3·2] (*relative use*)

> *If* **when** *follows a noun (e.g.* **day, time***) and defines the noun, translate using* **(en) que** *not* **cuando***:*

(en) que; **during the time ~ she lived abroad** durante el tiempo (en) que vivió en el extranjero; **the year ~ you were born** el año (en) que naciste; **she can't remember a time ~ she wasn't happy** no recuerda una época (en) que no fuese feliz; **there are times ~ I wish I'd never met him** hay momentos en los que desearía no haberlo conocido nunca

> *If the* **when** *clause following a noun provides additional information which does not define or restrict the noun — in English as in Spanish commas are obligatory here — translate using* **cuando***:*

cuando; **some days, ~ we're very busy, we don't finish work till very late** algunos días, cuando tenemos mucho trabajo, no acabamos hasta muy tarde

Ⓑ CONJUNCTION
[1] ***= at, during*** *or* ***after the time that***

> *As a conjunction,* **when** *can be translated by* **cuando** *(without an accent) followed by either the indicative or the subjunctive. Use the* **INDICATIVE** *when talking about the past or making general statements about the present. Use the* **SUBJUNCTIVE** *when the action is or was in the future:*

cuando; **~ I came in** cuando entré; **~ I was young** cuando era joven; **he had just sat down ~ the phone rang** acababa de sentarse cuando sonó el teléfono; **everything looks nicer ~ the sun is shining** todo está más bonito cuando brilla el sol; **he arrived at 8 o'clock, ~ traffic is at its peak** llegó a las ocho en punto, en lo peor del tráfico; **call me ~ you get there** llámame cuando llegues; **~ the bridge is built** cuando se construya el puente; **you can go ~ we have finished** puedes irte cuando hayamos terminado; **he said he'd tell me ~ I was older** dijo que me lo diría cuando fuera mayor

> *If* **when** + **VERB** *can be substituted by* **on** + *-ING in English and describes an action that takes place at the same time as another one or follows it very closely, you can use* **al** + **INFINITIVE***:*

be careful ~ crossing *or* **~ you cross the road** ten cuidado al cruzar la calle; **~ he went out he saw it was raining** al salir vio que estaba lloviendo; **~ a student at Oxford, she ...** cuando era estudiante *or* estudiaba en Oxford ...; **my father, ~ young, had a fine tenor voice** mi padre, de joven *or* cuando era joven, tenía una buena voz de tenor; **~ just three years old, he was ...** cuando tenía sólo tres años, era ...; **the floor is slippery ~ wet** el suelo resbala cuando está mojado; **hardly had the film begun ~ there was a power cut** apenas había empezado la película cuando se fue la corriente; **even ~** aun cuando
[2] ***= if*** si, cuando; **this sounds expensive ~ compared with other cars** éste parece caro si *or* cuando se compara con otros coches; **how can I relax ~ I've got loads of things to do?** ¿cómo puedo relajarme si *or* cuando tengo montones de cosas que hacer?; **I wouldn't walk ~ I could get the bus** no iría a pie si pudiese tomar el autobús
[3] ***= whereas*** cuando; **he thought he was recovering, ~ in fact ...** pensaba que se estaba recuperando, cuando de hecho ...; **she made us study ~ all we wanted to do was play** nos hacía estudiar cuando lo único que queríamos hacer era jugar

whence [wens] ADV [1] (*poet*) (= *from where*) de donde; (*interrog*) ¿de dónde?
[2] (*frm*) (= *from which*) por lo cual; (= *there-*

fore) y por consiguiente; **~ I conclude that ...** por lo cual concluyo que ...

whenever [wen'evəʳ] Ⓐ CONJ [1] (= *at whatever time*) cuando; **we can leave ~ it suits you** nos podemos ir cuando quieras; **come ~ you like** ven cuando quieras
[2] (= *every time*) siempre que, cuando, cada vez que, cada que (*Mex**); **~ I smell roses I think of Mary** siempre que *or* cada vez que *or* cuando huele a rosas me acuerdo de Mary; **~ you see one of those, stop** siempre que *or* cada vez que *or* cuando veas uno de esos, párate; **I go ~ I can** voy siempre que puedo; **we will help ~ possible** ayudaremos siempre cuando *or* que sea posible
Ⓑ ADV [1] **Monday, Tuesday, or ~** el lunes o el martes o cuando sea
[2] (*in questions*) cuándo; **~ did I say that?** ¿cuándo dije yo eso?; **~ can he have done it?** ¿cuándo demonios ha podido hacerlo?; **~ do I have the time for such things?** ¿cuándo crees que tengo tiempo para estas cosas?

where [wɛəʳ]

[A] ADVERB [B] CONJUNCTION

Ⓐ ADVERB
[1] ***in direct and indirect questions, reported speech***

Where *in direct questions as well as after report verbs and expressions of (un)certainty and doubt (e.g.* **no sé***) usually translates as* **dónde** *(with an accent), sometimes preceded by a preposition:*

dónde; **~ am I?** ¿dónde estoy?; **~ are you going (to)?** ¿a dónde *or* adónde vas?, ¿dónde vas?; **~ have you come from?** ¿de dónde has venido?; **~ can I have put my keys (down)?** ¿dónde *or* en dónde puedo haber puesto las llaves?; **~ should we be if ...?** ¿a dónde *or* adónde habríamos ido a parar si ...?; **~ did we go wrong?** ¿en qué nos equivocamos?; **can you tell me ~ there's a chemist's?** ¿puede decirme dónde hay una farmacia?; **I don't know ~ she lives** no sé dónde vive
[2] ***in other statements*** [2·1] (= *the place that*)

Where *in other statements is usually translated as* **donde** *(without an accent), again often preceded by a preposition:*

donde; **there's a telephone box near ~ I live** hay una cabina cerca de donde vivo; **this is ~ we found it** aquí es donde lo encontramos; **that's ~ we got to in the last lesson** hasta aquí llegamos en la última clase; **that's just ~ you're wrong!** ¡en eso te equivocas!, ¡ahí es donde te equivocas!; **that's ~ I disagree with you** en eso no estoy de acuerdo contigo, ahí es donde no estoy de acuerdo contigo; **~ this book is dangerous is in suggesting that ...** el aspecto peligroso de este libro es la sugerencia de que ...
[2·2] (*after noun*) donde; **this is the hotel ~ we stayed** éste es el hotel donde *or* en el que estuvimos; **the beach ~ we picnicked** la playa donde *or* a la que *or* adonde fuimos de picnic; **we went to visit the house ~ Diego was born** fuimos a visitar la casa (en) donde nació Diego
Ⓑ CONJUNCTION
[1] [= *if*] **~ husband and wife both work, benefits are ...** en el caso de que los dos esposos trabajen, los beneficios son ...; **~ possible** en lo posible
[2] [= *whereas*] mientras que, cuando; **sometimes a teacher will be listened to ~ a parent might not** a veces a un maestro se le hace caso, mientras que *or* cuando a un padre tal vez no

whereabouts Ⓐ [ˌwɛərə'baʊts] ADV dónde; **~ did you first see it?** ¿dónde lo viste por primera vez?
Ⓑ ['wɛərəbaʊts] NSING OR NPL paradero *msing*; **nobody knows his ~** se desconoce su paradero actual

whereas [wɛər'æz] CONJ (= *on the other hand*) mientras; (*Jur*) considerando que

whereat [wɛər'æt] ADV (*liter*) con lo cual

whereby [wɛə'baɪ] ADV (*frm*) por lo cual, por donde; **the rule ~ it is not allowed to** (+ *INFIN*) la regla según *or* mediante la cual no se permite + *infin*

wherefore†† ['wɛəfɔːʳ] (*also liter*) Ⓐ ADV (= *why*) por qué; (= *and for this reason*) y por tanto, por lo cual
Ⓑ N = **why C**

wherein [wɛər'ɪn] ADV (*frm or liter*) en donde

whereof [wɛər'ɒv] ADV (*frm or liter*) de que

whereon [wɛər'ɒn] ADV (*frm or liter*) en que

wheresoever [ˌwɛəsəʊ'evəʳ] ADV (*liter*) dondequiera que

whereto [ˌwɛə'tuː] ADV (*frm or liter*) adonde

whereupon ['wɛərəpɒn] ADV (*frm or liter*) con lo cual, después de lo cual

wherever [wɛər'evəʳ] Ⓐ CONJ [1] (= *no matter where*) dondequiera que; **he follows me ~ I go** me sigue dondequiera que *or* por donde vaya; **~ you go I'll go too** (a)dondequiera que vayas *or* vayas donde vayas yo te acompañaré; **~ I am** (esté) donde esté; **~ they went they were cheered** les recibían con aplausos dondequiera que fueran *or* fueran a donde fueran; **I'll buy them ~ they come from** los compraré no importa su procedencia, los compraré vengan de donde vengan
[2] (= *anywhere*) donde; **sit ~ you like** siéntate donde te parezca bien; **~ possible** donde sea posible
Ⓑ ADV [1] **in Madrid, London, or ~** en Madrid, Londres o donde sea; **he comes from Laxey, ~ that is** es de Laxey, a saber dónde está eso
[2] (*in questions*) ¿dónde demonios *or* diablos?; **~ did you put it?** ¿dónde demonios lo pusiste?; **~ can they have got to?** ¿dónde diablos se habrán metido?

wherewith [wɛə'wɪθ] ADV (*frm or liter*) con lo cual

wherewithal ['wɛəwɪðɔːl] N **the ~ (to do sth)** los medios (para hacer algo), los recursos (para hacer algo)

wherry ['werɪ] N chalana *f*

whet [wet] VT [+ *tool*] afilar, amolar; [+ *appetite, curiosity*] estimular, despertar

whether ['weðəʳ] CONJ si; **I don't know ~ ...** no sé si ...; **I doubt ~ ...** dudo que + *subjun*; **I am not certain ~ he'll come (or not)** no estoy seguro de que venga; **~ it is ... or not** sea ... o no (sea); **~ you like it or not** tanto si quieres como si no; **~ they come or not** vengan o no (vengan)

whetstone ['wetstəʊn] N piedra *f* de amolar, afiladera *f*

whew [hwjuː] EXCL ¡vaya!, ¡caramba!

whey [weɪ] N suero *m*

whey-faced ['weɪfeɪst] ADJ pálido

whf ABBR = **wharf**

which [wɪtʃ]

[A] PRONOUN [B] ADJECTIVE

Ⓐ PRONOUN
[1] ***in direct and indirect questions, reported speech***

Which/which one/which ones *in direct and indirect questions and after expressions of (un)certainty and doubt (e.g.* **no sé***) usually translate as* **cuál/cuáles**:

cuál; **~ do you want?** (*offering one*) ¿cuál quieres?; (*offering two or more*) ¿cuáles quieres?; **I can't tell ~ is ~** no sé cuál es cuál; **~ of you did it?** ¿cuál de vosotros lo hizo?; **~ of you is Kathleen?** ¿cuál de vosotras es Kathleen?; **I don't know ~ to choose** no sé cuál escoger; **tell me ~ you like best** dime cuáles te gustan más; **I don't mind ~** no me importa cuál
[2] ***relative*** [2·1] (*replacing noun*)

In relative clauses where **which** *defines the noun it refers to, you can usually translate it as* **que**. *Note that in this type of sentence* **which** *can be substituted by* **that** *in English:*

que; **the letter ~ came this morning was from my niece** la carta que llegó esta mañana era de mi sobrina; **it's an illness ~ causes nerve damage** es una enfermedad que daña los nervios; **do you remember the house ~ we saw last week?** ¿te acuerdas de la casa que vimos la semana pasada?; **the bear ~ I saw** el oso que vi

If **which** *is the object of a preposition, you can either translate it as* **que** *(usually preceded by the definite article) or as* ARTICLE + **cual/cuales**. *Use the second option particularly in formal language or after long prepositions or prepositional phrases:*

your letter, ~ I received this morning, cheered me up tu carta, que *or* (*more frm*) la cual he recibido esta mañana, me ha levantado el ánimo; **the bull ~ I'm talking about** el toro del que *or* (*more frm*) del cual estoy hablando; **the meeting ~ we attended** la reunión a la que *or* (*more frm*) a la cual asistimos; **the hotel at ~ we stayed** el hotel en el que *or* (*more frm*) en el cual nos hospedamos; **the cities to ~ we are going** las ciudades a las que *or* (*more frm*) a las cuales vamos; **he explained the means by ~ we could achieve our objective** explicó los medios a través de los cuales podíamos alcanzar nuestro objetivo

If instead of defining the noun the **which** *clause merely adds additional information, you can translate* **which** *using either* **que** *or* ARTICLE + **cual/cuales**:

the oak dining-table, ~ was a present from my father, seats 10 people comfortably la mesa de roble, que *or* la cual fue un regalo de mi padre, admite cómodamente diez comensales
[2·2] (*replacing clause*)

When **which** *refers to the whole of a preceding sentence or idea, translate as* **lo que** *or* **lo cual**:

it rained hard ~ upset her llovió mucho, lo que *or* lo cual le disgustó; **they left early, ~ my wife did not like at all** se marcharon pronto, lo cual *or* lo que no agradó nada a mi mujer

After a preposition only **lo cual** *can be used:*

after ~ we went to bed después de lo cual nos acostamos; **from ~ we deduce that ...** de lo cual deducimos que ...
Ⓑ ADJECTIVE
[1] ***in direct and indirect questions, reported speech***

When **which** *is used as an interrogative adjective, translate using* **qué** + NOUN *when the possibilities are very open or* **cuál/cuáles de** + ARTICLE + PLURAL NOUN *when the possibilities are limited:*

qué; **~ house do you live in?** ¿en qué casa vives?; **~ day are they coming?** ¿qué día vienen?; **I don't know ~ tie he wants** no sé qué corbata quiere; **~ picture do you prefer?** ¿qué cuadro prefieres?, ¿cuál de los cuadros prefieres?; **~ option do you prefer?** ¿cuál de las alternativas prefieres?; **~ way did she go?** ¿por dónde se fue?; **~ one?** ¿cuál?; **I don't know ~ one to choose** no sé cuál escoger; **tell me ~ ones you like best** dime cuáles te gustan más

2 *relative* **look ~ way you will ...** mires por donde mires ...; **he used "peradventure", ~ word is now archaic** (*frm*) dijo "peradventure", palabra que ha quedado ahora anticuada; **in ~ case** en cuyo caso; **he didn't get here till 10, by ~ time Jane had already left** no llegó hasta las 10 y para entonces Jane ya se había ido

whichever [wɪtʃˈevəʳ] Ⓐ PRON 1 (= *no matter which*) **~ of the methods you choose** cualquiera de los métodos que escojas, no importa el método que escojas

2 (= *the one which*) el/la que; **choose ~ is easiest** elige el que sea más fácil

Ⓑ ADJ 1 (= *no matter which*) **~ system you have there are difficulties** no importa el sistema que tengas, hay problemas, cualquiera que sea el sistema que tengas, hay problemas; **~ way you look at it** se mire como se mire

2 (= *any, the ... which*) el ... que/la ... que; **you can choose ~ system you want** puedes elegir el sistema que quieras

whiff [wɪf] Ⓐ N 1 (= *smell*) olorcito *m*; (= *nasty*) tufillo; **a faint ~ of mothballs** un leve olorcito a bolas de naftalina; **to catch a ~ of sth** oler algo; **a ~ of grapeshot** un poco de metralla; **what a ~!** ¡qué tufo!

2 (= *sniff, mouthful*) **to go out for a ~ of air** salir a tomar el fresco; **not a ~ of wind** ni el menor soplo de viento

3 (*fig*) [*of scandal, corruption*] indicio *m*

Ⓑ VI (*) oler (mal); **to ~ of** oler a; (= *stink of*) apestar a

Whig [wɪg] (*Pol, Hist*) Ⓐ N *político liberal de los siglos XVII y XVIII*

Ⓑ ADJ liberal

while [waɪl] Ⓐ N 1 **a ~** (= *some moments*) un ratito; (= *some minutes, hours*) un rato; (= *some weeks, months*) un tiempo; **after a ~** al cabo de un rato, al rato; **all the ~** todo el tiempo; **I lived in Paris for a ~** viví un tiempo en París; **let it simmer for a ~** deje que hierva un rato a fuego lento; **it will be a good ~ before he gets here** tardará (un rato) en venir aún, todavía falta (un rato) para que venga (*LAm*); **a little ~ ago** hace poco; **a long ~ ago** hace mucho; **once in a ~** de vez en cuando; **it takes quite a ~** lleva tiempo; **in a short ~** dentro de poco, al rato (*LAm*); **stay a ~ with us** quédate un rato con nosotros; **the ~** entretanto, mientras tanto; **he looked at me the ~** mientras tanto me estaba mirando

2 **it is worth ~ to ask whether ...** vale la pena preguntar si ...; **we'll make it worth your ~** te compensaremos generosamente; **it's not worth my ~** no me vale la pena

Ⓑ CONJ 1 (= *during the time that*) mientras; **~ this was happening** mientras pasaba esto; **she fell asleep ~ reading** se durmió mientras leía; **~ you are away** mientras estés fuera; **to drink ~ on duty** beber estando de servicio

2 (= *as long as*) mientras (que); **it won't happen ~ I'm here** no pasará mientras (que) yo esté aquí

3 (= *although*) aunque; **~ I admit it is awkward** aunque reconozco que es difícil

4 (= *whereas*) mientras que; **I enjoy sport, ~ he prefers reading** a mí me gusta el deporte, mientras que él prefiere la lectura

► **while away** VT + ADV **to ~ away the time** *or* **the hours** pasar el tiempo *or* el rato

whilst [waɪlst] CONJ (*esp Brit*) = **while B**

whim [wɪm] N capricho *m*, antojo *m*; **a passing ~** un capricho pasajero, un antojo; **it's just a ~ of hers** es un capricho suyo; **as the ~ takes me** según se me antoja

whimbrel [ˈwɪmbrəl] N zarapito *m*

whimper [ˈwɪmpəʳ] Ⓐ N [*from dog, sick person*] gemido *m*, quejido *m*; **without a ~** sin un quejido, sin una queja; *see also* **bang A**

Ⓑ VT **"yes," she ~ed** —sí —dijo lloriqueando *or* gimoteando

Ⓒ VI [*dog*] gemir, gimotear; [*sick person*] gemir; [*child*] lloriquear

whimpering [ˈwɪmpərɪŋ] Ⓐ ADJ [*dog*] que gime, que gimotea; [*sick person*] que gime; [*child*] lloriqueante

Ⓑ N [*of dog*] gemidos *mpl*, gimoteo *m*; [*of sick person*] gemidos *mpl*; [*of child*] lloriqueo *m*

whimsical [ˈwɪmzɪkəl] ADJ [*person*] caprichoso; [*idea, suggestion*] caprichoso, fantástico; [*smile*] enigmático; **to be in a ~ mood** estar de humor para dejar volar la fantasía

whimsicality [wɪmzɪˈkælɪtɪ] N [*of person*] capricho *m*, fantasía *f*; [*of idea*] lo fantástico; **a novel of a pleasing ~** una novela de agradable fantasía

whimsically [ˈwɪmzɪkəlɪ] ADV [*describe, muse*] caprichosamente; [*smile, laugh*] enigmáticamente

whimsy [ˈwɪmzɪ] N (= *whim*) capricho *m*, antojo *m*; (= *whimsicality*) fantasía *f*

whin [wɪn] N tojo *m*

whine [waɪn] Ⓐ N [*of dog*] gemido *m*; (*louder*) gañido *m*; [*of child*] quejido *m*; [*of siren, bullet*] silbido *m*; **... he said in a ~** [*child*] ... dijo lloriqueando; [*adult*] ... dijo quejumbroso *or* quejándose

Ⓑ VI 1 (= *make noise*) [*dog*] gemir; (*louder*) gañir; [*child*] lloriquear, gimotear; [*siren, bullet*] silbar

2 (*) (= *complain*) quejarse; **it's just a scratch, stop whining** no es más que un arañazo, deja de quejarte; **to ~ about sth** [*adult*] quejarse de algo; [*child*] lloriquear *or* gimotear por algo; **don't come whining to me about it** no vengas a quejarte a mí

Ⓒ VT [*adult*] decir quejumbroso *or* quejándose; [*child*] decir lloriqueando *or* gimoteando

whinge* [wɪndʒ] Ⓐ N **to have a ~ (about sth)** quejarse (de algo)

Ⓑ VI quejarse; **to ~ about sth** quejarse de algo

Ⓒ VT **"but I want to go too," he ~d** —pero yo también quiero ir —dijo en tono de queja

whingeing* [ˈwɪndʒɪŋ] (*Brit*) Ⓐ ADJ [*voice*] quejumbroso; [*person*] protestón, quejica*

Ⓑ N gimoteo *m*, lloriqueo *m*

whinger* [ˈwɪndʒəʳ] N (*Brit*) quejica* *mf*, llorica* *mf*

whining [ˈwaɪnɪŋ] Ⓐ ADJ 1 (= *complaining*) [*voice*] quejumbroso; [*person*] quejica*

2 **a ~ sound** (*made by engine, machine*) un sonido chirriante

Ⓑ N 1 (= *complaining*) quejidos *mpl*, gimoteo *m*

2 (= *sound*) [*of engine, machine*] chirrido *m*; [*of siren*] silbido *m*; [*of dog*] gemido(s) *m(pl)*; (*louder*) gañido(s) *m(pl)*

whinny [ˈwɪnɪ] Ⓐ N relincho *m*

Ⓑ VI relinchar

whip [wɪp] Ⓐ N 1 (*for training, driving animals*) látigo *m*; (= *riding crop*) fusta *f*, fuete *m* (*LAm*); (*for punishment*) azote *m*; **he was given 20 lashes of the ~** le dieron 20 latigazos con el azote; *see also* **crack C4**

2 (*Brit Parl*) 2·1 (= *person*) *diputado encargado de la disciplina del partido en el parlamento*; **chief ~** *diputado jefe encargado de la disciplina del partido en el parlamento*

2·2 (= *call*) **(two-line/three-line) ~** *citación (con subrayado doble/triple) para que un diputado acuda a votar en una cuestión importante*; → LEADER OF THE HOUSE

3 (*Culin*) batido *m* (*de claras de huevo o nata*)

Ⓑ VT 1 (*with whip, stick*) [+ *horse*] fustigar; [+ *person*] azotar; [+ *child*] dar un azote a, dar una paliza a; ✦*IDIOM* **to ~ into a frenzy**: **he was ~ping the crowd into a frenzy** estaba provocando el frenesí en la multitud; *see also* **shape A5**

2 (*liter*) [*wind*] azotar; **the wind ~ped her skirts around her legs** el viento hacía que la falda le azotara las piernas

3 (*Culin*) [+ *cream*] montar; [+ *mixture, egg white*] batir

4 (*) (= *defeat*) dar una paliza a*

5 (*) (= *remove*) **he ~ped a gun out of his pocket** en un abrir y cerrar de ojos sacó un revólver del bolsillo; **he ~ped the letter out of my hand** me quitó la carta de la mano de un tirón, me arrebató la carta

6 (= *rush*) **they ~ped her into hospital** la llevaron al hospital a toda prisa

7 (*Brit**) (= *steal*) mangar*, birlar*

8 (= *strengthen*) [+ *rope*] reforzar

9 (*Sew*) [+ *hem, seam*] sobrehilar

Ⓒ VI 1 (= *speed, rush*) **I ~ped into a parking space** me metí enseguida en un hueco para aparcar; **I'll just ~ into the chemist's** voy en un segundo a la farmacia

2 (= *lash*) **the rope broke and ~ped across his face** la cuerda se rompió y le azotó la cara

3 (= *flap*) batir; **the rigging was ~ping against the mast of the yacht** las jarcias batían contra el mástil del yate

Ⓓ CPD ► **whip hand** N ✦*IDIOMS* **to have the ~ hand** llevar la voz cantante; **to have the ~ hand over sb** llevar ventaja a algn

► **whip back** VI + ADV (= *return*) volverse de golpe; (= *bounce back*) rebotar de repente hacia atrás

► **whip in** VT + ADV 1 (*Hunting*) [+ *hounds*] llamar, reunir

2 (*Parl*) [+ *member*] llamar para que vote; [+ *electors*] hacer que acudan a las urnas

► **whip off** VT + ADV [+ *lid*] quitar con un movimiento brusco; [+ *dress, trousers, gloves*] quitarse rápidamente

► **whip on** VT + ADV [*lid*] poner con un movimiento brusco; [+ *dress, trousers, gloves*] ponerse rápidamente

► **whip out** VT + ADV sacar de repente; **we'll soon ~ that tooth out** te sacaremos ese diente antes de que te des cuenta; *see also* **whip B5**

► **whip round** VI + ADV (= *turn*) [*person*] volverse *or* darse la vuelta de repente; **his head ~ped round in astonishment** volvió *or* giró la cabeza asombrado

► **whip through** VI + PREP [+ *book*] leer rápidamente; [+ *task, homework*] realizar de un tirón

► **whip up*** VT + ADV 1 (= *make*) [+ *meal*] preparar rápidamente; [+ *dress*] hacer rápidamente

2 (*Culin*) [+ *cream*] montar; [+ *egg white*] batir

➤ LANGUAGE IN USE: **while B4** 5.1, 26.3

3 (= *stir up*) [+ *support*] procurar, conseguir; [+ *enthusiasm, interest, excitement*] despertar; [+ *hatred*] provocar; **I couldn't ~ up any enthusiasm for the idea** (*among other people*) no pude despertar entusiasmo por la idea; (*in myself*) la idea no me entusiasmaba; **the proposed measure has ~ped up a storm of protest among students** la medida propuesta ha levantado una ola de protestas entre los estudiantes
4 (= *rouse*) [+ *crowd*] exaltar; **he ~ped the crowd up into a frenzy of hate** exaltó a la multitud hasta despertar en ellos un odio febril
5 (= *spur on*) [+ *horses*] azotar
6 (= *lift*) [+ *dust*] levantar

> **WHIP**
> *En el Parlamento británico la disciplina de partido está a cargo de un grupo de parlamentarios llamados* **whips**, *encabezados por el* **Chief Whip**. *Su deber es informar a los miembros del partido de los asuntos del Parlamento, comunicar a los líderes del partido las opiniones de los parlamentarios y asegurarse de que todos ellos asistan a la Cámara de los Comunes* (**House of Commons**) *y emitan su voto en asuntos importantes. Este último aspecto puede ser crucial cuando el gobierno sólo posee una escasa mayoría. Tanto el gobierno como la oposición tienen sus propios* **whips** *y por lo general todos ellos tienen también altos cargos en la Administración del Estado si pertenecen al partido en el poder.*

whipcord ['wɪpkɔːd] N tralla *f*

whiplash ['wɪplæʃ] N 1 tralla *f*, latigazo *m*
2 (*Med*) (*also* **~ injury**) traumatismo *m* cervical

whipped [wɪpt] Ⓐ ADJ (*Culin*) batido
Ⓑ CPD ► **whipped cream** N nata *f* montada

whipper-in ['wɪpər'ɪn] N (*pl* **whippers-in**) (*Hunting*) montero/a *m/f* que cuida los perros de caza

whippersnapper ['wɪpəˌsnæpəʳ] N (*also* **young ~**) mequetrefe *m*

whippet ['wɪpɪt] N perro *m* lebrel

whipping ['wɪpɪŋ] Ⓐ N 1 (= *hiding*) tunda* *f*, azotaina* *f*; (*more serious*) paliza* *f*; **you'll get a ~ if your dad finds out** como tu padre se entere te van a dar una tunda *or* azotaina; **to give sb a ~** dar una tunda *or* azotaina a algn
2 (*) (= *defeat*) paliza* *f*
Ⓑ CPD ► **whipping boy** N cabeza *f* de turco, chivo *m* expiatorio ► **whipping cream** N nata *f* para montar ► **whipping post** N *poste donde se apoya el infractor para ser azotado* ► **whipping top** N peonza *f*, trompo *m*

whippy ['wɪpɪ] ADJ flexible, dúctil

whip-round* ['wɪpraʊnd] N colecta *f*; **to have a ~ (for sb)** hacer una colecta (para algn)

whipsaw ['wɪpsɔː] N sierra *f* cabrilla

whir [wɜːʳ] = **whirr**

whirl [wɜːl] Ⓐ N (= *spin*) giro *m*, vuelta *f*; [*of dust, water etc*] remolino *m*; [*of cream*] rizo *m*; **my head is in a ~** la cabeza me está dando vueltas; **the social ~** la actividad social; **a ~ of pleasures** un torbellino de placeres; ✦**IDIOM let's give it a ~*** ¡nada se pierde con intentar!
Ⓑ VT 1 (= *spin*) hacer girar; **he ~ed Anne round the dance floor** hizo girar a Anne por la pista; **as the wind ~ed leaves into the air** mientras el aire hacia revolotear *or* girar las hojas en el aire; **he ~ed his sword round his head** esgrimió su espada haciéndola girar sobre su cabeza
2 (*fig*) (= *transport*) llevar rápidamente; **the train ~ed us off to Paris** el tren nos llevó rápidamente a París; **he ~ed us off to the theatre** nos llevó volando al teatro
Ⓒ VI [*wheel, merry-go-round*] girar; [*leaves, dust, water*] arremolinarse; (*fig*) (= *move quickly*) **the dancers ~ed past** los bailarines pasaron girando vertiginosamente; **my head was ~ing** me daba vueltas la cabeza

►**whirl round** Ⓐ VI + ADV [*wheel, merry-go-round*] girar, dar vueltas; [*dust, water*] arremolinarse; **she ~ed round to face me** se volvió rápidamente para mirarme
Ⓑ VT + ADV hacer girar; **he was ~ing something round on the end of a string** hacía girar algo al extremo de un hilo
Ⓒ VT + PREP *see* **whirl B1**

whirligig ['wɜːlɪgɪg] N 1 (= *toy*) molinete *m*
2 (= *merry-go-round*) tiovivo *m*
3 (*also* **~ beetle**) girino *m*
4 (*fig*) vicisitudes *fpl*; (= *confusion*) movimiento *m* confuso

whirlpool ['wɜːlpuːl] N 1 (*lit*) remolino *m*; (*fig*) vorágine *f*
2 (*also* **~ bath**) (= *tub*) bañera *f* de hidromasaje; (= *pool*) piscina *f* de hidromasaje

whirlwind ['wɜːlwɪnd] Ⓐ N (*lit, fig*) torbellino *m*; ✦**IDIOMS like a ~** como un torbellino, como una tromba; **to reap the ~** segar lo que se ha sembrado, padecer las consecuencias
Ⓑ CPD [*romance*] apasionado, arrollador; **a ~ courtship** un noviazgo brevísimo; **they took us on a ~ tour** nos llevaron de gira relámpago

whirlybird* ['wɜːlɪbɜːd] N (*US*) helicóptero *m*

whirr [wɜːʳ] Ⓐ N [*of insect wings*] zumbido *m*; [*of machine*] (*quiet*) zumbido *m*, runrún *m*; (*louder*) rechino *m*
Ⓑ VI [*insect wings*] zumbar; [*machine*] (*quietly*) zumbar, runrunear; (*more loudly*) rechinar

whisk [wɪsk] Ⓐ N 1 (= *fly whisk*) matamoscas *m inv*
2 (*Culin*) (= *hand whisk*) batidor *m*; (= *electric whisk*) batidora *f*
Ⓑ VT 1 (*Culin*) batir
2 (*) (= *move quickly*) **they ~ed him off to a meeting** se lo llevaron volando a una reunión; **we were ~ed up in the lift to the ninth floor** el ascensor nos llevó con toda rapidez al piso nueve; *see also* **whisk off, whisk up**
Ⓒ VI (*) **he ~ed past me as I was coming in** cuando entraba, le vi pasar de largo a toda velocidad

►**whisk away** Ⓐ VT + ADV 1 (= *shake off*) [+ *dust*] quitar con un movimiento brusco; **the horse ~ed the flies away with its tail** el caballo ahuyentó las moscas con la cola
2 (= *take*) **the waiter ~ed the dishes away** el camarero se llevó los platos en seguida; **she ~ed it away from me** me lo arrebató
Ⓑ VI + ADV desaparecer de repente

►**whisk off** VT + ADV [+ *dust*] quitar con un movimiento brusco; *see also* **whisk B2**

►**whisk up** VT + ADV (*Culin*) batir; *see also* **whisk B2**

whisker ['wɪskəʳ] N [*of animal*] bigote *m*; (= *hair*) pelo *m*; **~s** (*Zool*) bigotes *mpl*; (= *side whiskers*) patillas *fpl*; (= *beard*) barba *fsing*; (= *moustache*) bigote(s) *m(pl)*; ✦**IDIOMS by a ~** por un pelo; **within a ~ of**: **he was within a ~ of falling down** le faltó un pelo para caer, faltó un pelo para que cayera

whiskered ['wɪskəd] ADJ bigotudo

whisky, whiskey (*US, Irl*) ['wɪskɪ] N whisky *m*; **~ and soda** whisky *m* con sifón, whisky *m* con soda

whisper ['wɪspəʳ] Ⓐ N 1 (*lit*) (= *low tone*) cuchicheo *m*, susurro *m*; [*of leaves*] susurro *m*; **to speak in a ~** hablar en voz baja, susurrar; **to say sth in a ~** decir algo en voz baja, susurrar algo; **her voice was scarcely more than a ~** su voz no era más que un susurro
2 (= *rumour*) rumor *m*, voz *f*; **there is a ~ that ...** corre el rumor *or* la voz de que ..., se rumorea que ...; **at the least ~ of scandal** al menor indicio del escándalo
Ⓑ VT 1 (*lit*) decir en voz baja, susurrar; **to ~ sth to sb** decir algo al oído de algn, susurrar algo a algn
2 (*fig*) **it is ~ed that ...** corre la voz de que ..., se rumorea que ...
Ⓒ VI (= *talk*) cuchichear, susurrar, hablar muy bajo; [*leaves*] susurrar; **to ~ to sb** cuchichear a algn; **it's rude to ~ in company** es de mala educación cuchichear en compañía, secretos en reunión es falta de educación; **stop ~ing!** ¡silencio!

whispering ['wɪspərɪŋ] Ⓐ N 1 (= *talking*) cuchicheo *m*; [*of leaves*] susurro *m*
2 (= *gossip*) chismes *mpl*, chismografía *f*; (= *rumours*) rumores *mpl*
Ⓑ CPD ► **whispering campaign** N campaña *f* de murmuraciones

whist [wɪst] Ⓐ N whist *m*
Ⓑ CPD ► **whist drive** N certamen *m* de whist

whistle ['wɪsl] Ⓐ N 1 (= *sound*) silbido *m*, chiflido *m* (*esp LAm*); **final ~** pitido *m* final
2 (= *instrument*) silbato *m*, pito *m*; **blast on the ~** pitido *m*; **the referee blew his ~** el árbitro pitó; ✦**IDIOM to blow the ~ on sb** (= *denounce*) delatar a algn; (= *put a stop to*) poner fin a las actividades de algn
Ⓑ VT silbar; **to ~ a tune** silbar una melodía; ✦**IDIOM I'm not just whistling Dixie** (*US*) no hablo en broma, no me estoy marcando ningún farol*
Ⓒ VI silbar, chiflar (*esp LAm*); (*Sport*) pitar, silbar; **the boys ~ at the girls** los chicos silban a las chicas; **the crowd ~d at the referee** el público silbó al árbitro; **he ~d for his dog** llamó a su perro con un silbido; **the referee ~d for a foul** el árbitro pitó una falta; **the bullet ~d past my ear** la bala pasó silbando muy cerca de mi oreja; ✦**IDIOM he can ~ for it*** lo pedirá en vano

►**whistle up** VT + ADV 1 **to ~ up one's dog** llamar a su perro con un silbido
2 (= *find*) encontrar, hacer aparecer
3 (= *rustle up*) [+ *meal*] preparar, servir
4 (= *get together*) [+ *people*] reunir

whistle-blower* ['wɪslbləʊəʳ] N *persona que tira de la manta, persona que desvela una situación ilegal*

whistle-stop ['wɪslstɒp] Ⓐ N (*US*) (= *station*) apeadero *m*
Ⓑ CPD ► **whistle-stop tour** N (*US Pol*) gira *f* electoral rápida; (*fig*) recorrido *m* rápido

Whit [wɪt] Ⓐ N Pentecostés *m*
Ⓑ CPD [*holiday, weekend*] de Pentecostés ► **Whit Monday** N lunes *m* de Pentecostés ► **Whit Sunday** N día *m* de Pentecostés ► **Whit week** N semana *f* de Pentecostés

whit [wɪt] N († *or liter*) **not a ~** ni un ápice; **without a ~ of** sin pizca de; **every ~ as good as** de ningún modo inferior a

white [waɪt] Ⓐ ADJ (*compar* **whiter**, *superl* **whitest**) 1 (*gen*) blanco; [*wine, grape, chocolate*] blanco; [*coffee*] (= *milky*) con leche; (= *with dash of milk*) cortado; **to go** *or* **turn ~** (*in face*) ponerse blanco *or* pálido, palidecer;

whiter than white [*person, way of life*] sin tacha, angelical; **"Bleacho" washes whiter than white** "Bleacho" deja la colada blanca como la nieve; **he went ~ at the age of 30** el pelo se le puso blanco a los 30 años, encaneció a los 30 años; **she was ~ with rage** estaba pálida de la rabia; ♦***IDIOMS*** **to show the ~ feather** mostrarse cobarde; **to be as ~ as a sheet** *or* **ghost** estar pálido como la muerte; *see also* **bleed B3**

[2] (*racially*) [*person*] blanco; [*area*] de raza blanca; [*vote*] de los blancos

Ⓑ N [1] (= *colour*) blanco *m*; **his face was a deathly ~** su rostro estaba blanco *or* pálido como la muerte; **the sheets were a dazzling ~** las sábanas eran de un blanco deslumbrante; **to be dressed in ~** ir vestido de blanco; *see also* **black A1, B1**

[2] (= *white person*) blanco/a *m/f*

[3] (*also* **~ wine**) blanco *m*; **a glass of ~** un blanco

[4] [*of egg*] clara *f*

[5] [*of eye*] blanco *m*

[6] **whites** (*Sport*) **cricket/tennis ~s** equipo *m* blanco de cricket/tennis

Ⓒ CPD ► **white blood cell** N glóbulo *m* blanco ► **white chocolate** N chocolate *m* blanco ► **white Christmas** N Navidades *fpl* blancas *or* con nieve ► **white coffee** N (*milky*) café *m* con leche; (*with dash of milk*) café *m* cortado ► **white dwarf** N (*Astron*) enana *f* blanca ► **white elephant** N (*fig*) elefante *m* blanco; **~ elephant stall** *tenderete donde se venden cachivaches* ► **white ensign** N (*Brit*) enseña *f* blanca ► **white flag** N (*Mil*) bandera *f* blanca ► **white fox** N = **arctic fox** ► **white gold** N oro *m* blanco ► **white goods** NPL electrodomésticos *mpl* ► **white grape** N uva *f* blanca ► **white heat** N (*Phys*) calor *m* blanco ► **white hope*** N **the great ~ hope** la gran esperanza dorada ► **white horses** NPL (*on waves*) cabrillas *fpl* ► **the White House** N (*in US*) la Casa Blanca ► **white knight** N (*Fin*) caballero *m* blanco ► **white lead** N (*Chem*) albayalde *m* ► **white lie** N mentira *f* piadosa; **to tell a ~ lie** decir una mentira piadosa ► **white light** N (*Phys*) luz *f* blanca ► **white magic** N magia *f* blanca ► **white meat** N (*Culin*) carne *f* blanca ► **White Nile** N = **Nile** ► **white noise** N (*Acoustics*) ruido *m* blanco *or* uniforme ► **white owl** N búho *m* blanco ► **White Paper** N (*Brit, Australia, Canada Parl*) libro *m* blanco ► **white pepper** N pimienta *f* blanca ► **White Russia** N (*Hist*) la Rusia Blanca ► **White Russian** N (*Hist*) ruso/a *m/f* blanco/a ► **white sale** N (*Comm*) rebajas *fpl* de ropa blanca ► **white sapphire** N zafiro *m* blanco ► **white sauce** N salsa *f* bechamel, besamel *f* ► **the White Sea** N el Mar Blanco ► **white shark** N tiburón *m* blanco ► **white slave trade** N trata *f* de blancas ► **white spirit** N (*Brit*) trementina *f* ► **white tie** N (= *tie*) pajarita *f* blanca; (= *outfit*) traje *m* de etiqueta con pajarita blanca; *see also* **white-tie** ► **white trash**** N (*US pej*) *término ofensivo contra la clase blanca pobre estadounidense* ► **white water** N aguas *fpl* rápidas; **~ water rafting** piragüismo *m* en aguas rápidas ► **white wedding** N **to have a ~ wedding** casarse de blanco (y por la iglesia) ► **white whale** N ballena *f* blanca ► **white wine** N vino *m* blanco ► **white wood** N madera *f* blanca; *see also* **supremacist**

whitebait ['waɪtbeɪt] N morralla *f*, pescadito *m* frito

whitebeam ['waɪtbiːm] N mojera *f*

whiteboard ['waɪtbɔːd] N pizarra *f* vileda®, pizarra *f* blanca

white-collar ['waɪt,kɒləʳ] ADJ **~ worker** oficinista *mf*; **~ crime** crímenes *mpl* de guante blanco

white-faced ['waɪt'feɪst] ADJ blanco (como papel)

whitefish ['waɪtfɪʃ] N (= *species*) corégono *m*; (*collectively*) pescado *m* magro, pescado *m* blanco

whitefly ['waɪt,flaɪ] N mosca *f* blanca

white-haired ['waɪt'hɛəd] ADJ canoso, con canas, de pelo cano

Whitehall [,waɪt'hɔːl] N *calle de Londres en la cual hay muchos ministerios*; (*fig*) el gobierno británico

WHITEHALL

***Whitehall** es la calle de Londres que va desde **Trafalgar Square** al Parlamento (**Houses of Parliament**), calle en la que se hallan la mayoría de los ministerios. Su nombre se usa con frecuencia para referirse conjuntamente a la Administración (**Civil Service**) y a los ministerios, cuando se trata de sus funciones administrativas.*

white-headed ['waɪt'hedɪd] ADJ canoso, con canas, de pelo cano; **~ boy*** (*fig*) favorito *m*, protegido *m*

white-hot ['waɪt'hɒt] ADJ [*metal*] calentado al blanco, candente

whiten ['waɪtn] Ⓐ VT blanquear

Ⓑ VI blanquear; [*person*] palidecer, ponerse pálido

whitener ['waɪtnəʳ] N blanqueador *m*

whiteness ['waɪtnɪs] N blancura *f*

whitening ['waɪtnɪŋ] N = **whiting²**

whiteout ['waɪtaʊt] N [1] (*Met*) resplandor *m* sin sombras

[2] (= *block*) bloqueo *m* total causado por la nieve

[3] (*fig*) masa *f* confusa

whitethorn ['waɪtθɔːn] N espino *m*

whitethroat ['waɪtθrəʊt] N curruca *f* zarcera

white-tie ['waɪt,taɪ] ADJ de etiqueta; **a ~ dinner** una cena de etiqueta; *see also* **white C**

whitewash ['waɪtwɒʃ] Ⓐ N [1] (*lit*) cal *f*, jalbegue *m*

[2] (*fig*) encubrimiento *m*

Ⓑ VT [1] (*lit*) encalar, enjalbegar

[2] (*fig*) encubrir

[3] (*Sport**) dejar en blanco, dar un baño a*

whither ['wɪðəʳ] ADV (*poet*) ¿adónde?

whiting¹ ['waɪtɪŋ] N (*pl* **whiting**) (= *fish*) pescadilla *f*

whiting² ['waɪtɪŋ] N (= *colouring*) tiza *f*, blanco *m* de España; (*for shoes*) blanco *m* para zapatos; (= *whitewash*) jalbegue *m*

whitish ['waɪtɪʃ] ADJ blanquecino, blancuzco

whitlow ['wɪtləʊ] N panadizo *m*

Whitsun ['wɪtsn] Ⓐ N Pentecostés *m*

Ⓑ CPD de Pentecostés

Whitsuntide ['wɪtsntaɪd] Ⓐ N Pentecostés *m*

Ⓑ CPD de Pentecostés

whittle ['wɪtl] VT [+ *wood, shape*] tallar (con cuchillo)

► **whittle away** Ⓐ VT + ADV (= *reduce*) [+ *savings, amount*] ir reduciendo; **our sovereignty is gradually being ~d away** poco a poco está mermando nuestra soberanía

Ⓑ VI + ADV **to ~ away at sth** (*lit*) tallar algo; (*fig*) ir reduciendo algo

► **whittle down** VT + ADV [+ *workforce, amount*] reducir; **the short-list has been ~d down to three** hemos reducido el número de candidatos preseleccionados a tres

whiz(z) [wɪz] Ⓐ N [1] (*) (= *ace*) as* *m*; **he's a ~ at tennis** es un as del tenis*

[2] (= *sound*) silbido *m*, zumbido *m*

Ⓑ VI **to ~ by** *or* **past** [*bullet, arrow*] pasar zumbando; [*car*] pasar a gran velocidad; **it whizzed past my head** pasó (silbando) muy cerca de mi cabeza; **to whizz along** ◊ **go whizzing along** ir como una bala; **the sledge whizzed down the slope** el trineo bajó la cuesta a gran velocidad

Ⓒ CPD ► **whiz(z) kid*** N prodigio *m*

WHO N ABBR (= **World Health Organization**) OMS *f*

who [huː] PRON [1] (*in direct and indirect questions*) quién *sing*, quiénes *pl*; **~ is it?** ¿quién es?; **~ are they?** ¿quiénes son?; **~ are you looking for?** ¿a quién buscas?; **~ does she think she is?*** ¿quién se cree que es?; **I know ~ it was** (yo) sé quién fue; **you'll soon find out ~'s ~** pronto sabrás quién es quién

[2] (*in exclamations*) quién; **guess ~!** ¡a ver si adivinas quién soy!; **~ should it be but Neil!** ¿a que no sabes quién era? ¡Neil!, ¡no era otro que Neil!

[3] (*relative*) que; (*after preposition*) el/la que, quien, el/la cual (*more frm*); **my cousin ~ lives in New York** mi primo que vive en Nueva York; **the girl ~ you saw** la chica que viste; **the girl ~ you spoke to has since left the company** la chica con la que *or* con quien *or* (*more frm*) con la cual hablaste ya no trabaja en la empresa; **those ~ can swim** los que saben nadar; **he ~ wishes to ...** el que desee ...; **deny it ~ may** aunque habrá quien lo niegue

whoa [wəʊ] EXCL ¡so!

who'd [huːd] = **who would, who had**

whodun(n)it* [huː'dʌnɪt] N novela *f* policíaca

whoever [huː'evəʳ] PRON [1] (= *no matter who, anyone that*) **it won't be easy, ~ does it** no será fácil, no importa quién lo haga; **~ finds it can keep it** quienquiera que lo encuentre puede quedarse con él, el/la que lo encuentre que se lo quede; **I'll talk to ~ it is** hablaré con quien sea; **ask ~ you like** pregúntaselo a cualquiera

[2] (= *the person that*) **~ said that is an idiot** quien haya dicho eso es un imbécil, quienquiera que haya dicho eso es un imbécil

[3] (*in questions*) quién; **~ told you that?** ¿quién te dijo eso?

whole [həʊl] Ⓐ N (= *complete unit*) todo *m*; **the ~ may be greater than the sum of the** *or* **its parts** el todo puede ser mayor que la suma de las partes; **four quarters make a ~** cuatro cuartos hacen una unidad; **as a ~**: **the estate is to be sold as a ~** la propiedad va a venderse como una unidad; **Europe should be seen as a ~** Europa debería considerarse como un todo *or* una unidad; **taken as a ~, the project is a success** si se considera en su totalidad, el proyecto es un éxito; **is this true just in India, or in the world as a ~?** ¿es ése el caso sólo en la India o en todo el mundo?; **the ~ of** todo; **the ~ of Glasgow was talking about it** todo Glasgow hablaba de ello; **the ~ of our output this year** toda nuestra producción de este año; **the ~ of July** todo el mes de julio; **the ~ of the time** todo el tiempo; **the ~ of Europe** toda Europa, Europa entera; **the ~ of the morning** toda la mañana, la mañana entera; **on the ~** en general

Ⓑ ADJ [1] (= *entire*) todo; **the ~ family was there** toda la familia estaba allí; **we spent**

WHO, WHOM

In direct and indirect questions

• In direct and indirect questions as well as after expressions of (un)certainty and doubt (e.g. **no sé**), translate **who** using **quién/quiénes** when it is the subject of a verb:

Who broke the window?
¿Quién rompió la ventana?
She had no idea who her real parents were
Ignoraba quiénes eran sus verdaderos padres

• When **who/whom** is the object of a verb or preposition, translate using **quién/quiénes** preceded by personal **a** or another preposition as relevant:

Who(m) did you call?
¿A quién llamaste?
Who(m) is she going to marry?
¿Con quién se va a casar?
You must tell me who you are going to go out with
Tienes que decirme con quién/quiénes vas a salir

In exclamations

• Translate using **quién/quiénes** with an accent as in the interrogative form:

Who would have thought it!
¡Quién lo hubiera pensado!

As relative

• When **who/whom** follows the noun it refers to, the most common translation is **que**:

Do you recognize the three girls who have just come in?
¿Reconoces a las tres chicas que acaban de entrar?
Peter, who was at the match, has told me all about it
Peter, que estuvo en el partido, me lo ha contado todo
That man (who) you saw wasn't my father
El hombre que viste no era mi padre

! Personal **a** is not used before **que**.

"Who" as subject of a verb

• When **who** is the subject, **que** can sometimes be substituted by **el cual/la cual** or **quien** (singular) and **los cuales/las cuales** or **quienes** (plural). This can help avoid ambiguity:

I bumped into Ian and Sue, who had just come back from Madrid
Me encontré con Ian y con Sue, la cual** or **quien acababa de regresar de Madrid

• Only **que** is possible in cases where subject **who** can be substituted by **that**, i.e. where **who** defines the person in question and the sentence does not make sense if you omit the **who** clause:

The little boy who won the cycle race is Sarah's nephew
El niñito que ganó la carrera ciclista es el sobrino de Sarah

"Who(m)" as object of a verb or preposition

• When **who(m)** is the object of a verb, you can translate it using **que** as above. Alternatively, especially in formal language, use personal **a** + **quien/quienes** or personal **a** + ARTICLE + **cual/cuales** *etc* or personal **a** + ARTICLE + **que**:

The woman (who *or* whom) you're describing is my music teacher
La señora que** or **a quien** or **a la cual** or **a la que describes es mi profesora de música

"Who(m)" as object of a preposition

• After prepositions, you should usually use **que** or **cual** preceded by the article, or **quien**:

This is the girl (who *or* whom) I talked to you about
Ésta es la chica de la que** or **de la cual** or **de quien te hablé

Para otros usos y ejemplos ver las entradas who *y* whom.

---

the ~ summer in Italy pasamos todo el verano *or* el verano entero en Italia; **a ~ hour** toda una hora, una hora entera; **it rained for three ~ days** llovió durante tres días enteros *or* seguidos; **~ towns were destroyed** pueblos enteros fueron destruidos; **along its ~ length** todo a lo largo; **I've never told anyone in my ~ life** nunca se lo he dicho a nadie en toda mi vida; **a ~ load of people were there*** había un montón de gente allí*; **he took the ~ lot*** se lo llevó todo; **I'm fed up with the ~ lot of them*** estoy harto de todos ellos; **a ~ lot better/worse*** muchísimo mejor/peor; **it's a ~ new world to me*** es un mundo completamente nuevo para mí; **I've bought myself a ~ new wardrobe*** me he comprado un vestuario completamente nuevo; **the ~ point was to avoid that happening** el propósito era evitar que eso pasara; **the ~ point of coming here was to relax** el objetivo de venir aquí era relajarse; **the figures don't tell the ~ story** las cifras no nos dicen toda la verdad; **let's forget the ~ thing** olvidemos todo el asunto, olvidémoslo todo; **he didn't tell the ~ truth** no dijo toda la verdad; **the ~ world** todo el mundo, el mundo entero; ✦***IDIOMS*** **to go the ~ hog*** liarse la manta a la cabeza*; **this is a ~ new ball game*** es una historia distinta por completo, es algo completamente distinto
2 (= *intact*) entero; **not a glass was left ~ following the party** no quedó ni un vaso entero tras la fiesta; **keep the egg yolks ~** procure que no se rompan las yemas de huevo; **the seal on the letter was still ~** el sello de la carta no estaba roto; **to make sth ~** (*liter*) (= *heal*) curar algo; **he swallowed it ~** se lo tragó entero
Ⓒ CPD ► **whole milk** N leche *f* entera ► **whole note** N (*US Mus*) semibreve *f* ► **whole number** N número *m* entero

wholefood(s) ['həʊlfuːd(z)] (*Brit*) Ⓐ N comida *f* naturista, alimentos *mpl* integrales
Ⓑ CPD ► **wholefood(s) restaurant** N restaurante *m* naturista

whole-grain ['həʊlgreɪn] ADJ [*bread, cereal*] integral

wholehearted ['həʊl'hɑːtɪd] ADJ [*approval, support*] incondicional

wholeheartedly ['həʊl'hɑːtɪdlɪ] ADV [*approve, support, accept*] incondicionalmente

wholeheartedness ['həʊl'hɑːtɪdnɪs] N entusiasmo *m*

wholemeal ['həʊlmiːl] ADJ [*bread, flour*] integral

wholeness ['həʊlnɪs] N (*gen*) totalidad *f*, integridad *f*; [*of mind, body*] integridad *f*

▼**wholesale** ['həʊlseɪl] Ⓐ ADJ 1 [*price, trade*] al por mayor
2 (*fig*) (= *on a large scale*) en masa; (= *indiscriminate*) general, total; **~ destruction** destrucción *f* total *or* sistemática
Ⓑ ADV 1 (*lit*) al por mayor; **to buy/sell ~** comprar/vender al por mayor
2 (*fig*) en masa; **the books were burnt ~** los libros fueron quemados en masa
Ⓒ N venta *f* al por mayor, mayoreo *m* (*Mex*)
Ⓓ CPD ► **wholesale dealer** N = **wholesaler** ► **wholesale price index** N índice *m* de precios al por mayor ► **wholesale trader** N = **wholesaler**

wholesaler ['həʊl,seɪləʳ] N comerciante *mf* al por mayor, mayorista *mf*

wholesaling ['həʊlseɪlɪŋ] N venta *f* al por mayor, mayoreo *m* (*Mex*)

wholesome ['həʊlsəm] ADJ sano, saludable

wholesomeness ['həʊlsəmnɪs] N lo sano, lo saludable

whole-wheat ['həʊlwiːt] ADJ (*esp US*) de trigo integral, hecho con trigo entero

who'll [huːl] = **who will**

wholly ['həʊlɪ] ADV totalmente, completamente; **not ~ successful** no todo un éxito, no un éxito completo

whom [huːm] PRON (*frm*) 1 (*in direct and indirect questions*) **~ did you see?** ¿a quién viste?; **from ~ did you receive it?** ¿de quién lo recibiste?; **I know of ~ you are talking** sé de quién hablas
2 (*relative*) **the gentleman ~ I saw** el señor a quien *or* al cual *or* al que vi, el señor que vi (*less frm*); **the lady ~ I saw** la señora a quien *or* a la cual *or* a la que vi, la señora que vi (*less frm*); **the lady with ~ I was talking** la señora con la que *or* con la cual *or* con quien hablaba; **three policemen, none of ~ wore a helmet** tres policías, ninguno de los cuales llevaba casco; **three policemen, two of ~ were drunk** tres policías, dos de los cuales estaban borrachos; **three policemen, all of ~ were drunk** tres policías, que estaban todos borrachos; → WHO, WHOM

whomever [huːm'evəʳ] PRON (*an accusative form*) *of* **whoever**

whomsoever [,huːmsəʊ'evəʳ] PRON (*an emphatic accusative form*) *of* **whosoever**

whoop [huːp] Ⓐ N grito *m*, alarido *m*; **with a ~ of joy** con un grito de alegría
Ⓑ VI gritar, dar alaridos; [*when coughing*] toser
Ⓒ VT **to ~ it up†*** (= *make merry*) divertirse ruidosamente; (= *let hair down*) echar una cana al aire

whoopee [wʊ'piː] Ⓐ EXCL ¡estupendo!
Ⓑ N **to make ~†*** divertirse una barbaridad*
Ⓒ CPD ► **whoopee cushion*** N cojín *m* de ventosidades

whooping cough ['huːpɪŋ,kɒf] N tos *f* ferina, coqueluche *f*

whoops [wuːps] EXCL ¡epa!, ¡lep!

whoosh [wʊ(ː)ʃ] N *ruido del agua que sale bajo presión, o del viento fuerte*; **it came out with a ~** salió con mucha fuerza

whop‡ [wɒp] VT pegar

whopper* ['wɒpəʳ] N 1 (= *big thing*) monstruo *m*; **that fish is a ~** ese pez es enorme; **what a ~!** ¡qué enorme!
2 (= *lie*) bola *f*

whopping* ['wɒpɪŋ] ADJ (*also* **~ great**) enorme, grandísimo

whore ['hɔːʳ] Ⓐ N (*pej*) puta *f*
Ⓑ VI (*also* **to go whoring**) putear, putañear††

who're [huːəʳ] = **who are**

whorehouse ['hɔːhaʊs] N (*pl* **whorehouses** ['hɔːhaʊzɪz]) (*US*) casa *f* de putas

whorl [wɜːl] N [*of shell*] espira *f*; [*of fingerprint*] espiral *m*; (*Bot*) verticilo *m*

whortleberry ['wɜːtl,bərɪ] N arándano *m*

who's [huːz] = **who is**, **who has**

whose [huːz] Ⓐ PRON (*in direct and indirect questions*) de quién; **~ is this?** ¿de quién es esto?; **~ are these?** (*1 owner expected*) ¿de

➤ LANGUAGE IN USE: wholesale A 20.1

quién son éstos?; (*2 or more owners expected*) ¿de quiénes son éstos?; **I don't know ~ it is** no sé de quién es

Ⓑ ADJ 1 (*in direct and indirect questions*) de quién; **~ purse is this?** ¿de quién es este monedero?; **~ cars are these?** (*1 owner expected*) ¿de quién son estos coches?; (*2 or more owners expected*) ¿de quiénes son estos coches?; **~ fault was it?** ¿quién tuvo la culpa?; **~ car did you go in?** ¿en qué coche fuiste?; **do you know ~ hat this is?** ¿sabes de quién es este sombrero?; **I don't know ~ watch this is** no sé de quién es este reloj

2 (*relative*) cuyo; **those ~ passports I have** aquellas personas cuyos pasaportes tengo, *or* de las que tengo pasaportes; **the man ~ hat I took** el hombre cuyo sombrero tomé; **the man ~ seat I sat in** el hombre en cuya silla me senté; **the cup ~ handle you broke** la taza a la que le rompiste el asa

WHOSE

In direct and indirect questions

- **Whose** in direct questions as well as after report verbs and expressions of (un)certainty and doubt (e.g. **no sé**) translates as **de quién/de quiénes**, (*never* **cuyo**):

  Whose coat is this?
  ¿De quién es este abrigo?
  He asked us whose coats they were
  Nos preguntó de quiénes eran los abrigos
  I don't know whose umbrella this is
  No sé de quién es este paraguas

As a relative

- In relative clauses **whose** can be translated by **cuyo/cuya/cuyos/cuyas** and must agree with the following noun:

  The man whose daughter is a friend of Emily's works for the Government
  El señor cuya hija es amiga de Emily trabaja para el Gobierno
  ...the house whose roof collapsed...
  ...la casa cuyo tejado se hundió...

NOTE: When **whose** refers to more than one noun, make **cuyo** agree with the first:

  ...a party whose policies and strategies are very extremist...
  ...un partido cuya política y tácticas son muy extremistas...

- However, **cuyo** is not much used in spoken Spanish. Try using another structure instead:

  ...the house whose roof collapsed...
  ...la casa a la que se le hundió el tejado...
  My daughter, whose short story won a prize in the school competition, wants to be a journalist
  Mi hija, a quien premiaron por su relato en el concurso de la escuela, quiere ser periodista

! There is no accent on **quien** here, as it is a relative pronoun.

For further uses and examples, see main entry.

whosis* ['hu:zɪs] N (*US*) 1 (*= thing*) chisme *m*, cosa *f*

2 (*= person*) fulano/a *m/f*, cómo-se-llame *mf*

whosoever [ˌhu:səʊ'evəʳ] = **whoever**

who've [hu:v] = **who have**

whozis* ['hu:zɪs] N (*US*) = **whosis**

whse ABBR = **warehouse**

why [waɪ] Ⓐ ADV por qué; **~ not?** ¿por qué no?; **~ on earth didn't you tell me?** ¿por qué demonios no me lo dijiste?; **I know ~ you did it** sé por qué lo hiciste; **~ he did it we shall never know** no sabremos nunca por qué razón lo hizo; **that's ~ I couldn't come** por eso no pude venir; **which is ~ I am here** que es por lo que estoy aquí

Ⓑ EXCL ¡toma!, ¡anda!; **~, it's you!** ¡toma, eres tú!, ¡anda, eres tú!; **~, what's the matter?** bueno, ¿qué pasa?; **~, there are 8 of us!** ¡si somos 8!; **~, it's easy!** ¡vamos, es muy fácil!

Ⓒ N **the ~s and (the) wherefores** el porqué

WHY

- **Why** can usually be translated by **por qué**:

  Why didn't you come?
  ¿Por qué no viniste?
  They asked her why she hadn't finished her report
  Le preguntaron por qué no había terminado el informe

! Remember the difference in spelling between **por qué** (why) and **porque** (because).

- To ask specifically about the *purpose* of something, you can translate **why** using **para qué**:

  Why go if we are not needed?
  ¿Para qué vamos a ir si no nos necesitan?

- In statements, you can translate (**the reason**) **why** using **por qué, la razón (por la que)** or **el motivo (por el que)**:

  Tell me (the reason) why you don't want to accept the proposal
  Dime por qué *or* ***la razón por la que*** *or* ***el motivo por el que no quieres aceptar la propuesta***

- Translate **that's why** using **por eso**:

  That's why they wouldn't pay
  Por eso no querían pagar

- Like all question words in Spanish, **porqué** can function as a masculine noun. Note that in **el porqué**, **porqué** is written as one word:

  I'd like to know why he's absent *or* the reason for his absence
  Me gustaría saber el porqué de su ausencia

For further uses and examples, see main entry.

whyever [ˌwaɪ'evəʳ] ADV **~ did you do it?** ¿por qué demonios lo hiciste?

WI Ⓐ ABBR 1 = **West Indies**

2 (*US*) = **Wisconsin**

Ⓑ N ABBR (*Brit*) (= **Women's Institute**) ≈ IM *m*

wick [wɪk] N mecha *f*; ✦**IDIOMS he gets on my ~*** me hace subir por las paredes*; **to dip one's ~**** echar un polvo**

wicked ['wɪkɪd] Ⓐ ADJ 1 (*= evil*) malvado, cruel; **that was a ~ thing to do** eso no se perdona

2 (*= naughty*) [*grin, look, suggestion*] pícaro; **he gave a ~ grin** sonrió con picardía; **a ~ sense of humour** un sentido del humor socarrón

3 (*) (*fig*) [*price*] escandaloso; [*satire*] muy mordaz, cruel; [*temper*] terrible; (*= very bad*) horroroso, horrible; **a ~ waste** un despilfarro escandaloso; **it's ~ weather** hace un tiempo horrible; **it's a ~ car to start** este coche es horrible para arrancar

4 (**) (*= brilliant*) de puta madre*, estupendo*, guay*

Ⓑ N ✦**IDIOM no rest** *or* **peace for the ~** no hay descanso para los malvados

wickedly ['wɪkɪdlɪ] ADV 1 (*= evilly*) [*behave, destroy*] malvadamente, cruelmente

2 (*= naughtily*) [*grin, laugh, suggest*] con picardía; **a ~ funny play** una obra para desternillarse de risa

wickedness ['wɪkɪdnɪs] N 1 (*= evil*) maldad *f*, crueldad *f*; **all manner of ~** toda clase de maldades

2 (*= naughtiness*) [*of grin, laugh, suggestion*] picardía *f*

wicker ['wɪkəʳ] Ⓐ N mimbre *m or f*

Ⓑ CPD de mimbre

wickerwork ['wɪkəwɜ:k] Ⓐ N 1 (*= objects*) artículos *mpl* de mimbre

2 [*of chair etc*] rejilla *f*

3 (*= craft*) cestería *f*

Ⓑ CPD de mimbre

wicket ['wɪkɪt] Ⓐ N 1 (*Cricket*) (*= stumps*) palos *mpl*; (*= pitch*) terreno *m*; (*= fallen wicket*) entrada *f*, turno *m*; ✦**IDIOM to be on a sticky ~** estar en un aprieto*; → CRICKET

2 (*also* **~ gate**) postigo *m*, portillo *m*

Ⓑ CPD ► **wicket keeper** N (*Cricket*) guardameta *mf*

wide [waɪd] (*compar* **wider**; *superl* **widest**) Ⓐ ADJ 1 [*street, river, trousers*] ancho; [*area*] extenso; [*ocean, desert*] vasto; [*space, circle, valley*] amplio; **he was a tall man with ~ shoulders** era un hombre alto de hombros anchos; **it's ten centimetres ~** tiene diez centímetros de ancho *or* de anchura; **a three-mile-~ crater** un cráter de tres millas de ancho *or* de anchura; **how ~ is it?** ¿cuánto tiene de ancho?, ¿qué anchura tiene?; **her eyes were ~ with amazement** tenía los ojos como platos de asombro*; ✦**IDIOM to give sb a ~ berth** evitar a algn

2 (*= extensive*) [*support, variety*] gran; [*range, selection*] amplio; **a ~ choice of bulbs is available** hay una gran variedad de bulbos donde escoger, hay una gran variedad de bulbos disponible; **there is a ~ choice of colours** hay muchos colores para escoger; **he has a ~ following** tiene un gran número de seguidores; **a ~ range of** una amplia gama de; **in the wider context of** dentro del contexto más amplio de; **the story received ~ coverage** el suceso recibió una amplia cobertura; **to have (a) ~ knowledge of sth** tener amplios conocimientos de algo; **this ruling could have wider implications** esta decisión podría tener implicaciones más amplias; **the incident raises wider issues** el incidente hace plantearse cuestiones de mayor envergadura

3 (*= large*) [*gap, differences*] grande; **to win by a ~ margin** ganar por un margen amplio

4 (*= off target*) **his first shot was ~** (*Ftbl*) su primer tiro *or* chute pasó de largo; (*Shooting*) su primer disparo no dio en el blanco; **to be ~ of the target** desviarse mucho del blanco; ✦**IDIOM to be ~ of the mark** encontrarse lejos de la realidad; **their accusations may not be so ~ of the mark** puede que sus acusaciones no se encuentren tan lejos de la realidad

Ⓑ ADV 1 (*= fully*) **he opened the window ~** abrió la ventana de par en par; **~ apart** bien separados; **to be ~ awake** (*lit*) estar completamente despierto; **we'll have to be ~ awake for this meeting** tendremos que estar con los ojos bien abiertos en esta reunión, tendremos que estar muy al tanto en esta reunión; **~ open** [*window, door*] de par en par, completamente abierto; **with his eyes (open) ~** *or* **~ open** con los ojos muy abiertos; **she went into marriage with her eyes ~ open** se casó sabiendo muy bien lo que hacía; **the ~ open spaces** los espacios abiertos; **we were left ~ open to attack** quedamos totalmente expuestos a un ataque

2 (*= off target*) **the shot went ~** (*Ftbl*) el tiro *or* chute pasó de largo; (*Shooting*) el disparo no dio en el blanco; **Fleming shot ~** (*Ftbl*) Fleming realizó un disparo que pasó de largo a la portería; *see also* **far A1**

➤ LANGUAGE IN USE: **why A** 1.1, 17.1, 26.3

Ⓒ N (*Cricket*) *pelota que el bateador no puede golpear porque la han lanzado muy lejos y que cuenta como una carrera para el equipo del bateador*

Ⓓ CPD ► **wide boy**‡ N buscón‡ *m*, ratero* *m*

-wide [waɪd] ADJ, ADV (*ending in compounds*) **a Community-wide ballot** una votación a escala comunitaria; *see also* **countrywide, nationwide**

wide-angle ['waɪd,æŋgl] ADJ **~ lens** gran angular *m*

wide-awake ['waɪdə'weɪk] ADJ 1 (*lit*) completamente *or* bien despierto

2 (*fig*) (= *on the ball*) despabilado; (= *alert*) vigilante, alerta

wide-bodied ['waɪd'bɒdɪd] ADJ (*Aer*) de fuselaje ancho

wide-eyed ['waɪd'aɪd] ADJ con los ojos muy abiertos, con los ojos como platos*; (*fig*) inocente, cándido

widely ['waɪdlɪ] ADV 1 (= *over wide area, far apart*) **debris from the blast was scattered ~** los restos de la explosión quedaron esparcidos por una amplia zona; **the trees were ~ spaced** los árboles estaban muy separados los unos de los otros

2 (= *extensively*) [*travel*] mucho; **to be ~ available** poder conseguirse con facilidad; **it is ~ believed that ...** mucha gente cree que ...; **the cabinet reshuffle had been ~ expected** la remodelación del gabinete ministerial había sido esperada por muchos; **a ~ held belief** una creencia generalizada; **to be ~ read** [*reader*] tener una amplia cultura, haber leído mucho; [*author*] contar con un gran número de lectores; **his books are ~ read** sus libros cuentan con un gran número de lectores, sus libros se leen mucho; **it is ~ regarded as ...** es considerado por la mayoría como ...; **to be ~ travelled** haber viajado mucho; **to be ~ used** ser de uso extendido *or* generalizado

3 (= *greatly*) [*vary, differ*] mucho

4 (= *broadly*) [*smile*] abiertamente

widen ['waɪdn] Ⓐ VT 1 (*lit*) [+ *road, river, sleeve*] ensanchar

2 (*fig*) [+ *knowledge, circle of friends*] extender, ampliar

Ⓑ VI 1 (*lit*) (*also* **~ out**) ensancharse; **the passage ~s out into a cave** el pasillo se ensancha para formar una caverna

2 (*fig*) **the gap between rich and poor has ~ed** ha aumentado la diferencia entre ricos y pobres; **the ~ing gap between the rich and the poor** el creciente abismo entre los ricos y los pobres

wideness ['waɪdnɪs] N anchura *f*, amplitud *f*

wide-ranging ['waɪd,reɪndʒɪŋ] ADJ [*survey, report*] de gran alcance; [*interests*] muy diversos

wide-screen ['waɪdskriːn] ADJ [*film*] para pantalla ancha; [*television set*] de pantalla ancha, con pantalla panorámica

widespread ['waɪdspred] ADJ [*use*] generalizado, extendido; [*belief, concern*] generalizado; [*support, criticism*] a nivel general; [*fraud, corruption*] muy extendido; **to become ~** extenderse, generalizarse; **rain will become ~ across the whole of the British Isles** las lluvias se extenderán por todas las Islas Británicas; **there is ~ fear that ...** muchos temen que ...

widgeon ['wɪdʒən] N ánade *m* silbón

widget* ['wɪdʒɪt] N (= *device*) artilugio *m*; (= *thingummy*) ingenio *m*, cacharro* *m*

widow ['wɪdəʊ] Ⓐ N 1 viuda *f*; **to be left a ~** quedar viuda, enviudar; **Widow Newson**†† la viuda de Newson; **~'s pension** viudedad *f*, pensión *f* de viudedad

2 (*fig*) **I'm a golf ~** paso mucho tiempo sola mientras mi marido juega al golf; **all the cricket ~s got together for tea** todas las mujeres cuyos maridos estaban jugando al críquet se reunieron para tomar el té

Ⓑ VT **to be ~ed** enviudar, quedar viudo/a; **she was twice ~ed** ha enviudado dos veces, quedó viuda dos veces; **she has been ~ed for five years** enviudó hace cinco años, quedó viuda hace cinco años

Ⓒ CPD ► **widow's peak** N pico *m* de viuda

widowed ['wɪdəʊd] ADJ viudo; **his ~ mother** su madre viuda

widower ['wɪdəʊəʳ] N viudo *m*

widowhood ['wɪdəʊhʊd] N viudez *f*

width [wɪdθ] N 1 [*of street, river*] ancho *m*, anchura *f*; **what ~ is the room?** ¿qué ancho *or* anchura tiene la habitación?; **it is five metres in ~** ◊ **it has a ~ of five metres** tiene cinco metros de ancho *or* anchura, tiene un ancho *or* una anchura de cinco metros

2 [*of fabric, swimming pool*] ancho *m*; **to swim a ~** hacer un ancho (de la piscina)

widthways ['wɪdθweɪz] ADV, **widthwise** ['wɪdθwaɪz] ADV a lo ancho

wield [wiːld] VT [+ *sword, axe, pen*] manejar; [+ *power, influence*] ejercer

wiener schnitzel ['viːnə'ʃnɪtsəl] N escalope *m* de ternera con guarnición

wienie ['wiːnɪ] N (*US Culin, Culin*) salchicha *f* de Frankfurt

wife [waɪf] Ⓐ N (*pl* **wives**) mujer *f*, esposa *f*; **this is my ~** ésta es mi esposa *or* mujer; **my boss and his ~** mi jefe y su esposa *or* mujer; **the ~*** la parienta*, la jefa*; **"The Merry Wives of Windsor"** "Las alegres comadres de Windsor"; **~'s earned income** ingresos *mpl* de la mujer; **to take a ~**† desposarse; **to take sb to ~**† desposarse con algn

Ⓑ CPD ► **wife beater** N *hombre que maltrata a su mujer* ► **wife swapping** N cambio *m* de pareja

wifely† ['waɪflɪ] ADJ de esposa

wig [wɪg] N peluca *f*

wigeon ['wɪdʒən] N ánade *m* silbón

wigging* ['wɪgɪŋ] N (*Brit*) rapapolvo* *m*, bronca *f*; **to give sb a ~** echar un rapapolvo *or* una bronca a algn*

wiggle ['wɪgl] Ⓐ N meneo *m*; **to walk with a ~** caminar contoneándose

Ⓑ VT [+ *toes, fingers*] mover (mucho); [+ *hips*] contonear, menear

Ⓒ VI [*person*] contonearse; [*hips*] contonearse, menearse

wiggly ['wɪglɪ] ADJ [*line*] ondulado

wight†† [waɪt] N (*hum*) criatura *f*; **luckless ~** ◊ **sorry ~** pobre hombre *m*

wigmaker ['wɪg,meɪkəʳ] N peluquero/a *m/f* (*que se dedica a hacer pelucas*)

wigwam ['wɪgwæm] N tipi *m*, tienda *f* india

wilco [,wɪl'kəʊ] ADV ABBR (*Telec*) (= **I will comply**) ¡procedo!

wild [waɪld] Ⓐ ADJ (*compar* **wilder**, *superl* **wildest**) 1 (= *not domesticated*) 1·1 [*animal, bird*] salvaje; (= *fierce*) feroz; **~ duck** pato *m* salvaje; ✦*IDIOM* **~ horses wouldn't drag me there** tendrían que llevarme a rastras, no iría ni por todo el oro del mundo

1·2 [*plant*] silvestre; **~ flowers** flores *fpl* silvestres; **~ strawberries** fresas *fpl* silvestres; ✦*IDIOM* **to sow one's ~ oats** correrla*

1·3 [*countryside*] salvaje, agreste; **a ~ stretch of coastline** un tramo salvaje *or* agreste de costa

2 (= *stormy*) [*wind*] furioso, violento; [*weather*] tormentoso; [*sea*] bravo; **it was a ~ night** fue una noche tormentosa *or* de tormenta

3 (= *unrestrained, disorderly*) [*party*] loco; [*enthusiasm*] desenfrenado; [*hair*] revuelto; [*appearance*] desastrado; [*look, eyes*] de loco; **he invited a bunch of his ~ friends round** invitó a un grupo de amigos locos; **he had a ~ youth** hizo muchas locuras en su juventud; **we had some ~ times together** ¡hicimos cada locura juntos!; ✦*IDIOM* **~ and woolly**: **a member of some ~ and woolly activist group** un miembro de un grupo de esos de activistas locos

4 (*) (*emotionally*) 4·1 (= *angry*) **it drives** *or* **makes me ~** me saca de quicio; **he went ~ when he found out** se puso como loco cuando se enteró; **to be ~ with sb** estar furioso con algn

4·2 (= *distraught*) **I was ~ with jealousy** estaba loco de celos

4·3 (= *ecstatic*) [*cheers, applause*] exaltado, apasionado; **to be ~ about sth/sb: he's just ~ about Inga** está loco por Inga; **I'm not exactly ~ about the idea** no es que la idea me entusiasme demasiado; **Anthea drives men ~ with desire** Anthea vuelve a los hombres locos de deseo; **the crowd went ~ (with excitement)** la multitud se puso loca de entusiasmo; **to be ~ with joy** estar loco de alegría

5 (= *crazy, rash*) [*idea, plan, rumour*] descabellado, disparatado; **it's a ~ exaggeration** es una enorme exageración; **they made some ~ promises** hicieron unas promesas disparatadas; **they have succeeded beyond their ~est dreams** han tenido más éxito del que jamás habían soñado; **never in my ~est dreams did I imagine winning this much** nunca imaginé, ni soñando, que ganaría tanto

6 (= *haphazard*) **it's just a ~ guess** no es más que una conjetura al azar *or* una suposición muy aventurada; **I made a ~ guess** dije lo primero que se me vino a la cabeza

7 (*Cards*) **aces are ~** los ases sirven de comodines

Ⓑ ADV 1 **to grow ~** crecer en estado silvestre

2 **to run ~** 2·1 (= *roam freely*) [*animal*] correr libremente; [*child*] corretear libremente

2·2 (= *get out of control*) **the garden had run ~** las plantas del jardín habían crecido de forma descontrolada; **Molly has let that girl run ~** Molly ha dejado que esa niña haga lo que quiera; **you've let your imagination run ~** te has dejado llevar por la imaginación; **the inevitable result of fanaticism run ~** la inevitable consecuencia del fanatismo desenfrenado

Ⓒ N 1 **the ~: animals caught in the ~** animales capturados en su hábitat natural; **untended fields returning to the ~** campos descuidados que vuelven a su estado silvestre; **the call of the ~** el atractivo de lo salvaje *or* de la naturaleza

2 **the ~s** tierras *fpl* inexploradas; **the ~s of Canada** las tierras inexploradas de Canadá; **to live out in the ~s** (*hum*) vivir en el quinto pino*; **they live out in the ~s of Berkshire** viven en lo más remoto de Berkshire

Ⓓ CPD ► **wild beast** N fiera *f*, bestia *f* salvaje ► **wild boar** N jabalí *m* ► **wild card** N (*Comput, Cards*) comodín *m*; (*Sport*) *invitación para participar en un torneo a pesar de no reunir los requisitos establecidos*; **the ~ card in the picture is Eastern Europe** la gran incógnita dentro de este conjunto es Europa Oriental ► **wild cherry** N cereza *f* silvestre ► **wild child** N (*Brit*) adolescente *mf* rebelde ► **wild goose chase** N **he sent me off on a ~**

goose chase me mandó de la Ceca a la Meca*; **it proved to be a ~ goose chase** resultó ser una búsqueda inútil ► **wild rice** N arroz *m* silvestre ► **the Wild West** N el oeste americano

wildcat ['waɪld'kæt] Ⓐ N (*pl* **wildcats** *or* **wildcat**) [1] (*Zool*) gato *m* montés
[2] (*for oil*) perforación *f* de sondaje en tierra virgen
Ⓑ VI (*US*) hacer perforaciones para extraer petróleo
Ⓒ CPD [*scheme, venture*] descabellado ► **wildcat strike** N huelga *f* salvaje *or* no autorizada

wildebeest ['wɪldɪbiːst] N (*pl* **wildebeests** *or* **wildebeest**) ñu *m*

wilderness ['wɪldənɪs] N (= *desert*) desierto *m*; (= *hills*) monte *m*; (= *virgin land*) tierra *f* virgen; **a ~ of ruins** un desierto de ruinas; **he spent four years in the ~ before returning to power** (*fig*) pasó cuatro años al margen de la política antes de volver al poder

wild-eyed ['waɪld'aɪd] ADJ de mirada salvaje

wildfire ['waɪld,faɪəʳ] N **to spread like ~** correr como un reguero de pólvora

wildfowl ['waɪldfaʊl] NPL (*gen*) aves *fpl* de caza; (= *ducks*) ánades *mpl*

wildfowler ['waɪld,faʊləʳ] N cazador(a) *m/f* de ánades

wildfowling ['waɪld,faʊlɪŋ] N caza *f* de ánades

wildlife ['waɪldlaɪf] Ⓐ N fauna *f*
Ⓑ CPD ► **wildlife preserve**, **wildlife reserve**, **wildlife sanctuary** N reserva *f* natural ► **wildlife trust** N asociación *f* protectora de la naturaleza

wildly ['waɪldlɪ] ADV [1] (= *ecstatically*) [*shout*] como loco; [*applaud*] a rabiar, como loco; **the Democrats were cheering ~ for their nominee** los demócratas vitoreaban como locos a su candidato nominado
[2] (= *frantically*) [*stare, look*] con cara de espanto; [*gesture*] como loco, violentamente; **the driver was gesticulating ~** el conductor gesticulaba como loco *or* violentamente
[3] (= *violently*) [*hit out, throw*] violentamente, como loco
[4] (= *crazily, rashly*) [*guess*] sin pensarlo mucho; [*promise*] en un arrebato; [*exaggerated*] muy
[5] (= *haphazardly*) [*shoot*] a lo loco, a tontas y a locas*; [*fluctuate, vary*] muchísimo
[6] (= *extremely*) **~ happy/enthusiastic** loco de felicidad/entusiasmo; **Naomi was ~ jealous of her sister** Naomi sentía unos celos locos de su hermana; **a ~ improbable story** una historia disparatadísima; **a ~ inaccurate estimate** un cálculo que dista/distaba muchísimo de la realidad

wildness ['waɪldnɪs] N [1] (= *undomesticated state*) [*of animal, tribe, landscape*] estado *m* salvaje, lo salvaje; [*of place*] estado *m* salvaje *or* agreste, lo salvaje, lo agreste
[2] (= *storminess*) [*of weather*] furia *f*; [*of sea*] bravura *f*
[3] (= *lack of restraint*) desenfreno *m*; [*of appearance*] lo desordenado; **there was a look of ~ in his eyes** había algo de locura en su mirada
[4] (= *craziness, rashness*) [*of idea, plan, rumour*] lo descabellado, lo disparatado
[5] (= *haphazardness*) [*of shot*] lo errático

wiles [waɪlz] NPL artimañas *fpl*, ardides *mpl*

wilful, **willful** (*US*) ['wɪlfʊl] ADJ [1] (= *obstinate*) testarudo, terco
[2] (= *deliberate*) intencionado, deliberado, premeditado; [*murder etc*] premeditado

wilfully, **willfully** (*US*) ['wɪlfəlɪ] ADV [1] (= *obstinately*) voluntariosamente, tercamente; **you have ~ ignored …** te has obstinado en no hacer caso de …
[2] (= *intentionally*) a propósito, adrede

wilfulness, **willfulness** (*US*) ['wɪlfʊlnɪs] N [1] (= *obstinacy*) testarudez *f*, terquedad *f*
[2] (= *premeditation*) lo intencionado, lo premeditado

wiliness ['waɪlɪnɪs] N astucia *f*

will¹ [wɪl] (*pt* **would**) Ⓐ AUX VB, MODAL AUX VB
[1] (*talking about the future*) [1·1] **I ~** *or* **I'll finish it tomorrow** lo terminaré mañana; **I ~** *or* **I'll have finished it by tomorrow** lo habré terminado para mañana; **"you won't lose it, ~ you?"** no lo perderás ¿verdad?; (*stronger*) no lo vayas a perder; **you ~ come to see us, won't you?** vendrás a vernos, ¿no?; **it won't take long** no llevará mucho tiempo; **we'll probably go out later** seguramente saldremos luego; **I'll always love you** te querré siempre; **what ~ you do?** ¿qué vas a hacer?; **we'll be having lunch late** vamos a comer tarde; **we'll talk about it later** hablamos luego
[1·2] (*emphatic language*) **I ~ do it!** ¡sí lo haré!; **no he won't!** ¡no lo hará!
[2] (*in conjectures*) **he ~** *or* **he'll be there by now** ya debe de haber llegado *or* ya habrá llegado; **she'll be about 50** tendrá como 50 años; **that ~ be the postman** será el cartero
[3] (*expressing willingness*) [3·1] (*in commands, insistence*) **~ you sit down!** ¡siéntate!; **~ you be quiet!** ¿te quieres callar?; **he ~ have none of it** no quiere ni siquiera pensarlo; **"I won't go" — "oh yes you ~"** —no voy —¿cómo que no?; **I ~ not** *or* **I won't put up with it!** ¡no lo voy a consentir!; **I ~ not have it that …** no permito que se diga que … + *subjun*; **I ~** (*marriage service*) sí quiero
[3·2] (*in offers, requests, invitations, refusals*) **come on, I'll help you** venga, te ayudo; **~ you help me?** ¿me ayudas?; **wait a moment, ~ you?** espera un momento, ¿quieres?; **~ you have some tea?** ¿quieres tomar un té?; **~ you sit down?** ¿quiere usted sentarse?, tome usted asiento (*more frm*); **won't you come with us?** ¿no quieres venir con nosotros?; **Tom won't help me** Tom no me quiere ayudar
[4] (*expressing habits*) [4·1] soler, acostumbrar a; **she ~ read for hours on end** suele leer *or* acostumbra a leer durante horas y horas
[4·2] (*expressing persistence*) **she ~ smoke, despite what the doctor says** a pesar de lo que dice el médico, se empeña en fumar; **accidents ~ happen** son cosas que pasan; **boys ~ be boys** así son los chicos; **he ~ keep leaving the door open** siempre tiene que dejar la puerta abierta; **if you ~ eat so much, you can hardly expect to be slim** si insistes en comer tanto, no pensarás adelgazar
[5] (*expressing capability*) **the car won't start** el coche no arranca; **the car ~ cruise at 100mph** el coche podrá alcanzar las 100 millas por hora; **a man who ~ do that ~ do anything** un hombre que es capaz de eso es capaz de todo
Ⓑ VI (= *wish*) querer; **(just) as you ~!** ¡como quieras!; **if God ~s** si lo quiere Dios; **say what you ~** di lo que quieras; **do as you ~** haz lo que quieras, haz lo que te parezca bien; **look where you ~, you won't find one** mires donde mires, no vas a encontrar uno

will² [wɪl] Ⓐ N [1] (= *inclination, wish*) voluntad *f*; **against sb's ~** contra la voluntad de algn; **at ~** a voluntad; **to do sb's ~** hacer la voluntad de algn; **Thy ~ be done** hágase tu voluntad; **to do sth of one's own free ~** hacer algo por voluntad propia; **the ~ of God** la voluntad de Dios; **iron ~** ◊ **~ of iron** voluntad *f* de hierro; **to have a ~ of one's own** tener voluntad propia; **it is my ~ that you should do it** (*frm*) quiero que lo hagas; **the ~ to win/live** el deseo de ganar/vivir; **to work with a ~** trabajar con ahinco; **with the best ~ in the world** por mucho que se quiera; ✦***PROV*** **where there's a ~ there's a way** querer es poder; *see also* **ill A2**
[2] (= *testament*) testamento *m*; **the last ~ and testament of …** la última voluntad de …; **to make a ~** hacer testamento
Ⓑ VT [1] (= *urge on by willpower*) lograr a fuerza de voluntad; **he ~ed himself to stay awake** consiguió quedarse despierto a fuerza de voluntad; **I was ~ing you to win** estaba deseando que ganaras
[2] (= *ordain*) ordenar, disponer; **God has so ~ed it** Dios lo ha ordenado así
[3] (= *leave in one's will*) **to ~ sth to sb** legar algo a algn, dejar algo (en herencia) a algn; **he ~ed his pictures to the nation** legó sus cuadros a la nación

Will [wɪl] N (*familiar form*) *of* **William**

willful ['wɪlfʊl] ADJ (*US*) = **wilful**

willfully ['wɪlfəlɪ] ADV (*US*) = **wilfully**

willfulness ['wɪlfʊlnɪs] N (*US*) = **wilfulness**

William ['wɪljəm] N Guillermo; **~ the Conqueror** Guillermo el Conquistador

willie* [wɪlɪ] N (*Brit*) = **willy**

willies* ['wɪlɪz] NPL **it gives me the ~** me da horror; **I get the ~ whenever I think about it** me horroriza pensar en ello

willing ['wɪlɪŋ] ADJ [1] (= *enthusiastic*) [*helper*] voluntarioso; **she proved to be a ~ helper in their campaign** demostró ser una ayudante voluntariosa en su campaña; **there were plenty of ~ hands** había mucha gente dispuesta a ayudar; **he was a ~ participant in the scheme** participó en el programa por su propia voluntad; **we're looking for a few ~ volunteers** estamos buscando unos cuantos voluntarios con buena disposición; **his pronouncements found a ~ audience** sus opiniones tuvieron una buena acogida
[2] (= *disposed*) **to be ~ to do sth** estar dispuesto a hacer algo; **are you ~?** ¿estás dispuesto (a hacerlo)?; **to show ~** mostrarse dispuesto; *see also* **god**

willingly ['wɪlɪŋlɪ] ADV [1] (= *with pleasure*) con gusto, de buena gana; **"will you help us?" — "willingly!"** —¿nos ayudas? —¡con mucho gusto! *or* ¡cómo no!
[2] (= *voluntarily*) por voluntad propia

willingness ['wɪlɪŋnɪs] N buena voluntad *f*, buena disposición *f*; **I don't doubt his ~, just his competence** no dudo de su buena voluntad *or* disposición, sólo de su capacidad; **I had to prove my ~ to work** tuve que probar mi buena disposición para trabajar; **I was grateful for his ~ to help** agradecí su interés por ayudar

will-o'-the-wisp ['wɪləðə'wɪsp] N (*lit*) fuego *m* fatuo; (*fig*) quimera *f*

willow ['wɪləʊ] Ⓐ N (*also* **~ tree**) sauce *m*
Ⓑ CPD ► **willow pattern** N *dibujos de aspecto chinesco para la cerámica*; *see also* **willow-pattern** ► **willow warbler** N mosquitero *m* musical

willowherb ['wɪləʊhɜːb] N adelfa *f*

willow-pattern ['wɪləʊ,pætən] ADJ **~ plate** plato *m* de estilo chino; *see also* **willow B**

willowy ['wɪləʊɪ] ADJ esbelto

➤ LANGUAGE IN USE: **will¹ A1** 4, 10.4 **A3** 10.4 **willing 2** 3, 11.2

willpower ['wɪlpaʊəʳ] N fuerza *f* de voluntad

Willy ['wɪlɪ] N (*familiar form*) *of* **William**

willy* ['wɪlɪ] N [1] (*Anat*) colita* *f*, pito* *m*
[2] **the willies** *see* **willies**

willy-nilly ['wɪlɪ'nɪlɪ] ADV [1] (= *unsystematically*) de cualquier manera
[2] (= *willingly or not*) quiérase o no, guste o no guste

wilt[1] [wɪlt] (A) VI [1] [*flower*] marchitarse
[2] (*fig*) (= *lose strength*) debilitarse; (= *lose courage*) perder el ánimo, desanimarse; **we were beginning to ~ in the heat** el calor estaba empezando a hacernos desfallecer
(B) VT [1] (*lit*) marchitar
[2] (*fig*) debilitar

wilt[2]†† [wɪlt] 2ND PERS (*thou form*) *of* **will**[1]

Wilts [wɪlts] N ABBR = **Wiltshire**

wily ['waɪlɪ] ADJ (*compar* **wilier**; *superl* **wiliest**) astuto, taimado

WIMP [wɪmp] ABBR (*Comput*) = **windows, icons, menu** *or* **mice, pointers**

wimp* [wɪmp] N **he's a ~** (*physically*) es un debilucho*; (*in character*) es un parado*

►**wimp out*** VI + ADV rajarse*

wimpish* ['wɪmpɪʃ] ADJ [*behaviour*] ñoño; [*person*] (*physically*) debilucho*; (*in character*) parado*

wimpishness* ['wɪmpɪʃnɪs] N debilidad *f*

wimple ['wɪmpl] N griñon *m*

wimpy ['wɪmpɪ] = **wimpish**

win [wɪn] (*vb: pt, pp* **won**) (A) N victoria *f*, triunfo *m*; **another ~ for Castroforte** otra victoria *or* otro triunfo para el Castroforte; **their fifth ~ in a row** su quinta victoria consecutiva, su quinto triunfo consecutivo; **last Sunday's ~ against** *or* **over Pakistan** la victoria del domingo frente a *or* sobre Pakistán; **to back a horse for a ~** apostar dinero por un caballo para que gane la/una carrera; **I had a ~ on the lottery** gané la lotería; *see also* **no-win**
(B) VT [1] (= *be victorious in*) [+ *competition, bet, war, election*] ganar; ✦*IDIOMS* **you can't ~ them all** no siempre se puede ganar; **to ~ the day** (*Mil*) triunfar; (*fig*) triunfar, imponerse; **pragmatism will probably ~ the day** al final triunfará *or* se impondrá el pragmatismo; **the government finally won the day after a heated debate** finalmente el gobierno triunfó *or* se impuso tras un debate acalorado; *see also* **spur A1**
[2] (= *be awarded*) [+ *cup, award, prize, title*] ganar; [+ *contract, order*] obtener, conseguir; **the party won a convincing victory at the polls** el partido consiguió *or* obtuvo una victoria convincente en las elecciones
[3] (= *obtain*) [+ *pay rise, promotion*] conseguir, ganarse; [+ *support, friendship, recognition*] ganarse; [+ *metal, ore*] extraer (**from** de); **how to ~ friends and influence people** cómo ganarse amigos e influenciar a las personas; **to ~ a reputation for honesty** granjearse *or* ganarse una reputación de persona honrada; **to ~ sb sth: it won him first prize** le valió *or* le ganó el primer premio; **this manoeuvre won him the time he needed** esta maniobra le ganó el tiempo que necesitaba; **to ~ sth from sb** ganar algo a algn; **he won five pounds from her at cards** le ganó cinco libras jugando a cartas; **new land won from the marshes** nuevas tierras ganadas a los pantanos; **to ~ sb's hand (in marriage)** obtener la mano de algn (en matrimonio) (*frm*); **to ~ sb's heart** conquistar a algn; **to ~ sb to one's cause** ganar a algn para la causa de uno, atraer a algn a la causa de uno
[4] (= *reach*) [+ *shore*] llegar a, alcanzar; [+ *goal*] conseguir; **he won his way to the top of his profession** (a base de trabajar duro) consiguió llegar a la cima de su profesión
[5] (*Mil*) (= *capture*) tomar
(C) VI (*in war, sport, competition*) ganar; **who's ~ning?** ¿quién va ganando?; **go in and ~!** ¡a ganar!; **he has a good chance of ~ning** tiene muchas posibilidades de hacerse con la victoria *or* de ganar; **OK, you ~*** vale, ganas tú; **Evans won 2-6, 6-4, 6-3** Evans ganó 2-6, 6-4, 6-3; **she always ~s at cards** siempre gana a las cartas; **to ~ by a head/a length** ganar por una cabeza/un largo; **to play to ~** jugar a ganar; ✦*IDIOMS* **you can't ~: whatever you say, you're always wrong, you can't ~** digas lo que digas, ellos siempre tienen razón, ¡no hay manera!; **to ~ hands down** ganar de forma aplastante

►**win back** VT + ADV [+ *trophy*] recobrar; [+ *support, confidence*] volver a ganarse; [+ *land*] reconquistar, volver a conquistar; [+ *gambling loss, job*] recuperar; [+ *voters, girlfriend, boyfriend*] volver a conquistar a; **I won the money back from him** recuperé el dinero que me ganó

►**win out** VI + ADV triunfar, imponerse; **tiredness won out** triunfó *or* se impuso el cansancio; **she won out over six other candidates** se impuso a otros seis candidatos

►**win over, win round** VT + ADV convencer; **eventually we won him over to our point of view** por fin lo convencimos de que teníamos razón; **they are hoping to ~ over undecided voters** esperan ganarse a los votantes indecisos

►**win through** VI + ADV [1] (= *succeed*) triunfar; **stick to your principles and you will ~ through** mantente firme a tus principios y al final triunfarás
[2] (*Sport*) **she won through to the second round** ganó y pasó a la segunda ronda

wince [wɪns] (A) N [*of revulsion*] mueca *f*; [*of pain*] mueca *f* de dolor; **he said with a ~** dijo con una mueca
(B) VI (= *shudder*) estremecerse; **he ~d in pain** hizo una mueca de dolor; **he ~d at the thought of dining with Camilla** la idea de cenar con Camilla le hacía estremecer

winceyette [,wɪnsɪ'et] N (*Brit*) franela *f* de algodón

winch [wɪntʃ] (A) N torno *m*, cabrestante *m*
(B) VT (*also* **~ up**) levantar (con un torno *or* cabrestante); **he was ~ed up by the helicopter** lo levantaron con el helicóptero; **to ~ sth down** bajar algo (con un torno *or* cabrestante)

Winchester disk® ['wɪntʃɪstə'dɪsk] N disco *m* Winchester®

wind[1] [wɪnd] (A) N [1] viento *m*; **which way is the ~ blowing?** ¿de dónde sopla el viento?; **against the ~** contra el viento; **to run before the ~** (*Naut*) navegar viento en popa; **high ~** viento fuerte; **into the ~** contra el viento; ✦*IDIOMS* **to see which way the ~ blows** esperar para ver por dónde van los tiros; **~s of change** aires *mpl* de cambio, aires *mpl* nuevos; **to get ~ of sth** enterarse de algo; **to get the ~ up*** preocuparse; **to have the ~ up*** estar preocupado; **there's something in the ~** algo se está cociendo; **to put the ~ up sb** (*Brit**) dar un susto a algn; **it really put the ~ up me** me dio un susto de los buenos; **to take the ~ out of sb's sails** cortar las alas a algn; ✦*PROV* **it's an ill ~ that blows nobody any good** no hay mal que por bien no venga; *see also* **sail A1**
[2] (*Physiol*) gases *mpl*; [*of baby*] flato *m*; **to break ~** ventosear; **to bring up ~** [*baby*] eructar
[3] (= *breath*) aliento *m*; **to be short of ~** estar sin aliento; *see also* **second**[1] **A1**
[4] (*) (= *talk*) **that's all a lot of ~** todo eso son chorradas*
[5] (*Mus*) **the ~(s)** los instrumentos *mpl* de viento
(B) VT **to ~ sb** (*with punch etc*) dejar a algn sin aliento; **to ~ a baby** hacer eructar a un niño; **to be ~ed by a ball** quedar sin aliento por el golpe de un balón; **to be ~ed after a race** quedar sin aliento después de una carrera
(C) CPD ► **wind chimes** NPL móvil *m* de campanillas ► **wind cone** N = **windsock** ► **wind energy** N = **wind power** ► **wind farm** N parque *m* eólico ► **wind instrument** N instrumento *m* de viento ► **wind machine** N máquina *f* de viento ► **wind power** N energía *f* eólica *or* del viento ► **wind tunnel** N túnel *m* aerodinámico *or* de pruebas aerodinámicas ► **wind turbine** N aerogenerador *m*

wind[2] [waɪnd] (*pt, pp* **wound** [waʊnd]) (A) VT [1] (= *roll, coil*) [+ *rope, wire*] enrollar; **the rope wound itself round a branch** la cuerda se enrolló en *or* alrededor de una rama; **with a rope wound tightly round his waist** con una cuerda que le ceñía estrechamente la cintura; **to ~ wool into a ball** ovillar lana, hacer un ovillo de lana; **~ this round your head** envuélvete la cabeza con esto, líate esto a la cabeza; **to ~ one's arms round sb** rodear a algn con los brazos, abrazar a algn estrechamente
[2] (*also* **~ up**) [+ *clock, watch, toy*] dar cuerda a; [+ *key, handle*] dar vueltas a
[3] (= *twist*) **the road ~s its way through the valley** la carretera serpentea por el valle
(B) VI (= *snake*) serpentear; **the road ~s up the valley** el camino serpentea por el valle; **the car wound slowly up the hill** el coche subió lentamente la sinuosa colina
(C) N [1] (= *bend*) curva *f*, recodo *m*
[2] **to give one's watch a ~** dar cuerda al reloj; **give the handle another ~** dale otra vuelta a la manivela

►**wind back** VT + ADV [+ *tape, film*] rebobinar

►**wind down** (A) VT + ADV [+ *car window*] bajar; (= *scale down*) [+ *production, business*] disminuir poco a poco, reducir poco a poco
(B) VI + ADV [1] (*lit*) [*clock*] pararse
[2] (*) (= *relax*) relajarse
[3] (*) (= *come to an end*) [*activity, event*] tocar a su fin

►**wind forward** VT + ADV [+ *tape, film*] correr

►**wind in** VT + ADV **to ~ in a fishing line** ir cobrando sedal

►**wind on** (A) VT + ADV [+ *film*] enrollar
(B) VI + ADV [*film*] enrollarse

►**wind up** (A) VT + ADV [1] (*lit*) [+ *car window*] subir; [+ *clock, toy*] dar cuerda a
[2] (= *close*) [+ *meeting, debate*] cerrar, dar por terminado; [+ *company*] liquidar; **he wound up his speech by saying that ...** terminó su discurso diciendo que ...
[3] **to be wound up** (= *tense*) estar tenso; **she's dreadfully wound up** está muy tensa; **it gets me all wound up (inside)** me pone nerviosísimo
[4] (*Brit**) **to ~ sb up** (= *provoke*) provocar a algn; (= *tease*) tomar el pelo a algn
(B) VI + ADV [1] (= *finish*) [*meeting, debate, speaker*] concluir, terminar; **how does the play ~ up?** ¿cómo concluye *or* termina la obra?
[2] (*) (= *end up*) acabar; **we wound up in Rome** acabamos en Roma, fuimos a parar a Roma

windbag* ['wɪndbæg] N (= *person*) hablador(a) *m/f*

windblown ['wɪndbləʊn] ADJ [*leaf etc*] llevado *or* arrancado por el viento; [*hair*] despeinado por el viento

windborne ['wɪndbɔːn] ADJ llevado por el viento

windbreak ['wɪndbreɪk] N (*natural*) abrigada *f*, barrera *f* contra el viento; (*for plants*) pantalla *f* cortavientos; (*at seaside*) cortavientos *m inv*

windbreaker ['wɪnd,breɪkəʳ] N (*esp US*) cazadora *f*

windburn ['wɪnd,bɜːn] N **to get ~** curtirse al viento

windcheater ['wɪnd'tʃiːtəʳ] N cazadora *f*

windchill ['wɪndtʃɪl] Ⓐ N sensación *f* térmica, *efecto térmico producido por un viento frío y una baja temperatura*
Ⓑ CPD ► **the windchill factor** N *factor que determina la sensación térmica producida por un viento frío y una baja temperatura*

winder ['waɪndəʳ] N (*on watch etc*) cuerda *f*

windfall ['wɪndfɔːl] Ⓐ N 1 (= *apple etc*) fruta *f* caída
2 (*fig*) dinero *m* caído del cielo
Ⓑ CPD ► **windfall profits** NPL beneficios *mpl* imprevistos ► **windfall tax** N *impuesto sobre determinados beneficios extraordinarios*

windgauge ['wɪndgeɪdʒ] N anemómetro *m*

winding ['waɪndɪŋ] Ⓐ ADJ [*road, path*] tortuoso, serpenteante
Ⓑ N [*of road*] tortuosidad *f*; **the ~s of a river** las vueltas *or* los meandros de un río
Ⓒ CPD ► **winding sheet** N mortaja *f* ► **winding staircase** N escalera *f* de caracol

winding-gear ['waɪndɪŋgɪəʳ] N manubrio *m*, cabrestante *m*

winding-up ['waɪndɪŋ'ʌp] N conclusión *f*; (*Comm*) liquidación *f*

windjammer ['wɪnd,dʒæməʳ] N buque *m* de vela (grande y veloz)

windlass ['wɪndləs] N torno *m*

windless ['wɪndlɪs] ADJ sin viento

windmill ['wɪndmɪl] N molino *m* de viento; (= *toy*) molinete *m*

window ['wɪndəʊ] Ⓐ N 1 (*gen, Comput*) ventana *f*; (= *shop window*) escaparate *m*, vitrina *f* (*LAm*), vidriera *f* (*S. Cone*); [*of booking office, car, envelope*] ventanilla *f*; **to lean out of the ~** asomarse a la ventana; **to look out of the ~** mirar por la ventana; **to break a ~** romper un cristal *or* (*LAm*) un vidrio; ✦**IDIOM to fly out of the ~: common sense flies out of the ~** el sentido común se va al traste, se pierde todo atisbo de sentido común
2 (= *period of time*) espacio *m*
Ⓑ CPD ► **window box** N jardinera *f* de ventana ► **window cleaner** N (= *liquid*) limpiacristales *m inv*; (= *person*) limpiacristales *mf inv* ► **window display** N escaparate *m* ► **window dresser** N escaparatista *mf*, decorador(a) *m/f* de escaparates ► **window dressing** N escaparatismo *m*, decoración *f* de escaparates; (*in accounts etc*) presentación *f* de información especiosa; **it's all just ~ dressing** (*fig*) es pura fachada ► **window envelope** N sobre *m* de ventanilla ► **window frame** N marco *m* de ventana ► **window ledge** N antepecho *m*, alféizar *m* de la ventana ► **window of opportunity** N excelente oportunidad *f*, oportunidad *f* única ► **window pane** N cristal *m*, vidrio *m* (*LAm*) ► **window seat** N asiento *m* junto a la ventana; (*Rail etc*) asiento *m* junto a una ventanilla

window-shop ['wɪndəʊʃɒp] VI ir a mirar escaparates

window-shopping ['wɪndəʊ,ʃɒpɪŋ] N **to go ~** ir a mirar escaparates; **I like ~** me gusta mirar escaparates

windowsill ['wɪndəʊsɪl] N antepecho *m*, alféizar *m* de la ventana

windpipe ['wɪndpaɪp] N tráquea *f*

wind-powered ['wɪnd,paʊəd] ADJ impulsado por el viento

windproof ['wɪndpruːf] ADJ a prueba de viento

windscreen ['wɪndskriːn], **windshield** ['wɪndʃiːld] (*US*) Ⓐ N parabrisas *m inv*
Ⓑ CPD ► **windscreen washer** N lavaparabrisas *m inv* ► **windscreen wiper** N limpiaparabrisas *m inv*

windsleeve ['wɪndsliːv] N = **windsock**

windsock ['wɪndsɒk] N (*Aer*) manga *f* (de viento)

windstorm ['wɪndstɔːm] N ventarrón *m*, huracán *m*

windsurf ['wɪndsɜːf] VI hacer windsurf

windsurfer ['wɪndsɜːfəʳ] N tablista *mf*, surfista *mf*

windsurfing ['wɪndsɜːfɪŋ] N windsurf *m*; **to go ~** hacer windsurf

windswept ['wɪndswept] ADJ [*place*] azotado por el viento; **he came in looking very ~** entró con el pelo muy revuelto

wind-up* ['waɪndʌp] N 1 (*Brit*) (= *joke*) tomadura *f* de pelo* 2 = **winding-up**

windward ['wɪndwəd] Ⓐ ADJ de barlovento
Ⓑ N barlovento *m*; **to ~** a barlovento

Windward Isles ['wɪndwəd,aɪlz] NPL Islas *fpl* de Barlovento

windy ['wɪndɪ] ADJ (*compar* **windier**; *superl* **windiest**) 1 [*day*] de mucho viento, ventoso; [*place*] (= *exposed to wind*) expuesto al viento; **it's ~ today** hoy hace viento; **Edinburgh's a very ~ city** en Edimburgo hace mucho viento; **the Windy City** Chicago *m*; → CITY NICKNAMES 2 (*Brit*†*) (= *afraid, nervous*) miedoso, temeroso (**about** por); **to be ~** pasar miedo; **to get ~** asustarse

wine [waɪn] Ⓐ N vino *m*; **red/white/rosé ~** vino tinto/blanco/rosado
Ⓑ VT **to ~ and dine sb** agasajar a algn
Ⓒ VI **to ~ and dine** comer y beber (en restaurantes)
Ⓓ CPD ► **wine bar** N bar *m* especializado en servir vinos ► **wine bottle** N botella *f* de vino ► **wine cask** N tonel *m* de vino, barril *m* de vino ► **wine cellar** N bodega *f* ► **wine grower** N viñador(a) *m/f* ► **wine growing** N vinicultura *f*; *see also* **wine-growing** ► **wine list** N lista *f or* carta *f* de vinos ► **wine merchant** N (*Brit*) vinatero/a *m/f* ► **wine press** N prensa *f* de uvas, lagar *m* ► **wine rack** N botellero *m* ► **wine taster** N catador(a) *m/f* de vinos ► **wine tasting** N cata *f* de vinos ► **wine vinegar** N vinagre *m* de vino ► **wine waiter** N sumiller *m*, escanciador *m*

winebibber ['waɪn,bɪbəʳ] N bebedor(a) *m/f*

wineglass ['waɪnglɑːs] N copa *f* (de vino)

wine-growing ['waɪn,grəʊɪŋ] ADJ vinícola; *see also* **wine D**

winemanship ['waɪnmən'ʃɪp] N pericia *f* en vinos, enofilia *f*

winery ['waɪnərɪ] N (*esp US*) bodega *f*

wineskin ['waɪnskɪn] N pellejo *m*, odre *m*

wing [wɪŋ] Ⓐ N 1 [*of bird*] ala *f*; **the bird spread its ~s** el pájaro extendió las alas; **to be on the ~** estar volando; **to shoot a bird on the ~** matar un pájaro al vuelo; **on the ~s of fantasy** en alas de la fantasía; **to take ~** (*liter*) irse volando, alzar el vuelo; ✦**IDIOMS to clip sb's ~s** cortar las alas a algn; **to do sth on a ~ and a prayer** hacer algo con Dios y ayuda; **to stretch** *or* **spread one's ~s** empezar a volar; **to take sb under one's ~** dar amparo a algn, tomar a algn bajo su protección
2 [*of chair*] orejera *f*, oreja *f*
3 (*Sport*) (= *position*) extremo *m*, ala *f*; (= *player*) extremo/a *m/f*, alero/a *m/f*
4 (*Archit*) ala *f*; **the east/west ~** el ala este/oeste
5 (= *section*) ala *f*; **the left ~ of the party** el ala izquierda del partido
6 (*Brit Aut*) aleta *f*
7 **wings** (*Theat*) bastidores *mpl*; ✦**IDIOM to be waiting in the ~s** esperar entre bastidores
Ⓑ VT 1 **to ~ one's way: soon they were airborne and ~ing their way south** poco tiempo después iban (transportados) por aire en dirección sur
2 (= *wound*) [+ *bird*] tocar en el ala, herir en el ala; [+ *person*] herir en el brazo/hombro
3 **to ~ it** (*Theat, fig**) improvisar sobre la marcha
Ⓒ CPD ► **wing case** N (*Zool*) élitro *m* ► **wing chair** N butaca *f* de orejas, butaca *f* orejera ► **wing collar** N cuello *m* de puntas ► **wing commander** N teniente *mf* coronel de aviación ► **wing mirror** N retrovisor *m* ► **wing nut** N tuerca *f* mariposa ► **wing tip** N punta *f* del ala

wingding* ['wɪŋ,dɪŋ] N (*US*) fiesta *f* animada, guateque *m* divertido

winged [wɪŋd] ADJ (*Zool*) alado; [*seed*] con alas

-winged [wɪŋd] ADJ (*ending in compounds*) de alas; **brown-winged** de alas pardas; **four-winged** de cuatro alas

winger ['wɪŋəʳ] N (*Sport*) extremo/a *m/f*, alero/a *m/f*

wingless ['wɪŋlɪs] ADJ sin alas

wingspan ['wɪŋspæn], **wingspread** ['wɪŋspred] N envergadura *f*

wink [wɪŋk] Ⓐ N 1 (= *blink*) pestañeo *m*; (*meaningful*) guiño *m*; **to give sb a ~** guiñar el ojo a algn; **he said with a ~** dijo guiñando el ojo; ✦**IDIOMS to have 40 ~s** echarse una siesta *or* cabezada; **to tip sb the ~*** avisar a algn secretamente
2 (= *instant*) **I didn't sleep a ~** ◊ **I didn't get a ~ of sleep** no pegué ojo
Ⓑ VI 1 (*meaningfully*) guiñar el ojo; **to ~ at sb** guiñar el ojo a algn; **to ~ at sth** (*fig*) hacer la vista gorda a algo
2 [*light, star*] centellear, parpadear
Ⓒ VT [+ *eye*] guiñar

winker ['wɪŋkəʳ] N (*Brit Aut*) intermitente *m*

winking ['wɪŋkɪŋ] Ⓐ N pestañeo *m*; ✦**IDIOM it was as easy as ~** era facilísimo
Ⓑ ADJ pestañeante

winkle ['wɪŋkl] Ⓐ N bígaro *m*, bigarro *m*
Ⓑ VT **to ~ a secret out of sb** sacar un secreto a algn

winkle-pickers* ['wɪnkl'pɪkəz] NPL (*Brit*) *zapatos o botas de puntera muy estrecha*

winner ['wɪnəʳ] N 1 (*in race, competition*) vencedor(a) *m/f*, ganador(a) *m/f*; [*of prize, lottery*] ganador(a) *m/f*; **~ takes all** el ganador se lo lleva todo
2 (*Ftbl*) (= *goal*) gol *m* de la victoria, gol *m* decisivo
3 (*fig*) 3·1 (*) (= *sth successful*) **this record is a ~!** ¡este disco es un exitazo!*; **I think you're on to a ~ there** creo que con esto tienes la ganancia asegurada
3·2 (= *beneficiary*) **the ~s will be the shareholders** los que saldrán ganando serán los accionistas

winning ['wɪnɪŋ] Ⓐ ADJ 1 [*person, horse, team*]

ganador, vencedor; [*number, entry*] ganador; [*goal, shot*] de la victoria, decisivo
[2] (= *engaging*) [*smile*] encantador, irresistible; [*personality*] encantador, cautivador
Ⓑ CPD ► **winning post** N meta *f*

winnings [ˈwɪnɪŋz] NPL ganancias *fpl*

winnow [ˈwɪnəʊ] VT aventar

winnower [ˈwɪnəʊəʳ], **winnowing machine** [ˈwɪnəʊɪŋməˌʃiːn] N aventadora *f*

wino* [ˈwaɪnəʊ] N alcohólico/a *m/f*

winsome [ˈwɪnsəm] ADJ encantador, cautivador

winsomely [ˈwɪnsəmlɪ] ADV de forma encantadora, de forma cautivadora

winsomeness [ˈwɪnsəmnɪs] N encanto *m*

winter [ˈwɪntəʳ] Ⓐ N invierno *m*; **in ~** en invierno; **I like to go skiing in (the) ~** me gusta ir a esquiar en invierno; **in the ~ of 1998** en el invierno de 1998; **a ~'s day** un día de invierno
Ⓑ VI invernar
Ⓒ CPD ► **winter clothes** NPL ropa *f* de invierno ► **winter Olympics** NPL Olimpiada *f* de invierno, Juegos *mpl* Olímpicos de invierno ► **winter quarters** NPL cuarteles *mpl* de invierno ► **winter solstice** N solsticio *m* de invierno ► **winter sports** NPL deportes *mpl* de invierno

wintergreen [ˈwɪntəgriːn] N gaulteria *f*; **oil of ~** aceite *m* de gaulteria

winterize [ˈwɪntəraɪz] VT (*US*) adaptar para el invierno

winterkill [ˈwɪntəˈkɪl] (*US*) Ⓐ VT matar de frío
Ⓑ VI perecer a causa del frío

wintertime [ˈwɪntətaɪm] N invierno *m*; **in (the) ~** en invierno

wintry, **wintery** [ˈwɪntrɪ] ADJ invernal; (*fig*) glacial

wipe [waɪp] Ⓐ N [1] (= *action*) **to give sth a ~ (down** *or* **over)** pasar un trapo a algo, dar una pasada con un trapo a algo
[2] (= *product*) toallita *f*; **baby ~s** toallitas *fpl* húmedas para el bebé; **face ~s** toallitas húmedas para la cara
Ⓑ VT [1] (= *clean, dry*) [+ *table, floor, surface*] pasar un trapo a, limpiar (con un trapo); [+ *blackboard*] borrar, limpiar; [+ *dishes*] secar; [+ *one's nose, shoes*] limpiarse; [+ *one's face, hands*] secarse; **to ~ one's eyes/one's brow** enjugarse *or* secarse las lágrimas/la frente; **~ your feet before you come in** límpiate los pies antes de entrar; **to ~ one's bottom** limpiarse el trasero; **to ~ sth clean** limpiar algo; **to ~ sth dry** secar algo (con un trapo/una toalla, etc); ✦***IDIOMS*** **to ~ the floor with sb*** dar una paliza a algn*; **to ~ the slate clean** hacer borrón y cuenta nueva
[2] (= *remove*) **she ~d the sweat from** *or* **off her face** se secó *or* se limpió el sudor de la cara; **she ~d the tears from her eyes** se secó *or* se limpió las lágrimas de los ojos; **he stood up, wiping the crumbs from around his mouth** se levantó, limpiándose *or* quitándose las migas de alrededor de la boca; **ten billion pounds was ~d off shares** el valor de las acciones bajó en diez mil millones de libras; ✦***IDIOM*** **that will ~ the smile off her face!*** ¡eso le quitará las ganas de sonreír!, ¡con eso se le quitarán las ganas de sonreír!
[3] (= *move, pass*) **to ~ sth over sth**: **he ~d a handkerchief over his forehead** se enjugó *or* se secó la frente con un pañuelo; **he ~d his hand across his eyes** se pasó la mano por los ojos
[4] (= *erase*) [+ *tape, disk, data*] borrar; **they had ~d what had happened from their minds** habían borrado de la memoria lo sucedido; **the village was ~d from** *or* **off the map in a bombing raid** los bombardeos borraron la aldea del mapa
Ⓒ VI secar; **you wash, I'll ~** tú friega, yo seco

►**wipe at** VI + PREP (= *dry*) secar; (= *clean*) limpiar; **she ~d at her nose with (the back of) her hand** se secó/limpió la nariz con (el dorso de) la mano

►**wipe away** VT + ADV [1] (*lit*) [+ *one's tears*] enjugarse, secarse; [+ *sb's tears*] enjugar, secar; [+ *marks*] quitar, limpiar; **he ~d away the blood with a handkerchief** limpió la sangre con un pañuelo
[2] (*fig*) [+ *guilt, hurt, memory*] borrar

►**wipe down** VT + ADV [+ *surface, wall*] limpiar

►**wipe off** Ⓐ VT + ADV (= *remove*) [+ *stain, marks*] quitar, limpiar; [+ *recording, data*] borrar Ⓑ VI + ADV [*stain, marks*] salir, limpiarse

►**wipe out** VT + ADV [1] (= *clean*) [+ *container*] limpiar
[2] (= *eliminate*) [+ *town, people, army*] aniquilar; [+ *species*] exterminar; [+ *disease*] erradicar; [+ *opposition*] derrotar de forma aplastante, aniquilar
[3] (= *erase*) [+ *past, memory*] borrar
[4] (= *cancel*) [+ *debt*] liquidar; [+ *gains*] cancelar
[5] (*) (= *exhaust*) dejar hecho polvo*
[6] (*) (= *bankrupt*) dejar en la ruina *or* bancarrota
[7] (*) (= *kill*) liquidar*, borrar del mapa*

►**wipe up** Ⓐ VT + ADV limpiar
Ⓑ VI + ADV [1] (= *dry the dishes*) secar
[2] (= *clean up*) limpiar

wipe-out [ˈwaɪpaʊt] N [1] (= *destruction*) [*of town*] destrucción *f*; [*of army, people*] aniquilación *f* [2] (*in competition, election*) derrota *f* aplastante [3] (*Surfing*) caída *f*

wiper [ˈwaɪpəʳ] N [1] (= *cloth*) paño *m*, trapo *m*
[2] (*Brit Aut*) limpiaparabrisas *m inv*

wire [ˈwaɪəʳ] Ⓐ N [1] (*metal*) alambre *m*; (*Elec*) cable *m*; **copper ~** hilo *m* de cobre; **the telephone ~** el cable del teléfono; ✦***IDIOMS*** **to get one's ~s crossed*** tener un malentendido; **to pull ~s** (*US**) tocar resortes; **he can pull ~s** (*US**) tiene enchufes*, tiene buenas agarraderas (*Chile**)
[2] (*US Telec*) telegrama *m*; **to send sb a ~** enviar un telegrama a algn
[3] (*Police*) (= *hidden microphone*) micrófono *m* oculto
Ⓑ VT [1] (*also* **~ up**) (*Elec*) [+ *house*] poner la instalación eléctrica en; [+ *fence*] electrificar; **it's ~d (up) for sound** tiene la instalación eléctrica para el sonido; **it's all ~d (up) for cable television** se ha completado la instalación eléctrica para la televisión por cable; **to be ~d up** (*US**) (= *tense*) estar tenso
[2] (*US Telec*) **to ~ sb** comunicar con algn (por telegrama); **to ~ money to sb** enviar un giro telegráfico a algn; **to ~ information to sb** enviar información a algn por telegrama
[3] (= *connect*) conectar (**to** a); **it's ~d to the alarm** está conectado a la alarma
Ⓒ CPD ► **wire brush** N cepillo *m* de alambre ► **wire cutters** NPL cortaalambres *m inv*, cizalla *fsing* ► **wire fence** N alambrado *m* ► **wire mesh**, **wire netting** N tela *f* metálica, malla *f* metálica ► **wire service** N (*esp US*) agencia *f* de noticias ► **wire wool** N lana *f* de alambre

►**wire up** VT + ADV *see* **wire B1**

wire-haired [ˈwaɪəhɛəd] ADJ [*dog*] de pelo áspero

wireless† [ˈwaɪəlɪs] (*esp Brit*) Ⓐ N radio *f*; **by ~** por radio; **to talk on the ~** hablar por radio
Ⓑ ADJ (= *without wires*) inalámbrico
Ⓒ CPD ► **Wireless Application Protocol** N (*Telec*) Protocolo *m* de aplicaciones inalámbricas ► **wireless message** N radiograma *m* ► **wireless operator** N radiotelegrafista *mf*, radio *mf* ► **wireless technology** N tecnología *f* inalámbrica ► **wireless station** N emisora *f*

wirepuller* [ˈwaɪəˌpʊləʳ] N (*US*) enchufista* *mf*

wirepulling* [ˈwaɪəˌpʊlɪŋ] N (*US*) empleo *m* de resortes, enchufismo* *m*

wiretap [ˈwaɪətæp] (*US*) Ⓐ VI intervenir las conexiones telefónicas, practicar escuchas telefónicas Ⓑ VT [+ *telephone*] intervenir; [+ *room*] poner escuchas telefónicas en

wiretapping [ˈwaɪəˈtæpɪŋ] N (*US*) intervención *f* electrónica

wirewalker [ˈwaɪəwɔːkəʳ] N (*US*) = **tightrope walker**

wireworm [ˈwaɪəwɜːm] N gusano *m* de elatérido

wiring [ˈwaɪərɪŋ] Ⓐ N (*Elec*) (= *wiring system*) instalación *f* eléctrica; (= *wires*) cables *mpl*; **the cause of the fire was faulty ~** la causa del incendio fue la instalación eléctrica defectuosa
Ⓑ CPD ► **wiring diagram** N diagrama *m* de la instalación eléctrica

wiry [ˈwaɪərɪ] ADJ (*compar* **wirier**, *superl* **wiriest**) [*person, animal, build*] enjuto y fuerte; [*hair*] áspero, tieso; [*hand*] nervudo

Wis., **Wisc.** ABBR (*US*) = **Wisconsin**

wisdom [ˈwɪzdəm] Ⓐ N sabiduría *f*; **he is a man of great ~** es un hombre de gran sabiduría; **I question the ~ of that decision** dudo que sea una decisión acertada; **I would question the ~ of attempting such a thing** no me parece acertado intentarlo; **in my ~, I decided to ignore their advice** (*iro*) dando muestras de mi gran sabiduría, decidí hacer caso omiso de su consejo
Ⓑ CPD ► **wisdom tooth** N muela *f* del juicio

▼ **wise**[1] [waɪz] Ⓐ ADJ (*compar* **wiser**, *superl* **wisest**)
[1] (= *learned*) [*person*] sabio; [*words*] sabio, acertado; **he's a very ~ man** es un hombre muy sabio; **the Three Wise Men** los Reyes Magos; **she's very ~ in the ways of the world** tiene mucha experiencia de la vida; **she had grown ~r with age** se había vuelto más prudente *or* juiciosa con los años; **to get ~** (*esp US**) darse cuenta, caer en la cuenta*; **the police got ~ to them** la policía los caló*; **to get ~ with sb** (*esp US**) hacerse el listo con algn; **a ~ move** una idea acertada; **I'm none the wiser** me he quedado igual; **nobody will be any the ~r** nadie se dará cuenta; **to put sb ~ to sth*** poner a algn al corriente *or* al tanto de algo; ✦***IDIOM*** **to be ~ after the event** criticar una vez que las cosas ya han pasado, criticar a posteriori
[2] (= *prudent*) [*precaution*] sabio; [*decision, choice*] sabio, acertado; **a map of the area would be a ~ investment** sería aconsejable comprar un mapa del área; **it would be ~ to** (+ *INFIN*) sería prudente + *infin*, sería aconsejable + *infin*; **you'd be ~ to accept** harías bien en aceptar; **he was ~ enough to refuse** tuvo la suficiente sensatez como para negarse
Ⓑ CPD ► **wise guy*** N listillo/a* *m/f* (*pej*); **~ guy, huh?** ¿tú te lo sabes todo, eh?, eres muy listo, ¿verdad? ► **wise man** N (= *sage*) sabio *m*; (= *witch doctor*) hechicero *m* ► **wise woman** N (= *sage*) sabia *f*; (= *witch doctor*) hechicera *f*

►**wise up*** VI + ADV espabilarse*, avisparse*; **~ up!** ¡espabílate!; **to ~ up to sth** caer en la cuenta de algo

wise[2]† [waɪz] N (*frm*) **in this ~** de esta guisa; **in no ~** de ningún modo

➤ LANGUAGE IN USE: wise[1] A2 2.2

-wise [waɪz] ADV (*ending in compounds*) en cuanto a, respecto a; **how are you off money-wise?** ¿de dinero cómo estás?

wiseacre ['waɪz,eɪkəʳ] N sabihondo/a *m/f*

wisecrack* ['waɪzkræk] Ⓐ N salida *f* graciosa; **to make a ~** tener una salida graciosa
Ⓑ VT **"you weigh a ton," he ~ed** —pesas más que un burro en brazos —dijo bromeando
Ⓒ VI bromear

wisely ['waɪzlɪ] ADV [1] (= *prudently*) sabiamente, prudentemente; **she chose ~** escogió sabiamente *or* prudentemente; **he had ~ brought an umbrella with him** había tenido la prudencia de traerse un paraguas
[2] (= *sagaciously*) sabiamente; **we all nodded ~** (*iro, hum*) todos asentimos con aire de entendidos

▼**wish** [wɪʃ] Ⓐ N [1] (= *desire, will*) deseo *m*; **they are sincere in their ~ to make amends for the past** son sinceros en su deseo de enmendar el pasado; **their ~ for peace is sincere** ◊ **they are sincere in their ~ for peace** son sinceros en sus deseos de paz; **it has long been my ~ to do that** desde hace mucho tiempo vengo deseando hacer eso; **he did it against my ~es** lo hizo en contra de mis deseos *or* mi voluntad; **to go against sb's ~es** ir en contra de los deseos *or* la voluntad de algn; **his ~ came true** su deseo se hizo realidad; **your ~ is my command** (*liter or hum*) sus deseos son órdenes para mí; **it is her dearest ~ to go there one day** su mayor deseo es ir allí un día; **his dying ~ was to be buried here** su última voluntad fue que lo enterraran aquí; **she expressed a ~ that the money be donated to charity** manifestó su deseo de que el dinero se donara a instituciones benéficas; **the fairy granted her three ~es** el hada le concedió tres deseos; **I have no great ~ to go** no tengo muchas ganas de ir, no me apetece mucho ir; **you shall have** *or* **get your ~** tu deseo se hará realidad, tu deseo se cumplirá; **to make a ~** pedir un deseo; ✦*PROV* **if ~es were horses, beggars would ride** no se puede pedir la luna; *see also* **death B**
[2] (*in letters, greetings*) **(with) best ~es** saludos, recuerdos; **with best ~es from Peter** recuerdos de Peter; **best ~es** *or* **all good ~es for a happy birthday** te deseamos un feliz cumpleaños, nuestros mejores deseos para un feliz cumpleaños; **(with) best ~es for Christmas and the New Year** (con) nuestros mejores deseos *or* (*frm*) augurios para la Navidad y el Año Nuevo; **please give him my best ~es** dale recuerdos míos; **I went to give him my best ~es** fui a darle la enhorabuena; **the Prime Minister has sent a message of good ~es to the French president** el Primer Ministro ha mandado un mensaje de buena voluntad al presidente francés
Ⓑ VT [1] **I ~** (= *if only*) [1·1] (*in unrealizable or unlikely situations*) **I ~ I were rich** ojalá fuese rico; **I ~ it weren't true** ojalá no fuera así; **I only ~ I'd known that before** ojalá lo hubiera sabido antes; **I ~ I could!** ¡ojalá pudiera!; **"did you go?" — "I ~ I had"** —¿fuiste? —¡ya me hubiera gustado! *or* —¡ojalá!; **I ~ I hadn't said that** siento haber dicho eso, ojalá no hubiera dicho eso
[1·2] (*when change is possible*) **I ~ you'd hurry up** a ver si te das prisa; **I do ~ you'd let me help** ¿por qué no me dejas que te ayude?; **I ~ you wouldn't shout** me gustaría que no gritaras, a ver si dejas de gritar
[2] (*other subjects, other tenses*) **she ~es that she could go to school like other children** le gustaría poder ir a la escuela como otros niños; **I bet you ~ you were still working here!** ¡apuesto a que te gustaría seguir trabajando aquí todavía!
[3] **to ~ sb sth: to ~ sb good luck/a happy Christmas** desear buena suerte/felices pascuas a algn; **~ me luck!** ¡deséame suerte!; **I ~ you all possible happiness** os/te deseo la más completa felicidad; **to ~ sb good morning** dar los buenos días a algn; **to ~ sb goodbye** despedirse de algn; **to ~ sb well/ill: we ~ her well in her new job** le deseamos todo lo mejor en su nuevo trabajo; **I don't ~ her ill** *or* **any harm** no le deseo ningún mal
[4] **to ~ sth on sb** desear algo a algn; **I wouldn't ~ that on anybody** eso no se lo desearía a nadie
[5] (*frm*) (= *want*) querer, desear (*frm*); **I do not ~ it** no lo quiero, no lo deseo (*frm*); **to ~ to do sth** querer *or* (*frm*) desear hacer algo; **I ~ to be alone** quiero *or* (*frm*) deseo estar solo; **I ~ to be told when he comes** quiero *or* (*frm*) deseo que se me avisen cuando llegue; **I don't ~ to sound mean, but ...** no quisiera parecer tacaño, pero ...; **without ~ing to be unkind, you must admit she's not the most interesting company** sin ánimo de ser cruel, tienes que admitir que no es una persona muy interesante; **to ~ sb to do sth** querer *or* (*frm*) desear que algn haga algo; **what do you ~ me to do?** ¿qué quieres *or* (*frm*) deseas que haga?
Ⓒ VI [1] (= *make a wish*) pedir un deseo; **to ~ for sth** desear algo; **she has everything she could ~ for** tiene todo lo que pudiera desear; **what more could one ~ for?** ¿qué más se puede pedir *or* desear?; **I couldn't have ~ed for a nicer birthday** no podía haber soñado con un día de cumpleaños mejor; **"of course you're earning a lot, aren't you?" — "I ~!"** —claro que ganas un montón, ¿verdad? —¡ojalá!
[2] (*frm*) (= *want*) **(just) as you ~** como quieras, como usted desee (*frm*); **you may stay here as long as you ~** te puedes quedar todo el tiempo que quieras *or* desees
Ⓓ CPD ► **wish fulfilment** N **daydreams are a sort of ~ fulfilment** las fantasías son una especie de satisfacción de los deseos ► **wish list** N lista *f* de deseos; **top of my ~ list is ...** mi deseo principal es ...

►**wish away** VT + ADV **these problems/people can't just be ~ed away** estos problemas/estas personas no desaparecen sólo con desearlo; **the son he would ~ away if he could** el hijo que desearía no haber tenido nunca

wishbone ['wɪʃbəʊn] N espoleta *f*

wishful ['wɪʃfʊl] Ⓐ ADJ **to be ~ to do** *or* **of doing sth** (*frm*) estar deseoso de hacer algo
Ⓑ CPD ► **wishful thinking** N ilusiones *fpl*; **that's just ~ thinking** eso es querer hacerse ilusiones

wishing well ['wɪʃɪŋ,wel] N pozo *m* de los deseos

wish-wash* ['wɪʃwɒʃ] N aguachirle *f*

wishy-washy* ['wɪʃɪ,wɒʃɪ] ADJ [*colour*] soso; [*beer*] insípido; [*answer, solution*] a medias; [*thinking, ideas*] vago; [*person*] sin carácter

wisp [wɪsp] N [*of hair*] mechón *m*; [*of cloud, smoke*] voluta *f*; [*of straw*] manojo *m*

wispy ['wɪspɪ] ADJ [*hair*] ralo, fino; [*cloud*] tenue

wisteria [wɪs'tɪərɪə] N glicina *f*, vistaria *f*

wistful ['wɪstfʊl] ADJ (= *thoughtful*) pensativo; (= *sad*) melancólico, triste

wistfully ['wɪstfəlɪ] ADV (= *thoughtfully*) pensativamente; (= *sadly*) con melancolía, tristemente; **she looked at me ~** (= *thoughtfully*) me miró pensativa; (= *sadly*) me miró melancólica *or* triste

wistfulness ['wɪstfʊlnɪs] N (= *thoughtfulness*) lo pensativo; (= *sadness*) melancolía *f*, tristeza *f*

wit¹ [wɪt] N [1] (= *understanding*) inteligencia *f*; **a battle of ~s** una contienda entre dos inteligencias; **to collect one's ~s** reconcentrarse; **to be at one's ~s' end** no saber qué hacer, estar desesperado; **to gather one's ~s** reconcentrarse; **to have** *or* **keep one's ~s about one** no perder la cabeza; **he hadn't the ~ to see that ...** no tenía bastante inteligencia para comprender que ...; **to live by one's ~s** vivir del cuento; **to be out of one's ~s** estar fuera de sí; **to be frightened** *or* **scared out of one's ~s** estar profundamente asustado; **to sharpen one's ~s** aguzar el ingenio, despabilarse; **to use one's ~s** usar su sentido común
[2] (= *humour, wittiness*) ingenio *m*, agudeza *f*; **in a flash of ~ he said ...** en un golpe de ingenio dijo ...; **to have a ready ~** ser ingenioso; **the ~ and wisdom of Joe Soap** las agudezas y sabiduría de Joe Soap; **a story told without ~** un cuento narrado sin gracia
[3] (= *person*) persona *f* ingeniosa; (*Hist*) ingenio *m*; **an Elizabethan ~** un ingenio de la época isabelina

wit² [wɪt] N (*frm*) (*also Jur*) **to wit ...** a saber ..., esto es ...

witch [wɪtʃ] Ⓐ N bruja *f*
Ⓑ CPD ► **witch doctor** N hechicero *m* ► **witch hazel** N olmo *m* escocés ► **witch hunt** N caza *f* de brujas

witchcraft ['wɪtʃkrɑːft] N brujería *f*

witchery ['wɪtʃərɪ] N [1] (*lit*) brujería *f*
[2] (*fig*) encanto *m*, magia *f*

witching hour ['wɪtʃɪŋ,aʊəʳ] N (*hum*) hora *f* de las brujas

with [wɪð, wɪθ] PREPOSITION

When **with** *is part of a set combination, eg* **good with, pleased with, to agree with**, *look up the other word.*

The commonest translation of **with** *is* **con**. *Note that whenever it combines with* **mí, ti** *or* **sí** *the forms* **conmigo, contigo, consigo** *are used.*

[1] con; **he had an argument ~ his brother** tuvo una discusión con su hermano; **she mixed the sugar ~ the eggs** mezcló el azúcar con los huevos; **I'll be ~ you in a moment** un momento y estoy con vosotros, en un momento *or* enseguida estoy con vosotros; **come ~ me!** ven conmigo; **he took it away ~ him** se lo llevó consigo; *BUT* **~ the Alcántara it is the biggest ship in** *or* **of its class** junto con el Alcántara es el mayor buque de esa clase; *see also* **down A7, A10, off A3, out A1**

◆ **along** *or* **together with** junto con; **he was arrested along** *or* **together ~ four other terrorists** fue detenido junto con otros cuatro terroristas

◆ **to be with sb** (= *in the company of*) estar con algn; **I was ~ him** yo estaba con él; **I'm ~ you there** en eso estoy de acuerdo contigo; **are you ~ us or against us?** ¿estás a favor nuestro o en contra?; **I'm not ~ you*** (= *able to understand*) no te entiendo *or* sigo; **are you ~ me?*** ¿me entiendes?; **it's a problem that will always be ~ us** es un problema que siempre nos va a afectar, es un problema que no se va a resolver

◆ **to be with it*** (= *up-to-date*) estar al tanto *or* al día; (= *fashionable*) [*person*] estar al tanto de lo que se lleva; [*thing*] estar de moda; (= *men-*

➤ LANGUAGE IN USE: **wish A2** 21.2, 23.1, 23.2, 23.3, 24.2 **B3** 23.1, 23.5 **B5** 8.4

tally alert) estar lúcido *or* despabilado; **sorry, I'm just not ~ it today** lo siento, hoy estoy atontado

◆ **to get with it*** *ponerse al día;* **get ~ it!** ¡ponte al día!

[2] *in descriptions* con; **we're looking for a house ~ a garden** buscamos una casa con jardín; **I don't like men ~ beards** no me gustan los hombres con barba; **a man ~ checked trousers** un hombre con pantalones de cuadros; **a car ~ the latest features** un coche con las últimas novedades *or* prestaciones; *BUT* **passengers ~ tickets** los pasajeros que tienen *or* con billetes; **you can't speak to the queen ~ your hat on** no se puede hablar con la reina con el sombrero puesto

Note: when the **with** *description pinpoints the particular person or thing you are talking about,* **with** *is usually translated by* **de**:

the man ~ the checked trousers el hombre de los pantalones de cuadros; **the girl ~ the blue eyes** la chica de los ojos azules

[3] *indicating manner, means* con; **to walk ~ a walking stick** andar con bastón; **to cut wood ~ a knife** cortar madera con un cuchillo; *BUT* **~ one blow** de un golpe; **she took off her shoes ~ a sigh** se quitó los zapatos dando un suspiro; **... and ~ these words of advice, he left us** ... y tras darnos este consejo nos dejó; **to fill a glass ~ wine** llenar una copa de vino; **~ no trouble at all** sin dificultad alguna, sin ninguna dificultad; **~ that, he closed the door** luego *or* a continuación, cerró la puerta

[4] *indicating cause* de; **to shiver ~ cold** tiritar *or* temblar de frío; **to shake ~ fear** temblar de miedo; **the hills are white ~ snow** las colinas están cubiertas de nieve; *BUT* **to be ill ~ measles** tener sarampión; **I spent a week in bed ~ flu** estuve una semana en (la) cama con la gripe

[5] *= as regards* con; **it's the same ~ most team sports** lo mismo ocurre con la mayoría de los deportes de equipo; *BUT* **it's a habit ~ him** es una costumbre que tiene, es algo típico de él; **how are things ~ you?** ¿qué tal?, ¿cómo te va? (*esp LAm*), ¿qué hubo? (*Mex, Chile*)

[6] *= owing to* con; **I couldn't see him ~ so many people there** no lo vi con tanta gente como había; **~ so much happening it was difficult to arrange a date** con todo lo que estaba pasando era difícil acordar una cita; *BUT* **~ the approach of winter, trade began to fall off** al acercarse el invierno, el comercio empezó a declinar

[7] *= according to* [*increase, change, improve*] con; **the risk of developing heart disease increases ~ the number of cigarettes smoked** el riesgo de sufrir enfermedades coronarias aumenta con el número de cigarrillos que se fume; *BUT* **it varies ~ the time of year** varía según la estación

[8] *= in the house of* con; **he lives ~ his aunt** vive con su tía; **she stayed ~ friends** se quedó con *or* en casa de unos amigos

[9] *= working for* **he's ~ IBM** trabaja para *or* en IBM; **a scientist ~ ICI** un científico de ICI; **I've been ~ this company for eight years** llevo ocho años en esta empresa

[10] *= in the care of* **to leave sth ~ sb** dejar algo en manos de algn *or* con algn; **to leave a child ~ sb** dejar a un niño al cuidado de algn *or* con algn

[11] *on, about* **he had no money ~ him** no llevaba dinero (encima); **luckily, she had an umbrella ~ her** afortunadamente, llevaba (encima) un paraguas

[12] *= in the same direction as* con; **I was swimming ~ the current** nadaba con *or* a favor de la corriente; *see also* **flow A**

[13] *= in spite of* con; **~ all his faults** con todos sus defectos

withal†† [wɪ'ðɔːl] ADV además, también

withdraw [wɪθ'drɔː] (*pt* **withdrew**; *pp* **withdrawn**) Ⓐ VT [1] (*= take out*) [*+ money*] retirar, sacar (**from** de)

[2] (*= recall*) [*+ troops, ambassador, team*] retirar (**from** de); [*+ product, advertisement, banknotes*] retirar (**from** de)

[3] (*= cancel*) [*+ application, permission, support, licence*] retirar; **to ~ one's labour** ponerse en huelga

[4] (*= retract*) [*+ words, remark*] retractarse de, retirar; [*+ charge*] retirar; **to ~ one's hand (from sth/sb)** apartar la mano (de algo/algn)

Ⓑ VI [1] (*= move away*) apartarse, alejarse

[2] (*= leave room*) retirarse

[3] (*= move back, retreat*) [*troops, forces, police*] retirarse (**from** de); **to ~ to a new position** retirarse a una nueva posición

[4] (*= pull out*) (*from deal, game, talks*) retirarse (**from** de)

[5] (*= withdraw application, candidacy*) retirarse (**from** de); **to ~ in favour of sb** retirarse en favor de algn

[6] (*during lovemaking*) dar marcha atrás*

[7] (*Psych*) **to ~ into o.s.** retraerse, encerrarse en sí mismo

withdrawal [wɪθ'drɔːəl] Ⓐ N [1] (*from bank*) **to make a ~** retirar dinero *or* fondos

[2] (*= recall, removal*) [*of troops, ambassador, team, services, advertisement*] retirada *f* (**from** de); [*of banknote*] retirada *f* de la circulación; **his party has announced its ~ of support for the government** su partido ha anunciado la retirada de su apoyo al gobierno; **they may be contemplating a partial ~ from the country** puede que estén considerando una retirada parcial del país

[3] (*= cancellation*) [*of application, permission, support, licence*] retirada *f*

[4] (*= retraction*) [*of allegation, remark*] retractación *f*; [*of charge*] retirada *f*

[5] (*Psych*) (*from sb, sth*) retraimiento *m* (**from** de)

[6] (*after drug addiction*) síndrome *m* de abstinencia; **to be suffering from ~** padecer el síndrome de abstinencia

[7] (*during lovemaking*) (*= act*) retirada *f* (del pene); (*as contraception*) marcha *f* atrás*, coitus *m* interruptus

Ⓑ CPD ► **withdrawal method** N método *m* de la marcha atrás*, coitus *m* interruptus ► **withdrawal notice** N (*Fin*) aviso *m* de retirada de fondos ► **withdrawal symptoms** NPL síndrome *msing* de abstinencia

withdrawn [wɪθ'drɔːn] Ⓐ PP *of* **withdraw**

Ⓑ ADJ (*= introverted*) reservado, introvertido; (*= detached, absent*) retraído, encerrado en sí mismo

withdrew [wɪθ'druː] PT *of* **withdraw**

withe [wɪθ] N mimbre *m or f*

wither ['wɪðəʳ] Ⓐ VT [*+ flower, plant*] marchitar; **to ~ sb with a look** aplastar *or* fulminar a algn con la mirada

Ⓑ VI [*flower, plant, beauty*] marchitarse; [*limb*] debilitarse, atrofiarse; [*person*] debilitarse; [*hope*] desvanecerse

►**wither away** VI + ADV [*flower, plant*] marchitarse; [*hope*] desvanecerse

withered ['wɪðəd] ADJ [*flower, plant*] marchito; [*limb*] debilitado, atrofiado

withering ['wɪðərɪŋ] ADJ [*heat*] abrasador; [*tone, look, remark*] fulminador

witheringly ['wɪðərɪŋlɪ] ADV [*say, look*] desdeñosamente

withers ['wɪðəz] NPL cruz *fsing* (de caballo)

withhold [wɪθ'həʊld] (*pt, pp* **withheld** [wɪθ'held]) VT [1] [*+ information*] ocultar; [*+ money*] retener; [*+ decision*] aplazar; **to ~ the truth from sb** no revelar la verdad a algn; **to ~ a pound of sb's pay** retener una libra del pago a algn

[2] (*= refuse*) negar; **to withold one's consent** negar el consentimiento; **a parent's right to grant or ~ permission** el derecho de un padre a dar o (de)negar su permiso; **to ~ one's help** negarse a ayudar a algn

withholding tax [wɪθ'həʊldɪŋ,tæks] N [1] *impuesto que se grava a aquellos que tienen una fuente de ingresos en el país pero residen en otro, y que se puede reclamar si existe un acuerdo entre ambos países*

[2] (*US*) *porción de los impuestos de un empleado que la empresa paga directamente al gobierno*

▼**within** [wɪð'ɪn] Ⓐ PREP dentro de; **I want it back ~ three days** quiero que me lo devuelvas dentro de tres días; **here ~ the town** aquí dentro de la ciudad; **to be ~ call** estar al alcance de la voz; **to live ~ one's income** vivir conforme a los ingresos; **to be ~ the law** no rebasar los límites de la ley, atenerse a la legalidad; **a voice ~ me said ...** una voz interior me dijo ...; **the police arrived ~ minutes** la policía llegó a los pocos minutos; **the village is ~ a mile of the river** el pueblo dista poco menos de una milla del pueblo; **we were ~ 100 metres of the summit** faltaban 100 metros para que llegáramos a la cumbre; **~ a year of her death** a poco menos de un año de su muerte; **~ a radius of ten kilometres** en un radio de diez kilómetros; **the shops are ~ easy reach** las tiendas están cerca; **~ the stipulated time** dentro del plazo señalado; **~ the week** antes de terminar la semana; ✦*IDIOM* **to be ~ an inch of** estar a dos dedos de

Ⓑ ADV dentro; **"car for sale - apply within"** "se vende coche - razón dentro *or* (*LAm*) infórmese adentro"; **from ~** desde dentro, desde el interior

without [wɪð'aʊt]

When **without** *is an element in a phrasal verb, eg* **do without**, **go without**, *look up the verb.*

Ⓐ PREP [1] sin; **~ a coat** sin abrigo; **three days ~ food** tres días sin comer; **~ speaking** sin hablar, sin decir nada; **he did it ~ telling me** lo hizo sin decírmelo; **~ my noticing it** sin verlo yo, sin que yo lo notase; **not ~ some difficulty** no sin cierta dificultad; **times ~ number** un sinfín de veces

[2] (††) (*= outside*) fuera de

Ⓑ ADV (*liter*) fuera; **from ~** desde fuera

with-profits ['wɪθ'prɒfɪts] ADJ **~ endowment assurance** seguro *m* dotal con beneficios

withstand [wɪθ'stænd] (*pt, pp* **withstood** [wɪθ'stʊd]) VT resistir, aguantar

withy ['wɪðɪ] N mimbre *m or f*

witless ['wɪtlɪs] ADJ estúpido, tonto; **to scare sb ~** dar un susto mortal a algn

witness ['wɪtnɪs] Ⓐ N [1] (*= person*) testigo *mf*; **eye ~** testigo ocular; **~ for the prosecution/defence** testigo de cargo/descargo; **there were no ~es** no hubo testigos; **to call sb as a ~** citar a algn como testigo; **we want no ~es to this** no queremos que nadie vea esto, no queremos que haya testigos; **I was (a) ~ to this event** yo presencié este suceso, yo fui testigo de este suceso

➤ LANGUAGE IN USE: **within A** 20.6, 20.7

2 (= *evidence*) testimonio *m*; **to give ~ for/against sb** atestiguar a favor de/en contra de algn; **to bear ~ to sth** (*lit*) atestiguar algo; (*fig*) demostrar *or* probar algo; **in ~ of** en fe de
Ⓑ VT 1 (= *be present at*) presenciar, asistir a; (= *see*) ver; **to ~ sb doing sth** ver a algn hacer algo, ver cómo algn hace algo; **the accident was ~ed by two people** hay dos testigos del accidente; **to ~ a document** firmar un documento como testigo; **this period ~ed important changes** (*liter*) este periodo fue testigo de cambios importantes
2 (= *attest by signature*) atestiguar la veracidad de
3 (= *consider as evidence*) ver, mirar
Ⓒ VI (= *testify*) dar testimonio, atestiguar; **to ~ to sth** dar testimonio de *or* atestiguar algo
Ⓓ CPD ► **witness box** (*Brit*), **witness stand** (*US*) N tribuna *f* de los testigos, estrado *m*

witter* ['wɪtəʳ] VI (*Brit*) parlotear; **to ~ on about sth** hablar de algo sin parar; **stop ~ing (on)!** ¿quieres callarte de una vez?

witticism ['wɪtɪsɪzəm] N dicho *m* ingenioso, agudeza *f*, ocurrencia *f*

wittily ['wɪtɪlɪ] ADV (= *cleverly*) ingeniosamente; (= *amusingly*) con gracia, de modo divertido

wittiness ['wɪtɪnɪs] N [*of person*] agudeza *f*, ingenio *m*; [*of remarks, script*] lo agudo, lo ingenioso; **I loved the ~ of the script** me encantó lo agudo *or* ingenioso del guión

wittingly ['wɪtɪŋlɪ] ADV (*frm*) a sabiendas

witty ['wɪtɪ] ADJ (*compar* **wittier**, *superl* **wittiest**) [*person, remark, speech*] agudo, ingenioso; **he's very ~** (= *clever*) es muy agudo *or* ingenioso; (= *funny*) tiene mucha gracia

wives [waɪvz] NPL *of* **wife**

wizard ['wɪzəd] Ⓐ N 1 (= *sorcerer*) mago *m*, brujo *m*, hechicero *m*
2 (*) (= *genius*) genio *mf*, as *m*; **he's a financial ~** es un genio de las finanzas; **he's a ~ at chess** es un genio jugando al ajedrez
Ⓑ ADJ (*esp Brit*†) estupendo*, maravilloso

wizardry ['wɪzədrɪ] N 1 (= *sorcery*) hechicería *f*, brujería *f*
2 (*) (= *skill*) **his financial ~** su genio financiero; **a piece of technical ~** una maravilla de la técnica

wizened ['wɪznd] ADJ arrugado, marchito

wk ABBR (= **week**) sem.

W/L ABBR = **wavelength**

WLTM* VT ABBR = **would like to meet**

Wm ABBR = **William**

WMD(s) NPL ABBR = **weapons of mass destruction**

WMO N ABBR (= **World Meteorological Organization**) OMM *f*

WNW ABBR (= **west-northwest**) ONO

WO N ABBR (*Mil*) = **warrant officer**

wo, woa [wəʊ] EXCL = **whoa**

woad [wəʊd] N hierba *f* pastel, glasto *m*

wobble ['wɒbl] Ⓐ N [*of chair, table etc*] tambaleo *m*, bamboleo *m*; [*of voice*] temblor *m*; **to walk with a ~** tambalearse al andar, andar tambaleándose Ⓑ VI 1 (= *move unsteadily*) tambalearse, bambolearse; [*voice*] temblar
2 (= *hesitate*) vacilar

wobbly ['wɒblɪ] Ⓐ ADJ (*compar* **wobblier**, *superl* **wobbliest**) [*chair, table*] cojo, que se tambalea; [*tooth, wheel*] flojo, que se mueve; [*cyclist*] inseguro; [*voice, jelly*] temblón; [*bottom, thighs*] flácido; **his legs are a bit ~** ◊ **he's a bit ~ on his legs** tiene las piernas un poco flojas; **she drew a ~ line** trazó una línea irregular Ⓑ N **to throw a ~*** ponerse histérico

➤ LANGUAGE IN USE: wonder C 16.1

wodge* [wɒdʒ] N trozo *m* grande

woe [wəʊ] N (*poet, hum*) desgracia *f*, aflicción *f*; **~ is me!** ¡ay de mí!; **~ betide you if you're lying!** ¡pobre de ti como sea mentira!; **a tale of ~** una historia triste

woebegone ['wəʊbɪ,gɒn] ADJ (*liter*) desconsolado, angustiado

woeful ['wəʊfʊl] ADJ 1 (= *lamentable*) [*lack, ignorance, state*] lamentable, deplorable
2 (*liter*) (= *sad*) [*person*] afligido, desconsolado; [*look, expression*] de desconsuelo, de congoja; [*tale*] triste

woefully ['wəʊfəlɪ] ADV 1 (= *lamentably*) **the level of funding is ~ inadequate** el nivel de financiación es de una insuficiencia lamentable *or* deplorable; **he is ~ out of touch with public opinion** está lamentablemente desconectado de la opinión pública; **to be ~ short of sth** andar sumamente escaso de algo
2 (*liter*) (= *sadly*) tristemente; **she shook her head ~** sacudió la cabeza afligida, sacudió la cabeza tristemente

Wog‡* [wɒg] N (*Brit offensive*) negro/a *m/f*

wok [wɒk] N *cazuela china de base redonda*

woke [wəʊk] PT *of* **wake**[3]

woken ['wəʊkn] PP *of* **wake**[3]

wold [wəʊld] N rasa *f* ondulada

wolf [wʊlf] Ⓐ N (*pl* **wolves** [wʊlvz]) 1 (= *animal*) lobo *m*; **lone ~** (*fig*) lobo *m* solitario; ✦*IDIOMS* **to cry ~** dar una falsa alarma; **to keep the ~ from the door** defenderse de *or* contra la miseria; **a ~ in sheep's clothing** un lobo disfrazado de cordero; **to throw sb to the wolves** arrojar a algn a los lobos
2 (*) (= *womanizer*) tenorio *m*
Ⓑ VT (*also* **~ down**) zamparse*, engullir
Ⓒ CPD ► **wolf whistle** N silbido *m* de admiración

wolfcub ['wʊlfkʌb] N lobato *m*

wolfhound ['wʊlfhaʊnd] N (*also* **Irish ~**) lebrel *m* irlandés

wolfish ['wʊlfɪʃ] ADJ lobuno

wolfpack ['wʊlfpæk] N manada *f* de lobos

wolfram ['wʊlfrəm] N volframio *m*, wolfram *m*

wolverine ['wʊlvəri:n] N carcayú *m*, glotón *m*

wolves [wʊlvz] NPL *of* **wolf**

woman ['wʊmən] Ⓐ N (*pl* **women** ['wɪmɪn]) mujer *f*; **~ is very different from man** la mujer es muy distinta del hombre; **I have a ~ who comes in to do the cleaning** tengo una mujer que me hace la limpieza; **the ~ in his life** su compañera; **his ~*** (= *lover*) su querida; **~ to ~** de mujer a mujer; **women's doubles** dobles *mpl* femeninos; **women's football** fútbol *m* femenino; **women's group** grupo *m* femenino; **women's lib*** la liberación de la mujer; **women's libber*** feminista *mf*; **women's movement** movimiento *m* feminista; **she's her own ~** es una mujer muy fiel a sí misma; **women's page** sección *f* femenina; **women's refuge** hogar *m* para mujeres maltratadas; **women's rights** derechos *mpl* de la mujer; **women's room** (*US*) servicio *m* de señoras; **women's studies** (*Univ*) estudios *mpl* de la mujer; **women's team** equipo *m* femenino; **~ of the town** (*euph*) prostituta *f*; **it's women's work** es un trabajo de mujeres; **a ~ of the world** una mujer de mundo; **young ~** joven *f*; *see also* **honest A1, little**[1] **A3, old A6**
Ⓑ CPD ► **woman doctor** N doctora *f* ► **woman driver** N conductora *f* ► **woman engineer** N ingeniera *f* ► **woman pilot** N piloto *f* ► **woman priest** N mujer *f* sacerdote ► **woman writer** N escritora *f*

woman-hater ['wʊmən,heɪtəʳ] N misógino *m*

womanhood ['wʊmənhʊd] N 1 (= *women in general*) mujeres *fpl*, sexo *m* femenino
2 (= *age*) edad *f* adulta (de mujer); **to reach ~** llegar a la edad adulta (de mujer)
3 (= *womanliness*) feminidad *f*

womanish ['wʊmənɪʃ] ADJ mujeril, propio de mujer; [*man*] afeminado

womanize ['wʊmənaɪz] VI dedicarse a la caza de mujeres

womanizer ['wʊmənaɪzəʳ] N mujeriego *m*, donjuán *m*

womankind ['wʊmən'kaɪnd] N mujeres *fpl*, sexo *m* femenino

womanlike ['wʊmənlaɪk] ADJ mujeril

womanliness ['wʊmənlɪnɪs] N feminidad *f*

womanly ['wʊmənlɪ] ADJ femenino

womb [wu:m] N matriz *f*, útero *m*; (*fig*) cuna *f*

wombat ['wɒmbæt] N wombat *m*

women ['wɪmɪn] NPL *of* **woman**

womenfolk ['wɪmɪnfəʊk] NPL mujeres *fpl*

won [wʌn] PT, PP *of* **win**

wonder ['wʌndəʳ] Ⓐ N 1 (= *feeling*) asombro *m*; **in ~** asombrado, maravillado; **to be lost in ~** quedar maravillado
2 (= *object of wonder*) maravilla *f*; (= *cause of wonder*) milagro *m*; **the ~s of science** las maravillas de la ciencia; **the Seven Wonders of the World** las Siete Maravillas del Mundo; **the ~ of it was that …** lo (más) asombroso fue que …; **a nine-day ~** un prodigio que deja pronto de serlo; **it's a ~ that …** es un milagro que …; **~s will never cease!** ¡todavía hay milagros!; **to do ~s** obrar milagros; **it did ~s for her health** obró milagros en su salud; **it's little** *or* **no** *or* **small ~ that he left** no es de extrañarse que se haya marchado; **no ~!** ¡no me extraña!; **he promised ~s** prometió el oro y el moro; **to work ~s** obrar milagros
Ⓑ VT preguntarse; **if you're ~ing how to do it** si te estás preguntando cómo hacerlo; **I was just ~ing if you knew …** me preguntaba si tu sabrías …; **I ~ what he'll do now** me pregunto qué hará ahora; **I ~ where Caroline is** ¿dónde estará Caroline?, ¿me pregunto dónde estará Caroline?; **I ~ whether the milkman's been** a ver si el lechero ha venido; **she ~ed whether to go on** no sabía si seguir adelante; **I ~ why she said that** ¿por qué diría eso?, me pregunto por qué dijo eso
Ⓒ VI 1 (= *ask o.s., speculate*) preguntarse, pensar; **"does she know about it?" — "I ~"** —¿se habrá enterado ella? —eso mismo me pregunto yo; **I ~ed about that for a long time** le di muchas vueltas a eso; **I was ~ing if you could help** te agradecería que me ayudaras; **I often ~** me lo pregunto a menudo; **it set me ~ing** me hizo pensar
2 (= *be surprised*) asombrarse, maravillarse; **to ~ at sth** asombrarse de algo, maravillarse de algo; **that's hardly to be ~ed at** eso no tiene nada de extraño, no hay que asombrarse de eso; **can you ~?** natural, ¿no?; **I shouldn't ~!** ¡sería lógico!; **I shouldn't ~ if …** no me sorprendería que + *subjun*; **she's married by now, I shouldn't ~** se habrá casado ya como sería lógico, cabe presumir que está casada ya
Ⓓ CPD ► **wonder boy** N joven *m* prodigio ► **wonder drug** N remedio *m* milagroso

wonderful ['wʌndəfʊl] ADJ 1 (= *excellent*) [*person, experience, surprise*] maravilloso, estupendo; [*painting, piece of music*] maravilloso, precioso; [*opportunity*] estupendo; [*feeling*] maravilloso; **it would be ~ to be able to sing well** sería maravilloso tener buena voz; **she**

looks ~ for her age está estupenda para la edad que tiene; **isn't it ~!** ◊ **how ~!** ¡qué estupendo!, ¡qué maravilla!; **we had a ~ time** (nos) lo pasamos de maravilla *or* estupendamente

2 (= *amazing*) [*memory, achievement*] increíble

wonderfully ['wʌndəfəlɪ] ADJ 1 (= *extremely*) **she was always ~ kind to me** siempre fue amabilísima conmigo; **it's a ~ funny play** es una obra increíblemente divertida, es una obra divertidísima; **he looks ~ well** está de maravilla, tiene un aspecto estupendo

2 (= *very well*) [*sleep, adapt, work*] de maravilla; **the doctor says she is doing ~** el médico dice que se está recuperando de maravilla *or* estupendamente

wondering ['wʌndərɪŋ] ADJ [*tone, look*] (= *questioning*) perplejo; (= *amazed*) sorprendido

wonderingly ['wʌndərɪŋlɪ] ADV **to look ~ at sb** (= *questioningly*) mirar a algn perplejo; (= *in amazement*) mirar a algn sorprendido

wonderland ['wʌndəlænd] N país *m* de la maravilla, país *m* de las aventuras; **a ~ of amusement parks** un paraíso de parques de atracciones

wonderment ['wʌndəmənt] N = **wonder A1**

wonderstruck ['wʌndəstrʌk] ADJ (*liter*) asombrado, pasmado

wonder-worker ['wʌndə,wɜːkəʳ] N (*Med*) remedio *m* milagroso

wondrous ['wʌndrəs] (*liter*) Ⓐ ADJ maravilloso
Ⓑ ADV (††) = **wondrously**

wondrously ['wʌndrəslɪ] ADV (*liter*) maravillosamente; **~ beautiful** extraordinariamente hermoso, hermoso en extremo

wonga‡ ['wɒŋgə] N (*Brit*) pasta* *f*, guita‡ *f*

wonky* ['wɒŋkɪ] ADJ (*compar* **wonkier**; *superl* **wonkiest**) (*Brit*) 1 (= *wobbly*) [*chair, table*] cojo, que se tambalea

2 (= *crooked*) torcido, chueco (*LAm*)

3 (= *broken down*) estropeado, descompuesto (*esp Mex*); **to go ~** [*car, machine*] estropearse; [*TV picture*] descomponerse

won't [wəʊnt] = **will not**

wont [wəʊnt] (*frm*) Ⓐ ADJ **to be ~ to do sth** soler hacer algo, acostumbrar a hacer algo; **as he was ~ (to)** como solía (hacer) *or* acostumbraba a hacer
Ⓑ N costumbre *f*; **as was my ~** como era mi costumbre, como solía hacer *or* acostumbraba a hacer; **it is his ~ to read after dinner** tiene por costumbre leer después de cenar, suele leer *or* acostumbra a leer después de cenar

wonted ['wəʊntɪd] ADJ (*liter*) acostumbrado

woo [wuː] VT 1 (*lit*) cortejar

2 (*fig*) buscarse

wood [wʊd] Ⓐ N 1 (= *material*) madera *f*; **it's made of ~** es de madera; **dead ~** (*lit*) ramas *fpl* muertas; **touch ~!** ¡toca madera!; *see also* **deadwood**

2 (= *firewood*) leña *f*

3 (= *forest*) bosque *m*; **woods** bosque *msing*; **we went for a walk in the ~(s)** fuimos a pasear por el bosque; **to take to the ~s** echarse al monte; ✦*IDIOMS* **we're not out of the ~(s) yet** aún no estamos fuera de peligro; **he can't see the ~ for the trees** (*Brit*) los árboles no le dejan ver el bosque, aún no le encuentra el chiste (*LAm*)

4 (*Golf*) palo *m* de madera

5 (*Bowls*) bola *f*

6 (*in brewing*) **beer drawn from the ~** cerveza *f* de barril

7 (*Mus*) **the ~s** los instrumentos de viento de madera

Ⓑ CPD ► **wood alcohol** N alcohol *m* metílico ► **wood anemone** N anémona *f* silvestre ► **wood block** N bloque *m* de madera; (= *woodcut*) grabado *m* en madera; (*in paving*) adoquín *m* de madera, tarugo *m* ► **wood carving** N talla *f* de madera ► **wood engraving** N grabado *m* en madera ► **wood pulp** N pasta *f* de madera ► **wood shavings** NPL virutas *fpl* ► **wood spirit** N = **wood alcohol**

woodbine ['wʊdbaɪn] N 1 (= *honeysuckle*) madreselva *f*

2 (*US*) (= *Virginia creeper*) viña *f* loca

woodchuck ['wʊdtʃʌk] N marmota *f* de América; → GROUNDHOG DAY

woodcock ['wʊdkɒk] N chocha *f* perdiz

woodcraft ['wʊdkrɑːft] N conocimiento *m* de la vida del bosque

woodcut ['wʊdkʌt] N grabado *m* en madera

woodcutter ['wʊd,kʌtəʳ] N leñador *m*

wooded ['wʊdɪd] ADJ arbolado

wooden ['wʊdn] Ⓐ ADJ 1 (= *made of wood*) de madera

2 (*fig*) (= *lacking expression*) [*actor, performance*] acartonado, inexpresivo; [*face, person*] rígido, inexpresivo; [*style*] seco, poco expresivo

Ⓑ CPD ► **wooden horse** N caballo *m* de madera ► **wooden leg** N pierna *f* de madera, pata *f* de palo* ► **wooden spoon** N cuchara *f* de palo; (*fig*) premio *m* de consolación

wooden-headed ['wʊdn'hedɪd] ADJ cabezahueca

woodenly ['wʊdnlɪ] ADV [*say, react*] de manera poco expresiva; [*act*] de forma acartonada

woodland ['wʊdlənd] Ⓐ N bosque *m*
Ⓑ CPD de los bosques

woodlark ['wʊdlɑːk] N totovía *f*, cogujada *f*

woodlouse ['wʊdlaʊs] N (*pl* **woodlice** ['wʊdlaɪs]) cochinilla *f*

woodman ['wʊdmən] N (*pl* **woodmen**) (= *woodcutter*) leñador *m*; (= *forester*) trabajador *m* forestal

woodpecker ['wʊd,pekəʳ] N pájaro *m* carpintero; **green ~** pito *m* real; **lesser spotted ~** pico *m* menor

woodpigeon ['wʊd,pɪdʒən] N paloma *f* torcaz

woodpile ['wʊdpaɪl] N montón *m* de leña

woodshed ['wʊdʃed] N leñera *f*

woodsy ['wʊdzɪ] ADJ (*US*) selvático

woodwind ['wʊdwɪnd] N **the ~s** ◊ **the ~ section** los instrumentos *mpl* de viento de madera

woodwork ['wʊdwɜːk] N 1 (= *craft*) carpintería *f*

2 (= *wooden parts*) enmaderado *m*, maderaje *m*; **they come crawling out of the ~** (*fig*) aparecen de no se sabe dónde

woodworm ['wʊdwɜːm] N carcoma *f*; **the table has ~** la mesa está carcomida

woody ['wʊdɪ] ADJ (*compar* **woodier**; *superl* **woodiest**) 1 [*plant, stem, texture*] leñoso; [*odour*] a madera

2 (= *wooded*) [*countryside*] lleno de bosque

woof¹ [wʊf] Ⓐ N (= *bark*) ladrido *m*
Ⓑ EXCL ¡guau!
Ⓒ VI ladrar

woof² [wuːf] N (*Tex*) trama *f*

woofer ['wuːfəʳ] N altavoz *m* para sonidos graves

woofter‡, **wooftah‡** ['wʊftə] N (*Brit pej*) marica‡ *m*

wooing ['wuːɪŋ] N galanteo *m*

wool [wʊl] Ⓐ N [*of sheep*] lana *f*; **all ~** ◊ **pure ~** lana pura; **it's made of ~** es de lana; ✦*IDIOM* **to pull the ~ over sb's eyes** dar a algn gato por liebre; *see also* **dyed-in-the-wool**

Ⓑ ADJ de lana

Ⓒ CPD ► **wool merchant** N comerciante *mf* de lanas, lanero/a *m/f* ► **wool trade** N comercio *m* de lana

woolen ['wʊlən] ADJ, N (*US*) = **woollen**

woolgathering ['wʊl,gæðərɪŋ] N (*fig*) **to be ~** andar distraído

wooliness ['wʊlɪnɪs] N (*US*) = **woolliness**

woollen, **woolen** (*US*) ['wʊlən] Ⓐ ADJ de lana
Ⓑ **woollens** NPL géneros *mpl* de lana
Ⓒ CPD ► **woollen industry** N industria *f* de la lana

woolliness, **wooliness** (*US*) ['wʊlɪnɪs] N 1 [*of material, garment, sheep*] lanosidad *f*, lo lanoso

2 (= *vagueness*) [*of ideas, thinking, essay*] vaguedad *f*, imprecisión *f*; [*of person*] confusión *f*

woolly, **wooly** (*US*) ['wʊlɪ] Ⓐ ADJ (*compar* **woollier**; *superl* **woolliest**) 1 [*jumper etc*] de lana; [*animal*] lanudo

2 (= *vague*) [*ideas, thinking, essay*] vago, impreciso; [*person*] confuso

Ⓑ N 1 (= *sweater*) jersey *m* de lana

2 **woollies*** **woolies** (*US**) (= *clothing*) ropa *f* de lana

woolly-minded ['wʊlɪ'maɪndɪd] ADJ confuso

woolman ['wʊlmæn] N (*pl* **woolmen**) (= *trader*) comerciante *m* en lanas; (= *manufacturer*) dueño *m* de una fábrica textil, lanero *m*

Woolsack ['wʊlsæk] N **the ~** (*Brit Parl*) saco *m* de lana (*silla del Gran Canciller en la Cámara de los Lores*)

wooly ['wʊlɪ] ADJ, N (*US*) = **woolly**

woops* [wʊps] = **whoops**

woozy* ['wuːzɪ] ADJ (*compar* **woozier**; *superl* **wooziest**) mareado

Wop** [wɒp] N (*offensive*) italiano/a *m/f*

Worcester sauce [,wʊstə'sɔːs], **Worcestershire sauce** [,wʊstəʃə'sɔːs] N salsa *f* Worcester, salsa *f* Worcestershire

Worcs. ABBR = **Worcestershire**

word [wɜːd] Ⓐ N 1 (*gen*) palabra *f*; (= *remark*) palabra *f*; (*Ling*) voz *f*, vocablo *m*; **I remember every ~ he said** recuerdo todas y cada una de sus palabras; **that's not the ~ I would have chosen** yo no me hubiera expresado así; **the ~s** (= *lyrics*) la letra; **I won't hear a ~ against him** no permito que se le critique; **a big ~*** una palabra difícil; **in ~ and deed** de palabra y hecho; **~s fail me** no me lo puedo creer; **~s failed me** me quedé sin habla; **a man of few ~s** un hombre nada locuaz; **I can't find (the) ~s to tell you ...** no encuentro palabras para decirte ...; **fine ~s** palabras elocuentes (pero quizá poco sinceras); **~ for ~** palabra por palabra; **too stupid for ~s** de lo más estúpido; **what's the ~ for "shop" in Spanish?** ¿cómo se dice "shop" en español?; **the Spanish have a ~ for it** en español existe una palabra para eso; **there is no other ~ for it** no se puede llamar de otro modo; **silly isn't the ~ for it** ¡llamarle estúpido es poco!; **I can't get a ~ out of him** no logro sacarle una palabra; **in a ~** en pocas palabras, en una palabra; **in other ~s** en otros términos, es decir, esto es; **in the ~s of Calderón** con palabras de Calderón, como dice Calderón; **in his own ~s** con sus propias palabras; **she didn't say so in so many ~s** no lo dijo exactamente así, no lo dijo así concretamente; **to have the last ~ in an argument** decir la última palabra en una discusión; **to measure one's ~s** medir las palabras; by ~ of mouth verbalmente, de palabra; a ~ of advice un consejo; a ~ of thanks unas palabras de agradecimiento; a ~ of warning una advertencia; I can't put my feelings into ~s no tengo palabras para expresar lo que siento; to put in a (good) ~ for sb avalar a algn, interceder por algn; don't say a ~ about it no digas nada de eso; he never said a ~ no dijo una sola palabra; he didn't say a ~ about it to me ni me lo mencionó; nobody had a good ~ to say about him nadie quería defenderle, nadie habló en su favor; I now call on Mr Allison to say a few ~s ahora le cedo la palabra al Sr. Allison, ahora le invito al Sr. Allison a hacer uso de la palabra; to weigh one's ~s medir las palabras; with these ~s, he sat down y tras pronunciar estas palabras se sentó; without a ~ sin decir palabra *or* ni pío; ✦*IDIOMS* from the ~ go desde el principio mismo; it's the last ~ in luxury es el último grito en lo que a lujo se refiere; you're putting ~s into my mouth te refieres a cosas que yo no he dicho; you took the ~s right out of my mouth me quitaste la palabra de la boca; the ~ on the street is that ... los que saben del tema dicen que ...; ✦*PROVS* many a true ~ is spoken in jest las bromas a veces pueden ser veras; a ~ to the wise (is sufficient) al buen entendedor pocas palabras le bastan; *see also* breathe A2, eat A, edgeways, mince A2

2 (= *talk*) to have a ~ with sb hablar (dos palabras) con algn, tener unas palabras con algn; I'll have a ~ with him about it lo hablaré con él, se lo mencionaré; could I have a (short) ~ with you? ¿puedo hablar un momento contigo?; I had a few ~s with him yesterday tuve unas palabras con él ayer; to have a ~ in sb's ear (*Brit*) decir algo a algn en confianza

3 (= *angry words*) to have ~s with sb reñir *or* (*esp LAm*) pelear(se) con algn; the referee had ~s with him el árbitro le dijo cuatro palabras; ~s passed between them cambiaron algunas palabras injuriosas

4 (*no pl*) (= *message*) recado *m*; (= *news*) noticia *f*, aviso *m*; to bring ~ of sth to sb informar a algn de algo; ~ came that ... llegó noticia de que ..., se supo que ...; if ~ gets out that ... si sale a la luz que ..., si llega a saberse que ...; the ~ is going round that ... se dice que ..., corre la voz de que ...; ~ has it that ... ◊ the ~ is that ... se dice que ...; to leave ~ (with/for sb) that ... dejar recado (con/para algn) de que ..., dejar dicho (con/para algn) que ...; there's still no ~ from John todavía no sabemos nada de John; pass the ~ that it's time to go diles que es hora de marcharnos; to send ~ mandar recado; to send sb ~ of sth avisar a algn de algo; to spread the ~ propagar la noticia

5 (*no pl*) (= *promise, assurance*) palabra *f* (de honor); it's his ~ against mine es su palabra contra la mía; to take sb at his ~ aceptar lo que algn dice; to break one's ~ faltar a *or* no cumplir la palabra; to give sb one's ~ (that ...) dar la palabra a algn (de que ...); to go back on one's ~ faltar a la palabra; you have my ~ tienes mi palabra; we only have *or* we've only got her ~ for it todo lo que sabemos es lo que ella dice; to hold *or* keep sb to his ~ hacer que algn cumpla su palabra; ~ of honour palabra *f*, palabra *f* de honor; to keep one's ~ cumplir (lo prometido); (upon) my ~! ¡caramba!; he's a man of his ~ es hombre de palabra; I take your ~ for it te creo, ¡basta con que me lo digas!*; take my ~ for it te lo aseguro; ✦*IDIOMS* his ~ is (as good as) his bond su palabra merece entera confianza; to be as good as one's ~ cumplir (lo prometido)

6 (*no pl*) (= *command*) orden *f*; to give the ~ to do sth dar la orden de hacer algo; you have only to say the ~ solamente hace falta que des la orden; his ~ is law su palabra es ley; ~ of command voz *f* de mando

7 (*Rel*) verbo *m*, palabra *f*; the Word of God el Verbo de Dios

Ⓑ VT [+ *letter etc*] redactar; it's not very clearly ~ed está mal redactado; how shall we ~ it? ¿cómo lo expresamos?; a simply ~ed refusal una negativa sencilla; a well ~ed declaration una declaración bien expresada

Ⓒ CPD ► word association N (*Psych*) asociación *f* de palabras ► word blindness N alexia *f* ► word class N categoría *f* gramatical (de las palabras) ► word count N recuento *m* de vocabulario ► word formation N formación *f* de palabras ► word game N juego *m* de formación de palabras ► word list N lista *f* de palabras, vocabulario *m* ► word order N orden *m* de palabras ► word picture N descripción *f* ► word processing N procesamiento *m* de textos ► word processor N procesador *m* de textos

wordage ['wɜːdɪdʒ] N número *m or* recuento *m* de palabras

word-blind ['wɜːdblaɪnd] ADJ aléxico

wordbook ['wɜːdbʊk] N vocabulario *m*

wordiness ['wɜːdɪnɪs] N verbosidad *f*, prolijidad *f*

wording ['wɜːdɪŋ] N the ~ is unclear está mal redactado

wordless ['wɜːdlɪs] ADJ 1 (= *silent*) silencioso 2 (= *without words*) sin palabras

word-of-mouth ['wɜːdəv'maʊθ] ADJ verbal, oral; *see also* word A1

word-perfect ['wɜːd'pɜːfɪkt] ADJ (*Brit*) sin falta de expresión; to be ~ saber perfectamente su papel

wordplay ['wɜːdpleɪ] N juego *m* de palabras

word-process ['wɜːd'prəʊses] VT pasar a máquina

wordsmith ['wɜːdsmɪθ] N (= *writer*) artífice *mf* de la palabra; (= *poet*) poeta *mf*

wordwrap ['wɜːdræp] N salto *m* de línea automático

wordy ['wɜːdɪ] ADJ (*compar* wordier; *superl* wordiest) verboso, prolijo

wore [wɔːʳ] PT *of* wear

work [wɜːk] Ⓐ N 1 (= *activity*) trabajo *m*; (= *effort*) esfuerzo *m*; "work in progress" "trabajo en curso"; to be at ~ on sth estar trabajando sobre algo; there are forces at ~ hay fuerzas en movimiento; ~ has begun on the new dam se han comenzado las obras del nuevo embalse; ~ has begun on the new project ha comenzado el trabajo en el nuevo proyecto; it's all in a day's ~ es pan de cada día; to do one's ~ hacer su trabajo; he did some good ~ at head office hizo un buen trabajo en la oficina central; the medicine had done its ~ la medicina había surtido efecto; to get some ~ done hacer algo (de trabajo); to get on with one's ~ seguir trabajando; good ~! (= *well done*) ¡buen trabajo!; it's hard ~ es mucho trabajo, cuesta (trabajo); he's hard ~* es una persona difícil; a piece of ~ un trabajo; she's put a lot of ~ into it le ha puesto grandes esfuerzos; to make quick ~ of sth/sb despachar algo/a algn con rapidez; to set to ~ ponerse a trabajar; to set sb to ~ poner a algn a trabajar; to make short ~ of sth/sb despachar algo/a algn con rapidez; to start ~ ponerse a trabajar; ✦*IDIOM* to have one's ~ cut out: I have my ~ cut out as it is ya tengo trabajo hasta por encima de las cejas; I had my ~ cut out to stop it me costó detenerlo; you'll have your ~ cut out trying to stop him te costará muchísimo trabajo impedirle; *see also* nasty A4

2 (= *employment, place of employment*) trabajo *m*; "~ wanted" (*US*) "demandas de empleo"; to be at ~ estar trabajando; accidents at ~ accidentes *mpl* laborales; to go to ~ ir a trabajar; to go out to ~ (= *have a job*) tener un trabajo; to be in ~ tener trabajo; she's looking for ~ está buscando trabajo; it's nice ~ if you can get it es muy agradable para los que tienen esa suerte; I'm off ~ for a week tengo una semana de permiso; a day off ~ un día libre; to take time off ~ tomarse tiempo libre; to be out of ~ estar desempleado *or* parado *or* en paro; to put sb out of ~ dejar a algn sin trabajo; on her way to ~ camino del trabajo

3 (= *product, deed*) obra *f*; (= *efforts*) trabajo; the ~s of God las obras de Dios; this is the ~ of a professional/madman esto es trabajo de un profesional/loco; what do you think of his work? ¿qué te parece su trabajo?; the dictator and all his ~s el dictador y todo lo suyo; good ~s obras *fpl* de caridad; his life's ~ el trabajo al que ha dedicado su vida

4 (*Art, Literat etc*) obra *f*; the ~s of Dickens las obras de Dickens; a ~ of art una obra de arte; a literary ~ una obra literaria; a ~ of reference un libro de consulta

5 works [*of machine, clock etc*] mecanismo *msing*; ✦*IDIOM* to bung *or* gum up the ~s fastidiarlo todo; *see also* spanner

6 works (*Mil*) obras *fpl*, fortificaciones *fpl*; road ~s obras; Ministry of Works Ministerio *m* de Obras Públicas

Ⓑ VI 1 (*gen*) trabajar; (= *be in a job*) tener trabajo; to ~ to achieve sth dirigir todos sus esfuerzos a lograr algo; he is ~ing at his German está dándole al alemán; to ~ hard trabajar mucho *or* duro; she ~s in a bakery trabaja en una panadería; he ~s in education/publishing trabaja en la enseñanza/el campo editorial; he prefers to ~ in wood/oils prefiere trabajar la madera/con óleos; to ~ to rule (*Ind*) estar en huelga de celo; to ~ towards sth trabajar *or* realizar esfuerzos para conseguir algo; ✦*IDIOM* to ~ like a slave *or* Trojan *etc* trabajar como un demonio

2 (= *function*) [*machine, car*] funcionar; the heating isn't ~ing la calefacción no funciona; it won't ~ no funciona; "not working" "no funciona"; my brain doesn't seem to be ~ing today (*hum*) mi cerebro no funciona hoy como es debido; it may ~ against us podría sernos desfavorable; this can ~ both ways esto puede ser un arma de doble filo; this may ~ in our favour puede que esto nos venga bien; to get sth ~ing hacer funcionar algo; it ~s off the mains funciona con la electricidad de la red; my plan ~ed perfectly mi plan funcionó a la perfección

3 (= *be effective*) [*plan*] salir, marchar; [*drug, medicine, spell*] surtir efecto, ser eficaz; [*yeast*] fermentar; how long does it take to ~? ¿cuánto tiempo hace falta para que empiece a surtir efecto?; the scheme won't ~ el proyecto no es práctico, esto no será factible; it won't ~, I tell you! ¡te digo que no se puede (hacer)!

4 [*mouth, face, jaws*] moverse, torcerse

5 (= *move gradually*) she ~ed methodically down the list repasó metódicamente la lista; to ~ loose desprenderse; to ~ round to a question preparar el terreno para preguntar algo; eventually he ~ed round to the price

➤ LANGUAGE IN USE: work B1 19.2

por fin llegó a mencionar el precio; **what are you ~ing round to?** ¿adónde va a parar todo esto?, ¿qué propósito tiene todo esto?

Ⓒ VT [1] (= *make work*) hacer trabajar; **he ~s his staff too hard** hace trabajar demasiado al personal; **to ~ o.s. to death** matarse trabajando

[2] (= *operate*) **can you ~ it?** ¿sabes manejarlo?; **it is ~ed by electricity** funciona con electricidad

[3] (= *achieve*) [+ *change*] producir, motivar; [+ *cure*] hacer, efectuar; [+ *miracle*] hacer; **he has managed to ~ his promotion*** ha conseguido asegurarse el ascenso; **they ~ed it so that she could come*** lo arreglaron para que viniera; *see also* **wonder A2**

[4] (*Sew*) coser; (*Knitting*) [+ *row*] hacer; **~ed with blue thread** bordado de hilo azul

[5] (= *shape*) [+ *dough, clay*] trabajar; [+ *stone, marble*] tallar, grabar; **~ed flint** piedra *f* tallada; **~ the butter and sugar together** amasar el azúcar y la mantequilla juntos

[6] (= *exploit*) [+ *mine*] explotar; [+ *land*] cultivar; **this land has not been ~ed for many years** estas tierras hace mucho tiempo que no se cultivan; **he ~s the eastern part of the province** trabaja en la parte este de la provincia

[7] (= *manoeuvre*) **he gradually ~ed the rope through the hole** poco a poco fue metiendo la cuerda por el agujero; **to ~ one's hands free** lograr soltar las manos; **he ~ed the lever up and down** movió la palanca hacia arriba y hacia abajo; **to ~ o.s. into a rage** ponerse furioso, enfurecerse; **he ~ed the crowd (up) into a frenzy** exaltó los ánimos de la multitud; **the screw had ~ed itself loose** el tornillo se había soltado solo; **to ~ one's way along** ir avanzando poco a poco; **to ~ one's way up a cliff** escalar poco a poco *or* a duras penas un precipicio; **to ~ one's way up to the top of a company** llegar a la dirección de una compañía por sus propios esfuerzos; **he ~ed his way up in the firm** ascendió en la compañía mediante sus propios esfuerzos

[8] (= *finance*) **to ~ one's passage on a ship** costearse un viaje trabajando; **to ~ one's way through college** costearse los estudios universitarios trabajando

Ⓓ CPD ► **work camp** N campamento *m* laboral ► **work ethic** N ética *f* del trabajo ► **work experience** N experiencia *f* laboral ► **work file** N fichero *m* de trabajo ► **work force** N (= *labourers*) mano *f* de obra; (= *personnel*) plantilla *f* ► **work permit** N permiso *m* de trabajo ► **work study** N práctica *f* estudiantil ► **work surface** N = **worktop** ► **work therapy** N laborterapia *f*, terapia *f* laboral ► **work week** N (*US*) semana *f* laboral

►**work away** VI + ADV seguir trabajando, trabajar sin parar; **to ~ away at sth** darle (duro) a algo*

►**work in** Ⓐ VI + ADV (= *fit in*) ajustarse a, cuadrar con; **it ~s in quite well with our plans** esto se ajusta bastante bien a nuestros planes, esto cuadra bastante bien con nuestros planes

Ⓑ VT + ADV [1] [+ *screw etc*] (*slowly*) introducir poco a poco; (*with difficulty*) meter con esfuerzo

[2] [+ *quotation, reference, subject*] meter; **we'll try to ~ in a reference somewhere** trataremos de meter una referencia en alguna parte

[3] (= *mix in*) agregar, añadir; **~ the flour in gradually** agregar *or* añadir la harina poco a poco

►**work off** Ⓐ VI + ADV [*nut, handle*] desprenderse, soltarse (con el uso)

Ⓑ VT + ADV [1] [+ *debt*] pagar con su trabajo

[2] **to ~ off one's feelings** desahogarse; **to ~ off surplus fat** quitarse las grasas excesivas trabajando; **I must try to ~ off all the weight I've put on** tengo que moverme para ver si adelgazo lo que he engordado

►**work on** VI + PREP [1] [+ *project etc*] trabajar en; **they're ~ing on the car now** están trabajando en el coche ahora; **they will get ~ing on it at once** se pondrán enseguida manos a la obra; **the police are ~ing on it** la policía lo está investigando

[2] (= *act on*) **we've no clues to ~ on** no tenemos pistas en qué basarnos; **we're ~ing on the principle that ...** nos atenemos al *or* nos basamos en el principio de que ...

[3] (= *try to persuade*) **he hasn't agreed yet but I'm ~ing on him** todavía no está de acuerdo pero le estoy tratando de convencer

►**work out** Ⓐ VT + ADV [1] (= *calculate*) [+ *cost, profit*] calcular; [+ *answer*] encontrar; **I ~ed it out in my head** lo calculé mentalmente

[2] (= *solve*) [+ *problem*] resolver; **things will ~ themselves out** al final, todo saldrá bien *or* se solucionará

[3] (= *devise*) idear; **to ~ out a plan** idear *or* (*frm*) urdir un plan

[4] (= *understand*) lograr entender; **I just couldn't ~ it out** no lograba entenderlo; **can you ~ out where we are on the map?** ¿puedes determinar *or* averiguar dónde estamos en el mapa?; **I can't ~ him out*** no puedo entenderle

[5] (= *exhaust*) [+ *mine, land*] agotar

[6] (*in job*) **to ~ out one's notice** trabajar hasta que se acabe el tiempo de preaviso

[7] (= *get rid of*) [+ *anger, frustration*] librarse de

Ⓑ VI + ADV [1] (= *allow solution*) resolverse; **it doesn't ~ out** [*sum*] no sale

[2] (= *amount to*) **the cost ~ed out at five pounds** los costos ascendieron a cinco libras; **how much does it ~ out at?** ¿cuánto suma?, ¿a cuánto sale?; **it ~s out at ten pounds each** sale a diez libras esterlinas por persona; **gas heating would ~ out cheaper** la calefacción de gas saldría más barata

[3] (= *succeed*) salir bien; **I hope it will ~ out well** espero que salga bien; **everything ~ed out well** todo *or* la cosa salió bien; **how did it ~ out?** ¿qué tal salió?; **it hasn't ~ed out that way** no ha sido así

[4] (= *exercise*) hacer ejercicio; **I ~ out twice a week** hago ejercicio dos veces a la semana

►**work over*** VT + ADV (= *beat up*) dar una paliza a

►**work through** VI + PREP (*Psych*) [+ *problem, conflict*] tratar

►**work up** VT + ADV [1] (= *develop*) [+ *energy, courage*] conseguir; **I can't ~ up much enthusiasm for the plan** no consigo entusiasmarme con el plan; **together they ~ed the business up from nothing** entre los dos levantaron el negocio de la nada; **you could ~ this story up into a film** podrías desarrollar este cuento para hacer una película; **to ~ up an appetite** abrir el apetito; **I've ~ed up quite a thirst, carrying those boxes** me ha entrado mucha sed cargando esas cajas

[2] (= *excite*) **he ~ed the crowd up into a frenzy** exaltó los ánimos de la multitud; **to ~ o.s. up into a rage** ponerse furioso, enfurecerse; **to be ~ed up** excitarse, exaltarse, emocionarse (*esp LAm*); **don't get all ~ed up!** ¡cálmate!

►**work up to** VI + PREP preparar el terreno para; **events were ~ing up to a crisis** los sucesos estaban preparando el terreno para una crisis; **what are you ~ing up to?** ¿qué propósito tiene todo esto?, ¿adónde va a parar todo esto?; **I thought he was ~ing up to a proposal** creía que estaba preparando el terreno para hacerme una declaración

workable ['wɜːkəbl] ADJ práctico, factible

workaday ['wɜːkədeɪ] ADJ rutinario

workaholic [ˌwɜːkə'hɒlɪk] N trabajador(a) *m/f* obsesivo/a, adicto/a *m/f* al trabajo

workbasket ['wɜːkˌbɑːskɪt] N neceser *m* de costura

workbench ['wɜːkbentʃ] N banco *m* de trabajo, mesa *f* de trabajo

workbook ['wɜːkbʊk] N libro *m* de trabajo; (*Scol*) cuaderno *m*

workbox ['wɜːkbɒks] N (*Sew*) neceser *m* de costura

workday ['wɜːkdeɪ] N (*US*) día *m* laborable

worker ['wɜːkər] Ⓐ N [1] (= *person*) (*gen*) trabajador(a) *m/f*; (*Agr, Ind*) obrero/a *m/f*; **he's a fast ~** trabaja deprisa; (*) (*euph*) va deprisa con las mujeres*; **she's a hard ~** es muy trabajadora; **she's a good ~** trabaja bien; *see also* **office B**, **research D**

[2] (= *ant, bee*) obrera *f*

Ⓑ CPD ► **worker ant** N hormiga *f* obrera ► **worker bee** N abeja *f* obrera ► **worker priest** N sacerdote *m* obrero

workflow ['wɜːkfləʊ] N volumen *m* de trabajo

workhorse ['wɜːkˌhɔːs] N caballo *m* de tiro; (*fig*) persona *f* muy trabajadora

workhouse ['wɜːkhaʊs] N (*pl* **workhouses** ['wɜːkhaʊzɪz]) (*Brit Hist*) asilo *m* de pobres

work-in ['wɜːkɪn] N encierro *m* (en una fábrica *etc*)

working ['wɜːkɪŋ] Ⓐ ADJ [1] (= *economically active*) [*person*] trabajador, que trabaja; [*population*] activo; **~ mothers** madres *fpl* trabajadoras, madres *fpl* que trabajan; **the ~ man** el hombre trabajador *or* que trabaja; **the ~ woman** la mujer trabajadora *or* que trabaja; **ordinary ~ people** gente trabajadora normal y corriente; **he's a ~ dog** es un perro de trabajo *or* labor

[2] (= *relating to work*) [*conditions, practice, environment, week*] laboral; [*life*] laboral, activo; [*day*] laborable; [*breakfast, lunch*] de trabajo; [*clothes*] de faena, de trabajo; **your order will be sent within three ~ days** (*Brit*) su pedido será despachado en un plazo de tres días laborables; **my ~ day begins at eight a.m.** mi jornada (laboral *or* de trabajo) empieza a las ocho de la mañana; **during ~ hours** durante horas de trabajo; **~ patterns** pautas *fpl* laborales, pautas *fpl* de trabajo

[3] (= *provisional*) [*title, definition*] momentáneo, provisional; **~ hypothesis** hipótesis *f inv* de trabajo

[4] (= *functioning*) [*farm, mill, steam train*] en funcionamiento; **to have a ~ knowledge of sth** tener conocimientos básicos de algo; **to be in ~ order** funcionar perfectamente

Ⓑ N [1] (= *operation*) [*of machine, engine, computer*] funcionamiento *m*; [*of mine*] explotación *f*

[2] **workings** [2·1] [*of organization, parliament*] forma *f* de funcionar; [*of machine, engine, computer*] (= *operation, way of working*) funcionamiento *m*; (= *mechanism*) mecanismo *m*; **the ~s of his mind** su forma de pensar

[2·2] (= *mine*) mina *fsing*; (= *excavations*) excavaciones *fpl*

Ⓒ CPD ► **working assets** NPL (*Comm, Fin*) activo *m* circulante ► **working capital** N (*Comm, Fin*) capital *m* circulante, capital *m* de explotación ► **the working class(es)** N(PL) la clase obrera, la clase trabajadora; *see also*

working-class ▸ **working expenses** NPL gastos *mpl* de explotación ▸ **working face** N cara *f* de trabajo ▸ **working group** N grupo *m* de trabajo (**on** sobre); ▸ **working holiday** N *vacaciones en las que se combina el trabajo con el ocio* ▸ **working majority** N (*Pol*) mayoría *f* suficiente ▸ **working model** N modelo *m* articulado ▸ **working paper** N documento *m* de trabajo ▸ **working parts** NPL partes *fpl* activas ▸ **working partner** N socio *m* activo ▸ **working party** N = **working group** ▸ **working relationship** N relación *f* de trabajo; **they have a good ~ relationship** tienen una buena relación de trabajo, trabajan bien juntos ▸ **working vacation** N (*US*) = **working holiday**

working-class ['wɜːkɪŋklɑːs] ADJ [*person, family*] de clase obrera, de clase trabajadora; [*neighbourhood*] obrero; **a self-educated man from a ~ background** un autodidacta de familia de clase obrera *or* trabajadora; **to be ~** ser de clase obrera *or* trabajadora; *see also* **working**

workload ['wɜːkləʊd] N cantidad *f* de trabajo, trabajo *m*; **we've taken on more staff to cope with the extra ~** hemos contratado más personal para dar abasto con el trabajo extra

workman ['wɜːkmən] N (*pl* **workmen**) obrero *m*; **to be a good ~** ser buen trabajador, trabajar bien; ✦*PROV* **a bad** *or* **poor ~ always blames his tools** el mal trabajador siempre echa la culpa a sus herramientas

workmanlike ['wɜːkmənlaɪk] ADJ competente, bien hecho

workmanship ['wɜːkmənʃɪp] N [*of craftsman*] (= *work*) trabajo *m*; (= *skill*) habilidad *f*; [*of artefact*] factura *f*, fabricación *f*; **he prides himself on the quality of his ~** presume de la calidad de su trabajo; **he has been accused of shoddy ~** le acusan de hacer un trabajo de mala calidad; **the chest was of Arab ~** el arcón era de factura *or* fabricación árabe; **the finish and ~ of the woodwork was excellent** el acabado y la factura *or* fabricación de la caja eran excelentes; **of fine ~** esmerado, exquisito; **this is just poor ~** esto no es más que un ejemplo de falta de habilidad profesional

workmate ['wɜːkmeɪt] N compañero/a *m/f* de trabajo

workout ['wɜːkaʊt] N (*Sport*) sesión *f* de ejercicios, sesión *f* de entrenamiento

workpeople ['wɜːkˌpiːpl] N (= *workers*) obreros *mpl*; (= *staff*) personal *m*, mano *f* de obra

workplace ['wɜːkˌpleɪs] N lugar *m* de trabajo

workroom ['wɜːkrʊm] N taller *m*

works [wɜːks] Ⓐ N (*pl inv*) [1] (*Brit*) (= *factory etc*) fábrica *f*
[2] **the ~*** (= *the lot*) todo, la totalidad; ✦*IDIOM* **to give sb the ~** (= *treat harshly*) dar a algn una paliza; (= *treat generously*) tratar a algn a cuerpo de rey
[3] (‡) (= *syringe*) chuta‡ *f*
Ⓑ CPD ▸ **works canteen** N comedor *m* de la fábrica ▸ **works council** N consejo *m* de obreros, comité *m* de empresa ▸ **works manager** N gerente *mf* de fábrica ▸ **works outing** N excursión *f* del personal

work-sharing ['wɜːkˌʃeərɪŋ] N repartimiento *m* del trabajo

worksheet ['wɜːkʃiːt] N [1] (*Ind*) hoja *f* de trabajo
[2] (*Scol*) hoja *f* de ejercicios

workshop ['wɜːkʃɒp] N taller *m*; **a music ~** un taller de música; **a drama ~** un taller de teatro

workshy ['wɜːkʃaɪ] ADJ perezoso, flojo (*esp LAm*)

workspace ['wɜːkspeɪs] N [1] (= *area to work in*) espacio *m* para trabajar
[2] (*Comput*) área *f* de trabajo

workstation ['wɜːkˌsteɪʃən] N (*Comput*) terminal *f* de trabajo

worktable ['wɜːkˌteɪbl] N mesa *f* de trabajo

worktop ['wɜːktɒp] N encimera *f*

work-to-rule ['wɜːktə'ruːl] N huelga *f* de brazos caídos

work-worn ['wɜːkwɔːn] ADJ agotado (por el trabajo)

world [wɜːld] Ⓐ N [1] (= *planet*) mundo *m*; **Australia is on the other side of the ~** Australia está al otro lado del mundo; **the ~ we live in** el mundo en el que vivimos; **the ~'s worst cook** el peor cocinero del mundo; **our company leads the ~ in shoe manufacturing** nuestra empresa es líder mundial en la confección de calzado; **since the ~ began** desde que el mundo es mundo; **in the best of all possible ~s** en el mejor de los mundos; **it's not the end of the ~!*** ¡no es el fin del mundo!; **the tallest man in the ~** el hombre más alto del mundo; **it's what he wants most in (all) the ~** es lo que más quiere en el mundo; **the New World** el Nuevo Mundo; **the Old World** el Viejo Mundo; **she has travelled all over the ~** ha viajado por todo el mundo; **people came from all over the ~** vino gente de todas partes del mundo; **it's the same the ~ over** es igual en todo el mundo, es igual vayas a donde vayas; **in a perfect ~ this would be possible** en un mundo ideal *or* perfecto esto sería posible; **you have to start living in the real ~** tienes que empezar a afrontar la vida *or* la realidad; **to go round the ~** dar la vuelta al mundo; **on a ~ scale** a escala mundial; **to see the ~** ver mundo; **to take the ~ as it is** aceptar la realidad, aceptar las cosas como son; **the worst of all possible ~s** el peor de todos los mundos posibles; ✦*IDIOMS* **to have the ~ at one's feet** tener el mundo a sus pies; **it's out of this ~*** es una maravilla; **to live in a ~ of one's own** vivir en su propio mundo; **you seem to be in a ~ of your own today** hoy parece que estás en otro mundo; **the ~ is your oyster** tienes el mundo a tus pies; **it's a small ~!** ¡el mundo es un pañuelo!; **to feel on top of the ~** sentirse de maravilla; *see also* **dead A1, money A1, third D**
[2] (= *realm*) mundo *m*; **the ~ of dreams** el mundo de los sueños; **the animal ~** el reino animal; **the Arab ~** el mundo árabe; **the business ~** el mundo de los negocios; **the English-speaking ~** el mundo de habla inglesa; **the plant ~** el reino vegetal; **the ~ of sport** el mundo deportivo, el mundo de los deportes; **the sporting ~** el mundo deportivo, el mundo de los deportes; **the Western ~** el mundo occidental
[3] (= *society*) mundo *m*; **her blouse was undone for all the ~ to see** tenía la blusa desabrochada a la vista de todo el mundo; **to be alone in the ~** estar solo en el mundo, no tener a nadie en el mundo; ✦*IDIOMS* **to come down in the ~** venir a menos; **to go up in the ~** prosperar, medrar; **the ~ and his wife** el ciento y la madre*, todo Dios*; *see also* **man A1, outside C1, way A2**
[4] (= *life*) mundo *m*; **in this ~** en esta vida, en este mundo; **to bring a child into the ~** traer a un niño al mundo; **to come into the ~** venir al mundo; **in the next ~** en la otra vida, en el otro mundo; **the other ~** el otro mundo; ✦*IDIOMS* **to have the best of both ~s** tenerlo todo; **he's not long for this ~** no le queda mucha vida, le queda poco de vida
[5] (*in emphatic expressions*) **for all the ~ as if it had never happened** como si nunca hubiera ocurrido; **she looked for all the ~ as if she were dead** cualquiera hubiera dicho que estaba muerta; **they're ~s apart** son totalmente opuestos *or* diferentes, no tiene nada que ver el uno con el otro; **they're ~s apart politically** políticamente los separa un abismo, mantienen posiciones políticas totalmente diferentes; **their views are ~s apart** sus opiniones son totalmente distintas; **there's a ~ of difference between ...** hay un mundo *or* abismo entre ...; **I'd give the ~ to know** daría todo el oro del mundo por saberlo; **it did him the ~ of good** le sentó de maravilla, le hizo la mar de bien*; **nothing in the ~ would make me do it** no lo haría por nada del mundo; **how in the ~ did you manage to do it?*** ¿cómo demonios *or* diablos conseguiste hacerlo?; **what in the ~ were you thinking of!*** ¡qué demonios *or* diablos estabas pensando!*; **where in the ~ has he got to?*** ¿dónde demonios *or* diablos se ha metido?*; **why in the ~ did you do that?*** ¿por qué demonios *or* diablos hiciste eso?*; **she means the ~ to me** ella significa muchísimo para mí; **not for all the ~** por nada del mundo; **he promised me the ~** me prometió la luna; **to think the ~ of sb** tener a algn en gran estima
Ⓑ CPD [*economy, proportions*] mundial; [*events, news*] internacional; [*trade*] internacional, mundial; [*tour*] mundial, alrededor del mundo ▸ **World Bank** N Banco *m* Mundial ▸ **world beater** N campeón(ona) *m/f* mundial ▸ **world champion** N campeón(ona) *m/f* del mundo, campeón(ona) *m/f* mundial ▸ **world championship** N campeonato *m* mundial, campeonato *m* del mundo ▸ **the World Council of Churches** N el Concilio Mundial de las Iglesias ▸ **the World Court** N el Tribunal Internacional de Justicia ▸ **the World Cup** N (*Ftbl*) la Copa Mundial, la Copa del Mundo ▸ **world fair** N feria *f* universal ▸ **the World Health Organization** N la Organización Mundial de la Salud ▸ **world language** N lengua *f* universal ▸ **world leader** N [*of country, company*] líder *m* mundial; (= *politician*) jefe/a *m/f* de estado ▸ **world market** N mercado *m* mundial ▸ **world market price** N precio *m* (del mercado) mundial ▸ **world order** N orden *m* mundial ▸ **world power** N (= *country*) potencia *f* mundial ▸ **world premiere** N estreno *m* mundial ▸ **world record** N récord *m* mundial ▸ **World Series** N (*US*) campeonato *m* mundial de béisbol; → BASEBALL ▸ **world title** N título *m* mundial ▸ **world view** N cosmovisión *f* ▸ **world war** N guerra *f* mundial; **World War One/Two** la Primera/Segunda Guerra Mundial

world-class ['wɜːldklɑːs] ADJ de talla mundial

world-famous ['wɜːld'feɪməs] ADJ de fama mundial, mundialmente conocido

worldliness ['wɜːldlɪnɪs] N mundanería *f*; (= *sophistication*) sofisticación *f*

worldly ['wɜːldlɪ] ADJ (*compar* **worldlier**; *superl* **worldliest**) [1] (= *material*) [*success, pleasures*] mundano, material; **all my ~ goods** todos mis bienes materiales
[2] (= *experienced*) con (mucho) mundo; **he was more ~ than other boys his age** tenía más mundo que otros muchachos de su edad; **~ wisdom** mundo *m*, saber *m* mundano
[3] (= *sophisticated*) sofisticado

worldly-wise ['wɜːldlɪ'waɪz] ADJ de mundo, que conoce mundo

world-shaking [ˈwɜːld,ʃeɪkɪŋ] ADJ pasmoso

world-shattering [ˈwɜːld,ʃætərɪŋ] ADJ = **world-shaking**

world-weariness [ˈwɜːldˈwɪərɪnɪs] N hastío *m*

world-weary [ˈwɜːldˈwɪərɪ] ADJ hastiado, cansado de la vida

worldwide [ˈwɜːldˈwaɪd] Ⓐ ADJ mundial, universal
Ⓑ ADV mundialmente, en todo el mundo; **it's known ~** es mundialmente conocido, es conocido en todo el mundo; **to travel ~** viajar por todo el mundo
Ⓒ CPD ► **the Worldwide Web** N (*Internet*) el World Wide Web, el WWW

WORM [wɜːm] ABBR = **write once read many times**

worm [wɜːm] Ⓐ N [1] (= *earthworm*) gusano *m*, lombriz *f*; ✦*IDIOM* **the ~ will turn** la paciencia tiene un límite; *see also* **glow**
[2] (*in fruit, vegetable*) gusano *m* (*also Comput*)
[3] (*Med*) **to have ~s** tener lombrices
[4] (*pej*) (= *person*) gusano *m*
Ⓑ VT [1] (= *wriggle*) **he ~ed his way out through the narrow window** salió arrastrándose por la estrecha ventana; **to ~ one's way into a group** (*pej*) infiltrarse en un grupo; **to ~ one's way into sb's confidence** (*pej*) ganarse la confianza de algn
[2] (*pej*) (= *extract*) **to ~ a secret out of sb** arrancarle un secreto a algn
[3] (= *treat*) [+ *dog, cat, horse*] desparasitar
Ⓒ CPD ► **worm powder** N polvos *mpl* antiparasitarios ► **worm tablet** N tableta *f* antiparasitaria

worm-eaten [ˈwɜːm,iːtn] ADJ [*wood*] carcomido, apolillado; [*cloth*] apolillado; [*fruit*] con gusanos

wormhole [ˈwɜːmhəʊl] N (*left by earthworm*) agujero *m* de gusano; (*left by woodworm*) agujero *m* de polilla

worming [ˈwɜːmɪŋ] CPD ► **worming powder** N polvos *mpl* antiparasitarios ► **worming tablet** N tableta *f* antiparasitaria

wormwood [ˈwɜːmwʊd] N [1] ajenjo *m*
[2] (*fig*) hiel *f*, amargura *f*

wormy [ˈwɜːmɪ] ADJ [1] (= *worm-eaten*) [*fruit*] con gusanos; [*furniture*] carcomido, apolillado
[2] (= *full of worms*) [*soil*] lleno de gusanos

worn [wɔːn] Ⓐ PP *of* **wear**
Ⓑ ADJ [1] (= *deteriorated*) [*garment, furniture, tyre, component*] gastado; [*steps, stone, surface*] desgastado; **the carpet is a bit ~** la moqueta está un poco gastada
[2] (= *tired*) [*person*] rendido, agotado; [*face*] cansado; **he's looking very ~** tiene aspecto de muy cansado

worn-out [ˈwɔːnˈaʊt] ADJ [1] [*garment, furniture, tyre, component*] gastado
[2] (= *exhausted*) [*person*] rendido, agotado; **we were worn out after the long walk** estábamos rendidos *or* agotados después de andar tanto
[3] (*fig*) [*argument, idea*] gastado

worried [ˈwʌrɪd] ADJ [1] (= *anxious*) [*person*] preocupado; [*look*] de preocupación; **to be ~** estar preocupado; **to be ~ about sth** estar preocupado por algo; **if I'm late he gets ~** si llego tarde se preocupa; **I was getting ~** estaba empezando a preocuparme; **you had me ~** me tenías preocupado; **to be ~ sick** *or* **to death (about sth)*** estar preocupadísimo *or* muy preocupado (por algo); **he was ~ that she would report him to the police** tenía miedo de que ella lo delatase a la policía
[2] (= *bothered*) **I'm not ~** me da igual*, me tiene sin cuidado; **I'm not ~ either way** me da igual una cosa que otra*

worrier [ˈwʌrɪəʳ] N **to be a ~** ser un/una agonías*, ser un preocupón/una preocupona*

worrisome [ˈwʌrɪsəm] ADJ (*esp US*) inquietante, preocupante

▼**worry** [ˈwʌrɪ] Ⓐ N [1] (= *thing to worry about*) preocupación *f*; **he hasn't any worries** no tiene ninguna preocupación; **his worries were completely unfounded** estaba preocupado sin razón; **he may have damaged his spine, which is a ~** puede que se haya dañado la columna, lo que es causa *or* motivo de preocupación; **my son has always been a ~ to me** mi hijo siempre me ha causado preocupaciones; **it's a great ~ to us all** es una gran preocupación para todos nosotros, nos preocupa mucho a todos; **financial worries** problemas *mpl* económicos, problemas *mpl* de dinero; **that's the least of my worries** eso es lo que menos me preocupa, eso es lo de menos
[2] (= *anxiety*) preocupación *f*, inquietud *f*; **she has caused me a great deal** *or* **a lot of ~** me ha tenido muy preocupado *or* inquieto, me ha dado muchas preocupaciones; **to make o.s. sick with ~** preocuparse muchísimo; **to be frantic** *or* **out of one's mind** *or* **sick with ~*** estar preocupadísimo; **source of ~** motivo *m* de preocupación
Ⓑ VT [1] (= *cause concern to*) preocupar; **what's ~ing you?** ¿qué es lo que te preocupa?; **that phone call has been ~ing me all day** esa llamada de teléfono me ha tenido preocupado todo el día; **that doesn't ~ me in the least** eso no me preocupa en absoluto; **to ~ o.s. about sth** preocupare por algo; **don't ~ your head!*** ¡no le des muchas vueltas!, ¡no te calientes la cabeza!*; **to ~ o.s. over sth** preocuparse por algo; **to ~ o.s. sick about sth*** preocuparse muchísimo por algo
[2] (= *bother*) molestar; **the cold doesn't ~ me** el frío no me molesta; **that doesn't ~ me in the least** eso me trae absolutamente sin cuidado; **I don't want to ~ you with my problems but …** no te quiero cargar *or* molestar con mis problemas pero …; **don't ~ yourself with the details** no te preocupes por los detalles
[3] (= *fear*) **they ~ that extremists might gain control** temen que los extremistas se hagan con el control, los preocupa que los extremistas se hagan con el control
[4] (= *play with, harry*) [*dog*] [+ *bone*] mordisquear, juguetear con; [+ *sheep*] acosar
[5] (= *fiddle with*) [+ *object*] juguetear con; [+ *problem*] dar vueltas a; **he kept ~ing the loose tooth with his tongue** no dejaba de toquetearse con la lengua el diente que tenía flojo
Ⓒ VI [1] (= *be anxious*) preocuparse; **he worries a lot** se preocupa mucho; **don't ~!** ¡no te preocupes!; **I'll punish him if I catch him, don't you ~!** ¡si lo pillo lo castigaré, que no te quepa duda!; **to ~ about sth/sb** preocuparse por algo/algn; **there's nothing to ~ about** no hay por qué preocuparse; **that's nothing to ~ about** no hay que preocuparse por eso; **don't ~ about me** no te preocupes por mí; **I've got quite enough to ~ about without that** tengo ya bastantes problemas para preocuparme por eso; **she worries about her health** le preocupa su salud; **not to ~!*** ¡no pasa nada!, ¡no te preocupes!; **to ~ over sth/sb** preocuparse por algo/algn
[2] (= *bother*) molestarse; **don't ~, I'll do it** no te molestes, yo lo haré
[3] **to ~ at sth** [*dog*] mordisquear algo, juguetear con algo; [*person*] (= *fiddle with*) juguetear con algo; **to ~ at a problem** dar vueltas a un problema
Ⓓ CPD ► **worry beads** NPL *sarta de cuentas con la que se juguetea para calmar los nervios* ► **worry lines** NPL *arrugas en la frente debidas a la preocupación*

worrying [ˈwʌrɪɪŋ] Ⓐ ADJ [*situation, news, sign*] preocupante, inquietante
Ⓑ N **all this ~ has aged him** todas estas preocupaciones lo han envejecido

▼**worse** [wɜːs] Ⓐ ADJ COMPAR *of* **bad** peor; **his essay is ~ than yours** su trabajo es peor que el tuyo; **it could be ~** podría ser peor; **it's even ~ than we'd predicted** es todavía peor de lo que habíamos pronosticado; **to get ~** [*weather, situation, crime*] empeorar; [*patient*] empeorar, ponerse peor; **my cold is getting ~** mi resfriado va a peor; **my eyesight is getting ~** mi vista va a peor, cada vez veo peor, cada vez tengo peor vista; **his behaviour is getting ~** su comportamiento es cada vez peor; **to get ~ and ~** ponerse cada vez peor, ir de mal en peor; **things will get ~ before they get better** las cosas empeorarán antes de que se les vea la punta; **it gets ~** (*preparing sb for bad news*) lo peor no es eso; **to make sth ~** empeorar algo; **it'll only make matters** *or* **things ~** sólo empeorará las cosas; **and, to make matters ~, …** y, para colmo de desgracia, …; **he appeared none the ~ for his ordeal** no parecía desmejorado a pesar de su terrible experiencia; **there's nothing ~ than …** no hay nada peor que …; **it's like last time, only ~** es como la última vez, sólo que peor; **to be the ~ for drink** ir cargado de copas*; **what was ~** para colmo (de males); *see also* **bad**, **bark**, **better**, **wear**
Ⓑ ADV COMPAR *of* **badly** peor; **I sang ~ than he did** *or* **than him** yo cantaba peor que él; **you could** *or* **might do ~ than give her a call** sería aconsejable que la llamarás
Ⓒ N **it's a change for the ~** es un cambio a peor; **there was ~ to come** ◊ **~ was to come** lo peor todavía estaba por verse, aún quedaba lo peor; *see also* **turn**

worsen [ˈwɜːsn] Ⓐ VT empeorar
Ⓑ VI empeorar

worsening [ˈwɜːsnɪŋ] Ⓐ ADJ [*situation*] que empeora, que va de mal en peor
Ⓑ N empeoramiento *m*

worship [ˈwɜːʃɪp] Ⓐ N [1] (= *adoration*) adoración *f*; (= *reverence*) veneración *f*; (= *organized worship*) culto *m*; **place of ~** lugar *m* de culto; **hours of ~** horario *m* de cultos
[2] (*Brit*) (*in titles*) **Your Worship** (*to judge*) su Señoría; (*to mayor*) señor(a) alcalde(sa); **His Worship the Mayor** el señor alcalde
Ⓑ VT [+ *God, money, success*] adorar, rendir culto a; [+ *film star, singer*] adorar, idolatrar; **she ~s her children** (*fig*) adora a sus hijos; ✦*IDIOM* **he ~ped the ground she walked on** besaba la tierra que ella pisaba, sentía verdadera adoración por ella
Ⓒ VI (*Rel*) hacer sus devociones

worshiper [ˈwɜːʃɪpəʳ] N (*US*) = **worshipper**

worshipful [ˈwɜːʃɪpfʊl] ADJ (*esp Brit*) (*in titles*) excelentísimo

worshipper, **worshiper** (*US*) [ˈwɜːʃɪpəʳ] N devoto/a *m/f*; **worshippers** (*collectively*) fieles *mpl*

worst [wɜːst] Ⓐ ADJ SUPERL *of* **bad** [1] (*gen*) peor; **it was the ~ film I've ever seen** fue la peor película de mi vida, fue la película más mala que he visto en mi vida; **~ of all** lo que es peor; **it was the ~ winter for 20 years** fue el peor invierno en 20 años; **the ~ storm in**

years la peor tormenta en años; **that's the ~ part (of it)** eso es lo peor; **at the ~ possible time** en el peor momento posible; **it was the ~ thing he ever did** fue lo peor que hizo nunca; *see also* **fear**

[2] (= *most badly affected*) [*victim*] más afectado; **the ~ sufferers are children** los más afectados son los niños

Ⓑ ADV SUPERL *of* **badly** [1] (*gen*) peor; **the ~-dressed man in England** el hombre peor vestido de Inglaterra; **they all sing badly but he sings ~ (of all)** todos cantan mal, pero él peor que nadie; **to come off ~: they had a punch-up and he came off ~** tuvieron una pelea y él fue el que salió peor parado

[2] [*affected, hit*] más; **he visited some of the ~ affected areas** visitó algunas de las zonas más afectadas

Ⓒ N [1] **the ~** lo peor; **the ~ that can happen is that ...** lo peor que puede pasar es que ...; **we threw away the ~ of them** los peores los tiramos a la basura; **to fear the ~** temerse lo peor; **the ~ of it is that ...** lo peor de todo es que ...; **that's not the ~ of it** eso no es lo peor; **to get the ~ of it*** llevarse la peor parte; ✦*IDIOM* **if the ~ comes to the ~** en el peor de los casos

[2] **at ~** en el peor de los casos; **at ~, they can only say no** en el peor de los casos, nos dirán que no; **the situation is at its ~ in urban centres** en los núcleos urbanos es donde la situación es más grave; **things** *or* **matters were at their ~** las cosas estaban peor que nunca; **he's at his ~ in the evenings** por las tardes es cuando está más insoportable

Ⓓ VT (†) [+ *person*] (*in fight*) derrotar; (*in conflict*) vencer

worsted ['wʊstɪd] N (= *cloth*) estambre *m*

worth [wɜːθ] Ⓐ ADJ [1] (= *equal in value to*) **to be ~ sth** valer algo; **it's ~ five pounds** vale cinco libras; **it's ~ a lot of money** vale mucho dinero; **what** *or* **how much is it ~?** ¿cuánto vale?; **it's not ~ much** no vale mucho; **it's ~ a great deal to me** (*sentimentally*) para mí tiene gran valor sentimental; **he was ~ a million when he died** murió millonario, murió dejando una fortuna de un millón; **what's the old man ~?** ¿cuánto dinero tiene el viejo?; **"don't tell anybody" — "what's it ~ to you?"*** —no se lo digas a nadie —¿cuánto me das si no digo nada?; **to run for all one is ~** correr como si le llevara a uno el diablo; **to sing for all one is ~** cantar con toda el alma; **it must be ~ a fortune** debe valer una fortuna; **it's more than my job's ~ to tell you** me costaría mi empleo decirte eso; **it's not ~ the paper it's written on** vale menos que el papel en que está escrito; **she's ~ ten of him** ella vale diez veces más que él; **I tell you this for what it's ~** te digo esto por si te interesa

[2] (= *deserving of*) **it's ~ reading** vale *or* merece la pena leerlo; **it's ~ the effort** vale *or* merece la pena molestarse en hacerlo; **it's ~ having** vale *or* merece la pena tenerlo; **it's (not) ~ it** (no) vale *or* merece la pena; **life isn't ~ living** la vida no tiene sentido para mí; **the cathedral is ~ a look** la catedral merece la pena, merece la pena ver la catedral; **it's ~ mentioning that ...** merece la pena mencionar que ..., es digno de mención el hecho de que ...; **it's ~ supporting** es digno de apoyo; **it's ~ thinking about** vale *or* merece la pena pensarlo; **it's not ~ the trouble** no vale *or* merece la pena; **the meal was ~ the wait** la comida estaba tan rica que mereció la pena esperar, la comida mereció *or* compensó la espera; **it's well ~ doing** bien vale *or* merece la pena hacerlo; *see also* **job, while**

Ⓑ N [*of thing*] valor *m*; [*of person*] valía *f*; **ten pounds' ~ of books** libros por valor de diez libras, diez libras de libros; **he had no chance to show his true ~** no tuvo oportunidad de mostrar su valía; *see also* **money A1**

worthily ['wɜːðɪlɪ] ADV dignamente; **he ~ represented his country** representó a su país dignamente; **to respond ~ to an occasion** estar a la altura de las circunstancias

worthiness ['wɜːðɪnɪs] N [*of person*] valía *f*; [*of cause*] mérito *m*

worthless ['wɜːθlɪs] ADJ (= *of no monetary value*) sin ningún valor; (= *useless*) inútil; (= *despicable*) despreciable; **the painting was quite ~** la pintura apenas tenía ningún valor; **a ~ individual** un tipo despreciable

worthlessness ['wɜːθlɪsnɪs] N [*of object*] (*in money terms*) falta *f* de valor; [*of effort, advice*] lo inútil; [*of person*] lo despreciable; **feelings of ~** sensación *f* de inutilidad

▼**worthwhile** ['wɜːθ'waɪl] ADJ [*activity, enterprise, job*] que vale la pena; [*cause*] loable; **a ~ film** una película seria *or* que merece atención; **it makes it all ~** le da sentido a todo; **to be ~** (= *worthy*) valer *or* merecer la pena; **it would be ~ seeing** *or* **to see him** convendría verlo; **I had nothing ~ to say** no tenía nada interesante que decir; *see also* **while A2**

worthy ['wɜːðɪ] Ⓐ ADJ (*compar* **worthier**; *superl* **worthiest**) [1] (= *deserving*) [*winner, champion*] merecido; [*successor*] digno; **she found a ~ opponent in Sabatini** encontró en Sabatini a una oponente de su categoría; **~ cause** buena causa *f*, causa *f* noble; **to be ~ of sth/sb** ser digno de algo/algn; **~ of attention** digno de atención; **a greatest hits album ~ of the name** un disco de grandes éxitos digno de su nombre; **she wanted so much to be ~ of her father** ansiaba ser digna hija de su padre; **that comment was not ~ of you** esa observación fue indigna de usted; **that remark is not ~ of a reply** ese comentario no (se) merece una respuesta

[2] (= *good*) [*person*] respetable; [*motive, aim*] encomiable

[3] (*iro*) [*person*] honorable, venerable

Ⓑ N (*hum*) ilustre personaje *m*

wot‡ [wɒt] PRON (*Brit*) = **what**

wotcha‡ ['wɒtʃə], **wotcher‡** ['wɒtʃəʳ] EXCL (*Brit*) ¡hola!

▼**would** [wʊd] AUX VB, MODAL AUX VB [1] (*conditional tense*) **if you asked him he ~ do it** si se lo pidieras lo haría; **if you had asked him he ~ have done it** si se lo hubieras pedido lo habría hecho; **you ~ never know she was not a native Spanish speaker** nadie diría que el español no es su lengua materna; **~ you go there by yourself?** ¿irías allí sola?; **I ~ have a word with him (if I were you)** sería aconsejable discutirlo con él; **I ~n't worry too much if I were you** yo en tu lugar no me preocuparía demasiado

[2] (*in indirect speech*) **I said I ~ do it** te dije que lo haría *or* hacía; **I thought you ~ want to know** pensé que querrías saber

[3] (*emphatic*) **you ~ be the one to forget!** ¡quién más si no tú se iba a olvidar!, ¡tú tenías que ser el que se olvidase!; **it ~ be you!** ¡tú tenías que ser!; **he ~ say that, ~n't he?** es lógico que dijera eso

[4] (*conjecture*) **what ~ this be?** ¿qué será esto?; **it ~ have been about eight o'clock** serían las ocho; **it ~ seem so** así parece ser

[5] (*indicating willingness*) [5·1] (*in invitations*) querer; **~ you like some tea?** ◊ **~ you care for some tea?** ¿quiere tomar un té?; **~ you come this way?** pase por favor *or* (*esp LAm*) si hace favor

[5·2] (*requests, wishes*) **~ you close the door please?** ¿puedes cerrar la puerta, por favor?; **please ~ you wake me up at seven o'clock?** ¿podría despertarme a las siete, por favor?; **~ you mind?** si no le importa, si no tiene inconveniente; **what ~ you have me do?** ¿qué quieres que haga?

[5·3] (*insistence*) **I told her not to but she ~ do it** le dije que no, pero insistió en hacerlo

[5·4] (*refusal*) **he ~n't do it** no quería hacerlo, se negó a hacerlo; **he ~n't say if it was true** no quiso decir si era verdad; **the car ~n't start** el coche se negó *or* negaba a arrancar, el coche no quería arrancar

[6] (*habit*) **he ~ paint it each year** solía pintarlo cada año, lo pintaba cada año

[7] (*in set expressions*) **~ that it were not so!** (†, *poet*) ¡ojalá (y) no fuera así!; **~ to God!** ◊ **~ to heaven!** (*liter*) ¡ojalá!; **try as he ~** por mucho que se esforzara, por más que intentase

would-be ['wʊdbiː] ADJ **a ~ poet/politician** un aspirante a poeta/político

wouldn't ['wʊdnt] = **would not**

would've ['wʊdəv] = **would have**

wound¹ [wuːnd] Ⓐ N herida *f*; **a bullet/knife ~** una herida de bala/cuchillo; **a chest/head ~** una herida en el pecho/la cabeza; ✦*IDIOMS* **to lick one's ~s** lamer sus heridas; **to open up old ~s** abrir viejas heridas; *see also* **salt A1**

Ⓑ VT herir; **he was ~ed in the leg** fue herido en la pierna; **to ~ sb's feelings** (*fig*) herir los sentimientos de algn; **she was deeply ~ed by this remark** (*fig*) su comentario la hirió profundamente

wound² [waʊnd] PT, PP *of* **wind²**

wounded ['wuːndɪd] Ⓐ ADJ herido; **there were six dead and fifteen ~** hubo seis muertos y quince heridos

Ⓑ NPL **the ~** los heridos

wounding ['wuːndɪŋ] ADJ [*remark, tone*] hiriente

wove [wəʊv] PT *of* **weave**

woven ['wəʊvən] PP *of* **weave**

wow* [waʊ] Ⓐ EXCL ¡vaya!, ¡anda!, ¡mira nomás! (*LAm*)

Ⓑ VT chiflar*, cautivar

Ⓒ N (*Acoustics*) lloro *m*, bajón *m* del volumen

WP Ⓐ N ABBR [1] = **word processing**

[2] = **word processor**

Ⓑ ABBR (= **weather permitting**) si lo permite el tiempo

wpb* N ABBR = **wastepaper basket**

WPC N ABBR = **Woman Police Constable**

WPI N ABBR = **wholesale price index**

wpm ABBR (= **words per minute**) p.p.m.

WR N ABBR (*Sport*) = **World Record**

WRAC [ræk] N ABBR (*Brit*) = **Women's Royal Army Corps**

wrack¹ [ræk] VT = **rack¹ B**

wrack² [ræk] N = **rack²**

wrack³ [ræk] N (*Bot*) fuco *m*, alga *f*

WRAF [wæf] N ABBR (*Brit*) = **Women's Royal Air Force**

wraith [reɪθ] N fantasma *m*

wrangle ['ræŋgl] Ⓐ N riña *f*, disputa *f*, pleito *m* (*esp LAm*); **legal ~** disputa *f* legal

Ⓑ VI **to ~ (about** *or* **over sth)** reñir *or* pelear (por *or* sobre algo)

wrangling ['ræŋglɪŋ] N riña *f*, discusión *f*

wrap [ræp] Ⓐ N [1] (= *garment*) chal *m*, rebozo *m* (*LAm*)

2 (*around parcel*) envoltorio *m*; **under ~s** (*fig*) en secreto, tapado (*esp LAm*); **to keep sth under ~s** (*fig*) guardar algo en secreto; **to take the ~s off sth** (*fig*) desvelar *or* revelar algo, sacar algo a la luz pública
Ⓑ VT 1 (*also* ~ **up**) envolver; **shall I ~ it for you?** ¿se lo envuelvo?; **she ~ped the child in a blanket** envolvió al niño en una manta; **the scheme is ~ped in secrecy** (*fig*) el proyecto está envuelto en el misterio
2 (= *coil*) **~ the rug round your legs** enróllate la manta alrededor de las piernas
►**wrap up** Ⓐ VT + ADV 1 = **wrap B1**
2 (*) (= *conclude*) concluir, poner punto final a; **that just about ~s it up** eso prácticamente lo concluye *or* le pone punto final; **to ~ up a deal** cerrar un trato
3 **to be ~ped up in sb/sth** estar embelesado con algn/absorto en algo; **they're ~ped up in each other** están embelesados el uno con el otro, están absortos el uno en el otro
Ⓑ VI + ADV 1 (= *dress warmly*) abrigarse; **~ up warm!** ¡abrígate bien!
2 (*) (= *be quiet*) callarse; **~ up!*** ¡cállate!
wraparound ['ræpəˌraʊnd] Ⓐ N reciclado *m*, bucle *m*
Ⓑ CPD ► **wraparound shades** NPL = **wraparound sunglasses** ► **wraparound skirt** N falda *f* cruzada ► **wraparound sunglasses** NPL gafas *fpl* de sol envolventes
wrapper ['ræpəʳ] N [*of goods*] envoltura *f*, envase *m*; [*of sweet*] envoltorio *m*; [*of book*] sobrecubierta *f*; (*postal: round newspaper*) faja *f*
wrapping ['ræpɪŋ] Ⓐ N envoltura *f*, envase *m*
Ⓑ CPD ► **wrapping paper** N (*gen*) papel *m* de envolver; (= *gift-wrap*) papel *m* de regalo
wrath [rɒθ] N (*poet*) [*of person*] cólera *f*; [*of storm*] ira *f*, furia *f*; *see also* **incur**
wrathful ['rɒθfʊl] ADJ (*liter*) colérico, iracundo
wrathfully ['rɒθfəlɪ] ADV (*liter*) coléricamente
wreak [riːk] VT [+ *destruction, vengeance*] hacer, causar; **to ~ havoc** causar estragos
wreath [riːθ] N (*pl* **wreaths** [riːðz]) [*of flowers*] guirnalda *f*; (*for funeral*) corona *f*; [*of smoke, mist*] espiral *m*; **laurel ~** corona *f* de laurel
wreathe [riːð] (*esp liter*) Ⓐ VT 1 (= *encircle*) ceñir, rodear (**with** de); **a face ~d in smiles** una cara muy risueña *or* sonriente; **trees ~d in mist** árboles *mpl* envueltos en niebla
2 (= *garland*) [+ *person*] engalanar, enguirnaldar (**with** con); **to ~ flowers into one's hair** ponerse flores en el pelo
Ⓑ VI [*smoke*] **to ~ upwards** elevarse en espirales
wreck [rek] Ⓐ N 1 (= *destruction*) [*of ship*] naufragio *m*; (*fig*) [*of hopes, plans*] fracaso *m*, frustración *f*
2 (= *wrecked ship*) restos *mpl* de un naufragio, buque *m* hundido
3 (*) (= *old car*) tartana* *f*; (= *old boat, plane*) cacharro* *m*; **that car is a ~!** ¡ese coche es una tartana!*; **the car was a complete ~** el coche estaba hecho polvo*; **I'm a ~** ◊ **I feel a ~** estoy hecho polvo*; **he's an old ~** es un carcamal*; **she's a nervous ~** tiene los nervios destrozados; **she looks a ~** está hecha una pena*
Ⓑ VT 1 (*Naut*) [+ *ship*] hundir, hacer naufragar; **to be ~ed** naufragar; **the ship was ~ed on those rocks** el buque naufragó en aquellas rocas
2 (= *break*) estropear, destrozar; (*into pieces*) destruir, hacer pedazos; **the explosion ~ed the whole house** la explosión destruyó toda la casa; **he ~ed his Dad's car** dejó el coche de su padre destrozado
3 (= *ruin*) [+ *health, happiness*] arruinar, hundir; [+ *marriage*] destrozar; **it ~ed my life** me arruinó la vida; **the bad weather ~ed our plans** el mal tiempo echó por tierra nuestros planes
wreckage ['rekɪdʒ] N 1 (= *remains*) [*of ship*] restos *mpl* de un naufragio, pecios *mpl* de un naufragio (*frm*); [*of car, aeroplane, train*] restos *mpl*; [*of house, building*] escombros *mpl*, ruinas *fpl*
2 (= *act*) [*of ship*] naufragio *m*; (*fig*) naufragio *m*, ruina *f*, destrucción *f*
wrecked [rekt] ADJ 1 (= *destroyed*) destruido; (= *broken down*) estropeado, averiado; [*ship*] naufragado, hundido
2 (‡) [*person*] (= *exhausted*) hecho polvo; (= *drunk*) cocido‡; (*from drugs*) (= *high*) colocado‡; **he got really ~ at the party** se cocío bien en la fiesta‡, se cogió una buena borrachera en la fiesta
wrecker ['rekəʳ] N 1 (= *destroyer*) (*gen*) destructor(a) *m/f*; (*Hist*) [*of ships*] saboteador(a) *m/f*, *persona que que se dedicaba a provocar naufragios*
2 (*US*) (= *breaker, salvager*) demoledor *m*
3 (*US*) (= *breakdown van*) camión-grúa *m*
wrecking ball ['rekɪŋˌbɔːl] N martillo *m* de demolición
Wren* [ren] N (*Brit Navy*) *miembro de la sección femenina de la marina británica*
wren [ren] N (*Orn*) reyezuelo *m*, troglodito *m*
wrench [rentʃ] Ⓐ N 1 (= *tug*) tirón *m*, jalón *m* (*LAm*); **to give sth a ~** tirar *or* (*LAm*) jalar algo (con violencia *or* fuerza)
2 (*Med*) torcedura *f*
3 (= *tool*) llave *f* inglesa, llave *f* de tuerca
4 (*fig*) **it was a ~ to see her go** dolió mucho verla partir
Ⓑ VT 1 **to ~ sth off/(away) from/out of** arrancar algo de; **he ~ed himself free** haciendo un gran esfuerzo se soltó; **to ~ a door open** abrir una puerta de un tirón *or* (*LAm*) jalón
2 (*Med*) torcerse
Ⓒ VI **he ~ed free** haciendo un gran esfuerzo se soltó
wrest [rest] VT **to ~ sth from sb** arrebatar *or* arrancar algo a algn; **to ~ gold from the rocks** extraer a duras penas oro de las rocas; **to ~ a living from the soil** vivir penosamente cultivando la tierra; **to ~ o.s. free** (lograr) liberarse tras grandes esfuerzos
wrestle ['resl] Ⓐ N **to have a ~ with sb** luchar con algn
Ⓑ VI luchar (a brazo partido); (*Sport, fig*) luchar (**with** con); **we are wrestling with the problem** estamos luchando con el problema; **the pilot ~d with the controls** el piloto luchaba con los mandos
Ⓒ VT (*Sport*) luchar con, luchar contra; **to ~ sb to the ground** tumbar a algn, derribar a algn
wrestler ['resləʳ] N (*Sport*) luchador(a) *m/f*
wrestling ['reslɪŋ] Ⓐ N (*Sport*) lucha *f* libre
Ⓑ CPD ► **wrestling match** N partido *m* de lucha libre
wretch [retʃ] N desgraciado/a *m/f*, miserable *mf*; **little ~** (*often hum*) pícaro/a *m/f*, granuja *mf*; **some poor ~** algún desgraciado, algún pobre diablo
wretched ['retʃɪd] ADJ 1 (= *unhappy*) desdichado, desgraciado
2 (= *abject, poor*) [*condition*] miserable, lamentable; [*slum*] lamentable; [*life, existence*] miserable, desgraciado, infeliz; **to live in ~ poverty** vivir en la miseria más absoluta
3 (*) (= *very bad*) horrible, espantoso; **what ~ luck!** ¡maldita la suerte!; **where's that ~ dog!** ¡dónde está ese maldito *or* condenado perro!; **to feel ~** (= *miserable*) sentirse infeliz; (= *ill*) sentirse muy mal
wretchedly ['retʃɪdlɪ] ADV 1 (*as intensifier*) terriblemente; **she felt ~ alone** se sentía terriblemente sola; **his marriage was ~ unhappy** era muy infeliz en su matrimonio; **to be ~ unlucky** tener malísima suerte; **to be ~ poor** vivir en la miseria más absoluta
2 (= *miserably*) **"I made it all up," she said ~** —me lo inventé todo —dijo desconsolada; **they treated her ~** la trataron de modo infame
3 (†*) (= *very badly*) [*play, sing etc*] pésimamente, fatal*
wretchedness ['retʃɪdnɪs] N 1 (= *unhappiness*) desdicha *f*
2 (= *abjectness*) [*of conditions*] miseria *f*; [*of life, existence*] desgracia *f*, infelicidad *f*; (= *poverty*) miseria *f*
wrick [rɪk] Ⓐ N torcedura *f*
Ⓑ VT (*Brit*) torcer; **to ~ one's neck** torcerse el cuello
wriggle ['rɪgl] Ⓐ VT mover; **to ~ one's toes/fingers** mover los dedos de los pies/de las manos; **to ~ one's way through sth** avanzar con dificultad a través de algo
Ⓑ VI (*also* ~ **about** *or* **around**) [*person, animal*] (*restlessly*) moverse, revolverse; (*in pain*) retorcerse; [*worm, snake, eel*] serpentear; [*fish*] colear; **to ~ along** moverse serpenteando; **to ~ away** escaparse serpenteando; **to ~ down** bajarse serpenteando; **to ~ free** escaparse, escurrirse; **to ~ through a hole** deslizarse por un agujero; **to ~ out of a difficulty** escabullirse, escaparse de un apuro
wriggly ['rɪglɪ] ADJ (*compar* **wrigglier**; *superl* **wriggliest**) sinuoso
wring [rɪŋ] (*pt, pp* **wrung**) Ⓐ VT 1 (*also* ~ **out**) [+ *clothes, washing*] escurrir
2 (= *twist*) torcer, retorcer; **I'll ~ your neck for that!*** ¡te voy a retorcer el pescuezo!*; **she wrung my hand** me dio un apretón de manos; ✦**IDIOM to ~ one's hands** (*in distress*) retorcerse las manos
3 (*fig*) **eventually we wrung the truth out of them** al final les sacamos la verdad; **to ~ money out of sb** sacar dinero a algn
Ⓑ N **to give the clothes a ~** escurrir la ropa
wringer ['rɪŋəʳ] N escurridor *m*
wringing ['rɪŋɪŋ] ADJ (*also* ~ **wet**) empapado
wrinkle[1] ['rɪŋkl] Ⓐ N arruga *f*
Ⓑ VT (*also* ~ **up**) [+ *fabric, clothes*] arrugar; [+ *brow, forehead*] fruncir
Ⓒ VI (*also* ~ **up**) arrugarse
wrinkle[2]‡ ['rɪŋkl] N (= *idea*) idea *f*, noción *f*; (= *tip*) indicación *f*; (= *dodge*) truco *m*
wrinkled ['rɪŋkld] ADJ arrugado
wrinkly ['rɪŋklɪ] Ⓐ ADJ (*compar* **wrinklier**; *superl* **wrinkliest**) = **wrinkled**
Ⓑ N (*Brit* pej*) viejo/a *m/f*
wrist [rɪst] Ⓐ N muñeca *f*
Ⓑ CPD ► **wrist joint** N articulación *f* de la muñeca
wristband ['rɪstbænd] N [*of shirt*] puño *m*; [*of watch*] pulsera *f*; (*Sport*) muñequera *f*
wristlet ['rɪstlɪt] Ⓐ N pulsera *f*, muñequera *f*, brazalete *m*
Ⓑ CPD ► **wristlet watch** N reloj *m* de pulsera
wristwatch ['rɪstwɒtʃ] N reloj *m* de pulsera
writ[1] [rɪt] N (*Jur*) mandato *m* judicial; **to serve a ~ on sb** notificar un mandato judicial a algn; **to issue a ~ against sb** demandar a algn
writ[2] [rɪt] Ⓐ PT, PP (††) *of* **write**
Ⓑ ADJ (*liter*) **it's just the old policy ~ large** es la misma política en forma exagerada; **guilt**

was ~ large on his face se hacía patente la culpa en su cara

write [raɪt] (*pt* **wrote**; *pp* **written**) Ⓐ VT [1] (*gen*) [+ *letter, book, essay, article*] escribir; [+ *music, song*] escribir, componer; **he's just written another novel** acaba de escribir otra novela; **~ your name here** escribe *or* pon tu nombre aquí; **how do you ~ his name?** ¿cómo se escribe su nombre?; **he's got an essay to ~** tiene que escribir una redacción; **she ~s that she is very happy in her new life** dice en la carta que está muy contenta con su nueva vida; **it is written that …** está escrito que …; **to ~ sb a cheque** hacer un cheque a algn, extender un cheque a algn (*more frm*); **to ~ a letter to sb** ◊ **~ sb a letter** escribir (una carta) a algn; **to ~ a note to/for sb** escribir una nota a algn; **to ~ sb a prescription** ◊ **~ a prescription for sb** hacer una receta a algn; **✦IDIOM to have sth written all over one: he had "policeman" written all over him*** se le notaba a la legua que era policía; **his guilt was written all over him*** se le veía *or* notaba en la cara que era culpable; **you're lying, it's written all over your face!*** estás mintiendo, se te nota a la legua *or* en la cara
[2] (= *write a letter to*) (*US*) **to ~ sb** escribir a algn
[3] (*Comput*) [+ *program, software*] escribir; **to ~ sth to disk** pasar algo a un disco
Ⓑ VI [1] (*in longhand*) escribir; **~ on both sides of the paper** escribe por los dos lados del papel; **this pen ~s well** esta pluma escribe muy bien
[2] (= *correspond*) escribir; **she wrote to say that she'd be late** escribió para avisar que llegaría tarde; **I am writing in reply to your advertisement** les escribo en respuesta a su anuncio; **I'll ~ for a catalogue** escribiré pidiendo un catálogo; **to ~ to sb** escribir a algn; **✦IDIOM it's nothing to ~ home about*** no es nada del otro mundo*
[3] (*as author, journalist*) escribir; **he ~s for a living** se gana la vida escribiendo; **he ~s about social policy** escribe sobre política social; **he ~s for the "Times"** escribe *or* colabora en el "Times"; **he ~s on foreign policy for the "Guardian"** escribe sobre política internacional para el "Guardian"

►**write away** VI + ADV **to ~ away for sth** escribir pidiendo algo

►**write back** VI + ADV **to ~ back to sb** contestar a algn; **he wrote in April but I still haven't written back** me escribió en abril pero aún no le he contestado

►**write down** VT + ADV [1] (= *note down*) [+ *address, number, details*] apuntar, anotar
[2] (= *decrease value of*) [+ *asset*] amortizar (por depreciación); [+ *value*] depreciar; [+ *goods*] rebajar el valor en libros

►**write in** Ⓐ VI + ADV escribir, mandar una carta; **a lot of people have written in to complain** mucha gente ha escrito *or* ha mandado cartas quejándose; **to ~ in for sth** escribir pidiendo algo
Ⓑ VT + ADV (= *include*) [+ *word, item, part, scene*] añadir, agregar; [+ *clause in contract*] incluir; (*US Pol*) [+ *candidate's name*] añadir a la lista oficial

►**write into** VT + PREP [1] (*Jur*) incluir en; **to ~ sth into an agreement/contract** (*at the outset*) incluir algo en un acuerdo/contrato; (*later*) añadir algo en un acuerdo/contrato
[2] [+ *character, scene, item*] incluir en

►**write off** Ⓐ VI + ADV **to ~ off for** [+ *information, application form, details, goods*] escribir pidiendo
Ⓑ VT + ADV [1] (*Fin*) [+ *debt*] cancelar (por considerarla incobrable); **to ~ £1000 off for depreciation** amortizar 1000 libras por depreciación; **to ~ sth off against tax** desgravar algo de los impuestos
[2] [+ *vehicle*] [*insurer*] declarar siniestro total; [*driver*] destrozar; **the car had to be written off** el coche fue declarado siniestro total; **he has just written off his new car** acaba de tener un accidente con el coche nuevo y ha quedado destrozado
[3] (= *reject*) [+ *idea, scheme*] desechar; **to ~ sth off as a total loss** considerar algo como totalmente perdido; **I've written off the whole thing as a dead loss** ese asunto lo considero un fracaso que es mejor olvidar; **it would be unwise to ~ off the former minister just yet** sería prematuro considerar acabado al anterior ministro; **many people wrote them off as cranks** mucha gente los rechazó considerándolos unos chalados
[4] (= *write quickly*) [+ *letter, postcard*] escribir (rápidamente)

►**write out** VT + ADV [1] (= *put on paper*) [+ *word, name, speech, list*] escribir
[2] (= *make out*) [+ *cheque*] hacer, extender (*more frm*); [+ *receipt*] hacer; [+ *prescription*] escribir
[3] (= *copy*) [+ *notes, essay*] pasar en limpio, pasar a limpio (*Sp*); [+ *recipe*] copiar
[4] (*of TV or radio series*) [+ *character, part*] suprimir; **he was written out of the series** suprimieron el papel que tenía en la serie, lo eliminaron de la serie

►**write up** VT + ADV [1] (= *make*) [+ *report*] redactar; [+ *notes*] pasar en limpio, pasar a limpio (*Sp*); [+ *diary*] poner al día
[2] (= *record*) [+ *experiment, one's findings, visit*] describir (por escrito)
[3] (= *report on*) [+ *event*] escribir una crónica sobre, hacer un reportaje sobre; **she wrote it up for the local paper** escribió una crónica *or* hizo un reportaje sobre ello en el periódico local
[4] (= *review*) escribir una reseña de, escribir una crítica de

write-off ['raɪtɒf] N [1] (= *vehicle*) siniestro *m* total; **his car was a complete ~** el coche fue declarado siniestro total, el coche quedó siniestro total
[2] (*Comm*) anulación *f* en libros, cancelación *f* en libros
[3] (*Fin*) cancelación *f* (*de una deuda considerada incobrable*); **he proposed a complete ~ of debt** propuso cancelar totalmente la deuda
[4] (= *disaster*) desastre *m*, fracaso *m*; **the whole afternoon was a ~** la tarde entera fue un desastre *or* fracaso

write-protect ['raɪtprə'tekt] VT proteger contra escritura

writer ['raɪtəʳ] N [*of letter, report*] escritor(a) *m/f*; (*as profession*) escritor(a) *m/f*, autor(a) *m/f*; **a ~ of detective stories** un escritor *or* autor de novelas policíacas; **to be a good ~** (*handwriting*) tener buena letra; (*content*) escribir bien, ser buen escritor/a; **to be a poor ~** (*handwriting*) tener mala letra; **~'s cramp** calambre *m* de los escribientes

write-up ['raɪtʌp] N [1] (= *report*) crónica *f*, reportaje *m*
[2] (= *review*) crítica *f*, reseña *f*

writhe [raɪð] VI retorcerse; **to ~ with** *or* **in pain** retorcerse de dolor; **to ~ with embarrassment** morirse de vergüenza *or* (*LAm*) pena

►**writhe about, writhe around** VI + ADV retorcerse

writing ['raɪtɪŋ] Ⓐ N [1] (= *handwriting*) letra *f*; **I can't read your ~** no entiendo tu letra
[2] (= *system*) escritura *f*; **before the invention of ~** antes de la invención de la escritura
[3] (= *letters, words*) **there was some ~ on the page** había algo escrito en la página; **I could see the ~ but couldn't read it** podía ver que había algo escrito pero no podía leerlo; **in ~** por escrito; **I'd like to have that in ~** me gustaría tenerlo por escrito; **to put sth in ~** poner algo por escrito; **✦IDIOM to see the ~ on the wall** vérsela venir*; **he had seen the ~ on the wall** vio lo que se le venía encima*; **the ~ is on the wall for the president/the company** el presidente/la compañia tiene los días contados
[4] (= *written work*) **the essay contains some imaginative ~** el ensayo tiene secciones redactadas con imaginación; **Aubrey's biographical ~s** las obras biográficas de Aubrey; **it's a brilliant piece of ~** está maravillosamente escrito
[5] (= *activity*) escritura *f*; **~ is his hobby** su hobby es la escritura, su hobby es escribir; **he earns quite a lot from ~** gana bastante escribiendo; **a course in novel ~** un curso sobre redacción de novelas
Ⓑ CPD ► **writing case** N estuche *m* para material de correspondencia ► **writing desk** N escritorio *m* ► **writing materials** NPL artículos *mpl* de escritorio ► **writing pad** N bloc *m* ► **writing paper** N papel *m* de escribir ► **writing table** N escritorio *m*

written ['rɪtn] Ⓐ PP *of* **write**
Ⓑ ADJ [*test, agreement, exam*] escrito; [*permission, guarantee, offer*] por escrito; **her ~ English is excellent** su inglés escrito es excelente; **Somali has been a ~ language for over 25 years** la lengua somalí ha tenido escritura desde hace más de 25 años; **the power of the ~ word** el poder de la palabra escrita; **~ statement** declaración *f* escrita; **~ evidence/proof** (*Admin*) pruebas *fpl* documentales

WRNS [renz] N ABBR (*Brit*) = **Women's Royal Naval Service**

wrong [rɒŋ] Ⓐ ADJ [1] (*morally*) (= *bad*) malo; (= *unfair*) injusto; **it's ~ to steal** ◊ **stealing is ~** robar está mal; **there's nothing ~ in that** no hay nada malo en eso; **that was very ~ of you** ahí *or* en eso has hecho muy mal; **you were ~ to do that** hacer eso estuvo mal por tu parte; **what's ~ with a drink now and again?** ¿qué tiene de malo tomarse una copa de vez en cuando?; **there's nothing ~ with that** no hay nada malo en eso
[2] (= *incorrect, mistaken*) [*answer*] incorrecto; [*calculation, belief*] equivocado; **the ~ answer** la respuesta incorrecta; **he made a number of ~ assumptions** se equivocó al hacer ciertas suposiciones; **to be ~** [*person*] equivocarse, estar equivocado; **that is ~** eso no es exacto *or* cierto; **the information they gave us was ~** la información que nos dieron era incorrecta; **you're ~ about that** ahí *or* en eso estás equivocado; **that clock is ~** ese reloj anda *or* marcha mal; **the letter has the ~ date on it** la carta tiene la fecha equivocada; **you've opened the packet at the ~ end** has abierto el paquete por el lado que no es, has abierto el paquete al revés; **I was ~ in thinking that …** me equivoqué al pensar que …; **I'm in the ~ job** tengo un puesto que no me conviene; **he's got the ~ kind of friends** no tiene los amigos apropiados; **that's the ~ kind of plug** se necesita otro tipo de enchufe; **she married the ~ man** se equivocó al casarse con él; **to play a ~ note**

➤ LANGUAGE IN USE: **write B2** 21.1, 21.2 **wrong A1** 14 **A2** 12.1, 18.3

tocar una nota falsa; **you have the ~ number** (*Telec*) se ha equivocado de número; **it's the ~ one** no es el/la que hace falta; **I think you're talking to the ~ person** creo que no es conmigo con quien debería hablar; **it's in the ~ place** está mal situado, está mal colocado; **is this the ~ road?** ¿nos habremos equivocado de camino?; **~ side** [*of cloth*] revés *m*, envés *m*; **he was driving on the ~ side (of the road)** iba por el carril contrario; **to say/do the ~ thing** decir/hacer algo inoportuno; **at the ~ time** inoportunamente; **we were on the ~ train** nos habíamos equivocado de tren; **the ~ way round** al revés; **to go the ~ way** (*on route*) equivocarse de camino; **that's the ~ way to go about it** ésa no es la forma de enfocarlo; **a piece of bread went down the ~ way** se me fue un pedazo de pan por el otro camino *or* por el camino viejo; *see also* **rub up**

[3] (= *amiss*) **is anything** *or* **something ~?** ¿pasa algo?; **what's ~?** ¿qué pasa?; **what's ~ with you?** ¿qué te pasa?; **what's ~ with the car?** ¿qué le pasa al coche?; **nothing's ~** ◊ **there's nothing ~** no pasa nada; **there's nothing ~ with it/him** no le pasa nada; **something's ~** ◊ **there's something ~** hay algo mal *or* que no está bien; **there's something ~ with my lights** ◊ **something's ~ with my lights** algo les pasa a mis faros; **something was very ~** había algo que no iba nada bien

[4] **to be ~ in the head*** estar chiflado*

Ⓑ ADV mal; **to answer ~** contestar mal, contestar incorrectamente; **you did ~ to insult him** hiciste mal en insultarle; **you're doing it all ~** lo estás haciendo todo mal; **you've done it ~** lo has hecho mal; **to get sth ~** equivocarse en algo; **the accountant got his sums ~*** el contable se equivocó al hacer las cuentas; **don't get me ~*** no me malinterpretes; **you've got it all ~*** (= *misunderstood*) no has entendido nada; **to go ~** [*person*] (*on route*) equivocarse de camino; (*in calculation*) equivocarse; (*morally*) ir por el mal camino; [*plan*] salir mal, malograrse (*Peru*), cebarse (*Mex**); (*Mech*) fallar, estropearse; **the robbery went ~ and they got caught** el atraco fracasó y los pillaron; **something went ~ with the gears** las marchas empezaron a funcionar mal; **something went ~ with their plans** algo falló en sus planes; **you can't go ~** (*with choice*) no te equivocarás, puedes estar seguro (**with** con); (*in directions*) no tiene pérdida; **well, in that case you thought ~** bueno, en ese caso pensaste mal

Ⓒ N mal *m*; **to do sb a ~** hacer mal a algn; **he can do no ~** es incapaz de hacer mal a nadie; **he did her ~** se portó mal con ella; **to be in the ~** (= *guilty*) obrar mal; (= *mistaken*) estar equivocado; **to put sb in the ~** dejar en mal lugar a algn, poner en evidencia a algn; **to right a ~** deshacer un agravio, acabar con un abuso; ✦*PROV* **two ~s don't make a right** no se subsana un error cometiendo otro; *see also* **right C1**

Ⓓ VT ser injusto con; **you ~ me** eso no es justo; **to feel that one has been ~ed** sentirse agraviado

wrongdoer ['rɒŋ,duːəʳ] N malhechor(a) *m/f*, delincuente *mf*

wrongdoing ['rɒŋ,duːɪŋ] N maldad *f*; (*Rel*) pecado *m*; **he will be punished for his ~s** se le castigará por su maldad

wrong-foot ['rɒŋ'fʊt] VT poner en situación violenta, poner en situación desfavorable; **that left us ~ed** eso nos dejó en una situación violenta

wrongful ['rɒŋfʊl] ADJ [1] (= *unjust*) injusto; **~ dismissal** despido *m* improcedente

[2] (= *unlawful*) ilegal; **~ arrest** arresto *m* ilegal

wrongfully ['rɒŋfəlɪ] ADV [1] [*accused, convicted*] injustamente

[2] [*arrested*] ilegalmente

wrong-headed ['rɒŋ'hedɪd] ADJ [*ideas, opinions, policies*] desatinado, desacertado; [*person*] obcecado

wrong-headedness ['rɒŋ'hedɪdnɪs] N obcecación *f*

wrongly ['rɒŋlɪ] ADV [1] (= *incorrectly*) [*believe, assume, diagnose*] equivocadamente; **you have been ~ informed** le han informado mal

[2] (= *unjustly*) [*accuse, convict*] injustamente; *see also* **rightly 2**

wrongness ['rɒŋnɪs] N [1] (= *unfairness*) injusticia *f*

[2] (= *incorrectness*) [*of answer*] lo incorrecto

[3] (= *evil*) maldad *f*

wrote [rəʊt] PT *of* **write**

wrought [rɔːt] Ⓐ (†† *or liter*) PT, PP *of* **work**; **great changes have been ~** se han efectuado grandes cambios; **destruction ~ by the floods** daños *mpl* causados por las inundaciones

Ⓑ ADJ **~ iron** hierro *m* forjado

wrought-up ['rɔːt'ʌp] ADJ **to be ~** estar nervioso

WRU N ABBR (*Wales*) = **Welsh Rugby Union**

wrung [rʌŋ] PT, PP *of* **wring**

WRVS N ABBR (*Brit*) = **Women's Royal Voluntary Service**

wry [raɪ] ADJ [*person, sense of humour, remark*] irónico; **to make a ~ face** hacer una mueca, torcer el gesto

wryly ['raɪlɪ] ADV irónicamente, con ironía

wryneck ['raɪnek] N torcecuello *m*

WS N ABBR (*Scot Jur*) = **Writer to the Signet**

WSW ABBR (= **west-southwest**) OSO

wt ABBR = **weight**

W/T ABBR (= **wireless telegraphy**) radiotelegrafía *f*

WTO N ABBR (= **World Trade Organization**) OMC *f*

WV ABBR (*US*) = **West Virginia**

W. Va. ABBR (*US*) = **West Virginia**

WWF N ABBR = **Worldwide Fund for Nature**

WWI N ABBR = **World War One**

WWII N ABBR = **World War Two**

WWW N ABBR (*Internet*) = **World Wide Web**; **the ~** el Web

WY ABBR (*US*) = **Wyoming**

wych-elm ['wɪtʃelm] N olmo *m* escocés, olmo *m* de montaña

Wyo. ABBR (*US*) = **Wyoming**

WYSIWYG ['wɪzɪ,wɪg] ABBR (*Comput*) = **what you see is what you get**

X x

X, **x** [eks] Ⓐ N (= *letter*) (*also Math*) X, x *f*; **if you have X dollars a year** si uno tiene X dólares al año; **for X number of years** durante X años; **X marks the spot** el sitio está señalado con una X; **X for Xmas** X de Xiquena
Ⓑ CPD ► **X chromosome** N cromosoma *m* X

Xavier ['zeɪvɪəʳ] N Javier

X-certificate ['eksə,tɪfɪkɪt] ADJ (*Brit Cine*) no apto para menores de 18 años

xenon ['zenɒn] N xenón *m*

xenophobe ['zenəfəʊb] N xenófobo/a *m/f*

xenophobia [,zenə'fəʊbɪə] N xenofobia *f*

xenophobic [,zenə'fəʊbɪk] ADJ xenófobo

Xenophon ['zenəfən] N Jenofonte

xerography [zɪə'rɒgrəfɪ] N xerografía *f*

Xerox® ['zɪərɒks] Ⓐ N (= *machine*) fotocopiadora *f*; (= *copy*) fotocopia *f*
Ⓑ VT fotocopiar

Xerxes ['zɜːksiːz] N Jerjes

XL ABBR = **extra large**

Xmas ['eksməs] N ABBR = **Christmas**

X-rated ['eks'reɪtɪd] ADJ (*US Cine*) = **X-certificate**

X-ray ['eks'reɪ] Ⓐ N (= *ray*) rayo-X *m*; (= *photo*) radiografía *f*; **I had an ~ taken** me hicieron una radiografía
Ⓑ VT hacer una radiografía a, radiografiar; **they ~ed my arm** me hicieron una radiografía del brazo, me radiografiaron el brazo
Ⓒ CPD ► **X-ray examination** N examen *m* con rayos X ► **X-ray photograph** N radiografía *f* ► **X-ray treatment** N tratamiento *m* de rayos X

xylograph ['zaɪləgrɑːf] N xilografía *f*, grabado *m* en madera

xylographic [zaɪlə'græfɪk] ADJ xilográfico

xylography [zaɪ'lɒgrəfɪ] N xilografía *f*

xylophone ['zaɪləfəʊn] N xilófono *m*

xylophonist [zaɪ'lɒfənɪst] N xilofonista *mf*

Y y

Y, y [waɪ] Ⓐ N (= *letter*) Y, y *f*; **Y for Yellow** Y de Yegua
Ⓑ CPD ► **Y chromosome** N cromosoma *m* Y; *see also* **Y-fronts**

Y2K [ˌwaɪtuːˈkeɪ] ABBR = **Year 2000**; **the Y2K problem** (*Comput*) el (problema del) efecto 2000

yacht [jɒt] Ⓐ N (*esp Sport*) barco *m* de vela, velero *m*; (*luxury*) yate *m*; (*small, model*) balandro *m*, balandra *f*
Ⓑ VI pasear a vela, navegar a vela; **to go ~ing** ir a pasear *or* navegar a vela
Ⓒ CPD ► **yacht club** N club *m* náutico ► **yacht race** N regata *f* de veleros

yachting [ˈjɒtɪŋ] N navegación *f* a vela, balandrismo *m*; **the ~ fraternity** los aficionados al deporte de la vela; **a ~ trip** una excursión en barco de vela

yachtsman [ˈjɒtsmən] N (*pl* **yachtsmen**) balandrista *m*, deportista *m* náutico

yachtsmanship [ˈjɒtsmənʃɪp] N arte *m* de navegar en yate *or* balandro

yachtswoman [ˈjɒtswʊmən] N (*pl* **yachtswomen**) balandrista *f*, deportista *f* náutica

yack* [jæk], **yackety-yak*** [ˈjækɪtɪˈjæk] Ⓐ N (= *chatter*) cháchara* *f*; **to have a ~** estar de cháchara*
Ⓑ VI (*pej*) hablar como una cotorra*

yah [jɑː] EXCL ¡bah!

yahoo Ⓐ [jɑːˈhuː] EXCL ¡yupi!
Ⓑ [ˈjɑːhuː] N (*Brit* pej*) niñato/a* *m/f*

yak [jæk] N (= *animal*) yac *m*, yak *m*

Yakuza [jəˈkuːzə] N **the ~** los yakuzas

Yale® [jeɪl] CPD ► **Yale key** N llave *f* de seguridad ► **Yale lock** N cerradura *f* de cilindro

yam [jæm] N ñame *m*; (= *sweet potato*) batata *f*, camote *m* (*LAm*)

yammer* [ˈjæməʳ] VI quejarse, gimotear

yang [jæŋ] N yang *m*

Yank* [jæŋk] N (*sometimes pej*) yanqui *mf*, gringo/a *m/f* (*LAm*)

yank [jæŋk] Ⓐ N tirón *m*, jalón *m* (*LAm*); **to give sth a ~** tirar de *or* (*LAm*) jalar algo
Ⓑ VT tirar de, jalar (*LAm*)

►**yank off*** VT + ADV (= *detach*) arrancar de un tirón; **he ~ed the button off** arrancó el botón de un tirón; **to ~ one's clothes off** quitarse la ropa precipitadamente; **to ~ sb off to jail** pillar *or* (*LAm*) agarrar y meter a algn en la cárcel

►**yank out*** VT + ADV sacar de un tirón; **to ~ a nail out** sacar un clavo de un tirón

Yankee [ˈjæŋkɪ] Ⓐ ADJ yanqui
Ⓑ N yanqui *mf*

> **YANKEE**
>
> *Aunque en los demás países se utiliza el término* **Yankee** *para referirse a los estadounidenses en general, en Estados Unidos un* **Yankee** *es un habitante de un estado del norte, sobre todo para los sureños, ya que en el norte se dice que un verdadero* **Yankee** *es el oriundo de Nueva Inglaterra. La primera vez que se utilizó fue en la canción* **Yankee Doodle***, escrita por un inglés para burlarse de los colonos americanos. Sin embargo, durante la revolución americana, los soldados del general Washington transformaron la canción de insulto en himno patriótico. Desde la guerra de Secesión los sureños han intentado distinguirse de los norteños llamándoles* **Yankees***. Los británicos usan el término peyorativo* **Yank** *para referirse a los estadounidenses.*

yap [jæp] Ⓐ N [*of dog*] pequeño ladrido *m*
Ⓑ VI [1] [*dog*] dar pequeños ladridos, ladrar
[2] (*) (= *chat*) charlar

yapping [ˈjæpɪŋ] N [1] (*of dog*) pequeños ladridos *mpl*
[2] (*) (= *chatting*) charla* *f*, palique* *m*

yard[1] [jɑːd] N (= *measure*) yarda *f* (*91,44cm*); **a few ~s off** ≈ a unos metros; **he pulled out ~s of handkerchief** sacó un enorme pañuelo; **with a face a ~ long** con una cara muy larga

yard[2] [jɑːd] N [1] (= *courtyard, farmyard*) patio *m*; (*US*) (= *garden*) jardín *m*; (*for livestock*) corral *m*; (*Scol*) patio *m* (de recreo); (= *worksite*) taller *m*; (*for storage*) depósito *m*, almacén *m*; (*for shipping, boats*) astillero *m*; (*Rail*) estación *f*; **the Yard** ◊ **Scotland Yard** (*Brit*) *oficina central de la policía de Londres*
[2] (*Naut*) (= *spar*) verga *f*

yardage [ˈjɑːdɪdʒ] N ≈ metraje *m*

yardarm [ˈjɑːdɑːm] N (*Naut*) verga *f*, penol *m*

yardstick [ˈjɑːdstɪk] N (*fig*) patrón *m*, criterio *m*, medida *f*

yarn [jɑːn] Ⓐ N [1] (= *wool*) hilo *m*
[2] (= *tale*) cuento *m*, historia *f*; ✦*IDIOM* **to spin a ~** soltar una historia; **she spun them a ~ about how she'd masterminded the whole project** les soltó una historia de cómo había estado al frente de todo el proyecto
Ⓑ VI contar historias

yarrow [ˈjærəʊ] N milenrama *f*

yashmak [ˈjæʃmæk] N velo *m* (de musulmana)

yaw [jɔː] (*Naut*) Ⓐ N guiñada *f*
Ⓑ VI guiñar, hacer una guiñada

yawl [jɔːl] N yol *m*, yola *f*

yawn [jɔːn] Ⓐ N bostezo *m*; **to give a ~** bostezar; **to say sth with a ~** decir algo bostezando; **it was a ~ from start to finish*** fue aburridísimo, fue un plomo*
Ⓑ VI bostezar; (*fig*) [*gap, abyss*] abrirse
Ⓒ VT **to ~ one's head off** bostezar mucho

yawning [ˈjɔːnɪŋ] ADJ (*fig*) [*gap, abyss*] enorme; **there is a ~ gap between the moderates and the left wing of the party** existe un enorme abismo entre los moderados y el ala izquierda del partido

yd ABBR (= **yard**) yda

ye [jiː] Ⓐ PRON (*liter, dial*) vosotros, vosotras
Ⓑ DEF ART (††) = **the**

yea†† [jeɪ] Ⓐ ADV (= *yes*) sí; (= *indeed*) sin duda, ciertamente; (= *moreover*) además
Ⓑ N (= *yes*) sí; **the ~s and the nays** los votos a favor y los votos en contra; **let your ~ be ~ and your nay be nay** sé consecuente con lo que dices

yeah* [jɛə] ADV = **yes**

year [ˈjɪəʳ] N [1] (= *twelve months*) año *m*; **it takes ~s** es cosa de años, se tarda años; **we waited ~s** esperamos una eternidad; **in the ~ (of our Lord) 1869** en el año (del Señor) 1869; **he died in his 89th ~** murió a los 89 años; **he got ten ~s** le condenaron a diez años de prisión; **three times a ~** tres veces al año; **100 dollars a ~** 100 dólares al año; **in after ~s** (*liter*) en los años siguientes, años después; **to reckon sth by the ~** calcular algo por años; **~ end** final *m* del año; **we never see her from one ~'s end to the other** no la vemos en todo el año; **~ of grace** año *m* de gracia; **~ in, ~ out** año tras año, todos los años sin falta; **to reckon sth in ~s** calcular algo por años; **last ~** el año pasado; **the ~ before last** el año antepasado; **next ~** (*looking to future*) el año que viene; **the next ~** (*in past time*) el año siguiente; **she's three ~s old** tiene tres años; **an eight-~-old child** un niño de ocho años; **the work has put ~s on him** el trabajo lo ha envejecido; **all (the) ~ round** durante todo el año; **that hairstyle takes ~s off you*** ese peinado te quita un montón de años*; ✦*IDIOM* **in the ~ dot** en el año de la nana*; **since the ~ dot** desde el año de la nana*, desde siempre
[2] (= *age*) **in my early ~s** en mi infancia, en mi juventud; **from her earliest ~s** desde muy joven; **he looks old/young for his ~s** aparenta más/menos años de los que tiene; **she's very spry for a woman of her ~s** para una mujer de su edad está muy ágil; **he's getting on in ~s** va para viejo; **in his later ~s** en sus últimos años
[3] (*Brit Scol, Univ*) curso *m*, año *m*; **she's in the fifth ~** está en quinto; **the kids in my ~** los chicos de mi curso; **he's in fourth ~ Law** estudia cuarto (curso de) de Derecho
[4] [*of wine*] cosecha *f*, vendimia *f*; **1982 was a good/bad ~** 1982 fue una buena/mala cosecha *or* vendimia, 1982 fue un buen/mal año

yearbook ['jɪəbʊk] N anuario *m*;
→ HIGH SCHOOL

YEARBOOK

*En los centros de educación secundaria (***high schools***) y universidades estadounidenses se suele publicar un anuario (***yearbook***) al final de cada curso académico, en el que se registran muchos aspectos de su vida académica y social. El libro contiene fotografías de cada uno de los alumnos, profesores y demás personal de la administración, además de fotografías de grupos y organizaciones estudiantiles. Una sección se dedica a las estudiantes más atractivas, entre las cuales se incluye la* **Homecoming Queen***, reina de las fiestas de antiguos alumnos. También hay secciones dedicadas a los estudiantes con más probabilidades de éxito en la vida y a aquellos que gozan de mayor popularidad. Es tradición que los estudiantes escriban dedicatorias en los anuarios de sus compañeros de clase.*
⇨ *Ver tb* HIGH SCHOOL

yearling ['jɪəlɪŋ] Ⓐ ADJ primal
Ⓑ N primal(a) *m/f*

yearlong ['jɪə'lɒŋ] ADJ que dura un año (entero); [*ban, moratorium*] de un año

yearly ['jɪəlɪ] Ⓐ ADJ anual; **~ payment** anualidad *f*
Ⓑ ADV anualmente, cada año; **(once) ~** una vez al año

yearn [jɜːn] VI **to ~ for** [+ *native land, person*] añorar; [+ *freedom*] anhelar; **to ~ to do sth** anhelar hacer algo, ansiar hacer algo

yearning ['jɜːnɪŋ] Ⓐ ADJ [*desire*] ansioso, vehemente; [*look, tone*] de ansia, anhelante
Ⓑ N (= *desire*) ansia *f*, anhelo *m*; (= *longing*) añoranza *f* (**for** de); **to have a ~ to do sth** tener ansias *or* muchas ganas de hacer algo, anhelar hacer algo (*liter*)

yearningly ['jɜːnɪŋlɪ] ADV con ansia, ansiosamente

year-round ['jɪə'raʊnd] ADJ que dura todo el año, de todo el año

yeast [jiːst] Ⓐ N levadura *f*
Ⓑ CPD ► **yeast extract** N extracto *m* de levadura

yeasty ['jiːstɪ] ADJ 1 [*smell, taste*] a levadura
2 (*fig*) frívolo, superficial

yell [jel] Ⓐ N grito *m*, chillido *m*; **to let out** *or* **give a ~** soltar *or* pegar un grito; **~s of laughter** carcajadas *fpl*
Ⓑ VI (*also* **to ~ out**) gritar, chillar
Ⓒ VT (*also* **to ~ out**) [+ *order, name*] gritar

yelling ['jelɪŋ] N gritos *mpl*, chillidos *mpl*

yellow ['jeləʊ] Ⓐ ADJ (*compar* **yellower**; *superl* **yellowest**) 1 (*in colour*) [*ribbon, paint, colour*] amarillo; [*hair*] rubio; [*teeth, fingers*] amarillo, amarillento; **to go** *or* **turn ~** volverse *or* ponerse amarillo, volverse *or* ponerse amarillento; **the fields were ~ with buttercups** los campos estaban amarillos, llenos de ranúnculos; **his fingers were ~ with nicotine** tenía los dedos amarillos *or* amarillentos de la nicotina
2 (*by race*) amarillo
3 (*) (= *cowardly*) gallina*, miedica*, cagueta‡; **to have a ~ streak** ser un poco gallina *or* miedica*
Ⓑ N 1 (= *colour*) amarillo *m*
2 (= *yolk*) yema *f*
Ⓒ VI volverse amarillo, ponerse amarillo; **the paper had ~ed with age** el papel se había vuelto *or* puesto amarillo con el paso del tiempo; **~ing leaves/pages** hojas *fpl* amarillentas
Ⓓ VT **~ed newspapers** periódicos amarillentos (por el paso del tiempo); **grass verges ~ed by weeks of sunshine** la hierba seca y amarillenta al borde del camino tras semanas de sol
Ⓔ CPD ► **yellow belly*** N gallina* *mf*, cagueta‡ *mf* ► **yellow card** N (*Ftbl*) tarjeta *f* amarilla ► **yellow fever** N fiebre *f* amarilla ► **yellow line** N línea *f* amarilla (de estacionamiento limitado); **a double ~ line** una línea amarilla doble; **a single ~ line** una línea amarilla ► **yellow ochre** N ocre *m* amarillo ► **Yellow Pages®** NPL (*Telec*) páginas *fpl* amarillas ► **the yellow peril*** N la amenaza amarilla ► **the yellow press** N la prensa amarilla, la prensa sensacionalista ► **the Yellow River** N el Río Amarillo ► **the Yellow Sea** N el Mar Amarillo ► **yellow wagtail** N lavandera *f* boyera

yellow-card ['jeləʊ,kɑːd] VT (*Sport*) amonestar, mostrar la tarjeta amarilla a

yellowhammer ['jeləʊ,hæmə^r] N escribano *m* cerillo

yellowish ['jeləʊɪʃ] ADJ amarillento

yellowness ['jeləʊnɪs] N color *m* amarillo, amarillez *f*

yellowy ['jeləʊɪ] ADJ amarillento, que tira a amarillo

yelp [jelp] Ⓐ N [*of animal*] gañido *m*; [*of person*] grito *m*, chillido *m*
Ⓑ VI [*animal*] gañir; [*person*] gritar, chillar

yelping ['jelpɪŋ] N [*of animal*] gañidos *mpl*; [*of person*] gritos *mpl*, chillidos *mpl*

Yemen ['jemən] N Yemen *m*

Yemeni ['jemənɪ] Ⓐ ADJ yemenita
Ⓑ N yemenita *mf*

yen [jen] N 1 (= *currency*) yen *m*
2 (*) **to have a ~ to do sth** morirse de ganas de hacer algo*, tener muchas ganas de hacer algo

yeoman ['jəʊmən] N (*pl* **yeomen**) (*Brit Hist*) 1 (*also* **~ farmer**) pequeño propietario *m*, terrateniente *m* rural
2 (*Mil*) soldado *m* (voluntario) de caballería; **~ of the guard** alabardero *m* de la Casa Real; ✦**IDIOM to give ~ service** prestar grandes servicios

yeomanry ['jəʊmənrɪ] N 1 (= *landowners*) pequeños propietarios *mpl*, terratenientes *mpl* rurales
2 (*Brit Mil*) caballería *f* voluntaria

yep* [jep] ADV (*esp US*) sí

yes [jes] Ⓐ ADV sí; **"I didn't say that!" — "oh, ~, you did"** —¡yo no he dicho eso! —sí, sí que lo has dicho; **"you're not going, are you?" — "~, I am"** —tú no vas, ¿verdad? —sí sí, (que) voy; **yes?** (*doubtfully*) ¿de verdad?, ¿ah sí?; (*awaiting further reply*) ¿y qué más?, y ¿luego? (*LAm*); (*answering knock at door*) ¿sí?, ¡adelante!; **to say ~** decir que sí, aceptar; (*to marriage proposal*) dar el sí; **he says ~ to everything** a todo dice que sí, se conforma con cualquier cosa; **~ and no** (= *sort of*) sí y no; **~ ~, but what if it doesn't?** de acuerdo, pero ¿y si no es así?
Ⓑ N sí *m*; **he gave a reluctant ~** asintió pero de mala gana
Ⓒ CPD ► **yes man*** N adulador *m*, pelotillero *m* (*Sp**)

yes-no question [,jes'nəʊ,kwestʃən] N pregunta *f* de sí o no

yesterday ['jestədeɪ] Ⓐ ADV ayer; **~ afternoon** ayer por la tarde; **~ morning/evening** ayer por la mañana/tarde; **all day ~** todo el día de ayer; **late ~** ayer a última hora; ✦**IDIOM I wasn't born ~** no me chupo el dedo*
Ⓑ N ayer *m*; **the day before ~** anteayer; **~ was Monday** ayer era lunes; **all our ~s** todos nuestros ayeres

yesteryear ['jestə'jɪə^r] ADV (*poet*) antaño

YET

In questions

- When **yet** is used in affirmative questions, translate using **ya**:

Is Mary here yet?
¿Está aquí María ya?
Have they arrived yet?
¿Han llegado ya?

In negatives

- When **not ... yet** is used in statements or questions, translate using **todavía no** or **aún no**, both of which can go at either the beginning or the end of the sentence:

My parents haven't got up yet
Mis padres no se han levantado todavía *or* ***aún, Todavía*** *or* ***Aún no se han levantado mis padres***
Haven't they done it yet?
¿No lo han hecho todavía *or* ***aún?, ¿Todavía*** *or* ***Aún no lo han hecho?***

Meaning "to date"

- When **yet** follows a superlative or **never** and means "to date", translate using **hasta ahora**:

It's the best (one) yet
Es el mejor hasta ahora
I've never been late yet
Hasta ahora no he llegado nunca con retraso

Meaning "still"
In predictions

- When **yet** is used in predictions about the future, translate using **todavía** or **aún**:

The economic crisis will go on for some time yet
La crisis económica continuará todavía *or* ***aún algún tiempo***
They will be a long time yet
Todavía *or* ***Aún tardarán bastante en venir***

With to-INFINITIVE

- When **yet** is followed by **to** + VERB, translate using **todavía por** or **sin** + INFINITIVE or **aún por** or **sin** + INFINITIVE:

The house is yet to be cleaned
La casa está todavía por *or* ***sin limpiar*** ◇ ***La casa está aún por*** *or* ***sin limpiar***

Meaning "even"

- When **yet** precedes a comparative and means "even", translate using **todavía** or **aún**:

There is yet more rain to come in the north
Todavía *or* ***Aún habrá más precipitaciones en el norte***
Yet bigger satellites will be sent up into orbit
Se pondrán en órbita satélites todavía *or* ***aún más grandes***

yet [jet] Ⓐ ADV 1 (= *now, up to now, by now*) todavía, aún; **he hasn't come ~** todavía *or* aún no ha llegado, no ha llegado todavía *or* aún; **don't go (just) ~** no te vayas todavía, quédate un rato; **need you go ~?** ¿tienes que irte ya?; **as ~** todavía, por ahora; **we haven't heard anything as ~** todavía *or* por ahora no sabemos nada; **not ~** todavía *or* aún no; **"are you coming?" — "not just ~"** —¿vienes? —todavía *or* aún no
2 (= *to date*) hasta ahora; **this is his best film ~** es su mejor película hasta ahora
3 (= *still*) todavía, aún; **there's hope for me**

~ todavía *or* aún tengo esperanzas; **that question is ~ to be decided** está todavía por *or* sin decidir, aún está por *or* sin decidir; **he may ~ succeed** todavía puede que lo consiga, puede que aún lo consiga; **it won't be dark for half an hour ~** todavía *or* aún queda media hora para que anochezca

[4] (= *even*) todavía, aún; **the queues are likely to grow longer ~** es probable que las colas se hagan aún *or* todavía más largas; **better ~, let him buy them for you for Christmas** mejor aún, deja que te los regale por Navidad; **~ again** otra *or* una vez más; **they are celebrating ~ another victory** están celebrando otra *or* una victoria más; **many were killed, ~ more have been left homeless** muchos resultaron muertos y aún *or* todavía más han perdido sus hogares

[5] (*frm*) **nor ~** ni

Ⓑ CONJ (= *in spite of everything*) sin embargo, con todo; (= *but*) pero; **I told him several times, ~ he still hasn't done it** se lo dije varias veces, (y) sin embargo no lo ha hecho; **a powerful ~ fragile piece of equipment** un equipo potente pero frágil

yeti ['jetɪ] N yeti *m*

yew [juː] N (*also* **~ tree**) tejo *m*

Y-fronts® ['waɪfrʌnts] NPL (*Brit*) calzoncillos *mpl*

YHA N ABBR (*Brit*) = **Youth Hostels Association**

Yid** [jɪd] N (*offensive*) judío/a *m/f*

Yiddish ['jɪdɪʃ] Ⓐ ADJ judío
Ⓑ N (*Ling*) yíd(d)ish *m*, judeo-alemán *m*

yield [jiːld] Ⓐ N (*from crop, mine, investment*) rendimiento *m*; **~ per hectare** el rendimiento por hectárea; **high-~ bonds** bonos *mpl* de alto rendimiento; **this year, grain ~s have trebled** este año la producción de cereales se ha triplicado; **how to improve milk ~s** cómo mejorar la producción de leche

Ⓑ VT [1] (= *produce*) [+ *crop, minerals, results*] producir; [+ *interest*] rendir, producir; [+ *profit, benefits*] producir, reportar; [+ *opportunity*] brindar, ofrecer; **the shares ~ five per cent** las acciones producen *or* reportan *or* rinden un cinco por ciento de beneficios

[2] (*frm*) (= *surrender*) [+ *territory, power, control*] ceder (**to** a); **to ~ the floor to sb** ceder la palabra a algn; **to ~ ground to sb** (*Mil, fig*) ceder terreno a algn; **to ~ the right of way to sb** (*US Aut*) ceder el paso a algn

Ⓒ VI [1] (*Agr*) (= *produce*) **land that ~s well/poorly** una tierra que produce mucho/poco; **a variety of strawberry that ~s well** una variedad de fresa que da mucha producción

[2] (*frm*) (= *surrender*) rendirse, ceder; **we shall never ~** nunca nos rendiremos, nunca cederemos; **to ~ to sth** ceder a *or* ante algo; **we will not ~ to threats** no vamos a ceder a *or* ante las amenazas; **he refused to ~ to temptation** se negó a caer en la tentación, se negó a ceder a *or* ante la tentación; **the disease ~ed to treatment** la enfermedad remitió con el tratamiento

[3] (= *give way*) [*ice, door, branch*] ceder; **he felt the floor ~ beneath his feet** notó cómo el suelo cedía *or* hundía bajo sus pies; **to ~ under pressure** ceder *or* hundirse ante la presión

[4] (*US Aut*) ceder el paso; **"yield"** "ceda el paso"

►**yield up** VT + ADV (*liter*) [+ *territory, power, control*] ceder (**to** a); [+ *secret*] revelar; **nature ~s up its bounty** (*liter*) la naturaleza da su recompensa

yielding ['jiːldɪŋ] ADJ [1] (= *soft*) [*ground, surface, substance*] flexible, blando

[2] (= *compliant, submissive*) [*person*] (*in temperament*) complaciente; (*physically*) tierno

yin [jɪn] N yin *m*

yippee* [jɪ'piː] EXCL yupi*

YMCA N ABBR = **Young Men's Christian Association**

yo ['jəʊ] EXCL (*as greeting*) ¡hola!; (*to attract attention*) ¡eh!, ¡oye!

yob* ['jɒb], **yobbo** ['jɒbəʊ] N (*Brit*) vándalo *m*, gamberro *m* (*Sp*)

yobbish ['jɒbɪʃ] ADJ (*Brit*) [*behaviour*] de gamberro; [*person*] salvaje, incívico

yod [jɒd] N yod *f*

yodel, yodle ['jəʊdl] Ⓐ VI cantar a la tirolesa
Ⓑ VT cantar a la tirolesa
Ⓒ N canto *m* a la tirolesa

yoga ['jəʊgə] Ⓐ N yoga *m*
Ⓑ CPD [*meditation, technique, position*] yóguico, de yoga

yoghurt ['jəʊgət] N = **yogurt**

yogi ['jəʊgɪ] N (*pl* **yogis** *or* **yogin** ['jəʊgɪn]) yogui *m*

yogurt ['jəʊgət] N yogur(t) *m*

yo-heave-ho [jəʊ'hiːv'həʊ] EXCL = **heave-ho**

yoke [jəʊk] Ⓐ N (*pl* **yokes** *or* **yoke**) [1] [*of oxen*] yunta *f*; (*carried on shoulder*) balancín *m*, percha *f*; (*fig*) yugo *m*; **under the ~ of the Nazis** bajo el yugo de los nazis; **to throw off the ~** sacudir el yugo

[2] (*on dress, blouse*) canesú *m*

Ⓑ VT (*also* **~ together**) [+ *oxen*] uncir; (*fig*) unir

yokel ['jəʊkəl] N palurdo/a *m/f*, pueblerino/a *m/f*

yolk [jəʊk] N yema *f* (de huevo)

Yom Kippur [ˌjɒmkɪ'pʊəʳ] N Yom Kip(p)ur *m*

yomp [jɒmp] VI *caminar penosamente (por un terreno difícil)*

yon [jɒn] ADV (*poet or dial*) aquel

yonder ['jɒndəʳ] Ⓐ ADJ aquel
Ⓑ ADV allá, a lo lejos; **(over) ~** allá

yonks* [jɒŋks] N (*Brit*) **for ~** hace siglos*; **I haven't seen you for ~** hace siglos que no te veo*

yoo-hoo* ['juː'huː] EXCL ¡yu-hu!*

yore [jɔːʳ] N (†† *or liter*) **of ~** de antaño, de otro tiempo, de hace siglos; **the days of ~** los tiempos de antaño, otros tiempos

YOU

When translating **you**, even though you often need not use the pronoun itself, you will have to choose between using familiar **tú**/**vosotros** verb forms and the polite **usted**/**ustedes** ones.

• In Spain, use **tú** and the plural **vosotros**/**vosotras** with anyone you call by their first name, with children and younger adults. Use **usted**/**ustedes** with people who are older than you, those in authority and in formal contexts.

• In Latin America usage varies depending on the country and in some places only the **usted** forms are used. Where the **tú** form does exist, only use it with people you know very well. In other areas **vos**, used with verb forms that are similar to the **vosotros** ones, often replaces **tú**. This is standard in Argentina and certain Central American countries while in other countries it is considered substandard. Use **ustedes** for all cases of **you** in the plural.

For further uses and examples, see main entry.

Yorks [jɔːks] N ABBR (*Brit*) = **Yorkshire**

Yorkshire pudding ['jɔːkʃɪə'pʊdɪŋ] N (*Brit*) *especie de buñuelo que se sirve acompañando al rosbif*

you [juː] PRON

Note that subject pronouns are used less in Spanish than in English - mainly for emphasis or to avoid ambiguity.

[1] (*sing*) [1·1] (*familiar*) (*as subject*) tú; (*as direct/indirect object*) te; (*after prep*) ti; **what do you think about it?** ¿y tú que piensas?; **~ and I will go** iremos tú y yo; **~'re very strong** eres muy fuerte; **~ don't understand me** no me entiendes; **I know ~** te conozco; **I'll send ~ a postcard** te mandaré una postal; **I gave the letter to ~ yesterday** te di la carta ayer; **I gave it to ~** te lo di; **I told you to do it** te dije a ti que lo hicieras, es a ti a quien dije que lo hicieras; **it's for ~** es para ti; **she's taller than ~** es más alta que tú; **can I come with ~** ¿puedo ir contigo?

[1·2] (*formal*) (*as subject*) usted, Ud, Vd; (*as direct object*) lo/la, le (*Sp*); (*as indirect object*) le; (*after prep*) usted, Ud, Vd; **~'re very kind** es usted muy amable; **I saw ~, Mrs Jones** la vi, señora Jones; **I gave ~ the keys** le di las llaves

Change **le** *to* **se** *before a direct object pronoun:*

I gave it to ~ se lo di; **I gave them to ~** se las di; **this is for ~** esto es para usted; **they're taller than ~** son más altos que usted

[2] (*pl*) [2·1] (*familiar*) (*as subject*) vosotros/as (*Sp*), ustedes (*LAm*); (*as direct object*) os (*Sp*), los/las (*LAm*); (*as indirect object*) os (*Sp*), les (*LAm*); (*after prep*) vosotros/as (*Sp*), ustedes (*LAm*); **~'ve got kids but we haven't** vosotros tenéis hijos pero nosotros no; **~'re sisters, aren't you?** vosotras sois hermanas, ¿no?; **~ have all been here before** todos (vosotros) habéis estado aquí antes; **~ all know why we are here** todos sabéis por qué estamos aquí; **~ stay here, and I'll go and get the key** (vosotros) quedaos aquí, que yo iré a por la llave; **I know ~ both** yo os conozco a los dos; **I gave it to ~** os lo di; **I gave them to ~** os los di; **I'd like to speak to ~** quiero hablar con vosotros; **I live upstairs from ~** vivo justo encima de vosotros; **they've done it better than ~** lo han hecho mejor que vosotros; **they'll go without ~** irán sin vosotros

[2·2] (*formal*) (*as subject*) ustedes, Uds, Vds; (*as direct object*) los/las, les (*Sp*); (*as indirect object*) les; (*after prep*) ustedes, Uds, Vds; **~ are very kind** son ustedes muy amables; **are ~ brothers?** ¿son (ustedes) hermanos?; **may I help ~?** ¿puedo ayudarlos?; **I gave ~ the keys** les di las llaves

Change **les** *to* **se** *before a direct object pronoun:*

I gave it to ~ se lo di; **I gave them to ~** se las di; **we arrived after ~** llegamos después de ustedes

[3] (*general*)

When **you** *means "one" or "people" in general, the impersonal* **se** *is often used:*

~ can't do that no se puede hacer eso, eso no se hace, eso no se permite; **~ can't smoke here** no se puede fumar aquí, no se permite fumar aquí, se prohíbe fumar aquí; **when ~ need one it's not here** cuando se necesita uno no está aquí; **~ never know** ◊ **~ never can tell** nunca se sabe

A further possibility is **uno**:

~ never know whether … uno nunca sabe si …

Impersonal constructions are also used:
~ need to check it every day hay que comprobarlo cada día, conviene comprobarlo cada día; **~ must paint it** hace falta pintarlo; **fresh air does ~ good** el aire puro (te) hace bien

4 (*phrases and special uses*) **~ Spaniards** vosotros los españoles; **~ doctors!** ¡vosotros, los médicos!; **between ~ and me** entre tú y yo; **~ fool!** ¡no seas tonto!; **that's lawyers for ~!** ¡para que te fíes de los abogados!; **there's a pretty girl for ~!** ¡mira que chica más guapa!; **if I were** *or* **was ~** yo que tú, yo en tu lugar; **~ there!** ¡oye, tú!; **that dress just isn't ~** ese vestido no te sienta bien; **poor ~!** ◊ **poor old ~!** ◊ **~ poor old thing!** ¡pobrecito!

you'd [ju:d] = **you would, you had**

you-know-who* [ˌju:nəʊ'hu:] N tú ya sabes quien, fulano

you'll [ju:l] = **you will, you shall**

young [jʌŋ] Ⓐ ADJ (*compar* **younger**; *superl* **youngest**) 1 (= *not old*) [*person, animal*] joven; [*child*] pequeño, de corta edad; **my ~er brother** mi hermano menor *or* pequeño; **she is two years ~er than me** es dos años más joven que yo, tiene dos años menos que yo; **if I were ten years ~er** si tuviera diez años menos, si fuera diez años más joven; **I'm not so ~ as I was, I'm not getting any ~er** los años no perdonan *or* no pasan en balde; **~ Britain** la juventud británica; **Pitt the ~er** Pitt el joven; **she started writing poetry at a very ~ age** comenzó a escribir poesía siendo muy joven; **at a very ~ age he was sent to boarding school** siendo muy pequeño lo mandaron a un internado; **in my ~(er) days** cuando era joven, en mi juventud; **they have a ~ family** tienen niños pequeños; **she looks quite ~ for her age** aparenta bastante menos edad de la que tiene, parece bastante más joven de lo que es; **the ~er generation** la generación de los más jóvenes; **the ~er generation of film-makers** la generación de cineastas jóvenes; **~ hopeful** joven aspirante *mf*; **a ~ lady** una joven; **why thank you, ~ lady!** ¡muchas gracias, señorita *or* joven!; **now look here, ~ lady!** ¡atiende, jovencita!; **a ~ man** un joven; **you've done well, ~ man** muy bien hecho, muchacho; **she's out with her ~ man** ha salido con su novio *or* chico*; **to marry ~** casarse joven; **it is enjoyed by millions, ~ and old** millones lo disfrutan, grandes y pequeños; **a ~ person** una persona joven; ✦***IDIOMS*** **you're as ~ as you feel** la edad se lleva dentro; **~ at heart** joven de espíritu; **the night is ~** la noche es joven; **you're only ~ once** sólo se vive una vez; *see also* **Turk**

2 (= *youthful*) **that dress is too ~ for her** ese vestido es para alguien más joven; **the family business was in need of ~ blood** el negocio familiar necesitaba savia nueva; **he has a very ~ outlook** piensa como los jóvenes, tiene mentalidad de joven

3 (= *new*) [*moon*] nuevo; [*plant, spinach, wheat*] tierno; [*wine, country*] joven; **the 20th century was still ~** el siglo XX estaba todavía en sus comienzos

Ⓑ NPL 1 (= *offspring*) [*of animals*] crías *fpl*; **a mother defending her ~** una madre protegiendo a sus crías; **to be with ~** estar preñada

2 (= *young people*) **the ~** los jóvenes, la juventud

Ⓒ CPD ► **young gun** N (= *actor, sportsman etc*) joven valor *m* ► **young offender** N (*Brit*) delincuente *mf* juvenil

youngish ['jʌŋɪʃ] ADJ bastante joven, más bien joven

young-looking ['jʌŋˌlʊkɪŋ] ADJ de aspecto joven

youngster ['jʌŋstəʳ] N joven *mf*

your ['jʊəʳ] POSS ADJ 1 (*belonging to one person*) 1·1 (*familiar*) (*with singular noun*) tu; (*with plural noun*) tus; **~ book/table** tu libro/mesa; **~ friends** tus amigos; **it's ~ go** te toca, es tu turno; **have you washed ~ hair?** ¿te has lavado el pelo?; **he's ~ son, not mine!** ¡es hijo tuyo, no mío!

1·2 (*formal*) (*with singular noun*) su; (*with plural noun*) sus; **~ book/table** su libro/mesa; **~ friends** sus amigos; **it's ~ go** es su turno, le toca a usted; **can I see ~ passport, sir?** ¿me enseña su pasaporte, señor?; **is this ~ luggage?** ¿es de usted este equipaje?

2 (*belonging to more than one person*) 2·1 (*familiar*) (*with singular noun*) vuestro/a (*Sp*), su (*LAm*); (*with plural noun*) vuestros/as (*Sp*), sus (*LAm*); **~ house** vuestra casa (*Sp*), su casa (*LAm*); **you can leave ~ bags in this room** podéis dejar las *or* vuestras bolsas en esta habitación (*Sp*), pueden dejar las *or* sus bolsas en esta habitación (*LAm*); **would you like to wash ~ hands?** ¿queréis lavaros las manos?

2·2 (*formal*) (*with singular noun*) su; (*with plural noun*) sus; **~ house** su casa; **you can leave ~ bags in this room** pueden dejar las *or* sus bolsas en esta habitación; **is this ~ dog?** ¿es de ustedes este perro?

3 (= *one's*) **it's bad for ~ health** perjudica la salud

you're ['jʊəʳ] = **you are**

yours ['jʊəz] POSS PRON 1 (*belonging to one person*) 1·1 (*familiar*) (*referring to singular possession*) (el/la) tuyo/a; (*referring to plural possession*) (los/las) tuyos/as; **is that box ~?** ¿esa caja es tuya?; **I've lost my pen, can I use ~?** he perdido el bolígrafo, ¿puedo usar el tuyo?; **that dog of ~!** ¡ese perro tuyo!; **which is ~?** ¿cuál es el tuyo?; **these are my keys and those are ~** éstas son mis llaves y ésas son las tuyas; **what's ~?*** (*offering drink*) ¿qué vas a tomar?

1·2 (*formal*) (*referring to singular possession*) (el/la) suyo/a, (el/la) de usted; (*referring to plural possession*) (los/las) suyos/as, (los/las) de usted; **you and ~** usted y los suyos; **is that box ~?** ¿esa caja es suya?; **I've lost my pen, can I use ~?** he perdido el bolígrafo, ¿puedo usar el suyo?; **these are my keys and those are ~** éstas son mis llaves y ésas son las suyas; **Yours** (*in letter*) le saluda atentamente; *see also* **truly**

2 (*belonging to more than one person*) 2·1 (*familiar*) (*referring to singular possession*) (el/la) vuestro/a, (el/la) suyo/a (*LAm*), (el/la) de ustedes (*LAm*); (*referring to plural possession*) (los/las) vuestros/as, (los/las) suyos/as (*LAm*), (los/las) de ustedes (*LAm*); **that's ~** eso es vuestro

2·2 (*formal*) (*referring to singular possession*) (el/la) suyo/a, (el/la) de ustedes; (*referring to plural possession*) (los/las) suyos/as, (los/las) de ustedes

yourself [jə'self] PRON (*pl* **yourselves** [jə'selvz]) 1 (*reflexive*) 1·1 (*familiar*) te; **have you hurt ~?** ¿te has hecho daño?

1·2 (*formal*) se; **have you hurt ~?** ¿se ha hecho daño?

2 (*for emphasis*) 2·1 (*familiar*) tú mismo/a; **you did it ~** tú mismo lo hiciste; **do it ~!** ¡hazlo tú mismo!; **you ~ said so** tú mismo lo dijiste

2·2 (*formal*) usted mismo/a; **you did it ~** usted mismo lo hizo; **you ~ said so** usted mismo lo dijo

3 (*after a preposition*) 3·1 (*familiar*) ti mismo/a; **you did it for ~** lo hiciste para ti mismo

3·2 (*formal*) usted mismo/a; **you did it for ~** lo hizo para usted mismo

3·3 (**all**) **by ~** sin ayuda de nadie; **did you come by ~?** ¿viniste solo?

4 = **oneself**

yourselves [jə'selvz] PRON 1 (*reflexive*) 1·1 (*familiar*) os (*Sp*), se (*LAm*); **did you enjoy ~?** ¿os divertisteis?, ¿se divirtieron? (*LAm*); **help ~ to vegetables** servíos las verduras

1·2 (*formal*) se; **help ~ to vegetables** sírvanse las verduras

2 (*after prep, for emphasis*) 2·1 (*familiar*) vosotros/as mismos/as, ustedes mismos/as (*LAm*); **you'll have to pay for taxis ~** vosotros mismos tendréis que pagar los taxis

2·2 (*formal*) ustedes mismos/as; **you'll have to pay for taxis ~** ustedes mismos tendrán que pagar los taxis

youth [ju:θ] Ⓐ N 1 (= *young age*) juventud *f*; **in my ~** en mi juventud

2 (*pl* **youths** [ju:ðz]) (= *boy*) joven *m*

3 (= *young people*) jóvenes *mpl*, juventud *f*; **the ~ of today** los jóvenes *or* la juventud de hoy

Ⓑ CPD ► **youth club** N club *m* juvenil ► **youth employment scheme** N plan *m* de empleo juvenil ► **youth hostel** N albergue *m* juvenil ► **youth hostelling** N **to go ~ hostelling** pasar las vacaciones en albergues juveniles ► **youth worker** N (*Brit*) (= *social worker*) *asistente social que se encarga de adolescentes menores de 18 años*; (= *community worker*) *empleado del municipio que trabaja con grupos de jóvenes en la comunidad*

youthful ['ju:θfʊl] ADJ [*looks, appearance*] joven, juvenil; [*enthusiasm, energy*] juvenil; [*ambition, indiscretion, inexperience*] de juventud; **a group of ~ newcomers** un grupo de jóvenes aún desconocidos; **to look ~** tener aspecto joven, parecer joven

youthfulness ['ju:θfʊlnɪs] N juventud *f*

you've [ju:v] = **you have**

yowl [jaʊl] Ⓐ N [*of animal*] aullido *m*; [*of person*] alarido *m*

Ⓑ VI [*animal*] aullar; [*person*] dar alaridos

yo-yo ['jəʊjəʊ] N (*pl* **yo-yos**) 1 ® (= *toy*) yoyó® *m*

2 (*US‡*) bobo/a *m/f*, imbécil *mf*

yr ABBR 1 = **year**

2 = **your**

yrs ABBR 1 = **years**

2 = **yours**

YT ABBR (*Canada*) = **Yukon Territory**

YTS N ABBR (*Brit*) (*formerly*) (= **Youth Training Scheme**) *plan de promoción de empleo para jóvenes*

ytterbium [ɪ'tɜ:bɪəm] N iterbio *m*, yterbio *m*

yttrium ['ɪtrɪəm] N itrio *m*

yuan ['ju:'æn] N yuan *m*

yucca ['jʌkə] N yuca *f*

yuck* [jʌk] EXCL ¡puaj!*

yucky* ['jʌkɪ] ADJ asqueroso

Yugoslav ['ju:gəʊ'slɑ:v] Ⓐ ADJ yugoeslavo, yugoslavo

Ⓑ N yugoeslavo/a *m/f*, yugoslavo/a *m/f*

Yugoslavia ['ju:gəʊ'slɑ:vɪə] N Yugoslavia *f*

Yugoslavian ['ju:gəʊ'slɑ:vɪən] ADJ yugoeslavo, yugoslavo

yuk* [jʌk] EXCL = **yuck**

Yule [ju:l] Ⓐ N († *or liter*) Navidad *f*

Ⓑ CPD ► **Yule log** N (= *wood*) leño *m* de Navidad; (= *cake*) tronco *m* de Navidad

Yuletide ['ju:ltaɪd] N († *or liter*) Navidad *f*; **at ~** por Navidades, en Navidad

yum* [jʌm] EXCL **yum yum!** ¡ñam ñam!*

yummy* [ˈjʌmɪ] ADJ (*compar* **yummier**; *superl* **yummiest**) de rechupete*

yup* [jʌp] ADV (*US*) sí

yuppie* [ˈjʌpɪ] Ⓐ N ABBR (= **young upwardly mobile professional**) yuppie *mf*

Ⓑ CPD [*car, clothes*] de yuppie; [*bar, restaurant, area*] de yuppies ► **yuppie flu** N síndrome *m* vírico

yuppified* [ˈjʌpɪˌfaɪd] ADJ [*bar, restaurant, area, flat*] de yuppies; **he is becoming more and more ~** se está haciendo cada vez más yuppie

yuppy* [ˈjʌpɪ] N = **yuppie**

YWCA N ABBR = **Young Women's Christian Association**

Z z

Z, **z** [zed] (*US*) [zi:] N (= *letter*) Z, z *f*; **Z for Zebra** Z de Zaragoza

zaftig* ['zæftɪg] ADJ (*US*) [*woman*] regordeta y mona

Zaire [zɑ:'i:əʳ] N Zaire *m*

Zairean [zɑ:'i:ərɪən] Ⓐ ADJ zaireño
Ⓑ N zaireño/a *m/f*

Zambesi [zæm'bi:zɪ] N Zambeze *m*

Zambia ['zæmbɪə] N Zambia *f*

Zambian ['zæmbɪən] Ⓐ ADJ zambiano
Ⓑ N zambiano/a *m/f*

zany ['zeɪnɪ] ADJ (*compar* **zanier**; *superl* **zaniest**) estrafalario, surrealista

Zanzibar ['zænzɪbɑ:ʳ] N Zanzíbar *m*

zap* [zæp] Ⓐ EXCL ¡zas!
Ⓑ VT [1] (= *destroy*) [+ *person*] cargarse*
[2] (*Comput*) (= *delete*) [+ *word, data*] borrar, suprimir
[3] (*TV*) **to ~ the TV channels** zapear
Ⓒ VI (= *move quickly*) ir corriendo

► **zap along*** VI + ADV ir a toda pastilla*

zappy* ['zæpɪ] ADJ [*car*] alegre, respondón; [*computer*] veloz; [*prose, style*] ágil; [*approach*] vivaz

Z-bed ['zedbed] N cama *f* plegable

zeal [zi:l] N celo *m*, entusiasmo *m* (**for** por)

zealot ['zelət] N fanático/a *m/f*

zealotry ['zelətrɪ] N fanatismo *m*

zealous ['zeləs] ADJ entusiasta (**for** de)

zealously ['zeləslɪ] ADV con entusiasmo

zebra ['zi:brə] Ⓐ N (*pl* **zebras** *or* **zebra**) cebra *f*
Ⓑ CPD ► **zebra crossing** N (*Brit*) paso *m* de peatones, paso *m* de cebra

zebu ['zi:bu:] N cebú *m*

zed [zed], **zee** [zi:] (*US*) N zeta *f*

Zen [zen] Ⓐ N Zen *m*
Ⓑ CPD ► **Zen Buddhism** N budismo *m* Zen ► **Zen Buddhist** N budista *mf* Zen

zenana [ze'nɑ:nə] N harén *m* indio

zenith ['zenɪθ] N [1] (*Astron*) cenit *m*
[2] (*fig*) cenit *m*, apogeo *m*; **to be at the ~ of one's power** estar en el apogeo de su poder

Zeno ['zɪ:nəʊ] N Zenón *m*

Zephaniah [,zefə'naɪə] N Sofonías *m*

zephyr ['zefəʳ] N céfiro *m*

zeppelin ['zeplɪn] N zepelín *m*

zero ['zɪərəʊ] Ⓐ N (*pl* **zeros** *or* **zeroes**) cero *m*; **absolute ~** cero *m* absoluto; **5° below ~** 5 grados bajo cero
Ⓑ CPD [*altitude*] cero; (*) [*interest, hope*] nulo ► **zero gravity** N gravedad *f* cero ► **zero growth** N crecimiento *m* cero ► **zero hour** N hora *f* cero, hora *f* H ► **zero option** N opción *f* cero ► **zero rating** N tasa *f* cero ► **zero tolerance** N tolerancia cero; **a policy of ~ tolerance** una política de tolerancia cero (*en el mantenimiento del orden público*)

► **zero in on** VI + PREP [1] (*Mil*) (= *aim at*) [+ *target*] apuntar a; (= *move in on*) dirigirse de cabeza a
[2] (*fig*) (= *identify*) identificar; (= *concentrate on*) dirigir todos sus esfuerzos a; **he raised the binoculars and ~ed in on an eleventh-floor room** elevó los prismáticos y los dirigió *or* enfocó hacia una habitación de la undécima planta; **he ~ed in on those who …** reservó sus críticas más acérrimas para los que …

> **ZERO**
>
> *Existen varias palabras que pueden usarse en lugar de* **zero** *según el contexto.* **Zero** *es el término más general en inglés americano, que se usa en la mayoría de los casos. En inglés británico se usa normalmente en matemáticas y ciencias para referirse a temperaturas u otras escalas de valores, como por ejemplo en las frases* **zero population growth** *(crecimiento de población cero), o* **zero inflation** *(índice de inflación cero).*
>
> **Nought** *se usa en inglés británico para leer números decimales, como por ejemplo* **nought point nought seven: 0.07** *(en inglés se usa el punto en vez de la coma como separador decimal) y en las calificaciones:* **nought out of ten** *(cero sobre diez).*
>
> **O** *(pronunciado igual que la letra* **o***) se usa en inglés británico en los números de teléfono:* **O one four one** *: 0141. También se usa en secuencias de dígitos que no representan cantidades numéricas, como por ejemplo en tarjetas de crédito o números de cuentas bancarias.*
>
> **Nil** *se usa normalmente en el Reino Unido en los tanteos deportivos:* **Liverpool won five nil** *(Liverpool ganó cinco a cero).*
>
> **Nothing** *es el equivalente americano de* **nil**, *aunque también se usa a veces en inglés británico.*

zero-rated ['zɪərəʊ,reɪtɪd] ADJ **to be ~ for VAT** tener tipo cero del IVA

zest [zest] N [1] (= *enthusiasm*) gusto *m*, entusiasmo *m* (**for** por); **to do sth with ~** hacer algo con entusiasmo; **to eat with ~** comer con gusto; **her ~ for life** sus ganas de vivir, su gusto por la vida [2] (= *excitement*) ánimo *m*

zestful ['zestfʊl] ADJ entusiasta

zestfully ['zestfəlɪ] ADV con entusiasmo

zesty ['zestɪ] ADJ [*wine*] garboso, enérgico

Zeus [zju:s] N Zeus

ZIFT [zɪft] N ABBR = **Zygote Intrafallopian Transfer**

ziggurat ['zɪgʊræt] N zigurat *m*

zigzag ['zɪgzæg] Ⓐ N zigzag *m* Ⓑ VI zigzaguear, serpentear Ⓒ ADJ en zigzag

zilch‡ [zɪltʃ] N nada de nada; **these shares are worth ~** estas acciones no valen nada de nada*, estas acciones no valen ni cinco*; **Mark knows ~ about art** Mark no sabe absolutamente nada sobre arte; **he's a real ~** (*US*) es un cero a la izquierda

zillion* ['zɪljən] Ⓐ ADJ **a ~ dollars** tropecientos dólares*; **a ~ problems** tropecientos problemas*, problemas a montones*
Ⓑ N (*pl* **zillions** *or* **zillion**) **~s of dollars** tropecientos dólares*

Zimbabwe [zɪm'bɑ:bwɪ] N Zimbabue *m*

Zimbabwean [zɪm'bɑ:bwɪən] Ⓐ ADJ zimbabuo
Ⓑ N zimbabuo/a *m/f*

Zimmer® ['zɪmə] N (*Brit*) (*also* **~ frame**) andador *m*

zinc [zɪŋk] Ⓐ N zinc *m*, cinc *m*
Ⓑ CPD ► **zinc ointment** N pomada *f* de zinc ► **zinc oxide** N óxido *m* de zinc

zine* [zi:n], **'zine*** N fanzine *m*, revistilla *f*

zing [zɪŋ] Ⓐ N [1] (= *noise of bullet*) silbido *m*, zumbido *m*
[2] (*) (= *zest*) gusto *m*, entusiasmo *m*
Ⓑ VI [*bullet, arrow*] silbar; **the bullet ~ed past his ear** la bala le pasó silbando cerca de la oreja; **the cars ~ed past** los coches pasaron estruendosamente

zinnia ['zɪnɪə] N rascamoño *m*, zinnia *f*

Zion ['zaɪən] N Sión *m*

Zionism ['zaɪənɪzəm] N sionismo *m*

Zionist ['zaɪənɪst] Ⓐ ADJ sionista
Ⓑ N sionista *mf*

zip [zɪp] Ⓐ N [1] (*Brit*) (*also* **~ fastener**) cremallera *f*, cierre *m* relámpago (*LAm*)
[2] (*) (= *energy*) vigor *m*, energía *f*
[3] (‡) (= *nothing*) nada de nada*; **I know ~ about it** no sé nada de nada sobre eso*
[4] (= *sound of bullet*) silbido *m*, zumbido *m*
Ⓑ VT [1] (= *close*) [+ *dress, bag*] cerrar la cremallera de
[2] **to ~ open** abrir la cremallera de
[3] (*Comput*) [+ *file*] comprimir
Ⓒ VI **to ~ in** entrar volando *or* zumbando; **to ~ past** pasar volando *or* zumbando
Ⓓ CPD ► **zip code** N (*US*) código *m* postal ► **zip-fastener** N cremallera *f*, cierre *m* relámpago (*LAm*) ► **zip file** (*Comput*) archivo *m* comprimido ► **zip gun** N (*US*) arma *f* de fuego de fabricación casera

► **zip up** Ⓐ VT + ADV [+ *dress, bag*] cerrar la cremallera de; **can you ~ me up please?** ¿me subes *or* cierras la cremallera?
Ⓑ VI + ADV cerrar

zipper ['zɪpəʳ] N (*esp US*) = **zip A1**

zippy* ['zɪpɪ] ADJ (*compar* **zippier**; *superl* **zippiest**) enérgico, vigoroso

zircon ['zɜːkən] N circón *m*

zirconium [zɜː'kəʊnɪəm] N circonio *m*

zit* [zɪt] N grano *m*

zither ['zɪðə^r] N cítara *f*

zloty ['zlɔːtɪ] N (*pl* **zlotys** *or* **zloty**) zloty *m*

zodiac ['zəʊdɪæk] N zodíaco *m*

zodiacal [zəʊ'daɪəkəl] ADJ zodiacal, del zodíaco

zombie ['zɒmbɪ] N [1] (= *monster*) zombi *m*
[2] (*fig*) zombi *mf*

zonal ['zəʊnl] ADJ zonal

zone [zəʊn] Ⓐ N (*gen*) zona *f*; **postal ~** (*US*) zona *f* postal
Ⓑ VT dividir en *or* por zonas, distribuir en zonas
Ⓒ CPD ► **zone therapy** N reflexoterapia *f*, reflejoterapia *f*

zoning ['zəʊnɪŋ] N división *f* por zonas, distribución *f* en zonas

zonked* [zɒŋkt] ADJ (*also* **~ out**) [1] (= *exhausted*) agotado, reventado*, hecho polvo*
[2] (*on drugs*) colgado*, colocado (*Sp**); (*on drink*) como una cuba*, curda *inv* (*Sp**)

zonk out* [zɒŋk'aʊt] VI + ADV quedarse como un tronco*

zoo [zuː] N zoo *m*, zoológico *m*, jardín *m* zoológico, parque *m* zoológico

zookeeper ['zuːkiːpə^r] N guarda *mf* de jardín zoológico, guarda *mf* de parque zoológico

zoological [ˌzəʊə'lɒdʒɪkəl] ADJ zoológico; **~ gardens** = **zoo**

zoologist [zəʊ'ɒlədʒɪst] N zoólogo/a *m/f*

zoology [zəʊ'ɒlədʒɪ] N zoología *f*

zoom [zuːm] Ⓐ N [1] (= *sound*) zumbido *m*
[2] (*Phot*) (*also* **~ lens**) zoom *m*
[3] (*Aer*) (= *upward flight*) empinadura *f*
Ⓑ VI [1] [*engine*] zumbar; **it ~ed past my ear** me pasó zumbando por la oreja
[2] (= *go fast*) ir zumbando*; **he ~ed past at 120kph** pasó zumbando a 120kph*
[3] (*Aer*) empinarse
Ⓒ CPD ► **zoom lens** N (*Phot*) zoom *m*

► **zoom in** VI + ADV (*Phot, Cine*) **to ~ in (on sb/sth)** enfocar (a algn/algo) con el zoom

► **zoom out** VI + ADV (*Cine*) pasar a un plano general con el zoom

zoomorph ['zəʊəʊmɒːf] N zoomorfo *m*

zoomorphic [ˌzəʊəʊ'mɒːfɪk] ADJ zoomórfico

zoophyte ['zəʊəˌfaɪt] N zoófito *m*

zooplankton [ˌzəʊəʊ'plæŋktən] N zooplancton *m*

zoot-suit* ['zuːtsuːt] N *traje de espaldas anchas y de pantalones anchos de los años 40*

Zoroaster [ˌzɒrəʊ'æstə^r] N Zoroastro

Zoroastrianism [ˌzɒrəʊ'æstrɪənˌɪzəm] N zoroastrismo *m*

zouk [zuːk] N (*Mus*) zouk *m*

zucchini [zuː'kiːnɪ] N (*pl* **zucchini** *or* **zucchinis**) (*US*) calabacín *m*, calabacita *f* (*LAm*)

Zulu ['zuːluː] Ⓐ ADJ zulú
Ⓑ N zulú *mf*

Zululand ['zuːluːlænd] N Zululandia *f*

Zürich ['zjʊərɪk] N Zurich *f*

zygote ['zaɪgəʊt] N cigoto *m*, zigoto *m*

The Spanish Verb

Each verb entry in the Spanish-English section of the Dictionary includes a reference by number and letter to the tables below, in which the simple tenses and parts of the three conjugations and of irregular verbs are set out. For verbs having only a slight irregularity the indication of it is given in the main text of the dictionary (*eg* **escribir** ▸conjug 3a◂ (*pp* **escrito**)), and is not repeated here. Certain other verbs have been marked in the main text as *defective* and in some cases indications of usage have been given there, but for further information it is best to consult a full grammar of the language.

Certain general points may be summarized here:

The **imperfect** is regular for all verbs except *ser* (*era* etc) and *ir* (*iba* etc).

The **conditional** is formed by adding to the stem of the future tense (in most cases the infinitive) the endings of the imperfect tense of *haber*: *contaría etc.* If the stem of the future tense is irregular, the conditional will have the same irregularity: *decir – diré, diría*; *poder – podré, podría*.

Compound tenses are formed with the auxiliary *haber* and the past participle:

perfect	he cantado (*subj*: haya cantado)
pluperfect	había cantado (*subj*: hubiera cantado, hubiese cantado)
future perfect	habré cantado
conditional perfect	habría cantado
perfect infinitive	haber cantado
perfect gerund	habiendo cantado

The **imperfect subjunctives** I and II can be seen as being formed from the 3rd person plural of the preterite, using as a stem what remains after removing the final *-ron* syllable and adding to it *-ra* (I) or *-se* (II), *eg*:

cantar: canta/ron – cantara, cantase
perder: perdie/ron – perdiera, perdiese
reducir: reduje/ron – redujera, redujese

The form of the **imperative** depends not only on number but also on whether the person(s) addressed is (are) treated in familiar or in formal terms. The 'true' imperative is used only in familiar address in the affirmative:

cantar: canta (tú), cantad (vosotros)
vender: vende (tú), vended (vosotros)
partir: parte (tú), partid (vosotros)

(There are a few irregular imperatives in the singular – *salir – sal, hacer – haz*, etc, but all the plurals are regular.) The imperative affirmative in formal address requires the subjunctive: *envíemelo, háganlo, conduzca Vd con más cuidado, ¡oiga!* The imperative negative in both familiar and formal address also requires the subjunctive: *no me digas, no os preocupéis, no grite tanto Vd, no se desanimen Vds.*

Continuous tenses are formed with *estar* and the gerund: *está leyendo, estaba lloviendo, estábamos hablando de eso*. Other auxiliary verbs may occasionally replace *estar* in certain senses: *según voy viendo, va mejorando, iba cogiendo flores, lo venía estudiando desde hacía muchos años*. Usage of the continuous tenses does not exactly coincide with that of English.

The **passive** is formed with tenses of *ser* and the past participle, which agrees in number and gender with the subject: *las casas fueron construidas, será firmado mañana el tratado, después de haber sido vencido*. The passive is much less used in Spanish than in English, its function often being taken over by a reflexive construction, by *uno*, etc.

SPANISH VERB CONJUGATIONS

INFINITIVE	PRESENT INDICATIVE	PRESENT SUBJUNCTIVE	PRETERITE
[1a] **cantar** (regular: see table at end of list)			
Gerund: *cantando*			
[1b] **cambiar**	cambio	cambie	cambié
i of the stem is not stressed and the verb is regular	cambias	cambie	cambiaste
Gerund: *cambiando*	cambia	cambie	cambió
	cambiamos	cambiemos	cambiamos
	cambiáis	cambiéis	cambiasteis
	cambian	cambien	cambiaron
[1c] **enviar**	env**í**o	env**í**e	envié
i of the stem stressed in parts of the present tenses	env**í**as	env**í**es	enviaste
Gerund: *enviando*	env**í**a	env**í**e	envió
	enviamos	enviemos	enviamos
	enviáis	enviéis	enviasteis
	env**í**an	env**í**en	enviaron
[1d] **evacuar**	evacuo	evacue	evacué
u of the stem is not stressed and the verb is regular	evacuas	evacues	evacuaste
Gerund: *evacuando*	evacua	evacue	evacuó
	evacuamos	evacuemos	evacuamos
	evacuáis	evacuéis	evacuasteis
	evacuan	evacuen	evacuaron
[1e] **situar**	sit**ú**o	sit**ú**e	situé
u of the stem stressed in parts of the present tenses	sit**ú**as	sit**ú**es	situaste
Gerund: *situando*	sit**ú**a	sit**ú**e	situó
	situamos	situemos	situamos
	situáis	situéis	situasteis
	sit**ú**an	sit**ú**en	situaron
[1f] **cruzar**	cruzo	cru**c**e	cru**c**é
Stem consonant **z** written **c** before **e**	cruzas	cru**c**es	cruzaste
Gerund: *cruzando*	cruza	cru**c**e	cruzó
	cruzamos	cru**c**emos	cruzamos
	cruzáis	cru**c**éis	cruzasteis
	cruzan	cru**c**en	cruzaron
[1g] **picar**	pico	pi**qu**e	pi**qu**é
Stem consonant **c** written **qu** before **e**	picas	pi**qu**es	picaste
Gerund: *picando*	pica	pi**qu**e	picó
	picamos	pi**qu**emos	picamos
	picáis	pi**qu**éis	picasteis
	pican	pi**qu**en	picaron
[1h] **pagar**	pago	pa**gu**e	pa**gu**é
Stem consonant **g** written **gu** (with **u** silent) before **e**	pagas	pa**gu**es	pagaste
Gerund: *pagando*	paga	pa**gu**e	pagó
	pagamos	pa**gu**emos	pagamos
	pagáis	pa**gu**éis	pagasteis
	pagan	pa**gu**en	pagaron
[1i] **averiguar**	averiguo	averi**gü**e	averi**gü**é
u of the stem written **ü** (so that it is pronounced) before **e**	averiguas	averi**gü**es	averiguaste
Gerund: *averiguando*	averigua	averi**gü**e	averiguó
	averiguamos	averi**gü**emos	averiguamos
	averiguáis	averi**gü**éis	averiguasteis
	averiguan	averi**gü**en	averiguaron
[1j] **cerrar**	c**ie**rro	c**ie**rre	cerré
Stem vowel **e** becomes **ie** when stressed	c**ie**rras	c**ie**rres	cerraste
Gerund: *cerrando*	c**ie**rra	c**ie**rre	cerró
	cerramos	cerremos	cerramos
	cerráis	cerréis	cerrasteis
	c**ie**rran	c**ie**rren	cerraron

INFINITIVE	PRESENT INDICATIVE	PRESENT SUBJUNCTIVE	PRETERITE
[1k] **errar**	**ye**rro	**ye**rre	erré
As [1j], but diphthong written **ye-** at the	**ye**rras	**ye**rres	erraste
start of the word	**ye**rra	**ye**rre	erró
Gerund: *errando*	erramos	erremos	erramos
	erráis	erréis	errasteis
	yerran	**ye**rren	erraron
[1l] **contar**	c**ue**nto	c**ue**nte	conté
Stem vowel **o** becomes **ue** when stressed	c**ue**ntas	c**ue**ntes	contaste
Gerund: *contando*	c**ue**nta	c**ue**nte	contó
	contamos	contemos	contamos
	contáis	contéis	contasteis
	c**ue**ntan	c**ue**nten	contaron
[1m] **agorar**	ag**üe**ro	ag**üe**re	agoré
As [1l], but diphthong written **üe** (so that the **u** is	ag**üe**ras	ag**üe**res	agoraste
pronounced)	ag**üe**ra	ag**üe**re	agoró
Gerund: *agorando*	agoramos	agoremos	agoramos
	agoráis	agoréis	agorasteis
	ag**üe**ran	ag**üe**ren	agoraron
[1n] **jugar**	j**ue**go	j**uegu**e	ju**gu**é
Stem vowel **u** becomes **ue** when stressed; stem	j**ue**gas	j**uegu**es	jugaste
consonant **g** written **gu** (with **u** silent) before **e**	j**ue**ga	j**uegu**e	jugó
Gerund: *jugando*	jugamos	ju**gu**emos	jugamos
	jugáis	ju**gu**éis	jugasteis
	j**ue**gan	j**uegu**en	jugaron
[1o] **estar**	estoy	esté	estuve
Irregular.	estás	estés	estuviste
Imperative: *está (tú)*	está	esté	estuvo
Gerund: *estando*	estamos	estemos	estuvimos
	estáis	estéis	estuvisteis
	están	estén	estuvieron
[1p] **andar**	ando	ande	anduve
Irregular.	andas	andes	anduviste
Gerund: *andando*	anda	ande	anduvo
	andamos	andemos	anduvimos
	andáis	andéis	anduvisteis
	andan	anden	anduvieron
[1q] **dar**	doy	dé	di
Irregular.	das	des	diste
Gerund: *dando*	da	dé	dio
	damos	demos	dimos
	dais	deis	disteis
	dan	den	dieron
[2a] **temer** (regular: see table at end of list)			
[2b] **vencer**	ven**z**o	ven**z**a	vencí
Stem consonant **c** written **z** before **a** and **o**	vences	ven**z**as	venciste
Gerund: *venciendo*	vence	ven**z**a	venció
	vencemos	ven**z**amos	vencimos
	vencéis	ven**z**áis	vencisteis
	vencen	ven**z**an	vencieron
[2c] **coger**	co**j**o	co**j**a	cogí
Stem consonant **g** written **j** before **a** and **o**	coges	co**j**as	cogiste
Gerund: *cogiendo*	coge	co**j**a	cogió
	cogemos	co**j**amos	cogimos
	cogéis	co**j**áis	cogisteis
	cogen	co**j**an	cogieron
[2d] **conocer**	cono**zc**o	cono**zc**a	conocí
Stem consonant **c** becomes **zc** before **a** and **o**	conoces	cono**zc**as	conociste
Gerund: *conociendo*	conoce	cono**zc**a	conoció
	conocemos	cono**zc**amos	conocimos
	conocéis	cono**zc**áis	conocisteis
	conocen	cono**zc**an	conocieron

INFINITIVE	PRESENT INDICATIVE	PRESENT SUBJUNCTIVE	PRETERITE
[2e] **leer**	leo	lea	leí
Unstressed **i** between vowels is written **y**	lees	leas	leíste
Past Participle: *leído*	lee	lea	le**yó**
Gerund: *leyendo*	leemos	leamos	leímos
	leéis	leáis	leísteis
	leen	lean	le**y**eron
[2f] **tañer**	taño	taña	tañí
Unstressed **i** after **ñ** (and also after **ll**) is omitted	tañes	tañas	tañiste
	tañe	taña	ta**ñó**
Gerund: *tañendo*	tañemos	tañamos	tañimos
	tañéis	tañáis	tañisteis
	tañen	tañan	ta**ñ**eron
[2g] **perder**	pi**e**rdo	pi**e**rda	perdí
Stem vowel **e** becomes **ie** when stressed	pi**e**rdes	pi**e**rdas	perdiste
Gerund: *perdiendo*	pi**e**rde	pi**e**rda	perdió
	perdemos	perdamos	perdimos
	perdéis	perdáis	perdisteis
	pi**e**rden	pi**e**rdan	perdieron
[2h] **mover**	mu**e**vo	mu**e**va	moví
Stem vowel **o** becomes **ue** when stressed	mu**e**ves	mu**e**vas	moviste
Gerund: *moviendo*	mu**e**ve	mu**e**va	movió
	movemos	movamos	movimos
	movéis	mováis	movisteis
	mu**e**ven	mu**e**van	movieron
[2i] **oler**	**hue**lo	**hue**la	olí
As [2h], but diphthong is written **hue-** at the start of the word	**hue**les	**hue**las	oliste
	huele	**hue**la	olió
Gerund: *oliendo*	olemos	olamos	olimos
	oléis	oláis	olisteis
	huelen	**hue**lan	olieron
[2j] **haber** (see table at end of list)			
[2k] **tener**	tengo	tenga	tuve
Irregular.	tienes	tengas	tuviste
Future: *tendré*	tiene	tenga	tuvo
Imperative: *ten (tú)*	tenemos	tengamos	tuvimos
Gerund: *teniendo*	tenéis	tengáis	tuvisteis
	tienen	tengan	tuvieron
[2l] **caber**	quepo	quepa	cupe
Irregular.	cabes	quepas	cupiste
Future: *cabré*	cabe	quepa	cupo
Gerund: *cabiendo*	cabemos	quepamos	cupimos
	cabéis	quepáis	cupisteis
	caben	quepan	cupieron
[2m] **saber**	sé	sepa	supe
Irregular.	sabes	sepas	supiste
Future: *sabré*	sabe	sepa	supo
Gerund: *sabiendo*	sabemos	sepamos	supimos
	sabéis	sepáis	supisteis
	saben	sepan	supieron
[2n] **caer**	caigo	caiga	caí
Unstressed **i** between vowels written **y**, as [2e]	caes	caigas	caíste
Past Participle: *caído*	cae	caiga	ca**yó**
Gerund: *cayendo*	caemos	caigamos	caímos
	caéis	caigáis	caísteis
	caen	caigan	ca**y**eron
[2o] **traer**	traigo	traiga	traje
Irregular.	traes	traigas	trajiste
Past Participle: *traído*	trae	traiga	trajo
Gerund: *trayendo*	traemos	traigamos	trajimos
	traéis	traigáis	trajisteis
	traen	traigan	trajeron

INFINITIVE	PRESENT INDICATIVE	PRESENT SUBJUNCTIVE	PRETERITE
[2p] **valer**	valgo	valga	valí
Irregular.	vales	valgas	valiste
Future: *valdré*	vale	valga	valió
Gerund: *valiendo*	valemos	valgamos	valimos
	valéis	valgáis	valisteis
	valen	valgan	valieron
[2q] **poner**	pongo	ponga	puse
Irregular.	pones	pongas	pusiste
Future: *pondré*	pone	ponga	puso
Past Participle: *puesto*	ponemos	pongamos	pusimos
Imperative: *pon (tú)*	ponéis	pongáis	pusisteis
Gerund: *poniendo*	ponen	pongan	pusieron
[2r] **hacer**	hago	haga	hice
Irregular.	haces	hagas	hiciste
Future: *haré*	hace	haga	hizo
Past Participle: *hecho*	hacemos	hagamos	hicimos
Imperative: *haz (tú)*	hacéis	hagáis	hicisteis
Gerund: *haciendo*	hacen	hagan	hicieron
[2s] **poder**	puedo	pueda	pude
Irregular.	puedes	puedas	pudiste
In present tenses like [2h]	puede	pueda	pudo
Future: *podré*	podemos	podamos	pudimos
Gerund: *pudiendo*	podéis	podáis	pudisteis
	pueden	puedan	pudieron
[2t] **querer**	quiero	quiera	quise
Irregular.	quieres	quieras	quisiste
In present tenses like [2g]	quiere	quiera	quiso
Future: *querré*	queremos	queramos	quisimos
Gerund: *queriendo*	queréis	queráis	quisisteis
	quieren	quieran	quisieron
[2u] **ver**	veo	vea	vi
Irregular.	ves	veas	viste
Imperfect: *veía*	ve	vea	vio
Past Participle: *visto*	vemos	veamos	vimos
Gerund: *viendo*	veis	veáis	visteis
	ven	vean	vieron

[2v] **ser** (see table at end of list)

[2w] **placer.** Exclusively 3rd person singular. Irregular forms: Present subj. *plazca* (less commonly *plega* or *plegue*); Preterite *plació* (less commonly *plugo*); Imperfect subj. I *placiera*, II *placiese* (less commonly *plugiera*, *plugiese*).

[2x] **yacer.** Archaic. Irregular forms: Present indic. *yazco* (less commonly *yazgo* or *yago*), *yaces* etc; Present subj. *yazca* (less commonly *yazga* or *yaga*), *yazcas* etc; Imperative *yace* (*tú*) (less commonly *yaz*).

[2y] **raer.** Present indic. usually *raigo*, *raes* etc (like *caer* [2n]), but *rayo* occasionally found; Present subj. usually *raiga*, *raigas* etc (also like *caer*), but *raya*, *rayas* etc occasionally found.

[2z] **roer.** Alternative forms in present tenses: Indicative, *roo*, *roigo* or *royo*; *roes*, *roe* etc. Subjunctive, *roa*, *roiga* or *roya*. First persons usually avoided because of the uncertainty. The gerund is *royendo*.

[3a] **partir** (regular: see table at end of list)

INFINITIVE	PRESENT INDICATIVE	PRESENT SUBJUNCTIVE	PRETERITE
[3b] **esparcir**	espar**z**o	espar**z**a	esparcí
Stem consonant **c** written **z** before **a** and **o**	esparces	espar**z**as	esparciste
Gerund: *esparciendo*	esparce	espar**z**a	esparció
	esparcimos	espar**z**amos	esparcimos
	esparcís	espar**z**áis	esparcisteis
	esparcen	espar**z**an	esparcieron
[3c] **dirigir**	diri**j**o	diri**j**a	dirigí
Stem consonant **g** written **j** before **a** and **o**	diriges	diri**j**as	dirigiste
Gerund: *dirigiendo*	dirige	diri**j**a	dirigió
	dirigimos	diri**j**amos	dirigimos
	dirigís	diri**j**áis	dirigisteis
	dirigen	diri**j**an	dirigieron

INFINITIVE	PRESENT INDICATIVE	PRESENT SUBJUNCTIVE	PRETERITE
[3d] **distinguir**	distin**g**o	distin**g**a	distinguí
u after the stem consonant **g** omitted before **a** and **o**	distingues	distin**g**as	distinguiste
Gerund: *distinguendo*	distingue	distin**g**a	distinguió
	distinguimos	distin**g**amos	distinguimos
	distinguís	distin**g**áis	distinguisteis
	distinguen	distin**g**an	distinguieron
[3e] **delinquir**	delin**c**o	delin**c**a	delinquí
Stem consonant **qu** written **c** before **a** and **o**	delinques	delin**c**as	delinquiste
Gerund: *delinquiendo*	delinque	delin**c**a	delinquió
	delinquimos	delin**c**amos	delinquimos
	delinquís	delin**c**áis	delinquisteis
	delinquen	delin**c**an	delinquieron
[3f] **lucir**	lu**zc**o	lu**zc**a	lucí
Stem consonant **c** becomes **zc** before **a** and **o**	luces	lu**zc**as	luciste
Gerund: *luciendo*	luce	lu**zc**a	lució
	lucimos	lu**zc**amos	lucimos
	lucís	lu**zc**áis	lucisteis
	lucen	lu**zc**an	lucieron
[3g] **huir**	hu**y**o	hu**y**a	huí
A **y** is inserted before endings not beginning with **i**	hu**y**es	hu**y**as	huiste
Gerund: *huyendo*	hu**y**e	hu**y**a	hu**y**ó
	huimos	hu**y**amos	huimos
	huís	hu**y**áis	huisteis
	hu**y**en	hu**y**an	hu**y**eron
[3h] **gruñir**	gruño	gruña	gruñí
Unstressed **i** after **ñ** (and also after **ch** and **ll**) omitted	gruñes	gruñas	gruñiste
Gerund: *gruñendo*	gruñe	gruña	gru**ñ**ó
	gruñimos	gruñamos	gruñimos
	gruñís	gruñáis	gruñisteis
	gruñen	gruñan	gru**ñ**eron
[3i] **sentir**	s**ie**nto	s**ie**nta	sentí
The stem vowel **e** becomes **ie** when stressed; **e** becomes **i** in 3rd persons of Preterite, 1st and 2nd persons pl. of Present Subjunctive.	s**ie**ntes	s**ie**ntas	sentiste
Gerund: *sintiendo*	s**ie**nte	s**ie**nta	s**i**ntió
In *adquirir* the stem vowel **i** becomes **ie** when stressed	sentimos	sintamos	sentimos
	sentís	sintáis	sentisteis
	s**ie**nten	s**ie**ntan	s**i**ntieron
[3j] **dormir**	d**ue**rmo	d**ue**rma	dormí
The stem vowel **o** becomes **ue** when stressed; **o** becomes **u** in 3rd persons of Preterite, 1st and 2nd persons pl. of Present Subjunctive.	d**ue**rmes	d**ue**rmas	dormiste
Gerund: *durmiendo*	d**ue**rme	d**ue**rma	d**u**rmió
	dormimos	d**u**rmamos	dormimos
	dormís	d**u**rmáis	dormisteis
	d**ue**rmen	d**ue**rman	d**u**rmieron
[3k] **pedir**	p**i**do	p**i**da	pedí
The stem vowel **e** becomes **i** when stressed, and in 3rd persons of Preterite, 1st and 2nd persons pl. of Present Subjunctive.	p**i**des	p**i**das	pediste
Gerund: *pidiendo*	p**i**de	p**i**da	p**i**dió
	pedimos	p**i**damos	pedimos
	pedís	p**i**dáis	pedisteis
	p**i**den	p**i**dan	p**i**dieron
[3l] **reír**	río	ría	reí
Irregular.	ríes	rías	reíste
Past Participle: *reído*	ríe	ría	rió
Gerund: *riendo*	reímos	riamos	reímos
Imperative: *ríe (tú)*	reís	riáis	reísteis
	ríen	rían	rieron
[3m] **erguir**	yergo	yerga	erguí
Irregular.	yergues	yergas	erguiste
Gerund: *irguiendo*	yergue	yerga	irguió
Imperative: *yergue (tú)* and less commonly *irgue (tú)*	erguimos	yergamos	erguimos
	erguís	yergáis	erguisteis
	yerguen	yergan	irguieron

INFINITIVE	PRESENT INDICATIVE	PRESENT SUBJUNCTIVE	PRETERITE
[3n] **reducir**	redu**zc**o	redu**zc**a	red**uj**e
The stem consonant **c** becomes **zc** before **a** and **o**	reduces	redu**zc**as	red**uj**iste
as [3f]; irregular preterite in **-uj-**	reduce	redu**zc**a	red**uj**o
Gerund: *reduciendo*	reducimos	redu**zc**amos	red**uj**imos
	reducís	redu**zc**áis	red**uj**isteis
	reducen	redu**zc**an	red**uj**eron
[3o] **decir**	digo	diga	dije
Irregular.	dices	digas	dijiste
Future: *diré*	dice	diga	dijo
Past Participle: *dicho*	decimos	digamos	dijimos
Gerund: *diciendo*	decís	digáis	dijisteis
Imperative: *di (tú)*	dicen	digan	dijeron
[3p] **oír**	oigo	oiga	oí
Irregular.	**oy**es	oigas	oíste
Unstressed **i** between vowels becomes **y**	**oy**e	oiga	**oy**ó
Past Participle: *oído*	oímos	oigamos	oímos
Gerund: *oyendo*	oís	oigáis	oísteis
	oyen	oigan	o**y**eron
[3q] **salir**	salgo	salga	salí
Irregular.	sales	salgas	saliste
Future: *saldré*	sale	salga	salió
Imperative: *sal (tú)*	salimos	salgamos	salimos
Gerund: *saliendo*	salís	salgáis	salisteis
	salen	salgan	salieron
[3r] **venir**	vengo	venga	vine
Irregular.	vienes	vengas	viniste
Future: *vendré*	viene	venga	vino
Gerund: *viniendo*	venimos	vengamos	vinimos
Imperative: *ven (tú)*	venís	vengáis	vinisteis
	vienen	vengan	vinieron
[3s] **ir**	voy	vaya	fui
Irregular.	vas	vayas	fuiste
Imperfect: *iba*	va	vaya	fue
Gerund: *yendo*	vamos	vayamos	fuimos
Imperative: *ve (tú), id (vosotros)*	vais	vayáis	fuisteis
	van	vayan	fueron

[1a] **cantar** (regular verb)

INDICATIVE

Present
canto
cantas
canta
cantamos
cantáis
cantan

Imperfect
cantaba
cantabas
cantaba
cantábamos
cantabais
cantaban

Preterite
canté
cantaste
cantó
cantamos
cantasteis
cantaron

Future
cantaré
cantarás
cantará
cantaremos
cantaréis
cantarán

Gerund
cantando

CONDITIONAL
cantaría
cantarías
cantaría
cantaríamos
cantaríais
cantarían

Imperative
canta (tú)
cantad (vosotros)

Past Participle
cantado

SUBJUNCTIVE

Present
cante
cantes
cante
cantemos
cantéis
canten

Imperfect
cantara/-ase
cantaras/-ases
cantara/-ase
cantáramos/-ásemos
cantarais/-aseis
cantaran/-asen

[2a] **temer** (regular verb)

INDICATIVE

Present
temo
temes
teme
tememos
teméis
temen

Imperfect
temía
temías
temía
temíamos
temíais
temían

Future
temeré
temerás
temerá
temeremos
temeréis
temerán

Preterite
temí
temiste
temió
temimos
temisteis
temieron

Gerund
temiendo

CONDITIONAL
temería
temerías
temería
temeríamos
temeríais
temerían

Imperative
teme (tú)
temed (vosotros)

Past Participle
temido

SUBJUNCTIVE

Present
tema
temas
tema
temamos
temáis
teman

Imperfect
temiera/-iese
temieras/-ieses
temiera/-iese
temiéramos/-iésemos
temierais/-ieseis
temieran/-iesen

[3a] **partir** (regular verb)

INDICATIVE

Present
parto
partes
parte
partimos
partís
parten

Imperfect
partía
partías
partía
partíamos
partíais
partían

Preterite
partí
partiste
partió
partimos
partisteis
partieron

Future
partiré
partirás
partirá
partiremos
partiréis
partirán

Gerund
partiendo

CONDITIONAL
partiría
partirías
partiría
partiríamos
partiríais
partirían

Imperative
parte (tú)
partid (vosotros)

Past Participle
partido

SUBJUNCTIVE

Present
parta
partas
parta
partamos
partáis
partan

Imperfect
partiera/-iese
partieras/-ieses
partiera/-iese
partiéramos/-iésemos
partierais/-ieseis
partieran/-iesen

[2j] **haber**

INDICATIVE

Present
he
has
ha
hemos
habéis
han

Imperfect
había
habías
había
habíamos
habíais
habían

Preterite
hube
hubiste
hubo
hubimos
hubisteis
hubieron

Future
habré
habrás
habrá
habremos
habréis
habrán

Gerund
habiendo

Past Participle
habido

CONDITIONAL
habría
habrías
habría
habríamos
habríais
habrían

SUBJUNCTIVE

Present
haya
hayas
haya
hayamos
hayáis
hayan

Imperfect
hubiera/-iese
hubieras/-ieses
hubiera/-iese
hubiéramos/-iésemos
hubierais/-ieseis
hubieran/-iesen

[2v] **ser**

INDICATIVE

Present
soy
eres
es
somos
sois
son

Imperfect
era
eras
era
éramos
erais
eran

Preterite
fui
fuiste
fue
fuimos
fuisteis
fueron

Future
seré
serás
será
seremos
seréis
serán

Gerund
siendo

Past Participle
sido

CONDITIONAL
sería
serías
sería
seríamos
seríais
serían

Imperative
sé (tú)
sed (vosotros)

SUBJUNCTIVE

Present
sea
seas
sea
seamos
seáis
sean

Imperfect
fuera/-ese
fueras/-eses
fuera/-ese
fuéramos/-ésemos
fuerais/-eseis
fueran/-esen

El verbo inglés

El verbo inglés es bastante más sencillo que el español, a lo menos en cuanto a su forma. Hay muchos verbos fuertes o irregulares (damos una lista de ellos a continuación) y varias clases de irregularidad ortográfica (véanse las notas al final); pero hay una sola conjugación, y dentro de cada tiempo no hay variación para las seis personas excepto en el presente (tercera persona de singular). Por tanto, no es necesario ofrecer para el verbo inglés los cuadros y paradigmas con que se suele explicar el verbo español; la estructura general y las formas del verbo inglés se resumen en las siguientes notas.

Indicativo

(a) Presente: tiene la misma forma que el infinitivo en todas las personas menos la tercera del singular; en ésta, se añade una **-s** al infinitivo, p.ej. **he sells**, o se añade **-es** si el infinitivo termina en sibilante (los sonidos [s], [z], [ʃ] y [tʃ]; en la escritura **-ss, -zz, -sh** y **-ch**, etc). Esta **-s** añadida tiene dos pronunciaciones: tras consonante sorda se pronuncia sorda [s], p.ej. **scoffs** [skɒfs], **likes** [laɪks], **taps** [tæps], **waits** [weɪts], **baths** [bɑːθs]; tras consonante sonora se pronuncia sonora, p.ej. **robs** [rɒbz], **bends** [bendz], **seems** [siːmz], **gives** [gɪvz], **bathes** ['beɪðz]; **-es** se pronuncia también sonora tras sibilante o consonante sonora, o letra final del infinitivo, p.ej. **races** ['reɪsɪz], **urges** ['ɜːdʒɪz], **lashes** ['læʃɪz], **passes** ['pɑːsɪz].

Los verbos que terminan en **-y** la cambian en **-ies** en la tercera persona del singular, p.ej. **tries, pities, satisfies**; pero son regulares los verbos que en el infinitivo tienen una vocal delante de la **-y**, p.ej. **pray – he prays, annoy – she annoys**.

El verbo **be** es irregular en todas las personas:

I am	we are
you are	you are
he is	they are

Cuatro verbos más tienen forma irregular en la tercera persona del singular:

do – he does [dʌz]	go – he goes [gəʊz]
have – he has [hæz]	say – he says [sez]

(b) Pretérito (o **pasado simple**) **y participio de pasado:** tienen la misma forma en inglés; se forman añadiendo **-ed** al infinitivo, p.ej. **paint – I painted – painted**, o bien añadiendo **-d** a los infinitivos terminados en **-e** muda, p.ej. **bare – I bared – bared, move – I moved – moved, revise – I revised – revised.** (Para los muchos verbos irregulares, véase la lista abajo.) Esta **-d** o **-ed** se pronuncia por lo general [t]: **raced** [reɪst], **passed** [pɑːst]; pero cuando se añade a un infinitivo terminado en consonante sonora o en **r**, se pronuncia [d], p.ej. **bared** [bɛəd], **moved** [muːvd], **seemed** [siːmd], **buzzed** [bʌzd]. Si el infinitivo termina en **-d** o **-t**, la desinencia **-ed** se pronuncia como una sílaba más, [ɪd], p.ej. **raided** ['reɪdɪd], **dented** ['dentɪd]. Para los verbos cuyo infinitivo termina en **-y**, véase **Verbos débiles** (**e**) abajo.

(c) Tiempos compuestos del pasado: se forman como en español con el verbo auxiliar **to have** y el participio de pasado: perfecto **I have painted**, pluscuamperfecto **I had painted**.

(d) Futuro y condicional (o **potencial**): se forma el futuro con el auxiliar **will** o **shall** y el infinitivo, p.ej. **I will do it, they shall not pass**; se forma el condicional (o potencial) con el auxiliar **would** o **should** y el infinitivo, p.ej. **I would go, if she should come**. Como en español y de igual formación existen los tiempos compuestos llamados futuro perfecto, p.ej. **I shall have finished**, y potencial compuesto, p.ej. **I would have paid**.

(e) Para cada tiempo del indicativo existe una forma continua que se forma con el tiempo apropiado del verbo **to be** (equivalente en este caso al español **estar**) y el participio de presente (véase abajo): **I am waiting, we were hoping, they will be buying it, they would have been waiting still, I had been painting all day.** Conviene subrayar que el modo de emplear estas formas continuas no corresponde siempre al sistema español.

Subjuntivo

Este modo tiene muy poco uso en inglés. En el presente tiene la misma forma que el infinitivo en todas las personas, **(that) I go**, **(that) she go** etc. En el pasado simple el único verbo que tiene forma especial es **to be**, que es **were** en todas las personas, **(that) I were**, **(that) we were** etc. En los demás casos donde la lógica de los tiempos en español pudiera parecer exigir una forma de subjuntivo en pasado, el inglés emplea el presente, p.ej. **he had urged that we do it at once**. El subjuntivo se emplea obligatoriamente en inglés en **if I were you, if he were to do it, were I to attempt it** (el indicativo **was** es tenido por vulgar en estas frases y análogas); se encuentra también en la frase fosilizada **so be it,** y en el lenguaje oficial de las actas, etc, p.ej. **it is agreed that nothing be done, it was resolved that the pier be painted** (pero son igualmente correctos **should be done, should be painted**).

Gerundio y participio de presente

Tienen la misma forma en inglés; se añade al infinitivo la desinencia **-ing**, p.ej. **washing, sending, passing**. Para las muchas irregularidades ortográficas de esta desinencia, véase la sección **Verbos débiles** abajo.

Voz pasiva

Se forma exactamente como en español, con el tiempo apropiado del verbo **to be** (equivalente en este caso a **ser**) y el participio de pasado: **we are forced to, he was killed, they had been injured, the company will be taken over, it ought to have been rebuilt, were it to be agreed**.

Imperativo

Hay solamente una forma, que es la del infinitivo: **tell me, come here, don't do that**.

VERBOS FUERTES (O IRREGULARES)

INFINITIVO	PRETÉRITO	PARTICIPIO DE PASADO
abide	abode *or* abided	abode *or* abided
arise	arose	arisen
awake	awoke *or* awaked	awoken *or* awaked
be	was, were	been
bear	bore	(*llevado*) borne, (*nacido*) born
beat	beat	beaten
become	became	become
beget	begot, (††) begat	begotten
begin	began	begun
bend	bent	bent
beseech	besought	besought
bet	bet *or* betted	bet *or* betted
bid (*ordenar*)	bade	bidden
(*licitar* etc)	bid	bid
bind	bound	bound
bite	bit	bitten
bleed	bled	bled
blow	blew	blown
break	broke	broken
breed	bred	bred
bring	brought	brought
build	built	built
burn	burned *or* burnt	burned *or* burnt
burst	burst	burst
buy	bought	bought
can	could	–
cast	cast	cast
catch	caught	caught
choose	chose	chosen
cleave[1] (*vt*)	clove *or* cleft	cloven *or* cleft
cleave[2] (*vi*)	cleaved, (††) clave	cleaved
cling	clung	clung
come	came	come
cost (*vt*)	costed	costed
(*vi*)	cost	cost
creep	crept	crept
cut	cut	cut
deal	dealt	dealt
dig	dug	dug
do	did	done
draw	drew	drawn
dream	dreamed *or* dreamt	dreamed *or* dreamt
drink	drank	drunk
drive	drove	driven
dwell	dwelt	dwelt
eat	ate	eaten
fall	fell	fallen
feed	fed	fed
feel	felt	felt
fight	fought	fought
find	found	found
flee	fled	fled
fling	flung	flung
fly	flew	flown
forbid	forbad(e)	forbidden
forget	forgot	forgotten
forsake	forsook	forsaken
freeze	froze	frozen
get	got	got, (*US*) gotten
gild	gilded	gilded *or* gilt
gird	girded *or* girt	girded *or* girt
give	gave	given
go	went	gone
grind	ground	ground
grow	grew	grown
hang	hung, (*Law*) hanged	hung, (*Law*) hanged
have	had	had
hear	heard	heard
heave	heaved, (*Naut*) hove	heaved, (*Naut*)hove
hew	hewed	hewed *or* hewn
hide	hid	hidden
hit	hit	hit
hold	held	held
hurt	hurt	hurt
keep	kept	kept
kneel	knelt	knelt
know	knew	known
lade	laded	laden
lay	laid	laid
lead	led	led
lean	leaned *or* leant	leaned *or* leant
leap	leaped *or* leapt	leaped *or* leapt
learn	learned *or* learnt	learned *or* learnt
leave	left	left
lend	lent	lent
let	let	let
lie	lay	lain
light	lit *or* lighted	lit *or* lighted
lose	lost	lost
make	made	made
may	might	–
mean	meant	meant
meet	met	met
mow	mowed	mown *or* mowed
pay	paid	paid
put	put	put
quit	quit *or* quitted	quit *or* quitted
read [ri:d]	read [red]	read [red]
rend	rent	rent
rid	rid	rid
ride	rode	ridden
ring	rang	rung
rise	rose	risen
run	ran	run
saw	sawed	sawed *or* sawn
say	said	said
see	saw	seen
seek	sought	sought
sell	sold	sold
send	sent	sent
set	set	set
sew	sewed	sewn
shake	shook	shaken
shave	shaved	shaved *or* shaven
shear	sheared	sheared *or* shorn
shed	shed	shed
shine	shone	shone
shoe	shod	shod
shoot	shot	shot
show	showed	shown *or* showed
shrink	shrank	shrunk
shut	shut	shut
sing	sang	sung
sink	sank	sunk
sit	sat	sat
slay	slew	slain
sleep	slept	slept

INFINITIVO	PRETÉRITO	PARTICIPIO DE PASADO	INFINITIVO	PRETÉRITO	PARTICIPIO DE PASADO
slide	slid	slid	**stride**	strode	stridden
sling	slung	slung	**strike**	struck	struck
slink	slunk	slunk	**string**	strung	strung
slit	slit	slit	**strive**	strove	striven
smell	smelled *or* smelt	smelled *or* smelt	**swear**	swore	sworn
smite	smote	smitten	**sweep**	swept	swept
sow	sowed	sowed *or* sown	**swell**	swelled	swollen
speak	spoke	spoken	**swim**	swam	swum
speed (*vt*)	speeded	speeded	**swing**	swung	swung
(*vi*)	sped	sped	**take**	took	taken
spell	spelled *or* spelt	spelled *or* spelt	**teach**	taught	taught
spend	spent	spent	**tear**	tore	torn
spill	spilled *or* spilt	spilled *or* spilt	**tell**	told	told
spin	spun, (††) span	spun	**think**	thought	thought
spit	spat	spat	**thrive**	throve *or* thrived	thriven *or* thrived
split	split	split	**throw**	threw	thrown
spoil	spoiled *or* spoilt	spoiled *or* spoilt	**thrust**	thrust	thrust
spread	spread	spread	**tread**	trod	trodden
spring	sprang	sprung	**wake**	woke *or* waked	woken *or* waked
stand	stood	stood	**wear**	wore	worn
stave	stove *or* staved	stove *or* staved	**weave**	wove	woven
steal	stole	stolen	**weep**	wept	wept
stick	stuck	stuck	**win**	won	won
sting	stung	stung	**wind**	wound	wound
stink	stank	stunk	**wring**	wrung	wrung
strew	strewed	strewed *or* strewn	**write**	wrote	written

N.B. No constan en esta lista los verbos compuestos con prefijo etc; para ellos véase el verbo básico, p.ej. para **forbear** véase **bear**, para **understand** véase **stand**.

VERBOS DÉBILES CON IRREGULARIDAD ORTOGRÁFICA

(a) Hay muchos verbos cuya ortografía varía ligeramente en el participio de pasado y en el gerundio. Son los que terminan en consonante simple precedida de vocal simple acentuada; antes de añadirles la desinencia **-ed** o **-ing**, se dobla la consonante:

Infinitivo	*Participio de pasado*	*Gerundio*
sob	sobbed	sobbing
wed	wedded	wedding
lag	lagged	lagging
control	controlled	controlling
dim	dimmed	dimming
tan	tanned	tanning
tap	tapped	tapping
prefer	preferred	preferring
pat	patted	patting

(pero **cook-cooked-cooking**, **fear-feared-fearing**, **roar-roared-roaring**, donde la vocal no es simple y por tanto no se dobla la consonante).

(b) Los verbos que terminan en **-c** la cambian en **-ck** al añadirse las desinencias **-ed**, **-ing**:

frolic	frolicked	frolicking
traffic	trafficked	trafficking

(c) Los verbos terminados en **-l**, **-p**, aunque precedida de vocal átona, tienen doblada la consonante en el participio de pasado y en el gerundio en el inglés británico, pero simple en el de Estados Unidos:

grovel	*(Brit)* grovelled *(US)* groveled	*(Brit)* grovelling *(US)* groveling
travel	*(Brit)* travelled *(US)* traveled	*(Brit)* travelling *(US)* traveling
worship	*(Brit)* worshipped *(US)* worshiped	*(Brit)* worshipping *(US)* worshiping

Nota – existe la misma diferencia en los sustantivos formados sobre tales verbos: *(Brit)* traveller = *(US)* traveler, *(Brit)* worshipper = *(US)* worshiper.

(d) Si el verbo termina en **-e** muda, se suprime ésta al añadir las desinencias **-ed**, **-ing**:

rake	raked	raking
care	cared	caring
smile	smiled	smiling
move	moved	moving
invite	invited	inviting

(Pero se conserva esta **-e** muda delante de **-ing** en los verbos **dye**, **singe** y otros, y en los pocos que terminan en **-oe**: **dyeing**, **singeing**, **hoeing**.)

(e) Si el verbo termina en **-y** (con las dos pronunciaciones de [ɪ] y [aɪ]) se cambia ésta en **-ied** (con las pronunciaciones respectivas de [ɪd] y [aɪd]) para formar el pretérito y el participio de pasado: **worry-worried-worried**; **pity-pitied-pitied**; **falsify-falsified-falsified**; **try-tried-tried**. El gerundio de tales verbos es regular: **worrying**, **trying** etc. Pero el gerundio de los verbos monosílabos **die**, **lie**, **vie** se escribe **dying**, **lying**, **vying**.

Aspects of Word Formation in Spanish

Processes of word formation in Spanish are in some respects far richer and more complex than those of English, and users of the dictionary may find the following notes of interest as guides which both draw together and extend information conveyed in the main alphabetic list.

1 Prefixes and prefixed elements

These very largely correspond to those of English when drawn, as so many are, from the common Graeco-Latin stock: **contra-**, **des-**, **dis-**, **ex-**, **hiper-**, **hipo-**, **para-**, **re-**, **ultra-** and so on, with **auto-** representing both English **auto-** and **self-**. There is normally total correspondence also in the immense range of scientific elements, allowance being made for phonetic and orthographic adjustments such as **lympho-/linfo-**. Elements may build up in blinding-with-science advertisements such as that for **electrofisiohidroterapias**. There are a few traditional Spanish intensifying prefixes which have no corresponding English forms: see **re-**, **requete-**, **recontra-**, also **archi-** which is much more used than **arch-** in English. These may be combined for exceptional emphasis: **archirrequetedicho** 'oft-repeated'.

2 Formation by suffix

(a) In both languages many suffixes of Latin origin correspond perfectly and will not be discussed here: **-al/-al**, **-ific(al)/-ífico**, **-ity/-idad**, **-ous/-oso**, **-tion/-ción**, and others. It is probable but not wholly predictable that in both languages on any one base the full range of forms can be built: for example **-izar**, **-izado**, **-izante**, **-izaje**, **-ización**, **-izacionar**, **-izacionismo**, though Spanish with its greater degree of latinity may much exceed English in this regard (**tecnocratizarse** 'to become technocratic'; 'to become dominated by technocrats'; **desgubernamentalización**, **destrascendentalización**). See further remarks below on **-able**, **-abilidad**.

(b) For other suffixes, hundreds of items have been listed in the main body of the dictionary because they are sufficiently common to warrant this. They are of two types. In the first group are those words which have become fully 'lexicalized' and need separate treatment, such as **lentillas**, **mesilla**, **mujerzuela**, **palabrota**, **plazoleta**. In the second group, an occasional series has been included in the main dictionary as an illustration of the process here under discussion: see for example **amigacho-amigazo-amiguete-amigote-amiguito**. In any case, the notion of what may be considered 'lexicalized' is very unsure.

(c) Identification of the base word is easy in most cases. Normally, but far from always, the suffixed form retains the gender of the original noun. Certain changes of what is or becomes with suffix a medial consonant need to be borne in mind: **lazo-lacito**, **voz-vocecita**, **barco-barquito**, **loco-loquillo**. Sometimes two or even more suffixes are built on a base: **facilonería** consists of **fácil** + **-ón** + **-ería**, **hombrachón** consists of **hombre** + **-acho** + **-ón**, **tristoncete** consists of **triste** + **-ón** + **ete**, **gentucilla** consists of **gente** + **-uza** + **-illa**, while real complexities are offered by **es una marisabidilla** and **hay peces pero son chiquititecillos**. The need for a compounding consonant is seen in some formations: **hombre** will not make ***hombrito** or ***hombrillo**, but **hombrecito**, **hombrecillo**.

(d) Nearly all the suffixes to be listed below are nouns and adjectives. There is little one can say about the formation of verbs except to note that it is less free than in English (in which one can all too readily say 'the troops will be helicoptered in', 'the match was weathered off', 'please have this text word-processed and the data accessed'). New verbs almost always belong to the first **-ar** conjugation (including **-ear**, **-ificar**, **-izar**) and may themselves be built on noun or adjectival suffixes or related to them (eg **mariconear** supposing noun suffix **-eo**).

(e) Few adverbs are listed below; they are readily formed in the standard way from the feminine form of the adjective + **-mente**. Speakers and writers of Spanish in ordinary colloquial registers tend to avoid these forms (this does not refer to such ordinary forms as eg **rápidamente**), preferring less pretentious circumlocutions ('de una manera ...', etc), but the **-mente** forms appear powerfully in literary and journalistic writing and are often much more expressive than the English adverbial form in **-ly**. Thus we find **obrar maquiavélicamente** 'to act in a Machiavellian fashion', **pintar goyescamente** 'to paint in the manner of Goya', **una fruta gustativamente superior** 'a fruit which is superior in terms of flavour', **generacionalmente hablando** 'speaking in terms of generations', **solicitar improrrogablemente** 'apply with no possible extension of the deadline', **una republiquilla organizada mafiosamente** 'a potty republic organized on Mafia lines', and even as an imaginative nonce-word **huyó gacelamente** 'she fled with the grace of a gazelle' (there being no base adjective ***gacelo**).

(f) The usage discussed below is that of Spain. Latin-American Spanish offers notable differences from this: some suffixes of Spain are hardly used in Latin America, while **-ito** is used far more and often without any perceptible diminutive or emotive function (eg **Con permiso** 'May I come in?' in Spain may be **Con permisito** in Venezuela). See eg **ahorita**, **lueguito**.

(g) While some of the suffixes listed below present no semantic problem, being wholly objective or neutral (when designating largeness or smallness), some of these and many others may carry an emotive charge (intensifying, belittling, self-deprecatory, ironical, admiring ...) for the speaker or writer and this is often a subtle one. It follows that to give an English translation or even an impression in a few words is difficult: the reader should try to form his own sense by inspecting a wide range of examples of the same suffix, including some which are cross-referenced to the main dictionary. The expressive wealth of formation by suffix can be illustrated by the following collection of forms all based on **rojo** in its political sense and gathered from the press in recent years: **rojamen**, **rojazo**, **rojeras**, **rojería**, **rojerío**, **rojete**, **rojillo**, **rojismo**, **rojista**, **rojoide**.

-able, -abilidad (*also* -ible, -ibilidad)

This suffix often expresses more than the corresponding English **-able**, **-ability** (or English does not tolerate the corresponding forms). Examples are **idolatrable** 'that can be idolatrized', **improrrogable** 'that cannot be extended', **jubilable** 'of pensionable age'. The latinate nature of Spanish permits such formations as **inasequibilidad**, **inconsultabilidad**, **la indescarrilabilidad del nuevo tren**.

-acho, -acha

Pejorative noun suffix: **vulgacho** 'the common herd'. Compare in the dictionary **hombracho**, **populacho**, **ricacho**.

-aco, -aca

Pejorative noun suffix: **hombraco** 'contemptible fellow, horrible chap', **tiparraco** 'odious individual, creep'. Compare in the dictionary **libraco**, **pajarraco**.

-ada

(i) A noun suffix expressing 'an act by or typical of': **carlistada** 'Carlist uprising', **payasada** 'clownish trick'; compare in the dictionary **bobada**, **perrada**, **puñalada**.

(ii) A noun suffix implying some notion of collectivity, as in **extranjerada** 'group of foreigners', **parrafada** 'good long chat', and compare in the dictionary **camada**, **hornada**, **indiada**, **muslada**. Beyond these one finds also an intensifying function, as in **gozada**, **liada**, **riada**, with which perhaps belong **panzada**, **tripada** 'bellyful'.

-ado, -aje

These noun suffixes of similar function are enjoying some popularity at the moment in new formations which express a process (often rendered by English **-ing**): **blanqueado** and **lavado (del dinero)** 'laundering (of money)', **lastrado** 'ballasting', **clonaje** 'cloning', **reciclaje** 'recycling'. A particular function of **-ado** is to express a collectivity, in English 'the body of...': see in the dictionary **alumnado**, **campesinado**, **estudiantado**, **profesorado**.

-ajo, -aja

Strongly pejorative noun suffix: **muñecajo** 'rotten old doll', **papelajo** 'dirty old bit of paper'; see further in the dictionary **pintarrajo**. Among adjectives one finds **pequeñajo** 'wretchedly small'.

-amen

A humorous augmentative: **barrigamen** 'grossly fat belly',

labiamen 'great red gash of a made-up mouth', **papelamen** 'lots of paper'. Compare in the dictionary **caderamen**, **culamen**, **tetamen**, whose tone is warmly appreciative.

-ante

A neutral adjectival suffix which generally corresponds to English **-ing**. Self-explanatory are eg **destripante**, **gimoteante**, **lastrante**, **masificante**, **mistificante**, **mitificante**: less transparent are the **crónicas masacrantes** 'vicious reports' which a journalist wrote about an event. Compare in the dictionary **golfante**, **hilarante**, **pimpante**, **preocupante**, and see also **-izante**.

-ata

See in the dictionary the group **bocata**, **drogata**, **fumata**, **tocata**, colloquial variations created by young people.

-azo, **-aza**

(i) Augmentative of more or less neutral tone: **animalazo** 'huge creature, whacking great brute', **generalazo** 'important general', **golpazo** 'heavy blow'.

(ii) Augmentative of favourable tone: **golazo** 'great goal', **morenazo** 'man with dark good looks'; 'man with a lovely tan', **talentazo** 'immense talent'.

(iii) Augmentative of unfavourable tone: **cochinaza** 'dirty sow of a woman', **locaza** 'outrageous old queen', **melenaza** 'great mop of long hair'.

(iv) The suffix may signify 'a blow with ...': **ladrillazo** 'blow with a brick', **misilazo** 'missile strike'; compare in the dictionary **aldabonazo**, **codazo**, etc.

(v) The suffix may signify 'a sound made with ...': **cornetazo** 'bugle-call, blast on the bugle'; compare in the dictionary **telefonazo** and (with probable sounds) **frenazo**.

(vi) The (attempted) blow may be a military one, a coup or attack: in the past a **gibraltarazo** may have been contemplated, and there was certainly a **malvinazo**. See in the dictionary **cuartelazo**, **decretazo**, **tejerazo**.

-e

This is increasingly used as a noun suffix to refer to a process: **manduque** 'eating', **tueste** 'roasting' (of coffee). Compare in the dictionary **cuelgue**, **derrame**, **desfase**, **desmadre**.

-ejo, **-eja**

Mostly a pejorative suffix: **discursejo** 'rotten speech', **grupejo** 'insignificant little group', **nos costó un milloncejo** 'it cost us all of a million', **todo por unas cuantas pesetejas** 'all for a few measly pesetas'. See in the dictionary **animalejo**, **caballejo**, **palabreja**. Sometimes the sense is simply diminutive, eg **gracejo**, **rinconcejo**.

-eo

This like **-e** refers to a process or continuing act, and is much commoner: **guitarreo** 'strumming on the guitar', **ligoteo** 'chatting-up', **mariposeo** 'flirting', **marisqueo** 'gathering shellfish'. See in the dictionary **cachondeo**, **gimoteo**, **musiqueo**, **papeleo**.

-eras

A strongly intensifying masculine singular suffix: **guarreras** 'filthy person', **macheras** 'over-the-top macho man'. Compare **boceras**, **golferas**, **guaperas**.

-ería

Among a very wide variety of applications of this common suffix one may distinguish a general notion of quality inherent in the base noun or adjective: **marchosería**, **matonería**, **mitinería**, **milagrería**, **pelmacería** (compare in the dictionary **chiquillería**, **nadería**, **patriotería**, **tontería**). The suffix may also indicate 'place where', as in **floristería**, **frutería**; a recent invention is **bocatería** 'sandwich bar'.

-ero

The wide application of this mainly adjectival suffix may be gauged from eg **cafetero**, **carero**, **faldero**, **futbolero**, **patriotero**, **pesetero** in the dictionary. A **barco atunero/bacaladero/camaronero/marisquero** will fish for tunny, cod, shrimps, and shellfish respectively.

-esco

English **-esque** is only a pale equivalent of this adjectival suffix. Self-explanatory are **chaplinesco**, **tarzanesco**, and in the dictionary **goyesco**, **mitinesco**, **oficinesco**.

-ete, **-eta**

Mildly diminutive noun and adjectival suffix: **alegrete** 'a bit merry', **guapete** 'quite handsome'; **unos duretes** 'a few measly pesetas', **tartaleta** 'small cake'. Compare in the dictionary **galancete**, **palacete**, **pobrete**.

-ez

A noun suffix which can often be translated by the English abstract **-ness**: **grisez**, **majez**, **menudez**, **modernez**, **muchachez**, and in the dictionary eg **gelidez**, **morenez**, **testarudez**.

-iano

A common adjectival suffix which English **-ian** might but usually cannot represent when attached to personal names: not only, in the dictionary, native **calderoniano**, **galdosiano**, **lorquiano**, but also **galbraithiano**, **goethiano**, **grouchiano**, **joyciano** (and **joyceano**), **una novela lampedusiana**. Some forms may puzzle foreign learners: eg **la poesía juanramoniana** refers to the work of the Spanish poet Juan Ramón Jiménez.

-ico, **-ica**

As an adjective, this is a regional (Aragon and Navarre, Granada, Murcia) variant of **-ito**: **me duele un tantico**, **¿te han dejado solico?** As a noun it is a contemptuous diminutive: **cobardica**, **llorica**, **miedica**, **mierdica**, **sólo me pidió medio milloncico**. Compare in the dictionary **acusica**, **roñica**.

-il

An adjectival suffix which is not specially pejorative but conveys a mildly ironical tone. Senses are transparent: **caciquil**, **curanderil**, **una dieta garbancil**, **machil** 'a bit too macho', **ministeril**, **ratonil**. Very expressive are **urraquil**, which depends on the word **urraca**, 'magpie', with its thievish propensities, and **sus encantos cleopatriles** 'her femme fatale (-like) charms'.

-illo, **-illa**

A noun and adjectival suffix, gently diminutive and often implying a degree of good-humoured condescension. For adjectives, consider **un vino ligerillo** 'a pleasantly light wine', **es dificilillo** 'it's a wee bit tricky'. For nouns, **un lugarcillo** 'a nice little place', **jefecillo** 'local boss, petty boss', **jequecillo** 'petty sheik', **un olorcillo a corrupción** 'a slight smell of corruption'. More plainly pejorative are **empleadillo**, **ministrillo**, **personajillo**.

-ín, **-ina**

A mildly approving suffix for nouns and adjectives, quite widely used but specially attached to Asturias and Granada: **guapín**, **guapina**, **jovencina**, **monín**, **pequeñín; cafetín** is in part demeaning but also affectionate, and **tontín** to a child will not cause alarm.

-ísimo

This suffix is not one of the degrees of comparison but implies 'very' with various nuances:

(i) 'Very', neutral in tone: **un asunto importantísimo** 'a very important matter, a most important matter'; **una cuestión discutidísima** 'a highly controversial question'; **un desarrolladísimo sentido de orgullo** 'a very highly developed sense of pride'; **es dificilísimo** 'it is extremely difficult'.

(ii) More emotionally: **es simpatiquísimo** 'he's terribly nice, he's awfully kind'; **es guapísima** 'she really is pretty'.

(iii) Exaggerating somewhat in order to impress: **un libro grandísimo** 'an enormous great book, a megatome'; **una comida costosísima**. There may be humour or irony, depending on context: **la superfinísima actriz**, **esta cursilísima costumbre**.

(iv) Passionately patriotic: **aquel españolísimo plato** 'that most Spanish of all dishes'; **la madrileñísima plaza de Santa Ana** 'St Anne's Square which is so (endearingly) typical of Madrid'.

(v) Exceptionally, one finds this suffix attached to a noun: **aquí ella es la jefísima** 'she's the only real boss round here'.

(vi) Adverbs may be formed in the usual way on some of these forms, eg **brillantísimamente**, **riquísimamente**.

-ismo

In hundreds of simple cases, Spanish words in **-ismo** naturally correspond to English **-ism**. But Spanish uses the suffix much more and in creations which English has to express in a circumlocutory way: while **japonesismo** might just be 'Japanese-ness', and **ilegalismo** is hardly more than **ilegalidad** 'illegality', **el guitarrismo moderno** has to be 'modern guitar-playing' and **gorilismo** 'rule by bully-boys'. **El felipismo** sums up criticism of the former Spanish Prime Minister Felipe González.

Real complications start with such examples as **gaudinismo** 'style and practices of the architect Gaudí', **gubernamentalismo** 'government interventionism, tendency for the government to intervene in everything', **el paragüismo de los gallegos** 'devotion of the Galicians to their umbrellas' and in America **quemimportismo** 'couldn't-care-less attitude'.

-ista

This forms nouns of common gender and adjectives also. Simple cases such as **comunista** again correspond precisely to English, but many do not: an **independentista** supports an independence movement, that is **un movimiento independentista**; a **madridista** is a supporter of Real Madrid football club, and many Spanish teams acquire similarly-designated supporters; a **plusmarquista** is a record-holder and a **mariposista** specializes in the butterfly stroke. Compare in the dictionary **congresista**, **juerguista**, **ordenancista**.

-itis

A few formations on this adopt the suffix of eg **bronquitis** and humorously imply a medical condition: **barriguitis** 'tendency to get a paunch, paunchiness', **concursitis** 'obsessive wish to enter competitions', **empatitis** 'tendency to draw games', **mudancitis** 'disease which leads one to move house perpetually'. See in the dictionary **gandulitis**, **holgazanitis**.

-ito, -ita

This suffix is the commonest of all. One can discern at least three categories:

(i) The purely diminutive: **Juanito** 'Johnny', **su hijito** 'her small son, her baby', **es más bien bajita** 'she's rather on the short side'. Among adverbs one finds **salimos tempranito**, **pues hazlo prontito**.

(ii) Diminutive with added affective (usually kindly) nuance: **jugosito** 'nice and juicy', **limpito** 'clean as a new pin', **un golito** 'a nice little goal', **iban cogiditos de la mano**, **¡pobrecito!** 'poor old chap!', 'poor little fellow!', etc. One may be self-deprecating: **te traigo un regalito**, **ofrecemos una fiestecita en casa**, or one may need to apologize for troubling others: **¿me echas una firmita aquí?** 'could you please sign here?' To small children it is natural to say **hay que ser educaditos** 'we must be on our best behaviour'.

(iii) Other uses express a kind of superlative: **ahora mismito** 'this very instant', **estaba solito** 'he was all on his own', **están calentitos** 'they're piping hot', **lo mejorcito que haya** 'the very best there is'.

-izante

This adjectival and noun suffix may correspond to English **-izing**, as in **medida liberalizante**, **tendencia modernizante**, but sometimes goes beyond this: **idiotizante** 'stupefying', **colores mimetizantes**, **hormona masculinizante**. Compare **teorizante** and others in the dictionary.

-izo

This adjectival suffix expresses the 'quality' of the base word: see in the dictionary eg **acomodadizo**, **huidizo**, **quebradizo**, **rollizo**.

-ocracia

Spanish **meritocracia** = English 'meritocracy', but Spanish seems to have a greater capacity for rather bitterly humorous formations with this suffix: **dedocracia**, **falocracia**, **yernocracia**.

-oide

This adjectival and noun suffix implies 'somewhat, rather', and is always pejorative: **extranjeroide** 'somewhat foreign', **liberaloide** 'pseudo-liberal', **estas tramas fascistoides** 'these quasi-fascist schemes'.

-ón, -ona

This very frequent noun and adjectival suffix has several differing connotations:

(i) purely augmentative: **muchachón**, **generalón** 'really important general', **pistolón**, **liberalón**, **lingotón** 'big shot of whisky' (etc); among adjectives, **grandón** 'tall and solidly built', **gastón** 'free-spending', **docilón** 'extremely placid'.

(ii) augmentative with a strongly approving tone: **mimosón**, **simpaticón**, **guapetón**

(iii) augmentative with unpleasant or strongly ironic nuances: **facilón** 'trite', **pegarse un madrugón** 'to get up at the crack of dawn', **hombrón** 'hulking great brute', **milagrón** 'great miracle', **movidón** (see **movida** in the dictionary).

-osis

Like **-itis**, this is for jocular formations which echo the common suffix of medical terms: **ligosis** 'obsessive womanizing'.

-ote, -ota

An adjectival and noun augmentative, with varying nuances. Among adjectives, **gordote**, **guapote**, **liberalote**, **mansote** (of a bull) carry little extra charge, as is the case also with nouns **drogota**, **muchachote**, **pasota**. Stronger feelings emerge with **presumidote** 'impossibly vain', **militarote** 'overblown braggart soldier'. One man who stole a glance at an attractive girl took a longer look, explaining that his **miradita** became a **miradota**.

-ucho, -ucha

Much like **-uco**, **-uca**, and commoner: **debilucho** 'weakish', **delicaducho** 'rather delicate', **delgaducho** 'terribly thin, scrawny', **morenucho** 'extremely swarthy'; a **hotelucho** would be classed as minus two stars. See in the dictionary **cuartucho**, **novelucha**.

-uco, -uca

This is a diminutive suffix, not common except perhaps in Santander province (**niñuco** 'very small boy'), and more especially a pejorative one: **frailuco** 'contemptible little priest', **mujeruca** 'very odd little woman'.

-udo, -uda

This adjectival suffix expresses the notion of 'possessing (the base quality) in abundance': **mostachudo**, **patilludo**, **talentudo; una caligrafía garrapatuda** 'nasty scrawled writing'. Compare in the dictionary **concienzudo**, **huesudo**, **linajudo**, **melenudo**, **suertudo**.

-uelo, -uela

A diminutive and sometimes affectionate suffix: **gordezuelo**, **pequeñuelo**, **muchachuelo**, **tontuela**.

-ujo, -uja

A strongly pejorative suffix for adjective and noun: **papelujo** 'wretched bit of paper'; **estrechujo**, **pequeñujo**.

-uzo, -uza

A very strongly pejorative suffix for adjective and noun: **marranuzo** 'filthy, stinking'; **carnuza** 'rotten awful meat'.

3 Designations of women in the professions etc.

(a) In recent decades the entry of women into many professions previously more or less closed to them has caused developments and problems for Spanish with its consistent gender-marking of nouns (in contrast to English with its very restricted perception of gender in such usages as 'she will dock tomorrow' and 'she's been a very good car', together, naturally, with the full range of biological pairs 'fox/vixen', 'bull/cow' and so on). What follows is an attempt to outline aspects of usage and problems in Spanish, without recommendations which it would be perilous to offer in a time of rapid change. Alternative possibilities have been offered in many entries in the main text of the dictionary. The remarks relate to Peninsular Spanish; usage in Latin America, especially in countries with strongly conservative social structures, is very varied and often different from that of Spain.

(b) There is generally no problem about the morphology (forms) of the feminine. A noun whose masculine ends in **-o** has a feminine in **-a: la médica**, **la ministra**, **la bióloga**, **la**

bioquímica. The same is true of **-or** and **-ora**: **la instructora**, **la lectora**, **la embajadora**, **la conductora**, and of other pairs such as **alcalde/alcaldesa**, **coronel/coronela**, **capitán/capitana**, **presidente/presidenta**, **jefe/jefa**, while all nouns in **-ista** are of common gender anyway: **el/la periodista** etc. (note however the special case of **el modisto**). There is doubt as between **la juez** and **la jueza**.

(c) Usage, however, often invalidates any automatic application of forms mentioned above. On the one hand, some women in the professions may feel that they have attained full status and equality with men colleagues only when the established standard word is applied to them: one may expect **la abogada** and this will often be correct, but sometimes a woman prefers to be **la médico** and equally **la arquitecto**, **la dramaturgo**.

As the presence of women increases in posts originally held only by men, the feminine form seems to take over the masculine when applied to women, becoming more acceptable and widely used.

(d) There is a special problem when a feminine form already exists in a pejorative sense which may for a time preclude, for some speakers and writers, its use about a woman with a newly-attained professional or other status: such words as **jefa** and **socia** are concerned here. It was noticed that the woman circulation manager of a Spanish newspaper sent out subscription forms for some years signing her name over the words **Jefe de Márketing** and then changing the first to **Jefa**. The women members of a society will more likely be **las miembros** but one notes a tendency for them to be **las socias**, showing that the old pejorative sense is no longer a bar to this. There is also a group of words for sciences whose existence may in some contexts cause doubt: because **la física** is 'physics' there may be uncertainty about whether a woman physicist should be **una física** or **una físico**. A few special cases cause difficulties of other kinds: since **la policía** is established as 'the police force', it is not readily applicable to a policewoman in case confusion should arise, and informants specify that while they will refer to **una policía** 'a policewoman' and **unas policías** 'several policewomen', they would avoid such usage with the definite article and say **la mujer policía** 'the policewoman' or possibly take refuge in the safely bi-gender **la agente**. If there is doubt a woman should naturally be asked which designation she herself prefers.

(e) In the category of military and similar ranks older senses have been relegated as archaisms: **la coronela** was 'the colonel's lady' but is now '(woman) colonel', **la embajadora** is not 'the ambassador's wife' but '(woman) ambassador', and **la alcaldesa** is '(woman) mayor'. A woman minister in a nonconformist church may safely be called **la pastora**, but it is wholly unsure by what term women priests in the Anglican Church are or will be known.

4 Attributive use of nouns

(a) Examples of such formations as **el patrón oro** go back to the 17th century, but remained rare until recent times when there has been an explosion of the attributive use of nouns (defined as the use of a noun in a qualifying or adjectival function but without concord of number or gender). Much of this is owed to the influence of English, but some formations now go well beyond any possible pattern existing in English. **Buque fantasma** translates English 'ghost ship' and **gobierno fantasma** was once formed as a calque on English 'shadow cabinet', but the usage then develops a momentum of its own in Spanish and we find **empresa fantasma**, **gol fantasma** and other expressive formations.

(b) Well-established usages are covered in many cases by entries in the dictionary. Such are **acuerdo marco**, **cuestión clave**, **cárcel modelo**, **emisión pirata**, **fecha límite**, **niño prodigio**, **país satélite**, **peso pluma**, **piso piloto**, **programa coloquio**, **reunión cumbre**. There is a range of attributives which may go with eg **efecto**: **efecto boomerang/dominó/embudo/escoba/invernadero**. Formations such as **faros antiniebla**, **manifestaciones antihuelga**, **medidas antipolución** are now standard, as are many others in the domains of fashion (**falda pantalón**, **falda tubo**) and cuisine, etc. These correspond closely to English models. Statements about colour in attributive form are also standard usage, eg **un vestido color lila**, **uniformes verde oliva**, **cortinas verde oscuro** (but naturally **cortinas verdes** with concord). The same is true of phrases with **modelo**, **tipo**, and similar words: **un coche modelo Tiburón 1500**, **aviones tipo Concorde**, **un sombrero estilo Bogart**, and also of biological definitions such as **el pájaro hembra**, **las musarañas macho**.

(c) Creativity in this aspect in journalistic Spanish has now gone well beyond any possible English model, however: examples are **un jugador promesa**, **horas punta**, **tecnología punta**, **el grupo revelación del año**, **una teoría puente**. Abbreviations may figure too in a kind of journalistic shorthand: **tres aviones USA**, **dos agentes CIA**.

(d) While the principle of non-concord is the soundest one, as above, speakers may occasionally treat the attributive element as an adjective and assign it concord for number (but never for gender): **hay dos palabras claves**, **pedimos pagos extras**. One finds both **hombres rana** and **hombres ranas**.

Note: *preceding a word denotes an invented form.

Numerals

Los números

CARDINAL NUMBERS — NÚMEROS CARDINALES

nought, zero	**0**	cero
one	**1**	(*m*) uno, (*f*) una
two	**2**	dos
three	**3**	tres
four	**4**	cuatro
five	**5**	cinco
six	**6**	seis
seven	**7**	siete
eight	**8**	ocho
nine	**9**	nueve
ten	**10**	diez
eleven	**11**	once
twelve	**12**	doce
thirteen	**13**	trece
fourteen	**14**	catorce
fifteen	**15**	quince
sixteen	**16**	dieciséis
seventeen	**17**	diecisiete
eighteen	**18**	dieciocho
nineteen	**19**	diecinueve
twenty	**20**	veinte
twenty-one	**21**	veintiuno (*see note* **B**)
twenty-two	**22**	veintidós
twenty-three	**23**	veintitrés
thirty	**30**	treinta
thirty-one	**31**	treinta y uno
thirty-two	**32**	treinta y dos
forty	**40**	cuarenta
fifty	**50**	cincuenta
sixty	**60**	sesenta
seventy	**70**	setenta
eighty	**80**	ochenta
ninety	**90**	noventa
ninety-nine	**99**	noventa y nueve
a (*or* one) hundred	**100**	cien, ciento (*see note* **C**)
a hundred and one	**101**	ciento uno
a hundred and two	**102**	ciento dos
a hundred and ten	**110**	ciento diez
a hundred and eighty-two	**182**	ciento ochenta y dos
two hundred	**200**	(*m*) doscientos, (*f*) –as
three hundred	**300**	(*m*) trescientos, (*f*) –as
four hundred	**400**	(*m*) cuatrocientos, (*f*) –as
five hundred	**500**	(*m*) quinientos, (*f*) –as
six hundred	**600**	(*m*) seiscientos, (*f*) –as
seven hundred	**700**	(*m*) setecientos, (*f*) –as
eight hundred	**800**	(*m*) ochocientos, (*f*) –as
nine hundred	**900**	(*m*) novecientos, (*f*) –as
a (*or* one) thousand	**1000**	mil
a thousand and two	**1002**	mil dos
two thousand	**2000**	dos mil
ten thousand	**10000**	diez mil
a (*or* one) hundred thousand	**100000**	cien mil
a (or one) million	**1000000**	un millón (*see note* **D**)
two million	**2000000**	dos millones (*see note* **D**)

Notes on usage of the cardinal numbers

Ⓐ **One,** and the other numbers ending in one, agree in Spanish with the noun (stated or implied): *una casa, un coche, si se trata de pagar en libras ello viene a sumar treinta y una, había ciento una personas.*

Ⓑ **21:** In Spanish there is some uncertainty when the number is accompanied by a feminine noun. In the spoken language both *veintiuna peseta* and *veintiuna pesetas* are heard; in 'correct' literary language only *veintiuna pesetas* is found. With a masculine noun the numeral is shortened in the usual way: *veintiún perros rabiosos.* These remarks apply also to 31, 41 etc.

Ⓒ **100:** When the number is spoken alone or in counting a series of numbers both *cien* and *ciento* are heard. When there is an accompanying noun the form is always *cien: cien hombres, cien chicas.* In the compound numbers note 101 = *ciento uno,* 110 = *ciento diez,* but 100000 = *cien mil.*

Ⓓ **1000000:** In Spanish the word *millón* is a noun, so the numeral takes *de* when there is a following noun: *un millón de fichas, tres millones de árboles quemados.*

Ⓔ In Spanish the cardinal numbers may be used as nouns, as in English; they are always masculine: *jugó el siete de corazones, el once nacional de Ruritania, éste es el trece y nosotros buscamos el quince.*

Ⓕ To divide the larger numbers clearly a point is used in Spanish where English places a comma: English 1,000 = Spanish 1.000, English 2,304,770 = Spanish 2.304.770. (This does not apply to dates: see below.)

ORDINAL NUMBERS — NÚMEROS ORDINALES

first	**1**	primero (*see note* **B**)
second	**2**	segundo
third	**3**	tercero (*see note* **B**)
fourth	**4**	cuarto
fifth	**5**	quinto
sixth	**6**	sexto
seventh	**7**	séptimo
eighth	**8**	octavo
ninth	**9**	noveno, nono
tenth	**10**	décimo
eleventh	**11**	undécimo
twelfth	**12**	duodécimo
thirteenth	**13**	decimotercio, decimotercero
fourteenth	**14**	decimocuarto
fifteenth	**15**	decimoquinto
sixteenth	**16**	decimosexto
seventeenth	**17**	decimoséptimo
eighteenth	**18**	decimoctavo
nineteenth	**19**	decimonoveno, decimonono
twentieth	**20**	vigésimo
twenty-first	**21**	vigésimo primero, vigésimo primo
twenty-second	**22**	vigésimo segundo
thirtieth	**30**	trigésimo
thirty-first	**31**	trigésimo primero, trigésimo primo
fortieth	**40**	cuadragésimo
fiftieth	**50**	quincuagésimo
sixtieth	**60**	sexagésimo

seventieth	**70**	septuagésimo
eightieth	**80**	octogésimo
ninetieth	**90**	nonagésimo
hundredth	**100**	centésimo
hundred and first	**101**	centésimo primero
hundred and tenth	**110**	centésimo décimo
two hundredth	**200**	ducentésimo
three hundredth	**300**	trecentésimo
four hundredth	**400**	cuadringentésimo
five hundredth	**500**	quingentésimo
six hundredth	**600**	sexcentésimo
seven hundredth	**700**	septingentésimo
eight hundredth	**800**	octingentésimo
nine hundredth	**900**	noningentésimo
thousandth	**1000**	milésimo
two thousandth	**2000**	dos milésimo
millionth	**1000000**	millonésimo
two millionth	**2000000**	dos millonésimo

Notes on usage of the ordinal numbers

Ⓐ All these numbers are adjectives in *-o*, and therefore agree with the noun in number and gender: *la quinta vez, en segundas nupcias, en octavo lugar.*

Ⓑ *Primero* and *tercero* are shortened to *primer, tercer* when they directly precede a masculine singular noun: *en el primer capítulo, el tercer hombre* (but *los primeros coches en llegar, el primero y más importante hecho*).

Ⓒ In Spanish the ordinal numbers from 1 to 10 are commonly used; from 11 to 20 rather less; above 21 they are rarely written and almost never heard in speech (except for *milésimo*, which is frequent). The custom is to replace the forms for 21 and above by the cardinal number: *en el capítulo treinta y seis, celebran el setenta aniversario* (or *el aniversario setenta*), *en el poste ciento cinco contando desde la esquina.*

Ⓓ **Kings, popes and centuries.** The ordinal numbers from 1 to 9 are employed for these in Spanish as in English: *en el siglo cuarto, Eduardo octavo, Pío nono, Enrique primero.* For 10 either the cardinal or the ordinal may be used: *siglo diez* or *siglo décimo, Alfonso diez* or *Alfonso décimo.* For 11 and above it is now customary to use only the cardinal number: *Alfonso once* (but *onceno* in the Middle Ages), *Juan veintitrés, en el siglo dieciocho.*

Ⓔ **Abbreviations.** English 1st, 2nd, 3rd, 4th, 5th etc = Spanish 1º or 1er, 2º, 3º or 3er, 4º, 5º and so on (*f*: 1era, 2a).

Ⓕ See also the notes on Dates, below.

DECIMALS — LAS DECIMALES

In Spanish a comma is written where English writes a point: English 3·56 (*three point five six*) = Spanish 3,56 (*tres coma cinco seis*); English ·07 (*point zero seven*) = Spanish ,07 (*coma cero siete*). The recurring decimal 3·3333 may be written in English as 3·3 and in Spanish as 3,3.

FRACTIONS — NÚMEROS QUEBRADOS

one half, a half	$\frac{1}{2}$	(m) *medio,* (f) *media*
one and a half helpings	$1\frac{1}{2}$	*(una) porción y media*
two and a half kilos	$2\frac{1}{2}$	*dos kilos y medio*
one third, a third	$\frac{1}{3}$	*un tercio, la tercera parte*
two thirds	$\frac{2}{3}$	*dos tercios, las dos terceras partes*
one quarter, a quarter	$\frac{1}{4}$	*un cuarto, la cuarta parte*
three quarters	$\frac{3}{4}$	*tres cuartos, las tres cuartas partes*
one sixth, a sixth	$\frac{1}{6}$	*un sexto, la sexta parte*
five and five sixths	$5\frac{5}{6}$	*cinco y cinco sextos*
one twelfth, a twelfth	$\frac{1}{12}$	*un duodécimo; un dozavo, la duodécima parte*
seven twelfths	$\frac{7}{12}$	*siete dozavos*
one hundredth, a hundredth	$\frac{1}{100}$	*un centésimo, una centésima parte*
one thousandth, a thousandth	$\frac{1}{1000}$	*un milésimo*

UNITS — NOMENCLATURA

3,684 is a four-digit number.	*3.684 es un número de cuatro dígitos (or guarismos).*
It contains 4 units, 8 tens, 6 hundreds and 3 thousands.	*Contiene 4 unidades, 8 decenas, 6 centenas y 3 unidades de millar.*
The decimal ·234 contains 2 tenths, 3 hundredths and 4 thousandths.	*La fracción decimal ,234 contiene 2 décimas, 3 centésimas y 4 milésimas.*

PERCENTAGES — LOS PORCENTAJES

2½% two and a half per cent	*2½ por 100,* (less frequently) *2½%; dos y medio por cien, dos y medio por ciento* (in spoken usage and among the authorities there is disagreement about *cien/ciento* here).
18% of the people here are over 65.	*El dieciocho por ciento de la gente aquí tienen mas de 65 años.*
Production has risen by 8%.	*La producción ha aumentado en un 8 por 100.*
(See also per, hundred *in the main text.)*	*(Véase también* por, cien/ciento *en el diccionario.)*

CALCULATIONS

8 + **6** = **14** eight and (*or* plus) six are (*or* make) fourteen
15 – **3** = **12** fifteen take away three are (*or* equals) twelve, three from fifteen leaves twelve
3 x **3** = **9** three threes are nine, three times three is nine
32 ÷ **8** = **4** thirty-two divided by eight is (*or* equals) four
$3^2 = 9$ three squared is nine
$2^5 = 32$ two to the fifth (*or* to the power of five) is (*or* equals) thirty-two
$\sqrt{16} = 4$ the square root of sixteen is four

EL CÁLCULO

8 + **6** = **14** *ocho y (*or* más) seis son catorce*
15 – **3** = **12** *quince menos tres resta doce, de tres a quince van doce*
3 x **3** = **9** *tres por tres son nueve*
32 ÷ **8** = **4** *treinta y dos dividido por ocho es cuatro*
$3^2 = 9$ *tres al cuadrado son nueve*
$2^5 = 32$ *dos a la quinta potencia son treinta y dos*
$\sqrt{16} = 4$ *la raíz cuadrada de dieciséis es cuatro.*

SIGNS

+ addition sign
+ plus sign (*eg* +7 = plus seven)
– subtraction sign
– minus sign (*eg* –3 = minus three)
x multiplication sign
÷ division sign
√ square root sign
∞ infinity
≡ sign of identity, is exactly equal to
= sign of equality, equals
≈ is approximately equal to
≠ sign of inequality, is not equal to
> is greater than
< is less than

LOS SIGNOS

+ signo de adición
+ signo de más (*p.ej.* +7 = 7 de más)
– signo de sustracción
– signo de menos (*p.ej.* –3 = 3 de menos)
x signo de multiplicación
: signo de división
√ signo de raíz cuadrada
∞ infinito
≡ signo de identidad, es exactamente igual a
= signo de igualdad, es igual a
≈ es aproximadamente igual a
≠ signo de no identidad, no es igual a
> es mayor que
< es menor que

METRIC SYSTEM — SISTEMA MÉTRICO

Measures formed with the following prefixes are mostly omitted:

Se omiten la mayor parte de las medidas formadas con los siguientes prefijos:

deca-	10 times	10 veces	*deca-*
hecto-	100 times	100 veces	*hecto-*
kilo-	1000 times	1000 veces	*kilo-*
deci-	one tenth	una décima	*deci-*
centi-	one hundredth	una centésima	*centi-*
mil(l)i-	one thousandth	una milésima	*mili-*

Linear measures — medidas de longitud

1 millimetre (milímetro)	=	0·03937 inch (pulgada)
1 centimetre (centímetro)	=	0·3937 inch (pulgada)
1 metre (metro)	=	39·37 inches (pulgadas)
	=	1·094 yards (yardas)
1 kilometre (kilómetro)	=	0·6214 mile (milla) *or* almost exactly five-eighths of a mile

Square measures — medidas cuadradas o de superficie

1 square centimetre (centímetro cuadrado)	=	0·155 square inch (pulgada cuadrada)
1 square metre (metro cuadrado)	=	10·764 square feet (pies cuadrados)
	=	1·196 square yards (yardas cuadradas)
1 square kilometre (kilómetro cuadrado)	=	0·3861 square mile (milla cuadrada)
	=	247·1 acres (acres)
1 are = 100 square metres (área)	=	119·6 square yards (yardas cuadradas)
1 hectare = 100 ares (hectárea)	=	2·471 acres (acres)

Cubic measures — medidas cúbicas

1 cubic centimetre (centímetro cúbico)	=	0·061 cubic inch (pulgada cubica)
1 cubic metre (metro cúbico)	=	35·315 cubic feet (pies cubicos)
	=	1·308 cubic yards (yardas cubicas)

Measures of capacity — medidas de capacidad

1 litre (litro) = 1000 cubic centimetres	=	1·76 pints (pintas)
	=	0·22 gallon (galón)

Weights — pesos

1 gramme (gramo)	=	15·4 grains (granos)
1 kilogramme (kilogramo)	=	2·2046 pounds (libras)
1 quintal (quintal métrico) = 100 kilogrammes	=	220·46 pounds (libras)
1 metric ton (tonelada métrica) = 1000 kilogrammes	=	0·9842 ton (tonelada)

BRITISH SYSTEM — SISTEMA BRITÁNICO

Linear measures — medidas de longitud

1 inch (pulgada)	=	2,54 centímetros
1 foot (pie) = 12 inches	=	30,48 centímetros
1 yard (yarda) = 3 feet	=	91,44 centímetros
1 furlong (estadio) = 220 yards	=	201,17 metros
1 mile (milla) = 1760 yards	=	1.609,33 metros
	=	1,609 kilómetros

Surveyors' measures — medidas de agrimensura

1 link = 7·92 inches	=	20,12 centímetros
1 rod (*or* pole, perch) = 25 links	=	5,029 metros
1 chain = 22 yards = 4 rods	=	20,12 metros

Square measures — medidas cuadradas o de superficie

1 square inch (pulgada cuadrada)	=	6,45 cm^2
1 square foot (pie cuadrado) = 144 square inches	=	929,03 cm^2
1 square yard (yarda cuadrada) = 9 square feet	=	0,836 m^2
1 square rod = 30·25 square yards	=	25,29 m^2
1 acre = 4840 square yards	=	40,47 areas
1 square mile (milla cuadrada) = 640 acres	=	2,59 km^2

Cubic measures — medidas cúbicas

1 cubic inch (pulgada cúbica)	=	16,387 cm^3
1 cubic foot (pie cúbico) = 1728 cubic inches	=	0,028 m^3
1 cubic yard (yarda cúbica) = 27 cubic feet	=	0,765 m^3
1 register ton (tonelada de registro) = 100 cubic feet	=	2,832 m^3

Measures of capacity — medidas de capacidad

(a) Liquid – para líquidos		
1 gill	=	0,142 litro
1 pint (pinta) = 4 gills	=	0,57 litro
1 quart = 2 pints	=	1,136 litros
1 gallon (galon) = 4 quarts	=	4,546 litros
(b) Dry – para áridos		
1 peck = 2 gallons	=	9,087 litros
1 bushel = 4 pecks	=	36,37 litros
1 quarter = 8 bushels	=	290,94 litros

Weights — pesos (Avoirdupois system — sistema avoirdupois)

1 grain (grano)	=	0,0648 gramo
1 drachm *or* dram = 27,34 grains	=	1,77 gramos
1 ounce (onza) = 16 dra(ch)ms	=	28,35 gramos
1 pound (libra) = 16 ounces	=	453,6 gramos
	=	0,453 kilogramo
1 stone = 14 pounds	=	6,35 kilogramos
1 quarter = 28 pounds	=	12,7 kilogramos
1 hundredweight = 112 pounds	=	50,8 kilogramos
1 ton (tonelada) = 2240 pounds = 20 hundredweight	=	1.016,06 kilogramos

US MEASURES — MEDIDAS NORTEAMERICANAS

In the US the same system as that which applies in Great Britain is used for the most part; the main differences are mentioned below.
En EE.UU. se emplea en general el mismo sistema que en Gran Bretaña; las principales diferencias son las siguientes:

Measures of capacity — medidas de capacidad

(a) Liquid – para líquidos		
1 US liquid gill	=	0,118 litro
1 US liquid pint = 4 gills	=	0,47 litro
1 US liquid quart = 2 pints	=	0,946 litro
1 US gallon = 4 quarts	=	3,785 litros
(b) Dry – para áridos		
1 US dry pint	=	0,550 litro
1 US dry quart = 2 dry pints	=	1,1 litros
1 US peck = 8 dry quarts	=	8,81 litros
1 US bushel = 4 pecks	=	35,24 litros

Weights — pesos

1 hundredweight (or short hundredweight) = 100 pounds	=	45,36 kilogramos
1 ton (or short ton) = 2000 pounds = 20 short hundredweights	=	907,18 kilogramos

TRADITIONAL SPANISH WEIGHTS AND MEASURES — PESOS Y MEDIDAS ESPAÑOLES TRADICIONALES

These are the measures which were standard until the introduction of the metric system in Spain in 1871, and they are still in use in some provinces and in agriculture.

Son éstas las medidas que se emplearon hasta la introducción del sistema métrico en España en 1871. Se emplean todavía en algunas provincias y en la agricultura.

Linear measures — medidas de longitud

1 vara	=	0·836 metre
1 braza	=	1·67 metres
1 milla	=	1·852 kilometres
1 legua	=	5·5727 kilometres

Square measure — medida cuadrada o de superficie

1 fanega = 6460 square metres = 1·59 acres

Measures of capacity — medidas de capacidad

(a) Liquid – para líquidos		
1 cuartillo	=	0·504 litre
1 azumbre = 4 cuartillos	=	2·016 litres
1 cántara = 8 azumbres	=	16·13 litres
(b) Dry – para áridos		
1 celemín	=	4·625 litres
1 fanega = 12 celemines	=	55·5 litres = 1·58 bushels

Weights — pesos

1 onza	=	28·7 grammes
1 libra = 16 onzas	=	460 grammes
1 arroba = 25 libras	=	11·502 kilogrammes = 25 pounds
1 quintal = 4 arrobas	=	46 kilogrammes

TIME	LA HORA
2 hours 33 minutes and 14 seconds	*2 horas 33 minutos y 14 segundos*
half an hour	*media hora*
a quarter of an hour	*un cuarto de hora*
three quarters of an hour	*tres cuartos de hora*
what's the time?	*¿qué hora es?*
what do you make the time?	*¿qué hora tienes?*
have you the right time?	*¿tiene Vd la hora exacta?*
I make it 2.20	*yo tengo las dos veinte*
my watch says 3.37	*mi reloj marca las tres treinta y siete*
it's 1 o'clock	*es la una*
it's 2 o'clock	*son las dos*
it's 5 past 4	*son las cuatro y cinco*
it's 10 to 6	*son las seis menos diez*
it's half-past 8	*son las ocho y media*
it's a quarter past 9	*son las nueve y cuarto*
it's a quarter to 2	*son las dos menos cuarto*
at 10 a.m.	*a las diez de la mañana*
at 4 p.m.	*a las cuatro de la tarde*
at 11 p.m.	*a las once de la noche*
at exactly 3 o'clock, at 3 sharp, at 3 on the dot	*a las tres en punto*
the train leaves at 19.32	*el tren sale a las diecinueve treinta y dos*
(at) what time does it start?	*¿a qué hora comienza?*
it is just after 3	*son un poco más de las tres*
it is nearly 9	*son casi las nueve*
about 8 o'clock	*cerca de las ocho, hacia las ocho, a eso de las ocho*
at (*or* by) 6 o'clock at the latest	*a las seis a más tardar*
have it ready for 5 o'clock	*téngalo listo para las cinco*
it is full each night from 7 to 9	*está lleno todas las noches de siete a nueve*
"closed from 1.30 to 4.30"	*"cerrado de 1.30 a 4.30"*
until 8 o'clock	*hasta las ocho*
it would be about 11	*serán las once*
it would have been about 10	*serían las diez*
at midnight	*a medianoche*
before midday, before noon	*antes del mediodía*

DATES — LAS FECHAS

N.B. The days of the week and the months are written with small letters in Spanish: *lunes, martes, febrero, mayo.*
N.B. *Los días de la semana y los meses empiezan con mayúscula en inglés*: Monday, Tuesday, February, May.

DATES	LAS FECHAS
the 1st of July, July 1st	*el 1° de julio, el primero de julio*
the 2nd of May, May 2nd	*el 2 de mayo, el dos de mayo* (the cardinal numbers are used in Spanish for dates from 2nd to 31st)
on the 21st (of) June	*el 21 de junio, el día veintiuno de junio*
on Monday	*el lunes*
he comes on Mondays	*viene los lunes*
"closed on Fridays"	*"cerrado los viernes"*
he lends it to me from Monday to Friday	*me lo presta de lunes a viernes*
from the 14th to the 18th	*desde el 14 hasta el 18, desde el catorce hasta el dieciocho*
what's the date?, what date is it today?	*¿qué día es hoy?*
today's the 12th	*hoy es el doce, estamos a doce*
one Thursday in October	*un jueves en octubre*
about the 4th of July	*hacia el cuatro de julio*
In letters: 19th May 1984	En cartas: *19 de mayo de 1984*
1975, nineteen (hundred and) seventy-five	*mil novecientos setenta y cinco*
4 BC, BC 4	*4 a. de C.*
70 AD, AD 70	*70 d. de C.*
in the 13th Century	*en el siglo XIII, en el siglo trece*
in (*or* during) the 1930s	*en el decenio de 1930 a 40, durante los años treinta*
in 1940 something	*en el año 1940 y tantos*

Abreviaturas e indicaciones semánticas y estilísticas		Abbreviations, field labels and style labels
abreviatura	*abr, abbr*	abbreviation
adjetivo	*adj*	adjective
administración	*Admin*	administration
adverbio	*adv*	adverb
aeronáutica	*Aer*	aeronautics
agricultura	*Agr*	agriculture
alguien	*algn*	somebody, someone
anatomía	*Anat*	anatomy
Andes	*And*	Andes
Antillas	*Ant*	Antilles
Arqueología	*Archeol*	Archeology
arquitectura	*Archit*	architecture
Argentina	*Arg*	Argentina
arquitectura	*Arquit*	architecture
artículo	*art*	article
astrología	*Astrol*	astrology
astronomía	*Astron*	astronomy
automóviles, automovilismo	*Aut*	automobiles
auxiliar	*aux*	auxiliary
las Islas Baleares	*Baleares*	Balearic Islands
biología	*Bio, Biol*	biology
Bolivia	*Bol*	Bolivia
botánica	*Bot*	botany
británico, Gran Bretaña	*Brit*	British, Great Britain
Centroamérica	*CAm*	Central America
química	*Chem*	chemistry
cine	*Cine*	cinema
Colombia	*Col*	Colombia
comercio	*Com, Comm*	commerce
comparativo	*compar*	comparative
informática	*Comput*	computing
condicional	*cond*	conditional
conjunción	*conj*	conjunction
conjugación	*conjug*	conjugation
construcción	*Constr*	construction
costura	*Cos*	sewing
compuesto	*cpd*	compound
Costa Rica	*C. Rica*	Costa Rica
culinario, cocina	*Culin*	culinary, cooking
definido	*def*	definite
demostrativo	*dem*	demonstrative
deportes	*Dep*	sport
derecho	*Der*	law
ecología	*Ecol*	ecology
economía	*Econ*	economy
Ecuador	*Ecu*	Ecuador
educación	*Educ*	education
Estados Unidos	*EEUU*	United States
por ejemplo	*eg*	for example
electricidad	*Elec*	electricity
escolar	*Escol*	school
España	*Esp*	Spain
especialmente	*esp*	especially
etcétera	*etc*	etcetera
eufemismo	*euf, euph*	euphemism
exclamación	*excl*	exclamation
femenino	*f*	feminine
farmacia	*Farm*	pharmacy
femenino	*fem*	feminine
ferrocarriles	*Ferro*	railways
figurado	*fig*	figurative
filosofía	*Fil*	philosophy
finanzas	*Fin*	finance
física	*Fís*	physics
fisiología	*Fisiol*	physiology
fotografía	*Fot*	photography
femenino plural	*fpl*	feminine plural
frecuentemente	*frec, freq*	frequently
uso formal	*frm*	formal usage
femenino singular	*fsing*	feminine singular
fútbol	*Ftbl*	football
generalmente	*gen*	generally
geografía	*Geog*	geography
geología	*Geol*	geology
geometría	*Geom*	geometry
gobierno	*Govt*	government
gramática	*Gram*	grammar
Guatemala	*Guat*	Guatemala
historia	*Hist*	history
Honduras	*Hond*	Honduras
horticultura	*Hort*	horticulture
humorístico	*hum*	humorous
impersonal	*impers*	impersonal
industria	*Ind*	industry
indefinido	*indef*	indefinite
indicativo	*indic*	indicative
infinitivo	*infin*	infinitive
informática	*Inform*	computing
Inglaterra	*Ingl*	England
interrogativo	*interrog*	interrogative
invariable	*inv*	invariable
Irlanda	*Irl*	Ireland
irónico	*iró, iro*	ironic
irregular	*irr*	irregular
derecho, jurídico	*Jur*	law, legal
Latinoamérica	*LAm*	Latin America
lingüística	*Ling*	linguistics
literalmente	*lit*	literally
literario	*liter*	literary
literatura	*Literat*	literature
masculino	*m, masc*	masculine